LONGMAN

PRONUNCIATION
DICTIONARY

J C Wells

PEARSON

Longman

Pearson Education Limited
Edinburgh Gate
Harlow
Essex CM20 2JE
England
and Associated Companies throughout the World

Visit our website: http://www.longman.com/dictionaries

First published 1990
This edition published 2000
Ninth impression 2007

ISBN 978-0-582-36467-7 (Paperback edition)
British Library Cataloguing-in-Publication Data
A catalogue record for this book is available from the British Library.

Designed by Helen Colman
Graphs by Robert Escott
Set in Times by Morton Word Processing Ltd, Scarborough, United Kingdom
Printed in China
SWTC/10

J.C. **Wells** occupies the Chair of Phonetics in the University of London. He was born in
Lancashire in 1939. Both at school and as an undergraduate at Cambridge he special-
ized in Classics, but switched to phonetics as a postgraduate at University College
London, where he became a member of the academic staff in 1962. There he teaches
English phonetics, both to native speakers and to EFL learners, as well as general
phonetics and phonology and the phonetics of various other languages.

Among the books he has written on the subject of phonetics and pronunciation are
Jamaican Pronunciation in London and, his best-known work, the three-volume **Accents
of English**. His first published book was an Esperanto dictionary.

For further information, visit his website at www.phon.ucl.ac.uk/home/wells/home.htm.

CONTENTS

Spelling-to-sound guidelines (grapheme-to-phoneme rules) for each letter of the alphabet are distributed throughout the dictionary, each at the head of the entries beginning with that letter.
(See also DOUBLE CONSONANT LETTERS; SHORT VOWEL, LONG VOWEL.)

Notes on pronunciation and phonetics

Index to notes on pronunciation and phonetics

Acknowledgements

I am fortunate in the many people who have been ready to help me as I planned and prepared this dictionary. My colleagues in Phonetics and Linguistics at University College London, including several now retired, have patiently tolerated my obsessive questioning: among them I would mention especially the late Prof. A.C. Gimson, with whom I held many discussions on the problems of compiling and maintaining a pronouncing dictionary and on the changing nature of RP (Received Pronunciation).

For detailed advice on American English, I am grateful to Linda Shockey; for checking the Russian transcriptions, to John Baldwin and Sue Barry; for the Arabic, to Janaan Dawood; for the Hindi, to Neil and Saras Smith; and the Japanese, to Kazuhiko Matsuno and Noriko Hattori. Thanks too to Graham Pointon of the BBC Pronunciation Unit. Jill House and Dinah Jackson made various helpful suggestions in the course of proof-reading. Any remaining errors are naturally my own responsibility.

I am of course greatly indebted to successive editions of Daniel Jones's *English Pronouncing Dictionary* (Dent, 12th edn, 1963; 13th edn revised by A.C. Gimson, 1967; 14th edn, 1977; reprinted with revisions and supplement by S.M. Ramsaran, 1988). *EPD* has set the standard against which other dictionaries must inevitably be judged. Other pronouncing dictionaries I have frequently consulted include *BBC Pronouncing Dictionary of British Names*, 2nd edn by G.E. Pointon (Oxford University Press, 1983); *NBC Handbook of Pronunciation*, 4th edn by Eugene Ehrlich and Raymond Hand, Jr. (Harper and Row, 1984); and *A Pronouncing Dictionary of American English* by J.S. Kenyon and T.A. Knott (Merriam, 1953). For American pronunciation I have also regularly explored *Webster's Ninth New Collegiate Dictionary* (Merriam-Webster, 1983), the *American Heritage Dictionary* (Houghton Mifflin, 1981), and *The Random House Dictionary*, 2nd edn (Random House, 1987). For Australian pronunciation I have used *The Macquarie Dictionary* (Macquarie Library, 1981), and for Indian words *Common Indian Words in English* by R.E. Hawkins (Delhi: Oxford University Press, 1984). I have taken certain medical terms from *Butterworths Medical Dictionary* (2nd edn Butterworth & Co, 1978). Not only for German, but also for information about proper names from a variety of foreign languages, *Duden Aussprachewörterbuch* by Max Mangold (2nd edn, Bibliographisches Institut Mannheim, 1974) has proved invaluable. For French I have drawn particularly on *Dictionnaire de la prononciation* by Alain Lerond (Larousse, 1980); for Italian on *Dizionario d'ortografia e di pronunzia* by Migliorini, Tagliavini & Fiorelli (ERI–Edizioni RAI, 1969). For the entries on affixes and the spelling-to-sound boxes I have taken advantage of ideas contained in *The Groundwork of English Stress* by Roger Kingdon (Longman, 1958), *English Word-Stress* by Erik Fudge (Allen & Unwin, 1984), *Rules of Pronunciation for the English Language* by Axel Wijk (Oxford University Press, 1966), and a number of works by Lionel Guierre, including *Drills in English Stress-Patterns* (4th edn Paris: Armand Colin–Longman, 1984).

Nearly three hundred native speakers of British English took the time and trouble to answer a detailed questionnaire about preferences in the pronunciation of particular words (see 1.7 below, Opinion polls). Thanks to all of them: their chief reward is to have their views recorded in the polling figures presented in this book.

My particular thanks go to Susan Maingay and Stephen Crowdy of Longman Dictionaries, who have been consistently supportive and cooperative, everything a publisher should be; and to Clare Fletcher, who made numerous suggestions for clearer or more felicitous wording and presentation.

John Wells

Note to the second edition

My thanks for helpful suggestions go to the many reviewers and friendly critics of the first edition of LPD, and in particular to Jack Windsor Lewis.

Since the first appearance of LPD there have been new editions of many of the works of reference listed above. I have made particular use of the invaluable Duden *Aussprachewörterbuch* (3rd edn, 1990) and – for Australian names – of *The Macquarie Dictionary* (2nd edn, Macquarie University NSW, 1991).

A much fuller treatment of English spelling-to-sound rules is now available in *A Survey of English Spelling* by Edward Carney (Routledge, 1994).

I have been stimulated by the radical revisions made in the fifteenth edition of the Daniel Jones *English Pronouncing Dictionary*, now edited by Peter Roach and James Hartman (Cambridge University Press, 1997).

For advice on Chinese names I am indebted to Siew-Yue Killingley, Cheung Kwan-Hin and John Maidment, and for further information on Japanese to Mitsuhiro Nakamura.

I am grateful to Rebecca Dauer for checking the 5,000 new entries from the point of view of American English. Particular thanks also to my graduate student Yuko Shitara for allowing me to include the findings of her 1993 AmE pronunciation preference survey.

Thanks are due to the volunteers who participated in the 1998 pronunciation preference poll – not 275 this time, but over 1900 – to Jonathan Wadman for turning questionnaire responses into computer files, and to my colleague Andy Faulkner for help with processing the data.

Longman have continued to be supportive in every way. Thanks particularly to Adam Gadsby, Emma Campbell, Emma Williams, Dinah Jackson and Sheila Dallas; and to Della Summers who commissioned both the first edition of this dictionary and this current revision.

John Wells
London, March 1999

A quick guide to the dictionary

British and American pronunciations

Where only one pronunciation is given this means that the word has a similar pronunciation in both British and American English.

The symbol ‖ is used to introduce American English pronunciations when these are different from British English forms.

Sometimes, when the American English pronunciation is different in only one part of a word, the dictionary shows only this part.

bad bæd — pronunciation used in both BrE and AmE

batter ˈbæt ə ‖ ˈbæt̬ ᵊr
    BrE   AmE

bender ˈbend ə ‖ -ᵊr — the AmE pronunciation is ˈbend ᵊr

Main pronunciations and alternatives

All main pronunciations (recommended as models for learners of English) are shown in colour. If there are alternative pronunciations, these are shown in black type.

Where only one pronunciation is given for the main pronunciation and for the alternative, this means that both have a similar pronunciation in British and American English.

Sometimes when an alternative pronunciation is different only in one part of a word, the dictionary shows only this part.

Pronunciations which are widespread among educated speakers of British English but which are not, however, considered to belong to RP (Received Pronunciation) are marked with the symbol §.

The dictionary also includes pronunciations which are generally considered to be incorrect.

main BrE   main AmE

baroque bə ˈrɒk bæ-, -ˈrəʊk ‖ -ˈroʊk -ˈrɑːk

alternative BrE   alternative AmE

bankrupt ˈbæŋk rʌpt -rəpt ~**ed** ɪd əd ~**ing** ɪŋ ~**s** s

pronunciation and alternative used in both BrE and AmE

bases *pl of* **base** ˈbeɪs ɪz-əz

an alternative pronunciation is ˈbeɪs əz

bath *n* bɑːθ §bæθ ‖ bæθ

the RP form is bɑːθ; in England bæθ is a localized northern form, though it is standard in AmE

grievous ˈgriːv əs △ˈgriːv i‿əs

be careful not to use this pronunciation

Pronunciations of foreign words

For words belonging to foreign languages, which are in use in English, the dictionary shows both their anglicized pronunciations and their pronunciations in the language of origin.

pronunciation in BrE and AmE

Benz benz —*Ger* [bɛnts]

original German pronunciation

Inflected and derived forms

Entries include information about the pronunciation of the different forms of headword (plurals, past tense forms, etc.)

Sometimes the different forms are shown in full.

Sometimes just the endings are shown.

blub blʌb **blubbed** blʌbd **blubbing** ˈblʌb ɪŋ **blubs** blʌbz

building ˈbɪld ɪŋ ~**s** z

the plural form **buildings** is pronounced ˈbɪld ɪŋz

Sometimes an ending is added not to the complete word but to just part of it. The symbol | is used to show exactly which part is concerned.

beef|y 'biːf |i **~ier** i‿ə ‖ i‿ºr **~iest** i‿ɪst i‿əst

beef + ier = _____↑   ↑__ beef + iest =
'biːfi‿ə   'biːfi‿ɪst

Stress marks

Words of more than one syllable are marked for stress. The LPD recognizes two types of stress. (See the note on 'Stress', p. 741.)

When alternative pronunciations are different only in the way in which they are stressed, the full pronunciation is not repeated but small blocks (··) are used to represent the syllables of the word.

secondary stress   primary stress

↓   ↓

interchangeability ˌɪnt ə ˌtʃeɪndʒ ə 'bɪl ət i -ɪt i

backslid|e 'bæk slaɪd ˌ·'·

an alternative stress pattern is ˌbæk 'slaɪd

Stress shift

Some words have different stress patterns according to whether they are being used alone or directly before a noun. (See the note on 'Stress shift', p. 742.) The symbol ◄ is used to show words which can behave in this way.

academic ˌæk ə 'dem ɪk ◄

Stress in compounds

The pronunciation of compound words can often be derived from their component parts. Stress patterns, however, are not always easy to predict and so important compounds and their patterns are listed after the main entry.

bee biː **bees, bee's** biːz
ˌbee's 'knees; 'bee sting

compounds showing stress patterns

Special notes

The dictionary makes use of some special symbols to help you to arrive at the right pronunciation.

! This symbol is a warning that the pronunciation is quite different from what the spelling might lead you to expect!

bury 'ber i *(! = berry)*

* This symbol is a warning that the British and American pronunciations are different in an important and unpredictable way.

baton 'bæt ɒn -ən ‖ bə 'tɑːn *(*)*

= This symbol draws attention to another word which has exactly the same pronunciation as the word looked up.

blew bluː *(= blue)*

→ This symbol shows that an alternative pronunciation is the result of a general rule which affects not just this word but a whole range of words and phrases in the language.

bridegroom 'braɪd gruːm →'braɪg-
(See the note on 'Assimilation', p. 49.)

For more detailed information see 'Index to notes on pronunciation and phonetics', p. v, and 'Symbols', pp. xxiii-xxvi.

Foreword to the second edition

Some 5,000 new entries have been added. They include

- words that have come into use, or into wider use, since the previous edition (*cashpoint, ciabatta, geek, karaoke, Netscape, website*)
- additional technical and scientific terms (*bergschrund, biohazard, Ethernet, pancreatitis*)
- additional proper names (*Charlottesville, Mandelson*), including in particular many Chinese and Australian toponyms (*Xinjiang, Wallerawang, Groote Eylandt, La Trobe*)
- words omitted by oversight from the previous edition (*accreditation, admiration, exemption, implementation, marathon*)
- inflected and derived forms previously missing (*adornment, berthed, expendable, fraudster*).

As well as numerous corrections and improvements in detail, two general adjustments to the transcription used in this edition deserve mention:

- The separate symbol for 'tertiary stress', which was not well received, has been replaced by the secondary stress mark. In place of *the ˌEuro ₒvision 'Song ₒContest* we now write *the ˌEuroˌvision 'Song ˌContest*.
- The AmE vowel in words such as *thought, law* is now transcribed ɔː (replacing the ɒː of the first edition). For the AmE minority who distinguish pairs such as *hoarse* and *horse*, the vowel of the first is now transcribed phonemically, as oʊ (rather than oː).

The findings of two new pronunciation preference polls have been incorporated.

A few minor changes have been made in the phonetic transcription of foreign languages. In particular,

- Tone 2 of Swedish, Norwegian, and Serbian/Croatian is now shown as [ˮ]
- the open schwa of Portuguese and German is now shown as [ɐ]
- The Russian sound commonly transliterated *shch* is now shown as [ɕtɕ]
- The Japanese pitch accent step-up (non-contrastive) is now shown as [ˌ] and the accent (contrastive, followed by step-down) as ['], these marks being placed before the mora in question
- the notation of clicks has been brought into line with the International Phonetic Association's 1989 decisions
- transcriptions of modern standard Chinese (Mandarin) have been added, in IPA as well as in the Pinyin romanization
- the tones of Chinese, Thai, and Vietnamese are shown by raised numerals; Chinese tones are also shown by Pinyin vowel diacritics.

Despite the place-of-articulation terms used in the current IPA chart, I have decided to retain the traditional labels *palato-alveolar* and *post-alveolar* for English ʃ and r respectively.

JCW, March 1999

1 Introduction

This is a specialist dictionary of **pronunciation**. It offers the user three kinds of information about English pronunciation that are not available in a general dictionary: information on **variants**, on **inflected** and **derived** forms, and on **proper names**. It covers both British and American English.

1.1 Variants. Many English words have a number of different possible pronunciations. Some of the users of LPD will be teachers and learners of EFL/ESL (English as a foreign or second language), and will look for advice on how to pronounce a given word. For them one **main pronunciation**, printed in colour, is given at each entry. This is the form recommended for EFL purposes. (See the CITATION FORM, DICTIONARY ENTRY AND CONNECTED SPEECH box for how to unpack the abbreviatory conventions.) If the British English (BrE) and American English (AmE) recommended forms are different from one another, then both are given in colour. Other users of LPD, especially those who are native speakers of English, will be interested not only to see what form is recommended but also what **variants** are recognized. Where pronunciations other than the main one are in common educated use, they too are included, but as **secondary pronunciations**, printed in black. Some pronunciations are controversial, and so as evidence for the selection of a main pronunciation, between 200 and 300 entries include a report of one or more **opinion polls** of pronunciation preferences (see 1.7 below).

The wide coverage of variants makes LPD suitable for use not only in speech production but also in speech recognition: not only for human speakers of English but also for computer applications.

1.2 Inflected and derived forms. As well as the uninflected forms of words, LPD systematically includes the plurals of nouns (and possessives if they are pronounced differently from plurals), the third person singular present tense (*s*-forms), present participles (*ing*-forms), past tenses and past participles (*ed*-forms) of verbs, the comparatives and superlatives of adjectives, and derivatives such as those in -*ly*, -*able*, -*er*, -*less*, -*ness*, -*ship*. Where the base form has only one syllable, pronunciations for inflected forms are given in full; otherwise they are usually cut back.

1.3 Proper names. LPD includes all the more commonly encountered proper names – **personal** names (first names, Christian names), **family** names (surnames, last names), names of **mythical** and **literary** characters, **place** names, and **commercial** names (particularly names of products). British names are covered as thoroughly as possible within the space available, while American, Irish, and Australian ones have not been neglected. Many names from other languages are also included, in most cases with their pronunciation in the language of origin as well as in an anglicized form.

1.4 Compounds and phrases. As well as all the above, LPD also includes a good selection of **compounds and phrases**, showing their stress patterns. Some of these illustrate the effect of the highly productive principle of STRESS SHIFT which affects many longer English words. The effects of affixes on word stress are discussed in the special entries devoted to affixes and word endings.

1.5 Spelling. English **spelling** is notorious for its shortcomings. Knowing the orthography of a word does not enable one to predict its pronunciation with any confidence. Nevertheless, certain general principles do govern the relationship between spelling and sound (grapheme and phoneme), even though they may be subject to exceptions and uncertainties. Although many handbooks of English pronunciation ignore them entirely, on the implicit grounds that these rules are so chaotic that it is better to learn the pronunciation of each new word separately, it nevertheless seemed helpful for LPD to offer the user something rather than nothing. Accordingly, guidelines designed to be useful particularly to the EFL learner are given at each letter of the alphabet.

1.6 Homophones. Learners and native speakers alike can reinforce their grasp of the distinction between sound and spelling by noting **homophones** (= words distinct in spelling but pronounced identically). LPD points them out in notes such as

    bear (= *bare*)   **write** (= *right*)

1.7 Opinion polls. For many words of uncertain pronunciation, LPD reports the preferences expressed in three opinion polls:
- a postal opinion poll carried out by the author in 1988 among a panel of 275 native speakers of BrE from throughout Britain;
- a postal opinion poll carried out by Yuko Shitara in 1993 among a panel of 400 native speakers of AmE from throughout the United States;
- an opinion poll carried out by the author in 1998 among a panel of 1,932 native speakers of BrE from throughout Britain, some of whom answered by postal questionnaire but others by e-mail or interactively through the World Wide Web.

Further details of the 1988 poll are to be found in the first edition of LPD, and in my paper 'Age grading in pronunciation preferences', *Proceedings of the XIIIth International Congress of Phonetic Sciences, Stockholm 1995,* vol. 3, pp. 696–699. The 1993 poll is described in Yuko Shitara, 'A survey of American pronunciation preferences', *Speech Hearing and Language 7,* 1993, pp. 201–232, Dept. of Phonetics and Linguistics, University College London. The 1998 poll is described in my paper 'Pronunciation preferences in British English: a new survey' in the *Proceedings* of the 14th ICPhS, San Francisco 1999, and on the UCL Phonetics and Linguistics website, www.phon.ucl.ac.uk.

The four age groups referred to in the graphs are different for the three surveys. In BrE88 the categories from oldest to youngest were those born respectively before 1923, in 1923–47, in 1948–62 and after 1962. In AmE93 they were born in or before 1927, in 1928–47, in 1948–67, and in or after 1968. In BrE98 they were born up to 1933, 1934–53, 1954–73, and since 1973.

2 Types of pronunciation recorded

2.1 British pronunciation. The model of British English pronunciation recorded in LPD is a modernized version of the type known as **Received Pronunciation**, or **RP**.

In England and Wales, RP is widely regarded as a model for correct pronunciation, particularly for educated formal speech. It is what was traditionally used by BBC news readers – hence the alternative name **BBC pronunciation**, although now that the BBC admits regional accents among its announcers this name has become less appropriate. It is the usual standard in teaching English as a foreign language, in all countries where the model is BrE rather than AmE.

RP itself inevitably changes as the years pass. There is also a measure of diversity within it. Furthermore, the democratization undergone by English society during the second half of the twentieth century means that it is nowadays necessary to define RP in a rather broader way than was once customary. LPD includes a number of pronunciations that diverge from traditional, 'classical' RP. The 'RP' transcriptions shown in LPD in fact cover very much more than a narrowly defined RP.

2.2 Other varieties of British English. British Received Pronunciation (RP) is not **localized** (= not associated with any particular city or region). It is to be heard in all parts of the country from those with the appropriate social or educational background. On the other hand, most people do have some degree of local colouring in their speech.

To a large extent, however, this is manifested in details of phonetic realization (use of particular allophones, for example [ʔ] rather than [t] for /t/ in certain positions – see PHONEME AND ALLOPHONE and GLOTTAL STOP) rather than in any substantial deviation from the RP system (= the inventory of vowel and consonant phonemes). Hence it is automatically covered by the transcription used in LPD.

Pronunciations widespread in England among educated speakers, but which are nevertheless judged to fall outside RP, are marked with the special sign §. Since LPD aims to portray the current state of the English language, we think it important not to ignore them, as other dictionaries do.

one	wʌn §wɒn	The general form is wʌn; wɒn is a localized northern form.
last	lɑːst §læst	The RP form is lɑːst. In England læst is a localized northern form (though it is standard in AmE).

Many other BrE 'educated non-RP' forms are not mentioned explicitly.

Speech with local features of the southeast of England is often referred to as **Estuary English**. This involves, in particular,

- frequent use of ʔ for syllable-final t (see GLOTTAL STOP).
- vocalization of l, i.e. the use of a vowel or semivowel of the o type in place of a dark l, thus **milk** mɪok, **table** ˈteɪb o.
- use of tʃ and dʒ in place of tj and dj, thus **tune** tʃuːn, **reduce** rɪ ˈdʒuːs (= yod coalescence, see ASSIMILATION).

Other widespread but local pronunciation characteristics from various parts of the British Isles include the following:

- ŋg for ŋ at the end of a stem: for example, **sing** sɪŋ is also regionally sɪŋg, and **singer** 'sɪŋ ə is also regionally 'sɪŋ gə.
- ɔə for ɔː in certain words: for example, **four** fɔː (also regionally, and formerly in RP, fɔə).
- use of vowel qualities closer to iː, uː than to ɪə, ʊə in words such as **periodic, purity**.
- ʌ and ə not distinguished in quality, both being like RP ə.
- r corresponding to spelling *r* before a consonant sound or at the end of a word: for example, **cart** kɑːt, regionally also kɑːrt (as in AmE).
- many other forms characteristic of Scottish or Irish pronunciation.

These and other pronunciation features associated with regional accents may often be inferred from LPD transcriptions. For example, broad local accents of the north of England have ʊ wherever LPD writes ʌ – for example **love** lʌv, regionally also lʊv. In London and increasingly elsewhere, some people replace θ and ð with f and v respectively, at least in casual speech.

For a few words, LPD includes a pronunciation variant that is not considered correct. These variants are included because of the fact that they are in widespread use. They are marked with the special sign △.

    grievous 'griːv əs △'griːv i‿əs

Australian pronunciation is phonemically similar to RP, though with certain important differences. See AUSTRALIAN ENGLISH. For detailed descriptions of many varieties of native English pronunciation throughout the world, see the author's *Accents of English* (three volumes and cassette, Cambridge University Press, 1982).

2.3 American pronunciation. The AmE pronunciations shown in LPD are those appropriate to the variety (accent) known as **General American**. This is what is spoken by the majority of Americans, namely those who do not have a noticeable eastern or southern accent. It is the appropriate model for EFL learners who wish to speak AmE rather than BrE.

    American pronunciation is shown in LPD entries after the mark ‖. If an entry contains no ‖, then the American pronunciation is the same as the British. If the pronunciation after ‖ is **not** in colour, then the main AmE pronunciation is the same as in BrE.

docile	'dəʊs aɪəl ‖ 'dɑːs əl	The AmE pronunciation is 'dɑːs əl.
crown	kraʊn	The AmE pronunciation is kraʊn, the same as in BrE.
tomato	tə 'mɑːt əʊ ‖ -'meɪt̬ oʊ	The AmE pronunciation is tə 'meɪt̬ oʊ.
ability	ə 'bɪl ət i ‖ -ət̬ i	The AmE pronunciation is ə 'bɪl ət̬ i.
tritium	'trɪt i‿əm ‖ 'trɪt̬- 'trɪʃ-	The AmE pronunciation is usually 'trɪt̬ i‿əm, less commonly 'trɪʃ i‿əm
thorax	'θɔːr æks ‖ 'θoʊr-	The AmE pronunciation is usually 'θɔːr æks, as in BrE. Less commonly it is 'θoʊr æks.

The mark (*), sparingly used, draws attention to cases where the BrE (RP) and AmE pronunciations differ in unpredictable or unexpected ways.

GenAm is not as tightly codified for EFL purposes as RP. Accordingly, some of the conventions followed in LPD need to be discussed.

There is considerable variability in GenAm vowels in the open back area. LPD follows tradition in continuing to distinguish the vowel of **lot** lɑːt from that of **thought** θɔːt. (Note, though, that books by American scholars generally do not use length marks.) However, fewer and fewer Americans distinguish these two vowel sounds from one another; so a secondary AmE pronunciation with ɑː is given for all words having ɔː (except before r).

LPD distinguishes between the vowels ʌ and ə, although in AmE they can generally be regarded as allophones of the same phoneme, and for some speakers are more or less identical phonetically too. Thus where LPD writes **above** ə ˈbʌv some speakers pronounce ə ˈbəv. Similarly LPD distinguishes between ɝː and ər, as in **further** ˈfɝːð ər, although many speakers have a similar syllabic [r] in both syllables. All these qualities arguably represent the same phoneme ə, with or without a following r.

Where RP has ʌr followed by a vowel sound, most Americans use ɝː, and that is what is shown in LPD entries: **courage** ˈkʌr ɪdʒ ‖ ˈkɝː- . It should be noted, however, that there are other Americans who use ʌr, as in RP.

AmE pronunciations **not** explicitly shown in LPD include the use of ɪ rather than e before a nasal, as when **ten** is pronounced tɪn. Although this is typically a 'southern' variant, it can also be heard elsewhere, for example in California.

For most Americans ə and ɪ are not distinct as weak vowels (so that **rabbit** rhymes with **abbot**). For AmE LPD follows the rule of showing ɪ before palato-alveolar and velar consonants (ʃ, tʃ, dʒ, k, g, ŋ), and in prefixes such as re-, e-, **de-**, but ə elsewhere. Where no separate indication is given for AmE, but both ɪ and ə variants are shown for an entry, it may be assumed that AmE prefers ɪ or ə according to this rule. The actual quality used by Americans for ə varies considerably, being typically more ɪ-like when followed by a consonant but more ʌ-like when at the end of a word.

3 The English phonemic system and its notation

3.1 Vowels and diphthongs. The English vowels and diphthongs are conveniently considered in five groups (A, B, C, D, E below). There are certain differences between RP and GenAm, both in realization (vowel quality) and in the system (vowel inventory).

The **short** vowels are:

A

ɪ	kit, bid
e	dress, bed
æ	trap, bad
ɒ	(RP) lot, odd
ʌ	strut, bud
ʊ	foot, good

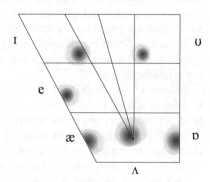

The **long vowels and diphthongs** are:

B

iː	fleece, see
eɪ	face, day
aɪ	price, high
ɔɪ	choice, boy

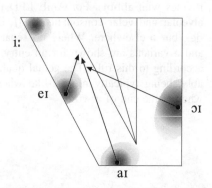

C-1 (RP)

uː	goose, two
əʊ	goat, show
aʊ	mouth, now
ɒʊ	*near-RP variant in* cold *(see 3.6)*

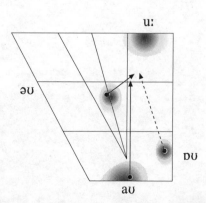

C-2 (GenAm)

uː	goose, two
oʊ	goat, show
aʊ	mouth, now

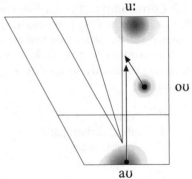

D-1 (RP)

ɪə	near, here
eə	square, fair
ɑː	start, father
ɔː	thought, law, north, war
ʊə	cure, jury, poor (*if not* ɔː)
ɜː	nurse, stir

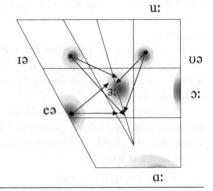

D-2 (GenAm)

ɑː	lot, odd, start, father
ɔː	thought, law (*if not* ɑː), north, war
ɝː	nurse, stir

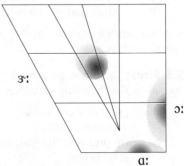

The **weak** vowels are:

E

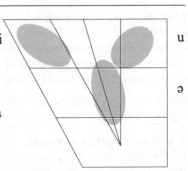

i	(happ)y, (rad)i(ation), (glor)i(ous)
ə	a(bout), (comm)a, (comm)o(n)
u	(infl)u(ence), (sit)u(ation), (biv)ou(ac)

—although the weak vowel system also includes

ɪ	i(ntend), (rabb)i(t) (*if not* ə)
ʊ	(stim)u(lus), (ed)u(cate) (*if not* ə *or* u)

and the syllabic consonants (see below).

See WEAK VOWELS.

3.2 Consonants. The English consonants are p, b, t, d, k, g, tʃ, dʒ, f, v, θ, ð, s, z, ʃ, ʒ, h, r, l, j, w, m, n, ŋ. For their classification by voicing, place, and manner, see the articles on VOICED AND VOICELESS and ARTICULATION.

The symbols p, b, t, d, k, f, v, h, r, l, w, m, n stand for the English consonant sounds usually so spelled. Keywords for the remaining consonant sounds are as follows:

		g	go, give, gag
tʃ	church	dʒ	judge
θ	thin, author, path	ð	this, other, smooth
s	cease, sister	z	zone, roses
ʃ	ship, ocean	ʒ	vision
j	yet	ŋ	sing, long, thanks

The GenAm transcriptions also make use of the symbol t̬, representing the often voiced alveolar tap used for t in certain positions, as in **atom, better**: see T-VOICING.

In words and names from foreign languages some speakers also use x (Scots *ch*, voiceless velar fricative) and ɬ (Welsh *ll*, voiceless alveolar lateral fricative), which can thus to some extent be considered marginal members of the English consonant system.

As explained at OPTIONAL SOUNDS, symbols written raised denote sounds that are sometimes optionally inserted. Likely syllabic consonants are shown in this way, since a syllabic consonant always has an optional variant involving ə and a non-syllabic consonant:

ᵊl	(midd)le, (tot)al
ᵊn	(sudd)en(ly), (serv)an(t)
ᵊr	AmE (fath)er, (stand)ar(d).

Symbols written in *italics* denote sounds sometimes omitted: hɪndʒ hinge. See OPTIONAL SOUNDS.

3.3 Stress is shown by a mark placed at the beginning of the syllable in question, as in the following examples. See further discussion in the article on STRESS.

ˈ	primary word stress	re ˈMEMber
ˌ	secondary stress	ˌACa ˈDEMic; ˈBUTter ˌFINgers
⁞	(in prefixes) stressed, but level undefined: primary or secondary as appropriate.	

LPD shows no stress mark
- on the final syllable of words such as **celebrate** ˈsel ə breɪt
- on the monosyllabic second element of an early-stressed compound or phrase, for example **selling price** ˈsel ɪŋ praɪs
- on entries that are words of one syllable, for example **time** taɪm.

Stress is always relative, and LPD's general principle is to mark it only in branching structures.

3.4 Transcription systems. There are various systems of transcription in use for English, including several which conform to the principles of the International Phonetic Alphabet. The differences between them are in many cases trivial. The system used in LPD conforms to the current de facto standard.

The user's attention is drawn to the abbreviatory conventions explained in the article on CITATION FORM, DICTIONARY ENTRY AND CONNECTED SPEECH. Other dictionaries use other abbreviatory conventions and may differ, for example, in how (if at all) syllable divisions are shown.

Early editions of Jones's *English Pronouncing Dictionary* (before 1977) used a typographically simpler, 'broad' transcription system for RP. In some parts of the world this system still persists. It involves

- i, ɔ, u for the short vowels LPD writes as ɪ, ɒ, ʊ;
- ei, ou, ai, au, ɔi, iə, ɛə, uə for the diphthongs LPD writes as eɪ, əʊ, aɪ, aʊ, ɔɪ, ɪə, eə, ʊə;
- ɔː for the long vowel LPD writes as ɜː.

The current, 15th edition of *EPD* (CUP, 1997) writes

- ɚ corresponding to LPD's ᵊr;
- ɜːr corresponding to LPD's ɜːꞏ.

For AmE, authors in the IPA tradition often use the Kenyon and Knott system, which involves

- no length marks
- ɛ for the vowel which LPD writes as e
- e, o for the normally diphthongal vowels LPD writes as eɪ, oʊ
- ɚ corresponding to LPD's ᵊr.

A different AmE tradition, that of Trager and Smith, involves

- š, ž, č, ǰ for the IPA ʃ, ʒ, tʃ, dʒ
- the representation of long vowels and diphthongs as sequences such as iy, ow, ɔh (= LPD iː, oʊ, ɔː)
- acute and grave marks over vowels (é, è) to show stress, corresponding to the IPA marks ', ˌ before the syllable.

3.5 Syllabification.
Syllable divisions are shown in LPD by spacing. This makes the transcriptions of long words easier to read and makes certain details of pronunciation more explicit.

The rhythm of a word or phrase is determined by the number and nature of the syllables it contains. Thus syllables 'carry' stress and intonation. (This is obviously particularly important for poetry and singing.) The division of a word into syllables is its **syllabification**.

The question of syllabification in English is controversial: different phoneticians hold very different views about it. The syllabification principles adopted in LPD are those which most helpfully predict the **distribution of allophones** (see PHONEME AND ALLOPHONE).

LPD assumes that there is a syllable boundary wherever there is a boundary between the elements of a compound: thus **playtime** is ˈpleɪ taɪm. It is also assumed that every word consists of whole syllables, and that a consonant cannot belong to two syllables at once. Thus **city** must be either ˈsɪt i or ˈsɪ ti – the t cannot be in both syllables. (In fact it must be the first, ˈsɪt i, because the t is pronounced in a way typical of final t: not aspirated like initial plosives, but on the contrary potentially subject to T-VOICING and glottalling (see GLOTTAL STOP).)

It is generally agreed that phonetic syllable divisions must as far as possible avoid creating consonant clusters which are not found at the edges of words. This is the **phonotactic** constraint. Thus **windy** might be ˈwɪn di or ˈwɪnd i, but it could not be ˈwɪ ndi (because English words cannot begin with nd). LPD takes the view that the syllabification of this word actually parallels its morphology: **wind+y**, 'wɪnd i. For the same reason, **language** must be 'læŋ gwɪdʒ, not 'læŋg wɪdʒ or 'læ ŋgwɪdʒ.

The principle that LPD adopts is that **consonants are syllabified with whichever of the two adjacent vowels is more strongly stressed**. If they are both unstressed, it goes with the leftward one. A **weak** vowel counts as 'less stressed' than an unstressed strong one.

In general, this principle is subject to the phonotactic constraint. However, there are some cases where correct prediction of allophones requires us to override it.

(i) Certain unstressed syllables end in a strong short vowel, even though words cannot. In **nostalgia** the t is unaspirated (as in **stack** stæk, not as in **tack** tæk), so the syllabification is (BrE) nɒ 'stældʒ ə.

(ii) r can end a syllable, even though in BrE it cannot end a word pronounced in isolation. The r in **starry** 'stɑːr i is like the r in **star is**, and different from the more forceful r in **star runner**. Likewise, ʒ can end a syllable: **vision** 'vɪʒ ᵊn.

(iii) Within a morpheme, tr and dr are not split. If **petrol** were 'pet rəl, as the phonotactic constraint leads us to expect (since English words do not end in tr), its t would likely be glottal and its r voiced (as in **rat-race** 'ræt reɪs). In fact, the tr in this word is pronounced as a voiceless affricate; so LPD syllabifies it 'petr əl.

For further discussion, please see the author's article 'Syllabification and allophony' in Ramsaran, S. (ed.), 1990, *Studies in the pronunciation of English*, London: Edward Arnold.

3.6 Phonological processes in speech.

The mark → precedes secondary pronunciations that can be regarded as derived by automatic rule from the main pronunciation. Examples of processes covered by such a rule include ASSIMILATION and the use of the special allophone ɒʊ before l in some varieties of (near-)RP:

include ɪn 'kluːd →ɪŋ 'kluːd
cold kəʊld →kɒʊld

For some speakers, a form shown with → may correspond to the way a word is stored in the mental lexicon, whereas for others the same form may be derived by phonological rule.

The mark → is not applied to phrases exemplifying STRESS SHIFT, since stress shift is shown by the symbol ◄.

In general, LPD shows results only of processes operating within the word, independently of the phonetic context afforded by surrounding words. Hence, for example, it does not show the optional variant of **ribbon** derived by perseverative ASSIMILATION ('rɪb m), since this form is restricted to cases where the following word does not begin with a vowel. But the corresponding variant of **vacant** ('veɪk ŋt) is included, since its occurrence is context-free.

4 Foreign languages

4.1 Names from foreign languages can either be pronounced in a way that imitates the foreign language or be integrated into the English sound system. Although this applies mainly to personal and geographical names, to some extent it applies to ordinary words too. Accordingly, for many such words LPD shows their pronunciation in the language of origin as well as their anglicized pronunciation. There are two reasons for this: the obvious one of giving the user information about the foreign-language pronunciation, and the less obvious one that those speakers of English who have some knowledge of the foreign language may well pronounce such words or names in a way that imitates the phonetics of the foreign language, or occupies some half-way stage between the foreign-language pronunciation and the anglicization.

Educated speakers of BrE usually know some French. So do Canadians. They will therefore try to pronounce French names in a French way. They may well use nasalized vowels (or attempts at them) and other characteristics of French pronunciation when they pronounce words they perceive as French. The sounds represented as ɒ̃, æ̃, ɔ̃ː (as in **bon, vingt-et-un**) may for this reason be regarded as marginal members of the RP vowel system. On the whole, though, it is only those whose knowledge of French goes beyond the average who succeed in differentiating the real-French vowels ɒ̃ and ɑ̃ (as in **bon** and **banc** respectively), or y and u (as in **rue** and **roue**) or in producing œ̃ rather than ɔ̃.

Educated speakers of AmE usually know some Spanish, and may incorporate some characteristics of Spanish phonetics when pronouncing Spanish words or names. Apart from Hispanics, though, most Americans would not distinguish between ɾ (**puro**) and rr (**burro**) in the way native speakers of Spanish do.

People living in Wales, whether or not they speak Welsh, can often pronounce the ɬ appropriate for many Welsh names; so can some other speakers of BrE, but usually not of AmE.

Ignorance may lead to surprising results. The German city of **München** (*Ger* ˈmʏn çən) has an English name **Munich** ˈmjuːn ɪk. But British people sometimes think that this is its German name, and attempt to pronounce it as German, producing the quite inappropriate ˈmjuːn ɪx.

Seeing the Pinyin spelling **Beijing** for the city whose traditional English name is **Peking** (Chinese ³pei ¹tɕiŋ), English speakers suppose that the letter **j** should have the same value as in French, ʒ, and say ˌbeɪ ˈʒɪŋ – whereas ˌbeɪ ˈdʒɪŋ would be much closer to the Chinese.

4.2 Transcriptions of foreign languages call for a number of phonetic symbols not included in the list of those used for English. More subtly, they call for certain differences of interpretation in some of the symbols that are also used for English. Thus the symbol t is used not only for the typically alveolar and often aspirated sound of English, but also for the typically dental and unaspirated sound of French. IPA symbols must always be allowed a certain leeway in their interpretation if the transcription is not to be intolerably burdened with diacritic details.

In transcriptions of German, Danish, Swedish, Norwegian, Icelandic, Welsh, Irish, Scottish Gaelic, and Japanese, voiceless plosives may be assumed to be aspirated, at least when at the beginning of a stressed syllable, much as in English.

Voiced obstruents in these languages, as in English, may be susceptible to devoicing. In all other foreign languages both plosives and affricates should be assumed to be unaspirated unless explicitly marked as aspirated. Thus both syllables in the Chinese pronunciation of **Beijing** [³pei ¹tɕiŋ] start with voiceless unaspirated consonants, which sound similar to the devoiced /b, dʒ/ of English. In certain cases, including notably Hindi, Chinese, and Korean, aspiration is distinctive in both plosives and affricates.

In general, the transcription LPD uses for foreign languages is a phonemic one for the language in question, sometimes modified in the direction of greater phonetic explicitness. Thus the French vowel of **vin** is shown as æ̃, rather than the more customary ɛ̃, because of the phonetic similarity to the vowel quality of English æ. In Spanish, LPD distinguishes between the plosive and the fricative/approximant allophones of b, d, g, since they sound so different to the English ear. Because LPD uses r for the English consonant as in **red**, it transcribes ɾ or ɾɾ in languages that typically have a tongue-tip tapped or rolled r-sound, and ʁ for those that typically have a uvular r-sound.

No stress-marks are used in the transcription of French and Hindi, since these languages have no lexical stress. Nevertheless, there may often appear to be stress on the final syllable of French words and on long vowels in Hindi words.

Japanese pitch-accent is shown in accordance with IPA principles, although this differs from notation that is customary among Japanese scholars. Namely, the accent, if there is one in the word, is shown by the mark ['] **before** the accented mora; this is the mora after which the pitch is typically lower. The pitch upstep that occurs automatically on the second mora of words not bearing an accent on the first two moras is shown as [ˌ]. This mark is not used before a moraic obstruent.

In transcriptions of Swedish and other languages with two types of word-stress, the mark '' denotes tone 2. In Chinese (Putonghua), the tones are as follows:

1.	high level	[¹ma]	mā *mother*
2.	rising	[²ma]	má *hemp*
3.	low fall-rise	[³ma]	mǎ *horse*
4.	falling	[⁴ma]	mà *to scold*

In Cantonese, they are

1.	high level/ high fall	[¹fan]	*to separate*
2.	high rise	[²fan]	*powder*
3.	mid level	[³fan]	*to sleep*
4.	low fall	[⁴fan]	*tomb*
5.	low rise	[⁵fan]	*to work hard*
6.	lowish level	[⁶fan]	*participation*

5 Symbols

5.1 Phonetic symbols This list includes both the symbols used for English and other symbols of the International Phonetic Alphabet that appear in LPD. These general-phonetic symbols are used for transcribing words in foreign languages and occasionally also for allophonic transcription of English. Their meaning is in most cases somewhat flexible: for example, the symbol e stands for a range of similar but not identical vowel qualities in Danish, German, French, Spanish, Japanese, and English.

For the meaning of the terms used in the definitions, see note at ARTICULATION. 'Chinese' means the Pinyin romanization.

a	open front unrounded vowel; also for open vowel between front and back; French/German/Italian/Spanish *a*; first element of English diphthongs in *price, high* (aɪ), and *mouth, how* (aʊ)
ɑ	open back unrounded vowel; English *father* (ɑː)
ɑ̃	nasalized open back unrounded vowel, French *an*
æ	raised open front unrounded vowel; English *trap, bad*
æ̃	nasalized raised open front unrounded vowel, French *in*
ɐ	open variety of [ə], German *-er*
b	voiced bilabial plosive, English *b*
β	voiced bilabial fricative, Spanish *b/v* between vowels
ɓ	voiced bilabial implosive (glottalic ingressive plosive), Zulu *b*
c	voiceless palatal plosive, like [kj]
ç	voiceless palatal fricative, German *ich*
d	voiced alveolar (sometimes: dental) plosive, English *d*
dʒ	voiced palato-alveolar affricate, English *j*
dr	voiced post-alveolar affricate, English *dr*
dʑ	voiced alveolo-palatal affricate, Japanese *j*
ð	voiced dental fricative, in English *father*
d̪	voiced dental plosive (where dentality is distinctive)
ɖ	voiced retroflex plosive
ðˤ	pharyngealized ('emphatic') [ð]
e	close-mid front unrounded vowel, French *é*; also for vowel between close-mid and open-mid, English *dress*; first element of English diphthongs in *face* (eɪ) and (RP) *square* (eə)
ɛ	open-mid front unrounded vowel, French *è*
ə	mid central unrounded vowel; English vowel at beginning of *about* and at end of *comma*; first element of RP diphthong in *goat, blow* (əʊ); second element of RP diphthongs in *near, square, cure*
ɚ	rhotacized [ə], in GenAm *better* (= syllabic [r])
ɜ	mid central unrounded vowel, RP *nurse, stir* (ɜː)
ɝ	rhotacized [ɜ], GenAm *nurse, stir* (ɝː)
f	voiceless labiodental fricative, English *f*
g	voiced velar plosive, English 'hard' *g*
ɣ	voiced velar fricative (= voiced [x])
h	voiceless glottal fricative, English *h*
ħ	voiceless pharyngeal fricative

h	aspiration
i	close front unrounded vowel, French *i*; English *fleece, key* (iː); English neutralization of iː-ɪ, *happy*
ɪ	lax (lowered-centralized) [i], English *kit*; second element of English diphthongs in *face, price, choice*
ɨ	close central unrounded vowel, Polish *y*, Russian ы, north Welsh *u*
i̥	voiceless [i]
j	voiced palatal approximant (semivowel), English *y* in *yet*
ɟ	voiced palatal plosive, like [ɡj]
ʲ	palatalized, [i]-coloured (e.g. tʲ = palatalized t)
k	voiceless velar plosive, English *k*
l	voiced alveolar lateral, English *l*
ɫ	velarized voiced alveolar lateral, English 'dark' l
ɬ	voiceless alveolar lateral fricative, Welsh *ll*
ʎ	voiced palatal lateral, Italian *gl*
m	voiced bilabial nasal, English *m*
m̥	voiceless bilabial nasal
n	voiced alveolar (sometimes: dental) nasal, English *n*
n̪	voiced dental nasal (where dentality is distinctive)
ŋ	voiced velar nasal, English *ng*
ɲ	voiced palatal nasal, Spanish *ñ*
ɳ	voiced retroflex nasal
N	voiced uvular nasal; Japanese *-n*, alternatively pronounced as a nasalized close back vowel
o	close-mid back rounded vowel, French *o*; also for back rounded vowel between close-mid and open-mid, Spanish *o*; first element of AmE diphthong in *goat, blow* (oʊ)
ɔ	open-mid back rounded vowel; English *north, thought*; first element of English diphthong in *choice*; French o in *pomme*
ɔ̃	nasalized open-mid back rounded vowel, French *on*
ɒ	open back rounded vowel; RP *lot*; first element of BrE diphthong variant in *cold* (ɒʊ)
ø	close-mid front rounded vowel, in French *deux*, German *schön*
œ	open-mid front rounded vowel, in French *neuf*, German *plötzlich*
œ̃	nasalized open-mid front rounded vowel, French *un*
p	voiceless bilabial plosive, English *p*
ɸ	voiceless bilabial fricative, Japanese *f*
q	voiceless uvular plosive, Arabic *q*
r	voiced post-alveolar approximant, English *red* (this differs from the usual IPA value, which is a trill, LPD's rr)
ɾ	voiced alveolar tap, Spanish single *r*
rr	voiced alveolar trill, Spanish initial *r* or double *rr*
ʈ	voiced retroflex flap
ʁ	voiced uvular fricative/approximant, French *r*
s	voiceless alveolar fricative, English *s*
ʃ	voiceless palato-alveolar fricative, English *sh*
ç	voiceless alveolo-palatal fricative, Japanese *sh*, Chinese *x*
ʂ	voiceless retroflex fricative, Chinese *sh*
sˤ	pharyngealized ('emphatic') [s]

t	voiceless alveolar (sometimes: dental) plosive, English *t*
t̬	alveolar tap, usually voiced, AmE *t* in *city*
tʃ	voiceless palato-alveolar affricate, English *ch*
tr	voiceless post-alveolar affricate, English *tr*
tɕ	voiceless alveolopalatal affricate, Japanese *ch*, Chinese *q*
t̪	voiceless dental plosive (where dentality is distinctive)
θ	voiceless dental fricative, English *th*
ʈ	voiceless retroflex plosive
tˁ	pharyngealized ('emphatic') [t]
u	close back rounded vowel, French *ou*; English *goose* (uː); English neutralization of uː-ʊ, *thank you*
ʊ	lax (lowered-centralized) [u], English *foot*; second element in English diphthongs in *mouth, goat*
ʉ	close central rounded vowel, Swedish *u*
ɯ	close back unrounded vowel, Japanese *u*
ɯ̥	voiceless [ɯ]
ɰ	voiced velar approximant (semivowel), Japanese *w*
v	voiced labiodental fricative, English *v*
ʋ	voiced labiodental approximant, Dutch *w*
ʌ	open-mid back unrounded vowel; also for open-mid unrounded vowel between back and front, English *strut, love*
w	voiced labial-velar approximant (semivowel), English *w*
ʍ	voiceless labial-velar fricative/approximant, Scottish *wh*
x	voiceless velar fricative, German *ach*, Spanish *jota*
χ	voiceless uvular fricative, Welsh *ch*
y	close front rounded vowel, in French *lune*, German *über*
ʏ	lax (lowered-centralized) [y], in German *hübsch*
ɥ	voiced labial-palatal approximant (semivowel), in French *huit*
z	voiced alveolar fricative, English *z*
ʒ	voiced palato-alveolar fricative, in English *measure*
ʑ	voiced alveopalatal fricative, second element of Japanese *j*
ʔ	glottal plosive, glottal stop
ʕ	voiced pharyngeal fricative/approximant, Arabic *'ayn*
|	voiceless dental click, Zulu *c*
‖	voiceless lateral click, Zulu *x*
ˈ	primary word stress (re 'MEMber)
ˌ	secondary stress (ˌACa 'DEMic)
ˌ	stress (= ' or ˌ as appropriate)
ː	length

5.2 Other symbols

‖	GenAm pronunciation follows (see p. xiv–xv)
§	BrE non-RP (see p. xiii)
⚠	pronunciation considered incorrect (see p. xiv)
◄	stress shift possible (see p. xx)
→	variant derived by rule (see p. xx)
‿	possible compression (see p. 165)
(!)	pronunciation unexpected for this spelling

(*)	RP and GenAm differ in an unpredictable and striking way
=	is pronounced the same as
+	(in prefix) attracts consonant from next syllable
~	recapitulates headword up to |, otherwise all of headword
|	end of part to be recapitulated
-	recapitulates as many syllables from the main or preceding pronunciation as it contains, minus the number of syllables preceding/following this mark (count syllables by counting spaces plus _ and • symbols)
•	recapitulates one syllable from the main or preceding pronunciation
/	the orthographic version with or without the part following this sign corresponds respectively to the pronunciation with or without the part following this sign

A a

a   Spelling-to-sound

1 Where the spelling is **a**, the pronunciation differs according to whether the vowel is short or long, followed or not by **r**, and strong or weak.

2 The 'strong' pronunciation is regularly
æ, as in **cat** kæt ('short A'), or
eɪ, as in **face** feɪs ('long A').

3 Where **a** is followed by **r**, the 'strong' pronunciation is
ɑː, as in **start** stɑːt ‖ stɑːrt, or
eə ‖ e, as in **square** skweə ‖ skwer;
or, indeed there may be the regular 'short' pronunciation
æ, as in **carol** 'kær əl (although in this position many speakers of GenAm use e, thus 'ker əl).

4 Less frequently, the 'strong' pronunciation is
ɑː, as in **father** 'fɑːð ə ‖ 'fɑːð ªr,
ɑː ‖ æ, as in **bath** bɑːθ ‖ bæθ,
ɒ ‖ ɑː, as in **watch** wɒtʃ ‖ wɑːtʃ (especially after w),
ɔː, as in **talk** tɔːk (especially before l), **warm** wɔːm ‖ wɔːrm.

5 The 'weak' pronunciation is
ə, as in **about** ə 'baʊt, or
ɪ, as in **village** 'vɪl ɪdʒ.
Because of COMPRESSION, **a** is usually silent in the ending **-ally**, as in **basically** 'beɪs ɪk li.
Note that where the spelling is **a** the pronunciation is never ʌ.

6 **a** also forms part of the digraphs **ai, au, aw, ay**.

ai, ay   Spelling-to-sound

1 Where the spelling is one of the digraphs **ai, ay**, the pronunciation is regularly
eɪ, as in **rain** reɪn, **day** deɪ;
or, before **r**,
eə ‖ e, as in **fair** feə ‖ fer.

2 Occasionally with these digraphs the pronunciation is 'weak':
ə, as in **curtain** 'kɜːt ªn ‖ 'kɜːt ªn (for a few speakers ɪ, thus 'kɜːt ɪn), or
i, as in **Murray** 'mʌr i ‖ 'mɜː i, when at the end of a word. (For **Monday**, etc., see note at **-day**.)

A

3 Note also the exceptional words **says, said, again, against**, usually pronounced with e.

au, aw   Spelling-to-sound

1 Where the spelling is one of the digraphs **au** and **aw**, the pronunciation is regularly
ɔː, as in **author** ˈɔːθ ə ‖ ˈɔːθ ᵊr, **law** lɔː.

2 In a few words, the pronunciation is
ɑː ‖ æ, as in **laugh** lɑːf ‖ læf;
or, in loanwords from foreign languages,
əʊ ‖ oʊ, as in **gauche**, or aʊ, as in **sauerkraut**;
or, in BrE only,
ɒ, as in **sausage** ˈsɒs ɪdʒ.

A, a *name of letter* eɪ **A's, As, a's** eɪz
—*Communications code name:* Alfa
ˌA'1◄, ˌA-'1; ˌA1(ˈM); ˌA, 30'3 —*These patterns apply to all British road numbers.*
ˌA'4◄; ˌA4 'paper
a *indef article, before a consonant sound, strong form* eɪ, *weak form* ə —*See also* an
a *Latin prep* eɪ ɑː —*See also phrases with this word*
a, à *French prep* æ ɑː —*See also phrases with this word*
a- *comb. form* ˈeɪ, eɪ, ˈæ, æ, ə —*When it has a negative meaning, this prefix is usually* eɪ
(ˌathe'istic), *though in some words there are alternative pronunciations with* æ *or* ə
(ₒa'moral), *and sometimes* ə *is the only form* (a'morphous). *With other meanings, the pronunciation is regularly* ə (a'way, a'spire), *unless stressed because of a suffix, in which case it is* ˈæ (ˌaspi'ration).
Aachen ˈɑːk ən —*Ger* [ˈʔɑː xən]
aah ɑː **aah'd, aahed** ɑːd **aahing, aah'ing** ˈɑːr ɪŋ ‖ ˈɑː ɪŋ **aahs, aah's** ɑːz
Aalborg ˈɔːl bɔːɡ ˈɑːl- ‖ -bɔːrɡ —*Danish* Ålborg [ˈʌl bɒːˀ]
Aalto ˈɑːlt əʊ ‖ -oʊ —*Finnish* [ˈɑːl to]
aardvark ˈɑːd vɑːk ‖ ˈɑːrd vɑːrk **~s** s
aard|wolf ˈɑːd ˌwʊlf ‖ ˈɑːrd- **~wolves** wʊlvz
Aarhus ˈɔː huːs ˈɑː-, -hʊs ‖ ˈɔːr- ˈɑːr- —*Danish* Århus [ˈɔː huːˀs]
Aaron (i) ˈeər ən ‖ ˈer ən, (ii) ˈær ən ‖ ˈer- —*In BrE traditionally (i), and still usually so for the biblical character; but the personal name may nowadays be either (i) or (ii)*
Aaronic ₍ₒₑə ˈrɒn ɪk ◄ ‖ æ ˈrɑːn ɪk e-
ab æb —*See also phrases with this word* **abs** æbz
AB ˌeɪ ˈbiː **~s, ~'s** z
ab- ₍ₒˈæb, əb —*As a true prefix meaning 'away', ab- is usually* æb, *though with unstressed and*

reduced-vowel variants (ab'duct). *It is always* ˈæb *when it means 'cgs unit'* ('abvolt, ˌab'coulomb). *With a vaguer meaning, it is mostly* əb (ab'stain) *unless stressed* ('abdicate, 'abstract).
aback ə ˈbæk
Abaco ˈæb ə kəʊ ‖ -koʊ
abacus ˈæb ək əs **~es** ɪz əz
Abadan ˌæb ə ˈdɑːn -ˈdæn
Abaddon ə ˈbæd ən
abaft ə ˈbɑːft §-ˈbæft ‖ ə ˈbæft
abalone ˌæb ə ˈləʊn i ‖ -ˈloʊn- **~s** z
abandon ə ˈbænd ən **~ed** d **~ing** ɪŋ **~s** z
abandonment ə ˈbænd ən mənt →ə̃m-
abase ə ˈbeɪs **abased** ə ˈbeɪst **abases** ə ˈbeɪs ɪz -əz **abasing** ə ˈbeɪs ɪŋ
abasement ə ˈbeɪs mənt
abash ə ˈbæʃ **abashed** ə ˈbæʃt **abashes** ə ˈbæʃ ɪz -əz **abashing** ə ˈbæʃ ɪŋ
abashment ə ˈbæʃ mənt
abate ə ˈbeɪt **abated** ə ˈbeɪt ɪd -əd ‖ ə ˈbeɪt̬ əd **abates** ə ˈbeɪts **abating** ə ˈbeɪt ɪŋ ‖ ə ˈbeɪt̬ ɪŋ
abatement ə ˈbeɪt mənt **~s** s
abatis, abattis ˈæb ət ɪs §-əs; ˌæb ə ˈtiː, ˈ•••‖ -ət̬ əs -ə tiː **~es** *pl after* s *forms* ɪz əz; *for those who pronounce* -iː, *the pl is written as the sing. but pronounced with added* z
abattoir ˈæb ə twɑː ‖ -twɑːr -twɔːr **~s** z
Abba ˈæb ə
abbac|y ˈæb əs li **~ies** iz
Abbado ə ˈbɑːd əʊ ‖ -oʊ —*It* [ab ˈbaː do]
Abbas (i) ˈæb əs, (ii) ə ˈbɑːs
Abbasid ə ˈbæs ɪd ˈæb əs-, §-əd **~s** z
abbatial ə ˈbeɪʃ ᵊl
abbe, abbé, A~ ˈæb eɪ ‖ æ ˈbeɪ ˈæb eɪ —*Fr* [a be] **~s** z
Abberton ˈæb ət ən ‖ -ᵊrt ᵊn
abbess ˈæb es -ɪs, §-əs; æ ˈbes ‖ -əs **~es** ɪz əz
Abbeville ˈæb vɪl ˈæb ɪ vɪl, -ə- ‖ æb ˈviːᵊl ˈæb i vɪl —*Fr* [ab vil]

A

Abbevillian ˌæb ˈvɪl i_ən ◄ ˌæb ɪ ˈvɪl-, §ˌæb ə-
abbey, Abbey ˈæb i ~s z
Abbie ˈæb i
abbot, Abbot ˈæb ət ~s s
Abbotsbury ˈæb əts bər_i ‖ -ˌber i
abbotship ˈæb ət ʃɪp ~s s
Abbott ˈæb ət
abbrevi|ate ə ˈbriːv i |eɪt ~ated eɪt ɪd -əd
  ‖ eɪt̬ əd ~ates eɪts ~ating eɪt ɪŋ ‖ eɪt̬ ɪŋ
abbreviation ə ˌbriːv i ˈeɪʃ ən ~s z
abbreviator ə ˈbriːv i eɪt ə ‖ -eɪt̬ ər ~s z
abbreviatory ə ˈbriːv i_ət_ər i ə ˌbriːv i ˈeɪt
  ər i ◄ ‖ -i_ə tɔːr i -tour i
Abbs æbz
Abby ˈæb i
ABC ˌeɪ biː ˈsiː ABCs ˌeɪ biː ˈsiːz
abdabs ˈæb dæbz
Abdela æb ˈdel ə
abdi|cate ˈæbd ɪ |keɪt -ə- ~cated keɪt ɪd -əd
  ‖ keɪt̬ əd ~cates keɪts ~cating
  keɪt ɪŋ ‖ keɪt̬ ɪŋ
abdication ˌæbd ɪ ˈkeɪʃ ən -ə- ~s z
abdomen ˈæbd əm ən ən -ɪn, -ə men; æb ˈdəʊm-
  ~s z
abdominal æb ˈdɒm ɪn əl əb-, -ən əl ‖ -ˈdɑːm-
  ~ly i ~s z
abduct ₍ˌ₎æb ˈdʌkt əb- ~ed ɪd əd ~ing ɪŋ ~s s
abduction ₍ˌ₎æb ˈdʌk ʃən əb- ~s z
abductor ₍ˌ₎æb ˈdʌkt ə əb- ‖ -ər ~s z
Abdul ˈæbd ʊl -əl
Abdulla, Abdullah æb ˈdʌl ə əb-, -ˈdʊl-
  —Arabic [ab ˈdʊɫ ɫah]
Abe short for Abraham eɪb
à Becket ə ˈbek ɪt §-ət
abed ə ˈbed
Abednego ˌæb ed ˈniːg əʊ ə ˈbed nɪ gəʊ, -nə-
  ‖ ə ˈbed nɪ goʊ
Abel ˈeɪb əl
Abelard ˈæb ə lɑːd -ɪ- ‖ -lɑːrd —Fr [a be laːʁ]
abele ə ˈbiːəl ˈeɪb əl
Abelian ə ˈbiːl i_ən
abelmosk ˈeɪb əl mɒsk ‖ -mɑːsk
Aber ˈæb ə ‖ -ər
Aberaeron, Aberayron ˌæb ər ˈaɪᵊr ən ‖ -ər-
  —Welsh [a ber ˈəi ron]
Aberavon ˌæb ər ˈæv ən ‖ -ər- —Welsh
  Aberafan [a ber ˈa van]
Abercon|way ˌæb ə ˈkɒn |weɪ ‖ -ər ˈkɑːn- ~wy
  wi
Abercorn ˈæb ə kɔːn ‖ -ər kɔːrn
Abercrombie, Abercromby (i) ˈæb ə ˌkrʌm bi
  ˌ•ˈ••• ‖ ˈæb ər-, (ii) -ˌkrɒm bi ˌ•ˈ•••
  ‖ -ˌkrɑːm-
Aberdare ˌæb ə ˈdeə ‖ -ər ˈdeʳr -ˈdæʳr
Aberdaron ˌæb ə ˈdær ən ‖ -ər- -ˈder-
Aberdeen place in Scotland ˌæb ə ˈdiːn ‖ -ər-
  —but places in the US are ˈ••• ~shire ʃə
  -ʃɪə, §-ʃɑr_ə ‖ ʃɪr -ʃʳr
Aberdonian ˌæb ə ˈdəʊn i_ən ◄ ‖ -ər ˈdoʊn- ~s
  z
Aberdour ˌæb ə ˈdaʊ_ə ‖ -ər ˈdaʊ_ər
Aberdovey ˌæb ə ˈdʌv i ‖ -ər-

Aberfan ˌæb ə ˈvæn ‖ -ᵊr- —also,
  inappropriately, -ˈfæn —Welsh [a ber ˈvan]
Aberfeldy ˌæb ə ˈfeld i ‖ -ᵊr-
Aberffraw ə ˈbeə frau ‖ -ˈber-
Aberfoyle ˌæb ə ˈfɔɪᵊl ‖ -ᵊr-
Abergavenny ˌæb ə gə ˈven i ‖ ˌæb ᵊr- —as a
  family name also ˌæb ə ˈgen i ‖ -ᵊr-
Abergele ˌæb ə ˈgel i -eɪ ‖ -ᵊr- —Welsh
  [a ber ˈge le]
Abermule ˌæb ə ˈmjuːl ‖ -ᵊr-
Abernethy, a~ ˌæb ə ˈneθ i -ˈniːθ- ‖ -ᵊr- ˈ••••
Aberporth ˌæb ə ˈpɔːθ ‖ -ᵊr ˈpɔːrθ
aberranc|e æ ˈber ən̩ts ə-, ˈæb ᵊr- ~es ɪz əz
  ~y i
aberrant æ ˈber ənt ə-, ˈæb ᵊr- ~ly li
aberration ˌæb ə ˈreɪʃ ən ~s z
Abersoch ˌæb ə ˈsəʊk -ˈsɒk ‖ -ᵊr ˈsouk —Welsh
  [a ber ˈsoːχ]
Abersychan ˌæb ə ˈsɪk ən -ˈsʌk- ‖ -ᵊr- —Welsh
  [a ber ˈsə χan]
Abertillery ˌæb ə tɪ ˈleər i -təˈ•- ‖ -ᵊr tə ˈler i
Aberystwyth ˌæb ə ˈrɪst wɪθ —Welsh
  [a ber ˈə sduɨθ]
abet ə ˈbet abets ə ˈbets abetted ə ˈbet ɪd
  -əd ‖ ə ˈbet̬ əd abetting ə ˈbet ɪŋ ‖ ə ˈbet̬ ɪŋ
abetment ə ˈbet mənt
abetter, abettor ə ˈbet ə ‖ ə ˈbet̬ ər ~s z
abey|ance ə ˈbeɪ |ən̩ts ~ant ənt
Ab Fab ˌæb ˈfæb
abhor əb ˈhɔː æb-, ə ˈbɔː ‖ æb ˈhɔːr əb-
  abhorred əb ˈhɔːd æb-, ə ˈbɔːd ‖ æb ˈhɔːrd
  əb- abhorring əb ˈhɔːr ɪŋ æb-, ə ˈbɔːr-
  ‖ æb- əb- abhors əb ˈhɔːz æb-, ə ˈbɔːz
  ‖ æb ˈhɔːrz əb-
abhorrence əb ˈhɒr ən̩ts æb-, ə ˈbɒr-
  ‖ æb ˈhɔːr ən̩ts əb-, -ˈhɑːr-
abhorrent əb ˈhɒr ənt æb-, ə ˈbɒr- ‖ æb ˈhɔːr
  ənt əb-, -ˈhɑːr- ~ly li
abide ə ˈbaɪd abided ə ˈbaɪd ɪd -əd abides
  ə ˈbaɪdz abiding/ly ə ˈbaɪd ɪŋ /li abode
  ə ˈbəʊd ‖ ə ˈboud
Abidjan ˌæb i ˈdʒɑːn -ˈdʒæn —Fr [a bid ʒɑ̃]
Abigail, a~ ˈæb ɪ geɪᵊl §-ə-
Abilene places in TX, KS ˈæb ə liːn -ɪ-
abilit|y ə ˈbɪl ət |i -ɪt- ‖ -ət̬ i ~ies iz
-ability ə ˈbɪl ət i -ɪt- ‖ -ət̬ i —A word with this
  suffix has a secondary stress in the same place
  as the primary stress in the corresponding word
  with -able (ˌcookaˈbility, ˌpreferaˈbility).
Abingdon ˈæb ɪŋ dən
Abinger ˈæb ɪndʒ ə ‖ -ər
ab initio ˌæb ɪ ˈnɪʃ i əʊ ˌ•ə-, -ˈnɪs- ‖ -ou
abiotic ˌeɪ baɪ ˈɒt ɪk ◄ ‖ -ˈɑːt̬ ɪk ◄
abject ˈæb dʒekt ~ly li
abjection æb ˈdʒek ʃən
abjuration ˌæb dʒʊ ˈreɪʃ ən -dʒɔː-, -dʒə-
  ‖ -dʒə-
abjure əb ˈdʒʊə æb-, -ˈdʒɔː ‖ æb ˈdʒʊʳr -d d
  ~s z abjuring əb ˈdʒʊər ɪŋ æb-, -ˈdʒɔːr-
  ‖ æb ˈdʒʊr ɪŋ
Abkhazi|a æb ˈkɑːz i_|ə -ˈkeɪz- ~an/s ən/z
ab|late ₍ˌ₎æb |ˈleɪt ~lated ˈleɪt ɪd -əd ‖ ˈleɪt̬ əd
  ~lates ˈleɪts ~lating ˈleɪt ɪŋ ‖ ˈleɪt̬ ɪŋ

A

ablation ₍ᵢ₎æb 'leɪʃ ᵊn
ablatival ˌæb lə 'taɪv ᵊl ◄
ablative *case* 'æb lət ɪv ‖ -lət̬- ~s z
    ˌablative 'absolute
ablative *'ablating'* ₍ᵢ₎æb 'leɪt ɪv ‖ -'leɪt̬ ɪv
ablaut 'æb laʊt —*Ger* ['ʔap laʊt]
ablaze ə 'bleɪz
able 'eɪb ᵊl   abler 'eɪb lə ‖ -lᵊr   ablest 'eɪb lɪst
    -ləst
-able əb ᵊl —*In general, this suffix is stress-neutral* (in'terpretable, de'sirable, com'municable). *There are, however, some important exceptions* ('admirable, 'preferable, 'reputable), *and speakers disagree for some words* (applicable, comparable, formidable, hospitable, irrevocable, lamentable, transferable) — *see individual entries.*
able-bodied ˌeɪb ᵊl 'bɒd id ◄ ‖ -'bɑːd-
ablution ə 'bluːʃ ᵊn æ- ~s z
ably 'eɪb li
-ably əb li —*The stress is always as in the corresponding* -able *form.*
abnegation ˌæb nɪ 'geɪʃ ᵊn -nə-, -ne-
Abner 'æb nə ‖ -nᵊr
Abney 'æb ni
abnormal ₍ᵢ₎æb 'nɔːm ᵊl əb- ‖ -'nɔːrm- ~ly i
abnormalit|y ˌæb nɔː 'mæl ət li ˌ•nə-, -ɪt i
    ‖ -nɔːr 'mæl ət̬ li ~ies iz
Abo, abo *'aboriginal'* 'æb əʊ ‖ -oʊ ~s z
ABO *blood type classification* ˌeɪ biː 'əʊ ‖ -'oʊ
aboard ə 'bɔːd ‖ ə 'bɔːrd -'boʊrd
abode ə 'bəʊd ‖ ə 'boʊd ~s z
abolish ə 'bɒl ɪʃ ‖ ə 'bɑːl- ~ed t ~es ɪz əz
    ~ing ɪŋ
abolition ˌæb ə 'lɪʃ ᵊn ~ism ˌɪz əm ~ist/s
    ˌɪst/s ˌəst/s
abomas|um ˌæb əʊ 'meɪs |əm ‖ -oʊ- ~a ə
A-bomb 'eɪ bɒm ‖ -bɑːm ~s z
abominab|le ə 'bɒm ɪn əb |ᵊl -ən̩ əb-
    ‖ ə 'bɑːm- ~ly li
    a ˌbominable 'snowman, •'•••, ••
abomi|nate ə 'bɒm ɪ |neɪt -ə- ‖ ə 'bɑːm-
    ~nated neɪt ɪd -əd ‖ neɪt̬ əd ~nates neɪts
    ~nating neɪt ɪŋ ‖ neɪt̬ ɪŋ
abomination ə ˌbɒm ɪ 'neɪʃ ᵊn -ə- ‖ ə ˌbɑːm-
    ~s z
aboriginal, A~ ˌæb ə 'rɪdʒ ᵊn_ᵊl ◄-ɪn ᵊl ~ly i
aboriginalit|y, A~ ˌæb ə ˌrɪdʒ ə 'næl ət li-ɪ-'•-, -ɪt li ‖ -ət̬ li ~ies iz
aborigine, A~ ˌæb ə 'rɪdʒ ᵊn_i-ɪn i ~s z
aborning ə 'bɔːn ɪŋ ‖ ə 'bɔːrn ɪŋ
abort ə 'bɔːt ‖ ə 'bɔːrt   aborted ə 'bɔːt ɪd-əd
    ‖ ə 'bɔːrt̬ əd   aborting ə 'bɔːt ɪŋ ‖ ə 'bɔːrt̬ ɪŋ
    aborts ə 'bɔːts ‖ ə 'bɔːrts
abortifacient ə ˌbɔːt ɪ 'feɪʃ ᵊnt §-ə-, -'feɪʃ i_ənt
    ‖ ə ˌbɔːrt̬ ə- ~s s
abortion ə 'bɔːʃ ᵊn ‖ ə 'bɔːrʃ- ~s z
abortionist ə 'bɔːʃ ᵊn_ɪst §_əst ‖ ə 'bɔːrʃ- ~s s
abortive ə 'bɔːt ɪv ‖ ə 'bɔːrt̬ ɪv ~ly li
abound ə 'baʊnd   abounded ə 'baʊnd ɪd-əd
    abounding/ly ə 'baʊnd ɪŋ /li   abounds
    ə 'baʊndz
about ə 'baʊt

about-fac|e ə ˌbaʊt 'feɪs •'•• ~ed t ~es ɪz əz
    ~ing ɪŋ
about-turn ə ˌbaʊt 'tɜːn ‖ -'tɜːrn ~ed d ~ing
    ɪŋ ~s z
above ə 'bʌv
aboveboard ə ˌbʌv 'bɔːd ◄ •'•• ‖ ə 'bʌv bɔːrd
    -boʊrd
above-mentioned ə ˌbʌv 'menʃ ᵊnd ◄
    the a ˌbove- ˌmentioned 'facts
Aboyne ə 'bɔɪn
abracadabra ˌæb rə kə 'dæb rə
abrad|e ə 'breɪd ~ed ɪd əd ~es z ~ing ɪŋ
Abraham 'eɪb rə hæm -həm ~s z
Abram *place in Greater Manchester* 'æb rəm
    'ɑːb-, -ræm
Abrams 'eɪb rəmz
Abramson 'eɪb rəm sən
abrasion ə 'breɪʒ ᵊn ~s z
abrasive ə 'breɪs ɪv -'breɪz- ~ly li ~s z
abraxas, A~ ə 'bræks əs
abreact ˌæb ri 'ækt ~ed ɪd əd ~ing ɪŋ ~s s
abreaction ˌæb ri 'æk ʃᵊn ~s z
abreast ə 'brest
abridg|e ə 'brɪdʒ ~ed d ~es ɪz əz ~ing ɪŋ
Abridge 'eɪ brɪdʒ
abridgement, abridgment ə 'brɪdʒ mənt ~s s
abroad ə 'brɔːd ‖ -'brɑːd *(!)*
abro|gate 'æb rə |geɪt ~gated geɪt ɪd-əd
    ‖ geɪt̬ əd ~gates geɪts ~gating
    geɪt ɪŋ ‖ geɪt̬ ɪŋ
abrogation ˌæb rə 'geɪʃ ᵊn
abrupt ə 'brʌpt ~ly li ~ness nəs nɪs
Abruzzi ə 'bruts i —*It* [a 'brut tsi]
ABS ˌeɪ biː 'es
Absalom 'æb səl əm
abscess 'æb ses -sɪs, §-səs ~ed t ~es ɪz əz
absciss|a æb 'sɪs |ə əb- ~ae iː ~as əz
abscission æb 'sɪʃ ᵊn -'sɪʒ-
abscond əb 'skɒnd æb- ‖ -'skɑːnd ~ed ɪd əd
    ~er/s ə/z ‖ ᵊr/z ~ing ɪŋ ~s z
Abse 'æbz i
abseil 'æb seɪᵊl 'æp-, -saɪᵊl ~ed d ~ing ɪŋ ~s
    z
absenc|e 'æb sᵊnts ~es ɪz əz
absent *adj* 'æb sᵊnt ~ly li
ab|sent *v* æb |'sent əb- ~sented 'sent ɪd-əd
    ‖ 'sent̬ əd ~senting 'sent ɪŋ ‖ 'sent̬ ɪŋ
    ~sents 'sents
absentee ˌæb sᵊn 'tiː ◄ ~s z
absenteeism ˌæb sᵊn 'tiː ˌɪz əm
absentia æb 'sent i_ə əb-, -'sentʃ-
absently 'æb sᵊnt li
absent-minded ˌæb sᵊnt 'maɪnd ɪd ◄-əd ~ly li
    ~ness nəs nɪs
    ˌabsent ˌminded pro'fessor
absinth, absinthe 'æb sɪntθ-sæ̃θ
absit omen ˌæb sɪt 'əʊm en ‖ -sɪt 'oʊm-
absolute 'æb sə luːt -ljuːt, ˌ••'•◄ ~ness nəs
    nɪs
absolutely 'æb sə luːt li-ljuːt li, ˌ••'••◄
    —*There are also casual rapid-speech forms*
    'æbs i, 'æbs li
absolution ˌæb sə 'luːʃ ᵊn -'ljuːʃ- ~s z

absolutism 'æb sə luːt ˌɪz əm -sə ljuːt-, ˌ•ˈ•'•-
‖ -luːtַ ˌɪz əm
absolutive ˌæb sə 'luːt ɪv ◄ -'ljuːt- ‖ -'luːtַ- ~**s**
z
absolv|e əb 'zɒlv §æb-, §-'zəʊlv ‖ -'zɑːlv
-'sɑːlv, -'zɔːlv, -'sɔːlv ~**ed** d ~**es** z ~**ing** ɪŋ

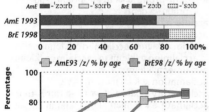

ABSORB

AmE ■-'zɔːrb ▨-'sɔːrb BrE ■-'zɔːb ▥-'sɔːb					

AmE 1993					
BrE 1998					
	0	20	40	60	80	100%

▨ AmE93 /z/ % by age ▨ BrE98 /z/ % by age

Percentage (vertical axis: 0, 40, 60, 80, 100)
Horizontal axis: Older ◄— Speakers —► Younger

absorb əb 'zɔːb æb-, -'sɔːb ‖ -'zɔːrb -'sɔːrb
~**ed** d ~**ing/ly** ɪŋ /li ~**s** z —*Poll panel*
preferences: AmE 1993, -'zɔːrb 75%, -'sɔːrb
25%; BrE 1998, -'zɔːb 83%, -'sɔːb 17%
absorbedly əb 'zɔːb ɪd li æb-, -'sɔːb-, -əd-;
-'zɔːbd li, -'sɔːbd li ‖ -'zɔːrb- -'sɔːrb-
absorbency əb 'zɔːb ən̩t s i æb-, -'sɔːb-
‖ -'zɔːrb- -'sɔːrb-
absorbent əb 'zɔːb ənt æb-, -'sɔːb- ‖ -'zɔːrb-
-'sɔːrb-
absorber əb 'zɔːb ə æb-, -'sɔːb- ‖ -'zɔːrb ər
-'sɔːrb- ~**s** z
absorption əb 'zɔːp ʃən æb-, -'sɔːp- ‖ -'zɔːrp-
-'sɔːrp-
absorptive əb 'zɔːpt ɪv æb-, -'sɔːpt- ‖ -'zɔːrpt-
-'sɔːrpt-
absorptivity ˌæb zɔːp 'tɪv ət i ˌ•sɔːp-, -ɪt i
‖ -zɔːrp 'tɪv ət̩ i ˌ•sɔːrp-
abstain əb 'steɪn æb- ~**ed** d ~**er/s** ə/z ‖ ər/z
~**ing** ɪŋ ~**s** z
abstemious əb 'stiːm i_əs æb- ~**ly** li ~**ness**
nəs nɪs
abstention əb 'stenʧ ən æb- ~**s** z
abstinence 'æb stɪn ən̩t s
abstinent 'æb stɪn ənt ~**ly** li
abstract *adj* 'æb strækt ‖ ₍ᵢ₎•'•
abstract *n* 'æb strækt ~**s** s
abstract *v 'remove'* ₍ᵢ₎æb 'strækt əb-, '•• ~**ed**
ɪd əd ~**ing** ɪŋ ~**s** s
abstract *v 'summarize'* 'æb strækt ~**ed** ɪd əd
~**er/s** ə/z ‖ ³r/z ~**ing** ɪŋ ~**s** s
abstraction ₍ᵢ₎æb 'stræk ʃən əb- ~**ism** ˌɪz əm
~**ist/s** _ɪst/s §_əst/s ~**s** z
abstractive ₍ᵢ₎æb 'strækt ɪv əb-
abstract|ly 'æb strækt| li ‖ ₍ᵢ₎•'•• ~**ness** nəs
nɪs
abstruse ₍ᵢ₎æb 'struːs əb- ~**ly** li ~**ness** nəs nɪs
abstrusity ₍ᵢ₎æb 'struːs ət i əb-, -ɪt- ‖ -ət̩ i

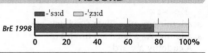

ABSURD

■-'sɜːd ▨-'zɜːd					
BrE 1998					
	0	20	40	60	80	100%

absurd, A~ əb 'sɜːd §æb-, -'zɜːd ‖ -'sɝːd
-'zɝːd ~**ism** ˌɪz əm ~**ist/s** ɪst/s §əst/s ~**ly** li
—*BrE 1998 poll panel preference:* -'sɜːd 77%,
-'zɜːd 23%
absurdit|y əb 'sɜːd ət li §æb-, -'zɜːd-, -ɪt-
‖ -'sɝːd ət̩ li -'zɝːd- ~**ies** iz
ABTA 'æb tə
Abu Dhabi ˌæb u 'dɑːb i ˌɑːb-, -'dæb- ‖ ˌɑːb-
—*Arabic* [a bu 'ðˤa bi]
Abuja ə 'buːdʒ ə ɑː-
abulia ə 'buːl i_ə eɪ-, -'bjuːl-
abundance ə 'bʌnd ən̩t s
abundant ə 'bʌnd ənt ~**ly** li
Abu Nidal ˌæb uː niː 'dɑːl ˌɑːb-, -'dæl ‖ ˌɑːb-
ˌæb-
abuse *v* ə 'bjuːz **abused** ə 'bjuːzd **abuses**
ə 'bjuːz ɪz -əz **abusing** ə 'bjuːz ɪŋ
abuse *n* ə 'bjuːs **abuses** ə 'bjuːs ɪz -əz *(NB
verb ≠ noun)*
abuser ə 'bjuːz ə ‖ -ªr ~**s** z
Abu Simbel ˌæb uː 'sɪm bªl ˌɑːb-, -bel ‖ ˌɑːb-
ˌæb-
abusive ə 'bjuːs ɪv -'bjuːz- ~**ly** li ~**ness** nəs
nɪs
abut ə 'bʌt **abuts** ə 'bʌts **abutted** ə 'bʌt ɪd
-əd ‖ ə 'bʌt̩ əd **abutting** ə 'bʌt ɪŋ ‖ ə 'bʌt̩ ɪŋ
abutilon ə 'bjuːt ɪl ən §-əl-, -ɪ lɒn, -ə lɒn, -ªl ɒn
‖ ə 'bjuːt̩ ªl ɑːn -ən ~**s** z
abutment ə 'bʌt mənt ~**s** s
abuttal ə 'bʌt ªl ‖ ə 'bʌt̩ ªl ~**s** z
abutt... —*see* **abut**
abuzz ə 'bʌz
Abydos ə 'baɪd ɒs -əs ‖ -ɑːs -ɔːs
abysm ə 'bɪz əm
abysmal ə 'bɪz mªl æ- ~**ly** i
abyss ə 'bɪs æ-, 'æb ɪs ~**es** ɪz əz
abyssal ə 'bɪs ªl æ-
Abyssini|a ˌæb ɪ 'sɪn i_ə ˌæb ə- ~**an/s** ən/z
AC ˌeɪ 'siː
a/c —*see* **account**
ac- *This prefix is a variant of* ad-. *Its*
pronunciation varies according to context. (1)
When followed in spelling by ce, ci, *it is usually*
ək (ac'celerate), *but* ¦æk *if stressed because of a*
suffix (ˌacci'dental) *and in a few two-syllable*
nouns ('access). (2) *Otherwise, it is* ə, *but* ¦æ *if*
stressed because of a suffix
(ac'claim; ˌaccla'mation).
-ac *This suffix and word-ending is mostly* æk
('cardiac, 'maniac); *but note* ˌele'giac *usually*
with ək.
acacia ə 'keɪʃ ə -'keɪs i_ə ~**s** z
academe, A~ 'æk ə diːm, ˌ•'•
academia ˌæk ə 'diːm i_ə
academic ˌæk ə 'dem ɪk ◄ ~**al/s** ªl/z ~**ally** ªl_i
~**s** s
ˌacaˌdemic 'freedom

A

academician ə ˌkæd ə 'mɪʃ ᵊn ˌæk əd-, -ɪ'•-,
-e'•- ~s z
academicism ˌæk ə 'dem ɪ ˌsɪz əm -ə,•-
academ|y, A~ ə 'kæd əm li ~**ies** iz
   A͵cademy a'ward
Acadi|a ə 'keɪd i ˌə ~**an/s** ən/z
acanth|us ə 'kæntᵊθ ləs ~**i** aɪ ~**uses** əs ɪz -əz
a cappella ˌæk ə 'pel ə ˌɑːk-, -æ- ‖ ˌɑː kə- —*It*
[ak kap 'pel la]
Acapulco ˌæk ə 'pʊlk əʊ ‖ ˌɑːk ə 'puːlk oʊ
-'pʊlk- —*Sp* [a ka 'pul ko]
acarid 'æk ər ɪd §-əd ~s z
ACAS 'eɪk æs
acatalectic ˌeɪ ˌkæt ə 'lekt ɪk ◄ •, •-, æ, •-, ə, •-
acced|e ək 'siːd æk-, ɪk- ~**ed** ɪd əd ~**es** z
~**ing** ɪŋ
accelerando æk ˌsel ə 'rænd əʊ ək-, ɪk-;
ə ˌtʃel- ‖ -'rɑːnd oʊ ɑː ˌtʃel- —*It*
[at tʃe le 'ran do]
accelerant ək 'sel ər ənt æk-, ɪk- ~s s
accele|rate ək 'sel ə ˌreɪt æk-, ɪk- ~**rated**
reɪt ɪd -əd ‖ reɪt̬ əd ~**rates** reɪts ~**rating**
reɪt ɪŋ ‖ reɪt̬ ɪŋ
acceleration ək ˌsel ə 'reɪʃ ᵊn æk-, ɪk- ~s z
accelerator ək 'sel ə reɪt ə æk-, ɪk- ‖ -reɪt̬ ᵊr
~s z
accelerometer ək ˌsel ə 'rɒm ɪt ə æk-, ɪk-,
-ət ə ‖ -'rɑːm ət̬ ᵊr ~s z
accent n 'æks ᵊnt 'æk sent ‖ 'æk sent ~s s
ac|cent v æk 'ˈsent ək-, ɪk-, 'æk ˌsent; 'æk ˌsᵊnt
‖ 'æk ˌsent •'• ~**cented** sent ɪd sᵊnt-, -əd
‖ sent̬ əd ~**centing** sent ɪŋ sᵊnt- ‖ sent̬ ɪŋ
~**cents** sents sᵊnts ‖ sents
accentor æk 'sent ə ək-, ɪk- ‖ -'sent̬ ᵊr ~s z
accentual ək 'sentʃ u ˌəl æk-, ɪk-, -'sent ju ˌ ~**ly**
i
accentu|ate ək 'sentʃ u ˌeɪt æk-, ɪk-, -'sent ju-
~**ated** eɪt ɪd -əd ‖ eɪt̬ əd ~**ates** eɪts ~**ating**
eɪt ɪŋ ‖ eɪt̬ ɪŋ
accentuation ək ˌsentʃ u 'eɪʃ ᵊn æk-, ɪk-,
-ˌsent ju-
accept ək 'sept æk-, ɪk- ~**ed** ɪd əd ~**ing** ɪŋ ~s
s
acceptability ək ˌsept ə 'bɪl ət i æk-, ɪk-, -ɪt i
‖ -ət̬ i
acceptab|le ək 'sept əb ləl æk-, ɪk- ~**ly** li
acceptanc|e ək 'sept ᵊnᵗs æk-, ɪk- ~**es** ɪz əz
acceptation ˌæks ep 'teɪʃ ᵊn
acceptor ək 'sept ə æk-, ɪk- ‖ -ᵊr ~s z
access v, n 'æk ses —*as a v, occasionally also*
•'• ~**ed** t ~**es** ɪz əz ~**ing** ɪŋ
   'access time
Access *tdmk* 'æk ses
accessibility ək ˌses ə 'bɪl ət i æk-, ɪk-, -, •ɪ-,
-ɪt i ‖ -ət̬ i
accessib|le ək 'ses əb ləl æk-, ɪk-, -ɪb- ~**leness**
ᵊl nəs -nɪs ~**ly** li
accession ək 'seʃ ᵊn æk-, ɪk- ~**ed** d ~**ing** ˌɪŋ
~s z
accessoris|e, accessoriz|e ək 'ses ə raɪz æk-,
ɪk- ~**ed** d ~**es** ɪz əz ~**ing** ɪŋ
accessor|y ək 'ses ər ˌi æk-, ɪk-, △ə- ~**ies** iz

acciaccatura ə ˌtʃæk ə 'tʊər ə △-ˌkætʃ-
‖ ɑː ˌtʃɑːk ə 'tʊr ə —*It* [at tʃak ka 'tuː ra]
accidence 'æks ɪd ᵊnᵗs -əd- ‖ -ə denᵗs
accident 'æks ɪd ᵊnt -əd- ‖ -ə dent ~s s
accidental ˌæks ɪ 'dent ᵊl ◄ -ə- ‖ -'dent̬ ᵊl ◄ ~**ly**
i ~**s** z
   ˌacci͵dental 'death
accident-prone 'æks ɪd ᵊnt prəʊn '•əd-
‖ -proʊn -ə dent-
accidie 'æks ɪd i -əd-
accipiter æk 'sɪp ɪt ə -ət- ‖ -ət̬ ᵊr ~s z
acclaim ə 'kleɪm   **acclaimed** ə 'kleɪmd
   acclaiming ə 'kleɪm ɪŋ   **acclaims** ə 'kleɪmz
acclaimer ə 'kleɪm ə ‖ -ᵊr ~s z
acclamation ˌæk lə 'meɪʃ ᵊn ~s z
acclamatory ə 'klæm ət ˌᵊr i ‖ -ə tɔːr i -toʊr i
accli|mate 'æk lɪ ˌmeɪt -lə-; ə 'klaɪm eɪt, -ət
~**mated** meɪt ɪd -əd ‖ meɪt̬ əd ~**mates** meɪts
~**mating** meɪt ɪŋ ‖ meɪt̬ ɪŋ
acclimation ˌæk lɪ 'meɪʃ ᵊn -lə-, -laɪ-
acclimatis... —*see* **acclimatiz...**
acclimatization ə ˌklaɪm ət aɪ 'zeɪʃ ᵊn -ɪ'•-
‖ -ət̬ ə-
acclimatiz|e ə 'klaɪm ə taɪz ~**ed** d ~**es** ɪz əz
~**ing** ɪŋ
acclivit|y ə 'klɪv ət i ‖ æ-, -ɪt- ‖ -ət̬ li ~**ies** iz
accolade 'æk ə leɪd -lɑːd, ,••'• ~s z
accommo|date ə 'kɒm ə ˌdeɪt ‖ ə 'kɑːm-
~**dated** deɪt ɪd -əd ‖ deɪt̬ əd ~**dates** deɪts
~**dating/ly** deɪt ɪŋ /li ‖ deɪt̬ ɪŋ /li
accommodation ə ˌkɒm ə 'deɪʃ ᵊn ‖ ə ˌkɑːm-
(not ˌæk ɒm-) ~s z
accompaniment ə 'kʌmp ᵊn ˌi mənt ~s s
accompanist ə 'kʌmp ᵊn ˌɪst §ˌəst ~s s
accompan|y ə 'kʌmp ᵊn ˌli ~**ied** id ~**ies** iz
~**ying** i ɪŋ
accomplic|e ə 'kʌmp lɪs ə 'kɒmp-, -ləs
‖ ə 'kɑːmp ləs ə 'kʌmp- ~**es** ɪz əz

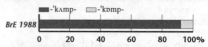

ACCOMPLISH

■-'kʌmp-   ▢-'kɒmp-

BrE 1988

| 0 | 20 | 40 | 60 | 80 | 100% |

accomplish ə 'kʌmp lɪʃ ə 'kɒmp- ‖ ə 'kɑːmp-
ə 'kʌmp- —*BrE poll 1988 panel preference:*
-'kʌmp- 92%, -'kɒmp- 8%. *In AmE, however,*
-'kɑːmp- *clearly predominates.* ~**ed** t ~**er/s**
ə/z ‖ ᵊr/z ~**es** ɪz əz ~**ing** ɪŋ ~**ment/s**
mənt/s
accord ə 'kɔːd ‖ ə 'kɔːrd ~**ed** ɪd əd ~**ing** ɪŋ
~s z
accordance ə 'kɔːd ᵊnᵗs ‖ ə 'kɔːrd ᵊnᵗs
accordant ə 'kɔːd ᵊnt ‖ ə 'kɔːrd ᵊnt ~**ly** li
according ə 'kɔːd ɪŋ ‖ ə 'kɔːrd ɪŋ ~**ly** li
accordion ə 'kɔːd i ˌən ‖ ə 'kɔːrd- ~**ist/s** ɪst/s
§əst/s ~s z
accost ə 'kɒst ‖ ə 'kɔːst ə 'kɑːst ~**ed** ɪd əd
~**ing** ɪŋ ~s s
accouchement ə 'kuːʃ mɒ̃ -mɑ̃: ‖ -mɑːnt
ˌæk uːʃ 'mɑ̃:
accoucheur ˌæk uː 'ʃɜː ‖ -'ʃɜ: ~s z
account ə 'kaʊnt   **accounted** ə 'kaʊnt ɪd -əd

‖ ə ˈkaʊn̩ əd **accounting**
ə ˈkaʊnt ɪŋ ‖ ə ˈkaʊn̩ ɪŋ
accountability ə ˌkaʊnt ə ˈbɪl ət i -ɪt i
‖ ə ˌkaʊn̩ ə ˈbɪl ət̬ i
accountable ə ˈkaʊnt əb əl ‖ ə ˈkaʊn̩- **~ness**
nəs nɪs
accountancy ə ˈkaʊnt ən‖s i ‖ -ən̩‖s i
accountant ə ˈkaʊnt ənt ‖ -ən̩t **~s** s
accoutered, accoutred ə ˈkuːt əd ‖ ə ˈkuːt̬ ərd
accouterment, accoutrement ə ˈkuːtr ə mənt
ə ˈkuːt- ‖ ə ˈkuːt̬ ər- ə ˈkuːtr ə- **~s** s
Accra ə ˈkrɑː ə-
accred|it ə ˈkred |ɪt §-ət ‖ -|ət **~ited** ɪt ɪd §ət-,
-əd ‖ ət̬ əd **~iting** ɪt ɪŋ §ət- ‖ ət̬ ɪŋ **~its** ɪts
§əts ‖ əts
accreditation ə ˌkred ɪ ˈteɪʃ ən-ə-
ac|crete ə |ˈkriːt æ- **~creted** ˈkriːt ɪd-əd
‖ ˈkriːt̬ əd **~cretes** ˈkriːts **~creting**
ˈkriːt ɪŋ ‖ ˈkriːt̬ ɪŋ
accretion ə ˈkriːʃ ən æ- **~s** z
Accrington ˈæk rɪŋ tən
accrual ə ˈkruː‿əl §ə ˈkruːl **~s** z
accrue ə ˈkruː **accrued** ə ˈkruːd **accrues**
ə ˈkruːz **accruing** ə ˈkruː‿ɪŋ
accultu|rate ə ˈkʌltʃ ə |reɪt æ- **~rated** reɪt ɪd
-əd ‖ reɪt̬ əd **~rates** reɪts **~rating**
reɪt ɪŋ ‖ reɪt̬ ɪŋ
acculturation ə ˌkʌltʃ ə ˈreɪʃ ən æ-
accumulable ə ˈkjuːm jəl əb əl -ˈ•jʊl-
accumu|late ə ˈkjuːm jə |leɪt -ju-, △-ə-
~lated leɪt ɪd-əd ‖ leɪt̬ əd **~lates** leɪts
~lating leɪt ɪŋ ‖ leɪt̬ ɪŋ
accumulation ə ˌkjuːm jə ˈleɪʃ ən-juˈ•-,
△-əˈ•- **~s** z
accumulative ə ˈkjuːm jəl ət ɪv-ˈ•jʊl-,
△-ˈ•əl-; -ˈ•jə leɪt ɪv, -ˈ•ju-, △-ˈ•ə-
‖ -jə leɪt̬ ɪv-jəl ət̬- **~ly** li **~ness** nəs nɪs
accumulator ə ˈkjuːm jə leɪt ə-ˈ•ju-, △-ˈ•ə-
‖ -leɪt̬ ər **~s** z
accurac|y ˈæk jər əs |i ˈ•jʊr-, -ɪs i **~ies** iz
accurate ˈæk jər ət -jʊr-, -ɪt **~ly** li **~ness** nəs
nɪs
Accurist tdmk ˈæk jʊr ɪst -jər-, §-əst
accursed ə ˈkɜːs ɪd -əd; ə ˈkɜːst ‖ ə ˈkɝːst
ə ˈkɝːs əd **~ly** li **~ness** nəs nɪs
accurst ə ˈkɜːst ‖ ə ˈkɝːst
accusal ə ˈkjuːz əl **~s** z
accusation ˌæk ju ˈzeɪʃ ən ‖ -jə- **~s** z
accusatival ə ˌkjuːz ə ˈtaɪv əl ◄
accusative ə ˈkjuːz ət ɪv ‖ -ət̬- **~ly** li **~s** z
accusatorial ə ˌkjuːz ə ˈtɔːr i‿əl ◄ ‖ -ˈtoʊr-
accusatory ə ˈkjuːz ə‿tər i ˌæk ju ˈzeɪt ər i
‖ -tɔːr i -toʊr i
accus|e ə ˈkjuːz **~ed** d **~es** ɪz əz **~ing/ly** ɪŋ /li
accuser ə ˈkjuːz ə ‖ -ər **~s** z
accustom ə ˈkʌst əm **~ed** d **~ing** ɪŋ **~s** z
AC/DC, ac-dc ˌeɪ siː ˈdiː siː ◄
ace eɪs **aced** eɪst **aces** ˈeɪs ɪz -əz **acing**
ˈeɪs ɪŋ
-acea ˈeɪs i‿ə ˈeɪʃ ə — **Crustacea** krʌ ˈsteɪs i‿ə
-ˈsteɪʃ ə
-aceae ˈeɪs i i iː ˈeɪʃ- — **Rosaceae** rəʊ ˈzeɪs i iː
-ˈzeɪʃ- ‖ roʊ-

Aceldama ə ˈkeld əm əə ˈseld-; ˌæk el ˈdɑːm ə
‖ ə ˈseld-
-aceous ˈeɪʃ əs— **rosaceous**
rəʊ ˈzeɪʃ əs ‖ roʊ-
acephalous ˌeɪ ˈsef əl əs ə-
acequia ə ˈseɪk i‿ɑː:- **~s** z
Acer tdmk ˈeɪs ə ‖ -ər
acerbic ə ˈsɜːb ɪk æ- ‖ -ˈsɝːb ɪk **~ally** əl‿i
acerbit|y ə ˈsɜːb ət i æ-, -ɪt- ‖ -ˈsɝːb ət̬ li **~ies**
iz
acetabul|um ˌæs ɪ ˈtæb jʊl |əm, -ˈ•ə-, -jəl əm
‖ -jəl |əm **~a** ə
acetaldehyde ˌæs ɪ ˈtæld ɪ haɪd, -ˈ•ə-, -ˈ•ə-
ən; ˌæs ɪt- ‖ ə ˌsiːt̬- ˌæs ət̬-
acetanilide ˌæs ɪ ˈtæn ə laɪd, -ˈ•ə-, -ˈ•ɪ-, -əl aɪd
‖ -əl aɪd-əd
acetate ˈæs ə teɪt-ɪ- **~s** s
acetic ə ˈsiːt ɪk ə ˈset- ‖ ə ˈsiːt̬ ɪk
a ˌcetic ˈacid
acetification ə ˌset ɪf ɪ ˈkeɪʃ ən-,siːt-, -, -əf-,
§-əˈ•- ‖ ə ˌset- ə ˌsiːt̬-
aceti|fy ə ˈset ɪ |faɪ ə ˈsiːt-, -ə- ‖ -ˈset̬- -ˈsiːt̬-
~fied faɪd **~fier/s** faɪ ə/z ‖ faɪ ər/z **~fies**
faɪz **~fying** faɪ ɪŋ
acetone ˈæs ə təʊn-ɪ- ‖ -toʊn
acetyl ˈæs ɪ taɪəl-ə-; -ɪt ɪl, -ət-, -əl; ə ˈsiːt aɪəl,
-ɪl, -əl ‖ ˈæs ət̬ əl‿ə ˈsiːt̬ əl, ˈæs ə tiːəl
acetylcholine ˌæs ɪ taɪəl ˈkəʊl iːn, -ˈ•ə-;
ˌæs ɪt ɪl-, ˌæs ət-, -əl‿ˈ•-; ə ˌsiːt aɪəl-, -, -ˈ•ɪl-,
-, -ˈ•əl-; -ɪn ‖ ə ˌsiːt̬ əl ˈkoʊl- ə ˌset̬-; ˌæs ət̬-,
ˌæs ə tiːəl-
acetylene ə ˈset ə liːn-ɪ-; -əl iːn; -əl ɪn, §-ən
‖ ə ˈset̬ əl iːn -ən
acetylsalicylic ˌæs ɪ taɪəl ˌsæl ə ˈsɪl ɪk ◄, -ˈ•ə-,
ˌæs ɪt ɪl-, ˌæs ət-, -əl‿, -ˈ•-; ə ˌsiːt aɪəl-, -, -ˈ•ɪl-,
-, -ˈ•əl-; -ɪˈ•- ‖ ə ˌsiːt̬ əl- ˌæs ət̬-
ach ɑːx æx —Ger [ʔax]
Achae|a ə ˈkiː‿ə **~an/s** ən/z
Achaemenid ə ˈkiːm ən ɪd -ˈkem-, -ɪn-, §-əd
~s z
Achai|a ə ˈkaɪ‿ə **~an/s** ən/z
Achates ə ˈkeɪt iːz -ˈkɑːt- ‖ ə ˈkeɪt̬ iːz
ache eɪk (!) **ached** eɪkt **aches** eɪks **aching/ly**
ˈeɪk ɪŋ /li
Achebe ə ˈtʃeɪb i -eɪ
Achelous ˌæk ə ˈləʊ əs -ɪ- ‖ -ˈloʊ-
achene ə ˈkiːn eɪ- **~s** z
Acheron ˈæk ər ən -ə rɒn ‖ -ə rɑːn
Acheson ˈætʃ ɪs ən -əs-
Acheulian ə ˈʃuːl i‿ən -ˈtʃuːl-
achieve ə ˈtʃiːv **achieved** ə ˈtʃiːvd **achieves**
ə ˈtʃiːvz **achieving** ə ˈtʃiːv ɪŋ
achievement ə ˈtʃiːv mənt **~s** s
aˈchievement test
Achill ˈæk ɪl -əl
achillea ˌæk ɪ ˈliː‿ə -ə- **~s** z
Achilles, -ˈ ə ˈkɪl iːz
Aˌchilles' ˈheel; Aˌchilles' ˈtendon
Achitophel ə ˈkɪt ə fel ‖ ə ˈkɪt̬-
ach-laut ˈæx laʊt ˈæk- ‖ ˈɑːx- —Ger Ach-Laut
[ˈʔax laʊt] **~s** s
Achnasheen ˌæk nə ˈʃiːn ˌæx-

A

achondroplasia ˌeɪ ˌkɒndr əʊ 'pleɪz i̯ə
ə ˌkɒndr- ‖ ˌeɪ ˌkɑːndr ə -'pleɪʒ ə
achondroplastic ˌeɪ ˌkɒndr əʊ 'plæst ɪk
ə ˌkɒndr-, -'plɑːst- ‖ ˌeɪ ˌkɑːndr ə-
achoo ə 'tʃuː
achromatic ˌæk rəʊ 'mæt ɪk ◄ ˌeɪ krəʊ-
‖ ˌæk rə 'mæt̬ ɪk ◄ ~ally əl̩_i
achromatism ə 'krəʊm ə ˌtɪz əm ₍ᵢ₎æ-, ₍ᵢ₎eɪ-
‖ ₍ᵢ₎eɪ 'kroʊm-
achtung ˌæx 'tʊŋ ˌɑːx-, '•• ‖ ˌɑːx- —Ger A~
['ʔax tʊŋ]
achy 'eɪk i
ach-y-fi ˌæx ə 'viː ˌʌx-, ˌæk-, ˌʌk- —Welsh
[aːχ ə 'viː]
acicul|a ə 'sɪk jʊl ə -jəl- ‖ -jəl lə ~ae iː ~ar
ə ‖ ᵊr
acid 'æs ɪd §-əd ~ly li ~ness nəs nɪs ~s z
ˌacid 'rain; ˌacid 'rock; ˌacid 'test
acidhead 'æs ɪd hed §-əd- ~s z
acidic ə 'sɪd ɪk æ-
acidification ə ˌsɪd ɪf ɪ 'keɪʃ ᵊn -ˌəf-, §-ə'•-
acidi|fy ə 'sɪd ɪ |faɪ æ-, -ə- ~fied faɪd ~fier/s
faɪ_ə/z ‖ faɪ_ᵊr/z ~fies faɪz ~fying faɪ ɪŋ
acidity ə 'sɪd ət i æ-, -ɪt- ‖ -ət̬ i
acidophilus ˌæs ɪ 'dɒf ɪl əs ˌ•ə-, -əl_əs ‖ -'dɑːf-
acidu|late ə 'sɪd ju |leɪt æ-, -jə-; -'sɪdʒ u-, -ə-
‖ ə 'sɪdʒ ə- ~lated leɪt ɪd -əd ‖ leɪt̬ əd
~lates leɪts ~lating leɪt ɪŋ ‖ leɪt̬ ɪŋ
acidulous ə 'sɪd jʊl əs æ-, -'sɪdʒ ʊl- ‖ ə 'sɪdʒ
əl əs
acing 'eɪs ɪŋ
ac|inus 'æs |ɪn əs -ən- ~ini ɪ naɪ ə-
Acis 'eɪs ɪs §-əs
ack-ack 'æk æk ˌ•'•
ackee 'æk i -iː ~s z
Ackerley 'æk əl i ‖ -ᵊr li
Ackerman 'æk ə mən ‖ -ᵊr-
Ackland 'æk lənd
acknowledg|e ək 'nɒl ɪdʒ æk-, ɪk- ‖ -'nɑːl-
~ed d ~es ɪz əz ~ing ɪŋ
acknowledgement, acknowledgment
ək 'nɒl ɪdʒ mənt æk-, ɪk- ‖ -'nɑːl- ~s s
Ackroyd 'æk rɔɪd
Acland 'æk lənd
Acle 'eɪk ᵊl
acme 'æk mi ~s z
acne 'æk ni ~d d
Acol, acol (i) 'æk ᵊl, (ii) 'eɪk ɒl ‖ -ɑːl —The
place in Kent is 'eɪk ɒl
acolyte 'æk ə laɪt -ᵊl aɪt ~s s
Acomb 'eɪk əm
Aconcagua ˌæk ən 'kæg wə →-əŋ-, -ɒn-
‖ -'kɑːg- ˌɑːk- —Sp [a koŋ 'ka ɣwa]
aconite 'æk ə naɪt ~s s
acorn 'eɪk ɔːn ‖ 'eɪk ɔːrn -ᵊrn ~s z
acotyledon ˌeɪ ˌkɒt ɪ 'liːd ᵊn ə ˌkɒt-, æ-, -ə'•-,
-ᵊl 'iːd- ‖ ˌeɪ ˌkɑːt̬ ᵊl 'iːd ᵊn -s z
A'Court 'eɪ kɔːt ‖ 'eɪ kɔːrt -koʊrt
acoustic ə 'kuːst ɪk -'kʊst- —formerly also
-'kaʊst- ~s s
acoustical ə 'kuːst ɪk ᵊl ~ly_i
acoustician ˌæk u 'stɪʃ ᵊn ~s z

acquaint ə 'kweɪnt acquainted ə 'kweɪnt ɪd
-əd ‖ ə 'kweɪnt̬ əd acquainting
ə 'kweɪnt ɪŋ ‖ ə 'kweɪnt̬ ɪŋ acquaints
ə 'kweɪnts
acquaintanc|e ə 'kweɪnt ᵊnts ‖ -ᵊnts ~es ɪz əz
acquaintanceship ə 'kweɪnt ᵊn ʃɪp -ᵊnts-,
→-ᵊntʃ- ‖ -ᵊnts- ~s s
acquiesc|e ˌæk wi 'es ~ed t ~es ɪz əz ~ing ɪŋ
acquiescence ˌæk wi 'es ᵊnts
acquiescent ˌæk wi 'es ᵊnt ◄ ~ly li
acquire ə 'kwaɪ_ə ‖ ə 'kwaɪ_ᵊr ~d d ~ment/s
mənt/s ~s z acquiring
ə 'kwaɪ_ər ɪŋ ‖ ə 'kwaɪ_ᵊr ɪŋ
acquisition ˌæk wɪ 'zɪʃ ᵊn -wə- ~s z
acquisitive ə 'kwɪz ət ɪv -ɪt- ‖ -ət̬ ɪv ~ly li
~ness nəs nɪs
acquit ə 'kwɪt acquits ə 'kwɪts acquitted
ə 'kwɪt ɪd -əd ‖ ə 'kwɪt̬ əd acquitting
ə 'kwɪt ɪŋ ‖ ə 'kwɪt̬ ɪŋ
acquittal ə 'kwɪt ᵊl ‖ ə 'kwɪt̬ ᵊl ~s z
acre, Acre 'eɪk ə ‖ 'eɪk ᵊr ~d d ~s z
ˌAcre 'Lane
Acre place in Israel 'eɪk ə 'ɑːk- ‖ -ᵊr
acreag|e 'eɪk ᵊr_ɪdʒ ~es ɪz əz
acrid 'æk rɪd §-rəd ~ly li ~ness nəs nɪs
acridity æ 'krɪd ət i ə-, -ɪt- ‖ -ət̬ i
acriflavine ˌæk rɪ 'fleɪv iːn -rə-, -ɪn, §-ᵊn
Acrilan tdmk 'æk rɪ læn -rə-, -lən
acrimonious ˌæk rɪ 'məʊn i_əs ◄ ˌ•rə-
‖ -'moʊn- ~ly li ~ness nəs nɪs
acrimony 'æk rɪm ən i '•rəm- ‖ -ə moʊn i
acro- comb. form
with stress-neutral suffix ¦æk rəʊ ‖ ¦æk rə -roʊ
— acrophobia ˌæk rəʊ 'fəʊb i_ə ‖ -rə 'foʊb-
with stress-imposing suffix ə 'krɒ+ ‖ ə 'krɑː+
— acropetal ə 'krɒp ɪt ᵊl §-ət-
‖ ə 'krɑːp ət̬ ᵊl
acrobat 'æk rə bæt ~s s
acrobatic ˌæk rə 'bæt ɪk ◄ ‖ -'bæt̬ ɪk ◄ ~ally əl_i
~s s
acrolect 'æk rəʊ lekt ‖ -roʊ- -rə- ~s s
acrolectal ˌæk rəʊ 'lekt ᵊl ‖ -roʊ- -rə-
acromegalic ˌæk rəʊ mə 'gæl ɪk ◄ -mɪ'•-
‖ ˌæk roʊ-
acromegaly ˌæk rəʊ 'meg əl i ‖ ˌæk roʊ-
acronym 'æk rə nɪm ~s z
acrophob|ia ˌæk rəʊ 'fəʊb i_ə ‖ -rə 'foʊb- ~ic
ɪk ◄
acropolis ə 'krɒp əl ɪs §-əs ‖ -'krɑːp-
across ə 'krɒs ‖ ə 'krɔːs -'krɑːs
across-the-board
ə ˌkrɒs ðə 'bɔːd ◄ ‖ ə ˌkrɔːs ðə 'bɔːrd ◄
ə ˌkrɑːs-, -'boʊrd
an əˌcross-the-ˌboard 'increase
acrostic ə 'krɒst ɪk ‖ ə 'krɔːst ɪk -'krɑːst-
~ally əl_i ~s s
acrylic ə 'krɪl ɪk æ- ~s s
act ækt acted 'ækt ɪd -əd acting 'ækt ɪŋ
acts, Acts ækts
ˌact of 'God
Actaeon æk 'tiː_ən
ACTH ˌeɪ siː tiː 'eɪtʃ ækθ
actinic æk 'tɪn ɪk

actinide 'ækt ɪ naɪd §-ə- ~s z
actinism 'ækt ɪ ˌnɪz əm §-ə-
actinium æk 'tɪn i_əm
actinometer ˌækt ɪ 'nɒm ɪt ə §,•ə-, -ət ə
‖ -'nɑːm ət ªr ~s z
action 'æk ʃªn ~ed d ~ing ɪŋ ~s z
'action man; ˌaction 'replay; 'action
ˌstations, ˌ•• '••
actionab|le 'æk ʃªn_əb |ªl ~ly li
action-packed 'æk ʃªn pækt →-ʃªm-
Actium 'ækt i_əm
acti|vate 'ækt ɪ |veɪt -ə- ~vated veɪt ɪd -əd
‖ veɪt̬ əd ~vates veɪts ~vating
veɪt ɪŋ ‖ veɪt̬ ɪŋ
activation ˌækt ɪ 'veɪʃ ªn -ə- ~s z
activator 'ækt ɪ veɪt ə ‖ -veɪt̬ ªr ~s z
active 'ækt ɪv ~ly li ~ness nəs nɪs ~s z
Activex 'ækt ɪ veks
activism 'ækt ɪv ˌɪz əm §-əv-
activist 'ækt ɪv ɪst §-əv-, §-əst ~s s
activit|y æk 'tɪv ət li -ɪt- ‖ -ət̬ li ~ies iz
Acton 'ækt ən
actor 'ækt ə ‖ -ªr —There is also a mannered
pronunciation -ɔː ‖ -ɔːr ~s z
actress 'æk trəs -trɪs, -tres ~es ɪz əz
actressy 'æk trəs i -trɪs-
actual 'æk tʃu_əl 'æk tʃəl, 'æk ʃu_əl, 'æk ʃªl,
'ækt ju_əl
actualis... —see **actualiz...**
actualité ˌækt ju 'æl ɪ teɪ ˌæk tʃu-, -ə•
‖ ˌɑːk tʃu ɑːl ə 'teɪ ˌæk- —Fr [ak ty al i te]
actualit|y ˌæk tʃu 'æl ət li ˌ•tju-, ˌ•ʃu-, -ɪt i
‖ -ət̬ li ~ies iz
actualization ˌæk tʃu_əl aɪ 'zeɪʃ ªn ˌ•tju_,
ˌ•ʃu_, -ɪ'•- ‖ -ə'•-
actualiz|e 'æk tʃu_ə laɪz 'ækt ju_, 'æk ʃu_ ~ed
d ~es ɪz əz ~ing ɪŋ
actually 'æk tʃu_əl i 'æk tʃªl i, 'æk ʃu_əl i,
'æk ʃªl_i, 'ækt ju_əl i —There is also a very
casual form 'æk ʃi
actuarial ˌæk tʃu 'eər i_əl ◄ ˌækt ju-, ˌæk ʃu-
‖ -'er- ~ly i
actuar|y 'æk tʃu_ər li 'ækt ju_, 'æk ʃu_ ‖ -er li
~ies iz
actu|ate 'æk tʃu eɪt 'ækt ju-, 'æk ʃu- ~ated
eɪt ɪd -əd ‖ eɪt̬ əd ~ates eɪts ~ating
eɪt ɪŋ ‖ eɪt̬ ɪŋ
actuation ˌæk tʃu 'eɪʃ ªn ˌækt ju-, ˌæk ʃu-
actuator 'æk tʃu eɪt ə 'ækt ju-, 'æk ʃu-
‖ -eɪt̬ ªr
acuity ə 'kjuː_ət i ˌ_ɪt- ‖ -ət̬ i
acumen 'æk jum ən -jəm-; -ju men, -jə-;
ə 'kjuː_m en, -ən ‖ ə 'kjuː_m ən 'æk jəm-
acuminate ə 'kjuː_m ɪn ət -ən-, -ɪt; -ə neɪt, -ə-
acupuncture 'æk ju ˌpʌŋk tʃə -jə-, §-ə-,
△-wə-, -ʃə ‖ -jə ˌpʌŋk tʃªr
acupuncturist 'æk ju ˌpʌŋk tʃər ɪst '•jə-,
§'•ə-, △'•wə-, ˌ•'••, -ʃər ɪst, §-əst
‖ 'æk jə- ~s s
acute ə 'kjuːt ~ly li ~ness nəs nɪs
aˌcute 'accent
-acy əs i —Words with this suffix are stressed in
the same way as the corresponding form with

-ate, if there is one (le'gitimacy). Otherwise, the
stem keeps its usual stress, though sometimes
with a vowel change (su'preme — su'premacy).
See also -cracy.
acyclic ₍ₐ₎eɪ 'saɪk lɪk -'sɪk-
ad æd (= add) **ads** ædz —See also phrases with
this word
ad- əd, ₍ₐ₎æd —This prefix is strong ˌæd when
stressed, (1) because of a suffix (ˌadap'tation),
and (2) in some two-syllable nouns ('adverb).
Otherwise, in RP and GenAm, it is usually
unstressed and weak (a'dapt), although some
speakers use a strong vowel if the following
stem begins with a consonant (ad'mit). Before a
stem with initial d or dʒ the prefix regularly
loses its d (ad'diction). Note the irregularly
stressed word 'adjective.
-ad æd, əd — octad 'ɒkt æd -əd ‖ 'ɑːkt-
AD ˌeɪ 'diː
Ada 'eɪd ə
adag|e 'æd ɪdʒ ~es ɪz əz
adagio ə 'dɑːdʒ i_əʊ -'dɑːʒ-, -'dɑːdʒ əʊ
‖ ə 'dɑːdʒ oʊ -'dɑːdʒ i_oʊ ~s z
Adair ə 'deə ‖ ə 'deªr -'dæªr
Adam 'æd əm —'s z —but for the French
composer, æ 'dɒ̃ ‖ ɑː 'dɑːm —Fr [a dɑ̃]
ˌAdam's 'apple ‖ '•• ˌ••
adamancy 'æd əm ən°s i
adamant 'æd əm ənt ~ly li
adamantine ˌæd ə 'mænt aɪn ◄ ‖ -iːn -aɪn, -ªn
Adamawa ˌæd ə 'mɑː wə
Adamic ə 'dæm ɪk æ-
Adams 'æd əmz
Adamsez 'æd əmz ɪz -əz; -əm sez
Adamson 'æd əm sən
adapt ə 'dæpt **adapted** ə 'dæpt ɪd -əd
adapting ə 'dæpt ɪŋ **adapts** ə 'dæpts
adaptability ə ˌdæpt ə 'bɪl ət i -ɪt i ‖ -ət̬ i
adaptab|le ə 'dæpt əb |ªl ~ly li
adaptation ˌæd æp 'teɪʃ ªn -əp- ~s z
adapter ə 'dæpt ə ‖ -ªr ~s z
adaptive ə 'dæpt ɪv ~ly li ~ness nəs nɪs
adaptor ə 'dæpt ə ‖ -ªr ~s z
Adare ə 'deə ‖ ə 'deªr -'dæªr
ADC ˌeɪ diː 'siː ~s, ~'s z
Adcock 'æd kɒk →'æg- ‖ -kɑːk
add æd **added** 'æd ɪd -əd **adding** 'æd ɪŋ
adds ædz
ADD 'attention deficit disorder' ˌeɪ diː 'diː
Addams 'æd əmz
addax 'æd æks
addend|um ə 'dend |əm ~a ə
adder 'æd ə ‖ 'æd ªr ~s z
addict v ə 'dɪkt **addicted** ə 'dɪkt ɪd -əd
addicting ə 'dɪkt ɪŋ **addicts** ə 'dɪkts
addict n 'æd ɪkt **addicts** 'æd ɪkts
addiction ə 'dɪk ʃªn ~s z
addictive ə 'dɪkt ɪv ~ly li ~ness nəs nɪs
Addie 'æd i
Addington 'æd ɪŋ tən
Addis 'æd ɪs §-əs
ˌAddis 'Ababa 'æb əb ə
Addiscombe 'æd ɪs kəm §-əs-

A

Addison 'æd ɪs ən §-əs- ~'s z
'Addison's di‚sease
addition ə 'dɪʃ ən ~s z
additional ə 'dɪʃ ən_əl ~ly i
additive 'æd ət ɪv -ɪt- ǁ -əţ ɪv ~s z
addle 'æd əl addled 'æd əld addles 'æd əlz
addling 'æd əl_ɪŋ
Addlebrough 'æd əl bər_ə ǁ -,bɝː oʊ
Addlestone 'æd əl stəʊn ǁ -stoʊn
add-on 'æd ɒn ǁ -ɑːn -ɔːn ~s z

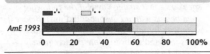

ADDRESS

AmE 1993

0   20   40   60   80   100%

address n ə 'dres ǁ 'ædr es ~es ɪz əz —AmE
    1993 poll panel preference: •'• 58%, '•• 42%.
    Some AmE speakers use '•• in the sense of
    'destination, location', but •'• in other senses.
address v ə 'dres æ- ~ed t ~es ɪz əz ~ing ɪŋ
addressable ə 'dres əb əl
addressee ,ædr es 'iː ə ,dres 'iː ~s z
Addressograph tdmk ə 'dres əʊ grɑːf -græf
    ǁ -ə græf
adduc|e ə 'djuːs æ-, →§-'dʒuːs ǁ ə 'duːs -'djuːs
    ~ed t ~es ɪz əz ~ing ɪŋ
adduct ə 'dʌkt æ- ~ed ɪd əd ~ing ɪŋ ~s s
adduction ə 'dʌk ʃən
adductor ə 'dʌkt ə ǁ -ər ~s z
Addy 'æd i
-ade eɪd —This suffix is usually stressed
    (,lemo'nade, ,harlequi'nade). When -ade is not a
    true suffix it may be stressed or unstressed,
    taking one of the forms eɪd, 'eɪd, ɑːd, 'ɑːd,
    depending on the particular word ('marmelade;
    ,prome'nade, '•••): see individual entries.
Adel 'æd əl
Adela 'æd ɪl ə -əl-; ə 'deɪl ə
Adelaide 'æd ə leɪd -ɪ-, →-əl eɪd
Adele, Adèle ə 'del
Adelie, Adélie ə 'deɪl i -'diːl-, 'æd ɪl i, -əl i
Adelina ,æd ə 'liːn ə -ɪ-; -əl 'iːn-
Adeline 'æd ə laɪn -ɪ-, -liːn; -əl aɪn, -iːn
Adelphi ə 'delf i
Aden 'eɪd ən —Arabic ['ʔa dan]
Adenauer 'æd ə naʊ_ə 'ɑːd-, →-ən aʊ_ ǁ _ər
    —Ger ['ʔaː də naʊ ɐ]
Adeney 'eɪd ən_i
adenine 'æd ə niːn -naɪn, -nɪn ǁ -ən iːn
adenoid 'æd ɪ nɔɪd -ə-, →-ən ɔɪd ǁ -ən ɔɪd ~s z
adenoidal ,æd ɪ 'nɔɪd əl ◄ -ə-, →-ən 'ɔɪd-
    ǁ ,æd ən 'ɔɪd əl ◄ ~ly i
adenom|a ,æd ɪ 'nəʊm ǀə -ə-, →-ən 'əʊm-
    ǁ ,æd ən 'oʊm ǀə ~as əz ~ata ət ə ǀ ət ə
adenopathy ,æd ɪ 'nɒp əθ i ,•ə-, →-ən 'ɒp-
    ǁ ,æd ən 'ɑːp-
adenosine ə 'den əʊ siːn ə-; ,æd ɪ 'nəʊs iːn, -ə-
    ǁ -ə siːn -əs ən
adept n 'æd ept ə 'dept, æ 'dept ~s s
adept adj ə 'dept æ-, 'æd ept ~ly li ~ness nəs
    nɪs
adequacy 'æd ɪk wəs i '•ək-, -wɪs i

adequate 'æd ɪk wət -ək-, -wɪt ~ly li ~ness
    nəs nɪs
adessive æ 'des ɪv ə- ~s z
adeste fideles æd ,est i fɪ 'deɪl eɪz əd-, -eɪs
à deux æ 'dɜː ɑː- ǁ -'dʌ —Fr [a dø]
Adger 'ædʒ ə ǁ -ər
adhere əd 'hɪə ‚ææd- ǁ -'hɪər ~d d ~s z
    adhering əd 'hɪər ɪŋ ‚ææd- ǁ -'hɪr ɪŋ
adherence əd 'hɪər ənts ‚ææd-, -'her- ǁ -'hɪr-
adherent əd 'hɪər ənt ‚ææd-, -'her- ǁ -'hɪr- ~ly
    li ~s s
adhesion əd 'hiːʒ ən ‚ææd-
adhesive əd 'hiːs ɪv ‚ææd-, -'hiːz- ~ly li ~ness
    nəs nɪs ~s z
ad hoc ‚ææd 'hɒk ◄ -'həʊk ǁ -'hɑːk ,ɑːd-, -'hoʊk
adhoc-ery, adhockery ,æd 'hɒk ər i -'həʊk-
    ǁ -'hɑːk- ,ɑːd-, -'hoʊk-
ad hominem ‚ææd 'hɒm ɪ nem -ə- ǁ -'hɑːm-
    ,ɑːd-, -ən əm
adiabatic ,æd i_ə 'bæt ɪk ◄ ,eɪ ,daɪ_ə-,
    ǁ -'bæţ ɪk ◄ ~ally əl_i
Adidas tdmk 'æd ɪ dæs -ə-, ə 'diːd æs, -əz
    ǁ 'ɑːd ə- ə 'diːd əz, -əs
Adie 'eɪd i
Adiemus ,æd i 'eɪm əs
adieu ə 'djuː æ-, →§-'dʒuː, -'djɜː ǁ -'duː -'djuː
    —Fr [a djø] ~s z ~x z —or as sing.
ad infinitum ,æd ,ɪn fɪ 'naɪt əm •,•-, -fə'•-
    ǁ -'naɪţ əm ,ɑːd-
adios ,æd i 'ɒs ǁ -'oʊs ,ɑːd- —Sp [a 'ðjos]
adipocere 'æd ɪ pəʊ sɪə -ə-, -pə-, ,•••'•
    ǁ -ə poʊ sɪr
adipose 'æd ɪ pəʊs -ə-, -pəʊz ǁ -poʊs ~ness
    nəs nɪs
adiposity ,æd ɪ 'pɒs ət i ,•ə-, -ɪt i ǁ -'pɑːs əţ i
Adirondack ,æd ə 'rɒnd æk -ɪ- ǁ -'rɑːnd-
adit 'æd ɪt §-ət ~s s
adjacency ə 'dʒeɪs ənts i
adjacent ə 'dʒeɪs ənt ~ly li
adjectival ,ædʒ ɪk 'taɪv əl ◄ -ek-, -ək- ~ly i ~s
    z
adjective 'ædʒ ɪkt ɪv -ekt-, -əkt- ǁ △-əţ- ~s z
adjoin ə 'dʒɔɪn æ- ~ed d ~ing ɪŋ ~s z
adjourn ə 'dʒɜːn ǁ ə 'dʒɝːn ~ed d ~ing ɪŋ ~s
    z
adjournment ə 'dʒɜːn mənt →-'dʒɜːm-
    ǁ -'dʒɝːn- ~s s
adjudg|e ə 'dʒʌdʒ æ- ~ed d ~es ɪz əz ~ing
    ɪŋ
adjudi|cate ə 'dʒuːd ɪ ǀkeɪt -ə- ~cated keɪt ɪd
    -əd ǁ keɪţ əd ~cates keɪts ~cating
    keɪt ɪŋ ǁ keɪţ ɪŋ
adjudication ə ,dʒuːd ɪ 'keɪʃ ən -ə'•- ~s z
adjudicator ə 'dʒuːd ɪ keɪt ə -ə-'•-ə- ǁ -keɪţ ər ~s
    z
adjunct 'ædʒ ʌŋkt ~s s
adjunction ə 'dʒʌŋk ʃən æ-, ,æd-
adjunctive ə 'dʒʌŋkt ɪv æ-, ,æd-
adjuration ,ædʒ uə 'reɪʃ ən -ə- ~s z
adjure ə 'dʒʊə -'dʒɔː ǁ ə 'dʒʊər ~d d ~s z
    adjuring ə 'dʒʊər ɪŋ -'dʒɔːr- ǁ ə 'dʒʊər ɪŋ
adjust ə 'dʒʌst ~ed ɪd əd ~ing ɪŋ ~s s
adjustab|le ə 'dʒʌst əb ǀəl ~ly li

adjuster ə 'dʒʌst ə ‖ -ᵊr ~s z
adjustment ə 'dʒʌst mənt ~s s
adjutancy 'ædʒ ʊt ənts i
adjutant 'ædʒ ʊt ənt -ət- ~s s
Adkins 'æd kınz →'æg-
Adlai 'æd leı -laı
Adlard 'æd lɑːd -ləd ‖ -lɑːrd
Adler *(i)* 'æd lə ‖ -lᵊr, *(ii)* 'ɑːd- —*Ger* ['ʔɑːd lɐ]
Adlerian æd 'lıər i_ən ‖ -'ler- ~s z
Adlestrop 'æd ᵊl strɒp ‖ -strɑːp
ad lib ˌæd 'lıb
ad-lib ˌæd 'lıb ◄ ~bed d ~bing ıŋ ~s z
ad|man 'æd |mæn -mən ~**men** men mən
admass 'æd mæs
admeasure æd 'meʒ ə əd- ‖ -ᵊr -'meıʒ- ~s z
admen 'æd men -mən
Admetus æd 'miːt əs ‖ -'miːṭ-
admin 'æd mın ˌ•'•
administer əd 'mın ıst ə æd-, →əb-, -əst- ‖ -ᵊr
  ~**ed** d **administering** əd 'mın ıst ər ıŋ
  -'•əst-; →-'•ıs trıŋ, →-'•əs trıŋ ~**s** z
admini|strate əd 'mın ı |streıt æd-, →əb-, -ə-
  ~**strated** streıt ıd -əd ‖ streıṭ əd ~**strates**
  streıts ~**strating** streıt ıŋ ‖ streıṭ ıŋ
administration əd ˌmın ı 'streıʃ ᵊn æd-, →əb-,
  -ə- ~**s** z
administrative əd 'mın ıs trət ıv æd-, →əb-,
  -'•əs-; -'•ı streıt-, -'•ə- ‖ -ə streıṭ ıv
  -əs trəṭ ıv ~**ly** li
administrator əd 'mın ı streıt ə æd-, →əb-,
  -'•ə- ‖ -streıṭ ᵊr ~**s** z
admirable 'æd mᵊr_əb ᵊl →'æb- ~**ness** nəs nıs
admirably 'æd mᵊr_əb li →'æb-
admiral 'æd mᵊr_əl →'æb- ~**s** z
admiral|ty 'æd mᵊr_əl |ti →'æb- ~**ties** tiz
  ˌAdmiralty 'Arch
admiration ˌæd mə 'reıʃ ᵊn →ˌæb-, -mı-
admire əd 'maı_ə §æd-, →əb- ‖ əd 'maı_ᵊr ~**d**
  d ~**s** z **admiring/ly** əd 'maı_ər ıŋ /li §æd-
  ‖ əd 'maı_ᵊr ıŋ /li
admirer əd 'maı_ər ə §æd-, →əb- ‖ əd 'maı_ᵊr
  ᵊr ~**s** z
admissibility əd ˌmıs ə 'bıl ət i æd-, →əb-,
  -ˌ•ı-, -ıt i ‖ -əṭ i
admissib|le əd 'mıs əb ᵊl æd-, →əb-, -ıb- ~**ly**
  li
admission əd 'mıʃ ᵊn æd-, →əb- ~**s** z
ad|mit əd |'mıt æd-, →əb- ~**mits** 'mıts
  ~**mitted** 'mıt ıd -əd ‖ 'mıṭ əd ~**mitting**
  'mıt ıŋ ‖ 'mıṭ ıŋ
admittance əd 'mıt ᵊnts æd-, →əb-
admitted əd 'mıt ıd æd-, →əb-, -əd ‖ -'mıṭ əd
  ~**ly** li
admixture əd 'mıks tʃə æd-, →əb- ‖ -tʃᵊr ~**s**
  z
admonish əd 'mɒn ıʃ æd-, →əb- ‖ -'mɑːn-
  ~**ed** t ~**es** ız əz ~**ing** ıŋ ~**ment/s** mənt/s
admonition ˌæd mə 'nıʃ ᵊn→ˌæb- ~**s** z
admonitory əd 'mɒn ıt_ər i æd-, →əb-, -'•ə-
  ‖ -'mɑːn ə tɔːr i -tour i
ad nauseam ˌæd 'nɔːz i æm -'nɔːs-,
  -əm ‖ -'nɑːz-

adnominal ₍ᵢ₎æd 'nɒm ın ᵊl -ən-, -ᵊn_ᵊl
  ‖ -'nɑːm- ~**s** z
ado ə 'duː
adobe ə 'dəʊb i ‖ ə 'doʊb i
adolescence ˌæd ə 'les ᵊnts -ᵊl 'es-
adolescent ˌæd ə 'les ᵊnt ◄ -ᵊl 'es- ~**s** s
Adolf 'æd ɒlf ‖ 'eıd ɑːlf 'æd-
Adolfo ə 'dɒlf əʊ ‖ ə 'dɑːlf oʊ
Adolph 'æd ɒlf ‖ 'eıd ɑːlf 'æd-
Adolphus ə 'dɒlf əs ‖ ə 'dɑːlf əs
Adonai ˌæd əʊ 'naı '•••, -ɒ-, ˌ••'neı aı;
  ə 'dəʊn i_aı ‖ ˌɑːd ə 'naı -'nɔı
Adonis ə 'dəʊn ıs -'dɒn-, -əs ‖ -'doʊn- -'dɑːn-
adopt ə 'dɒpt ‖ ə 'dɑːpt ~**ed** ıd əd ~**er/s** ə/z
  ‖ ᵊr/z ~**ing** ıŋ ~**s** s
adoption ə 'dɒp ʃᵊn ‖ ə 'dɑːp- ~**s** z
adoptive ə 'dɒpt ıv ‖ ə 'dɑːpt- ~**ly** li
adorab|le ə 'dɔːr əb ᵊl ‖əl ‖ -'dour- ~**leness** ᵊl nəs
  -nıs ~**ly** li
adoration ˌæd ə 'reıʃ ᵊn -ɔː-
adore ə 'dɔː ‖ ə 'dɔːr -'dour **adored**
  ə 'dɔːd ‖ ə 'dɔːrd -'dourd **adores**
  ə 'dɔːz ‖ ə 'dɔːrz -'dourz **adoring/ly**
  ə 'dɔːr ıŋ /li ‖ -'dour-
adorer ə 'dɔːr ə ‖ -ᵊr -'dour- ~**s** z
adorn ə 'dɔːn ‖ ə 'dɔːrn ~**ed** d ~**ing** ıŋ ~**s** z
adornment ə 'dɔːn mənt →-'dɔːm- ‖ -'dɔːrn-
  ~**s** s
adrenal ə 'driːn ᵊl
adrenalin, A~ *tdmk*, **adrenaline** ə 'dren ᵊl ın
  -'driːn-, §-ən
adrenocorticotrophic ə ˌdriːn əʊ ˌkɔːt ık əʊ
  'trɒf ık ◄ ‖ -oʊ ˌkɔːrṭ ık oʊ 'troʊf ık ◄ -'trɑːf-
Adrian 'eıdr i_ən
Adriana ˌeıdr i 'ɑːn ə
Adriatic ˌeıdr i 'æt ık ◄ ‖ -'æṭ-
  ˌAdri,atic 'Sea
Adrienne 'eıdr i_ən ˌ••'en
adrift ə 'drıft
adroit ə 'drɔıt ~**ly** li ~**ness** nəs nıs
adsorb ₍ᵢ₎æd 'sɔːb əd-, -'zɔːb ‖ -'sɔːrb -'zɔːrb
  ~**ed** d ~**ing** ıŋ ~**s** z
adsorption ₍ᵢ₎æd 'sɔːp ʃᵊn əd-, -'zɔːp-
  ‖ -'sɔːrp- -'zɔːrp-
adstrate 'æd streıt
adsum 'æd sʊm -sʌm
aduki ə 'duːk i
adu|late 'æd ju |leıt 'ædʒ u-, 'ædʒ ə- ‖ 'ædʒ ə-
  'æd jə-, 'æd ə- ~**lated** leıt ıd -əd ‖ leıṭ əd
  ~**lates** leıts ~**lating** leıt ıŋ ‖ leıṭ ıŋ
adulation ˌæd ju 'leıʃ ᵊn ˌædʒ u-, ˌædʒ ə-
  ‖ ˌædʒ ə- ˌæd jə-, ˌæd ə-
adulator 'æd ju leıt ə 'ædʒ u-, 'ædʒ ə-
  ‖ 'ædʒ ə leıṭ ᵊr 'æd jə-, 'æd ə- ~**s** z
adulatory ˌæd ju 'leıt ər i ◄ ˌædʒ u-, ˌædʒ ə-,
  '••••; 'ædʒ ʊl ət_ər i ‖ 'ædʒ əl ə tɔːr i
  'æd jəl-, 'æd ᵊl-, -tour i
Adullam ə 'dʌl əm
Adullamite ə 'dʌl ə maıt ~**s** s
adult *adj, n* 'æd ʌlt ə 'dʌlt ‖ ə 'dʌlt 'æd ʌlt ~**s**
  s —*AmE 1993 poll panel preference (noun):*
  •'• 88%, '•• 12%
adulterant ə 'dʌlt ər ənt ~**s** s

A

adulte|rate ə 'dʌlt ə |reɪt   ~**rated** reɪt ɪd -əd
   ‖ reɪt̬ əd   ~**rates** reɪts   ~**rating**
   reɪt ɪŋ ‖ reɪt̬ ɪŋ
adulteration ə ˌdʌlt ə 'reɪʃ ³n   ~s z
adulterator ə 'dʌlt ə reɪt ə ‖ -reɪt̬ ³r   ~s z
adulterer ə 'dʌlt ³r ə ‖ _³r ³r   ~s z
adulteress ə 'dʌlt ³r es -ɪs, -əs ‖ -əs   ~es ɪz əz
adulterous ə 'dʌlt ³r əs   ~ly li
adulter|y ə 'dʌlt ³r |i   ~ies iz
adulthood 'æd ʌlt hʊd ə 'dʌlt- ‖ ə 'dʌlt-
   'æd ʌlt-
adum|brate 'æd ʌm |breɪt -əm-; ə 'dʌm-
   ~**brated** breɪt ɪd -əd ‖ breɪt̬ əd   ~**brates**
   breɪts   ~**brating** breɪt ɪŋ ‖ breɪt̬ ɪŋ
adumbration ˌæd ʌm 'breɪʃ ³n -əm-
Adur 'eɪd ə ‖ -³r
ad valorem ˌæd və 'lɔːr em -væ-, -əm ‖ -əm
   -'loʊr-
advanc|e əd 'vɑːnᵗs §₍ᵢ₎æd-, §-'vænᵗs ‖ -'vænᵗs
   ~**ed** t   ~**ement/s** mənt/s   ~**es** ɪz əz   ~**ing** ɪŋ
advantag|e əd 'vɑːnt ɪdʒ §æd-, §-'vænt-
   ‖ -'vænt̬-   —*When explicitly opposed to*
   disadvantage, *sometimes contrastively stressed*
   '•••. *In public tennis scoring often*
   æd 'vɑːnt eɪdʒ ‖ -'vænt-   ~**ed** d   ~**es** ɪz əz
advantageous ˌæd vən 'teɪdʒ əs ◄ -væn-,
   -vɑːn-   ~**ly** li   ~**ness** nəs nɪs
advent, Advent 'æd vent -v³nt
Advent|ism 'æd vənt ˌɪz əm -vent-;
   əd 'vent, ••, æd- ‖ 'æd vent̬ ˌ|- əd 'vent̬ ˌ,••,
   æd-   ~**ist/s** ɪst/s §əst/s
adventitious ˌæd vən 'tɪʃ əs ◄ -ven-   ~**ly** li
   ~**ness** nəs nɪs
adventive əd 'vent ɪv æd- ‖ -'vent̬-   ~**ly** li
adventure əd 'ventʃ ə §æd- ‖ -³r   ~**d** d   ~**s** z
   adventuring əd 'ventʃ ³r_ɪŋ §æd-
adventurer əd 'ventʃ ³r_ə §æd- ‖ _³r   ~**s** z
adventuress əd 'ventʃ ³r_əs §æd-, -ɪs, -ə res
   ~**es** ɪz əz
adventurous əd 'ventʃ ³r_əs §æd-   ~**ly** li
   ~**ness** nəs nɪs
adverb 'æd vɜːb ‖ -vɜːb   ~**s** z
adverbial əd 'vɜːb i_əl æd- ‖ -'vɜːb-   ~**ly** i   ~**s**
   z
adversarial ˌæd vɜː 'seər i_əl ◄, •və-
   ‖ -v³r 'ser- , •və-   ~**ly** i
adversar|y 'æd vəs ³r_|i -er i; §əd 'vɜːs ər |i,
   §æd- ‖ 'æd v³r ser |i '•və-   ~**ies** iz
adversative əd 'vɜːs ət ɪv æd- ‖ -'vɜːs ət̬-   ~**ly**
   li   ~**s** z
adverse 'æd vɜːs əd 'vɜːs, ˌæd- ‖ æd 'vɜːs '••
   ~**ly** li   ~**ness** nəs nɪs
adversit|y əd 'vɜːs ət i li æd-, -ɪt-
   ‖ əd 'vɜːs ət̬ li   ~**ies** iz
advert *n* 'æd vɜːt ‖ -vɜːt   ~**s** s
ad|vert *v* əd |'vɜːt æd- ‖ æd |'vɜːt   ~**verted**
   'vɜːt ɪd -əd ‖ 'vɜːt̬ əd   ~**verting**
   'vɜːt ɪŋ ‖ 'vɜːt̬ ɪŋ   ~**verts** 'vɜːts ‖ 'vɜːts
advertis|e 'æd və taɪz ‖ -v³r-   ~**ed** d   ~**es** ɪz əz
   ~**ing** ɪŋ
advertisement əd 'vɜːt ɪs mənt -ɪz-, -əs-, -əz-;
   §'æd və taɪz mənt, §,••'•••

‖ ˌæd v³r 'taɪz mənt əd 'vɜːt̬ əs-, -əz- *(*)* ~**s**
   s
advertorial ˌæd və 'tɔːr i_əl -vɜː- ‖ -v³r-
   -'toʊr-   ~**s** z
advice əd 'vaɪs §æd-
Advil *tdmk* 'æd vɪl -v³l
advisability əd ˌvaɪz ə 'bɪl ət i §æd-, -ɪti ‖ -ət̬ i
advisab|le əd 'vaɪz əb |³l §æd-   ~**ly** li
advis|e əd 'vaɪz §æd-   ~**ed** d   ~**es** ɪz əz   ~**ing** ɪŋ
advisedly əd 'vaɪz ɪd li §æd-, -əd-
advisor|y əd 'vaɪz ³r_|i §æd-   ~**ies** iz
advocaat 'æd vəʊ kɑː; -kɑːt ‖ -voʊ-
advocacy 'æd vək əs i
advocate *n* 'æd vək ət -ɪt; -və keɪt   ~**s** s
advo|cate *v* 'æd və |keɪt   ~**cated** keɪt ɪd -əd
   ‖ keɪt̬ əd   ~**cates** keɪts   ~**cating**
   keɪt ɪŋ ‖ keɪt̬ ɪŋ
advokaat 'æd vəʊ kɑː; -kɑːt ‖ -voʊ-
advowson əd 'vaʊz ³n æd-   ~**s** z
Adwick-le-Street ˌæd wɪk li 'striːt
adz, adze ædz   **adzed** ædzd   **adzes** 'ædz ɪz -əz
   adzing 'ædz ɪŋ
adzuki æd 'zuːk i —*Jp* [a ˌdzɯ 'ki]
   ad'zuki bean
aedes, Aedes, Aëdes eɪ 'iːd iːz
aedile 'iːd aɪ³l ‖ -³l   ~**s** z   ~**ship/s** ʃɪp/s
Aegean ɪ 'dʒiː_ən iː-
   Ae,gean 'Sea
Aegina ɪ 'dʒaɪn ə -'giːn- —*ModGk* ['e ji na]
aegis 'iːdʒ ɪs §-əs
Aegisthus ɪ 'dʒɪs θəs
aegrotat 'aɪg rəʊ tæt 'iːg-; i 'grəʊt æt ‖ -roʊ-
   ~**s** s
Aelfric, Ælfric 'ælf rɪk
-aemia *comb. form* 'iːm i_ə— **septicaemia**
   ˌsept ɪ 'siːm i_ə ,•ə-
Aeneas i 'niː_əs -'neɪ-, -æs
Aeneid 'iːn i_ɪd i 'niː ɪd
Aeolian i 'əʊl i_ən eɪ- ‖ i 'oʊl-   ~**s** z
Aeolic i 'ɒl ɪk -'əʊl- ‖ i 'ɑːl-
Aeolus 'iː_əl əs i 'əʊl-
aeon 'iː_ən 'iː ɒn ‖ -ɑːn   ~**s** z
aepyornis ˌiːp i 'ɔːn ɪs §-əs ‖ -'ɔːrn-
aer|ate 'eər |eɪt △'eər i |eɪt ‖ 'er- 'ær-   ~**ated**
   eɪt ɪd -əd ‖ eɪt̬ əd   ~**ates** eɪts   ~**ating**
   eɪt ɪŋ ‖ eɪt̬ ɪŋ
aeration ₍ᵢ₎eə 'reɪʃ ³n ‖ ₍ᵢ₎e- ₍ᵢ₎æ-
aerator 'eər eɪt ə △'eər i •• ‖ 'er eɪt̬ ³r 'ær-   ~**s**
   z
aerial 'eər i_əl ‖ 'er- 'ær-; eɪ 'ɪr- —*in RP*
   formerly also eɪ 'ɪər i_əl   ~**s** z
aerialist 'eər i_əl ɪst §-əst ‖ 'er- 'ær-   ~**s** s
aerie 'ɪər i 'eər-, 'aɪ³r- ‖ 'er i 'ær-, 'ɪr-; 'eɪ ri   ~**s**
   z
Aer Lingus *tdmk* ˌeə 'lɪŋ gəs ‖ ˌer- ˌær-
aero, Aero 'eər əʊ ‖ 'er oʊ 'ær-   ~**s** z
aero- *comb. form*
   with stress-neutral suffix ¦eər əʊ ‖ ¦er oʊ ¦ær-,
   -ə — **aerobiosis** ˌeər əʊ baɪ 'əʊs ɪs §-əs
   ‖ ˌer oʊ baɪ 'oʊs əs ˌær-
   with stress-imposing suffix ₍ᵢ₎eə 'rɒ+ ‖ ₍ᵢ₎e 'rɑː+
   ₍ᵢ₎æ- — **aerography**
   ₍ᵢ₎eə 'rɒg rəf i ‖ ₍ᵢ₎e 'rɑːg- ₍ᵢ₎æ-

aerobatic ˌeər əʊ 'bæt ɪk ◂ ‖ ˌer ə 'bæt̬ ɪk ◂
ˌær- **~ally** ᵊl‿i **~s** s
aerobic ⁽ˌ⁾eə 'rəʊb ɪk ‖ ⁽ˌ⁾e 'roʊb ɪk ⁽ˌ⁾æ- **~ally**
ᵊl‿i **~s** s
aerodrome 'eər ə drəʊm ‖ 'er ə droʊm 'ær- **~s**
z
aerodynamic ˌeər əʊ daɪ 'næm ɪk ◂-dɪ'·-
‖ ˌer oʊ- ˌær- **~ally** ᵊl‿i **~s** s
aerodyne 'eər əʊ daɪn ‖ 'er ə- 'ær- **~s** z
Aeroflot tdmk 'eər əʊ flɒt ‖ 'er ə floʊt 'ær-,
-flɑːt —Russ [ʌ ɪ rʌ 'flɔt]
aerofoil 'eər əʊ fɔɪᵊl ‖ 'er oʊ- 'ær- **~s** z
aerogram, aerogramme 'eər əʊ græm ‖ 'er ə-
'ær- **~s** z
aerolite 'eər əʊ laɪt ‖ 'er ə- 'ær- **~s** s
aerolith 'eər əʊ lɪθ ‖ 'er ə- 'ær- **~s** s
aeronaut 'eər əʊ nɔːt ‖ 'er ə- 'ær-, -nɑːt **~s** s
aeronautic ˌeər əʊ 'nɔːt ɪk ◂ ‖ ˌer ə 'nɔːt̬ ɪk ◂
ˌær-, -'nɑːt̬- **~al** ᵊl **~ally** ᵊl‿i **~s** s
Aeronwy aɪᵊ 'rɒn wi ‖ -'rɑːn- —Welsh
[əi 'rɔn ui, -wi]
aeroplane 'eər ə pleɪn ‖ 'er- 'ær- **~s** z
aerosol 'eər əʊ sɒl ‖ 'er ə sɑːl 'ær-, -sɔːl **~s** z
aerospace 'eər əʊ speɪs ‖ 'er oʊ- 'ær-
aerostatic ˌeər əʊ 'stæt ɪk ◂ ‖ ˌer oʊ 'stæt̬ ɪk ◂
ˌær- **~ally** ᵊl‿i **~s** s
aertex, A~ tdmk 'eə teks ‖ 'er- 'ær-
aer|y 'nest, high place' 'ɪər li 'eər-, 'aɪᵊr- ‖ 'er li
'ær-, 'ɪr-; 'eɪ r|i **~ies** iz
aery 'ethereal' 'eər i ‖ 'er i 'ær-; 'eɪ ər i
Aeschines 'iːsk ɪ niːz-ə- ‖ 'esk- 'iːsk-
Aeschylus 'iːsk əl əs-ɪl- ‖ 'esk- 'iːsk-
Aesculapi|an ˌiːsk ju 'leɪp i‿|ən ˌjə- ‖ ˌesk jə-
ˌ·ə- **~us** əs
Aesop 'iːs ɒp ‖ -ɑːp-əp
Aesopian iː 'səʊp i‿ən -'sɒp- ‖ -'soʊp- -'sɑːp-
aesthete 'iːs θiːt ‖ 'es- (*) **~s** s
aesthetic iːs 'θet ɪk-s, eɪs- ‖ es 'θet̬ ɪk ɪs-
~ally ᵊl‿i **~s** s
aestheticism iːs 'θet ɪ ˌsɪz əm-ə- ‖ es 'θet̬ ə-
ɪs-
aestival iː 'staɪv ᵊl ‖ 'est əv ᵊl
aesti|vate 'iːst ɪ |veɪt 'est-, -ə- ‖ 'est- **~vated**
veɪt ɪd-əd ‖ veɪt̬ əd **~vates** veɪts **~vating**
veɪt ɪŋ ‖ veɪt̬ ɪŋ
aestivation ˌiːst ɪ 'veɪʃ ᵊn ˌest-, -ə- ‖ ˌest- **~s**
z
Æthelbert 'eθ ᵊl bɜːt ‖ -bɝːt
Æthelred 'eθ ᵊl red
aether, Aether 'iːθ ə ‖ -ᵊr (= ether)
Aetherius iː 'θɪər i‿əs ɪ- ‖ 'θɪr-
aetiological ˌiːt i‿ə 'lɒdʒ ɪk ᵊl ◂ ‖ ˌiːt̬ i‿ə 'lɑːdʒ-
~ly ‿i
aetiolog|y ˌiːt i 'ɒl ədʒ li ‖ ˌiːt̬ i 'ɑːl- **~ies** iz
Aetna 'et nə
Aetoli|a i 'təʊl i‿|ə ‖ -'toʊl- **~an/s** ən/z
af- ə, æ —This variant of ad- is usually ə
(af'firm); but if stressed because of a suffix it is
ˌæ (ˌaffir'mation).
afar ə 'fɑː ‖ ə 'fɑːr
Afar African people 'æf ɑː æ 'fɑː, ə- ‖ 'ɑːf ɑːr
~s z
affability ˌæf ə 'bɪl ət i-ɪt i ‖ -ət̬ i

affab|le 'æf əb |ᵊl **~ly** li
affair ə 'feə ‖ ə 'feᵊr ə 'fæᵊr **~s** z
affaire ə 'feə ‖ ə 'feᵊr ə 'fæᵊr —Fr [a fɛːʁ] **~s** z
affect v ə 'fekt —Also, to highlight the contrast
with effect, sometimes ⁽ˌ⁾æ- **~ed** ɪd əd **~ing** ɪŋ
~s s
affect n 'æf ekt ə 'fekt **~s** s
affectation ˌæf ek 'teɪʃ ᵊn-ɪk- **~s** z
affected ə 'fekt ɪd-əd **~ly** li **~ness** nəs nɪs
affection ə 'fek ʃᵊn **~s** z
affectionate ə 'fek ʃᵊn‿ət ‿ɪt **~ly** li **~ness** nəs
nɪs
affective æ 'fekt ɪv
affenpinscher 'æf ᵊn ˌpɪntʃ ə ‖ -ᵊr **~s** z
afferent 'æf ər ənt
affianc|e ə 'faɪ‿ᵊnts æ- **~ed** t **~es** ɪz əz **~ing**
ɪŋ
affidavit ˌæf ɪ 'deɪv ɪt-ə-, §-ət **~s** s
affili|ate v ə 'fɪl i |eɪt **~ated** eɪt ɪd-əd ‖ eɪt̬ əd
~ates eɪts **~ating** eɪt ɪŋ ‖ eɪt̬ ɪŋ
affiliate n, adj ə 'fɪl i‿ət ‿ɪt, -eɪt **~s** s
affiliation ə ˌfɪl i 'eɪʃ ᵊn **~s** z
af,fili'ation ,order
affinit|y ə 'fɪn ət i li-ɪt- ‖ -ət̬ i **~ies** iz
affirm ə 'fɜːm ‖ ə 'fɝːm **~ed** d **~ing** ɪŋ **~s** z
affirmation ˌæf ə 'meɪʃ ᵊn ‖ -ᵊr- **~s** z
affirmative ə 'fɜːm ət ɪv ‖ ə 'fɝːm ət̬ ɪv **~ly** li
affix v ə 'fɪks æ- **~ed** t **~es** ɪz əz **~ing** ɪŋ
affix n 'æf ɪks **~es** ɪz əz
affixation ˌæf ɪk 'seɪʃ ᵊn
afflatus ə 'fleɪt əs æ- ‖ -'fleɪt̬-
afflict ə 'flɪkt **~ed** ɪd əd **~ing** ɪŋ **~s** s
affliction ə 'flɪk ʃᵊn **~s** z
afflictive ə 'flɪkt ɪv **~ly** li
affluence 'æf lu‿ᵊnts
affluent 'æf lu‿ənt **~ly** li
afflux 'æf lʌks **~es** ɪz əz
afford ə 'fɔːd ‖ ə 'fɔːrd -'foʊrd **~ed** ɪd əd
~ing ɪŋ **~s** z
affordability ə ˌfɔːd ə 'bɪl ət i-ɪt-
‖ ə ˌfɔːrd ə 'bɪl ət̬ i-ˌfoʊrd-
affordab|le ə 'fɔːd əb |ᵊl ‖ -'fɔːrd- -'foʊrd-
~ly li
afforest ə 'fɒr ɪst æ-, -əst ‖ -'fɔːr əst -'fɑːr-
~ed ɪd əd **~ing** ɪŋ **~s** s
afforestation ə ˌfɒr ɪ 'steɪʃ ᵊn æ-, -ə-
‖ -ˌfɔːr ə- -ˌfɑːr-; ˌæ,·· '·· ·
affray ə 'freɪ **~s** z
Affric 'æf rɪk
affricate n 'æf rɪk ət-rək-, -ɪt; -rɪ keɪt, -rə- **~s**
s
affri|cate v 'æf rɪ |keɪt-rə- **~cated** keɪt ɪd-əd
‖ keɪt̬ əd **~cates** keɪts **~cating**
keɪt ɪŋ ‖ keɪt̬ ɪŋ
affrication ˌæf rɪ 'keɪʃ ᵊn-rə-
affricative æ 'frɪk ət ɪv ə-; 'æf rɪ keɪt-, '·rə-
‖ -ət̬- **~ly** li
affright ə 'fraɪt
affront n, v ə 'frʌnt **affronted** ə 'frʌnt ɪd-əd
‖ ə 'frʌnt̬ əd **affronting** ə 'frʌnt ɪŋ ‖ ə 'frʌnt̬
ɪŋ **affronts** ə 'frʌnts
Afghan, a~ 'æf gæn-gɑːn, -gən **~s** z
afghani æf 'gɑːn i-'gæn- **~s** z

A

A

Afghanistan æf ˈɡæn ɪ stɑːn -ə-, -stæn, •ˌ••ˈ•, ˌ•••ˈ• ‖ -ə stæn
aficionado ə ˌfɪʃ iˌə ˈnɑːd əʊ ə ˌfɪs-, ə ˌfɪʃ əˈ•- ‖ -ˈnɑːd oʊ —*Sp* [a fi θjo ˈna ðo, -sjo•-] ~s z
afield ə ˈfiːˀld
afire ə ˈfaɪ‿ə ‖ ə ˈfaɪ‿ᵊr
aflame ə ˈfleɪm
aflatoxin ˌæf lə ˈtɒks ɪn §-ᵊn ‖ -ˈtɑːks ᵊn ~s z
AFL-CIO ˌeɪ ef ˈel ˌsiː aɪ ˈəʊ ‖ -ˈoʊ
afloat ə ˈfləʊt ‖ ə ˈfloʊt
aflutter ə ˈflʌt ə ‖ ə ˈflʌt ᵊr
Afon ˈæv ᵊn -ɒn ‖ -ɑːn —*Welsh* [ˈa von]
afoot ə ˈfʊt
afore ə ˈfɔː ‖ ə ˈfɔːr -ˈfoʊr
aforementioned ə ˌfɔː ˈmentʃ ᵊnd ◄ •ˈ•, •• ‖ ə ˌfɔːr- -ˌfoʊr-
aforesaid ə ˈfɔː sed ‖ ə ˈfɔːr- -ˈfoʊr-
aforethought ə ˈfɔː θɔːt ‖ ə ˈfɔːr- -ˈfoʊr-, -θɑːt
aforetime ə ˈfɔː taɪm ‖ ə ˈfɔːr- -ˈfoʊr-
a fortiori ˌeɪ ˌfɔːt i ˈɔːr aɪ ˌɑː-, -i ‖ ˌeɪ ˌfɔːrʃ i ˈɔːr i -ˌfɔːrt̮-, -ˈoʊr-, -aɪ
afoul ə ˈfaʊl
afraid ə ˈfreɪd
A-frame ˈeɪ freɪm ~s z
afresh ə ˈfreʃ
Africa ˈæf rɪk ə
African ˈæf rɪk ᵊn ~s z
African-American ˌæf rɪk ᵊn ə ˈmer ɪk ᵊn ◄ ~s z
Africanis... *see* **Africaniz...**
Africanist ˈæf rɪk ᵊn ɪst §-əst ~s s
Africanization ˌæf rɪk ᵊn aɪ ˈzeɪʃ ᵊn ˌ•rək-, -ɪˈ•- ‖ -ə•ˈ•- ~s z
Africaniz|e ˈæf rɪk ə naɪz ˈ•rək- ~ed d ~es ɪz əz ~ing ɪŋ
Afrikaans ˌæf rɪ ˈkɑːnˣs ◄ -rə-, -ˈkɑːnz ‖ ˌɑːf-
Afrikaner ˌæf rɪ ˈkɑːn ə ◄ -rə- -ˈ•r ˌɑːf- ~dom dəm ~s z
Afro, afro ˈæf rəʊ ‖ -roʊ ~s z
Afro- *comb. form* ˈæf rəʊ ‖ -roʊ — **Afro-Cuban** ˌæf rəʊ ˈkjuːb ən ◄ ‖ -roʊ-
Afro-Asiatic ˌæf rəʊ ˌeɪʃ i ˈæt ɪk ◄ -ˌeɪz-, -ˌeɪʒ-, -ˌeɪs- ‖ -roʊ ˌeɪʒ i ˈæt̮ ɪk ◄
Afro-Caribbean ˌæf rəʊ ˌkær ə ˈbiːᵊn ◄ -ˌɪ-; -kə ˈrɪb iˌən ‖ -ˌker-; -kə ˈrɪb iˌən ~s z
afrormosia ˌæf rɔː ˈməʊz iˌə ‖ ˌæf rɔːr ˈmoʊʒ ə
aft ɑːft §æft ‖ æft
after ˈɑːft ə §ˈæft- ‖ ˈæft ᵊr ~s z
after- ˈɑːft ə §ˈæft ə ‖ ˈæft ᵊr —*Compounds with this prefix are almost always early-stressed* (ˈafter,burner). *There is one important exception:* ˌafterˈnoon.
afterbirth ˈɑːft ə bɜːθ §ˈæft- ‖ ˈæft ᵊr bɜːθ ~s s
afterburner ˈɑːft ə ˌbɜːn ə §ˈæft- ‖ ˈæft ᵊr ˌbɜːn ᵊr ~s z
aftercare ˈɑːft ə keə §ˈæft- ‖ ˈæft ᵊr ker -kær
aftereffect ˈɑːft ər ɪ ˌfekt §ˈæft-, ˈ•ˌᵊr-, -ə,• ‖ ˈæft ᵊr- ~s s
afterglow ˈɑːft ə gləʊ §ˈæft- ‖ ˈæft ᵊr gloʊ
afterlife ˈɑːft ə laɪf §ˈæft- ‖ ˈæft ᵊr-

aftermath ˈɑːft ə mæθ §ˈæft-, -mɑːθ ‖ ˈæft ᵊr-
afternoon ˌɑːft ə ˈnuːn ◄ §ˌæft-, §-ˈnʊn, -ᵊn ˈuːn ‖ ˌæft ᵊr- ~s z
   ˌafternoon ˈtea
after-sales ˌɑːft ə ˈseɪᵊlz ◄ §ˌæft- ‖ ˌæft ᵊr-
aftershave ˈɑːft ə ʃeɪv §ˈæft-, ˌ•ˈ•ˈ ‖ ˈæft ᵊr- ~s z
   ˈaftershave ˌlotion, ˌ••ˈ•, ˌ••
aftershock ˈɑːft ə ʃɒk §ˈæft- ‖ ˈæft ᵊr ʃɑːk ~s s
aftertaste ˈɑːft ə teɪst §ˈæft- ‖ ˈæft ᵊr- ~s s
afterthought ˈɑːft ə θɔːt §ˈæft- ‖ ˈæft ᵊr- -θɑːt ~s s
afterward ˈɑːft ə wəd §ˈæft- ‖ ˈæft ᵊr wᵊrd ~s z
Afton ˈæft ən
ag- ə-, æ —*This variant of ad- is usually* ə (agˈgression), *but* ˌæ *if stressed because of a suffix* (ˈaggravate).
Aga, aga ˈɑːg ə
   ˌAga ˈKhan
Agadir ˌæg ə ˈdɪə ‖ ˌɑːg ə ˈdɪᵊr ˌæg-
Agag ˈeɪg æg
again ə ˈgen ə ˈgeɪn —*BrE 1988 poll panel preference:* -ˈgen 80%, -ˈgeɪn 20%. *Many BrE speakers use both pronunciations. AmE 1993 poll panel preference:* -ˈgen 97%, -ˈgeɪn 3%.
against ə ˈgenᵗst ə ˈgeɪnᵗst
agama ˈæg əm ə ə ˈgɑːm ə ~s z
Agamemnon ˌæg ə ˈmem nən -nɒn ‖ -nɑːn
agapanthus ˌæg ə ˈpænᵗθ əs ~es ɪz əz
agape *adv, adj* ˈwide open' ə ˈgeɪp
agape *n* ˈlove, love feast' ˈæg əp i -eɪ; ə ˈgɑːp i ‖ ɑː ˈgɑːp eɪ ˈɑːg ə peɪ
agar ˈeɪg ə -ɑː ‖ ˈɑːg ᵊr ˈeɪg-, -ɑːr
Agar *family name (i)* ˈeɪg ə ‖ -ᵊr, *(ii)* -ɑː ‖ -ɑːr
agar-agar ˌeɪg ᵊr ˈeɪg ə ‖ ˌɑːg ᵊr ˈɑːg ᵊr
agaric ˈæg ᵊr ɪk ə ˈgær- ~s s
Agassi, Agassiz ˈæg əs i
agate ˈæg ət -ɪt
Agate *family name (i)* ˈæg ət, *(ii)* ˈeɪg ət
Agatha ˈæg əθ ə
agave ə ˈgeɪv i ə ˈgɑːv i, ˈæg eɪv ‖ ə ˈgɑːv i ~s z
age eɪdʒ **aged** *past, pp* eɪdʒd **ageing, aging** ˈeɪdʒ ɪŋ **ages** ˈeɪdʒ ɪz -əz
   ˌage of conˈsent
-age ɪdʒ, (ˌ)ɑːʒ —*In most words -age is pronounced* ɪdʒ (perˈcentage), *although some recent French borrowings are pronounced with* ɑːʒ, *stressed in AmE and sometimes in BrE* (ˌentouˈrage). *Some words have two or more competing variants* (garage), *and there are exceptions* (outrage).
aged ˈvery old' ˈeɪdʒ ɪd -əd; §eɪdʒd
aged ˈhaving a specified age'; *past and pp of* **age** eɪdʒd
Agee ˈeɪdʒ iː
ageism ˈeɪdʒ ˌɪz əm
ageist ˈeɪdʒ ɪst §-əst ~s s
ageless ˈeɪdʒ ləs -lɪs ~ly li ~ness nəs nɪs
age-long ˌeɪdʒ ˈlɒŋ ◄ ‖ ˈeɪdʒ lɔːŋ ◄ -lɑːŋ
agenc|y ˈeɪdʒ ᵊnᵗs li ~ies iz

Affricates

1 An **affricate** is a complex consonant sound consisting of a plosive that is immediately followed by a fricative (see ARTICULATION) made at the same place of articulation. It can therefore also be described as a plosive that has a slow release.

2 English has two affricate phonemes: tʃ, as in **church** tʃɜːtʃ ‖ tʃɝːtʃ, and dʒ, as in **judge** dʒʌdʒ. Their place of articulation is palato-alveolar. In addition to this pair, the clusters tr and dr are pronounced as affricates in RP and GenAm, as in **try** traɪ and **dream** driːm. Their place of articulation is post-alveolar.

3 Affricates always belong together in the same syllable: **achieve** ə ˈtʃiːv, **address** ə ˈdres, **natural** ˈnætʃ rəl.

4 Other affricate-like sequences of consonants are found in words such as **obvious** ˈɒb vi‿əs ‖ ˈɑːb vi‿əs, **eighth** eɪtθ, **cats** kæts, **rides** raɪdz; but we do not usually list bv, tθ, ts, dz among the English affricates. Notice also that the t followed by ʃ in **nutshell** ˈnʌt ʃel is not an affricate.

---

agenda ə ˈdʒend ə ~**s** z
agene ˈeɪdʒ iːn
agent ˈeɪdʒ ənt ~**s** s —*See also phrases with this word*
agent provocateur ˌæʒ ɒ̃ prə ˌvɒk ə ˈtɜː ˌeɪdʒ ənt- ‖ ˌɑːʒ ɑ̃ː prou ˌvɑːk ə ˈtɜː -ˈtʊᵊr —*Fr* [a ʒɑ̃ pʁɔ vɔ ka tœːʁ] **agents provocateurs** *same pronunciation, or* -z
agentive ˈeɪdʒ ənt ɪv
age-old ˌeɪdʒ ˈəʊld ◄ →-ˈɒʊld ‖ -ˈoʊld ◄
-ageous ˈeɪdʒ əs —*This suffix may impose rhythmic stress on the preceding stem* (ˌadvanˈtageous).
ageratum ˌædʒ ə ˈreɪt əm ‖ -ˈreɪt̬- ~**s** z
Agfa *tdmk* ˈæg fə
Agg æg
Aggett ˈæg ɪt -ət
Aggie ˈæg i
aggiornamento ə ˌdʒɔːn ə ˈment əʊ ˌæ- ‖ ə ˌdʒɔːrn ə ˈment ou —*It* [ad dʒor na ˈmen to]
agglome|rate v ə ˈglɒm ə ˌreɪt ‖ ə ˈglɑːm- ~**rated** reɪt ɪd -əd ‖ reɪt̬ əd ~**rates** reɪts ~**rating** reɪt ɪŋ ‖ reɪt̬ ɪŋ
agglomerate *adj, n* ə ˈglɒm ər ət -ɪt, -ə reɪt ‖ ə ˈglɑːm- ~**s** s
agglomeration ə ˌglɒm ə ˈreɪʃ ən ‖ ə ˌglɑːm- ~**s** z
aggluti|nate v ə ˈgluːt ɪ ˌneɪt -ə- ‖ -əⁿ eɪt ~**nated** neɪt ɪd -əd ‖ neɪt̬ əd ~**nates** neɪts ~**nating** neɪt ɪŋ ‖ neɪt̬ ɪŋ
agglutinate *adj, n* ə ˈgluːt ɪn ət -ən-, -ɪt; -ɪ neɪt, -ə- ‖ -ⁿn- ~**s** s
agglutination ə ˌgluːt ɪ ˈneɪʃ ən -ə- ‖ -ⁿn ˈeɪʃ-
agglutinative ə ˈgluːt ɪn ət ɪv •ˈ•ən-; -ɪ neɪt-, -ə neɪt-, -ⁿn eɪt- ‖ -ⁿn eɪt̬ ɪv -ⁿn ət̬ ɪv ~**ly** li

aggrandis... —*see* **aggrandiz...**
aggrandiz|e ə ˈgrænd aɪz ˈæg rən daɪz ~**ed** d ~**es** ɪz əz ~**ing** ɪŋ
aggrandizement ə ˈgrænd ɪz mənt -əz-, -aɪz-
aggra|vate ˈæg rə ˌveɪt ~**vated** veɪt ɪd -əd ‖ veɪt̬ əd ~**vates** veɪts ~**vating/ly** veɪt ɪŋ /li ‖ veɪt̬ ɪŋ /li
aggravation ˌæg rə ˈveɪʃ ən ~**s** z
aggregate *adj, n* ˈæg rɪg ət -rəg-, -ɪt; -rɪ geɪt, -rə- ~**s** s
aggre|gate v ˈæg rɪ ˌgeɪt -rə- ~**gated** geɪt ɪd -əd ‖ geɪt̬ əd ~**gates** geɪts ~**gating** geɪt ɪŋ ‖ geɪt̬ ɪŋ
aggregation ˌæg rɪ ˈgeɪʃ ən -rə- ~**s** z
aggression ə ˈgreʃ ən
aggressive ə ˈgres ɪv ~**ly** li ~**ness** nəs nɪs
aggressor ə ˈgres ə ‖ -ᵊr ~**s** z
aggrieved ə ˈgriːvd
aggro ˈæg rəʊ ‖ -roʊ
Agha- *comb. form in Irish place names* ˌæx ə — **Aghacully** ˌæx ə ˈkʌl i
aghast ə ˈgɑːst §-ˈgæst ‖ ə ˈgæst
agile ˈædʒ aɪᵊl ‖ -ᵊl -aɪᵊl ~**ly** li ~**ness** nəs nɪs
agility ə ˈdʒɪl ət i -ɪt i ‖ -ət̬ i
agin ə ˈgɪn
Agincourt ˈædʒ ɪn kɔː ˈæʒ-, §-ən-, -kɔːt ‖ -kɔːrt -kourt
agio ˈædʒ i‿əʊ ‖ -ou ~**s** z
agiotage ˈædʒ ət ɪdʒ ˈædʒ i‿ət ɪdʒ, ə ˈtɑːʒ ‖ ˈædʒ i‿ət̬ ɪdʒ ˌæʒ ə ˈtɑːʒ
agist v ə ˈdʒɪst ~**ed** ɪd əd ~**ing** ɪŋ ~**ment/s** mənt/s ~**s** s
agi|tate ˈædʒ ɪ ˌteɪt -ə- ~**tated/ly** teɪt ɪd /li -əd /li ‖ teɪt̬ əd /li ~**tates** teɪts ~**tating** teɪt ɪŋ ‖ teɪt̬ ɪŋ
agitation ˌædʒ ɪ ˈteɪʃ ən -ə- ~**s** z

A

agitato ˌædʒ ɪ 'tɑːt əʊ -ə- ‖ -oʊ
agitator 'ædʒ ɪ teɪt ə '•ə- ‖ -teɪt̬ ər ~s z
agitprop 'ædʒ ɪt prɒp §-ət-, ˌ•'• ‖ -prɑːp
Aglaia ə 'glaɪ_ə -'gleɪ ə
agleam ə 'gliːm
aglet 'æg lət -lɪt ~s s
agley ə 'gleɪ -'glaɪ, -'gliː
aglimmer ə 'glɪm ə ‖ -ər
aglitter ə 'glɪt ə ‖ ə 'glɪt̬ ər
aglow ə 'gləʊ ‖ ə 'gloʊ
AGM ˌeɪ dʒiː 'em ~s, ~'s z
agma 'æg mə 'æŋ- ~s z
agnail 'æg neɪəl ~s z
agnate 'æg neɪt ~s s
Agnes 'æg nɪs -nəs
Agnew 'æg njuː ‖ -nuː
Agni 'æg ni 'ʌg- —Hindi [əg n̩i]
agnomen æg 'nəʊm en ‖ -'noʊm ən
agnosia æg 'nəʊz i_ə ‖ -'noʊʒ ə -'noʊʃ-
agnostic ₍ᵢ₎æg 'nɒst ɪk əg- ‖ -'nɑːst- ~ally ᵊl_i
~s s
agnosticism ₍ᵢ₎æg 'nɒst ɪ ˌsɪz əm əg-, -ə-
‖ -'nɑːst-
Agnus Dei ˌæg nəs 'deɪ_iː ˌɑːg-, -nʊs-,
ˌɑːn jʊs-, -'diː aɪ
ago ə 'gəʊ ‖ ə 'goʊ
agog ə 'gɒg ‖ ə 'gɑːg
-agogic ə 'gɒdʒ ɪk -'gəʊdʒ- ‖ -'gɑːdʒ-
-'goʊdʒ- — hypnagogic ˌhɪp nə 'gɒdʒ ɪk ◄
-'gəʊdʒ- ‖ -'gɑːdʒ- -'goʊdʒ-
a-go-go, à gogo ə 'gəʊ gəʊ ‖ ɑː 'goʊ goʊ —Fr
[a go go]
-agogue stress-imposing ə gɒg ‖ ə gɑːg —
galactogogue gə 'lækt ə gɒg ‖ -gɑːg
-agogy ə gɒdʒ i -gɒg-, -gəʊg- ‖ ə gɑːdʒ i
-gɑːg-, -goʊg- — pedagogy 'ped ə gɒdʒ i
-gɒg i ‖ -gɑːdʒ i -gɑːg i
agoni... —see agony
agonis... —see agonize
agonist 'æg ən ɪst §-əst ~s s
Agonistes ˌæg əʊ 'nɪst iːz ‖ -ə-
agoniz|e 'æg ə naɪz ~ed d ~es ɪz əz ~ing/ly
ɪŋ /li
agon|y 'æg ən li ~ies iz
'agony aunt; 'agony ˌcolumn
agora, Agora 'æg ər ə ~s z
agoraphobia ˌæg ər_ə 'fəʊb i_ə ‖ -'foʊb-
agoraphobic ˌæg ər_ə 'fəʊb ɪk ◄ ‖ -'foʊb- ~s s
agouti ə 'guːt i ‖ ə 'guːt̬ i ~es, ~s z
Agra 'ɑːg rə 'æg-
agranulocytosis ə ˌgræn jʊl əʊ saɪ 'təʊs ɪs
ˌeɪ, •-, -jəl •-'•-, §-əs
‖ ə ˌgræn jə loʊ saɪ 'toʊs əs
agrapha 'æg rəf ə
agraphia ₍ᵢ₎eɪ 'græf i_ə æ-
agrarian ə 'greər i_ən æ- ‖ ə 'grer- ə 'grær-
~ism ˌɪz əm ~s z
agree ə 'griː agreed ə 'griːd agrees ə 'griːz
agreeing ə 'griː_ɪŋ
agreeab|le ə 'griː_əb |əl ~leness ᵊl nəs -nɪs
~ly li
agreement ə 'griː mənt ~s s
agribusiness 'æg ri ˌbɪz nəs -nɪs

Agricola ə 'grɪk əl ə æ-
agricultural ˌæg rɪ 'kʌltʃ ər_əl ◄ , •rə- ~ly i
agriculturalist ˌæg rɪ 'kʌltʃ ər_əl ɪst , •rə-, §-əst
~s s
agriculture 'æg rɪ ˌkʌltʃ ə -rə-, ˌ•'•• ◄ ‖ -ər
agriculturist ˌæg rɪ 'kʌltʃ ər ɪst , •rə-, §-əst ~s
s
Agrigento ˌæg rɪ 'dʒent əʊ -rə- ‖ -oʊ —It
[a gri 'dʒɛn to]
agrimony 'æg rɪm ən i '•rəm- ‖ -ə moʊn i
Agrippa ə 'grɪp ə
Agrippina ˌæg rɪ 'piːn ə -rə-
agro- comb. form
with stress-neutral suffix ¦æg rəʊ ‖ -roʊ —
agrobiology
ˌæg rəʊ baɪ 'ɒl ədʒ i ‖ -roʊ baɪ 'ɑːl-
with stress-imposing suffix ə 'grɒ+ æ-
‖ -'grɑː+ — agrology ə 'grɒl ədʒ i æ-
‖ -'grɑːl-
agronomic ˌæg rəʊ 'nɒm ɪk ◄ ‖ -rə 'nɑːm-
~al/ly ᵊl /_i ~s s
agronomist ə 'grɒn əm ɪst §-əst ‖ ə 'grɑːn- ~s
s
agronomy ə 'grɒn əm i ‖ ə 'grɑːn-
aground ə 'graʊnd
aguardiente
ˌæg wɑːd i 'ent i ‖ ˌɑːg wɑːrd i 'ent̬ i -'ent eɪ
—Sp [a ɣwar 'ðjen te]
ague 'eɪg juː ~s z
Aguecheek 'eɪg juː tʃiːk
aguish 'eɪg ju ɪʃ ~ly li ~ness nəs nɪs
Agulhas ə 'gʌl əs
Agutter (i) 'æg ət ə ‖ -ət̬ ər , (ii)
ə 'gʌt ə ‖ ə 'gʌt̬ ər
aha ɑː
aha ɑː 'hɑː ə-
Ahab 'eɪ hæb
Ahasuerus ˌeɪ hæz ju 'ɪər əs ə ˌhæz-, -'eər-
‖ -'ɪr-
ahead ə 'hed
ahem [ʔm ʔm:] said with tense voice; also
[m 'm̩m]; also spelling pronunciation ə 'hem
Ahenobarbus ə ˌhiːn əʊ 'bɑːb əs -ˌhen-
‖ -oʊ 'bɑːrb-
Ahern, Aherne (i) ə 'hɜːn ‖ ə 'hɝːn , (ii)
'eɪ hɜːn ‖ -hɝːn
ahimsa ə 'hɪm sɑː
ahistorical ˌeɪ hɪ 'stɒr ɪk ᵊl ‖ -'stɔːr- -'stɑːr-
~ly_i
Ahithophel ə 'hɪθ ə fel
Ahmadabad 'ɑːm əd ə bæd '•ɪd-, -bɑːd
Ahmed 'ɑːm ed
Ahmedabad 'ɑːm əd ə bæd '•ɪd-, '•ed-, -bɑːd
ahoy ə 'hɔɪ
Ahura Mazda ə ˌhʊər ə 'mæz də ‖ ə ˌhʊr- ɑː-,
-'mɑːz-
AI ˌeɪ 'aɪ
ai 'three-toed sloth' 'aɪ i 'ɑː i, aɪ ais 'aɪ iz 'ɑː iz,
aɪz
aid eɪd aided 'eɪd ɪd -əd aiding 'eɪd ɪŋ aids
eɪdz
AID ˌeɪ aɪ 'diː
Aida, Aïda aɪ 'iːd ə ɑː- —It [a 'i: da]

Aidan 'eɪd ᵊn

aide eɪd (= *aid*) **aides** eɪdz

aide|-de-camp ˌeɪd‖ də 'kɑːmp -'kɒ̃, -'kɑ̃ː
‖ -'kæmp —*Fr* [ɛd də kɑ̃] **aides~** ˌeɪd-
ˌeɪdz- —*Fr* [ɛd də kɑ̃]

aide-memoire, aide-mémoire ˌeɪd mem 'wɑː
ˌ•'•• ‖ -'wɑːr —*Fr* [ɛd me mwaːʁ]

AIDS, Aids eɪdz
'AIDS ˌpatient

aigrette 'eɪg ret eɪ 'gret ~s s

aiguille 'eɪg wiːl -wɪl ‖ ˌeɪ 'gwiːᵊl —*Fr* [e ɡɥij]
~s z *or as sing.*

aiguillette ˌeɪg wɪ 'let -wə- ~s s

Aiken 'eɪk ᵊn

aikido aɪ 'kiːd əʊ 'aɪk ɪ dəʊ ‖ aɪ 'kiːd oʊ
ˌaɪk ɪ 'doʊ —*Jp* [a,i 'ki doo]

ail eɪᵊl (= *ale*) **ailed** eɪᵊld **ailing** 'eɪᵊl ɪŋ **ails**
eɪᵊlz

ailanthus eɪ 'lænᵗθ əs ~**es** ɪz əz

Ailbhe 'ælv ə

Aileen *(i)* 'eɪl iːn ‖ eɪ 'liːn, *(ii)* 'aɪl iːn ‖ aɪ 'liːn

aileron 'eɪl ə rɒn ‖ -rɑːn ~**s** z

ailment 'eɪᵊl mənt ~**s** s

Ailsa 'eɪᵊls ə 'eɪᵊlz ə
ˌAilsa 'Craig

ailuro- *comb. form* aɪ ˌl̩ʊər əʊ eɪ-, -ˌljʊər-;
ˌeɪl jʊᵊr əʊ ‖ aɪ ˌlʊr ə — **ailurophobia**
aɪ ˌlʊər əʊ 'fəʊb i ə eɪ-, -ˌljʊər-; ˌeɪl jʊᵊr-
‖ aɪ ˌlʊr ə 'foʊb-

aim eɪm **aimed** eɪmd **aiming** 'eɪm ɪŋ **aims**
eɪmz

Aimee, Aimée 'eɪm eɪ -i ‖ e 'meɪ eɪ- —*Fr*
[ɛ me]

aimless 'eɪm ləs -lɪs ~**ly** li ~**ness** nəs nɪs

ain eɪn

Ainscough, Ainscow 'eɪnz kəʊ ‖ -koʊ

Ainsdale 'eɪnz deɪᵊl

Ainsley, Ainslie 'eɪnz li

Ainsworth 'eɪnz wɜːθ -wəθ ‖ -wᵊrθ

ain't eɪnt

Aintree 'eɪn triː 'eɪntr i

Ainu 'aɪn uː ~**s** z

aioli, aïoli aɪ 'əʊl i eɪ- ‖ -'oʊl i —*It* [a 'jɔ li]

air eə ‖ eᵊr æᵊr **aired** eəd ‖ eᵊrd æᵊrd **airing**
'eər ɪŋ ‖ 'er ɪŋ 'ær- **airs** eəz ‖ eᵊrz æᵊrz
'air ˌchamber; air chief 'marshal◄; air
'commodore◄; 'air freight; air 'marshal◄;
'air raid; 'air ˌrifle; 'air ˌterminal; ˌair
ˌtraffic con'trol, ˌ• '•• •ˌ•, '•ˌ•• •ˌ•; ˌair
vice-'marshal◄

airbag 'eə bæg ‖ 'er- 'ær- ~**s** z

airbas|e 'eə beɪs ‖ 'er- 'ær- ~**es** ɪz əz

airbed 'eə bed ‖ 'er- 'ær- ~**s** z

airbladder 'eə ˌblæd ə ‖ 'er ˌblæd ᵊr 'ær- ~**s** z

airborne 'eə bɔːn ‖ 'er bɔːrn 'ær-, -boʊrn

airbrake 'eə breɪk ‖ 'er- 'ær- ~**s** s

airbrick 'eə brɪk ‖ 'er- 'ær- ~**s** s

airbrush 'eə brʌʃ ‖ 'er- 'ær- ~**ed** t ~**es** ɪz əz
~**ing** ɪŋ

airburst 'eə bɜːst ‖ 'er bɜːst 'ær- ~**s** s

airbus, A~ *tdmk* 'eə bʌs ‖ 'er- 'ær- ~**es** ɪz əz

air-condition 'eə kən ˌdɪʃ ᵊn ˌ•• '•• ‖ 'er- 'ær-
~**ed** d ~**ing** ˌɪŋ ~**s** z

air-cool 'eə kuːl ‖ 'er- 'ær- ~**ed** d ~**ing** ɪŋ ~**s**
z

aircraft 'eə krɑːft §-kræft ‖ 'er kræft 'ær-
'aircraft ˌcarrier

aircraft|man 'eə krɑːft |mən §-kræft-
‖ 'er kræft- 'ær- ~**men** mən ~**woman**
ˌwʊm ən ~**women** ˌwɪm ɪn §-ən

aircrafts|man 'eə krɑːfts |mən §-kræfts-
‖ 'er kræfts- 'ær- ~**men** mən ~**woman**
ˌwʊm ən ~**women** ˌwɪm ɪn §-ən

aircrew 'eə kruː ‖ 'er- 'ær- ~**s** z

aircushion 'eə ˌkʊʃ ᵊn ‖ 'er- 'ær- ~**s** z

Airdrie 'eədr i ‖ 'erdr i

air-drie... —*see* **air-dry**

Airdrieonian ˌeədr i 'əʊn i ˌən ◄ ‖ ˌerdr i 'oʊn-
~**s** z

airdrop 'eə drɒp ‖ 'er drɑːp 'ær- ~**ped** t
~**ping** ɪŋ ~**s** s

air-|dry 'eə |draɪ ‖ 'er- 'ær- ~**dries** draɪz
~**dried** draɪd ~**drying** draɪ ɪŋ

Aire eə ‖ eᵊr æᵊr

Airedale 'eə deɪᵊl ‖ 'er- 'ær- ~**s** z

airer 'eər ə ‖ 'er ᵊr 'ær- ~**s** z

Airey 'eər i ‖ 'er i 'ær i

airfare 'eə feə ‖ 'er fer 'ær fær ~**s** z

airfield 'eə fiːᵊld ‖ 'er- 'ær- ~**s** z

airflow 'eə fləʊ ‖ 'er floʊ 'ær- ~**s** z

airforc|e 'eə fɔːs ‖ 'er fɔːrs 'ær-, -foʊrs ~**es** ɪz
əz

airframe 'eə freɪm ‖ 'er- 'ær- ~**s** z

airgun 'eə gʌn ‖ 'er- 'ær- ~**s** z

airhead 'eə hed ‖ 'er- 'ær- ~**s** z

airhole 'eə həʊl →-hɒʊl ‖ 'er hoʊl 'ær- ~**s** z

airhostess 'eə ˌhəʊst es -ɪs, -əs ‖ 'er ˌhoʊst əs
'ær- ~**es** ɪz əz

airi... —*see* **airy**

airily 'eər ᵊl i -ɪ li ‖ 'er- 'ær-

airiness 'eər i nəs -nɪs ‖ 'er- 'ær-

airing 'eər ɪŋ ‖ 'er ɪŋ 'ær- ~**s** z
'airing ˌcupboard

air-intake 'eᵊr ˌɪn teɪk ‖ 'er- 'ær- ~**s** s

airlane 'eə leɪn ‖ 'er- 'ær- ~**s** z

airless 'eə ləs -lɪs ‖ 'er- 'ær- ~**ness** nəs nɪs

airletter 'eə ˌlet ə ‖ 'er ˌleṭ ᵊr 'ær- ~**s** z

airlift 'eə lɪft ‖ 'er- 'ær- ~**ed** ɪd əd ~**ing** ɪŋ ~**s**
s

airline 'eə laɪn ‖ 'er- 'ær- ~**s** z

airliner 'eə ˌlaɪn ə ‖ 'er ˌlaɪn ᵊr 'ær- ~**s** z

airlock 'eə lɒk ‖ 'er laːk 'ær- ~**s** s

airmail 'eə meɪᵊl ‖ 'er- 'ær- ~**ed** d ~**ing** ɪŋ ~**s**
z

air|man 'eə |mən -mæn ‖ 'er- 'ær- ~**men** mən
men

airmobile ˌeə 'məʊb aɪᵊl ◄ '•ˌ•• ‖ 'er ˌmoʊb ᵊl
'ær-, -iːᵊl, -aɪᵊl; -moʊ ˌbiːᵊl

airplane 'eə pleɪn ‖ 'er- 'ær- ~**s** z

airplay 'eə pleɪ ‖ 'er- 'ær-

airpocket 'eə ˌpɒk ɪt §-ət ‖ 'er ˌpaːk ət 'ær- ~**s**
s

airport 'eə pɔːt ‖ 'er pɔːrt 'ær-, -poʊrt ~**s** s

airscrew 'eə skruː ‖ 'er- 'ær- ~**s** z

air-sea ˌeə 'siː ◄ ‖ ˌer- ˌær-
ˌair-sea 'rescue

A

airshaft 'eə ʃɑːft §-ʃæft ‖ 'er ʃæft 'ær- ~s s
airship 'eə ʃɪp ‖ 'er- 'ær- ~s s
airsick 'eə sɪk ‖ 'er- 'ær- ~ness nəs nɪs
airside 'eə saɪd ‖ 'er- 'ær-
airspace 'eə speɪs ‖ 'er- 'ær-
airspeed 'eə spiːd ‖ 'er- 'ær- ~s z
airstream 'eə striːm ‖ 'er- 'ær- ~s z
  'airstream ˌmechanism
airstrike 'eə straɪk ‖ 'er- 'ær- ~s s
airstrip 'eə strɪp ‖ 'er- 'ær- ~s s
airtight 'eə taɪt ‖ 'er- 'ær-
airtime 'eə taɪm ‖ 'er- 'ær-
air-to-air ˌeə tu 'eə ◂ -tə- ‖ ˌer tə 'er ◂
  ˌær tə 'ær, -tu-
airwaves 'eə weɪvz ‖ 'er- 'ær-
airway 'eə weɪ ‖ 'er- 'ær- ~s z
air|woman 'eə ˌwʊm ən ‖ 'er- 'ær- ~women
  ˌwɪm ɪn §-ən
airworth|y 'eə ˌwɜːð li ‖ 'er ˌwɜːð li 'ær-
  ~iness i nəs i nɪs
air|y, Air|y 'eər li ‖ 'er li 'ær i ~ier i‿ə ‖ i‿ər
  ~iest i‿ɪst i‿əst
airy-fairy ˌeər i 'feər i ◂ ‖ ˌer i 'fer i ◂
  ˌær i 'fær i
Aisha (i) aɪ 'iːʃ ə ɑː-, eɪ-, (ii) 'eɪʃ ə 'aɪʃ ə
aisle aɪəl (= isle) aisles aɪəlz
Aisling 'æʃ lɪŋ
Aisne eɪn —Fr [ɛn]
ait eɪt (= eight) aits eɪts
aitch eɪtʃ aitches 'eɪtʃ ɪz -əz
aitch-bone 'eɪtʃ bəʊn ‖ -boʊn ~s z
Aitchison 'eɪtʃ ɪs ən -əs-
Aithne 'eθ nə -ni
Aitken, Aitkin (i) 'eɪt kɪn, (ii) 'eɪk ɪn
Aiwa 'aɪ wə —Jp [a,i wa]
Aix eɪks eks —Fr [ɛks]
Aix-en-Provence ˌeɪks ɒn prə 'vɒnˡs ˌeks-,
  →, ˈɒm- ‖ -ɑːn proʊ 'vɑːs —Fr
  [ɛk sɑ̃ pʁɔ vɑ̃ːs]
Aix-la-Chapelle ˌeɪks lɑː ʃæ 'pel ˌeks-, ˌˈlæ-,
  ˌˈlə- ‖ -ʃɑː 'pel —Fr [ɛks la ʃa pɛl]
Aix-les-Bains ˌeɪks leɪ 'bæ̃ ˌeks-, -'bæn —Fr
  [ɛks le bæ̃]
Ajaccio æ 'dʒæs i əʊ -'ʒæks- ‖ ɑː 'jɑːtʃ oʊ
  -i oʊ —Fr [a ʒak sjo]
ajar ə 'dʒɑː ‖ ə 'dʒɑːr
Ajax (i) 'eɪdʒ æks, (ii) 'aɪ æks —The scouring
  powder (tdmk) is (i), the Dutch football team (ii)
aka —see also known as; sometimes said aloud
  as 'æk ə or ˌeɪ keɪ 'eɪ
Akabusi ˌæk ə 'buːs i
Akai tdmk 'æk aɪ ‖ ə 'kaɪ
Akan ə 'kæn ‖ 'ɑːk ɑːn —Akan [a kã]
Akbar 'æk bɑː ‖ -bɑːr
Akela ɑː 'keɪl ə
Akerman (i) 'æk ə mən ‖ -ər-, (ii) 'eɪk-
Akihito ˌæk i 'hiːt əʊ ‖ ˌɑːk i 'hiːt oʊ —Jp
  [a 'ki çi to]
akimbo ə 'kɪm bəʊ -boʊ
akin ə 'kɪn
Akins 'eɪk ɪnz §-ənz
Akita, akita ə 'kiːt ə ‖ ə 'kiːt̬ ə —Jp ['a kị ta]
  ~s z

Akkad 'æk æd ‖ 'ɑːk ɑːd
Akkadian ə 'keɪd i‿ən æ-, -'kæd-
Akron 'æk rɒn -rən ‖ -rən
Akrotiri ˌæk rəʊ 'tɪər i ‖ ˌɑːk roʊ 'tɪr i
Al æl
al æl —It, Arabic [al] —See also phrases with this
  word
al- ə, æ —This variant of ad- is usually ə (al'lot),
  but æ if stressed because of a suffix
  (ˌallo'cation).
-al əl, əl —When forming an adjective, this suffix
  imposes stress one or two syllables back
  (ˌuni'versal, 'personal). When forming a noun, it
  is stress-neutral (ˌdisap'proval).
al|a 'eɪl ə ~ae iː
a la, à la ˌæl ɑː -ə, ˌɑː lɑː ‖ ˌɑː lɑː, ˌɑːl ə, ˌæl ə
  —Fr [a la]
  ˌa la 'carte, ˌà la 'carte kɑːt ‖ kɑːrt —Fr
  [kaʁt]; ˌa la 'grecque, ˌà la 'grecque grek
  —Fr [gʁɛk]; ˌa la 'mode, ˌà la 'mode
  məʊd ‖ moʊd —Fr [mɔd]
Alabam|a ˌæl ə 'bæm lə ◂ -'bɑːm- ~an/s ən/z
  ~ian/s i‿ən/z
alabaster 'æl ə bɑːst ə -bæst ə, ˌ•ˈ••
  ‖ -bæst ər
alack ə 'læk
alackaday ə ˌlæk ə 'deɪ •ˈ•••
alacrity ə 'læk rət i -rɪt- ‖ -rət̬ i
Aladdin ə 'læd ɪn §-ən
Alaister 'æl ɪst ə -əst- ‖ -ər
alameda, A~ ˌæl ə 'miːd ə -'meɪd- —Sp
  [a la 'me ða] ~s z
Alamein 'æl ə meɪn ,•ˈ•
Alamo 'æl ə məʊ ‖ -moʊ
Alamogordo ˌæl əm ə 'gɔːd əʊ ‖ -'gɔːrd oʊ
Alan 'æl ən
Alana ə 'læn ə -'lɑːn-
Alanbrooke 'æl ən brʊk →-əm-
Aland, Åland 'ɔː lənd 'ɑː- —Swed ['oː land]
alanine 'æl ə niːn -naɪn
alar 'eɪl ə -ɑː ‖ -ər
Alaric 'æl ər ɪk
alarm ə 'lɑːm ‖ ə 'lɑːrm ~ed d ~ing ɪŋ ~s z
  a'larm clock
alarm|ism ə 'lɑːm ˌɪz əm ‖ ə 'lɑːrm- ~ist/s
  ɪst/s §əst/s
alarum ə 'lær əm -'lɑːr-, -'leər- ‖ -'ler- ~s z
alas ə 'læs -'lɑːs
Alasdair 'æl əst ə -ə steə ‖ -ər
Alask|a, a~ ə 'læsk lə ~an/s ən/z
Alastair 'æl əst ə -ə steə ‖ -ər
alate 'eɪl eɪt ~s s
alb ælb albs ælbz
Alba, alba 'ælb ə
albacore 'ælb ə kɔː ‖ -kɔːr -koʊr ~s z
Alban 'ɔːlb ən 'ɒlb- ‖ 'ɑːlb-
Albani|a æl 'beɪn i‿ə ɔːl- ~an/s ən/z
Albany 'ɔːlb ən i 'ɒlb-, §'ælb- ‖ 'ɑːlb-
albatross 'ælb ə trɒs -trɑːs -trɔːs ~es ɪz əz
albedo æl 'biːd əʊ ‖ -oʊ ~s z
Albee (i) 'ɔːlb iː ‖ 'ɔːlb i 'ɑːlb-, (ii) 'ælb iː
albeit ˌɔːl 'biː‿ɪt §ˌɒl-, ət ‖ ˌɑːl-, ˌæl-

Albemarle 'ælb ə mɑːl ‖ -mɑːrl
    ˌAlbemarle ' Sound
Albeniz, Albéniz æl 'beɪn ɪθ ‖ ɑːl 'beɪn iːs —*Sp*
    [al 'βe niθ]
Alberich 'ælb ə rɪk -rɪx —*Ger* ['al bə ʁɪç]
Albert, a~ 'ælb ət ‖ -ərt —*but as a French name,*
    æl 'beə ‖ ɑːl 'beər —*Fr* [al bɛːʁ] ~**s**, ~'s s
Alberta æl 'bɜːt ə ‖ -'bɝːt̬ ə
Albertina ˌælb ə 'tiːn ə ‖ -ər-
Albertine 'ælb ə tiːn ˌ•'• ‖ -ər-
albescence æl 'bes ənts
albescent æl 'bes ənt
Albigenses ˌælb ɪ 'dʒenˈs iːz -ə-, -'genˈs-
Albigensian ˌælb ɪ 'dʒenˈs i‿ən ◂ ˌ•ə-, -'genˈs-
    ‖ -'dʒenˈʃ ən ◂ ~**s** z
albinism 'ælb ɪ ˌnɪz əm -ə-
albino æl 'biːn əʊ ‖ -'baɪn oʊ *(*)* ~**s** z
Albinoni ˌælb ɪ 'nəʊn i §-ə- ‖ -'noʊn i —*It*
    [al bi 'noː ni]
Albion 'ælb i‿ən
albite 'ælb aɪt
Alborg 'ɔːl bɔːg 'ɑːl- ‖ -bɔːrg —*Danish* Ålborg
    ['ʌl bɔː']
Albright 'ɔːl braɪt 'ɒl- ‖ 'ɑːl-
Albrow 'ɔːl braʊ ‖ 'ɑːl-
album 'ælb əm ~**s** z
albumen 'ælb jum ɪn -jəm-, -ən; -ju men, -jə-
    ‖ æl 'bjuːm ən
albumin 'ælb jum ɪn -jəm-, -ən ‖ æl 'bjuːm ən
albuminous æl 'bjuːm ɪn əs -ən-
albuminuria æl ˌbjuːm ɪ 'njʊər i‿ə -,•ə-
    ‖ -'nʊr- -'njʊr-
Albuquerque 'ælb ə kɜːk i ˌ•'•• ‖ -kɝːk i
Albury 'ɔːl bər‿i 'ɒl-, 'ɔː- ‖ 'ɔːl ˌber i 'ɑːl-
Alcaeus æl 'siː‿əs
Alcaic, a~ æl 'keɪ ɪk ~**s** s
alcalde æl 'kæld i ‖ -'kɑːld-, -eɪ ~**s** z
Alcan *tdmk* 'æl kæn
Alcatraz 'ælk ə træz ˌ•'•
Alcazar, a~ ˌælk ə 'zɑː æl 'kæz ə ‖ 'ælk ə zɑːr
    æl 'kæz ər, -'kɑːz- —*Sp* Alcázar [al 'ka θaɾ]
    ~**s** z
Alceste æl 'sest
Alcester 'ɔːlst ə ‖ -ər 'ɑːlst-
Alcestis æl 'sest ɪs §-əs
alchemist 'ælk əm ɪst -ɪm-, §-əst ~**s** s
alchemy 'ælk əm i -ɪm-
alcheringa ˌælt̬ʃ ə 'rɪŋ gə
Alcibiades ˌæls ɪ 'baɪ‿ə diːz ˌ•ə-
Alcinous æl 'sɪn əʊ əs ‖ -oʊ-
Alcmene ælk 'miːn i
Alcoa *tdmk* æl 'kəʊ ə ‖ -'koʊ-
Alcock *(i)* 'æl kɒk ‖ -kɑːk , *(ii)* 'ɔːl- 'ɒl- ‖ 'ɑːl-
alcohol 'ælk ə hɒl ‖ -hɔːl -hɑːl ~**s** z
alcoholic ˌælk ə 'hɒl ɪk ◂ ‖ -'hɑːl- -'hɔːl- ~**s** s
alcoholism 'ælk ə hɒl ˌɪz əm -həl, • - ‖ -hɑːl ˌɪz
    əm -hɔːl, • -
Alconbury 'ɔːlk ən bər‿i 'ɔːk-, 'ɒlk-, →'•əm-
    ‖ 'ɔːlk ən ˌber i 'ɑːlk-
alcopop 'ælk əʊ pɒp ‖ -oʊ pɑːp   ~**s** s
Alcott *(i)* 'ɔːlk ət 'ɒlk-, -ɒt ‖ 'ɔːlk ɑːt 'ɑːlk-, *(ii)*
    'ælk-
alcove 'ælk əʊv ‖ -oʊv ~**s** z

Alcuin 'ælk wɪn §-wən
Alcyone æl 'saɪˌən i -'siːˌ
Alda 'ɔːld ə
Aldabra (ˌ)æl 'dæbr ə
Aldebaran æl 'deb ər̩ən -ə ræn
Aldeburgh 'ɔːld bər̩ə 'ɒld- ‖ 'ɔːld ˌbɝː oʊ
    'ɑːld-
aldehyde 'æld ɪ haɪd -ə- ~**s** z
Alden 'ɔːld ən 'ɒld- ‖ 'ɑːld-
Aldenham 'ɔːld ən̩əm 'ɒld- ‖ 'ɑːld-
al dente (ˌ)æl 'dent i -eɪ ‖ (ˌ)ɑːl- —*It* [al 'dɛn te]
alder, Alder 'ɔːld ə 'ɒld- ‖ 'ɔːld ər 'ɑːld- ~**s** z
Aldergrove 'ɔːld ə grəʊv 'ɒld- ‖ 'ɔːld ər groʊv
    'ɑːld-
Alderley 'ɔːld ə li 'ɒld-, -əl i ‖ -ər- 'ɑːld-
alder|man 'ɔːld ə |mən 'ɒld- ‖ -ər- 'ɑːld-
    ~**men** mən
aldermanic ˌɔːld ə 'mæn ɪk ◂ ˌɒld- ‖ -ər-, ˌɑːld-
Aldermaston 'ɔːld ə ˌmɑːst ən 'ɒld-, §-ˌmæst-
    ‖ -ər ˌmæst- 'ɑːld-
Alderney 'ɔːld ən i 'ɒld- ‖ -ərn i 'ɑːld-
Aldersgate 'ɔːld əz geɪt 'ɒld-, -gɪt, -gət ‖ -ərz-
    'ɑːld-
Aldershot 'ɔːld ə ʃɒt 'ɒld- ‖ 'ɔːld ər ʃɑːt 'ɑːld-
Alderson 'ɔːld əs ən 'ɒld- ‖ -ərs- 'ɑːld-
Alderton 'ɔːld ət ən 'ɒld- ‖ 'ɔːld ərt ən 'ɑːld-
Aldgate 'ɔːl*d* gɪt 'ɒld-, -geɪt, -gət ‖ 'ɔːl*d* geɪt
    'ɑːl*d*-
Aldhelm 'ɔːld helm 'ɒld- ‖ 'ɑːld-
Aldine 'ɔːld aɪn 'ɒld-, -iːn ‖ 'ɑːld-
Aldington 'ɔːld ɪŋ tən 'ɒld- ‖ 'ɑːld-
Aldis, Aldiss 'ɔːld ɪs 'ɒld-, §-əs ‖ 'ɑːld-
aldol 'æld ɒl ‖ -ɑːl -ɔːl, -oʊl
aldosterone æl 'dɒst ə rəʊn ˌæld əʊ 'stɪər əʊn
    ‖ -'dɑːst ə roʊn ˌæld oʊ stə 'roʊn
Aldous 'ɔːld əs 'ɒld- ‖ 'ɑːld-
Aldrich 'ɔːld rɪtʃ 'ɒld-, -rɪdʒ ‖ 'ɑːld-
Aldridge 'ɔːld rɪdʒ 'ɒld- ‖ 'ɑːld-
Aldrin, a~ 'ɔːldr ɪn 'ɒldr-, §-ən ‖ 'ɑːldr-
Aldus 'ɔːld əs 'ɒld-, 'æld- ‖ 'ɑːld-
Aldwych 'ɔːld wɪtʃ 'ɒld- ‖ 'ɑːld-
ale eɪ*ə*l **ales** eɪ*ə*lz
aleatoric ˌæl i‿ə 'tɒr ɪk ◂ ˌeɪl- ‖ -'tɔːr- -'tɑːr-
    ~**ally** *ə*l_i
aleatory ˌæl i 'eɪt ər i 'eɪl i‿ət̩ər i
    ‖ 'eɪl i‿ə tɔːr i -toʊr i
Alec, Aleck, a~ 'æl ɪk -ek
Alecto ə 'lekt əʊ æ- ‖ -oʊ
Aled 'æl ed -ɪd —*Welsh* ['a led]
ale|house 'eɪ*ə*l |haʊs ~**houses** haʊz ɪz -əz
Alemannic ˌæl ə 'mæn ɪk ◂ -ɪ-
alembic ə 'lem bɪk ~**s** s
Alencon, Alençon 'æl ən sɒ̃ ‖ ˌæl ɑːn 'soʊn
    —*Fr* [a lɑ̃ sɔ̃]
aleph 'æl ef 'ɑːl-, -ɪf, §-əf ‖ 'ɑːl əf -ef ~**s** s
Aleppo ə 'lep əʊ ‖ -oʊ
alert ə 'lɜːt ‖ ə 'lɝːt **alerted** ə 'lɜːt ɪd -əd
    ‖ ə 'lɝːt̬ əd **alerting** ə 'lɜːt ɪŋ ‖ ə 'lɝːt̬ ɪŋ
    alerts ə 'lɜːts ‖ ə 'lɝːts
alert|ly ə 'lɜːt| li ‖ ə 'lɝːt| li ~**ness** nəs nɪs
Aleut 'æl i uːt ˌ•'•• ; æ 'luːt, ə-, -'ljuːt ‖ ə 'luːt
    ~**s** s
Aleutian ə 'luːʃ ən -'ljuːʃ-, -'•i‿ən ~**s** z

A

A-level 'eɪ ˌlev ᵊl ~s z
ale|wife 'eɪᵊl |waɪf ~wives waɪvz
Alex 'æl ɪks -eks
Alexander ˌæl ɪg 'zɑːnd ə -eg-, -ɪk-, -'zænd-
 ‖ -'zænd ᵊr —There is also a Scottish form
 'elʃ ɪnd ə ‖ -ᵊr
alexanders ˌæl ɪg 'zɑːnd əz -eg-, -ɪk-, -'zænd-
 ‖ -'zænd ᵊrz
Alexandra ˌæl ɪg 'zɑːndr ə -eg-, -ɪk-, -'zændr-
 ‖ -'zændr ə
Alexandretta ˌæl ɪg zɑːn 'dret ə ˌ•eg-, ˌ•ɪk-,
 -zæn'•- ‖ -zæn 'dreṭ ə
Alexandria ˌæl ɪg 'zɑːndr i‿ə ˌ•eg-, ˌ•ɪk-,
 -'zændr- ‖ -'zændr-
Alexandrian, a~ ˌæl ɪg 'zɑːndr i‿ən ◂ ˌ•eg-,
 ˌ•ɪk-, -'zændr- ‖ -'zændr- ~s z
alexandrine ˌæl ɪg 'zændr aɪn -eg-, -ɪk-,
 -'zɑːndr-, -iːn, -ɪn ~s z
alexia ˌeɪ 'leks i‿ə ə'•-
Alexis ə 'leks ɪs §-əs
Alf ælf
alfa, Alfa 'ælf ə ~s z
Alfa-Laval ˌælf ə lə 'væl ‖ -'vɑːl
alfalfa æl 'fælf ə
Alfa-Romeo tdmk ˌælf ə rəʊ 'meɪ əʊ -'rəʊm i əʊ
 ‖ -roʊ 'meɪ oʊ ~s z
Al-Fayed æl 'faɪ ed
Alfie 'ælf i
Alfonso æl 'fɒnz əʊ -'fɒnᵗs- ‖ -'fɑːnᵗs oʊ —Sp
 [al 'fon so]
Alford (i) 'ɔːl fəd 'ɒl- ‖ 'ɔːl fᵊrd 'ɑːl-, (ii) 'æl-
Alfred 'ælf rɪd -rəd
Alfreda æl 'friːd ə
alfresco æl 'fresk əʊ ‖ -oʊ
Alfreton 'ɔːlf rɪt ən 'ɒlf-, 'ælf-, -rət-
 ‖ 'ɔːlf rət ᵊn 'ɑːlf-, 'ælf-
alga 'ælg ə algae 'ældʒ iː 'ælg-, -aɪ
Algarve æl 'gɑːv '•• ‖ ɑːl 'gɑːrv ə —Port
 [aɫ 'gar və]
algebra 'ældʒ ɪb rə -əb- ~s z
algebraic ˌældʒ ɪ 'breɪ ɪk ◂ -ə- ~al ᵊl ~ally ᵊl‿i
algebraist ˌældʒ ɪ 'breɪ ɪst -ə-, §-əst ~s s
Algeciras ˌældʒ ɪ 'sɪər əs -ə-, -e-, -'sɪr- ‖ -'sɪr-
 —Sp [al xe 'θi ɾas]
Algeo 'ældʒ i əʊ ‖ -oʊ
Alger 'ældʒ ə ‖ -ᵊr
Algeri|a æl 'dʒɪər i‿|ə ‖ -'dʒɪr- ~an/z ən/z
Algernon 'ældʒ ən ən ‖ -ᵊrn-
Algie 'ældʒ i
Algiers ⑴æl 'dʒɪəz '•• ‖ -'dʒɪᵊrz
alginate 'ældʒ ɪ neɪt -ə- ~s s
Algipan tdmk 'ældʒ ɪ pæn -ə-
Algoa æl 'gəʊ ə ‖ -'goʊ-
Algol, ALGOL 'ælg ɒl ‖ -ɑːl -ɔːl
algolagnia ˌælg əʊ 'læg ni‿ə ‖ ˌælg oʊ-
Algonkian æl 'gɒŋk i‿ən -wi‿ən ‖ -'gɑːŋk- ~s z
Algonquian æl 'gɒŋk wi‿ən -i‿ən ‖ -'gɑːŋk- ~s
 z
Algonquin æl 'gɒŋk wɪn -ɪn, §-wən, §-ən
 ‖ -'gɑːŋk- ~s z
algorithm 'ælg ə ˌrɪð əm ~s z
algorithmic ˌælg ə 'rɪð mɪk ◂ ~ally ᵊl‿i
Algy 'ældʒ i

Alhambra æl 'hæm brə əl-; ə 'læm- —Sp
 [a 'lam bra]
Ali 'æl i 'ɑːl- ‖ 'ɑːl i —but the former boxer
 Muhammad Ali pronounces ɑː 'liː —Arabic
 ['ʕa li]
 ˌAli 'Baba 'bɑːb ɑː
alias 'eɪl i‿əs -æs ~es ɪz əz ~ing ɪŋ
alibi 'æl ə baɪ -ɪ- ~ed d ~ing ɪŋ ~s z
Alicante ˌæl ɪ 'kænt i -ə-, -eɪ ‖ -'kænṭ i
 ˌɑːl ə 'kɑːnṭ- —Sp [a li 'kan te]
Alice 'æl ɪs §-əs ~'s ɪz əz
 ˌAlice 'Springs
Alicia ə 'lɪʃ ə ə 'lɪs i‿ə, -'lɪʃ i‿ə
Alick 'æl ɪk
alidade 'æl ɪ deɪd -ə- ~s z
alien 'eɪl i‿ən ~s z
alienable 'eɪl i‿ən əb ᵊl
alie|nate 'eɪl i‿ə |neɪt ~nated neɪt ɪd -əd
 ‖ neɪṭ əd ~nates neɪts ~nating
 neɪt ɪŋ ‖ neɪṭ ɪŋ
alienation ˌeɪl i‿ə 'neɪʃ ᵊn ~s z
alienist 'eɪl i‿ən ɪst §-əst ~s s
alight ə 'laɪt alighted ə 'laɪt ɪd -əd ‖ ə 'laɪṭ əd
 alighting ə 'laɪt ɪŋ ‖ ə 'laɪṭ ɪŋ alights
 ə 'laɪts alit ə 'lɪt
align ə 'laɪn aligned ə 'laɪnd aligning
 ə 'laɪn ɪŋ aligns ə 'laɪnz
alignment ə 'laɪn mənt ~s s
alike ə 'laɪk
alimentary ˌæl ɪ 'ment ᵊr i ◂ ˌ•ə-
alimentation ˌæl ɪ men 'teɪʃ ᵊn ˌ•ə-, -mən'•-
alimon|y 'æl ɪ mən li '•ə- ‖ -moʊn li ~ies iz
aliphatic ˌæl ɪ 'fæt ɪk ◂ -ə- ‖ -'fæṭ-
aliquot 'æl ɪ kwɒt -ə- ‖ -kwɑːt -kwət
Alisha ə 'lɪʃ ə
Alison, a~ 'æl ɪs ən -əs-
Alistair 'æl ɪst ə -əst-; -ɪ steə, -ə- ‖ -ə ster
 -əst ᵊr
alit ə 'lɪt
Alitalia tdmk ˌæl ɪ 'tæl i‿ə -'tɑːl- ‖ ˌɑːl ɪ 'tɑːl-
 —It [a li 'ta: lja]
alive ə 'laɪv
alizarin ə 'lɪz ᵊr ɪn in §-ən
alkali 'ælk ə laɪ ~s z
alkaline 'ælk ə laɪn
alkalinity ˌælk ə 'lɪn ət i -ɪt i ‖ -əṭ i
alkaloid 'ælk ə lɔɪd ~s z
alkane 'ælk eɪn ~s z
alkanet 'ælk ə net ~s s
Alka-Seltzer tdmk ˌælk ə 'selts ə '•••, •••
 ‖ 'ælk ə ˌselts ᵊr ~s z
alkene 'ælk iːn ~s z
alkyd 'ælk ɪd §-əd
alkyl 'ælk ɪl -aɪᵊl, §-ᵊl ‖ -ᵊl ~s z
alkyne 'ælk aɪn ~s z
all ɔːl ‖ ɑːl
 ˌall 'clear; ˌAll 'Saints; ˌAll 'Saints' Day; ˌAll
 'Souls'; ˌall the 'same
all- ˌɔːl ‖ ˌɑːl — all-important
 ˌɔːl ɪm 'pɔːt ᵊnt ◂ ‖ -'pɔːrt ᵊnt ◂ ˌɑːl-
alla 'æl ə 'ɑːl-, -ɑː ‖ 'ɑːl ə 'æl ə —It ['al la]
 ˌalla 'breve 'breɪv i -'brev-, -eɪ; 'brev —It
 ['bre: ve]

Allah 'æl ə ə 'lɑː; æ 'lɑː, ə-
Allahabad ˌæl ə hə 'bɑːd -'bæd —*Hindi/Urdu*
[ɪ la: ha: baːd̪]
allamanda ˌæl ə 'mænd ə ~s z
all-American ˌɔːl ə 'mer ɪk ən ◄ ‖ ˌɑːl-
ˌall-Aˌmerican 'athlete
Allan 'æl ən
Allan-a-Dale ˌæl ən ə 'deɪəl
Allandale 'æl ən deɪəl
allanto|in ə 'lænt əʊl ɪn ˌæl ən 'təʊl-, §-ən
‖ -oʊl- ~is ɪs §əs
all-around ˌɔːl ə 'raʊnd ◄‖ ˌɑːl-
Allardice 'æl ə daɪs ‖ -ər-
Allason 'æl əs ən
allative 'æl ət ɪv ‖ -əṭ- ~s z
Allaun ə 'lɔːn ‖ -'lɑːn
allay ə 'leɪ ~ed d ~ing ɪŋ ~s z
Allbeury ɔːl 'bjʊər i ‖ ɔːl 'bjʊr i ɑːl-
All-Black 'ɔːl blæk ‖ 'ɑːl- ~s s
All-Bran *tdmk* 'ɔːl brænǁ 'ɑːl-
all-day ˌɔːl 'deɪ ◄ ‖ ˌɑːl-
ˌall-day 'meeting
Allder 'ɔːld ə 'ɒld- ‖ 'ɔːld ər ɑːld- ~'s z
allegation ˌæl ə 'geɪʃ ən-ɪ- ~s z
alleg|e ə 'ledʒ ˌ(ˌ)æ- ~ed d ~es ɪz əz ~ing ɪŋ
allegedly ə 'ledʒ ɪd li -əd-
Alleghany, Allegheny ˌæl ɪ 'geɪn i -ə-, -'gen-
allegianc|e ə 'liːdʒ ənts ~es ɪz əz
allegorical ˌæl ə 'gɒr ɪk əl ◄ˌˌɪ- ‖ -'gɔːr-
-'gɑːr- ~ly i
allegor|y 'æl əg ər_li ˌˌɪg- ‖ -ə gɔːr li -goʊr i
~ies iz ~ist/s ɪst/s §əst/s
allegretto ˌæl ə 'gret əʊ-ɪ- ‖ -'greṭ oʊ ~s z
Allegri ə 'leɪg riː -'leg-, -ri
allegro ə 'leg rəʊ -'leɪg- ‖ -roʊ ~s z
allele ə 'liːəl ~s z
all-electric ˌɔːl ə 'lek trɪk ◄-ɪ- ‖ ˌɑːl-
allelic ə 'liːl ɪk
alleluia ˌæl ə 'luː jə ◄-ɪ-, -eɪ- —*In hymns also
occasionally* æ ˌleɪ lu: 'ja: *(where final stress is
called for)* ~s z
allemande 'æl ə mænd -ɪ-, -maːnd ‖ -mæn,
-maːnd, ˌˌˌ◄ —*Fr* [al mã:d] ~s z
all-embracing ˌɔːl ɪm 'breɪs ɪŋ ◄-əm-,
-em- ‖ ˌɑːl-
Allen 'æl ən -ɪn
Allenby 'æl ən bi→-əm-
Allendale 'æl ən deɪəl -ɪn-
Allende aɪ 'end i -'jend-, -eɪ ‖ ɑ 'jend- ˌɑːl-
—*Sp* [a 'ʎen de, -'jen-]
Allentown 'æl ən taʊn
allergen 'æl ə dʒen -ɜ:-, -ədʒ ən ‖ -ər- ~s z
allergenic ˌæl ə 'dʒen ɪk ◄-ɜː- ‖ -ər-
allergic ə 'lɜːdʒ ɪk ‖ ə 'lɜ·ːdʒ ɪk
allerg|y 'æl ədʒ li ‖ -ərdʒ li ~ies iz ~ist/s ɪst/s
§əst/s
Allerton 'æl ət ən ‖ -ərt ən—*but some places of
this name in Yks are* 'ɒl-
allevi|ate ə 'liːv i eɪt ~ated eɪt ɪd-əd ‖ eɪṭ əd
~ates eɪts ~ating eɪt ɪŋ ‖ eɪṭ ɪŋ
alleviation ə ˌliːv i 'eɪʃ ən
alley 'æl i ~s z
Alleyn 'æl ɪn-ən

Alleyne (i) æ 'leɪn, (ii) -'liːn, (iii) 'æl ən -ɪn
alleyway 'æl i weɪ ~s z
Allhallows ₍ˌ₎ɔːl 'hæl əʊz ‖ -oʊz ₍ˌ₎ɑːl-
allheal 'ɔːl hiːəl ‖ 'ɑːl-
allianc|e ə 'laɪ_ənts ~es ɪz əz
Allie 'æl i
allied *adj* 'æl aɪd ə 'laɪd
allies *n* 'æl aɪz ə 'laɪz, *v* ə 'laɪz 'æl aɪz
alligator 'æl ɪ geɪt ə ˌˌə- ‖ -geɪṭ ər ~s z
all-in ˌɔːl 'ɪn ◄ ‖ ˌɑːl-
ˌall-in 'wrestling
all-inclusive ˌɔːl ɪn 'kluːs ɪv ◄→-ɪŋ-,
§-'kluːz- ‖ ˌɑːl-
All-India ˌɔːl 'ɪnd i_ə ◄ ‖ ˌɑːl-
ˌAll-ˌIndia 'Radio
Allingham 'æl ɪŋ əm
all-in-one ˌɔːl ɪn 'wʌn ◄-ən-, §-'wɒn ‖ ˌɑːl-
Allinson 'æl ɪn sən §-ən-
Allison 'æl ɪs ən -əs-
allite|rate ə 'lɪt ə ǀreɪt ə 'lɪṭ ə- ~rated reɪt ɪd
-əd ‖ reɪṭ əd ~rates reɪts ~rating
reɪt ɪŋ ‖ reɪṭ ɪŋ
alliteration ə ˌlɪt ə 'reɪʃ ən ‖ ə ˌlɪṭ- ~s z
alliterative ə 'lɪt_ər ət ɪv-ə reɪt ɪv ‖ ə 'lɪṭ
ər əṭ ɪv-ə reɪṭ ɪv ~ly li ~ness nəs nɪs
allium 'æl i_əm
all-night ˌɔːl 'naɪt ◄ ‖ ˌɑːl-
ˌall-night 'party
all-nighter ˌɔːl 'naɪt ə ◄ ‖ ˌɔːl 'naɪṭ ər ˌɑːl- ~s z
allo- *comb. form*
with stress-neutral suffix ǀæl əʊ ‖ ǀæl ə -oʊ —
allotrope 'æl əʊ trəʊp ‖ -ə troʊp
with stress-imposing suffix ə 'lɒ+ æ 'lɒ+
‖ -'lɑ:+ — allotropy ə 'lɒtr əp i æ-
‖ ə 'lɑːtr-
'allo *non-standard interjection* ə 'ləʊ æ- ‖ -'loʊ
Alloa 'æl əʊ ə ‖ -oʊ ə
allo|cate 'æl ə ǀkeɪt ~cated keɪt ɪd-əd
‖ keɪṭ əd ~cates keɪts ~cating
keɪt ɪŋ ‖ keɪṭ ɪŋ
allocation ˌæl ə 'keɪʃ ən ~s z
allochthonous æ 'lɒk θən əs ə- ‖ -'lɑːk- ~ly li
allocution ˌæl ə 'kjuːʃ ən ~s z
allograph 'æl əʊ grɑːf -græf ‖ -ə græf ~s s
allographic ˌæl əʊ 'græf ɪk ◄ ‖ -ə- ~ally əl_i
allomorph 'æl əʊ mɔːf ‖ -ə mɔːrf ~s s
allomorphic ˌæl əʊ 'mɔːf ɪk ◄ ‖ -ə 'mɔːrf-
~ally əl_i
allomorph|ism 'æl əʊ mɔːf ǀɪz əm ‖ -ə mɔːrf-
~y i
allopathic ˌæl ə 'pæθ ɪk ◄ ~ally əl_i
allopathy ə 'lɒp əθ i æ- ‖ ə 'lɑːp-
allophone 'æl ə fəʊn ‖ -foʊn ~s z
allophonic ˌæl ə 'fɒn ɪk ◄ ‖ -'fɑːn- ~ally əl_i
allophony æ 'lɒf ən i ə-; 'æl ə fəʊn i ‖ ə 'lɑːf
ən i 'æl ə foʊn i
all-or-nothing ˌɔːl ɔː 'nʌθ ɪŋ ◄ ‖ ˌɔːl ər- ˌɑːl-,
-ɔːr-
allot ə 'lɒt ‖ ə 'lɑːt allots ə 'lɒts ‖ ə 'lɑːts
allotted ə 'lɒt ɪd-əd ‖ ə 'lɑːṭ əd allotting
ə 'lɒt ɪŋ ‖ ə 'lɑːṭ ɪŋ
allotment ə 'lɒt mənt ‖ ə 'lɑːt- ~s s
allotone 'æl əʊ təʊn ‖ -ə toʊn ~s z

A

allotrope 'æl ə trəʊp ‖ -troʊp ~s s
allott... —see allot ·
Allott 'æl ət
all-out ˌɔːl 'aʊt ◄ ‖ ˌɑːl-
  ˌall-out 'effort
allow ə 'laʊ allowed ə 'laʊd (= aloud)
  allowing ə 'laʊ_ɪŋ allows ə 'laʊz
allowable ə 'laʊ_əb əl
allowanc|e ə 'laʊ_ənts ~es ɪz əz
Alloway 'æl ə weɪ
allowedly ə 'laʊ ɪd li -əd-
alloy n 'æl ɔɪ ə 'lɔɪ ~s z
alloy v ə 'lɔɪ 'æl ɔɪ ~ed d ~ing ɪŋ ~s z
all-powerful ˌɔːl 'paʊ_ə fəl ◄ -fʊl ‖ -'paʊ_ər- ˌɑːl-
all-purpose ˌɔːl 'pɜːp əs ◄ ‖ -'pɜː:p- ˌɑːl-
all-round ˌɔːl 'raʊnd ◄ ‖ ˌɑːl-
  ˌall-round 'athlete
all-rounder ˌɔːl 'raʊnd ə ‖ -ər ˌɑːl- ~s z
Allsop, Allsopp 'ɔːl sɒp 'ɒl- ‖ 'ɔːl sɑːp 'ɑːl-
allsort 'ɔːl sɔːt ‖ 'ɔːl sɔːrt ˌɑːl- ~s s
allspice 'ɔːl spaɪs ‖ 'ɑːl-
all-star adj ˌɔːl 'stɑː ◄ '·· ‖ -'stɑːr ◄ ˌɑːl-
  ˌall-star 'cast
all-star n 'ɔːl stɑː ‖ -stɑːr 'ɑːl- ~s z
Allston 'ɔːlst ən 'ɒlst- ‖ 'ɑːlst-
all-time ˌɔːl 'taɪm ◄ ‖ ˌɑːl-
  ˌall-time 'greats
allud|e ə 'luːd ə 'ljuːd ~ed ɪd əd ~es z ~ing ɪŋ
allure ə 'lʊə -'ljʊə, -'ljɔː ‖ ə 'lʊər ~d d
  ~ment/s mənt/s ~s z alluring/ly
  ə 'lʊər ɪŋ /li -'ljʊər-, -'ljɔːr- ‖ ə 'lʊr ɪŋ /li
allusion ə 'luːʒ ən -'ljuːʒ- ~s z
allusive ə 'luːs ɪv -'ljuːs- ‖ -'luːz- ~ly li ~ness nəs nɪs
alluvi|al ə 'luːv i_əl -'ljuːv- ~a ə ~on ən ~um əm
all-weather ˌɔːl 'weð ə ◄ ‖ -ər ◄ ˌɑːl-
  ˌall-ˌweather 'garments
Allworthy 'ɔːl ˌwɜːð i ‖ 'ɔːl ˌwɜːð i 'ɑːl-

ALLY

AmE 1993

0 20 40 60 80 100%

ally v ə 'laɪ 'æl aɪ allied ə 'laɪd 'æl aɪd —but in
  allied forces usually 'æl aɪd allies ə 'laɪz
  'æl aɪz allying ə 'laɪ ɪŋ 'æl aɪ- —AmE 1993
  poll panel preference: •'• 50%, '•• 50%
ally n 'æl aɪ ə 'laɪ allies 'æl aɪz ə 'laɪz
Ally personal name 'æl i
-ally əl i —but -ically is usually reduced by
  COMPRESSION to ɪk li
allyl 'æl aɪəl -ɪl, §-əl ‖ -əl
Alma 'ælm ə —See also phrases with this word
Alma Ata æl ˌmɑː ə 'tɑː
almagest, A~ 'ælm ə dʒest
alma mater ˌælm ə 'mɑːt ə -'meɪt- ‖ -'mɑːt̬ ər
almanac, almanack 'ɔːlm ə næk 'ɒlm-,
  'ælm- ‖ 'ɑːlm-, 'ælm- ~s s
almandine 'ælm ən diːn 'ɑːm-, 'ɑːlm-, -dɪn,
  -daɪn; ˌ··'• ~s z

Alma-Tadema ˌælm ə 'tæd ɪm ə §-əm ə
Almeida æl 'miːd ə
Almeria ˌælm ə 'riː_ə —Sp Almería [al me 'ri a]
almight|y (ˌ)ɔːl 'maɪt li ‖ ɔːl 'maɪt̬ li ɑːl- ~ily ɪ li
  əl i ‖ əl i
almond, A~ 'ɑːm ənd §'ɑːlm-, §'ælm-, §'ɒlm-
  ~s z
almond-eyed ˌɑːm ənd 'aɪd ◄ §ˌɑːlm-, ˌælm-,
  ˌɒlm-
Almondsbury 'ɑːm əndz bər_i §'ɑːlm-, §'ælm-,
  §'ɒlm- ‖ -ˌber i —in Avon locally also
  'eɪmz bər_i
almoner 'ɑːm ən ə 'ælm-, §'ɒlm- ‖ 'ælm ən ər
  'ɑːm- ~s z
almon|ry 'ɑːm ən| ri ~ries riz
almost 'ɔːl məʊst 'ɒl-, ˌ•'•◄ ‖ 'ɔːl moʊst 'ɑːl-
alms ɑːmz §ɑːlmz, §ɒlmz ‖ ɔːlmz
alms-|house 'ɑːmz haʊs §'ɑːlmz-,
  §'ɒlmz- ‖ 'ɔːlmz- ~houses haʊz ɪz əz
Alne (i) ɔːn ‖ ɑːn, (ii) ɔːln ‖ ɑːln, (iii) æln
Alnmouth 'æln maʊθ →'ælm-, 'eɪl-
Alnwick 'æn ɪk
aloe 'æl əʊ ‖ -oʊ ~s z
aloft ə 'lɒft ‖ ə 'lɑːft -'lɔːft
aloha ə 'ləʊ hə -hɑː ‖ ə 'loʊ hɑː ɑː-
alone ə 'ləʊn ‖ ə 'loʊn
along ə 'lɒŋ ‖ ə 'lɔːŋ -'lɑːŋ
alongside ə ˌlɒŋ 'saɪd ◄ •'•• ‖ ə 'lɔːŋ saɪd
  -'lɑːŋ-, •,•'•
Alonso ə 'lɒnz əʊ -'lɒnts- ‖ ə 'lɑːnz oʊ -'lɑːnts-
  —Sp [a 'lon so]
Alonzo ə 'lɒnz əʊ ‖ ə 'lɑːnz oʊ —Sp [a 'lon θo,
  -so]
aloof ə 'luːf
alopecia ˌæl ə 'piːʃ ə -'piːʃ i_ə
aloud ə 'laʊd
Aloysius ˌæl əʊ 'ɪʃ əs -'ɪs i_əs ‖ ˌæl ə 'wɪʃ əs
alp ælp alps, Alps ælps
alpaca æl 'pæk ə ~s z
Alpen tdmk 'ælp ən
alpenglow 'ælp ən gləʊ →-əŋ- ‖ -gloʊ
alpenhorn 'ælp ən hɔːn ‖ -hɔːrn ~s z
alpenstock 'ælp ən stɒk ‖ -stɑːk ~s s
Alperton 'ælp ət ən ‖ -ərt ən
Alph ælf
alpha, Alpha 'ælf ə ~s z
  ˌAlpha Cen'tauri sen 'tɔːr i ken-, -'taʊər-;
  'alpha ˌparticle; 'alpha ˌrhythm
alphabet 'ælf ə bet -bɪt, §-bət ~s s
alphabetic ˌælf ə 'bet ɪk ◄ -'bet̬- ~al əl ~ally
  əl_i
alphabetis... —see alphabetiz...
alphabetization ˌælf ə bet aɪ 'zeɪʃ ən ˌ•·bɪt-,
  -ɪ'•- ‖ -bet̬ ə 'zeɪʃ-
alphabetiz|e 'ælf ə bet aɪz -bə taɪz, -bɪ taɪz
  ‖ -bə taɪz ~ed d ~es ɪz əz ~ing ɪŋ
alphanumeric ˌælf ə nju 'mer ɪk ◄ §-nu'•-
  ‖ -nu 'mer- -nju'•-
Alphege 'ælf ɪdʒ
Alphonso æl 'fɒnz əʊ -'fɒnts- ‖ -'fɑːnts oʊ
  —Sp [al 'fon so]
alpine 'ælp aɪn ~s z
alpin|ism 'ælp ɪn ˌɪz əm -ən- ~ist/s ɪst/s əst/s

A

Alport 'ɔːl pɔːt ‖ -pɔːrt 'ɑːl-, -poʊrt
Alps ælps
already ɔːl 'red i ɒl-, ˌˑ- ‖ ɑːl-
Alresford 'ɔːlz fəd ‖ -fərd 'ɑːlz- —*but places of this name are locally also* 'ɑːlz-, 'ɑːls-, 'eɪəls-
alright ˌɔːl 'raɪt ◄ ‖ ˌɔːl- ˌɑːl-
Alsace æl 'sæs -'zæs; 'ælz æs —*Fr* [al zas]
Alsager (i) ɔːl 'seɪdʒ ə ‖ -ər ɑːl-, (ii) 'ɔːls ədʒ ə -ɪdʒ- ‖ -ər 'ɑːls-
Alsatian æl 'seɪʃ ən ˌˑ-, -'ˑi_ən
alsike 'æls ɪk -aɪk
also 'ɔːls əʊ 'ɒls- ‖ 'ɔːls oʊ 'ɑːls-
Alsop 'ɔːl sɒp 'ɒl- ‖ 'ɔːl saɪp 'ɑːl-
also-ran 'ɔːls əʊ ræn 'ɒls-, ˌˑˑ'ˑ ‖ -oʊ- 'ɑːls-
Alston 'ɔːlst ən 'ɒlst- ‖ 'ɑːlst-
alt *musical term* ælt ‖ ɑːlt
Alt *name of river* ɔːlt ɒlt ‖ ɑːlt
Altai ˌˌɑːl 'taɪ
Altaic æl 'teɪ ɪk
Altair 'ælt eə æl 'teə ‖ æl 'teər -'tæər, -'taɪər, 'ˑˑ; -'tɑː ər
Altamira ˌælt ə 'mɪər ə ‖ ˌɑːlt ə 'mɪr ə —*Sp* [al ta 'mi ra]
altar 'ɔːlt ə 'ɒlt- ‖ 'ɔːlt ər 'ɑːlt- (*= alter*) ~s z
　'altar boy
Altarnun ˌɔːlt ə 'nʌn ˌɒlt- ‖ -ər- ˌɑːlt-
altarpiec|e 'ɔːlt ə piːs 'ɒlt- ‖ -ər- 'ɑːlt- ~es ɪz əz
Altavista *tdmk* ˌælt ə 'vɪst ə
altazimuth ælt 'æz ɪm əθ §-əm-
Altdorfer 'ælt dɔːf ə ‖ -dɔːrf ər 'ɑːlt- —*Ger* ['ʔalt dɔʁf ɐ]
alter *v* 'ɔːlt ə 'ɒlt- ‖ 'ɔːlt ər 'ɑːlt- ~**ed** d
　altering 'ɔːlt_ər ɪŋ 'ɒlt_ ‖ 'ɑːlt_ ~**s** z —*See also phrases with this word*
alteration ˌɔːlt ə 'reɪʃ ən ˌɒlt- ‖ ˌɑːlt- ~**s** z
altercation ˌɔːlt ə 'keɪʃ ən ˌɒlt- ‖ -ər- ˌɑːlt- ~**s** z
alter ego ˌælt ər 'iːg əʊ ˌɔːlt-, ˌɒlt-, -'eg- ‖ ˌɑːlt ər 'iːg oʊ ˌɒlt- ~**s** z
alternant ɔːl 'tɜːn ənt ɒl- ‖ 'ɔːlt ərn ənt 'ɑːlt- ~**s** s
alternate *adj, n* ɔːl 'tɜːn ət ɒl-, -ɪt ‖ 'ɔːlt ərn ət 'ɑːlt- (*) ~**ly** li ~**s** s
alter|nate *v* 'ɔːlt ə |neɪt 'ɒlt- ‖ -ər- 'ɑːlt- ~**nated** neɪt ɪd -əd ‖ neɪt əd ~**nates** neɪts ~**nating** neɪt ɪŋ ‖ neɪt ɪŋ
　ˌalternating 'current
alternation ˌɔːlt ə 'neɪʃ ən ˌɒlt- ‖ -ər- ˌɑːlt- ~**s** z
alternative ɔːl 'tɜːn ət ɪv ɒl- ‖ ɔːl 'tɜːn əţ ɪv ɑːl-, æl- ~**ly** li ~**s** z
alternator 'ɔːlt ə neɪt ə 'ɒlt- ‖ 'ɔːlt ər neɪţ ər 'ɑːlt-, 'ælt- ~**s** z
althaea, althea *'hollyhock'* æl 'θiː_ə ~**s** z
Althea *personal name* 'æltθ i_ə
Althorp (i) 'ɔːl θɔːp ‖ -θɔːrp 'ɑːl-, (ii) 'æl- —*but the place in Northants is locally also* 'ɔːltr əp, *as is Viscount A~*
although ɔːl 'ðəʊ ɒl-, ˌˑ-, §-'θəʊ ‖ ɔːl 'ðoʊ ɑːl-
Althusser ˌælt u 'seə ‖ ˌɑːlt u: 'seər —*Fr* [al ty sɛːʁ]

altimeter 'ælt ɪ ˌmiːt ə 'ɔːlt-, 'ɒlt-, -ə-; æl 'tɪm ɪt ə, -ət- ‖ æl 'tɪm əţ ər 'ælt ə ˌmiːţ ər ~**s** z
Altiplano ˌælt ɪ 'plɑːn əʊ ‖ -oʊ ˌɑːlt- —*Sp* [al ti 'pla no]
altissimo æl 'tɪs ɪ məʊ -ə- ‖ -moʊ ɑːl-
altitude 'ælt ɪ tjuːd 'ɔːlt-, 'ɒlt-, -ə-, →§-tʃuːd ‖ -tuːd -tjuːd ~**s** z
Altman 'ɔːlt mən‖ 'ɑːlt-

　　■ 'ælt-　□ 'ɒlt-　■ 'ɔːlt-　▨ 'ɑːlt-

BrE 1998

0　20　40　60　80　100%

alto 'ælt əʊ 'ɒlt-, 'ɔːlt-, 'ɑːlt- ‖ 'ælt oʊ ~**s** z —*BrE 1998 poll panel preference:* 'ælt- *71%,* 'ɒlt- *14%,* 'ɔːlt- *8%,* 'ɑːlt- *7%*
altocumulus ˌælt əʊ 'kjuːm jʊl əs -jəl əs ‖ -oʊ 'kjuːm jəl-
altogether ˌɔːl tə 'geð ə ◄ 'ˑˑˑˑ ‖ -ər ◄ ˌɑːl-
Alton 'ɔːlt ən 'ɒlt- ‖ 'ɔːlt ən 'ɑːlt-
Altoona æl 'tuːn ə
alto-relievo ˌælt əʊ rɪ 'liː vəʊ -rə'ˑ- ‖ -oʊ rɪ 'liːv oʊ ˌɑːlt-
altostratus ˌælt əʊ 'streɪt əs -'strɑːt- ‖ -oʊ 'streɪţ əs -'stræţ-
altricial æl 'trɪʃ əl
Altrincham 'ɔːltr ɪŋ əm 'ɒltr- ‖ 'ɑːltr-
altruism 'æltr u ˌɪz əm
altruist 'æltr u ɪst §-əst ~**s** s
altruistic ˌæltr u 'ɪst ɪk ◄ ~**ally** əl_i
alum 'æl əm
alumina ə 'luːm ɪn ə -'ljuːm-
aluminium ˌæl ə 'mɪn i_əm ◄, ˑu-, ˑju-, ˑjə-
aluminous ə 'luːm ɪn əs -'ljuːm-, -ən-
aluminum ə 'luːm ɪn əm -'ljuːm-, -ən-
alum|na ə 'lʌm |nə ~**nae** niː ~**ni** naɪ ~**nus** nəs
Alun 'æl ɪn —*Welsh* ['a lɪn, -lɪn]
Alva 'ælv ə
Alvar 'ælv ɑː -ə ‖ -ɑːr -ər
Alvarez (i) æl 'vɑːr ez, (ii) 'ælv ə rez —*Sp* Álvarez ['al βa reθ]
alveolar ˌælv i 'əʊl ə ◄ æl 'viː_əl ə, 'ælv i_əl ə ‖ æl 'viː əl ər ~**s** z
alveolaris... —*see* **alveolariz...**
alveolarity ˌælv i_ə 'lær ət i æl ˌviː_ə-, -ɪt i ‖ æl ˌvi: ə 'lær əţ i -'ler-
alveolarization ˌælv i ˌəʊl ər əz 'zeɪʃ ən æl ˌviː_əl-, ˌælv i_əl-, -ɪ'ˑ- ‖ æl ˌviː əl ər ə-
alveolariz|e ˌælv i 'əʊl ə raɪz æl 'viː_əl-, 'ælv i_əl- ‖ æl 'vi: əl ə raɪz ~**ed** d ~**es** ɪz əz ~**ing** ɪŋ
alveole 'ælv i əʊl →-ɒʊl ‖ -oʊl ~**s** z
alveol|us ˌælv i 'əʊl əs æl 'viː_əl əs, 'ælv i_əl əs ‖ æl 'vi: əl- ~**i** aɪ iː
Alvey 'ælv i
Alvin 'ælv ɪn §-ən
Alvis 'ælv ɪs §-əs
always 'ɔːl weɪz §'ɒl-, -wɪz, -wəz ‖ 'ɑːl-
Alwyn (i) 'ɔːl wɪn ‖ 'ɑːl-, (ii) 'æl-
Alyn 'æl ɪn -ən
Alyson 'æl ɪs ən -əs-

A

alyssum 'æl ıs əm -əs- ‖ ə 'lıs əm
Alzheimer 'ælts haım ə 'ælz- ‖ 'ɑːlts haım ᵊr
—Ger ['ʔalts haim ɐ] ~'s z
'Alzheimer's di͵sease
am from be, strong form æm, weak form əm
—see I'm, 'm
AM, am, a.m. 'amplitude modulation'; 'ante
meridiem' ͵eı 'em ◄
AMA ͵eı em 'eı
Amadeus ͵æm ə 'deı əs ‖ ͵ɑːm ə 'deı ʊs -əs
amadou 'æm ə du:
amah 'ɑːm ə 'æm-, -ɑː ~s z
Amahl 'æm ɑːl ‖ ə 'mɑːl
Amalekite ə 'mæl ə kaıt ‖ 'æm ə lek aıt,
͵•••• ~s s
Amalfi ə 'mælf i ‖ ə 'mɑːlf i —It [a 'mal fi]
amalgam ə 'mælg əm ~s z
amalga|mate ə 'mælg ə |meıt ~mated
meıt ıd -əd ‖ meıt əd ~mates meıts
~mating meıt ıŋ ‖ meıt ıŋ
amalgamation ə ͵mælg ə 'meı ʃ ᵊn ~s z
Amanda ə 'mænd ə
amanita ͵æm ə 'naıt ə -'niːt- ‖ -'naıt̬ ə -'niːt̬ ə
~s z
amanuens|is ə ͵mæn ju 'enᵗs |ıs §-əs —es iːz
amaranth 'æm ə rænᵗθ ~s s
amaranthine ͵æm ə 'rænᵗθ aın ◄ ‖ -ᵊn ◄ -aın
amarett|o ͵æm ə 'ret| əʊ ‖ -'ret̬ ı oʊ ~i iː
Amarillo ͵æm ə 'rıl əʊ ‖ -oʊ
amaryllis, A~ ͵æm ə 'rıl ıs §-əs —es ız əz
amass ə 'mæs amassed ə 'mæst amasses
ə 'mæs ız -əz amassing ə 'mæs ıŋ
amassment ə 'mæs mənt
amateur 'æm ət ə 'æm ə t ʃʊə, -t ʃə, -t jʊə;
͵æm ə 'tɜː ◄ ‖ 'æm ə t ʃʊr -əƫ ᵊr, -ə t jʊr ~s z
amateurish 'æm ət ᵊr ı ʃ -ət ʃ ᵊr-, -ə tʊər-;
͵æm ə 't jʊər ı ʃ ◄, -'tɜːr- ‖ ͵æm ə 'tʊr ı ʃ ◄
-'t ʃʊr-, -'tɜː:-, -'t jʊr- ~ly li ~ness nəs nıs
amateurism 'æm ət ᵊr ͵ız əm '•ət ʃ-, -ə tɜːr-,
-ə t ʃʊər-, -ə t jʊər- ‖ 'æm ə t ʃʊr- -əƫ ᵊr-,
-ə t jʊr-
Amati ə 'mɑːt i æ- —It [a 'mɑː ti]
amatol 'æm ə tɒl ‖ -tɑːl -tɔːl, -toʊl
amatory 'æm ət͵ᵊr i ‖ -ə tɔːr i -toʊr i
amaurosis ͵æm ɔː 'rəʊs ıs §-əs ‖ -'roʊs əs -ɑː-
amaze ə 'meız amazed ə 'meızd amazes
ə 'meız ız -əz amazing ə 'meız ıŋ
amazed|ly ə 'meız ıdl li -'•əd- ~ness nəs nıs
amazement ə 'meız mənt
amazing ə 'meız ıŋ ~ly li
amazon, Amazon 'æm əz ən ‖ -ə zɑːn -əz ən
~s z
Amazonia ͵æm ə 'zəʊn i͵ə ‖ -'zoʊn-
amazonian, A~ ͵æm ə 'zəʊn i͵ən ◄ -'zoʊn- ~s
z
Amazulu ͵æm ə 'zuːl uː
ambassador æm 'bæs əd ə -ıd- ‖ -ᵊr ~s z
ambassadorial æm ͵bæs ə 'dɔːr i əl ◄, ͵•••,
-ı'•- ‖ -'doʊr-
ambassadorship æm 'bæs əd ə ʃıp -'•ıd-
‖ -ᵊr ʃıp ~s s
ambassadress æm 'bæs ə dres -ədr ıs, -əs;
•͵•ə 'dres ‖ -ədr əs —es ız əz

amber, Amber 'æm bə ‖ -bᵊr
ambergris 'æm bə griːs -griː, -grıs ‖ -grıs
-griːs
Ambi tdmk 'æm bi
ambi- comb. form ͵æm bi-
ambiance 'æm bi͵ənᵗs 'ɒm-, -ɒnᵗs,
-ɒ̃s ‖ ͵ɑːm bi 'ɑːnᵗs —Fr [ɑ̃ bjɑ̃ːs]
ambidexterity ͵æm bi dek 'ster ət i -ıt i ‖ -ət̬ i
ambidextrous ͵æm bi 'deks trəs ◄ ~ly li
ambience 'æm bi͵ənᵗs 'ɒm-, -ɒnᵗs,
-ɒ̃s ‖ ͵ɑːm bi 'ɑːnᵗs —Fr ambiance [ɑ̃ bjɑ̃ːs]
ambient 'æm bi͵ənt
ambiguit|y ͵æm bı 'gjuː ət li, •bə-, -ıt i ‖ ət̬ li
~ies iz
ambiguous æm 'bıg ju͵əs ~ly li ~ness nəs
nıs
ambisyllabic ͵æm bi sı 'læb ık ◄ -sə-
ambisyllabicity ͵æm bi ͵sıl ə 'bıs ət i -ıt i ‖ -ət̬ i
ambit 'æm bıt -bət ~s s
ambition æm 'bıʃ ᵊn ~s z
ambitious æm 'bıʃ əs ~ly li ~ness nəs nıs
ambivalence æm 'bıv əl ənᵗs ͵æm bi 'veıl ᵊnᵗs
ambivalent æm 'bıv əl ənt ͵æm bi 'veıl ənt ◄
~ly li
amble 'æm bᵊl ambled 'æm bᵊld ambles
'æm bᵊlz ambling 'æm bᵊl ıŋ
Ambler 'æm blə ‖ 'æm blᵊr
Ambleside 'æm bᵊl saıd
amblyopia ͵æm bli 'əʊp i͵ə ‖ -'oʊp-
ambo, Ambo 'æm bəʊ ‖ -boʊ
Amboina, a~ æm 'bɔın ə
Amboinese ͵æm bɔı 'niːz ◄ ‖ -'niːs ◄
amboyna æm 'bɔın ə
Ambridge 'æm brıdʒ
Ambrose 'æm brəʊz -brəʊs ‖ -broʊz
ambrosi|a æm 'brəʊz i͵ə • 'brəʊʒ ə
‖ æm 'broʊʒ ə -al əl ~an ən
ambsace 'eımz eıs 'æmz-
ambulac|rum ͵æm bju 'leık |rəm -'læk- ‖ -bjə-
~ra rə
ambulanc|e 'æm bjəl ənᵗs -bjʊl-, §-bəl- ~es ız
əz
ambulance|man 'æm bjəl ənᵗs |mæn '•bjʊl-,
§'•bəl- ~men men
ambulant 'æm bjəl ənt -bjʊl-
ambu|late 'æm bju |leıt -bjə- ‖ -bjə- ~lated
leıt ıd -əd ‖ leıt̬ əd ~lates leıts ~lating
leıt ıŋ ‖ leıt̬ ıŋ
ambulation ͵æm bju 'leıʃ ᵊn -bjə- ‖ -bjə- ~s
z
ambulator|y 'æm bju 'leıt ər li ◄, •bjə-,
'•'•lət͵ᵊr i ‖ 'æm bjəl ə tɔːr li-toʊr i ~ies iz
ambuscad|e ͵æm bə 'skeıd ‖ 'æm bə skeıd
~ed ıd əd ~es z ~ing ıŋ
ambush 'æm bʊʃ ~ed t ~es ız əz ~ing ıŋ
ambystoma æm 'bıst əm ə ~s z
Amdahl tdmk 'æm dɑːl
ameb|a ə 'miːb |ə ~ae iː ~as əz
amebiasis ͵æm iː 'baı͵əs ıs §-əs
amebic ə 'miːb ık
ameboid ə 'miːb ɔıd
Ameche ə 'miːtʃ i
Amelia ə 'miːl i͵ə

amelio|rate ə 'miːl i‿ə |reɪt ~rated reɪt ɪd -əd
‖ reɪt̬ əd ~rates reɪts ~rating
reɪt ɪŋ ‖ reɪt̬ ɪŋ
amelioration ə ˌmiːl i‿ə 'reɪʃ ᵊn ~s z
ameliorative ə 'miːl i‿ə reɪt ɪv -rət ɪv ‖ -reɪt̬ ɪv
ameliorator ə 'miːl i‿ə reɪt ə ‖ -reɪt̬ ᵊr ~s z
amen ˌɑː 'men ◂ ˌeɪ- —Although ˌɑː- is the
usual form among Protestants in Britain, ˌeɪ- is
preferred by Roman Catholics and also in non-
religious contexts, as in ˌAmen 'Corner. In AmE,
ˌeɪ- predominates in speech, but ˌɑː- is
preferred in singing. ~s z
amenability ə ˌmiːn ə 'bɪl ət i -ˌmen-, -ɪt i
‖ -ət̬ i
amenab|le ə 'miːn əb |ᵊl -'men- ~ly li
amend ə 'mend amended ə 'mend ɪd -əd
amending ə 'mend ɪŋ amends ə 'mendz
amendment ə 'mend mənt →-'mem- ~s s
amenit|y ə 'miːn ət i -'men-, -ɪt- ‖ -ət̬ i ~ies
iz
amenorrhea, amenorrhoea ˌeɪ ˌmen ə 'riː‿ə
ˌæ-, •ˌ•- ‖ eɪ ˌmen- ɑː-
ament 'catkin' 'æm ənt 'eɪm- ~s s
ament 'mentally deficient person' 'eɪ ment
-mənt; æ 'ment ~s s
amentia ₍ᵢ₎eɪ 'menʃ ə ₍ᵢ₎æ-, -'menʃ i‿ə
America ə 'mer ɪk ə -ək- —also sometimes
⚠-'mər-; so also in derivatives ~s, ~'s z
Aˌmerica On 'Line tdmk, •ˌ••• '• •
American ə 'mer ɪk ən -ək- ~s z
Aˌmerican 'English; Aˌmerican Ex'press
tdmk; Aˌmerican 'Indian
Americana ə ˌmer ɪ 'kɑːn ə -ˌ•ə- ‖ -'kæn-
americanis... —see americaniz...
Americanism ə 'mer ɪk ən ˌɪz əm -'•ək- ~s z
americanization ə ˌmer ɪk ən aɪ 'zeɪʃ ᵊn
-ˌ•ək-, -ɪ'•- ‖ -ə 'zeɪʃ-
americaniz|e ə 'mer ɪk ə naɪz -'•ək- ~ed d
~es ɪz əz ~ing ɪŋ
americium ˌæm ə 'rɪs i‿əm -'rɪʃ-
Amerind 'æm ə rɪnd ~s z
Amerindian ˌæm ə 'rɪnd i‿ən ◂ ~s z
Amersham 'æm əʃ əm ‖ -ᵊrʃ-
Amery 'eɪm ər i
Ames eɪmz
Amesbury 'eɪmz bər‿i ‖ -ˌber i
Ameslan 'æm ə slæn 'æm slæn
amethyst 'æm əθ ɪst -ɪθ-, §-əst ~s s
amethystine ˌæm ə 'θɪst aɪn ◂ -ɪ- ‖ -ən -aɪn
Amex tdmk 'æm eks
Amharic æm 'hær ɪk əm- ‖ ɑːm 'hɑːr-
Amherst (i) 'æm əst ‖ -ᵊrst , (ii) -hɜːst ‖ -hɝːst
— (i) is the traditional form in both BrE and
AmE, and hence appropriate for Baron A~, the
18th-century general, and for the place in MA.
amiability ˌeɪm i‿ə 'bɪl ət i -ɪt i ‖ -ət̬ i
amiab|le 'eɪm i‿əb |ᵊl —leness ᵊl nəs -nɪs ~ly li
amicability ˌæm ɪk ə 'bɪl ət i ‚•ək-, -ɪt i ‖ -ət̬ i
amicab|le 'æm ɪk əb |ᵊl '•ək-; ə 'mɪk- ~leness
ᵊl nəs -nɪs ~ly li
amic|e 'æm ɪs §-əs ~es ɪz əz
Amice 'eɪm ɪs §-əs

amicus ə 'maɪk əs æ-, -'miːk-, -ʊs
aˌmicus 'curiae 'kjʊər i i: -aɪ ‖ 'kjʊr- 'kʊr-
amid ə 'mɪd
amide 'æm aɪd 'eɪm- ‖ -əd ~s z
Amidol tdmk 'æm ɪ dɒl §-ə- ‖ -dɑːl -dɔːl, -doʊl
amidships ə 'mɪd ʃɪps
amidst ə 'mɪdst -'mɪtst
Amiens 'æm i‿ɒ̃ -æ̃, -ənz —formerly, and as an
English-language name, and for the Dublin
street, 'eɪm i‿ənz; in Shakespeare 'æm i‿ənz
—Fr [a mjæ̃]
Amies 'eɪm iz
Amiga tdmk ə 'miːg ə
amigo ə 'miːg əʊ æ- ‖ -oʊ ɑː- —Sp [a 'mi ɣo]
Amin ₍ᵢ₎ɑː 'miːn ₍ᵢ₎æ-
amine 'æm iːn -ɪn, §-ən; ə 'miːn ‖ ə 'miːn
'æm iːn, -ən ~s z
amino ə 'miːn əʊ -'maɪn-; 'æm ɪn əʊ, -ən-
‖ -oʊ
aˌmino 'acid
amir ə 'mɪə ‖ ə 'mɪᵊr ~s z
Amis 'eɪm ɪs §-əs
Amish 'ɑːm ɪʃ 'æm-
amiss ə 'mɪs
Amistad 'æm ɪ stæd -ə- ‖ 'ɑːm ə stɑːd
amit|y 'æm ət i -ɪt i ‖ -ət̬ i ~ies iz
Amlwch 'æm lʊk -lʊx —Welsh ['am lʊχ]
Amman place in Jordan ə 'mɑːn æ-, -'mæn,
‖ 'ɑːm ɑːn —Arabic [ʕam 'maːn]
Amman river in Wales 'æm ən
ammeter 'æm iːt ə -ɪt-, -ˌmiːt- ‖ -iːt̬ ᵊr ~s z
ammo 'æm əʊ ‖ -oʊ
Ammon 'æm ən
ammonia ə 'məʊn i‿ə ‖ ə 'moʊn-
ammoniac ə 'məʊn i æk ‖ ə 'moʊn-
ammoniated ə 'məʊn i eɪt ɪd -əd
‖ ə 'moʊn i eɪt̬ əd
ammonite, A~ 'æm ə naɪt ~s s
ammonium ə 'məʊn i‿əm ‖ ə 'moʊn-
ammunition ˌæm ju 'nɪʃ ᵊn -jə- ‖ -jə-
amnesia æm 'niːz i‿ə -'niːʒ ə ‖ -'niːʒ ə
amnesiac æm 'niːz i æk ‖ -'niːʒ- ~s s
amnesic æm 'niːz ɪk -'niːs- ~s s
amnest|y, A~ 'æm nəst |i -nɪst- ~ies iz
ˌAmnesty ˌInter'national
amniocentesis ˌæm ni‿əʊ sen 'tiːs ɪs §-əs
‖ ˌæm ni oʊ-
amnion 'æm ni‿ən -ɒn ‖ -ɑːn -ən ~s z
amniote 'æm ni əʊt ‖ -oʊt ~s s
amniotic ˌæm ni 'ɒt ɪk ◂ ‖ -'ɑːt̬ ɪk ◂
Amoco tdmk 'æm ə kəʊ ‖ -koʊ
amoeb|a ə 'miːb ə ~ae iː ~as əz
amoebiasis ˌæm i: 'baɪ‿əs ɪs §-əs
amoebic ə 'miːb ɪk
amoeboid ə 'miːb ɔɪd
amok ə 'mɒk ə 'mʌk, 'ɑːm əʊ ‖ ə 'mʌk -'mɑːk
among ə 'mʌŋ §-'mɒŋ
amongst ə 'mʌŋkst §-'mɒŋkst
amontillado ˌæm ɒnt ɪ 'lɑːd əʊ ə ˌmɒnt-, -ə'•-
‖ ə ˌmɑːnt ə 'lɑːd oʊ —Sp [a mon ti 'ʎa ðo,
-'ja-] ~s z
amoral ˌeɪ 'mɒr əl ◂ ₍ᵢ₎æ- ‖ -'mɔːr- -'mɑːr- ~ly
i

A

amorality ˌeɪ mɒ 'ræl ət i ˌæ-, -ˌmə-, -ɪt i
‖ ˌeɪ mə 'ræl ət̬ i ˌ•mɔː-
amorett|o, A~ ˌæm ə 'ret ləʊ ‖ -'ret̬ loʊ ˌɑːm-
~ii
Amorite 'æm ə raɪt ~s s
amoroso ˌæm ə 'rəʊs əʊ ‖ ˌɑːm ə 'roʊs oʊ
amorous 'æm ər_əs ~ly li ~ness nəs nɪs
amorphous ə 'mɔːf əs ‖ ə 'mɔːrf- ~ly li ~ness
nəs nɪs
amortis... —see amortiz...
amortizable ə 'mɔːt aɪz əb əl‖ 'æm ər taɪz-
ə 'mɔːr-
amortization ə ˌmɔːt aɪ 'zeɪʃ ən -ɪ-
‖ ˌæm ər̬t ə- ə ˌmɔːrt̬ ə-
amortiz|e ə 'mɔːt aɪz ‖ 'æm ər taɪz ə 'mɔːr-
~ed d ~ement/s mənt/s ~es ɪz əz ~ing ɪŋ
Amory 'eɪm ər i
Amos 'eɪm ɒs ‖ -əs
amount ə 'maʊnt amounted ə 'maʊnt ɪd -əd
‖ ə 'maʊnt̬ əd amounting
ə 'maʊnt ɪŋ ‖ ə 'maʊnt̬ ɪŋ amounts
ə 'maʊnts
amour ə 'mʊə ˌæ- ‖ ə 'mʊər ɑː- ~s z
amour-propre ˌæm ʊə 'prɒp_rə
‖ ˌɑːm ʊr 'proʊp_rə ˌæm- —Fr
[a muʁ pʁɔpχ]
Amoy ə 'mɔɪ ɑː-, æ- —Chinese Xiàmén
[⁴çja²mən]
amp æmp amps æmps
ampelopsis ˌæmp ɪ 'lɒps ɪs -ə-, §-əs ‖ -'lɑːps-
amperag|e 'æmp ər_ɪdʒ -ɪər- ‖ -ɪr- ~es ɪz əz
ampere, ampère, A~ 'æmp eə ‖ -ɪr -er —Fr
[ɑ̃ pɛːʁ] ~s z
ampersand 'æmp ə sænd ‖ -ər- ~s z
Ampex tdmk 'æmp eks
amphetamine æm 'fet ə miːn -mɪn, §-mən
‖ -'fet̬- ~s z
amphi- comb. form
with stress-neutral suffix ¦æmpf i —
amphipathic ˌæmpf i 'pæθ ɪk ◂
with stress-imposing suffix æm 'fɪ+ —
amphitropous æm 'fɪtr əp əs
amphibian ₍ᵢ₎æm 'fɪb i_ən ~s z
amphibious ₍ᵢ₎æm 'fɪb i_əs ~ly li ~ness nəs
nɪs
amphibole mineral 'æmpf ɪ bəʊl §-ə-, →-bɒʊl
‖ -boʊl ~s z
amphibolite æm 'fɪb ə laɪt ~s s
amphibolog|y ˌæmpf i 'bɒl ədʒ| i ‖ -'bɑːl-
~ies iz
amphibrach 'æmpf i bræk ~s s
amphictyonic, A~ æm ˌfɪkt i 'ɒn ɪk ◂ ‖ -'ɑːn-
amphimacer æm 'fɪm əs ə ‖ -ər ~s z
amphisbaena ˌæmpf ɪs 'biːn ə §-əs- ~s z
amphitheater, amphitheatre 'æmpf i ˌθɪət ə
§'••θi ˌet ə ‖ 'æmpf ə ˌθiː ət̬ ər △'æmp- ~s z
Amphitrite ˌæmpf i 'traɪt i '••, •• -ə 'traɪt̬ i
Amphitryon æm 'fɪtr i_ən
amph|ora 'æmpf |ər ə ~orae ə riː ~oras ər əz
ampicillin ˌæmp ɪ 'sɪl ɪn -ə-, §-ən
ample 'æmp əl ampler 'æm plə ‖ -plər
amplest 'æm plɪst -pləst
Ampleforth 'æmp əl fɔːθ ‖ -fɔːrθ -foʊrθ

Amplex tdmk 'æmp leks
amplexicaul æm 'pleks ɪ kɔːl §-ə- ‖ -kɑːl
amplification ˌæmp lɪf ɪ 'keɪʃ ən ˌ•ləf-, §-ə'•-
~s z
ampli|fy 'æmp lɪ |faɪ -lə- ~fied faɪd ~fier/s
faɪ_ə/z ‖ faɪ_ər/z ~fies faɪz ~fying faɪ ɪŋ
amplitude 'æmp lɪ tjuːd -lə-, →§-tʃuːd ‖ -tuːd
-tjuːd ~s z
amply 'æmp li
Ampney (i) 'æmp ni, (ii) 'æm ni
ampoule 'æmp uːl -juːl ~s z
Ampthill 'æmpt hɪl -ɪl
ampule 'æmp juːl ~s z
ampull|a æm 'pʊl ə -'pʌl- ~ae iː -as əz
ampu|tate 'æmp ju |teɪt §-jə- ‖ -jə- ~tated
teɪt ɪd -əd ‖ teɪt̬ əd ~tates teɪts ~tating
teɪt ɪŋ ‖ teɪt̬ ɪŋ
amputation ˌæmp ju 'teɪʃ ən §-jə- ‖ -jə- ~s z
amputee ˌæmp ju 'tiː §-jə- ‖ -jə- ~s z
Amritsar æm 'rɪts ə əm-, -ɑː- ‖ -ər —Hindi
[əm rɪt̬ sər]
Amsterdam 'æmᵖst ə dæm ˌ•'• ◂ ‖ -ər- —Du
[ˌam stər 'dam]
Amstrad tdmk 'æm stræd ~s, ~'s z
Amtrak tdmk 'æm træk
amuck ə 'mʌk
Amu Darya ˌæm ə muː 'dɑːr i_ə ə ˌmuː-
amulet 'æm jʊl ət §-jəl-, -ɪt, -ju let ‖ -jəl- ~s s
Amundsen 'ɑːm ənd sən 'æm-, -ʊnd- —Norw
['ɑː mun sən]
Amur ə 'mʊə 'æm ʊə ‖ ɑː 'mʊər —Russ
[ʌ 'mur]
amuse ə 'mjuːz amused ə 'mjuːzd amuses
ə 'mjuːz ɪz -əz amusing ə 'mjuːz ɪŋ
amusement ə 'mjuːz mənt ~s s
a'musement ar̩ cade; a'musement park
amusing ə 'mjuːz ɪŋ ~ly li ~ness nəs nɪs
Amway tdmk 'æm weɪ
Amy 'eɪm i
Amyas 'eɪm i_əs
amygdaloid ə 'mɪgd ə lɔɪd
amyl 'æm əl 'eɪm-, -aɪəl, -ɪl
ˌamyl 'nitrite
amytal, A~ tdmk 'æm ɪ tæl -ə- ‖ -tɑːl -tɔːl
an strong form æn, weak form ən —see also a
an- ₍ᵢ₎æn, æ ən —When it is a variant of ad-, this
prefix is usually ə (an'nul), but æ if stressed
because of a suffix ('annotate). As a negative
prefix, it is usually æn (ˌan'oxia), undergoing
reduction to ən only in a few better-known
words (a'nonymous).
ana 'ɑːn ə
ana- comb. form
before stress-neutral suffix ¦æn ə —
Anabaptist ˌæn ə 'bæpt ɪst §-əst
before stress-imposing suffix ə 'næ+ —
anadromous ə 'nædr əm əs
Anabaptist ˌæn ə 'bæpt ɪst ◂ §-əst ~s s
anabasis ə 'næb əs ɪs §-əs
anabatic ˌæn ə 'bæt ɪk ◂ ‖ -'bæt̬-
anabolic ˌæn ə 'bɒl ɪk ◂ ‖ -'bɑːl-
ˌana̩bolic 'steroid
anachronism ə 'næk rə ˌnɪz əm ~s z

A

anachronistic ə ˌnæk rə 'nɪst ɪk ◄ ~**ally** ᵊl_i
Anacin *tdmk* 'æn ə sɪn
anacoluth|on ˌæn ək ə 'luːθ |ᵊn -'ljuːθ-, -ˌɒn
‖ -ˈlɑːn ~**a** ə ~**ons** ᵊnz ɒnz ‖ ɑːnz
anaconda, A~ ˌæn ə 'kɒnd ə ‖ -'kɑːnd ə ~**s** z
Anacreon ə 'næk ri_ən -ɒn ‖ -ɑːn
anacrus|is ˌæn ə 'kruːs |ɪs §-əs ~**es** iːz
anacrustic ˌæn ə 'krʌst ɪk ◄
Anadin *tdmk* 'æn ə dɪn
anaemia ə 'niːm i_ə
anaemic ə 'niːm ɪk ~**ally** ᵊl_i
anaerobic ˌæn ə 'rəʊb ɪk ◄ -eə- ‖ -'roʊb- -e-
~**ally** ᵊl_i ~**s** s
anaesthesia ˌæn əs 'θiːz i_ə ˌ•iːs-, ˌ•ɪs-, -'θiːʒ ə
‖ -'θiːʒ ə
anaesthesiologist ˌæn əs ˌθiːz i 'ɒl ədʒ ɪst
§-əst ‖ -'ɑːl- ~**s** s
anaesthesiology ˌæn əs ˌθiːz i 'ɒl ədʒ i ‖ -'ɑːl-
anaesthetic ˌæn əs 'θet ɪk ◄ -iːs-, -ɪs- ‖ -'θeṭ-
~**s** s
anaesthetis... —*see* **anaesthetiz...**
anaesthetist ə 'niːs θət ɪst æ-, -θɪt-, §-əst
‖ ə 'nes θəṭ əst *(*)* ~**s** s
anaesthetization ə ˌniːs θət aɪ 'zeɪʃ ᵊn -ɪ'•-
‖ ə ˌnes θəṭ ə-
anaesthetiz|e ə 'niːs θə taɪz -θɪ- ‖ ə 'nes- *(*)*
~**ed** d ~**es** ɪz əz ~**ing** ɪŋ
anaglyph 'æn ə glɪf ~**s** s
anaglypta, A~ *tdmk* ˌæn ə 'glɪpt ə
anagram 'æn ə græm ~**med** d ~**ming** ɪŋ ~**s** z
anagrammatic ˌæn ə grə 'mæt ɪk ◄ ‖ -'mæṭ-
~**ally** ᵊl_i
Anaheim 'æn ə haɪm
Anais, Anaïs ˌæn aɪ 'iːs ◄ ə 'naɪ_əs
anal 'eɪn ᵊl ~**ly** i
analect 'æn ə lekt -ᵊl ekt ~**s** s
analecta ˌæn ə 'lekt ə
analemma ˌæn ə 'lem ə
analemmatic ˌæn ə le 'mæt ɪk ◄ ‖ -'mæṭ-
analeptic ˌæn ə 'lept ɪk ◄
analgesia ˌæn ᵊl 'dʒiːz i_ə ˌ•æl-,
-'dʒiːs- ‖ -'dʒiːʒ ə
analgesic ˌæn ᵊl 'dʒiːz ɪk ◄ -æl-, -'dʒiːs- ~**s** s
analog 'æn ə lɒg -ᵊl ɒg ‖ 'æn ᵊl ɔːg -ɑːg ~**s** z
analogical ˌæn ə 'lɒdʒ ɪk ᵊl ◄ -ᵊl 'ɒdʒ-
‖ -ᵊl 'ɑːdʒ- ~**ly** i
analogis|e, analogiz|e ə 'næl ə dʒaɪz ~**ed** d
~**es** ɪz əz ~**ing** ɪŋ
analogous ə 'næl əg əs -ədʒ- ~**ly** li
analogue 'æn ə lɒg -ᵊl ɒg ‖ 'æn ᵊl ɔːg -ɑːg ~**s**
z
analog|y ə 'næl ədʒ |i ~**ies** iz
analphabetic ˌæn ælf ə 'bet ɪk ◄ •, •- ‖ -'beṭ-
anal-retentive ˌeɪn ᵊl rɪ 'tent ɪv -rə'•-, §-riː'•
‖ -'tenṭ-
analysable 'æn ə laɪz əb ᵊl →'æn ᵊl aɪz-;
ˌ••'•••
analysand ə 'næl ɪ sænd -ə- ~**s** z
analys|e 'æn ə laɪz -ᵊl aɪz ~**ed** d ~**er/s** ə/z
‖ ᵊr/z ~**es** vɪz əz ~**ing** ɪŋ
analysis ə 'næl əs ɪs -ɪs ɪs, §-əs **analyses** *n*
ə 'næl ə siːz -ɪ-
analyst 'æn ᵊl ɪst §-əst ~**s** s

analytic ˌæn ə 'lɪt ɪk ◄ -ᵊl 'ɪt- ‖ -ᵊl 'ɪṭ ɪk ◄ ~**al**
ᵊl ~**ally** ᵊl_i
analyzable 'æn ə laɪz əb ᵊl →'æn ᵊl aɪz-;
ˌ••'•••
analyz|e 'æn ə laɪz -ᵊl aɪz ~**ed** d ~**er/s** ə/z
‖ ᵊr/z ~**es** ɪz əz ~**ing** ɪŋ
anamnesis ˌæn æm 'niːs ɪs §-əs
Anancy ə 'nænⁱs i
Ananda ə 'nænd ə -'nʌnd-
Ananias ˌæn ə 'naɪ_əs
anapaest, anapest 'æn ə piːst -pest ‖ -pest ~**s**
s
anapaestic, anapestic ˌæn ə 'piːst ɪk ◄ -'pest-
‖ -'pest-
anaphor 'æn ə fɔː -əf ə ‖ -fɔːr ~**s** z
anaphora ə 'næf ᵊr ə
anaphoric ˌæn ə 'fɒr ɪk ◄ ‖ -'fɔːr- -'fɑːr- ~**ally**
ᵊl_i
anaphylactic ˌæn ə fɪ 'lækt ɪk -ə fə- ~**ally** ᵊl_i
anaphylaxis ˌæn ə fɪ 'læks ɪs -ə fə-, §-əs
anaptyctic ˌæn əp 'tɪkt ɪk ◄ -æp-
anaptyxis ˌæn əp 'tɪks ɪs -æp-, §-əs
anarch 'æn ɑːk ‖ -ɑːrk ~**s** s
anarchic æ 'nɑːk ɪk ə- ‖ -'nɑːrk- -**al** ᵊl ~**ally**
ᵊl_i
anarchism 'æn ə ˌkɪz əm -ɑː- ‖ -ᵊr- -ɑːr-
anarchist 'æn ək ɪst -ɑːk-, §-əst ‖ -ᵊrk- -ɑːrk-
~**s** s
anarchistic ˌæn ə 'kɪst ɪk ◄ -ɑː- ‖ -ᵊr- -ɑːr-
anarchy 'æn ək i -ɑːk- ‖ -ᵊrk i -ɑːrk-
anarthria æn 'ɑːθ ri_ə ‖ -'ɑːrθ-
anarthric æn 'ɑːθ rɪk ‖ -'ɑːrθ-
Anastasia ˌæn ə 'steɪz i_ə -'stɑːz- ‖ -'steɪʒ ə
-'stɑːʒ ə
anastigmat æn 'æst ɪg mæt ən-; ˌæn ə 'stɪg-
~**s** s
anastigmatic ˌæn ə stɪg 'mæt ɪk ◄ æn ˌæst ɪg-,
ən- ‖ -'mæṭ-
anastomos|e ə 'næst ə məʊz æ- ‖ -moʊz
-moʊs ~**ed** d ~**es** ɪz əz ~**ing** ɪŋ
anastomos|is ə ˌnæst ə 'məʊs |ɪs æ-, ˌæn əst-,
§-əs ‖ -'moʊs- ~**es** iːz
anathema ə 'næθ əm ə -ɪm- ~**s** z
anathematis|e, anathematiz|e
ə 'næθ əm ə taɪz -'•ɪm- ~**ed** d ~**es** ɪz əz
~**ing** ɪŋ
Anatole 'æn ə təʊl →-tɒʊl ‖ -toʊl —*Fr*
[a na tɔl]
Anatoli|a ˌæn ə 'təʊl i_|ə ‖ -'toʊl- ~**an/s** ən/z
anatomical ˌæn ə 'tɒm ɪk ᵊl ◄ ‖ -'tɑːm- ~**ly** i
anatomis|e ə 'næt ə maɪz ‖ ə 'næṭ- ~**ed** d ~**es**
ɪz əz ~**ing** ɪŋ
anatomist ə 'næt əm ɪst §-əst ‖ ə 'næṭ- ~**s** s
anatomiz|e ə 'næt ə maɪz ‖ ə 'næṭ- ~**ed** d ~**es**
ɪz əz ~**ing** ɪŋ
anatom|y ə 'næt əm |i ‖ ə 'næṭ- ~**ies** iz
Anaxagoras ˌæn æk 'sæg ᵊr əs -ə ræs
ANC ˌeɪ en 'siː
-ance ᵊnⁱs —*Words with this suffix are stressed
like words in -ant. Examples:* con'trive —
con'trivance; re'luctant, re'luctance. *Exception:*
re'connaissance.
ancestor 'ænⁱs est ə -ɪst-, -əst- ‖ -ᵊr ~**s** z

A

ancestral æn 'ses trəl **~ly** i
ancestress 'æn^t s es tres -ɪs-, -əs-, -trəs, -trɪs ‖ -trəs **~es** ɪz əz
ances|try 'æn^t s es ˌtri -ɪs-, -əs- **~tries** triz
Anchises æn 'kaɪs iːz →æŋ-
anchor 'æŋk ə ‖ 'æŋk ər **~ed** d **anchoring** 'æŋk ər ɪŋ **~s** z
anchorag|e, A~ 'æŋk ər ɪdʒ **~es** ɪz əz
anchoress 'æŋk ər ɪs -əs, -ə res **~es** ɪz əz
anchorite 'æŋk ə raɪt **~s** s
anchor|man 'æŋk ə ˌmæn ‖ -ər- **~men** men **~person** ˌpɜːs ən ‖ ˌpɝːs ən **~woman** ˌwʊm ən **~women** ˌwɪm ɪn §-ən
anchov|y 'æntʃ əv ˌi æn 'tʃəʊv ˌi ‖ 'æn tʃoʊv ˌi •'•• **~ies** iz
ancien regime, ancien régime ˌɒn^t s i æn reɪ 'ʒiːm ˌɑːn^t s-, ˌ••ɒn-; ɑːn ˌsjæn•'• ‖ ˌɑːn^t s jæn •'• —*Fr* [ɑ̃ sjæ̃ ʁe ʒim]
ancient 'eɪn^t ʃ ənt **~ness** nəs nɪs
ˌ**Ancient** ˈ**Greek**; ˌ**ancient** ˈ**monument**
ancillar|y æn 'sɪl ər ˌi ⚠-'sɪl i‿ər ˌi ‖ 'æn^t s ə ler ˌi *(*)* **~ies** iz
Ancoats 'æŋ kəʊts ‖ -koʊts
Ancona æŋ 'kəʊn ə ‖ -'koʊn ə —*It* [aŋ 'koː na]
Ancram 'æŋk rəm
Ancren Riwle ˌæŋk ren 'riː ʊl i, •rɪn-, ˌ•rən-, -ə
-ancy ən^t s i —*Words with this suffix are stressed like words in* -ant. *Example:* 'hesitant, 'hesitancy
and *strong form* ænd, *weak forms* ənd, ən —*The presence or absence of* d *in the weak form is not sensitive to phonetic context: the choice depends on the fact that the weak form* ənd *is slightly more formal than* ən. *From* ən, *regular processes of SYLLABIC CONSONANT formation and ASSIMILATION produce the phonetic variants* m, n, ŋ *(all syllabic, though they can lose their syllabicity by COMPRESSION before a weak vowel) and* əm, əŋ.
and ˈ**so on**
Andalusi|a ˌænd ə 'luːs i‿ə -'luːz-, -lu 'siː‿ə ‖ -'luːʒ ə —*Sp* Andalucía [an da lu 'θi a] **~an/s** ən/z ‖ ən/z
Andaman 'ænd əm ən -ə mæn **~s** z
Andamanese ˌænd əm ə 'niːz ◂ ‖ -'niːs ◂
andante æn 'dænt i -eɪ ‖ ɑːn 'dɑːnt eɪ æn 'dænt̬ i —*It* [an 'dan te]
andantino ˌænd æn 'tiːn əʊ ‖ ˌɑːnd ɑːn 'tiːn oʊ —*It* [an dan 'tiː no]
Andean æn 'diː‿ən 'ænd i‿ən **~s** z
Andersen, Anderson 'ænd əs ən ‖ -ərs-
Andersonstown 'ænd əs ənz taʊn ‖ '•ərs-
Andes 'ænd iːz
andesite 'ænd ɪ zaɪt -ə-, -saɪt
Andhra Pradesh ˌændr ə prɑː 'deʃ ˌɑːndr-, -'deɪʃ —*Hindi* [aːndʰr prə deːʃ]
andiron 'ænd ˌaɪ‿ən ‖ -ˌaɪ‿ərn **~s** z
and/or ˌænd 'ɔː ◂ ‖ -'ɔːr
ˌ**apples** ˌ**and/or** ˈ**pears**
Andorr|a æn 'dɔːr ə -'dɒr- ‖ -'dɑːr ə —*Catalan* [ən 'dɔ rrə] **~an/s** ən/z
Andover 'ænd əʊv ə ‖ -oʊv ər
Andre, André 'ɒndr eɪ 'ændr-, 'ɑːndr- ‖ 'ɑːndr- —*Fr* [ɑ̃ dʁe]
Andrea 'ændr i‿ə —*but as an Italian name,* æn 'dreɪ ə —*It* [an 'drɛː a]
Anˌ**drea del** ˈ**Sarto** del 'sɑːt əʊ ‖ -'sɑːrt oʊ —*It* [del 'sar to]
Andreas 'ændr i‿əs, -æs —*but the place in the Isle of Man is* 'ændr əs; *as a Spanish name,* æn 'dreɪ əs —*Sp* [an 'dre as]
Andrei 'ɒndr eɪ 'ændr-, 'ɑːndr- ‖ 'ɑːndr- —*Russ* [ʌn 'drʲej]
Andrew 'ændr uː
Andrewes, Andrews 'ændr uːz
Andrex *tdmk* 'ændr eks
Andria 'ændr i‿ə
andro- *comb. form*
with stress-neutral suffix ˌændr əʊ ‖ -ə — **androcentric** ˌændr əʊ 'sentr ɪk ◂ ‖ -ə-
with stress-imposing suffix æn 'drɒ+ ‖ -'drɑː+ — **androgyny** æn 'drɒdʒ ən i -ɪn- ‖ -'drɑːdʒ-
Androcles 'ændr ə kliːz
androgen 'ændr ədʒ ən -ə dʒen **~s** z
androgynous æn 'drɒdʒ ən əs -ɪn- ‖ -'drɑːdʒ-
androgyny æn 'drɒdʒ ən i -ɪn- ‖ -'drɑːdʒ-
android 'ændr ɔɪd **~s** z
Andromache æn 'drɒm ək i ‖ -'drɑːm-
Andromeda æn 'drɒm ɪd ə -əd- ‖ -'drɑːm-
Andronicus *(i)* æn 'drɒn ɪk əs ‖ -'drɑːn-; *(ii)* ˌændr ə 'naɪk əs —*in Shakespeare's* Titus A~, *(i)*
Andropov æn 'drɒp ɒf 'ændr ə pɒf ‖ ɑːn 'droʊp ɔːf -'drɑːp-, -ɑːf —*Russ* [ʌn 'dro pəf]
Andros 'ændr ɒs ‖ -əs -ɑːs
-androus 'ændr əs — **polyandrous** ˌpɒl i 'ændr əs ◂ ‖ ˌpɑːl-
-andry 'ændr i — **polyandry** ˌpɒl i 'ændr i ‖ ˌpɑːl-
Andy 'ænd i
-ane eɪn — **pentane** 'pent eɪn
anecdotage 'æn ɪk dəʊt ɪdʒ '•ek-, '•ək- ‖ -doʊt̬ ɪdʒ
anecdotal ˌæn ɪk 'dəʊt əl ◂ -ek-, -ək- ‖ -'doʊt̬-
anecdote 'æn ɪk dəʊt -ek-, -ək- ‖ -doʊt **~s** s
anecdotist 'æn ɪk dəʊt ɪst -ek-, -ək-, §-əst ‖ -doʊt̬ əst **~s** s
anechoic ˌæn ɪ 'kəʊ ɪk ◂ -e-, -ə- ‖ -'koʊ-
Aneirin ə 'naɪər ɪn -ən —*Welsh* [a 'nəi rin]
anemia ə 'niːm i‿ə
anemic ə 'niːm ɪk **~ally** əl‿i
anemometer ˌæn ɪ 'mɒm ɪt ə ˌ•ə-, -ət ə ‖ -'mɑːm ət̬ ər **~s** z
anemone ə 'nem ən i ⚠ə 'nen əm i **~s** z
anencephalic ˌæn en ke 'fæl ɪk ◂ →ˌ•eŋ-, ˌ•en sɪ-, ˌ•en sə-
anencephaly ˌæn en 'kef əl i →ˌ•eŋ-, -en 'sef-
anent ə 'nent
aneroid 'æn ə rɔɪd
anesthesia ˌæn əs 'θiːz i‿ə ˌ•iːs-, ˌ•ɪs-, -'θiːʒ ə ‖ -'θiːʒ ə
anesthesiologist ˌæn əs ˌθiːz i 'ɒl ədʒ ɪst §-əst ‖ -'ɑːl- **~s** s

anesthesiology ˌæn əs ˌθiːz i 'ɒl ədʒ i ‖ -'ɑːl-
anesthetic ˌæn əs 'θet ɪk ◂ -iːs-, -ɪs- ‖ -'θeṭ-
~s s
anesthetist ə 'niːs θət ɪst æ-, -θɪt-, §-əst
‖ ə 'nes θəṭ əst (*) ~s s
anesthetization ə ˌniːs θət aɪ 'zeɪʃ ən -ɪ'•-
‖ ə ˌnes θəṭ ə-
anesthetiz|e ə 'niːs θə taɪz -θɪ- ‖ ə 'nes- (*)
~ed d ~es ɪz əz ~ing ɪŋ
aneurin 'thiamine' ə 'njʊər ɪn §-'nʊər-;
'æn jʊr-, -ən ‖ 'æn jər ən
Aneurin ə 'naɪ°r ɪn -ən —Welsh [a 'nəi rin,
-'nəi]
aneurism, aneurysm 'æn jə ˌrɪz əm -juə- ~s z
aneurismal, aneurysmal ˌæn jə 'rɪz məl ◂ -juə-
anew ə 'njuː ‖ ə 'nuː- -'njuː
Anfield 'æn fiː°ld
anfractuosit|y ˌæn frækt ju 'ɒs ət ‖i -fræk tʃu-,
•ˌ•-, -ɪt i ‖ æn ˌfræk tʃu 'ɑːs əṭ ‖i ~ies iz
anfractuous ₍ᵢ₎æn 'frækt ju_əs -'fræk tʃu‿
‖ -'fræk tʃu‿əs
angary 'æŋ gər i
angel, Angel 'eɪndʒ əl —but as a Spanish name,
'ɑːn hel —Sp Ángel ['aŋ xel] ~s z
Angela 'ændʒ əl ə -ɪl-
Angeleno ˌændʒ ə 'liːn əʊ ‖ -oʊ —Sp Angeleño
[aŋ xe 'le ɲo] ~s z
angelfish 'eɪndʒ əl fɪʃ
angelic æn 'dʒel ɪk ~ally ᵊl i
angelica, A~ æn 'dʒel ɪk ə
Angelico æn 'dʒel ɪ kəʊ ‖ -koʊ ɑːn-, -'dʒeɪl-
—It [an 'dʒɛː li ko]
Angelina ˌændʒ ə 'liːn ə -e-, -ɪ-
Angell 'eɪndʒ əl
Angelo, Angelou 'ændʒ ə ləʊ -ɪ- ‖ -loʊ
angelus, A~ 'ændʒ əl əs -ɪl- ~es ɪz əz
anger 'æŋ gə ‖ 'æŋ gər angered
'æŋ gəd ‖ -gərd angering 'æŋ gər‿ɪŋ
angers 'æŋ gəz ‖ -gərz
Angers place in France ˌɑːn 'ʒeɪ ˌɒ̃- —Fr [ɑ̃ ʒe]
Angevin 'ændʒ əv ɪn -ɪv-, §-ən
Angharad æn 'hær əd æn- ‖ -'her- —Welsh
[aŋ 'ha rad]
angi- comb. form before vowel ¦ændʒ i —
angioma ˌændʒ i 'əʊm ə ‖ -'oʊm-
Angie 'ændʒ i
angina æn 'dʒaɪn ə
an ˌgina 'pectoris 'pekt ər ɪs §-əs
angio- comb. form
with stress-neutral suffix ¦ændʒ i_əʊ ‖ -ə —
angiogram 'ændʒ i_əʊ græm ‖ ə græm
with stress-imposing suffix ˌændʒ i 'ɒ+ ‖ -'ɑː+
— angiography ˌændʒ i 'ɒg rəf i ‖ -'ɑːg-
angioplasty 'ændʒi_əʊ ˌplæst i ‖ -i_ə-
angiosperm 'ændʒ i əʊ spɜːm ‖ -ə spɝːm ~s z
Angkor 'æŋ kɔː ‖ -kɔːr
ˌAngkor 'Wat
angle, Angle 'æŋ gᵊl angled 'æŋ gᵊld angles,
Angles 'æŋ gᵊlz angling 'æŋ glɪŋ 'æŋ gᵊl‿ɪŋ
'angle ˌbracket
Anglepoise tdmk 'æŋ gᵊl pɔɪz
angler 'æŋ glə ‖ -glᵊr ~s z
Anglesey 'æŋ gᵊls i -iː

anglesite 'æŋ gᵊl saɪt
Angli|a 'æŋ gli_ə ~an/s ən/z
Anglican 'æŋ glɪk ən ~ism ˌɪz əm ~s z
anglice, A~ 'æŋ glɪs i -gləs-
anglicis... —see angliciz...
anglicism, A~ 'æŋ glɪ ˌsɪz əm -glə-
anglicization, A~ ˌæŋ glɪs aɪ 'zeɪʃ ən ˌ•gləs-,
-ɪ'•- ‖ -ə 'zeɪʃ- ~s z
angliciz|e, A~ 'æŋ glɪ saɪz -glə- ~ed d ~es ɪz
əz ~ing ɪŋ
angling 'æŋ glɪŋ
Anglo 'æŋ gləʊ ‖ -gloʊ ~s z
Anglo- ¦æŋ gləʊ ‖ -gloʊ — Anglo-Spanish
ˌæŋ gləʊ 'spæn ɪʃ ◂ ‖ -gloʊ-
Anglo-American ˌæŋ gləʊ ə 'mer ɪk ən ◂ -ək
ən ‖ ˌ•gloʊ- ~s z
Anglo-Catholic ˌæŋ gləʊ 'kæθ lɪk ◂ -'kæθ əl ɪk,
-'kɑːθ- ‖ -gloʊ- ~s s
Anglo-Catholicism ˌæŋ gləʊ kə 'θɒl ə ˌsɪz əm
-ɪ,•- ‖ -gloʊ kə 'θɑːl-
Anglo-French ˌæŋ gləʊ 'frentʃ ◂ ‖ -gloʊ-
Anglo-Indian ˌæŋ gləʊ 'ɪnd i_ən ◂ ‖ ˌ•gloʊ- ~s
z
Anglo-Irish ˌæŋ gləʊ 'aɪᵊr ɪʃ ◂ ‖ -gloʊ-
the ˌAnglo-ˌIrish A'greement
anglophile 'æŋ gləʊ faɪᵊl ‖ -glə- ~s z
anglophilia ˌæŋ gləʊ 'fɪl i_ə ‖ ˌ•glə-
anglophobe 'æŋ gləʊ fəʊb ‖ -glə foʊb ~s z
anglophobia ˌæŋ gləʊ 'fəʊb i_ə ‖ -glə 'foʊb-
Anglophone, a~ 'æŋ glə fəʊn ‖ -foʊn
Anglo-Saxon ˌæŋ gləʊ 'sæks ən ◂ ‖ -gloʊ- ~s z
Angmering 'æŋ mər ɪŋ
Angol|a 'gəʊl ə ‖ -'goʊl ə ~an/s ən/z
angora, A~ æŋ 'gɔːr ə ‖ -'goʊr-
angostura, A~ ˌæŋ gə 'stjʊər ə ◂ -gɒ-, -'stʊər-,
-'stjɔːr- ‖ -'stʊr ə ◂ —Sp [aŋ go 'stu ra]
ˌAngoˌstura 'bitters
Angouleme, Angoulême ˌɒŋ gu 'lem ‖ ˌɑːŋ-
—Fr [ɑ̃ gu lɛm]
angry 'æŋ gri angrier 'æŋ gri_ə ‖ _ʳr angriest
'æŋ gri_ɪst _əst angrily 'æŋ grəl i -grɪ li
angst æŋkst ‖ ɑːŋkst —Ger [ʔaŋst]
angstrom, A~ 'æŋks trəm -trʌm —Swedish
Ångström ['ɒŋ strœm] ~s z
'angstrom ˌunit
Anguill|a æŋ 'gwɪl ə -ə 'gwiːl- ~an/s ən/z
anguish 'æŋ gwɪʃ ~ed t ~es ɪz əz ~ing ɪŋ
angular 'æŋ gjʊl ə -gjəl- ‖ -gjəl ᵊr ~ly li
~ness nəs nɪs
angularit|y ˌæŋ gju 'lær ət ‖i -ˌgjə-, -ɪt i
‖ -gjə 'lær əṭ ‖i -'ler- ~ies iz
Angus 'æŋ gəs
anharmonic ˌæn hɑː 'mɒn ɪk ◂ ‖ -hɑːr 'mɑːn-
anhinga æn 'hɪŋ gə ~s z
Anhui ˌæn 'hweɪ ‖ ˌɑːn- —Chinese Ānhuī [¹an
¹xwei]
anhydride ₍ᵢ₎æn 'haɪdr aɪd ~s z
anhydrite ₍ᵢ₎æn 'haɪdr aɪt ~s z
anhydrous ₍ᵢ₎æn 'haɪdr əs
ani bird 'ɑːn i anis 'ɑːn iz
aniconic ˌæn aɪ 'kɒn ɪk ◂ ‖ -'kɑːn-
anil 'æn ɪl -ᵊl
Anil ə 'niːl

A

aniline 'æn əl ın -ıl-, -iːn, §-ən
anilingus ,eın i 'lıŋ gəs
anima 'æn ım ə §-əm-
animadversion ,æn ım æd 'vɜːʃ ən §,•əm-,
-əd'•-, -'vɜːʒ- ‖ -'vɜːʒ- -'vɜːʃ- ~s z
animad|vert ,æn ım æd |'vɜːt §,•əm-, -'be'•
‖ -|'vɜːt ~verted 'vɜːt ıd -əd ‖ 'vɜːt̬ əd
~verting 'vɜːt ıŋ ‖ 'vɜːt̬ ıŋ ~verts
'vɜːts ‖ 'vɜːts
animal 'æn ım əl -əm- ~s z
    ,animal 'husbandry
animalcule ,æn ı 'mæl kjuːl -ə- ~s z
animalism 'æn ım əl ,ız əm
animalistic ,æn ım ə 'lıst ık ◄ -əl 'ıst-
animality ,æn ı 'mæl ət i ,•ə-, -ıt i ‖ -ət̬ i
animate adj 'æn ım ət -əm-, -ıt; -ı meıt, -ə-
    ~ness nəs nıs
ani|mate v 'æn ı |meıt -ə- ~mated/ly
    meıt ıd /li -əd ‖ meıt̬ əd /li ~mates meıts
    ~mating meıt ıŋ ‖ meıt̬ ıŋ
animation ,æn ı 'meıʃ ən -ə- ~s z
animator 'æn ı meıt ə '•ə- ‖ -meıt̬ ər ~s z
animatronic ,æn ım ə 'trɒn ık ◄ ,•əm-
    ‖ -'trɑːn- ~s s
anime, animé 'æn ı meı -ə- ~s z
animism 'æn ı ,mız əm -ə-
animist 'æn ım ıst -əm-, §-əst ~s s
animosit|y ,æn ı 'mɒs ət li ,•ə-, -ıt i
    ‖ -'mɑːs ət̬ li ~ies iz
animus 'æn ım əs -əm-
anion 'æn ,aı ən ~s z
anionic ,æn aı 'ɒn ık ◄ ‖ -'ɑːn-
anis 'æn iː -iːs; æ 'niːs ‖ ɑː 'niːs -'niː —Fr [a ni,
    -nis], Sp anís [a 'nis]
anise 'æn ıs §-əs
aniseed 'æn ı siːd -ə-
anisette ,æn ı 'zet §-ə-, -'set ~s s
anisogamy ,æn aı 'sɒg əm i ‖ -'saːg-
anisomorphic æn ,aıs əʊ 'mɔːf ık ◄ ,•,•-
    ‖ -ə 'mɔːrf- ~ally əl_i
anisotropic æn ,aıs əʊ 'trɒp ık ◄ ,•,•-, -'trəʊp-
    ‖ -ə 'traːp- -ə 'trəʊp-
Anita ə 'niːt ə ‖ ə 'niːt̬ ə
Anjou ,ɑːn 'ʒuː ,ɒ̃- ‖ 'ɑːndʒ uː —Fr [ɑ̃ ʒu]
Ankara 'æŋk ər ə ‖ 'ɑːŋk- —Turkish ['aŋ ka
    ra]
ankh æŋk ɑːŋk ankhs æŋks ɑːŋks
ankle 'æŋk əl ~s z
    'ankle sock
anklet 'æŋk lət -lıt ~s s
ankylos|e 'æŋk ı ləʊz -ə-, -ləʊs ‖ -loʊs -loʊz
    ~ed d ‖ t ~es ız əz ~ing ıŋ
ankylosis ,æŋk ı 'ləʊs ıs -ə-, §-əs ‖ -'loʊs-
Anlaby 'æn ləb i
Ann æn
    (ı)Ann 'Arbor
Anna, anna 'æn ə ~'s, ~s z
Annabel 'æn ə bel
Annabella ,æn ə 'bel ə
Annalisa ,æn ə 'liːz ə -'liːs-
annalist 'æn əl ıst §-əst (= analyst) ~s s
annals 'æn əlz
Annam (ı)æ 'næm 'æn æm

Annamarie, Anna-Marie ,æn ə mə 'riː
Annamese ,æn ə 'miːz ◄ -'miːs ◄
Annan 'æn ən —but the African Secretary-
    General of the UN is -æn
Annapolis ə 'næp əl ıs §-əs
Annapurna ,æn ə 'pɜːn ə -'pʊən- ‖ -'pʊrn ə
    -'pɜːn-
annatto, A~ ə 'næt əʊ ‖ ə 'naːt̬ oʊ
Anne æn
anneal ə 'niːəl annealed ə 'niːəld annealing
    ə 'niːəl ıŋ anneals ə 'niːəlz
Anneka 'æn ık ə -ək-
annelid 'æn ə lıd §-əl əd ~s z
Annemarie, Anne-Marie ,æn mə 'riː →,æm-
Annesley (i) 'ænz li , (ii) 'æn ız li -əz-
Annet, Annett 'æn ıt -ət
Annette ə 'net æ-
annex v ə 'neks æ- ~ed t ~es ız əz ~ing ıŋ
annex n 'æn eks ~es ız əz
annexation ,æn ek 'seıʃ ən -ık- ~s z
annex|e 'æn eks ~es ız əz
annexure 'æn ek ʃʊə ‖ -ʃʊr ~s z
Annie 'æn i
Annigoni ,æn i 'gəʊn i ‖ -'goʊn i —It
    [an ni 'go: ni]
annihi|late ə 'naı_ə |leıt ,ı•• ~lated leıt ıd -əd
    ‖ leıt̬ əd ~lates leıts ~lating leıt ıŋ ‖ leıt̬ ıŋ
annihilation ə ,naı_ə 'leıʃ ən ,ı-
Annika 'æn ık ə
Annis 'æn ıs §-əs
Anniston 'æn ıst ən §-əst-
anniversar|y ,æn ı 'vɜːs ər_li ◄ ,•ə- ‖ -'vɜːs-
    ~ies iz
Anno Domini ,æn əʊ 'dɒm ı naı -ə•, -niː
    ‖ ,æn oʊ 'daːm ə niː -'doʊm-, -naı
anno|tate 'æn əʊ |teıt ‖ -ə- ~tated teıt ıd -əd
    ‖ teıt̬ əd ~tates teıts ~tating
    teıt ıŋ ‖ teıt̬ ıŋ
annotation ,æn əʊ 'teıʃ ən ‖ -ə- ~s z
annotator 'æn əʊ teıt ə ‖ -ə teıt̬ ər ~s z
annotative 'æn əʊ teıt ıv ‖ -ə teıt̬-
announc|e ə 'naʊn̩s ~ed t ~es ız əz ~ing ıŋ
announcement ə 'naʊn̩s mənt ~s s
announcer ə 'naʊn̩s ə ‖ -ər ~s z
annoy ə 'nɔı annoyed ə 'nɔıd annoying/ly
    ə 'nɔı ıŋ /li annoys ə 'nɔız
annoyanc|e ə 'nɔı ən̩s ~es ız əz
annual 'æn ju_əl -jul ~ly i ~s z
annualised, annualized 'æn ju_ə laızd '•ju•
annuitant ə 'njuː_ıt ənt ət- ‖ ə 'nuː ət ənt
    -'njuː- ~s s
annuit|y ə 'njuː_ət li -ıt- ‖ ə 'nuː ət̬ li -'njuː-
    ~ies iz
annul ə 'nʌl ~led d ~ling ıŋ ~s z
annular 'æn jʊl ə -jəl- ‖ -jəl ər
annu|late 'æn ju |leıt -jə- ‖ -jə- ~lated leıt ıd
    -əd ‖ leıt̬ əd
annuli 'æn ju laı ‖ -jə-
annull... —see annul
annulment ə 'nʌl mənt ~s s
annulus 'æn jʊl əs -jəl- ‖ -jəl- annuli
    'æn ju laı ‖ -jə-
annum 'æn əm

annunci|ate ə 'nʌnts i eɪt ə 'nʌntʃ- **~ated** eɪt ɪd -əd ‖ eɪt əd **~ates** eɪts **~ating** eɪt ɪŋ ‖ eɪt ɪŋ
annunciation, A~ ə ˌnʌnts i 'eɪʃ ən ə ˌnʌntʃ- **~s** z
annunciative ə 'nʌnts i‿ət ɪv ə 'nʌntʃ-, -eɪt ɪv; -'nʌntʃ ət ɪv ‖ -eɪt ɪv
annunciator ə 'nʌnts i eɪt ə ə 'nʌntʃ- ‖ -eɪt ər **~s** z
annunciatory ə 'nʌnts i‿ət‿ər i ə 'nʌntʃ-, •ˌ• • 'eɪt ər i; ə 'nʌntʃ ət‿ər i ‖ -ə tɔːr i -toʊr i
annus 'æn əs -ʊs ‖ 'ɑːn-
ˌ**annus mi'rabilis** mɪ 'rɑːb əl ɪs mə-, -'ræb-, -ɪl-, §-əs
Anny 'æn i
anoa ə 'nəʊ ə ‖ ə 'noʊ ə **anoas** ə 'nəʊ əz ‖ -'noʊ-
anode 'æn əʊd ‖ -oʊd **~s** z
anodic æ 'nɒd ɪk ‖ ə 'nɑːd ɪk
anodis|e, anodiz|e 'æn əʊ daɪz ‖ -ə- **~ed** d **~es** ɪz əz **~ing** ɪŋ
anodyne 'æn əʊ daɪn ‖ -ə- **~s** z
anoint ə 'nɔɪnt **anointed** ə 'nɔɪnt ɪd -əd ‖ ə 'nɔɪnt əd **anointing** ə 'nɔɪnt ɪŋ ‖ ə 'nɔɪnt ɪŋ **anoints** ə 'nɔɪnts
anointment ə 'nɔɪnt mənt **~s** s
anole ə 'nəʊl i ‖ -'noʊl- **~s** z
anomalistic ə ˌnɒm ə 'lɪst ɪk ◂ ‖ ə ˌnɑːm- **~ally** əl‿i
anomalous ə 'nɒm əl əs ‖ ə 'nɑːm- **~ly** li **~ness** nəs nɪs
anomal|y ə 'nɒm əl |i ‖ ə 'nɑːm- **~ies** iz
anomic ə 'nɒm ɪk æ-, -'nəʊm- ‖ -'nɑːm- -'noʊm-
anomie, anomy 'æn əʊm i ‖ -əm i
anon ə 'nɒn ‖ ə 'nɑːn
Anona ə 'nəʊn ə ‖ ə 'noʊn ə
anonymity ˌæn ə 'nɪm ət i ˌæn ɒ-, -ɪt i ‖ -əṭ i
anonymous ə 'nɒn ɪ məs -ə- ‖ ə 'nɑːn- **~ly** li
anopheles, A~ ə 'nɒf ə liːz -ɪ- ‖ ə 'nɑːf-
anorak 'æn ə ræk **~s** s
anorectic ˌæn ə 'rekt ɪk ◂ **~s** s
anorexia ˌæn ə 'reks i‿ə ◂ ˌæn ɒ- **~s** z
ˌ**anoˌrexia ner'vosa** nɜː 'vəʊs ə -'vəʊz- ‖ nər 'voʊs ə -'voʊz-
anorexic ˌæn ə 'reks ɪk ◂ **~s** s
anosmia æn 'ɒz mi‿ə -'ɒs- ‖ -'ɑːz- -'ɑːs-
another ə 'nʌð ə ‖ -ər —*There is also an occasional emphatic form* ˌeɪ- **~'s** z
A.N.Other ˌeɪ ˌen 'ʌð ə ‖ -ər
Anouilh 'æn u iː 'ɒn-, ˌ• • '•; æ 'nuː‿i ‖ ɑː 'nuː jə æ-, -i; ˌ• • 'iː —*Fr* [a nuj]
ANOVA ˌæn əʊ 'vɑː '• • • ‖ -oʊ-
anoxia (ˌ)æn 'ɒks i‿ə ‖ -'ɑːks-
ansaphone *tdmk* 'ɑːnts ə fəʊn §'ænts- ‖ 'ænts ə foʊn **~s** z
Ansbacher 'ænz bæk ə ‖ -ər
Anschluss, a~ 'æn ʃlʊs ‖ 'ɑːn- —*Ger formerly* Anschluß ['ʔan ʃlʊs]
Anscombe 'ænts kəm
Ansell 'ænts əl
Anselm 'ænts elm
anserine 'ænts ə raɪn -riːn, -rɪn
Ansermet 'ɒnts ə meɪ 'ɑːnts-, 'ɒ̃- ‖ ˌɑːnts ər 'meɪ —*Fr* [ɑ̃ sɛʁ mɛ]
Ansett 'æn set
Anshun ˌæn 'ʃʊn ‖ ˌɑːn 'ʃuːn —*Chinese* Ānshùn [1an 4ʂwən]
ANSI 'ænts i
Anson 'ænts ən
Anstey 'æntst i
Anstruther 'ænts trʌð ə ‖ -ər —*The place in Fife is locally also* 'eɪntst ə ‖ -ər
Ansty 'æntst i
answer 'ɑːnts ə §'ænts ə ‖ 'ænts ər *(!)* **~ed** d **answering** 'ɑːnts ər‿ɪŋ §'ænts- ‖ 'ænts- **~s** z
'**answering maˌchine;** '**answering** ˌ**service**
answerability ˌɑːnts ər‿ə 'bɪl ət i §ˌænts-, -ɪt i ‖ ˌænts ər‿ə 'bɪl əṭ i
answerab|le 'ɑːnts ər‿əb |əl §'ænts- ‖ 'ænts- **~ly** li
answerphone 'ɑːnts ə fəʊn §'ænts- ‖ 'ænts ər foʊn **~s** z
ant ænt **ants** ænts
ant- *comb. form before vowel* ¦ænt, ænt — **antacid** (ˌ)ænt 'æs ɪd §-əd, **antonym** 'ænt ən ɪm §-əm
-ant ənt —*When attached to an independent stem, this suffix is usually stress-neutral* (ac'count — ac'countant; in'habit — in'habitant). *Otherwise, it imposes stress: on the antepenultimate syllable if the penultimate is weak* ('arrogant, 'applicant, sig'nificant), *but on the penultimate itself if it is strong* (flam'boyant, re'luctant). *There are several exceptions: note* ex'ecutant,'ignorant, 'Protestant.
Antabuse *tdmk* 'ænt ə bjuːs -bjuːz
antacid (ˌ)ænt 'æs ɪd §-əd **~s** z
Antaeus æn 'tiː‿əs -'teɪ-
antagonis... —*see* **antagoniz...**
antagonism æn 'tæg ə ˌnɪz əm **~s** z
antagonist æn 'tæg ən ɪst §-əst **~s** s
antagonistic æn ˌtæg ə 'nɪst ɪk ◂ ˌænt æg- **~ally** əl‿i
antagoniz|e æn 'tæg ə naɪz **~ed** d **~es** ɪz əz **~ing** ɪŋ
Antalya æn 'tæl jə ‖ ɑːn 'tɑːl jə —*Turkish* [an 'tal ja]
Antananarivo ˌænt ə ˌnæn ə 'riːv əʊ ‖ -oʊ
antarctic, A~ (ˌ)ænt 'ɑːkt ɪk ⚠-'ɑːt- ‖ (ˌ)ænt 'ɑːrkt- -'ɑːrt-
Antˌarctic '**Circle**, ˌ•ˌ•-
Antarctica (ˌ)ænt 'ɑːkt ɪk ə ⚠-'ɑːt- ‖ -'ɑːrkt- -'ɑːrt-
Antares æn 'teər iːz ‖ -'ter- -'tær-
ant-bear 'ænt beə ‖ -ber -bær **~s** z
ante 'ænt i ‖ 'ænt i **~d, ~ed** d **~ing** ‿ɪŋ **~s** z
ˌ**ante me'ridiem** mə 'rɪd i‿əm -em
ante- *comb. form with stress-neutral suffix* ¦ænt i ‖ ¦ænt i *(= anti-)* — **antebellum** ˌænt i 'bel əm ◂ ‖ ˌænt i-
anteater 'ænt ˌiːt ə ‖ 'ænt ˌiːt ər **~s** z
antecedence ˌænt ɪ 'siːd ənts -ə- ‖ ˌænt ə-
antecedent ˌænt ɪ 'siːd ənt ◂ -ə- ‖ ˌænt ə- **~s** s

antechamber 'ænt i ,tʃeɪm bə ‖ 'ænt̬
   i ,tʃeɪm bᵊr ~s z
ante|date ,ænt i 'deɪt ◄'••• ‖ 'ænt̬ i |deɪt
   ~dated deɪt ɪd -əd ‖ deɪt̬ əd ~dates deɪts
   ~dating deɪt ɪŋ ‖ deɪt̬ ɪŋ
antediluvian ,ænt i dɪ 'luːv i‿ən ◄ -də'•-,
   -daɪ'•-, -'ljuːv- ‖ ,ænt̬ i- ~s z
antelope 'ænt ɪ ləʊp -ə- ‖ 'ænt̬ ə loʊp ~s s
antenatal ,ænt i 'neɪt ᵊl ◄ ‖ ,ænt̬ i 'neɪt̬ ᵊl ◄ ~s
   z
antenn|a æn 'ten |ə ~ae iː ~as əz
antepenult ,ænt i pɪ 'nʌlt -pə'•, -pe'• ‖ ,ænt̬
   i 'piːn ʌlt -pɪ 'nʌlt ~s s
antepenultimate ,ænt i pɪ 'nʌlt ɪm ət ◄ -pə'•-,
   -pe'•-, -əm ət, -ɪt ‖ ,ænt̬ i- ~ly li ~s s
anterior æn 'tɪər i‿ə ‖ -'tɪr i‿ᵊr ~ly li
anteriority æn ,tɪər i 'ɒr ət i -ɪt i
   ‖ æn ,tɪr i 'ɔːr ət̬ i
anteroom 'ænt i ruːm -rʊm ‖ 'ænt̬ i- ~s z
Anthea 'ænt̬θ i‿ə
anthelion ænt 'hiːl i‿ən æn 'θiːl- ~s z
anthelminthic ,ænt̬θ el 'mɪnt̬θ ɪk ◄ ,ænt hel-
   ~s s
anthelmintic ,ænt̬θ el 'mɪnt ɪk ◄ ,ænt hel-
   ‖ -'mɪnt̬- ~s s
anthem 'ænt̬θ əm ~s z
anther 'ænt̬θ ə ‖ -ᵊr ~s z
anthill 'ænt hɪl ~s z
anthologis... —see anthologiz...
anthologist æn 'θɒl ədʒ ɪst §-əst ‖ -'θɑːl- ~s s
anthologiz|e æn 'θɒl ə dʒaɪz ‖ -'θɑːl- ~ed d
   ~es ɪz əz ~ing ɪŋ
antholog|y æn 'θɒl ədʒ li ‖ -'θɑːl- ~ies iz
Anthony (i) 'ænt ən i, (ii) 'ænt̬θ- —in BrE (i)
   predominates, in AmE (ii).
anthracite 'ænt̬θ rə saɪt
anthracnose æn 'θræk nəʊs -nəʊz ‖ -noʊs
anthrax 'ænt̬θ ræks
anthropic æn 'θrɒp ɪk ‖ -'θrɑːp-
anthropo- comb. form
   with stress-neutral suffix 'ænt̬θ rəʊp əʊ
   ‖ 'ænt̬θ rəp ə — anthropophobia
   ,ænt̬θ rəʊp əʊ 'fəʊb i‿ə ‖ ,ænt̬θ rəp ə 'foʊb-
   with stress-imposing suffix ,ænt̬θ rə 'pɒ+
   'pɒ+ ‖ ,ænt̬θ rə 'pɑː+ — anthroposcopy
   ,ænt̬θ rəʊ 'pɒsk əp i ‖ -rə 'pɑːsk-
anthropocentric ,ænt̬θ rəʊp əʊ
   'sentr ɪk ◄ ‖ -rəp ə- ~ally ᵊl‿i
anthropoid 'ænt̬θ rəʊ pɔɪd ‖ -rə- ~s z
anthropological ,ænt̬θ rəʊp ə 'lɒdʒ ɪk ᵊl ◄
   ‖ -rəp ə 'lɑːdʒ- ~ly‿i
anthropologist ,ænt̬θ rə 'pɒl ədʒ ɪst §-əst
   ‖ -'pɑːl- ~s s
anthropology ,ænt̬θ rə 'pɒl ədʒ i ‖ -'pɑːl-
anthropometry ,ænt̬θ rəʊ 'pɒm ətr i -ɪtr i
   ‖ -rə 'pɑːm-
anthropomorphic ,ænt̬θ rəʊp əʊ
   'mɔːf ɪk ◄ ‖ -rəp ə 'mɔːrf- ~ally ᵊl‿i
anthropomorphism ,ænt̬θ rəʊp əʊ 'mɔːf ,ɪz
   əm ‖ -rəp ə 'mɔːrf-
anthropophagi ,ænt̬θ rəʊ 'pɒf ə dʒaɪ -gaɪ
   ‖ -rə 'pɑːf-

anthropophagous ,ænt̬θ rəʊ 'pɒf əg əs
   ‖ -rə 'pɑːf-
anthropophagy ,ænt̬θ rəʊ 'pɒf ədʒ i
   ‖ -rə 'pɑːf-
anthroposophy ,ænt̬θ rəʊ 'pɒs əf i ‖ -rə 'pɑːs-
anthurium æn 'θjʊər i‿əm -'θʊər- ‖ -'θʊr-
   -'θjʊr-
anti 'ænt i ‖ 'ænt̬ i 'ænt aɪ ~s z
anti- comb. form
   with stress-neutral suffix ¦ænt i ‖ ¦ænt̬ i ¦ænt aɪ
   — antibacterial
   ,ænt i bæk 'tɪər i‿əl ◄ ‖ ,ænt̬ i bak 'tɪr-
   ,ænt aɪ-
   with stress-imposing suffix æn 'tɪ+ —
   antiphony æn 'tɪf ᵊn i
antiabortion
   ,ænt i ə 'bɔːʃ ᵊn ‖ ,ænt̬ i ə 'bɔːrʃ ᵊn ,ænt aɪ-
   ~ist/s ɪst/s §əst/s
antiaircraft, anti-aircraft ,ænt i 'eə krɑːft ◄
   §-kræft ‖ ,ænt̬ i 'er kræft ◄ ,ænt aɪ-, -'ær-
antialias ,ænt i 'eɪl i‿əs ‖ ,ænt̬ i- ,ænt aɪ- ~ed
   t ~es ɪz əz ~ing ɪŋ
antiballistic ,ænt i bə 'lɪst ɪk ◄ ‖ ,ænt̬ i-
   ,ænt aɪ-
   ,antibal,listic 'missile
Antibes ɒn 'tiːb ɑːn-, æn- ‖ ɑːn- —Fr [ɑ̃ tib]
antibiotic ,ænt i baɪ 'ɒt ɪk ◄ ‖ ,ænt̬
   i baɪ 'ɑːt̬ ɪk ◄ ,ænt aɪ- ~ally ᵊl‿i ~s s
antibod|y 'ænt i ,bɒd li ‖ 'ænt̬ i ,bɑːd li 'ænt aɪ-
   ~ies iz
antic 'ænt ɪk ‖ 'ænt̬ ɪk ~s s
anticholinergic ,ænt i ,kəʊl ɪ 'nɜːdʒ ɪk -,kɒl-,
   -ə'•- ‖ ,ænt̬ i ,koʊl ə 'nɜːdʒ ɪk ,ænt aɪ-
Antichrist, a- 'ænt i kraɪst ‖ 'ænt̬ i- 'ænt aɪ-
antici|pate æn 'tɪs ɪ |peɪt ◄ -ə- ~pated peɪt ɪd
   -əd ‖ peɪt̬ əd ~pates peɪts ~pating
   peɪt ɪŋ ‖ peɪt̬ ɪŋ
anticipation æn ,tɪs ɪ 'peɪʃ ᵊn ,•••, -ə'•- ~s z
anticipatory æn 'tɪs ɪp ət̬ər i -'•əp-; •, •ɪ 'peɪt
   ər i, ,•••-, -ə'•- ‖ æn 'tɪs əp ə tɔːr i -toʊr i
anticlerical ,ænt i 'kler ɪk ᵊl ◄ ‖ ,ænt̬ i- ,ænt aɪ-
   ~ism ,ɪz əm
anticlimactic ,ænt i klaɪ 'mækt ɪk ◄ -klɪ'•-,
   -klə'•- ‖ ,ænt̬ i- ,ænt aɪ- ~ally ᵊl‿i
anticlimax ,ænt i 'klaɪm æks ‖ ,ænt̬ i- ,ænt aɪ-
   ~es ɪz əz
anticline 'ænt i klaɪn ‖ 'ænt̬ i- 'ænt aɪ- ~s z
anticlockwise ,ænt i 'klɒk waɪz ◄ ‖ ,ænt̬
   i 'klɑːk- ,ænt aɪ-
anticoagulant ,ænt i kəʊ 'æg jʊl ənt ◄ -jəl ənt
   ‖ ,ænt̬ i koʊ 'æg jəl ənt ,ænt aɪ- ~s s
anticonvulsant ,ænt i kən 'vʌls ᵊnt ◄ §-kɒn'•-
   ‖ ,ænt̬ i- ,ænt aɪ- ~s s
Anticosti ,ænt ɪ 'kɒst i -ə- ‖ ,ænt̬ ə 'kɑːst i
   -'kɔːst-
anticyclone ,ænt i 'saɪk ləʊn ‖ ,ænt̬ i 'saɪk loʊn
   ,ænt aɪ- ~s z
anticyclonic ,ænt i saɪ 'klɒn ɪk ◄ ‖ ,ænt̬
   i saɪ 'klɑːn ɪk ◄ ,ænt aɪ-
antidepressant ,ænt i dɪ 'pres ᵊnt ◄ -də'•-,
   §-diː'•- ‖ ,ænt̬ i- ,ænt aɪ- ~s s
antidote 'ænt i dəʊt ‖ 'ænt̬ i doʊt ~s s
Antietam æn 'tiːt əm ‖ -'tiːt̬-

antiformant 'ænt· i ˌfɔːm ənt ‖ 'ænʈ i ˌfɔːrm-
ˌænt aɪ- ~s s
antifouling ˌænt i 'faʊl ɪŋ ‖ ˌænʈ i- ˌænt aɪ-
antifreeze 'ænt i friːz ˌ•·'• ‖ 'ænʈ i-
anti-g ˌænt i 'dʒiː ‖ ˌænʈ i- ˌænt aɪ-
antigen 'ænt ɪdʒ ən -ədʒ-, -i dʒen ‖ 'ænʈ- ~s z
Antigone æn 'tɪg ən i
Antigonus æn 'tɪg ən əs
Antigu|a æn 'tiːg |ə —there is also an occasional
spelling pronunciation -w|ə ~an/s ən/z
antihero 'ænt i ˌhɪər əʊ ‖ ˌænʈ i ˌhɪr oʊ
ˌænt aɪ-, -ˌhiː roʊ ~es z
antihistamine ˌænt i 'hɪst ə miːn -mɪn, -mən
‖ ˌænʈ i- ˌænt ə-
antiknock ˌænt i 'nɒk ‖ ˌænʈ i 'nɑːk ˌænt aɪ-
Antillean æn 'tɪl i_ən ~s z
Antilles æn 'tɪl iːz
antilock ˌænt i 'lɒk ◄ ‖ ˌænʈ i 'lɑːk ◄ ˌænt aɪ-
antilog 'ænt i lɒg ‖ 'ænʈ i lɔːg 'ænt aɪ-, -lɑːg
~s z
antilogarithm ˌænt i 'lɒg ə rɪð əm -rɪθ• ‖ ˌænʈ
i 'lɔːg- ˌænt aɪ-, -'lɑːg- ~s z
antimacassar ˌænt i mə 'kæs ə ‖ ˌænʈ
i mə 'kæs ər ˌænt aɪ- ~s z
antimagnetic ˌænt i mæg 'net ɪk ◄-məg'•-
‖ ˌænʈ i mæg 'neʈ ɪk ◄ ˌænt aɪ-
antimalarial ˌænt i mə 'leər i_əl ◄ ‖ ˌænʈ
i mə 'ler- ˌænt aɪ- ~s z
antimatter 'ænt i ˌmæt ə ‖ 'ænʈ i ˌmæʈ ər
'ænt aɪ-
antimissile ˌænt i 'mɪs aɪəl ◄ ‖ ˌænʈ i 'mɪs əl ◄
ˌænt aɪ- ~s z
antimony 'ænt ɪ mən i '•ə- ‖ 'ænʈ ə moʊn i
anting 'ænt ɪŋ ‖ 'ænʈ ɪŋ
antinomian ˌænt i 'nəʊm i_ən ◄ ‖ ˌænʈ i 'noʊm-
ˌænt aɪ- ~ism ˌɪz əm
antinomy æn 'tɪn əm i
Antinous æn 'tɪn əʊ əs ‖ -oʊ-
antinovel 'ænt i ˌnɒv əl ‖ 'ænʈ i ˌnɑːv əl
'ænt aɪ-
antinuclear ˌænt i 'njuːk li_ə ◄ §-'nuːk-,
△-jəl ə ‖ ˌænʈ i 'nuːk li_ər◄ ˌænt aɪ-, -'njuːk-,
△-jəl ər
Antioch 'ænt i ɒk ‖ 'ænʈ i ɑːk
Antiochus æn 'taɪ_ək əs
antioxidant ˌænt i 'ɒks ɪd ənt -əd ənt ‖ ˌænʈ
i 'ɑːks- ˌænt aɪ- ~s s
antiparticle 'ænt i ˌpɑːt ɪk əl ‖ 'ænʈ i ˌpɑːrt-
'ænt aɪ- ~s z
Antipas 'ænt i pæs ‖ 'ænʈ i-
antipasto 'ænt i ˌpæst əʊ -ˌpɑːst-, ˌ••'•·
‖ ˌænʈ i 'pɑːst oʊ -'pæst-
Antipater æn 'tɪp ət ə ‖ -əʈ ər
antipathetic ˌænt i pə 'θet ɪk ◄ æn ˌtɪp ə-
‖ ˌænʈ i pə 'θeʈ ɪk ◄ ~ally əl_i
antipath|y æn 'tɪp əθ |i ~ies iz
antipersonnel ˌænt i ˌpɜːs ə 'nel ‖ ˌænʈ i ˌpɝːs-
ˌænt aɪ-
ˌanti ˌperson'nel mine
antiperspirant ˌænt i 'pɜːsp ər ənt -ɪr ənt
‖ ˌænʈ i 'pɝːsp- ˌænt aɪ- ~s s
antiphon 'ænt ɪf ən §-əf-; -ɪ fɒn, -ə- ‖ 'ænʈ
ə fɑːn -əf ən ~s z

antiphonal æn 'tɪf ən əl ~ly i
antiphrasis æn 'tɪf rəs ɪs §-əs
antipodal æn 'tɪp əd əl
antipodean, A~ æn ˌtɪp ə 'diː_ən ˌ•·- ~s z
antipodes, A~ æn 'tɪp ə diːz
antipyretic ˌænt i paɪ 'ret ɪk ◄ ‖ ˌænʈ
i paɪ 'reʈ ɪk ◄ ˌænt aɪ- ~s s
antiquarian ˌænt ɪ 'kweər i_ən ◄, •ə- ‖ ˌænʈ
ə 'kwer- ~ism ˌɪz əm ~s z
antiquar|y 'ænt ɪk wər |i '•ək- ‖ 'ænʈ ə kwer |i
~ies iz
antiquated 'ænt ɪ kweɪt ɪd '•ə-, -əd ‖ 'ænʈ
ə kweɪʈ əd ~ness nəs nɪs
antique (ˌ)æn 'tiːk —formerly also 'ænt ɪk ~ly li
~ness nəs nɪs
antiquit|y æn 'tɪk wət |i -wɪt- ‖ -wəʈ |i ~ies iz
anti-rac|ism ˌænt i 'reɪs ˌɪz əm ‖ ˌænʈ i-
ˌænt aɪ- ~ist/s ɪst/s əst/s
antirrhinum ˌænt ɪ 'raɪn əm -ə- ‖ ˌænʈ ə- ~s z
antiscorbutic ˌænt i skɔː 'bjuːt ɪk ◄ ‖ ˌænʈ
i skɔːr 'bjuːʈ ɪk ◄ ˌænt aɪ- ~s s
anti-Semite ˌænt i 'siːm aɪt -'sem- ‖ ˌænʈ
i 'sem- ˌænt aɪ- ~s s
anti-Semitic ˌænt i sə 'mɪt ɪk ◄-sɪ'•- ‖ ˌænʈ
i sə 'mɪʈ ɪk ◄ ˌænt aɪ-
anti-Semitism ˌænt i 'sem ə ˌtɪz əm-'•ɪ-
‖ ˌænʈ i- ˌænt aɪ-
antisepsis ˌænt i 'seps ɪs ◄-ə-, §-əs ‖ ˌænʈ ə-
antiseptic ˌænt i 'sept ɪk ◄-ə- ‖ ˌænʈ ə- ~ally
əl_i ~s s
antisocial ˌænt i 'səʊʃ əl ◄ ‖ ˌænʈ i 'soʊʃ əl ◄
ˌænt aɪ- ~ly i
antispasmodic ˌænt i spæz 'mɒd ɪk ◄ ‖ ˌænʈ
i spæz 'mɑːd- ˌænt aɪ-
antistatic ˌænt i 'stæt ɪk ◄ ‖ ˌænʈ i 'stæʈ ɪk ◄
ˌænt aɪ-
Antisthenes æn 'tɪs θə niːz -θɪ-
antistrophe æn 'tɪs trəf i
antitank ˌænt i 'tæŋk ‖ ˌænʈ i- ˌænt aɪ-
antith|esis æn 'tɪθ |əs ɪs -ɪs-, §-əs ~eses ə siːz
-ɪ-
antithetic ˌænt ɪ 'θet ɪk ◄-ə- ‖ ˌænʈ ə 'θeʈ ɪk ◄
~al əl ~ally əl_i
antitoxin ˌænt i 'tɒks ɪn §-ən ‖ ˌænʈ i 'tɑːks ən
ˌænt aɪ- ~s z
antitrust ˌænt i 'trʌst ‖ ˌænʈ i- ˌænt aɪ-
antitussive ˌænt i 'tʌs ɪv ‖ ˌænʈ i- ˌænt aɪ- ~s
z
antiviral ˌænt i 'vaɪər əl ‖ ˌænʈ i- ˌænt aɪ-
antivivisection|ism ˌænt i ˌvɪv ɪ 'sek ʃən| ˌɪz
əm §-, •ə- ‖ ˌænʈ i- ˌænt aɪ- ~ist/s ˌɪst/s
ˌəst/s
antler 'ænt lə ‖ -lər ~ed d ~s z
antlike 'ænt laɪk
antlion 'ænt ˌlaɪ_ən ~s z
Antofagasta ˌænt əf ə 'gæst ə —Sp
[an to fa 'ɣas ta]
Antoine ɒn 'twaːn aːn-, -'twæn, '•·
‖ aːn 'twaːn —Fr [ɑ̃ twan]
Antoinette ˌænt wə 'net ˌaːnt-, -waː- —Fr
[ɑ̃ twa nɛt]
Anton 'ænt ɒn ‖ -aːn
Antonia æn 'təʊn i_ə ‖ -'toʊn-

A

Antonian æn 'təʊn i_ən ‖ -'toʊn- ~s z
Antonine 'ænt ə naɪn ‖ 'ænt̬-
Antoninus ˌænt ə 'naɪn əs ◀ ‖ ˌænt̬-
  ˌAntoˌninus 'Pius
Antonio æn 'təʊn i_əʊ ‖ -'toʊn i_oʊ
Antonioni ˌænt əʊn i 'əʊn i æn ˌtəʊn-
  ‖ ˌɑːnt oʊn 'joʊn i —It [an to 'njo: ni]
Antonius æn 'təʊn i_əs ‖ -'toʊn-
antonomasia ˌænt ə nəʊ 'meɪz i_ə æn ˌtɒn əʊ-,
  -'meɪʒ- ‖ -noʊ 'meɪʒ i_ə -'meɪʒ ə
Antonov æn 'tɒn ɒf ‖ -'tɔːn ɔːf -'taːn aːf,
  -'toʊn- —Russ [ʌn 'to nəf]
Antony 'ænt ən i ‖ -ᵊn i
antonym 'ænt ə nɪm ‖ -ᵊn ɪm ~s z
antonym|ous æn 'tɒn əm |əs -ɪm- ‖ -'taːn- ~y
  i
Antrim 'æntr ɪm -əm
Antrobus 'æntr əb əs
antr|um 'æntr| əm ~a ə
antsy 'ænts i
Antwerp 'ænt wɜːp ‖ -wɜːp —Dutch
  Antwerpen ['ɑnt wɛrp ən]
Anubis ə 'njuːb ɪs §-əs ‖ ə 'nuːb- ə 'njuːb-
anuresis ˌæn juə 'riːs ɪs §-əs
anuria ₍ᵢ₎æn 'jʊər i_ə ˌæn juə 'riː_ə ‖ -'jʊr-
anus 'eɪn əs ~es ɪz əz
anvil 'æn vɪl -vᵊl ~s z
Anwar 'æn wɑː ‖ 'ɑːn wɑːr
Anwen 'æn wen
Anwyl 'æn wɪl -wəl
anxiet|y æŋ 'zaɪ_ət li §æŋg-, -ɪt- ‖ -ət̬ li ~ies iz
anxious 'æŋkʃ əs ~ly li ~ness nəs nɪs
any strong form 'en i (!); occasional weak form
  ən i → ᵊn_i —In Irish English, any and its
  compounds are often 'æn i
Anyang ˌæn 'jæŋ ‖ ˌɑːn 'jɑːŋ —Chinese Ānyáng
  [¹an ²jaŋ]
anybody 'en i bɒd i 'en ə-, -bəd i ‖ -baːd i
  —also weak form ən-
anyhow 'en i haʊ -ə-
anymore ˌen i 'mɔː ‖ -'mɔːr -'moʊr
anyone 'en i wʌn -ə-, §-wɒn, -wən —also weak
  form ən-
anyplace 'en i pleɪs -ə- —also weak form ən-
anyroad 'en i rəʊd -ə- ‖ -roʊd
anything 'en i θɪŋ -ə-; △-θɪŋk —also weak form
  ən-
anyway 'en i weɪ -ə- ~s z
anywhere 'en i weə -ə-, -hweə ‖ -hwer -hwær,
  -hwᵊr —also weak form ən-
Anzac 'ænz æk
Anzio 'ænz i əʊ ‖ -oʊ 'ɑːnz- —It ['an tsio]
ANZUS 'ænz əs -ʊs
AOB ˌeɪ əʊ 'biː ‖ -oʊ-
A-OK, A-Okay ˌeɪ əʊ 'keɪ ‖ -oʊ-
AOL tdmk ˌeɪ əʊ 'el ‖ -oʊ-
aorist 'eər ɪst 'eɪ ər ɪst, -əst ‖ 'eɪ ər əst ~s s
aoristic ₍ᵢ₎eə 'rɪst ɪk ◀ ˌeɪ ə'•- ‖ ˌeɪ ə 'rɪst-
  ~ally ᵊl_i
aort|a eɪ 'ɔːt ə ‖ -'ɔːrt̬ ə ~al ᵊl ~as əz ~ic ɪk
Aotearoa ˌaː əʊ tiː_ə 'rəʊ ə ‖ ˌaː oʊ tiː ə 'roʊ ə
aoudad 'aʊd æd 'aː u dæd ~s z
Ap in Welsh names æp

ap- ə, æ —This variant of ad- is usually ə
  (ap'pear), but æ if stressed because of a suffix
  (ˌappa'rition).
apace ə 'peɪs
Apache ə 'pætʃ i ~s z —for the obsolete sense
  'ruffian', the pronunciation was ə 'pæʃ —Fr
  [a paʃ]
Apalachicola ˌæp ə lætʃ ɪ 'kəʊl ə ◀ -ə'•-
  ‖ -'koʊl-
apanage 'æp ən ɪdʒ
apart ə 'pɑːt ‖ ə 'pɑːrt
apartheid ə 'pɑːt heɪt -haɪt, -eɪt, -aɪt, -aɪd
  ‖ ə 'pɑːrt eɪt -aɪt —Afrikaans [a 'part heɪt]
apartment ə 'pɑːt mənt ‖ ə 'pɑːrt- ~s s
  a'partment ˌbuilding; a'partment house
apathetic ˌæp ə 'θet ɪk ◀ ‖ -'θet̬- ~ally ᵊl_i
apathy 'æp əθ i
apatite 'æp ə taɪt
ape eɪp aped eɪpt apes eɪps aping 'eɪp ɪŋ
apelike 'eɪp laɪk
ape|man 'eɪpl mæn ~men men
Apennines 'æp ə naɪnz -ɪ-, -e-
aperçu ˌæp 3ː 'sjuː -ə-, -'suː ‖ -ər 'suː ˌaːp-
  —Fr [a pɛʁ sy] ~s z —or as singular
aperient ə 'pɪər i_ənt ‖ ə 'pɪr- ~s s
aperiodic ˌeɪ ˌpɪər i 'ɒd ɪk ‖ -ˌpɪr i 'aːd- ~ally
  ᵊl_i
aperiodicity ˌeɪ ˌpɪər i_ə 'dɪs ət i -ˌ•i ɒ-, -ɪt i
  ‖ -ˌpɪr i_ə 'dɪs ət̬ i
aperitif, apéritif ə ˌper ə 'tiːf æ-, -ɪ-,
  •'••tɪf ‖ aː- —Fr [a pe ʁi tif] ~s s
aperture 'æp ə tʃə -tjʊə, -tʃʊə ‖ -ər tʃʊr -tʃᵊr,
  -tjʊr ~s z
apeshit 'eɪp ʃɪt
apex, Apex, APEX 'eɪp eks ~es ɪz əz
apfelstrudel 'æp fᵊl ˌstruːd ᵊl -ˌʃtruːd-, ˌ••'••
  —Ger ['apf ᵊl ˌʃtʁuːd ᵊl] ~s z
aphaeresis æ 'fɪər əs ɪs ə-, -ɪs ɪs, §-əs ‖ ə 'fer-
aphasia ə 'feɪz i_ə eɪ-, æ-, -'feɪʒ ə, -'feɪʒ i_ə
  ‖ ə 'feɪʒ ə
aphasic ə 'feɪz ɪk eɪ-, æ-
aphelion æ 'fiːl i_ən æp 'hiːl-
apheresis æ 'fɪər əs ɪs ə-, -ɪs ɪs, §-əs ‖ ə 'fer-
aphesis 'æf əs ɪs -ɪs -ɪs ɪs, §-əs
aphetic ə 'fet ɪk æ- ‖ -'fet̬- ~ally ᵊl_i
aphid 'eɪf ɪd 'æf-, §-əd ~s z
aph|is 'eɪf |ɪs 'æf-, §-əs ~ides ɪ diːz §ə-
aphonia ₍ᵢ₎eɪ 'fəʊn i_ə ‖ -'foʊn-
aphorism 'æf ə ˌrɪz əm ~s z
aphorist 'æf ər ɪst §-əst ~s s
aphoristic ˌæf ə 'rɪst ɪk ◀ ~ally ᵊl_i
Aphra 'æf rə
aphrodisiac ˌæf rə 'dɪz i æk ‖ -'diːz- ~s s
Aphrodite ˌæf rə 'daɪt i ‖ -'daɪt̬ i
aphtha 'æfθ ə
aphthous 'æfθ əs
Apia aː 'piː_ə ə-, -aː
apian 'eɪp i_ən
apiar|y 'eɪp i_ər li ‖ -er li ~ies iz ~ist/s ɪst/s
  §əst/s
apical 'æp ɪk ᵊl 'eɪp-
apices 'eɪp ɪ siːz 'æp-, -ə-
apiculture 'eɪp i ˌkʌltʃ ə §-ə- ‖ -ᵊr

A

apiece ə 'piːs
aping 'eɪp ɪŋ
Apis sacred bull 'æp ɪs 'ɑːp-, 'eɪp-, §-əs
apish 'eɪp ɪʃ ~ly li ~ness nəs nɪs
aplastic (ˌ)eɪ 'plæst ɪk -'plɑːst-
aplenty ə 'plent i ‖ ə 'plent̬ i
aplomb ə 'plɒm æ- ‖ -'plɑːm -'plʌm
apnea, apnoea æp 'niːˌə 'æp niˌə
apo- comb. form
  with stress-neutral suffix ¦æp əʊ ‖ ¦æp ə —
  apogamic ˌæp əʊ 'gæm ɪk ◄ ‖ -ə-
  with stress-imposing suffix ə 'pɒ+ æ 'pɒ+
  ‖ ə 'pɑː+ — apogamous ə 'pɒg əm əs æ-
  ‖ -'pɑːg-
apocalyps|e, A~ ə 'pɒk ə lɪps ‖ ə 'pɑːk- ~es ɪz
  əz
apocalyptic ə ˌpɒk ə 'lɪpt ɪk ◄ ‖ ə ˌpɑːk- ~ally
  əl_i
apocope ə 'pɒk əp i ‖ ə 'pɑːk- (!)
apocrypha, A~ ə 'pɒk rəf ə -rɪf ə ‖ ə 'pɑːk-
apocryphal ə 'pɒk rəf əl -rɪf əl ‖ ə 'pɑːk- ~ly i
apodosis ə 'pɒd əs ɪs §-əs ‖ ə 'pɑːd-
apogee 'æp əʊ dʒiː ‖ -ə-
apolitical ˌeɪ pə 'lɪt ɪk əl ◄ ‖ -'lɪt̬- ~ly _i
Apollinaire ə ˌpɒl ɪ 'neə -ə- ‖ ə ˌpɑːl ə 'neər
  -'næər —Fr [a pɔ li nɛːʁ]
Apollinaris ə ˌpɒl ɪ 'neər ɪs -ə-, -'nɑːr-, §-əs
  ‖ ə ˌpɑːl ə 'ner əs
Apollo, a~ ə 'pɒl əʊ ‖ ə 'pɑːl oʊ
Apollodorus ə ˌpɒl ə 'dɔːr əs ‖ ə ˌpɑːl- -'dour-
Apollonian ˌæp ə 'ləʊn iˌən ‖ -'loʊn-
Apollonius ˌæp ə 'ləʊn iˌəs ‖ -'loʊn-
Apollyon ə 'pɒl iˌən ‖ ə 'pɑːl jən
apologetic
  ə ˌpɒl ə 'dʒet ɪk ◄ ‖ ə ˌpɑːl ə 'dʒet̬ ɪk ◄ ~ally
  əl_i ~s s
apologia ˌæp ə 'ləʊdʒ iˌə -'ləʊdʒ ə ‖ -'loʊdʒ-
apologies ə 'pɒl ədʒ ɪz ‖ ə 'pɑːl-
apologis... —see apologiz...
apologist ə 'pɒl ədʒ ɪst §-əst ‖ ə 'pɑːl- ~s s
apologiz|e ə 'pɒl ə dʒaɪz ‖ ə 'pɑːl- ~ed d ~es
  ɪz əz ~ing ɪŋ
apologue 'æp əʊ lɒg ‖ ə lɔːg -lɑːg ~s z
apolog|y ə 'pɒl ədʒ |i ‖ ə 'pɑːl- ~ies ɪz
apophthegm 'æp ə θem ~s z
apoph|ysis ə 'pɒf ləs ɪs -ɪs ɪs, §-əs ‖ ə 'pɑːf-
  ~yses ə siːz ɪ-
apoplectic ˌæp ə 'plekt ɪk ◄ ~ally əl_i
apoplexy 'æp ə pleks i
apoptosis ˌæp əp 'təʊs ɪs ˌeɪ pɒp-, §-əs
  ‖ -'touss- ˌeɪ pɑːp-
aport ə 'pɔːt ‖ ə 'pɔːrt -'pourt
aposiopesis ˌæp əʊ ˌsaɪˌə 'piːs ɪs §-əs ‖ ˌæp ə-
apostas|y ə 'pɒst əs li ‖ ə 'pɑːst- ~ies ɪz
apostate ə 'pɒst eɪt -ət, -ɪt ‖ ə 'pɑːst- (!) ~s s
apostatis|e, apostatiz|e
  ə 'pɒst ə taɪz ‖ ə 'pɑːst- ~ed d ~es ɪz əz
  ~ing ɪŋ
a posteriori ˌeɪ pɒ ˌster i 'ɔːr aɪ ˌɑː-, -ˌstɪər-, -i
  ‖ ˌɑː poʊ ˌstɪr i 'ɔːr i ˌeɪ-, ˌˌpɑː-, -'our i
apostle ə 'pɒs əl ‖ ə 'pɑːs əl ~s, ~s' z ~ship
  ʃɪp
  Aˌpostles' 'Creed

apostolate ə 'pɒst ə leɪt ‖ ə 'pɑːst-
apostolic ˌæp ə 'stɒl ɪk ◄ -ɒ- ‖ -'stɑːl- ~ally
  əl_i
  ˌapoˌstolic suc'cession
apostrophe ə 'pɒs trəf i ‖ ə 'pɑːs- ~s z
apostrophis|e, apostrophiz|e
  ə 'pɒs trə faɪz ‖ ə 'pɑːs- ~ed d ~es ɪz əz
  ~ing ɪŋ
apothecar|y ə 'pɒθ ək ər_|i -'•ɪk-
  ‖ ə 'pɑːθ ə ker |i ~ies, ~ies' ɪz
apothegm 'æp ə θem ~s z
apotheosis ə ˌpɒθ i 'əʊs ɪs ◄ ˌæp əθ-, §-əs
  ‖ ə ˌpɑːθ i 'ous əs ˌæp əθ-
apotheosis|e, apotheosiz|e ə ˌpɒθ i 'əʊs aɪz
  ˌæp əθ-‖ ə ˌpɑːθ i 'ous aɪz ˌæp əθ- ~ed d
  ~es ɪz əz ~ing ɪŋ
app æp apps æps
appal ə 'pɔːl ‖ -'pɑːl ~led d ~ling ɪŋ ~s z
Appalach|ia ˌæp ə 'leɪtʃ iˌə -'leɪtʃ |ə; -'leɪʃ-
  ~ian/s iˌən/z ən/z
appall ə 'pɔːl ‖ -'pɑːl ~ed d ~ing ɪŋ ~s z
Appaloosa, a~ ˌæp ə 'luːs ə ~s z
appanag|e 'æp ən ɪdʒ ~es ɪz əz
apparat ˌæp ə 'rɑːt ‖ ˌɑːp- 'æp ə ræt
apparatchik ˌæp ə 'ræt tʃɪk -'rɑːt-, -'rætʃ ɪk,
  -'rɑːtʃ ɪk ‖ ˌɑːp ə 'rɑːt- -'rɑːtʃ ɪk ~s s
apparatus sing., pl ˌæp ə 'reɪt əs -'rɑːt-, -'ræt-
  ‖ -'ræt̬ əs -'reɪt̬- ~es ɪz əz
apparel n, v ə 'pær əl ‖ -'per- ~ed, ~led d
  ~ing, ~ling ɪŋ ~s z
apparent ə 'pær ənt -'peər- ‖ -'per- ~ly li
  ~ness nəs nɪs
apparition ˌæp ə 'rɪʃ ən ~s z
appassionata ə ˌpæs iˌə 'nɑːt ə ‖ ə -'nɑːt̬ ə
  -ˌpɑːs-
appeal ə 'piːəl appealed ə 'piːəld
  appealing/ly ə 'piːəl ɪŋ/ li appeals ə 'piːəlz
appear ə 'pɪə ‖ ə 'pɪər appeared
  ə 'pɪəd ‖ ə 'pɪərd appearing
  ə 'pɪər ɪŋ ‖ ə 'pɪr ɪŋ appears
  ə 'pɪəz ‖ ə 'pɪərz
appearanc|e ə 'pɪər ənts ‖ ə 'pɪr- ~es ɪz əz
appeas|e ə 'piːz ~ed d ~ement mənt ~er/s
  ə/z ‖ ər/z ~es ɪz əz ~ing ɪŋ
appellant ə 'pel ənt ~s s
appellate ə 'pel ət -ɪt, -eɪt
appellation ˌæp ə 'leɪʃ ən -ɪ-, -e- ~s z
  appellation contrôlée
  ˌæp ə ˌlæs i ɒ kɒn 'trəʊl eɪ
  ‖ -ˌlɑːs i oun ˌkɑːn trou 'leɪ —Fr
  [a pe la sjɔ̃ kɔ̃ tʁɔ le]
appellative ə 'pel ət ɪv æ- ‖ -ət̬ ɪv ~ly li
appellee ˌæp el 'iː -ə 'liː- ~s z
append ə 'pend ~ed ɪd əd ~ing ɪŋ ~s z
appendag|e ə 'pend ɪdʒ ~es ɪz əz
appendectom|y ˌæp ən 'dekt əm |i →ˌæp m-;
  ˌæp en- ~ies ɪz
appendicectom|y ə ˌpend ɪ 'sekt əm |i -ˌ•ə-
  ~ies ɪz
appendices ə 'pend ɪ siːz -ə-
appendicitis ə ˌpend ə 'saɪt ɪs -ˌ•ɪ-, §-əs
  ‖ -'saɪt̬ əs

A

append|ix ə 'pend |ɪks ~ices ɪ siːz ə- ~ixes
ɪks ɪz -əz
apperceiv|e ˌæp ə 'siːv ‖ -ᵊr- ~ed d ~es z
~ing ɪŋ
apperception ˌæp ə 'sep ʃən ‖ -ᵊr- ~s z
apperceptive ˌæp ə 'sept ɪv ◀ ‖ -ᵊr-
Apperley 'æp əl i ‖ -ᵊr li
appertain ˌæp ə 'teɪn ‖ -ᵊr- ~ed d ~ing ɪŋ ~s
z
appestat 'æp ɪ stæt -ə- ~s s
appetenc|e 'æp ɪt ənᵗs -ət- ~y i
appetent 'æp ɪt ənt -ət-
appetis|e 'æp ɪ taɪz -ə- ~er/s ə/z ‖ ᵊr/z ~ing/
ly ɪŋ /li
appetite 'æp ɪ taɪt -ə- ~s s
appetiz|e 'æp ɪ taɪz -ə- ~er/s ə/z ‖ ᵊr/z ~ing/
ly ɪŋ /li
Appian 'æp i ˌən
ˌAppian 'Way
applaud ə 'plɔːd ‖ -'plɑːd ~ed ɪd əd ~ing ɪŋ
~s z
applause ə 'plɔːz ‖ -'plɑːz
apple 'æp əl ~s z
ˌapple ˌblossom; ˌapple 'green◀; ˌapple
'pie; ˌapple 'sauce ‖ '• • •; 'apple tree
Appleby 'æp əl bi
applecart 'æp əl kɑːt ‖ -kɑːrt ~s s
Appledore 'æp əl dɔː ‖ -dɔːr
Applegarth 'æp əl gɑːθ ‖ -gɑːrθ
applejack 'æp əl dʒæk
apple-pie ˌæp əl 'paɪ ◀
ˌapple-pie 'order
Appleseed 'æp əl siːd
applet 'æp lət -lɪt ~s s
Appleton 'æp əl tən
Appleyard 'æp əl jɑːd ‖ -jɑːrd
applianc|e ə 'plaɪ ənᵗs ~es ɪz əz
applicability ə ˌplɪk ə 'bɪl ət i ˌæp lɪk-, -ɪt i
‖ -əṭ i

APPLICABLE

■ə'plɪk- ▭'æp lɪk-

	0	20	40	60	80	100%
BrE 1988						
AmE 1993						
BrE 1998						

---

applicab|le ə 'plɪk əb |əl 'æp lɪk əb |əl ~ly li
—Poll panel preferences: BrE 1988, ə'plɪk-
77%, 'æplɪk- 23%; AmE 1993, 'æplɪk- 64%,
ə'plɪk- 36%; BrE 1998, ə'plɪk- 84%, 'æplɪk-
16%.
applicant 'æp lɪk ənt -lək- ~s s
application ˌæp lɪ 'keɪʃ ən -lə- ~s z
applicator 'æp lɪ keɪt ə '•lə- ‖ -keɪṭ ᵊr ~s z
applie... —see apply
appliqué ə 'pliːk eɪ æ- ‖ ˌæp lə 'keɪ ~d d
~ing ɪŋ ~s z
apply ə 'plaɪ applied ə 'plaɪd applies ə 'plaɪz
applying ə 'plaɪ ɪŋ
appoggiatura ə ˌpɒdʒ ə 'tʊər ə -ˌ•i_ə'••,
-'tjʊər- ‖ ə ˌpɑːdʒ ə 'tʊr ə ~s z
appoint ə 'pɔɪnt appointed ə 'pɔɪnt ɪd -əd
‖ ə 'pɔɪnṭ əd appointing
ə 'pɔɪnt ɪŋ ‖ ə 'pɔɪnṭ ɪŋ appoints ə 'pɔɪnts

appointee ə ˌpɔɪn 'tiː ˌæp ɔɪn- ~s z
appointive ə 'pɔɪnt ɪv ‖ ə 'pɔɪnṭ ɪv
appointment ə 'pɔɪnt mənt ~s s
Appomattox ˌæp ə 'mæt əks ‖ -'mæṭ-
apport ə 'pɔːt ‖ ə 'pɔːrt -'poʊrt
apportion ə 'pɔːʃ ən ‖ ə 'pɔːrʃ ən -'poʊrʃ- ~ed
d ~ing ˌ ɪŋ ~ment/s mənt/s ~s z
appos|e æ 'pəʊz ə- ‖ -'poʊz ~ed d ~es ɪz əz
~ing ɪŋ
apposite 'æp əz ɪt -ət; -ə zaɪt ~ly li ~ness nəs
nɪs
apposition ˌæp ə 'zɪʃ ən
appositional ˌæp ə 'zɪʃ ən_əl ◀ ~ly i
appositive ə 'pɒz ət ɪv æ-, -ɪt- ‖ -'pɑːz əṭ- ~ly
li
appraisal ə 'preɪz əl ~s z
apprais|e ə 'preɪz ~ed d ~es ɪz əz ~ing ɪŋ
appraisement ə 'preɪz mənt ~s s
appreciab|le ə 'priːʃ əb |əl -'•i_əb-,
ə 'priːs i_ ‖ ə 'priːʃ- ~ly li
appreci|ate ə 'priːʃ i eɪt ə 'priːs- ‖ ə 'priːʃ-
~ated eɪt ɪd -əd ‖ eɪṭ əd ~ates eɪts ~ating
eɪt ɪŋ ‖ eɪṭ ɪŋ
appreciation ə ˌpriːʃ i 'eɪʃ ən -ˌpriːs- ‖ ə ˌprɪʃ-
appreciative ə 'priːʃ i_ət ɪv -'priːs-, -eɪt-;
-'priːʃ ət ɪv ‖ ə 'priːʃ əṭ ɪv ə 'prɪʃ-; -'•i eɪṭ-
~ly li ~ness nəs nɪs
appreciatory ə 'priːʃ i_ət_ər i -'priːs-, •, ••'eɪt
ər i ◀ ‖ ə 'priːʃ ə tɔːr i -'prɪʃ-, -toʊr i
apprehend ˌæp rɪ 'hend ◀ -rə- ~ed ɪd əd ~ing
ɪŋ ~s z
apprehensibility ˌæp rɪ ˌhenᵗs ə 'bɪl ət i ˌ•rə-,
-, •ə-, -ɪt i ‖ -əṭ i
apprehensib|le ˌæp rɪ 'henᵗs əb |əl ˌ•rə-, -ɪb əl
~ly li
apprehension ˌæp rɪ 'henᵗʃ ən -rə- ~s z
apprehensive ˌæp rɪ 'henᵗs ɪv -rə- ~ly li
~ness nəs nɪs
apprentic|e ə 'prent ɪs -əs ‖ ə 'prenṭ- ~ed t
~es ɪz əz ~ing ɪŋ
apprenticeship ə 'prent ɪs ʃɪp →-ɪʃ•, -ɪ•,
§-əs• ‖ ə 'prenṭ əs- →-əʃ•, -ə• ~s s
appris|e, appriz|e ə 'praɪz ~ed d ~es ɪz əz
~ing ɪŋ
appro 'æp rəʊ ‖ -roʊ
approach v, n ə 'prəʊtʃ ‖ ə 'proʊtʃ ~ed t ~es
ɪz əz ~ing ɪŋ
approachability ə ˌprəʊtʃ ə 'bɪl ət i -ɪt i
‖ ə ˌproʊtʃ ə 'bɪl əṭ i
approachab|le ə 'prəʊtʃ əb |əl ‖ ə 'proʊtʃ- ~ly
li
appro|bate 'æp rəʊ |beɪt ‖ -rə- ~bated beɪt ɪd
-əd ‖ beɪṭ əd ~bates beɪts ~bating
beɪt ɪŋ ‖ beɪṭ ɪŋ
approbation ˌæp rəʊ 'beɪʃ ən ‖ -rə-
approbative 'æp rəʊ beɪt ɪv ‖ -rə beɪṭ ɪv
approbatory ˌæp rəʊ 'beɪt ər i ◀
‖ ə 'proʊb ə tɔːr i ˌæp rəb-, -toʊr i
appropriacy ə 'prəʊp ri_əs i ‖ ə 'proʊp-
appropri|ate v ə 'prəʊp ri eɪt ‖ ə 'proʊp-
~ated eɪt ɪd -əd ‖ eɪṭ əd ~ates eɪts ~ating
eɪt ɪŋ ‖ eɪṭ ɪŋ

appropriate *adj* ə 'prəʊp ri‿ət ‿ɪt ‖ ə 'proʊp-
~ly li ~ness nəs nɪs
appropriation ə ˌprəʊp ri 'eɪʃ ᵊn ‖ ə ˌproʊp-
~s z
approval ə 'pruːv ᵊl ~s z
approv|e ə 'pruːv ~ed d ~es z ~ing ɪŋ
approximant ə 'prɒks ɪm ənt -əm-
‖ ə 'prɑːks- ~s s
approximate *adj* ə 'prɒks ɪm ət -əm-, -ɪt
‖ ə 'prɑːks- ~ly li
approxi|mate *v* ə 'prɒks ɪ |meɪt -ə- ‖ -'prɑːks-
~mated meɪt ɪd -əd ‖ meɪt̬ əd ~mates meɪts
~mating meɪt ɪŋ ‖ meɪt̬ ɪŋ
approximation ə ˌprɒks ɪ 'meɪʃ ᵊn -ə-
‖ -ˌprɑːks- ~s z
approximative ə 'prɒks ɪm ət ɪv -'•əm-;
§-ɪ meɪt ɪv, §-ə•• ‖ ə 'prɑːks ə meɪt̬ ɪv ~ly li
Apps æps
appurtenanc|e ə 'pɜːt ɪn ən⁀s -ən-
‖ ə 'pɝːt ᵊn_ən⁀s ~es ɪz əz
appurtenant ə 'pɜːt ɪn ənt -ən-
‖ ə 'pɝːt ᵊn_ənt
APR ˌeɪ piː 'ɑː ‖ -'ɑːr
Aprahamian ˌæp rə 'heɪm i_ən
apraxia ₍ₐ₎eɪ 'præks i_ə ə-, æ-
apres, après 'æp reɪ ‖ ˌɑː 'preɪ ◂ ˌæ- —*Fr*
[a pʁɛ]
apres-ski, après-ski ˌæp reɪ 'skiː ◂ ‖ ˌɑːp- ˌæp-
apricot 'eɪp rɪ kɒt -rə- ‖ -kɑːt 'æp- ~s s
April 'eɪp rᵊl -rɪl
ˌApril 'fool, ˌApril 'Fools' Day
a priori ˌeɪ praɪ 'ɔːr aɪ ˌɑː-, -pri-, -i
‖ ˌɑː pri 'ɔːr i ˌeɪ-, ˌæp ri-, -'oʊr-
aprioristic ˌeɪ ˌpraɪ_ə 'rɪst ɪk ˌɑː-, -ˌpriːˌ, -ɔː'•-
~ally ᵊl_i
apriority ˌeɪ praɪ 'ɒr ət i -ɪt i ‖ ˌɑː pri 'ɔːr ət̬ i
ˌeɪ-, ˌæp ri-
apron 'eɪp rən ‖ -ᵊrn ~ed d ~ing ɪŋ ~s z
'apron strings
apropos ˌæp rə 'pəʊ ◂ '••• ‖ -'poʊ ◂
apse æps apses 'æps ɪz -əz
apsidal 'æps ɪd ᵊl §-əd-; æp 'saɪd ᵊl
Apsley 'æps li
apt æpt apter 'æpt ə ‖ -ᵊr aptest 'æpt ɪst
§-əst
Apted 'æpt ɪd -əd
apterous 'æpt ᵊr əs
apteryx 'æpt ə rɪks
apt|ly 'æpt |li ~ness nəs nɪs
aptitude 'æpt ɪ tjuːd -ə-, →§-tʃuːd ‖ -tuːd
-tjuːd ~s z
'aptitude test
Apuleius ˌæp ju 'liːˌəs -'leɪ- ‖ -jə-
Apulia ə 'pjuːl i_ə —*It* Puglia ['puʎ ʎa]
Apus 'eɪp əs
Aqaba, 'Aqaba 'æk əb ə ‖ 'ɑːk ə bɑː 'æk-,
-əb ə —*Arabic* ['ʕa qɑ bah]
aq|ua 'æk |wə ‖ 'ɑːk- 'æk- ~uae wiː waɪ, weɪ
—*see also phrases with this word*
ˌaqua 'fortis
aquacade 'æk wə keɪd ‖ 'ɑːk- 'æk- ~s z
aquaculture 'æk wə ˌkʌltʃ ə ‖ 'ɑːk wə ˌkʌltʃ ᵊr
'æk-

aqualung, Aqua-Lung *tdmk* 'æk wə lʌŋ ‖ 'ɑːk-
'æk- ~s z
aquamarine ˌæk wə mə 'riːn ◂ ‖ ˌɑːk- ˌæk- ~s
z
aquanaut 'æk wə nɔːt ‖ 'ɑːk- 'æk-, -nɑːt ~s s
aquaplan|e 'æk wə pleɪn ‖ 'ɑːk- 'æk- ~ed d
~es z ~ing ɪŋ
aqua regia ˌæk wə 'riːdʒ i_ə -'riːdʒ ə ‖ ˌɑːk-
ˌæk-
aquarelle ˌæk wə 'rel ‖ ˌɑːk- ˌæk- ~s z
aquarellist ˌæk wə 'rel ɪst §-əst ‖ ˌɑːk- ˌæk-
~s s
aquaria ə 'kweər i_ə ‖ ə 'kwer- ə 'kwær-
Aquarian ə 'kweər i_ən ‖ ə 'kwer- ə 'kwær-
~s z
aquarist 'æk wər ɪst §-əst ‖ ə 'kwer- ə 'kwær-
*(*) ~s s
aquari|um ə 'kweər i_|əm ‖ ə 'kwer- ə 'kwær-
~a ə ~ums əmz
Aquarius ə 'kweər i_əs ‖ ə 'kwer- ə 'kwær-
Aquascutum *tdmk* ˌæk wə 'skjuːt əm ‖ -'skjuːt̬-
aquatic ə 'kwæt ɪk -'kwɒt- ‖ ə 'kwɑːt̬ ɪk
-'kwæt̬- ~ally ᵊl_i ~s s
aquatint 'æk wə tɪnt ‖ 'ɑːk- 'æk- ~s s
aquavit 'æk wə vɪt -viːt ‖ 'ɑːk wə viːt ~s s
aqua vitae ˌæk wə 'vaɪt iː -'viːt aɪ
‖ ˌɑːk wə 'vaɪt̬ i ˌæk-
aqueduct 'æk wɪ dʌkt -wə- ~s s
aqueous 'eɪk wi əs 'æk-
aquifer 'æk wɪf ə -wəf- ‖ -ᵊr ~s z
Aquila 'æk wɪl ə -wəl-; ə 'kwɪl ə
aquilegia ˌæk wɪ 'liːdʒ i_ə ˌ•wə-, -'liːdʒ ə ~s z
aquiline 'æk wɪ laɪn -wə- ‖ -wəl ən
Aquinas ə 'kwaɪn əs æ-, -æs
Aquino ə 'kiːn əʊ ‖ -oʊ —*Sp* [a 'ki no]
Aquitaine ˌæk wɪ 'teɪn -wə-, '••• —*Fr*
[a ki tɛn]
Aquitania ˌæk wɪ 'teɪn i_ə ˌ•wə-
aquiver ə 'kwɪv ə ‖ -ᵊr
ar- ə, æ —*This variant of* ad- *is usually* ə
(ar'range), *but* æ *if stressed because of a suffix*
('arrogant).
-ar ə, ɑː ‖ ᵊr, ɑːr —*In most words this ending is*
pronounced weak, ə ‖ ᵊr ('cedar,'stellar). *In a*
few rarer or newer words it is pronounced
strong, ɑː ‖ ɑːr, *either as an alternative or as*
the only form ('lumbar,'radar).
Arab 'ær əb ~s z
Arabella ˌær ə 'bel ə ‖ ˌer-
arabesque ˌær ə 'besk ◂ ‖ ˌer- ~s s
Arabia ə 'reɪb i_ə
Arabian ə 'reɪb i_ən ~s z
A,rabian 'Nights
Arabic 'ær əb ɪk ‖ 'er-
ˌArabic 'numeral
arabica ə 'ræb ɪk ə ~s z
arabinose ə 'ræb ɪ nəʊz §-ə-, -nəʊs ‖ -noʊs
-noʊz
arabis 'ær əb ɪs §-əs ‖ 'er-
Arabist 'ær əb ɪst §-əst ‖ 'er- ~s s
arable 'ær əb ᵊl ‖ 'er-
Araby 'ær əb i ‖ 'er-
arachnid ə 'ræk nɪd §-nəd ~s z

A

arachnoid ə 'ræk nɔɪd ~s z
arachnophobia ə ‚ræk nəʊ
  'fəʊb i‿ə ‖ -nə 'foʊb-
Arafat 'ær ə fæt ‖ 'er-, -fɑːt —Arabic
  [ʕa ra 'faːt]
Arafura ‚ær ə 'fʊər ə -'fjʊər- ‖ ‚ɑːr ə 'fʊr ə
Aragon 'ær əg ən ‖ -ə gɑːn -əg ən —Sp Aragón
  [a ra 'ɣon] —but as a Fr family name,
  -ə gɒ̃‖ -ə gɔːn, Fr [a ʁa gɔ̃]
aragonite ə 'ræg ə naɪt 'ær əg-
arak 'ær ək -æk ‖ 'er-; ə 'ræk
Aral 'ær əl 'ɑːr-, 'eər- ‖ 'er-
Araldite tdmk 'ær əl daɪt ‖ 'er-
aralia ə 'reɪl i‿ə ~s z
Aramaic ‚ær ə 'meɪ ɪk ◄ ‚er-
Araminta ‚ær ə 'mɪnt ə ‖ -'mɪnt̬ ə ‚er-
Aran 'ær ən ‖ 'er-
Aranda 'ær ənd ə ə 'rʌnt ə
Arapaho ə 'ræp ə həʊ ‖ -hoʊ
Ararat 'ær ə ræt ‖ 'er-
Araucania ‚ær ɔː 'keɪn i‿ə ‖ ‚er-, ‚•ɑː-; ə ‚rɔː-,
  ə ‚rɑː-
araucaria ‚ær ɔː 'keər i‿ə ‖ -'ker-, ‚er-, ‚•ɑː-,
  -'kær- ~s z
Arawak 'ær ə wæk ‖ -wɑːk 'er- ~an ən ~s s
arbalest, arbalist 'ɑːb əl ɪst -əst ‖ 'ɑːrb- ~s s
Arbela ɑː 'biːl ə ‖ ɑːr-
arbiter, A~ 'ɑːb ɪt ə -ət- ‖ 'ɑːrb ət̬ ər ~s z
arbitrage 'ɑːb ɪ trɑːʒ -ə-, -trɪdʒ, ‚•‧'trɑːʒ
  ‖ 'ɑːrb-
arbitrageur ‚ɑːb ɪ trɑː 'ʒɜː ‚•ə-, -trə'•, -'ʒʊə
  ‖ ‚ɑːrb ə trɑː 'ʒɜ˞- ~s z
arbitral 'ɑːb ɪtr əl -ətr- ‖ 'ɑːrb-
arbitrament ɑː 'bɪtr ə mənt ‖ ɑːr- ~s s
arbitrarily 'ɑːb ɪtr ər əl i ‚•ətr-, -ɪ li; ⚠'•‧•ə li;
  ‚ɑːb ə 'treər•‧, -'trer-, §-'trær-
  ‖ ‚ɑːr bə 'trer əl i
arbitrar|y 'ɑːb ɪtr ər|i ‚•ətr-; ⚠'•‧•li
  ‖ 'ɑːrb ə trerl i ~iness i nəs i nɪs
arbi|trate 'ɑːb ɪ |treɪt -ə- ‖ 'ɑːrb- ~trated
  treɪt ɪd -əd ‖ treɪt̬ əd ~trates treɪts
  ~trating treɪt ɪŋ ‖ treɪt̬ ɪŋ
arbitration ‚ɑːb ɪ 'treɪʃ ᵊn -ə- ‖ ‚ɑːrb- ~s z
arbitrator 'ɑːb ɪ treɪt ə ‚•‧ə- ‖ 'ɑːrb ə treɪt̬ ər
  ~s z
Arblaster 'ɑːb lɑːst ə §-læst- ‖ 'ɑːrb læst ər
arbor 'arbour'; 'shaft' 'ɑːb ə ‖ 'ɑːrb ər ~s z
arbor 'tree' 'ɑːb ə -ɔː; ‖ 'ɑːrb ər ~s z
  ‚arbor 'vitae 'vaɪt iː 'viːt aɪ ‖ 'vaɪt̬ i
Arbor 'ɑːb ə ‖ 'ɑːrb ər
  'Arbor Day
arboraceous ‚ɑːb ə 'reɪʃ əs ◄ -ɔː- ‖ ‚ɑːrb-
arbore|al ɑː 'bɔːr i‿|əl ‖ ɑːr- -'boʊr- ~ally əl‿i
  ~ous əs
arboresc|ence ‚ɑːb ə 'res |ᵊnts ◄ ‖ ‚ɑːrb- ~ent
  ᵊnt
arboret|um ‚ɑːb ə 'riːt əm ‖ ‚ɑːrb ə 'riːt̬ əm
  ~a ə
Arborfield 'ɑːb ə fiːᵊld ‖ 'ɑːrb ər-
arboriculture 'ɑːb ər i ‚kʌltʃ ə ‚•‧•‧•;
  ɑː 'bɒr-, ‧, •‧'•‧• ‖ 'ɑːrb ər i ‚kʌltʃ ər
  ɑːr 'bɔːr-, -'boʊr-
Arborite tdmk 'ɑːb ə raɪt ‖ 'ɑːrb-

arbour 'ɑːb ə ‖ 'ɑːrb ᵊr ~s z
arbovirus 'ɑːb əʊ ‚vaɪᵊr əs ‖ 'ɑːrb oʊ- ~es ɪz
  əz
Arbroath ɑː 'brəʊθ ‖ ɑːr 'broʊθ
Arbuckle 'ɑː ‚bʌk ᵊl ‚•'•• ‖ 'ɑːr-
Arbuthnot ɑː 'bʌθ nət ə-, -nɒt ‖ ɑːr-
arbutus ɑː 'bjuːt əs ‖ ɑːr 'bjuːt̬ əs ~es ɪz əz
arc ɑːk ‖ ɑːrk (=ark) arced, arcked
  ɑːkt ‖ ɑːrkt arcing, arcking
  'ɑːk ɪŋ ‖ 'ɑːrk ɪŋ arcs ɑːks ‖ ɑːrks —See also
  phrases with this word
arcad|e ‚ɑː 'keɪd ‖ ɑːr- ~ed ɪd əd ~es z
Arcadi|a ɑː 'keɪd i‿|ə ‖ ɑːr- ~an/s ən/z
Arcady 'ɑːk əd i ‖ 'ɑːrk-
arcana ɑː 'keɪnə -'kɑːn- ‖ ɑːr-
arcane ‚ᵤɑː 'keɪn ‖ ɑːr-
arcan|um ɑː 'keɪn |əm -'kɑːn- ‖ ɑːr- ~a ə
Arc de Triomphe ‚ɑːk də 'triː ɒmpf -əʊmpf
  ‖ ‚ɑːrk də tri 'ɑːmpf -'ɔːmpf —Fr
  [aʁk də tʁi ɔ̃ːf]
arced ɑːkt ‖ ɑːrkt
arch, Arch ɑːtʃ ‖ ɑːrtʃ arched ɑːtʃt ‖ ɑːrtʃt
  arches 'ɑːtʃ ɪz -əz‖ 'ɑːrtʃ- arching
  'ɑːtʃ ɪŋ ‖ 'ɑːrtʃ-
arch- ¦ɑːtʃ ‖ ¦ɑːrtʃ- — archfool
  ‚ɑːtʃ 'fuːl ‚ɑːrtʃ- —Note however the
  exception archangel ¦ɑːk- ‖ ¦ɑːrk-, and compare
  archi-
-arch ɑːk ‖ ɑːrk — ecclesiarch
  ɪ 'kliːz i ɑːk ‖ -ɑːrk —but in monarch usually
  ək in RP.
Archaean ɑː 'kiː‿ən ‖ ɑːr-
archaeo- comb. form
  with stress-neutral suffix ¦ɑːk i əʊ ‖ ¦ɑːrk i oʊ
  — archaeoastronomy ‚ɑːk i əʊ
  ə 'strɒn əm i ‖ ‚ɑːrk i oʊ ə 'strɑːn-
  with stress-imposing suffix
  ¦ɑːk i 'ɒ+ ‖ ¦ɑːrk i 'ɑː+ — archaeopteryx
  ‚ɑːk i 'ɒpt ə rɪks ‖ ‚ɑːrk i 'ɑːpt-
archaeological ‚ɑːk i‿ə 'lɒdʒ ɪk ᵊl ◄ ‖
  ‚ɑːrk i‿ə 'lɑːdʒ- ~ly ‿i
archaeologist ‚ɑːk i 'ɒl ədʒ ɪst §-əst
  ‖ ‚ɑːrk i 'ɑːl- ~s s
archaeology ‚ɑːk i 'ɒl ədʒ i ‖ ‚ɑːrk i 'ɑːl-
archaeopteryx ‚ɑːk i 'ɒpt ə rɪks ‖ ‚ɑːrk i 'ɑːpt-
Archaeozoic, a- ‚ɑːk i‿ə 'zəʊ ɪk ◄
  ‖ ‚ɑːrk i‿ə 'zoʊ ɪk ◄
archaic ‚ᵤɑː 'keɪ ɪk ‖ ɑːr- ~ally ᵊl‿i
archais... —see archaiz...
archaism 'ɑːk eɪ ‚ɪz əm ‖ 'ɑːrk i- '•eɪ- ~s z
archaiz|e 'ɑːk eɪ aɪz -i- ‖ 'ɑːrk i- -eɪ- ~ed d
  ~es ɪz əz ~ing ɪŋ
archangel, A~ 'ɑːk ‚eɪndʒ əl ‚•'•• ‖ 'ɑːrk- ~s
  z
archbishop ‚ᵤɑːtʃ 'bɪʃ əp ‖ ‚ᵤɑːrtʃ- ~s s
archbishopric ‚ᵤɑːtʃ 'bɪʃ əp rɪk ‖ ‚ᵤɑːrtʃ- ~s s
Archbold 'ɑːtʃ bəʊld →-bɒʊld ‖ 'ɑːrtʃ boʊld
archdeacon, A~ ‚ᵤɑːtʃ 'diːk ən ‖ ‚ᵤɑːrtʃ- ~s z
archdeacon|ry ‚ᵤɑːtʃ 'diːk ən |ri ‖ ‚ᵤɑːrtʃ-
  ~ries riz
archdi|ocese ‚ɑːtʃ 'daɪ_ləs ɪs §-əs; ə siːz, -siːs
  ‖ ‚ɑːrtʃ 'daɪ ləs əs ~oceses ə siːz əs ɪs ɪz,
  -əs-, -əz; ə siːz ɪz, -siːs-, -əz ‖ ə səs əz, -iːz

archducal ˌɑːtʃ 'djuːk ᵊl ◄→§-'dʒuːk-
‖ ˌɑːrtʃ 'duːk ᵊl ◄-'djuːk-
archduchess ˌɑːtʃ 'dʌtʃ ɪs -əs ‖ ˌɑːrtʃ- ~es ɪz
əz
archduch|y ˌɑːtʃ 'dʌtʃ |i i ‖ ˌɑːrtʃ- ~ies iz
archduke ˌɑːtʃ 'djuːk ◄→§-'dʒuːk
‖ ˌɑːrtʃ 'duːk ◄-'djuːk ~s s
Archean ɑː 'kiːˌən ‖ ɑːr-
arched ɑːtʃt ‖ ɑːrtʃt
Archelaus ˌɑːk ɪ 'leɪ əs -ə- ‖ ˌɑːrk-
archenem|y ˌɑːtʃ 'en əm |i -ɪm- ‖ ˌɑːrtʃ- ~ies
iz
archeo- comb. form
  with stress-neutral suffix ⫦ɑːk i əʊ ‖ ⫦ɑːrk i oʊ
  — archaeoastronomy ˌɑːk i əʊ
  ə 'strɒn əm i ‖ ˌɑːrk i oʊ ə 'strɑːn-
  with stress-imposing suffix
  ˌɑːk i 'ɒ+ ‖ ˌɑːrk i 'ɑː+— archaeopteryx
  ˌɑːk i 'ɒpt ə rɪks ‖ ˌɑːrk i 'ɑːpt-
archeological
  ˌɑːk iˌə 'lɒdʒ ɪk ᵊl ◄ ˌɑːrk iˌə 'lɑːdʒ- ~ly ˌi
archeologist ˌɑːk i 'ɒl ədʒ ɪst §-əst
  ‖ ˌɑːrk i 'ɑːl- ~s s
archeology ˌɑːk i 'ɒl ədʒ i ‖ ˌɑːrk i 'ɑːl-
archeopteryx ˌɑːk i 'ɒpt ə rɪks ‖ ˌɑːrk i 'ɑːpt-
Archeozoic, a~ ˌɑːk iˌə 'zəʊ ɪk ◄
  ‖ ˌɑːrk iˌə 'zoʊ ɪk ◄
archer, A~ 'ɑːtʃ ə ‖ 'ɑːrtʃ ᵊr ~s z
archery 'ɑːtʃ ər i ‖ 'ɑːrtʃ-
arches, A~ 'ɑːtʃ ɪz -əz ‖ 'ɑːrtʃ-
archetypal ˌɑːk i 'taɪp ᵊl ◄'••,•• ‖ ˌɑːrk- ~ly i
archetype 'ɑːk i taɪp ‖ 'ɑːrk- ~s s
archetypical ˌɑːk i 'tɪp ɪk ᵊl ◄,•ə- ‖ ˌɑːrk- ~ly
ˌi
archi- ⫦ɑːk i-ɪ ‖ ⫦ɑːrk i-ə — archicarp
  'ɑːk i kɑːp ‖ 'ɑːrk i kɑːrp
Archibald 'ɑːtʃ ɪ bɔːld -ə- ‖ 'ɑːrtʃ ə- -bɑːld
-archic comb. form 'ɑːk ɪk ‖ 'ɑːrk-—
  heptarchic hep 'tɑːk ɪk ‖ -'tɑːrk-
Archie 'ɑːtʃ i ‖ 'ɑːrtʃ i
archimandrite ˌɑːk i 'mændr aɪt ◄ ‖ ˌɑːrk ə-
  ~s s
Archimedean ˌɑːk ɪ 'miːd iˌən -'meɪd-;
  -mi: 'diːˌən ‖ ˌɑːrk-
Archimedes ˌɑːk ɪ 'miːd iːz ◄-ə-, -'meɪd-
  ‖ ˌɑːrk-
arching 'ɑːtʃ ɪŋ ‖ 'ɑːrtʃ-
archipelago ˌɑːk ɪ 'pel ə gəʊ ,•ə-, -ɪ gəʊ
  ‖ ˌɑːrk ə 'pel ə goʊ ~es, ~s z
archiphoneme 'ɑːk i ˌfəʊn iːm ,••'••
  ‖ 'ɑːrk i ˌfoʊn- ~s z
archiphonemic ˌɑːk i fəʊ
  'niːm ɪk ◄ ‖ ˌɑːrk i foʊ- ~ally ᵊlˌi
architect 'ɑːk ɪ tekt -ə- ‖ 'ɑːrk- ~s s
architectonic ˌɑːk ɪ tek 'tɒn ɪk ◄,•ə-
  ‖ ˌɑːrk ə tek 'tɑːn- ~ally ᵊlˌi ~s s
architectural ˌɑːk ɪ 'tek tʃ ᵊr ᵊl ◄,•ə- ‖ ˌɑːrk-
  ~ly i
architecture 'ɑːk ɪ tek tʃə'•ə-
  ‖ 'ɑːrk ə tek tʃᵊr
architrave 'ɑːk ɪ treɪv -ə- ‖ 'ɑːrk- ~s z
archival ɑː 'kaɪv ᵊl ‖ ɑːr-
archiv|e 'ɑːk aɪv ‖ 'ɑːrk- ~ed d ~es z ~ing ɪŋ

archivist 'ɑːk ɪv ɪst -əv-, §-əst ‖ 'ɑːrk- -aɪv-
  ~s s
archon 'ɑːk ən -ɒn ‖ 'ɑːrk ɑːn ~s z ~ship ʃɪp
archway 'ɑːtʃ weɪ ‖ 'ɑːrtʃ- ~s z
-archy ɑːk i ‖ ɑːrk i— heptarchy
  'hept ɑːk i ‖ -ɑːrk i—but in
  'anarchy,'monarchy usually ək i ‖ ᵊrk i
arcing, arck... —see arc
arco, Arco tdmk 'ɑːk əʊ ‖ 'ɑːrk oʊ
arcsin, arcsine 'ɑːk saɪn ,•'• ‖ 'ɑːrk-
arctan 'ɑːk tæn ,•'• ‖ 'ɑːrk-
arctic, A~ 'ɑːkt ɪk △'ɑːt- ‖ 'ɑːrkt- 'ɑːrt̮- ~ally
  ᵊlˌi
  Arctic 'Circle
Arcturus ɑːk 'tjʊər əs ‖ ɑːrk 'tʊr-
arc-weld ˌɑːk 'weld ‖ ˌɑːrk- ~ed ɪd əd ~ing ɪŋ
  ~s z
ard ɑːd ‖ ɑːrd ards ɑːdz ‖ ɑːrdz
-ard əd, ɑːd ‖ ᵊrd, ɑːrd—In well-known words
  this ending is əd ‖ ᵊrd ('standard, 'custard,
  'wizard, 'Edward). In less familiar words
  ɑːd ‖ ɑːrd is an alternative or sometimes the
  only pronunciation, often through the influence
  of the spelling ('bollard, 'mansard). The suffix
  -ward(s) is usually wəd(z) ‖ wᵊrd(z), but -yard
  is jɑːd ‖ jɑːrd except usually in 'vineyard.
Ardagh 'ɑːd ə-ɑː: ‖ 'ɑːrd ə
Ardeche, Ardèche ɑː 'deʃ ‖ ɑːr- —Fr [aʁ dɛʃ]
Ardee ɑː 'diː ‖ ɑːr-
Arden 'ɑːd ᵊn ‖ 'ɑːrd-
ardency 'ɑːd ᵊnts i ‖ 'ɑːrd-
Ardennes ɑː 'den-'denz ‖ ɑːr- —Fr [aʁ dɛn]
ardent 'ɑːd ᵊnt ‖ 'ɑːrd- ~ly li
ard fhéis ˌɑːd 'eɪʃ ˌɔːd- ‖ ˌɑːrd-—Irish
  [ɒʳd 'eːʃ]
Arding 'ɑːd ɪŋ ‖ 'ɑːrd-
Ardingly 'ɑːd ɪŋ laɪ ,•'• ‖ 'ɑːrd-
Ardizzone ˌɑːd ɪ 'zəʊn i -ə- ‖ ˌɑːrd ə 'zoʊn i
Ardmore ɑːd 'mɔː —ɑː:b- ‖ ɑːrd 'mɔːr -'moʊr
Ardnamurchan ˌɑːd nə 'mɜːk ən -'mɜːx-
  ‖ ˌɑːrd nə 'mɝːk ən
ardor, ardour 'ɑːd ə ‖ 'ɑːrd ᵊr
Ardoyne ɑː 'dɔɪn ‖ ɑːr-
Ardrishaig ɑː 'drɪʃ ɪg -eɪg ‖ ɑːr-
Ardrossan ɑː 'drɒs ᵊn ‖ ɑːr 'drɑːs ᵊn -'drɔːs-
Ards ɑːdz ‖ ɑːrdz
arduous 'ɑːd juˌəs 'ɑːdʒ uˌ ‖ 'ɑːrdʒ uˌəs ~ly li
  ~ness nəs nɪs
Ardwick 'ɑːd wɪk ‖ 'ɑːrd-
are v from be, strong form ɑː ‖ ɑːr, weak form
  ə ‖ ᵊr
are n ' 100 m² ' eə ɑː ‖ eᵊr æᵊr, ɑːr
area 'eər iˌə ‖ 'er- 'ær- ~s z
  'area code
areca ə 'riːk ə 'ær ɪk ə ~s z
arena ə 'riːn ə ~s z
Arenig ə 'ren ɪg —Welsh [a 're nɪg]
aren't ɑːnt ‖ ɑːrnt
are|ola ə 'riːˌl əl əæ- ~olae ə liː ~olas əl əz
areometer ˌeər i 'ɒm ɪt ə ,ær-, -ət ə
  ‖ ˌer i 'ɑːm ət̮ ᵊr ,ær- ~s z
Areopagite ˌær i 'ɒp ə gaɪt -dʒaɪt ‖ ˌær i 'ɑːp-
  ˌer- ~s s

A

Areopagitic ˌær i ɒp ə 'dʒɪt ɪk -'gɪt-
‖ ˌær i ɑːp ə 'dʒɪt̬ ɪk ˌer- ~a ə
Areopagus ˌær i 'ɒp əg əs ‖ -'ɑːp- ˌer-
Ares 'eər iːz ‖ 'er- 'ær-
arete, arête ə 'reɪt æ-, -'ret —Fr [a ʁɛt] ~s s
Aretha ə 'riːθ ə
Arethusa ˌær ɪ 'θjuːz ə -ə-, -e-, -'θuːz-
‖ -'θuːz ə ˌer-
Arfon 'ɑːv ən -ɒn ‖ 'ɑːrv- -ɑːn —Welsh
['ar von]
argali 'ɑːg əl i ‖ 'ɑːrg- ~s z
Argand, a~ 'ɑːg ænd -ənd ‖ ˌɑːr 'gɑːn ◂ -'gæn
—Fr [aʁ gɑ̃]
argent, A~ 'ɑːdʒ ənt ‖ 'ɑːrdʒ-
Argentina ˌɑːdʒ ən 'tiːn ə ‖ ˌɑːrdʒ-
Argentine country 'ɑːdʒ ən taɪn -tiːn ‖ 'ɑːrdʒ-
Argentine inhabitant 'ɑːdʒ ən tiːn -taɪn
‖ 'ɑːrdʒ- ~s z
Argentinian ˌɑːdʒ ən 'tɪn i ən ◂ ‖ ˌɑːrdʒ- ~s z
Argie 'ɑːdʒ i ‖ 'ɑːrdʒ i ~s z
argillaceous ˌɑːdʒ ɪ 'leɪʃ əs ◂ -ə- ‖ ˌɑːrdʒ-
arginine 'ɑːdʒ ɪ niːn -ə-, -naɪn ‖ 'ɑːrdʒ-
Argive 'ɑːg aɪv 'ɑːdʒ- ‖ 'ɑːrdʒ- 'ɑːrg- ~s z
Argo 'ɑːg əʊ ‖ 'ɑːrg oʊ
argol 'ɑːg ɒl -əl ‖ 'ɑːrg ɑːl -ɔːl, -əl
Argolis 'ɑːg ə lɪs ‖ 'ɑːrg-
argon 'ɑːg ɒn -ən ‖ 'ɑːrg ɑːn
Argonaut 'ɑːg ə nɔːt ‖ 'ɑːrg- -nɑːt ~s s
Argos 'ɑːg ɒs ‖ 'ɑːrg ɑːs -əs
argos|y 'ɑːg əs |i ‖ 'ɑːrg- ~ies iz
argot 'ɑːg əʊ -ət, -ɒt ‖ 'ɑːrg oʊ -ət
arguab|le 'ɑːg ju_əb |ᵊl ‖ 'ɑːrg- ~ly li
argu|e 'ɑːg juː ‖ 'ɑːrg- ~ed d ~es z ~ing ɪŋ
argument 'ɑːg ju mənt -jə- ‖ 'ɑːrg jə- ~s s
argumentation ˌɑːg ju men 'teɪʃ ən ˌ•jə-,
-mən'•- ‖ ˌɑːrg jə mən- -men'•-
argumentative ˌɑːg ju 'ment ət ɪv ◂ ˌ•jə-
‖ ˌɑːrg jə 'ment̬ ət ɪv ◂ ~ly li ~ness nəs nɪs
argus, Argus 'ɑːg əs ‖ 'ɑːrg-
argy-bargy ˌɑːdʒ i 'bɑːdʒ i ‖ ˌɑːrdʒ i 'bɑːrdʒ i
Argyle, a~, Argyll ₍ₐₐₐ₎ɑː 'gaɪᵊl ‖ ₍ₐₐₐ₎ɑːr- '•• —For
the name of the type of sock and sock pattern,
AmE prefers the stressing '••
Argyrol tdmk 'ɑːdʒ ə rɒl -ɪ- ‖ 'ɑːrdʒ ə roʊl
-rɑːl, -rɔːl
Arhus 'ɔː huːs 'ɑː-, -hʊs ‖ 'ɑːr- 'ɔːr- —Danish
Århus ['ɔː huːˀs]
aria 'ɑːr i_ə ~s z
Ariadne ˌær i 'æd ni ‖ ˌer-, -'ɑːd-
Arial 'eər i_əl ‖ 'er- 'ær-
Arian 'eər i_ən ‖ 'er- 'ær- ~s z
-arian comb. form 'eər i_ən ‖ 'er- 'ær- —
libertarian ˌlɪb ə 'teər i_ən ‖ -ᵊr 'ter- -'tær-
Ariane ˌær i 'æn ‖ ˌɑːr i 'ɑːn —Fr [aʁ jan]
Arianna ˌær i 'æn ə ‖ ˌer-
arid 'ær ɪd §-əd ‖ 'er- ~ly li ~ness nəs nɪs
aridit|y ə 'rɪd ət |i æ-, -ɪt i ‖ -ət̬ |i ~ies iz
Ariel, ariel 'eər i_əl ‖ 'er- 'ær-
Arien 'eər i_ən ‖ 'er- 'ær-
Aries 'eər iːz 'eər i iːz ‖ 'er iːz 'ær-, '•i iːz
arietta ˌær i 'et ə ‖ ˌɑːr i 'et̬ ə ˌær-, ˌer- —It
[a ri 'et ta] ~s z
aright ə 'raɪt

aril 'ær əl -ɪl ‖ 'er- ~s z
-arily ᵊr_əl i ər_ɪ li; 'er•••, §'ær•• ‖ 'er əl i
—Compare -ary. The traditional RP form is now
increasingly replaced by 'er-,
giving a mismatch between adjective and
adverb; see necessarily, primarily
Arimathaea, Arimathea ˌær ɪm ə 'θiː_ə
ˌ•əm- ‖ ˌer-
arioso ˌɑːr i 'əʊz əʊ ˌær-, -'əʊs- ‖ -'oʊs oʊ
-'oʊz- ~s z
Ariosto ˌær i 'ɒst əʊ ‖ ˌɑːr i 'ɑːst oʊ -'ɔːst-,
-'oʊst- —It [a 'rjɔs to]
arise ə 'raɪz arisen ə 'rɪz ən (!) arises
ə 'raɪz ɪz -əz arising ə 'raɪz ɪŋ arose
ə 'rəʊz ‖ ə 'roʊz
Aristaeus ˌær i 'stiː_əs -ə- ‖ er-
Aristarchus ˌær ɪ 'stɑːk əs -ə- ‖ -'stɑːrk- ˌer-
Aristides ˌær ɪ 'staɪd iːz -ə- ‖ ˌer-
Aristippus ˌær ɪ 'stɪp əs -ə- ‖ ˌer-
aristo ə 'rɪst əʊ ‖ -oʊ ~s z
Aristoc tdmk 'ær ɪ stɒk -ə- ‖ -stɑːk 'er-
aristocrac|y ˌær ɪ 'stɒk rəs |i ˌ•ə- ‖ -'stɑːk-
ˌer- ~ies iz
aristocrat 'ær ɪst ə kræt '•əst-, ə 'rɪst-
‖ ə 'rɪst- ~s s
aristocratic ˌær ɪst ə 'kræt ɪk ◂ ˌ•əst-, ə ˌrɪst-
‖ ə ˌrɪst ə 'kræt̬ ɪk ◂ ~ally ᵊl_i
Aristophanes ˌær ɪ 'stɒf ə niːz ˌ•ə- ‖ -'stɑːf-
ˌer-
Aristophanic ˌær ɪst ə 'fæn ɪk ◂ ˌ•əst-,
-ᴅ'•- ‖ ˌer-
Aristotelian ˌær ɪst ə 'tiːl i_ən ◂ ˌ•əst-, -ᴅ'•-,
-'tel- ‖ ˌer- ~s z
ˌAristoˌtelian 'logic
Aristotle 'ær ɪ stɒt ᵊl '•ə- ‖ -stɑːt̬ ᵊl 'er-
arithmetic n ə 'rɪθ mə tɪk
arithmetic adj ˌær ɪθ 'met ɪk ◂ -əθ- ‖ -'met̬ ɪk ◂
ˌer- ~al ᵊl ~ally ᵊl_i
ˌarithˌmetic pro'gression
arithmetician ə ˌrɪθ mə 'tɪʃ ən ˌær ɪθ-, ˌær əθ-
~s z
-arium comb. form 'eər i_əm ‖ 'er- 'ær- —
planetarium ˌplæn ə 'teər i_əm ˌ•ɪ- ‖ -'ter-
-'tær-
Arizon|a ˌær ɪ 'zəʊn |ə ◂ -ə- ‖ -'zoʊn |ə ◂ ˌer-
~an/s ən/z ~ian/s i_ən/z
Arjuna 'ɑːdʒ ʊn ə ‖ 'ɑːrdʒ- —Hindi [ər dʒʊn]
ark, Ark ɑːk ‖ ɑːrk arks ɑːks ‖ ɑːrks
Arkansan ɑː 'kænz ən ‖ ɑːr- ~s z
Arkansas 'ɑːk ən sɔː ‖ 'ɑːrk- -sɑː —but the A~
River is also ɑː 'kænz əs ‖ ɑːr-
Arkell (i) 'ɑːk ᵊl ‖ 'ɑːrk-, (ii) ɑː 'kel ‖ ɑːr-
Arkhangelsk ˌɑːk æŋ 'gelsk ɑː 'kæŋ gelsk
‖ ɑːr 'kɑːn gelsk —Russ [ʌr 'xan gɪlʲsk]
Arkle 'ɑːk ᵊl ‖ 'ɑːrk-
Arklow 'ɑːk ləʊ ‖ 'ɑːrk loʊ
Arkwright 'ɑːk raɪt ‖ 'ɑːrk-
Arlen 'ɑːl ən ‖ 'ɑːrl-
Arlene 'ɑːl iːn ɑː 'liːn ‖ 'ɑːrl 'liːn
Arles ɑːlz ɑːl ‖ ɑːrl —Fr [aʁl]
Arlette ₍ₐₐ₎ɑː 'let ‖ ɑːr-
Arlington 'ɑːl ɪŋ tən ‖ 'ɑːrl-
Arlott 'ɑːl ət ‖ 'ɑːrl-

arm ɑːm ‖ ɑːrm **armed** ɑːmd ‖ ɑːrmd **arming**
'ɑːm ɪŋ ‖ 'ɑːrm ɪŋ **arms** ɑːmz ‖ ɑːrmz
armada ɑː 'mɑːd ə ‖ ɑːr- —*formerly* -'meɪd-
~s z
Armadale 'ɑːm ə deɪᵊl ‖ 'ɑːrm-
armadillo ˌɑːm ə 'dɪl əʊ ‖ ˌɑːrm ə 'dɪl oʊ ~s z
Armageddon ˌɑːm ə 'ged ᵊn ‖ ˌɑːrm-
Armagh ˌɑː 'mɑː ◄ ‖ ˌɑːr-
Armagnac, a- 'ɑːm ən jæk ‖ ˌɑːrm ən 'jæk
-'jɑːk —*Fr* [aʁ ma njak]
Armalite, ArmaLite *tdmk* 'ɑːm ə laɪt ‖ 'ɑːrm-
~s s
armament 'ɑːm ə mənt ‖ 'ɑːrm- ~s s
armamentarium ˌɑːm ə men 'teər iˌəm
-mən'•- ‖ ˌɑːrm ə men 'ter-
Armand 'ɑːm ənd ‖ ɑːr 'mɑːn —*Fr* [aʁ mɑ̃]
Armani ɑː 'mɑːn i ‖ ɑːr- —*It* [ar 'mɑː ni]
Armathwaite 'ɑːm ə θweɪt ‖ 'ɑːrm-
Armatrading ˌɑːm ə 'treɪd ɪŋ ‖ ˌɑːrm-
armature 'ɑːm ətʃ ə -ə tjʊə, -ə tʃʊə
‖ 'ɑːrm ə tʃʊr -tʊr, -ətʃ ᵊr ~s z
armband 'ɑːm bænd ‖ 'ɑːrm- ~s z
armchair 'ɑːm tʃeə ˌ•'• ‖ 'ɑːrm tʃer -tʃær ~s
z
armed ɑːmd ‖ ɑːrmd
ˌarmed 'forces
Armeni|a ɑː 'miːn iˌə ‖ ɑːr- ~an/s ən/z
Armentieres, Armentières 'ɑːm ən tɪəz ˌ•••
‖ ˌɑːrm ən 'tjeᵊr —*Fr* [aʁ mɑ̃ tjɛːʁ]
armeria ɑː 'mɪər iˌə ‖ ɑːr 'mɪr-
Armfield 'ɑːm fiːᵊld ‖ 'ɑːrm-
armful 'ɑːm fʊl ‖ 'ɑːrm- ~s z
armhole 'ɑːm həʊl →-hɒʊl ‖ 'ɑːrm hoʊl ~s z
Armidale 'ɑːm ɪ deɪᵊl -ə- ‖ 'ɑːrm-
armie... —*see* **army**
armiger, A~ 'ɑːm ɪdʒ ə §-ədʒ- ‖ 'ɑːrm ɪdʒ ᵊr
~s z
armigerous ɑː 'mɪdʒ ᵊr əs ‖ ɑːr-
armillary ɑː 'mɪl ər i 'ɑːm ɪl- ‖ 'ɑːrm ə ler i
ɑːr 'mɪl ər i
Arminian ɑː 'mɪn iˌən ‖ ɑːr- ~ism ˌɪz ᵊm ~s z
Arminius ɑː 'mɪn iˌəs ‖ ɑːr-
Armistead 'ɑːm ɪ sted -stɪd ‖ 'ɑːrm-
armistic|e 'ɑːm ɪst ɪs -əst-, §-əs; §ɑː 'mɪst ɪs
‖ 'ɑːrm- ~es ɪz əz
'Armistice ˌDay
Armitage 'ɑːm ɪt ɪdʒ -ət- ‖ 'ɑːrm ət̬-
armlet 'ɑːm lət -lɪt ‖ 'ɑːrm- ~s s
Armley 'ɑːm li ‖ 'ɑːrm-
armlock 'ɑːm lɒk ‖ 'ɑːrm lɑːk ~s s
armor, A~ 'ɑːm ə ‖ 'ɑːrm ᵊr ~ed d **armoring**
'ɑːm ᵊr ɪŋ ‖ 'ɑːrm- ~s z
ˌarmored 'car; ˌarmor 'plate ‖ '•••
armorer 'ɑːm ᵊr ə ‖ 'ɑːrm ᵊr ᵊr ~s z
armorial ɑː 'mɔːr iˌəl ‖ ɑːr- -'moʊr- ~s z
Armoric|a ɑː 'mɒr ɪk ‖ə ‖ ɑːr 'mɔːr- -'mɑːr-
~an/s ən/z
armor|y 'ɑːm ᵊr ‖i i ‖ 'ɑːrm- ~ies iz
armour, A~ 'ɑːm ə ‖ 'ɑːrm ᵊr ~ed d
armouring 'ɑːm ᵊr ɪŋ ‖ 'ɑːrm- ~s z
ˌarmoured 'car; ˌarmour 'plate ‖ '•••
armourer 'ɑːm ᵊr ə ‖ 'ɑːrm ᵊr ᵊr ~s z
armour|y 'ɑːm ᵊr ‖i i ‖ 'ɑːrm- ~ies iz

armpit 'ɑːm pɪt ‖ 'ɑːrm- ~s s
armrest 'ɑːm rest ‖ 'ɑːrm- ~s s
arms ɑːmz ‖ ɑːrmz
'arms ˌrace
Armstrong 'ɑːm strɒŋ ‖ 'ɑːrm strɔːŋ -strɑːŋ
arm|y 'ɑːm ‖i i ‖ 'ɑːrm ‖i i ~ies iz
ˌarmy 'officer
Arndale 'ɑːn deɪᵊl ‖ 'ɑːrn-
Arne ɑːn ‖ ɑːrn
Arnhem 'ɑːn əm ‖ 'ɑːrn- —*Dutch* ['ɑrn hɛm,
-əm]
'Arnhem ˌLand
arnica 'ɑːn ɪk ə ‖ 'ɑːrn-
Arno 'ɑːn əʊ ‖ 'ɑːrn oʊ —*It* ['ar no]
Arnold 'ɑːn ᵊld ‖ 'ɑːrn-
Arnot, Arnott 'ɑːn ət -ɒt ‖ 'ɑːrn- -ɑːt
A-road 'eɪ rəʊd ‖ -roʊd ~s z
aroint ə 'rɔɪnt
aroma ə 'rəʊm ə ‖ ə 'roʊm ə ~s z
aromatherapy ə ˌrəʊm ə 'θer əp i •'•••, •••
‖ -ˌroʊm-
aromatic ˌær ə 'mæt ɪk ◄ -əʊ- ‖ -'mæt̬- ˌer-
~ally ᵊlˌi
aromaticity ˌær ə mæ 'tɪs ət i -mə'••-,
ə ˌrəʊm ə-, -ɪt i ‖ -ət̬ i ˌer-; ə ˌroʊm ə-
aromatis|e, aromatiz|e
ə 'rəʊm ə taɪz ‖ ə 'roʊm- ~ed d ~es ɪz əz
~ing ɪŋ
Aronowitz ə 'rɒn ə wɪts ‖ ə 'rɑːn-
arose ə 'rəʊz ‖ ə 'roʊz
around ə 'raʊnd
arousal ə 'raʊz ᵊl ~s z
arous|e ə 'raʊz ~ed d ~es ɪz əz ~ing ɪŋ
Arp ɑːp ‖ ɑːrp
arpeggio ɑː 'pedʒ i əʊ -'pedʒ əʊ
‖ ɑːr 'pedʒ i oʊ -'pedʒ oʊ ~ed d ~s z
arquebus 'ɑːk wɪb əs -wəb- ‖ 'ɑːrk- ~es ɪz əz
arrack 'ær ək -æk ‖ 'er-; ə 'ræk
arraign ə 'reɪn ~ed d ~ing ɪŋ ~ment/s
mənt/s ~s z
Arran 'ær ən ‖ 'er-
arrange ə 'reɪndʒ **arranged** ə 'reɪndʒd
arranges ə 'reɪndʒ ɪz -əz **arranging**
ə 'reɪndʒ ɪŋ
arrangement ə 'reɪndʒ mənt ~s s
arranger ə 'reɪndʒ ə ‖ -ᵊr ~s z
arrant 'ær ənt ‖ 'er- ~ly li
arras 'ær əs ‖ 'er- ~es ɪz əz
Arras 'ær əs ‖ 'er- —*Fr* [a ʁɑːs]
Arrau ə 'raʊ —*Sp* [a 'rrau]
array ə 'reɪ **arrayed** ə 'reɪd **arraying** ə 'reɪ ɪŋ
arrays ə 'reɪz
arrear ə 'rɪə ‖ ə 'rɪᵊr ~s z
arrearag|e ə 'rɪər ɪdʒ ‖ ə 'rɪr- ~es ɪz əz
Arrecife ˌær ə 'siːf eɪ -ɪ-, -e- ‖ ˌɑːr- —*Sp*
[a rre 'θi fe, -'si-]
arrest *v, n* ə 'rest ~ed ɪd əd ~ing/ly ɪŋ /li ~s s
arrestable ə 'rest əb ᵊl
arrester, arrestor ə 'rest ə ‖ -ᵊr ~s z
arrhythmia ə 'rɪð mi ə eɪ-
Arrian 'ær iˌən ‖ 'er-
arriere-pensee, arrière-pensée

A

,ær i eə 'pɒnˑs eɪ -pɒn 'seɪ ‖ -,er paɪn 'seɪ
,er- —*Fr* [aʁ jɛʁ pɑ̃ se]
arris 'ær ɪs §-əs ‖ 'er- ~**es** ɪz əz
arrival ə 'raɪv ᵊl ~**s** z
  ar'rival time
arrive ə 'raɪv **arrived** ə 'raɪvd **arrives** ə 'raɪvz
  arriving ə 'raɪv ɪŋ
arrivederci ə ,riːv ə 'dɔːtʃ i -'deətʃ- ‖ -'dertʃ i
  —*It* [aˑr ri ve 'der tʃi]
arriving ə 'raɪv ɪŋ
arriviste, ~s ,ær iː 'viːst -'vɪst; ə 'riːv ɪst ‖ ,er-
  —*Fr* [a ʁi vist]
Arrochar 'ær ək ə -əx- ‖ -ᵊr 'er-
arrogance 'ær əg ənˑs ‖ 'er-
arrogant 'ær əg ənt ‖ 'er- ~**ly** li
arro|gate 'ær ə |geɪt ‖ 'er- ~**gated** geɪt ɪd -əd
  ‖ geɪt̬ əd ~**gates** geɪts ~**gating**
  geɪt ɪŋ ‖ geɪt̬ ɪŋ
arrogation ,ær ə 'geɪʃ ᵊn ‖ ,er- ~**s** z
arrondissement
  ,ær ɒn 'diːs mɒ̃ ‖ æ ,raɪnd iːs 'maːn ə- —*Fr*
  [a ʁɔ̃ dis mɑ̃]
arrow 'ær əʊ ‖ -oʊ 'er- ~**ed** d ~**ing** ɪŋ ~**s** z
arrowhead 'ær əʊ hed ‖ -oʊ- 'er- ~**s** z
arrowroot 'ær əʊ ruːt ‖ -oʊ- 'er-
Arrowsmith 'ær əʊ smɪθ ‖ -oʊ- 'er-
arrowwood 'ær əʊ wʊd ‖ -oʊ- 'er-
arroyo ə 'rɔɪ əʊ ‖ -oʊ —*Sp* [a 'rro jo] ~**s** z
ars ɑːz ‖ ɑːrs
  ,ars po'etica pəʊ 'et ɪk ə ‖ poʊ 'et̬-
arse ɑːs ‖ æs ɑːrs **arsed** ɑːst ‖ æst ɑːrst **arses**
  'ɑːs ɪz -əz ‖ 'æs- 'ɑːrs- **arsing** 'ɑːs ɪŋ ‖ 'æs-
  'ɑːrs-
arsehole 'ɑːs həʊl →-hɒʊl ‖ 'æs hoʊl 'ɑːrs- ~**d**
  d ~**s** z
arsenal, A~ 'ɑːs ᵊn‿ᵊl ‖ 'ɑːrs- ~**s, ~'s** z
arsenate 'ɑːs ə neɪt -ɪ-; -ᵊn ət, -ɪn-, -ɪt ‖ 'ɑːrs-
  ~**s** s
arsenic *n* 'ɑːs ᵊn‿ɪk ‖ 'ɑːrs-
arsenic *adj* ɑː 'sen ɪk ‖ ɑːr- ~**al/s** ᵊl/z
arsenide 'ɑːs ə naɪd -ɪ- ‖ 'ɑːrs- ~**s** z
arsine 'ɑːs iːn ‖ 'ɑːrs- ɑːr 'siːn
arsis 'ɑːs ɪs §-əs ‖ 'ɑːrs-
arson 'ɑːs ᵊn ‖ 'ɑːrs-
arsonist 'ɑːs ᵊn ɪst §-əst ‖ 'ɑːrs- ~**s** s
art *n* ɑːt ‖ ɑːrt —*but in certain French phrases*
  also ɑː ‖ ɑːr **arts** ɑːts ‖ ɑːrts —*See also*
  phrases with this word
  'art form; ,arts and 'crafts; 'Arts ,Faculty
art *v, from* **be**, *usual form* ɑːt ‖ ɑːrt, *occasional*
  weak form ət ‖ ᵊrt
Art *name* ɑːt ‖ ɑːrt
Artaxerxes ,ɑːt ə 'zɜːks iːz -əg-, -ək-, '•‿•,••
  ‖ ,ɑːrt̬ ə 'zɜːks iːz
art deco, Art Deco ,ɑːt 'dek əʊ ,ɑː-, -'deɪk-
  ‖ ,ɑːrt̬ deɪ 'koʊ ,ɑːr-, -'deɪk oʊ —*Fr* Art Déco
  [aʁ de ko]
artefact 'ɑːt ɪ fækt -ə- ‖ 'ɑːrt̬- ~**s** s
Artemis 'ɑːt ɪm ɪs -əm-, §-əs ‖ 'ɑːrt̬-
artemisia ,ɑːt ɪ 'mɪz i‿ə ,•ə-, -'miːz-
  ‖ ,ɑːrt̬ ə 'mɪʒ ə -'mɪʒ i‿ə, -'mɪz- ~**s** z
Artemus 'ɑːt ɪm əs -əm- ‖ 'ɑːrt̬-
arterial ɑː 'tɪər i‿əl ‖ ɑːr 'tɪr- ~**ly** i

arteries 'ɑːt ər iz ‖ 'ɑːrt̬-
arteriole ɑː 'tɪər i‿əʊl →-ɒʊl ‖ ɑːr 'tɪr i oʊl ~**s**
  z
arteriosclerosis ɑː ,tɪər i əʊ sklə 'rəʊs ɪs
  -sklɪə'•-, -sklɪ'•-, §-əs
  ‖ ɑːr ,tɪr i oʊ sklə 'roʊs əs
Arterton 'ɑːt ət ᵊn ‖ 'ɑːrt̬ ᵊrt ᵊn
arter|y 'ɑːt ər li ‖ 'ɑːrt̬- ~**ies** iz
artesian ɑː 'tiːz i‿ən -'tiːʒ-; -'tiːʒ ᵊn
  ‖ ɑːr 'tiːʒ ᵊn
  ar,tesian 'well
Artex *tdmk* 'ɑːt eks ‖ 'ɑːrt-
artful 'ɑːt fᵊl -fʊl ‖ 'ɑːrt- ~**ly** ‿i
  ,Artful 'Dodger
Arthington *(i)* 'ɑːð ɪŋ tən ‖ 'ɑːrð-, *(ii)*
  'ɑːθ- ‖ 'ɑːrθ-
arthr- *comb. form before vowel*
  with stressed suffix ɑː θr+ ‖ ɑːr θr+ —
  arthralgia ɑː 'θrældʒ i‿ə ‖ ɑːr-
  with unstressed suffix |ɑːθ r+ ‖ |ɑːrθ r+ —
  arthrous 'ɑːθ rəs ‖ 'ɑːrθ-
arthritic ɑː 'θrɪt ɪk ‖ ɑːr 'θrɪt̬ ɪk ~**ally** ᵊl‿i
arthritis ɪs ⚠,ɑːθ ə 'raɪt-, §-əs
  ‖ ɑːr 'θraɪt̬ əs
arthro- *comb. form*
  with stress-neutral suffix |ɑːθ rəʊ ‖ |ɑːrθ rə —
  arthrospore 'ɑːθ rəʊ spɔː ‖ 'ɑːrθ rə spɔːr
  -spoʊr
  with stress-imposing suffix
  ɑː 'θrɒ+ ‖ ɑːr 'θrɑː+ — **arthropodous**
  ɑː 'θrɒp əd əs ‖ ɑːr 'θrɑːp-
arthropod 'ɑːθ rə pɒd ‖ 'ɑːrθ rə pɑːd ~**s** z
Arthur 'ɑːθ ə ‖ 'ɑːrθ ᵊr
Arthurian ɑː 'θjʊər i‿ən -'θʊər- ‖ ɑːr 'θʊr-
artic *'articulated vehicle'* ɑː 'tɪk 'ɑːt ɪk ‖ ɑːr- ~**s**
  s
artichoke 'ɑːt ɪ tʃəʊk -ə- ‖ 'ɑːrt̬ ə tʃoʊk ~**s** s
article 'ɑːt ɪk ᵊl ‖ 'ɑːrt̬- ~**d** d ~**s** z
articulate *adj* ɑː 'tɪk jʊl ət -jəl-, -ɪt
  ‖ ɑːr 'tɪk jəl ət ~**ly** li ~**ness** nəs nɪs
articu|late *v* ɑː 'tɪk ju |leɪt -jə- ‖ ɑːr 'tɪk jə-
  ~**lated** leɪt ɪd -əd ‖ leɪt̬ əd ~**lates** leɪts
  ~**lating** leɪt ɪŋ ‖ leɪt̬ ɪŋ
articulation ɑː ,tɪk ju 'leɪʃ ᵊn -jə- ‖ ɑːr ,tɪk jə-
  ~**s** z
articulative ɑː 'tɪk jʊl ət ɪv -ju leɪt ɪv
  ‖ ɑːr 'tɪk jəl ət̬ ɪv -jə leɪt̬-
articulator ɑː 'tɪk ju leɪt ə -'•jə-
  ‖ ɑːr 'tɪk jə leɪt̬ ᵊr
articulator|y ɑː 'tɪk jʊl ət‿ᵊr li -'•jəl-;
  ɑː ,tɪk ju 'leɪt ᵊr li, -, •jə-, •'••••
  ‖ ɑːr 'tɪk jəl ə tɔːr li -toʊr i ~**ily** ᵊl i ɪ li
arti... —*see* **arty**
artifact 'ɑːt ɪ fækt -ə- ‖ 'ɑːrt̬- ~**s** s
artific|e 'ɑːt ɪf ɪs -əf-, §-əs ‖ 'ɑːrt̬- ~**es** ɪz əz
artificer ɑː 'tɪf ɪs ə -əs- ‖ ɑːr 'tɪf əs ᵊr ~**s** z
artificial ,ɑːt ɪ 'fɪʃ ᵊl ◄ -ə-, ‖ ,ɑːrt̬- ~**ly** i
  ,arti,ficial in'telligence; ,arti,ficial 'kidney;
  ,arti,ficial ,respi'ration
artificiality ,ɑːt ɪ ,fɪʃ i 'æl ət i ,•ə-, -ɪt i
  ‖ ,ɑːrt̬ ə ,fɪʃ i 'æl ət̬ i
artillery ɑː 'tɪl ər‿i ‖ ɑːr-

Articulation

1 Articulation is the production of speech sounds by using the speech organs to modify the air stream set in motion by the lungs. (Regularly in some languages, and very occasionally in English, the air may be set in motion in a way not involving the lungs. This applies, for example, in CLICKS.)
Consonants are classified according to their **place** and **manner** of articulation.

2 English consonant sounds have the following **places of articulation**:

p, b, m	are **bilabials**,	articulated by the lower lip against the upper lip
f, v	are **labiodentals**,	articulated by the lower lip against the upper teeth
θ, ð	are **dentals**,	articulated by the tongue tip against the upper teeth
t, d, n, l, s, z	are **alveolars**,	articulated by the tongue tip or blade against the alveolar ridge
r, tr, dr	are **post-alveolars**,	articulated by raising the tongue tip towards the rear of the alveolar ridge
ʃ, ʒ, tʃ, dʒ	are **palato-alveolars**,	articulated by the retracted blade of the tongue against the alveolar ridge and hard palate (usually accompanied by some lip-rounding)
j	is a **palatal**,	articulated by raising the front of the body of the tongue towards the hard palate
k, g, ŋ	are **velars**,	articulated by the back of the tongue against the soft palate
w	is a **labial-velar**,	articulated by raising the back of the tongue towards the soft palate and rounding the lips
ʔ	is a **glottal**	(see GLOTTAL STOP)

3 Note that in some other languages there are also

- **alveolo-palatals**, articulated by the front of the body of the tongue against the hard palate, together with raising the blade of the tongue towards the alveolar ridge (e.g. the Japanese *sh* ç)
- **labial-palatals**, articulated like palatals but with rounding of the lips (e.g. the French ɥ in *juin* ʒɥ æ̃)
- **retroflexes**, articulated by curling the tongue tip back against the alveolar ridge or hard palate (e.g. the Hindi *ʈ* ʈ)
- **uvulars**, articulated by the extreme back of the tongue against the uvula (e.g. the French *r* ʁ)
- **pharyngals**, articulated by squeezing the pharynx (e.g. the Arabic ' ʕ)

A

▶ *Articulation*

4 English consonants have the following typical **manners of articulation**:

p, t, k, b, d, g	are **plosives**,	articulated with a complete obstruction of the mouth passage, entirely blocking the air-flow for a moment
f, v, θ, ð, s, z, ʃ, ʒ	are **fricatives**,	articulated by narrowing the mouth passage so as to make the air-flow turbulent, while allowing it to pass through continuously
tʃ, dʒ (and also usually tr, dr)	are **affricates**,	articulated with first a complete obstruction and then a narrowing of the mouth passage (see AFFRICATES)
m, n, ŋ	are **nasals**,	articulated by completely obstructing the mouth passage but allowing the air to pass out through the nose
r, l	are **liquids**,	articulated by diverting or modifying the air-flow through the mouth
j, w	are **semivowels**,	articulatorily like vowels, but functioning as consonants because they are not syllabic

Plosives, fricatives and affricates are all **obstruents**; nasals, liquids and semivowels are **sonorants**. Liquids and semivowels are usually **approximants** (= the air escapes freely through the mouth with no turbulence).

---

artillery|man ɑː 'tɪl ər_i |mən -mæn ‖ ɑːr-
  ~men mən men
artisan ˌɑːt ɪ 'zæn -ə-, '••• ‖ 'ɑːrt̬ əz ən -əs-
  (*) ~s z
artisanate ˌɑːt ɪ 'zæn eɪt -ə- ‖ 'ɑːrt̬ əz ə neɪt
  '•əs-
artist 'ɑːt ɪst §-əst ‖ 'ɑːrt̬ əst ~s s
artiste ɑː 'tiːst ‖ ɑːr- —Fr [aʁ tist] ~s s
artistic ɑː 'tɪst ɪk ‖ ɑːr- ~ally əl_i
artistry 'ɑːt ɪst ri §-əst- ‖ 'ɑːrt̬-
artless 'ɑːt ləs -lɪs ‖ 'ɑːrt- ~ly li ~ness nəs nɪs
art nouveau, Art Nouveau ˌɑːt nuː 'vəʊ ˌɑː-
  ‖ ˌɑːrt nuː 'voʊ ˌɑːr- —Fr [aʁ nu vo]
Artois ɑː 'twɑː ‖ ɑːr- —Fr [aʁ twa]
artsy-craftsy ˌɑːts i 'krɑːfts i ◄ §-'kræfts-
  ‖ ˌɑːrts i 'kræfts i ◄
Arturo ɑː 'tʊər əʊ ‖ ɑːr 'tʊr oʊ —It [ar 'tuː ro]
artwork 'ɑːt wɜːk ‖ 'ɑːrt wɜ˞ːk
art|y 'ɑːt |i ‖ 'ɑːrt̬ |i ~ier i_ə ‖ i_ər ~iest i_ɪst
  i_əst ~ily ɪ li əl i ~iness i nəs i nɪs
arty-crafty ˌɑːt i 'krɑːft i ◄ §-'kræft-
  ‖ ˌɑːrt̬ i 'kræft i ◄
arty-farty ˌɑːt i 'fɑːt i ◄ ‖ ˌɑːrt̬ i 'fɑːrt̬ i ◄
Arub|a ə 'ruːb |ə —Dutch [ɑ 'ry: baː] ~an/s
  ən/z
arugula ə 'ruːg əl ə -jʊl-, -jəl-

arum 'eər əm ‖ 'er- 'ær-
Arun 'ær ən ‖ 'er-
Arundel (i) 'ær ənd əl ‖ 'er-, (ii) ə 'rʌnd əl —The
  place in Sussex is (i), that in MD (ii).
arvo 'ɑːv əʊ ‖ -oʊ ~s z
Arwel 'ɑː wel ‖ 'ɑːr- —Welsh ['ar wel]
Arwyn 'ɑː wɪn ‖ 'ɑːr- —Welsh ['ar win, -wɪn]
-ary əri, eri —In words of three syllables this
  suffix is usually weak, ər i ('binary, 'glossary).
  In longer words it is usually weak in BrE, ər i
  (frequently reduced to ri); but strong in AmE,
  er i : thus 'arbitrary 'ɑːb ɪtr ər i ‖ 'ɑːrb ə trer i,
  'customary 'kʌst əm ər_i ‖ 'kʌst ə mer i. The
  stress may fall either one or two syllables
  further back (ex'emplary, ˌanni'versary;
  'mercenary, ˌinter'planetary). A few words differ
  in stress as between BrE and AmE (co'rollary
  ‖ 'corollary).
Aryan 'eər i_ən 'ɑːr- ‖ 'er- 'ær-, 'ɑːr- ~s z
aryl 'ær ɪl -əl ‖ 'er-
arytenoid ˌær ɪ 'tiːn ɔɪd ◄-ə- ‖ ə 'rɪt ən ɔɪd
  ˌær ə 'tiːn ɔɪd, ˌer- (*) ~s z
  ˌary,tenoid 'cartilage ‖ •,••••-
as strong form æz, weak form əz
as- This variant of ad- is usually ə, but æ if

A

stressed because of a suffix (as'sign; ˌassig'nation).
Asa *(i)* 'eɪs ə, *(ii)* 'eɪz ə, *(iii)* 'ɑːs ə
asafetida, asafoetida ˌæs ə 'fet ɪd ə -'fiːt-, §-əd- ‖ -'feṭ əd ə
asap *'as soon as possible'* ˌeɪ es eɪ 'piː —*sometimes spoken as* 'eɪs æp, 'æs-
Asaph 'æs əf
asarabacca ˌæs ər ə 'bæk ə
asbestos æs 'best əs æz-, -ɒs
asbestosis ˌæs be 'stəʊs ɪs ˌæz-, §-əs ‖ -'stoʊs-
Asbury 'æz bər_i ‖ 'æz ˌber i -bər_i
ˌAsbury 'Park
ascarid 'æsk ə rɪd ~s z
Ascalon 'æsk ə lɒn -əl ən ‖ -lɑːn
ascend ə 'send —*also, when in contrast with* descend, ˌæ- ~**ed** ɪd əd ~**ing** ɪŋ ~s z
ascendanc|e ə 'send ən¹s ~**y** i
ascendant ə 'send ənt
ascendenc|e ə 'send ən¹s ~**y** i
ascendent ə 'send ənt
ascender ə 'send ə ‖ -ᵊr ~s z
ascension, A~ ə 'sen¹ʃ ən
As'cension Day
Ascensiontide ə 'sen¹ʃ ən taɪd
ascent ə 'sent —*also, when in contrast with* descent, ˌæ- (= *assent*) ~s s
ascertain ˌæs ə 'teɪn ‖ -ᵊr- ~**ed** d ~**ing** ɪŋ ~s z
ascertainable ˌæs ə 'teɪn əb ᵊl ◄ ‖ -ᵊr-
ascertainment ˌæs ə 'teɪn mənt →-'teɪm- ‖ -ᵊr-
ascetic ə 'set ɪk æ- ‖ -'seṭ ɪk ~**ally** ᵊl_i ~s s
asceticism ə 'set ɪ ˌsɪz əm æ-, -ə, •- ‖ -'seṭ-
Asch æʃ
Ascham 'æsk əm
Ascherson 'æʃ əs ən ‖ -ᵊrs-
asci 'æsk aɪ 'æs-, -iː
ascidian ə 'sɪd i_ən ~s z
ASCII 'æsk i
ASCIIzation ˌæsk i aɪ 'zeɪʃ ᵊn -i_ɪ- ‖ -i_ə- ~s z
Asclepius ə 'skliːp i_əs æ-
Ascomycetes, a~ ˌæsk əʊ maɪ 'siːt iːz ‖ -ou maɪ 'siːṭ iːz
Ascona æ 'skəʊn ə ‖ -'skoʊn- —*It* [as 'koː na]
ascorbic ə 'skɔːb ɪk æ- ‖ -'skɔːrb-
Ascot, ascot 'æsk ət §-ɒt ‖ -ɑːt ~'s, ~s s
ascribable ə 'skraɪb əb ᵊl
ascrib|e ə 'skraɪb ~**ed** d ~**es** z ~**ing** ɪŋ
ascription ə 'skrɪp ʃᵊn æ- ~s z
ascus 'æsk əs **asci** 'æsk aɪ 'æs-, -iː
Asda *tdmk* 'æz də
asdic 'æz dɪk ~s s
-ase eɪz eɪs — **oxidase** 'ɒks ɪ deɪz -ə-, -deɪs ‖ 'ɑːks-
ASEAN 'æz i_ən 'æs-
asepsis ₍ᵢ₎eɪ 'seps ɪs ə-, æ-
aseptic ₍ᵢ₎eɪ 'sept ɪk ə-, æ-
asexual ₍ᵢ₎eɪ 'sek ʃu_əl æ-, -'seks ju_əl, -'sek ʃᵊl ~**ly** i
Asfordby 'æs fəd bi 'æz-, →-fəb- ‖ -fᵊrd-
Asgarby 'æz gə bi ‖ -gᵊr-
Asgard 'æs gɑːd 'æz- ‖ -gɑːrd

ash, Ash æʃ **ashes** 'æʃ ɪz -əz
ˌAsh 'Wednesday
ashamed ə 'ʃeɪmd
Ashanti ə 'ʃænt i ‖ -'ʃɑːnt-
Ashbee 'æʃ bi -biː
ashbin 'æʃ bɪn ~s z
Ashbourne 'æʃ bɔːn ‖ -bɔːrn -boʊrn
Ashburton æʃ 'bɜːt ᵊn 'æʃ ˌbɜːt-, -bət- ‖ 'æʃ ˌbɜːt ᵊn
Ashby 'æʃ bi
Ashby-de-la-Zouch ˌæʃ bi də lə 'zuːʃ ˌ•・'•, -lɑː' •
ashcan 'æʃ kæn ~s z
Ashcombe 'æʃ kəm
Ashcroft 'æʃ krɒft ‖ -krɔːft -krɑːft
Ashdod 'æʃ dɒd ‖ -dɑːd
Ashdown 'æʃ daʊn
Ashe æʃ
ashen 'æʃ ᵊn
Asher 'æʃ ə ‖ -ᵊr
ashes, Ashes 'æʃ ɪz -əz
Asheville 'æʃ vɪl
Ashfield 'æʃ fiːᵊld
Ashford 'æʃ fəd ‖ -fᵊrd
ashi... —*see* **ashy**
Ashington 'æʃ ɪŋ tən
Ashkenaz|i, ~y ˌæʃ kə 'nɑːz i -kɪ- ‖ -ɑːʃ- ~**im** ɪm §-əm
Ashkhabad 'æʃ kə bæd -bɑːd; ˌ•・'•, ˌɑːʃ- ‖ ˌɑːʃ kə 'bɑːd '•・• —*Russ* [əʃ xʌ 'bat]
ashlar 'æʃ lə ‖ -lᵊr ~s z
Ashleigh, Ashley, Ashlie 'æʃ li
Ashman 'æʃ mən
Ashmole 'æʃ məʊl →-mɒʊl ‖ -moʊl
Ashmolean æʃ 'məʊl i_ən ‖ -'moʊl-
Ashmore 'æʃ mɔː ‖ -mɔːr -moʊr
ashore ə 'ʃɔː ‖ ə 'ʃɔːr -'ʃoʊr
ashplant 'æʃ plɑːnt §-plænt ‖ -plænt ~s s
ashram 'æʃ rəm 'ɑːʃ-, -ræm ~s z
Ashton 'æʃt ən
Ashton-in-Makerfield ˌæʃt ən ɪn 'meɪk ə fiːᵊld →-ɪm'•- ‖ -ᵊr fiːᵊld
Ashton-under-Lyne ˌæʃt ən ˌʌnd ə 'laɪn ˌ•・'•・• ‖ -ˌʌnd ᵊr-
Ashtoreth 'æʃt ə reθ
ashtray 'æʃ treɪ ~s z
Ashurst 'æʃ hɜːst -ɜːst ‖ -hɜːst
Ashwell 'æʃ wəl -wel
Ashworth 'æʃ wɜːθ ‖ -wɜːθ
ash|y 'æʃ li ~**ier** i_ə ‖ i_ᵊr ~**iest** i_ɪst i_əst

ASIA

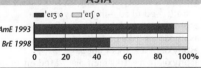

	■'eɪʒ ə □'eɪʃ ə				
AmE 1993					
BrE 1998					
0	20	40	60	80	100%

Asia 'eɪʒ ə 'eɪʃ ə —*Poll panel preferences: AmE 1993,* 'eɪʒ ə *91%,* 'eɪʃ ə *9%; BrE 1998,* 'eɪʃ ə *49%,* 'eɪʒ ə *51%.*
ˌAsia 'Minor
Asiago ˌæz i 'ɑːg əʊ ‖ ˌɑːs i 'ɑːg ou ˌɑːz-, ˌɑːʃ-, ˌɑːʒ- —*It* [a 'zjaː go]
Asian 'eɪʒ ᵊn 'eɪʃ- ~s z

Asiana *tdmk* ˌæs i ˈɑːn ə
Asian-American ˌeɪʒ ᵊn_ə ˈmer ɪk ᵊn ◄ ˌeɪʃ-
Asiatic ˌeɪʒ i ˈæt ɪk ◄ ˌeɪz-, ˌeɪʃ-, ˌeɪs-
‖ -ˈæt̬ ɪk ◄ ~s s
Asics *tdmk* ˈæz ɪks ˈæs-
aside ə ˈsaɪd ~s z
Asimov ˈæs ɪ mɒv ˈæz-, -ə- ‖ ˈæz ə mɑːf -mɔːf
asinine ˈæs ɪ naɪn -ə- ~ly li
asininity ˌæs ɪ ˈnɪn ət i, •ə-, -ɪt i ‖ -ət̬ i
ask ɑːsk §æsk, Δɑːks ‖ æsk asked ˈɑːskt
§æskt, Δɑːkst ‖ æskt asking ˈɑːsk ɪŋ
§ˈæsk-, Δˈɑːks- ‖ ˈæsk ɪŋ asks ɑːsks §æsks,
Δˈɑːks ɪz ‖ æsks
 ˈasking price
askance ə ˈskænts -ˈskɑːnts ‖ ə ˈskænts
askari æ ˈskɑːr i ə- ~s z
Aske æsk
Askelon ˈæsk əl ən -ɪl-, -ə lɒn, -ɪ- ‖ -ə lɑːn
askew *adv* ə ˈskjuː
Askew *family name* ˈæsk juː
Askey ˈæsk i
Askham ˈæsk əm
Askrigg ˈæsk rɪg
aslant ə ˈslɑːnt §-ˈslænt ‖ ə ˈslænt
asleep ə ˈsliːp
ASLEF ˈæz lef
A/S level ˌeɪ ˈes ˌlev ᵊl ~s z
ASLIB ˈæz lɪb
Asmara ˌæs ˈmɑːr ə æz- ‖ -ˈmær-, -ˈmer-
Asmodeus æs ˈməʊd i_əs ˌæs məʊ ˈdiːˌəs
‖ ˌæz mə ˈdiːˌəs
asocial ₍ˌ₎eɪ ˈsəʊʃ ᵊl ‖ -ˈsoʊʃ-
Asoka ə ˈsəʊk ə -ˈʃəʊk- ‖ ə ˈsoʊk ə —*Hindi*
[ə ʃoːk]
asp æsp asps æsps
asparagus ə ˈspær əg əs -ˈsper-
aspartame ˈæsp ə teɪm ə ˈspɑːt eɪm ‖ -ᵊr-
aspartic ə ˈspɑːt ɪk ‖ ə ˈspɑːrt̬-
Aspasia æ ˈspeɪz i_ə ə-, -ˈspeɪʒ- ‖ æ ˈspeɪʒ ə
Aspatria ə ˈspeɪtr i_ə æ-
aspect ˈæsp ekt ~s s
 ˈaspect ˌratio
aspectual ə ˈspek tʃu_əl ə-, -tju_ ~ly i
Aspel, Aspell ˈæsp ᵊl
aspen, Aspen ˈæsp ən ~s z
Asperges, a~ æ ˈspɜːdʒ iːz ə- ‖ -ˈspɜːdʒ-
asperit|y æ ˈsper ət i ə-, -ɪt- ‖ -ət̬ i ~ies iz
aspersion ə ˈspɜːʃ ᵊn æ-, §-ˈspɜːʒ- ‖ -ˈspɜːʒ-
-ˈspɜːʃ- ~s z
asphalt ˈæs fælt ˈæʃ-, -fɒlt, Δ-felt ‖ -fɔːlt
-fɑːlt ~ed ɪd əd ~ing ɪŋ ~s s
asphodel ˈæs fə del ˈæʃ- ~s z
asphyxia æs ˈfɪks i_ə əs-
asphyxiant æs ˈfɪks i_ənt əs-
asphyxi|ate æs ˈfɪks i_eɪt əs- ~ated eɪt ɪd -əd
‖ eɪt̬ əd ~ates eɪts ~ating eɪt ɪŋ ‖ eɪt̬ ɪŋ
asphyxiation æs ˌfɪks i_ˈeɪʃ ᵊn əs- ~s z
aspic ˈæsp ɪk
aspidistra ˌæsp ɪ ˈdɪs trə -ə- ~s z
Aspinall ˈæsp ɪn ᵊl -ən-; -ɪ nɔːl, -ə-
aspirant ˈæsp ᵊr ənt -ɪr-; ə ˈspaɪᵊr- ~s s
aspi|rate *v* ˈæsp ə ǀreɪt -ɪ- ~rated reɪt ɪd -əd

‖ reɪt̬ əd ~rates reɪts ~rating
reɪt ɪŋ ‖ reɪt̬ ɪŋ
aspirate *n* ˈæsp ᵊr_ət -ɪr-, ˌɪt ~s s
aspiration ˌæsp ə ˈreɪʃ ᵊn -ɪ- ~al ᵊl ~s z
aspirator ˈæsp ə reɪt ə ˈ•ɪ- ‖ -reɪt̬ ᵊr ~s z
aspire ə ˈspaɪ_ə ‖ ə ˈspaɪ_ᵊr ~d d ~s z
 aspiring ə ˈspaɪ_ər ɪŋ ‖ ə ˈspaɪ_ᵊr ɪŋ
aspirin ˈæsp rɪn -rən; ˈæsp ᵊr ᵊn, -ɪn ~s z
aspiring ə ˈspaɪ_ər ɪŋ ‖ ə ˈspaɪ_ᵊr ɪŋ ~ly li
asplenium æ ˈspliːn i_əm ə- ~s z
Aspley ˈæsp li
Asprey ˈæsp ri
Aspro *tdmk* ˈæsp rəʊ ‖ -roʊ ~s z
Asquith ˈæsk wɪθ
ass æs —*As a term of abuse, in BrE also* ɑːs
*(which may however be taken as a
pronunciation rather of* arse) asses ˈæs ɪz -əz
assagai ˈæs ə gaɪ ~s z
assai æ ˈsaɪ —*It* [as ˈsai]
assail ə ˈseɪᵊl ~ed d ~ing ɪŋ ~s z
assailant ə ˈseɪl ənt ~s s
Assam æ ˈsæm ˈæs æm
Assamese ˌæs ə ˈmiːz ◄ -æ- ‖ -ˈmiːs
assassin ə ˈsæs ɪn -ᵊn ~s z
assassi|nate ə ˈsæs ɪ ǀneɪt -ə- ~nated neɪt ɪd
-əd ‖ neɪt̬ əd ~nates neɪts ~nating
neɪt ɪŋ ‖ neɪt̬ ɪŋ
assassination ə ˌsæs ɪ ˈneɪʃ ᵊn -ə- ~s z
assault ə ˈsɔːlt -ˈsɒlt ‖ -ˈsɑːlt ~ed ɪd əd ~ing
ɪŋ ~s s
 as'sault course
assay *n* ə ˈseɪ æ-; ˈæs eɪ ‖ ˈæs eɪ æ ˈseɪ ~s z
assay *v* ə ˈseɪ æ- ~ed d ~ing ɪŋ ~s z
assegai ˈæs ɪ gaɪ -ə- ~s z
assemblag|e ə ˈsem blɪdʒ —*but with reference
to wine blending,* ˌæs ɒm ˈblɑːʒ ‖ ˌɑːs ɑːm-
—*Fr* [a sɑ̃ blaːʒ] ~es ɪz əz
assembl|e ə ˈsem bᵊl ~ed d ~er/s _ə/z ǀ_ᵊr/z
~es z ~ing _ɪŋ
assem|bly ə ˈsem ǀbli ~blies bliz
 as'sembly ˌlanguage; as'sembly line
assembly|man ə ˈsem bli ǀmən ~men mən
men ~woman ˌwʊm ən ~women ˌwɪm ɪn
§-ən
assent *n, v* ə ˈsent (= *ascent*) assented
ə ˈsent ɪd -əd ‖ ə ˈsent̬ əd assenting
ə ˈsent ɪŋ ‖ ə ˈsent̬ ɪŋ assents ə ˈsents
Asser ˈæs ə ‖ -ᵊr
assert ə ˈsɜːt ‖ ə ˈsɜːt asserted ə ˈsɜːt ɪd -əd
‖ ə ˈsɜːt̬ əd asserting ə ˈsɜːt ɪŋ ‖ ə ˈsɜːt̬ ɪŋ
asserts ə ˈsɜːts ‖ ə ˈsɜːts
assertion ə ˈsɜːʃ ᵊn ‖ ə ˈsɜː ᵊn ~s z
assertive ə ˈsɜːt ɪv ‖ ə ˈsɜːt̬ ɪv ~ly li ~ness
nəs nɪs
assess ə ˈses ~ed t ~es ɪz əz ~ing ɪŋ
assessment ə ˈses mənt ~s s
assessor ə ˈses ə ‖ -ᵊr ~s z
asset ˈæs et -ɪt ~s s
asset-strip|per/s ˈæs et ˌstrɪp ǀə/z -ɪt- ‖ -ᵊr/z
~ping ɪŋ
asseve|rate ə ˈsev ə ǀreɪt æ- ~rated reɪt ɪd -əd
‖ reɪt̬ əd ~rates reɪts ~rating
reɪt ɪŋ ‖ reɪt̬ ɪŋ

Aspiration

A

An **aspirated** consonant is one that is accompanied by a brief [h]-sound.
In certain environments the English plosives p, t, k are aspirated. That is to say,
there is a delay between the release of the primary closure of the articulators and
the beginning of voicing for the sound that follows. In the word **pan** pæn, for
example, the voicing for æ does not begin immediately after the lips separate for
the end of the p. There is a moment's delay, during which the air escapes freely
through the mouth, impeded neither by the lips nor by the vocal folds. This
constitutes the aspiration of the p. It is one of the ways we recognize the plosive
as being a p rather than a b.
We can distinguish three possibilities for the aspiration of English p, t, k,
depending on their position.

1 They are **aspirated**
when they occur at the **beginning of a syllable** in which the vowel is strong,
as in
pin pɪn (like pʰɪn),
tail teɪᵊl,
come kʌm,
appeal ə ˈpiːᵊl,
retain rɪ ˈteɪn,
maritime ˈmær ɪ taɪm.
If one of l, r, w, j comes between the plosive and the vowel, then aspiration
takes the form of making this consonant voiceless, as in
play pleɪ (here the l is voiceless),
approve ə ˈpruːv (the r is voiceless).
twin twɪn (the w is voiceless),
accuse ə ˈkjuːz (the j is voiceless).

2 They are **unaspirated**
• when preceded by s at the beginning of a syllable, as in **spin** spɪn (the ɪ
starts immediately upon the release of the p), **stack** stæk, **school** skuːl,
screen skriːn (the r may be voiced);
• when followed by any FRICATIVE, as in **lapse** læps, **depth** depθ, **sets** sets,
fix fɪks;
• if immediately followed by another plosive, as with the k in **doctor** ˈdɒktə
‖ ˈdɑːkt ᵊr. The release stage of the first plosive is then usually inaudible
('masked').

3 Otherwise, they are unaspirated or just slightly aspirated. For example:
ripe raɪp, **shut** ʃʌt, **lake** leɪk;
happy ˈhæp i, **writer** ˈraɪt ə (BrE), **lucky** ˈlʌk i;
wasp wɒsp ‖ wɑːsp, **resting** ˈrest ɪŋ, **Oscar** ˈɒsk ə ‖ ˈɑːsk ᵊr, **lifted**
ˈlɪft ɪd;
today tə ˈdeɪ (note that the t, although at the beginning of a syllable, is
followed by a WEAK vowel).

A

asseveration ə ˌsev ə 'reɪʃ ᵊn æ- ~s z
assez 'æs eɪ ‖ ɑː 'seɪ —Fr [a se]
asshole 'ɑːs həʊl 'æs-, →-hʊol ‖ 'æs hoʊl ~s z
assibi|late ə 'sɪb ə ǁeɪt æ-, -ɪ- ~lated leɪt ɪd
-əd ‖ leɪt̬ əd ~lates leɪts ~lating
leɪt ɪŋ ‖ leɪt̬ ɪŋ
assibilation ə ˌsɪb ə 'leɪʃ ᵊn æ-, -ɪ- ~s z
assiduit|y ˌæs ɪ 'djuː ət li ǀ•ə-, →§-'dʒuː-, ˌɪt i
‖ -'duː ət̬ li -'dʒuː- ~ies iz
assiduous ə 'sɪd juˍəs §-'sɪdʒ uˍ ‖ ə 'sɪdʒ uˍəs
~ly li ~ness nəs nɪs
assign ə 'saɪn ~ed d ~ing ɪŋ ~s z
assignab|le ə 'saɪn əb ᵊl ~ly li
assignat/s 'æs ɪg næt/s ˌæs iː 'njɑː/z —Fr
[a si nja]
assignation ˌæs ɪg 'neɪʃ ᵊn ~s z
assignee ˌæs aɪ 'niː -ɪ-, §-ə- ‖ ə ˌsaɪ 'niː
ˌæs ə 'niː ~s z
assignment ə 'saɪn mənt →-'saɪm- ~s s
assimilable ə 'sɪm əl əb ᵊl -'•ɪl-
assimi|late ə 'sɪm ə ǁeɪt -ɪ- ~lated leɪt ɪd -əd
‖ leɪt̬ əd ~lates leɪts ~lating leɪt ɪŋ ‖ leɪt̬ ɪŋ
assimilation ə ˌsɪm ə 'leɪʃ ᵊn -ɪ- ~s z
assimilative ə 'sɪm əl ət ɪv -ə leɪt ɪv ‖ -ə leɪt̬ ɪv
-əl ət̬- ~ly li
assimilatory ə 'sɪm əl ət ˌər i -'•ɪl-; •ˌ•ə 'leɪt
ər i, -ˌ•ɪ- ‖ -ə tɔːr i -toʊr i
Assiniboine ə 'sɪn ɪ bɔɪn -ə- ~s z
Assisi ə 'siːs i æ-, -'siːz- ‖ -'sɪs- —It [a 'siː zi]
assist ə 'sɪst ~ed ɪd əd ~ing ɪŋ ~s s
assistance ə 'sɪst ᵊns
assistant ə 'sɪst ᵊnt ~s s
As,sistant Pro'fessor; As,sistant 'Secretary
assiz|e ə 'saɪz ~es ɪz əz

BrE 1998

associ|ate v ə 'səʊs i‿ˌeɪt -'səʊʃ- ‖ ə 'soʊʃ-
ə 'soʊs- ~ated eɪt ɪd -əd ‖ eɪt̬ əd ~ates eɪts
~ating eɪt ɪŋ ‖ eɪt̬ ɪŋ —BrE 1998 poll panel
preference: -'səʊs- 69%, -'səʊʃ- 31%
associate n, adj ə 'səʊs i‿ət -'səʊʃ-, -ɪt, -eɪt
‖ ə 'soʊʃ- ə 'soʊs- ~s s

ASSOCIATION

BrE 1998

association ə ˌsəʊs i 'eɪʃ ᵊn ǀ -ˌsəʊʃ- ‖ ə ˌsoʊs-
ə ˌsoʊʃ- ~s z —BrE 1998 poll panel
preference: -ˌsəʊs- 78%, -ˌsəʊʃ- 22%
As,soci,ation 'football
associative ə 'səʊs i‿ət ɪv -'səʊʃ-, -eɪt ɪv
‖ ə 'soʊʃ i eɪt̬ ɪv -'soʊs-, ət̬ ɪv ~ly li
associativity ə ˌsəʊs iˍə 'tɪv ət i -ˌsəʊʃ-, -ɪt i
‖ ə ˌsoʊʃ iˍə 'tɪv ət̬ i -ˌsoʊs-
assonanc|e 'æs ᵊn ᵊnᵗs ~es ɪz əz
assonant 'æs ᵊn ənt ~s s
assort ə 'sɔːt ‖ ə 'sɔːrt assorted ə 'sɔːt ɪd -əd

‖ ə 'sɔːɾt əd assorting ə 'sɔːt ɪŋ ‖ ə 'sɔːrt̬ ɪŋ
assorts ə 'sɔːts ‖ ə 'sɔːrts
assortment ə 'sɔːt mənt ‖ ə 'sɔːrt- ~s s
Assouan, Assuan ˌæs 'wɑːn ◂ ˌɑːs-, -'wæn, '••
—Arabic [ʔa 'sˤwɑːn]
assuag|e ə 'sweɪdʒ ~ed d ~er/s ə/z ‖ ᵊr/z ~es
ɪz əz ~ement mənt ~ing ɪŋ
assuasive ə 'sweɪs ɪv -'sweɪz-

-'sjuːm -'suːm -'ʃuːm

BrE 1988

0   20   40   60   80   100%

assum|e ə 'sjuːm -'suːm, §-'ʃuːm ‖ ə 'suːm
—BrE 1988 poll panel preference: -'sjuːm
84%, -'suːm 11%, -'ʃuːm 5%. ~ed d ~es z
~ing/ly ɪŋ /li
assumption, A~ ə 'sʌmp ʃᵊn ~s z
assumptive ə 'sʌmp tɪv
assuranc|e ə 'ʃɔːr ᵊnᵗs -'ʃʊər- ‖ ə 'ʃʊr- -'ʃɝ:-
~es ɪz əz
assur|e ə 'ʃɔː- -'ʃʊə ‖ ə 'ʃʊᵊr -'ʃɝː ~ed d ~es z
assuring ə 'ʃɔːr ɪŋ -'ʃʊər- ‖ ə 'ʃʊr ɪŋ -'ʃɝː-
assuredly ə 'ʃɔːr ɪd li -'ʃʊər-, -əd- ‖ ə 'ʃʊr-
-'ʃɝː-
Assyri|a ə 'sɪr iˍə ~an/s ən/z
Assyriologist, a~ ə ˌsɪr i 'ɒl ədʒ ɪst §-əst
‖ -'ɑːl- ~s s
Assyriology ə ˌsɪr i 'ɒl ədʒ i ‖ -'ɑːl-
Asta 'æst ə
astable ˌₐeɪ 'steɪb ᵊl
Astaire ə 'steə ‖ ə 'steᵊr -'stæᵊr
Astarte æ 'stɑːt i ə- ‖ -'stɑːrt̬-
astatine 'æst ə tiːn -tɪn
Astbury 'æst bər‿i ‖ -ˌber i
aster 'æst ə ‖ -ᵊr ~s z
asterisk n, v 'æst ə rɪsk ⚠-rɪks ~ed t ~ing ɪŋ
~s s
asterism 'æst ə ˌrɪz ᵊm ~s z
Asterix 'æst ə rɪks
astern ə 'stɜːn ‖ ə 'stɝːn
asteroid 'æst ə rɔɪd ~s z
asthenia æs 'θiːn iˍə
asthenic æs 'θen ɪk ~al ᵊl
asthma 'æs mə 'æsθ- ‖ 'æz- (*)
asthmatic æs 'mæt ɪk æsθ- ‖ æz 'mæt̬ ɪk ~ally
ᵊl‿i ~s s
Asti 'æst i -iː ‖ 'ɑːst i —It ['as ti]
ˌAsti spu'mante spu 'mænt i ‖ spu 'mɑːnt i
—It [spu 'man te]
astigmatic ˌæst ɪg 'mæt ɪk ◂ ‖ -'mæt̬- ~ally ᵊl‿i
astigmatism ə 'stɪg mə ˌtɪz ᵊm æ- ~s z
astilbe ə 'stɪlb i ~s z
astir ə 'stɜː ‖ ə 'stɝː
Astle (i) 'æst ᵊl, (ii) 'æs ᵊl
Astley 'æst li
Aston 'æst ᵊn
ˌAston 'Martin tdmk; ˌAston 'Villa
astonish ə 'stɒn ɪʃ ‖ ə 'stɑːn ɪʃ ~ed t ~es ɪz
əz ~ing/ly ɪŋ /li
astonishment ə 'stɒn ɪʃ mənt ‖ -'stɑːn-
Astor 'æst ə ‖ -ᵊr
Astoria ə 'stɔːr iˍə æ-

Assimilation

1 **Assimilation** is a type of COARTICULATION. It is the alteration of a speech sound to make it more similar to its neighbours. In English it mainly affects PLACE OF ARTICULATION.

2 The alveolar consonants t, d, n, when they occur at the end of a word or syllable, can optionally assimilate to the place of articulation of the next syllable ('regressive' assimilation).

Thus n can become m before p, b, m, as in the examples

ten men ,ten 'men → ,tem 'men
downbeat 'daʊn biːt → 'daʊm biːt.

Similarly, n can become ŋ before k, g, as in

fine grade ,faɪn 'greɪd → ,faɪŋ 'greɪd
incredible ɪn 'kred əb ᵊl → ɪŋ 'kred əb ᵊl.

In the same way d can change to b and g respectively, as in

red paint ,red 'peɪnt → ,reb 'peɪnt
admit əd 'mɪt → əb 'mɪt
bad guys 'bæd gaɪz → 'bæg gaɪz.

It is also possible for t to change to p and k, though a more frequent possibility is for t, when followed by another consonant, to be realized as a GLOTTAL STOP.

eight boys ,eɪt 'bɔɪz → ,eɪp 'bɔɪz
or, more usually, → ,eɪʔ 'bɔɪz.

3 In the same way s and z can change to ʃ and ʒ respectively, but only before ʃ or j at the beginning of the next syllable. In **you, your** the j may then disappear.

this shape ,ðɪs 'ʃeɪp → ,ðɪʃ 'ʃeɪp
these shoes ,ðiːz 'ʃuːz → ,ðiːʒ 'ʃuːz
this unit ,ðɪs 'juːn ɪt → ,ðɪʃ 'juːn ɪt
unless you... ən 'les ju → ən 'leʃ (j)u
as you see ,æz ju 'siː → ,æʒ (j)u 'siː

4 Assimilation can also sometimes operate in the other direction: that is, a consonant can assimilate to the place of articulation of the consonant at the end of the preceding syllable ('progressive' assimilation). In English this applies only to SYLLABIC n, changing it to syllabic m or ŋ as appropriate.

ribbon ('rɪb ən →) 'rɪb n̩ → 'rɪb m̩
bacon ('beɪk ən →) 'beɪk n̩ → 'beɪk ŋ̍
up and down (,ʌp ən 'daʊn →) ,ʌp n̩ 'daʊn → ,ʌp m̩ 'daʊn

This assimilation can operate only if the words are said without a phonetic ə between the plosive and the nasal. Furthermore, it cannot apply if the sound after the nasal is a vowel.

happens ('hæp ənz →) 'hæp n̩z → 'hæp m̩z
happened ('hæp ənd →) 'hæp n̩d → 'hæp m̩d
happening ('hæp ən ɪŋ →) 'hæp n̩ ɪŋ (cannot assimilate further).

A

▶ *Assimilation*

5 Yod coalescence (or 'coalescent' assimilation) is the process which changes
t or d plus j into tʃ or dʒ respectively. Across word boundaries it mainly
affects phrases involving **you** or **your**.

> **let you out** ˌlet ju 'aʊt → ˌletʃ u 'aʊt
> **would you try** ˌwʊd ju 'traɪ → ˌwʊdʒ u 'traɪ
> **get your bags** ˌget jɔː 'bægz → ˌgetʃ ɔː 'bægz ‖ ˌget jᵊr 'bægz →
> ˌgetʃ ᵊr 'bægz

6 Within a word, the status of yod coalescence depends on whether the
following vowel is STRONG or WEAK.

- Where the vowel is strong, i.e. uː or ʊə, yod coalescence can frequently be
  heard in BrE, although not in careful RP. (In AmE there is usually no j, so
  the possibility does not arise.)
  > **tune** tjuːn → §tʃuːn
  > **endure** ɪn 'djʊə → §ɪn 'dʒʊə
- Where the vowel is weak, i.e. u or ə, assimilation is often variable in BrE,
  but obligatory in AmE.
  > **factual** 'fækt ju‿əl → 'fæk tʃu‿əl
  > **educate** 'ed ju keɪt -jə- → 'edʒ u keɪt -ə-

7 Historically, a process of yod coalescence is the origin of the tʃ used by all
speakers in words such as **nature**, and of the dʒ in words such as **soldier**.
Similarly, yod coalescence involving fricatives (sj → ʃ, zj → ʒ) explains the
ʃ in words such as **pressure, delicious, patient, Russian**, and the ʒ in words
such as **measure**. For example, **delicious** came to English from Latin via the
French **délicieux** de li sjø, but in English the sj coalesced into ʃ several
centuries ago.

8 Some speakers of BrE assimilate s to ʃ before tr and tʃ, thus **strong** strɒŋ→
ʃtrɒŋ, **student** 'stjuːd ᵊnt→ 'stʃuːd- → 'ʃtʃuːd-. This is not shown in LPD.
The EFL learner should not imitate it.

---

astound ə 'staʊnd **~ed** ɪd əd **~ing/ly** ɪŋ /li **~s**
z

astra, Astra 'æs trə

astragal 'æs trəg ᵊl -trɪg- **~s** z

astrag|alus ə 'stræg ləl əs **~ali** ə laɪ

astrakhan, A~ ˌæs trə 'kæn ◄ -'kɑːn —*Russ*
['as trə xᵊnʲ]

astral 'æs trᵊl **~ly** i

astray ə 'streɪ

Astrid 'æs trɪd

astride ə 'straɪd

astringency ə 'strɪndʒ ᵊn¦s i

astringent ə 'strɪndʒ ᵊnt **~ly** li **~s** s

astro- *comb. form*
> *with stress-neutral suffix* ˌæs trəʊ ‖ -trə —
> **astrosphere** 'æs trəʊ sfɪə ‖ -trə sfɪr
> *with stress-imposing suffix* ə 'strɒ+ æ 'strɒ+
> ‖ ə 'strɑː+ — **astrophorous** ə 'strɒf ᵊr əs
> æ- ‖ -'strɑːf-

astrodome, A~ 'æs trəʊ dəʊm ‖ -trə doʊm

astrolabe 'æs trəʊ leɪb ‖ -trə- **~s** z

astrologer ə 'strɒl ədʒ ə æ- ‖ ə 'strɑːl ədʒ ᵊr
~s z

astrological ˌæs trə 'lɒdʒ ɪk ᵊl ◄ ‖ -'lɑːdʒ- **~ly**
‿i

astrology ə 'strɒl ədʒ i æ- ‖ -'strɑːl-

astronaut 'æs trə nɔːt ‖ -nɑːt **~s** s

astronautical ˌæs trə 'nɔːt ɪk ᵊl ◄ ‖ -'nɔːt̮-
-'nɑːt̮- **~ly** ‿i

astronautics ˌæs trə 'nɔːt ɪks ‖ -'nɔːt̮- -'nɑːt̮-

astronomer ə 'strɒn əm ə ‖ ə 'strɑːn əm ᵊr **~s**
z

astronomic ˌæs trə 'nɒm ɪk ◄ ‖ -'nɑːm- **~al** ᵊl
~ally ᵊl‿i

astronomy ə 'strɒn əm i ‖ -'strɑːn-

astrophys|ical ˌæs trəʊ 'fɪz ɪk ᵊl ◄ ‖ ˌæs trə-
ˌ•troʊ- **~icist/s** ɪs ɪst/s -əs-, §-əst/s **~ics** ɪks

astroturf, AstroTurf *tdmk*
'æs trəʊ tɜːf ‖ -troʊ tɜ͟ːf   **~ed** t
Asturias æ 'stʊər i æs ə-, -'stjʊər-, -əs ‖ -'stʊr-
—*Sp* [as 'tur jas]
astute ə 'stjuːt æ-, →§-'stʃuːt ‖ ə 'stuːt
ə 'stjuːt   **~ly** li   **~ness** nəs nɪs
Astyanax æ 'staɪ ə næks ə-
Asuncion, Asunción æ ˌsʊnˢts i 'ɒn -'əʊn,
•'•• ‖ ɑː ˌsuːnˢts i 'oʊn ˌ•• —*AmSp*
[a sun 'sjon]
asunder ə 'sʌnd ə ‖ -ə͟r
Aswad 'æz wɒd ‖ -wɑːd
Aswan ˌæs 'wɑːn ◄ ˌɑːs-, -'wæn, '•• —*Arabic*
[ʔa 'sˤwaːn]
asyl|um ə 'saɪl ləm   **~a** ə   **~ums** əmz
asymmetric ˌeɪ sɪ 'metr ɪk ◄ ˌeɪ sə-, ˌæs ɪ-,
ˌæs ə-   **~al** əl   **~ally** əl_i
asymmetry ⁽ᵢ⁾æ 'sɪm ətr i ˌeɪ-, -ɪtr- ‖ ˌeɪ-
asymptote 'æs ɪmp təʊt -əmp- ‖ -toʊt   **~s** s
asymptotic ˌæs ɪmp 'tɒt ɪk ◄ -əmp-
‖ -'taːt̬ ɪk ◄   **~ally** əl_i
asynchronous ⁽ᵢ⁾eɪ 'sɪŋk rən əs -'sɪn krən-   **~ly** li
asyndetic ˌæs ɪn 'det ɪk ◄ §-ən-; ˌeɪ sɪn-
‖ -'det̬ ɪk ◄
asyndeton æ 'sɪnd ɪt ən ə-, §-ət-; -ɪ tɒn, -ə-
‖ ə 'sɪnd ə tɑːn ˌeɪ-
at *strong form* æt , *weak form* ət —*The phrase* at
all *'in any degree, ever' is usually syllabified*
irregularly as ə 'tɔːl *in BrE and sometimes as*
ə 'tɔːl, ə 'tɑːl *in AmE.*
at- *This variant of* ad- *is usually* ə (at'tach), *but* ˌæ
if stressed because of a suffix (ˌattri'bution).
atabrin, atabrine, A~ *tdmk* 'æt əb rɪn §-rən,
-ə briːn ‖ 'æt̬-
Atack 'eɪt æk
Atahualpa ˌæt ə 'waːlp ə -'wælp- ‖ ˌæt̬-
Atalanta ˌæt ə 'lænt ə ‖ ˌæt̬ ə 'lænt̬ ə
AT&T *tdmk* ˌeɪ ˌtiː ən 'tiː
Atari *tdmk* ə 'taːr i æ-
Ataturk, Atatürk 'æt ə tɜːk ‖ 'æt̬ ə tɜ͟ːk
—*Turkish* [a ta 'tyrk]
atavism 'æt ə ˌvɪz əm ‖ 'æt̬-
atavistic ˌæt ə 'vɪst ɪk ◄ ‖ ˌæt̬-   **~ally** əl_i
ataxia ə 'tæks i ə ⁽ᵢ⁾eɪ-, æ-
ataxic ə 'tæks ɪk   **~s** s
ataxy ə 'tæks i
Atchison 'ætʃ ɪs ən -əs-
atchoo ə 'tʃuː
Atco *tdmk* 'æt kəʊ ‖ -koʊ
ate *past of* **eat** et eɪt ‖ eɪt ▵et —*BrE 1988 poll*
panel preference: et 55%, eɪt 45%. *In AmE,*
however, et *is considered non-standard.*
Ate *Greek goddess* 'aːt i 'eɪt-, -iː ‖ 'eɪt̬ i
-ate eɪt ˌət ɪt ˌ|eɪt —*This suffix is regularly*
strong, eɪt , *in verbs, but often weakened to* ət ,
ɪt *in nouns and adjectives. Its influence on stress*
depends on the length of the word. (1) *In two-*
syllable verbs stress usually falls on the suffix in
BrE (vi'brate, cre'ate), *but on the stem in AmE*
('vibrate, 'create). (2) *In longer verbs, the stress*
generally falls on the antepenultimate
('demonstrate, dis'criminate, as'sociate). *There*

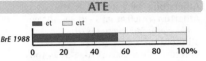

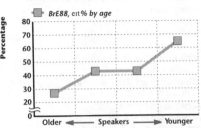

are a few exceptions and cases where speakers
disagree ('sequestrate *or* se'questrate). (3) *In*
nouns and adjectives the suffix is unstressed
('private, 'climate), *and in longer words the*
primary stress generally falls two syllables back
from the suffix ('delegate, 'vertebrate,
ap'propriate; *important exceptions are* in'nate,
or'nate, se'date). *The suffix vowel is generally*
weak in familiar words ('climate, 'private),
though in some words speakers vary ('candidate,
'magistrate). *In more technical words a strong*
vowel is retained ('sulphate, 'caudate). (4) *Note*
the distinction between verb and noun/adj in
cases such as 'separate, as'sociate, 'moderate,
'delegate.

A-team 'eɪ tiːm
atebrin *tdmk* 'æt əb rɪn §-rən, -ə briːn ‖ 'æt̬-
atelier ə 'tel i ˌeɪ æ-; 'æt əl jeɪ ‖ ˌæt̬ əl 'jeɪ —*Fr*
[a tə lje]   **~s** z
a tempo ⁽ᵢ⁾aː 'temp əʊ ‖ -oʊ
Athabasc|a, Athabask|a ˌæθ ə 'bæsk ə   **~an**
ən
Athanasian ˌæθ ə 'neɪʃ ən ◄ -'neɪʒ-; -'neɪʃ i ən,
-'neɪs-, -'neɪz- ‖ -'neɪʒ-
   the ˌAthə nasian' creed
Athanasius ˌæθ ə 'neɪʃ əs ◄ -'neɪʒ-; -'neɪʃ i əs,
-'neɪs-, -'neɪz- ‖ -'neɪʒ-
Athapascan, Athapaskan ˌæθ ə 'pæsk ən ◄
Athawes (i) 'æθ ɔːz ‖ -aːz, (ii) 'æt hɔːz ‖ -haːz
atheism 'eɪθ i ˌɪz əm
atheist 'eɪθ i ɪst §-əst   **~s** s
atheistic ˌeɪθ i 'ɪst ɪk ◄   **~al** əl   **~ally** əl_i
atheling 'æθ əl ɪŋ   **~s** z
Athelstan 'æθ əl stən -stæn —*in Old English*
was 'æð əl staːn
athematic ˌæθ iː 'mæt ɪk ◄ -ɪ-, -ə-; ˌeɪ θiː-, -θɪ-,
-θə- ‖ -'mæt̬-
Athena ə 'θiːn ə
Athenaeum ˌæθ ə 'niːˌəm -ə-
Athene ə 'θiːn i -iː
Athenian ə 'θiːn i ən   **~s** z
Athens 'æθ ɪnz -ənz
atherom|a ˌæθ ə 'rəʊm ə ‖ -'roʊm ə   **~as** əz
   ~ata ə ‖ ət̬ ə
atheroscle|rosis ˌæθ ə rəʊ sklə 'rəʊs ɪs
-sklе'••-, -sklɪ'••-, §-əs ‖ -roʊ sklə 'roʊs əs
   ~rotic 'rɒt ɪk ◄ ‖ 'raːt̬ ɪk ◄

Atherstone 'æθ ə stəʊn ‖ -ᵊr stoʊn
Atherton (i) 'æθ ət ᵊn ‖ -ᵊrt ᵊn, (ii) 'æð- —the
place near Manchester is (ii).
athetoid 'æθ ə tɔɪd -ɪ-
athetosis ,æθ ə 'təʊs ɪs -ɪ-, §-əs ‖ -'toʊs-
Athey 'æθ i
athirst ə 'θɜːst ‖ ə 'θɝːst
athlete 'æθ liːt ⚠'æθ ə liːt ~s, ~'s s
  ,athlete's 'foot
athletic æθ 'let ɪk əθ-; ⚠,æθ ə 'let- ‖ -'let̬-
  ~ally ᵊl_i
athleticism æθ 'let ɪ ,sɪz əm əθ-, -'•ə-;
  ⚠,æθ ə 'let- ‖ -'let̬-
Athlone ₍ᵢ₎æθ 'ləʊn ‖ -'loʊn
Athol place in MA 'æθ ɒl ‖ -aːl -ɔːl, -ᵊl
Atholl place in Scotland 'æθ ᵊl
at-home ət 'həʊm æt-; ə 'təʊm ‖ -'hoʊm ~s z
Athos 'æθ ɒs 'eɪθ- ‖ -aːs —ModGk ['a θɔs]
athwart ə 'θwɔːt ‖ ə 'θwɔːrt
-ation 'eɪʃ ᵊn —This suffix bears the primary
  word stress. In words of four or more syllables,
  a further rhythmic (secondary) stress falls two
  syllables further back (,conso'lation,
  con,side'ration, ne,goti'ation, as,soci'ation).
  Words in -isation/-ization, however, have the
  secondary stress earlier if possible, namely in
  the same place as the primary stress of the
  corresponding -ise/-ize word (,organi'zation,
  ,atomi'zation, ,dramati'zation, ,actuali'zation).
atishoo ə 'tɪʃ uː
Ativan tdmk 'æt ɪ væn §-ə- ‖ 'æt̬ ə-
-ative ət ɪv, eɪt ɪv ‖ ət̬ ɪv, eɪt̬ ɪv —In words of
  three syllables, the first receives the stress, and
  the suffix vowel is weak ('fricative, 'vocative,
  'laxative, 'narrative; exception cre'ative). In
  longer words, the stress usually falls on the
  same syllable as in the underlying stem:
  ac'cusative, con'sultative, pre'servative;
  'operative, 'qualitative, ag'glutinative,
  ,argu'mentative; ad'ministrative. There is
  sometimes a vowel change (de'rive —
  de'rivative), and there are several exceptional
  cases (com'bine — 'combinative, 'alternate —
  al'ternative, in'terrogate — ,inter'rogative,
  'demonstrate — de'monstrative). Where the
  primary stress is on the last syllable of the stem,
  the suffix has a reduced vowel (,inter'rogative);
  but otherwise in these longer words the choice between
  weak-vowelled ət ɪv ‖ ət̬ ɪv and strong-vowelled
  eɪt ɪv ‖ eɪt̬ ɪv depends partly on social or
  regional factors, with BrE RP tending to prefer
  ət ɪv, AmE eɪt̬ ɪv: see individual entries.
Atka 'æt kə ‖ 'aːt-
Atkins 'æt kɪnz
Atkinson 'æt kɪnᵗs ᵊn
Atlanta ət 'lænt ə æt- ‖ æt 'lænt̬ ə ət-
Atlantean ,æt læn 'tiː_ən ◂ æt 'lænt i_ən, ət-
atlantes ət 'lænt iːz æt-
Atlantic, a~ ət 'lænt ɪk §₍ᵢ₎æt- ‖ -'lænt̬-
  At,lantic 'City; At,lantic 'Ocean
Atlantis ət 'lænt ɪs ₍ᵢ₎æt-, §-əs ‖ -'lænt̬-
atlas, Atlas 'æt ləs ~es ɪz əz

ATM ,eɪ tiː 'em ~s z
atman 'aːt mən
atmosphere 'æt məs fɪə ‖ -fɪr ~s z
atmospheric ,æt məs 'fer ɪk ◂ ‖ -'fɪr- ~al ᵊl
  ~ally ᵊl_i ~s s
  ,atmos,pheric 'pressure
atoll 'æt ɒl ə 'tɒl ‖ 'æt ɔːl -aːl ~s z
atom 'æt əm ‖ 'æt̬ əm ~s z
  'atom bomb
atomic ə 'tɒm ɪk ‖ ə 'taːm- ~ally ᵊl_i
  a,tomic 'bomb; a,tomic 'energy
atomis... —see atomiz...
atomism 'æt ə ,mɪz əm ‖ 'æt̬-
atomistic ,æt ə 'mɪst ɪk ◂ ,æt̬- ~ally ᵊl_i
atomiz|e 'æt ə maɪz ‖ 'æt̬ ə- ~ed d ~er/s ə/z
  ‖ ᵊr/z ~es ɪz əz ~ing ɪŋ
atonal ₍ᵢ₎eɪ 'təʊn ᵊl æ-, ə- ‖ -'toʊn- ~ism ,ɪz
  əm ~ly i
atonality ,eɪ təʊ 'næl ət i ,æ-, ,•tə-, -ɪt i
  ‖ -toʊ 'næl ət̬ i
aton|e ə 'təʊn ‖ ə 'toʊn ~ed d ~es z ~ing ɪŋ
atonement ə 'təʊn mənt ‖ ə 'toʊn- ~s s
atoneness ₍ᵢ₎æt 'wʌn nəs -nɪs
atonic ₍ᵢ₎eɪ 'tɒn ɪk ₍ᵢ₎æ-, ə- ‖ -'taːn-
atoning ə 'təʊn ɪŋ ‖ ə 'toʊn ɪŋ
atony 'æt ən i ‖ 'æt̬ ən i
atop ə 'tɒp ‖ ə 'taːp
atopic ,eɪ 'tɒp ɪk ◂ -'taːp- -'toʊp- ~ally ᵊl_i
atopy 'æt əp i
-ator eɪt ə ‖ eɪt̬ ᵊr —Stress falls on the same
  syllable(s) as for the corresponding verb in -ate
  — radiator 'reɪd i eɪt ə ‖ -eɪt̬ ᵊr
Atora tdmk ə 'tɔːr ə
-atory The BrE and AmE pronunciations of this
  suffix differ. In BrE the vowel of the penultimate
  syllable is always weak: the suffix is either
  ət_ᵊr i or eɪt ᵊr i and, if the latter, may be
  stressed. Different speakers often pronounce
  differently. Thus ar'ticulatory may have
  -jʊl ət_ᵊr i or -ju leɪt ᵊr i, or alternatively may
  be stressed ar,ticu'latory◂. In AmE the suffix
  always has a strong vowel, ə tɔːr i ə toʊr i,
  stress remaining as for the corresponding verb
  in -ate: ar'ticulatory, 'mandatory.
ATP ,eɪ tiː 'piː
atrabilious ,ætr ə 'bɪl i_əs ◂ ~ness nəs nɪs
atresia ə 'triːz i_ə æ-, -'triːʒ-, -'triːʒ ə
  ‖ ə 'triːʒ ə
Atreus 'eɪtr i əs -uːs; 'eɪtr uːs
at-risk ₍ᵢ₎æt 'rɪsk ət-
atri|um 'eɪtr i ləm 'ætr- ~a ə ~al əl
atrocious ə 'trəʊʃ əs ‖ ə 'troʊʃ əs ~ly li ~ness
  nəs nɪs
atrocit|y ə 'trɒs ət li -ɪt i ‖ ə 'traːs ət̬ li ~ies iz
atrophic æ 'trɒf ɪk ₍ᵢ₎eɪ-, ə- ‖ -'traːf-
atr|ophy n, v 'ætr ləf i ⚠-ə faɪ ~ophied əf id
  ⚠ə faɪd ~ophies əf iz ⚠ə faɪz ~ophying
  əf i ɪŋ ⚠ə faɪ ɪŋ
atropine 'ætr ə piːn -əp ɪn, §-əp ən
Atropos 'ætr ə pɒs -əp əs ‖ -paːs
attaboy 'æt ə bɔɪ ‖ 'æt̬-
attach ə 'tætʃ attached ə 'tætʃt attaches
  ə 'tætʃ ɪz əz attaching ə 'tætʃ ɪŋ

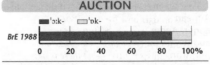

attaché ə 'tæʃ eɪ -i ‖ ˌæt̬ ə 'ʃeɪ ˌæt æ- *(*)* ~s z
   at'taché case ‖ ˌatta'ché case
attachment ə 'tætʃ mənt ~s s
attack ə 'tæk **attacked** ə 'tækt **attacking**
   ə 'tæk ɪŋ **attacks** ə 'tæks
attacker ə 'tæk ə ‖ -ᵊr ~s z
attain ə 'teɪn ~ed d ~ing ɪŋ ~s z
attainability ə ˌteɪn ə 'bɪl ət i -ɪt i ‖ -ət̬ i
attainable ə 'teɪn əb ᵊl
attainder ə 'teɪnd ə ‖ -ᵊr
attainment ə 'teɪn mənt →-'teɪm- ~s s
attar 'æt ə -ɑː ‖ 'æt̬ ᵊr 'æt ɑːr ~s z
attempt ə 'tempt ~ed ɪd əd ~ing ɪŋ ~s s
Attenborough 'æt ᵊn bər_ə →'•əm-, §-ˌbʌr ə
   ‖ -ˌbɝː oʊ
attend ə 'tend ~ed ɪd əd ~ing ɪŋ ~s z
attendanc|e ə 'tend ᵊnᵗs ~es ɪz əz
attendant ə 'tend ənt ~s s
attendee ə ˌten 'diː ˌæt en- ~s z
attention ə 'tenᵗʃ ᵊn ~s z
attentive ə 'tent ɪv ‖ ə 'tent̬ ɪv ~ly li ~ness
   nəs nɪs
attenu|ate v ə 'ten ju |eɪt ~ated eɪt ɪd -əd
   ‖ eɪt̬ əd ~ates eɪts ~ating eɪt ɪŋ ‖ eɪt̬ ɪŋ
attenuate adj ə 'ten ju_ət _ɪt, -eɪt
attenuation ə ˌten ju 'eɪʃ ᵊn ~s z
attenuator ə 'ten ju eɪt ə ‖ -eɪt̬ ᵊr ~s z
Attercliffe 'æt ə klɪf ‖ 'æt̬ ᵊr-
attest ə 'test ~ed ɪd əd ~ing ɪŋ ~s s
attestation ˌæt e 'steɪʃ ᵊn -ə- ~s z
attestor ə 'test ə ‖ -ᵊr ~s z
attic, Attic 'æt ɪk ‖ 'æt̬- ~s s
Attica 'æt ɪk ə ‖ 'æt̬-
Atticism 'æt ɪ ˌsɪz əm §-ə- ‖ 'æt̬-
Attila ə 'tɪl ə 'æt ɪl-
attire ə 'taɪ_ə ‖ ə 'taɪ_ᵊr ~d d ~s z **attiring**
   ə 'taɪ_ər ɪŋ ‖ ə 'taɪ_ᵊr ɪŋ

ATTITUDE

■ -tuːd	▭ -tjuːd				
AmE 1993					
0	20	40	60	80	100%

attitude 'æt ɪ t juːd -ə-, →§-'tʃuːd ‖ 'æt̬ ə tuːd
   -tjuːd ~s z —*AmE 1993 poll panel preference:*
   -tuːd *88%*, -tjuːd *12%*.
attitudinal ˌæt ɪ 'tjuːd ɪn ᵊl ◄, •ə-, →§-'tʃuːd-,
   -ᵊn_əl ‖ ˌæt̬ ə 'tuːd ᵊn_əl ◄-'tjuːd- ~ly i
attitudinis|e, attitudiniz|e ˌæt ɪ 'tjuːd ɪ naɪz
   ˌ•ə-, →§-'tʃuːd-, -ə naɪz, -ᵊn aɪz
   ‖ ˌæt̬ ə 'tuːd ᵊn aɪz -'tjuːd- ~ed d ~es ɪz əz
   ~ing ɪŋ
Attleborough 'æt ᵊl bər_ə ‖ 'æt̬ ᵊl ˌbɝː oʊ
Attlee 'æt li
atto- ˌæt əʊ ‖ ˌæt̬ oʊ — **attogram**
   'æt əʊ græm ‖ 'æt̬ oʊ-
attorney ə 'tɜːn i ‖ ə 'tɝːn i *(!)* ~ship/s ʃɪp/s
   ~s z
   at,torney 'general
attract ə 'trækt ~ed ɪd əd ~ing ɪŋ ~s s
attractant ə 'trækt ᵊnt ~s s
attraction ə 'træk ʃᵊn ~s z
attractive ə 'trækt ɪv ~ly li ~ness nəs nɪs
attractor ə 'trækt ə ‖ -ᵊr ~s z

attributab|le ə 'trɪb jʊt əb |ᵊl -'•jət-, -'•juːt-
   ‖ -'trɪb jət̬- ~ly li
attribute n 'ætr ɪ bjuːt -ə- ~s s
attribute v ə 'trɪb juːt §'ætr ɪ bjuːt, §-ə-
   ‖ ə 'trɪb jət -juːt **attributed** ə 'trɪb jʊt ɪd
   'ætr ɪ bjuːt-, '•ə-, -əd ‖ ə 'trɪb jət̬ əd -juːt̬ əd
attributes v ə 'trɪb juːts §'ætr ɪ bjuːts, §-ə-
   ‖ ə 'trɪb jəts -juːts **attributing** ə 'trɪb jʊt ɪŋ
   'ætr ɪ bjuːt-, '•ə- ‖ ə 'trɪb jət̬ ɪŋ -juːt̬ ɪŋ
attribution ˌætr ɪ 'bjuːʃ ᵊn -ə- ~s z
attributive ə 'trɪb jʊt ɪv -jət ɪv, -juːt ɪv;
   §'ætr ɪ bjuːt ɪv, §'•ə- ‖ -jət̬ ɪv ~ly li ~ness
   nəs nɪs
attrition ə 'trɪʃ ᵊn æ-
Attu 'æt uː
Attucks 'æt əks ‖ 'æt̬-
attun|e ə 'tjuːn æ-, →§-'tʃuːn ‖ ə 'tuːn ə 'tjuːn
   ~ed d ~es z ~ing ɪŋ
Attw... —*see* **Atw...**
ATV ˌeɪ tiː 'viː ~s z
Atwater 'æt ˌwɔːt ə ‖ -ˌwɔːt̬ ᵊr -ˌwɑːt̬ ᵊr
Atwell 'æt wel
atwitter ə 'twɪt ə ‖ ə 'twɪt̬ ᵊr
Atwood 'æt wʊd
atypical ˌeɪ 'tɪp ɪk ᵊl ~ly i
au əʊ ‖ oʊ —*Fr* [o] —*See also phrases with this*
   word
aubade əʊ 'bɑːd ‖ oʊ- —*Fr* [o bad] ~s z
auberge, ~s ˌəʊ 'beəʒ ‖ ˌoʊ 'beᵊrʒ —*Fr*
   [o bɛʁʒ]
aubergine 'əʊb ə ʒiːn -dʒiːn ‖ 'oʊb ᵊr- ~s z
Auberon 'ɔːb ᵊr_ən 'əʊb-, -ə rɒn, '•rɒn ‖ 'ɑːb-,
   -ə rɑːn —*The writer* A~ Waugh *pronounces*
   'ɔːb-
Aubrey 'ɔːb ri ‖ 'ɑːb-
aubrietia ɔː 'briːʃ ə -'briːʃ i_ə ‖ ɑː-, oʊ- ~s z
auburn, A~ 'ɔːb ən 'ɔː bɜːn ‖ 'ɔːb ᵊrn 'ɑːb-
Aubusson 'əʊb ju sɒn ‖ ˌoʊb ə 'saːn -'soʊn
   —*Fr* [o by sɔ̃]
Auchinleck 'ɔːk ɪn lek 'ɒx-, -ən-, ˌ•'• ‖ 'ɑːk-
Auchterarder ˌɒxt ər 'ɑːd ə ˌɒxt- ‖ ˌɔːkt
   ər 'ɑːrd ᵊr ˌɑːkt-
Auchtermuchty ˌɔːkt ə 'mʌkt i ˌɒxt-;
   ˌɒxt ə 'mʌxt i ‖ -ᵊr- ˌɑːkt-
Auckland 'ɔːk lənd ‖ 'ɑːk-
au contraire ˌəʊ kɒn 'treə ‖ ˌoʊ kɑːn 'treᵊr
   -'træᵊr —*Fr* [o kɔ̃ tʁɛːʁ]
au courant əʊ 'kʊr ᵊ̃ ‖ ˌoʊ ku 'rɑːn —*Fr*
   [o ku ʁɑ̃]

AUCTION

■ 'ɔːk-	▭ 'ɒk-				
BrE 1988					
0	20	40	60	80	100%

auction 'ɔːk ʃᵊn 'ɒk- ‖ 'ɑːk- —*BrE poll 1988*
   panel preference: 'ɔːk- *87%*, 'ɒk- *13%*. ~ed d
   ~ing ˌɪŋ ~s z
auctioneer ˌɔːk ʃə 'nɪə ◄ ˌɒk- ‖ -'nɪᵊr ˌɑːk- ~s
   z
auctorial ɔːk 'tɔːr i_əl ‖ ɑːk-, -'toʊr-
audacious ɔː 'deɪʃ əs ‖ ɑː- ~ly li ~ness nəs
   nɪs
audacit|y ˌ(ˌ)ɔː 'dæs ət i -ɪt i ‖ -ət̬ i ˌ(ˌ)ɑː- ~ies ɪz

A

Auden 'ɔːd ən ‖ 'ɑːd-
Audenshaw 'ɔːd ən ʃɔː ‖ 'ɑːd ən ʃɑː
Audi tdmk 'aʊd i 'ɔːd- ‖ 'ɔːd-, 'ɑːd-
audibility ˌɔːd ə 'bɪl ət i ˌ•ɪ-, -ɪt i ‖ -əṭ i ˌɑːd-
audib|le 'ɔːd əb |əl -ɪb- ‖ 'ɑːd- ~ly li
Audie 'ɔːd i ‖ 'ɑːd-
audienc|e 'ɔːd i_ənts ‖ 'ɑːd- ~es ɪz əz
audile 'ɔːd aɪəl -ɪl ‖ 'ɑːd-
audio 'ɔːd i_əʊ ‖ _oʊ 'ɑːd- ~s z
  ˌaudio casˈsette
audiolingual ˌɔːd i_əʊ 'lɪŋ gwəl ◀ -'lɪŋ gju_əl
  ‖ _oʊ- ˌɑːd- ~ly i
audiological ˌɔːd i_ə 'lɒdʒ ɪk əl ◀ -'lɑːdʒ-
  ˌɑːd- ~ly i
audiologist ˌɔː di 'ɒl ədʒ ɪst §-əst ‖ -'ɑːl- ˌɑːd-
  ~s s
audiology ˌɔːd i 'ɒl ədʒ i ‖ -'ɑːl- ˌɑːd-
audiometer ˌɔːd i 'ɒm ɪt ə -ət ə ‖ -'ɑːm əṭ ər
  ˌɑːd- ~s z
audiometry ˌɔːd i 'ɒm ətr i -ɪtr i ‖ -'ɑːm- ˌɑːd-
audiophile 'ɔːd i_əʊ faɪl ‖ _oʊ- 'ɑːd- ~s z
audiotape 'ɔːd i_əʊ teɪp ‖ _oʊ- 'ɑːd- ~s s
audiotyp|ing 'ɔːd i_əʊ ˌtaɪp ɪŋ ‖ _oʊ- 'ɑːd-
  ~ist/s ɪst/s əst/s
audiovisual ˌɔːd i_əʊ 'vɪʒ u_əl ◀ -'vɪz ju_əl,
  -'vɪʒ əl ‖ _oʊ- ˌɑːd-, -'vɪʒ əl ~ly i
  ˌaudio ˌvisual ˈaids
aud|it 'ɔːd |ɪt §-ət ‖ 'ɔːd |ət 'ɑːd- ~ited ɪt ɪd
  §ət-, -əd ‖ əṭ əd ~iting ɪt ɪŋ §ət- ‖ əṭ ɪŋ ~its
  ɪts §əts ‖ əts
audition ɔː 'dɪʃ ən ‖ ɑː- ~ed d ~ing ɪŋ ~s z
auditor 'ɔːd ɪt ə -ət- ‖ -əṭ ər 'ɑːd- ~s z
auditori|um ˌɔːd i 'tɔːr i_|əm ˌ•ə- ‖ ˌɑːd-,
  -'toʊr- ~a ə ~ums əmz
auditor|y 'ɔːd ɪt_ər i ˌ•ət_ ‖ 'ɔːd ə tɔːr li 'ɑːd-,
  -toʊr i ~ily əl i ɪ li
Audlab tdmk 'ɔːd læb ‖ 'ɑːd-
Audlem 'ɔːd ləm ‖ 'ɑːd-
Audley 'ɔːd li ‖ 'ɑːd-
Audrey 'ɔːdr i ‖ 'ɑːdr-
Audubon 'ɔːd ə bɒn -əb ən ‖ -bɑːn 'ɑːd-, -əb
  ən
AUEW ˌeɪ juː ˌiː 'dʌb əl ju
auf German prepn aʊf —Ger [aʊf] —See also
  phrases with this word
au fait (ˌ)əʊ 'feɪ ‖ (ˌ)oʊ- —Fr [o fɛ]
au fond (ˌ)əʊ 'fɒ̃ ‖ (ˌ)oʊ 'foʊn -'fɔː- —Fr [o fɔ̃]
auf Wiedersehen (ˌ)aʊf 'viːd ə zeɪn -'wiːd-,
  -'••ˌzeɪ ən ‖ -ər- —Ger [aʊf 'viː dɐ ˌzeː ən]
Augean ɔː 'dʒiː_ən ‖ ɑː-
auger, Auger 'ɔːg ə ‖ -ər 'ɑːg- ~s z
aught ɔːt ‖ ɑːt (= ought)
Aughton 'ɔːt ən ‖ 'ɑːt- —but there is one
  village of this name, near Lancaster, which is
  'æft ən
augite 'ɔːdʒ aɪt ‖ 'ɑːdʒ-
aug|ment v (ˌ)ɔːg |'ment ‖ ɑːg- ~mented
  'ment ɪd -əd ‖ 'menṭ əd ~menting
  'ment ɪŋ ‖ 'menṭ ɪŋ ~ments 'ments
augment n 'ɔːg ment -mənt ‖ 'ɑːg- ~s s
augmentation ˌɔːg men 'teɪʃ ən -mən- ‖ ˌɑːg-
  ~s z

augmentative ɔːg 'ment ət ɪv ‖ -'menṭ əṭ ɪv
  ɑːg- ~s z
au gratin əʊ 'græt æn ‖ oʊ 'grɑːt ən —Fr
  [o gʁa tæ̃]
Augsburg 'aʊgz bɜːg 'aʊks-, -bʊəg ‖ -bɜ˞ːg
  'ɑːgz-, -bʊrg —Ger ['aʊks bʊʁk]
augur n, v 'ɔːg ə -jə ‖ -ər 'ɑːg- ~ed d
  auguring 'ɔːg ər ɪŋ -jər- ‖ 'ɑːg- ~s z
augur|y 'ɔːg jʊr |i -jər-, -ər- ‖ -jər li 'ɑːg-, -ər-
  ~ies iz
august adj (ˌ)ɔː 'gʌst ‖ (ˌ)ɑː-; '•• ~ly li ~ness
  nəs nɪs
August n, name of month 'ɔːg əst ‖ 'ɑːg-
August personal name, august n 'clown'
  'aʊg ʊst ~s s
Augusta ɔː 'gʌst ə ə- ‖ ɑː-
Augustan ɔː 'gʌst ən ə- ‖ ɑː- ~s z
Augustine ɔː 'gʌst ɪn ə-, §-ən ‖ 'ɔːg ə stiːn
  'ɑːg- (*)
Augustinian ˌɔːg ə 'stɪn i_ən ◀ ˌ•ʌ- ‖ ˌɑːg- ~s
  z
Augustus ɔː 'gʌst əs ə- ‖ ɑː-
au jus əʊ 'ʒuː -'ʒuːs ‖ oʊ- —Fr [o ʒy]
auk ɔːk ‖ ɑːk auks ɔːks ‖ ɑːks
auklet 'ɔːk lət -lɪt ‖ 'ɑːk- ~s s
aul|a 'ɔːl |ə 'aʊl- ‖ 'ɑːl- ~ae iː
au lait əʊ 'leɪ ‖ oʊ- —Fr [o lɛ]
auld, Auld ɔːld ‖ ɑːld
  ˌauld ˌlang ˈsyne zaɪn saɪn; ˌAuld ˈReekie
  'riːk i
Aulis 'ɔːl ɪs 'aʊl-, §-əs ‖ 'ɑːl-
Aum ɔːm ‖ ɑːm
au naturel əʊ ˌnæt ju 'rel -ˌnæt̬ ʃ ə-, -ˌnæt jə-,
  ˌ•ˌ•- ‖ oʊ ˌnɑːtʃ ə 'rel —Fr [o na ty ʁɛl]

AUNT

	ænt	ɑːnt			
AmE 1993					
	0 20 40 60 80 100%				

aunt ɑːnt §ænt ‖ ænt ɑːnt aunts ɑːnts §ænts
  ‖ ænts ɑːnts —AmE 1993 poll panel
  preference: ænt 70%, ɑːnt 30%.
  ˌAunt ˈSally
aunt|ie, aunt|y, Aunt|y 'ɑːnt li §'ænt- ‖ 'ænt̬ li
  'ɑːnt- ~ies iz
au pair (ˌ)əʊ 'peə ‖ (ˌ)oʊ 'peər -'pæər —Fr
  [o pɛʁ] ~s z
au poivre əʊ 'pwɑːv -'•rə ‖ oʊ- —Fr
  [o pwavʁ]
aur|a 'ɔːr |ə ~ae iː
aural 'ɔːr əl —Sometimes 'aʊər əl, to avoid
  confusion with oral ~ly i
aureate 'ɔːr i eɪt -ət, -ɪt ‖ -ly li ~ness nəs nɪs
Aurelian ɔː 'riːl i_ən
Aurelius ɔː 'riːl i_əs
aureola ɔː 'riːəl ə ə ˌɔːr i 'əʊl ə,
  ˌɒr- ˌɔːr i 'oʊl ə ~s z
aureole 'ɔːr i əʊl -oʊl ~s z
aureomycin, A~ tdmk ˌɔːr i əʊ 'maɪs ɪn §-ən
  ‖ -oʊ'•-
au revoir ˌəʊ rə 'vwɑː -rɪ-, §-riː-
  ‖ oʊ rə 'vwɑːr —Fr [oʁ vwaʁ]
auricle 'ɔːr ɪk əl 'ɒr- ~s z

A

auricul|a ɔː 'rɪk jʊl ə ɒ-, -jəl- ‖ -jəl lə **~ar**
ə ‖ ᵊr **~as** əz
Auriel 'ɔːr i‿əl
auriferous ɔː 'rɪf ᵊr‿əs
Auriga ɔː 'raɪg ə ‖ ɑː-
Aurignacian ˌɔːr ɪg 'neɪʃ ᵊn ◂ -iːn 'jeɪʃ-
aurochs 'ɔːr ɒks 'aʊᵊr- ‖ -ɑːks **~es** ɪz əz
auror|a, A~ ə 'rɔːr lə ɔː- **~ae** iː **~as** əz
   au,rora au'stralis ɒ 'streɪl ɪs ɔː-, ə-, -'strɑːl-,
   §-əs ‖ ɔː 'streɪl əs ɑː-; **au,rora ,bore'alis**
Auschwitz 'aʊʃ wɪts -vɪts —*Ger* ['aʊʃ vɪts]
auscultation ˌɔːsk ᵊl 'teɪʃ ᵊn ˌɒsk-, -ʌl- ‖ ˌɑːsk-
auslese, A~ 'aʊs leɪz ə —*Ger* ['aʊs leː zə]
auspices 'ɔːsp ɪs ɪz 'ɒsp-, -əs-, -əz, -iːz ‖ 'ɑːsp-
auspicious ɔː 'spɪʃ əs ɒ- ‖ ɑː- **~ly** li **~ness** nəs
   nɪs
Aussie 'ɒz i ‖ 'ɔːs i 'ɑːs-, 'ɔːz-, 'ɑːz- **~s** z
Aust ɔːst ‖ ɑːst
Austell 'ɒst ᵊl 'ɔːst-‖ 'ɑːst- — St A~'s *in*
   Cornwall is locally also -'ɔːs ᵊlz
Austen 'ɒst ɪn 'ɔːst-, §-ən ‖ 'ɑːst-
Auster 'ɔːst ə ‖ -ᵊr 'ɑːst-
austere ɔː 'stɪə ɒ- ‖ ɔː 'stɪᵊr ɑː-, -'steᵊr **~ly** li
austerit|y ɔː 'ster ət li ɒ-, -ɪt i ‖ ɔː 'ster əţ li ɑː-,
   -'stɪr- **~ies** ɪz
Austerlitz 'ɔːst ə lɪts 'aʊst- ‖ -ᵊr- 'ɑːst-
Austick 'ɔːst ɪk ‖ 'ɑːst-
Austin 'ɒst ɪn 'ɔːst-, §-ən ‖ 'ɑːst-
austral 'ɔːs trəl 'ɒs- ‖ 'ɑːs-
Austra|lasia ˌɒs trə 'leɪʒ ə ◂ ˌɔːs-, -'leɪʃ-,
   -l'leɪz i‿ə ‖ ˌɔːs- ˌɑːs- **~lasian/s** 'leɪʒ ən/z
   'leɪʃ-, 'leɪʃ i‿ən/z
Australi|a ɒ 'streɪl i‿ə ɔː-, ə- ‖ ɔː- ɑː-, ə-
   ~an/s ən/z —*locally* ə-
Australoid 'ɒs trə lɔɪd 'ɔːs- ‖ 'ɔːs- 'ɑːs- **~s** z
australopithecine ˌɒs trəl əʊ 'pɪθ ə saɪn ˌɔːs-,
   -ɪ•, -siːn ‖ ɔː ˌstreɪl oʊ- ɑː- **~s** z
australopithecus ˌɒs trəl əʊ 'pɪθ ɪk əs -ək əs
   ‖ ɔː ˌstreɪl oʊ '•- ɑː-
Austri|a 'ɒs tri‿ə 'ɔːs- ‖ 'ɔːs- 'ɑːs- **~an/s** ən/z
Austro- *comb. form* 'ɒs trəʊ 'ɔːs trəʊ ‖ 'ɔːs troʊ
   'ɑːs troʊ — **Austro-Hungarian**
   ˌɒs trəʊ hʌŋ 'geər i‿ən ◂ ˌɔːs-
   ‖ ˌɔːs troʊ hʌŋ 'ger- ˌɑːs-, -'gær-
Austronesi|a ˌɒs trəʊ 'niːz i‿ə ◂ ˌɔːs-, -'niːʒ lə,
   -'niːs i‿lə, -'niːʃ i‿lə ‖ ˌɔːs troʊ 'niːʒ lə ˌɑːs-,
   -'niːʃ- **~an/s** ən/z
Austyn 'ɒst ɪn 'ɔːst-, §-ən ‖ 'ɔːst- ɑːst-
AUT ˌeɪ juː 'tiː
autarchic ɔː 'tɑːk ɪk ‖ -'tɑːrk- ɑː- **~al** ᵊl
autarchy 'ɔːt ɑːk i ‖ -ɑːrk i 'ɑːt-
autarkic ɔː 'tɑːk ɪk ‖ -'tɑːrk- ɑː- **~al** ᵊl
autarky 'ɔːt ɑːk i ‖ -ɑːrk i 'ɑːt-
auteur ɔː 'tɜː ₍ᵤ₎əʊ- ‖ oʊ 'tɜːː —*Fr* [o tœːʁ]
authentic ɔː 'θent ɪk ‖ -'θenţ ɪk ɑː- **~ally** ᵊl‿i
authenti|cate ɔː 'θent ɪ |keɪt §-ə- ‖ -'θenţ- ɑː-
   ~cated keɪt ɪd -əd ‖ keɪţ əd **~cates** keɪts
   ~cating keɪt ɪŋ ‖ keɪţ ɪŋ **~cator/s** keɪt ə/z
   ‖ keɪţ ᵊr/s
authentication ɔː ˌθent ɪ 'keɪʃ ᵊn §-ə- ‖ -ˌθenţ-
   ɑː- **~s** z
authenticity ˌɔːθ en 'tɪs ət i, •ᵊn-, -ɪt i ‖ -əţ i
   ˌɑːθ-, ˌ•ᵊn-

author 'ɔːθ ə ‖ 'ɔːθ ᵊr 'ɑːθ- **~ed** d **authoring**
   'ɔːθ ər‿ɪŋ ‖ 'ɑːθ- **~s** z
authoress 'ɔːθ ə res -ᵊr ɪs, -ᵊr əs, ˌɔːθ ə 'res
   ‖ 'ɔːθ ᵊr əs 'ɑːθ- **~es** ɪz əz
authorial ɔː 'θɔːr i‿əl ‖ ɑː- **~ly** i
authoris... —*see* **authoriz...**
authoritarian ɔː ˌθɒr ɪ 'teər i‿ən ◂ -ə'•-
   ‖ -ˌθɔːr ə 'ter- ɑː-, ə- **~ism** ˌɪz əm **~s** z
authoritative ɔː 'θɒr ɪt ət ɪv -'•ət-; -ɪ teɪt ɪv,
   -ə•• ‖ ə 'θɔːr ə teɪţ ɪv ɔː-, ɑː- **~ly** li **~ness**
   nəs nɪs
authorit|y ɔː 'θɒr əţ li ə-, -ɪt i ‖ ə 'θɔːr əţ li ɔː-,
   ɑː- **~ies** ɪz
authorization ˌɔːθ ər‿aɪ 'zeɪʃ ᵊn -ər‿ɪ- ‖ ˌ•ə-
   ˌɑːθ- **~s** z
authoriz|e 'ɔːθ ə raɪz ‖ 'ɑːθ- **~ed** d **~es** ɪz əz
   ~ing ɪŋ
   Authorized 'Version
authorship 'ɔːθ ə ʃɪp ‖ -ᵊr- 'ɑːθ-
autism 'ɔːt ˌɪz əm ‖ 'ɑːt-
autistic ɔː 'tɪst ɪk ‖ ɑː- **~ally** ᵊl‿i
auto 'ɔːt əʊ ‖ 'ɔːţ oʊ 'ɑːţ- **~s** z
auto- *comb. form*
   with stress-neutral suffix 'ɔːt əʊ ‖ 'ɔːţ oʊ 'ɑːţ-
   — **autoimmune** ˌɔːt əʊ ɪ 'mjuːn ‖ ˌɔːţ oʊ-
   ˌɑːţ-
   with stress-imposing suffix ɔː 'tɒ+ ‖ ɔː 'tɑː+
   ɑː- — **autolysis** ɔː 'tɒl əs ɪs -ɪs-, §-əs
   ‖ ɔː 'tɑːl- ɑː-
autobahn 'ɔːt əʊ bɑːn 'aʊt- ‖ 'ɔːţ oʊ- 'ɑːţ-
   —*Ger* ['au to baːn] **~s** z
autobiographer ˌɔːt əʊ
   baɪ 'ɒg rəf ə ‖ ˌɔːţ ə baɪ 'ɑːg rəf ᵊr ˌɑːţ- **~s** z
autobiographic ˌɔːt əʊ ˌbaɪ‿ə 'græf ɪk ◂
   -ˌbaɪ əʊ ə ˌbaɪ ə- ˌɑːţ- **~al** ᵊl **~ally** ᵊl‿i
autobiograph|y ˌɔːt əʊ
   baɪ 'ɒg rəf li i ‖ ˌɔːţ ə baɪ 'ɑːg- ˌɑːţ- **~ies** ɪz
autocar, A~ 'ɔːt əʊ kɑː ‖ 'ɔːţ oʊ kɑːr 'ɑːţ- **~s** z
autochang|e 'ɔːt əʊ tʃeɪndʒ ‖ 'ɔːţ oʊ- 'ɑːţ-
   ~es ɪz əz
autochanger
   'ɔːt əʊ ˌtʃeɪndʒ ə ‖ 'ɔːţ oʊ ˌtʃeɪndʒ ᵊr 'ɑːţ- **~s**
   z
autochthon ɔː 'tɒk θᵊn -θɒn ‖ -'tɑːk- ɑː-,
   -θɑːn **~s** z
autochthonous ɔː 'tɒk θən əs ‖ -'tɑːk- ɑː- **~ly**
   li
autoclav|e 'ɔːt əʊ kleɪv ‖ 'ɔːţ oʊ- 'ɑːţ- **~ed** d
   ~es z **~ing** ɪŋ
autocorrelation ˌɔːt əʊ ˌkɒr ə 'leɪʃ ᵊn -ɪ'•-
   ‖ ˌɔːţ oʊ ˌkɔːr- ˌɑːţ-, -ˌkɑːr-
autocrac|y ɔː 'tɒk rəs li i ‖ -'tɑːk- ɑː- **~ies** ɪz
autocrat 'ɔːt ə kræt ‖ 'ɔːţ ə- 'ɑːţ- **~s** s
autocratic ˌɔːt ə 'kræt ɪk ◂ ‖ ˌɔːţ ə 'kræţ ɪk ◂
   ˌɑːţ- **~al** ᵊl **~ally** ᵊl‿i
autocross 'ɔːt əʊ krɒs ‖ 'ɔːţ oʊ krɔːs 'ɑːţ-,
   -krɑːs
autocue, A~ *tdmk* 'ɔːt əʊ kjuː ‖ 'ɔːţ oʊ- 'ɑːţ-
   ~s z
autocycle 'ɔːt əʊ ˌsaɪk ᵊl ‖ 'ɔːţ oʊ- 'ɑːţ- **~s** z
auto-da-fé ˌɔːt əʊ də 'feɪ ˌaʊt-, -dɑː'• ‖ ˌɔːţ oʊ-
   ˌɑːţ- —*Port* [au tu da 'fe]

A

autodestruct ˌɔːt əʊ dɪ 'strʌkt -də'•, §-diː'•
‖ ˌɔːṭ oʊ- ˌaːṭ- ~ed ɪd əd ~ing ɪŋ ~s s
autodidact 'ɔːt əʊ dɪ ˌdækt -ˌdaɪd ækt, ˌ••'•••
‖ ˌɔːṭ oʊ 'daɪd ækt ˌaːṭ-, -də 'dækt ~s s
autodidactic ˌɔːt əʊ dɪ 'dækt ɪk ◄-daɪ'•-
‖ ˌɔːṭ oʊ daɪ- ˌaːṭ-, ˌ••də- ~ally ᵊl_i
autoerotic ˌɔːt əʊ ɪ 'rɒt ɪk ◄-ə'•-
‖ ˌɔːṭ oʊ ɪ 'raːṭ ɪk ◄ˌaːṭ-
autoeroticism ˌɔːt əʊ ɪ 'rɒt ɪ ˌsɪz əm -ə'•-,
-ə,•- ‖ ˌɔːṭ oʊ ɪ 'raːṭ ə- ˌaːṭ-
autoerotism ˌɔːt əʊ 'er ə ˌtɪz əm ‖ ˌɔːṭ oʊ-
ˌaːṭ-
autogiro ˌɔːt əʊ 'dʒaɪᵊr əʊ ‖ ˌɔːṭ oʊ 'dʒaɪᵊr oʊ
ˌaːṭ- ~s z
autograph 'ɔːt ə grɑːf -græf ‖ 'ɔːṭ ə græf 'aːṭ-
~ed t ~ing ɪŋ ~s s
autogyro ˌɔːt əʊ 'dʒaɪᵊr əʊ ‖ ˌɔːṭ oʊ 'dʒaɪᵊr oʊ
ˌaːṭ- ~s z
autoharp, A~ tdmk 'ɔːt əʊ hɑːp ‖ 'ɔːṭ oʊ hɑːrp
'aːṭ- ~s s
autoimmun|e ˌɔːt əʊ ɪ 'mjuːn ◄ ‖ ˌɔːṭ oʊ- ˌaːṭ-
~ity ət i ɪt i ‖ əṭ i
autoload ˌɔːt əʊ 'ləʊd '••• ‖ ˌɔːṭ oʊ 'loʊd ˌaːṭ-
~ed ɪd əd ~ing ɪŋ ◄ ~s z
autologous ɔː 'tɒl əg əs ‖ -'tɑːl- ɑː- ~ly li
Autolycus ɔː 'tɒl ɪk əs ‖ -'tɑːl- ɑː-
automaker 'ɔːt əʊ ˌmeɪk ə ‖ 'ɔːṭ oʊ ˌmeɪk ᵊr
'aːṭ- ~s z
automat, A~ tdmk 'ɔːt ə mæt ‖ 'ɔːṭ- 'aːṭ- ~s s
automata ɔː 'tɒm ət ə ‖ ɔː 'tɑːm əṭ ə ɑː-
auto|mate 'ɔːt ə ˌmeɪt ‖ 'ɔːṭ- 'aːṭ- ~mated
meɪt ɪd -əd ‖ meɪṭ əd ~mates meɪts
~mating meɪt ɪŋ ‖ meɪṭ ɪŋ
automatic ˌɔːt ə 'mæt ɪk ◄ ‖ ˌɔːṭ ə 'mæṭ ɪk ◄
ˌaːṭ- ~ally ᵊl_i
ˌauto,matic 'pilot
automation ˌɔːt ə 'meɪʃ ᵊn ‖ ˌɔːṭ- ˌaːṭ-
automatism ɔː 'tɒm ə ˌtɪz əm ‖ ɔː 'tɑːm- ɑː-
autom|aton ɔː 'tɒm |ət ən ‖ ɔː 'tɑːm |ət ᵊn ɑː-,
-lə taːn ~ata ət ə ‖ əṭ ə ~atons ət
ənz ‖ ət ᵊnz
automobile 'ɔːt ə məʊ ˌbiːᵊl ,••'••
‖ 'ɔːt ə moʊ ˌbiːᵊl 'aːṭ-; ˌ•••'•; ˌ••'••• ~s z
automotive ˌɔːt əʊ
'məʊt ɪv ◄ ‖ ˌɔːṭ ə 'moʊṭ ɪv ◄ ˌaːṭ-
autonomic ˌɔːt ə 'nɒm ɪk ◄ ‖ ˌɔːṭ ə 'naːm ɪk ◄
ˌaːṭ- ~ally ᵊl_i
ˌauto,nomic 'nervous ˌsystem
autonomous ɔː 'tɒn əm əs ‖ ɔː 'taːn- ɑː- ~ly
li
autonom|y ɔː 'tɒn əm li ‖ ɔː 'taːn- ɑː- ~ies ɪz
autopilot 'ɔːt əʊ ˌpaɪl ət ‖ 'ɔːṭ oʊ- 'aːṭ- ~s s
autops|y 'ɔːt ɒps li -əps-; ɔː 'tɒps li
‖ 'ɔːt aːps li 'aːṭ-; 'ɔːṭ əps i, 'aːṭ- ~ies ɪz
autoreverse ˌɔːt əʊ rɪ 'vɜːs -rə'•, §-riː'•
‖ ˌɔːṭ oʊ rɪ 'vɝːs ˌaːṭ-
autoroute 'ɔːt əʊ ruːt ‖ 'ɔːṭ oʊ- 'aːṭ- —Fr
[o ʁut] ~s s
autosegmental ˌɔːt əʊ seg 'ment ᵊl ◄ -səg'•-,
-sɪg'•- ‖ ˌɔːṭ oʊ seg 'menṭ ᵊl ◄ ˌaːṭ- ~ly i
autostrada 'ɔːt əʊ ˌstrɑːd ə 'aut- ‖ 'aʊṭ oʊ-
'ɔːṭ-, 'aːṭ- —It [au to 'stra: da] ~s z

autosuggestion ˌɔːt əʊ sə 'dʒes tʃən -'dʒes-
‖ ˌɔːṭ oʊ səg 'dʒes tʃən ˌaːṭ-
Autrey 'ɔːtr i ‖ 'aːtr-
autumn, A~ 'ɔːt əm ‖ 'ɔːṭ əm 'aːṭ- ~s z
autumnal ɔː 'tʌm nᵊl ‖ ɑː- ~ly i
Auty 'ɔːt i ‖ 'ɔːṭ i 'aːṭ i
Auvergne əʊ 'veən -'vɜːn ‖ oʊ 'veᵊrn -'vɝːn
—Fr [o vɛʁnj, ɔ-]
au vin əʊ 'væ̃ -'væn ‖ oʊ- —Fr [o væ̃]
AUX ɔːks ‖ aːks
'AUX ˌnode
auxiliar|y ɔːg 'zɪl i_ər li ɔːk-, ɔːk 'sɪl-,
△-'•ər li ‖ ɑːg-, -'zɪl ər li ~ies ɪz
auxin 'ɔːks ɪn §-ən ‖ 'aːks- ~s z
Ava (i) 'aːv ə, (ii) 'eɪv ə
avail ə 'veɪᵊl ~ed d ~ing ɪŋ ~s z
availabilit|y ə ˌveɪl ə 'bɪl ət li -ɪt i ‖ -əṭ li ~ies
ɪz
availab|le ə 'veɪl əb |ᵊl ~ly li
avalanch|e 'æv ə lɑːntʃ §-læntʃ ‖ -læntʃ ~es ɪz
əz
Avalon 'æv ə lɒn ‖ -laːn
avant-garde ˌæv ɒŋ 'gaːd ◄ -ᵊnt-, -ɒ̃-
‖ ˌaːv aːn 'gaːrd ◄ ˌæv-; ə 'vaːnt gaːrd —Fr
[a vɑ̃ gaʁd]
Avar 'æv aː 'eɪv- ‖ -aːr
avarice 'æv ᵊr_ɪs §_əs
avaricious ˌæv ə 'rɪʃ əs ◄ ~ly li ~ness nəs nɪs
avast ə 'vaːst §-'væst ‖ ə 'væst
avatar 'æv ə taː, ˌ••'• ‖ -taːr ~s z
avaunt ə 'vɔːnt ‖ -'vaːnt
ave, Ave 'hail'; 'prayer' 'aːv eɪ -i
ˌAve Ma'ria; ˌAve Ma,ria 'Lane
Ave. —see Avenue; sometimes spoken as æv
Avebury 'eɪv bᵊr_i ‖ -ˌber i —locally also 'eɪb
ᵊr_i
avenge ə 'vendʒ avenged ə 'vendʒd avenges
ə 'vendʒ ɪz -əz avenging/ly ə 'vendʒ ɪŋ /li
avenger ə 'vendʒ ə ‖ -ᵊr ~s z
avens 'eɪv ᵊnz 'æv-, -ɪnz ‖ 'æv-
aventurine ə 'ventʃ ə riːn -ər ɪn, -ᵊr ən
avenue 'æv ə njuː -ɪ- ‖ -nuː -njuː ~s z
aver ə 'vɜː ‖ ə 'vɝː averred ə 'vɜːd ‖ ə 'vɝːd
averring ə 'vɜːr ɪŋ ‖ ə 'vɝː ɪŋ avers
ə 'vɜːz ‖ ə 'vɝːz
averag|e 'æv ᵊr_ɪdʒ ~ed d ~es ɪz əz ~ing ɪŋ
Averil, Averill 'æv ᵊr_ɪl -ᵊr_əl
Avernus ə 'vɜːn əs ‖ ə 'vɝːn əs
Averroes, Averroës ə 'ver əʊ iːz ˌæv ə 'rəʊ-
‖ -oʊ-
averr... —see aver
averse ə 'vɜːs ‖ ə 'vɝːs ~ly li ~ness nəs nɪs
aversion ə 'vɜːʃ ᵊn §-'vɜːʒ- ‖ ə 'vɝːʒ ᵊn
-'vɝːʃ- ~s z
a'version ˌtherapy
aversive ə 'vɜːs ɪv §-'vɜːz- ‖ ə 'vɝːs ɪv -'vɝːz-
avert ə 'vɜːt ‖ ə 'vɝːt averted ə 'vɜːt ɪd -əd
‖ ə 'vɝːṭ əd averting ə 'vɜːt ɪŋ ‖ ə 'vɝːṭ ɪŋ
averts ə 'vɜːts ‖ ə 'vɝːts
Avery 'eɪv ᵊr_i
Aves, aves 'eɪv iːz
Avesta ə 'vest ə
Avestan ə 'vest ᵊn

Australian English

The pronunciation of English in **Australia** is generally similar to BrE rather than AmE. Some of the points of difference are as follows:

- If there is a choice between ɪ and ə as a weak vowel, Australian English prefers ə.
  valid 'væl əd (rhymes with **salad** 'sæl əd)
  boxes 'bɒks əz (sounds just like **boxers**).
- Australian English uses fewer GLOTTAL STOPs than BrE. When t is between vowels it is often voiced as in AmE; and, as in AmE, it may be elided after n (see T-VOICING).
  better 'beṱ ə
  entertain ˌenṱ ə 'teɪn .
- The vowels ɪ, e and æ tend to be closer than in BrE RP; ɑː tends to be fronter; ɪə and eə are monophthongal (like ɪː, eː); and the diphthongs eɪ and əʊ tend to be wider (almost like aɪ and aʊ), while aɪ and aʊ sound more like ɑɪ, æʊ.

---

avgolemono ˌæv gəʊ
  'lem ə nəʊ ‖ ˌɑːv goʊ 'lem ə noʊ —*Gk*
  [av ɣɔ 'lɛ mɔ nɔ]
Avia *tdmk* 'eɪv i‿ə
avian 'eɪv i‿ən
aviar|y 'eɪv i‿ər li ‖ -er li ~**ies** iz
aviation ˌeɪv i 'eɪʃ ən
aviator 'eɪv i eɪt ə ‖ -eɪṱ ər ~**s** z
Avicenna ˌæv ɪ 'sen ə §-ə-
avid 'æv ɪd §-əd ~**ly** li
avidity ə 'vɪd ət i æ-, -ɪt- ‖ -əṱ i
Aviemore ˌæv i 'mɔː ‖ -'mɔːr -'moʊr
avifauna 'eɪv ɪ ˌfɔːn ə 'æv-, §-ə- ‖ -ˌfɑːn-
Avignon ˌæv iːn jɔ̃ ‖ ˌæv iːn 'joʊn -'jɑːn, -'jɔːn
  —*Fr* [a vi njɔ̃]
Avila 'æv ɪl ə -əl- ‖ 'ɑːv- —*Sp* ['a βi la]
avionic ˌeɪv i 'ɒn ɪk ◄ ‖ -'ɑːn- ~**s** s
avirulent ˌeɪ 'vɪr ʊl ənt ◄ ə'•-, jʊl-, -jəl-, -əl-
  ‖ -əl- -jəl-
Avis 'eɪv ɪs §-əs
Avoca ə 'vəʊk ə ‖ ə 'voʊk ə
avocado ˌæv ə 'kɑːd əʊ ◄ ‖ -oʊ ◄ ˌɑːv- ~**s** z
  ˌavoˌcado 'pear
avocation ˌæv əʊ 'keɪʃ ən ‖ -ə- ~**al** ‿əl ~**s** z
avocet 'æv ə set ~**s** s
Avogadro ˌæv əʊ 'gɑːdr əʊ -'gædr-
  ‖ -ə 'gɑːdr oʊ ˌɑːv-, -'gædr- —*It*
  [a vo 'ga: dro] ~**'s** z
  ˌAvoˌgadro('s) 'number
avoid ə 'vɔɪd **avoided** ə 'vɔɪd ɪd -əd
  avoiding ə 'vɔɪd ɪŋ **avoids** ə 'vɔɪdz
avoidab|le ə 'vɔɪd əb |əl ‖ -**ly** li
avoidance ə 'vɔɪd ənts
avoirdupois ˌæv wɑː dju 'pwɑː ◄ -'• •,
  ˌæv ə də 'pɔɪz ◄ ‖ æv ər də 'pɔɪz '• • •,•
Avon (i) 'eɪv ən -ɒn ‖ -ɑːn, (ii) 'æv ən, (iii) ɑːn
  —*In most senses, (i), though the brand of
  cosmetics is usually* -ɒn ‖ -ɑːn; *the river in*

*Devon is (ii), while the river and loch in
Grampian are (iii).*
Avonmouth 'eɪv ən maʊθ
Avory 'eɪv ər‿i
avow ə 'vaʊ **avowed** ə 'vaʊd **avowing**
  ə 'vaʊ‿ɪŋ **avows** ə 'vaʊz
avowal ə 'vaʊ‿əl ə 'vaʊl ~**s** z
avowedly ə 'vaʊ ɪd li -əd-
Avril 'æv rəl -rɪl
avuncular ə 'vʌŋk jʊl ə -jəl- ‖ -jəl ər
aw ɔː ‖ ɑː
AWACS, Awacs 'eɪ wæks
await ə 'weɪt **awaited** ə 'weɪt ɪd -əd
  ‖ ə 'weɪṱ əd **awaiting** ə 'weɪt ɪŋ ‖ ə 'weɪṱ ɪŋ
  awaits ə 'weɪts
awake ə 'weɪk **awaked** ə 'weɪkt **awakes**
  ə 'weɪks **awaking** ə 'weɪk ɪŋ **awoke**
  ə 'wəʊk ‖ ə 'woʊk **awoken** ə 'wəʊk
  ən ‖ ə 'woʊk ən
awaken ə 'weɪk ən ~**ed** d ~**ing/s**‿ɪŋ/z ~**s** z
award ə 'wɔːd ‖ ə 'wɔːrd ~**ed** ɪd əd ~**er/s** ə/
  z ‖ ər/z ~**ing** ɪŋ ~**s** z
awardable ə 'wɔːd əb əl ‖ ə 'wɔːrd-
aware ə 'weə ‖ ə 'weər
awareness ə 'weə nəs -nɪs ‖ -'wer-
awash ə 'wɒʃ ‖ ə 'wɔːʃ -'wɑːʃ
away ə 'weɪ
Awbery 'ɔː bər‿i ‖ 'ɔː ˌber i 'ɑː-
awe, Awe ɔː ‖ ɑː **awed** ɔːd ‖ ɑːd
aweigh ə 'weɪ (= *away*)
awe-inspiring
  'ɔːr ɪn ˌspaɪ‿ər ɪŋ ‖ 'ɔː ɪn ˌspaɪ‿ər ɪŋ 'ɑː- ~**ly**
  li
awesome 'ɔː səm ‖ 'ɑː- ~**ly** li ~**ness** nəs nɪs
awestricken 'ɔː ˌstrɪk ən ‖ 'ɑː-
awestruck 'ɔː strʌk ‖ 'ɑː-
awful 'ɔːf əl -ʊl ‖ 'ɑːf- —*but in the literal*

A

meaning 'awe-inspiring', 'ɔː ful ‖ 'ɔː-, 'ɑː-
~ness nəs nɪs
awfully 'ɔːf li 'ɔːf əl‿i, -ʊl i ‖ 'ɑːf-
awhile ə 'waɪəl -'hwaɪəl ‖ ə 'hwaɪəl
awkward 'ɔːk wəd ‖ -wərd 'ɑːk- ~**ly** li ~**ness**
nəs nɪs
awl ɔːl ‖ ɑːl (= all) **awls** ɔːlz ‖ ɑːlz
awn ɔːn ‖ ɑːn **awns** ɔːnz ‖ ɑːnz
awning 'ɔːn ɪŋ ‖ 'ɑːn- ~**s** z
awoke ə 'wəʊk ‖ ə 'woʊk
awoken ə 'wəʊk ən ‖ ə 'woʊk ən
AWOL 'eɪ wɒl ‖ -waːl -wɔːl —*or as letters*
ˌeɪ ˌdʌb əl ju ˌəʊ 'el ‖ -ˌoʊ-
awry ə 'raɪ —*jocularly, or by confusion, also*
'ɔːr i
ax, axe æks **axes** 'æks ɪz -əz
axel, Axel 'æks əl (= axle) ~**s** z
axe|man 'æks |mən-mæn ~**men** mən men
axes *from* **ax, axe** 'æks ɪz -əz
axes *pl of* **axis** 'æks iːz
Axholme 'æks həʊm ‖ -hoʊm
axial 'æks i‿əl ~**ly** i
axil 'æks ɪl -əl ~**s** z
axill|a æk 'sɪl |ə ~**ae** iː
axiom 'æks i‿əm ~**s** z
axiomatic ˌæks i‿ə 'mæt ɪk ◀ ‖ -'mæt̬- ~**al** əl
~**ally** əl‿i
axis 'æks ɪs §-əs **axes** 'æks iːz
axle 'æks əl ~**s** z
ax|man 'æks |mən -mæn ~**men** mən men
Axminster 'æks ˌmɪntst ə ‖ -ər ~**s** z
axolotl ˌæks ə 'lɒt əl '••••‖ 'æks ə laːt̬ əl ~**s** z
axon 'æks ɒn ‖ -aːn ~**s** z
axonometric ˌæks ən əʊ 'metr ɪk ◀ ‖ -ən oʊ-
~**ally** əl‿i
ay '*always*' eɪ aɪ
ay '*yes*' aɪ (= I, eye)
ayah 'aɪ ə ~**s** z
ayatollah ˌaɪ‿ə 'tɒl ə ‖ -'toʊl ə ˌaː jə- ~**s** z
Ayckbourn 'eɪk bɔːn ‖ -bɔːrn -boʊrn
Aycliffe 'eɪ klɪf
aye '*always*' eɪ aɪ
aye '*yes*' aɪ (= I, eye) **ayes** aɪz
aye-aye *n* 'aɪ aɪ ~**s** z
Ayenbite of Inwyt
ˌeɪ ən baɪt əv 'ɪn wɪt ‖ ˌ•• baɪt-
Ayer eə ‖ eər æər
Ayers eəz ‖ eərz æərz
ˌAyers 'Rock
Ayesha aɪ 'iːʃ ə ɑː-; 'aɪʃ ə

Aylesbury 'eɪəlz bər‿i ‖ -ˌber i
Aylesford 'eɪəlz fəd 'eɪəls- ‖ -fərd
Aylesham *place in Kent* 'eɪəl ʃəm
Ayling 'eɪl ɪŋ
Aylmer 'eɪəl mə ‖ -mər
Aylsham *place in Nfk* 'eɪəl ʃəm —*locally also*
-səm; 'aːl ʃəm
Aylward 'eɪəl wəd -wɔːd ‖ -wərd -wɔːrd
Aymara ˌaɪm ə 'rɑː ◀ '•••; aɪ 'mɑːr ə —*Sp*
Aymará [aɪ ma 'ra] ~**s** z
Aynho 'eɪn həʊ ‖ -hoʊ
Ayot 'eɪ ət
Ayr eə ‖ eər æər
Ayrshire 'eə ʃə -ʃɪə, §'eə ˌʃaɪ‿ə ‖ 'er ʃər 'ær-,
-ˌʃɪr, -ˌʃaɪ‿ər
Ayrton 'eət ən ‖ 'ert ən 'ært-
Aysgarth 'eɪz gɑːθ ‖ -gɑːrθ
Ayto 'eɪt əʊ ‖ -oʊ
Ayton, Aytoun 'eɪt ən
ayurved|a, A~ ˌaɪ‿ə 'veɪd ə -ʊə-, ˌɑː juə-,
-'viːd- ‖ ˌɑː jʊr- ~**ic** ɪk ◀
A-Z ˌeɪ tə 'zed ‖ ˌeɪt̬ ə 'ziː-
azalea ə 'zeɪl i‿ə ~**s** z
Azani|a ə 'zeɪn i‿ə ~**an/s** ən/z
Azariah ˌæz ə 'raɪ‿ə
azathioprine ˌæz ə 'θaɪ əʊ priːn ‖ -ə priːn
Azerbaijan ˌæz ə baɪ 'dʒɑːn -'ʒɑːn ‖ ˌɑːz ər-
—*Russ* [ʌ zɪr bʌj 'dʒan]
Azerbaijani ˌæz ə baɪ 'dʒɑːn i ◀ -'ʒɑːn-
‖ ˌɑːz ər- ~**s** z
Azeri æ 'zeər i ə- ‖ ɑː 'zer i ˌæ- ~**s** z
azide 'eɪz aɪd ~**s** z
azimuth 'æz ɪm əθ -əm- ~**s** s
azimuthal ˌæz ɪ 'mʌθ əl ◀ -ə-, -'mjuː θ- ~**ly** i
Aziz ə 'ziːz -'zɪz
Aznavour ˌæz nə vʊə -vɔː ‖ ˌɑːz nə 'vʊər -'vɔːr
—*Fr* [az na vuːʁ]
azo 'eɪz əʊ 'æz- ‖ -oʊ
azo- *comb. form* ¦eɪz əʊ ¦æz əʊ ‖ -oʊ —
azobenzene ˌeɪz əʊ 'benz iːn ˌæz- ‖ -oʊ-
azoic ˌₐeɪ 'zəʊ ɪk ‖ -'zoʊ-
Azores ə 'zɔːz ‖ 'eɪz ɔːrz -oʊrz (*)
Azov 'eɪz ɒv 'ɑːz-, 'æz- ‖ -ɑːv -ɔːv —*Russ*
[ʌ 'zɔf]
AZT *tdmk* ˌeɪ zed 'tiː ‖ -ziː-
Aztec 'æz tek ~**s** s
Aztecan 'æz tek ən •'••
azure 'æʒ ə 'eɪʒ-, -ʊə, -jʊə; 'æz jʊə, 'eɪz-;
ə 'zjʊə ‖ 'æʒ ər
azygous 'æz ɪg əs ˌₐeɪ 'zaɪg əs, ə-

B b

b Spelling-to-sound

1 Where the spelling is **b**, the pronunciation is regularly b, as in **baby** 'beɪb i.

2 Where the spelling is double **bb**, the pronunciation is again b, as in **shabby** 'ʃæb i.

3 b is silent in two groups of words:
(i) before **t** in **debt** det, **doubt**, **subtle**;
(ii) after **m** at the end of a word or stem, as in **climb** klaɪm, **lamb**, **thumb**, **bomber**.

B, b biː **Bs, B's, b's** biːz —*Communications code name:* Bravo
ˌB and ˈB, ˌb and ˈb
BA ˌbiː ˈeɪ
baa bɑː ‖ bæ bɑː **baaed** bɑːd ‖ bæd bɑːd
  baaing 'bɑːʳ ɪŋ ‖ 'bæ ɪŋ 'bɑː ɪŋ **baas** bɑːz ‖ bæz bɑːz
Baader-Meinhof
  ˌbɑːd ə 'maɪn hɒf ‖ -ʳr 'maɪn hoʊf —*Ger* [ˌba: dɐ 'maɪn hoːf]
Baal 'beɪ əl beɪˀl, bɑːl
baa-lamb 'bɑː læm ‖ 'bæ- ~s z
Baalbek, Ba'albek 'bɑːl bek —*Arabic* [ba 'ʕal bak]
baas '*master*' bɑːs
baas *from* **baa** bɑːz ‖ bæz bɑːz
Ba'ath bɑːθ —*Arabic* [baʕθ]
Bab *religious leader* bɑːb
baba 'bɑːb ɑː -ə ~s z
  ˌbaba ga'nush gə 'nʊʃ
babaco bə 'bɑːk əʊ ‖ -oʊ ~s z
Babar 'bɑːb ɑː ‖ -ɑːr 'bæb-
Babbage 'bæb ɪdʒ
Babbitt, b~ 'bæb ɪt §-ət
Babbittry 'bæb ɪtr i §-ətr-
babbl|e 'bæb ᵊl **~ed** d **~er/s** _ə/z ‖ _ᵊr/z **~es** z **~ing** _ɪŋ
Babcock 'bæb kɒk ‖ -kɑːk
babe beɪb **babes** beɪbz
Babel, babel 'beɪb ᵊl ‖ 'bæb-
babi... —*see* **baby**
Babington 'bæb ɪŋ tən
Babinski bə 'bɪn ski
babiroussa, babirussa ˌbæb ɪ 'ruːs ə ˌbɑːb-, -ə- ~s z
Babi Yar ˌbɑːb i 'jɑː ‖ -'jɑːr —*Russ* [ˌba bʲi 'jar]
baboon bə 'buːn ‖ bæ- ~s z
Babs bæbz
babu, Babu 'bɑːb uː —*Hindi* [ba: buː]
babushka bə 'buːʃ kə bæ-, -'bʊʃ- —*Russ* ['ba buʃ kə]

baby, Baby 'beɪb i **babied** 'beɪb id **babies** 'beɪb iz **babying** 'beɪb i ɪŋ
  ˌbaby 'blue◄; 'baby ˌboomer; ˌbaby 'boy; 'baby buggy; 'baby ˌcarriage; ˌbaby 'girl; ˌbaby 'grand; 'baby talk; 'baby tooth
baby-bouncer, B~ *tdmk* 'beɪb i ˌbaʊn‿s ə ‖ -ʳr ~s z
Babycham *tdmk* 'beɪb i ʃæm
baby-faced 'beɪb i feɪst
Babygro *tdmk* 'beɪb i grəʊ ‖ -groʊ ~s z
babyhood 'beɪb i hʊd
babyish 'beɪb i_ɪʃ **~ly** li **~ness** nəs nɪs
Babylon 'bæb ɪl ən -əl-; -ɪ lɒn, -ə- ‖ -ə lɑːn -əl ən
Babyloni|a ˌbæb ɪ 'ləʊn i_ə ˌ•ə- ‖ -'loʊn- **~an/s** ən/z
baby-mind|er/s 'beɪb i ˌmaɪnd ə/z ‖ -ᵊr/z **~ing** ɪŋ
baby-|sit 'beɪb i ǀsɪt **~sitter/s** sɪt ə/z ‖ sɪt̬ ᵊr/z **~sitting** sɪt ɪŋ ‖ sɪt̬ ɪŋ
baby-walker 'beɪb i ˌwɔːk ə ‖ -ᵊr ~s z
BAC ˌbiː eɪ 'siː
Bacall bə 'kɔːl ‖ -'kɑːl
Bacardi *tdmk* bə 'kɑːd i ‖ -'kɑːrd- —*Sp* Bacardí [ba kar 'ði] ~s z
baccalaureate ˌbæk ə 'lɔːr i_ət ˌ_ɪt ‖ -'lɑːr- ~s z
baccara, baccarat 'bæk ə rɑː ˌ••'• ‖ 'bɑːk-, ˌbæk- —*Fr* [ba ka ʁa]
baccate 'bæk eɪt
Bacchae 'bæk iː -aɪ
bacchanal ˌbæk ə 'næl '•••; 'bæk ən ᵊl ‖ ˌbɑːk- ~s z
bacchanalia, B~ ˌbæk ə 'neɪl i_ə
bacchanalian ˌbæk ə 'neɪl i_ən ◄
bacchant 'bæk ənt →-ŋt ‖ bə 'kænt -'kɑːnt; 'bæk ənt ~s s
bacchante/s bə 'kænt i/z bə 'kænt/s ‖ -'kænt̬ i/z -'kɑːnt̬-; bə 'kɑːnt/s
Bacchic, b~ 'bæk ɪk
Bacchus 'bæk əs
bacciferous bæk 'sɪf ᵊr_əs

baccy 'bæk i

Bach, bach bɑːk bɑːx —*Ger* [bax]; *Welsh* [baːχ] —*but the floral remedy firm* Dr Bach *is* bætʃ

Bacharach 'bæk ə ræk

bachelor, B~ 'bætʃ əl_ə -ɪl ə ‖ -əl_ər ~hood hud ~ship ʃɪp ~s z
  'bachelor girl; Bachelor of 'Arts; 'bachelor's de,gree

bacillar bə 'sɪl ə 'bæs ɪl ə, -əl- ‖ -ər

bacillary bə 'sɪl ər i 'bæs ɪl-, '•əl- ‖ 'bæs ə ler i bə 'sɪl ər i

bacilliform bə 'sɪl ɪ fɔːm bæ-, -ə• ‖ -fɔːrm

bacill|us bə 'sɪl ləs ~i aɪ iː

bacitracin ˌbæs ɪ 'treɪs ɪn -ə-, §-ən

back bæk backed bækt backing 'bæk ɪŋ
  backs bæks
  'back ˌcountry; ˌback 'door◄; 'back for,mation; ˌback 'garden; ˌback 'number; ˌback 'passage; ˌback 'seat; ˌback street; 'back talk; ˌback 'up; ˌback 'yard

backache 'bæk eɪk ~s s

backbench ˌbæk 'bentʃ ◄ '••

backbencher ˌbæk 'bentʃ ə ◄ '•••‖ -ər ~s z

backbit|er/s 'bæk baɪt |ə/z ‖ -baɪt̬ |ər/z ~ing ɪŋ

backblocks 'bæk blɒks ‖ -blɑːks

backboard 'bæk bɔːd ‖ -bɔːrd -boʊrd ~s z

backbone 'bæk bəʊn ‖ -boʊn ~d d ~s z

backbreak|er/s 'bæk ˌbreɪk |ə/z ‖ -|ər/z ~ing ɪŋ

backchat 'bæk tʃæt

backcloth 'bæk klɒθ ‖ -klɔːθ -klɑːθ

backcomb 'bæk kəʊm ‖ -koʊm ~ed d ~ing ɪŋ ~s z

back|date ˌbæk |'deɪt ◄ '•• ‖ 'bæk |deɪt ~dated deɪt ɪd -əd ‖ deɪt̬ əd ~dates deɪts ~dating deɪt ɪŋ ‖ deɪt̬ ɪŋ

backdrop 'bæk drɒp ‖ -drɑːp ~s s

backer, B~ 'bæk ə ‖ -ər ~s z

backfill 'bæk fɪl ~ed d ~ing ɪŋ ~s z

backfire n 'bæk ˌfaɪ_ə ‖ -ˌfaɪ_ər ~s z

backfire v ˌbæk 'faɪ_ə ◄ '•, •• ‖ 'bæk ˌfaɪ_ər ~d d ~s z backfiring ˌbæk 'faɪ_ər ɪŋ '•, •- ‖ 'bæk ˌfaɪ_ər ɪŋ

backflip 'bæk flɪp ~s s

back-formation 'bæk fɔː ˌmeɪʃ ən ‖ -fɔːr- ~s z

backgammon 'bæk ˌgæm ən •'••

background 'bæk graʊnd ~s z

backhand 'bæk hænd ~ed v ɪd əd ~ing ɪŋ ~s z

backhanded adj ˌbæk 'hænd ɪd ◄ -əd ‖ 'bæk hænd əd ~ly li ~ness nəs nɪs

backhander 'bæk hænd ə ˌ•'•• ‖ -ər ~s z

backhoe 'bæk həʊ ‖ -hoʊ ~s z

Backhouse, b~ 'bæk haʊs -əs

backing 'bæk ɪŋ
  'backing store

backlash 'bæk læʃ

backless 'bæk ləs -lɪs

backlighting ˌbæk 'laɪt ɪŋ '•, •• ‖ 'bæk ˌlaɪt̬ ɪŋ ˌ•'••

backlist 'bæk lɪst ~s s

backlit ˌbæk 'lɪt ◄ '••

backlog 'bæk lɒg ‖ -lɔːg -lɑːg ~s z

backmost 'bæk məʊst ‖ -moʊst

backpack 'bæk pæk ~ed t ~er/s ə/z ‖ -ər/z ~ing ɪŋ ~s s

backpedal, back-pedal ˌbæk 'ped əl ◄ '•, •• ‖ 'bæk ˌped əl ~ed, ~led d ~ing, ~ling ɪŋ ~s z

backra 'bʌk rə 'bæk- ‖ 'bæk- 'buk-

backrest 'bæk rest ~s s

backroom 'bæk ruːm -rum ~s z
  'backroom boys

Backs bæks

backscratcher 'bæk ˌskrætʃ ə ‖ -ər ~s z

back-seat ˌbæk 'siːt ◄
  ˌback-seat 'driver

backsheesh ˌbæk 'ʃiːʃ '••

backside 'bæk saɪd ˌ•'• ~s z

backsight 'bæk saɪt ~s s

backslapping 'bæk ˌslæp ɪŋ ~s z

backslash 'bæk slæʃ ~es ɪz əz

backslid|e 'bæk slaɪd ˌ•'• ~er/s ə/z ‖ -ər/z ~ing ɪŋ

backspac|e n 'bæk speɪs ~es ɪz əz

backspac|e v ˌbæk 'speɪs ◄ '•• ~ed t ~es ɪz əz ~ing ɪŋ

backspin 'bæk spɪn

backstage ˌbæk 'steɪdʒ ◄
  ˌbackstage 'workers

backstair ˌbæk 'steə ◄ ‖ 'bæk ster ~s z
  ˌbackstairs 'influence

backstay 'bæk steɪ ~s z

backstitch 'bæk stɪtʃ ~ed t ~es ɪz əz ~ing ɪŋ

backstop 'bæk stɒp ‖ -stɑːp ~s s

backstreet 'bæk striːt

backstroke 'bæk strəʊk ‖ -stroʊk ~s s

back-to-back ˌbæk tə 'bæk ◄
  ˌback-to-back 'housing

backtrack 'bæk træk ˌ•'• ~ed t ~ing ɪŋ ~s s

backup 'bæk ʌp ~s s

backward 'bæk wəd ‖ -wərd ~ly li ~ness nəs nɪs

backwardation ˌbæk wə 'deɪʃ ən ‖ -wər-

backwards 'bæk wədz ‖ -wərdz

backwash 'bæk wɒʃ ‖ -wɔːʃ -wɑːʃ ~es ɪz əz

backwater 'bæk ˌwɔːt ə ‖ -ˌwɔːt̬ ər -ˌwɑːt̬ ər ~s z

backwoods 'bæk wudz

backwoods|man 'bæk wudz |mən ˌ•'•- ~men mən men

backyard ˌbæk 'jɑːd ◄ ‖ -'jɑːrd ◄ ~s z

Bacofoil tdmk 'beɪk əʊ fɔɪ_əl ‖ -oʊ-

bacon, Bacon 'beɪk ən ~s z
  ˌbacon 'sandwich

Baconian beɪ 'kəʊn i_ən bə- ‖ -'koʊn- ~s z

bacteria bæk 'tɪər i_ə ‖ -'tɪr-

bacterial bæk 'tɪər i_əl ‖ -'tɪr- ~ly i

bactericidal bæk ˌtɪər ɪ 'saɪd əl ◄ -ə- ‖ -ˌtɪr ə- ~ly i

bactericide bæk 'tɪər ɪ saɪd -ə- ‖ -'tɪr ə- ~s z

bacteriological bæk ˌtɪər i_ə 'lɒdʒ ɪk əl ◄ ‖ -ˌtɪr i_ə 'lɑːdʒ- ~ly _i

bacteriologist bæk ˌtɪər i 'ɒl ədʒ ɪst §-əst
‖ -ˌtɪr i 'ɑːl- ~s s
bacteriology bæk ˌtɪər i 'ɒl ədʒ i ‖ -ˌtɪr i 'ɑːl-
bacteriophag|e bæk 'tɪər i‿əʊ feɪdʒ ‖ -'tɪr i‿ə-
~es ɪz əz
bacterium bæk 'tɪər i‿əm ‖ -'tɪr-
Bactria 'bæk tri‿ə
Bactrian 'bæk tri‿ən ~s z
Bacup 'beɪk əp -ʌp
bad bæd
ˌbad 'blood; ˌbad 'debt; ˌbad 'faith; ˌbad
'feeling; ˌbad 'form; ˌbad 'news
Bad in German placenames bæd bɑːd ‖ bɑːd
—Ger [baːt] —See also phrases with this word
Badajoz ˌbæd ə 'hɒz -'həʊz, '•••
‖ ˌbɑːd ə 'hoʊs —Sp [ba ða 'xoθ]
badass 'bæd æs ~es ɪz əz
Badcock 'bæd kɒk →'bæg- ‖ -kɑːk
Baddeley 'bæd əl‿i
Baddesley (i) 'bæd ɪz li -əz-, (ii) 'bædz li
baddie, baddy 'bæd i baddies 'bæd iz
Baddiel bə 'diːəl
baddish 'bæd ɪʃ
bade bæd beɪd
Badedas tdmk 'bɑːd ə dæs -ɪ-; bə 'deɪd æs, -əs
Badel bə 'del
Baden British or American name 'beɪd ən
Baden places in German-speaking countries
'bɑːd ən —Ger ['baː dən]
Baden-Baden ˌbɑːd ən 'bɑːd ən —Ger
[ˌbaː dən 'baː dən]
Baden-Powell ˌbeɪd ən 'pəʊ əl -'paʊ‿əl, -el, -ɪl,
-'paʊl ‖ -'poʊ əl
Bader 'bɑːd ə ‖ -ər
badge bædʒ badges 'bædʒ ɪz -əz
badger 'bædʒ ə ‖ -ər ~ed d badgering 'bædʒ
ər‿ɪŋ ~s z
Bad Godesberg ˌbæd 'gəʊd əz bɜːg -beəg;
-'gəʊdz• ‖ ˌbɑːt 'goʊd əz bɜːg -berg —Ger
[ˌbaːt 'goː dəs bɛʁk]
badinage 'bæd ɪ nɑːʒ -ə-, -nɑːdʒ, ˌ••'• —Fr
[ba di naʒ]
badlands 'bæd lændz
badly 'bæd li
badly-off ˌbæd li 'ɒf ◄ -'ɔːf ‖ -'ɔːf ◄ -'ɑːf
badminton, B~ 'bæd mɪn tən →'bæb-, △-mɪŋ-
bad-|mouth 'bæd maʊθ →'bæb-, -maʊð
~mouthed maʊθt maʊðd ~mouthing
maʊθ ɪŋ maʊð ɪŋ ~mouths v maʊθs maʊðz
badness 'bæd nəs -nɪs
Badoit tdmk 'bæd wɑː ‖ bɑː 'dwɑː —Fr
[ba dwa]
bad-tempered ˌbæd 'temp əd ◄ ‖ -ərd ◄ '•••
~ly li
Baedeker 'beɪd ɪk ə -ək-, -ek- ‖ -ər ~s z —Ger
['bɛː də kɐ]
Baer beə ‖ beər
Baerlein 'beə laɪn ‖ 'ber-
Baez 'baɪ ez •'• —but the singer Joan Baez
prefers baɪz
Baffin 'bæf ɪn §-ən
baffl|e 'bæf əl ~ed d ~es z ~ing‿ɪŋ
bafflement 'bæf əl mənt

BAFTA 'bæft ə
bag bæg bagged bægd bagging 'bæg ɪŋ
bags bægz
'bag ˌlady
Baganda bə 'gænd ə -'gɑːnd-
bagasse bə 'gæs bæ-, -'gɑːs
bagatelle ˌbæg ə 'tel ~s z
Bagdad ˌbæg 'dæd '•• ‖ 'bæg dæd —Arabic
[baɣ 'daːd]
Bagehot (i) 'bædʒ ət, (ii) 'bæg ət —The
economist Walter B~ was (i).
bagel 'beɪg əl ~s z
bagful 'bæg fʊl ~s z bagsful 'bægz fʊl
baggag|e 'bæg ɪdʒ ~es ɪz əz
'baggage ˌcar; 'baggage ˌroom; 'baggage
ˌtag
Baggally 'bæg əl i
bagg... —see bag
Baggie tdmk 'bæg i ~s z
Baggins 'bæg ɪnz §-ənz
bagg|y 'bæg li ~ier i‿ə ‖ i‿ər ~iest i‿ɪst i‿əst
~ily ɪ li əl i ~iness i nəs -nɪs
Baghdad ˌbæg 'dæd '•• ‖ 'bæg dæd —Arabic
[baɣ 'daːd]
Bagley 'bæg li
bag|man 'bæg |mən ~men mən men
Bagnall, Bagnell 'bæg nəl
bagnio 'bæn jəʊ 'bɑːn- ‖ 'bɑːn joʊ ~s z
Bagnold 'bæg nəʊld →-nɒʊld ‖ -noʊld
bagpip|e 'bæg paɪp ~er/s ə/z ‖ ər/z ~es s
~ing ɪŋ
bagsful 'bægz fʊl
Bagshaw 'bæg ʃɔː ‖ -ʃɑː
Bagshot 'bæg ʃɒt ‖ -ʃɑːt
baguette bæ 'get bə- ~s s —Fr [ba ɡɛt]
Baguley 'bæg əl‿i -jʊl-
bagwash 'bæg wɒʃ ‖ -wɔːʃ -wɑːʃ ~s ɪz əz
bah bɑː ‖ bæ (= baa)
bahadur bə 'hɑːd ə -ʊə ‖ -ər -ʊr ~s z
Bahai, Baha'i, Bahá'í bə 'haɪ bɑː-, -'hɑː i,
-'haɪ i ~s z —Persian [ba hɑː ʔiː]
Baha|ism bə 'haɪ |ˌɪz əm bɑː-, -'hɑː- ~ist/s
ɪst/s əst/s
Bahama bə 'hɑːm ə ~s z
Bahamian bə 'heɪm i‿ən -'hɑːm- ~s z
Bahasa bə 'hɑːs ə bɑː-
Baha'ullah, Bahá'u'lláh ˌbɑː hɑː 'ʊl ə
bə ˌhɑː ʊ 'lɑː
Bahia bə 'hiː‿ə bɑː 'iː ə —Port [bɐ 'i ɐ]
Bahrain, Bahrein ˌbɑː 'reɪn ˌbɑːx-;
ˌbɑː hə 'reɪn —Arabic [baħ 'reːn] ~i/s i/z
baht bɑːt bahts bɑːts
bahuvrihi ˌbɑː huː 'vriː hi
Baikal baɪ 'kæl -'kɑːl, '•• —Russ [bʌj 'kał]
bail beɪəl bailed beɪəld bailing 'beɪəl ɪŋ bails
beɪəlz
bailable 'beɪəl əb əl
Baildon 'beɪəld ən
Baile Atha Cliath, Baile Átha Cliath ˌblɑː 'kliə
ˌblɔː- ‖ -'kliː ə ˌblɔː- —Irish [bɫɑː 'kliə]
bailee ˌbeɪ 'liː ˌbeɪəl 'iː ~s z
bailey, B~ 'beɪl i ~s, ~'s z
ˌBailey 'bridge, '•••

bailie 'beɪl i ~s z
bailiff 'beɪl ɪf §-əf ~s s
bailiwick 'beɪl ɪ wɪk §-ə- ~s s
Baillie 'beɪl i
Baillieu 'beɪl ju:
Bailly 'beɪl i
bailment 'beɪəl mənt
bailor ˌbeɪ 'lɔ: 'beɪəl ə, ˌbeɪəl 'ɔ: ‖ -'lɔ:r ~s z
bailout 'beɪəl aʊt ~s s
bails|man 'beɪəlz |mən ~men mən men
Baily 'beɪl i ~'s z
Bain beɪn
Bainbridge 'beɪn brɪdʒ →'beɪm-
Baines beɪnz
bain-marie ˌbæn mə 'ri: →ˌbæm-, -mæ- ~s z
—Fr [bæ ma ʁi]
Bairam baɪ 'rɑːm -'ræm; 'baɪər əm ~s z
Baird beəd ‖ beərd
bairn beən ‖ beərn **bairns** beənz ‖ beərnz
Bairnsfather 'beənz ˌfɑːð ə ‖ 'bernz ˌfɑːð ər
Bairstow 'beə stəʊ ‖ 'ber stoʊ
bait beɪt **baited** 'beɪt ɪd -əd ‖ 'beɪt̬ əd **baiting**
'beɪt ɪŋ ‖ 'beɪt̬ ɪŋ **baits** beɪts
baize beɪz (= bays)
Baja 'bɑː hɑː —Sp ['ba xa]
ˌBaja ˌCali'fornia
Bajan 'beɪdʒ ən ~s z
bajra 'bɑːdʒ rə
bake beɪk **baked** beɪkt **bakes** beɪks **baking**
'beɪk ɪŋ
ˌbaked 'beans
bake|house 'beɪk| haʊs ~houses haʊz ɪz -əz
bakelite, B~ tdmk 'beɪk ə laɪt 'beɪk laɪt
baker, Baker 'beɪk ə ‖ -ər ~s z
ˌbaker's 'dozen; 'Baker Street
bakeries 'beɪk ər_iz
Bakerloo ˌbeɪk ə 'lu: ‖ -ər-
ˌBaker'loo line
Bakersfield 'beɪk əz fi:əld ‖ -ərz-
baker|y 'beɪk ər_|i ~ies iz
Bakewell 'beɪk wel -wəl
ˌBakewell 'tart
baking 'beɪk ɪŋ
'baking ˌpowder
baklava 'bɑːk lə vɑː; bæk- ~s z
baksheesh ˌbæk 'ʃiːʃ '··
Bakst bækst ‖ bɑːkst —Russ [bakst]
Baku ⑴bɑː 'ku: bæ-
Bakunin bə 'kuːn ɪn bɑː-, §-ən —Russ
[bʌ 'ku nʲɪn]
Bala 'bæl ə 'bɑːl ə
Balaam 'beɪl əm -æm
balaclava, B~ ˌbæl ə 'klɑːv ə ◄ —Russ
[bə ɫʌ 'kɫa və] ~s z
balalaika ˌbæl ə 'laɪk ə —Russ [bə ɫʌ 'ɫaj kə]
~s z
balanc|e 'bæl ənᵗs ~ed t ~es ɪz əz ~ing ɪŋ
ˌbalanced 'diet; ˌbalance of 'power;
'balance sheet; 'balance wheel
Balanchine 'bæl ən tʃiːn -ʃiːn
balas 'bæl əs -beɪl-
balata 'bæl ət ə bə 'lɑːt ə ‖ bə 'lɑːt̬ ə ~s z

Balaton 'bæl ə tɒn 'bɒl- ‖ 'bɑːl ə tɑːn 'bæl-,
-toʊn —Hung ['bɒ lɒ ton]
Balboa, b~ bæl 'bəʊ ə ‖ -'boʊ- ~s z —Sp
[bal 'βo a]
Balbriggan, b~ bæl 'brɪg ən
Balbus 'bælb əs
Balchin 'bɔːltʃ ɪn 'bɒltʃ-, §-ən ‖ 'bɑːltʃ-
Balcomb, Balcombe 'bɔːlk əm 'bɒlk- ‖ 'bɑːlk-
Balcon 'bɔːlk ən 'bɒlk- ‖ 'bɑːlk-
balcon|y 'bælk ən |i ~ies iz
bald bɔːld §bɒld ‖ bɑːld (= bawled) **balder**
'bɔːld ə §'bɒld- ‖ 'bɔːld ər 'bɑːld- **baldest**
'bɔːld ɪst §'bɒld-, -əst ‖ 'bɑːld-
baldachin, baldaquin 'bɔːld ək ɪn §'bɒld-,
§-ən ‖ 'bɑːld-
Balder name 'bɔːld ə 'bɒld- ‖ 'bɔːld ər 'bɑːld-
balderdash 'bɔːld ə dæʃ §'bɒld- ‖ -ər- 'bɑːld-
bald-faced ˌbɔːld 'feɪst ◄ §ˌbɒld- ‖ ˌbɑːld-
baldhead 'bɔːld hed §'bɒld- ‖ 'bɑːld- ~s z
baldheaded ˌbɔːld 'hed ɪd ◄ §ˌbɒld-,
-əd ‖ ˌbɑːld-
baldie 'bɔːld i §'bɒld i ‖ 'bɑːld i ~s z
balding 'bɔːld ɪŋ §'bɒld- ‖ 'bɑːld-
baldish 'bɔːld ɪʃ §'bɒld- ‖ 'bɑːld-
bald|ly 'bɔːld |li §'bɒld- ‖ 'bɑːld- ~ness nəs nɪs
Baldock 'bɔːld ɒk 'bɒld- ‖ -ɑːk 'bɑːld-
baldric 'bɔːld rɪk §'bɒldr- ‖ 'bɑːldr-
Baldry 'bɔːldr i 'bɒldr i ‖ 'bɑːldr i
Baldwin 'bɔːld wɪn §'bɒld-, §-wən ‖ 'bɑːld-
bale beɪəl (= bail) **baled** beɪəld **bales** beɪəlz
baling 'beɪəl ɪŋ
Bale family name beɪəl
Bale, Bâle place in Switzerland bɑːl —Fr [bɑl]
Balearic ˌbæl i 'ær ɪk ◄ bə 'lɪər ɪk ‖ -'er- ~s s
baleen bə 'liːn bæ-, beɪ-
baleful 'beɪəl fəl -fʊl -ly i ~ness nəs nɪs
Balenciaga bə ˌlenᵗs i 'ɑːg ə bæ- —Sp
[ba len 'θja ɣa]
baler 'beɪəl ə ‖ -ər ~s z
Balfe bælf
Balfour (i) 'bælf ə ‖ -ər, (ii) 'bæl fɔː ‖ -fɔːr -foʊr
the ˌBalfour ˌdecla'ration
Balham 'bæl əm
Bali 'bɑːl i
Balinese ˌbɑːl ɪ 'niːz ◄ -ə- ‖ -'niːs
Baliol 'beɪl i_əl
balk bɔːk bɔːlk ‖ bɑːk **balked** bɔːkt
bɔːlkt ‖ bɑːkt **balking** 'bɔːk ɪŋ 'bɔːlk-
‖ 'bɑːk- **balks** bɔːks bɔːlks ‖ bɑːks
Balkan 'bɔːlk ən 'bɒlk- ‖ 'bɑːlk- ~s z
Balkanis..., b~ —see Balkaniz...
Balkanization, b~ ˌbɔːlk ən aɪ 'zeɪʃ ən ˌbɒlk-,
-ɪ'·· ‖ -ə'·· ˌbɑːlk-
Balkaniz|e, b~ 'bɔːlk ə naɪz 'bɒlk- ‖ 'bɑːlk-
~ed d ~es ɪz əz ~ing ɪŋ
balk|y 'bɔːk |i ‖ 'bɑːk- ~ier i_ə ‖ i_ər ~iest i_ɪst
i_əst
ball, Ball bɔːl ‖ bɑːl **balled** bɔːld ‖ bɑːld (=
bald) **balling** 'bɔːl ɪŋ ‖ 'bɑːl- **balls** bɔːlz
‖ bɑːlz
'ball boy; 'ball games; 'ball park
Ballachulish ˌbæl ə 'huːl ɪʃ
ballad 'bæl əd ~s z

ballade bæ 'lɑːd bə- ~s z —*Fr* [ba lad]
balladeer ˌbæl ə 'dɪə ‖ -'dɪˀr ~s z
Ballance 'bæl ənts
ball-and-socket ˌbɔːl ən 'sɒk ɪt -ənd-, §-ət
‖ -'sɑːk ət ˌbɑːl-
Ballantine 'bæl ən taɪn
Ballantrae ˌbæl ən 'treɪ
Ballantyne 'bæl ən taɪn
Ballarat 'bæl ə ræt ˌ•••
Ballard 'bæl ɑːd -əd ‖ -ɑːrd -ˀrd
ballast 'bæl əst ~ed ɪd əd ~ing ɪŋ ~s s
Ballater 'bæl ət ə ‖ -ət̬ ˀr
ballbearing ˌbɔːl 'beər ɪŋ ‖ -'ber- ˌbɑːl-, -'bær-
~s z
ballcock 'bɔːl kɒk ‖ -kɑːk 'bɑːl- ~s s
ballerina ˌbæl ə 'riːn ə ~s z
Ballesteros ˌbæl ɪ 'stɪər ɒs -ə-, -e-, -'steər-,
-'ster- ‖ ˌbaɪ ə 'ster oʊs ˌbæl- —*Sp*
[ba ʎe 'ste ros, ba je-]
ballet 'bæl eɪ ‖ bæ 'leɪ 'bæl eɪ ~s z
'ballet ˌdancer ‖ •'• ˌ••
balletic bæ 'let ɪk bə- ‖ -'let̬-
balletomane 'bæl ɪt əʊ meɪn '•ət-, '•et-;
bə 'let • •, bæ- ‖ bə 'let̬ ə meɪn
balletomania ˌbæl ɪt əʊ 'meɪn i‿ə ˌ•ət-, ˌ•et-
‖ ˌlet̬ ə 'meɪn i‿ə *(*)*
Balliol 'beɪl i‿əl
ballist|a bə 'lɪst ə ~ae iː ~as əz
ballistic bə 'lɪst ɪk ~ally ᵊl‿i ~s s
Balloch 'bæl ək -əx —*but the place in Highland
region is* bæ 'lɒx
ballock 'bɒl ək ‖ 'bɔːl- 'bɑːl- ~s s
balloon bə 'luːn ~ed d ~ing ɪŋ ~s z
balloonist bə 'luːn ɪst §-əst ~s s
ballot 'bæl ət **balloted** 'bæl ət ɪd -əd
‖ 'bæl ət̬ əd **balloting** 'bæl ət ɪŋ ‖ 'bæl ət̬ ɪŋ
ballots 'bæl əts
'ballot box; 'ballot ˌpaper
ballpark 'bɔːl pɑːk ‖ -pɑːrk 'bɑːl- ~s s
ball-peen, ball-pein 'bɔːl piːn ‖ 'bɑːl- ~s z
ballplayer 'bɔːl ˌpleɪ ə ‖ -ˀr 'bɑːl- ~s z
ballpoint 'bɔːl pɔɪnt ‖ 'bɑːl- ~s s
ballroom 'bɔːl ruːm -rʊm ‖ 'bɑːl- ~s z
ˌballroom 'dancing
balls, Balls bɔːlz ‖ bɑːlz **ballsed** bɔːlzd
‖ bɑːlzd **ballses** 'bɔːlz ɪz -əz ‖ 'bɑːlz-
ballsing 'bɔːlz ɪŋ ‖ 'bɑːlz- —*These are parts
of the slang verb* to balls up
balls-up *n* 'bɔːlz ʌp ‖ 'bɑːlz- ~s s
balls|y 'bɔːlz |i ‖ 'bɑːlz- ~ier i‿ə ‖ i‿ˀr ~iest
i‿ɪst i‿əst ~iness i nəs i nɪs
bally, Bally 'bæl i —*but the tdmk for shoes is
properly Fr* [ba ji]
Ballycastle ˌbæl i 'kɑːs ᵊl §-'kæs- ‖ -'kæs-
ballyhoo ˌbæl i 'huː ‖ 'bæl i huː ~ed d ~ing ɪŋ
~s z
Ballymacarrett ˌbæl i mə 'kær ət -ɪt ‖ -'ker-
Ballymena ˌbæl i 'miːn ə
Ballymoney ˌbæl i 'mʌn i
balm bɑːm §bɑːlm, §bɒlm **balms** bɑːmz
§bɑːlmz, §bɒlmz
Balmain *(i)* ˌbæl 'meɪn; *(ii)* 'bæl mæ̃ -mæn
‖ -meɪn •'• —*Fr* [bal mæ̃] —*as an English or*

*Scottish name, and for the place in Australia,
(i); as a French name, (ii)*
Balmoral, b~ bæl 'mɒr əl ˌ•- ‖ -'mɔːr- -'mɑːr-
balm|y 'bɑːm |i §'bɑːlm-, §'bɒlm- ~ier
i‿ə ‖ i‿ˀr ~iest i‿ɪst i‿əst ~ily ɪ li əl i ~iness
i nəs -nɪs
balneal 'bæln i‿əl
balneology ˌbæln i 'ɒl ədʒ i ‖ -'ɑːl-
Balniel bæl 'niː²l
Balogh 'bæl ɒg ‖ -ɑːg
baloney bə 'ləʊn i ‖ -'loʊn-
Baloo bə 'luː 'bɑːl u:
BALPA 'bælp ə
Balquhidder bæl 'wɪd ə -'hwɪd-, -'kwɪd-
‖ -'hwɪd ˀr
balsa 'bɔːls ə -'bɒls- ‖ 'bɑːls- ~s s
Balsall 'bɔːls ᵊl 'bɒls- ‖ -ɔːl 'bɑːls ɑːl
balsam 'bɔːls əm 'bɒls- ‖ 'bɑːls- ~s z
balsamic bɔːl 'sæm ɪk bɒl- ‖ bɑːl-
Balt bɔːlt bɒlt ‖ bɑːlt **Balts** bɔːlts
bɒlts ‖ bɑːlts
Balthazar bæl 'θæz ə 'bælθ ə zɑː, ˌ•••
‖ bæl 'θeɪz ˀr —*in Shakespeare* ˌbælθ ə 'zɑː,
'••• ‖ -'zɑːr
balti 'bɔːlt i 'bɒlt-, 'bælt- ‖ 'bɑːlt i 'bɔːlt-
Baltic 'bɔːlt ɪk 'bɒlt-‖ 'bɑːlt-
ˌBaltic 'Sea
Baltimore 'bɔːlt ɪ mɔː 'bɒlt-, -ə- ‖ -ə mɔːr
'bɑːlt-, -moʊr; -əm ˀr
Balto-Slavic ˌbɔːlt əʊ 'slɑːv ɪk ◂ ˌbɒlt-
‖ -oʊ 'slæv- ˌbɑːlt-, -'slɑːv-
Balto-Slavonic ˌbɔːlt əʊ slə 'vɒn ɪk ◂ ˌbɒlt-
‖ -oʊ slə 'vɑːn- ˌbɑːlt-
Baluchi bə 'luːtʃ i ~s z
Baluchistan bə ˌluːtʃ ɪ 'stɑːn -ə-, -'stæn, •'•••
‖ -ə 'stæn
baluster 'bæl əst ə ‖ -ˀr ~s z
balustrade ˌbæl ə 'streɪd ‖ 'bæl ə streɪd ~s z
Balzac 'bælz æk ⚠'bɔːlz-, ⚠'bɒlz-; bæl 'zæk
‖ 'bɔːlz- 'bɑːlz-, -ɑːk —*Fr* [bal zak]
Bamako ˌbæm ə 'kəʊ '••• ‖ -'koʊ ˌbɑːm-
Bamber 'bæm bə ‖ -bˀr
Bamberg 'bæm bɜːg ‖ -bɝːg 'bɑːm-, -berg
—*Ger* ['bam bɛʁk]
Bambi 'bæm bi
bambin|o bæm 'biːn |əʊ ‖ -|oʊ bɑːm- ~i i ~os
əʊz ‖ oʊz —*It* [bam 'biː no]
bamboo ˌbæm 'buː ◂ ~s z
ˌbamboo 'furniture
bamboozl|e ₍ᵢ₎bæm 'buːz ᵊl ~ed d ~es z ~ing
‿ɪŋ
Bamburgh 'bæm bər‿ə
Bamford 'bæm fəd ‖ -fˀrd
Bamforth 'bæm fɔːθ ‖ -fɔːrθ -foʊrθ
ban bæn **banned** bænd *(= band)* **banning**
'bæn ɪŋ **bans** bænz
banal bə 'nɑːl bæ-, -'næl, §'beɪn ᵊl ~ly li
banalit|y bə 'næl ət |i bæ-, beɪ-, -ɪt i ‖ -ət̬ |i
~ies iz
banana bə 'nɑːn ə ‖ -'næn- ~s z
ba'nana oil; ba'nana skin; baˌnana 'split
Bananarama
bə ˌnɑːn ə 'rɑːm ə ‖ bə ˌnæn ə 'ræm ə

B

Banaras bə 'nɑːr əs
banausic bə 'nɔːz ɪk -'nɔːs- ‖ -'nɔːs- -'nɑːs-, -'nɔːz-, -'nɑːz-
Banbridge bæn 'brɪdʒ →bæm-, '••
Banbury 'bæn bər_i →'bæm- ‖ -ˌber i
    ˌBanbury 'Cross
Banchory 'bæŋk ər i 'bæŋx-
banco 'bæŋk əʊ ‖ -oʊ ~s z
Bancroft 'bæn krɒft →'bæŋ- ‖ -krɔːft -krɑːft
band bænd **banded** 'bænd ɪd -əd **banding**
    'bænd ɪŋ **bands** bændz
    'band saw
Banda 'bænd ə ‖ 'bɑːnd-
bandag|e 'bænd ɪdʒ ~ed d ~es ɪz əz ~ing ɪŋ
Band-Aid *tdmk*, **band-aid** 'bænd eɪd ~s z
bandana, bandanna ⑴bæn 'dæn ə ~s z
Bandaranaike ˌbænd ər ə 'naɪ ɪk ə -'naɪk ə
    ‖ ˌbɑːnd-
Bandar Seri Begawan
    ˌbænd ə ˌser i bə 'gɑː wən ˌ•ɑː-, -be'•-,
    -bɪ'•-, -ˌgaʊ ən ‖ ˌbɑːnd ər-
bandbox 'bænd bɒks →'bæm- ‖ -bɑːks ~es ɪz
    əz
bandeau 'bænd əʊ ‖ bæn 'doʊ ~s, ~x z —*Fr*
    [bɑ̃ do]
banderol, banderole 'bænd ə rəʊl →-rɒʊl
    ‖ -roʊl ~s z
bandicoot 'bænd i kuːt ~s s
bandie... —*see* **bandy**
bandit 'bænd ɪt §-ət ~s s
banditry 'bænd ɪtr i -ətr-
banditti bæn 'dɪt i ‖ -'dɪt̬-
bandleader 'bænd ˌliːd ə ‖ -ᵊr ~s z
bandmaster 'bænd ˌmɑːst ə §-ˌmæst ə
    ‖ -ˌmæst ᵊr ~s z
bandoleer, bandolier ˌbænd ə 'lɪə ‖ -'lɪᵊr ~s z
bandore bæn 'dɔː 'bænd ɔː ‖ 'bænd ɔːr -oʊr
    ~s z
band-pass 'bænd pɑːs §-pæs ‖ -pæs ~es ɪz əz
bandsaw 'bænd sɔː ‖ -sɑː ~s z
bands|man 'bændz |mən ~men mən men
bandstand 'bænd stænd ~s z
Bandung 'bæn dʊŋ ,•'• ‖ 'bɑːn-
bandwagon 'bænd ˌwæg ən ~s z
bandwidth 'bænd wɪdθ -wɪtθ ~s s
band|y 'bænd |i ~ied id ~ies iz ~ying i_ɪŋ
bandy-legged ˌbænd i 'legd ◄ -'leg ɪd, -'leg əd
bane beɪn **banes** beɪnz
baneful 'beɪn fᵊl -fʊl ~ly i
Banff bæntᶠf →bæmᵖf
Banfield 'bæn fiːᵊld
bang bæŋ **banged** bæŋd **banging** 'bæŋ ɪŋ
    bangs bæŋz
Bangalore ˌbæŋ gə 'lɔː ‖ -'lɔːr -'loʊr, '•••
banger 'bæŋ ə ‖ -ᵊr ~s z
Bangkok, b~ ˌbæŋ 'kɒk '•• ‖ 'bæŋ kɑːk ~'s,
    ~s s
Bangladesh ˌbæŋ glə 'deʃ ◄ -'deɪʃ ‖ ˌbɑːŋ-
Bangladeshi ˌbæŋ glə 'deʃ i ◄ -'deɪʃ- ‖ ˌbɑːŋ-
    ~z z
bangle 'bæŋ gᵊl ~s z
bang-on ˌbæŋ 'ɒn ‖ -'ɔːn -'ɑːn

Bangor *(i)* 'bæŋ gə △'bæŋ ə ‖ -gᵊr, *(ii)*
    -gɔː ‖ -gɔːr —*Welsh* ['baŋ gɔr] —*The places
    in the UK are usually (i), but the place in ME is
    usually (ii).*
Bangui ˌbɒŋ 'giː ˌbɑːŋ- ‖ ˌbɑːŋ- —*Fr* [bɑ̃ gi]
bang-up ˌbæŋ 'ʌp ◄
Banham 'bæn əm
banian 'bæn i_ən 'bæn jæn ~s z
banish 'bæn ɪʃ ~ed t ~es ɪz əz ~ing ɪŋ
banister 'bæn ɪst ə -əst ə ‖ -ᵊr ~s z
Banja Luka ˌbæn jə 'luːk ə ˌbɑːn- ‖ ˌbɑːn-
    —*Serbian* ['ba: ɲa: "lu: ka]
banjax 'bæn dʒæks ~ed t
banjo 'bæn dʒəʊ ˌ•'• ‖ -dʒoʊ ~es, ~s z ~ist/s
    ɪst/s §əst/s
Banjul bæn 'dʒuːl ‖ 'bɑːn dʒuːl
bank bæŋk **banked** bæŋkt **banking** 'bæŋk ɪŋ
    banks bæŋks
    'bank acˌcount; 'bank ˌbalance; 'bank
    draft; ˌbank 'holiday; 'bank loan; 'bank
    ˌmanager; 'bank rate; 'bank ˌstatement
bankable 'bæŋk əb ᵊl
bankbill 'bæŋk bɪl ~s z
bankbook 'bæŋk bʊk ~s s
banker 'bæŋk ə ‖ -ᵊr ~s z
    'banker's card; ˌbanker's 'order
Bankes bæŋks
Bankhead 'bæŋk hed
banknote 'bæŋk nəʊt ‖ -noʊt ~s s
bankroll 'bæŋk rəʊl →-rɒʊl ‖ -roʊl ~ed d
    ~ing ɪŋ ~s z
bankrupt 'bæŋk rʌpt -rəpt ~ed ɪd əd ~ing ɪŋ
    ~s s
bankrupt|cy 'bæŋk rʌpt |si -rəpt- ~cies siz
Banks bæŋks **Banks's** 'bæŋks ɪz -əz
banksia 'bæŋks i_ə ~s z
Ban-Lon *tdmk* 'bæn lɒn ‖ -lɑːn
Bann bæn
bann... —*see* **ban**
banner, B~ 'bæn ə ‖ -ᵊr ~s z
    ˌbanner 'headline
Bannerman 'bæn ə mən ‖ -ᵊr-
Banning 'bæn ɪŋ
Bannister 'bæn ɪst ə §-əst- ‖ -ᵊr
bannock 'bæn ək ~s s
Bannockburn 'bæn ək bɜːn ‖ -bɝːn
banns bænz (= *bans*)
banq|uet 'bæŋk |wɪt §-wət ‖ -|wət -wet
    ~ueted wɪt ɪd wət əd ‖ wət əd wet əd
    ~ueter/s wɪt ə/z wət- ‖ wət ᵊr/z wet-
    ~ueting wɪt ɪŋ wət- ‖ wət̬ ɪŋ wet- ~uets
    wɪts wəts ‖ wət̬s wets
banquette ⑴bæŋ 'ket ~s s
Banquo 'bæŋk wəʊ ‖ -woʊ ~'s z
banshee, banshie 'bæn ʃiː •'• ~s z
Banstead 'bæn̩st ɪd §-əd, 'bæn sted
bantam, B~ 'bænt əm ‖ 'bænt̬- ~s z
bantamweight 'bænt əm weɪt ‖ 'bænt̬- ~s s
banter 'bænt ə ‖ 'bænt̬ ᵊr ~ed d **bantering/ly**
    'bænt ər ɪŋ /li ‖ 'bænt̬ ər ɪŋ /li ~s z
banterer 'bænt ər ə ‖ 'bænt̬ ər ᵊr ~s z
Banting, b~ 'bænt ɪŋ ‖ 'bænt̬ ɪŋ
Bantoid 'bænt ɔɪd 'bɑːnt-

B

Bantry 'bæntr i
 ,Bantry 'Bay
Bantu ,bæn 'tu: ◀ ,ba:n-, '•• ~s z
 ,Bantu 'languages
bantustan, B~ ,bæn tu: 'sta:n ,ba:n-, -'stæn,
 '••• ~s z
banyan 'bæn jən -i_ən, -jæn ~s z
 'banyan tree
banzai ₍ₒ₎bæn 'zaɪ ◀ ₍ₒ₎ba:n-, '•• ‖ ₍ₒ₎ba:n- ~s z
 —Jp [ba,n 'dzai]
baobab 'beɪ əʊ bæb 'baʊ bæb ‖ -ə- ~s z
 'baobab tree
BAOR ,bi: eɪ əʊ 'a: ‖ -oʊ 'a:r ~'s z
bap bæp **baps** bæps
baptis... —see **baptiz...**
baptism 'bæpt ,ɪz əm ~s z
baptismal ₍ₒ₎bæp 'tɪz məl ~ly i
Baptist 'bæpt ɪst §-əst ~s s
baptister|y 'bæpt ɪst ər_li i §'•əst- ~ies iz
baptis|try 'bæpt ɪs |tri §-əs- ~tries triz

BAPTIZE

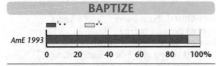

AmE 1993

| 0 | 20 | 40 | 60 | 80 | 100% |

baptiz|e bæp 'taɪz ,•'• ‖ 'bæpt aɪz bæp 'taɪz
 ~ed d ~er/s ə/z ‖ ər/z ~es ɪz əz ~ing ɪŋ
 —AmE 1993 poll panel preference: '•• 92%,
 •'• 8%
bar, Bar ba: ‖ ba:r **barred** ba:d ‖ ba:rd (=
 bard) **barring** 'ba:r ɪŋ **bars** ba:z ‖ ba:rz
 ,bar 'billiards; 'bar chart; 'bar graph; ,bar
 'none; ,bar 'sinister
Barabbas bə 'ræb əs
barathea ,bær ə 'θi:_ə ‖ ,ber-
barb ba:b ‖ ba:rb **barbed** ba:bd ‖ ba:rbd
 barbing 'ba:b ɪŋ ‖ 'ba:rb ɪŋ **barbs**
 ba:bz ‖ ba:rbz
 ,barbed 'wire
Barbadian ba: 'beɪd i_ən -'beɪdʒ ən ‖ ba:r- ~s
 z
Barbados ba: 'beɪd ɒs -əʊz, -əs, -əʊs
 ‖ ba:r 'beɪd oʊs ~'s ɪz əz
Barbara 'ba:b rə 'ba:b ər ə ‖ 'ba:rb- ~'s z
barbarian ba: 'beər i_ən ‖ ba:r 'ber i_ən -'bær-
 ~s z
barbaric ba: 'bær ɪk ‖ ba:r- -'ber- ~ally əl_i
barbaris... —see **barbariz...**
barbarism 'ba:b ə ,rɪz əm ‖ 'ba:rb- ~s z
barbarit|y ba: 'bær ət i -ɪt- ‖ ba:r 'bær ət li
 -'ber- ~ies iz
barbariz|e 'ba:b ə raɪz ‖ 'ba:rb- ~ed d ~es ɪz
 əz ~ing ɪŋ
Barbarossa ,ba:b ə 'rɒs ə ‖ ,ba:rb ə 'rɔːs ə
 -'ra:s-
barbarous 'ba:b ər_əs ‖ 'ba:rb- ~ly li ~ness
 nəs nɪs
Barbary 'ba:b ər_i ‖ 'ba:rb-
 ,Barbary 'ape
barbate 'ba:b eɪt ‖ 'ba:rb-
barbecu|e 'ba:b ɪ kju: -ə- ‖ 'ba:rb- ~ed d
 ~es z ~ing ɪŋ
barbel 'ba:b əl ‖ 'ba:rb- ~s z

barbell 'ba: bel ‖ 'ba:r- ~s z
barbequ|e 'ba:b ɪ kju: -ə- ‖ 'ba:rb- ~ed d
 ~es z ~ing ɪŋ
barber, B~ 'ba:b ə ‖ 'ba:rb ər ~ed d
 barbering 'ba:b ər ɪŋ ‖ 'ba:rb ər ɪŋ ~s z
barberr|y 'ba:b ər_li i ‖ 'ba:r ,ber li ~ies iz
barbershop 'ba:b ə ʃɒp ‖ 'ba:rb ər ʃɑːp ~s s
barbet 'ba:b ɪt §-ət ‖ 'ba:rb ət ~s s
barbette ba: 'bet ‖ ba:r- ~s s
barbican, B~ 'ba:b ɪk ən -ək- ‖ 'ba:rb- ~s z
Barbie, b~ 'ba:b i ‖ 'ba:rb i
 'Barbie doll
Barbirolli ,ba:b ɪ 'rɒl i -ə- ‖ ,ba:rb ə 'ra:l i
 -'rɔːl-
barbital 'ba:b ɪt əl -ət- ‖ 'ba:rb ə ta:l -tɔːl
barbitone 'ba:b ɪ təʊn -ə- ‖ 'ba:rb ə toʊn
barbiturate ba: 'bɪtʃ ʊr ət -'bɪtʃ ər_ət,
 -'bɪt jʊr-, -ɪt, -jə reɪt, -juə- ‖ ba:r 'bɪtʃ ər_ət,
 ,ba:rb ə 'tjʊr ət, -eɪt ~s s
Barbizon 'ba:b ɪ zɒn §-ə- ‖ ,ba:rb ə 'zoʊn
 -'za:n —Fr [baʁ bi zɔ̃]
Barbour 'ba:b ə ‖ 'ba:rb ər
bar-b-que 'ba:b ɪ kju: -ə- ‖ 'ba:rb- ~s z
Barbra 'ba:b rə ‖ 'ba:rb-
Barbuda ba: 'bju:d ə ‖ ba:r- -'bu:d-
barbule 'ba:b ju:l ‖ 'ba:rb ju:əl
barbwire ,ba:b 'waɪ_ə ◀ ‖ ,ba:rb 'waɪ_ər ◀ '••
barcarole, barcarolle ,ba:k ə 'rəʊl →-'rɒʊl,
 '••• ‖ 'ba:rk ə roʊl ~s z
Barcelona ,ba:s ɪ 'ləʊn ə ◀ -ə-
 ‖ ,ba:rs ə 'loʊn ə ◀ —Sp [bar θe 'lo na],
 Catalan [bər sə 'lo nə]
Barchester 'ba: tʃɪst ə -tʃəst-, ,tʃest ə
 ‖ 'ba:r ,tʃest ər -tʃəst-
Barclay 'ba:k li -leɪ ‖ 'ba:rk- ~'s z
Barclaycard tdmk 'ba:k li ka:d -leɪ-
 ‖ 'ba:rk li ka:rd -leɪ- ~s z
barcod|e 'ba: kəʊd ‖ 'ba:r koʊd ~ed ɪd əd
 ~es z ~ing ɪŋ
Barcoo ,ba: 'ku: ◀ ‖ ,ba:r-
 ,Barcoo 'dog
bard ba:d ‖ ba:rd **barded** 'ba:d ɪd -əd
 ‖ 'ba:rd əd **barding** 'ba:d ɪŋ ‖ 'ba:rd ɪŋ
 bards ba:dz ‖ ba:rdz
Bardell (i) ba: 'del ‖ ba:r-, (ii) 'ba:d əl -el
 ‖ 'ba:rd-
bardic 'ba:d ɪk ‖ 'ba:rd ɪk
bardolater ba: 'dɒl ət ə ‖ ba:r 'da:l ət ər ~s z
bardolatry ba: 'dɒl ətr i ‖ ba:r 'da:l-
Bardolph 'ba:d ɒlf ‖ 'ba:rd a:lf
Bardon 'ba:d ən ‖ 'ba:rd ən
Bardot ba: 'dəʊ ‖ ba:r 'doʊ —Fr [baʁ do]
Bardsey 'ba:d si ‖ 'ba:rd-
Bardsley 'ba:dz li ‖ 'ba:rdz-
bard|y 'ba:d|i i ‖ 'ba:rd|i i ~ies iz
bare beə ‖ beər bæ:r (= bear) **bared**
 beəd ‖ beərd bæ:rd **barer** 'beər ə ‖ 'ber ər
 'bær- **bares** beəz ‖ beərz bæ:rz **barest**
 'beər ɪst -əst ‖ 'ber əst 'bær- **baring**
 'beər ɪŋ ‖ 'ber ɪŋ 'bær-
bareback 'beə bæk ‖ 'ber- 'bær-
barebacked ,beə 'bækt ◀ ‖ 'ber bækt 'bær-
Barebones 'beə bəʊnz ‖ 'ber boʊnz 'bær-

B

barefaced ˌbeə ˈfeɪst ◄ ‖ ˌber- ˌbær-
barefacedly ˌbeə ˈfeɪst li ◄ -ˈfeɪs ɪd-, -əd-; ˈ•••
‖ ˌber- ˌbær-
bare|foot ˈbeə |fʊt ˌ•ˈ• ‖ ˈber- ˈbær- ~footed
fʊt ɪd -əd ‖ fʊt əd
bareheaded ˌbeə ˈhed ɪd ◄ -əd ‖ ˌber- ˌbær-
barelegged ˌbeə ˈlegd ◄ -ˈleg ɪd, -əd ‖ ˌber-
ˌbær-
barely ˈbeə li ‖ ˈber li ˈbær-
Barenboim ˈbær ən bɔɪm ˈbeər-, →-əm-
‖ ˈber- ˈbær-
bareness ˈbeə nəs -nɪs ‖ ˈber- ˈbær-
Barents ˈbær ənts ‖ ˈber- ˈbær-, ˈbɑːr-
barf bɑːf ‖ bɑːrf barfed bɑːft ‖ bɑːrft
barfing ˈbɑːf ɪŋ ‖ ˈbɑːrf ɪŋ barfs
bɑːfs ‖ bɑːrfs
bar|fly ˈbɑː |flaɪ ‖ ˈbɑːr- ~flies flaɪz
Barford ˈbɑː fəd ‖ ˈbɑːr fərd
bargain ˈbɑːg ɪn -ən ‖ ˈbɑːrg- ~ed d ~er/s ə/z
‖ ər/z ~ing ɪŋ ~s z
ˈbargaining ˌcounter
barge bɑːdʒ ‖ bɑːrdʒ barged
bɑːdʒd ‖ bɑːrdʒd barges ˈbɑːdʒ ɪz -əz
‖ ˈbɑːrdʒ əz barging ˈbɑːdʒ ɪŋ ‖ ˈbɑːrdʒ ɪŋ
bargeboard ˈbɑːdʒ bɔːd ‖ ˈbɑːrdʒ bɔːrd
-boʊrd ~s z
bargee ˌbɑː ˈdʒiː ‖ ˌbɑːr- ~s z
barge|man ˈbɑːdʒ |mən -mæn ‖ ˈbɑːrdʒ-
~men mən men
bargepole ˈbɑːdʒ pəʊl →-pɒʊl ‖ ˈbɑːrdʒ poʊl
~s z
barging ˈbɑːdʒ ɪŋ ‖ ˈbɑːrdʒ ɪŋ
Bargoed ˈbɑː gɔɪd ‖ ˈbɑːr-
Barham (i) ˈbɑːr əm, (ii) ˈbær əm ‖ ˈber-
Barhaugh ˈbɑː hʌf ‖ ˈbɑːr-
Bari ˈbɑːr i —It [ˈbaː ri]
baric ˈbeər ɪk ˈbær- ‖ ˈber ɪk
baring ˈbeər ɪŋ ‖ ˈber ɪŋ ˈbær-
Baring (i) ˈbeər ɪŋ ‖ ˈber-, (ii) ˈbær ɪŋ ‖ ˈber-
Baring-Gould ˌbeər ɪŋ ˈguːld ‖ ˌber- ˌbær-
baritone ˈbær ɪ təʊn -ə- ‖ ˈbær ə toʊn ˈber- ~s
z
barium ˈbeər i_əm ‖ ˈber- ˈbær-
ˌbarium ˈmeal
bark bɑːk ‖ bɑːrk barked bɑːkt ‖ bɑːrkt
barking ˈbɑːk ɪŋ ‖ ˈbɑːrk ɪŋ barks
bɑːks ‖ bɑːrks
barkeep ˈbɑː kiːp ‖ ˈbɑːr- ~er/s ə/z ‖ ər/z ~s
s
barker, B~ ˈbɑːk ə ‖ ˈbɑːrk ər ~s z
Barking ˈbɑːk ɪŋ ‖ ˈbɑːrk ɪŋ ~'s z
Barkley, Barkly ˈbɑːk li ‖ ˈbɑːrk-
Barkston ˈbɑːkst ən ‖ ˈbɑːrkst-
Barlaston ˈbɑːl əst ən ‖ ˈbɑːrl-
barley ˈbɑːl i ‖ ˈbɑːrl i
ˈbarley ˌsugar, ˈbarley ˌwater, ˌbarley
ˈwine
barleycorn, B~ ˈbɑːl i kɔːn ‖ ˈbɑːrl i kɔːrn
Barlinnie bɑː ˈlɪn i ‖ bɑːr-
Barlow, Barlowe ˈbɑːl əʊ ‖ ˈbɑːrl oʊ
barm bɑːm ‖ bɑːrm
ˈbarm cake
barmaid ˈbɑː meɪd ‖ ˈbɑːr-

bar|man ˈbɑː |mən -mæn ‖ ˈbɑːr- ~men mən
men
Barmecide ˈbɑːm ɪ saɪd -ə- ‖ ˈbɑːrm-
barmecidal, B~ ˌbɑːm ɪ ˈsaɪd əl ◄ -ə- ‖ ˌbɑːrm-
barmi... —see barmy
bar mitz|vah, bar miz|vah
ˌ(ˌ)bɑː ˈmɪts |və ‖ ˌ(ˌ)bɑːr- ~vahed vəd
~vahing vər ɪŋ ‖ və ɪŋ ~vahs vəz
Barmouth ˈbɑː məθ ‖ ˈbɑːr-
barm|y ˈbɑːm i ‖ ˈbɑːrm i ~ier i_ə ‖ i_ər ~iest
i_ɪst i_əst ~iness i nəs -nɪs
barn bɑːn ‖ bɑːrn barns bɑːnz ‖ bɑːrnz
ˈbarn dance; ˌbarn ˈdoor; ˌbarn ˈowl
Barnabas ˈbɑːn əb əs -ə bæs ‖ ˈbɑːrn-
Barnaby ˈbɑːn əb i ‖ ˈbɑːrn-
barnacle ˈbɑːn ək əl -ɪk- ‖ ˈbɑːrn- ~d d ~s z
ˈbarnacle goose
Barnard (i) ˈbɑːn əd ‖ ˈbɑːrn ərd, (ii)
-ɑːd ‖ -ɑːrd, (iii) bə ˈnɑːd ‖ bər ˈnɑːrd
Barnardo bə ˈnɑːd əʊ bɑː- ‖ bər ˈnɑːrd oʊ ~'s
z
Barnehurst ˈbɑːn hɜːst ‖ ˈbɑːrn hɝːst
Barnes bɑːnz ‖ bɑːrnz
Barnet ˈbɑːn ɪt §-ət ‖ ˈbɑːrn-
Barnett (i) ˈbɑːn ɪt §-ət ‖ ˈbɑːrn ət, (ii)
bɑː ˈnet ‖ bɑːr-
barney, B~ ˈbɑːn i ‖ ˈbɑːrn i ~ed d ~ing ɪŋ
~s z
Barnoldswick bɑː ˈnəʊldz wɪk →-ˈnɒʊldz-
‖ bɑːr ˈnoʊldz- —locally also ˈbɑːl ɪk
Barnsley ˈbɑːnz li ‖ ˈbɑːrnz-
Barnstable ˈbɑːnˈst əb əl ‖ ˈbɑːrnˈst-
Barnstaple ˈbɑːnˈst əp əl ‖ ˈbɑːrnˈst-
barnstorm ˈbɑːn stɔːm ‖ ˈbɑːrn stɔːrm ~ed d
~ing ɪŋ ~s z
Barnum ˈbɑːn əm ‖ ˈbɑːrn-
barnyard ˈbɑːn jɑːd ‖ ˈbɑːrn jɑːrd ~s z
baro- comb. form
with stress-neutral suffix ˌbær ə ‖ ˌber- —
barogram ˈbær ə græm ‖ ˈber-
with stress-imposing suffix bə ˈrɒ+ ‖ bə ˈrɑː+
— barometry bə ˈrɒm ətr i -ɪtr- ‖ bə ˈrɑːm-
Baroda bə ˈrəʊd ə ‖ -ˈroʊd-
barograph ˈbær ə grɑːf -græf ‖ -græf ˈber- ~s
s
barographic ˌbær ə ˈgræf ɪk ◄ ‖ ˌber- ~al əl
~ally əl_i
barometer bə ˈrɒm ɪt ə -ət- ‖ -ˈrɑːm ət ər
barometric ˌbær ə ˈmetr ɪk ◄ ‖ ˌber- ~al əl
~ally əl_i
baron ˈbær ən ‖ ˈber- (= barren) ~s z
Baron (i) ˈbær ən ‖ ˈber-, (ii) ˈbeər ən ‖ ˈber-
baronag|e ˈbær ən ɪdʒ ‖ ˈber- ~es ɪz əz
baroness ˈbær ə nes ˌ•ˈ•◄; ˈbær ən ɪs,
-əs ‖ ˈber- ~es ɪz əz
baronet ˈbær ən ɪt -ət; -ə net,
ˌbær ə ˈnet ‖ ˈber- ~s s
baronetag|e ˈbær ən ɪt ɪdʒ -ət ɪdʒ; -ə net-,
ˌbær ə ˈnet- ‖ -ət ɪdʒ ˈber- ~es ɪz əz
baronet|cy ˈbær ən ɪt |si -ət si; -ə net- ‖ ˈber-
~cies siz
baronial bə ˈrəʊn i_əl ‖ -ˈroʊn- ~ly i
baron|y ˈbær ən |i ‖ ˈber- ~ies iz

baroque bə 'rɒk bæ-, -'rəʊk ‖ -'roʊk -'rɑːk
Barossa bə 'rɒs ə ‖ -'rɑːs- -'rɔːs-
Barotse bə 'rɒts i ‖ -'rɑːts- ~land lænd
barouch|e bə 'ruːʃ bæ- ~es ɪz əz
barque bɑːk ‖ bɑːrk (= bark) barques
bɑːks ‖ bɑːrks
barquentine 'bɑːk ən tiːn →-ŋ- ‖ 'bɑːrk-
Barr bɑː ‖ bɑːr
Barra 'bær ə ‖ 'ber-
barrack 'bær ək ‖ 'ber- ~s s
Barraclough 'bær ə klʌf ‖ 'ber-
barracoon ˌbær ə 'kuːn ‖ ˌber- ~s z
barracouta ˌbær ə 'kuːt ə ‖ -'kuːt̬ ə ˌber- ~s z
barracuda ˌbær ə 'kjuːd ə -'kuːd- ‖ -'kuːd ə
ˌber- ~s z
barrag|e 'dam' 'bær ɑːʒ -ɑːdʒ ‖ 'bɑːr ɪdʒ (*)
~es ɪz əz
barrag|e 'artillery fire' 'bær ɑːʒ -ɑːdʒ ‖ bə 'rɑːʒ
-'rɑːdʒ ~es ɪz əz
'barrage balˌloon ‖ •'• •ˌ•
barramunda ˌbær ə 'mʌnd ə ‖ ˌber- ~s z
barramundi ˌbær ə 'mʌnd i ‖ ˌber- ~s z
Barranquilla ˌbær ən 'kiːl jə ‖ ˌbɑːr ən 'kiː jə
ˌbær-, ˌber- —AmSp [ba rraŋ 'ki ja]
Barrat, Barratt 'bær ət ‖ 'ber-
barratry 'bær ətr i ‖ 'ber-
barre bɑː ‖ bɑːr —Fr [baːʁ] ~s z
barré 'bær eɪ ‖ bɑː 'reɪ —Fr [ba ʁe]
barred bɑːd ‖ bɑːrd
barrel 'bær əl ‖ 'ber- ~ed, ~led d ~ing, ~ling
ɪŋ ~s z
'barrel ˌorgan
barrel-chested ˌbær əl 'tʃest ɪd ◄ -əd,
'•• ,•• ‖ ˌber-
barrelhouse 'bær əl haʊs ‖ 'ber-
Barrell 'bær əl ‖ 'ber-
barren 'bær ən ‖ 'ber- ~ly li ~ness nəs nɪs
Barrett 'bær ət -ɪt ‖ 'ber-
barrette bə 'ret bɑː- ~s s
Barri 'bær i ‖ 'ber-
barricad|e ˌbær ɪ 'keɪd -ə-, '••• ‖ 'bær ə keɪd
'ber-, ˌ•'• ~ed ɪd əd ~es z ~ing ɪŋ
Barrie 'bær i ‖ 'ber-
barrier 'bær i‿ə ‖ _ər 'ber- ~s z
'barrier cream; ˌbarrier 'reef, '••••
barring "bɑːr ɪŋ
Barrington 'bær ɪŋ tən ‖ 'ber-
barrio 'bær i‿əʊ ‖ 'bɑːr i oʊ 'bær-, 'ber- —Sp
['ba rrjo] ~s z —Sp [s]
barrister 'bær ɪst ə -əst- ‖ -ər 'ber- ~s z
Barron 'bær ən ‖ 'ber-
barroom 'bɑː ruːm -rʊm ‖ 'bɑːr- ~s z
barrow, B~ 'bær əʊ ‖ -oʊ 'ber- ~s z
'barrow boy
Barrow-in-Furness ˌbær əʊ ɪn 'fɜːn ɪs §-ən'•-,
-əs ‖ ˌbær oʊ ən 'fɜːn əs ˌber-
Barry 'bær i ‖ 'ber-
Barrymore 'bær i mɔː ‖ -mɔːr 'ber-, -moʊr
Barsac, b~ 'bɑːs æk ‖ bɑːr 'sæk —Fr [baʁ sak]
Barset 'bɑːs ɪt -ət, -et ‖ 'bɑːrs- ~shire ʃə ʃɪə
‖ ʃər ʃɪr
Barsham 'bɑːʃ əm ‖ 'bɑːrʃ-
Barstow 'bɑːst əʊ ‖ 'bɑːr stoʊ

Bart, bart, BART bɑːt ‖ bɑːrt —see also baronet
bartender 'bɑː ˌtend ə ‖ 'bɑːr ˌtend ər ~s z
barter 'bɑːt ə ‖ 'bɑːrt̬ ər ~ed d bartering
'bɑːt ər ɪŋ ‖ 'bɑːrt̬ ər ɪŋ ~s z
Barth bɑːt ‖ bɑːrt —Ger [baʁt, baːɐ̯t]
Bartholdi bɑː 'tɒld i -'θɒld- ‖ bɑːr 'θɑːld i
-'tɑːld-, -'θɔːld-, -'tɔːld- —Fr [baʁ tɔl di]
Bartholin 'bɑːt θ əl ɪn 'bɑːt-, §-ən ‖ 'bɑːrθ-
'bɑːrt̬-
Bartholomew bɑː 'θɒl ə mjuː bə- ‖ bɑːr 'θɑːl-
bər-
Bartle 'bɑːt əl ‖ 'bɑːrt̬ əl
Bartlett 'bɑːt lət -lɪt ‖ 'bɑːrt-
Bartok, Bartók 'bɑːt ɒk ‖ 'bɑːrt ɑːk -ɔːk
—Hungarian ['bɒr toːk]
Bartolommeo bɑː ˌtɒl ə 'meɪ əʊ ,•••'••
‖ bɑːr ˌtɑːl ə 'meɪ oʊ -ˌtɔːl- —It
[bar to lom 'meː o]
Barton 'bɑːt ən ‖ 'bɑːrt ən
Barts, Bart's bɑːts ‖ bɑːrts
bartsia 'bɑːts i‿ə ‖ 'bɑːrts- ~s z
Baruch name in the Bible (Apocrypha) 'bɑːr ʊk
'beər-, -ək ‖ bə 'ruːk 'bɑːr uːk, 'ber-, -ək
Baruch family name bə 'ruːk
Barugh bɑːf ‖ bɑːrf
Barwick 'bær ɪk 'bɑː wɪk ‖ 'bɑːr wɪk
baryon 'bær i ɒn ‖ -ɑːn 'ber- ~s z
Baryshnikov bə 'rɪʃ nɪ kɒf -nə• ‖ -kɑːf -kɔːf
—Russ [bʌ 'rɨʃ nʲɪ kəf]
barysphere 'bær ɪ sfɪə -ə- ‖ -sfɪr 'ber-
baryta bə 'raɪt ə ‖ -'raɪt̬-
barytes bə 'raɪt iːz
barytone 'bær ɪ təʊn -ə- ‖ -toʊn 'ber- ~s z
basal 'beɪs əl §'beɪz-
ˌbasal 'ganglia; ˌbasal me'tabo.lism
basalt 'bæs ɔːlt -ɒlt; bə 'sɔːlt, -'sɒlt ‖ bə 'sɔːlt
-'sɑːlt; 'beɪs ɔːlt, -ɑːlt ~s s
basaltic bə 'sɔːlt ɪk -'sɒlt- ‖ -'sɑːlt-
Basan 'beɪs æn
bascule 'bæsk juːl ~s z
base beɪs based beɪst bases 'beɪs ɪz -əz
basing 'beɪs ɪŋ
ˌbase 'metal; 'base rate
baseball 'beɪs bɔːl ‖ -bɑːl ~s z
'baseball bat; 'baseball cap
baseboard 'beɪs bɔːd ‖ -bɔːrd -boʊrd ~s z
base-born 'beɪs bɔːn ,•'• ‖ ˌbeɪs 'bɔːrn ◄
Basel 'bɑːz əl —Ger ['baː zəl]
baseless 'beɪs ləs -lɪs ~ly li ~ness nəs nɪs
baseline 'beɪs laɪn ~s z
basement 'beɪs mənt ~s s
basenji bə 'sendʒ i ~s z
baseplate 'beɪs pleɪt ~s s
baser 'beɪs ə ‖ -ər
bases pl of base 'beɪs ɪz -əz
bases pl of basis 'beɪs iːz
basest 'beɪs ɪst -əst
Basford (i) 'beɪs fəd ‖ -fərd, (ii) 'bæs- —The
place in Notts is (i); those in Cheshire and Staffs
are (ii)
bash bæʃ bashed bæʃt bashes 'bæʃ ɪz -əz
bashing/s 'bæʃ ɪŋ/z
Bashan 'beɪʃ æn

B

bashful 'bæʃ fᵊl -fʊl **~ly** ˌi **~ness** nəs nɪs
-bashing ˌbæʃ ɪŋ — **square-bashing**
'skweə ˌbæʃ ɪŋ ‖ 'skwer-
Bashir bə 'ʃɪə ‖ -'ʃɪᵊr
Bashkir ₍ₗ₎bæʃ 'kɪə ‖ bɑːʃ 'kɪᵊr **~s** z
Bashkiria ₍ₗ₎bæʃ 'kɪər i_ə -'kɪr- ‖ bɑːʃ 'kɪr-
basho 'bæʃ əʊ ‖ bɑː 'ʃoʊ **~s** z —*Jp* [ba ˌɕo]
basic, BASIC 'beɪs ɪk **~ally** li ᵊl_i **~s** s
ˌBasic 'English
basidiomycete bə ˌsɪd i_əʊ maɪ 'siːt
•ˌ•••'maɪs iːt ‖ -oʊ 'maɪs iːt •ˌ•••maɪ 'siːt
basidi|um bə 'sɪd il_əm bæ- **~a** _ə **~al** _ᵊl
Basie 'beɪs i
basil, Basil 'bæz ᵊl -ɪl ‖ 'beɪz ᵊl 'beɪs-, 'bæs-
basilar 'bæz ɪl ə 'bæs-, -ᵊl- ‖ -ᵊr
Basildon 'bæz ᵊl dən
basilect 'bæz ɪ lekt 'beɪs-, -ə- **~s** s
basilectal ˌbæz ɪ 'lekt ᵊl ◂ ˌbeɪs-, -ə- **~ly** i
basilica bə 'zɪl ɪk ə -'sɪl- ‖ -'sɪl- **~s** z
basilisk 'bæz ə lɪsk 'bæs-, -ɪ- **~s** s
basin 'beɪs ᵊn **~s** z
basinet 'bæs ɪ net -ə-, -nɪt, ˌ••'net
basing *pr ptcp of* **base** 'beɪs ɪŋ
Basing *name* 'beɪz ɪŋ
Basinger 'beɪs ɪndʒ ə 'bæs-, -ənʤ- ‖ -ᵊr
Basingstoke 'beɪz ɪŋ stəʊk ‖ -stoʊk
basis 'beɪs ɪs §-əs **bases** 'beɪs iːz
-basis *stress-imposing* bəs ɪs §-əs — **anabasis**
ə 'næb əs ɪs §-əs
bask bɑːsk §bæsk ‖ bæsk **basked** bɑːskt
§bæskt ‖ bæskt **basking** 'bɑːsk ɪŋ §'bæsk-
‖ 'bæsk ɪŋ **basks** bɑːsks §bæsks ‖ bæsks
Baskerville 'bæsk ə vɪl ‖ -ᵊr- **~s** z
basket 'bɑːsk ɪt §'bæsk-, -ət ‖ 'bæsk ət **~s** s
'basket case
basketball 'bɑːsk ɪt bɔːl §'bæsk-, -ət-
‖ 'bæsk ət bɔːl -bɑːl
basketful 'bɑːsk ɪt fʊl §'bæsk-, -ət- ‖ 'bæsk-
basketry 'bɑːsk ɪtr i §'bæsk-, -ətr- ‖ 'bæsk-
basketwork 'bɑːsk ɪt wɜːk §'bæsk-, §-ət-
‖ 'bæsk ət wɜːk
Baskin 'bæsk ɪn §-ən
Baskin-Robbins *tdmk* ˌbæsk ɪn 'rɒb ɪnz §-ən-,
§-ənz ‖ -'rɑːb-
Basle bɑːl —*Ger* Basel ['bɑː zᵊl]
Baslow 'bæz ləʊ ‖ -loʊ
basmati, B~ bæz 'mɑːt i bæs-, bəz-, bəs-,
-'mæt- —*Hindi* [ba: smə ʈi:]
Basnett 'bæz nɪt -nət, -net
basophil 'beɪs əʊ fɪl 'beɪz- ‖ -ə-
basophilic ˌbeɪs əʊ 'fɪl ɪk ◂ ˌbeɪz- ‖ -ə-
Basotho bə 'suːt uː -'səʊt əʊ ‖ -'soʊt oʊ
Basque, basque bæsk bɑːsk **Basques,**
basques bæsks bɑːsks
Basra, Basrah 'bæz rə 'bɑːz- ‖ 'bɑːs rə 'bæs-,
'bɑːz-, 'bæz- —*Arabic* ['basˤ ra]
bas-relief ˌbɑː ri 'liːf ◂ ˌbæs-, -rə- **~s** s
bass *in music* beɪs (= *base*) **basses** 'beɪs ɪz -əz
ˌbass 'clef; ˌbass 'fiddle; ˌbass gui'tar
bass *'fish'; 'bast'* bæs **basses** 'bæs ɪz -əz
Bass *family name; place name element; beer tdmk*
bæs **Basses, Bass's** 'bæs ɪz -əz
ˌBass 'Rock

Bassanio bə 'sɑːn i_əʊ bæ- ‖ -oʊ
Bassenthwaite 'bæs ᵊn θweɪt
basset, B~ 'bæs ɪt -ət **~s** s
ˌbasset 'horn; 'basset hound
Basseterre ˌbæs 'teə ‖ -'teᵊr
Bassetlaw ˌbæs ɪt 'lɔː -ət- ‖ -'lɑː
Bassett 'bæs ɪt -ət
Bassey 'bæs i
bassinet, bassinette ˌbæs ɪ 'net -ə- **~s** s
Bassingbourn 'bæs ɪŋ bɔːn ‖ -bɔːrn -boʊrn
bassist 'beɪs ɪst §-əst **~s** s
basso 'bæs əʊ 'bɑːs- ‖ -oʊ —*It* ['bas so] **~s** z
ˌbasso pro'fundo prəʊ 'fʌnd əʊ -'fund-
‖ -proʊ 'fʌnd oʊ —*It* [pro 'fun do]
bassoon bə 'suːn bæ- **~ist/s** ɪst/s §əst/s **~s** z
basswood 'bæs wʊd
bast bæst
Bastable 'bæst əb ᵊl
bastard 'bɑːst əd 'bæst- ‖ 'bæst ᵊrd **~s** z
bastardis... —*see* **bastardiz...**
bastardization ˌbɑːst əd aɪ 'zeɪʃ ᵊn ˌbæst-,
-ɪ'•- ‖ ˌbæst ᵊrd ə-
bastardiz|e 'bɑːst ə daɪz 'bæst- ‖ 'bæst ᵊr-
~ed d **~es** ɪz əz **~ing** ɪŋ
bastard|y 'bɑːst əd |i 'bæst- ‖ 'bæst ᵊrd |i **~ies**
iz
baste beɪst (= *based*) **basted** 'beɪst ɪd -əd
bastes beɪsts **basting** 'beɪst ɪŋ
Bastedo bə 'stiːd əʊ ‖ -oʊ
Basten 'bæst ᵊn -ɪn
Bastille, b~ ₍ₗ₎bæ 'stiː|ᵊl —*Fr* [ba stij]
Bastin 'bæst ɪn §-ən
bastinado ˌbæst ɪ 'neɪd əʊ -ə-, -'nɑːd- ‖ -oʊ
bastion 'bæst i_ən ‖ 'bæs tʃən **~s** z
Basuto bə 'suːt əʊ ‖ -oʊ
Basutoland bə 'suːt əʊ lænd ‖ -'suːt oʊ-
bat bæt **bats** bæts **batted** 'bæt ɪd -əd
‖ 'bæt̬ əd **batting** 'bæt ɪŋ ‖ 'bæt̬ ɪŋ
Bata *tdmk* 'bɑːt ə ‖ 'bɑːt̬ ə
Batavia bə 'teɪv i_ə
batboy 'bæt bɔɪ **~s** z
batch bætʃ **batches** 'bætʃ ɪz -əz
ˌbatch 'processing
Batchelor 'bætʃ əl_ə -ɪl- ‖ -ᵊl_ər
bate, Bate beɪt **bated** 'beɪt ɪd -əd ‖ 'beɪt̬ əd
bates beɪts **bating** 'beɪt ɪŋ ‖ 'beɪt̬ ɪŋ
ˌbated 'breath
bateleur ˌbæt ə 'lɜː →-ᵊl 'ɜː; '••• ‖ ˌbæt̬ ᵊl 'ɜː
'••• **~s** z
Bately 'beɪt li
Bateman 'beɪt mən
Bates beɪts
Batesian 'beɪts i_ən
Bateson 'beɪt sən
Batey 'beɪt i ‖ 'beɪt̬ i

BATH						
■ -ðz □ -θs						
BrE 1988						
AmE 1993						
0	20	40	60	80	100%	

bath *n* bɑːθ §bæθ ‖ bæθ **baths** bɑːðz §bɑːθs,
§bæθs, §bæðz ‖ bæðz bæθs —*Poll panel*

*preferences: BrE 1988, -ðz 50%, -θs 50%; AmE
1993, -ðz 50%, -θs 50%. Surprisingly, exactly
half of each panel preferred the -θs form,
traditionally considered non-standard. Some
people differentiate between 'acts of bathing',
with -θs, and 'bathtubs, bathhouses', with -ðz.*
bath's bɑːθs §bæθs ‖ bæθs
'bath mat; 'bath night; 'bath salts
bath *v* bɑːθ §bæθ ‖ bæθ **bathed** bɑːθt §bæθt
‖ bæθt **bathing** 'bɑːθ ɪŋ §'bæθ- ‖ 'bæθ ɪŋ
baths bɑːθs §bæθs ‖ bæθs —*This verb is not
current in AmE.*
Bath *place name* bɑːθ §bæθ ‖ bæθ
‚Bath 'bun; ‚Bath 'chair; '‧ ‧
bathe beɪð **bathed** beɪðd **bathes** beɪðz
bathing 'beɪð ɪŋ
bathed *past & pp of* **bath** bɑːθt §bæθt ‖ bæθt
bathed *past & pp of* **bathe** beɪðd
bathetic bə 'θet ɪk bæ- ‖ -'θeṭ ɪk
bath|house 'bɑːθ| haʊs §'bæθ|- ‖ 'bæθ|-
~**houses** haʊz ɪz -əz
bathing *from* **bath** 'bɑːθ ɪŋ §'bæθ- ‖ 'bæθ ɪŋ
bathing *from* **bathe** 'beɪð ɪŋ
'bathing ‚beauty; 'bathing ‚costume;
'bathing ma‚chine; 'bathing suit
Batho *(i)* 'bæθ əʊ ‖ -oʊ, *(ii)* 'beɪθ-
bathos 'beɪθ ɒs ‖ -ɑːs -ɔːs, -oʊs
bathrobe 'bɑːθ rəʊb §'bæθ- ‖ 'bæθ roʊb ~**s** z
bathroom 'bɑːθ ruːm §'bæθ-, -rʊm ‖ 'bæθ- ~**s**
z
Bathsheba 'bæθ ʃɪb ə ‚bæθ 'ʃiːb-
bathtub 'bɑːθ tʌb §'bæθ- ‖ 'bæθ- ~**s** z
Bathurst 'bæθ ɜːst 'bɑːθ-, -əst, -hɜːst ‖ -ɚːst
bathy- *comb. form*
with stress-neutral suffix |bæθ ɪ —
bathymetric ‚bæθ ɪ 'metr ɪk ◀
with stress-imposing suffix bə 'θɪ+ bæ- —
bathymetry bə 'θɪm ətr i bæ-, -ɪtr i
bathyal 'bæθ i‿əl
bathypelagic ‚bæθ ɪ pə 'lædʒ ɪk ◀
bathyscaphe 'bæθ ɪ skeɪf §-ə- ‖ -s-
bathysphere 'bæθ ɪ sfɪə -ə- ‖ -sfɪr ~**s** z
batik bə 'tiːk bæ-; 'bæt ɪk, 'bɑːt ɪk ~**s** s
bating 'beɪt ɪŋ ‖ 'beɪṭ ɪŋ
batiste bæ 'tiːst bə- ~**s** s
Batley 'bæt li
batman '*army servant*' 'bæt mən **batmen**
'bæt mən -men
Batman *cartoon character* 'bæt mæn
baton 'bæt ɒn -ən ‖ bə 'tɑːn *(*)* —*See also
phrases with this word* ~**s** z
Baton Rouge ‚bæt ən 'ruːʒ
bats bæts
Batsford 'bæts fəd ‖ -fᵊrd
bats|man 'bæts| mən ~**men** mən
Batson 'bæts ən
batt, Batt bæt
battalion bə 'tæl jən -'tæl i‿ən ~**s** z
batt... —*see* **bat**
battels 'bæt ᵊlz ‖ 'bæṭ-
batten, B~ 'bæt ᵊn ~**ed** d ~**ing**‿ɪŋ ~**s** z
Battenberg 'bæt ᵊn bɜːg ‖ -bɝːg —*Ger*

['bat ᵊn bɛʁk]
‚Battenberg 'cake
batter 'bæt ə ‖ 'bæṭ ᵊr ~**ed** d **battering/s**
'bæt‿ᵊr ɪŋ/z ‖ 'bæṭ ᵊr ɪŋ/z ~**s** z
'battering ram
Battersby 'bæt əz bi ‖ 'bæṭ ᵊrz-
batteries —*see* **battery**
Battersea 'bæt əs i -ə siː ‖ 'bæṭ ᵊr siː
batter|y 'bæt r|i 'bæt ᵊr|i ‖ 'bæṭ ᵊr |i →'bætr |i
~**ies** iz
batti... —*see* **batty**
batting 'bæt ɪŋ ‖ 'bæṭ ɪŋ
'batting ‚average
Battisford 'bæt ɪs fəd §-əs- ‖ 'bæṭ əs fᵊrd
battl|e, B~ 'bæt ᵊl ‖ 'bæṭ ᵊl ~**ed** d ~**es** z ~**ing**
‿ɪŋ
'battle ‚cruiser; 'battle cry; 'battle fa‚tigue;
‚battle 'royal
battleax, battleax|e 'bæt ᵊl æks ‖ 'bæṭ- ~**es** ɪz
əz
battledore 'bæt ᵊl dɔː ‖ 'bæṭ ᵊl dɔːr -doʊr ~**s** z
battledress 'bæt ᵊl dres ‖ 'bæṭ-
battlefield, B~ 'bæt ᵊl fiːᵊld ‖ 'bæṭ- ~**s** z
battleground 'bæt ᵊl graʊnd ‖ 'bæṭ- ~**s** z
battlement 'bæt ᵊl mənt ‖ 'bæṭ- ~**ed** ɪd əd ~**s**
s
battleship 'bæt ᵊl ʃɪp ‖ 'bæṭ- ~**s** s
‚battleship 'grey
battue bæ 'tuː -'tjuː —*Fr* [ba ty]
batt|y 'bæt li ‖ 'bæṭ li ~**ier** i‿ə ‖ i‿ᵊr ~**iest** i‿ɪst
i‿əst ~**iness** i nəs -nɪs
Batty, Battye 'bæt i ‖ 'bæṭ i
batwing 'bæt wɪŋ ~**s** z
bauble 'bɔːb ᵊl ‖ 'bɑːb- ~**s** z
Baucis 'bɔːs ɪs §-əs ‖ 'bɑːs-
baud bɔːd bɑʊd ‖ bɑːd
Baudelaire 'bəʊd ə leə -ᵊl eə, ‚‧‧'‧
‖ ‚boʊd ᵊl 'eᵊr —*Fr* [bod lɛːʁ]
Bauer 'baʊ‿ə ‖ 'baʊ‿ᵊr —*Ger* ['bau ɐ]
Baugh bɔː ‖ bɑː
Baughan *(i)* bɔːn ‖ bɑːn, *(ii)* 'bɒf ᵊn ‖ 'bɑːf-
'bɔːf-
Bauhaus 'baʊ haʊs —*Ger* ['bau haus]
bauhinia bəʊ 'hɪn i‿ə bɔː- ‖ bɔː- bɑː-
Baulch bɒlʃ ‖ bɑːlʃ bɔːlʃ
baulk bɔːk bɑːlk ‖ bɑːk **baulked** bɔːkt
bɔːlkt ‖ bɑːkt **baulking** 'bɔːk ɪŋ 'bɔːlk-
‖ 'bɑːk- **baulks** bɔːks bɔːlks ‖ bɑːks
Baum baʊm —*as an American family name, also*
bɑːm, bɔːm
Baumé 'bəʊm eɪ ‖ boʊ 'meɪ —*Fr* [bo me]
bauxite 'bɔːks aɪt ‖ 'bɑːks-
Bavari|a bə 'veər i‿ə ‖ -'ver- -'vær- ~**an/s**
ən/z
bavarois|e ‚bæv ə 'wɑːz -ɑː- ‖ -ɑːr- ~**es** ɪz əz
—*Fr* [ba va ʁwaːz]
Baverstock 'bæv ə stɒk ‖ -ᵊr stɑːk
Baw Baw 'bɔː bɔː ‖ 'bɑː bɑː
bawbee ‚bɔː 'biː 'bɔːb i ‖ 'bɔːb i 'bɑːb-;
‚bɔː'biː;, ‚bɑː- ~**s** z
bawd bɔːd ‖ bɑːd **bawds** bɔːdz ‖ bɑːdz
Bawden 'bɔːd ᵊn ‖ 'bɑːd-

B

B

bawd|y 'bɔːd |i ‖ 'bɑːd- **~ier** i_ə ‖ i_ᵊr **~iest**
i_ɪst i_əst **~ily** ɪ li əl i **~iness** i nəs i nɪs
bawdyhouse 'bɔːd i haʊs ‖ 'bɑːd-
bawl bɔːl ‖ bɑːl (= *ball*) **bawled** bɔːld ‖ bɑːld
 bawling 'bɔːl ɪŋ ‖ 'bɑːl- **bawls** bɔːlz ‖ bɑːlz
Bawtree, Bawtry 'bɔːtr i ‖ 'bɑːtr-
Bax bæks
Baxendale 'bæks ᵊn deɪᵊl
Baxter 'bækst ə ‖ -ᵊr
bay beɪ **bays** beɪz (= *baize*)
 **'bay leaf; ,bay 'rum; 'Bay Stater; 'Bay
 Street; 'bay tree; ,bay 'window**
bayadere ,baɪ_ə 'dɪə -'deə ‖ 'baɪ ə dɪr
Bayard, b~ 'beɪ ɑːd -əd ‖ -ᵊrd -aːrd
bayberry 'beɪ ,ber i
Bayer *tdmk* 'beɪ ə ‖ -ᵊr
Bayes beɪz
Bayesian 'beɪz i_ən ‖ 'beɪʒ ᵊn
Bayeux ₍ᵢ₎baɪ 'ɜː, ₍ᵢ₎beɪ-, -'jɜː: ‖ 'beɪ u 'baɪ- —*Fr*
 [ba jø]
Bayley 'beɪl i
Baylis, Bayliss 'beɪl ɪs §-əs
Bayne beɪn
Baynes beɪnz
bay|onet 'beɪ |ən ɪt -ət; -ə net, ,••'• ‖ -lən ət
 -ə net, ,••'net **~oneted, ~onetted** ən ɪt ɪd
 -ət-, -əd; ə net-, ,••'•• ‖ ən ət əd ə net-,
 ,••'•• **~oneting, ~onetting** ən ɪt ɪŋ -ət-;
 ə net-, ,••'•• ‖ ən ət ɪŋ ə net-, ,••'••
 ~onets ən ɪts -əts; ə nets, ,••'• ‖ ən əts
 ə nets, ,•ə 'nets
Bayonne *place in France* baɪ 'ɒn ‖ -'ɔːn -'oʊn,
 -'ɑːn —*Fr* [ba jɔn]
Bayonne *place in NJ* beɪ 'oʊn ‖ -'oʊn
bayou 'baɪ uː -juː: ‖ -oʊ -uː -oʊ
Bayreuth ,baɪᵊ 'rɔɪt 'baɪᵊr ɔɪt —*Ger* [baɪ 'ʁɔʏt]
Bayswater 'beɪz ,wɔːt ə ‖ -,wɔːt ᵊr -,wɑːt-
Baywatch 'beɪ wɒtʃ ‖ -wɑːtʃ
Baz bæz
bazaar, bazar bə 'zɑː ‖ -'zɑːr **~s** z
Bazalgette 'bæz ᵊl dʒet
Bazell bə 'zel
bazooka bə 'zuːk ə **~s** z
BBC ,bi: bi: 'si: ◂ ,bi:b i-
 ,BBC-'2; ,BBC ,World 'Service, ,••• '• ,••
BBQ 'bɑːb ɪ kjuː -ə- ‖ 'bɑːrb-
bdellium 'del i_əm bə 'del-
be *strong form* biː:, *weak form* bi —*For* am, are,
 aren't, art, been, being, is, isn't, was, wasn't,
 wast, were, weren't, *see separate entries*
be- bɪ bə *This prefix is always unstressed:*
 be'neath, be'friend.
Bea biː
beach biːtʃ **beached** biːtʃt **beaches** 'biːtʃ ɪz
 -əz **beaching** 'biːtʃ ɪŋ
 'beach ball; 'beach ,buggy
beachchair 'biːtʃ tʃeə ‖ -tʃer **~s** z
beachcomber 'biːtʃ ,kəʊm ə ‖ -,koʊm ᵊr **~s** z
beachhead 'biːtʃ hed **~s** z
Beach-la-Mar, beach-la-mar
 ,biːtʃ lə 'mɑː: ‖ -'mɑːr
beachwear 'biːtʃ weə ‖ -wer

Beachy 'biːtʃ i
 ,Beachy 'Head
beacon, B~ 'biːk ᵊn **~s** z
Beaconsfield (i) 'bek ᵊnz fiːᵊld (ii) 'biːk- —*The
 place in Bucks is (i); Disraeli's title and the
 places in Tasmania and Canada are (ii)*
bead biːd **beaded** 'biːd ɪd -əd **beading/s**
 'biːd ɪŋ/z **beads** biːdz
beadi... —*see* **beady**
beadle, B~ 'biːd ᵊl **~s** z
beadwork 'biːd wɜːk ‖ -wɜːk
bead|y 'biːd li **~ier** i_ə ‖ i_ᵊr **~iest** i_ɪst i_əst
 ~ily ɪ li əl i **~iness** i nəs -nɪs
beady-eyed ,biːd i 'aɪd ◂
beagle 'biːg ᵊl **~s** z **beagling** 'biːg ᵊl ɪŋ
beak biːk **beaked** biːkt **beaks** biːks
Beaken 'biːk ᵊn
beaker 'biːk ə ‖ -ᵊr **~s** z
 'Beaker Folk
beakerful 'biːk ə fʊl ‖ -ᵊr-
beaklike 'biːk laɪk
Beal, Beale biːᵊl
be-all and end-all ,biː ɔːl ən 'end ɔːl
 -ənd'•- ‖ -ɑːl ən 'end ɑːl
beam biːm **beamed** biːmd **beaming** 'biːm ɪŋ
 beams biːmz
beam-ends ,biːm 'endz
Beamer 'biːm ə ‖ -ᵊr **~s** z
Beaminster 'bem ɪn'st ə ‖ -ᵊr —*There is also a
 spelling pronunciation* 'biːm-
Beamish 'biːm ɪʃ
bean, Bean biːn **beans** biːnz
 'bean curd
beanbag 'biːn bæg →'biːm- **~s** z
beanfeast 'biːn fiːst **~s** s
beanie 'biːn i **~s** z
 'beanie ,baby
beano, Beano 'biːn əʊ ‖ -oʊ **~s** z
beanpole 'biːn pəʊl →'biːm-, →-pɒʊl ‖ -poʊl
 ~s z
beanshoot 'biːn ʃuːt **~s** s
beansprout 'biːn spraʊt **~s** s
beanstalk 'biːn stɔːk ‖ -stɑːk **~s** s
bear *n, v* beə ‖ beᵊr bæᵊr (= *bare*) **bearing**
 'beᵊr ɪŋ ‖ 'ber ɪŋ 'bær- **bears** beəz ‖ beᵊrz
 bæᵊrz **bore** bɔː ‖ bɔːr boʊr **borne**
 bɔːn ‖ bɔːrn boʊrn
 'bear ,garden; 'bear hug; 'bear ,market;
 ,bear 'up
bearab|le 'beᵊr əb |ᵊl ‖ 'ber- 'bær- **~ly** li
bear-baiting 'beə ,beɪt ɪŋ ‖ 'ber ,beɪt ɪŋ 'bær-
beard, Beard bɪəd ‖ bɪᵊrd **bearded** 'bɪəd ɪd
 -əd **bearding** 'bɪəd ɪŋ ‖ 'bɪᵊrd ɪŋ
 beards bɪədz ‖ bɪᵊrdz
beardless 'bɪəd ləs -lɪs ‖ 'bɪᵊrd ləs **~ness** nəs
 nɪs
Beardsall, Beardsell 'bɪəd sᵊl ‖ 'bɪᵊrd-
Beardsley 'bɪədz li ‖ 'bɪᵊrdz-
Beare bɪə ‖ bɪr —*but* ,Beare 'Green *in Surrey is*
 beə
bearer 'beᵊr ə ‖ 'ber ᵊr **~s** z
bearhug 'beə hʌg ‖ 'ber- **~s** z
bearing 'beᵊr ɪŋ ‖ 'ber ɪŋ 'bær- **~s** z

bearish 'beər ɪʃ ‖ 'ber ɪʃ 'bær- **~ly** li **~ness**
nəs nɪs
bearnaise, béarnaise, B~ ˌbeɪ ə 'neɪz ◄ -ɑː-,
-'nez ‖ 'beɪ ər neɪz -ɑːr- —*Fr* [be aʁ nɛːz]
Bearsden ₍ᵢ₎beəz 'den ‖ ₍ᵢ₎berz-
bearskin 'beə skɪn ‖ 'ber- **~s** z
Bearsted (i) 'bɜː sted ‖ 'bɜː-, (ii) 'beə- ‖ 'ber-
Beasant 'bez ənt
beast biːst beasts biːsts
ˌbeast of 'burden
beastie 'biːst i **~s** z
beast|ly 'biːst ‖li **~liness** li nəs -nɪs
beat biːt beaten 'biːt ən beating
'biːt ɪŋ ‖ 'biːṭ ɪŋ beats biːts
beater 'biːt ə ‖ 'biːṭ ər **~s** z
beatific ˌbiːˌə 'tɪf ɪk ◄ **~ally** əlᵢi
beatification bi ˌæt ɪ fɪ 'keɪʃ ən -ˌ•ə-, §-fə'•-
‖ -ˌæt̬-
beati|fy bi 'æt ɪ |faɪ -ə- ‖ -'æt̬- **~fied** faɪd
~fies faɪz **~fying** faɪ ɪŋ
beating 'biːt ɪŋ ‖ 'biːṭ ɪŋ **~s** z
beatitude, B~ bi 'æt ɪ tjuːd -ə-, →-tʃuːd
‖ -'æt̬ ə tuːd -tjuːd **~s** z
Beatle 'biːt əl ‖ 'biːṭ əl (= beetle) **~s** z
beatnik 'biːt nɪk **~s** s
Beaton 'biːt ən
Beatrice 'bɪətr ɪs -əs ‖ 'biː ətr əs —also, in
imitated Italian, ˌbeɪ ə 'triːtʃ eɪ, -ɑː-, -i
—Italian [be a 'tri: tʃe]
Beatrix 'bɪətr ɪks ‖ 'biː ə trɪks
Beattie 'biːt i ‖ 'biːṭ i
Beattock 'biːt ək ‖ 'biːṭ ək
Beatty (i) 'biːt i ‖ 'biːṭ i, (ii) 'beɪt i ‖ 'beɪṭ i
—The film actor Warren B~ is (ii)
beau bəʊ ‖ boʊ —Fr [bo] beaus, beaux bəʊz
bəʊ ‖ boʊz —See also phrases with this word
Beaucaire ˌbəʊ 'keə ‖ ˌboʊ 'keᵊr
Beauchamp 'biːtʃ əm
Beauclerk 'bəʊ kleə •'• ‖ 'boʊ klɜːk
Beaufort (i) 'bəʊ fət -fɔːt ‖ 'boʊ fərt, (ii) 'bjuː-
—The British dukedom, the personal and family
name, the places in NC and Australia, the Arctic
sea, and the wind scale are (i); the place in SC
is (ii).
'Beaufort scale; ˌBeaufort 'Sea
beau geste ˌbəʊ 'ʒest ‖ ˌboʊ- —Fr [bo ʒɛst]
ˌBeaujolais nou'veau nu 'vəʊ ‖ -'voʊ —Fr
[nu vo]
Beaulieu 'bjuːl i (!)
Beauly 'bjuːl i
Beaumaris bəʊ 'mær ɪs bjuː-, §-əs ‖ boʊ-
-'mer-
beau monde ˌbəʊ 'mɒnd ‖ ˌboʊ 'mɔːnd
-'mɑːnd —Fr [bo mɔ̃ːd]
Beaumont 'bəʊ mənt -mɒnt ‖ 'boʊ mɑːnt ˌ•'•
—but the place in Cumbria is 'biː-
Beaune bəʊn ‖ boʊn —Fr [bon]
beaut bjuːt beauts bjuːts
beauteous 'bjuːt i_əs ‖ 'bjuːṭ- **~ly** li
beautician bjuː 'tɪʃ ən **~s** z
beauties 'bjuːt iz ‖ 'bjuːṭ iz

beautification ˌbjuːt ɪf ɪ 'keɪʃ ən ˌ•əf-, §-ə'•-
‖ ˌbjuːṭ-
beautifi... —see beautify
beautiful 'bjuːt əf əl -ɪf-; -ɪ fʊl, -ə- ‖ 'bjuːṭ-
beautifully 'bjuːt əf li -ɪf-; -ɪ fʊl i, -ə fʊl i
‖ 'bjuːṭ-
beauti|fy 'bjuːt ɪ |faɪ -ə- ‖ 'bjuːṭ- **~fied** faɪd
~fies faɪz **~fying** faɪ ɪŋ
beauty 'bjuːt i ‖ 'bjuːṭ i beauties
'bjuːt iz ‖ 'bjuːṭ iz
'beauty ˌcontest; 'beauty ˌparlour; 'beauty
queen; 'beauty ˌsalon ‖ -•,•; 'beauty
sleep; 'beauty spot
Beauvais ₍ᵢ₎bəʊ 'veɪ ‖ ₍ᵢ₎boʊ- —Fr [bo vɛ]
Beauvoir 'bəʊv wɑː ‖ boʊv 'wɑːr —Fr
[bo vwaːʁ]
beaux bəʊz bəʊ ‖ boʊz
beaux-arts ₍ᵢ₎bəʊ 'zɑː ‖ ₍ᵢ₎boʊ 'zɑːr —Fr
[bo zaːʁ]
Beavan 'bev ən
beaver, B~ 'biːv ə ‖ -ər **~ed** d beavering 'biːv
ər_ɪŋ **~s** z
Beaverbrook 'biːv ə brʊk ‖ -ər-
Beavis 'biːv ɪs §-əs
Beazley 'biːz li
Bebb beb
Bebbington, Bebington 'beb ɪŋ tən
bebop 'biː bɒp ‖ -bɑːp
bebopper 'biː bɒp ə ‖ -bɑːp ər **~s** z
becalm bɪ 'kɑːm bə-, §biː-, -'kɑːlm, §-'kɒlm
~ed d **~ing** ɪŋ **~s** z
became bɪ 'keɪm bə-, §biː-

BECAUSE

AmE 1993	■-'kʌz	□-'kɔːz	■-'kɔːs or -'kɑːs
0 20 40 60 80 100%			

because bɪ 'kɒz bə-, §biː-, -'kəz, -kəz, §-'kɔːz,
§-'kɒs, §-'kɔːs ‖ -'kʌz -'kɔːz, -'kɑːz, -'kəz,
-kəz —Many speakers use bɪ kəz (or bə kəz)
as the weak form, bɪ 'kɒz ‖ -'kɔːz (etc.) as the
strong form. Some, though, also use an irregular
strong form bɪ 'kʌz, bə 'kʌz. There are also
casual variants kɒz, kəz (etc.) — see **cos**.
—AmE 1993 poll panel preference: -'kʌz 57%,
-'kɔːz or -'kɑːz 41%, -'kɔːs or -'kɑːs 2%
Beccles 'bek əlz
bechamel, béchamel ˌbeɪʃ ə 'mel ◄ —Fr
[be ʃa mɛl]
beche-de-mer, bêche-de-mer ˌbeʃ də 'meə
ˌbeɪʃ- ‖ -'meᵊr —This is not a true French
expression.
Becher's 'biːtʃ əz ‖ -ᵊrz
Bechet 'beʃ eɪ
Bechstein 'bek staɪn
Bechtel 'bekt el
Bechuana ˌbetʃ u 'ɑːn ə △ˌbek ju- **~land**
lænd
beck, Beck bek becks beks
Beckenbauer 'bek ən baʊ_ə ‖ -baʊ_ər —Ger
['bɛk ən bau ɐ]
Beckenham 'bek ən_əm
Becker 'bek ə ‖ -ər —Ger ['bɛk ɐ]

Becket, Beckett 'bek ɪt §-ət
Beckford 'bek fəd ‖ -fərd
Beckham 'bek əm
Beckinsale 'bek ɪn seɪəl §-ən-
Beckmann 'bek mən —*Ger* ['bɛk man]
beckon 'bek ən ~ed d ~ing/ly ɪŋ /li ~s z
Beckton 'bekt ən
Beckwith 'bek wɪθ
Becky 'bek i
becloud bɪ 'klaʊd bə-, §biː- ~ed ɪd əd ~ing
ɪŋ ~s z
be|come bɪ |'kʌm bə-, §biː- ~came 'keɪm
~comes 'kʌmz ~coming 'kʌm ɪŋ
becoming bɪ 'kʌm ɪŋ bə-, §biː- ~ly li
Becontree 'bek ən triː
Becquerel, b~ 'bek ər_əl ˌbek ə 'rel —*Fr*
[bɛk ʁɛl] ~s z
Becton 'bekt ən
bed bed bedded 'bed ɪd -əd bedding 'bed ɪŋ
beds bedz
ˌbed and 'breakfast; 'bed ˌlinen
BEd ˌbiː 'ed
bedad bɪ 'dæd bə-
Bedale *place in NYks* 'biːd əl 'biː deɪəl
Bedales 'biː deɪəlz
bedaub bɪ 'dɔːb bə-, §biː- ‖ -'dɑːb ~ed d ~ing
ɪŋ ~s z
bedazzl|e bɪ 'dæz əl bə-, §biː- ~ed d ~es z
~ing ɪŋ
bedbug 'bed bʌg →'beb- ~s z
bedchamber 'bed ˌtʃeɪm bə ‖ -bər ~s z
bedclothes 'bed kləʊðz -kləʊz ‖ -kloʊz
-kloʊðz
beddable 'bed əb əl
bedd... —*see* bed
Beddau 'beð aɪ —*Welsh* ['be ðai, -ðe]
bedder 'bed ə ‖ -ər ~s z
Beddgelert beð 'gel ət bed-, beɪð- ‖ -ərt
—*Welsh* [ˌbeːð 'ge lert]
bedding, B~ 'bed ɪŋ
'bedding plant
Beddoes, Beddowes, Beddows
'bed əʊz ‖ -oʊz
beddy-byes 'bed i baɪz
Bede biːd
bedeck bɪ 'dek bə-, §biː- ~ed t ~ing ɪŋ ~s s
bedel, bedell 'biːd əl ~s z
Bedevere 'bed ə vɪə -ɪ- ‖ -vɪr
bedevil bɪ 'dev əl bə-, §biː- ~ed, ~led d ~ing,
~ling ɪŋ ~ment mənt ~s z
bedew bɪ 'djuː bə-, §biː-, →§-'dʒuː ‖ -'duː
-'djuː ~ed d ~ing ɪŋ ~s z
bedfellow 'bed ˌfel əʊ ‖ -oʊ ~s z
Bedford 'bed fəd ‖ -fərd
Bedfordshire 'bed fəd ʃə -ʃɪə ‖ -fərd ʃər -ʃɪr
bedhead 'bed hed ~s z
bedim bɪ 'dɪm bə-, §biː- ~med d ~ming ɪŋ
~s z
Bedivere 'bed ə vɪə -ɪ- ‖ -vɪr
bedizen bɪ 'daɪz ən bə-, §biː-, -'dɪz- ~ed d
~ing ɪŋ ~s z
bedjacket 'bed ˌdʒæk ɪt §-ət ~s s
bedlam 'bed ləm

bedlinen 'bed ˌlɪn ɪn §-ən
Bedlington 'bed lɪŋ tən
bedmaker 'bed ˌmeɪk ə →'beb- ‖ -ər ~s z
bedouin, B~ 'bed u ɪn -æ̃, -ən ~s z
bedpan 'bed pæn →'beb- ~s z
bedpost 'bed pəʊst →'beb- ‖ -poʊst ~s s
bedraggl|e bɪ 'dræg əl bə-, §biː- ~ed d ~es z
~ing ɪŋ
bedridden 'bed ˌrɪd ən
bedrock 'bed rɒk ‖ -rɑːk

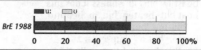

BrE 1988

0   20   40   60   80   100%

bedroom 'bedr uːm 'bedr ʊm, 'bed ruːm, -rʊm
—*BrE 1988 poll panel preference:* uː: *63%,* ʊ
37%. ~s z
ˌbedroom 'slippers
Beds bedz —*see also* Bedfordshire
bedside 'bed saɪd
ˌbedside 'manner
bedsit, bed-sit ˌbed 'sɪt '·· ~s s
bedsitter, bed-sitter ˌbed 'sɪt ə ‖ -'sɪt̬ ər ~s z
bed-sitting room ˌbed 'sɪt ɪŋ ruːm -rʊm ‖ -'sɪt̬-
~s z
bedsock 'bed sɒk ‖ -sɑːk ~s s
bedsore 'bed sɔː ‖ -sɔːr -soʊr ~s z
bedspread 'bed spred ~s z
bedstead 'bed sted ~s z
bedstraw 'bed strɔː ‖ -strɑː ~s z
bedtime 'bed taɪm ~s z
ˌbedtime 'story
Bedwell 'bed wəl -wel
Bedwellty bed 'welt i -'welt- —*Welsh*
[bed 'weɬ ti]
bed-wett|er/s 'bed ˌwet| ə/z ‖ -ˌwet̬| ər/z
~ing ɪŋ
bee biː bees, bee's biːz
ˌbee's 'knees; 'bee sting
Beeb biːb
beech, Beech biːtʃ *(= beach)* beeches 'biːtʃ ɪz
-əz
Beecham 'biːtʃ əm
Beecher 'biːtʃ ə ‖ -ər
Beeching 'biːtʃ ɪŋ
beechnut 'biːtʃ nʌt ~s s
beechwood 'biːtʃ wʊd
bee-eater 'biː ˌiːt ə ‖ -ˌiːt̬ ər ~s z
beef biːf beefed biːft beefing 'biːf ɪŋ beefs
biːfs beeves biːvz
ˌbeef 'tea
beefburger 'biːf ˌbɜːg ə ‖ -ˌbɜːɡ ər ~s z
beefcake 'biːf keɪk
beefeater 'biːf ˌiːt ə ‖ -ˌiːt̬ ər ~s z
beefi... —*see* beefy
beefsteak 'biːf steɪk ~s s
beefwood 'biːf wʊd
beef|y 'biːf |i ~ier i_ə ‖ i_ər ~iest i_ɪst i_əst
Bee Gee 'biː dʒiː ~s z
beehive 'biː haɪv ~s z
beekeep|er/s 'biː ˌkiːp ə/z ‖ -ər/z ~ing ɪŋ
beeline 'biː laɪn

Beelzebub bi 'elz ɪ bʌb -ə-

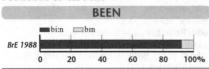

BEEN

| ■ biːn | ▢ bɪn |

BrE 1988

0   20   40   60   80   100%

been biːn bɪn ‖ bɪn —*Some BrE speakers have*
biːn *as strong form,* bɪn *as weak form.* —*BrE*
1988 poll panel preference (for strong form):
biːn 92%, bɪn 8%.

beep biːp **beeped** biːpt **beeping** 'biːp ɪŋ
beeps biːps
beeper 'biːp ə ‖ -ᵊr ~s z
beer, Beer bɪə ‖ bɪᵊr **beers** bɪəz ‖ bɪᵊrz
Beerbohm 'bɪə bəʊm ‖ 'bɪr boʊm
beeri... —*see* **beery**
Beersheba bɪə 'ʃiːb ə 'bɪəʃ ɪb ə ‖ bɪr-
beer|y, Beery 'bɪər |i ‖ 'bɪr |i ~**ier** i‿ə ‖ i‿ᵊr
~**iest** i‿ɪst i‿əst
beestings '*colostrum*' 'biːst ɪŋz
Beeston 'biːst ən
beeswax 'biːz wæks
beeswing 'biːz wɪŋ
beet biːt *(= beat)* **beets** biːts
Beethoven 'beɪt həʊv ən -əʊv- ‖ 'beɪt oʊv ən
—*Ger* ['beːt hoː fən] ~'s z
beetl|e 'biːt ᵊl ‖ 'biːṭ ᵊl ~**ed** d ~**es** z ~**ing** ɪŋ
Beeton 'biːt ən
beetroot 'biːtr uːt 'biːt ruːt ~s s
beeves biːvz
beezer 'biːz ə ‖ -ᵊr
befall bɪ 'fɔːl bə-, §biː- ‖ -'fɑːl ~**en** ən ~**ing** ɪŋ
~**s** z **befell** bɪ 'fel bə-, §biː-
be|fit bɪ |'fɪt bə-, §biː- ~**fits** 'fɪts ~**fitted**
'fɪt ɪd -əd ‖ 'fɪṭ əd ~**fitting/ly** 'fɪt ɪŋ /
li ‖ 'fɪṭ ɪŋ /li
befog bɪ 'fɒg bə-, §biː- ‖ -'fɔːg -'fɑːg ~**ged** d
~**ging** ɪŋ ~**s** z
before bɪ 'fɔː bə-, §biː- ‖ -'fɔːr -'foʊr
beforehand bɪ 'fɔː hænd bə-, §biː- ‖ -'fɔːr-
-'foʊr-
befoul bɪ 'faʊl bə-, §biː- ~**ed** d ~**ing** ɪŋ ~**s** z
befriend bɪ 'frend bə-, §biː- ~**ed** ɪd əd ~**ing**
ɪŋ ~**s** z
befuddl|e bɪ 'fʌd ᵊl bə-, §biː- ~**ed** d ~**ement**
mənt ~**es** z ~**ing** ɪŋ
beg beg **begged** begd **begging** 'beg ɪŋ
begs begz
begad bɪ 'gæd bə-
began bɪ 'gæn bə-, §biː-
be|get bɪ |'get bə-, §biː- ~**gat/s** 'gæt/s ~**gets**
'gets ~**getting** 'get ɪŋ ‖ 'geṭ ɪŋ ~**got**
'gɒt ‖ 'gɑːt ~**gotten** 'gɒt ən ‖ 'gɑːt ən
begetter bɪ 'get ə bə-, §biː- ‖ -'geṭ ᵊr ~**s** z
beggar 'beg ə ‖ -ᵊr ~**ed** d **beggaring** 'beg
ᵊr‿ɪŋ ~**s** z
beggar|ly 'beg ə |li -ᵊl i ‖ -ᵊr- ~**liness** li nəs
-nɪs
beggar-my-neighb|our, ~or ˌbeg ə mi 'neɪb ə
-maɪ'•- ‖ ˌbeg ᵊr maɪ 'neɪb ᵊr
beggary 'beg ᵊr i
be|gin bɪ |'gɪn bə-, §biː- ~**gan** 'gæn ~**ginning**
'gɪn ɪŋ ~**gins** 'gɪnz ~**gun** 'gʌn

Begin *Israeli name* 'beɪg ɪn 'beg-
beginner bɪ 'gɪn ə bə-, §biː- ‖ -ᵊr ~**s** z
beˌginner's 'luck
beginning bɪ 'gɪn ɪŋ bə-, §biː- ~**s** z
begone bɪ 'gɒn bə-, §biː-, §-'gɑːn, §-'gɔːn
‖ -'gɔːn -'gɑːn
begonia bɪ 'gəʊn i‿ə bə- ‖ -'goʊn jə ~**s** z
begorra bɪ 'gɒr ə bə- ‖ -'gɔːr- -'gɑːr-
begot bɪ 'gɒt bə-, §biː- ‖ -'gɑːt ~**ten** ᵊn
begrim|e bɪ 'graɪm bə-, §biː- ~**ed** d ~**es** z
~**ing** ɪŋ
begrudg|e bɪ 'grʌdʒ bə-, §biː- ~**ed** d ~**es** ɪz
əz ~**ing** ɪŋ
beguil|e bɪ 'gaɪᵊl bə-, §biː- ~**ed** d ~**es** z ~**ing**
ɪŋ
beguine '*dance*', '*music*' bɪ 'giːn bə- ~**s** z
Beguine '*member of sisterhood*' 'beg iːn 'beɪg-;
bi 'giːn, bə-, ˌbeɪ- ~**s** z
begum, Begum 'beɪg əm 'biːg- ~**s** z
begun bɪ 'gʌn bə-, §biː-
behalf bɪ 'hɑːf bə-, §biː- ‖ -'hæf
Behan 'biː ən
behav|e bɪ 'heɪv bə-, §biː- ~**ed** d ~**es** z ~**ing**
ɪŋ
behavior, behaviour bɪ 'heɪv jə bə-, §biː-
‖ -jᵊr ~**s** z
be'havio(u)r ˌpattern; be'havio(u)r
ˌtherapy
behavior|al, behaviour~ bɪ 'heɪv jᵊr əl ~**ism**
ˌɪz əm ~**ist/s** ɪst/s §əst/s
behavio|ristic, behaviou~ bɪ ˌheɪv jə 'rɪst ɪk ◂
bə-, §biː-
behead bɪ 'hed bə-, §biː- ~**ed** ɪd əd ~**ing** ɪŋ
~**s** z
beheld bɪ 'held bə-, §biː-
behemoth, B~ bɪ 'hiːm ɒθ bə-, -əθ ‖ -ɑːθ -əθ
behest bɪ 'hest bə-, §biː-
behind bɪ 'haɪnd bə-, §biː- ~**s** z
behindhand bɪ 'haɪnd hænd bə-, §biː-
Behn ben
behold bɪ 'həʊld bə-, §biː-, →-'hɒʊld ‖ -'hoʊld
~**ing** ɪŋ ~**s** z
beholden bɪ 'həʊld ən bə-, §biː-, →-'hɒʊld-
‖ -'hoʊld-
beholder bɪ 'həʊld ə bə-, §biː-, →'hɒʊld-
‖ -'hoʊld ᵊr ~**s** z
behoov|e bɪ 'huːv bə-, §biː- ~**ed** d ~**es** z
~**ing** ɪŋ
behov|e bɪ 'həʊv bə-, §biː- ‖ -'hoʊv ~**ed** d
~**es** z ~**ing** ɪŋ
Behrens 'beər ənz ‖ 'ber- —*Ger* ['beːʁ əns]
Beiderbecke 'baɪd ə bek ‖ -ᵊr-
beige beɪʒ beɪdʒ
Beighton *(i)* 'beɪt ən, *(ii)* 'baɪt ən
beignet 'beɪn jeɪ ', •'• ~**s** z —*Fr* [bɛ njɛ]
Beijing ˌbeɪ 'dʒɪŋ -'ʒɪŋ —*Note: there is no*
justification in Chinese for the -'ʒɪŋ
pronunciation frequently heard in English.
—*Chi* Běijīng [³peɪ ¹tɕiŋ]
being 'biː ɪŋ ~**s** z
Beinn *in ScGaelic names* ben
Beira 'baɪᵊr ə ‖ 'beɪ rə —*Port* ['bɐi ʁɐ]
Beirut ˌbeɪ 'ruːt ◂ ˌbeə- —*Arabic* [bej 'ruːt]

B

Beit baɪt

Beith biːθ —*but the place in Strathclyde is* biːð

Bejam *tdmk* 'biː dʒæm 'biːdʒ əm

bejeweled, bejewelled bɪ 'dʒuː‿əld bə-, §biː-, -'dʒuːld

Bekonscot 'bek ənz kɒt ‖ -kɑːt

bel, Bel bel *(= bell)* —*It* [bɛl] **bels** belz
  ,bel **'canto** 'kænt əʊ ‖ 'kɑːnt oʊ —*It* ['kan to]; ,Bel **Pa'ese** paɪ 'eɪz i pɑː- —*It* [pa 'eː ze]

belabor, belabour bɪ 'leɪb ə bə-, §biː- ‖ -ᵊr
  ~**ed** d **belaboring, belabouring** bɪ 'leɪb ər‿ɪŋ ~**s** z

Belafonte ,bel ə 'fɒnt i ‖ -'fɑːnt̬ i -eɪ

Belarius bɪ 'leər i‿əs bə-, -'lɑːr- ‖ -'ler- -'lær-

Belarus ,bel ə 'ruːs —*Belorussian* [,bʲe ła 'rus], *Russian* [,bʲe łɐ 'rus]

belated bɪ 'leɪt ɪd bə-, §biː-, -əd ‖ -'leɪt̬- ~**ly** li ~**ness** nəs nɪs

Belau bə 'laʊ bɪ-, be-; 'bel aʊ

belay bɪ 'leɪ bə-, §biː- ~**ed** d ~**ing** ɪŋ ~**s** z
  be'laying pin

belch, Belch beltʃ **belched** beltʃt **belching** 'beltʃ ɪŋ **belches** 'beltʃ ɪz -əz

Belcher 'beltʃ ə 'belʃ- ‖ -ᵊr

beldam, beldame 'beld əm 'bel dæm, -dɑːm

beleaguer bɪ 'liːg lə bə-, §biː- ‖ -ᵊr ~**ered** əd ‖ ᵊrd ~**ering** ər ɪŋ ~**ers** əz ‖ ᵊrz

Belem be 'lem bə- —*Port* [bə 'lẽɪ, be 'lẽi]

belemnite 'bel əm naɪt ~**s** z

Belfast ,bel 'fɑːst ◂ '•• , §-'fæst ‖ 'bel fæst ,•'•

belfry 'belf |ri ~**ries** riz

Belgae 'belg aɪ 'beldʒ iː

Belgian 'beldʒ ən ~**s** z

Belgic 'beldʒ ɪk

Belgium 'beldʒ əm

Belgrade ,bel 'greɪd ‖ '••

Belgrano bel 'grɑːn əʊ ‖ -oʊ —*Sp* [bel 'ɣra no]

Belgrave 'bel greɪv
  ,Belgrave **'Square**

Belgravia bel 'greɪv i‿ə

Belial 'biːl i‿əl

be|lie bɪ |'laɪ bə-, §biː- ~**lied** 'laɪd ~**lies** 'laɪz ~**lying** 'laɪ ɪŋ

belief bɪ 'liːf bə-, §biː- ~**s** s

believab|le bɪ 'liːv əb |əl bə-, §biː- ~**ly** li

believ|e bɪ 'liːv bə-, §biː- ~**er/s** ə/z ‖ ᵊr/z ~**ed** d ~**es** z ~**ing** ɪŋ

Belinda bə 'lɪnd ə bɪ-

Belisarius ,bel ɪ 'sɑːr i‿əs, •ə-, -'seər- ‖ -'ser-

Belisha bə 'liːʃ ə bɪ-
  Be,lisha **'beacon**

belittl|e bɪ 'lɪt əl bə-, §biː- ‖ -'lɪt̬- ~**ed** d ~**es** z ~**ing** ɪŋ

Belize bə 'liːz bə-, be-

Belizean bɪ 'liːz i‿ən bə-, be-, -'lɪz- ~**s** z

bell, Bell bel **belled** beld **belling** 'bel ɪŋ **bells** belz
  'bell jar; ,Bell 'Rock; 'bell tent

Bella 'bel ə
  ,Bella **'Coola** 'kuːl ə

belladonna ,bel ə 'dɒn ə ‖ -'dɑːn-

Bellamy 'bel əm i

bellbird, B~ 'bel bɜːd ‖ -bɝːd ~**s** z

bell-bottom 'bel ,bɒt əm ‖ -,bɑːt̬ əm ~**s** z

bellboy 'bel bɔɪ ~**s** z

belle, Belle bel *(= bell)* **belles** belz
  ,belle é'poque eɪ 'pɒk ‖ -'pɔːk -'pɑːk —*Fr* [bɛ le pɔk]; ,Belle **'Fourche** *river in US* fuːʃ

Belleek bə 'liːk bɪ-

Bellenden Ker ,bel ənd ən 'kɜː ‖ -'kɝː

Bellerophon bə 'ler əf ən bɪ-

belles-lettres ,bel 'letr ə —*Fr* [bɛl lɛtχ]

Belleville 'bel vɪl

Bellevue ,bel 'vjuː ‖ 'bel vjuː

Bellew 'bel juː

bellflower, B~ 'bel ,flaʊ‿ə ‖ -,flaʊ‿ᵊr ~**s** z

bellhop 'bel hɒp ‖ -hɑːp ~**s** s

bellicose 'bel ɪ kəʊs -ə-, -kəʊz ‖ -koʊs ~**ly** li ~**ness** nəs nɪs

bellicosity ,bel ɪ 'kɒs ət i ,•ə-, -ɪt i ‖ -'kɑːs ət̬ i

bellie... —*see* **belly**

belligerenc|e bə 'lɪdʒ ᵊr‿ənts bɪ- ~**y** i

belligerent bə 'lɪdʒ ᵊr‿ənt bɪ-

Belling 'bel ɪŋ

Bellingham *(i)* 'bel ɪŋ əm -həm, *(ii)* -ɪndʒ əm, *(iii)* -ɪŋ hæm —*The place in Greater London is (i), that in Northumberland (ii), and that in Washington State (iii). The family name may be any of the three.*

Bellingshausen 'bel ɪŋz ,haʊz ᵊn

Bellini be 'liːn i bə- —*It* [bel 'liː ni]

bell|man 'bel |mən ~**men** mən men

Bellmawr ₍₎bel 'mɔː ‖ ₍₎bel 'mɑːr -'mɔːr

Belloc 'bel ɒk -ək ‖ -ɑːk

Bellona be 'ləʊn ə ‖ -'loʊn-

bellow, B~ 'bel əʊ ‖ -oʊ ~**ed** d ~**ing** ɪŋ ~**s** z

Bellows 'bel əʊz ‖ -oʊz

bellring|er/s 'bel ,rɪŋ ə/z ‖ -ᵊr/z ~**ing** ɪŋ

bellwether 'bel ,weð ə ,•'•• ‖ -ᵊr ~**s** z

bell|y 'bel |i ~**ied** id ~**ies** iz ~**ying** i‿ɪŋ
  'belly ,button; 'belly flop; 'belly laugh

bellyach|e 'bel i eɪk ~**ed** t ~**es** s ~**ing** ɪŋ

belly-danc|e 'bel i dɑːnts §-dænts ‖ -dænts ~**er/s** ə/z ‖ ᵊr/z ~**ing** ɪŋ

bellyful 'bel i fʊl

belly-landing 'bel i ,lænd ɪŋ ~**s** z

Belmondo bel 'mɒnd əʊ ‖ -'mɑːnd oʊ —*Fr* [bɛl mɔ̃ do]

Belmont 'bel mɒnt -mənt ‖ -mɑːnt

Belmopan ,belm əʊ 'pæn ‖ -oʊ-

Belmore 'bel mɔː ‖ -mɔːr -moʊr

Beloff 'bel ɒf ‖ -ɑːf

Belo Horizonte ,bel əʊ ,hɒr ɪ 'zɒnt i ,beɪl-, -ə'•-, -eɪ ‖ -oʊ ,hɔːr ə 'zɑːnt i —*Port* [,bɛ lo ri 'zõ ti]

belong bɪ 'lɒŋ bə-, §biː- ‖ -'lɔːŋ -'lɑːŋ ~**ed** d ~**ing/s** ɪŋ/z ~**s** z

Belorussia ,bel əʊ 'rʌʃ ə bi ,el-, -'ruːs i‿ə

Belorussian ,bel əʊ 'rʌʃ ən bi ,el-, -'ruːs i‿ən ~**s** z

beloved bɪ 'lʌv ɪd bə-, §biː-, -əd, -'lʌvd —*but predicatively always* -'lʌvd

below bɪ 'ləʊ bə-, §biː- ‖ -'loʊ

Belper 'belp ə ‖ -ᵊr

Belsen 'bels ᵊn —*Ger* ['bɛl zᵊn]

Belshazzar bel ˈʃæz ə ‖ -ᵊr
Belsize ˈbel saɪz
 ˌBelsize ˈPark
Belstead ˈbel stɪd -sted, §-stəd
belt belt **belted** ˈbelt ɪd -əd **belting** ˈbelt ɪŋ
 belts belts
 ˈbelt drive
Beltane ˈbelt eɪn -ən
beltway ˈbelt weɪ ~s z
beluga bə ˈluːɡ ə bɪ-, be- ~s z
belvedere, B~ ˈbelv ə dɪə -ɪ-, ˌ•• ˈ•‖ -dɪr ~s z
Belvoir place in Leics; family name ˈbiːv ə ‖ -ᵊr
 (!)
bem|a ˈbiːm |ə ~**as** əz ~**ata** ət ə ‖ ət̬ ə
Bemba ˈbem bə ~s z
Bembo ˈbem bəʊ ‖ -boʊ
Bembridge ˈbem brɪdʒ
bemoan bɪ ˈməʊn bə-, §biː- ‖ -ˈmoʊn ~**ed** d
 ~**ing** ɪŋ ~s z
bemus|e bɪ ˈmjuːz bə-, §biː- ~**ed** d ~**es** ɪz əz
 ~**ing** ɪŋ
Ben, ben ben **bens** benz —See also phrases
 with this word
benadryl, B~ tdmk ˈben ə drɪl ~s z
Benares bɪ ˈnɑːr ɪz bə-, be-, -əz
Benaud ˈben əʊ ‖ -oʊ
Benbecula ben ˈbek jʊl ə →bem-
Benbow ˈben bəʊ →ˈbem- ‖ -boʊ
Bence benˈs
bench bentʃ **benched** bentʃt **benches**
 ˈbentʃ ɪz -əz **benching** ˈbentʃ ɪŋ
bencher ˈbentʃ ə ‖ -ᵊr ~s z
Benchley ˈbentʃ li
benchmark ˈbentʃ mɑːk ‖ -mɑːrk ~**ed** t ~**ing**
 ɪŋ ~s s
bend bend **bended** ˈbend ɪd -əd **bending**
 ˈbend ɪŋ **bends** bendz **bent** bent
 ˌbend ˈover; ˌbend ˈsinister
bender ˈbend ə ‖ -ᵊr ~s z
Bendigo ˈbend ɪ ɡəʊ -ə- ‖ -ɡoʊ
Bendix ˈbend ɪks
bend|y ˈbend li ~**ier** i_ə ‖ i_ᵊr ~**iest** i_ɪst i_əst
 ~**iness** i nəs -nɪs
beneath bɪ ˈniːθ bə-, §biː-
Benedicite, b~ ˌben ɪ ˈdaɪs ət i ˌ•ə-, -ˈdiːtʃ-,
 -ɪt i; -ɪ teɪ, -ə teɪ -ət̬ i ~s z
Benedick, b~ ˈben ɪ dɪk -ə-
Benedict ˈben ɪ dɪkt -ə- —The former
 pronunciation ˈben ɪt is nowadays spelt
 correspondingly as Bene't or Benet.
benedictine, B~ ˈliqueur' ˌben ɪ ˈdɪkt iːn ◀
 -ə- ‖ -dɪk ˈtiːn ~s z
Benedictine ˈmonk', ˌben ɪ ˈdɪkt ɪn ◀ -ə-, -iːn,
 -aɪn ~s z
benediction ˌben ɪ ˈdɪkʃ ən -ə- ~s z
Benedictus ˌben ɪ ˈdɪkt əs -ə-, -ʊs
benefaction ˌben ɪ ˈfæk ʃən -ə- ~s z
benefactive ˌben ɪ ˈfækt ɪv -ə-, ˈ•••• ~s z
benefactor ˈben ɪ fækt ə ˈ•ə- ‖ -ᵊr ~s z
benefactress ˈben ɪ fæk trəs ˈ•ə-, -trɪs, ˌ••ˈ••
 ~**es** ɪz əz
benefice ˈben ɪf ɪs -əf-, §-əs ~**ed** t ~s ɪz əz
beneficence bə ˈnef ɪs ənˈs bɪ-, -əs-

beneficent bə ˈnef ɪs ənt bɪ-, -əs-, ~**ly** li
beneficial ˌben ɪ ˈfɪʃ əl ◀ -ə- ~**ly** i ~**ness** nəs
 nɪs
beneficiar|y ˌben ɪ ˈfɪʃ ər_|i ˌ•ə-, -ˈfɪʃ i_ər |i
 ‖ -ˈfɪʃ i er |i -ˈ• ər_|i ~**ies** iz
bene|fit ˈben ɪ |fɪt -ə-, §-fət ~**fited, ~fitted**
 fɪt ɪd §fət-, -əd ‖ fɪt̬ əd ~**fiting, ~fitting**
 fɪt ɪŋ §fət- ‖ fɪt̬ ɪŋ ~**fits** fɪts §fəts
Benelux ˈben ɪ lʌks -ə-
 the ˈBenelux ˌcountries
Benenden ˈben ənd ən —formerly also
 ˌben ən ˈden
Benet, Bene't ˈben ɪt §-ət
Benét American family name bə ˈneɪ be-
Benetton tdmk ˈben ɪt ən -ət-; -ɪ tɒn,
 -ə- ‖ -ə tɑːn
benevolence bə ˈnev əl_ənˈs bɪ-
benevolent bə ˈnev əl_ənt bɪ- ~**ly** li
Benfleet ˈben fliːt
BEng ˌbiː ˈendʒ
Bengal ˌben ˈɡɔːl ◀ →ˌbeŋ-, -ˈɡɑːl
Bengali ben ˈɡɔːl i →beŋ-, -ˈɡɑːl-, ˌ•ˈ••◀ ~s z
Benghazi ben ˈɡɑːz i →beŋ- —Arabic
 [ˌba ni ˈɣaː zi]
Benguela ben ˈɡwel ə →beŋ-, -ˈɡweɪl-, -ˈɡel-,
 -ˈɡeɪl- —Port [beŋ ˈɡwɛ lɐ]
Ben Gurion, Ben-Gurion ben ˈɡʊər i_ən
 →beŋ- ‖ -ˈɡʊr-, ˌben ɡʊr ˈjaːn, -ˈjɔːn
Ben Hur, Ben-Hur ˌben ˈhɜː ‖ -ˈhɜ˞ː
Benidorm ˈben ɪ dɔːm -ə- ‖ -dɔːrm
benighted bɪ ˈnaɪt ɪd bə-, §biː-, -əd ‖ -ˈnaɪt̬-
 ~**ly** li ~**ness** nəs nɪs
benign bə ˈnaɪn bɪ- ~**ly** li
benignanc|y bə ˈnɪɡ nənˈs li ~**ies** iz
benignant bə ˈnɪɡ nənt bɪ- ~**ly** li
benignit|y bə ˈnɪɡ nət li bɪ-, -nɪt i ‖ -nət̬ li ~**ies**
 iz
Benin be ˈniːn bɪ-, bə-, -ˈnɪn
Beninese ˌben ɪ ˈniːz ◀ be ˌniː-, bɪ-, bə-, -ˌnɪ-
benison ˈben ɪz ən -ɪs-, -əz-, -əs- ~s z
Benita be ˈniːt ə bɪ-, bə- ‖ -ˈniːt̬-
Benito be ˈniːt əʊ bɪ-, bə- ‖ -ˈniːt̬ oʊ
Benjamin, b~ ˈbendʒ əm_ɪn ən
Ben Macdhui ˌben mək ˈduː i
Benn ben
Bennelong ˈben ɪ lɒŋ -ə- ‖ -lɔːŋ -lɑːŋ
Bennet, Bennett ˈben ɪt §-ət
Ben Nevis ˌben ˈnev ɪs §-əs
Bennie, b~ ˈben i ~s z
Bennington ˈben ɪŋ tən
Benn|y, benn|y ˈben li ~**ies**, ~**y's** iz
Benoni bə ˈnəʊn i bɪ-, be- ‖ -ˈnoʊn-
Ben Rhydding ˌben ˈrɪd ɪŋ
Benson ˈbenˈs ən
bent bent **bents** bentˈs
Bentall ˈbent ɔːl -ɒːl ‖ -ɔːl -ɑːl ~ˈs z
Bentham ˈbent̬ əm ˈbent-
Benthamism ˈbent̬ ə ˌmɪz əm ˈbent-
Benthamite ˈbent̬ ə maɪt ˈbent-
benthic ˈbent̬ ɪk
benthos ˈbent̬ ɒs ‖ ˈben θɑːs
Bentinck ˈbent ɪŋk
Bentine ben ˈtiːn ˈ••

B

Bentley 'bent li ~s z
Benton 'bent ən ‖ -ᵊn
bentonite 'bent ə naɪt ‖ -ᵊn aɪt
ben trovato ,ben trəʊ 'vɑːt əʊ ‖ -troʊ 'vɑːt̬ oʊ
—*It* [,bɛn tro 'vaː to]
Bentsen 'bents ən
bentwood 'bent wʊd
Benue 'ben u eɪ ‖ 'beɪn weɪ
Benue-Congo
,ben u eɪ 'kɒŋ gəʊ ‖ ,beɪn weɪ 'kɑːŋ goʊ
benumb bɪ 'nʌm bə-, §biː:- ~ed d ~ing ɪŋ ~s
z
Benylin *tdmk* 'ben ɪ lɪn -ə-, -ᵊl ɪn
Benyon 'ben jən
Benz benz —*Ger* [bɛnts]
benzedrine, B~ *tdmk* 'benz ə driːn -ɪ-, -drɪn ~s
z
benzene 'benz iːn ben 'ziːn
,benzene 'ring
benzidine 'benz ɪ diːn -ə-, -dɪn
benzine 'benz iːn ben 'ziːn
benzo- *comb. form*
with stress-neutral suffix ˌbenz əʊ ‖ -oʊ —
benzosulfate, benzosulphate
,benz əʊ 'sʌlf eɪt ‖ -oʊ-
benzocaine 'benz əʊ keɪn ‖ -ə-
benzodiazepine ,benz əʊ daɪ 'eɪz ə piːn -di'•-,
-pɪn; ,benz əʊ 'deɪz-, -'dæz- ‖ ,benz oʊ-
benzoic ben 'zəʊ ɪk ‖ -'zoʊ-
benzoin 'benz əʊ ɪn ben 'zəʊ•, §-ən; 'benz ɔɪn
‖ -oʊ- —*Some people claim to distinguish*
'benz əʊ ɪn *etc.* 'phenyl benzoyl carbinol' *from*
'benz ɔɪn 'gum benjamin'
benzol 'benz ɒl ‖ -oʊl -ɑːl, -ɔːl
benzole 'benz əʊl →-ɒʊl ‖ -oʊl
benzoyl 'benz əʊ ɪl §-əl ‖ -oʊ-
benzpyrene ,benz 'paɪᵊr iːn
benzyl 'benz ɪl -ᵊl ‖ -iːᵊl -ᵊl
Beowulf 'beɪ əʊ wʊlf ‖ -ə-

BEQUEATH

	■-'kwiːð	▭'kwiːθ			
BrE 1988					
0	20	40	60	80	100%

be|queath bɪ ǀ'kwiːð bə-, §biː:-, -'kwiːθ —*BrE*
1988 poll panel preference: -'kwiːð 58%,
-'kwiːθ 42%. **~queathed** 'kwiːðd 'kwiːθt
~queathes 'kwiːðz 'kwiːθs **~queathing**
'kwiːð ɪŋ 'kwiːθ ɪŋ
bequest bɪ 'kwest bə-, §biː:- ~s s
Bequia *Caribbean island* 'bek wi -weɪ *(!)*
be|rate bɪ ǀ'reɪt bə-, §biː:- **~rated** 'reɪt ɪd -əd
‖ 'reɪt̬ əd **~rates** 'reɪts **~rating**
'reɪt ɪŋ ‖ 'reɪt̬ ɪŋ
Berber 'bɜːb ə ‖ 'bɝːb ᵊr ~s z
Berbera 'bɜːb ər ə ‖ 'bɝːb-
berberis 'bɜːb ər ɪs §-əs ‖ 'bɝːb- **~es** ɪz əz
Berbice bɜː 'biːs 'bɜːb ɪs ‖ bɝː-
berceuse beə 'sɜːz ‖ ber 'sʊz -'sɜ:z —*Fr*
[bɛʁ søːz]
Berchtesgaden 'beəkt əz gɑːd ᵊn 'beəxt-
‖ 'berkt- —*Ger* [ˈbɛʁç təs gaːd ᵊn]
Bere bɪə ‖ bɪᵊr

bereav|e bɪ 'riːv bə-, §biː:- **~ed** d **~ement/s**
mənt/s **~es** z **~ing** ɪŋ
bereft bɪ 'reft bə-, §biː:-
Berengaria ,ber əŋ 'geər i_ə ,•ɪŋ-, ,•eŋ-
‖ -'ger-
Berenice ,ber ɪ 'naɪs i -ə-, -'naɪk-, -iː:; -'niːtʃ eɪ,
-i; -'niːs
Berenson 'ber ᵊn's ən
Beresford 'ber ɪs fəd -əs-, -ɪz-, -əz- ‖ -fᵊrd
beret 'ber eɪ -i; bə 'reɪ ‖ bə 'reɪ —*Formerly also*
'ber ɪt. ~s z
berg, Berg bɜːg ‖ bɝːg —*Ger* [bɛʁk] **bergs**
bɜːgz ‖ bɝːgz
Bergamo 'bɜːg ə məʊ ‖ 'bɝːg ə moʊ —*It* ['bɛr
ga mo]
bergamot 'bɜːg ə mɒt ‖ 'bɝːg ə mɑːt ~s s
'bergamot oil
Bergen 'bɜːg ən 'beəg- ‖ 'bɝːg- —*Norw*
['bær gən, 'bæʁ-]
Berger *(i)* 'bɜːdʒ ə ‖ 'bɝːdʒ ᵊr, *(ii)*
'bɜːg ə ‖ 'bɝːg ᵊr —*as a British name, (i); as*
an American name, (ii)
Bergerac 'bɜːʒ ə ræk ‖ ,berʒ ə 'ræk -'rɑːk
Bergman 'bɜːg mən ‖ 'bɝːg-
bergschrund 'bɜːg ʃrund ‖ 'bɝːg- ~s z —*Ger*
B~ ['bɛʁk ʃʁʊnt]
Bergson 'bɜːg sᵊn ‖ 'bɝːg- —*Fr* [bɛʁk sɔn]
Bergsonian bɜːg 'səʊn i_ən‖ bɝːg 'soʊn-
berg- ~s z
beribboned bɪ 'rɪb ᵊnd bə-, §biː:-
beriberi ,ber i 'ber i '•• ,••
Bering 'beər ɪŋ 'ber- ‖ 'bɪr ɪŋ 'ber- —*Danish*
['beː ʁeŋ]
,Bering 'Sea, ,Bering 'Strait
Berisford 'ber ɪs fəd -əs-, -ɪz-, -əz- ‖ -fᵊrd
berk bɜːk ‖ bɝːk **berks** bɜːks ‖ bɝːks
Berkeley *(i)* 'bɑːk li ‖ 'bɑːrk-, *(ii)*
'bɜːk li ‖ 'bɝːk- —*British and Irish places and*
names are (i), American places and names are
(ii).
berkelium bɜː 'kiːl i_əm bə-, 'bɜːk li_əm
‖ 'bɝːk li_əm
Berkhamsted 'bɜːk əm sted 'bɑːk-, -əm'st ɪd,
-əd ‖ 'bɝːk-
Berkley *place in Michigan* 'bɜːk li ‖ 'bɝːk-
Berks *name of county* bɑːks §bɜːks ‖ bɝːks
bɑːrks —*see also* Berkshire
Berkshire *(i)* 'bɑːk ʃə -ʃɪə ‖ 'bɑːrk ʃᵊr -ʃɪr, *(ii)*
'bɜːk- ‖ 'bɝːk- —*The English county is (i),*
though with a non-standard variant (ii). The
hills in MA are (ii). ~s z
Berlei *tdmk* 'bɜːl i -aɪ ‖ 'bɝːl-
Berlin (ₗ)bɜː 'lɪn ‖ (ₗ)bɝː:- —*Ger* [bɛʁ 'liːn] —*but*
the town in New Hampshire is 'bɜːl ən
Berliner (ₗ)bɜː 'lɪn ə ‖ bɝː 'lɪn ᵊr ~s z
Berlioz 'beəl i əʊz 'bɜːl- ‖ 'berl i oʊz —*Fr*
[bɛʁ ljoːz]
Berlitz 'bɜːl ɪts §-əts ‖ 'bɝːl ɪts bɝː 'lɪts
berm, berme bɜːm ‖ bɝːm **bermes, berms**
bɜːmz ‖ bɝːmz
Bermondsey 'bɜːm əndz i ‖ 'bɝːm-
Bermuda bə 'mjuːd ə ‖ bᵊr- ~s z
Ber,muda 'shorts; Ber,muda 'Triangle

Bermudan bə 'mjuːd ⁿn ‖ bᵊr- ~s z

Bern bɜːn beən ‖ bɝːn bern —*Ger* [bɛʁn]

Bernadette ˌbɜːn ə 'det ‖ ˌbɝːn-

Bernadotte ˌbɜːn ə 'dɒt '•• ‖ 'bɝːn ə dɑːt

Bernal (i) bə 'næl ‖ bᵊr-, (ii) 'bɜːn ᵊl ‖ 'bɝːn-

Bernard (i) 'bɜːn əd ‖ 'bɝːn ᵊrd, (ii)
bə 'nɑːd ‖ bᵊr 'nɑːrd —*As a British name
usually* (i), *as an American name usually* (ii).

Bernardette ˌbɜːn ə 'det ‖ ˌbɝːn ᵊr- -ə-

Bernardine 'bɜːn ə dɪn -diːn ‖ 'bɝːn ᵊr-

Berne bɜːn beən ‖ bɝːn bern —*Fr* [bɛʁn]

Berners 'bɜːn əz ‖ 'bɝːn ᵊrz

Bernese ˌbɜː 'niːz ◄ ‖ ˌbɝː- -'niːs

Bernhardt 'bɜːn hɑːt ‖ 'bɝːn hɑːrt —*Fr*
[bɛʁ nɑːʁ]

Bernice (i) 'bɜːn ɪs -əs ‖ 'bɝːn-, (ii) bə 'niːs
bɜː- ‖ bᵊr-, (iii) bɜː 'naɪs i ‖ bᵊr- —*In AmE
usually* (ii).

Bernini bɜː 'niːn i bə- ‖ bᵊr- —*It* [ber 'niː ni]

Bernoulli bɜː 'nuːl i bə- ‖ bᵊr- —*Fr*
[bɛʁ nu ji], *Ger* [bɛʁ 'nʊl i]
Ber'nouilli ef ˌfect

Bernstein (i) 'bɜːn staɪn ‖ 'bɝːn-, (ii) -stiːn

Be-Ro *tdmk* 'biː rəʊ ‖ -roʊ

Berol *tdmk* 'biː rɒl -rəʊl ‖ -rɑːl -rɔːl, -roʊl

Berridge 'ber ɪdʒ

Berriew 'ber i uː

berr|y 'ber li ~ied id ~ies iz ~ying i ɪŋ

Berry 'ber i

Berryman 'ber i mən

berserk bə 'zɜːk bɜː-, -'sɜːk; 'bɜːs ɜːk, 'bɜːz-
‖ bᵊr 'sɝːk -'zɝːk ~er/s ə/z ‖ ᵊr/z

Bert bɜːt ‖ bɝːt

Bertelsmann *tdmk* 'bɜːt ᵊlz mæn -mən ‖ 'bɝːt̬-
—*Ger* ['bɛʁ tᵊls man]

berth bɜːθ ‖ bɝːθ (= *birth*) berthed
bɜːθt ‖ bɝːθt berthing 'bɜːθ ɪŋ ‖ 'bɝːθ ɪŋ
berths bɜːθs bɜːðz ‖ bɝːθs

Bertha 'bɜːθ ə ‖ 'bɝːθ ə

Bertie 'bɜːt i ‖ 'bɝːt̬ i —*but as a family name in
BrE*, 'bɑːt i

Bertolucci ˌbɜːt ə 'lʊtʃ i-'luːtʃ-
‖ ˌbɜːt̬ ə 'luːtʃ i —*It* [ber to 'lut tʃi]

Bertram 'bɜːtr əm ‖ 'bɝːtr-

Bertrand 'bɜːtr ənd ‖ 'bɝːtr-

Berwick 'ber ɪk

Berwick-on-Tweed ˌber ɪk ɒn 'twiːd ‖ -ɑːn• -ɔːn•

Berwickshire 'ber ɪk ʃə -ʃɪə; '•• ˌʃaɪ_ə ‖ -ʃɪr
-ʃᵊr; '•• ˌʃaɪ_ᵊr

Berwyn 'beə wɪn 'bɜː- ‖ 'bɝː-

beryl, Beryl 'ber əl -ɪl ~s z

beryllium bə 'rɪl i_əm be-

Berzelius bə 'ziːl i_əs -'zeɪl- ‖ bᵊr- —*Swed*
[bær 'seː li ʊs]

Besancon, Besançon bə 'zɒs ɒ̃ ‖ -'zɑːn soʊn
-'zænts ᵊn —*Fr* [bə zɑ̃ sɔ̃]

Besant (i) 'bes ᵊnt 'bez-, (ii) bɪ 'zænt bə-

beseech bɪ 'siːtʃ bə-, §biː- ~ed t ~es ɪz əz
~ing/ly ɪŋ /li besought bɪ 'sɔːt bə-, §biː- ‖
-'sɑːt

beseem bɪ 'siːm bə-, §biː- ~ed d ~ing ɪŋ ~s z

be|set bɪ l'set bə-, §biː- ~sets 'sets ~setting
'set ɪŋ ‖ 'set̬ ɪŋ

beside bɪ 'saɪd bə-, §biː- ~s z

besieg|e bɪ 'siːdʒ bə-, §biː-, -'siːʒ ~ed d
~ement mənt ~er/s ə/z ‖ ᵊr/z ~es ɪz əz
~ing ɪŋ

be|smear bɪ l'smɪə bə-, §biː- ‖ -l'smɪᵊr
~smeared smɪəd ‖ 'smɪᵊrd ~smearing
'smɪər ɪŋ ‖ 'smɪr ɪŋ ~smears
'smɪəz ‖ 'smɪᵊrz

besmirch bɪ 'smɜːtʃ bə-, §biː- ‖ -l'smɝːtʃ ~ed
t ~ment mənt ~es ɪz əz ~ing ɪŋ

besom 'biːz əm ~ed d ~ing ɪŋ ~s z

besotted bɪ 'sɒt ɪd bə-, §biː-, -'zɒt-, -əd
‖ -'sɑːt̬ əd

besought bɪ 'sɔːt bə-, §biː- ‖ -'sɑːt

bespangl|e bɪ 'spæŋ gᵊl bə-, §biː- ~ed d ~es z
~ing ˌɪŋ

bespatt|er bɪ 'spæt ə bə-, §biː- ‖ -l'spæt̬ ᵊr
~ered əd ‖ ᵊrd ~ering ˌər ɪŋ ‖ ᵊr ɪŋ ~ers
əz ‖ ᵊrz

be|speak bɪ l'spiːk bə-, §biː- ~speaking
'spiːk ɪŋ ~speaks 'spiːks ~spoke
'spəʊk ‖ 'spoʊk ~spoken 'spəʊk ən ‖ 'spoʊk
ən

bespectacled bɪ 'spekt ək ᵊld bə-, §biː-, -ɪk-

bespok|e bɪ 'spəʊk bə-, §biː- ‖ -'spoʊk ~en
ən

besprinkl|e bɪ 'sprɪŋk ᵊl bə-, §biː- ~ed d ~es z
~ing ˌɪŋ

Bess bes Bess's 'bes ɪz-əz

Bessarabi|a ˌbes ə 'reɪb i_ə ~an/s ən/z ◄

Bessborough 'bez bᵊr_ə ‖ -ˌbɜː oʊ

Bessbrook 'bes brʊk

Bessel, Bessell 'bes ᵊl
'Bessel ˌfunction

Bessemer 'bes ɪm ə -əm- ‖ -ᵊr
ˌBessemer con'verter

Besses o' th' Barn ˌbes ɪz əð 'bɑːn ˌ•əz-
‖ -'bɑːrn

Bessey, Bessie, Bessy 'bes i

best, Best best bested 'best ɪd -əd besting
'best ɪŋ bests bests
ˌbest 'man

bestial 'best i_əl ‖ 'bes tʃəl→'beʃ-, 'biːs- ~ly i
(*)

bestialit|y ˌbest i 'æl ət i-ɪt i ‖ ˌbes tʃi 'æl ət̬ li
→ˌbeʃ-, ˌbiːs- (*) ~ies iz

bestiar|y 'best i_ər li ‖ 'bes tʃi er li→'beʃ-,
'biːs- (*) ~ies iz

be|stir bɪ l'stɜː bə-, §biː- ‖ -l'stɝː ~stirred
'stɜːd ‖ 'stɝːd ~stirring 'stɜːr ɪŋ ‖ 'stɝː ɪŋ
~stirs 'stɜːz ‖ 'stɝːz

bestow bɪ 'stəʊ bə-, §biː- ‖ -'stoʊ ~ed d
~ing ɪŋ ~s z

bestowal bɪ 'stəʊ əl bə-, §biː- ‖ -'stoʊ-

bestrew bɪ 'struː bə-, §biː-

bestrewn bɪ 'struːn bə-, §biː-

be|stride bɪ l'straɪd bə-, §biː- ~strides 'straɪdz
~stridden 'strɪd ᵊn ~strode
'strəʊd ‖ 'stroʊd

bestseller, best-seller ˌbest 'sel ə ◄ ‖ -ᵊr
~dom dəm ~s z

B

bestselling, best-selling ˌbes*t* 'sel ɪŋ ◄
Beswick 'bez ɪk
bet, Bet bet betted 'bet ɪd -əd ‖ 'bet̬-
  betting 'bet ɪŋ ‖ 'bet̬- bets bets
beta, Beta 'bi:t ə ‖ 'beɪt̬ ə *(*)* ~s z
  ' beta ˌparticle; ' beta ˌrhythm
beta-blocker 'bi:t ə ˌblɒk ə ‖ 'beɪt̬ ə ˌblɑ:k ər
  ~s z
betaine 'bi:t ə i:n -ɪn; bɪ 'teɪ-, bə- ‖ 'bi:t̬-
be|take bɪ |'teɪk bə-, §bi:- ~taken 'teɪk ən
  ~takes 'teɪks ~taking 'teɪk ɪŋ ~took 'tʊk
Betamax *tdmk* 'bi:t ə mæks ‖ 'beɪt̬-
betatron 'bi:t ə trɒn ‖ 'beɪt̬ ə trɑ:n ~s z
betcha 'betʃ ə
betel 'bi:t əl ‖ 'bi:t̬ əl *(= beetle)*
  ' betel nut
Betelgeuse 'bi:t əl dʒɜ:z -ɜ:z, -dʒu:z, ˌ•••
  ‖ 'bi:t̬ əl dʒu:s 'bet̬-, -dʒu:z
bete noire, bête noir, bete-noire, bête-noire
  ˌbeɪt 'nwɑː ˌbet- ‖ ˌbet nə 'wɑːr ˌbeɪt- —*Fr*
  [bet nwaːʁ] betes noires, bêtes noires,
  betes-noires, bêtes-noires ˌbeɪt 'nwɑːz
  ˌbet-, 'nwɑː ‖ ˌbet nə 'wɑːrz ˌbeɪt- —*Fr*
  [bet nwaːʁ]
beth *Hebrew letter* bet beθ ‖ beɪt beɪθ, beɪs
Beth *personal name* beθ
Beth-Ann, Bethanne, Beth-Anne ˌbeθ 'æn
Bethany 'beθ ən i
Bethel, bethel 'beθ əl ~'s, ~s z
Bethell *(i)* 'beθ əl, *(ii)* be 'θel
Bethesda be 'θezd ə bɪ-, bə-
be|think bɪ |'θɪŋk bə-, §bi:- ~thinking 'θɪŋk ɪŋ
  ~thinks 'θɪŋks ~thought 'θɔːt ‖ 'θɑːt
Bethlehem 'beθ lɪ hem -lə-, -li_əm
Bethnal 'beθ nəl
  ˌBethnal ' Green
bethought bɪ 'θɔːt bə-, §bi:- ‖ -'θɑːt
Bethune, Béthune be 'θjuːn bɪ-, bə-, -'tjuːn,
  -'tuːn ‖ -'θuːn —*Fr* [be tyn] —*As a family
  name, also* 'biːt ən ‖ bə 'θuːn
betid|e bɪ 'taɪd bə-, §bi:- ~ed ɪd əd ~es z
  ~ing ɪŋ
betimes bɪ 'taɪmz bə-, §bi:-
betise, bêtise be 'tiːz ₍ᵢ₎beɪ- —*Fr* [bɛ tiːz] ~s
  same pronunciation
Betjeman 'betʃ ə mən -ɪ-
betoken bɪ 'təʊk ən bə-, §bi:- ‖ -'toʊk- ~ed d
  ~er/s _ə/z ‖ _ər/z ~ing _ɪŋ ~s z
beton|y 'bet ən li ~ies iz
betook bɪ 'tʊk bə-, §bi:-
betray bɪ 'treɪ bə-, §bi:- ~ed d ~er/s ə/z ‖ ər/z
  ~ing ɪŋ ~s z
betrayal bɪ 'treɪ əl bə-, §bi:-
betrayment bɪ 'treɪ mənt bə-, §bi:- ~s s
be|troth bɪ |'trəʊð bə-, §bi:-, -'trəʊθ ‖ -|'troʊð
  -'trɑːθ ~trothed 'trəʊðd 'trəʊθt ‖ -'troʊðd
  -'trɑːθt ~trothing 'trəʊð ɪŋ 'trəʊθ-
  ‖ -'troʊð ɪŋ -'trɑːθ- ~troths 'trəʊðz 'trəʊθs
  ‖ -'troʊðz -'trɑːθs
betrothal bɪ 'trəʊð əl bə-, §bi:-, -'trəʊθ-
  ‖ -'troʊð- -'trɑːθ- ~s z
Betsy 'bets i
Bettany 'bet ən i

Bette 'bet i bet
bett... —*see* bet
Bettelheim 'bet əl haɪm ‖ 'bet̬-
better 'bet ə ‖ 'bet̬ ər ~ed d bettering
  'bet_ər ɪŋ ‖ 'bet̬ ər ɪŋ ~s z
betterment 'bet ə mənt ‖ 'bet̬ ər-
better-off ˌbet ər 'ɒf -'ɔːf ‖ ˌbet̬ ər 'ɔːf -'ɑːf
Betterton 'bet ət ən ‖ 'bet̬ ərt ən
Betteshanger 'bets ˌhæŋ ə ‖ -ər
Bettina be 'tiːn ə bə, bɪ-
betting 'bet ɪŋ ‖ 'bet̬ ɪŋ
  ' betting shop
Betton 'bet ən
bettor 'bet ə ‖ 'bet̬ ər ~s z
Bettws 'bet əs -ʊs ‖ 'bet̬- —*Welsh* ['bet us]
Bettws... —*see* Betws...
Betty 'bet i ‖ 'bet̬ i ~'s z
between bɪ 'twiːn bə-, §bi:-
betweentimes bɪ 'twiːn taɪmz bə-, §bi:-
betwixt bɪ 'twɪkst bə-, §bi:-
Betws-y-Coed ˌbet əs i 'kɔɪd ˌ•ʊs-, -'kəʊ ɪd,
  -ed ‖ ˌbet̬- —*Welsh* [ˌbet us ə 'koːid]
Betws-yn-Rhos ˌbet əs ɪn 'rəʊs ˌ•ʊs-, -ən•
  ‖ ˌbet̬ əs ən 'roʊs —*Welsh* [ˌbet us ən 'hroːs]
Beulah 'bjuːl ə
Bevan 'bev ən
bevatron 'bev ə trɒn ‖ -trɑːn ~s z
bevel 'bev əl ~ed, ~led d ~ing, ~ling ɪŋ ~s z
  ' bevel gear
beverag|e 'bev ər_ɪdʒ ~es ɪz əz
Beveridge 'bev ər_ɪdʒ
Beverley, Beverly 'bev əl i ‖ -ər li
  ˌBeverly ' Hills
Bevin 'bev ɪn §-ən
Bevis *(i)* 'bev ɪs §-əs, *(ii)* 'biːv-
bevv|y 'bev li ~ied id ~ies iz
bev|y 'bev li *(= bevvy)* ~ies iz
bewail bɪ 'weɪəl bə-, §bi:- ~ed d ~ing ɪŋ ~s z
beware bɪ 'weə bə-, §bi:- ‖ -'weər -'wæər
Bewdley 'bjuːd li
Bewes bjuːz
bewhiskered bɪ 'wɪsk əd bə-, §bi:-, -'hwɪsk-
  ‖ -'hwɪsk ərd
Bewick, Bewicke 'bjuː_ɪk
bewigged bɪ 'wɪgd bə-
bewild|er bɪ 'wɪld lə bə-, §bi:- ‖ -lər ~ered
  əd ‖ ərd ~ering/ly _ər ɪŋ /li ~erment
  ə mənt ‖ ər mənt ~ers əz ‖ ərz
bewitch bɪ 'wɪtʃ bə-, §bi:- ~ed t ~er/s ə/z
  ‖ ər/z ~es ɪz əz ~ing/ly ɪŋ /li ~ment/s
  mənt/s
Bewley 'bjuːl i
Bexar *county in TX* beə ‖ beər
Bexhill ˌbeks 'hɪl ◄
  ˌBexhill-on-ˌ Sea
Bexley 'beks li
Bexleyheath ˌbeks li 'hiːθ
bey, Bey beɪ *(= bay)* beys, Beys beɪz
Beyfus 'beɪf əs 'baɪf-
Beynon 'baɪn ən 'beɪn-
beyond bɪ 'jɒnd bə-, §bi:-; bi 'ɒnd ‖ bi 'ɑːnd
bezant, B~ 'bez ənt ~s s
bezel 'bez əl ~s z

Beziers, Béziers 'bez i eɪ —Fr [be zje]
bezique bɪ 'ziːk bə- ~s s
bezoar 'biːz ɔː ‖ -ɔːr -oʊr ~s z
Bhagavad-Gita ˌbʌg əv əd 'giːt ə ˌbæg-,
  -ə væd- ‖ ˌbaːg ə ˌvaːd-
bhagwan, B~ 'bæg waːn bʌ 'gwaːn —Hindi
  [bhəg ʋaːn]
bhaji 'baːdʒ i ~s z —Hindi [bha: dʒi]
bhajia 'baːdʒ i‿ə
bhang bæŋ —Hindi [bha:ŋ]
bhangra 'bæŋ grə 'baːŋ- —Hindi [bha:ŋgr]
bharal 'bʌr əl ‖ 'bɜː‿əl ~s z —Hindi [bhə rəl]
bhikku 'bɪk uː
bhindi 'bɪnd i —Hindi [bhɪŋ ɖi]
Bhopal ₍ˌ₎bəʊ 'paːl ‖ ₍ˌ₎boʊ-
Bhreathnach 'vræn ɒk ‖ -aːk
Bhutan ˌbuː 'taːn -'tæn
Bhutanese ˌbuːt ə 'niːz ◂ ‖ -'niːs
Bhutto 'buːt əʊ 'bʊt- ‖ 'buːt̬ oʊ
bi baɪ
bi- comb. form ₍ˌ₎baɪ — biaxial ₍ˌ₎baɪ 'æks i‿əl
Biaf|ra bi 'æf |rə baɪ- ~ran/s rən/z
Bialystok bi 'æl ɪ stɒk -'‿ə-; ˌbiː‿ə 'lɪst ɒk
  ‖ bi 'aːl ə staːk —Polish Białystok [bja 'wɨ
  stɔk]
Bianca bi 'æŋk ə
biannual ˌbaɪ 'æn ju‿əl ~ly i ~s z
Biarritz ˌbɪə 'rɪts '•• ‖ ˌbiː ə 'rɪts '••• —Fr
  [bja ʁits]
bias, Bias 'baɪ‿əs ~ed, ~sed t ~es, ~ses ɪz əz
  ~ing, ~sing ɪŋ
  ˌbias 'binding
biathlete baɪ 'æθ liːt ~s z
biathlon baɪ 'æθ lən -lɒn ‖ -laːn ~s z
bib bɪb bibbed bɪbd bibbing 'bɪb ɪŋ bibs
  bɪbz
Bibb bɪb
bibb... —see bib
Bibby 'bɪb i ~'s z
bibelot 'bɪb ləʊ ‖ 'biːb ə loʊ ~s z —or as sing.
bible, Bible 'baɪb əl ~s z
  'Bible belt; 'Bible ˌstudy
biblical, B~ 'bɪb lɪk əl ~ly ‿i
biblio- comb. form
  with stress-neutral suffix ˈbɪb li əʊ ‖ -ə •-
  bibliomania ˌbɪb li əʊ 'meɪn i‿ə ‖ -ə '•-
  with stress-imposing suffix ˌbɪb li 'ɒ+ ‖ -'aː+ —
  bibliolatry ˌbɪb li 'ɒl ətr i ‖ -'aːl-
bibliographer ˌbɪb li 'ɒg rəf ə ‖ -'aːg rəf ər ~s
  z
bibliographic ˌbɪb li‿ə 'græf ɪk ◂ ~al əl ~ally
  əl‿i
bibliograph|y ˌbɪb li 'ɒg rəf |i ‖ -'aːg- ~ies iz
bibliophile 'bɪb li‿ə faɪəl ~s z
bibulous 'bɪb jʊl əs -jəl- ‖ -jəl- ~ly li ~ness
  nəs nɪs
Bic, BiC tdmk bɪk Bics, BiCs bɪks
bicameral ₍ˌ₎baɪ 'kæm ər‿əl
bicameralism ₍ˌ₎baɪ 'kæm ər‿ə ˌlɪz əm
bicarb 'baɪ kaːb ˌ•'• ‖ -kaːrb
bicarbonate ₍ˌ₎baɪ 'kaːb ən‿ət -ɪt, -eɪt
  ‖ -'kaːrb-
  biˌcarbonate of 'soda

bice baɪs
  ˌbice 'green
bicentenar|y ˌbaɪ sen 'tiːn ər‿|i -'ten-;
  ₍ˌ₎baɪ 'sent ɪn ər‿li, -'sent ən- ‖ -'ten-
  ₍ˌ₎•'sent ən er |i ~ies iz
bicentennial ˌbaɪ sen 'ten i‿əl ~s z
biceps 'baɪ seps ~es ɪz əz
Bicester 'bɪst ə ‖ -ər (!)
Biche-la-mar ˌbiːtʃ lə 'maː ˌbiːʃ-, -læ- ‖ -'maːr
bichromate ₍ˌ₎baɪ 'krəʊm eɪt -ət, -ɪt ‖ -'kroʊm-
bicker 'bɪk ə ‖ -ər ~ed d bickering 'bɪk ər ɪŋ
  ~s s
Bickerstaff, Bickerstaffe 'bɪk ə staːf §-stæf
  ‖ -ər stæf
Bickersteth 'bɪk ə steθ -stɪθ ‖ -ər-
Bickerton 'bɪk ət ən ‖ -ərt ən
Bickford 'bɪk fəd ‖ -fərd
bickie 'bɪk i ~s z
Bickley 'bɪk li
Bicknell 'bɪk nəl
bicoastal ₍ˌ₎baɪ 'kəʊst əl ‖ -'koʊst-
bicolor, bicolour 'baɪ ˌkʌl ə ‖ -ər
biconcave ₍ˌ₎baɪ 'kɒŋ keɪv -'kɒn-,
  ˌbaɪ kɒn 'keɪv ‖ ₍ˌ₎baɪ 'kaːn-
biconcavity ˌbaɪ kɒn 'kæv ət i -ɪt i
  ‖ ˌbaɪ kaːn 'kæv ət̬ i
biconvex ₍ˌ₎baɪ 'kɒn veks ˌbaɪ kɒn 'veks
  ‖ ₍ˌ₎baɪ 'kaːn-
biconvexity ˌbaɪ kɒn 'veks ət i -ɪt i
  ‖ ˌbaɪ kaːn 'veks ət̬ i
bicuspid ˌbaɪ 'kʌsp ɪd §-əd ~s z
bicuspidate ˌbaɪ 'kʌsp ɪ deɪt §-ə-
bicycl|e 'baɪs ɪk əl -ək- ~ed d ~es z ~ing ‿ɪŋ
  'bicycle clip; 'bicycle pump
bicyclist 'baɪs ɪk lɪst -ək-, §-ləst ~s s
bid bɪd bade bæd beɪd bidden 'bɪd ən
  bidding 'bɪd ɪŋ bids bɪdz
  'bid price
biddable 'bɪd əb əl
Biddell (i) 'bɪd əl, (ii) bɪ 'del
bidden 'bɪd ən
bidder, B~ 'bɪd ə ‖ -ər ~s z
Biddie 'bɪd i
bidding 'bɪd ɪŋ
Biddle 'bɪd əl
Biddulph 'bɪd ʌlf
Biddy, biddly 'bɪd li ~ies iz
bide, Bide baɪd bided 'baɪd ɪd -əd biding
  'baɪd ɪŋ bides baɪdz bode bəʊd ‖ boʊd
Bideford 'bɪd ɪ fəd -ə- ‖ -fərd (!)
Biden 'baɪd ən
bidet 'biːd eɪ ‖ bɪ 'deɪ —Fr [bi dɛ] (*) ~s z
bidialectal ˌbaɪ ˌdaɪ‿ə 'lekt əl
bidialectalism ˌbaɪ ˌdaɪ‿ə 'lekt ə ˌlɪz əm -əl ˌɪz-
bidirectional ˌbaɪ daɪ‿ə 'rek ʃən‿əl ◂ ˌ•də-, ˌ•dɪ-
  ~ly i
Bidwell 'bɪd wel
Bieber 'biːb ə ‖ -ər
Biedermeier 'biːd ə ˌmaɪ‿ə ‖ -ər ˌmaɪ‿ər —Ger
  ['biː dɐ ˌmai ɐ]
Bielefeld 'biːl ə feld -felt —Ger ['biː lə fɛlt]
biennial baɪ 'en i‿əl ~ly i

B

bien-pensant ˌbjæ ˈpɒ̃s õ ‖ -pɑ̃ː ˈsɑ̃ː —*Fr*
[bjæ pɑ̃ sɑ̃]
bier bɪə ‖ bɪ^ər *(= beer)* **biers** bɪəz ‖ bɪ^ərz
Bierce bɪəs ‖ bɪ^ərs
bierkeller ˈbɪə ˌkel ə ‖ ˈbɪr ˌkel ^ər —*Ger* B~
[ˈbiːɐ ˌkɛl ɐ] ~s z
biff bɪf **biffed** bɪft **biffing** ˈbɪf ɪŋ **biffs** bɪfs
Biffen ˈbɪf ɪn §-^ən
Biffo ˈbɪf əu ‖ -ou
bifid ˈbaɪ fɪd ~**ly** li
bifocal ˌbaɪ ˈfəuk ^əl ◄ ‖ -ˈfouk- ~s z
bifoliate ˌbaɪ ˈfəul i eɪt -i_ət, ˌɪt ‖ -ˈfoul-
bifur|cate v ˈbaɪ fə |keɪt -fɜː- ‖ -ˈf^ər- ~**cated**
keɪt ɪd -əd ‖ keɪt̬ əd ~**cates** keɪts ~**cating**
keɪt ɪŋ ‖ keɪt̬ ɪŋ
bifurcate adj ˌbaɪ ˈfɜːk eɪt -ət, -ɪt; ˈbaɪ fə keɪt,
-kət, -kɪt ‖ -ˈfɜːk- ~**ly** li
bifurcation ˌbaɪ fə ˈkeɪʃ ^ən -fɜː- ‖ -ˈf^ər- ~s z
big bɪg **bigger** ˈbɪg ə ‖ -^ər **biggest** ˈbɪg ɪst
-əst
ˌBig ˈApple; ˌbig ˈbang ˌtheory; ˌBig ˈBen;
ˌBig ˈBrother; ˌbig ˈbusiness; ˌbig ˈdeal;
ˌbig ˈgame; ˌbig ˈstick; Big ˈSur sɜː ‖ sɜˈ;
ˈbig time, ˌ·ˈ·; ˌbig ˈtop; ˌbig ˈwheel
bigami... —*see* **bigamy**
bigamist ˈbɪg əm ɪst §-əst ~s s
bigamous ˈbɪg əm əs ~**ly** li
bigam|y ˈbɪg əm li ~**ies** iz
Bigbury ˈbɪg b^ər_i ‖ ˈbɪg ˌber i
Bigelow ˈbɪg ə ləu -ɪ- ‖ -lou
Bigfoot ˈbɪg fut
Biggar ˈbɪg ə ‖ -^ər
bigg... —*see* **big**
biggie ˈbɪg i ~s z
Biggin ˈbɪg ɪn §-^ən
biggish ˈbɪg ɪʃ
Biggles ˈbɪg ^əlz
Biggleswade ˈbɪg ^əlz weɪd
Biggs bɪgz
bigg|y ˈbɪg|i ~**ies** iz
bighead ˈbɪg hed ~s z
bigheaded ˌbɪg ˈhed ɪd ◄ -əd ~**ly** li ~**ness** nəs
nɪs
big-hearted ˌbɪg ˈhɑːt ɪd ◄ -əd ‖ -ˈhɑːrt̬- ~**ly** li
~**ness** nəs nɪs
bighorn ˈbɪg hɔːn ‖ -hɔːrn ~s z
bight baɪt *(= bite, byte)* **bighted** ˈbaɪt ɪd -əd
‖ ˈbaɪt̬- **bighting** ˈbaɪt ɪŋ ‖ ˈbaɪt̬- **bights**
baɪts
bigmouth ˈbɪg mauθ ~s s
bigmouthed ˌbɪg ˈmauðd ◄ -ˈmauθt, ˈ··
Bignell ˈbɪg n^əl
bigness ˈbɪg nəs -nɪs
bignonia bɪg ˈnəun i_ə ‖ -ˈnoun- ~s z
bigot ˈbɪg ət ~s s
bigoted ˈbɪg ət ɪd -əd ‖ -ət̬ əd ~**ly** li ~**ness**
nəs nɪs
bigotr|y ˈbɪg ətr li ~**ies** iz
big-time ˈbɪg taɪm
bigwig ˈbɪg wɪg ~s z
Bihar bɪ ˈhɑː ‖ -ˈhɑːr —*Hindi* [bɪ ɦɑːr]
Bihari bɪ ˈhɑːr i ~s z
bijou ˈbiːʒ uː biː ˈʒuː ~s, ~x z

bijouterie biː ˈʒuːt ər i ‖ -ˈʒuːt̬- —*Fr* [bi ʒu tʁi]
bike baɪk **biked** baɪkt **bikes** baɪks **biking**
ˈbaɪk ɪŋ
biker, Biker ˈbaɪk ə ‖ -^ər ~s z
bikini, B~ bɪ ˈkiːn i bə- ~s z
Biko ˈbiːk əu ‖ -ou
bilabial _(ˌ)baɪ ˈleɪb i_əl ~**ly** i ~s z
bilateral _(ˌ)baɪ ˈlæt_^ər əl ‖ -ˈlæt̬ ər əl →-ˈlætr əl
~**ly** i ~**ness** nəs nɪs
Bilbao bɪl ˈbau -ˈbɑː ‖ əu ‖ -ˈbɑː ou —*Sp*
[bil ˈβa o]
bilberr|y ˈbɪl b^ər_li ‖ -ˌber li ~**ies** iz
bilbo, Bilbo ˈbɪlb əu ‖ -ou ~**es**, ~s z
Bildungsroman ˈbɪld uŋz rəu ˌmɑːn ‖ -rou, ·
—*Ger* [ˈbɪld ʊŋs ʁo ˌmaːn]
bile baɪ^əl
ˈbile duct
bilge bɪldʒ **bilged** bɪldʒd **bilges** ˈbɪldʒ ɪz -əz
bilging ˈbɪldʒ ɪŋ
bilgy ˈbɪldʒ i
bilharzia bɪl ˈhɑːz i_ə -ˈhɑːts- ‖ -ˈhɑːrz-
biliary ˈbɪl i_ər i ‖ -er i
bilingual _(ˌ)baɪ ˈlɪŋ gwəl -ˈlɪŋ gju_əl ~**ism** ˌɪz
əm ~**ly** i ~s z
bilious ˈbɪl i_əs ~**ly** li ~**ness** nəs nɪs
bilirubin ˌbɪl i ˈruːb ɪn ˌbaɪl-, §-^ən
-**bility** bɪl ət i -ɪt- ‖ -ət̬-
bilk bɪlk **bilked** bɪlkt **bilker/s** ˈbɪlk ə/z ‖ -^ər/z
bilking ˈbɪlk ɪŋ **bilks** bɪlks
bill, Bill bɪl **billed** bɪld **billing** ˈbɪl ɪŋ **bills** bɪlz
ˌbill of ˈfare; ˌbill of ˈrights; ˌbill of ˈsale
billable ˈbɪl əb ^əl
billabong ˈbɪl ə bɒŋ ‖ -bɔːŋ -bɑːŋ ~s z
billboard ˈbɪl bɔːd ‖ -bɔːrd -bourd ~s z
Billerica ˌbɪl ˈrɪk ə ˌbel ə ˈ··
Billericay ˌbɪl ə ˈrɪk i
bill|et ˈbɪl |ɪt -ət ‖ -ət ~**eted** ɪt ɪd ət-, -əd
‖ ət̬ əd ~**eting** ɪt ɪŋ ət- ‖ ət̬ ɪŋ ~**ets** ɪts əts
billet-doux ˌbɪl eɪ ˈduː -i- —*Fr* [bi je du]
billets-doux ˌbɪl eɪ ˈduːz -i-, -ˈduː —*Fr*
[bi je du]
Billett ˈbɪl ɪt §-ət
billettee ˌbɪl ɪ ˈtiː -ə- ~s z
billeter ˈbɪl ɪt ə -ət- ‖ -ət̬ ^ər ~s z
billfold ˈbɪl fəuld →-fɒuld ‖ -fould ~s z
billhook ˈbɪl huk §-huːk ~s s
billiard ˈbɪl jəd ˈbɪl i_əd ‖ -j^ərd ~s z
ˈbilliard ball; ˈbilliard ˌtable
Billie ˈbɪl i
Billie-Jean ˌbɪl i ˈdʒiːn ◄
billies —*see* **billy**
Billinge ˈbɪl ɪndʒ
Billingham ˈbɪl ɪŋ əm -həm
Billings ˈbɪl ɪŋz
Billingsgate ˈbɪl ɪŋz geɪt
Billingshurst ˈbɪl ɪŋz hɜːst ‖ -hɜˈːst
Billingsley ˈbɪl ɪŋz li
billion ˈbɪl jən ˈbɪl i_ən ~s z
billionaire ˌbɪl jə ˈneə ◄ ‖ -ˈne^ər ◄ ~s z
billionth ˈbɪl jən^tθ ˈbɪl i_ən^tθ ~s z
billow ˈbɪl əu ‖ -ou ~**ed** d ~**ing** ɪŋ ~s z
billowy ˈbɪl əu i ‖ -ou-
billposter ˈbɪl ˌpəust ə ‖ -ˌpoust ^ər ~s z

B

billposting 'bɪl ˌpəʊst ɪŋ ‖ -ˌpoʊst-
billsticker 'bɪl ˌstɪk ə ‖ -ᵊr ~s z
Billy, billy 'bɪl i Billy's, billies 'bɪl iz
'billy goat
billy-can 'bɪl i kæn ~s z
billycock 'bɪl i kɒk ‖ -kɑːk ~s s
billy-o, billy-oh 'bɪl i əʊ ‖ -oʊ
Biloxi bɪ 'lʌks i bə-, -'lɒks- ‖ -'lɑːks- —In MS,
locally -'lʌks-
Bilston 'bɪlst ən
Biltmore 'bɪlt mɔː ‖ -mɔːr -moʊr
biltong 'bɪl tɒŋ ‖ -tɔːŋ -tɑːŋ
Bim bɪm
bimbo 'bɪm bəʊ ‖ -boʊ ~s z
bimetallic ˌbaɪ me 'tæl ɪk ◄ -mə-, -mɪ-
ˌbimeˌtallic 'strip
bimetallism ˌbaɪ 'met ᵊl ˌɪz əm -əl ˌɪz- ‖ -'meţ-
bimilleni|al ˌbaɪ mɪ 'len i_ˌəl ˌ•mə- ~um əm
Bimini, b~ 'bɪm ən i -ɪn- ~s z
bimodal ₍ᵢ₎baɪ 'məʊd ᵊl ‖ -'moʊd-
bimodality ˌbaɪ məʊ 'dæl ət i -ɪt i
‖ -moʊ 'dæl əţ i
bimonth|ly ˌbaɪ 'mʌntᵊθ |li ~lies liz
bin bɪn bins bɪnz
Bina (i) 'baɪn ə, (ii) 'biːn ə
binar|y 'baɪn ᵊr i ~ies iz
binaural ₍ᵢ₎baɪ 'nɔːr ᵊl bɪ-
Binchy 'bɪntʃ i
bind baɪnd binding 'baɪnd ɪŋ binds baɪndz
bound baʊnd
binder, B~ 'baɪnd ə ‖ -ᵊr ~s z
binder|y 'baɪnd ᵊr li ~ies iz
binding 'baɪnd ɪŋ ~ly li ~ness nəs nɪs ~s z
bindweed 'baɪnd wiːd
bine baɪn bines baɪnz
Binet 'biːn eɪ ‖ bɪ 'neɪ —Fr [bi nɛ]
Binet-Simon
ˌbiːn eɪ 'saɪm ən ‖ bɪ ˌneɪ siː 'moʊn
bing, Bing bɪŋ bings, Bing's bɪŋz
binge, Binge bɪndʒ binged bɪndʒd
bingeing, binging 'bɪndʒ ɪŋ binges
'bɪndʒ ɪz -əz
Bingen 'bɪŋ ən —Ger ['bɪŋ ən]
Bingham 'bɪŋ əm
Binghamton 'bɪŋ əm tən
Bingley 'bɪŋ li
bingo, Bingo 'bɪŋ gəʊ ‖ -goʊ
'bingo hall
Binks bɪŋks
bin-liner 'bɪn ˌlaɪn ə ‖ -ᵊr ~s z
bin|man 'bɪn |mæn →'bɪm-, -mən ~men men
-mən
binnacle 'bɪn ək ᵊl -ɪk- ~s z
Binney, Binnie 'bɪn i
Binns bɪnz
Binoche bɪ 'nɒʃ bə- ‖ -'noʊʃ —Fr [bi nɔʃ]
binocular n bɪ 'nɒk jʊl ə bə-, baɪ-, -jəl-
‖ -'nɑːk jəl ᵊr ~s z
binocular adj baɪ 'nɒk jʊl ə bɪ-, bə-
‖ -'nɑːk jəl ᵊr ~ly li
biˌnocular 'vision
binocularity baɪ ˌnɒk ju 'lær ət i bɪ-, bə-,
-ˌ•jə-, -ɪt i ‖ -ˌnɑːk jə 'lær əţ i -'ler-

binomial ₍ᵢ₎baɪ 'nəʊm i_əl ‖ -'noʊm- ~ly i ~s z
biˈnomial ˌtheorem
bint bɪnt bints bɪnts
binturong 'bɪnt ju rɒŋ -jə- ‖ bɪn 'tʊr ɔːŋ -ɑːŋ
~s z
Binyon 'bɪn jən
bio, Bio 'baɪ əʊ ‖ -oʊ
bio- comb. form
with stress-neutral suffix ˌbaɪ əʊ ‖ -oʊ —In
some well-known words, the weakening of the
second diphthong to ə has become thoroughly
established, with the consequence in RP that
SMOOTHING from ˌbaɪ_ə to ˌbaə is also heard.
But in some other cases, where the separateness
of the prefix is strongly felt, əʊ ‖ oʊ remains
strong. — biolytic ˌbaɪ əʊ
'lɪt ɪk ◄ ‖ ˌbaɪ oʊ 'lɪţ ɪk ◄
with stress-imposing suffix baɪ 'ɒ+ ‖ -'ɑː+ —
biolysis baɪ 'ɒl əs ɪs -ɪs-, §-əs ‖ -'ɑːl-
biochemical ˌbaɪ əʊ 'kem ɪk ᵊl ◄ ‖ ˌ•oʊ- ~ly_i
~s z
biochemist ˌbaɪ əʊ 'kem ɪst §-əst ‖ -oʊ- ~s s
biochemistry ˌbaɪ əʊ 'kem ɪs tri -əs tri ‖ ˌ•oʊ-
biodata 'baɪ əʊ ˌdeɪt ə -ˌdɑːt- ‖ -oʊ ˌdæţ ə
biodegradability ˌbaɪ əʊ dɪ ˌɡreɪd ə 'bɪl ət i
-də,•-, -ɪt i ‖ ˌbaɪ oʊ dɪ ˌɡreɪd ə 'bɪl əţ i
biodegradab|le ˌbaɪ əʊ dɪ 'ɡreɪd əb |ᵊl ◄ -də'•-
‖ ˌ•oʊ- ~ly li
biodegradation ˌbaɪ əʊ ˌdeɡ rə 'deɪʃ ᵊn
‖ ˌ•oʊ-
biodegrad|e ˌbaɪ əʊ dɪ 'ɡreɪd -də'•, §-diː'•
‖ ˌbaɪ oʊ- ~ed ɪd əd ~es z ~ing ɪŋ
biodiversity ˌbaɪ əʊ daɪ 'vɜːs ət i -dɪ'•-, -ɪt i
‖ ˌbaɪ oʊ də 'vɜːs əţ i -daɪ'•-
bioengineering ˌbaɪ əʊ ˌendʒ ɪ 'nɪər ɪŋ -,•ə-
‖ -oʊ ˌendʒ ə 'nɪr-
biofeedback ˌbaɪ əʊ 'fiːd bæk →'fiːb- ‖ -oʊ-
biographer baɪ 'ɒɡ rəf ə ‖ -'ɑːɡ rəf ᵊr ~s z
biographic ˌbaɪ_ə 'ɡræf ɪk ◄ ~al ᵊl ~ally ᵊl_i
biograph|y baɪ 'ɒɡ rəf li i ‖ -'ɑːɡ- ~ies iz
biohazard 'baɪ əʊ ˌhæz əd ‖ -oʊ ˌhæz ᵊrd ~s z
Bioko bi 'əʊk əʊ ‖ -'oʊk oʊ
biological ˌbaɪ_ə 'lɒdʒ ɪk ᵊl ◄ ‖ -'lɑːdʒ- ~ly_li
ˌbioˌlogical 'clock
biologist baɪ 'ɒl ədʒ ɪst §-əst ‖ -'ɑːl- ~s s
biology baɪ 'ɒl ədʒ i ‖ -'ɑːl-
biomass 'baɪ əʊ mæs ‖ -oʊ-
biome 'baɪ əʊm ‖ -oʊm ~s z
biometric ˌbaɪ əʊ 'metr ɪk ◄ ‖ -oʊ- ~al ᵊl ~s
s
Bion 'baɪ_ən -ɒn ‖ 'baɪ ɑːn
bionic ₍ᵢ₎baɪ 'ɒn ɪk ‖ -'ɑːn- ~s s
biophysical ˌbaɪ əʊ 'fɪz ɪk ᵊl ◄ ‖ ˌ•oʊ- ~ly_i
biophysicist ˌbaɪ əʊ 'fɪz ɪs ɪst -əs ɪst, §-əst
‖ ˌ•oʊ- ~s s
biophysics ˌbaɪ əʊ 'fɪz ɪks ‖ -oʊ-
biopic 'baɪ əʊ pɪk ‖ -oʊ- ~s s
bioprogram 'baɪ əʊ ˌprəʊ ɡræm ˌ•'•'••
‖ -oʊ ˌproʊ- ~s z
biops|y 'baɪ ɒps li •'•• ‖ -'ɑːps- ~ies iz
biorhythm 'baɪ əʊ ˌrɪð əm ‖ -oʊ- ~s z
biorhythmic ˌbaɪ əʊ 'rɪð mɪk ◄ ‖ -oʊ-
bioscope 'baɪ_ə skəʊp ‖ -skoʊp ~s s

B

biosphere 'baɪ əʊ sfɪə ‖ -ə sfɪr ~s z
Bio-Strath tdmk 'baɪ əʊ stræθ ‖ -oʊ-
biota baɪ 'əʊt ə ‖ -'oʊt̬-
biotech 'baɪ əʊ tek ‖ -oʊ-
biotechnology
ˌbaɪ əʊ tek 'nɒl ədʒ i ‖ -oʊ tek 'nɑːl-
biotic baɪ 'ɒt ɪk ‖ -'ɑːt̬-
bipartisan ˌbaɪ ˌpɑːt ɪ 'zæn -ə-; (ᵢ)•'•••, -ɪz ən,
  -əz- ‖ (ᵢ)baɪ 'pɑːrt̬ əz ən -əs- ~ship ʃɪp
bipartite (ᵢ)baɪ 'pɑːt aɪt '•••‖-'pɑːrt- ~ly li
bipartition ˌbaɪ pɑː 'tɪʃ ᵊn -pə- ‖ -pɑːr-
biped 'baɪ ped ~s z
bipedal ˌbaɪ 'piːd ᵊl ◂ -'ped- ~ly i
biplane 'baɪ pleɪn ~s z
bipod 'baɪ pɒd ‖ -pɑːd ~s z
bipolar ˌbaɪ 'pəʊl ə ◂ ‖ -'poʊl ᵊr ◂
bipolarity ˌbaɪ pəʊ 'lær ət i -ɪt i ‖ -poʊ 'lær ət̬ i
  -'ler-
biquadratic ˌbaɪ kwɒ 'dræt ɪk ◂ ‖ -kwɑː 'dræt̬-
birch, Birch bɜːtʃ ‖ bɜ˞ːtʃ birches, Birch's
  'bɜːtʃ ɪz -əz ‖ 'bɜ˞ːtʃ-
Birchall (i) 'bɜːtʃ ɔːl ‖ 'bɜ˞ːtʃ- -ɑːl, (ii) -ᵊl
Bircher 'bɜːtʃ ə ‖ 'bɜ˞ːtʃ ᵊr
Birchington 'bɜːtʃ ɪŋ tən ‖ 'bɜ˞ːtʃ-
bird, Bird bɜːd ‖ bɜ˞ːd birding
  'bɜːd ɪŋ ‖ 'bɜ˞ːd ɪŋ birds bɜːdz ‖ bɜ˞ːdz
  'bird ˌfancier; ˌbird of 'passage; ˌbird of
  'prey; 'bird ˌtable
birdbath 'bɜːd bɑːθ →'bɜːb-, §-bæθ
  ‖ 'bɜ˞ːd bæθ
bird-brained 'bɜːd breɪnd →'bɜːb- ‖ 'bɜ˞ːd-
birdcag|e 'bɜːd keɪdʒ →'bɜːg- ‖ 'bɜ˞ːd- ~es ɪz
  əz
birder 'bɜːd ə ‖ 'bɜ˞ːd ᵊr ~s z
birdie, B~ 'bɜːd i ‖ 'bɜ˞ːd i ~s z
birdlike 'bɜːd laɪk ‖ 'bɜ˞ːd-
birdlim|e 'bɜːd laɪm ‖ 'bɜ˞ːd- ~ed d ~ing ɪŋ
  ~s z
bird|man 'bɜːd |mæn →'bɜːb-, -mən ‖ 'bɜ˞ːd-
  ~men men -mən
Birdsall (i) 'bɜːd sɔːl ‖ 'bɜ˞ːd- -sɑːl, (ii) -sᵊl
birdseed 'bɜːd siːd ‖ 'bɜ˞ːd-
bird's-eye, Birdseye 'bɜːdz aɪ ‖ 'bɜ˞ːdz-
bird's-foot 'bɜːdz fʊt ‖ 'bɜ˞ːdz- ~s s
bird's-nest 'bɜːdz nest ‖ 'bɜ˞ːdz- ~s s
birdsong 'bɜːd sɒŋ ‖ 'bɜ˞ːd sɔːŋ -sɑːŋ ~s z
bird-watch|er/s 'bɜːd ˌwɒtʃ |ə/z
  ‖ 'bɜ˞ːd ˌwɑːtʃ |ᵊr/z -ˌwɔːtʃ- ~ing ɪŋ
birefring|ence ˌbaɪ rɪ 'frɪndʒ |ᵊn|ts -rə-, §-riː-
  ~ent ənt
bireme 'baɪ riːm ~s z
biretta bə 'ret ə bɪ- ‖ -'ret̬- ~s z
Birgit 'bɪəg ɪt 'bɜːg-, §-ət ‖ 'bɪrg-
Birgitta bɪə 'gɪt ə ‖ bɪr 'gɪt̬ ə —Swedish
  [bɪr ˈɡit a]
biriani ˌbɪr i 'ɑːn i ~s z
Birkbeck 'bɜːk bek ‖ 'bɜ˞ːk- —but as a family
  name sometimes 'bɜː bek ‖ 'bɜ˞ː-
Birkenhead ˌbɜːk ən 'hed '•••‖ˌbɜ˞ːk-
Birkenshaw 'bɜːk ən ʃɔː ‖ 'bɜ˞ːk- -ʃɑː
Birkenstock 'bɜːk ən stɒk ‖ 'bɜ˞ːk ən stɑːk ~s
  s
Birkett 'bɜːk ɪt §-ət ‖ 'bɜ˞ːk-

birl bɜːl ‖ bɜ˞ːl birled bɜːld ‖ bɜ˞ːld birling
  'bɜːl ɪŋ ‖ 'bɜ˞ːl- birls bɜːlz ‖ bɜ˞ːlz
Birley 'bɜːl i ‖ 'bɜ˞ːl i
Birling 'bɜːl ɪŋ ‖ 'bɜ˞ːl ɪŋ
Birmingham (i) 'bɜːm ɪŋ əm -həm ‖ 'bɜ˞ːm-,
  (ii) -hæm —The place in England is (i), but
  places in the US are (ii).
Birnam 'bɜːn əm ‖ 'bɜ˞ːn-
Birney, Birnie 'bɜːn i ‖ 'bɜ˞ːn i
biro, Biro tdmk 'baɪᵊr əʊ ‖ -oʊ —Hungarian Biró
  ['bi roː] ~s z
Birobidzhan ˌbɪr əʊ bɪ 'dʒɑːn ‖ ˌ•oʊ- —Russ
  [bʲɪ rə bʲɪ 'dʒan]
birr bɜː ‖ bɜ˞ː birred bɜːd ‖ bɜ˞ːd birring
  'bɜːr ɪŋ ‖ 'bɜ˞ː- birrs bɜːz ‖ bɜ˞ːz
Birrane bɪ 'reɪn bə-
Birrell 'bɪr ᵊl
Birt bɜːt ‖ bɜ˞ːt
birth bɜːθ ‖ bɜ˞ːθ birthed bɜːθt ‖ bɜ˞ːθt
  birthing 'bɜːθ ɪŋ ‖ 'bɜ˞ːθ- births
  bɜːθs ‖ bɜ˞ːθs
  'birth ˌcerˌtificate; 'birth conˌtrol
birthday 'bɜːθ deɪ -di ‖ 'bɜ˞ːθ- —See note at
  -day ~s z
  'birthday cake; 'birthday card; ˌBirthday
  'honours; 'birthday ˌparty; 'birthday
  ˌpresent; 'birthday suit
birthmark 'bɜːθ mɑːk ‖ 'bɜ˞ːθ mɑːrk ~s s
birthplace 'bɜːθ pleɪs ‖ 'bɜ˞ːθ- ~s ɪz əz
birthrate 'bɜːθ reɪt ‖ 'bɜ˞ːθ- ~s s
birthright 'bɜːθ raɪt ‖ 'bɜ˞ːθ- ~s s
birthroot 'bɜːθ ruːt ‖ 'bɜ˞ːθ-
birthstone 'bɜːθ stəʊn ‖ 'bɜ˞ːθ stoʊn ~s z
birthwort 'bɜːθ wɜːt §-wɔːt ‖ 'bɜ˞ːθ wɜ˞ːt
  -wɔːrt ~s s
Birtles 'bɜːt ᵊlz ‖ 'bɜ˞ːt̬-
Birtwhistle 'bɜːt ˌwɪs ᵊl -ˌhwɪs- ‖ 'bɜ˞ːt ˌhwɪs-
biryani ˌbɪr i 'ɑːn i ~s z
bis bɪs
Biscay 'bɪsk eɪ -i
Biscayne ˌbɪ 'skeɪn ◂
  ˌBiscayne 'Boulevard
biscuit 'bɪsk ɪt §-ət ~s s
bisect (ᵢ)baɪ 'sekt '•• ‖ '•• ~ed ɪd əd ~ing ɪŋ
  ~s s
bisection (ᵢ)baɪ 'sek ʃᵊn '•,•• ‖ '•,•• ~al ᵊl
  ~ally ᵊl i
bisector (ᵢ)baɪ 'sekt ə ‖ 'baɪ ˌsekt ᵊr ~s z
bisexual ˌbaɪ 'sek ʃu ᵊl ◂ -'seks ju ᵊl, -'sekʃ ᵊl
  ~ly i ~s z
bisexuality ˌbaɪ ˌsek ʃu 'æl ət i -ˌseks ju-, -ɪt i
  ‖ -ət̬ i
bish bɪʃ bishes 'bɪʃ ɪz -əz
bishop, B~ 'bɪʃ əp ~s s
  ˌBishop's 'Stortford
bishophood 'bɪʃ əp hʊd
bishopric 'bɪʃ əp rɪk ~s s
Bishopsgate 'bɪʃ əps geɪt
Bishopston 'bɪʃ əps tən
Bisley 'bɪz li
Bismag tdmk 'bɪz mæg
Bismarck 'bɪz mɑːk ‖ -mɑːrk —Ger ['bɪs maʁk]
bismuth 'bɪz məθ

bismuthic bɪz ˈmjuːθ ɪk -ˈmʌθ-; ˈbɪz məθ-
BiSoDol _tdmk_ ˈbaɪ saʊ dɒl ‖ -soʊ dɑːl -dɔːl
bison ˈbaɪs ᵊn ‖ ˈbaɪz- ~s z
Bispham ˈbɪsp əm —_but as a family name sometimes_ ˈbɪs fəm
bisque bɪsk —_Fr_ [bisk] **bisques** bɪsks
Bissau bɪ ˈsaʊ ˈbɪs aʊ —_Port_ [bi ˈsau]
Bissell ˈbɪs ᵊl
Bisset, Bissett (i) ˈbɪs ɪt §-ət, (ii) ˈbɪz-
bissextile bɪ ˈsekst aɪᵊl ‖ -ᵊl
bistable ˌbaɪ ˈsteɪb ᵊl
bister ˈbɪst ə ‖ -ᵊr ~ed d
Bisto _tdmk_ ˈbɪst əʊ ‖ -oʊ
bistort ˈbɪst ɔːt ‖ -ɔːrt ~s s
bistour|y ˈbɪst ər |i ~ies iz
bistre ˈbɪst ə ‖ -ᵊr ~d d
bistro ˈbiːs trəʊ ˈbɪs- ‖ -troʊ —_Fr (usually_ bistrot) [bis tʁo] ~s z
bit bɪt **bits** bɪts
   ˈbit part
bitch bɪtʃ **bitched** bɪtʃt **bitches** ˈbɪtʃ ɪz -əz
   bitching ˈbɪtʃ ɪŋ
bitch|y ˈbɪtʃ |i ~ier i‿ə ‖ i‿ᵊr ~iest i‿ɪst i‿əst
   ~ily ɪ li əl i ~iness i nəs i nɪs
bite baɪt **bit** bɪt **bites** baɪts **biting**
   ˈbaɪt ɪŋ ‖ ˈbaɪt̬ ɪŋ **bitten** ˈbɪt ᵊn
biter ˈbaɪt ə ‖ ˈbaɪt̬ ᵊr ~s z
bite-size ˈbaɪt saɪz
Bithell (i) ˈbɪθ ᵊl, (ii) bɪ ˈθel
Bithynia baɪ ˈθɪn i‿ə bɪ-
bitmap ˈbɪt mæp ~ped t ~ping ɪŋ ~s s
bitt bɪt (= bit) **bitts** bɪts
bitten ˈbɪt ᵊn
bitt|er ˈbɪt ə ‖ ˈbɪt̬ |ᵊr ~erer ər ə ‖ ᵊr ər
   ~erest ər ɪst -əst ~ers əz ‖ ᵊrz
   ˌbitter ˈend; ˌbitter ˈlemon
bittercress ˈbɪt ə kres ‖ ˈbɪt̬ ᵊr-
bitterly ˈbɪt ə li -ᵊl i ‖ ˈbɪt̬ ᵊr li
bittern ˈbɪt ᵊn -ɜːn ‖ ˈbɪt̬ ᵊrn ~s z
bitterness ˈbɪt ə nəs -nɪs; -ᵊn əs, -ɪs ‖ ˈbɪt̬ ᵊr-
bitternut ˈbɪt ə nʌt ‖ ˈbɪt̬ ᵊr- ~s s
bittersweet ˈbɪt ə swiːt ˌ•ˈ•‿ ‖ ˈbɪt̬ ᵊr-
bitt|y ˈbɪt |i ‖ ˈbɪt̬ li ~iness i nəs i nɪs
bitumen ˈbɪtʃ ʊm ɪn -əm-, -ən; -ʊ men, -ə-;
   ˈbɪt jʊm ɪn ‖ bə ˈtuːm ən bɪ-, baɪ-, -ˈtjuːm-
   (*)
bituminiz|e bɪ ˈtjuːm ɪ naɪz bə-, →§-ˈtʃuːm-,
   -ə-; ˈbɪtʃ ʊm ɪ-, ˈ•əm-, ˈ••ə- ‖ bə ˈtuːm- bɪ-,
   baɪ-, -ˈtjuːm- ~ed d ~es ɪz əz ~ing ɪŋ
bituminous bɪ ˈtjuːm ɪn əs bə-, →§-ˈtʃuːm-,
   -ən əs ‖ -ˈtuːm- -ˈtjuːm-
biunique ˌbaɪ juː ˈniːk ◄ ~ly li ~ness nəs nɪs
bivalenc|e ₍ᵢ₎baɪ ˈveɪl ən̍s ◄ ˈbɪv əl ən̍s ~y i
bivalent ₍ᵢ₎baɪ ˈveɪl ənt ◄ ˈbɪv əl ənt
bivalve ˈbaɪ vælv ~s z
bivouac ˈbɪv u‿æk ~ked t ~king ɪŋ ~s s
bivv|y ˈbɪv |i ~ies iz
biweek|ly ₍ᵢ₎baɪ ˈwiːk |li ~lies liz
biz bɪz
bizarre bɪ ˈzɑː bə- ‖ -ˈzɑːr ~ly li ~ness nəs
   nɪs
Bizet ˈbiːz eɪ ‖ biː ˈzeɪ —_Fr_ [bi zɛ] ~'s z
Bjelke-Petersen ˌbjelk i ˈpiːt əs ən ‖ -ˈpiːt̬ ᵊrs-

Björk bjɔːk bjɜːk, bi ˈɔːk ‖ bjɔːrk bjɝːk
   —_Icelandic_ [bjœr̥k]
Bjorn, Björn bi ˈɔːn bjɜːn ‖ bi ˈɔːrn bjɝːn
   —_Swedish_ [bjœɳ]
blab blæb **blabbed** blæbd **blabbing** ˈblæb ɪŋ
   blabs blæbz
blabb|er ˈblæb |ə ‖ -|ᵊr ~ered əd ‖ ᵊrd ~ering
   ər‿ɪŋ ~ers əz ‖ ᵊrz
blabber|mouth ˈblæb ə |maʊθ ‖ -ᵊr- ~mouths
   maʊðz maʊθs
blabby ˈblæb i
Blaby ˈbleɪb i
black, Black blæk **blacked** blækt **blacker**
   ˈblæk ə ‖ -ᵊr **blackest** ˈblæk ɪst -əst
   blacking ˈblæk ɪŋ **blacks, Blacks** blæks
   ˌblack and ˈblue◄; ˌblack and ˈwhite◄;
   ˈBlack ˌCountry; ˌBlack ˈDeath; ˌblack ˈeye;
   ˌBlack ˈForest; ˌblack ˈhole; ˌblack ˈice;
   ˌblack ˈmagic; ˌBlack Maˈria; ˌblack
   ˈmarket; ˌblack ˌmarkeˈteer; ˌBlack ˈMass;
   ˌblack ˌpeople; ˌblack ˈpower; ˌblack
   ˈpudding; ˌBlack ˈSea; ˈblack spot
Blackadder ˈblæk ˌæd ə ‚•ˈ••; ˈblæk əd ə ‖ -ᵊr
Blackall ˈblæk ɔːl ‖ -ɑːl
blackamoor ˈblæk ə mɔː -mʊə ‖ -mʊr ~s z
black-and-white ˌblæk ən ˈwaɪt ◄ -ənd-, →-ŋ-,
   -ˈhwaɪt ‖ -ˈhwaɪt ◄
blackball ˈblæk bɔːl ‖ -bɑːl ~ed d ~ing ɪŋ ~s
   z
blackberr|y ˈblæk bər‿li ‖ -ˌber li -ˌier i ~ied id ~ies
   iz ~ying i ɪŋ
blackbird ˈblæk bɜːd ‖ -bɝːd ~s z
blackboard ˈblæk bɔːd ‖ -bɔːrd -boʊrd ~s z
   ˌblackboard ˈjungle
Blackburn ˈblæk bɜːn -bən ‖ -bɝːn —_locally_
   also ˈblæg-
blackcap ˈblæk kæp ~s s
blackcock ˈblæk kɒk ‖ -kɑːk
blackcurrant ˌblæk ˈkʌr ənt ◄ ‚•ˈ••, ˈ•‚••
   ‖ ˈblæk ˌkɝː ənt ~s s
blacken ˈblæk ᵊn ~ed d ~ing ‿ɪŋ ~s z
Blacket, Blackett ˈblæk ɪt §-ət
black-eyed ˌblæk ˈaɪd ◄
   ˌblack-eyed ˈSusan
blackface ˈblæk feɪs
black|fly ˈblæk |flaɪ ~flies flaɪz
Blackfoot ˈblæk fʊt
Blackford ˈblæk fəd ‖ -fᵊrd
Blackfriars ˌblæk ˈfraɪ‿əz ◄ ˈ•‚••, ‖ -ˈfraɪ‿ᵊrz ◄
   ˌBlack‚friars ˈBridge
blackguard ˈblæg ɑːd -əd ‖ -ɑːrd -ᵊrd ~ly li ~s
   z
blackhead ˈblæk hed ~s z
Blackheath ˌblæk ˈhiːθ ◄
Blackie (i) ˈblæk i, (ii) ˈbleɪk i
blacking ˈblæk ɪŋ ~s z
blackish ˈblæk ɪʃ ~ly li
blackjack ˈblæk dʒæk ~ed t ~ing ɪŋ ~s s
blacklead ˈblæk led ˌ•ˈ• ~ed ɪd əd ~ing ɪŋ
   ~s z
blackleg ˈblæk leg ~ged d ~ging ɪŋ ~s z
Blackley ˈblæk li —_but the place in Manchester is_
   ˈbleɪk-

B

B

blacklist 'blæk lɪst ~ed ɪd əd ~ing ɪŋ ~s s
Blacklock 'blæk lɒk ‖ -lɑːk
blackly 'blæk li
blackmail 'blæk meɪəl ~ed d ~er/s ə/z ‖ ər/z
  ~ing ɪŋ ~s z
Blackman 'blæk mən
Blackmore 'blæk mɔː ‖ -mɔːr -moʊr
blackness 'blæk nəs -nɪs
blackout 'blæk aʊt ~s s
Blackpool 'blæk puːl
Blackshirt 'blæk ʃɜːt ‖ -ʃɝːt ~s s
blacksmith 'blæk smɪθ ~ing ɪŋ ~s s
Blackstone 'blæk stən -stən ‖ -stoʊn -stən
blackthorn 'blæk θɔːn ‖ -θɔːrn ~s z
black-tie ˌblæk 'taɪ ◄
blacktop 'blæk tɒp ‖ -tɑːp
Blacktown 'blæk taʊn
Blackwall 'blæk wɔːl ‖ -wɑːl
  ˌBlackwall 'Tunnel
blackwater, B~ 'blæk ˌwɔːt ə ‖ -ˌwɔːt̬ ər -ˌwɑːt̬-
Blackwell 'blæk wəl -wel
Blackwood, b~ 'blæk wʊd —but the place in
  Gwent is ˌ•'•
bladder 'blæd ə ‖ -ər ~s z
bladderwort 'blæd ə wɜːt §-wɔːt ‖ -ər wɝːt
  -wɔːrt ~s s
bladderwrack 'blæd ə ræk ‖ -ər-
blade bleɪd bladed 'bleɪd ɪd -əd blades
  bleɪdz
Bladon 'bleɪd ən
blaeberry 'bleɪ bər_i ‖ -ˌber i
Blaenau 'blaɪn aɪ ⚠-aʊ; 'bleɪn i —Welsh ['bləɪ
  naɪ, 'bləɪ-, -na, -ne]
  ˌBlaenau 'Gwent
blag blæg blagged blægd blagging
  'blæg ɪŋ blags blægz
Blagden, Blagdon 'blægd ən
blagger 'blæg ə ‖ -ər ~s z
blah blɑː
blain, Blain, Blaine bleɪn blains, Blaine's
  bleɪnz
Blair bleə ‖ bleər
Blairgowrie ˌbleə 'gaʊər i ‖ ˌbler-
Blairite 'bleər aɪt ‖ 'bler- ~s s
Blaise bleɪz
Blake bleɪk Blake's bleɪks
Blakemore 'bleɪk mɔː ‖ -mɔːr -moʊr
Blakeney 'bleɪk ni
Blakenham 'bleɪk ən_əm
blame bleɪm blamed bleɪmd blames bleɪmz
  blaming 'bleɪm ɪŋ
blameless 'bleɪm ləs -lɪs ~ly li ~ness nəs nɪs
blameworth|y 'bleɪm ˌwɜːð li ‖ -ˌwɝːð li
  ~iness i nəs i nɪs
Blanc blɒ̃ ‖ blɑ̃: —Fr [blɑ̃]
blanch, B~ blɑːntʃ §blæntʃ ‖ blæntʃ blanched
  blɑːntʃt §blæntʃt ‖ blæntʃt blanches
  'blɑːntʃ ɪz §'blæntʃ-, -əz ‖ 'blæntʃ əz
  blanching 'blɑːntʃ ɪŋ §'blæntʃ- ‖ 'blæntʃ ɪŋ
Blanchard 'blæntʃ əd -ɑːd ‖ -ərd -ɑːrd
Blanche blɑːntʃ ‖ blæntʃ
Blanchflower 'blɑːntʃ ˌflaʊ_ə §'blæntʃ-
  ‖ 'blæntʃ ˌflaʊ_ər

blancmang|e blə 'mɒndʒ ‖ -'mɑːndʒ (!) ~es ɪz
  əz
blanco, B~ tdmk 'blæŋk əʊ ‖ -oʊ ~ed d ~s z
  ~ing ɪŋ
bland, Bland blænd blander 'blænd ə ‖ -ər
  blandest 'blænd ɪst -əst
Blandford 'blænd fəd ‖ -fərd
blandish 'blænd ɪʃ ~ed t ~es ɪz əz ~ing ɪŋ
  ~ment/s mənt/s
bland|ly 'blænd |li ~ness nəs nɪs
blank blæŋk blanked blæŋkt blanking
  'blæŋk ɪŋ blanks blæŋks
  ˌblank 'cartridge; ˌblank 'cheque or 'check;
  ˌblank 'verse
blank|et 'blæŋk |ɪt §-ət ‖ -|ət ~eted ɪt ɪd §ət-,
  -əd ‖ ət̬ əd ~eting ɪt ɪŋ ‖ ət̬ ɪŋ ~ets ɪts §əts
  ‖ əts
blank|ly 'blæŋk |li ~ness nəs nɪs
blanquette (ˌ)blɒŋ 'ket (ˌ)blæŋ- ‖ (ˌ)blɑːŋ- —Fr
  [blɑ̃ kɛt]
  blanˌquette de 'veau vəʊ ‖ voʊ —Fr [vo]
Blantyre 'blæn ˌtaɪ_ə ˌblæn 'taɪ_ə ‖ ˌblæn 'taɪər
blare bleə ‖ bleər blared bleəd ‖ bleərd
  blares bleəz ‖ bleərz blaring
  'bleər ɪŋ ‖ 'bler ɪŋ
blarney, B~ 'blɑːn i ‖ 'blɑːrn i ~ed d ~s z
  ~ing ɪŋ
blase, blasé 'blɑːz eɪ ‖ ˌblɑː 'zeɪ —Fr [blɑ ze]
blasphem|e (ˌ)blæs 'fiːm (ˌ)blɑːs- ‖ '•• ~ed d
  ~er/s ə/z ‖ ər/z ~es z ~ing ɪŋ
blasphemi... —see blasphemy
blasphemous 'blæs fəm əs 'blɑːs-, -fɪm- ~ly li
blasphem|y 'blæs fəm |i 'blɑːs-, -fɪm- ~ies iz
blast blɑːst §blæst ‖ blæst blasted 'blɑːst ɪd
  §'blæst-, -əd ‖ 'blæst əd blasting 'blɑːst ɪŋ
  §'blæst- ‖ 'blæst ɪŋ blasts blɑːsts §blæsts
  ‖ blæsts
  'blast ˌfurnace
blasto- comb. form
  with stress-neutral suffix ˌblæst əʊ ‖ -ə —
  blastopore 'blæst əʊ pɔː ‖ -ə pɔːr -poʊr
  with stress-imposing suffix blæ 'stɒ+ ‖ -'stɑː+
  — blastolysis blæ 'stɒl əs ɪs -ɪs, §-əs
  ‖ -'stɑːl-
blast-off 'blɑːst ɒf §'blæst-, -ɔːf ‖ 'blæst ɔːf
  -ɑːf
blat blæt blats blæts blatted 'blæt ɪd -əd
  ‖ 'blæt̬- blatting 'blæt ɪŋ ‖ 'blæt̬-
blatancy 'bleɪt ənts i
blatant 'bleɪt ənt ~ly li
Blatchford 'blætʃ fəd ‖ -fərd
blath|er 'blæð |ə ‖ -|ər ~ered əd ‖ ərd ~ering
  ər_ɪŋ ~ers əz ‖ ərz
Blavatsky blə 'væt ski ‖ -'vɑːt-
Blawith (i) blɑː ð, (ii) 'bleɪ wɪθ —The places in
  Cumbria are (i).
Blaydes bleɪdz
Blaydon 'bleɪd ən
blaze bleɪz blazed bleɪzd blazes 'bleɪz ɪz -əz
  blazing/ly 'bleɪz ɪŋ /li
blazer 'bleɪz ə ‖ -ər ~s z
blazon 'bleɪz ən ~ed d ~ing ɪŋ ~ment/s
  mənt/s ~s z

blazon|ry 'bleɪz ᵊn |ri ~ries riz
Blea bliː
bleach bliːtʃ bleached bliːtʃt bleaches
'bliːtʃ ɪz -əz bleaching 'bliːtʃ ɪŋ
bleacher 'bliːtʃ ə ‖ -ᵊr ~s z
bleak bliːk bleaker 'bliːk ə ‖ -ᵊr bleakest
'bliːk ɪst -əst
bleak|ly 'bliːk |li ~ness nəs nɪs
blear blɪə ‖ blɪᵊr bleared blɪəd ‖ blɪᵊrd
blearing 'blɪər ɪŋ ‖ 'blɪr ɪŋ blears
blɪəz ‖ blɪᵊrz
blear|y 'blɪər |i ‖ 'blɪr |i ~ier i_ə ‖ i_ᵊr ~iest
i_ɪst i_əst ~ily əl i ɪ li ~iness i nəs i nɪs
bleary-eyed ˌblɪər i 'aɪd ◂ ‖ ˌblɪr-
Bleasdale 'bliːz deɪᵊl
bleat bliːt bleated 'bliːt ɪd -əd ‖ 'bliːt̬ əd
bleats bliːts bleating 'bliːt ɪŋ ‖ 'bliːt̬ ɪŋ
bleb bleb blebs blebz
bled, Bled bled
Bleddyn 'bleð ɪn
Bledisloe 'bled ɪs ləʊ -əs-, -ɪz- ‖ -loʊ
bleed bliːd bled bled bleeding 'bliːd ɪŋ
bleeds bliːdz
bleeder 'bliːd ə ‖ -ᵊr ~s z
bleep bliːp bleeped bliːpt bleeping 'bliːp ɪŋ
bleeps bliːps
bleeper 'bliːp ə ‖ -ᵊr ~s z
blemish 'blem ɪʃ ~ed t ~es ɪz əz ~ing ɪŋ
Blencathra blen 'kæθ rə
blench blentʃ blenched blentʃt blenches
'blentʃ ɪz -əz blenching 'blentʃ ɪŋ
blend blend blended 'blend ɪd -əd blending
'blend ɪŋ blends blendz
blende blend (= blend)
blender 'blend ə ‖ -ᵊr ~s z
Blenheim 'blen ɪm -əm
Blenkinsop 'bleŋk ɪn sɒp -ən- ‖ -sɑːp
Blennerhassett ˌblen ə 'hæs ɪt §-ət, '• • • •
‖ -ᵊr-
blenn|y 'blen |i ~ies iz
blent blent
blepharitis ˌblef ə 'raɪt ɪs §-əs ‖ -'raɪt̬ əs
blepharo- comb. form
with stress-neutral suffix ˈblef ə rəʊ ‖ -ᵊr ə —
blepharoplasty 'blef ə rəʊ ˌplæst i ‖ 'blef
ᵊr ə-
with stress-imposing suffix ˌblef ə 'rɒ+ ‖ -'rɑː+
— blepharotomy ˌblef ə 'rɒt əm i ‖ -'rɑːt̬-
Bleriot, Blériot 'bler i əʊ ‖ ˌbler i 'oʊ '• • • —Fr
[ble ʁjo]
Bles bles
blesbok 'bles bɒk -bʌk ‖ -bɑːk ~s s
blesbuck 'bles bʌk ~s s
bless bles blesses 'bles ɪz -əz blessing
'bles ɪŋ blest blest
blessed past & pp of bless blest
blessed adj, B~ 'bles ɪd -əd ~ly li ~ness nəs
nɪs
blessing 'bles ɪŋ ~s z
Blessington 'bles ɪŋ tən
blest blest
blet blet
Bletchingley 'bletʃ ɪŋ li

Bletchley 'bletʃ li
bleth|er 'bleð |ə ‖ -|ᵊr ~ered əd ‖ ᵊrd ~ering
ᵊr_ɪŋ ~ers əz ‖ ᵊrz
blew bluː (= blue)
Blewett 'bluː_ɪt §_ət
blewits 'bluː_ɪts §_əts
Blewitt 'bluː_ɪt §_ət
Bligh blaɪ
blight blaɪt blighted 'blaɪt ɪd -əd ‖ 'blaɪt̬ əd
blighting 'blaɪt ɪŋ ‖ 'blaɪt̬ ɪŋ blights blaɪts
blighter 'blaɪt ə ‖ 'blaɪt̬ ᵊr ~s z
Blighty 'blaɪt i ‖ 'blaɪt̬ i
blimey 'blaɪm i
blimp, Blimp blɪmp blimps blɪmps
blimpish 'blɪmp ɪʃ
blind blaɪnd blinded 'blaɪnd ɪd -əd blinder
'blaɪnd ə ‖ -ᵊr blindest 'blaɪnd ɪst -əst
blinding/ly 'blaɪnd ɪŋ /li blinds blaɪndz
ˌblind 'alley; ˌblind 'date; ˌblind 'drunk;
ˌblind man's 'buff; 'blind spot
blinder 'blaɪnd ə ‖ -ᵊr ~s z
blindfold 'blaɪnd fəʊld →-fɒʊld ‖ -foʊld
Blindley 'blaɪnd li
blindly 'blaɪnd li
blindness 'blaɪnd nəs -nɪs
blindworm 'blaɪnd wɜːm ‖ -wɝːm ~s z
blini 'blɪn i 'bliːn- ~s z
blink blɪŋk blinked blɪŋkt blinking 'blɪŋk ɪŋ
blinks blɪŋks
blinker 'blɪŋk ə ‖ -ᵊr ~ed d ~s z
blinks blɪŋks
blintz blɪnts blintzes 'blɪnts ɪz -əz
blip blɪp blipped blɪpt blipping 'blɪp ɪŋ
blips blɪps
bliss, Bliss blɪs
Blissett 'blɪs ɪt §_ət
blissful 'blɪs fᵊl -fʊl ~ly _i ~ness nəs nɪs
blist|er 'blɪst |ə ‖ -|ᵊr ~ered əd ‖ ᵊrd ~ering/
ly ᵊr_ɪŋ /li ~ers əz ‖ -ᵊrz
'blister pack
BLit ˌbiː 'lɪt
blithe blaɪð ‖ blaɪθ
blithe|ly 'blaɪð |li ‖ 'blaɪθ- ~ness nəs nɪs
blithering 'blɪð ᵊr_ɪŋ
blithesome 'blaɪð səm §'blaɪθ- ~ly li ~ness
nəs nɪs
Blithfield 'blɪθ fiːᵊld —locally also 'blɪf iːᵊld
BLitt ˌbiː 'lɪt
blitz blɪts blitzed blɪtst blitzes 'blɪts ɪz -əz
blitzing 'blɪts ɪŋ
blitzkrieg 'blɪts kriːg —Ger B~ ['blɪts kʁiːk]
~s z
Blixen 'blɪks ᵊn
blizzard 'blɪz əd ‖ -ᵊrd ~s z
bloat bləʊt ‖ bloʊt bloated 'bləʊt ɪd -əd
‖ 'bloʊt̬ əd bloating 'bləʊt ɪŋ ‖ 'bloʊt̬ ɪŋ
bloats bləʊts ‖ bloʊts
bloater 'bləʊt ə ‖ 'bloʊt̬ ᵊr ~s z
blob blɒb ‖ blɑːb blobs blɒbz ‖ blɑːbz
bloc blɒk ‖ blɑːk (= block) blocs
blɒks ‖ blɑːks
Bloch blɒk blɒx ‖ blɑːk

block blɒk ‖ blɑːk **blocked** blɒkt ‖ blɑːkt
blocking 'blɒk ɪŋ ‖ 'blɑːk ɪŋ **blocks**
blɒks ‖ blɑːks
ˌblock and 'tackle; ˌblock 'letters; ˌblock
re'lease; ˌblock 'vote
blockad|e blɒ 'keɪd ‖ blɑː- ~**ed** ɪd əd ~**er/s**
ə/z ‖ ər/z ~**es** z ~**ing** ɪŋ
blockag|e 'blɒk ɪdʒ ‖ 'blɑːk- ~**es** ɪz əz
blockboard 'blɒk bɔːd ‖ 'blɑːk bɔːrd -boʊrd
blockbuster 'blɒk ˌbʌst ə ‖ 'blɑːk ˌbʌst ər ~**s** z
blockhead 'blɒk hed ‖ 'blɑːk- ~**s** z
block|house 'blɒk |haʊs ‖ 'blɑːk- ~**houses**
haʊz ɪz -əz
Blodwen 'blɒd wɪn -wen ‖ 'blɑːd- —*Welsh*
['blod wen]
Bloemfontein 'bluːm fən ˌteɪn -fɒn- ‖ -fɑːn-
Blofeld 'bləʊ feld ‖ 'bloʊ-
bloke bləʊk ‖ bloʊk **blokes** bləʊks ‖ bloʊks
blokeish, blokish 'bləʊk ɪʃ ‖ 'bloʊk- ~**ness**
nəs nɪs
Blom blɒm ‖ blɑːm
Blomefield 'bluːm fiːəld
Blomfield 'blɒm fiːəld 'blʌm-, 'blʊm-, 'bluːm-
‖ 'blɑːm-
blond, blonde blɒnd ‖ blɑːnd **blondes,**
blonds blɒndz ‖ blɑːndz
blondie, B~ 'blɒnd i ‖ 'blɑːnd i
Blondel ˌblɒn 'del ‖ ˌblɑːn- —*Fr* [blɔ̃ dɛl]
Blondin 'blɒnd ɪn ‖ blɑːn 'dæn —*Fr* [blɔ̃ dæ̃]
blondish 'blɒnd ɪʃ ‖ 'blɑːnd-
blood, Blood blʌd **blooded** 'blʌd ɪd -əd
blooding 'blʌd ɪŋ **bloods** blʌdz
'blood bank; ˌblood 'brother; 'blood
count; 'blood ˌdonor; 'blood group;
'blood lust; 'blood ˌmoney; 'blood
ˌplasma; 'blood ˌpoisoning; 'blood
ˌpressure; ˌblood 'red◂; 'blood re,lation,
ˌ· ·'··; 'blood sports; 'blood transˌfusion;
'blood type; 'blood ˌvessel
blood-and-thunder ˌblʌd ən 'θʌnd ə ‖ -ər
blood|bath 'blʌd| bɑːθ →'blʌb-, §-bæθ ‖ -bæθ
~**baths** bɑːðz §bɑːθs, §bæθs, §bæðz ‖ bæðz
bæθs
-blooded 'blʌd ɪd ◂ -əd — **hot-blooded**
ˌhɒt 'blʌd ɪd ◂ -əd ‖ ˌhɑːt-
bloodhound 'blʌd haʊnd ~**s** z
bloodi... —*see* **bloody**
bloodless 'blʌd ləs -lɪs ~**ly** li ~**ness** nəs nɪs
bloodletting 'blʌd ˌlet ɪŋ ‖ -ˌleţ-
bloodline 'blʌd laɪn
bloodshed 'blʌd ʃed
bloodshot 'blʌd ʃɒt ‖ -ʃɑːt
bloodstain 'blʌd steɪn ~**ed** d ~**s** z
bloodstock 'blʌd stɒk ‖ -stɑːk
bloodstream 'blʌd striːm
bloodsucker 'blʌd ˌsʌk ə ‖ -ər ~**s** z
bloodsucking 'blʌd ˌsʌk ɪŋ
bloodthirst|y 'blʌd ˌθɜːst |i ‖ -ˌθɝːst i ~**ily** ɪ li
əl i ~**iness** i nəs i nɪs
blood|y 'blʌd |i ~**ied** id ~**ier** i‿ə ‖ i‿ər ~**ies** iz
~**iest** i‿ɪst i‿əst ~**ily** ɪ li əl i ~**iness** i nəs i nɪs
ˌBloody 'Mary
bloody-minded ˌblʌd i 'maɪnd ɪd ◂ -əd ~**ly** li

bloom, Bloom bluːm **bloomed** bluːmd
blooming 'bluːm ɪŋ **blooms** bluːmz
Bloomberg 'bluːm bɜːg ‖ -bɝːg
bloomer, B~ 'bluːm ə ‖ -ər ~**s** z
blooming *euphemistic intensifier* 'bluːm ɪŋ
'blʊm-, -ɪn, -ən ~**ly** li ~**ness** nəs nɪs —*The*
forms with final n, although non-standard, are
sometimes used in RP for jocular effect
Bloomfield 'bluːm fiːəld
Bloomingdale 'bluːm ɪŋ deɪəl ~'**s** z
Bloomington 'bluːm ɪŋ tən
Bloomsbury 'bluːmz bər‿i ‖ -ˌber i
'Bloomsbury Group
bloop bluːp **blooped** bluːpt **blooping**
'bluːp ɪŋ **bloops** bluːps
blooper 'bluːp ə ‖ -ər ~**s** z
Bloor, Blore blɔː ‖ blɔːr bloʊr
Blorenge 'blɒr ɪndʒ ‖ 'blɔːr-
blossom, B~ 'blɒs əm ‖ 'blɑːs- ~**ed** d ~**ing** ɪŋ
~**s** z
blot blɒt ‖ blɑːt **blots** blɒts ‖ blɑːts **blotted**
'blɒt ɪd -əd ‖ 'blɑːţ əd **blotting**
'blɒt ɪŋ ‖ 'blɑːţ ɪŋ
'blotting ˌpaper
blotch blɒtʃ ‖ blɑːtʃ **blotched** blɒtʃt ‖ blɑːtʃt
blotch|y 'blɒtʃ |i ‖ 'blɑːtʃ |i ~**ier** i‿ə ‖ i‿ər
~**iest** i‿ɪst i‿əst ~**ily** ɪ li əl i ~**iness** i nəs i nɪs
blott... *see* **blot**
blotter 'blɒt ə ‖ 'blɑːţ ər ~**s** z
blotto 'blɒt əʊ ‖ 'blɑːţ oʊ
Blount (*i*) blʌnt, (*ii*) blaʊnt
blouse blaʊz ‖ blaʊs (***) —*in RP formerly also*
bluːz **blouses** 'blaʊz ɪz -əz ‖ 'blaʊs-
blouson 'bluːz ɒn ‖ 'blaʊs ɑːn 'bluːs-, 'blaʊz-,
'bluːz-, -oʊn —*Fr* [blu zɔ̃] ~**s** z
blow bləʊ ‖ bloʊ **blew** bluː **blowed**
bləʊd ‖ bloʊd **blowing** 'bləʊ ɪŋ ‖ 'bloʊ ɪŋ
blown bləʊn §'bləʊ ən ‖ bloʊn **blows**
bləʊz ‖ bloʊz
blowback 'bləʊ bæk ‖ 'bloʊ- ~**s** s
blow-by-blow
ˌbləʊ baɪ 'bləʊ ◂ ‖ ˌbloʊ baɪ 'bloʊ ◂
ˌblow-by-ˌblow ac'count
blow-drier 'bləʊ draɪ‿ə, ˌ·'·· ‖ 'bloʊ draɪ‿ər
blow-dry 'bləʊ draɪ ˌ·'· ‖ 'bloʊ-
blower 'bləʊ ə ‖ 'bloʊ ər ~**s** z
blowfish 'bləʊ fɪʃ ‖ 'bloʊ- ~**es** ɪz əz
blow|fly 'bləʊ |flaɪ ‖ 'bloʊ- ~**flies** flaɪz
blowgun 'bləʊ gʌn ‖ 'bloʊ- ~**s** z
blowhard 'bləʊ hɑːd ‖ 'bloʊ hɑːrd ~**s** z
blowhole 'bləʊ həʊl →-hɒʊl ‖ 'bloʊ hoʊl ~**s** z
blowlamp 'bləʊ læmp ‖ 'bloʊ- ~**s** s
blown bləʊn §'bləʊ ən ‖ bloʊn
blowout 'bləʊ aʊt ‖ 'bloʊ- ~**s** s
blowpipe 'bləʊ paɪp ‖ 'bloʊ- ~**s** s
blows|y 'blaʊz |i ~**ier** i‿ə ‖ i‿ər ~**iest** i‿ɪst i‿əst
~**ily** ɪ li əl i
blowtorch 'bləʊ tɔːtʃ ‖ 'bloʊ tɔːrtʃ ~**es** ɪz əz
blow-up 'bləʊ ʌp ‖ 'bloʊ- ~**s** s
blow|y 'bləʊ |i ‖ 'bloʊ |i ~**ier** i‿ə ‖ i‿ər ~**iest**
i‿ɪst i‿əst
blowz|y 'blaʊz |i ~**ier** i‿ə ‖ i‿ər ~**iest** i‿ɪst i‿əst
~**ily** ɪ li əl i

Bloxham 'blɒks əm ‖ 'blɑːks-
blub blʌb blubbed blʌbd blubbing 'blʌb ɪŋ
blubs blʌbz
blubb|er 'blʌb |ə ‖ -|ᵊr ~ered əd ‖ ᵊrd ~ering
ər_ɪŋ ~ers əz ‖ ᵊrz
Blucher, Blücher, b~ 'bluːk ə 'bluːtʃ- ‖ -ᵊr
—Ger ['bly: çɐ]
bludge blʌdʒ bludged blʌdʒd bludges
'blʌdʒ ɪz -əz bludging 'blʌdʒ ɪŋ
bludgeon 'blʌdʒ ən ~ed d ~ing ɪŋ ~s z
bludger 'blʌdʒ ə ‖ -ᵊr ~s z
blue, Blue bluː blued bluːd blueing, bluing
'bluː_ɪŋ bluer 'bluː_ə ‖ _ᵊr blues bluːz
bluest 'bluː_ɪst _əst
ˌblue 'blood; ˌblue 'moon; ˌblue 'peter
bluebag 'bluː bæg
bluebeard, B~ 'bluː bɪəd ‖ -bɪrd
bluebell, B~ 'bluː bel ~s z
blueberr|y 'bluː bər_li -ˌber i ‖ -ˌber li ~ies iz
ˌblueberry 'pie
bluebird 'bluː bɜːd ‖ -bɝːd ~s z
blue-black ˌbluː 'blæk ◄
ˌblue-black 'ink
blue-blooded ˌbluː 'blʌd ɪd ◄ -əd
bluebook 'bluː bʊk §-buːk ~s s
bluebottle 'bluː ˌbɒt ᵊl ‖ -ˌbɑːt̬- ~s z
bluecoat 'bluː kəʊt ‖ -koʊt ~s s
Bluecol tdmk 'bluː kɒl ‖ -kɑːl
blue-collar ˌbluː 'kɒl ə ◄ ‖ -'kɑːl ᵊr
blue-eyed ˌbluː 'aɪd ◄
ˌblue-eyed 'boy
Bluefields 'bluː fiːᵊldz
bluefish 'bluː fɪʃ
bluegrass 'bluː grɑːs §-græs ‖ -græs
blue-green ˌbluː 'griːn ◄
ˌblue-green 'algae
blueish 'bluː_ɪʃ ~ness nəs nɪs
bluejacket 'bluː ˌdʒæk ɪt §-ət ~s s
bluejay 'bluː dʒeɪ ~s z
blueness 'bluː nəs -nɪs
bluenose 'bluː nəʊz ‖ -noʊz
blue-pencil ˌbluː 'pen¹s ᵊl -ɪl ~ed, ~led d
~ing, ~ling _ɪŋ ~s z
blue|print 'bluː |prɪnt ~printed prɪnt ɪd -əd
‖ 'bluː ˌprɪnt̬ əd ~printing prɪnt ɪŋ ‖ prɪnt̬ ɪŋ
~prints prɪnts
blue-ribbon ˌbluː 'rɪb ən ◄
blues bluːz
blue-sky ˌbluː 'skaɪ ◄
bluestocking 'bluː ˌstɒk ɪŋ ‖ -ˌstɑːk- ~s z
bluesy 'bluːz i
bluet 'bluː_ɪt §-ət
bluethroat 'bluː θrəʊt ‖ -θroʊt ~s s
bluetit 'bluː tɪt ~s s
Bluett 'bluː_ɪt §_ət
bluey 'bluː_i ~s z
bluff blʌf bluffed blʌft bluffer 'blʌf ə ‖ -ᵊr
bluffest 'blʌf ɪst -əst bluffing 'blʌf ɪŋ
bluffs blʌfs
bluffer 'blʌf ə ‖ -ᵊr ~s z
bluff|ly 'blʌf |li ~ness nəs nɪs
bluing 'bluː_ɪŋ
bluish 'bluː_ɪʃ ~ness nəs nɪs

Blum bluːm
Blundell 'blʌnd ᵊl
Blundellsands ˌblʌnd ᵊl 'sændz
Blunden 'blʌnd ən
blund|er 'blʌnd |ə ‖ -|ᵊr ~ered əd ‖ ᵊrd
~ering/ly ᵊr ɪŋ /li ~ers əz ‖ ᵊrz
blunderer 'blʌnd ᵊr ə ‖ ᵊr ᵊr ~s z
blunderbuss 'blʌnd ə bʌs ‖ -ᵊr- ~s ɪz əz
blunge blʌndʒ blunged blʌndʒd blunges
'blʌndʒ ɪz -əz blunging 'blʌndʒ ɪŋ
blunt, Blunt blʌnt blunted 'blʌnt ɪd -əd
‖ 'blʌnt̬ əd blunter 'blʌnt ə ‖ 'blʌnt̬ ᵊr
bluntest 'blʌnt ɪst -əst ‖ 'blʌnt̬ əst
blunting 'blʌnt ɪŋ ‖ 'blʌnt̬ ɪŋ blunts blʌnts
blunt|ly 'blʌnt |li ~ness nəs nɪs
blur, Blur blɜː ‖ blɝː blurred blɜːd ‖ blɝːd
blurring 'blɜːr ɪŋ ‖ 'blɝː ɪŋ blurs
blɜːz ‖ blɝːz
blurb blɜːb ‖ blɝːb blurbs blɜːbz ‖ blɝːbz
blurr... —see blur
blurt blɜːt ‖ blɝːt blurted 'blɜːt ɪd -əd
‖ 'blɝːt̬ əd blurting 'blɜːt ɪŋ ‖ 'blɝːt̬ ɪŋ
blurts blɜːts ‖ blɝːts
blush blʌʃ blushed blʌʃt blushes 'blʌʃ ɪz -əz
blushing/ly 'blʌʃ ɪŋ /li
blusher 'blʌʃ ə ‖ -ᵊr ~s z
blust|er 'blʌst |ə ‖ -|ᵊr ~ered əd ‖ ᵊrd
~ering/ly ᵊr_ɪŋ /li ~ers əz ‖ ᵊrz
blusterous 'blʌst ᵊr_əs ~ly li
blustery 'blʌst ᵊr_i
Blu-Tack tdmk 'bluː tæk
Bly blaɪ
Blyth (i) blaɪð, (ii) blaɪθ, (iii) blaɪ —The place in
Northumberland is (i).
Blythe blaɪð
Blyton 'blaɪt ən
B-movie 'biː ˌmuːv i
BMus ˌbiː 'mʌz
BMW tdmk ˌbiː em 'dʌb ᵊl ju ~s, ~'s z
BMX ˌbiː em 'eks
B'nai B'rith bə ˌneɪ bə 'riːθ •ˌ•ˈbrɪθ
BNOC 'biː nɒk ‖ -nɑːk
bo, Bo bəʊ ‖ boʊ
BO ˌbiː 'əʊ ‖ -'oʊ
boa 'bəʊ ə ‖ 'boʊ ə —in RP formerly also bɔː
boas 'bəʊ əz ‖ 'boʊ əz
Boadicea ˌbəʊ əd ɪ 'siː_ə -ə'•• ‖ ˌboʊ-
Boakes, Boaks bəʊks ‖ boʊks
Boanerges ˌbəʊ ə 'nɜːdʒ iːz ‖ ˌboʊ ə 'nɝːdʒ-
boar bɔː ‖ bɔːr boʊr (= bore) boars
bɔːz ‖ bɔːrz boʊrz
board bɔːd ‖ bɔːrd boʊrd boarded 'bɔːd ɪd
-əd ‖ 'bɔːrd əd 'boʊrd- boarding
'bɔːd ɪŋ ‖ 'bɔːrd ɪŋ 'boʊrd- boards
bɔːdz ‖ bɔːrdz boʊrdz
'boarding card; 'boarding school
boarder 'bɔːd ə ‖ 'bɔːrd ᵊr 'boʊrd- ~s z
boarding|house 'bɔːd ɪŋ |haʊs ‖ 'bɔːrd-
'boʊrd- ~houses haʊz ɪz -əz
Boardman 'bɔːd mən →'bɔːb- ‖ 'bɔːrd-
'boʊrd-
boardroom 'bɔːd ruːm -rʊm ‖ 'bɔːrd- 'boʊrd-
~s z

boardwalk 'bɔːd wɔːk ‖ 'bɔːrd- 'bourd-, -waːk
~s s
Boas 'bəʊ æz -æs, -əz, -əs ‖ 'boʊ-
boast bəʊst ‖ boʊst **boasted** 'bəʊst ɪd -əd
‖ 'boʊst- **boasting/ly** 'bəʊst ɪŋ /li ‖ 'boʊst-
boasts bəʊsts ‖ boʊsts
boaster 'bəʊst ə ‖ 'boʊst ᵊr ~s z
boastful 'bəʊst fᵊl -fʊl ‖ 'boʊst- **~ly** i **~ness**
nəs nɪs
boat bəʊt ‖ boʊt **boated** 'bəʊt ɪd -əd
‖ 'boʊt̮ əd **boating** 'bəʊt ɪŋ ‖ 'boʊt̮ ɪŋ **boats**
bəʊts ‖ boʊts
'boat ˌpeople; 'boat race; 'boat train
boatel ₍ₒ₎bəʊ 'tel ‖ ₍ₒ₎boʊ- ~s z
Boateng 'bwaːt eŋ —*but popularly usually*
'bəʊt- ‖ 'boʊt-
boater 'bəʊt ə ‖ 'boʊt̮ ᵊr ~s z
boathook 'bəʊt hʊk §-huːk ‖ 'boʊt- ~s s
boat|house 'bəʊt |haʊs ‖ 'boʊt- **~houses**
haʊz ɪz -əz
boatload 'bəʊt ləʊd ‖ 'boʊt loʊd ~s z
boat|man 'bəʊt |mən ‖ 'boʊt- **~men** mən men
boatshed 'bəʊt ʃed ‖ 'boʊt- ~s z
boatswain 'bəʊs ᵊn ‖ 'boʊs ᵊn —*There is also a*
spelling pronunciation 'bəʊt sweɪn ‖ 'boʊt-
~s z
boatyard 'bəʊt jɑːd ‖ 'boʊt jɑːrd ~s z
Boaz 'bəʊ æz ‖ 'boʊ-
bob, Bob bɒb ‖ baːb **bobbed** bɒbd ‖ baːbd
bobbing 'bɒb ɪŋ ‖ 'baːb ɪŋ **bobs, Bob's**
bɒbz ‖ baːbz
Bobbie 'bɒb i ‖ 'baːb i
bobbi... —*see* **bobby**
bobbin 'bɒb ɪn §-ən ‖ 'baːb ən ~s z
Bobbitt 'bɒb ɪt §-ət ‖ 'baːb ət
bobble 'bɒb ᵊl ‖ 'baːb ᵊl ~s z
bobby, Bobby 'bɒb i ‖ 'baːb i **bobbies,**
Bobby's 'bɒb iz ‖ 'baːb-
'bobby pin; 'bobby socks
bobby-soxer 'bɒb i sɒks ə ‖ 'baːbi saːks ᵊr
bobcat 'bɒb kæt ‖ 'baːb- ~s s
bobolink 'bɒb ə lɪŋk ‖ 'baːb- ~s s
bobsled 'bɒb sled ‖ 'baːb- ~s z
bobsleigh 'bɒb sleɪ ‖ 'baːb- ~s z
bobstay 'bɒb steɪ ‖ 'baːb- ~s z
bobtail 'bɒb teɪᵊl ‖ 'baːb- **~ed** d **~ing** ɪŋ ~s z
Boca Raton ˌbəʊk ə rə 'təʊn ‖ ˌboʊk ə rə 'toʊn
Boccaccio bɒ 'kaːtʃ i‿əʊ bə-, -'kætʃ-
‖ boʊ 'kaːtʃ i‿oʊ —*It* [bo 'kat tʃo]
Boccherini ˌbɒk ə 'riːn i ‖ ˌbaːk- ˌboʊk- —*It*
[bok ke 'riː ni]
Boche, boche bɒʃ ‖ baːʃ boʊʃ
Bochum 'bəʊk əm ‖ 'boʊk- —*Ger* ['boːx ʊm]
bock, Bock bɒk ‖ baːk **bocks** bɒks ‖ baːks
ˌbock 'beer
bod bɒd ‖ baːd **bods** bɒdz ‖ baːdz
bodacious bəʊ 'deɪʃ əs ‖ boʊ- **~ly** li
Boddington 'bɒd ɪŋ tən ‖ 'baːd-
bode bəʊd ‖ boʊd **boded** 'bəʊd ɪd -əd
‖ 'boʊd əd **bodes** bəʊdz ‖ boʊdz **boding**
'bəʊd ɪŋ ‖ 'boʊd ɪŋ
bodega bəʊ 'diːg ə -'deɪg- ‖ boʊ 'deɪg ə —*Sp*

[bo 'ðe ɣa] ~s z
Boˌdega 'Bay
bodge bɒdʒ ‖ baːdʒ **bodged** bɒdʒd ‖ baːdʒd
bodges 'bɒdʒ ɪz -əz ‖ 'baːdʒ əz **bodging**
'bɒdʒ ɪŋ ‖ 'baːdʒ ɪŋ
bodger 'bɒdʒ ə ‖ 'baːdʒ ᵊr ~s z
bodgie 'bɒdʒ i ~s z
Bodhisattva ˌbɒd ɪ 'sæt və ˌbəʊd-, §-ə-, -'sʌt-,
-'saːt-, -wə ‖ ˌboʊd ə 'sʌt və
bodhran, bodhrán 'bɔːr aːn baʊ 'raːn
Bodiam (i) 'bəʊd i‿əm ‖ 'boʊd-, (ii)
'bɒd- ‖ 'baːd-
bodic|e 'bɒd ɪs -əs ‖ 'baːd- **~es** ɪz əz
Bodie 'bəʊd i ‖ 'boʊd i
bodie... —*see* **body**
-bodied 'bɒd id ◄ ‖ -'baːd id ◄ — **full-bodied**
ˌfʊl 'bɒd id ◄ ‖ -'baːd-
bodily 'bɒd ɪ li -əl i ‖ 'baːd ᵊl i
bodkin, B~ 'bɒd kɪn ‖ 'baːd- ~s z
Bodleian bɒd 'liː‿ən 'bɒd li‿ən ‖ baːd-
Bodley 'bɒd li ‖ 'baːd-
Bodmer 'bɒd mə ‖ 'baːd mᵊr
Bodmin 'bɒd mɪn →'bɒb-, §-mən ‖ 'baːd-
Bodnant 'bɒd nænt ‖ 'baːd-
Bodoni bə 'dəʊn i ‖ -'doʊn- —*It* [bo 'do: ni]
body, Body 'bɒd i ‖ 'baːd i **bodies**
'bɒd iz ‖ 'baːd iz
'body blow; 'body ˌbuilding; 'body count;
'body ˌdouble; 'body ˌlanguage; 'body
ˌpopping; 'body ˌsnatcher; 'body
ˌstocking; 'body ˌwarmer
bodycheck 'bɒd i tʃek ‖ 'baːd- ~s s
bodyguard 'bɒd i gaːd ‖ 'baːd i gaːrd ~s z
bodyline 'bɒd i laɪn ‖ 'baːd- ~s z
bodywork 'bɒd i wɜːk ‖ 'baːd i wɜːk
Boehm (i) bəʊm 'bəʊ əm ‖ boʊm, (ii) biːm, (iii)
bɜːm ‖ bɝːm (iv) beɪm —*Ger* [bøːm]
boehmite 'bɜːm aɪt ‖ 'beɪm- 'boʊm- (*)
Boeing tdmk 'bəʊ ɪŋ ‖ 'boʊ ɪŋ
Boeotia bi 'əʊʃ ə -i‿ə ‖ -'oʊʃ ə
Boeotian bi 'əʊʃ ᵊn -i‿ən ‖ -'oʊʃ ᵊn ~s z
Boer bɔː 'bəʊ ə, bʊə ‖ bɔːr boʊr, bʊᵊr **Boers**
bɔːz 'bəʊ əz, bʊəz ‖ bɔːrz boʊrz, bʊᵊrz
Boethius bəʊ 'iːθ i‿əs ‖ boʊ-
boeuf bɜːf ‖ bʊf bʌf, boʊf —*Fr* [bœf]
ˌboeuf ˌbourgui'gnon ˌbʊəg iːn 'jɒn ˌbɔːg-,
-ɪn-, -ən- ‖ ˌbʊrg iːn 'jaːn -'jɔːn, -'joʊn —*Fr*
[buʁ gi njɔ̃]
boff bɒf ‖ baːf **boffed** bɒft ‖ baːft **boffing**
'bɒf ɪŋ ‖ 'baːf ɪŋ **boffs** bɒfs ‖ baːfs
boffin 'bɒf ɪn §-ən ‖ 'baːf- ~s z
boffo 'bɒf əʊ ‖ 'baːf oʊ
Bofors 'bəʊf əz ‖ 'boʊ fɔːrz -fɔːrs —*Swed*
[buː 'fɒʂ]
bog bɒg ‖ baːg bɔːg **bogged** bɒgd ‖ baːgd
bɔːgd **bogging** 'bɒg ɪŋ ‖ 'baːg ɪŋ 'bɔːg-
bogs bɒgz ‖ baːgz bɔːgz
Bogalusa place in LA ˌbəʊg ə 'luːs ə ‖ ˌboʊg-
Bogarde 'bəʊg aːd ‖ 'boʊg aːrd
Bogart 'bəʊg aːt ‖ 'boʊg aːrt
bogbean 'bɒg biːn ‖ 'baːg- 'bɔːg-
Bogdanov bɒg 'daːn əv ‖ baːg-
bogey, Bogey 'bəʊg i ‖ 'boʊg i ~s z

bogey|man 'bəʊg i |mæn ‖ 'boʊg- **~men** men
boggie... —*see* **boggy**
bogginess 'bɒg i nəs -nɪs ‖ 'bɑːg- 'bɔːg-
Boggis 'bɒg ɪs §-əs ‖ 'bɑːg-
boggl|e 'bɒg əl ‖ 'bɑːg əl **~ed** d **~es** z **~ing** _ɪŋ
boggly 'bɒg li ‖ 'bɑːg li 'bɔːg- **~ier** i_ə ‖ i_ər **~iest** i_ɪst i_əst
bogie 'bəʊg i ‖ 'boʊg i (= *bogey*) **~s** z
Bognor 'bɒg nə ‖ 'bɑːg nər
Bogota, Bogotá ,bɒg ə 'tɑː ,bəʊg-
‖ ,boʊg ə 'tɑː '••• —*Sp* [bo ɣo 'ta] —*but the place in NJ is* bə 'goʊt̬ ə
bogus 'bəʊg əs ‖ 'boʊg-
bogy 'bəʊg i ‖ 'boʊg i (= *bogey*)
bohea bəʊ 'hiː ‖ boʊ-
Boheme, Bohème, b~ bəʊ 'em -'eɪm ‖ boʊ-
Bohemia bəʊ 'hiːm i_ə ‖ boʊ-
bohemian, B~ bəʊ 'hiːm i_ən ‖ boʊ- **~s** z
Bohm, Böhm bɜːm ‖ boʊm —*Ger* [bøːm]
Bohr bɔː ‖ bɔːr boʊr —*Danish* [boːʁ]
Bohun (i) buːn, (ii) 'bəʊ ən ‖ 'boʊ-
bohunk 'bəʊ hʌŋk ‖ 'boʊ- **~s** s
boil bɔɪəl **boiled** bɔɪəld **boiling** 'bɔɪl ɪŋ **boils** bɔɪəlz
Boileau 'bɔɪl əʊ bwæ 'ləʊ ‖ bwɑː 'loʊ —*Fr* [bwa lo]
boiler 'bɔɪl ə ‖ -ər **~s** z
'boiler suit
boilermak|er/s 'bɔɪl ə ,meɪk |ə/z ‖ -ər ,meɪk |ər/z **~ing** ɪŋ
boilerplate 'bɔɪl ə pleɪt ‖ -ər- **~s** s
boiling 'bɔɪəl ɪŋ
'boiling point; ,boiling 'water
boil-in-the-bag ,bɔɪəl ɪn ðə 'bæg ◀
boing bɔɪŋ
boink bɔɪŋk
Bois bɔɪz —*but in French placenames* bwɑː
Boise *place in ID* 'bɔɪz i 'bɔɪs i
boisterous 'bɔɪst ər əs →'bɔɪs trəs **~ly** li **~ness** nəs nɪs
Bokhara bɒ 'kɑːr ə bəʊ- ‖ boʊ- —*Russ* [bu 'xa rə]
Bokmål 'bʊk mɔːl 'buːk- ‖ -mɑːl —*Norw* ['buːk mɔːl]
bola 'bəʊl ə ‖ 'boʊl ə —*Sp* ['bo la] **~s** z
Bolam 'bəʊl əm ‖ 'boʊl-
Bolan 'bəʊl ən ‖ 'boʊl-
bolas 'bəʊl əs ‖ 'boʊl- —*Sp* ['bo las]
bold, Bold bəʊld →bɒʊld ‖ boʊld **bolder** 'bəʊld ə →'bɒʊld ə ‖ 'boʊld ər **boldest** 'bəʊld ɪst →'bɒʊld-, -əst ‖ 'boʊld əst
boldface 'bəʊld feɪs →'bɒʊld-, ,•'• ‖ 'boʊld- **~d** t
bold|ly 'bəʊld |li →'bɒʊld- ‖ 'boʊld- **~ness** nəs nɪs
Boldre 'bəʊld ə →'bɒʊld- ‖ 'boʊld ər
bole bəʊl →bɒʊl ‖ boʊl (= *bowl*) **boles** bəʊlz ‖ boʊlz
Boleat, Boléat 'bəʊl i_ət -i ɑː ‖ 'boʊl-
bolero *'dance'* bə 'leər əʊ ‖ -'ler oʊ **~s** z
bolero *'garment'* 'bɒl ə rəʊ bə 'leər əʊ ‖ bə 'ler oʊ **~s** z

bo|letus bəʊ |'liːt əs ‖ boʊ |'liːt̬ əs **~leti** 'liːt aɪ -iː **~letuses** 'liːt əs ɪz -əz ‖ 'liːt̬-
Boleyn (i) bə 'lɪn, (ii) 'bʊl ɪn, (iii) bʊ 'liːn
Bolger 'bɒldʒ ə 'bɒldʒ- ‖ 'boʊldʒ ər 'bɑːldʒ-
bolide 'bəʊl aɪd -ɪd, §-əd ‖ 'boʊl- **~s** z
Bolingbroke 'bɒl ɪŋ brʊk 'bʊl- ‖ 'bɑːl-
Bolinger 'bɒl ɪndʒ ə -əndʒ- ‖ 'bɑːl əndʒ ər
Bolitho bə 'laɪθ əʊ ‖ -oʊ
Bolivar, b~ 'bɒl ɪ vɑː: -ə-; bɒ 'liːv ɑː ‖ 'bɑːl əv ər bə 'liːv ɑːr —*Sp* Bolívar [bo 'li βar]
Bolivia bə 'lɪv i_ə
Bolivian bə 'lɪv i_ən **~s** z
boliviano bə ,lɪv i 'ɑːn əʊ bɒ- ‖ -oʊ **~s** z
boll bəʊl →bɒʊl; bɒl ‖ boʊl (= *bowl*) **bolls** bəʊlz →bɒʊlz; bɒlz ‖ boʊlz
,boll 'weevil
bollard 'bɒl ɑːd -əd ‖ 'bɑːl ərd **~s** z
Bollin 'bɒl ɪn §-ən ‖ 'bɑːl-
Bollinger 'bɒl ɪndʒ ə -əndʒ- ‖ 'bɑːl əndʒ ər
bollix 'bɒl ɪks **~ed** t **~es** ɪz əz **~ing** ɪŋ
bollock 'bɒl ək ‖ 'bɑːl- **~ed** t **~ing/s** ɪŋ/z **~s** s
bollocks-up 'bɒl əks ʌp ‖ 'bɑːl-
Bollywood 'bɒl i wʊd ‖ 'bɑːl-
Bologna bə 'ləʊn jə -'lɒn- ‖ -'loʊn- —*It* [bo 'loɲ ɲa]
bologna *'sausage'* bə 'ləʊn i ‖ bə 'loʊn i
bolognaise, bolognese ,bɒl ə 'neɪz ◀ △-əg-, -'nez ‖ ,boʊl ən 'jeɪz ◀
,bolognaise ' sauce
boloney bə 'ləʊn i ‖ bə 'loʊn i
Bolshevik 'bɒlʃ ə vɪk -ɪ- ‖ 'boʊlʃ- **~s** s
Bolshevism 'bɒlʃ ə ,vɪz əm -ɪ- ‖ 'boʊlʃ-
Bolshevist 'bɒlʃ əv ɪst -ɪv-, §-əst ‖ 'boʊlʃ- **~s** s
Bolshevistic ,bɒlʃ ə 'vɪst ɪk ◀ -ɪ- ‖ ,boʊlʃ-
bolshie 'bɒlʃ i ‖ 'boʊlʃ i **~s** z
Bolshoi, Bolshoy ,bɒl 'ʃɔɪ ◀ ‖ ,boʊl- —*Russ* [bʌlʲ 'ʃɔj]
,Bolshoi ' Ballet ‖ ,•• •'•
bolshy 'bɒlʃ i ‖ 'boʊlʃ i
Bolsover 'bɒls ,əʊv ə 'bəʊlz- ‖ 'boʊls ,oʊv ər —*The place in Derbyshire is locally* 'bəʊlz-, →'bɒʊlz-
bolst|er, B~ 'bəʊlst |ə →'bɒʊlst-; §'bɒlst- ‖ 'boʊlst |ər **~ered** əd ‖ ərd **~ering** ər_ɪŋ **~ers** əz ‖ ərz
bolt, Bolt bəʊlt →bɒʊlt, §bɒlt ‖ boʊlt **bolted** 'bəʊlt ɪd →'bɒʊlt-, §'bɒlt-, -əd ‖ 'boʊlt əd **bolting** 'bəʊlt ɪŋ →'bɒʊlt-, §'bɒlt- ‖ 'boʊlt ɪŋ **bolts, Bolt's** bəʊlts →bɒʊlts, §bɒlts ‖ boʊlts
bolter 'bəʊlt ə →'bɒʊlt-, §'bɒlt- ‖ 'boʊlt ər **~s** z
bolthole 'bəʊlt həʊl →'bɒʊlt hɒʊl, §'bɒlt- ‖ 'boʊlt hoʊl **~s** z
Bolton 'bəʊlt ən →'bɒʊlt- ‖ 'boʊlt- **~s** z
Bolton-le-Sands ,bəʊlt ən li 'sændz →,bɒʊlt-, -lə'• ‖ ,boʊlt-
Boltzmann 'bɒlts mən 'bəʊlts- ‖ 'boʊlts- —*Ger* ['bɔlts man]
bolus 'bəʊl əs ‖ 'boʊl- **~es** ɪz əz
bomb bɒm ‖ bɑːm **bombed** bɒmd ‖ bɑːmd **bombing** 'bɒm ɪŋ ‖ 'bɑːm ɪŋ **bombs**

B

bɒmz ‖ baːmz
'bomb di,sposal
bombard v bɒm 'baːd ‖ baːm 'baːrd **~ed** ɪd
əd **~ing** ɪŋ **~s** z
bombardier ,bɒm bə 'dɪə ◄ ‖ ,baːm bᵊr 'dɪᵊr
-bə- **~s** z
bombardment bɒm 'baːd mənt →-'baːb-
‖ baːm 'baːrd- **~s** s
bombasine ,bɒm bə ziːn ,• • '• ‖ ,baːm bə 'ziːn
bombast 'bɒm bæst ‖ 'baːm-
bombastic bɒm 'bæst ɪk ‖ baːm- **~ally** ᵊl_i
Bombay ,bɒm 'beɪ ◄ ‖ ,baːm-
,**Bombay** 'duck
bombazine 'bɒm bə ziːn ,• • '• ‖ ,baːm bə 'ziːn
bombe bɒm bɒmb ‖ baːm —Fr [bɔ̃ːb]
bombes bɒmz bɒmbz ‖ baːmz
bomber 'bɒm ə ‖ 'baːm ᵊr **~s** z
bomblet 'bɒm lət -lɪt ‖ 'baːm- **~s** s
bombproof 'bɒm pruːf §-prʊf ‖ 'baːm- **~ed** t
bombshell 'bɒm ʃel ‖ 'baːm- **~s** z
bombsight 'bɒm saɪt ‖ 'baːm- **~s** s
bombsite 'bɒm saɪt ‖ 'baːm- **~s** s
Bompas 'bʌmp əs
bon bɒn bɔ̃ ‖ baːn —Fr [bɔ̃] —See also phrases
with this word
bona 'bəʊn ə ‖ 'boʊn ə
,**bona** 'fide 'faɪd i 'fiːd eɪ; ,**bona** 'fides
'faɪd iːz 'fiːd eɪz, -eɪs
Bonaire bɒn 'eə ‖ bə 'neᵊr
Bonallack bə 'næl ək
bonanza bə 'nænz ə **~s** z
Bonaparte 'bəʊn ə paːt ‖ 'boʊn ə paːrt —Fr
[bɔ na paʁt]
Bonapartism 'bəʊn ə paːt ,ɪz
əm ‖ 'boʊn ə paːrt̩-
Bonapartist 'bəʊn ə paːt ɪst §-əst
‖ 'boʊn ə paːrt̩ əst **~s** s
Bonar (i) 'bəʊn ə ‖ 'boʊn ᵊr, (ii)
'bɒn ə ‖ 'baːn ᵊr
Bonaventure 'bɒn ə ,ventʃ ə ,• • '• •
‖ 'baːn ə ,ventʃ ᵊr ,• • '• •
bonbon 'bɒn bɒn →'bɒm- ‖ 'baːn baːn **~s** z
bonce bɒnᵗs ‖ baːnᵗs **bonces** 'bɒnᵗs ɪz -əz
‖ 'baːnᵗs-
bond, Bond bɒnd ‖ baːnd **bonded** 'bɒnd ɪd
-əd ‖ 'baːnd əd **bonding**
'bɒnd ɪŋ ‖ 'baːnd ɪŋ **bonds, Bond's**
bɒndz ‖ baːndz
bondage 'bɒnd ɪdʒ ‖ 'baːnd-
Bondfield 'bɒnd fiːᵊld ‖ 'baːnd-
bondholder 'bɒnd ,həʊld ə →-,hɒʊld-
‖ 'baːnd ,hoʊld ᵊr **~s** z
Bondi place in Australia 'bɒnd aɪ ‖ 'baːnd-
bondservant 'bɒnd ,sɜːv ᵊnt ‖ 'baːnd ,sɜːv ᵊnt
~s s
bonds|man 'bɒndz mən ‖ 'baːndz- **~men**
mən men
bone, Bone bəʊn ‖ boʊn **boned**
bəʊnd ‖ boʊnd **boning** 'bəʊn ɪŋ ‖ 'boʊn ɪŋ
bones bəʊnz ‖ boʊnz
,**bone** 'china; 'bone ,marrow; 'bone meal
bone-dry ,bəʊn 'draɪ ◄ ‖ ,boʊn-
bonehead 'bəʊn hed ‖ 'boʊn- **~s** z

bone-idle ,bəʊn 'aɪd ᵊl ◄ ‖ ,boʊn-
bone-lazy ,bəʊn 'leɪz i ◄ ‖ ,boʊn-
bonemeal 'bəʊn miːᵊl →-'bəʊm- ‖ 'boʊn-
boner 'bəʊn ə ‖ 'boʊn ᵊr **~s** z
bone-setter 'bəʊn ,set ə ‖ 'boʊn ,set̬ ᵊr **~s** z
bone-shaker 'bəʊn ,ʃeɪk ə ‖ 'boʊn ,ʃeɪk ᵊr **~s**
z
Bo'ness ,bəʊ 'nes ‖ ,boʊ-
bonfire 'bɒn ,faɪ_ə ‖ 'baːn ,faɪ_ᵊr **~s** z
bong bɒŋ ‖ baːŋ bɔːŋ **bonged** bɒŋd ‖ baːŋd
bɔːŋd **bonging** 'bɒŋ ɪŋ ‖ 'baːŋ ɪŋ 'bɔːŋ-
bongs bɒŋz ‖ baːŋz bɔːŋz
bongo 'bɒŋ gəʊ ‖ 'baːŋ goʊ 'bɔːŋ- **~s** z
Bonham 'bɒn əm ‖ 'baːn-
Bonham-Carter
,bɒn əm 'kaːt ə ‖ ,baːn əm 'kaːrt̬ ᵊr
Bonhoeffer 'bɒn ,hɜːf ə ‖ 'baːn ,hoʊf ᵊr —Ger
['boːn hœf ɐ, 'bɔn-]
bonhomie 'bɒn əm i -ɒm-, -iː ‖ ,baːn ə 'miː
'• • •
boni... —see **bony**
Boniface 'bɒn ɪ feɪs -ə- ‖ 'baːn-
Bonington 'bɒn ɪŋ tən ‖ 'baːn-
Bonio tdmk 'bəʊn i əʊ ‖ 'boʊn i oʊ **~s** z
Bonita bə 'niːt ə ‖ -'niːt̬-
bonito bə 'niːt əʊ ‖ -'niːt̬ oʊ -ə- **~s** z
Bon Jovi ,bɒn 'dʒəʊv i ‖ ,baːn 'dʒoʊv i
bonk bɒŋk ‖ baːŋk **bonked** bɒŋkt ‖ baːŋkt
bonking 'bɒŋk ɪŋ ‖ 'baːŋk ɪŋ **bonks**
bɒŋks ‖ baːŋks
bonkers 'bɒŋk əz ‖ 'baːŋk ᵊrz
bon mot ,bɔ̃ 'məʊ ,bɒn- ‖ ,baːn 'moʊ ,bɔːn-
—Fr [bɔ̃ mo] **~s** z
Bonn bɒn ‖ baːn —Ger [bɔn]
bonne bɒn ‖ baːn bɔːn, bʌn —Fr [bɔn]
,**bonne** 'bouche buːʃ —Fr [buʃ]; ,**bonne**
'femme fæm —Fr [fam]
bonnet 'bɒn ɪt §-ət ‖ 'baːn- **~s** s
Bonneville 'bɒn ə vɪl ‖ 'baːn-
Bonnie 'bɒn i ‖ 'baːn i
,**Bonnie** ,**Prince** 'Charlie
bonn|y, Bonny 'bɒn li i ‖ 'baːn li i **~ier** i_ə ‖ i_ᵊr
~iest i_ɪst i_əst **~ily** ɪ li əl i **~iness** i nəs i nɪs
bonobo bə 'nəʊb əʊ 'bɒn ə bəʊ ‖ bə 'noʊb oʊ
~s z
bonsai 'bɒn saɪ 'bəʊn- ‖ ,baːn 'saɪ ,boʊn-, '• •
—Jp [bo,n sai] **~s** z
Bonser, Bonsor 'bɒnᵗs ə ‖ 'baːnᵗs ᵊr
bonus 'bəʊn əs ‖ 'boʊn- **~es** ɪz əz
bon vivant ,bɔ̃ 'viːv ð̃ -viː 'vð̃
‖ ,baːn viː 'vaːnt —Fr [bɔ̃ vi vɑ̃]
bon viveur ,bɔ̃ viː 'vɜː ‖ ,baːn viː 'vɜːː —not a
true French expression **~s** z
bon voyage ,bɔ̃ vwaɪ 'aːʒ, • '• • ‖ ,baːn-
,bɔːn- —Fr [bɔ̃ vwa ja:ʒ]
bon|y 'bəʊn li i ‖ 'boʊn li i **~ier** i_ə ‖ i_ᵊr **~iest**
i_ɪst i_əst **~ily** ɪ li əl i **~iness** i nəs i nɪs
Bonython bə 'naɪθ ᵊn
bonze bɒnz ‖ baːnz **bonzes** 'bɒnz ɪz -əz
‖ 'baːnz əz
bonzer 'bɒnz ə ‖ 'baːnz ᵊr
Bonzo 'bɒnz əʊ ‖ 'baːnz oʊ

boo buː **booed** buːd **booing** ˈbuːˌɪŋ **boos**
   buːz
boob buːb **boobed** buːbd **boobing** ˈbuːb ɪŋ
   boobs buːbz
boo-boo ˈbuː buː ~s z
booby ˈbuːb i **boobies** ˈbuːb iz
   ˈbooby hatch; ˈbooby prize; ˈbooby trap
booby-trap ˈbuːb i træp ~ped t ~ping ɪŋ ~s
   s
boodl|e, B~ ˈbuːd ᵊl ~ed d ~es, ~e's z ~ing
   ˌɪŋ
booger ˈbʊg ə ˈbuːg- ‖ -ᵊr ~s z
boogie ˈbuːg i ˈbʊg i ‖ ˈbʊg i ˈbuːg i ~d d
   ~ing ɪŋ ~s z
boogie-woogie ˌbuːg i ˈwuːg i ˌbʊg i ˈwʊg i
   ‖ ˌbʊg i ˈwʊg i ˌbuːg i ˈwuːg i
boohoo ˌbuː ˈhuː ~ed d ~ing ɪŋ ~s z
boojum ˈbuːdʒ əm
book bʊk §buːk **booked** bʊkt §buːkt
   booking ˈbʊk ɪŋ §ˈbuːk- **books** bʊks §buːks
   ˈbook club; ˈbook shelf; ˈbook ˌtoken
bookable ˈbʊk əb ᵊl §ˈbuːk-
bookbinder ˈbʊk ˌbaɪnd ə §ˈbuːk- ‖ -ᵊr ~s z
bookbinder|y ˈbʊk ˌbaɪnd ᵊr‿li §ˈbuːk- ~ies iz
bookbinding ˈbʊk ˌbaɪnd ɪŋ §ˈbuːk-
bookcas|e ˈbʊk keɪs §ˈbuːk- ~es ɪz əz
bookend ˈbʊk end §ˈbuːk-, ˌˈ• ~s z
Booker, b~ ˈbʊk ə §ˈbuːk- ‖ -ᵊr
Bookham ˈbʊk əm
bookie ˈbʊk i §ˈbuːk- ~s z
bookish ˈbʊk ɪʃ §ˈbuːk- ~ly li ~ness nəs nɪs
bookkeep|er/s ˈbʊk ˌkiːp lə/z §ˈbuːk- ‖ -lᵊr/z
   ~ing ɪŋ
booklet ˈbʊk lət §ˈbuːk-, -lɪt ~s s
booklover ˈbʊk ˌlʌv ə §ˈbuːk- ‖ -ᵊr ~s z
bookmaker ˈbʊk ˌmeɪk ə §ˈbuːk- ‖ -ᵊr ~s z
book|man ˈbʊkl mən §ˈbuːkl-, -mæn ~men
   mən men
bookmark ˈbʊk mɑːk §ˈbuːk- -mɑːrk ~s s
bookmobile ˈbʊk məʊ ˌbiːl §ˈbuːk- ~s z
bookplate ˈbʊk pleɪt §ˈbuːk- ~s s
bookseller ˈbʊk ˌsel ə §ˈbuːk- ‖ -ᵊr ~s z
book|shelf ˈbʊk lʃelf §ˈbuːk- ~shelves ʃelvz
bookshop ˈbʊk ʃɒp §ˈbuːk- ‖ -ʃɑːp ~s s
bookstall ˈbʊk stɔːl §ˈbuːk- ‖ -stɑːl ~s z
bookstore ˈbʊk stɔː §ˈbuːk- ‖ -stɔːr -stoʊr ~s
   z
bookwork ˈbʊk wɜːk §ˈbuːk- ‖ -wɝːk
bookworm ˈbʊk wɜːm §ˈbuːk- ‖ -wɝːm ~s z
Boole buːl
Boolean, b~ ˈbuːl i‿ən ~s z
boom, Boon buːm **boomed** buːmd **booming**
   ˈbuːm ɪŋ **booms** buːmz
   ˈboom town
boomer, B~ ˈbuːm ə ‖ -ᵊr ~s z
boomerang ˈbuːm ə ræŋ ~ed d ~ing ɪŋ ~s z
boomlet ˈbuːm lət -lɪt ~s s
boomslang ˈbuːm slæŋ ~s z
boon, Boon buːn **boons** buːnz
boondocks ˈbuːn dɒks ‖ -dɑːks
boondoggl|e ˈbuːn ˌdɒg ᵊl ‖ -ˌdɑːg- -ˌdɔːg-
   ~ed d ~es z ~ing ˌɪŋ

Boone buːn
boong bʊŋ **boongs** bʊŋz
boonies ˈbuːn iz
boor bʊə bɔː ‖ bʊᵊr bɔːr **boors** bʊəz bɔːz
   ‖ bʊᵊrz bɔːrz
boorish ˈbʊər ɪʃ ˈbɔːr- ‖ ˈbʊr- ˈbɔːr- ~ly li
   ~ness nəs nɪs
Boosey ˈbuːz i
boost buːst **boosted** ˈbuːst ɪd -əd **boosting**
   ˈbuːst ɪŋ **boosts** buːsts
booster ˈbuːst ə ‖ -ᵊr ~s z
boot, Boot buːt **booted** ˈbuːt ɪd -əd ‖ ˈbuːt̬ əd
   booting ˈbuːt ɪŋ ‖ ˈbuːt̬ ɪŋ **boots, Boots**
   buːts
   ˈboot camp
bootable ˈbuːt əb ᵊl ‖ ˈbuːt̬-
bootblack ˈbuːt blæk ~s s
bootee ˈbuːt iː ₍ˌ₎buː ˈtiː ‖ ₍ˌ₎buː ˈtiː ˈbuːt̬ i ~s z
Bootes, Boötes bəʊ ˈəʊt iːz ‖ boʊ ˈoʊt iːz

BOOTH

■ buːð □ buːθ

BrE 1998

0 20 40 60 80 100%

BrE98 /ð/ by region

South of England, North of England, Wales, Scotland

booth, Booth buːð buːθ ‖ buːθ **booths,**
   Booth's buːðz buːθs ‖ buːθs —BrE 1998 poll
   panel preference: buːð 62%, buːθ 38%
Bootham ˈbuːð əm
Boothby ˈbuːð bi
Boothe buːð buːθ ‖ buːθ
Boothia ˈbuːθ i‿ə
Boothroyd ˈbuːθ rɔɪd ˈbuːð-
bootjack ˈbuːt dʒæk ~s s
bootlac|e ˈbuːt leɪs ~es ɪz əz
Bootle ˈbuːt ᵊl ‖ ˈbuːt̬ ᵊl
bootleg ˈbuːt leg ~ged d ~ging ɪŋ ~s z
bootlegger ˈbuːt leg ə ‖ -ᵊr ~s z
bootless ˈbuːt ləs -lɪs
Boots tdmk buːts
bootstrap ˈbuːt stræp ~ped t ~ping ɪŋ ~s s
boot|y ˈbuːt li ‖ ˈbuːt̬ li ~ies iz
booze buːz **boozed** buːzd **boozes** ˈbuːz ɪz
   -əz **boozing** ˈbuːz ɪŋ
boozer ˈbuːz ə ‖ -ᵊr ~s z
booze-up ˈbuːz ʌp ~s z
booz|y ˈbuːz li ~ier i‿ə ‖ i‿ᵊr ~iest i‿ɪst ‿əst
   ~ily ɪ li əl i ~iness i nəs -nɪs
bop bɒp ‖ bɑːp **bopped** bɒpt ‖ bɑːpt
   bopping ˈbɒp ɪŋ ‖ ˈbɑːp ɪŋ **bops**
   bɒps ‖ bɑːps

bo-peep, B~ ₍ᵢ₎bəʊ 'piːp ‖ ₍ᵢ₎boʊ-
Bophuthatswana ˌbɒp uːt ət 'swaːn ə
ˌ•ʊ tæt'•-; bɒ ˌpuːt ət'•-, bəʊ-
‖ ˌboʊ ˌpuːʈ ət- -ˌpuːt aːt-
bopp... —*see* **bop**
bopper 'bɒp ə ‖ 'baːp ᵊr ~s z
boracic bə 'ræs ɪk bɒ-
borage 'bɒr ɪdʒ 'bʌr- ‖ 'bɔːr- 'baːr-
borate 'bɔːr eɪt -ət, -ɪt ‖ 'boʊr- ~s s
borax 'bɔːr æks ‖ 'boʊr-
borborygmus ˌbɔːb ə 'rɪg məs ‖ ˌbɔːrb-
Bordeaux ₍ᵢ₎bɔː 'dəʊ ◄ ‖ ₍ᵢ₎bɔːr 'doʊ —*Fr*
[bɔʁ do]
Bor'deaux ˌmixture
Bordelaise, b~ ˌbɔːd ə 'leɪz -ᵊl 'eɪz ‖ ˌbɔːrd-
—*Fr* [bɔʁ də lɛːz]
bordello bɔː 'del əʊ ‖ bɔːr 'del oʊ ~s z
border, B~ 'bɔːd ə ‖ 'bɔːrd ᵊr ~ed d
bordering 'bɔːd‿ᵊr ɪŋ ‖ 'bɔːrd‿ᵊr ɪŋ ~s z
'border ˌterrier
borderer 'bɔːd ᵊr ə ‖ 'bɔːrd ᵊr ᵊr ~s z
borderland 'bɔːd ə lænd -ᵊl ænd ‖ 'bɔːrd ᵊr-
~s z
borderline 'bɔːd ə laɪn -ᵊl aɪn ‖ 'bɔːrd ᵊr- ~s z
bore bɔː ‖ bɔːr boʊr **bored** bɔːd ‖ bɔːrd boʊrd
bores bɔːz ‖ bɔːrz boʊrz **boring** 'bɔːr ɪŋ
‖ 'boʊr-
boreal 'bɔːr i‿əl ‖ 'boʊr-
borealis ˌbɔːr i 'eɪl ɪs -'aːl-, §-əs ‖ -'æl əs ˌboʊr-
Boreas 'bɒr i æs 'bɔːr-, əs ‖ 'bɔːr- 'boʊr-
boredom 'bɔː dəm ‖ 'bɔːr- 'boʊr-
Boreham 'bɔːr əm ‖ 'boʊr-
Borehamwood ˌbɔːr əm 'wʊd ‖ ˌboʊr-
borehole 'bɔː həʊl →-hɒʊl ‖ 'bɔːr hoʊl 'boʊr-
~s z
borer 'bɔːr ə ‖ -ᵊr 'boʊr- ~s z
Borg bɔːg ‖ bɔːrg —*Swedish* [bɔrj]
Borges 'bɔːx es 'bɔːg- ‖ 'bɔːr hes —*Sp*
['bor xes]
Borgia 'bɔːdʒ i‿ə 'bɔːʒ-; '•ə ‖ 'bɔːrdʒ- 'bɔːrʒ-
—*It* ['bɔr dʒa]
boric 'bɔːr ɪk 'bɒr- ‖ 'boʊr-
Boris 'bɒr ɪs §-əs ‖ 'bɔːr- —*Russ* [bʌ 'rʲis]
Bork bɔːk ‖ bɔːrk
Borland 'bɔː lənd ‖ 'bɔːr-
Borlotti, b~ bɔː 'lɒt i ‖ bɔːr 'laːʈ i —*It*
[bor 'lɔt ti]
Bormann 'bɔː mæn -mən ‖ 'bɔːr- —*Ger*
['boːʁ man]
born bɔːn ‖ bɔːrn
-born 'bɔːn ◄ ‖ 'bɔːrn ◄ — **free-born**
ˌfriː 'bɔːn ◄ ‖ -'bɔːrn ◄
born-again ˌbɔːn ə 'gen ◄ -'geɪn ‖ ˌbɔːrn-
ˌborn-aˌgain 'Christian
borne bɔːn ‖ bɔːrn boʊrn
Borneo 'bɔːn i əʊ ‖ 'bɔːrn i oʊ
Bornholm 'bɔːn həʊm -hɒlm ‖ 'bɔːrn hoʊm
—*Danish* [bɔʁn 'hɔlˀm]
Borodin 'bɒr ə dɪn ‖ 'bɔːr ə diːn 'baːr- —*Russ*
[bə rʌ 'dʲin]
Borodino ˌbɒr ə 'diːn əʊ ‖ ˌbɔːr ə 'diːn oʊ
ˌbaːr- —*Russ* [bə rə dʲɪ 'nɔ]
boron 'bɔːr ɒn ‖ -aːn 'boʊr-

borough 'bʌr ə ‖ 'bɝː oʊ (*) ~s z
borrow, B~ 'bɒr əʊ ‖ 'bɔːr oʊ 'baːr- ~ed d
~ing ɪŋ ~s z
Borrowdale 'bɒr əʊ deɪᵊl ‖ 'bɔːr oʊ- 'baːr-
borsch bɔːʃ ‖ bɔːrʃ
borscht, borshch bɔːʃt bɔːʃtʃ ‖ bɔːrʃt —*Russ*
[borɕtɕ]
Borsley 'bɔːz li ‖ 'bɔːrz-
borstal, B~ 'bɔːst ᵊl ‖ 'bɔːrst- ~s z
bort bɔːt ‖ bɔːrt
Borth bɔːθ ‖ bɔːrθ
Borthwick 'bɔːθ wɪk ‖ 'bɔːrθ-
Borussia bəʊ 'ruːs i‿ə ‖ boʊ- —*Ger*
[bo 'ʁʊs i‿a]
borzoi 'bɔːz ɔɪ ˌbɔː 'zɔɪ ‖ 'bɔːrz- ~s z
Bosanquet 'bəʊz ᵊn ket →-ᵊŋ-, -kɪt ‖ 'boʊz-
boscage 'bɒsk ɪdʒ ‖ 'baːsk-
Boscastle 'bɒs ˌkaːs ᵊl -ˌkæs- ‖ 'baːs ˌkæs-
Boscawen (i) bɒ 'skaʊ ən bə-, -'skɔː-
‖ baː 'skoʊ ən, (ii) 'bɒsk wɪn -§wən, -waɪn,
-ə wən ‖ 'baːsk- —*The British family name is
usually* (i); *the place in NH is* (ii).
Bosch bɒʃ ‖ baːʃ bɔːʃ —*Dutch* [bɔs]; *Ger* [bɔʃ]
Boscobel 'bɒsk ə bel ‖ 'baːsk-
Bose (i) bəʊz ‖ boʊz, (ii) bəʊs ‖ boʊs
bosh bɒʃ ‖ baːʃ
Bosham 'bɒz əm ‖ 'baːz- —*There is also a
spelling pronunciation* 'bɒʃ- ‖ 'baːʃ-
Bosie 'bəʊz i ‖ 'boʊz i
boskiness 'bɒsk i nəs -nɪs ‖ 'baːsk-
bosky 'bɒsk i ‖ 'baːsk i
Bosley 'bɒz li ‖ 'baːz-
bos'n, bo's'n 'bəʊs ᵊn ‖ 'boʊs-
Bosnia 'bɒz ni‿ə ‖ 'baːz- ~n/s n/z
bosom 'bʊz əm §'buːz- ~s z
bosomy 'bʊz əm i 'buːz-
boson 'bəʊs ɒn 'bəʊz- ‖ 'boʊs aːn 'boʊz-
Bosphorus 'bɒsp ᵊr‿əs 'bɒs fᵊr‿ ‖ 'baːsp-
'baːs fᵊr‿
Bosporus 'bɒsp ᵊr‿əs ‖ 'baːsp-
boss bɒs ‖ bɔːs baːs **bossed** bɒst ‖ bɔːst baːst
bosses 'bɒs ɪz -əz ‖ 'bɔːs əz 'baːs- **bossing**
'bɒs ɪŋ ‖ 'bɔːs ɪŋ 'baːs-
ˌboss 'shot
bossa nova ˌbɒs ə 'nəʊv ə ‖ ˌbaːs ə 'noʊv ə
boss-eyed 'bɒs aɪd ˌ•'•◄ ‖ 'baːs- 'bɔːs-
bossi... —*see* **bossy**
Bossom 'bɒs əm ‖ 'baːs-
bossly 'bɒs li ‖ 'bɔːs li 'baːs- ~ier i‿ə ‖ i‿ᵊr
~iest i‿ɪst i‿əst ~ily ɪ li əl i ~iness i nəs i nɪs
Bostik *tdmk* 'bɒst ɪk ‖ 'baːst-
Bostock 'bɒst ɒk ‖ 'baːst aːk 'baːst-
Boston, b~ 'bɒst ən ‖ 'bɔːst- 'baːst-
ˌBoston 'Tea ˌParty
bosun 'bəʊs ᵊn ‖ 'boʊs- ~s z
Boswell 'bɒz wᵊl -wel ‖ 'baːz-
Bosworth 'bɒz wəθ -wɜːθ ‖ 'baːz wᵊrθ -wɜːθ
ˌBosworth 'Field
bot bɒt ‖ baːt **bots** bɒts baːts **botted**
'bɒt ɪd -əd ‖ 'baːʈ- **botting** 'bɒt ɪŋ ‖ 'baːʈ ɪŋ
botanic bə 'tæn ɪk bɒ- ~al ᵊl ~ally ᵊl‿i
botanis... —*see* **botaniz...**
botanist 'bɒt ᵊn ɪst §-əst ‖ 'baːt ᵊn‿əst ~s s

B

botaniz|e 'bɒt ə naɪz -ᵊn aɪz ‖ 'baːt ᵊn aɪz ~ed
  d ~er/s ə/z ‖ ᵊr/z ~es ɪz əz ~ing ɪŋ
botany 'bɒt ᵊn i ‖ 'baːt ᵊn i
  ˌBotany 'Bay
botch bɒtʃ ‖ baːtʃ botched bɒtʃt ‖ baːtʃt
  botches 'bɒtʃ ɪz -əz ‖ 'baːtʃ əz botching
  'bɒtʃ ɪŋ ‖ 'baːtʃ ɪŋ
botcher 'bɒtʃ ə ‖ 'baːtʃ ᵊr ~s z
botch-up 'bɒtʃ ʌp ‖ 'baːtʃ- ~s s
botch|y 'bɒtʃ li ‖ 'baːtʃ li ~ier i ə ‖ i ᵊr ~iest
  i ɪst i əst ~ily ɪ li əl i
botel ₍ˌ₎bəʊ 'tel ‖ ₍ˌ₎boʊ- ~s z
bot|fly 'bɒt |flaɪ ‖ 'baːt- ~flies flaɪz
both bəʊθ ‖ boʊθ
Botha 'bəʊt ə 'bʊət- ‖ 'boʊt ə —Afrikaans
  ['buə ta]
Botham (i) 'bəʊθ əm ‖ 'boʊθ-, (ii) 'bɒθ
  əm ‖ 'baːθ- —The cricketer Ian B~ is (i).
bother 'bɒð ə ‖ 'baːð ᵊr ~ed d bothering
  'bɒð ᵊr ɪŋ ‖ 'baːð ᵊr ɪŋ ~s z
botheration ˌbɒð ə 'reɪʃ ᵊn ‖ ˌbaːð-
bothersome 'bɒð ə səm ‖ 'baːð ᵊr-
bothi... —see bothy
Bothnia 'bɒθ ni ə ‖ 'baːθ-
Bothwell 'bɒθ wəl 'bɒð-, -wel ‖ 'baːθ- 'baːð-
both|y 'bɒθ li ‖ 'baːθ li ~ies iz
Botley 'bɒt li ‖ 'baːt-
Botolph 'bɒt ɒlf ‖ 'baːt aːlf
botryoid 'bɒtr i ɔɪd ‖ 'baːtr-
botryoidal ˌbɒtr i 'ɔɪd ᵊl ◂ ‖ ˌbaːtr-
botrytis bɒ 'traɪt ɪs bə-, §-əs ‖ boʊ 'traɪt̬ əs
Botswan|a bɒt 'swaːn |ə ‖ baːt- —Tswana
  [bʊ 'tswa: na] ~an/s ən/z
Bott, bott bɒt ‖ baːt
bott... —see bot
Botticelli ˌbɒt ɪ 'tʃel i §-ə- ‖ ˌbaːt̬ ə- —It
  [bot ti 'tʃɛl li]
bottl|e 'bɒt ᵊl ‖ 'baːt̬ ᵊl ~ed d ~es z ~ing ˌɪŋ
  'bottle bank; ˌbottle 'green◂; 'bottle
  ˌparty
bottlebrush 'bɒt ᵊl brʌʃ ‖ 'baːt̬- ~es ɪz əz
bottled-up ˌbɒt ᵊld 'ʌp ◂ ‖ ˌbaːt̬-
bottle-|feed 'bɒt ᵊl |fiːd ‖ 'baːt̬- ~fed fed
  ~feeding fiːd ɪŋ ~feeds fiːdz
bottleful 'bɒt ᵊl fʊl ‖ 'baːt̬- ~s z
bottleneck 'bɒt ᵊl nek ‖ 'baːt̬-
bottlenose 'bɒt ᵊl nəʊz ‖ 'baːt̬ ᵊl noʊz ~d d
bottler 'bɒt ᵊl ə ‖ 'baːt̬ ᵊl ᵊr ~s z
bottle-washer 'bɒt ᵊl ˌwɒʃ ə ‖ 'baːt̬ ᵊl ˌwaːʃ ᵊr
  -ˌwɔːʃ- ~s z
bottom, B~ 'bɒt əm ‖ 'baːt̬- ~ed d ~ing ɪŋ ~s
  z
  ˌbottom 'drawer; ˌbottom 'line
Bottome bə 'təʊm ‖ -'toʊm
bottomless 'bɒt əm ləs -lɪs ‖ 'baːt̬-
Bottomley 'bɒt əm li ‖ 'baːt̬-
bottommost 'bɒt əm məʊst ‖ 'baːt̬ əm moʊst
bottomry 'bɒt əm ri ‖ 'baːt̬-
botulin 'bɒt jʊl ɪn 'bɒtʃ əl-, §-ən ‖ 'baːtʃ əl ən
botulinus ˌbɒt ju 'laɪn əs ˌbɒtʃ u-, ˌbɒtʃ ə-,
  -'liːn- ‖ ˌbaːtʃ ə-
botulism 'bɒt ju ˌlɪz əm 'bɒtʃ u-, 'bɒtʃ ə-
  ‖ 'baːtʃ ə-

bouchee, bouchée 'buːʃ eɪ buː 'ʃeɪ ‖ buː 'ʃeɪ
  —Fr [bu ʃe] ~s z
Boucher (i) 'baʊtʃ ə ‖ -ᵊr, (ii) 'buːʃ eɪ buː 'ʃeɪ
Boucicault 'buːs i kəʊ ‖ -koːlt -kaːlt, -koʊ
boucle, bouclé, bouclee, bouclée
  'buːk leɪ ‖ buː 'kleɪ
Boudicca 'buːd ɪk ə bəʊ 'dɪk ə ‖ buː 'dɪk ə
Boudin 'buːd æ̃ ‖ buː'dæn —Fr [bu dæ̃]
boudoir 'buːd wɑː -wɔː ‖ 'buːd wɑːr 'buːd- ~s
  z
bouffant 'buːf ɒ̃ -ɒŋ, -ɒnt ‖ buː 'faːnt
  'buːf aːnt
Bougainville 'buːg ən vɪl →-ŋ- —in Australian
  English, 'bɔʊg- —Fr [bu gæ̃ vil]
bougainvillaea, bougainvillea ˌbuːg ən 'vɪl i ə
  ˌbɔʊg- ‖ ˌboʊg-, ˌbʊg-, →, •ŋ- ~s z
bough 'branch' baʊ (= bow 'bend') boughed
  baʊd boughs baʊz
Bough name (i) bɒf ‖ bɔːf baːf, (ii) baʊ
  bought bɔːt ‖ baːt
Boughton (i) 'baʊt ᵊn, (ii) 'bɔːt ᵊn ‖ 'baːt-
bougie 'buːʒ iː 'buːdʒ-, buː 'ʒiː —Fr [bu ʒi] ~s
  z
bouillabaisse ˌbuː jə 'bes -'beɪs, '•••—Fr
  [bu ja bɛs]
bouillon 'buː jɒn 'bwiː-, -jɒ̃ ‖ 'bʊl jaːn —Fr
  [bu jɔ̃]
  'bouillon cube
Boulby 'bəʊl bi →'bɒʊl- ‖ 'boʊl-
boulder, B~ 'bəʊld ə →'bɒʊld- ‖ 'boʊld ᵊr (=
  bolder) ~s z
  'boulder clay
boule 'council in ancient Athens' 'buːl eɪ 'baʊl-,
  -iː
boule 'gem' buːl boules 'gems' buːlz
boules game buːl —Fr [bul]
boulevard 'buːl ə vɑːd 'buːl vɑːd, -vɑː
  ‖ 'bʊl ə vaːrd (*) ~s z
boulevardier ₍ˌ₎buːl 'vɑːd i eɪ ˌbuːl əˈ••-
  ‖ ˌbʊl ə vaːr 'dɪᵊr ˌbuːl-, -'djeɪ ~s z
Boulez 'buːl ez -eɪ ‖ buː 'lez —Fr [bu lɛːz]
Boulogne bu 'lɔɪn bə- ‖ -'loʊn -'lɔɪn —Fr
  [bu lɔnj]
Boult bəʊlt →bɒʊlt ‖ boʊlt
Boulter 'bəʊlt ə →'bɒʊlt- ‖ 'boʊlt ᵊr
Boulting 'bəʊlt ɪŋ →'bɒʊlt- ‖ 'boʊlt ɪŋ
Boulton 'bəʊlt ᵊn →'bɒʊlt- ‖ 'boʊlt ᵊn
bounce baʊn̩ts bounced baʊn̩tst bounces
  'baʊn̩ts ɪz -əz bouncing 'baʊn̩ts ɪŋ
bouncer 'baʊn̩ts ə ‖ -ᵊr ~s z
bounc|y 'baʊn̩ts li ~ier i ə ‖ i ᵊr ~iest i ɪst
  i əst ~ily ɪ li əl i ~iness i nəs i nɪs
bound, Bound bounded 'baʊnd ɪd -əd
  bounding 'baʊnd ɪŋ bounds baʊndz
  ˌbound 'form
-bound baʊnd — southbound 'saʊθ baʊnd
boundar|y 'baʊnd ᵊr_i li ~ies iz
  'boundary ˌlayer
bounden 'baʊnd ən
bounder 'baʊnd ə ‖ -ᵊr ~s z
boundless 'baʊnd ləs -lɪs ~ly li ~ness nəs nɪs
bounteous 'baʊnt i_əs ‖ 'baʊnt̬- ~ly li ~ness
  nəs nɪs

bounti... —*see* **bounty**
bountiful ˈbaʊnt ɪf əl -əf-; -ɪ fʊl, -ə- ‖ ˈbaʊnt̬-
~**ly** ͵i ~**ness** nəs nɪs
bount|y, B~ ˈbaʊnt |i ‖ ˈbaʊnt̬ |i ~**ies** iz
ˈbounty ͵hunter

B

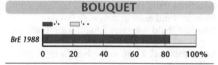

BOUQUET

BrE 1988

| 0 | 20 | 40 | 60 | 80 | 100% |

bouquet bu ˈkeɪ bəʊ-, ˈbuːk eɪ ‖ boʊ- —*BrE
1988 poll panel preference:* •ˈ• 83%, ˈ• • 17%.
Some people say bu- *for the aroma,* bəʊ- ‖ boʊ-
for the flowers. ~**s** z
bouˌquet garˈni gɑː ˈniː ‖ gɑːr-, ͵• •-
bourbon *drink* ˈbɜːb ən ˈbʊəb- ‖ ˈbɝːb- ~**s** z
Bourbon *dynasty* ˈbʊəb ən ˈbɔːb-, -ɒn ‖ ˈbʊrb
ən ˈbɔːrb-, ˈbʊərb- —*Fr* [buʁ bɔ̃] ~**s** z —*in
French pronounced as the sing.*
bourdon, B~ ˈbʊəd ən ˈbɔːd- ‖ ˈbʊrd- ~**s** z
bourgeois, B~ ˈbʊəʒ wɑː ˈbɔːʒ-, ͵•ˈ• ‖ ˈbʊrʒ-
͵•ˈ• —*Fr* [buʁ ʒwa] —*In the noun the plural
(spelt identically with the sing.) is pronounced
either with* z *or, as in French, identically with
the sing.* —*But the type size is* bɜː ˈdʒɔɪs ‖bɝː-
bourgeoisie ͵bʊəʒ wɑː ˈziː ͵bɔːʒ- ‖ ͵bʊrʒ-
—*Fr* [buʁ ʒwa zi]
Bourke bɜːk ‖ bɝːk
bourn, Bourn, bourne bɔːn bʊən ‖ bɔːrn
bʊərn, bʊʊrn **bourns, bournes** bɔːnz bʊənz
‖ bɔːrnz bʊərnz, bʊʊrnz
Bourne *(i)* bɔːn ‖ bɔːrn bʊʊrn, *(ii)*
bʊən ‖ bʊərn, *(iii)* bɜːn ‖ bɝːn
Bournemouth ˈbɔːn məθ →ˈbɔːm- ‖ ˈbɔːrn-
ˈbʊrn-, ˈbʊʊrn-
Bournville ˈbɔːn vɪl ‖ ˈbɔːrn- ˈbʊrn-, ˈbʊʊrn-
Bournvita *tdmk* ͵bɔːn ˈviːt ə ‖ ͵bɔːrn ˈviːt̬ ə
͵bʊrn-, ͵bʊʊrn-
bourree, bourrée ˈbʊr eɪ ˈbʊər- ‖ bʊ ˈreɪ —*Fr*
[bu ʁe] ~**s** z
bourse, B~ bʊəs bɔːs ‖ bʊʊrs **bourses** ˈbʊəs ɪz
ˈbɔːs-, -əz ‖ ˈbʊrs əz
Bourton ˈbɔːt ən ‖ ˈbɔːrt ən ˈbʊʊrt-
boustrophedon ͵buːs trə ˈfiːd ən ͵baʊs-, -ɒn
‖ -ɑːn
bout baʊt **bouts** baʊts
boutique buː ˈtiːk ~**s** s
boutonniere bu ͵tɒn i ˈeə ͵bʊt ɒn ˈjeə, ͵buːt-
‖ ͵buːt ən ˈɪʳr (*) ~**s** z
Boutros ˈbuːtr ɒs ‖ -oʊs
͵Boutros ˈGhali ˈgɑːl i
Bouverie ˈbuːv ər i
bouzouki bu ˈzuːk i bə- —*Gk* [bu ˈzu ci] ~**s** z
Bovary ˈbəʊv ər i ‖ ˈboʊv- —*Fr* [bo va ʁi]
Bovey *family name (i)* ˈbəʊv i ‖ ˈboʊv i *(ii)*
ˈbuːv- *(iii)* ˈbʌv-
Bovey Tracey ͵bʌv i ˈtreɪs i
bovine ˈbəʊv aɪn ‖ ˈboʊv- -iːn ~**s** z
Bovingdon ˈbɒv ɪŋ dən ˈbʌv- ‖ ˈbɑːv-
Bovington ˈbɒv ɪŋ tən ‖ ˈbɑːv-
Bovis ˈbəʊv ɪs §-əs ‖ ˈboʊv-
Bovril *tdmk* ˈbɒv rəl -rɪl ‖ ˈbɑːv-

bovver ˈbɒv ə ‖ ˈbɑːv ər
ˈbovver boots; ˈbovver boy
bow *v* ʻ*bend the head/body forward*ʼ baʊ **bowed**
baʊd **bowing** ˈbaʊ ɪŋ **bows** baʊz
bow *v* ʻ*play a stringed instrument*ʼ; ʻ*curve*ʼ
bəʊ ‖ boʊ **bowed** bəʊd ‖ boʊd **bowing**
ˈbəʊ ɪŋ ‖ ˈboʊ ɪŋ **bows** bəʊz ‖ boʊz
bow *n* (ʻ*act of bending*ʼ; *of boat or ship*) baʊ
bows baʊz
bow *n* (*for arrows,* ʻ*knot*ʼ, *for violin*) bəʊ ‖ boʊ
bows bəʊz ‖ boʊz
͵bow ˈlegs
Bow *place name* bəʊ ‖ boʊ
Bowater ˈbəʊ ͵wɔːt ə ‖ ˈboʊ ͵wɔːt̬ ər -͵wɑːt̬-
Bowden *(i)* ˈbəʊd ən ‖ ˈboʊd ən, *(ii)* ˈbaʊd ən
Bowdler ˈbaʊd lə ‖ -lər
bowdleris... —*see* **bowdleriz...**
bowdlerism ˈbaʊd lər ͵ɪz əm ‖ ˈboʊd-
bowdlerization ͵baʊd lər aɪ ˈzeɪʃ ən -ɪ ʼ•-
‖ -ə ˈzeɪʃ-, ͵boʊd-
bowdleriz|e ˈbaʊd lə raɪz ‖ ˈboʊd- ~**ed** d
~**er/s** ə/z ‖ ər/z ~**es** ɪz əz ~**ing** ɪŋ
Bowdoin, Bowdon ˈbəʊd ən ‖ ˈboʊd-
Bowe bəʊ ‖ boʊ
bowel ˈbaʊ͜əl baʊl ‖ ˈbaʊ͜əl ~**s** z
ˈbowel ͵movement
Bowen ˈbəʊ ɪn §-ən ‖ ˈboʊ-
bower, Bower ˈbaʊ͜ə ‖ ˈbaʊ͜ər ~**ed** d
bowering ˈbaʊ͜ər ɪŋ ‖ ˈbaʊ͜ər ɪŋ ~**s** z
bowerbird ˈbaʊ͜ə bɜːd ‖ ˈbaʊ͜ər bɝːd ~**s** z
Bowers ˈbaʊ͜əz ‖ ˈbaʊ͜ərz
Bowery, b~ ˈbaʊ͜ər i ‖ ˈbaʊ͜ər i
Bowes bəʊz ‖ boʊz
Bowie *name (i)* ˈbaʊ i, *(ii)* ˈbəʊ i ‖ ˈboʊ i, *(iii)*
ˈbuː͵i —*in* ˈbowie knife, *(ii) or (iii)*
Bowker ˈbaʊk ə ‖ -ər
bowl bəʊl →bɒʊl ‖ boʊl **bowled** bəʊld
→bɒʊld ‖ boʊld **bowling** ˈbəʊl ɪŋ →ˈbɒʊl-
‖ ˈboʊl ɪŋ **bowls** bəʊlz →bɒʊlz ‖ boʊlz
Bowland ˈbəʊ lənd ‖ ˈboʊ-
Bowlby ˈbəʊl bi →ˈbɒʊl- ‖ ˈboʊl-
bow-legged ͵bəʊ ˈleg ɪd ◂ -əd, ʼ•͵••;
͵bəʊ ˈlegd, ʼ• • ‖ ˈboʊ ͵leg əd ˈboʊ legd
bowler, B~ ˈbəʊl ə →ˈbɒʊl- ‖ ˈboʊl ər ~**s** z
Bowles bəʊlz →bɒʊlz ‖ boʊlz
bowlful ˈbəʊl fʊl →ˈbɒʊl- ‖ ˈboʊl-
bowline ˈbəʊl ɪn §-ən, §ˈbəʊ laɪn ‖ ˈboʊl-
ˈboʊ laɪn ~**s** z
bowling, B~ ˈbəʊl ɪŋ →ˈbɒʊl- ‖ ˈboʊl ɪŋ
ˈbowling ͵alley; ˈbowling ͵average;
ˈbowling green
bow|man ʻ*archer*ʼ , **B~** ˈbəʊ |mən ‖ ˈboʊ-
~**men** mən men
bow|man ʻ*oarsman*ʼ ˈbaʊ |mən ~**men** mən
men
Bown baʊn
Bowness bəʊ ˈnes ‖ boʊ-
Bowra ˈbaʊ͜ər ə
Bowring ˈbaʊ͜ər ɪŋ
bowsaw ˈbəʊ sɔː ‖ ˈboʊ- -sɑː ~**s** z
bowser, B~ ˈbaʊz ə ‖ -ər ~**s** z
bowshot ˈbəʊ ʃɒt ‖ ˈboʊ ʃɑːt
bowsprit ˈbəʊ sprɪt ‖ ˈboʊ- ~**s** s

bowstring ˈbəʊ strɪŋ ‖ ˈboʊ- ~s z
bow tie ˌbəʊ ˈtaɪ ‖ ˌboʊ-
bow window ˌbəʊ ˈwɪnd əʊ ‖ ˌboʊ ˈwɪnd oʊ
bowwow *interj* ˌbaʊ ˈwaʊ
bowwow *n* ˈbaʊ waʊ ~s z
bowyang ˈbəʊ jæŋ ‖ ˈboʊ- ~s z
bowyer, B~ ˈbəʊ jə ‖ ˈboʊ jər
box, Box bɒks ‖ bɑːks **boxed** bɒkst ‖ bɑːkst
  boxes ˈbɒks ɪz -əz ‖ ˈbɑːks əz **boxing**
  ˈbɒks ɪŋ ‖ ˈbɑːks ɪŋ
  ˌBox and ˈCox; ˈbox ˌcamera; ˌbox end
  ˈwrench; ˈbox ˌjunction; ˈbox ˌnumber
boxcar ˈbɒks kɑː ‖ ˈbɑːks kɑːr ~s z
boxer, Boxer ˈbɒks ə ‖ ˈbɑːks ər ~s z
boxful ˈbɒks fʊl ‖ ˈbɑːks- ~s z
boxing ˈbɒks ɪŋ ‖ ˈbɑːks-
  ˈBoxing Day; ˈboxing gloves; ˈboxing ring
box-offic|e ˈbɒks ˌɒf ɪs §-əs ‖ ˈbɑːks ˌɔːf əs
  -ˌɑːf- ~es ɪz əz
boxroom ˈbɒks ruːm -rʊm ‖ ˈbɑːks- ~s z
boxwood ˈbɒks wʊd ‖ ˈbɑːks-
boxy ˈbɒks i ‖ ˈbɑːks i
boy, Boy bɔɪ **boys** bɔɪz
  ˌboy ˈscout ‖ ˈ• •
-boy bɔɪ — **schoolboy** ˈskuːl bɔɪ
boyar ˈbɔɪ ə -ɑː; ˈbəʊ jɑː, •ˈ• ‖ boʊ ˈjɑːr ˈbɔɪ ər
  ~s z
Boyce bɔɪs
boy|cott, B~ ˈbɔɪ |kɒt -kət ‖ -|kɑːt ~cotted
  kɒt ɪd kət-, -əd ‖ kɑːt əd ~cotting kɒt ɪŋ
  kət- ‖ kɑːt̬ ɪŋ ~cotts kɒts kəts ‖ kɑːts
Boyd bɔɪd
boyfriend ˈbɔɪ frend ~s z
boyhood ˈbɔɪ hʊd
boyish ˈbɔɪ ɪʃ ~ly li ~ness nəs nɪs
Boyle bɔɪəl
Boyne bɔɪn
boyo ˈbɔɪ əʊ ‖ -oʊ ~s z
boysenberr|y ˈbɔɪz ən bər_li →ˈ•ˌm-, -ˌber li
  ‖ -ˌber li ~ies iz
Boyson ˈbɔɪs ən
Boyzone ˈbɔɪ zəʊn ‖ -zoʊn
Boz bɒz ‖ bɑːz —*Dickens apparently pronounced*
  bəʊz
bozo ˈbəʊz əʊ ‖ ˈboʊz oʊ ~s z
BP ˌbiː ˈpiː
BPhil ˌbiː ˈfɪl
BR ˌbiː ˈɑː ‖ -ˈɑːr
bra brɑː **bras** brɑːz
Brabant brə ˈbænt —*Dutch* [ˈbraː bɑnt]; *Fr*
  [bʁa bã]
Brabantio brə ˈbænt i_əʊ -ˈbæntʃ- ‖ -_oʊ
Brabazon ˈbræb əz ən -ə zɒn ‖ -ə zɑːn
Brabham ˈbræb əm
Brabin ˈbreɪb ɪn §-ən
Brabourne ˈbreɪ bɔːn -bən ‖ -bɔːrn -boʊrn
brace breɪs **braced** breɪst **braces** ˈbreɪs ɪz
  -əz **bracing** ˈbreɪs ɪŋ
  ˌbrace and ˈbit
Bracegirdle ˈbreɪs ˌgɜːd əl ‖ -ˌgɜːd-
bracelet ˈbreɪs lət -lɪt ~s s
brachial ˈbreɪk i_əl ˈbræk-
brachiate *adj* ˈbreɪk i eɪt _ət, _ɪt

brachi|ate *v* ˈbreɪk i |eɪt ~ated eɪt ɪd -əd
  ‖ eɪt̬ əd ~ates eɪts ~ating eɪt ɪŋ ‖ eɪt̬ ɪŋ
brachiation ˌbreɪk i ˈeɪʃ ən
brachiopod ˈbreɪk i_ə pɒd ˈbræk- ‖ -pɑːd ~s z
brachiosaur|us ˌbreɪk i_ə ˈsɔːr əs ˌbræk- ~i aɪ
  ~uses əs ɪz əs əz
brachy- *comb. form*
  with stress-neutral suffix ˌbræk i —
  brachyglossal ˌbræk i ˈglɒs əl ◂ ‖ -ˈglɑːs-
  with stress-imposing suffix bræ ˈkɪ+ —
  brachylogy bræ ˈkɪl ədʒ i
brachycephalic ˌbræk i sə ˈfæl ɪk ◂ -sɪ- •-
bracken ˈbræk ən
Brackenbury ˈbræk ən bər_i →ˈ• əm- ‖ -ˌber i
brack|et ˈbræk |ɪt §-ət ‖ -ət ~eted ɪt ɪd §ət-,
  -əd ‖ ət̬ əd ~eting ɪt ɪŋ §ət- ‖ ət̬ ɪŋ ~ets ɪts
  §əts ‖ əts
brackish ˈbræk ɪʃ ~ness nəs nɪs
Brackley ˈbræk li
Brackman ˈbræk mən
Bracknell ˈbræk nəl
bract brækt **bracts** brækts
bracteole ˈbrækt i əʊl →-ɒʊl ‖ -oʊl ~s z
brad, Brad bræd **brads** brædz
bradawl ˈbræd ɔːl ‖ -ɑːl ~s z
Bradbourne ˈbræd bɔːn →ˈbræb- ‖ -bɔːrn
  -boʊrn
Bradbrook ˈbræd brʊk →ˈbræb-
Bradbury ˈbræd bər_i →ˈbræb- ‖ -ˌber i
Braddock ˈbræd ək
Braddon ˈbræd ən
Braden ˈbreɪd ən
Bradenton ˈbreɪd ən tən
Bradfield ˈbræd fiːld
Bradford ˈbræd fəd ‖ -fərd —*in WYks locally*
  also ˈbræt-
Bradlaugh ˈbræd lɔː ‖ -lɑː
Bradley *(i)* ˈbræd li, *(ii)* ˈbreɪd li
Bradman ˈbræd mən →ˈbræb-
Bradshaw ˈbræd ʃɔː ‖ -ʃɑː
Bradwell ˈbræd wəl -wel
Brady ˈbreɪd i
brady- *comb. form* ˌbræd i -ə — **bradycardia**
  ˌbræd i ˈkɑːd i_ə ˌ•ə- ‖ -ˈkɑːrd-
bradykinin ˌbræd ɪ ˈkaɪn ɪn ˌbreɪd-, §-ən
brae breɪ *(= bray)* **braes** breɪz
Braemar ˌbreɪ ˈmɑː ◂ ‖ -ˈmɑːr ◂
Braeuisge breɪ ˈwɪsk i
brag bræg **bragged** brægd **bragging/ly**
  ˈbræg ɪŋ /li **brags** brægz
Bragg bræg
braggadocio ˌbræg ə ˈdəʊtʃ i_əʊ -ˈdəʊʃ-
  ‖ -ˈdoʊʃ i_oʊ -ˈdoʊs- ~s z
braggart ˈbræg ət -ɑːt ‖ -ərt ~s s
bragg... —*see* **brag**
Brahe ˈbrɑː hə -ə, -hi —*Danish* [ˈbʁaː ə]
Brahma ˈbrɑːm ə —*but as the name of a breed of*
  fowl or cattle, also ˈbreɪm ə
Brahmanic brɑː ˈmæn ɪk
Brahmaputra ˌbrɑːm ə ˈpuːtr ə —*Hindi*
  [brəhm pʊt̪r]
brahmin, B~ ˈbrɑːm ɪn §-ən ~s z
Brahminism ˈbrɑːm ɪn ˌɪz əm §-ən-

B

Brahms brɑːmz —*Ger* [bʁɑːms]
Brahui brɑː ˈhuːi̯i
braid, Braid breɪd braided ˈbreɪd ɪd -əd
braiding ˈbreɪd ɪŋ braids breɪdz
braider ˈbreɪd ə ‖ -ᵊr ~s z
brail breɪᵊl brailed breɪᵊld brailing ˈbreɪᵊl ɪŋ
brails breɪᵊlz
braille, B~ breɪᵊl —*Fr* [bʁaj]
brailler ˈbreɪᵊl ə ‖ -ᵊr ~s z
brain, Brain breɪn brained breɪnd braining
ˈbreɪn ɪŋ brains breɪnz
ˈbrain ˌdamage; ˈbrain drain; ˈbrain(s)
trust
brain|child ˈbreɪn |tʃaɪᵊld ~children tʃɪldr ən
Braine breɪn
braini... —*see* brainy
brainless ˈbreɪn ləs -lɪs ~ness nəs nɪs
brainpan ˈbreɪn pæn →ˈbreɪm- ~s z
brainstem ˈbreɪn stem ~s z
brainstorm ˈbreɪn stɔːm ‖ -stɔːrm ~ed d
~ing ɪŋ ~s z
brainteaser ˈbreɪn ˌtiːz ə ‖ -ᵊr ~s z
Braintree ˈbreɪn triː ˈbreɪntr i
brainwash ˈbreɪn wɒʃ ‖ -wɔːʃ -wɑːʃ ~ed t
~es ɪz əz ~ing/s ɪŋ/z
brainwave ˈbreɪn weɪv ~s z
brain|y ˈbreɪn |i ~ier i_ə ‖ i_ᵊr ~iest i_ɪst i_əst
~ily ɪ li əl i ~iness i nəs i nɪs
braise breɪz (= *brays*) braised breɪzd braises
ˈbreɪz ɪz -əz braising ˈbreɪz ɪŋ
Braithwaite ˈbreɪθ weɪt
brake, Brake breɪk (= *break*) braked breɪkt
brakes breɪks braking ˈbreɪk ɪŋ
ˈbrake ˌfluid; ˈbrake shoe
brake|man ˈbreɪk |mən ~men mən men
braless ˈbrɑː ləs -lɪs
Bram bræm
Bramah (*i*) ˈbrɑːm ə, (*ii*) ˈbræm ə
Bramall ˈbræm ɔːl ‖ -ɑːl
Brambell ˈbræm bᵊl
bramble, B~ ˈbræm bᵊl ~s z
brambling ˈbræm blɪŋ ~s z
Bramhope ˈbræm həʊp ‖ -hoʊp
Bramley ˈbræm li ~s z
Brammer ˈbræm ə ‖ -ᵊr
Brampton ˈbræmpt ən
Bramwell ˈbræm wəl -wel
bran bræn
ˈbran tub
Branagh ˈbræn ə
branch brɑːntʃ §bræntʃ ‖ bræntʃ branched
brɑːntʃt §bræntʃt ‖ bræntʃt branches
ˈbrɑːntʃ ɪz §ˈbræntʃ-, -əz ‖ ˈbræntʃ əz
branching ˈbrɑːntʃ ɪŋ §ˈbræntʃ- ‖ ˈbræntʃ ɪŋ
-branch bræŋk — lamellibranch
lə ˈmel ɪ bræŋk §-ə-
branchi|a ˈbræŋk i_|ə ~ae iː ~al əl
brand, Brand brænd branded ˈbrænd ɪd -əd
branding ˈbrænd ɪŋ brands, Brand's
brændz
ˈbrand name
Brandeis ˈbrænd aɪs

Brandenburg ˈbrænd ən bɜːg →-əm- ‖ -bɜːg
—*Ger* [ˈbʁan dᵊn bʊʁk] ~s z
ˌBrandenburg Conˈcerto; ˌBrandenburg
ˈGate
Brander ˈbrænd ə ‖ -ᵊr
Brandi ˈbrænd i
brandi... —*see* brandy
brandish ˈbrænd ɪʃ ~ed t ~er/s ə/z ‖ ᵊr/z ~es
ɪz əz ~ing ɪŋ
brandling ˈbrænd lɪŋ ~s z
brand-new ˌbrænd ˈnjuː ◄ ‖ -ˈnuː ◄ -ˈnjuː ◄
ˌbrand-new ˈclothes
Brando ˈbrænd əʊ ‖ -oʊ
Brandon ˈbrænd ən
Brandreth ˈbrænd rɪθ -əθ, -eθ
Brandt brænt —*Ger* [bʁant]
brand|y, B~ ˈbrænd |i ~ied id ~ies iz ~ying
i ɪŋ
Brangwyn ˈbræŋ gwɪn
Braniff ˈbræn ɪf §-əf
Branigan, Brannigan ˈbræn ɪg ən §-əg-
branks bræŋks
Branksome ˈbræŋk səm
Branson ˈbrænts ᵊn
Branston ˈbrænᵗst ən
brant, Brant brænt brants bræn/s
Branwell ˈbræn wəl -wel
Braque brɑːk bræk —*Fr* [bʁak]
Brasenose ˈbreɪz nəʊz ‖ -noʊz
brash bræʃ brasher ˈbræʃ ə ‖ -ᵊr brashest
ˈbræʃ ɪst -əst
Brasher *family name* ˈbreɪʃ ə ‖ -ᵊr
brash|ly ˈbræʃ |li ~ness nəs nɪs
Brasilia brə ˈzɪl i_ə —*Port* Brasília [bʁɐ ˈzi ljɐ]
brass, Brass brɑːs §bræs ‖ bræs brassed
brɑːst §bræst ‖ bræst brasses ˈbrɑːs ɪz
§ˈbræs-, -əz ‖ ˈbræs əz
ˌbrass ˈband; ˌbrassed ˈoff; ˌbrass ˈhat;
ˌbrass ˈknuckles; ˌbrass ˈtacks
brassard ˈbræs ɑːd ‖ -ɑːrd brə ˈsɑːrd ~s z
brassbound, B~ ˈbrɑːs baʊnd §ˈbræs-
brasserie ˈbræs ər i ˌbræs ə ˈriː ‖ ˌbræs ə ˈriː
~s z
brassica ˈbræs ɪk ə ~s z
brassie ˈbrɑːs i ˈbræs- ‖ ˈbræs i ~s z
brassi- —*see* brassy
brassie ˈbrɑːs i §ˈbræs- ‖ ˈbræs i ~s z
brassiere ˈbræz i_ə ˈbræs-, -i eə ‖ brə ˈzɪᵊr (*)
~s z
Brassington ˈbræs ɪŋ tən
brass-monkey ˌbrɑːs ˈmʌŋk i ◄ §ˌbræs-
‖ ˌbræs-
ˌbrass-ˈmonkey ˌweather
Brasso *tdmk* ˈbrɑːs əʊ §ˈbræs- ‖ ˈbræs oʊ
brass|y ˈbrɑːs |i §ˈbræs- ‖ ˈbræs |i ~ier
i_ə ‖ i_ᵊr ~iest i_ɪst i_əst ~ily ɪ li əl i ~iness
i nəs i nɪs
Brasted ˈbreɪst ed -ɪd, -əd
brat bræt brats bræts
Bratby ˈbræt bi
Bratislava ˌbræt ɪ ˈslɑːv ə -ə-, ˈ•••• ‖ ˌbrɑːt̬-
ˌbræt̬- —*Slovak* [ˈbra ti̯ sla va]
brattish ˈbræt ɪʃ ‖ ˈbræt̬-

B

Brattleboro 'bræt əl bər_ə ‖ 'bræʈ əl ˌbɜ: oʊ
Bratton 'bræt ən
bratwurst 'bræt wɜːst 'braːt- ‖ 'braːt wɜ˞ːst
—Ger B~ ['bʀaːt vʊʀst]
Braun (i) brɔːn ‖ braːn, (ii) braʊn —As a tdmk,
(i)
Braunton 'brɔːnt ən ‖ 'brɔːnt ən 'braːnt-
bravado brə 'vaːd əʊ ‖ -oʊ —es, ~s z
brave breɪv braved breɪvd braver
'breɪv ə ‖ -ər braves breɪvz bravest
'breɪv ɪst -əst braving 'breɪv ɪŋ
brave|ly 'breɪv |li ~ness nəs nɪs
braver|y 'breɪv ər_|i ~ies iz
Bravington 'bræv ɪŋ tən
bravo name for letter B, b 'braːv əʊ ‖ -oʊ
bravo interj; n 'shout of approval' ⑴braː 'vəʊ
'braːv əʊ ‖ 'braːv oʊ braː 'voʊ ~s z
bravo n 'assassin' 'braːv əʊ ‖ -oʊ ~es, ~s z
Bravo 'braːv əʊ ‖ -oʊ
bravura brə 'vjʊər ə -'vʊər- ‖ -'vjʊr- -'vʊr-
braw brɔː ‖ braː
Brawdy 'brɔːd i ‖ 'braːd-
brawl brɔːl ‖ braːl brawled brɔːld ‖ braːld
brawling/ly 'brɔːl ɪŋ /li ‖ 'braːl- brawls
brɔːlz ‖ braːlz
brawler 'brɔːl ə ‖ -ər 'braːl- ~s z
brawn brɔːn ‖ braːn
brawn|y 'brɔːn |i ‖ 'braːn- ~ier i_ə ‖ i_ər ~iest
i_ɪst i_əst ~ily ɪ li əl i ~iness i nəs i nɪs
Braxton 'brækst ən
bray, Bray breɪ brayed breɪd (= braid)
braying 'breɪ ɪŋ brays breɪz
braze breɪz (= braise, brays) brazed breɪzd
brazes 'breɪz ɪz -əz brazing 'breɪz ɪŋ
brazen 'breɪz ən ~ed d ~ing ɪŋ ~ly li ~ness
nəs nɪs ~s z
brazer 'breɪz ə ‖ -ər ~s z
brazier, B~ 'breɪz i_ə 'breɪʒ ə, 'breɪʒ i_ə
‖ 'breɪʒ ər ~s z
Brazil country, b~ 'nut', 'wood', 'dye' brə 'zɪl
Bra'zil nut
Brazil family name (i) 'bræz əl -ɪl, (ii) brə 'zɪl
Brazilian brə 'zɪl i_ən ~s z
Brazzaville 'bræz ə vɪl 'braːz- —Fr
[bʀa za vil]
Brčko 'bɜːtʃ kəʊ ‖ 'bɜ˞ːtʃ koʊ —Serbian
['bᵊrtʃ kɔː]
breach, B~ briːtʃ (= breech) breached briːtʃt
breaches 'briːtʃ ɪz -əz breaching 'briːtʃ ɪŋ
bread bred (= bred) breaded 'bred ɪd -əd
breading 'bred ɪŋ breads bredz
'bread bin; 'bread box; ˌbread 'pudding;
ˌbread 'sauce
Breadalbane brə 'dɔːlb ɪn brɪ-, -'dælb-,
-ən ‖ -'daːlb-
bread-and-butter ˌbred ən 'bʌt ə ◄ →-əm-,
→ˌbreb m- ‖ -'bʌʈ ər ◄
ˌbread-and'butter ˌissues
breadbasket 'bred ˌbaːsk ɪt →'breb-, §-ˌbæsk-,
§-ət ‖ -ˌbæsk ət ~s s
breadboard 'bred bɔːd →'breb- ‖ -bɔːrd
-boʊrd ~s z
breadcrumb 'bred krʌm →'breg- ~s z
breadfruit 'bred fruːt ~s s
bread|knife 'bred| naɪf ~knives naɪvz
breadline 'bred laɪn ~s z
breadnut 'bred nʌt ~s s
breadth bredθ bretθ, §breθ breadths bredθs
bretθs, §breθs
breadth|ways 'bredθ |weɪz 'bretθ-, §'breθ-
~wise waɪz
breadwinner 'bred ˌwɪn ə ‖ -ər ~s z
break breɪk (= brake) breaking 'breɪk ɪŋ
breaks breɪks broke brəʊk ‖ broʊk broken
'brəʊk ən ‖ 'broʊk ən
breakable 'breɪk əb əl ~s z
breakag|e 'breɪk ɪdʒ ~es ɪz əz
breakaway 'breɪk ə ˌweɪ ~s z
breakdown 'breɪk daʊn ~s z
breaker 'breɪk ə ‖ -ər ~s z
break-even, breakeven ˌbreɪk 'iːv ən '•• , ••
breakfast 'brek fəst §'breɪk- ~ed ɪd əd ~er/s
ə/z ‖ ər/z ~ing ɪŋ ~s s
breakfront 'breɪk frʌnt
break-in 'breɪk ɪn ~s z
breaking 'breɪk ɪŋ
ˌbreaking and 'entering; 'breaking point
breakneck 'breɪk nek
breakout 'breɪk aʊt ~s s
breakpoint 'breɪk pɔɪnt ~s s
Breakspear 'breɪk spɪə ‖ -spɪr
breakthrough 'breɪk θruː ~s z
breakup 'breɪk ʌp ~s s
breakwater 'breɪk ˌwɔːt ə ‖ -ˌwɔːʈ ər -ˌwaːʈ- ~s
z
bream, Bream briːm
Brean briːn
Brearley 'brɪə li ‖ 'brɪr-
breast brest breasted 'brest ɪd -əd breasting
'brest ɪŋ breasts brests
breastbone 'brest bəʊn ‖ -boʊn ~s z
breast-|feed 'brest |fiːd ~fed fed ~feeding
fiːd ɪŋ ~feeds fiːdz
breastplate 'brest pleɪt ~s s
breaststroke 'brest strəʊk ‖ -stroʊk
breastwork 'brest wɜːk ‖ -wɜ˞ːk ~s s
breath breθ breaths breθs (!)
'breath test
breathalys|e, breathalyz|e 'breθ ə laɪz
→-əl aɪz ~ed d ~er/s tdmk ə/z ‖ ər/z ~es ɪz
əz ~ing ɪŋ
breathe briːð breathed briːðd (!) breathes
briːðz (!) breathing 'briːð ɪŋ
breathed adj 'having breath; voiceless' breθt
briːðd
breathed past and pp of breathe briːðd
breather 'briːð ə ‖ -ər ~s z
breathi... —see breathy
breathing 'briːð ɪŋ
'breathing space
breathless 'breθ ləs -lɪs ~ly li ~ness nəs nɪs
breathtaking 'breθ ˌteɪk ɪŋ ~ly li
breath|y 'breθ |i ~ier i_ə ‖ i_ər ~iest i_ɪst i_əst
~ily ɪ li əl i ~iness i nəs i nɪs
breathy-voiced ˌbreθ i 'vɔɪst ◄
Brebner 'breb nə ‖ -nᵊr

breccia 'bretʃ i‿ə 'bretʃ ə
brecciated 'bretʃ i eɪt ɪd -əd ‖ -eɪţ-
Brechin 'briːk ɪn 'briːx-, §-ən
Brecht brext brekt —*Ger* [bʁɛçt]
Brechtian 'brext i‿ən 'brekt- ~s z
Breckenridge 'brek ən rɪdʒ →-ŋ-
Breckland 'brek lənd -lænd
Brecknock 'brek nɒk -nək ‖ -nɑːk -nək
Brecon 'brek ən
bred bred (= *bread*)
Breda 'briːd ə 'breɪd ə, breɪ 'dɑː —*Dutch*
[bʁe 'daː, bʁə-]
Bredon 'briːd ən
breech briːtʃ **breeches** *pl of* **breech** 'briːtʃ ɪz
-əz
'**breeches buoy**
breeches '*trousers*' 'brɪtʃ ɪz 'briːtʃ-, -əz
breeching 'brɪtʃ ɪŋ 'briːtʃ-
breech-load|er/s 'briːtʃ ‚ləʊd lə/z ‚•'••
‖ -‚loʊd lər/z ~**ing** ɪŋ
breed briːd **bred** bred **breeding** 'briːd ɪŋ
breeds briːdz
breeder 'briːd ə ‖ -ər ~s z
breeding-ground 'briːd ɪŋ graʊnd ~s z
breeks briːks
Breen briːn
breeze, B~ briːz **breezed** briːzd **breezes**
'briːz ɪz -əz **breezing** 'briːz ɪŋ
breezeblock 'briːz blɒk ‖ -blɑːk ~s s
breezeway 'briːz weɪ ~s z
breez|y 'briːz li ~**ier** i‿ə ‖ i‿ər ~**iest** i‿ɪst i‿əst
~**ily** ɪ li əl i ~**iness** i nəs i nɪs
Breitling 'braɪt lɪŋ
Brekkies *tdmk* 'brek ɪz
Bremen 'breɪm ən 'brem- —*Ger* ['bʁeː mən]
—*but the places in the USA are* 'briːm ən
Bremerhaven 'breɪm ə hɑːv ən 'brem- ‖ '•‚ər-
—*Ger* [bʁeːm ɐ 'haːf ən]
Bremner 'brem nə ‖ -nər
Bren bren
'**Bren gun**
Brend brend
Brenda 'brend ə
Brendan 'brend ən
Brennan 'bren ən
Brenner 'bren ə ‖ -ər —*Ger* ['bʁɛn ɐ]
‚**Brenner ' Pass**
Brent, brent brent
Brentford 'brent fəd ‖ -fərd
Brenton 'brent ən
Brentwood 'brent wʊd
bre'r, br'er breə brɜː ‖ brɜː brer
Brereton (i) 'brɪət ən ‖ 'brɪrt ən, (ii)
'breət ən ‖ 'brert ən
Brest brest —*Fr* [bʁɛst]
Brest-Litovsk ‚brest lɪ 'tɒfsk -'tɒvsk ‖ -'tɔːfsk
-'tɑːfsk, -'toʊfsk —*Russ* [‚brʲest lʲɪ 'tofsk]
brethren 'breð rən -rɪn
Breton 'bret ɒn -ən, -ɔ̃ ‖ -ən —*Fr* [bʁə tɔ̃] ~s z
Brett bret
Bretton 'bret ən
Breughel 'brɔɪg əl 'brɜːg- ‖ 'bruːg- —*Dutch*
['brøː xəl] ~s, ~'s z

breve briːv ‖ brev **breves** briːvz ‖ brevz
brevet 'brev ɪt §-ət ~s s
breviar|y 'brev i‿ər i ‖ 'briːv-, '•‚ər li ‖ -i er li
~**ies** iz
brevier brə 'vɪə brɪ- ‖ -'vɪər
brevity 'brev ət i -ɪt- ‖ -əţ-
brew bruː **brewed** bruːd (= *brood*) **brewing**
'bruː‿ɪŋ **brews** bruːz (= *bruise*)
brewer, B~ 'bruː‿ə ‖ -‿ər ~s, ~'s z
brewer|y 'bruː‚ər i ~**ies** iz
Brewster 'bruːst ə ‖ -ər
brew-up 'bruː ʌp
Brezhnev 'breʒ nef —*Russ* ['brʲeʒ nʲɪf]
Brian 'braɪ‿ən —*occasionally also* 'briː‿ən
‚**Brian Bo'ru** bə 'ruː
briar 'braɪ‿ə ‖ 'braɪ‿ər ~s z
briarroot 'braɪ‿ə ruːt ‖ 'braɪ‿ər- -rʊt
bribable 'braɪb əb əl
bribe braɪb **bribed** braɪbd **bribes** braɪbz
bribing 'braɪb ɪŋ
briber 'braɪb ə ‖ -ər ~s z
briber|y 'braɪb ər i ~**ies** iz
bric-a-brac, bric-à-brac 'brɪk ə bræk
Brice braɪs
bricht brɪxt —*The StdEng equivalent of this*
Scots dialect word is **bright** braɪt
brick brɪk **bricked** brɪkt **bricking** 'brɪk ɪŋ
bricks brɪks
brickbat 'brɪk bæt ~s s
brickfield 'brɪk fiːəld ~s z
brickie 'brɪk i ~s z
bricklay|er/s 'brɪk ‚leɪ lə/z ‖ -lər/z ~**ing** ɪŋ
brick-red ‚brɪk 'red ◄
brickwork 'brɪk wɜːk ‖ -wɝːk ~s s
bridal 'braɪd əl (= *bridle*)
bride, Bride braɪd **brides** braɪdz
'**bride price**
bridegroom 'braɪd gruːm →'braɪg-, -grʊm ~s
z
Brideshead 'braɪdz hed
bridesmaid 'braɪdz meɪd ~s z
bride-to-be ‚braɪd tə 'biː -tu- **brides-to-be**
‚braɪdz tə 'biː -tu-
Bridewell, b~ 'braɪd wəl -wel
bridge, Bridge brɪdʒ **bridged** brɪdʒd
bridges 'brɪdʒ ɪz -əz **bridging** 'brɪdʒ ɪŋ
'**bridge ‚player**
bridgeable 'brɪdʒ əb əl
bridgehead 'brɪdʒ hed ~s z
Bridgeman 'brɪdʒ mən
Bridgend ‚brɪdʒ 'end '•• —*The town in Mid*
Glam is locally brɪ 'dʒend
Bridgeport 'brɪdʒ pɔːt ‖ -pɔːrt -poʊrt
Bridger 'brɪdʒ ə ‖ -ər
Bridges 'brɪdʒ ɪz -əz
Bridget 'brɪdʒ ɪt -ət
Bridgetown 'brɪdʒ taʊn —*but in Barbados*
locally §-tʌn
Bridgewater 'brɪdʒ ‚wɔːt ə ‖ -‚wɔːţ ər -‚wɑːţ-
bridgework 'brɪdʒ wɜːk ‖ -wɝːk ~s s
bridging 'brɪdʒ ɪŋ
'**bridging loan**
Bridgman 'brɪdʒ mən

Breaking

When a vowel is followed in the same syllable by r or l, a glide sound ə may develop before the liquid. The vowel then becomes a diphthong, and is said to undergo **breaking**.

Two types of breaking are particularly frequent in English, and are shown explicitly in this dictionary:

- **feel** fiːᵊl Besides the traditional pronunciation fiːl, the form fiːəl (or fɪəl) is often to be heard, especially in BrE. This happens when l follows iː, eɪ, aɪ, ɔɪ, and is termed **pre-l breaking**. (Some speakers of GenAm have pre-l breaking after uː, oʊ, aʊ, thus **rule** ruːᵊl. This is **not** shown in LPD.)
- **fear** fɪə ‖ fɪᵊr In AmE, the usual pronunciation involves the phoneme ɪ. (Unlike BrE, AmE has no phoneme ɪə.) However, this word may actually sound more like fɪər or fɪər, especially if said slowly. This is due to **pre-r breaking**, which arises in GenAm when r follows ɪ, e, æ.

Both kinds of breaking are particularly common in the last syllable of a stressed word (including words of one syllable).

B

Bridgnorth 'brɪdʒ nɔːθ ‖ -nɔːrθ
Bridgwater 'brɪdʒ ˌwɔːt ə ‖ -ˌwɔːt̬ ər -ˌwɑːt̬-
Bridie, b~ 'braɪd i ~s, ~'s z
bridl|e, B~ 'braɪd ᵊl ~ed d ~es z ~ing ˌɪŋ
  'bridle path
Bridlington 'brɪd lɪŋ tən
bridoon brɪ 'duːn ~s z
Bridport 'brɪd pɔːt →'brɪb- ‖ -pɔːrt -poʊrt
Brie, brie briː —*Fr* [bʁi]
brief briːf **briefed** briːft **briefer** 'briːf ə ‖ -ər
  briefest 'briːf ɪst -əst **briefing** 'briːf ɪŋ
  briefs briːfs
briefcas|e 'briːf keɪs ~es ɪz əz
brief|ly 'briːf lli ~ness nəs nɪs
brier 'braɪ‿ə ‖ 'braɪ‿ər ~s z
Brierley, Brierly (i) 'braɪ‿ə li ‖ 'braɪ‿ər-, (ii) 'brɪə li ‖ 'brɪr-
Briers 'braɪ‿əz ‖ 'braɪ‿ərz
brig brɪg **brigs** brɪgz
brigade brɪ 'geɪd brə- ~s z
brigadier ˌbrɪg ə 'dɪə ◂ ‖ -'dɪᵊr ◂ ~s z
brigadier-general
  ˌbrɪg ə ˌdɪə 'dʒen ᵊr‿əl ‖ -ˌdɪr- ~s z
Brigadoon ˌbrɪg ə 'duːn
brigalow 'brɪg ə ləʊ ‖ -loʊ
brigand 'brɪg ənd ~s z
brigandage 'brɪg ənd ɪdʒ
brigantine 'brɪg ən tiːn -taɪn ~s z
Brigg brɪg
Briggs brɪgz
Brigham 'brɪg əm
Brighouse 'brɪg haʊs
bright, Bright braɪt **brighter**
  'braɪt ə ‖ 'braɪt̬ ər **brightest** 'braɪt ɪst -əst
  ‖ 'braɪt̬ əst **brights** braɪts
  ˌbright 'lights; 'Bright's di‚sease; ˌbright
  'spark
brighten 'braɪt ᵊn ~ed d ~ing ˌɪŋ ~s z

bright-eyed ˌbraɪt 'aɪd ◂ ‖ ˌbraɪt̬-
Brightlingsea 'braɪt lɪŋ siː
bright|ly 'braɪt lli ~ness nəs nɪs
Brighton 'braɪt ᵊn (= *brighten*)
brightwork 'braɪt wɜːk ‖ -wɜ˞ːk
Brigid 'brɪdʒ ɪd §-əd
Briginshaw 'brɪg ɪn ʃɔː ‖ -ʃɑː
Brigitte brɪ 'ʒiːt 'brɪʒ ɪt —*Fr* [bʁi ʒit]
brill, Brill brɪl **brills** brɪlz
brillianc|e 'brɪl jənts 'brɪl i‿ənts ~y i
brilliant 'brɪl jənt 'brɪl i‿ənt ~ly li ~ness nəs
  nɪs
brilliantine 'brɪl jən tiːn ˌ•••ᵊ ~d d
Brillo *tdmk* 'brɪl əʊ ‖ -oʊ
  'Brillo pad
brim brɪm **brimmed** brɪmd **brimming**
  'brɪm ɪŋ **brims** brɪmz
Brimble 'brɪm bᵊl
brimful, brimfull ˌbrɪm 'fʊl ◂ '••
-brimmed 'brɪmd — **wide-brimmed**
  ˌwaɪd 'brɪmd ◂
brimstone 'brɪm stəʊn -stən ‖-stoʊn
Brindisi 'brɪnd ɪz i -əz- —*It* ['brin di zi]
brindle 'brɪnd ᵊl ~d d
Brindley 'brɪnd li
brine braɪn **brined** braɪnd **brines** braɪnz
  brining 'braɪn ɪŋ
Brinell brɪ 'nel brə-
  Bri'nell ‚number
bring brɪŋ **bringing** 'brɪŋ ɪŋ **brings** brɪŋz
  brought brɔːt △bɒːt ‖ brɑːt
  ˌbring-and-'buy sale
bringer 'brɪŋ ə ‖ -ər ~s z
brini... —*see* **briny**
brinjal 'brɪndʒ əl
brink, Brink brɪŋk **brinks** brɪŋks
brinkmanship 'brɪŋk mən ʃɪp
brinksmanship 'brɪŋks mən ʃɪp

B

Brinks-Mat *tdmk* ˌbrɪŋks 'mæt
Brinley 'brɪn li
Brinton 'brɪnt ən ‖ -ᵊn
brin|y 'braɪn li ~ier i_ə ‖ i_ᵊr ~iest i_ɪst i_əst
~iness i nəs i nɪs
Bri-Nylon *tdmk* ˌbraɪ 'naɪl ɒn ‖ -ɑːn
brio, Brio 'briː əʊ ‖ -oʊ
brioch|e bri 'ɒʃ -'əʊʃ, 'ˌ• • ‖ -'oʊʃ —*Fr* [bʁi ɔʃ]
~es ɪz əz
briolette ˌbriː əʊ 'let ‖ -ə- ~s s
briony, B~ 'braɪ_ən i
briquet, briquette brɪ 'ket ~s s
Brisbane 'brɪz bən -beɪn
Brisco, Briscoe 'brɪsk əʊ ‖ -oʊ
Briseis braɪ 'siː ɪs §-əs
brisk brɪsk brisker 'brɪsk ə ‖ -ᵊr briskest
'brɪsk ɪst -əst
brisket 'brɪsk ɪt §-ət
brisk|ly 'brɪsk |li ~ness nəs nɪs
brisling 'brɪz lɪŋ 'brɪs- ~s z
bristl|e 'brɪs ᵊl ~ed d ~es z ~ing _ɪŋ
bristlecone 'brɪs ᵊl kəʊn ‖ -koʊn
bristletail 'brɪs ᵊl teɪᵊl ~s z
bristl|y 'brɪs ᵊl_i ~iness i nəs -nɪs
Bristol 'brɪst ᵊl
ˌBristol 'Channel; 'Bristol ˌfashion
Bristolian brɪs 'təʊl i_ən ‖ -'toʊl- ~s z
Bristow, Bristowe 'brɪst əʊ ‖ -oʊ
Brit, brit brɪt Brits, brits brɪts
Britain 'brɪt ᵊn ~'s z
Britannia brɪ 'tæn jə brə-
Britannic brɪ 'tæn ɪk brə-
Britax *tdmk* 'brɪt æks
britches 'brɪtʃ ɪz -əz
Briticism 'brɪt ɪ ˌsɪz əm -ə- ‖ 'brɪt̬- ~s z
British 'brɪt ɪʃ ‖ 'brɪt̬ ɪʃ
ˌBritish 'English; ˌBritish 'Isles; ˌBritish
'Summer Time
Britisher 'brɪt ɪʃ ə ‖ 'brɪt̬ ɪʃ ᵊr ~s z
Britishness 'brɪt ɪʃ nəs -nɪs ‖ 'brɪt̬-
Britoil *tdmk* 'brɪt ɔɪᵊl
Briton 'brɪt ᵊn *(= Britain)* ~s z
Britt brɪt
Brittain, Brittan 'brɪt ᵊn
Brittany 'brɪt ən i ‖ -ᵊn-
Britten 'brɪt ᵊn
brittl|e 'brɪt ᵊl ‖ 'brɪt̬ ᵊl ~er ə ‖ ᵊr ~eness nəs
nɪs ~est ɪst əst
brittle-star 'brɪt ᵊl stɑː ‖ 'brɪt̬ ᵊl stɑːr ~s z
Britvic *tdmk* 'brɪt vɪk
Brix brɪks
Brixham 'brɪks əm
Brixton 'brɪkst ən
Brize Norton ˌbraɪz 'nɔːt ᵊn ‖ -'nɔːrt-
Brno 'bɜːn əʊ brə 'nəʊ ‖ 'bɜ˞ːn oʊ —*Czech*
['bᵊr no]
Bro., bro. —*see* Brother
bro brəʊ ‖ broʊ
broach brəʊtʃ ‖ broʊtʃ broached
brəʊtʃt ‖ broʊtʃt broaches 'brəʊtʃ ɪz -əz
‖ 'broʊtʃ əz broaching
'brəʊtʃ ɪŋ ‖ 'broʊtʃ ɪŋ
Broackes brəʊks ‖ broʊks

broad, Broad brɔːd ‖ brɑːd *(!)* broader
'brɔːd ə ‖ -ᵊr 'brɑːd- broadest 'brɔːd ɪst -əst
‖ 'brɑːd- broads, Broads brɔːdz ‖ brɑːdz
ˌbroad 'beans; 'broad jump
B-road 'biː rəʊd ‖ -roʊd
broadband 'brɔːd bænd →'brɔːb- ‖ 'brɑːd-
Broadbent 'brɔːd bent →'brɔːb- ‖ 'brɑːd-
Broadbridge 'brɔːd brɪdʒ →'brɔːb- ‖ 'brɑːd-
broadcast 'brɔːd kɑːst →'brɔːg-, §-kæst
‖ -kæst 'brɑːd- ~er/s ə/z ‖ ᵊr/z ~ing ɪŋ ~s s
broadcloth 'brɔːd klɒθ →'brɔːg-, -klɔːθ
‖ -klɔːθ 'brɑːd-, -klɑːθ
broaden 'brɔːd ᵊn ‖ 'brɑːd- ~ed d ~ing _ɪŋ
~s z
Broadhead 'brɔːd hed ‖ 'brɑːd-
Broadhurst 'brɔːd hɜːst ‖ -hɜ˞ːst 'brɑːd-
broad-leaved ˌbrɔːd 'liːvd ◄ ‖ ˌbrɑːd-
broadloom 'brɔːd luːm ‖ 'brɑːd-
broadly 'brɔːd li ‖ 'brɑːd-
broadminded ˌbrɔːd 'maɪnd ɪd ◄ →ˌbrɔːb-,
-əd ‖ ˌbrɑːd- ~ly li ~ness nəs nɪs
Broadmoor 'brɔːd mɔː →'brɔːb-, -mʊə ‖ -mʊr
'brɑːd-, -mɔːr
broadness 'brɔːd nəs -nɪs ‖ 'brɑːd-
Broadribb 'brɔːd rɪb ‖ 'brɑːd-
broadsheet 'brɔːd ʃiːt ‖ 'brɑːd- ~s s
broadside 'brɔːd saɪd ‖ 'brɑːd- ~s z
broad-spectrum ˌbrɔːd 'spek trəm ◄ ‖ ˌbrɑːd-
Broadstairs 'brɔːd steəz ‖ -sterz 'brɑːd-
broadsword 'brɔːd sɔːd ‖ -sɔːrd 'brɑːd-,
-soʊrd ~s z
Broadwater 'brɔːd ˌwɔːt ə ‖ -ˌwɔːt̬ ᵊr 'brɑːd-,
-ˌwɑːt̬-
broadway, B~ 'brɔːd weɪ ‖ 'brɑːd- ~s z
broadwise 'brɔːd waɪz ‖ 'brɑːd-
Broadwood 'brɔːd wʊd ‖ 'brɑːd-
Brobat *tdmk* 'brəʊb æt ‖ 'broʊb-
Brobdingnag 'brɒbd ɪŋ næg ‖ 'brɑːbd-
Brobdingnagian
ˌbrɒbd ɪŋ 'næg i_ən ◄ ‖ ˌbrɑːbd-
Broca 'brəʊk ə ‖ 'broʊk ə —*Fr* [bʁɔ ka] ~'s z
brocad|e brə 'keɪd brəʊ- ‖ broʊ- ~ed ɪd əd
~es z ~ing ɪŋ
brocatel, brocatelle ˌbrɒk ə 'tel ‖ ˌbrɑːk-
broccoli 'brɒk ᵊl i §-ə laɪ ‖ 'brɑːk-
broch brɒk brɒx ‖ brɑːx brochs brɒks brɒxs
‖ brɑːxs

BROCHURE

BrE 1988

0   20   40   60   80   100%

brochure 'brəʊʃ ə -ʊə, -jʊə; brɒ 'ʃʊə, brə-
‖ broʊ 'ʃʊᵊr —*BrE* 1988 *poll panel preference:*
'•• 90%, •'• 10%. ~s z
brock, Brock brɒk ‖ brɑːk brocks, Brock's
brɒks ‖ brɑːks
Brocken 'brɒk ᵊn ‖ 'brɑːk- —*Ger* ['bʁɔk ᵊn]
ˌBrocken 'spectre
Brockenhurst 'brɒk ᵊn hɜːst ‖ 'brɑːk ᵊn hɜ˞ːst
brocket 'brɒk ɪt §-ət ‖ 'brɑːk ət ~s s
Brocklebank 'brɒk ᵊl bæŋk ‖ 'brɑːk-
Brockley 'brɒk li ‖ 'brɑːk-

Brockway 'brɒk weɪ ‖ 'brɑːk-
Brockwell 'brɒk wəl -wel ‖ 'brɑːk-
Broderick 'brɒd_ər ɪk ‖ 'brɑːd_
broderie anglaise ˌbrəʊd ər i 'ɒŋ gleɪz ˌbrɒd-,
 -'ɑːŋ-, -glez, ˌ • • • ₍ᵢ₎•'•
 ‖ ˌbrəʊd ə ˌriː ɑːŋ 'gleɪz —Fr
 [bʁɔd ʁi ɑ̃ glɛːz]
Brodick 'brɒd ɪk ‖ 'brɑːd-
Brodie, b~ 'brəʊd i ‖ 'broʊd i
Brodsky 'brɒd ski ‖ 'brɑːd- —Russ ['brɒt skʲij]
Broederbond 'bruː d ə bɒnd 'brʊd-, -bɒnt,
 -bɔːnt ‖ -ər bɑːnt -bɔːnt —Afrikaans
 ['bru dɑr bɔnt]
Brogan, b~ 'brəʊg ən ‖ 'broʊg-
brogue brəʊg ‖ broʊg **brogues**
 brəʊgz ‖ broʊgz
broil brɔɪəl **broiled** brɔɪəld **broiling** 'brɔɪəl ɪŋ
 broils brɔɪəlz
broiler 'brɔɪəl ə ‖ -ər ~**s** z
Brokaw 'brəʊk ɔː ‖ 'broʊk ɔː -ɑː
broke brəʊk ‖ broʊk
Broke brʊk
broken 'brəʊk ən ‖ 'broʊk-
 ˌBroken 'Hill
broken-down ˌbrəʊk ən 'daʊn ◄ ‖ ˌbroʊk-
broken-hearted ˌbrəʊk ən 'hɑːt ɪd ◄ -əd
 ‖ ˌbroʊk ən 'hɑːrt̬ əd ◄
 ˌbroken-ˌhearted 'lover
brok|er 'brəʊk lə ‖ 'broʊk lər ~**ering** ər ɪŋ
 ~**ers** əz ‖ ərz
brokerage 'brəʊk ər ɪdʒ ‖ 'broʊk-
Brolac tdmk 'brəʊ læk ‖ 'broʊ-
broll|y 'brɒl li ‖ 'brɑːl li ~**ies** iz
bromate 'brəʊm eɪt ‖ 'broʊm-
brome brəʊm ‖ broʊm
Brome (i) brəʊm ‖ broʊm, (ii) bruːm
bromegrass 'brəʊm grɑːs §-græs
 ‖ 'broʊm græs
bromeliad brəʊ 'miːl i æd ‖ broʊ- ~**s** z
Bromfield 'brɒm fiːəld ‖ 'brɑːm-
bromic 'brəʊm ɪk ‖ 'broʊm-
bromide 'brəʊm aɪd ‖ 'broʊm- ~**s** z
bromidic brəʊ 'mɪd ɪk ‖ broʊ-
bromine 'brəʊm iːn -ɪn, -aɪn ‖ 'broʊm-
Bromley (i) 'brɒm li ‖ 'brɑːm li, (ii) 'brʌm li
 —The places in London are (i), but were
 formerly also (ii). The family name may be
 either.
bromoform 'brəʊm əʊ fɔːm ‖ 'broʊm ə fɔːrm
Brompton 'brɒmpt ən 'brʌmpt- ‖ 'brɑːmpt ən
Bromsgrove 'brɒmz grəʊv ‖ 'brɑːmz groʊv
Bromwich 'brɒm ɪtʃ 'brʌm-, -ɪdʒ ‖ 'brɑːm-
Bromyard 'brɒm jɑːd -jəd ‖ 'brɑːm jɑːrd
bronchi 'brɒŋk aɪ -iː ‖ 'brɑːŋk-
bronchia 'brɒŋk i‿ə ‖ 'brɑːŋk-
bronchial 'brɒŋk i‿əl ‖ 'brɑːŋk-
bronchiole 'brɒŋk i əʊl →-ɒʊl ‖ 'brɑːŋk i oʊl
 ~**s** z
bronchitic brɒŋ 'kɪt ɪk brɒn- ‖ brɑːŋ 'kɪt̬ ɪk
 brɑːn-
bronchitis ₍ᵢ₎brɒŋ 'kaɪt ɪs ₍ᵢ₎brɒn-, §-əs
 ‖ brɑːŋ 'kaɪt̬ əs brɑːn-

broncho- comb. form
 with stress-neutral suffix ˌbrɒŋk əʊ ‖ ˌbrɑːŋk ə
 -oʊ — **bronchogram** 'brɒŋk əʊ
 græm ‖ 'brɑːŋk ə-
 with stress-imposing suffix brɒŋ 'kɒ+ brɒn-
 ‖ brɑːŋ 'kɑː+ brɑːn- — **bronchography**
 brɒŋ 'kɒg rəf i ‖ brɑːŋ 'kɑːg-
bronchodilator ˌbrɒŋk əʊ daɪ 'leɪt ə -dɪ'•-,
 -də'•- ‖ ˌbrɑːŋk oʊ daɪ 'leɪt̬ ər -'daɪl eɪt̬ ər ~**s**
 z
bronch|us 'brɒŋk ləs ‖ 'brɑːŋk- ~**i** aɪ iː
bronco 'brɒŋk əʊ ‖ 'brɑːŋk oʊ ~**s** z
Bronski 'brɒn ski ‖ 'brɑːn-
Bronson 'brɒnts ən ‖ 'brɑːnts ən
Bronstein 'brɒn stiːn ‖ 'brɑːn-
Bronte, Brontë 'brɒnt i -eɪ ‖ 'brɑːnt̬ i
 'brɑːnt eɪ ~**s**, ~'**s** z
brontosaur 'brɒnt ə sɔː ‖ 'brɑːnt̬ ə sɔːr
brontosaur|us ˌbrɒnt ə 'sɔːr ləs ◄ ‖ ˌbrɑːnt̬- ~**i**
 aɪ ~**uses** əs ɪz əs əz
Bronwen 'brɒn wen -wən, -wɪn ‖ 'brɑːn-
Bronx brɒŋks ‖ brɑːŋks
 ˌBronx 'cheer
bronze brɒnz ‖ brɑːnz **bronzed**
 brɒnzd ‖ brɑːnzd **bronzes** 'brɒnz ɪz -əz
 ‖ 'brɑːnz əz **bronzing** 'brɒnz ɪŋ ‖ 'brɑːnz ɪŋ
 'Bronze Age; ˌbronze 'medal
bronzer 'brɒnz ə ‖ 'brɑːnz ər ~**s** z
bronzy 'brɒnz i ‖ 'brɑːnz i
brooch brəʊtʃ ‖ broʊtʃ bruːtʃ (!) **brooches**
 'brəʊtʃ ɪz -əz ‖ 'broʊtʃ əz 'bruːtʃ-
brood bruːd **brooded** 'bruːd ɪd -əd
 brooding/ly 'bruːd ɪŋ /li **broods** bruːdz
brooder 'bruːd ə ‖ -ər ~**s** z
brood|y 'bruːd li ~**ier** i‿ə ‖ i‿ər ~**iest** i‿ɪst
 i‿əst ~**ily** ɪ li əl i ~**iness** i nəs i nɪs
brook brʊk §bruːk **brooked** brʊkt §bruːkt
 brooking 'brʊk ɪŋ §'bruːk- **brooks** brʊks
 §bruːks
Brook, Brooke brʊk §bruːk
Brookeborough 'brʊk bər_ə
Brookes brʊks §bruːks
Brookfield 'brʊk fiːəld §'bruːk-
Brooking 'brʊk ɪŋ §'bruːk- ~**s** z
Brook|land 'brʊk lland §'bruːk- ~**lands** ləndz
brooklime 'brʊk laɪm §'bruːk- ~**s** z
Brookline 'brʊk laɪn
Brooklyn 'brʊk lɪn -lən
 ˌBrooklyn 'Bridge
Brookner 'brʊk nə ‖ -nər
Brooks brʊks §bruːks
Brookside ˌbrʊk 'saɪd §ˌbruːk-
brookweed 'brʊk wiːd
Brookwood 'brʊk wʊd

BROOM

	■ bruːm □ brʊm	

BrE 1988	
0 20 40 60 80 100%	

broom bruːm brʊm —BrE 1988 poll panel
 preference: bruːm 92%, brʊm 8%. **brooms**
 bruːmz brʊmz
Broom, Broome bruːm brʊm

B

Broomfield 'brʊm fiːˀld 'bruːm-
broomrape 'bruːm reɪp 'brʊm- ~s s
broomstick 'bruːm stɪk 'brʊm- ~s s
Brophy 'brəʊf i ‖ 'brouf i
Bros brɒs brɒz ‖ brɔːs braːs —or see Brothers
brose brəʊz ‖ brouz
Brosnahan (i) 'brɒz nə hən ‖ 'braːz-, (ii)
  'brɒs- ‖ 'braːs-
broth brɒθ brɔːθ ‖ brɔːθ braːθ broths brɒθs
  brɔːθs, brɔːðz ‖ brɔːθs braːθs
brotha non-standard variant of brother 'brʌð ə
  ~s z
brothel 'brɒθ ᵊl ‖ 'braːθ- 'brɔːθ-, 'braːð-,
  'brɔːð- ~s z
brother, B~ 'brʌð ə ‖ -ᵊr ~s z
  ,Brother 'Jonathan
brotherhood 'brʌð ə hʊd ‖ -ᵊr- ~s z
broth|er-in-law 'brʌð |ər ɪn ‚lɔː ' • ə-,
  ‚ən ‚lɔː ‖ -‚lɑː ~ers-in-law əz ɪn ‚lɔː §-ən,•
  ‖ ᵊrz ən- -‚lɑː
brother|ly 'brʌð ə |li ‖ -ᵊr- ~liness li nəs li nɪs
brothers-in-law 'brʌð əz ɪn ‚lɔː §-ən,• ‖ -ᵊrz
  ən- -‚lɑː
Brotherton 'brʌð ət ən ‖ -ᵊrt ᵊn
Brough brʌf —but the place in Highland,
  Scotland, is brɒx ‖ brɔːx, braːx
brougham 'bruː‚əm bruːm ~s z
Brougham (i) brʊm, (ii) bruːm, (iii) brɔːm
  ‖ braːm, (iv) 'bruː‚əm, (v) 'brəʊ əm ‖ 'brou-
brought brɔːt △boːt ‖ braːt
Broughton (i) 'brɔːt ᵊn ‖ 'braːt-, (ii) 'braʊt ᵊn,
  (iii) 'brʌft ᵊn —Most places with this name are
  (i), but the place in Northants is (ii) and places
  in Wales are (iii).
brouhaha 'bruː hɑː hɑː •'••• ~s z
brow braʊ brows braʊz (= browse)
brow|beat 'braʊ |biːt ~beaten biːt ᵊn
  ~beating biːt ɪŋ ‖ biːt̬ ɪŋ ~beats biːts
brown, Brown braʊn browned braʊnd
  browner 'braʊn ə ‖ -ᵊr brownest 'braʊn ɪst
  -əst browning 'braʊn ɪŋ browns braʊnz
  ,brown 'Betty; ,brown 'rat; ,brown 'rice;
  ,brown 'sugar
Browne braʊn
browned-off ‚braʊnd 'ɒf ◂ -'ɔːf ◂ ‖ -'ɔːf ◂ -'ɑːf
Brownhills 'braʊn hɪlz
Brownian 'braʊn i‚ən
brownie, B~ 'braʊn i ~s z
  'Brownie Guide; 'brownie point
Browning, b~ 'braʊn ɪŋ
brownish 'braʊn ɪʃ
Brownjohn 'braʊn dʒɒn ‖ -dʒaːn
Brownlee, Brownlie 'braʊn li -liː
Brownlow 'braʊn ləʊ ‖ -loʊ
brownness 'braʊn nəs -nɪs
brown-nos|e ‚braʊn 'nəʊz '•• ‖ -'noʊz ~ed d
  ~es ɪz əz ~ing ɪŋ
brownout 'braʊn aʊt ~s s
Brownrigg 'braʊn rɪg
brownshirt, B~ 'braʊn ʃɜːt ‖ -ʃɝːt ~s s
brownstone 'braʊn stəʊn ‖ -stoʊn ~s z
browse braʊz browsed braʊzd browses
  'braʊz ɪz -əz browsing 'braʊz ɪŋ

browser 'braʊz ə ‖ -ᵊr ~s z
Broxbourne 'brɒks bɔːn ‖ 'braːks bɔːrn -boʊrn
Brubeck 'bruː bek
Bruce bruːs
brucellosis ‚bruːs ɪ 'ləʊs ɪs -ə-, §-əs ‖ -'loʊs-
Bruch brʊk brʊx —Ger [bʁʊx]
Bruckner 'brʊk nə ‖ -nᵊr —Ger ['bʁʊk nɐ]
  —but as an American name, 'brʌk-
Bruegel, Brueghel 'brɔɪg ᵊl 'brɜːg-,
  'brɜːx- ‖ 'bruːg- —Dutch ['brøː xəl]
Bruford 'bruː fəd ‖ -fᵊrd
Bruges bruːʒ bruːdʒ —Fr [bʁyːʒ], Flemish
  Brugge ['brʏɣə]
Bruin, bruin 'bruː‚ɪn §‚ən ~s, ~'s z
bruise bruːz bruised bruːzd bruises 'bruːz ɪz
  -əz bruising/ly 'bruːz ɪŋ /li
bruiser 'bruːz ə ‖ -ᵊr ~s z
bruit bruːt (= brute) bruited 'bruːt ɪd -əd
  ‖ 'bruːt̬ əd bruiting 'bruːt ɪŋ ‖ 'bruːt̬ ɪŋ
  bruits bruːts
Brum brʌm
brumal 'bruːm ᵊl
brum|by, B~ 'brʌm|bi ~bies biz
Brummagem, b~ 'brʌm ədʒ əm
Brummell 'brʌm ᵊl
Brumm|ie, Brumm|y, b~ 'brʌm li ~ies iz
brunch brʌntʃ brunches 'brʌntʃ ɪz -əz
Brundisium brʌn 'dɪz i‚əm brʊn- ‖ -'dɪʒ-
Brunei 'bruːn aɪ bru 'naɪ
Brunel bru 'nel
brunet, brunette bru 'net ~s s
Brunnhilde, Brünnhilde brʊn 'hɪld ə '•‚••
  —Ger [bʁʏn 'hɪl də]
Bruno 'bruːn əʊ ‖ -oʊ
Brunson 'brʌntˢ ᵊn
Brunswick 'brʌnz wɪk
brunt, Brunt brʌnt
Brunton 'brʌnt ᵊn ‖ -ᵊn
brush brʌʃ brushed brʌʃt brushes 'brʌʃ ɪz
  -əz brushing 'brʌʃ ɪŋ
brushi... —see brushy
brush-off 'brʌʃ ɒf -ɔːf ‖ -ɔːf -aːf
brush-up 'brʌʃ ʌp
brushwood 'brʌʃ wʊd
brushwork 'brʌʃ wɜːk ‖ -wɝːk
brush|y 'brʌʃ li ~ier i‚ə ‖ i‚ᵊr ~iest i‚ɪst i‚əst
  ~iness i nəs i nɪs
brusque brʊsk bruːsk, brʌsk ‖ brʌsk
brusque|ly 'brʊsk |li 'bruːsk-, 'brʌsk- ‖ 'brʌsk-
  ~ness nəs nɪs
Brussels, b~ 'brʌs ᵊlz —Fr Bruxelles [bʁy sɛl],
  Dutch Brussel ['brʏs əl]
  ,brussels 'sprouts
brut bruːt —Fr [bʁyt]
Brut tdmk bruːt
brutal 'bruːt ᵊl ‖ 'bruːt̬ ᵊl ~ly i
brutalis... —see brutaliz...
brutalism 'bruːt ᵊl ‚ɪz əm -ə ‚lɪz- ‖ 'bruːt̬-
brutalist 'bruːt ᵊl ɪst §-əst ‖ 'bruːt̬- ~s s
brutalit|y bru 'tæl ət li -ɪt- ‖ -ət̬ li ~ies iz
brutalization ‚bruːt ᵊl aɪ 'zeɪʃ ᵊn -ɪ'•-
  ‖ ‚bruːt̬ ᵊl ə-

B

brutaliz|e 'bruːt ə laɪz -ᵊl aɪz ‖ 'bruːt̬ ᵊl aɪz
~**ed** d ~**es** ɪz əz ~**ing** ɪŋ
brute bruːt **brutes** bruːts
brutish 'bruːt ɪʃ ‖ 'bruːt̬- ~**ly** li ~**ness** nəs nɪs
Bruton 'bruːt ən
Brutus 'bruːt əs ‖ 'bruːt̬-
bruxism 'bruks ˌɪz əm 'brʌks-
Bryan 'braɪ_ən
Bryant 'braɪ_ənt
Bryce braɪs
Bryden, Brydon 'braɪd ən
Brylcreem *tdmk* 'brɪl kriːm ~**ed** d
Brymon *tdmk* 'braɪm ən -ɒn ‖ -ɑːn
Bryn brɪn
Brynley 'brɪn li
Brynmawr *place in Gwent* brɪn 'mau_ə →brɪm-
‖ -'mau_ʲr —*Welsh* [brɪn 'maur, brɪn-]
Bryn Mawr *place in USA* ˌbrɪn 'mɔː →ˌbrɪm-
‖ -'mɑːr
Brynmor 'brɪn mɔː →'brɪm- ‖ -mɔːr
bryon|y, B~ 'braɪ_ən li ~**ies** iz
bryophyte 'braɪ əʊ faɪt ‖ -ə- ~**s** s
bryozoan ˌbraɪ əʊ 'zəʊ ən ‖ -ə 'zoʊ- ~**s** z
Bryson 'braɪs ən
Brythonic brɪ 'θɒn ɪk brə- ‖ -'θɑːn-
Brzezinski brə 'ʒɪnˈsk i
BSc, B.Sc. ˌbiː es 'siː
BSE ˌbiː es 'iː
B-side 'biː saɪd ~**s** z
BSkyB *tdmk* ˌbiː skaɪ 'biː
BST ˌbiː es 'tiː
bub bʌb **bubs** bʌbz
bubal 'bjuːb ᵊl ~**s** z
bubbl|e 'bʌb ᵊl ~**ed** d ~**es** z ~**ing** _ɪŋ
ˌbubble and 'squeak; 'bubble bath;
'bubble ˌchamber; 'bubble gum; 'bubble
sort; 'bubble wrap
bubbl|y 'bʌb ᵊl_i ~**ier** _i ə ‖ _i ᵊr ~**iest** _i ɪst
_i əst
bubo 'bjuːb əʊ 'buːb- ‖ -oʊ ~**s** z
bubonic bju 'bɒn ɪk bu- ‖ -'bɑːn-
buˌbonic 'plague
buccal 'bʌk ᵊl *(= buckle)*
buccaneer ˌbʌk ə 'nɪə ‖ -'nɪʳr ~**neered**
'nɪəd ‖ 'nɪʳrd ~**neering** 'nɪər ɪŋ ‖ 'nɪr ɪŋ
~**neers** 'nɪəz ‖ 'nɪrz
buccinator 'bʌks ɪ neɪt ə ‖ ˈ•ə- ‖ -neɪt̬ ᵊr ~**s** z
Buccleuch bə 'kluː *(!)*
Bucephalus bju 'sef ᵊl əs
Buchan 'bʌk ən 'bʌx-
Buchanan bju 'kæn ən bə- —*In Scotland
usually* bə-
Bucharest ˌbuːk ə 'rest ˌbjuːk-, ˌbuk-, ˌbuːx-,
'••• ‖ 'buːk ə rest —*Romanian* Bucureşti
[bu ku reʃ ti]
Buchenwald 'buːk ən væld ‖ -wɑːld -wɔːld
—*Ger* ['buː xᵊn valt]
Buchman *(i)* 'bʌk mən, *(ii)* 'buk-
Buchmanism 'bʌk mən ˌɪz əm 'buk-
buck, Buck bʌk **bucked** bʌkt **bucking**
'bʌk ɪŋ **bucks** bʌks
buckaroo ˌbʌk ə 'ruː '••• ~**s** z
buckbean 'bʌk biːn ~**s** z

buckboard 'bʌk bɔːd ‖ -bɔːrd -boʊrd ~**s** z
Buckden 'bʌk dən
bucker 'bʌk ə ‖ -ᵊr ~**s** z
buck|et 'bʌk |ɪt §-ət ‖ -|ət ~**eted** ɪt ɪd §ət-, -əd
‖ ət̬ əd ~**eting** ɪt ɪŋ §ət- ‖ ət̬ ɪŋ ~**ets** ɪts
§əts ‖ əts
'bucket seat; 'bucket shop
bucketful 'bʌk ɪt fʊl §-ət- ~**s** z
buckeye 'bʌk aɪ ~**s** z
Buckfastleigh ˌbʌk fɑːst 'liː §-'fæst- ‖ -'fæst-
Buckhurst 'bʌk hɜːst -ɜːst ‖ -hɜːst
Buckie 'bʌk i
Buckingham 'bʌk ɪŋ əm △-ən_əm, §-həm
~**shire** ʃə ʃɪə ‖ ʃʳr ʃɪr
ˌBuckingham 'Palace
buckish 'bʌk ɪʃ ~**ly** li ~**ness** nəs nɪs
Buckland 'bʌk lənd
buckl|e 'bʌk ᵊl ~**ed** d ~**es** z ~**ing** _ɪŋ
buckler, B~ 'bʌk lə ‖ -lᵊr ~**s** z
Buckley 'bʌk li
buckling 'bʌk lɪŋ ~**s** z
Buckmaster 'bʌk ˌmɑːst ə §-ˌmæst-
‖ -ˌmæst ᵊr
Buckminster 'bʌk ˌmɪntˈst ə ‖ -ᵊr
Bucknall, Bucknell 'bʌk nᵊl
buckram 'bʌk rəm
Bucks, Bucks. bʌks
bucksaw 'bʌk sɔː ‖ -sɑː ~**s** z
buckshee ˌbʌk 'ʃiː ◂ '•• ‖ 'bʌk ʃiː
buckshot 'bʌk ʃɒt ‖ -ʃɑːt
buckskin 'bʌk skɪn
buckteeth ˌbʌk 'tiːθ
buckthorn 'bʌk θɔːn ‖ -θɔːrn ~**s** z
Buckton 'bʌkt ən
buck|tooth ˌbʌk |'tuːθ §-'tʊθ ~**teeth** 'tiːθ
buckwheat 'bʌk wiːt -hwiːt ‖ -*h*wiːt
buckyball 'bʌk i bɔːl ‖ -bɑːl ~**s** z
bucolic bju 'kɒl ɪk ‖ -'kɑːl- ~**ally** ᵊl_i
Buczacki bu 'tʃæt ski bju-
bud, Bud bʌd **budded** 'bʌd ɪd -əd **budding**
'bʌd ɪŋ **buds** bʌdz
Budapest ˌbjuːd ə 'pest ◂ ˌbuːd-, ˌbud-, '•••
‖ 'buːd ə pest —*Hung* ['bu dɒ pɛʃt]
budd... —*see* bud
Budd bʌd
Buddha, b~ 'bʊd ə ‖ 'buːd ə —*Hindi* [bʊd̪d̪ʰ]
~**s** z
Buddhism 'bʊd ˌɪz əm ‖ 'buːd-
Buddhist 'bʊd ɪst §-əst ‖ 'buːd-
Buddhistic bu 'dɪst ɪk
buddi... —*see* buddy
Buddig 'bɪð ɪg —*Welsh* ['bɪ ðɪg, 'bi-]
buddleia 'bʌd li_ə bʌd 'liː_ə ~**s** z
budd|y 'bʌd li ~**ied** id ~**ies** iz ~**ying** i_ɪŋ
buddy-buddy ˌbʌd i 'bʌd i '••, ••
Bude bjuːd
budge, Budge bʌdʒ **budged** bʌdʒd **budges**
'bʌdʒ ɪz -əz **budging** 'bʌdʒ ɪŋ
budgerigar 'bʌdʒ ər_i gɑː ‖ -gɑːr ~**s** z
budg|et, B~ 'bʌdʒ |ɪt §-ət ‖ -|ət ~**eted** ɪt ɪd
§ət-, -əd ‖ ət̬ əd ~**eting** ɪt ɪŋ §ət- ‖ ət̬ ɪŋ
~**ets** ɪts §əts ‖ əts
'budget acˌcount; 'Budget Day

budgetary 'bʌdʒ ɪt_ər i '•ət_ ‖ -ə ter i
budgie, B~ 'bʌdʒ i ~s z
Budleigh 'bʌd li
Budweiser tdmk 'bʌd waɪz ə ‖ -ər
Buenos Aires ˌbweɪn ɒs 'aɪər iz ˌbwen-, -əs-, -əz-, -'eər-, -iːz, ˌ•'eəz ‖ ˌbweɪn əs- —Spanish [ˌbwe nos 'ai res], locally also [-noh 'ai re]
Buerk bɜːk ‖ bɝːk
buff bʌf buffed bʌft buffing 'bʌf ɪŋ buffs bʌfs
buffalo, B~ 'bʌf ə ləʊ -əl əʊ ‖ -loʊ ~es, ~s z
  'buffalo grass
buffer 'bʌf ə ‖ -ər ~ed d buffering 'bʌf ər_ɪŋ ~s z
  'buffer state; 'buffer stock; 'buffer zone
buff|et v, n 'blow' 'bʌf |ɪt §-ət ‖ -|ət ~eted ɪt ɪd ət-, -əd ‖ əт əd ~eting/s ɪt ɪŋ/z ət- ‖ əт ɪŋ/z ~ets ɪts §əts ‖ əts
buffet n 'meal, sideboard, counter' 'bʊf eɪ 'bʌf-, -i ‖ bə 'feɪ bu- (*)
  'buffet car ‖ •'••
bufflehead 'bʌf əl hed ~ed ɪd əd ~s z
buffo 'bʊf əʊ ‖ 'buːf oʊ —It ['buf fo]
buffoon bə 'fuːn bʌ- ~s z
buffooner|y bə 'fuːn ər li bʌ- ~ies iz
Buffs bʌfs
bug bʌg bugged bʌgd bugging 'bʌg ɪŋ bugs bʌgz
  ˌBugs 'Bunny
Bug river buːg —Russ, Polish [buk]
bugaboo 'bʌg ə buː
Buganda bu 'gænd ə
Bugatti bju 'gæt i bu- ‖ -'gɑːt̬-
bugbear 'bʌg beə ‖ -ber ~s z
bug-eyed ˌbʌg 'aɪd ◂ '•• ‖ '••
  ˌbug-eyed 'monster
bugg... —see bug
bugger 'bʌg ə ‖ -ər ~ed d buggering 'bʌg ər_ɪŋ ~s z
bugger-all, bugger all ˌbʌg ər 'ɔːl ◂ ‖ -ər- -'ɑːl
buggery 'bʌg ər i
buggi... —see buggy
Buggins 'bʌg ɪnz §-ənz ~'s ɪz -əz
  'Buggins'(s) turn
bugg|y 'bʌg li ~ier i_ə ‖ i_ər ~ies iz ~iest i_ɪst i_əst ~iness i nəs i nɪs
bug|house 'bʌg |haʊs ~houses haʊz ɪz -əz
bugl|e, Bugle 'bjuːg əl ~ed d ~es z ~ing _ɪŋ
bugler 'bjuːg lə ‖ -lər ~s z
bugloss 'bjuː glɒs ‖ -glɑːs -glɔːs ~es ɪz -əz
Bugner (i) 'bʌg nə ‖ -nər, (ii) 'bʊg-
bugrake 'bʌg reɪk ~s s
buhl buːl
Buick tdmk 'bjuːˌɪk ~s s
build bɪld building 'bɪld ɪŋ builds bɪldz
  built bɪlt
builder 'bɪld ə ‖ -ər ~s z
building 'bɪld ɪŋ ~s z
  'building block; 'building so,ciety
buildup 'bɪld ʌp ~s s
built bɪlt

Builth bɪlθ
  ˌBuilth 'Wells
built-in ˌbɪlt 'ɪn ◂
  ˌbuilt-in 'cupboards
built-up ˌbɪlt 'ʌp ◂
  ˌbuilt-up 'area
Buist (i) bjuːst, (ii) 'bjuːˌɪst
Buitoni tdmk bju 'təʊn i ‖ -'toʊn-
Bujumbura ˌbuːdʒ əm 'bʊər ə -ʊm- ‖ -'bʊr-
Bukhara bu 'kɑːr ə -'xɑːr- —Russ [bu 'xa rə]
Bukta tdmk 'bʌkt ə
Bulawayo ˌbʊl ə 'weɪ əʊ ˌbuːl- ‖ -oʊ —Ndebele [ɓu la 'wa: jɔ]
bulb bʌlb bulbs bʌlbz
bulbar 'bʌlb ə ‖ -ər -ɑːr
bulbil 'bʌlb ɪl §-əl ~s z
bulbous 'bʌlb əs ~ly li
bulbul 'bʊl bʊl ~s z
Bulgar, b~ 'bʌlg ɑː 'bʊlg-, -ə ‖ -ɑːr -ər ~s z
Bulgari|a bʌl 'geər i_ə bʊl- ‖ -'ger- -'gær- ~an/s ən/z
bulge bʌldʒ bulged bʌldʒd bulges 'bʌldʒ ɪz -əz bulging 'bʌldʒ ɪŋ
bulg|y 'bʌldʒ li ~ier i_ə ‖ i_ər ~iest i_ɪst i_əst ~iness i nəs i nɪs
bulimi|a bu 'lɪm| i_ə bju-, -'liːm|- ~ic ɪk
bulk bʌlk bulked bʌlkt bulking 'bʌlk ɪŋ bulks bʌlks
bulkhead 'bʌlk hed ~s z
bulk|y 'bʌlk li ~ier i_ə ‖ i_ər ~iest i_ɪst i_əst ~ily ɪ li əl i ~iness i nəs i nɪs
bull, Bull bʊl bulls bʊlz
  ˌbull 'terrier
bull|a 'bʊl lə 'bʌl- ~ae iː
bullac|e 'bʊl ɪs -əs ~es ɪz əz
Bullard (i) 'bʊl ɑːd ‖ -ɑːrd, (ii) -əd ‖ -ərd
bulldog 'bʊl dɒg ‖ -dɔːg -dɑːg ~s z
  'bulldog clip
bulldoz|e 'bʊl dəʊz ‖ -doʊz ~ed d ~es ɪz əz ~ing ɪŋ
bulldozer 'bʊl ˌdəʊz ə ‖ -ˌdoʊz ər ~s z
Bullen 'bʊl ən -ɪn
Buller 'bʊl ə ‖ -ər
bullet 'bʊl ɪt -ət ~s s
bullet-headed ˌbʊl ɪt 'hed ɪd ◂-ət-, -əd
bulletin 'bʊl ət ɪn -ɪt-, §-ən ‖ -ən ~s z
  'bulletin board
bulletproof 'bʊl ɪt pruːf §-ət-, §-prʊf
bullfight 'bʊl faɪt ~s s
bullfight|er/s 'bʊl ˌfaɪt ə/z ‖ -ˌfaɪt̬ ər/z ~ing ɪŋ
bullfinch 'bʊl fɪntʃ ~es ɪz əz
bullfrog 'bʊl frɒg ‖ -frɑːg -frɔːg ~s z
bullhead 'bʊl hed ~s z
bullheaded ˌbʊl 'hed ɪd ◂-əd ~ly li ~ness nəs nɪs
bullhorn 'bʊl hɔːn ‖ -hɔːrn ~s z
bulli... —see bully
bullion 'bʊl i_ən
bullish 'bʊl ɪʃ ~ly li ~ness nəs nɪs
bullnecked ˌbʊl 'nekt ◂
bullnose 'bʊl nəʊz ‖ -noʊz ~d d
bullock, B~ 'bʊl ək ‖-ɑːk ~s s

B

Bullokar 'bʊl ə kɑː -ək ə ‖ -ə kɑːr -ək ər
Bullough 'bʊl əʊ ‖ -oʊ
bullpen 'bʊl pen ~s z
bullring 'bʊl rɪŋ ~s z
bullroarer 'bʊl ˌrɔːr ə ‖ -ər -ˌroʊr- ~s z
bull's-eye 'bʊlz aɪ ~s z
bull|shit 'bʊl |ʃɪt ~shitter/s ʃɪt ə/z ‖ ʃɪt̬ ər/z
  ~shitting ʃɪt ɪŋ ‖ ʃɪt̬ ɪŋ ~shits ʃɪts
bullwhip 'bʊl wɪp -hwɪp ‖ -hwɪp ~ped t
  ~ping ɪŋ ~s s
bull|y 'bʊl |i ~ied id ~ies iz ~ying i_ɪŋ
  ˌbully' beef, '···
bullyboy 'bʊl i bɔɪ
bully-off 'bʊl i ɒf ‖ -ɔːf -ɑːf
bullyrag 'bʊl i ræg ~ged d ~ging ɪŋ ~s z
Bulmer 'bʊlm ə ‖ -ər
Bulow, Bülow 'bjuːl əʊ ‖ -oʊ —Ger ['byː lo]
bulrush 'bʊl rʌʃ ~es ɪz əz
Bulstrode (i) 'bʊl strəʊd ‖ -stroʊd, (ii) 'bʌl-
Bultitude 'bʌlt ɪ tjuːd -ə-, →§-tʃuːd ‖ -tuːd
  -tjuːd
bulwark 'bʊl wək 'bʌl-, -wɜːk ‖ -wərk ~s s
Bulwer 'bʊl wə ‖-wər
bum bʌm **bummed** bʌmd **bumming** 'bʌm ɪŋ
  bums bʌmz
  ˌbum's' rush
bumbag 'bʌm bæg ~s z
bumbl|e 'bʌm bəl ~ed d ~es z ~ing/ly ɪŋ /li
bumblebee 'bʌm bəl biː ~s z
bumbledom 'bʌm bəl dəm
bumble-puppy 'bʌm bəl ˌpʌp i
bumbler 'bʌm blə ‖ ər ~s z
bumboat 'bʌm bəʊt ‖ -boʊt ~s s
bumf bʌmpf
bumfuzzled bʌm 'fʌz əld
Bumiputra ˌbuːm ɪ 'puːtr ə
bummalo 'bʌm ə ləʊ ‖ -loʊ
bummaree ˌbʌm ə 'riː '··· ~s z
bummer 'bʌm ə ‖ -ər ~s z
bump bʌmp **bumped** bʌmpt **bumping**
  'bʌmp ɪŋ **bumps** bʌmps
  ˌbump' start
bumper 'bʌmp ə ‖ -ər ~s z
bumper-to-bumper
  ˌbʌmp ə tə 'bʌmp ə ◄ ‖ -ər tə 'bʌmp ər ◄
bumph bʌmpf
bumpi... —see **bumpy**
bumpkin 'bʌmp kɪn ~s z
bumptious 'bʌmp ʃəs ~ly li ~ness nəs nɪs
Bumpus 'bʌmp əs
bump|y 'bʌmp |i ~ier i_ə ‖ i_ər ~iest i_ɪst
  i_əst ~ily ɪ li əl i ~iness i nəs i nɪs
bun bʌn **buns** bʌnz
Buna tdmk 'buːn ə 'bjuːn-
Bunbury 'bʌn bər_i →'bʌm- ~ed d ~ing ɪŋ
  ~ish ɪʃ ~ist/s ɪst/s §əst/s
bunch, Bunch bʌntʃ **bunched** bʌntʃt
  bunches 'bʌntʃ ɪz -əz **bunching** 'bʌntʃ ɪŋ
Bunche bʌntʃ
bunco 'bʌŋk əʊ ‖ -oʊ ~ed d ~ing ɪŋ ~s z
Buncombe 'bʌŋk əm
bund, Bund bʌnd **bunds** bʌndz

Bundes|bank 'bʊnd əz |bæŋk 'bʌnd- —Ger
  ['bʊn dəs ˌbaŋk] ~rat rɑːt —Ger [ʁaːt] ~tag
  tɑːg —Ger [taːk] ~wehr veə ‖ ver —Ger
  [veːɐ]
bundl|e 'bʌnd əl ~ed d ~es z ~ing ɪŋ
Bundy 'bʌnd i
bunfight 'bʌn faɪt ~s s
bung bʌŋ **bunged** bʌŋd **bunging** 'bʌŋ ɪŋ
  bungs bʌŋz
bungalow 'bʌŋ gə ləʊ ‖ -loʊ ~s z
Bungay 'bʌŋ gi
bungee 'bʌndʒ i -iː
  'bungee ˌjumping
bunghole 'bʌŋ həʊl →-hɒʊl ‖ -hoʊl ~s z
bungl|e 'bʌŋ gəl ~ed d ~er/s ə/z ‖ ər/z ~es z
  ~ing/ly ɪŋ /li
bunion 'bʌn jən ~s z
bunk bʌŋk **bunked** bʌŋkt **bunking** 'bʌŋk ɪŋ
  bunks bʌŋks
bunker, B~ 'bʌŋk ə ‖ -ər ~ed d **bunkering**
  'bʌŋk ər_ɪŋ ~s z
bunk|house 'bʌŋk |haʊs ~houses haʊz ɪz -əz
bunko 'bʌŋk əʊ ‖ -oʊ ~ed d ~ing ɪŋ ~s z
bunkum 'bʌŋk əm
bunk-up 'bʌŋk ʌp
bunn|y, Bunny 'bʌn |i ~ies iz
  'bunny ˌgirl
bunsen, B~ 'bʌnⁿs ən —Ger ['bʊn zⁿn] ~s z
  ˌBunsen' burner ‖ '·· ,··
bunt bʌnt **bunted** 'bʌnt ɪd -əd ‖ 'bʌnt̬ əd
  bunting 'bʌnt ɪŋ ‖ 'bʌnt̬ ɪŋ **bunts** bʌnts
Bunter 'bʌnt ə ‖ 'bʌnt̬ ər
bunting, B~ 'bʌnt ɪŋ ‖ 'bʌnt̬ ɪŋ ~s z
Bunty 'bʌnt i ‖ 'bʌnt̬ i
Buñuel 'buːn ju el ,···· ‖ ˌbuːn 'wel —Sp
  [bu 'ɲwel]
bunya 'bʌn jə ~s z
Bunyan 'bʌn jən
Bunyanesque ˌbʌn jə 'nesk ◄
bunyip 'bʌn jɪp ~s s
buoy bɔɪ ‖ 'buː i bɔɪ (in BrE = boy) **buoyed**
  bɔɪd ‖ 'buː id bɔɪd **buoying**
  'bɔɪ ɪŋ ‖ 'buː i ɪŋ 'bɔɪ ɪŋ **buoys**
  bɔɪz ‖ 'buː iz bɔɪz
buoyancy 'bɔɪ ənts i ‖ 'buː jənts i
buoyant 'bɔɪ ənt ‖ 'buː jənt ~ly li
BUPA 'buːp ə 'bjuːp-
bur bɜː ‖ bɝː **burs** bɜːz ‖ bɝːz
Burbage 'bɜːb ɪdʒ ‖ 'bɝːb-
Burbank 'bɜː bæŋk ‖ 'bɝː-
Burberr|y 'bɜː bər_li ‖ 'bɝː- -ˌber li ~ies iz
burbl|e 'bɜːb əl ‖ 'bɝːb- ~ed d ~es z ~ing ɪŋ
Burbury 'bɜː bər_i ‖ 'bɝː- -ˌber i
burbot 'bɜːb ət ‖ 'bɝːb- ~s s
Burch bɜːtʃ ‖ bɝːtʃ
Burchell 'bɜːtʃ əl ‖ 'bɝːtʃ-
Burcher 'bɜːtʃ ə ‖ 'bɝːtʃ ər
Burchill 'bɜːtʃ əl -ɪl ‖ 'bɝːtʃ-
Burco tdmk 'bɜːk əʊ ‖ 'bɝːk oʊ
burden, B~ 'bɜːd ən ‖ 'bɝːd ən ~ed d ~ing
  _ɪŋ ~s z
burdensome 'bɜːd ən səm ‖ 'bɝːd- ~ly li
  ~ness nəs nɪs

B

Burdett *(i)* 'bɜːd et ‖ 'bɜːːd-, *(ii)* ˌbɜː 'det bə-
‖ bəⁱ 'det
burdock 'bɜː dɒk ‖ 'bɜːː dɑːk ~s s
Burdon 'bɜːd ³n ‖ 'bɜːːd-
Bure bjʊə ‖ bjʊⁱr
bure *'Fijian cottage'* 'bʊr eɪ 'bjʊər- ~s z
bureau 'bjʊər əʊ 'bjɔːr-; bjʊⁱ 'rəʊ ‖ 'bjʊr oʊ
—*Fr* [ʁo] ~s, ~x z —*or as sing.*
ˌbureau de 'change ʃɒndʒ ʃɒ̃ʒ, ʃɑːndʒ
‖ ʃɑːndʒ —*Fr* [ʃɑ̃ːʒ]
bureaucrac|y bjʊⁱ 'rɒk rəs |i bjɔː-, bjə-
‖ -'rɑːk- ~ies iz
bureaucrat 'bjʊər ə kræt 'bjɔːr- ‖ 'bjʊr- ~s s
bureaucratic ˌbjʊər ə 'kræt ɪk ◂ ˌbjɔːr-
‖ ˌbjʊr ə 'kræt ɪk ◂ ~ally ³l_i
bureaux 'bjʊər əʊz 'bjɔːr-, -əʊ; bjʊⁱ 'rəʊz,
-'rəʊ ‖ 'bjʊr oʊz
burette bjʊⁱ 'ret ~s s
Burford 'bɜː fəd ‖ 'bɜːː fⁱrd
burg, Burg bɜːg ‖ bɜːːg **burgs** bɜːgz ‖ bɜːːgz
Burge bɜːdʒ ‖ bɜːːdʒ
burgee 'bɜːdʒ iː ‖ 'bɜːːdʒ iː ~s z
burgeon 'bɜːdʒ ³n ‖ 'bɜːːdʒ- ~ed d ~ing ɪŋ
~s z
burger, B~ 'bɜːg ə ‖ 'bɜːːg ⁱr ~s z
burgess, B~ 'bɜːdʒ ɪs -əs, -es ‖ 'bɜːːdʒ- ~es ɪz
əz
burgh 'bʌr ə ‖ 'bɜːː oʊ *(= borough)* ~s z
Burgh *(i)* 'bʌr ə ‖ 'bɜːː oʊ, *(ii)* bɜːg ‖ bɜːːg, *(iii)*
bɜː ‖ bɜːː
Burgh-by-Sands *place in Cumbria*
ˌbrʌf baɪ 'sændz
Burghclere 'bɜː kleə ‖ 'bɜːː kler
burgher 'bɜːg ə ‖ 'bɜːːg ⁱr ~s z
Burghfield 'bɜː fiːⁱld ‖ 'bɜːː-
Burghley 'bɜːl i ‖ 'bɜːːl i
burglar 'bɜːg lə ‖ 'bɜːːg lⁱr ~s z
'burglar aˌlarm
burglari... —*see* **burglary**
burglaris|e, burglariz|e 'bɜːg lə raɪz ‖ 'bɜːːg-
~ed d ~es ɪz əz ~ing ɪŋ
burglar|y 'bɜːg lər |i △-³l r|i ‖ 'bɜːːg- ~ies iz
burgl|e 'bɜːg ³l ‖ 'bɜːːg ³l ~ed d ~es z ~ing
ɪŋ
burgomaster 'bɜːg əʊ ˌmɑːst- § -ˌmæst-
‖ 'bɜːːg ə ˌmæst ⁱr ~s z
burgoo 'bɜːg uː ‖ 'bɜːːg- bⁱr 'guː
Burgos 'bʊəg ɒs ‖ 'bʊr goʊs -gɑːs —*Sp* ['bur
ɣos]
Burgoyne 'bɜːg ɔɪn bɜː 'gɔɪn ‖ bⁱr 'gɔɪn
Burgundian bɜː 'gʌnd i_ən bə- ‖ bⁱr- ~s z
Burgund|y, b~ 'bɜːg ənd |i →-ŋd- ‖ 'bɜːːg-
~ies iz
Burhop 'bʌr əp ‖ 'bɜːː-
burial 'ber i_əl *(!)* ~s z
Buridan 'bjʊər ɪd ³n -əd- ‖ 'bjʊr-
buri... —*see* **bury**
Buriat ˌbʊr i 'ɑːt ◂ ˌbʊər-, -'æt; ˌbʊə 'jɑːt
‖ ˌbʊr 'jɑːt ◂ ~s s
burin 'bjʊər ɪn -ən ‖ 'bjʊr- 'bɜːː- ~s z
burk bɜːk ‖ bɜːːk ~s s
Burke, burke bɜːk ‖ bɜːːk **burked**

bɜːkt ‖ bɜːːkt **burking** 'bɜːk ɪŋ ‖ 'bɜːːk ɪŋ
burkes bɜːks ‖ bɜːːks
Burkina Faso
bɜː ˌkiːn ə 'fæs əʊ ‖ bⁱr ˌkiːn ə 'fɑːs oʊ bʊr-
Burkitt 'bɜːk ɪt §-ət ‖ 'bɜːːk- ~'s s
burl, Burl bɜːl ‖ bɜːːl **burled** bɜːld ‖ bɜːːld
burling 'bɜːl ɪŋ ‖ 'bɜːːl ɪŋ **burls**
bɜːlz ‖ bɜːːlz
burlap 'bɜː læp ‖ 'bɜːː-
Burleigh 'bɜːl i ‖ 'bɜːːl i
burlesqu|e bɜː 'lesk ‖ bɜːː- ~ed t ~ely li ~es
s ~ing ɪŋ
Burley 'bɜːl i ‖ 'bɜːːl i
burli... —*see* **burly**
Burlington 'bɜːl ɪŋ tən ‖ 'bɜːːl-
burl|y, Burly 'bɜːl |i ‖ 'bɜːːl |i ~ier i_ə ‖ i_ⁱr
~iest i_ɪst i_əst ~ily ɪ li əl i ~iness i nəs i nɪs
Burma 'bɜːm ə ‖ 'bɜːːm ə
Burmah 'bɜːm ə ‖ 'bɜːːm ə
Burman 'bɜːm ən ‖ 'bɜːːm ən ~s z
Burmese ˌbɜː 'miːz ◂ ‖ ˌbɜːː- -'miːs
burn, Burn bɜːn ‖ bɜːːn **burned**
bɜːnd ‖ bɜːːnd **burning** 'bɜːn ɪŋ ‖ 'bɜːːn ɪŋ
burns bɜːnz ‖ bɜːːnz **burnt** bɜːnt ‖ bɜːːnt
Burnaby 'bɜːn əb i ‖ 'bɜːːn-
Burnage 'bɜːn ɪdʒ ‖ 'bɜːːn-
Burnaston 'bɜːn əst ən ‖ 'bɜːːn-
Burne bɜːn ‖ bɜːːn
burned-out ˌbɜːnd 'aʊt ◂ ‖ ˌbɜːːnd-
Burne-Jones ˌbɜːn 'dʒəʊnz ‖ ˌbɜːːn 'dʒoʊnz
Burnell bɜː 'nel ‖ bⁱr-
burner 'bɜːn ə ‖ 'bɜːːn ⁱr ~s z
burnet 'bɜːn ɪt §-ət ‖ bⁱr 'net 'bɜːːn ət ~s s
Burnet, Burnett *(i)* bə 'net bɜː:- ‖ bⁱr-, *(ii)*
'bɜːn ɪt §-ət ‖ 'bɜːːn-
Burney 'bɜːn i ‖ 'bɜːːn i
Burnham 'bɜːn əm ‖ 'bɜːːn-
Burnham-on-Crouch
ˌbɜːn əm ɒn 'kraʊtʃ ‖ ˌbɜːːn əm ɑːn- ˌ‧‧'ɔːn-
burning 'bɜːn ɪŋ ‖ 'bɜːːn ɪŋ ~ly li ~s z
ˌburning 'bush
burnish 'bɜːn ɪʃ ‖ 'bɜːːn ɪʃ ~ed t ~er/s ə/
z ‖ ⁱr/z ~es ɪz əz ~ing ɪŋ
Burnley 'bɜːn li ‖ 'bɜːːn-
burnoos|e, burnous, burnous|e bɜː 'nuːs
-'nuːz ‖ bⁱr- ~es ɪz əz
burnout 'bɜːn aʊt ‖ 'bɜːːn- ~s s
Burns bɜːnz ‖ bɜːːnz —*In Scottish*
pronunciation, bʌrnz
'Burns night
Burnside 'bɜːn saɪd ‖ 'bɜːːn- **b~s** z
burnt bɜːnt ‖ bɜːːnt
ˌburnt 'offering
Burntisland bɜːnt 'aɪl ənd ‖ bɜːːnt̮-
burnt-out ˌbɜːnt 'aʊt ◂ ‖ ˌbɜːːnt̮-
ˌburnt-out 'case
Burntwood 'bɜːnt wʊd ‖ 'bɜːːnt-
burn-up 'bɜːn ʌp ‖ 'bɜːːn-
buroo bə 'ruː bruː ~s z
burp bɜːp ‖ bɜːːp **burped** bɜːpt ‖ bɜːːpt
burping 'bɜːp ɪŋ ‖ 'bɜːːp- **burps**
bɜːps ‖ bɜːːps
Burpham 'bɜːf əm ‖ 'bɜːːf-

burr, Burr bɜː ‖ bɜ˞ː burred bɜːd ‖ bɜ˞ːd (= bird) burring 'bɜːr ɪŋ ‖ 'bɜ˞ː ɪŋ burrs bɜːz ‖ bɜ˞ːz
burrawang 'bʌr ə wæŋ ~s z
Burrell 'bʌr əl ‖ 'bɜ˞ː-
Burren 'bʌr ən ‖ 'bɜ˞ː-
burrito bə 'riːt əʊ bʊ- ‖ bə 'riːt̬ oʊ —Sp [bu 'rri to] ~s z —Sp [-s]
burro 'bʊr əʊ ‖ 'bɜ˞ː oʊ 'bʊr- —Sp ['bu rro] ~s z
Burrough 'bʌr əʊ ‖ 'bɜ˞ː oʊ -ə
Burroughes, Burroughs 'bʌr əʊz ‖ 'bɜ˞ː oʊz
burrow, B~ 'bʌr əʊ ‖ 'bɜ˞ː oʊ -ed d ~ing ɪŋ ~s z
Burrows 'bʌr əʊz ‖ 'bɜ˞ː oʊz
burry adj 'prickly' 'bɜːr i ‖ 'bɜ˞ː i
burry n 'aboriginal' 'bʊr i
Burry family name 'bʌr i ‖ 'bɜ˞ː i
burs|a 'bɜːs |ə ‖ 'bɜ˞ːs |ə ~ae iː ~al əl ~as əz
bursar 'bɜːs ə ‖ 'bɜ˞ːs ər -ɑːr ~s z
bursarial bɜː 'seər i_əl ‖ bər 'ser-
bursarship 'bɜːs ə ʃɪp ‖ 'bɜ˞ːs ər- ~s s
bursar|y 'bɜːs ər_li ‖ 'bɜ˞ːs- ~ies iz
Burscough 'bɜːsk əʊ ‖ 'bɜ˞ːsk oʊ
burse bɜːs ‖ bɜ˞ːs burses 'bɜːs ɪz -əz ‖ 'bɜ˞ːs əz
bursitis bɜː 'saɪt ɪs §-əs ‖ bər 'saɪt̬-
Burslem 'bɜːz ləm ‖ 'bɜ˞ːz-
burst bɜːst ‖ bɜ˞ːst bursting 'bɜːst ɪŋ ‖ 'bɜ˞ːst ɪŋ bursts bɜːsts ‖ bɜ˞ːsts
Burstall 'bɜːst ɔːl ‖ 'bɜ˞ːst- -ɑːl
Burt bɜːt ‖ bɜ˞ːt
burthen 'bɜːð ən ‖ 'bɜ˞ːð- -ed d ~ing ɪŋ ~s z
Burton, b~ 'bɜːt ən ‖ 'bɜ˞ːt- ~s, ~'s z
Burtonwood ˌbɜːt ən 'wʊd ‖ ˌbɜ˞ːt-
Burundi bʊ 'rʊnd i bə- ~an/s _ən/z
Burwash place in Sussex 'bɜː wɒʃ ‖ 'bɜ˞ː wɑːʃ —locally also 'bʌr əʃ
Burwell 'bɜː wel -wəl ‖ 'bɜ˞ː-
bury 'ber i (! = berry) buried 'ber id buries 'ber iz burying 'ber i_ɪŋ
Bury 'ber i —As a family name, also 'bjʊər i ‖ 'bjʊr i
  ˌBury St 'Edmunds
Buryat ˌbʊr i 'ɑːt ◂ ˌbʊər-, -'æt; ˌbʊə 'jɑːt ‖ ˌbʊr 'jɑːt ◂ ~s s
bus bʌs bused, bussed bʌst (= bust) buses, busses 'bʌs ɪz -əz busing, bussing 'bʌs ɪŋ
  'bus bar; 'bus boy; 'bus ˌshelter; 'bus ˌstation; 'bus stop
busbar 'bʌs bɑː ‖ -bɑːr ~s z
bus|by, Busby 'bʌz |bi ~bies biz
Busch bʊʃ
Buse bjuːz
bush, Bush bʊʃ bushed bʊʃt bushes, Bush's 'bʊʃ ɪz -əz bushing 'bʊʃ ɪŋ
  ˌbush 'telegraph
bushbab|y 'bʊʃ ˌbeɪb li ~ies iz
bushbuck 'bʊʃ bʌk
bushcraft 'bʊʃ krɑːft §-kræft ‖ -kræft
bushel 'bʊʃ əl ~s z
Bushell (i) 'bʊʃ əl (ii) bʊ 'ʃel
Bushey 'bʊʃ i

bushfire 'bʊʃ ˌfaɪ_ə ‖ -ˌfaɪ_ər ~s z
bushhammer 'bʊʃ ˌhæm ə ‖ -ər ~s z
Bushido bu 'ʃiːd əʊ ˌbʊʃ i 'dəʊ ‖ 'buːʃ i doʊ 'bʊʃ- —Jp [bu 'çi doo]
bushi... —see bushy
Bushire bu 'ʃaɪ_ə bju-, -'ʃɪə ‖ bu 'ʃɪər
bush|man, B~ 'bʊʃ |mən ~men mən men
Bushmills 'bʊʃ mɪlz
Bushnell 'bʊʃ nəl
bushranger 'bʊʃ ˌreɪndʒ ə ‖ -ər ~s z
bushveld, B~ 'bʊʃ felt -velt
bushwhack 'bʊʃ wæk -hwæk ‖ -hwæk ~ed t ~er/s ə/z ‖ ər/z ~ing ɪŋ ~s s
bush|y 'bʊʃ li ~ier i_ə ‖ i_ər ~iest i_ɪst i_əst ~ily ɪ li əl i ~iness i nəs i nɪs
bushy-tailed ˌbʊʃ i 'teɪəld ◂
busi... —see busy
business 'bɪz nəs -nɪs ~es ɪz əz
  'business card; 'business class; 'business end; 'business hours, ˌ•• '•; 'business suit
businesslike 'bɪz nəs laɪk -nɪs-
business|man 'bɪz nəs |mæn -nɪs-, -mən ~men men mən ~woman ˌwʊm ən ~women ˌwɪm ɪn §-ən
busk, Busk bʌsk busked bʌskt busking 'bʌsk ɪŋ busks bʌsks
busker 'bʌsk ə ‖ -ər ~s z
buskin 'bʌsk ɪn §-ən -ed d ~s z
bus|man 'bʌs |mən -mæn ~men mən men
  ˌbusman's 'holiday
buss, Buss bʌs bussed bʌst busses 'bʌs ɪz -əz bussing 'bʌs ɪŋ
buss... —see bus
bust bʌst busted 'bʌst ɪd -əd busting 'bʌst ɪŋ busts bʌsts
bustard 'bʌst əd ‖ -ərd ~s z
buster, B~ 'bʌst ə ‖ -ər ~s z
-buster ˌbʌst ə ‖ -ər — pricebuster 'praɪs ˌbʌst ə ‖ -ər
bustier 'bʌst i eɪ 'bʊst-, -i_ə ‖ ˌbuːst i 'eɪ ˌbʌst- ~s z
bustl|e 'bʌs əl ~ed d ~es z ~ing/ly ɪŋ /li
bust-up 'bʌst ʌp ~s s
bust|y 'bʌst li ~ier i_ə ‖ i_ər ~iest i_ɪst i_əst ~iness i nəs i nɪs
bus|y 'bɪz li ~ier i_ə ‖ i_ər ~iest i_ɪst i_əst ~ily ɪ li əl i ~yness əz i nəs i nɪs
  ˌbusy 'Lizzie
busybod|y 'bɪz i ˌbɒd li ‖ -ˌbɑːd li ~ies iz
busywork 'bɪz i wɜːk ‖ -wɜ˞ːk
but strong form bʌt, weak form bət
butadiene ˌbjuːt ə 'daɪ iːn -•'•• ‖ ˌbjuːt̬-
butane 'bjuːt eɪn bju: 'teɪn
butanoic ˌbjuːt ə 'nəʊ ɪk ◂ -ən 'əʊ- ‖ ˌbjuːt ən 'oʊ ɪk ◂
butanol 'bjuːt ə nɒl -ən ɒl ‖ -ən oʊl -ɑːl, -ɔːl
butanone 'bjuːt ə nəʊn -ən əʊn ‖ -ən oʊn
butch, Butch bʊtʃ
butch|er, B~ 'bʊtʃ lə ‖ -lər ~ered əd ‖ ərd ~ering ər ɪŋ ~ers əz ‖ ərz
butcherbird 'bʊtʃ ə bɜːd ‖ -ər bɜ˞ːd ~s z
butcher|y 'bʊtʃ ər li ~ies iz
Bute bjuːt

B

butene 'bjuːt iːn

Buthelezi ˌbuːt ə 'leɪz i ‖ ˌbuːt̬- —Zulu [bu te 'leˈ zi]

butler, B~ 'bʌt lə ‖ -lᵊr ~s z

Butlin 'bʌt lɪn -lən ~'s z

Butskellite 'bʌts kə laɪt -kɪ- ~s s

butt, Butt bʌt butted 'bʌt ɪd -əd ‖ 'bʌt̬ əd butting 'bʌt ɪŋ ‖ 'bʌt̬ ɪŋ butts bʌts

butte, Butte bjuːt

butter 'bʌt ə ‖ 'bʌt̬ ᵊr ~ed d buttering 'bʌt̬ ˌər ɪŋ ‖ 'bʌt̬ ᵊr ɪŋ ~s z ˌbutter 'bean; ˌbutter 'icing; 'butter ˌmountain

butterball 'bʌt ə bɔːl ‖ 'bʌt̬ ᵊr- -bɑːl ~s z

butterbur 'bʌt ə bɜː ‖ 'bʌt̬ ᵊr bɝː ~s z

buttercup 'bʌt ə kʌp ‖ 'bʌt̬ ᵊr- ~s s

butterfat 'bʌt ə fæt ‖ 'bʌt̬ ᵊr- ~s s

Butterfield 'bʌt ə fiːᵊld ‖ 'bʌt̬ ᵊr-

butterfingers 'bʌt ə ˌfɪŋ gəz ‖ 'bʌt̬ ᵊr ˌfɪŋ gᵊrz

butter|fly 'bʌt ə |flaɪ ‖ 'bʌt̬ ᵊr- ~flies flaɪz ˈbutterfly bush; ˈbutterfly stroke; ˈbutterfly valve

butteri... —see buttery

Butterkist tdmk 'bʌt ə kɪst ‖ 'bʌt̬ ᵊr-

Buttermere 'bʌt ə mɪə ‖ 'bʌt̬ ᵊr mɪr

buttermilk 'bʌt ə mɪlk ‖ 'bʌt̬ ᵊr-

butternut 'bʌt ə nʌt ‖ 'bʌt̬ ᵊr- ~s s

Butters 'bʌt əz ‖ 'bʌt̬ ᵊrz

butterscotch 'bʌt ə skɒtʃ ‖ 'bʌt̬ ᵊr skɑːtʃ

Butterwick 'bʌt ə wɪk -ᵊr ɪk ‖ 'bʌt̬ ᵊr wɪk

butterwort 'bʌt ə wɜːt §-wɔːt ‖ 'bʌt̬ ᵊr wɝːt -wɔːrt ~s s

Butterworth 'bʌt ə wəθ -wɜːθ ‖ 'bʌt̬ ᵊr wᵊrθ ~'s s

butter|y 'bʌt ᵊr li ‖ 'bʌt̬- ~ies iz

Butthead 'bʌt hed

butti... —see butty

buttock 'bʌt ək ‖ 'bʌt̬- ~s s

button, B~ 'bʌt ᵊn ~ed d ~ing ˌɪŋ ~s z

button-down ˌbʌt ᵊn 'daʊn ◄ ˌbutton-down 'collar

buttonhol|e 'bʌt ᵊn həʊl →-hɒʊl ‖ -hoʊl ~ed d ~es z ~ing ɪŋ

buttonhook 'bʌt ᵊn hʊk §-huːk ~s s

buttress 'bʌtr əs -ɪs ~ed t ~es ɪz əz ~ing ɪŋ

butt|y 'bʌt li ‖ 'bʌt̬ li ~ies iz

butyl 'bjuːt aɪᵊl -ɪl, §-ᵊl ‖ 'bjuːt̬ ᵊl

butyric bju 'tɪr ɪk

buxom 'bʌks əm ~ly li ~ness nəs nɪs

Buxted 'bʌkst ɪd -əd, -ed

Buxtehude ˌbʊkst ə 'huːd ə ' • • • • —Ger [bʊks tə 'huː də], Danish [bʊks də 'huː ðə]

Buxton 'bʌkst ən

buy baɪ (= by) bought bɔːt ‖ bɑːt buying 'baɪ ɪŋ buys baɪz

buyback 'baɪ bæk ~s s

buyer 'baɪ ə ‖ 'baɪ ᵊr ~s z ˌbuyer's 'market, ' • • , • •

buyout 'baɪ aʊt ~s s

Buys Ballot ˌbaɪs bə 'lɒt ˌbɔɪs-, ˌbaɪz-, -'bæl ət ‖ -'lɑːt —Dutch [ˌbœys bɑ 'lɔt]

Buzby 'bʌz bi

Buzfuz 'bʌz fʌz

buzz bʌz buzzed bʌzd buzzes 'bʌz ɪz -əz buzzing 'bʌz ɪŋ

buzzard, B~ 'bʌz əd ‖ -ᵊrd ~s z

buzzer 'bʌz ə ‖ -ᵊr ~s z

buzzword 'bʌz wɜːd ‖ -wɝːd ~s z

BVD tdmk ˌbiː viː 'diː ~'s z

bwana 'bwɑːn ə — ˈbwɑːn ə

BWIA tdmk 'biː wiː —or as ˌB ˌW ˌI 'A

Bwlch bʊlk bʊlx —Welsh [bʊlχ]

by baɪ —This word normally has no weak form. However there is an occasional weak form bi, bə, which is stylistically marked and in RP restricted to set phrases. The EFL learner should always use the pronunciation baɪ.

Byatt 'baɪ ət

by-blow 'baɪ bləʊ -bloʊ ~s z

Bydgoszcz 'bɪd gɒʃ ‖ -gɔːʃ -goʊʃ —Polish ['bɪd gɔʃtʃ]

bye, Bye baɪ (= by, buy) byes baɪz

bye- comb. form ˌbaɪ — bye-election 'baɪ ɪ ˌlek ʃᵊn -ə-

bye-bye interj (ˌ)baɪ 'baɪ

bye-byes n ˌbaɪ baɪz

byelaw 'baɪ lɔː ‖ -lɑː ~s z

by-election 'baɪ ɪ ˌlek ʃᵊn -ə- ~s z

Byeloruss|ia bi ˌel əʊ 'rʌʃ lə ˌbel əʊ' • -, -'ruːs li ə -oʊ 'rʌʃ lə —Also, inappropriately, ˌbaɪ əʊ ləʊ- ~ian/s ᵊn/z i ən/z

Byers 'baɪ əz ‖ 'baɪ ᵊrz

Byfield 'baɪ fiːᵊld

Byfleet 'baɪ fliːt

bygone 'baɪ gɒn §-gɑːn ‖ -gɔːn -gɑːn ~s z

Bygraves 'baɪ greɪvz

Byker 'baɪk ə ‖ -ᵊr

bylaw 'baɪ lɔː ‖ -lɑː ~s z

byline 'baɪ laɪn ~s z

Byng bɪŋ

BYO ˌbiː waɪ 'əʊ ‖ -'oʊ

BYOB ˌbiː waɪ əʊ 'biː ‖ -oʊ 'biː

bypass 'baɪ pɑːs §-pæs ‖ -pæs ~ed t ~es ɪz əz ~ing ɪŋ 'bypass ˌsurgery

by|path 'baɪ |pɑːθ §-pæθ ‖ -|pæθ ~paths pɑːðz pɑːθs, §pæðz, §pæθs ‖ -pæðz -pæθs

byplay 'baɪ pleɪ

byproduct 'baɪ ˌprɒd ʌkt ‖ -ˌprɑːd əkt ~s s

Byrd bɜːd ‖ bɝːd

byre 'baɪ ə ‖ 'baɪ ᵊr byres 'baɪ əz ‖ 'baɪ ᵊrz

Byrne bɜːn ‖ bɝːn

byroad 'baɪ rəʊd ‖ -roʊd ~s z

Byrom 'baɪᵊr əm

Byron 'baɪᵊr ən ~'s z

Byronic baɪᵊ 'rɒn ɪk ‖ -'rɑːn- ~ally ᵊl_i

Bysshe bɪʃ

byssinosis ˌbɪs ɪ 'nəʊs ɪs -ə-, §-əs ‖ -'noʊs-

byss|us 'bɪs |əs ~i aɪ ~uses əs ɪz -əz

bystander 'baɪ ˌstænd ə ‖ -ᵊr ~s z

byte baɪt (= bite) bytes baɪts

byway 'baɪ weɪ ~s z

Byward 'baɪ wəd ‖ -wᵊrd

byword 'baɪ wɜːd ‖ -wɝːd ~s z

by-your-leave ˌbaɪ jɔː 'liːv -jʊə-, -jə- ‖ -jᵊr-

Byzantian bɪ 'zænt i‿ən bə-, baɪ-, -'zæntʃ ən
~s z
Byzantine, b~ bɪ 'zænt aɪn bə-, baɪ-, -iːn;
'bɪz ən taɪn, -tiːn ‖ 'bɪz ən tiːn -taɪn ~s z
Byzantium bɪ 'zænt i‿əm bə-, baɪ-, -'zæntʃ-
‖ -'zæntʃ- -'zænt̮-

Cc

c	Spelling-to-sound

1 Where the spelling is **c**, the pronunciation is regularly
  k, as in **cut** kʌt ('hard C'), or
  s, as in **nice** naɪs ('soft C').
  Less frequently, it is
  ʃ, as in **ocean** 'əʊʃ ᵊn ‖ 'oʊʃ ᵊn.
  c may also form part of the digraphs **ch** and **ck**.

2 The pronunciation is regularly k when **c**
  • is at the end of a word, as in **basic** 'beɪs ɪk, or
  • is followed by one of **a, o, u**, as in **camp** kæmp, **copy** 'kɒp i ‖ 'kɑːp i, **curl** kɜːl ‖ kɝːl, or
  • is followed by a consonant letter, as in **cry** kraɪ.

3 The pronunciation is regularly s when **c**
  • is followed by one of **e, i, y**, as in **central** 'sentr əl, **city** 'sɪt i, **cycle** 'saɪk ᵊl, **face** feɪs.
  Note also **Caesar** 'siːz ə ‖ -ᵊr.

4 Where **c** at the end of a stressed syllable is followed by **e** or **i** plus a vowel within a word, the pronunciation is regularly ʃ, as in **precious** 'preʃ əs, **special** 'speʃ ᵊl, **musician** mju 'zɪʃ ᵊn. In these cases the **e** or **i** is silent, as usually applies when the following vowel is weak; but when the vowel after the **e** or **i** is strong, the pronunciation is i, as in **speciality** ˌspeʃ i 'æl ət i ‖ -ət̬ i. Sometimes there is an alternative possibility with s, as in **appreciate, associate, oceanic**; and where there is another ʃ in the same word, as in **association, pronunciation**, many speakers prefer s.

5 Correspondingly, where the spelling is double **cc**, the pronunciation is
  k in most positions, as in **account** ə 'kaʊnt; but
  ks when followed by one of **e, i, y**, as in **accept** ək 'sept.

6 Correspondingly, too, where the spelling is **sc** the pronunciation is
  sk in most positions, as in **describe** dɪ 'skraɪb; but
  s when followed by one of **e, i, y**, as in **scent** sent, **disciple** dɪ 'saɪp ᵊl;
  ʃ when at the end of a stressed syllable and followed by **i** plus a vowel within a word, as in **luscious** 'lʌʃ əs.
  sc may also form part of the trigraph **sch** (see **ch** 4).

7 **c** is silent in one or two exceptional words, including **muscle** 'mʌs ᵊl, **indict** ɪn 'daɪt, **Connecticut** kə 'net ɪk ət ‖ -'net̬-.

ch   Spelling-to-sound

1 Where the spelling is the digraph **ch**, the pronunciation is regularly
tʃ, as in **chip** tʃɪp, or
ʃ, as in **machine** mə ˈʃiːn, or
k, as in **chemistry** ˈkem ɪs tri.
ch may also form part of the trigraph **sch** (see 4).

2 Where the spelling is the trigraph **tch**, the pronunciation is regularly tʃ, as in **fetch** fetʃ.

3 Otherwise, there is no reliable rule for choosing between the three possibilities for **ch**. In general,
tʃ is the pronunciation in long-established words, as **cheese, chain, coach**;
ʃ is the pronunciation in recent loanwords from French, as **champagne, parachute**; nʃ is also a less usual option in place of ntʃ at the end of a syllable, as in **lunch**;
k is the pronunciation in words of Greek origin, as **chaos, monarch**. Where **ch** is followed by a consonant letter, the pronunciation is always k, as in **Christmas** ˈkrɪs məs, **technical** ˈtek nɪk ᵊl.

4 After **s**, the pronunciation is usually k, as in **school**. Occasionally, **sch** is a trigraph, and the pronunciation is ʃ; this applies in words borrowed from German, certain proper names, and the traditional BrE pronunciation of **schedule**.

5 Occasionally, the pronunciation is
dʒ, as in the usual version of **sandwich** ˈsæn wɪdʒ and some other British place-names ending in **-ich**; or
x, in certain words from foreign languages, as **loch** (with k as an anglicizing alternative).

6 **ch** is silent in one or two exceptional words, including **yacht** jɒt ‖ jɑːt.

7 The sound tʃ is also sometimes written **t**, as in **question, natural**; and **c**, as in **cello**.

ck   Spelling-to-sound

Where the spelling is the digraph **ck**, the pronunciation is always k, as in **back** bæk, **acknowledge** ək ˈnɒl ɪdʒ ‖ ək ˈnɑːl ɪdʒ.

C, c siː   **C's, Cs, c's** siːz —*Communications code name:* Charlie
ˌC of ˈE
C++ ˌsiː plʌs ˈplʌs
CAA ˌsiː eɪ ˈeɪ
cab kæb   **cabs** kæbz
   ˈcab rank
cabal kə ˈbæl ‖ -ˈbɑːl   ~**s** z
cabala kə ˈbɑːl ə kæ-   ~**s** z

cabalism ˈkæb ə ˌlɪz əm
cabalistic ˌkæb ə ˈlɪst ɪk ◄
Caballé kə ˈbaɪ eɪ kæ- ‖ ˌkæb ɑː ˈjeɪ -ɑːl- —*Sp* [ka ˈβa ʎe, -je]
caballero ˌkæb ə ˈleər əʊ ‖ -ˈjer oʊ ˌkæb ᵊl- —*Sp* [ka βa ˈʎe ro, -ˈje-]
cabana kə ˈbɑːn ə ‖ kə ˈbæn ə -ˈbɑːn-, -jə —*Sp* cabaña [ka ˈβa ɲa]
cabaret ˈkæb ə reɪ ˌ•ˈ•ˈ•   ~**s** z

C

cabbage 'kæb ɪdʒ ~s ɪz əz
　,cabbage 'white
cabbala kə 'baːl ə kæ- ~s z
cabbalism 'kæb ə ˌlɪz əm
cabbalistic ˌkæb ə 'lɪst ɪk ◂
cabbie, cabby 'kæb i **cabbies** 'kæb iz
cabdriver 'kæb ˌdraɪv ə ‖ -ər ~s z
caber 'keɪb ə ‖ -ər 'kɑːb- ~s z
cabernet sauvignon, C~ S~
　ˌkæb ə neɪ ˌsəuv iːn 'jɒn -'jɔ̃, -'‧ ‧ ‧
　‖ ˌkæb ər ˌneɪ ˌsouv iːn 'joun —Fr
　[ka bɛʁ nɛ so vi njɔ̃]
cabin 'kæb ɪn §-ən ~s z
　'cabin boy; 'cabin class; 'cabin crew;
　'cabin ˌcruiser; 'cabin ˌfever
Cabinda kə 'bɪnd ə -'biːnd- —Port [kɐ 'βin dɐ]
cabinet 'kæb ɪn ət -ən ˌət, -ɪt ~s s
cabinet-mak|er/s 'kæb ɪn ət ˌmeɪk ə/z -ən ˌət-,
　-ɪn ɪt- ‖ -ər/z **~ing** ɪŋ
cabl|e 'keɪb əl **~ed** d **~es** z **~ing** ɪŋ
　'cable car; ˌcable 'tele,vision, ˌ‧ ‧ ‧ '‧ ‧,
　'‧ ‧ ˌ‧ ‧ ‧
cablegram 'keɪb əl græm ~s z
cableway 'keɪb əl weɪ ~s z
cab|man 'kæb mən **~men** mən men
cabochon 'kæb ə ʃɒn ‖ -ʃɑːn —Fr [ka bɔ ʃɔ̃]
caboodle kə 'buːd əl
caboos|e kə 'buːs **~es** ɪz əz
Caborn 'keɪ bɔːn ‖ -bɔːrn
Cabot 'kæb ət ~s s
cabotage 'kæb ə tɑːʒ -ət ɪdʒ
Cabrillo kə 'brɪl əʊ ‖ -'briː jou —AmSp
　[ka 'βɾi jo]
cabriole 'kæb ri əʊl →-ɒul, ˌ‧ ‧ '‧ ‖ -oul
cabriolet 'kæb ri ə leɪ -ri əʊ-, ˌ‧ ‧ '‧
　‖ ˌkæb ri ə 'leɪ ~s z
cabstand 'kæb stænd ~s z
ca'canny ˌkɔː 'kæn i ‖ ˌkɑː-
cacao kə 'kaʊ -'kaː əʊ, -'keɪ əʊ ‖ -oʊ
Caccia, c~ 'kætʃ ə '‧i_ə ‖ 'kɑːtʃ-
cacciatore ˌkætʃ ə 'tɔːr i ˌkɑːtʃ-, -eɪ ‖ ˌkɑːtʃ-
　-'tour- —It [kat tʃa 'toː re]
cachalot 'kæʃ ə lɒt ‖ -lou -lɑːt
cache kæʃ (= cash) **cached** kæʃt **caches**
　'kæʃ ɪz -əz **caching** 'kæʃ ɪŋ
cachectic kæ 'kekt ɪk kə-
cachepot 'kæʃ pəʊ -pɒt, ˌ‧'‧ ‖ 'kæʃ pɑːt -pou
cache-sexe ˌkæʃ 'seks
cachet 'kæʃ eɪ kæ 'ʃeɪ ‖ kæ 'ʃeɪ ~s z
cachexia kæ 'keks i_ə kə-
cachexy kæ 'keks i kə-
cachin|nate 'kæk ɪ ˌneɪt -ə- **~nated** neɪt ɪd
　-əd ˌneɪt əd **~nates** neɪts **~nating**
　neɪt ɪŋ ‖ neɪt̬ ɪŋ
cachinnation ˌkæk ɪ 'neɪʃ ən -ə- ~s z
cachou kə 'ʃuː kæ-; 'kæʃ uː ~s z
cacique kæ 'siːk kə- ‖ kə- ~s s
cack-handed ˌkæk 'hænd ɪd ◂ -əd **~ly** li
cackl|e 'kæk əl **~ed** d **~er/s** ə/z ‖ ˌər/z **~es** z
　~ing ɪŋ
caco- comb. form
　with stress-neutral suffix ˌkæk əʊ ‖ -ə —
　cacographic ˌkæk əʊ 'græf ɪk ◂ ‖ -ə-

　with stress-imposing suffix kæ 'kɒ+ kə-
　‖ kæ 'kɑː+ — **cacography** kæ 'kɒg rəf i kə-
　‖ -'kɑːg-
cacoethes ˌkæk əʊ 'iːθ iːz ‖ -oʊ-
cacophoni... —see **cacophony**
cacophonous kə 'kɒf ən əs kæ- ‖ kæ 'kɑːf-
　~ly li
cacophon|y kə 'kɒf ən ļi kæ- ‖ kæ 'kɑːf- **~ies**
　iz
cact|us 'kækt ļəs **~i** aɪ iː **~uses** əs ɪz əs əz
cacuminal kæ 'kjuːm ɪn əl kə-, -ən- ~s z
cad, CAD kæd **cads** kædz
cadastral kə 'dæs trəl
cadaver kə 'dæv ə -'dɑːv-, -'deɪv- ‖ -ər ~s z
cadaveric kə 'dæv ər ɪk
cadaverous kə 'dæv ər əs **~ly** li **~ness** nəs nɪs
Cadbury 'kæd bər i →'kæb- ‖ -ˌber i ~'s z
Cadby 'kæd bi →'kæb-
CAD-CAM, CAD/CAM 'kæd kæm
caddie 'kæd i ~s z
caddis 'kæd ɪs §-əs
　'caddis fly
caddish 'kæd ɪʃ **~ly** li **~ness** nəs nɪs
cadd|y 'kæd ļi **~ies** iz
cade, Cade keɪd
Cadeby 'keɪd bi →'keɪb-
Cadell (i) kə 'del, (ii) 'kæd əl
cadenc|e 'keɪd ənts **~ed** t **~es** ɪz əz
cadency 'keɪd ənts i
cadent 'keɪd ənt
cadenza kə 'denz ə ~s z
Cader Idris ˌkæd ər 'ɪdr ɪs ‖ ˌkɑːd ər- —Welsh
　[ˌka der 'i dris]
cadet kə 'det ~s s
　ca'det corps
cadetship kə 'det ʃɪp ~s s
cadge kædʒ **cadged** kædʒd **cadges** 'kædʒ ɪz
　-əz **cadging** 'kædʒ ɪŋ
cadger 'kædʒ ə ‖ -ər ~s z
cadi 'kɑːd i 'keɪd i ~s z
Cadillac tdmk 'kæd ɪ læk -ə-, -əl æk ~s s
Cadiz place in Spain kə 'dɪz —Sp Cádiz ['ka ðiθ]
Cadmean kæd 'miː_ən
cadmic 'kæd mɪk →'kæb-
cadmium 'kæd mi_əm →'kæb-
Cadmus 'kæd məs →'kæb-
Cadogan kə 'dʌg ən
cadre 'kɑːd ə 'keɪd-, -rə ‖ 'kædr i 'kɑːdr-, -eɪ
　(*) ~s z
caduce|us kə 'djuːs i_əs →-'dʒuːs- ‖ -'duːs-
　-'duːʃ ļəs, -'djuːʃ- **~i** aɪ
caducous kə 'djuːk əs →-'dʒuːk- ‖ -'duːk-
　-'djuːk-
Cadwallader kæd 'wɒl əd ə ‖ -'waːl əd ər
caec|um 'siːk ļəm **~a** ə **~al** əl
Caedmon 'kæd mən →'kæb-
Caen kɒ̃ kaːn ‖ kaːn —Fr [kɑ̃]
Caerau 'kaɪ ˌr aɪ —Welsh ['kəi raɪ, -rai, -re]
Caerleon kɑː 'liː_ən ˌkaɪ_ə- ‖ kɑːr-
Caernarfon, Caernarvon
　kə 'nɑːv ən ‖ kɑːr 'nɑːrv- —Welsh
　[kəir 'nar von] **~shire** ʃə ʃɪə ‖ ʃər ʃɪr

C

Caerphilly kə 'fɪl i keə-, kɑː- ‖ kɑːr- —*Welsh*
 [kəir 'fil i, kar-]
Caersws ˌkaɪ_ə 'suːs ‖ ˌkaɪ_ᵊr- —*Welsh*
 [kəir 'suːs]
Caesar 'siːz ə ‖ -ᵊr —*Classical Latin* ['kai sar]
 ~s, ~s z
Caesarea ˌsiːz ə 'riː_ə
caesarean, caesarian sɪ 'zeər i_ən sə-, siː-
 ‖ -'zer- -'zær-
 cae ˌsarean ' section
caesium 'siːz i_əm 'siːs-
caesur|a sɪ 'zjʊər |ə sə-, siː-, -'zjɔːr-, -'ʒʊər-
 ‖ -'zʊr- **~ae** iː aɪ **~as** əz
cafe, café 'kæf eɪ -i; kæ 'feɪ ‖ kæ 'feɪ kə- —*Fr*
 [ka fe] —*Sometimes also (but in RP only
 facetiously)* kæf, keɪf **~s** z
 ˌcafé au 'lait, •ˌ•- əʊ 'leɪ ‖ oʊ- —*Fr* [o lɛ]
cafeteria ˌkæf ə 'tɪər i_ə ‖ -'tɪr- **~s** z
cafetière ˌkæf ti 'eə ˌ•ə ti'• ‖ ˌkæf ə 'tɪᵊr —*Fr*
 [kaf tjɛːʁ] **~s** z —*or as sing.*
caff kæf **caffs** kæfs
caffeine 'kæf iːn ‖ kæ 'fiːn *(*)*
Caffin, Caffyn 'kæf ɪn §-ᵊn
CAFOD, Cafod 'kæf ɒd ‖ -ɑːd
caftan 'kæft æn -aːn ‖ 'kæft ən kæf 'tæn **~s** z
cage, Cage keɪdʒ **caged** keɪdʒd **cages**
 'keɪdʒ ɪz -əz **caging** 'keɪdʒ ɪŋ
 ' cage bird
cag|ey 'keɪdʒ |i **~ier** i_ə ‖ i_ᵊr **~iest** i_ɪst i_əst
 ~ily ɪ li -əl i **~iness** i nəs -nɪs
Cagliari ˌkæl i 'ɑːr i 'kæl jər i —*It* ['kaʎ ʎa ri]
Cagliostro ˌkæl i 'ɒs trəʊ ‖ kæl 'jɑːs troʊ kaːl-,
 -'jɔːs- —*It* [kaʎ 'ʎɔs tro]
Cagney 'kæg ni
cagoule kə 'guːl kæ- **~s** z
cag|y 'keɪdʒ |i **~ier** i_ə ‖ i_ᵊr **~iest** i_ɪst i_əst
 ~ily ɪ li -əl i **~iness** i nəs -nɪs
Cahill *(i)* 'kɑː hɪl, *(ii)* 'keɪ hɪl
cahoots kə 'huːts
Caiaphas 'kaɪ_ə fæs
Caicos 'keɪk əs -ɒs
caiman 'keɪm ən keɪ 'mæn, kaɪ- **~s** z
Cain, Caine keɪn (= *cane*) —*but* Cain *as a Welsh
 female name is* kaɪn
caique, caïque kaɪ 'iːk kɑː- **~s** s
Caird keəd ‖ keᵊrd
Cairene 'kaɪᵊr iːn
cairn keən ‖ keᵊrn **cairned** keənd ‖ keᵊrnd
 cairns keənz ‖ keᵊrnz
 ˌcairn ' terrier
Cairncross 'keən krɒs →'keəŋ-, -krɔːs, ˌ•'•
 ‖ 'kern krɔːs -krɑːs
Cairngorm, c~ ˌkeən 'gɔːm →ˌkeəŋ-, '••
 ‖ 'kern gɔːrm
Cairns keənz ‖ keᵊrnz —*but in Australia the
 town in Queensland is usually* kænz
Cairo *in Egypt* 'kaɪᵊr əʊ ‖ -oʊ —*but places in the
 USA are* 'ker oʊ, 'keɪ roʊ. —*Arabic* El Qahira
 [el 'qɑː hi rɑ, il qɑ 'hi rɑ]
caisson 'keɪs ᵊn -ɒn; kə 'suːn ‖ 'keɪs ɑːn -ᵊn **~s**
 z
Caister, Caistor 'keɪst ə ‖ -ᵊr
Caithness 'keɪθ nes -nɪs, -nəs, ˌ•'nes

caitiff 'keɪt ɪf §-əf ‖ 'keɪt̮ əf **~s** s
Caitlin 'keɪt lɪn 'kæt liːn
Caius 'kaɪ_əs ‖ 'keɪ əs —*but as a family name
 and for the Cambridge college,* kiːz
cajol|e kə 'dʒəʊl →-'dʒɒʊl ‖ -'dʒoʊl **~ed** d
 ~es z **~ing/ly** ɪŋ /li
cajoler|y kə 'dʒəʊl ər| i ‖ -'dʒoʊl- **~ies** iz
Cajun 'keɪdʒ ən **~s** z
cajuput 'kædʒ ə pʊt -pət **~s** s
cake keɪk **caked** keɪkt **cakes** keɪks **caking**
 'keɪk ɪŋ
cakewalk 'keɪk wɔːk ‖ -wɑːk **~s** s
CAL kæl ˌsi: eɪ 'el
Calabar ˌkæl ə 'bɑː ◄ '•••‖ -'bɑːr ◄
 ˌCalabar 'bean
calabash 'kæl ə bæʃ **~es** ɪz əz
calaboos|e 'kæl ə buːs ˌ••'•‖ **~es** ɪz əz
calabrese 'kæl ə briːs -briːz
Calabri|a kə 'læb ri_ə -'lɑːb- ‖ -'leɪb- -'lɑːb-
 —*It* [ka 'la: bria] **~an/s** ən/z
caladium kə 'leɪd i_əm **~s** z
Calais 'kæl eɪ -i ‖ kæ 'leɪ —*Fr* [ka lɛ]
calaloo, calalu 'kæl ə luː
calamari ˌkæl ə 'mɑːr i ‖ ˌkɑː-l- —*It* [ka la 'ma:
 ri]
calami 'kæl ə maɪ
calamine 'kæl ə maɪn
 'calamine ˌlotion, ˌ••• '••
calamint 'kæl ə mɪnt
calamitous kə 'læm ɪt əs -ət- ‖ -ət̮ əs **~ly** li
 ~ness nəs nɪs
calamit|y kə 'læm ət |i -ɪt- ‖ -ət̮ i **~ies** iz
 Ca,lamity 'Jane
cal|amus 'kæl |əm əs **~ami** ə maɪ
calathea ˌkæl ə 'θiː_ə
calcane|us kæl 'keɪn i|_əs **~a** _ə **~al** _əl **~i** aɪ
 ~um _əm
calcareous kæl 'keər i_əs ‖ -'ker- -'kær-
calceolaria ˌkæls i_ə 'leər i_ə ‖ -'ler- **~s** z
calciferol kæl 'sɪf ə rɒl ‖ -roʊl -raːl, -rɔːl
calciferous kæl 'sɪf ər_əs
calcification ˌkæls ɪf ɪ 'keɪʃ ᵊn, ˌ•əf-, §-ə'•-
calcifi... —*see* **calcify**
calcifug|e 'kæls ɪ fjuːdʒ §-ə- **~es** ɪz əz
calci|fy 'kæls ɪ |faɪ -ə- **~fied** faɪd **~fies** faɪz
 ~fying faɪ ɪŋ
calcination ˌkæls ɪ 'neɪʃ ᵊn -ə-
calcin|e 'kæl saɪn -sɪn **~ed** d **~es** z **~ing** ɪŋ
calcite 'kæls aɪt **~s** s
calcitic kæl 'sɪt ɪk ‖ -'sɪt̮-
calcium 'kæls i_əm
 ˌcalcium ' carbonate
Calcot, Calcott *(i)* 'kælk ət -ɒt ‖ -ɑːt, *(ii)*
 'kɔːlk- 'kɒlk- ‖ 'kɑːlk-
calculability ˌkælk jʊl ə 'bɪl ət i, ˌ•jəl-, -ɪt i
 ‖ -jəl ə 'bɪl ət̮ i
calculable 'kælk jʊl əb ᵊl '•jəl- ‖ 'kælk jəl-
calcu|late 'kælk ju |leɪt -jə- ‖ -jə- **~lated/ly**
 leɪt ɪd /li -əd /li ‖ leɪt̮ əd /li **~lates** leɪts
 ~lating/ly leɪt ɪŋ /li ‖ leɪt̮ ɪŋ /li
calculation ˌkælk ju 'leɪʃ ᵊn -jə- ‖ -jə- **~s** z
calculative 'kælk jʊl ət ɪv '•jəl-, -ju leɪt-
 ‖ -jə leɪt̮-

calculator 'kælk ju leɪt ə ˈ•jə- ‖ -jə leɪt̬ ᵊr ~**s** z

calc|ulus 'kælk |jʊl əs -jəl- ‖ -jəl əs ~**uli** ju laɪ jə- ‖ jə laɪ

Calcutta ₍ₒ₎kæl 'kʌt ə ‖ -'kʌt̬-

Caldecote 'kɔːld ɪk ət 'kɒld-, -ək- ‖ 'kɔːld ə koʊt 'kɑːld-

Caldecott 'kɔːld ɪ kɒt 'kɒld-, -ə-, -kət ‖ 'kɔːld ə kɑːt 'kɑːld-

Calder 'kɔːld ə 'kɒld- ‖ 'kɔːld ᵊr 'kɑːld-

caldera kæl 'deər ə 'kɔːld ər ə ‖ kæl 'der ə ~**s** z

Calderdale 'kɔːld ə deɪᵊl 'kɒld- ‖ -ᵊr- 'kɑːld-

caldron 'kɔːldr ən 'kɒldr- ‖ 'kɑːldr- ~**s** z

Caldwell 'kɔːld wel 'kɒld- ‖ 'kɑːld-

Caldy 'kɔːld i 'kɒld- ‖ 'kɑːld-

Cale keɪᵊl

Caleb 'keɪl eb ‖ -əb

Caledon 'kæl ɪd ən -əd-

Caledoni|a ˌkæl ɪ 'dəʊn i̯ə ˌ•ə- ‖ -'doʊn- ~**an/s** ən/z

calefacient ˌkæl ɪ 'feɪʃ i̯ənt -'feɪʃ ᵊnt

calefaction ˌkæl ɪ 'fæk ʃᵊn -ə-

calefactory ˌkæl ɪ 'fæk tᵊr i̯

calendar 'kæl ənd ə -ɪnd- ‖ -ᵊr ~**s** z

ˌcalendar 'month

calend|er 'kæl ənd |ə -ɪnd- ‖ -|ᵊr *(= calendar)* ~**ered** əd ‖ ᵊrd ~**ering** ər ɪŋ ~**ers** əz ‖ ᵊrz

calendrical kə 'lendr ɪk ᵊl kæ-

calends 'kæl endz 'keɪl-, -ɪndz, -əndz

calendula kæ 'lend jʊl ə kə-, -jəl- ‖ -'lendʒ əl ə ~**s** z

calf kɑːf ‖ kæf **calves** kɑːvz ‖ kævz

ˈcalf love

calfskin 'kɑːf skɪn ‖ 'kæf-

Calgary 'kælg ər i

Calhoun *(i)* kæl 'huːn, *(ii)* kə 'huːn

Caliban 'kæl ə bæn -ɪ-

caliber 'kæl əb ə -ɪb-; kə 'liːb ə, -'laɪb- ‖ -ᵊr

cali|brate 'kæl ə |breɪt -ɪ- ~**brated** breɪt ɪd -əd ‖ breɪt̬ əd ~**brates** breɪts ~**brating** breɪt ɪŋ ‖ breɪt̬ ɪŋ

calibration ˌkæl ə 'breɪʃ ᵊn -ɪ- ~**s** z

calibrator 'kæl ə breɪt ə ˈ•ɪ- ‖ -breɪt̬ ᵊr ~**s** z

calibre 'kæl əb ə -ɪb-; kə 'liːb ə, -'laɪb- ‖ -ᵊr

calico 'kæl ɪ kəʊ -ə- ‖ -koʊ ~**es**, ~**s** z

Calicut 'kæl ɪk ət -ɪ kʌt

California ˌkæl ə 'fɔːn i̯ə ˌ•ɪ- ‖ -'fɔːrn jə

Californian ˌkæl ə 'fɔːn i̯ən ◄ ˌ•ɪ- ‖ -'fɔːrn jən ◄ ~**s** z

ˌCaliˌfornian 'Desert

californium ˌkæl ə 'fɔːn i̯əm ˌ•ɪ- ‖ -'fɔːrn-

Caligula kə 'lɪg jʊl ə -jəl-

caliper 'kæl ɪp ə -əp- ‖ -ᵊr ~**ed** d ~**s** z

caliph 'keɪl ɪf 'kæl-, -əf; kæ 'liːf ~**s** s

caliphate 'kæl ɪ feɪt 'keɪl-, -ə- -ət ~**s** s

calisthenic ˌkæl ɪs 'θen ɪk ◄ -əs- ~**s** s

Calistoga ˌkæl ɪ 'stəʊg ə -ə- ‖ -'stoʊg ə

calk kɔːk ‖ kɑːk **calked** kɔːkt ‖ kɑːkt **calking** 'kɔːk ɪŋ ‖ 'kɑːk- **calks** kɔːks ‖ kɑːks

Calke kɔːk ‖ kɑːk

call kɔːl ‖ kɑːl **called** kɔːld ‖ kɑːld **calling** 'kɔːl ɪŋ ‖ 'kɑːl- **calls** kɔːlz ‖ kɑːlz

'call box; 'call girl; 'call sign

calla 'kæl ə ~**s** z

Callaghan 'kæl ə hən -hæn

Callander 'kæl ənd ə ‖ -ᵊr

Callard 'kæl ɑːd ‖ -ɑːrd

Callas 'kæl əs -æs

Callaway 'kæl ə weɪ

callboy 'kɔːl bɔɪ ‖ 'kɑːl- ~**s** z

caller *'one that calls'* 'kɔːl ə ‖ 'kɔːl ᵊr 'kɑːl- ~**s** z

calligrapher kə 'lɪg rəf ə kæ- ‖ -ᵊr ~**s** z

calligraphic ˌkæl ɪ 'græf ɪk ◄ -ə- ~**ally** ᵊl_i

calligraphist kə 'lɪg rəf ɪst kæ-, §-əst ~**s** s

calligraphy kə 'lɪg rəf i kæ-

Callil kə 'lɪl

Callimachus kə 'lɪm ək əs

call-in 'kɔːl ɪn ‖ 'kɑːl-

calling 'kɔːl ɪŋ ‖ 'kɑːl- ~**s** z

'calling card

Calliope, c~ kə 'laɪ_əp i kæ- ~**s** z

calliper 'kæl ɪp ə -əp- ‖ -ᵊr ~**ed** d ~**s** z

callipygian ˌkæl ɪ 'pɪdʒ i̯ən ◄ ˌ•ə-

callipygous ˌkæl ɪ 'paɪg əs ◄ -ə-

callisthenic ˌkæl ɪs 'θen ɪk ◄ -əs- ~**s** s

Callisto kə 'lɪst əʊ kæ- ‖ -oʊ

callosit|y kə 'lɒs ət |i kæ-, -ɪt- ‖ -'lɑːs ət̬ |i ~**ies** iz

callous 'kæl əs ~**ed** t ~**ly** li ~**ness** nəs nɪs

callout 'kɔːl aʊt ‖ 'kɑːl- ~**s** s

callow, C~ 'kæl əʊ ‖ -oʊ ~**ness** nəs nɪs

Calloway 'kæl ə weɪ

Callum 'kæl əm

call-up 'kɔːl ʌp ‖ 'kɑːl- ~**s** s

callus 'kæl əs *(= callous)* ~**es** ɪz əz

calm kɑːm ‖ kɑːlm, §kɒlm **calmer** 'kɑːm ə 'kɑːlm-, §'kɒlm- ‖ -ᵊr **calmest** 'kɑːm ɪst 'kɑːlm-, §'kɒlm-, -əst

Calman 'kæl mən

calmative 'kælm ət ɪv 'kɑːm- ‖ -ət̬- ~**s** z

calm|ly 'kɑːm |li 'kɑːlm-, §'kɒlm- ~**ness** nəs nɪs

Calne kɑːn §kɑːln, §kɒln

calomel 'kæl ə mel -əm ᵊl

calor, Calor *tdmk* 'kæl ə ‖ -ᵊr

'Calor gas

caloric kə 'lɒr ɪk kæ-; 'kæl ər- ‖ -'lɔːr- -'lɑːr-

calorie, C~ 'kæl ər i ~**s** z

'calorie ˌcounting

calorific ˌkæl ə 'rɪf ɪk ◄

calorimeter ˌkæl ə 'rɪm ɪt ə -ət ə ‖ -ət̬ ᵊr ~**s** z

calotte kə 'lɒt ‖ -'lɑːt ~**s** s

Calpurnia kæl 'pɜːn i̯ə ‖ -'pɜ͡ːn-

calque kælk **calqued** kælkt **calques** kælks **calquing** 'kælk ɪŋ

Calthorpe *(i)* 'kæl θɔːp ‖ -θɔːrp, *(ii)* 'kɔːl- 'kɒl- ‖ 'kɑːl-

Calton 'kɔːlt ən ‖ 'kɑːlt- —*but in Strathclyde locally* 'kælt-

caltrap, caltrop 'kæltr əp 'kɔːltr- ~**s** s

Calum 'kæl əm

calumet 'kæl ju met -jə-, ˌ••ˈ• ~**s** s

C

calumni|ate kə 'lʌm ni |eɪt ~ated eɪt ɪd -əd
‖ eɪt̬ əd ~ates eɪts ~ating eɪt ɪŋ ‖ eɪt̬ ɪŋ
calumniation kə ˌlʌm ni 'eɪʃ ᵊn ~s z
calumnious kə 'lʌm ni‿əs ~ly li
calum|ny 'kæl əm |ni ~nies niz
Calvados, c~ 'kælv ə dɒs ‖ ˌkælv ə 'doʊs
ˌkɑːlv- —Fr [kal va doːs]
Calvar|y, c~ 'kælv ər |i ~ies iz
calve kɑːv ‖ kæv (in RP = carve) calved
kɑːvd ‖ kævd calves kɑːvz ‖ kævz calving
'kɑːv ɪŋ ‖ 'kæv-
Calverley 'kɑːv ə li 'kælv- ‖ -ᵊr-
Calvert (i) 'kælv ət ‖ -ᵊrt, (ii) 'kɔːlv- ‖ 'kɑːlv-
Calverton (i) 'kælv ət ən ‖ -ᵊrt ᵊn, (ii) 'kɑːv-
calves from calf, calve kɑːvz ‖ kævz
Calvin 'kælv ɪn §-ən
Calvinism 'kælv ə ˌnɪz əm -ɪ-
Calvinist, c~ 'kælv ən ɪst §-ɪn-, §-əst ~s s
Calvinistic ˌkælv ə 'nɪst ɪk ◂ -ɪ- ~al ᵊl
Calvocoressi ˌkælv ə kə 'res i
calx kælks calxes 'kælks ɪz -əz
calyces 'keɪl ɪ siːz 'kæl-, -ə-
Calydon 'kæl ɪd ən -əd-
calypso, C~ kə 'lɪps əʊ ‖ -oʊ ~s z
calypsonian ˌkæl ɪp 'səʊn i‿ən ‖ -'soʊn- ~s z
calyx 'keɪl ɪks 'kæl- ~es ɪz əz
calzone kæl 'zəʊn i -eɪ ‖ -'zoʊn -'zoʊn i;
ˌkælt 'soʊn i ~s z —It [kal 'tsoː ne]
cam, Cam kæm cams kæmz
camaraderie ˌkæm ə 'rɑːd ər i -'ræd-, -ə ri:
‖ ˌkɑːm-
Camargue kæ 'mɑːɡ kə- ‖ -'mɑːrɡ —Fr
[ka maʁɡ]
camarilla ˌkæm ə 'rɪl ə -jə ‖ -'riː jə —Sp
[ka ma 'ri ʎa, -ja] ~s z
Camay tdmk kæ 'meɪ 'kæm eɪ
cam|ber, C~ 'kæm |bə ‖ -bᵊr ~bered
bəd ‖ bᵊrd ~bering bər ɪŋ ~bers bəz ‖ bᵊrz
Camberley 'kæm bə li -bᵊl i ‖ -bᵊr-
Camberwell 'kæm bə wᵊl -wel ‖ -bᵊr-
ˌCamberwell 'beauty
cambium 'kæm bi‿əm
Cambodi|a kæm 'bəʊd i‿|ə ‖ -'boʊd- ~an/s
ən/z
Camborne 'kæm bɔːn ‖ -bɔːrn -boʊrn
Cambray 'kɒm breɪ 'kɒ̃- ‖ kɑːm 'breɪ —Fr
[kɑ̃ bʁɛ]
Cambri|a 'kæm bri‿|ə 'keɪm- ~an/s ən/z
Cambridge 'keɪm brɪdʒ ~shire ʃə ʃɪə ‖ ʃᵊr ʃɪr
cambric 'keɪm brɪk ~s s
Cambuslang ˌkæm bəs 'læŋ
Cambyses kæm 'baɪs iːz
camcorder 'kæm ˌkɔːd ə ˌ•'•• ‖ -ˌkɔːrd ᵊr ~s
z
Camden 'kæm dən
ˌCamden 'Town
came keɪm
camel 'kæm ᵊl ~s z
Camelford 'kæm ᵊl fəd ‖ -fᵊrd
camelhair 'kæm ᵊl heə ‖ -her
Camelia kə 'miːl i‿ə
camellia kə 'miːl i‿ə -'mel- ~s z
Camelot 'kæm ə lɒt -ɪ- ‖ -lɑːt

Camembert 'kæm əm beə -bɜːt ‖ -ber -bɜːt
—Fr [ka mɑ̃ bɛːʁ] ~s z
cameo 'kæm i əʊ ‖ -oʊ ~s z
camera 'kæm ər‿ə ~s z
cameral 'kæm ər əl
camera|man 'kæm rə |mæn -mən ~men men
mən
camera obscura ˌkæm ər ər əb 'skjʊər ə -ɒb'•-
‖ -ə əb 'skjʊr ə
camera-ready ˌkæm rə 'red i ◂
ˌcamera-ˌready 'copy
camera-shy 'kæm rə ʃaɪ -ər‿ə-
Cameron 'kæm ər‿ən
Cameronian ˌkæm ə 'rəʊn i‿ən ‖ -'roʊn- ~s z
Cameroon ˌkæm ə 'ruːn '••• ~s z
Cameroonian ˌkæm ə 'ruːn i‿ən ~s z
camiknicker 'kæm i ˌnɪk ə ˌ••'••• ‖ -ᵊr ~s z
camiknicks 'kæm i nɪks
Camilla kə 'mɪl ə
Camille kə 'mɪl -'miːᵊl
camisole 'kæm ɪ səʊl -ə-, →-sɒʊl ‖ -soʊl ~s z
camlet 'kæm lət -lɪt
Camoens, Camoëns 'kæm əʊ enz -enᵗs ‖ -oʊ-
—Port Camões [kɐ 'mõĩʃ]
camomile 'kæm ə maɪᵊl ~s z
ˌcamomile 'tea
camouflag|e 'kæm ə flɑːʒ -u-, -flɑːdʒ ~ed d
~es ɪz əz ~ing ɪŋ
Camoys (i) 'kæm ɔɪz, (ii) kə 'mɔɪz
camp, Camp kæmp camped kæmpt
camping 'kæmp ɪŋ camps kæmps
ˌcamp 'bed; ˌCamp 'David; ˌcamp
'follower; ˌ•ˌ•••
campaign ₍₎kæm 'peɪn ~ed d ~er/s ə/z ‖ ᵊr/z
~ing ɪŋ ~s z
campanile ˌkæmp ə 'niːl i -eɪ; -'niːᵊl i ˌkɑːmp-
~s z
campanologist ˌkæmp ə 'nɒl ədʒ ɪst §-əst
‖ -'nɑːl- ~s s
campanology ˌkæmp ə 'nɒl ədʒ i ‖ -'nɑːl-
campanula kæm 'pæn jʊl ə kəm-, -jəl- ~s z
Campari kæm 'pɑːr i ‖ kɑːm- —It [kam 'pɑː
ri]
Campbell 'kæm bᵊl ~s, 's z
Campbeltown 'kæm bᵊl taʊn
Campden 'kæm dən 'kæmp-
camper 'kæmp ə ‖ -ᵊr ~s z
campfire 'kæmp ˌfaɪə ‖ -ˌfaɪ‿ᵊr ~s z
campground 'kæmp graʊnd ~s z
camphor 'kæmᵖf ə ‖ -ᵊr
campho|rate 'kæmᵖf ə |reɪt ~rated reɪt ɪd -əd
‖ reɪt̬ əd
camping 'kæmp ɪŋ
campion, C~ 'kæmp i‿ən ~s z
Campling 'kæmp lɪŋ
Campsie 'kæmps i
campsite 'kæmp saɪt ~s s
campus 'kæmp əs ~es ɪz əz
campylobacter ˌkæmp ɪl əʊ 'bækt ə ˌ•əl-,
kæm ˌpɪl-, '•••ˌ•• ‖ -oʊ 'bækt ᵊr
CAMRA 'kæm rə
Camrose 'kæm rəʊz ‖ -roʊz
camshaft 'kæm ʃɑːft §-ʃæft ‖ -ʃæft ~s s

Camus kæ 'muː kə-, kɑː- —*Fr* [ka my]

can *v 'be able' strong form* kæn, *weak form* kən

can *n, v 'tin'* kæn **canned** kænd **canning**
'kæn ɪŋ **cans** kænz

Cana 'keɪn ə

Canaan 'keɪn ən 'keɪn i‿ən

Canaanite 'keɪn ə naɪt -i‿ə- ~s s

Canada 'kæn əd ə §-ɪd- ~'s z

Canadian kə 'neɪd i‿ən ~s z

canal kə 'næl ~s z
ca'nal boat

Canaletto ˌkæn ə 'let əʊ →‿əl 'et- ‖ -əl 'et oʊ
—*It* [ka na 'let to] ~s, ~'s z

canalis... — see canaliz...

canalization ˌkæn əl aɪ 'zeɪʃ ᵊn -ɪ'•-
‖ -əl ə 'zeɪʃ-

canaliz|e 'kæn ə laɪz -əl aɪz ‖ -əl aɪz ~ed d ~es
ɪz əz ~ing ɪŋ

canape, canapé 'kæn ə peɪ -əp i ~s z

canard 'kæn ɑːd kæ 'nɑːd, kə- ‖ kə 'nɑːrd
—*Fr* [ka naːʁ] ~s z

canar|y, C~ kə 'neər |i ‖ -'ner |i ~ies iz

canasta kə 'næst ə

Canavan 'kæn əv ən

Canaveral kə 'næv ᵊr‿əl

Canberra 'kæn bər‿ə →'kæm- ‖ -ber ə

cancan 'kæn kæn →'kæŋ-

cancel 'kæn͡ts ᵊl ~ed, ~led d ~ing, ~ling ͜ɪŋ
~s z

cancela... — see cancella...

cancellable 'kæn͡ts ᵊl‿əb ᵊl

canc|ellate 'kæn͡ts|ᵊl ət -ɪt; '•ə leɪt ~ellated
ə leɪt ɪd -əd; →'əl eɪt- ᵊl eɪt əd

cancellation ˌkæn͡ts ə 'leɪʃ ᵊn -ɪ-; -əl 'eɪʃ- ~s z

cancellous 'kæn͡ts ᵊl əs

cancer, C~ 'kæn͡ts ə ‖ -ᵊr ~s z

Cancerian ₍ₒ₎kæn 'sɪər i‿ən -'seər- ‖ -'sɪr- ~s z

cancerous 'kæn͡ts ᵊr‿əs ~ly li

cancroid 'kæŋk rɔɪd ~s z

Cancun, Cancún kæn 'kuːn ‖ kɑːn- —*Sp*
Cancún [kaŋ 'kun]

Candace 'kænd ɪs -əs; kæn 'deɪs i

candela kæn 'diːl ə -'del-, -'deɪl- ~s z

candelab|ra ˌkænd ə 'lɑːb |rə -ɪ-, -'læb- ~ras
rəz ~rum/s rəm/z

Canderel *tdmk* 'kænd ə rel ˌ•'•

Candi 'kænd i

Candia 'kænd i‿ə

Candice 'kænd ɪs -əs

candid 'kænd ɪd §-əd ~ly li ~ness nəs nɪs

Candida, c~ 'kænd ɪd ə §-əd-

candidac|y 'kænd ɪd əs |i '•əd- ‖ 'kæn- ~ies iz

candidate 'kænd ɪ deɪt -ə-; -ɪd ət, -əd-,
-ɪt ‖ 'kæn- ~s s

candidature 'kænd ɪd ət ʃ ə '•əd-, -ɪt ʃ-;
-ɪ deɪt ʃ-, -ə deɪt ʃ- ‖ 'kænd əd ə t ʃʊr 'kæn-,
-ət ʃ ᵊr ~s z

Candide ₍ₒ₎kɒn 'diːd kɒ̃- ‖ ₍ₒ₎kɑːn- —*Fr*
[kɑ̃ did]

candidiasis ˌkænd ɪ 'daɪ‿ə sɪs ˌ•ə-, §-əs

candi... —*see* candy

candle 'kænd ᵊl ~s z

candle|light 'kænd ᵊl| laɪt ~lit lɪt

Candlemas 'kænd ᵊl mæs -məs

candlepower 'kænd ᵊl ˌpaʊ‿ə ‖ -ˌpaʊ‿ᵊr

Candler 'kænd lə ‖ -lᵊr

candlestick 'kænd ᵊl stɪk ~s s

candlewick 'kænd ᵊl wɪk

Candlin 'kænd lɪn -lən

can-do ˌkæn 'duː ◂

candor, candour 'kænd ə ‖ -ᵊr

cand|y, Candy 'kænd |i ~ied id ~ies iz
~ying i ɪŋ
'candy stripe; 'candy ˌstriper

candyfloss 'kænd i flɒs ‖ -flɔːs -flɑːs

candy-striped 'kænd i straɪpt

candytuft 'kænd i tʌft

cane, Cane keɪn **caned** keɪnd **canes** keɪnz
caning 'keɪn ɪŋ

canebrake 'keɪn breɪk →'keɪm-

Canes Venatici ˌkeɪn iːz vɪ 'næt ɪ saɪ ˌkɑːn-,
ˌ•eɪz-, -və'•-, ve'•-, -ə•-, -kiː

Canewdon kə 'njuːd ᵊn

Canfield, c~ 'kæn fiːᵊld

Canicula kə 'nɪk jʊl ə -jəl-

canicular kə 'nɪk jʊl ə -jəl- ‖ -jəl ᵊr

canine 'keɪn aɪn 'kæn- ~s z

caning 'keɪn ɪŋ ~s z

Canis 'keɪn ɪs 'kæn-, §-əs

canister 'kæn ɪst ə -əst- ‖ -ᵊr ~s z

cank|er 'kæŋk |ə ‖ -|ᵊr ~ered əd ‖ ᵊrd ~ering
ər ɪŋ ~ers əz ‖ ᵊrz

cankerous 'kæŋk ᵊr əs

Cann kæn

canna 'kæn ə ~s z

cannabis 'kæn əb ɪs §-əs

Cannae 'kæn iː

cann... —*see* can

cannel 'kæn ᵊl

cannelloni, canneloni ˌkæn ə 'ləʊn i -ɪ-;
-əl 'əʊn- ‖ -əl 'oʊn i —*It* [kan nel 'lo ni]

canner, C~ 'kæn ə ‖ -ᵊr

canner|y 'kæn ᵊr |i ~ies iz

Cannes kæn kænz —*Fr* [kan]

cannibal 'kæn ɪb ᵊl -əb- ~s z

cannibalis... —*see* cannibaliz...

cannibalism 'kæn ɪb ə ˌlɪz əm '•əb-, -əl ˌɪz-

cannibalistic ˌkæn ɪb ə 'lɪst ɪk ◂ ˌ•əb-, -əl 'ɪst-

cannibalization ˌkæn ɪb ᵊl aɪ 'zeɪʃ ᵊn ˌ•əb-,
-ɪ'•- ‖ -ə 'zeɪʃ-

cannibaliz|e 'kæn ɪb ə laɪz '•əb-, -əl aɪz ~ed d
~es ɪz əz ~ing ɪŋ

canni... — see canny

cannikin 'kæn ɪk ɪn -ək-, §-ən ~s z

Canning 'kæn ɪŋ

Cannizzaro ˌkæn ɪ 'zɑːr əʊ -ə- ‖ -oʊ —*It*
[kan nit 'tsa ro]

Cannock 'kæn ək

cannon, C~ 'kæn ən ~ed d ~ing ɪŋ ~s z
'cannon ˌfodder

cannonad|e ˌkæn ə 'neɪd ~ed ɪd əd ~es z
~ing ɪŋ

cannonball 'kæn ən bɔːl →-əm- ‖ -bɑːl ~s z

cannot 'kæn ɒt -ət; §kæ 'nɒt, kə- ‖ 'kæn ɑːt
kə 'nɑːt, kæ- —*see also* can't

cann|ula 'kæn |jʊl ə -jəl- ‖ -|jəl ə **~ulae** ju liː
jə-, -laɪ ‖ jə- **~ulas** jʊl əz jəl- ‖ jəl əz
cann|y 'kæn |i **~ier** i‿ə ‖ i‿ʳr **~iest** i‿ɪst i‿əst
~ily ɪ li əl i **~iness** i nəs i nɪs
canoe kə 'nuː **~d** d **~ing** ɪŋ **~s** z
canoeist kə 'nuː‿ɪst §‿əst **~s** s
canola kə 'nəʊl ə ‖ -'noʊl-
canon, Canon 'kæn ən *(= cannon)* **~s** z
,canon' law
cañon 'kæn jən —*AmSp* cañón [ka 'ɲon] **~s** z
Canonbury 'kæn ən bər‿i →'•əm- ‖ -ˌber i
canoness ˌkæn ə 'nes 'kæn ən ɪs, §-əs, -ə nes
‖ 'kæn ən əs **~es** ɪz əz
canonical kə 'nɒn ɪk əl ‖ -'nɑːn- **~ly**‿i **~s** z
canonicity ˌkæn ə 'nɪs ət i ,•ɒ-, -ɪt i ‖ -ət̬ i
canonis... —*see* **canoniz...**
canonization ˌkæn ən aɪ 'zeɪʃ ən -ɪ'•-
‖ -ə 'zeɪʃ- **~s** z
canoniz|e 'kæn ə naɪz **~ed** d **~es** ɪz əz **~ing**
ɪŋ
canon|ry 'kæn ən |ri **~ries** riz
canoodl|e kə 'nuːd əl **~ed** d **~es** z **~ing**‿ɪŋ
can-opener 'kæn ˌəʊp ən‿ə ‖ -ˌoʊp ən‿ʳr **~s** z
Canopic kə 'nəʊp ɪk kæ-, -'nɒp- ‖ -'noʊp-
-'nɑːp-
canopi... —*see* **canopy**
Canopus kə 'nəʊp əs kæ- ‖ -'noʊp-
canop|y 'kæn əp |i **~ied** id **~ies** iz
Canossa kə 'nɒs ə kæ- ‖ -'nɑːs- —*It*
[ka 'nos sa]
canst *strong form* kænst , *weak form* kən‹t›st
cant, Cant kænt **canted** 'kænt ɪd -əd
‖ 'kænt̬ əd **canting/ly** 'kænt ɪŋ /li ‖ 'kænt̬-
cants kænts
can't kɑːnt ‖ kænt △keɪnt —*Before a*
consonant (less frequently before a vowel) also
kɑːn ‖ kæn. Unlike can, this word has no weak
form.
Cantab 'kænt æb
cantabile kæn 'tɑːb ɪ leɪ -ə leɪ; -əl i, -ɪl i
Cantabrian kæn 'teɪb ri‿ən **~s** z
Cantabrigian ˌkænt ə 'brɪdʒ i‿ən ◂ **~s** z
cantaloup, cantaloupe
'kænt ə luːp ‖ 'kænt̬ ə loʊp *(*)* **~s** s
cantankerous kæn 'tæŋk ər‿əs kən- **~ly** li
~ness nəs nɪs
cantata kæn 'tɑːt ə kən- ‖ kən 'tɑːt̬ ə **~s** z
canteen₍ᵢ₎ kæn 'tiːn **~s** z
canter, C~ 'kænt ə ‖ 'kænt̬ ʳr **~ed** d
cantering 'kænt ər‿ɪŋ ‖ 'kænt̬ ʳr ɪŋ **~s** z
Canterbury, c~ 'kænt ə bər‿i -ˌber i
‖ 'kænt̬ ʳr ˌber i
cantharides kæn 'θær ɪ diːz -ə- ‖ -'θer-
canth|us 'kænt θ |əs **~i** aɪ
canticle 'kænt ɪk əl §-ək- ‖ 'kænt̬ ək əl **~s** z
cantilena ˌkænt ɪ 'leɪn ə -ə-, -'liːn- ‖ ˌkænt̬-
~s z
cantilev|er 'kænt ɪ liːv ə '•ə-; -əl iːv-
‖ 'kænt̬ əl iːv |ʳr -ev ʳr **~ered** əd ‖ ʳrd
~ering ər‿ɪŋ **~ers** əz ‖ ʳrz
canto 'kænt əʊ ‖ -oʊ **~s** z
canton *'political division, esp. Swiss'* 'kænt ɒn
₍ᵢ₎ kæn 'tɒn ‖ 'kænt ɑːn -ən; kæn 'tɑːn **~s** z

canton *in heraldry; on flag* 'kænt ən **~ed** d
~ing ɪŋ **~s** z
Canton *place in China* ˌkæn 'tɒn ◂ ‖ -'tɑːn ◂
—*Chi* Guǎngzhōu [³kwaŋ ¹t͡sou]
Canton *places in UK, US; family name* 'kænt ən
canton *v 'quarter (soldiers)'* kæn 'tuːn kən-
‖ -'tɑːn -'toʊn **~ed** d **~ing** ɪŋ **~s** z
Cantona ˌkænt ə 'nɑː —*Fr* [kɑ̃ to na]
cantonal 'kænt ən əl kæn 'təʊn əl, -'tɒn-
‖ 'kænt ən əl kæn 'tɑːn əl
Cantonese ˌkænt ə 'niːz ◂ ‖ -ən 'iːz ◂ -'iːs
cantonment kæn 'tuːn mənt kən-, →-'tuːm-
‖ -'tɑːn- -'toʊn- **~s** z
cantor, C~ 'kænt ɔː -ə ‖ -ʳr
cantorial kæn 'tɔːr i‿əl ‖ -'toʊr-
cantoris kæn 'tɔːr ɪs §-əs ‖ -'toʊr-
Cantuar 'kænt ju ɑː ‖ -ɑːr
Canuck kə 'nʌk **~s** s
can|ula 'kæn |jʊl ə -jəl- ‖ -|jəl ə **~ulae** ju liː
jə-, -laɪ ‖ jə- **~ulas** jʊl əz jəl- ‖ jəl əz
Canute kə 'njuːt -'nuːt ‖ -'nuːt -'njuːt
canvas 'kænv əs **~es** ɪz əz
canvasback 'kænv əs bæk **~s** s
canvass 'kænv əs **~ed** t **~er/s** ə/z ‖ ʳr/z **~es**
ɪz əz **~ing** ɪŋ
Canvey 'kænv i
canyon 'kæn jən **~s** z
,Canyon de' Chelly *place in AZ* də 'ʃeɪ
cap kæp **capped** kæpt **capping** 'kæp ɪŋ **caps**
kæps
CAP ˌsiː eɪ 'piː
capabilit|y ˌkeɪp ə 'bɪl ət i -ɪt i ‖ -ət̬ i **~ies** iz
capable 'keɪp əb əl **~ness** nəs nɪs
capably 'keɪp əb li
capacious kə 'peɪʃ əs **~ly** li **~ness** nəs nɪs
capacitanc|e kə 'pæs ɪt ən‹t›s -ət- **~es** ɪz əz
capacitor kə 'pæs ɪt ə -ət- ‖ -ət̬ ʳr **~s** z
capacit|y kə 'pæs ət |i -ɪt- ‖ -ət̬ i **~ies** iz
cap-a-pie, cap-a-pie ˌkæp ə 'piː -'peɪ
caparison kə 'pær ɪs ən -əs- ‖ -'per- **~ed** d
~ing‿ɪŋ **~s** z
cape, Cape keɪp **capes** keɪps —*See also*
phrases with this word
,Cape Ca' naveral; ,Cape' Horn; ,Cape of
,Good' Hope; ,Cape' Province; 'Cape
Town
Cape Girardeau *place in MO*
ˌkeɪp dʒə 'rɑːd əʊ ‖ -'rɑːrd oʊ
Capel 'keɪp əl —*but in Welsh place names* 'kæp-
—*Welsh* ['kap el]
,Capel' Curig 'kɪr ɪg -'kjʊər- —*Welsh*
['kɪ rig, 'ke-]
capelin 'keɪp əl‿ɪn §‿ən
Capell 'keɪp əl
Capella kə 'pel ə
Capenhurst 'keɪp ən hɜːst ‖ -hɝːst
cap|er 'keɪp |ə ‖ -ʳr **~ered** əd ‖ ʳrd **~ering**
ər‿ɪŋ **~ers** əz ‖ ʳrz
capercaillie, capercailzie ˌkæp ə 'keɪl i -ji
‖ -ʳr- **~s** z
Capernaum kə 'pɜːn i‿əm -eɪ-; •'•əm
‖ -'pɝːn-
Capetian kə 'piːʃ ən **~s** z

Cape Verd|e ˌkeɪp 'vɜːd-'veəd ‖ -'vɝːd
~ean/s i_ən/z
capful 'kæp fʊl ~s z
capillarit|y ˌkæp ɪ 'lær ət li ˌ•ə-, -ɪt i ‖ -əţ li
-'ler- ~ies iz
capillar|y kə 'pɪl ər li ‖ 'kæp ə ler li(*) ~ies iz
Capistrano ˌkæp ɪ 'strɑːn əʊ §-ɑ- ‖ -oʊ
capital 'kæp ɪt ³l -ət- ‖ -əţ- ~s z
ˌcapital 'gain; ˌcapital 'punishment
capital-intensive ˌkæp ɪt ³l ɪn 'ten¹s ɪv ◄ ˌ•ət-,
§-ən' •- ‖ ˌkæp əţ- ~ly li
capitalis... —see capitaliz...
capitalism 'kæp ɪt ə ˌlɪz əm'•ət-, -³l ˌɪz-;
kæ 'pɪt-, kə- ‖ -əţ ³l ˌɪz-
capitalist 'kæp ɪt ³l ɪst '•ət-, kæ 'pɪt-, kə 'pɪt-,
§-əst ‖ 'kæp əţ ³l əst ~s s
capitalistic ˌkæp ɪt ə 'lɪst ɪk ◄ˌ•ət-, -³l 'ɪst-
‖ -əţ ³l 'ɪst- ~ally ³l_i
capitalization ˌkæp ɪt ³l aɪ 'zeɪʃ ³n ˌ•ət-, -ɪ'•-;
kæ 'pɪt-, kə- ‖ -əţ ³lə 'zeɪʃ- ~s z
capitaliz|e 'kæp ɪt ə laɪz'•ət-, -³l aɪz; kæ 'pɪt-,
kə- ‖ -əţ ³l aɪz ~ed d ~es ɪz əz ~ing ɪŋ
capitation ˌkæp ɪ 'teɪʃ ³n -ə-
capitol, C~ 'kæp ɪt ³l -ət-; -ɪ tɒl, -ə- ‖ -əţ ³l
-ə tɑːl (usually = capital) ~s z
Capitoline kə 'pɪt əʊ laɪn 'kæp ɪt-, '•ət-, -³l aɪn
‖ 'kæp əţ ³l aɪn
capitul|a kə 'pɪt jʊl lə -jəl- ‖ -'pɪtʃ əl lə ~ar
ə ‖ ³r
capitu|late kə 'pɪt ju lleɪt -jə-; -'pɪtʃ u-, -ə-
‖ -'pɪtʃ ə- ~lated leɪt ɪd-əd ‖ leɪţ əd ~lates
leɪts ~lating leɪt ɪŋ ‖ leɪţ ɪŋ
capitulation kə ˌpɪt ju 'leɪʃ ³n -jə-; -ˌpɪtʃ u-,
-ə- ‖ -ˌpɪtʃ ə- ~s z
capitul|um kə 'pɪt jʊl ləm-jəl- ‖ -'pɪtʃ əl- ~a
ə
Caplan 'kæp lən
caplet, C~ tdmk 'kæp lət -lɪt
capo for guitar 'kæp əʊ 'keɪp- ‖ 'keɪp oʊ ~s z
capo 'Mafia leader' 'kɑːp əʊ 'kæp- ‖ -oʊ ~s z
Capodimonte, Capo-di-Monte
ˌkæp əʊ di 'mɒnt eɪ ˌkɑːp-, -i
‖ ˌkɑːp oʊ diː 'mɑːnt eɪ —It
[ˌkaː po di 'mon te]
capon, Capon 'keɪp ən -ɒn ‖ -ɑːn -ən ~s z
Capone kə 'pəʊn ‖ -'poʊn
capote kə 'pəʊt ‖ -'poʊt —Fr [ka pɔt] ~s s
Capote kə 'pəʊt i ‖ -'poʊţ i
Capp kæp
Cappa, Cappagh 'kæp ə
Cappadoci|a ˌkæp ə 'dəʊs i_ə-'dəʊʃ-,
-'dəʊʃ lə ‖ -'doʊʃ- ~an/s ən/z
capp... —see cap
capper, C~ 'kæp ə ‖ -³r
cappuccino ˌkæp u 'tʃiːn əʊ -ə-
‖ ˌkɑːp ə 'tʃiːn oʊ -jə- ~s z
Capri kə 'priː kæ-; 'kæp riː —It ['kaː pri]
capric 'kæp rɪk
capriccio kə 'priːtʃ i_əʊ -'prɪtʃ- ‖ _oʊ ~s z
capriccioso kə ˌpriːtʃ i 'əʊs əʊ -ˌprɪtʃ-, -'əʊz-
‖ -'oʊs oʊ
capric|e kə 'priːs ~es ɪz əz

capricious kə 'prɪʃ əs ‖ -'priːʃ- ~ly li ~ness
nəs nɪs
Capricorn 'kæp rɪ kɔːn -rə- ‖ -kɔːrn ~s z
Capricorn|ian ˌkæp rɪ 'kɔːn i_ən ◄ ˌ•rə-
‖ -'kɔːrnl- ~ians i_ənz ~us əs
caprine 'kæp raɪn
capriol|e 'kæp ri əʊl→-ɒʊl ‖ -oʊl ~ed d ~es z
~ing ɪŋ
Caprivi kə 'priːv i kæ-
caproic kə 'prəʊ ɪk kæ- ‖ -'proʊ-
capsicum 'kæps ɪk əm-ək- ~s z

CAPSIZE

AmE 1993

▮ ••	▭ •'•

0   20   40   60   80   100%

capsiz|e (ˌ)kæp 'saɪz ‖ 'kæps aɪz—AmE 1993
poll panel preference: '•• 93%, •'• 7%. ~ed
d ~es ɪz əz ~ing ɪŋ
capstan 'kæpst ən ‖ -æn ~s z
'capstan lathe
capstone 'kæp stəʊn ‖ -stoʊn ~s z
capsular 'kæps jʊl ə-jəl- ‖ -³l ³r
capsule 'kæps juːl-³l ‖ -³l-uːl ~s z
captain 'kæpt ɪn -ən ‖ -ən—also, particularly
nautical or as a vocative, 'kæp ən ; with this
pronunciation also spelt cap'n ~ed d ~ing ɪŋ
~s z
captain|cy 'kæpt ən lsi-ɪn- ~cies siz
captainship 'kæpt ɪn ʃɪp-ən-
caption 'kæp ʃ³n ~ed d ~ing ɪŋ ~s z
captious 'kæp ʃəs ~ly li ~ness nəs nɪs
capti|vate 'kæpt ɪ lveɪt -ə- ~vated veɪt ɪd-əd
‖ veɪţ əd ~vates veɪts ~vating
veɪt ɪŋ ‖ veɪţ ɪŋ
captivation ˌkæpt ɪ 'veɪʃ ³n -ə-
captivator 'kæpt ɪ veɪt ə '•ə- ‖ -veɪţ ³r ~s z
captive 'kæpt ɪv ~s z
captivit|y kæp 'tɪv ət li -ɪt- ‖ -əţ li ~ies iz
captor 'kæpt ə ‖ -³r-ɔːr ~s z
cap|ture 'kæp tʃə-ʃə ‖ -ltʃ³r-ʃ³r ~tured tʃəd
ʃəd ‖ tʃ³rd ʃ³rd ~tures tʃəz ʃəz ‖ tʃ³rz ʃ³rz
~turing tʃər ɪŋ ʃər-
Capua 'kæp ju_ə—It ['ka pu a]
capuch|e kə 'puːʃ-'puːtʃ ~es ɪz əz
capuchin 'kæp jʊtʃ ɪn-juʃ-, §-ən; kə 'puːtʃ-,
-'puːʃ- ‖ 'kæp jəʃ ³n kə 'pjuːtʃ ən ~s z
Capulet 'kæp ju let -lət, -lɪt ‖ -jəl ət ~s s
capybara ˌkæp i 'bɑːr ə ‖ -'bær-, -'ber- ~s z
car kɑː ‖ kɑːr cars kɑːz ‖ kɑːrz
'car park; 'car pool; 'car wash
Cara 'kɑːr ə ‖ kær-, 'ker-
carabiner ˌkær ə 'biːn ə ‖ -³r ˌker- ~s z
carabinieri ˌkær ə bɪn i 'eər i ‖ ˌkær əb ən ən 'jer i
ˌker- —It [ka ra bi 'nje: ri]
caracal 'kær ə kæl ‖ 'ker- ~s z
Caracalla ˌkær ə 'kæl ə ‖ ˌker-
caracara ˌkær ə 'kɑːr ə ˌkɑːr- ‖ ˌker-, -kə 'rɑː
~s z
Caracas kə 'ræk əs -'rɑːk- ‖ -'rɑːk- —Sp
[ka 'ra kas]
caracol|e 'kær ə kəʊl→-kɒʊl ‖ -koʊl 'ker- ~ed
d ~es z ~ing ɪŋ

Caractacus kə ˈrækt ək əs
caracul ˈkær ə kʌl -ək ᵊl ‖ -ˈker-
Caradoc kə ˈræd ɒk -ək ‖ -ɑːk
Caradog kə ˈræd ɒg ‖ -ɑːg -ɔːg
　—*Welsh*[ka ˈra dog]
Caradon ˈkær əd ən ‖ ˈker-
carafe kə ˈræf -ˈrɑːf ~s s
carambola ˌkær əm ˈbəʊl ə ‖ -ˈboʊl ə ˌker- ~s
　z
caramel ˈkær ə mel -əm ᵊl ‖ -əm ᵊl ker-, -ə mel;
　ˈkɑːrm ᵊl ~s z
caramelis|e, carameliz|e ˈkær əm ə laɪz -ᵊl aɪz;
　-ə mel aɪz ‖ ˈker-; ˈkɑːrm ə laɪz ~ed d ~es
　ɪz əz ~ing ɪŋ
Caran d'Ache *tdmk* ˌkær ən ˈdæʃ ‖ ˌkɑːr
　ən ˈdɑːʃ ˌkær-, ˌker-
carapac|e ˈkær ə peɪs ‖ ˈker- ~es ɪz əz
carat ˈkær ət ‖ ˈker- (= *carrot*) ~s s
Caravaggio ˌkær ə ˈvædʒ i əʊ ˌkɑːr-, -ˈvɑːdʒ-
　‖ ˌkær ə ˈvɑːdʒ oʊ ˌker- —*It* [ka ra ˈvad dʒo]
caravan ˈkær ə væn ˌ•ˈ•ᵊ• ‖ ˈker- ~er/s,
　~ner/s ə/z ‖ ᵊr/z ~ing, ~ning ɪŋ ~s z
caravansary ˌkær ə ˈvæn sər i ‖ ˌker-
caravanserai ˌkær ə ˈvæn sə raɪ -reɪ,
　-sər i ‖ ˌker- ~s z
caravel ˈkær ə vel ˌ•ˈ•ᵊ•; ˈkær əv ᵊl ‖ ˈker- ~s z
caraway ˈkær ə weɪ ‖ ˈker-
carb kɑːb ‖ kɑːrb **carbs** kɑːbz ‖ kɑːrbz
carbamate ˈkɑːb ə meɪt ‖ ˈkɑːrb-
carbazole ˈkɑːb ə zəʊl →-zɒʊl ‖ ˈkɑːrb ə zoʊl
carbide ˈkɑːb aɪd ‖ ˈkɑːrb- ~s z
carbine ˈkɑːb aɪn ‖ ˈkɑːrb iːn -aɪn ~s z
carbineer ˌkɑːb ɪ ˈnɪə -ə- ‖ ˌkɑːrb ə ˈnɪᵊr ~s z
Carbis ˈkɑːb ɪs §-əs ‖ ˈkɑːrb-
carbohydrate ˌkɑːb əʊ ˈhaɪdr eɪt ‖ ˌkɑːrb oʊ-
　-ə- ~s s
carbolic kɑː ˈbɒl ɪk ‖ kɑːr ˈbɑːl ɪk
carbon ˈkɑːb ən ‖ ˈkɑːrb- ~s z
　ˌcarbon ˈcopy; ˌcarbon ˈdating; ˌcarbon
　diˈoxide; ˈcarbon ˌpaper
carbonade ˌkɑːb ə ˈneɪd -ˈnɑːd, ˈ•ˈ• ‖ ˌkɑːrb-
　~s z
carbonado ˌkɑːb ə ˈneɪd əʊ -ˈnɑːd-
　‖ ˌkɑːrb ə ˈneɪd oʊ ~es, ~s z
carbo|nate *v* ˈkɑːb ə |neɪt ‖ ˈkɑːrb- ~nated
　neɪt ɪd -əd ‖ neɪt̬ əd ~nates neɪts ~nating
　neɪt ɪŋ ‖ neɪt̬ ɪŋ
carbonate *n* ˈkɑːb ə neɪt -ən ət, -ɪt ‖ ˈkɑːrb-
　~s s
carbonation ˌkɑːb ə ˈneɪʃ ᵊn ‖ ˌkɑːrb-
carbonic kɑː ˈbɒn ɪk ‖ kɑːr ˈbɑːn ɪk
carboniferous, C~ ˌkɑːb ə ˈnɪf ᵊr_əs ◀ ‖ ˌkɑːrb-
carbonis... —see **carboniz...**
carbonization ˌkɑːb ən aɪ ˈzeɪʃ ᵊn -ɪˈ•-
　‖ ˌkɑːrb ən ə- ~s z
carboniz|e ˈkɑːb ə naɪz ‖ ˈkɑːrb- ~ed d ~es ɪz
　əz ~ing ɪŋ
carbonyl ˈkɑːb ə naɪ ᵊl -nɪl, -ən ᵊl ‖ ˈkɑːrb ə nɪl
　-niːᵊl, ˌ•ˈ•ᵊ•
carborundum, C~ *tdmk* ˌkɑːb ə ˈrʌnd əm
　‖ ˌkɑːrb-
Carbost ˈkɑːb ɒst ‖ ˈkɑːrb ɔːst -ɑːst

carboxyl kɑː ˈbɒks ɪl -aɪᵊl, §-ᵊl ‖ kɑːr ˈbɑːks ᵊl
carboy ˈkɑːb ɔɪ ‖ ˈkɑːrb- ~s z
carbuncle ˈkɑːb ʌŋk ᵊl ‖ ˈkɑːrb- ~s z
carburant ˈkɑːb jʊr ənt -jər-, -ər- ‖ ˈkɑːrb ər-
　-jər- ~s s
carburation ˌkɑːb ju ˈreɪʃ ᵊn -jə-, -ə-
　‖ ˌkɑːrb ə- -jə-
carburetor, carburetter, carburettor
　ˌkɑːb ə ˈret ə -juᵊ-, ˈ•••ᵊ ‖ ˈkɑːrb ə reɪt̬ ᵊr
　(*) ~s z
carcajou ˈkɑːk ə dʒuː -ʒuː ‖ ˈkɑːrk- ~s z
carcas|e, carcass ˈkɑːk əs ‖ ˈkɑːrk- ~es ɪz əz
Carcassonne ˌkɑːk ə ˈsɒn ‖ ˌkɑːrk ə ˈsɑːn
　-ˈsɔːn —*Fr* [kaʁ ka sɔn]
Carchemish ˈkɑːk ə mɪʃ -ɪ-; kɑː ˈkiːm ɪʃ
　‖ ˈkɑːrk- kɑːr ˈkiːm ɪʃ
carcinogen kɑː ˈsɪn ədʒ ən ˈkɑːs ɪn-, -ə dʒen
　‖ kɑːr- ˈkɑːrs ᵊn ə dʒen ~s z
carcinogenic ˌkɑːs ɪn ə ˈdʒen ɪk ◀ ˌ•ən-;
　kɑː ˌsɪn- ‖ ˌkɑːrs ᵊn oʊ- kɑːr ˌsɪn-, -əˈ••-
carcinoma ˌkɑːs ɪ ˈnəʊm ə -ə-, -ᵊn ˈəʊm-
　‖ ˌkɑːrs ᵊn ˈoʊm ə ~s z
card kɑːd ‖ kɑːrd **carded** ˈkɑːd ɪd -əd ‖ˈkɑːrd-
　carding ˈkɑːd ɪŋ ‖ ˈkɑːrd- **cards**
　kɑːdz ‖ kɑːrdz
　ˌcard ˈindex, ˈ• ˌ••
cardamom, cardamum ˈkɑːd əm əm ‖ ˈkɑːrd-
　-ə mɑːm
cardan, C~ ˈkɑːd ᵊn -æn ‖ ˈkɑːrd-
cardboard ˈkɑːd bɔːd →ˈkɑːb- ‖ ˈkɑːrd bɔːrd
　-boʊrd
card-carrying ˈkɑːd ˌkær i_ɪŋ →ˈkɑːg-
　‖ ˈkɑːrd- -ˌker-
Cardew ˈkɑː djuː ‖ ˈkɑːr duː
cardi- *comb. form* ˈkɑːd i ‖ ˈkɑːrd i —
　cardialgia ˌkɑːd i ˈæld ʒi_ə -ˈæld ʒ ə ‖ ˌkɑːrd-
cardiac ˈkɑːd i æk ‖ ˈkɑːrd-
cardie ˈkɑːd i ‖ ˈkɑːrd i ~s z
Cardiff ˈkɑːd ɪf §-əf ‖ ˈkɑːrd əf
cardigan, C~ ˈkɑːd ɪg ən ‖ ˈkɑːrd- ~s z
Cardin ˈkɑːd æ̃ -æn ‖ kɑːr ˈdæn —*Fr* [kaʁ dæ̃]
cardinal ˈkɑːd ɪn ᵊl -ᵊn_ᵊl ‖ ˈkɑːrd- ~s z
　ˌcardinal ˈpoint; ˌcardinal ˈvowel
cardinality ˌkɑːd ɪ ˈnæl ət i ˌ•ə-, -ᵊn ˈæl-, -ɪt i
　‖ ˌkɑːrd ᵊn ˈæl ət̬ i
cardio- *comb. form*
　with stress-neutral suffix
　ˈkɑːd i_əʊ ‖ ˈkɑːrd i_oʊ ə —
　cardiomyopathy
　ˌkɑːd i_əʊ maɪ ˈɒp əθ i ‖ ˌkɑːrd i_oʊ maɪ ˈɑːp-
　with stress-imposing suffix
　ˌkɑːd i ˈɒ+ ‖ ˌkɑːrd i ˈɑː+ — **cardiography**
　ˌkɑːd i ˈɒg rəf i ‖ ˌkɑːrd i ˈɑːg-
cardiogram ˈkɑːd i_əʊ græm ‖ ˈkɑːrd i_ə- ~s z
cardioid ˈkɑːd i ɔɪd ‖ ˈkɑːrd- ~s z
cardiological
　ˌkɑːd i_ə ˈlɒdʒ ɪk ᵊl ◀ ˌkɑːrd i_ə ˈlɑːdʒ- ~ly
　_i
cardiologist ˌkɑːd i ˈɒl ədʒ ɪst §-əst
　‖ ˌkɑːrd i ˈɑːl- ~s s
cardiology ˌkɑːd i ˈɒl ədʒ i ‖ ˌkɑːrd i ˈɑːl-
cardiovascular ˌkɑːd i_əʊ ˈvæsk jʊl ə ◀ -jəl ə
　‖ ˌkɑːrd i oʊ ˈvæsk jəl ᵊr

cardoon ₍ᵢ₎kɑː ˈduːn ‖ ₍ᵢ₎kɑːr- **~s** z
cardpunch ˈkɑːd pʌntʃ →ˈkɑːb- ‖ ˈkɑːrd- **~es**
  ɪz əz
cardsharp ˈkɑːd ʃɑːp ‖ ˈkɑːrd ʃɑːrp **~ing** ɪŋ
  ~s s
cardsharper ˈkɑːd ˌʃɑːp ə ‖ ˈkɑːrd ˌʃɑːrp ər **~s**
  z
Cardus ˈkɑːd əs ‖ ˈkɑːrd-
card|y ˈkɑːd| i ‖ ˈkɑːrd| i **~ies** iz
care keə ‖ keər kæər **cared** keəd ‖ keərd kæərd
  cares keəz ‖ keərz kæərz **caring**
  ˈkeər ɪŋ ‖ ˈker ɪŋ ˈkær-
careen kə ˈriːn **~ed** d **~ing** ɪŋ **~s** z
career kə ˈrɪə ‖ -ˈrɪər **careered**
  kə ˈrɪəd ‖ -ˈrɪərd **careering**
  kə ˈrɪər ɪŋ ‖ -ˈrɪr ɪŋ **careers** kə ˈrɪəz ‖ -ˈrɪərz
careerism kə ˈrɪər ˌɪz əm ‖ -ˈrɪr-
careerist kə ˈrɪər ɪst §-əst ‖ -ˈrɪr- **~s** s
carefree ˈkeə friː ˌ•ˈ• ‖ ˈker- ˈkær-
careful ˈkeəf ᵊl -ʊl ‖ ˈkerf- ˈkærf- **~ly** ̩i
  ~ness nəs nɪs
caregiver ˈkeə ˌɡɪv ə ‖ ˈker ˌɡɪv ər ˈkær- **~s** z
careless ˈkeə ləs -lɪs ‖ ˈker- ˈkær- **~ly** li **~ness**
  nəs nɪs —*See poll figures at* **-less**
carer ˈkeər ə ‖ ˈker ər ˈkær- **~s** z
caress kə ˈres **~ed** t **~es** ɪz əz **~ing** ɪŋ
caret ˈkær ɪt -ət, -et ‖ ˈker- **~s** s
caretaker ˈkeə ˌteɪk ə ‖ ˈker ˌteɪk ər ˈkær- **~s** z
  ˈcaretaker ˌgovernment
Carew *family name (i)* kə ˈruː, *(ii)* ˈkeər i ‖ ˈker i
Carew *place in Dyfed* ˈkeər uː -i ‖ ˈker-
careworn ˈkeə wɔːn ‖ ˈker wɔːrn -woʊrn
Carey ˈkeər i ‖ ˈker i
carfare ˈkɑː feə ‖ ˈkɑːr fer
Carfax ˈkɑː fæks ‖ ˈkɑːr-
Cargill *(i)* ˈkɑː ɡɪl ‖ ˈkɑːr-, *(ii)* ˈɡɪl ‖ kɑːr-
cargo ˈkɑːɡ əʊ ‖ ˈkɑːrɡ oʊ **~es, ~s** z
Carholme ˈkɑː həʊm ‖ ˈkɑːr houm
carhop ˈkɑː hɒp ‖ ˈkɑːr hɑːp **~s** s
Caria ˈkeər i‿ə ‖ ˈker- ˈkær-
Carib ˈkær ɪb §-əb ‖ ˈker- **~s** z

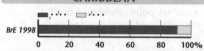

CARIBBEAN

BrE 1998

0   20   40   60   80   100%

Caribbean ˌkær ə ˈbiː‿ən ◄ -ɪ-;
  kə ˈrɪb i‿ən ‖ ˌker- —*BrE 1998 poll panel*
  preference: ˌ•ˈ•ˈ•• 91%, •ˈ•ˈ•• 9%
  ˌCarib ˌbean ˈSea, •ˌ•ˈ•• ˈ•
caribou ˈkær ə buː -ɪ- ‖ ˈker- **~s** z
caricatur|e ˈkær ɪk ə tʃʊə ˈ•ək-, -tjʊə, -tʃɔː,
  -tjɔː; ˌ•••ˈ• ‖ -tʃʊr ˈker-, -tʊr, -tjʊr; -ətʃ ər
  ~ed d **~es** z **caricaturing** ˈkær ɪk ə tʃʊər ɪŋ
  ˈ•ək-, -tjʊər ɪŋ, -tʃɔː ɪŋ, -tjɔː ɪŋ; ˌ•••ˈ••
  ‖ -tʃʊr ɪŋ ˈker-, -tʊr ɪŋ, -tjʊr ɪŋ; -ətʃ ər ɪŋ
caricaturist ˈkær ɪk ə tʃʊər ɪst ˈ•ək-, -tjʊər•,
  -tʃɔːr•, -tjɔːr•, §-əst; ˌ•••ˈ•• ‖ -tʃʊr əst
  ˈker-, -tʊr•, -tjʊr•, -tʃ‿ər• **~s** s
CARICOM ˈkær ɪ kɒm -ə- ‖ ˈkɑːm ˈker-
caries ˈkeər iz -iːz; ˈkeər i iːz ‖ ˈker- ˈkær-
carillon kə ˈrɪl jən -ɒn; ˈkær ɪl-, -əl-
  ‖ ˈkær ə lɑːn ˈker- **~s** z

carin|a, C~ kə ˈriːn lə -ˈraɪn- **~ae** iː aɪ **~as** əz
caring ˈkeər ɪŋ ‖ ˈker ɪŋ ˈkær- **~ly** li
Carinthi|a kə ˈrɪntⁱθ i‿|ə **~an/s** ən/z
carioca, C~ ˌkær i ˈəʊk ə ‖ -ˈouk ə ˌker- **~s** z
carious ˈkeər i‿əs ‖ ˈker- ˈkær-
Carisbrooke ˈkær ɪz brʊk -ɪs-, -əz-, -əs- ‖ ˈker-
Carl kɑːl ‖ kɑːrl
Carla ˈkɑːl ə ‖ ˈkɑːrl ə
Carleen, Carlene ˈkɑːl iːn ‖ ˈkɑːrl-
Carleton ˈkɑːlt ən ‖ ˈkɑːrlt-
carline, C~ ˈkɑːl aɪn -ɪn, §-ən ‖ ˈkɑːrl ən **~s** z
Carling ˈkɑːl ɪŋ ‖ ˈkɑːrl ɪŋ
Carlingford ˈkɑːl ɪŋ fəd ‖ ˈkɑːrl ɪŋ fᵊrd
Carlisle *(i)* ₍ᵢ₎kɑː ˈlaɪᵊl ‖ ₍ᵢ₎kɑːr- kᵊr-, *(ii)*
  ˈkɑː laɪᵊl ‖ ˈkɑːr- —*In BrE usually (i),*
  although the place in Cumbria is locally (ii); in
  AmE usually (ii).
Carlist ˈkɑːl ɪst §-əst ‖ ˈkɑːrl- **~s** s
Carlo ˈkɑːl əʊ ‖ ˈkɑːrl oʊ **~'s** z
carload ˈkɑː ləʊd ‖ ˈkɑːr loud **~s** z
Carlos ˈkɑːl ɒs ‖ ˈkɑːrl ous -əs —*Sp* [ˈkar los]
Carlotta kɑː ˈlɒt ə ‖ kɑːr ˈlɑːt ə
Carlovingian ˌkɑːl əʊ ˈvɪndʒ i‿ən ◄ -ˈvɪndʒ ən
  ‖ ˌkɑːrl ə- **~s** z
Carlow ˈkɑːl əʊ ‖ ˈkɑːrl oʊ
Carlsbad ˈkɑːlz bæd ‖ ˈkɑːrlz-
Carlsberg ˈkɑːlz bɜːɡ ‖ ˈkɑːrlz bɜːɡ **~s, 's** z
Carlson ˈkɑːls ən ‖ ˈkɑːrls-
Carlton ˈkɑːlt ən ‖ ˈkɑːrlt-
Carlyle ₍ᵢ₎kɑː ˈlaɪᵊl ‖ ₍ᵢ₎kɑːr- ˈ••
Carman ˈkɑːm ən ‖ ˈkɑːrm-
Carmarthen kə ˈmɑːð ᵊn ‖ kɑːr ˈmɑːrð-
Carmel *(i)* ˈkɑːm el -ᵊl ‖ ˈkɑːrm-, *(ii)*
  ₍ᵢ₎kɑː ˈmel ‖ ₍ᵢ₎kɑːr- —*The mountain is usually*
  (i); the place in California is (ii).
Carmelle ₍ᵢ₎kɑː ˈmel ‖ ₍ᵢ₎kɑːr-
Carmelite ˈkɑːm ə laɪt -ɪ-; -el aɪt ‖ ˈkɑːrm- **~s**
  s
Carmen ˈkɑːm en ‖ ˈkɑːrm ən —*Sp* [ˈkar men]
Carmichael kɑː ˈmaɪk ᵊl -ˈmɪx-, ˈ•ˌ•• ‖
  ‖ ˈkɑːr ˌmaɪk ᵊl
Carmina Burana ˌkɑːm ɪn ə bə ˈrɑːn ə §,•ən-,
  kɑː ˌmiːn ə-, -bu ˈrɑːn- ‖ ˌkɑːrm ən-
  kɑːr ˌmiːn-
carminative ˈkɑːm ɪn ət ɪv ˈ•ən-
  ‖ kɑːr ˈmɪn əṭ ɪv ˈkɑːrm ə neɪṭ- **~s** z
carmine ˈkɑːm aɪn -ɪn, §-ən ‖ ˈkɑːrm- **~s** z
Carmody ˈkɑːm əd i ‖ ˈkɑːrm-
Carnaby ˈkɑːn əb i ‖ ˈkɑːrn-
Carnac ˈkɑːn æk ‖ kɑːr ˈnæk —*Fr* [kaʁ nak]
carnage ˈkɑːn ɪdʒ ‖ ˈkɑːrn-
Carnaghan ˈkɑːn əɡ ən ‖ ˈkɑːrn- -ə hæn
carnal ˈkɑːn ᵊl ‖ ˈkɑːrn ᵊl **~ly** i
carnality kɑː ˈnæl ət i -ɪt- ‖ kɑːr ˈnæl əṭ i
carnallite ˈkɑːn ə laɪt -ᵊl aɪt ‖ ˈkɑːrn ᵊl aɪt
Carnap ˈkɑːn æp ‖ ˈkɑːrn-
Carnarvon kə ˈnɑːv ᵊn ‖ kᵊr ˈnɑːrv-
carnassial kɑː ˈnæʃ i‿əl ‖ kɑːr-
Carnatic kɑː ˈnæt ɪk ‖ kɑːr ˈnæṭ ɪk
carnation kɑː ˈneɪʃ ᵊn ‖ kɑːr- **~s** z
carnauba kɑː ˈnɔːb ə -ˈnaʊb- ‖ kɑːr- -ˈnɑːb-
Carnegie *(i)* kɑː ˈneɡ i ‖ kɑːr-, *(ii)* -ˈneɪɡ-, *(iii)*

C

-'niːg-, *(iv)* 'kɑːn əg i ‖ 'kɑːrn- —*Andrew C~*
was (ii); but C~ Hall is usually (iv).
carnelian kɑː 'niːl iˌən kə- ‖ kɑːr- ~s z
carnet 'kɑːn eɪ ‖ kɑːr 'neɪ —*Fr* [kaʁ nɛ] ~s z
Carney 'kɑːn i ‖ 'kɑːrn i
Carnforth 'kɑːn fɔːθ -fəθ ‖ 'kɑːrn fɔːrθ -foʊrθ
carnie 'kɑːn i ‖ 'kɑːrn i   ~s z
carnival 'kɑːn ɪv əl -əv- ‖ 'kɑːrn- ~s z
carnivore 'kɑːn ɪ vɔː -ə- ‖ 'kɑːrn ə vɔːr -voʊr
  ~s z
carnivorous kɑː 'nɪv ər_əs ‖ kɑːr- ~ly li ~ness
  nəs nɪs
Carnochan 'kɑːn ək ən -əx- ‖ 'kɑːrn-
Carnot 'kɑːn əʊ ‖ kɑːr 'noʊ —*Fr* [kaʁ no]
Carnoustie kɑː 'nuːst i ‖ kɑːr-
carob 'kær əb ‖ 'ker- ~s z
carol, Carol 'kær əl ‖ 'ker- ~ed, ~led d ~ing,
  ~ling ɪŋ ~s z
Carola 'kær əl ə ‖ 'ker-
Carole 'kær əl ‖ 'ker-
Carolina ˌkær ə 'laɪn ə ◂ ‖ ˌker- ~s, ~'s z
Caroline *(i)* 'kær ə laɪn ‖ 'ker-, *(ii)* -əl ɪn §-ən
Carolingian ˌkær ə 'lɪndʒ iˌən ◂ ‖ ˌker- ~s z
Carolinian ˌkær ə 'lɪn iˌən ◂ ‖ ˌker- ~s z
Carolyn 'kær əl ɪn §-ən ‖ 'ker-
carom 'kær əm ‖ 'ker- ~ed d ~ing ɪŋ ~s z
caron 'kær ən ‖ 'ker- ~s z
Caron *(i)* 'kær ən ‖ 'ker-, *(ii)* kə 'rɒn ‖ -'rɑːn
  -'rɔːn
carotene 'kær ə tiːn ‖ 'ker-
carotid kə 'rɒt ɪd §-əd ‖ -'rɑːt̬- ~s z
carousal kə 'raʊz əl ~s z
carous|e kə 'raʊz ~ed d ~es ɪz əz ~ing ɪŋ
carousel ˌkær ə 'sel -u-, -'zel ‖ ˌker-, '• • • ~s z
carp kɑːp ‖ kɑːrp **carped** kɑːpt ‖ kɑːrpt
  carping 'kɑːp ɪŋ ‖ 'kɑːrp- **carps**
  kɑːps ‖ kɑːrps
carpaccio kɑː 'pætʃ i əʊ -'pɑːtʃ-; •'•əʊ
  ‖ kɑːr 'pɑːtʃ oʊ —*It* [kaʁ 'pat tʃo]
carpal 'kɑːp əl ‖ 'kɑːrp- ~s z
Carpathian kɑː 'peɪθ iˌən ‖ kɑːr- ~s z
carpe diem ˌkɑːp i 'diː em ‖ ˌkɑːrp-
carpel 'kɑːp əl -el ‖ 'kɑːrp- ~s z
Carpentaria ˌkɑːp ən 'teər iˌə → •m-, •ˌen-
  ‖ ˌkɑːrp ən 'ter-
carpenter, C~ 'kɑːp ənt ə -ɪnt-, →-mt-
  ‖ 'kɑːrp ənt̬ ər →-mt̬- ~ed d **carpentering**
  'kɑːp ənt_ər ɪŋ -ɪnt-, →mt_ ‖ 'kɑːrp ənt̬
  ər ɪŋ→'•əntr ɪŋ, →-mtr- ~s z
carpentry 'kɑːp əntr i -ɪntr i, →-m tri ‖ 'kɑːrp-
carp|et 'kɑːp |ɪt §-ət ‖ 'kɑːrp |ət ~eted ɪt ɪd
  §ət-, -əd ‖ ət̬ əd ~eting ɪt ɪŋ §ət- ‖ ət̬ ɪŋ
  ~ets ɪts §əts ‖ əts
  'carpet ˌbeetle; 'carpet ˌbombing; 'carpet
  ˌslippers
carpetbag 'kɑːp ɪt bæg §-ət- ‖ 'kɑːrp- ~ger/s
  ə/z ‖ ər/z ~ging ɪŋ ~s z
carpet-sweeper 'kɑːp ɪt ˌswiːp ə §-ət-
  ‖ 'kɑːrp ət ˌswiːp ər ~s z
carpi 'kɑːp aɪ ‖ 'kɑːrp-
carping 'kɑːp ɪŋ ‖ 'kɑːrp ɪŋ ~ly li
carpo- *comb. form*
  with stress-neutral suffix ˌkɑːp əʊ ‖ ˌkɑːrp ə —

carpophore 'kɑːp əʊ fɔː ‖ 'kɑːrp ə fɔːr
  with stress-imposing suffix
  kɑ 'pɒ+ ‖ kɑːr 'pɑː+ — **carpophagous**
  kɑː 'pɒf əg əs ‖ kɑːr 'pɑːf-
carport 'kɑː pɔːt ‖ 'kɑːr pɔːrt -poʊrt ~s s
-carpous 'kɑːp əs ‖ 'kɑːrp- — **polycarpous**
  ˌpɒl i 'kɑːp əs ◂ ‖ ˌpɑːl i 'kɑːrp-
carp|us 'kɑːp |əs ‖ 'kɑːrp- ~i aɪ iː
carr, Carr kɑː ‖ kɑːr ~s z
carrageen, carragheen 'kær ə giːn
  ˌ••'• ‖ 'ker-
Carrantuohill, Carrauntoohill ˌkær ən 'tuːˌəl
  ‖ ˌker-
Carrara kə 'rɑːr ə —*It* [kaʁ 'ra ra]
Carrbridge ˌkɑː 'brɪdʒ ‖ ˌkɑːr-
carrel 'kær əl ‖ 'ker- (= *carol*) ~s z
Carrhae 'kær iː ‖ 'ker-
Carriacou ˌkær iˌə 'kuː '•••• ‖ ˌker-
carriag|e 'kær ɪdʒ ‖ 'ker- ~es ɪz əz
carriageway 'kær ɪdʒ weɪ ‖ 'ker- ~s z
Carrick, c~ 'kær ɪk ‖ 'ker-
Carrickfergus ˌkær ɪk 'fɜːg əs ‖ -'fɝːg əs ˌker-
Carrie 'kær i ‖ 'ker-
carri... —*see* **carry**
carrier 'kær iˌə ‖ 'kær iˌər 'ker- ~s z
  'carrier bag, ˌ••• '•; ˌcarrier 'pigeon,
  '••• ˌ••; 'carrier wave
Carrington 'kær ɪŋ tən ‖ 'ker-
carrion 'kær iˌən ‖ 'ker-
  ˌcarrion 'crow, '••• •
Carrol, Carroll 'kær əl ‖ 'ker-
Carron 'kær ən ‖ 'ker-
carrot 'kær ət ‖ 'ker-
carroty 'kær ət i ‖ -ət̬ i 'ker-
carrousel ˌkær ə 'sel -u-, -'zel ‖ ˌker-, '••• ~s
  z
Carruthers kə 'rʌð əz ‖ -ərz
carry, Carry 'kær i ‖ 'ker- **carried** 'kær id
  ‖ 'ker- **carries** 'kær iz 'ker- **carrying**
  'kær iˌɪŋ ‖ 'ker-
carryall 'kær i ɔːl ‖ 'ker-, -ɑːl ~s z
carrycot 'kær i kɒt ‖ -kɑːt 'ker- ~s s
carrying 'kær iˌɪŋ ‖ 'ker-
  'carrying case; 'carrying charge
carryings-on ˌkær iˌɪŋz 'ɒn ‖ -'ɑːn ˌker-, -'ɔːn
carry-on 'kær i ɒn ˌ••'•◂ ‖ -ɑːn 'ker-, -ɔːn ~s
  z
carryout 'kær i aʊt ‖ 'ker- ~s s
carry-over 'kær iˌəʊv ə ‖ -ˌoʊv ər 'ker- ~s z
Carse kɑːs ‖ kɑːrs
Carshalton kɑː 'ʃɔːlt ən kə- ‖ kɑːr- -'ʃɑːlt-
  —*formerly also* keɪs 'hɔːt ən
carsick 'kɑː sɪk ‖ 'kɑːr-
Carson 'kɑːs ən ‖ 'kɑːrs ən
  ˌCarson 'City
Carstairs ˌkɑː 'steəz '•• ‖ 'kɑːr sterz
cart kɑːt ‖ kɑːrt **carted** 'kɑːt ɪd -əd ‖ 'kɑːrt̬ əd
  carting 'kɑːt ɪŋ ‖ 'kɑːrt̬ ɪŋ **carts**
  kɑːts ‖ kɑːrts
  'cart track
Carta 'kɑːt ə ‖ 'kɑːrt̬ ə
cartage 'kɑːt ɪdʒ ‖ 'kɑːrt̬-

C

Cartagena ˌkɑːt ə ˈdʒiːn ə ‖ ˌkɑːrʈ ə ˈheɪn ə
-ˈgeɪn- —*Sp* [kar ta ˈxe na]
carte blanche ˌkɑːt ˈblɑːntʃ -ˈblɒʃ ‖ ˌkɑːrt-
—*Fr* [kaʁ tə blɑ̃ːʃ]
cartel kɑː ˈtel ‖ kɑːr- ~s z
carter, C~ ˈkɑːt ə ‖ ˈkɑːrʈ ər ~s z
Carteret ˈkɑːt ə ret -rɪt, -rət ‖ ˈkɑːrʈ-, ˌ•• ˈret
Cartesian kɑː ˈtiːz i_ən -ˈtiːʒ ən ‖ kɑːr ˈtiːʒ ən
~s z
Carthage ˈkɑːθ ɪdʒ ‖ ˈkɑːrθ-
Carthaginian ˌkɑːθ ə ˈdʒɪn i_ən ◄ ‖ ˌkɑːrθ- ~s
z
Carthew ˈkɑːθ juː ‖ ˈkɑːrθ uː
carthors|e ˈkɑːt hɔːs ‖ ˈkɑːrt hɔːrs ~es ɪz əz
Carthusian kɑː ˈθjuːz i_ən -ˈθuːz-
‖ kɑːr ˈθuːʒ ən -ˈθjuːʒ- ~s z
Cartier ˈkɑːt i eɪ ‖ ˈkɑːrʈ- —*but as a French or
French Canadian name,* ˌ•• ˈ•. —*Fr* [kaʁ tje]
~ˈs z
cartilage ˈkɑːt əl_ɪdʒ -ɪl- ‖ ˈkɑːrʈ- ~es ɪz əz
cartilaginous ˌkɑːt ə ˈlædʒ ɪn əs ◄ ˌ•ɪ-,
-əl ˈædʒ-, -ən əs ‖ ˌkɑːrʈ əl ˈædʒ ən əs◄
Cartland ˈkɑːt lənd ‖ ˈkɑːrt-
cartload ˈkɑːt ləʊd ‖ ˈkɑːrt loʊd ~s z
Cartmel ˈkɑːt məl -mel ‖ ˈkɑːrt-
cartographer kɑː ˈtɒg rəf ə ‖ kɑːr ˈtɑːg rəf ər
~s z
cartographic ˌkɑːt ə ˈgræf ɪk ◄ ‖ ˌkɑːrʈ- ~al əl
~ally əl_i
cartography kɑː ˈtɒg rəf i ‖ kɑːr ˈtɑːg-
cartomancy ˈkɑːt əʊ ˌmænts i ‖ ˈkɑːrʈ ə-
carton, C~ ˈkɑːt ən ‖ ˈkɑːrt ən ~s z
cartoon kɑː ˈtuːn ‖ kɑːr- ~s z
cartoonist kɑː ˈtuːn ɪst §-əst ‖ kɑːr- ~s s
cartophilist kɑː ˈtɒf əl ɪst -ɪl-, §-əst
‖ kɑːr ˈtɑːf- ~s s
cartophily kɑː ˈtɒf əl i -ɪl- ‖ kɑːr ˈtɑːf-
cartouch|e kɑː ˈtuːʃ ‖ kɑːr- ~es ɪz əz
cartridg|e ˈkɑːtr ɪdʒ ‖ ˈkɑːrtr- §ˈkætr- ~es ɪz
əz
'cartridge belt; 'cartridge ˌpaper
cartwheel ˈkɑːt wiː əl -hwiː əl ‖ ˈkɑːrt hwiː əl
~ed d ~ing ɪŋ ~s z
Cartwright, c~ ˈkɑːt raɪt ‖ ˈkɑːrt-
caruncle ˈkærˌʌŋk əl kæ-; ˈkær əŋk- ~s z
Caruso kə ˈruːs əʊ -ˈruːz- ‖ -oʊ —*It*
[ka ˈru: so]
Caruthers kə ˈrʌð əz ‖ -ərz
carve kɑːv ‖ kɑːrv carved kɑːvd ‖ kɑːrvd
carves kɑːvz ‖ kɑːrvz carving
ˈkɑːv ɪŋ ‖ ˈkɑːrv ɪŋ
carvel ˈkɑːv əl -el ‖ ˈkɑːrv- ~s z
carvel-built ˈkɑːv əl bɪlt -el- ‖ ˈkɑːrv-
carver, C~ ˈkɑːv ə ‖ ˈkɑːrv ər ~s z
carver|y ˈkɑːv ər i i ‖ ˈkɑːrv- ~ies iz
carve-up ˈkɑːv ʌp ‖ ˈkɑːrv-
carving ˈkɑːv ɪŋ ‖ ˈkɑːrv ɪŋ ~s z
'carving knife
Carwardine ˈkɑː wə diːn ‖ ˈkɑːr wər-
Cary *personal name* ˈkær i ˈkeər- ‖ ˈker-
Cary *family name* ˈkeər i ‖ ˈker i ˈkær-
caryatid ˌkær i ˈæt ɪd §-əd; ˈkær i_ə tɪd
‖ -ˈæt əd ˌker-; ˈkær i_ə tɪd, ˈker- ~s z

Caryl ˈkær əl -ɪl ‖ ˈker-
Carysfort ˈkær ɪs fɔːt -əs- ‖ -fɔːrt ˈker-, -foʊrt
carzey ˈkɑːz i ‖ — ~s z
Casablanca ˌkæs ə ˈblæŋk ə
ˌkæz- ‖ ˌkɑːs ə ˈblɑːŋk ə —*Fr* [ka za blɑ̃ ka]
Casals kə ˈsælz ‖ -ˈsɑːlz kɑː- —*Sp* [ka ˈsals],
Catalan [kə ˈzals]
Casanova ˌkæs ə ˈnəʊv ə ˌkæz-
‖ ˌkæz ə ˈnoʊv ə ˌkæs- —*It* [ka sa ˈnɔː va]
Casaubon kə ˈsɔːb ən ˈkæz ə bɒn ‖ -ˈsɑːb-;
ˈkæz ə bɑːn —*Fr* [ka zo bɔ̃]
casbah ˈkæz bɑː -bə ‖ ˈkɑːz-
cascad|e, C~ ₍ₒ₎kæ ˈskeɪd ~ed ɪd əd ~es z
~ing ɪŋ
cascara kæ ˈskɑːr ə ‖ -ˈskær- -ˈsker-
cascarilla ˌkæsk ə ˈrɪl ə ‖ -ˈriː jə, -ˈrɪl jə
case, Case keɪs cased keɪst cases ˈkeɪs ɪz -əz
casing keɪs ɪŋ
'case ˌending; ˌcase 'history; 'case ˌstudy
casebook ˈkeɪs bʊk §-buːk ~s s
casebound ˈkeɪs baʊnd
case-harden ˈkeɪs ˌhɑːd ən ‖ -ˌhɑːrd- ~ed d
~ing ˌɪŋ ~s z
casein ˈkeɪs i ɪn ˈkeɪs iːn ‖ keɪ ˈsiːn
caseload ˈkeɪs ləʊd ‖ -loʊd ~s z
casemate ˈkeɪs meɪt ~s s
casement, C~ ˈkeɪs mənt ~ed ɪd əd ~s s
ˌcasement 'window
casework ˈkeɪs wɜːk ‖ -wɜːːk
caseworker ˈkeɪs ˌwɜːk ə ‖ -ˌwɜːːk ər ~s z
Casey ˈkeɪs i
cash, Cash kæʃ cashed kæʃt cashes ˈkæʃ ɪz
-əz cashing ˈkæʃ ɪŋ
'cash card; 'cash crop; ˌcash 'discount;
'cash diˌspenser; 'cash flow; 'cash
maˌchine; 'cash ˌregister
cash-and-carry ˌkæʃ ən ˈkær i →- əŋ- ‖ -ˈker-
cashbook ˈkæʃ bʊk ~s s
cashew ˈkæʃ uː kæ ˈʃuː, kə- ~s z
ca|shier kæ ‖ˈʃɪə kə- ‖ -ˈʃɪər ~shiered
ˈʃɪəd ‖ ˈʃɪərd ~shiering ˈʃɪər ɪŋ ‖ ˈʃɪr ɪŋ
~shiers ˈʃɪəz ‖ ˈʃɪərz
Cashin ˈkæʃ ɪn §-ən
cashless ˈkæʃ ləs -lɪs
Cashman ˈkæʃ mən
cashmere ˈkæʃ mɪə ˌ•ˈ• ‖ ˈkæʒ mɪr ˈkæʃ- ~s z
cashpoint ˈkæʃ pɔɪnt ~s s
casing ˈkeɪs ɪŋ ~s z
casino kə ˈsiːn əʊ ‖ -oʊ ~s z
Casio *tdmk* ˈkæs i_əʊ ‖ oʊ
cask kɑːsk §kæsk ‖ kæsk casks kɑːsks
§kæsks ‖ kæsks
casket ˈkɑːs kɪt §ˈkæs-, §-ət ‖ ˈkæsk ət ~s s
Caslon ˈkæz lɒn -lən ‖ -lɑːn -lən
Caspar ˈkæsp ə -ɑː ‖ -ər -ɑːr
Caspian ˈkæsp i_ən
casque kæsk kɑːsk ‖ kæsk casques kæsks
kɑːsks ‖ kæsks
Cass kæs
Cassandra kə ˈsændr ə -ˈsɑːndr- ~s, ~'s z
cassareep ˈkæs ə riːp
cassata kə ˈsɑːt ə kæ- ‖ -ˈsɑːʈ ə —*It*
[kas ˈsa: ta]

cassava kə 'saːv ə

Cassel, Cassell 'kæs ᵊl —*but as a French name,* kæ 'sel —*Fr* [ka sɛl]

casserol|e 'kæs ə rəʊl →-rɒʊl ‖ -rəʊl 'kæz- ~**ed** d ~**es** z ~**ing** ɪŋ

cassette kə 'set kæ- ~**s** s
  cas'sette re,corder

cassia 'kæs i_ə ‖ 'kæʃ ə (*)

Cassidy 'kæs əd i -ɪd-

Cassie 'kæs i

Cassillis 'kæs ᵊlz

Cassio 'kæs i_əʊ ‖ _oʊ

Cassiopeia ,kæs i əʊ 'piː_ə -'peɪ ə ‖ -i_ə-

cassis kæ 'siːs kɑː-; 'kæs iːs —*Fr* [ka sis]

cassiterite kə 'sɪt ə raɪt ‖ -'sɪt̬-

Cassius 'kæs i_əs ‖ 'kæʃ əs -i_əs (*)

Cassivelaunus ,kæs ɪv ə 'lɔːn əs ,•əv-, -ɪ'•-, -'laʊn- ‖ -'lɑːn-

cassock 'kæs ək ~**s** s

Casson 'kæs ᵊn

cassoulet ,kæs u 'leɪ -ə-, '•••‖ -ə- —*Fr* [ka su lɛ] ~**s** z

cassowar|y 'kæs ə weər li -wər i ‖ -wer li ~**ies** iz

cast kɑːst §kæst ‖ kæst **casting** 'kɑːst ɪŋ §'kæst- ‖ 'kæst ɪŋ **casts** kɑːsts §kæsts ‖ kæsts

Castali|a kæ 'steɪl i_ə —**an** ən

castanet ,kæst ə 'net ~**s** s

castaway 'kɑːst ə ,weɪ §'kæst- ‖ 'kæst- ~**s** z

caste kɑːst §kæst ‖ kæst (= *cast*) **castes** kɑːsts §kæsts ‖ kæsts

Castel Gandolfo ,kæst el gæn 'dɒlf əʊ ‖ -'dɑːlf oʊ —*It* [kas ,tel gan 'dɔl fo]

castellated 'kæst ə leɪt ɪd '•ɪ-, -ᵊl eɪt-, -əd ‖ -leɪt̬ əd

caster 'kɑːst ə §'kæst- ‖ 'kæst ᵊr ~**s** z
  'caster ,sugar, ,•• '••

Casterbridge 'kɑːst ə brɪdʒ §'kæst- ‖ 'kæst ᵊr-

casti|gate 'kæst ɪ |geɪt -ə- ~**gated** geɪt ɪd -əd ‖ geɪt̬- ~**gates** geɪts ~**gating** geɪt ɪŋ ‖ geɪt̬ ɪŋ

castigation ,kæst ɪ 'geɪʃ ᵊn -ə- ~**s** z

castigator 'kæst ɪ geɪt ə '•ə- ‖ -geɪt̬ ᵊr ~**s** z

Castile kæ 'stiːᵊl —*but the place in NY is* -'staɪᵊl

Castilian kæ 'stɪl i_ən ~**s** z

casting 'kɑːst ɪŋ §'kæst- ‖ 'kæst ɪŋ ~**s** z
  ,casting 'vote

cast-iron ,kɑːst 'aɪ_ən ◄ §,kæst- ‖ ,kæst 'aɪ_ᵊrn ◄

castl|e, C~ 'kɑːs ᵊl §'kæs- ‖ 'kæs ᵊl ~**ed** d ~**es** z ~**ing** _ɪŋ

Castlebar ,kɑːs ᵊl 'bɑː: §,kæs- ‖ ,kæs ᵊl 'bɑːr

Castleford 'kɑːs ᵊl fəd §'kæst- ‖ 'kæs ᵊl fᵊrd

Castlemaine 'kɑːs ᵊl meɪn §'kæs- ‖ 'kæs-

Castlenau 'kɑːs ᵊl nɔː: §'kæs-, -nəʊ ‖ 'kæs- -nɑː:

Castlerea, Castlereagh 'kɑːs ᵊl reɪ §'kæs-, ,•• '• ‖ 'kæs-

Castleton 'kɑːs ᵊl tən §'kæs- ‖ 'kæs-

Castlewellan ,kɑːs ᵊl 'wel ən §,kæs- ‖ ,kæs-

castoff, cast-off 'kɑːst ɒf §'kæst-, -ɔːf ‖ 'kæst ɔːf -ɑːf ~**s** s

castor, C~ 'kɑːst ə §'kæst- ‖ 'kæst ᵊr (= *caster*) ~**s** z
  ,castor 'oil; 'castor ,sugar, ,••'••

castrate kæ 'streɪt ‖ 'kæs treɪt (*) **castrated** kæ 'streɪt ɪd -əd ‖ 'kæs treɪt̬ əd **castrates** kæ 'streɪts ‖ 'kæs treɪts **castrating** kæ 'streɪt ɪŋ ‖ 'kæs treɪt̬ ɪŋ

castration kæ 'streɪʃ ᵊn ~**s** z

castrat|o kæ 'strɑːt |əʊ kə- ‖ -|oʊ ~**i** iː

Castries kæ 'striːz -'striːs

Castro 'kæs trəʊ ‖ -troʊ —*Sp* ['kas tro]

Castrol *tdmk* 'kæs trɒl ‖ -troʊl -trɑːl, -trɔːl

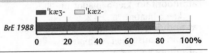

CASUAL

	'kæʒ-		'kæz-
BrE 1988			

0   20   40   60   80   100%

casual 'kæʒ u_əl -juˌ, 'kæz juˌ; 'kæʒ ᵊl —*BrE poll 1988 panel preference:* 'kæʒ- 77%, 'kæz- 23%. ~**ly** i ~**ness** nəs nɪs ~**s** z

casual|ty 'kæʒ u_əl |ti '•juˌ, 'kæz juˌ; 'kæʒ ᵊl |ti ~**ties** tiz
  'casualty ward

casuarina ,kæz ju_ə 'riːn ə ,kæʒ juˌ, ,kæʒ uˌ, ,kæʒ ə 'riːn ə; -'raɪn- ‖ ,kæʒ uˌ ~**s** z

casuist 'kæz ju_ɪst 'kæʒ juˌ, 'kæʒ uˌ, §_əst ‖ 'kæʒ u_əst ~**s** s

casuistic ,kæz ju 'ɪst ɪk ◄ ,kæʒ ju-, ,kæʒ u- ‖ ,kæʒ u- ~**ally** ᵊl_i

casuis|try 'kæz ju_ɪs |tri 'kæʒ juˌ, 'kæʒ uˌ, §_əs• ‖ 'kæʒ u_əs- ~**tries** triz

casus belli ,kɑːs ʊs 'bel iː -əs-; ,keɪs əs 'bel aɪ

cat kæt **cats** kæts
  'cat ,burglar; 'cat ,cracker; 'cat door; 'cat flap; ,cat's 'cradle; ,cat's 'whisker

CAT kæt
  'CAT scan, 'CAT ,scanner

cata- *comb. form*
  with stress-neutral suffix ,kæt ə ‖ ,kæt̬ ə —
  cataclastic ,kæt ə 'klæst ɪk ◄ ‖ ,kæt̬-
  with stress-imposing suffix kə 'tæ+ —
  catadromous kə 'tædr əm əs

catabolic ,kæt ə 'bɒl ɪk ◄ ‖ ,kæt̬ ə 'bɑːl- ~**ally** ᵊl_i

catabolism kə 'tæb ə ,lɪz əm

catachresis ,kæt ə 'kriːs ɪs §-əs ‖ ,kæt̬-

catachrestic ,kæt ə 'krest ɪk ◄ ‖ ,kæt̬-

cataclysm 'kæt ə ,klɪz əm ‖ 'kæt̬- ~**s** z

cataclysmal ,kæt ə 'klɪz mᵊl ‖ ,kæt̬- ~**ly** i

cataclysmic ,kæt ə 'klɪz mɪk ◄ ‖ ,kæt̬- ~**ally** ᵊl_i

catacomb 'kæt ə kuːm -kəʊm ‖ 'kæt̬ ə koʊm ~**s** z

catafalque 'kæt ə fælk ‖ 'kæt̬ ə fɔːk -fɑːk, -fɔːlk, -fælk ~**s** s

Catalan 'kæt ə læn -ᵊl ən, ᵊl æn; ,kæt ə 'læn ‖ 'kæt̬ ᵊl ən -æn, ,kɑːt ə 'lɑːn ~**s** z

catalectic ,kæt ə 'lekt ɪk ◄ -ᵊl 'ekt- ‖ ,kæt̬ ᵊl 'ekt ɪk ◄

catalepsy 'kæt ə leps i -ᵊl eps- ‖ 'kæt̬ ᵊl eps i

cataleptic ,kæt ə 'lept ɪk ◄ -ᵊl 'ept- ‖ ,kæt̬ ᵊl 'ept ɪk ◄

Catalina ˌkæt ə 'liːn ə -ᵊl 'iːn- ‖ ˌkæt̮ ᵊl 'iːn ə

catalog, catalogu|e 'kæt ə lɒg -ᵊl ɒg
‖ 'kæt̮ ᵊl ɔːg -aːg ~ed d ~ing ɪŋ catalogs,
catalogues 'kæt ə lɒgz -ᵊl ɒgz ‖ 'kæt̮ ᵊl ɔːgz
-aːgz

Catalonia ˌkæt ə 'ləun i_ə -ᵊl 'əun-
‖ ˌkæt̮ ᵊl 'oun-

catalpa kə 'tælp ə ‖ -'taːlp-, -'tɔːlp- ~s z

catalysis kə 'tæl əs ɪs §-əs

catalyst 'kæt ᵊl ɪst §-əst ‖ 'kæt̮- ~s s

catalytic ˌkæt ə 'lɪt ɪk ◄ -ᵊl 'ɪt- ‖ ˌkæt̮ ᵊl 'ɪt̮ ɪk ◄
~ally ᵊl_i

catamaran ˌkæt əm ə 'ræn '•••• ‖ ˌkæt̮- ~s z

catamite 'kæt ə maɪt ‖ 'kæt̮- ~s s

catamount 'kæt ə maunt ‖ 'kæt̮- ~s s

catamountain ˌkæt ə 'maunt ɪn -ən
‖ ˌkæt̮ ə 'maunt̮ ᵊn ~s z

cat-and-dog ˌkæt ᵊn 'dɒg ◄ ‖ -'dɔːg -'daːg

cat-and-mouse ˌkæt ᵊn 'maus ◄

cataphora kə 'tæf ər ə

cataphoresis ˌkæt ə fə 'riːs ɪs -fɒ'•-, §-əs
‖ ˌkæt̮-

cataphoretic ˌkæt ə fə 'ret ɪk ◄ -fɒ'•-
‖ ˌkæt̮ ə fə 'ret̮ ɪk ◄ ~ally ᵊl_i

cataphoric ˌkæt ə 'fɒr ɪk ◄ ‖ ˌkæt̮ ə 'fɔːr ɪk ◄
-'faːr- ~ally ᵊl_i

cataplasm 'kæt ə ˌplæz əm ‖ 'kæt̮- ~s z

cataplexy 'kæt ə pleks i ‖ 'kæt̮-

catapult 'kæt ə pʌlt §-pult ‖ 'kæt̮- ~ed ɪd -əd
~ing ɪŋ ~s s

cataract 'kæt ə rækt ‖ 'kæt̮- ~s s

catarrh kə 'taː ‖ -'taːr

catarrhal kə 'taːr əl

catarrhine 'kæt ə raɪn ‖ 'kæt̮- ~s z

catastasis kə 'tæst əs ɪs §-əs

catastrophe kə 'tæs trəf i ~s z

catastrophic ˌkæt ə 'strɒf ɪk ◄ ‖ ˌkæt̮ ə 'straːf-
~ally ᵊl_i
ˌcata strophic 'failure

catastrophism kə 'tæs trə ˌfɪz əm

catatonia ˌkæt ə 'təun i_ə ‖ ˌkæt̮ ə 'toun-

catatonic ˌkæt ə 'tɒn ɪk ◄ ‖ ˌkæt̮ ə 'taːn- ~ally
ᵊl_i

Catawba, c~ kə 'tɔːb ə ‖ -'taːb-

catbird 'kæt bɜːd ‖ -bɜːd ~s z

catcall 'kæt kɔːl ‖ -kaːl ~s z

catch kætʃ △ketʃ catches 'kætʃ ɪz △'ketʃ-,
-əz catching 'kætʃ ɪŋ △'ketʃ- caught kɔːt
‖ kaːt
'catch crop

catch-22 ˌkætʃ ˌtwent i 'tuː △ˌketʃ-, △-ˌtwen-
‖ -ˌtwent̮-

catch-all 'kætʃ ɔːl △'ketʃ- ‖ -aːl

catch-as-catch-can ˌkætʃ əz ˌkætʃ 'kæn
△ˌketʃ əz ˌketʃ-

catcher 'kætʃ ə △'ketʃ- ‖ -ᵊr ~s z

catch|fly 'kætʃ |flaɪ △'ketʃ- ~flies flaɪz

catchi... —see catchy

catchment 'kætʃ mənt △'ketʃ-
'catchment ˌarea

catchpenny 'kætʃ ˌpen i △'ketʃ-

catchphras|e 'kætʃ freɪz △'ketʃ- ~es ɪz əz

Catchpole, c~ 'kætʃ pəul →-pɒul ‖ -poul ~s z

catchweight 'kætʃ weɪt △'ketʃ- ~s s

catchword 'kætʃ wɜːd △'ketʃ- ‖ -wɜːd ~s z

catch|y 'kætʃ |i △'ketʃ- ~ier i_ə ‖ i_ᵊr ~iest
i_ɪst i_əst

cate keɪt cates keɪts

catechesis ˌkæt ɪ 'kiːs ɪs -ə-, §-əs ‖ ˌkæt̮-

catechis... —see catechiz...

catechism 'kæt ə ˌkɪz əm -ɪ- ‖ 'kæt̮- ~s z

catechist 'kæt ək ɪst -ɪk-, §-əst ‖ 'kæt̮- ~s s

catechiz|e 'kæt ə kaɪz -ɪ- ‖ 'kæt̮- ~ed d ~er/s
ə/z ‖ ᵊr/z ~es ɪz əz ~ing ɪŋ

catechu 'kæt ə tʃuː -ɪ-, -ʃuː ‖ 'kæt̮-

catechumen ˌkæt ə 'kjuːm en -ɪ-, -ɪn, -ən
‖ ˌkæt̮- ~s z

categorial ˌkæt ə 'gɔːr i_əl ˌ•ɪ- ‖ ˌkæt̮- -'gour-
~ly i

categoric ˌkæt ə 'gɒr ɪk ◄ -ɪ- ‖ ˌkæt̮ ə 'gɔːr ɪk ◄
-'gaːr-

categorical ˌkæt ə 'gɒr ɪk ᵊl ◄ ˌ•ɪ-
‖ ˌkæt̮ ə 'gɔːr ɪk ᵊl ◄ -'gaːr- ~ly_i
ˌcate gorical de'nial

categori... —see category

categoris... —see categoriz...

categorization ˌkæt ɪg ər_aɪ 'zeɪʃ ᵊn -ɪ'•-
‖ ˌkæt̮ ɪg ər ə-

categoriz|e 'kæt ɪg ə raɪz '•əg- ‖ 'kæt̮- ~ed d
~es ɪz əz ~ing ɪŋ

categor|y 'kæt əg ər_i '•ɪg- ‖ 'kæt̮ ə gɔːr li
-gour- (*) ~ies iz

catenar|y kə 'tiːn ər li ‖ 'kæt̮ ᵊn er li (*) ~ies iz

cate|nate v 'kæt ɪ |neɪt -ə-; -ᵊln eɪt
‖ 'kæt̮ ᵊln eɪt ~nated neɪt ɪd -əd ‖ neɪt̮ əd
~nates neɪts ~nating neɪt ɪŋ ‖ neɪt̮ ɪŋ

catenation ˌkæt ɪ 'neɪʃ ᵊn -ə-; -ᵊn 'eɪʃ-
‖ ˌkæt̮ ᵊn 'eɪʃ ᵊn ~s z

cater, Cater 'keɪt ə ‖ 'keɪt̮ ᵊr ~ed d catering
'keɪt_ᵊr ɪŋ ‖ 'keɪt̮ ᵊr ɪŋ ~s z

cater-cornered
ˌkæt ə 'kɔːn əd ◄ ‖ ˌkæt̮ ə 'kɔːrn ᵊrd ◄ -ɪ-, -ᵊr-,
'•••

caterer 'keɪt_ᵊr ə ‖ 'keɪt̮ ᵊr ᵊr ~s z

Caterham 'keɪt_ᵊr əm ‖ 'keɪt̮ ᵊr hæm

Caterina ˌkæt ə 'riːn ə ‖ ˌkæt̮-

caterpillar 'kæt ə pɪl ə ‖ 'kæt̮ ᵊr pɪl ᵊr ~s z

caterwaul 'kæt ə wɔːl ‖ 'kæt̮ ᵊr wɔːl -waːl ~ed
d ~ing ɪŋ ~s z

Catesby 'keɪts bi

catfish 'kæt fɪʃ ~es ɪz əz

catfood 'kæt fuːd

Catford 'kæt fəd ‖ -fᵊrd

catgut 'kæt gʌt

Cath kæθ Cath's kæθs —but St Catherine's
College, Cambridge, is colloquially known as
kæts

Cathar 'kæθ ə -aː ‖ -aːr ~s z

Catharine 'kæθ ᵊr_ɪn ən

Catharism 'kæθ ə ˌrɪz əm

Catharist 'kæθ ᵊr ɪst §-əst ~s s

cathars|is kə 'θaːs ɪs kæ-, §-əs ‖ -'θaːrs- ~es
iːz

cathartic kə 'θaːt ɪk kæ- ‖ -'θaːrt̮- ~s s

Cathay ‿'China'‿ kæ 'θeɪ kə-
ˌCathay Pa'cific tdmk, •,• •ʹ••

Cathays *place in SGlam* kə 'teɪz
Cathcart 'kæθ kɑːt ˌ•'• ‖ -kɑːrt —*The place in Strathclyde is* ˌ•'•
cathedra kə 'θiːdr ə -'θedr-, -'tedr-
cathedral kə 'θiːdr əl ~s z
Cather 'kæð ə ‖ -ər
Catherine, c~ 'kæθ ər_ɪn ˌ_ən ~'s z
  'catherine wheel
Catherwood 'kæθ ə wʊd 'kæð- ‖ -ər-
catheter 'kæθ ɪt ə -ət- ‖ 'kæθ ət ̬ ər 'kæθt ər ~s z
catheteris... —*see* **catheteriz...**
catheterization ˌkæθ ɪt ̬ ər aɪ 'zeɪʃ ən ˌ•ət ̬ _, -ɪ'•- ‖ ˌkæθ ət ̬ ər ə- ˌkæθt ər ə'•-
catheteriz|e 'kæθ ɪt ə raɪz '•ət- ‖ 'kæθ ət ̬- 'kæθ ə raɪz ~ed d ~es ɪz əz ~ing ɪŋ
cathexis kæ 'θeks ɪs kə-, §-əs
Cathleen 'kæθ liːn ˌ•'•
cathode 'kæθ əʊd ‖ -oʊd ~s z
  ˌcathode 'ray
cathode-ray tube ˌkæθ əʊd 'reɪ tjuːb →§-tʃuːb ‖ -oʊd 'reɪ tuːb -tjuːb
cathodic kæ 'θɒd ɪk kə-, -'θəʊd- ‖ -'θɑːd-
catholic, C~ 'kæθ lɪk 'kæθ əl ɪk, §'kæːθ- ~s s
Catholicism, c~ kə 'θɒl ə ˌsɪz əm -ɪ- ‖ -'θɑːl-
catholicity, C~ ˌkæθ ə 'lɪs ət i -ɪt i ‖ -ət ̬ i
Cathrine 'kæθ rɪn -rən
Cathy 'kæθ i
Catiline 'kæt ə laɪn -ɪ-, -əl aɪn ‖ 'kæt ̬ əl aɪn
cation 'kæt ˌaɪ_ən ‖ 'kæt ̬- ~s z
catkin 'kæt kɪn §-kən ~s z
Catling, c~ 'kæt lɪŋ
catmint 'kæt mɪnt ~s s
catnap 'kæt næp ~s s
catnip 'kæt nɪp ~s s
Cato 'keɪt əʊ ‖ 'keɪt ̬ oʊ ~'s z
Caton 'keɪt ən
cat-o'-nine tails ˌkæt ə 'naɪn teɪəlz ‖ ˌkæt ̬-
Catrina kə 'triːn ə
Catrine 'kætr iːn
Catriona kə 'triː_ən ə kæ-; -'triːn ə; ˌkætr i 'əʊn ə ‖ -'oʊn-
cat's-ear 'kæts ɪə ‖ -ɪr ~s z
cat's-eye, Catseye *tdmk* 'kæts aɪ ~s z
Catskill 'kæts kɪl ~s z
cat's-paw 'kæts pɔː ‖ -pɑː ~s z
catsuit 'kæt suːt -sjuːt ~s s
catsup 'kæts əp 'ketʃ-, 'kætʃ- —*see also* ketchup ~s s
Catterick 'kæt ˌər ɪk ‖ 'kæt ̬ ər ɪk
catter|y 'kæt ər i ‖ 'kæt ̬- ~ies iz
cattish 'kæt ɪʃ ‖ 'kæt ̬ ɪʃ ~ly li ~ness nəs nɪs
cattle 'kæt əl ‖ 'kæt ̬ əl
  'cattle cake; 'cattle grid; 'cattle truck
cattleya 'kæt li_ə ~s z
Catto 'kæt əʊ ‖ 'kæt ̬ oʊ
Catton 'kæt ən
catt|y 'kæt i ‖ 'kæt ̬ i ~ier i_ə ‖ i_ər ~iest i_ɪst i_əst ~ily ɪ li əl i ‖ əl i ~iness i nəs -nɪs
Catullus kə 'tʌl əs
catwalk 'kæt wɔːk ‖ -wɑːk ~s s
Caucasian kɔː 'keɪz i_ən -'keɪʒ-, -'keɪʒ ən ‖ kɔː 'keɪʒ ən kɑː-, -'kæʒ- ~s z

Caucasoid 'kɔːk ə sɔɪd -zɔɪd ‖ 'kɑːk-
Caucasus 'kɔːk əs əs ‖ 'kɑːk-
caucus 'kɔːk əs ‖ 'kɑːk- ~es ɪz əz
caudal 'kɔːd əl ‖ 'kɑːd- ~ly i
caudate 'kɔːd eɪt ‖ 'kɑːd-
caudillo kɔː 'diːl jəʊ kaʊ-, -'dɪl əʊ ‖ kaʊ 'diː joʊ -'dɪl- —*Sp* [kau 'ði ʎo, -jo] ~s z
Caudine 'kɔːd aɪn ‖ 'kɑːd-
caudle, C~ 'kɔːd əl ‖ 'kɑːd- ~s z
caught kɔːt ‖ kɑːt
caul kɔːl ‖ kɑːl (= call) ~s z
cauldron 'kɔːldr ən 'kɒldr- ‖ 'kɑːldr- ~s z
Caulfield 'kɔːl fiːəld 'kɔː- ‖ 'kɑːl-, 'kɔː-
cauliflower 'kɒl i ˌflaʊ_ə ‖ 'kɑː li ˌflaʊ_ər 'kɔːl- ~s z
  ˌcauli flower 'cheese; ˌcauli flower 'ear
caulk kɔːk ‖ kɑːk **caulked** kɔːkt ‖ kɑːkt
  caulking 'kɔːk ɪŋ ‖ 'kɑːk- **caulks** kɔːks ‖ kɑːks
Caunce (i) kɔːnts ‖ kɑːnts; (ii) kɒnts ‖ kɑːnts
causal 'kɔːz əl ‖ 'kɑːz- ~ly i
causalit|y kɔː 'zæl ət i -ɪt- ‖ -ət ̬ i kɑː- ~ies iz
causation kɔː 'zeɪʃ ən ‖ kɑː- ~s z
causative 'kɔːz ət ɪv -ət ̬- ‖ 'kɑːz- ~ly li ~s z
cause kɔːz ‖ kɑːz **caused** kɔːzd ‖ kɑːzd
  causes 'kɔːz ɪz -əz ‖ 'kɑːz- **causing** 'kɔːz ɪŋ ‖ 'kɑːz- —*See also phrases with this word*
cause celebre, cause célèbre ˌkɔːz sə 'leb ˌkɔːz-, -se-, -sɪ-, ˌ•'•rə ‖ ˌkɔːz sə 'leb rə ˌkɑːz-, ˌkoʊz- —*Fr* [koz se lɛbʁ]
causerie 'kəʊz ər i ‖ ˌkoʊz ə 'riː —*Fr* [koz ʁi] ~s z
causeway 'kɔːz weɪ ‖ 'kɑːz- ~s z
caustic 'kɔːst ɪk 'kɒst- ‖ 'kɑːst- ~ally əl_i ~s s
causticity kɔː 'stɪs ət i kɒ-, -ɪt- ‖ -ət ̬ i kɑː-
Caute kaʊt ‖ koʊt
cauteri... —*see* **cautery**
cauteris... —*see* **cauteriz...**
cauterization ˌkɔːt ər aɪ 'zeɪʃ ən -ɪ'•- ‖ ˌkɔːt ̬ ər ə- ˌkɑːt ̬- ~s z
cauteriz|e 'kɔːt ə raɪz ‖ 'kɔːt ̬- 'kɑːt ̬- ~ed d ~es ɪz əz ~ing ɪŋ
cauter|y 'kɔːt ər i ‖ 'kɔːt ̬- 'kɑːt ̬- ~ies iz
Cauthen 'kɔːθ ən ‖ 'kɑːθ-
caution 'kɔːʃ ən ‖ 'kɑːʃ- ~ed d ~ing ˌɪŋ ~s z
cautionary 'kɔːʃ ən ər_i -ən_ər i ‖ 'kɔːʃ ə ner i 'kɑːʃ-
cautious 'kɔːʃ əs ‖ 'kɑːʃ- ~ly li ~ness nəs nɪs
cavalcade ˌkæv əl 'keɪd ◄ '••• ~s z
cavalier ˌkæv ə 'lɪə ◄ ‖ -'lɪər◄ ~ly li ~s z
cavalla kə 'væl ə ~s z
Cavalleria Rusticana ˌkæv əl ə 'riː_ə ˌrʊst i 'kɑːn ə kə ˌvæl-, -, rʌst- —*It* [ka val le 'ri a ʁus ti 'ka na]
cavall|y kə 'væl li ~ies iz
caval|ry 'kæv əl ri ~ries riz
cavalry|man 'kæv əl ri |mən -mæn ~men mən men
Cavan 'kæv ən
Cavanagh (i) 'kæv ən ə, (ii) kə 'væn ə
cavatina ˌkæv ə 'tiːn ə ‖ ˌkɑːv-

cave *n, v* '*hollow*' keɪv **caved** keɪvd **caves**
keɪvz **caving** 'keɪv ɪŋ
'**cave ,painting**
cave *n* '*watch*' 'keɪv i
cave *interj* ,keɪ 'viː 'keɪv i
Cave *name* keɪv
caveat 'kæv i æt 'keɪv-, -ət ‖ 'kɑːv i ɑːt 'kæv-,
-æt ~s s
,**caveat 'emptor** 'em*p*t ɔː -ə ‖ -ɔːr -ᵊr
cave-in 'keɪv ɪn ~s z
Cavell *(i)* 'kæv ᵊl; *(ii)* kə 'vel —*Nurse* Edith C~
was (i).
cave|man 'keɪv |mæn ~**men** men
Cavendish, c~ 'kæv ᵊnd ɪʃ
caver 'keɪv ə ‖ -ᵊr ~s z
cavern 'kæv ᵊn ‖ -ᵊrn **-ed** d **~ing** ɪŋ ~s z
cavernous 'kæv ᵊn əs ‖ -ᵊrn- **~ly** li
Caversham 'kæv əʃ əm ‖ -ᵊrʃ-

CAVIAR

BrE 1988
0 20 40 60 80 100%

caviar, caviare 'kæv i ɑː ,•'•• ‖ -ɑːr 'kɑːv- ~s
z —*BrE 1988 poll panel preference:* '••• 77%,
,••'• 23%.
cavi... —*see* **cavy**
cavil 'kæv ᵊl -ɪl **~ed, ~led** d **~ing, ~ling** ɪŋ ~s
z
cavitation ,kæv ɪ 'teɪʃ ᵊn -ə- ~s z
cavit|y 'kæv ət |i -ɪt- ‖ -əţ |i **~ies** iz
ca|vort kə |'vɔːt ‖ -|'vɔːrt **~vorted** 'vɔːt ɪd -əd
‖ 'vɔːrţ əd **~vorting** 'vɔːt ɪŋ ‖ 'vɔːrţ ɪŋ
~vorts 'vɔːts ‖ 'vɔːrts
Cavour kə 'vʊə -'vɔː ‖ -'vʊᵊr —*It* [ka 'vuːr]
cavy 'keɪv i **cavies** 'keɪv iz
caw kɔː ‖ kɑː **cawed** kɔːd ‖ kɑːd **cawing**
'kɔːr ɪŋ ‖ 'kɔː ɪŋ 'kɑː- **caws** kɔːz ‖ kɑːz *(=*
cause)
Cawdor 'kɔːd ə -ɔː ‖ -ᵊr 'kɑːd-, -ɔːr
Cawdrey 'kɔːdr i ‖ 'kɑːdr-
Cawley 'kɔːl i ‖ 'kɑːl-
Cawnpore ,kɔːn 'pɔː ‖ 'kɔːn pɔːr 'kɑːn-
Cawood 'keɪ wʊd
Caxton 'kækst ᵊn
cay kiː keɪ **cays** kiːz keɪz
cayenne, C~ ₍ᵢ₎keɪ 'en ₍ᵢ₎kaɪ- —*Fr* [ka jɛn]
Cayley 'keɪl i
cayman, C~ 'keɪm ᵊn ~s z
'**Cayman ,Islands** ‖ ,•• '••
Cayuga ki 'uːg ə keɪ-, kaɪ- ~s z
Cazenove 'kæz ə nəʊv -ɪ- ‖ -noʊv —*but the*
road in north London is usually 'keɪz nəʊv
CB ,siː 'biː **~er/s** ə/z ‖ ᵊr/z
CBE ,siː biː 'iː
CBS ,siː biː 'es ◄
CD ,siː 'diː ~s z
,**C'D ,player**
CD-ROM ,siː diː 'rɒm ‖ -'rɑːm ~s z
céad míle fáilte ,keɪd ,miːl ə 'fɔːltʃ ə ‖ -'fɑːltʃ-
—*Irish* [ˌkʲeːd ˌmʲiːlʲə 'fɑːlʲ tʲə]
ceanothus ,siː‿ə 'nəʊθ əs ‖ -'noʊθ- **~es** ɪz əz

cease siːs **ceased** siːst **ceases** 'siːs ɪz -əz
ceasing 'siːs ɪŋ
cease-fire 'siːs ,faɪ‿ə ,•'•• ‖ -,faɪ‿ᵊr ~s z
ceaseless 'siːs ləs -lɪs **~ly** li
Ceausescu tʃaʊ 'ʃesk uː -'tʃesk-, -juː
—*Romanian* Ceauşescu [tʃau 'ʃes ku]
cecal 'siːk ᵊl
Cecil *(i)* 'ses ᵊl -ɪl, *(ii)* 'siːs-, *(iii)* 'sɪs- —*In BrE*
usually (i), though the English landed family is
(iii). In AmE usually (ii).
Cecile 'ses iːᵊl -ᵊl, -ɪl; se 'siːᵊl ‖ se 'siːᵊl
Cecilia sə 'siːl i‿ə sɪ-, -'sɪl- ‖ -'siːl jə -'sɪl-
Cecily *(i)* 'sɪs ᵊl i -ɪl-, *(ii)* 'ses-
cecum 'siːk əm **ceca** 'siːk ə
cedar 'siːd ə ‖ -ᵊr *(= seeder)* ~s z
,**Cedar 'Rapids**
cedarwood 'siːd ə wʊd ‖ -ᵊr- ~s z
cede siːd *(= seed)* **ceded** 'siːd ɪd -əd **cedes**
siːdz **ceding** 'siːd ɪŋ
cedi 'siːd i *(= seedy)* ~s z
cedilla sə 'dɪl ə sɪ- ~s z
Cedric *(i)* 'sedr ɪk, *(ii)* 'siːdr ɪk —*Usually (i) in*
BrE, (ii) in AmE
Ceefax 'siː fæks
Cefn 'kev ᵊn
ceili, ceilidh 'keɪl i ~s z
ceiling 'siːl ɪŋ *(usually = sealing)* ~s z
Ceinwen 'kaɪn wen —*Welsh* ['kəin wen]
celadon 'sel əd ᵊn -ə dɒn ‖ -ə dɑːn
'**celadon ware**
celandine 'sel ən daɪn -diːn ~s z
Celanese *tdmk* ,sel ə 'niːz
-cele siːᵊl — **hydrocele** 'haɪdr ə siːᵊl
celeb sə 'leb sɪ- ~s z
Celebes sə 'liːb iz se-, sɪ-, -'leɪb-; 'sel ɪ biːz, -ə-
celebrant 'sel əb rᵊnt -ɪb- ~s s
cele|brate 'sel ə |breɪt -ɪ- **~brated** breɪt ɪd -əd
‖ breɪţ əd **~brates** breɪts **~brating**
breɪt ɪŋ ‖ breɪţ ɪŋ
celebration ,sel ə 'breɪʃ ᵊn -ɪ- ~s z
celebrator 'sel ə breɪt ə '••ɪ- ‖ -breɪţ ᵊr ~s z
celebratory ,sel ə 'breɪt ᵊr i ◄ ,•ɪ-, '•••••,
'••brət ᵊr i ‖ 'sel əb rə tɔːr i sə 'leb-, -toʊr i
celebrit|y sə 'leb rət i sɪ-, -rɪt- ‖ -rəţ i **~ies** iz
celeriac sə 'ler i‿æk sɪ-
celerity sə 'ler ət i sɪ-, -ɪt- ‖ -əţ i
celery 'sel ᵊr i
celesta sə 'lest ə sɪ- ~s z
Celeste, c~ sə 'lest sɪ- **~'s, ~s** s
celestial sə 'lest i‿ᵊl sɪ- ‖ -'les tʃᵊl →-'leʃ- **~ly**
i
celestite 'sel ə staɪt -ɪ-; sə 'lest aɪt, sɪ-
Celia 'siːl i‿ə
celiac 'siːl i‿æk
celibacy 'sel əb əs i '•ɪb-
celibate 'sel əb ət -ɪb-, -ɪt ~s s
Celine, Céline se 'liːn sə-, sɪ-, seɪ-
cell sel *(= sell)* **celled** seld **cells** selz
cell|ar 'sel |ə ‖ -|ᵊr *(= seller)* **~ared** əd ‖ ᵊrd
~aring ᵊr ɪŋ **~ars** əz ‖ ᵊrz
cellarage 'sel ᵊr ɪdʒ
cellarer 'sel ᵊr ə ‖ -ᵊr ᵊr ~s z
cellaret, cellarette ,sel ə 'ret ~s s

cellar|man 'sel ə mən -mæn ‖ -ᵊr- **~men** mən
  men
Cellini tʃe 'liːn i tʃɪ-, tʃə- —*It* [tʃel 'liː ni]
cellist 'tʃel ɪst §-əst **~s** s
cellmate 'sel meɪt **~s** s
Cellnet *tdmk* 'sel net
cello 'tʃel əʊ ‖ -oʊ **~s** z
cellophane, C~ *tdmk* 'sel ə feɪn
cellphone 'sel fəʊn ‖ -foʊn **~s** z
cellular 'sel jʊl ə -jəl- ‖ -jəl ᵊr
cellularity ˌsel ju 'lær ət i ˌ•jə-, -ɪt i
  ‖ -jə 'lær ət̬ i -'ler-
cellule 'sel juːl **~s** z
cellulite 'sel ju laɪt -jə-, ˌ•• 'liːt ‖ -jə-
celluloid, C~ *tdmk* 'sel ju lɔɪd -jə- ‖ -jə- -ə-
cellulose 'sel ju ləʊs -jə-, -ləʊz ‖ -jə loʊs
Celsius 'sels i_əs ‖ 'selʃ əs
celt *'stone implement'* selt **celts** selts
Celt *(i)* kelt, *(ii)* selt **Celts** *(i)* kelts, *(ii)* selts
  —*In England and Wales usually (i), in Scotland*
  (ii)
Celtic *(i)* 'kelt ɪk, *(ii)* 'selt ɪk —*The sea is (i), the*
  football, baseball and basketball teams are (ii).
  The languages are usually (i).
Cemaes Bay ˌkem aɪs 'beɪ
cembalo 'tʃem bə ləʊ ‖ -loʊ **~s** z
cement *n, v* sə 'ment sɪ- **cemented**
  sə 'ment ɪd sɪ-, -əd ‖ -'ment̬ əd **cementing**
  sə 'ment ɪŋ sɪ- ‖ -'ment̬ ɪŋ **cements**
  sə 'men/s sɪ-
  ce'ment ˌmixer
cementation ˌsiːm en 'teɪʃ ᵊn -ən-
cementite sə 'ment aɪt sɪ-
cementum sə 'ment əm sɪ- ‖ -'ment̬-
cemeter|y 'sem ətr li -ɪtr-; ˌ•ət̬_ər li, ˌ•ɪt̬_
  ‖ 'sem ə ter li **~ies** iz
Cemmaes 'kem aɪs
Cenci 'tʃentʃ i —*It* ['tʃen tʃi]
CEng ˌsiː 'endʒ
Cenis sə 'niː se- —*Fr* [sə_ni]
cenobite 'siːn əʊ baɪt 'sen- ‖ -ə- **~s** s
cenotaph, C~ 'sen ə tɑːf -tæf ‖ -tæf **~s** s
Cenozoic ˌsiːn əʊ 'zəʊ ɪk ◂ ‖ -ə 'zoʊ- ˌsen-
cense sen/s *(= sense)* **censed** sentst **censes**
  'sen/s ɪz -əz **censing** 'sen/s ɪŋ
censer 'sen/s ə ‖ -ᵊr *(= censor, sensor)* **~s** z
cens|or 'sen/s ‖ə ‖ -ɪ-ᵊr **~ored** əd ‖ ᵊrd **~oring**
  ᵊr ɪŋ **~ors** əz ‖ ᵊrz
censorial sen 'sɔːr i_əl ‖ -'soʊr-
censorious sen 'sɔːr i_əs ‖ -'soʊr- **~ly** li
  ~ness nəs nɪs
censorship 'sen/s ə ʃɪp ‖ -ᵊr-
censurab|le 'sen/ʃ ᵊr_əb |ᵊl **~ly** li
censure 'sen/ʃ ə 'sen/s jʊə ‖ 'sen/ʃ ᵊr
  censured 'sen/ʃ əd 'sen/s jʊəd ‖ 'sen/ʃ ᵊrd
  censures 'sen/ʃ əz 'sen/s jʊəz ‖ 'sen/ʃ ᵊrz
  censuring 'sen/ʃ ᵊr ɪŋ 'sen/s jʊər ɪŋ
census 'sen/s əs **~es** ɪz əz
cent sent *(= sent)* **cents** sen/s
cental 'sent ᵊl **~s** z
centaur 'sent ɔː ‖ -ɔːr **~s** z
Centaur|us sen 'tɔːr |əs **~i** aɪ iː
centaury 'sent ɔːr i

centavo sen 'tɑːv əʊ ‖ -oʊ —*Sp* [sen 'ta βo] **~s**
  z
centenarian ˌsent ɪ 'neər i_ən ˌ•ə-
  ‖ ˌsent ᵊn 'er- **~s** z
centenar|y ₍ᵢ₎sen 'tiːn ᵊr li sᵊn-, -'ten- ‖ -'ten-
  'sent ᵊn er li **~ies** iz
centennial sen 'ten i_əl sᵊn- **~ly** i **~s** z
center 'sent ə ‖ 'sent̬ ᵊr **~ed** d **centering**
  'sent ᵊr ɪŋ →'sentr ɪŋ ‖ 'sent̬ ᵊr ɪŋ **~s** z
centerboard 'sent ə bɔːd ‖ 'sent̬ ᵊr bɔːrd
  -boʊrd **~s** z
centerfold 'sent ə fəʊld →-foʊld ‖ 'sent̬
  ᵊr foʊld **~s** z
centerpiec|e 'sent ə piːs ‖ 'sent̬ ᵊr- **~es** ɪz əz
centesimal sen 'tes əm ᵊl -ɪm- **~ly** i
centi- ˌsent i -ə ‖ ˌsent̬ ə ˌsɑːnt̬ ə
centigrade 'sent ɪ greɪd -ə- ‖ 'sent̬ ə- 'sɑːnt̬-
centigram, centigramme 'sent ɪ græm -ə-
  ‖ 'sent̬ ə- 'sɑːnt̬- **~s** z
centiliter, centilitre 'sent ɪ ˌliːt ə -ə- ‖ 'sent̬
  ə ˌliːt̬ ᵊr 'sɑːnt̬- **~s** z
centime 'sɒnt iːm 'sɑːnt- ‖ 'sɑːnt- 'sent-
  —*Fr* [sɑ̃ tim] **~s** z
centimeter, centimetre 'sent ɪ ˌmiːt ə -ə-
  ‖ 'sent̬ ə ˌmiːt̬ ᵊr 'sɑːnt̬- **~s** z
centipede 'sent ɪ piːd -ə- ‖ 'sent̬ ə- **~s** z
centner 'sent nə ‖ -nᵊr —*Ger* Zentner
  ['tsent nɐ] **~s** z
cento 'sent əʊ ‖ -oʊ **~s** z
central, C~ 'sentr əl
  ˌCentral 'Africa; ˌCentral ˌAfrican
  Re'public; ˌcentral 'heating; ˌcentral
  'nervous ˌsystem; ˌcentral 'processing
  ˌunit; ˌcentral ˌreser'vation; 'Central Time
centralis... —*see* **centraliz...**
centralism 'sentr ə ˌlɪz əm
centralist 'sentr əl ɪst -əst
centralistic ˌsentr ə 'lɪst ɪk ◂
centralit|y sen 'træl ət li -ɪt- ‖ -ət̬ li **~ies** iz
centralization ˌsentr əl aɪ 'zeɪʃ ᵊn -ɪ'•- ‖ -əl ə-
centraliz|e 'sentr ə laɪz **~ed** d **~er/s** ə/z ‖ ᵊr/z
  ~es ɪz əz **~ing** ɪŋ
centrally 'sentr əl i
centre 'sent ə ‖ 'sent̬ ᵊr **~d** d **centring**
  'sent_ər ɪŋ ‖ 'sent̬ ər ɪŋ **~s** z
  'centre bit; ˌcentre 'forward
centreboard 'sent ə bɔːd ‖ 'sent̬ ᵊr bɔːrd
  -boʊrd **~s** z
centrefold 'sent ə fəʊld →-foʊld ‖ 'sent̬
  ᵊr foʊld **~s** z
centrepiec|e 'sent ə piːs ‖ 'sent̬ ᵊr- **~es** ɪz əz
-centric 'sentr ɪk — **heliocentric**
  ˌhiːl i_əʊ 'sentr ɪk ◂ ‖ -oʊ 'sentr-
centrifugal ˌsentr ɪ 'fjuːg ᵊl ◂ -ə-;
  sen 'trɪf jʊg ᵊl, -jəg- ‖ sen 'trɪf jəg ᵊl -əg-
  ~ly i
centrifugation ˌsentr ɪ fju 'geɪʃ ᵊn
  ˌ•ə- ‖ -fjə'••-
centrifug|e 'sentr ɪ fjuːdʒ -ə-, -fjuːʒ **~ed** d
  ~es ɪz əz **~ing** ɪŋ
centripetal sen 'trɪp ɪt ᵊl -ət-; ˌsentr ɪ 'piːt ᵊl,
  -ə- ‖ -ət̬ ᵊl **~ly** i
centrist 'sentr ɪst §-əst **~s** s

centro- *comb. form*
  with stress-neutral suffix ¦sentr əʊ ‖ -ə —
  centrosome 'sentr əʊ səʊm ‖ -ə səʊm
centroid 'sentr ɔɪd ~s z
centromere 'sentr əʊ mɪə ‖ -ə mɪr ~s z
centum 'kent əm
centupl|e 'sent jʊp əl -jəp-; sen 'tjuːp-
  ‖ sen 'tuːp əl -'tjuːp-, -'tʌp- ~**ed** d ~**es** z
  ~**ing** ɪŋ
centurion sen 'tjʊər i‿ən -'tʃʊər-, -'tjɔːr-,
  -'tʃɔːr- ‖ -'tʊr- -'tjʊr- ~**s** z
century 'sentʃ ər‿i
CEO ˌsiː iː 'əʊ ‖ -'oʊ ~**s** z
ceorl tʃeəl ‖ 'tʃeɪ ɔːrl
cep, cèpe sep **ceps, cèpes** seps
cephalic sə 'fæl ɪk sɪ-, ke-, kɪ- —*In words
  containing (-)cephal-, the medical profession in
  Britain generally prefers* k. *The alternative
  pronunciation with* s *is nevertheless widespread,
  and preferred in AmE.*
Cephalonia ˌkef ə 'ləʊn i‿ə ˌsef- ‖ -'loʊn-
  —*ModGk* Kefallinía [cɛ fa li 'ni a]
cephalopod 'sef əl ə pɒd ‖ -pɑːd ~**s** z
cephalosporin ˌsef əl əʊ 'spɔːr ɪn ˌkef-, §-ən
  ‖ -ə 'spɔːr ən -'spoʊr-
cephalothorax ˌsef əl əʊ 'θɔːr æks ‖ -əl oʊ-
  -'θoʊr-
-cephalous 'sef əl əs 'kef- — **autocephalous**
  ˌɔːt əʊ 'sef əl əs ◂ ‖ ˌɔːt̬ ə- ˌɑːt̬-
-cephaly 'kef əl i 'sef- — **microcephaly**
  ˌmaɪk rəʊ 'kef əl i -'sef- ‖ ˌ•oʊ-
Cephas 'siːf æs
Cepheid, c~ 'siːf i ɪd 'sef-, §-əd
Cepheus 'siːf juːs 'siːf i‿əs
cepstral 'keps trəl
cepstrum 'keps trəm ~**s** z
ceramic sə 'ræm ɪk sɪ-, kə-, kɪ-, ke- ~**s** s
cerastes sə 'ræst iːz sɪ-, se-
Cerberus 'sɜːb ər‿əs ‖ 'sɜ·b-
cercaria sɜː 'keər i‿ə sə- ‖ sər 'ker-
cere sɪə ‖ sɪʳr (= *sere*) **cered** sɪəd ‖ sɪʳrd
cereal 'sɪər i‿əl ‖ 'sɪr- (= *serial*) ~**s** z
cerebell|um ˌser ə 'bel |əm -ɪ- ~**a** ə ~**ar** ə ‖ əʳr
Cerebos *tdmk* 'ser ə bɒs -ɪ- ‖ -bɑːs -boʊs
cerebral 'ser əb rəl -ɪ-; sə 'riːb rəl, sɪ- ~**ly** i
cere|brate 'ser ə |breɪt -ɪ- ~**brated** breɪt ɪd
  -əd ‖ breɪt̬ əd ~**brates** breɪts ~**brating**
  breɪt ɪŋ ‖ breɪt̬ ɪŋ
cerebration ˌser ə 'breɪʃ ən -ɪ- ~**s** z
cerebra sə 'riːb rə sɪ-; 'ser əb rə, -ɪb-
cerebrospinal ˌser əb rəʊ 'spaɪn əl ◂ ˌ•ɪb-;
  sə ˌriːb- ‖ -əb roʊ-
cerebrovascular ˌser əb rəʊ 'væsk jʊl ə ◂
  ˌ•ɪb-, -jəl ə; sə ˌriːb- ‖ -roʊ 'væsk jəl əʳr ◂
cerebrum sə 'riːb rəm sɪ-; 'ser əb-, -ɪb-
Ceredig kə 'red ɪg —*Welsh* [ke 're dig]
Ceredigion ˌker ə 'dɪg i ɒn ‖ -ɑːn —*Welsh*
  [ke re 'dig jɔn]
cerement 'sɪə mənt 'ser ə mənt ‖ 'sɪr- ~**s** s
ceremonial ˌser ə 'məʊn i‿əl ◂ ˌ•ɪ- ‖ -'moʊn-
  ~**ism** ˌɪz əm ~**ist/s** ɪst/s əst/s ~**ly** i
ceremonious ˌser ə 'məʊn i‿əs ◂ ˌ•ɪ-
  ‖ -'moʊn- ~**ly** li ~**ness** nəs nɪs

ceremon|y 'ser əm ən |i, ˌ•ɪm- ‖ -ə moʊn |i
  ~**ies** iz
Ceres 'sɪər iːz ‖ 'sɪr-
Cerf sɜːf ‖ sɜ·f
Ceri 'ker i
cerise sə 'riːz sɪ-, -'riːs
cerium 'sɪər i‿əm ‖ 'sɪr-
CERN sɜːn ‖ sɜ·n
Cerne Abbas ˌsɜːn 'æb əs ‖ ˌsɜ·n-
Cerrig-y-Drudion ˌker ɪg ə 'drɪd jɒn ‖ -jɑːn
  -jɔːn
cert sɜːt ‖ sɜ·t **certs** sɜːts ‖ sɜ·ts
certain 'sɜːt ən -ɪn ‖ 'sɜ·t-
certainly 'sɜːt ən li -ɪn- ‖ 'sɜ·t-
certain|ty 'sɜːt ən |ti -ɪn- ‖ 'sɜ·t- ~**ties** tiz
CertEd ˌsɜːt 'ed ‖ ˌsɜ·t-
certes 'sɜːt ɪz -əz, -iːz; sɜːts ‖ 'sɜ·t̬ iːz sɜ·ts
certifiab|le 'sɜːt ɪ faɪˌəb |əl ˌ•'ə-, ˌ•'•
  ‖ 'sɜ·t̬- ~**ly** li
certificate *n* sə 'tɪf ɪk ət -ək-, -ɪt ‖ sər- ~**s** s
certifi|cate *v* sə 'tɪf ɪ |keɪt -ə- ‖ sər- ~**cated**
  keɪt ɪd -əd ‖ keɪt̬ əd ~**cates** keɪts ~**cating**
  keɪt ɪŋ ‖ keɪt̬ ɪŋ
certification ˌsɜːt ɪf ɪ 'keɪʃ ən, ˌ•əf-, -ə'•-
  ‖ ˌsɜ·t̬- —*Occasionally also* sə ˌtɪf- ‖ sər-, *but
  only in the sense 'certificating', not in the sense
  'certifying'*
certi|fy 'sɜːt ɪ |faɪ -ə- ‖ 'sɜ·t̬- ~**fied** faɪd ~**fies**
  faɪz ~**fying** faɪ ɪŋ
certiorari ˌsɜːt ɪ‿ə 'reər aɪ ˌsɜːt-, -i ɔː-, -'rɑːr i
  ‖ ˌsɜ·ʃ ɪ‿ə 'rer i, ˌ•ə'••
certitude 'sɜːt ɪ tjuːd -ə-, →-tʃuːd
  ‖ 'sɜ·t̬ ə tuːd -tjuːd ~**s** z
cerulean sə 'ruːl i‿ən sɪ-
cerumen sə 'ruːm en sɪ-, -ən
Cervantes sɜː 'vænt iːz -ɪz ‖ sər- —*Sp*
  [θer 'βan tes]
cervelat ˌsɜːv ə 'lɑːt -'lɑː, -'læt, '•••
  ‖ 'sɜ·v ə lɑːt -lɑː, -læt
cervical 'vaɪk əl sɜː-; 'sɜːv ɪk əl ‖ 'sɜ·v ɪk əl
cervices sə 'vaɪs iːz sɜː-; 'sɜːv ɪ siːz, -ə- ‖ sər-
  'sɜ·v ə siːz
cervine 'sɜːv aɪn ‖ 'sɜ·v-
cervix 'sɜːv ɪks ‖ 'sɜ·v- ~**es** ɪz əz
Cesar, César 'seɪz ɑː ‖ seɪ 'zɑːr —*Fr* [se zaːʁ]
cesarean, cesarian sɪ 'zeər i‿ən sə-, siː-
  ‖ -'zer- -'zær-
Cesarewitch sɪ 'zær ə wɪtʃ sə-, -ɪ- ‖ -'zer-
cesium 'siːz i‿əm 'siːs-
cess ses
cessation se 'seɪʃ ən sɪ-, sə-
cession 'seʃ ən (= *session*) ~**s** z
Cessna *tdmk* 'ses nə ~**s**, ~'**s** z
cesspit 'ses pɪt ~**s** s
cesspool 'ses puːl ~**s** z
c'est la vie ˌseɪ lɑː 'viː -lə- —*Fr* [sɛ la vi]
cesta 'sest ə ~**s** z
cestode 'sest əʊd ‖ -oʊd ~**s** z
cestus 'sest əs ~**es** ɪz əz
cesur|a sɪ 'zjʊər |ə sə-, siː-, -'zjɔːr-, -'ʒʊər-
  ‖ -'zʊr- ~**ae** iː aɪ ~**as** əz
cetacean sɪ 'teɪʃ ən sə-, -'teɪʃ i‿ən, -'teɪs i‿ən
  ~**s** z

cetane 'siːt eɪn
  'cetane ˌnumber
ceteris paribus ˌket ə riːs 'pær ɪb əs ˌkeɪt-,
  ˌset-, -ər ɪs-, -'paːr-, -əb-, -ʊs ‖ ˌkeɪt̬ ər əs-
  -'per-
Ceti 'siːt aɪ
cetological ˌsiːt ə 'lɒdʒ ɪk ᵊl ◄ ‖ ˌsiːt̬ ə 'laːdʒ-
cetolog|ist/s siː 'tɒl ədʒ ɪst/s sɪ-, §-əst/s
  ‖ -'taːl- **~y** i
cetrimide 'setr ɪ maɪd -ə-
Cetshwayo ketʃ 'waɪ əʊ ‖ -oʊ —*Zulu*
  [ɪɛ 'tʃwa: jɔ]
Cetus 'siːt əs ‖ 'siːt̬-
cetyl 'siːt ɪl -ᵊl ‖ 'siːt̬ ᵊl
Ceuta 'sjuːt ə 'suːt- ‖ 'seɪ uːt̬ ə —*Sp* ['θeu ta,
  'seu-]
Cevennes, Cévennes sɪ 'ven seɪ-, sə- —*Fr*
  [se vɛn]
ceviche sɪ 'viːtʃ eɪ sə-, seɪ-, -i; seɪ 'viːʃ —*AmSp*
  [se 'vi tʃe]
Ceylon sɪ 'lɒn sə- ‖ -'laːn
Ceylonese ˌsel ə 'niːz ◄ ˌsiːl- ‖ -'niːs
Cezanne, Cézanne sɪ 'zæn seɪ-, sə-
  ‖ seɪ 'zaːn —*Fr* [se zan]
cf —*see* **compare**
Chablis, c~ 'ʃæb liː 'ʃaːb-, -li ‖ ʃæ 'bliː ʃaː-, ʃə-
  —*Fr* [ʃa bli]
Chabrier 'ʃæb ri eɪ 'ʃaːb-; ʃaː 'briː-
  ‖ ˌʃaːb ri 'eɪ —*Fr* [ʃa bʁi je]
Chabrol ʃæ 'brɒl ʃə- ‖ ʃaː 'broʊl —*Fr*
  [ʃa bʁɔl]
cha-cha 'tʃaː tʃaː ~**ed** d **cha-chaing**
  'tʃaː tʃaːr ɪŋ ‖ -tʃaː ɪŋ ~**s** z
cha-cha-cha ˌtʃaː tʃaː 'tʃaː
chacma 'tʃæk mə ‖ 'tʃaːk- ~**s** z
chaconne ʃə 'kɒn ʃæ- ‖ ʃaː 'kaːn -'kɔːn —*Fr*
  [ʃa kɔn]
chacun à son goût ˌʃæk ɜːn ˌaː sɒŋ 'guː -ˌæ-
  ‖ ʃaː ˌkuːn aː saːn- -sɔːn'• —*Fr*
  [ʃa kœ̃ a sɔ̃ gu]
Chad, chad tʃæd
Chadband 'tʃæd bænd →'tʃæb-
Chadburn 'tʃæd bɜːn 'tʃæb- ‖ -bɜ·n
Chadderton 'tʃæd ət ᵊn ‖ -ᵊrt ᵊn
Chadian 'tʃæd i_ən ~**s** z
Chadic 'tʃæd ɪk
chador 'tʃaːd ɔː 'tʃʌd-, -ə ‖ -ɔːr
Chadwick 'tʃæd wɪk
chaebol 'tʃeɪ bɒl ‖ -bɔːl -baːl, -boʊl —*Kor*
  [tʃɛ bol]
Chaeronea ˌkaɪᵊr ə 'niː_ə ˌkɪər-, ˌker-
chaeto- *comb. form*
  with stress-neutral suffix ˌkiːt əʊ ‖ kiːt̬ ə —
    chaetopod 'kiːt əʊ pɒd ‖ 'kiːt̬ ə paːd
  with stress-imposing suffix kiː 'tɒ+ ‖ -'taː+ —
    chaetophorous kiː 'tɒf ər əs ‖ -'taːf-
chafe tʃeɪf **chafed** tʃeɪft **chafes** tʃeɪfs
  chafing 'tʃeɪf ɪŋ
chafer 'tʃeɪf ə ‖ -ᵊr ~**s** z
chaff tʃaːf tʃæf **chaffed** tʃaːft tʃæft
  ‖ tʃæft **chaffing** 'tʃaːf ɪŋ 'tʃæf- ‖ 'tʃæf-
  chaffs tʃaːfs tʃæfs ‖ tʃæfs

chaffer 'tʃæf ə ‖ -ᵊr ~**ed** d **chaffering** 'tʃæf
  ᵊr ɪŋ ~**s** z
Chaffey 'tʃæf i
chaffinch 'tʃæf ɪntʃ ~**es** ɪz əz
chafing 'tʃeɪf ɪŋ
  'chafing dish
Chagall ʃæ 'gæl ʃə-, -'gaːl —*Fr* [ʃa gall] ~**s**, ~'**s**
  z
Chagas 'ʃaːg əs —*Port* ['ʃa ɣɐʃ] —*The*
  possessive form ~' *has the same pronunciation,*
  or sometimes an extra ɪz, əz.
  'Chagas' diˌsease
Chagford 'tʃæg fəd ‖ -fᵊrd
chagrin 'ʃæg rɪn -rən ‖ ʃə 'grɪn (*) ~**ed** d
Chagrin 'ʃæg ræ ‖ ʃa: 'græn —*Fr* [ʃa gʁæ̃]
Chaim haɪm xaɪm —*Hebrew* ['xa jim, xa 'jiːm]
chain, Chain tʃeɪn **chained** tʃeɪnd **chaining**
  'tʃeɪn ɪŋ **chains** tʃeɪnz
  'chain gang; 'chain ˌletter; ˌchain link
  'fencing; ˌchain re'action; 'chain stitch;
  'chain store
chainsaw 'tʃeɪn sɔː ‖ -saː ~**s** z
chain-smok|e 'tʃeɪn sməʊk ‖ -smoʊk ~**ed** t
  ~**er/s** ə/z ‖ ᵊr/z ~**es** s ~**ing** ɪŋ
chair tʃeə ‖ tʃeᵊr **chaired** tʃeəd ‖ tʃeᵊrd
  chairing 'tʃeər ɪŋ ‖ 'tʃer ɪŋ **chairs**
  tʃeəz ‖ tʃeᵊrz
  'chair lift
chairbound 'tʃeə baʊnd ‖ 'tʃer-
chair|man 'tʃeə |mən ‖ 'tʃer- ~**men** mən men
  ~**manship/s** mən ʃɪp/s ~**person/s** ˌpɜːs ᵊn/
  z ‖ ˌpɜ·ːs ᵊn/z ~**woman** ˌwʊm ən ~**women**
  ˌwɪm ɪn §-ən
chaise ʃeɪz ‖ tʃeɪs **chaises** 'ʃeɪz ɪz -əz;
  ʃeɪz ‖ tʃeɪs əz
  ˌchaise 'longue lɒŋ ‖ lɔːŋ laːŋ —*Fr*
  [ʃez lɔ̃ːg] —*The plural,* ~(**s**) **longues**, *is*
  pronounced identically with the singular, or
  sometimes with added z. *Particularly in AmE,*
  longue *is sometimes changed by popular*
  etymology to **lounge**.
chakra 'tʃʌk rə 'tʃæk-, 'tʃaːk-
chalaz|a kə 'leɪz lə ~**ae** iː ~**as** əz
Chalcedon 'kæls ɪd ᵊn -əd-; -ɪ dɒn, -ə-
  ‖ -ə daːn
chalcedon|y kæl 'sed ᵊn |i ‖ 'kæls ə doʊn i
  ~**ies** iz
Chalcidice kæl 'sɪd əs i -ɪs-
Chalcis 'kæls ɪs §-əs
chalcopyrite ˌkælk əʊ 'paɪᵊr aɪt ‖ -ə-
Chalde|a kæl 'diː_lə kɔːl- ‖ kɔːl-, kaːl- ~**an/s**
  ən/z
Chaldee kæl 'diː kɔːl-, '•• ‖ kɔːl-, kaːl- ~**s** z
Chaldon 'tʃɔːld ᵊn 'tʃɒld- ‖ 'tʃaːld-
chaldron 'tʃɔːldr ᵊn ‖ 'tʃaːldr- ~**s** z
chalet 'ʃæl eɪ -i ‖ ʃæ 'leɪ (*) ~**s** z
Chalfont 'tʃæl fɒnt 'tʃælf ᵊnt ‖ -faːnt —*locally*
  also 'tʃɑːf ᵊnt
chalic|e 'tʃæl ɪs -əs ~**es** ɪz əz
chalk, Chalk tʃɔːk ‖ tʃaːk **chalked** tʃɔːkt
  ‖ tʃaːkt **chalking** 'tʃɔːk ɪŋ ‖ 'tʃaːk- **chalks**
  tʃɔːks ‖ tʃaːks

C

C

chalkboard 'tʃɔːk bɔːd ‖ -bɔːrd 'tʃɑːk-, -boʊrd
~s z
Chalker 'tʃɔːk ə ‖ -ər 'tʃɑːk-
chalkface 'tʃɔːk feɪs ‖ 'tʃɑːk-
chalkstripe 'tʃɔːk straɪp ‖ 'tʃɑːk- ~s s
chalk|y 'tʃɔːk |i ‖ 'tʃɑːk- ~ier i̯ə ‖ i̯ər ~iest
i̯ɪst i̯əst ~iness i nəs i nɪs
challah 'hɑːl ə xɑː 'lɑː ~s z challoth
xɑː 'lɒt ‖ -'loʊt
challeng|e 'tʃæl ɪndʒ -əndʒ ~ed d ~es ɪz əz
~ing ɪŋ
challenger, C~ 'tʃæl ɪndʒ ə -əndʒ- ‖ -ər ~s z
Challenor 'tʃæl ən ə -ɪn- ‖ -ər
Challes, Challis 'tʃæl ɪs -əs
Challock 'tʃɒl ək ‖ 'tʃɑːl-
Challoner 'tʃæl ən ə ‖ -ər
Chalmers (i) 'tʃɑːm əz 'tʃɑːlm- ‖ -ərz, (ii)
'tʃælm-
chalybeate kə 'lɪb i̯ət ɪt, -eɪt ‖ -'liːb-
cham kæm chams kæmz
chamber 'tʃeɪm bə ‖ -bər ~ed d ~s z
'chamber ˌmusic; 'chamber ˌorchestra;
'chamber pot
chamberlain 'tʃeɪm bə lɪn -lən ‖ -bər- ~s z
Chamberlain, Chamberlaine, Chamberlayne
(i) 'tʃeɪm bə lɪn -lən ‖ -bər-, (ii) -leɪn
chambermaid 'tʃeɪm bə meɪd ‖ -bər- ~s z
Chambers 'tʃeɪm bəz ‖ -bərz
Chambourcy tdmk ʃæm 'buəs i ‖ ˌʃɑːm bʊr 'siː
—Fr [ʃɑ̃ buʁ si]
chambray 'ʃæm breɪ -bri
chambré 'ʃɒm breɪ ‖ ˌʃɑːm 'breɪ —Fr [ʃɑ̃ bʁe]
chameleon kə 'miːl i̯ən ~s z
chameleonic kə ˌmiːl i 'ɒn ɪk ◂ ‖ -'ɑːn-
chameleon-like kə 'miːl i̯ən laɪk
chamfer 'tʃæmᵖf ə 'ʃæmᵖf- ‖ -ər 'tʃæmᵖ- ~ed
d chamfering 'tʃæmᵖf ər_ɪŋ 'ʃæmᵖf- ‖
'tʃæmᵖ- ~s z
chamm|y 'ʃæm |i ~ies ɪz
chamois (i) 'ʃæm wɑː ‖ ʃæm 'wɑː, (ii) 'ʃæm i
—(ii) is used mainly in reference to chamois
leather, and is then alternatively spelt chammy,
shammy. The plural may have z, or may —
particularly in reference to the goats — be
pronounced identically with the singular.
chamomile 'kæm ə maɪ_əl -miːəl
Chamonix 'ʃæm ə niː -ɒ- ‖ ˌʃæm ə 'niː —Fr
[ʃa mɔ ni]
champ tʃæmp champed tʃæmpt champing
'tʃæmp ɪŋ champs tʃæmps
champagne, C~ ˌʃæm 'peɪn ◂ —Fr [ʃɑ̃ panj]
ˌchampagne 'cocktail
champak 'tʃʌmp ək 'tʃæmp æk
Champernowne 'tʃæmp ə naʊn ‖ -ər-
champers 'ʃæmp əz ‖ -ərz
champerty 'tʃæmp ət i -ɜːt- ‖ -ərt̬ i
champignon 'ʃæmp iːn jɒ̃ ˌ•'••; ʃæm 'pɪn jən
‖ ʃæm 'pɪn jən tʃæm- —Fr [ʃɑ̃ pi njɔ̃] ~s z
—or as singular
champion, C~ 'tʃæmp jən -i̯ən ~ed d ~ing
ɪŋ ~s z
championship 'tʃæmp jən ʃɪp -i̯ən- ~s s
Champlain ₍ₗ₎ʃæm 'pleɪn —Fr [ʃɑ̃ plæ̃]

Champneys 'tʃæmp nɪz
Champs Elysees, Champs Elysées
ˌʃɒnz ə 'liːz eɪ ˌʃɒmz-, ˌʃɒ̃z-, -ɪ-, -eɪ-
‖ ˌʃɑːnz ˌeɪl i 'zeɪ —Fr [ʃɑ̃ ze li ze]
Chan tʃæn —Cantonese [⁴tsʰɐn]

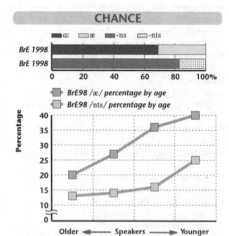

CHANCE

■ ɑː	▢ æ	■ -ns	▨ -nts		

BrE 1998

BrE 1998

0   20   40   60   80   100%

◆ BrE98 /æ/ percentage by age
◆ BrE98 /nts/ percentage by age

Older ◄— Speakers —► Younger

chance tʃɑːnts §tʃænts ‖ tʃænts —BrE 1998
poll panel preference (not restricted to RP): ɑː
69%, æ 31%; -ns 83%, -nts 17%. chanced
tʃɑːntst §tʃæntst ‖ tʃæntst chances
'tʃɑːnts ɪz §'tʃænts-, -əz ‖ 'tʃænts əz
chancing 'tʃɑːnts ɪŋ §'tʃænts- ‖ 'tʃænts ɪŋ
chancel 'tʃɑːnts əl §'tʃænts- ‖ 'tʃænts əl ~s z
chanceller|y 'tʃɑːnts əl_ər li §'tʃænts-, '•əl ər_li
‖ 'tʃænts- ~ies iz
chancellor, C~ 'tʃɑːnts əl_ə §'tʃænts-
‖ 'tʃænts əl_ər ~s z
chancer|y 'tʃɑːnts ər_li §'tʃænts- ‖ 'tʃænts-
~ies iz
Chanctonbury 'tʃæŋkt ən bər_i →'•əm-,
-ˌber i ‖ -ˌber i
chancre 'ʃæŋk ə ‖ -ər ~s z
chancroid 'ʃæŋk rɔɪd ~s z
chanc|y 'tʃɑːnts |i §'tʃænts i ‖ 'tʃænts |i ~ier
i̯ə ‖ i̯ər ~iest i̯ɪst i̯əst
chandelier ˌʃænd ə 'lɪə ˌʃɒnd-, -əl 'ɪə ‖ -əl 'ɪər
~s z
chandelle ʃæn 'del ʃɑːn- ~s z
Chandigarh ˌtʃʌnd i 'gɜː ˌtʃænd-, -'gɑː, '•••gə
‖ -'gɜːː -'gɑːr
chandler, C~ 'tʃɑːnd lə §'tʃænd- ‖ 'tʃænd lər
~s z
chandler|y 'tʃɑːnd lər li §'tʃænd-, §-əl r|i
‖ 'tʃænd- ~ies iz
Chandos (i) 'ʃænd ɒs ‖ -ɑːs, (ii) 'tʃænd-
Chanel ʃə 'nel ʃæ- —Fr [ʃa nɛl]
Chang tʃæŋ ‖ dʒɑːŋ —Chi Zhāng [¹tʂaŋ]
Changchun ˌtʃæŋ 'tʃʊn ‖ ˌtʃɑːŋ- —Chi
Chángchūn [²tʂʰaŋ ¹tʂʰwən]
change tʃeɪndʒ changed tʃeɪndʒd changes
'tʃeɪndʒ ɪz -əz changing 'tʃeɪndʒ ɪŋ
'change ˌringing
changeability ˌtʃeɪndʒ ə 'bɪl ət i -ɪt i ‖ -ət̬ i

changeab|le 'tʃeɪndʒ əb |əl ~leness əl nəs -nɪs
~ly li
changeless 'tʃeɪndʒ ləs -lɪs ~ly li ~ness nəs
nɪs
changeling 'tʃeɪndʒ lɪŋ ~s z
changeover n 'tʃeɪndʒ ˌəʊv ə ‖ -ˌoʊv ər ~s z
changer 'tʃeɪndʒ ə ‖ -ər ~s z
changeround 'tʃeɪndʒ raʊnd ~s z
Changi place in Singapore 'tʃæŋ i
changing 'tʃeɪndʒ ɪŋ
'changing room
channel, C~ 'tʃæn əl ~ed, ~led d ~ing, ~ling
ɪŋ ~s z
'Channel ˌIslands ‖ ˌ• • ' • •
Channing 'tʃæn ɪŋ
Channon (i) 'tʃæn ən, (ii) 'ʃæn ən
chanson 'ʃɒ̃ sɒ̃ 'ʃɒn-, -sɒn ‖ ʃɑːn 'sɔːn -'soʊn,
-'sɑːn; 'ʃænts ən —Fr [ʃɑ̃ sɔ̃] ~s z —or as
singular
chant, Chant tʃɑːnt §tʃænt ‖ tʃænt chanted
'tʃɑːnt ɪd §'tʃænt- -əd ‖ 'tʃænt̬ əd chanting
'tʃɑːnt ɪŋ §'tʃænt- ‖ 'tʃænt̬ ɪŋ
Chantal ˌʃɑːn 'tæl ˌʃɒn-, ˌʃæn-, -'tɑːl
‖ ʃɑːn 'tɑːl —Fr [ʃɑ̃ tal]
Chantelle ˌʃɑːn 'tel ˌʃɒn-, ˌʃæn- —Fr [ʃɑ̃ tɛl]
chanter, C~ 'tʃɑːnt ə §'tʃænt- ‖ 'tʃænt̬ ər ~s z
chanterelle ˌʃɒnt ə 'rel ˌʃænt-, ˌtʃænt- ‖ ˌʃænt̬-
ˌʃɑːnt̬- ~s z
chanteus|e ˌʃɒn 'tɜːz ˌʃɑːn- ‖ ʃɑːn 'tuːz ˌʃæn-
(*) —Fr [ʃɑ̃ tøːz] ~es ɪz əz —or as singular
chanti... —see chanty
Chanticleer, c~ 'ʃɑːnt ə kliə 'ʃɒnt-, 'tʃɑːnt-,
'tʃænt-, -ɪ-, ˌ• • ' • ‖ 'tʃænt̬ ə klɪr ~s, ~'s z
Chantilly ʃæn 'tɪl i ʃɒn- ‖ ˌʃɑːnt i 'jiː —Fr
[ʃɑ̃ ti ji]
chantr|y, C~ 'tʃɑːntr li §'tʃæntr- ‖ 'tʃæntr li
~ies iz
'chantry ˌchapel
chant|y 'ʃænt li 'tʃænt-, 'tʃɑːnt- ‖ 'ʃænt̬ li
~ies iz
Chanukah 'hɑːn ək ə 'hɒn-, 'kɑːn-, -ʊk-, -ɑː
—Hebrew [xa nu 'ka]
Chao tʃaʊ
ˌChao ˌYuen 'Ren ˌjuː en 'ren —Chi Zhào
Yuánrèn [⁴tʂɐu ²ɥɛn ⁴z̩ən]
chaology keɪ 'ɒl ədʒ i ‖ -'ɑːl-
chaos 'keɪ ɒs ‖ -ɑːs
chaotic keɪ 'ɒt ɪk ‖ -'ɑːt̬- ~ally əl_i
chap tʃæp chapped tʃæpt chapping
'tʃæp ɪŋ chaps tʃæps
chaparral ˌʃæp ə 'ræl ˌtʃæp-, -'rɑːl
chapati, chapatti tʃə 'pɑːt i -'pæt- —Hindi
[tʃə pɑː ʈi] ~s z
chapbook 'tʃæp bʊk §-buːk ~s s
chapel, C~ 'tʃæp əl ~s z
Chapel-en-le-Frith ˌtʃæp əl ˌen lə 'frɪθ
-əl ən lə-
chapelgo|er/s 'tʃæp əl ˌgəʊ |ə/z ‖ -ˌgoʊ |ər/z
~ing ɪŋ
Chapeltown 'tʃæp əl taʊn
chaperon, chaperon|e 'ʃæp ə rəʊn ‖ -roʊn
~ed d ~es, ~s z ~ing ɪŋ
chapfallen 'tʃæp ˌfɔːl ən ‖ -ˌfɑːl-

chaplain 'tʃæp lɪn -lən ~s z
chaplain|cy 'tʃæp lən |si -lɪn- ~cies siz
chaplet 'tʃæp lət -lɪt ~s s
Chaplin 'tʃæp lɪn -lən
Chaplinesque ˌtʃæp lɪ 'nesk ◂ -lə-
Chapman 'tʃæp mən
chappal 'tʃʌp əl ~s z
Chappaquiddick ˌtʃæp ə 'kwɪd ɪk
chapp... —see chap
Chappell 'tʃæp əl
chappie, C~ tdmk 'tʃæp i ~s z
chaps tʃæps
chapstick 'tʃæp stɪk ~s s
chaptalis... —see chaptaliz...
chaptalization ˌtʃæpt əl aɪ 'zeɪʃ ən ˌʃæpt-,
-ɪ' • - ‖ -əl ə-
chaptaliz|e 'tʃæpt ə laɪz 'ʃæpt- ~ed d ~es ɪz
əz ~ing ɪŋ
chapter 'tʃæpt ə ‖ -ər ~s z
ˌchapter and 'verse; 'chapter house
char tʃɑː ‖ tʃɑːr charred tʃɑːd ‖ tʃɑːrd
charring 'tʃɑːr ɪŋ chars tʃɑːz ‖ tʃɑːrz
charabanc 'ʃær ə bæŋ -bɒŋ ‖ 'ʃer- ~s z
character 'kær əkt ə -ɪkt- ‖ -ər 'ker- ~s z
'character ˌsketch
characteris... —see characteriz...
characteristic ˌkær əkt ə 'rɪst ɪk ◂
ˌ• 'ɪkt- ‖ ˌker- ~ally əl_i ~s s
characterization ˌkær əkt ər_aɪ 'zeɪʃ ən ˌ• ɪkt-,
ɪ' • - ‖ -ɪkt ər_ə- ˌker-
characteriz|e 'kær əkt ə raɪz ' • ɪkt- ‖ 'ker-
~ed d ~es ɪz əz ~ing ɪŋ
characterless 'kær əkt ə ləs ' • ɪkt-, -lɪs ‖ -ər ləs
'ker- ~ly li
charade ʃə 'rɑːd -'reɪd ‖ -'reɪd ~s z —The
-'reɪd form, previously only AmE, is now
occasionally also heard in BrE
charbroil 'tʃɑː brɔɪəl ‖ 'tʃɑːr- ~ed d ~ing ɪŋ
~s z
charcoal 'tʃɑː kəʊl →-kɒʊl ‖ 'tʃɑːr koʊl ~ed d
~ing ɪŋ ~s z
charcoal-burner 'tʃɑː kəʊl ˌbɜːn ə →-kɒʊl-
‖ 'tʃɑːr koʊl ˌbɜːn ər ~s z
charcuterie ʃɑː 'kuːt ər i -'kjuːt-
‖ ʃɑːr ˌkuːt̬ ə 'riː - ' • • —Fr [ʃaʁ ky tʁi]
chard, Chard tʃɑːd ‖ tʃɑːrd
Chardonnay, c~ 'ʃɑːd ə neɪ →-ən eɪ
‖ ˌʃɑːrd ən 'eɪ ~s z —Fr Chardonnet
[ʃaʁ dɔ nɛ]
charge tʃɑːdʒ ‖ tʃɑːrdʒ charged
tʃɑːdʒd ‖ tʃɑːrdʒd charges 'tʃɑːdʒ ɪz -əz
‖ 'tʃɑːrdʒ əz charging
'tʃɑːdʒ ɪŋ ‖ 'tʃɑːrdʒ ɪŋ
'charge acˌcount; 'charge card; 'charge
hand; 'charge nurse; 'charge sheet
chargeable 'tʃɑːdʒ əb əl ‖ 'tʃɑːrdʒ-
chargé d'affaires ˌʃɑːʒ eɪ dæ 'feə -də' •
‖ ʃɑːr ˌʒeɪ də 'feər -dæ' • —Fr
[ʃaʁ ʒe da fɛːʁ] —The plural, chargés
d'affaires, is pronounced identically with the
singular, as in French; or, alternatively, as
ˌ• eɪz- ‖ • ˌʒeɪz-
charger 'tʃɑːdʒ ə ‖ 'tʃɑːrdʒ ər ~s z

Chari 'tʃɑːr i
chari... —see chary
Charing 'tʃær ɪŋ 'tʃeər- ‖ 'tʃer-
,Charing 'Cross
chari|ot 'tʃær i‿ət ‖ 'tʃer- ~oted ət ɪd -əd
‖ ət əd ~oting ət ɪŋ ‖ ət ɪŋ ~ots əts
charioteer ,tʃær i‿ə 'tɪə ‖ -'tɪ°r ,tʃer- ~s z
charisma kə 'rɪz mə charismata kə 'rɪz mət ə
,kær ɪz 'mɑːt ə, -əz- ‖ kə 'rɪz mət ə
charismatic ,kær ɪz 'mæt ɪk ◄ -əz- ‖ -'mæt̬-
,ker- ~ally ᵊl‿i
charitab|le 'tʃær ɪt əb |ᵊl '•ət- ‖ 'tʃær ət̬-
'tʃer- ~leness ᵊl nəs -nɪs ~ly li
charit|y, C~ 'tʃær ət |i -ɪt- ‖ -ət̬ li 'tʃer- ~ies iz
charivari ,ʃɑːr ɪ 'vɑːr i ,ʃær-, -ə- ‖ ʃə ,rɪv ə 'riː
,ʃɪv ə 'riː (*)
charivaria ,ʃɑːr ɪ 'vɑːr i‿ə ,ʃær-, '•ə-
charka 'tʃɜːk ɑː 'tʃɑːk-, -ə ‖ 'tʃɜːk- ~s z
charlad|y 'tʃɑː ,leɪd |i ‖ 'tʃɑːr- ~ies iz
charlatan 'ʃɑːl ət ən -ə tæn ‖ 'ʃɑːrl ət ᵊn ~ism
,ɪz əm ~ry ri ~s z
Charlbury 'tʃɑːl bər‿i ‖ 'tʃɑːrl ,ber i
Charlecote 'tʃɑːl kəʊt ‖ 'tʃɑːrl koʊt
Charleen (i) 'tʃɑːl iːn ₍ₒ₎tʃɑː 'liːn ‖ 'tʃɑːrl-, (ii)
'ʃɑːl iːn ₍ₒ₎ʃɑː 'liːn ‖ 'ʃɑːrl iːn ₍ₒ₎ʃɑːr 'liːn
Charlemagne 'ʃɑːl ə meɪn -maɪn, ,•••
‖ 'ʃɑːrl- —Fr [ʃaʁ lə manj]
Charlene (i) 'tʃɑːl iːn ₍ₒ₎tʃɑː 'liːn ‖ 'tʃɑːrl-, (ii)
'ʃɑːl iːn ₍ₒ₎ʃɑː 'liːn ‖ 'ʃɑːrl iːn ₍ₒ₎ʃɑːr 'liːn
Charles tʃɑːlz ‖ tʃɑːrlz —but as a French name,
ʃɑːl ‖ ʃɑːrl, Fr [ʃaʁl] Charles', Charles's
'tʃɑːlz ɪz -əz; tʃɑːlz ‖ 'tʃɑːrlz əz tʃɑːrlz
Charleston, c~ 'tʃɑːlst ən 'tʃɑːlz tən ‖ 'tʃɑːrlst
ən ~s z
Charlestown 'tʃɑːlz taʊn ‖ 'tʃɑːrlz-
Charley, Charlie, c~ 'tʃɑːl i ‖ 'tʃɑːrl i
'charley horse
Charlie, c~ 'tʃɑːl i ‖ 'tʃɑːrl i ~s, ~'s z
charlock 'tʃɑː lɒk ‖ 'tʃɑːr lɑːk
charlotte, C~ 'ʃɑːl ət -ɒt ‖ 'ʃɑːrl- ~s, ~'s s
,Charlotte A'malie ə 'mɑːl i‿ə ‖ ə 'mɑːl jə;
,charlotte 'russe ruːs
Charlottenburg
ʃɑː 'lɒt ən bɜːg ‖ ʃɑːr 'lɑːt ᵊn bɜːg —Ger
[ʃaʁ 'lɔt ᵊn bʊʁk]
Charlottesville 'ʃɑːl əts vɪl ‖ 'ʃɑːrl- -vᵊl
Charlottetown 'ʃɑːl ət taʊn ‖ 'ʃɑːrl-
Charlton 'tʃɑːlt ən ‖ 'tʃɑːrlt-
charm tʃɑːm ‖ tʃɑːrm charmed
tʃɑːmd ‖ tʃɑːrmd charming
'tʃɑːm ɪŋ ‖ 'tʃɑːrm ɪŋ charms
tʃɑːmz ‖ tʃɑːrmz
Charmaine ₍ₒ₎ʃɑː 'meɪn ‖ ʃɑːr-
charmer 'tʃɑːm ə ‖ 'tʃɑːrm ᵊr ~s z
Charmian (i) 'tʃɑːm i‿ən ‖ 'tʃɑːrm-, (ii)
'ʃɑːm- ‖ 'ʃɑːrm-, (iii) 'kɑːm- ‖ 'kɑːrm-
charming 'tʃɑːm ɪŋ ‖ 'tʃɑːrm ɪŋ ~ly li
charnel 'tʃɑːn ᵊl ‖ 'tʃɑːrn ᵊl
'charnel house
Charnock 'tʃɑːn ɒk -ək ‖ 'tʃɑːrn ɑːk
Charnwood 'tʃɑːn wʊd ‖ 'tʃɑːrn-
Charolais, Charollais 'ʃær ə leɪ ‖ ,ʃær ə 'leɪ
,ʃer-, ,ʃɑːr- —As a pl n, also with final z

Charon 'keər ən -ɒn ‖ 'ker- 'kær-
charpoy 'tʃɑːp ɔɪ ‖ 'tʃɑːrp- ~s z
Charrington 'tʃær ɪŋ tən ‖ 'tʃer-
chart, Chart tʃɑːt ‖ tʃɑːrt charted 'tʃɑːt ɪd
-əd ‖ 'tʃɑːrt̬ əd charting 'tʃɑːt ɪŋ ‖ 'tʃɑːrt̬ ɪŋ
charter 'tʃɑːt ə ‖ 'tʃɑːrt̬ ᵊr ~ed d chartering
'tʃɑːt ᵊr ɪŋ ‖ 'tʃɑːrt̬ ᵊr ɪŋ ~s z
,chartered ac'countant; 'charter flight;
,charter 'member
Charterhouse 'tʃɑːt ə haʊs ‖ 'tʃɑːrt̬ ᵊr-
Charteris (i) 'tʃɑːt ər ɪs -əs ‖ 'tʃɑːrt̬-, (ii)
'tʃɑːt əz ‖ 'tʃɑːrt̬ ᵊrz
Chartham 'tʃɑːt əm ‖ 'tʃɑːrt̬-
Chartism 'tʃɑːt ,ɪz əm ‖ 'tʃɑːrt̬-
Chartist 'tʃɑːt ɪst §-əst ‖ 'tʃɑːrt̬- ~s s
Chartres place in France 'ʃɑːtr ə ʃɑːtr, ʃɑːt
‖ 'ʃɑːrtr ə —Fr [ʃaʁtʁ]
chartreuse, C~ tdmk ʃɑː 'trɜːz ‖ ʃɑːr 'truːz
-'truːs (*) —Fr [ʃɑʁ tʁøːz]
Chartwell 'tʃɑːt wel -wəl ‖ 'tʃɑːrt-
char|woman 'tʃɑː ‖ ,wʊm ən ‖ 'tʃɑːr- ~women
,wɪm ɪn §-ən
char|y 'tʃeər |i ‖ 'tʃer |i 'tʃær- ~ier i‿ə ‖ i‿ᵊr
~iest i‿ɪst i‿əst ~ily ᵊl i ɪl i ~iness i nəs i nɪs
Charybdis kə 'rɪbd ɪs §-əs
Chas. tʃæz tʃæs —or see Charles
chase, Chase tʃeɪs chased tʃeɪst (= chaste)
chases 'tʃeɪs ɪz -əz chasing 'tʃeɪs ɪŋ
chaser 'tʃeɪs ə ‖ -ᵊr ~s z
chasm 'kæz əm (!) ~s z
chassé 'ʃæs eɪ ‖ ʃæ 'seɪ ~d d ~ing ɪŋ ~s z
chasseur ₍ₒ₎ʃæ 'sɜː ‖ -'sɜːː —Fr [ʃa sœːʁ]
chassis sing. 'ʃæs i ‖ 'tʃæs-, ⚠-əs chassis pl
'ʃæs iz -i ‖ 'tʃæs-
chaste tʃeɪst (= chased) chaster 'tʃeɪst ə ‖ -ᵊr
chastest 'tʃeɪst ɪst -əst
chastely 'tʃeɪst li
chasten 'tʃeɪs ᵊn ~ed d ~ing ɪŋ ~s z
chasteness 'tʃeɪst nəs -nɪs
chastis|e ₍ₒ₎tʃæ 'staɪz ‖ 'tʃæst aɪz ~ed d ~es
ɪz əz ~ing ɪŋ
chastisement tʃæ 'staɪz mənt 'tʃæst ɪz mənt,
-əz- ‖ 'tʃæst aɪz- ~s s
chastiser ₍ₒ₎tʃæ 'staɪz ə ‖ -ᵊr ~s z
chastity, C~ 'tʃæst ət i -ɪt- ‖ -ət̬ i
'chastity belt
chasuble 'tʃæz jʊb ᵊl -jəb- ‖ -jəb- -əb- ~s z
chat tʃæt chats tʃæts chatted 'tʃæt ɪd -əd
‖ 'tʃæt̬ əd chatting 'tʃæt ɪŋ ‖ 'tʃæt̬ ɪŋ
'chat show
Chataway 'tʃæt ə weɪ ‖ 'tʃæt̬-
chateau, château 'ʃæt əʊ ‖ ʃæ 'toʊ —Fr
[ʃa to] ~s z
Chateaubriand, c~ ,ʃæt əʊ bri 'ɒn ◄ -'ɒ̃, -'ɒnd;
-'briː•; ʃæ 'təʊb ri• ‖ ʃæ ,toʊ bri 'ɑːn ◄ —Fr
[ʃa to bri jɑ̃]
Châteauneuf-du-Pape ,ʃæt əʊ nɜːf dju 'pæp
-du'•, -'pɑːp ‖ ʃæ ,toʊ nʌf du 'pɑːp —Fr
[ʃa to nœv dy pap]
chateaux, châteaux 'ʃæt əʊz -əʊ ‖ ʃæ 'toʊz
-'toʊ —Fr [ʃa to]
chatelain, châtelain 'ʃæt ə leɪn -ᵊl eɪn
‖ 'ʃæt̬ ᵊl eɪn —Fr [ʃat lɛ̃] ~s z

chatelaine, châtelaine 'ʃæt ə leɪn -ᵊl eɪn ‖ ˌʃæt ᵊl eɪn —*Fr* [ʃat lɛn] ~s z
Chater 'tʃeɪt ə ‖ 'tʃeɪt ᵊr
Chatham 'tʃæt əm ‖ 'tʃæt̬-
chatline 'tʃæt laɪn ~s z
Chatsworth 'tʃæts wəθ -wɜːθ ‖ -wᵊrθ
Chattahoochee ˌtʃæt ə 'huːtʃ i ◄ ‖ ˌtʃæt̬-
ˌChatta,hoochee 'River
Chattanooga ˌtʃæt ᵊn 'uːg ə ˌtʃæt ə 'nuːg ə
ˌChatta,nooga 'choo-choo
chatt... —*see* chat
chattel 'tʃæt ᵊl ‖ 'tʃæt̬- ~s z
chatter 'tʃæt ə ‖ 'tʃæt̬ ᵊr ~ed d **chattering**
'tʃæt ᵊr ɪŋ ‖ 'tʃæt̬ ᵊr ɪŋ ~s z
chatterbox 'tʃæt ə bɒks ‖ 'tʃæt̬ ᵊr baːks ~es
ɪz əz
chatterer 'tʃæt ᵊr ə ‖ 'tʃæt̬ ᵊr ᵊr ~s z
Chatteris 'tʃæt ᵊr ɪs §-əs ‖ 'tʃæt̬-
Chatterjee, Chatterji 'tʃæt ə dʒiː ‖ 'tʃæt̬ ᵊr-
Chatterley 'tʃæt ə li -ᵊl i ‖ 'tʃæt̬ ᵊr- ~'s z
Chatterton 'tʃæt ət ᵊn ‖ 'tʃæt̬ ᵊrt ᵊn
chattie... —*see* chatty
Chatto 'tʃæt əʊ ‖ 'tʃæt̬ oʊ
chatt|y 'tʃæt |i ‖ 'tʃæt̬ |i ~ier i‿ə ‖ i‿ᵊr ~iest
i‿ɪst i‿əst ~ily ɪ li əl i ~iness i nəs i nɪs
Chatwin 'tʃæt wɪn
Chaucer 'tʃɔːs ə ‖ -ᵊr 'tʃɑːs-
Chaucerian tʃɔː 'sɪər i‿ən ‖ -'sɪr- tʃɑː- ~s z
chaudfroid 'ʃəʊ fwɑː -frwɑː ‖ 'ʃoʊ- —*Fr*
[ʃo fʁwa]
Chaudhuri, Chaudhury 'tʃaʊd‿ᵊr i
chauffeur 'ʃəʊf ə ʃəʊ 'fɜː, ʃə- ‖ ʃoʊ 'fɝː ~s z
chaulmoog|ra tʃɔːl 'muːg rə tʃəʊl- ‖ tʃɑːl-
~ric rɪk
Chauncey, Chauncy 'tʃɔːnᵗs i ‖ 'tʃɑːnᵗs-
chausses ʃəʊs ‖ ʃoʊs
chautauqua, C~ ʃə 'tɔːk wə ‖ -'tɑːk- ~s z
chauvinism 'ʃəʊv ɪ ˌnɪz əm -ɪ- ‖ 'ʃoʊv-
chauvinist 'ʃəʊv ᵊn ˌɪst -ɪn-, ˌəst ‖ 'ʃoʊv- ~s s
chauvinistic ˌʃəʊv ə 'nɪst ɪk ◄ -ɪ- ‖ ˌʃoʊv-
~ally ᵊl‿i
Chavasse ʃə 'væs
Chavez 'tʃæv es ‖ 'tʃɑːv ez ʃɑːv-, -es —*Sp*
Chávez ['tʃa βeθ, -βes]
Chavon, Chavonne ʃə 'vɒn ‖ -'vɑːn
Chawton 'tʃɔːt ᵊn ‖ 'tʃɑːt-
Chay tʃeɪ
Chayefsky tʃaɪ 'ef ski
chayote tʃaɪ 'əʊt i ‖ -'oʊt̬- ~s z
Chaz tʃæz
Che tʃeɪ
Cheadle 'tʃiːd ᵊl
Cheam tʃiːm
cheap tʃiːp **cheaper** 'tʃiːp ə ‖ -ᵊr **cheapest**
'tʃiːp ɪst -əst
cheapen 'tʃiːp ᵊn ~ed d ~ing ɪŋ ~s z
cheapie 'tʃiːp i ~s z
cheap-jack 'tʃiːp dʒæk ~s s
cheap|ly 'tʃiːp |li ~ness nəs nɪs
cheapo 'tʃiːp əʊ ‖ -oʊ
Cheapside 'tʃiːp saɪd ˌ•'•
cheapskate 'tʃiːp skeɪt ~s s

cheat tʃiːt **cheated** 'tʃiːt ɪd -əd ‖ 'tʃiːt̬ əd
cheating/ly 'tʃiːt ɪŋ /li ‖ 'tʃiːt̬ ɪŋ /li **cheats**
tʃiːts
cheater 'tʃiːt ə ‖ 'tʃiːt̬ ᵊr ~s z
Cheatham 'tʃiːt əm ‖ 'tʃiːt̬-
Chechen 'tʃetʃ en -ən; tʃɪ 'tʃen, tʃe-
Chechenia tʃɪ 'tʃen jə tʃe-
Chechnya tʃetʃ 'njɑː 'tʃetʃ ni‿ə
check tʃek **checked** tʃekt **checking** 'tʃek ɪŋ
checks tʃeks
'checking ac,count
checkbook 'tʃek bʊk §-buːk (*NB not* 'tʃeg-) ~s
s
checkbox 'tʃek bɒks ‖ -bɑːks ~es ɪz əz
checker, C~ 'tʃek ə ‖ -ᵊr ~ed d **checkering**
'tʃek ᵊr‿ɪŋ ~s z
checkerboard 'tʃek ə bɔːd ‖ -ᵊr bɔːrd -boʊrd
~s z
check-in 'tʃek ɪn ~s z
Checkland 'tʃek lənd
Checkley 'tʃek li
checklist 'tʃek lɪst ~s s
check|mate 'tʃek |meɪt ˌ•'• ~mated meɪt ɪd
-əd ‖ meɪt̬ əd ~mates meɪts ~mating
meɪt ɪŋ ‖ meɪt̬ ɪŋ
checkout 'tʃek aʊt ~s s
checkpoint 'tʃek pɔɪnt ~s s
checkrail 'tʃek reɪᵊl ~s z
checkrein 'tʃek reɪn ~s z
checkroom 'tʃek ruːm -rʊm ~s z
checkup 'tʃek ʌp ~s s
Cheddar, c~ 'tʃed ə ‖ -ᵊr
ˌCheddar 'cheese
Chedzoy 'tʃedz ɔɪ
cheek, Cheek tʃiːk **cheeked** tʃiːkt **cheeking**
'tʃiːk ɪŋ **cheeks** tʃiːks
cheekbone 'tʃiːk bəʊn ‖ -boʊn (*NB not* 'tʃiːg-)
~s z
-cheeked 'tʃiːkt — **rosy-cheeked**
ˌrəʊz i 'tʃiːkt ◄ ‖ ˌroʊz-
cheek|y 'tʃiːk |i ~ier i‿ə ‖ i‿ᵊr ~iest i‿ɪst i‿əst
~ily ɪ li əl i ~iness i nəs i nɪs
cheep tʃiːp (= *cheap*) **cheeped** tʃiːpt
cheeping 'tʃiːp ɪŋ **cheeps** tʃiːps
cheer tʃɪə ‖ tʃɪ³r **cheered** tʃɪəd ‖ tʃɪ³rd
cheering 'tʃɪər ɪŋ ‖ 'tʃɪr ɪŋ **cheers**
tʃɪəz ‖ tʃɪ³rz
cheerful 'tʃɪəf ᵊl -ʊl ‖ 'tʃɪrf- ~ly‿i
cheeri... —*see* cheery
cheerio, C~ ˌtʃɪər i 'əʊ ◄ ‖ ˌtʃɪr i 'oʊ '••• ~s z
cheerleader 'tʃɪə ˌliːd ə ‖ 'tʃɪr ˌliːd ᵊr ~s z
cheerless 'tʃɪə ləs -lɪs ‖ 'tʃɪr- ~ly li ~ness nəs
nɪs
cheers tʃɪəz ‖ tʃɪ³rz
cheer|y 'tʃɪər |i ‖ 'tʃɪr |i ~ier i‿ə ‖ i‿ᵊr ~iest
i‿ɪst i‿əst ~ily əl i ɪl i ~iness i nəs i nɪs
cheese tʃiːz **cheesed** tʃiːzd **cheeses** 'tʃiːz ɪz
-əz
ˌcheesed 'off; ˌcheese 'straw
cheeseboard 'tʃiːz bɔːd ‖ -bɔːrd -boʊrd ~s z
cheeseburger 'tʃiːz ˌbɜːg ə ‖ -ˌbɝːg ᵊr ~s z
cheesecake 'tʃiːz keɪk ~s s
cheesecloth 'tʃiːz klɒθ -klɔːθ ‖ -klɔːθ -klɑːθ

C

Cheeseman 'tʃiːz mən
cheesemonger 'tʃiːz ˌmʌŋ gə ‖ -gʳ -ˌmɑːŋ-
~s z
cheeseparing 'tʃiːz ˌpeər ɪŋ ‖ -ˌper- -ˌpær-
Cheesewright 'tʃiːz raɪt
Cheesman 'tʃiːz mən
cheesy 'tʃiːz i
cheetah 'tʃiːt ə ‖ 'tʃiːt̬ ə ~s z
Cheetham 'tʃiːt əm ‖ 'tʃiːt̬-
Cheever 'tʃiːv ə ‖ -ʳr
chef ʃef chefs ʃefs —*but in French phrases*
both sing. and pl are ʃeɪ —*See also phrases*
with this word
chef d'oeuvre, chefs d'oeuvre ˌʃeɪ 'dɜːv rə
-'dɜːv ‖ ˌʃeɪ 'dʌv —*Fr* [ʃɛ dœːvʁ]
Chegwin 'tʃeg wɪn
Chek Lap Kok ˌtʃek læp 'kɒk ‖ -lɑːp 'koʊk
—*Cantonese* [³tsʰɛːk ⁶laːp ³kɔːk]
Cheke tʃiːk
Chekhov 'tʃek ɒf -ɒv ‖ -ɔːf -ɑːf —*Russ*
['tʃɛ xəf]
Chekhovian tʃe 'kəʊv i_ən -'kɒv- ‖ -'koʊv-
chel‖a '*claw*' 'kiːl ǀ ə ~ae iː
chela '*disciple*' 'tʃeɪl ə —*Hindi* [tʃe: laː] ~s z
chelate *n, adj* 'kiːl eɪt 'tʃiːl- ~s s
chelate *v* ki: 'leɪt kɪ-, kə-, tʃiː-; 'kiːl eɪt, 'tʃiːl-
‖ 'kiːl eɪt chelated ki: 'leɪt ɪd kɪ-, kə-, tʃiː-,
-əd; 'kiːl eɪt-, 'tʃiːl- ‖ 'kiːl eɪt̬ əd
chelation ki: 'leɪʃ ən kɪ-, kə-, tʃiː-
Chelmer 'tʃelm ə ‖ -ʳr
Chelmsford 'tʃelmz fəd 'tʃelm's- ‖ -fʳrd
—*locally also* 'tʃemz-, 'tʃɒmz-
Chelsea 'tʃels i
ˌChelsea 'bun
Cheltenham 'tʃelt ən_əm
ˌCheltenham 'Spa
chemical 'kem ɪk ᵊl ~ly_i ~s z
ˌchemical ˌengi'neering
chemin de fer ʃə ˌmæn də 'feə ‖ -'feʳr —*Fr*
[ʃə mæt fɛːʁ, ʃmæt fɛːʁ]
chemis‖e ʃə 'miːz ~es ɪz əz
chemist 'kem ɪst §-əst ~s, ~'s s
chemis‖try 'kem ɪs ǀtri -əs- ~tries triz
Chemnitz 'kem nɪts —*Ger* ['kɛm nɪts]
chemo- *comb. form*
with stress-neutral suffix ǀkiːm əʊ ǀkem əʊ
‖ -oʊ — chemosynthesis ˌkiːm əʊ
'sɪntᵊθ əs ɪs ˌkem-, -ɪs ɪs, §-əs ‖ ˌˑoʊ-
with stress-imposing suffix ki: 'mɒ+ ke 'mɒ+
‖ -'mɑː+ — chemolysis ki: 'mɒl əs ɪs ke-,
-ɪs ɪs, §-əs ‖ -'mɑːl-
chemotherapy ˌkiːm əʊ 'θer əp i ˌkem-
‖ ˌˑoʊ-
Chenevix (i) 'tʃen ə vɪks, (ii) 'ʃen-
Cheney (i) 'tʃeɪn i, (ii) 'tʃiːn i
Chengdu ˌtʃʌŋ 'duː —*Chinese* Chéngdū
[²tsʰəŋ ¹tu]
Chenies (i) 'tʃeɪn iz, (ii) 'tʃiːn iz —*The place in*
Bucks may be either (i) or (ii).
chenille ʃə 'niːᵊl
cheongsam ˌtʃɒŋ 'sæm tʃi ˌɒŋ- ‖ 'tʃɔːŋ saːm
'tʃɑːŋ- ~s z
Cheops 'kiː ɒps ‖ -ɑːps

Chepstow 'tʃep stəʊ ‖ -stoʊ
cheque tʃek (= *check*) cheques tʃeks
'cheque card
chequebook 'tʃek bʊk §-buːk (*NB not* 'tʃeg-)
~s s
chequer 'tʃek ə ‖ -ʳr (= *checker*) ~ed d
chequering 'tʃek ər_ɪŋ ~s z
Chequers 'tʃek əz ‖ -ʳrz
Cher ʃeə ‖ ʃeʳr
Cherbourg 'ʃeə bʊəg 'ʃɜː-, -bɔːg, -bɜːg
‖ 'ʃer bʊrg —*Fr* [ʃɛʁ buːʁ]
cherchez la femme ˌʃeəʃ eɪ læ 'fæm -lɑː' ·
‖ ˌʃer ˌʃeɪ- —*Fr* [ʃɛʁ ʃe la fam]
Cheremis, Cheremiss 'tʃer ə mɪs -miːs, ˌˑˑ' ·
Cherenkov tʃə 'reŋk ɒf tʃɪ-, -ɒv ‖ -ɑːf —*Russ*
[tʃɪ 'rjɛn kəf]
Cherie, Chérie ʃə 'riː ʃe-
Cherilyn (i) 'tʃer əl ɪn -ɪl-, -ən, (ii) 'ʃer-
cherimoya ˌtʃer ɪ 'mɔɪ ə -ə-
cherish 'tʃer ɪʃ ~ed t ~es ɪz əz ~ing ɪŋ
Cheriton 'tʃer ɪt ən -ət- ‖ -ᵊn
Chernobyl tʃɜː 'nəʊb ᵊl tʃə-, -'nɒb-, -ɪl;
'tʃɜːn əb- ‖ tʃʳr 'noʊb- —*Russ* [tʃɪr 'no bilʲ]
Chernomyrdin ˌtʃɜːn ə 'mɪəd ɪn -'mɜːd-, -ᵊn
‖ ˌtʃʳrn ə 'mɪrd- ˌtʃʒːn- —*Russ* [tʃɪr
nʌ 'mɪr dʲin]
chernozem 'tʃɜːn əʊ zem ˌˑˑ'zjɒm
‖ ˌtʃʒːn ə 'zem -'ʒɑːm, -'ʒɔːm —*Russ*
[tʃɪr nʌ 'zʲom]
Cherokee 'tʃer ə kiː ˌˑˑ' · ~s z
cheroot ʃə 'ruːt ~s s
cherr‖y, C~ 'tʃer i ~ies ɪz
cherry-pick 'tʃer i pɪk ~ed t ~ing ɪŋ ~s s
Chersonese, c~ 'kɜːs ə niːs -niːz, ˌˑˑ' ·
‖ 'kɜːs-
chert tʃɜːt ‖ tʃɜːt cherts tʃɜːts ‖ tʃʒːts
Chertsey 'tʃɜːts i ‖ 'tʃʒːts i
cherub 'tʃer əb ~s z
cherubic tʃə 'ruːb ɪk tʃe- ~ally ᵊl_i
cherubim 'tʃer ə bɪm 'ker-, -u-
Cherubini ˌker u 'biːn i -ə-, -iː —*It*
[ke ʁu 'bi ni]
chervil 'tʃɜːv ᵊl -ɪl ‖ 'tʃʒːv-
Cherwell 'tʃɑː wəl -wel ‖ 'tʃɑːr-
Cheryl (i) 'tʃer ᵊl -ɪl, (ii) 'ʃer-
Chesapeake 'tʃes ə piːk
ˌChesapeake 'Bay
Chesebrough 'tʃiːz brə ‖ -broʊ
Chesham 'tʃeʃ əm —*formerly* 'tʃes-
Cheshire 'tʃeʃ ə -ɪə ‖ -ʳr
ˌCheshire 'cat, ˌCheshire 'cheese
Cheshunt 'tʃeʃ ᵊnt 'tʃeʃ-
Chesil 'tʃez ᵊl
ˌChesil 'Beach
Chesney (i) 'tʃez ni, (ii) 'tʃes ni
chess tʃes
chessboard 'tʃes bɔːd ‖ -bɔːrd -boʊrd ~s z
chess‖man 'tʃes ǀmæn -mən ~men men mən
chest tʃest chested 'tʃest ɪd -əd chests
tʃests
ˌchest of 'drawers
-chested 'tʃest ɪd -əd
Chester 'tʃest ə ‖ -ʳr

Chesterfield, c~ 'tʃest ə fiːəld ‖ -ər- **~s** z
Chester-le-Street ˌtʃest ə li 'striːt -əl i- ‖ ˌ•ər-
Chesterton 'tʃest ət ən ‖ -ərt ən
chestnut, C~ 'tʃes nʌt 'tʃest- **~s** s
ˈ**chestnut tree**
chest|y 'tʃest |i **~ier** i‿ə ‖ i‿ər **~iest** i‿ɪst i‿əst **~iness** i nəs i nɪs
Chet tʃet
Chetham *(i)* 'tʃiːt əm ‖ 'tʃiːt̬-, *(ii)* 'tʃet- ‖ 'tʃet̬-
Chetnik 'tʃet nɪk **~s** s
Chetwode 'tʃet wʊd
Chetwyn 'tʃet wɪn
Chetwynd 'tʃet wɪnd
Cheung tʃʌŋ —*Cantonese* [¹tsœːŋ]
cheval glass ʃə 'væl glɑːs §-glæs ‖ -glæs
chevalier *n* ˌʃev ə 'lɪə ‖ -'lɪər **~s** z
Chevalier *name* ʃə 'væl i‿eɪ ʃɪ-
Chevening 'tʃiːv nɪŋ
Chevette *tdmk* ʃə 'vet ʃe- **~s** s
Chevington 'tʃev ɪŋ tən
Cheviot 'tʃiːv i‿ət 'tʃev- ‖ 'ʃev- —*locally* 'tʃiːv- **~s** s
Chevon, Chevonne ʃə 'vɒn ʃɪ- ‖ -'vɑːn
chèvre 'ʃev rə 'ʃeəv- —*Fr* [ʃɛːvʁ]
Chevrolet *tdmk* 'ʃev rə leɪ ˌ••'• ‖ ˌʃev rə 'leɪ **~s** z
chevron 'ʃev rən -rɒn **~s** z
chevv|y, chev|y *v* 'tʃev |i **~ied** id **~ies** iz **~ying** i‿ɪŋ
Chevvy, Chevy *n 'Chevrolet'* 'ʃev i
chew tʃuː **chewed** tʃuːd **chewing** 'tʃuː‿ɪŋ **chews** tʃuːz
ˈ**chewing gum**
Chewton 'tʃuːt ən
chew|y 'tʃuː|‿i **~iness** i nəs -nɪs
Cheyenne ˌʃaɪ 'æn ◂ -'en **~s** z
Cheyne *(i)* 'tʃeɪn i, *(ii)* tʃeɪn, *(iii)* tʃiːn
Cheyne-Stokes ˌtʃeɪn 'stəʊks ‖ -'stoʊks
chez ʃeɪ —*Fr* [ʃe]
₍ₗ₎**chez 'nous** nuː —*Fr* [nu]
chi *Greek letter* kaɪ **chis** kaɪz
Chiang Kaishek ˌtʃæŋ kaɪ 'ʃek tʃiˌæŋ- ‖ tʃiˌɑːŋ- —*Chi* Jiǎng Jièshí [³tɕjaŋ ⁴tɕjɛ ²ʂɯr]
Chiang Mai tʃi ˌæŋ 'maɪ ‖ -ˌɑːŋ-
Chianti, c~ ki 'ænt i ‖ -'ɑːnt̬ i —*It* ['kjan ti] **~shire** ʃə ʃɪə, ˌʃaɪ‿ə ‖ ʃər ʃɪr, ˌʃaɪ‿ər
Chiapas tʃi 'æp əs ‖ -'ɑːp- —*Sp* ['tʃja pas]
chiaroscuro ki ˌɑːr ə 'skʊər əʊ -'skjʊər- ‖ -'skʊr oʊ -'skjʊr- —*It* [kja ros 'kuː ro] **~s** z
chias|ma kaɪ 'æz |mə **~mas** məz **~mata** mət ə ‖ mət̬ ə
chiasmus kaɪ 'æz məs
Chibcha 'tʃɪb tʃə
Chibchan 'tʃɪb tʃən
chibouk tʃɪ 'buːk tʃə- **~s** s
chic ʃiːk ʃɪk
Chicago ʃɪ 'kɑːg əʊ ʃə- ‖ -oʊ —*locally also* -'kɔːg-
Chicana, c~ tʃɪ 'kɑːn ə ʃɪ-, tʃə-, ʃə- ‖ -'kæn- —*Sp* [tʃi 'ka na] **~s** z
chican|e ʃɪ 'keɪn ʃə- **~ed** d **~es** z **~ing** ɪŋ
chicaner|y ʃɪ 'keɪn ər |i ʃə- **~ies** iz
Chicano, c~ tʃɪ 'kɑːn əʊ ʃɪ-, tʃə-, ʃə- ‖ -oʊ -'kæn- —*Sp* [tʃi 'ka no] **~s** z
Chichele 'tʃɪtʃ əl i -ɪl-
Chichén Itzá tʃɪ ˌtʃen ɪt 'sɑː -iːt- —*AmSp* [tʃi ˌtʃe nit 'sa]
Chichester 'tʃɪtʃ ɪst ə -əst- ‖ -ər —*but the place in upstate NY is* 'tʃaɪ ˌtʃest ər
Chichewa tʃɪ 'tʃeɪ wə
chi-chi 'ʃiː ʃiː 'tʃiː tʃiː
chick, Chick tʃɪk **chicks** tʃɪks
chickabidd|y 'tʃɪk ə bɪd |i **~ies** iz
chickadee 'tʃɪk ə diː ˌ••'• **~s** z
chickaree 'tʃɪk ə riː **~s** z
Chickasaw 'tʃɪk ə sɔː ‖ -sɑː **~s** z
chicken 'tʃɪk ɪn -ən **~ed** d **~ing** ɪŋ **~s** z
ˈ**chicken pox,** ˈ**chicken** ˌ**wire**
chickenfeed 'tʃɪk ɪn fiːd -ən-
chickenhearted ˌtʃɪk ɪn 'hɑːt ɪd ◂ -ən-, -əd ‖ -'hɑːrt̬ əd ◂
chickenlivered ˌtʃɪk ɪn 'lɪv əd ◂ -ən- ‖ -ərd ◂ '•• ˌ••
chickenshit 'tʃɪk ɪn ʃɪt -ən-
chickpea 'tʃɪk piː **~s** z
chickweed 'tʃɪk wiːd
chicle 'tʃɪk əl
chicory 'tʃɪk ər i
chid... —*see* **chide**
Chiddingly *place in Sussex* ˌtʃɪd ɪŋ 'laɪ
chide tʃaɪd **chid** tʃɪd **chidden** 'tʃɪd ən **chided** 'tʃaɪd ɪd -əd **chides** tʃaɪdz
chief tʃiːf **chiefly** 'tʃiːf li **chiefs** tʃiːfs
ˌ**chief** ˈ**constable;** ˌ**Chief E**ˈ**xecutive;** ˌ**chief in**ˈ**spector**◂**;** ˌ**Chief** ˈ**Justice**◂**;** ˌ**chief of** ˈ**staff;** ˌ**chief** ˌ**superin**ˈ**tendent**◂
chieftain 'tʃiːft ən -ɪn **~s** z
chieftain|cy 'tʃiːft ən |si -ɪn- **~cies** siz
chiffchaff 'tʃɪf tʃæf **~s** s
chiffon 'ʃɪf ɒn ʃɪ 'fɒn ‖ ʃɪ 'fɑːn **~s** z
chiffonier, chiffonnier ˌʃɪf ə 'nɪə ‖ -'nɪər **~s** z
chigger 'tʃɪg ə 'dʒɪg- ‖ -ər **~s** z
chignon 'ʃiːn jɒn -jɒ̃ ‖ -jɑːn —*Fr* [ʃi ɲɔ̃] **~s** z
chigoe 'tʃɪg əʊ ‖ -oʊ 'tʃiːg- **~s** z
Chigwell 'tʃɪg wəl -wel
chihuahua, C~ tʃɪ 'wɑː wə tʃə-, ʃɪ-, ʃə-, -wɑː; -'waʊ ə —*Sp* [tʃi 'wa wa] **~s** z
chilblain 'tʃɪl bleɪn **~ed** d **~s** z
child, Child tʃaɪəld **children** 'tʃɪldr ən 'tʃʊldr- ‖ 'tʃɪld ərn **children's** 'tʃɪldr ənz 'tʃʊldr- ‖ 'tʃɪld ərnz **child's** tʃaɪə*l*dz
ˈ**child a**ˌ**buse;** ˈ**child care;** ˈ**child's play;** ˌ**child** ˈ**prodigy**
childbearing 'tʃaɪə*ld* ˌbeər ɪŋ ‖ -ˌber- -ˌbær-
childbed 'tʃaɪə*ld* bed
childbirth 'tʃaɪə*ld* bɜːθ ‖ -bɜ˞ːθ
Childe, c~ 'tʃaɪəld
childermas, C~ 'tʃɪld ə mæs ‖ -ər-
Childers 'tʃɪld əz ‖ -ərz
childhood 'tʃaɪəld hʊd
childish 'tʃaɪəld ɪʃ **~ly** li **~ness** nəs nɪs
childless 'tʃaɪ*ld* ləs -lɪs **~ness** nəs nɪs
childlike 'tʃaɪə*ld* laɪk

childmind|er 'tʃaɪld ˌmaɪnd| ə ‖ -ᵊr ~ers
 əz ‖ -ᵊrz ~ing ɪŋ
childproof 'tʃaɪᵊld pruːf §-prʊf
children 'tʃɪldr ən 'tʃʊldr- ‖ 'tʃɪld ᵊrn ~'s z
 'children's home
Childs tʃaɪᵊldz
Childwall 'tʃɪl wɔːl 'tʃɪld- ‖ -wɑːl
Chile, chile 'tʃɪl i i ‖ -eɪ —Sp ['tʃi le]
 ˌchile con 'carne kɒn 'kɑːn i →kɒŋ-, kən-,
 -eɪ ‖ kɑːn 'kɑːrn i kən-
Chilean 'tʃɪl i‿ən ‖ tʃɪ 'liː ən, -'leɪ- ~s z
chili 'tʃɪl i i (= chilly) ~es z
 'chili dog
chiliad 'kɪl i æd 'kaɪl-, -əd ~s z
chiliasm 'kɪl i ˌæz əm
chiliast 'kɪl i æst ~s s
chiliastic ˌkɪl i 'æst ɪk ◄
Chilkoot 'tʃɪl kuːt
chill tʃɪl chilled tʃɪld chilling 'tʃɪl ɪŋ chills
 tʃɪlz
chiller 'tʃɪl ə ‖ -ᵊr ~s z
chilli 'tʃɪl i i (= chilly) ~es z
 ˌchilli con 'carne kɒn 'kɑːn i →kɒŋ-, kən-,
 -eɪ ‖ kɑːn 'kɑːrn i kən-; 'chilli ˌpowder
chilling 'tʃɪl ɪŋ ~ly li
chillness 'tʃɪl nəs -nɪs
Chillon ʃɪ 'lɒn ʃə-; 'tʃɪl ən, -ɒn ‖ ʃə 'lɑːn —Fr
 [ʃi jɔ̃]
chillum 'tʃɪl əm
chill|y 'tʃɪl i ~ier i‿ə ‖ i‿ᵊr ~iest i‿ɪst i‿əst
 ~ily ɪ li əl i ~iness i nəs i nɪs
Chilpruf tdmk 'tʃɪl pruːf §-prʊf
Chiltern 'tʃɪlt ən ‖ -ᵊrn ~s z
 ˌChiltern 'Hills; ˌChiltern 'Hundreds
Chilton 'tʃɪlt ən ‖ -ᵊn
Chilver 'tʃɪlv ə ‖ -ᵊr ~s z
chimaera kaɪ 'mɪər ə kɪ-, kə-, ʃɪ-, ʃə-, -'meər-;
 'kɪm ər ə, 'ʃɪm- ‖ -'mɪr ə ~s z
Chimborazo ˌtʃɪm bə 'rɑːz əʊ ˌʃɪm- ‖ -oʊ
 —AmSp [tʃim bo 'ra so]
chime tʃaɪm chimed tʃaɪmd chimes tʃaɪmz
 chiming 'tʃaɪm ɪŋ
chimer 'tʃaɪm ə ‖ -ᵊr ~s z
chimera kaɪ 'mɪər ə kɪ-, kə-, ʃɪ-, ʃə-, -'meər-;
 'kɪm ər ə, 'ʃɪm- ‖ -'mɪr ə ~s z
chimeric kaɪ 'mer ɪk kɪ-, kə-, ʃɪ- ~al ᵊl ~ally
 ᵊl i
chimney 'tʃɪm ni ~s z
chimneybreast 'tʃɪm ni brest ~s s
chimneypiec|e 'tʃɪm ni piːs ~es ɪz əz
chimneypot 'tʃɪm ni pɒt ‖ -pɑːt ~s s
chimneystack 'tʃɪm ni stæk ~s s
chimneysweep 'tʃɪm ni swiːp ~s s
chimneysweeper 'tʃɪm ni ˌswiːp ə ‖ -ᵊr ~s z
chimp tʃɪmp chimps tʃɪmps
chimpanzee ˌtʃɪmp æn 'ziː ◄ -ən- ‖ ˌʃɪmp-;
 tʃɪm 'pænz i ~s z
chin tʃɪn chinned tʃɪnd chinning 'tʃɪn ɪŋ
 chins tʃɪnz
China, china 'tʃaɪn ə
China|man, c~ 'tʃaɪn ə |mən ~men mən men
Chinatown 'tʃaɪn ə taʊn
chinaware 'tʃaɪn ə weə ‖ -wer

chinch tʃɪntʃ chinches 'tʃɪntʃ ɪz -əz
 'chinch bug
chincherinchee ˌtʃɪntʃ ə 'rɪntʃ i -rɪn 'tʃiː,
 -rən 'tʃiː ~s z
chinchilla tʃɪn 'tʃɪl ə ~s z
chin-chin ˌtʃɪn 'tʃɪn
Chincoteague ˌʃɪŋ kə 'tiːg
Chindit 'tʃɪnd ɪt §-ət ~s s
chine tʃaɪn chines tʃaɪnz
Chinese ˌtʃaɪ 'niːz ◄ ‖ -'niːs ◄
 ˌChinese 'chequers; ˌChinese 'gooseberry;
 ˌChinese 'restaurant
Chingford 'tʃɪŋ fəd ‖ -fᵊrd
chink tʃɪŋk chinked tʃɪŋkt chinking 'tʃɪŋk ɪŋ
 chinks tʃɪŋks
chinless 'tʃɪn ləs -lɪs
 ˌchinless 'wonder
Chinnor 'tʃɪn ə ‖ -ᵊr
chino 'tʃiːn əʊ 'ʃiːn- ‖ -oʊ ~s z
chinoiserie ʃɪn 'wɑːz ər i ⑴ʃiːn-, -ˌwɑːz ə 'riː
 —Fr [ʃi nwa zʁi]
chinook, C~ ⑴tʃɪ 'nuːk ʃɪ-, §tʃə-, -'nʊk
 ‖ ʃə 'nʊk ʃɪ- ~s s
chinquapin 'tʃɪŋk ə pɪn -ɪ- ~s z
chinstrap 'tʃɪn stræp ~s s
chintz tʃɪnts chintzes 'tʃɪnts ɪz -əz
chintz|y 'tʃɪnts li ~ier i‿ə ‖ i‿ᵊr ~iest i‿ɪst
 i‿əst
chinwag 'tʃɪn wæg ~s z
chinwagging 'tʃɪn ˌwæg ɪŋ
chionodoxa kaɪ ˌɒn ə 'dɒks ə -ˌəʊn-, ˌkaɪ‿ən-
 ‖ kaɪ ˌoʊn ə 'dɑːks ə ~s z
Chios 'kaɪ ɒs 'kiː- ‖ -ɑːs
chip tʃɪp chipped tʃɪpt chipping 'tʃɪp ɪŋ
 chips tʃɪps
 'chip ˌbasket; 'chip shot
chipboard 'tʃɪp bɔːd ‖ -bɔːrd -boʊrd
chipmunk 'tʃɪp mʌŋk ~s s
chipolata ˌtʃɪp ə 'lɑːt ə ‖ -'lɑːt̬ ə ~s z
chipp... —see chip
Chippendale 'tʃɪp ən deɪᵊl →-m-
Chippenham 'tʃɪp ən‿əm
chipper 'tʃɪp ə ‖ -ᵊr
Chippewa 'tʃɪp ɪ wɑː -ə-, -wə
chippi... —see chip; chippy
chipping, C~ 'tʃɪp ɪŋ
 ˌChipping 'Sodbury 'sɒd bər‿i →'sɒb-
 ‖ 'sɑːd ˌber i -bər‿i
chipp|y 'tʃɪp li ~ies iz
Chirac 'ʃɪr æk ‖ ʃɪ 'rɑːk —Fr [ʃi ʁak]
chiral 'kaɪᵊr əl
chirality kaɪ 'ræl ət i -ɪt- ‖ -ət̬ i
Chirk tʃɜːk ‖ tʃɝːk
chiromancy 'kaɪᵊr əʊ ˌmænts i ‖ -ə-
Chiron 'kaɪᵊr ən -ɒn ‖ -ɑːn
chiropodist kɪ 'rɒp əd ɪst kə-, ʃɪ-, ʃə-, §-əst
 ‖ kə 'rɑːp- —formerly also kaɪᵊ- ~s s
chiropody kɪ 'rɒp əd i kə-, ʃɪ-, ʃə- ‖ kə 'rɑːp-
 —formerly also kaɪᵊ-
chiropractic ˌkaɪᵊr əʊ 'prækt ɪk ◄ '•ˌ••,•ˌ••
 ‖ 'kaɪᵊr ə ˌprækt ɪk
chiropractor 'kaɪᵊr əʊ ˌprækt ə ‖ -ə ˌprækt ᵊr
 ~s z

chirp tʃɜːp ‖ tʃɝːp **chirped** tʃɜːpt ‖ tʃɝːpt
  chirping 'tʃɜːp ɪŋ ‖ 'tʃɝːp ɪŋ **chirps**
  tʃɜːps ‖ tʃɝːps
chirper 'tʃɜːp ə ‖ 'tʃɝːp ᵊr ~s z
chirp|y 'tʃɜːp |i ‖ 'tʃɝːp |i ~**ier** i‿ə ‖ i‿ᵊr ~**iest**
  i‿ɪst i‿əst ~**ily** ɪ li əl i ~**iness** i nəs i nɪs
chirr tʃɜː ‖ tʃɝː **chirred** tʃɜːd ‖ tʃɝːd
  chirring 'tʃɜːr ɪŋ ‖ 'tʃɝː ɪŋ **chirrs**
  tʃɜːz ‖ tʃɝːz
chirrup 'tʃɪr əp ‖ 'tʃɝː- ~**ed** t ~**ing** ɪŋ ~**s** s
chisel 'tʃɪz ᵊl ~**ed**, ~**led** d ~**ing**, ~**ling** ‿ɪŋ ~**s**
  z
chiseler, chiseller 'tʃɪz ᵊl‿ə ‖ ᵊr ~s z
Chisholm 'tʃɪz əm
Chislehurst 'tʃɪz ᵊl hɜːst ‖ -hɝːst
chi-square 'kaɪ skweə ‖ -skwer ~**d** d
  'chi-square test
Chiswick 'tʃɪz ɪk §-ək
chit tʃɪt **chits** tʃɪts
chitchat 'tʃɪt tʃæt
chitin 'kaɪt ɪn -ᵊn ‖ -ᵊn
chitinous 'kaɪt ɪn əs -ən- ‖ -ᵊn-
chiton 'kaɪt ᵊn -ɒn ‖ -ɑːn ~s z
Chittagong 'tʃɪt ə gɒŋ ‖ 'tʃɪt̬ ə gɔːŋ -gɑːŋ
Chittenden 'tʃɪt ᵊnd ən
chitterling 'tʃɪt ə lɪŋ →-ᵊl ɪŋ ‖ 'tʃɪt̬ ᵊr lɪŋ
  'tʃɪt lən ~s z
Chitty, c~ 'tʃɪt i ‖ 'tʃɪt̬ i
chiv tʃɪv ʃɪv **chivs** tʃɪvz ʃɪvz
chivalric 'ʃɪv ᵊl rɪk ʃə 'væl-
chivalrous 'ʃɪv ᵊl rəs ~**ly** li ~**ness** nəs nɪs
chival|ry 'ʃɪv ᵊl |ri ~**ries** riz
Chivas (i) 'ʃɪv æs, (ii) 'ʃiːvəs
chive tʃaɪv **chives** tʃaɪvz
Chivers 'tʃɪv əz ‖ -ᵊrz
chivv|y, chiv|y 'tʃɪv |i ~**ied** id ~**ies** iz ~**ying**
  i‿ɪŋ
chiz, chizz tʃɪz
chlamydi|a klə 'mɪd i‿ə ~**ae** iː ~**al** ᵊl
Chloe, Chloë 'kləʊ i ‖ 'kloʊ i
chloracne ˌklɔːr 'æk ni ‖ ˌkloʊr-
chloral 'klɔːr ᵊl ‖ 'kloʊr-
chlorambucil klɔːr 'æm bju sɪl ‖ -bjə- kloʊr-
chloramine 'klɔːr ə miːn
  ˌklɔːr 'æm iːn ‖ 'kloʊr-
chloramphenicol ˌklɔːr æm 'fen ɪ kɒl ˌ•əm-,
  §-ə kɒl ‖ -koʊl ˌkloʊr-, -kɑːl, -kɔːl
chlorate 'klɔːr eɪt ‖ 'kloʊr- ~s s
chlordane 'klɔːd eɪn ‖ 'klɔːrd- 'kloʊrd-
chloric 'klɔːr ɪk 'klɒr- ‖ 'kloʊr-
chloride 'klɔːr aɪd ‖ 'kloʊr- ~s z
chlori|nate 'klɔːr ɪ |neɪt 'klɒr-, -ə- ‖ 'kloʊr-
  ~**nated** neɪt ɪd -əd ‖ neɪt̬ əd ~**nates** neɪts
  ~**nating** neɪt ɪŋ ‖ neɪt̬ ɪŋ
chlorination ˌklɔːr ɪ 'neɪʃ ᵊn ˌklɒr-, -ə- ‖ ˌkloʊr-
chlorine 'klɔːr iːn -ɪn, §-ᵊn ‖ 'kloʊr-
chlorite 'klɔːr aɪt ‖ 'kloʊr-
chloro- *comb. form*
  with stress-neutral suffix ¦klɔːr əʊ ¦klɒr-
  ‖ ¦klɔːr ə ¦kloʊr- — **chlorobenzene**
  ˌklɔːr əʊ 'benz iːn ˌklɒr- ‖ ˌklɔːr ə- ˌkloʊr-
chlorodyne 'klɔːr ə daɪn 'klɒr- ‖ 'kloʊr-

chloroform 'klɒr ə fɔːm 'klɔːr- ‖ 'klɔːr ə fɔːrm
  'kloʊr- ~**ed** d ~**ing** ɪŋ ~**s** z
chlorophyl, chlorophyll 'klɒr ə fɪl 'klɔːr-
  ‖ 'klɔːr- 'kloʊr-
chloroquine, C~ 'klɔːr ə kwɪn 'klɒr-, -kwiːn
  ‖ 'klɔːr ə kwiːn 'kloʊr-
chlorosis klɔː 'rəʊs ɪs §-əs ‖ klə 'roʊs-
chlorpromazine ˌklɔː 'prəʊm ə ziːn -'prɒm-
  ‖ ˌklɔːr 'prɑːm ə ziːn ˌkloʊr-
Choat, Choate tʃəʊt ‖ tʃoʊt
Chobham 'tʃɒb əm ‖ 'tʃɑːb-
choc tʃɒk ‖ tʃɑːk (= *chock*) **chocs**
  tʃɒks ‖ tʃɑːks
chocaholic ˌtʃɒk ə 'hɒl ɪk ◄ ‖ ˌtʃɑːk ə 'hɑːl ɪk ◄
  ˌtʃɔːk-, -'hɔːl- ~**s** s
choc-bar 'tʃɒk bɑː ‖ 'tʃɑːk bɑːr ~**s** z
chocho 'tʃəʊ tʃəʊ ‖ 'tʃoʊ tʃoʊ ~**s** z
choc-ice 'tʃɒk aɪs ‖ 'tʃɑːk- ~**es** ɪz əz
chock tʃɒk ‖ tʃɑːk **chocked** tʃɒkt ‖ tʃɑːkt
  chocking 'tʃɒk ɪŋ ‖ 'tʃɑːk ɪŋ **chocks**
  tʃɒks ‖ tʃɑːks
chock-a-block ˌtʃɒk ə 'blɒk ◄ ‖ 'tʃɑːk ə blɑːk
chock-full ˌtʃɒk 'fʊl ◄ ‖ ˌtʃɑːk- tʃʌk-
chocoholic ˌtʃɒk ə 'hɒl ɪk ◄ ‖ ˌtʃɑːk ə 'hɑːl ɪk ◄
  ˌtʃɔːk-, -'hɔːl- ~**s** s
chocolate 'tʃɒk lət -lɪt; 'tʃɒk ᵊl ət, -ɪt ‖ 'tʃɔːk-
  'tʃɑːk- ~**s** s
  ˌchocolate 'biscuit; 'chocolate cake, ˌ•• '•;
  ˌchocolate 'pudding
chocolate-box 'tʃɒk lət bɒks -lɪt-
  ‖ 'tʃɔːk lət bɑːks 'tʃɑːk-
Choctaw, c~ 'tʃɒkt ɔː ‖ 'tʃɑːkt ɔː -ɑː ~s z
CHOGM 'tʃɒg əm ‖ 'tʃɑːg-
choice tʃɔɪs **choicer** 'tʃɔɪs ə ‖ -ᵊr **choices**
  'tʃɔɪs ɪz -əz **choicest** 'tʃɔɪs ɪst -əst
choicely 'tʃɔɪs li **choiceness** 'tʃɔɪs nəs -nɪs
choir 'kwaɪ‿ə ‖ 'kwaɪ‿ᵊr (! = *quire*) **choirs**
  'kwaɪ‿əz ‖ 'kwaɪ‿ᵊrz
  'choir school
choirboy 'kwaɪ‿ə bɔɪ ‖ 'kwaɪ‿ᵊr- ~**s** z
choirmaster 'kwaɪ‿ə ˌmɑːst ə §-ˌmæst-
  ‖ 'kwaɪ‿ᵊr ˌmæst ᵊr ~**s** z
choke tʃəʊk ‖ tʃoʊk **choked** tʃəʊkt ‖ tʃoʊkt
  choking 'tʃəʊk ɪŋ ‖ 'tʃoʊk ɪŋ **chokes**
  tʃəʊks ‖ tʃoʊks
chokeberr|y 'tʃəʊk ˌber| i ‖ 'tʃoʊk- ~**ies** iz
chokecherr|y 'tʃəʊk ˌtʃer| i ‖ 'tʃoʊk- ~**ies** iz
choker 'tʃəʊk ə ‖ 'tʃoʊk ᵊr ~**s** z
chokey, choky 'tʃəʊk i ‖ 'tʃoʊk i
cholecystectom|y ˌkɒl ɪ sɪst 'ekt əm |i ˌ•ə-
  ‖ ˌkoʊl ə- ~**ies** iz
choler 'kɒl ə ‖ 'kɑːl ᵊr 'koʊl- (*usually* = *collar*)
cholera 'kɒl ər ə ‖ 'kɑːl-
choleraic ˌkɒl ə 'reɪ ɪk ◄ ‖ ˌkɑːl-
choleric 'kɒl ər ɪk kɒ 'ler- ‖ 'kɑːl- kə 'ler-
  ~**ally** ᵊl i
cholesterol kə 'lest ə rɒl kɒ-, -ᵊr‿ᵊl ‖ -roʊl
  -rɑːl, -rɔːl
choline 'kəʊl iːn ‖ 'koʊl-
cholinergic ˌkəʊl ɪ 'nɜːdʒ ɪk ◄ ˌkɒl-, -ə-
  ‖ ˌkoʊl ə 'nɝːdʒ ɪk ◄
cholinesterase ˌkəʊl ɪ 'nest ə reɪz ˌkɒl-, ˌ•ə-,
  -reɪs ‖ ˌkoʊl-

C

cholla 'tʃɒl ə ~s z
Cholmeley 'tʃʌm li
Cholmondeley 'tʃʌm li
chomp tʃɒmp ‖ tʃɑːmp **chomped**
tʃɒm*p*t ‖ tʃɑːm*p*t **chomping**
'tʃɒmp ɪŋ ‖ 'tʃɑːmp ɪŋ **chomps**
tʃɒm*p*s ‖ tʃɑːm*p*s
Chomsky 'tʃɒmᵖsk i ‖ 'tʃɑːmᵖsk i
Chomskyan 'tʃɒmᵖsk i‿ən ‖ 'tʃɑːmᵖsk- ~s z
chondroma kɒn 'drəʊm ə ‖ kɑːn 'droʊm ə ~s
z
Chongqing ˌtʃʊŋ 'tʃɪŋ —*Chi* Chóngqìng
[²tʂʰʊŋ ⁴tɕʰiŋ]
choo-choo 'tʃuː tʃuː ~s z
chook tʃʊk **chooks** tʃʊks
choose tʃuːz (= *chews*) **chooses** 'tʃuːz ɪz -əz
choosing 'tʃuːz ɪŋ **chose** tʃəʊz ‖ tʃoʊz
chosen 'tʃəʊz ən ‖ 'tʃoʊz ən
chooser 'tʃuːz ə ‖ -ər ~s z
choos|y 'tʃuːz |i ~ier i‿ə ‖ i‿ər ~iest i‿ɪst i‿əst
~iness i nəs i nɪs
chop tʃɒp ‖ tʃɑːp **chopped** tʃɒpt ‖ tʃɑːpt
chopping 'tʃɒp ɪŋ ‖ 'tʃɑːp ɪŋ **chops**
tʃɒps ‖ tʃɑːps
ˌchop 'suey 'suːˌi
chop-chop ˌtʃɒp 'tʃɒp ‖ 'tʃɑːp tʃɑːp ˌ•'•
chopfallen 'tʃɒp ˌfɔːl ən ‖ 'tʃɑːp- -ˌfɑːl-
chop|house 'tʃɒp |haʊs ‖ 'tʃɑːp- ~houses
haʊz ɪz -əz
Chopin 'ʃɒp æ̃ 'ʃəʊp- ‖ 'ʃoʊp æn —*Fr* [ʃɔ pæ̃]
chopp... —*see* chop
chopper 'tʃɒp ə ‖ 'tʃɑːp ər ~s z
chopp|y 'tʃɒp |i ‖ 'tʃɑːp |i ~ier i‿ə ‖ i‿ər ~iest
i‿ɪst i‿əst ~ily ɪ li əl i ~iness i nəs -nɪs
chopstick 'tʃɒp stɪk ‖ 'tʃɑːp- ~s s
choral 'kɔːr əl ‖ 'koʊr- ~ly i
chorale kɒ 'rɑːl kɔː-, kə- ‖ kə 'ræl -'rɑːl ~s z
chord kɔːd ‖ kɔːrd (= *cord*) **chords**
kɔːdz ‖ kɔːrdz
-chord kɔːd ‖ kɔːrd — **octachord**
'ɒkt ə kɔːd ‖ 'ɑːkt ə kɔːrd
chordal 'kɔːd əl ‖ 'kɔːrd-
chordate 'kɔːd eɪt -ɪt, -ət ‖ 'kɔːrd- ~s s
chore tʃɔː ‖ tʃɔːr tʃoʊr **chores** tʃɔːz ‖ tʃɔːrz
tʃoʊrz
chorea kɒ 'rɪə kɒ-, kə- ‖ kə 'riːə
choreograph 'kɒr i‿ə grɑːf 'kɔːr-, -græf
‖ 'kɔːr i‿ə græf 'koʊr- ~ed t ~ing ɪŋ ~s s
choreographer ˌkɒr i 'ɒg rəf ə ˌkɔːr-
‖ ˌkɔːr i 'ɑːg rəf ər ˌkoʊr- ~s z
choreographic ˌkɒr i‿ə 'græf ɪk ◄ ˌkɔːr-
‖ ˌkɔːr- ˌkoʊr- ~ally əlˌi
choreography ˌkɒr i 'ɒg rəf i ˌkɔːr-
‖ ˌkɔːr i 'ɑːg- ˌkoʊr-
choriamb 'kɒr i æmb 'kɔːr-, -æm ‖ 'kɔːr-
'koʊr- ~s z
choriambic ˌkɒr i 'æm bɪk ◄ ˌkɔːr- ‖ ˌkɔːr-
ˌkoʊr-
choriambus ˌkɒr i 'æm bəs ˌkɔːr- ‖ ˌkɔːr-
ˌkoʊr-
choric 'kɒr ɪk ‖ 'kɔːr ɪk 'kɑːr-, 'koʊr-
chorine 'kɔːr iːn ‖ 'koʊr- ~s z
chorion 'kɔːr i‿ən -ɒn ‖ -i ɑːn 'koʊr-

chorionic ˌkɔːr i 'ɒn ɪk ◄ ‖ -'ɑːn- ˌkoʊr-
chorister 'kɒr ɪst ə -əst- ‖ 'kɔːr əst ər 'kɑːr-,
'koʊr- ~s z
chorizo tʃə 'riːz əʊ tʃɒ-, -'rɪts- ‖ -oʊ -'riːs-
—*Sp* [tʃo 'ri θo, -so] ~s z
Chorley 'tʃɔːl i ‖ 'tʃɔːrl i
Chorleywood ˌtʃɔːl i 'wʊd ‖ ˌtʃɔːrl-
Chorlton 'tʃɔːlt ən ‖ 'tʃɔːrlt ən
Chorlton-cum-Hardy ˌtʃɔːlt ən kʌm 'hɑːd i
→, •əŋ- ‖ ˌtʃɔːrlt ən kʌm 'hɑːrd i
choroid 'kɔːr ɔɪd ‖ 'koʊr-
chortl|e 'tʃɔːt əl ‖ 'tʃɔːrt̬ əl ~ed d ~es z ~ing
ˌɪŋ
chorus 'kɔːr əs ‖ 'koʊr- ~ed t ~es ɪz əz ~ing
ɪŋ
'chorus girl
chose tʃəʊz ‖ tʃoʊz
chosen 'tʃəʊz ən ‖ 'tʃoʊz ən
chota 'tʃəʊt ə ‖ 'tʃoʊt̬ ə
Chou En-lai ˌtʃəʊ en 'laɪ -ən- ‖ ˌtʃoʊ- —*Chi*
Zhōu Ēnlái [¹tʂou ¹ən ²lai]
chough tʃʌf **choughs** tʃʌfs
choux ʃuː (= *shoe*)
chow tʃaʊ **chows** tʃaʊz
'chow chow; ˌchow 'mein meɪn
Chow tʃaʊ —*Cantonese* [¹tsɐw]
chow-chow 'tʃaʊ tʃaʊ ~s z
chowder 'tʃaʊd ə ‖ -ər ~s z
chrestomath|y kre 'stɒm ə θ li ‖ -'stɑːm- ~ies
iz
Chrimbo 'krɪm bəʊ ‖ -boʊ
Chris krɪs **Chris's** 'krɪs ɪz -əz
chrism 'krɪz əm
chrisom 'krɪz əm ~s z
Chrissie, Chrissy 'krɪs i
Christ kraɪst **Christ's** kraɪsts
Christabel 'krɪst ə bel
Christadelphian ˌkrɪst ə 'delf i‿ən ◄ ~s z
Christchurch 'kraɪst tʃɜːtʃ ‖ -tʃɝːtʃ
christen 'krɪs ən ~ed d ~ing ˌɪŋ ~s z
Christendom 'krɪs ən dəm
christening 'krɪs ənˌɪŋ ~s z
'christening robe
Christi 'krɪst i
Christian 'krɪs tʃən →'krɪʃ-; 'krɪst i‿ən ~s z
'Christian name; ˌChristian 'Science
Christiana ˌkrɪst i 'ɑːn ə ˌkrɪs tʃi- ‖ -'æn ə
christiania, C~ ˌkrɪst i 'ɑːn i‿ə ~s z
Christianis... —*see* Christianiz...
Christianit|y ˌkrɪst i 'æn ət li ˌkrɪs tʃi-,
→ˌkrɪʃ tʃi-, -ɪt i ‖ ˌkrɪs tʃi 'æn ət li ~ies iz
Christianization ˌkrɪs tʃən aɪ 'zeɪʃ ən →ˌkrɪʃ-,
-ɪ'•-; ˌkrɪst i‿ən aɪ 'zeɪʃ- ‖ -ə 'zeɪʃ-
Christianiz|e 'krɪs tʃə naɪz →'krɪʃ-;
'krɪst i‿ə naɪz ~ed d ~er/s ə/z ‖ ər/z ~es ɪz
əz ~ing ɪŋ
Christianly 'krɪs tʃən li →'krɪʃ-; 'krɪst i‿ən li
Christie, c~ 'krɪst i ~s, ~'s z
Christina krɪ 'stiːn ə
Christine 'krɪst iːn
Christlike 'kraɪst laɪk ~ness nəs nɪs
Christmas 'krɪs məs §'krɪz- —*in very careful
speech sometimes* 'krɪst- ~es ɪz əz

'Christmas box; 'Christmas cake;
'Christmas card; ˌChristmas 'cracker;
ˌChristmas 'Day; ˌChristmas 'Eve;
'Christmas ˌIsland ‖ ˌ•• '••; 'Christmas
ˌpresent; ˌChristmas 'pudding; ˌChristmas
'stocking; 'Christmas tree
Christmassy 'krɪs məs i
Christmastide 'krɪs məs taɪd 'krɪst-
Christmastime 'krɪs məs taɪm 'krɪst-
Christobel 'krɪst ə bel
Christophe krɪ 'stɒf ‖ kriː 'stɑːf -'stɔːf —*Fr*
[kʁi stɔf]
christophene 'krɪst ə fiːn ~s z
Christopher 'krɪst əf ə ‖ -ʳr
Christopherson krɪ 'stɒf əs ən ‖ -'stɑːf ʳrs-
Christy, c~ 'krɪst i
chroma 'krəʊm ə ‖ 'kroʊm ə
chromate 'krəʊm eɪt ‖ 'kroʊm- ~s s
chromatic krə 'mæt ɪk krəʊ- ‖ kroʊ 'mæt̬ ɪk
~**ally** ᵊl_i ~**ness** nəs nɪs
chromaticity ˌkrəʊm ə 'tɪs ət i -ɪt i
‖ ˌkroʊm ə 'tɪs ət̬ i
chromatid 'krəʊm ət ɪd §-əd ‖ 'kroʊm ət̬ əd
-ə tɪd ~s z
chromatin 'krəʊm ət ɪn §-ən ‖ 'kroʊm- ~s z
chromatogram 'krəʊm ət ə græm krəʊ 'mæt-
‖ kroʊ 'mæt̬ ə græm krə- ~s z
chromatographic
ˌkrəʊm ət ə 'græf ɪk ◂ ‖ kroʊ ˌmæt̬ ə- krə-
chromatography
ˌkrəʊm ə 'tɒg rəf i ‖ ˌkroʊm ə 'tɑːg-
chrome krəʊm ‖ kroʊm **chromed**
krəʊmd ‖ kroʊmd **chromes**
krəʊmz ‖ kroʊmz **chroming**
'krəʊm ɪŋ ‖ 'kroʊm ɪŋ
ˌchrome 'yellow
chrominance 'krəʊm ɪn ənᵗs §-ən- ‖ 'kroʊm-
chromite 'krəʊm aɪt ‖ 'kroʊm-
chromium 'krəʊm i_əm ‖ 'kroʊm-
chromo 'krəʊm əʊ ‖ 'kroʊm oʊ ~s z
chromolithograph ˌkrəʊm əʊ 'lɪθ ə grɑːf
-græf ‖ ˌkroʊm ə 'lɪθ ə græf ~s s
chromolithographic
ˌkrəʊm əʊ ˌlɪθ ə 'græf ɪk ‖ ˌkroʊm ə-
chromolithography
ˌkrəʊm əʊ lɪ 'θɒg rəf i ‖ ˌkroʊm ə lɪ 'θɑːg-
chromosomal
ˌkrəʊm ə 'səʊm ᵊl ◂ ‖ ˌkroʊm ə 'soʊm ᵊl ◂
~**ly** i
chromosome 'krəʊm ə səʊm ‖ 'kroʊm ə soʊm
~**s** z
chromosphere 'krəʊm ə sfɪə ‖ 'kroʊm ə sfɪr
chronax|ie, chronax|y 'krəʊn æks |i
krɒn 'æks i ‖ 'kroʊn- 'krɑːn- ~**ies** iz
chroneme 'krəʊn iːm ‖ 'kroʊn- ~s z
chronemic krəʊ 'niːm ɪk ‖ kroʊ-
chronic 'krɒn ɪk ‖ 'krɑːn ɪk ~**ally** ᵊl_i
chronicl|e, C~ 'krɒn ɪk ᵊl ‖ 'krɑːn- ~**ed** d ~**es**
z ~**ing** _ɪŋ
chronicler 'krɒn ɪk lə ‖ 'krɑːn ɪk lᵊr ~s z
chrono- *comb. form*
with stress-neutral suffix ˌkrɒn əˌkrəʊn əʊ
‖ ˌkrɑːn əˌkroʊn ə— **chronoscopic**

ˌkrɒn ə 'skɒp ɪk ◂ ˌkrəʊn-
‖ ˌkrɑːn ə 'skɑːp ɪk ◂ ˌkroʊn-
with stress-imposing suffix
krə 'nɒ+ ‖ krə 'nɑː+ — **chronoscopy**
krə 'nɒsk əp i ‖ -'nɑːsk-
chronograph 'krɒn ə grɑːf 'krəʊn-, -græf
‖ 'krɑːn ə græf 'kroʊn- ~s s
chronological ˌkrɒn ə 'lɒdʒ ɪk ᵊl ◂ ˌkrəʊn-,
-ᵊl 'ɒdʒ- ‖ ˌkrɑːn ᵊl 'ɑːdʒ ɪk ᵊl ◂ ˌkroʊn- ~**ly**
ˌi
chronolog|y krə 'nɒl ədʒ |i krɒ-, krəʊ-
‖ -'nɑːl- ~**ies** iz
chronometer krə 'nɒm ɪt ə krɒ-, krəʊ-, -ət-
‖ -'nɑːm ət̬ ᵊr ~s z
chronometric ˌkrɒn ə 'metr ɪk ◂ ˌkrəʊn-
‖ ˌkrɑːn- ˌkroʊn- ~**al** ᵊl ~**ally** ᵊl_i
chronometry krə 'nɒm ətr i krɒ-, krəʊ-, -ɪtr-
‖ -'nɑːm-
chrysalid 'krɪs ᵊl ɪd §-əd ~s z
chrysalides krɪ 'sæl ɪ diːz krə-, -ə-
chrysalis 'krɪs ᵊl ɪs §-əs ~**es** ɪz əz
chrysanth krə 'sænᵗθ krɪ-, -'zænᵗθ ~s s

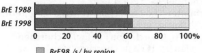

CHRYSANTHEMUM

■ -'sænᵗθ- ☐ -'zænᵗθ-

	0	20	40	60	80	100%
BrE 1988						
BrE 1998						

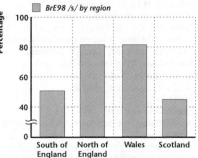

BrE98 /s/ by region

Percentage — 0, 20, 40, 60, 80, 100

South of England, North of England, Wales, Scotland

chrysanthemum krə 'sænᵗθ ɪm əm krɪ-,
-'zænᵗθ-, -əm_əm —*BrE poll panel
preferences: 1988,* -'sænᵗθ- *61%,* -'zænᵗθ-
39%; 1998, -'sænᵗθ- *63%,* -'zænᵗθ- *37%* . ~**s** z
chryselephantine ˌkrɪs ˌel ɪ 'fænt aɪn -ə-
Chryseis kraɪ 'siːˌɪs §ˌəs
Chrysler *tdmk* 'kraɪz lə ‖ 'kraɪs lᵊr ~**s** z
chrysolite 'krɪs ə laɪt
chrysoprase 'krɪs ə preɪz
Chrysostom 'krɪs əst əm
chrysotile 'krɪs ə taɪᵊl -tɪl, §-tᵊl
chthonian 'θəʊn i_ən 'kθəʊn- ‖ 'θoʊn-
chthonic 'θɒn ɪk 'kθɒn- ‖ 'θɑːn-
chub tʃʌb **chubs** tʃʌbz
Chubb tʃʌb
chubb|y 'tʃʌb |i ~**ier** i_ə ‖ i_ᵊr ~**iest** i_ɪst i_əst
~**iness** i nəs i nɪs
chuck, Chuck tʃʌk **chucked** tʃʌkt **chucking**
'tʃʌk ɪŋ **chucks** tʃʌks
chucker-out ˌtʃʌk ər 'aʊt ‖ -ᵊr- **chuckers-out**
ˌtʃʌk əz 'aʊt ‖ -ᵊrz-

chuckl|e 'tʃʌk əl ~ed d ~es z ~ing _ɪŋ
chuckwalla 'tʃʌk wɒl ə ‖ -wɑːl ə ~s z
chuff tʃʌf chuffed tʃʌft chuffing 'tʃʌf ɪŋ
  chuffs tʃʌfs
chug tʃʌg chugged tʃʌgd chugging 'tʃʌg ɪŋ
  chugs tʃʌgz
chugalug 'tʃʌg ə lʌg ~ged d ~ging ɪŋ ~s z
Chukchee, Chukchi 'tʃʊk tʃi: 'tʃʌk- ~s z
chukka, chukker 'tʃʌk ə ‖ -ər ~s z
Chula Vista ,tʃuːl ə 'vɪst ə
chum tʃʌm chummed tʃʌmd chumming
  'tʃʌm ɪŋ chums tʃʌmz
Chumbawamba ,tʃʌm bə 'wɑːm bə -'wʌm-
chumm|y 'tʃʌm |i ~ier i_ə ‖ i_ər ~iest i_ɪst
  i_əst ~ily ɪ li əl i ~iness i nəs i nɪs
chump tʃʌmp chumps tʃʌmps
chunder 'tʃʌnd ə ‖ -ər ~ed d chundering
  'tʃʌnd_ər ɪŋ ~s z
Chungking ,tʃʊŋ 'kɪŋ ,tʃʌŋ- —Chi Chóngqìng
  [²tsʰʊŋ ⁴tɕʰiŋ]
chunk tʃʌŋk chunked tʃʌŋkt chunking
  'tʃʌŋk ɪŋ chunks tʃʌŋks
chunk|y 'tʃʌŋk |i ~ier i_ə ‖ i_ər ~iest i_ɪst
  i_əst ~iness i nəs i nɪs
chunnel, C~ 'tʃʌn əl
chunter 'tʃʌnt ə ‖ 'tʃʌntʃ ər ~ed d chuntering
  'tʃʌnt_ər ɪŋ ‖ 'tʃʌntʃər ɪŋ ~s z
church, Church tʃɜːtʃ ‖ tʃɝːtʃ churched
  tʃɜːtʃt ‖ tʃɝːtʃt churches 'tʃɜːtʃ ɪz -əz
  ‖ 'tʃɝːtʃ əz churching 'tʃɜːtʃ ɪŋ ‖ 'tʃɝːtʃ ɪŋ
  church's, C~ 'tʃɜːtʃ ɪz -əz ‖ 'tʃɝːtʃ əz
  ,Church 'Army; ,Church Com'missioners;
  ,Church 'militant; ,Church Sla'vonic
Churchdown 'tʃɜːtʃ daʊn ‖ 'tʃɝːtʃ-
churchgo|er/s 'tʃɜːtʃ ,gəʊ |ə/z
  ‖ 'tʃɝːtʃ ,goʊ |ər/z ~ing ɪŋ
Churchill 'tʃɜːtʃ ɪl ‖ 'tʃɝːtʃ-
Churchillian tʃɜː 'tʃɪl i_ən ‖ tʃɝː-
church|man, C~ 'tʃɜːtʃ |mən ‖ 'tʃɝːtʃ- ~men
  mən men
churchwarden ,tʃɜːtʃ 'wɔːd ən ◀
  ‖ 'tʃɜːtʃ ,wɔːrd ən ~s z
church|y 'tʃɜːtʃ|i i ‖ 'tʃɝːtʃ|i i ~iness i nəs -nɪs
churchyard 'tʃɜːtʃ jɑːd ‖ 'tʃɝːtʃ jɑːrd ~s z
churl tʃɜːl ‖ tʃɝːl churls tʃɜːlz ‖ tʃɝːlz
churlish 'tʃɜːl ɪʃ ‖ 'tʃɝːl- ~ly li ~ness nəs nɪs
churn tʃɜːn ‖ tʃɝːn churned tʃɜːnd ‖ tʃɝːnd
  churning 'tʃɜːn ɪŋ ‖ 'tʃɝːn ɪŋ churns
  tʃɜːnz ‖ tʃɝːnz
chute ʃuːt (= shoot) chutes ʃuːts
Chuter 'tʃuːt ə ‖ 'tʃuːt ər
chutney 'tʃʌt ni
chutzpah 'hʊts pə 'xʊts-, -pɑː
Chuvash 'tʃuːv æʃ tʃu 'vɑːʃ ~es ɪz əz
Chuzzlewit 'tʃʌz əl wɪt
chyle kaɪəl
chyme kaɪm
chymotrypsin ,kaɪm əʊ 'trɪps ɪn §-ən ‖ -oʊ-
chypre 'ʃiːp rə —Fr [ʃipχ]
CIA ,si: aɪ 'eɪ
ciabatta tʃə 'bæt ə -'bɑːt- —It [tʃa 'bat ta]
ciao tʃaʊ
Ciaran 'kɪər ən ‖ 'kɪr-

Ciba tdmk 'si:b ə —Ger ['tsi: ba]
Ciba-Geigy tdmk ,si:b ə 'gaɪg i
Cibber 'sɪb ə ‖ -ər
cibori|um sɪ 'bɔːr i_|əm sə- ‖ -'boʊr- ~a ə
cicada sɪ 'kɑːd ə sə- ‖ -'keɪd ə saɪ-, -'kɑːd- ~s
  z
cicala sɪ 'kɑːl ə sə- ~s z
cicatric|e 'sɪk ətr ɪs §-əs ~es ɪz əz
cicatris... —see cicatriz...
cicatrix 'sɪk ə trɪks sə 'keɪtr ɪks, sɪ- cicatrices
  ,sɪk ə 'traɪs iːz
cicatrization ,sɪk ətr aɪ 'zeɪʃ ən -ətr ɪ- ‖ -ətr ə-
cicatriz|e 'sɪk ə traɪz ~ed d ~es ɪz əz ~ing ɪŋ
cicely, C~ 'sɪs əl_i -ɪl-
Cicero, c~ 'sɪs ə rəʊ ‖ -roʊ
ciceron|e ,tʃɪtʃ ə 'rəʊn li ,sɪs- ‖ -'roʊn li ~i iː
Ciceronian ,sɪs ə 'rəʊn i_ən ◀ ‖ -'roʊn- ~s z
cichlid 'sɪk lɪd §-ləd ~s z
cicisbe|o ,tʃɪtʃ ɪz 'beɪ ləʊ ‖ -loʊ —It
  [tʃit tʃiz 'bɛː o] ~i iː
Cid sɪd
CID ,si: aɪ 'di:
-cidal 'saɪd əl — genocidal ,dʒen ə 'saɪd əl ◀
-cide saɪd — insecticide ɪn 'sekt ɪ saɪd -ə-
cider 'saɪd ə ‖ -ər ~s z
cig sɪg cigs sɪgz
cigar sɪ 'gɑː sə- ‖ -'gɑːr ~s z

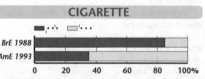

CIGARETTE

cigaret, cigarette ,sɪg ə 'ret '··· ‖ '··· ,··'·
  ~s s —Poll panel preferences: BrE 1988, ,··'·
  85%, '··· 15%; AmE 1993, '··· 65%, ,··'·
  35%.
  ,ciga'rette ,holder, '····-; ,ciga'rette
  ,lighter, '····-
cigarillo ,sɪg ə 'rɪl əʊ ‖ -'ri: joʊ ~s z
cigg|ie, cigg|y 'sɪg |i ~ies iz
ciguatera ,sɪg wə 'teər ə ,si:g-, -'tɪər- ‖ -'ter-
  —AmSp [si ɣwa 'te ra]
cilantro sɪ 'læntr əʊ sə- ‖ -'lɑːntr oʊ -'læntr-
  —AmSp [si 'lan tro]
Cilcennin kɪl 'ken ɪn §-ən
Cilento sɪ 'lent əʊ sə- ‖ -oʊ
cilia 'sɪl i_ə 'si:l-
ciliary 'sɪl i_ər i ‖ -i er i
Cilic|ia saɪ 'lɪs |i_ə sɪ-, sə-, -'lɪʃ- ‖ sə 'lɪʃ |ə
  ~ian/s i_ən/z ‖ ən/z
ciliat|e 'sɪl i eɪt -i_ət, -i_ɪt ~ed ɪd əd ~es s
cili|um 'sɪl i_|əm ~a ə
cill sɪl (= sill) cills sɪlz
Cilla 'sɪl ə
Cimabue ,tʃɪm ə 'buː eɪ ,tʃiːm-, -i —It
  [tʃi ma 'bu: e]
cimetidine saɪ 'met ɪ diːn sɪ-, sə-, -ə-
  ‖ -'met ə-
Cimmerian sɪ 'mɪər i_ən sə-, -'mer- ‖ -'mɪr-
  ~s z
C-in-C ,si: ɪn 'si: §-ən- ~s z

cinch sɪntʃ **cinched** sɪntʃt **cinches** 'sɪntʃ ɪz
-əz **cinching** 'sɪntʃ ɪŋ
cinchona sɪŋ 'kəʊn ə ‖ -'koʊn- ~**s** z
Cincinnati ˌsɪnˈts ə 'næt i ◄ -ɪ- ‖ -'næt̬ i
Cincinnatus ˌsɪnˈts ə 'nɑːt əs ◄ -ɪ-, -'neɪt-
‖ -'næt̬-
cincture 'sɪŋk tʃə ‖ -tʃʳr ~**s** z
cinder 'sɪnd ə ‖ -ʳr ~**s** z
Cinderella ˌsɪnd ə 'rel ə ◄ §sɪn 'drel ə
Cindy 'sɪnd i
cine 'sɪn i
cine- ˌsɪn i — **cinephotography** ˌsɪn i fəʊ
'tɒg rəf i ‖ -fə 'tɑːg-
cineaste, cinéaste 'sɪn i æst -eɪ-, ˌ•••◄ ~**s** s
cinecamera 'sɪn i ˌkæm ʳr ə ˌ••'••• ~**s** z
cinefilm 'sɪn i fɪlm ~**s** z
cinema 'sɪn əm ə -ɪm-; -ɪ mɑː, -ə- ~**s** z
cinemago|er/s 'sɪn əm ə ˌgəʊ ə/z '•ɪm-
‖ -ˌgoʊ ʳr/z ~**ing** ɪŋ
cinemascope, CinemaScope *tdmk*
'sɪn əm ə skəʊp '•ɪm- ‖ -skoʊp
cinematic ˌsɪn ə 'mæt ɪk ◄ -ə- ‖ -'mæt̬- ~**ally**
əl_i
cinematograph ˌsɪn ə 'mæt ə grɑːf ˌ•ɪ-, -græf
‖ -'mæt̬ ə græf ~**s** s
cinematography ˌsɪn əm ə 'tɒg rəf i ˌ•ɪm-
‖ -'tɑːg-
cinema verite, cinéma vérité
ˌsɪn əm ə 'ver ɪ teɪ ˌ•ɪm-, -ɪ mɑː:-, -ə mɑː:-,
-ə teɪ ‖ -ˌver ə 'teɪ —*Fr* [si ne ma ve ʁi te]
cine-projector 'sɪn i prə ˌdʒekt ə ‖ -ʳr ~**s** z
cineradiography ˌsɪn i ˌreɪd i 'ɒg rəf i ‖ -'ɑːg-
cineradiographic ˌsɪn i ˌreɪd i_ə 'græf ɪk ~**ally**
əl_i
Cinerama *tdmk* ˌsɪn ə 'rɑːm ə -ɪ-
cineraria ˌsɪn ə 'reər i_ə ‖ -'rer- ~**s** z
Cinna 'sɪn ə
cinnabar 'sɪn ə bɑː ‖ -bɑːr
cinnamon 'sɪn əm ən
cinque, C~ sɪŋk (= *sink*)
ˌCinque ' Ports, '••
cinquecento ˌtʃɪŋk wɪ 'tʃent əʊ §-wə- ‖ -oʊ
—*It* [tʃiŋ kwe 'tʃen to]
cinquefoil 'sɪŋk fɔɪʳl 'sæŋk- ~**s** z
Cinzano *tdmk* tʃɪn 'zɑːn əʊ sɪn-; tʃɪnt 'sɑːn-,
sɪnt- ‖ -oʊ ~**s** z
cipher 'saɪf ə ‖ -ʳr ~**ed** d **ciphering** 'saɪf
ʳr_ɪŋ ~**s** z
Cipriani ˌsɪp ri 'ɑːn i
circa 'sɜːk ə ‖ 'sɜˑk ə
circadian sɜː 'keɪd i_ən ‖ sʳr-
Circassian sə 'kæs i_ən sɜː- ‖ sʳr 'kæʃ ən -i_ən
~**s** z
Circe 'sɜːs i ‖ 'sɜˑs i
circl|e 'sɜːk ᵊl ‖ 'sɜˑk ᵊl ~**ed** d ~**es** z ~**ing** ɪŋ
circlet 'sɜːk lət -lɪt ‖ 'sɜˑk- ~**s** s
circlip 'sɜːk lɪp ‖ 'sɜˑk- ~**s** s
circs sɜːks ‖ sɜˑks
circu|it 'sɜːk ɪt §-ət ‖ 'sɜˑk ət ~**ited** ɪt ɪd
§ət-, -əd ‖ ət̬ əd ~**iting** ɪt ɪŋ §ət- ‖ ət̬ ɪŋ ~**its**
ɪts §əts ‖ əts
ˈcircuit ˌbreaker; ˈcircuit ˌdiagram; ˈcircuit
ˌjudge

circuitous sɜː 'kjuː ɪt əs sə-, -ət-
‖ sʳr 'kjuː ət̬ əs ~**ly** li ~**ness** nəs nɪs
circuitry 'sɜːk ətr i -ɪtr- ‖ 'sɜˑk-
circuity sɜː 'kjuː ət i sə-, -ɪt i ‖ sʳr 'kjuː ət̬ i
circular 'sɜːk jʊl ə -jəl- ‖ 'sɜˑk jəl ʳr ~**s** z
ˌcircular ' saw
circularit|y ˌsɜːk jʊ 'lær ət li ˌ•jə-, -ɪt i
‖ ˌsɜˑk jə 'lær ət̬ li -'ler- ~**ies** iz
circularis... —*see* **circulariz...**
circularization ˌsɜːk jʊl ər aɪ 'zeɪʃ ᵊn ˌ•jəl-,
-ɪ'•- ‖ ˌsɜˑk jəl ʳr ə-
circulariz|e 'sɜːk jʊl ə raɪz '•jəl- ‖ 'sɜˑk jəl-
~**ed** d ~**es** ɪz əz ~**ing** ɪŋ
circu|late 'sɜːk jʊ |leɪt -jə- ‖ 'sɜˑk jə- ~**lated**
leɪt ɪd -əd ‖ leɪt̬ əd ~**lates** leɪts ~**lating**
leɪt ɪŋ ‖ leɪt̬ ɪŋ
circulation ˌsɜːk jʊ 'leɪʃ ᵊn -jə- ‖ ˌsɜˑk jə- ~**s**
z
circulator 'sɜːk jʊ leɪt ə '•jə- ‖ 'sɜˑk jə leɪt̬ ʳr
~**s** z
circulatory ˌsɜːk jʊ 'leɪt_ər i ˌ•jə-;
'sɜːk jʊl ət_ʳr i, '•jəl- ‖ 'sɜˑk jəl ə tɔːr i
-toʊr i
circum- *comb. form* ˌsɜːk əm ˈsɜˑk əm —
circumlunar ˌsɜːk əm 'luːn ə ◄ -'ljuːn-
‖ ˌsɜˑk əm 'luːn ʳr ◄
circumcis|e 'sɜːk əm saɪz ‖ 'sɜˑk- ~**ed** d
~**er/s** ə/z ‖ ʳr/z ~**es** ɪz əz ~**ing** ɪŋ
circumcision ˌsɜːk əm 'sɪʒ ᵊn ‖ ˌsɜˑk- ~**s** z
circumferenc|e sə 'kʌmpf ʳr_ᵊnts ‖ sʳr- sə-
~**es** ɪz əz
circumferential sə ˌkʌmpf ə 'rentʃ ᵊl ◄ ‖ sʳr-
sə-
circumflex 'sɜːk əm fleks ‖ 'sɜˑk- ~**ed** t ~**es**
ɪz əz ~**ing** ɪŋ
circumlocution
ˌsɜːk əm lə 'kjuːʃ ᵊn ‖ ˌsɜˑk əm loʊ- ~**s** z
circumlocutory ˌsɜːk əm 'lɒk jʊt_ər i -'•jət_,
-lə 'kjuːt ʳr i ‖ ˌsɜˑk əm 'lɑːk jə tɔːr i -toʊr i
circumnavi|gate ˌsɜːk əm 'næv ɪ |geɪt -'•ə-
‖ ˌsɜˑk- ~**gated** geɪt ɪd -əd ‖ geɪt̬ əd
~**gates** geɪts ~**gating** geɪt ɪŋ ‖ geɪt̬ ɪŋ
circumnavigation ˌsɜːk əm ˌnæv ɪ 'geɪʃ ᵊn
-ˌ•ə- ‖ ˌsɜˑk- ~**s** z
circumscrib|e 'sɜːk əm skraɪb ˌ•••◄ ‖ 'sɜˑk-
~**ed** d ~**es** z ~**ing** ɪŋ
circumscription ˌsɜːk əm 'skrɪp ʃᵊn ‖ ˌsɜˑk-
~**s** z
circumspect 'sɜːk əm spekt ‖ 'sɜˑk- ~**ly** li
~**ness** nəs nɪs
circumspection ˌsɜːk əm 'spek ʃᵊn ‖ ˌsɜˑk-
circumstanc|e 'sɜːk əm stænᵗs -stɑːnᵗs, -stᵊnᵗs
‖ 'sɜˑk əm stænᵗs ~**ed** t ~**es** ɪz əz —*BrE*
1998 poll panel preference: -stænᵗs 66%,
-stɑːnᵗs 24%, -stᵊnᵗs 11%
circumstantial ˌsɜːk əm 'stæntʃ ᵊl ◄ -'stɑːntʃ-
‖ ˌsɜˑk- ~**ly** i
circumvallation ˌsɜːk əm və 'leɪʃ ᵊn -væ'•-
‖ ˌsɜˑk- ~**s** z
circum|vent ˌsɜːk əm ǀ'vent ˌ••• ‖ ˌsɜˑk-
~**vented** 'vent ɪd -əd ‖ 'vent̬ əd ~**venting**
'vent ɪŋ ‖ 'vent̬ ɪŋ ~**vents** 'venᵗs

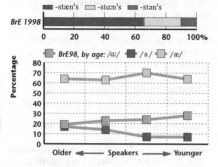

CIRCUMSTANCE

-stæn's   -staːn's   -stən's

BrE 1998

0   20   40   60   80   100%

BrE98, by age: /ɑː/   /ə/   /æ/

Percentage: 80 70 60 50 40 30 20 10 0

Older ◄—— Speakers ——► Younger

C

circumvention ˌsɜːk əm 'ventʃ ᵊn ‖ ˌsɝːk- ~s z

circumventive
  ˌsɜːk əm 'vent ɪv ◄ ‖ ˌsɝːk əm 'venṭ ɪv ◄

circus 'sɜːk əs ‖ 'sɝːk- ~es ɪz əz

Cirencester 'saɪᵊr ən ˌsest ə ‖ -ᵊr —*formerly, and occasionally still*, 'sɪs ɪt ə ‖ -əṭ ᵊr

Ciro 'sɪər əʊ ‖ 'sɪr oʊ

cirque sɜːk ‖ sɝːk **cirques** sɜːks ‖ sɝːks

cirrhosis sə 'rəʊs ɪs sɪ-, §-əs ‖ -'roʊs-

cirri 'sɪr aɪ

cirrocumulus ˌsɪr əʊ 'kjuːm jʊl əs -jəl əs
  ‖ ˌsɪr oʊ 'kjuːm jəl əs

cirrostratus ˌsɪr əʊ 'straːt əs -'streɪt-
  ‖ ˌsɪr oʊ 'streɪt əs -'stræṭ-

cirr|us 'sɪr |əs ~i aɪ

cis- *comb. form* ˌsɪs — **cis-butadiene**
  ˌsɪs ˌbjuːt ə 'daɪ iːn ‖ -ˌbjuːṭ-

Cisalpine ₍ₗ₎sɪs 'ælp aɪn

cisco 'sɪsk əʊ ‖ -oʊ ~es, ~s z

Ciskei ˌsɪs 'kaɪ '••

cisplatin ₍ₗ₎sɪs 'plæt ɪn -ᵊn

Cissie 'sɪs i

cissoid 'sɪs ɔɪd ~s z

cissus 'sɪs əs

ciss|y, Cissy 'sɪs li ~ies iz

Cistercian sɪ 'stɜːʃ ᵊn sə- ‖ -'stɝːʃ- ~s z

cistern 'sɪst ən ‖ -ᵊrn ~s z

cis-trans ˌsɪs 'trænz ◄ -'traːnz

cistron 'sɪs trən -trɒn ‖ -traːn ~s z

cistus 'sɪst əs

citadel 'sɪt əd ᵊl -ə del ‖ 'sɪṭ- ~s z

citation saɪ 'teɪʃ ᵊn sɪ- ~s z
  ci'**tation form**

cite saɪt (= *sight, site*) **cited** 'saɪt ɪd -əd
  ‖ 'saɪṭ əd **cites** saɪts **citing** 'saɪt ɪŋ ‖ 'saɪṭ ɪŋ

cithara 'sɪθ ər ə ~s z

cither 'sɪθ ə ‖ -ᵊr ~s z

Citibank *tdmk* 'sɪt i bæŋk ‖ 'sɪṭ-

Citicorp *tdmk* 'sɪt i kɔːp ‖ 'sɪṭ i kɔːrp

citified 'sɪt i faɪd ‖ 'sɪṭ-

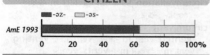

CITIZEN

-əz-   -əs-

AmE 1993

0   20   40   60   80   100%

---

citizen 'sɪt ɪz ən -əz- ‖ 'sɪṭ əz ən -əs- ~s z
  —*AmE 1993 poll panel preference:* -əz- 64%,
  -əs- 36%.
  ˌCitizens Ad'vice ˌBureau

citizenry 'sɪt ɪz ən ri '•əz- ‖ 'sɪṭ-

citizenship 'sɪt ɪz ən ʃɪp '•əz- ‖ 'sɪṭ- ~s s

citral 'sɪtr əl -æl

citrate 'sɪtr eɪt 'saɪtr-, -ət, -ɪt ~s s

citric 'sɪtr ɪk
  ˌcitric 'acid

citrine 'sɪtr ɪn -iːn, §-ən

Citrine sɪ 'triːn sə-

Citroen, Citroën *tdmk* 'sɪtr əʊ ən 'sɪtr ən
  ‖ ˌsɪtr oʊ 'en —*Fr* [si tʁɔ ɛn] ~s z

citron 'sɪtr ən ~s z

citronella ˌsɪtr ə 'nel ə

citrous 'sɪtr əs (= *citrus*)

citrus 'sɪtr əs ~es ɪz əz

cittern 'sɪt ɜːn -ᵊn ‖ 'sɪt ᵊrn ~s z

cit|y 'sɪt li ‖ 'sɪṭ li ~ies iz
  'city ˌeditor; ˌcity 'fathers; ˌcity 'hall

cityscape 'sɪt i skeɪp ‖ 'sɪṭ- ~s s

city-state ˌsɪt i 'steɪt ‖ ˌsɪṭ- '••• ~s s

Ciudad θju 'daːd ˌθiːˌu 'daːd ‖ sju 'daːd
  ˌsiːˌu 'daːd —*Sp* [θju 'ðað, sju-]

civet 'sɪv ɪt §-ət ~s s

civic 'sɪv ɪk ~s s

civies 'sɪv iz

civil 'sɪv ᵊl -ɪl
  ˌcivil de'fence; ˌcivil ˌengi'neering; ˌcivil
  'liberties; 'civil list; ˌcivil 'rights; ˌcivil
  'servant; ˌcivil 'war

civilian sə 'vɪl i‿ən sɪ- ~s z

civilis... —*see* **civiliz...**

civilit|y sə 'vɪl ət li sɪ-, -ɪt- ‖ -əṭ li ~ies iz

civilization ˌsɪv ᵊl aɪ 'zeɪʃ ᵊn ˌ•ɪl-, -ɪ'• ‖ -ᵊl ə-
  ~s z

civiliz|e 'sɪv ə laɪz -ɪ-; -ᵊl aɪz ~ed d ~er/s ə/
  z ‖ ᵊr/z ~es ɪz əz ~ing ɪŋ

civilly 'sɪv ᵊl i -ɪl-

civv|y 'sɪv li ~ies iz
  'civvy street

clachan, C~ 'klæx ən 'klæk-, 'klɑːx-

clack klæk **clacked** klækt **clacking** 'klæk ɪŋ
  clacks klæks

Clackmannan klæk 'mæn ən ~shire ʃə ʃɪə,
  ˌʃaɪ‿ə ‖ ʃᵊr ʃɪr, ˌʃaɪ‿ᵊr

Clacton 'klækt ən

clad klæd **cladding/s** 'klæd ɪŋ/z **clads** klædz

clade kleɪd **clades** kleɪdz

cladist 'kleɪd ɪst -əst ~s s

cladistics klə 'dɪst ɪks klæ-

Clady 'klæd i

clag klæg **clagged** klægd **clagging** 'klæg ɪŋ
  clags klægz

claggy 'klæg i

Claiborne 'kleɪ bɔːn ‖ -bɔːrn

claim kleɪm **claimed** kleɪmd **claiming**
  'kleɪm ɪŋ **claims** kleɪmz

claimable 'kleɪm əb ᵊl

claimant 'kleɪm ənt ~s s

claimer 'kleɪm ə ‖ -ᵊr ~s z

Clair kleə ‖ kleᵊr klæᵊr

Citation form, dictionary entry and connected speech

1 LPD, like other dictionaries, makes use of various **abbreviatory conventions**. This enables the dictionary to show a number of possible pronunciations with a single transcription of a word. However, it means that if you want to convert a passage in ordinary spelling into phonetic transcription you must 'unpack' these conventions.

2 For example, some phonetic symbols in LPD are written in *italic* or raised, to denote OPTIONAL SOUNDS. If you are writing a transcription, you should choose either to include the sound or to omit it. The simplest rule is to convert italic symbols into roman (= plain), and to omit raised symbols.

dictionary entry	**glimpse**	glɪm*p*s
you can write		glɪmps
dictionary entry	**fail**	feɪᵊl
you can write		feɪl

3 LPD uses spaces to show SYLLABIFICATION. You will probably want to omit these spaces in your transcription.

dictionary entry	**running**	'rʌn ɪŋ
you can write		'rʌnɪŋ

4 The LPD mark ‿, too, shows a syllable boundary, though it is a boundary that may be removed by COMPRESSION. You can ignore this mark.

dictionary entry	**hideous**	'hɪd i‿əs
you can write		'hɪdiəs
dictionary entry	**listening**	'lɪs ᵊn‿ɪŋ
you can write		'lɪsnɪŋ

5 Carrying out the procedure described above will give you a possible **citation form** (= dictionary pronunciation) for a word. This is the way the word might typically be pronounced if spoken in isolation. However, when a word occurs in a phrase or sentence, its pronunciation may sometimes be different from this. Some of the special phonetic characteristics of **connected speech** are discussed in the articles on ASSIMILATION, COMPOUNDS AND PHRASES, DOUBLE CONSONANTS, ELISION, R LIAISON, STRESS SHIFT, T-VOICING, and WEAK FORMS.

---

clairaudi|ence ₍ₗ₎kleər 'ɔːd i‿ənts ‖ ₍ₗ₎kler-
  ₍ₗ₎klær-, -'ɑːd- **~ent/s** ənt/s
Claire kleə ‖ kleᵊr klæᵊr
Clairol *tdmk* 'kleər ɒl ‖ 'kler ɔːl 'klær-, -ɑːl
clairvoyance ₍ₗ₎kleə 'vɔɪ ənts ‖ ₍ₗ₎kler- ₍ₗ₎klær-
clairvoyant ₍ₗ₎kleə 'vɔɪ ənt ‖ ₍ₗ₎kler- ₍ₗ₎klær- **~ly**
  li **~s** s
clam klæm **clammed** klæmd **clamming**
  'klæm ɪŋ **clams** klæmz
  ˌclam 'chowder
clamant 'kleɪm ənt 'klæm-
clambake 'klæm beɪk **~s** s
clamber 'klæm bə ‖ -bᵊr **~ed** d **clambering**
  'klæm bᵊr‿ɪŋ **~s** z

clamm|y 'klæm |i **~ier** i‿ə ‖ i‿ᵊr **~iest** i‿ɪst
  i‿əst **~ily** ɪ li əl i **~iness** i nəs i nɪs
clamor 'klæm ə ‖ -ᵊr **~ed** d **clamoring** 'klæm
  ər ɪŋ **~s** z
clamorous 'klæm ər‿əs **~ly** li **~ness** nəs nɪs
clamour 'klæm ə ‖ -ᵊr **~ed** d **clamouring**
  'klæm ər ɪŋ **~s** z
clamp, Clamp klæmp **clamped** klæm*p*t
  clamping 'klæmp ɪŋ **clamps** klæm*p*s
clampdown 'klæmp daʊn **~s** z
clamshell 'klæm ʃel **~s** z
clan klæn **clans** klænz
Clancarty klæn 'kɑːt i →klæŋ- ‖ -'kɑːr̬t i
Clancey, Clancy 'klænᵗs i

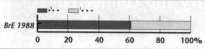

CLANDESTINE

BrE 1988

| 0 | 20 | 40 | 60 | 80 | 100% |

clandestine klæn 'dest ɪn -aɪn, §-ən;
'klænd e staɪn, -ɪ-, -ə-, -stɪn —*BrE 1988 poll
panel preference:* •'•• 61%, '••• 39%. **~ly** li
~ness nəs nɪs
clang klæŋ **clanged** klæŋd **clanging** 'klæŋ ɪŋ
clangs klæŋz
clanger 'klæŋ ə ǁ -ər **~s** z
clangor 'klæŋ gə -ə ǁ -ər -gər
clangorous 'klæŋ gər əs -ər- **~ly** li
clangour 'klæŋ gə -ə ǁ -ər -gər
clank klæŋk **clanked** klæŋkt **clanking**
'klæŋk ɪŋ **clanks** klæŋks
Clanmaurice, Clanmorris (ˌ)klæn 'mɒr ɪs
→(ˌ)klæm-, §-əs ǁ -'mɔːr- -'maːr-
clannish 'klæn ɪʃ **~ly** li **~ness** nəs nɪs
Clanricarde *(i)* (ˌ)klæn 'rɪk əd ǁ -ərd, *(ii)*
ˌklæn rɪ 'kɑːd ◄ ǁ -'kɑːrd ◄
clanship 'klæn ʃɪp
clans|man 'klænz |mən **~men** mən men
~woman ˌwʊm ən **~women** ˌwɪm ɪn §-ən
clap klæp **clapped** klæpt **clapping** 'klæp ɪŋ
claps klæps
clapboard 'klæp bɔːd 'klæb əd ǁ 'klæb ərd
'klæp bɔːrd, -bourd
Clapham 'klæp əm
ˌClapham 'Junction
clapp... —*see* **clap**
clapped-out ˌklæpt 'aʊt ◄
clapper 'klæp ə ǁ -ər **~s** z
clapperboard 'klæp ə bɔːd ǁ -ər bɔːrd-bourd
~s z
Clapton 'klæpt ən
claptrap 'klæp træp
claque klæk (= *clack*) **claques** klæks
Clara 'kleər ə ǁ 'kler ə'klær- —*As a foreign
name, also* 'klɑːr ə
clarabella, C~ ˌklær ə 'bel əǁ ˌkler-
Clare kleə ǁ kleərklæər
Claremont 'kleə mɒnt-mənt ǁ 'kler maːnt
'klær-
Clarence 'klær ənˈsǁ 'kler-
Clarenceux 'klær ən suː-sjuː ǁ 'kler-
Clarendon, c~ 'klær ənd ənǁ 'kler-
claret 'klær ət-ɪt ǁ 'kler- **~s** s
Clarges 'klɑːdʒ ɪz-əz ǁ 'klɑːrdʒ əz
Clarice 'klær ɪs§-əs ǁ 'kler-
Claridg|e 'klær ɪdʒǁ 'kler- **~e's** ɪzəz
clarification ˌklær əf ɪ 'keɪʃ ən, •ɪf-,
§-ə'•- ǁ ˌkler- **~s** z
clarificatory ˌklær əf ɪ 'keɪt ər i ◄, •ɪf-, §-ə'•-;
'klær əf ɪ kət ˌər i, ˌ•ɪf-, §'••ə-
ǁ 'klær əf ɪk ə tɔːr i'kler-, klə 'rɪf-, -toʊr i *(*)
clari|fy 'klær ə |faɪ-ɪ- ǁ 'kler- **~fied** faɪd
~fier/s faɪ ˌə/z ǁ faɪ ˌər/z **~fies** faɪz **~fying**
faɪ ɪŋ
Clarinda klə 'rɪnd əklæ-
clarinet ˌklær ə 'net-ɪ- ǁ ˌkler- **~s** s

clarinetist, clarinettist ˌklær ə 'net ɪst -ɪ-,
§-əst ǁ -'net- ˌkler- **~s** s
clarion 'klær i_ən ǁ 'kler- **~s** z
Clarissa klə 'rɪs ə
clarity 'klær ət i -ɪt- ǁ -ət i 'kler-
Clark, Clarke klɑːk ǁ klɑːrk
clarkia 'klɑːk i_ə ǁ 'klɑːrk- **~s** z
Clarkson 'klɑːks ən ǁ 'klɑːrks ən
Claro 'kleər əʊ ǁ 'kler oʊ
Clarrie 'klær i ǁ 'kler-
clart klɑːt ǁ klɑːrt **clarts** klɑːts ǁ klɑːrts
clarty 'klɑːt i ǁ 'klɑːrt i
clar|y, Clary 'kleər |i ǁ 'kler |i 'klær- **~ies** iz
-clase kleɪz kleɪs — **orthoclase** 'ɔːθ əʊ kleɪz
-kleɪs ǁ 'ɔːrθ ə-
clash klæʃ **clashed** klæʃt **clashes** 'klæʃ ɪz -əz
clashing 'klæʃ ɪŋ
clasp klɑːsp §klæsp ǁ klæsp **clasped** klɑːspt
§klæspt ǁ klæspt **clasping** 'klɑːsp ɪŋ
§'klæsp- ǁ 'klæsp ɪŋ **clasps** klɑːsps §klæsps
ǁ klæsps
'clasp knife
class klɑːs §klæs ǁ klæs **classed** klɑːst §klæst
ǁ klæst **classes** 'klɑːs ɪz §'klæs-, -əz ǁ 'klæs-
classing 'klɑːs ɪŋ §'klæs- ǁ 'klæs ɪŋ
ˌclass 'action; 'class ˌsystem; ˌclass
'struggle, '• ˌ••; ˌclass 'war, '• •
class-conscious ˌklɑːs 'kɒntʃ əs ◄ §ˌklæs-
ǁ 'klæs ˌkaːntʃ əs **~ness** nəs nɪs
classic 'klæs ɪk **~s** s
classical 'klæs ɪk əl **~ly** _i **~ism** ˌɪz əm
ˌClassical 'Latin
classicism 'klæs ɪ ˌsɪz əm-ə-
classicist 'klæs ɪs ɪst -əs-, §-əst **~s** s
classi... —*see* **classy**
classifiable 'klæs ɪ faɪ ˌəb əl'••ə-, ••'••••
classification ˌklæs ɪf ɪ 'keɪʃ ən, •əf-, -ə'•- **~s**
z
classificatory ˌklæs ɪf ɪ 'keɪt ər i ◄, •əf-, §-ə'•-;
'••ɪk ət ər i ǁ 'klæs əf ɪk ə tɔːr ikləˈsɪf-,
klæ 'sɪf-, -toʊr i *(*)
classifier 'klæs ɪ faɪ ˌə§'•ə- ǁ -faɪ ˌər **~s** z
classi|fy 'klæs ɪ |faɪ-ə- **~fied** faɪd **~fies** faɪz
~fying faɪ ɪŋ
classism 'klɑːs ˌɪz əm§'klæs- ǁ 'klæs-
classless 'klɑːs ləs§'klæs-, -lɪs ǁ 'klæs- **~ness**
nəsnɪs
classmate 'klɑːs meɪt§'klæs- ǁ 'klæs- **~s** s
classroom 'klɑːs ruːm§'klæs-, -rʊm ǁ 'klæs-
~s z
classwork 'klɑːs wɜːk§'klæs- ǁ 'klæs wɜːk
class|y 'klɑːs |i§'klæs- ǁ 'klæs |i **~ier** i_ə ǁ i_ər
~iest i_ɪst i_əst
clast klæst **clasts** klæsts
clastic 'klæst ɪk
clathrate 'klæθ reɪt **~s** s
clatter 'klæt ə ǁ 'klæt ər **~ed** d **clattering**
'klæt_ər ɪŋ ǁ 'klæt ər ɪŋ **~s** z
Claud klɔːdǁ klɑːd
Claude *(i)* klɔːd ǁ kloʊd *(ii)* klɔːdǁ klɑːd —*Fr*
[klod]
Claudette (ˌ)klɔː 'detǁ (ˌ)klɑː-
Claudia 'klɔːd i_əǁ 'klɑːd-

C

Claudian 'klɔːd i_ən ‖ 'klɑːd-
claudication ˌklɔːd ɪ 'keɪʃ ən -ə- ‖ ˌklɑːd-
Claudius 'klɔːd i_əs ‖ 'klɑːd-
Claughton 'klɔːt ən ‖ 'klɑːt- —*but places with this spelling in Lancashire are* 'klæft ən *(near Lancaster) and* 'klaɪt ən *(near Preston)*
clausal 'klɔːz əl ‖ 'klɑːz-
clause klɔːz ‖ klɑːz *(= claws)* **clauses** 'klɔːz ɪz -əz ‖ 'klɑːz-
Clausewitz 'klauz ə vɪts 'klaus- —*Ger* ['klau zə vɪts]
claustrophobia ˌklɔːs trə 'fəub i_ə ˌklɒs- ‖ -'foub- ˌklɑːs-
claustrophobic ˌklɔːs trə 'fəub ɪk ◂ ˌklɒs- ‖ -'foub- ˌklɑːs- ~**ally** əl_i ~s s
clave kleɪv klɑːv **claves** kleɪvz klɑːvz
Claverhouse 'kleɪv ə haus ‖ -ər-
Clavering *(i)* 'kleɪv ər ɪŋ, *(ii)* 'klæv-
Claverton 'klæv ət ən ‖ -ərt ən
clavichord 'klæv ɪ kɔːd -ə- ‖ -kɔːrd ~s z
clavicle 'klæv ɪk əl ~s z
clavier klə 'vɪə 'klæv i_ə ‖ -'vɪər ~s z
claviform 'klæv ɪ fɔːm §-ə- ‖ -fɔːrm
Clavius 'kleɪv i_əs
claw klɔː ‖ klɑː **clawed** klɔːd ‖ klɑːd **clawing** 'klɔːˌ ɪŋ ‖ 'klɔːˌ ɪŋ 'klɑː- **claws** klɔːz ‖ klɑːz
　'claw ˌhammer
clawback 'klɔː bæk ‖ 'klɑː- ~s s
Claxton 'klækst ən
clay, Clay kleɪ **clays** kleɪz
　ˌclay 'pigeon, ˌclay 'pigeon ˌshooting
Claydon 'kleɪd ən
clayey 'kleɪ i
claymore 'kleɪ mɔː ‖ -mɔːr -mour ~s z
claypan 'kleɪ pæn ~s z
Clayton 'kleɪt ən
claytonia kleɪ 'təun i_ə ‖ -'toun- ~s z
clean kliːn **cleaned** kliːnd **cleaning** 'kliːn ɪŋ **cleans** kliːnz
clean-cut ˌkliːn 'kʌt ◂ →ˌkliːŋ-
cleaner 'kliːn ə ‖ -ər ~s, ~'s z
cleanli... —*see* **cleanly**
clean-limbed ˌkliːn 'lɪmd ◂
　ˌclean-limbed 'heroes
cleanliness 'klen li nəs -nɪs
clean|ly *adj* 'kliːn |li §'kliːn- ~**lier** li_ə ‖ li_ər ~**liest** li_ɪst li_əst
cleanly *adv* 'kliːn li
cleanse klenz **cleansed** klenzd **cleansing** 'klenz ɪŋ **cleanses** 'klenz ɪz -əz
clean-shaven ˌkliːn 'ʃeɪv ən ◂
Cleanthes kli 'æntθ iːz
cleanup 'kliːn ʌp ~s s
clear klɪə ‖ klɪər **cleared** klɪəd ‖ klɪərd **clearer** 'klɪər ə ‖ 'klɪr ər **clearest** 'klɪər ɪst -əst ‖ 'klɪr əst **clearing** 'klɪər ɪŋ ‖ 'klɪr ɪŋ
clearanc|e 'klɪər ənts ‖ 'klɪr- ~**es** ɪz əz
　'clearance ˌsale
Clearasil *tdmk* 'klɪər ə sɪl ‖ 'klɪr-
clearcole 'klɪə kəul →-kɒul ‖ 'klɪr koul
clear-cut ˌklɪə 'kʌt ◂ ‖ ˌklɪr-
　ˌclear-cut de'cision
clearer 'klɪər ə ‖ 'klɪr ər ~s z

clear-headed ˌklɪə 'hed ɪd ◂ -əd ‖ ˌklɪr- ~**ly** li ~**ness** nəs nɪs
　ˌclear-ˌheaded 'attitude
clearing 'klɪər ɪŋ ‖ 'klɪr ɪŋ ~s z
　'clearing ˌbank
clearing|house 'klɪər ɪŋ |haus ‖ 'klɪr- ~**houses** hauz ɪz -əz
clear|ly 'klɪə |li ‖ 'klɪr |li ~**ness** nəs nɪs
clearout 'klɪər aut ‖ 'klɪr- ~s s
clear-sighted ˌklɪə 'saɪt ɪd ◂ -əd ‖ ˌklɪr- 'saɪt̬ əd ◂ ~**ly** li ~**ness** nəs nɪs
clear-up 'klɪər ʌp ‖ 'klɪr- ~s s
clearway 'klɪə weɪ ‖ 'klɪr- ~s z
cleat kliːt **cleated** 'kliːt ɪd -əd ‖ 'kliːt̬ əd **cleats** kliːts
Cleator 'kliːt ə ‖ 'kliːt̬ ər
cleavag|e 'kliːv ɪdʒ ~**es** ɪz əz
cleave, C~ kliːv **cleaved** kliːvd **cleaves** kliːvz **cleaving** 'kliːv ɪŋ **cleft** kleft **clove** kləuv ‖ klouv **cloven** 'kləuv ən ‖ 'klouv ən
cleaver, C~ 'kliːv ə ‖ -ər ~s z
Cleckheaton ₍ₒ₎klek 'hiːt ən
Cleddau 'kleð aɪ —*Welsh* ['kle ðai, -ðe]
Cledwyn 'kled wɪn
Clee kli
cleek kliːk **cleeks** kliːks
Cleese kliːz
Cleethorpes 'kli θɔːps ‖ -θɔːrps
clef klef **clefs** klefs
cleft kleft **clefts** klefts
　ˌcleft 'palate; ˌcleft 'stick
cleg kleg **clegs** klegz
Clegg kleg
Cleisthenes 'klaɪsθ ə niːz -ɪ-
cleistogamy klaɪ 'stɒg əm i ‖ -'stɑːg-
Cleland *(i)* 'klel ənd, *(ii)* 'kliːl ənd
Clem, clem klem
clematis 'klem ət ɪs §-əs; klə 'meɪt-, klɪ- ‖ 'klem ət̬ əs klɪ 'mæt̬-, -'meɪt̬-, -'mɑːt̬- ~**es** ɪz əz
Clemence 'klem ənts
clemenc|y, C~ 'klem ənts li ~**ies** iz
Clemens 'klem ənz
clement, C~ 'klem ənt ~**ly** li
Clementina ˌklem ən 'tiːn ə
clementine, C~ 'klem ən taɪn -tiːn ~s z
clench klentʃ **clenched** klentʃt **clenches** 'klentʃ ɪz -əz **clenching** 'klentʃ ɪŋ
Cleo 'kliː əu ‖ -ou
Cleobury *places in Shropshire* 'klɪb ər i 'kleb-, 'klɪəb-
Cleobury *family name (i)* 'kləu bər_i ‖ 'klou ˌber i, *(ii)* 'kliː-
Cleon 'kliːˌən -ɒn ‖ -ɑːn
Cleopatra, c~ ˌkliːˌə 'pætr ə -'pɑːtr- ‖ ~'s z
clepsydr|a 'kleps ɪdr ə -ədr-; klep 'sɪdr ə ~**ae** iː ~**as** əz
clerestor|y 'klɪə ˌstɔːr li 'klɪəst ər_li ‖ 'klɪr- -ˌstour- ~**ies** iz
clerg|y 'klɜːdʒ |i ‖ 'klɜːdʒ li ~**ies** iz
clergy|man 'klɜːdʒ i |mən ‖ 'klɜːdʒ- ~**men** mən ~**woman** ˌwum ən ~**women** ˌwɪm ɪn §-ən

cleric 'kler ɪk ~s s
clerical 'kler ɪk əl ~ly _i
clericalism 'kler ɪk ə ˌlɪz əm -əl ˌɪz-
clerihew, C~ 'kler i hjuː -ə- ~s z
clerisy 'kler əs i -ɪs-
clerk, Clerk klɑːk ‖ klɝːk (*) clerked
klɑːkt ‖ klɝːkt clerking 'klɑːk ɪŋ ‖ 'klɝːk ɪŋ
clerks klɑːks ‖ klɝːks
Clerkenwell 'klɑːk ən wel -wəl ‖ 'klɝːk-
'klɑːrk-
Clermont 'kleə mɒnt 'klɜː-, -mənt
‖ 'kler mɑːnt 'klɝː-
Clery 'klɪər i ‖ 'klɪr i
Clevedon 'kliːv dən
Cleveland 'kliːv lənd
Cleveleys 'kliːv liz
clever 'klev ə ‖ -ər cleverer 'klev ər ə ‖ -ər ər
cleverest 'klev ər ɪst -əst ~ly li ~ness nəs
nɪs
'clever dick, ˌ·· '·
clever-clever ˌklev ə 'klev ə ◄ ‖ -ər 'klev ər
Cleverdon 'klev əd ən ‖ -ərd-
Cleves kliːvz —Fr Clèves [klɛːv], Ger Kleve
['kleː və]
clevis 'klev ɪs §-əs ~es ɪz əz
clew kluː (= clue) clewed kluːd clewing
'kluː ɪŋ clews kluːz
Clewer 'kluː ə ‖ -ər
Clewes, Clews kluːz
Cley (i) kleɪ, (ii) klaɪ
Clibborn 'klɪb ən ‖ -ərn
Cliburn 'klaɪ bɜːn ‖ -bɝːn
cliche, cliché 'kliːʃ eɪ ‖ kliː 'ʃeɪ (*) ~d, ~'d d
~s z
click klɪk clicked klɪkt clicking 'klɪk ɪŋ clicks
klɪks
'click ˌbeetle; 'click ˌlanguage
clickety-click ˌklɪk ət i 'klɪk ‖ ˌklɪk ət̬-
client 'klaɪ ənt ~s s
clientele ˌkliː ɒn 'tel -ð-, -ɑːn-, ˌkliː ən-
‖ ˌklaɪ ən- ~s z
Clifden 'klɪft ən
cliff klɪf cliffs klɪfs
'cliff ˌdweller
Cliff, Cliffe klɪf
cliffhanger 'klɪf ˌhæŋ ə ‖ -ər ~s z
Clifford 'klɪf əd ‖ -ərd
Clift klɪft
Clifton 'klɪft ən
Cliftonville 'klɪft ən vɪl
climacteric klaɪ 'mækt ər ɪk ˌklaɪ mæk 'ter ɪk
~s s
climactic klaɪ 'mækt ɪk ~ally əl_i
climate 'klaɪm ət -ɪt ~s s
climatic klaɪ 'mæt ɪk ‖ -'mæt̬- ~ally əl_i
climatologic
ˌklaɪm ət ə 'lɒdʒ ɪk ◄ ‖ -ət̬ ə 'lɑːdʒ- ~al əl
~ally əl_i
climatolog|ist/s ˌklaɪm ə 'tɒl ədʒ ɪst/s §-əst/s
‖ -'tɑːl- ~y i
climax 'klaɪm æks climaxed 'klaɪm ækst
climaxes 'klaɪm æks ɪz -əz climaxing
'klaɪm æks ɪŋ

climb klaɪm (= clime) climbed klaɪmd
climbing 'klaɪm ɪŋ climbs klaɪmz
climbable 'klaɪm əb əl
climb-down 'klaɪm daʊn ~s z
climber 'klaɪm ə ‖ -ər ~s z
climbing 'klaɪm ɪŋ
'climbing frame; 'climbing ˌirons
clime klaɪm climes klaɪmz
clinch, Clinch klɪntʃ clinched klɪntʃt clinches
'klɪntʃ ɪz -əz clinching 'klɪntʃ ɪŋ
clincher 'klɪntʃ ə ‖ -ər ~s z
cline, Cline klaɪn clines klaɪnz
cling klɪŋ clinging 'klɪŋ ɪŋ clings klɪŋz
clung klʌŋ
clingfilm 'klɪŋ fɪlm
clingstone 'klɪŋ stəʊn ‖ -stoʊn
cling|y 'klɪŋ |i ~ier i_ə ‖ i_ər ~iest i_ɪst i_əst
~iness i nəs -nɪs
clinic 'klɪn ɪk ~s s
clinical 'klɪn ɪk əl ~ly _i
clinician klɪ 'nɪʃ ən klə- ~s z
clink klɪŋk clinked klɪŋkt clinking 'klɪŋk ɪŋ
clinks klɪŋks
clinker 'klɪŋk ə ‖ -ər ~ed d clinkering
'klɪŋk ər ɪŋ ~s z
clinker-built ˌklɪŋk ə 'bɪlt ◄ ‖ -ər-
clinkety-clank ˌklɪŋk ət i 'klæŋk ‖ -ət̬ i-
clinometer klaɪ 'nɒm ɪt ə klɪ-, -ət-
‖ -'nɑːm ət̬ ər ~s z
clint, Clint klɪnt clints klɪnts
Clinton 'klɪnt ən ‖ -ən
Clio (i) 'klaɪ əʊ ‖ -oʊ, (ii) 'kliː- —The muse is
usually (i), the model of car (ii).
cliometric ˌklaɪ əʊ 'metr ɪk ◄ ‖ -ə- ~s s
clip klɪp clipped klɪpt clipping 'klɪp ɪŋ clips
klɪps
'clip joint
clipboard 'klɪp bɔːd ‖ -bɔːrd -boʊrd ~s z
clip-clop 'klɪp klɒp ˌ·'· ‖ -klɑːp ~ped t
~ping ɪŋ ~s s
clip-on 'klɪp ɒn ‖ -ɑːn -ɔːn
clipper 'klɪp ə ‖ -ər ~s z
clippie 'klɪp i ~s z
clipping 'klɪp ɪŋ ~s z
Clipsham 'klɪp ʃəm
Clipstone 'klɪp stəʊn ‖ -stoʊn
clique kliːk §klɪk cliques kliːks §klɪks
cliquey 'kliːk i §'klɪk i
cliquish 'kliːk ɪʃ §'klɪk ɪʃ ~ly li ~ness nəs nɪs
cliquy 'kliːk i §'klɪk i
Clissold 'klɪs əʊld →-ɒʊld, -əld ‖ -oʊld
Clitheroe 'klɪð ə rəʊ ‖ -roʊ
clitic 'klɪt ɪk ‖ 'klɪt̬ ɪk ~s s
cliticis... —see cliticiz...
cliticization ˌklɪt ɪs aɪ 'zeɪʃ ən ˌ·əs-, -ɪ'·-
‖ ˌklɪt̬ əs ə-
cliticiz|e 'klɪt ɪ saɪz -ə- ‖ 'klɪt̬- ~ed d ~es ɪz
əz ~ing ɪŋ
clitoral 'klɪt ər əl 'klaɪt- ‖ 'klɪt̬-
clitoridectom|y ˌklɪt ər ɪ 'dekt əm |i -ə'·-
‖ ˌklɪt̬- ~ies iz
clitoris 'klɪt ər ɪs 'klaɪt-, §-əs ‖ 'klɪt̬-
Clive klaɪv

Clicks

A **click** is a speech sound made with an air stream set in motion within the mouth rather than by the lungs.

In English, isolated clicks are sometimes used as meaningful noises, but they are not part of the phoneme system and do not form part of the pronunciation of words.

An alveolar click ǀ can be used as a sign of disapproval (see the entry **tut-tut**). If accompanied by a breathy-voiced ŋ, it is a kind of sneer. A lateral click ǁ can be used to encourage horses.

C

Cliveden 'klɪvd ən
clivia 'klaɪv i̯ə 'klɪv- ~s z
cloac|a kləʊ 'eɪk |ə ‖ kloʊ- ~ae iː
cloak kləʊk ‖ kloʊk **cloaked** kləʊkt ‖ kloʊkt
  cloaking 'kləʊk ɪŋ ‖ 'kloʊk ɪŋ **cloaks**
  kləʊks ‖ kloʊks
cloak-and-dagger ˌkləʊk ən 'dæg ə →-ŋ-
  ‖ ˌkloʊk ən 'dæg ᵊr
cloakroom 'kləʊk ruːm -rʊm ‖ 'kloʊk-
clobber 'klɒb ə ‖ 'klɑːb ᵊr ~ed d **clobbering**
  'klɒb ᵊr ɪŋ ‖ 'klɑːb- ~s z
cloche klɒʃ kləʊʃ ‖ kloʊʃ **cloches** 'klɒʃ ɪz
  'kləʊʃ-, -əz ‖ 'kloʊʃ əz
clock klɒk ‖ klɑːk **clocked** klɒkt ‖ klɑːkt
  clocking 'klɒk ɪŋ ‖ 'klɑːk ɪŋ **clocks**
  klɒks ‖ klɑːks
  ˌclock ' radio; ' clock ˌtower
clock-watch|er/s 'klɒk ˌwɒtʃ |ə/z
  ‖ 'klɑːk ˌwɑːtʃ |ᵊr/z ~ing ɪŋ
clockwise 'klɒk waɪz ‖ 'klɑːk-
clockwork 'klɒk wɜːk ‖ 'klɑːk wɜ˞ːk
clod klɒd ‖ klɑːd **clods** klɒdz ‖ klɑːdz
Clodagh 'kləʊd ə ‖ 'kloʊd ə
cloddish 'klɒd ɪʃ ‖ 'klɑːd ɪʃ ~ness nəs nɪs
clodhopper 'klɒd ˌhɒp ə ‖ 'klɑːd ˌhɑːp ᵊr ~s z
clog klɒg ‖ klɑːg klɔːg **clogged**
  klɒgd ‖ klɑːgd klɔːgd **clogging**
  'klɒg ɪŋ ‖ 'klɑːg ɪŋ 'klɔːg- **clogs**
  klɒgz ‖ klɑːgz klɔːgz
  ' clog dance
cloggy 'klɒg i ‖ 'klɑːg i 'klɔːg-
Clogher 'klɒx ə 'klɒ hə; klɔː ‖ klɔːr
cloisonne, cloisonné klwɑ: 'zɒn eɪ klwʌ-
  ‖ ˌklɔːz ə 'neɪ
cloister 'klɔɪst ə ‖ -ᵊr ~ed d **cloistering**
  'klɔɪst ᵊr_ɪŋ ~s z
cloistral 'klɔɪs trəl
clomp klɒmp ‖ klɑːmp **clomped**
  klɒmpt ‖ klɑːmpt **clomping**
  'klɒmp ɪŋ ‖ 'klɑːmp ɪŋ **clomps**
  klɒmps ‖ klɑːmps
clonal 'kləʊn ᵊl ‖ 'kloʊn ᵊl ~ly i
clone kləʊn ‖ kloʊn **cloned** kləʊnd ‖ kloʊnd
  clones kləʊnz ‖ kloʊnz **cloning**
  'kləʊn ɪŋ ‖ 'kloʊn ɪŋ
Clones place in Ireland 'kləʊn ɪs -əs ‖ 'kloʊn-

clonic 'klɒn ɪk ‖ 'klɑːn ɪk
clonk klɒŋk ‖ klɑːŋk klɔːŋk **clonked**
  klɒŋkt ‖ klɑːŋkt klɔːŋkt **clonking**
  'klɒŋk ɪŋ ‖ 'klɑːŋk ɪŋ 'klɔːŋk- **clonks**
  klɒŋks ‖ klɑːŋks klɔːŋks
Clonmel, Clonmell ˌklɒn 'mel →ˌklɒm-, '··
  ‖ ˌklɑːn-
clonus 'kləʊn əs ‖ 'kloʊn əs ~es ɪz əz
clop klɒp ‖ klɑːp **clopped** klɒpt ‖ klɑːpt
  clopping 'klɒp ɪŋ ‖ 'klɑːp ɪŋ **clops**
  klɒps ‖ klɑːps
Clophill 'klɒp hɪl ‖ 'klɑːp-
clopp... —see **clop**
close adj, adv kləʊs ‖ kloʊs **closer**
  'kləʊs ə ‖ 'kloʊs ᵊr **closest** 'kləʊs ɪst -əst
  ‖ 'kloʊs əst
  ˌclose ' call; ˌclose ' quarters; ˌclose ' shave;
  ˌclose ' thing
close v kləʊz ‖ kloʊz **closed** kləʊzd ‖ kloʊzd
  closes 'kləʊz ɪz -əz ‖ 'kloʊz əz **closing**
  'kləʊz ɪŋ ‖ 'kloʊz ɪŋ
  ˌclosed ' book; ˌclosed ˌcircuit ' tele ˌvision;
  ˌclosed ' shop
close n 'courtyard' kləʊs ‖ kloʊs **closes**
  'kləʊs ɪz -əz ‖ 'kloʊs əz
close n 'end' kləʊz ‖ kloʊz **closes** 'kləʊz ɪz -əz
  ‖ 'kloʊz əz
Close family name kləʊs ‖ kloʊs
close-cropped
  ˌkləʊs 'krɒpt ◄ ‖ ˌkloʊs 'krɑːpt ◄
close-cut ˌkləʊs 'kʌt ◄ ‖ ˌkloʊs-
closed-door ˌkləʊzd 'dɔː ◄ ‖ ˌkloʊzd 'dɔːr ◄
  -'doʊr
closedown 'kləʊz daʊn ‖ 'kloʊz-
closefisted ˌkləʊs 'fɪst ɪd ◄ -əd ‖ ˌkloʊs-
close-grained ˌkləʊs 'greɪnd ◄ ‖ ˌkloʊs-
close-hauled ˌkləʊs 'hɔːld ◄ ‖ ˌkloʊs- -'hɑːld
close-knit ˌkləʊs 'nɪt ◄ ‖ ˌkloʊs-
close-lipped ˌkləʊs 'lɪpt ◄ ‖ ˌkloʊs-
closely 'kləʊs li ‖ 'kloʊs-
closely-knit ˌkləʊs li 'nɪt ◄ ‖ ˌkloʊs-
  ˌclosely-knit ' group
closeness 'kləʊs nəs -nɪs ‖ 'kloʊs-
closeout 'kləʊz aʊt ‖ 'kloʊz-
closer n 'kləʊz ə ‖ 'kloʊz ᵊr ~s z
closer comparative adj 'kləʊs ə ‖ 'kloʊs ᵊr

close season 'kləus ˌsiːz ən ˌ•'•• ‖ 'klouzd-
close-set ˌkləus 'set ◀ ‖ ˌklous-
ˌclose-set 'eyes
clos|et 'klɒz |ɪt §-ət ‖ 'klɑːz |ət ~eted ɪt ɪd
§ət-, -əd ‖ əţ əd ~eting ɪt ɪŋ §ət- ‖ əţ ɪŋ
~ets ɪts §-əts ‖ əts
close-up 'kləus ʌp ‖ 'klous- ~s s
closing 'kləuz ɪŋ ‖ 'klouz ɪŋ
'closing date; 'closing price; 'closing time
clostridi|um klɒ 'strɪd i_|əm ‖ klɑː- ~a ə
closure 'kləuʒ ə ‖ 'klouʒ ər ~d d closuring
'kləuʒ ər ɪŋ ‖ 'klouʒ- ~s z
clot klɒt ‖ klɑːt clots klɒts ‖ klɑːts clotted
'klɒt ɪd -əd ‖ 'klɑːţ əd clotting
'klɒt ɪŋ ‖ 'klɑːţ ɪŋ
ˌclotted 'cream
cloth klɒθ klɔːθ ‖ klɔːθ klɑːθ cloths klɒθs
klɒðz, klɔːðz, klɔːθs ‖ klɔːðz klɔːθs, klɑːðz,
klɑːθs
clothbound 'klɒθ baund 'klɔːθ- ‖ 'klɔːθ-
'klɑːθ-
clothe v kləuð ‖ klouð clothed
kləuðd ‖ klouðd clothes kləuðz ‖ klouðz
clothing 'kləuð ɪŋ ‖ 'klouð ɪŋ
cloth-eared ˌklɒθ 'ɪəd ◀ ˌklɔːθ- ‖ ˌklɔːθ 'ɪ°rd ◀
ˌklɑːθ-
clothes n kləuðz kləuz ‖ klouz klouðz
'clothes ˌhanger; 'clothes moth; 'clothes
peg
clothesbasket 'kləuðz ˌbɑːsk ɪt 'kləuz-,
§-,bæsk-, §-ət ‖ 'klouz ˌbæsk ət 'klouðz- ~s
s
clotheshors|e 'kləuðz hɔːs 'kləuz-
‖ 'klouz hɔːrs 'klouðz- ~es ɪz əz
clothesline 'kləuðz laɪn 'kləuz- ‖ 'klouz-
'klouðz- ~s z
clothespin 'kləuðz pɪn 'kləuz- ‖ 'klouz-
'klouðz- ~s z
clothier, C~ 'kləuð i_ə ‖ 'klouð i_°r ~s z
clothing 'kləuð ɪŋ ‖ 'klouð ɪŋ
Clotho 'kləuθ əu ‖ 'klouθ ou
clott... —see clot
cloture 'kləutʃ ə ‖ 'kloutʃ °r ~s z
cloud klaud clouded 'klaud ɪd -əd clouding
'klaud ɪŋ clouds klaudz
'cloud ˌchamber; ˌcloud 'nine
cloudbank 'klaud bæŋk →'klaub- ~s s
cloudberr|y 'klaud bər_|i →'klaub-, -ˌber li
‖ -ˌber li ~ies iz
cloudburst 'klaud bɜːst →'klaub- ‖ -bɝːst ~s
s
cloud-capped ˌklaud 'kæpt ◀→ˌklaug-, '••
ˌcloud-capped 'mountains
cloud-cuckoo-land ˌklaud 'kuk uː lænd
→ˌklaug- ‖ -'kuːk-
Cloudesley 'klaudz li
cloudi... —see cloudy
cloudless 'klaud ləs-lɪs ~ly li
cloudscape 'klaud skeɪp ~s s
cloud|y 'klaud |i ~ier i_ə ‖ i_°r ~iest i_ɪst i_əst
~ily ɪ li əl i ~iness i nəs i nɪs
clough, Clough klʌf—but the place in Co.
Down is klɒx

Clouseau 'kluːz əu ‖ klu: 'zou —Fr [klu zo]
clout, Clout klaut clouted 'klaut ɪd -əd
‖ 'klauţ əd clouting 'klaut ɪŋ ‖ 'klauţ ɪŋ
clouts klauts
Clouzot 'kluːz əu ‖ klu: 'zou —Fr [klu zo]
clove kləuv ‖ klouv cloves kləuvz ‖ klouvz
ˌclove 'hitch, '••
Clovelly klə 'vel i
cloven 'kləuv ən ‖ 'klouv ən
cloven-footed ˌkləuv ən 'fut ɪd ◀ -əd
‖ ˌklouv ən 'fuţ əd ◀
cloven-hoofed ˌkləuv ən 'huːft ◀ -'huft
‖ ˌklouv ən 'huft ◀ -'huːft, -'huvd, -'huːvd
clover 'kləuv ə ‖ 'klouv °r ~s z
clover|leaf 'kləuv ə |liːf ‖ 'klouv °r- ~leafs
liːfs ~leaves liːvz
Clovis 'kləuv ɪs §-əs ‖ 'klouv-
Clowes (i) klauz, (ii) kluːz
clown klaun clowned klaund clowning
'klaun ɪŋ clowns klaunz
clownery 'klaun ər i
clownish 'klaun ɪʃ ~ly li ~ness nəs nɪs
cloy klɔɪ cloyed klɔɪd cloying/ly 'klɔɪ ɪŋ /li
cloys klɔɪz
cloze kləuz ‖ klouz
club klʌb clubbed klʌbd clubbing 'klʌb ɪŋ
clubs klʌbz
ˌClub 'Med; ˌclub 'sandwich; ˌclub 'soda
clubbable 'klʌb əb əl
clubb... —see club
club|foot ˌklʌb |'fut '•• ~feet 'fiːt ~footed
'fut ɪd ◀-əd ‖ 'fuţ əd◀
club|house 'klʌb |haus ~houses hauz ɪz -əz
clubland 'klʌb lænd -lənd
clubmate 'klʌb meɪt ~s s
club|man 'klʌb |mən -mæn ~men mən men
clubs klʌbz
cluck klʌk clucked klʌkt clucking 'klʌk ɪŋ
clucks klʌks
clue kluː clued kluːd clueing, cluing 'kluː_ɪŋ
clues kluːz
Cluedo tdmk 'kluːd əu ‖ -ou
clueless 'kluː ləs -lɪs ~ly li ~ness nəs nɪs
Cluj kluːʒ —Romanian [kluʒ]
Clumber, c~ 'klʌm bə ‖ -bər
clump klʌmp clumped klʌmpt clumping
'klʌmp ɪŋ clumps klʌmps
clums|y 'klʌmz |i ~ier i_ə ‖ i_°r ~iest i_ɪst
i_əst ~ily ɪ li əl i ~iness i nəs i nɪs
Clun klʌn
Clunes kluːnz
clung klʌŋ
Clunie 'kluːn i
Clunies 'kluːn iz
clunk klʌŋk clunked klʌŋkt clunking
'klʌŋk ɪŋ clunks klʌŋks
Cluny 'kluːn i —Fr [kly ni]
clupeid 'kluːp i ɪd §-əd ~s z
clupeoid 'kluːp i ɔɪd
cluster 'klʌst ə ‖ -°r ~ed d clustering 'klʌst
ər_ɪŋ ~s z
'cluster bomb; 'cluster pine

Clipping

1 A **clipped** vowel is one that is pronounced more quickly than an unclipped vowel. For example, **rice** raɪs has a quick aɪ (and a slow s) when compared with **rise** raɪz (slow aɪ, quicker z).

In English, a vowel (or vowel plus nasal, or vowel plus LIQUID) is clipped when it is followed by one of the consonants p, t, ţ, k, tʃ, f, θ, s, ʃ within the same syllable (when 'syllable' is determined as in this dictionary). These are the FORTIS consonants, and we call this phenomenon **pre-fortis clipping**. It is particularly noticeable with long vowels and diphthongs when they are stressed.

The vowels have pre-fortis clipping in the words
feet fiːt (compare **feed** fiːd),
loose luːs (compare **lose** luːz),
rate reɪt (compare **raid** reɪd).

So do the vowels in the stressed syllables in the words
seeking 'siːk ɪŋ (compare **intriguing** ɪn 'triːg ɪŋ),
paper 'peɪp ə ‖ 'peɪp ªr (compare **labo(u)r** 'leɪb ə ‖ -ªr),
total 'təʊt ªl ‖ 'toʊţ ªl (compare **modal** 'məʊd ªl ‖ 'moʊd ªl).

The eɪ in **plating** 'pleɪt ɪŋ ‖'pleɪţ ɪŋ has pre-fortis clipping, but the eɪ in **play-time** does not, since here the t is in a different syllable.

2 Clipping does not involve any change of vowel quality ('timbre'). Clipped iː in **teach** tiːtʃ does not sound like ɪ in **rich** rɪtʃ.

3 Both the e and the n of **tent** tent are affected by pre-fortis clipping: compare **tend** tend with no clipping. Both the ɪ and the l of **milk** mɪlk are clipped. In **fierce**, clipping affects the ɪə of BrE fɪəs and the ɪªr of AmE fɪªrs: compare **fears** fɪəz ‖ fɪªrz, where there is no clipping.

4 Another, less noticeable, kind of clipping in English depends on the presence within a word of one or more unstressed syllables after the stressed syllable. The iː in **leader** 'liːd ə ‖ 'liːd ªr is somewhat clipped in comparison with the iː in **lead** liːd, because in **leader** an unstressed syllable follows. The iː in **leadership** 'liːd ə ʃɪp ‖ 'liːd ªr ʃɪp is rather more clipped, because two unstressed syllables follow. This kind of clipping is called **rhythmic clipping**.

5 In **teacher** 'tiːtʃ ə ‖ 'tiːtʃ ªr the iː is affected both by pre-fortis clipping (because of the tʃ) and by rhythmic clipping (because of the **-er**). As a result, it is phonetically quite short. (We still call it a long vowel, because it is still an allophone of the phoneme iː.)

6 The contrary process to clipping may be called **stretching**. This tends to affect the vowel of the last syllable a speaker makes before taking a breath or stopping talking.

clutch klʌtʃ **clutched** klʌtʃt **clutches**
ˈklʌtʃ ɪz -əz **clutching** ˈklʌtʃ ɪŋ
ˈclutch bag

clutter ˈklʌt ə ‖ ˈklʌt̮ ər **~ed** d **cluttering**
ˈklʌt ̮ər ɪŋ ‖ ˈklʌt̮ ər ɪŋ **~s** z

Clutterbuck ˈklʌt ə bʌk ‖ ˈklʌt̮ ər-

Clutton ˈklʌt ən

Clwyd ˈkluː ɪd —*Welsh* [klu‍ɪd, klʊid]

Clwydian klu ˈɪd i ̩ən

Clydach ˈklɪd əx ˈklʌd-, -ək

Clyde klaɪd

Clydebank ˈklaɪd bæŋk →ˈklaɪb-

Clydella *tdmk* klaɪ ˈdel ə

Clydesdale ˈklaɪdz deɪ ᵊl

Clydeside ˈklaɪd saɪd

Clyne klaɪn

Clyro ˈklaɪᵊr əʊ ‖ -oʊ

Clyst klɪst

clyster ˈklɪst ə ‖ -ᵊr **~s** z

Clytemnestra ˌklaɪt əm ˈniːs trə ˌklɪt-, -ɪm-,
-em-, -ˈnes- ‖ ˌklaɪt̮-

cm —*see* centimeter/s

cʹmon kəm ˈɒn ‖ -ˈɑːn -ˈɔːn

CND ˌsiː en ˈdiː

Cnidus ˈnaɪd əs ˈknaɪd-

CNN ˌsiː en ˈen

Cnut kə ˈnjuːt

co- ˌkəʊ ‖ ˌkoʊ —*New compounds in co- vary
between early and late stress, with a preference
for late* (ˌco-arˈranger) *except when the second
element has only one syllable* (ˈco-heir). *In
established words, note however* ˈco,pilot,
ˈcosine.

Co. kəʊ ‖ koʊ —*or see* Company, County

co *WWW and e-mail* kəʊ ‖ koʊ

CO ˌsiː ˈəʊ ◂ ‖ -ˈoʊ

c/o ˌsiː ˈəʊ ◂ ‖ -ˈoʊ —*or see* care of, carried over

coach kəʊtʃ ‖ koʊtʃ **coached** kəʊtʃt ‖ koʊtʃt
coaches ˈkəʊtʃ ɪz -əz ‖ ˈkoʊtʃ əz **coaching**
ˈkəʊtʃ ɪŋ ‖ ˈkoʊtʃ ɪŋ
ˈcoach ˌstation

coachbuilder ˈkəʊtʃ ˌbɪld ə ‖ ˈkoʊtʃ ˌbɪld ᵊr **~s**
z

Coachella kəʊ ˈtʃel ə ‖ koʊ- kə-

coach|man ˈkəʊtʃ |mən ‖ ˈkoʊtʃ- **~men** mən
men

coachwork ˈkəʊtʃ wɜːk ‖ ˈkoʊtʃ wɜːk

Coad, Coade kəʊd ‖ koʊd

coadjutor kəʊ ˈædʒ ʊt ə -ət- ‖ koʊ ˈædʒ ət̮ ᵊr
ˌkoʊ ə ˈdʒuːt̮ ᵊr **~s** z

coagulant kəʊ ˈæg jʊl ənt -jəl- ‖ koʊ ˈæg jəl-
~s s

coagu|late kəʊ ˈæg jʊ |leɪt -jə- ‖ koʊ ˈæg jə-
~lated leɪt ɪd -əd ‖ leɪt̮ əd **~lates** leɪts
~lating leɪt ɪŋ ‖ leɪt̮ ɪŋ

coagulation kəʊ ˌæg jʊ ˈleɪʃ ᵊn -jə-
‖ koʊ ˌæg jə-

Coahuila ˌkəʊ ə ˈwiːl ə ‖ ˌkoʊ- —*AmSp*
[ko a ˈwi la]

coal kəʊl →kɒʊl ‖ koʊl **coaled** kəʊld →kɒʊld
‖ koʊld *(= cold)* **coaling** ˈkəʊl ɪŋ →ˈkɒʊl-
‖ ˈkoʊl ɪŋ **coals** kəʊlz →kɒʊlz ‖ koʊlz
ˈcoal gas; ˈcoal tar; ˈcoal tit

Coalbrookdale ˌkəʊl brʊk ˈdeɪᵊl→ˌkɒʊl-,
§-bruːk- ‖ ˌkoʊl-

coalbunker ˈkəʊl ˌbʌŋk ə→ˈkɒʊl-
‖ ˈkoʊl ˌbʌŋk ᵊr **~s** z

coalesc|e ˌkəʊ ə ˈles ‖ ˌkoʊ- **~ed** t **~es** ɪz əz
~ing ɪŋ

coalescenc|e ˌkəʊ ə ˈles ᵊn|s ‖ ˌkoʊ- **~es** ɪz əz

coalescent ˌkəʊ ə ˈles ᵊnt ◂ ‖ ˌkoʊ-

coalfac|e ˈkəʊl feɪs→ˈkɒʊl- ‖ ˈkoʊl- **~es** ɪz əz

coalfield ˈkəʊl fiːᵊld→ˈkɒʊl- ‖ ˈkoʊl- **~s** z

coalfish ˈkəʊl fɪʃ→ˈkɒʊl- ‖ ˈkoʊl-

coalhole ˈkəʊl həʊl→ˈkɒʊl hɒʊl ‖ ˈkoʊl hoʊl
~s z

coal|house ˈkəʊl |haʊs→ˈkɒʊl- ‖ ˈkoʊl-
~houses haʊz ɪz -əz

Coalisland kəʊl ˈaɪl ənd ‖ koʊl-

Coalite *tdmk* ˈkəʊl aɪt ‖ ˈkoʊl-

coalition ˌkəʊ ə ˈlɪʃ ᵊn ‖ ˌkoʊ- **~s** z

coal|man ˈkəʊl mən→ˈkɒʊl-, -mæn ‖ ˈkoʊl-
~men mən men

coalmine ˈkəʊl maɪn→ˈkɒʊl- ‖ ˈkoʊl- **~s** z

coalminer ˈkəʊl ˌmaɪn ə→ˈkɒʊl-
‖ ˈkoʊl ˌmaɪn ᵊr **~s** z

coalpit ˈkəʊl pɪt→ˈkɒʊl- ‖ ˈkoʊl- **~s** s

Coalport ˈkəʊl pɔːt→ˈkɒʊl- ‖ ˈkoʊl pɔːrt
-poʊrt

Coalsack ˈkəʊl sæk→ˈkɒʊl- ‖ ˈkoʊl-

coalscuttle ˈkəʊl ˌskʌt ᵊl→ˈkɒʊl-
‖ ˈkoʊl ˌskʌt̮ ᵊl **~s** z

Coalville ˈkəʊl vɪl→ˈkɒʊl-, -vᵊl ‖ ˈkoʊl-

coaming ˈkəʊm ɪŋ ‖ ˈkoʊm ɪŋ **~s** z

coarse kɔːs ‖ kɔːrs koʊrs *(= course)* **coarser**
ˈkɔːs ə ‖ ˈkɔːrs ᵊr ˈkoʊrs- **coarsest** ˈkɔːs ɪst
-əst ‖ ˈkɔːrs əst ˈkoʊrs-

coarse-grained ˌkɔːs ˈɡreɪnd ◂ ‖ ˌkɔːrs-
ˌkoʊrs-

coarsely ˈkɔːs li ‖ ˈkɔːrs- ˈkoʊrs-

coarsen ˈkɔːs ᵊn ‖ ˈkɔːrs ᵊn ˈkoʊrs- **~ed** d
~ing ˌɪŋ **~s** z

coarseness ˈkɔːs nəs -nɪs ‖ ˈkɔːrs- ˈkoʊrs-

coarticu|late ˌkəʊ ɑː ˈtɪk ju |leɪt -jə-
‖ ˌkoʊ ɑːr ˈtɪk jə- **~lated** leɪt ɪd -əd ‖ leɪt̮ əd
~lates leɪts **~lating** leɪt ɪŋ ‖ leɪt̮ ɪŋ

coarticulation ˌkəʊ ɑː ˌtɪk ju ˈleɪʃ ᵊn -jə-
‖ ˌkoʊ ɑːr ˌtɪk jə- **~s** z

coarticulatory ˌkəʊ ɑː ˈtɪk jʊl ət̮ ᵊr i -ˈʼ•jəl-;
-ˌtɪk ju ˈleɪt ᵊr i, -ˌ•jə-, ˌ•ʼ•••••
‖ ˌkoʊ ɑːr ˈtɪk jəl ə tɔːr i -toʊr i

coast kəʊst ‖ koʊst **coasted** ˈkəʊst ɪd -əd
‖ ˈkoʊst əd **coasting** ˈkəʊst ɪŋ ‖ ˈkoʊst ɪŋ
coasts kəʊsts ‖ koʊsts

coastal ˈkəʊst ᵊl ‖ ˈkoʊst-

coaster ˈkəʊst ə ‖ ˈkoʊst ᵊr **~s** z

coastguard ˈkəʊst ɡɑːd ‖ ˈkoʊst ɡɑːrd **~s** z

coastguards|man ˈkəʊst ɡɑːdz |mən ‖ ˈkoʊst
ɡɑːrdz- **~men** mən men

coastline ˈkəʊst laɪn ‖ ˈkoʊst-

coastward ˈkəʊst wəd ‖ ˈkoʊst wᵊrd **~s** z

coastwise ˈkəʊst waɪz ‖ ˈkoʊst-

coat kəʊt ‖ koʊt **coated** ˈkəʊt ɪd -əd
‖ ˈkoʊt̮ əd **coating** ˈkəʊt ɪŋ ‖ ˈkoʊt̮ ɪŋ **coats**
kəʊts ‖ koʊts
ˈcoat ˌhanger

Coarticulation

1 Speech sounds tend to be influenced by the speech sounds that surround them. **Coarticulation** is the retention of a phonetic feature that was present in a preceding sound, or the anticipation of a feature that will be needed for a following sound. Most ALLOPHONIC variation – though not all – is coarticulatory.

2 For example, a vowel or liquid that is adjacent to a nasal tends to be somewhat nasalized. This **coarticulation of nasality** applies to the vowels in **money** 'mʌn i, and to the l in **elm** elm.

3 The English LENIS ('voiced') obstruents tend to lose their voicing when adjacent to a voiceless consonant or to a pause. For example, this applies to the consonants in **good** gʊd when said in isolation, or in a phrase such as **the first good thing**. This is **coarticulation of voicing** (see VOICED AND VOICELESS).

4 Many consonants vary somewhat, depending on which vowel comes after them. Thus the ʃ in **sheep** ʃiːp is more iː-like, the ʃ in **short** ʃɔːt ‖ ʃɔːrt is more ɔː-like. This is **coarticulation of place of articulation**. Other examples are the d in **dream** driːm (post-alveolar because of the r) and the b in **obvious** 'ɒb vi̯ əs ‖ 'ɑːb vi̯ əs (sometimes labiodental because of the v).

5 For cases where coarticulation is variable, and may result in what sounds like a different phoneme, see ASSIMILATION.

C

Coatbridge 'kəʊt brɪdʒ ˌ•'• ‖ 'koʊt- —*locally* ˌ•'•
coatee ˌkəʊt iː ‖ ˌkəʊ 'tiː ‖ ˌkoʊ 'tiː ~s z
Coates, Coats kəʊts ‖ koʊts
coati kəʊ 'ɑːt i ‖ koʊ 'ɑːt̬ i ~s z
coati-mundi kəʊ ˌɑːt i 'mʌnd i -'mʊnd- ‖ koʊ ˌɑːt̬-
coating 'kəʊt ɪŋ ‖ 'koʊt̬ ɪŋ ~s z
coat-tail 'kəʊt teɪəl ‖ 'koʊt- ~s z
coauthor ˌkəʊ 'ɔːθ ə '•ˌ•• ‖ ˌkoʊ 'ɔːθ ər -'ɑːθ- ~ed d **coauthoring** ˌkəʊ 'ɔːθ ər ɪŋ ‖ ˌkoʊ- -'ɑːθ- ~s z
coax v kəʊks ‖ koʊks (= *cokes*) **coaxed** kəʊkst ‖ koʊkst **coaxes** 'kəʊks ɪz -əz ‖ 'koʊks əz **coaxing** 'kəʊks ɪŋ ‖ 'koʊks ɪŋ
coax n 'cable' 'kəʊ æks ‖ 'koʊ- ~es ɪz əz
coaxial ˌ(ˌ)kəʊ 'æks i̯ əl ˌ(ˌ)koʊ- ~ly i
cob kɒb ‖ kɑːb **cobs** kɒbz ‖ kɑːbz
Cobain kəʊ 'beɪn ‖ koʊ- '••
cobalt 'kəʊb ɔːlt -ɒlt ‖ 'koʊb- -ɑːlt
Cobb kɒb ‖ kɑːb
cobber 'kɒb ə ‖ 'kɑːb ər ~s z
Cobbett 'kɒb ɪt §-ət ‖ 'kɑːb-
cobble 'kɒb əl ‖ 'kɑːb- ~s z
Cobbleigh 'kɒb li ‖ 'kɑːb li
cobbler 'kɒb lə ‖ 'kɑːb lər ~s z
cobblestone 'kɒb əl stəʊn ‖ 'kɑːb əl stoʊn ~s z
Cobbold 'kɒb əʊld →-ɒʊld ‖ 'kɑːb oʊld

Cobden 'kɒb dən ‖ 'kɑːb-
cobelligerent ˌkəʊ bə 'lɪdʒ ər_ənt ◂ -bɪ- ‖ ˌkoʊ- ~s s
Cobh, Cóbh kəʊv ‖ koʊv —*Irish* [koːv]
Cobham 'kɒb əm ‖ 'kɑːb-
coble 'kəʊb əl 'kɒb- ‖ 'koʊb- ~s z
Cobleigh, Cobley 'kɒb li ‖ 'kɑːb-
Coblenz kəʊ 'blents ‖ koʊ- —*Ger* Koblenz ['koː blɛnts]
cobnut 'kɒb nʌt ‖ 'kɑːb- ~s s
COBOL, Cobol 'kəʊb ɒl ‖ 'koʊb ɔːl -ɑːl
cobra 'kəʊb rə 'kɒb- ‖ 'koʊb- ~s z
coburg, C~ 'kəʊ bɜːg ‖ 'koʊ bɜːg —*Ger* ['koː bʊʁk]
cobweb 'kɒb web ‖ 'kɑːb- ~s z
coca 'kəʊk ə ‖ 'koʊk ə
Coca-Cola *tdmk* ˌkəʊk ə 'kəʊl ə ‖ ˌkoʊk ə 'koʊl ə
cocaine ˌ(ˌ)kəʊ 'keɪn kə- ‖ ˌ(ˌ)koʊ- '••
coccal 'kɒk əl ‖ 'kɑːk əl
cocci 'kɒks aɪ ‖ 'kɒk- ‖ 'kɑːks-
coccidiosis kɒk ˌsɪd i 'əʊs ɪs -ˌkɒks ɪd-, §-əs ‖ kɑːk ˌsɪd i 'oʊs əs ˌkɑːks ɪd-
coccus 'kɒk əs ‖ 'kɑːk-
coccyx 'kɒks ɪks ‖ 'kɑːks- **coccyges** kɒk 'saɪdʒ iːz ‖ kɑːk-
Coch *in Welsh names* kəʊx kəʊk ‖ koʊk —*Welsh* [koːχ]

co|chair ˌkəʊ ˈtʃeə ˈˌ•• ‖ ˌkoʊ ˈtʃeᵊr —*Some speakers stress the v* ˌ•ˈ• *but the n* ˈ••. ~chaired ˈtʃeəd ‖ ˈtʃeᵊrd ~chairing ˈtʃeər ɪŋ ‖ ˈtʃer ɪŋ ~chairs ˈtʃeəz ‖ ˈtʃeᵊrz

Cochin ˈkəʊtʃ ɪn ˈkɒtʃ-, §-ən ‖ ˈkoʊtʃ-

cochineal ˌkɒtʃ ɪ ˈniːᵊl -ə-, ˈ••• ‖ ˌkɑːtʃ- ˌkoʊtʃ-

cochle|a ˈkɒk li‿|ə ‖ ˈkoʊk- ˈkɑːk- ~ae iː ~ar ə ‖ ᵊr

Cochran, Cochrane ˈkɒk rən ˈkɒx- ‖ ˈkɑːk-

cock kɒk ‖ kɑːk cocked kɒkt ‖ kɑːkt cocking ˈkɒk ɪŋ ‖ ˈkɑːk ɪŋ cocks kɒks ‖ kɑːks (= cox) ˌcocked ˈhat

cockad|e kɒ ˈkeɪd ‖ kɑː- ~ed ɪd əd ~es z

cock-a-doodle-doo ˌkɒk ə ˌduːd ᵊl ˈduː ‖ ˌkɑːk-

cock-a-hoop ˌkɒk ə ˈhuːp ‖ ˌkɑːk-

Cockaigne kɒ ˈkeɪn kə- ‖ kɑː-

cock-a-leekie ˌkɒk ə ˈliːk i ‖ ˌkɑːk-

cockalorum ˌkɒk ə ˈlɔːr əm ‖ ˌkɑːk- -ˈloʊr- ~s z

cockamamie, cockamamy ˌkɒk ə ˈmeɪm i ◂ ‖ ˌkɑːk-

cock-and-bull ˌkɒk ən ˈbʊl →-ŋ-, →-əm- ‖ ˌkɑːk-

cockateel, cockatiel ˌkɒk ə ˈtiːᵊl ‖ ˌkɑːk- ~s z

cockatoo ˌkɒk ə ˈtuː ˈ••• ‖ ˈkɑːk ə tuː ~s z

cockatric|e ˈkɒk ə traɪs -trɪs, -trəs ‖ ˈkɑːk- ~es ɪz əz

Cockayne kɒ ˈkeɪn kə- ‖ kɑː-

Cockburn ˈkəʊb ən -ɜːn ‖ ˈkoʊ bɜːn (!)

cockchafer ˈkɒk ˌtʃeɪf ə ‖ ˈkɑːk ˌtʃeɪf ᵊr ~s z

Cockcroft (i) ˈkɒk krɒft -rɒft ‖ ˈkɑːk krɔːft -rɔːft, -krɑːft, -rɑːft; (ii) ˈkəʊ krɒft ‖ ˈkoʊ krɔːft -krɑːft

cockcrow ˈkɒk krəʊ ‖ ˈkɑːk kroʊ

cocker, C~ ˈkɒk ə ‖ ˈkɑːk ᵊr ~s z ˌcocker ˈspaniel

cockerel ˈkɒk ᵊr_əl ‖ ˈkɑːk- ~s z

Cockermouth ˈkɒk ə maʊθ -məθ ‖ ˈkɑːk ᵊr-

cockeyed ˌkɒk ˈaɪd ◂ ˈ•• ‖ ˌkɑːk-

Cockfield ˈkəʊ fiːᵊld ‖ ˈkoʊ- (!)

cockfight ˈkɒk faɪt ‖ ˈkɑːk- ~s s

cockfighting ˈkɒk ˌfaɪt ɪŋ ‖ ˈkɑːk ˌfaɪt ɪŋ

Cockfosters ˈkɒk fɒst əz ˌ•ˈ•• ‖ ˈkɑːk fɔːst ᵊrz -fɑːst-, ˌ•ˈ••

cockhorse ˌkɒk ˈhɔːs ◂ ‖ ˌkɑːk ˈhɔːrs ◂

cockieleekie ˌkɒk i ˈliːk i -ə- ‖ ˌkɑːk-

cockle ˈkɒk ᵊl ‖ ˈkɑːk ᵊl ~s z

cockleshell ˈkɒk ᵊl ʃel ‖ ˈkɑːk- ~s z

cockney, C~ ˈkɒk ni ‖ ˈkɑːk- ~ism/s ˌɪz əm/z ~s z

cock-of-the-rock ˌkɒk əv ðə ˈrɒk ‖ ˌkɑːk əv ðə ˈrɑːk

cockpit ˈkɒk pɪt ‖ ˈkɑːk- ~s s

cockroach ˈkɒk rəʊtʃ ‖ ˈkɑːk roʊtʃ ~es ɪz əz

Cockroft (i) ˈkɒk rɒft ‖ ˈkɑːk rɔːft -rɑːft, (ii) ˈkəʊ krɒft ‖ ˈkoʊ krɔːft -krɑːft

Cocks kɒks ‖ kɑːks

cockscomb ˈkɒks kəʊm ‖ ˈkɑːks koʊm ~s z

cocksfoot ˈkɒks fʊt ‖ ˈkɑːks- ~s s

cock|shy ˈkɒk |ʃaɪ ‖ ˈkɑːk- ~shies ʃaɪz

cockspur ˈkɒk spɜː ‖ ˈkɑːk spɜː: ~s z

cocksucker ˈkɒk ˌsʌk ə ‖ ˈkɑːk ˌsʌk ᵊr ~s z

cocksure ˌkɒk ˈʃɔː ◂ -ˈʃʊə ‖ ˌkɑːk ˈʃʊᵊr ◂ -ˈʃɜː: ~ly li ~ness nəs nɪs

cocktail ˈkɒk teɪᵊl ‖ ˈkɑːk- ~s z ˈcocktail lounge; ˈcocktail ˌparty; ˈcocktail stick

cock-up ˈkɒk ʌp ‖ ˈkɑːk- ~s s

cock|y ˈkɒk |i ‖ ˈkɑːk li ~ier i_ə ‖ i_ᵊr ~iest i_ɪst i_əst ~ily ɪ li əl i ~iness i nəs i nɪs

cocky-leeky ˌkɒk i ˈliːk i -ə- ‖ ˌkɑːk-

coco, Coco ˈkəʊk əʊ ‖ ˈkoʊk oʊ ˌcoco de ˈmer meə ‖ meᵊr

cocoa ˈkəʊk əʊ ‖ ˈkoʊk oʊ ~s z

coconut ˈkəʊk ə nʌt ‖ ˈkoʊk- ~s s ˌcoconut ˈmatting; ˈcoconut shy

cocoon kə ˈkuːn ~ed d ~ing ɪŋ ~s z

Cocos ˈkəʊk əs -ɒs ‖ ˈkoʊk əs -oʊs

cocotte kə ˈkɒt kɒ-, kəʊ- ‖ koʊ ˈkɑːt kɑː-, -ˈkɔːt —*Fr* [kɔ kɔt] ~s s

cocoyam ˈkəʊk əʊ jæm ‖ ˈkoʊk oʊ- ~s z

Cocteau ˈkɒkt əʊ ‖ kɑːk ˈtoʊ kɔːk- —*Fr* [kɔk to]

cod kɒd ‖ kɑːd codded ˈkɒd ɪd -əd ‖ ˈkɑːd əd codding ˈkɒd ɪŋ ‖ ˈkɑːd ɪŋ cods kɒdz ‖ kɑːdz

COD ˈcash on delivery ˌsiː əʊ ˈdiː ‖ -oʊ-

coda ˈkəʊd ə ‖ ˈkoʊd ə ~s z

coddl|e ˈkɒd ᵊl ‖ ˈkɑːd- ~ed d ~es z ~ing ˌɪŋ

code kəʊd ‖ koʊd coded ˈkəʊd ɪd -əd ‖ ˈkoʊd əd codes kəʊdz ‖ koʊdz coding/s ˈkəʊd ɪŋ/z ‖ ˈkoʊd ɪŋ/z

codeine ˈkəʊd iːn ‖ ˈkoʊd-

coder ˈkəʊd ə ‖ ˈkoʊd ᵊr ~s z

codeword ˈkəʊd wɜːd ‖ ˈkoʊd wɜːd ~s z

codex ˈkəʊd eks ‖ ˈkoʊd- ~es ɪz əz codices ˈkəʊd ɪ siːz ˈkɒd-, -ə- ‖ ˈkoʊd ə- ˈkɑːd-

codfish ˈkɒd fɪʃ ‖ ˈkɑːd-

codger ˈkɒdʒ ə ‖ ˈkɑːdʒ ᵊr ~s z

codice... —*see* codex

codicil ˈkəʊd ɪ sɪl ˈkɒd-, -ə- ‖ ˈkɑːd ə sɪl -əs ᵊl ~s z

codification ˌkəʊd ɪf ɪ ˈkeɪʃ ᵊn ˌ•əf-, §-ə-ˈ•- ‖ ˌkɑːd- ˌkoʊd- ~s z

codi|fy ˈkəʊd ɪ |faɪ -ə- ‖ ˈkɑːd- ˈkoʊd- ~fied faɪd ~fier/s faɪ_ə/z ‖ faɪ_ᵊr/z ~fies faɪz ~fying faɪ ɪŋ

coding ˈkəʊd ɪŋ ‖ ˈkoʊd- ~s z

codlin ˈkɒd lɪn §-lən ‖ ˈkɑːd- ~s z

codling ˈkɒd lɪŋ ‖ ˈkɑːd- ~s z

cod-liver oil ˌkɒd lɪv ər ˈɔɪᵊl ◂ ‖ ˈkɑːd lɪv ᵊr ˌɔɪᵊl ◂

codomain ˌkəʊ də ˈmeɪn -dəʊ-, ˈ•••• ‖ ˌkoʊ doʊ- ~s z

codon ˈkəʊd ɒn ‖ ˈkoʊd ɑːn ~s z

codpiec|e ˈkɒd piːs →ˈkɒb- ‖ ˈkɑːd- ~es ɪz əz

Codrington ˈkɒdr ɪŋ tən ‖ ˈkɑːdr-

codriver ˈkəʊ ˌdraɪv ə ˌ•ˈ•• ‖ ˈkoʊ ˌdraɪv ᵊr ~s z

codswallop ˈkɒdz ˌwɒl əp ‖ ˈkɑːdz ˌwɑːl-

Cody ˈkəʊd i ‖ ˈkoʊd i

Coe kəʊ ‖ koʊ

coed ˈkəʊ ed ˌ•ˈ• ‖ ˈkoʊ- ~s z

Coed *in Welsh placenames* kɔɪd —*Welsh* [kɔid, koːd, koid]
coeducation ˌkəʊ ˌed ju ˈkeɪʃ ᵊn -ˌedʒ u-
‖ ˌkoʊ ˌedʒ ə-
coeducational ˌkəʊ ˌed ju ˈkeɪʃ ᵊn‿əl ◂ -ˌedʒ u-
‖ ˌkoʊ ˌedʒ ə- **~ly** i
coefficient ˌkəʊ ɪ ˈfɪʃ ᵊnt ◂ -ə- ‖ ˌkoʊ- **~s** s
ˌcoefˌficient of ˈfriction
coelacanth ˈsiːl ə kænᵗθ **~s** s
coelenterate sɪ ˈlent ə reɪt sə-, siː-, -ər ət,
-ər ɪt ‖ -ˈlenţ- **~s** s
coeliac ˈsiːl i æk
ˈcoeliac diˌsease
coenobite ˈsiːn əʊ baɪt ‖ -ə- **~s** s
coequal ₍ₒ₎kəʊ ˈiːk wəl ‖ ₍ₒ₎koʊ- **~ly** i **~s** z
coerc|e kəʊ ˈɜːs ‖ koʊ ˈɝːs **~ed** t **~er/s** ə/z
‖ ᵊr/z **~es** ɪz əz **~ing** ɪŋ
coercible kəʊ ˈɜːs əb ᵊl -ɪb ᵊl ‖ koʊ ˈɝːs-
coercion kəʊ ˈɜːʃ ᵊn ‖ koʊ ˈɝːʃ ᵊn -ˈɝːʒ-
coercive kəʊ ˈɜːs ɪv ‖ koʊ ˈɝːs- **~ly** li **~ness**
nəs nɪs
coercivity ˌkəʊ ɜː ˈsɪv ət i -ɪt i
‖ ˌkoʊ ɝː ˈsɪv əţ i
coeternal ˌkəʊ ɪ ˈtɜːn ᵊl ◂ -iː-
‖ ˌkoʊ ɪ ˈtɝːn ᵊl ◂ **~ly** i
Coetzee ₍ₒ₎kuːt ˈsɪə -ˈsiː- —*Afrikaans* [ku ˈtsɪə]
Coeur d'Alene ˌkɜː də ˈleɪn -dᵊl ˈeɪn
‖ ˌkɝːd ᵊl ˈeɪn
Coeur de Lion ˌkɜː də ˈliː ɒ̃ ˌkɜːd ᵊl ˈiː-, -ɒn,
-ᵊn ‖ ˌkɝː də ˈlaɪ ən ˌkɝːd ᵊl ˈaɪ ən —*Fr*
[kœʁ də ljɔ̃]
coeval kəʊ ˈiːv ᵊl ‖ koʊ- **~ly** i **~s** z
coexist ˌkəʊ ɪg ˈzɪst -ɪk-, -əg-, -ək-, -eg-, -ek-
‖ ˌkoʊ- **~ed** ɪd əd **~ing** ɪŋ **~s** s
coexist|ence ˌkəʊ ɪg ˈzɪst ᵊnᵗs -ɪk-, -əg-, -ək-,
-eg-, -ek- ‖ ˌkoʊ- **~ent/ly** ᵊnt /li
coextensive ˌkəʊ ɪk ˈstenᵗs ɪv -ek-, -ək-
‖ ˌkoʊ- **~ly** li **~ness** nəs nɪs
cofactor ˈkəʊ ˌfækt ə ‖ ˈkoʊ ˌfækt ᵊr **~s** z
CofE ˌsiː‿əv ˈiː

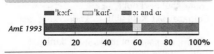

COFFEE

■ˈkɔːf- ▨ˈkɑːf- ▤ˈɔː and ɑː

AmE 1993					
0	20	40	60	80	100%

coffee ˈkɒf i ‖ ˈkɔːf i ˈkɑːf- **~s** z —*AmE 1993*
poll panel preference: ˈkɔːf- 57%, ˈkɑːf- 6%;
no distinction made between ɔː *and* ɑː, 37%.
ˈcoffee bar; ˈcoffee break; ˈcoffee cup;
ˈcoffee klatch klætʃ ‖ klɑːtʃ, klʌtʃ; ˈcoffee
house; ˈcoffee ˌmorning; ˈcoffee shop;
ˈcoffee ˌtable
coffeemaker ˈkɒf i ˌmeɪk ə ‖ ˈkɔːf i ˌmeɪk ᵊr
ˈkɑːf- **~s** z
coffeepot ˈkɒf i pɒt ‖ ˈkɔːf i pɑːt ˈkɑːf- **~s** s
coffee-table book ˈkɒf i teɪb ᵊl ˌbʊk §-ˌbuːk
‖ ˈkɔːf- ˈkɑːf-
coffer ˈkɒf ə ‖ ˈkɔːf ᵊr ˈkɑːf- **~s** z
cofferdam ˈkɒf ə dæm ‖ ˈkɔːf ᵊr- ˈkɑːf- **~s** z
Coffey ˈkɒf i ‖ ˈkɔːf i ˈkɑːf-
coffin, C~ ˈkɒf ɪn §-ᵊn ‖ ˈkɔːf ᵊn ˈkɑːf- **~s** z
coffle ˈkɒf ᵊl ‖ ˈkɔːf- ˈkɑːf- **~s** z
cog kɒg ‖ kɑːg **cogs** kɒgz ‖ kɑːgz

Cogan ˈkəʊg ən ‖ ˈkoʊg ən
cogency ˈkəʊdʒ ᵊnᵗs i ‖ ˈkoʊdʒ-
cogent ˈkəʊdʒ ᵊnt ‖ ˈkoʊdʒ- **~ly** li
Coggan ˈkɒg ən ‖ ˈkɑːg-
Coggeshall *(i)* ˈkɒg ɪʃ ᵊl ˈkɒks ᵊl ‖ ˈkɑːg-, *(ii)*
ˈkɒgz ɔːl ‖ ˈkɑːgz- -ɑːl —*The place in Essex
is (i). the family name (ii)*
Coghill ˈkɒg hɪl -ɪl ‖ ˈkɑːg-
Coghlan *(i)* ˈkəʊl ən ‖ ˈkoʊl-, *(ii)* ˈkɒx lən ˈkɒg-
‖ ˈkɔːk- ˈkɑːk-
cogi|tate ˈkɒdʒ ɪ |teɪt -ə- ‖ ˈkɑːdʒ- **~tated**
teɪt ɪd -əd ‖ teɪţ əd **~tates** teɪts **~tating**
teɪt ɪŋ ‖ teɪţ ɪŋ
cogitation ˌkɒdʒ ɪ ˈteɪʃ ᵊn -ə- ‖ ˌkɑːdʒ-
cogitative ˈkɒdʒ ɪt ət ɪv ˈ•ət-; -ɪ teɪt-, -ə teɪt-
‖ ˈkɑːdʒ ə teɪţ ɪv **~ly** li **~ness** nəs nɪs
cogito ergo sum ˌkɒg ɪt əʊ ˌɜːg əʊ ˈsʊm
§ˌ•ət-, -ˈsʌm ‖ ˌkoʊg ə toʊ ˌɝːg oʊ ˈsʊm
-ˌerg-
cognac, C~ ˈkɒn jæk ‖ ˈkoʊn- —*Fr* [kɔ njak]
~s s
cognate ˈkɒg neɪt ₍ₒ₎•ˈ• ‖ ˈkɑːg- **~ly** li **~s** s
cognis... —*see* **cogniz...**
cognition kɒg ˈnɪʃ ᵊn ‖ kɑːg-
cognitive ˈkɒg nət ɪv -nɪt- ‖ ˈkɑːg nəţ ɪv **~ly** li
cogniz|ance ˈkɒg nɪz ᵊnᵗs -nəz-; kɒg ˈnaɪz-;
ˈkɒn ɪz-, -əz- ‖ ˈkɑːg- **~ant** ᵊnt
cognomen ₍ₒ₎kɒg ˈnəʊm en -ən
‖ ₍ₒ₎kɑːg ˈnoʊm ən ˈkɑːg nəm-
cognoscent|e ˌkɒg nə ˈʃent| i -nəʊ-, -ˈsent-, -iː;
ˌkɒn jəʊ- ‖ ˌkɑːn jə ˈʃenţ i -ə- **~i** i iː
cogwheel ˈkɒg wiːᵊl -hwiːᵊl ‖ ˈkɑːg ʰwiːᵊl **~s** z
cohab|it ₍ₒ₎kəʊ ˈhæb |ɪt §-ət ‖ ₍ₒ₎koʊ ˈhæb |ət
~ited ɪt ɪd əd §ət-, -əd ‖ əţ əd **~iting** ɪt ɪŋ §ət-
‖ əţ ɪŋ **~its** ɪts §əts ‖ əts
cohabitation kəʊ ˌhæb ɪ ˈteɪʃ ᵊn ˌ•ˌ•-, -əˈ•-
‖ koʊ-
cohabitee kəʊ ˌhæb ɪ ˈtiː, ˌ•ˌ•-, -əˈ• ‖ koʊ- **~s**
z
Cohen ˈkəʊ ɪn §-ən ‖ ˈkoʊ ən
coher|e kəʊ ˈhɪə ‖ koʊ ˈhɪᵊr **~ed** d **~es** z
cohering kəʊ ˈhɪər ɪŋ ‖ koʊ ˈhɪr ɪŋ
coherenc|e kəʊ ˈhɪər ᵊnᵗs ‖ koʊ ˈhɪr- **~y** i
coherent kəʊ ˈhɪər ᵊnt ‖ koʊ ˈhɪr- **~ly** li
cohesion kəʊ ˈhiːʒ ᵊn ‖ koʊ-
cohesive kəʊ ˈhiːs ɪv -ˈhiːz- ‖ koʊ- **~ly** li
~ness nəs nɪs
coho ˈkəʊ həʊ ‖ ˈkoʊ hoʊ
coho|bate ˈkəʊ həʊ |beɪt ‖ ˈkoʊ hoʊ- **~bated**
beɪt ɪd -əd ‖ beɪţ əd **~bates** beɪts **~bating**
beɪt ɪŋ ‖ beɪţ ɪŋ
cohobation ˌkəʊ həʊ ˈbeɪʃ ᵊn ‖ ˌkoʊ hoʊ-
Cohoes kə ˈhəʊz ‖ -ˈhoʊz
cohort ˈkəʊ hɔːt ‖ ˈkoʊ hɔːrt **~s** s
cohosh ˈkəʊ hɒʃ ‖ ˈkoʊ hɑːʃ **~es** ɪz əz
COHSE ˈkəʊz i ‖ ˈkoʊz i
coif *'headdress'* kɔɪf **coifs** kɔɪfs
coif *'coiffure'* kwɑːf kwæf **coiffed** kwɑːft
kwæft **coiffing** ˈkwɑːf ɪŋ ˈkwæf- **coifs**
kwɑːfs kwæfs
coiffeur kwɑː ˈfɜː kwɒ-, kwæ-, kwʌ- ‖ -ˈfɝː
—*Fr* [kwa fœːʁ] **~s** z

C

coiffure kwɑː ˈfjʊə kwɒ-, kwæ-, kwʌ- ‖ -ˈfjʊ⁰r
—*Fr* [kwa fyːʁ] ~**d** d ~**s** z
coign kɔɪn (= *coin*)
coil kɔɪ⁰l **coiled** kɔɪ⁰ld **coiling** ˈkɔɪl ɪŋ **coils**
kɔɪ⁰lz
ˈ**coil spring**
Coimbra ˈkwɪm brə ˈkwiːm- —*Port*
[ˈkwĩ bɾɐ]
coin kɔɪn ˈkɔɪ ɪn **coined** kɔɪnd ˈkɔɪ ɪnd
coining ˈkɔɪn ɪŋ ˈkɔɪ ɪn ɪŋ **coins** kɔɪnz
ˈkɔɪ ɪnz
coinag|e ˈkɔɪn ɪdʒ ~**es** ɪz əz
coincid|e ˌkəʊ ɪn ˈsaɪd -ən- ‖ ˌkoʊ- ~**ed** ɪd əd
~**es** z ~**ing** ɪŋ
coincidenc|e kəʊ ˈɪnⁱs ɪd ənⁱs -əd- ‖ koʊ-
-ə denⁱs ~**es** ɪz əz
coincident kəʊ ˈɪnⁱs ɪd ənt -əd- ‖ koʊ- -ə dent
coincidental kəʊ ˌɪnⁱs ɪ ˈdent ᵊl ◄ , •••-, -ə’ ••
‖ koʊ ˌɪnⁱs ə ˈdent̮ ᵊl , ••• ~**ly** i
coin-op ˈkɔɪn ɒp ‖ -ɑːp ~**s** s
Cointreau *tdmk* ˈkwɒntr əʊ ˈkwɑːntr-,
ˈkwæntr- ‖ kwɑːn ˈtroʊ —*Fr* [kwɛ̃ tʁo] ~**s**
z
coir ˈkɔɪ ə ‖ kɔɪ⁰r
coit, Coit kɔɪt
coital ˈkəʊ ɪt ᵊl §-ət-; ˈkɔɪt ᵊl ‖ ˈkoʊ ət̮ ᵊl
coition kəʊ ˈɪʃ ᵊn ‖ koʊ-
coitus ˈkəʊ ɪt əs §-ət-; ˈkɔɪt əs ‖ ˈkoʊ ət̮ əs
ˈkɔɪt̮ əs
ˌcoitus ˌinter’ruptus ˌɪnt ə ˈrʌpt əs ‖ ˌɪnt̮-;
ˌcoitus ˌreser’vatus ˌrez ə ˈvɑːt əs , •ɜː-,
-ˈveɪt- ‖ -ᵊr ˈveɪt əs
cojones kə ˈhəʊn ɪz -eɪz ‖ -ˈhoʊn- -eɪs —*Sp*
[ko ˈxo nes]
coke kəʊk ‖ koʊk **coked** kəʊkt koʊkt **cokes**
kəʊks ‖ koʊks **coking** ˈkəʊk ɪŋ ‖ ˈkoʊk ɪŋ
Coke *family name* (i) kʊk §kuːk, (ii)
kəʊk ‖ koʊk
Coke *tdmk* kəʊk ‖ koʊk **Cokes** kəʊks ‖ koʊks
Coker ˈkəʊk ə ‖ ˈkoʊk ᵊr
col, Col kɒl ‖ kɑːl **cols** kɒlz ‖ kɑːlz
col., Col. → **colonel, column**
col- ˌkɒ, kə ‖ ˌkɑː, kə —*This prefix, found only*
before l, *is pronounced stressed* ˈkɒ ‖ ˌkɑː: *(1) if*
the following syllable is unstressed
(ˌcolloˈcation), *(2) in a few two-syllable nouns*
(ˈcolleague; *but* colˈlapse *with* kə-); *and (3)*
occasionally, in context, when contrastively
stressed (to select and ˈcollect). *Otherwise it is*
usually weak kə (colˈlision).
cola ˈkəʊl ə ‖ ˈkoʊl ə ~**s** z
colander ˈkʌl ənd ə ˈkɒl-, -ɪnd- ‖ -ᵊr ˈkɑːl- ~**s**
z
Colby (i) ˈkəʊl bi →ˈkɒʊl- ‖ ˈkoʊl-, (ii)
ˈkɒl- ‖ ˈkɑːl-
Colchester ˈkəʊltʃ ɪst ə →ˈkɒʊltʃ-, §ˈkɒltʃ-,
-əst- ‖ ˈkoʊl ˌtʃest ᵊr
colchicum ˈkɒltʃ ɪk əm ˈkɒlk- ‖ ˈkɑːltʃ- ~**s** z
Colchis ˈkɒlk ɪs §-əs ‖ ˈkɑːlk-
cold kəʊld →kɒʊld ‖ koʊld **colder** ˈkəʊld ə
→ˈkɒʊld- ‖ ˈkoʊld ᵊr **coldest** ˈkəʊld ɪst
→ˈkɒʊld, -əst ‖ ˈkoʊld- **colds** kəʊldz
→kɒʊldz ‖ koʊldz

ˌcold ˈchisel; ˌcold ˈcomfort; ˈcold cream;
ˌcold ˈcuts, , • ˈ•; ˌcold ˈfeet; ˌcold ˈfish;
ˌcold ˈframe; ˌcold ˈfront, ˈ• •; ˈcold snap;
ˌcold ˈsore; ˌcold ˈsteel; ˈcold ˈstorage;
ˌcold ˈsweat; ˌcold ˈturkey; ˌcold ˈwar◄
cold-blooded ˌkəʊld ˈblʌd ɪd ◄ →ˌkɒʊld-, -əd
‖ ˌkoʊld- ~**ly** li ~**ness** nəs nɪs
cold-drawn ˌkəʊld ˈdrɔːn ◄ →ˌkɒʊld- ‖ ˌkoʊld-
-ˈdrɑːn
Coldfield ˈkəʊld fiː⁰ld →ˈkɒʊld- ‖ ˈkoʊld-
cold-hearted ˌkəʊld ˈhɑːt ɪd ◄ →ˌkɒʊld-, -əd
‖ ˌkoʊld ˈhɑːrt̮ əd ◄
coldish ˈkəʊld ɪʃ →ˈkɒʊld- ‖ ˈkoʊld ɪʃ
Colditz ˈkəʊld ɪts →ˈkɒʊld-, ˈkɒld-, §-əts
‖ ˈkoʊld- ˈkɑːld- —*Ger* [ˈkɔl dɪts]
cold|ly ˈkəʊld |li →ˈkɒʊld- ‖ ˈkoʊld- ~**ness** nəs
nɪs
cold-shoulder ˌkəʊld ˈʃəʊld ə →ˌkɒʊld ˈʃoʊld-
‖ ˌkoʊld ˈʃoʊld ᵊr ~**ed** d
Coldstream ˈkəʊld striːm →ˈkɒʊld- ‖ ˈkoʊld-
cole, Cole kəʊl →kɒʊl koʊl (= *coal*)
Colebrook ˈkəʊl brʊk →ˈkɒʊl- ‖ ˈkoʊl-
Coleclough (i) ˈkəʊl klʌf →ˈkɒʊl- ‖ ˈkoʊl-, (ii)
-klaʊ
colectom|y kəʊ ˈlekt əm |i ‖ koʊ- ~**ies** iz
Coleford ˈkəʊl fəd →ˈkɒʊl- ‖ ˈkoʊl fᵊrd
Coleherne ˈkəʊl hɜːn →ˈkɒʊl- ‖ ˈkoʊl hɜːn
• ˈ•
Coleman ˈkəʊl mən →ˈkɒʊl- ‖ ˈkoʊl-
Colenso kə ˈlenz əʊ ‖ -oʊ
coleoptera ˌkɒl i ˈɒpt ᵊr ə ‖ ˌkɑːl i ˈɑːpt-
coleopterous ˌkɒl i ˈɒpt ᵊr əs ◄ ‖ ˌkɑːl i ˈɑːpt-
Coleraine (ᵢ)ˌkəʊl ˈreɪn →(ᵢ)ˌkɒʊl- ‖ (ᵢ)ˌkoʊl-
Coleridge ˈkəʊl ᵊr ɪdʒ ‖ ˈkoʊl- ~ˈ**s** ɪz əz
Colerne (i) kə ˈlɜːn ‖ -ˈlɜːrn ; (ii)
ˈkɒl ən ‖ ˈkɑːl ᵊrn , (iii) ˈkʌl ən ‖ -ᵊrn
coleslaw ˈkəʊl slɔː →ˈkɒʊl- ‖ ˈkoʊl- -slɑː ~**s** z
Colet ˈkɒl ɪt -ət ‖ ˈkɑːl-
Colette kɒ ˈlet kə-, ˌkɒ- ‖ koʊ- —*Fr* [kɔ lɛt]
coleus ˈkəʊl i‿əs ‖ ˈkoʊl-
coley ˈkəʊl i ‖ ˈkoʊl i ~**s** z
Colgate *tdmk* ˈkəʊl geɪt →ˈkɒʊl-, ˈkɒl-, -gət,
-gɪt ‖ ˈkoʊl- -geɪt
colibri, C~ *tdmk* ˈkɒl ɪb ri -əb- ‖ ˈkɑːl-
colic ˈkɒl ɪk ‖ ˈkɑːl- ~**s** s
colicky ˈkɒl ɪk i ‖ ˈkɑːl-
coliform ˈkəʊl ɪ fɔːm ˈkɒl- ‖ ˈkoʊl ə fɔːrm
ˈkɑːl-
Colima kə ˈliːm ə —*Sp* [ko ˈli ma]
Colin (i) ˈkɒl ɪn -ən ‖ ˈkɑːl-, (ii) ˈkəʊl lɪn ‖ ˈkoʊ-
—*as a British name*, (i).
Colindale ˈkɒl ɪn deɪᵊl -ən- ‖ ˈkɑːl-
Coliseum ˌkɒl ə ˈsiː‿əm -ɪ- ‖ ˌkɑːl-
colitis kəʊ ˈlaɪt ɪs kɒ-, §-əs ‖ koʊ ˈlaɪt̮ əs kə-
Coll kɒl ‖ kɑːl
collabo|rate kə ˈlæb ə |reɪt ~**rated** reɪt ɪd -əd
‖ reɪt̮ əd ~**rates** reɪts ~**rating**
reɪt ɪŋ ‖ reɪt̮ ɪŋ
collaboration kə ˌlæb ə ˈreɪʃ ᵊn ~**s** z
collaborative kə ˈlæb ᵊr_ət ɪv -ə reɪt-
‖ -ə reɪt̮ ɪv -ᵊr_ət̮- ~**ly** li
collaborator kə ˈlæb ə reɪt ə ‖ -reɪt̮ ᵊr ~**s** z

collag|e kɒ 'lɑːʒ kə-; 'kɒl ɑːʒ ‖ kə- kɑː-, kɔː-, koʊ- —*Fr* [kɔ laːʒ] ~es ɪz əz
collagen 'kɒl ədʒ ən -ɪn ‖ 'kɑːl-
collaps|e kə 'læps ~ed t ~es ɪz əz ~ing ɪŋ
collapsibility kə ˌlæps ə 'bɪl ət i -ˌı-, -ɪt i ‖ -əɾ i
collapsible kə 'læps əb əl -ɪb-
collar 'kɒl ə ‖ 'kɑːl ər ~ed d collaring 'kɒl ər ɪŋ ‖ 'kɑːl- ~s z
'collar stud
collarbone 'kɒl ə bəʊn ‖ 'kɑːl ər boʊn ~s z
collard 'kɒl əd ‖ 'kɑːl ərd ~s z
collarette ˌkɒl ə 'ret ‖ ˌkɑːl- ~s s
col|late kə 'leɪt kɒ-, kəʊ- ‖ kɑː-, koʊ-, 'kɑːl eɪt ~lated 'leɪt ɪd -əd ‖ 'leɪɾ əd ~lates 'leɪts ~lating 'leɪt ɪŋ ‖ 'leɪɾ ɪŋ
collateral kə 'læt_ər əl kɒ- ‖ -'læɾ ər əl →-'lætr əl ~ly i
collation kə 'leɪʃ ən kɒ-, kəʊ- ‖ kɑː-, koʊ- ~s z
collator kə 'leɪt ə kɒ-, kəʊ-; 'kɒl eɪt ə, 'kəʊl- ‖ kə 'leɪɾ ər kɑː-, koʊ-, 'kɑːl eɪɾ ər ~s z
colleague 'kɒl iːg ‖ 'kɑːl- -ɪg ~s z
collect *v, adj, adv* kə 'lekt ~ed ɪd əd ~ing ɪŋ ~s s
collect *n 'prayer'* 'kɒl ekt -ɪkt ‖ 'kɑːl- ~s s
collectable kə 'lekt əb əl -ɪb- ~s z
collectanea ˌkɒl ek 'teɪn i_ə ‖ ˌkɑːl-
collected kə 'lekt ɪd -əd ~ly li ~ness nəs nɪs
collectible kə 'lekt əb əl -ɪb- ~s z
collection kə 'lek ʃən ~s z
collective kə 'lekt ɪv ~ly li ~ness nəs nɪs ~s z
col,lective 'farm
collectivis... —*see* collectiviz...
collectivism kə 'lekt ɪ ˌvɪz əm -ə-
collectivist kə 'lekt ɪv ɪst -əv ɪst, §-əst ~s s
collectivistic kə ˌlekt ɪ 'vɪst ɪk ◂ -ə-
collectivit|y ˌkɒl ek 'tɪv ət i kə ˌlek-, -ɪt i ‖ kə ˌlek 'tɪv əɾ li ˌkɑːl ek- ~ies iz
collectivization kə ˌlekt ɪv aɪ 'zeɪʃ ən -ɪ, •əv-, -ɪ'•- ‖ -ɪv ə- ~s z
collectiviz|e kə 'lekt ɪ vaɪz -ə- ~ed d ~es ɪz əz ~ing ɪŋ
collector kə 'lekt ə ‖ -ər ~s z
col,lector's ˌitem
colleen, C~ kɒ 'liːn 'kɒl iːn ‖ kɑː 'liːn 'kɑːl iːn ~s z
colleg|e 'kɒl ɪdʒ ‖ 'kɑːl- ~es ɪz əz
collegial kə 'liːdʒ i_əl -'liːg-
collegiality kə ˌliːdʒ i 'æl ət i -ɪt i ‖ -əɾ i
collegian kə 'liːdʒ i_ən -'liːdʒ ən ~s z
collegiate kə 'liːdʒ i_ət kɒ-, _ɪt; -'liːdʒ ət, -ɪt
collegium kə 'liːdʒ i_əm -'leg-; -'liːdʒ əm ~s z
collenchyma kə 'leŋk ɪm ə kɒ-, §-əm-
Colles 'kɒl ɪs -əs ‖ 'kɑːl- Colles' *as nominative, or with added* ɪz, əz
ˌColles' 'fracture
collet, Collet, Collett 'kɒl ɪt -ət ‖ 'kɑːl- ~s s
Colley 'kɒl i ‖ 'kɑːl i
collid|e kə 'laɪd ~ed ɪd əd ~es z ~ing ɪŋ
collie 'kɒl i ‖ 'kɑːl i ~s z
collier, C~ 'kɒl i_ə ‖ 'kɑːl jər ~s z
collier|y 'kɒl jər li ‖ 'kɑːl- ~ies iz

colli|gate 'kɒl ɪ ˌgeɪt -ə- ‖ 'kɑːl- ~gated geɪt ɪd -əd ‖ geɪɾ əd ~gates geɪts ~gating geɪt ɪŋ ‖ geɪɾ ɪŋ
colligation ˌkɒl ɪ 'geɪʃ ən -ə- ‖ ˌkɑːl- ~s z
colligative kə 'lɪg ət ɪv ‖ 'kɑːl ə geɪɾ ɪv
colli|mate 'kɒl ɪ ˌmeɪt -ə- ‖ 'kɑːl- ~mated meɪt ɪd -əd ‖ meɪɾ əd ~mates meɪts ~mating meɪt ɪŋ ‖ meɪɾ ɪŋ
collimation ˌkɒl ɪ 'meɪʃ ən -ə- ‖ ˌkɑːl- ~s z
collimator 'kɒl ɪ meɪt ə ' • ə- ‖ 'kɑːl ə meɪɾ ər ~s z
Collin 'kɒl ɪn -ən ‖ 'kɑːl-
collinear kɒ 'lɪn i_ə kə-, kəʊ- ‖ kə 'lɪn i_ər kɑː-
Collinge 'kɒl ɪndʒ -əndʒ ‖ 'kɑːl-
Collingham 'kɒl ɪŋ əm ‖ 'kɑːl-
Collingwood 'kɒl ɪŋ wʊd ‖ 'kɑːl-
Collins, c~ 'kɒl ɪnz -ənz ‖ 'kɑːl-
Collinson 'kɒl ɪnts ən -ənts- ‖ 'kɑːl-
Collis 'kɒl ɪs -əs ‖ 'kɑːl-
collision kə 'lɪʒ ən ~s z
col'lision ˌcourse
collo|cate *v* 'kɒl ə ˌkeɪt -əʊ- ‖ 'kɑːl- ~cated keɪt ɪd -əd ‖ keɪɾ əd ~cates keɪts ~cating keɪt ɪŋ ‖ keɪɾ ɪŋ
collocate *n* 'kɒl ək ət -ɪt; -ə keɪt ‖ 'kɑːl- ~s s
collocation ˌkɒl ə 'keɪʃ ən -əʊ- ‖ ˌkɑːl- ~s z
collocutor kə 'lɒk jʊt ə -jət-; 'kɒl ə kjuːt ə ‖ -'lɑːk jəɾ ər ~s z
collodi|on kə 'ləʊd i_ən ‖ -'loʊd- ~um əm
colloid 'kɒl ɔɪd ‖ 'kɑːl- ~s z
colloidal kə 'lɔɪd əl kɒ-
collop 'kɒl əp ‖ 'kɑːl- ~s s
colloquia kə 'ləʊk wi_ə ‖ -'loʊk-
colloquial kə 'ləʊk wi_əl ‖ -'loʊk- ~ly i
colloquialism kə 'ləʊk wi_ə ˌlɪz əm ‖ -'loʊk- ~s z
colloquium kə 'ləʊk wi_əm ‖ -'loʊk- ~s z
colloq|uy 'kɒl ək| wi ‖ 'kɑːl- ~uies wiz
collotype 'kɒl əʊ taɪp ‖ 'kɑːl ə- ~s s
Colls kɒlz ‖ kɑːlz
collud|e kə 'luːd kɒ-, -'ljuːd ~ed ɪd əd ~es z ~ing ɪŋ
collusion kə 'luːʒ ən kɒ-, -'ljuːʒ- ~s z
collusive kə 'luːs ɪv kɒ-, -'ljuːs-, -'luːz-, -'ljuːz- ~ly li ~ness nəs nɪs
colluvi|um kə 'luːv i_əm kɒ-, -'ljuːv- ~a ə ~ums əmz
colly, Colly 'kɒl i ‖ 'kɑːl i
collyri|um kə 'lɪr i_əm ~a ə
collywobbles 'kɒl i ˌwɒb əlz ‖ 'kɑːl i ˌwɑːb əlz
Colman (*i*) 'kəʊl mən →'kɒʊl- ‖ 'koʊl-, (*ii*) 'kɒl- ‖ 'kɑːl-
Colnaghi kɒl 'nɑːg i ‖ kɑːl-
Colnbrook 'kəʊln brʊk →'kɒʊln-, 'kəʊn- ‖ 'koʊln-
Colne kəʊn kəʊln ‖ koʊn
Colney 'kəʊn i 'kəʊln i ‖ 'koʊn i
colobus 'kɒl əb əs ‖ 'kɑːl- ~es ɪz əz
colocynth 'kɒl ə sɪntθ ‖ 'kɑːl- ~s s
cologne, C~ kə 'ləʊn ‖ -'loʊn ~s, C~'s z
Colombi|a kə 'lɒm bi_ə -'lʌm- ‖ -'lʌm- -'loʊm- ~an/s ən/z

Colombo kə ˈlʌm bəʊ -ˈlɒm- ‖ -boʊ
  Coˈlombo Plan
colon *'punctuation mark'; 'part of intestine'*
  ˈkəʊl ən -ɒn ‖ ˈkoʊl ən ~s z
colon *'colonial farmer'* kɒ ˈlɒn kə- ‖ kə ˈloʊn
  koʊ- —*Fr* [kɔ lɔ̃] ~s z
Colon, Colón *place in Panama,* **colon, colón**
  currency unit kɒ ˈlɒn kə- ‖ kə ˈloʊn koʊ-
  —*Sp* [ko ˈlon]
colonel, C~ ˈkɜːn əl ‖ ˈkɜːn əl (= *kernel*) ~s z
  ˌColonel ˈBlimp
colonel|cy ˈkɜːn əl |si ‖ ˈkɜːn- ~cies siz
colonial kə ˈləʊn i‿əl ‖ -ˈloʊn- ~ly i ~s z
colonialism kə ˈləʊn i‿ə ˌlɪz əm ‖ -ˈloʊn-
colonialist kə ˈləʊn i‿əl ɪst §-əst ‖ -ˈloʊn- ~s s
coloni... —*see* **colony**
colonic kəʊ ˈlɒn ɪk kə- ‖ koʊ ˈlɑːn-
colonis... —*see* **coloniz...**
colonist ˈkɒl ən ɪst §-əst ‖ ˈkɑːl- ~s s
colonization ˌkɒl ən aɪ ˈzeɪʃ ᵊn -ən ɪ-
  ‖ ˌkɑːl ən ə- ~s z
coloniz|e ˈkɒl ə naɪz ‖ ˈkɑːl- ~ed d ~es ɪz əz
  ~ing ɪŋ
colonizer ˈkɒl ə naɪz ə ‖ ˈkɑːl ə naɪz ᵊr ~s z
colonnad|e ˌkɒl ə ˈneɪd ˈ• • • ‖ ˌkɑːl- ~ed ɪd
  əd ~es z
colonoscope kə ˈlɒn ə skəʊp ‖ -ˈlɑːn ə skoʊp
  ~s s
Colonsay ˈkɒl ənz eɪ -ən seɪ ‖ ˈkɑːl-
Colonus kə ˈləʊn əs -ˈlɒn- ‖ -ˈloʊn-
colon|y ˈkɒl ən |i ‖ ˈkɑːl- ~ies iz
colophon ˈkɒl ə fɒn -əf ᵊn ‖ ˈkɑːl ə fɑːn -əf ən
  ~s z
colophony kɒ ˈlɒf ᵊn i kə- ‖ kə ˈlɑːf-
color ˈkʌl ə ‖ -ᵊr **colored** ˈkʌl əd ‖ -ᵊrd
  coloring ˈkʌl ər ɪŋ **colors** ˈkʌl əz ‖ -ᵊrz
  ˈcolor bar, ˈcolor line; ˈcolor scheme;
  ˌcolor ˈsupplement
Colorado, c~ ˌkɒl ə ˈrɑːd əʊ◀
  ‖ ˌkɑːl ə ˈræd oʊ ◀ -ˈrɑːd-
  ˌColoˌrado ˈbeetle; ˌColoˌrado ˈSprings
colorant ˈkʌl ər ᵊnt ~s s
coloration ˌkʌl ə ˈreɪʃ ᵊn ~s z
coloratura ˌkɒl ər ə ˈtʊər ə -ˈtjʊər- ‖ ˌkʌl
  ər ə ˈtʊr ə -ˈtjʊr-
color-blind ˈkʌl ə blaɪnd ‖ -ᵊr- ~ness nəs nɪs
color-cod|e ˌkʌl ə ˈkəʊd ˈ• • • ‖ ˌkʌl ᵊr ˈkoʊd
  ~ed ɪd əd ~ing ɪŋ ~es z
colored ˈkʌl əd ‖ -ᵊrd ~s z
colorfast ˈkʌl ə fɑːst §-fæst ‖ -ᵊr fæst ~ness
  nəs nɪs
colorful ˈkʌl ə fᵊl -fʊl ‖ -ᵊr- ~ly i
colorimeter ˌkʌl ə ˈrɪm ɪt ə -ət ə ‖ -ət ᵊr ~s z
colorimetry ˌkʌl ə ˈrɪm ətr i -ɪtr i
coloring ˈkʌl ər ɪŋ
  ˈcoloring ˌmatter
colorist ˈkʌl ər ɪst §-əst ~s s
colorless ˈkʌl ə ləs -lɪs ‖ -ᵊr- ~ly li ~ness nəs
  nɪs
Coloroll *tdmk* ˈkʌl ə rəʊl →-rɒʊl ‖ -roʊl
colorwash ˈkʌl ə wɒʃ ‖ -ᵊr wɔːʃ -wɑːʃ ~ed t
  ~es ɪz əz ~ing ɪŋ
colorway ˈkʌl ə weɪ ‖ -ᵊr- ~s z

Colossae kə ˈlɒs iː -aɪ ‖ -ˈlɑːs-
colossal kə ˈlɒs ᵊl ‖ -ˈlɑːs- ~ly i
Colosseum, c~ ˌkɒl ə ˈsiː əm ‖ ˌkɑːl-
colossi kə ˈlɒs aɪ ‖ -ˈlɑːs-
Colossian kə ˈlɒʃ ᵊn kə ˈlɒs i‿ən, -ˈlɒʃ- ‖ -ˈlɑːʃ-
  ~s z
coloss|us kə ˈlɒs |əs ‖ -ˈlɑːs- ~i aɪ ~uses əs ɪz
  -əz
colostom|y kə ˈlɒst əm |i ‖ -ˈlɑːst- ~ies iz
  coˈlostomy bag
colostrum kə ˈlɒs trəm ‖ -ˈlɑːs-
colour ˈkʌl ə ‖ -ᵊr **coloured** ˈkʌl əd ‖ -ᵊrd
  colouring ˈkʌl ər ɪŋ **colours** ˈkʌl əz ‖ -ᵊrz
  ˈcolour bar, ˈcolor line; ˈcolour scheme;
  ˌcolour ˈsupplement
colour-blind ˈkʌl ə blaɪnd ‖ -ᵊr- ~ness nəs nɪs
color-cod|e ˌkʌl ə ˈkəʊd ˈ• • • ‖ ˌkʌl ᵊr ˌkoʊd
  ˌ• •ˈ• ~ed ɪd ◀ əd ~ing ɪŋ ~es z
coloured ˈkʌl əd ‖ -ᵊrd ~s z
colourfast ˈkʌl ə fɑːst §-fæst ‖ -ᵊr fæst ~ness
  nəs nɪs
colourful ˈkʌl ə fᵊl -fʊl ‖ -ᵊr- ~ly i
colouring ˈkʌl ər ɪŋ
  ˈcolouring ˌmatter
colourist ˈkʌl ər ɪst §-əst ~s s
colourless ˈkʌl ə ləs -lɪs ‖ -ᵊr- ~ly li ~ness nəs
  nɪs
colourwash ˈkʌl ə wɒʃ ‖ -ᵊr wɔːʃ -wɑːʃ ~ed t
  ~es ɪz əz ~ing ɪŋ
colourway ˈkʌl ə weɪ ‖ -ᵊr- ~s z
-colous *stress-imposing* kəl əs — **sanguicolous**
  sæŋ ˈɡwɪk əl əs
colpitis kɒl ˈpaɪt ɪs §-əs ‖ kɑːl ˈpaɪt̬ əs
colpo- *comb. form*
  with stress-neutral suffix ˌkɒlp əʊ ‖ ˌkɑːlp oʊ
  — **colpomycosis** ˌkɒlp əʊ maɪ ˈkəʊs ɪs §-əs
  ‖ ˌkɑːlp oʊ maɪ ˈkoʊs əs
  with stress-imposing suffix
  kɒl ˈpɒ+ ‖ kɑːl ˈpɑː+ — **colporrhaphy**
  kɒl ˈpɒr əf i ‖ kɑːl ˈpɑːr-
colporteur ˌkɒl pɔː ˈtɜː ˌkəʊl-; ˌkɒl ˈpɔːt ə,
  ˈkəʊl-, ˌ•ˈ• • ‖ ˌkɑːl pɔːr ˈtɜː -poʊr-;
  ˈkɑːl ˌpɔːrt̬ ᵊr, -ˌpoʊrt̬- —*Fr* [kɔl pɔʁ tœːʁ]
  ~s z
colposcope ˈkɒlp ə skəʊp ‖ ˈkɑːlp ə skoʊp ~s
  s
Colquhoun kə ˈhuːn
Colson ˈkəʊls ᵊn →ˈkɒʊls- ‖ ˈkoʊls-
Colston ˈkəʊlst ən →ˈkɒʊlst- ‖ ˈkoʊlst-
colt, Colt kəʊlt →kɒʊlt ‖ koʊlt **colts, Colts**
  kəʊlts →kɒʊlts ‖ koʊlts
colter ˈkəʊlt ə →ˈkɒʊlt-, §ˈkuːt- ‖ ˈkoʊlt̬ ᵊr ~s
  z
coltish ˈkəʊlt ɪʃ →ˈkɒʊlt-, ‖ ˈkoʊlt̬- ~ly li
  ~ness nəs nɪs
Coltrane kɒl ˈtreɪn ‖ koʊl-
coltsfoot ˈkəʊlts fʊt →ˈkɒʊlts- ‖ ˈkoʊlts- ~s s
colubrine ˈkɒl ju braɪn -brɪn, -brən ‖ ˈkɑːl ə-
  -jə-
Colum, Columb ˈkɒl əm ‖ ˈkɑːl-
Columba kə ˈlʌm bə ~'s z
columbari|um ˌkɒl əm ˈbeər i‿|əm
  ‖ ˌkɑːl əm ˈber i‿|əm -ˈbær- ~a ə

Columbia kə ˈlʌm bi_ə
Columbian kə ˈlʌm bi_ən   ~s z
columbine, C~ ˈkɒl əm baɪn ‖ ˈkɑːl-   ~s z
columbite kə ˈlʌm baɪt ˈkɒl əm- ‖ ˈkɑːl əm-
columbium kə ˈlʌm bi_əm
Columbo kə ˈlʌm bəʊ ‖ -boʊ
Columbus kə ˈlʌm bəs
column ˈkɒl əm ‖ ˈkɑːl əm   ~ed d   ~s z
columnar kə ˈlʌm nə ‖ -nᵊr
columnist ˈkɒl əm nɪst -ɪst, §-nəst, §-əst
   ‖ ˈkɑːl-   ~s s
colure kə ˈlʊə -ˈljʊə; ˈkəʊ· ‖ -ˈlʊᵊr   ~s z
Colville ˈkɒl vɪl ‖ ˈkoʊl-
Colvin ˈkɒlv ɪn §-ən ‖ ˈkoʊlv ən
Colwich ˈkɒl wɪtʃ ‖ ˈkɑːl- —*formerly* -ɪtʃ
Colwyn ˈkɒl wɪn -wən ‖ ˈkɑːl-
   ˌColwyn ˈBay
Colyer ˈkɒl jə ‖ ˈkɑːl jᵊr
Colyton ˈkɒl ɪt ən -ət- ‖ ˈkɑːl ət ᵊn
colza ˈkɒlz ə ‖ ˈkɑːlz ə ˈkoʊlz-
com- *This prefix is pronounced stressed*
   kɒm ‖ kɑːm *(1) if the following syllable is*
   unstressed (ˌcombiˈnation); *(2) in many*
   disyllabic nouns (ˈcombine; *but* comˈmand); *and*
   (3) occasionally, in context, when contrastively
   stressed (ˌdepartments and ˈcompartments).
   Otherwise it is usually weak kəm *in RP and GA,*
   though strong in some regional British speech
   (comˈputer). *Before a stem beginning* m, *one* m
   is lost (ˈcommerce, comˈmit).
com *WWW and e-mail* kɒm ‖ kɑːm
coma ˈkəʊm ə ‖ ˈkoʊm ə   ~s z
Comanche kə ˈmænʧ i   ~s z
comatose ˈkəʊm ə təʊs -təʊz ‖ ˈkoʊm ə toʊs
   ~ly li
comb kəʊm ‖ koʊm   **combed** kəʊmd ‖ koʊmd
   combing ˈkəʊm ɪŋ ‖ ˈkoʊm ɪŋ   **combs**
   kəʊmz ‖ koʊmz
combat *n, adj* ˈkɒm bæt ˈkʌm-, -bət ‖ ˈkɑːm-
   ˈcombat faˌtigue
com|bat *v* ˈkɒm |bæt ˈkʌm-, -bət; kəm ˈbæt,
   ₍ˌ₎kɒm- ‖ kəm ˈbæt ˈkɑːm bæt   ~**bated,**
   ~**batted** bæt ɪd -əd ‖ ˈbæt əd   ~**bating,**
   ~**batting** bæt ɪŋ ‖ ˈbæt ɪŋ   ~**bats**
   bæts ‖ ˈbæts
combatant ˈkɒm bət ənt ˈkʌm-; kəm ˈbæt ᵊnt,
   ₍ˌ₎kɒm- ‖ kəm ˈbæt ᵊnt   ~s s
combative ˈkɒm bət ɪv ˈkʌm-; kəm ˈbæt ɪv,
   ₍ˌ₎kɒm- ‖ kəm ˈbæt ɪv   ~**ly** li   ~**ness** nəs nɪs
Combe, combe kuːm —*as a family name, also*
   kəʊm ‖ koʊm
comber *'thing that combs'* ˈkəʊm ə ‖ ˈkoʊm ᵊr
   ~s z
comber *fish* ˈkɒm bə ‖ ˈkɑːm bᵊr   ~s z
combination ˌkɒm bɪ ˈneɪʃ ᵊn -bə- ‖ ˌkɑːm-
   . ~s z
   ˌcombiˈnation lock
combinative ˈkɒm bɪ nət ɪv ˌ•bə-, -neɪt ɪv
   ‖ ˈkɑːm bə neɪt ɪv kəm ˈbaɪn ət-
combinatorial ˌkɒm bɪn ə ˈtɔːr i_əl ◄ ˌ•bən-
   ‖ ˌkɑːm- kəm ˌbaɪn-, -ˈtoʊr-
combin|e *v 'join, unite'* kəm ˈbaɪn §₍ˌ₎kɒm-   ~**ed**

d   ~**er/s** ə/z ‖ ᵊr/z   ~**es** z   ~**ing** ɪŋ
   comˈbining form
combin|e *v 'harvest'* ˈkɒm baɪn ‖ ˈkɑːm-   ~**ed** d
   ~**es** z   ~**ing** ɪŋ
combine *n* ˈkɒm baɪn ‖ ˈkɑːm-   ~s z
   ˌcombine ˈharvester
combing ˈkəʊm ɪŋ ‖ ˈkoʊm ɪŋ   ~s z
combo ˈkɒm bəʊ ‖ ˈkɑːm boʊ   ~s z
comb-out ˈkəʊm aʊt ‖ ˈkoʊm-   ~s s
combust kəm ˈbʌst §₍ˌ₎kɒm-   ~**ed** ɪd əd   ~**ing**
   ɪŋ   ~s s
combustibility kəm ˌbʌst ə ˈbɪl ət i §kɒm-,
   §ˌkɒm bʌst-, -ɪˈ•-, -ɪt i ‖ -ət i
combustib|le kəm ˈbʌst əb ᵊl §₍ˌ₎kɒm-, -ɪb-
   ~**ly** li
combustion kəm ˈbʌs tʃən §₍ˌ₎kɒm-
   comˈbustion ˌchamber
combustive kəm ˈbʌst ɪv §₍ˌ₎kɒm-
come kʌm —*There is also an occasional weak*
   form kəm. *See* cˈmon   **came** keɪm   **comes**
   kʌmz   **coming** ˈkʌm ɪŋ
come-all-ye kʌm ˈɔːl ji kə ˈmɔːl-, -jə ‖ -ˈɑːl-
come-at-able ˌkʌm ˈæt əb ᵊl ‖ -ˈæt̬-
comeback ˈkʌm bæk   ~s s
Comecon ˈkɒm i kɒn ‖ ˈkɑːm i kɑːn
comedian kə ˈmiːd i_ən   ~s z
comedic kə ˈmiːd ɪk   ~**ally** ᵊl_i
comedienne kə ˌmiːd i ˈen   ~s z
comedi... —*see* **comedy**
comedo ˈkɒm ɪ dəʊ -ə-; kə ˈmiːd əʊ
   ‖ ˈkɑːm ə doʊ   ~s z   **comedones**
   ˌkɒm ɪ ˈdəʊn iːz -ə- ‖ ˌkɑːm ə ˈdoʊn iːz
comedown ˈkʌm daʊn   ~s z
comed|y ˈkɒm əd li -ɪd- ‖ ˈkɑːm-   ~**ies** iz
come-hither ₍ˌ₎kʌm ˈhɪð ə ‖ -ᵊr -ˈhɪθ-
come|ly ˈkʌm |li   ~**lier** li_ə li_ᵊr   ~**liest** li_ɪst
   li_əst   ~**liness** li nəs li nɪs
Comenius kə ˈmeɪn i_əs kɒ-, -ˈmiːn-
come-on ˈkʌm ɒn ‖ -ɑːn -ɔːn   ~s z
comer ˈkʌm ə ‖ -ᵊr   ~s z
Comer *family name* ˈkəʊm ə ‖ ˈkoʊm ᵊr
-comer ˌkʌm ə ‖ -ᵊr — **late-comer**
   ˈleɪt ˌkʌm ə ‖ -ᵊr   ~s z
comestible kə ˈmest əb ᵊl -ɪb-   ~s z
comet ˈkɒm ɪt §-ət ‖ ˈkɑːm-   ~s s
comeuppanc|e ˌkʌm ˈʌp ᵊnᵗs →-mᵖs   ~**es** ɪz
   əz
comfit ˈkʌmᵖf ɪt ˈkɒmᵖf-, §-ət ‖ ˈkɑːmᵖf-   ~s s
comf|ort, C~ ˈkʌmᵖf |ət ‖ -|ᵊrt   ~**orted** ət ɪd
   -əd ‖ ᵊrt̬ əd   ~**orting** ət ɪŋ ‖ ᵊrt̬ ɪŋ   ~**orts**
   əts ‖ ᵊrts
   ˈcomfort ˌstation
comfortab|le ˈkʌmᵖft əb ᵊl
   ˈkʌmᵖf ət əb ᵊl ‖ -ᵊrb-, ˈkʌmᵖf ət̬ əb ᵊl, ˈ•ᵊrt̬-
   ~**ly** li   ~**ness** nəs nɪs
   ˌcomfortably ˈoff
comforter ˈkʌmᵖf ət ə ‖ -ᵊrt̬ ᵊr -ət̬-   ~s z
comfortless ˈkʌmᵖf ət ləs -lɪs ‖ -ᵊrt-
comfrey ˈkʌmᵖf ri   ~s z
comf|y ˈkʌmᵖf li   ~**ier** i_ə ‖ i_ᵊr   ~**iest** i_ɪst i_əst
comic ˈkɒm ɪk ‖ ˈkɑːm-   ~s s
   ˌcomic ˈopera; ˈcomic ˌstrip

comical 'kɒm ɪk ᵊl ‖ 'kɑːm- **~ly** _i **~ness** nəs
nɪs
Cominform 'kɒm ɪn ˌfɔːm -ən-
‖ 'kɑːm ən ˌfɔːrm
coming 'kʌm ɪŋ **~s** z
coming-out ˌkʌm ɪŋ 'aʊt
Comintern 'kɒm ɪn ˌtɜːn -ən- ‖ 'kɑːm ən ˌtɝːn
comit|y 'kɒm ət li -ɪt- ‖ 'kɑːm əţ li 'koʊm-
~ies iz
comma 'kɒm ə ‖ 'kɑːm ə **~s** z
command kə 'mɑːnd §-'mænd ‖ -'mænd **~ed**
ɪd əd **~ing** ɪŋ **~s** z
com'mand ˌmodule; com,mand
per'formance
commandant 'kɒm ən dænt -dɑːnt, ˌ••'•
‖ 'kɑːm- **~s** s
comman|deer ˌkɒm ən l'dɪə -ɑːn-, §-æn-
‖ ˌkɑːm ən l'dɪᵊr **~deered** 'dɪəd ‖ 'dɪᵊrd
~deering 'dɪər ɪŋ ‖ 'dɪr ɪŋ **~deers**
'dɪəz ‖ 'dɪᵊrz
commander kə 'mɑːnd ə §-'mænd-
‖ -'mænd ᵊr **~s** z
com,mander in 'chief
commanding kə 'mɑːnd ɪŋ §-'mænd-
‖ -'mænd- **~ly** li
com,manding 'officer
commandment kə 'mɑːn_d mənt →-'mɑːm-,
§-'mænd- ‖ -'mænd- **~s** s
commando kə 'mɑːnd əʊ §-'mænd-
‖ -'mænd oʊ **~s** z
Comme des Garçons _tdmk_ ˌkɒm deɪ 'gɑːs ɒ̃
-gɑː 'sɒ̃ ‖ ˌkɑːm deɪ gɑːr 'soʊn—_Fr_
[kɔm de gaʁ sɔ̃]
commedia dell'arte kɒ ˌmeɪd i ə del 'ɑːt eɪ
kə-, -ˌmed- ‖ kə ˌmeɪd i ə del 'ɑːrţ i -ˌmed-
—_It_ [kɔm 'meː dia del 'lar te]
comme il faut ˌkɒm iːᵊl 'fəʊ ‖ ˌkʌm iːᵊl 'foʊ
ˌkɑːm-, ˌkɔːm- —_Fr_ [kɔm il fo]
commemo|rate kə 'mem ə lreɪt **~rated** reɪt ɪd
-əd ‖ reɪţ əd **~rates** reɪts **~rating**
reɪt ɪŋ ‖ reɪţ ɪŋ **~rator/s** reɪt ə/z ‖ reɪţ ᵊr/z
commemoration kə ˌmem ə 'reɪʃ ᵊn **~s** z
commemorative kə 'mem ər_ət ɪv -ə reɪt-
‖ əţ ɪv -ə reɪţ- **~s** z
commenc|e kə 'men¹s **~ed** t **~es** ɪz əz **~ing**
ɪŋ
commencement kə 'men¹s mənt **~s** s
commend kə 'mend **~ed** ɪd əd **~ing** ɪŋ **~s** z
commendab|le kə 'mend əb ᵊl **~ly** li
commendation ˌkɒm en 'deɪʃ ᵊn -ən-
‖ ˌkɑːm ən- -en- **~s** z
commendatory kə 'mend ə_tər i ˌkɒm en 'deɪt
ər i, ˌ•ən- ‖ -ə tɔːr i -toʊr i
commensal kə 'men¹s ᵊl **~ism** ˌɪz əm **~ly** i **~s**
z
commensurability kə ˌmen¹ʃ ər_ə 'bɪl ət i
-ˌmen¹s-, -ˌjər ə-, -ɪt i ‖ kə ˌmen¹s ər_ə 'bɪl əţ i
commensurab|le kə 'men¹ʃ ər_əb ᵊl -'men¹s-,
-jər əb- ‖ -'men¹s- **~ly** li
commensurate kə 'men¹ʃ ər_ət -'men¹s-, -jər-,
-ɪt ‖ -'men¹s- **~ly** li
comment _n_ 'kɒm ent ‖ 'kɑːm- **~s** s

comm|ent _v_ 'kɒm lent §kɒ 'ment, kə-
‖ 'kɑːm- **~ented** ent ɪd -əd ‖ enţ əd
~enting ent ɪŋ ‖ enţ ɪŋ **~ents** en¹s
commentar|y 'kɒm ənt_ər li ‖ 'kɑːm ən ter li
~ies iz
commen|tate 'kɒm ən lteɪt -en- ‖ 'kɑːm-
~tated teɪt ɪd -əd ‖ teɪţ əd **~tates** teɪts
~tating teɪt ɪŋ ‖ teɪţ ɪŋ
commentator 'kɒm ən teɪt ə ¹•en-
‖ 'kɑːm ən teɪţ ᵊr **~s** z
Commer _tdmk_ 'kɒm ə ‖ 'kɑːm ᵊr **~s** z
commerce 'kɒm ɜːs ‖ 'kɑːm ᵊrs kə 'mɝːs
commercial kə 'mɜːʃ ᵊl ‖ -'mɝːʃ- **~ly** i **~s** z
com,mercial 'traveller
commercialis... —_see_ **commercializ...**
commercialism kə 'mɜːʃ ə ˌlɪz əm -ᵊl ˌɪz-
‖ -'mɝːʃ-
commerciality kə ˌmɜːʃ i 'æl ət i -ɪt i
‖ kə ˌmɝːʃ i 'æl əţ i
commercialization kə ˌmɜːʃ ᵊl aɪ 'zeɪʃ ᵊn -ᵊl ɪ-
‖ -ˌmɝːʃ ᵊl ə-
commercializ|e kə 'mɜːʃ ə laɪz -ᵊl aɪz
‖ -'mɝːʃ- **~ed** d **~es** ɪz əz **~ing** ɪŋ
commie 'kɒm i ‖ 'kɑːm i **~s** z
commination ˌkɒm ɪ 'neɪʃ ᵊn -ə- ‖ ˌkɑːm-
commingl|e kɒ 'mɪŋ gᵊl kə- ‖ kə- kɑː- **~ed** d
~es z **~ing** _ɪŋ
commi|nute 'kɒm ɪ lnjuːt §-ə- ‖ 'kɑːm ə lnuːt
-njuːt **~nuted** njuːt ɪd -əd ‖ nuːţ əd njuːţ-
~nutes njuːts ‖ nuːts njuːts **~nuting**
njuːt ɪŋ ‖ nuːţ ɪŋ njuːţ-
comminution ˌkɒm ɪ 'njuːʃ ᵊn §-ə-
‖ ˌkɑːm ə 'nuːʃ- -'njuːʃ-
commis 'kɒm i -ɪs ‖ ˌkɑː 'miː ◄ kə-
'commis chef, ˌcommis 'chef
commise|rate kə 'mɪz ə lreɪt **~rated** reɪt ɪd
-əd ‖ reɪţ əd **~rates** reɪts **~rating**
reɪt ɪŋ ‖ reɪţ ɪŋ
commiseration kə ˌmɪz ə 'reɪʃ ᵊn **~s** z
commiserative kə 'mɪz ər_ət ɪv -ə reɪt ɪv
‖ -ə reɪţ ɪv **~ly** li
commissar ˌkɒm ɪ 'sɑː -ə-, '••• ‖ 'kɑːm ə sɑːr
~s z
commissariat ˌkɒm ɪ 'seər i ət, ¹•ə-, -'sær-,
-'sɑːr-, -æt ‖ ˌkɑːm ə 'ser- **~s** s
commissar|y 'kɒm ɪs ər li ¹•ᵊs- ‖ 'kɑːm ə ser li
~ies iz
commission kə 'mɪʃ ᵊn **~ed** d **~ing** _ɪŋ **~s** z
com'mission ˌagent
commissionaire kə ˌmɪʃ ə 'neə -ᵊn 'eə ‖ -'neᵊr
~s z
commissional kə 'mɪʃ ᵊn_ᵊl
commissionary kə 'mɪʃ ᵊn_ər i ‖ -ə ner i
commissioner kə 'mɪʃ ᵊn_ə ‖ _ᵊr **~s** z
commissure 'kɒm ɪ sjʊə -ə-, -ʃʊə ‖ 'kɑːm ə ʃʊr
~s z
commit kə 'mɪt **commits** kə 'mɪts
committed kə 'mɪt ɪd -əd ‖ -'mɪţ əd
committing kə 'mɪt ɪŋ ‖ -'mɪţ ɪŋ
commitment kə 'mɪt mənt **~s** s
committable kə 'mɪt əb ᵊl ‖ -'mɪţ-
committal kə 'mɪt ᵊl ‖ -'mɪţ- **~s** z

Combining forms

1 Many literary and scientific words are composed of **combining forms** derived from Greek or Latin. Typically, they consist of a first element and a second element. For example, **microscopic** consists of **micro-** plus **-scopic**. LPD has entries for these separate elements, which makes it possible to work out the pronunciation of many rare or new words not listed in the dictionary.

2 One problem is that of deciding the stress pattern of such a word. Most combining form **suffixes** (= second elements) are **stress-neutral** (= they preserve the location of stresses in the first element; the suffix may well be stressed itself). Others are **stress-imposing** (= they cause the main stress to fall on a particular syllable of the first element).

For example, **-graphic** ˈgræf ɪk is stress-neutral, but **-graphy** is stress-imposing (as in **epigraphy** e ˈpɪg rəf i).

3 A first element usually has two different pronunciations, one used with stress-neutral suffixes, the other with stress-imposing suffixes. For the pronunciation of the whole word, the pronunciation for the suffix must be combined with the appropriate pronunciation for the first element.

4 The mark ¦ in the pronunciation of a first element means a stress. This will be a secondary stress (ˌ) if the suffix includes a main stress; if not, it will be a main stress (ˈ). In general, suffixes of two or more syllables are stressed, but those of one syllable are not.

5 For example, take the first element **cata-**.
- With a stress-neutral suffix, it is pronounced ¦kæt ə. Combining this with **-graphic** ˈgræf ɪk we get **catagraphic** ˌkæt ə ˈgræf ɪk. Combining it with **-phyte** faɪt we get **cataphyte** ˈkæt ə faɪt.
- With a stress-imposing suffix, it is pronounced kə ˈtæ+. (The sign + is a reminder that this syllable is incomplete and must attract at least one consonant from the suffix.) Combining **cata-** with **-logy** lədʒ i (stress-imposing) we get **catalogy** kə ˈtæl ədʒ i.

(The words **catagraphic, cataphyte, catalogy** do not exist. But if they did, we know that this is how they would be pronounced.)

C

committee kə ˈmɪt i ‖ -ˈmɪt̮ i —*but* ˌkɒm ɪ ˈtiː ‖ ˌkɑːm- *in the obsolete sense 'person to whom someone or something is committed'* ~s z
com¦ mittee stage

committee|man kə ˈmɪt i ǀmən mæn ‖ -ˈmɪt̮-
~**men** mən men ~**woman** ˌwʊm ən
~**women** ˌwɪm ɪn §-ən

commode kə ˈməʊd ‖ -ˈmoʊd ~s z

commodification kə ˌmɒd ɪf ɪ ˈkeɪʃ ən -ə-, •əf-,
§-əˈ•- ‖ -ˌmɑːd-

commodi|fy kə ˈmɒd ɪ ǀfaɪ -ə- ‖ -ˈmɑːd-
~**fied** faɪd ~**fies** faɪz ~**fying** faɪ ɪŋ

commodious kə ˈməʊd i‿əs ‖ -ˈmoʊd- ~**ly** li
~**ness** nəs nɪs

commodit|y kə ˈmɒd ət li -ɪt- ‖ -ˈmɑːd ət̮ li
~**ies** iz

commodore ˈkɒm ə dɔː ‖ ˈkɑːm ə dɔːr -doʊr
~**s** z

Commodus ˈkɒm əd əs kə ˈmoʊd- ‖ ˈkɑːm-

common ˈkɒm ən ‖ ˈkɑːm- ~**er** ə ‖ ər ~**est** ɪst
əst ~**ly** li ~**ness** nəs nɪs
ˌcommon deˈ nominator; ˌ Common
ˈ Market; ˌcommon ˈ noun; ˈcommon room;
ˌcommon ˈ sense

commonage ˈkɒm ən ɪdʒ ‖ ˈkɑːm-

commonalit|y ˌkɒm ə ˈnæl ət li -ɪt i
‖ ˌkɑːm ə ˈnæl ət̮ li ~**ies** iz

commonal|ty ˈkɒm ən əl ti ‖ ˈkɑːm- ~**ties** tiz

commoner ˈkɒm ən ə ‖ ˈkɑːm ən ər ~**s** z

common-law ˌkɒm ən ˈlɔː ◀ ‖ ˌkɑːm- -ˈlɑː
  ˌcommon-lawˈ marriage
common-or-garden ˌkɒm ən ɔː ˈgɑːd ən ◀
  -əˈ•- ‖ ˌkɑːm ən ər ˈgɑːrd ən ◀
commonplac|e ˈkɒm ən pleɪs →-əm- ‖ ˈkɑːm-
  ~es ɪz əz
commonsense ˌkɒm ən ˈsenᵗs ◀ ‖ ˌkɑːm-
  ˌcommonsense deˈcision
commonsensical
  ˌkɒm ən ˈsenᵗs ɪk əl ◀ ‖ ˌkɑːm- ~ly_i
commonsensicality ˌkɒm ən ˌsenᵗs ɪ ˈkæl ət i
  -ˌ•ə-, -ɪt i ‖ ˌkɑːm ən ˌsenᵗs ɪ ˈkæl ət̬ i
commonweal ˈkɒm ən wiːᵊl ‖ ˈkɑːm-
commonwealth, C~ ˈkɒm ən welθ ‖ ˈkɑːm-
commotion kə ˈməʊʃ ᵊn ‖ -ˈmoʊʃ- ~s z
commotional kə ˈməʊʃ ᵊn_əl ‖ -ˈmoʊʃ-
comms kɒmz ‖ kɑːmz

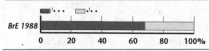

COMMUNAL

	◨'··· ▱·'··				
BrE 1988					
	0	20 40	60	80	100%

communal ˈkɒm jʊn ᵊl -jən-; kə ˈmjuːn ᵊl
  ‖ kə ˈmjuːn ᵊl ˈkɑːm jən- —BrE 1988 poll
  panel preference: ˈ•·· 68%, •ˈ•· 32%. ~ly i
communality ˌkɒm ju ˈnæl ət i -ɪt i
  ‖ ˌkɑːm ju ˈnæl ət̬ i
communard, C~ ˈkɒm ju nɑːd -nɑː:
  ‖ ˈkɑːm ju nɑːrd -nɑːr ~s z
commun|e v kə ˈmjuːn ˈkɒm juːn ~ed d ~es
  z ~ing ɪŋ
commune, C~ n ˈkɒm juːn ‖ ˈkɑːm- kə ˈmjuːn
  ~s z
communicability kə ˌmjuːn ɪk ə ˈbɪl ət i -ɪt i
  ‖ -ət̬ i
communicable kə ˈmjuːn ɪk əb ᵊl ~ness nəs
  nɪs
communicant kə ˈmjuːn ɪk ənt ~s s
communi|cate kə ˈmjuːn ɪ ˈkeɪt -ə- ~cated
  keɪt ɪd -əd ‖ keɪt̬ əd ~cates keɪts ~cating
  keɪt ɪŋ ‖ keɪt̬ ɪŋ
communication kə ˌmjuːn ɪ ˈkeɪʃ ᵊn -ə- ~s z
  comˌmuniˈcation cord; comˌmuniˈcations
  ˌsatellite
communicative kə ˈmjuːn ɪk ət ɪv -ˈ•ək-;
  -ɪ keɪt-, -ə keɪt- ‖ -ə keɪt̬ ɪv -ɪk ət̬- ~ly li
  ~ness nəs nɪs
  comˌmunicative ˈcompetence
communicator kə ˈmjuːn ɪ keɪt ə ‖ -keɪt̬ ər
communion, C~ kə ˈmjuːn i_ən ~s z
  comˈmunion rail
communique, communiqué kə ˈmjuːn ɪ keɪ
  -ə- ~s z
communism, C~ ˈkɒm ju ˌnɪz əm -jə-
  ‖ ˈkɑːm jə-
communist, C~ ˈkɒm jʊn ɪst -jən-, -juːn-,
  §-əst ‖ ˈkɑːm jən əst ~s s
communitarian kə ˌmjuːn ɪ ˈteər i_ən ◀-əˈ•-
  ‖ -ˈter- ~s z
communit|y kə ˈmjuːn ət i -ɪt- ‖ -ət̬ i ~ies iz
  comˈmunity ˌcentre; comˈmunity chest,
  •ˌ••• ˈ•; comˈmunity medicine;
  comˌmunity ˈsinging

commutability kə ˌmjuːt ə ˈbɪl ət i -ɪt i
  ‖ kə ˌmjuːt̬ ə ˈbɪl ət̬ i
commutable kə ˈmjuːt əb ᵊl ‖ -ˈmjuːt̬-
commu|tate ˈkɒm ju ˌteɪt ‖ ˈkɑːm jə- ~tated
  teɪt ɪd -əd ‖ teɪt̬ əd ~tates teɪts ~tating
  teɪt ɪŋ ‖ teɪt̬ ɪŋ
commutation ˌkɒm ju ˈteɪʃ ᵊn ‖ ˌkɑːm jə- ~s
  z
  ˌcommuˈtation ˌticket
commutative kə ˈmjuːt ət ɪv ˈkɒm ju teɪt ɪv
  ‖ ˈkɑːm jə teɪt̬ ɪv kə ˈmjuːt̬ ət̬ ɪv ~ly li
commutator ˈkɒm ju teɪt ə ‖ ˈkɑːm jə teɪt̬ ər
  ~s z
commute kə ˈmjuːt **commuted** kə ˈmjuːt ɪd
  -əd ‖ -ˈmjuːt̬ əd **commutes** kə ˈmjuːts
  commuting kə ˈmjuːt ɪŋ ‖ -ˈmjuːt̬ ɪŋ
commuter kə ˈmjuːt ə ‖ -ˈmjuːt̬ ər ~s z
Como ˈkəʊm əʊ ‖ ˈkoʊm oʊ —It [ˈkɔː mo]
Comoro ˈkɒm ə rəʊ ‖ ˈkɑːm ə roʊ ~s z
comp kɒmp ‖ kɑːmp ~s s
compact adj kəm ˈpækt ₍ₗ₎kɒm- ‖ ₍ₗ₎kɑːm- —In
  stress-shifting environments usually
  ˌkɒm pækt ‖ ˌkɑːm-, as if underlyingly
  ˌkɒm ˈpækt ◀ ‖ ˌkɑːm- (even for speakers who
  otherwise say kəm ˈpækt) ~ly li ~ness nəs
  nɪs
  ˌcompact ˈdisc/ˈdisk
compact n ˈkɒm pækt ‖ ˈkɑːm-
compact v 'press together' kəm ˈpækt
  ₍ₗ₎kɒm- ‖ ₍ₗ₎kɑːm- ~ed ɪd əd ~ing ɪŋ ~s s
compact v 'make an agreement'
  ˈkɒm pækt ‖ ˈkɑːm- ~ed ɪd əd ~ing ɪŋ ~s s
compaction kəm ˈpæk ʃᵊn §₍ₗ₎kɒm-
compactor kəm ˈpækt ə §₍ₗ₎kɒm- ‖ -ᵊr ~s z
companion kəm ˈpæn jən §₍ₗ₎kɒm-, -ˈpæn i_ən
  ~able əb ᵊl ~ably əb li ~ate ət ɪt ~s z
  ~ship ʃɪp ~way/s weɪ/z
compan|y ˈkʌmp ᵊn_li ~ies iz
  ˌcompany ˈsecretary
Compaq tdmk ˈkɒm pæk ‖ ˈkɑːm-
comparability ˌkɒmp ᵊr_ə ˈbɪl ət i -ɪt i;
  kəm ˌpær ə-, §kɒm-, -ˌpeər- ‖ ˌkɑːmp
  ᵊr_ə ˈbɪl ət̬ i kəm ˌper ə-, -ˌpær-
comparab|le ˈkɒmp ᵊr_əb ᵊl kəm ˈpær əb ᵊl,
  §₍ₗ₎kɒm-, -ˈpeər- ‖ ˈkɑːmp- kəm ˈper-, -ˈpær-
  ~ly li
comparative kəm ˈpær ət ɪv §₍ₗ₎kɒm- ‖ -ət̬-
  -ˈper- ~ly li
comparator kəm ˈpær ət ə §₍ₗ₎kɒm- ‖ -ət̬ ᵊr
  -ˈper- ~s z
com|pare kəm |ˈpeə §₍ₗ₎kɒm- ‖ -|ˈpeᵊr -ˈpæᵊr
  ~pared ˈpeəd ‖ ˈpeᵊrd ˈpæᵊrd ~pares
  ˈpeəz ‖ ˈpeᵊrz ˈpæᵊrz ~paring
  ˈpeər ɪŋ ‖ ˈper ɪŋ ˈpær-
comparison kəm ˈpær ɪs ᵊn §₍ₗ₎kɒm-, -əs-,
  §-ɪz-, §-əz- ‖ -ˈper- ~s z
compartment n kəm ˈpɑːt mənt §₍ₗ₎kɒm-
  ‖ -ˈpɑːrt- ~s s
compartmentalization
  ˌkɒm pɑːt ˌment ᵊl aɪ ˈzeɪʃ ᵊn-əl ɪ-
  ‖ kəm ˌpɑːrt ˌment̬ ᵊl ə- ˌkɑːm pɑːrt-
compartmentaliz|e ˌkɒm pɑːt ˈment ᵊl aɪz

-ə laɪz ‖ kəm ˌpɑːrt ˈmen*t̬* ᵊl aɪz ˌkɑːm pɑːrt-
~ed d **~es** ɪz əz **~ing** ɪŋ
compass ˈkʌmp əs §ˈkɒmp- ‖ ˈkɑːmp- **~ed** t
~es ɪz əz **~ing** ɪŋ
ˈcompass point
compassion kəm ˈpæʃ ᵊn §$_{(ı)}$kɒm-
compassionate kəm ˈpæʃ ᵊn‿ət §$_{(ı)}$kɒm-, ‿ɪt
~ly li **~ness** nəs nɪs
compatibility kəm ˌpæt ə ˈbɪl ət i §kɒm-,
§ˌkɒm pæt-, -ɪˈ••-, -ɪt i ‖ -ˌpæt̬ ə ˈbɪl ət̬ i
compatib|le kəm ˈpæt əb |ᵊl §$_{(ı)}$kɒm-, -ɪb-
‖ -ˈpæt̬- **~ly** li
compatriot kəm ˈpætr i‿ət $_{(ı)}$kɒm- ‖ -ˈpeɪtr-
$_{(ı)}$kɑːm-, -ɑːt *(*)* **~s** s
compeer ˈkɒm pɪə •ˈ• ‖ kəm ˈpɪᵊr $_{(ı)}$kɑːm-,
ˈkɑːm pɪr **~s** z
compel kəm ˈpel §$_{(ı)}$kɒm- **~led** d **~ling/ly**
ɪŋ /li **~s** z
compellab|le kəm ˈpel əb |ᵊl §$_{(ı)}$kɒm- **~ly** li
compendious kəm ˈpend i‿əs §$_{(ı)}$kɒm- **~ly** li
~ness nəs nɪs
compendium kəm ˈpend i‿əm §$_{(ı)}$kɒm- **~s** z
compensable kəm ˈpenᵗs əb ᵊl
compen|sate ˈkɒmp *ə*n |seɪt -en- ‖ ˈkɑːmp-
~sated seɪt ɪd -əd ‖ seɪt̬ əd **~sates** seɪts
~sating seɪt ɪŋ ‖ seɪt̬ ɪŋ
compensation ˌkɒmp *ə*n ˈseɪʃ ᵊn -en-
‖ ˌkɑːmp- **~s** z
compensatory ˌkɒmp *ə*n ˈseɪt‿*ə*r i ◂ ˌ•en-,
ˈ•••••; kəm ˈpenᵗs ət‿*ə*r i, §$_{(ı)}$kɒm-
‖ kəm ˈpenᵗs ə tɔːr i -tour i
compere, compère ˈkɒm peə ‖ ˈkɑːm per **~d**
d **~s** z **compering, compèring**
ˈkɒm peər ɪŋ ‖ ˈkɑːm per ɪŋ
com|pete kəm |ˈpiːt §$_{(ı)}$kɒm- **~peted** ˈpiːt ɪd
-əd ‖ ˈpiːt̬ əd **~petes** ˈpiːts **~peting**
ˈpiːt ɪŋ ‖ ˈpiːt̬ ɪŋ
competenc|e ˈkɒmp ɪt *ə*nᵗs -ət-
‖ ˈkɑːmp ət ᵊnᵗs **~y** i
competent ˈkɒmp ɪt *ə*nt -ət- ‖ ˈkɑːmp ət ᵊnt
~ly li
competition ˌkɒmp ə ˈtɪʃ ᵊn -ɪ- ‖ ˌkɑːmp- **~s**
z
competitive kəm ˈpet ət ɪv §$_{(ı)}$kɒm-, -ɪt-
‖ -ˈpet̬ ət̬- **~ly** li **~ness** nəs nɪs
competitor kəm ˈpet ɪt ə §$_{(ı)}$kɒm-, -ət-
‖ -ˈpet̬ ət̬ ᵊr **~s** z
compilation ˌkɒmp ɪ ˈleɪʃ ᵊn -ə-, -aɪ- ‖ ˌkɑːmp-
~s z
compil|e kəm ˈpaɪᵊl §$_{(ı)}$kɒm- **~ed** d **~es** z
~ing ɪŋ
compiler kəm ˈpaɪl ə $_{(ı)}$kɒm- ‖ -ᵊr **~s** z
complacenc|e kəm ˈpleɪs ᵊnᵗs §$_{(ı)}$kɒm- **~y** i
complacent kəm ˈpleɪs ᵊnt §$_{(ı)}$kɒm- **~ly** li
complain kəm ˈpleɪn §$_{(ı)}$kɒm- **~ed** d **~er/s** ə/
z ‖ ᵊr/z **~ing/ly** ɪŋ /li **~s** z
complainant kəm ˈpleɪn ənt §$_{(ı)}$kɒm- **~s** s
complaint kəm ˈpleɪnt §$_{(ı)}$kɒm- **~s** s
complaisance kəm ˈpleɪz ᵊnᵗs §$_{(ı)}$kɒm-
‖ -ˈpleɪs- -ˈpleɪz-; ˌkɑːm pleɪ ˈzænᵗs, -plə-,
-ˈzɑːnᵗs, ˈ••• *(*)*
complaisant kəm ˈpleɪz ᵊnt §$_{(ı)}$kɒm- ‖ -ˈpleɪs-
-ˈpleɪz-; ˌkɑːm pleɪ ˈzænt, -plə-, -ˈzɑːnt, ˈ•••
(*) **~ly** li
compleat kəm ˈpliːt $_{(ı)}$kɒm-
complected kəm ˈplekt ɪd §$_{(ı)}$kɒm-, -əd
complement *n* ˈkɒmp lɪ mənt -lə- ‖ ˈkɑːmp lə-
(= compliment) **~s** s
comple|ment *v* ˈkɒmp lɪ |ment -lə-, ˌ••ˈ•
‖ ˈkɑːmp lə- *(= compliment) —see note at* -ment **~mented** ment ɪd -əd ‖ men*t̬* əd
~menting ment ɪŋ ‖ men*t̬* ɪŋ **~ments** men*t*s
complemental ˌkɒmp lɪ ˈment ᵊl ◂ -lə-
‖ ˌkɑːmp lə ˈmen*t̬* ᵊl ◂
complementarity ˌkɒmp lɪ men ˈtær ət i ˌ•lə-,
-mən ˈ•-, -ɪt i ‖ ˌkɑːmp lə men ˈtær ət̬ i
-mən ˈ•-, -ˈter-
complementary ˌkɒmp lɪ ˈment‿*ə*r i ◂ ˌ•lə-
‖ ˌkɑːmp lə ˈmen*t̬* *ə*r i ◂ →-ˈmentr i *(= complimentary)*
ˌcompleˌmentary ˈcolours
complementation ˌkɒmp lɪ men ˈteɪʃ ᵊn ˌ•lə-,
-mən ˈ•- ‖ ˌkɑːmp lə-
complementiser, complementizer
ˈkɒmp lɪ ment aɪz ə ˈ•lə-, -mən taɪz ə
‖ ˈkɑːmp lə ment aɪz ᵊr -mən taɪz ᵊr **~s** z
com|plete kəm |ˈpliːt §$_{(ı)}$kɒm- **~pleted**
ˈpliːt ɪd -əd ‖ ˈpliːt̬ əd **~pletes** ˈpliːts
~pleting ˈpliːt ɪŋ ‖ ˈpliːt̬ ɪŋ
completion kəm ˈpliːʃ ᵊn §$_{(ı)}$kɒm- **~s** z
completive kəm ˈpliːt ɪv ˌ(§)kɒm- ‖ -ˈpliːt̬-

COMPLEX

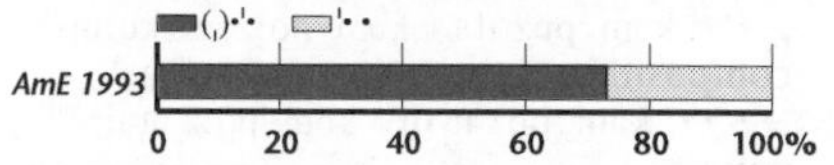

$_{(ı)}$•ˈ•
ˈ••
AmE 1993
0
20
40
60
80
100%

complex *adj* ˈkɒm pleks kəm ˈpleks, ˌkɒm-
‖ ˌkɑːm ˈpleks ◂ kəm-, ˈkɑːm pleks **~ly** li
—AmE 1993 poll panel preference: $_{(ı)}$•ˈ• *73%,* ˈ•• *27%.*
ˌcomplex ˈnumber; ˌcomplex ˈsentence
complex *n* ˈkɒm pleks ‖ ˈkɑːm- **~es** ɪz əz
complexion kəm ˈplekʃ ᵊn §$_{(ı)}$kɒm- **~ed** d **~s**
z
complexit|y kəm ˈpleks ət |i §$_{(ı)}$kɒm-, -ɪt-
‖ -ət̬ |i **~ies** iz
complianc|e kəm ˈplaɪ‿ənᵗs §$_{(ı)}$kɒm- **~es** ɪz əz
~y i
compliant kəm ˈplaɪ‿ənt §$_{(ı)}$kɒm- **~ly** li
compli|cate ˈkɒmp lɪ |keɪt -lə- ‖ ˈkɑːmp lə-
~cated keɪt ɪd -əd ‖ keɪt̬ əd **~cates** keɪts
~cating keɪt ɪŋ ‖ keɪt̬ ɪŋ
complicated ˈkɒmp lɪ keɪt ɪd -əd
‖ ˈkɑːmp lə keɪt̬ əd **~ly** li **~ness** nəs nɪs
complication ˌkɒmp lɪ ˈkeɪʃ ᵊn -lə-
‖ ˌkɑːmp lə- **~s** z
complicity kəm ˈplɪs ət i §$_{(ı)}$kɒm-, -ɪt- ‖ -ət̬ i
complie... *—see* **comply**
compliment *n* ˈkɒmp lɪ mənt -lə- ‖ ˈkɑːmp lə-
~s s
compli|ment *v* ˈkɒmp lɪ |ment -lə-, ˌ••ˈ•
‖ ˈkɑːmp lə- *—see note at* -ment **~mented**
ment ɪd -əd ‖ men*t̬* əd **~menting**
ment ɪŋ ‖ men*t̬* ɪŋ **~ments** men*t*s

C

complimentar|y ˌkɒmp lɪ 'ment_ər li ◄, •lə-
 ‖ ˌkɑːmp lə 'menˈ ər li ◄→-'mentr li ~ies iz
 ~ily əl i ɪ li ~iness i nəs i nɪs
complin 'kɒmp lɪn -lən ‖ 'kɑːmp-
compline 'kɒmp lɪn -lən, -laɪn ‖ 'kɑːmp-
com|ply kəm |'plaɪ §₍ᵢ₎kɒm- ~plied 'plaɪd
 ~plies 'plaɪz ~plying 'plaɪ ɪŋ
compo 'kɒmp əʊ ‖ 'kɑːmp oʊ
component kəm 'pəʊn ənt §₍ᵢ₎kɒm- ‖ -'poʊn-
 ~s s
 com ˌponent 'parts
componential ˌkɒmp əʊ 'nenʧ əl ◄ ‖ ˌkɑːmp ə-
com|port v kəm |'pɔːt §₍ᵢ₎kɒm- ‖ -|'pɔːrt
 -'poʊrt ~ported 'pɔːt ɪd -əd ‖ 'pɔːrʈ əd
 'poʊrʈ- ~porting 'pɔːt ɪŋ ‖ 'pɔːrʈ ɪŋ 'poʊrʈ-
 ~ports 'pɔːts ‖ 'pɔːrts 'poʊrts
comportment kəm 'pɔːt mənt §₍ᵢ₎kɒm-
 ‖ -'pɔːrt- -'poʊrt-
compos|e kəm 'pəʊz §₍ᵢ₎kɒm- ‖ -'poʊz ~ed d
 ~es ɪz əz ~ing ɪŋ
composedly kəm 'pəʊz ɪd li §₍ᵢ₎kɒm-, -əd •
 ‖ -'poʊz-
composer kəm 'pəʊz ə §₍ᵢ₎kɒm- ‖ -'poʊz ər ~s
 z
composite adj 'kɒmp əz ɪt -əs-, §-ət; -ə zaɪt,
 -saɪt ‖ kəm 'paːz ət kɑːm- ~s s
composite v 'kɒmp ə zaɪt -saɪt, ˌ• •'•;
 kəm 'pɒz ɪt ‖ kəm 'paːz ət kɑːm-
 composited 'kɒmp ə zaɪt ɪd -saɪt ɪd, -əd,
 ˌ• •'••; kəm 'pɒz ɪt- ‖ kəm 'paːz əʈ əd
 kɑːm- composites 'kɒmp ə zaɪts -saɪts,
 ˌ• •'•; kəm 'pɒz ɪts ‖ kəm 'paːz əts kɑːm-
 compositing 'kɒmp ə zaɪt ɪŋ -saɪt ɪŋ,
 ˌ• •'••; kəm 'pɒz ɪt ɪŋ ‖ kəm 'paːz əʈ ɪŋ
 kɑːm-
Compositae kəm 'pɒz ɪ taɪ §₍ᵢ₎kɒm-, -ə-, -tiː
 ‖ -'paːz-
composition ˌkɒmp ə 'zɪʃ ən ‖ ˌkɑːmp- ~s z
compositional ˌkɒmp ə 'zɪʃ ən_əl ◄ ‖ ˌkɑːmp-
compositor kəm 'pɒz ɪt ə §₍ᵢ₎kɒm-, -ət-
 ‖ -'paːz əʈ ər ~s z
compos mentis ˌkɒmp əs 'ment ɪs ˌkɒm pɒs-,
 §-əs ‖ ˌkɑːmp əs 'menʈ əs ˌkoʊm poʊs-
compost 'kɒmp ɒst ‖ 'kɑːm poʊst (*) ~ed ɪd
 əd ~ing ɪŋ ~s s
composure kəm 'pəʊʒ ə §₍ᵢ₎kɒm- ‖ -'poʊʒ ər
compote 'kɒm pəʊt -pɒt ‖ 'kɑːm poʊt ~s s
compound v kəm 'paʊnd ₍ᵢ₎kɒm-, '•• ~ed ɪd
 əd ~ing ɪŋ ~s z
compound n 'kɒm paʊnd ‖ 'kɑːm- ~s z
compound adj 'kɒm paʊnd ‖ 'kɑːm-
 kəm 'paʊnd, ˌkɑːm 'paʊnd ◄
 ˌcompound 'fracture; ˌcompound
 'interest; ˌcompound 'tense
comprehend ˌkɒmp rɪ 'hend -rə- ‖ ˌkɑːm-
 ~ed ɪd əd ~ing ɪŋ ~s z
comprehensibility ˌkɒmp rɪ ˌhenˈs ə 'bɪl ət i
 ˌ• rə-, -, •ɪ-, -ɪt i ‖ ˌkɑːmp rɪ ˌhenˈs ə 'bɪl əʈ i
comprehensib|le ˌkɒmp rɪ 'henˈs əb |əl ˌ• rə-,
 -ɪb əl ‖ ˌkɑːmp- ~ly li
comprehension ˌkɒmp rɪ 'henʧ ən -rə-
 ‖ ˌkɑːmp-

comprehensive ˌkɒmp rɪ 'henˈs ɪv ◄ -rə-
 ‖ ˌkɑːmp- ~ly li ~s z
comprehensivis... —see comprehensiviz...
comprehensivization
 ˌkɒmp rɪ ˌhenˈs ɪv aɪ 'zeɪʃ ən ˌ• rə-, -ɪ' •-
 ‖ ˌkɑːmp rɪ ˌhenˈs ɪv ə-
comprehensiviz|e ˌkɒmp rɪ 'henˈs ɪ vaɪz ˌ• rə-
 ‖ ˌkɑːmp- ~ed d ~es ɪz əz ~ing ɪŋ
compress v kəm 'pres §₍ᵢ₎kɒm- ~ed t ~es ɪz
 əz ~ing ɪŋ
 com ˌpressed 'air
compress n 'kɒm pres ‖ 'kɑːm- ~es ɪz əz
compressibility kəm ˌpres ə 'bɪl ət i §kɒm-,
 §ˌkɒm pres-, -, •ɪ-, -ɪt i ‖ -əʈ i
compressible kəm 'pres əb əl §₍ᵢ₎kɒm-
compression kəm 'preʃ ən §₍ᵢ₎kɒm- ~s z
compressor kəm 'pres ə §₍ᵢ₎kɒm- ‖ -ər ~s z
compris|e kəm 'praɪz §₍ᵢ₎kɒm- ~ed d ~es ɪz
 əz ~ing ɪŋ
compromis|e 'kɒmp rə maɪz ‖ 'kɑːmp- ~ed d
 ~es ɪz əz ~ing ɪŋ
comptometer, C~ tdmk ˌkɒmp 'tɒm ɪt ə -ət-
 ‖ ˌkɑːmp 'tɑːm əʈ ər ~s z
Compton (i) 'kɒmpt ən ‖ 'kɑːmpt ən, (ii)
 'kʌmpt ən
comptroller kən 'trəʊl ə kəmp-, ₍ᵢ₎kɒmp-,
 §₍ᵢ₎kɒn- ‖ -'troʊl ər kɑːmp-, '• • • ~s z
compulsion kəm 'pʌlʃ ən §₍ᵢ₎kɒm- ~s z
compulsive kəm 'pʌls ɪv §₍ᵢ₎kɒm- ~ly li ~ness
 nəs nɪs
compulsor|y kəm 'pʌls ər_li ~ily əl i ɪ li
 ~iness i nəs i nɪs
compunction kəm 'pʌŋk ʃən §₍ᵢ₎kɒm-
Compuserve tdmk
 'kɒmp ju sɜːv ‖ 'kɑːmp jə sɜːv
computability kəm ˌpjuːt ə 'bɪl ət i §kɒm-,
 §ˌkɒm pjuːt-, ˌkɒm pjʊt-, -ɪt i
 ‖ -ˌpjuːʈ ə 'bɪl əʈ i
computable kəm 'pjuːt əb əl 'kɒm pjʊt-
 ‖ -'pjuːʈ-
computation ˌkɒm pju 'teɪʃ ən ‖ ˌkɑːm- ~s z
computational ˌkɒm pju 'teɪʃ ən_əl ◄ ‖ ˌkɑːm-
 ~ly i
com|pute kəm |'pjuːt §₍ᵢ₎kɒm- ~puted
 'pjuːt ɪd -əd ‖ 'pjuːʈ əd ~putes 'pjuːts
 ~puting 'pjuːt ɪŋ ‖ 'pjuːʈ ɪŋ
computer kəm 'pjuːt ə §₍ᵢ₎kɒm- ‖ -'pjuːʈ ər ~s
 z
 com 'puter ˌlanguage
computerate kəm 'pjuːt ər ət §₍ᵢ₎kɒm-, -ɪt
 ‖ -'pjuːʈ-
computeris... —see computeriz...
computerization kəm ˌpjuːt ə raɪ 'zeɪʃ ən
 §₍ᵢ₎kɒm-, -ər ɪ- ‖ -ˌpjuːʈ ər ə-
computeriz|e kəm 'pjuːt ə raɪz §₍ᵢ₎kɒm-
 ‖ -'pjuːʈ- ~ed d ~es ɪz əz ~ing ɪŋ
comrade 'kɒm reɪd 'kʌm-, -rɪd, -rəd
 ‖ 'kɑːm ræd -rəd (*) ~s z ~ship ʃɪp
Comrie 'kɒm ri ‖ 'kɑːm-
coms kɒmz ‖ kɑːmz
comsat, C~ tdmk 'kɒm sæt ‖ 'kɑːm- ~s s
Comstock 'kɒm stɒk 'kʌm- ‖ 'kɑːm stɑːk

Compounds and phrases

1 A two-element **compound** is typically pronounced with **early** stress: that is to say, its first element has more stress than its second.

　'bedtime 'bed taɪm
　'block‚buster 'blɒk ‚bʌst ə ‖ 'blɑːk ‚bʌst ᵊr.

Although many compounds are written as single words, others are written as two words.

　'Christmas card
　'visitors' book
　'music ‚lessons
　'beauty ‚contest

2 On the other hand, a **phrase** is typically pronounced with **late** stress: that is to say, the second of two words has more stress than the first.

　‚next 'time
　‚printed 'cards
　‚several 'books
　‚weekly 'lessons

3 These stress patterns, and all others, can be changed if the speaker wants to emphasize a particular contrast (to focus on a particular element).

　I ‚don't want ‚music 'lessons — ‚just some ‚time to 'practise!
　It ‚wasn't a ‚beauty 'contest — ‚more a ‚beauty com'mercial.

The stress patterns shown in this dictionary are those that apply if no special emphasis (no contrastive focus) is required.

4 Some expressions, grammatically compounds, are nevertheless pronounced with late stress (= as if they were phrases). Among them are compounds in which the first element names the **material or ingredient** of which a thing is made.

　a ‚rubber 'duck
　‚paper 'plates
　‚cheese 'sandwiches
　a ‚pork 'pie
　a ‚gold 'ring

However, expressions involving **cake, juice** and **water** take early stress.

　'almond cake
　'orange juice
　'barley ‚water.

5 Names of roads and streets all take late stress except those involving **street** itself, which take early stress.

　‚Melrose 'Road
　‚Lavender 'Crescent
　‚Oxford 'Square
　‚King's 'Avenue
　but 'Gower Street.

comstockery 'kɒm stɒk ər i 'kʌm-, ˌˌ•'••
‖ 'kɑːm stɑːk-

Comte kɒnt kɔːnt ‖ koʊnt —Fr [kɔ̃ːt]

Comus 'kəʊm əs ‖ 'koʊm-

Comyn 'kʌm ɪn §-ən

Comyns 'kʌm ɪnz §-ənz

con, Con kɒn ‖ kɑːn —but as an Italian prepn,
in AmE also kɔːn, koʊn **conned**
kɒnd ‖ kɑːnd **conning** 'kɒn ɪŋ ‖ 'kɑːn ɪŋ
cons kɒnz ‖ kɑːnz —see also phrases with this
word.

con- This prefix is pronounced stressed
kɒn ‖ kɑːn (1) if the following syllable is
unstressed (ˌconfronˈtation), (2) in many two-
syllable nouns ('contract, but conˈtrol); and (3)
in context, when contrastively stressed
(ˌuniˌformity and 'conˌformity). Otherwise it is
usually weak kən in RP and GenAm, though
strong in some regional British speech
(conˈsider). Before a stem beginning n, one n is
lost (conˈnect, ˌconnoˈtation).

Cona tdmk 'kəʊn ə ‖ 'koʊn ə

conacre 'kɒn ˌeɪk ə kən 'eɪk ə ‖ 'kɑːn ˌeɪk ər
~s z

Conakry ˌkɒn ə 'kriː ‖ 'kɑːn ə kriː —Fr
[kɔ na kʁi]

con amore ˌkɒn ə 'mɔːr eɪ -i ‖ ˌkɑːn- ˌkɔːn,
ˌkoʊn-, -'moʊr-

Conan (i) 'kəʊn ən ‖ 'koʊn-, (ii) 'kɒn- ‖ 'kɑːn-
—For Sir A. Conan Doyle, (i)

conation kəʊ 'neɪʃ ən ‖ koʊ-

Concannon kɒn 'kæn ən ‖ kɑːn-

concate|nate kən 'kæt ə ǀneɪt →kəŋ-, ₍ˌ₎kɒn-,
→₍ˌ₎kɒŋ-, -ɪ-, -əǀn eɪt ‖ kɑːn 'kæt əǀn eɪt
~nated neɪt ɪd -əd ‖ neɪt̬ əd **~nates** neɪts
~nating neɪt ɪŋ ‖ neɪt̬ ɪŋ

concatenation kən ˌkæt ə 'neɪʃ ən →kəŋ-,
kɒn-, ˌkɒn kæt-, -ɪ'••-, -ən 'eɪʃ-
‖ kɑːn ˌkæt ən 'eɪʃ ən ˌ••- ~s z

concatenative kən 'kæt ən_ət ɪv →kəŋ-,
₍ˌ₎kɒn-, →₍ˌ₎kɒŋ-, -'•ɪn-, -ə neɪt-, -ɪ neɪt-
‖ ₍ˌ₎kɑːn 'kæt ən eɪt̬ ɪv

concave ₍ˌ₎kɒn 'keɪv ◄ →₍ˌ₎kɒŋ-, kən-, →kəŋ-,
'•• ‖ ₍ˌ₎kɑːn- ~ly li ~ness nəs nɪs

concavit|y ₍ˌ₎kɒn 'kæv ət li →₍ˌ₎kɒŋ-, kən-,
→kəŋ-, -ɪt- ‖ kɑːn- **~ies** iz

concavo-concave kɒn ˌkeɪv əʊ kɒn 'keɪv ◄
kən-, -kən'• ‖ kɑːn ˌkeɪv oʊ kɑːn 'keɪv

concavo-convex kɒn ˌkeɪv əʊ kɒn 'veks ◄
kən-, -kən'• ‖ kɑːn ˌkeɪv oʊ kɑːn 'veks

conceal kən 'siːl §₍ˌ₎kɒn- **~ed** d **~ing** ɪŋ
~ment mənt **~s** z

conced|e kən 'siːd §₍ˌ₎kɒn- **~ed** ɪd əd **~es** z
~ing ɪŋ

conceit kən 'siːt §₍ˌ₎kɒn- **~s** s

conceited kən 'siːt ɪd §₍ˌ₎kɒn-, -əd ‖ -'siːt̬ əd
~ly li **~ness** nəs nɪs

conceivab|le kən 'siːv əb |əl §₍ˌ₎kɒn- **~ly** li

conceiv|e kən 'siːv §₍ˌ₎kɒn- **~ed** d **~er/s** ə/
z ‖ ər/z **~es** z **~ing** ɪŋ

concele|brate ˌkɒn 'sel ə ǀbreɪt kən-, -ɪ-
‖ ˌkɑːn- **~brated** breɪt ɪd -əd ‖ breɪt̬ əd
~brates breɪts **~brating** breɪt ɪŋ ‖ breɪt̬ ɪŋ

concelebration ˌkɒn ˌsel ə 'breɪʃ ən kən ˌsel-,
-ɪ'••- ‖ ˌkɑːn- **~s** z

concen|trate 'kɒnᵗs ən ǀtreɪt -en- ‖ 'kɑːnᵗs-
~trated treɪt ɪd -əd ‖ treɪt̬ əd **~trates** treɪts
~trating treɪt ɪŋ ‖ treɪt̬ ɪŋ

concentration ˌkɒnᵗs ən 'treɪʃ ən -en-
‖ ˌkɑːnᵗs- **~s** z
  ˌconcen'tration camp

concentrator 'kɒnᵗs ən treɪt ə '•en-
‖ 'kɑːnᵗs ən treɪt̬ ər **~s** z

concentric kən 'sentr ɪk ₍ˌ₎kɒn- ‖ ₍ˌ₎kɑːn- **~ally**
əl_i

concept 'kɒn sept ‖ 'kɑːn- **~s** s

conception kən 'sep ʃən §₍ˌ₎kɒn- **~s** z

conceptual kən 'sep tʃu_əl §₍ˌ₎kɒn-, -ʃu_əl;
-'sept juː ‖ kɑːn-, -'sep tʃəl

conceptualis... —see **conceptualiz...**

conceptualization kən ˌsep tʃu_əl aɪ 'zeɪʃ ən
§kɒn-, -, •ʃu_əl-, -ˌsept juː-, -ɪ'••- ‖ -ə 'zeɪʃ-
kɑːn-, -ˌsep tʃəl ə 'zeɪʃ- **~s** z

conceptualiz|e kən 'sep tʃu_ə laɪz §₍ˌ₎kɒn-,
-'sept juː; -'sep tʃu laɪz,
-'sep tʃə laɪz ‖ kɑːn-, -'sep ʃu_ **~ed** d **~es** ɪz
əz **~ing** ɪŋ

conceptually kən 'sep tʃu_əl i §₍ˌ₎kɒn-, -ʃu_əl i;
-'sept juː ‖ kɑːn-, -'sep tʃəl i

concern kən 'sɜːn §₍ˌ₎kɒn- ‖ -'sɝːn **~ed** d
~ing ɪŋ **~s** z

concerned|ly kən 'sɜːn ɪd ǀli §₍ˌ₎kɒn-, -əd-;
-'sɜːnd ǀli ‖ -'sɝːn əd- **~ness** nəs nɪs

concert n 'musical performance'
'kɒnᵗs ət ‖ 'kɑːnᵗs ərt **~s** s
  ˌconcert 'grand

concert n 'agreement' 'kɒnᵗs ət 'kɒn sɜːt
‖ 'kɑːnᵗs ərt 'kɑːn sɝːt

con|cert v kən ǀ'sɜːt §₍ˌ₎kɒn- ‖ -ǀ'sɝːt **~certed**
'sɜːt ɪd -əd ‖ -'sɝːt̬ əd **~certing**
'sɜːt ɪŋ ‖ -'sɝːt̬ ɪŋ **~certs** 'sɜːts ‖ -'sɝːts

concertante ˌkɒntʃ ə 'tænt eɪ -i
‖ ˌkoʊn tʃər 'tɑːnt eɪ

concerted kən 'sɜːt ɪd §₍ˌ₎kɒn-, -əd ‖ -'sɝːt̬ əd
~ly li

Concertgebouw ₍ˌ₎kɒn 'sɜːt gə baʊ kən-,
-gɪ baʊ ‖ kɑːn 'sɝːt- —Dutch
[kɒn 'sɛrt xə ˌbɒu]

concertgo|er/s 'kɒnᵗs ət ˌgəʊ ə/z
‖ 'kɑːnᵗs ərt ˌgoʊ ǀər/z **~ing** ɪŋ

concerti kən 'tʃeət iː §₍ˌ₎kɒn-, -'tʃɜːt-
‖ -'tʃert̬ iː
  conˌcerti 'grossi 'grɒs iː ‖ 'groʊs iː

concertina ˌkɒnᵗs ə 'tiːn ə ‖ ˌkɑːnᵗs ər- **~ed** d
concertinaing
ˌkɒnᵗs ə 'tiːn ər ɪŋ ‖ ˌkɑːnᵗs ər 'tiːn ə ɪŋ **~s** z

concertin|o
ˌkɒntʃ ə 'tiːn ǀəʊ ‖ ˌkɑːntʃ ər 'tiːn ǀoʊ **~i** iː
~os əʊz ‖ oʊz

concertmaster 'kɒnᵗs ət ˌmɑːst ə §-ˌmæst-
‖ 'kɑːnᵗs ərt ˌmæst ər **~s** z

concert|o kən 'tʃeət ǀəʊ §₍ˌ₎kɒn-, -'tʃɜːt-
‖ -'tʃert̬ ǀoʊ **~i** iː **~os** əʊz ‖ oʊz
  conˌcerto 'grosso 'grɒs əʊ ‖ 'groʊs oʊ

concession kən 'seʃ ən §₍ˌ₎kɒn- **~s** z

Compression

1 Sometimes a sequence of sounds has two possible pronunciations: either as two separate syllables, or **compressed** into a single syllable. Possible compressions are shown in LPD by the symbol ‿ between the syllables affected.

lenient	'liːn i‿ənt	Two pronunciations are possible: a slower one 'liːn i ənt, and a faster one 'liːn jənt.
maddening	'mæd ᵊn‿ɪŋ	Two pronunciations are possible: a slower one with three syllables, 'mæd n ɪŋ or 'mæd ən ɪŋ and a faster one with two syllables, 'mæd nɪŋ.
diagram	'daɪ‿ə græm	Two pronunciations are possible: a slower one 'daɪ ə græm, and a faster one 'daə græm.

2 Generally the uncompressed version is more usual
- in rarer words
- in slow or deliberate speech
- the first time a word is used in a given discourse.

The compressed version is more usual
- in frequently used words
- in fast or casual speech
- if the word has already been used in the discourse.

3 When a syllable is compressed, one of the following phonetic changes takes place. (They are also exemplified in 1 above.)
- A weak vowel i or u is changed into the corresponding semivowel, j or w, producing in combination with the following vowel a crescendo DIPHTHONG.
  influence 'ɪn flu‿ən^ts (= 'ɪn.flu.ən^ts or 'ɪn.flwən^ts)
- A syllabic consonant is changed into a plain non-syllabic consonant. (See SYLLABIC CONSONANTS for LPD's use of superscript schwa (ᵊ) to indicate a potential syllabic consonant.)
  doubling 'dʌb ᵊl‿ɪŋ (= 'dʌb.l.ɪŋ or 'dʌb.lɪŋ)
- A long vowel or diphthong changes: iː becomes ɪ, uː becomes ʊ, and a diphthong loses its second element, so that aɪ and aʊ become a. In LPD this possibility is shown by printing the length-mark or the second element in italics (*iː, aɪ, aʊ*). These changes, known as **smoothing**, are often to be heard in BrE RP, but not in GenAm.
  agreeable ə 'griː‿əb ᵊl (= ə.'griː.əb.l or ə.'grɪəb.l)
  ruinous 'ruː ɪn‿əs (= 'ruː.ɪn.əs or 'rʊɪn.əs)
  scientist 'saɪ‿ənt ɪst (= 'saɪ.ənt.ɪst or 'saənt.ɪst)
  nowadays 'naʊ‿ə deɪz (= 'naʊ.ə.deɪz or 'naə.deɪz)

4 In the case of two potential syllabic consonants, it is always the one **before** the mark ‿ that can lose its syllabicity through compression.
  national 'næʃ ᵊn‿əl (= 'næʃ.n.əl or 'næʃ.nəl)
  liberal 'lɪb ᵊr‿əl (= 'lɪb.r.əl or 'lɪb.rəl)

► *Compression*

5 Sometimes a pronunciation that was originally the result of compression has become the only possibility. For example, the comparative of **simple** 'sɪmp ᵊl might be expected to be **simpler** 'sɪmp ᵊl ə ‖ -ᵊr (three syllables). In fact it is always 'sɪmp lə ‖ -lᵊr (two syllables). There are also words where speakers differ: most people always pronounce **factory** 'fæk tri with two syllables, but a few may sometimes say it with three, 'fækt ᵊr i.

Many historical compressions are shown as such in the spelling: **angry, disastrous, remembrance**. In such words an uncompressed pronunciation (e.g. rɪ 'mem bᵊr ᵊnᵗs) is not considered standard.

concessionaire kən ˌseʃ ə 'neə §₍ᵢ₎kɒn- ‖ -'neᵊr
~s z
concessionary kən 'seʃ ᵊn ᵊr‿i -ᵊn‿ᵊr i
‖ -ə ner i
concessive kən 'ses ɪv §₍ᵢ₎kɒn-
conch kɒŋk kɒntʃ ‖ kɑːŋk kɑːntʃ, kɔːŋk
conches 'kɒntʃ ɪz -əz ‖ 'kɑːntʃ ɪz **conchs**
kɒŋks ‖ kɑːŋks kɔːŋks
conch|a 'kɒŋk lə ‖ 'kɑːŋk lə ~ae iː
conchie 'kɒnᵗʃ i ‖ 'kɑːnᵗʃ i ~s z
Conchobar 'kɒn u‿ə 'kɒŋk əʊ ə ‖ 'kɑːn u‿ᵊr
'kɑːŋk oʊ ᵊr
conchoid 'kɒŋk ɔɪd ‖ 'kɑːŋk- ~s z
conchoidal kɒŋ 'kɔɪd ᵊl ‖ kɑːŋ-
conchological
ˌkɒŋk ə 'lɒdʒ ɪk ᵊl ◄ ‖ ˌkɑːŋk ə 'lɑːdʒ- ~ly‿i
conchologist ₍ᵢ₎kɒŋ 'kɒl ədʒ ɪst ₍ᵢ₎kɒn-, §-əst
‖ ₍ᵢ₎kɑːŋ 'kɑːl- ~s s
conchology ₍ᵢ₎kɒŋ 'kɒl ədʒ i ₍ᵢ₎kɒn-
‖ ₍ᵢ₎kɑːŋ 'kɑːl-
concierg|e kɒn si eəʒ 'kõ-, ˌ•'•
‖ koʊn 'sjeᵊrʒ —*Fr* [kɔ̃ sjɛʁʒ] ~es ɪz əz
conciliar kən 'sɪl i‿ə §₍ᵢ₎kɒn- ‖ -‿ᵊr
concili|ate kən 'sɪl i eɪt §₍ᵢ₎kɒn- ~ated eɪt ɪd
-əd ‖ eɪt̬ əd ~ates eɪts ~ating eɪt ɪŋ ‖ eɪt̬ ɪŋ
conciliation kən ˌsɪl i 'eɪʃ ᵊn §₍ᵢ₎kɒn- ~s z
conciliator kən 'sɪl i eɪt ə -eɪt̬ ᵊr ~s z
conciliatory kən 'sɪl i‿ət‿ᵊr i §₍ᵢ₎kɒn-, -i eɪt ᵊr i;
kən ˌsɪl i 'eɪt ᵊr i ‖ -i‿ə tɔːr i -tour i
concise kən 'saɪs §₍ᵢ₎kɒn- ~ly li ~ness nəs nɪs
concision kən 'sɪʒ ᵊn §₍ᵢ₎kɒn-
conclave 'kɒŋ kleɪv 'kɒn- ‖ 'kɑːn- ~s z
conclud|e kən 'kluːd →kəŋ-, §₍ᵢ₎kɒn- ~ed ɪd
əd ~es z ~ing ɪŋ
conclusion kən 'kluːʒ ᵊn →kəŋ-, §₍ᵢ₎kɒn- ~s z
conclusive kən 'kluːs ɪv →kəŋ-, §₍ᵢ₎kɒn-,
§-'kluːz- ~ly li ~ness nəs nɪs
conclusory kən 'kluːs ər i →kəŋ-, §₍ᵢ₎kɒn-,
-'kluːz-
concoct kən 'kɒkt →kəŋ-, §₍ᵢ₎kɒn- ‖ -'kɑːkt
~ed ɪd əd ~ing ɪŋ ~s s
concoction kən 'kɒk ʃᵊn →kəŋ-, §₍ᵢ₎kɒn-
‖ -'kɑːk- ~s z
concomitanc|e kən 'kɒm ɪt ᵊnᵗs →kəŋ-,
§₍ᵢ₎kɒn-, -ət- ‖ -'kɑːm ət ᵊnᵗs ~y i

concomitant kən 'kɒm ɪt ᵊnt →kəŋ-, §₍ᵢ₎kɒn-,
-ət- ‖ -'kɑːm ət ᵊnt ~ly li ~s s
concord 'kɒŋ kɔːd 'kɒn- ‖ 'kɑːn kɔːrd
→'kɑːŋ- ~s z
Concord (i) 'kɒŋ kɔːd 'kɒn- ‖ 'kɑːn kɔːrd
→'kɑːŋ-, (ii) 'kɒŋk əd 'kɒn kɔːd, 'kɒŋ-
‖ 'kɑːŋk ᵊrd —*The place in NC is* (i), *that in
MA* (ii). *Authorities disagree about the places in
CA and NH.*
concordanc|e kən 'kɔːd ᵊnᵗs →kəŋ-, §₍ᵢ₎kɒn-
‖ -'kɔːrd- kɑːn- ~ed t ~es ɪz əz ~ing ɪŋ
concordant kən 'kɔːd ᵊnt →kəŋ-, §₍ᵢ₎kɒn-
‖ -'kɔːrd ᵊnt ~ly li
concordat kən 'kɔːd æt →kɒŋ-, kən-, →kəŋ-
‖ kən 'kɔːrd æt ~s s
Concorde *aircraft* 'kɒŋ kɔːd 'kɒn- ‖'kɑːn kɔːrd
→'kɑːŋ-, •'• ~s z
concours 'kɒŋ kʊə ‖ koʊn 'kʊᵊr —*Fr* [kɔ̃ kuːʁ]
ˌconcours/conˌcours d'ele'gance, c~
d'élé'gance ˌdel eɪ 'gɒnᵗs ‖ ˌdeɪ leɪ 'gɑːnᵗs
—*Fr* [de le gɑ̃ːs]
concours|e 'kɒŋ kɔːs 'kɒn- ‖ 'kɑːn kɔːrs
→'kɑːŋ-, -kours ~es ɪz əz
concrete *n; adj 'made of ~'* 'kɒŋ kriːt 'kɒn-
‖ 'kɑːn- ₍ᵢ₎•'•
ˌconcrete 'jungle; 'concrete ˌmixer
concrete *adj 'not abstract'* 'kɒŋ kriːt 'kɒn-
‖ ₍ᵢ₎kɑːn 'kriːt '••, kən 'kriːt ~ly li ~ness
nəs nɪs
con|crete *v 'cover with ~'* 'kɒŋ |kriːt 'kɒn-
‖ 'kɑːn- ₍ᵢ₎•'• ~creted kriːt ɪd -əd ‖ kriːt̬ əd
~cretes kriːts ~creting kriːt ɪŋ ‖ kriːt̬ ɪŋ
con|crete *v 'solidify'* kən |'kriːt →kəŋ-, ₍ᵢ₎kɒn-
‖ 'kɑːn |kriːt ₍ᵢ₎•'• ~creted 'kriːt ɪd -əd
‖ kriːt̬ əd ~cretes 'kriːts ‖ kriːts ~creting
'kriːt ɪŋ ‖ kriːt̬ ɪŋ
concretion kən 'kriːʃ ᵊn →kəŋ-, ₍ᵢ₎kɒn- ‖ kɑːn-
kən- ~s z
concretis... —*see* **concretiz...**
concretization
ˌkɒŋ kriːt aɪ 'zeɪʃ ᵊn ‖ kɑːn ˌkriːt̬ ə-, ˌ••-
concretiz|e 'kɒŋ kriːt aɪz ‖ kɑːn 'kriːt aɪz '••-
~ed d ~es ɪz əz ~ing ɪŋ
concubinage kɒn 'kjuːb ɪn ɪdʒ →kɒŋ-, kən-,
→kəŋ-, -ᵊn- ‖ kɑːn-

concubine 'kɒŋ kju baɪn 'kɒn-, -kjə- ‖ 'kɑːŋ-
~s z

concupiscence kən 'kjuːp ɪs ənts →kəŋ-, kɒn-,
→kɒŋ-, §-əs-; ˌkɒŋ kju 'pɪs- ‖ kɑːn-

concupiscent kən 'kjuːp ɪs ənt →kəŋ-, kɒn-,
→kɒŋ-, §-əs-; ˌkɒŋ kju 'pɪs- ‖ kɑːn-

con|cur kən ‖'kɜː →kəŋ-, §(ˌ)kɒn- ‖ -‖'kɜː:
kɑːn- ~curred 'kɜːd ‖ 'kɜːːd ~curring
'kɜːr ɪŋ ‖ 'kɜː: ɪŋ ~curs 'kɜːz ‖ 'kɜː:z

concurrence kən 'kʌr ənts →kəŋ-, §(ˌ)kɒn-
‖ -'kɜː:- kɑːn-

concurrent kən 'kʌr ənt →kəŋ-, §(ˌ)kɒn-
‖ -'kɜː:- kɑːn- ~ly li

concuss kən 'kʌs →kəŋ-, §(ˌ)kɒn- ~ed t ~es ɪz
əz ~ing ɪŋ

concussion kən 'kʌʃ ən →kəŋ-, §(ˌ)kɒn-

concussive kən 'kʌs ɪv →kəŋ-, §(ˌ)kɒn-

Conde, Condé 'kɒnd eɪ ‖ kɑːn 'deɪ —Fr
[kɔ̃ de]
ˌCondé 'Nast nɑːst næst ‖ næst

condemn kən 'dem §(ˌ)kɒn- ~ed d ~ing ɪŋ ~s
z
con'demned cell, • , • ' •

condemnable kən 'dem nəb əl

condemnation ˌkɒn dem 'neɪʃ ən -dəm-
‖ ˌkɑːn- ~s z

condemnatory kən 'dem nət_ər i §(ˌ)kɒn-;
ˌkɒn dem 'neɪt ər i ◂, • dəm-
‖ kən 'dem nə tɔːr i -tour i

condensate 'kɒn dents eɪt 'kɒnd ən seɪt;
kən 'dents eɪt ‖ 'kɑːn- ~s s

condensation ˌkɒn den 'seɪʃ ən -dən- ‖ ˌkɑːn-
~s z

condens|e kən 'dents §(ˌ)kɒn- ~ed t ~es ɪz əz
~ing ɪŋ
con,densed 'milk

condenser kən 'dents ə §(ˌ)kɒn- ‖ -ər ~s z

condescend ˌkɒn dɪ 'send -də- ‖ ˌkɑːn- ~ed
ɪd əd ~ing/ly ɪŋ /li ~s z

condescension ˌkɒn dɪ 'sentʃ ən -də- ‖ ˌkɑːn-

condign kən 'daɪn 'kɒn daɪn ‖ 'kɑːn daɪn ~ly
li

condiment 'kɒnd ɪ mənt -ə- ‖ 'kɑːnd- ~s s

condition kən 'dɪʃ ən §(ˌ)kɒn- ~ed d ~ing _ɪŋ
~s z
con,ditioned 'reflex

conditional kən 'dɪʃ ən_əl §(ˌ)kɒn- ~ly i

conditionality kən ˌdɪʃ ə 'næl ət i §kɒn-,
§ˌkɒn ˌdɪʃ-, -ɪt i ‖ -əţ i

conditioner kən 'dɪʃ ən_ə §(ˌ)kɒn- ‖ -ər ~s z

condo 'kɒnd əu ‖ 'kɑːnd ou ~s z

condol|e kən 'dəul §(ˌ)kɒn-, →-'dɒul ‖ -'doul
~ed d ~es z ~ing ɪŋ

condolenc|e kən 'dəul ənts §(ˌ)kɒn- ‖ -'doul-
~es ɪz əz

condom 'kɒnd əm 'kɒn dɒm ‖ 'kʌnd əm
'kɑːnd- ~s z

condominium ˌkɒnd ə 'mɪn i_əm ‖ ˌkɑːnd- ~s
z

Condon 'kɒnd ən -ɒn ‖ 'kɑːnd ən

condonation ˌkɒnd ə 'neɪʃ ən ˌkɒn dəu-
‖ ˌkɑːnd- ˌkɑːn dou-

condon|e kən 'dəun §(ˌ)kɒn- ‖ -'doun ~ed d
~es z ~ing ɪŋ

condor 'kɒnd ɔː -ə ‖ 'kɑːnd ər -ɔːr ~s z

condottier|e ˌkɒn ˌdɒt i 'eər eɪ kən ˌdɒt-
‖ ˌkɑːn də 'tjer li ˌkɑːn ˌdaːţ i 'er li —It
[kɒn dɒt 'tjeːr e] ~i iː

Condover 'kʌnd əuv ə ‖ -ouv ər

conduc|e kən 'djuːs §(ˌ)kɒn-, →§-'dʒuːs
‖ -'duːs -'djuːs ~ed t ~es ɪz əz ~ing ɪŋ

conducive kən 'djuːs ɪv §(ˌ)kɒn-, →§-'dʒuːs-
‖ -'duːs- -'djuːs- ~ness nəs nɪs

conduct n 'kɒn dʌkt -dəkt ‖ 'kɑːn- ~s s

conduct v kən 'dʌkt §(ˌ)kɒn- ~ed ɪd əd ~ing
ɪŋ ~s s

conductance kən 'dʌkt ənts §(ˌ)kɒn-

conduction kən 'dʌk ʃən §(ˌ)kɒn-

conductive kən 'dʌkt ɪv §(ˌ)kɒn- ~ly li

conductivity ˌkɒn dʌk 'tɪv ət i , • dək-, -ɪt i
‖ ˌkɑːn dʌk 'tɪv əţ i kən ˌdʌk 'tɪv-

conductor kən 'dʌkt ə §(ˌ)kɒn- ‖ -ər ~s z
~ship/s ʃɪp/s
con'ductor rail

conductress kən 'dʌk trəs §(ˌ)kɒn-, -trɪs, -tres
~es ɪz əz

conduit 'kɒn djuː_ɪt 'kʌn-, -duː_ɪt, →§-dʒuː_ɪt,
§_ət; 'kɒnd ɪt, 'kʌnd-, §-ət ‖ 'kɑːn duː_ət
-djuː_ ~s s

Condy 'kɒnd i ‖ 'kɑːnd i

condyle 'kɒn daɪəl -dɪl, §-dəl ‖ 'kɑːn- ~s z

condylom|a ˌkɒnd ɪ 'ləum ə -ə-
‖ ˌkɑːnd ə 'loum ə -ata ət ə ‖ əţ ə ~as əz

cone kəun ‖ koun coned kəund ‖ kound
coning 'kəun ɪŋ ‖ 'koun ɪŋ cones
kəunz ‖ kounz

Conestoga ˌkɒn ɪ 'stəug ə -ə-
‖ ˌkɑːn ə 'stoug ə

coney, Coney 'kəun i ‖ 'koun i ~s z
ˌConey 'Island

confab n 'kɒn fæb kən 'fæb ‖ 'kɑːn- ~s s

confab v kən 'fæb 'kɒn fæb ‖ 'kɑːn fæb ~bed
d ~bing ɪŋ ~s z

confabu|late kən 'fæb ju leɪt (ˌ)kɒn- ‖ -jə-
~lated leɪt ɪd-əd ‖ leɪţ əd ~lates leɪts
~lating leɪt ɪŋ ‖ leɪţ ɪŋ

confabulation kən ˌfæb ju 'leɪʃ ən (ˌ)kɒn-
‖ -jə- ~s z

confect v kən 'fekt §(ˌ)kɒn- ~ed ɪd əd ~ing ɪŋ
~s s

confection kən 'fek ʃən §(ˌ)kɒn- ~s z

confectioner kən 'fek ʃən_ə §(ˌ)kɒn- ‖ _ər ~s z

confectioner|y kən 'fek ʃən_ər li §(ˌ)kɒn-, -ʃən
ər_li i ‖ -ʃə ner li ~ies iz

confederac|y, C~ kən 'fed_ər əs li §(ˌ)kɒn-
~ies iz

confederate adj, n kən 'fed_ər ət §(ˌ)kɒn-, -ɪt
~s s

confede|rate v kən 'fed ə ˌreɪt §(ˌ)kɒn- ~rated
reɪt ɪd-əd ‖ reɪţ əd ~rates reɪts ~rating
reɪt ɪŋ ‖ reɪţ ɪŋ

confederation, C~ kən ˌfed ə 'reɪʃ ən §kɒn-,
§ˌkɒn, • - ~s z

con|fer kən ‖'fɜː §(ˌ)kɒn- ‖ -‖'fɜː: ~ferred

'fɜːd ‖ 'fɜːd **~ferring** 'fɜːr ɪŋ ‖ 'fɜː ɪŋ **~fers**
'fɜːz ‖ 'fɜːz
conferee ˌkɒn fə 'riː -fɜː- ‖ ˌkɑːn- **~s** z
conferenc|e 'kɒn fᵊr_ᵊnᵗs ‖ 'kɑːn- **~es** ɪz əz
conferral kən 'fɜːr əl §(ˌ)kɒn- ‖ -'fɜː- **~s** z
conferv|a kən 'fɜːv lə (ˌ)kɒn- ‖ -'fɜːv lə **~ae** iː
~as əz
confess kən 'fes §(ˌ)kɒn- **~ed** t **~es** ɪz əz
~ing ɪŋ
confession kən 'feʃ ᵊn §(ˌ)kɒn- **~s** z
confessional kən 'feʃ ᵊn_əl §(ˌ)kɒn- **~s** z
confessor kən 'fes ə (ˌ)kɒn-, -ɔː ‖ -ᵊr 'kɑːn fes-,
-ɔːr **~s** z
confetti kən 'fet i kɒn- ‖ -'feṭ i
confidant, confidante 'kɒn fɪ dænt -fə-, ˌ•• ' • ˈ•,
ˌ••'dɑːnt, '••dənt ‖ 'kɑːn- -dɑːnt **~s** s
confid|e kən 'faɪd §(ˌ)kɒn- **~ed** ɪd əd **~er/s** ə/
z ‖ ᵊr/z **~es** z **~ing** ɪŋ
confidence 'kɒn fɪd ᵊnᵗs -fəd- ‖ 'kɑːn- **~es** ɪz
əz
'confidence ˌlimit; 'confidence ˌtrick
confident 'kɒn fɪd ᵊnt -fəd- ‖ 'kɑːn- **~ly** li
confidential ˌkɒn fɪ 'denᵗʃ ᵊl ◄ -fə- ‖ ˌkɑːn-
~ly i
confidentiality ˌkɒn fɪ ˌdenᵗʃ i 'æl ət i, •fə-
‖ ˌkɑːn fə ˌdenᵗʃ i 'æl əṭ i
confiding kən 'faɪd ɪŋ §(ˌ)kɒn- **~ly** li
configuration kən ˌfɪg jə 'reɪʃ ᵊn ˌkɒn ˌfɪg-,
-juᵊ-, -ə- ‖ ˌkɑːn ˌfɪg- **~al/ly** ᵊl /i **~s** z
configure kən 'fɪg ə §(ˌ)kɒn- ‖ -jᵊr (*) **~ed** d
~es z **configuring** kən 'fɪg ᵊr ɪŋ (ˌ)kɒn-
‖ -jər ɪŋ
confin|e v kən 'faɪn §(ˌ)kɒn- **~ed** d **~es** z
~ing ɪŋ
confine n 'kɒn faɪn ‖ 'kɑːn- **~s** z
confinement kən 'faɪn mənt §(ˌ)kɒn-, →-'faɪm-
~s s
confirm kən 'fɜːm §(ˌ)kɒn- ‖ -'fɜːm **~ed** d
~ing ɪŋ **~s** z
confirmation ˌkɒn fə 'meɪʃ ᵊn ‖ ˌkɑːn fᵊr- **~s** z
confirmatory kən 'fɜːm ət_ᵊr i ˌkɒn fə 'meɪt
ᵊr i ◄, '••••• ‖ -'fɜːm ə tɔːr i -toʊr i
con|firmed kən I'fɜːmd §(ˌ)kɒn- ‖ -I'fɜːmd
~firmedly 'fɜːm ɪd li -əd- ‖ 'fɜːm əd li
confi|scate v 'kɒn fɪ Iskeɪt -fə- ‖ 'kɑːn-
~scated skeɪt ɪd -əd ‖ skeɪṭ əd **~scates**
skeɪts **~scating** skeɪt ɪŋ ‖ skeɪṭ ɪŋ
confiscation ˌkɒn fɪ 'skeɪʃ ᵊn -fə- ‖ ˌkɑːn- **~s**
z
confiscatory kən 'fɪsk ət_ᵊr i kɒn-;
ˌkɒn fɪ 'skeɪt ᵊr i, •'fə-, '••••• ‖ -ə tɔːr i
-toʊr i
Confiteor kɒn 'fɪt i ɔː kən- ‖ kən 'fɪṭ i ɔːr
-'fiːt-, -i_ᵊr
conflagration ˌkɒn flə 'greɪʃ ᵊn ‖ ˌkɑːn- **~s** z
con|flate kən I'fleɪt (ˌ)kɒn- **~flated** 'fleɪt ɪd -əd
‖ 'fleɪṭ əd **~flates** 'fleɪts **~flating**
'fleɪt ɪŋ ‖ 'fleɪṭ ɪŋ
conflation kən 'fleɪʃ ᵊn (ˌ)kɒn- **~s** z
conflict n 'kɒn flɪkt ‖ 'kɑːn- **~s** s
conflict v kən 'flɪkt §(ˌ)kɒn-;
'kɒn flɪkt ‖ 'kɑːn flɪkt **~ed** ɪd əd **~ing/ly**
ɪŋ /li **~s** s

confluenc|e 'kɒn flu_ᵊnᵗs ‖ 'kɑːn- **~es** ɪz əz
confluent 'kɒn flu_ᵊnt ‖ 'kɑːn- **~s** s
conform kən 'fɔːm §(ˌ)kɒn- ‖ -'fɔːrm **~ed** d
~ing ɪŋ **~s** z
conformab|le kən 'fɔːm əb |ᵊl §(ˌ)kɒn-
‖ -'fɔːrm- **~leness** ᵊl nəs -nɪs **~ly** li
conformal kən 'fɔːm ᵊl (ˌ)kɒn- ‖ -'fɔːrm-
(ˌ)kɑːn- **~ly** i
conformance kən 'fɔːm ᵊnᵗs §(ˌ)kɒn-
‖ -'fɔːrm-
conformation ˌkɒn fɔː 'meɪʃ ᵊn -fə-
‖ ˌkɑːn fɔːr- -fᵊr-
conformer kən 'fɔːm ə §(ˌ)kɒn- ‖ -'fɔːrm ᵊr **~s**
z
conformist kən 'fɔːm ɪst §(ˌ)kɒn-, §-əst
‖ -'fɔːrm- **~s** s
conformit|y kən 'fɔːm ət li §(ˌ)kɒn-, -ɪt-
‖ -'fɔːrm əṭ li **~ies** iz
confound kən 'faʊnd (ˌ)kɒn- ‖ (ˌ)kɑːn- **~ed** ɪd
əd **~ing** ɪŋ **~s** z
confounded kən 'faʊnd ɪd (ˌ)kɒn-, -əd ‖ (ˌ)kɑːn-
~ly li **~ness** nəs nɪs
confraternity ˌkɒn frə 'tɜːn ət i -ɪt i
‖ ˌkɑːn frə 'tɜːn əṭ i
confrere, confrère 'kɒn freə ‖ 'kɑːn frer
'koʊn-, •'• —Fr [kɔ̃ fʁɛːʁ] **~s** z
con|front kən I'frʌnt §(ˌ)kɒn- **~fronted**
'frʌnt ɪd -əd ‖ 'frʌnṭ əd **~fronting**
'frʌnt ɪŋ ‖ 'frʌnṭ ɪŋ **~fronts** 'frʌnᵗs
confrontation ˌkɒn frʌn 'teɪʃ ᵊn -frən-
‖ ˌkɑːn-
confrontational ˌkɒn frʌn 'teɪʃ ᵊn_əl ◄, •frən-
‖ ˌkɑːn- **~ly** i
confrontationist ˌkɒn frʌn 'teɪʃ ᵊn_ɪst, •frən-,
§-əst ‖ ˌkɑːn- **~s** s
Confucian kən 'fjuːʃ ᵊn (ˌ)kɒn-, -'fjuːʃ i_ən
~ism ɪz əm
Confucius kən 'fjuːʃ əs (ˌ)kɒn-, -'fjuːʃ i_əs
—Chi Kǒng Fūzǐ [³kʰʊŋ ¹fu ³tsɨ]
confus|e kən 'fjuːz §(ˌ)kɒn- **~ed** d **~es** ɪz əz
~ing/ly ɪŋ /li
confused|ly kən 'fjuːz ɪd lli §(ˌ)kɒn-, -əd-;
-'fjuːzd lli **~ness** nəs nɪs
confusion kən 'fjuːʒ ᵊn §(ˌ)kɒn- **~s** z
confutation ˌkɒn fju 'teɪʃ ᵊn ‖ ˌkɑːn- **~s** z
con|fute kən I'fjuːt §(ˌ)kɒn- **~futed** 'fjuːt ɪd
-əd ‖ 'fjuːṭ əd **~futes** 'fjuːts **~futing**
'fjuːt ɪŋ ‖ 'fjuːṭ ɪŋ
conga 'kɒŋ gə ‖ 'kɑːŋ gə **~ed** d **congaing**
'kɒŋ gəʳ ɪŋ ‖ 'kɑːŋ gə ɪŋ **~s** z
congé 'kɒn ʒeɪ 'kɒ̃- ‖ koʊn 'ʒeɪ kɑːn-, kɔːn-;
'kɑːn ʒeɪ —Fr [kɔ̃ ʒe] **~s** z
congeal kən 'dʒiːᵊl §(ˌ)kɒn- **~ed** d **~ing** ɪŋ **~s**
z
congelation ˌkɒn dʒɪ 'leɪʃ ᵊn-dʒə- ‖ ˌkɑːn-
congener kən 'dʒiːn ə kɒn-; 'kɒndʒ ɪn ə, -ᵊn-
‖ 'kɑːndʒ ᵊn ᵊr kən 'dʒiːn ᵊr **~s** z
congenial kən 'dʒiːn i_əl §(ˌ)kɒn- **~ly** i
congeniality kən ˌdʒiːn i 'æl ət i §ˌkɒn dʒiːn-,
-ɪt i ‖ -əṭ i
congenital kən 'dʒen ɪt ᵊl §(ˌ)kɒn-, §-ət- ‖ -əṭ-
~ly i

C

conger 'kɒŋ gə ‖ 'kɑːŋ g‿r ~**s** z
  ˌconger 'eel
congeries kɒn 'dʒɪər iːz kən-, -'dʒer-, -ɪz,
  -'dʒer i iːz ‖ 'kɑːnʤ ə riːz
congest kən 'dʒest §₍ᵢ₎kɒn- ~**ed** ɪd əd ~**ing** ɪŋ
  ~**s** s
congestion kən 'dʒes tʃən §₍ᵢ₎kɒn-, →-'dʒeʃ-
Congleton 'kɒŋ gəl tən ‖ 'kɑːŋ-
conglomerate adj, n kən 'glɒm ər‿ət →kəŋ-,
  §₍ᵢ₎kɒn-, ɪt, -ə reɪt ‖ -'glɑːm- ~**s** s
conglome|rate v kən 'glɒm ə |reɪt →kəŋ-
  ~**rated** reɪt ɪd -əd ‖ reɪt əd ~**rating**
  reɪt ɪŋ ‖ reɪt ɪŋ ~**rates** reɪts
conglomeration kən ˌglɒm ə 'reɪʃ ᵊn →kəŋ-,
  §kɒn-, §ˌkɒn ˌglɒm- ‖ -ˌglɑːm- ˌkɑːn ˌglɑːm-
  ~**s** z
Congo 'kɒŋ gəʊ ‖ 'kɑːŋ goʊ
Congolese ˌkɒŋ gə 'liːz ◀ ‖ ˌkɑːŋ- -'liːs
congrats kən 'græts →kəŋ-, §₍ᵢ₎kɒn-
congratters kən 'græt əz →kəŋ-, §₍ᵢ₎kɒn-
  ‖ -'græt ᵊrz

CONGRATULATE

■ -'grædʒ- ▢ -'grætʃ-
AmE 1993
0   20   40   60   80   100%

Percentage
◆ AmE93 /dʒ/ by age
80
70
60
50
40
30
20
0
Older ◀— Speakers —▶ Younger

congratu|late kən 'grætʃ u |leɪt →kəŋ-,
  §₍ᵢ₎kɒn-, -ə-; -'græt ju- ‖ -'grædʒ ə |leɪt
  -'grætʃ- —AmE 1993 poll panel preference:
  -'grædʒ- 58%, -'grætʃ- 42%. ~**lated** leɪt ɪd
  -əd ‖ leɪt əd ~**lates** leɪts ~**lating**
  leɪt ɪŋ ‖ leɪt ɪŋ
congratulation kən ˌgrætʃ u 'leɪʃ ᵊn →kəŋ-,
  §kɒn-, §ˌkɒn ˌgrætʃ-, -ə-; -ˌgræt ju-
  ‖ kən ˌgrætʃ ə- -ˌgrædʒ- ~**s** z
congratulatory kən ˌgrætʃ u 'leɪt ər i ◀→kəŋ-,
  §kɒn-, §ˌkɒn ˌgrætʃ-, -ə'•-; -ˌgræt ju-;
  kən 'grætʃ əl ət‿ər i, -'•ʊl- ‖ kən 'grætʃ
  əl‿ə tɔːr i -'grædʒ-, -tʊʊr i (*)
congregant 'kɒŋ grɪg ᵊnt -grəg- ‖ 'kɑːŋ- ~**s** s
congre|gate v 'kɒŋ grɪ |geɪt -grə- ‖ 'kɑːŋ-
  ~**gated** geɪt ɪd -əd ‖ geɪt əd ~**gates** geɪts
  ~**gating** geɪt ɪŋ ‖ geɪt ɪŋ
congregation ˌkɒŋ grɪ 'geɪʃ ᵊn -grə- ‖ ˌkɑːŋ-
  ~**s** z
congregational, C~ ˌkɒŋ grɪ 'geɪʃ ᵊn‿əl ◀
  ˌ•grə- ‖ ˌkɑːŋ-
Congregationalism ˌkɒŋ grɪ 'geɪʃ ᵊn‿ə ˌlɪz əm
  ˌ•grə-, əl ˌɪz- ‖ ˌkɑːŋ-
Congregationalist ˌkɒŋ grɪ 'geɪʃ ᵊn‿əl ɪst
  ˌ•grə-, §-əst ‖ ˌkɑːŋ- ~**s** s

Congresbury 'kɒŋz bər‿i 'kuːmz-
  ‖ 'kɑːŋz ber i
congress 'kɒŋ gres ‖ 'kɑːŋ grəs -rəs ~**es** ɪz əz
congressional kən 'greʃ ᵊn‿əl →kəŋ-, ₍ᵢ₎kɒn-,
  →₍ᵢ₎kɒŋ- ‖ ₍ᵢ₎kɑːn-
congress|man 'kɒŋ gres |mən -grɪs-, -grəs-
  ‖ 'kɑːŋ grəs- ~**men** mən men ~**woman**
  ˌwʊm ən ~**women** ˌwɪm ɪn §-ən
Congreve 'kɒŋ griːv ‖ 'kɑːn- →'kɑːŋ-
congruenc|e 'kɒŋ gru‿ənts ‖ 'kɑːŋ- kən 'gruː‿
  ~**es** ɪz əz ~**y** i
congruent 'kɒŋ gru‿ənt ‖ 'kɑːŋ- kən 'gruː‿
  ~**ly** li
congruential ˌkɒŋ gru 'entʃ ᵊl ◀ ‖ ˌkɑːŋ-
congruit|y kən 'gruː‿ət i →kəŋ-, ₍ᵢ₎kɒn-,
  →₍ᵢ₎kɒŋ-, ‿ɪt- ‿ət li ₍ᵢ₎kɑːn- ~**ies** iz
congruous 'kɒŋ gru‿əs ‖ 'kɑːŋ- ~**ly** li ~**ness**
  nəs nɪs
conic 'kɒn ɪk ‖ 'kɑːn ɪk ~**s** s
  ˌconic 'section
conical 'kɒn ɪk ᵊl ‖ 'kɑːn-
conidi|um kəʊ 'nɪd i‿ləm ‖ kə- ~**a** ə ~**al** əl
conie... —see **cony**
conifer 'kɒn ɪf ə 'kəʊn-, -əf- ‖ 'kɑːn əf ‿r ~**s** z
coniferous kəʊ 'nɪf ər‿əs kɒ- ‖ koʊ- kə-
coning 'kəʊn ɪŋ ‖ 'koʊn ɪŋ
Coningham 'kʌn ɪŋ əm ‖ -hæm
Coningsby 'kɒn ɪŋz bi 'kʌn- ‖ 'kʌn-
Conisborough, Conisbrough 'kɒn ɪs bər‿ə
  '•əs- ‖ 'kɑːn əs ˌbɝː oʊ
Coniston 'kɒn ɪst ən §-əst- ‖ 'kɑːn-
conium 'kəʊn i‿əm ‖ 'koʊn-
conjectural kən 'dʒek tʃᵊr‿əl §₍ᵢ₎kɒn-, -ʃᵊr‿əl
  ~**ly** i
conjecture kən 'dʒek tʃə §₍ᵢ₎kɒn-, -ʃə ‖ -tʃᵊr
  ~**d** d ~**s** z **conjecturing** kən 'dʒek tʃər ɪŋ
  §₍ᵢ₎kɒn-, -ʃᵊr-
conjoin kən 'dʒɔɪn ₍ᵢ₎kɒn- ‖ ₍ᵢ₎kɑːn- ~**ed** d
  ~**ing** ɪŋ ~**s** z
conjoint kən 'dʒɔɪnt ₍ᵢ₎kɒn-, '•• ‖ ₍ᵢ₎kɑːn- ~**ly**
  li
conjugal 'kɒndʒ ʊg ᵊl -əg- ‖ 'kɑːndʒ əg ᵊl
  kən 'dʒuːg- ~**ly** i
conjugality ˌkɒndʒ u 'gæl ət i -ɪt i
  ‖ ˌkɑːndʒ ə 'gæl ət i, •u-
conju|gate v 'kɒndʒ u |geɪt -ə- ‖ 'kɑːndʒ ə-
  ~**gated** geɪt ɪd -əd ‖ geɪt əd ~**gates** geɪts
  ~**gating** geɪt ɪŋ ‖ geɪt ɪŋ
conjugate adj, n 'kɒndʒ ʊg ət -əg-, -ɪt; -u geɪt
  ‖ 'kɑːndʒ əg ət -ə geɪt ~**ly** li ~**s** s
conjugation ˌkɒndʒ u 'geɪʃ ᵊn -ə- ‖ ˌkɑːndʒ ə-
  ~**al/ly** ᵊl /i ~**s** z
conjunct 'kɒn dʒʌŋkt kən 'dʒʌŋkt, ₍ᵢ₎kɒn-
  ‖ 'kɑːn- ~**ly** li ~**s** s
conjunction kən 'dʒʌŋk ʃᵊn §₍ᵢ₎kɒn- ~**al/ly**
  ᵊl /i ~**s** z
conjunctiv|a ˌkɒn dʒʌŋk 'taɪv |ə ‖ ˌkɑːn-
  kən ˌdʒʌŋk'taɪv |ə ~**ae** iː ~**al** əl ~**as** z
conjunctivitis kən ˌdʒʌŋkt ɪ 'vaɪt ɪs §kɒn-,
  §ˌkɒn dʒʌŋkt ɪ '•-, -ə'•-, §-əs ‖ -'vaɪt̬ əs
conjuncture kən 'dʒʌŋk tʃə §₍ᵢ₎kɒn- ‖ -tʃᵊr ~**s**
  z

C

conjuration ˌkɒn dʒu 'reɪʃ ᵊn ˌkʌndʒ ə-
‖ ˌkɑːndʒ ə-
conjure '*do magic; evoke*' 'kʌndʒ ə ‖ 'kɑːndʒ ᵊr
~d d ~s z conjuring 'kʌndʒ ᵊr ɪŋ ‖ 'kɑːndʒ-
conjure '*ask solemnly*' kən 'dʒʊə ₍ᵢ₎kɒn-, -'dʒɔː
‖ -'dʒʊᵊr ~d d ~s z conjures kən 'dʒʊəz
₍ᵢ₎kɒn-, -'dʒɔːz ‖ -'dʒʊᵊrz
conjurer, conjuror 'kʌndʒ ᵊr_ə ‖ 'kɑːndʒ ᵊr ər
'kʌndʒ- ~s z
conk kɒŋk ‖ kɑːŋk kɔːŋk conked
kɒŋkt ‖ kɑːŋkt kɔːŋkt conking
'kɒŋk ɪŋ ‖ 'kɑːŋk ɪŋ 'kɔːŋk- conks
kɒŋks ‖ kɑːŋks kɔːŋks
conked-out ˌkɒŋkt 'aʊt ◂ ‖ ˌkɑːŋkt- ˌkɔːŋkt-
conker 'kɒŋk ə ‖ 'kɑːŋk ᵊr ~s z
Conleth 'kɒn ləθ ‖ 'kɑːn-
con|man 'kɒn |mæn ‖ 'kɑːn- ~men men
con moto ₍ᵢ₎kɒn 'məʊt əʊ ‖ ₍ᵢ₎kɑːn 'moʊt̬ oʊ
₍ᵢ₎koʊn-
Connacht 'kɒn ɔːt -ət' ‖ 'kɑːn ɔːt -ɑːt
Connah 'kɒn ə ‖ 'kɑːn ə
connate 'kɒn eɪt kɒ 'neɪt ‖ 'kɑːn- kɑː 'neɪt
~ly li
Connaught 'kɒn ɔːt ‖ 'kɑːn ɔːt -ɑːt
connect kə 'nekt ~ed/ly ɪd /li əd /li ~ing ɪŋ
~s s
conˌnected 'speech; conˈnecting rod
Connecticut kə 'net ɪk ət §-ək- ‖ -'net̬- (!)
connection kə 'nek ʃᵊn ~al _əl ~ism ˌɪz əm
~ist/s ɪst/s §əst/s ‖ əst/s ~s z
connective kə 'nekt ɪv ~ly li
connectivity ˌkɒn ek 'tɪv ət i kə ˌnek '•-, -ɪt i
‖ ˌkɑːn ek 'tɪv ət̬ i
connector kə 'nekt ə ‖ -ᵊr ~s z
conned kɒnd ‖ kɑːnd
Connell (i) 'kɒn ᵊl ‖ 'kɑːn ᵊl; (ii) kə 'nel
Connemara ˌkɒn ɪ 'mɑːr ə -ə- ‖ ˌkɑːn-
Connery 'kɒn ər i ‖ 'kɑːn-
Connex *tdmk* 'kɒn eks kə 'neks ‖ 'kɑːn-
connexion kə 'nek ʃᵊn ~al _əl ~s z
Connibere 'kɒn ɪ bɪə -ə- ‖ 'kɑːn ə bɪr
Connie 'kɒn i ‖ 'kɑːn i
conning 'kɒn ɪŋ ‖ 'kɑːn ɪŋ
'conning ˌtower
conniption kə 'nɪp ʃᵊn
connivance kə 'naɪv ᵊnts
conniv|e kə 'naɪv ~ed d ~er/s ə/z ‖ ᵊr/z ~es
z ~ing ɪŋ
connoisseur ˌkɒn ə 'sɜː -ɪ- ‖ ˌkɑːn ə 'sɝː -'sʊᵊr
~s z ~ship ʃɪp
Connolly 'kɒn əl i ‖ 'kɑːn-
Connor 'kɒn ə ‖ 'kɑːn ᵊr
Connors 'kɒn əz ‖ 'kɑːn ᵊrz
connotation ˌkɒn ə 'teɪʃ ᵊn -əʊ-, △-ju-
‖ ˌkɑːn- ~s z
connotative 'kɒn ə teɪt ɪv '•əʊ-, △'•ju-;
kə 'nəʊt ət ɪv, kɒ- ‖ 'kɑːn ə teɪt̬ ɪv
kə 'noʊt̬ ət̬ ɪv ~ly li
con|note kə |'nəʊt kɒ- ‖ -|'noʊt kɑː- ~noted
'nəʊt ɪd -əd ‖ 'noʊt̬ əd ~notes
'nəʊts ‖ 'noʊts ~noting 'nəʊt ɪŋ ‖ 'noʊt̬ ɪŋ
connubial kə 'njuːb i_əl kɒ- ‖ -'nuːb- -'njuːb-
~ly i

connubiality kə ˌnjuːb i 'æl ət i kɒ-
‖ -ˌnuːb i 'æl ət̬ i -ˌnjuːb-
conoid 'kəʊn ɔɪd ‖ 'koʊn- ~s z
Conor 'kɒn ə ‖ 'kɑːn ᵊr
conquer 'kɒŋk ə ‖ 'kɑːŋk ᵊr (= *conker*) ~ed d
conquering 'kɒŋk ᵊr ɪŋ ‖ 'kɑːŋk- ~s z
conqueror 'kɒŋk ər_ə ‖ 'kɑːŋk ᵊr_ər ~s z
conquest, C~ 'kɒŋ kwest ‖ 'kɑːn kwest
→'kɑːŋ-, -kwəst ~s s
conquistador kɒn 'kwɪst ə dɔː →kɒŋ-, ˌ•••'•,
•ˌ••'• ‖ kɑːn 'kiːst ə dɔːr kən-, kɔːŋ-,
-'kwɪst- —*Sp* [koŋ kis ta 'ðor]
conquistadores kɒn ˌkwɪst ə 'dɔːr eɪz
→kɒŋ-, ˌ•••'•• ‖ kɑːn- kən-, kɔːŋ-, -ˌkiːst-,
-'doʊr-, -eɪs —*Sp* [koŋ kis ta 'ðo res]
Conrad 'kɒn ræd ‖ 'kɑːn-
Conrail, ConRail *tdmk* 'kɒn reɪᵊl ˌ•'• ‖ 'kɑːn-
Conran 'kɒn rən -ræn ‖ 'kɑːn-
Conroy 'kɒn rɔɪ ‖ 'kɑːn-
consanguineous
ˌkɒn sæŋ 'gwɪn i_əs ◂ ‖ ˌkɑːn- ˌ•sæn- ~ly li
consanguinity ˌkɒn sæŋ 'gwɪn ət i -ɪt i
‖ ˌkɑːn sæŋ 'gwɪn ət̬ i ˌ•sæn-
conscienc|e 'kɒntʃ ᵊnts ‖ 'kɑːntʃ ᵊnts ~es ɪz əz
'conscience clause; 'conscience ˌmoney
conscienceless 'kɒntʃ ᵊnts ləs -lɪs ‖ 'kɑːntʃ-
conscience-stricken 'kɒntʃ ᵊnts ˌstrɪk
ᵊn ‖ 'kɑːntʃ-
conscientious ˌkɒntʃ i 'entʃ əs ◂ ˌkɒnts-
‖ ˌkɑːntʃ- ~ly li ~ness nəs nɪs
ˌconsciˌentious obˈjector
conscionable 'kɒntʃ ᵊn_əb ᵊl ‖ 'kɑːntʃ-
conscious 'kɒntʃ əs ‖ 'kɑːntʃ əs ~ly li
consciousness 'kɒntʃ əs nəs -nɪs ‖ 'kɑːntʃ-
'consciousness ˌraising
conscript *n* 'kɒn skrɪpt ‖ 'kɑːn- ~s s
conscript *v* kən 'skrɪpt §₍ᵢ₎kɒn- ~ed ɪd əd
~ing ɪŋ ~s s
conscription kən 'skrɪp ʃᵊn §₍ᵢ₎kɒn-
conse|crate 'kɒnts ɪ |kreɪt -ə- ‖ 'kɑːnts ə-
~crated kreɪt ɪd -əd ‖ kreɪt̬ əd ~crates
kreɪts ~crating kreɪt ɪŋ ‖ kreɪt̬ ɪŋ
consecration ˌkɒnts ɪ 'kreɪʃ ᵊn -ə- ‖ ˌkɑːnts ə-
consecrator 'kɒnts ɪ kreɪt ə '•ə-
‖ 'kɑːnts ə kreɪt̬ ᵊr ~s z
consecutive kən 'sek jʊt ɪv §₍ᵢ₎kɒn-, -jət-, §-ət-
‖ -jət̬ ɪv -ət̬- ~ly li ~ness nəs nɪs
consensual kən 'sents ju_əl ₍ᵢ₎kɒn-, -'sentʃ u_əl
‖ -'sentʃ u_əl -'sentʃ əl ~ly i
consensus kən 'sents əs §₍ᵢ₎kɒn-
con|sent *v, n* kən |'sent §₍ᵢ₎kɒn- ~sented
'sent ɪd -əd ‖ 'sent̬ əd ~senting
'sent ɪŋ ‖ 'sent̬ ɪŋ ~sents 'sents
consequenc|e 'kɒnts ɪk wənts -ək-; §-ɪ kwents,
§-ə- ‖ 'kɑːnts ə kwents -ɪk wənts ~es ɪz əz
consequent 'kɒnts ɪk wənt -ək-; §-ɪ kwent,
§-ə- ‖ 'kɑːnts ə kwent -ɪk wənt ~ly li
consequential ˌkɒnts ɪ 'kwentʃ ᵊl ◂ -ə-
‖ ˌkɑːnts- ~ly i
conservanc|y kən 'sɜːv ᵊnts i §₍ᵢ₎kɒn- ‖ -'sɝːv-
~ies iz
conservation ˌkɒnts ə 'veɪʃ ᵊn ‖ ˌkɑːnts ᵊr- ~al
_əl ◂

conservationism ˌkɒnts ə 'veɪʃ ə ˌnɪz əm
-ən ˌɪz- ‖ ˌkɑːnts ər-
conservationist ˌkɒnts ə 'veɪʃ ən_ɪst əst
‖ ˌkɑːnts ər- ~s s
conservatism kən 'sɜːv ə ˌtɪz əm §ᵤkɒn-
‖ -'sɜːv-
conservative, C~ kən 'sɜːv ət ɪv §ᵤkɒn-
‖ -'sɜːv əṯ ɪv ~ly li ~s z
  Con'servative ˌParty
conservatoire kən 'sɜːv ə twɑː ᵤkɒn-
‖ -'sɜːv ə twɑːr •ˌ••'• ~s z
conservator kən 'sɜːv ət ə §ᵤkɒn-;
  'kɒnts ə veɪt ə ‖ -'sɜːv əṯ ər -ə tɔːr;
  'kɑːnts ər veɪt ər ~s z
conservator|y kən 'sɜːv ətr li -'sɜːv ət ər li
‖ kən 'sɜːv ə tɔːr li -toʊr i ~ies iz
conserv|e v kən 'sɜːv §ᵤkɒn- ‖ -'sɜːv ~ed d
~es z ~ing ɪŋ
conserve n 'kɒn sɜːv kən 'sɜːv ‖ 'kɑːn sɜːv ~s
z
Consett 'kɒnts ɪt -ət, -et ‖ 'kɑːnts-
consider kən 'sɪd ə §ᵤkɒn- ‖ -ᵊr ~ed d
  considering kən 'sɪd_ər ɪŋ ~s z
considerab|le kən 'sɪd_ər əb lᵊl §ᵤkɒn- ~ly li
considerate kən 'sɪd_ər ət §ᵤkɒn-, -ɪt ~ly li
~ness nəs nɪs
consideration kən ˌsɪd ə 'reɪʃ ən §ᵤkɒn- ~s z
Considine 'kɒnts ɪ daɪn -ə- ‖ 'kɑːnts-
consign kən 'saɪn §ᵤkɒn- ~ed d ~ing ɪŋ ~s z
consignee ˌkɒnts aɪ 'niː -ɪ-, -ə- ‖ ˌkɑːnts- ~s z
consignment kən 'saɪn mənt §ᵤkɒn-,
→-'saɪm- ~s s
consignor kən 'saɪn ə §ᵤkɒn-; ˌkɒnts aɪ 'nɔː,
kən ˌsaɪ 'nɔː ‖ -ᵊr ˌkɑːnts aɪ 'nɔːr, -ə-;
kən ˌsaɪ 'nɔːr ~s z
consist kən 'sɪst §ᵤkɒn- ~ed ɪd əd ~ing ɪŋ
~s s
consistence kən 'sɪst ənts §ᵤkɒn-
consistenc|y kən 'sɪst ənts li §ᵤkɒn- ~ies iz
consistent kən 'sɪst ənt ~ly li
consistorial ˌkɒn sɪ 'stɔːr i_əl ‖ ˌkɑːn- -'stoʊr-
consistor|y kən 'sɪst ər_li ~ies iz
consolation ˌkɒnts ə 'leɪʃ ən ‖ ˌkɑːnts- ~s z
  ˌconso'lation prize
consolatory kən 'sɒl ət_ər i §ᵤkɒn-, -'səʊl-
‖ -'soʊl ə tɔːr i -'sɑːl-, -toʊr i
consol|e v kən 'səʊl §ᵤkɒn-, →-'sɒʊl ‖ -'soʊl
~ed d ~es z ~ing/ly ɪŋ /li
console n 'kɒn səʊl →-sɒʊl ‖ 'kɑːn soʊl ~s z
consoli|date kən 'sɒl ɪ deɪt §ᵤkɒn-, -ə-
‖ -'sɑːl- ~dated deɪt ɪd -əd ‖ deɪṯ əd ~dates
deɪts ~dating deɪt ɪŋ ‖ deɪṯ ɪŋ
consolidation kən ˌsɒl ɪ 'deɪʃ ən §kɒn-,
§ˌkɒn ˌsɒl-, -ə'•- ‖ -ˌsɑːl-
consolidator kən 'sɒl ɪ deɪt ə §ᵤkɒn-, -'•ə-
‖ -'sɑːl ə deɪṯ ər
consols kən 'sɒlz 'kɒnts ɒlz, -ᵊlz ‖ -'sɑːlz
consomme, consommé kɒn 'sɒm eɪ kən-,
  'kɒnts ə meɪ, -ɒ- ‖ ˌkɑːnts ə 'meɪ (*) —Fr
  [kɔ̃ sɔ me] ~s z
consonance 'kɒnts ən_ənts ‖ 'kɑːnts-
consonant 'kɒnts ən_ənt ‖ 'kɑːnts- ~s s

consonantal
ˌkɒnts ə 'nænt ᵊl ◂ ‖ ˌkɑːnts ə 'nænt̬ ᵊl ◂ ~ly i
consort n 'kɒn sɔːt ‖ 'kɑːn sɔːrt ~s s
con|sort v kən ‖'sɔːt ᵤkɒn- ‖ -‖'sɔːrt ᵤkɑːn-,
'•• ~sorted 'sɔːt ɪd -əd ‖ 'sɔːrt̬ əd ~sorting
'sɔːt ɪŋ ‖ 'sɔːrt̬ ɪŋ ~sorts 'sɔːts ‖ 'sɔːrts
consorti|um kən 'sɔːt i_ləm §ᵤkɒn-, -'sɔːʃ-,
-'sɔːʃ ləm ‖ -'sɔːrt̬ i_ləm -'sɔːrʃ-; -'sɔːrʃ ləm
~a ə
conspecific ˌkɒn spə 'sɪf ɪk ◂ -spɪ- ‖ ˌkɑːn-
conspectus kən 'spekt əs §ᵤkɒn- ~es ɪz əz
conspicuous kən 'spɪk ju_əs §ᵤkɒn- ~ly li
~ness nəs nɪs
conspirac|y kən 'spɪr əs li §ᵤkɒn- ~ies iz
conspirator kən 'spɪr ət ə §ᵤkɒn- ‖ -əṯ ər ~s z
conspiratorial kən ˌspɪr ə 'tɔːr i_əl ◂
ᵤkɒn- ‖ -'toʊr- ~ly i
conspire kən 'spaɪ_ə §ᵤkɒn- ‖ -'spaɪ_ᵊr ~d d
~s z **conspiring** kən 'spaɪər ɪŋ §ᵤkɒn-
‖ -'spaɪ_ᵊr ɪŋ
constable, C~ 'kʌnt st əb ᵊl 'kɒnt st- ‖ 'kɑːnt st-
  'kʌnt st- ~s z —The painter John C~ was
  'kʌnt st-
constabular|y kən 'stæb jʊl ər li §ᵤkɒn-,
-'•jəl- ‖ -jə ler li ~ies iz
Constance 'kɒnt st ənts ‖ 'kɑːnt st-
constancy 'kɒnt st ənts i ‖ 'kɑːnt st-
constant, C~ 'kɒnt st ənt ‖ 'kɑːnt st- ~ly li
Constanta, Constantsa kən 'stænt s ə kɒn-
‖ -'stɑːnt s ə —Romanian Constanţa
  [kon 'stan tsa]
Constantine 'kɒnt st ən taɪn -tiːn ‖ 'kɑːnt st-
Constantinople ˌkɒn ˌstænt ɪ 'nəʊp ᵊl -ə-
‖ ˌkɑːn ˌstænt ᵊn 'oʊp ᵊl
constatation ˌkɒnt st ə 'teɪʃ ən ‖ ˌkɑːnt st- ~s s
constellation ˌkɒnt st ə 'leɪʃ ən -ɪ- ‖ ˌkɑːnt st-
~s z
consternation ˌkɒnt st ə 'neɪʃ ən ‖ ˌkɑːnt st ər-
consti|pate 'kɒnt st ɪ ǀpeɪt -ə- ‖ 'kɑːnt st-
~pated peɪt ɪd -əd ‖ peɪt̬ əd ~pates peɪts
~pating peɪt ɪŋ ‖ peɪt̬ ɪŋ
constipation ˌkɒnt st ɪ 'peɪʃ ən -ə- ‖ ˌkɑːnt st-
constituenc|y kən 'stɪt ju_ənts li §ᵤkɒn-,
-'stɪtʃ u_ ‖ -'stɪtʃ u_ ~ies iz
constituent kən 'stɪt ju_ənt §ᵤkɒn-, -'stɪtʃ u_
‖ -'stɪtʃ u_ ~s s
  conˌstituent asˈsembly
consti|tute 'kɒnt st ɪ ǀtjuːt -ə-, →§-tʃuːt
‖ 'kɑːnt st ə ǀtuːt -tjuːt ~tuted tjuːt ɪd
→§tʃuːt-, -əd ‖ tuːt̬ əd tjuːt̬- ~tutes tjuːts
→§tʃuːts ‖ tuːts tjuːts ~tuting tjuːt ɪŋ
→§tʃuːt- ‖ tuːt̬ ɪŋ tjuːt̬ ɪŋ
constitution ˌkɒnt st ɪ 'tjuːʃ ən -ə-, →§-'tʃuːʃ-
‖ ˌkɑːnt st ə 'tuːʃ ən -'tjuːʃ- ~s z
constitutional ˌkɒnt st ɪ 'tjuːʃ ən_əl ◂ ˌ•ə-,
→§-'tʃuːʃ- ‖ ˌkɑːnt st ə 'tuːʃ- -'tjuːʃ- ~ly i
constitutionalism ˌkɒnt st ɪ 'tjuːʃ ən_ə ˌlɪz əm
ˌ•ə-, →§-'tʃuːʃ-, -əl ˌɪz- ‖ ˌkɑːnt st ə 'tuːʃ-
-'tjuːʃ-
constitutionalist ˌkɒnt st ɪ 'tjuːʃ ən_əl ɪst ˌ•ə-,
→§-'tʃuːʃ- ‖ ˌkɑːnt st ə 'tuːʃ- -'tjuːʃ-, §-əst
~s s

C

constitutionality ˌkɒnˈstɪ ɪ ˌtjuːʃ ə ˈnæl ət i
ˌˈ•ə-, →§-ˌtʃuːʃ-, -ɪt i
‖ ˌkɑːnˈtst ə ˌtuːʃ ə ˈnæl əʈ i -ˌtjuːʃ-

constitutive kən ˈstɪt jʊt ɪv §₍ᵢ₎kɒn-, -ˈstɪtʃ ət-;
ˈkɒnˈtst ɪ tjuːt ɪv, ˌˈ•ə-, -tʃuːt ɪv
‖ ˈkɑːnˈtst ə tuːʈ ɪv -tjuːʈ ɪv; kən ˈstɪtʃ əʈ- **~ly**
li

constrain kən ˈstreɪn §₍ᵢ₎kɒn- **~ed** d **~ing** ɪŋ
~s z

constraint kən ˈstreɪnt §₍ᵢ₎kɒn- **~s** s

constrict kən ˈstrɪkt §₍ᵢ₎kɒn- **~ed** ɪd əd **~ing**
ɪŋ **~s** s

constriction kən ˈstrɪk ʃən §₍ᵢ₎kɒn- **~s** z

constrictive kən ˈstrɪkt ɪv §₍ᵢ₎kɒn- **~ly** li

constrictor kən ˈstrɪkt ə §₍ᵢ₎kɒn- ‖ -ər **~s** z

construct v kən ˈstrʌkt §₍ᵢ₎kɒn- **~ed** ɪd əd
~ing ɪŋ **~s** s

construct n ˈkɒn strʌkt ‖ ˈkɑːn- **~s** s

construction kən ˈstrʌk ʃən §₍ᵢ₎kɒn- **~s** z

constructional kən ˈstrʌk ʃən əl §₍ᵢ₎kɒn- **~ly** i

constructionist kən ˈstrʌk ʃən ɪst §₍ᵢ₎kɒn-,
§ əst **~s** s

constructive kən ˈstrʌkt ɪv §₍ᵢ₎kɒn- **~ly** li
~ness nəs nɪs

constructiv|ism kən ˈstrʌkt ɪv ˌɪz əm §₍ᵢ₎kɒn-
~ist/s ɪst/s §əst/s

constructor kən ˈstrʌkt ə §₍ᵢ₎kɒn- ‖ -ər **~s** z

construe kən ˈstruː §₍ᵢ₎kɒn- **~d** d **~s** z
construing kən ˈstruːˌɪŋ §₍ᵢ₎kɒn-

consubstantial ˌkɒn səb ˈstæntʃ əl ◂ §-sʌb-,
-ˈstɑːntʃ- ‖ ˌkɑːn-

consubstantiation ˌkɒn səb ˌstæntʃ i ˈeɪʃ ən
§ˌ•sʌb-, -ˌstænts-, -ˌstɑːntʃ-, -ˌstɑːnts-
‖ ˌkɑːn-

consuetude ˈkɒns wɪ tjuːd -wə-, →-tʃuːd
‖ ˈkɑːns wɪ tuːd kən ˈsuː əˈ•, -tjuːd

consul ˈkɒns əl ‖ ˈkɑːns əl **~s** z
ˌconsul ˈgeneral

consular ˈkɒns jʊl ə -jəl- ‖ ˈkɑːns əlˌər (*)

consulate ˈkɒns jʊl ət -jəl-, -ɪt ‖ ˈkɑːns əlˌət
~s s

consulship ˈkɒns əl ʃɪp ‖ ˈkɑːns- **~s** s

consult v kən ˈsʌlt §₍ᵢ₎kɒn- **~ed** ɪd əd **~ing** ɪŋ
~s s
conˈsulting room

consult n kən ˈsʌlt §₍ᵢ₎kɒn-; ˈkɒn sʌlt **~s** s

consultanc|y kən ˈsʌlt ənts li §₍ᵢ₎kɒn- **~ies** iz

consultant kən ˈsʌlt ənt §₍ᵢ₎kɒn- **~s** s

consultation ˌkɒnts əl ˈteɪʃ ən -ʌl- ‖ ˌkɑːnts-
~s z

consultative kən ˈsʌlt ət ɪv §₍ᵢ₎kɒn- ‖ -əʈ ɪv
ˈkɑːnts əl teɪʈ ɪv

consultatory kən ˈsʌlt ət ˌər i §₍ᵢ₎kɒn-
‖ -ə tɔːr i -toʊr i

consumable kən ˈsjuːm əb əl §₍ᵢ₎kɒn-, -ˈsuːm-,
§-ˈʃuːm- ‖ -ˈsuːm- **~s** z

consum|e kən ˈsjuːm §₍ᵢ₎kɒn-, -ˈsuːm, §-ˈʃuːm
‖ -ˈsuːm **~ed** d **~es** z **~ing** ɪŋ

consumer kən ˈsjuːm ə §₍ᵢ₎kɒn-, -ˈsuːm-,
§-ˈʃuːm- ‖ -ˈsuːm ər **~s** z
conˌsumer ˈdurable; conˈsumer goods

consumerism kən ˈsjuːm ə ˌrɪz əm §₍ᵢ₎kɒn-,
-ˈsuːm-, §-ˈʃuːm-, -ər ˌɪz- ‖ -ˈsuːm-

consuming kən ˈsjuːm ɪŋ §₍ᵢ₎kɒn-, -ˈsuːm-,
§-ˈʃuːm- ‖ -ˈsuːm-

consummate adj kən ˈsʌm ət §₍ᵢ₎kɒn-, -ɪt;
ˈkɒnts əm-, -jʊm-, -ju:m- ‖ ˈkɑːnts əm- **~ly** li

consum|mate v ˈkɒnts ə ˌmeɪt -jʊ- ‖ ˈkɑːnts-
~mated meɪt ɪd -əd ‖ meɪʈ əd **~mates** meɪts
~mating meɪt ɪŋ ‖ meɪʈ ɪŋ

consummation ˌkɒnts ə ˈmeɪʃ ən -ju-
‖ ˌkɑːnts- **~s** z

consumption kən ˈsʌmp ʃən §₍ᵢ₎kɒn-

consumptive kən ˈsʌmpt ɪv §₍ᵢ₎kɒn- **~ly** li **~s**
z

Contac tdmk ˈkɒn tæk ‖ ˈkɑːn-

contact n ˈkɒn tækt ‖ ˈkɑːn- **~s** s
ˈcontact lens, ˌ•• ˈ•

contact v ˈkɒn tækt kən ˈtækt, ₍ᵢ₎kɒn- ‖ ˈkɑːn-
~ed ɪd əd **~ing** ɪŋ **~s** s

contagion kən ˈteɪdʒ ən §₍ᵢ₎kɒn-, -ˈteɪdʒ iˌən
~s z

contagious kən ˈteɪdʒ əs §₍ᵢ₎kɒn-, -ˈteɪdʒ iˌəs
~ly li **~ness** nəs nɪs

contain kən ˈteɪn §₍ᵢ₎kɒn- **~ed** d **~ing** ɪŋ **~s** z

container kən ˈteɪn ə §₍ᵢ₎kɒn- ‖ -ər **~s** z

containeris... —see **containeriz...**

containerization kən ˌteɪn ər aɪ ˈzeɪʃ ən §kɒn-,
ˌkɒn ˌteɪn-, -ər ɪ- ‖ -ər ə-

containeriz|e kən ˈteɪn ə raɪz §₍ᵢ₎kɒn- **~ed** d
~es ɪz əz **~ing** ɪŋ

containment kən ˈteɪn mənt §₍ᵢ₎kɒn-, →-ˈteɪm-

contaminant kən ˈtæm ɪn ənt §₍ᵢ₎kɒn-, -ən- **~s**
s

contami|nate kən ˈtæm ɪ ˌneɪt §₍ᵢ₎kɒn-, -ə-
~nated neɪt ɪd -əd ‖ neɪʈ əd **~nates** neɪts
~nating neɪt ɪŋ ‖ neɪʈ ɪŋ

contamination kən ˌtæm ɪ ˈneɪʃ ən §₍ᵢ₎kɒn-, -ə-

contango kən ˈtæŋ gəʊ kɒn- ‖ -goʊ **~s** z

conte 'story' kɒnt ‖ koʊnt —Fr [kɔ̃ːt] **~s** s

conté 'crayon' ˈkɒnt eɪ -i ‖ ˈkɑːnt- —Fr [kɔ̃ te]
~s z

Conteh ˈkɒnt eɪ ‖ ˈkɑːnt-

contemn kən ˈtem §₍ᵢ₎kɒn- **~ed** d **~ing** ɪŋ **~s**
z

contem|plate ˈkɒnt əm ˌpleɪt ˈkɒn tem-
‖ ˈkɑːnʈ əm- ˈkɑːn tem- **~plated** pleɪt ɪd -əd
‖ pleɪʈ əd **~plates** pleɪts **~plating**
pleɪt ɪŋ ‖ pleɪʈ ɪŋ

contemplation ˌkɒnt əm ˈpleɪʃ ən ˌkɒn tem-
‖ ˌkɑːnʈ əm- ˌkɑːn tem-

contemplative kən ˈtemp lət ɪv §₍ᵢ₎kɒn-;
ˈkɒnt əm pleɪt ɪv, ˈkɒn tem-, -plət ɪv ‖ -lət-
ˈkɑːnʈ əm pleɪʈ ɪv, ˈkɑːn tem- —Some
speakers may distinguish between •ˈ••• *(with
reference to monks and nuns) and* ˈ•••
'pensive'. **~ly** li **~ness** nəs nɪs **~s** z

contemporaneity kən ˌtemp ər ə ˈniːˌət i
kɒn-, ˌkɒn ˌtemp-, -ˈneɪ-, ˌɪt i ‖ -əʈ i

contemporaneous kən ˌtemp ə ˈreɪn iˌəs kɒn-,
ˌkɒn ˌtemp- **~ly** li **~ness** nəs nɪs

contemporar|y kən ˈtemp ər_ˌər li §₍ᵢ₎kɒn-
‖ -ə rer li —casually also -ˈtemp rˈli **~ies** iz

contempt kən ˈtempt §₍ᵢ₎kɒn- **~s** s

contemptibility kən ˌtempt ə ˈbɪl ət i §₍ᵢ₎kɒn-,
-ɪt i ‖ -əʈ i

contemptib|le kən 'tempt əb |əl §₍₎kɒn-
~**leness** əl nəs -nɪs ~**ly** li
contemptuous kən 'tempt ju‿əs §₍₎kɒn-,
-'tempt ʃu‿ ‖ -'temp t ʃu‿əs -ʃu‿əs ~**ly** li
~**ness** nəs nɪs
contend kən 'tend §₍₎kɒn- ~**ed** ɪd əd ~**er/s**
ə/z ‖ -ər/z ~**ing** ɪŋ ~**s** z
con|tent adj, v, n 'contentment' kən |'tent
§₍₎kɒn- ~**tented** 'tent ɪd -əd ‖ 'tenṯ əd
~**tenting** 'tent ɪŋ ‖ 'tenṯ ɪŋ ~**tents** 'tents
content n 'matter contained' 'kɒn tent ‖ 'kɑːn-
~**s** s
contented kən 'tent ɪd §₍₎kɒn-, -əd ‖ -'tenṯ əd
~**ly** li ~**ness** nəs nɪs
contention kən 'tentʃ ən §₍₎kɒn- ~**s** z
contentious kən 'tentʃ əs §₍₎kɒn- ~**ly** li ~**ness**
nəs nɪs
contentment kən 'tent mənt §₍₎kɒn-
conterminous kɒn 'tɜːm ɪn əs kən-, -ən-
‖ -'tɜː·m- ₍₎kɑːn- ~**ly** li
contessa kɒn 'tes ə ‖ kɑːn- —It [kon 'tes sa]
contest v kən 'test §₍₎kɒn-;
'kɒn test ‖ 'kɑːn test ~**ed** ɪd əd ~**ing** ɪŋ ~**s**
s
contest n 'kɒn test ‖ 'kɑːn- ~**s** s
contestant kən 'test ənt §₍₎kɒn- ~**s** s
contestation ˌkɒnt e 'steɪʃ ən ‖ ˌkɑːnt-
context 'kɒn tekst ‖ 'kɑːn- ~**s** s
context-free ˌkɒn tekst 'friː ◄ ‖ ˌkɑːn-
context-sensitive ˌkɒn tekst 'sents ət ɪv ◄
-ɪt ɪv ‖ ˌkɑːn tekst 'sents əṯ ɪv ◄
contextual kən 'tekst ju‿əl §₍₎kɒn-, -'teks tʃu‿
‖ kɑːn 'teks tʃu‿əl kən-, -'teks tʃəl ~**ly** i
contextualis... —see **contextualiz...**
contextualization kən ˌtekst ju‿əl aɪ 'zeɪʃ ən
§₍₎kɒn-, -ˌteks tʃu‿, -ɪ'• -
‖ kɑːn ˌteks tʃu‿əl ə 'zeɪʃ ən kən-,
-ˌteks tʃəl ə 'zeɪʃ-
contextualiz|e kən 'tekst ju‿ə laɪz §₍₎kɒn-,
-'teks tʃu‿ ‖ kɑːn 'teks tʃu‿ə laɪz kən-,
-'teks tʃə laɪz ~**ed** d ~**es** ɪz əz ~**ing** ɪŋ
Contiboard tdmk 'kɒnt i bɔːd ‖ 'kɑːnṯ i bɔːrd
-bourd
contiguit|y ˌkɒnt ɪ 'gjuː‿ət li ˌ•ə-, -ɪt i ‖ ˌkɑːnṯ
ə 'gjuː əṯ li ~**ies** iz
contiguous kən 'tɪg ju‿əs §₍₎kɒn- ~**ly** li
~**ness** nəs nɪs
Contin 'kɒnt ɪn §-ən ‖ 'kɑːnt-
continence 'kɒnt ɪn ənts -ən- ‖ 'kɑːnt ən-
continent 'kɒnt ɪn ənt -ən- ‖ 'kɑːnt ən‿ənt
~**ly** li ~**s** s
continental ˌkɒnt ɪ 'nent əl ◄ -ə-
‖ ˌkɑːnt ən 'enṯ əl ◄ ~**ly** i
ˌconti·nental 'breakfast; ˌconti·nental
'shelf
contingenc|y kən 'tɪndʒ ənts li §₍₎kɒn- ~**ies** iz
contingent kən 'tɪndʒ ənt §₍₎kɒn- ~**ly** li ~**s** s
continua kən 'tɪn ju‿ə §₍₎kɒn-
continual kən 'tɪn ju‿əl §₍₎kɒn- ~**ly** i
continuance kən 'tɪn ju‿ənts §₍₎kɒn-
continuant kən 'tɪn ju‿ənt §₍₎kɒn- ~**s** s
continuation kən ˌtɪn ju 'eɪʃ ən §₍₎kɒn- ~**s** z

continuative kən 'tɪn ju‿ət ɪv -eɪt ɪv ‖ -eɪṯ ɪv
~**ly** li
continu|e kən 'tɪn juː §₍₎kɒn-, -ju ‖ -ju ~**ed** d
~**es** z ~**ing** ‿ɪŋ
continuit|y ˌkɒnt ɪ 'njuː‿ət li ˌ•ə-, -ɪt i
‖ ˌkɑːnt ən 'uː əṯ li -'juː- ~**ies** iz
continuo kən 'tɪn ju əʊ ₍₎kɒn-, -u- ‖ -oʊ ~**s** z
continuous kən 'tɪn ju‿əs §₍₎kɒn- ~**ly** li
~**ness** nəs nɪs
continu|um kən 'tɪn ju‿əm §₍₎kɒn- ~**a** ə
contoid 'kɒnt ɔɪd ‖ 'kɑːnt- ~**s** z
contoidal kɒn 'tɔɪd əl ‖ kɑːn-
con|tort kən |'tɔːt §₍₎kɒn- -|'tɔːrt ~**torted**
'tɔːt ɪd -əd ‖ 'tɔːrṯ əd ~**torting**
'tɔːt ɪŋ ‖ 'tɔːrṯ ɪŋ ~**torts** 'tɔːts ‖ 'tɔːrts
contorted kən 'tɔːt ɪd §₍₎kɒn-, -əd ‖ 'tɔːrṯ əd
~**ly** li ~**ness** nəs nɪs
contortion kən 'tɔːʃ ən §₍₎kɒn- ‖ -'tɔːrʃ ən ~**s**
z
contortionist kən 'tɔːʃ ən‿ɪst ₍₎kɒn-, §‿əst
‖ -'tɔːrʃ- ~**s** s
contour 'kɒn tʊə -tɔː ‖ 'kɑːn tʊr ~**ed** d
contouring 'kɒn tʊər ɪŋ -tɔːr-
‖ 'kɑːn tʊr ɪŋ ~**s** z
'contour line
contra- comb. form ¦kɒntr ə ‖ ¦kɑːntr ə —
contraposition ˌkɒntr ə pə 'zɪʃ ən ‖ ˌkɑːntr-
contra, C~ 'kɒntr ə -ɑː ‖ 'kɑːntr ə ~**s** z
contraband 'kɒntr ə bænd ‖ 'kɑːntr- ~**ist/s**
ɪst/s §əst/s ‖ əst/s
contrabass ˌkɒntr ə 'beɪs '•‿• ‖ 'kɑːntr ə beɪs
~**ist/s** ɪst/s §əst/s ‖ əst/s
contraception ˌkɒntr ə 'sep ʃən ‖ ˌkɑːntr-
contraceptive ˌkɒntr ə 'sept ɪv ◄ ‖ ˌkɑːntr- ~**s**
z
contract n 'kɒn trækt ‖ 'kɑːn- ~**s** s
contract v kən 'trækt §₍₎kɒn- —but in the
meaning 'agree under contract, make a
contract' sometimes 'kɒn trækt ‖ 'kɑːn- ~**ed**
ɪd əd ~**ing** ɪŋ ~**s** s
contractible kən 'trækt əb əl §₍₎kɒn-
contractile kən 'trækt aɪəl §₍₎kɒn- ‖ -əl -aɪəl
contractility ˌkɒn træk 'tɪl ət i -ɪt i
‖ ˌkɑːn træk 'tɪl əṯ i
contraction kən 'træk ʃən §₍₎kɒn- ~**s** z
contractor kən 'trækt ə §₍₎kɒn-; 'kɒn trækt ə
‖ 'kɑːn trækt ᵊr ~**s** z
contractual kən 'træk tʃu‿əl §₍₎kɒn-,
-'trækt ju‿ ‖ kɑːn-, -'træk tʃəl ~**ly** i
contracture kən 'træk tʃə §₍₎kɒn-, -tjʊə, -ʃə
‖ -tʃᵊr ~**s** z
contradict ˌkɒntr ə 'dɪkt ‖ ˌkɑːntr- ~**ed** ɪd əd
~**ing** ɪŋ ~**s** s
contradiction ˌkɒntr ə 'dɪk ʃən ‖ ˌkɑːntr- ~**s** z
contradictor|y ˌkɒntr ə 'dɪkt ər‿li ◄ ‖ ˌkɑːntr-
~**ies** iz ~**ily** əl i ɪ li ~**iness** i nəs i nɪs
contradistinction ˌkɒntr ə dɪ 'stɪŋk ʃən -ə də-
‖ ˌkɑːntr-
contradistinctive ˌkɒntr ə dɪ 'stɪŋkt ɪv ◄ -ə də-
‖ ˌkɑːntr- ~**ly** li
contrafactual ˌkɒntr ə 'fæk tʃu‿əl ◄ -ʃu‿əl;
-'fækt ju‿ ‖ ˌkɑːntr- ~**ly** i ~**s** z

C

contraflow 'kɒntr ə fləʊ ˌ•·'•‖ 'kɑːntr ə floʊ
~s z

contrail 'kɒn treɪəl ‖ 'kɑːn- ~s z

contraindi|cate ˌkɒntr ə ˈɪnd ɪ |keɪt →ˌ•ər-
‖ ˌkɑːntr- ~**cated** keɪt ɪd -əd ‖ keɪt̬ əd
~**cates** keɪts ~**cating** keɪt ɪŋ ‖ keɪt̬ ɪŋ

contraindication ˌkɒntr ə ˌɪnd ɪ ˈkeɪʃ ən
→ˌ•ər-, -ˌ•ə- ‖ ˌkɑːntr- ~s z

contralateral ˌkɒntr ə ˈlæt̬ ər
əl ◄ ‖ ˌkɑːntr ə ˈlæt̬ ər əl →-ˈlætr əl

contralto kən ˈtrɑːlt əʊ §ₗₙkɒn-, -ˈtrælt-
‖ -ˈtrælt oʊ ~s z

contraption kən ˈtræp ʃən §ₗₙkɒn- ~s z

contrapuntal ˌkɒntr ə ˈpʌnt əl ◄
‖ ˌkɑːntr ə ˈpʌnt̬ əl ◄ ~**ly** i

contrari... —*see* **contrary**

contrariet|y ˌkɒntr ə ˈraɪ_ət ‖i -ɪt i
‖ ˌkɑːntr ə ˈraɪ ət̬ ‖i ~**ies** iz

contrarily kən ˈtreər əl i -ɪ li; 'kɒntr ər-
‖ 'kɑːn trer əl i ˌ•'•-

contrariwise kən ˈtreər i waɪz §ₗₙkɒn-; 'kɒntr
ər- ‖ 'kɑːn trer- kən 'trer-

contrar|y *n; adj 'different, opposed'* 'kɒntr
ər ‖i ‖ 'kɑːn trer ‖i ~**ies** iz ~**iness** i nəs i nɪs

contrar|y *adj 'perverse, obstinate'* kən 'treər ‖i
§ₗₙkɒn- ‖ -'trer ‖i 'kɑːn trer ‖i ~**iness** i nəs
i nɪs

contrast *n* 'kɒn trɑːst §-træst ‖ 'kɑːn træst ~s
s

contrast *v* kən 'trɑːst §ₗₙkɒn-, §-'træst;
'kɒn trɑːst, §-træst ‖ -'træst 'kɑːn træst
—*The* -'træst *form was apparently used in RP
until at least the 1940's.* ~**ed** ɪd əd ~**ing** ɪŋ
~s s

contrasty 'kɒn trɑːst i §-'træst- ‖ 'kɑːn træst i

contraven|e ˌkɒntr ə 'viːn ‖ ˌkɑːntr- ~**ed** d
~**es** z ~**ing** ɪŋ

contravention ˌkɒntr ə 'ventʃ ən ‖ ˌkɑːntr- ~s
z

contretemps 'kɒntr ə tɒ̃ -tɒŋ, -tɒm
‖ 'kɑːntr ə tɑ̃: —*Fr* [kɔ̃ tʁə tɑ̃] —*The plural
(spelled identically) is pronounced with* -z *or, as
in French, like the singular.*

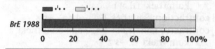

contribute kən 'trɪb juːt §ₗₙkɒn-;
'kɒntr ɪ bjuːt, -ə- ‖ kən 'trɪb jət -juːt —*BrE
1988 poll panel preference:* •'•• 73%, '•••
27%. **contributed** kən 'trɪb jʊt ɪd §ₗₙkɒn-;
'kɒntr ɪ bjuːt ɪd, '•ə-, -əd ‖ -'trɪb jət̬ əd -ət-,
-juːt̬- **contributes** kən 'trɪb juːts §ₗₙkɒn-;
'kɒntr ɪ bjuːts, -ə- ‖ -'trɪb jəts -juːts
contributing kən 'trɪb jʊt ɪŋ -jət-, §-juːt-;
'kɒntr ɪ bjuːt ɪŋ, '•ə- ‖ -'trɪb jət̬ ɪŋ -ət-,
-juːt̬-

contribution ˌkɒntr ɪ 'bjuːʃ ən -ə- ‖ ˌkɑːntr-
~s z

contributive kən 'trɪb jʊt ɪv §ₗₙkɒn-, -jət-,
§-juːt-; 'kɒntr ɪ bjuːt-, '•ə- ‖ -jət̬ ɪv -ət̬- ~**ly**
li ~**ness** nəs nɪs

contributor kən 'trɪb jʊt ə §ₗₙkɒn-, -jət-,
§-juːt-; 'kɒntr ɪ bjuːt ə, '•ə- ‖ -jət̬ ər -ət̬- ~s
z

contributor|y kən 'trɪb jʊ_tər ‖i §ₗₙkɒn-, -'•jə-,
§-'•juː;, ˌkɒntr ɪ 'bjuːt ər ‖i, ˌ•ə- ‖ -jə tɔːr ‖i
-tʊr i ~**ies** iz

contrite 'kɒn traɪt kən 'traɪt ‖ kən 'traɪt
'kɑːn traɪt ~**ly** li ~**ness** nəs nɪs

contrition kən 'trɪʃ ən §ₗₙkɒn-

contrivanc|e kən 'traɪv ənts §ₗₙkɒn- ~**es** ɪz əz

contriv|e kən 'traɪv §ₗₙkɒn- ~**ed** d ~**es** z
~**ing** ɪŋ

control kən 'trəʊl §ₗₙkɒn-, →-'trɒʊl ‖ -'troʊl
~**led** d ~**ling** ɪŋ ~s z
con'trol freak; con'trol group; con'trol
room; con'trol ˌtower

controller kən 'trəʊl ə §ₗₙkɒn-, →-'trɒʊl-
‖ -'troʊl ər ~s z

controversial ˌkɒntr ə 'vɜːʃ əl ◄ -'vɜːs i_əl
‖ ˌkɑːntr ə 'vɜːːʃ əl◄ -'vɜːs i_əl ~**ist/s** ɪst/s
§əst/s ‖ əst/s ~**ly** i

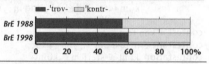

	-'trɒv-	'kɒntr-			
BrE 1988					
BrE 1998					
0	20	40	60	80	100%

controvers|y 'kɒntr ə vɜːs ‖i -vəs ‖i;
kən 'trɒv əs ‖i, §ₗₙkɒn- ‖ 'kɑːntr ə vɜːːs ‖i
~**ies** iz —*Among RP speakers the* 'kɒntr- *form
perhaps still predominates; but in BrE in
general the* -'trɒv- *form is now clearly more
widespread. BrE poll panel preferences: 1988,
-'trɒv- 56%, 'kɒntr- 44%; 1998, -'trɒv- 60%,
'kɒntr- 40%. In AmE* 'kɑːntr- *is the only
possibility.*

contro|vert ˌkɒntr ə ‖'vɜːt ◄ '•••
‖ 'kɑːntr ə ‖vɜːːt ˌ•••'• ~**verted** 'vɜːt ɪd -əd
‖ vɜːːt̬ əd ~**verting** 'vɜːt ɪŋ ‖ vɜːːt̬ ɪŋ ~**verts**
'vɜːts ‖ vɜːːts

contumacious ˌkɒn tju 'meɪʃ əs ◄ ˌkɑːn tə-
-tjə, -tʃə- ~**ly** li ~**ness** nəs nɪs

contumac|y 'kɒnt jʊm əs ‖i '•jəm-
‖ kən 'tuːm əs ‖i -'tjuːm- ~**ies** iz

contumelious ˌkɒn tju 'miːl i_əs ◄ ‖ ˌkɑːn tə-
ˌ•tjə-, ˌ•tʃə- ~**ly** li

contumely 'kɒn tjuːm li -tjʊm ɪl i, -əl i;
kən 'tjuːm əl_i, -ɪl i ‖ kən 'tuːm əl i kən-,
-'tjuːm-; 'kɑːn tə miːl i, '•tjə-, '•tʃə-

contus|e kən 'tjuːz §ₗₙkɒn-, →§-'tʃuːz ‖ -'tuːz
-'tjuːz ~**ed** d ~**es** ɪz əz ~**ing** ɪŋ

contusion kən 'tjuːʒ ən §ₗₙkɒn-, →§-'tʃuːʒ-
‖ -'tuːʒ- -'tjuːʒ- ~s z

conundrum kə 'nʌndr əm ~s z

conurbation ˌkɒn ɜː 'beɪʃ ən -ə- ‖ ˌkɑːn ər- ~s
z

conure 'kɒn jʊə ‖ 'kɑːn jʊr ~s z

Convair *tdmk* 'kɒn veə ‖ 'kɑːn ver

convalesc|e ˌkɒn və 'les ‖ ˌkɑːn- ~**ed** t ~**es** ɪz
əz ~**ing** ɪŋ

convalescence ˌkɒn və 'les ənts ‖ ˌkɑːn-

convalescent ˌkɒn və 'les ənt ◄ ‖ ˌkɑːn- ~s s

convection kən 'vek ʃən §ₗₙkɒn-

convective kən 'vekt ɪv §(ˌ)kɒn- ~**ly** li
convector kən 'vekt ə §(ˌ)kɒn- ‖ -ᵊr ~**s** z
conven|e kən 'viːn §(ˌ)kɒn- ~**ed** d ~**es** z ~**ing** ɪŋ
convenienc|e kən 'viːn i_ənts §(ˌ)kɒn- ~**es** ɪz əz
con'venience food
convenient kən 'viːn i_ənt §(ˌ)kɒn- ~**ly** li
convenor kən 'viːn ə §(ˌ)kɒn- ‖ -ᵊr ~**s** z
convent 'kɒn vənt ‖ 'kaːn- -vent ~**s** s
conventicle kən 'vent ɪk ᵊl §(ˌ)kɒn- ‖ -'vent̮- ~**s** z
convention kən 'ventʃ ᵊn §(ˌ)kɒn- ~**s** z
conventional kən 'ventʃ ᵊn_əl §(ˌ)kɒn- ~**ism** ɪz əm ~**ly** i
conventionalis... —see **conventionaliz...**
conventionality kən ,ventʃ ə 'næl ət i §(ˌ)kɒn-, -ɪt i ‖ -ət̮ i
conventionalized kən 'ventʃ ᵊn_ə laɪzd §(ˌ)kɒn-
converb 'kɒn vɜːb ‖ 'kaːn vɜ·ːb ~**s** z
converg|e kən 'vɜːdʒ (ˌ)kɒn- ‖ -'vɜ·ːdʒ —but in contrast to diverge, 'kɒn vɜːdʒ ‖ 'kaːn vɜ·ːdʒ ~**ed** d ~**es** ɪz əz ~**ing** ɪŋ
convergenc|e kən 'vɜːdʒ ᵊnts §(ˌ)kɒn- ‖ -'vɜ·ːdʒ- —but in contrast to divergence, 'kɒn vɜːdʒ- ‖ 'kaːn vɜ·ːdʒ- ~**es** ɪz əz ~**ies** ɪz ~**y** i
convergent kən 'vɜːdʒ ᵊnt §(ˌ)kɒn- ‖ -'vɜ·ːdʒ- —but in contrast to divergent, 'kɒn vɜːdʒ- ‖ 'kaːn vɜ·ːdʒ- ~**ly** li
conversab|le kən 'vɜːs əb ᵊl ‖ -'vɜ·ːs- ~**leness** ᵊl nəs -nɪs ~**ly** li
conversant kən 'vɜːs ᵊnt §(ˌ)kɒn- ‖ -'vɜ·ːs- 'kaːn vɜ·ːs- ~**ly** li
conversation ,kɒn və 'seɪʃ ᵊn ‖ ,kaːn vᵊr- ~**s** z
,conver'sation piece
conversational ,kɒn və 'seɪʃ ᵊn_əl ◂ ‖ ,kaːn vᵊr- ~**ly** i
conversationalist ,kɒn və 'seɪʃ ᵊn_əl ɪst §-əst ‖ ,kaːn vᵊr- ~**s** s
conversazion|e ,kɒn və sæts i 'əʊn li ‖ ,kaːn vᵊr saːts i 'oʊn li ,koʊn- —It [kon ver sat 'tsjoː ne] ~**es** ɪz ~**i** iː
convers|e v kən 'vɜːs §(ˌ)kɒn- ‖ -'vɜ·ːs ~**ed** t ~**es** ɪz əz ~**ing** ɪŋ
converse n 'kɒn vɜːs ‖ 'kaːn vɜ·ːs
converse adj 'kɒn vɜːs kən 'vɜːs ‖ kən 'vɜ·ːs 'kaːn vɜ·ːs ~**ly** li
conversion kən 'vɜːʃ ᵊn §(ˌ)kɒn-, §-'vɜːʒ- ‖ -'vɜ·ːʒ- -'vɜ·ːʃ- ~**s** z
con'version ,factor
con|vert v kən |'vɜːt §(ˌ)kɒn- ‖ -|'vɜ·ːt ~**verted** 'vɜːt ɪd -əd ‖ 'vɜ·ːt̮ əd ~**verts** 'vɜːts ‖ 'vɜ·ːts ~**verting** 'vɜːt ɪŋ ‖ 'vɜ·ːt̮ ɪŋ
convert n 'kɒn vɜːt ‖ 'kaːn vɜ·ːt ~**s** s
converter kən 'vɜːt ə §(ˌ)kɒn- ‖ -'vɜ·ːt̮ ᵊr ~**s** z
convertibility kən ,vɜːt ə 'bɪl ət i §kɒn-, §,kɒn ,vɜːt-, -ɪ'•-, -ɪt i ‖ -,vɜ·ːt̮ ə 'bɪl ət̮ i
convertible kən 'vɜːt əb ᵊl §(ˌ)kɒn-, -ɪb- ‖ -'vɜ·ːt̮-
convertor kən 'vɜːt ə §(ˌ)kɒn- ‖ -'vɜ·ːt̮ ᵊr ~**s** z

convex ,kɒn 'veks ◂ kən- ‖ ,kaːn- kən-; 'kaːn veks ~**ly** li
convexit|y kən 'veks ət i ,kɒn-, -ɪt- ‖ -ət̮ i ,kaːn- ~**ies** ɪz
convexo-concave kən ,veks əʊ kɒn 'keɪv ◂ kɒn-, ,kɒn,•-, →-kɒŋ'•, -kən'• ‖ -oʊ kaːn-
convexo-convex kən ,veks əʊ kɒn 'veks ◂ kɒn-, ,kɒn,•-, -kən'• ‖ -oʊ kaːn-
convey kən 'veɪ §(ˌ)kɒn- ~**ed** d ~**ing** ɪŋ ~**s** z
conveyanc|e kən 'veɪ ᵊnts §(ˌ)kɒn- ~**ed** t ~**er/s** ə/z ‖ ᵊr/z ~**es** ɪz əz ~**ing** ɪŋ
conveyer, conveyor kən 'veɪ ə §(ˌ)kɒn- ‖ -ᵊr ~**s** z
con'veyor belt
convict v kən 'vɪkt §(ˌ)kɒn- ~**ed** ɪd əd ~**ing** ɪŋ ~**s** s
convict n 'kɒn vɪkt ‖ 'kaːn- ~**s** s
conviction kən 'vɪk ʃᵊn §(ˌ)kɒn- ~**s** z
convinc|e kən 'vɪnts §(ˌ)kɒn- ~**ed** t ~**es** ɪz əz ~**ing/ly** ɪŋ /li
convivial kən 'vɪv i_əl §(ˌ)kɒn- ~**ly** i
conviviality kən ,vɪv i 'æl ət i §(ˌ)kɒn-, -ɪt i ‖ -ət̮ i
convocation, C~ ,kɒn və 'keɪʃ ᵊn ‖ ,kaːn- ~**s** z
convok|e kən 'vəʊk §(ˌ)kɒn- ‖ -'voʊk ~**ed** t ~**es** s ~**ing** ɪŋ
convoluted 'kɒn və ,luːt ɪd -,ljuːt-, -əd, ,•'•• ◂ ‖ 'kaːn və ,luːt̮ əd ~**ly** li
convolution ,kɒn və 'luːʃ ᵊn -'ljuːʃ- ‖ ,kaːn- ~**s** z
convolv|e kən 'vɒlv §-'vəʊlv ~**ed** d ~**es** z ~**ing** ɪŋ
convolv|ulus kən 'vɒlv |jʊl əs §(ˌ)kɒn-, -jəl- ‖ -'vaːlv |jəl- -'vɔːlv-, -'vaːlv-, -'vɔːv- ~**uli** ju laɪ jə- ‖ jə laɪ ~**uluses** jʊl əs ɪz jəl-, -əz ‖ jəl əs əz
convoy n 'kɒn vɔɪ ‖ 'kaːn- ~**s** z
convoy v 'kɒn vɔɪ ‖ 'kaːn- kən 'vɔɪ ~**ed** d ~**ing** ɪŋ ~**s** z
convulsant kən 'vʌls ᵊnt §(ˌ)kɒn- ~**s** s
convuls|e kən 'vʌls §(ˌ)kɒn- ~**ed** t ~**es** ɪz əz ~**ing** ɪŋ
convulsion kən 'vʌlʃ ᵊn §(ˌ)kɒn- ~**s** z
convulsive kən 'vʌls ɪv §(ˌ)kɒn- ~**ly** li ~**ness** nəs nɪs
Conway 'kɒn weɪ ‖ 'kaːn-
Conwy 'kɒn wi ‖ 'kaːn- —Welsh ['kɒn uɨ]
con|y 'kəʊn |i ‖ 'koʊn |i —formerly 'kʌn i ~**ies** iz
Conybeare (i) 'kɒn i bɪə ‖ 'kaːn i bɪr, (ii) 'kʌn-
coo kuː **cooed** kuːd **cooing** 'kuː ɪŋ **coos** kuːz
Coober Pedy ,kuːb ə 'piːd i ‖ -ᵊr-
Cooch kuːtʃ
cooee, cooey 'kuː iː ,•'•; 'kuː i ~**s** z
Coogan 'kuːg ᵊn
cook, Cook kʊk §kuːk **cooked** kʊkt §kuːkt **cooking** 'kʊk ɪŋ §'kuːk- **cooks** kʊks §kuːks
'cook book
cook-chill ,kʊk 'tʃɪl ◂ §,kuːk- ~**ed** d ~**ing** ɪŋ ~**s** z
Cooke kʊk §kuːk
Cookeen tdmk (ˌ)kʊ 'kiːn

cooker 'kʊk ə §'kuːk- ‖ -ᵊr ~s z
cookery 'kʊk ər_i §'kuːk-
  'cookery book
cook|house 'kʊk |haʊs §'kuːk- ~houses
  haʊz ɪz -əz
cookie 'kʊk i ~s z
cooking 'kʊk ɪŋ §'kuːk-
  'cooking ˌapple
cookout 'kʊk aʊt §'kuːk- ~s s
Cookson 'kʊks ən
Cooktown 'kʊk taʊn
cook|y 'kʊk |i ~ies iz
cool kuːl cooled kuːld cooler 'kuːl ə ‖ -ᵊr
  coolest 'kuːl ɪst -əst cooling 'kuːl ɪŋ cools
  kuːlz
  'cooling ˌtower
coolabah 'kuːl ə bɑː ~s z
coolamon 'kuːl ə mɒn ‖ -mɑːn
Coolangatta ˌkuːl əŋ 'gæt ə -ən- ‖ -'gæţ ə
coolant 'kuːl ənt ~s s
cooler 'kuːl ə ‖ -ᵊr ~s z
Cooley 'kuːl i
Coolgardie kuːl 'gaːd i ‖ -'gaːrd i
cool-headed ˌkuːl 'hed ɪd ◄ -əd
coolibah, coolibar 'kuːl ə baː -ɪ- ~s z
Coolidge 'kuːl ɪdʒ
coolie 'kuːl i ~s z
Coolin 'kuːl ɪn §-ən
cooling-off ˌkuːl ɪŋ 'ɒf -'ɔːf ‖ -'ɔːf -'ɑːf
  ˌcooling-'off ˌperiod
coolly 'kuːl li -i
Cooloola kə 'luːl ə
coolth kuːlθ
coomb, coombe, C~ kuːm coombs kuːmz
Coombes, Coombs, Coomes kuːmz
coon kuːn coons kuːnz
Coonawarra ˌkuːn ə 'wɒr ə ‖ -'wɑːr ə -'wɔːr ə
cooncan 'kuːn kæn →'kuːŋ-
Cooney 'kuːn i
coonskin 'kuːn skɪn ~s z
coontie 'kuːnt i ~s z
coop kuːp ‖ kʊp cooped kuːpt ‖ kʊpt
  cooping 'kuːp ɪŋ ‖ 'kʊp- coops kuːps
  ‖ kʊps
Co-op, co-op 'kəʊ ɒp ‖ 'koʊ aːp ~s s
Coope kuːp
cooper, C~ 'kuːp ə ‖ -ᵊr 'kʊp- ~ed d
  coopering 'kuːp ər ɪŋ ‖ 'kʊp- ~s z
cooperage 'kuːp ər ɪdʒ 'kʊp-
coope|rate, co-ope|rate kəʊ 'ɒp ə |reɪt
  ‖ koʊ 'aːp- ~rated reɪt ɪd -əd ‖ reɪţ əd
  ~rates reɪts ~rating reɪt ɪŋ ‖ reɪţ ɪŋ
cooperation, co-operation kəʊ ˌɒp ə 'reɪʃ ᵊn
  ˌkəʊ ˌɒp- ‖ koʊ ˌaːp- ˌkoʊ ˌaːp-
cooperative, co-operative, C~ kəʊ 'ɒp
  ər_ət ɪv ‖ koʊ 'aːp ər_əţ ɪv -ə reɪţ- ~ly li
  ~ness nəs nɪs
coopt, co-opt kəʊ 'ɒpt ‖ koʊ 'aːpt ~ed ɪd əd
  ~ing ɪŋ ~s s
cooptation, co-optation
  ˌkəʊ ɒp 'teɪʃ ᵊn ‖ ˌkoʊ aːp- ~s z
cooption, co-option kəʊ 'ɒp ʃᵊn ‖ koʊ 'aːp-
  ~s z

coordinate, co-ordinate adj, n kəʊ 'ɔːd ɪn ət
  -ᵊn_ət, -ɪt ‖ koʊ 'ɔːrd ᵊn_ət -eɪt ~ly li ~ness
  nəs nɪs ~s s
coordin|ate, co-ordin|ate v kəʊ 'ɔːd ɪ n|eɪt -ə-,
  -ᵊn |eɪt ‖ koʊ 'ɔːrd ᵊn |eɪt ~ated eɪt ɪd -əd
  ‖ eɪţ əd ~ates eɪts ~ating eɪt ɪŋ ‖ eɪţ ɪŋ
coordination, co-ordination
  kəʊ ˌɔːd ɪ 'neɪʃ ᵊn ˌkəʊ ˌɔːd-, -ə-, -ᵊn 'eɪʃ-
  ‖ koʊ ˌɔːrd ᵊn_ 'eɪʃ ᵊn ˌkoʊ ˌɔːrd-
coordinator, co-ordinator kəʊ 'ɔːd ɪ neɪt ə
  -'•ə-, -ᵊn eɪt- ‖ koʊ 'ɔːrd ᵊn eɪţ ᵊr ~s z
Coors tdmk kɔːz kʊəz ‖ kʊᵊrz
coot kuːt coots kuːts
Coot, Coote kuːt
Cootamundra ˌkuːt ə 'mʌndr ə ◄ ‖ ˌkuːţ-
  ˌCoota ˌmundra 'wattle
cootie 'kuːt i ‖ 'kuːţ i ~s z
co-own ˌkəʊ 'əʊn ‖ ˌkoʊ 'oʊn ~ed d ~er/s
  ə/z ‖ -ᵊr/z ~ership ə ʃɪp ‖ -ᵊr ʃɪp ~ing ɪŋ
  ~s z
cop kɒp ‖ kaːp copped kɒpt ‖ kaːpt
  copping 'kɒp ɪŋ ‖ 'kaːp ɪŋ cops
  kɒps ‖ kaːps
Copacabana ˌkəʊp ə kə 'bæn ə ‖ ˌkoʊp- —Sp
  [ko pa ka 'βa na], BrazPort [kɔ pa ka 'bɐ na]
copacetic ˌkəʊp ə 'siːt ɪk ◄ ‖ ˌkoʊp ə 'seţ ɪk ◄
  -'siːţ-
copaiba kəʊ 'paɪb ə kɒ- ‖ koʊ-
copal 'kəʊp ᵊl -æl ‖ 'koʊp-
copartner ˌkəʊ 'paːt nə ‖ ˌkoʊ 'paːrt nᵊr ~s z
  ~ship/s ʃɪp/s
cope, Cope kəʊp ‖ koʊp coped
  kəʊpt ‖ koʊpt copes kəʊps ‖ koʊps coping
  'kəʊp ɪŋ ‖ 'koʊp ɪŋ
-cope stress-imposing kəp i— apocope
  ə 'pɒk əp i ‖ -'paːk-
copeck 'kəʊp ek ‖ 'koʊp- ~s s
Copeland 'kəʊp lənd ‖ 'koʊp-
Copenhagen ˌkəʊp ᵊn 'heɪg ᵊn ◄ -'haːg-,
  '•••, •• ‖ 'koʊp ᵊn ˌheɪg ᵊn, ••'••, -'haːg ᵊn
  —Danish København [køb ᵊn 'haʊʔn]
coper 'kəʊp ə ‖ 'koʊp ᵊr ~s z
Copernic|an kəʊ 'pɜːn ɪk |ən ‖ koʊ 'pɜːn- kə-
  ~us əs
Copestake 'kəʊp steɪk ‖ 'koʊp-
copestone 'kəʊp stəʊn ‖ 'koʊp stoʊn ~s z
copi... —see copy
copier 'kɒp i_ə ‖ 'kaːp i_ᵊr ~s z
copilot 'kəʊ ˌpaɪl ət ,•'•• ‖ 'koʊ- ~s s
coping 'kəʊp ɪŋ ‖ 'koʊp ɪŋ
copingstone 'kəʊp ɪŋ stəʊn ‖ 'koʊp ɪŋ stoʊn
  ~s z
copious 'kəʊp i_əs ‖ 'koʊp- ~ly li ~ness nəs
  nɪs
copita kəʊ 'piːt ə kɒ- ‖ koʊ 'piːţ ə —Sp
  [ko 'pi ta] ~s z —Sp [s]
Copland (i) 'kəʊp lənd ‖ 'koʊp-, (ii)
  'kɒp- ‖ 'kaːp- —The composer, Aaron C~, is
  (i)
Copley 'kɒp li ‖ 'kaːp-
copolymer ₍ₒ₎kəʊ 'pɒl ɪm ə -əm-
  ‖ ₍ₒ₎koʊ 'paːl əm ᵊr ~s z
cop-out, copout 'kɒp aʊt ‖ 'kaːp- ~s s

copp... —*see* cop
copper 'kɒp ə ‖ 'kɑːp ᵊr ~ed d ~s z
  ,copper 'beech; 'Copper Belt; ,copper
  'sulphate
copperas 'kɒp ər əs ‖ 'kɑːp-
copper-bottomed ,kɒp ə 'bɒt əmd◄
  ‖ ,kɑːp ᵊr 'bɑːt̬ əmd ◄
Copperfield 'kɒp ə fiːᵊld ‖ 'kɑːp ᵊr-
copperhead 'kɒp ə hed ‖ 'kɑːp ᵊr- ~s z
coppermine, C~ 'kɒp ə maɪn ‖ 'kɑːp ᵊr- ~s z
copperplate 'kɒp ə pleɪt ,•••‖ 'kɑːp ᵊr-
coppersmith, C~ 'kɒp ə smɪθ ‖ 'kɑːp ᵊr- ~s s
coppery 'kɒp ər i ‖ 'kɑːp-
coppic|e 'kɒp ɪs §-əs ‖ 'kɑːp əs ~ed t ~es ɪz
  əz ~ing ɪŋ
Coppola 'kɒp əl ə ‖ 'koʊp- 'kɑːp-
Coppull 'kɒp ᵊl ‖ 'kɑːp-
copra 'kɒp rə ‖ 'koʊp- 'kɑːp-
copro- *comb. form*
  with stress-neutral suffix ¦kɒp rəʊ ‖ ¦kɑːp rə-
  — coprophilia ,kɒp rəʊ 'fɪl i̯ə ‖ ,kɑːp rə-
  with stress-imposing suffix
  kɒ 'prɒ+ ‖ kɑː 'prɑː+ — coprophagous
  kɒ 'prɒf əg əs ‖ kɑː 'prɑːf-
coprocessor, co-processor ,kəʊ 'prəʊs es ə
  '•,•••‖ ,koʊ 'prɑːs es ᵊr -'prɑːs- ~s z
coproduc|e ,kəʊ prə 'djuːs §-'duːs, →§-'dʒuːs
  ‖ ,koʊ prə 'duːs -'djuːs ~ed t ~es ɪz əz
  ~ing ɪŋ
coproduction ,kəʊ prə 'dʌk ʃᵊn ‖ ,koʊ-
copse kɒps ‖ kɑːps (= *cops*) copses 'kɒps ɪz
  -əz ‖ 'kɑːps əz
Copt kɒpt ‖ kɑːpt Copts kɒpts ‖ kɑːpts
copter, 'copter 'kɒpt ə ‖ 'kɑːpt ᵊr ~s z
Copthall 'kɒpt ɔːl -hɔːl ‖ 'kɑːpt ɔːl -hɔːl, -ɑːl,
  -hɑːl
Coptic 'kɒpt ɪk ‖ 'kɑːpt-
cop|ula 'kɒp |jʊl ə -jəl- ‖ 'kɑːp |jəl ə ~ulae
  ju liː -jəˌ -leɪ ‖ jə liː ~ulas jʊl əz jəl-
  ‖ jəl əz
copu|late 'kɒp ju |leɪt -jə- ‖ 'kɑːp jə- ~lated
  leɪt ɪd -əd ‖ leɪt̬ əd ~lates leɪts ~lating
  leɪt ɪŋ ‖ leɪt̬ ɪŋ
copulation ,kɒp ju 'leɪʃ ᵊn -jə- ‖ ,kɑːp jə- ~s
  z
copulative 'kɒp jʊl ət ɪv '•jəl-; -ju leɪt-,
  -jə leɪt- ‖ 'kɑːp jəl ət̬ ɪv -jə leɪt̬- ~ly li
cop|y 'kɒp |i ‖ 'kɑːp |i ~ied id ~ies iz ~ying
  i̯ɪŋ
  'copy ,taster; 'copy ,typist
copybook 'kɒp i bʊk §-buːk ‖ 'kɑːp- ~s s
copyboy 'kɒp i bɔɪ ‖ 'kɑːp- ~s z
copycat 'kɒp i kæt ‖ 'kɑːp- ~s s
copydesk 'kɒp i desk ‖ 'kɑːp- ~s s
Copydex *tdmk* 'kɒp i deks ‖ 'kɑːp-
copy-ed|it 'kɒp i ˌed |ɪt §-ət ‖ 'kɑːp i ˌed |ət
  ~ited ɪt ɪd §ət-, -əd ‖ ət̬ əd ~iting ɪt ɪŋ §ət-
  ‖ ət̬ ɪŋ ~its ɪts §əts ‖ əts
copygirl 'kɒp i ɡɜːl ‖ 'kɑːp i ɡɜːl ~s z
copyhold 'kɒp i həʊld →-hɒʊld ‖ 'kɑːp i hoʊld
  ~s z
copyholder 'kɒp i ˌhəʊld ə →-ˌhɒʊld-
  ‖ 'kɑːp i ˌhoʊld ᵊr ~s z

copyist 'kɒp i ɪst §-əst ‖ 'kɑːp- ~s s
copyreader 'kɒp i ˌriːd ə ‖ 'kɑːp i ˌriːd ᵊr ~s z
copy|right 'kɒp i |raɪt ‖ 'kɑːp- ~righted
  raɪt ɪd -əd ‖ raɪt̬ əd ~righting
  raɪt ɪŋ ‖ raɪt̬ ɪŋ ~rights raɪts
copywrit|er/s 'kɒp i ˌraɪt ə/z ‖ 'kɑːp i ˌraɪt̬ ᵊr/
  z ~ing ɪŋ
coq au vin ,kɒk əʊ 'væn -'væ̃ ‖ ,koʊk oʊ-
  ,kɑːk- —*Fr* [kɔ ko vɛ̃]
co|quet kɒ |'ket kəʊ- ‖ koʊ |'ket ~quets 'kets
  ~quetted 'ket ɪd -əd ‖ 'ket̬ əd ~quetting
  'ket ɪŋ ‖ 'ket̬ ɪŋ
Coquet 'kəʊk ɪt §-ət ‖ 'koʊk-
coquetr|y 'kɒk ɪtr |i 'kəʊk-, -ətr- ‖ 'koʊk-
  koʊ 'ketr |i ~ies iz
coquette kɒ 'ket kəʊ- ‖ koʊ- ~s s
coquettish kɒ 'ket ɪʃ kəʊ- ‖ koʊ 'ket̬ ɪʃ ~ly li
  ~ness nəs nɪs
coquille kɒ 'kiː ‖ koʊ 'kiːᵊl —*Fr* [kɔ kij]
  co,quilles ,St 'Jacques ,sæn 'ʒæk -,sæ̃-
  ‖ ,sɑːn 'ʒɑːk —*Fr* [sæ̃ ʒak]
coquina kəʊ 'kiːn ə ‖ koʊ-
cor kɔː ‖ kɔːr —*See also phrases with this word*
  ,cor 'blimey
Cora 'kɔːr ə ‖ 'koʊr-
coracle 'kɒr ək ᵊl ‖ 'kɔːr- 'kɑːr- ~s z
coral, Coral 'kɒr əl ‖ 'kɔːr- 'kɑːr- ~s z
  ,Coral 'Sea; 'coral snake
coralline 'kɒr ə laɪn ‖ 'kɔːr- 'kɑːr- ~s z
coralroot 'kɒr əl ruːt ‖ 'kɔːr- 'kɑːr- ~s s
Coram 'kɔːr əm
cor anglais ,kɔːr 'ɒŋ ɡleɪ -'ɑːŋ-
  ‖ ,kɔːr ɑːŋ 'ɡleɪ ,koʊr-, -ɔːŋ- cors anglais
  ,kɔːz- ‖ ,kɔːrz- ,koʊrz-
corban 'kɔː bæn 'kɔːb ən ‖ 'kɔːr-
corbel 'kɔːb ᵊl ‖ 'kɔːrb- ~ed, ~led d ~ing,
  ~ling ɪŋ ~s z
Corbet, Corbett 'kɔːb ɪt §-ət ‖ 'kɔːrb-
Corbin 'kɔːb ɪn §-ᵊn ‖ 'kɔːrb-
Corbishley 'kɔːb ɪʃ li ‖ 'kɔːrb-
Corbridge 'kɔː brɪdʒ ‖ 'kɔːr-
Corbusier kɔː 'buːz i eɪ -'bjuːz-
  ‖ ,kɔːrb uːz 'jeɪ -uːs- —*Fr* [kɔʁ by zje]
Corby 'kɔːb i ‖ 'kɔːrb i
Corbyn 'kɔːb ɪn §-ᵊn ‖ 'kɔːrb ən
Corcoran 'kɔːk ᵊr_ᵊn ‖ 'kɔːrk-
Corcyra kɔː 'saɪᵊr ə ‖ kɔːr- —*ModGk* Kérkira
  ['cɛr ci ra]
cord kɔːd ‖ kɔːrd corded 'kɔːd ɪd -əd ‖ 'kɔːrd-
  cording 'kɔːd ɪŋ ‖ 'kɔːrd- cords
  kɔːdz ‖ kɔːrdz
cordage 'kɔːd ɪdʒ ‖ 'kɔːrd-
cordate 'kɔːd eɪt ‖ 'kɔːrd- ~ly li
Cordelia kɔː 'diːl i̯ə ‖ kɔːr-
cordelier, C~ ,kɔːd ə 'lɪə -ɪ- ‖ ,kɔːrd ə 'lɪᵊr ~s
  z
Cordell ,kɔː 'del ‖ ,kɔːr-
cordial 'kɔːd i̯əl ‖ 'kɔːrdʒ əl (*) ~ly i ~s z
cordiality ,kɔːd i 'æl ət i -ɪt i ‖ ,kɔːrdʒ i 'æl ət̬ i
  kɔːr 'dʒæl ət̬ i (*)
cordillera ,kɔːd ɪl 'jeər ə -əl- ‖ ,kɔːrd ᵊl 'jer ə
  kɔːr 'dɪl ᵊr ə —*Sp* [kor ði ˈʎe ra, -ˈje-]
cordite 'kɔːd aɪt ‖ 'kɔːrd-

cordless 'kɔːd ləs -lɪs ‖ 'kɔːrd-
cordoba, córdoba, C~ 'kɔːd əb ə ‖ 'kɔːrd-
—Sp Córdoba ['kor ðo βa]
cordon 'kɔːd ᵊn ‖ 'kɔːrd ᵊn ~s z —but in
French words -ō̃, -ɒn, -ɒŋ ‖ kɔːr 'dɔ̃ː, -'dɑːn,
-'dɔːn —See also phrases with this word
cordon bleu ˌkɔːd õ̃ 'blɜː ◄ -ɒn-, -ɒm-, -ɒŋ-
‖ kɔːr ˌdɔ̃ː 'blʊ —Fr [kɔʁ dɔ̃ blø]
cordon sanitaire ˌkɔːd õ̃ ˌsæn ɪ 'teə ˌ•ɒn-, -ə'•
‖ kɔːr ˌdɔ̃ː ˌsɑːn i 'teᵊr —Fr
[kɔʁ dɔ̃ sa ni tɛːʁ]
Cordova 'kɔːd əv ə ‖ 'kɔːrd- —Sp Córdoba
['kor ðo βa]
cordovan 'kɔːd əv ᵊn ‖ 'kɔːrd-
corduroy 'kɔːd ə rɔɪ -jʊ-, -jə-; 'kɔːdʒ ə-, -ʊ-;
ˌ•'•, 'kɔːdr ɔɪ ‖ 'kɔːrd- ~ed d ~s z
cordwain 'kɔːd weɪn ‖ 'kɔːrd- ~er/s ə/z ‖ ᵊr/z
core kɔː ‖ kɔːr koʊr cored kɔːd ‖ kɔːrd koʊrd
cores kɔːz ‖ kɔːrz koʊrz coring 'kɔːr ɪŋ
‖ 'koʊr-
'core time
coreferential ˌkəʊ ˌref ə 'rentʃ ᵊl ◄ ‖ ˌkoʊ- ~ly
i
Corel tdmk kə 'rel kɒ-; 'kɒr ᵊl ‖ 'kɔːr ᵊl, 'kɑːr-
core‖late 'kɒr ə ‖leɪt -ɪ-; 'kəʊ rɪ-, -rə-, ˌ•'•
‖ 'koʊ rɪ- ~lated leɪt ɪd -əd ‖ leɪt̬ əd ~lates
leɪts ~lating leɪt ɪŋ ‖ leɪt̬ ɪŋ
Coreldraw, CorelDraw! tdmk kə ˌrel 'drɔː ˌkɒr
əl '• ‖ -'drɑː
coreligionist, co-religionist ˌkəʊ rɪ 'lɪdʒ ᵊn ɪst
ˌ•rə-, §ˌ•riː-, §ˌ•əst ‖ ˌkoʊ- ~s s
Corelli kə 'rel i kɒ- ‖ koʊ- —It [ko 'rɛl li]
Coren 'kɒr ən ‖ 'kɔːr-
coreopsis ˌkɒr i 'ɒps ɪs §-əs ‖ ˌkɔːr i 'ɑːps-
ˌkoʊr-
corer 'kɔːr ə ‖ -ᵊr 'koʊr- ~s z
corespondent, co-respondent ˌkəʊ rɪ 'spɒnd
ənt -rə-, §-riː- ‖ ˌkoʊ rɪ 'spɑːnd- ~s s
Corey 'kɔːr i ‖ 'koʊr-
corf kɔːf ‖ kɔːrf corves kɔːvz ‖ kɔːrvz
Corfam tdmk 'kɔː fæm ‖ 'kɔːr-
Corfe kɔːf ‖ kɔːrf
Corfu ˌkɔː 'fuː -'fjuː ‖ 'kɔːr fuː -fjuː, ˌ•'•
—ModGk Kérkira ['cɛr ci ra]
ˌCorfu 'Channel
corgi, Corgi 'kɔːg i ‖ 'kɔːrg i ~s z
coriander ˌkɒr i 'ænd ə '•••• ‖ 'kɔːr i ænd ᵊr
'koʊr-, ˌ•'•••
Corin 'kɒr ɪn -ən ‖ 'kɔːr-
Corinne kə 'rɪn
Corinth place in Greece 'kɒr ɪntθ -əntθ ‖ 'kɔːr-
'kɑːr- —but places in the US are kə 'rɪntθ
Corinthian kə 'rɪntθ i_ən ‖ 'kɔːr-
Coriolanus ˌkɒr i_əʊ 'leɪn əs kə ˌraɪ_ə-, -'lɑːn-
‖ ˌkɔːr i_ə- ˌkɑːr-
Coriolis ˌkɒr i 'əʊl ɪs §-əs ‖ ˌkɔːr i 'oʊl əs
ˌkoʊr-, -ə 'liːs —Fr [kɔ jɔ lis]
cork, Cork kɔːk ‖ kɔːrk corked kɔːkt ‖ kɔːrkt
corking 'kɔːk ɪŋ ‖ 'kɔːrk ɪŋ corks
kɔːks ‖ kɔːrks
corkage 'kɔːk ɪdʒ ‖ 'kɔːrk-
corkboard 'kɔːk bɔːd ‖ 'kɔːrk bɔːrd -boʊrd
corker 'kɔːk ə ‖ 'kɔːrk ᵊr ~s z

corkscrew 'kɔːk skruː ‖ 'kɔːrk- ~ed d ~ing ɪŋ
~s z
corkwood 'kɔːk wʊd ‖ 'kɔːrk-
cork‖y 'kɔːk ‖i ‖ 'kɔːrk ‖i ~ier i_ə ‖ i_ᵊr ~iest
i_ɪst i_əst ~iness i nəs i nɪs
Corlett 'kɔːl ɪt -ət ‖ 'kɔːrl-
Corley 'kɔːl i ‖ 'kɔːrl i
corm kɔːm ‖ kɔːrm corms kɔːmz ‖ kɔːrmz
Cormac, Cormack 'kɔːm æk -ək ‖ 'kɔːrm-
cormel 'kɔːm ᵊl ‖ 'kɔːrm ᵊl kɔːr 'mel ~s z
cormorant 'kɔːm ᵊr_ənt ‖ 'kɔːrm- -ə rænt ~s
s
corn kɔːn ‖ kɔːrn corned kɔːnd ‖ kɔːrnd
corning 'kɔːn ɪŋ ‖ 'kɔːrn ɪŋ corns
kɔːnz ‖ kɔːrnz
'corn bread; ˌcorned 'beef◄; ˌcorned beef
'sandwich; 'corn exˌchange; 'Corn Laws
cornball 'kɔːn bɔːl →'kɔːm- ‖ 'kɔːrn- -bɑːl
~s z
corncob 'kɔːn kɒb →'kɔːŋ- ‖ 'kɔːrn kɑːb ~s z
corncockle 'kɔːn ˌkɒk ᵊl →'kɔːŋ-
‖ 'kɔːrn ˌkɑːk ᵊl ~s z
corncrake 'kɔːn kreɪk →'kɔːŋ- ‖ 'kɔːrn- ~s s
corne‖a 'kɔːn i_ə kɔː 'niː_ə ‖ 'kɔːrn i_ə ~ae iː
~al ᵊl ~as əz
cornel 'kɔːn ᵊl -el ‖ 'kɔːrn ᵊl -el ~s z
Corneille kɔː 'neɪ -'neᵊl ‖ kɔːr- —Fr [kɔʁ nɛj]
Cornelia kɔː 'niːl i_ə ‖ kɔːr-
cornelian kɔː 'niːl i_ən ‖ kɔːr- ~s z
Cornelius kɔː 'niːl i_əs ‖ kɔːr-
Cornell ˌkɔː 'nel ‖ ˌkɔːr-
corner, C~ 'kɔːn ə ‖ 'kɔːrn ᵊr 'kɔːn- ~ed d
cornering 'kɔːn ᵊr ɪŋ ‖ 'kɔːrn ᵊr ɪŋ 'kɔːn- ~s
z
ˌcorner 'shop, '•••
-cornered 'kɔːn əd ‖ 'kɔːrn ᵊrd 'kɔːn- —
three-cornered ˌθriː 'kɔːn əd ◄ ‖ -'kɔːrn ᵊrd
-'kɔːn-
cornerstone 'kɔːn ə stəʊn ‖ 'kɔːrn ᵊr stoʊn
'kɔːn- ~s z
cornet 'kɔːn ɪt §-ət ‖ kɔːr 'net (*) ~s s
cornetto, C~ tdmk ₍ₒ₎kɔː 'net əʊ ‖ ₍ₒ₎kɔːr 'net̬ oʊ
~s z
cornfield 'kɔːn fiː_əld ‖ 'kɔːrn- ~s z
cornflakes 'kɔːn fleɪks ‖ 'kɔːrn-
cornflour 'kɔːn ˌflaʊ_ə ‖ 'kɔːrn ˌflaʊ_ᵊr
cornflower 'kɔːn ˌflaʊ_ə ‖ 'kɔːrn ˌflaʊ_ᵊr ~s z
Cornford 'kɔːn fəd ‖ 'kɔːrn fᵊrd
Cornhill ˌkɔːn 'hɪl '•• ‖ 'kɔːrn hɪl
cornic‖e 'kɔːn ɪs §-əs ‖ 'kɔːrn əs -ɪs ~es ɪz əz
cornich‖e, C~ ₍ₒ₎kɔː 'niːʃ 'kɔːn iːʃ, -ɪʃ ‖ ₍ₒ₎kɔːr-
~es ɪz əz
Cornish 'kɔːn ɪʃ ‖ 'kɔːrn-
ˌCornish 'pasty
Cornish‖man 'kɔːn ɪʃ ‖mən ‖ 'kɔːrn- ~men
mən men ~woman ˌwʊm ən ~women
ˌwɪm ɪn §-ən
corn pone 'kɔːn pəʊn ‖ 'kɔːrn poʊn
cornrow 'kɔːn rəʊ ‖ 'kɔːrn roʊ ~s z
cornstarch 'kɔːn stɑːtʃ ‖ 'kɔːrn stɑːrtʃ
cornucopia ˌkɔːn ju 'kəʊp i_ə ‖ ˌkɔːrn ə 'koʊp-
ˌ•jə- ~s z
Cornwall 'kɔːn wɔːl -wəl ‖ 'kɔːrn wɑːl -wɔːl

Cornwallis kɔːn 'wɒl ɪs §-əs ‖ kɔːrn 'waːl-
corn|y 'kɔːn li ‖ 'kɔːrn li ~ier i_ə ‖ i_ər ~iest
i_ɪst i_əst
corolla, C~ kə 'rɒl ə ‖ -'roʊl ə -'raːl ə
corollar|y kə 'rɒl ər li ‖ 'kɔːr ə ler li 'kaːr- (*)
~ies iz
Coromandel ˌkɒr əʊ 'mænd əl ‖ ˌkɔːr ə- ˌkaːr-
coron|a, C~ kə 'rəʊn lə ‖ -'roʊn lə ~ae iː ~s z
coronach 'kɒr ən ək -əx ‖ 'kɔːr- 'kaːr- ~s s
coronal 'kɒr ən əl kə 'rəʊn əl ‖ 'kɔːr- 'kaːr-;
kə 'roʊn- ~s z
coronar|y 'kɒr ən ər_li ‖ 'kɔːr ə ner li 'kaːr-
~ies iz
coronation ˌkɒr ə 'neɪʃ ən ◄ ‖ ˌkɔːr- ˌkaːr- ~s
z
coroner 'kɒr ən ə ‖ 'kɔːr ən ər 'kaːr- ~s z
coronet 'kɒr ən ɪt -ət; -ə net, ˌ•• 'net
‖ ˌkɔːr ə 'net ˌkaːr- ~s s
Corot 'kɒr əʊ ‖ kaː 'roʊ kɔː-, kə- —Fr [kɔ ʁo]
Corp. kɔːp ‖ kɔːrp —or see Corporal
corpora 'kɔːp ər_ə -ə raː ‖ 'kɔːrp-
ˌcorpora cal'losa kə 'ləʊs ə ‖ -'loʊs-;
ˌcorpora 'lutea 'luːt i_ə ‖ 'luːt̬- ; ˌcorpora
stri'ata straɪ 'eɪt ə ‖ -'eɪt̬-
corporal 'kɔːp ər_əl ‖ 'kɔːrp- ~s z
corporate 'kɔːp ər_ət _ɪt ‖ 'kɔːrp- ~ly li
corporation ˌkɔːp ə 'reɪʃ ən ◄ ‖ ˌkɔːrp- ~s z
ˌcorpo'ration tax
corporeal kɔː 'pɔːr i_əl ‖ kɔːr- -'poʊr- ~ly i
corps sing. kɔː ‖ kɔːr koʊr (= core) corps pl
kɔːz ‖ kɔːrz koʊrz
ˌcorps de 'ballet ‖ ˌ•• •'•
corpse kɔːps ‖ kɔːrps corpsed
kɔːpst ‖ kɔːrpst corpsing
'kɔːps ɪŋ ‖ 'kɔːrps ɪŋ corpses 'kɔːps ɪz -əz
‖ 'kɔːrps əz
corpulenc|e 'kɔːp jʊl ən̩ts -jəl- ‖ 'kɔːrp jəl-
~y i
corpulent 'kɔːp jʊl ənt -jəl- ‖ 'kɔːrp jəl- ~ly li
corpus, Corpus 'kɔːp əs ‖ 'kɔːrp- ~es ɪz əz
ˌcorpus cal'losum kə 'ləʊs əm ‖ -'loʊs-;
ˌCorpus 'Christi 'krɪst i ; ˌcorpus de'licti
dɪ 'lɪkt aɪ də-, §diː-, -iː; ˌcorpus 'luteum
'luːt i_əm ‖ 'luːt̬- ; ˌcorpus stri'atum
straɪ 'eɪt əm ‖ -'eɪt̬-
corpuscle 'kɔːp ʌs əl kɔː 'pʌs əl ‖ 'kɔːrp- ~s z
corpuscular kɔː 'pʌsk jʊl ə -jəl-
‖ kɔːr 'pʌsk jəl ər
corpus-based 'kɔːp əs beɪst ˌ•'•◄ ‖ 'kɔːrp-
Corr kɔː ‖ kɔːr Corrs kɔːz ‖ kɔːrz
corral kə 'raːl kɒ- ‖ -'ræl (may = chorale) ~led
d ~ling ɪŋ ~s z
correct kə 'rekt ~ed ɪd əd ~ing ɪŋ ~ly li
~ness nəs nɪs ~s s
correction kə 'rek ʃən ~s z
correctional kə 'rek ʃən_əl
correctitude kə 'rekt ɪ tjuːd §-ə-, →§-tʃuːd
‖ -tuːd -tjuːd
corrective kə 'rekt ɪv ~ly li ~s z
corrector kə 'rekt ə ‖ -ər ~s z
Correggio kɒ 'redʒ i_əʊ kə-, -'redʒ əʊ
‖ kə 'redʒ i_oʊ -'redʒ oʊ —It [kor 'red dʒo]
~s, ~'s z

correlate n 'kɒr ə leɪt -ɪ-; -əl ət, -ɪt ‖ 'kɔːr-
'kaːr- ~s s
corre|late v 'kɒr ə |leɪt -ɪ- ‖ 'kɔːr- 'kaːr-
~lated leɪt ɪd -əd ‖ leɪt̬ əd ~lates leɪts
~lating leɪt ɪŋ ‖ leɪt̬ ɪŋ
correlation ˌkɒr ə 'leɪʃ ən -ɪ- ‖ ˌkɔːr- ˌkaːr- ~s
z
ˌcorre'lation coef'ficient
correlative kə 'rel ət ɪv kɒ- ‖ -ət̬ ɪv ~ly li
~ness nəs nɪs ~s z
correspond ˌkɒr ə 'spɒnd -ɪ- ‖ ˌkɔːr ə 'spaːnd
ˌkaːr- ~ed ɪd əd ~ing/ly ɪŋ /li ~s z
correspondenc|e ˌkɒr ə 'spɒnd ən̩ts -ɪ-
‖ ˌkɔːr ə 'spaːnd- ˌkaːr- ~es ɪz əz
ˌcorre'spondence course
correspondent ˌkɒr ə 'spɒnd ənt -ɪ-
‖ ˌkɔːr ə 'spaːnd- ˌkaːr- ~ly li ~s s
corrida kɒ 'riːd ə kə- ‖ kɔː 'riːð ə —Sp
[ko 'rri ða] ~s z
corridor 'kɒr ɪ dɔː -ə-; -ɪd ə, -əd- ‖ 'kɔːr əd ər
'kaːr-, -ə dɔːr ~s z
corrie, C~ 'kɒr i ‖ 'kɔːr i 'kaːr i ~s z
Corriedale 'kɒr i deɪəl ‖ 'kɔːr- 'kaːr- ~s z
Corrigan 'kɒr ɪg ən -əg- ‖ 'kɔːr- 'kaːr-
corrigend|um ˌkɒr ɪ 'dʒend əm -ə-, -'gend-
‖ ˌkɔːr- ˌkaːr- ~a ə
Corris 'kɒr ɪs §-əs ‖ 'kɔːr- 'kaːr-
corrobo|rate kə 'rɒb ə |reɪt ‖ -'raːb- ~rated
reɪt ɪd -əd ‖ reɪt̬ əd ~rates reɪts ~rating
reɪt ɪŋ ‖ reɪt̬ ɪŋ
corroboration kə ˌrɒb ə 'reɪʃ ən ‖ -ˌraːb- ~s z
corroborative kə 'rɒb ər_ət ɪv -ə reɪt-
‖ -'raːb ə reɪt̬ ɪv -ər_ət̬ ɪv ~ly li
corroborator kə 'rɒb ə reɪt ə ‖ -'raːb ə reɪt̬ ər
~s z
corroboree kə 'rɒb ər i -ə riː ‖ -'raːb- ~s z
corrod|e kə 'rəʊd ‖ -'roʊd ~ed ɪd əd ~es z
~ing ɪŋ
corrodible kə 'rəʊd əb əl -ɪb- ‖ -'roʊd-
corrosion kə 'rəʊʒ ən ‖ -'roʊʒ-
corrosive kə 'rəʊs ɪv -'rəʊz- ‖ -'roʊs- -'roʊz-
~ly li ~ness nəs nɪs
corru|gate 'kɒr ə |geɪt -ʊ-, -ju- ‖ 'kɔːr- 'kaːr-
~gated geɪt ɪd -əd ‖ geɪt̬ əd ~gates geɪts
~gating geɪt ɪŋ ‖ geɪt̬ ɪŋ
corrugation ˌkɒr ə 'geɪʃ ən -ʊ-, -ju- ‖ ˌkɔːr-
ˌkaːr- ~s z
corrupt kə 'rʌpt ~ed ɪd əd ~ing ɪŋ ~s s
corruptibility kə ˌrʌpt ə 'bɪl ət i -ˌ•ɪ-, -ɪt i
‖ -ət̬ i
corruptib|le kə 'rʌpt əb əl -ɪb- ~ly li
corruption kə 'rʌp ʃən ~s z
corruptor kə 'rʌpt ə ‖ -ər ~s z
corruptive kə 'rʌpt ɪv ~ly li
Corsa tdmk 'kɔːs ə ‖ 'kɔːrs ə
corsag|e (ˌ)kɔː 'saːʒ '•• ‖ (ˌ)kɔːr- -'saːdʒ, '••
~es ɪz əz
corsair 'kɔːs eə (ˌ)kɔː 'seə ‖ 'kɔːrs er
(ˌ)kɔːr 'seər ~s z
corselet 'kɔːs lət -lɪt ‖ 'kɔːrs- —but for the
undergarment, properly Corselette tdmk,
ˌkɔːs ə 'let ‖ ˌkɔːrs- ~s s

cors|et 'kɔːs ɪt §-ət ‖ 'kɔːrs ‖ət ~eted ɪt ɪd §ət-, -əd ‖ ‖ət əd ~eting ɪt ɪŋ §ət- ‖ ‖ət ɪŋ ~ets ɪts §əts ‖ əts
corsetry 'kɔːs ɪtr i §-ətr- ‖ 'kɔːrs-
Corsica 'kɔːs ɪk ə ‖ 'kɔːrs-
Corsican 'kɔːs ɪk ən ‖ 'kɔːrs- ~s s
Corstorphine kə 'stɔːf ɪn §-ən ‖ kər 'stɔːrf-
cortegl|e, cortègl|e ₍ₒ₎kɔː 'teɪʒ -'teʒ, ' ‧ ‧ ‖ ₍ₒ₎kɔːr 'teʒ —Fr [kɔʁ tɛːʒ] ~es ɪz əz
Cortes 'parliament' 'kɔːt ez -ɪz, -es ‖ 'kɔːrt-
Cortes, Cortés 'kɔːt ez kɔː 'tez ‖ kɔːr 'tez —Sp Cortés [kor 'tes]
cortex 'kɔːt eks ‖ 'kɔːrt- ~es ɪz əz cortices 'kɔːt ɪ siːz -ə- ‖ 'kɔːrt̬-
Cortez 'kɔːt ez kɔː 'tez ‖ kɔːr 'tez —Sp Cortés [kor 'tes]
Corti 'kɔːt i ‖ 'kɔːrt̬ i —It ['kor ti]
cortical 'kɔːt ɪk əl ‖ 'kɔːrt̬-
cortices 'kɔːt ɪ siːz -ə- ‖ 'kɔːrt̬-
corticosteroid ˌkɔːt ɪk əʊ 'stɪər ɔɪd ‖ ˌkɔːrt̬ ɪ koʊ 'stɪr ɔɪd ~s z
corticosterone ˌkɔːt ɪk əʊ 'stɪər əʊn -ɪ 'kɒst ə rəʊn ‖ ˌkɔːrt̬ ɪ koʊ 'stɪr oʊn -'kɑːst ə roʊn
Cortina kɔː 'tiːn ə ‖ kɔːr- ~s z
cortisone, C~ 'kɔːt ɪ zəʊn -ə-, -səʊn ‖ 'kɔːrt̬ ə zoʊn -soʊn
Cortland 'kɔːt lənd ‖ 'kɔːrt-
Corton 'kɔːt ən ‖ 'kɔːrt ən
corundum kə 'rʌnd əm
Corunna kə 'rʌn ə kɒ- —Sp La Coruña [la ko 'ru ɲa], Galician A Corunha [a ko 'ru ɲa]
coru|scate 'kɒr ə |skeɪt ‖ 'kɔːr- 'kɑːr- ~scated skeɪt ɪd -əd ‖ skeɪt̬ əd ~scates skeɪts ~scating skeɪt ɪŋ ‖ skeɪt̬ ɪŋ
coruscation ˌkɒr ə 'skeɪʃ ən ‖ ˌkɔːr- ˌkɑːr- ~s z
corvee, corvée 'kɔːv eɪ ‖ ₍ₒ₎kɔːr 'veɪ ' ‧ ‧ —Fr [kɔʁ ve] ~s z
corvette ₍ₒ₎kɔː 'vet ‖ ₍ₒ₎kɔːr- ~s s
corvine 'kɔːv aɪn ‖ 'kɔːrv-
Corvo 'kɔːv əʊ ‖ 'kɔːrv oʊ
Corvus 'kɔːv əs ‖ 'kɔːrv-
Corwen 'kɔː wən ‖ 'kɔːr- —Welsh ['kor wen]
Cory 'kɔːr i
corybant, C~ 'kɒr ɪ bænt -ə- ‖ 'kɔːr- ~s s corybantes, C~ ˌkɒr ɪ 'bænt iːz -ə- ‖ ˌkɔːr-
Corydon 'kɒr ɪd ən -əd, -ɒn ‖ 'kɔːr-
corymb 'kɒr ɪmb -ɪm, §-əm ‖ 'kɔːr- 'kɑːr- ~s z
coryphae|us ˌkɒr ɪ 'fiː ̠ləs -ə- ‖ ˌkɔːr- ˌkɑːr- ~i aɪ iː
Coryton (i) 'kɒr ɪt ən -ət- ‖ 'kɔːr ət ən, (ii) 'kɔːr- —in Devon, (i); in Essex, (ii)
coryza kə 'raɪz ə
cos 'because' kəz kəs, occasional strong form kɒz kɒs ‖ kɑːz kɔːz
cos 'cosine' kɒz kɒs ‖ kɑːs
cos 'lettuce' kɒs kɒz ‖ koʊs
Cos island in Greece kɒs ‖ kɑːs koʊs
Cosa Nostra ˌkəʊz ə 'nɒs trə ‖ ˌkoʊs ə 'noʊs-
Cosby 'kɒz bi ‖ 'kɑːz bi
cosec 'kəʊ sek ‖ 'koʊ-

cosecant ˌkəʊ 'siːk ənt ‖ ˌkoʊ- -ænt ~s s
cosech 'kəʊ seʃ ‖ 'koʊ- —or as cosec h
coset 'kəʊ set ‖ 'koʊ- ~s s
Cosford 'kɒs fəd ‖ 'kɑːs fərd
Cosgrave 'kɒz greɪv ‖ 'kɑːz-
cosh 'bludgeon' kɒʃ ‖ kɑːʃ coshed kɒʃt ‖ kɑːʃt coshes 'kɒʃ ɪz -əz ‖ 'kɑːʃ əz coshing 'kɒʃ ɪŋ ‖ 'kɑːʃ ɪŋ
cosh 'hyperbolic cosine' kɒʃ ‖ kɑːʃ —or as cos h
Cosham 'kɒs əm ‖ 'kɑːs əm
Cosi Fan Tutte, Così Fan Tutte ˌkəʊs i ˌfæn 'tʊt i ˌkəʊz-, kəʊ ˌsiː- ‖ koʊ ˌsiː faːn 'tʊt eɪ -'tuːt- —It [ko ˌsif fan 'tut te]
cosignator|y ˌkəʊ 'sɪg nət ər i ‖ ˌkoʊ 'sɪg nə tɔːr i -toʊr i ~ies iz
cosine 'kəʊ saɪn ‖ 'koʊ- ~s z
CoSIRA kəʊ 'saɪər ə ‖ koʊ-
cosmetic kɒz 'met ɪk ‖ kaːz 'met̬ ɪk ~ally ̠l_i ~s s
cos,metic 'surgery
cosmetician ˌkɒz mə 'tɪʃ ən -mɪ- ‖ ˌkaːz- ~s z
cosmetologist ˌkɒz mə 'tɒl ədʒ ɪst -me-, §-əst ‖ ˌkaːz mə 'taːl- ~s s
cosmic 'kɒz mɪk ‖ 'kaːz- ~ally ̠l_i
ˌcosmic 'ray
Cosmo 'kɒz məʊ ‖ 'kaːz moʊ
cosmo- comb. form
with stress-neutral suffix ˌkɒz məʊ ‖ ˌkaːz mə -moʊ — cosmographic ˌkɒz məʊ 'græf ɪk ◄ ‖ ˌkaːz mə-
with stress-imposing suffix kɒz 'mɒ+ ‖ kaːz 'maː+ — cosmographer kɒz 'mɒg rəf ə ‖ kaːz 'maːg rəf ər
cosmogon|y kɒz 'mɒg ən li ‖ kaːz 'maːg- ~ies iz
cosmography kɒz 'mɒg rəf i ‖ kaːz 'maːg-
cosmological ˌkɒz məʊ 'lɒdʒ ɪk ̠l ‖ ˌkaːz mə 'laːdʒ- ~ly ̠i
cosmolog|y kɒz 'mɒl ədʒ li ‖ kaːz 'maːl- ~ies iz
cosmonaut 'kɒz mə nɔːt ‖ 'kaːz- -naːt ~s s
cosmopolitan ˌkɒz mə 'pɒl ɪt ən ◄ ‖ ˌkaːz mə 'paːl ət ən ◄ ~ism ˌɪz əm ~s z
cosmos 'kɒz mɒs ‖ 'kaːz məs -moʊs, -maːs
Cossack 'kɒs æk ‖ 'kaːs- -ək ~s s
coss|et 'kɒs ɪt §-ət ‖ 'kaːs lət ~eted ɪt ɪd §ət-, -əd ‖ ‖ət əd ~eting ɪt ɪŋ §ət- ‖ ‖ət ɪŋ ~ets ɪts §əts ‖ əts
cossie 'kɒz i ‖ 'kaːz i ~s z
cost kɒst kɔːst ‖ kɔːst kaːst costed 'kɒst ɪd 'kɔːst-, -əd ‖ 'kɔːst əd 'kaːst- costing/s 'kɒst ɪŋ/z 'kɔːst- ‖ 'kɔːst ɪŋ/z 'kaːst- costs kɒsts kɔːsts ‖ kɔːsts kaːsts
ˌcost of 'living, ˌcost of 'living ˌindex; ˌcost 'price
costa, Costa 'kɒst ə ‖ 'koʊst ə 'kaːst ə, 'kɔːst ə —See also phrases with this word —Sp ['kos ta] ~s z
ˌCosta 'Blanca 'blæŋk ə ‖ 'blaːŋk ə —Sp [-'βlaŋ ka];
ˌCosta 'Brava 'braːv ə —Sp [-'βra βa];

ˌCosta del ˈSol del ˈsɒl ‖ -ˈsoʊl —Sp
[-ðel ˈsol]
Costain (i) ˈkɒst eɪn ‖ ˈkɑːst-, (ii)
kɒ ˈsteɪn ‖ kɑː-
costal ˈkɒst ᵊl ‖ ˈkɑːst ᵊl
co-star ˈkəʊ stɑː ‖ ˈkoʊ stɑːr ~red d co-
starring ˈkəʊ stɑːr ɪŋ ‖ ˈkoʊ- ~s z
costard ˈkʌst əd ˈkɒst- ‖ ˈkɑːst ᵊrd ~s z
Costard ˈkɒst əd -ɑːd ‖ ˈkɑːst ᵊrd
Costa Ric|a ˌkɒst ə ˈriːk |ə ‖ ˌkoʊst-, ˌkɔːst-,
ˌkɑːst- —Sp [ˌkos ta ˈrri ka] ~an/s ən/z
cost-effective ˌkɒst ɪ ˈfekt ɪv ◂ ˌkɔːst-, -ə-,
ˈ• •, • • ‖ ˌkɔːst- ˌkɑːst- ~ly li ~ness nəs nɪs
Costello (i) kɒ ˈstel əʊ kə- ‖ kɑː ˈstel oʊ, (ii)
ˈkɒst əl əʊ -ɪl- ‖ ˈkɑːst ə loʊ —In Ireland
usually (ii), elsewhere (i)
costermonger
ˈkɒst ə ˌmʌŋ gə ‖ ˈkɑːst ᵊr ˌmʌŋ gᵊr -ˌmɑːŋ-
~s z
Costessey place in Norfolk ˈkɒs i ‖ ˈkɑːs i (!)
costive ˈkɒst ɪv ‖ ˈkɑːst- ˈkɔːst- ~ly li ~ness
nəs nɪs
cost|ly ˈkɒst |li ˈkɔːst- ‖ ˈkɔːst |li ˈkɑːst- ~lier
li‿ə ‖ li‿ᵊr ~liest li‿ɪst li‿əst ~liness li nəs
li nɪs
costmary ˈkɒst ˌmeər i ‖ ˈkɔːst ˌmer i ˈkɑːst-
Costner ˈkɒst nə ‖ ˈkɑːst nᵊr
cost-plus ˌkɒst ˈplʌs ◂ ˌkɔːst- ‖ ˌkɔːst- ˌkɑːst-
cost-push ˌkɒst ˈpʊʃ ˌkɔːst- ‖ ˌkɔːst- ˌkɑːst-

COSTUME

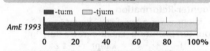

AmE 1993

■-tuːm   ▢-tjuːm

0   20   40   60   80   100%

costume n, adj ˈkɒs tjuːm →§ˈkɒs tʃuːm
‖ ˈkɑːs tuːm -tjuːm ~d d ~s z —AmE 1993
poll panel preference: -tuːm 75%, -tjuːm 25%.
ˈcostume ˌjewellery
costumier kɒ ˈstjuːm i‿ə →§-ˈstʃuːm-, -i eɪ
‖ kɑː ˈstuːm i eɪ -ˈstjuːm-, -ᵊr ~s z
cos|y ˈkəʊz |i ‖ ˈkoʊz |i ~ier i‿ə ‖ i‿ᵊr ~ies iz
~iest i‿ɪst i‿əst ~ily ɪ li əl i ~iness i nəs i nɪs
cot kɒt ‖ kɑːt cots kɒts ‖ kɑːts
ˈcot death
cotan ˈkəʊ tæn ‖ ˈkoʊ-
cotangent ˌkəʊ ˈtændʒ ənt ˈ•‿•, • • ‖ ˌkoʊ- ~s s
cotanh ˈkəʊ θæn -tænʃ ‖ ˈkoʊ- —or as cotan h
cote kəʊt ‖ koʊt (= coat) —formerly also
kɒt ‖ kɑːt cotes kəʊts ‖ koʊts
Cote d'Azur, Côte d'Azur ˌkəʊt də ˈzjʊə -dæ-
‖ ˌkoʊt də ˈzʊᵊr —Fr [kot da zyːʁ]
Cote d'Ivoire, Côte d'Ivoire
ˌkəʊt diː ˈvwɑː ‖ ˌkoʊt diː ˈvwɑːr —Fr
[kot di vwaːʁ]
coterie ˈkəʊt ᵊr i ˌkəʊt ə ˈriː ‖ ˈkoʊt ᵊr i
ˌkoʊt ə ˈriː ~s z
coterminous ₍ᵢ₎kəʊ ˈtɜːm ɪn əs -ən-
‖ ₍ᵢ₎koʊ ˈtɜːm- ~ly li
coth kɒθ ‖ kɑːθ —or as cot h
Cothi ˈkɒθ i ‖ ˈkɑːθ i ˈkɔːθ-
cothurn|us kəʊ ˈθɜːn |əs kɒ- ‖ koʊ ˈθɜːn |əs
~i aɪ
cotillion kə ˈtɪl i‿ən kəʊ-, kɒ- ‖ koʊ- ~s z

cotinga kəʊ ˈtɪŋ gə ‖ koʊ-
Coton ˈkəʊt ᵊn ‖ ˈkoʊt ᵊn
cotoneaster kə ˌtəʊn i ˈæst ə ‖ -ˈtoʊn i ˌæst ᵊr
—There is also a spelling pronunciation,
considered incorrect,
ˌkɒt ᵊn ˈiːst ə ‖ ˈkɑːt ᵊn ˌiːst ᵊr ~s z
Cotopaxi ˌkɒt ə ˈpæks i ˌkəʊt-, -əʊ- ‖ ˌkoʊt ə-
-ˈpɑːks i —Sp [ko to ˈpak si]
Cotswold ˈkɒts wəʊld →-wɒʊld, -wəld
‖ ˈkɑːts woʊld ~s z
cotta ˈkɒt ə ‖ ˈkɑːt̬ ə ~s z
cottag|e ˈkɒt ɪdʒ ‖ ˈkɑːt̬ ɪdʒ ~ed d ~es ɪz əz
~ing ɪŋ
ˌcottage ˈcheese ‖ ˈ•‿• •; ˌcottage
ˈhospital; ˌcottage ˈindustry; ˌcottage
ˈloaf; ˌcottage ˈpie
cottager ˈkɒt ɪdʒ ə ‖ ˈkɑːt̬ ɪdʒ ᵊr ~s z
cottar ˈkɒt ə ‖ ˈkɑːt̬ ᵊr ~s z
Cottenham ˈkɒt ᵊn_əm ‖ ˈkɑːt ᵊn_əm
cotter, C~ ˈkɒt ə ‖ kɑːt̬ ᵊr ~s z
Cotterell ˈkɒtr əl ‖ ˈkɑːtr-
Cottesloe ˈkɒts ləʊ ˈkɒt əz ləʊ ‖ ˈkɑːts loʊ
ˈkɑːt̬ əz loʊ
Cottesmore ˈkɒts mɔː ‖ ˈkɑːts mɔːr -moʊr
Cottle ˈkɒt ᵊl ‖ ˈkɑːt̬ ᵊl
cotton, C~ ˈkɒt ᵊn ‖ ˈkɑːt ᵊn ~s z
ˌcotton ˈcandy; ˈcotton gin; ˈcotton grass;
ˌcotton ˈwaste; ˌcotton ˈwool◂
cotton-picking ˈkɒt ᵊn ˌpɪk ɪŋ ‖ ˈkɑːt-
cottonseed ˈkɒt ᵊn siːd ‖ ˈkɑːt-
cottontail ˈkɒt ᵊn teɪᵊl ‖ ˈkɑːt- ~s z
cottonwood ˈkɒt ᵊn wʊd ‖ ˈkɑːt- ~s z
cottony ˈkɒt ᵊn i ‖ ˈkɑːt-
cotyledon ˌkɒt ɪ ˈliːd ᵊn -ə-; -ᵊl ˈiːd-
‖ ˌkɑːt ᵊl ˈiːd ᵊn ~ous əs ~s z
coucal ˈkuːk ᵊl ˈkʊk-, -æl, -ɑːl ~s z
couch kaʊtʃ —but ˈcouch grass is also kuːtʃ
couched kaʊtʃt couches ˈkaʊtʃ ɪz -əz
couching ˈkaʊtʃ ɪŋ
Couch kuːtʃ
couchant ˈkaʊtʃ ənt ˈkuːʃ ənt
couchette ₍ᵢ₎kuː ˈʃet ~s s
Coué ˈkuː eɪ ‖ kuː ˈeɪ —Fr [kwe, ku e]
cougar ˈkuːg ə -ɑː ‖ -ᵊr ~s z
cough kɒf ‖ kɔːf kɑːf coughed kɒft
kɔːft ‖ kɔːft kɑːft coughing ˈkɒf ɪŋ ˈkɔːf-
‖ ˈkɔːf ɪŋ ˈkɑːf- coughs kɒfs kɔːfs ‖ kɔːfs
kɑːfs
ˈcough drop; ˈcough ˌmixture
Coughlan (i) ˈkɒf lən ˈkɒx-, ˈkɒk- ‖ ˈkɔːf-
ˈkɑːf-, ˈkoʊk-, (ii) ˈkɒg lən ‖ ˈkɔːg- ˈkɑːg-,
(iii) ˈkəʊl ən ‖ ˈkoʊl ən
Coughton (i) ˈkəʊt ᵊn ‖ ˈkoʊt-, (ii) ˈkaʊt ᵊn
could strong form kʊd, occasional weak form kəd
couldn't ˈkʊd ᵊnt —There is also a form ˈkʊd ᵊn,
in standard speech used mainly before a
consonant. This word has no weak form.
couldst kʊdst
coulee ˈkuːl i -eɪ ~s z
coulis sing. ˈkuːl i ‖ ku ˈliː coulis pl ˈkuːl iz -i
‖ ku ˈliːz -ˈliː —Fr [ku li]
coulomb, C~ ˈkuːl ɒm ‖ -ɑːm -oʊm —Fr
[ku lɔ̃] ~s z

C

Coulsdon 'kuːlz dən 'kəʊlz-
Coulson (i) 'kəʊls ən →'kɒʊls- ‖ 'kəʊls ən, (ii) 'kuːls ən
Coulston 'kuːlst ən
coulter 'kəʊlt ə →'kɒʊlt-, 'kuːt- ‖ 'kəʊlt ər ~s z
Coulthard (i) 'kuːlt ɑːd ‖ -ɑːrd, (ii) 'kəʊlθ- →'kɒʊlθ- ‖ 'kəʊlθ-
Coulton 'kəʊlt ən →'kɒʊlt- ‖ 'kəʊlt ən
coumarin 'kuːm ər ɪn §-ən
council 'kaʊns əl -ɪl (usually = counsel) ~s z
,Council 'Bluffs; 'council house; 'council tax
council|man 'kaʊns əl |mən -ɪl-, -mæn ~men mən men
councillor 'kaʊns əl_ə -ɪl- ‖ _ər ~s z
counsel 'kaʊns əl ~ed, ~led d ~ing, ~ling _ɪŋ ~s z
counsellor, counselor 'kaʊns əl_ə ‖ _ər ~s z ~ship ʃɪp
count kaʊnt counted 'kaʊnt ɪd -əd ‖ 'kaʊnṭ əd counting 'kaʊnt ɪŋ ‖ 'kaʊnṭ ɪŋ counts kaʊnts
'count noun
countab|le 'kaʊnt əb |əl ‖ 'kaʊnṭ- ~ly li
countdown 'kaʊnt daʊn ~s z
countenanc|e 'kaʊnt ən ənts -ɪn- ‖ -ən_ənts ~ed t ~es ɪz əz ~ing ɪŋ
counter 'kaʊnt ə ‖ 'kaʊnṭ ər ~ed d countering 'kaʊnt_ər ɪŋ ‖ 'kaʊnṭ ər ɪŋ ~s z
counter- prefix ¦kaʊnt ə ‖ ¦kaʊnṭ ər —In context, this prefix often bears a contrastive nuclear accent (not shown in the entries below).
counteract ,kaʊnt ər 'ækt -ə 'rækt ‖ ,kaʊnṭ ər- ~ed ɪd əd ~ing ɪŋ ~s s
counteraction ,kaʊnt ər 'æk ʃən -ə 'ræk-, '•••,•• ‖ ,kaʊnṭ ər- ~s z
counterattack v, n 'kaʊnt ər ə ,tæk ,•••'• ‖ 'kaʊnṭ ər- ~ed t ~ing ɪŋ ~s s
counterattraction ,kaʊnt ər ə 'træk ʃən '•••,•• ‖ ,kaʊnṭ ər- ~s z
counterbalanc|e n 'kaʊnt ə ,bæl ənts ‖ 'kaʊnṭ ər- ~es ɪz əz
counterbalanc|e v ,kaʊnt ə 'bæl ənts ‖ ,kaʊnṭ ər- ~ed t ~es ɪz əz ~ing ɪŋ
counterblast 'kaʊnt ə blɑːst §-blæst ‖ 'kaʊnṭ ər blæst ~s s
countercharg|e v, n 'kaʊnt ə tʃɑːdʒ ‖ 'kaʊnṭ ər tʃɑːrdʒ ~ed d ~es ɪz əz ~ing ɪŋ
counterclaim v, n 'kaʊnt ə kleɪm ‖ 'kaʊnṭ ər- ~ed d ~ing ɪŋ ~s z
counterclockwise ,kaʊnt ə 'klɒk waɪz ‖ ,kaʊnṭ ər 'klɑːk-
counterespionage ,kaʊnt ər 'esp i_ə nɑːʒ -nɑːdʒ, -nɪdʒ ‖ ,kaʊnṭ ər-
counterfactual ,kaʊnt ə 'fæk tʃu_əl -'fæk tju_əl ‖ ,kaʊnṭ ər- -ʃu_əl, -'fæk tʃəl ~ly i
counter|feit 'kaʊnt ə |fɪt -fiːt ‖ 'kaʊnṭ ər- ~feited fɪt ɪd fiːt-, -əd ‖ fɪṭ əd ~feiting fɪt ɪŋ fiːt- ‖ fɪṭ ɪŋ ~feits fɪts fiːts
counterfoil 'kaʊnt ə fɔɪəl ‖ 'kaʊnṭ ər- ~s z

counterinsurgency ,kaʊnt ər ɪn 'sɜːdʒ ənts i ‖ ,kaʊnṭ ər ɪn 'sɝːdʒ-
counterintelligence ,kaʊnt ər ɪn 'tel ɪdʒ ənts -ədʒ ənts, '•••,••• ‖ ,kaʊnṭ ər-
counterintuitive ,kaʊnt ər ɪn 'tjuː_ət ɪv ◀ →§-'tʃuː_ ‖ ,kaʊnṭ ər ɪn 'tuː_əṭ ɪv -'tjuː_ ~ly li
counterirritant ,kaʊnt ər 'ɪr ɪt ənt §-ət ənt ‖ ,kaʊnṭ ər 'ɪr ət ənt ~s s
countermand ,kaʊnt ə 'mɑːnd §-'mænd, '••• ‖ 'kaʊnṭ ər mænd ,•••• ~ed ɪd əd ~ing ɪŋ ~s z
countermarch 'kaʊnt ə mɑːtʃ ‖ 'kaʊnṭ ər mɑːrtʃ ~ed t ~es ɪz əz ~ing ɪŋ
countermeasure 'kaʊnt ə ,meʒ ə ‖ 'kaʊnṭ ər ,meʒ ər -,meɪʒ- ~s z
counteroffensive ,kaʊnt ər ə 'fents ɪv '•••,•• ‖ 'kaʊnṭ ər ə ,fents ɪv ~s z
counterpane 'kaʊnt ə peɪn ‖ 'kaʊnṭ ər- ~s z
counterpart 'kaʊnt ə pɑːt ‖ 'kaʊnṭ ər pɑːrt ~s s
counter|point 'kaʊnt ə |pɔɪnt ‖ 'kaʊnṭ ər- ~pointed pɔɪnt ɪd -əd ‖ pɔɪnṭ əd ~pointing pɔɪnt ɪŋ ‖ pɔɪnṭ ɪŋ ~points pɔɪnts
counterpois|e 'kaʊnt ə pɔɪz ‖ 'kaʊnṭ ər- ~ed d ~es ɪz əz ~ing ɪŋ
counterproductive ,kaʊnt ə prə 'dʌkt ɪv ◀ ‖ ,kaʊnṭ ər- ~ly li ~ness nəs nɪs
counterproposal 'kaʊnt ə prə ,pəʊz əl ‖ 'kaʊnṭ ər prə ,poʊz əl ~s z
Counter-Reformation ,kaʊnt ə ,ref ə 'meɪʃ ən ‖ ,kaʊnṭ ər ,ref ər-
counterrevolution ,kaʊnt ə ,rev ə 'luːʃ ən -'ljuːʃ-, '••••,•• ‖ ,kaʊnṭ ər- ~s z
counterrevolutionar|y ,kaʊnt ə ,rev ə 'luːʃ ən_ər |i -'ljuːʃ-, -ən ər_|i, '••••,•- ‖ ,kaʊnṭ ər ,rev ə 'luːʃ ə ner |i ~ies iz
countersank 'kaʊnt ə sæŋk ,•••'• ‖ 'kaʊnṭ ər-
countershaft 'kaʊnt ə ʃɑːft §-ʃæft ‖ 'kaʊnṭ ər ʃæft ~s s
countersign v 'kaʊnt ə saɪn ,••'• ‖ 'kaʊnṭ ər- ~ed d ~ing ɪŋ ~s z
countersign n 'kaʊnt ə saɪn ‖ 'kaʊnṭ ər- ~s z
counter|sink 'kaʊnt ə sɪŋk ,••'• ‖ 'kaʊnṭ ər- ~sank sæŋk ~sinking sɪŋk ɪŋ ~sunk sʌŋk
countertenor ,kaʊnt ə 'ten ə '••,•• ‖ 'kaʊnṭ ər ,ten ər ~s z
countervail ,kaʊnt ə 'veɪəl '••• ‖ ,kaʊnṭ ər- ~ed d ~ing ɪŋ ~s z
counterweight 'kaʊnt ə weɪt ‖ 'kaʊnṭ ər- ~s s
countess 'kaʊnt ɪs -es, -əs, ,kaʊn 'tes ‖ 'kaʊnṭ əs ~es ɪz əz
counti... —see county
counting|house 'kaʊnt ɪŋ |haʊs ‖ 'kaʊnṭ ɪŋ- ~houses haʊz ɪz -əz
countless 'kaʊnt ləs -lɪs
countrified 'kʌntr i faɪd
countr|y 'kʌntr |i ~ies iz
,country and 'western; ,country 'bumpkin; 'country club; ,country 'cousin; ,country 'dance ‖ '•• •; ,country 'house; ,country 'seat

country|man 'kʌntr i |mən **~men** mən
countryside 'kʌntr i saɪd
countrywide ˌkʌntr i 'waɪd ◄ '•••
country|woman 'kʌntr i |ˌwʊm ən **~women**
　ˌwɪm ɪn §-ən
count|y 'kaʊnt i ‖ 'kaʊnt̬ i **~ies** iz
　ˌcounty 'council; ˌcounty 'court; ˌcounty
　'town
coup kuː (!) **coups** kuːz —See also phrases
　with this word
coup de grace, coup de grâce ˌkuː də 'grɑːs
　—Fr [kud gʁas]
coup d'état ˌkuː deɪ 'tɑː —Fr [ku de ta]
coup de théâtre ˌkuː də teɪ 'ɑːtr_ə —Fr
　[kud te aːtχ]
coupe 'dish' kuːp **~s** s
coupe, coupé 'vehicle' 'kuːp eɪ ‖ kuː 'peɪ kuːp
　coupes, coupés 'kuːp eɪz ‖ kuː 'peɪz kuːps
Couper 'kuːp ə ‖ -ᵊr
Couperin 'kuːp ə ræn -ræ —Fr [ku pʁæ]
Coupland (i) 'kuːp lənd, (ii) 'kəʊp- ‖ 'koʊp-
coupl|e 'kʌp ᵊl **~ed** d **~es** z **~ing** ◌ɪŋ
coupler 'kʌp lə ‖ -lᵊr **~s** z
couplet 'kʌp lət -lɪt **~s** s
coupling pres ptcp of **couple** 'kʌp ᵊl◌ɪŋ
coupling n 'kʌp lɪŋ **~s** z

COUPON

coupon 'kuːp ɒn ʌ△'kjuːp- ‖ -aːn 'kjuːp- **~s** z
　—Poll panel preferences: AmE 1993, 'kuːp-
　52%, 'kjuːp- 48%; BrE 1998, 'kuːp- 94%,
　'kjuːp- 6%
coups kuːz —In French phrases usually kuː:, as
　singular —Fr [ku]. See **coup**
courage, C~ 'kʌr ɪdʒ ‖ 'kɝː ɪdʒ
courageous kə 'reɪdʒ əs **~ly** li **~ness** nəs nɪs
courgette (ˌ)kɔː 'ʒet (ˌ)kʊə- ‖ kʊr- **~s** s
courier 'kʊr i_ə 'kʊər-, 'kʌr- ‖ 'kɝː i_ᵊr 'kʊr-
　~s z
Courland 'kʊə lənd -lænd ‖ 'kʊr-
Courrèges ku 'reʒ -'reɪʒ —Fr [ku ʁɛːʒ]
course kɔːs ‖ kɔːrs koʊrs (= coarse) **coursed**
　kɔːst ‖ kɔːrst koʊrst **courses** 'kɔːs ɪz -əz
　‖ 'kɔːrs əz 'koʊrs- **coursing**
　'kɔːs ɪŋ ‖ 'kɔːrs ɪŋ 'koʊrs-
courser 'kɔːs ə ‖ 'kɔːrs ᵊr 'koʊrs- **~s** z
coursework 'kɔːs wɜːk ‖ 'kɔːrs wɝːk 'koʊrs-
court, Court kɔːt ‖ kɔːrt koʊrt **courted**
　'kɔːt ɪd -əd ‖ 'kɔːrt̬ əd 'koʊrt̬- **courting**
　'kɔːt ɪŋ ‖ 'kɔːrt̬ ɪŋ 'koʊrt̬- **courts**
　kɔːts ‖ kɔːrts koʊrts
　'court card; ˌcourt 'circular; 'court shoe
Courtauld 'kɔːt əʊld →-ɒuld, -əʊ ‖ 'kɔːrt oʊld
　'koʊrt-
court-bouillon ˌkɔːt 'buː jɒn ˌkʊət-, ˌkʊə-
　‖ ˌkɔːr 'buːl jɑːn —Fr [kuʁ bu jɔ̃]
Courtelle tdmk (ˌ)kɔː 'tel ‖ (ˌ)kɔːr- (ˌ)koʊr-
Courtenay 'kɔːt ni ‖ 'kɔːrt- 'koʊrt-

courteous 'kɜːt i_əs 'kɔːt- ‖ 'kɝː t̬- **~ly** li
　~ness nəs nɪs
courtesan ˌkɔːt ɪ 'zæn -ə-, '••• ‖ 'kɔːrt̬ əz ən
　'koʊrt̬-, -ə zæn **~s** z
courtes|y 'kɜːt əs li 'kɔːt-, -ɪs- ‖ 'kɝː t̬- **~ies** iz
　'courtesy car; 'courtesy light; 'courtesy
　ˌtitle
court|house 'kɔːt |haʊs ‖ 'kɔːrt- 'koʊrt-
　~houses haʊz ɪz -əz
courtier 'kɔːt i_ə 'kɔːt jə ‖ 'kɔːrt̬ i_ᵊr 'koʊrt̬-;
　'kɔːrtʃ ᵊr, 'koʊrtʃ- **~s** z
court|ly 'kɔːt |li ‖ 'kɔːrt- 'koʊrt- **~liness** li nəs
　li nɪs
court-martial ˌkɔːt 'mɑːʃ ᵊl ◄ ‖ 'kɔːrt ˌmɑːrʃ ᵊl
　'koʊrt-, ˌ•'•• **courts-martial**
　ˌkɔːts 'mɑːʃ ᵊl ‖ 'kɔːrts ˌmɑːrʃ ᵊl 'koʊrts-,
　ˌ•'••
Courtneidge 'kɔːt nɪdʒ ‖ 'kɔːrt- 'koʊrt-
Courtney 'kɔːt ni ‖ 'kɔːrt- 'koʊrt-
courtroom 'kɔːt ruːm -rʊm ‖ 'kɔːrt- 'koʊrt-
　~s z
courtship 'kɔːt ʃɪp ‖ 'kɔːrt- 'koʊrt-
courts-martial —see **court-martial**
courtyard 'kɔːt jɑːd ‖ 'kɔːrt jɑːrd 'koʊrt- **~s** z
Courvoisier tdmk (ˌ)kʊə 'vwæz i eɪ -'vwɑːz-
　‖ ˌkɔːrv waːs i 'eɪ —Fr [kuʁ vwa zje] **~s** z
couscous 'kuːs kuːs
cousin 'kʌz ᵊn **~s** z
Cousins 'kʌz ᵊnz
Cousteau 'kuːst əʊ ‖ ku 'stoʊ —Fr [ku sto]
couth kuːθ
Coutts kuːts
couture ku 'tjʊə -'tʊə, →§-'tʃʊə ‖ -'tʊr -'tjʊr
　—Fr [ku tyːʁ]
couturier ku 'tjʊər i eɪ -'tʊər-, →§-'tʃʊər-, -i_ə
　‖ -'tʊr- -i_ᵊr **~s** z
couvade (ˌ)kuː 'vɑːd
covalenc|y ˌkəʊ 'veɪl ᵊn̩ts li '•,••• ‖ ˌkoʊ-
　~ies iz
covalent ˌkəʊ 'veɪl ᵊnt ◄ ‖ ˌkoʊ-
　ˌcoˌvalent 'bond
covariance ˌkəʊ 'veər i_ᵊn̩ts '•,•••
　‖ ˌkoʊ 'ver- -'vær-
cove, Cove kəʊv ‖ koʊv **coves** kəʊvz ‖ koʊvz
coven 'kʌv ᵊn **~s** z
covenant n 'kʌv ᵊn_ᵊnt **~s** s
coven|ant v 'kʌv ᵊn_|ᵊnt -ə n|ænt **~anted**
　ᵊnt ɪd -əd ‖ ᵊnt̬ əd ænt̬ əd **~anting**
　ᵊnt ɪŋ ‖ ᵊnt̬ ɪŋ ænt̬ ɪŋ **~ants** ᵊnts ‖ ænts
covenanter, covenantor, C~ 'kʌv ᵊn_ᵊnt ə
　ˌkʌv ə 'nænt ə, ˌkʌv ə næn 'tɔː ‖ 'kʌv ə nænt̬
　ᵊr, ˌ•'••, ˌkʌv ə næn 'tɔːr **~s** z
Covent 'kɒv ᵊnt 'kʌv- ‖ 'kʌv- 'kɑːv-
　ˌCovent 'Garden◄
Coventry 'kɒv ᵊntr i 'kʌv- ‖ 'kʌv- 'kɑːv-
cover 'kʌv ə ‖ -ᵊr **covered** 'kʌv əd ‖ -ᵊrd
　covering 'kʌv ᵊr_ɪŋ **covers** 'kʌv əz ‖ -ᵊrz
　'cover ˌcharge; ˌcovered 'wagon; 'cover
　girl; 'cover ˌletter; 'cover note; ˌcover
　'point
Coverack (i) 'kʌv ə ræk -ᵊr ək, (ii)
　'kɒv- ‖ 'kɑːv-
coverage 'kʌv ᵊr_ɪdʒ

C

coverall 'kʌv ər ɔːl ‖ -ər ɔːl -ɑːl ~s z
Coverdale 'kʌv ə deɪəl ‖ -ər-
covering 'kʌv ər_ɪŋ ~s z
  covering 'letter
cover|let 'kʌv ə |lət -lɪt ‖ -ər- -lɪd ~lets ləts
  lɪts ‖ lɪdz
Coverley 'kʌv ə li ‖ -ər-

COVERT

BrE ▬'kʌv- ▭'kəʊ- ▨,kəʊ 'vɜːt
AmE ▨'koʊ vɜːt ▬,koʊ 'vɜːt ▨'kʌv-

BrE 1988
AmE 1993

0   20   40   60   80   100%

covert n 'kʌv ət -ə ‖ -ərt 'koʊ vɜːt ~s s
covert adj 'kʌv ət ,kəʊ vɜːt ,kəʊ 'vɜːt ◄
  ‖ 'koʊ vɜːt ,•'•; 'kʌv ərt —Poll panel
  preferences: BrE 1988, 'kʌv- 54%, 'kəʊ- 37%,
  ,kəʊ 'vɜːt 9%; AmE 1993, 'koʊ vɜːt 53%,
  ,koʊ 'vɜːt 40%, 'kʌv- 7%. ~ly li ~ness nəs
  nɪs
cover-up 'kʌv ər ʌp ‖ -ər ʌp ~s s
cov|et 'kʌv |ɪt -ət ‖ -|ət ~eted ɪt ɪd §ət-, -əd
  ‖ ət əd ~eting ɪt ɪŋ §ət- ‖ ət ɪŋ ~ets ɪts
  §əts ‖ əts
covetable 'kʌv ɪt əb əl '•ət- ‖ '•ət̬-
covetous 'kʌv ɪt əs -ət- ‖ -ət̬ əs ~ly li ~ness
  nəs nɪs
covey 'kʌv i ~s z
coving 'kəʊv ɪŋ ‖ 'koʊv ɪŋ
cow, Cow kaʊ cows kaʊz
  ,cow 'parsley
cowabunga ,kaʊ ə 'bʌŋ gə
cowage 'kaʊ ɪdʒ
Cowan 'kaʊ ən
coward, C~ 'kaʊ əd ‖ 'kaʊ ərd ~s z
cowardice 'kaʊ əd ɪs §-əs ‖ 'kaʊ ərd-
coward|ly 'kaʊ əd |li ‖ 'kaʊ ərd- ~liness li nəs
  li nɪs
cowbell 'kaʊ bel ~s z
cowberr|y 'kaʊ bər_li -,ber |i ‖ -,ber li ~ies iz
cowbird 'kaʊ bɜːd ‖ -bɜ:d ~s z
cowboy 'kaʊ bɔɪ ~s z
Cowbridge 'kaʊ brɪdʒ
cowcatcher 'kaʊ ,kætʃ ə ‖ -ər §-,ketʃ- ~s z
Cowdenbeath ,kaʊd ən 'bi:θ
Cowdray, Cowdrey 'kaʊdr i -eɪ
Cowell (i) 'kaʊ əl kaʊl ‖ 'kaʊ əl, (ii)
  'kəʊ əl ‖ 'koʊ əl
Cowen (i) 'kaʊ ən -ɪn, (ii) 'kəʊ- ‖ 'koʊ-
cower 'kaʊ ə ‖ 'kaʊ ər cowered
  'kaʊ əd ‖ 'kaʊ ərd cowering
  'kaʊ ər ɪŋ ‖ 'kaʊ ər ɪŋ cowers
  'kaʊ əz ‖ 'kaʊ ərz
Cowes kaʊz
Cowgill 'kaʊ gɪl
cowgirl 'kaʊ gɜːl ‖ -gɜ:l ~s z
cowhand 'kaʊ hænd ~s z
cowheel 'kaʊ hi:əl
cowherd 'kaʊ hɜːd ‖ -hɜ:d ~s z
cowhide 'kaʊ haɪd ~s z
Cowie 'kaʊ i

cowl kaʊl cowled kaʊld cowling 'kaʊl ɪŋ
  cowls kaʊlz
Cowley 'kaʊl i
cowlick 'kaʊ lɪk ~s s
cowling, C~ 'kaʊl ɪŋ ~s z
cow|man 'kaʊ |mən -mæn ~men mən men
co-worker ,kəʊ 'wɜːk ə '•,•• ‖ 'koʊ ,wɜ:k ər
  ~s z
cowpat 'kaʊ pæt ~s s
Cowper (i) 'ku:p ə ‖ -ər, (ii) 'kaʊp-
cowpoke 'kaʊ pəʊk ‖ -poʊk ~s s
cowpox 'kaʊ pɒks ‖ -pɑ:ks
cowrie, cowry 'kaʊər i cowries 'kaʊər iz
cowshed 'kaʊ ʃed ~s z
cowslip 'kaʊ slɪp ~s s
cox, Cox kɒks ‖ kɑ:ks (= cocks) coxed
  kɒkst ‖ kɑ:kst coxes 'kɒks ɪz -əz
  ‖ 'kɑ:ks əz coxing 'kɒks ɪŋ ‖ 'kɑ:ks ɪŋ
  Cox's 'kɒks ɪz -əz ‖ 'kɑ:ks əz
coxalgia kɒk 'sældʒ ə -'sældʒ i_ə ‖ kɑ:k-
coxcomb 'kɒks kəʊm ‖ 'kɑ:ks koʊm ~s z
Coxe kɒks ‖ kɑ:ks
Coxsackie place in NY kɒk 'sæk i kʊk 'sɑ:k i
  ‖ kɑ:k-
  Cox'sackie ,virus
coxswain 'kɒks ən -weɪn ‖ 'kɑ:ks- ~s z
coy kɔɪ coyer 'kɔɪ ə ‖ -ər coyest 'kɔɪ ɪst -əst
  coyly 'kɔɪ li coyness 'kɔɪ nəs -nɪs
Coyle kɔɪəl
coyote kɔɪ 'əʊt i kaɪ-; 'kɔɪ əʊt, 'kaɪ-
  ‖ kaɪ 'oʊt̬ i 'kaɪ oʊt coyotes kɔɪ 'əʊt iz kaɪ-;
  'kɔɪ əʊts, 'kaɪ- ‖ kaɪ 'oʊt̬ iz 'kaɪ oʊts
coypu 'kɔɪp u: -ju:, kɔɪ 'pu:- ~s z
coz kʌz
cozen 'kʌz ən ~ed d ~ing ɪŋ ~s z
Cozens 'kʌz ənz
coz|ly 'kəʊz li ‖ 'koʊz li ~ier i_ə ‖ i_ər ~iest
  i_ɪst i_əst ~ily ɪ li əl i ~iness i nəs i nɪs
CPA ,si: pi: 'eɪ ~s z
CP'er ,si: 'pi: ə ‖ -ər ~s z
CP/M ,si: pi: 'em
CPU ,si: pi: 'ju: ~s z
crab, Crab kræb crabbing 'kræb ɪŋ crabs
  kræbz
  'crab ,apple; 'crab louse; ,Crab 'Nebula;
  ,crab 'paste
Crabb, Crabbe kræb
crabbed 'kræb ɪd -əd; kræbd ~ly li ~ness nəs
  nɪs
crabb|ly 'kræb li ~ier i_ə ‖ i_ər ~iest i_ɪst i_əst
crabgrass 'kræb grɑːs §-græs ‖ -græs
crabtree, C~ 'kræb tri: ~s z
crabways 'kræb weɪz
crabwise 'kræb waɪz
crack kræk cracked krækt cracking 'kræk ɪŋ
  cracks kræks
crackbrained 'kræk breɪnd
crackdown 'kræk daʊn ~s z
cracker 'kræk ə ‖ -ər ~s z
cracker-barrel 'kræk ə ,bær əl ‖ -ər- -,ber-
crackerjack 'kræk ə dʒæk ‖ -ər-
crackhead 'kræk hed ~s z
Crackington 'kræk ɪŋ tən

crackjaw 'kræk dʒɔː‖ -dʒɑː
crackl|e 'kræk ᵊl ~ed d ~es z ~ing ɪŋ
crackleware 'kræk ᵊl weə ‖ -wer -wær
crackling *ptcp, verbal n* 'kræk ᵊl ɪŋ
crackling *n 'crisp pork skin'* 'kræk lɪŋ -lən
crackly 'kræk ᵊl i
cracknel 'kræk nᵊl ~s z
Cracknell 'kræk nᵊl
crackpot 'kræk pɒt ‖ -pɑːt ~s s
cracks|man 'kræks |mən ~men mən men
crackup 'kræk ʌp ~s s
Cracow 'kræk aʊ -əʊ, -ɒf ‖ 'krɑːk aʊ —*Polish*
Kraków ['kra kuf]
-cracy *stress-imposing* krəs i — plutocracy
plu: 'tɒk rəs i ‖ -'tɑːk-
Craddock 'kræd ək
cradl|e 'kreɪd ᵊl ~ed d ~es z ~ing ɪŋ
cradle-snatch|er/s 'kreɪd ᵊl ˌsnætʃ |ə/z ‖ -ᵊr/z
~ing ɪŋ
Cradley *(i)* 'kreɪd li, *(ii)* 'kræd-
craft krɑːft §kræft ‖ kræft crafted 'krɑːft ɪd
§'kræft, -əd ‖ 'kræft əd crafting 'krɑːft ɪŋ
§'kræft- ‖ 'kræft ɪŋ crafts krɑːfts §kræfts
‖ kræfts
'craft ˌunion
-craft krɑːft §kræft ‖ kræft — woodcraft
'wʊd krɑːft §-kræft ‖ -kræft
crafts|man 'krɑːfs |mən §'kræfts- ‖ 'kræfs-
~men mən men
craftsmanship 'krɑːfs mən ʃɪp §'kræfts-
‖ 'kræfs-
craft|y 'krɑːft |i §'kræft- ‖ 'kræft li ~ier
i̯ə ‖ i̯ᵊr ~iest i̯ɪst i̯əst ~ily ɪ li əl i ~iness
i nəs i nɪs
crag kræg crags krægz
Cragg kræg
Craggs krægz
cragg|y 'kræg |i ~ier i̯ə ‖ i̯ᵊr ~iest i̯ɪst i̯əst
~ily ɪ li əl i ~iness i nəs i nɪs
Craig kreɪg
Craigavon ˌkreɪg 'æv ᵊn
Craigie 'kreɪg i
Craignure ₍ᵢ₎kreɪg 'njʊə ‖ -'nʊᵊr -'njʊᵊr
crake kreɪk crakes kreɪks
cram, Cram kræm crammed kræmd
cramming 'kræm ɪŋ crams kræmz
crambo 'kræm bəʊ ‖ -boʊ
cram-full ˌkræm 'fʊl ◄
crammer 'kræm ə ‖ -ᵊr ~s z
Cramond 'kræm ənd 'krɑːm-
cramp kræmp cramped kræmpt cramping
'kræmp ɪŋ cramps kræmps
crampon 'kræmp ɒn -ən ‖ -ɑːn ~s s
cran, Cran kræn crans krænz
cranage 'kreɪn ɪdʒ
cranberr|y 'kræn bər |i →'kræm- ‖ -ˌber i
~ies iz
Cranborne, Cranbourn, Cranbourne
'kræn bɔːn →'kræm- ‖ -bɔːrn -boʊrn
Cranbrook 'kræn brʊk →'kræm-
crane, Crane kreɪn craned kreɪnd craning
'kreɪn ɪŋ cranes kreɪnz
'crane fly

cranesbill 'kreɪnz bɪl ~s z
Cranfield 'kræn fiːᵊld
Cranford 'kræn fəd ‖ -fᵊrd
crania 'kreɪn i̯ə
cranial 'kreɪn i̯əl
cranio- *comb. form*
with stress-neutral suffix ¦kreɪn i̯əʊ ‖ oʊ —
craniometric ˌkreɪn i̯əʊ 'metr ɪk ◄ ‖ -oʊ' ◄ -
with stress-imposing suffix ˌkreɪn i 'ɒ+ ‖ -'ɑː+
— craniotomy ˌkreɪn i 'ɒt əm i ‖ -'ɑːt̬-
crani|um 'kreɪn i̯əm ~a ə
crank, Crank kræŋk cranked kræŋkt
cranking 'kræŋk ɪŋ cranks kræŋks
crankcas|e 'kræŋk keɪs ~es ɪz əz
cranki... —*see* cranky
Cranko 'kræŋk əʊ ‖ -oʊ
crankpin 'kræŋk pɪn ~s z
crankshaft 'kræŋk ʃɑːft §-ʃæft ‖ -ʃæft ~s s
Crankshaw 'kræŋk ʃɔː ‖ -ʃɑː
crank|y 'kræŋk |i ~ier i̯ə ‖ i̯ᵊr ~iest i̯ɪst
i̯əst ~ily ɪ li əl i ~iness i nəs i nɪs
Cranleigh, Cranley 'kræn li
Cranmer 'kræn mə →'kræm- ‖ -mᵊr
crannog 'kræn əg ~s z
crann|y 'kræn li ~ied id ~ies iz
Cranston 'kræntˢt ən
Cranwell 'kræn wəl -wel
crap kræp crapped kræpt crapping 'kræp ɪŋ
craps kræps
crape kreɪp
crapper 'kræp ə ‖ -ᵊr ~s z
crappie, crappy 'kræp i crappies 'kræp iz
crapp|y 'kræp| i ~ier i̯ə ‖ i̯ᵊr ~iest i̯ɪst
i̯əst ~ily ɪ li əl i ~iness i nəs i nɪs
craps kræps
crapshoot 'kræp ʃuːt ~s s
crapshooter 'kræp ˌʃuːt̬ ᵊr ~s z
crapulence 'kræp jʊl ənˢt -jəl- ‖ -jəl-
crapulent 'kræp jʊl ənt -jəl- ‖ -jəl- ~ly li
crapulous 'kræp jʊl əs -jəl- ‖ -jəl- ~ness nəs
nɪs
craquelure 'kræk ə lʊə -ljʊə ‖ -lʊr
crases 'kreɪs iːz
crash kræʃ crashed kræʃt crashes 'kræʃ ɪz
-əz crashing 'kræʃ ɪŋ
'crash ˌbarrier; 'crash ˌhelmet
Crashaw 'kræʃ ɔː ‖ -ɑː
crash-div|e 'kræʃ daɪv ˌ•'• ~ed d ~es z ~ing
ɪŋ crash-dove 'kræʃ dəʊv ‖ -doʊv
crash-land 'kræʃ lænd ˌ•'• ~ed ɪd əd ~s z
~ing/s ɪŋ/z
crasis 'kreɪs ɪs §-əs crases 'kreɪs iːz
crass kræs crasser 'kræs ə ‖ -ᵊr crassest
'kræs ɪst -əst
crass|ly 'kræs |li ~ness nəs nɪs
Crassus 'kræs əs
-crat kræt — plutocrat 'pluːt əʊ
kræt ‖ 'pluːt̬ ə-
Cratchit 'krætʃ ɪt §-ət
crate kreɪt crated 'kreɪt ɪd -əd ‖ 'kreɪt̬ əd
crates kreɪts crating 'kreɪt ɪŋ ‖ 'kreɪt̬ ɪŋ
crater 'kreɪt ə ‖ 'kreɪt̬ ᵊr ~ed d cratering
'kreɪt ər ɪŋ ‖ 'kreɪt̬ ər ɪŋ ~s z

Crathes 'kræθ ɪz -əz

Crathy 'kræθ i

Crathorn, Crathorne 'kreɪ θɔːn ‖ -θɔːrn

-cratic 'kræt ɪk ‖ 'kræt̬ ɪk — plutocratic
,pluːt əʊ 'kræt ɪk ◄ ‖ ,pluːt̬ ə 'kræt̬ ɪk ◄

cra|vat krə|'væt ~vats 'væts~vatted 'væt ɪd
-əd ‖ 'væt̬ əd

crave kreɪv craved kreɪvd craves kreɪvz
craving 'kreɪv ɪŋ

craven, Craven 'kreɪv ən ~ly li ~ness nəs nɪs

craving 'kreɪv ɪŋ ~s z

craw krɔː ‖ krɑː craws krɔːz ‖ krɑːz

crawfish 'krɔː fɪʃ ‖ 'krɑː-

Crawford 'krɔː fəd ‖ -fərd 'krɑː-

crawl krɔːl ‖ krɑːl crawled krɔːld ‖ krɑːld
crawling 'krɔːl ɪŋ ‖ 'krɑːl- crawls krɔːlz
‖ krɑːlz

crawler 'krɔːl ə ‖ -ər 'krɑːl- ~s z

Crawley 'krɔːl i i ‖ 'krɑːl-

crawl|y 'krɔːl li ‖ 'krɑːl- ~ier i‿ə ‖ i‿ər ~iest
i‿ɪst i‿əst

Crawshaw 'krɔː ʃɔː ‖ 'krɑː ʃɑː

Crawshay 'krɔː ʃeɪ ‖ 'krɑː-

Cray kreɪ

crayfish 'kreɪ fɪʃ

Crayford 'kreɪ fəd ‖ -fərd

Crayola tdmk kreɪ 'əʊl ə ‖ -'oʊl-

crayon 'kreɪ ɒn -ən ‖ -ɑːn -ən; kræn ~ed d
~ing ɪŋ ~s z

craze kreɪz crazed kreɪzd crazes 'kreɪz ɪz
-əz crazing 'kreɪz ɪŋ

craz|y 'kreɪz li ~ier i‿ə ‖ i‿ər ~iest i‿ɪst i‿əst
~ily ɪ li əl i ~iness i nəs i nɪs
,Crazy 'Horse, ,crazy 'paving

CRE ,si: aɪr 'iː ‖ -aːr-

Creagh kreɪ

creak kriːk creaked kriːkt creaking 'kriːk ɪŋ
creaks kriːks

creak|y 'kriːk li ~ier i‿ə ‖ i‿ər ~iest i‿ɪst i‿əst
~ily ɪ li əl i ~iness i nəs i nɪs

cream kriːm creamed kriːmd creaming
'kriːm ɪŋ creams kriːmz
,cream 'cheese; ,cream 'cracker; ,cream
'puff; ,cream 'sauce; ,cream 'soda; ,cream
'tea

creamer 'kriːm ə ‖ -ər ~s z

creamer|y 'kriːm ər i ~ies iz

cream|y 'kriːm li ~ier i‿ə ‖ i‿ər ~iest i‿ɪst
i‿əst ~ily ɪ li əl i ~iness i nəs i nɪs

crease kriːs creased kriːst creases 'kriːs ɪz
-əz creasing 'kriːs ɪŋ

crease-resistant 'kriːs rɪ ,zɪst ənt -rə-, §-riː-,
ˌ • • ' • • ◄

Creasey, Creasy 'kriːs i

CREATE

AmE 1993

0   20   40   60   80   100%

cre|ate kri |'eɪt ,kriː-, ' • • —AmE 1993 poll
panel preference: • ' • 87%, ' • • 13%. ~ated
'eɪt ɪd -əd ‖ 'eɪt̬ əd ~ates 'eɪts ~ating
'eɪt ɪŋ ‖ 'eɪt̬ ɪŋ

creatine 'kriː‿ə tiːn -tɪn, §-ət ən

creatinine kri 'æt ə niːn -ɪ-; ən iːn; ən ɪn, -ɪn ɪn,
§-ən ən ‖ -ən iːn -ən

creation kri 'eɪʃ ən ,kriː- ~s z

creationism kri 'eɪʃ ən ,ɪz əm ,kriː-

creationist kri 'eɪʃ ən‿ɪst ,kriː-, §_əst ~s s

creative kri 'eɪt ɪv ,kriː- ‖ -'eɪt̬ ɪv ~ly li ~ness
nəs nɪs

creativity ,kriː eɪ 'tɪv ət i ,kriː‿ə-, -ɪt i ‖ -ət̬ i

creator kri 'eɪt ə ,kriː-; 'kriː eɪt ə ‖ -'eɪt̬ ər ~s z

creature 'kriːtʃ ə ‖ -ər ~s z
,creature 'comforts ‖ • • • , • •

creche, crèche kreʃ kreɪʃ —Fr [kʁɛʃ]
creches, crèches 'kreʃ ɪz 'kreɪʃ-, -əz

Crecy, Crécy 'kres i i ‖ kreɪ 'siː —Fr [kʁe si]

cred kred

Creda tdmk 'kriːd ə

credal 'kriːd əl

credenc|e 'kriːd ənts ~es ɪz əz

credential krə 'dentʃ əl krɪ- ~s z

credenza krə 'denz ə krɪ- ~s z

credibility ,kred ə 'bɪl ət i , • ɪ-, -ɪt i ‖ -ət̬ i
,credi'bility gap

credib|le 'kred əb |əl -ɪb- ~ly li

cred|it 'kred |ɪt §-ət ‖ -|ət ~ited ɪt ɪd §ət-, -əd
‖ ət̬ əd ~iting ɪt ɪŋ §ət- ‖ ət̬ ɪŋ ~its ɪts §əts
‖ ət̬s
'credit ac,count; 'credit card; 'credit ,limit;
'credit note; 'credit squeeze

creditab|le 'kred ɪt əb |əl §' • ət- ‖ 'kred ət̬- ~ly
li

Crediton 'kred ɪt ən §-ət- ‖ -ət ən

creditor 'kred ɪt ə §-ət- ‖ -ət̬ ər ~s z

creditworth|y 'kred ɪt ,wɜːð i §-ət-
‖ -,wɜːð i ~iness i nəs i nɪs

credo, Credo 'kreɪd əʊ 'kriːd- ‖ -oʊ ~s z

credulity krə 'djuːl ət i krɪ-, kre-, →§-'dʒuːl-,
-ɪt- ‖ -'duːl ət̬ i -'djuːl-

credulous 'kred jʊl əs -jəl- ‖ 'kredʒ əl əs ~ly
li ~ness nəs nɪs

Cree kriː Crees kriːz

creed, Creed kriːd creeds kriːdz

CREEK

        ■ kriːk   ☐ krɪk

AmE 1993

0   20   40   60   80   100%

creek kriːk ‖ krɪk —AmE 1993 poll panel
preference: kriːk 98%, krɪk 2%. creeks kriːks
‖ krɪks

Creek kriːk (= creak) Creeks kriːks

creel kriːəl creels kriːəlz

Creeley 'kriːl i

creep kriːp creeping 'kriːp ɪŋ creeps kriːps
crept krept

creeper 'kriːp ə ‖ -ər ~s z

creep|y 'kriːp li ~ier i‿ə ‖ i‿ər ~iest i‿ɪst i‿əst
~ily ɪ li əl i ~iness i nəs i nɪs

creepy-crawl|y ,kriːp i 'krɔːl li ' • • , • • ‖ -'krɑːl-
~ies iz

Creevey 'kriːv i

Creighton (i) 'kraɪt ən, (ii) 'kreɪt-

Creigiau 'kraɪg ə —Welsh ['krəɪg jai, -je]

cremate krə 'meɪt krɪ- ‖ 'kriːm eɪt **cremated**
  krə 'meɪt ɪd krɪ-, -əd ‖ 'kriːm eɪt̬ əd
  cremates krə 'meɪts krɪ- ‖ 'kriːm eɪts
  cremating krə 'meɪt ɪŋ krɪ- ‖ 'kriːm eɪt̬ ɪŋ
cremation krə 'meɪʃ ən krɪ- ‖ krɪ- ~**s** z
crematori|um ˌkrem ə 'tɔːr i̯_ləm ‖ ˌkriːm-
  ˌkrem-, -'toʊr- ~**a** ə
cremator|y 'krem ət̬_ər li ‖ 'kriːm ə tɔːr li
  'krem-, -toʊr- ~**ies** iz
creme, crème krem kreɪm, kriːm —*Fr* [kʁɛm]
  cremes, crèmes kremz kreɪmz, kriːmz —*Fr*
  [kʁɛm] —*See also phrases with this word*
Creme kriːm
creme brulee, crème brûlée ˌkrem bruː 'leɪ
  ˌkreɪm-, ˌ • ' • • —*Fr* [kʁɛm bʁy le]
creme caramel, crème caramel
  ˌkrem ˌkær ə 'mel ˌkreɪm- ‖ -ˌker-; ˌ•'•••
creme de la creme, crème de la crème
  ˌkrem də lɑː 'krem ˌkreɪm-, -'kreɪm —*Fr*
  [kʁɛm də la kʁɛm]
creme de menthe, crème de menthe
  ˌkrem də 'mɒntθ ˌkreɪm-, -'mɑːnt ‖ -'mɑːnt
  —*Fr* [kʁɛm də mɑ̃ːt]
creme fraiche, crème fraîche ˌkrem 'freʃ
  ˌkreɪm-, -'freɪʃ —*Fr* [kʁɛm fʁɛʃ]
Cremona krɪ 'məʊn ə krə- ‖ -'moʊn ə —*It*
  [kre 'mo: na]
Cremora *tdmk* krɪ 'mɔːr ə krə-
crenate 'kriːn eɪt
crenel|late, crenell|ate 'kren ə l|eɪt -əl |eɪt
  ‖ -əl |eɪt ~**ated** eɪt ɪd -əd ‖ eɪt̬ əd ~**ates**
  eɪts ‖ eɪts ~**ating** eɪt ɪŋ ‖ eɪt̬ ɪŋ
crenelation, crenellation ˌkren ə 'leɪʃ ən
  -əl 'eɪʃ- ‖ ˌkren əl 'eɪʃ ən ~**s** z
creole, Creole 'kriː əʊl 'kreɪ-, →-ʊol ‖ -oʊl ~**s**
  z
creolis... —*see* **creoliz...**
creolization ˌkriː əl aɪ 'zeɪʃ ən ˌkreɪ-, ˌ•əʊl-,
  -ɪ'•- ‖ -əl ə-
creoliz|e 'kriː ə laɪz 'kreɪ-, -əʊ- ~**ed** d ~**es** ɪz
  əz ~**ing** ɪŋ
Creon 'kriː ən -ɒn ‖ -ɑːn
creosol 'kriː ə sɒl ‖ -soʊl -sɑːl, -sɔːl
creo|sote 'kriː ə |səʊt ‖ -|soʊt ~**soted** səʊt ɪd
  -əd ‖ soʊt̬ əd ~**sotes** səʊts ‖ soʊts ~**soting**
  səʊt ɪŋ ‖ soʊt̬ ɪŋ
  '**creosote bush**
crepe, crêpe kreɪp krep —*Fr* [kʁɛp] **crepes,**
  crêpes kreɪps kreps
  ˌcrepe de 'Chine ʃiːn —*Fr* [də ʃin]; ˌcrepe
  '**paper** ‖ '• ˌ•••; ˌcrepe su'zette, ˌcrepes
  su'zettes su 'zet —*Fr* [sy zɛt]
crepi|tate 'krep ɪ |teɪt §-ə- ~**tated** teɪt ɪd -əd
  ‖ teɪt̬ əd ~**tates** teɪts ~**tating**
  teɪt ɪŋ ‖ teɪt̬ ɪŋ
crepitation ˌkrep ɪ 'teɪʃ ən §-ə- ~**s** z
crept krept
crepuscular krɪ 'pʌsk jʊl ə krə-, kre-, -jəl-
  ‖ -jəl ər
crescend|o krə 'ʃend |əʊ krɪ- ‖ -|oʊ ~**i** iː ~**os**
  əʊz ‖ oʊz
crescent 'krez ənt 'kres- ‖ 'kres- —*BrE 1988*

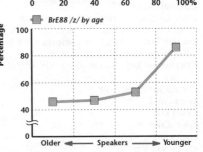

CRESCENT

■ 'krez-   ▨ 'kres-

BrE 1988

0   20   40   60   80   100%

▨ BrE88 /z/ by age

Percentage (y-axis): 0, 40, 60, 80, 100

Older ◄— Speakers —► Younger

poll panel preference: 'krez- 55%, 'kres- 45%.
  ~**s** s
cresol 'kriːs ɒl ‖ -ɑːl -ɔːl, -oʊl
cress kres
cresset 'kres ɪt §-ət ~**s** s
Cressida 'kres ɪd ə -əd-
Cresswell 'kres wel 'krez-, -wəl
crest krest **crested** 'krest ɪd -əd **cresting**
  'krest ɪŋ **crests** krests
Cresta 'krest ə
crestfallen 'krest ˌfɔːl ən ‖ -ˌfɑːl-
Creswell 'kres wel 'krez-, -wəl
cretaceous, C~ krɪ 'teɪʃ əs krə-, kre-,
  -'teɪʃ i̯_əs
Cretan 'kriːt ən ~**s** z
Crete kriːt
cretic 'kriːt ɪk ‖ 'kriːt̬ ɪk ~**s** s
cretin 'kret ɪn -ən ‖ 'kriːt ən (*) ~**ism** ˌɪz əm
  ~**s** z
cretinous 'kret ɪn əs -ən- ‖ 'kriːt ən əs (*)
cretonne kre 'tɒn krə-, krɪ-; 'kret ɒn
  ‖ 'kriːt ɑːn krɪ 'tɑːn
Creutzfeldt-Jakob
  ˌkrɔɪts felt 'jæk ɒb ‖ -'jɑːk oʊb
  ˌCreutzfeldt-'Jakob diˌsease
crevass|e krə 'væs krɪ- ~**es** ɪz əz
crevic|e 'krev ɪs §-əs ~**ed** t ~**es** ɪz əz
crew kruː **crewed** kruːd (= *crude*) **crewing**
  'kruː ɪŋ **crews** kruːz
  '**crew cut**; ˌcrew 'neck, '• •
Crewe kruː
crewel 'kruː əl ɪl
Crewkerne 'kruː kɜːn ‖ -kɝːn
crew|man 'kruː |mən -mæn ~**men** mən men
crewmember 'kruː ˌmem bə ‖ -bᵊr ~**s** z
cri kriː **cris** kriː kriːz
  ˌcri de 'coeur də 'kɜː ‖ də 'kɝː —*Fr*
  [kʁid kœːʁ]
Crianlarich ˌkriː ən 'lær ɪx -ɪk ‖ -'ler-
crib krɪb **cribbed** krɪbd **cribbing** 'krɪb ɪŋ
  cribs krɪbz
  '**crib death**
Cribb krɪb
cribbage 'krɪb ɪdʒ
cribb... —*see* **crib**
cribber 'krɪb ə ‖ -ᵊr ~**s** z

C

Cribbins 'krɪb ɪnz §-ənz
Criccieth 'krɪk i‿əθ -eθ —Welsh ['krik jeθ]
Crich kraɪtʃ
Crichel 'krɪtʃ əl
Crichton 'kraɪt ən
crick, Crick krɪk cricked krɪkt cricking
'krɪk ɪŋ cricks, Crick's krɪks
crick|et 'krɪk ɪt §-ət ‖ -lət ~eter/s ɪt ə/z §ət-
‖ əṭ ər/z ~eting ɪt ɪŋ ət- ‖ əṭ ɪŋ
Crickhowell krɪk 'haʊ‿əl -'haʊl; krɪ 'kaʊ‿əl,
-'kaʊl
cricoid 'kraɪk ɔɪd ~s z
cried kraɪd
Crieff kri:f
crier, Crier 'kraɪ‿ə ‖ 'kraɪ‿ər ~s z
cries kraɪz
crikey 'kraɪk i
crime kraɪm —but in French expressions kri:m
    crimes kraɪmz —See also phrases with this
    word
Crimea kraɪ 'mɪə -'mi: ə ‖ -'mi: ə
Crimean kraɪ 'mɪən -'mi: ən ‖ -'mi: ən ~s z
crime passionnel ,kri:m ,pæs i‿ə 'nel
    -,pæʃ ə 'nel —Fr [kʁim pa sjɔ nɛl]
criminal 'krɪm ɪn əl -ən- ~ly i ~s z
criminalis... —see criminaliz...
criminalit|y ,krɪm ɪ 'næl ət i ,•ə-, -ɪt i ‖ -əṭ li
    ~ies iz
criminaliz|e 'krɪm ɪn əl aɪz -ən‿əl- ~ed d ~es
    ɪz əz ~ing ɪŋ
criminalization ,krɪm ɪn əl aɪ 'zeɪʃ ən -ən‿əl-,
    -ɪ'•- ‖ -ə 'zeɪʃ-
crimini 'kri:m ɪ ni: 'krɪm-, -ə-
criminological ,krɪm ɪn ə 'lɒdʒ ɪk əl ◂ ,•ən-
    ‖ -'la:dʒ- ~ly i
criminologist ,krɪm ɪ 'nɒl ədʒ ɪst ,•ə-, §-əst
    ‖ -'na:l- ~s s
criminology ,krɪm ɪ 'nɒl ədʒ i ,•ə- ‖ -'na:l-
Crimond 'krɪm ənd
crimp krɪmp crimped krɪmpt crimping
    'krɪmp ɪŋ crimps krɪmps
crimplene, C~ tdmk 'krɪmp li:n
crimson 'krɪmz ən ~ed d ~ing ɪŋ ~s z
cringe krɪndʒ cringed krɪndʒd cringes
    'krɪndʒ ɪz -əz cringing 'krɪndʒ ɪŋ
cringer 'krɪndʒ ə ‖ -ər ~s z
cringle 'krɪŋ ɡəl ~s z
crinkl|e 'krɪŋk əl ~ed d ~es z ~ing ‿ɪŋ
crinkly 'krɪŋk li
crinoid 'kraɪn ɔɪd 'krɪn- ~s z
crinoline 'krɪn əl ɪn -ən ~s z
cripes kraɪps
Crippen 'krɪp ɪn -ən
cripp|le 'krɪp əl ~ed d ~es z ~ing ‿ɪŋ
Cripplegate 'krɪp əl ɡeɪt
Cripps krɪps
Crisco tdmk 'krɪsk əʊ ‖ -oʊ
crisis 'kraɪs ɪs §-əs crises 'kraɪs i:z
crisp, Crisp krɪsp crisped krɪspt crisping
    'krɪsp ɪŋ crisps krɪsps
crispbread 'krɪsp bred ~s z
Crispian 'krɪsp i‿ən
Crispin 'krɪsp ɪn §-ən

crisply 'krɪsp li
crispness 'krɪsp nəs -nɪs
crisp|y 'krɪsp li ~ier i‿ə ‖ i‿ər ~iest i‿ɪst i‿əst
    ~ily ɪ li əl i ~iness i nəs i nɪs
crisscross 'krɪs krɒs -krɔ:s ‖ -krɔ:s -kra:s ~ed
    t ~es ɪz əz ~ing ɪŋ
Cristobal, Cristóbal krɪ 'stəʊb əl ‖ -'stoʊb-
    —Sp [kris 'to βal]
Critchley 'krɪtʃ li
criteri|on kraɪ 'tɪər i‿ən ‖ -'tɪr- ~a ə ~al əl
critic 'krɪt ɪk ‖ 'krɪṭ ɪk ~s s
critical 'krɪt ɪk əl ‖ 'krɪṭ- ~ly ‿i
    ,critical 'mass
criticality ,krɪt ɪ 'kæl ət i ,•ə-, -ɪt i
    ‖ ,krɪṭ ə 'kæl əṭ i
criticism 'krɪt ɪ ,sɪz əm -ə- ‖ 'krɪṭ ə- ~s z
criticis|e, criticiz|e 'krɪt ɪ saɪz -ə- ‖ 'krɪṭ ə-
    ~ed d ~es ɪz əz ~ing ɪŋ
critique krɪ 'ti:k krə- ~s s
Crittall 'krɪt ɔ:l ‖ -a:l
critter 'krɪt ə ‖ 'krɪṭ ər ~s z
CRO ,si: a:r 'əʊ ‖ -'oʊ
croak krəʊk ‖ kroʊk croaked krəʊkt ‖ kroʊkt
    croaking/s 'krəʊk ɪŋ/z ‖ 'kroʊk ɪŋ/z croaks
    krəʊks ‖ kroʊks
croak|y 'krəʊk li ‖ 'kroʊk li ~ily ɪ li əl i ~iness
    i nəs i nɪs
Croat 'krəʊ æt -ət ‖ 'kroʊ- ~s s
Croatia krəʊ 'eɪʃ ə ‖ kroʊ-
Croatian krəʊ 'eɪʃ ən ‖ kroʊ- ~s z
crochet 'krəʊʃ eɪ -i, §-ə ‖ kroʊ 'ʃeɪ ~ed d
    ~ing ɪŋ ~s z
crocidolite krəʊ 'sɪd ə laɪt ‖ kroʊ-
crock krɒk ‖ kra:k crocked krɒkt ‖ kra:kt
    crocks krɒks ‖ kra:ks
Crocker 'krɒk ə ‖ 'kra:k ər
crockery 'krɒk ər i ‖ 'kra:k-
crocket 'krɒk ɪt §-ət ‖ 'kra:k- ~s s
Crockett 'krɒk ɪt §-ət ‖ 'kra:k-
Crockford 'krɒk fəd ‖ 'kra:k fərd
crocodile 'krɒk ə daɪəl ‖ 'kra:k- ~s z
    'crocodile clip; 'crocodile tears, ,•••'•
crocodilian ,krɒk ə 'dɪl i‿ən ‖ ,kra:k- ~s z
crocus 'krəʊk əs ‖ 'kroʊk əs ~es ɪz əz
Croes- in Welsh place names krɔɪs — Croeserw
    krɔɪs 'er u:
Croesus 'kri:s əs
croft, Croft krɒft krɔ:ft ‖ krɔ:ft kra:ft
    crofting 'krɒft ɪŋ 'krɔ:ft- ‖ 'krɔ:ft ɪŋ
    'kra:ft- crofts krɒfts krɔ:fts ‖ krɔ:fts
    kra:fts
crofter 'krɒft ə 'krɔ:ft- ‖ 'krɔ:ft ər 'kra:ft- ~s
    z
Crofton 'krɒft ən 'krɔ:ft- ‖ 'krɔ:ft- 'kra:ft-
Crohn krəʊn ‖ kroʊn
    'Crohn's di,sease
croiss|ant 'kwæs lõ 'krwæs-, 'krwʌs-, 'kwa:s-
    ‖ kwa: 'slɑ̃ krə-, krwa:-, -'sla:nt —Fr
    [kʁwa sɑ̃] ~ants õz|l ɑ̃: ɑ:nts
Croix krwa: kwa: —but in the name of the island
    St Croix, krɔɪ —Fr [kʁwa]
    ,Croix de 'Guerre də 'ɡeə ‖ -'geər —Fr
    [kʁwad ɡɛːʁ]

Croker 'krəʊk ə ‖ 'kroʊk ᵊr
Cro-Magnon ₍ᵢ₎krəʊ 'mæn jɒn -jən; -'mæg nən, -nɒn ‖ ₍ᵢ₎kroʊ 'mæg nən -nɑːn —*Fr* [kʁɔ ma njɔ̃]
Cromartie, Cromarty 'krɒm ət i ‖ 'krɑːm ᵊrt̬ i
Crombie *(i)* 'krɒm bi ‖ 'krɑːm-, *(ii)* 'krʌm-
Crome krəʊm ‖ kroʊm
Cromer 'krəʊm ə ‖ 'kroʊm ᵊr
Cromford 'krɒm fəd ‖ 'krɑːm fᵊrd
cromlech 'krɒm lek ‖ 'krɑːm- **~s** s
Crompton *(i)* 'krɒm*p*t ən ‖ 'krɑːm*p*t-, *(ii)* 'krʌm*p*t-
Cromwell 'krɒm wəl -wel ‖ 'krɑːm- *—formerly* 'krʌm-, -ᵊl
Cromwellian ₍ᵢ₎krɒm 'wel i‿ən ‖ ₍ᵢ₎krɑːm-
crone krəʊn ‖ kroʊn **crones** krəʊnz ‖ kroʊnz
Cronin 'krəʊn ɪn §-ən ‖ 'kroʊn-
cronk krɒŋk ‖ krɑːŋk
Cronkite 'krɒŋk aɪt ‖ 'krɑːn kaɪt 'krɑːŋk aɪt
cron|y 'krəʊn |i ‖ 'kroʊn |i **~ies** iz **~ism** ˌɪz əm
crook, Crook krʊk §kruːk **crooks** krʊks §kruːks
crookback, C~ 'krʊk bæk §'kruːk- **~ed** t **~s** s
Crooke krʊk §kruːk
crooked 'krʊk ɪd §'kruːk-, -əd **~er** ə ‖ ᵊr **~est** ɪst əst **~ly** li **~ness** nəs nɪs
Crookes krʊks §kruːks
Croom, Croome kruːm
croon kruːn **crooned** kruːnd **crooning** 'kruːn ɪŋ **croons** kruːnz
crooner 'kruːn ə ‖ -ᵊr **~s** z
crop krɒp ‖ krɑːp **cropped** krɒpt ‖ krɑːpt **cropping** 'krɒp ɪŋ ‖ 'krɑːp ɪŋ **crops** krɒps ‖ krɑːps
'crop ˌspraying
cropper 'krɒp ə ‖ 'krɑːp ᵊr **~s** z
croquet 'krəʊk i -eɪ ‖ kroʊ 'keɪ
croquette krɒ 'ket krəʊ- ‖ kroʊ 'ket **~s** s
crore krɔː ‖ krɔːr kroʊr **crores** krɔːz ‖ krɔːrz kroʊrz
Crosbie, Crosby 'krɒz bi 'krɒs- ‖ 'krɔːz bi 'krɑːz-
crosier, C~ 'krəʊz i‿ə 'krəʊʒ ə ‖ 'kroʊʒ ᵊr **~s** z
Crosland 'krɒs lənd ‖ 'krɔːs- 'krɑːs-
cross, Cross krɒs krɔːs ‖ krɔːs krɑːs **crossed** krɒst krɔːst ‖ krɔːst krɑːst **crosses** 'krɒs ɪz 'krɔːs-, -əz ‖ 'krɔːs əz 'krɑːs- **crossing** 'krɒs ɪŋ 'krɔːs- ‖ 'krɔːs ɪŋ 'krɑːs-
ˌcrossed 'line
cross- ¦krɒs ¦krɔːs ‖ ¦krɔːs ¦krɑːs — **cross-cultural** ˌkrɒs 'kʌltʃ ᵊr‿əl ◂ ˌkrɔːs- ‖ ˌkrɔːs- ˌkrɑːs-
crossbar 'krɒs bɑː 'krɔːs- ‖ 'krɔːs bɑːr 'krɑːs- **~s** z
crossbeam 'krɒs biːm 'krɔːs- ‖ 'krɔːs- 'krɑːs- **~s** z
crossbench 'krɒs ben*t*ʃ 'krɔːs-, ˌ•'• ‖ 'krɔːs- 'krɑːs- **~er/s** ə/z ‖ ᵊr/z **~es** ɪz əz
crossbill 'krɒs bɪl 'krɔːs- ‖ 'krɔːs- 'krɑːs- **~s** z
crossbones 'krɒs bəʊnz 'krɔːs- ‖ 'krɔːs boʊnz 'krɑːs-
crossbow 'krɒs bəʊ 'krɔːs- ‖ 'krɔːs boʊ 'krɑːs- **~s** z
crossbred 'krɒs bred 'krɔːs- ‖ 'krɔːs- 'krɑːs-
crossbreed 'krɒs briːd 'krɔːs- ‖ 'krɔːs- 'krɑːs- **~s** z
crosscheck *n* 'krɒs tʃek 'krɔːs-, ˌ•'• ‖ 'krɔːs- 'krɑːs- **~s** s
crosscheck *v* ˌkrɒs 'tʃek ˌkrɔːs-, '•• ‖ ˌkrɔːs- ˌkrɑːs- **~ed** t **~ing** ɪŋ **~s** s
cross-country ˌkrɒs 'kʌntr i ◂ ˌkrɔːs- ‖ ˌkrɔːs- ˌkrɑːs-
ˌcross-ˌcountry 'running
crosscourt 'krɒs kɔːt 'krɔːs- ‖ 'krɔːs kɔːrt 'krɑːs-, -koʊrt
crosscurrent 'krɒs ˌkʌr ənt 'krɔːs- ‖ 'krɔːs ˌkɝː ənt 'krɑːs- **~s** s
crosscut *n* 'krɒs kʌt 'krɔːs- ‖ 'krɔːs- 'krɑːs- **~s** s
cross|cut *v, adj* 'krɒs |kʌt 'krɔːs-, ˌ•'• ‖ 'krɔːs- 'krɑːs- **~cuts** kʌts **~cutting** kʌt ɪŋ ‖ kʌt̬ ɪŋ
cross-dress|er/s ˌkrɒs 'dres |ə/z ˌkrɔːs- ‖ ˌkrɔːs 'dres |ᵊr/z ˌkrɑːs- **~ing** ɪŋ
crosse krɒs ‖ krɔːs krɑːs
cross-examination ˌkrɒs ɪg ˌzæm ə 'neɪʃ ᵊn ˌkrɔːs-, ˌ•ɪk-, ˌ•əg-, ˌ•ək-, ˌ•eg-, ˌ•ek-, -ɪ'•- ‖ ˌkrɔːs- ˌkrɑːs- **~s** z
cross-examin|e ˌkrɒs ɪg 'zæm ɪn ˌkrɔːs-, -ɪk-, -əg-, -ək-, -eg-, -ek-, §-ən ‖ ˌkrɔːs- ˌkrɑːs- **~ed** d **~es** z **~ing** ɪŋ
cross-eyed ˌkrɒs 'aɪd ◂ ˌkrɔːs-, '•• ‖ 'krɔːs aɪd 'krɑːs-, ˌ•'•
cross-fertilis... *—see* **cross-fertiliz...**
cross-fertilization ˌkrɒs ˌfɜːt ᵊl aɪ 'zeɪʃ ᵊn ˌkrɔːs-, -ɪl aɪ-, -ɪ'•-, -ə'•- ‖ ˌkrɔːs ˌfɝːt̬ ᵊl ə- ˌkrɑːs-
cross-fertiliz|e ˌkrɒs 'fɜːt ə laɪz ˌkrɔːs-, -ɪ-, -ᵊl aɪz ‖ ˌkrɔːs 'fɝːt̬ ᵊl aɪz ˌkrɑːs- **~ed** d **~es** ɪz əz **~ing** ɪŋ
crossfire 'krɒs ˌfaɪ‿ə 'krɔːs- ‖ 'krɔːs ˌfaɪ‿ᵊr 'krɑːs-
cross-grained ˌkrɒs 'greɪnd ◂ ˌkrɔːs- ‖ ˌkrɔːs- ˌkrɑːs-
cross-hatching 'krɒs ˌhætʃ ɪŋ 'krɔːs- ‖ 'krɔːs- 'krɑːs-
cross-index ˌkrɒs 'ɪnd eks ˌkrɔːs- ‖ ˌkrɔːs- ˌkrɑːs- **~ed** t **~es** ɪz əz **~ing** ɪŋ
crossing 'krɒs ɪŋ 'krɔːs- ‖ 'krɔːs ɪŋ 'krɑːs- **~s** z
crossjack 'krɒs dʒæk 'krɔːs- ‖ 'krɔːs- 'krɑːs- *—nautically also* 'krɔːdʒ ɪk, 'krɒdʒ-, -ək ‖ 'krɑːdʒ-, 'krɔːdʒ- **~s** s
cross-legged ˌkrɒs 'legd ◂ ˌkrɔːs-, '••; -'leg ɪd, -əd ‖ 'krɔːs legd 'krɑːs-, ˌ•'•
Crossley 'krɒs li 'krɔːs- ‖ 'krɔːs- 'krɑːs-
Crossmaglen ˌkrɒs mə 'glen ˌkrɔːs- ‖ ˌkrɔːs- ˌkrɑːs-
Crossman 'krɒs mən 'krɔːs- ‖ 'krɔːs- 'krɑːs-
crossmatch ˌkrɒs 'mætʃ ˌkrɔːs-, '•• ‖ ˌkrɔːs- ˌkrɑːs- **~ed** t **~es** ɪz əz **~ing** ɪŋ
crossover 'krɒs ˌəʊv ə 'krɔːs- ‖ 'krɔːs ˌoʊv ᵊr 'krɑːs- **~s** z
crosspatch 'krɒs pætʃ 'krɔːs- ‖ 'krɔːs- 'krɑːs- **~es** ɪz əz

C

crosspiec|e 'krɒs piːs 'krɔːs- ‖ 'krɔːs- 'krɑːs-
  ~es ɪz əz
cross|ply 'krɒs |plaɪ 'krɔːs- ‖ 'krɔːs- 'krɑːs-
  ~plies plaɪz
cross-pollination ˌkrɒs ˌpɒl ə 'neɪʃ ᵊn ˌkrɔːs-,
  -ɪ- ‖ ˌkrɔːs ˌpɑːl- ˌkrɑːs-
cross-polli|nate ˌkrɒs 'pɒl ə |neɪt ˌkrɔːs-, -ɪ-
  ‖ ˌkrɔːs 'pɑːl- ˌkrɑːs- **~nated** neɪt ɪd -əd
  ‖ neɪt̬ əd **~nates** neɪts **~nating**
  neɪt ɪŋ ‖ neɪt̬ ɪŋ
cross-purposes ˌkrɒs 'pɜːp əs ɪz ˌkrɔːs-, -əz
  ‖ ˌkrɔːs 'pɜːp- ˌkrɑːs-, '•,• • •
cross-question ˌkrɒs 'kwes tʃən ˌkrɔːs-,
  →-'kweʃ- ‖ ˌkrɔːs- ˌkrɑːs- **~ed** d **~ing** ɪŋ
  ~s z
cross-re|fer ˌkrɒs rɪ |'fɜː ˌkrɔːs-, -rə-, §-riː-
  ‖ ˌkrɔːs rɪ |'fɝː ˌkrɑːs- **~ferred** 'fɜːd ‖ 'fɝːd
  ~ferring 'fɜːr ɪŋ ‖ 'fɝː ɪŋ **~fers** 'fɜːz ‖ 'fɝːz
cross-referenc|e ˌkrɒs 'ref ᵊr_ᵊnts ˌkrɔːs-
  ‖ ˌkrɔːs-, ˌkrɑːs-, '•,• • • **~ed** t **~es** ɪz əz
  ~ing ɪŋ
crossroad 'krɒs rəʊd 'krɔːs- ‖ 'krɔːs roʊd
  'krɑːs- **~s** z
cross-section 'krɒs ˌsek ʃᵊn 'krɔːs-, ˌ•'•
  ‖ 'krɔːs- 'krɑːs- **~ed** d **~s** z
cross-sectional ˌkrɒs 'sek ʃᵊn_ᵊl ◂ ˌkrɔːs-
  ‖ ˌkrɔːs-, ˌkrɑːs-
cross-stitch 'krɒs stɪtʃ 'krɔːs- ‖ 'krɔːs- 'krɑːs-
crosstalk 'krɒs tɔːk 'krɔːs- ‖ 'krɔːs tɔːk
  'krɑːs tɑːk
crosstown ˌkrɒs 'taʊn ◂ ˌkrɔːs- ‖ ˌkrɔːs-
  ˌkrɑːs-
crosstree 'krɒs triː 'krɔːs- ‖ 'krɔːs- 'krɑːs- **~s**
  z
crosswalk 'krɒs wɔːk 'krɔːs- ‖ 'krɔːs wɔːk
  'krɑːs wɑːk **~s** s
crosswind 'krɒs wɪnd 'krɔːs- ‖ 'krɔːs- 'krɑːs-
  ~s z
crosswise 'krɒs waɪz 'krɔːs- ‖ 'krɔːs- 'krɑːs-
crossword 'krɒs wɜːd 'krɔːs- ‖ 'krɔːs wɝːd
  'krɑːs- **~s** z
  'crossword ˌpuzzle
crosswort 'krɒs wɜːt 'krɔːs-, §-wɔːt
  ‖ 'krɔːs wɝːt 'krɑːs-, -wɔːrt
Crosthwaite 'krɒs θweɪt 'krɔːs- ‖ 'krɔːs-
  'krɑːs-
crostini krɒ 'stiːn i ‖ krɑː- —*It* [kro 'stiː ni]
crotch krɒtʃ ‖ krɑːtʃ **crotched**
  krɒtʃt ‖ krɑːtʃt **crotches** 'krɒtʃ ɪz -əz
  ‖ 'krɑːtʃ əz
crotchet 'krɒtʃ ɪt -ət ‖ 'krɑːtʃ ət **~s** s
crotchet|y 'krɒtʃ ət |i -ɪt- ‖ 'krɑːtʃ ət̬ |i **~iness**
  i nəs i nɪs
croton, Croton 'krəʊt ᵊn ‖ 'kroʊt- **~s** z
crouch, Crouch kraʊtʃ —*but the place in Kent
  is* kruːtʃ **crouched** kraʊtʃt **crouches**
  'kraʊtʃ ɪz -əz **crouching** 'kraʊtʃ ɪŋ
Crouchback 'kraʊtʃ bæk
croup kruːp
croupier 'kruːp i_ə -i eɪ ‖ -_ᵊr **~s** z
croupy 'kruːp i
crouton 'kruːt ɒn -ð ‖ -ɑːn kruː 'tɑːn —*Fr*
  [kʁu tɔ̃] **~s** z

crow, Crow krəʊ ‖ kroʊ **crew** kruː **crowed**
  krəʊd ‖ kroʊd **crowing** 'krəʊ ɪŋ ‖ 'kroʊ ɪŋ
  crows krəʊz ‖ kroʊz
crowbar 'krəʊ bɑː ‖ 'kroʊ bɑːr **~s** z
Crowborough 'krəʊ bᵊr_ə ‖ 'kroʊ ˌbɝː oʊ
crowd kraʊd **crowded** 'kraʊd ɪd -əd
  crowding 'kraʊd ɪŋ **crowds** kraʊdz
  ˌcrowded 'out
crowdedness 'kraʊd ɪd nəs -əd-, -nɪs
Crowe krəʊ ‖ kroʊ
crowfoot 'krəʊ fʊt ‖ 'kroʊ- **~s** s
Crowhurst 'krəʊ hɜːst ‖ 'kroʊ hɝːst
Crowley *(i)* 'krəʊ li ‖ 'kroʊ li, *(ii)* 'kraʊ-
crown kraʊn **crowned** kraʊnd **crowning**
  'kraʊn ɪŋ **crowns** kraʊnz
  ˌcrown 'colony; ˌcrown 'court; ˌCrown
  'Derby; ˌcrowned 'head; ˌcrown 'jewels;
  ˌcrown 'prince◂, ˌCrown Prince 'George
Crowndale 'kraʊn deɪᵊl
crown-of-thorns ˌkraʊn əv 'θɔːnz ‖ -'θɔːrnz
crow's-|foot 'krəʊz| fʊt ‖ 'kroʊz- **~feet** fiːt
crow's-nest 'krəʊz nest ‖ 'kroʊz- **~s** s
Crowther 'kraʊð ə ‖ -ᵊr
Crowthorne 'krəʊ θɔːn ‖ 'kroʊ θɔːrn
Croxford 'krɒks fəd ‖ 'krɑːks fᵊrd
Croyde krɔɪd
Croydon 'krɔɪd ᵊn
crozier, C~ 'krəʊz i_ə 'krəʊʒ ə ‖ 'kroʊʒ ᵊr **~s** z
cru kruː —*Fr* [kʁy]
cruces 'kruːs iːz
crucial 'kruːʃ ᵊl 'kruːʃ i_ᵊl **~ly** i
cruciality ˌkruːʃ i 'æl ət i -ɪt i ‖ -ət̬ i
crucian 'kruːʃ ᵊn
cruciate 'kruːʃ i eɪt 'kruːs-, -_ət, -ɪt
crucible 'kruːs əb ᵊl -ɪb- **~s** z
crucifer 'kruːs ɪf ə -əf- ‖ -əf ᵊr **~s** z
Cruciferae kruː 'sɪf ə riː
cruciferous kruː 'sɪf ᵊr əs
crucifix 'kruːs ə fɪks -ɪ- **~es** ɪz əz
crucifixion ˌkruːs ə 'fɪk ʃᵊn -ɪ- **~s** z
cruciform 'kruːs ɪ fɔːm -ə- ‖ -fɔːrm
cruci|fy 'kruːs ɪ |faɪ -ə- **~fied** faɪd **~fier/s**
  faɪ_ə/z ‖ faɪ_ᵊr/z **~fies** faɪz **~fying** faɪ ɪŋ
cruck krʌk **crucks** krʌks
crud krʌd
cruddy 'krʌd i
crude kruːd **cruder** 'kruːd ə ‖ -ᵊr **crudest**
  'kruːd ɪst -əst
crudely 'kruːd li
Cruden 'kruːd ᵊn **~'s** z
crudeness 'kruːd nəs -nɪs
crudites, crudités 'kruːd ɪ teɪ -ə-
  ‖ ˌkruːd ɪ 'teɪ —*Fr* [kʁy di te]
crudit|y 'kruːd ət |i -ɪt- ‖ -ət̬ |i **~ies** iz
cruel 'kruː_ᵊl kruːl **crueler, crueller** 'kruː_ᵊl ə
  'kruːl ə ‖ -ᵊr **cruelest, cruellest** 'kruː_ᵊl ɪst
  -əst; 'kruːl ɪst, -əst
cruelly 'kruː_ᵊl i -li; 'kruːl i, -li
cruel|ty 'kruː_ᵊl |ti 'kruːl |ti **~ties** tiz
cruet 'kruː_ɪt §-ət **~s** s
Cruft krʌft **Crufts, Cruft's** krʌfts
Cruickshank, Cruikshank 'krʊk ʃæŋk §'kruːk-

cruise kru:z (= *crews*) **cruised** kru:zd **cruises**
　'kru:z ɪz -əz **cruising** 'kru:z ɪŋ
　ˌcruise 'missile ‖ '• ，• •
cruiser 'kru:z ə ‖ -ər ~s z
cruiserweight 'kru:z ə weɪt ‖ -ər- ~s s
cruising 'kru:z ɪŋ
　'cruising speed
cruller 'krʌl ə ‖ -ər ~s z
crumb krʌm **crumbed** krʌmd **crumbing**
　'krʌm ɪŋ **crumbs** krʌmz
crumbl|e 'krʌm bəl ~ed d ~es z ~ing ˌɪŋ
crum|bly 'krʌm ǀbli ~blier bli_ə ‖ bli_ər
　~bliest bli_ɪst bli_əst
crumb|y 'krʌm ǀi ~ier i_ə ‖ i_ər ~iest i_ɪst
　i_əst
crumhorn 'krʌm hɔ:n ‖ -hɔ:rn
Crumlin 'krʌm lɪn -lən
Crummock 'krʌm ək
crumm|y 'krʌm ǀi ~ier i_ə ‖ i_ər ~iest i_ɪst
　i_əst
crump, Crump krʌmp **crumped** krʌmpt
　crumping 'krʌmp ɪŋ **crumps, Crump's**
　krʌmps
crumpet 'krʌmp ɪt §-ət ~s s
crumpl|e 'krʌmp əl ~ed d ~es z ~ing ˌɪŋ
crunch krʌntʃ **crunched** krʌntʃt **crunches**
　'krʌntʃ ɪz -əz **crunching** 'krʌntʃ ɪŋ
Crunchie *tdmk* 'krʌntʃ i ~s z
crunchy 'krʌntʃ i
crupper 'krʌp ə ‖ -ər
crusad|e kru: 'seɪd ~ed ɪd əd ~es z ~ing ɪŋ
crusader kru: 'seɪd ə ‖ -ər ~s z
cruse, Cruse kru:z ‖ kru:s (*usually* = *cruise*)
　cruses 'kru:z ɪz -əz ‖ 'kru:s-
crush krʌʃ **crushed** krʌʃt **crushes** 'krʌʃ ɪz
　-əz **crushing/ly** 'krʌʃ ɪŋ /li
　'crush ˌbarrier
crushable 'krʌʃ əb əl
Crusoe 'kru:s əʊ 'kru:z- ‖ -oʊ
crust krʌst **crusted** 'krʌst ɪd -əd **crusting**
　'krʌst ɪŋ **crusts** krʌsts
crustacean krʌ 'steɪʃ ən -'steɪʃ i_ən ~s z
crustal 'krʌst əl
crust|y 'krʌst ǀi ~ier i_ə ‖ i_ər ~iest i_ɪst i_əst
　~ily i li əl i ~iness i nəs i nɪs
crutch, Crutch krʌtʃ **crutched** krʌtʃt
　crutches 'krʌtʃ ɪz -əz **crutching** 'krʌtʃ ɪŋ
Cruttenden 'krʌt ənd ən
Cruttwell, Crutwell 'krʌt wəl
crux krʌks kruks **cruces** 'kru:s i:z **cruxes**
　'krʌks ɪz -əz
Cruyff krɔɪf kraɪf —*Dutch* [krœyf]
Cruz kru:z —*Sp* [kruθ], *AmSp* [krus], *Port*
　[kruʃ], *BrazPort* [krus]
cruzeiro kru 'zeər əʊ ‖ -'zer oʊ —*Port*
　[kru 'zei ru] ~s z
crwth kru:θ
cry kraɪ **cried** kraɪd **cries** kraɪz **crying**
　'kraɪ ɪŋ
crybab|y 'kraɪ ˌbeɪb i ~ies iz
Cryer 'kraɪ_ə ‖ 'kraɪ_ər
cryo- *comb. form*
　with stress-neutral suffix ǀkraɪ əʊ -ə ‖ -ə -oʊ —

cryoscopic ˌkraɪ əʊ
　'skɒp ɪk ◀ ‖ -ə 'ska:p ɪk ◀
　with stress-imposing suffix kraɪ 'ɒ+ ‖ -'a:+ —
　cryoscopy kraɪ 'ɒsk əp i ‖ -'a:sk-
cryogenic ˌkraɪ əʊ 'dʒen ɪk ◀ ‖ -ə- ~s s
cryonic kraɪ 'ɒn ɪk ‖ -'a:n- ~s s
cryostat 'kraɪ_ə stæt ~s s
cryotron 'kraɪ_ə trɒn ‖ -tra:n ~s z
crypt krɪpt **crypts** krɪpts
crypt- *comb. form before vowel* ǀkrɪpt —
　cryptanalysis ˌkrɪpt ə 'næl əs ɪs -ɪs ɪs, §-əs
cryptic 'krɪpt ɪk ~ally əl_i
crypto 'krɪpt əʊ ‖ -oʊ ~s z
crypto- *comb. form before consonant*
　with stress-neutral suffix ǀkrɪpt əʊ ‖ -oʊ —
　crypto-Fascist ˌkrɪpt əʊ 'fæʃ ɪst §-əst ‖ -oʊ-
　with stress-imposing suffix krɪp 'tɒ+ ‖ -'ta:+
　— **cryptogamous** krɪp 'tɒg əm əs ‖ -'ta:g-
cryptogam 'krɪpt ə gæm ~s z
cryptogram 'krɪpt ə græm ~s z
cryptographer krɪp 'tɒg rəf ə ‖ -'ta:g rəf ər
　~s z
cryptographic ˌkrɪpt ə 'græf ɪk ◀ ~ally əl_i
cryptography krɪp 'tɒg rəf i ‖ -'ta:g-
cryptorchidism krɪp 'tɔ:k ɪ ˌdɪz əm -'•ə-
　‖ -'tɔ:rk-
crystal, C~ 'krɪst əl ~s z
　ˌcrystal 'ball; ˌcrystal 'clear◀; 'crystal
　ˌgazing; ˌCrystal 'Palace; 'crystal set
crystaliz... —*see* **crystalliz...**
crystalline 'krɪst ə laɪn -li:n; -əl aɪn, -i:n
　‖ -əl ən -ə laɪn, -ə li:n
crystallis... —*see* **crystalliz...**
crystallization ˌkrɪst əl aɪ 'zeɪʃ ən -əl ɪ-, -əl ə-
　‖ -əl ə-
crystalliz|e 'krɪst ə laɪz -əl aɪz ~ed d ~es ɪz əz
　~ing ɪŋ
crystallographer ˌkrɪst ə 'lɒg rəf ə -əl 'ɒg-
　‖ -əl 'a:g rəf ər ~s z
crystallographic ˌkrɪst əl ə 'græf ɪk ◀ ~al əl
　~ally əl_i
crystallography ˌkrɪst ə 'lɒg rəf i -əl 'ɒg-
　‖ -əl 'a:g-
csardas, csárdás 'tʃa:d æʃ -a:ʃ; 'za:d əs
　‖ 'tʃa:rd a:ʃ —*Hung* ['tʃa:r da:ʃ]
CSE ˌsi: es 'i: ~s, 's z
ctenoid 'ti:n ɔɪd 'ten-
cub kʌb **cubbing** 'kʌb ɪŋ **cubs** kʌbz
　'Cub Scout
Cuba 'kju:b ə —*Sp* ['ku βa]
Cuban 'kju:b ən ~s z
cubbyhole 'kʌb i həʊl →-hɒʊl ‖ -hoʊl ~s z
cube kju:b **cubed** kju:bd **cubes** kju:bz
　cubing 'kju:b ɪŋ
　ˌcube 'root ‖ '• •
cubeb 'kju:b eb ~s z
cubic 'kju:b ɪk
cubical 'kju:b ɪk əl (= *cubicle*) ~ly _i
cubicle 'kju:b ɪk əl ~s z
cubism 'kju:b ˌɪz əm
cubist 'kju:b ɪst §-əst ~s s
cubit 'kju:b ɪt §-ət ~s s
Cubitt 'kju:b ɪt §-ət

Cublington 'kʌb lɪŋ tən
cuboid 'kjuːb ɔɪd ~s z
Cuckfield 'kʊk fiːld
cucking-stool 'kʌk ɪŋ stuːl ~s z
Cuckmere 'kʊk mɪə ǁ -mɪr
Cuckney 'kʌk ni
cuckold 'kʌk əʊld →-ɒʊld, -əld ǁ -oʊld -əld ~ed ɪd əd ~er/s ə/z ǁ -ᵊr/z ~ing ɪŋ ~s z
cuckoldry 'kʌk əld ri -əʊld- ǁ -oʊld-
cuckoo 'kʊk uː ǁ 'kuːk- 'kʊk- ~s z
　'cuckoo clock
cuckoopint 'kʊk uː paɪnt -pɪnt ǁ 'kuːk- 'kʊk- ~s s
cuckoo-spit 'kʊk uː spɪt ǁ 'kuːk- 'kʊk-
cucumber 'kjuːk ʌm bə -bər ǁ -bər ~s z
cucurbit kju 'kɜːb ɪt §-ət ǁ -'kɝːb- ~s s
cud kʌd
cudbear 'kʌd beə →'kʌb- ǁ -ber
Cuddesdon 'kʌdz dən
cuddl|e 'kʌd ᵊl ~ed d ~es z ~ing ɪŋ
cuddlesome 'kʌd ᵊl səm
cuddly 'kʌd ᵊl_i
Cuddy, cudd|y 'kʌd li ~ies iz
cudgel 'kʌdʒ əl ~ed, ~led d ~ing, ~ling ɪŋ ~s z
Cudlipp 'kʌd lɪp
cudweed 'kʌd wiːd
Cudworth 'kʌd wəθ -wɜːθ ǁ -wᵊrθ —locally also -əθ
cue kjuː **cued** kjuːd **cueing, cuing** 'kjuː_ɪŋ **cues** kjuːz
　'cue ball
cuff, Cuff kʌf **cuffed** kʌft **cuffing** 'kʌf ɪŋ **cuffs** kʌfs
Cuffley 'kʌf li
cufflink 'kʌf lɪŋk ~s s
cui bono ˌkuː_i 'bəʊn əʊ ˌkwiː'•-, -'bɒn- ǁ ˌkwiː 'boʊn oʊ
Cuillin 'kuːl ɪn -ən
cuirass kwɪ 'ræs kwə-, kjuə- ~ed t ~es ɪz əz
cuirassier ˌkwɪr ə 'sɪə ˌkjʊər- ǁ -'sɪᵊr ~s z
Cuisenaire, c~ ˌkwiːz ə 'neə ǁ -'neᵊr —Fr [kɥi nɛːʁ]
cuisine kwɪ 'ziːn kwə-, △kju- —Fr [kɥi zin]
　cui,sine min'ceur mæn 'sɜː ǁ -'sɝː —Fr [mæ sœːʁ]
cuisse kwɪs **cuisses** 'kwɪs ɪz -əz
Culbertson 'kʌlb ət sən ǁ -ᵊrt-
Culcheth 'kʌltʃ əθ -ɪθ
cul-de-sac 'kʌl də sæk 'kʊl-, ˌ•••• —Fr [kyd sak, kyt-] ~s s
Culham 'kʌl əm
culinary 'kʌl ɪn ər_i 'kjuːl-, '•ən- ǁ -ə ner i
Culkin 'kʌlk ɪn §-ən
cull kʌl **culled** kʌld **culling** 'kʌl ɪŋ **culls** kʌlz
Cullen 'kʌl ən -ɪn
cullender 'kʌl ənd ə -ɪnd- ǁ -ᵊr ~s z
culler, C~ 'kʌl ə ǁ -ᵊr ~s z
cullet 'kʌl ɪt -ət
Cullinan 'kʌl ɪn ən -ən-
Culloden kə 'lɒd ᵊn kʌ-, -'ləʊd- ǁ -'lɑːd- -'lɒʊd-
　Cul,loden 'Moor

Cullompton kə 'lʌmpt ən 'kʌl əmpt-
culm, Culm kʌlm
culmi|nate 'kʌlm ɪ |neɪt -ə- ~nated neɪt ɪd -əd ǁ neɪt̬ əd ~nates neɪts ~nating neɪt ɪŋ ǁ neɪt̬ ɪŋ
culmination ˌkʌlm ɪ 'neɪʃ ᵊn -ə- ~s z
culminative 'kʌlm ɪn ət ɪv '•ən-; -ɪ neɪt ɪv, -ə•• ǁ -ə neɪt̬ ɪv ~ly li
culotte kju 'lɒt ku- ǁ 'kuːl ɑːt 'kjuːl-; ku 'lɑːt, kju- —Fr [ky lɔt] ~s s
culpa 'kʊlp ə -ɑː
culpability ˌkʌlp ə 'bɪl ət i -ɪt i ǁ -ət̬ i
culpab|le 'kʌlp əb |ᵊl ~ly li
Culpeper, Culpepper 'kʌl ˌpep ə ǁ -ᵊr
culprit 'kʌlp rɪt -rət ~s s
Culross (i) 'kʌl rɒs ˌ•'•; 'kuːl-, -rəs ǁ -rɔːs -rɑːs, (ii) 'kuː- —In Scotland, (ii); otherwise usually (i)
culs-de-sac 'kʌl də sæk 'kʊl-, ˌ•••• —Fr [kyd sak, kyt-]
Culshaw 'kʌl ʃɔː ǁ -ʃɑː
cult kʌlt **cults** kʌlts
Culter 'kuːt ə ǁ 'kuːt̬ ᵊr (!)
cultic 'kʌlt ɪk
cultism 'kʌlt ˌɪz ᵊm
cultist 'kʌlt ɪst §-əst ~s s
cultivable 'kʌlt ɪv əb ᵊl '•əv-
cultivar 'kʌlt ɪ vɑː -ə- ǁ -vɑːr ~s z
culti|vate 'kʌlt ɪ |veɪt -ə- ~vated veɪt ɪd -əd ǁ veɪt̬ əd ~vates veɪts ~vating veɪt ɪŋ ǁ veɪt̬ ɪŋ
cultivation ˌkʌlt ɪ 'veɪʃ ᵊn -ə- ~s z
cultivator 'kʌlt ɪ veɪt ə '•ə- ǁ -veɪt̬ ᵊr ~s z
cultural 'kʌltʃ ᵊr_əl ~ly li
culture 'kʌltʃ ə ǁ -ᵊr ~d d ~s z **culturing** 'kʌltʃ ᵊr_ɪŋ
　'culture ˌmedium; 'culture shock
Culver 'kʌlv ə ǁ -ᵊr
culvert 'kʌlv ət ǁ -ᵊrt ~s s
Culzean kə 'leɪn
cum 'come' kʌm
cum, -cum- Latin prepn kʌm kʊm —may be stressed or unstressed —See also phrases with this word
Cumae 'kjuːm iː
cumber 'kʌm bə ǁ -bᵊr ~ed d **cumbering** 'kʌm bᵊr_ɪŋ ~s z
Cumberland 'kʌm bə lənd ǁ -bᵊr-
Cumberledge 'kʌm bə ledʒ -lɪdʒ ǁ -bᵊr-
Cumbernauld ˌkʌm bə 'nɔːld '••• ǁ -bᵊr- -'nɑːld
cumbersome 'kʌm bə səm ǁ -bᵊr- ~ly li ~ness nəs nɪs
Cumbrae 'kʌm breɪ
Cumbria 'kʌm bri_ə
Cumbrian 'kʌm bri_ən ~s z
cumbrous 'kʌm brəs
cum grano salis kʌm ˌgreɪn əʊ 'seɪl ɪs kʊm-, -ˌgrɑːn-, -'sɑːl-, -'sæl-, §-əs ǁ kʊm ˌgrɑːn oʊ 'sɑːl əs
cumin 'kʌm ɪn 'kuːm-, 'kjuːm-, §-ən
cum laude ˌ⁽ˌ⁾kʌm 'laʊd eɪ ˌ⁽ˌ⁾kʊm-, 'lɔːd-, -i ǁ kʊm 'laʊd i -ə

C

cummerbund 'kʌm ə bʌnd ‖ -ᵊr- **~s** z
cummin, C~ 'kʌm ɪn §-ən
Cummings, cummings 'kʌm ɪŋz
Cumnock 'kʌm nək
Cumnor 'kʌm nə ‖ -nᵊr
cumquat 'kʌm kwɒt ‖ -kwɑːt **~s** s
cumshaw 'kʌm ʃɔː ‖ -ʃɑː **~s** z
cumulative 'kjuːm jʊl ət ɪv '•jəl-; -ju leɪt-,
　-jə leɪt- ‖ -jəl ət̬ ɪv -jə leɪt̬ ɪv **~ly** li **~ness**
　nəs nɪs
cumulonimbus ˌkjuːm jʊl əʊ 'nɪm bəs ˌ•jəl-
　‖ -jə loʊ-
cumulostratus ˌkjuːm jʊl əʊ 'streɪt əs ˌ•jəl-,
　-'strɑːt- ‖ -jə loʊ 'streɪt̬ əs -'stræt̬-
cumulus 'kjuːm jʊl əs -jəl- ‖ -jəl əs
Cunard ₍ᵢ₎kjuː 'nɑːd ‖ -'nɑːrd ˌkuː- **~er/s** ə/
　z ‖ -ᵊr/z
cunctation ₍ᵢ₎kʌŋk 'teɪʃ ᵊn
cunctator ₍ᵢ₎kʌŋk 'teɪt ə ‖ -'teɪt̬ ᵊr **~s** z
Cundy 'kʌnd i
cuneal 'kjuːn i‿əl
cuneate 'kjuːn i eɪt ‿ət, -ɪt
cuneiform 'kjuːn ɪ fɔːm 'kjuːn i‿ɪ fɔːm, -i‿ə-;
　kju 'neɪ ɪ fɔːm, -'niː-, -ə fɔːm ‖ -fɔːrm
Cuningham, Cuninghame 'kʌn ɪŋ əm ‖ -hæm
Cunliffe 'kʌn lɪf
cunnilinctus ˌkʌn ɪ 'lɪŋkt əs -ə-
cunnilingus ˌkʌn ɪ 'lɪŋ gəs -ə-
cunning 'kʌn ɪŋ **~ly** li **~ness** nəs nɪs
Cunningham 'kʌn ɪŋ əm ‖ -hæm
Cunobelin, Cunobeline kju 'nɒb əl ɪn §-ən
　‖ -'noʊb-
Cunobelinus ˌkjuːn əʊ bə 'laɪn əs -bɪ'•-, -'liːn-
　‖ ˌkjuːn oʊ-
cunt kʌnt **cunts** kʌnts
Cunynghame 'kʌn ɪŋ əm ‖ -hæm
Cuomo 'kwəʊm əʊ ‖ 'kwoʊm oʊ
cup kʌp **cupped** kʌpt **cupping** 'kʌp ɪŋ **cups**
　kʌps
　'cup ˌfinal, ˌ•'•‿•
Cupar 'kuːp ə ‖ -ᵊr
cupbearer 'kʌp ˌbeər ə ‖ -ˌber ᵊr **~s** z
cupboard 'kʌb əd ‖ -ᵊrd **~s** z
　'cupboard ˌlove
cupcake 'kʌp keɪk **~s** s
cupful 'kʌp fʊl **~s** z
cupid, Cupid 'kjuːp ɪd §-əd **~s**, **~'s** z
cupidity kju 'pɪd ət i -ɪt- ‖ -ət̬ i
Cupit, Cupitt 'kjuːp ɪt §-ət
cupola 'kjuːp əl ə **~s** z
cuppa 'kʌp ə
cupreous 'kjuːp ri‿əs
cupric 'kjuːp rɪk
Cuprinol tdmk 'kjuːp rɪ nɒl -rə- ‖ -nɑːl -nɔːl,
　-noʊl
cupronickel ˌkjuːp rəʊ 'nɪk ᵊl ˌkuːp- ‖ -roʊ-
cuprous 'kjuːp rəs
cup-tie 'kʌp taɪ **~s** z
cupule 'kjuːp juːl **~s** z
cur kɜː ‖ kɜː: **curs** kɜːz ‖ kɜː:z
curable 'kjʊər əb ᵊl 'kjɔːr- ‖ 'kjʊr-
curacao, curaçao, C~ 'kjʊər ə səʊ 'kjɔːr-,
　ˌ••'•‖ 'kjʊr ə soʊ 'kʊr-, -saʊ, ˌ••'•

curac|y 'kjʊər əs li 'kjɔːr- ‖ 'kjʊr- **~ies** iz
curare, curari kjʊ 'rɑːr i
curassow 'kjʊər ə səʊ 'kjɔːr- ‖ 'kjʊr ə soʊ **~s**
　z
curate 'kjʊər ət 'kjɔːr-, -ɪt ‖ 'kjʊr- -eɪt **~s** s
　ˌcurate's 'egg
curative 'kjʊər ət ɪv 'kjɔːr- ‖ 'kjʊr ət̬ ɪv **~ly** li
　~ness nəs nɪs
curator kjʊə 'reɪt ə ‖ 'kjʊr eɪt̬ ᵊr -ət̬-;
　kju 'reɪt̬ ᵊr **~s** z
curb kɜːb ‖ kɜː:b **curbed** kɜːbd ‖ kɜː:bd
　curbing 'kɜːb ɪŋ ‖ 'kɜː:b ɪŋ **curbs**
　kɜːbz ‖ kɜː:bz
curbstone 'kɜːb stəʊn ‖ 'kɜː:b stoʊn **~s** z
curd kɜːd ‖ kɜː:d **curds** kɜːdz ‖ kɜː:dz
　ˌcurd 'cheese, ˌ•‿•
curdl|e 'kɜːd ᵊl ‖ 'kɜː:d ᵊl **~ed** d **~es** z **~ing**
　_ɪŋ
cure kjʊə kjɔː ‖ kjʊᵊr **cured** kjʊəd kjɔːd
　‖ kjʊᵊrd **cures** kjʊəz kjɔːz ‖ kjʊᵊrz **curing**
　'kjʊər ɪŋ 'kjɔːr- ‖ 'kjʊr ɪŋ
curé 'kjʊər eɪ 'kjɔːr- ‖ kjuː 'reɪ 'kjʊr eɪ —Fr
　[ky ʁe] **~s** z
cure-all 'kjʊər ɔːl 'kjɔːr- ‖ 'kjʊr ɔːl -ɑːl **~s** z
curettage kjʊə 'ret ɪdʒ ˌkjʊər ɪ 'tɑːʒ, -ə-
　‖ ˌkjʊr ə 'tɑːʒ
curette kjʊə 'ret **~s** s
curfew 'kɜːf juː ‖ 'kɜː:f- **~s** z
cur|ia 'kjʊər li‿ə 'kjɔːr-, 'kʊər- ‖ 'kjʊr- **~iae**
　i iː i aɪ
Curie, curie 'kjʊər i -iː ‖ 'kjʊr i kju 'riː —Fr
　[ky ʁi] **~s** z
curing —see **cure**
curio 'kjʊər i əʊ 'kjɔːr- ‖ 'kjʊr i oʊ
curiosa ˌkjʊər i 'əʊs ə ‖ ˌkjʊr i 'oʊs ə -'oʊz-
curiosity ˌkjʊər i 'ɒs ət i ˌkjɔːr-, -ɪt i
　‖ ˌkjʊr i 'ɑːs ət̬ i
curious 'kjʊər i‿əs 'kjɔːr- ‖ 'kjʊr- **~er** ə ‖ ᵊr
　~ly li **~ness** nəs nɪs
curium 'kjʊər i‿əm 'kjɔːr- ‖ 'kjʊr-
curl kɜːl ‖ kɜː:ᵊl **curled** kɜːld ‖ kɜː:ᵊld **curling**
　'kɜːl ɪŋ ‖ 'kɜː:l ɪŋ **curls** kɜːlz ‖ kɜː:ᵊlz
curler 'kɜːl ə ‖ 'kɜː:l ᵊr **~s** z
curlew 'kɜːl juː -uː ‖ 'kɜː:l- **~s** z
curlicue 'kɜːl i kjuː ‖ 'kɜː:l- **~s** z
curling 'kɜːl ɪŋ ‖ 'kɜː:l ɪŋ
curl|y 'kɜːl li ‖ 'kɜː:l li **~ier** i‿ə ‖ i‿ᵊr **~ies** iz
　~iest i‿ɪst i‿əst **~iness** i nəs i nɪs
curlycue 'kɜːl i kjuː ‖ 'kɜː:l- **~s** z
curmudgeon kɜː 'mʌdʒ ən kə- ‖ kᵊr- **~ly** li
　~s z
Curr kɜː ‖ kɜː:
curragh, C~ 'kʌr ə -əx ‖ 'kɜː: ə **~s** z
Curran 'kʌr ən ‖ 'kɜː:-
currant 'kʌr ənt ‖ 'kɜː:- (= current) **~s** s
　ˌcurrant 'bun
currawong 'kʌr ə wɒŋ ‖ 'kɜː: ə wɑːŋ **~s** z
currenc|y 'kʌr ənts li ‖ 'kɜː:- **~ies** iz
current 'kʌr ənt ‖ 'kɜː:- **~ly** li **~ness** nəs nɪs
　~s s
　ˌcurrent af'fairs
curricul|um kə 'rɪk jʊl əm -jəl- ‖ -jəl- **~a** ə

C

cur,riculum 'vitae 'viːt aɪ -eɪ; 'vaɪt iː ‖ 'vaɪt̬ i 'wiːt aɪ
Currie 'kʌr i ‖ 'kɜː i
currier 'kʌr i‿ə ‖ 'kɜː i‿ər ~s z
currish 'kɜːr ɪʃ ‖ 'kɜː-
curr|y, Curry 'kʌr |i ‖ 'kɜː |i ~ied id ~ies iz ~ying i‿ɪŋ
'curry ˌpowder
curse kɜːs ‖ kɜːs cursed kɜːst ‖ kɜːst curses 'kɜːs ɪz -əz ‖ 'kɜːs əz cursing 'kɜːs ɪŋ ‖ 'kɜːs ɪŋ curst kɜːst ‖ kɜːst
cursed adj 'kɜːs ɪd -əd; kɜːst ‖ 'kɜːs əd kɜːst ~ly li ~ness nəs nɪs
cursed past, pp kɜːst ‖ kɜːst
cursive 'kɜːs ɪv ‖ 'kɜːs ɪv ~ly li ~s z
cursor 'kɜːs ə ‖ 'kɜːs ər ~s z
cursorial kɜː 'sɔːr i‿əl ‖ kər- -'sour-
cursor|y 'kɜːs ər‿|i ‖ 'kɜːs- ~ily əl i ɪ li ~iness i nəs i nɪs
curst kɜːst ‖ kɜːst
curt, Curt kɜːt ‖ kɜːt
curtail kɜː 'teɪəl kə- ‖ kər- ~ed d ~ing ɪŋ ~ment mənt ~s z
curtain 'kɜːt ən ‖ 'kɜːt- ~ed d ~ing ˌɪŋ ~s z
'curtain call
curtain-raiser 'kɜːt ən ˌreɪz ə ‖ 'kɜːt ən ˌreɪz ər ~s z
curtain-up ˌkɜːt ən 'ʌp ‖ ˌkɜːt-
curtilage 'kɜːt əl ɪdʒ -ɪl- ‖ 'kɜːt əl-
Curtin 'kɜːt ɪn §-ən ‖ 'kɜːt ən
Curtis, Curtiss 'kɜːt ɪs §-əs ‖ 'kɜːt̬-
Curtius 'kɜːt i‿əs ‖ 'kɜːt̬- —but as a German name sometimes 'kɜːts- ‖ 'kɜːts- —Ger ['kʊʁ tsi ʊs]
curtly 'kɜːt li ‖ 'kɜːt-
curtness 'kɜːt nəs -nɪs ‖ 'kɜːt-
curts|ey, curts|y 'kɜːts li ‖ 'kɜːts li ~eyed, ~ied id ~eying, ~ying i‿ɪŋ ~eys, ~ies iz
curvaceous, curvacious kɜː 'veɪʃ əs ‖ kər- ~ly li ~ness nəs nɪs
curvature 'kɜːv ətʃ ə -ə tjʊə ‖ 'kɜːv ə tʃʊr -tʃər, -tʊr, -tjʊr
curve kɜːv ‖ kɜːv curved kɜːvd ‖ kɜːvd curves kɜːvz ‖ kɜːvz curving 'kɜːv ɪŋ ‖ 'kɜːv-
curvet kɜː 'vet ‖ kər- 'kɜːv ət curveted, curvetted kɜː 'vet ɪd -əd ‖ kər 'vet̬ əd 'kɜːv ət̬ əd curveting, curvetting kɜː 'vet ɪŋ ‖ kər 'vet̬ ɪŋ 'kɜːv ət̬ ɪŋ curvets kɜː 'vets ‖ kər- 'kɜːv əts
curvilinear ˌkɜːv ɪ 'lɪn i‿ə ◂ ˌ•ə- ‖ ˌkɜːv ə 'lɪn i‿ər ◂ ~ly li
Curwen 'kɜː wɪn -wən ‖ 'kɜː-
Curzon 'kɜːz ən ‖ 'kɜːz-
Cusack (i) 'kjuːs æk, (ii) 'kjuːz-
cuscus 'kʌs kʌs 'kʌsk əs ~es ɪz əz
Cush kʌʃ kʊʃ
Cushing 'kʊʃ ɪŋ
cushion 'kʊʃ ən ~ed d ~ing ˌɪŋ ~s z
Cushite 'kʌʃ aɪt 'kʊʃ- ~s s
Cushitic kʌ 'ʃɪt ɪk kʊ- ‖ -'ʃɪt̬-
cush|y 'kʊʃ |i ~ier i‿ə ‖ i‿ər ~iest i‿ɪst i‿əst
cusp kʌsp cusped kʌspt cusps kʌsps

cuspid 'kʌsp ɪd §-əd
cuspidor 'kʌsp ɪ dɔː §-ə- ‖ -dɔːr -doʊr ~s z
cuss kʌs cussed kʌst cusses 'kʌs ɪz -əz cussing 'kʌs ɪŋ
cussed adj 'kʌs ɪd -əd ~ly li ~ness nəs nɪs
cussed past, pp kʌst
Cusson 'kʌs ən
custard 'kʌst əd ‖ -ərd ~s z
ˌcustard 'apple; ˌcustard 'pie; 'custard ˌpowder
Custer 'kʌst ə ‖ -ər ~'s z
custodial kʌ 'stəʊd i‿əl ‖ -'stoʊd-
custodian kʌ 'stəʊd i‿ən ‖ -'stoʊd- ~ship ʃɪp
custod|y 'kʌst əd |i ~ies iz
custom 'kʌst əm ~s z
'custom(s) house
customable 'kʌst əm əb əl
customarily 'kʌst əm ər‿əl i ‿ɪ li, ˌkʌst ə 'mer- ‖ ˌkʌst ə 'mer əl i
customary 'kʌst əm ər‿i ‖ -ə mer i
custom-built ˌkʌst əm 'bɪlt ◂ '•••
customer 'kʌst əm ə ‖ -ər ~s z
customis|e, customiz|e 'kʌst ə maɪz ~ed d ~es ɪz əz ~ing ɪŋ
custom-made ˌkʌst əm 'meɪd ◂ '•••
cut kʌt cuts kʌts cutting 'kʌt ɪŋ ‖ 'kʌt̬ ɪŋ
ˌcut 'glass ◂, ˌcut glass 'bowls
cut-and-cover ˌkʌt ən 'kʌv ə ◂ ‖ -ər
cut-and-dried ˌkʌt ən 'draɪd ◂
cut-and-dry ˌkʌt ən 'draɪ
cutaneous kju 'teɪn i‿əs ~ly li
cutaway 'kʌt ə ˌweɪ ‖ 'kʌt̬- ~s z
cutback 'kʌt bæk ~s s
cutch, Cutch kʌtʃ
cute kjuːt cuter 'kjuːt ə ‖ 'kjuːt̬ ər cutest 'kjuːt ɪst -əst ‖ 'kjuːt̬ əst
cute|ly 'kjuːt |li ~ness nəs nɪs
cutesy 'kjuːts i
Cutex tdmk 'kjuːt eks
Cutforth 'kʌt fɔːθ ‖ -fɔːrθ -foʊrθ
Cuthbert 'kʌθ bət ‖ -bərt
Cuthbertson 'kʌθ bət sən ‖ -bərt-
cuticle 'kjuːt ɪk əl ‖ 'kjuːt̬- ~s z
Cuticura tdmk ˌkjuːt ɪ 'kjʊər ə -ə-, -'kjɔːr- ‖ ˌkjuːt̬ ə 'kjʊr ə
cutie 'kjuːt i ‖ 'kjuːt̬ i ~s z
cutis 'kjuːt ɪs §-əs ‖ 'kjuːt̬-
cutlass, cutlass 'kʌt ləs ~es ɪz əz
cutler, C~ 'kʌt lə ‖ -lər ~s z
cutlery 'kʌt lər i -ler i
cutlet 'kʌt lət -lɪt ~s s
cutoff 'kʌt ɒf -ɔːf ‖ 'kʌt̬ ɔːf -ɑːf ~s s
cutout 'kʌt aʊt ‖ 'kʌt̬- ~s s
cut-price ˌkʌt 'praɪs ◂
cutpurse 'kʌt pɜːs ‖ -pɜːs ~es ɪz əz
cut-rate ˌkʌt 'reɪt ◂
cutter, C~ 'kʌt ə ‖ 'kʌt̬ ər ~s z
cutthroat 'kʌt θrəʊt ‖ -θroʊt ~s s
cutting 'kʌt ɪŋ ‖ 'kʌt̬ ɪŋ ~ly li ~s z
ˌcutting 'edge
cuttle 'kʌt əl ‖ 'kʌt̬ əl
cuttlebone 'kʌt əl bəʊn ‖ 'kʌt̬ əl boʊn
cuttlefish 'kʌt əl fɪʃ ‖ 'kʌt̬- ~es ɪz əz

Cutty Sark ˌkʌt i 'sɑːk ‖ 'kʌt̬ i sɑːrk
cutup 'kʌt ʌp ‖ 'kʌt̬- ~s s
cutwater 'kʌt ˌwɔːt ə ‖ -ˌwɔːt̬ ər -ˌwɑːt̬ ər ~s z
cutworm 'kʌt wɜːm ‖ -wɝːm ~s z
Cuvier 'kjuːv i eɪ ‖ ˌ•'• —Fr [ky vje]
Cuxhaven 'kʊks ˌhɑːv ən —Ger [kʊks 'haːf ən]
Cuyahoga ˌkaɪ‿ə 'həʊg ə ◄ -'hɒg- ‖ -'hoʊg ə ◄
    -'hɔːg-, -'hɑːg-; kə'••
    ˌCuyaˌhoga 'River
Cuyp kaɪp kɔɪp —Dutch [kœyp]
Cuzco 'kʊsk əʊ ‖ 'kuːsk oʊ —AmSp ['kus ko]
CV ˌsiː 'viː ~s, ~'s z
CVA ˌsiː viː 'eɪ ~s, ~'s z
cwm, Cwm kʊm kuːm —Welsh [kʊm] cwms
    kʊmz kuːmz
    (ₗ)Cwm 'Rhondda
Cwmbran, Cwmbrân kʊm 'brɑːn kuːm-
Cwmyoy kʊm 'jɔɪ
cwt —see hundredweight
Cy saɪ
cy pres, cy près ˌsiː 'preɪ ˌsaɪ-
-cy si — bankruptcy 'bæŋk rʌpts i -rəpts-
cyan 'saɪ‿ən -æn
cyanamid saɪ 'æn əm ɪd §-əd; 'saɪ‿ən-
cyanamide saɪ 'æn ə maɪd -əm ɪd, §-əm əd;
    'saɪ‿ən- ‖ -əm əd
cyanate 'saɪ‿ə neɪt ~s s
cyanic saɪ 'æn ɪk
cyanide 'saɪ‿ə naɪd ~s z
cyano 'saɪ‿ə nəʊ saɪ 'æn əʊ ‖ 'saɪ ə noʊ
cyanogen saɪ 'æn ədʒ ən -ɪn, -en
cyanosis ˌsaɪ‿ə 'nəʊs ɪs §-əs ‖ -'noʊs-
Cybele 'sɪb əl i -ɪl-
cybercafe, cybercafé 'saɪb ə ˌkæf eɪ -i
    ‖ -ər kæ ˌfeɪ ˌ•••'• ~s z
cybernetic ˌsaɪb ə 'net ɪk ◄ -ər 'net̬- ~ally əl_i
    ~s s
cyber|punk 'saɪb ə |pʌŋk ‖ -ər- ~punks pʌŋks
cyberspace 'saɪb ə speɪs ‖ -ər-
cyborg 'saɪb ɔːg ‖ -ɔːrg ~s z
cycad 'saɪk æd -əd ~s z
Cyclades 'sɪk lə diːz
cyclamate 'saɪk lə meɪt 'sɪk- ~s s
cyclamen 'sɪk ləm ən 'saɪk-, -lə men ~s z
cycle 'saɪk əl —In the senses 'bicycle', 'ride a
    bicycle' only, there is also an AmE
    pronunciation 'sɪk- cycled 'saɪk əld cycles
    'saɪk əlz cycling 'saɪk əl_ɪŋ
    'cycle track
cyclic 'saɪk lɪk 'sɪk-

CYCLICAL

cyclical 'sɪk lɪk əl 'saɪk- —BrE 1988 poll panel
    preference: 'sɪk- 58%, 'saɪk- 42%. ~ly _i
cycling 'saɪk lɪŋ
cyclist 'saɪk lɪst §-ləst ~s s
cyclo- comb. form
    with stress-neutral suffix ˌsaɪk ləʊ ˌsɪk ləʊ
    ‖ -loʊ — cyclohexane ˌsaɪk ləʊ 'heks eɪn
    ˌsɪk- ‖ -loʊ-

with stress-imposing suffix saɪ 'klɒ+ ‖ -'klɑː+
    — cyclometer saɪ 'klɒm ɪt ə -ət-
    ‖ -'klɑːm ət̬ ər
cyclo-cross 'saɪk ləʊ krɒs -krɔːs ‖ -loʊ krɔːs
    -krɑːs
cycloid 'saɪk lɔɪd ~s z
cyclometer saɪ 'klɒm ɪt ə -ət- ‖ -'klɑːm ət̬ ər
    ~s z
cyclone 'saɪk ləʊn ‖ -loʊn ~s z
cyclonic saɪ 'klɒn ɪk ‖ -'klɑːn- ~al əl
cyclopaedia ˌsaɪk ləʊ 'piːd i‿ə ‖ ˌ•lə- ~s z
cyclopaedic ˌsaɪk ləʊ 'piːd ɪk ◄ ‖ -lə- ~ally əl_i
Cyclopean, c~ ˌsaɪk ləʊ 'piː‿ən ◄
    saɪ 'kləʊp i‿ən ‖ -lə-
cyclopedia ˌsaɪk ləʊ 'piːd i‿ə ‖ ˌ•lə- ~s z
cyclopedic ˌsaɪk ləʊ 'piːd ɪk ◄ ‖ -lə- ~ally əl_i
cyclopes, C~ saɪ 'kləʊp iːz ‖ -'kloʊp-
cyclops, C~ 'saɪk lɒps ‖ -lɑːps
cyclorama ˌsaɪk ləʊ 'rɑːm ə ‖ -lə 'ræm ə
    -'rɑːm- ~s z
cyclosporin ˌsaɪk ləʊ 'spɔːr ɪn §-ən ‖ -loʊ-
    -'spoʊr-
cyclostyl|e 'saɪk ləʊ staɪəl ‖ -lə- ~ed d ~es z
    ~ing ɪŋ
cyclothym|ia ˌsaɪk ləʊ 'θaɪm i‿ə ˌsɪk- ‖ ˌ•lə-
    ~ic ɪk ◄
cyclotron 'saɪk ləʊ trɒn ‖ -lə traːn ~s z
cyder 'saɪd ə ‖ -ər ~s z
Cydrax tdmk 'saɪdr æks
Cyfeiliog kə 'vaɪl ɪ ɒg ‖ -ɑːg -ɔːg —Welsh
    [kə 'vəil jog]
cygnet 'sɪg nət -nɪt (= signet) ~s s
Cygnus 'sɪg nəs
cylinder 'sɪl ɪnd ə -ənd- ‖ -ər ~s z
cylindrical sə 'lɪndr ɪk əl sɪ-, -ək- ~ly _i
cyma 'saɪm ə
cymbal 'sɪm bəl (= symbol) ~s z
cymbalist 'sɪm bəl ɪst §-əst ~s s
cymbalo 'sɪm bə ləʊ ‖ -loʊ ~s z
Cymbeline 'sɪm bə liːn -bɪ-
cymbidium sɪm 'bɪd i‿əm ~s z
cyme saɪm cymes saɪmz
Cymric 'kɪm rɪk 'kʌm-
Cymru, Cymry 'kʌm ri △'kʊm-, 'kɪm- —Other
    pronunciations may be heard from those
    unfamiliar with Welsh. —Welsh ['kəm ri, -ri]
    (in Welsh these two words are homophones)
    ˌCymru am 'byth æm 'bɪθ —Welsh [am 'bɪθ,
    -'bɪːθ]
Cynan 'kʌn ən —Welsh ['kə nan]
Cynara 'sɪn ər ə sɪ 'nɑːr ə
Cyncoed kɪn 'kɔɪd →kɪŋ-
Cynewulf 'kɪn ɪ wʊlf -ə-
cynghanedd kəŋ 'hæn eð kʌŋ-, -'hɑːn-
    —Welsh [kəŋ 'ha neð]
cynic, Cynic 'sɪn ɪk ~s s
cynical 'sɪn ɪk əl ~ly _i ~ness nəs nɪs
cynicism 'sɪn ɪ ˌsɪz əm -ə-
Cynon 'kʌn ən —Welsh ['kə nɒn]
cynosure 'saɪn ə sjʊə 'sɪn-, -zjʊə, -ʃʊə, -ʒʊə
    ‖ -ʃʊr ~s z
Cynthia 'sɪntθ i‿ə
cypher 'saɪf ə ‖ -ər ~s z

cy pres, cy près ˌsiː ˈpreɪ ˌsaɪ-
cypress ˈsaɪp rəs -rɪs **~es** ɪz əz
Cyprian ˈsɪp ri_ən
Cypriot ˈsɪp ri_ət **~s** s
Cypriote ˈsɪp ri əʊt ‖ -oʊt **~s** s
cypripedium ˌsɪp rɪ ˈpiːd i_əm ˌ•rə- **~s** z
Cyprus ˈsaɪp rəs
Cyrano de Bergerac ˌsɪr ə nəʊ də ˈbɜːʒ ə ræk
  -ˈbeəʒ- ‖ -noʊ də ˈbɝːʒə- -rɑːk —Fr
  [si ʁa nod bɛʁ ʒə ʁak]
Cyrenaic ˌsaɪᵊr ə ˈneɪ ɪk ◄ ˌsɪr-, -ɪ- ‖ ˌsɪr-
Cyrenaica ˌsaɪᵊr ə ˈneɪ ɪk ə ˌsɪr-, -ɪ-, -ˈnaɪ-
  ‖ ˌsɪr-
Cyrene saɪᵊ ˈriːn i
Cyrenian saɪᵊ ˈriːn i_ən **~s** z
Cyriac ˈsɪr i æk
Cyriax ˈsɪr i æks
Cyril ˈsɪr əl -ɪl
Cyrillic sə ˈrɪl ɪk sɪ-, kɪ-
Cyrus ˈsaɪᵊr əs
cyst sɪst **cysts** sɪsts
-cyst sɪst — **otocyst** ˈəʊt əʊ sɪst ‖ ˈoʊt̬ oʊ-
cystectom|y sɪ ˈstekt əm |i **~ies** iz
cysteine ˈsɪst i iːn -ɪn; ˈsɪst eɪn ‖ -ə-
cystic ˈsɪst ɪk
cystine ˈsɪst iːn -ɪn
cystitis sɪ ˈstaɪt ɪs §-əs ‖ -ˈstaɪt̬-
cysto- comb. form
  with stress-neutral suffix ¦sɪst ə — **cystoscope**
  ˈsɪst ə skəʊp ‖ -skoʊp
  with stress-imposing suffix sɪ ˈstɒ+ sə-
  ‖ -ˈstɑː+ — **cystoscopy**
  sɪ ˈstɒsk əp i ‖ -ˈstɑːsk-

Cythera sɪ ˈθɪər ə sə- ‖ -ˈθɪr ə
Cytherea ˌsɪθ ə ˈriː_ə
-cyte saɪt — **leucocyte** ˈluːk ə saɪt ˈljuːk-
cyto- comb. form
  with stress-neutral suffix ¦saɪt əʊ ‖ ¦saɪt̬ ə -oʊ
   — **cytolytic** ˌsaɪt əʊ ˈlɪt ɪk ◄ ‖ ˌsaɪt̬ ə ˈlɪt̬-
  with stress-imposing suffix saɪ ˈtɒ+ ‖ -ˈtɑː+ —
cytolysis saɪ ˈtɒl əs ɪs -ɪs-, §-əs ‖ -ˈtɑːl-
cytogenetic ˌsaɪt əʊ dʒə ˈnet ɪk ◄ -dʒɪˈ•-
  ‖ ˌsaɪt̬ oʊ dʒə ˈnet̬- **~s** s **~ally** əl_i **~s** s
cytological ˌsaɪt ə ˈlɒdʒ ɪk əl ◄ ‖ ˌsaɪt̬ ə ˈlɑːdʒ-
  ~ly _i
cytologist saɪ ˈtɒl ədʒ ɪst §-əst ‖ -ˈtɑːl- **~s** s
cytology saɪ ˈtɒl ədʒ i ‖ -ˈtɑːl-
cytomegalovirus ˌsaɪt əʊ ˈmeg ə ləʊ ˌvaɪᵊr əs
  -əl əʊ- ‖ ˌsaɪt̬ ə ˈmeg ə loʊ-
cytoplasm ˈsaɪt əʊ ˌplæz əm ‖ ˈsaɪt̬ ə-
cytoplasmic ˌsaɪt əʊ ˈplæz mɪk ◄ ‖ ˌsaɪt̬ ə-
cytosine ˈsaɪt əʊ siːn ‖ ˈsaɪt̬ ə-
cytotoxic ˌsaɪt əʊ ˈtɒks ɪk ◄ ‖ ˌsaɪt̬ ə ˈtɑːks-
cytotoxin ˌsaɪt əʊ ˈtɒks ɪn §-ᵊn
  ‖ ˌsaɪt̬ ə ˈtɑːks- ᵊn **~s** z
czar zɑː tsɑː ‖ zɑːr tsɑːr **czars** zɑːz tsɑːz
  ‖ zɑːrz tsɑːrz
czardas ˈtʃɑːd æʃ -ɑːʃ; ˈzɑːd əs ‖ ˈtʃɑːrd ɑːʃ
  —Hung csárdás [ˈtʃɑːr daːʃ]
czardom ˈzɑː dəm ˈtsɑː- ‖ ˈzɑːr- ˈtsɑːr-
czarina zɑː ˈriːn ə tsɑː- **~s** z
Czech tʃek (= check) **Czechs** tʃeks
Czechoslovak ˌtʃek əʊ
  ˈsləʊv æk ◄ ‖ -oʊ ˈsloʊv- -əˌ, -ɑːk **~s** s
Czechoslovaki|a ˌtʃek əʊ sləʊ ˈvæk i_|ə -ˈvɑːk-
  ‖ -ə sloʊ ˈvɑːk- -ˈvæk- **~an/s** ən/z

Dd

d	Spelling-to-sound

1 Where the spelling is **d**, the pronunciation is regularly d, as in **dead** ded.

2 Where the spelling is double **dd**, the pronunciation is again d, as in **middle** 'mɪd ᵊl.

3 Less frequently, the pronunciation is dʒ, as in **gradual** 'grædʒ u‿əl, **procedure** prə 'siːdʒ ə ‖ -ᵊr. This pronunciation comes about through yod coalescence (see ASSIMILATION), and applies only where the spelling is **du**, most typically where **u** counts as a weak vowel.

4 The verb ending **-ed** has three regular pronunciations (see alphabetic entry at **-ed**). Note that after a voiceless consonant the pronunciation is regularly t, as in **clapped** klæpt.

5 **d** is usually silent in **sandwich** and **Wednesday**.

D, d diː **D's, d's, Ds** diːz —*Communications code name:* Delta

-d —*see* **-ed**

-'d d —*This contracted form of* had *and* would *is used only after words (usually pronouns) ending in a vowel sound:* he'd hiːd, I'd aɪd, she'd ʃiːd, they'd ðeɪd, we'd wiːd, you'd juːd, who'd huːd, Joe'd dʒəʊd ‖ dʒoʊd. *After a word ending in a consonant the spelling* 'd *implies merely a weak form,* əd : it'd ɪt əd ‖ ɪt̬ əd. *The occasional contracted form of* did *(esp. AmE) is pronounced in the same way.*

d' d —*This contracted form of* do *is found principally in* d'you djuː, →dʒuː, dʒə

da *in Italian phrases* daː: də —*It* [da] —*See also phrases with this word*

DA ˌdiː 'eɪ

dab dæb **dabbed** dæbd **dabbing** 'dæb ɪŋ **dabs** dæbz

ˌdab 'hand

dabbl|e 'dæb ᵊl **~ed** d **~er/s** ‿ə/z ‖ ‿ᵊr/z **~es** z **~ing** ‿ɪŋ

dabchick 'dæb tʃɪk **~s** s

D'Abernon 'dæb ən ən 'daːb- ‖ -ᵊrn-

dabster 'dæb stə ‖ -stᵊr **~s** z

da capo daː 'kaːp əʊ də- ‖ -oʊ —*It* [dak 'kaː po]

Dacca 'dæk ə —*see* Dhaka

dace deɪs **daces** 'deɪs ɪz -əz

dacha 'dætʃ ə ‖ 'daːtʃ ə —*Russ* ['da tʃə] **~s** z

Dachau 'dæk aʊ 'dæx- ‖ 'daːk- —*Ger* ['dax aʊ]

dachshund 'dæks ᵊnd 'dæʃ-, -hʊnd, -hʊnt ‖ 'daːks hʊnd —*Ger* ['daks hʊnt] **~s** z

Dacia 'deɪs i‿ə 'deɪʃ ə, 'deɪʃ i‿ə

Dacian 'deɪs i‿ən 'deɪʃ ᵊn, 'deɪʃ i‿ən **~s** z

dacoit də 'kɔɪt **~s** s

Dacre 'deɪk ə ‖ -ᵊr

dacron, D~ *tdmk* 'dæk rɒn 'deɪk- ‖ 'deɪk raːn 'dæk-

dactyl 'dækt ɪl -ᵊl **~s** z

dactylic dæk 'tɪl ɪk **~ally** ᵊl‿i

dactylogram dæk 'tɪl ə græm **~s** z

dactylographic dæk ˌtɪl ə 'græf ɪk ◂

dactylography ˌdækt ɪ 'lɒg rəf i ˌ•ə- ‖ -'laːg-

-dactylous 'dækt ɪl əs -ᵊl- — **polydactylous** ˌpɒl i 'dækt ɪl əs ◂ -ᵊl əs ‖ ˌpaːl-

dad, Dad dæd **dads, Dad's** dædz

dada, Dada 'daːd aː

dadaism, D~ 'daːd aːʳ ˌɪz əm ‖ -aː-

dadaist, D~ 'daːd aːʳ ɪst §-əst ‖ -aː- **~s** s

dadaistic, D~ ˌdaːd aːʳ 'ɪst ɪk ◂ ‖ -aː-

daddy, Daddy 'dæd i **daddies, Daddy's** 'dæd iz

ˌdaddy 'longlegs 'lɒŋ legz ‖ 'lɔːŋ- 'laːŋ-

Dade deɪd

dado 'deɪd əʊ ‖ -oʊ **~s** z

Daedalus 'diːd ᵊl əs ‖ 'ded- (*)

daemon 'diːm ən 'daɪm-, 'deɪm- **~s** z

daemonic dɪ 'mɒn ɪk də-, diː- ‖ -'maːn- **~ally** ᵊl‿i

Daewoo 'deɪ uː ‖ ˌdaɪ 'wuː —*Korean* [dɛ u]

DAF, Daf *tdmk* dæf

daff, Daff dæf **daffs** dæfs

daffodil 'dæf ə dɪl **~s** z

daff|y, Daffy 'dæf |i **~ier** i‿ə ‖ i‿ᵊr **~iest** i‿ɪst i‿əst

daft dɑːft §dæft ‖ dæft **dafter** 'dɑːft ə §'dæft-
‖ 'dæft ər **daftest** 'dɑːft ɪst §'dæft-, -əst
‖ 'dæft-
daft|ly 'dɑːft |li §'dæft- ‖ 'dæft- **~ness** nəs nɪs
Dafydd 'dæv ɪð 'dɑːv- —*Also sometimes* 'dæf-,
-ɪd *by those not familiar with Welsh.* —*Welsh*
['da vɪð, -vɪð]
Dafydd ap 'Gwilym æp 'gwɪl ɪm ɑːp-
dag dæg **dags** dægz
da Gama də 'gɑːm ə ‖ -'gæm- —*Port*
[dɐ 'ɣɐ mɐ]
Dagenham 'dæg ən̩ əm
Dagestan ˌdɑːg ɪ 'stɑːn -ə-
Dagg dæg
dagga 'dæx ə 'dæg-, 'dʌx-, 'dɑːg-
dagger 'dæg ə ‖ -ər **~s** z
Daggett 'dæg ɪt §-ət
dagg|y 'dæg |i **~ier** i ̯ə ‖ i ̯ər **~iest** i ̯ɪst i ̯əst
Daglish 'dæg lɪʃ
daglock 'dæg lɒk ‖ -lɑːk **~s** s
Dagmar 'dæg mɑː ‖ -mɑːr
dago 'deɪg əʊ ‖ -oʊ **-es**, **~s** z
Dagon 'deɪg ɒn -ən ‖ -ɑːn
daguerreotype, daguerrotype də 'ger əʊ
taɪp ‖ -ə- **~s** s
Dagwood 'dæg wʊd
Dahl dɑːl
dahlia, D~ 'deɪl i ̯ə ‖ 'dæl jə 'dɑːl- (*) **~s** z
Dahomey də 'həʊm i ‖ -'hoʊm i
Dahrendorf 'dær ən dɔːf 'dɑːr- ‖ -dɔːrf —*Ger*
['daː ʁən dɔʁf]
Dai daɪ
Daiches (i) 'deɪʃ ɪz -əz, -ɪs, -əs, (ii) 'deɪtʃ-, (iii)
'daɪx-
Daihatsu *tdmk* daɪ 'hæts uː ‖ -'hɑːts- —*Jp*
[da,i ha tsɯ]
Dail, Dáil dɔɪəl dɔːl, daɪəl —*Irish* [dɑːlʲ]
Dail 'Eireann, Dáil 'Éireann 'eər
ən ‖ 'eɪ rən 'er- —*Irish* ['eː rʲən]
dail|y 'deɪl li **~ies** iz
daily 'bread
Daimler 'deɪm lə ‖ -lər —*Ger* ['daɪm lɐ] **~s** z
daimon 'daɪm ɒn -ən ‖ -oʊn
daimyo 'daɪm jəʊ ‖ -joʊ —*Jp* [da,i 'mjoo]
daint|y, D~ 'deɪnt li i ‖ 'deɪnt̬ li **~ier** i ̯ə ‖ i ̯ər
~ies iz **~iest** i ̯ɪst i ̯əst **~ily** ɪ li əl i **~iness**
i nəs i nɪs
daiquiri, D~ 'daɪk ər i 'dæk-, -ɪr- **~s** z
dair|y 'deər li i ‖ 'der li 'dær- **~ies** iz
'dairy ˌcattle; 'dairy ˌfarmer
Dairylea *tdmk* ˌdeər i 'liː ◀ '•••' ‖ ˌder-
dairymaid 'deər i meɪd ‖ 'der- 'dær- **~s** z
dairy|man 'deər i |mən -mæn ‖ 'der- 'dær-
~men mən men
dais 'deɪ ɪs §-əs; deɪs ‖ 'daɪ- **daises** 'deɪ ɪs ɪz
§-əs-, -əz; 'deɪs ɪz, -əz ‖ 'daɪ-
daisy, Daisy 'deɪz i **daisies, Daisy's** 'deɪz iz
'daisy ˌchain; 'daisy ˌwheel
Daiwa *tdmk* 'daɪ wɑː —*Jp* [da,i ɯa]
dak dɑːk dɔːk, dæk —*Hindi* [d̪ɑːk]
Dakar 'dæk ɑː -ə ‖ də 'kɑːr —*Fr* [da kaːʁ]
Dakin 'deɪk ɪn §-ən
Dakota də 'kəʊt ə ‖ -'koʊt̬ ə **~s** z

Dakotan də 'kəʊt ən ‖ -'koʊt̬- **~s** z
DAKS *tdmk* dæks
dal *'pulse'* dɑːl
dal *in Italian phrases* dæl dɑːl ‖ dɑːl —*It* [dal]
Dalai Lama ˌdæl aɪ 'lɑːm ə ˌdɑːl- ‖ ˌdɑːl-
Dalaman 'dæl ə mæn ˌ•'•• —*Turkish*
[dɑ lɑ 'man]
dalasi də 'lɑːs i
Dalbeattie dæl 'biːt i dəl- ‖ -'biːt̬ i —*locally*
dəl-
Dalberg 'dæl bɜːg ‖ -bɜːrg
Dalby (i) 'dɔːl bi 'dɒl- ‖ 'dɑːl-, (ii) 'dæl bi
dale, Dale deɪəl **dales, Dales** deɪəlz
Dalek 'dɑːl ek **~s** s
dales|man 'deɪəlz |mən -mæn **~men** mən men
~woman ˌwʊm ən **~women** ˌwɪm ɪn §-ən
Daley 'deɪl i
Dalgarno dæl 'gɑːn əʊ ‖ -'gɑːrn oʊ
Dalgetty, Dalgety ˌ(ˌ)dæl 'get i dəl- ‖ -'get̬ i
Dalgleish, Dalglish dæl 'gliːʃ dəl-
Dalhousie (i) dæl 'haʊz i, (ii) -'huːz i —(i) *is*
appropriate for the current Earl of D~. The
19th-century governor of Canada is often
referred to as (ii).
Dali 'dɑːl i —*Sp* Dalí [da 'li], *Catalan* [də 'li]
Dalian ˌdɑː li 'æn —*Chi* Dàlián [⁴da ²ljɛn]
Dalkeith dæl 'kiːθ
Dalkey 'dɔːk i 'dɔːlk- ‖ 'dɔːlk i 'dɑːlk i
Dallaglio də 'læl i əʊ ‖ -oʊ -'lɑːl-
Dallapiccola ˌdæl ə 'pɪk əl ə —*It*
[dal la 'pik ko la]
Dallas 'dæl əs
Dallasite 'dæl ə saɪt **~s** s
Dalles dælz
dalliance 'dæl i ̯ən̩ts **~es** ɪz əz
Dalloway 'dæl ə weɪ
dall|y 'dæl li **~ied** id **~ies** iz
Dalmatia dæl 'meɪʃ ə -'meɪʃ i ̯ə
dalmatian, D~ dæl 'meɪʃ ən̩ -'meɪʃ i ̯ən **~s** z
dalmatic dæl 'mæt ɪk ‖ -'mæt̬- **~s** s
Dalmeny dæl 'men i dəl-
Dalry dəl 'raɪ dæl-
Dalrymple dæl 'rɪmp əl, '•••, dəl 'rɪmp-
dal segno ˌ(ˌ)dæl 'sen jəʊ ˌ(ˌ)dɑːl-
‖ ˌ(ˌ)dɑːl 'seɪn joʊ —*It* [dal 'seɲ ɲo]
Dalston 'dɔːlst ən 'dɒlst- ‖ 'dɑːlst-
Dalton, d~ 'dɔːlt ən 'dɒlt- ‖ 'dɑːlt- **~ism** ˌɪz
əm
Daltrey, Daltry 'dɔːltr i 'dɒltr- ‖ 'dɑːltr-
Dalwhinnie dæl 'wɪn i dəl-, -'hwɪn- ‖ -'hwɪn i
—*locally* dəl 'hwɪn i
Daly 'deɪl i
Dalyell (i) di 'el daɪ-, (ii) 'dæl jəl
Dalzell (i) di 'el, (ii) 'dæl zel
Dalziel (i) di 'el, (ii) 'dæl ziːəl
dam dæm **dammed** dæmd **damming**
'dæm ɪŋ **dams** dæmz
damag|e 'dæm ɪdʒ **~ed** d **~es** ɪz əz **~ing/ly**
ɪŋ /li
Daman 'deɪm ən
Damara də 'mɑːr ə **~s** z
Damaraland də 'mɑːr ə lænd
Damart *tdmk* 'dæm ɑːt 'deɪm- ‖ -ɑːrt

damascene, D~ 'dæm ə siːn ˌ•• '• ~**dd** ~**s** z
Damascus də 'mæsk əs -'mɑːsk- —*Arabic*
  Dimashq [di 'maʃq]
damask 'dæm əsk ~**ed** t ~**s** s
D'Amato də 'mɑːt əʊ ‖ -oʊ
dame, Dame deɪm **dames** deɪmz
Damen 'deɪm ən
Damian, Damien, Damion 'deɪm i‿ən —*As a*
  French name, Damien *is* [da mjæ̃]
damm... —*see* **dam**
dammar 'dæm ə ‖ -ər
dammit 'dæm ɪt §-ət
damn dæm (= *dam*) **damned** dæmd
  damning 'dæm ɪŋ -nɪŋ **damns** dæmz
damnab|le 'dæm nəb |əl ~**ly** li
damnation ₍ᵢ₎dæm 'neɪʃ ᵊn
damnedest 'dæmd ɪst -əst
Damoclean ˌdæm ə 'kliː‿ən ◂
Damocles 'dæm ə kliːz
Damon 'deɪm ən
damosel, damozel ˌdæm ə 'zel ~**s** z
damp dæmp **damped** dæmpt **damper**
  'dæmp ə ‖ -ər **dampest** 'dæmp ɪst -əst
  damping 'dæmp ɪŋ **damps** dæmps
  '**damp course**; ˌ**damp 'squib**
dampen 'dæmp ən ~**ed** d ~**ing** ɪŋ ~**s** z
damper, D~ 'dæmp ə ‖ -ər ~**s** z
Dampier 'dæmp i‿ə 'dæmp ɪə ‖ -ər
dampish 'dæmp ɪʃ
damp|ly 'dæmp |li ~**ness** nəs nɪs
damp-proof 'dæmp pruːf §-pruf
damsel 'dæmz ᵊl 'dæmps ᵊl ~**s** z
damsel|fly 'dæmz ᵊl |flaɪ ~**flies** flaɪz
damson 'dæmz ᵊn ~**s** z
Dan dæn
dan dæn —*Jp* ['daɴ]
Dana (i) 'dɑːn ə, (ii) 'deɪn ə, (iii) 'dæn ə
  —*Generally (i) in BrE, (ii) in AmE.*
Danae, Danaë 'dæn i‿iː -eɪ-
Danaides, Danaïdes də 'neɪ ɪ diːz dæ-, -ə-
Dan-Air tdmk ˌdæn 'eə ‖ -'eᵊr -'æᵊr
Da Nang ˌdɑː 'næŋ ‖ də 'nɑːŋ ₍ᵢ₎dɑː-, -'næŋ
Danaus, Danaüs 'dæn i‿əs -eɪ-
Danbury 'dæn bər‿i →'dæm- ‖ -ˌber i
Danby 'dæn bi →'dæm-
dance, Dance dɑːnᵗs §dænᵗs ‖ dænᵗs **danced**
  dɑːnᵗst §dænᵗst ‖ dænᵗst **dances** 'dɑːnᵗs ɪz
  §'dænᵗs-, -əz ‖ 'dænᵗs- **dancing/ly**
  'dɑːnᵗs ɪŋ /li §'dænᵗs- ‖ 'dænᵗs ɪŋ /li
dancer, D~ 'dɑːnᵗs ə §'dænᵗs- ‖ 'dænᵗs ər ~**s** z
Dancy 'dænᵗs i
dandelion 'dænd i laɪ‿ən '•-, -əl aɪ‿ ‖ -əl aɪ ən
  ~**s** z
Dandenong 'dænd ə nɒŋ ‖ -nɑːŋ
dander 'dænd ə ‖ -ər
Dandie 'dænd i
  ˌDandie 'Dinmont 'dɪn mənt →-'dɪm-,
  -mɒnt
dandi... —*see* **dandy**
dandi|fy 'dænd ɪ |faɪ §-ə- ~**fied** faɪd ~**fier/s**
  faɪ‿ə/z ‖ faɪ‿ər/z ~**fies** faɪz ~**fying** faɪ ɪŋ
Dandini dæn 'diːn i
dandl|e 'dænd ᵊl ~**ed** d ~**es** z ~**ing** ɪŋ

Dando 'dænd əʊ ‖ -oʊ
dandruff 'dændr əf -ʌf
dand|y, Dandy 'dænd |i ~**ies** iz
Dane deɪn **Danes** deɪnz
Danegeld 'deɪn geld →'deɪŋ-
Danelagh, Danelaw 'deɪn lɔː ‖ -lɑː
dang dæŋ
danger 'deɪndʒ ə ‖ -ər ~**s** z
  'danger ˌmoney
Dangerfield 'deɪndʒ ə fiːᵊld ‖ -ər-
dangerous 'deɪndʒ ᵊr_əs ~**ly** li
dangl|e 'dæŋ gᵊl ~**ed** d ~**er/s** _ə/z ‖ _ᵊr/z ~**es**
  z ~**ing** ɪŋ
dangly 'dæŋ gli
Daniel, Daniell 'dæn jəl
Daniella ˌdæn i 'el ə dæn 'jel ə
Danielle ˌdæn i 'el dæn 'jel
Daniels 'dæn jᵊlz
danio, Danio 'deɪn i‿əʊ ‖ -oʊ
Danish, d~ 'deɪn ɪʃ
  ˌDanish 'blue; ˌDanish 'pastry
dank dæŋk **danker** 'dæŋk ə ‖ -ər **dankest**
  'dæŋk ɪst -əst **dankly** 'dæŋk li **dankness**
  'dæŋk nəs -nɪs
Dankworth 'dæŋk wɜːθ -wəθ ‖ -wᵊrθ
Dannie 'dæn i
Dannimac tdmk 'dæn i mæk
d'Annunzio dæ 'nʊnᵗs i‿əʊ ‖ dɑː 'nʊnᵗs i oʊ
  —*It* [dan 'nun tsjo]
Danny 'dæn i
Dano-Norwegian ˌdeɪn əʊ nɔː 'wiːdʒ
  ən ◂ ‖ -oʊ nɔːr-
danse dɒnᵗs dɑːnᵗs ‖ dɑːnᵗs —*Fr* [dɑ̃ːs]
danseur ₍ᵢ₎dɒn 'sɜː ₍ᵢ₎dɑːn- ‖ ₍ᵢ₎dɑːn 'sʊᵊr -'sɜː
  —*Fr* [dɑ̃ sœːʁ] ~**s** z
danseuse ₍ᵢ₎dɒn 'sɜːz ₍ᵢ₎dɑːn- ‖ ₍ᵢ₎dɑːn 'suːz
  -'sʊz —*Fr* [dɑ̃ søːz] ~**s** *same pronunciation*
Dante 'dænt i 'dɑːnt-, -eɪ 'dɑːnt eɪ —*It*
  ['dan te]
Dantean 'dænt i‿ən 'dɑːnt-; dæn 'tiː‿ən, dɑːn-
  ~**s** z
Dantesque ₍ᵢ₎dæn 'tesk ₍ᵢ₎dɑːn-
Danton 'dænt ɒn -ən; dɔ̃ 'tɔ̃ -ᵊn ˌdɑːn 'toʊn
  —*Fr* [dɑ̃ tɔ̃]
Danube 'dæn juːb
Danubian dæ 'njuːb i‿ən də-
Danvers 'dæn vəz ‖ -vᵊrz
Danville 'dæn vɪl -vᵊl
Danzig 'dænts ɪg -ɪk —*Ger* ['dan tsɪç], *Polish*
  Gdańsk [gdaˈjsk]
Danziger 'dænts ɪg ə ‖ -ər
dap dæp **daps** dæps
daphne, D~ 'dæf ni
daphnia 'dæf ni‿ə
Daphnis 'dæf nɪs §-nəs
dapper 'dæp ə ‖ -ər ~**ly** li ~**ness** nəs nɪs
dappl|e 'dæp ᵊl ~**ed** d ~**es** z ~**ing** ɪŋ
dapple-gray, dapple-grey ˌdæp ᵊl 'greɪ ◂
dapsone 'dæps əʊn ‖ -oʊn
Dar dɑː ‖ dɑːr —*See also phrases with this word*
DAR ˌdiː‿eɪ 'ɑː ‖ -'ɑːr
Darbishire 'dɑːb i ʃə -ʃɪə ‖ 'dɑːrb i ʃᵊr -ʃɪr
d'Arblay 'dɑːb leɪ ‖ 'dɑːrb-

D

Darby 'dɑːb i ‖ 'dɑːrb i
  ,Darby and 'Joan club
d'Arc dɑːk ‖ dɑːrk
Darcus 'dɑːk əs ‖ 'dɑːrk-
Darcy, D'Arcy 'dɑːs i ‖ 'dɑːrs i
Dardanelles ,dɑːd ə 'nelz -ən 'elz
  ‖ ,dɑːrd ən 'elz
Dardanus 'dɑːd ən əs ‖ 'dɑːrd-
Dardic 'dɑːd ɪk ‖ 'dɑːrd-
dare, Dare deə ‖ deər dæər **dared**
  deəd ‖ deərd dæərd **dares** deəz ‖ deərz
  dæərz **daring** 'deər ɪŋ ‖ 'der ɪŋ 'dær-
daredevil 'deə ,dev əl ‖ 'der- 'dær- ~ry ri ~s z
Darent 'dær ənt ‖ 'der-
daren't deənt §'deər ənt ‖ 'der ənt 'dær-
Darenth 'dær ənᵗθ ‖ 'der-
daresay ,deə 'seɪ ◄ 'des eɪ ‖ ,der- ,dær- —*The*
  'des eɪ *form is not used at the end of a sentence.*
Daresbury 'dɑːz bər_i ‖ 'dɑːrz- -,ber i
Dar es Salaam, Dar-es-Salaam
  ,dɑːr es sə 'lɑːm ͵•ɪs-, ͵•ez-, ͵•ɪz-
darg dɑːg ‖ dɑːrg **dargs** dɑːgz ‖ dɑːrgz
daric 'dær ɪk ‖ 'der- ~s s
Darien 'deər i_ən 'dær- ‖ ,der i 'en ,dær-,
  ,dɑːr- —*Sp* Darién [da 'rjen]
Darin 'dær ən -ɪn ‖ 'der-
daring 'deər ɪŋ ‖ 'der- 'dær- ~ly li ~ness nəs
  nɪs
dariole 'dær i əʊl →-ɒʊl ‖ -oʊl 'der-, 'dɑːr- ~s
  z
Darius *(i)* də 'raɪ_əs, *(ii)* 'deər i_əs 'dær-
  ‖ 'der-, *(iii)* 'dɑːr- —*(i) is appropriate for the*
  ancient Persian king
Darjeeling dɑː 'dʒiːl ɪŋ ‖ dɑːr-
dark dɑːk ‖ dɑːrk **darker** 'dɑːk ə ‖ 'dɑːrk ər
  darkest 'dɑːk ɪst -əst ‖ 'dɑːrk-
  'Dark ,Ages, ͵• '• •; ,dark 'glasses; ,dark
  'horse
darken 'dɑːk ən ‖ 'dɑːrk- ~ed d ~ing _ɪŋ ~s
  z
darkey 'dɑːk i ‖ 'dɑːrk i ~s z
darkie 'dɑːk i ‖ 'dɑːrk i ~s z
darkish 'dɑːk ɪʃ ‖ 'dɑːrk-
darkling 'dɑːk lɪŋ ‖ 'dɑːrk-
dark|ly 'dɑːk |li ‖ 'dɑːrk- ~ness nəs nɪs
darkroom 'dɑːk ruːm -rʊm ‖ 'dɑːrk- ~s z
dark|y 'dɑːk |i ‖ 'dɑːrk |i ~ies iz
Darlaston 'dɑːl əst ən ‖ 'dɑːrl-
Darleen, Darlene 'dɑːl iːn ‖ ,dɑːr 'liːn
Darley 'dɑːl i ‖ 'dɑːrl i
darling, D~ 'dɑːl ɪŋ ‖ 'dɑːrl- ~s z
Darlington 'dɑːl ɪŋ tən ‖ 'dɑːrl-
Darmstadt 'dɑːm stæt ‖ 'dɑːrm- —*Ger*
  ['daʁm ʃtat]
darn dɑːn ‖ dɑːrn **darned** dɑːnd ‖ dɑːrnd
  darning 'dɑːn ɪŋ ‖ 'dɑːrn- **darns**
  dɑːnz ‖ dɑːrnz
  'darning ,needle
darnel 'dɑːn əl ‖ 'dɑːrn- ~s z
Darnley 'dɑːn li ‖ 'dɑːrn-
darner 'dɑːn ə ‖ 'dɑːrn ər ~s z
Darrel, Darrell 'dær əl ‖ 'der-
Darren, Darron 'dær ən ‖ 'der-

Darrow 'dær əʊ ‖ -oʊ 'der-
Darryl 'dær əl -ɪl ‖ 'der-
dart, Dart dɑːt ‖ dɑːrt **darted** 'dɑːt ɪd -əd
  ‖ 'dɑːrt̬ əd **darting** 'dɑːt ɪŋ ‖ 'dɑːrt̬ ɪŋ **darts**
  dɑːts ‖ dɑːrts
D'Artagnan, Dartagnan dɑː 'tæn jɒn -jən
  ‖ ,dɑːrt ən 'jɑːn —*Fr* [daʁ ta njɑ̃]
dartboard 'dɑːt bɔːd ‖ 'dɑːrt bɔːrd -boʊrd ~s
  z
darter 'dɑːt ə ‖ 'dɑːrt̬ ər ~s z
Dartford 'dɑːt fəd ‖ 'dɑːrt fərd
Darth Vader ,dɑːθ 'veɪd ə ‖ ,dɑːrθ 'veɪd ər
Dartmoor 'dɑːt mɔː -mʊə ‖ 'dɑːrt mʊr -mɔːr
Dartmouth 'dɑːt məθ ‖ 'dɑːrt-
dartre 'dɑːt ə ‖ 'dɑːrt̬ ər *(= darter)*
Darwen 'dɑː wɪn §-wən ‖ 'dɑːr- —*locally also*
  'dær ən
Darwin 'dɑː wɪn §-wən ‖ 'dɑːr-
Darwinian dɑː 'wɪn i_ən ‖ dɑːr- ~s z
Darwinism 'dɑː wɪn ,ɪz əm -wən- ‖ 'dɑːr-
Daryll 'dær əl -ɪl ‖ 'der-
dash, Dash dæʃ **dashed** dæʃt **dashes** 'dæʃ ɪz
  -əz **dashing** 'dæʃ ɪŋ
dashboard 'dæʃ bɔːd ‖ -bɔːrd -boʊrd ~s z
dasheen dæ 'ʃiːn 'dæʃ iːn
dashiki də 'ʃiːk i dɑː-, dæ- ~s z
dashing 'dæʃ ɪŋ ~ly li ~ness nəs nɪs
dashpot 'dæʃ pɒt ‖ -pɑːt ~s s
Dashwood 'dæʃ wʊd
dassie 'dæs i 'dʌs i ~s z
dastardly 'dæst əd li 'dɑːst- ‖ -ᵊrd-
dasyure 'dæs i jʊə 'dæz- ‖ -jʊr ~s z
DAT dæt ,diː eɪ 'tiː

DATA

BrE	■'deɪt ə	▨'dɑːt ə	▥'dæt ə
AmE	■'deɪt̬ ə	■'dæt̬ ə	▨'dɑːt̬ ə

BrE 1988					
AmE 1993					
0	20	40	60	80	100%

---

data 'deɪt ə 'dɑːt ə, §'dæt ə ‖ 'deɪt̬ ə 'dæt̬ ə,
  'dɑːt̬ ə —*Poll panel preferences: BrE 1988*,
  'deɪt ə 92%, 'dɑːt ə 6%, 'dæt ə 2%; *AmE*
  1993, 'deɪt̬ ə 64%, 'dæt̬ ə 35%, 'dɑːt̬ ə 1%.
  'data bus; 'data ,capture; ,data
  'processing
databank 'deɪt ə bæŋk 'dɑːt- ‖ 'deɪt̬- 'dæt̬-,
  'dɑːt̬- ~s s
database 'deɪt ə beɪs 'dɑːt- ‖ 'deɪt̬- 'dæt̬-,
  'dɑːt̬- ~es ɪz əz
datafile 'deɪt ə faɪᵊl 'dɑːt- ‖ 'deɪt̬- 'dæt̬-, 'dɑːt̬-
  ~s z
Datapost *tdmk* 'deɪt ə pəʊst 'dɑːt-
  ‖ 'deɪt̬ ə poʊst 'dæt̬-, 'dɑːt̬-
Datchet 'dætʃ ɪt §-ət
date deɪt **dated** 'deɪt ɪd -əd ‖ 'deɪt̬ əd **dates**
  deɪts **dating** 'deɪt ɪŋ ‖ 'deɪt̬ ɪŋ
  'date palm; 'dating ,agency
dateline 'deɪt laɪn ~d d ~s z
date-stamp 'deɪt stæmp ~ed t ~ing ɪŋ ~s s
datival də 'taɪv əl deɪ- ~ly i ~s z
dative 'deɪt ɪv ‖ 'deɪt̬- ~s z

Datsun *tdmk* 'dæts ᵊn ‖ 'dɑːts- —*Jp*
[dat 'to saṇ] ~s z
datum 'deɪt əm 'dɑːt- ‖ 'deɪṭ- 'dæṭ-, 'dɑːṭ-
datura də 'tjʊər ə ‖ -'tʊr- -'tjʊr- ~s z
daub dɔːb ‖ dɑːb **daubed** dɔːbd ‖ dɑːbd
   daubs dɔːbz ‖ dɑːbz **daubing** 'dɔːb ɪŋ
   ‖ 'dɑːb-
daube dəʊb ‖ doʊb —*Fr* [doːb] ~s z
Daubeney, Daubney 'dɔːb ni ‖ 'dɑːb-
Daudet 'dəʊd eɪ ‖ doʊ 'deɪ —*Fr* [do dɛ]
daughter 'dɔːt ə ‖ 'dɔːṭ ᵊr 'dɑːṭ- ~**ly** li ~s z
daughter-in-law 'dɔːt ər ɪn ˌlɔː →ʼdɔːtr•ˌ•,
   -ən,• ‖ 'dɔːṭ ᵊr_ən ˌlɔː 'dɑːṭ ᵊr_ən ˌlɑː ~s z
daughters-in-law 'dɔːt əz ɪn ˌlɔː -ən,•
   ‖ 'dɔːṭ ᵊrz ən ˌlɔː 'dɑːṭ ᵊrz ən ˌlɑː
daunt, Daunt dɔːnt ‖ dɑːnt **daunted** 'dɔːnt ɪd
   -əd ‖ 'dɔːnṭ əd 'dɑːnṭ- **daunting/ly**
   'dɔːnt ɪŋ /li ‖ 'dɔːnṭ ɪŋ /li 'dɑːnṭ- **daunts**
   dɔːnts ‖ dɑːnts
dauntless 'dɔːnt ləs -lɪs ‖ 'dɑːnt- ~**ly** li ~**ness**
   nəs nɪs
dauphin, D~ 'dɔːf ɪn 'dəʊf-, §-ᵊn, -æ
   ‖ doʊ 'fæn 'doʊf ᵊn —*Fr* [do fæ̃] ~s z
dauphine, D~ 'dɔːf iːn 'dəʊf- ‖ doʊ 'fiːn —*Fr*
   [do fin] ~s z
Dave deɪv
davenport, D~ 'dæv ᵊn pɔːt →ʼ-ᵊm- ‖ -pɔːrt
   -poʊrt ~s s
Daventry 'dæv ᵊntr i —*formerly also* 'deɪntr i
Davey 'deɪv i
David 'deɪv ɪd §-əd —*but as a non-English name
   also* dæ 'viːd
Davidson 'deɪv ɪd sᵊn §-əd-
Davie 'deɪv i
Davies 'deɪv ɪs §-əs, -iːz
Davina də 'viːn ə
da Vinci də 'vɪntʃ i —*It* [dav 'vin tʃi]
Davis 'deɪv ɪs §-əs
Davison 'deɪv ɪs ᵊn §-əs-
davit 'dæv ɪt 'deɪv-, §-ət ~s s
Davos dæ 'vəʊs 'dɑːv ɒs ‖ dɑː 'voʊs —*Ger*
   [da 'voːs]
Davro 'dæv rəʊ ‖ -roʊ
Davy 'deɪv i
   ˌDavy ˌJones's 'locker; 'Davy lamp
Davyhulme 'deɪv i hjuːm
daw, Daw dɔː ‖ dɑː **daws, Daw's** dɔːz ‖ dɑːz
dawdl|e 'dɔːd ᵊl ‖ 'dɑːd- ~**ed** d ~**er/s** _ə/
   z ‖ _ᵊr/z ~**es** z ~**ing/ly** _ɪŋ /li
Dawe dɔː ‖ dɑː
Dawes dɔːz ‖ dɑːz
Dawkins 'dɔːk ɪnz §-ᵊnz ‖ 'dɑːk-
Dawlish 'dɔːl ɪʃ ‖ 'dɑːl-
dawn, Dawn dɔːn ‖ dɑːn **dawned** dɔːnd
   ‖ dɑːnd **dawning** 'dɔːn ɪŋ ‖ 'dɑːn- **dawns**
   dɔːnz ‖ dɑːnz
   ˌdawn 'chorus; ˌdawn 'redwood
Dawnay 'dɔːn i ‖ 'dɑːn-
Dawson 'dɔːs ᵊn ‖ 'dɑːs-
Dax dæks
day, Day deɪ **days** deɪz
   'day bed; ˌDay 'Lewis; 'day ˌnursery; ˌday

of 'reckoning; ˌday re'lease course; ˌday
re'turn; 'day school
-day deɪ, di —*Although RP and GenAm are both
   traditionally considered to prefer* di, *most
   speakers in practice use both pronunciations for
   this suffix, often in a strong form—weak form
   relationship. The* deɪ *form is generally preferred
   in exposed positions, for example at the end of a
   sentence:* I'll do it on Monday 'mʌn deɪ; *the* di
   *form is preferred in close-knit expressions such
   as* Monday morning
   ˌmʌnd i 'mɔːn ɪŋ ‖ -'mɔːrn-.
Dayak 'daɪ æk ~s s
Dayan daɪ 'æn -'ɑːn ‖ dɑː 'jɑːn
daybook 'deɪ bʊk §-buːk ~s s
dayboy 'deɪ bɔɪ ~s z
daybreak 'deɪ breɪk
day-care 'deɪ keə ‖ -ker -kær
daydream 'deɪ driːm ~**er/s** ə/z ‖ ᵊr/z ~**ing** ɪŋ
   ~s z
daygirl 'deɪ gɜːl ‖ -gɝːl ~s z
dayglo, Day-Glo *tdmk* 'deɪ gləʊ ‖ -gloʊ
Day-Lewis ˌdeɪ 'luː_ɪs §_əs
daylight 'deɪ laɪt ~s s
   ˌdaylight 'robbery; ˌdaylight 'saving
dayroom 'deɪ ruːm -rʊm ~s z
dayspring 'deɪ sprɪŋ
daystar 'deɪ stɑː ‖ -stɑːr
daytime 'deɪ taɪm
day-to-day ˌdeɪ tə 'deɪ ◀ ‖ ˌdeɪṭ ə-
   ˌday-to-ˌday 'running
Dayton 'deɪt ᵊn
Daytona deɪ 'təʊn ə ‖ -'toʊn ə
   Dayˌtona 'Beach
Daz *tdmk* dæz
daze deɪz **dazed** deɪzd **dazes** 'deɪz ɪz -əz
   dazing 'deɪz ɪŋ
dazzl|e 'dæz ᵊl ~**ed** d ~**er/s** _ə/z ‖ ᵊr/z ~**es** z
   ~**ing/ly** _ɪŋ /li
DC ˌdiː 'siː
DC10 ˌdiː siː 'ten ~s, ~'s z
D-day 'diː deɪ
DDT ˌdiː diː 'tiː
de *in French phrases* də dɪ —*Fr* [də]
de *in Latin phrases* deɪ diː
De, de *in English family names* də
de- ˌdiː:, dɪ, də —*Attached to free forms, meaning
   'do the opposite of' or 'remove', this prefix is
   usually pronounced strong,* (ˌ)diː: (ˌde'nasalized).
   *With these meanings it is freely productive, and
   most words made this way are not included in
   the dictionary. Otherwise the prefix is usually
   weak,* dɪ (de'cide, de'pend), *with variants*
   də, §diː:; *but strong* ˌdiː+ *before an unstressed
   syllable* ('deference, ˌdere'liction).
deacon, D~ 'diːk ᵊn ~s z
deaconess ˌdiːk ə 'nes '•••; 'diːk ᵊn_ɪs, əs
   ‖ 'diːk ᵊn əs ~**es** ɪz əz
deacti|vate di 'ækt ɪ ˌveɪt ˌdiː:-, -ə- ~**vated**
   veɪt ɪd -əd ‖ veɪṭ əd ~**vates** veɪts ~**vating**
   veɪt ɪŋ ‖ veɪṭ ɪŋ
deactivation di ˌækt ɪ 'veɪʃ ᵊn ˌdiː:,•-, -ə-

dead ded **deader** 'ded ə ‖ -ᵊr **deadest**
'ded ɪst -əst
,dead 'centre; ,dead 'duck; ,dead 'end;
,dead 'heat; ,dead 'letter; ,dead 'loss;
'dead march; 'dead ,nettle; ,dead
'reckoning; ,dead 'ringer; ,Dead 'Sea◄;
,Dead Sea 'Scrolls; ,dead 'weight
dead-and-alive ,ded ən_ə 'laɪv ◄ -ᵊnd ə-
deadbeat n 'ded biːt →'deb- ~s s
dead beat adj ,ded 'biːt ◄ →,deb-
deadbolt 'ded bəʊlt →'deb-, →-bɒʊlt ‖ -boʊlt
~s s
deaden 'ded ən ~ed d ~ing _ɪŋ ~s z
deadeye 'ded aɪ
deadhead ,ded 'hed '•• ‖ '•• ~ed ɪd əd
~ing ɪŋ ~s z
deadli... —see deadly
deadlight 'ded laɪt ~s s
deadline 'ded laɪn ~s z
deadliness 'ded li nəs -nɪs
deadlock 'ded lɒk ‖ -lɑːk ~ed t ~s s
dead|ly 'ded ‖li ~lier li_ə ‖ li_ᵊr ~liest li_ɪst
li_əst
,deadly 'nightshade; ,deadly 'sin
deadman 'ded mæn →'deb-
,deadman's 'fingers
deadpan 'ded pæn →'deb-
deadwood 'ded wʊd ,•'•
deaf def **deafer** 'def ə ‖ -ᵊr **deafest** 'def ɪst
-əst
deaf-aid 'def eɪd ~s z
deaf-and-dumb ,def ən 'dʌm ◄
deafen 'def ən ~ed d ~ing _ɪŋ ~s z
deafly 'def li
deaf-mute ,def 'mjuːt ◄ ~s s
deafness 'def nəs -nɪs
Deakin 'diːk ɪn §-ən
deal, Deal diːᵊl **dealing/s** 'diːᵊl ɪŋ/z **deals**
diːᵊlz **dealt** delt (!)
dealer 'diːᵊl ə ‖ -ᵊr ~s z ~ship/s ʃɪp/s
dealt delt
dean, Dean diːn **deans, Dean's** diːnz
Deana (i) di 'æn ə, (ii) 'diːn ə
Deane (i) diːn, (ii) di 'æn
deaner|y 'diːn ər li ~ies iz
deanship 'diːn ʃɪp ~s s
dear, Dear dɪə ‖ dɪᵊr **dearer** 'dɪər ə ‖ 'dɪr ᵊr
dearest 'dɪər ɪst -əst ‖ 'dɪr- **dears**
dɪəz ‖ dɪᵊrz
Dearborn 'dɪə bɔːn -bən ‖ 'dɪr bɔːrn -bᵊrn
Deare dɪə ‖ dɪᵊr
dearie 'dɪər i ‖ 'dɪr i ~s z
Dearing 'dɪər ɪŋ ‖ 'dɪr ɪŋ
dearly 'dɪə li ‖ 'dɪr li
Dearne dɜːn ‖ dɝːn
dearness 'dɪə nəs -nɪs ‖ 'dɪr-
dearth dɜːθ ‖ dɝːθ **dearths** dɜːθs ‖ dɝːθs
deary 'dɪər i ‖ 'dɪr i
death deθ **deaths** deθs
'death camp; 'death cell; 'death
cer,tificate; 'death ,duties; 'death knell;
'death mask; 'death ,penalty; 'death rate;
'death ,rattle; 'death 'row; 'death squad;

'death tax; 'death toll; 'death trap; ,Death
'Valley; 'death ,warrant; 'death wish
DeAth, De'ath di 'æθ deɪ-, -'ɑːθ; deɪθ, deθ,
diːθ
deathbed 'deθ bed ~s z
deathblow 'deθ bləʊ ‖ -bloʊ ~s z
death-dealing 'deθ ,diːᵊl ɪŋ
deathless 'deθ ləs -lɪs ~ly li ~ness nəs nɪs
deathlike 'deθ laɪk
death|ly 'deθ ‖li ~liness li nəs -nɪs
death's-head 'deθs hed ~s z
deathwatch 'deθ wɒtʃ ‖ -wɑːtʃ ~es ɪz əz
,deathwatch 'beetle
Deauville 'dəʊ vɪl -viːᵊl ‖ 'doʊ- —Fr [do vil]
Deayton 'diːt ən
deb deb **debs** debz
debacle, débâcle deɪ 'bɑːk ᵊl di-, də-; -'bɑːkl;
'deɪb ɑːk ᵊl; △'deb ək ᵊl —Fr [de bɑːkl] ~s z
—or as sing.
debag ,diː 'bæg ~ged d ~ging ɪŋ ~s z
de|bar dɪ ‖'bɑː də-, ₍ᵢ₎diː- ‖ -ᵊ'bɑːr ~barred
'bɑːd ‖ 'bɑːrd ~barring 'bɑːr ɪŋ ~bars
'bɑːz ‖ 'bɑːrz
debark 'disembark' dɪ 'bɑːk ,diː-, də- ‖ -'bɑːrk
~ed t ~ing ɪŋ ~s s
debark 'strip the bark from (wood)', 'disable
vocal cords of (dog)' ,diː 'bɑːk ‖ -'bɑːrk ~ed t
~ing ɪŋ ~s s
debarkation ,diː bɑː 'keɪʃ ᵊn ‖ -bɑːr- ~s z
debarment dɪ 'bɑː mənt də-, ₍ᵢ₎diː- ‖ -'bɑːr-
debarr... —see debar
debas|e dɪ 'beɪs də-, §diː- ~ed t ~ement/s
mənt/s ~er/s ə/z ‖ ᵊr/z ~es ɪz əz ~ing ɪŋ
debatab|le dɪ 'beɪt əb ᵊl də-, §diː- ‖ -'beɪt̬-
~ly li
de|bate dɪ ‖'beɪt də-, §diː- ~bated 'beɪt ɪd -əd
‖ 'beɪt̬ əd ~bater/s 'beɪt ə/z ‖ 'beɪt̬ ᵊr/z
~bates 'beɪts ~bating 'beɪt ɪŋ ‖ 'beɪt̬ ɪŋ
debauch dɪ 'bɔːtʃ də-, §diː- ‖ -'bɑːtʃ ~ed t
~es ɪz əz ~ing ɪŋ
debauchee ,deb ɔː 'tʃiː -'ʃiː; dɪ ,bɔː-, də- ‖ -ɑː-
~s z
debaucher|y dɪ 'bɔːtʃ ᵊr_li də-, §diː- ‖ -'bɑːtʃ-
~ies iz
Debbie, Debby 'deb i
De Beauvoir də 'bəʊ vwɑː ‖ -,boʊ 'vwɑːr —Fr
[də bo vwaːʁ]
De Beer də 'bɪə ‖ -'bɪᵊr
Deben 'diːb ᵊn
Debenham 'deb ᵊn_əm
debenture dɪ 'bentʃ ə də-, §diː- ‖ -ᵊr ~s z
debili|tate dɪ 'bɪl ɪ ‖teɪt də-, -ə- ~tated
teɪt ɪd -əd ‖ teɪt̬ əd ~tates teɪts ~tating
teɪt ɪŋ ‖ teɪt̬ ɪŋ
debilitation dɪ ,bɪl ɪ 'teɪʃ ᵊn də-, §diː-, -ə-
debilit|y dɪ 'bɪl ət li də-, §diː-, -ɪt- ‖ -ət̬ li ~ies
iz
deb|it 'deb ‖ɪt §-ət ‖ -ət ~ited ɪt ɪd §ət-, -əd
‖ ət̬ əd ~iting ɪt ɪŋ §ət- ‖ ət̬ ɪŋ ~its ɪts §əts
‖ əts
debonair, debonaire ,deb ə 'neə ◄ ‖ -'neᵊr ◄
-'næᵊr ~ly li ~ness nəs nɪs

debon|e ˌdiː 'bəʊn ‖ -'boʊn **~ed** d **~es** z **~ing** ɪŋ

de Bono də 'bəʊn əʊ ‖ -'boʊn oʊ

Deborah 'deb ər_ə

debouch dɪ 'baʊtʃ də-, ₍ᵤ₎diː-, -'buːʃ **~ed** t **~es** ɪz əz **~ing** ɪŋ

Debra 'deb rə

Debrett də 'bret dɪ- **~'s** s

debridement, débridement dɪ 'briːd mənt də-, ₍ᵤ₎diː-, deɪ-, •, •'mɒ̃ —*Fr* [de bʁid mɑ̃]

debrief ˌdiː 'briːf **~ed** t **~ing** ɪŋ **~s** s

debris, débris 'deb riː 'deɪb- ‖ də 'briː 'deɪb riː *(*)*

De Broglie də 'brəʊg li ‖ də 'brɔɪ —*Fr* [də bʁɔj, də bʁɔ gli]

Debs debz

debt det *(!)* **debts** dets

debtor 'det ə ‖ 'det̬ ər **~s** z

debug ˌdiː 'bʌg **~ged** d **~ging** ɪŋ **~s** z

de|bunk ˌdiː ‖'bʌŋk **~bunked** 'bʌŋkt **~bunking** 'bʌŋk ɪŋ **~bunks** 'bʌŋks

De Burgh də 'bɜːg ‖ -'bɝːg

Debussy də 'buːs i -'bjuːs-, -'bʊs-; 'deɪb juːs i ‖ ˌdeɪb ju 'siː —*Fr* [də by si]

DEBUT

	'deɪb-	'deb-
BrE 1988		
	0 20 40 60 80 100%	

debut, début 'deɪb juː -uː; 'deb juː ‖ deɪ 'bjuː —*BrE 1988 poll panel preference:* 'deɪb- *69%,* 'deb- *31%.* —*Fr* [de by] **~s** z

debutant, débutant 'deb ju tɒ̃ 'deɪb- —*Fr* [de by tɑ̃]

debutante, débutante 'deb ju tɑːnt 'deɪb-, -tænt, -tɒnt —*Fr* [de by tɑ̃ːt] **~s** s

DEC *tdmk* dek

Dec —*see* **December**

deca- *comb. form*
  with stress-neutral suffix ˌdek ə — **decagram** 'dek ə græm
  with stress-imposing suffix dɪ 'kæ+ də- — **Decapolis** dɪ 'kæp əl ɪs də-, §-əs

DECADE

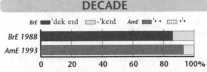

	BrE	'dek eɪd	-'keɪd	AmE		••		•'•
BrE 1988								
AmE 1993								
	0 20 40 60 80 100%							

decade 'dek eɪd dɪ 'keɪd, de-; 'dek əd —*Poll panel preferences: BrE 1988,* 'dek eɪd *86%,* -'keɪd *14%; AmE 1993,* '•• *93%,* •'• *7%. The form* 'dek əd *is associated mainly with the religious sense, 'part of the rosary, set of ten Hail Marys'.* **~s** z

decadence 'dek əd ən̩ts

decadent 'dek əd ənt **~ly** li **~s** s

decaf, decaff 'diː kæf **~s** s

decaffei|nate ˌdiː 'kæf ɪ ‖neɪt dɪ-, -ə- **~nated** neɪt ɪd -əd ‖ neɪt̬ əd **~nates** neɪts **~nating** neɪt ɪŋ ‖ neɪt̬ ɪŋ

decagon 'dek əg ən -ə gɒn ‖ -ə gɑːn **~s** z

decahedr|on ˌdek ə 'hiːdr |ən -'hedr-; '••,•• **~a** ə **~ons** ənz

decal dɪ 'kæl 'diː kæl ‖ 'diː kæl dɪ 'kæl **~s** z

decalcomania dɪ ˌkælk ə 'meɪn i_ə

Decalogue 'dek ə lɒg ‖ -lɔːg -lɑːg

Decameron dɪ 'kæm ər_ən də-, de-

decamp dɪ 'kæmp ˌdiː- **~ed** t **~ing** ɪŋ **~s** s

decanal dɪ 'keɪn ᵊl də-; 'dek ən ᵊl **~ly** i

decane 'dek eɪn

decani dɪ 'keɪn aɪ

de|cant dɪ ‖'kænt ˌdiː-, də- **~canted** 'kænt ɪd -əd ‖ 'kænt̬ əd **~canting** 'kænt ɪŋ ‖ 'kænt̬ ɪŋ **~cants** 'kænts

decanter dɪ 'kænt ə də-, ˌdiː- ‖ -'kænt̬ ər **~s** z

decapitation dɪ ˌkæp ɪ 'teɪʃ ᵊn ˌdiːˌkæp-, -ə- **~s** z

decapi|tate dɪ 'kæp ɪ ‖teɪt də-, ₍ᵤ₎diː-, -ə- **~tated** teɪt ɪd -əd ‖ teɪt̬ əd **~tates** teɪts **~tating** teɪt ɪŋ ‖ teɪt̬ ɪŋ

decapod 'dek ə pɒd ‖ -pɑːd **~s** z

decarbonis... —*see* **decarboniz...**

decarbonization ˌdiː ˌkɑːb ən aɪ 'zeɪʃ ᵊn •,•-, -ɪ'•• ‖ ˌdiː ˌkɑːrb ən ə- **~s** z

decarboniz|e ₍ᵤ₎diː 'kɑːb ə naɪz ‖ -'kɑːrb- **~ed** d **~es** ɪz əz **~ing** ɪŋ

decasyllabic ˌdek ə sɪ 'læb ɪk ◂ -sə'•• •-

decasyllable 'dek ə ˌsɪl əb ᵊl ,••'••• ◂ **~s** z

decathlete dɪ 'kæθ liːt de-, də- **~s** s

decathlon dɪ 'kæθ lɒn de-, də-, -lən ‖ -lɑːn -lən **~s** z

Decatur dɪ 'keɪt ə də- ‖ -'keɪt̬ ər

decay dɪ 'keɪ də-, §diː- **~ed** d **~ing** ɪŋ **~s** z

Decca *tdmk* 'dek ə

Deccan 'dek ən —*Hindi* [d̪ək kʰɪŋ, d̪eː kən]

deceas|e dɪ 'siːs də-, §diː- **~ed** t **~es** ɪz əz **~ing** ɪŋ

decedent dɪ 'siːd ᵊnt də-, §diː- **~s** s

deceit dɪ 'siːt də-, §diː- **~s** s

deceitful dɪ 'siːt fᵊl də-, §diː-, -fʊl **~ly** ˌi **~ness** nəs nɪs

deceiv|e dɪ 'siːv də-, §diː- **~ed** d **~es** z **~ing** ɪŋ

decele|rate ˌdiː 'sel ə ‖reɪt **~rated** reɪt ɪd -əd ‖ reɪt̬ əd **~rates** reɪts **~rating** reɪt ɪŋ ‖ reɪt̬ ɪŋ

deceleration ˌdiː ˌsel ə 'reɪʃ ᵊn •,•- **~s** z

December dɪ 'sem bə də-, §diː-, §-'zem- ‖ -bᵊr

Decembrist dɪ 'sem brɪst də-, §diː-, §-brəst **~s** s

decenc|y 'diːs ᵊnts |i **~ies** iz

decennial dɪ 'sen i_əl də-, de-, diː- **~ly** i

decent 'diːs ᵊnt **~ly** li **~ness** nəs nɪs

decentralis... —*see* **decentraliz...**

decentralization ˌdiː ˌsentr əl aɪ 'zeɪʃ ᵊn •,•-, -ɪ'•• ‖ -əl ə- **~s** z

decentraliz|e ₍ᵤ₎diː 'sentr ə laɪz **~ed** d **~es** ɪz əz **~ing** ɪŋ

deception dɪ 'sep ʃᵊn də-, §diː- **~s** z

deceptive dɪ 'sept ɪv də-, §diː- **~ly** li **~ness** nəs nɪs

deci- ˌdes i ‖ ˌdes ə — **decimetre** 'des i ˌmiːt ə ‖ -ə ˌmiːt̬ ᵊr

decibel 'des ɪ bel -ə-; -ɪb ᵊl, -əb- **~s** z

D

decid|e dɪ ˈsaɪd də-, §diː- ~**ed** ɪd əd ~**er/s** ə/
z ‖ ᵊr/z ~**es** z ~**ing** ɪŋ
decided|ly dɪ ˈsaɪd ɪd ǁli də-, §diː-, -əd- ~**ness**
nəs nɪs
deciduous dɪ ˈsɪd ju̯_əs də-, §diː-
‖ dɪ ˈsɪdʒ u̯_əs ~**ly** li ~**ness** nəs nɪs
decile ˈdes aɪᵊl -ɪl ~**s** z
Decima ˈdes ɪm ə -əm-
decimal ˈdes ᵊm ᵊl -ɪm- ~**ly** i ~**s** z
  ˌdecimal ˈpoint; ˈdecimal ˌsystem
decimalis... —*see* **decimaliz...**
decimalization ˌdes ᵊm ᵊl aɪ ˈzeɪʃ ᵊn ˌ•ɪm-,
  -ɪˈ•- ‖ -ə ˈzeɪʃ-
decimaliz|e ˈdes ᵊm ə laɪz ˈ•ɪm-, -ᵊl aɪz ~**ed** d
  ~**es** ɪz əz ~**ing** ɪŋ
deci|mate ˈdes ɪ |meɪt -ɪ- ~**mated** meɪt ɪd -əd
  ‖ meɪt̬ əd ~**mates** meɪts ~**mating**
  meɪt ɪŋ ‖ meɪt̬ ɪŋ
decimation ˌdes ə ˈmeɪʃ ᵊn -ɪ- ~**s** z
Decimus ˈdes ɪm əs -əm-
decipher dɪ ˈsaɪf ə də-, ₍ₒ₎diː- ‖ -ᵊr ~**ed** d
  deciphering dɪ ˈsaɪf ᵊr_ɪŋ də-,₍ₒ₎diː- ~**s** z
decipherable dɪ ˈsaɪf ᵊr_əb ᵊl də-, ₍ₒ₎diː-
decipherer dɪ ˈsaɪf ᵊr_ə də-, ₍ₒ₎diː- ‖ -ᵊr_ər ~**s**
z
decipherment dɪ ˈsaɪf ə mənt də-, ₍ₒ₎diː- ‖ -ᵊr-
  ~**s** s
decision dɪ ˈsɪʒ ᵊn də-, §diː-, -ˈzɪʃ-, -ˈzɪʒ-, -ˈsɪʃ-
  ~**s** z
decision-mak|er/s dɪ ˈsɪʒ ᵊn ˌmeɪk lə/z də-,
  §diː-, -ˈzɪʃ-, -ˈzɪʒ-, -ˈsɪʃ- ‖ -lᵊr/z ~**ing** ɪŋ
decisive dɪ ˈsaɪs ɪv də-, §diː-, -ˈsaɪz- ~**ly** li
  ~**ness** nəs nɪs
deck dek **decked** dekt **decking** ˈdek ɪŋ
  decks deks
deckchair ˈdek tʃeə ˌ•ˈ• ‖ -tʃer -tʃær ~**s** z
Decker ˈdek ə ‖ -ᵊr
-decker ˈdek ə ‖ -ᵊr — **single-decker**
  ˌsɪŋ gᵊl ˈdek ə ◂ ‖ -ᵊr
deckhand ˈdek hænd ~**s** z
deckhouse ˈdek haʊs
deckle ˈdek ᵊl ~**s** z
  ˌdeckle ˈedge
deckle-edged ˌdek ᵊl ˈedʒd ◂
declaim dɪ ˈkleɪm də-, §diː- ~**ed** d ~**ing** ɪŋ ~**s**
z
declamation ˌdek lə ˈmeɪʃ ᵊn ~**s** z
declamator|y dɪ ˈklæm ət_ᵊr li də-, §diː-
  ‖ -ə tɔːr li -toʊr i ~**ily** ᵊl ɪ ɪ li
Declan ˈdek lən
declarable dɪ ˈkleər əb ᵊl də-, §diː- ‖ -ˈkler-
  -ˈklær-
declaration ˌdek lə ˈreɪʃ ᵊn ~**s** z
declarative dɪ ˈklær ət ɪv də-, §diː-, -ˈkleər-
  ‖ -ət̬ ɪv -ˈkler- ~**ly** li
declaratory dɪ ˈklær ət_ᵊr i də-, §diː-, -ˈkleər-
  ‖ -ə tɔːr i -ˈkler-, -toʊr i
declare dɪ ˈkleə də-, §diː- ‖ dɪ ˈkleᵊr -ˈklæᵊr
  ~**d** d ~**s** z **declaring** dɪ ˈkleər ɪŋ də-, §diː-
  ‖ dɪ ˈkler ɪŋ -ˈklær-
declaredly dɪ ˈkleər ɪd li də-, §diː-, -əd-
  ‖ -ˈkler- -ˈklær-

declasse, déclassé, declassee, déclassée
  deɪ ˈklæs eɪ -ˈklɑːs-, ˌ•ˈ•ᵊ• ‖ ˌdeɪ klæ ˈseɪ
  -klɑː- —*Fr* [de kla se]
declassifiable ₍ₒ₎diː ˈklæs ɪ faɪˌəb ᵊl -ˈ•ə-,
  ˌ•ˌ•ˈ•ᵊ•-
declassification ˌdiː ˌklæs ɪf ɪ ˈkeɪʃ ᵊn •ˌ•-,
  -əf ɪˈ•-, §-ᵊˈ•-
declassi|fy ₍ₒ₎diː ˈklæs ɪ |faɪ -ə- ~**fied** faɪd
  ~**fies** faɪz ~**fying** faɪ ɪŋ
declension dɪ ˈklentʃ ᵊn də-, §diː- ~**al** _ᵊl ~**s** z
declinable dɪ ˈklaɪn əb ᵊl də-, §diː-
declination ˌdek lɪ ˈneɪʃ ᵊn -lə- ~**al** _ᵊl ~**s** z
declin|e v dɪ ˈklaɪn də-, §diː- ~**ed** d ~**es** z
  ~**ing** ɪŋ
decline n dɪ ˈklaɪn də-, §diː-; ˈdiː klaɪn ~**s** z
declivit|y dɪ ˈklɪv ət li də-, §diː-, -ɪt- ‖ -ət̬ li
  ~**ies** iz
declutch ₍ₒ₎diː ˈklʌtʃ dɪ-, də- ~**ed** t ~**es** ɪz əz
  ~**ing** ɪŋ
decoct dɪ ˈkɒkt də-, §diː- ‖ -ˈkɑːkt ~**ed** ɪd əd
  ~**ing** ɪŋ ~**s** s
decoction dɪ ˈkɒk ʃᵊn də-, §diː- ‖ -ˈkɑːk- ~**s** z
decod|e ₍ₒ₎diː ˈkəʊd ‖ -ˈkoʊd ~**ed** ɪd əd ~**er/s**
  ə/z ‖ ᵊr/z ~**es** z ~**ing** ɪŋ
decok|e v dɪ ˈkəʊk dɪ-, də- ‖ -ˈkoʊk ~**ed** t
  ~**es** s ~**ing** ɪŋ
decoke n ˈdiː kəʊk ˌ•ˈ• ‖ -koʊk ~**s** s
decolletage, décolletage ˌdeɪ kɒl ˈtɑːʒ
  deɪ ˈkɒl ɪ tɑːʒ, -ə- ‖ -kɑːl-, ˌ•ˈ•ᵊ•, ˌdek
  əl ə'• —*Fr* [de kɔl ta:ʒ]
decollete, décolleté deɪ ˈkɒl teɪ -ˈkɒl ɪ teɪ,
  -ə teɪ ‖ ˌdeɪ kɑːl ˈteɪ, ˌ•ˈ•ᵊ• —*Fr* [de kɔl te]
decolonis... —*see* **decoloniz...**
decolonization ˌdiː ˌkɒl ən aɪ ˈzeɪʃ ᵊn •ˌ•-,
  -ɪˈ•- ‖ ˌdiː ˌkɑːl ən ə- ~**s** z
decoloniz|e ₍ₒ₎diː ˈkɒl ə naɪz ‖ -ˈkɑːl- ~**ed** d
  ~**es** ɪz əz ~**ing** ɪŋ
decommission ˌdiː kə ˈmɪʃ ᵊn ~**ed** d ~**ing** _ɪŋ
  ~**s** z
decomposable ˌdiː kəm ˈpəʊz əb ᵊl ‖ -ˈpoʊz-
decompos|e ˌdiː kəm ˈpəʊz §-kɒm- ‖ -ˈpoʊz
  ~**ed** d ~**es** ɪz əz ~**ing** ɪŋ
decomposition ˌdiː ˌkɒmp ə ˈzɪʃ ᵊn ‖ -ˌkɑːmp-
decompress ˌdiː kəm ˈpres §-kɒm- ~**ed** t ~**es**
  ɪz əz ~**ing** ɪŋ
decompression ˌdiː kəm ˈpreʃ ᵊn §-kɒm- ~**s** z
  ˌdecom'pression ˌchamber
decongestant ˌdiː kən ˈdʒest ᵊnt §-kɒn- ~**s** s
deconse|crate ˌdiː ˈkɒns ɪ |kreɪt -ə-
  ‖ -ˈkɑːnˈts- ~**crated** kreɪt ɪd -əd ‖ kreɪt̬ əd
  ~**crates** kreɪts ~**crating** kreɪt ɪŋ ‖ kreɪt̬ ɪŋ
deconsecration ˌdiː ˌkɒnˈts ɪ ˈkreɪʃ ᵊn •ˌ•-
  ‖ -ˌkɑːnˈts- ~**s** z
deconstruct ˌdiː kən ˈstrʌkt §-kɒn- ~**ed** ɪd əd
  ~**ing** ɪŋ ~**s** s
deconstruction ˌdiː kən ˈstrʌk ʃᵊn §-kɒn-
  ~**ism** ˌɪz əm ~**ist/s** ɪst/s §əst/s ‖ əst/s ~**s** z
decontami|nate ˌdiː kən ˈtæm ɪ |neɪt §ˌ•kɒn-,
  -ə neɪt ~**nated** neɪt ɪd -əd ‖ neɪt̬ əd ~**nates**
  neɪts ~**nating** neɪt ɪŋ ‖ neɪt̬ ɪŋ
decontamination ˌdiː kən ˌtæm ɪ ˈneɪʃ ᵊn
  §ˌ•kɒn-, -əˈ•- ~**s** z

decontrol ˌdiː kən ˈtrəʊl §-kɒn-, →-ˈtrɒʊl
‖ -ˈtrɒʊl ~led d ~ling ɪŋ ~s z
decor, décor ˈdeɪk ɔː ˈdek- ‖ deɪ ˈkɔːr
ˈdeɪk ɔːr ~s z
deco|rate ˈdek ə |reɪt ~rated reɪt ɪd -əd
‖ reɪt̮ əd ~rates reɪts ~rating
reɪt ɪŋ ‖ reɪt̮ ɪŋ
decoration ˌdek ə ˈreɪʃ ən ~s z
decorative ˈdek ər_ət ɪv ‖ _ət̮ ɪv -ə reɪt̮- ~ly li
~ness nəs nɪs
decorator ˈdek ə reɪt ə ‖ -reɪt̮ ər ~s z
decorous ˈdek ər əs —formerly dɪ ˈkɔːr əs ~ly
li ~ness nəs nɪs
decorti|cate ˌdiː ˈkɔːt ɪ |keɪt §-ə- ‖ -ˈkɔːrt̮-
~cated keɪt ɪd -əd ‖ keɪt̮ əd ~cates keɪts
~cating keɪt ɪŋ ‖ keɪt̮ ɪŋ
decortication ˌdiː ˌkɔːt ɪ ˈkeɪʃ ən §-ə-
‖ diː ˌkɔːrt̮ ə- ~s z
decorum dɪ ˈkɔːr əm də- ‖ -ˈkoʊr-
decoupage, découpage ˌdeɪ ku ˈpɑːʒ —Fr
[de ku paʒ]
decoupl|e (ˌ)diː ˈkʌp əl ~ed d ~es z ~ing ˌɪŋ
De Courcey, De Courcy (i) də ˈkɔːs i ‖ -ˈkɔːrs i
-ˈkoʊrs-, (ii) -ˈkʊəs i ‖ -ˈkʊrs i, (iii)
-ˈkɜːs i ‖ -ˈkɜːs i
decoy n ˈkɔɪ dɪ ˈkɔɪ, də-, §diː- ~s z
decoy v dɪ ˈkɔɪ də-, §diː- ~ed d ~ing ɪŋ ~s z
decreas|e v ˌdiː ˈkriːs ◂ dɪ-, də-, ˈ•• ~ed t ~es
ɪz əz ~ing/ly ɪŋ /li
decreas|e n ˈdiː kriːs dɪ ˈkriːs, də-, ˌdiː- ~es ɪz
əz
decree dɪ ˈkriː də-, §diː- ~d d ~ing ɪŋ ~s z
de cree ˈnisi
decrement n ˈdek rɪ mənt -rə- ~s s
decre|ment v ˈdek rɪ |ment -rə- —See note at
-ment ~mented ment ɪd -əd ‖ ment̮ əd
~menting ment ɪŋ ‖ ment̮ ɪŋ ~ments ments
decreolis... —see decreoliz...
decreolization ˌdiː ˌkriː_əl aɪ ˈzeɪʃ ən -ˌkreɪ-,
-ˌ•əʊl-, -ɪˈ•- ‖ -ə ˈzeɪʃ-
decreoliz|e ˌdiː ˈkriː_ə laɪz -ˈkreɪ-, -əʊ- ~ed d
~es ɪz əz ~ing ɪŋ
decrepit dɪ ˈkrep ɪt də-, §-ət ~ly li
decrepi|tate dɪ ˈkrep ɪ |teɪt də-, §diː-, -ə-
~tated teɪt ɪd -əd ‖ teɪt̮ əd ~tates teɪts
~tating teɪt ɪŋ ‖ teɪt̮ ɪŋ
decrepitude dɪ ˈkrep ɪ t juːd də-, §diː-, -ə-,
→§-tʃuːd ‖ -tuːd -tjuːd
decrescendo ˌdiː krə ˈʃend əʊ ˌdeɪ-, -krɪ- ‖ -oʊ
~s z
De Crespigny (i) də ˈkrep ɪn i -ən-, (ii) -ˈkresp-
decretal dɪ ˈkriːt əl də-, §diː- ‖ -ˈkriːt̮ əl ~s z
decri... —see decry
decriminalis... —see decriminaliz...
decriminalization ˌdiː ˌkrɪm ɪn əl aɪ ˈzeɪʃ ən
-ˌ•ən_əl-, •, •-, -ɪˈ•- ‖ -ə ˈzeɪʃ-
decriminaliz|e (ˌ)diː ˈkrɪm ɪn ə laɪz -ən_ə-,
-əl aɪz ~ed d ~es ɪz əz ~ing ɪŋ
de|cry dɪ |ˈkraɪ də-, §diː- ~cried ˈkraɪd ~cries
ˈkraɪz ~crying ˈkraɪ ɪŋ
decrypt (ˌ)diː ˈkrɪpt ~ed ɪd əd ~ing ɪŋ ~s s
decryption (ˌ)diː ˈkrɪp ʃən ~s z
decubitus dɪ ˈkjuːb ɪt əs də-, §diː-, -ət- ‖ -ət̮-

decumbent dɪ ˈkʌm bənt də-, §diː-
decurion de ˈkjʊər i_ən dɪ- ‖ -ˈkjʊr- ~s z
decurrent dɪ ˈkʌr ənt də-, ˌdiː- ‖ -ˈkɜː- ~ly li
decuss|ate v dɪ ˈkʌs |eɪt ˌdiː-; ˈdek əs-, ~ated
eɪt ɪd -əd ‖ eɪt̮ əd ~ates eɪts ~ating
eɪt ɪŋ ‖ eɪt̮ ɪŋ
decussate adj ˈkʌs eɪt ˌdiː-, -ət, -ɪt ~ly li
Dedalus ˈdiːd əl əs ‖ ˈded-
Deddington ˈded ɪŋ tən
Dedham ˈded əm
dedi|cate ˈded ɪ |keɪt §-ə- ~cated/ly keɪt ɪd /li
-əd /li ‖ keɪt̮ əd /li ~cates keɪts ~cating
keɪt ɪŋ ‖ keɪt̮ ɪŋ
dedicatee ˌded ɪk ə ˈtiː, ˌ•ək- ~s z
dedication ˌded ɪ ˈkeɪʃ ən §-ə- ~s z
dedicator ˈded ɪ keɪt ə §ˈ•ə- ‖ -keɪt̮ ər ~s z
dedicatory ˈded ɪk ət_ər i -ɪ keɪt ər i ‖ -ə tɔːr i
-toʊr i
deduc|e dɪ ˈdjuːs də-, §diː-, →§-ˈdʒuːs ‖ -ˈduːs
-ˈdjuːs ~ed t ~es ɪz əz ~ing ɪŋ
deducible dɪ ˈdjuːs əb əl də-, §diː-, →§-ˈdʒuːs-,
-ɪb- ‖ -ˈduːs- -ˈdjuːs-
deduct dɪ ˈdʌkt də-, §diː- ~ed ɪd əd ~ing ɪŋ
~s s
deductible dɪ ˈdʌkt əb əl də-, §diː-, -ɪb- ~s z
deduction dɪ ˈdʌk ʃən də-, §diː- ~s z
deductive dɪ ˈdʌkt ɪv də-, §diː- ~ly li
Dee diː
deed diːd deeded ˈdiːd ɪd -əd deeding
ˈdiːd ɪŋ deeds diːdz
ˈdeed poll
Deedes diːdz
deejay ˈdiː dʒeɪ ˌ•ˈ• ~s z
Deekes, Deeks diːks
Deeko tdmk ˈdiːk əʊ ‖ -oʊ
deem diːm deemed diːmd deeming ˈdiːm ɪŋ
deems diːmz
Deemer ˈdiːm ə ‖ -ər
Deeming ˈdiːm ɪŋ
de-emphasis|e, de-emphasiz|e
ˌdiː ˈemp f ə saɪz ~ed d ~es ɪz əz ~ing ɪŋ
deemster ˈdiːm stə ‖ -stər ~s z
deep diːp deeper ˈdiːp ə ‖ -ər deepest
ˈdiːp ɪst -əst deeps diːps
ˌdeep ˈend; ˌDeep ˈSouth; ˌdeep ˈspace;
ˌdeep ˈwater
deep-dyed ˌdiːp ˈdaɪd ◂
deepen ˈdiːp ən ~ed d ~ing ˌɪŋ ~s z
deep-freez|e n, Deepfreeze tdmk
ˌdiːp ˈfriːz ‖ ˈdiːp friːz ~es ɪz əz
deep-freez|e v ˌdiːp ˈfriːz ~er/s ə/z ‖ ər/z ~es
ɪz əz ~ing ɪŋ
deep-frozen ˌdiːp ˈfrəʊz ən ◂ ‖ -ˈfroʊz-
deep-|fry ˌdiːp |ˈfraɪ ˈ•• ~fried ˈfraɪd ~fries
ˈfraɪz ~frying ˈfraɪ ɪŋ
Deeping ˈdiːp ɪŋ
deep-laid ˌdiːp ˈleɪd ◂
deep|ly ˈdiːp |li ~ness nəs nɪs
deep-rooted ˌdiːp ˈruːt ɪd ◂ -əd ‖ -ˈruːt̮- ~ness
nəs nɪs
deep-sea ˌdiːp ˈsiː ◂
deep-seated ˌdiːp ˈsiːt ɪd ◂ -əd ‖ -ˈsiːt̮-
deer dɪə ‖ dɪªr (= dear)

D

Deer, Deere dɪə ‖ dɪəʳr
deerhound 'dɪə haʊnd ‖ 'dɪr- ~s z
deerskin 'dɪə skɪn ‖ 'dɪr- ~s z
deerstalker 'dɪə ˌstɔːk ə ‖ 'dɪr ˌstɔːk əʳr -ˌstɑːk-
  ~s z
de-esca|late ₍ᵢ₎di: 'esk ə ‖leɪt **~lated** leɪt ɪd -əd
  ‖ leɪṭ əd **~lates** leɪts **~lating** leɪt ɪŋ ‖ leɪṭ ɪŋ
de-escalation ˌdi: ˌesk ə 'leɪʃ ən •ˌ•- ~s z
Deeside 'di: saɪd
defac|e dɪ 'feɪs də-, §di:- **~ed** t **~es** ɪz əz
  ~ing ɪŋ
defacement dɪ 'feɪs mənt də-, §di:- ~s s
de facto ₍ᵢ₎deɪ 'fækt əʊ di- ‖ -oʊ
defalc|ate 'di:f ælk leɪt -ɔːlk- ‖ dɪ 'fælk-
  -'fɔːlk-; 'def əl k|eɪt **~ated** eɪt ɪd -əd ‖ eɪṭ əd
  ~ates eɪts **~ating** eɪt ɪŋ ‖ eɪṭ ɪŋ
defalcation ˌdi:f æl 'keɪʃ ən -ɔːl- ‖ ˌdef əl- ~s z
defamation ˌdef ə 'meɪʃ ən ˌdi:f- ~s z
defamator|y dɪ 'fæm ə_təʳr li də-, §di:-
  ‖ -ə tɔːr li -toʊr i **~ily** əl i ɪ li
defam|e dɪ 'feɪm də-, §di:- **~ed** d **~es** z **~ing**
  ɪŋ
default v dɪ 'fɔːlt də-, §di:-, -'fɒlt ‖ -'fɑːlt **~ed**
  ɪd əd **~er/s** ə/z ‖ ʳr/z **~ing** ɪŋ **~s** s
default n dɪ 'fɔːlt də-, §di:-, -'fɒlt; 'di:• ‖ -'fɑːlt
  ~s s
defeasance dɪ 'fi:z ənts də-, §di:-
defeasible dɪ 'fi:z əb əl də-, §di:-, -ɪb-
de|feat v, n dɪ |'fi:t də-, §di:- **~feated** 'fi:t ɪd
  -əd ‖ 'fi:ṭ əd **~feating** 'fi:t ɪŋ ‖ 'fi:ṭ ɪŋ
  ~feats 'fi:ts
defeatism dɪ 'fi:t ˌɪz əm də-, §di:- ‖ -'fi:ṭ-
defeatist dɪ 'fi:t ɪst də-, §di:-, §-əst ‖ -'fi:ṭ- **~s**
  s
defe|cate 'def ə |keɪt 'di:f-, -ɪ- **~cated** keɪt ɪd
  -əd ‖ keɪṭ əd **~cates** keɪts **~cating**
  keɪt ɪŋ ‖ keɪṭ ɪŋ
defecation ˌdef ə 'keɪʃ ən ˌdi:f-, -ɪ- ~s z

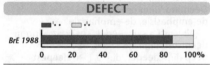

DEFECT

BrE 1988

0   20   40   60   80   100%

defect n 'di: fekt dɪ 'fekt, də-, §di:- —*BrE*
  1988 poll panel preference: '•• *86%,* •'• *14%.*
  ~s s
defect v dɪ 'fekt də-, §di:- **~ed** ɪd əd **~ing** ɪŋ
  ~s s
defection dɪ 'fek ʃən də-, §di:- ~s z
defective dɪ 'fekt ɪv də-, §di:- **~ly** li **~ness**
  nəs nɪs
defector dɪ 'fekt ə də-, §di:- ‖ -ʳr ~s z
defenc|e dɪ 'fents də-, §di:- **~es** ɪz əz
defenceless dɪ 'fents ləs də-, §di:-, -lɪs **~ly** li
  ~ness nəs nɪs
defence|man dɪ 'fents| mən də-, §di:- **~men**
  mən
defend dɪ 'fend də-, §di:- **~ed** ɪd əd **~ing** ɪŋ
  ~s z
defendant dɪ 'fend ənt də-, §di:- ‖ -ænt ~s s
defender dɪ 'fend ə də-, §di:- ‖ -ʳr ~s z
defenestration ˌdi: ˌfen ɪ 'streɪʃ ən -ə'•-
  ‖ •ˌ•- ~s z

defene|strate ₍ᵢ₎di: 'fen ɪ |streɪt -ə- **~strated**
  streɪt ɪd -əd ‖ streɪṭ əd **~strates** streɪts
  ~strating streɪt ɪŋ ‖ streɪṭ ɪŋ
defens|e dɪ 'fents də-, §di:- ‖ 'di:• **~es** ɪz əz
defenseless dɪ 'fents ləs də-, §di:-, -lɪs **~ly** li
  ~ness nəs nɪs
defense|man dɪ 'fents| mən də-, §di:- **~men**
  mən
defensibility dɪ ˌfents ə 'bɪl ət i də-, §di:-, -, •ɪ-,
  -ɪt i ‖ -əṭ i
defensib|le dɪ 'fents əb |əl də-, §di:-, -ɪb- **~ly** li
defensive dɪ 'fents ɪv də-, §di:- **~ly** li **~ness**
  nəs nɪs
de|fer dɪ |'fɜː də-, §di:- ‖ -|'fɝː **~ferred**
  'fɜːd ‖ 'fɝːd **~ferring** 'fɜːr ɪŋ ‖ 'fɝː ɪŋ **~fers**
  'fɜːz ‖ 'fɝːz
deference 'def əʳr_ənts
deferent 'def əʳr_ənt
deferential ˌdef ə 'rentʃ əl ◄ **~ly** i
deferment dɪ 'fɜː mənt də-, §di:- ‖ -'fɝː- ~s s
deferrer dɪ 'fɜːr ə də-, §di:- ‖ -'fɝː ʳr ~s z
defiance dɪ 'faɪ_ənts də-, §di:-
defiant dɪ 'faɪ_ənt də-, §di:- **~ly** li
defibril|late ₍ᵢ₎di: 'fɪb rɪ |leɪt -'faɪb-, -rə-
  ~lated leɪt ɪd -əd ‖ leɪṭ əd **~lates** leɪts
  ~lating leɪt ɪŋ ‖ leɪṭ ɪŋ
defibrillation di: ˌfɪb rɪ 'leɪʃ ən -ˌfaɪb-, ˌ•ˌ•-,
  -rə'•-
defibrillator ₍ᵢ₎di: 'fɪb rɪ leɪt ə -'faɪb-, -'•rə-
  ‖ -leɪṭ ʳr ~s z
deficienc|y dɪ 'fɪʃ ənts li də-, §di:- **~ies** ɪz
  de'ficiency di,sease
deficient dɪ 'fɪʃ ənt də-, §di:- **~ly** li
deficit 'def əs ɪt -ɪs-, -ət; dɪ 'fɪs-, də-, §di:-
  —*formerly also* 'di:f- ~s s
de fide dɪ 'faɪd i ˌdi:-; ˌdeɪ 'fi:d eɪ
defie... —*see* **defy**
defilad|e ˌdef ɪ 'leɪd -ə-, '••• **~ed** ɪd əd **~es** z
  ~ing ɪŋ
defil|e v dɪ 'faɪəl də-, §di:- **~ed** d **~es** z **~ing**
  ɪŋ
defile n dɪ 'faɪəl də-, §di:-; 'di: faɪəl ~s z
defilement dɪ 'faɪəl mənt də-, §di:- ~s s
definab|le dɪ 'faɪn əb |əl də-, §di:- **~ly** li
defin|e dɪ 'faɪn də-, §di:- **~ed** d **~er/s** ə/
  z ‖ -ʳr/z **~es** z **~ing** ɪŋ
definite 'def ən_ət -ɪn-, -ɪt **~ly** li **~ness** nəs
  nɪs
  ˌdefinite 'article
definition ˌdef ə 'nɪʃ ən -ɪ- **~al** əl
definitive dɪ 'fɪn ət ɪv də-, §di:-, -ɪt- ‖ -əṭ ɪv
  ~ly li **~ness** nəs nɪs
de|flate ˌdi: |'fleɪt dɪ-, də- **~flated** 'fleɪt ɪd -əd
  ‖ 'fleɪṭ əd **~flates** 'fleɪts **~flating**
  'fleɪt ɪŋ ‖ 'fleɪṭ ɪŋ
deflation ˌdi: 'fleɪʃ ən dɪ-, də- ~s z
deflationary ˌdi: 'fleɪʃ ən əʳr_i dɪ-, də-, -ən_əʳr i
  ‖ -ə ner i
deflator dɪ 'fleɪt ə də- ‖ -'fleɪṭ ʳr ~s z
deflect dɪ 'flekt də-, §di:- **~ed** ɪd əd **~ing** ɪŋ
  ~s s
deflection dɪ 'flek ʃən də-, §di:- ~s z

D

defloration ˌdiː flɔː 'reɪʃ ᵊn ˌdef lɔː- ‖ ˌdef lə-
ˌdiːf- ~s z
deflower ˌdiː 'flaʊ‿ə dɪ-, də- ‖ -'flaʊ‿ᵊr ~ed d
   deflowering ˌdiː 'flaʊ‿ər ɪŋ dɪ-, də-
   ‖ -'flaʊ‿ᵊr ɪŋ ~s z
Defoe dɪ 'fəʊ də-, §diː- ‖ -'foʊ
defoliant ₍ᵢ₎diː 'fəʊl iˌənt dɪ-, də- ‖ -'foʊl- ~s s
defoli|ate ₍ᵢ₎diː 'fəʊl i |eɪt dɪ-, də- ‖ -'foʊl-
   ~ated eɪt ɪd -əd ‖ eɪţ əd ~ates eɪts ~ating
   eɪt ɪŋ ‖ eɪţ ɪŋ
defoliation diː ˌfəʊl i 'eɪʃ ᵊn dɪ-, də-, ˌdiː ˌfəʊl-
   ‖ -ˌfoʊl- ~s z
deforest ˌdiː 'fɒr ɪst dɪ-, də-, -əst ‖ -'fɔːr-
   -'fɑːr- ~ed ɪd əd ~ing ɪŋ ~s s
deforestation diː ˌfɒr ɪ 'steɪʃ ᵊn dɪ-, də-,
   ˌdiː ˌfɒr-, -ə- ‖ -ˌfɔːr- -ˌfɑːr- ~s s
deform dɪ 'fɔːm də-, ˌdiː- ‖ -'fɔːrm ~ed d
   ~ing ɪŋ ~s z
deformation ˌdiː fɔː 'meɪʃ ᵊn ˌdef ə-
   ‖ ˌdiː fɔːr- ˌdef ᵊr- ~s z
deformit|y dɪ 'fɔːm ət li i də-, §diː-, -ɪt-
   ‖ -'fɔːrm əţ li ~ies iz
defraud dɪ 'frɔːd də-, ˌdiː- ‖ -'frɑːd ~ed ɪd əd
   ~er/s ə/z ‖ ᵊr/z ~ing ɪŋ ~s z
defraudation ˌdiː frɔː 'deɪʃ ᵊn ‖ -frɑː- ~s s
defray dɪ 'freɪ də-, §diː- ~ed d ~ing ɪŋ ~s z
defrayal dɪ 'freɪ əl də-, §diː- ~s z
De Freitas də 'freɪt əs ‖ -'freɪţ-
defrock ˌdiː 'frɒk ‖ -'frɑːk ~ed t ~ing ɪŋ ~s s
defrost ˌdiː 'frɒst dɪ-, də-, -'frɔːst ‖ -'frɔːst
   -'frɑːst ~ed ɪd əd ~ing ɪŋ ~s s
deft deft **defter** 'deft ə ‖ -ᵊr **deftest** 'deft ɪst
   -əst **deftly** 'deft li **deftness** 'deft nəs -nɪs
defunct dɪ 'fʌŋkt də-, §diː-; 'diː fʌŋkt ~ness
   nəs nɪs
defus|e ˌdiː 'fjuːz dɪ-, də- —*Several 1988 poll
   panel members expressed spontaneous
   disapproval of the pronunciation* dɪ-, *which can
   lead to confusion with* diffuse. ~ed d ~es ɪz
   əz ~ing ɪŋ
de|fy dɪ |'faɪ də-, §diː- ~fied 'faɪd ~fier/s
   'faɪ‿ə/z ‖ 'faɪ‿ᵊr/z ~fies 'faɪz ~fying 'faɪ ɪŋ
degage, dégagé ˌdeɪ gɑː 'ʒeɪ -gæ-;
   ₍ᵢ₎deɪ 'gɑːʒ eɪ
Deganwy dɪ 'gæn wi də- —*Welsh* [de 'ga nui,
   -nuɪ]
Degas 'deɪg ɑː ‖ də 'gɑː —*Fr* [də 'ga]
De Gaulle də 'gəʊl di-, →-'gɒʊl, -'gɔːl ‖ -'gɔːl
   -'goʊl —*Fr* [də gol]
degauss ˌdiː 'gaʊs -'gɔːs ~ed t ~es ɪz əz
   ~ing ɪŋ
degemi|nate ˌdiː 'dʒem ɪ |neɪt -ə- ~nated
   neɪt ɪd -əd ‖ neɪţ əd ~nates neɪts ~nating
   neɪt ɪŋ ‖ neɪţ ɪŋ
degemination ˌdiː ˌdʒem ɪ 'neɪʃ ᵊn -ə- ~s z
degenerac|y dɪ 'dʒen ᵊr_əs li i də-, §diː- ~ies iz
degenerate *adj, n* dɪ 'dʒen ᵊr_ət də-, §diː-, -ɪt
   ~ly li ~ness nəs nɪs ~s s
degene|rate *v* dɪ 'dʒen ə |reɪt də-, §diː-
   ~rated reɪt ɪd -əd ‖ reɪţ əd ~rates reɪts
   ~rating reɪt ɪŋ ‖ reɪţ ɪŋ
degeneration dɪ ˌdʒen ə 'reɪʃ ᵊn də-, §diː- ~s
   z

degenerative dɪ 'dʒen ᵊr_ət ɪv də-, §diː-,
   -ə reɪt ɪv ‖ _əţ ɪv -ə reɪţ ɪv ~ly li
DeGeneres də 'dʒen ᵊr əs dɪ-
deglutition ˌdiː glu 'tɪʃ ᵊn
degradability dɪ ˌgreɪd ə 'bɪl ət i də-, §diː-,
   -ɪt i ‖ -əţ i
degradable dɪ 'greɪd əb ᵊl də-, §diː-
degradation ˌdeg rə 'deɪʃ ᵊn ~s z
degrad|e dɪ 'greɪd də-, §diː- ~ed ɪd əd ~es z
   ~ing/ly ɪŋ /li
de|grease ˌdiː |'griːs -'griːz ~greased 'griːst
   'griːzd ~greases 'griːs ɪz 'griːz-, -əz
   ~greasing 'griːs ɪŋ 'griːz-
degree dɪ 'griː də-, §diː- ~s z
De Havilland dɪ 'hæv ɪl ənd də-, -ᵊl-
dehisc|e dɪ 'hɪs də-, §diː- ~ed t ~es ɪz əz
   ~ing ɪŋ
dehiscence dɪ 'hɪs ᵊnᵗs də-, §diː-
dehiscent dɪ 'hɪs ᵊnt də-, §diː-
dehorn ˌdiː 'hɔːn ‖ -'hɔːrn ~ed d ~ing ɪŋ ~s
   z
Dehra Dun ˌdeər ə 'duːn ‖ ˌder-
dehumanis... —*see* **dehumaniz...**
dehumanization diː ˌhjuːm ən aɪ 'zeɪʃ ᵊn
   ˌ•ˌ•-, -ən ɪ- ‖ -ən ə- -ˌjuːm-
dehumaniz|e ₍ᵢ₎diː 'hjuːm ə naɪz ‖ -'juːm- ~ed
   d ~es ɪz əz ~ing ɪŋ
dehumidi|fy ˌdiː hju 'mɪd ɪ |faɪ ˌ•ju-, ˌ•'•ə-
   ~fied faɪd ~fier/s faɪ‿ə/z ‖ faɪ‿ᵊr/z ~fies
   faɪz ~fying faɪ ɪŋ
dehydr|ate ₍ᵢ₎diː 'haɪdr |eɪt ◄ -haɪ 'dr|eɪt; '•••
   ~ated eɪt ɪd -əd ‖ eɪţ əd ~ates eɪts ~ating
   eɪt ɪŋ ‖ eɪţ ɪŋ
dehydration ˌdiː haɪ 'dreɪʃ ᵊn ~s z
dehydrogenase ˌdiː haɪ 'drɒdʒ ə neɪz
   ˌdiː 'haɪdr ədʒ-, -neɪs ‖ -'drɑːdʒ-
Deianira ˌdeɪ ə 'naɪᵊr ə ˌdiː_
deic|e, de-ic|e ˌdiː 'aɪs ~ed t ~es ɪz əz ~ing
   ɪŋ
deicide 'deɪ ɪ saɪd 'diː_, -ə- ~s z
deictic 'daɪkt ɪk 'deɪkt- —*Also sometimes, by
   misanalysis,* di 'ɪkt ɪk, deɪ- ~ally ᵊl_i ~s s
deification ˌdeɪ ɪf ɪ 'keɪʃ ᵊn ˌdiː_, ˌ•əf-, §-ə'•-
   ~s z
dei|fy 'deɪ ɪ |faɪ 'diː_, -ə- ~fied faɪd ~fier/s
   faɪ‿ə/z ‖ faɪ‿ᵊr/z ~fies faɪz ~fying faɪ ɪŋ
Deighton *(i)* 'deɪt ᵊn, *(ii)* 'daɪt ᵊn, *(iii)* 'diːt ᵊn
deign deɪn *(= Dane)* **deigned** deɪnd
   deigning 'deɪn ɪŋ **deigns** deɪnz
Dei gratia ˌdeɪ iː 'grɑːt i‿ə ˌdiː aɪ 'greɪʃ-
Deimos 'deɪm ɒs 'daɪm- ‖ -ɑːs
deindustriali|sation, ~zation
   ˌdiː ɪn ˌdʌs tri_əl aɪ 'zeɪʃ ᵊn -ɪ'•- ‖ -ə'•-
Deirdre 'dɪədr i ‖ 'dɪrdr i —*but in Ireland* -ə
   —*Ir* ['dierʲ dirʲe]
deism 'deɪ ˌɪz əm 'diː- ‖ 'diː- 'deɪ-
deist 'deɪ ɪst 'diː-, §-əst ‖ 'diː- 'deɪ- ~s s

DEITY

	'deɪ-	'diː-
BrE 1988		

0   20   40   60   80   100%

D

deit|y 'deɪ ət |i 'diː_, -ɪt- ‖ 'diː ət̮ |i 'deɪ- —*BrE 1988 poll panel preference:* 'deɪ- 80%, 'diː- 20%. ~ies iz

deixis 'daɪks ɪs 'deɪks-, §-əs —*Also sometimes, by misanalysis,* di 'ɪks ɪs, deɪ-, §-əs

deja vu, déjà vu ˌdeɪ ʒɑː 'vuː -'vjuː —*Fr* [de ʒa vy]

dejected dɪ 'dʒekt ɪd də-, §diː-, -əd ~ly li ~ness nəs nɪs

dejection dɪ 'dʒek ʃən də-, §diː- ~s z

De Jong, De Jongh də 'jɒŋ ‖ -'jɔːŋ -'jɑːŋ, -'dʒɔːŋ, -'dʒɑːŋ

de jure ₍ˌ₎deɪ 'dʒʊər i di-, -'jʊər-, -eɪ ‖ ₍ˌ₎diː 'dʒʊr i ₍ˌ₎deɪ 'jʊr eɪ

de Keyser də 'kaɪz ə ‖ -ər

Dekker 'dek ə ‖ -ər

dekko 'dek əʊ ‖ -oʊ ~s z

de Klerk də 'kleək ‖ -'kleərk —*Afrikaans* [də 'klɛrk]

De Kooning də 'kuːn ɪŋ

del, Del del

Delacour 'del ə kʊə -kɔː ‖ -kʊr

Delacourt 'del ə kɔːt ‖ -kɔːrt -koʊrt

Delacroix 'del ə krwɑː ˌ••'• —*Fr* [də la krwa]

Delagoa ˌdel ə 'gəʊ ə ◂ ‖ -'goʊ ə ˌDelaˌgoa 'Bay

Delahaye 'del ə heɪ

Delafield 'del ə fiːˀld

de la Mare ˌdel ə 'meə də lɑː-; 'del ə meə ‖ -'meᵊr -'mæᵊr

Delamere 'del ə mɪə ˌ••'• ‖ -mɪr

Delancey də 'lænˑs i

Delaney də 'leɪn i dɪ-

Delano (i) 'del ə nəʊ ‖ -noʊ, (ii) də 'leɪn əʊ ‖ -oʊ —*Franklin D~ Roosevelt was (i); the place in CA is (ii).*

De-La-Noy 'del ə nɔɪ

Delany də 'leɪn i dɪ-

de la Renta ˌdel ə 'rent ə dəl-

Delargy də 'lɑːg i ‖ -'lɑːrg i

De La Rue, de la Rue ˌdel ə 'ruː dəl ə-; 'del ə ruː

delation dɪ 'leɪʃ ən də-, §diː- ~s z

Delaware 'del ə weə ‖ -wer -wær

De La Warr 'del ə weə ‖ -wer -wær

delay dɪ 'leɪ də-, §diː- ~ed d ~er/s ə/z ‖ -ər/z ~ing ɪŋ ~s z

Delbert 'delb ət ‖ -ərt

Delbridge 'del brɪdʒ

del credere ˌdel 'kreɪd ər i -'kred- ~s z

Delderfield 'deld ə fiːˀld ‖ -ər-

dele 'diːl i: -i ~d d ~ing ɪŋ ~s z

delectab|le dɪ 'lekt əb |əl də-, §diː- ~ly li

delectation ˌdiː lek 'teɪʃ ən

delegac|y 'del ɪg əs i ‖ '•əg- ~ies iz

delegate n 'del ɪg ət -əg-, -ɪt; -ɪ geɪt, -ə- ~s s

dele|gate v 'del ɪ |geɪt -ə- ~gated geɪt ɪd -əd ‖ geɪt̮ əd ~gates geɪts ~gating geɪt ɪŋ ‖ geɪt̮ ɪŋ

delegation ˌdel ɪ 'geɪʃ ən -ə- ~s z

de|lete dɪ |'liːt də-, §diː- ~leted 'liːt ɪd -əd ‖ 'liːt̮ əd ~letes 'liːts ~leting 'liːt ɪŋ ‖ 'liːt̮ ɪŋ

deleterious ˌdel ɪ 'tɪər i_əs ◂ ˌdiːl-, ˌ•ə- ‖ -'tɪr- ~ly li ~ness nəs nɪs

deletion dɪ 'liːʃ ən də-, §diː- ~s z

delf delf

Delfont 'del fɒnt ‖ -fɑːnt

delft, Delft delft

delftware 'delft weə ‖ -wer -wær

Delgado del 'gɑːd əʊ ‖ -oʊ

Delhi 'del i

deli 'del i ~s z

Delia 'diːl i_ə

Delian 'diːl i_ən ~s z

deliberate adj dɪ 'lɪb ər_ət də-, §diː-, ˌɪt ~ly li ~ness nəs nɪs

delibe|rate v dɪ 'lɪb ə |reɪt də-, §diː- ~rated reɪt ɪd -əd ‖ reɪt̮ əd ~rates reɪts ~rating reɪt ɪŋ ‖ reɪt̮ ɪŋ

deliberation dɪ ˌlɪb ə 'reɪʃ ən də-, §diː- ~s z

deliberative dɪ 'lɪb ər_ət ɪv də-, §diː- ‖ -ə reɪt̮ ɪv -ər_ət̮- ~ly li ~ness nəs nɪs

Delibes də 'liːb dɪ- —*Fr* [də lib]

delicac|y 'del ɪk əs |i '•ək- ~ies iz

delicate 'del ɪk ət -ək-, -ɪt ~ly li ~ness nəs nɪs

delicatessen ˌdel ɪk ə 'tes ən, '•ək- ~s z

delicious dɪ 'lɪʃ əs də-, §diː- ~ly li ~ness nəs nɪs

de|light n, v dɪ |'laɪt də-, §diː- ~lighted 'laɪt ɪd -əd ‖ 'laɪt̮ əd ~lighting 'laɪt ɪŋ ‖ 'laɪt̮ ɪŋ ~lights 'laɪts

delighted dɪ 'laɪt ɪd də-, §diː-, -əd ‖ -'laɪt̮ əd ~ly li ~ness nəs nɪs

delightful dɪ 'laɪt fˀl də-, §diː-, -fʊl ~ly ˌi ~ness nəs nɪs

Delilah dɪ 'laɪl ə də-

delim|it ₍ˌ₎diː 'lɪm |ɪt dɪ-, də-, §-ət ‖ -ɪt -ited ɪt ɪd §ət-, -əd ‖ ət̮ əd ~iting ɪt ɪŋ §ət- ‖ ət̮ ɪŋ ~its ɪts §əts ‖ əts

delimi|tate dɪ 'lɪm ɪ |teɪt də-, ˌdiː- ~tated teɪt ɪd -əd ‖ teɪt̮ əd ~tates teɪts ~tating teɪt ɪŋ ‖ teɪt̮ ɪŋ

delimitation dɪ ˌlɪm ɪ 'teɪʃ ən də-, ˌdiː- ~s z

delimitative dɪ 'lɪm ɪt ət ɪv də-, §diː-, §-'•ət-; -ɪ teɪt ɪv, -ə•• ‖ -ə teɪt̮ ɪv

deline|ate dɪ 'lɪn i |eɪt də-, §diː- ~ated eɪt ɪd -əd ‖ eɪt̮ əd ~ates eɪts ~ating eɪt ɪŋ ‖ eɪt̮ ɪŋ

delineation dɪ ˌlɪn i 'eɪʃ ən də-, §diː- ~s z

delineator dɪ 'lɪn i eɪt ə də-, §diː- ‖ -eɪt̮ ər ~s z

delinquenc|y dɪ 'lɪŋk wənˑs |i də-, §diː- ~ies iz

delinquent dɪ 'lɪŋk wənt də-, §diː- ~ly li ~s s

deliquesc|e ˌdel ɪ 'kwes -ə- ~ed t ~es ɪz əz ~ing ɪŋ

deliquescence ˌdel ɪ 'kwes ənˑs -ə-

deliquescent ˌdel ɪ 'kwes ənt ◂ -ə-

delirious dɪ 'lɪr i_əs də-, §diː-, 'lɪər- —*BrE poll panel preferences: 1988,* -'lɪr- 54%, -'lɪər- 46%; *1998,* -'lɪr- 46%, -'lɪər- 54% *(those born since 1973: 80%).* ~ly li ~ness nəs nɪs

deliri|um dɪ 'lɪr i_|əm də-, §diː-, 'lɪər- ~a ə ~ums əmz

de|lirium 'tremens 'triːm enz 'trem-, -ənz

De Lisle, De L'Isle də 'laɪˀl

Delius 'diːl i_əs

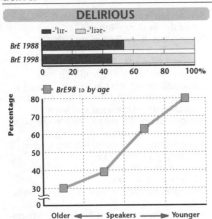

DELIRIOUS

-'lɪr- -'lɪər-

BrE 1988

BrE 1998

0 20 40 60 80 100%

BrE98 ɪə by age

Percentage

80
70
60
50
40
30
0

Older ← Speakers → Younger

---

deliver dɪ 'lɪv ə də-, §diː- ‖ -ər ~**ed** d
  delivering dɪ 'lɪv ər_ɪŋ ~**s** z
deliverability dɪ ˌlɪv ər_ə 'bɪl ət i də-, §diː-, -ɪt i
  ‖ -əṭ i
deliverable dɪ 'lɪv ər_əb əl də-, §diː- ~**s** z
deliverance dɪ 'lɪv ər_ənts də-, §diː-
deliverer dɪ 'lɪv ər_ə də-, §diː- ‖ -ər_ər ~**s** z
deliver|y dɪ 'lɪv ər_li də-, §diː- ~**ies** iz
delivery|man dɪ 'lɪv ər_i |mæn də-, §diː-, -mən
  ~**men** men mən
dell, Dell del **dells, Dell's** delz
Della 'del ə
Deller 'del ə ‖ -ər
Dellums 'del əmz
Delmar, Del Mar del 'mɑː ' • • ‖ 'del mɑːr • '•
Delmarva del 'mɑːv ə ‖ -'mɑːrv ə
Delmonico del 'mɒn ɪ kəʊ ‖ -'mɑːn ɪ koʊ
Del Monte *tdmk* del 'mɒnt eɪ -i ‖ -'mɑːnt-
Deloitte də 'lɔɪt
Delorean də 'lɔːr i_ən
Delores də 'lɔːr ɪz dɪ-, -əz ‖ -ɪs
Delors də 'lɔː ‖ -'lɔːr —*Fr* [də lɔːʁ]
Delos 'diːl ɒs ‖ -ɑːs
de|louse ˌdiː |'laʊs -'laʊz ~**loused** 'laʊst 'laʊzd
  ~**louses** 'laʊs ɪz 'laʊz-, -əz ~**lousing** 'laʊs ɪŋ
  'laʊz-
Delph delf
Delphi 'delf aɪ -i —*Mod Gk* [ðel 'fi]
Delphian 'delf i_ən
Delphic 'delf ɪk
Delphine del 'fiːn
delphinium del 'fɪn i_əm ~**s** z
Delphinus del 'faɪn əs
Delroy 'del rɔɪ
Delsey *tdmk* 'dels i
delta, Delta 'delt ə ~**s** z
deltaic del 'teɪ ɪk
delta-winged ˌdelt ə 'wɪŋd ◄
deltic 'delt ɪk
deltiology ˌdelt i 'ɒl ədʒ i ‖ -'ɑːl-
deltoid 'delt ɔɪd ~**s** z
delud|e dɪ 'luːd də-, §diː-, -'ljuːd ~**ed** ɪd əd
  ~**es** z ~**ing** ɪŋ
delug|e *n, v* 'del juːdʒ -juːʒ ~**ed** d ~**es** ɪz əz
  ~**ing** ɪŋ

delusion dɪ 'luːʒ ən də-, §diː-, -'ljuːʒ- ~**al** _əl
  ~**s** z
delusive dɪ 'luːs ɪv də-, §diː-, -'ljuːs-, §-'luːz-,
  §-'ljuːz- ~**ly** li ~**ness** nəs nɪs
delusory dɪ 'luːs ər i də-, §diː-, -'ljuːs-, -'luːz-,
  -'ljuːz-
deluxe, de luxe də 'lʌks dɪ-, §diː-, -'lʊks,
  -'luːks —*Fr* [də lyks]
delve delv **delved** delvd **delver/s** 'delv ə/
  z ‖ -ər/z **delves** delvz **delving** 'delv ɪŋ
Delwyn 'del wɪn
Delyn 'del ɪn
Delyth 'del ɪθ
Dem dem —*or as* Democrat, Democratic
demagnetis... —*see* **demagnetiz...**
demagnetization ˌdiː ˌmæg nət aɪ 'zeɪʃ ən
  •ˌ•-, -nɪt•ˌ'•-, -ɪ'•- ‖ -nəṭ ə-
demagnetiz|e ₍ᵢ₎diː 'mæg nə taɪz -nɪ- ~**ed** d
  ~**es** ɪz əz ~**ing** ɪŋ
demagog 'dem ə gɒg ‖ -gɑːg ~**s** z
demagogic ˌdem ə 'gɒg ɪk ◄ -'gɒdʒ- ‖ -'gɑːg-
  -'gɑːdʒ-, -'goʊdʒ- ~**ally** əl_i
demagogue 'dem ə gɒg ‖ -gɑːg ~**s** z
demagoguer|y 'dem ə gɒg ər i |ˌ••'•- ‖ -gɑːg
  ər li ~**ies** iz
demagogy 'dem ə gɒg i -gɒdʒ- ‖ -gɑːg i
  -gɑːdʒ-, -goʊdʒ-
deman ˌdiː 'mæn ~**ned** d ~**ning** ɪŋ ~**s** z
demand *n, v* dɪ 'mɑːnd də-, §diː-, §-'mænd
  ‖ -'mænd ~**ed** ɪd əd ~**ing/ly** ɪŋ /li ~**s** z
de Manio də 'mæn i əʊ ‖ -oʊ
demarc|ate 'diː mɑːk eɪt ‖ dɪ 'mɑːrk eɪt
  'diː mɑːrk eɪt ~**ated** eɪt ɪd -əd ‖ eɪṭ əd
  ~**ates** eɪts ~**ating** eɪt ɪŋ ‖ eɪṭ ɪŋ
demarcation ˌdiː mɑː 'keɪʃ ən ‖ -mɑːr-
  ˌdemar'cation di,spute, -,••
demarcative dɪ 'mɑːk ət ɪv ˌdiː-
  ‖ -'mɑːrk əṭ ɪv
demarcator 'diː mɑːk eɪt ə ‖ dɪ 'mɑːrk eɪṭ ər
  'diː mɑːrk eɪṭ ər ~**s** z
demarch|e, démarch|e 'deɪ mɑːʃ ,•'•
  ‖ deɪ 'mɑːrʃ dɪ- ~**es** ɪz əz —*or as sing.* —*Fr*
  [de maʁʃ]
dematerialis... —*see* **dematerializ...**
dematerialization ˌdiː mə ˌtɪər i_əl aɪ 'zeɪʃ ən
  -ɪ'•- ‖ -ˌtɪr i_əl ə- ~**s** z
dematerializ|e ˌdiː mə 'tɪər i_ə laɪz ‖ -'tɪr-
  ~**ed** d ~**es** ɪz əz ~**ing** ɪŋ
deme diːm **demes** diːmz
demean dɪ 'miːn də-, §diː- ~**ed** d ~**ing** ɪŋ ~**s**
  z
demeanor, demeanour dɪ 'miːn ə də-, §diː-
  ‖ -ər ~**s** z
de|ment *v, n* dɪ |'ment də-, §diː- ~**mented**
  'ment ɪd -əd ‖ 'menṭ əd ~**menting**
  'ment ɪŋ ‖ 'menṭ ɪŋ ~**ments** 'ments 'menṭs
demented dɪ 'ment ɪd də-, ₍ᵢ₎diː-, -əd ‖ -'menṭ
  əd ~**ly** li ~**ness** nəs nɪs
dementia dɪ 'mentʃ ə də-, ₍ᵢ₎diː-, -'mentʃ i_ə,
  -'ment i_ə ~**s** z
  de,mentia 'praecox
demerara, D~ ˌdem ə 'reər ə ◄ -'rɑːr- ‖ -'rer ə

-'rɑːr ə
ˌdemeˌrara 'sugar
demerg|e ˌdiː 'mɜːdʒ ‖ -'mɝːdʒ ~ed d ~es ɪz
əz ~ing ɪŋ
demerger ˌdiː 'mɜːdʒ ə dɪ '•• ‖ -'mɝːdʒ ᵊr ~s
z
demerit ₍ᵢ₎diː 'mer ɪt §-ət ~s s —*but, with
contrastive stress*, (ˌmerits and) 'deˌmerits
Demerol *tdmk* 'dem ə rɒl ‖ -roʊl -rɑːl, -rɔːl
demersal dɪ 'mɜːs ᵊl də-, §diː- ‖ -'mɝːs-
demesne dɪ 'meɪn də-, §diː-, -'miːn ~s z
Demeter dɪ 'miːt ə də- ‖ -'miːt̬ ᵊr
Demetrius dɪ 'miːtr i‿əs də-
demi- ¦dem i
demie... —*see* demy
demigod 'dem i gɒd ‖ -gɑːd ~s z
demigoddess 'dem i ˌgɒd es -ɪs, -əs ‖ -ˌgɑːd əs
~es ɪz əz
demijohn 'dem i dʒɒn ‖ -dʒɑːn ~s z
demilitaris... —*see* demilitariz...
demilitarization ˌdiː ˌmɪl ɪt‿ər aɪ 'zeɪʃ ᵊn •ˌ•ˌ-,
-ət‿ər aɪ-, -ɪ'•- ‖ -ət‿ər ə- ~s z
demilitariz|e ₍ᵢ₎diː 'mɪl ɪt ə raɪz -'•ət- ~ed d
~es ɪz əz ~ing ɪŋ
de Mille də 'mɪl
demilune 'dem i luːn -ljuːn ~s z
demimondaine ˌdem i mɒn 'deɪn -'mɒnd eɪn
‖ -mɑːn 'deɪn -'mɑːnd eɪn —*Fr*
[də mi mɔ̃ dɛn] ~s z
demimonde ˌdem i 'mɒnd '•••
‖ 'dem i mɑːnd —*Fr* [də mi mɔ̃ːd]
de minimis ₍ᵢ₎deɪ 'mɪn ɪ mɪs -ə-
demis|e dɪ 'maɪz də-, §diː-, -'miːz ~ed d ~es
ɪz əz ~ing ɪŋ
demisemiquaver 'dem i sem i ˌkweɪv ə ˌ•••'•-
‖ -ᵊr ~s z
demist ˌdiː 'mɪst ~ed ɪd əd ~ing ɪŋ ~s s
demister ˌdiː 'mɪst ə ‖ -ᵊr ~s z
demitasse 'dem i tæs -tɑːs, ˌ••'• —*Fr*
[də mi tas]
demiurge 'dem i ɜːdʒ 'diːm- ‖ -ɝːdʒ
demo 'dem əʊ ‖ -oʊ ~s z
demo- *comb. form*
with stress-neutral suffix ¦dem ə ¦diːm ə —
demographic ˌdem ə 'græf ɪk ◄ ˌdiːm-
with stress-imposing suffix dɪ 'mɒ+ də-, diː-
‖ -'mɑː+ — demography dɪ 'mɒg rəf i də-,
diː- ‖ -'mɑːg-
demob ₍ᵢ₎diː 'mɒb ‖ -'mɑːb ~bed d ~bing ɪŋ
~s z
demobilis... —*see* demobiliz...
demobilization dɪ ˌməʊb əl aɪ 'zeɪʃ ᵊn diː-,
ˌdiː, •-, -ɪl aɪ-, -ɪ'•- ‖ -ˌmoʊb əl ə- ~s z
demobiliz|e dɪ 'məʊb ə laɪz ₍ᵢ₎diː-, -ɪ-, -ᵊl aɪz
‖ -'moʊb- ~ed d ~es ɪz əz ~ing ɪŋ
democrac|y dɪ 'mɒk rəs |i də- ‖ -'mɑːk- ~ies
ɪz
democrat 'dem ə kræt ~s s
democratic ˌdem ə 'kræt ɪk ◄ ‖ -'kræt̬ ɪk ◄
~ally ᵊl‿i
democratis... —*see* democratiz...
democratization dɪ ˌmɒk rət aɪ 'zeɪʃ ᵊn də-,
-ɪ'•- ‖ -ˌmɑːk rət̬ ə-

democratiz|e dɪ 'mɒk rə taɪz də- ‖ -'mɑːk-
~ed d ~es ɪz əz ~ing ɪŋ
Democritus dɪ 'mɒk rɪt əs də-, -rət-
‖ -'mɑːk rət̬ əs
demode, démodé ₍ᵢ₎deɪ 'məʊd eɪ
‖ ˌdeɪ moʊ 'deɪ —*Fr* [de mɔ de]
demodu|late ˌdiː 'mɒd ju ‖leɪt dɪ-, -'mɒdʒ u-
‖ -'mɑːdʒ ə- ~lated leɪt ɪd -əd ‖ leɪt̬ əd
~lates leɪts ~lating leɪt ɪŋ ‖ leɪt̬ ɪŋ
demodulation ˌdiː ˌmɒd ju 'leɪʃ ᵊn -ˌmɒdʒ u-;
dɪ ˌmɒd- ‖ -ˌmɑːdʒ ə- dɪ ˌmɑːdʒ ə- ~s z
demodulator ˌdiː 'mɒd ju leɪt ə dɪ-, -'mɒdʒ u-
‖ -'mɑːdʒ ə leɪt̬ ᵊr ~s z
demographer dɪ 'mɒg rəf ə də-, diː-
‖ -'mɑːg rəf ᵊr ~s z
demographic ˌdem ə 'græf ɪk ◄ ˌdiːm- ~ally
ᵊl‿i
demography dɪ 'mɒg rəf i də-, diː- ‖ -'mɑːg-
demoiselle ˌdem wɑː 'zel -wə- —*Fr*
[də mwa zɛl] ~s z —*or as sing.*
demolish dɪ 'mɒl ɪʃ də-, §diː- ‖ -'mɑːl- ~ed t
~es ɪz əz ~ing ɪŋ
demolition ˌdem ə 'lɪʃ ᵊn ˌdiːm- ~s z
demolitionist ˌdem ə 'lɪʃ ᵊn‿ɪst ˌdiːm-, §_əst
~s s
demon 'diːm ən ~s z
demonetis|e, demonetiz|e ₍ᵢ₎diː 'mʌn ɪ taɪz
-'mɒn-, -ə- ‖ -'mɑːn- -'mʌn- ~ed d ~es ɪz
əz ~ing ɪŋ
demoniac dɪ 'məʊn i æk də-, diː- ‖ -'moʊn-
~s s
demoniacal ˌdiːm əʊ 'naɪ‿ək ᵊl ◄ ‖ ˌ•ə-
demonic dɪ 'mɒn ɪk də-, diː- ‖ -'mɑːn-
demonis... —*see* demoniz...
demonization ˌdiːm ən aɪ 'zeɪʃ ᵊn -ɪ'•- ‖ -ə'•
demoniz|e 'diːm ən aɪz ~ed d ~es ɪz əz
~ing ɪŋ
demonology ˌdiːm ə 'nɒl ədʒ i ‖ -'nɑːl-
demonstrability dɪ ˌmɒnˢt trə 'bɪl ət i də-,
-ɪt i; ˌdem ənˢt- ‖ dɪ ˌmɑːnˢt trə 'bɪl ət̬ i

DEMONSTRABLE

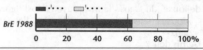

	■ ·¦···	▭¦····	
BrE 1988			
0	20 40	60 80	100%

demonstrab|le dɪ 'mɒnˢt trəb |ᵊl də-;
'dem ənˢt- ‖ dɪ 'mɑːnˢt- —*BrE 1988 poll
panel preference:* •'•••• 63%, '•••• 37%. ~ly
li
demon|strate 'dem ən ‖streɪt ~strated
streɪt ɪd -əd ‖ streɪt̬ əd ~strates streɪts
~strating streɪt ɪŋ ‖ streɪt̬ ɪŋ
demonstration ˌdem ən 'streɪʃ ᵊn ~s z
demonstrative dɪ 'mɒnˢt trət ɪv də-
‖ -'mɑːnˢt trət̬ ɪv ~ly li ~ness nəs nɪs
demonstrator 'dem ən streɪt ə ‖ -streɪt̬ ᵊr ~s z
de Montfort də 'mɒnt fət -fɔːt ‖ dɪ 'mɑːnt fᵊrt
demoralis... —*see* demoraliz...
demoralization dɪ ˌmɒr əl aɪ 'zeɪʃ ᵊn ˌdiː, •-,
-ɪ'•- ‖ dɪ ˌmɔːr əl ə-, -ˌmɑːr-
demoraliz|e dɪ 'mɒr ə laɪz ₍ᵢ₎diː- ‖ -'mɔːr-
-'mɑːr- ~ed d ~es ɪz əz ~ing ɪŋ
Demos 'diːm ɒs ‖ -ɑːs

Demosthenes dɪ 'mɒsθ ə niːz də-, -ɪ-
‖ -'mɑːsθ-
de|mote ˌdiː ǀ'məʊt dɪ-, də- ‖ -ǀ'moʊt
~**moted** 'məʊt ɪd -əd ‖ 'moʊt̬ əd ~**motes**
'məʊts ‖ 'moʊts ~**moting**
'məʊt ɪŋ ‖ 'moʊt̬ ɪŋ
demotic dɪ 'mɒt ɪk də-, diː- ‖ -'mɑːt̬ ɪk
demotion ˌdiː 'məʊʃ ən dɪ-, də- ‖ -'moʊʃ ən
~**s** z
demoti|vate ˌdiː 'məʊt ɪ ǀveɪt -ə- ‖ -ǀ'moʊt̬ ə-
~**vated** veɪt ɪd -əd ‖ veɪt̬ əd ~**vates** veɪts
~**vating** veɪt ɪŋ ‖ veɪt̬ ɪŋ
demotivation ˌdiː ˌməʊt ɪ 'veɪʃ ən -ə-
‖ diː ˌmoʊt̬ ə-
Dempsey 'demps i
Dempster, d~ 'dempst ə ‖ -ər
demulcent dɪ 'mʌls ənt də, diː:- ~**s** s
de|mur v, n dɪ ǀ'mɜː də-, §diː:- ‖ -ǀ'mɜː:
~**murred** 'mɜːd ‖ 'mɜː:d ~**murring**
'mɜːr ɪŋ ‖ 'mɜː: ɪŋ ~**murs** 'mɜːz ‖ 'mɜː:z
de|mure dɪ ǀ'mjʊə də-, §diː:- ‖ -ǀ'mjʊər
~**murer** 'mjʊər ə ‖ 'mjʊr ər ~**murest**
'mjʊər ɪst -əst ‖ 'mjʊr əst ~**murely**
'mjʊə li ‖ 'mjʊr li ~**mureness** 'mjʊə nəs nɪs
‖ 'mjʊr-
demurrage dɪ 'mʌr ɪdʒ də-, §diː:- ‖ -'mɜː:-
demurral dɪ 'mʌr əl də-, §diː:- ‖ -'mɜː:- ~**s** z
demurr... —see **demur**
demurrer 'objection' dɪ 'mʌr ə də-, §diː:-
‖ -'mɜː: ər
demurrer 'objector' dɪ 'mɜː:r ə də-, §diː:-
‖ -'mɜː: ər
de|my dɪ ǀ'maɪ də- ~**mies** 'maɪz
demystification ˌdiː ˌmɪst ɪf ɪ 'keɪʃ ən •ǀ•-,
-əf ɪ-, §-ə' •- ‖ diː ˌmɪst-
demysti|fy ₍ₙ₎diː 'mɪst ɪ ǀfaɪ -ə- ~**fied** faɪd
~**fier/s** faɪ_ə/z ‖ faɪ_ər/z ~**fies** faɪz ~**fying**
faɪ ɪŋ
demythologis... —see **demythologiz...**
demythologization ˌdiː mɪ ˌθɒl ədʒ aɪ 'zeɪʃ ən
ˌ•mə-, -ɪ'•- ‖ -ˌθɑːl ədʒ ə-
demythologiz|e ˌdiː mɪ 'θɒl ə dʒaɪz •ǀmə-
‖ -'θɑːl- ~**ed** d ~**es** ɪz əz ~**ing** ɪŋ
den, Den den **dens, Den's** denz
Dena 'diːn ə
Denaby 'den əb i
denari|us dɪ 'neər iǀ_əs də-, -'nɑːr- ‖ -'ner-
-'nær- ~**i** aɪ iː
denary 'diːn ər i 'den-
denationalis... —see **denationaliz...**
denationalization ˌdiː ˌnæʃ ən_əl aɪ 'zeɪʃ ən
•ǀ, •-, -ɪ'•- ‖ diː ˌnæʃ ən_əl ə- ~**s** z
denationaliz|e ₍ₙ₎diː 'næʃ ən_ə laɪz _əl aɪz ~**ed**
d ~**es** ɪz əz ~**ing** ɪŋ
denature ₍ₙ₎diː 'neɪtʃ ə ‖ -ər ~**d** d ~**s** z
denaturing ₍ₙ₎diː 'neɪtʃ ər ɪŋ
denaturiz|e ₍ₙ₎diː 'neɪtʃ ə raɪz ~**ed** d ~**es** ɪz əz
~**ing** ɪŋ
Denbigh, Denby 'den bi →'dem-
Dench dentʃ
dendrite 'dendr aɪt ~**s** s
dendritic ₍ₙ₎den 'drɪt ɪk ‖ -'drɪt̬ ɪk ~**ally** əl_i

dendrochronology ˌdendr əʊ krə 'nɒl ədʒ i
ˌ•• krɒ- ‖ -oʊ krə 'nɑːl-
dendrogram 'dendr ə græm ~**s** z
dendroid 'dendr ɔɪd
dendrology den 'drɒl ədʒ i ‖ -'drɑːl-
dene, Dene British name diːn **denes** diːnz
'dene hole
Dene, Déné Canadian Indian people 'den i -eɪ
Deneb 'den eb
Denebola dɪ 'neb əl ə də-, de-
dengue 'deŋ gi -geɪ
Deng Xiaoping ˌdʌŋ ʃaʊ 'pɪŋ ˌdeŋ- —Chi
Dēng Xiǎopíng [¹təŋ ³çjɐu ²pʰiŋ]
Den Haag den 'hɑːg dən- —Dutch [dɛn 'haːx]
Denham, Denholm, Denholme 'den əm —but
Denholme, W.Yks., is usually -hɒlm ‖ -hoʊlm
denial dɪ 'naɪ_əl də-, §diː:- ~**s** z
denie... —see **deny**
denier measure of fineness 'den i_ə -eɪ ‖ 'den jər
denier coin 'den i_ə -eɪ; də 'nɪə ‖ də 'nɪər —Fr
[də nje] ~**s** z
denier 'one that denies' dɪ 'naɪ_ə də-, §diː:-
‖ -'naɪ_ər ~**s** z
deni|grate 'den ɪ ǀgreɪt -ə-; 'diː naɪ ˌgreɪt
~**grated** greɪt ɪd -əd ‖ greɪt̬ əd ~**grates**
greɪts ~**grating** greɪt ɪŋ ‖ greɪt̬ ɪŋ
denigration ˌden ɪ 'greɪʃ ən -ə-; ˌdiː naɪ- ~**s** z
denigratory ˌden ɪ 'greɪt ər i ◂ , •ə-; '•••••
‖ 'den ɪg rə tɔːr i -toʊr i (*)
denim 'den ɪm -əm ~**ed** d ~**s** z
De Niro də 'nɪər əʊ ‖ -'nɪr oʊ
Denis 'den ɪs §-əs ~**'s** ɪz əz
Denise də 'niːz de-, dɪ-, -'niːs
Denison 'den ɪs ən -əs-
denizen 'den ɪz ən -əz-~ **s** z
Denmark 'den mɑːk →'dem- ‖ -mɑːrk
Denne den
Dennie 'den i
Denning 'den ɪŋ
Dennis 'den ɪs §-əs
Dennison 'den ɪs ən §-əs-
Denny 'den i
denominable dɪ 'nɒm ɪn əb əl də-, §diː:-, -'•ən-
‖ -'nɑːm-
denomi|nate v dɪ 'nɒm ɪ ǀneɪt də-, §diː:-, -ə-
‖ -'nɑːm- ~**nated** neɪt ɪd -əd ‖ neɪt̬ əd
~**nates** neɪts ~**nating** neɪt ɪŋ ‖ neɪt̬ ɪŋ
denominate adj dɪ 'nɒm ɪn ət də-, §diː:-, -ən-,
-ɪt; -ɪ neɪt, -ə- ‖ -'nɑːm-
denomination dɪ ˌnɒm ɪ 'neɪʃ ən də-, §diː:-, -ə-
‖ -ˌnɑːm- ~**s** z
denominational dɪ ˌnɒm ɪ 'neɪʃ ən_əl ◂ də-,
§diː:-, -, •ə- ‖ -ˌnɑːm- ~**ism** ˌɪz əm ~**ly** i
denominative dɪ 'nɒm ɪn ət ɪv ˌdiː:-, -ən_ət-
‖ -'nɑːm ən_ət̬ ɪv ~**s** z
denominator dɪ 'nɒm ɪ neɪt ə də-, §diː:-, -'•ə-
‖ -ˌnɑːm ə neɪt̬ ər ~**s** z
denotation ˌdiː nəʊ 'teɪʃ ən ‖ -noʊ- ~**s** z
denotative dɪ 'nəʊt ət ɪv ˌdiː:-, də-;
'diː nəʊteɪt ɪv ‖ 'diː noʊ teɪt̬ ɪv dɪ 'noʊt̬ ət̬ ɪv
~**ly** li
de|note dɪ ǀ'nəʊt də-, §diː:- ‖ -ǀ'noʊt ~**noted**

D

'nəʊt ɪd -əd ‖ 'noʊt̬ əd ~notes
'nəʊts ‖ 'noʊts ~noting 'nəʊt ɪŋ ‖ 'noʊt̬ ɪŋ
denouement, dénouement deɪ 'nu: mɒ̃ dɪ-,
də- ‖ ˌdeɪ nu: 'mɑ̃: —Fr [de nu mɑ̃] ~s z
—or as sing.
denounc|e dɪ 'naʊnts də-, §di:- ~ed t ~er/s
ə/z ‖ -ᵊr/z ~es ɪz əz ~ing ɪŋ
de novo ₍ᵢ₎deɪ 'nəʊv əʊ di:-, dɪ-, də ‖ -'noʊv oʊ
Denovo tdmk dɪ 'nəʊv əʊ də-, di:-, ₍ᵢ₎deɪ-
‖ -'noʊv oʊ
dense dens denser 'dents ə ‖ -ᵊr densest
'dents ɪst -əst densely 'dents li denseness
'dents nəs -nɪs
Denselow 'denz ə ləʊ ‖ -loʊ
densit|y 'dents ət |i -ɪt- ‖ -ət̬ i ~ies iz
dent, Dent dent dented 'dent ɪd -əd ‖ 'dent̬
əd denting 'dent ɪŋ ‖ 'dent̬ ɪŋ dents dents
dental 'dent ᵊl ‖ 'dent̬ ᵊl ~ly i ~s z
ˌdental 'floss; ˌdental 'surgeon, ˈ•• ˌ••
dentate 'dent eɪt ~ly li
denticle 'dent ɪk ᵊl ‖ 'dent̬- ~s z
denticulate den 'tɪk jʊl ət -jəl-, -ɪt; -ju leɪt,
-jə- ‖ -jəl ət ~ly li
dentiform 'dent ɪ fɔːm §-ə- ‖ 'dent̬ ə fɔːrm
dentifric|e 'dent ɪf rɪs -əf-, §-rəs ‖ 'dent̬ əf-
~es ɪz əz
dentil 'dent ɪl -ᵊl ‖ 'dent̬ ᵊl ~s z
dentilabial ˌdent i 'leɪb i‿əl ◂ ‖ ˌdent̬- ~s z
dentilingual ˌdent i 'lɪŋ gwəl ◂ -'lɪŋ gju‿əl
‖ ˌdent̬- ~s z
dentine 'dent i:n ˌden 'ti:n
dentist 'dent ɪst §-əst ‖ 'dent̬ əst ~s s
dentistry 'dent ɪst ri -əst- ‖ 'dent̬-
dentition den 'tɪʃ ᵊn
Denton 'dent ᵊn ‖ -ᵊn
D'Entrecasteaux ˌdɒntr ə kæ 'stəʊ ◂
ˌ•• 'kæst əʊ ‖ ˌdɑːntr ə kæ 'stoʊ ◂
ˌ•• 'kæst oʊ —Fr [dɑ̃ tʁə ka sto]
denture 'dentʃ ə ‖ -ᵊr ~s z
denudation ˌdi: nju 'deɪʃ ᵊn §-nu-; ˌden ju-
‖ -nu- -nju- ~s z
denud|e dɪ 'nju:d də-, di:-, §-'nu:d ‖ -'nu:d
-'nju:d ~ed ɪd əd ~es z ~ing ɪŋ
denumerability dɪ ˌnju:m ᵊr‿ə 'bɪl ət i də-,
§di:-, §-ˌnu:m-, -ɪti ‖ -ˌnu:m ᵊr‿ə 'bɪl ət̬ i
-ˌnju:m-
denumerab|le dɪ 'nju:m ᵊr‿əb |ᵊl də-, §di:-,
§-'nu:m- ‖ -'nu:m- -'nju:m- ~ly li
denunciation dɪ ˌnʌnts i 'eɪʃ ᵊn də-, §di:- ~s z
denunciatory dɪ 'nʌnts i‿ət‿ər i də-, §di:-,
-'nʌntʃ- ‖ ‿ə tɔːr i -toʊr-
Denver 'den və ‖ -vᵊr
de|ny dɪ |'naɪ də-, §di:- ~nied 'naɪd ~nies
'naɪz ~nying 'naɪ ɪŋ
Denys 'den ɪs §-əs
Denzil 'denz ᵊl -ɪl
Deo 'deɪ əʊ 'di:- ‖ -oʊ —See also phrases with
this word
deoch an doris, deoch an doruis ˌdɒx
ən 'dɒr ɪs ˌdjɒx-, -əs ‖ —
deodand 'di: əʊ dænd ‖ -ə- ~s z
deodar 'di: əʊ dɑ: ‖ -ə dɑːr ~s z
deodorant di 'əʊd‿ᵊr ənt ‖ -'oʊd‿ ~s s

deodoris|e, deodoriz|e di 'əʊd ə raɪz -ᵊr aɪz
‖ -'oʊd- ~ed d ~er/s ə/z ‖ -ᵊr/z ~es ɪz əz
~ing ɪŋ
deo gratias ˌdeɪ əʊ 'grɑːt i‿əs ˌdi:-, -æs, -ɑːs
‖ ˌ•'oʊ-
deontic di 'ɒnt ɪk ˌdi:- ‖ -'ɑːnt̬-
deontological di ˌɒnt ə 'lɒdʒ ɪk ᵊl ◂ ˌdi:-
‖ -ˌɑːnt̬ ə 'lɑːdʒ- ~ly ‿i
deontology ˌdi: ɒn 'tɒl ədʒ i ‖ -ɑːn 'tɑːl-
deo volente ˌdeɪ əʊ və 'lent i ˌdi:-, -vɒ'•-, -eɪ
‖ ˌ•'oʊ-
deoxy- ˌdi: ɒks i di ˌɒks i ‖ di ˌɑːks i —
deoxycorticosterone
ˌdi: ɒks i ˌkɔːt ɪ kəʊ 'stɪər əʊn di ˌɒks-,
-'kɒst ə rəʊn ‖ di ˌɑːks i ˌkɔːrt̬ ɪ 'kɑːst ə roʊn
-'koʊst-
deoxyge|nate ˌdi: 'ɒks ɪdʒ ə |neɪt di-,
§-'‿ədʒ-; ˌdi: ɒk 'sɪdʒ- ‖ -'ɑːks- ~nated
neɪt ɪd -əd ‖ neɪt̬ əd ~nates neɪts ~nating
neɪt ɪŋ ‖ neɪt̬ ɪŋ
deoxyribonucleic
ˌdi: ɒks i ˌraɪb əʊ nju 'kli: ɪk ◂ di ˌɒks-,
-'kleɪ- ‖ di ˌɑːks i ˌraɪb oʊ nu- -nju'•-,
-'kleɪ-
ˌdeoxyˌribonuˌcleic 'acid
dep —see depart, departure
Depardieu 'dep ɑː djɜ: ˌ•'•◂ ‖ -ɑːr 'djʌ —Fr
[də paʁ djø]
de|part dɪ |'pɑːt də-, §di:- ‖ -|'pɑːrt ~parted
'pɑːt ɪd -əd ‖ 'pɑːrt̬ əd ~parts
'pɑːts ‖ 'pɑːrts ~parting 'pɑːt ɪŋ ‖ 'pɑːrt̬ ɪŋ
department dɪ 'pɑːt mənt də-, §di:- ‖ -'pɑːrt-
~s s
de'partment store
departmental ˌdi: pɑːt 'ment ᵊl ◂ dɪ ˌpɑːt-,
də-, §di:- ‖ ˌdi: pɑːrt 'ment̬ ᵊl dɪ ˌpɑːrt- ~ly i
departure dɪ 'pɑːtʃ ə də-, §di:- ‖ -'pɑːrtʃ ᵊr ~s
z
de'parture lounge; de'parture time
Depeche Mode dɪ ˌpeʃ 'məʊd də-, §di:-
‖ -'moʊd
depend dɪ 'pend də-, §di:- ~ed ɪd əd ~ing ɪŋ
~s z
dependability dɪ ˌpend ə 'bɪl ət i də-, §di:-,
-ɪt i ‖ -ət̬ i
dependab|le dɪ 'pend əb |ᵊl də-, §di:- ~ly li
dependanc... —see dependenc...
dependant dɪ 'pend ənt də-, §di:- ~s s
dependence dɪ 'pend ᵊnts də-, §di:- ~es ɪz əz
dependenc|y dɪ 'pend ᵊnts |i də-, §di:- ~ies iz
dependent dɪ 'pend ənt də-, §di:- ~s s
depict dɪ 'pɪkt də-, §di:- ~ed ɪd əd ~ing ɪŋ
~s s
depiction dɪ 'pɪk ʃᵊn də-, §di:- ~s z
depi|late 'dep ɪ |leɪt -ə- ~lated leɪt ɪd -əd
‖ leɪt̬ əd ~lates leɪts ~lating leɪt ɪŋ ‖ leɪt̬ ɪŋ
depilation ˌdep ɪ 'leɪʃ ᵊn -ə-
depilator|y dɪ 'pɪl ət‿ᵊr |i də-, §di:- ‖ -ə tɔːr |i
-toʊr i ~ies iz
de|plete dɪ |'pli:t də-, §di:- ~pleted 'pli:t ɪd
-əd ‖ 'pli:t̬ əd ~pletes 'pli:ts ~pleting
'pli:t ɪŋ ‖ 'pli:t̬ ɪŋ
depletion dɪ 'pli:ʃ ᵊn də-, §di:- ~s z

deplorab|le dɪ ˈplɔːr əb |ᵊl də-, §diː- ‖ -ˈploʊr-
  ~ly li
deplore dɪ ˈplɔː də-, §diː- ‖ -ˈplɔːr -ˈploʊr ~**d**
  d ~**s** z **deploring** dɪ ˈplɔːr ɪŋ də-,
  §diː- ‖ -ˈploʊr-
deploy dɪ ˈplɔɪ də-, §diː- ~**ed** d ~**ing** ɪŋ
  ~**ment** mənt ~**s** z
deponent dɪ ˈpəʊn ənt də-, §diː- ‖ -ˈpoʊn- ~**s**
  s
Depo-Provera *tdmk* ˌdep əʊ prəʊ
  ˈvɪər ə ‖ -oʊ proʊ ˈver ə
depopu|late ₍ˌ₎diː ˈpɒp ju |leɪt -jə- ‖ -ˈpɑːp jə-
  ~**lated** leɪt ɪd -əd ‖ leɪt̬ əd ~**lates** leɪts
  ~**lating** leɪt ɪŋ ‖ leɪt̬ ɪŋ
depopulation ˌdiː ˌpɒp ju ˈleɪʃ ᵊn •ˌ•-, -jə-ˈ•-
  ‖ diː ˌpɑːp jə-
de|port dɪ ‖ˈpɔːt də-, §diː- ‖ -‖ˈpɔːrt -ˈpoʊrt
  ~**ported** ˈpɔːt ɪd -əd ‖ ˈpɔːrt̬ əd ˈpoʊrt̬-
  ~**porting** ˈpɔːt ɪŋ ‖ ˈpɔːrt̬ ɪŋ ˈpoʊrt̬- ~**ports**
  ˈpɔːts ‖ ˈpɔːrts ˈpoʊrts
deportation ˌdiː pɔː ˈteɪʃ ᵊn ‖ -pɔːr- -pᵊr-,
  -poʊr- ~**s** z
deportee ˌdiː pɔː ˈtiː ‖ -pɔːr- -poʊr- ~**s** z
deportment dɪ ˈpɔːt mənt də-, §diː- ‖ -ˈpɔːrt-
  -ˈpoʊrt-
depos|e dɪ ˈpəʊz də-, §diː- ‖ -ˈpoʊz ~**ed** d
  ~**es** ɪz əz ~**ing** ɪŋ
depos|it dɪ ˈpɒz ɪt də-, §diː-, §-ət ‖ -ˈpɑːz |ət
  ~**ited** ɪt ɪd §ət-, -əd ‖ ət̬ əd ~**iting** ɪt ɪŋ §ət-
  ‖ ət̬ ɪŋ ~**its** ɪts §əts ‖ əts
  deˈposit acˌcount
depositar|y dɪ ˈpɒz ɪt‿ər |i də-, §diː-, -ˈ•ət‿
  ‖ -ˈpɑːz ə ter |i ~**ies** ɪz
deposition ˌdep ə ˈzɪʃ ᵊn ˌdiː pə- ~**s** z
depositor dɪ ˈpɒz ɪt ə də-, §diː-, -ət-
  ‖ -ˈpɑːz ət̬ ᵊr ~**s** z
depositor|y dɪ ˈpɒz ɪt‿ər |i də-, §diː-, -ˈ•ət‿
  ‖ -ˈpɑːz ə tɔːr i -toʊr i ~**ies** ɪz

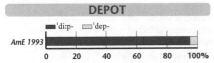

DEPOT

AmE 1993

ˈdiːp-   ˈdep-

0   20   40   60   80   100%

depot ˈdep əʊ ‖ -oʊ —*but in AmE generally*
  ˈdiːp- *in the sense 'bus station, train station'*
  (AmE 1993 poll panel preference: ˈdiːp- *95%,*
  ˈdep- *5%).* ~**s** z
depravation ˌdep rə ˈveɪʃ ᵊn
deprav|e dɪ ˈpreɪv də-, §diː- ~**ed** d ~**es** z
  ~**ing** ɪŋ
depravit|y dɪ ˈpræv ət |i də-, §diː-, -ɪt- ‖ -ət̬ |i
  ~**ies** ɪz
depre|cate ˈdep rə |keɪt -rɪ- ~**cated** keɪt ɪd
  -əd ‖ keɪt̬ əd ~**cates** keɪts ~**cating/ly**
  keɪt ɪŋ /li ‖ keɪt̬ ɪŋ /li
deprecation ˌdep rə ˈkeɪʃ ᵊn -rɪ-
deprecatory ˈdep rə keɪt ər i ˈ•rɪ-, ˌ••ˈ•••;
  -kət‿ər i ‖ -kə tɔːr i -toʊr i
depreci|ate dɪ ˈpriːʃ i |eɪt də-, §diː-, -ˈpriːs-
  ~**ated** eɪt ɪd -əd ‖ eɪt̬ əd ~**ates** eɪts ~**ating**
  eɪt ɪŋ ‖ eɪt̬ ɪŋ
depreciation dɪ ˌpriːʃ i ˈeɪʃ ᵊn də-, §diː-,
  -ˌpriːs-

depreciatory dɪ ˈpriːʃ i‿ət‿ər i də-, §diː-,
  -ˈpriːs-, -ˈpriːʃ ət‿ər i ‖ ə tɔːr i -toʊr i
depre|date ˈdep rə |deɪt -rɪ- ~**dated** deɪt ɪd
  -əd ‖ deɪt̬ əd ~**dates** deɪts ~**dating**
  deɪt ɪŋ ‖ deɪt̬ ɪŋ
depredation ˌdep rə ˈdeɪʃ ᵊn -rɪ- ~**s** z
depredatory dɪ ˈpred ət‿ər i də-, §diː-;
  ˌdep rə ˈdeɪt ər i, ˌ•rɪ-, ˈ••• - ‖ -ə tɔːr i
  -toʊr i
depress dɪ ˈpres də-, §diː- ~**ed** t ~**es** ɪz əz
  ~**ing/ly** ɪŋ /li
depressant dɪ ˈpres ᵊnt də-, §diː- ~**s** s
depression dɪ ˈpreʃ ᵊn də-, §diː- ~**s** z
depressive dɪ ˈpres ɪv də-, §diː- ~**ly** li ~**ness**
  nəs nɪs ~**s** z
depressor dɪ ˈpres ə də-, §diː- ‖ -ᵊr ~**s** z
depressuris... —*see* **depressuriz...**
depressurization dɪ ˌpreʃ ər aɪ ˈzeɪʃ ᵊn •ˌ•-,
  dɪ, •-, -ɪˈ• - ‖ dɪ ˌpreʃ ər‿ə- ~**s** z
depressuriz|e ₍ˌ₎diː ˈpreʃ ə raɪz dɪ- ~**ed** d ~**es**
  ɪz əz ~**ing** ɪŋ

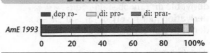

DEPRIVATION

ˌdep rə-   ˌdiː prə-   ˌdiː praɪ-

AmE 1993

0   20   40   60   80   100%

deprivation ˌdep rɪ ˈveɪʃ ᵊn -rə-; ˌdiː prə-, -prɪ-,
  -praɪ- —*AmE 1993 poll panel preference:*
  ˌdep rə- *93%,* ˌdiː prə- *4%,* ˌdiː praɪ- *3%.*
  ~**s** z
depriv|e dɪ ˈpraɪv də-, §diː- ~**ed** d ~**es** z ~**ing**
  ɪŋ
de profundis ˌdeɪ prə ˈfʊnd iːs ˌdiː-, -prɒ-,
  -ˈfʌnd-, -ɪs ‖ -proʊ-
depside ˈdeps aɪd -ɪd, §-əd ~**s** z
dept —*see* **department**
Deptford ˈdet fəd ˈdep*t*- ‖ -fᵊrd
depth depθ **depths** depθs
  ˈdepth charge
deputation ˌdep ju ˈteɪʃ ᵊn -jə- ‖ -jə- ~**s** z
de|pute dɪ ‖ˈpjuːt də-, §diː- ~**puted** ˈpjuːt ɪd
  -əd ‖ ˈpjuːt̬ əd ~**putes** ˈpjuːts ~**puting**
  ˈpjuːt ɪŋ ‖ ˈpjuːt̬ ɪŋ
deputi... —*see* **deputy**
deputis|e, deputiz|e ˈdep ju taɪz -jə- ‖ -jə-
  ~**ed** d ~**es** ɪz əz ~**ing** ɪŋ
deput|y ˈdep jut li -jət- ‖ -jət̬ li ~**ies** ɪz
De Quincey də ˈkwɪnts i
derail ₍ˌ₎diː ˈreɪᵊl dɪ- ~**ed** d ~**ing** ɪŋ ~**s** z
derailleur dɪ ˈreɪl jə də-, ₍ˌ₎diː-, -ə ‖ -ᵊr ~**s** z
derailment ₍ˌ₎diː ˈreɪᵊl mənt dɪ- ~**s** s
derang|e dɪ ˈreɪndʒ də-, §diː- ~**ed** d ~**es** ɪz əz
  ~**ing** ɪŋ
derangement dɪ ˈreɪndʒ mənt də-, §diː-
de|rate ˌdiː ‖ˈreɪt ~**rated** ˈreɪt ɪd -əd ‖ ˈreɪt̬ əd
  ~**rates** ˈreɪts ~**rating** ˈreɪt ɪŋ ‖ ˈreɪt̬ ɪŋ
derb|y ˈdɑːb li §ˈdɜːb- ‖ ˈdɝːb li (*) ~**ies** ɪz
Derby (i) ˈdɑːb i, (ii) ˈdɜːb i ‖ ˈdɝːb i
  —*For the place in England, usually* (i)*; for*
  places in the US, (ii)
Derbyshire ˈdɑːb i ʃə §ˈdɜːb-, -ʃɪə ‖ ˈdɑːrb i ʃᵊr
  ˈdɝːb-, -ʃɪr

D

deregu|late ˌdiː 'reg ju ǁeɪt dɪ-, -jə- ǁ -jə-
~**lated** leɪt ɪd -əd ǁ leɪt̬ əd ~**lates** leɪts
~**lating** leɪt ɪŋ ǁ leɪt̬ ɪŋ
deregulation ˌdiː ˌreg ju 'leɪʃ ən -jə-
ǁ diː ˌreg jə- ˌˌˌˈˌˌˌˈˌ
Dereham 'dɪər əm ǁ 'dɪr-
Derek 'der ɪk
derelict 'der ə lɪkt -ɪ- ~**s** s
dereliction ˌder ə 'lɪk ʃən -ɪ- ~**s** z
derestrict ˌdiː rɪ 'strɪkt -rə-, §-riː- ~**ed** ɪd əd
~**ing** ɪŋ ~**s** s
derestriction ˌdiː rɪ 'strɪk ʃən -rə-, §-riː- ~**s** z
De Reszke də 'resk i
Derg dɜːg ǁ dɝːg
derid|e dɪ 'raɪd də-, §diː- ~**ed** ɪd əd ~**es** z
~**ing** ɪŋ
de rigueur ˌˌdə riː 'gɜː ˌˌdeɪ-, ˌˌdiː-, -riː-
ǁ -'gɝː —*Fr* [də ʁi gœːʁ]
derision dɪ 'rɪʒ ən də-, §diː-
derisive dɪ 'raɪs ɪv də-, §diː-, -'raɪz-, -'rɪz- ~**ly**
li ~**ness** nəs nɪs
deris|ory dɪ 'raɪs |ər_i də-, §diː-, -'raɪz- ~**orily**
ər_əl i ər_ɪ li
derivable dɪ 'raɪv əb əl də-, §diː-
derivation ˌder ɪ 'veɪʃ ən -ə- ~**al** _əl ~**s** z
derivative dɪ 'rɪv ət ɪv də-, §diː- ǁ -ət̬ ɪv ~**ly** li
~**s** z
deriv|e dɪ 'raɪv də-, §diː- ~**ed** d ~**es** z ~**ing** ɪŋ
d'Erlanger 'deəl õʒ eɪ ǁ ˌderl ɑːn 'ʒeɪ
derm dɜːm ǁ dɝːm
-derm dɜːm ǁ dɝːm — **periderm**
'per i dɜːm ǁ -dɝːm
dermal 'dɜːm əl ǁ 'dɝːm-
-dermal 'dɜːm əl ǁ 'dɝːm əl — **peridermal**
ˌper i 'dɜːm əl ◂ ǁ -'dɝːm-
dermatitis ˌdɜːm ə 'taɪt ɪs §-əs
ǁ ˌdɝːm ə 'taɪt̬ əs
dermatologist ˌdɜːm ə 'tɒl ədʒ ɪst §-əst
ǁ ˌdɝːm ə 'tɑːl- ~**s** s
dermatology ˌdɜːm ə 'tɒl ədʒ i ǁ ˌdɝːm ə 'tɑːl-
dermis 'dɜːm ɪs §-əs ǁ 'dɝːm-
Dermod 'dɜːm əd ǁ 'dɝːm-
Dermot, Dermott 'dɜːm ət ǁ 'dɝːm-
dernier cri ˌdɜːn i eɪ 'kriː ǁ ˌdɝːn- —*Fr*
[dɛʁ nje kʁi]
dero|gate 'der ə |geɪt 'diː rəʊˌ|geɪt ~**gated**
geɪt ɪd -əd ǁ geɪt̬ əd ~**gates** geɪts ~**gating**
geɪt ɪŋ ǁ geɪt̬ ɪŋ
derogation ˌder ə 'geɪʃ ən ˌdiː rəʊ- ~**s** z
derogator|y dɪ 'rɒg ət_ər li də-
ǁ -'rɑːg ə tɔːr li -toʊr i ~**ily** əl i ɪl i ~**iness**
i nəs i nɪs
Deronda də 'rɒnd ə dɪ- ǁ -'rɑːnd ə
derrick, D~ 'der ɪk ~**s** s
Derrida də 'riːd ə de-; 'der ɪd ə, -əd-
ǁ ˌder i 'dɑː ˈˌˌˈ —*Fr* [dɛ ʁi da]
Derrie 'der i
derriere, derrière 'der i eə ˌˌˈˈ ǁ ˌder i 'eʳr
—*Fr* [dɛʁ jɛːʁ] ~**s** z —*or as sing.*
derring-do ˌder ɪŋ 'duː ˌdeər-, ˌdɜːr-
derringer, D~ 'der ɪndʒ ə -əndʒ- ǁ -ʳr ~**s** z
derris 'der ɪs §-əs
Derry, derry 'der i

derv dɜːv ǁ dɝːv
dervish 'dɜːv ɪʃ ǁ 'dɝːv- ~**es** ɪz əz
Dervla 'dɜːv lə ǁ 'dɝːv-
Derwent 'dɜː wənt -went ǁ 'dɝː- —*but Baron
D~ is* 'dɑː-
Derwentwater 'dɜː wənt ˌwɔːt ə -went-
ǁ 'dɝː wənt ˌwɔːt̬ ʳr -ˌwɑːt̬ ʳr
Deryck 'der ɪk
Deryn 'der ɪn §-ən
Des dez ǁ des —*See also phrases with this word*
DES ˌdiː iː 'es
Desai de 'saɪ 'deɪs aɪ
De Sales də 'sɑːlz
desali|nate ˌˌdiː 'sæl ɪ |neɪt -ə- ~**nated** neɪt ɪd
-əd ǁ neɪt̬ əd ~**nates** neɪts ~**nating**
neɪt ɪŋ ǁ neɪt̬ ɪŋ
desalination ˌdiː ˌsæl ɪ 'neɪʃ ən -ə- ǁ diː ˌsæl ə-
desalinis... —*see* **desaliniz...**
desalinization ˌdiː ˌsæl ɪn aɪ 'zeɪʃ ən diː ˌsæl-,
-ən aɪ-, -ɪ'ˌˈ ǁ -ən ə-
desaliniz|e ˌˌdiː 'sæl ɪ naɪz -ə- ~**ed** d ~**es** ɪz
əz ~**ing** ɪŋ
De Salis *(i)* də 'sæl ɪs §-əs, *(ii)* -'seɪl-, *(iii)*
də 'sɑːlz
desalt ˌdiː 'sɒlt -'sɔːlt ǁ -'sɔːlt -'sɑːlt ~**ed** ɪd
əd ~**ing** ɪŋ ~**s** s
De Saumarez, De Sausmarez də 'sɒm ər ɪz
-ə rez ǁ -'sɑːm-
Desborough 'dez bər_ə ǁ -ˌbɝː oʊ
descal|e ˌdiː 'skeɪʳl ~**ed** d ~**es** z ~**ing** ɪŋ
descant *n* 'desk ænt ~**s** s
de|scant *v* dɪ |'skænt də-, de- ~**scanted**
'skænt ɪd -əd ǁ 'skænt̬ əd ~**scanting**
'skænt ɪŋ ǁ 'skænt̬ ɪŋ ~**scants** 'skænts
Descartes 'deɪ kɑːt ˈˌˈ ǁ deɪ 'kɑːrt —*Fr*
[de kaʁt]
descend dɪ 'send də-, §diː- ~**ed** ɪd əd ~**ing** ɪŋ
~**s** z
descendant dɪ 'send ənt də-, §diː- ~**s** s
descender dɪ 'send ə də-, §diː- ǁ -ʳr ~**s** z
descent dɪ 'sent də-, §diː- ~**s** s
describable dɪ 'skraɪb əb əl də-, §diː-
describ|e dɪ 'skraɪb də-, §diː- ~**ed** d ~**er/s** ə/
z ǁ ʳr/z ~**es** z ~**ing** ɪŋ
descrie... —*see* **descry**
description dɪ 'skrɪp ʃən də-, §diː- ~**s** z
descriptive dɪ 'skrɪpt ɪv də-, §diː- ~**ly** li ~**ness**
nəs nɪs
descriptiv|ism dɪ 'skrɪpt ɪv |ˌɪz əm də-, §diː-
~**ist/s** ɪst/s §-əst/s
descriptor dɪ 'skrɪpt ə də-, §diː- ǁ -ʳr ~**s** z
de|scry dɪ |'skraɪ də-, §diː- ~**scried** 'skraɪd
~**scries** 'skraɪz ~**scrying** 'skraɪ ɪŋ
Desdemona ˌdez dɪ 'məʊn ə -də- ǁ -'moʊn-
dese|crate 'des ɪ |kreɪt -ə- ~**crated** kreɪt ɪd
-əd ǁ kreɪt̬ əd ~**crates** kreɪts ~**crating**
kreɪt ɪŋ ǁ kreɪt̬ ɪŋ
desecration ˌdes ɪ 'kreɪʃ ən -ə- ~**s** z
deseed ˌdiː 'siːd ~**ed** ɪd əd ~**ing** ɪŋ ~**s** s
desegre|gate ˌˌdiː 'seg rɪ |geɪt -rə- ~**gated**
geɪt ɪd -əd ǁ geɪt̬ əd ~**gates** geɪts ~**gating**
geɪt ɪŋ ǁ geɪt̬ ɪŋ

desegregation ˌdiː ˌseg rɪ ˈgeɪʃ ᵊn -rə-
‖ diː ˌseg-
deselect ˌdiː sə ˈlekt -sɪ- **~ed** ɪd əd **~ing** ɪŋ
~s s
deselection ˌdiː sə ˈlek ʃᵊn -sɪ- **~s** z
de Selincourt də ˈsel ɪn kɔːt →-ɪŋ- ‖ -kɔːrt
-koʊrt
desensitis... —*see* **desensitiz...**
desensitization ˌdiː ˌsenᵗs ət aɪ ˈzeɪʃ ᵊn -ɪt aɪ-,
-ɪˈ•- ‖ diː ˌsenᵗs ət̬ ə- **~s** z
desensitiz|e ₍ᵢ₎diː ˈsenᵗs ə taɪz -ɪ- **~ed** d **~es** ɪz
əz **~ing** ɪŋ
desert *n 'arid place'* ˈdez ət ‖ -ᵊrt **~s** s
ˌdesert ˈrat
desert *n 'what is deserved'* dɪ ˈzɜːt də-. §diː-
‖ -ˈzɝːt **~s** s
de|sert *v* dɪ |ˈzɜːt də-, §diː- ‖ -|ˈzɝːt **~serted**
ˈzɜːt ɪd -əd ‖ ˈzɝːt̬ əd **~serting**
ˈzɜːt ɪŋ ‖ ˈzɝːt̬ ɪŋ **~serts** ˈzɜːts ‖ ˈzɝːts
deserter dɪ ˈzɜːt ə də-, §diː- ‖ -ˈzɝːt̬ ᵊr **~s** z
desertification dɪ ˌzɜːt ɪf ɪ ˈkeɪʃ ᵊn də-,
ˌdez ət-, -əf•ˈ•-, §-əˈ•- ‖ -ˌzɝːt̬ əf-
desertion dɪ ˈzɜːʃ ᵊn də-, §diː- ‖ -ˈzɝːʃ- **~s** z
deserv|e dɪ ˈzɜːv də-, §diː- ‖ -ˈzɝːv **~ed** d
~es z **~ing** ɪŋ
deserved|ly dɪ ˈzɜːv ɪd |li də-, §diː-, -əd-
‖ -ˈzɝːv- **~ness** nəs nɪs
deshabille ˌdez ə ˈbiːᵊl ˌdeɪz-, ˌdes-, -æ-
déshabillé ˌdez ə ˈbiː eɪ ˌdeɪz-, ˌdes-, -æ-; -ˈbiːᵊl
—*Fr* [de za bi je]
desiccant ˈdes ɪk ᵊnt -ək- **~s** s
desic|cate ˈdes ɪ |keɪt -ə- **~cated** keɪt ɪd -əd
‖ keɪt̬ əd **~cates** keɪts **~cating**
keɪt ɪŋ ‖ keɪt̬ ɪŋ
desiccation ˌdes ɪ ˈkeɪʃ ᵊn -ə- **~s** z
desiccator ˈdes ɪ keɪt ə ˈ•ə- ‖ -keɪt̬ ᵊr **~s** z
desiderata dɪ ˌzɪd ə ˈrɑːt ə də-, -ˌsɪd-, -ˈreɪt-
‖ -ˈrɑːt̬ ə -ˈreɪt̬-
desiderative dɪ ˈzɪd ᵊr ət ɪv də- ‖ -ə reɪt̬ ɪv
ᵊr ət̬ ɪv **~s** z
desiderat|um dɪ ˌzɪd ə ˈrɑːt ləm də-, -ˌsɪd-,
-ˈreɪt- ‖ -ˈrɑːt̬- -ˈreɪt̬- **~a** ə
design dɪ ˈzaɪn də-, §diː- **~ed** d **~ing/ly** ɪŋ /li
~s z
desig|nate *v* ˈdez ɪg |neɪt **~nated** neɪt ɪd -əd
‖ neɪt̬ əd **~nates** neɪts **~nating**
neɪt ɪŋ ‖ neɪt̬ ɪŋ
designate *adj* ˈdez ɪg nət -nɪt, -neɪt
designation ˌdez ɪg ˈneɪʃ ᵊn **~s** z
designator ˈdez ɪg neɪt ə ‖ -neɪt̬ ᵊr **~s** z
designedly dɪ ˈzaɪn ɪd li də-, §diː-, -əd-
designer dɪ ˈzaɪn ə də-, §diː- ‖ -ᵊr **~s** z
de,signer ˈjeans
desinenc|e ˈdez ɪn ᵊnᵗs ˈdes-, -ən- **~es** ɪz əz
desinential ˌdez ɪ ˈnenᵗʃ ᵊl ◄ ˌdes-, -ə-
desirability dɪ ˌzaɪ̯ᵊr ə ˈbɪl ət i də-, §diː-, -ɪt i
‖ -ˌzaɪ̯ᵊr ə ˈbɪl ət̬ i
desirab|le dɪ ˈzaɪ̯ᵊr əb |ᵊl də-, §diː- ‖ -ˈzaɪ̯ᵊr-
~leness ᵊl nəs -nɪs **~les** ᵊlz **~ly** li
desire dɪ ˈzaɪ̯ə də-, §diː- ‖ -ˈzaɪ̯ᵊr **~d** d **~s** z
desiring dɪ ˈzaɪ̯ᵊr ɪŋ də-, §diː- ‖ -ˈzaɪ̯ᵊr ɪŋ
Desiree, Désirée deɪ ˈzɪᵊr eɪ de-, dɪ-
‖ ˌdez ə ˈreɪ

desirous dɪ ˈzaɪ̯ᵊr əs də-, §diː- ‖ -ˈzaɪ̯ᵊr- **~ly**
li **~ness** nəs nɪs
desist dɪ ˈzɪst də-, §diː-, -ˈsɪst **~ed** ɪd əd **~ing**
ɪŋ **~s** s
desk desk **desks** desks
deskill ˌdiː ˈskɪl **~ed** d **~ing** ɪŋ **~s** z
desktop ˈdesk tɒp ˌ•ˈ• ‖ -tɑːp **~s** s
deskwork ˈdesk wɜːk ‖ -wɝːk
desman ˈdes mən ˈdez- **~s** z
desmid ˈdez mɪd §-məd **~s** z
desmoid ˈdez mɔɪd ˈdes- **~s** z
Des Moines də ˈmɔɪn dɪ-
Desmond ˈdez mənd
desolate *adj* ˈdes əl ət ˈdez-, -ɪt **~ly** li
deso|late *v* ˈdes ə |leɪt ˈdez- **~lated** leɪt ɪd -əd
‖ leɪt̬ əd **~lates** leɪts **~lating** leɪt ɪŋ ‖ leɪt̬ ɪŋ
desolation ˌdes ə ˈleɪʃ ᵊn ˌdez-
De Soto də ˈsəʊt əʊ ‖ -ˈsoʊt oʊ —*Sp*
[de ˈso to]
Desoutter dɪ ˈsuːt ə də- ‖ -ˈsuːt̬ ᵊr
De Souza də ˈsuːz ə
desoxy- ˌdez ˌɒks i ‖ -ˌɑːks-
desoxymorphine ˌdez ˌɒks i ˈmɔːf iːn
‖ ˌdez ˌɑːks i ˈmɔːrf-
despair dɪ ˈspeə də- ‖ -ˈspeᵊr -ˈspæᵊr **~ed** d
despairing/ly dɪ ˈspeər ɪŋ /li də- ‖ -ˈsper-
-ˈspær- **~s** z
Despard ˈdesp ɑːd ‖ -ɑːrd
despatch *v* dɪ ˈspætʃ də- **~ed** t **~es** ɪz əz
~ing ɪŋ
despatch *n* dɪ ˈspætʃ də-; ˈdɪs pætʃ **~es** ɪz əz
Despenser dɪ ˈspenᵗs ə də- ‖ -ᵊr
desperado ˌdesp ə ˈrɑːd əʊ ‖ -oʊ -ˈreɪd- **~es,**
~s z
desperate ˈdesp ᵊr ət -ɪt **~ly** li **~ness** nəs nɪs
desperation ˌdesp ə ˈreɪʃ ᵊn
despicability dɪ ˌspɪk ə ˈbɪl ət i də-, §diː-,
ˌdesp ɪk-, -ɪt i ‖ -ət̬ i
despicab|le dɪ ˈspɪk əb |ᵊl də-, §diː-; ˈdesp ɪk-
~leness ᵊl nəs -nɪs **~ly** li
despis|e dɪ ˈspaɪz də-, §diː- **~ed** d **~es** ɪz əz
~ing ɪŋ
despite dɪ ˈspaɪt də-, §diː-
Des Plaines *place in IL* des ˈpleɪnz
despoil dɪ ˈspɔɪᵊl də-, §diː- **~ed** d **~ing** ɪŋ **~s**
z
despoliation dɪ ˌspəʊl i ˈeɪʃ ᵊn də-, §diː-
‖ -ˌspoʊl-
despond dɪ ˈspɒnd də-, §diː-; ˈdesp ɒnd
‖ -ˈspɑːnd **~ed** ɪd əd **~ing** ɪŋ **~s** z
despondenc|e dɪ ˈspɒnd ᵊnᵗs də-, §diː-
‖ -ˈspɑːnd- **~ies** iz **~y** i
despondent dɪ ˈspɒnd ᵊnt də-, §diː-
‖ -ˈspɑːnd- **~ly** li
despot ˈdesp ɒt -ət ‖ -ɑːt -ət **~s** s
despotic dɪ ˈspɒt ɪk də-, de- ‖ -ˈspɑːt̬ ɪk **~ally**
ᵊl_i
despotism ˈdesp ə ˌtɪz əm
des res ˌdez ˈrez
dessert dɪ ˈzɜːt də- ‖ -ˈzɝːt **~s** s
des'sert wine
dessertspoon dɪ ˈzɜːt spuːn də- ‖ -ˈzɝːt- **~s** z

D

dessert|spoonful dɪ 'zɜːt |spuːn fʊl də-
‖ -'zɜːt- • , • ' • • **~spoonsful** spuːnz fʊl
destabilis... —*see* **destabiliz...**
destabilization ˌdiː ˌsteɪb ᵊl aɪ 'zeɪʃ ᵊn
dɪ ˌsteɪb-, -ɪl • ' • -, -ɪ' • - ‖ diː ˌsteɪb ᵊl̩_ə- **~s** z
destabiliz|e ˌdiː 'steɪb ə laɪz də-, -ɪ-, -ᵊl aɪz
~ed d **~es** ɪz əz **~ing** ɪŋ
deStalinis... —*see* **deStaliniz...**
deStalinization ˌdiː ˌstɑːl ɪn aɪ 'zeɪʃ ᵊn -ˌstæl-,
-, -•ən-, -ɪ' • - ‖ diː ˌstɑːl ən ə- -ˌstæl-
deStaliniz|e ˌdiː 'stɑːl ɪ naɪz -'stæl-, -ə- **~ed** d
~es ɪz əz **~ing** ɪŋ
De Stijl də 'staɪᵊl —*Dutch* [də 'steɪl]
destination ˌdest ɪ 'neɪʃ ᵊn -ə- **~s** z
destine 'dest ɪn -ən **~d** d **~s** z
destin|y 'dest ᵊn |i -ɪn- **~ies** iz
destitute 'dest ɪ tjuːt -ə-, →§-tʃuːt ‖ -tuːt
-tjuːt
destitution ˌdest ɪ 'tjuːʃ ᵊn -ə-, →§-'tʃuːʃ-
‖ -'tuːʃ ᵊn -'tjuːʃ-
destroy dɪ 'strɔɪ də-, §diː- **~ed** d **~ing** ɪŋ **~s** z
destroyer dɪ 'strɔɪ ə də-, §diː- ‖ -ᵊr **~s** z
destruct dɪ 'strʌkt də-, §diː- **~ed** ɪd əd **~ing**
ɪŋ **~s** s
destructib|le dɪ 'strʌkt əb |ᵊl də-, §diː-, -ɪb-
~leness ᵊl nəs -nɪs **~ly** li
destruction dɪ 'strʌk ʃᵊn də-, §diː- **~s** z
destructive dɪ 'strʌkt ɪv də-, §diː- **~ly** li
~ness nəs nɪs
destructor dɪ 'strʌkt ə də-, §diː- ‖ -ᵊr **~s** z
Destry 'des tri
desuetude 'des wɪ tjuːd →§-tʃuːd; dɪ 'sjuːː_ɪ-,
də-, ₍ₗ₎diː-, -'suːː_ə- ‖ -tuːd -tjuːd; dɪ 'suː ə-
desultor|y 'des ᵊlt _ər |i 'dez- ‖ -ᵊl tɔːr |i -tour i
~ily əl i i li **~iness** i nəs i nɪs
detach dɪ 'tætʃ də-, §diː- **~ed** t **~es** ɪz əz
~ing ɪŋ
detachedly dɪ 'tætʃ ɪd li də-, -əd-;
-'tætʃt li
detachment dɪ 'tætʃ mənt də-, §diː- **~s** s
detail *n, v* 'diː teɪᵊl ; dɪ 'teɪᵊl, də-, §diː- **~ed** d
~ing ɪŋ **~s** z —*AmE 1993 poll panel
preference:* ' • • 75%, • ' • 25%.
detain dɪ 'teɪn də-, §diː- **~ed** d **~ing** ɪŋ **~s** z
detainee ˌdiː teɪ 'niː ; dɪ ˌteɪ-, də-, §diː-;
ˌdɪt eɪ- **~s** z
detect dɪ 'tekt də-, §diː- **~ed** ɪd əd **~ing** ɪŋ
~s s
detectab|le, detectib|le dɪ 'tekt əb |ᵊl də-,
§diː-, -ɪb- **~ly** li
detection dɪ 'tek ʃᵊn də-, §diː-
detective dɪ 'tekt ɪv də-, §diː- **~s** z
detector dɪ 'tekt ə də-, §diː- ‖ -ᵊr **~s** z
de'tector van
detent dɪ 'tent də-, §diː- **~s** s
detente, détente ˌdeɪ tɒnt -tɑːnt; deɪ 'tɒnt,
-'tɑːnt ‖ deɪ 'tɑːnt —*Fr* [de tɑ̃ːt]
detention dɪ 'tenᵗʃ ᵊn də-, §diː- **~s** z
de'tention ˌcentre
deter dɪ 'tɜː də-, §diː- ‖ -'tɜː- **~red** d
deterring dɪ 'tɜːr ɪŋ də-, §diː- ‖ -'tɜː ɪŋ **~s**
z
Deterding 'det əd ɪŋ ‖ -ᵊrd-

detergent dɪ 'tɜːdʒ ᵊnt də-, §diː- ‖ -'tɜːdʒ-
~s s
deterior|ate dɪ 'tɪər i_ə r|eɪt də-, §diː-,
⚠-'tɪər ə r|eɪt, ⚠-'tɪər i |eɪt ‖ -'tɪr- **~ated**
eɪt ɪd -əd ‖ eɪţ əd **~ates** eɪts **~ating**
eɪt ɪŋ ‖ eɪţ ɪŋ
deterioration dɪ ˌtɪər i_ə 'reɪʃ ᵊn də-, §diː-,
⚠-,tɪər ə 'reɪʃ ᵊn, ⚠-,tɪər i 'eɪʃ ᵊn ‖ -,tɪr- **~s**
z
determinable dɪ 'tɜːm ɪn əb ᵊl də-, §diː-,
-ən_əb- ‖ -'tɜːm-
determinant dɪ 'tɜːm ɪn ənt də-, §diː-, -ən-
‖ -'tɜːm- **~s** s
determinate dɪ 'tɜːm ɪn ət də-, §diː-, -ən-, -ɪt
‖ -'tɜːm- **~ly** li **~ness** nəs nɪs
determination dɪ ˌtɜːm ɪ 'neɪʃ ᵊn də-, §diː-, -ə-
‖ -,tɜːm- **~s** z
determinative dɪ 'tɜːm ɪn ət ɪv də-, §diː-,
-ən_ət- ‖ -'tɜːm ə neɪţ ɪv -ən_əţ- **~ness** nəs
nɪs **~s** z
determin|e dɪ 'tɜːm ɪn də-, §diː-, -ən ‖ -'tɜːm-
~ed/ly d /li **~es** z **~ing** ɪŋ
determiner dɪ 'tɜːm ɪn ə də-, §diː-, -ən-
‖ -'tɜːm ən ᵊr **~s** z
determinism dɪ 'tɜːm ɪ ˌnɪz əm də-, §diː-, -ə-
‖ -'tɜːm-
deterministic dɪ ˌtɜːm ɪ 'nɪst ɪk ◄ də-, §diː-, -ə-
‖ -,tɜːm- **~ally** ᵊl_i
deterrence dɪ 'ter ᵊnts də-, §diː-, §-'tɜːr-
‖ -'tɜː- -'ter-
deterrent dɪ 'ter ᵊnt də-, §diː-, §-'tɜːr- ‖ -'tɜː-
-'ter- **~s** s
detest dɪ 'test də-, §diː- **~ed** ɪd əd **~ing** ɪŋ **~s**
s
detestab|le dɪ 'test əb |ᵊl də-, §diː- **~leness**
ᵊl nəs -nɪs **~ly** li
detestation ˌdiː te 'steɪʃ ᵊn
dethron|e dɪ 'θrəʊn də-, ₍ₗ₎diː- ‖ -'θroʊn **~ed** d
~ement mənt **~es** z **~ing** ɪŋ
Detmold 'det məʊld →-mɒʊld ‖ -moʊld —*Ger*
['dɛt mɔlt]
deton|ate 'det ə n|eɪt -ᵊn |eɪt ‖ 'det ᵊn |eɪt
'deţ ə n|eɪt **~ated** eɪt ɪd -əd ‖ eɪţ əd **~ates**
eɪts **~ating** eɪt ɪŋ ‖ eɪţ ɪŋ
detonation ˌdet ə 'neɪʃ ᵊn -ᵊn 'eɪʃ-
‖ ˌdet ᵊn 'eɪʃ ᵊn ˌdeţ ə 'neɪʃ- **~s** z
detonator 'det ə neɪt ə -ᵊn eɪt- ‖ 'det ᵊn eɪţ ᵊr
'deţ ə neɪţ ᵊr **~s** z
detour 'diː tʊə 'deɪ-, -tɔː; ˌdeɪ 'tʊə, dɪ-, də-,
-'tɔː ‖ -tʊr dɪ 'tʊᵊr **~ed** d **~s** z
detox ˌdiː 'tɒks dɪ-; 'diː tɒks ‖ -'tɑːks
detoxi|cate ˌdiː 'tɒks ɪ |keɪt dɪ-, -ə- ‖ -'tɑːks-
~cated keɪt ɪd -əd ‖ keɪţ əd **~cates** keɪts
~cating keɪt ɪŋ ‖ keɪţ ɪŋ
detoxication ˌdiː ˌtɒks ɪ 'keɪʃ ᵊn dɪ ˌtɒks-, -ə-
‖ diː ˌtɑːks-
detoxification ˌdiː ˌtɒks ɪf ɪ 'keɪʃ ᵊn dɪ ˌtɒks-,
-əf • ' • •, §-ə' • • ‖ -,tɑːks-
detoxi|fy ˌdiː 'tɒks ɪ faɪ dɪ-, -ə- ‖ -'tɑːks-
~fied faɪd **~fies** faɪz **~fying** faɪ ɪŋ
detract dɪ 'trækt də-, ₍ₗ₎diː- **~ed** ɪd əd **~ing** ɪŋ
~s s
detraction dɪ 'træk ʃᵊn də-, ₍ₗ₎diː- **~s** z

detractor dɪ 'trækt ə də-, ₍ᵢ₎diː- ‖ -ᵊr ~s z
detrain ˌdiː 'treɪn ~ed d ~ing ɪŋ ~s z
detribalis... —*see* **detribaliz...**
detribalization ˌdiː ˌtraɪb ᵊl aɪ 'zeɪʃ ᵊn
dɪ ˌtraɪb-, -ᵊl ɪ- ‖ -ᵊl ə-
detribaliz|e ˌdiː 'traɪb ə laɪz dɪ-, -ᵊl aɪz ~**ed** d
~**es** ɪz əz ~**ing** ɪŋ
detriment 'detr ɪ mənt -ə-
detrimental ˌdetr ɪ 'ment ᵊl ◄ -ə- ‖ -'menṯ ᵊl ◄
~**ly** i
detritus dɪ 'traɪt əs də-, §diː- ‖ -'traɪṯ əs
Detroit dɪ 'trɔɪt də-, §diː-
de trop də 'trəʊ ‖ -'troʊ —*Fr* [də tʁo]
Dettol 'det ɒl -ᵊl ‖ -ɑːl
detumesc|ence ˌdiː tju 'mes ᵊnts →§-tʃu-
‖ -tu- -tju- ~**ent** ᵊnt
Deucalion dju 'keɪl i_ən →dʒu- ‖ du- dju-
deuce djuːs →§dʒuːs ‖ duːs djuːs **deuces**
'djuːs ɪz →§dʒuːs-, -əz ‖ 'duːs- 'djuːs-
deuced djuːst →§dʒuːst; 'djuːs ɪd, →§'dʒuːs-,
-əd ‖ duːst djuːst
deucedly 'djuːs ɪd li →§'dʒuːs-, -əd- ‖ 'duːs-
'djuːs-
deus, Deus 'deɪ ʊs 'diː̯ əs
ˌdeus ex 'machina 'mæk ɪn ə 'mɑːk-, §-ən-;
-mə 'ʃiːn ə ‖ -'mɑːk ɪ nɑː- -'mæk-, -ən ə
deuterium dju 'tɪər i_əm →§dʒu- ‖ du 'tɪr-
dju-
deutero- ¦djuːt ə rəʊ →§¦dʒuːt- ‖ ¦duːt ə roʊ
— **Deutero-Isaiah** ˌdjuːt ə rəʊ aɪ 'zaɪ̯ ə
→§ˌdʒuːt- ‖ ˌduːt ə roʊ aɪ 'zeɪ ə
deuteron 'djuːt ə rɒn →§'dʒuːt- ‖ 'duːṯ ə rɑːn
'djuːṯ- ~s z
Deuteronomy ˌdjuːt ə 'rɒn əm i →§ˌdʒuːt-;
'djuːt ər_ə nɒm i, →§'dʒuːt- ‖ ˌduːṯ ə 'rɑːn-
ˌdjuːṯ-
Deutsch dɔɪtʃ
Deutsche Mark ˌdɔɪtʃ ə 'mɑːk ‖ -'mɑːrk —*Ger*
[ˌdɔy tʃə 'maʁk]
Deutschland 'dɔɪtʃ lənd -lænd —*Ger*
['dɔytʃ lant]
deutschmark, D~ 'dɔɪtʃ mɑːk ‖ -mɑːrk
deutzia 'djuːts i_ə →§'dʒuːts-; 'dɔɪts-
‖ 'duːts- 'djuːts- ~s z
deva 'deɪv ə 'diːv- —*Hindi* [ɖeːʋ]
De Valera də və 'leər ə ˌdev ə-, -'lɪər- ‖ -'ler ə
-'lɪr-
de Valois də 'væl wɑː
devaluation ˌdiː ˌvæl ju 'eɪʃ ᵊn dɪ ˌvæl-
‖ diː ˌvæl- ~s z
devalue ˌdiː 'væl juː dɪ- ~**d** d ~**s** z **devaluing**
ˌdiː 'væl juː̯ ɪŋ dɪ-
Devanagari ˌdeɪv ə 'nɑːg ər_i ˌdev-
Devaney dɪ 'veɪn i də-
deva|state 'dev ə ǀsteɪt ~**stated** steɪt ɪd -əd
‖ steɪṯ əd ~**states** steɪts ~**stating/ly**
steɪt ɪŋ /li ‖ steɪṯ ɪŋ /li
devastation ˌdev ə 'steɪʃ ᵊn
develop dɪ 'vel əp də-, §diː- ~**ed** t ~**er/s** ə/
z ‖ ᵊr/z ~**ing** ɪŋ ~**s** s
de'veloping ˌcountry, •ˌ•••ˈ••
development dɪ 'vel əp mənt də-, §diː- ~**s** s
de'velopment ˌarea

developmental dɪ ˌvel əp 'ment ᵊl ◄ də-, §diː-
‖ -'menṯ ᵊl ◄ ~**ly** i
deverbal ˌdiː 'vɜːb ᵊl ◄ ‖ -'vɜ·ːb- ~**s** z
deverbative ˌdiː 'vɜːb ət ɪv dɪ- ‖ -'vɜ·ːb əṯ ɪv
~**s** z
De Vere də 'vɪə dɪ- ‖ -'vɪᵊr
Devereux *(i)* 'dev ə ruːks, *(ii)* -rɜː -ᵊr ə ‖ -ᵊr ə,
(iii) -reks, *(iv)* -ruː, *(v)* -rəʊ ‖ -roʊ
devianc|e 'diːv i_ᵊnts ~**y** i
deviant 'diːv i_ənt ~**ly** li ~**s** s
devi|ate v 'diːv i ǀeɪt ~**ated** eɪt ɪd -əd ‖ eɪṯ əd
~**ates** eɪts ~**ating** eɪt ɪŋ ‖ eɪṯ ɪŋ
deviate n 'diːv i_ət -ɪt ~**s** s
deviation ˌdiːv i 'eɪʃ ᵊn ~**ism** ˌɪz əm ~**ist/s**
ɪst/s §-əst/s ~**s** z
deviator 'diːv i eɪt ə ‖ -eɪṯ ᵊr ~**s** z
devic|e dɪ 'vaɪs də-, §diː- ~**es** ɪz əz
devil 'dev ᵊl -ɪl ~**ed**, ~**led** d ~**ing**, ~**ling** ɪŋ ~**s**
z
ˌdevil's 'advocate; 'devil's food cake,
ˌ•• ' • •; ˌdevils-on-'horseback
devilish 'dev ᵊl_ɪʃ ~**ly** li ~**ness** nəs nɪs
de Villiers də 'vɪl jəz ‖ -jᵊrz
devil-may-care ˌdev ᵊl meɪ 'keə ◄ ‖ -'keᵊr◄
-'kæᵊr
devilment 'dev ᵊl mənt
devil|ry 'dev ᵊl |ri ~**ries** riz
Devine *(i)* dɪ 'viːn də-, *(ii)* -'vaɪn
devious 'diːv i_əs ~**ly** li ~**ness** nəs nɪs
devis|e dɪ 'vaɪz də-, §diː- ~**ed** d ~**er/s** ə/
z ‖ ᵊr/z ~**es** ɪz əz ~**ing** ɪŋ
devitalis... —*see* **devitaliz...**
devitalization ˌdiː ˌvaɪt ᵊl aɪ 'zeɪʃ ᵊn -ᵊl ɪ-
‖ diː ˌvaɪt ᵊl ə-
devitaliz|e ˌdiː 'vaɪt ə laɪz -ᵊl aɪz ‖ -'vaɪṯ ᵊl aɪz
~**ed** d ~**es** ɪz əz ~**ing** ɪŋ
Devizes dɪ 'vaɪz ɪz də-, -əz
Devlin 'dev lɪn -lən
devoic|e ₍ᵢ₎diː 'vɔɪs ~**ed** t ~**es** ɪz əz ~**ing** ɪŋ
devoid dɪ 'vɔɪd də-, §diː-
devolution ˌdiːv ə 'luːʃ ᵊn ˌdev-, -'ljuːʃ-
‖ ˌdev- ~**s** z
devolv|e dɪ 'vɒlv də-, ₍ᵢ₎diː-, §-'vəʊlv ‖ -'vɑːlv
~**ed** d ~**es** ɪz əz ~**ing** ɪŋ ~**ement** mənt
Devon 'dev ᵊn —*but the river in Notts. is* 'diːv-
Devonian de 'vəʊn i_ən də-, dɪ- ‖ -'voʊn- ~**s** z
Devonish 'dev ᵊn_ɪʃ
Devonport 'dev ᵊn pɔːt →-ᵊm- ‖ -pɔːrt -poʊrt
Devonshire 'dev ᵊn ʃə -ʃɪə ‖ -ʃᵊr -ʃɪr
de|vote dɪ ǀ'vəʊt də-, §diː- ‖ -ǀ'voʊt ~**voted**
'vəʊt ɪd -əd ‖ 'voʊṯ əd ~**votes**
'vəʊts ‖ 'voʊts ~**voting** 'vəʊt ɪŋ ‖ 'voʊṯ ɪŋ
devoted|ly dɪ 'vəʊt ɪd ǀli də-, §diː-, -əd-
‖ -'voʊṯ əd- ~**ness** nəs nɪs
devotee ˌdev əʊ 'tiː -ə 'tiː -'teɪ ~**s** z
devotion dɪ 'vəʊʃ ᵊn də-, §diː- ‖ -'voʊʃ- ~**s** z
devotional dɪ 'vəʊʃ ᵊn_əl də-, §diː- -'voʊʃ-
~**ly** i
devour dɪ 'vaʊ_ə də-, §diː- ‖ -'vaʊ_ᵊr ~**ed** d
devouring dɪ 'vaʊ_ər ɪŋ də-, §diː-
‖ -'vaʊᵊr ɪŋ ~**s** z
devout dɪ 'vaʊt də-, §diː- ~**ly** li ~**ness** nəs nɪs
De Vries *(i)* də 'vriːs, *(ii)* -'vriːz

dew dju: →§dʒu: ‖ du: dju: **dewed** dju:d
→§dʒu:d ‖ du:d dju:d **dewing** 'dju: ɪŋ
→§'dʒu:- ‖ 'du: ɪŋ 'dju:- **dews** dju:z
→§dʒu:z ‖ du:z dju:z
   'dew point
Dewar, dewar 'dju:ᵊ_ə →§'dʒu:ᵊ_ə ‖ 'du: ᵊr
   'dju: ᵊr ~s z
dewberr|y 'dju: bᵊr_|i →§'dʒu:- ‖ 'du: ˌber |i
   'dju:- ~ies iz
dewclaw 'dju: klɔ: →§'dʒu:- ‖ 'du:- 'dju:-,
   -klɑ: ~s z
dewdrop 'dju: drɒp →§'dʒu:- ‖ 'du: drɑ:p
   'dju:- ~s z
Dewey 'dju:ᵊ_i →§'dʒu:ᵊ_i ‖ 'du: i 'dju: i
   ˌDewey 'decimal ˌsystem
Dewhurst 'dju: hɜːst →§'dʒu:- ‖ 'du: hɜ·ːst
   'dju:-
Dewi 'de wi —this Welsh name is occasionally
   anglicized as 'dju:ᵊ_i
dewi... —see **dewy**
de Wint də 'wɪnt
dewlap 'dju: læp →§'dʒu:- ‖ 'du:- 'dju:- ~s s
dewpond 'dju: pɒnd →§'dʒu:- ‖ 'du: pɑ:nd
   'dju:- ~s z
Dewsbury 'dju:z bᵊr_i →§'dʒu:z-
   ‖ 'du:z ˌber i 'dju:z-
dew-worm 'dju: wɜːm →§'dʒu:- ‖ 'du: wɜ·ːm
   'dju:- ~s z
dew|y 'dju:ᵊ_|i →§'dʒu:ᵊ_i ‖ 'du: |i 'dju: i ~ier
   i_ə ‖ i_ᵊr ~iest i_ɪst i_əst ~ily ᵊl i əl i ~iness
   i nəs i nɪs
dewy-eyed ˌdju:ᵊ_i 'aɪd ◄ →§,dʒu:ᵊ_ ‖ ,du:-
   ,dju:-
Dexedrine *tdmk* 'deks ɪ dri:n -ə-
Dexter, d- 'dekst ə ‖ -ᵊr
dexterity dek 'ster ət i -ɪt- ‖ -ət̬ i
dexterous 'deks tᵊr_əs ~ly li ~ness nəs nɪs
dextral 'deks trəl ~ly i
dextrality dek 'stræl ət i -ɪt- ‖ -ət̬ i
dextrin 'deks trɪn
dextro- ˌdeks trəʊ ‖ -troʊ
dextrorotatory ˌdeks trəʊ rəʊ 'teɪt ər i ◄
   -'rəʊt ət_ər i ‖ -troʊ 'roʊt̬ ə tɔːr i ◄ -toʊr i (*)
dextrorse 'deks trɔːs ₍ₒ₎dek 'strɔːs ‖ -trɔːrs ~ly
   li
dextrose 'deks trəʊz -trəʊs ‖ -troʊs -troʊz
dextrous 'deks trəs ~ly li ~ness nəs nɪs
dey deɪ (= day) **deys** deɪz
De Zoete də 'zu:t
Dhahran ˌdɑ: 'ræn -'rɑ:n ‖ -'rɑ:n —Arabic
   [ðˤɑh 'rɑːn]
Dhaka 'dæk ə
dhal dɑ:l —Hindi [ɖɑːl]
dhansak dʌn 'sɑːk —Hindi [ɖəɳ sɑːk]
dharma 'dɑːm ə ‖ 'dɑːrm ə —Hindi [dʱərm]
Dharug, Dharuk, Dharruk dɑː 'ruːɡ 'dʌr ʊk
Dhekelia dɪ 'keɪl i_ə də-
dhobi 'dəʊb i ‖ 'doʊb i —Hindi ['dʱoː bi] ~s z
   'dhobi('s) itch
dhole dəʊl →dɒʊl ‖ doʊl (= dole) **dholes**
   dəʊlz →dɒʊlz ‖ doʊlz
dhoti 'dəʊt i ‖ 'doʊt̬ i —Hindi ['dʱoː t̪i] ~s z
dhow daʊ **dhows** daʊz

dhurrie 'dʌr i ~s z
Di daɪ **Di's** daɪz
di- ˌdaɪ — **dimorphemic**
   ˌdaɪ mɔː 'fiːm ɪk ◄ ‖ -mɔːr-
dia- comb. form
   with stress-neutral suffix ˌdaɪ_ə — **diatropic**
   ˌdaɪ_ə 'trɒp ɪk ◄ ‖ -'trɑːp-
   with stress-imposing suffix daɪ 'æ+ —
   diatropism daɪ 'ætr ə ˌpɪz əm
diabetes ˌdaɪ_ə 'biːt iːz ◄ -ɪs, §-əs ‖ -'biːt̬ əs -iːz
   ˌdiaˌbetes in'sipidus ɪn 'sɪp ɪd əs §-əd əs;
   ˌdiaˌbetes mel'litus mə 'laɪt əs mɪ-, me-
   ‖ -'laɪt̬- 'mel ət̬ əs
diabetic ˌdaɪ_ə 'bet ɪk ◄ ‖ -'bet̬- ~s s
diablerie di 'ɑːb lər i —Fr [dja blə ʁi]
diabolic ˌdaɪ_ə 'bɒl ɪk ◄ ‖ -'bɑːl- ~al ᵊl ~ally
   ᵊl_i
diabolism daɪ 'æb ə ˌlɪz əm
diabolo daɪ 'æb ə ləʊ di- ‖ -loʊ ~s z
diachronic ˌdaɪ_ə 'krɒn ɪk ◄ ‖ -'krɑːn- ~ally
   ᵊl_i
diachrony daɪ 'æk rən i
diacidic ˌdaɪ_ə 'sɪd ɪk ◄
diaconal daɪ 'æk ən ᵊl di-
diaconate daɪ 'æk ə neɪt di-, -ən ət, -ən ɪt
diacritic ˌdaɪ_ə 'krɪt ɪk ‖ -'krɪt̬- ~al ᵊl ~ally ᵊl_i
   ~s s
diadem 'daɪ_ə dem -əd əm ~ed d ~s z
Diadochi daɪ 'æd ə kaɪ
diaer|esis daɪ 'ɪər |əs ɪs -'er-, -ɪs ɪs, §-əs ‖ -'er-
   ~eses ə siːz ɪ-
Diaghilev di 'æɡ ə lef -ɪ-
diagnos|e 'daɪ_əɡ nəʊz -nəʊs, ˌ•ᵊ'•
   ‖ ˌ•ᵊ 'noʊs -'noʊz, '••• —AmE 1993 poll
   panel preference: ˌ•ᵊ'•noʊs 58%, '••noʊs
   32%, '••noʊz 7%, ˌ•ᵊ'•noʊz 3%. ~ed d ~es
   v ɪz əz ~ing ɪŋ
diagnos|is ˌdaɪ_əɡ 'nəʊs |ɪs -'nəʊz-, §-əs
   ‖ -'noʊs- ~es nˌiːz
diagnostic ˌdaɪ_əɡ 'nɒst ɪk ◄ ‖ -'nɑːst- ~ally
   ᵊl_i ~s s
diagnostician ˌdaɪ_əɡ nɒ 'stɪʃ ᵊn ‖ -nɑː'•• ~s
   z
diagonal daɪ 'æɡ ᵊn_əl ~ly i ~s z
diagram 'daɪ_ə ɡræm ~ed d ~ing ɪŋ ~med d
   ~ming ɪŋ ~s z
diagrammatic ˌdaɪ_ə ɡrə 'mæt ɪk ◄ ‖ -'mæt̬-
   ~al ᵊl ~ally ᵊl_i
dial 'daɪ_əl daɪᵊl **dialed, dialled** 'daɪ_əld
   daɪᵊld **dialing, dialling** 'daɪ_əl ɪŋ 'daɪᵊl ɪŋ
   dials 'daɪ_əlz daɪᵊlz
   'dialling ˌcode; 'dialling ˌtone; 'dial ˌtone
dialect 'daɪ_ə lekt ~s s
dialectal ˌdaɪ_ə 'lekt ᵊl ◄ ~ly i
dialectic ˌdaɪ_ə 'lekt ɪk ◄ ~al ᵊl ~ally ᵊl_i ~s s
dialectician ˌdaɪ_ə lek 'tɪʃ ᵊn ~s z
dialectological
   ˌdaɪ_ə lekt ə 'lɒdʒ ɪk ᵊl ◄ ‖ -'lɑːdʒ- ~ly _i
dialectologist ˌdaɪ_ə lek 'tɒl ədʒ ɪst §-əst
   ‖ -'tɑːl- ~s s
dialectology ˌdaɪ_ə lek 'tɒl ədʒ i ‖ -'tɑːl-
dialog, dialogue 'daɪ_ə lɒɡ ‖ -lɔːɡ -lɑːɡ ~s z
dialup 'daɪ_əl ʌp 'daɪᵊl ʌp

dialys|e 'daɪ‿ə laɪz ~**ed** d ~**es** ɪz əz ~**ing** ɪŋ
dialyses *from v* 'daɪ‿ə laɪz ɪz -əz
dialyses *n pl* daɪ 'æl ə siːz -ɪ-
dial|ysis daɪ 'æl |əs ɪs -ɪs-, §-əs ~**yses** ə siːz -ɪ-
diamagnetic ˌdaɪ‿ə mæg 'net ɪk ◄ -məg'• - ‖ -'næg-
diamante, diamanté ˌdiː‿ə 'mɒnt eɪ ˌdaɪ‿, -'mænt-, -i ‖ -maːn 'teɪ
diameter daɪ 'æm ɪt ə -ət- ‖ -ət̬ ər ~**s** z
diametral daɪ 'æm ɪtr əl -ətr-
diametric ˌdaɪ‿ə 'metr ɪk ◄ ~**al** əl ~**ally** əl‿i
   ˌdiaˌmetrically op'posed
diamond, D~ 'daɪ‿əm ənd §'daɪm ənd ‖ 'daɪm ənd ~**ed** ɪd əd ~**s** z
   ˌdiamond 'jubilee; ˌdiamond 'wedding (anniˌversary)
diamondback 'daɪ‿əm ənd bæk §'daɪm • • ‖ 'daɪm • • ~**s** s
Dian ₍ᵢ₎daɪ 'æn di-
Diana daɪ 'æn ə
Diane ₍ᵢ₎daɪ 'æn di-
dianetics *tdmk* ˌdaɪ‿ə 'net ɪks ‖ -'net̬-
dianoetic ˌdaɪ‿ə nəʊ 'et ɪk ◄ ‖ -noʊ 'et̬-
dianthus daɪ 'ænᵗθ əs ~**es** ɪz əz
diapason ˌdaɪ‿ə 'peɪz ən -'peɪs- ~**s** z
diaper 'daɪ‿əp ə §'daɪp ə ‖ 'daɪp ər ~**ed** d
   diapering 'daɪ‿əp ər‿ɪŋ §'daɪp ər‿ɪŋ ‖ 'daɪp ər‿ɪŋ ~**s** z
diaphanous daɪ 'æf ən əs ~**ly** li ~**ness** nəs nɪs
diaphone 'daɪ‿ə fəʊn ‖ -foʊn ~**s** z
diaphoneme 'daɪ‿ə ˌfəʊn iːm ‖ -ˌfoʊn- ~**s** z
diaphonemic ˌdaɪ‿ə fəʊ 'niːm ɪk ‖ -fə'• - ~**ally** əl‿i
diaphonic ˌdaɪ‿ə 'fɒn ɪk ◄ -'fɑːn- ~**ally** əl‿i
diaphoresis ˌdaɪ‿ə fə 'riːs ɪs -fɒ'• -, -fɔː'• -, §-əs
diaphoretic ˌdaɪ‿ə fə 'ret ɪk ◄ -fɒ'• -, -fɔː'• - ‖ -'ret̬ ɪk ◄ ~**s** s
diaphragm 'daɪ‿ə fræm ~**s** z
diaphragmatic ˌdaɪ‿ə fræg 'mæt ɪk ◄ ‖ -'mæt̬- ~**ally** əl‿i
diaph|ysis daɪ 'æf |əs ɪs -ɪs ɪs, §-əs ~**yses** ə siːz ɪ-
diarch|y 'daɪ‿ɑːk |i ‖ -ɑːrk |i ~**ies** ɪz
diaries 'daɪ‿ər iz
diarist 'daɪ‿ər ɪst §-əst; △'daɪ‿ər ɪ ɪst ~**s** s
diarrhea, diarrhoea ˌdaɪ‿ə 'rɪə §-'riː‿ə ‖ -'riː ə
diar|y 'daɪ‿ər |i ~**ies** ɪz
Dias 'diː‿əs —*Port* ['di ɐʃ]
Diaspora, d~ daɪ 'æsp ər ə ~**s** z
diaspore 'daɪ‿ə spɔː ‖ -spɔːr -spoʊr
diastase 'daɪ‿ə steɪz -steɪs
diastole daɪ 'æst əl i
diastolic ˌdaɪ‿ə 'stɒl ɪk ◄ ‖ -'stɑːl-
diathermy 'daɪ‿ə ˌθɜːm i ‖ -ˌθɝːm i
diath|esis daɪ 'æθ |əs ɪs -ɪs ɪs, §-əs ~**eses** ə siːz ɪ-
diatom 'daɪ‿ə tɒm ˌət əm ‖ -tɑːm ~**s** z
diatomaceous ˌdaɪ‿ə tɒm ə 'meɪʃ əs ‖ -ət̬ ə-
diatomic ˌdaɪ‿ə 'tɒm ɪk ◄ ‖ -'tɑːm-
diatomite daɪ 'æt ə maɪt ‖ -'æt̬-
diatonic ˌdaɪ‿ə 'tɒn ɪk ◄ ‖ -'tɑːn- ~**ally** əl‿i
   ˌdiaˌtonic 'scale
diatribe 'daɪ‿ə traɪb ~**s** z

Diaz 'diː æs -æθ ‖ -ɑːs —*Sp* Díaz ['di aθ], *AmSp* [-as]; *Port* Diaz ['di ɐʃ]
diazepam daɪ 'eɪz ə pæm -'æz-, -ɪ- ‖ -'æz-
diazo ₍ᵢ₎daɪ 'eɪz əʊ -'æz- ‖ -'æz oʊ
diazonium ˌdaɪ‿ə 'zəʊn i‿əm ‖ -'zoʊn-
dib dɪb **dibbed** dɪbd **dibbing** 'dɪb ɪŋ **dibs** dɪbz
dibber 'dɪb ə ‖ -ər ~**s** z
dibbl|e, D~ 'dɪb əl ~**ed** d ~**er/s** ə/z ‖ ər/z ~**es** z ~**ing** ˌɪŋ
Dibden 'dɪb dən
dibs dɪbz
DiCaprio di 'kæp ri əʊ ‖ -oʊ
dicast 'dɪk æst ~**s** s
Diccon 'dɪk ən
dice daɪs **diced** daɪst **dices** 'daɪs ɪz -əz **dicing** 'daɪs ɪŋ
dicentra ₍ᵢ₎daɪ 'sentr ə ~**s** z
dic|ey 'daɪs |i ~**ier** i‿ə ‖ i‿ər ~**iest** i‿ɪst i‿əst
dichlorvos daɪ 'klɔː vɒs ‖ -'klɔːr voʊs -'kloʊr-
dichotic ₍ᵢ₎daɪ 'kɒt ɪk dɪ- ‖ -'kɑːt̬ ɪk
dichotom|y daɪ 'kɒt əm li dɪ- ‖ -'kɑːt̬- ~**ies** iz
Dick, dick dɪk **Dick's, dicks** dɪks
Dicken 'dɪk ɪn §-ən
Dickens, d~ 'dɪk ɪnz §-ənz **D~'** ɪz əz —*or as nominative*
Dickensian dɪ 'kenz i‿ən də- ~**s** z
dicker, D~ 'dɪk ə ‖ -ər ~**ed** d **dickering** 'dɪk ər‿ɪŋ ~**s** z
Dickerson 'dɪk əs ən ‖ -ərs-
dickey, dickie, D~ 'dɪk i ~**s** z
dickhead 'dɪk hed ~**s** z
Dickie 'dɪk i
Dickins 'dɪk ɪnz §-ənz
Dickinson 'dɪk ɪn sən §-ən-
Dickon 'dɪk ən
Dickson 'dɪks ən
dick|y, Dicky 'dɪk |i ~**ies**, ~**y's** iz
dickybird 'dɪk i bɜːd ‖ -bɝːd ~**s** z
dicotyledon ˌdaɪ ˌkɒt ɪ 'liːd ən -ə-, -əl 'iːd- ‖ -ˌkɑːt̬ əl 'iːd ən •, • - ~**s** z
dicoumarol ₍ᵢ₎daɪ 'kuːm ə rɒl ‖ -roʊl -rɑːl, -rɔːl
dicta 'dɪkt ə
dictaphone, D~ *tdmk* 'dɪkt ə fəʊn ‖ -foʊn ~**s** z
dict|ate *v* ₍ᵢ₎dɪk 'teɪt ‖ 'dɪkt eɪt dɪk 'teɪt ~**ated** ɪd əd ‖ eɪt̬ əd ~**ates** eɪts ~**ating** eɪt ɪŋ ‖ eɪt̬ ɪŋ
dictate *n* 'dɪkt eɪt ~**s** s
dictation dɪk 'teɪʃ ən ~**s** z
dictator dɪk 'teɪt ə ‖ 'dɪkt eɪt̬ ər dɪk 'teɪt̬ ər ~**s** z
dictatorial ˌdɪkt ə 'tɔːr i‿əl ◄ ‖ -'toʊr- ~**ly** i ~**ness** nəs nɪs
dictatorship dɪk 'teɪt ə ʃɪp ‖ 'dɪkt eɪt̬ ər ʃɪp dɪk 'teɪt̬ ər- ~**s** s
diction 'dɪk ʃən
dictionar|y 'dɪk ʃən ər‿li 'dɪk ʃən‿ər li, §-ʃə ner li ‖ 'dɪk ʃə ner li ~**ies** iz
dict|um 'dɪkt |əm ~**a** ə ~**ums** əmz
did dɪd *occasional weak forms* §dəd, d — *see* 'd
didactic daɪ 'dækt ɪk dɪ-, də- ~**ally** əl‿i ~**s** s
didacticism daɪ 'dækt ɪ ˌsɪz əm dɪ-, də-, -ə-
Didcot 'dɪd kət →'dɪg-, -kɒt ‖ -kɑːt

diddl|e 'dɪd ᵊl ~ed d ~es z ~ing _ɪŋ
diddly 'dɪd ᵊl_i
diddlysquat ˌdɪd ᵊl_i 'skwɒt '••••
‖ '••• skwɑːt ˌ•••'•
diddums 'dɪd əmz
diddy 'dɪd i
Diderot 'diːd ə rəʊ ‖ ˌdiːd ə 'rəʊ —Fr [di dʁo]
didgeridoo ˌdɪdʒ ᵊr_i 'duː ~s z
didicoy, didikoi 'dɪd ɪ kɔɪ -ə- ~s z
Didier 'dɪd i eɪ —Fr [di dje]
didn't 'dɪd ᵊnt △'dɪt- —non-final also 'dɪd ᵊn
Dido, dido 'daɪd əʊ ‖ -oʊ
didst dɪdst
did|y 'daɪd |i ~ies iz
didymous, Didymus 'dɪd ɪm əs -əm-
die daɪ died daɪd dieing 'daɪ ɪŋ dies daɪz
dying 'daɪ ɪŋ
dieback 'daɪ bæk
die-cast 'daɪ kɑːst §-kæst ‖ -kæst ~ing ɪŋ ~s
s
dieffenbachia ˌdiːf ᵊn 'bæk i_ə →ˌ•əm-
‖ -'bɑːk- ~s z
Diego di 'eɪg əʊ ‖ -oʊ —Sp ['dje ɣo]
diehard 'daɪ hɑːd ‖ -hɑːrd ~s z
dieldrin 'diːᵊldr ɪn -ᵊn
dielectric ˌdaɪ ɪ 'lek trɪk ◄ -ə- ~ally ᵊl_i ~s s
diene, -diene 'daɪ iːn
Dieppe di 'ep ˌdiː- —Fr [djɛp]
dier|esis daɪ 'ɪər |əs ɪs -'er-, -ɪs ɪs, §-əs ‖ -'er-
~eses ə siːz ɪ-
dies from die daɪz
dies Latin, 'day' 'diː eɪz 'daɪ iːz ‖ -eɪs —See also
phrases with this word
diesel, D~ 'diːz ᵊl ‖ 'diːs- ~s z
'diesel ˌengine; 'diesel ˌfuel; 'diesel oil
diesel-electric ˌdiːz ᵊl ɪ 'lek trɪk ◄ -ə'•- ‖ ˌdiːs-
~s s
dieselisation, dieselization ˌdiːz ᵊl aɪ 'zeɪʃ ᵊn
-ᵊl ɪ- ‖ -ᵊl ə- ˌdiːs-
Dies Irae ˌdiː eɪz 'ɪər aɪ -ez-, -es-, -eɪ
‖ -eɪs 'ɪr eɪ
di|esis 'daɪ_|əs ɪs ɪs _ɪs ɪs, §-əs ~eses ə siːz ɪ-
dies non ˌdaɪ ɪz 'nɒn ˌdiː eɪz-, -'nəʊn ‖ -'nɑːn
ˌdiː eɪs-, -'noʊn
di|et 'daɪ_|ət ~eted ət ɪd -əd ‖ ət əd ~eting
ət ɪŋ ‖ ət ɪŋ ~ets əts
dietar|y 'daɪ_ət_ər |i ‖ 'daɪ ə ter |i ~ies iz
dieter 'one that diets' 'daɪ_ət ə ‖ 'daɪ ət ᵊr ~s z
Dieter name 'diːt ə ‖ 'diːt̬ ᵊr —Ger ['diː tɐ]
dietetic ˌdaɪ_ə 'tet ɪk ◄ ɪ- ‖ -'tet̬- ~ally ᵊl_i ~s
s
diethylstil|bestrol, ~boestrol
ˌdaɪ ˌeθ ᵊl stɪl 'biːs trɒl -ˌiːθ-, -, -ɪl-, -'bes-,
-trəl ‖ daɪ ˌeθ ᵊl stɪl 'bes troʊl -trɑːl, -trɔːl
dietician, dietitian ˌdaɪ_ə 'tɪʃ ᵊn ~s z
Dietrich 'diːtr ɪk 'diːətr-, -ɪx, -ɪʃ —Ger
['diː tʁɪç]
Dieu et mon droit
ˌdjɜːʳ eɪ mɒn 'drwɑː ‖ ˌdjʊ eɪ mɔːn 'dwɑː
—Fr [djø e mɔ̃ dʁwa]
differ 'dɪf ə ‖ -ᵊr ~ed d differing 'dɪf ᵊr_ɪŋ
~s z

differenc|e 'dɪf rᵊn's 'dɪf ᵊr_ᵊnts ‖ 'dɪf ᵊr_ᵊnts
~ed t ~es ɪz əz ~ing ɪŋ
different 'dɪf rᵊnt 'dɪf ᵊr_ᵊnt ‖ 'dɪf ᵊr_ᵊnt ~ly
li ~ness nəs nɪs
different|ia ˌdɪf ə 'rentʃ i_ə ~iae i iː i aɪ, i eɪ
differential ˌdɪf ə 'rentʃ ᵊl ◄ ~ly i ~s z
ˌdiffeˌrential 'calculus; ˌdiffeˌrential
e'quation; ˌdiffeˌrential 'gear
differenti|ate ˌdɪf ə 'rentʃ i eɪt ~ated eɪt ɪd
-əd ‖ eɪt̬ əd ~ates eɪts ~ating eɪt ɪŋ ‖ eɪt̬ ɪŋ
differentiation ˌdɪf ə ˌrentʃ i 'eɪʃ ᵊn ~s z
difficult 'dɪf ɪk ᵊlt -ək-; §-ɪ kʌlt, -ə- ~ly li
difficult|y 'dɪf ɪk ᵊlt li '•ək-; §-ɪ kʌlt, §-ə kʌlt-
~ies iz
diffidence 'dɪf ɪd ᵊn's -əd-
diffident 'dɪf ɪd ᵊnt -əd- ~ly li
diffract dɪ 'frækt də- ~ed ɪd əd ~ing ɪŋ ~s s
diffraction dɪ 'fræk ʃᵊn də- ~s z
diffuse adj dɪ 'fjuːs də-, daɪ- ~ly li ~ness nəs
nɪs
diffus|e v dɪ 'fjuːz də- ~ed d ~es ɪz əz ~ing
ɪŋ
diffuser n dɪ 'fjuːz ə də- ‖ -ᵊr ~s z
diffusion dɪ 'fjuːʒ ᵊn də- ~s z
diffusive dɪ 'fjuːs ɪv də-, §-'fjuːz- ~ly li ~ness
nəs nɪs
diffusivity ˌdɪf ju 'sɪv ət i dɪ ˌfjuː-, də ˌfjuː-,
-ɪt i ‖ -ət̬ i
dig dɪg digging 'dɪg ɪŋ digs dɪgz dug dʌg
digamma ˌdaɪ ˌgæm ə ₍ᵢ₎•'•• ~s z
Digbeth 'dɪg bəθ
Digby 'dɪg bi
digest n 'daɪ dʒest ~s s
digest v daɪ 'dʒest dɪ-, də- ~ed ɪd əd ~ing ɪŋ
~s s
digestant daɪ 'dʒest ᵊnt dɪ-, də- ~s s
digestibility daɪ ˌdʒest ə 'bɪl ət i dɪ-, də-, -, •ɪ-,
-ɪt i ‖ -ət̬ i
digestib|le daɪ 'dʒest əb |ᵊl dɪ-, də-, -ɪb- ~ly li
digestif dɪ 'ʒest iːf ˌdiːʒ es 'tiːf —Fr
[di ʒɛ stif] ~s s
digestion daɪ 'dʒes tʃən dɪ-, də-, →-'dʒeʃ- ~s
z
digestive daɪ 'dʒest ɪv dɪ-, də- ~ly li ~s z
digger, D~ 'dɪg ə ‖ -ᵊr ~s z
digging 'dɪg ɪŋ ~s z
Diggle 'dɪg ᵊl
dight daɪt
digit 'dɪdʒ ɪt §-ət ~s s
digital 'dɪdʒ ɪt ᵊl -ət- ‖ -ət̬ ᵊl ~ly i ~s z
digitalin ˌdɪdʒ ɪ 'teɪl ɪn -ə-, §-ᵊn ‖ -'tæl-
digitalis ˌdɪdʒ ɪ 'teɪl ɪs -ə-, §-əs ‖ -'tæl- (*)
digitis... —see digitiz...
digitization ˌdɪdʒ ɪt aɪ 'zeɪʃ ᵊn ˌ•ət-, -ɪ'•-
‖ -ət̬ ə-
digitiz|e 'dɪdʒ ɪ taɪz -ə- ~ed d ~er/s ə/z ‖ ᵊr/z
~es ɪz əz ~ing ɪŋ
diglossia ₍ᵢ₎daɪ 'glɒs i_ə ‖ -'glɑːs- -'glɔːs-
diglossic ₍ᵢ₎daɪ 'glɒs ɪk ‖ -'glɑːs- -'glɔːs-
diglot 'daɪ glɒt ‖ -glɑːt ~s s
digni|fy 'dɪg nɪ |faɪ -nə- ~fied/ly faɪd /li ~fies
faɪz ~fying faɪ ɪŋ

dignitar|y 'dɪg nət‿ər |i |•nɪt‿ ‖ -nə ter |i ~ies
iz
dignity 'dɪg nət |i -nɪt- ‖ -nəţ |i ~ies iz
digraph 'daɪ grɑf -græf ‖ -græf ~s s
digress daɪ 'gres ~ed t ~es ɪz əz ~ing ɪŋ
digression daɪ 'greʃ ən ~s z
digressive daɪ 'gres ɪv ~ly li ~ness nəs nɪs
dihedral ₍ᵢ₎daɪ 'hiːdr əl ~s z
Dijkstra 'daɪks trə —Dutch ['dɛik strɑ]
Dijon 'diːʒ ɒ̃ -ɒn ‖ diː 'ʒɑːn -'ʒɔːn, -'ʒoʊn —Fr
[di ʒɔ̃]
dik-dik 'dɪk dɪk ~s s
dike daɪk diked daɪkt dikes daɪks diking
'daɪk ɪŋ
diktat 'dɪkt æt -ɑːt ‖ dɪk 'tɑːt ~s s
dilapi|date dɪ 'læp ɪ |deɪt də-, -ə- ~dated
deɪt ɪd -əd ‖ deɪţ əd ~dates deɪts ~dating
deɪt ɪŋ ‖ deɪţ ɪŋ
dilapidation dɪ ˌlæp ɪ 'deɪʃ ən də-, -ə- ~s z
dilatation ˌdaɪl eɪ 'teɪʃ ən ˌdɪl-, -ə- ~s z
di|late daɪ 'leɪt dɪ-, də- ‖ 'daɪ |leɪt ~lated
leɪt ɪd -əd ‖ leɪţ əd ~lates leɪts ~lating
leɪt ɪŋ ‖ leɪţ ɪŋ
dilation daɪ 'leɪʃ ən dɪ-, də- ~s z
dilator daɪ 'leɪt ə dɪ-, də- ‖ -'leɪţ ər 'daɪ leɪţ ər
~s z
dilator|y 'dɪl ət‿ər |i ‖ -ə tɔːr |i -toʊr i ~ily əl i
ɪ li ~iness i nəs i nɪs
Dilbert 'dɪl bət -bɜːt ‖ -bərt
dildo, dildoe 'dɪld əʊ ‖ -oʊ ~s z
dildonics dɪl 'dɒn ɪks ‖ -'dɑːn-
dilemma dɪ 'lem ə daɪ-, də- ~s z
dilet|tante ˌdɪl ə |'tænt i -ɪ- ‖ -|'tɑːnt '•••
~tantes 'tænt iz ‖ 'tɑːnts ~tanti
'tænt iː ‖ -'tɑːnţ i
dilettantism ˌdɪl ə 'tænt ˌɪz əm -ɪ- ‖ -'tɑːnt-
'•••‿
Dilhorne 'dɪl ən -ɔːn ‖ -ᵊrn -hɔːrn
diligenc|e 'dɪl ɪdʒ ənts -ədʒ- ~es ɪz əz
diligent 'dɪl ɪdʒ ənt -ədʒ- ~ly li
Dilke dɪlk
dill, Dill dɪl
ˌdill 'pickle
Diller 'dɪl ə ‖ -ᵊr
dilli... —see dilly
Dillon 'dɪl ən
Dillwyn 'dɪl wɪn -ɪn
dill|y, Dilly 'dɪl |i ~ies iz
'dilly bag
dilly-dall|y 'dɪl i ˌdæl |i ˌ•• ‣•• ~ied id ~ies iz
~ying i‿ɪŋ
diluent 'dɪl ju‿ənt ~s s
di|lute v, adj ₍ᵢ₎daɪ |'luːt dɪ-, də-, -'ljuːt ~luted
'luːt ɪd -'ljuːt-, -əd ‖ 'luːţ əd ~lutes 'luːts
'ljuːts ~luting 'lut ɪŋ 'ljuːt- ‖ 'luːţ ɪŋ
dilution ₍ᵢ₎daɪ 'luːʃ ən dɪ-, də-, -'ljuːʃ- ~s z
diluvi|al daɪ 'luːv i‿|əl dɪ-, də-, -'ljuːv- ~an ən
~um əm
Dilworth 'dɪl wɜːθ -wəθ ‖ -wᵊrθ
Dilwyn 'dɪl wɪn
Dilys 'dɪl ɪs §-əs
dim dɪm dimmed dɪmd dimmer 'dɪm ə ‖ -ᵊr

dimmest 'dɪm ɪst §-əst dimming 'dɪm ɪŋ
dims dɪmz —See also phrases with this word
DiMaggio dɪ 'mædʒ i əʊ ‖ -oʊ •'•oʊ
Dimbleby 'dɪm bᵊl bi
dime daɪm dimes daɪmz
dimension daɪ 'menʧ ᵊn dɪ-, də- ‖ də- ~ed d
~ing ‿ɪŋ ~s z
dimensional daɪ 'menʧ ᵊn‿əl dɪ-, də- ‖ də-
~ly i
dimensionality daɪ ˌmenʧ ə 'næl ət i dɪ-, də-,
-ɪt i ‖ -əţ i
Diment 'daɪm ənt
dimer 'daɪm ə 'daɪ mɜː ‖ -ᵊr ~s z
dimercaprol ˌdaɪ mɜː 'kæp rɒl -mə-
‖ -mᵊr 'kæp roʊl -rɑːl, -rɔːl
dimerism 'dɪm ər ˌɪz əm
dimerous 'dɪm ər əs
dimeter 'dɪm ɪt ə -ət- ‖ -əţ ᵊr ~s z
diminish dɪ 'mɪn ɪʃ də- ~ed t ~es ɪz əz ~ing
ɪŋ ~ment mənt
diˌminished reˌsponsiˈbility; diˌminishing
reˈturns
diminuendo dɪ ˌmɪn ju 'end əʊ də- ‖ -oʊ ~es,
~s z
diminution ˌdɪm ɪ 'njuːʃ ᵊn -ə-, ⚠-ju- ‖ -'nuːʃ-
-'njuːʃ- ~s z
diminutive dɪ 'mɪn jut ɪv də-, -jət- ‖ -jəţ ɪv
~ly li ~ness nəs nɪs ~s z
dimit|ly, D~ 'dɪm ət |i -ɪt- ‖ -əţ |i ~ies iz
dimly 'dɪm li
dimmer 'dɪm ə ‖ -ᵊr ~s z
'dimmer switch
dimmish 'dɪm ɪʃ
Dimmock 'dɪm ək
dimness 'dɪm nəs -nɪs
dimorph|ism ₍ᵢ₎daɪ 'mɔːf ˌɪz əm ‖ -'mɔːrf-
~ous əs
dimout 'dɪm aʊt ~s s
dimpl|e 'dɪmp ᵊl ~ed d ~es z ~ing ‿ɪŋ
Dimplex tdmk 'dɪmp ĺeks
dimply 'dɪmp li
dim sum ˌdɪm 'sʌm -'sʊm —Cantonese
[²dim ¹sam]
dimwit 'dɪm wɪt ~s s
dim-witted ˌdɪm 'wɪt ɪd ◂ -əd ‖ -'wɪţ əd ◂ ~ly
li ~ness nəs nɪs
din, DIN dɪn dinned dɪnd dinning 'dɪn ɪŋ
dins dɪnz
Dina (i) 'diːn ə, (ii) 'daɪn-
Dinah 'daɪn ə
dinar 'diːn ɑː ‖ dɪ 'nɑːr 'diːn ɑːr ~s z
Dinaric dɪ 'nær ɪk də-, daɪ- ‖ -'ner-
Diˌnaric ˈAlps
Dinas 'diːn æs
din-din 'dɪn dɪn ~s z
dine daɪn dined daɪnd dines daɪnz dining
'daɪn ɪŋ
Dineen dɪ 'niːn də-
Dinefwr dɪ 'nev ʊə ‖ -ʊr
diner 'daɪn ə ‖ -ᵊr ~s z
Dinesen 'dɪn ɪs ᵊn 'diːn-, -əs-, -ɪn
dinette ₍ᵢ₎daɪ 'net ~s s

ding dɪŋ **dinged** dɪŋd **dinging** 'dɪŋ ɪŋ **dings**
dɪŋz —*See also phrases with this word*
Dingaan 'dɪŋ gɑːn
dingaling ˌdɪŋ ə 'lɪŋ '••• ~s z
Ding an sich ˌdɪŋ æn 'sɪk -'sɪx ‖ -ɑːn 'zɪk
—*Ger* [ˌdɪŋ an 'zɪç]
dingbat 'dɪŋ bæt ~s s
dingdong 'dɪŋ dɒŋ ˌ•'•◄ ‖ -dɔːŋ -dɑːŋ ~s z
dinge dɪndʒ **dinges** 'dɪndʒ ɪz -əz
dinger 'dɪŋ ə ‖ -ər ~s z
dingh|y 'dɪŋ li 'dɪŋ g|i ~ies iz
dingi... —*see* dingy
dingle, D~ 'dɪŋ gəl ~s z
Dingley 'dɪŋ li
dingo 'dɪŋ gəʊ ‖ -goʊ ~es z
dingus 'dɪŋ əs -gəs ~es ɪz əz
Dingwall 'dɪŋ wɔːl -wəl ‖ -wɑːl
dingl|y 'dɪndʒ li ~ier i_ə ‖ i_ər ~iest i_ɪst i_əst
~ily ɪ li əl i ~iness i nəs i nɪs
dining 'daɪn ɪŋ
'dining car; 'dining room; 'dining ˌtable
dink dɪŋk **dinks** dɪŋks
Dinka 'dɪŋk ə ~s z
dinki... —*see* dinky
Dinkins 'dɪŋk ɪnz §-ənz ‖ 'dɪn kɪnz
dinkum 'dɪŋk əm
dink|y 'dɪŋk li ~ier i_ə ‖ i_ər ~ies iz ~iest i_ɪst
i_əst
dinner 'dɪn ə ‖ -ər ~s z
'dinner bell; 'dinner ˌjacket; 'dinner
ˌparty; 'dinner plate; 'dinner ˌservice;
'dinner set; 'dinner ˌtable
dinnertime 'dɪn ə taɪm ‖ -ər- ~s z
dinoflagellate ˌdaɪn əʊ 'flædʒ ə leɪt -'•ɪ-;
-əl ət, -ɪt ‖ ˌ•oʊ- ~s s
Dinorwic dɪ 'nɔː wɪk də- ‖ -'nɔːr-
dinosaur 'daɪn ə sɔː ‖ -sɔːr ~s z
dinosaurian ˌdaɪn ə 'sɔːr i_ən ◄ ~s z
dinothere 'daɪn əʊ θɪə ‖ -ə θɪr ~s z
Dinsdale 'dɪnz deɪəl
dint dɪnt
Dinwiddie, Dinwiddy *(i)* dɪn 'wɪd i, *(ii)*
'dɪn wɪd i
Dio 'daɪ əʊ ‖ -oʊ
diocesan daɪ 'ɒs ɪs ən -əs-, -ɪz-, -əz- ‖ -'ɑːs-
~s z
di|ocese 'daɪ_ləs ɪs §-əs; lə siːz, -siːs ~oceses
ə siːz əs ɪs ɪz, -əz; ə siːz ɪz, ə siːs ɪz, -əz
Diocletian ˌdaɪ_ə 'kliːʃ ən -'kliːʃ i_ən
diode 'daɪ əʊd ‖ -oʊd ~s z
Diodorus ˌdaɪ_ə 'dɔːr əs ‖ -'doʊr-
ˌDioˌdorus 'Siculus 'sɪk jʊl əs ‖ -jəl əs
dioecious daɪ 'iːʃ əs ~ly li
Diogenes daɪ 'ɒdʒ ə niːz -ɪ- ‖ -'ɑːdʒ-
Diomede 'daɪ_ə miːd
Diomedes ˌdaɪ_ə 'miːd iːz
Dion *classical name* 'daɪ_ən
Dion *modern name* di 'ɒn 'diː_ən -ɒn ‖ di 'oʊn
—*Fr* [djɔ̃]
Dione daɪ 'əʊn i ‖ -'oʊn i
Dionne ˌdi: 'ɒn di- ‖ -'ɑːn
Dionysia ˌdaɪ_ə 'nɪz i_ə -'nɪs- ‖ -'nɪʃ-
Dionysiac ˌdaɪ_ə 'nɪz i æk ◄ -'nɪs- ‖ -'nɪʃ-

Dionysian ˌdaɪ_ə 'nɪz i_ən ◄ -'nɪs-, -'naɪs-
‖ -'nɪʃ ən -'naɪs i_ən ~s z
Dionysius ˌdaɪ_ə 'nɪz i_əs -'nɪs- ‖ -'nɪʃ- (*)
Dionysus ˌdaɪ_ə 'naɪs əs -'niːs-
Diophantine ˌdaɪ_əʊ 'fænt aɪn ◄ ‖ -ə- -ən
Diophantus ˌdaɪ_əʊ 'fænt əs ‖ -ə 'fænt̮ əs
diopside daɪ 'ɒps aɪd ‖ -'ɑːps-
dioptase daɪ 'ɒpt eɪz -eɪs ‖ -'ɑːpt-
diopter, dioptre daɪ 'ɒpt ə ‖ -'ɑːpt ər ~s z
Dior 'diː ɔː •'• ‖ di 'ɔːr —*Fr* [djɔːʁ]
diorama ˌdaɪ_ə 'rɑːm ə ‖ -'ræm ə -'rɑːm ə
dioramic ˌdaɪ_ə 'ræm ɪk ◄
diorite 'daɪ_ə raɪt
Dioscuri 'ɒsk jʊr i -aɪ; ˌdaɪ ə 'skjʊər-, -ɒ-
‖ ˌdaɪ ə 'skjʊr aɪ
diotic daɪ 'əʊt ɪk -'ɒt- ‖ -'oʊt ɪk -'ɑːt̮- ~ally əl_i
dioxide ˌdaɪ 'ɒks aɪd ‖ -'ɑːks- ~s z
dioxin daɪ 'ɒks ɪn §-ən ‖ -'ɑːks-
dip, DIP dɪp **dipped** dɪpt **dipping** 'dɪp ɪŋ
dips dɪps
'DIP switch
diphenylamine ˌdaɪ ˌfiːn aɪəl 'æm iːn -ˌfen-,
-əl-, -ɪn, -ən, -ə 'miːn ‖ daɪ ˌfen əl ə 'miːn
-'æm ən
diphone 'daɪ fəʊn ‖ -foʊn ~s z
diphtheria dɪf 'θɪər i_ə dɪp- ‖ -'θɪr-
diphthong 'dɪf θɒŋ 'dɪp- ‖ -θɔːŋ -θɑːŋ ~ed d
~ing ɪŋ ~s z
diphthongal ˌ(ˌ)dɪf 'θɒŋ gəl ˌ(ˌ)dɪp- ‖ -'θɔːŋ-
-'θɑːŋ- ~ly i
diphthongis... —*see* diphthongiz...
diphthongization ˌdɪf θɒŋ gaɪ 'zeɪʃ ən ˌdɪp-,
-aɪ'•-, -gɪ'•-, -ɪ'•- ‖ -θɔːŋ ə- -θɑːŋ ə-, -gə'•-
~s z
diphthongiz|e 'dɪf θɒŋ gaɪz 'dɪp-, -aɪz
‖ -θɔːŋ aɪz -θɑːŋ-, -gaɪz ~ed d ~es ɪz əz
~ing ɪŋ
diplo- *comb. form*
with stress-neutral suffix ˈdɪp ləʊ ‖ -lə —
diplocardiac ˌdɪp ləʊ
'kɑːd i æk ◄ ‖ -lə 'kɑːrd-
Diplock 'dɪp lɒk ‖ -lɑːk
diplodocus dɪ 'plɒd ək əs daɪ-; ˌdɪp ləʊ
'dəʊk əs ‖ -'plɑːd- ~es ɪz əz
diploid 'dɪp lɔɪd ~s z
diploma dɪ 'pləʊm ə də- ‖ -'ploʊm ə ~s z
diplomac|y dɪ 'pləʊm əs li də- ‖ -'ploʊm- ~ies
iz
diplomat 'dɪp lə mæt ~s s
diplomate 'dɪp lə meɪt ~s s
diplomatic ˌdɪp lə 'mæt ɪk ◄ ‖ -'mæt̮ ɪk ◄ ~ally
əl_i
ˌdiploˌmatic 'bag; ˌdiplo'matic corps;
ˌdiploˌmatic imˈmunity
diplomatist dɪ 'pləʊm ət ɪst də-, §-əst
‖ -'ploʊm ət̮- ~s s
diplophonia ˌdɪp ləʊ 'fəʊn i_ə ‖ -lə 'foʊn-
diplosis dɪ 'pləʊs ɪs §də-, §-əs ‖ -'ploʊs-
dipole 'daɪ pəʊl →-pɒʊl ‖ -poʊl ~s z
dipp.. —*see* dip
dipper, D~ 'dɪp ə ‖ -ər ~s z
dipp|y 'dɪp li ~ier i_ə ‖ i_ər ~iest i_ɪst i_əst
dipsomania ˌdɪps əʊ 'meɪn i_ə ‖ ˌ•ə-

Diphthongs

1 A **diphthong** is a complex vowel: a sequence of two vowel qualities within a single syllable. Compare **monophthong**, a vowel whose quality remains constant (as is the case with most vowels).

2 Several English vowel phonemes are diphthongal. The aɪ of **time** taɪm, for example, involves a movement of the tongue from a starting-point a towards an endpoint ɪ.

3 Ordinary diphthongs are **diminuendo** (or **falling**), in that the prominence decreases as we pass from the first element to the second. The a part of aɪ is more prominent than the ɪ part. Compare sequences such as the je in **yes** jes, which is a kind of **crescendo** (**rising**) diphthong (see also COMPRESSION).

4 In English, the distinction between diphthong and monophthong is not always clear-cut. For example, some speakers pronounce eə as a monophthong, ɛː. In some positions iː and uː may be somewhat diphthongal, ii, ʊu.

D

dipsomaniac ˌdɪps əʊ 'meɪn i æk ‖ ˌ•ə- ~s s
dipstick 'dɪp stɪk ~s s
dipswitch 'dɪp swɪtʃ ~es ɪz əz
Dipsy 'dɪps i
dipter|al 'dɪpt ər əl ~an ən ~ous əs
diptych 'dɪp tɪk ~s s
Dirac dɪ 'ræk də-; 'dɪr æk
dire 'daɪ_ə ‖ 'daɪ_ər **direr** 'daɪ_ər ə ‖ 'daɪ_ʳr ər
direst 'daɪ_ər ɪst -əst ‖ 'daɪ_ʳr əst
direct v, adj, adv (ˌ)daɪə 'rekt də-, dɪ- ‖ də- daɪ-
  ~ed ɪd əd ~ing ɪŋ ~s s —In the case of
  direct, the stress-shifted form ˌdaɪə rekt is
  frequent in BrE in phrases such as ˌdirect 'debit;
  but the weak-vowelled variant is also heard,
  də 'rekt, dɪ-, with no stress shift, thus di,rect
  'debit. —AmE 1993 poll panel preference: də-
  78%, daɪ- 22%.
  ˌdirect 'debit, •ˌ•-; ˌdirect 'method, •ˌ•-;
  ˌdirect 'object, •ˌ•-; ˌdirect 'speech, •ˌ•-;
  ˌdirect 'tax, •ˌ•-
direction daɪə 'rek ʃən də-, dɪ- ‖ də- daɪ- ~s z
  —BrE 1998 poll panel preference: daɪ- 54%,
  daɪə- 15%, dɪ- 15%, də- 15%
directional daɪə 'rek ʃən_əl də-, dɪ- ‖ də- daɪ-
  ~ly i
directionality daɪə ˌrek ʃə 'næl ət i də-, dɪ-,
  -ɪt i; ˌdaɪə•ˌ•'•- ‖ də ˌrek ʃə 'næl əţ i daɪ-
directive daɪə 'rekt ɪv də-, dɪ- ‖ də- daɪ- ~s z
directly daɪə 'rekt li də-, dɪ- ‖ də- daɪ- —In
  the senses 'immediately, as soon as' there is
  also a casual form 'drek li, becoming old-
  fashioned
Directoire, d~ ˌdɪr ek 'twɑː ˌdɪər-, ˌdiː rek-;
  də 'rekt wɑː, dɪ-, daɪə- ‖ ˌdiː rek 'twɑːr —Fr
  [di ʁɛk twaːʁ]
director daɪə 'rekt ə də-, dɪ- ‖ 'rekt ʳr daɪ-
  ~s z
directorate daɪə 'rekt ər_ət də-, dɪ-, ˌ_ɪt ‖ də-
  daɪ- ~s s

directorial ˌdaɪər ek 'tɔːr i_əl ◄ də ˌrek-,
  dɪ- ‖ -'toʊr-
directorship daɪə 'rekt ə ʃɪp də-, dɪ-
  ‖ də 'rekt ʳr- daɪ- ~s s
director|y daɪə 'rekt ər_|i də-, dɪ- ‖ də- daɪ-
  ~ies iz
directrix daɪə 'rek trɪks də-, dɪ-
direful 'daɪ_ə fəl -fʊl ‖ 'daɪ_ʳr- ~ly i ~ness nəs
  nɪs
dire|ly 'daɪ_ə |li ‖ 'daɪ_ʳr |li ~ness nəs nɪs
dirge dɜːdʒ ‖ dɜːːdʒ **dirges** 'dɜːdʒ ɪz -əz
  ‖ 'dɜːːdʒ-
dirham 'dɪər æm 'dɪr-, -əm ‖ də 'ræm ~s z
dirigible 'dɪr ɪdʒ əb əl '•ədʒ-, -ɪb əl; də 'rɪdʒ-,
  dɪ- ~s z
dirigisme 'dɪr ɪ ˌʒɪz əm -ə- —Fr [di ʁi ʒism]
dirigiste ˌdɪr ɪ 'ʒiːst ◄ -ə-, 'dɪr ɪʒ ɪst, -əst —Fr
  [di ʁi ʒist] ~s s —or as sing.
diriment 'dɪr ɪm ənt -əm-
dirk, Dirk dɜːk ‖ dɜːːk **dirks, Dirk's**
  dɜːks ‖ dɜːːks
dirndl 'dɜːnd əl ‖ 'dɜːːnd- ~s z
dirt dɜːt ‖ dɜːːt
  ˌdirt 'cheap; 'dirt ˌfarmer; ˌdirt 'road, '• •;
  'dirt track
dirt|y 'dɜːt li ‖ 'dɜːːt li ~ied id ~ier i_ə ‖ i_ʳr
  ~ies iz ~iest i_ɪst i_əst ~ily ɪ li əl i ~iness
  i nəs i nɪs ~ying i_ɪŋ
  ˌdirty old 'man; ˌdirty 'trick; ˌdirty 'word;
  'dirty work
Dis dɪs
dis dɪs **dissed** dɪst **disses** 'dɪs ɪz -əz
  dissing 'dɪs ɪŋ
dis- (ˌ)dɪs —Stressed when followed by an
  unstressed syllable, and often even when not:
  ˌdisaf'firm, (ˌ)dis'relish.
disabilit|y ˌdɪs ə 'bɪl ət li -ɪt i ‖ -əţ li ~ies iz
disabl|e dɪs 'eɪb əl §dɪz- ~ed d ~ement mənt
  ~es z ~ing_ɪŋ

D

disabus|e ˌdɪs ə 'bjuːz ~**ed** d ~**es** ɪz əz ~**ing** ɪŋ

disadvantag|e ˌdɪs əd 'vɑːnt ɪdʒ §-æd-, §-'vænt- ‖ -'vænt̬- ~**ed** d ~**es** ɪz əz ~**ing** ɪŋ

disadvantageous ˌdɪs ˌæd vən 'teɪdʒ əs •, •-, -væn'•-, -vɑːn'•- ~**ly** li ~**ness** nəs nɪs

disaffected ˌdɪs ə 'fekt ɪd -əd ~**ly** li

disaffection ˌdɪs ə 'fek ʃən

disaffili|ate ˌdɪs ə 'fɪl i |eɪt ~**ated** eɪt ɪd -əd ‖ eɪt̬ əd ~**ates** eɪts ~**ating** eɪt ɪŋ ‖ eɪt̬ ɪŋ

disaffiliation ˌdɪs ə ˌfɪl i 'eɪʃ ən ~**s** z

disafforest ˌdɪs ə 'fɒr ɪst -əst ‖ -'fɔːr- -'fɑːr- ~**ed** ɪd əd ~**ing** ɪŋ ~**s** s

disafforestation ˌdɪs ə ˌfɒr ɪ 'steɪʃ ən -ə'•- ‖ -ˌfɔːr- -ˌfɑːr- ~**s** z

disagree ˌdɪs ə 'griː —*Often with contrastive stress:* Do you agree or 'dɪs ə ˌgriː ? ~**d** d ~**ing** ɪŋ ~**s** z

disagreeab|le ˌdɪs ə 'griː əb |əl ◀ ~**ly** li

disagreement ˌdɪs ə 'griː mənt ~**s** s

disallow ˌdɪs ə 'laʊ ~**ed** d ~**ing** ɪŋ ~**s** z

disambigu|ate ˌdɪs æm 'bɪg ju |eɪt ~**ated** eɪt ɪd -əd ‖ eɪt̬ əd ~**ates** eɪts ~**ating** eɪt ɪŋ ‖ eɪt̬ ɪŋ

disambiguation ˌdɪs æm ˌbɪg ju 'eɪʃ ən ~**s** z

disappear ˌdɪs ə 'pɪə ‖ -'pɪ³r ~**ed** d

disappearing ˌdɪs ə 'pɪər ɪŋ ‖ -'pɪr ɪŋ ~**s** z

disappearanc|e ˌdɪs ə 'pɪər ənts ‖ -'pɪr- ~**es** ɪz əz

disap|point ˌdɪs ə |'pɔɪnt ~**pointed/ly** 'pɔɪnt ɪd /li -əd /li ‖ 'pɔɪnt̬ əd /li ~**pointing/ly** 'pɔɪnt ɪŋ /li ‖ 'pɔɪnt̬ ɪŋ /li ~**points** 'pɔɪnts

disappointment ˌdɪs ə 'pɔɪnt mənt ~**s** s

disapprobation ˌdɪs ˌæp rəʊ 'beɪʃ ən ‖ -ə-

disapproval ˌdɪs ə 'pruːv əl ~**s** z

disapprov|e ˌdɪs ə 'pruːv ~**ed** d ~**es** z ~**ing/ly** ɪŋ /li

disarm dɪs 'ɑːm dɪz- ‖ -'ɑːrm ~**ed** d ~**ing/ly** ɪŋ /li ~**s** z

disarmament dɪs 'ɑːm ə mənt dɪz- ‖ -'ɑːrm- ~**s** s

disarrang|e ˌdɪs ə 'reɪndʒ ~**ed** d ~**ement** mənt ~**es** ɪz əz ~**ing** ɪŋ

disarray ˌdɪs ə 'reɪ ~**ed** d ~**ing** ɪŋ ~**s** z

disassoci|ate ˌdɪs ə 'səʊʃ i |eɪt -'səʊs- ‖ -'soʊʃ- -'soʊs- ~**ated** eɪt ɪd -əd ‖ eɪt̬ əd ~**ates** eɪts ~**ating** eɪt ɪŋ ‖ eɪt̬ ɪŋ

disaster dɪ 'zɑːst ə də-, §-'zæst- ‖ -'zæst ³r ~**s** z
di'saster ˌarea

disastrous dɪ 'zɑːs trəs də-, §-'zæs-, △-'zæst ³r əs ‖ -'zæs- ~**ly** li ~**ness** nəs nɪs

disavow ˌdɪs ə 'vaʊ ~**ed** d ~**ing** ɪŋ ~**s** z

disavowal ˌdɪs ə 'vaʊ̯ əl -'vaʊl ~**s** z

disband dɪs 'bænd ~**ed** ɪd əd ~**ing** ɪŋ ~**s** z

disbandment dɪs 'bænd mənt ~**s** s

dis|bar dɪs |'bɑː ‖ -|'bɑːr ~**barred** 'bɑːd ‖ 'bɑːrd ~**barring** 'bɑːr ɪŋ ~**bars** 'bɑːz ‖ 'bɑːrz

disbarment dɪs 'bɑː mənt ‖ -'bɑːr- ~**s** s

disbelief ˌdɪs bɪ 'liːf -bə-, §-biː-

disbeliev|e ˌdɪs bɪ 'liːv -bə-, §-biː- ~**ed** d ~**er/s** ə/z ‖ ³r/z ~**es** z ~**ing/ly** ɪŋ /li

disbud ₍ₗ₎dɪs 'bʌd ~**ded** ɪd əd ~**ding** ɪŋ ~**s** z

disburden dɪs 'bɜːd ³n ‖ -'bɝːd- ~**ed** d ~**ing** ˌɪŋ ~**s** z

disburs|e dɪs 'bɜːs ‖ -'bɝːs ~**ed** t ~**es** ɪz əz ~**ing** ɪŋ

disbursement dɪs 'bɜːs mənt ‖ -'bɝːs- ~**s** s

disc dɪsk **discs** dɪsks
'disc brakes; 'disc ˌharrow; 'disc ˌjockey

discalced dɪs 'kælst

discard v dɪs 'kɑːd ˌ•- ‖ -'kɑːrd ~**ed** ɪd əd ~**ing** ɪŋ ~**s** z

discard n 'dɪs kɑːd ‖ -kɑːrd ~**s** z

discern dɪ 'sɜːn də-, -'zɜːn ‖ -'sɝːn -'zɝːn ~**ed** d ~**ing/ly** ɪŋ /li ~**s** z

discernib|le dɪ 'sɜːn əb |əl də-, -'zɜːn-, -ɪb- ‖ -'sɝːn- -'zɝːn- ~**ly** li

discernment dɪ 'sɜːn mənt də-, -'zɜːn- ‖ -'sɝːn- -'zɝːn-

discharg|e v dɪs 'tʃɑːdʒ ˌ•-, '•• ‖ -'tʃɑːrdʒ ~**ed** d ~**es** ɪz əz ~**ing** ɪŋ

discharg|e n 'dɪs tʃɑːdʒ •'• ‖ -'tʃɑːrdʒ ~**es** ɪz əz

disci 'dɪsk aɪ 'dɪs-

disciple dɪ 'saɪp əl də- ~**s** z ~**ship** ʃɪp

disciplinarian ˌdɪs ə plɪ 'neər i_ən ˌ•ɪ-, -plə'•- ‖ -'ner- ~**s** z

disciplinary 'dɪs ə plɪn ər_i '•ɪ-, '••plən-, ˌ••'plɪn ər i ‖ -plə ner i

disciplin|e n, v 'dɪs əp lɪn -ɪp-, -lən; §dɪ 'sɪp-, də- ~**ed** d ~**es** z ~**ing** ɪŋ

disclaim dɪs 'kleɪm ~**ed** d ~**ing** ɪŋ ~**s** z

disclaimer dɪs 'kleɪm ə ‖ -³r ~**s** z

disclos|e dɪs 'kləʊz ‖ -'kloʊz ~**ed** d ~**es** ɪz əz ~**ing** ɪŋ

disclosure dɪs 'kləʊʒ ə ‖ -'kloʊʒ ³r ~**s** z

disco 'dɪsk əʊ ‖ -oʊ ~**s** z

discob|olus dɪ 'skɒb |əl əs ‖ -'skɑːb- ~**oli** ə laɪ əl aɪ

discograph|y dɪ 'skɒg rəf i ‖ -'skɑːg- ~**ies** iz

discolor ₍ₗ₎dɪs 'kʌl ə ‖ -³r ~**ed** d **discoloring** dɪs 'kʌl ³r ɪŋ ~**s** z

discoloration dɪs ˌkʌl ə 'reɪʃ ən ˌ•, •- ~**s** z

discolour ₍ₗ₎dɪs 'kʌl ə ‖ -³r ~**ed** d **discolouring** dɪs 'kʌl ³r ɪŋ ~**s** z

discombobu|late ˌdɪsk əm 'bɒb ju |leɪt -jə- ‖ -'bɑːb jə- ~**lated** leɪt ɪd -əd ‖ leɪt̬ əd ~**lates** leɪts ~**lating** leɪt ɪŋ ‖ leɪt̬ ɪŋ

discomf|it dɪs 'kʌmᵖf |ɪt -ət -|ət ~**ited** ɪt ɪd §ət-, -əd ‖ ət̬ əd ~**iting** ɪt ɪŋ §ət- ‖ ət̬ ɪŋ ~**its** ɪts §əts ‖ ət̬s

discomfiture dɪs 'kʌmᵖf ɪtʃ ə -ətʃ- ‖ -³r ~**s** z

discomfort dɪs 'kʌmᵖf ət ‖ -³rt

discommod|e ˌdɪs kə 'məʊd ‖ -'moʊd ~**ed** ɪd əd ~**es** z ~**ing** ɪŋ

discompos|e ˌdɪs kəm 'pəʊz §-kɒm- ‖ -'poʊz ~**ed** d ~**es** z ~**ing/ly** ɪŋ /li

discomposure ˌdɪs kəm 'pəʊʒ ə §-kɒm- ‖ -'poʊʒ ³r

discon|cert ˌdɪs kən |'sɜːt §-kɒn- ‖ -|'sɝːt ~**certed** 'sɜːt ɪd -əd ‖ 'sɝːt̬ əd ~**certing/ly** 'sɜːt ɪŋ /li ‖ 'sɝːt̬ ɪŋ /li ~**certs** 'sɜːts ‖ 'sɝːts

disconfirm ˌdɪs kən 'fɜːm §-kɒn- ‖ -'fɝːm ~**ed** d ~**ing** ɪŋ ~**s** z

disconformit|y ˌdɪs kən ˈfɔːm ət li §ˌˈkɒn-,
-ɪt i ‖ -ˈfɔːrm əṭ li **~ies** iz
disconnect v ˌdɪs kə ˈnekt **~ed/ly** ɪd /li əd /li
~ing ɪŋ **~s** s
disconnect n ˌdɪs kə ˈnekt ˈ•• ,•
disconnection, disconnexion ˌdɪs kə ˈnek ʃən
~s z
disconsolate dɪs ˈkɒnᵗs əl ət -ɪt ‖ -ˈkɑːnᵗs- **~ly**
li **~ness** nəs nɪs
discon|tent ˌdɪs kən |ˈtent §-kɒn- **~tented**
ˈtent ɪd -əd ‖ ˈtenṭ əd **~tenting**
ˈtent ɪŋ ‖ ˈtenṭ ɪŋ **~tents** tenᵗs
discontented ˌdɪs kən ˈtent ɪd -əd ‖ -ˈtenṭ əd
~ly li **~ness** nəs nɪs
discontinuance ˌdɪs kən ˈtɪn ju‿ənᵗs §ˌˈkɒn-
discontinuation ˌdɪs kən ˌtɪn ju ˈeɪʃ ən
§ˌˈkɒn-
discontinu|e ˌdɪs kən ˈtɪn juː §-kɒn-, -ju **~ed**
d **~es** z **~ing** ɪŋ
discontinuit|y ˌdɪs ˌkɒnt ɪ ˈnjuːᵊ ət li-əˈ•‿, -ɪt i
‖ dɪs ˌkɑːnt ən ˈuː əṭ li -ˈjuː- **~ies** iz
discontinuous ˌdɪs kən ˈtɪn ju‿əs ◂ §ˌˈkɒn-
~ly li **~ness** nəs nɪs
discord n ˈdɪs kɔːd ‖ -kɔːrd **~s** z
discordanc|e dɪs ˈkɔːd ənᵗs ‖ -ˈkɔːrd ənᵗs **~es**
ɪz əz
discordant dɪs ˈkɔːd ənt ‖ -ˈkɔːrd ənt **~ly** li
discotheque ˈdɪsk ə tek ˌ••ˈ• **~s** s
discount n ˈdɪs kaʊnt **~s** s
ˈdiscount house; ˈdiscount store
dis|count v ˈdɪs |kaʊnt •ˈ• —AmE 1993 poll
panel preference: ˈ•• 82%, •ˈ• 18%.
~counted kaʊnt ɪd -əd ‖ kaʊnṭ əd
~counting kaʊnt ɪŋ ‖ kaʊnṭ ɪŋ **~counts**
kaʊnᵗs
discountenanc|e dɪs ˈkaʊnt ɪn ənᵗs -ən-
‖ -ˈkaʊnt ən- **~ed** t **~es** ɪz əz **~ing** ɪŋ
discourag|e dɪs ˈkʌr ɪdʒ ‖ -ˈkɝː- **~ed** d **~es** ɪz
əz **~ing/ly** ɪŋ /li
discouragement dɪs ˈkʌr ɪdʒ mənt ‖ -ˈkɝː- **~s**
s
discours|e n ˈdɪs kɔːs •ˈ• ‖ -kɔːrs -koʊrs **~es**
ɪz əz
discours|e v dɪs ˈkɔːs ‖ -ˈkɔːrs -ˈkoʊrs **~ed** t
~es ɪz əz **~ing** ɪŋ
discourteous dɪs ˈkɜːt i‿əs ‖ -ˈkɝːṭ- **~ly** li
~ness nəs nɪs
discourtes|y dɪs ˈkɜːt əs li -i ‖ -ˈkɝːṭ- **~ies** iz
discover dɪ ˈskʌv ə də- ‖ -ᵊr **~ed** d
discovering dɪ ˈskʌv ər‿ɪŋ **~s** z
discoverable dɪ ˈskʌv ər‿əb ᵊl
discoverer dɪ ˈskʌv ər‿ə də- ‖ -ᵊr‿ᵊr **~s** z
discover|y dɪ ˈskʌv ər‿li də- **~ies** iz
discred|it v, n ₍ᵢ₎dɪs ˈkred |ɪt §-ət ‖ -|ət **~ited**
ɪt ɪd §ət-, -əd ‖ əṭ əd **~iting** ɪt ɪŋ §ət- ‖ əṭ ɪŋ
~its ɪts §əts ‖ əts
discreditab|le ₍ᵢ₎dɪs ˈkred ɪt əb ᵊl §-ət əb-
‖ -əṭ əb- **~ly** li
discreet dɪ ˈskriːt də- **~ly** li **~ness** nəs nɪs
discrepanc|y dɪs ˈkrep ənᵗs i **~ies** iz
discrepant dɪs ˈkrep ənt -wə‿l
discrete dɪ ˈskriːt ˌdɪs ˈkriːt ◂ (usually =
discreet) **~ly** li **~ness** nəs nɪs

discretion dɪ ˈskreʃ ᵊn
discretionar|y dɪ ˈskreʃ ᵊn ᵊr‿li-ᵊn‿ər li
‖ -ə ner li -ily əl i ɪ li
discriminant dɪ ˈskrɪm ɪn ənt də-, -ən‿ənt **~s** s
discrimi|nate dɪ ˈskrɪm ɪ |neɪt də-, -ə- **~nated**
neɪt ɪd -əd ‖ neɪṭ əd **~nates** neɪts **~nating**
neɪt ɪŋ ‖ neɪṭ ɪŋ
discrimination dɪ ˌskrɪm ɪ ˈneɪʃ ᵊn də-, -ə- **~s**
z
discriminative dɪ ˈskrɪm ɪn ət ɪv də-, -ən‿ət-;
-ɪ neɪt ɪv, -ə•• ‖ -ə neɪṭ ɪv -ən‿əṭ ɪv **~ly** li
discriminator dɪ ˈskrɪm ɪ neɪt ə də-, -ˈ•ə-
‖ -neɪṭ ᵊr **~s** z
discriminator|y dɪ ˈskrɪm ɪn ət‿ər li də-, -ˈ•ən-;
-ˌskrɪm ɪ ˈneɪt ər li, -,•ə- ‖ -ə tɔːr li -toʊr i
~ily əl i ɪ li
discursive dɪs ˈkɜːs ɪv ‖ -ˈkɝːs- **~ly** li **~ness**
nəs nɪs
discus ˈdɪsk əs **disci** ˈdɪsk aɪ ˈdɪs aɪ **~es** ɪz əz
discuss dɪ ˈskʌs də- **~ed** t **~es** ɪz əz **~ing** ɪŋ
discussable dɪ ˈskʌs əb ᵊl
discussant dɪ ˈskʌs ᵊnt də- **~s** s
discussion dɪ ˈskʌʃ ᵊn də- **~s** z
disdain n, v dɪs ˈdeɪn dɪz- **~ed** d **~ing** ɪŋ **~s** z
disdainful dɪs ˈdeɪn fᵊl dɪz-, -fʊl **~ly** ‿i
diseas|e dɪ ˈziːz də- **~ed** d **~es** ɪz əz
disembark ˌdɪs ɪm ˈbɑːk -əm-, -em- ‖ -ˈbɑːrk
~ed t **~ing** ɪŋ **~s** s
disembarkation ˌdɪs ˌem bɑː ˈkeɪʃ ᵊn ,•ɪm-,
ˌ,•əm- ‖ -bɑːr- dɪs ˌem- **~s** z
disembarrass ˌdɪs ɪm ˈbær əs -əm-,
-em- ‖ -ˈber- **~ed** t **~es** ɪz əz **~ing** ɪŋ
~ment mənt
disembod|y ˌdɪs ɪm ˈbɒd li -əm-, -em-
‖ -ˈbɑːd li **~ied** ɪd **~ies** iz **~iment** i mənt
~ying i‿ɪŋ
disembogu|e ˌdɪs ɪm ˈbəʊg -əm-, -em-
‖ -ˈboʊg **~ed** d **~es** z **~ing** ɪŋ
disembowel ˌdɪs ɪm ˈbaʊ‿əl -əm-, -em-,
ˌ,••ˈbaʊl ‖ -ˈbaʊ‿əl **~ed**, **~led** d **~ing**, **~ling**
ɪŋ **~ment** mənt **~s** z
disembroil ˌdɪs ɪm ˈbrɔɪᵊl -əm-, -em- **~ed** d
~ing ɪŋ **~s** z
disen|chant ˌdɪs ɪn |ˈtʃɑːnt -ən, -en-, §-|ˈtʃænt
‖ -|ˈtʃænt **~chanted** ˈtʃɑːnt ɪd §ˈtʃænt-, -əd
‖ ˈtʃænṭ əd **~chanting** ˈtʃɑːnt ɪŋ §ˈtʃænt-
‖ ˈtʃænṭ ɪŋ **~chants** ˈtʃɑːnᵗs §ˈtʃænᵗs
‖ ˈtʃænts
disencum|ber ˌdɪs ɪn ˈkʌm |bə→-ɪŋ-, -ən-,
-en- ‖ -|bᵊr **~bered** bəd ‖ bᵊrd **~bering**
bᵊr‿ɪŋ **~bers** bəz ‖ bᵊrz
disendow ˌdɪs ɪn ˈdaʊ -ən-, -en- **~ed** d **~ing**
ɪŋ **~ment** mənt **~s** z
disenfranchis|e ˌdɪs ɪn ˈfræntʃ aɪz -ən-, -en-
~ed d **~ement** mənt **~es** ɪz əz **~ing** ɪŋ
disengag|e ˌdɪs ɪn ˈgeɪdʒ -ən-, -en- **~ed** d
~ement mənt **~es** ɪz əz **~ing** ɪŋ
disentangl|e ˌdɪs ɪn ˈtæŋ gᵊl -ən-, -en- **~ed** d
~ement mənt **~es** z **~ing** ‿ɪŋ
disequilibrium ˌdɪs ˌiːk wɪ ˈlɪb ri‿əm -ˌek-,
-wəˈ•- ‖ dɪs ˌek-
disestablish ˌdɪs ɪ ˈstæb lɪʃ -ə-, -e- **~ed** t **~es**
ɪz əz **~ing** ɪŋ **~ment** mənt

D

disestablishmentarian
ˌdɪs ɪ ˌstæb lɪʃ mən 'teər i‿ən ˌ•ə-, ˌ•e-
‖ -'ter- ~s z

disfav|or, disfav|our ₍ₗ₎dɪs 'feɪv |ə ‖ -|ªr ~ored,
~oured əd ‖ ªrd ~oring, ~ouring ər‿ɪŋ
~ors, ~ours əz ‖ ªrz

disfig|ure dɪs 'fɪg |ə ‖ -|jªr *(*)* ~ured əd ‖ jªrd
~ures əz ‖ jªrz ~uring ər‿ɪŋ ‖ jər ɪŋ

disfigurement dɪs 'fɪg ə mənt ‖ -jªr- ~s z

disforest ₍ₗ₎dɪs 'fɒr ɪst -əst ‖ -'fɔ:r- -'fɑ:r- ~ed
ɪd əd ~ing ɪŋ ~s s

disforestation ˌdɪs ˌfɒr ɪ 'steɪʃ ən •ˌ•-, -ə-
‖ ˌdɪs ˌfɔ:r- -ˌfɑ:r-

disfranchis|e dɪs 'fræntʃ aɪz ~ed d ~es ɪz əz
~ing ɪŋ

disfranchisement dɪs 'fræntʃ ɪz mənt -əz-,
-aɪz- ~s s

disfrock ˌdɪs 'frɒk ‖ -'frɑ:k ~ed t ~ing ɪŋ ~s
s

disgorg|e dɪs 'gɔ:dʒ ‖ -'gɔ:rdʒ ~ed d ~es ɪz
əz ~ing ɪŋ

disgrac|e *v, n* dɪs 'greɪs dɪz-, dəs- ~ed t ~es
ɪz əz ~ing ɪŋ

disgraceful dɪs 'greɪs fªl dɪz-, dəs-, -fʊl ~ly ‿i

disgruntled dɪs 'grʌnt ªld ‖ -'grʌnt̬-

disgruntlement dɪs 'grʌnt ªl mənt ‖ -'grʌnt̬-

disguis|e *v, n* dɪs 'gaɪz dɪz-, dəs- ~ed d ~er/s
ə/z ‖ ªr/z ~es ɪz əz ~ing ɪŋ

disgust *n, v* dɪs 'gʌst dɪz-, dəs- ~ed/ly ɪd /li
əd /li ~ing/ly ɪŋ /li ~s s

dish dɪʃ **dished** dɪʃt **dishes** 'dɪʃ ɪz -əz
dishing 'dɪʃ ɪŋ
'dish ˌtowel

dishabille ˌdɪs ə 'bi:ªl -æ-

disharmonious ˌdɪs hɑ: 'məʊn i‿əs
‖ -hɑ:r 'moʊn- ~ly li

disharmon|y ₍ₗ₎dɪs 'hɑ:m ən |i ‖ -'hɑ:rm- ~ies
iz

dish|cloth 'dɪʃ |klɒθ -klɔ:θ ‖ -|klɔ:θ -klɑ:θ
~cloths klɒθs klɒðz, klɔ:θs, klɔ:ðz ‖ klɔ:ðz
klɔ:θs, klɑ:ðz, klɑ:θs

dishearten dɪs 'hɑ:t ªn ‖ -'hɑ:rt- ~ed d
~ing/ly ‿ɪŋ /li ~ment mənt ~s z

dishevel dɪ 'ʃev ªl ~ed, ~led d ~ing, ~ling ɪŋ
~ment mənt ~s z

Dishforth 'dɪʃ fəθ -fɔ:θ ‖ -fªrθ -fɔ:rθ —*The*
place in N Yks is locally -fəθ

dishful 'dɪʃ fʊl ~s z

dishi... —*see* dishy

dishonest ₍ₗ₎dɪs 'ɒn ɪst dɪz-, -əst ‖ -'ɑ:n- ~ly li

dishonest|y ₍ₗ₎dɪs 'ɒn əst i dɪz-, -ɪst- ‖ -'ɑ:n-
~ies iz

dishon|or, dishon|our *n, v* dɪs 'ɒn ə dɪz-
‖ -'ɑ:n ªr ~ored, ~oured əd ‖ ªrd ~oring,
~ouring ər‿ɪŋ ~ors, ~ours əz ‖ ªrz

dishonorab|le, dishonourab|le dɪs 'ɒn
ər‿əb |ªl dɪz- ‖ -'ɑ:n- ~ly li

dishpan 'dɪʃ pæn ~s z

dishwasher 'dɪʃ ˌwɒʃ ə ‖ -ˌwɔ:ʃ ªr -ˌwɑ:ʃ ªr ~s
z

dishwater 'dɪʃ ˌwɔ:t ə ‖ -ˌwɔ:t̬ ªr -ˌwɑ:t̬ ªr

dish|y 'dɪʃ |i ~ier i‿ə ‖ i‿ªr ~iest i‿ɪst i‿əst

disillusion ˌdɪs ɪ 'lu:ʒ ən -ə-, -'lju:ʒ- ~ed d
~ing ‿ɪŋ ~ment/s mənt/s ~s z

disincentive ˌdɪs ɪn 'sent ɪv ‖ -'sent̬ ɪv ~s z

disinclination ˌdɪs ˌɪn klɪ 'neɪʃ ən →-ˌɪŋ-, ˌ•ən-,
-klə'•- ~s z

disinclin|e ˌdɪs ɪn 'klaɪn →-ɪŋ-, -ən- ~ed d
~es z ~ing ɪŋ

disinfect ˌdɪs ɪn 'fekt -ən- ~ed ɪd əd ~ing ɪŋ
~s s

disinfectant ˌdɪs ɪn 'fekt ənt -ən- ~s s

disinfection ˌdɪs ɪn 'fek ʃən -ən- ~s z

disinfest ˌdɪs ɪn 'fest -ən- ~ed ɪd əd ~ing ɪŋ
~s s

disinfestation ˌdɪs ˌɪn fe 'steɪʃ ən ˌ•ən- ~s z

disinflationary ˌdɪs ɪn 'fleɪʃ ən‿ər i ˌ•ən-,
-'fleɪʃ ªn ri ‖ -ə ner i

disinformation ˌdɪs ˌɪn fə 'meɪʃ ən ˌ••-, ˌ•ən-
‖ -fªr'•-

disingenuous ˌdɪs ɪn 'dʒen ju‿əs ◂ ˌ•ən- ~ly li
~ness nəs nɪs

disinher|it ˌdɪs ɪn 'her |ɪt -ən-, -ət ‖ -|ət ~ited
ɪt ɪd ət-, -əd ‖ ət̬ əd ~iting ɪt ɪŋ ət- ‖ ət̬ ɪŋ
~its ɪts əts ‖ əts

disinheritance ˌdɪs ɪn 'her ɪt ªnts ˌ•ən-
‖ -ət ªnts

disinte|grate dɪs 'ɪnt ɪ |greɪt -ə- ‖ -'ɪnt̬ ə-
~grated greɪt ɪd -əd ‖ greɪt̬ əd ~grates
greɪts ~grating greɪt ɪŋ ‖ greɪt̬ ɪŋ

disintegration dɪs ˌɪnt ɪ 'greɪʃ ən ˌ•ˌ•-, ˌ•ənt-,
-ə'•- ‖ -ˌɪnt̬ ə- ~s z

disin|ter ˌdɪs ɪn |'tɜ: -ən- ‖ -|'tɜ·: ~terred
'tɜ:d ‖ 'tɜ·:d ~terring 'tɜ:r ɪŋ ‖ 'tɜ·: ɪŋ
~ters 'tɜ:z ‖ 'tɜ·:z

disinterest ₍ₗ₎dɪs 'ɪntr əst -ɪst, -est;
-'ɪnt ə rest ‖ -'ɪnt̬ ər əst, -ə rest

disinterested ₍ₗ₎dɪs 'ɪntr əst ɪd -ɪst-, -est-, -əd;
-'ɪnt ə rest ɪd, -əd ‖ -'ɪnt̬ ər əst əd, -ə rest əd
~ly li ~ness nəs nɪs

disinterment ˌdɪs ɪn 'tɜ: mənt -ən- ‖ -'tɜ·:- ~s
s

disinvest ˌdɪs ɪn 'vest -ən- ~ed ɪd əd ~ing ɪŋ
~ment/s mənt/s ~s s

disjoin ₍ₗ₎dɪs 'dʒɔɪn ~ed d ~ing ɪŋ ~s z

disjoint dɪs 'dʒɔɪnt ~ly li

disjointed dɪs 'dʒɔɪnt ɪd -əd ‖ -'dʒɔɪnt̬ əd ~ly
li ~ness nəs nɪs

disjunct dɪs 'dʒʌŋkt '•• ~ly li ~s s

disjunction ₍ₗ₎dɪs 'dʒʌŋk ʃən ~s z

disjunctive ₍ₗ₎dɪs 'dʒʌŋkt ɪv ~ly li ~s z

disk dɪsk **disks** dɪsks
'disk drive

diskette dɪ 'sket ˌdɪsk 'et ~s s

Disley 'dɪz li

dislik|e *v, n* ₍ₗ₎dɪs 'laɪk —*but with contrastive*
stress, ˌlikes and 'dislikes ~ed t ~es s ~ing
ɪŋ

dislo|cate 'dɪs lə |keɪt -ləʊ- ‖ dɪs 'loʊ|k eɪt
~cated keɪt ɪd -əd ‖ keɪt̬ əd ~cates keɪts
~cating keɪt ɪŋ ‖ keɪt̬ ɪŋ

dislocation ˌdɪs lə 'keɪʃ ən -ləʊ- ‖ -loʊ- ~s z

dislodg|e dɪs 'lɒdʒ ‖ -'lɑ:dʒ ~ed d ~es ɪz əz
~ing ɪŋ

dislodgement, dislodgment
  dɪs ˈlɒdʒ mənt ‖ -ˈlɑːdʒ- ~s s
disloyal ₍ˌ₎dɪs ˈlɔɪ‿əl ~ly i
disloyal|ty ₍ˌ₎dɪs ˈlɔɪ‿əl |ti ~ties tiz
dismal ˈdɪz məl ~ly i ~ness nəs nɪs
dismantl|e dɪs ˈmænt əl ~ed d ~ement/s
  mənt/s ~es z ~ing ‿ɪŋ
dismast ˌdɪs ˈmɑːst §-ˈmæst ‖ -ˈmæst ~ed ɪd
  əd ~ing ɪŋ ~s s
dismay v, n dɪs ˈmeɪ dɪz- ~ed d ~ing ɪŋ ~s z
dismember ₍ˌ₎dɪs ˈmem bə ‖ -bər ~ed d
  dismembering ₍ˌ₎dɪs ˈmem bər‿ɪŋ ~s z
dismemberer ₍ˌ₎dɪs ˈmem bər‿ə ‖ -bər‿ər ~s z
  s
dismiss dɪs ˈmɪs §₍ˌ₎dɪz- ~ed t ~es ɪz əz ~ing
  ɪŋ
dismissal dɪs ˈmɪs əl §dɪz- ~s z
dismissive dɪs ˈmɪs ɪv §dɪz- ~ly li ~ness nəs
  nɪs
dis|mount ₍ˌ₎dɪs |ˈmaʊnt ~mounted ˈmaʊnt ɪd
  -əd ‖ ˈmaʊnt̬ əd ~mounting
  ˈmaʊnt ɪŋ ‖ ˈmaʊnt̬ ɪŋ ~mounts ˈmaʊnts
Disney ˈdɪz ni
  ˌDisney ˈWorld tdmk, ˈ• •
Disneyland tdmk ˈdɪz ni lænd
disobedience ˌdɪs ə ˈbiːd i‿ənts ˌ•‿əʊ-
disobedient ˌdɪs ə ˈbiːd i‿ənt ◄ ˌ•‿əʊ- ~ly li
disobey ˌdɪs ə ˈbeɪ -əʊ- ~ed d ~ing ɪŋ ~s z
disoblig|e ˌdɪs ə ˈblaɪdʒ §-əʊ- ~ed d ~es ɪz əz
  ~ing/ly ɪŋ /li
disord|er dɪs ˈɔːd lə dɪz- ‖ -ˈɔːrd lər ~ered
  əd ‖ ərd ~ering ər‿ɪŋ ~ers əz ‖ ərz
disorder|ly dɪs ˈɔːd ə |li dɪz-, -əll i ‖ -ˈɔːrd ər-
  ~liness li nəs -nɪs
  dis,orderly ˈconduct; dis,orderly ˈhouse
disorganis... —see **disorganiz...**
disorganization dɪs ˌɔːg ən aɪ ˈzeɪʃ ən dɪz-,
  ˌ•ˌ•-, -ɪˈ•- ‖ -ˌɔːrg ən‿ə-
disorganiz|e dɪs ˈɔːg ə naɪz dɪz-, ˌ•- ‖ -ˈɔːrg-
  ~ed d ~es ɪz əz ~ing ɪŋ
disori|ent ₍ˌ₎dɪs ˈɔːr i |ent ‿ənt ‖ -ˈoʊr- ~ented
  ent ɪd ənt-, -əd ‖ ent̬ əd ~enting ent ɪŋ ənt-
  ‖ ent̬ ɪŋ ~ents ents ənts
disorien|tate ₍ˌ₎dɪs ˈɔːr i‿ən |teɪt -ˈɒr-,
  -i en- ‖ -ˈoʊr- ~tated teɪt ɪd -əd ‖ teɪt̬ əd
  ~tates teɪts ~tating teɪt ɪŋ ‖ teɪt̬ ɪŋ
disorientation dɪs ˌɔːr i‿ən ˈteɪʃ ən -ˌɒr-, ˌ•ˌ•-,
  -i en- ‖ -ˌoʊr-
disown dɪs ˈəʊn ˌ•- ‖ -ˈoʊn ~ed d ~ing ɪŋ ~s
  z
disparag|e dɪ ˈspær ɪdʒ də- ‖ -ˈsper- ~ed d
  ~ement/s mənt/s ~es ɪz əz ~ing/ly ɪŋ /li
disparate ˈdɪsp ər‿ət -ɪt; -ə reɪt ‖ dɪs ˈpær-,
  -ˈper- ~ly li ~ness nəs nɪs
disparit|y ₍ˌ₎dɪs ˈpær ət li -ɪt- ‖ -ət̬ li -ˈper- ~ies
  ɪz
dispassionate dɪs ˈpæʃ ən‿ət ‿ɪt ~ly li ~ness
  nəs nɪs
dispatch v dɪ ˈspætʃ də- ~ed t ~er/s ə/z ‖ ər/z
  ~es ɪz əz ~ing ɪŋ
dispatch n dɪ ˈspætʃ də-; ˈdɪs pætʃ ~es ɪz əz
  diˈspatch box; diˈspatch ˌrider

dispel dɪ ˈspel ~led d ~ling ɪŋ ~s z
dispensable dɪ ˈspents əb əl ~ness nəs nɪs
dispensar|y dɪ ˈspents ər‿li ~ies iz
dispensation ˌdɪsp ən ˈseɪʃ ən -en- ~s z
dispens|e dɪ ˈspents ~ed t ~er/s ə/z ‖ ər/z
  ~es ɪz əz ~ing ɪŋ
dispersal dɪ ˈspɜːs əl də- ‖ -ˈspɝːs- ~s z
dispersant dɪ ˈspɜːs ənt də- ‖ -ˈspɝːs- ~s s
dispers|e dɪ ˈspɜːs də- ‖ -ˈspɝːs ~ed t ~es ɪz
  əz ~ing ɪŋ
dispersion, D~ dɪ ˈspɜːʃ ən də-, §-ˈspɜːʒ-
  ‖ -ˈspɝːʒ- -ˈspɝːʃ- ~s z
dispersive dɪ ˈspɜːs ɪv də- ‖ -ˈspɝːs- -ˈspɝːz-
dispir|it dɪ ˈspɪr lɪt -ət ‖ -lət ~ited/ly ɪt ɪd /li
  ət-, -əd /li ‖ ət̬ əd /li ~iting ɪt ɪŋ ət- ‖ ət̬ ɪŋ
  ~its ɪts əts ‖ əts
displac|e ₍ˌ₎dɪs ˈpleɪs ~ed t ~es ɪz əz ~ing ɪŋ
  ˌdisplaced ˈperson, •ˌ•-
displacement ₍ˌ₎dɪs ˈpleɪs mənt ~s s
display dɪ ˈspleɪ ~ed d ~ing ɪŋ ~s z
displeas|e ₍ˌ₎dɪs ˈpliːz ~ed d ~es ɪz əz ~ing/
  ly ɪŋ /li
displeasure ₍ˌ₎dɪs ˈpleʒ ə ‖ -ər
di|sport dɪ ˈspɔːt -ˈspɔːrt -ˈspoʊrt
  ~sported ˈspɔːt ɪd -əd ‖ ˈspɔːrt̬ əd ˈspoʊrt-
  ~sporting ˈspɔːt ɪŋ ‖ ˈspɔːrt̬ ɪŋ ˈspoʊrt̬-
  ~sports ˈspɔːts ‖ ˈspɔːrts ˈspoʊrts
disposability dɪ ˌspəʊz ə ˈbɪl ət i də-, -ɪt i
  ‖ -ˌspoʊz ə ˈbɪl ət̬ i
disposable dɪ ˈspəʊz əb əl də- ‖ -ˈspoʊz-
disposal dɪ ˈspəʊz əl də- ‖ -ˈspoʊz- ~s z
dispos|e dɪ ˈspəʊz də- ‖ -ˈspoʊz ~ed d ~es ɪz
  əz ~ing ɪŋ
disposition ˌdɪsp ə ˈzɪʃ ən ~s z
dispossess ˌdɪs pə ˈzes ~ed t ~es ɪz əz ~ing
  ɪŋ
dispossession ˌdɪs pə ˈzeʃ ən ~s z
Disprin tdmk ˈdɪsp rɪn -rən ~s z
disproof ₍ˌ₎dɪs ˈpruːf §-ˈprʊf ~s s
disproportion ˌdɪs prə ˈpɔːʃ ən ‖ -ˈpɔːrʃ ən
  -ˈpoʊrʃ- ~al/ly əl /i ~ed d ~ing ‿ɪŋ ~s z
disproportionate ˌdɪs prə ˈpɔːʃ ən‿ət ◄ ‿ɪt
  ‖ -ˈpɔːrʃ- -ˈpoʊrʃ- ~ly li ~ness nəs nɪs
disprov|e ₍ˌ₎dɪs ˈpruːv ~ed d ~es z ~ing ɪŋ
disputab|le dɪ ˈspjuːt əb əl də-; ˈdɪs pjʊt-
  ‖ dɪ ˈspjuːt̬ əb əl ˈdɪs pjət̬- ~ly li
disputant dɪ ˈspjuːt ənt də-; ˈdɪs pjʊt
  ənt ‖ ˈdɪs pjət ənt ~s s
disputation ˌdɪs pju ˈteɪʃ ən ‖ -pjə- ~s z
disputatious ˌdɪs pju ˈteɪʃ əs ◄ ‖ -pjə- ~ly li
  ~ness nəs nɪs
di|spute v dɪ ˈspjuːt də- ~sputed ˈspjuːt ɪd
  -əd ‖ ˈspjuːt̬ əd ~sputes ˈspjuːts ~sputing
  ˈspjuːt ɪŋ ‖ ˈspjuːt̬ ɪŋ
dispute n dɪ ˈspjuːt də-; ˈdɪs pjuːt —BrE 1988
  poll panel preference: •ˈ• 62%, ˈ•• 38%. ~s s
disqualification dɪs ˌkwɒl ɪf ɪ ˈkeɪʃ ən ˌ•ˌ•-,
  -əf ɪ-, ˌ•ˌkwɑː l- ‖ -ˌkwɑːl-
disquali|fy dɪs ˈkwɒl ɪ |faɪ ˌdɪs-, -ə- ‖ -ˈkwɑːl-
  ~fied faɪd ~fies faɪz ~fying faɪ ɪŋ
disqui|et dɪs ˈkwaɪ‿lət ~eted ət ɪd -əd ‖ ət̬ əd
  ~eting ət ɪŋ ‖ ət̬ ɪŋ ~ets əts

disquietude dɪs 'kwaɪ‿ə tjuːd -ɪ-, →§-tʃuːd
‖ -tuːd -tjuːd
disquisition ˌdɪs kwɪ 'zɪʃ ᵊn -kwə- ~al ‿əl ~s z
Disraeli dɪz 'reɪl i dɪs-
disregard v, n ˌdɪs rɪ 'gɑːd -rə-, §-riː- ‖ -'gɑːrd
~ed ɪd əd ~ing ɪŋ ~s z
disrelish ₍ₒ₎dɪs 'rel ɪʃ ~ed t ~es ɪz əz ~ing ɪŋ
disremem|ber ˌdɪs rɪ 'mem |bə -rə-, §-riː-
‖ -|bᵊr ~bered bəd ‖ bᵊrd ~bering bᵊr‿ɪŋ
~bers bəz ‖ bᵊrz
disrepair ˌdɪs rɪ 'peə -rə-, §-riː- ‖ -'peᵊr -'pæᵊr
disreputab|le dɪs 'rep jʊt əb ᵊl -jət əb-
‖ -jəʈ əb- ~leness ᵊl nəs -nɪs ~ly li
disrepute ˌdɪs rɪ 'pjuːt -rə-, §-riː-
disrespect ˌdɪs rɪ 'spekt -rə-, §-riː- ~ed ɪd əd
~ing ɪŋ ~s s
disrespectful ˌdɪs rɪ 'spekt fᵊl ◄ -rə-, §-riː-, -fʊl
~ly ‿i ~ness nəs nɪs
disrob|e ₍ₒ₎dɪs 'rəʊb ‖ -'roʊb ~ed d ~es z
~ing ɪŋ
disrupt dɪs 'rʌpt ~ed ɪd əd ~er/s ə/z ‖ ᵊr/z
~ing ɪŋ ~s s
disruption dɪs 'rʌp ʃn ~s z
disruptive dɪs 'rʌpt ɪv ~ly li ~ness nəs nɪs
disruptor dɪs 'rʌpt ə ‖ -ᵊr ~s z
Diss dɪs
diss dɪs dissed dɪst disses 'dɪs ɪz -əz
dissing 'dɪs ɪŋ
dissatisfaction ˌdɪs ˌsæt ɪs 'fæk ʃn ˌdɪs æt-,
dɪ ˌsæt-, -əs'•- ‖ ˌdɪs ˌsæʈ əs- ˌdɪs æʈ-,
dɪ ˌsæʈ- ~s z
dissatis|fy ˌdɪs 'sæt ɪs |faɪ ₍ₒ₎dɪ-, -əs- ‖ -'sæʈ-
~fied/ly faɪd /li ~fies faɪz ~fying faɪ ɪŋ
dissect dɪ 'sekt də-, daɪ- ~ed ɪd əd ~ing ɪŋ
~s s
dissection dɪ 'sek ʃn də-, daɪ- ~s z
dissemblance dɪ 'sem blənts də-
dissembl|e dɪ 'sem bᵊl də- ~ed d ~er/s ‿ə/z ‖
ᵊr/z ~es z ~ing ‿ɪŋ
dissemi|nate dɪ 'sem ɪ |neɪt də-, -ə- ~nated
neɪt ɪd -əd ‖ neɪʈ əd ~nates neɪts ~nating
neɪt ɪŋ ‖ neɪʈ ɪŋ
dissemination dɪ ˌsem ɪ 'neɪʃ ᵊn də-, -ə-
disseminator dɪ 'sem ɪ neɪt ə də-, -'•ə-
‖ -neɪʈ ᵊr ~s z
dissension dɪ 'sentʃ ᵊn də- ~s z
dis|sent v, n dɪ ‖'sent də- (usually = descent)
~sented 'sent ɪd -əd ‖ 'senʈ əd ~senting/ly
'sent ɪŋ /li ‖ 'senʈ ɪŋ /li ~sents 'sents
dissenter, D~ dɪ 'sent ə də- ‖ -'senʈ ᵊr ~s z
dissentient dɪ 'sentʃ i ənt də-, -'sentʃ ᵊnt ~s s
dissertation ˌdɪs ə 'teɪʃ ᵊn -ɜː- ‖ -ᵊr- ~s z
disservic|e dɪ 'sɜːv ɪs ₍ₒ₎dɪs-, §-əs ‖ -'sɜːv- ~es
ɪz əz
dissev|er dɪ 'sev lə ‖ -|ᵊr ~ered əd ‖ ᵊrd
~ering ᵊr‿ɪŋ ~ers əz ‖ ᵊrz
dissidence 'dɪs ɪd ᵊnts -əd-
dissident 'dɪs ɪd ᵊnt -əd- ~s s
dissimilar ₍ₒ₎dɪ 'sɪm ɪl ə ₍ₒ₎dɪs-, -ᵊl- ‖ -ᵊr ~ly li
dissimilarit|y ˌdɪs ɪm ɪ 'lær ət i ‿i, •əm-, dɪ ˌsɪm-,
ˌdɪs ˌsɪm-, -ə'•-, -ɪt i ‖ -'læʈ i -'ler- ~ies iz
dissimi|late ₍ₒ₎dɪ 'sɪm ɪ |leɪt -ə- ~lated leɪt ɪd

-əd ‖ leɪʈ əd ~lates leɪts ~lating
leɪt ɪŋ ‖ leɪʈ ɪŋ
dissimilation ˌdɪs ɪm ɪ 'leɪʃ ᵊn dɪ ˌsɪm-,
ˌdɪs ˌsɪm-, -ə'•- ‖ dɪ ˌsɪm- ~s z
dissimilitude ˌdɪs ɪ 'mɪl ɪ tjuːd ,•ə-, ,•sɪ-,
ˌ•sə-, -ə-, →§-tʃuːd ‖ -tuːd -tjuːd ~s z
dissimu|late dɪ 'sɪm ju |leɪt də-, -jə- ‖ -jə-
~lated leɪt ɪd -əd ‖ leɪʈ əd ~lates leɪts
~lating leɪt ɪŋ ‖ leɪʈ ɪŋ
dissimulation dɪ ˌsɪm ju 'leɪʃ ᵊn də-, -jə- ‖ -jə-
~s z
dissi|pate 'dɪs ɪ |peɪt -ə- ~pated peɪt ɪd -əd
‖ peɪʈ əd ~pates peɪts ~pating
peɪt ɪŋ ‖ peɪʈ ɪŋ
dissipation ˌdɪs ɪ 'peɪʃ ᵊn -ə- ~s z
dissoci|ate dɪ 'səʊs i |eɪt -'səʊʃ- ‖ -'soʊʃ-
-'soʊs- ~ated eɪt ɪd -əd ‖ eɪʈ əd ~ates eɪts
~ating eɪt ɪŋ ‖ eɪʈ ɪŋ
dissociation dɪ ˌsəʊʃ i 'eɪʃ ᵊn -ˌsəʊs- ‖ -ˌsoʊʃ-
-ˌsoʊs- ~s z
dissolubility dɪ ˌsɒl ju 'bɪl ət i -ˌ•jə-, -ɪt i
‖ dɪ ˌsɑːl jə 'bɪl əʈ i
dissoluble dɪ 'sɒl jʊb ᵊl -jəb- ‖ dɪ 'sɑːl jəb ᵊl
~ness nəs nɪs
dissolute 'dɪs ə luːt -ljuːt ~ly li ~ness nəs nɪs
dissolution ˌdɪs ə 'luːʃ ᵊn -'ljuːʃ- ~s z
dissolv|e dɪ 'zɒlv də-, §-'zəʊlv ‖ -'zɑːlv ~ed d
~es z ~ing ɪŋ
dissonanc|e 'dɪs ᵊn ᵊnts ~es ɪz əz
dissonant 'dɪs ᵊn ᵊnt ~ly li
dissuad|e dɪ 'sweɪd ~ed ɪd əd ~es z ~ing ɪŋ
dissuasion dɪ 'sweɪʒ ᵊn ~s z
dissuasive dɪ 'sweɪs ɪv -'sweɪz- ~ly li ~ness
nəs nɪs
dissy... —see disy...
distaff 'dɪst ɑːf §-æf ‖ -æf ~s s
distal 'dɪst ᵊl ~ly i
distanc|e 'dɪst ᵊnts ~ed t ~es ɪz əz ~ing ɪŋ
distant 'dɪst ᵊnt ~ly li
distaste ₍ₒ₎dɪs 'teɪst ~s s
distasteful ₍ₒ₎dɪs 'teɪst fᵊl -fʊl ~ly ‿i ~ness nəs
nɪs
distemp|er dɪ 'stemp lə də- ‖ -|ᵊr ~ered
əd ‖ ᵊrd ~ering ᵊr‿ɪŋ ~ers əz ‖ ᵊrz
distend dɪ 'stend də- ~ed ɪd əd ~ing ɪŋ ~s z
distension dɪ 'stentʃ ᵊn də-
distich 'dɪst ɪk ~s s
di|stil, di|still dɪ ‖'stɪl də- ~stilled 'stɪld
~stilling 'stɪl ɪŋ ~stills, ~stils 'stɪlz
distillate 'dɪst ɪl ət -ᵊl-, -ɪt; -ɪ leɪt, -ə- ~s s
distillation ˌdɪst ɪ 'leɪʃ ᵊn -ə-, -ᵊl 'eɪʃ- ~s z
ˌdistil'lation ˌcolumn
distiller dɪ 'stɪl ə də- ‖ -ᵊr ~s z
distiller|y dɪ 'stɪl ər i də- ~ies iz
distinct dɪ 'stɪŋkt də- ~ly li ~ness nəs nɪs
distinction dɪ 'stɪŋk ʃᵊn də- ~s z
distinctive dɪ 'stɪŋkt ɪv də- ~ly li ~ness nəs
nɪs
distingué dɪ 'stæŋ geɪ də- ‖ ˌdiːst æŋ 'geɪ
ˌdɪst- —Fr [di stæ ge]
distinguish dɪ 'stɪŋ gwɪʃ də-, -wɪʃ ~ed t ~es
ɪz əz ~ing ɪŋ

distinguishab|le dɪ 'stɪŋ gwɪʃ əb |əl də-,
-'•wɪʃ- **~ly** li
di|stort dɪ |'stɔːt də- ‖ -|'stɔːrt **~storted**
'stɔːt ɪd -əd ‖ 'stɔːrt̬ əd **~storting**
'stɔːt ɪŋ ‖ 'stɔːrt̬ ɪŋ **~storts** 'stɔːts ‖ 'stɔːrts
distortion dɪ 'stɔːʃ ᵊn də- ‖ -'stɔːrʃ ᵊn **~s** z
distract dɪ 'strækt də- **~ed/ly** ɪd /li əd /li
~ing/ly ɪŋ /li **~s** s
distraction dɪ 'stræk ʃᵊn də- **~s** z
distractor dɪ 'strækt ə də- ‖ -ᵊr **~s** z
distrain dɪ 'streɪn də- **~ed** d **~ing** ɪŋ **~s** z
distraint dɪ 'streɪnt də-
distrait ˌdɪs treɪ dɪ 'streɪ, də- ‖ dɪ 'streɪ —*Fr*
[di stʁɛ]
distraught dɪ 'strɔːt də- ‖ -'strɑːt **~ly** li
distress dɪ 'stres də- **~ed** t **~es** ɪz əz **~ing/ly**
ɪŋ /li
distressful dɪ 'stres fᵊl də-, -fʊl **~ly** i **~ness**
nəs nɪs
distribute dɪ 'strɪb juːt də-; 'dɪs trɪ bjuːt, -trə-
‖ -jət —*The stressing* '•••, *although disliked
by many, is widely used in BrE. BrE 1988 poll
panel preference:* •'••• 74%, '•••• 26%.
distributed dɪ 'strɪb jʊt ɪd də-, -jət-, -əd;
'dɪs trɪ bjuːt ɪd, '•trə-, -əd ‖ -jət̬ əd
distributes dɪ 'strɪb juːts də-; 'dɪs trɪ bjuːts,
-trə- ‖ -jəts **distributing** dɪ 'strɪb jʊt ɪŋ
də-, -jət-; 'dɪs trɪ bjuːt ɪŋ, '•trə- ‖ -jət̬ ɪŋ
distribution ˌdɪs trɪ 'bjuːʃ ᵊn -trə- **~s** z
distributional ˌdɪs trɪ 'bjuːʃ ᵊn_əl **~ly** i
distributive dɪ 'strɪb jʊt ɪv də-, -jə-,
§'dɪs trɪ bjuːt ɪv, '•trə- ‖ -jət̬ ɪv **~ly** li
~ness nəs nɪs
distributor dɪ 'strɪb jʊt ə də-, -jət ə;
§'dɪs trɪ bjuːt ə, '•trə- ‖ -jət̬ ᵊr **~s** z
ˌdistrict at'torney; ˌdistrict 'nurse; ˌDistrict
of Co'lumbia
distrust ₍ᵢ₎dɪs 'trʌst **~ed** ɪd əd **~ing** ɪŋ **~s** s
distrustful ₍ᵢ₎dɪs 'trʌst fᵊl -fʊl **~ly** i **~ness** nəs
nɪs
disturb dɪ 'stɜːb də- ‖ -'stɝːb **~ed** d **~ing/ly**
ɪŋ /li **~s** z
disturbanc|e dɪ 'stɜːb ᵊnts də-, →-mᵖs
‖ -'stɝːb- **~es** ɪz əz
disunion ₍ᵢ₎dɪs 'juːn i_ən →§₍ᵢ₎dɪʃ-
disu|nite ˌdɪs ju |'naɪt →§₍ᵢ₎dɪʃ- **~nited** 'naɪt ɪd
-əd ‖ 'naɪt̬ əd **~nites** 'naɪts **~niting**
'naɪt ɪŋ ‖ 'naɪt̬ ɪŋ
disunit|y ₍ᵢ₎dɪs 'juːn ət li →§₍ᵢ₎dɪʃ-, -ɪt- ‖ -ət̬ li
~ies iz
disuse *n* ₍ᵢ₎dɪs 'juːs →§₍ᵢ₎dɪʃ-
disused ˌdɪs 'juːzd ◂ dɪs-, →§₍ᵢ₎dɪʃ-
ˌdisused 'railway
disyllabic ˌdaɪ sɪ 'læb ɪk ◂ -sə-; ˌdɪs ɪ-, -ə- **~ally**
ᵊl_i
disyllable ˌdaɪ 'sɪl əb ᵊl ₍ᵢ₎dɪ-, '•,••• **~s** z
dit dɪt **dits** dɪts
ditch dɪtʃ **ditched** dɪtʃt **ditches** 'dɪtʃ ɪz -əz
ditching 'dɪtʃ ɪŋ
ditcher 'dɪtʃ ə ‖ -ᵊr **~s** z
Ditchling 'dɪtʃ lɪŋ
ditchwater 'dɪtʃ ˌwɔːt ə ‖ -ˌwɔːt̬ ᵊr -ˌwɑːt̬ ᵊr

dith|er 'dɪð |ə ‖ -|ᵊr **~ered** əd ‖ ᵊrd **~ering**
ᵊr_ɪŋ **~ers** əz ‖ ᵊrz
ditherer 'dɪð ᵊr_ə ‖ -ᵊr_ᵊr **~s** z
dithery 'dɪð ᵊr_i
dithyramb 'dɪθ ɪ ræm -ə-, -ræmb **~s** z
dithyrambic ˌdɪθ ɪ 'ræm bɪk ◂ -ə-
ditransitive ˌdaɪ 'trænᵗs ət ɪv -'trɑːnᵗs-,
-'trænz-, -'trɑːnz-, -ɪt- ‖ -'trænᵗs ət̬ ɪv
-'trænz- **~ly** li **~s** z
dits|y 'dɪts |i **~ier** i_ə ‖ i_ᵊr **~iest** i_ɪst i_əst
~iness i nəs i nɪs
dittander dɪ 'tænd ə §də- ‖ -ᵊr
dittany 'dɪt ᵊn i ‖ 'dɪt̬ ᵊn i
ditto 'dɪt əʊ ‖ 'dɪt̬ oʊ **~ed** d **~ing** ɪŋ **~s** z
Ditton 'dɪt ᵊn
ditt|y 'dɪt i ‖ 'dɪt̬ i **~ies** iz
ditz|y 'dɪts |i **~ier** i_ə ‖ i_ᵊr **~iest** i_ɪst i_əst
~iness i nəs nɪs
diuresis ˌdaɪ juᵊ 'riːs ɪs §-əs ‖ -jə-
diuretic ˌdaɪ juᵊ 'ret ɪk ◂ ‖ -jə 'ret̬ ɪk◂ **~s** s
diurnal daɪ 'ɜːn ᵊl ‖ -'ɝːn ᵊl **~ly** i
diva 'diːv ə **~s** z
diva|gate 'daɪv ə |geɪt 'daɪ veɪ-, 'dɪv ə-
~gated geɪt ɪd -əd ‖ geɪt̬ əd **~gates** geɪts
~gating geɪt ɪŋ ‖ geɪt̬ ɪŋ
divagation ˌdaɪv ə 'geɪʃ ᵊn ˌdaɪ veɪ-, ˌdɪv ə- **~s**
z
divalent ₍ᵢ₎daɪ 'veɪl ənt '•,••
Divali dɪ 'vɑːl i
divan dɪ 'væn də-, ₍ᵢ₎daɪ-, 'daɪv æn **~s** z
dive daɪv **dived** daɪvd **dives** daɪvz **diving**
'daɪv ɪŋ **dove** dəʊv ‖ doʊv
dive-bomb 'daɪv bɒm ‖ -bɑːm **~ed** d **~er/s**
ə/z ‖ ᵊr/z **~ing** ɪŋ **~s** z
diver, Diver 'daɪv ə ‖ -ᵊr **~s** z
diverg|e daɪ 'vɜːdʒ dɪ-, də- ‖ də 'vɝːdʒ daɪ-
~ed d **~es** ɪz əz **~ing** ɪŋ
divergenc|e daɪ 'vɜːdʒ ᵊnts dɪ-, də-
‖ də 'vɝːdʒ- daɪ- **~es** ɪz əz
divergent ₍ᵢ₎daɪ 'vɜːdʒ ənt dɪ-, də-
‖ də 'vɝːdʒ- daɪ- —*but with contrastive
stress, against* convergent, 'daɪˌ•• **~ly** li
divers 'daɪv əz -ɜːz; ₍ᵢ₎daɪ 'vɜːs, '•• ‖ -ᵊrz
diverse daɪ 'vɜːs ˌdaɪ-, '•• ‖ də 'vɝːs daɪ-,
'daɪ vɝːs **~ly** li **~ness** nəs nɪs
diversification daɪ ˌvɜːs ɪf ɪ 'keɪʃ ᵊn dɪ-, də-,
-ˌ•əf-, §-ə'•- ‖ də ˌvɝːs- daɪ- **~s** z
diversi|fy daɪ 'vɜːs ɪ |faɪ -ə- ‖ də 'vɝːs- daɪ-
~fied faɪd **~fies** faɪz **~fying** faɪ ɪŋ
diversion daɪ 'vɜːʃ ᵊn dɪ-, də-, §-'vɜːʒ-
‖ də 'vɝːʒ ᵊn daɪ-, -'vɝːʃ- **~ist/s** ɪst/s §əst/s
~s z
diversionary daɪ 'vɜːʃ ᵊn ᵊr_i dɪ-, də-, §-'vɜːʒ-,
-ᵊn_ᵊr- ‖ də 'vɝːʒ ᵊn er i daɪ-
diversit|y daɪ 'vɜːs ət i dɪ-, də-, -ɪt-
‖ də 'vɝːs ət̬ i daɪ- **~ies** iz
di|vert daɪ |'vɜːt dɪ-, də- ‖ də |'vɝːt daɪ-
~verted 'vɜːt ɪd -əd ‖ 'vɝːt̬ əd **~verting**
'vɜːt ɪŋ ‖ 'vɝːt̬ ɪŋ **~verts** 'vɜːts ‖ 'vɝːts
diverticulitis ˌdaɪv ə ˌtɪk ju 'laɪt ɪs ˌ•'ɜː-, §-əs
‖ ˌdaɪv ᵊr ˌtɪk jə 'laɪt̬ əs
diverticul|um ˌdaɪv ə 'tɪk jʊl əm ˌ•'ɜː-, -jəl əm
‖ ˌdaɪv ᵊr 'tɪk jəl əm **~a** ə

divertiment|odɪ ˌvɜːt ɪ 'ment ləu -ˌveət-, -ə-
‖ dɪ ˌvɜːʈ ɪ 'ment loʊ **~i**iː
divertissementˌdiː veə 'tiːs mɒ̃
dɪ 'vɜːt ɪs mənt, -əs-, -mɒ̃ ‖ dɪ 'vɜːʈ əs mənt
—*Fr* [di vɛʁ tis mɑ̃]
Dives *name* ˈdaɪv ɪz
divestdaɪ 'vest dɪ-, də- **~ed**ɪd əd **~ing**ɪŋ **~s**
s
divestituredaɪ 'vest ɪtʃ ə dɪ-, də- ‖ -ᵊr -ə tʃʊr
~sz
divestmentdaɪ 'vest mənt dɪ-, də- **~s**s
divid|edɪ 'vaɪd də- **~ed**ɪd əd **~es**z **~ing**ɪŋ
dividendˈdɪv ɪ dend -ə-; -ɪd ənd, -əd- **~s**z
dividerdɪ 'vaɪd ə də- ‖ -ᵊr **~s**z
divi-diviˌdɪv i 'dɪv i ˌdiːv i 'diːv i **~s**z
divinationˌdɪv ɪ 'neɪʃ ᵊn -ə- **~s**z
divin|e *adj, n, v*, **D~**dɪ 'vaɪn də- **~ed**d **~ely**li
~enessnəs nɪs **~er/s**ə/z ‖ ᵊr/z **~est**ɪst əst
~ingɪŋ
diˌvine 'right; Diˌvine 'Service; diˈvining
rod
diving ˈdaɪv ɪŋ
ˈdiving bell; ˈdiving suit
divingboard ˈdaɪv ɪŋ bɔːd ‖ -bɔːrd -bʊʊrd **~s**
z
divinit|y, D~dɪ 'vɪn ət i li də-, -ɪt- ‖ -əṭ li **~ies**
iz
Divis ˈdɪv ɪs §-əs
divisibilitydɪ ˌvɪz ə 'bɪl ət i də-, -ˌ•ɪ-, -ɪt i
‖ -əṭ i
divisib|ledɪ 'vɪz əb |əl də-, -ɪb- **~ly**li
divisiondɪ 'vɪʒ ᵊn də- **~al**ᵊl **~s**z
diˈvision ˌlobby
divisivedɪ 'vaɪs ɪv də-, §-'vaɪz-, §-'vɪz-, §-'vɪs-
~lyli **~ness**nəs nɪs
divisordɪ 'vaɪz ə də- ‖ -ᵊr (= *deviser*) **~s**z
divorc|e *n, v*dɪ 'vɔːs də- ‖ -'vɔːrs -'vʊʊrs **~ed**
t **~es**ɪz əz **~ing**ɪŋ
divorcé, divorcee, divorcéedɪ ˌvɔː 'siː də-,
-'seɪ; ˌdɪv ɔː-, ˌdiːv ɔː-, -'seɪ; dɪ 'vɔːs iː, də-,
-eɪ ‖ də ˌvɔːr 'seɪ -ˌvʊʊr-, -'siː; -'vɔːrs iː,
-'vʊʊrs-, -eɪ **~s**z
divot ˈdɪv ət **~s**s
divulg|edaɪ 'vʌldʒ dɪ-, də- ‖ də- daɪ- **~ed**d
~esɪz əz **~ing**ɪŋ
divulgenc|edaɪ 'vʌldʒ ᵊnts dɪ-, də- ‖ də- daɪ-
~esɪz əz
divv|y ˈdɪv li **~ied**id **~ies**iz **~ying**i ɪŋ
Diwalidɪ 'wɑːl i
Dixdɪks
Dixey, Dixie, d~ ˈdɪks i
ˈDixie Cup *tdmk*
Dixiecrat ˈdɪks i kræt **~s**s
Dixieland, d~ ˈdɪks i lænd
Dixon ˈdɪks ᵊn
DIY, diyˌdiː aɪ 'waɪ
ˌDIˈY shop
dizygoticˌdaɪ zaɪ 'gɒt ɪk ◂ ‖ -'gɑːʈ-
dizz|y ˈdɪz li **~ied**id **~ier**i‿ə ‖ i‿ᵊr **~ies**iz
~iesti‿ɪst i‿əst **~ily**ɪ li‿i **~iness**i nəs i nɪs
~ying/lyi‿ɪŋ /li
DJ, D.J.ˌdiː 'dʒeɪ ‖ '• • **DJs, D.J.s**
ˌdiː 'dʒeɪz ‖ '• •

Djakartadʒə 'kɑːt ə ‖ -'kɑːrṭ ə
djellaba, djellabah'dʒel əb ə dʒə 'lɑːb ə **~s**z
Djiboutidʒɪ 'buːt i dʒə- ‖ -'buːʈ i
djinndʒɪn **djinns**dʒɪnz
DLit, DLittˌdiː 'lɪt **~s, ~'s**s
DNAˌdiː en 'eɪ
Dneper, Dnieper'niːp ə 'dniːp- ‖ -ᵊr —*Russ*
[dnʲiepr]
Dnepropetrovskˌnep rəʊ pe 'trɒfsk -pɪ'•,
-pə'• ‖ -roʊ pə 'trɔːfsk -'trɑːvsk —*Russ*
[dnʲiɪ prə pʲi 'trɔfsk]
Dniester 'niːst ə 'dniːst- ‖ -ᵊr —*Russ* [dnʲiestr]
D-notic|e'diː ˌnəʊt ɪs §-əs ‖ -ˌnoʊṭ- **~es**ɪz əz
do *v, strong form*duː, *weak forms*du, də, d **did**
dɪd **didn't**'dɪd ᵊnt **does**dʌz (*see*) **doesn't**
'dʌz ᵊnt **doing**'duː ɪŋ **done**dʌn **don't**
dəʊnt ‖ doʊnt
do *n 'musical note'*dəʊ ‖ doʊ **dos**dəʊz ‖ doʊz
do *n, other senses*duː **dos, do's**duːz
DOAˌdiː əʊ 'eɪ ‖ -oʊ-
doable 'duː əb ᵊl
Doanedəʊn ‖ doʊn
dobbin, D~'dɒb ɪn §-ᵊn ‖ 'dɑːb- **~s, ~'s**z
Dobbsdɒbz ‖ dɑːbz
Dobell (*i*)dəʊ 'bel ‖ doʊ-, (*ii*) 'dəʊb ᵊl ‖ 'doʊb-
Doberman, d~'dəʊb ə mən ‖ 'doʊb ᵊr mən **~s**
z
ˌDoberman 'pinscher 'pɪntʃ ə ‖ ᵊr
Dobie 'dəʊb i ‖ 'doʊb i
Dobson 'dɒb sᵊn ‖ 'dɑːb-
doc, Docdɒk ‖ dɑːk **docs, Doc's**dɒks ‖ dɑːks
Docetismdəʊ 'siːt ˌɪz əm 'dəʊs ɪ ˌtɪz əm, -ə-
‖ doʊ 'siːṭ-
Docherty 'dɒx ət i 'dɒk- ‖ 'dɑːk ᵊrṭ i
docile 'dəʊs aɪᵊl ‖ 'dɑːs ᵊl (*) **~ly**li
docilitydəʊ 'sɪl ət i də-, -ɪt- ‖ dɑː 'sɪl əṭ i doʊ-
dockdɒk ‖ dɑːk **docked**dɒkt ‖ dɑːkt
docking 'dɒk ɪŋ ‖ 'dɑːk ɪŋ **docks**
dɒks ‖ dɑːks
docker, D~ 'dɒk ə ‖ 'dɑːk ᵊr **~s**z
dock|et 'dɒk |ɪt §-ət ‖ 'dɑːk |ət **~eted**ɪt ɪd
§ət-, -əd ‖ əṭ əd **~eting**ɪt ɪŋ §ət- ‖ əṭ ɪŋ
~etsɪts §əts ‖ əts
dockland, D~ 'dɒk lənd -lænd ‖ 'dɑːk- **~s**z
dockside 'dɒk saɪd ‖ 'dɑːk-
dockyard 'dɒk jɑːd ‖ 'dɑːk jɑːrd **~s**z
doctor, D~ 'dɒkt ə ‖ 'dɑːkt ᵊr **~ed**d
doctoring 'dɒkt ᵊr ɪŋ ‖ 'dɑːkt- **~s**z
doctoral 'dɒkt ᵊr əl →'dɒk trᵊl; dɒk 'tɔːr əl
‖ 'dɑːkt-
doctorate 'dɒkt ᵊr ət -ɪt; →'dɒk trət, -trɪt
‖ 'dɑːkt- **~s**s
Doctorow 'dɒkt ə rəʊ ‖ 'dɑːkt ə roʊ
doctrinaireˌdɒk trɪ 'neə ◂ -trə-
‖ ˌdɑːk trə 'neᵊr◂ -'næᵊr **~s**z
doctrinaldɒk 'traɪn ᵊl 'dɒk trɪn ᵊl, -trən-
‖ 'dɑːk trən ᵊl **~ly**i
doctrinarianˌdɒk trɪ 'neər i‿ən ◂ ˌ•trə-
‖ ˌdɑːk trə 'ner- **~s**z
doctrine 'dɒk trɪn -trən ‖ 'dɑːk- **~s**z
docudrama 'dɒk ju ˌdrɑːm ə ‖ 'dɑːk jə-
-ˌdræm ə **~s**z
document *n* 'dɒk ju mənt -jə- ‖ 'dɑːk jə- **~s**s

docu|ment v'dɒk ju |ment ‖ 'dɑːk jə- —*See note at* -ment **~mented**ment ɪd -əd‖ menʇ əd **~menting**ment ɪŋ ‖ menʇ ɪŋ **~ments** ments

documentar|y
,dɒk ju 'ment‿ər |i ‖ ,dɑːk jə 'menʇ ər i
→‿'mentr |i **~ies**iz

documentation,dɒk ju men 'teɪʃ ᵊn -mən'•-
‖ ,dɑːk jə-

Docwra'dɒk rə ‖ 'dɑːk-

Dod, Dodddɒd ‖ dɑːd

dodd|er'dɒd |ə ‖ 'dɑːd |ᵊr **~ered**əd ‖ ᵊrd **~ering/ly**ər ɪŋ /li **~ers**əz ‖ ᵊrz

doddery'dɒd ər i ‖ 'dɑːd-

Doddington'dɒd ɪŋ tən ‖ 'dɑːd-

doddle'dɒd ᵊl ‖ 'dɑːd- **~s**z

dodeca- *comb. form*
with stress-neutral suffix
¦dəʊ ¦dek ə ‖ dəʊ ¦dek ə — **dodecasyllable** ,dəʊ ,dek ə 'sɪl əb ᵊl ‖ dəʊ ,dek-
with stress-imposing suffix,dəʊd ɪ 'kæ+ -e-, -ə-
‖ ,dəʊd- — **dodecagonal**,dəʊd ɪ 'kæg ən ᵊl ◂ ,•e-, ,•ə- ‖ ,dəʊd- **~ly**i

dodecagon,dəʊ 'dek əg ən -ə gɒn‖ dəʊ- **~s**z

dodecahedr|on,dəʊ ,dek ə 'hiːdr |ən -'hedr- ‖ dəʊ ,dek- **~a**ə **~ons**ənz

Dodecanese,dəʊd ɪk ə 'niːz ◂,•ek-, §-'niːs ‖ dəʊ 'dek ə niːz -niːs, •,••'•

dodecaphonic,dəʊd ek ə 'fɒn ɪk ◂ ,•ɪk-, ,•ək- ‖ dəʊ ,dek ə 'fɑːn ɪk ◂

dodge, Dodgedɒdʒ ‖ dɑːdʒ **dodged** dɒdʒd ‖ dɑːdʒd **dodges**'dɒdʒ ɪz -əz ‖ 'dɑːdʒ- **dodging**'dɒdʒ ɪŋ ‖ 'dɑːdʒ ɪŋ

dodgem, D~ *tdmk*'dɒdʒ əm ‖ 'dɑːdʒ- **~s**z
' **dodgem cars**

dodger'dɒdʒ ə ‖ 'dɑːdʒ ᵊr **~s**z

Dodgson (i)'dɒdʒ sᵊn ‖ 'dɑːdʒ- , (ii) 'dɒd sᵊn ‖ 'dɑːd- —*Lewis Carroll (Charles D~) reportedly was* (ii)

dodg|y'dɒdʒ |i ‖ 'dɑːdʒ |i **~ier**‿ə ‖ i‿ᵊr **~iest** i‿ɪst i‿əst

Dodi'dəʊd i ‖ 'dəʊd i

dodo'dəʊd əʊ ‖ 'dəʊd oʊ **~es, ~s**z

Dodoma *place in Tanzania*'dəʊd əm ə -ə mɑː ‖ 'dəʊd-

Dodona *place in Greece*dəʊ 'dəʊn ə ‖ də 'dəʊn ə

Dodson'dɒd sᵊn ‖ 'dɑːd-

doe, Doedəʊ ‖ dəʊ **does**dəʊz ‖ dəʊz

doer'duː‿ə ‖ 'duː‿ᵊr **~s**z

-doer,duː‿ə ‖ 'duː‿ᵊr — **wrong-doer** 'rɒŋ ,duː‿ə ‖ ,rɔːŋ 'duː ᵊr ,rɑːŋ-

does *from* **do**, *strong form*dʌz , *weak forms*dəz , dz

does n, 'female animals'dəʊz ‖ dəʊz

doeskin'dəʊ skɪn ‖ 'dəʊ- **~s**z

doesn't'dʌz ᵊnt —*also, when non-final,* 'dʌz ᵊn

doeth'duː‿ɪθ ‿əθ

doffdɒf ‖ dɔːf **doffed**dɒft ‖ dɔːft dɑːft **doffing**'dɒf ɪŋ ‖ 'dɔːf ɪŋ 'dɑːf- **doffs** dɒfs ‖ dɔːfs dɑːfs

dogdɒg ‖ dɔːg dɑːg **dogged**dɒgd ‖ dɔːgd dɑːgd **dogging**'dɒg ɪŋ ‖ 'dɔːg ɪŋ 'dɑːg-

dogsdɒgz ‖ dɔːgz dɑːgz
' **dog**, biscuit;' **dog**, collar;' **dog days;**, **dog in the**' manger;' **dog**, paddle;' **dog rose;** , **dog's**' breakfast;' **dog tag**

Dogberry'dɒg ,ber i -bər‿i‖ 'dɔːg- 'dɑːg-

dogcart'dɒg kɑːt ‖ 'dɔːg kɑːrt 'dɑːg- **~s**s

dogcatcher'dɒg ,kætʃ ə §-,ketʃ- ‖ 'dɔːg ,kætʃ ᵊr 'dɑːg- **~s**z

dogedəʊdʒ dəʊʒ‖ dəʊdʒ **doges**'dəʊdʒ ɪz 'dəʊʒ-, -əz‖ 'dəʊdʒ-

dog-eared'dɒg ɪəd ,•'• ‖ 'dɔːg ɪrd 'dɑːg-

dog-eat-dog,dɒg iːt 'dɒg ‖ ,dɔːg iːt 'dɔːg ,dɑːg iːt 'dɑːg

dog-end,dɒg 'end '•• ‖ ,dɔːg- ,dɑːg- **~s**z

dogfight'dɒg faɪt ‖ 'dɔːg- 'dɑːg- **~s**s

dogfish'dɒg fɪʃ ‖ 'dɔːg- 'dɑːg- **~es**ɪz əz

dogfood'dɒg fuːd ‖ 'dɔːg- 'dɑːg- **~s**z

dogged adj'dɒg ɪd -əd‖ 'dɔːg- 'dɑːg- **~ly**li **~ness**nəs nɪs

dogged past & pp of **dog**dɒgd ‖ dɔːgd dɑːgd

dogger, D~'dɒg ə ‖ 'dɔːg ᵊr 'dɑːg ᵊr **~s**z

doggerel'dɒg ᵊr‿əl ‖ 'dɔːg- 'dɑːg-

doggie'dɒg i ‖ 'dɔːg i 'dɑːg i **~s**z

doggish'dɒg ɪʃ ‖ 'dɔːg- 'dɑːg- **~ly**li

doggo'dɒg əʊ ‖ 'dɔːg oʊ 'dɑːg-

doggone'dɒg ɒn ‖ ,dɑːg 'gɑːn ◂ ,dɔːg-, -'gɔːn **~d**d

dogg|y'dɒg |i ‖ 'dɔːg |i 'dɑːg- **~ier**i‿ə ‖ i‿ᵊr **~iest**i‿ɪst i‿əst
' **doggy bag;**' **doggy**, paddle

dog|house'dɒg |haʊs ‖ 'dɔːg- 'dɑːg- **~houses**haʊz ɪz -əz

dogie'dəʊg i ‖ 'dəʊg i **~s**z

dogleg'dɒg leg ‖ 'dɔːg- 'dɑːg- **~s**z

doglegged,dɒg 'leg ɪd ◂ -əd; -'legd‖ ,dɑːg- ,dɔːg-

dogma'dɒg mə ‖ 'dɔːg- 'dɑːg- **~s**z

dogmaticdɒg 'mæt ɪk ‖ dɔːg 'mæʇ ɪk dɑːg- **~ally**ᵊl i

dogmatism'dɒg mə ,tɪz əm ‖ 'dɔːg- 'dɑːg-

dogmatist'dɒg mət ɪst §-əst‖ 'dɔːg məʇ əst 'dɑːg- **~s**s

Dogon'dəʊg ɒn ‖ 'dəʊg ɑːn

do-good|er/s,du:' gʊd |ə/z ‖ ,du: gʊd |ᵊr/z **~ing**ɪŋ

dogsbod|y'dɒgz ,bɒd |i ‖ 'dɔːgz ,bɑːd |i 'dɑːgz- **~ies**iz

dogsled'dɒg sled ‖ 'dɔːg- 'dɑːg- **~s**z

dog's-tail'dɒgz teɪᵊl ‖ 'dɔːgz- 'dɑːgz- **~s**z

dog-tired,dɒg 'taɪ‿əd ◂ ‖ ,dɔːg 'taɪ‿ᵊrd ◂ ,dɑːg-

dogtooth'dɒg tuːθ §-tʊθ‖ 'dɔːg- 'dɑːg-

dogtrot'dɒg trɒt ‖ 'dɔːg traːt 'dɑːg-

dogwatch'dɒg wɒtʃ ‖ 'dɔːg waːtʃ 'dɑːg-, -wɔːtʃ **~es**ɪz əz

dogwood'dɒg wʊd ‖ 'dɔːg- 'dɑːg- **~s**z

dohdəʊ ‖ dəʊ (= doe) **dohs**dəʊz ‖ dəʊz

Doha'dəʊ hɑː: 'dəʊ əl‖ 'dəʊ-

Doherty (i)'dɒ hət i 'dɒx ət i‖ 'dɑː: hᵊrʇ i , (ii) 'dəʊ hət i -ət i‖ 'dəʊ ᵊrʇ i

Dohnanyi, Dohnányidɒk 'nɑːn ji dɒx-, -jiː ‖ 'dəʊn ɑːn ji —*Hung* ['doh na: ɲi]

Doig (i)dɔɪg , (ii)'dəʊ ɪg ‖ 'dəʊ-

doil|y 'dɔɪl |i ~ies iz
doing 'duː ɪŋ ~s z
doit dɔɪt doits dɔɪts
do-it-yourself ˌduː ɪt jə 'self ◄ →ˌɪt ʃ ə-, -jɔː' •, -jʊə' •; §, • ət-, §-ət ʃ ə- ‖ ˌduː ət ʃ ər- ~er/s ə/z ‖ ər/z
dojo 'dəʊ dʒəʊ ‖ 'doʊ dʒoʊ —Jp ['doo dzoo]
Doktorow 'dɒkt ər əʊ ‖ 'daːkt ər oʊ
Dolan 'dəʊl ən ‖ 'doʊl-
Dolby 'dɒl bi ‖ 'doʊl- 'dɔːl-, 'daːl-
dolce 'dɒltʃ i -eɪ ‖ 'doʊltʃ eɪ —It ['dɔl tʃe]
ˌdolce ˌfar ni'ente ˌfɑː ni 'ent i -eɪ ‖ ˌfɑːr- —It [ˌfar 'njɛn te]; ˌdolce 'vita 'viːt ə ‖ 'viːt̬ ə —It ['viː ta]
Dolcis tdmk 'dɒls ɪs 'dɒltʃ-, §-əs ‖ 'daːls-
doldrums 'dɒldr əmz 'dəʊldr- ‖ 'doʊldr- 'daːldr-, 'dɔːldr-
dole dəʊl →dɒʊl ‖ doʊl doled dəʊld →dɒʊld ‖ doʊld doles dəʊlz →dɒʊlz ‖ doʊlz doling 'dəʊl ɪŋ →'dɒʊl- ‖ 'doʊl ɪŋ
doleful 'dəʊl fəl →'dɒʊl-, -fʊl ‖ 'doʊl- ~ly i ~ness nəs nɪs
dolerite 'dɒl ə raɪt ‖ 'daːl-
Dolgellau, Dolgelley dɒl 'geθ li -laɪ ‖ daːl- —Welsh [dɔl 'ge ɬaɪ, -ɬa, -ɬe]
dolichocephalic ˌdɒl ɪ kəʊ sɪ 'fæl ɪk ◄ -sə' •-, -ke' •-, -kɪ' •- ‖ ˌdaːl ɪ koʊ-
dolichosaur|us ˌdɒl ɪ kəʊ 'sɔːr |əs ‖ ˌdaːl ɪ koʊ- ~i aɪ
Dolin 'dɒl ɪn §-ən ‖ 'doʊl-
dolina dɒ 'liːn ə dəʊ- ‖ doʊ- ~s z
doline dɒ 'liːn dəʊ- ‖ doʊ- ~s z
doli... —see dole
Dolittle 'duː ˌlɪt əl ‖ -ˌlɪt̬-
doll, Doll dɒl ‖ daːl dɔːl dolled dɒld ‖ daːld dɔːld dolling 'dɒl ɪŋ ‖ 'daːl ɪŋ 'dɔːl- dolls, doll's dɒlz ‖ daːlz dɔːlz
'doll's house
dollar, D~ 'dɒl ə ‖ 'daːl ər ~s z
ˌdollar 'bill; 'dollar sign
doll|house 'dɒl ˌhaʊs ‖ 'daːl- 'dɔːl- ~houses haʊz ɪz -əz
dollie, D~ 'dɒl i ‖ 'daːl i 'dɔːl i ~s z
Dollond 'dɒl ənd ‖ 'daːl- 'dɔːl-
dollop 'dɒl əp ‖ 'daːl- ~s s
doll|y, Dolly 'dɒl |i ‖ 'daːl |i 'dɔːl- ~ies, ~y's iz
'dolly bird; 'dolly ˌmixture
dolma 'dɒlm ə -ɑː ‖ 'daːlm- 'dɔːlm- —Turkish [doɫ 'ma] ~s z dolmades dɒl 'mɑːð ez -'mɑːd iːz ‖ daːl- dɔːl- —ModGk [dol 'ma ðes]
dolman 'dɒlm ən ‖ 'doʊlm- ~s z
dolmen 'dɒl men -mən ‖ 'doʊlm ən ~s z
Dolmetsch 'dɒl metʃ ‖ 'daːl- 'dɔːl-
Dolmio tdmk dɒl 'miː əʊ ‖ daːl 'miː oʊ
dolomite, D~ 'dɒl ə maɪt ‖ 'doʊl- 'daːl- ~s s
dolor 'dɒl ə ‖ 'doʊl ər 'daːl- ~s z
Dolores də 'lɔːr es dɒ-, -ɪs, -əs, -ez, -ɪz, -əz ‖ -əs -'loʊr- —Sp [do 'lo res]
doloroso ˌdɒl ə 'rəʊs əʊ -'rəʊz- ‖ ˌdoʊl ə 'roʊs oʊ —It [do lo 'ro: so]
dolorous 'dɒl ər əs ‖ 'doʊl- 'daːl- ~ly li ~ness nəs nɪs

dolour 'dɒl ə ‖ 'doʊl ər 'daːl- ~s z
dolphin, D~ 'dɒlf ɪn §-ən ‖ 'daːlf- 'dɔːlf- ~s z
dolphinarium ˌdɒlf ɪ 'neər i_əm ˌ•ə- ‖ ˌdaːlf ə 'ner- ˌdɔːlf- ~s z
Dolphus 'dɒlf əs ‖ 'daːlf-
dolt dəʊlt →dɒʊlt ‖ doʊlt dolts dəʊlts →dɒʊlts ‖ doʊlts
doltish 'dəʊlt ɪʃ →'dɒʊlt- ‖ 'doʊlt- ~ly li ~ness nəs nɪs
dom, Dom dɒm ‖ daːm
-dom dəm — martyrdom 'mɑːt ə dəm ‖ 'mɑːrt̬ ər dəm
domain dəʊ 'meɪn ‖ doʊ- də- ~s z
Dombey 'dɒm bi ‖ 'daːm-
dome dəʊm ‖ doʊm domed dəʊmd ‖ doʊmd domes dəʊmz ‖ doʊmz
Domecq dəʊ 'mek ‖ doʊ-
Domesday 'duːmz deɪ (= Doomsday)
'Domesday Book
domestic də 'mest ɪk ~ally əl_i ~s s
doˌmestic 'science; doˌmestic 'service
domesti|cate də 'mest ɪ |keɪt ~cated keɪt ɪd -əd ‖ keɪt̬ əd ~cates keɪts ~cating keɪt ɪŋ ‖ keɪt̬ ɪŋ
domestication də ˌmest ɪ 'keɪʃ ən
domesticity ˌdəʊm e 'stɪs ət i ˌdɒm-, , • ə-, -ɪt i ‖ ˌdoʊm e 'stɪs ət̬ i ˌdaːm-, , • ə-; də ˌme-
Domestos tdmk də 'mest ɒs dəʊ- ‖ -oʊs
domicil|e 'dɒm ɪ saɪəl 'dəʊm-, -ə-, -əs ɪl, §-əs əl ‖ 'daːm- 'doʊm-, -əs əl ~ed d ~es z ~ing ɪŋ
domiciliary ˌdɒm ɪ 'sɪl i_ər i , • ə-, -'sɪl ər i ‖ ˌdaːm ə 'sɪl i er i ˌdoʊm-
dominance 'dɒm ɪn ənts -ən- ‖ 'daːm-
dominant 'dɒm ɪn ənt -ən- ‖ 'daːm- ⚠-ət ~s s
domi|nate 'dɒm ɪ |neɪt -ə- ‖ 'daːm- ~nated neɪt ɪd -əd ‖ neɪt̬ əd ~nates neɪts ~nating neɪt ɪŋ ‖ neɪt̬ ɪŋ
domination ˌdɒm ɪ 'neɪʃ ən -ə- ‖ ˌdaːm- ~s z
dominatr|ix ˌdɒm ɪ 'neɪtr |ɪks -ə- ‖ ˌdaːm- ~ices i siːz ə- ~ixes ɪks ɪz -əz
domineer ˌdɒm ɪ 'nɪə -ə- ‖ ˌdaːm ə 'nɪər ~ed d domineering/ly ˌdɒm ɪ 'nɪər ɪŋ /li , • ə- ‖ ˌdaːm ə 'nɪr ɪŋ /li ~s z
Domingo də 'mɪŋ gəʊ dɒʊ-, dɒ- ‖ -goʊ —Sp [do 'miŋ go]
Dominic 'dɒm ɪ nɪk -ə- ‖ 'daːm-
Dominica in the Leeward Islands ˌdɒm ɪ 'niːk ə -ə- ‖ ˌdaːm- —but often called də 'mɪn ɪk ə by those not familiar with the name
dominical də 'mɪn ɪk əl dɒ-, dəʊ-
Dominican 'of the D~ Republic'; religious də 'mɪn ɪk ən ~s z
Doˌminican Re'public
Dominican 'of Dominica' ˌdɒm ɪ 'niːk ən -ə- ‖ ˌdaːm- —see note at Dominica ~s z
Dominick 'dɒm ɪ nɪk -ə-
dominie 'dɒm ɪn i -ən- ‖ 'daːm- ~s z
dominion də 'mɪn jən -'mɪn i_ən ~s z
Dominique ˌdɒm ɪ 'niːk -ə-, '• • • ‖ ˌdaːm- —Fr [dɔ mi nik]

domino, D~ 'dɒm ɪ nəʊ -ə- ‖ 'dɑːm ə noʊ
~es, ~s z
'domino ef,fect; 'domino ,theory
Dominus 'dɒm ɪn ʊs -ən-, -əs ‖ 'doʊm ɪ nuːs
'dɑːm-, -ə-
,dominus vo'biscum vəʊ 'bɪsk ʊm -əm
‖ voʊ-
Domitian də 'mɪʃ ən dəʊ-, dɒ-, -'mɪʃ i_ən
Domremy, Domrémy
dɒm 'reɪm i ‖ ,doʊm reɪ 'miː —*Fr* [dɔ̃ ʁe mi]
don, Don dɒn ‖ dɑːn —*See also phrases with
this word* **donned** dɒnd ‖ dɑːnd **donning**
'dɒn ɪŋ ‖ 'dɑːn ɪŋ **dons** dɒnz ‖ dɑːnz
Donaghadee ,dɒn ə hə 'diː ◂ ,•ək- ‖ ,dɑːn-
Donal 'dəʊn əl ‖ 'doʊn əl
Donald 'dɒn əld ‖ 'dɑːn əld
Donaldson 'dɒn əld sən ‖ 'dɑːn-
Donat 'dəʊn æt ‖ 'doʊn-
donate dəʊ 'neɪt ‖ 'doʊn eɪt doʊ 'neɪt —*AmE
1993 poll panel preference:* '•• 88%, •'• 12%.
donated dəʊ 'neɪt ɪd -əd ‖ 'doʊn eɪt̬ əd
doʊ 'neɪt̬- **donates** dəʊ 'neɪts ‖ 'doʊn eɪts
doʊ 'neɪts **donating** dəʊ
'neɪt ɪŋ ‖ 'doʊn eɪt̬ ɪŋ doʊ 'neɪt̬-
Donatello ,dɒn ə 'tel əʊ ‖ ,dɑːn ə 'tel oʊ
,doʊn- —*It* [do na 'tɛl lo] **~s, ~'s** z
donation dəʊ 'neɪʃ ən ‖ doʊ- **~s** z
Donatist 'dəʊn ət ɪst 'dɒn-, §-əst ‖ 'doʊn ət̬ əst
'dɑːn- **~s** z
donative 'dəʊn ət ɪv 'dɒn- ‖ 'doʊn ət̬ ɪv 'dɑːn-
~s z
donator dəʊ 'neɪt ə ‖ 'doʊn eɪt̬ ᵊr doʊ 'neɪt̬-
~s z
Don Carlos ,dɒn 'kɑːl ɒs →,dɒŋ-
‖ ,dɑːn 'kɑːrl oʊs -əs —*It, Sp* [doŋ 'kaɾ los]
Doncaster 'dɒŋk əst ə 'dɒŋ ,kɑːst ə, -,kæst-
‖ 'dɑːŋ ,kæst ᵊr 'dɑːn-, -kəst-
done dʌn (= *dun*)
donee ₍₎dəʊ 'niː ‖ doʊ- **~s** z
Donegal ,dɒn ɪ 'gɔːl ◂ ,dʌn-, -ə-, '••• ‖ ,dɑːn-
-'gɑːl, '•••
Donegan 'dɒn ɪg ən -əg-
Donelly 'dɒn əl i ‖ 'dɑːn-
Doner, Döner 'dɒn ə ‖ 'doʊn ᵊr —*Turkish*
[dø 'neɾ]
,doner ke'bab
dong dɒŋ ‖ dɑːŋ dɔːŋ **donged** dɒŋd ‖ dɑːŋd
dɔːŋd **donging** 'dɒŋ ɪŋ ‖ 'dɑːŋ ɪŋ 'dɔːŋ-
dongs dɒŋz ‖ dɑːŋz dɔːŋz
donga 'dɒŋ gə ‖ 'dɑːŋ- 'dɔːŋ- **~s** z
Don Giovanni ,dɒn dʒəʊ 'vɑːn i -'væn i
‖ ,dɑːn dʒi_ə 'vɑːn i —*It* [don dʒo 'van ni]
dongle 'dɒŋ gᵊl ‖ 'dɑːŋ- **~s** z
Donington 'dɒn ɪŋ tən 'dʌn- ‖ 'dɑːn-
Donizetti ,dɒn ɪ 'zet i -ə-, -ɪd- ‖ ,dɑːn ə 'zet̬ i
—*It* [do nid 'dzet ti]
donjon 'dɒndʒ ən 'dʌndʒ- ‖ 'dɑːndʒ- **~s** z
Don Juan (i) ,dɒn 'dʒuː_ən ‖ ,dɑːn-, (ii) -'wɑːn
-'hwɑːn —*Sp* [doŋ 'xwan] —*in English
literature, including Byron, and usually when
used metaphorically, BrE prefers (i); in imitated
Spanish, and generally in AmE, (ii) is preferred.*

donkey 'dɒŋk i ‖ 'dɑːŋk i 'dʌŋk-, 'dɔːŋk- **~s** z
'donkey ,engine; 'donkey ,jacket;
'donkey's years
donkeywork 'dɒŋk i wɜːk ‖ 'dɑːŋk i wɝːk
'dʌŋk-, 'dɔːŋk-
Donkin 'dɒŋk ɪn ‖ 'dɑːŋk-
Donleavy, Donlevy (i) dɒn 'liːv i ‖ dɑːn-, (ii)
-'lev i
Donna, donna 'dɒn ə ‖ 'dɑːn ə —*It* ['dɔn na]
Donne (i) dʌn, (ii) dɒn ‖ dɑːn —*The poet John
Donne was probably* (i).
donn... —*see* **don**
Donnegan 'dɒn ɪg ən -əg- ‖ 'dɑːn-
Donnell 'dɒn əl ‖ 'dɑːn-
Donnelly 'dɒn əl i ‖ 'dɑːn-
Donner, d~ 'dɒn ə ‖ 'dɑːn ᵊr
donnish 'dɒn ɪʃ ‖ 'dɑːn- **~ly** li **~ness** nəs nɪs
Donny 'dɒn i ‖ 'dɑːn i
Donnybrook, d~ 'dɒn i brʊk §-bruːk ‖ 'dɑːn-
~s s
Donoghue, Donohue 'dɒn ə hju: 'dʌn-, -hu:
‖ 'dɑːn-
donor 'dəʊn ə ‖ 'doʊn ᵊr —*but in contrast with*
donee *also* -ɔː, ₍₎dəʊ 'nɔː ‖ -ɔːr, ₍₎doʊ 'nɔːr
~s z
Donovan (i) 'dɒn əv ən ‖ 'dɑːn-, (ii) 'dʌn-
Don Pasquale ,dɒn pæ 'skwɑːl eɪ →,dɒm-, -i
‖ ,dɑːn pə- —*It* [dom pa 'skwɑː le]
Don Quixote ,dɒn 'kwɪks ət →,dɒŋ-,
,•kɪ 'həʊt i ‖ ,dɑːn-, ,•kiː 'hoʊt eɪ —*Sp*
[doŋ ki 'xo te]
don't dəʊnt ‖ doʊnt —*also, non-finally, esp.
before a consonant sound,* dəʊn ‖ doʊn. *This
word has no weak form except occasionally* də
in don't mind, don't know (*see* dunno). **don'ts**
dəʊnts ‖ doʊnts
,don't 'knows
do|nut 'dəʊ |nʌt ‖ 'doʊ- **~nuts** nʌts **~nutted**
nʌt ɪd -əd ‖ nʌt̬ əd **~nutting** nʌt ɪŋ ‖ nʌt̬ ɪŋ
doodad 'duː dæd **~s** z
doodah 'duː dɑː **~s** z
doodl|e 'duːd ᵊl **~ed** d **~es** z **~ing** _ɪŋ
doodlebug 'duːd ᵊl bʌg **~s** z
doohickey 'duː ,hɪk i **~s** z
Doolan 'duːl ən
Dooley 'duːl i
Doolittle 'duː ,lɪt ᵊl ‖ -,lɪt̬ ᵊl
doom duːm **doomed** duːmd **dooming**
'duːm ɪŋ **dooms** duːmz
doom-laden 'duːm ,leɪd ən
Doomsday, d~ 'duːmz deɪ
doomster 'duːm stə ‖ -stᵊr **~s** z
doomwatch 'duːm wɒtʃ ‖ -wɔːtʃ -wɑːtʃ **~er/s**
ə/z ‖ ᵊr/z **~es** ɪz əz
Doon, Doone duːn
Doonesbury 'duːnz bᵊr_i ‖ -,ber i
door dɔː ‖ dɔːr doʊr **doors** dɔːz ‖ dɔːrz doʊrz
doorbell 'dɔː bel ‖ 'dɔːr- 'doʊr- **~s** z
doorcas|e 'dɔː keɪs ‖ 'dɔːr- 'doʊr- **~es** ɪz əz
do-or-die ,duː ɔː 'daɪ ◂ ‖ -ᵊr- -ɔːr-
doorframe 'dɔː freɪm ‖ 'dɔːr- 'doʊr- **~s** z
doorjamb 'dɔː dʒæm ‖ 'dɔːr- 'doʊr- **~s** z

D

D

doorkeeper 'dɔː ˌkiːp ə ‖ 'dɔːr ˌkiːp ʰr 'dour-
~s z
doorknob 'dɔː nɒb ‖ 'dɔːr nɑːb 'dour- ~s z
doorknocker 'dɔː ˌnɒk ə ‖ 'dɔːr ˌnɑːk ʰr 'dour-
~s z
door|man 'dɔː |mən -mæn ‖ 'dɔːr- 'dour-
~**men** mən men
doormat 'dɔː mæt ‖ 'dɔːr- 'dour- ~s s
doornail 'dɔː neɪ⁰l ‖ 'dɔːr- 'dour- ~s z
doorplate 'dɔː pleɪt ‖ 'dɔːr- 'dour- ~s s
doorpost 'dɔː pəʊst ‖ 'dɔːr poust 'dour- ~s s
doorscraper 'dɔː ˌskreɪp ə ‖ 'dɔːr ˌskreɪp ʰr
'dour- ~s z
doorstep 'dɔː step ‖ 'dɔːr- 'dour- ~**ped** t
~**ping** ɪŋ ~s s
doorstop 'dɔː stɒp ‖ 'dɔːr stɑːp 'dour- ~**per/s**
ə/z ‖ ʰr/z ~s z
door-to-door ˌdɔː tə 'dɔː ◄ ‖ ˌdɔːr tə 'dɔːr ◄
ˌdour tə 'dour
doorway 'dɔː weɪ ‖ 'dɔːr- 'dour- ~s z
dopa 'dəʊp ə ‖ 'doup ə -ɑː
dopamine 'dəʊp ə miːn -mɪn ‖ 'doup-
dopant 'dəʊp ənt ‖ 'doup- ~s s
dope dəʊp ‖ doup **doped** dəʊpt ‖ doupt
dopes dəʊps ‖ doups **doping**
'dəʊp ɪŋ ‖ 'doup ɪŋ
'**dope fiend**; '**dope ˌpeddler**; '**dope sheet**
dop|ey 'dəʊp |i ‖ 'doup |i ~**ier** i̯ə ‖ i̯ʰr ~**iest**
i̯ɪst i̯əst
doppelganger, doppelgänger 'dɒp ⁰l ˌgæŋ ə
-ˌgeŋ- ‖ 'dɑːp ⁰l ˌgæŋ ʰr —Ger
['dɔp ⁰l ˌgɛŋ ʁ] ~s z
Doppler 'dɒp lə ‖ 'dɑːp lʰr
'**Doppler efˌfect**
dopy —see **dopey**
Dora 'dɔːr ə ‖ 'dour-
Dorabella ˌdɔːr ə 'bel ə ‖ ˌdour-
dorado də 'rɑːd əʊ dɒ- ‖ -ou ~s z
Doran 'dɔːr ən ‖ 'dour-
Dorcas 'dɔːk əs ‖ 'dɔːrk-
Dorchester 'dɔːtʃ ɪst ə §-est- ‖ 'dɔːr tʃest ʰr
'dɔːrtʃ əst ʰr
Dordogne ₍ₗ₎dɔː 'dɔɪn ‖ dɔːr 'doun —Fr
[dɔʁ dɔnj]
Dore dɔː ‖ dɔːr dour
Doré 'dɔːr eɪ ‖ dɔː 'reɪ —Fr [dɔ ʁe]
Doreen 'dɔːr iːn dɒ 'riːn, dɒ-, də- ‖ ˌdɔː 'riːn
Doria 'dɔːr i̯ə ‖ 'dour-
Dorian 'dɔːr i̯ən ‖ 'dour-
Doric 'dɒr ɪk ‖ 'dɔːr- 'dɑːr-
dorie... —see **dory**
Dorinda də 'rɪnd ə dɔː-, dɒ-
Doris personal name 'dɒr ɪs -əs ‖ 'dɔːr- 'dɑːr-,
'dour-
Doris in Greece 'dɔːr ɪs 'dɒr-, -əs ‖ 'dɑːr-,
'dour-
dork dɔːk ‖ dɔːrk **dorks** dɔːks ‖ dɔːrks
Dorking 'dɔːk ɪŋ ‖ 'dɔːrk-
Dorland-Kindersley
ˌdɔː lənd 'kɪnd əz li ‖ ˌdɔːr lənd 'kɪnd ʰrz li
dorm dɔːm ‖ dɔːrm **dorms** dɔːmz ‖ dɔːrmz
Dorman 'dɔːm ən ‖ 'dɔːrm-
dormanc|y 'dɔːm ən⸱s li ‖ 'dɔːrm- ~**ies** iz

dormant 'dɔːm ənt ‖ 'dɔːrm-
dormer, D~ 'dɔːm ə ‖ 'dɔːrm ʰr ~s z
dormie 'dɔːm i ‖ 'dɔːrm i
dormition dɔː 'mɪʃ ʰn ‖ dɔːr-
dormitor|y 'dɔːm ətr |i -ɪtr-; '•ət⸱ʰr li, '•ɪt⸱
‖ 'dɔːrm ə tɔːr li ~**ies** iz
'**dormitory ˌsuburb**
Dormobile tdmk 'dɔːm əʊ biːʰl ‖ 'dɔːrm ə- ~s z
dor|mouse 'dɔː |maʊs ‖ 'dɔːr- ~**mice** maɪs
dormy 'dɔːm i ‖ 'dɔːrm i
Dornoch 'dɔːn ɒk -ɒx, -ək, -əx ‖ 'dɔːrn ɑːk
—locally -əx
Dorothea ˌdɒr ə 'θɪə -'θiː ə ‖ ˌdɔːr ə 'θiː ə
ˌdɑːr-
Dorothy 'dɒr əθ i ‖ 'dɔːr- 'dɑːr- —formerly
-ət-
Dorow, Dorrow 'dɒr əʊ ‖ 'dɔːr ou 'dɑːr-
dorp dɔːp ‖ dɔːrp **dorps** dɔːps ‖ dɔːrps
Dorr dɔː ‖ dɔːr
Dorrington 'dɒr ɪŋ tən ‖ 'dɔːr- 'dɑːr-
Dorrit 'dɒr ɪt §-ət ‖ 'dɔːr- 'dɑːr-
Dors dɔːz ‖ dɔːrz
dorsal 'dɔːs ⁰l ‖ 'dɔːrs- ~**ly** i
Dorset 'dɔːs ɪt -ət ‖ 'dɔːrs-
Dorsey 'dɔːs i ‖ 'dɔːrs i
dorsum 'dɔːs əm ‖ 'dɔːrs-
Dortmund 'dɔːt mənd -mund ‖ 'dɔːrt- —Ger
['dɔʁt munt]
dor|y, Dory 'dɔːr |i ‖ 'dour- ~**ies** iz
DOS dɒs ‖ dɑːs dɔːs
do's duːz
dosag|e 'dəʊs ɪdʒ §'dəʊz- ‖ 'dous- ~**es** ɪz əz
dose dəʊs §dəʊz ‖ dous **dosed** dəʊst §dəʊzd
‖ doust **doses** 'dəʊs ɪz §'dəʊz-, -əz
‖ 'dous əz **dosing** 'dəʊs ɪŋ §'dəʊz-
‖ 'dous ɪŋ
dosh dɒʃ ‖ dɑːʃ
do-si-do ˌdəʊs i 'dəʊ ˌdəʊ saɪ 'dəʊ
‖ ˌdou siː 'dou ~s z
dosimeter dəʊ 'sɪm ɪt ə -ət- ‖ dou 'sɪm ət ʰr
~s z
dosimetry dəʊ 'sɪm ətr i -ɪtr- ‖ dou-
Dos Passos ₍ₗ₎dɒs 'pæs ɒs ‖ dous 'pæs ous dəs-,
-əs
doss dɒs ‖ dɑːs **dossed** dɒst ‖ dɑːst **dosses**
'dɒs ɪz -əz ‖ 'dɑːs əz **dossing**
'dɒs ɪŋ ‖ 'dɑːs ɪŋ
dosser 'dɒs ə ‖ 'dɑːs ʰr ~s z
doss|house 'dɒs |haʊs ‖ 'dɑːs- -**houses**
haʊz ɪz -əz
dossier 'dɒs i eɪ -i̯ə ‖ 'dɔːs i eɪ 'dɑːs-, -i̯ʰr
—Fr [do sje] ~s z
dost from **do** dʌst, weak form dəst
Dostoevski, Dostoevsky, Dostoyevski,
Dostoyevsky ˌdɒst ɔɪ 'ef ski ‖ ˌdɑːst ə 'jef-
ˌdʌst- —Russ [də stʌ 'jef skiɪj]
dot, Dot dɒt ‖ dɑːt **dots** dɒts ‖ dɑːts **dotted**
'dɒt ɪd -əd ‖ 'dɑːt̬ əd **dotting**
'dɒt ɪŋ ‖ 'dɑːt̬ ɪŋ
ˌdotted 'line
dotage 'dəʊt ɪdʒ ‖ 'dout̬-
dotard 'dəʊt əd -ɑːd ‖ 'dout̬ ʰrd ~s z

D

dote dəʊt ‖ doʊt **doted** 'dəʊt ɪd -əd ‖ 'doʊt̬ əd
  dotes dəʊts ‖ doʊts **doting**
  'dəʊt ɪŋ ‖ 'doʊt̬ ɪŋ
doth *from* **do** dʌθ, *weak form* dəθ
Dotheboys 'du: ðə ˌbɔɪz
doting 'dəʊt ɪŋ ‖ 'doʊt̬ ɪŋ **~ly** li
dot-matrix ˌdɒt 'meɪtr ɪks '•ˌ•• ‖ ˌdɑːt-
Dotrice də 'triːs dɒ-
dott... —*see* **dot**
dotterel 'dɒtr əl ‖ 'dɑːtr- **~s** z
Dottie 'dɒt i ‖ 'dɑːt̬ i
dottle 'dɒt əl ‖ 'dɑːt̬ əl
dott|y 'dɒt li ‖ 'dɑːt̬ li **~ier** i_ə ‖ i_ər **~iest** i_ɪst
  i_əst **~ily** ɪ li əl i **~iness** i nəs i nɪs
Douai 'daʊ i 'duːˌ, -eɪ ‖ du: 'eɪ —*but the place*
  in France is 'du: eɪ •'• —*Fr* [dwe, du e]
Douala du 'ɑːl ə —*Fr* [dwa la]
  'dʌb əl **~ed** d **~es** z **~ing** ˌɪŋ **~y** ˌi
  ˌdouble 'agent, ˌdouble 'bar; ˌdouble
  'bass; ˌdouble 'bed; ˌdouble 'bind; ˌdouble
  'bluff —*but* ˌbluff and 'double bluff;
  ˌdouble 'chin; ˌdouble 'cream; ˌdouble
  'date; ˌdouble 'fault; ˌdouble 'feature;
  ˌdouble 'figures; ˌDouble 'Gloucester;
  'doubles match; ˌdouble 'take, '•• •;
  ˌdouble 'time
double-barreled, double-barrelled
  ˌdʌb əl 'bær əld ◄ -'ber-
double-bedded ˌdʌb əl 'bed ɪd ◄ -əd
double-blind ˌdʌb əl 'blaɪnd ◄
double-breasted ˌdʌb əl 'brest ɪd ◄ -əd
double-check ˌdʌb əl 'tʃek '••• **~ed** t **~ing**
  ɪŋ **~s** s
double-clutch 'dʌb əl klʌtʃ **~ed** t **~es** ɪz əz
  ~ing ɪŋ
double-cross ˌdʌb əl 'krɒs -'krɔːs ‖ -'krɔːs
  -'krɑːs **~ed** t **~er/s** ə/z ‖ ər/z **~es** ɪz əz
  ~ing ɪŋ
Doubleday 'dʌb əl deɪ
double-deal|er/s ˌdʌb əl 'diːəl ə/z ‖ -ər/z
  ~ing ɪŋ
double-decker ˌdʌb əl 'dek ə ◄ ‖ -ər **~s** z
double-declutch ˌdʌb əl di: 'klʌtʃ -dɪ'•, -də'•
  ~ed t **~es** ɪz əz **~ing** ɪŋ
double-digit ˌdʌb əl 'dɪdʒ ɪt ◄ §-ət
double-dotted ˌdʌb əl 'dɒt ɪd ◄ -əd
  ‖ -'dɑːt̬ əd ◄
double-dutch ˌdʌb əl 'dʌtʃ
double-dyed ˌdʌb əl 'daɪd ◄
double-edged ˌdʌb əl 'edʒd ◄
  ˌdouble-edged 'compliment
double entendre ˌduːb əlˌɒn 'tɒnd rə ˌdʌb-
  ‖ ˌɑːn 'tɑːnd rə —*as if Fr* [du blɑ̃ tɑ̃ːdʀ]
double-entry ˌdʌb əl 'entr i ◄
double-glaz|e ˌdʌb əl 'gleɪz **~ed** d **~es** ɪz əz
  ~ing ɪŋ
double-header ˌdʌb əl 'hed ə ‖ -ər
double-jointed ˌdʌb əl 'dʒɔɪnt ɪd ◄ -əd
  ‖ -'dʒɔɪnt̬ əd ◄
double-park ˌdʌb əl 'pɑːk ‖ -'pɑːrk **~ed** t
  ~ing ɪŋ **~s** s
double-quick ˌdʌb əl 'kwɪk ◄
  ˌdouble-quick 'time

doubler 'dʌb əl_ə ‖ -ər **~s** z
double-spac|e ˌdʌb əl 'speɪs **~ed** t **~es** ɪz əz
  ~ing ɪŋ
double-stop ˌdʌb əl 'stɒp ‖ -'stɑːp **~ped** t
  ~ping ɪŋ **~s** s
doublet 'dʌb lət -lɪt **~s** s
double-talk 'dʌb əl tɔːk ‖ -tɑːk **~ed** t **~er/s**
  ə/z ‖ ər/z **~ing** ɪŋ **~s** s
doublethink 'dʌb əl θɪŋk
doubleton 'dʌb əl tən **~s** z
double-tongu|e ˌdʌb əl 'tʌŋ §-'tɒŋ **~ing** ɪŋ
doubling 'dʌb əl_ɪŋ **~s** z
doubloon dʌ 'bluːn **~s** z
doubly 'dʌb li
doubt daʊt **doubted** 'daʊt ɪd -əd ‖ 'daʊt̬ əd
  doubting 'daʊt ɪŋ ‖ 'daʊt̬ ɪŋ **doubts** daʊts
  ˌdoubting 'Thomas
doubter 'daʊt ə ‖ 'daʊt̬ ər **~s** z
doubtful 'daʊt fəl -fʊl **~ly** ˌi
doubtless 'daʊt ləs -lɪs **~ly** li
douceur duː 'sɜː ‖ -'sɝː —*Fr* [du sœːʀ] **~s** z
douche duːʃ **douched** duːʃt **douches**
  'duːʃ ɪz -əz **douching** 'duːʃ ɪŋ
Doug dʌg
Dougal, Dougall 'duːg əl
Dougan 'duːg ən
dough dəʊ ‖ doʊ (= *doe*) **doughs** dəʊz ‖ doʊz
doughboy 'dəʊ bɔɪ ‖ 'doʊ- **~s** z
Dougherty (i) 'dɒx ət i 'dɒk- ‖ 'dɑːk ərt̬ i, (ii)
  'dəʊ- ‖ 'doʊ- 'dɔːrt̬ i, (iii) 'dɑʊ-
dough|nut 'dəʊ nʌt ‖ 'doʊ- **~nuts** nʌts
  ~nutted nʌt ɪd -əd ‖ nʌt̬ əd **~nutting**
  nʌt ɪŋ ‖ nʌt̬ ɪŋ
dought|y, D~ 'daʊt li 'daʊt̬ li **~ier** i_ə ‖ i_ər
  ~iest i_ɪst i_əst **~ily** ɪ li əl i **~iness** i nəs i nɪs
dough|y 'dəʊ li ‖ 'doʊ li **~ier** i_ə ‖ i_ər **~iest**
  i_ɪst i_əst **~iness** i nəs i nɪs
Dougie 'dʌg i
Douglas 'dʌg ləs
Douglas-Home ˌdʌg ləs 'hjuːm
Doukhobor 'duːk ə bɔː ‖ -bɔːr **~s** z
Doulton 'dəʊlt ən →'dɒʊlt- ‖ 'doʊlt ən
Doune duːn
Dounreay 'duːn reɪ ˌ•'•
dour dʊə 'daʊ_ə ‖ dʊər daʊ_ər
dourine 'dʊər iːn ‖ dʊ 'riːn
dour|ly 'dʊə lli 'daʊ_ə lli ‖ 'dʊər- 'daʊ_ər-
  ~ness nəs nɪs
Douro 'dʊər əʊ ‖ 'dʊr oʊ —*Port* ['do ru]
douse daʊs **doused** daʊst **douses** 'daʊs ɪz
  -əz **dousing** 'daʊs ɪŋ
Douwe Egberts *tdmk* ˌdaʊ 'eg bəts -bɜːts
  ‖ -bərts
dove *n* dʌv **doves** dʌvz
dove *v from* **dive** dəʊv ‖ doʊv
dovecot 'dʌv kɒt ‖ -kɑːt **~s** s
dovecote 'dʌv kəʊt -kɒt ‖ -koʊt **~s** s
Dovedale 'dʌv deɪəl
dovekey, dovekie 'dʌv ki **~s** z
Dover 'dəʊv ə ‖ 'doʊv ər
  ˌDover 'sole
Dovercourt 'dəʊv ə kɔːt ‖ 'doʊv ər kɔːrt
  -koʊrt

Doveridge 'dʌv ər_ɪdʒ
dovetail *n, v* 'dʌv teɪəl ~ed d ~ing ɪŋ ~s z
Dovey 'dʌv i —*Welsh* Dyfi ['də vi]
Dow daʊ
dowager 'daʊ_ədʒ ə _ɪdʒ- ‖ -ər ~s z
Dowd daʊd
Dowdeswell 'daʊdz wəl -wel
Dowding 'daʊd ɪŋ
dowd|y 'daʊd |i ~ier i_ə ‖ i_ər ~ies iz ~iest
i_ɪst i_əst ~ily ɪ li əl i ~iness i nəs i nɪs
dowel 'daʊ_əl daʊl ‖ 'daʊ_əl doweled,
dowelled 'daʊ_əld daʊld ‖ 'daʊ_əld
doweling, dowelling 'daʊ_əl ɪŋ 'daʊl ɪŋ
‖ 'daʊ_əl ɪŋ dowels 'daʊəlz daʊlz ‖ 'daʊ_əlz
Dowell 'daʊ_əl daʊl ‖ 'daʊ_əl
dower, Dower 'daʊ_ə ‖ 'daʊ_ər ~s z
dowitcher 'daʊ_ɪtʃ ə ‖ -ər ~s z
Dow-Jones ˌdaʊ 'dʒəʊnz ◄ ‖ -'dʒoʊnz ◄
ˌDow-Jones 'average
Dowlais 'daʊ laɪs -ləs
Dowland 'daʊ lənd
down, Down daʊn downed daʊnd downing
'daʊn ɪŋ downs, Down's daʊnz
ˌdown 'payment; 'Down's ˌsyndrome
down- ˌdaʊn
down-and-out ˌdaʊn ən 'aʊt ◄ -ənd- ~s s
down-at-heel ˌdaʊn ət 'hiːəl ◄
downbeat 'daʊn biːt →'daʊm- ~s s
downcast 'daʊn kɑːst →'daʊŋ-, §-kæst ‖ -kæst
downdraft, downdraught 'daʊn drɑːft
§-dræft ‖ -dræft ~s s
downdrift 'daʊn drɪft
Downe daʊn
downer 'daʊn ə ‖ -ər ~s z
Downes daʊnz
Downey 'daʊn i
downfall 'daʊn fɔːl ‖ -fɑːl ~s z
downgrad|e *v* ˌdaʊn 'greɪd →ˌdaʊŋ-; '•• ~ed
ɪd əd ~es z ~ing ɪŋ
downgrade *n* 'daʊn greɪd →'daʊŋ- ~s z
Downham 'daʊn əm
downhearted ˌdaʊn 'hɑːt ɪd ◄ -əd
‖ -'hɑːrṭ əd ◄ ~ly li ~ness nəs nɪs
downhill ˌdaʊn 'hɪl ◄ ~er/s ə/z ‖ -ər/z
down-home ˌdaʊn 'həʊm ◄ ‖ -'hoʊm ◄
downi... —*see* downy
Downie 'daʊn i
Downing 'daʊn ɪŋ
'Downing Street
downland, D~ 'daʊn lænd -lənd ~s z
download ˌdaʊn 'ləʊd '•• ‖ 'daʊn loʊd ~ed ɪd
əd ~ing ɪŋ ~s z
downloadable ˌdaʊn 'ləʊd əb əl ◄ '••••
‖ 'daʊn loʊd əb əl
downmarket ˌdaʊn 'mɑːk ɪt ◄ →ˌdaʊm-, §-ət
‖ -'mɑːrk-
Downpatrick ˌdaʊn 'pætr ɪk →ˌdaʊm-
downpipe 'daʊn paɪp →'daʊm- ~s s
downplay ˌdaʊn 'pleɪ ~ed d ~ing ɪŋ ~s z
downpour 'daʊn pɔː →'daʊm- ‖ -pɔːr -pour
~s z
downrange ˌdaʊn 'reɪndʒ ◄
downright 'daʊn raɪt

downriver ˌdaʊn 'rɪv ə ◄ ‖ -ər ◄
Downs daʊnz
downscale ˌdaʊn 'skeɪəl ◄
Downside, d~ 'daʊn saɪd
downsiz|e 'daʊn saɪz ,•'• ~ed d ~es ɪz əz
~ing ɪŋ
downspout 'daʊn spaʊt ~s s
downstage ˌdaʊn 'steɪdʒ ◄
downstairs ˌdaʊn 'steəz ◄ ‖ -'steərz ◄ -'stæərz
downstate *adj, adv* ˌdaʊn 'steɪt ◄
downstate *n* 'daʊn steɪt
downstream ˌdaʊn 'striːm ◄
downswing 'daʊn swɪŋ ~s z
downtime 'daʊn taɪm
down-to-earth ˌdaʊn tu 'ɜːθ ◄ ‖ -'ɜːθ ◄
downtown ˌdaʊn 'taʊn ◄
downtrend 'daʊn trend ~s z
downtrodden 'daʊn ˌtrɒd ən ,•'•• ‖ -ˌtrɑːd-
downturn 'daʊn tɜːn ‖ -tɜːn ~s z
downward 'daʊn wəd ‖ -wərd ~ly li ~s z
downwash 'daʊn wɒʃ ‖ -wɔːʃ -wɑːʃ
downwind ˌdaʊn 'wɪnd ◄
down|y 'daʊn |i ~ier i_ə ‖ i_ər ~iest i_ɪst i_əst
dowr|y 'daʊər |i ~ies iz
dowse *'seek underground water or minerals'*
daʊz dowsed daʊzd dowses 'daʊz ɪz əz
dowsing 'daʊz ɪŋ
dowse *'drench', 'extinguish'* daʊs dowsed
daʊst dowses 'daʊs ɪz -əz dowsing
'daʊs ɪŋ
Dowse *name* daʊs
dowser 'daʊz ə ‖ -ər ~s z
Dowsing 'daʊz ɪŋ
dowsing rod 'daʊz ɪŋ rɒd ‖ -rɑːd
Dowson 'daʊs ən
doxastic dɒk 'sæst ɪk ‖ dɑːk-
doxolog|y dɒk 'sɒl ədʒ |i ‖ dɑːk 'sɑːl- ~ies iz
dox|y 'dɒks |i ‖ 'dɑːks |i ~ies iz
doyen 'dɔɪ ən -en —*Fr* [dwa jæ̃] ~s z
doyenne ˌdɔɪ 'en —*Fr* [dwa jɛn] ~s z
Doyle dɔɪəl
doyley, D'Oyley, doyly, D'Oyly 'dɔɪl i ~s z
doze dəʊz ‖ doʊz (= *doughs*) dozed
dəʊzd ‖ doʊzd dozes 'dəʊz ɪz -əz
‖ 'doʊz əz dozing 'dəʊz ɪŋ ‖ 'doʊz ɪŋ
dozen 'dʌz ən ~s z
dozer 'dəʊz ə ‖ 'doʊz ər ~s z
doz|y 'dəʊz |i ‖ 'doʊz |i ~ier i_ə ‖ i_ər ~iest
i_ɪst i_əst ~ily ɪ li əl i ~iness i nəs i nɪs
DPhil ˌdiː 'fɪl
Dr *'doctor'* 'dɒkt ə ‖ 'dɑːkt ər
Dr *'debtor'* 'det ə ‖ 'deṭ ər
drab dræb drabber 'dræb ə ‖ -ər drabbest
'dræb ɪst -əst drabs dræbz
Drabble 'dræb əl
drably 'dræb li
drabness 'dræb nəs -nɪs
dracaena drə 'siːn ə ~s z
drachm dræm (= *dram*) drachms dræmz
drach|ma 'dræk |mə ~mae miː meɪ ~mas
məz
Draco 'dreɪk əʊ ‖ -oʊ
draconian drə 'kəʊn i_ən dreɪ- ‖ -'koʊn-

Double consonant letters

1 Double **consonant** letters in English spelling normally correspond to a single sound in pronunciation. So **happy** is pronounced ˈhæp i (not ˈhæp pi); **rabbit** rhymes perfectly with **habit**, **Ellen** rhymes perfectly with **Helen**. For double **vowel** letters, see **ee** (under **e**), **oo** (under **o**).

2 An exception arises in a few words with **cc** before **i** or **e**, for example **succeed** sək ˈsiːd . See also the article on **s, ss**.

3 The other important exception is where the two letters in question belong to two different parts of a compound word, or one to a stem and one to an affix. Then the two letters usually correspond to two phonemes (see DOUBLE CONSONANT SOUNDS). Examples: **nighttime** ˈnaɪt taɪm, **unnamed** ˌʌn ˈneɪmd, **meanness** ˈmiːn nəs.
Adverbs in **-ly**, however, usually drop one l sound when attached to a stem ending in l: **fully** ˈfʊl i .

D

draconic drə ˈkɒn ɪk dreɪ- ‖ -ˈkɑːn ɪk **~ally** ᵊl_i
Dracula ˈdræk jʊl ə -jəl- ‖ -jəl ə
draff dræf
draft drɑːft §dræft ‖ dræft **drafted** ˈdrɑːft ɪd §ˈdræft-, -əd ‖ ˈdræft əd **drafting** ˈdrɑːft ɪŋ §ˈdræft- ‖ ˈdræft ɪŋ **drafts** drɑːfts §dræfts ‖ dræfts
   ˈdraft ˌdodger
draftee ₍ᵢ₎drɑːf ˈtiː §₍ᵢ₎dræf- ‖ ₍ᵢ₎dræf- **~s** z
drafts|man ˈdrɑːfts |mən §ˈdræfts- ‖ ˈdræfts- **~manship** mən ʃɪp **~men** mən men
draft|y ˈdrɑːft |i §ˈdræft- ‖ ˈdræft |i **~ier** i_ə ‖ i_ᵊr **~iest** i_ɪst i_əst **~iness** i nəs i nɪs
drag dræg **dragged** drægd **dragging** ˈdræg ɪŋ **drags** drægz
   ˈdrag ˌartist; ˈdrag race
Drage dreɪdʒ
dragee, dragée dræ ˈʒeɪ **~s** z
draggled ˈdræg ᵊld
dragg|ly ˈdræg |i **~ier** i_ə ‖ i_ᵊr **~iest** i_ɪst i_əst
dragline ˈdræg laɪn **~s** z
dragnet ˈdræg net **~s** s
drago|man ˈdræg ə |mən -mæn **~mans** mənz mænz **~men** mən men
dragon ˈdræg ən **~s** z
dragonet ˈdræg ən ɪt -ət, -ə net **~s** s
dragon|fly ˈdræg ən |flaɪ →-ŋ- **~flies** flaɪz
dragonnad|e ˌdræg ə ˈneɪd **~ed** ɪd əd **~es** z **~ing** ɪŋ
dragoon drə ˈguːn **~ed** d **~ing** ɪŋ **~s** z
dragster ˈdræg stə ‖ -stᵊr **~s** z
drail dreɪᵊl **drails** dreɪᵊlz
drain dreɪn **drained** dreɪnd **draining** ˈdreɪn ɪŋ **drains** dreɪnz
   ˈdraining board
drainage ˈdreɪn ɪdʒ
drainer ˈdreɪn ə ‖ -ᵊr **~s** z
drainpipe ˈdreɪn paɪp →ˈdreɪm- **~s** s

drake, Drake dreɪk **drakes, Drake's** dreɪks
Drakelow ˈdreɪk ləʊ ‖ -loʊ —*locally also* ˈ•ə•
Drakensberg ˈdrɑːk ənˈs bɜːg ˈdræk-, -ənz- ‖ -bɜˑg
Dralon *tdmk* ˈdreɪl ɒn ‖ -ɑːn
dram dræm **drams** dræmz
drama ˈdrɑːm ə ‖ ˈdræm ə —*AmE 1993 poll panel preference:* ˈdrɑːm- 88%, ˈdræm- 11%, ˈdreɪm- 1%. **~s** z
drama-doc ˌdrɑːm ə ˈdɒk ‖ -ˈdɑːk ˌdræm- **~s** s
Dramamine *tdmk* ˈdræm ə miːn -mɪn **~s** z
dramatic drə ˈmæt ɪk ‖ -ˈmæt̬- **~ally** ᵊl_i **~s** s
dramatis... —*see* **dramatiz...**
dramatis personae ˌdræm ət ɪs pɜː ˈsəʊn aɪ ˌdrɑːm-, drə ˈmæt-, -iː ‖ -ət̬ əs pᵊr ˈsoʊn iː -aɪ
dramatist ˈdræm ət ɪst ˈdrɑːm-, §-əst ‖ -ət̬ əst **~s** s
dramatization ˌdræm ət aɪ ˈzeɪʃ ᵊn ˌdrɑːm-, -ət ɪ- ‖ -ət̬ ə- **~s** z
dramatiz|e ˈdræm ə taɪz ˈdrɑːm- **~ed** d **~es** ɪz əz **~ing** ɪŋ
dramaturg|e ˈdræm ə tɜːdʒ ˈdrɑːm- ‖ -tɜˑdʒ **~es** ɪz əz
dramaturgic ˌdræm ə ˈtɜːdʒ ɪk ◄ ˌdrɑːm- ‖ -ˈtɜˑdʒ- **~al** ᵊl
dramaturgy ˈdræm ə tɜːdʒ i ˈdrɑːm- ‖ -tɜˑdʒ i
Drambuie dræm ˈbjuːˌi -ˈbuːˌi **~s** z
drank dræŋk
drape dreɪp **draped** dreɪpt **drapes** dreɪps **draping** ˈdreɪp ɪŋ
draper, D~ ˈdreɪp ə ‖ -ᵊr **~s** z
draper|y ˈdreɪp ᵊr |i **~ies** iz
drastic ˈdræst ɪk ˈdrɑːst- —*BrE 1988 poll panel preference:* ˈdræst- 88% (*southerners* 92%), ˈdrɑːst- 12% (*southerners* 8%). *In AmE always* ˈdræst-. **~ally** ᵊl_i
drat dræt **dratted** ˈdræt ɪd -əd ‖ ˈdræt̬ əd
draught drɑːft §dræft ‖ dræft **~s** s
   ˈdraught exˌcluder

Double consonant sounds

1 Double consonant sounds ('geminates') are found in English only across grammatical boundaries: where two words occur next to one another in connected speech, or in the two parts of a compound word, or a stem and an affix. They always straddle a syllable boundary, too. Examples are **a nice sight** ə ˌnaɪs 'saɪt, **midday** ˌmɪd 'deɪ, **soulless** 'səʊl ləs ‖ 'soʊl ləs.

2 Although cases like these consist of two identical phonemes in succession, they are not usually pronounced as two distinct complete sounds. The details depend on their manner of ARTICULATION.

- **Fricatives, nasals, liquids**: a geminate is pronounced like a single sound, except that it lasts longer. In **this set** ˌðɪs 'set the two s's come together to make a long sː between the two vowels, straddling the syllable boundary. In **ten names** ˌten 'neɪmz we get a long nː.
- **Plosives**: a geminate is pronounced like a single sound, with just one sequence of approach—hold—release (see PLOSIVES); but in a geminate the hold is longer. In **big game** ˌbɪg 'geɪm there is a single phonetic gː between the two vowels, straddling the syllable boundary. Exceptionally, because of the possibility of a GLOTTAL STOP, a geminated t may consist phonetically of ʔt: **that time** ˌðæt 'taɪm; but a single long alveolar tː is also possible.
- **Affricates** are the only case where two successive complete consonant sounds are pronounced independently, one after the other. In **rich choice** ˌrɪtʃ 'tʃɔɪs the fricative part of the first tʃ can be separately heard before the beginning of the second tʃ. In **orange juice** there are two separate dʒ's.

D

draughtboard 'drɑːft bɔːd §'dræft- ‖ 'dræft bɔːrd -bourd ~s z
draughts|man 'drɑːfts |mən §'dræfts- ‖ 'dræfts- ~**manship** mən ʃɪp ~**men** mən men
draught|y 'drɑːft |i §'dræft- ‖ 'dræft |i ~**ier** i‿ə ‖ i‿ər ~**iest** i‿ɪst i‿əst ~**iness** i nəs i nɪs
Drava 'drɑːv ə
Dravidian drə 'vɪd i‿ən ~s z
draw drɔː ‖ drɑː **drawing** 'drɔːr ɪŋ ‖ 'drɔː ɪŋ 'drɑː- **drawn** drɔːn ‖ drɑːn **draws** drɔːz ‖ drɑːz
drawback 'drɔː bæk ‖ 'drɑː- ~s s
drawbar 'drɔː bɑː ‖ -bɑːr 'drɑː- ~s z
drawbridg|e 'drɔː brɪdʒ ‖ 'drɑː- ~**es** ɪz əz
drawee ₍ˌ₎drɔːˈiː ‖ drɔː 'iː drɑː- ~s z
drawer *'sliding container'* drɔː ‖ drɔːr ~s z
drawer *'one that draws'* 'drɔːr ə ‖ 'drɔː‿ər 'drɑː‿ər ~s z
drawers *'undergarment'* drɔːz ‖ drɔːrz
drawing 'drɔːr ɪŋ ‖ 'drɔː ɪŋ 'drɑː- ~s z
  'drawing board; 'drawing pin; 'drawing room *also* 'drɔːɪŋ-
drawl drɔːl ‖ drɑːl **drawled** drɔːld ‖ drɑːld **drawling** 'drɔːl ɪŋ ‖ 'drɑːl- **drawls** drɔːlz ‖ drɑːlz
drawn drɔːn ‖ drɑːn

drawsheet 'drɔː ʃiːt ‖ 'drɑː- ~s s
drawstring 'drɔː strɪŋ ‖ 'drɑː- ~s z
Drax dræks
dray, Dray dreɪ **drays** dreɪz
Draycott *(i)* 'dreɪk ət, *(ii)* 'dreɪ kɒt ‖ -kɑːt
Drayton 'dreɪt ən
dread dred **dreaded** 'dred ɪd -əd **dreading** 'dred ɪŋ **dreads** dredz
dreadful 'dred fəl -fʊl ~**ly** ‿i ~**ness** nəs nɪs
dreadlock 'dred lɒk ‖ -lɑːk ~**ed** t ~s s
dreadnaught, dreadnought, D~ 'dred nɔːt ‖ -nɑːt ~s s
dream driːm **dreamed** dremᵖt driːmd ‖ driːmd **dreaming** 'driːm ɪŋ **dreams** driːmz **dreamt** dremᵖt
  'dream world
dreamboat 'driːm bəʊt ‖ -boʊt ~s s
dreamer 'driːm ə ‖ -ər ~s z
dreamland 'driːm lænd
dreamless 'driːm ləs -lɪs ~**ly** li
dreamlike 'driːm laɪk
dreamt dremᵖt
Dreamtime, d~ 'driːm taɪm
dream|y 'driːm |i ~**ier** i‿ə ‖ i‿ər ~**iest** i‿ɪst i‿əst ~**ily** ɪ li əl i ~**iness** i nəs i nɪs
drear drɪə ‖ drɪ‿ər

D

drear|y 'drɪər |i ‖ 'drɪr |i **~ier** i_ə ‖ i_ᵊr **~iest**
 i_ɪst i_əst **~ily** əl i ɪ li **~iness** i nəs i nɪs
dreck drek
dredge dredʒ **dredged** dredʒd **dredges**
 'dredʒ ɪz -əz **dredging** 'dredʒ ɪŋ
dredger 'dredʒ ə ‖ -ᵊr **~s** z
dree driː **dreed** driːd **dreeing** 'driː ɪŋ **drees**
 driːz
Dreena 'driːn ə
Dreft tdmk dreft
dreg dreg **dregs** dregz
Dreiser (i) 'draɪs ə ‖ -ᵊr, (ii) 'draɪz ə ‖ -ᵊr
drench drentʃ **drenched** drentʃt **drenches**
 'drentʃ ɪz -əz **drenching** 'drentʃ ɪŋ
Drene tdmk driːn
Dresden 'drezd ən —Ger ['dʁeːs dᵊn]
dress dres **dressed** drest **dresses** 'dres ɪz -əz
 dressing 'dres ɪŋ
 ˌdress 'circle, '• ˌ••; ˌdress re'hearsal;
 'dress shield; ˌdress 'suit ‖ '• •
dressage 'dres ɑːʒ -ɑːdʒ, -ɪdʒ, dre 'sɑːʒ
 ‖ drə 'sɑːʒ dre-
dresser 'dres ə ‖ -ᵊr **~s** z
dressing 'dres ɪŋ **~s** z
 'dressing room; 'dressing ˌtable
dressing-down ˌdres ɪŋ 'daʊn
dressing-gown 'dres ɪŋ gaʊn **~s** z
dressmaker 'dres ˌmeɪk ə ‖ -ᵊr **~s** z
dressmaking 'dres ˌmeɪk ɪŋ
dress|y 'dres |i **~ier** i_ə ‖ i_ᵊr **~iest** i_ɪst i_əst
 ~ily ɪ li əl i **~iness** i nəs i nɪs
drew, Drew druː:
Drexel 'dreks əl
drey dreɪ **dreys** dreɪz
Dreyfus 'dreɪf əs 'draɪf-, -ʊs —Fr [dʁɛ fys]
Drian 'driː_ən
dribbl|e 'drɪb əl **~ed** d **~er/s** _ə/z ‖ _ᵊr/z **~es**
 z **~ing** _ɪŋ
Driberg 'draɪ bɜːg ‖ -bɜ˞ːg
driblet 'drɪb lət -lɪt **~s** s
dribs and drabs ˌdrɪbz ən 'dræbz
dried draɪd
dried-up ˌdraɪd 'ʌp ◄
drier 'draɪ_ə ‖ 'draɪ_ᵊr **~s** z
dries draɪz
driest 'draɪ ɪst 'draɪ_əst
Driffield 'drɪf iːᵊld
drift drɪft **drifted** 'drɪft ɪd -əd **drifting**
 'drɪft ɪŋ **drifts** drɪfts
 'drift ice
driftage 'drɪft ɪdʒ
drifter 'drɪft ə ‖ -ᵊr **~s** z
driftnet 'drɪft net **~s** s
driftwood 'drɪft wʊd
Drighlington 'drɪg lɪŋ tən 'drɪl ɪŋ-
drill drɪl **drilled** drɪld **drilling** 'drɪl ɪŋ **drills**
 drɪlz
drillstock 'drɪl stɒk ‖ -stɑːk **~s** s
drily 'draɪ li
drink drɪŋk **drank** dræŋk **drinking** 'drɪŋk ɪŋ
 drinks drɪŋks **drunk** drʌŋk
 'drinking ˌfountain; 'drinking ˌwater
drinkable 'drɪŋk əb əl **~s** z

drink-driv|er ˌdrɪŋk 'draɪv| ə ‖ -ᵊr **~ers**
 əz ‖ ᵊrz **~ing** ɪŋ
drinking-up ˌdrɪŋk ɪŋ 'ʌp
 ˌdrinking-'up time
Drinkwater 'drɪŋk ˌwɔːt ə ‖ -ˌwɔːt̬ ᵊr -ˌwɑːt̬-
drip drɪp **dripped** drɪpt **dripping** 'drɪp ɪŋ
 drips drɪps
 'drip feed; 'drip pan
drip-|dry v 'drɪp |draɪ ˌ•'|• ◄ **~dried** draɪd
 ~dries draɪz **~drying** draɪ ɪŋ
drip-dry adj ˌdrɪp 'draɪ ◄
 ˌdrip-dry 'shirts
drip-|feed 'drɪp| fiːd ˌ•'|• ◄ **~fed** fed
 ~feeding fiːd ɪŋ **~feeds** fiːdz
drip-mat 'drɪp mæt **~s** s
dripping 'drɪp ɪŋ
dripp|y 'drɪp |i **~ier** i_ə ‖ i_ᵊr **~iest** i_ɪst i_əst
Driscoll 'drɪsk əl
drive draɪv **driven** 'drɪv ən **drives** draɪvz
 driving 'draɪv ɪŋ **drove** drəʊv ‖ droʊv
 'drive shaft; 'driving ˌlicence; 'driving
 seat; 'driving test
drive-by 'draɪv baɪ
drive-in 'draɪv ɪn **~s** s
drivel 'drɪv əl **~ed, ~led** d **~ing, ~ling** ɪŋ **~s** z
driveler, driveller 'drɪv əl_ə ‖ _ᵊr **~s** z
driven 'drɪv ən
driver, D~ 'draɪv ə ‖ -ᵊr **~s** z
 'driver ant; 'driver's ˌlicense; 'driver's seat
driveway 'draɪv weɪ **~s** z
Driza-bone tdmk 'draɪz ə bəʊn ‖ -boʊn
drizzl|e 'drɪz əl **~ed** d **~es** z **~ing** _ɪŋ
drizzly 'drɪz əl_i
Drogheda 'drɒɪ ɪd ə 'drɒh-, -əd-
drogue drəʊg ‖ droʊg **drogues**
 drəʊgz ‖ droʊgz
droid drɔɪd **droids** drɔɪdz
droit de seigneur ˌdrwɑː də seɪn 'jɜː: -sen'•,
 -siːn'• ‖ -'jɜ˞ː: —Fr [dʁwad sɛ njœːʁ]
Droitwich 'drɔɪt wɪtʃ
droll drəʊl →drɒʊl ‖ droʊl **drolls** drəʊlz
 →drɒʊlz ‖ droʊlz
droller|y 'drəʊl ər |i →'drɒʊl- ‖ 'droʊl- **~ies** iz
drollness 'drəʊl nəs →'drɒʊl-, -nɪs ‖ 'droʊl-
drolly 'drəʊl li →'drɒʊl- ‖ 'droʊl-
-drome drəʊm ‖ droʊm — **palindrome**
 'pæl ɪn drəʊm -ən- ‖ -droʊm
dromedar|y 'drɒm əd_ər |i 'drʌm-, '•ɪd_;
 -ə der i, -ɪ•• ‖ 'drɑːm ə der li 'drʌm- **~ies** iz
Dromio 'drəʊm i_əʊ 'drɒm- ‖ 'droʊm i oʊ
Dromore drə 'mɔː ‖ -'mɔːr -'moʊr
-dromous stress-imposing drəm əs —
 catadromous kə 'tædr əm əs
drone drəʊn ‖ droʊn **droned** drəʊnd ‖ droʊnd
 drones drəʊnz ‖ droʊnz **droning**
 'drəʊn ɪŋ ‖ 'droʊn ɪŋ
Dronfield 'drɒn fiːᵊld ‖ 'drɑːn-
drongo 'drɒŋ gəʊ ‖ 'drɑːŋ goʊ **~es, ~s** z
Drood druːd
drool druːl **drooled** druːld **drooling** 'druːl ɪŋ
 drools druːlz
droop druːp **drooped** druːpt **drooping/ly**
 'druːp ɪŋ /li **droops** druːps

droop|y 'druːp|i ~**ier** i‿ə ‖ i‿ər ~**iest** i‿ɪst
i‿əst ~**ily** ɪ li əl i ~**iness** i nəs -nɪs
drop drɒp ‖ drɑːp **dropped** drɒpt ‖ drɑːpt
dropping 'drɒp ɪŋ ‖ 'drɑːp ɪŋ **drops**
drɒps ‖ drɑːps
'**drop scone**; '**drop shot**
drophead 'drɒp hed ‖ 'drɑːp- ~**s** z
drop-in 'drɒp ɪn ‚•'• ‖ 'drɑːp-
dropkick 'drɒp kɪk ‖ 'drɑːp- ~**ed** t ~**ing** ɪŋ ~**s**
s
drop-leaf 'drɒp liːf ‖ 'drɑːp-
droplet 'drɒp lət -lɪt ‖ 'drɑːp- ~**s** s
drop-off 'drɒp ɒf -ɔːf ‖ 'drɑːp ɔːf -ɑːf ~**s** s
dropout 'drɒp aʊt ‖ 'drɑːp- ~**s** s
dropper 'drɒp ə ‖ 'drɑːp ər ~**s** z
dropping 'drɒp ɪŋ ‖ 'drɑːp- ~**s** z
dropsical 'drɒps ɪk əl ‖ 'drɑːps- ~**ly** i
dropsy 'drɒps i ‖ 'drɑːps i
dropwort 'drɒp wɜːt §-wɔːt ‖ 'drɑːp wɜ˞ːt
-wɔːrt ~**s** s
drosh|ky 'drɒʃ |ki ‖ 'drɑːʃ- ~**kies** kiz
drosophila drɒ 'sɒf ɪl ə drə-, -əl- ‖ drə 'sɑːf
əl ə drɑː- ~**s** z
dross drɒs ‖ drɑːs drɔːs
drought draʊt ‖ △draʊθ **droughts** draʊts
‖ △draʊθs —*The pronunciation with* θ
*properly belongs with a now archaic doublet
spelled* drouth.
drove drəʊv ‖ droʊv **droves** drəʊvz ‖ droʊvz
drover 'drəʊv ə ‖ 'droʊv ər ~**s** z
drown draʊn **drowned** draʊnd **drowning**
'draʊn ɪŋ **drowns** draʊnz
drowse draʊz **drowsed** draʊzd **drowses**
'draʊz ɪz -əz **drowsing** 'draʊz ɪŋ
drows|y 'draʊz |i ~**ier** i‿ə ‖ i‿ər ~**iest** i‿ɪst
i‿əst ~**ily** ɪ li əl i ~**iness** i nəs i nɪs
Droylsden 'drɔɪəlz dən
drub drʌb **drubbed** drʌbd **drubbing** 'drʌb ɪŋ
drubs drʌbz
Druce druːs
drudge drʌdʒ **drudged** drʌdʒd **drudges**
'drʌdʒ ɪz -əz **drudging/ly** 'drʌdʒ ɪŋ /li
drudger|y 'drʌdʒ ər‿|i ~**ies** iz
drug drʌg **drugged** drʌgd **drugging** 'drʌg ɪŋ
drugs drʌgz
'**drug ˌaddict**
drugget 'drʌg ɪt §-ət ~**s** s
druggie 'drʌg i ~**s** z
druggist 'drʌg ɪst §-əst ~**s** s
drugg|y 'drʌg |i ~**ies** iz
drugstore 'drʌg stɔː ‖ -stɔːr -stoʊr ~**s** z
Druid, druid 'druː‿ɪd ~**s** z
druidic dru 'ɪd ɪk ~**al** əl
drum drʌm **drummed** drʌmd **drumming**
'drʌm ɪŋ **drums** drʌmz
ˌdrum '**major** ‖ '• ‚•‚•; ˌdrum ˌmajo'**rette**
‖ '• • •‚•
Drumalbyn drʌm 'ælb ɪn §-ən
drumbeat 'drʌm biːt ~**s** s
drumfire 'drʌm ˌfaɪ‿ə ‖ -ˌfaɪ‿ər
drumhead 'drʌm hed ~**s** z
drumlin 'drʌm lɪn -lən ~**s** z
drummer 'drʌm ə ‖ -ər ~**s** z

drumm... —*see* **drum**
Drummond 'drʌm ənd
Drumnadrochit ˌdrʌm nə 'drɒx ɪt -'drɒk-, §-ət
‖ -'drɑːk-
Drumochter drə 'mɒxt ə -'mɒkt- ‖ -'mɑːkt ər
drumstick 'drʌm stɪk ~**s** s
drunk drʌŋk **drunks** drʌŋks
drunkard 'drʌŋk əd ‖ -ərd ~**s** z
drunken 'drʌŋk ən ~**ly** li ~**ness** nəs nɪs
drunkometer drʌŋ 'kɒm ɪt ə -ət-
‖ -'kɑːm ət ər 'drʌŋk ə ˌmiːt ər ~**s** z
drupe druːp (= *droop*) **drupes** druːps
Drury 'drʊər i ‖ 'drʊr i
Druse, druse druːz **Druses, druses** 'druːz ɪz
-əz
Drusilla dru 'sɪl ə
druther 'drʌð ə ‖ -ər ~**s** z
Druze druːz **Druzes** 'druːz ɪz -əz
dry draɪ **dried** draɪd **drier, dryer**
'draɪ‿ə ‖ 'draɪ‿ər **dries** draɪz **driest, dryest**
'draɪ ɪst 'draɪ‿əst **drying** 'draɪ ɪŋ
'**dry ˌbattery**, ‚• '••; ˌdry '**cleaner's**; '**dry
ˌdock**, ‚• '••; '**dry ˌgoods**; ˌdry '**ice**; ˌdry
'**land**; ˌdry '**rot**; ˌdry '**run**
dryad 'draɪ æd 'draɪ‿əd **dryades** 'draɪ‿ə diːz
dryads 'draɪ ædz 'draɪ‿ədz
Dryburgh 'draɪ bər‿ə ‖ 'draɪ bɜ˞ːg
dry-clean ˌdraɪ 'kliːn ◄ ~**ed** d ~**ing** ɪŋ ~**s** z
Dryden 'draɪd ən
dryer 'draɪ‿ə ‖ 'draɪ‿ər **dryest** 'draɪ ɪst
'draɪ‿əst
dry-eyed ˌdraɪ 'aɪd ◄
dryish 'draɪ ɪʃ
dryly 'draɪ li
dryness 'draɪ nəs -nɪs
drypoint 'draɪ pɔɪnt ~**s** s
Drysdale 'draɪz deɪəl
dry-shod ˌdraɪ 'ʃɒd ◄ ‖ 'draɪ ʃɑːd
dry-stone 'draɪ stəʊn ‚•'• ‖ -stoʊn
drywall 'draɪ wɔːl ‖ -wɑːl
DTI ˌdiː tiː 'aɪ
DTs, d t's, DT's ˌdiː 'tiːz
Du *in names* (i) dju →§'dʒu, (ii) du —*See also
phrases with this word* —*This prefix is
unstressed.*
dual 'djuː‿əl →§'dʒuː‿; djuːl, →§dʒuːl ‖ 'duː əl
'djuː- ~**s** z
ˌdual '**carriageway**
Duala du 'ɑːl ə
dualism 'djuː‿əl ˌɪz əm →§'dʒuː‿ ‖ 'duː- 'djuː-
~**s** z
dualist 'djuː‿əl ɪst →§'dʒuː‿, §-əst ‖ 'duː-
'djuː- ~**s** s
dualistic ˌdjuː‿ə 'lɪst ɪk ◄ →§ˌdʒuː‿ ‖ ˌduː-
ˌdjuː- ~**ally** əl‿i
dualit|y dju 'æl ət |i →§'dʒu-, -ɪt- ‖ du 'æl ət̬ i
dju- ~**ies** iz
dual-purpose ˌdjuː‿əl 'pɜːp əs ◄ →§ˌdʒuː‿;
ˌdju:l'••-, →§ˌdʒuː l- ‖ ˌduː əl 'pɜ˞ːp əs ◄
ˌdjuː-
Duane ₍ᵢ₎du: eɪn dweɪn
dub dʌb **dubbed** dʌbd **dubbing** 'dʌb ɪŋ
dubs dʌbz

Dubai ˌdu: 'baɪ ˌdju:-, →§ˌdʒu:-, du-, dju-,
   →§dʒu-; -'baɪ i
Dubarry dju 'bær i du- ‖ du- dju-, -'ber i
dubbin 'dʌb ɪn §-ən ~ed d ~s z
Dubček 'dʊb tʃek ‖ 'du:b- —Slovak ['dup tʃek]

dubiet|y dju 'baɪ‿ət |i →§dʒu-, -ɪt-
   ‖ du 'baɪ əṭ |i dju- ~ies iz
dubious 'dju:b i‿əs →§'dʒu:b- ‖ 'du:b-
   'dju:b- ~ly li ~ness nəs nɪs
Dublin 'dʌb lɪn §-lən
   ˌDublin ' Bay, ˌDublin Bay ' prawn
Dubliner 'dʌb lɪn ə §-lən- ‖ -ᵊr ~s z
Dubois, Du Bois American family name du 'bɔɪs
   də-, -'bɔɪz
Dubois French or Dutch family name du 'bwɑ:
   dju- —Fr [dy bwa]
Dubonnet tdmk, d~ du 'bɒn eɪ dju-, →§dʒu-
   ‖ ˌdu:b ə 'neɪ —Fr [dy bɔ nɛ] ~s z
Dubrovnik du 'brɒv nɪk dju- ‖ -'brɑ:v-
   —Croatian ["du brɔːv niːk]
Dubuque də 'bju:k
ducal 'dju:k ᵊl →§'dʒu:k- ‖ 'du:k ᵊl 'dju:k-
   ~ly i
Du Cane dju 'keɪn du-
Du Cann dju 'kæn du-
ducat 'dʌk ət ~s s
duce 'du:tʃ eɪ —It ['dut tʃe]
Duchamp 'dju: ʃɒ̃ 'du:-, -ʃɒm ‖ du 'ʃɑ̃: -'ʃɑ:m
   —Fr [dy ʃɑ̃]
Duchenne du 'ʃen dju-
Duchesne dju 'ʃeɪn du-
duchess 'dʌtʃ ɪs -əs, -es, ˌdʌtʃ 'es ~es ɪz əz
duchesse dju 'ʃes du- —Fr [dy ʃɛs]
duch|y 'dʌtʃ |i ~ies iz
Ducie 'dju:s i →§'dʒu:s- ‖ 'du:s i 'dju:s-
duck, Duck dʌk ducked dʌkt (= duct)
   ducking 'dʌk ɪŋ ducks dʌks
   'ducking stool; ˌducks and ' drakes
duckbill 'dʌk bɪl ~ed d ~s z
   ˌduckbilled ' platypus
duckboard 'dʌk bɔ:d ‖ -bɔ:rd -boʊrd ~s z
duck-egg 'dʌk eg ~s z
Duckett 'dʌk ɪt §-ət
Duckham 'dʌk əm ~'s z
duckie 'dʌk i ~s z
duckling 'dʌk lɪŋ ~s z
duckweed 'dʌk wi:d
Duckworth 'dʌk wəθ -wɜ:θ ‖ -wᵊrθ
duck|y 'dʌk |i ~ier i‿ə ‖ i‿ᵊr ~ies iz ~iest i‿ɪst
   i‿əst
duct dʌkt ducted 'dʌkt ɪd -əd ducting
   'dʌkt ɪŋ ducts dʌkts
ductile 'dʌkt aɪᵊl ‖ -ᵊl
ductility dʌk 'tɪl ət i -ɪt- ‖ -əṭ i
ductless 'dʌkt ləs -lɪs
dud dʌd duds dʌdz
Dudden, Duddon 'dʌd ᵊn
dude du:d dju:d dudes du:dz dju:dz
   'dude ranch
dudgeon 'dʌdʒ ən
Dudley 'dʌd li

due dju: →§dʒu: ‖ du: dju: —AmE 1993 poll
   panel preference: du: 91%, dju: 9%. dues
   dju:z →§dʒu:z ‖ du:z dju:z
duel 'dju:_əl →§'dʒu:‿; dju:l, →§dʒu:l ‖ 'du: əl
   'dju:- (= dual) ~ed, ~led d ~er/s, ~ler/s ə/
   z ‖ ᵊr/z ~ing, ~ling ɪŋ ~s z
duelist, duellist 'dju:_əl ɪst →§'dʒu:‿, §-əst;
   'dju:l•, →§'dʒu:l• ‖ 'du: əl əst 'dju:- ~s s
duenna dju 'en ə du- ‖ du- dju- ~s z
Duerden 'djʊəd ᵊn ‖ 'dʊrd ᵊn 'djʊrd-
duet dju 'et →§dʒu- ‖ du- dju- ~s s
duettist dju 'et ɪst →§dʒu-, §-əst ‖ du 'eṭ ɪst
   dju- ~s s
duff, Duff dʌf duffed dʌft duffing 'dʌf ɪŋ
   duffs dʌfs
duffel, D~ tdmk 'dʌf ᵊl
duffer 'dʌf ə ‖ -ᵊr ~s z
Dufferin 'dʌf ᵊr_ɪn -ᵊr_ən
Duffey, Duffie 'dʌf i
Duffield 'dʌf i:ᵊld
duffle 'dʌf ᵊl
   'duffle bag; ' duffle coat
Duffy 'dʌf i
Dufton 'dʌf tən
Dufy 'du:f i ‖ du 'fi: —Fr [dy fi]
dug dʌg dugs dʌgz
Dugald 'du:g ᵊld
Dugan 'du:g ən
Dugdale 'dʌg deɪᵊl
Duggan 'dʌg ən
Duggleby 'dʌg ᵊl bi
dugong 'du: gɒŋ 'dju:- ‖ -gɑ:ŋ -gɔ:ŋ ~s z
dugout 'dʌg aʊt ~s s
Duguid 'dju:g ɪd 'du:g-
duiker 'daɪk ə ‖ -ᵊr ~s z
Duisenberg 'daɪz ᵊn bɜːg 'dɔɪz-
   ‖ 'du:z ᵊn bɜ·ːg —Dutch ['dœy sᵊn bɛrx]
Duisburg 'dju:z bɜːg 'dju:s- ‖ 'du:s bɜ·ːg
   'du:z- —Ger ['dy:s bʊʁk]
Dukakis du 'kɑːk ɪs dju-, də-, §-əs
Dukas 'dju:k ɑ: 'du:k- ‖ du 'kɑ: dju- —Fr
   [dy ka]
duke, Duke dju:k →§dʒu:k ‖ du:k dju:k
   dukes, Duke's dju:ks →§dʒu:ks ‖ du:ks
   dju:ks
dukedom 'dju:k dəm →§'dʒu:k- ‖ 'du:k-
   'dju:k- ~s z
Dukeries 'dju:k ᵊr iz →§'dʒu:k- ‖ 'du:k-
   'dju:k-
Dukhobor 'du:k ə bɔ: -əʊ- ‖ -bɔ:r ~s z
Dukinfield 'dʌk ɪn fi:ᵊld -ən-
Dulais 'dɪl aɪs -əs
dulcet 'dʌls ɪt -ət
dulciana ˌdʌls i 'ɑ:n ə ‖ -'æn ə -'ɑ:n ə
Dulcie 'dʌls i
dulcimer 'dʌls ɪm ə -əm- ‖ -ᵊr ~s z
Dulcinea ˌdʌls ɪ 'ni:‿ə -ə-, -'neɪ ə
Dulcy 'dʌls i
dulia du 'laɪ ə dju-; 'dju:l i‿ə, 'du:l-
dull dʌl dulled dʌld duller 'dʌl ə ‖ -ᵊr
   dullest 'dʌl ɪst -əst dulling 'dʌl ɪŋ dulls
   dʌlz
dullard 'dʌl əd ‖ -ᵊrd ~s z

Dulles 'dʌl ɪs -əs

dullish 'dʌl ɪʃ

dullness 'dʌl nəs -nɪs

dullsville 'dʌlz vɪl §-vəl ~s z

dull-witted ˌdʌl 'wɪt ɪd ◄ -əd ‖ -'wɪt̮ əd ◄
~ness nəs nɪs

dully 'dʌl li 'dʌl i

dulness 'dʌl nəs -nɪs

dulse dʌls

Duluth də 'luːθ du-, dju-

Dulux tdmk 'djuː lʌks →§'dʒuː- ‖ 'duː- 'djuː-

Dulverton 'dʌlv ət ən ‖ -ərt ən

Dulwich 'dʌl ɪdʒ -ɪtʃ

duly 'djuː li →§'dʒuː- ‖ 'duː li 'djuː-

Duma, duma 'duːm ə

Dumaresq, d~ dju 'mer ɪk ‖ du- dju-

Dumas 'djuːm ɑː 'duːm-; dju 'mɑː ‖ du 'mɑː
—Fr [dy ma]

Du Maurier du 'mɒr i eɪ dju- ‖ də 'mɔːr-

dumb dʌm dumbed dʌmd dumber
'dʌm ə ‖ -ər dumbest 'dʌm ɪst -əst
dumbing 'dʌm ɪŋ dumbs dʌmz
'dumb show

Dumbarton ˌ(ˌ)dʌm 'bɑːt ən dəm- ‖ -'bɑːrt ən
ˌDumˌbarton 'Oaks

dumbbell 'dʌm bel ~s z

dumbfound ˌ(ˌ)dʌm 'faʊnd '•• ~ed ɪd əd ~ing
ɪŋ ~s z

dumb|ly 'dʌm |li ~ness nəs nɪs

Dumbo 'dʌm bəʊ ‖ -boʊ

dumbstruck 'dʌm strʌk

dumbwaiter ˌdʌm 'weɪt ə ‖ -'weɪt̮ ər ~s z

dumdum, dum-dum 'dʌm dʌm

dumfound ˌ(ˌ)dʌm 'faʊnd '•• ~ed ɪd əd ~ing
ɪŋ ~s z

Dumfries ˌ(ˌ)dʌm 'friːs dəm-, -'friːz

Dummer 'dʌm ə ‖ -ər

dumm|y 'dʌm |i ~ies iz

dump dʌmp dumped dʌmpt dumping
'dʌmp ɪŋ dumps dʌmps
'dump truck

dumper 'dʌmp ə ‖ -ər ~s z

dumpi... —see dumpy

dumpling 'dʌmp lɪŋ ~s z

dumpster, D~ tdmk 'dʌmpst ə ‖ -ər ~s z

dump|y 'dʌmp |i ~ier i_ə ‖ i_ər ~iest i_ɪst
i_əst ~ily ɪ li əl i ~iness i nəs i nɪs

dun, Dun dʌn dunned dʌnd dunner
'dʌn ə ‖ -ər dunnest 'dʌn ɪst -əst dunning
'dʌn ɪŋ duns dʌnz —See also phrases with
this word

Dunaway 'dʌn ə weɪ

Dunbar dʌn 'bɑː →dʌm- ‖ -'bɑːr '••

Dunblane dʌn 'bleɪn →dʌm-

Duncan 'dʌŋk ən

Duncannon dʌn 'kæn ən →dʌŋ-

dunce dʌnts dunces, dunce's 'dʌnts ɪz -əz
'dunce's cap

Dunciad 'dʌnts i æd

Dundalk in Ireland ˌ(ˌ)dʌn 'dɔːk -'dɔːlk ‖ -'dɑːk
—but the place in MD is '••

Dundas dʌn 'dæs 'dʌnd əs

Dundee ˌ(ˌ)dʌn 'diː
ˌ(ˌ)Dun'dee cake; ˌDundee U'nited, •, •-

dunderhead 'dʌnd ə hed ‖ -ər- ~ed ɪd əd ~s z

Dundonald dʌn 'dɒn əld ‖ -'dɑːn-

Dundonian dʌn 'dəʊn i_ən ‖ -'doʊn- ~s z

Dundrear|y, d~ dʌn 'drɪər li ‖ -'drɪr li ~ies iz

dune djuːn →§dʒuːn ‖ duːn djuːn dunes
djuːnz →§dʒuːnz ‖ duːnz djuːnz
'dune ˌbuggy

Dunedin dʌn 'iːd ɪn -ən —in NZ -ən

Dunfermline dʌn 'fɜːm lɪn -lən ‖ -'fɜːm-

dung dʌŋ dunged dʌŋd dunging 'dʌŋ ɪŋ
dungs dʌŋz
'dung ˌbeetle

Dungannon dʌn 'gæn ən →dʌŋ-

dungaree ˌdʌŋ gə 'riː '••• ~s z

Dungeness ˌdʌndʒ_ə 'nes ◄
ˌDungeness 'B; ˌDungeness 'crab

dungeon 'dʌndʒ ən ~s z

dunghill 'dʌŋ hɪl ~s z

Dunhill 'dʌn hɪl ~s, ~'s z

dunk dʌŋk dunked dʌŋkt dunking 'dʌŋk ɪŋ
dunks dʌŋks

Dunkeld dʌn 'keld →dʌŋ-

Dunkirk ˌ(ˌ)dʌn 'kɜːk →ˌ(ˌ)dʌŋ- ‖ 'dʌn kɜːk —Fr
Dunkerque [dœ̃ kɛʁk]

Dunkley 'dʌŋk li

Dunkling 'dʌŋk lɪŋ

Dun Laoghaire, Dún Laoghaire, Dún Laoire
ˌ(ˌ)dʌn 'lɪər i ˌ(ˌ)duːn-, -'leər-, -ə ‖ -'ler- —Irish
[dun 'ɬeː rʲe]

dunlin 'dʌn lɪn -lən ~s z

Dunlop 'dʌn lɒp ‖ -lɑːp —but as placename and
family name, in BrE usually •'•

Dunmail ˌdʌn 'meɪəl →ˌdʌm-
ˌDunmail 'Raise

Dunmow 'dʌn məʊ →'dʌm- ‖ -moʊ

Dunn, Dunne dʌn

dunn... —see dun

dunnage 'dʌn ɪdʒ

Dunnet, Dunnett 'dʌn ɪt §-ət
ˌDunnet 'Head

dunno 'don't know' də 'nəʊ ˌ(ˌ)dʌ- ‖ -'noʊ

dunnock 'dʌn ək ~s s

dunn|y 'dʌn li ~ies iz

Dunoon dʌn 'uːn də 'nuːn

Duns dʌnz
ˌDuns 'Scotus 'skəʊt əs 'skɒt- ‖ 'skoʊt̮-

Dunsany dʌn 'seɪn i -'sæn-

Dunsinane dʌn 'sɪn ən —but in Shakespeare's
'Macbeth' ˌdʌnts ɪ 'neɪn, -ə-, '•••

Dunstable 'dʌnts əb əl

Dunstan 'dʌntst ən

Dunster 'dʌntst ə ‖ -ər

Dunwoody dʌn 'wʊd i

duo 'djuː əʊ →§'dʒuː- ‖ 'duː oʊ 'djuː- ~s z

duodecimal ˌdjuː əʊ 'des ɪm əl ◄ →§ˌdʒuː-,
-'•əm- ‖ ˌduː oʊ- ˌdjuː- ~ly i ~s z

duodecimo ˌdjuː əʊ 'des ɪ məʊ →§ˌdʒuː-, -'•ə-
‖ ˌduː oʊ 'des ə moʊ ˌdjuː-

duoden|um ˌdjuː əʊ 'diːn |əm →§ˌdʒuː-
‖ ˌduː ə- ˌdjuː- ~a ə ~al əl ◄ ~ums əmz
ˌduoˌdenal 'ulcer

duologue 'dju:_ə lɒg →'dʒu:_ ‖ 'du: ə lɔ:g
'dju:-, -lɑ:g ~s z
duopol|y dju 'ɒp əl |i →§dʒu- ‖ du 'ɑ:p- dju-
~ies iz
dupe dju:p →§dʒu:p ‖ du:p dju:p **duped**
dju:pt →§dʒu:pt ‖ du:pt dju:pt **dupes**
dju:ps →§dʒu:ps ‖ du:ps dju:ps **duping**
'dju:p ɪŋ →§'dʒu:p- ‖ 'du:p ɪŋ 'dju:p-
duple 'dju:p əl →§'dʒu:p- ‖ 'du:p əl 'dju:p-
duplex 'dju:p leks →§'dʒu:p- ‖ 'du:p- 'dju:p-
~es ɪz əz
duplicate adj, n 'dju:p lɪk ət →§'dʒu:p-, -lək-,
-ɪt ‖ 'du:p- 'dju:p- ~s s
dupli|cate v 'dju:p lɪ |keɪt →§'dʒu:p-, -lə-
‖ 'du:p- 'dju:p- ~cated keɪt ɪd -əd ‖ keɪt̮ əd
~cates keɪts ~cating keɪt ɪŋ ‖ keɪt̮ ɪŋ
duplication ,dju:p lɪ 'keɪʃ ən →§,dʒu:p-, -lə-
‖ ,du:p- ,dju:p- ~s z
duplicator 'dju:p lɪ keɪt ə →§'dʒu:p-, '•lə-
‖ 'du:p lɪ keɪt̮ ər 'dju:p- ~s z
duplicitous dju 'plɪs ɪt əs →§dʒu-, -ət-
‖ du 'plɪs ət̮ əs dju- ~ly li
duplicity dju 'plɪs ət i →dʒu-, -ɪt-
‖ du 'plɪs ət̮ i dju-
Dupont (i) dju 'pɒnt →dʒu- ‖ du 'pɑːnt dju-,
(ii) 'dju: pɒnt →§'dʒu:- ‖ 'du: pɑːnt 'dju:-
—Fr [dy pɔ̃]
Dupré, Duprée, Duprez du 'preɪ dju- —but as
an English name, also -'pri:
Dupuytren du 'pwi:tr ən dju-; 'dju:p i trō,
,••'• —Fr [dy pɥi tʁæ̃]
Duquesne du 'keɪn dju- —Fr [dy kɛn]
durability ,djʊər ə 'bɪl ət i ,djɔːr-, →§,dʒʊər-,
-ɪt i ‖ ,dʊr ə 'bɪl ət̮ i ,djʊr-
durab|le 'djʊər əb |əl 'djɔːr-, →§'dʒʊər-
‖ 'dʊr- 'djʊr- ~leness əl nəs -nɪs ~ly li
Duracell tdmk 'djʊər ə sel →§'dʒʊər- ‖ 'dʊr-
'djʊr-
Durack 'djʊər æk ‖ 'dʊr- 'djʊr-
Duraglit tdmk 'djʊər ə glɪt →§'dʒʊər- ‖ 'dʊr-
'djʊr-
duralumin, D~ tdmk djuə 'ræl jʊ mɪn →§dʒuə-,
-jə-, §-mən ‖ du 'ræl jəm ən dju-
dura mater ,djʊər ə 'meɪt ə →§,dʒʊər-
‖ ,dʊr ə 'mɑːt̮ ər ,djʊr-, '•• ,•••
Duran djuə 'ræn duə-
durance 'djʊər əns 'djɔːr-, →§'dʒʊər- ‖ 'dʊr-
'djʊr-
Durango dju 'ræŋ gəʊ →§dʒu-, də-
‖ du 'ræŋ goʊ dju-, də-
duration djuə 'reɪʃ ən djɔː-, →§dʒuə- ‖ du-
dju- ~s z
durative 'djʊər ət ɪv 'djɔːr-, →§'dʒʊər-
‖ 'dʊr ət̮ ɪv 'djʊr-
Durban 'dɜːb ən ‖ 'dɝː b-
durbar 'dɜːb ɑː ,dɜː 'bɑː ‖ 'dɝː b ɑːr ~s z
Durbin 'dɜːb ɪn §-ən ‖ 'dɝː b-
Durbridge 'dɜː brɪdʒ ‖ 'dɝː-
Durer, Dürer 'djʊər ə ‖ 'dʊr ər —Ger ['dy: ʁɐ]
duress djuə 'res →§dʒuə-, 'djʊər es ‖ dʊ 'res
durex, Durex tdmk 'djʊər eks 'djɔːr-,
→§'dʒʊər- ‖ 'dʊr- 'djʊr- ~es ɪz əz
Durham 'dʌr əm ‖ 'dɝː-

durian 'dʊər i_ən 'djʊər-, -i ɑːn ‖ 'dʊr- ~s z
Durie 'djʊər i ‖ 'dʊr i 'djʊər-
during 'djʊər ɪŋ 'dʒʊər-, 'djɔːr-, -'dʒɜːr-,
'dʒɔːr-, 'dʒɜːr- ‖ 'dɝː ɪŋ 'dʊr-, 'djʊr- —BrE
1998 poll panel preference: 'dj- 65%, 'dʒ-
34%, 'd- 2%; ʊə 87%, ɔː 7%, ɜː 6%
Durkheim 'dɜːk haɪm ‖ 'dɝː k- —Fr [dyʁ kɛm]
durmast 'dɜː mɑːst §-mæst ‖ 'dɝː mæst ~s s
Durness 'dɜːn əs -ɪs ‖ 'dɝː n-
Durrant (i) 'dʌr ənt ‖ 'dɝː-, (ii) də 'rænt
Durrell 'dʌr əl ‖ 'dʊr- 'dɝː-
Durrenmatt, Dürrenmatt 'djʊər ən mæt
'dʊər- ‖ 'dʊr ən mɑːt —Ger ['dyʁ ən mat]
durr|ie, durr|y 'dʌr li ‖ 'dɝː li ~ies iz
durst dɜːst ‖ dɝːst **durstn't** 'dɜːs ənt ‖ 'dɝːs-
durum 'djʊər əm ‖ 'dʊr- 'djʊr-, 'dɝː-
dusk dʌsk **dusked** dʌskt **dusking** 'dʌsk ɪŋ
dusks dʌsks
dusk|y 'dʌsk li ~ier i_ə ‖ i_ər ~iest i_ɪst i_əst
~ily ɪ li əl i ~iness i nəs i nɪs
Dusseldorf, Düsseldorf
'dʊs əl dɔːf ‖ 'du:s əl dɔːrf 'dʊs- —Ger
['dʏs əl dɔʁf]
dust dʌst **dusted** 'dʌst ɪd -əd **dusting**
'dʌst ɪŋ **dusts** dʌsts
'dust ˌcover; 'dust ˌdevil; 'dusting
ˌpowder; 'dust ˌjacket; 'dust storm
dustbin 'dʌst bɪn ~s z
dustbowl 'dʌst bəʊl —→bɒʊl ‖ -boʊl ~s z
dustcart 'dʌst kɑːt ‖ -kɑːrt ~s s
dustcoat 'dʌst kəʊt ‖ -koʊt ~s s
duster 'dʌst ə ‖ -ər ~s z
dusti... —see dusty
Dustin 'dʌst ɪn §-ən
dust|man 'dʌst |mən ~men mən men
dustpan 'dʌst pæn ~s z
dustsheet 'dʌst ʃiːt →'dʌʃ- ~s s
dustup 'dʌst ʌp ~s s
dust|y, Dusty 'dʌst li ~ier i_ə ‖ i_ər ~iest i_ɪst
i_əst ~ily ɪ li əl i ~iness i nəs i nɪs
Dutch, dutch dʌtʃ
ˌDutch 'auction; ˌDutch 'courage; ˌDutch
'elm diˌsease; ˌDutch 'oven; ˌDutch 'treat;
ˌDutch 'uncle
Dutch|man 'dʌtʃ |mən ~men mən men
duteous 'dju:t i_əs →§'dʒu:t- ‖ 'du:t̮ i_əs
'dju:t̮- ~ly li ~ness nəs nɪs
Duthie 'dʌθ i
dutiable 'dju:t i_əb əl →§'dʒu:t- ‖ 'du:t̮-
'dju:t̮-
duti... —see duty
dutiful 'dju:t ɪ fəl →§'dʒu:t-, -ə-, -fʊl ‖ 'du:t̮-
'dju:t̮- ~ly _i ~ness nəs nɪs
Du Toit dju 'twɑ: du-
Dutton 'dʌt ən
dut|y 'dju:t li →§'dʒu:t i ‖ 'du:t̮ li 'dju:t̮ i ~ies
iz
duty-free ,dju:t i 'fri: ◄ →§,dʒu:t- ‖ ,du:t̮- ,dju:t̮-
,duty-'free shop, ,duty-free 'whisky
duum|vir dju 'ʌm |və du-, -'ʊm- ‖ du 'ʌm |vər
~virate vər ət vɪr-, -ɪt; -və reɪt, vɪ- ~viri
və ri: vɪ-, -raɪ

Duvalier du 'væl i eɪ dju- ‖ ˌdu: vɑːl 'jeɪ •'••
—*Fr* [dy va lje]
duvet 'du:v eɪ 'dju:v- ‖ du 'veɪ ~s z
dux dʌks
Duxford 'dʌks fəd ‖ -fərd
duyker 'daɪk ə ‖ -ər ~s z
DVD ˌdi: vi: 'di: ~s z
Dvorak, Dvořák 'dvɔːʒ æk 'vɔːʒ-, -ɑːk
‖ 'dvɔːʒ ɑːk —*Czech* ['dvɔ rʒaːk] ([rʒ] =
voiced alveolar fricative trill) —*but as an
American family name, and for the keyboard
design, also* 'dvɔːr æk
dwale dweɪˀl
dwarf dwɔːf ‖ dwɔːrf dwarfed
dwɔːft ‖ dwɔːrft dwarfing
'dwɔːf ɪŋ ‖ 'dwɔːrf ɪŋ dwarfs
dwɔːfs ‖ dwɔːrfs dwarves
dwɔːvz ‖ dwɔːrvz
dwarfish 'dwɔːf ɪʃ ‖ 'dwɔːrf-
dwarfism 'dwɔːf ˌɪz əm
dwarves dwɔːvz ‖ dwɔːrvz
Dwayne dweɪn
dweeb dwi:b dweebs dwi:bz
dwell dwel dwelled dweld dwelt dwelling
'dwel ɪŋ dwells dwelz dwelt dwelt
dweller 'dwel ə ‖ -ər ~s z
dwelling 'dwel ɪŋ ~s z
'dwelling house
dwelt dwelt
Dwight dwaɪt
dwindl|e 'dwɪnd ˀl ~ed d ~es z ~ing ˌɪŋ
Dworkin 'dwɔːk ɪn §-ən ‖ 'dwɔːrk-
Dwyer 'dwaɪ_ə ‖ _ər
Dwynwen 'du:_ɪn wen
dyad 'daɪ æd ~s z
dyadic daɪ 'æd ɪk ~s s
Dyak 'daɪ æk -ək ~s s
dyarch|y 'daɪ ɑːk |i ‖ -ɑːrk |i ~ies iz
dybbuk 'dɪb ək di: 'bu:k ~ed t ~s s
Dyce daɪs
dye daɪ (= *die*) dyed daɪd dyes daɪz dyeing
'daɪ ɪŋ
dyed-in-the-wool ˌdaɪd ɪn ðə 'wʊl ◂ •ən-
dyer, Dyer 'daɪ_ə ‖ 'daɪ_ər ~s z
dyestuff 'daɪ stʌf ~s s
dyeworks 'daɪ wɜːks ‖ -wɜːks
Dyfed 'dʌv ɪd -ed, -əd —*Welsh* ['də ved]
—*Also, by those not familiar with the name,*
'dɪf-
Dyffryn 'dʌf rɪn -rən —*Welsh* ['dəf rin, -rin]
Dyfrig 'dʌv rɪg —*Welsh* ['dəv rig]
dying 'daɪ ɪŋ
Dyirbal 'dʒɪəb ɑːl ‖ 'dʒɪrb-
dyke daɪk (= *dike*) dyked daɪkt dykes daɪks
dyking 'daɪk ɪŋ
Dykes daɪks

Dylan 'dɪl ən 'dʌl- —*Welsh* ['də lan]
Dymchurch 'dɪm tʃɜːtʃ ‖ -tʃɜːtʃ
dymo, Dymo *tdmk* 'daɪm əʊ ‖ -oʊ ~'d, ~ed d
~s z ~ing ɪŋ
Dymock, Dymoke 'dɪm ək
Dympna 'dɪmp nə
dynamic daɪ 'næm ɪk dɪ-, də- ~ally ˀl_i ~s s
dynamism 'daɪn ə ˌmɪz əm ~s z
dyna|mite 'daɪn ə ˌmaɪt ~mited maɪt ɪd -əd
‖ maɪt̬ əd ~mites maɪts ~miting
maɪt ɪŋ ‖ maɪt̬ ɪŋ
dynamo 'daɪn ə məʊ ‖ -moʊ ~s z
dynamometer ˌdaɪn ə 'mɒm ɪt ə -ət ə
‖ -'mɑːm ət̬ ər ~s z
dynast 'dɪn əst 'daɪn-, -æst ‖ 'daɪn æst -əst ~s
s
dynastic dɪ 'næst ɪk də-, daɪ- ‖ daɪ- ~ally ˀl_i
dynast|y 'dɪn əst |i ‖ 'daɪn- (*) ~ies iz
dyne daɪn (= *dine*) dynes daɪnz
Dynevor 'dɪn ɪv ə -əv- ‖ -ər —*but in Wales
often* dɪ 'nev ə. *Welsh* Dinefwr [di 'ne vur]
d'you dju:, dju, djə →dʒu:, →dʒu, →dʒə
dys- ˌ(ˌ)dɪs — dysfunction ˌ(ˌ)dɪs 'fʌŋk ʃən
Dysart 'daɪz ət 'daɪs-, -ɑːt ‖ -ɑːrt
dysarthria dɪs 'ɑːθ ri_ə ‖ -'ɑːrθ-
dysentery 'dɪs ən tr i 'dɪs ənt ər i, §-ən ter i
‖ 'dɪs ən ter i
dysfunction ˌ(ˌ)dɪs 'fʌŋk ʃən ~al ˌəl ~s z
dyslalia dɪs 'leɪl i_ə -'læl- ~s z
dyslectic ˌ(ˌ)dɪs 'lekt ɪk ~s s
dyslexia ˌ(ˌ)dɪs 'leks i_ə
dyslexic ˌ(ˌ)dɪs 'leks ɪk ~s s
dysmenorrhea, dysmenorrhoea
ˌdɪs ˌmen ə 'rɪə ‖ -'ri: ə
Dyson 'daɪs ən
dyspepsia dɪs 'peps i_ə ‖ -'pep ʃə
dyspeptic dɪs 'pept ɪk ~ally ˀl_i ~s s
dysphagia dɪs 'feɪdʒ i_ə -'feɪdʒ ə
dysphasia dɪs 'feɪz i_ə -'feɪʒ-, -'feɪʒ ə ‖ -'feɪʒ ə
-'feɪz i_ə, -'feɪz i_ə
dysphasic dɪs 'feɪz ɪk ~s s
dysphonia dɪs 'fəʊn i_ə ‖ -'foʊn-
dysphonic dɪs 'fɒn ɪk ‖ -'fɑːn ɪk ~s s
dysplasia dɪs 'pleɪz i_ə ‖ -'pleɪʒ ə -'pleɪʒ i_ə,
-'pleɪz i_ə
dyspnea, dyspnoea dɪsp 'ni:_ə
dyspraxia dɪs 'præks i_ə
dyspraxic dɪs 'præks ɪk
dysprosium dɪs 'prəʊz i_əm -'prəʊs- ‖ -'proʊz-
-'proʊʒ-, -'proʊs-, -'proʊʃ-
dystopia ˌ(ˌ)dɪs 'təʊp i_ə ‖ -'toʊp- ~s z
dystrophy 'dɪs trəf i
dysuria dɪs 'jʊər i_ə ˌdɪs juˀ 'rɪː_ə ‖ -'jʊr- dɪʃ-
dziggetai 'dʒɪg ə taɪ 'dzɪg-, 'zɪg-, -ɪ-, ˌ••'• ~s
z

E e

e   Spelling-to-sound

1 Where the spelling is **e**, the pronunciation differs according to whether the vowel is short or long, followed or not by **r**, and strong or weak.

2 The 'strong' pronunciation is regularly
e, as in **dress** dres ('short E'), or
iː, as in **cathedral** kə 'θiːdr əl ('long E').

3 Where **e** is followed by **r**, the 'strong' pronunciation is
ɜː ‖ ɜˑ, as in **serve** sɜːv ‖ sɝˑv, or
ɪə ‖ ɪ, as in **severe** sə 'vɪə ‖ sə 'vɪr;
or, indeed, there may be the regular 'short' pronunciation
e, as in **very** 'ver i.

4 The 'weak' pronunciation is
ɪ, as in **review** rɪ 'vjuː (although some speakers use ə instead, thus rə 'vjuː);
or
ə, as in **agent** 'eɪdʒ ənt (especially where the spelling is **el, ence, ent, er**).

5 Less frequently, the 'strong' pronunciation is
ɪ in the exceptional words **pretty, England, English**;
eə ‖ e in **where, there** (strong forms) and a few others;
eɪ, in foreign borrowings such as **suede** sweɪd, and often also in words ending in **-eity, -eic**, as **deity** 'deɪ ət i ‖ 'deɪ ət̬ i (also 'diː-), **nucleic**.
and, in BrE only, ɑː in **clerk, Derby** and a few others.

6 **e** is frequently silent. At the end of a word, for example, it is silent if it follows a consonant letter, as in **make** meɪk, **life, these, notice, orange, face, huge, collapse, twelve**. In this position it may have the function of indicating that the vowel before the consonant is long (**make, life, these**); or that **c** or **g** is 'soft' (**notice, orange**); or both of these (**face, huge**); or neither (**collapse, twelve**).

7 In a few cases at the end of a word after a consonant, the pronunciation is i, as in **apostrophe** ə 'pɒs trəf i ‖ ə 'pɑːs trəf i.

8 **e** also forms part of the digraphs **ea, ee, ei, eu, ew, ey**.

ea   Spelling-to-sound

1 Where the spelling is the digraph **ea**, there are several different pronunciations. The most usual are
iː, as in **tea** tiː, and
e, as in **bread** bred.

Less frequent are

eɪ, notable in **great** greɪt, **steak, break**;

ɪə ‖ iːə, notably in **idea** aɪ 'dɪə ‖ aɪ 'diː ə, **theatre**.

2 Where **ea** is followed by **r**, the pronunciation is regularly

ɪə ‖ ɪ, as in **near** nɪə ‖ nɪr.

Less frequently it is

ɜː ‖ ɜˑ, as in **early** 'ɜːl i ‖ 'ɜˑːl i and several others;

ɑː, notably in **heart** hɑːt ‖ hɑːrt, **hearth**;

eə ‖ e, notably in **bear** beə ‖ ber, **pear, swear, wear** and one meaning of **tear**.

3 **ea** is not a digraph in words such as **creation, react, area**.

ee   Spelling-to-sound

1 Where the spelling is the digraph **ee**, the pronunciation is regularly

iː, as in **tree** triː,

or, before **r**,

ɪə ‖ ɪ, as in **beer** bɪə ‖ bɪr.

2 Exceptionally, the pronunciation is ɪ in AmE **been** bɪn (sometimes also in BrE) and sometimes in **Greenwich** (although here many speakers use e).

ei, ey   Spelling-to-sound

1 Where the spelling is one of the digraphs **ei, ey**, the pronunciation is most frequently

eɪ, as in **veil** veɪl, **convey** kən 'veɪ.

2 Less frequently, it is

iː, as in **receive** rɪ 'siːv, **key** kiː,

and in a few words

aɪ, as in **height** haɪt, **eye** aɪ, or

e, as in **heifer** 'hef ə ‖ 'hef ᵊr, **Reynolds** 'ren ᵊldz.

3 Where the spelling is **ei** before **r**, the pronunciation is either

eə ‖ e, as in **their** ðeə ‖ ðer, or

ɪə ‖ ɪ, as in **weird** wɪəd ‖ wɪrd.

4 The exceptional **either, neither** may have aɪ or iː, with BrE preferring the former and AmE the latter.

5 **ei** is not a digraph in words such as **atheism, deity**.

eu, ew   Spelling-to-sound

1 Where the spelling is one of the digraphs **eu, ew**, the pronunciation is regularly

juː, as in **feudal** 'fjuːd ᵊl, **few** fjuː, or

uː, as in **rheumatism** 'ruːm ə tɪz əm, **crew** kruː.
(For the dropping of j, see **u**, 3.)

2 Exceptionally, it is also
əʊ ‖ oʊ, as in **sew** səʊ ‖ soʊ,
ɜː ‖ uː, in French words, as **masseuse** mæ 'sɜːz ‖ mə 'suːs, or
ɔɪ, in German-derived words, as **Freudian** 'frɔɪd i‿ən.
Note also **lieutenant**, BrE lef 'ten ənt.

3 Where the spelling is **eu** before **r**, the pronunciation is regularly
jʊə ‖ jʊ, as in **Europe** 'jʊər əp ‖ 'jʊr əp.
In words borrowed from French, it may also be
ɜː ‖ ɝː, as in **masseur** mæ 'sɜː ‖ mə 'sɝː.

E, e *name of letter* iː **Es, E's, e's** iːz
  —*Communications code name:* Echo
  'E ˌnumber
e *Latin prepn* eɪ iː —*See also phrases with this word*
e-mail 'iː meɪəl ~ed d ~ing ɪŋ ~s z
each iːtʃ
  ˌeach 'other; ˌeach 'way ◂
Eadie 'iːd i
Eads iːdz
Eady 'iːd i
eager 'iːg ə ‖ -ər ~ly li ~ness nəs nɪs
  ˌeager 'beaver
eagle, Eagle 'iːg əl ~s z
eagle-eyed ˌiːg əl 'aɪd ◂
eaglet 'iːg lət -lɪt ~s s
eagre 'eɪg ə 'iːg- ‖ -ər ~s z
Eakins 'eɪk ɪnz §-ənz
Eakring 'iːk rɪŋ
Ealing 'iːl ɪŋ
Eames *(i)* iːmz, *(ii)* eɪmz
Eamon, Eamonn 'eɪm ən
-ean 'iː‿ən, i‿ən —*In some words this suffix is stressed* (ˌEuro'pean), *but in others stress-imposing* (Shake'spearean). *Both possibilities are heard in Caribbean.*
ear ɪə ‖ ɪər **eared** ɪəd ‖ ɪərd **earing**
  'ɪər ɪŋ ‖ 'ɪr ɪŋ **ears** ɪəz ‖ ɪərz
  'ear ˌtrumpet
earache 'ɪər eɪk ‖ 'ɪr-
Eardley 'ɜːd li ‖ 'ɝːd-
eardrop 'ɪə drɒp ‖ 'ɪr drɑːp ~s s
eardrum 'ɪə drʌm ‖ 'ɪr- ~s z
eared ɪəd ‖ ɪərd
-eared 'ɪəd ‖ 'ɪərd
earflap 'ɪə flæp ‖ 'ɪr- ~s s
earful 'ɪə fʊl ‖ 'ɪr-
Earhart 'eə hɑːt ‖ 'er hɑːrt
earl, Earl ɜːl ‖ ɝːl **earls, Earl's** ɜːlz ‖ ɝːlz
  ˌEarl's 'Court; ˌEarl 'Grey
earldom 'ɜːl dəm ‖ 'ɝːl- ~s z
Earle ɜːl ‖ ɝːl
earless 'ɪə ləs -lɪs ‖ 'ɪr-
Earley 'ɜːl i ‖ 'ɝːl i

earli... —*see* **early**
earlobe 'ɪə ləʊb ‖ 'ɪr loʊb ~s z
early 'ɜːl i ‖ 'ɝːl i ~ier i‿ə ‖ i‿ər ~iest i‿ɪst
  i‿əst ~iness i nəs i nɪs ~ies iz
  ˌearly 'bird, ˌ• • '•; ˌearly 'closing day;
  ˌEarly 'English; ˌearly 'warning ˌsystem
earmark 'ɪə mɑːk ‖ 'ɪr mɑːrk ~ed t ~ing ɪŋ
  ~s s
earmuff 'ɪə mʌf ‖ 'ɪr- ~s s
earn, Earn ɜːn ‖ ɝːn (= *urn*) **earned** ɜːnd ɜːnt
  ‖ ɝːnd **earning/s** 'ɜːn ɪŋ/z ‖ 'ɝːn ɪŋ/z **earns**
  ɜːnz ‖ ɝːnz
earnest 'ɜːn ɪst -əst ‖ 'ɝːn- ~ly li ~ness nəs
  nɪs ~s s
Earnshaw 'ɜːn ʃɔː ‖ 'ɝːn- -ʃɑː
Earp ɜːp ‖ ɝːp
earphone 'ɪə fəʊn ‖ 'ɪr foʊn ~s z
earpiec|e 'ɪə piːs ‖ 'ɪr- ~es ɪz əz
earplug 'ɪə plʌg ‖ 'ɪr- ~s z
earring 'ɪə rɪŋ 'ɪər ɪŋ ‖ 'ɪr ɪŋ -rɪŋ ~s z
earshot 'ɪə ʃɒt ‖ 'ɪr ʃɑːt
ear-splitting 'ɪə ˌsplɪt ɪŋ ‖ 'ɪr ˌsplɪt̬ ɪŋ ~ly li
earth ɜːθ ‖ ɝːθ **earthed** ɜːθt ‖ ɝːθt **earthing**
  'ɜːθ ɪŋ ‖ 'ɝːθ ɪŋ **earths** *v* ɜːθs ‖ ɝːθs **earths**
  n pl ɜːθs ɜːðz ‖ ɝːθs **earth's** ɜːθs ‖ ɝːθs
  'earth ˌcloset; 'earth ˌsatellite; 'earth
  ˌscience
Eartha 'ɜːθ ə ‖ 'ɝːθ ə
earthborn 'ɜːθ bɔːn ‖ 'ɝːθ bɔːrn
earthbound 'ɜːθ baʊnd ‖ 'ɝːθ-
earthen 'ɜːθ ən 'ɜːð- ‖ 'ɝːθ-
earthenware 'ɜːθ ən weə 'ɜːð- ‖ 'ɝːθ ən wer
  -wær
earthi... —*see* **earthy**
earthling 'ɜːθ lɪŋ ‖ 'ɝːθ- ~s z
earthly 'ɜːθ li ‖ 'ɝːθ-
earth|man 'ɜːθ |mæn ‖ 'ɝːθ- ~men men
earthnut 'ɜːθ nʌt ‖ 'ɝːθ- ~s s
earthquake 'ɜːθ kweɪk ‖ 'ɝːθ- ~s s
earthshaking 'ɜːθ ˌʃeɪk ɪŋ ‖ 'ɝːθ-
earthshattering 'ɜːθ ˌʃæt‿ər ɪŋ ‖ 'ɝːθ ˌʃæt̬
  ər ɪŋ ~ly li
earthstar 'ɜːθ stɑː ‖ 'ɝːθ stɑːr ~s z
earthward 'ɜːθ wəd ‖ 'ɝːθ wərd ~s z

E

earthwork 'ɜːθ wɜːk ‖ 'ɜ·θ wɜ·k ~s s
earthworm 'ɜːθ wɜːm ‖ 'ɜ·θ wɜ·m ~s z
earth|ly 'ɜːθ li ‖ 'ɜ·θ li ~ier i‿ə ‖ i‿ər ~iest i‿ɪst
   i‿əst ~iness i nəs i nɪs
earwax 'ɪə wæks ‖ 'ɪr-
earwig 'ɪə wɪg ‖ 'ɪr- ~s z
Easdale 'iːz deɪəl
ease iːz eased iːzd eases 'iːz ɪz -əz easing
   'iːz ɪŋ
easeful 'iːz fəl -fʊl ~ly i ~ness nəs nɪs
easel 'iːz əl ~s z
easement 'iːz mənt ~s s
easi... —see easy
easily 'iːz ɪ li -əl i
Easington 'iːz ɪŋ tən
Eason 'iːs ən
east, East iːst
   ˌEast 'Anglia; ˌEast 'End; ˌEast 'Indies; ˌEast
   'London
eastbound 'iːst baʊnd
Eastbourne 'iːst bɔːn ‖ -bɔːrn -boʊrn
Eastcheap 'iːst tʃiːp
East Ender, Eastender ˌiːst 'end ə ‖ -ər ~s z
Easter 'iːst ə ‖ -ər ~s z
   ˌEaster 'Day; 'Easter egg; 'Easter ˌIsland
   ‖ ˌ•• '••; ˌEaster 'Sunday
Easterbrook 'iːst ə brʊk §-bruːk ‖ -ər-
easter|ly 'iːst əl i ‖ -ər li easterlies 'iːst
   əl iz ‖ -ər liz
eastern 'iːst ən ‖ -ərn
Easterner, e~ 'iːst ən ə ‖ -ərn ər -ən ər ~s z
easternmost 'iːst ən məʊst →-əm-
   ‖ -ərn moʊst
Eastertide 'iːst ə taɪd ‖ -ər- ~s z
easting 'iːst ɪŋ ~s z
Eastleigh ˌiːst 'liː ◂ '••
Eastman 'iːst mən
east-northeast ˌiːst nɔːθ 'iːst ‖ -nɔːrθ- —also
   naut -nɔːr- ‖ -nɔːr-
Easton 'iːst ən
east-southeast ˌiːst saʊθ 'iːst —also naut -saʊ-
eastward 'iːst wəd ‖ -wərd ~ly li ~s z
East-West ˌiːst 'west ◂
Eastwood 'iːst wʊd
eas|y 'iːz |i ~ier i‿ə ‖ i‿ər ~iest i‿ɪst i‿əst ~ily
   ɪ li əl i ~iness i nəs i nɪs
   ˌeasy 'chair, '•• •; 'easy street; ˌeasy
   'terms; ˌeasy 'virtue
easygoing ˌiːz i 'gəʊ ɪŋ ◂ ‖ -'goʊ ɪŋ ◂
easyJet tdmk 'iːz i dʒet
eat iːt ate et eɪt ‖ eɪt △et eaten 'iːt ən
   eating 'iːt ɪŋ ‖ 'iːt ɪŋ eats iːts
   'eating ˌapple; 'eating disˌorder
eatable 'iːt əb əl ‖ 'iːt̬- ~s z
eaten 'iːt ən
eater 'iːt ə ‖ 'iːt̬ ər ~s z
eater|y 'iːt ər |i ‖ 'iːt̬- ~ies iz
eating-|house 'iːt ɪŋ |haʊs ‖ 'iːt̬- ~houses
   haʊz ɪz -əz
eating-plac|e 'iːt ɪŋ pleɪs ‖ 'iːt̬- ~es ɪz əz
Eaton 'iːt ən
   ˌEaton 'Socon 'səʊk ən ‖ 'soʊk-

eau əʊ ‖ oʊ —Fr [o]
   ˌeau de co'logne də kə 'ləʊn di- ‖ -'loʊn
   —Fr [od kə lɔnj]; ˌeau de 'nil də 'niːl —Fr
   [od nil]; ˌeau de 'vie də 'viː —Fr [od vi]
eaves, Eaves iːvz
eavesdrop 'iːvz drɒp ‖ -drɑːp ~ped t ~per/s
   ə/z ᵊr/z ~ping ɪŋ ~s s
ebb eb ebbed ebd ebbing 'eb ɪŋ ebbs ebz
   ˌebb 'tide, '• •
Ebbsfleet 'ebz fliːt
Ebbw 'eb u -ə
   ˌEbbw 'Vale
EBCDIC 'eb si dɪk
Ebenezer ˌeb ə 'niːz ə ◂ -ɪ- ‖ -ər '•••
Eblis 'eb lɪs §-ləs
ebon 'eb ən
ebonite 'eb ə naɪt
ebon|y, Ebony 'eb ən |i ~ies iz
Ebor 'iːb ɔː ‖ -ɔːr
Eboracum ɪ 'bɒr ək əm iː-, ˌiːb ɔː 'rɑːk-
   ‖ ɪ 'bɔːr- ɪ 'bɑːr-
Ebro 'iːb rəʊ 'eb- ‖ -roʊ 'eɪb- —Sp ['e βro]
ebullience ɪ 'bʌl i‿ən¦s ə-, -'bʊl-
ebullient ɪ 'bʌl i‿ənt ə-, -'bʊl- ~ly li
ebullition ˌeb ə 'lɪʃ ən -ʊ-
Ebury 'iːb ər‿i
EC ˌiː 'siː
ecarte, écarté eɪ 'kɑːt eɪ ‖ ˌeɪ kɑːr 'teɪ —Fr
   [e kaʁ te]
Ecbatana ek 'bæt ən ə ˌek bə 'tɑːn ə
   ‖ ek 'bæt ən ə
Ecce Homo ˌek eɪ 'həʊm əʊ ˌeks-, ˌetʃ-, -i-,
   -'hɒm- ‖ -'hoʊm oʊ
eccentric ɪk 'sentr ɪk ek-, ək- ~ally əl‿i ~s s
eccentricit|y ˌeks en 'trɪs ət |i ˌ•ən-, -ɪt i ‖ -əṯ |i
   ~ies iz
Ecclefechan ˌek əl 'fek ən -'fex-
Eccles 'ek əlz
   'Eccles cake
ecclesia ɪ 'kliːz i‿ə
Ecclesiastes ɪ ˌkliːz i 'æst iːz ə-
ecclesiastic ɪ ˌkliːz i 'æst ɪk ◂ ə- ~al əl ~ally
   əl‿i ~s s
ecclesiasticism ɪ ˌkliːz i 'æst ɪ ˌsɪz əm ə-, -'•ə-
Ecclesiasticus ɪ ˌkliːz i 'æst ɪk əs ə-
ecclesio- comb. form
   with stress-neutral suffix ɪ ˌkliːz i‿ə ə- —
   ecclesiological ɪ ˌkliːz i‿ə 'lɒdʒ ɪk əl ◂ ə-
   ‖ -'lɑːdʒ-
   with stress-imposing suffix ɪ ˌkliːz i 'ɒ+ ə-
   ‖ ɪ ˌkliːz i 'ɑː+ — ecclesiology
   ɪ ˌkliːz i 'ɒl ədʒ i ə- ‖ -'ɑːl-
Eccleston 'ek əlst ən
eccrine 'ek rɪn -riːn, -rən, -raɪn
ecdysiast ek 'dɪz i æst ~s s
ECG ˌiː siː 'dʒiː ~s, ~'s z
echelon 'eʃ ə lɒn 'eɪʃ- ‖ -lɑːn ~ed d ~ing ɪŋ
   ~s z
echeveria, E~ ˌetʃ ɪ 'vɪər i‿ə ˌ•ə-
   ‖ ˌetʃ əv ə 'riː ə ˌeɪtʃ- ~s z
echid|na ɪ 'kɪd |nə ə-, e- ~nae niː ~nas nəz
echinacea ˌek ɪ 'neɪʃ ə ˌ•ə-, ˌ••'eɪs i‿ə

echinoderm ɪ 'kaɪn əʊ dɜːm ə-, -'kɪn-
‖ -ə dɜːm ~s z
echin|us ɪ 'kaɪn |əs ə-, e-; 'ek ɪn-, -ən- ~i aɪ
echo, Echo 'ek əʊ ‖ -oʊ ~ed d ~er/s ə/z ‖ ər/z
~es z ~ing ɪŋ
echoey 'ek əʊ i ‖ -oʊ i
echoic e 'kəʊ ɪk i-, ə- ‖ -'koʊ- ~ally əl_i
echolalia ˌek əʊ 'leɪl i‿ə ‖ , •oʊ-
echolocation ˌek əʊ ləʊ 'keɪʃ ən ‖ -oʊ loʊ-
echt ext ekt —Ger ['ʔɛçt]
Eckersley 'ek əz li ‖ -ərz-
Eckhart 'ek hɑːt ‖ -hɑːrt —Ger ['ʔɛk haʁt]
eclair, éclair ɪ 'kleə eɪ-, 'eɪk leə ‖ eɪ 'kleər ɪ-,
-'klæər —Fr [e klɛːʁ] ~s z
eclampsia ɪ 'klæmps i‿ə e-, ə-
eclat, éclat eɪ 'klɑː 'eɪk lɑː —Fr [e kla]
eclectic ɪ 'klekt ɪk e-, ə- ~ally əl_i ~s s
eclecticism ɪ 'klekt ɪ ˌsɪz əm e-, ə-, -ə-
eclips|e ɪ 'klɪps ə-, iː- ~ed t ~es ɪz əz ~ing ɪŋ
eclipsis ɪ 'klɪps ɪs ə-, iː-, §-əs
ecliptic ɪ 'klɪpt ɪk ə-, iː- ~s s
eclogue 'ek lɒg ‖ -lɔːg -lɑːg ~s z
Eco 'ek əʊ ‖ -oʊ —It ['ɛː ko]
eco- comb. form 'iːk əʊ ˌek əʊ ‖ 'iːk oʊ ˌek-, -ə
— **ecocide** 'iːk əʊ saɪd 'ek- ‖ -ə-
E. coli ˌiː 'kəʊl aɪ ‖ -'koʊl-
ecological ˌiːk ə 'lɒdʒ ɪk əl ◄ ˌek- ‖ -'lɑːdʒ-
~ly i
ecologist ɪ 'kɒl ədʒ ɪst e-, ə-, iː- ‖ -'kɑːl- ~s s
ecology ɪ 'kɒl ədʒ i e-, ə-, iː- ‖ -'kɑːl-
econometric ɪ ˌkɒn ə 'metr ɪk ◄ ə-, iː-
‖ -ˌkɑːn- ~al əl ~s s
econometrician ɪ ˌkɒn ə me 'trɪʃ ən ə-, iː-,
-mə' •- ‖ -ˌkɑːn ə mə- ~s z

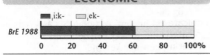
ECONOMIC
BrE 1988
■ iːk- ▨ ek-
0 20 40 60 80 100%

economic ˌiːk ə 'nɒm ɪk ◄ ˌek- ‖ -'nɑːm- ~al əl
~s s —BrE 1988 poll panel preference: ˌiːk-
62%, ˌek- 38%.
economie... —see economy
economise —see economize
economist ɪ 'kɒn əm ɪst ə-, §iː-, §-əst ‖ -'kɑːn-
~s s
economiz|e ɪ 'kɒn ə maɪz ə-, §iː- ‖ -'kɑːn-
~ed d ~er/s ə/z ‖ ər/z ~es ɪz əz ~ing ɪŋ
econom|y ɪ 'kɒn əm |i ə-, §iː- ‖ -'kɑːn- ~ies iz
e'conomy class
ecorche, écorché ˌeɪk ɔː 'ʃeɪ ‖ -ɔːr-
Ecorse place in MI 'iː kɔːs ɪ 'kɔːs ‖ 'iː kɔːrs
ɪ 'kɔːrs
ecosphere 'iːk əʊ sfɪə 'ek- ‖ -oʊ sfɪr
ecosystem 'iːk əʊ ˌsɪst əm 'ek-, -ɪm ‖ -oʊ- ~s z
—BrE 1998 poll panel preference: 'iːk- 88%,
'ek- 12%
ecraseur, écraseur ˌeɪk rɑː 'zɜː ‖ -'zɝː —Fr
[e kʁa zœːʁ] ~s z
ecru, écru 'eɪk ruː 'ek-
ecstas|y 'ekst əs |i ~ies iz
ecstatic ɪk 'stæt ɪk ek-, ək- ‖ -'stæt ɪk ~ally
əl_i ~s s

ECOSYSTEM

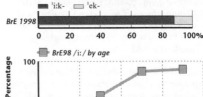
■ 'iːk- ▨ 'ek-
BrE 1998
0 20 40 60 80 100%

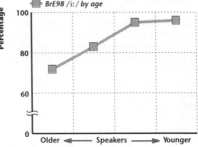
▦ BrE98 /iː/ by age
Percentage
100
80
60
0
Older ◄——— Speakers ———► Younger

ECT ˌiː siː 'tiː
ecto- comb. form
with stress-neutral suffix ˌekt əʊ ‖ ˌekt oʊ -ə —
ectogenic ˌekt əʊ 'dʒen ɪk ◄ ‖ -oʊ- -ə-
with stress-imposing suffix ek 'tɒ+ ‖ ek 'tɑː+
— **ectogenous** ek 'tɒdʒ ən əs -ɪn-
‖ -'tɑːdʒ-
ectomorph 'ekt əʊ mɔːf ‖ -ə mɔːrf ~s s
ectomorphic ˌekt əʊ 'mɔːf ɪk ◄ ‖ -ə 'mɔːrf-
-ectomy 'ekt əm i — **gastrectomy**
gæ 'strekt əm i
ectopic ˌ(ˌ)ek 'tɒp ɪk ‖ -'tɑːp-
ectoplasm 'ekt əʊ ˌplæz əm ‖ -ə-
ectype 'ek taɪp ~s s
ecu, e.c.u., ECU 'European currency unit'
'ek juː 'eɪk-, 'iːk-; ˌiː siː 'juː ‖ eɪ 'kuː —Fr
[e ky] ~s, ~'s z
ecu, écu old coin, 'shield' 'eɪk juː eɪ 'kjuː
‖ eɪ 'kjuː —Fr [e ky] ~s z
Ecuador 'ek wə dɔː ‖ -dɔːr —Sp [e kwa 'ðoɾ]
Ecuadoran ˌek wə 'dɔːr ən ◄ ~s z
Ecuadorean, Ecuadorian ˌek wə 'dɔːr i‿ən ◄
~s z
ecumenical ˌiːk ju 'men ɪk əl ◄ ˌek- ‖ ˌek jə-
~ly i
ecumenicism ˌiːk ju 'men ɪ ˌsɪz əm -'•ə-
‖ ˌek jə-
ecumenism ɪ 'kjuːm ə ˌnɪz əm iː-, 'ek jum-
eczema 'eks ɪm ə -əm‿ə; 'ek zɪm ə ‖ ɪg 'ziːm ə
'egz əm ə, 'eks-
eczematous ek 'sem ət əs ɪk-, -'siːm-; 'zem-,
-'ziːm-, ɪg- ‖ ɪg 'zem ət̬ əs -'ziːm-
Ed ed
-ed, -d t, d, ɪd əd —This unstressed ending has
three regular pronunciations:
1. After t or d it is pronounced ɪd or, less
commonly in BrE but regularly in AmE, əd, as
hated 'heɪt ɪd ‖ 'heɪt̬ əd, needed 'niːd ɪd ‖ -əd.
(In singing, exceptionally, a strong-vowelled
variant ed is usual, as 'niːd ed.)
2. After the other VOICED consonants or a
vowel sound, it is pronounced d, as called kɔːld,
seemed siːmd, vowed vaʊd, tied taɪd, feared
fɪəd ‖ fɪrd.
3. After the other VOICELESS consonants

E

(p, k, tʃ, f, θ, s, ʃ), *it is pronounced* t, *as* gripped grɪpt, patched pætʃt, knifed naɪft. *Certain adjectives have* ɪd, əd *against these rules, as* wicked 'wɪk ɪd, -əd. *The same applies also to most words in* -edly, *as* markedly 'mɑːk ɪd li, -əd- ‖ 'mɑːrk əd li. *This 'syllabic' pronunciation of the ending formerly applied to all* -ed *formations, and is still heard when people recite older literature, where it may be required for scansion purposes: thus (only in imitated old pronunciation)* seemed 'siːm ɪd.

Edale 'iː deɪəl
Edam 'iːd æm -əm —*Dutch* [eː 'dɑm]
edaphic ɪ 'dæf ɪk ə-, iː- **~ally** əl_i
Edda 'ed ə **~s** z
Eddic 'ed ɪk
Eddie 'ed i
eddie... —*see* **eddy**
Eddington 'ed ɪŋ tən
eddo 'ed əʊ ‖ -oʊ **~es** z
edd|y, Eddy 'ed |i **~ied** id **~ies** iz **~ying** i_ɪŋ
Eddystone 'ed ɪst ən -əst-; -i stəʊn ‖ -i stoʊn
Ede *family name* iːd
edelweiss 'eɪd əl vaɪs ⚠'aɪd-, -waɪs —*Ger* Edelweiß ['ʔeː dəl vaɪs]
edema ɪ 'diːm ə ə-, iː- **~s** z
edematous ɪ 'diːm ət əs ə-, iː- ‖ -əţ əs
Eden 'iːd ən
Edenbridge 'iːd ən brɪdʒ
Edenfield 'iːd ən fiːəld
edentate ɪ 'dent eɪt iː- **~s** s
Edessa ɪ 'des ə iː-
Edgar 'ed gə →'eg- ‖ -gər
Edgbaston 'edʒ bəst ən -bæst-
edge, Edge edʒ **edged** edʒd **edges** 'edʒ ɪz -əz **edging** 'edʒ ɪŋ
Edgecomb, Edgecombe 'edʒ kəm
-edged edʒd — **blunt-edged** ˌblʌnt 'edʒd ◄
Edgehill ˌedʒ 'hɪl —*but as a family name,* '••
Edgerton 'edʒ ət ən ‖ -ərt ən
edgeways 'edʒ weɪz
edgewise 'edʒ waɪz
Edgeworth 'edʒ wɜːθ -wəθ ‖ -wɝːθ
edging 'edʒ ɪŋ **~s** z
Edgware 'edʒ weə ‖ -wer
edg|y 'edʒ |i **~ier** i_ə ‖ i_ər **~iest** i_ɪst i_əst **~ily** ɪ li əl i **~iness** i nəs i nɪs
edh eð **edhs** eðz
edibility ˌed ə 'bɪl ət i ˌ•ɪ-, -ɪt i ‖ -əţ i
edible 'ed əb əl -ɪb-
edict 'iːd ɪkt **~s** s
Edie 'iːd i
edification ˌed ɪf ɪ 'keɪʃ ən ˌ•əf-, §-ə'•-
edific|e 'ed ɪf ɪs -əf-, §-əs **~es** ɪz əz
edi|fy 'ed ɪ |faɪ -ə- **~fied** faɪd **~fier/s** faɪ_ə/z ‖ faɪ_ər/z **~fies** faɪz **~fying** faɪ ɪŋ
Edina (i) e 'diːn ə ɪ-, (ii) ɪ 'daɪn ə iː- —*The place in MI is* (ii)
Edinburgh 'ed ɪn bər_ə →'•ɪm-, '•ən-, §-ˌbʌr ə ‖ -ˌbɜː ə -oʊ —*but the place in TX is locally* 'ed ən bɜːg
Edington 'ed ɪŋ tən
Edison 'ed ɪs ən -əs-

edit 'ed ɪt §-ət **edited** 'ed ɪt ɪd §-ət-, -əd ‖ -əţ- **editing** 'ed ɪt ɪŋ §-ət- ‖ -əţ- **edits** 'ed ɪts §-əts
Edith 'iːd ɪθ -əθ **~'s** s
edition ɪ 'dɪʃ ən ə- **~s** z
editor 'ed ɪt ə §-ət- ‖ -əţ ər **~s** z
editorial ˌed ɪ 'tɔːr i_əl ◄ ˌ•ə- ‖ -'toʊr- **~ly** i **~s** z
editorialis... —*see* **editorializ...**
editorialization ˌed ɪ ˌtɔːr i_əl aɪ 'zeɪʃ ən ˌ•ə-, -ɪ'•- ‖ -ə 'zeɪʃ- -ˌtoʊr- **~s** z
editorializ|e ˌed ɪ 'tɔːr i_ə laɪz ˌ•ə- ‖ -'toʊr- **~ed** d **~er/s** ə/z ‖ ər/z **~es** ɪz əz **~ing** ɪŋ
editorship 'ed ɪt ə ʃɪp ‖ -əţ ər- **~s** s
-edly ɪd li əd li — **designedly** dɪ 'zaɪn ɪd li də-, §diː-, -əd-
Edmead, Edmeade 'ed miːd →'eb-
Edmond 'ed mənd →'eb-
Edmonds 'ed məndz →'eb-
Edmondson 'ed mənd sən →'eb-
Edmonton 'ed mən tən →'eb-
Edmund 'ed mənd →'eb- **~s** z
Edmundson 'ed mənd sən →'eb-
Edna 'ed nə
Ednyfed 'ed nʌv ɪd -ed, §-əd —*Welsh* [ed 'nə ved]
Edo 'ed əʊ ‖ -oʊ —*Jp* [e ˌdo]
Edom 'iːd əm
Edomite 'iːd ə maɪt **~s** s
Edrich 'edr ɪtʃ
Edridge 'edr ɪdʒ
Edsel 'ed səl
educability ˌed jʊk ə 'bɪl ət i ˌedʒ ʊk-, §ˌedʒ ək-, -ɪt i ‖ ˌedʒ ək ə 'bɪl əţ i
educable 'ed jʊk əb əl 'edʒ ʊk-, §'edʒ ək- ‖ 'edʒ ək-
edu|cate 'ed ju |keɪt 'edʒ u-, §'edʒ ə- ‖ 'edʒ ə- **~cated** keɪt ɪd -əd ‖ keɪţ əd **~cates** keɪts **~cating** keɪt ɪŋ ‖ keɪţ ɪŋ
education ˌed ju 'keɪʃ ən ˌedʒ u-, §ˌedʒ ə- ‖ ˌedʒ ə- **~s** z
educational ˌed ju 'keɪʃ ən_əl ◄ ˌedʒ u-, §ˌedʒ ə- ‖ ˌedʒ ə- **~ly** i
educationalist ˌed ju 'keɪʃ ən_əl ɪst ˌedʒ u-, §ˌedʒ ə-, §-əst ‖ ˌedʒ ə- **~s** s
educative 'ed jʊk ət ɪv 'edʒ ʊk-, §'edʒ ək-; 'ed ju keɪt ɪv, 'edʒ u-, §'edʒ ə- ‖ 'edʒ ə keɪţ ɪv
educator 'ed ju keɪt ə 'edʒ u-, §'edʒ ə- ‖ 'edʒ ə keɪţ ər **~s** z
educ|e ɪ 'djuːs ə-, iː-, ‖ §-'dʒuːs ‖ -'duːs -'djuːs **~ed** t **~es** ɪz əz **~ing** ɪŋ
eduction ɪ 'dʌk ʃən ə-, iː- **~s** z
Edward 'ed wəd ‖ -wərd
Edwardes 'ed wədz ‖ -wərdz
Edwardian ed 'wɔːd i_ən -'wɑːd- ‖ -'wɔːrd- -'wɑːrd-
Edwards 'ed wədz ‖ -wərdz
Edwin 'ed wɪn §-wən
Edwina ed 'wiːn ə
Edwinstowe 'ed wɪn stəʊ §-wən- ‖ -stoʊ

-ee iː, eɪ, i —*Where this is a genuine suffix, it is usually stressed, as* ˌpay'ee, ˌabsen'tee. *In words*

*spelt -ee where it is not a genuine suffix, it may
be stressed* (ˌrefeˈree); *or unstressed but strong*
(ˈpedigree -griː *); or weak* (committee
kə ˈmɪt i ‖ -ˈmɪt̬ i). *If alternatively spelt -ée, it
is pronounced* eɪ *(see next entry).*

-ee, -ée eɪ —*Often unstressed in BrE, but usually
stressed in AmE, as* matinee 'ˈ• • • ‖ ˌ• •ˈ•,
fiancee •ˈ• • ‖ ˌ• •ˈ•

EEC ˌiː iː ˈsiː

eek iːk

eel iːᵊl   **eels** iːᵊlz

eelgrass 'ˈiːᵊl grɑːs §-græs ‖ -græs

eelpout 'ˈiːᵊl paʊt   ~s s

eelworm 'ˈiːᵊl wɜːm ‖ -wɝːm   ~s z

-een 'ˈiːn — velveteen ˌvelv ə ˈtiːn -ə-

e'en iːn

eeny meeny miny mo
  ˌiːn i ˌmiːn i ˌmaɪn i ˈməʊ ‖ -ˈmoʊ

-eer ˈɪə ‖ ˈɪᵊr — *This suffix is stressed:*
  mountaineer ˌmaʊnt ɪ ˈnɪə -ə- ‖ -ᵊn ˈɪᵊr

e'er eə ‖ eᵊr æᵊr (= *air*)

eer|ie ˈɪər li ‖ ˈɪr li **~ier** i_ə ‖ i_ᵊr **~iest** i_ɪst
  i_əst **~ily** əl i ɪ li **~iness** i nəs i nɪs

Eeyore 'ˈiː ɔː ‖ -ɔːr

eff ef   **effed** eft   **effing** 'ˈef ɪŋ   **effs** efs

effable 'ˈef əb ᵊl

effac|e ɪ ˈfeɪs e-, ə-   **~ed** t   **~es** ɪz əz   **~ing** ɪŋ

effaceable ɪ ˈfeɪs əb ᵊl e-, ə-

effacement ɪ ˈfeɪs mənt e-, ə-

effect ɪ ˈfekt ə-   **~ed** ɪd əd   **~ing** ɪŋ   **~s** s

effective ɪ ˈfekt ɪv ə- **~ly** li

effectual ɪ ˈfek tʃu_əl ə-, -tju_əl **~ly** i

effectu|ate ɪ ˈfek tʃu |eɪt ə-, -tju- **~ated** eɪt ɪd
  -əd ‖ eɪt̬ əd **~ates** eɪts **~ating** eɪt ɪŋ ‖ eɪt̬ ɪŋ

effectuation ɪ ˌfek tʃu 'ˈeɪʃ ᵊn ə-, -tju-

effeminacy ɪ ˈfem ɪn əs i ə-, e-, -ˈ•ən-

effeminate ɪ ˈfem ɪn ət ə-, e-, -ˈ•ən-, -ɪt **~ly** li
  ~s s

effendi, E~ e ˈfend ɪ ɪ-, ə-   **~s** z

efferent 'ˈef ər ənt 'ˈiːf-, -er-

effervesc|e ˌef ə ˈves ‖ -ᵊr-   **~ed** t   **~es** ɪz əz
  ~ing ɪŋ

effervescence ˌef ə ˈves ᵊn s ‖ -ᵊr-

effervescent ˌef ə ˈves ᵊnt ◂ ‖ -ᵊr- **~ly** li

effete ɪ ˈfiːt e-, ə- **~ly** li **~ness** nəs nɪs

efficacious ˌef ɪ ˈkeɪʃ əs ◂ -ə- **~ly** li **~ness** nəs
  nɪs

efficacity ˌef ɪ ˈkæs ət i ˌ•ə-, -ɪt i ‖ -ət̬ i

efficacy 'ˈef ɪk əs i 'ˈ•ək-

efficienc|y ɪ ˈfɪʃ ᵊnt s li ə- **~ies** ɪz
  ef'ficiency bar

efficient ɪ ˈfɪʃ ᵊnt ə- **~ly** li

Effie 'ˈef i

effig|y 'ˈef ɪdʒ li -ədʒ- **~ies** ɪz

Effingham *(i)* 'ˈef ɪŋ əm §-həm, *(ii)* -hæm —*The
place in England is (i), those in the USA (ii)*

effleurage 'ˈef lɜː rɑːʒ -lə-, ˌ•ˈ•ˈ• ‖ ˌef lə ˈrɑːʒ
  —*Fr* [ɛ flœ ʁaːʒ]

effloresc|e ˌef lə ˈres -lɔː-   **~ed** t   **~es** ɪz əz
  ~ing ɪŋ

efflorescenc|e ˌef lə ˈres ᵊnt s -lɔː-   **~es** ɪz əz

efflorescent ˌef lə ˈres ᵊnt ◂ -lɔː-

effluence 'ˈef lu_ᵊnt s

effluent 'ˈef lu_ᵊnt   **~s** s

effluvi|um ɪ ˈfluːv i_|əm e-, ə- **~a** ə **~al** əl
  ~ums əmz

efflux 'ˈef lʌks   **~es** ɪz əz

effort 'ˈef ət ‖ -ᵊrt -ɔːrt   **~s** s

effortless 'ˈef ət ləs -lɪs ‖ -ᵊrt- **~ly** li **~ness** nəs
  nɪs

effronter|y ɪ ˈfrʌnt ər li e-, ə- ‖ -ˈfrʌnt̬- **~ies** ɪz

effulgence ɪ ˈfʌldʒ ᵊnt s e-, ə-, -ˈfʊldʒ-

effulgent ɪ ˈfʌldʒ ᵊnt e-, ə-, -ˈfʊldʒ- **~ly** li

effusion ɪ ˈfjuːʒ ᵊn e-, ə- **~s** z

effusive ɪ ˈfjuːs ɪv e-, ə-, §-ˈfjuːz- **~ly** li **~ness**
  nəs nɪs

Efik 'ˈef ɪk   **~s** s

EFL ˌiː ef ˈel

eft eft   **efts** efts

EFTA 'ˈeft ə

e.g. ˌiː ˈdʒiː *or as* for example

egad ɪ ˈgæd

egalitarian ɪ ˌgæl ɪ ˈteər i_ən ə-, -ə'ˈ•-; ˌiːg æl-
  ‖ -ˈter- **~ism** ˌɪz ᵊm **~s** z

Egan 'ˈiːg ən

Egbert 'ˈeg bɜːt -bət ‖ -bɝːt

Egeria ɪ ˈdʒɪər i_ə iː- ‖ -ˈdʒɪr-

Egerton 'ˈedʒ ət ᵊn ‖ -ᵊrt ᵊn

egest ɪ ˈdʒest iː-   **~ed** ɪd əd   **~ing** ɪŋ   **~s** s

Egeus ɪ ˈdʒiː_əs iː-; ˈiːdʒ uːs, -juːs

egg eg   **egged** egd   **egging** 'ˈeg ɪŋ   **eggs** egz
  ˌegg and ˈspoon race; ˌegg ˈroll ‖ 'ˈ• •;
  'ˈegg ˌtimer; 'ˈegg white

eggar, Eggar 'ˈeg ə ‖ -ᵊr **~s** z

eggbeater 'ˈeg ˌbiːt ə ‖ -ˌbiːt̬ ᵊr **~s** z

egg-bound 'ˈeg baʊnd

eggcup 'ˈeg kʌp **~s** s

egghead 'ˈeg hed **~s** z

Egginton 'ˈeg ɪn tən

Eggleton 'ˈeg ᵊl tən

eggnog ˌeg ˈnɒg 'ˈ• • ‖ 'ˈeg nɑːg **~s** z

eggplant 'ˈeg plɑːnt §-plænt ‖ -plænt **~s** s

eggshell 'ˈeg ʃel **~s** z

eggwhisk 'ˈeg wɪsk -hwɪsk ‖ -hwɪsk **~s** s

Egham 'ˈeg əm

egis 'ˈiːdʒ ɪs §-əs

eglantine 'ˈeg lən taɪn -tiːn ‖ -n **~s** z

Eglon 'ˈeg lɒn ‖ -lɑːn

Eglwys 'ˈeg lu ɪs 'ˈeg lɔɪs —*Welsh* ['ˈe glujs]

Egmont 'ˈeg mɒnt -mənt ‖ -mɑːnt

ego 'ˈiːg əʊ 'ˈeg- ‖ -oʊ **~s** z
  'ˈego trip

egocentric ˌiːg əʊ ˈsentr ɪk ◂ ˌeg- ‖ -oʊ- **~ally**
  ᵊl_i

egocentricity ˌiːg əʊ sen ˈtrɪs ət i ˌeg-, -sᵊn'ˈ•-,
  -ɪt i ‖ -oʊ sen ˈtrɪs ət̬ i

egocentrism ˌiːg əʊ ˈsentr ˌɪz ᵊm ˌeg- ‖ -oʊ-

egoism 'ˈiːg əʊ ˌɪz ᵊm 'ˈeg- ‖ -oʊ-

egoist 'ˈiːg əʊ ɪst 'ˈeg-, §-əst ‖ -oʊ- **~s** s

egoistic ˌiːg əʊ ˈɪst ɪk ◂ ˌeg- ‖ -oʊ- **~ally** ᵊl_i

egomania ˌiːg əʊ ˈmeɪn i_ə ˌeg- ‖ ˌ•oʊ-

egomaniac ˌiːg əʊ ˈmeɪn i æk ˌeg- ‖ ˌ•oʊ- **~s**
  s

egomaniacal ˌiːg əʊ mə ˈnaɪ_ək ᵊl ◂ ˌeg-, -ɪk ᵊl
  ‖ ˌ•oʊ-

Egon 'ˈiːg ɒn 'ˈeg-, -ᵊn ‖ 'ˈeɪg ɑːn

E

egotism 'eg əʊ ,tɪz əm 'iːg- ‖ 'iːg ə-
egotist 'eg əʊt ɪst 'iːg-, §-əst ‖ 'iːg ət̬ əst ~s s
egotistic ,eg əʊ 'tɪst ɪk ◄ ,iːg- ‖ ,iːg ə- ~al əl
~ally əl_i
egregious ɪ 'griːdʒ əs ə-, -'griːdʒ i_əs ~ly li
~ness nəs nɪs
Egremont 'eg rə mənt -rɪ-, -mɒnt ‖ -mɑːnt
egress 'iː gres
egressive i 'gres ɪv —in contrast to ingressive,
also ,iː-
egret 'iːg rət -rɪt, -ret ‖ 'eg-; iː 'gret, ɪ- ~s s
Egypt 'iːdʒ ɪpt §-əpt
Egyptian ɪ 'dʒɪp ʃən ə-, iː- ~s z
Egyptological ,iːdʒ ɪpt ə 'lɒdʒ ɪk əl ◄ §,•əpt-;
ɪ ,dʒɪpt- ‖ -'lɑːdʒ-
Egyptologist ,iːdʒ ɪp 'tɒl ədʒ ɪst §,•əp-, §-əst
‖ -'tɑːl- ~s s
Egyptology ,iːdʒ ɪp 'tɒl ədʒ i §,•əp- ‖ -'tɑːl-
eh eɪ
Ehrlich 'eə lɪk -lɪx ‖ 'er- —Ger ['ʔeːɐ lɪç] —but
as an American family name, 'ɜː- ‖ 'ɝː-
Eichmann 'aɪk mən 'aɪx- —Ger ['ʔaɪç man]
Eid iːd
eider 'aɪd ə ‖ -ᵊr ~s z
eiderdown 'aɪd ə daʊn ‖ -ᵊr- ~s z
eidetic aɪ 'det ɪk ‖ -'det̬ ɪk ~ally əl_i
Eifel, Eiffel 'aɪf əl —Ger ['ʔai fəl], Fr [ɛ fɛl]
,Eiffel 'Tower
Eifion 'aɪv i ɒn ‖ -ɑːn —Welsh ['əiv jon]
eigenfunction 'aɪg ən ,fʌŋk ʃən →-ŋ- ~s z
eigenvalue 'aɪg ən ,væl juː →-ŋ- ~s z
Eiger 'aɪg ə ‖ -ᵊr —Ger ['ʔai gɐ]
Eigg eg
eight eɪt eights eɪts
eighteen ,eɪ 'tiːn ◄ §,eɪt-, §,eɪt 'iːn
,eighteen 'months
eighteenth ,eɪ 'tiːntθ ◄ §,eɪt-, §,eɪt 'iːntθ ~s s
,eighteenth 'century
eightfold 'eɪt fəʊld →-fɒʊld ‖ -foʊld
eighth eɪtθ ‖ eɪθ eighths eɪtθs ‖ eɪθs
'eighth note
eighti... —see eighty
eightieth 'eɪt i_əθ §-ti-, _ɪθ ‖ 'eɪt̬ i_əθ ~s s
eightsome 'eɪt səm ~s z
,eightsome 'reel
eight|ly 'eɪt li §'eɪt t li ‖ 'eɪt̬ li ~ies iz
,eighty-'four◄
Eilat eɪ 'lɑːt
Eilean 'el ən
,Eilean 'Donan 'dɒn ən ‖ -'doʊn-
Eileen 'aɪl iːn ‖ ,aɪ 'liːn ,eɪ-
Eilidh 'eɪl i
Eiloart 'aɪl əʊ ɑːt ‖ -oʊ ɑːrt
Eindhoven 'aɪnd həʊv ən 'aɪnt- ‖ -hoʊv-
—Dutch ['ɛint hoː vən]
einkorn 'aɪn kɔːn →'aɪŋ- ‖ -kɔːrn
Einstein 'aɪn staɪn —Ger ['ʔain ʃtain]
einsteinium aɪn 'staɪn i_əm
Eire, Éire 'eər ə ‖ 'er ə 'ær-; 'eɪ rə —Irish
['eː rʲə]
eirenicon aɪᵊ 'riːn ɪ kɒn -'ren- ‖ -kɑːn
Eirian 'aɪᵊr i_ən —Welsh ['əir jan]
Eirlys 'aɪ_ə lɪs ‖ 'aɪᵊr• —Welsh ['əir lis, -lis]

Eisenhower 'aɪz ən ,haʊ_ə ‖ -,haʊ_ᵊr
Eisenstein 'aɪz ən staɪn -ʃtaɪn —Russ
['ɛj zjɪn ʃtijn]
eisteddfod aɪ 'sted fəd ɪ-, ə-, -'steð vɒd
‖ -vɑːd —Welsh [əi 'sdeð vod] ~s z

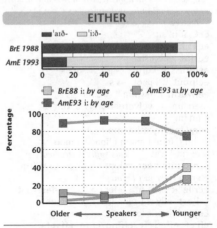

EITHER

	■ 'aɪð- □ 'iːð-
BrE 1988	
AmE 1993	

0 20 40 60 80 100%

■ BrE88 i: by age ■ AmE93 aɪ by age
■ AmE93 i: by age

Percentage
100
80
60
40
20
0

Older ◄—— Speakers ——► Younger

either 'aɪð ə 'iːð- ‖ 'iːð ᵊr 'aɪð- —Poll panel
preferences: BrE 1988, 'aɪð- 88%, 'iːð- 13%;
AmE 1993, 'iːð- 84%, 'aɪð- 16%.
either-or ,aɪð ər 'ɔː ,iːð- ‖ ,iːð ər 'ɔːr ,aɪð-
Eithne 'eθ ni —Irish ['e hə nə]
ejacu|late v ɪ 'dʒæk ju |leɪt ə-, iː-, -jə- ‖ -jə-
~lated leɪt ɪd -əd ‖ leɪt̬ əd ~lates leɪts
~lating leɪt ɪŋ ‖ leɪt̬ ɪŋ
ejaculate n ɪ 'dʒæk jʊl ət ə-, iː-, -jəl-, -ɪt;
-ju leɪt, -jə- ‖ -jəl- ~s s
ejaculatio ɪ ,dʒæk ju 'leɪʃ i əʊ iː-
‖ -jə 'leɪʃ i oʊ
ejaculation ɪ ,dʒæk ju 'leɪʃ ən ə-, iː-, -jə- ‖ -jə-
~s z
eject ɪ 'dʒekt ə-, iː- ~ed ɪd əd ~ing ɪŋ ~s s
ejecta ɪ 'dʒekt ə ə-, iː-
ejection ɪ 'dʒek ʃən ə-, iː- ~s z
e'jection seat
ejective ɪ 'dʒekt ɪv ə-, iː- ~ly li ~s z
ejectment ɪ 'dʒekt mənt ə-, iː- ~s s
ejector ɪ 'dʒekt ə ə-, iː- ‖ -ᵊr ~s z
e'jector seat
Ekco tdmk 'ek əʊ ‖ -oʊ
eke iːk eked iːkt ekes iːks eking 'iːk ɪŋ
EKG ,iː keɪ 'dʒiː ~s z
ekistics ɪ 'kɪst ɪks ə-, iː-
Ektachrome tdmk 'ekt ə krəʊm ‖ -kroʊm
el el —See also phrases with this word
elaborate adj ɪ 'læb ər_ət _ə-, _ɪt ~ly li ~ness
nəs nɪs
elabo|rate v ɪ 'læb ə |reɪt ə-, §iː- ~rated
reɪt ɪd -əd ‖ reɪt̬ əd ~rates reɪts ~rating
reɪt ɪŋ ‖ reɪt̬ ɪŋ
elaboration ɪ ,læb ə 'reɪʃ ən ə-, §iː- ~s z
Elaine ɪ 'leɪn e-, ə-
El Al tdmk ,el 'æl
El Alamein ⱥel 'æl ə meɪn •,••'•
Elam 'iːl əm
Elamite 'iːl ə maɪt ~s s

elan, élan eɪ ˈlɒ̃ ɪ-, -ˈlɑːn, -ˈlæn; ˈeɪl ɒn
  ‖ eɪ ˈlɑːn —*Fr* [e lɑ̃]
é|lan vi'tal viː ˈtæl -ˈtɑːl —*Fr* [vi tal]
Elan *tdmk for car* ɪ ˈlæn eɪ-
Elan *valley in Wales* ˈiːl ən
eland ˈiːl ənd ~s z
elapid ˈel ə pɪd §-əp əd ~s z
elaps|e ɪ ˈlæps ə- ~ed t ~es ɪz əz ~ing ɪŋ
elastic ɪ ˈlæst ɪk ə-, -ˈlɑːst- ~ally ᵊl_i ~s s
  e,lastic 'band
elasti|cate ɪ ˈlæst ɪ ǀkeɪt ə-, -ˈlɑːst- ~cated
  keɪt ɪd -əd ‖ keɪt̬ əd ~cates keɪts ~cating
  keɪt ɪŋ ‖ keɪt̬ ɪŋ
elasticity ˌiːl æ ˈstɪs ət i ˌel-, ˌ•ɑː-, -ɪt i; ɪ ˌlæ-,
  ə-, -ˌlɑː- ‖ -ət̬ i
Elastoplast *tdmk* ɪ ˈlæst əʊ plɑːst ə-, -ˈlɑːst-,
  -plæst ‖ -ə plæst
e|late ɪ ǀˈleɪt ə-, iː- ~lated ˈleɪt ɪd -əd ‖ ˈleɪt̬ əd
  ~lates ˈleɪts ~lating ˈleɪt ɪŋ ‖ ˈleɪt̬ ɪŋ
elated ɪ ˈleɪt ɪd ə-, iː-, -əd ‖ -ˈleɪt̬ əd ~ly li
  ~ness nəs nɪs
elation ɪ ˈleɪʃ ᵊn ə-, iː-
elative ˈiːl ət ɪv ɪ ˈleɪt-, iː- ‖ -ət̬- ~s z
Elba ˈelb ə —*It* [ˈel ba]
Elbe elb —*Ger* [ˈʔɛl bə]
Elbert ˈelb ət ‖ -ᵊrt
elbow ˈel bəʊ ‖ -boʊ ~ed d ~ing ɪŋ ~s z
  'elbow grease
elbowroom ˈel bəʊ ruːm -rʊm ‖ -boʊ-
El Cajon ˌel kə ˈhəʊn ‖ -ˈhoʊn —*Sp* El Cajón
  [el ka ˈxon]
elder, Elder ˈeld ə ‖ -ᵊr ~s z
  ˌelder 'brother; ˌelder 'statesman
elderberr|y ˈeld ə ˌber li -bᵊrˌli ‖ -ᵊr ˌber li
  ~ies iz
  ˌelderberry 'wine
elderflower ˈeld ə ˌflaʊ_ə ‖ -ᵊr ˌflaʊ_ᵊr ~s z
elder|ly ˈeld ᵊl li ‖ -ᵊr lli ~iness i nəs i nɪs
eldership ˈeld ə ʃɪp ‖ -ᵊr- ~s s
eldest ˈeld ɪst -əst
Eldon ˈeld ən
El Dorado ˌel də ˈrɑːd əʊ ‖ -oʊ -ˈreɪd-
Eldred ˈeldr ɪd -ed, -əd
eldrich ˈeldr ɪtʃ ˈel rɪtʃ
Eldridge ˈeldr ɪdʒ
Elea ˈiːl i_ə
Eleanor ˈel ən ə -ɪn- ‖ -ᵊr -ə nɔːr
Eleanora ˌel i_ə ˈnɔːr ə
Eleatic ˌel i ˈæt ɪk ◄ ˌiːl- ‖ -ˈæt̬-
Eleazar ˌel i ˈeɪz ə ‖ -ᵊr
elecampane ˌel i kæm ˈpeɪn ˌ•ə-
elect *adj, n, v* ɪ ˈlekt ə- ~ed ɪd əd ~ing ɪŋ ~s s
election ɪ ˈlek ʃᵊn ə- ~s z
electio|neer ɪ ˌlek ʃə ǀˈnɪə ə- -ǀˈnɪᵊr ~neered
  ˈnɪəd ‖ ˈnɪᵊrd ~neering ˈnɪər ɪŋ ‖ ˈnɪr ɪŋ
  ~neers ˈnɪəz ‖ ˈnɪᵊrz
elective ɪ ˈlekt ɪv ə- ~ly li
elector ɪ ˈlekt ə ə- ‖ -ᵊr ~s z
electoral ɪ ˈlekt ᵊr ᵊl ə-, →-ˈlek trᵊl; §-ˌlek ˈtɔːr
  ᵊl ◄ ~ly i
  e,lectoral 'college
electorate ɪ ˈlekt ᵊr_ət ə-, ‿ɪt ~s s

Electra ɪ ˈlek trə ə-
  E'lectra ˌcomplex
electret ɪ ˈlek trət ə-, -trɪt, -tret ~s s
electric ɪ ˈlek trɪk ə- ~s s
  e,lectric 'blanket; e,lectric 'chair; e,lectric
  'eel; e,lectric 'eye; e,lectric gui'tar;
  e,lectric 'shock, e,lectric 'shock ,therapy
electrical ɪ ˈlek trɪk ᵊl ə- ~ly _i
  e,lectrical ,engi'neering
electrician ɪ ˌlek ˈtrɪʃ ᵊn ə-, ˌel ek-, ˌel ɪk-,
  ˌɪl ek-, ˌiːl ek-, -ˈtrɪʒ- ~s z
electricity ɪ ˌlek ˈtrɪs ət i ə-, ˌel ek-, ˌel ɪk-,
  ˌɪl ek-, ˌiːl ek-, -ˈtrɪz-, -ɪt i ‖ -ət̬ i
electrification ɪ ˌlek trɪf ɪ ˈkeɪʃ ᵊn ə-, -, •trəf-,
  §-ə' • - ~s z
electri|fy ɪ ˈlek trɪ ǀfaɪ ə-, -trə- ~fied faɪd
  ~fier/s faɪ_ə/z ‖ faɪ_ᵊr/z ~fies faɪz ~fying
  faɪ ɪŋ
electro- *comb. form*
  with stress-neutral suffix ɪ ǀlek trəʊ ə-
  ‖ ɪ ǀlek troʊ -trə — **electrographic**
  ɪ ˌlek trəʊ ˈgræf ɪk ◄ ə- ‖ -troʊ- -trə-
  with stress-imposing suffix ɪ ˌlek ˈtrɒ+ ə-,
  ˌel ek-, ˌel ɪk-, ˌɪl ek-, ˌiːl ek- ‖ ɪ ˌlek ˈtrɑː+
  — **electrography** ɪ ˌlek ˈtrɒg rəf i ə-,
  ˌel ek-, ˌel ɪk-, ˌɪl ek-, ˌiːl ek- ‖ -ˈtrɑːg-
electrocardiogram ɪ ˌlek trəʊ ˈkɑːd i_əʊ græm
  ə- ‖ -troʊ ˈkɑːrd i_ə- ~s z
electrocardiograph ɪ ˌlek trəʊ ˈkɑːd i_əʊ grɑːf
  ə-, -græf ‖ -troʊ ˈkɑːrd i_ə græf ~s s
electrocardiography
  ɪ ˌlek trəʊ ˌkɑːd i ˈɒg rəf i ə-
  ‖ -troʊ ˌkɑːrd i ˈɑːg-
electroconvulsive ɪ ˌlek trəʊ kən ˈvʌls ɪv ə-
  ‖ -, • troʊ-
  e,lectrocon,vulsive 'therapy
electro|cute ɪ ˈlek trə ǀkjuːt ə- ~cuted
  kjuːt ɪd -əd ‖ kjuːt̬ əd ~cutes kjuːts
  ~cuting kjuːt ɪŋ ‖ kjuːt̬ ɪŋ
electrocution ɪ ˌlek trə ˈkjuːʃ ᵊn ə- ~s z
electrode ɪ ˈlek trəʊd ə- ‖ -troʊd ~s z
electrodynamic ɪ ˌlek trəʊ daɪ ˈnæm ɪk ◄ ə-,
  dɪ' • - ‖ -, • troʊ- ~ally ᵊl_i ~s s
electroencephalogram ɪ ˌlek trəʊ ɪn ˈsef
  ᵊl_ə græm ə-, -en' • -, -ˈkef-, -əʊ • ‖ -, • troʊ-
  ~s z
electroencephalograph ɪ ˌlek trəʊ ɪn ˈsef
  ᵊl_ə grɑːf ə-, -en' • -, -ˈkef-, -əʊ • , -græf
  ‖ -troʊ ɪn ˈsef ᵊl_ə græf ~s s
electrolier ɪ ˌlek trəʊ ˈlɪə ə- ‖ -trə ˈlɪᵊr ~s z
Electrolux *tdmk* ɪ ˈlek trəʊ lʌks ə- ‖ -troʊ-
electrolysis ɪ ˌlek ˈtrɒl əs ɪs ə-, ˌel ek-, ˌel ɪk-,
  ˌɪl ek-, ˌiːl ek-, -ɪs ɪs, §-əs ‖ -ˈtrɑːl-
electrolyte ɪ ˈlek trəʊ laɪt ‖ -trə- ~s s
electrolytic ɪ ˌlek trəʊ ˈlɪt ɪk ◄ ‖ -trə ˈlɪt̬-
electromagnet ɪ ˌlek trəʊ ˈmæg nɪt ə-, -nət
  ‖ -troʊ- ~s s
electromagnetic ɪ ˌlek trəʊ mæg ˈnet ɪk ◄ ə-,
  -məg' • - ‖ -troʊ mæg ˈnet̬- ~ally ᵊl_i
  e,lectromag,netic 'spectrum
electromagnetism ɪ ˌlek trəʊ ˈmæg nə ˌtɪz əm
  ə-, -' • nɪ- ‖ -, • troʊ-

E

electromotive ɪ ˌlek trəʊ ˈməʊt ɪv ◂ ə-
‖ -troʊ ˈmoʊt̮ ɪv ◂ -trə-
  e͵lectro͵motive ˈforce

electromyogram ɪ ˌlek trəʊ ˈmaɪˌə ɡræm ə-
‖ -ˌ•ˌtroʊ-

electromyography ɪ ˌlek trəʊ maɪ ˈɒɡ rəf i ə-
‖ -troʊ maɪ ˈɑːɡ-

electron ɪ ˈlek trɒn ə- ‖ -trɑːn ~s z
  e͵lectron ˈmicroscope ‖ •ˈ•• ͵•••

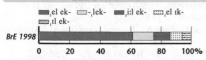

ELECTRONIC

■ˌel ek- □ -ˌlek- ■ˌiːl ek- ▨ˌel ɪk-
▨ˌɪl ek-

BrE 1998

0   20   40   60   80   100%

electronic ˌel ek ˈtrɒn ɪk ◂ ɪ ͵lek-, ə-; ͵el ɪk-,
ˌɪl ek-, ˌiːl ek- ‖ ɪ ˌlek ˈtrɑːn ɪk ◂ ~ally ᵊl‿i
~s s —BrE 1998 poll panel preference: ˌel ek-
61%, -ˌ lek- 14%, ˌiːl ek- 11%, ˌel ɪk- 8%,
ˌɪl ek- 6%

electropalatogram ɪ ˌlek trəʊ ˈpæl ət ə ɡræm
ə-, -ˈ•ə təʊ- ‖ -troʊ ˈpæl ət̮ ə-

electropalatography
  ɪ ˌlek trəʊ ͵pæl ə ˈtɒɡ rəf i ə-
‖ -troʊ ͵pæl ə ˈtɑːɡ-

electro|plate ɪ ˈlek trəʊ |pleɪt ə-, •ˌ•••ˈ• ‖ -trə-
~plated pleɪt ɪd -əd ‖ pleɪt̮ əd ~plates pleɪts
~plating pleɪt ɪŋ ‖ pleɪt̮ ɪŋ

electroscope ɪ ˈlek trəʊ skəʊp ə- ‖ -trə skoʊp
~s s

electroshock ɪ ˈlek trəʊ ʃɒk ə- ‖ -troʊ ʃɑːk
-trə-

electrostatic ɪ ͵lek trəʊ ˈstæt ɪk ◂ ə-
‖ -trə ˈstæt̮ ɪk ◂ ~ally ᵊl‿i ~s s

electrotyp|e ɪ ˈlek trəʊ taɪp ə- ‖ -trə- ~ed t
~es s ~ing ɪŋ

electrum ɪ ˈlek trəm ə-

electuar|y ɪ ˈlekt ju‿ər li ə- ‖ ɪ ˈlek tʃu er li
~ies iz

eleemosynary ˌel i iː ˈmɒz ɪn ər‿i ͵el i: ˈmɒz-,
ˌ•ɪ-, -ˈmɒs-, -ˈməʊz-, -ˈ•ən-
‖ ͵el ə ˈmɑːs ə ner i ˌ•ɪ-, -ˈmɑːz-, -ˈmoʊs-

elegance ˈel ɪɡ ən¹s -əɡ-

elegant ˈel ɪɡ ənt -əɡ- ~ly li

elegiac ͵el ɪ ˈdʒaɪˌək ◂ ə-, -æk ~s s
  ele͵giac ˈcouplet

elegis|e, elegiz|e ˈel ə dʒaɪz -ɪ- ~ed d ~es ɪz
əz ~ing ɪŋ

elegist ˈel ədʒ ɪst -ɪdʒ-, §-əst ~s s

eleg|y ˈel ədʒ li -ɪdʒ- ~ies iz

element ˈel ɪ mənt -ə- ~s s

elemental ͵el ɪ ˈment ᵊl ◂ -ə- ‖ -ˈment̮ ᵊl ◂ ~ly
i

elementar|y ͵el ɪ ˈment‿ər li ◂ ͵•ˌ•ə- ‖ -ˈment̮
ər li ◂→-ˈmentr li ~ily ᵊl i ɪ li ~iness i nəs
i nɪs
  ele͵mentary ˈparticle; ele͵mentary ˈschool

elenchus ɪ ˈleŋk əs ə-

Eleonora ͵el iˌə ˈnɔːr ə ɪ ͵leɪ ə-

elephant ˈel ɪf ənt -əf- ~s s

elephantiasis ͵el ɪf ən ˈtaɪˌəs ɪs -əf ən-,
-ɪ fæn-, -ə fæn-, §-əs

elephantine ͵el ɪ ˈfænt aɪn ◂ -ə- ‖ -iːn ◂ -aɪn;
ˈel əf ən tiːn, -taɪn

Eleusinian ͵el ju ˈsɪn iˌən ◂ ͵•u- ~s z

Eleusis ɪ ˈljuːs ɪs e-, ə-, -ˈluːs-, §-əs ‖ -ˈluːs-

Eleuthera ɪ ˈluːθ ər‿ə ə-, e-, -ˈljuːθ-

ele|vate ˈel ɪ |veɪt -ə- ~vated veɪt ɪd -əd
‖ veɪt̮ əd ~vates veɪts ~vating
veɪt ɪŋ ‖ veɪt̮ ɪŋ

elevation ͵el ɪ ˈveɪʃ ᵊn -ə- ~s z

elevator ˈel ɪ veɪt ə ͵•ˈ•ə- ‖ -veɪt̮ ᵊr ~s z
  ˈelevator ͵operator

eleven ɪ ˈlev ᵊn ə- ~s z

eleven-plus ɪ ͵lev ᵊn ˈplʌs ə-, →-ᵊm-

elevenses ɪ ˈlev ᵊnz ɪz ə-, -əz

eleventh ɪ ˈlev ᵊnᵗθ ə- ~s s
  e͵leventh ˈhour

elf, Elf elf elf's elfs elves elvz

Elfed ˈelv ed

elfin ˈelf ɪn §-ən

elfish ˈelf ɪʃ ~ly li ~ness nəs nɪs

Elfreda, Elfrida el ˈfriːd ə

Elgar ˈelɡ ɑː -ə ‖ -ɑːr -ᵊr

Elgin (i) ˈelɡ ɪn §-ən, (ii) ˈeldʒ ɪn -ən —For the
place in Scotland, and as a British name, (i); for
the place in IL, and as an American name, (ii).

El Greco el ˈɡrek əʊ ‖ -oʊ

Eli ˈiːl aɪ

Elia ˈiːl iˌə

Elias ɪ ˈlaɪˌəs ə-, -æs

elic|it ɪ ˈlɪs |ɪt ə-, iː-, §-lət ‖ -lət (usually = illicit)
~ited ɪt ɪd §ət-, -əd ‖ ət̮ əd ~iting ɪt ɪŋ §ət-
‖ ət̮ ɪŋ ~its ɪts §əts ‖ əts

elicitation ɪ ͵lɪs ɪ ˈteɪʃ ᵊn ə-, iː-, -ə- ~s z

elid|e ɪ ˈlaɪd ə-, iː- ~ed ɪd əd ~es z ~ing ɪŋ

eligibility ͵el ɪdʒ ə ˈbɪl ət i ͵•ˌədʒ-, -ɪˈ•-, -ɪt i
‖ -ət̮ i

eligib|le ˈel ɪdʒ əb |ᵊl ˈ•ədʒ-, -ɪb- ~ly li

Elihu ɪ ˈlaɪ hjuː e-, ə- ‖ ˈel ə hjuː

Elijah ɪ ˈlaɪdʒ ə ə-

Elim ˈiːl ɪm §-əm

elimi|nate ɪ ˈlɪm ɪ |neɪt ə-, §iː-, -ə- ~nated
neɪt ɪd -əd ‖ neɪt̮ əd ~nates neɪts ~nating
neɪt ɪŋ ‖ neɪt̮ ɪŋ

elimination ɪ ͵lɪm ɪ ˈneɪʃ ᵊn ə-, §iː-, -ə- ~s z

eliminator ɪ ˈlɪm ɪ neɪt ə ə-, §iː-, -ˈ•ə-
‖ -ˈneɪt̮ ᵊr ~s z

Elin ˈel ɪn -ən

Elinor ˈel ən ə -ɪn- ‖ -ən ᵊr -ə nɔːr

Eliot, Eliott ˈel iˌət

Elis ˈiːl ɪs §-əs

Elisabeth ɪ ˈlɪz əb əθ ə-

Elise ɪ ˈliːz ə-, e-

Elisha ɪ ˈlaɪʃ ə ə-

elision ɪ ˈlɪʒ ᵊn ə-, §iː- ~s z

elite, élite ɪ ˈliːt ₍ᵢ₎eɪ-, ə-, §iː- ~s s

elitism, élitism ɪ ˈliːt ͵ɪz əm eɪ-, ə-, §iː- ‖ -ˈliːt̮-

elitist, élitist ɪ ˈliːt ɪst ə-, §iː-, §-əst ‖ -ˈliːt̮- ~s s

elixir ɪ ˈlɪks ə e-, ə-, iː-, -ɪə; ˈel ɪk sɪə ‖ -ᵊr ~s z

Eliza ɪ ˈlaɪz ə ə-

Elizabeth ɪ ˈlɪz əb əθ ə- ~s, ~'s s

Elizabethan ɪ ͵lɪz ə ˈbiːθ ᵊn ◂ ə- ~s z

elk elk elks elks

Elkan (i) ˈelk ən, (ii) -ɑːn

Elision

1 **Elision** is the eliding (= omission, deletion) of a sound that would otherwise be present. It is particularly characteristic of rapid or casual speech. It is not random, but follows certain rules, which differ from one language to another.

2 Some types of possible elision can occur within words in isolation. They are shown in LPD by the use of *italic* symbols (or occasionally by raised symbols or by transcribing a second pronunciation). In English they include

- the elision of the middle part of ntʃ and ndʒ. For example, **lunch** lʌntʃ is pronounced lʌntʃ or, alternatively, lʌnʃ; **strange** streɪndʒ is streɪndʒ or streɪnʒ.
- the elision of the middle part of mps, mpt, nts, ŋks, ŋkt. For example, **jumped** dʒʌmpt is pronounced dʒʌmpt or, alternatively, dʒʌmt; **lynx** lɪŋks is lɪŋks or lɪŋs.

3 Other types of possible elision apply in compound words and in connected speech. They are shown in LPD for compounds, but naturally cannot be shown for connected speech. They include the elision of t and d at the end of a word, before a consonant at the beginning of the next word. Then

- t may be elided in ft, st, and less commonly in pt, kt, tʃt, θt, ʃt;
- d may be elided in ld, nd, and less commonly in bd, gd, dʒd, vd, ðd, zd, md, ŋd.

next	nekst	In isolation, or before a vowel sound, this word is pronounced nekst. But in a phrase such as **next thing**, **next question** it is often pronounced neks, with elision of the t.
stand	stænd	In isolation, or before a vowel sound, this word is pronounced stænd. But in a phrase such as **stand clear**, **stand firm** it is often pronounced stæn, with elision of the d.

4 The contracted negative **n't** ənt is a special case. Its t may be elided in connected speech, no matter what kind of sound follows. Thus when **didn't** ˈdɪd ənt is followed by another word or phrase, it is sometimes pronounced ˈdɪd ən.

5 The consonant h is often elided in unstressed syllables, and especially in weak forms of function words. Thus **him** is hɪm in isolation, or if stressed, but often ɪm when unstressed in a phrase such as **tell him**.

6 The vowel ə is subject to elision as follows.

- often (though not always) when it is followed by a nasal or liquid and then a WEAK vowel. There are two stages: first, the ə combines with the nasal or liquid, making the latter syllabic (see SYLLABIC CONSONANTS); then, the nasal or liquid may become non-syllabic (see COMPRESSION), in which case all trace of the ə has disappeared.

E

E

▶ *Elision*

camera 'kæm The full form is 'kæm.ər.ə. If ə is elided, in the first
ər_ə instance it makes the r syllabic: 'kæm.r̩.ə. This is usually
compressed to give 'kæm.rə. All three possibilities occur.

- sometimes, in casual speech, in the first syllable of a word in which the second syllable is stressed and begins with a liquid. The first syllable then undergoes compression. Thus **terrific** tə 'rɪf ɪk sometimes becomes 'trɪf ɪk, or **collide** kə 'laɪd becomes klaɪd. Since they are not found except in casual speech, these forms are not shown in LPD. The same applies to cases of apparent elision of ə in some speakers' occasional pronunciation of words such as **incident** 'ɪnᵗs əd ənt, **capacity** kə 'pæs ət i, where there seems to be a compensatory lengthening of the preceding consonant, giving the effect of 'ɪnᵗs: dənt, kə 'pæs: t i.

7 A pronunciation that originated through elision may become the only possibility for some speakers. Some people have 'kæm rə as the only pronunciation for **camera**, or pliːs as the only form for **police**. For many people it would feel very artificial to pronounce a t in **postman** 'pəʊs mən ‖ 'poʊs mən.

---

elkhound 'elk haʊnd ~s z
Elkie 'elk i
Elkins 'elk ɪnz
ell el **ells** elz
Ella 'el ə
Elland 'el ənd
Ellen 'el ən -ɪn
Ellery 'el ər i
Ellesmere 'elz mɪə ‖ -mɪr
  ˌEllesmere 'Port
Ellice 'el ɪs §-əs
Ellie 'el i
Ellington 'el ɪŋ tən
Elliot, Elliott 'el i_ət
ellips|e ɪ 'lɪps ə-, e- ~es ɪz əz
ellipses *pl of* **ellipse** ɪ 'lɪps ɪz ə-, e-, -əz
ellipses *pl of* **ellipsis** ɪ 'lɪps iːz ə-, e-
ellips|is ɪ 'lɪps ‖ɪs ə-, e-, §-əs ~es iːz
ellipsoid ɪ 'lɪps ɔɪd ə-, e- ~s z
ellipsoidal ˌel ɪp 'sɔɪd ᵊl ◂ ɪ ˌlɪp-, ə-, e-
ellipt ɪ 'lɪpt ə-, e- ~ed ɪd əd ~ing ɪŋ ~s s
elliptic ɪ 'lɪpt ɪk ə-, e- ~al ᵊl ~ally ᵊl_i
Ellis 'el ɪs §-əs
Ellison 'el ɪs ən -əs-
Ellsworth 'elz wɜːθ -wəθ ‖ -wɜːθ
elm elm **elms** elmz
Elmer 'elm ə ‖ -ᵊr
Elmes elmz
Elmet 'elm et -ɪt, §-ət
Elmhurst 'elm hɜːst ‖ -hɜːst
Elmira el 'maɪᵊr ə
Elmo 'elm əʊ ‖ -oʊ
El Monte el 'mɒnt i ‖ -'mɑːnt i —*Sp* [el 'mon te]

Elmwood 'elm wʊd
El Niño el 'niːn jəʊ ‖ -joʊ —*Sp* [el 'ni ɲo]
elocution ˌel ə 'kjuːʃ ᵊn
elocutionary ˌel ə 'kjuːʃ ᵊn ər_i ◂ -'•ᵊn_ər i
  ‖ -ə ner i
elocutionist ˌel ə 'kjuːʃ ᵊn_ɪst §_əst ~s s
Elohim e 'ləʊ hɪm ɪ-, ə-; ˌel əʊ 'hiːm ‖ -'loʊ-
  ˌel oʊ 'hiːm
Eloise ˌel əʊ 'iːz ‖ -oʊ- '•••
elon|gate 'iː lɒŋ ˌgeɪt ‖ ɪ 'lɔːŋ ˌgeɪt -'lɑːŋ- (*)
  ~gated geɪt ɪd -əd ‖ geɪt̬ əd ~gates geɪts
  ~gating geɪt ɪŋ ‖ geɪt̬ ɪŋ
elongation ˌiː lɒŋ 'geɪʃ ᵊn ‖ ɪ ˌlɔːŋ 'geɪʃ ᵊn
  -ˌlɑːŋ-; ˌiː lɔːŋ-, -lɑːŋ- ~s z
elop|e ɪ 'ləʊp ə-, §i:- ‖ -'loʊp ~ed t ~ement/
  s mənt/s ~es s ~ing ɪŋ
eloquence 'el ək wənᵗs
eloquent 'el ək wənt ~ly li ~ness nəs nɪs
El Paso el 'pæs əʊ ‖ -oʊ —*Sp* [el 'pa so]
Elphick 'elf ɪk
Elphinstone 'elf ɪn stən §-ᵊn-, -stəʊn ‖ -stoʊn
El Portal ˌel pɔː 'tæl ‖ -pɔːr-
Elroy 'el rɔɪ
Elsa 'els ə —*but as a German name, also* 'elz-
  —*Ger* ['ʔɛl za]
El Salvador ₍ˌ₎el 'sælv ə dɔː ‖ -dɔːr —*Sp*
  [el sal βa 'ðor]
Elsan *tdmk* 'el sæn
Elsbeth 'els bəθ
else, Else els
elsewhere ˌels 'weə -'hweə, '•• ‖ 'els ʰwer
  -ʰwær
Elsie 'els i

Elsinore 'els ɪ nɔː -ə-, ˌ•'•'• ‖ ˌels ə 'nɔːr -'nour
—*Danish* Helsingør [hɛl seŋ 'ø:ʔʁ]
Elspeth 'els pəθ
Elstow 'el stəʊ ‖ -stoʊ
Elstree 'els triː 'elz-, -tri
Elswick 'elz ɪk 'els-, -wɪk —*In Tyne and Wear,
locally* -ɪk
Elsworthy 'elz ˌwɜːð i ‖ -ˌwɝːð i
ELT ˌiː el 'tiː
Eltham (i) 'elt əm, (ii) 'elθ əm —*The place in
London is (i); those in Australia and NZ, (ii)*
Elton 'elt ən
eluci|date ɪ 'luːs ɪ ˌdeɪt ə-, iː-, -'ljuːs-, -ə-
~dated deɪt ɪd -əd ‖ deɪt̬ əd **~dates** deɪts
~dating deɪt ɪŋ ‖ deɪt̬ ɪŋ
elucidation ɪ ˌluːs ɪ 'deɪʃ ən ə-, iː-, -, ljuːs-, -ə-
~s z
elucidatory ɪ 'luːs ɪ deɪt ər i ə-, iː-, •, ••'••• •
‖ -əd ə tɔːr i -toʊr i
elud|e ɪ 'luːd ə-, iː-, -'ljuːd **~ed** ɪd əd **~es** z
~ing ɪŋ
Eluned e 'lɪn ed -'liːn-
elusive ɪ 'luːs ɪv ə-, iː-, -'ljuːs- **~ly** li **~ness**
nəs nɪs
elusory ɪ 'luːs ər i ə-, iː-, -'ljuːs-
elute ɪ 'luːt ə-, iː-, -'ljuːt **eluted** ɪ 'luːt ɪd ə-,
iː-, -'ljuːt-, -əd ‖ -'luːt̬- **~s** s **eluting**
ɪ 'luːt ɪŋ ə-, iː-, -'ljuːt- ‖ -'luːt̬-
elusion ɪ 'luːʃ ən ə-, iː-, -'ljuːʃ-
Elva 'elv ə
elver 'elv ə ‖ -ər **~s** z
elves elvz
Elvin 'elv ɪn §-ən
Elvira (i) el 'vɪər ə ‖ -'vɪr ə, (ii) -'vaɪər ə
Elvis 'elv ɪs §-əs
elvish 'elv ɪʃ
Elwes 'el wɪz -wəz
Elwyn 'el wɪn
Ely *place name* 'iːl i
Ely *American personal name* 'iːl aɪ
Elyot 'el i ̩ət
Elysee, Elysée eɪ 'liːz eɪ ɪ-, ə- ‖ ˌeɪl i: 'zeɪ —*Fr*
[e li ze]
Elysian, e~ ɪ 'lɪz i ̩ən ə-, iː- ‖ ɪ 'lɪʒ ən -'liːʒ-
Elysium ɪ 'lɪz i ̩əm ə-, iː- ‖ ɪ 'lɪʒ- -'liːʒ-, -'lɪz-
elytron 'el ɪ trɒn -ə-; -ɪtr ən, -ətr- ‖ -ə traːn
Elzevier, Elzevir 'elz ə vɪə 'els- ‖ -vɪr —*Dutch*
['ɛl zə viːr]
em em
em- ɪm, (ˌ)em —*This prefix is stressed* ˌem *if the
following syllable is unstressed* (ˌembroˈcation).
Otherwise it is unstressed (emˈbalm). *When it is
unstressed, a weak-vowel form* ɪm *is preferred
in RP, although some speakers, particularly
regional ones, use a strong-vowel form* em.
'em *pronoun* əm —*This variant of* them *has no
strong form.*
emaci|ate ɪ 'meɪʃ i ̩eɪt ə-, iː-, -'meɪs- **~ated**
eɪt ɪd -əd ‖ eɪt̬ əd **~ates** eɪts **~ating**
eɪt ɪŋ ‖ eɪt̬ ɪŋ
emaciation ɪ ˌmeɪʃ i 'eɪʃ ən ə-, iː-, -, meɪs-
e-mail 'iː meɪəl **~ed** d **~ing** ɪŋ **~s** z

ema|nate 'em ə ˌneɪt **~nated** neɪt ɪd -əd
‖ neɪt̬ əd **~nates** neɪts **~nating**
neɪt ɪŋ ‖ neɪt̬ ɪŋ
emanation ˌem ə 'neɪʃ ən **~s** z
emanative 'em ə neɪt ɪv -nət ɪv ‖ -neɪt̬ ɪv
emanatory 'em ə neɪt ər i , ••'•••;
'em ən ət ̩ər i ‖ -ən ə tɔːr i -toʊr i
emanci|pate ɪ 'mæn⁀s ɪ ˌpeɪt ə-, §iː-, -ə-
~pated peɪt ɪd -əd ‖ peɪt̬ əd **~pates** peɪts
~pating peɪt ɪŋ ‖ peɪt̬ ɪŋ
emancipation ɪ ˌmæn⁀s ɪ 'peɪʃ ən ə-, §iː-, -ə-
~s z
emancipator ɪ 'mæn⁀s ɪ peɪt ə ə-, §iː-, -'•ə-
‖ -peɪt̬ ər **~s** z
Emanuel ɪ 'mæn ju ̩əl ə- —*but in singing
usually* -el
emascu|late v ɪ 'mæsk ju ˌleɪt ə-, iː- ‖ -jə-
~lated leɪt ɪd -əd ‖ leɪt̬ əd **~lates** leɪts
~lating leɪt ɪŋ ‖ leɪt̬ ɪŋ
emasculate *adj* ɪ 'mæsk jʊl ət ə-, iː-, -ɪt,
-ju leɪt ‖ -jəl-
emasculation ɪ ˌmæsk ju 'leɪʃ ən ə-, iː- ‖ -jə-
~s z
embalm ɪm 'baːm em-, §-'baːlm **~ed** d **~er/s**
ə/z ‖ ər/z **~ing** ɪŋ **~s** z
embalmment ɪm 'baːm mənt em-, §-'baːlm-
~s s
embankment ɪm 'bæŋk mənt em- **~s** s
embarcadero, E~ em ˌbaːk ə 'deər əʊ ɪm-, əm-
‖ -ˌbaːrk ə 'der oʊ **~s** z
embargo ɪm 'baːg əʊ em- ‖ -'baːrg oʊ **~ed** d
~es z **~ing** ɪŋ
embark ɪm 'baːk em- ‖ -'baːrk **~ed** t **~ing** ɪŋ
~s s
embarkation ˌem baː 'keɪʃ ən ‖ -baːr- **~s** z
embarras de richesses
ɒm ˌbær aː də ri: 'ʃes ˌɑːm baː ˌraː- —*Fr*
[ɑ̃ ba ʁa dʁi ʃɛs]
embarrass ɪm 'bær əs em- ‖ -'ber- **~ed** t **~es**
ɪz əz **~ing/ly** ɪŋ /li **~ment/s** mənt/s
embass|y 'em bəs li **~ies** iz
embattl|e ɪm 'bæt əl em- ‖ -'bæt̬ əl **~ed** d **~es**
z **~ing** ̩ɪŋ
embed ɪm 'bed em- **~ded** ɪd əd **~ding** ɪŋ **~s**
z
embellish ɪm 'bel ɪʃ em- **~ed** t **~es** ɪz əz
~ing ɪŋ **~ment/s** mənt/s
ember, Ember 'em bə ‖ -bər **~s** z
'Ember day
embezzl|e ɪm 'bez əl em- **~ed** d **~es** z **~ing**
̩ɪŋ
embezzlement ɪm 'bez əl mənt em- **~s** s
embezzler ɪm 'bez əl̩ə em- ‖ -̩ər **~s** z
embitter ɪm 'bɪt ə em- ‖ -'bɪt̬ ər **~ed** d
embittering ɪm 'bɪt̩ər ɪŋ em- ‖ -'bɪt̬ ər- **~s**
z
embitterment ɪm 'bɪt ə mənt em- ‖ -'bɪt̬ ər-
emblazon ɪm 'bleɪz ən em- **~ed** d **~ing** ̩ɪŋ
~ment mənt **~s** z
emblem 'em bləm -blɪm **~s** z
emblematic ˌem blə 'mæt ɪk ◄ -blɪ- ‖ -'mæt̬-
~ally əl̩i
emblement 'em blə mənt -bəl- **~s** s

embodiment ɪm 'bɒd i mənt em- ‖ -'bɑːd- ~s
s
embod|ly ɪm 'bɒd li em- ‖ -'bɑːd li ~ied ɪd
~ies ɪz ~ying i_ɪŋ
embolden ɪm 'bəʊld ən em-, →-'bɒʊld-
‖ -'boʊld- ~ed d ~ing ɪŋ ~s z
emboli 'em bə laɪ
embolic em 'bɒl ɪk ‖ -'bɑːl-
embolism 'em bə ˌlɪz əm ~s z
em|bolus 'em |bəl əs ~boli bə laɪ
embonpoint ˌɒm bɒn 'pwæ̃ ˌ-ɒ̃-, →-bɒm-, -bɒ̃-,
-'pwɒ̃ ‖ ˌɑːm boʊn 'pwæn —Fr [ɑ̃ bɔ̃ pwæ̃]
embosomed ɪm 'bʊz əmd em-, §-'buːz-
emboss ɪm 'bɒs em- ‖ -'bɑːs -'bɔːs ~ed t ~es
ɪz əz ~ing ɪŋ
embouchure ˌɒm bu 'ʃʊə '··· ‖ ˌɑːm bu 'ʃʊ∘r
'ɑːm bə ʃʊr —Fr [ɑ̃ bu ʃyːʁ] ~s z
embourgeoisement
ˌɒm bʊəʒ 'waːz mɒ̃ ‖ em 'bʊrʒ waːz mɑːnt
ɑːm-, -mənt —Fr [ɑ̃ buʁ ʒwaz mɑ̃]
embowered ɪm 'baʊ_əd em- ‖ -'baʊ_∘rd
embrac|e ɪm 'breɪs em- ~ed t ~er/s ə/z ‖ ∘r/z
~es ɪz əz ~ing ɪŋ
embrasure ɪm 'breɪʒ ə em- ‖ -∘r ~s z
embrocation ˌem brə 'keɪʃ ən ~s z
embroider ɪm 'brɔɪd ə em- ‖ -∘r ~ed d
embroidering ɪm 'brɔɪd_ər ɪŋ em- ~s z
embroider|y ɪm 'brɔɪd_ər li em- ~ies ɪz
embroil ɪm 'brɔɪ∘l em- ~ed d ~ing ɪŋ ~s z
embryo 'em bri əʊ ‖ -oʊ ~s z
embryo- comb. form
with stress-neutral suffix ¦em bri əʊ ‖ -ə —
embryotome 'em bri əʊ təʊm ‖ -ə toʊm
with stress-imposing suffix ˌem bri 'ɒ+ ‖ -'ɑː+
— embryotomy ˌem bri 'ɒt əm i ‖ -'ɑːt̬-
embryology ˌem bri 'ɒl ədʒ i ‖ -'ɑːl-
embryonic ˌem bri 'ɒn ɪk ◄ ‖ -'ɑːn- ~ally ∘l_i
Emburey, Embury 'em bər i -bjʊr-
embus ɪm 'bʌs em- ~ed, ~sed t ~es, ~ses ɪz
əz ~ing, ~sing ɪŋ
emcee ˌem 'siː ~d d ~ing ɪŋ ~s z
-eme iːm — grapheme 'græf iːm —Although
strong-vowelled, this suffix is unstressed.
Emeline 'em ə liːn -ɪ-
emend ɪ 'mend ə-, iː- ~ed ɪd əd ~ing ɪŋ ~s z
emendation ˌiːm en 'deɪʃ ən ˌem-, -ən- ~s z
Emeney, Emeny 'em ən i
emerald 'em ∘r_əld ~s z
emerg|e ɪ 'mɜːdʒ ə-, iː- ‖ -'mɝːdʒ ~ed d ~es
ɪz əz ~ing ɪŋ
emergenc|e ɪ 'mɜːdʒ ənᵗs ə-, iː- ‖ -'mɝːdʒ-
~es ɪz əz
emergenc|y ɪ 'mɜːdʒ ənᵗs li ə-, §iː- ‖ -'mɝːdʒ-
~ies ɪz
emergent ɪ 'mɜːdʒ ənt ə-, iː- ‖ -'mɝːdʒ-
emeritus ɪ 'mer ɪt əs ə-, iː-, -ət- ‖ -ət̬ əs
Emerson 'em əs ən ‖ -∘rs-
emery, Emery 'em ∘r_i
'emery ˌpaper
emetic ɪ 'met ɪk ə-, iː- ‖ -'met̬ ɪk ~ally ∘l_i ~s
s
emetine 'em ɪ tiːn -ə-, -tɪn, -taɪn
EMF, emf ˌiː em 'ef

EMG ˌiː em 'dʒiː
EMI tdmk ˌiː em 'aɪ
emic 'iːm ɪk ~ally ∘l_i
emigrant 'em ɪg rənt -əg- ~s s
emi|grate 'em ɪ |greɪt -ə- ~grated greɪt ɪd -əd
‖ greɪt̬ əd ~grates greɪts ~grating
greɪt ɪŋ ‖ greɪt̬ ɪŋ
emigration ˌem ɪ 'greɪʃ ən -ə-
emigre, emigré, émigré 'em ɪ greɪ -ə- ~s z
Emil e 'miː∘l eɪ- —Ger ['ʔeː miːl]
Emile, Émile e 'miː∘l eɪ- —Fr [e 'mil]
Emily 'em əl i -ɪl-
eminenc|e, E~ 'em ɪn ənᵗs -ən- ~es ɪz əz —but
as a French word see next entry
eminence grise, éminence grise, éminences
grises ˌem i nɒ̃s 'griːz ‖ ˌeɪm i nɑːs- —Fr
[e mi nɑ̃s griːz]
eminent 'em ɪn ənt -ən- ~ly li
emir e 'mɪə ɪ-, ə-, eɪ-; 'em ɪə ‖ -'mɪ∘r ~s z
emirate 'em ∘r ət -ɪər-, -ɪt, -eɪt; e 'mɪər-,
i- ‖ ɪ 'mɪr- ~s s
emissar|y 'em ɪs ∘r_i ‖ -ə ser li ~ies ɪz
emission ɪ 'mɪʃ ∘n ə-, iː- ~s z
emissive ɪ 'mɪs ɪv ə-, iː-
emissivity ˌiːm ɪ 'sɪv ət i ˌem-, ˌ•ə-, -ɪt i ‖ -ət̬ i
e|mit ɪ |'mɪt ə-, iː- ~mits 'mɪts ~mitted
'mɪt ɪd -əd ‖ 'mɪt̬ əd ~mitting
'mɪt ɪŋ ‖ 'mɪt̬ ɪŋ
Emley 'em li
Emlyn 'em lɪn §-lən
Emma 'em ə
Emmanuel ɪ 'mæn ju_əl ə-
Emmaus ɪ 'meɪ əs e-, ə-
Emmeline 'em ə liːn -ɪ-
emmenagogue ɪ 'men ə gɒg ə-, e-, -'miːn-
‖ -gɑːg ~s z
Emmental, Emmenthal 'em ən tɑːl ‖ -∘r/s ə/
z ‖ -∘r/z
emmer 'em ə ‖ -∘r
Emmerdale 'em ə deɪ∘l ‖ -∘r-
Emmerson 'em əs ən ‖ -∘rs-
emmet, Emmet, Emmett 'em ɪt §-ət ~s s
emmetropia ˌem ɪ 'trəʊp i_ə ˌ•ə- ‖ -'troʊp-
emmetropic ˌem ɪ 'trɒp ɪk ◄-ə- ‖ -'trɑːp-
Emmie, Emmy 'em i ~s z
emollient ɪ 'mɒl i_ənt ə-, iː- ‖ -'mɑːl- ~s s
emolument ɪ 'mɒl ju mənt ə-, §iː- ‖ -'mɑːl jə-
Emory 'em ∘r i
e|mote ɪ |'məʊt ə-, iː- ‖ -l'moʊt ~moted
'məʊt ɪd -əd ‖ 'moʊt̬ əd ~motes
'məʊts ‖ 'moʊts ~moting
'məʊt ɪŋ ‖ 'moʊt̬ ɪŋ
emoticon ɪ 'məʊt ɪ kɒn ə-, iː-, -'mɒt-, -ɪk ən,
-,aɪk ɒn ‖ -'moʊt̬ ɪ kɑːn ~s z
emotion ɪ 'məʊʃ ∘n ə-, §iː- ‖ -'moʊʃ- ~s z
emotional ɪ 'məʊʃ ∘n_əl ə-, §iː- ‖ -'moʊʃ-
~ism ˌɪz əm ~ly i
emotive ɪ 'məʊt ɪv ə-, iː- ‖ -'moʊt̬ ɪv ~ly li
~ness nəs nɪs
empanel ɪm 'pæn ∘l em- ~ed, ~led d ~ing,
~ling ɪŋ ~s z
empathetic ˌemp ə 'θet ɪk ◄ ‖ -'θet̬- ~ally ∘l_i

E-mail and the WWW

In an e-mail address the character @ is read as *at*. In an e-mail address or a URL (= an address on the World Wide Web), the punctuation mark <.> is read as *dot*. The punctuation mark </> is usually read as *slash* or *forward slash*, and <#> as *hash* (BrE) or *pound sign* (AmE).

Thus <someone@shopping.com> would be read as *someone at shopping dot com*; <staff@retail.co.uk> would be read as *staff at retail dot co dot you kay*.

empathis|e, empathiz|e 'emp ə θaɪz ~**ed** d
~**es** ɪz əz ~**ing** ɪŋ
empathy 'emp əθ i
Empedocles em 'ped ə kliːz ɪm-
emperor 'emp ər_ə ‖ -ʲr_ʲr ~**s** z ~**ship** ʃɪp
emph|asis 'empf |əs ɪs §-əs ~**ases** ə siːz
emphasis|e, emphasiz|e 'empf ə saɪz ~**ed** d
~**es** ɪz əz ~**ing** ɪŋ
emphatic ɪm 'fæt ɪk em- ‖ -'fæt̮ ɪk ~**ally** ᵊl_i
~**s** s
emphysema ˌempf ɪ 'siːm ə -ə-, -aɪ-, -'ziːm-;
△-'ziːm i_ə
emphysematous ˌempf ɪ 'sem ət əs ◂-ə-,
-'siːm-
empire, E~ 'emp aɪ_ə ‖ 'emp aɪʳr ~**s** z
ˌEmpire 'State ˌBuilding
empire-builder 'emp aɪ_ə ˌbɪld ə
‖ 'emp aɪʳr ˌbɪld ʳr ~**s** z
empiric ɪm 'pɪr ɪk em- ~**s** s
empirical ɪm 'pɪr ɪk ᵊl em- ~**ly** _i
empiricism ɪm 'pɪr ɪ ˌsɪz əm em-, -'•ə-
emplacement ɪm 'pleɪs mənt em- ~**s** s
emplan|e ɪm 'pleɪn em- ~**ed** d ~**es** z ~**ing** ɪŋ
employ ɪm 'plɔɪ em-, əm- ~**ed** d ~**ing** ɪŋ ~**s** z
employee ɪm 'plɔɪ iː em-, əm-; ˌem plɔɪ 'iː,
ˌɪm- ‖ •, •'• ~**s** z
employer ɪm 'plɔɪ ə em-, əm- ‖ -ʲr ~**s** z
employment ɪm 'plɔɪ mənt em-, əm- ~**s** s
em'ployment ˌagency
empori|um em 'pɔːr i_|əm ɪm- ‖ -'poʊr- ~**a** ə
~**ums** əmz
empower ɪm 'paʊ_ə em- ‖ -'paʊ_ʳr ~**ed** d
em**powering** ɪm 'paʊ_ʳr ɪŋ em-
‖ -'paʊ_ʳr ɪŋ ~**ment** mənt ~**s** z
empress 'emp rəs -rɪs ~**es** ɪz əz
Empson 'emps ᵊn
empt|y 'empt |i ~**ied** id ~**ier** i_ə ‖ i_ʲr ~**ies** iz
~**iest** i_ɪst i_əst ~**ily** ɪ li əl i ~**iness** i nəs i nɪs
~**ying** i_ɪŋ
empty-handed ˌempt i 'hænd ɪd ◂-əd
empty-headed ˌempt i 'hed ɪd ◂-əd ~**ness**
nəs nɪs
empurpled ɪm 'pɜːp ᵊld em- ‖ -'pɜˑːp-
empyema ˌemp aɪ 'iːm ə
empyre|al ˌemp ɪ 'riː_ᵊl ◂-aɪʳ-, -ə- ~**an** ən
Emrys 'em rɪs —*Welsh* ['em ris, -ris]
Ems emz —*Ger* [ʔɛms]
EMS ˌi: em 'es
Emsworth 'emz wəθ -wɜːθ ‖ -wɜˑːθ

emu 'iːm juː ~**s** z
EMU ˌi: em 'juː 'iːm juː
emu|late 'em ju |leɪt -jə- ‖ -jə- ~**lated** leɪt ɪd
-əd ‖ leɪt̮ əd ~**lates** leɪts ~**lating**
leɪt ɪŋ ‖ leɪt̮ ɪŋ
emulation ˌem ju 'leɪʃ ᵊn -jə- ‖ -jə- ~**s** z
emulator 'em ju leɪt ə '•jə- ‖ -jə leɪt̮ ʳr ~**s** z
emulous 'em jʊl əs -jəl- ‖ -jəl- ~**ly** li ~**ness**
nəs nɪs
emulsification ɪ ˌmʌls ɪf ɪ 'keɪʃ ᵊn ə-, -ˌ•əf-,
§-ə'•
emulsi|fy ɪ 'mʌls ɪ |faɪ ə-, -ə- ~**fied** faɪd
~**fier/s** faɪ_ə/z ‖ faɪ_ʳr/z ~**fies** faɪz ~**fying**
faɪ ɪŋ
emulsion ɪ 'mʌl ʃᵊn ə- ~**ed** d ~**ing** _ɪŋ ~**s** z
e'mulsion paint
Emyr 'em ɪə ‖ -ɪr —*Welsh* ['em ir, -ir]
en *printer's measure* en **ens** enz
en *in French phrases* ɒ̃ ɒn, ɑːn ‖ ɑ̃: ɑːn —*Fr* [ɑ̃]
—*See also phrases with this word*
en- ɪn ən, (ˌ)en —*This prefix is stressed* ˌen *if the
following syllable is unstressed* (ˌenhar'monic).
*Otherwise the prefix is unstressed, and the
weak-vowel form* ɪn *is preferred in RP*
(en'large), *although some speakers, in Britain
particularly regional ones, use* en *or* ən.
-en ᵊn, ən, ɪn— **wooden** 'wʊd ᵊn **blacken**
'blæk ᵊn **woollen** 'wʊl ən
Ena 'iːn ə
enabl|e ɪn 'eɪb ᵊl en-, ən- ~**ed** d ~**ement**
mənt ~**er/s** _ə/z ‖ _ʲr/z ~**es** z ~**ing** _ɪŋ
enact ɪn 'ækt en-, ən- ~**ed** ɪd əd ~**ing** ɪŋ
~**ment/s** mənt/s ~**s** s
enamel ɪ 'næm ᵊl ə- ~**ed**, ~**led** d ~**er/s**, ~**ler/s**
ə/z ‖ ʲr/z ~**ing**, ~**ling** ɪŋ ~**ist/s**, ~**list/s** ɪst/s
§-əst/s ~**s** z
enamelware ɪ 'næm ᵊl weə ə- ‖ -wer
enamor, enamour ɪn 'æm ə en-, ən- ‖ -ʲr ~**ed**
d
enantio- *comb. form*
with stress-neutral suffix en ˌænt i_əʊ ɪn-
‖ ˌænt̮ i_ə— **enantiomorph** en 'ænt i əʊ
mɔːf ɪn- ‖ ɪn 'ænt̮ i_ə mɔːrf
with stress-imposing suffix en ˌænt i 'ɒ+ ɪn-
‖ ɪn ˌænt̮ i 'ɑː+— **enantiopathy**
en ˌænt i 'ɒp əθ i ɪn- ‖ ɪn ˌænt̮ i 'ɑːp-
enarthrosis ˌen ɑː 'θrəʊs ɪs §-əs ‖ -ɑːr 'θroʊs-
en bloc ˌɒ̃ 'blɒk ˌɒn-, →ˌɒm-, ˌɑːn-, →ˌɑːm-
‖ ˌɑ̃: 'blɑːk ˌɑːn- —*Fr* [ɑ̃ blɔk]

E

en brochette ˌɒ̃ brɒ ˈʃet ˌɒn-, →ˌɒm-
‖ ˌɑ̃: broʊ- —*Fr* [ɑ̃ bʁɔ ʃɛt]
en brosse ˌɒ̃ ˈbrɒs ˌɒn-, →ˌɒm- ‖ ˌɑːn ˈbrɔːs
-ˈbrɑːs —*Fr* [ɑ̃ bʁɔs]
encaenia, E~ en ˈsiːn i‿ə
encamp ɪn ˈkæmp en-, →ɪŋ-, →eŋ- **~ed** t
~ing ɪŋ **~ment/s** mənt/s **~s** s
encapsu|late ɪn ˈkæps ju lleɪt en-, ən-, →ɪŋ-,
→eŋ-, →əŋ-, §-ə-, §-ˈkæp ʃə- ‖ -ə- **~lated**
leɪt ɪd -əd ‖ leɪt̮ əd **~lates** leɪts **~lating**
leɪt ɪŋ ‖ leɪt̮ ɪŋ
encapsulation ɪn ˌkæps ju ˈleɪʃ ən en-, ən-,
→ɪŋ-, →eŋ-, →əŋ-, §-ə-, §-ˌkæp ʃə- ‖ -ə- **~s**
z
Encarta *tdmk* ɪn ˈkɑːt ə en-, →ɪŋ-, →eŋ-
‖ -ˈkɑːrt̮ ə
encas|e ɪn ˈkeɪs en-, →ɪŋ-, →eŋ- **~ed** t
~ement mənt **~es** ɪz əz **~ing** ɪŋ
encash ɪn ˈkæʃ en-, →ɪŋ-, →eŋ- **~able** əb əl
~ed t **~es** ɪz əz **~ing** ɪŋ **~ment/s** mənt/s
encaustic ɪn ˈkɔːst ɪk en-, →ɪŋ-, →eŋ-, -ˈkɒst-
‖ -ˈkɔːst- -ˈkɑːst- **~s** s
-ence ənts —*The two possible stress-effects of
this suffix are illustrated in* ˌcorreˈspondence
and maˈlevolence. *In a few words it triggers a
vowel change and shift of stress in the stem, as*
prevail prɪ ˈveɪəl → prevalence ˈprev əl ənts,
confide kən ˈfaɪd → confidence ˈkɒn fɪd ənts.
There is fluctuation in precedence, subsidence.
enceinte ˌ(ˌ)ɒn ˈsænt ˌ(ˌ)ɒ̃- ‖ ˌ(ˌ)ɑ̃ː- —*Fr* [ɑ̃ sæ̃t]
Enceladus en ˈsel əd əs
encephalic ˌen kɪ ˈfæl ɪk ◀→ˌeŋ-, -kə-, -ke-;
ˌen sɪ-, -sə-, -se- ‖ -sə-
encepha|litic en ˌkef ə lˈlɪt ɪk ◀→eŋ-, en ˌsef-,
ɪn-, ˌen kef-, ˌen sef- ‖ ɪn ˌsef ə lˈlɪt̮ ɪk ◀
~litis ˈlaɪt ɪs §-əs ‖ ˈlaɪt̮ əs
encephalo- *comb. form*
with stress-neutral suffix en ˌkef əl əʊ →eŋ-,
ɪn-, →ɪŋ-, en ˌsef-, ɪn ˌsef- ‖ ɪn ˌsef əl ə
encephalogram en ˈkef əl əʊ græm →eŋ-,
ɪn-, →ɪŋ-, en ˈsef-, ɪn ˈsef- ‖ ɪn ˈsef
əl ə græm
with stress-imposing suffix en ˌkef ə ˈlɒ+ →eŋ-,
en ˌsef-, ˌ• •-, ɪn, •- ‖ ɪn ˌsef ə ˈlɑː+ —
encephalopathy en ˌkef ə ˈlɒp əθ i →eŋ-,
en ˌsef-, ˌ• •-, ɪn, •- ‖ ɪn ˌsef ə ˈlɑːp-
encephalomyelitis en ˌkef ə ləʊ ˌmaɪ‿ə ˈlaɪt ɪs
→eŋ-, en ˌsef-, ˌ• •-, ɪn, •-
‖ ɪn ˌsef ə loʊ ˌmaɪ‿ə ˈlaɪt̮ əs
enchain ɪn ˈtʃeɪn en-, ən- **~ed** d **~ing** ɪŋ
~ment mənt **~s** z
en|chant ɪn lˈtʃɑːnt en-, ən-, §-ˈtʃænt
‖ -lˈtʃænt **~chanted** ˈtʃɑːnt ɪd §ˈtʃænt-, -əd
‖ ˈtʃænt̮ əd **~chanting** ˈtʃɑːnt ɪŋ §ˈtʃænt-
‖ ˈtʃænt̮ ɪŋ
enchanter ɪn ˈtʃɑːnt ə en-, ən-, §-ˈtʃænt-
‖ -ˈtʃænt̮ ər **~s** z
enchanting ɪn ˈtʃɑːnt ɪŋ en-, ən-, §ˈtʃænt-
‖ -ˈtʃænt̮ ɪŋ **~ly** li
enchantment ɪn ˈtʃɑːnt mənt §-ˈtʃænt-
‖ -ˈtʃænt- **~s** s
enchantress ɪn ˈtʃɑːntr əs en-, ən-, §-ˈtʃæntr-,
-ɪs, -es ‖ -ˈtʃæntr- **~es** ɪz əz

enchilada ˌen tʃɪ ˈlɑːd ə -tʃə- **~s** z
Encinitas ˌents ɪ ˈniːt əs -ə- ‖ -ˈniːt̮-
enciph|er ɪn ˈsaɪf lə en-, ən- ‖ -lər **~ered**
əd ‖ ərd **~ering** ər ɪŋ **~ers** əz ‖ ərz
encircl|e ɪn ˈsɜːk əl en-, ən- ‖ -ˈsɜːk- **~ed** d
~ement/s mənt/s **~es** z **~ing** ɪŋ
enclasp ɪn ˈklɑːsp en-, ən-, →ɪŋ-, →eŋ-, →əŋ-,
§-ˈklæsp ‖ -ˈklæsp **~ed** t **~ing** ɪŋ **~s** s
enclave ˈen kleɪv →ˈeŋ-, ˈɒŋ-, •ˈ• ‖ ˈɑːn- **~s** z
enclitic ɪn ˈklɪt ɪk en-, →ɪŋ-, →eŋ- ‖ -ˈklɪt̮ ɪk
~s s
enclos|e ɪn ˈkləʊz en-, ən-, →ɪŋ-, →eŋ-, →əŋ-
‖ -ˈkloʊz **~ed** d **~es** ɪz əz **~ing** ɪŋ
enclosure ɪn ˈkləʊʒ ə en-, ən-, →ɪŋ-, →eŋ-,
→əŋ- ‖ -ˈkloʊʒ ər **~s** z
encod|e ɪn ˈkəʊd ₍ᵢ₎en-, →ɪŋ-, →₍ᵢ₎eŋ- ‖ -ˈkoʊd
~ed ɪd əd **~er/s** ə/z ‖ ər/z **~es** z **~ing** ɪŋ
encomiast ɪn ˈkəʊm i æst en-, ən-, →ɪŋ-,
→eŋ-, →əŋ-, -əst ‖ -ˈkoʊm- **~s** s
encomi|um ɪn ˈkəʊm i‿ləm en-, ən-, →ɪŋ-,
→eŋ-, →əŋ- ‖ -ˈkoʊm- **~a** ə **~ums** əmz
encompass ɪn ˈkʌmp əs en-, ən-, →ɪŋ-, →eŋ-,
→əŋ- ‖ -ˈkɑːmp- **~ed** t **~es** ɪz əz **~ing** ɪŋ
~ment mənt
encore ˈɒŋ kɔː •ˈ• ‖ ˈɑːn kɔːr -koʊr
encounter ɪn ˈkaʊnt ə en-, ən-, →ɪŋ-, →eŋ-,
→əŋ- ‖ -ˈkaʊnt̮ ər **~ed** d **encountering**
ɪn ˈkaʊnt̮ ər ɪŋ en-, ən-, →ɪŋ-, →eŋ-, →əŋ-
‖ -ˈkaʊnt̮ ər ɪŋ →-ˈkaʊntr ɪŋ **~s** z
enˈcounter group
encourag|e ɪn ˈkʌr ɪdʒ en-, ən-, →ɪŋ-, →eŋ-,
→əŋ- ‖ -ˈkɝː- **~ed** d **~ement/s** mənt/s
~es ɪz əz **~ing/ly** ɪŋ /li
encroach ɪn ˈkrəʊtʃ en-, ən-, →ɪŋ-, →eŋ-,
→əŋ- ‖ -ˈkroʊtʃ **~ed** t **~es** ɪz əz **~ing** ɪŋ
~ment/s mənt/s
en croute, en croûte ˌɒn ˈkruːt →ˌɒŋ- ‖ ˌɑːn-
—*Fr* [ɑ̃ kʁut]
encrust ɪn ˈkrʌst en-, ən-, →ɪŋ-, →eŋ-, →əŋ-
~ed ɪd əd **~ing** ɪŋ **~s** s
encrypt ɪn ˈkrɪpt en-, ən-, →ɪŋ-, →eŋ-, →əŋ-
~ed ɪd əd **~ing** ɪŋ **~s** s
encryption ɪn ˈkrɪp ʃən en-, ən-, →ɪŋ-, →eŋ-,
→əŋ- **~s** z
encum|ber ɪn ˈkʌm lbə en-, ən-, →ɪŋ-, →eŋ-,
→əŋ- ‖ -lbər **~bered** bəd ‖ bərd **~bering**
bər ɪŋ **~bers** bəz ‖ bərz
encumbranc|e ɪn ˈkʌm brənts en-, ən-, →ɪŋ-,
→eŋ-, →əŋ- **~s** z
-ency ənts i —*Stress always as in the
corresponding* -ent *word:* sufˈficiency, ˈurgency,
ˈexcellency.
encyclical ɪn ˈsɪk lɪk əl en-, ən- **~s** z
encyclopaed... —*see* **encycloped...**
encyclopedia ɪn ˌsaɪk lə ˈpiːd i‿ə en-, ən- **~s** z
encyclopedic ɪn ˌsaɪk lə ˈpiːd ɪk ◀ en-, ən-
~ally əl‿i
encyclopedist ɪn ˌsaɪk lə ˈpiːd ɪst en-, ən-,
§-əst **~s** s
encyst en ˈsɪst **~ed** ɪd əd **~ing** ɪŋ **~s** s
end end **ended** ˈend ɪd -əd **ending** ˈend ɪŋ
ends endz

'end ˌmatter; 'end ˌproduct, ˌ• '••; 'end
ˌuser, ˌ• '•• •

endangler ɪn 'deɪndʒ lə en-, ən- ‖ -lᵊr ~ered
əd ‖ ᵊrd ~ering ᵊr_ɪŋ ~ers əz ‖ ᵊrz

endear ɪn 'dɪə en-, ən- ‖ -'dɪᵊr ~ed d
endearing/ly ɪn 'dɪər ɪŋ /li en-, ən-
‖ -'dɪr ɪŋ /li ~ment/s mənt/s ~s z

endeavor, endeavour ɪn 'dev ə en-, ən- ‖ -ᵊr
~ed d endeavoring, endeavouring ɪn 'dev
ᵊr_ɪŋ en-, ən- ~s z

Endell 'end ᵊl

endemic en 'dem ɪk ɪn- ~al ᵊl ~ally ᵊl_i

Enderby 'end ə bi ‖ -ᵊr-
'Enderby Land

Enders 'end əz ‖ -ᵊrz

endgame 'end geɪm →'eŋ- ~s z

Endicott 'end ɪ kɒt -ə-; -ɪk ət, -ək- ‖ -kɑːt

ending 'end ɪŋ ~s z

endive 'end ɪv -aɪv ‖ 'end aɪv 'ɑːnd iːv ~s z

endless 'end ləs -lɪs ~ly li ~ness nəs nɪs

endo- comb. form
  with stress-neutral suffix ˌend əʊ ‖ ˌend ə -oʊ
  — endocranial ˌend əʊ 'kreɪn i_əl ◄ ‖ ˌ•ə-
  with stress-imposing suffix en 'dɒ+ ‖ en 'dɑː+
  — endogenous en 'dɒdʒ ən əs -ɪn-
  ‖ -'dɑːdʒ-

endocarditis ˌend əʊ kɑː 'daɪt ɪs §-əs
  ‖ -oʊ kɑːr 'daɪt̬ əs

endocarp 'end əʊ kɑːp ‖ -ə kɑːrp ~s s

endocentric ˌend əʊ 'sentr ɪk ◄ ‖ -oʊ- ~ally
ᵊl_i

endocrine 'end əʊ kraɪn -krɪn, -kriːn, §-krən
  ‖ -ə- ~s z

endocrinology ˌend əʊ krɪ 'nɒl ədʒ i -kraɪ'•-
  ‖ -oʊ krɪ 'nɑːl-

endogamlous en 'dɒɡ əm ləs ‖ -'dɑːɡ- ~y i

endogenous en 'dɒdʒ ən əs ɪn-, -ɪn- ‖ -'dɑːdʒ-
~ly li

endometriosis ˌend əʊ ˌmiːtr i 'əʊs ɪs §-əs
  ‖ -oʊ ˌmiːtr i 'oʊs əs

endometrilum ˌend əʊ 'miːtr i_əm ‖ ˌ•oʊ- ~a
ə ~al əl

endomorph 'end əʊ mɔːf ‖ -ə mɔːrf ~s s

endomorphlic ˌend əʊ 'mɔːf ɪk◄ ‖ -ə 'mɔːrf-
~ism ˌɪz əm

endoplasm 'end əʊ ˌplæz əm ‖ -ə-

endoplasmic ˌend əʊ 'plæz mɪk ◄ ‖ -oʊ-

Endor 'end ɔː ‖ -ɔːr

endorphin en 'dɔːf ɪn §-ən ‖ -'dɔːrf- ~s z

endorsable ɪn 'dɔːs əb ᵊl en-, ən- ‖ -'dɔːrs-

endorsle ɪn 'dɔːs en-, ən- ‖ -'dɔːrs -'foʊrs ~ed t
~ment/s mənt/s ~er/s ə/z ‖ ᵊr/z ~es ɪz əz
~ing ɪŋ

endorsee ˌen dɔː 'siː ‖ -dɔːr- ~s z

endoscope 'end ə skəʊp ‖ -skoʊp ~s s

endoscopic ˌend ə 'skɒp ɪk ◄ ‖ -'skɑːp- ~ally
ᵊl_i

endoscoply en 'dɒsk əp li ‖ -'dɑːsk- ~ies iz

endosmosis ˌend ɒz 'məʊs ɪs -ɒs-, §-əs
  ‖ -ɑːz 'moʊs- -ɑːs-

endosperm 'end əʊ spɜːm ‖ -oʊ spɜːm

endothermic ˌend əʊ 'θɜːm ɪk ◄ ‖ -ə 'θɜːm-
~ally ᵊl_i

endow ɪn 'daʊ en-, ən- ~ed d ~ing ɪŋ
~ment/s mənt/s ~s z
en'dowment ˌmortgage; en'dowment
ˌpolicy

endpaper 'end ˌpeɪp ə →'em- ‖ -ᵊr ~s z

endplay 'end pleɪ →'em- ~ed d ~ing ɪŋ ~s z

Endsleigh 'endz li -liː

end-stopped 'end stɒpt ˌ•'• ‖ -stɑːpt

endule ɪn 'djuː en-, ən-, →§-'dʒuː ‖ -'duː -'djuː
~ed d ~es z ~ing ɪŋ

endurance ɪn 'djʊər ᵊn's en-, ən-, -'djɔːr-,
  →§-'dʒʊər- ‖ -'dʊr- -'djʊr-, -'dʒɝ-

endure ɪn 'djʊə en-, ən-, -'djɔː, →§-'dʒʊə
  ‖ -'dʊr -'djʊr-, -'dʒɝː ~d d ~s z enduring/
ly ɪn 'djʊər ɪŋ /li en-, ən-, -'djɔːr-,
  →§-'dʒʊər- ‖ -'dʊr ɪŋ /li -'djʊr-, -'dʒɝː-

endways 'end weɪz

endwise 'end waɪz

Endymion en 'dɪm i_ən ɪn-

-ene iːn — toluene 'tɒl ju iːn ‖ 'tɑːl-
  —Although strong-vowelled, this suffix is
  unstressed.

Eneas iː 'niːˌəs ɪ-, -'neɪ-, -æs

Eneid 'iːn i_ɪd ɪ 'niː-, §-əd

enema 'en əm ə -ɪm- ~s z

enemly 'en əm li -ɪm- ~ies iz
ˌenemy 'alien

Energen tdmk 'en ədʒ ən ‖ -ᵊrdʒ-

energetic ˌen ə 'dʒet ɪk ◄ ‖ -ᵊr 'dʒet̬ ɪk ◄ ~ally
ᵊl_i ~s s

Energis tdmk 'en ədʒ ɪs §-əs ‖ -ᵊrdʒ-

energisle, energizle 'en ə dʒaɪz ‖ -ᵊr- ~ed d
~es ɪz əz ~ing ɪŋ

energly 'en ədʒ li ‖ -ᵊrdʒ li ~ies iz

enerlvate 'en ə ˌveɪt -ɜː- ‖ -ᵊr- ~vated veɪt ɪd
-əd ‖ veɪt̬ əd ~vates veɪts ~vating
veɪt ɪŋ ‖ veɪt̬ ɪŋ

enervation ˌen ə 'veɪʃ ᵊn -ɜː- ‖ -ᵊr-

en famille ˌɒ̃ fæ 'miː ˌɒn-, ˌɑːn- ‖ ˌɑːn fə- —Fr
[ɑ̃ fa mij]

enfant terrible ˌɒ̃f ɒ̃ te 'riːb_lə ˌɒn fɒn-,
  ˌɑːn fɑːn-, -te'•- ‖ ɑːn ˌfɑːn- —Fr
[ɑ̃ fɑ̃ tɛ ʁibl] enfants terribles as singular

enfeeblle ɪn 'fiːb ᵊl en-, ən- ~ed d ~ement/s
mənt/s ~es z ~ing _ɪŋ

enfeoff ɪn 'fiːf en-, ən-, -'fef ~ed t ~ing ɪŋ
~s s

en fete, en fête ₍ₒ₎ɒ̃ 'feɪt ₍ₒ₎ɒn-, -'fet ‖ ₍ₒ₎ɑː- —Fr
[ɑ̃ fɛt]

Enfield 'en fiːᵊld

enfiladle v ˌen fɪ 'leɪd -fə-, '•• • ‖ 'en fə leɪd
-lɑːd ~ed ɪd əd ~es z ~ing ɪŋ

enfilade n 'en fɪ leɪd -fə-, ˌ••'• ‖ -lɑːd ~s z

enfold ɪn 'fəʊld en-, ən-, →-'fɒʊld ‖ -'foʊld
~ed ɪd əd ~ing ɪŋ ~s z

enforcle ɪn 'fɔːs en-, ən- ‖ -'fɔːrs -'foʊrs ~ed
t ~es ɪz əz ~ing ɪŋ

enforceablle ɪn 'fɔːs əb ᵊl en-, ən- ‖ -'fɔːrs-
-'foʊrs- ~ly li

enforcement ɪn 'fɔːs mənt en-, ən- ‖ -'fɔːrs-
-'foʊrs-

enfranchisle ɪn 'fræntʃ aɪz en-, ən- ~ed d ~es
ɪz əz ~ing ɪŋ

enfranchisement ɪn 'frænɪʃ ɪz mənt en-, ən-,
-əz- ‖ -aɪz- -əz- ~s s
Eng Lit ˌɪŋ 'lɪt
Engadine 'eŋ gə diːn ˌ• •ʼ•
engag|e ɪn 'geɪdʒ en-, ən-, →ɪŋ-, →eŋ-, →əŋ-
~ed d ~es ɪz əz ~ing/ly ɪŋ /li
engagé ˌɒŋ gæ 'ʒeɪ -gɑː- ‖ ˌɑːŋ gɑː- —Fr
[ã ga ʒe]
engagement ɪn 'geɪdʒ mənt en-, ən-, →ɪŋ-,
→eŋ-, →əŋ- ~s s
en'gagement book; en'gagement ring
en garde ˌ(ˌ)ɒ̃ 'gɑːd ˌ(ˌ)ɒn-, →ˌ(ˌ)ɒŋ- ‖ ˌ(ˌ)ɑːn 'gɑːrd
—Fr [ã gaʁd]
Engelbert 'eŋ gəl bɜːt ‖ -bɜ͟ːt —Ger
[ˈʔɛŋ əl bɛʁt]
Engels 'eŋ gəlz —Ger [ˈʔɛŋ əls]
engender ɪn 'dʒend ə en-, ən- ‖ -ər ~ed d
engendering ɪn 'dʒend ər ɪŋ ~s z
engine 'endʒ ɪn §ˈɪndʒ-, -ən ~s z
'engine ˌdriver
-engined 'endʒ ɪnd §ˈɪndʒ-, -ənd — twin-
engined ˌtwɪn 'endʒ ɪnd ◀ §-ˈɪndʒ-, -ənd
engi|neer ˌendʒ ɪ 'nɪə §ˌɪndʒ-, -ə- ‖ -ˈnɪər
~neered 'nɪəd ‖ 'nɪərd ~neering
'nɪər ɪŋ ‖ 'nɪr ɪŋ ~neers 'nɪəz ‖ 'nɪərz
England 'ɪŋ glənd -lənd ~ʼs z
Englefield 'eŋ gəl fiːəld
Englewood 'eŋ gəl wʊd
English 'ɪŋ glɪʃ -lɪʃ ~man mən ~men mən
men ~ness nəs nɪs ~woman ˌwʊm ən
~women ˌwɪm ɪn §-ən
ˌEnglish 'Channel; ˌEnglish 'literature
Eng. lit. ˌɪŋ 'lɪt ˌen-
engorg|e ɪn 'gɔːdʒ en-, ən-, →ɪŋ-, →eŋ-, →əŋ-
‖ -'gɔːrdʒ ~ed d ~ement mənt ~es ɪz əz
~ing ɪŋ
engraft ɪn 'grɑːft en-, ən-, →ɪŋ-, →eŋ-, →əŋ-,
§-'græft ‖ -'græft ~ed ɪd əd ~ing ɪŋ ~s s
engram 'en græm →'eŋ- ~s z
engrav|e ɪn 'greɪv en-, ən-, →ɪŋ-, →eŋ-, →əŋ-
~ed d ~er/s ə/z ‖ ər/z ~es z ~ing/s ɪŋ/z
engross ɪn 'grəʊs en-, ən-, →ɪŋ-, →eŋ-, →əŋ-,
§-'grɒs ‖ -'groʊs ~ed t ~es ɪz əz ~ing ɪŋ
engulf ɪn 'gʌlf en-, ən-, →ɪŋ-, →eŋ-, →əŋ-
~ed t ~ing ɪŋ ~s s
enhanc|e ɪn 'hɑːnts en-, ən-, -'hænts ‖ -'hænts
~ed t ~ement/s mənt/s ~er/s ə/z ‖ ər/z
~es ɪz əz ~ing ɪŋ
enharmonic ˌen hɑː 'mɒn ɪk ◀ ‖ -hɑːr 'mɑːn-
~ally əl_i
Enid 'iːn ɪd §-əd —but in Wales sometimes 'en-
enigma ɪ 'nɪg mə e-, ə- ~s z
enigmatic ˌen ɪg 'mæt ɪk ◀ ‖ -'mæt̬ ɪk ◀ ~ally
əl_i
enjambment ɪn 'dʒæm mənt en-, ən-,
-'dʒæmb- —Fr enjambement [ã ʒãb mã] ~s s
enjoin ɪn 'dʒɔɪn en-, ən- ~ed d ~ing ɪŋ ~s z
enjoy ɪn 'dʒɔɪ en-, ən- ~ed d ~ing ɪŋ ~s z
enjoyab|le ɪn 'dʒɔɪ əb |əl en-, ən- ~ly li
enjoyment ɪn 'dʒɔɪ mənt en-, ən- ~s s
enlarg|e ɪn 'lɑːdʒ en-, ən- ‖ -'lɑːrdʒ ~ed d
~ement/s mənt/s ~er/s ə/z ‖ ər/z ~es ɪz əz
~ing ɪŋ

enlighten ɪn 'laɪt ən en-, ən- ~ed d ~ing ɪŋ
~s z
enlightenment, E~ ɪn 'laɪt ən mənt en-, ən-
enlist ɪn 'lɪst en-, ən- ~ed ɪd əd ~ing ɪŋ ~s s
en'listed man
enlistment ɪn 'lɪst mənt en-, ən- ~s s
enliven ɪn 'laɪv ən en-, ən- ~ed d ~ing ɪŋ ~s
z
en masse ˌ(ˌ)ɒ̃ 'mæs ˌ(ˌ)ɒn-, →ˌ(ˌ)ɒm- ‖ ˌ(ˌ)ɑːn-
-'mɑːs —Fr [ã mas]
enmesh ɪn 'meʃ en-, ən-, →ɪm-, →em-, →əm-
~ed t ~es ɪz əz ~ing ɪŋ
enmit|y 'en mət |i →'em-, -mɪt-; ⚠'em nət i
‖ 'en mət̬ |i ~ies iz
Ennals 'en əlz
enneahedr|on ˌen i_ə 'hiːdr |ən -'hedr- ~a ə
Ennerdale 'en ə deɪəl ‖ -ər-
Ennis 'en ɪs §-əs
Enniskillen ˌen ɪs 'kɪl ən ◀ -əs-, -ɪn
Ennius 'en i_əs
ennobl|e ɪ 'nəʊb əl e-, ə-, ɪn-, en-, ən-
‖ -'noʊb- ~ed d ~ement mənt ~es z ~ing
ɪŋ
ennui 'ɒn wiː •ʼ• ‖ ˌɑːn 'wiː —Fr [ã nɥi]
Eno 'iːn əʊ ‖ -oʊ ~ʼs z
Enola Gay ɪ ˌnəʊl ə 'geɪ ‖ -ˌnoʊl-
enology iː 'nɒl ədʒ i ‖ -'nɑːl-
Enone iː 'nəʊn i ‖ -'noʊn i
enophile 'iːn əʊ faɪəl ‖ 'iːn ə- ~s z
Enoch 'iːn ɒk ‖ -ək -ɑːk
enormit|y ɪ 'nɔːm ət |i ə-, -ɪt- ‖ ɪ 'nɔːrm ət̬ |i
~ies iz
enormous ɪ 'nɔːm əs ə- ‖ ɪ 'nɔːrm- ~ly li
~ness nəs nɪs
Enos 'iːn ɒs ‖ -ɑːs
enosis 'en əʊs ɪs §-əs ‖ ɪ 'noʊs-
enough ɪ 'nʌf ə 'nʌf —After t, d (and sometimes
other obstruents) the ə and n may combine to
give a syllabic consonant, thus good enough
ˌgʊd n 'ʌf.
enounc|e ɪ 'naʊnts iː- ~ed t ~es ɪz əz ~ing
ɪŋ
enow ɪ 'naʊ ə-
en passant ˌɒn 'pæs ɒn →-, ɒm-, ˌɒ̃-, -ɒnt, -ɑːnt,
-ɒ̃; -pæ 'sɒnt, -'sɑːnt ‖ ˌɑːn pɑː 'sɑːn -pə-
—Fr [ã pa sã]
enplan|e ɪn 'pleɪn en-, →ɪm-, →em- ~ed d
~es z ~ing ɪŋ
enquire ɪn 'kwaɪ_ə en-, ən-, →ɪŋ-, →eŋ-, →əŋ-
‖ -'kwaɪ_ər ~d d ~s z enquiring/ly
ɪn 'kwaɪ_ər ɪŋ /li en-, ən-, →ɪŋ-, →eŋ-, →əŋ-
‖ -'kwaɪ_ər ɪŋ /li
enquir|y ɪn 'kwaɪ_ər |i en-, ən-, →ɪŋ-, →eŋ-,
→əŋ- ‖ ɪn 'kwaɪ_ər |i '•••; 'ɪŋk wər |i
~ies iz
enrag|e ɪn 'reɪdʒ en-, ən- ~ed d ~es ɪz əz
~ing ɪŋ
enrapture ɪn 'ræp tʃə en-, ən- ‖ -tʃər ~d d ~s
z enrapturing ɪn 'ræp tʃər ɪŋ en-, ən-
enrich ɪn 'rɪtʃ en-, ən- ~ed t ~er/s ə/z ‖ ər/z
~es ɪz əz ~ing ɪŋ ~ment/s mənt/s
Enrico en 'riːk əʊ ‖ -oʊ —It [en ' riː ko]
Enright 'en raɪt

enrob|e ɪn ˈrəʊb en-, ən- ‖ -ˈroʊb **~ed** d **~es**
z **~ing** ɪŋ
enrol, enroll ɪn ˈrəʊl en-, ən-, →-ˈrɒʊl ‖ -ˈroʊl
~ed d **~ing** ɪŋ **~ment/s** mənt/s **~s** z
en route ˌɒn ˈruːt ˌɒ̃- ‖ ˌɑːn- —*Fr* [ɑ̃ ʁut]
ENSA ˈents ə
ensanguined ɪn ˈsæŋ gwɪnd en-, ən-
Enschede ˈents kə deɪ —*Dutch* [ˈɛn sxə de]
ensconc|e ɪn ˈskɒnts en-, ən- ‖ -ˈskɑːnts **~ed** t
~es ɪz əz **~ing** ɪŋ
ensemble ɒn ˈsɒm bəl ɒ̃-, -ˈsɒ̃- ‖ ɑːn ˈsɑːm-
—*Fr* [ɑ̃ sɑ̃ːbl] **~s** z
enshrin|e ɪn ˈʃraɪn en-, ən- **~ed** d **~ement**
mənt **~es** z **~ing** ɪŋ
enshroud ɪn ˈʃraʊd en-, ən- **~ed** ɪd əd **~ing** ɪŋ
~s z
ensign ˈen saɪn —*but in the sense 'flag', naut,
usually* ˈents ən **~s** z
ensilag|e ˈents əl ɪdʒ -ɪl-; ɪn ˈsaɪl-, en-, ən- **~ed**
d **~es** ɪz əz **~ing** ɪŋ
ensil|e en ˈsaɪəl ˈents aɪəl, -əl **~ed** d **~es** z
~ing ɪŋ
enslav|e ɪn ˈsleɪv en-, ən- **~ed** d **~ement/s**
mənt/s **~er/s** ə/z ‖ ər/z **~es** z **~ing** ɪŋ
ensnare ɪn ˈsneə en-, ən- ‖ -ˈsneər -ˈsnæər **~d**
d **~ment/s** mənt/s **~s** z **ensnaring**
ɪn ˈsneər ɪŋ en-, ən- ‖ -ˈsner ɪŋ -ˈsnær-
Ensor ˈents ɔː -ə ‖ -ɔːr -ər
enstatite ˈents tə taɪt
ensu|e ɪn ˈsjuː en-, ən-, -ˈsuː ‖ -ˈsuː **~ed** d **~es**
z **~ing** ɪŋ
en suite ˌɒ̃ ˈswiːt ˌɒn-, ˌɑːn- ‖ ˌɑːn- —*Fr*
[ɑ̃ sɥit]
ensure ɪn ˈʃɔː en-, ən-, -ˈʃʊə, -ˈsjʊə ‖ -ˈʃʊər
-ˈʃɜː- **~d** d **~s** z **ensuring** ɪn ˈʃɔːr ɪŋ en-,
ən-, -ˈʃʊər-, -ˈsjʊər- ‖ -ˈʃʊr ɪŋ -ˈʃɜː-
ENT ˌiː en ˈtiː
　ˌEN'T ˌspecialist
-ent ənt —*This suffix has the same stress-effects
as -ence, thus* adˈjacent, inˈtelligent, ˈeminent;
note apˈparent. *It triggers a vowel change and
change of stress in the stem of some words, as*
exceˈl ɪk ˈsel → excellent ˈeks əl ənt, provide
prəˈvaɪd → provident ˈprɒv ɪd ənt ‖ ˈprɑːv-.
Note change of vowel but not of stress in apˈpear
→apˈparent.
entablature en ˈtæb lətʃ ə ɪn-, -lɪtʃ-; -lɪ tʃʊə,
lə- ‖ -lə tʃʊr -tʊr; -lətʃ ər **~s** z
entail ɪn ˈteɪəl en-, ən- **~ed** d **~ing** ɪŋ
~ment/s mənt/s **~s** z
entameb|a, entamoeb|a ˌent ə ˈmiːb |ə ‖ ˌent̬-
~ae iː **~as** əz
entangl|e ɪn ˈtæŋ ɡəl en-, ən- **~ed** d
~ement/s mənt/s **~es** z **~ing** ɪŋ
entasis ˈent əs ɪs §-əs ‖ ˈent̬-
Entebbe en ˈteb i ɪn-, ən-
entelech|y en ˈtel ək li ɪn-, ən- **~ies** ɪz
entendre —*see* double entendre
entente ₍ₒₙ ˈtɒnt ₍ₒ̃- ‖ ₍ₐːn ˈtɑːnt —*Fr*
[ɑ̃ tɑ̃ːt]
　ˌentente ˌcordiˈale, •ˌ•- ˌkɔːd i ˈɑːl
‖ ˌkɔːrd- —*Fr* [kɔʁ djal]

enter ˈent ə ‖ ˈent̬ ər **entered** ˈent əd ‖ ˈent̬ ərd
entering ˈent ər ɪŋ ‖ ˈent̬ ər ɪŋ →ˈentr ɪŋ
enters ˈent əz ‖ ˈent̬ ərz
enteric en ˈter ɪk
enteritis ˌent ə ˈraɪt ɪs §-əs ‖ ˌent̬ ə ˈraɪt̬ əs
entero- *comb. form*
　with stress-neutral suffix ˌent ər əʊ ‖ ˌent̬
　ə roʊ- — **enterobacterium**
　ˌent ər əʊ bæk ˈtɪər i ˌəm ‖ ˌent̬
　ə roʊ bæk ˈtɪr-
　with stress-imposing suffix ˌent ə ˈrɒ+ ‖ ˌent̬
　ə ˈrɑː+ — **enterostomy**
　ˌent ə ˈrɒst əm i ‖ ˌent̬ ə ˈrɑːst-
enterpris|e ˈent ə praɪz ‖ ˈent̬ ər- **~es** ɪz əz
~ing/ly ɪŋ /li
entertain ˌent ə ˈteɪn ‖ ˌent̬ ər- **~ed** d **~er/s**
ə/z ‖ ər/z **~ing/ly** ɪŋ /li **~s** z
entertainment ˌent ə ˈteɪn mənt →-ˈteɪm-
‖ ˌent̬ ər- **~s** s
enthalpy ˈen θælp i -θəlp-; en ˈθælp i, ɪn-, ən-
enthral, enthral|l ɪn ˈθrɔːl en-, ən- ‖ -ˈθrɑːl
~led d **~ling** ɪŋ **~ment** mənt **~s** z
enthron|e ɪn ˈθrəʊn en-, ən- ‖ -ˈθroʊn **~ed** d
~es z **~ement** mənt **~ing** ɪŋ
enthus|e ɪn ˈθjuːz en-, ən-, -ˈθuːz ‖ -ˈθuːz **~ed**
d **~es** ɪz əz **~ing** ɪŋ
enthusiasm ɪn ˈθjuːz i ˌæz əm en-, ən-, -ˈθuːz-,
§-əz- ‖ -ˈθuːz- **~s** z
enthusiast ɪn ˈθjuːz i æst en-, ən-, -ˈθuːz-,
§-əst ‖ -ˈθuːz- **~s** s
enthusiastic ɪn ˌθjuːz i ˈæst ɪk ◀ en-, ən-,
-ˌθuːz- ‖ -ˌθuːz- **~ally** əl_i
entia ˈent i_ə ˈent̬ʃ-
entic|e ɪn ˈtaɪs en-, ən- **~ed** t **~ement/s**
mənt/s **~er/s** ə/z ‖ ər/z **~es** ɪz əz **~ing/ly**
ɪŋ/ li
entire ɪn ˈtaɪ_ə en-, ən-, §ˌen-, §ˌɪn- ‖ -ˈtaɪ_ər
~ly li **~ness** nəs nɪs
entiret|y ɪn ˈtaɪ_ər ət |i en-, ən-, -ɪt i, -ˈtaɪ_ət li
‖ -ˈtaɪ_ərt̬ |i -ˈtaɪ_ər ət̬ |i **~ies** ɪz
entiti... —*see* entity
entitl|e ɪn ˈtaɪt əl en-, ən- ‖ -ˈtaɪt̬ əl **~ed** d
~ement/s mənt/s **~es** z **~ing** ɪŋ
entit|y ˈent ət |i -ɪt- ‖ ˈent̬ ət̬ |i **~ies** ɪz
entomb ɪn ˈtuːm en-, ən- **~ed** d **~ing** ɪŋ
~ment mənt **~s** z
entomological ˌent əm ə ˈlɒdʒ ɪk ə ◀ ‖ ˌent̬
əm ə ˈlɑːdʒ- **~ly** _i
entomologist ˌent ə ˈmɒl ədʒ ɪst §-əst ‖ ˌent̬
ə ˈmɑːl- **~s** s
entomology ˌent ə ˈmɒl ədʒ i ‖ ˌent̬ ə ˈmɑːl-
entourag|e ˈɒn tʊ rɑːʒ ˈɒ̃-, ˌ•• ̍•
‖ ˌɑːn tu ˈrɑːʒ —*Fr* [ɑ̃ tu ʁaːʒ] **~es** ɪz əz
entracte, entr'acte ˈɒntr ækt ˈɒ̃tr-, •ˈ•
‖ ˈɑːntr- —*Fr* [ɑ̃ tʁakt] **~s** s
entrails ˈentr eɪ_lz ‖ ˈentr əlz
entrain ɪn ˈtreɪn en-, ən- **~ed** d **~ing** ɪŋ
~ment mənt **~s** z
entrammel ɪn ˈtræm əl en-, ən- **~ed, ~led** d
~ing, ~ling ɪŋ **~s** z
entranc|e *n 'way in'* ˈentr ənts **~es** ɪz əz
entranc|e *v 'charm'* ɪn ˈtrɑːnts en-, ən-,

§-'trænᵗs ‖ -'trænᵗs ~ed t ~ement/s mənt/s
~es ɪz əz ~ing/ly ɪŋ /li
entrant 'entr ənt ~s s
entrap ɪn 'træp en-, ən- ~ment/s mənt/s
~ped t ~ping ɪŋ ~s s
en|treat ɪn ǀ'triːt en-, ən- ~treated 'triːt ɪd -əd
‖ 'triːt̬ əd ~treating/ly 'triːt ɪŋ /li ‖ 'triːt̬ ɪŋ /
li ~treats 'triːts
entreatment ɪn 'triːt mənt en-, ən- ~s s
entreat|y ɪn 'triːt li en-, ən- ‖ -'triːt̬ li ~ies iz
entrechat 'ɒntr ə ʃɑː 'ɒ̃tr-, 'ɑːntr-, ‚•ꞏ•
‖ ‚ɑːntr ə 'ʃɑː —Fr [ɑ̃ tʁə ʃa] ~s z
entrecote, entrecôte 'ɒntr ə kəʊt ‚•ꞏ•
‖ 'ɑːntr ə koʊt ‚•ꞏ• —Fr [ɑ̃ tʁə kot] ~s s
Entre-Deux-Mers ‚ɒntr ə ‚dɜː 'meə
‖ ‚ɑːntr ə ‚du: 'meᵊr —Fr [ɑ̃ tʁə dø mɛːʁ]
entree, entrée 'ɒntr eɪ 'ɒ̃tr- ‖ 'ɑːntr- —Fr
[ɑ̃ tʁe] ~s z
entremets sing. 'ɒntr ə meɪ 'ɒ̃tr-, 'ɑːntr-, ‚•ꞏ•
‖ 'ɑːntr- —Fr [ɑ̃ tʁə mɛ] ~ pl z
entrench ɪn 'trentʃ en-, ən- ~ed t ~es ɪz əz
~ing ɪŋ ~ment/s mənt/s
entre nous ‚ɒntr ə 'nu: ‚ɒ̃tr-, ‚ɑːntr- ‖ ‚ɑːntr-
—Fr [ɑ̃ tʁə nu]
entrepot, entrepôt 'ɒntr ə pəʊ 'ɒ̃tr-
‖ 'ɑːntr ə poʊ —Fr [ɑ̃ tʁə po] ~s z
entrepreneur ‚ɒntr ə prə 'nɜː ‚ɒ̃tr-, -pre'•,
-'njʊə ‖ ‚ɑːntr ə prə 'nɜꞏː -pə'•, -'nʊᵊr —Fr
[ɑ̃ tʁə pʁə nœːʁ] ~s z
entrepreneurial ‚ɒntr ə prə 'nɜːr i‿əl ◂ ‚ɒ̃tr-,
-pre'•-, -'njʊər- ‖ ‚ɑːntr ə prə 'nɜꞏ:- -'nʊr-
~ly i
entresol 'ɒntr ə sɒl 'ɒ̃tr- ‖ 'ɑːntr ə saːl —Fr
[ɑ̃ tʁə sɔl] ~s z
entries 'entr iz
entropic en 'trɒp ɪk ‖ -'trɑːp- ~ally əl‿i
entropy 'entr əp i
entrust ɪn 'trʌst en-, ən- ~ed ɪd əd ~ing ɪŋ
~ment mənt ~s s
entr|y 'entr li ~ies iz
    'entry cer‚tificate
entryism 'entr i ‚ɪz əm
entryist 'entr i ɪst §-əst ~s s
entryphone 'entr i fəʊn ‖ -foʊn ~s z
entryway 'entr i weɪ ~s z
entwin|e ɪn 'twaɪn en-, ən- ~ed d ~es z ~ing
ɪŋ
Entwistle 'ent wɪs əl
enucle|ate v ɪ 'njuːk li |eɪt i:-, ə- ‖ ɪ 'nuːk-
ɪ 'njuːk- ~ated eɪt ɪd -əd ‖ eɪt̬ əd ~ates eɪts
~ating eɪt ɪŋ ‖ eɪt̬ ɪŋ
enucleate adj ɪ 'njuːk li ət i:-, ə-, -ɪt, -eɪt
‖ ɪ 'nuːk- ɪ 'njuːk-
Enugu e 'nuːg uː ɪ-
enumerable ɪ 'njuːm ər‿əb əl ə-, §-'nuːm-
‖ ɪ 'nuːm- ɪ 'njuːm- (usually = innumerable)
enume|rate ɪ 'njuːm ə |reɪt ə-, §-'nuːm-
‖ ɪ 'nuːm- ɪ 'njuːm- ~rated reɪt ɪd -əd
‖ reɪt̬ əd ~rates reɪts ~rating
reɪt ɪŋ ‖ reɪt̬ ɪŋ
enumeration ɪ ‚njuːm ə 'reɪʃ ᵊn ə-, §-‚nuːm-
‖ ɪ ‚nuːm- ɪ ‚njuːm- ~s z

enumerator ɪ 'njuːm ə reɪt ə ə-, §-'nuːm-
‖ ɪ 'nuːm ə reɪt̬ ᵊr ɪ 'njuːm- ~s z
enunci|ate ɪ 'nʌnᵗs i |eɪt ə-, -'nʌntʃ- ~ated
eɪt ɪd -əd ‖ eɪt̬ əd ~ates eɪts ~ating
eɪt ɪŋ ‖ eɪt̬ ɪŋ
enunciation ɪ ‚nʌnᵗs i 'eɪʃ ᵊn ə-, -‚nʌntʃ- ~s z
enunciative ɪ 'nʌnᵗs i‿ət ɪv ə-, -'nʌntʃ-, -eɪt-
‖ -i eɪt̬ ɪv ~ly li
enunciator ɪ 'nʌnᵗs i eɪt ə ə-, -'nʌntʃ- ‖ -eɪt̬ ᵊr
~s z
enuresis ‚en ju‿ 'riːs ɪs §-əs ‖ -jə-
envelop v ɪn 'vel əp en-, ən- ~ed t ~er/s ə/
z ‖ ᵊr/z ~ing ɪŋ ~s s

ENVELOPE

■ 'en-   ☐ 'ɒn-

BrE 1988

0	20	40	60	80	100%

envelope n 'en və ləʊp 'ɒn- ‖ -loʊp 'ɑːn-
—BrE 1988 poll panel preference: 'en- 78%,
'ɒn- 22%. ~s s
envelopment ɪn 'vel əp mənt en-, ən-
envenom ɪn 'ven əm en-, ən- ~ed d ~ing ɪŋ
~s z
enviab|le 'en vi‿əb |əl ǀᵊl ~ly li
envie... —see **envy**
envious 'en vi‿əs ~ly li ~ness nəs nɪs
environ v ɪn 'vaɪᵊr ən en-, ən- ~ed d ~ing ɪŋ
~s z
environment ɪn 'vaɪᵊr ən mənt en-, ən-,
→-əm-, -ə- ~s s
environmental ɪn ‚vaɪᵊr ən 'ment ᵊl ◂ en-, ən-,
→-əm-, -ə- ‖ -'ment̬ ᵊl ◂ ~ism ‚ɪz əm ~ist/s
ɪst/s §əst/s ~ly i
environs n ɪn 'vaɪᵊr ənz en-, ən-; 'en vɪr-, -vər-
envisag|e ɪn 'vɪz ɪdʒ en-, ən- ~ed d ~es ɪz əz
~ing ɪŋ
envision ɪn 'vɪʒ ᵊn en-, ən- ~ed d ~ing ‿ɪŋ ~s
z
envoi, envoy 'en vɔɪ ‖ 'ɑːn- ~s z
en|vy 'en |vi ~vied vid ~vies viz ~vying/ly
vi‿ɪŋ /li
enwrap ɪn 'ræp en-, ən- ~ped t ~ping ɪŋ ~s
s
enwreath|e ɪn 'riːð en-, ən- ~ed d ~es z
~ing ɪŋ
enzyme 'en zaɪm ~s z
Eocene 'iː əʊ siːn ‖ -ə-
eohippus ‚iː əʊ 'hɪp əs ‖ -oʊ-
Eoin (i) 'əʊ ɪn -ən ‖ 'oʊ ən, (ii) jəʊn ‖ joʊn
eolian i 'əʊl i‿ən ‖ i 'oʊl-
Eolic i 'ɒl ɪk -'əʊl- ‖ i 'ɑːl ɪk
eolith 'iː əʊ lɪθ ‖ -ə- ~s s
eolithic, e- ‚iː əʊ 'lɪθ ɪk ◂ ‖ -ə-
eon 'iː‿ən -ɒn ‖ -ɑːn ~s z
Eos 'iː ɒs ‖ -ɑːs
eosin 'iː əʊs ɪn §-ən ‖ -əs-
eosinophil ‚i: əʊ 'sɪn əʊ fɪl ‖ ‚i: ə 'sɪn ə fɪl ~s z
Eothen 'iː əʊ θen i 'əʊθ en ‖ -ə-
-eous i‿əs — **piteous** 'pɪt i‿əs —This suffix
imposes stress on the preceding syllable:
cou'rageous. In some words its compressed form

jəs *has coalesced with the final consonant of the stem:* gorgeous 'gɔːdʒ əs ‖ 'gɔːrdʒ əs

EP ˌiː 'piː ~**s** , ~**'s** z

epact 'iːp ækt 'ep- ~**s** s

Epaminondas e ˌpæm ɪ 'nɒnd æs ɪ-, -ə- ‖ -'naːnd əs

eparch 'ep ɑːk ‖ -ɑːrk ~**s** s

eparch|y 'ep ɑːk |i ‖ -ɑːrk |i ~**ies** iz

epaulet, epaulette ˌep ə 'let -ɔː-, '••• ~**s** s

Epcot *tdmk* 'ep kɒt ‖ -kaːt

epee, épée 'ep eɪ 'eɪp-; e 'peɪ ‖ eɪ 'peɪ 'ep eɪ —*Fr* [e pe] ~**ist/s** ɪst/s §əst/s ~**s** z

epenthesis e 'penᵗθ əs ɪs ɪ-, ə-, §-əs

epenthesis|e, epenthesiz|e e 'penᵗθ ə saɪz ~**ed** d ~**es** ɪz əz ~**ing** ɪŋ

epenthetic ˌep en 'θet ɪk ◄ -ən-, →-m- ‖ -'θeṭ- ~**ally** əl_i

epergne ɪ 'pɜːn e-, -'peən ‖ ɪ 'pɜːn eɪ- —*not actually a French word* ~**s** z

epexegesis e ˌpeks ɪ 'dʒiːs ɪs ɪ-, ə-, -ə-, §-əs

epexegetic e ˌpeks ɪ 'dʒet ɪk ◄ ɪ-, ə-, -ə- ‖ -'dʒeṭ- ~**ally** əl_i

epha, ephah 'iːf ə ‖ 'ef ə ~**s** z

ephebe 'ef iːb ɪ 'fiːb, e- ~**s** z

ephedrine 'ef ɪ driːn -ə-; -ɪdr ɪn, -ədr-, -ən; ɪ 'fedr ɪn, -ən ‖ ɪ 'fedr ən e-

ephemera ɪ 'fem ər_ə e-, ə-, -'fiːm- ~**s** z

EPHEMERAL

	■-'fem- □-'fiːm-	
BrE 1998		
0	20 40 60 80	100%

ephemeral ɪ 'fem ər_əl e-, ə-, -'fiːm- ~**ly** i —*BrE 1998 poll panel preference:* -'fem- *86%,* -'fiːm- *14%*

ephemerality ɪ ˌfem ə 'ræl ət i e-, ə-, -ˌfem- ‖ -əṭ i

ephemeris ɪ 'fem ər ɪs e-, ə-, -'fiːm-, §-əs
  ephemerides ˌef ɪ 'mer ɪ diːz ˌ•ə-, -'•ə-

Ephesian ɪ 'fiːʒ ən e-, ə-, -'fiːʒ i_ən ~**s** z

Ephesus 'ef ɪs əs -əs-

Ephialtes ˌef i 'ælt iːz

ephod 'iːf ɒd 'ef- ‖ -aːd ~**s** z

ephor 'iːf ɔː 'ef-, -ə ‖ -ɔːr -ᵊr ~**s** z

Ephraim 'iːf reɪ ɪm -ri_, -əm; 'iːf rəm ‖ 'iːf ri_əm

epi- *comb. form*
  with stress-neutral suffix ˈep i ˈep ə —
    epistatic ˌep ɪ 'stæt ɪk ◄ -ə- ‖ -'stæṭ-
  with stress-imposing suffix ɪ 'pɪ+ e- —
    epistasis ɪ 'pɪst əs ɪs e-, §-əs

epic 'ep ɪk ~**s** s

epicanth|ic ˌep ɪ 'kænᵗθ |ɪk ◄ §-ə- ‖ -əl
  epi,canthic 'fold

epicene 'ep ɪ siːn §-ə- ~**s** z

epicenter, epicentre 'ep ɪ ˌsent ə §-ə- ‖ -ˌsenṭ ᵊr ~**s** z

epiclesis ˌep ɪ 'kliːs ɪs §-ə-, -əs

Epictetus ˌep ɪk 'tiːt əs ‖ -'tiːṭ-

epicure 'ep ɪ kjʊə §-ə-, -kjɔː ‖ -kjʊr ~**s** z

epicurean, E~ ˌep ɪ kjuə 'riː_ən §ˌ•ə- ~**s** z

Epicurus ˌep ɪ 'kjʊər əs §-ə-, -'kjɔːr- ‖ -'kjʊr-

epicycle 'ep ɪ ˌsaɪk əl §-ə- ~**s** z

epicyclic ˌep ɪ 'saɪk lɪk ◄ §-ə-, -'sɪk-
  epi,cyclic 'train

epicycloid ˌep ɪ 'saɪk lɔɪd §-ə- ~**s** z

Epidaurus ˌep ɪ 'dɔːr əs §-ə- —*ModGk* Epidhavros [ɛ 'pi ða vrɔs]

epideictic ˌep ɪ 'daɪkt ɪk ◄ -ə-

epidemic ˌep ɪ 'dem ɪk ◄ §-ə- ~**ally** əl_i ~**s** s

epidemiological ˌep ɪ ˌdiːm i_ə 'lɒdʒ ɪk əl §ˌ•ə-, -ˌdem- ‖ -'laːdʒ- ~**ly** _i

epidemiologist ˌep ɪ ˌdiːm i 'ɒl ədʒ ɪst §ˌ•ə-, -ˌdem-, §-əst ‖ -'aːl- ~**s** s

epidemiology ˌep ɪ ˌdiːm i 'ɒl ədʒ i §ˌ•ə-, -ˌdem- ‖ -'aːl-

epidermis ˌep ɪ 'dɜːm ɪs §-ə-, §-əs ‖ -'dɜːm-

epidiascope ˌep ɪ 'daɪ_ə skəʊp §ˌ•ə- ‖ -skoʊp ~**s** s

epi|didymis ˌep ɪ |'dɪd əm ɪs §ˌ•ə-, -ɪm ɪs, §-əs
  ~**didymides** dɪ 'dɪm ɪ diːz §də-, -ə-; 'dɪd əm ɪ diːz, -ə•

epidote 'ep ɪ dəʊt §-ə- ‖ -doʊt

epidural ˌep ɪ 'djʊər əl ◄ §-ə-, -'djɔːr-, →§-'dʒʊər- ‖ -'dʊr- -'djʊr- ~**ly** i ~**s** z

epigastrium ˌep ɪ 'gæs tri_əm §ˌ•ə-

epiglottal ˌep ɪ 'glɒt əl ◄ -ə- ‖ -'glaːṭ əl ◄

epiglottis ˌep ɪ 'glɒt ɪs -ə-, §-əs, '•••,•• ‖ -'glaːṭ- ~**es** ɪz əz

epigone 'ep ɪ gəʊn -ə- ‖ -goʊn ~**s** z

Epigoni e 'pɪg ə naɪ ɪ-, -iː

epigram 'ep ɪ græm -ə- ~**s** z

epigrammatic ˌep ɪ grə 'mæt ɪk ◄ ˌ•ə- ‖ -'mæṭ- ~**ally** əl_i

epigrammatist ˌep ɪ 'græm ət ɪst ˌ•ə-, §-əst ‖ -əṭ- ~**s** s

epigraph 'ep ɪ grɑːf -ə-, -græf ‖ -græf ~**s** s

epigrapher e 'pɪg rəf ə ɪ- ‖ -ᵊr ~**s** z

epigraphic ˌep ɪ 'græf ɪk ◄ -ə- ‖ -əl əl ~**ally** əl_i

epigraphy e 'pɪg rəf i ɪ-

epilepsy 'ep ɪ leps i '•ə-

epileptic ˌep ɪ 'lept ɪk ◄ -ə- ~**s** s
  epi,leptic 'fit

epilog, epilogue 'ep ɪ lɒg -ə- ‖ -lɔːg -laːg ~**s** z

epiphan|y, E~ ɪ 'pɪf ən |i ə- ~**ies** iz

epiphenom|enon ˌep ɪ fɪ 'nɒm |ɪn ən -fə'•-, -'•ən- ‖ -'naːm |ə naːn -ən ən ~**ena** ɪn ə ən- ‖ ən ə ~**enal** ɪn əl ən- ‖ ən əl

epiph|ysis e 'pɪf |əs ɪs ɪ-, §-əs ~**yses** ə siːz ɪ-

epiphyte 'ep ɪ faɪt -ə- ~**s** s

epiphytic ˌep ɪ 'fɪt ɪk ◄ -ə- ‖ -'fɪṭ-

Epirus ɪ 'paɪᵊr əs e-, ə-

episcopac|y ɪ 'pɪsk əp əs |i e-, ə- ~**ies** iz

episcopal ɪ 'pɪsk əp əl e-, ə- ~**ly** i

episcopalian, E~ ɪ ˌpɪsk ə 'peɪl i_ən ◄ e-, ə- ~**s** z

episcopate ɪ 'pɪsk əp ət e-, ə-, -ɪt, -eɪt ~**s** s

episcope *'projector'* 'ep ɪ skəʊp ‖ -skoʊp ~**s** s

episiotom|y ɪ ˌpɪz i 'ɒt əm |i e-, ə-, -ˌpiːz-, ˌep ɪz- ‖ -'aːṭ əm |i ~**ies** iz

episode 'ep ɪ səʊd -ə- ‖ -soʊd ~**s** z

episodic ˌep ɪ 'sɒd ɪk ◄ -ə- ‖ -'saːd- ~**ally** əl_i

epistemic ˌep ɪ 'stiːm ɪk ◄ -ə-, -'stem-

epistemological ɪ ˌpɪst ɪ mə 'lɒdʒ ɪk əl ◄ e-, ə-, -ˌ•ə-, -ˌ•iː- ‖ -'laːdʒ- ~**ly** _i

E

E

epistemology ɪ ˌpɪst ɪ 'mɒl ədʒ i e-, ə-, -ˌ•'ə-,
-ˌ•i:- ‖ -'mɑːl-
epistle, E~ ɪ 'pɪs ᵊl ə- ~s z
epistolary ɪ 'pɪst əl ər i e-, ə-; ˌep ɪ 'stɒl ər i ◂,
§ˌ•ə- ‖ -ə ler i
epistyle 'ep ɪ staɪᵊl -ə- ~s z
epitaph 'ep ɪ tɑːf -ə-, -tæf ‖ -tæf ~s s
epitaxial ˌep ɪ 'tæks i_əl ◂ ˌ•ə-
epithalami|um ˌep ɪθ ə 'leɪm i_|əm ˌ•əθ- ~a ə
epithelium ˌep ɪ 'θiːl i_əm ˌ•ə-
epithet 'ep ɪ θet -ə- ~s s
epitome ɪ 'pɪt əm i ə- ‖ ɪ 'pɪṭ əm i ~s z
epitomis|e, epitomiz|e ɪ 'pɪt ə maɪz ə-
‖ ɪ 'pɪṭ ə- ~ed d ~es ɪz əz ~ing ɪŋ
epizootic ˌep ɪ zəʊ 'ɒt ɪk ◂ ‖ -zoʊ 'ɑːṭ ɪk ◂ ~s s
e pluribus unum eɪ ˌplʊər ɪb əs 'uːn əm iː-,
-ˌplɔːr-, ˌ•ˌ•-, -əb•'•-, -ʊs'•-, -'juːn-, -ʊm
‖ -ˌplʊr-
epoch 'iːp ɒk ‖ 'ep ək -ɑːk (*) ~s s
epochal 'ep ɒk ᵊl 'iːp-, -ək-; ɪ 'pɒk ᵊl
‖ 'ep ək ᵊl
epoch-making 'iːp ɒk ˌmeɪk ɪŋ ‖ 'ep ək-
epode 'ep əʊd ‖ -oʊd ~s z
eponym 'ep ə nɪm ~s z
eponymous ɪ 'pɒn ɪm əs ə-, -əm- ‖ ɪ 'pɑːn-
~ly li
epos 'ep ɒs ‖ -ɑːs
EPOS 'iː pɒs ‖ -pɑːs
epoxide ɪ 'pɒks aɪd e-, ə- ‖ e 'pɑːks- ɪ- ~s z
epox|y ɪ 'pɒks |i e-, ə- ‖ e 'pɑːks |i ɪ- ~ies ɪz
eˌpoxy 'resin
Epping 'ep ɪŋ
ˌEpping 'Forest
EPROM 'iː prɒm ‖ -prɑːm ~s z
epsilon ep 'saɪl ən ɪp-, -ɒn; 'eps ɪ lɒn, -ə-, -lən
‖ 'eps ə lɑːn -əl ən (*) ~s z
Epsom 'eps əm
ˌEpsom 'Downs; ˌEpsom 'salts ‖ '••
Epson tdmk 'eps ɒn -ən ‖ -ɑːn
Epstein 'ep staɪn
Epstein-Barr ˌep staɪn 'bɑː →-staɪm- ‖ -'bɑːr
epylli|on e 'pɪl i_|ən ɪ-, ə- ~a ə
equability ˌek wə 'bɪl ət i -ɪt i ‖ -əṭ i
equab|le 'ek wəb |ᵊl ~leness ᵊl nəs -nɪs ~ly li
equal 'iːk wəl ~ed, ~led d ~ing, ~ling ɪŋ ~ly
i ~s z
ˌEqual 'Rights Aˌmendment; 'equal(s) sign
equalis... —see equaliz...
equalitarian ɪ ˌkwɒl ɪ 'teər i_ən ◂ iː-, ə-, -ˌ•'ə-
‖ ɪ ˌkwɒːl ə 'ter i_ən ◂ -ˌkwɑːl-, -'tær- ~s z
equalit|y ɪ 'kwɒl ət |i iː-, ə-, -ɪt- ‖ -'kwɑːl əṭ-
~ies ɪz
equalization ˌiːk wəl aɪ 'zeɪʃ ᵊn -ɪ'•- ‖ -ə'•-
~s z
equaliz|e 'iːk wə laɪz ~ed d ~er/s ə/z ‖ ər/z
~es ɪz əz ~ing ɪŋ
equally 'iːk wəl i
equanimity ˌek wə 'nɪm ət i ˌiːk-, -ɪti ‖ -əṭ i
equanimous iː 'kwæn ɪm əs iː-, e-, -'kwɒn-,
-əm- ~ly li
equatable ɪ 'kweɪt əb ᵊl iː-, ə- ‖ -'kweɪṭ-
e|quate ɪ |'kweɪt iː-, ə- ~quated 'kweɪt ɪd -əd

‖ 'kweɪṭ əd ~quates 'kweɪts ~quating
'kweɪt ɪŋ ‖ 'kweɪṭ ɪŋ

equation ɪ 'kweɪʒ ᵊn ə-, -'kweɪʃ- —AmE 1993
poll panel preference: -'kweɪʒ- 90%, -'kweɪʃ-
10%. ~s z
equative ɪ 'kweɪt ɪv iː-, ə- ‖ -'kweɪṭ- ~s z
equator, E~ ɪ 'kweɪt ə ə- ‖ ɪ 'kweɪṭ ᵊr ~s z
equatorial ˌek wə 'tɔːr i_əl ◂ ˌiːk- ‖ ˌiːk-
-'toʊr- ~ly i
ˌEquaˌtorial 'Guinea
equerr|y ɪ 'kwer |i ə-; 'ek wər |i ‖ 'ek wər |i
—at court, ɪ 'kwer i ~ies ɪz
equestrian ɪ 'kwes tri_ən e-, ə- ~ism ˌɪz əm
~s z
equestrienne ɪ ˌkwes tri 'en e-, ə- ~s z
equi 'ek wi 'iːk-
equi- comb. form
with stress-neutral suffix |iːk wɪ |ek-, -wə- —
equiprobable ˌiːk wɪ 'prɒb əb ᵊl ◂ ˌek-,
ˌ•wə- ‖ -'prɑːb-
equidistant ˌiːk wɪ 'dɪst ənt ◂ ˌek-, -wə- ~ly li
equilateral ˌiːk wɪ 'læt ᵊr əl ◂ ˌ•wə- ‖ -'læt ər
əl →-'lætr əl ~ly i
ˌequiˌlateral 'triangle
equilib|rate ˌiːk wɪ 'laɪb |reɪt ˌek-, -wə-, -'lɪb-;
iː 'kwɪl ɪ b|reɪt ɪ-, ə-, -ə- ‖ ɪ 'kwɪl ə b|reɪt
~rated reɪt ɪd -əd ‖ reɪṭ əd ~rates reɪts
~rating reɪt ɪŋ ‖ reɪṭ ɪŋ
equilibration ˌiːk wɪ laɪ 'breɪʃ ᵊn ˌek-, ˌ•wə-,
-lɪ'•-; iː ˌkwɪl ɪ-, ɪ-, -ə'•- ‖ ɪ ˌkwɪl ə-
equilibrium ˌiːk wɪ 'lɪb ri_əm ˌek-, ˌ•wə-
equine 'ek waɪn 'iːk- ‖ 'iːk- 'ek- ~s z
equinoctial ˌiːk wɪ 'nɒk ʃᵊl ◂ ˌek-, -wə-
‖ -'nɑːk- ~s z
ˌequiˌnoctial 'gales

equinox 'ek wɪ nɒks 'iːk-, -wə- ‖ -nɑːks ~es
ɪz əz —BrE 1998 poll panel preference: 'ek-
92%, 'iːk- 8%
equip ɪ 'kwɪp ə- ~ped t ~ping ɪŋ ~s s
equipag|e 'ek wɪp ɪdʒ -wəp- ~es ɪz əz
equipment ɪ 'kwɪp mənt ə-
equipoise 'ek wɪ pɔɪz 'iːk-, -wə- ~d d
equipollent ˌiːk wɪ 'pɒl ənt ◂ ˌek-, -wə-
‖ -'pɑːl-
equitab|le 'ek wɪt əb |ᵊl '•wət- ‖ -wəṭ əb-
~leness ᵊl nəs -nɪs ~ly li
equitation ˌek wɪ 'teɪʃ ᵊn -wə-
equit|y, E~ 'ek wət |i -wɪt- ‖ -wəṭ |i ~ies ɪz
equivalenc|e ɪ 'kwɪv ᵊl ᵊn|s ə- ~es ɪz əz ~ies
ɪz ~y i
equivalent ɪ 'kwɪv ᵊl ənt ə- ~ly li ~s s

equivocal ɪ ˈkwɪv ək ᵊl ə-, -ɪk ᵊl ~**ly** ̣i ~**ness**
  nəs nɪs
equivo|cate ɪ ˈkwɪv ə |keɪt ə- ~**cated** keɪt ɪd
  -əd ‖ keɪt̬ əd ~**cates** keɪts ~**cating**
  keɪt ɪŋ ‖ keɪt̬ ɪŋ
equivocation ɪ ˌkwɪv ə ˈkeɪʃ ᵊn ə- ~**s** z
equus, Equus ˈek wəs
er *hesitation noise, BrE* ɜː ə —*The AmE*
  equivalent is written uh
-er ə ‖ ᵊr — **dirtier** ˈdɜːt i ̣ə ‖ ˈdɝːt̬ i ̣ᵊr —*On*
  rare occasions this suffix receives contrastive
  stress, and is then pronounced ˈɜː ‖ ˈɝː, *thus*
  not early, but earliER ˌɜːl i ˈɜː ‖ ˌɝːl i ˈɝː
ER ˌi: ˈɑː ‖ -ˈɑːr
era ˈɪər ə ‖ ˈɪr ə ˈer ə, ˈi: rə ~**s** z
ERA ˌi: ɑːr ˈei
eradi|cate ɪ ˈræd i |keɪt ə-, §-ə- ~**cated** keɪt ɪd
  -əd ‖ keɪt̬ əd ~**cates** keɪts ~**cating**
  keɪt ɪŋ ‖ keɪt̬ ɪŋ
eradication ɪ ˌræd i ˈkeɪʃ ᵊn ə-, §-ə- ~**s** z
eradicator ɪ ˈræd i keɪt ə ə-, §-ˈ•ə- ‖ -keɪt̬ ᵊr
  ~**s** z
erase ɪ ˈreɪz ə- ‖ ɪ ˈreɪs (*) **erased** ɪ ˈreɪzd ə-
  ‖ ɪ ˈreɪst **erases** ɪ ˈreɪz ɪz ə-, -əz ‖ ɪ ˈreɪs əz
  erasing ɪ ˈreɪz ɪŋ ə- ‖ ɪ ˈreɪs ɪŋ
eraser ɪ ˈreɪz ə ə- ‖ ɪ ˈreɪs ᵊr ~**s** z
Erasmian ɪ ˈræz mi ̣ən e-, ə-, ~**s** z
Erasmus ɪ ˈræz məs e-, ə-
Erastian ɪ ˈræst i ̣ən e-, ə-, ‖ -ˈræs tʃən ~**ism**
  ˌɪz əm ~**s** z
erasure ɪ ˈreɪʒ ə ə- ‖ ɪ ˈreɪʃ ᵊr ~**s** z
Erato ˈer ə təʊ ‖ -toʊ
Eratosthenes ˌer ə ˈtɒsθ ə niːz ‖ -ˈtɑːsθ-
erbium ˈɜːb i ̣əm ‖ ˈɝːb-
Erdington ˈɜːd ɪŋ tən ‖ ˈɝːd-
ere *'before'* eə ‖ eᵊr æᵊr (= *air*)
'ere *'here'* ɪə ‖ ɪᵊr —*a nonstandard form of* here
Erebus ˈer ɪb əs -əb-
Erechtheum ˌer ek ˈθiː ̣əm -ɪk-,
  -ək- ‖ ɪ ˈrek θi ̣əm
Erechtheus ɪ ˈrek θjuːs e-, ə-, -ˈ•θi ̣əs
  ‖ -ˈrek θi ̣əs
erect *adj, v* ɪ ˈrekt ə- ~**ed** ɪd əd ~**ing** ɪŋ ~**ly** li
  ~**ness** nəs nɪs ~**s** s
erectile ɪ ˈrekt aɪᵊl ə- ‖ -ᵊl -aɪᵊl
erection ɪ ˈrek ʃᵊn ə- ~**s** z
erector ɪ ˈrekt ə ə- ‖ -ᵊr ~**s** z
eremite ˈer ə maɪt -ɪ- ~**s** s
eremitic ˌer ə ˈmɪt ɪk ◄ -ɪ- ‖ -ˈmɪt̬- ~**al** ᵊl
erethism ˈer ə ˌθɪz əm -ɪ-
Eretz ˈer ets -ɪts, §-əts —*Hebrew* [ˈɛ rets]
Erewhon ˈer ɪ wɒn -ə-, -hwɒn ‖ -hwɑːn -hwʌn,
  -wɑːn, -wʌn
Erfurt ˈeə fɜːt ‖ ˈer- —*Ger* [ˈɛʁ fʊʁt]
erg ɜːg ‖ ɝːg **ergs** ɜːgz ‖ ɝːgz
ergative ˈɜːg ət ɪv ‖ ˈɝːg ət̬ ɪv ~**ly** li ~**s** z
ergativity ˌɜːg ə ˈtɪv ət i -ɪt i ‖ ˌɝːg ə ˈtɪv ət̬ i
ergo ˈɜːg əʊ ˈeəg- ‖ ˈerg oʊ ˈɝːg-
ergonomic ˌɜːg ə ˈnɒm ɪk ◄ ‖ ˌɝːg ə ˈnɑːm ɪk ◄
  ~**ally** ᵊl ̣i ~**s** s
ergonomist ɜː ˈgɒn əm ɪst §-əst ‖ ɝː ˈgɑːn-
  ~**s** s

ergosterol ɜː ˈgɒst ə rɒl ‖ ɝː ˈgɑːst ə roʊl -rɔːl,
  -rɑːl
ergot ˈɜːg ət -ɒt ‖ ˈɝːg- -ɑːt
ergotism ˈɜːg ə ˌtɪz əm ‖ ˈɝːg-
Eric ˈer ɪk
Erica, erica ˈer ɪk ə ~**s**, ~ˈs z
ericaceous ˌer ɪ ˈkeɪʃ əs ◄ -ə-
Ericsson *tdmk* ˈer ɪks ᵊn —*Swed* [ˈeː rɪk sɔn]
Eridan|us e ˈrɪd ᵊn |əs ɪ-, ə- ~**i** aɪ
Erie ˈɪər i ‖ ˈɪr i
  ˌErie Caˈnal
Erik ˈer ɪk
Erika ˈer ɪk ə
Erin ˈer ɪn ˈɪər-, ˈeər-, §-ᵊn
Eris ˈer ɪs §-əs
eristic e ˈrɪst ɪk ɪ-, ə- ~**s** s
Erith ˈɪər ɪθ §-əθ ‖ ˈɪr-
Eritre|a ˌer ɪ ˈtreɪ ə -ə-, -ˈtriː ̣ə ‖ -ˈtriː ̣ə
  ~**an/s** ən/z
erk ɜːk ‖ ɝːk (= *irk*) **erks** ɜːks ‖ ɝːks
Erle ɜːl ‖ ɝːl
erlking ˈɜːl kɪŋ ‖ ˈɝːl-
ERM ˌi: ɑːr ˈem ‖ -ˈɑːr-
ermine ˈɜːm ɪn §-ᵊn ‖ ˈɝːm- ~**d** d ~**s** z
erne, Erne ɜːn ‖ ɝːn (= *earn*) **ernes**
  ɜːnz ‖ ɝːnz
Ernest ˈɜːn ɪst -əst ‖ ˈɝːn-
Ernestina ˌɜːn ɪ ˈstiːn ə -ə-, ‖ ˌɝːn-
Ernie ˈɜːn i ‖ ˈɝːn i
Ernle ˈɜːn li ‖ ˈɝːn-
Ernst eənˈtst ɜːnˈtst ‖ ɝːnˈtst —*Ger* [ʔɛʁnst]
erod|e ɪ ˈrəʊd ə- ‖ ɪ ˈroʊd ~**ed** ɪd əd ~**es** z
  ~**ing** ɪŋ
erogenous ɪ ˈrɒdʒ ᵊn əs e-, ə-, -ɪn- ‖ ɪ ˈrɑːdʒ-
Eroica ɪ ˈrəʊ ɪk ə e-, ə- ‖ ɪ ˈroʊ-
Eros ˈɪər ɒs ˈer-, -əʊz ‖ ˈer ɑːs ˈɪr-
erosion ɪ ˈrəʊʒ ᵊn ə- ‖ ɪ ˈroʊʒ ᵊn ~**s** z
erosive ɪ ˈrəʊs ɪv ə- ‖ ɪ ˈroʊs- ~**ly** li
erotic ɪ ˈrɒt ɪk ə- ‖ ɪ ˈrɑːt̬ ɪk ~**ally** ᵊl ̣i
erotica ɪ ˈrɒt ɪk ə ə- ‖ ɪ ˈrɑːt̬ ɪk ə
eroticis... —*see* **eroticiz...**
eroticism ɪ ˈrɒt ɪ ˌsɪz əm ə-, -ə- ‖ ɪ ˈrɑːt̬ ə-
eroticization ɪ ˌrɒt ɪs aɪ ˈzeɪʃ ᵊn ə-, ˌ•əs-, -ɪˈ•-
  ‖ ɪ ˈrɑːt̬ əs ə-
eroticiz|e ɪ ˈrɒt ɪ saɪz ə-, -ə- ‖ ɪ ˈrɑːt̬ ə- ~**ed** d
  ~**es** ɪz əz ~**ing** ɪŋ
erotogenic ɪ ˌrɒt ə ˈdʒen ɪk ◄ ə-, ˌrəʊt-
  ‖ ɪ ˌroʊt̬ ə- ɪ ˌrɑːt̬ ə- ~**ally** ᵊl ̣i
erotoman|ia ɪ ˌrɒt əʊ ˈmeɪn i ̣ə ə-, -ˌrəʊt-
  ‖ ɪ ˌroʊt̬ ə- ɪ ˌrɑːt̬ ə- ~**iac/s** i æk/s
Erpingham ˈɜːp ɪŋ əm ‖ ˈɝːp ɪŋ hæm
err ɜː §eə ‖ eᵊr ɝː **erred** ɜːd §eəd ‖ eᵊrd ɝːd
  erring ˈɜːr ɪŋ §ˈeᵊr-, §ˈeər- ‖ ˈer ɪŋ ˈɝː- **errs**
  ɜːz §eəz ‖ eᵊrz ɝːz
errancy ˈer ᵊnts i
errand ˈer ᵊnd ~**s** z
errant ˈer ᵊnt ~**ly** li
errata e ˈrɑːt ə ɪ-, ə-, -ˈreɪt- ‖ e ˈrɑːt̬ ə -ˈreɪt̬-,
  -ˈræt̬-
erratic ɪ ˈræt ɪk e-, ə- ‖ ɪ ˈræt̬ ɪk ~**ally** ᵊl ̣i ~**s** s
errat|um e ˈrɑːt ləm ɪ-, ə-, -ˈreɪt- ‖ e ˈrɑːt̬ ləm
  -ˈreɪt̬-, -ˈræt̬- ~**a** ə
errhine ˈer aɪn -ɪn

E

erring 'ɜːr ɪŋ §'er-, §'eər- ‖ 'er- 'ɜ·:- **~ly** li
Errol, Erroll 'er əl
erroneous ɪ 'rəʊn i‿əs e-, ə- ‖ ɪ 'roʊn- **~ly** li
  ~ness nəs nɪs
error 'er ə ‖ -ᵊr **~s** z
ersatz 'eə zæts 'ɜː-, -sæts, -zɑːts, •'•
  ‖ 'er zɑːts 'ɜː-, -sɑːts, -sæts, •'• —Ger
  [ʔɛʁ 'zats]
Erse ɜːs ‖ ɜːs
Erskine 'ɜːsk ɪn §-ən ‖ 'ɜːsk-
erstwhile 'ɜːst waɪᵊl -hwaɪᵊl ‖ 'ɜːst hwaɪᵊl
erubescence ,er u 'bes ᵊnts
erubescent ,er u 'bes ᵊnt **~ly** li
eructation ,iː rʌk 'teɪʃ ᵊn ɪ ,rʌk-; ,er ʌk-, -ək-
  ~s z
erudite 'er u daɪt -ju- ‖ -jə- -ə- **~ly** li **~ness**
  nəs nɪs
erudition ,er u 'dɪʃ ᵊn -ju- ‖ -jə- -ə-
erupt ɪ 'rʌpt ə- **~ed** ɪd əd **~ing** ɪŋ **~s** s
eruption ɪ 'rʌp ʃᵊn ə- **~s** z
eruptive ɪ 'rʌpt ɪv ə- **~ly** li
Ervine 'ɜːv ɪn §-ən, -aɪn ‖ 'ɜː·v-
-ery ər i —This stress-neutral suffix is used only
  after a strong-vowelled syllable (ma'chinery);
  after a weak-vowelled syllable the variant -ry ri
  is used instead ('dentistry).
Erymanthian ,er ɪ 'mænt θ i‿ən ◄
erysipelas ,er ɪ 'sɪp əl əs , •ə-, -ɪl əs
erythema ,er ɪ 'θiːm ə -ə-
erythrocyte ɪ 'rɪθ rəʊ saɪt ə- ‖ -rə- **~s** s
erythromycin ɪ ,rɪθ rəʊ 'maɪs ɪn ə-, §-ᵊn ‖ -rə-
erythropoietic ɪ ,rɪθ rəʊ pɔɪ 'et ɪk ◄ ə-
  ‖ -rə pɔɪ 'eʈ-
-es ending of pl or 3rd person sing., **-es'**
  possessive pl ending —There are two
  pronunciations: 1. After a sibilant sound
  (s, z, ʃ, ʒ, tʃ, dʒ) the ending is pronounced ɪz
  or, less commonly in BrE but regularly in AmE,
  əz, as pushes 'pʊʃ ɪz, -əz, churches'
  'tʃɜːtʃ ɪz, -əz. (In singing a strong-vowelled
  variant ez is occasionally used.) 2. Where the
  spelling y is changed to i, this ending is
  pronounced z, as cry — cries kraɪz. See also
  -s.
Esau 'iːs ɔː ‖ -ɑː
Esbjerg 'es bjɜːg ‖ -bjɜ·:g —Dan ['ɛs bjɛʁ?]
escalad|e ,esk ə 'leɪd '••• **~ed** ɪd əd **~es** z
  ~ing ɪŋ
esca|late 'esk ə |leɪt **~lated** leɪt ɪd -əd ‖ leɪʈ əd
  ~lates leɪts **~lating** leɪt ɪŋ ‖ leɪʈ ɪŋ
escalation ,esk ə 'leɪʃ ᵊn **~s** z
escalator 'esk ə leɪt ə ⚠•jə- ‖ -leɪʈ ᵊr **~s** z
escallonia ,esk ə 'ləʊn i‿ə ‖ -'loʊn-
escallop, escalope 'esk ə lɒp ◄, •'•'•;
  e 'skæl əp, -ɒp ‖ ɪ 'skæl əp (*) **~s** s
escapade ,esk ə 'peɪd '••• ‖ 'esk ə peɪd **~s** z
escap|e ɪ 'skeɪp e-, ə- **~ed** t **~es** s **~ing** ɪŋ
  e'scape road; e'scape ve,locity; e'scape
  wheel
escapee ɪ ,skeɪ 'piː ,esk eɪ 'piː **~s** z
escapement ɪ 'skeɪp mənt e-, ə- **~s** s
escapism ɪ 'skeɪp ,ɪz əm e-, ə-
escapist ɪ 'skeɪp ɪst e-, ə-, §-əst **~s** s

escapologist ,esk ə 'pɒl ədʒ ɪst , •eɪ-, §-əst
  ‖ -'pɑːl- **~s** z
escapology ,esk ə 'pɒl ədʒ i , •eɪ- ‖ -'pɑːl-
escargot ɪ 'skɑːg əʊ e- ‖ ,esk ɑːr 'goʊ (*) —Fr
  [ɛ skaʁ go] **~s** z
escarpment ɪ 'skɑːp mənt e-, ə- ‖ ɪ 'skɑːrp-
  ~s s
-esce 'es — **opalesce** ,əʊp ə 'les ‖ ,oʊp-
-escence 'es ᵊnts — **phosphorescence**
  ,fɒs fə 'res ᵊnts ‖ ,fɑːs-
-escent 'es ᵊnt — **frutescent** fruː 'tes ᵊnt
eschatological ,esk ət ə 'lɒdʒ ɪk ᵊl ◄, •æt-
  ‖ -əʈ ə 'lɑːdʒ- **~ly** ‿i
eschatology ,esk ə 'tɒl ədʒ i ‖ -'tɑːl-
es|cheat ɪs 'tʃiːt es-, əs- **~cheated** 'tʃiːt ɪd
  -əd ‖ 'tʃiːʈ əd **~cheating** 'tʃiːt ɪŋ ‖ 'tʃiːʈ ɪŋ
  ~cheats 'tʃiːts
Escher 'eʃ ə ‖ -ᵊr —Dutch ['ɛʃ ər]
escherichia ,eʃ ə 'rɪk i‿ə
eschew ɪs 'tʃuː es-, əs-; ⚠ɪ 'ʃuː **~ed** d **~ing**
  ɪŋ **~s** z
eschscholtzia ɪ 'ʃɒlts i‿ə e-, ə-, -'skɒlts-;
  -'skɒlʃ ə, -'skɒltʃ ə ‖ ɪ 'ʃɑːlts- **~s** z
Escoffier ɪ 'skɒf i eɪ e-, ə- ‖ ,esk ɑːf 'jeɪ —Fr
  [ɛ skɔ fje]
Escondido ,esk ən 'diːd əʊ ‖ -oʊ -ɑːn-
Escorial e 'skɔːr i æl -ɑːl, -i‿əl, ,esk ɒr ɪ 'ɑːl
  ‖ -i‿əl -'skoʊr- —Sp [es ko 'rjal]
escort n 'esk ɔːt ‖ -ɔːrt **~s** s
e|scort v ɪ 'skɔːt e-, ə-; 'eɪsk ɔːt ‖ ɪ 'skɔːrt e-
  ~scorted skɔːt ɪd -əd ‖ skɔːrʈ əd **~scorting**
  skɔːt ɪŋ ‖ skɔːrʈ ɪŋ **~scorts** skɔːts ‖ skɔːrts
escritoire ,esk rə 'twɑː -riː-, -rɪ- ‖ -'twɑːr **~s** z
escrow 'esk rəʊ es 'krəʊ ‖ 'esk roʊ es 'kroʊ
escudo ɪ 'ʃkuːd əʊ e-, ə-, -'skuːd-, -'skjuːd-
  ‖ -oʊ —Port [ɪ 'ʃku ðu] **~s** z
esculent 'es kjʊl ənt ‖ -jəl-
escutcheon ɪ 'skʌtʃ ən e- **~s** z
Esda 'es də 'ez-
Esdras 'ez dræs -drəs ‖ -drəs
-ese 'iːz ‖ -'iːs — **journalese**
  ,dʒɜːn ə 'liːz ◄ ‖ ,dʒɜ·:n- -'liːs **Japanese**
  ,dʒæp ə 'niːz ◄ ‖ -'niːs
Esher 'iːʃ ə ‖ -ᵊr
Esk esk
Eskdale 'esk deɪᵊl
esker 'esk ə ‖ -ᵊr **~s** z
Eskimo 'esk ɪ məʊ -ə- ‖ -moʊ **~s** z
ESL ,iː es 'el
Esme, Esmé 'ez mi
Esmeralda ,ez mə 'ræld ə
Esmond 'ez mənd
ESN ,iː es 'en
ESOL 'iːs ɒl ‖ -ɑːl
esophageal iː ,sɒf ə 'dʒiː‿əl ◄ ɪ-, ə-, ,iːs ɒf-
  ‖ ɪ ,sɑːf-
esophagus iː 'sɒf əg əs ɪ-, ə- ‖ ɪ 'sɑːf- **~es** ɪz
  əz
esoteric ,es əʊ 'ter ɪk ◄ ,iːs- ‖ ,es ə- **~ally** əl‿i
ESP ,iː es 'piː
espadrille ,esp ə 'drɪl '••• ‖ 'esp ə drɪl **~s** z
espalier ɪ 'spæl i eɪ e-, ə-, -i‿ə ‖ -'spæl jᵊr -jeɪ
  ~s z

esparto e ˈspɑːt əʊ ɪ- ‖ ɪ ˈspɑːṛṭ oʊ
especial ɪ ˈspeʃ ᵊl e-, ə-, ⚠ɪk-, ⚠ək- ~**ly** i
Esperantist ˌesp ə ˈrænt ɪst ◄ -ˈrɑːnt-, §-əst
  ‖ -ˈrɑːnṭ- ~**s** s
Esperanto ˌesp ə ˈrænt əʊ -ˈrɑːnt- ‖ -ˈrɑːnṭ oʊ
  —*Esperanto* [es pe ˈran to]
espial ɪ ˈspaɪ_əl e-, ə-
espie... —*see* **espy**
espionage ˈesp i_ə nɑːʒ -nɑːdʒ, ˌ•••ˈ•,
  ˈesp i_ən ɪdʒ
esplanade ˌesp lə ˈneɪd -ˈnɑːd, ˈ•••
  ‖ ˈesp lə nɑːd -neɪd ~**s** z
Esposito ˌesp ə ˈziːt əʊ -ˈsiːt- ‖ -ˈziːṭ oʊ -ˈsiːṭ-
  —*Sp* [es po ˈsi to]
espousal ɪ ˈspaʊz ᵊl e-, ə- ~**s** z
espouse ɪ ˈspaʊz e-, ə-, §-ˈspaʊs **espoused**
  ɪ ˈspaʊzd e-, ə-, §-ˈspaʊst **espouses**
  ɪ ˈspaʊz ɪz e-, ə-, §-ˈspaʊs-, -əz **espousing**
  ɪ ˈspaʊz ɪŋ e-, ə-, §-ˈspaʊs-
espresso e ˈspres əʊ ‖ -oʊ —*It* [e ˈsprɛs so] ~**s**
  z
esprit, E~ e ˈspriː ɪ-, ə- —*See also phrases with
  this word*
esprit de corps e ˌspriː də ˈkɔː ɪ-, ə-; ˌesp riː-
  ‖ -ˈkɔːr -ˈkoʊr —*Fr* [ɛs pʁid kɔːʁ]
esprit d'escalier e ˌspriː des ˈkæl i eɪ ɪ-, ə-
  ‖ e ˌspriː ˌdesk aːl ˈjeɪ —*Fr*
  [ɛs pʁi dɛs kal je]
e|spy ɪ ˈspaɪ e-, ə- ~**spied** ˈspaɪd ~**spies**
  ˈspaɪz ~**spying** ˈspaɪ ɪŋ
Espy ˈesp i
Esq. —*see* **Esquire**
-esque ˈesk — **Chaplinesque** ˌtʃæp lɪn ˈesk ◄
  -lən-
Esquiline ˈesk wɪ laɪn -wə-
Esquimalt ɪ ˈskwaɪm ɔːlt e-, ə-, -ɒlt ‖ -ɑːlt
esquire ɪ ˈskwaɪ_ə e-, ə- ‖ ˈesk waɪ_ᵊr
  ɪ ˈskwaɪ_ᵊr, e- ~**s** z
ESRC ˌiː es ɑː ˈsiː ‖ -ɑːr ˈ•
-ess ˈes, es, ɪs əs —*There is great inter-speaker
  variability in the treatment of this suffix. See
  individual entries.*
essay *n* 'piece of writing' ˈes eɪ ~**s** z
essay *n* 'attempt' ˈes eɪ e ˈseɪ ~**s** z
essay *v* e ˈseɪ ˈes eɪ ~**ed** d ~**ing** ɪŋ ~**s** z
essayist ˈes eɪ ɪst §-əst ~**s** s
esse ˈes i
Essen ˈes ᵊn —*Ger* [ˈʔɛs ᵊn]
essenc|e ˈes ᵊnts ~**es** ɪz əz
Essendon ˈes ᵊn dən
Essene ˈes iːn e ˈsiːn ‖ ɪ ˈsiːn e-; ˈes iːn ~**s** z
essential ɪ ˈsentʃ ᵊl e-, ə- ~**ly** i ~**ness** nəs nɪs
  ~**s** z
essentialit|y ɪ ˌsentʃ i ˈæl ət i e-, ə-, -ɪt li
  ‖ -əṭ li ~**ies** iz
Essex ˈes ɪks -əks
essive ˈes ɪv ~**s** z
Essling ˈes lɪŋ
Esso *tdmk* ˈes əʊ ‖ -oʊ
Essoldo e ˈsɒld əʊ ɪ-, ə- ‖ -ˈsɑːld oʊ
-est *superlative ending* ɪst əst — **biggest**
  ˈbɪg ɪst -əst, **nicest** ˈnaɪs ɪst -əst

-est *archaic and liturgical second person sing.
  ending* — **sendest** ˈsend ɪst -əst, **takest**
  ˈteɪk ɪst -əst
establish ɪ ˈstæb lɪʃ e-, ə- ~**ed** t ~**er/s** ə/
  z ‖ ᵊr/z ~**es** ɪz əz ~**ing** ɪŋ
  e, stablished ˈchurch
establishment, E~ ɪ ˈstæb lɪʃ mənt e-, ə- ~**s** s
establishmentarian
  ɪ ˌstæb lɪʃ mən ˈteər i_ən ◄ e-, ə- ‖ -ˈter- ~**s**
  z
estaminet e ˈstæm ɪ neɪ ɪ-, -ə-
  ‖ e ˌstaːm iː ˈneɪ —*Fr* [ɛs ta mi ne] ~**s** z
estancia ɪ ˈstænts i_ə e- ‖ e ˈstaːnts- —*AmSp*
  [es ˈtan sja] ~**s** z
estate ɪ ˈsteɪt e-, ə- ~**s** s
  e' state ˌagent; e' state ˈcar
Estcourt ˈesʈ kɔːt ‖ -kɔːrt -koʊrt
Este ˈest i —*It* [ˈɛs te]
Estee, Estée ˈest eɪ -i
esteem ɪ ˈstiːm e-, ə- ~**ed** d ~**ing** ɪŋ ~**s** z
Estefan ˈest ə fæn -ɪ-
Estella ɪ ˈstel ə e-, ə-
Estelle ɪ ˈstel e-, ə-
ester ˈest ə ‖ -ᵊr ~**s** z
esteras|e ˈest ə reɪz -reɪs ~**es** ɪz əz
Esterhazy ˈest ə haːz i ‖ ˈ•ᵊr- —*Hung*
  Eszterházy [ˈɛs tɛr haː zi]
Esther ˈest ə ˈesθ- ‖ -ᵊr
esthete ˈiːs θiːt ‖ ˈes- *(*)* ~**s** s
esthetic iːs ˈθet ɪk ɪs- ‖ es ˈθeṭ ɪk ~**al** ᵊl ~**ally**
  ᵊl_i ~**s** s
estheticism iːs ˈθet ɪ ˌsɪz əm -ə- ‖ es ˈθeṭ ə-
  ɪs-
Esthwaite ˈes θweɪt
estimab|le ˈest ɪm əb ᵊl ˈ•əm- ~**leness** ᵊl nəs
  -nɪs ~**ly** li
esti|mate *v* ˈest ɪ meɪt -ə-, -mət ~**mated**
  meɪt ɪd -əd ‖ meɪṭ əd ~**mates** meɪts
  ~**mating** meɪt ɪŋ ‖ meɪṭ ɪŋ
estimate *n* ˈest ɪm ət -əm-, -ɪt; -ɪ meɪt, -ə- ~**s** s
estimation ˌest ɪ ˈmeɪʃ ᵊn -ə- ~**s** z
estimator ˈest ɪ meɪt ə ˈ•ə- ‖ -meɪṭ ᵊr ~**s** z
estival i ˈstaɪv ᵊl ‖ ˈest əv ᵊl
esti|vate ˈiːst ɪ |veɪt ˈest-, -ə- ~**vated** veɪt ɪd
  -əd ‖ veɪṭ əd ~**vates** veɪts ~**vating**
  veɪt ɪŋ ‖ veɪṭ ɪŋ
estivation ˌiːst ɪ ˈveɪʃ ᵊn ˌest-, -ə- ~**s** z
Estoni|a e ˈstəʊn i_ə ɪ-, ə- ‖ -ˈstoʊn- ~**an/s**
  ən/z
estop ɪ ˈstɒp e-, ə- ‖ e ˈstaːp ~**ped** t ~**ping**
  ɪŋ ~**s** s
estoppel ɪ ˈstɒp ᵊl e-, ə- ‖ e ˈstaːp-
Estoril ˌest ə ˈrɪl ˈ••• —*Port* [ɪʃ tu ˈril]
estovers ɪ ˈstəʊv əz e-, ə- ‖ e ˈstoʊv ᵊrz ɪ-
estrade e ˈstraːd ɪ-, ə- ~**s** z
estradiol ˌes trə ˈdaɪ ɒl ˌiːs- ‖ -oʊl -ɔːl, -aːl
estragon, E~ ˈes trə gɒn ‖ -gaːn —*Fr*
  [ɛs tʁa gɔ̃]
estrang|e ɪ ˈstreɪndʒ e-, ə- ~**ed** d ~**es** ɪz əz
  ~**ing** ɪŋ
estrangement ɪ ˈstreɪndʒ mənt e-, ə- ~**s** s
estreat ɪ ˈstriːt e- ~**s** s
estrogen ˈiːs trədʒ ən ˈes- ‖ ˈes-

estrous, estrus 'iːs trəs 'es- ‖ 'es-
estuarine 'est ju_ə raɪn -rɪn ‖ 'es tʃu‿
estuar|y 'est jʊr li '•‿ju_ər li; 'es tʃʊr li, 'eʃ-
‖ 'es tʃu er li ~ies iz
esurienc|e ɪ 'sjʊər i_ənts ‖ ɪ 'sʊr- ~y i
esurient ɪ 'sjʊər i_ənt ‖ ɪ 'sʊr- ~ly li
et et —See also phrases with this word
ET ˌiː 'tiː
eta Greek letter 'iːt ə ‖ 'eɪt ə 'iːt̬ ə (*)
ETA 'estimated time of arrival' ˌiː tiː 'eɪ
ETA Basque organization 'et ə
etagere, étagère ˌeɪt ə 'ʒeə, et-, -æ-, -ɑː-
‖ -'ʒeᵊr —Fr [e ta ʒɛːʁ] ~s z
et al, et al. ˌ(ˌ)et 'æl ‖ ˌ(ˌ)et̬ 'ɑːl -'æl, -'ɔːl
Etam tdmk 'iːt æm
etc., etcetera, et cetera ˌ(ˌ)et 'setr ə ɪt-, ət-,
⚠ˌ(ˌ)ek-, -'set̬ ər ə ‖ -'set̬ ər ə →-'setr ə
etch etʃ etched etʃt etches 'etʃ ɪz -əz
etching/s 'etʃ ɪŋ/z
etch-a-sketch 'etʃ ə sketʃ
etcher/s 'etʃ ə/z ‖ -ᵊr/z
Etchingham ˌetʃ ɪŋ 'hæm
Eteocles 'et i_ə kliːz ɪ 'tiː_ə- ‖ ɪ 'tiː ə-
eternal ɪ 'tɜːn ᵊl iː-, ə- ‖ ɪ 'tɜːn ᵊl ~ly i
    e,ternal 'triangle
eternalis|e, eternaliz|e ɪ 'tɜːn ə laɪz iː-, ə-,
-ᵊl aɪz ‖ ɪ 'tɜːn- ~ed d ~es ɪz əz ~ing ɪŋ
etern|ity ɪ 'tɜːn ət li iː-, ə-, -ɪt- ‖ ɪ 'tɜːn ət̬ li
~ies iz
    e'ternity ring
Etesian ɪ 'tiːʒ i_ən -'tiːz-; -'tiːʒ ən ‖ ɪ 'tiːʒ ən
eth letter name eð
Eth woman's name eθ
-eth archaic and liturgical third person sing.
    ending ɪθ əθ — sendeth 'send ɪθ -əθ,
    taketh 'teɪk ɪθ -əθ
Ethan 'iːθ ən
ethane 'iːθ eɪn 'eθ- ‖ 'eθ-
ethanoic ˌeθ ə 'nəʊ ɪk ◄ ˌiːθ- ‖ -'noʊ-
ethanol 'eθ ə nɒl 'iːθ- ‖ -nɒʊl -nɔːl, -nɑːl
Ethel 'eθ ᵊl
Ethelbert 'eθ ᵊl bɜːt ‖ -bɜːt
Ethelberta ˌeθ ᵊl 'bɜːt ə ‖ -'bɜːt̬ ə
Ethelburga ˌeθ ᵊl 'bɜːg ə ‖ -'bɜːg ə
Etheldreda 'eθ ᵊl driːd ə
Ethelred 'eθ ᵊl red
ether 'iːθ ə ‖ -ᵊr
ethereal ɪ 'θɪər i_əl iː-, ə- ‖ ɪ 'θɪr- ~ly i ~ness
    nəs nɪs
etherealis|e, etherealiz|e ɪ 'θɪər i_ə laɪz iː-, ə-
‖ ɪ 'θɪr- ~ed d ~es ɪz əz ~ing ɪŋ
Etheredge, Etherege, Etheridge 'eθ ᵊr ɪdʒ
Ethernet, e~ tdmk 'iːθ ə net ‖ -ᵊr-
ethic 'eθ ɪk ~s s
ethical 'eθ ɪk ᵊl ~ly _i ~ness nəs nɪs
Ethiop 'iːθ i ɒp ‖ -ɑːp ~s s
Ethiope 'iːθ i əʊp ‖ -oʊp ~s s
Ethiopi|a ˌiːθ i 'əʊp i_ə ‖ -'oʊp- ~an/s ən/z
Ethiopic ˌiːθ i 'ɒp ɪk ◄ -'əʊp- ‖ -'ɑːp- -'oʊp-
ethmoid 'eθ mɔɪd ~s z
ethnarch 'eθ nɑːk ‖ -nɑːrk ~s s
Ethne 'eθ ni
ethnic 'eθ nɪk ~ally ᵊl_i ~s s

ethnicity eθ 'nɪs ət i -ɪt- ‖ -ət̬ i
ethno- comb. form
    with stress-neutral suffix ˌeθ nəʊ ‖ ˌeθ noʊ —
    ethnobotany ˌeθ nəʊ 'bɒt
    ən i ‖ ˌeθ noʊ 'bɑːt ən i
    with stress-imposing suffix eθ 'nɒ+ ‖ eθ 'nɑː+
    — ethnogeny eθ 'nɒdʒ ən i ‖ -'nɑːdʒ-
ethnocentric ˌeθ nəʊ 'sentr ɪk ◄ -noʊ-
ethnocentrism ˌeθ nəʊ 'sentr ˌɪz əm ‖ -noʊ-
ethnocentricity ˌeθ nəʊ sen 'trɪs ət i -ɪt i
‖ -noʊ sen 'trɪs ət̬ i
ethnographer eθ 'nɒg rəf ə ‖ -'nɑːg rəf ᵊr ~s
    z
ethnographic ˌeθ nə 'græf ɪk ◄ ~al ᵊl ~ally
    ᵊl_i
ethnography eθ 'nɒg rəf i ‖ -'nɑːg-
ethnological ˌeθ nə 'lɒdʒ ɪk ᵊl ◄ ‖ -'lɑːdʒ- ~ly
    _i
ethnologist eθ 'nɒl ədʒ ɪst §-əst ‖ -'nɑːl- ~s s
ethnology eθ 'nɒl ədʒ i ‖ -'nɑːl-
ethnomethodolog|ist/s
    ˌeθ nəʊ ˌmeθ ə 'dɒl ədʒ ɪst/s §-əst/s
‖ -noʊ ˌmeθ ə 'dɑːl- ~y i
ethnomusicological
    ˌeθ nəʊ ˌmjuːz ɪk ə 'lɒdʒ ɪk ᵊl
‖ -noʊ ˌmjuːz ɪk ə 'lɑːdʒ- ~ly _i
ethnomusicolog|ist/s
    ˌeθ nəʊ ˌmjuːz ɪ 'kɒl ədʒ ɪst/s -, •ə-, §-əst/s
‖ -noʊ ˌmjuːz ɪ 'kɑːl- ~y i
ethological ˌeθ ə 'lɒdʒ ɪk ᵊl ◄ ˌiːθ- ‖ -'lɑːdʒ-
    ~ly _i
etholog|ist/s iː 'θɒl ədʒ ɪst/s ɪ-, §-əst/s
‖ -'θɑːl- ~y i
ethos 'iːθ ɒs -ɑːs 'eθ-, -oʊs
ethyl 'eθ ᵊl -ɪl; 'iːθ aɪᵊl
    ˌethyl 'alcohol
ethylene 'eθ ə liːn -ɪ-
    ˌethylene 'glycol
etic 'et ɪk ‖ 'et̬ ɪk ~ally ᵊl_i
Etienne ˌet i 'en —Fr [e tjɛn]
etio|late 'iːt i_ə |leɪt -i əʊ- ‖ 'iːt̬- ~lated leɪt ɪd
    -əd ‖ leɪt̬ əd ~lates leɪts ~lating
    leɪt ɪŋ ‖ leɪt̬ ɪŋ
etiolation ˌiːt i_ə 'leɪʃ ən -i əʊ- ‖ ˌiːt̬-
etiological ˌiːt i_ə 'lɒdʒ ɪk ᵊl ◄ ˌiːt̬ i_ə 'lɑːdʒ-
    ~ly _i
etiolog|y ˌiːt i 'ɒl ədʒ li i ‖ ˌiːt̬ i 'ɑːl- ~ies iz
etiquette 'et ɪ ket -ɪk ət, ˌet ɪ 'ket ‖ 'et̬ ɪk ət
    -ɪ ket ~s s
Etive 'et ɪv ‖ 'et̬-
Etna 'et nə
Eton 'iːt ᵊn (= eaten)
    ˌEton 'collar
Etonian iː 'təʊn i_ən ɪ- ‖ -'toʊn- ~s z
Etruria ɪ 'trʊər i_ə ə- ‖ ɪ 'trʊr-
Etruscan ɪ 'trʌsk ən ə- ~s z
-ette 'et — lecturette ˌlek tʃə 'ret
Ettie 'et i ‖ 'et̬ i
Ettrick 'etr ɪk
Etty 'et i ‖ 'et̬ i
etude, étude 'eɪ tjuːd •'• ‖ eɪ 'tuːd -'tjuːd,
    '•• —Fr [e tyd] ~s z
etui, étui e 'twiː ‖ eɪ- —Fr [e tɥi] ~s z

Etwall 'et wɔ:l ‖ -wɑ:l
etyma 'et ɪm ə -əm- ‖ 'eṭ-
etymological ˌet ɪm ə 'lɒdʒ ɪk əl ◄ ˌ•əm-
  ‖ ˌeṭ əm ə 'lɑːdʒ- ~ly ˌi
etymologis... —see etymologiz...
etymologist ˌet ɪ 'mɒl ədʒ ɪst ˌ•ə-, §-əst
  ‖ ˌeṭ ə 'mɑːl- ~s s
etymologiz|e ˌet ɪ 'mɒl ə dʒaɪz ˌ•ə-
  ‖ ˌeṭ ə 'mɑːl- ~ed d ~es ɪz əz ~ing ɪŋ
etymolog|y ˌet ɪ 'mɒl ədʒ |i ˌ•ə- ‖ ˌeṭ ə 'mɑːl-
  ~ies iz
ety|mon 'et ɪ |mɒn -ə- ‖ 'eṭ ə |mɑːn ~ma mə
EU ˌi: 'ju:
eu- ˌju:ˌ ju — eubacteria
  ˌju: bæk 'tɪər i‿ə ‖ -'tɪr- eupeptic
  ju 'pept ɪk
Euan 'ju:‿ən
Eubank 'ju: bæŋk
Euboea ju: 'bɪə jʊ-, -'bi: ə ‖ -'bi: ə
eucalypt 'ju:k ə lɪpt ~s s
eucalypt|us ˌju:k ə 'lɪpt |əs ~i aɪ ~uses əs ɪz
  -əz
eucharist, E~ 'ju:k ər ɪst §-əst ~s s
eucharistic, E~ ˌju:k ə 'rɪst ɪk ◄
euch|re 'ju:k |ə ‖ -|ər ~red əd ‖ ərd ~res
  əz ‖ ərz ~ring ər ɪŋ
Euclid 'ju:k lɪd §-ləd
Euclidean, Euclidian, e~ ju: 'klɪd i‿ən ~s z
Eucryl tdmk 'ju:k rɪl -rəl
eudiometer ˌju:d i 'ɒm ɪt ə -ət ə ‖ -'ɑːm əṭ ər
  ~s z
Eudora ju 'dɔːr ə ‖ -'dour-
Eudoxus ju 'dɒks əs ‖ -'dɑːks-
Euen 'ju:‿ən
Eugene 'ju: dʒiːn -ʒiːn, •'•; ju 'ʒeɪn
eugenic ju 'dʒen ɪk ~ally əl‿i ~s s
Eugenie, Eugénie ju 'ʒeɪn i -'ʒiːn-, -'dʒiːn-
  —Fr [ø ʒe ni]
eukaryote ju 'kær i əʊt -ɒt, -i‿ət ‖ -oʊt -'ker-
  ~s s
Eulalia ju 'leɪl i‿ə
Euler 'ɔɪl ə 'ju:l- ‖ -ər —Ger ['ʔɔy lɐ]
eulogies 'ju:l ədʒ iz
eulogis|e 'ju:l ə dʒaɪz ~ed d ~es ɪz əz ~ing
  ɪŋ
eulogist 'ju:l ədʒ ɪst §-əst ~s s
eulogistic ˌju:l ə 'dʒɪst ɪk ◄ ~ally əl‿i
eulogi|um ju 'ləʊdʒ i‿|əm ‖ -'loʊdʒ- ~a ə
  ~ums əmz
eulogiz|e 'ju:l ə dʒaɪz ~ed d ~es ɪz əz ~ing
  ɪŋ
eulog|y 'ju:l ədʒ |i ~ies iz
Eumenides ju 'men i diːz -ə-
Eunice 'ju:n ɪs -əs, ju 'naɪs i
Eunson 'ju:n sən
eunuch 'ju:n ək ~s s
euonymus ju 'ɒn ɪm əs -əm- ‖ -'ɑːn- ~es ɪz
  əz
Eupen 'ɜːp ən 'ju:p-, 'ɔɪp- ‖ 'ɔɪp- —Fr
  [ø pɛn], Ger ['ʔɔy pən]
eupeptic ju 'pept ɪk
Euphemia ju 'fiːm i‿ə
euphemism 'ju:f ə ˌmɪz əm -ɪ- ~s s

euphemistic ˌju:f ə 'mɪst ɪk ◄ -ɪ- ~ally əl‿i
euphonic ju 'fɒn ɪk ‖ -'fɑːn- ~ally əl‿i
euphonious ju 'fəʊn i‿əs ‖ -'foʊn- ~ly li
  ~ness nəs nɪs
euphonium ju 'fəʊn i‿əm ‖ -'foʊn- ~s z
euphon|y 'ju:f ən |i ~ies iz
euphorbia ju 'fɔːb i‿ə ‖ -'fɔːrb- ~s z
euphorbiaceous ju ˌfɔːb i 'eɪʃ əs ◄ ‖ -ˌfɔːrb-
euphoria ju 'fɔːr i‿ə -'fɒr- ‖ -'four-
euphoric ju 'fɒr ɪk ‖ -'fɔːr- -'fɑːr- ~ally əl‿i
Euphrates ju 'freɪt iːz
Euphrosyne ju 'frɒz ɪ niː -ə- ‖ -'frɑːs- -'frɑːz-
Euphues 'ju:f ju iːz
euphuism 'ju:f ju ˌɪz əm ~s z
euphuistic ˌju:f ju 'ɪst ɪk ◄
euploid 'ju:p lɔɪd ~s z
Eurailpass 'jʊər eɪəl pɑːs 'jɔːr-, §-pæs;
  jʊə 'reɪəl- ‖ 'jʊr eɪəl pæs ~es ɪz əz
Eurasia juə 'reɪʒ ə -'reɪʃ-
Eurasian juə 'reɪʒ ən -'reɪʃ- ~s z
Euratom juər 'æt əm ‖ -'æṭ-
eureka juə 'ri:k ə
eurhythmic juə 'rɪð mɪk -'rɪθ- ~ally əl‿i ~s s
Eurig 'aɪər ɪg —Welsh ['əɪrɪg, 'əi-]
Euripides juə 'rɪp ɪ diːz -ə-
euripus, E~ juə 'raɪp əs
euro 'jʊər əʊ 'jɔːr- ‖ 'jʊr oʊ ~s z
Euro- comb. form
  with stress-neutral suffix ˌjʊər əʊ ˌjɔːr-
  ‖ 'jʊr ə -oʊ — Eurocrat 'jʊər əʊ kræt 'jɔːr-
  ‖ 'jʊr ə-
  with stress-imposing suffix juə 'rɒ+ ‖ juə 'rɑː+
  — Eurocracy juə 'rɒk rəs i ‖ -'rɑːk-
Eurocheque 'jʊər əʊ tʃek 'jɔːr- ‖ 'jʊr oʊ- ~s
  s
Eurocommunism 'jʊər əʊ ˌkɒm ju nɪz əm
  ˌjɔːr-, -, ˌ•jə-, ˌ••'••, •• ‖ 'jʊr oʊ ˌkɑːm jə-
Eurocommunist 'jʊər əʊ ˌkɒm jʊn ɪst 'jɔːr-,
  -ˌ•jən-, §-əst; ˌ••'•- ‖ 'jʊr oʊ ˌkɑːm jən əst
  ~s s
Eurodisney tdmk 'jʊər əʊ ˌdɪz ni 'jɔːr-
  ‖ 'jʊr oʊ-
Eurodollar 'jʊər əʊ ˌdɒl ə 'jɔːr-, ˌ••'••
  ‖ 'jʊr oʊ ˌdɑːl ər ~s z
Euroland 'jʊər əʊ lænd 'jɔːr- ‖ 'jʊr oʊ-
Europa ju 'rəʊp ə ‖ -'roup ə
Europe 'jʊər əp 'jɔːr- ‖ 'jʊr əp 'jɝː-
European ˌjʊər ə 'pi:‿ən ◄ ˌjɔːr- ‖ ˌjʊr- ˌjɝː-
  ~s z
  ˌEuroˌpean Com'munities; ˌEuroˌpean
  'Parliament; ˌEuroˌpean plan
europium juə 'rəʊp i‿əm ‖ -'roup-
Europoort, Europort 'jʊər əʊ pɔːt 'jɔːr-
  ‖ 'jʊr oʊ pɔːrt -pourt —Dutch ['ø: ro: pɔːrt]
Eurostar tdmk 'jʊər əʊ stɑː 'jɔːr-
  ‖ 'jʊr oʊ stɑːr ~s z
Eurotra juə 'rəʊtr ə ‖ -'routr ə
Eurotrash 'jʊər əʊ træʃ 'jɔːr- ‖ 'jʊr oʊ-
Eurotunnel tdmk 'jʊər əʊ ˌtʌn əl 'jɔːr-
  ‖ 'jʊr oʊ-
Eurovision 'jʊər əʊ ˌvɪʒ ən 'jɔːr- ‖ 'jʊr oʊ-
  ˌEuroˌvision 'Song ˌContest
Eurus 'jʊər əs 'jɔːr- ‖ 'jʊr-

E

Eurydice juə 'rɪd ɪs i -əs-, -iː —*Also, where appropriate, pronounced in imitated Italian:* ˌjuər ɪ 'diːtʃ i, -eɪ ‖ ˌjur- —*It* [eu ri 'di tʃe]

eurythmic juə 'rɪð mɪk -'rɪθ- **~ally** ᵊl̩_i **~s** s

Eusebius ju 'siːb i_əs

Eustace 'juːst əs -ɪs

eustachian, E~ ju 'steɪʃ ᵊn -'steɪʃ i_ən; ju 'steɪk i_ən
Eu,stachian 'tube

Euston 'juːst ən

eutectic ju 'tekt ɪk **~s** s

Eutelsat *tdmk* 'juːt ᵊl sæt 'ju: tel- ‖ 'juːt̬-

Euterpe ju 'tɜːp i ‖ -'tɜːp i

euthanasia ˌjuːθ ə 'neɪz i_ə -'neɪʒ i_ə, -'neɪʒ ə ‖ -'neɪʒ ə

eutrophic ju 'trɒf ɪk -'trəʊf- ‖ -'troʊf-

eutrophication ju ˌtrɒf ɪ 'keɪʃ ᵊn ˌjuː-, -ə- ‖ -ˌtroʊf-

Euxine 'juːks aɪn ‖ -ᵊn

Euxton 'ekst ən

Eva 'iːv ə —*as a foreign name also* 'eɪv ə *or (esp AmE)* 'ev ə

evacu|ate ɪ 'væk ju leɪt ə- **~ated** eɪt ɪd -əd ‖ eɪt̬ əd **~ates** eɪts **~ating** eɪt ɪŋ ‖ eɪt̬ ɪŋ

evacuation ɪ ˌvæk ju 'eɪʃ ᵊn ə- **~s** z

evacuee ɪ ˌvæk ju 'iː ə- **~s** z

evad|e ɪ 'veɪd ə- **~ed** ɪd əd **~er/s** ə/z ‖ ᵊr/z **~es** z **~ing** ɪŋ

Evadne ɪ 'væd ni

evalu|ate ɪ 'væl ju leɪt ə- **~ated** eɪt ɪd -əd ‖ eɪt̬ əd **~ates** eɪts **~ating** eɪt ɪŋ ‖ eɪt̬ ɪŋ

evaluation ɪ ˌvæl ju 'eɪʃ ᵊn ə- **~s** z

evaluative ɪ 'væl ju_ət ɪv ə-, -ju eɪt- ‖ -ju eɪt̬ ɪv **~ly** li

Evan 'ev ᵊn

Evander ɪ 'vænd ə ə- ‖ -ᵊr

evanescence ˌev ə 'nes ᵊnᵗs ˌiːv-

evanescent ˌev ə 'nes ᵊnt ◄ ˌiːv- **~ly** li

evangel ɪ 'vændʒ ᵊl -el **~s** z

evangelic ˌiːv æn 'dʒel ɪk ◄ ‖ ˌev ᵊn- **~s** s

evangelical ˌiːv æn 'dʒel ɪk ᵊl ◄ ‖ ˌev ᵊn- **~ly** _i **~s** s

Evangeline ɪ 'vændʒ ə liːn -ɪ-, -laɪn

evangelis... —*see* **evangeliz...**

evangelism ɪ 'vændʒ ə ˌlɪz ᵊm ə-, -ɪ-

evangelist ɪ 'vændʒ ᵊl ɪst ə-, -ɪl-, §-əst **~s** s

evangelistic ɪ ˌvændʒ ə 'lɪst ɪk ◄ ə-, -ɪ- **~ally** ᵊl_i

evangelization ɪ ˌvændʒ ᵊl aɪ 'zeɪʃ ᵊn ə-, -ˌɪl-, -ɪ'•- ‖ -ᵊl_ə-

evangeliz|e ɪ 'vændʒ ə laɪz ə-, -ɪ- **~ed** d **~es** ɪz əz **~ing** ɪŋ

Evans 'ev ᵊnz

Evanston 'ev ᵊnst ən

Evansville 'ev ᵊnz vɪl

evapo|rate ɪ 'væp ə |reɪt ə- **~rated** reɪt ɪd -əd ‖ reɪt̬ əd **~rates** reɪts **~rating** reɪt ɪŋ ‖ reɪt̬ ɪŋ
e,vaporated 'milk

evaporation ɪ ˌvæp ə 'reɪʃ ᵊn ə- **~s** z

evaporator ɪ 'væp ə reɪt ə ə- ‖ -reɪt̬ ᵊr **~s** z

evasion ɪ 'veɪʒ ᵊn ə- **~s** z

evasive ɪ 'veɪs ɪv ə-, §-'veɪz- **~ly** li **~ness** nəs nɪs

Evatt 'ev ət

eve, Eve iːv

Evelina ˌev ə 'liːn ə -ɪ-

Eveline 'iːv lɪn -lən

Evelyn *(i)* 'iːv lɪn -lən, *(ii)* 'ev- 'ev ə- —*As a man's name, and as an English family name, (i); as a woman's name, either. In AmE usually (ii).*

even 'iːv ᵊn **~ed** d **~ing** _ɪŋ **~s** z

even-handed ˌiːv ᵊn 'hænd ɪd ◄ -əd **~ly** li **~ness** nəs nɪs

evening *n 'period between afternoon and night'* 'iːv nɪŋ **~s** z
'evening dress, ˌ• • '•; **,evening 'prayer; ,evening 'star**

evening *v 'making even'* 'iːv ᵊn_ɪŋ

Evenki ɪ 'veŋk i ə-

Evenlode 'iːv ᵊn ləʊd ‖ -loʊd

evenness 'iːv ᵊn nəs -nɪs

evensong 'iːv ᵊn sɒŋ ‖ -sɔːŋ -sɑːŋ

e|vent ɪ |'vent ə- **~vented** 'vent ɪd -əd ‖ 'vent̬ əd **~venting** 'vent ɪŋ ‖ 'vent̬ ɪŋ **~vents** 'venᵗs

even-tempered ˌiːv ᵊn 'temp əd ◄ ‖ -ᵊrd ◄ **~ly** li **~ness** nəs nɪs

eventer ɪ 'vent ə ə- ‖ ɪ 'vent̬ ᵊr **~s** z

eventful ɪ 'vent fᵊl ə-, -fʊl **~ly** _i **~ness** nəs nɪs

eventide 'iːv ᵊn taɪd

eventual ɪ 'ventʃ u_əl ə-, -'ventʃ əl —*In formal style also* -'vent ju_əl

eventualit|y ɪ ˌventʃ u 'æl ət i ə-, -ˌvent ju-, -ɪt i ‖ -ət̬ li **~ies** iz

eventually ɪ 'ventʃ u_əl i ə-, -'ventʃ əl_i —*In formal style also* -'vent ju_əl i

eventu|ate ɪ 'ventʃ u leɪt ə-, -'vent ju- **~ated** eɪt ɪd -əd ‖ eɪt̬ əd **~ates** eɪts **~ating** eɪt ɪŋ ‖ eɪt̬ ɪŋ

ever 'ev ə ‖ -ᵊr

Everage 'ev ᵊr_ɪdʒ

Everard 'ev ə rɑːd ‖ -rɑːrd

ever-changing ˌev ə 'tʃeɪndʒ ɪŋ ◄ ‖ -ᵊr- **~ly** li

Everest 'ev ᵊr ɪst -əst, -ə rest

Everett 'ev ᵊr ɪt -ət, -ə ret

Everglades 'ev ə gleɪdz ‖ -ᵊr-

evergreen 'ev ə griːn ‖ -ᵊr- **~s** z

everlasting ˌev ə 'lɑːst ɪŋ ◄ §-'læst- ‖ -ᵊr 'læst- **~ly** li **~ness** nəs nɪs **~s** z
,ever,lasting 'life

Everley, Everly 'ev ə li ‖ -ᵊr-

evermore ˌev ə 'mɔː ◄ ‖ -ᵊr 'mɔːr -'moʊr

everpresent ˌev ə 'prez ᵊnt ◄ ‖ -ᵊr-

EverReady *tdmk* ˌev ə 'red i ◄ '•••, •• ‖ '•ᵊr, ••

Evers 'ev əz ‖ -ᵊrz

Evershed 'ev ə ʃed ‖ -ᵊr-

Eversholt 'ev ə ʃɒlt -ʃəʊlt ‖ -ᵊr ʃoʊlt

eversion ɪ 'vɜːʃ ᵊn iː-, ə-, -'vɜːʒ- ‖ -'vɜːʒ ᵊn -'vɜːʃ-

e|vert ɪ 'vɜːt iː-, ə- ‖ ɪ 'vɜːt **~verted** 'vɜːt ɪd -əd ‖ 'vɜːt̬ əd **~verting** 'vɜːt ɪŋ ‖ 'vɜːt̬ ɪŋ **~verts** 'vɜːts ‖ 'vɜːts

Evert 'ev ət ‖ -ᵊrt

Everton 'ev ət ən ‖ -ᵊrt ᵊn
every 'ev ri —*In very formal style occasionally
also* 'ev ər i *(and in compounds too)*
  every 'which way
everybody 'ev ri ˌbɒd i ‖ -ˌbɑːd i
everyday ˌev ri 'deɪ ◂
Everyman 'ev ri mæn
everyone 'ev ri wʌn §-wɒn
everyplace 'ev ri pleɪs
everything 'ev ri θɪŋ △-θɪŋk
everywhere 'ev ri weə -hweə ‖ -ʰwer -ʰwær
Evesham 'iːv ʃəm 'iːv ɪʃ əm, 'iːs əm
Evett 'ev ɪt -ət
Evian *tdmk* 'ev i ɒ̃ ‖ ˌeɪv i 'ɑːn —*Fr* Évian
  [e vjɑ̃]
evict ɪ 'vɪkt ə- ~**ed** ɪd əd ~**ing** ɪŋ ~**s** s
eviction ɪ 'vɪk ʃən ə- ~**s** z
evidenc|e *n, v* 'ev ɪd ənᵗs -əd-; §-ɪ denᵗs, §-ə-
  ~**ed** t ~**es** ɪz əz ~**ing** ɪŋ
evident 'ev ɪd ənt -əd-; §-ɪ dent, §-ə- ~**ly** li
evidential ˌev ɪ 'denᵗʃ ᵊl ◂-ə- ~**ly** i
evil 'iːv ᵊl -ɪl ~**s** z
  evil 'eye; 'Evil One
evildoer 'iːv ᵊl ˌduː_ə -ɪl-, ˌ•'•• ‖ ˌ_ᵊr ~**s** z
evilly 'iːv ᵊl i -ɪl i
evil-minded ˌiːv ᵊl 'maɪnd ɪd ◂-ɪl-, -əd ~**ly** li
  ~**ness** nəs nɪs
evilness 'iːv ᵊl nəs -ɪl-, -nɪs
evil-tempered ˌiːv ᵊl 'temp əd ◂-ɪl- ‖ -ᵊrd ~**ly**
  li ~**ness** nəs nɪs
evinc|e ɪ 'vɪnᵗs ə- ~**ed** t ~**es** ɪz əz ~**ing** ɪŋ
evisce|rate ɪ 'vɪs ə ˌreɪt iː-, ə- ~**rated** reɪt ɪd
  -əd ‖ reɪt̬ əd ~**rates** reɪts ~**rating**
  reɪt ɪŋ ‖ reɪt̬ ɪŋ
evisceration ɪ ˌvɪs ə 'reɪʃ ᵊn iː-, ə- ~**s** z
Evita e 'viːt ə e-, ə- —*Sp* [e 'βi ta]
evocation ˌiːv əʊ 'keɪʃ ᵊn ˌev- ‖ ˌiːv oʊ- ˌev ə-
  ~**s** z
evocative ɪ 'vɒk ət ɪv ə- ‖ -'vɑːk ət̬ ɪv ~**ly** li
  ~**ness** nəs nɪs
evok|e ɪ 'vəʊk iː-, ə- ‖ -'voʊk ~**ed** t ~**es** s
  ~**ing** ɪŋ
evolute 'iːv ə luːt 'ev-, -ljuːt ‖ 'ev-

EVOLUTION

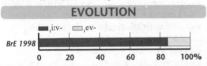

‖ iːv-   ‖ ev-

BrE 1998

0   20   40   60   80   100%

---

evolution ˌiːv ə 'luːʃ ᵊn ˌev-, -'ljuːʃ- ‖ ˌev- ~**s**
  z —*BrE 1998 poll panel preference:* ˌiːv- 85%,
  ˌev- 15%
evolutionar|y ˌiːv ə 'luːʃ ᵊn_ər li ◂ ˌev-, -'ljuːʃ-,
  -ᵊn ᵊr_li ‖ ˌev ə 'luːʃ ə ner li -ily ᵊl i ɪ li
evolutive ɪ 'vɒl jʊt ɪv iː-, ə-, -jət-
  ‖ -'vɑːl jət ɪv
evolv|e ɪ 'vɒlv iː-, ə-, §-'vəʊlv ‖ -'vɑːlv ~**ed** d
  ~**es** z ~**ing** ɪŋ
Evonne ˌi: 'vɒn ɪ-, ə- ‖ -'vɑːn
Evo-stik *tdmk* 'iːv əʊ stɪk ‖ -oʊ-
evzone 'ev zəʊn ‖ -zoʊn ~**s** z
Ewan 'juː_ən
Ewart 'juː_ət ‖ ᵊrt
Ewbank 'juː bæŋk

---

ewe juː §jəʊ *(= yew, you)* **ewes** juːz §jəʊz
Ewe *loch in Scotland* juː
Ewe *African people and language* 'e weɪ 'eɪ-
Ewell 'juː_əl juːl
Ewelme 'juː elm
Ewen 'juː_ən -ɪn
ewer 'juː_ə ‖ _ᵊr ~**s** z
Ewhurst 'juː hɜːst ‖ -hɝːst
Ewing 'juː_ɪŋ
Ewins 'juː_ɪnz
Ewyas 'juː_əs
ex eks —*See also phrases with this word* **exes,
  ex's** 'eks ɪz -əz
ex- ˌeks, ɪks, əks, eks —*or with* gz, kz —*This
  prefix is always stressed* ˌeks *when it has the
  specific meaning 'formerly'* (ˌex-'chairman).
  *When it has no such specific meaning, it is still
  stressed* ˌeks, ˌegz *(1) if the following syllable
  is unstressed* (ˌexca'vation), *and (2) in some
  disyllabic nouns and adjectives* ('extract).
  *Otherwise, in RP, the prefix is usually
  unstressed and weak* ɪks, ɪgz (ex'pect). *But both
  vowel and consonants are subject to variation:
  some speakers use the weak vowel* ə *rather than*
  ɪ, *though others (particularly BrE regional
  speakers) have strong* e *and may even stress it.
  The forms with* ks *are used before a following
  consonant sound, those with* gz *before a vowel
  sound* (exact ɪg 'zækt, exhaust ɪg 'zɔːst). *
  (However some speakers voice only the second
  consonant, thus* ɪk 'zækt, ɪk 'zɔːst.) *In words
  with the spellings* exce-, exci- *the consonants
  are simplified to* ks (excite ɪk 'saɪt). *Several
  words are irregular, as shown in the entries
  below.*
exacer|bate ɪg 'zæs ə ˌbeɪt eg-, əg-, ɪk-, ek-,
  ək-; ek 'sæs- ‖ -ᵊr- ~**bated** beɪt ɪd -əd
  ‖ beɪt̬ əd ~**bates** beɪts ~**bating**
  beɪt ɪŋ ‖ beɪt̬ ɪŋ
exacerbation ɪg ˌzæs ə 'beɪʃ ᵊn eg-, əg-, ɪk-,
  ek-, ək-; ek ˌsæs- ‖ -ᵊr-
exact *adj, v* ɪg 'zækt eg-, əg-, ɪk-, ek-, ək- ~**ed**
  ɪd əd ~**ing** ɪŋ ~**s** s
exacting ɪg 'zækt ɪŋ eg-, əg-, ɪk-, ek-, ək- ~**ly**
  li ~**ness** nəs nɪs
exaction ɪg 'zæk ʃᵊn eg-, əg-, ɪk-, ek-, ək- ~**s** z
exactitude ɪg 'zækt ɪ tjuːd eg-, əg-, ɪk-, ek-,
  ək-, -ə-, §→-tʃuːd ‖ -tuːd -tjuːd
exactly ɪg 'zækt li eg-, əg-, ɪk-, ek-, ək- —*In
  rapid casual speech this word may lose its
  initial vowel or even the whole initial syllable.*
exactness ɪg 'zækt nəs eg-, əg-, ɪk-, ek-, ək-,
  -nɪs
exactor *'one that exacts'* ɪg 'zækt ə eg-, əg-, ɪk-,
  ek-, ək- ‖ -ᵊr ~**s** z
ex-actor *'former actor'* ˌeks 'ækt ə ‖ -ᵊr ~**s** z
exagge|rate ɪg 'zædʒ ə ˌreɪt eg-, əg-, ɪk-, ek-,
  ək- ~**rated/ly** reɪt ɪd /li -əd /li ‖ reɪt̬ əd /li
  ~**rates** reɪts ~**rating** reɪt ɪŋ ‖ reɪt̬ ɪŋ
exaggeration ɪg ˌzædʒ ə 'reɪʃ ᵊn eg-, əg-, ɪk-,
  ek-, ək- ~**s** z
exalt ɪg 'zɔːlt eg-, əg-, ɪk-, ek-, ək-,
  -'zɒlt ‖ -'zɑːlt ~**ed** ɪd əd ~**ing** ɪŋ ~**s** s

exaltation ˌegz ɔːl 'teɪʃ ᵊn ˌeks-, -ɒl- ‖ -ɑːl-
exalted ɪg 'zɔːlt ɪd eg-, əg-, ɪk-, ek-, ək-,
 -'zɒlt-, -əd ‖ -'zɑːlt- ~ly li ~ness nəs nɪs
exam ɪg 'zæm eg- əg-, ɪk-, ek-, ək-; §'egz æm
 ~s z
 e'xam ˌpaper
examination ɪg ˌzæm ɪ 'neɪʃ ᵊn eg-, əg-, ɪk-,
 ek-, ək-, -ə- ~s z
 eˌxami'nation ˌpaper
examin|e ɪg 'zæm ɪn eg-, əg-, ɪk-, ek-, ək-, §-ən
 ~ed d ~es z ~ing ɪŋ
examinee ɪg ˌzæm ɪ 'niː eg-, əg-, ɪk-, ek-, ək-,
 -ə- ~s z
example ɪg 'zɑːmp ᵊl eg-, əg-, ɪk-, ek-, ək-,
 §-'zæmp- ‖ -'zæmp- ~s z
exanthema ˌeks æn 'θiːm ə ‖ ˌegz æn-
exarch 'eks ɑːk ‖ -ɑːrk ~s s
exarchate 'eks ɑːk eɪt ‖ -ɑːrk- ~s s

EXASPERATE

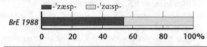

■-'zæsp- □-'zɑːsp-

BrE 1988

| 0 | 20 | 40 | 60 | 80 | 100% |

exaspe|rate ɪg 'zæsp ə |reɪt eg-, əg-, ɪk-, ek-,
 ək-, -'zɑːsp- —BrE 1988 poll panel
 preference: -'zæsp- 54% (southerners 33%),
 -'zɑːsp- 46% (southerners 67%). In AmE
 always -'zæsp-. ~rated/ly reɪt ɪd /li -əd /li
 ‖ reɪt̬ əd /li ~rates reɪts ~rating/ly reɪt ɪŋ /
 li ‖ reɪt̬ ɪŋ /li
exasperation ɪg ˌzæsp ə 'reɪʃ ᵊn eg-, əg-, ɪk-,
 ek-, ək-, -ˌzɑːsp-
Excalibur ek 'skæl ɪb ə -əb- ‖ -ᵊr
ex cathedra ˌeks kə 'θiːdr ə -'θedr-, -'tedr-
exca|vate 'eks kə |veɪt ~vated veɪt ɪd -əd
 ‖ veɪt̬ əd ~vates veɪts ~vating
 veɪt ɪŋ ‖ veɪt̬ ɪŋ
excavation ˌeks kə 'veɪʃ ᵊn ~s z
excavator 'eks kə veɪt ə ‖ -veɪt̬ ᵊr ~s z
exceed ɪk 'siːd ek-, ək- ~ed ɪd əd ~ing/ly
 ɪŋ /li ~s z
excel ɪk 'sel ek-, ək- ~led d ~ling ɪŋ ~s z
excellence 'eks ᵊl_ənts
Excellenc|y, e~ 'eks ᵊl_ənts li ~ies iz
excellent 'eks ᵊl_ənt ~ly li
excelsior ek 'sels i ɔː ɪk-, -i_ə ‖ -i_ᵊr -i ɔːr
except v, prep, conj ɪk 'sept ek-, ək- ~ed ɪd əd
 ~ing ɪŋ ~s s
exception ɪk 'sep ʃᵊn ek-, ək- ~s z
exceptionab|le ɪk 'sep ʃᵊn_əb |ᵊl ek-, ək- ~ly li
exceptional ɪk 'sep ʃᵊn_əl ek-, ək- ~ly i
excerpt n 'eks ɜːpt ek 'sɜːpt, 'egz ɜːpt
 ‖ 'eks ɝːpt 'egz ɝːpt ~s s
excerpt v ek 'sɜːpt ɪk-, ək-; ɪg 'zɜːpt
 ‖ ek 'sɝːpt eg 'zɝːpt, '•• ~ed ɪd əd ~ing
 ɪŋ ~s s
excess n ɪk 'ses ek-, ək-; 'eks es ~es ɪz əz —In
 stress-shifting environments usually ˌeks es, as
 if underlyingly ˌek 'ses ◂: ˌexcess 'baggage (see
 excess adj)
excess adj 'eks es ek 'ses, ɪk-, ək-
excessive ɪk 'ses ɪv ek-, ək- ~ly li

exchang|e n, v ɪks 'tʃeɪndʒ eks-, əks-, ~ed d
 ~es ɪz əz ~ing ɪŋ
 ex'change rate
exchangeable ɪks 'tʃeɪndʒ əb ᵊl eks-, əks-
exchequer ɪks 'tʃek ə eks-, əks- ‖ -ᵊr ~s z
excipient ɪk 'sɪp i_ənt ek-, ək- ~s s
excise n 'tax' 'eks aɪz ɪk 'saɪz, ek-, ək-
excis|e v 'remove' ɪk 'saɪz ₍ᵢ₎ek-, ək- ~ed d ~es
 ɪz əz ~ing ɪŋ
excision ɪk 'sɪʒ ᵊn ek-, ək- ~s z
excitability ɪk ˌsaɪt ə 'bɪl ət i ek-, ək-, -ɪt i
 ‖ -ˌsaɪt̬ ə 'bɪl ət̬ i
excitab|le ɪk 'saɪt əb |ᵊl ek-, ək- ‖ -'saɪt̬ əb-
 ~leness ᵊl nəs -nɪs ~ly li
excitation ˌeks ɪ 'teɪʃ ᵊn -ə-, -aɪ- ~s z
ex|cite ɪk |'saɪt ek-, ək- ~cited/ly 'saɪt ɪd /li
 əd /li ‖ 'saɪt̬ əd /li ~cites 'saɪts ~citing/ly
 'saɪt ɪŋ /li ‖ 'saɪt̬ ɪŋ /li
excitement ɪk 'saɪt mənt ek-, ək- ~s s
exciter, excitor ɪk 'saɪt ə ek-, ək- ‖ -'saɪt̬ ᵊr ~s
 z
exclaim ɪk 'skleɪm ek-, ək- ~ed d ~er/s ə/
 z ‖ ᵊr/z ~ing ɪŋ ~s z
exclamation ˌeks klə 'meɪʃ ᵊn ~s z
 ˌexcla'mation mark; ˌexcla'mation point
exclamator|y ɪk 'sklæm ət_ᵊr i ek-, ək-
 ‖ -ə tɔːr li -tour i ~ily əl ɪ i li
exclave 'eks kleɪv ~s z
exclud|e ɪk 'skluːd ek-, ək- ~ed ɪd əd ~er/s
 ə/z ‖ ᵊr/z ~es z ~ing ɪŋ
exclusion ɪk 'skluːʒ ᵊn ek-, ək- ~s z
exclusive ɪk 'skluːs ɪv ek-, ək-, §-'skluːz- ~ly li
 ~ness nəs nɪs
exclusivity ˌeks klu 'sɪv ət i -ɪt i ‖ -ət̬ i
excogi|tate eks 'kɒdʒ ɪ |teɪt ɪks-, -ə-
 ‖ -'kɑːdʒ- ~tated teɪt ɪd -əd ‖ teɪt̬ əd ~tates
 teɪts ~tating teɪt ɪŋ ‖ teɪt̬ ɪŋ
excogitation ˌeks ˌkɒdʒ ɪ 'teɪʃ ᵊn •ˌ•-,
 ɪks ˌkɒdʒ- ‖ eks ˌkɑːdʒ- ~s z
excommuni|cate v ˌeks kə 'mjuːn ɪ |keɪt -'••ə-
 ~cated keɪt ɪd -əd ‖ keɪt̬ əd ~cates keɪts
 ~cating keɪt ɪŋ ‖ keɪt̬ ɪŋ
excommunicate n, adj ˌeks kə 'mjuːn ɪk ət -ɪt,
 -ɪ keɪt ~s s
excommunication ˌeks kə ˌmjuːn ɪ 'keɪʃ ᵊn
 -ˌ•ə- ~s z
ex-con ˌeks 'kɒn ‖ -'kɑːn ~s z
ex-convict ˌeks 'kɒn vɪkt ‖ -'kɑːn- ~s s
excori|ate ɪk 'skɔːr i |eɪt ek-, ək-,
 -'skɒr- ‖ -'skour- ~ated eɪt ɪd -əd ‖ eɪt̬ əd
 ~ates eɪts ~ating eɪt ɪŋ ‖ eɪt̬ ɪŋ
excoriation ɪk ˌskɔːr i 'eɪʃ ᵊn ek-, ək-,
 -ˌskɒr- ‖ -ˌskour- ~s z
excrement 'eks krɪ mənt -krə-
excremental ˌeks krɪ 'ment ᵊl ◂ -krə- ‖ -'ment̬
 ᵊl ◂
excrescenc|e ɪk 'skres ᵊnts ek-, ək- ~es ɪz əz
excrescent ɪk 'skres ᵊnt ek-, ək- ~ly li
excreta ɪk 'skriːt ə ek-, ək- ‖ -'skriːt̬ ə
ex|crete ɪk |'skriːt ek-, ək- ~creted 'skriːt ɪd
 -əd ‖ 'skriːt̬ əd ~cretes 'skriːts ~creting
 'skriːt ɪŋ ‖ 'skriːt̬ ɪŋ
excretion ɪk 'skriːʃ ᵊn ek-, ək-

excretive ɪk 'skriːt ɪv ek-, ək- ‖ -'skriːt̬ ɪv
excretory ɪk 'skriːt ər i ek-, ək-
  ‖ 'eks krə tɔːr i -tour i
excruciating ɪk 'skruːʃ i eɪt ɪŋ ek-, ək-
  ‖ -eɪt̬ ɪŋ **~ly** li
exculp|ate 'eks kʌlp |eɪt ɪks 'kʌlp-, eks-
  ~ated eɪt ɪd -əd ‖ eɪt̬ əd **~ates** eɪts **~ating**
  eɪt ɪŋ ‖ eɪt̬ ɪŋ
exculpation ˌeks kʌl 'peɪʃ ən **~s** z
excursion ɪk 'skɜːʃ ən ek-, ək-, -'skɜːʒ-
  ‖ -'skɝːʒ ən **~s** z
  ex'cursion train
excursive ɪk 'skɜːs ɪv ek-, ək-, §-'skɜːz-
  ‖ -'skɝːs- **~ly** li **~ness** nəs nɪs
excursus ek 'skɜːs əs ɪk- ‖ -'skɝːs- **~es** ɪz əz
excusab|le ɪk 'skjuːz əb |əl ek-, ək- **~ly** li
excusatory ɪk 'skjuːz ət ər i ek-, ək-;
  ˌeks kjuː 'zeɪt ər i ‖ -'skjuːz ə tɔːr i -tour i
excus|e v ɪk 'skjuːz ek-, ək- **~ed** d **~er/s** ə/
  z ‖ ər/z **~es** ɪz əz **~ing** ɪŋ
excus|e n ɪk 'skjuːs ek-, ək- (!) **~es** ɪz əz
excuse-me ɪk 'skjuːz mi ek-, ək-, -miː **~s, ~'s**
  z
ex-directory ˌeks də 'rekt ər_i ˌ•dɪ-, ˌ•daɪə-
Exe eks
exeat 'eks i æt -eɪ- **~s** s
exec ɪg 'zek eg-, əg-, ɪk-, ek-, ək- **~s** s
execrab|le 'eks ɪk rəb |əl ‖ '•ək- **~ly** li
exe|crate 'eks ɪ |kreɪt -ə- **~crated** kreɪt ɪd -əd
  ‖ kreɪt̬ əd **~crates** kreɪts **~crating**
  kreɪt ɪŋ ‖ kreɪt̬ ɪŋ
execration ˌeks ɪ 'kreɪʃ ən -ə- **~s** z
executable 'eks ɪ kjuːt əb əl ‖ -kjuːt̬ əb əl
executant ɪg 'zek jut ənt eg-, əg-, ɪk-, ek-, ək-,
  -jət-, §-ət- ‖ -jət ənt -ət- **~s** s
exe|cute 'eks ɪ |kjuːt -ə- **~cuted** kjuːt ɪd -əd
  ‖ 'kjuːt̬ əd **~cutes** kjuːts **~cuting**
  kjuːt ɪŋ ‖ kjuːt̬ ɪŋ
execution ˌeks ɪ 'kjuːʃ ən -ə- **~s** z
executioner ˌeks ɪ 'kjuːʃ ən_ə ˌ•ə- ‖ _ər **~s** z
executive ɪg 'zek jut ɪv eg-, əg-, ɪk-, ek-, ək-,
  -jət-, §-ət- ‖ -jət̬ ɪv -ət̬- **~s** z
  e͵xecutive 'officer
executor ɪg 'zek jut ə eg-, əg-, ɪk-, ek-, ək-,
  -jət-, §-ət- ‖ -jət ər -ət̬ ər —but in the sense
  'performer' also 'eks ɪ kjuːt ə ‖ -kjuːt̬ ər **~s** z
executrix ɪg 'zek ju trɪks eg-, əg-, ɪk-, ek-, ək-
  ‖ -jə- -ə-
exeges|is ˌeks ɪ 'dʒiːs |ɪs -ə-, §-əs **~es** iːz
exegete 'eks ɪ dʒiːt -ə- **~s** s
exegetic ˌeks ɪ 'dʒet ɪk ◀ -ə- ‖ -'dʒet̬- **~al** əl
  ~s s
exemplar ɪg 'zemp lɑː eg-, əg-, ɪk-, ek-, ək-, -lə
  ‖ -lɑːr -lər **~s** z
exemplary ɪg 'zemp lər i eg-, əg-, ɪk-, ek-, ək-
exemplification ɪg ˌzemp lɪf ɪ 'keɪʃ ən eg-, əg-,
  ɪk-, ek-, ək-, -, •ləf-, §-ə'•- **~s** z
exempli|fy ɪg 'zemp lɪ |faɪ eg-, əg-, ɪk-, ek-,
  ək-, -lə- **~fied** faɪd **~fier/s** faɪ_ə/z ‖ faɪ_ər/z
  ~fies faɪz **~fying** faɪ ɪŋ
exempli gratia eg ˌzemp liː 'grɑːt i ɑː ɪg-, əg-;
  -laɪ 'greɪʃ i_ə, -eɪ

exempt adj, v ɪg 'zempt eg-, əg-, ɪk-, ek-, ək-
  ~ed ɪd əd **~ing** ɪŋ **~s** s
exemption ɪg 'zemp ʃən eg-, əg-, ɪk-, ek-, ək-
  ~s z
exequatur ˌeks ɪ 'kweɪt ə -ə- ‖ -'kweɪt̬ ər **~s** z
exequies 'eks ɪk wiz -ək-
exercis|e n, v 'eks ə saɪz ‖ -ər- **~ed** d **~er/s** ə/
  z ‖ ər/z **~es** ɪz əz **~ing** ɪŋ
  'exercise bike; 'exercise book
exergue ek 'sɜːg 'eks ɜːg ‖ 'eks ɝːg 'egz- **~s** z
ex|ert ɪg |'zɜːt eg-, əg-, ɪk-, ek-, ək- ‖ -|'zɝːt
  ~erted 'zɜːt ɪd -əd ‖ 'zɝːt̬ əd **~erting**
  'zɜːt ɪŋ ‖ 'zɝːt̬ ɪŋ **~erts** 'zɜːts ‖ 'zɝːts
exertion ɪg 'zɜːʃ ən eg-, əg-, ɪk-, ek-, ək-
  ‖ -'zɝːʃ ən **~s** z
Exeter 'eks ɪt ə -ət- ‖ -ət̬ ər
exeunt 'eks ɪ ʌnt -eɪ-, -ʊnt, -i_ənt
  ˌexeunt 'omnes ˈɒm neɪz -niːz ‖ 'ɑːm- 'ɔːm-
exfoli|ate ˌ(ɪ)eks 'fəʊl i |eɪt ‖ -'foʊl- **~ated**
  eɪt ɪd -əd ‖ eɪt̬ əd **~ates** eɪts **~ating**
  eɪt ɪŋ ‖ eɪt̬ ɪŋ
ex gratia ˌ(ɪ)eks 'greɪʃ ə -'greɪʃ i_ə
exhalation ˌeks hə 'leɪʃ ən -ə- **~s** z
exhalatory eks 'heɪl ət ər i ɪks-, əks-, -'hæl-
  ‖ -ə tɔːr i -tour i
exhal|e eks 'heɪəl ɪks-, əks-; eg 'zeɪəl, ɪg-, əg-
  ~ed d **~es** z **~ing** ɪŋ
exhaust v ɪg 'zɔːst eg-, əg-, ɪk-, ek-,
  ək- ‖ -'zɑːst **~ed** ɪd əd **~ing** ɪŋ **~s** s
exhaust n ɪg 'zɔːst eg-, əg-, ɪk-, ek-, ək-,
  §'eg zɔːst ‖ -'zɑːst **~s** s
  ex'haust pipe
exhaustion ɪg 'zɔːs tʃən eg-, əg-, ɪk-, ek-,
  ək- ‖ -'zɑːs-
exhaustive ɪg 'zɔːst ɪv eg-, əg-, ɪk-, ek-,
  ək- ‖ -'zɑːst- **~ly** li **~ness** nəs nɪs
exhib|it v ɪg 'zɪb |ɪt eg-, əg-, ɪk-, ek-, ək-, §-ət
  ‖ -|ət **~ited** ɪt ɪd §ət-, -əd ‖ ət̬ əd **~iting**
  ɪt ɪŋ §ət- ‖ ət̬ ɪŋ **~its** ɪts §əts ‖ əts
exhibit n ɪg 'zɪb ɪt eg-, əg-, ɪk-, ek-, ək-, §-ət;
  'eks ɪb-, -əb- **~s** s
exhibition ˌeks ɪ 'bɪʃ ən -ə- **~s** z
exhibitioner ˌeks ɪ 'bɪʃ ən_ə ˌ•ə- ‖ _ər **~s** z
exhibitionism ˌeks ɪ 'bɪʃ ən ˌɪz əm ˌ•ə-
exhibitionist ˌeks ɪ 'bɪʃ ən_ɪst ˌ•ə-, §_əst **~s** s
exhibitionistic ˌeks ɪ ˌbɪʃ ə 'nɪst ɪk ˌ•ə- **~ally**
  əl_i
exhibitor ɪg 'zɪb ɪt ə eg-, əg-, §-ət- ‖ -ət̬ ər **~s**
  z
exhila|rate ɪg 'zɪl ə |reɪt eg-, əg-, ɪk-, ek-, ək-,
  ek 'sɪl- **~rated** reɪt ɪd -əd ‖ reɪt̬ əd **~rates**
  reɪts **~rating/ly** reɪt ɪŋ /li ‖ reɪt̬ ɪŋ /li
exhilaration ɪg ˌzɪl ə 'reɪʃ ən eg-, əg-, ɪk-, ek-,
  ək-, ek ˌsɪl- **~s** z
ex|hort ɪg |'zɔːt eg-, əg-, ɪk-, ek-, ək- ‖ -|'zɔːrt
  ~horted 'zɔːt ɪd -əd ‖ 'zɔːrt̬ əd **~horting**
  'zɔːt ɪŋ ‖ 'zɔːrt̬ ɪŋ **~horts** 'zɔːts ‖ 'zɔːrts
exhortation ˌegz ɔː 'teɪʃ ən ˌeks- ‖ -ɔːr- -ər-
  ~s z
exhortative ɪg 'zɔːt ət ɪv eg-, əg-, ɪk-, ek-, ək-
  ‖ -'zɔːrt̬ ət̬ ɪv
exhortatory ɪg 'zɔːt ət_ər i eg-, əg-, ɪk-, ek-,
  ək- ‖ -'zɔːrt̬ ə tɔːr i -tour i

E

exhumation ˌeks hju 'meɪʃ ən -ju- ‖ ˌegz ju- ~s z

exhum|e eks 'hjuːm ɪg 'zjuːm, eg-, əg-, ɪk-, ek-, ək-, -'zuːm ‖ ɪg 'zuːm -'zjuːm, eks 'hjuːm ~ed d ~es z ~ing ɪŋ

ex hypothesi ˌeks haɪ 'pɒθ ə saɪ -əs i ‖ -'paːθ-

Exide tdmk 'eks aɪd

exigenc|e 'eks ɪdʒ ənts 'egz-, -ədʒ- ~es ɪz əz

exigenc|y 'eks ɪdʒ ənts li 'egz-, '•ədʒ-; ɪg 'zɪdʒ-, eg-, əg-, ɪk-, ek-, ək- ~ies iz

exigent 'eks ɪdʒ ənt 'egz-, -ədʒ- ~ly li

exiguity ˌeks ɪ 'gjuːˌət i _ɪt i ‖ ˌegz ɪ 'gjuː ət i

exiguous ɪg 'zɪg juˌəs eg-, əg-, ɪk-, ek-, ək-; ek 'sɪg-, ɪk-, ək- ~ly li ~ness nəs nɪs

exil|e n, v 'eks aɪəl 'egz- ~ed d ~es z ~ing ɪŋ

exist ɪg 'zɪst eg-, əg-, ɪk-, ek-, ək- ~ed ɪd əd ~ing ɪŋ ~s s

existence ɪg 'zɪst ənts eg-, əg-, ɪk-, ek-, ək-

existent ɪg 'zɪst ənt eg-, əg-, ɪk-, ek-, ək-

existential ˌegz ɪ 'stentʃ əl ◂ ˌeks-, -ə- ~ism ˌɪz əm ~ist/s ɪst/s §əst/s ~ly i

EXIT

ex|it 'eks ɪt 'egz-, §-ət ‖ -ət —*Poll panel preferences: BrE 1988,* 'eks- *55%,* 'egz- *45%; AmE 1993,* 'eks- *48%,* 'egz- *52%.* ~ited ɪt ɪd §ət-, -əd ‖ əţ əd ~iting ɪt ɪŋ §ət- ‖ əţ ɪŋ ~its ɪts §əts ‖ əts

'exit poll

Ex-lax tdmk 'eks læks

ex libris ˌeks 'liːb rɪs -'laɪb-, -riːs, §-rəs

Exmoor 'eks mʊə -mɔː ‖ -mʊr

ˌExmoor 'pony

Exmouth 'eks məθ -maʊθ

exo- comb. form
with stress-neutral suffix ˈeks əʊ ‖ ˈeks oʊ — exosphere 'eks əʊ sfɪə ‖ -oʊ sfɪr
with stress-imposing suffix ek 'sɒ+ ‖ ek 'saː+ — exogenous ek 'sɒdʒ ən əs -ɪn- ‖ -'saːdʒ-

exocentric ˌeks əʊ 'sentr ɪk ◂ ‖ -oʊ- ~ally əlˌi

Exocet tdmk 'eks əʊ set ‖ -oʊ- ~s s

exocrine 'eks əʊ kraɪn -krɪn, §-ək rən ‖ -ək rən

exodus, E~ 'eks əd əs §'egz- ~es ɪz əz

ex-officio, ex officio ˌeks ə 'fɪʃ i əʊ ◂, '•ɒ-, -'fɪs- ‖ -oʊ

exogamous ek 'sɒg əm əs ‖ -'saːg- ~ly li

exogamy ek 'sɒg əm i ‖ -'saːg-

exogenous ek 'sɒdʒ ən əs ɪk-, -ɪn- ‖ -'saːdʒ- ~ly li

exon 'eks ɒn ‖ -aːn ~s z

exone|rate ɪg 'zɒn ə |reɪt eg-, əg-, ɪk-, ek-, ək- ‖ -'zaːn- ~rated reɪt ɪd -əd ‖ reɪţ əd ~rates reɪts ~rating reɪt ɪŋ ‖ reɪţ ɪŋ

exoneration ɪg ˌzɒn ə 'reɪʃ ən eg-, əg-, ɪk-, ək- ‖ -ˌzaːn- ~s z

exonym 'eks əʊ nɪm ‖ -ə- ~s z

exophora ek 'sɒf ər ə ‖ -'saːf-

exophoric ˌeks əʊ 'fɒr ɪk ◂ ‖ -ə 'fɔːr- -'faːr-

exophthalm|ic ˌeks ɒf 'θælm lɪk ◂ -əf-, -ɒp- ‖ -aːf- -əf-, -aːp- ~os əs ɒs ‖ aːs

ˌexophˌthalmic 'goitre

exorbitance ɪg 'zɔːb ɪt ənts eg-, əg-, ɪk-, ek-, ək-, -ət- ‖ -'zɔːrb ət ənts

exorbitant ɪg 'zɔːb ɪt ənt eg-, əg-, ɪk-, ek-, ək-, -ət- ‖ -'zɔːrb ət ənt ~ly li

exorcis... —see exorciz...

exorcism 'eks ɔː ˌsɪz əm 'egz-, -ə- ‖ -ɔːr- -ər- ~s z

exorcist 'eks ɔːs ɪst 'egz-, -əs-, §-əst ‖ -ɔːrs- -ərs- ~s s

exorciz|e 'eks ɔːs aɪz 'egz-, -ə saɪz ‖ -ɔːrs aɪz -ər saɪz ~ed d ~es ɪz əz ~ing ɪŋ

exordi|um ek 'sɔːd iˌləm eg 'zɔːd- ‖ eg 'zɔːrd- ~a ə ~ums əmz

exotic ɪg 'zɒt ɪk eg-, əg-, ɪk-, ek-, ək-; ek 'sɒt ɪk ‖ -'zaːţ ɪk ~a ə ~ally əlˌi ~ness nəs nɪs

exoticism ɪg 'zɒt ɪ ˌsɪz əm eg-, əg-, ɪk-, ek-, ək-, -ə- ‖ -'zaːţ ə- ~s z

exp *'exponential'* eksp

expand ɪk 'spænd ek-, ək- ~ed ɪd əd ~er/s ə/ z ‖ ər/z ~ing ɪŋ ~s z

expans|e ɪk 'spænts ek-, ək- ~es ɪz əz

expansibility ɪk ˌspænts ə 'bɪl ət i -,•ɪ-, -ɪt i ‖ -əţ i

expansible ɪk 'spænts əb əl ek-, ək-, -ɪb-

expansion ɪk 'spæntʃ ən ek-, ək- ~s z

ex'pansion bolt

expansionary ɪk 'spæntʃ ən ˌər i ek-, ək- ‖ -ə ner i

expansion|ism ɪk 'spæntʃ ənl ˌɪz əm ek-, ək- ~ist/s ɪst/s §əst/s

expansive ɪk 'spænts ɪv ek-, ək- ~ly li ~ness nəs nɪs

ex parte ˌeks 'paːt i -eɪ ‖ -'paːrţ i

expat, ex-pat ˌeks 'pæt ◂ ~s s

expati|ate ek 'speɪʃ i |eɪt ɪk-, əks- ~ated eɪt ɪd -əd ‖ eɪţ əd ~ates eɪts ~ating eɪt ɪŋ ‖ eɪţ ɪŋ

expatri|ate v ˌ(ˌ)eks 'pætr i |eɪt ɪks-, -'peɪtr- ‖ -'peɪtr- ~ated eɪt ɪd -əd ‖ eɪţ əd ~ates eɪts ~ating eɪt ɪŋ ‖ eɪţ ɪŋ

expatriate n, adj ˌ(ˌ)eks 'pætr iˌət ɪks-, -'peɪtr-, _ɪt, -eɪt ‖ -'peɪtr- ~s s

expatriation eks ˌpætr i 'eɪʃ ən ɪks-, -ˌpeɪtr-, ˌeks ˌpeɪtr- ‖ -ˌpeɪtr-

expect ɪk 'spekt ˌ(ˌ)ek-, ək- ~ed ɪd əd ~ing ɪŋ ~s s

expectanc|e ɪk 'spekt ənts ek-, ək- ~es ɪz əz ~ies iz ~y i

expectant ɪk 'spekt ənt ek-, ək- ~ly li

expectation ˌeks pek 'teɪʃ ən ~s z

expectorant ɪk 'spekt ər ənt ek-, ək- ~s s

expecto|rate ɪk 'spekt ə |reɪt ek-, ək- ~rated reɪt ɪd -əd ‖ reɪţ əd ~rates reɪts ~rating reɪt ɪŋ ‖ reɪţ ɪŋ

expectoration ɪk ˌspekt ə 'reɪʃ ən ek-, ək- ~s z

expedienc|e ɪk 'spiːd iˌənts ek-, ək- ~es ɪz əz ~ies iz ~y i

expedient ɪk 'spiːd iˌənt ek-, ək- ~ly li

expe|dite 'eks pə ǀdaɪt -pɪ- ~**dited** daɪt ɪd -əd
ǁ daɪt̬ əd ~**diter/s** daɪt ə/z ǁ daɪt̬ ər/z ~**dites**
daɪts ~**diting** daɪt ɪŋ ǁ daɪt̬ ɪŋ
expedition ˌeks pə 'dɪʃ ən -pɪ- ~**s** z
expeditionary ˌeks pə 'dɪʃ ən ər_i ◂ ǀ•pɪ-,
-ən_ər i ǁ -ə ner i
expeditious ˌeks pə 'dɪʃ əs ◂ -pɪ- ~**ly** li ~**ness**
nəs nɪs
expel ɪk 'spel ek-, ək- ~**led** d ~**ling** ɪŋ ~**s** z
expellee ɪk ˌspel 'iː ek-, ək-; ˌeks pel- ~**s** z
expend ɪk 'spend ek-, ək- ~**ed** ɪd əd ~**ing** ɪŋ
~**s** z
expendab|le ɪk 'spend əb| əl ek-, ək- ~**ly** li
expenditure ɪk 'spend ɪtʃ ə ek-, ək- ǁ -ər
-ə tʃʊr ~**s** z
expens|e ɪk 'spen⟨t⟩s ek-, ək- ~**es** ɪz əz
ex'pense acˌcount
expensive ɪk 'spen⟨t⟩s ɪv ek-, ək- ~**ly** li ~**ness**
nəs nɪs
experienc|e n, v ɪk 'spɪər i_ən⟨t⟩s ek-, ək-
ǁ -'spɪr- ~**ed** t ~**es** ɪz əz ~**ing** ɪŋ
experiential ɪk ˌspɪər i 'entʃ əl ◂ ek-, ək-
ǁ -ˌspɪr- ~**ly** i
experiment n ɪk 'sper ɪ mənt ek-, ək-,
-ə- ǁ -'spɪr- ~**s** s
experi|ment v ɪk 'sper ɪ ǀment ek-, ək-,
-ə- ǁ -'spɪr- —See note at -ment ~**mented**
ment ɪd -əd ǁ ment̬ əd ~**menting**
ment ɪŋ ǁ ment̬ ɪŋ ~**ments** men⟨t⟩s
experimental ɪk ˌsper ɪ 'ment əl ◂ ⟨ᵤ⟩ek-, ək-,
-ə- ǁ -'ment̬ əl ◂ -ˌspɪr- ~**ism** ˌɪz əm ~**ist/s**
ɪst/s §əst/s ~**ly** i
experimentation ɪk ˌsper ɪ men 'teɪʃ ən ek-,
ək-, -ˌ•ə-, -mən⟨t⟩'•- ǁ -ˌspɪr- ~**s** z
expert 'eks pɜːt ˌek 'spɜːt, ɪk-, ək- ǁ 'eks pɝːt
ɪk 'spɝːt ~**ly** li ~**ness** nəs nɪs ~**s** s
ˌexpert 'system
expertise n ˌeks pɜː 'tiːz -pə-, '••• ǁ -pər 'tiːz
-'tiːs
expertis|e, expertiz|e v 'eks pə taɪz -pɜːt aɪz
ǁ -pər- ~**ed** d ~**es** ɪz əz ~**ing** ɪŋ
expiable 'eks pi_əb əl
expi|ate 'eks pi ǀeɪt ~**ated** eɪt ɪd -əd ǁ eɪt̬ əd
~**ates** eɪts ~**ating** eɪt ɪŋ ǁ eɪt̬ ɪŋ
expiation ˌeks pi 'eɪʃ ən ~**s** z
expiatory 'eks pi_ət_ər i -eɪt ər i, ˌeks pi 'eɪt
ər i ǁ ə tɔːr i -toʊr i
expiration ˌeks pə 'reɪʃ ən -pɪ-, -paɪ°- ~**s** z
expiratory ɪk 'spaɪ°r ət_ər i ⟨ᵤ⟩ek-, ək-, -'spɪr-
ǁ -ə tɔːr i -toʊr i
expir|e ɪk 'spaɪ_ə ⟨ᵤ⟩ek-, ək- ǁ ɪk 'spaɪ_ər ~**ed** d
~**es** ɪz əz ~**ing** ɪŋ
expir|y ɪk 'spaɪ_ər li ek-, ək- ǁ ɪk 'spaɪ_ər li
'eks pər li ~**ies** ɪz
ex'piry date
explain ɪk 'spleɪn ek-, ək- ~**ed** d ~**ing** ɪŋ ~**s** z
explainable ɪk 'spleɪn əb əl ek-, ək-
explanation ˌeks plə 'neɪʃ ən ~**s** z
explanator|y ɪk 'splæn ət_ər li ek-, ək-
ǁ -ə tɔːr li -toʊr i ~**ily** əl i ɪ ɪ li
expletive ɪk 'spliːt ɪv ek-, ək-; 'eks plət-
ǁ 'eks plət̬ ɪv ~**s** z
explicable ɪk 'splɪk əb əl ek-, ək-; 'eks plɪk-

expli|cate 'eks plɪ ǀkeɪt -plə- ~**cated** keɪt ɪd
-əd ǁ keɪt̬ əd ~**cates** keɪts ~**cating**
keɪt ɪŋ ǁ keɪt̬ ɪŋ
explication ˌeks plɪ 'keɪʃ ən -plə- —also as a
French word, Fr [ɛks pli ka sjɔ̃] ~**s** z
explicative ek 'splɪk ət ɪv ɪk-, ək-; 'eks plɪk-
ǁ -ət̬ ɪv
explicatory ek 'splɪk ət_ər i ɪk-, ək-;
ˌeks plɪ 'keɪt ər i ◂ ǁ -ə tɔːr i 'eks plɪk-,
-ə toʊr i
explicature ˌeks 'plɪk ətʃ ə -ə tjʊə; ɪk 'splɪk-,
ək-, ek- ǁ -ər ~**s** z
explicit ɪk 'splɪs ɪt ek-, ək-, §-ət —For contrast
with implicit, also ˌeks 'plɪs-, '•, •- ~**ly** li
~**ness** nəs nɪs
explod|e ɪk 'spləʊd ek-, ək- ǁ -'sploʊd ~**ed** ɪd
əd ~**er/s** ə/z ǁ ər/z ~**es** z ~**ing** ɪŋ
exploit n 'eks plɔɪt ~**s** s
ex|ploit v ɪk ǀ'splɔɪt ⟨ᵤ⟩ek-, ək- ~**ploited**
'plɔɪt ɪd -əd ǁ 'plɔɪt̬ əd ~**ploiting**
'plɔɪt ɪŋ ǁ 'plɔɪt̬ ɪŋ ~**ploits** 'plɔɪts
exploitation ˌeks plɔɪ 'teɪʃ ən ~**s** z
exploitative ɪk 'splɔɪt ət ɪv ⟨ᵤ⟩ek-, ək-
ǁ -'splɔɪt̬ ət̬ ɪv ~**ly** li
exploration ˌeks plə 'reɪʃ ən -plɔː- ~**s** z
explorative ɪk 'splɒr ət ɪv ek-, ək-, -'splɔːr-
ǁ -'splɔːr ət̬ ɪv -'sploʊr- ~**ly** li
exploratory ɪk 'splɒr ət_ər i ek-, ək-, -'splɔːr-
ǁ -'splɔːr ə tɔːr i -'sploʊr ə toʊr i
explore ɪk 'splɔː ek-, ək- ǁ -'splɔːr -'sploʊr ~**d**
d ~**s** z **exploring** ɪk 'splɔːr ɪŋ ek-,
ək- ǁ -'sploʊr-
explorer ɪk 'splɔːr ə ek-, ək- ǁ -'splɔːr ər
-'sploʊr- ~**s** z
explosion ɪk 'spləʊʒ ən ek-, ək- ǁ -'sploʊʒ ən
~**s** z
explosive ɪk 'spləʊs ɪv ek-, ək-, -'spləʊz-
ǁ -'sploʊs- ~**ly** li ~**ness** nəs nɪs ~**s** z
expo, Expo 'eks pəʊ ǁ -poʊ ~**s** z
exponent ɪk 'spəʊn ənt ek-, ək- ǁ ɪk 'spoʊn-
'eks poʊn- ~**s** s
exponential ˌeks pə 'nentʃ əl ◂ -pəʊ- -poʊ-
~**ly** i
ˌexpo nential 'growth
exponenti|ate ˌeks pə 'nentʃ i ǀeɪt
ˌ•pəʊ- ǁ ˌ•poʊ- ~**ated** eɪt ɪd -əd ǁ eɪt̬ əd
~**ates** eɪts ~**ating** eɪt ɪŋ ǁ eɪt̬ ɪŋ
exponentiation ˌeks pə ˌnentʃ i 'eɪʃ ən
ˌ•pəʊ- ǁ ˌ•poʊ- ~**s** z
ex|port v ɪk ǀ'spɔːt ek-, ək-; ˌeks 'pɔːt, '••
ǁ ɪk ǀ'spɔːrt ek-, -'spoʊrt; 'eks pɔːrt, -poʊrt
~**ported** 'spɔːt ɪd -əd ǁ 'spɔːrt̬ əd -'spoʊrt̬-
~**porting** 'spɔːt ɪŋ ǁ 'spɔːrt̬ ɪŋ -'spoʊrt̬-
~**ports** 'spɔːts ǁ 'spɔːrts -'spoʊrts
export n 'eks pɔːt -pɔːrt -poʊrt ~**s** s
exportable ɪk 'spɔːt əb əl ek-, ək-; ˌeks 'pɔːt-,
'••- ǁ ɪk 'spɔːrt̬ əb əl ek-, -'spoʊrt̬-;
'eks pɔːrt̬-, -poʊrt̬-
exportation ˌeks pɔː 'teɪʃ ən ǁ -pɔːr- -poʊr-,
-pər- ~**s** z
expos|e v ɪk 'spəʊz ek-, ək- ǁ -'spoʊz ~**ed** d
~**es** ɪz əz ~**ing** ɪŋ

exposé *n* ek ˈspəʊz eɪ ɪk-, ək- ‖ ˌeks poʊ ˈzeɪ
—*Fr* [ɛk spo ze] ~s z
exposition ˌeks pə ˈzɪʃ ᵊn ~s z
expositor ɪk ˈspɒz ət ə ek-, ək-, -ɪt-
‖ -ˈspɑːz ət̬ ᵊr ~s z
expository ɪk ˈspɒz ət_ər i ek-, ək-, -ˈ•ɪt_
‖ -ˈspɑːz ə tɔːr i -toʊr i
ex post facto ˌeks ˌpəʊst ˈfækt əʊ •ˌ•-
‖ -ˌpoʊst ˈfækt oʊ
expostu|late ɪk ˈspɒs tju ‖leɪt ek-, ək-, -tʃu-
‖ -ˈspɑːs tʃə- ~**lated** leɪt ɪd -əd ‖ leɪt̬ əd
~**lates** leɪts ~**lating** leɪt ɪŋ ‖ leɪt̬ ɪŋ
expostulation ɪk ˌspɒs tju ˈleɪʃ ᵊn ek-, ək-,
-tʃu- ‖ -ˌspɑːs tʃə- ~s z
exposure ɪk ˈspəʊʒ ə ek-, ək- ‖ -ˈspoʊʒ ᵊr
—*There is also an occasional very careful form*
-ˈspəʊʒ jə ‖ -ˈspoʊʒ jᵊr ~s z
ex¦posure ˌmeter
expound ɪk ˈspaʊnd ek-, ək- ~**ed** ɪd əd ~**ing**
ɪŋ ~s z
express ɪk ˈspres ek-, ək- —*In a stress-shifting
environment the adj or n is sometimes*
ˌeks pres, *as if underlyingly* ˌeks ˈpres ◂:
ˌExpress ˈDairies. *There is usually no stress-
shifting in the v:* to exˌpress ˈsympathy ~**ed** t
~**es** ɪz əz ~**ing** ɪŋ ~**ly** li
expressible ɪk ˈspres əb ᵊl -ɪb-
expression ɪk ˈspreʃ ᵊn ek-, ək- ~**ism** ˌɪz əm
~**ist/s** ɪst/s §əst/s ~s z
expressionistic ɪk ˌspreʃ ə ˈnɪst ɪk ◂ ek-, ək-,
→-ᵊn ˈɪst- ~**ally** ᵊl_i
expressionless ɪk ˈspreʃ ᵊn ləs ek-, ək-, -lɪs
~**ly** li ~**ness** nəs nɪs
expressive ɪk ˈspres ɪv ek-, ək- ~**ly** li ~**ness**
nəs nɪs
expressivity ˌeks pre ˈsɪv ət i -ɪt i ‖ -ət̬ i
expressway ɪk ˈspres weɪ ek-, ək- ~s z
expropri|ate ɪk ˈsprəʊp ri ‖eɪt (ˌ)ek-, ək-
‖ -ˈsproʊp- ~**ated** eɪt ɪd -əd ‖ eɪt̬ əd ~**ates**
eɪts ~**ating** eɪt ɪŋ ‖ eɪt̬ ɪŋ
expropriation ɪk ˌsprəʊp ri ˈeɪʃ ᵊn ek-, ək-,
ˌeks ˌprəʊp- ‖ -ˌsproʊp- ~s z
expulsion ɪk ˈspʌlʃ ᵊn ek-, ək- ~s z
expung|e ɪk ˈspʌndʒ (ˌ)ek-, ək- ~**ed** d ~**es** ɪz
əz ~**ing** ɪŋ
expur|gate ˈeks pə ‖geɪt -pɜː- ‖ -pᵊr- ~**gated**
geɪt ɪd -əd ‖ geɪt̬ əd ~**gates** geɪts ~**gating**
geɪt ɪŋ ‖ geɪt̬ ɪŋ
expurgation ˌeks pə ˈgeɪʃ ᵊn -pɜː- ‖ -pᵊr- ~s z
expurgatory ek ˈspɜːg ət_ər i ‖ -ə tɔːr i -toʊr i
exquisite ɪk ˈskwɪz ɪt ek-, ək-, ˈeks kwɪz-, -ət
—*Poll panel preferences: BrE 1988,* •ˈ•• 69%,
ˈ••• 31%; *AmE 1993,* •ˈ•• 76%, ˈ••• 24%.
~**ly** li ~**ness** nəs nɪs
ex-service ˌeks ˈsɜːv ɪs ◂ ˌek-, §-əs ‖ -ˈsɜːv əs
ex-service|man ˌeks ˈsɜːv ɪs ‖mən ˌek-, -əs-
‖ -ˈsɜːv- ~**men** mən men ~**woman**
ˌwʊm ən ~**women** ˌwɪm ɪn §-ən
extant (ˌ)ek ˈstænt ɪk-, ək-; ˈekst ənt
Extel *tdmk* ˈeks tel
extemporaneous ɪk ˌstemp ə ˈreɪn i_əs ◂ (ˌ)ek-,
ək- ~**ly** li ~**ness** nəs nɪs
extempore ɪk ˈstemp ər i (ˌ)ek-, ək-

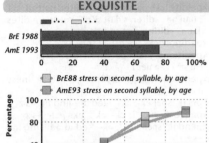

EXQUISITE

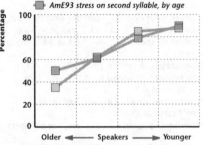

BrE88 stress on second syllable, by age
AmE93 stress on second syllable, by age

Percentage

Older ◀━━━ Speakers ━━━▶ Younger

extemporis... —*see* **extemporiz...**
extemporization ɪk ˌstemp ər aɪ ˈzeɪʃ ᵊn ek-,
ək-, -ər ɪ- ‖ -ᵊr ə- ~s z
extemporiz|e ɪk ˈstemp ə raɪz ek-, ək- ~**ed** d
~**es** ɪz əz ~**ing** ɪŋ
extend ɪk ˈstend ek-, ək- ~**ed** ɪd əd ~**ing** ɪŋ
~s z
exˌtended ˈfamily
extender ɪk ˈstend ə ek-, ək- ‖ -ᵊr ~s z
extensibility ɪk ˌsten⟨t⟩s ə ˈbɪl ət i -ˌ•ɪ-, -ɪt i
‖ -ət̬ i
extensible ɪk ˈsten⟨t⟩s əb ᵊl ek-, ək-, -ɪb-
extension ɪk ˈsten⟨t⟩ʃ ᵊn ek-, ək- ~s z
extensional ɪk ˈsten⟨t⟩ʃ ᵊn_əl ek-, ək-
extensionality ɪk ˌsten⟨t⟩ʃ ə ˈnæl ət i ek-, ək-,
-ɪt i ‖ -ət̬ i
extensive ɪk ˈsten⟨t⟩s ɪv ek-, ək- ~**ly** li ~**ness**
nəs nɪs
extensor ɪk ˈsten⟨t⟩s ə ek-, ək-, -ɔː ‖ -ᵊr ~s z
extent ɪk ˈstent ek-, ək- ~s s
extenu|ate ɪk ˈsten ju ‖eɪt ek-, ək- ~**ated**
eɪt ɪd -əd ‖ eɪt̬ əd ~**ates** eɪts ~**ating**
eɪt ɪŋ ‖ eɪt̬ ɪŋ
extenuation ɪk ˌsten ju ˈeɪʃ ᵊn ek-, ək- ~s z
exterior ɪk ˈstɪər i_ə (ˌ)ek-, ək- ‖ -ˈstɪr i_ᵊr ~**ly**
li ~s z
exterioris... —*see* **exterioriz...**
exteriority ɪk ˌstɪər i ˈɒr ət i ek-, ək-, ˌekst ɪər-,
-ɪt i ‖ -ˌstɪr i ˈɔːr ət̬ i -ˈɑːr-
exteriorization ɪk ˌstɪər i_ər aɪ ˈzeɪʃ ᵊn ek-,
ək-, ˌekst ɪər-, -ɪˈ•- ‖ -ˌstɪr i_ᵊr ə- ~s z
exterioriz|e ɪk ˈstɪər i_ə raɪz (ˌ)ek-, ək- ‖ -ˈstɪr-
~**ed** d ~**es** ɪz əz ~**ing** ɪŋ
extermi|nate ɪk ˈstɜːm ɪ ‖neɪt ek-, ək-, -ə-
‖ -ˈstɜːm- ~**nated** neɪt ɪd -əd ‖ neɪt̬ əd
~**nates** neɪts ~**nating** neɪt ɪŋ ‖ neɪt̬ ɪŋ
extermination ɪk ˌstɜːm ɪ ˈneɪʃ ᵊn ek-, ək-, -ə-
‖ -ˌstɜːm- ~s z
exterminator ɪk ˈstɜːm ɪ neɪt ə ek-, ək-, -ˈ•ə-
‖ -ˈstɜːm ə neɪt̬ ᵊr ~s z
extern ˈeks tɜːn ‖ -tɜːn ~s z
external ɪk ˈstɜːn ᵊl (ˌ)ek-, ək- ‖ -ˈstɜːn ᵊl ~**ly** i
~s z

externalis... —*see* **externaliz...**
externalit|y ,ekst ɜː 'næl ət |i -ɪt i
‖ ,ekst ɝː 'næl əṭ |i **~ies** iz
externalization ɪk ,stɜːn əl aɪ 'zeɪʃ ᵊn ek-, ək-,
,ekst ɜːn-, -əl ɪ- ‖ -,stɝːn əl ə- **~s** z
externaliz|e ɪk 'stɜːn ə laɪz ₍ᵢ₎ek-, ək-, -əl aɪz
‖ -'stɝːn- **~ed** d **~es** ɪz əz **~ing** ɪŋ
exterritorial ,eks ,ter ɪ 'tɔːr i̯əl ◄ ‖ -'toʊr- **~ly**
i
extinct ɪk 'stɪŋkt ₍ᵢ₎ek-, ək-
extinction ɪk 'stɪŋk ʃᵊn ₍ᵢ₎ek-, ək- **~s** z
extinguish ɪk 'stɪŋ gwɪʃ ek-, ək-, §-wɪʃ **~ed** t
~er/s ə/z ‖ ᵊr/z **~es** ɪz əz **~ing** ɪŋ
extir|pate 'ekst ɜː |peɪt -ə- ‖ -ᵊr- **~pated**
peɪt ɪd -əd ‖ peɪṭ əd **~pates** peɪts **~pating**
peɪt ɪŋ ‖ peɪṭ ɪŋ
extirpation ,ekst ɜː 'peɪʃ ᵊn -ə- ‖ -ᵊr- **~s** z
extol, extol|l ɪk 'stəʊl ek-, ək-, →-'stɒʊl, -'stɒl
‖ -'stoʊl **~led** d **~ling** ɪŋ **~s** z
Exton 'ekst ᵊn
ex|tort ɪk |'stɔːt ek-, ək- ‖ -|'stɔːrt **~storted**
'stɔːt ɪd -əd ‖ 'stɔːrṭ əd **~storting**
'stɔːt ɪŋ ‖ 'stɔːrṭ ɪŋ **~storts** 'stɔːts ‖ 'stɔːrts
extortion ɪk 'stɔːʃ ᵊn ek-, ək- ‖ -'stɔːrʃ ᵊn **~s**
z
extortionate ɪk 'stɔːʃ ᵊn̯ət ek-, ək-, ‿ɪt
‖ -'stɔːrʃ- **~ly** li
extortioner ɪk 'stɔːʃ ᵊn̯ə ek-, ək-
‖ -'stɔːrʃ ᵊn̯ᵊr **~s** z
extortionist ɪk 'stɔːʃ ᵊn̯ɪst ek-, ək-, §‿əst
‖ -'stɔːrʃ- **~s** s
extra 'eks trə **~s** z
,extra 'cover
extra- *comb. form*
with stress-neutral suffix |eks trə —
extracanonical
,eks trə kə 'nɒn ɪk ᵊl ◄ ‖ -'nɑːn-
with stress-imposing suffix ɪk 'stræ+ ek-, ək-
— **extrapolate** ɪk 'stræp ə leɪt ek-, ək-
extract *v* ɪk 'strækt ek-, ək- —*In AmE, in the*
sense 'select and cite excerpts' also 'eks trækt
~ed ɪd əd **~ing** ɪŋ **~s** s
extract *n* 'eks trækt **~s** s
extraction ɪk 'stræk ʃᵊn ek-, ək- **~s** z
extractive ɪk 'strækt ɪv ek-, ək-
extractor ɪk 'strækt ə ek-, ək- ‖ -ᵊr **~s** z
ex'tractor fan
extracurricular ,eks trə kə 'rɪk jʊl ə ◄ -jəl ə
‖ -jəl ᵊr
extraditable 'eks trə daɪt əb ᵊl ,•••••
‖ -daɪṭ əb ᵊl
extra|dite 'eks trə |daɪt **~dited** daɪt ɪd -əd
‖ daɪṭ əd **~dites** daɪts **~diting**
daɪt ɪŋ ‖ daɪṭ ɪŋ
extradition ,eks trə 'dɪʃ ᵊn **~s** z
extrados *sing.* ek 'streɪd ɒs ‖ 'eks trə dɑːs **~es**
ɪz əz **extrados** *pl* ek 'streɪd əʊz
‖ 'eks trə doʊz
extragalactic ,ek strə gə 'lækt ɪk ◄
extrajudicial ,eks trə dʒu 'dɪʃ ᵊl ◄ **~ly** i
extramarital ,eks trə 'mær ɪt ᵊl ◄ -ət ᵊl
‖ -əṭ ᵊl ◄ -'mer- **~ly** i
extrametrical ,eks trə 'metr ɪk ᵊl ◄

extramural ,eks trə 'mjʊər əl ◄ -'mjɔːr-
‖ -'mjʊr əl **~ly** i
extraneous ɪk 'streɪn i̯əs ek-, ək- **~ly** li
~ness nəs nɪs
extraordinaire ɪk ,strɔːd ɪ 'neə ek-, ək-, -ə-,
-ᵊn 'eə ‖ ɪk ,strɔːrd ᵊn 'eᵊr —*Fr*
[ɛk stʁa ɔʁ di nɛːʁ]

EXTRAORDINARILY

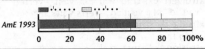

AmE 1993
0   20   40   60   80   100%

extraordinarily ɪk 'strɔːd ᵊn ᵊr̯əl i ek-, ək-,
-'•ɪn-, -ᵊn̯ᵊr əl i, §-,strɔːd ᵊn 'er əl i◄, -ɪ li;
,eks trə 'ɔːd ᵊn ᵊr̯əl i◄, -ᵊn̯ᵊr əl i, -ɪ li
‖ ɪk ,strɔːrd ᵊn 'er əl i ◄ •'•••••• —*AmE*
1993 poll panel preference: •'•••••• *63%,*
•,••'••• *37% (figures perhaps unreliable*
because of confusion over possible stress
shifting).
extraordinary ɪk 'strɔːd ᵊn ᵊr̯i ek-, ək-, -'•ɪn-,
§-er i, -ᵊn̯ᵊr i, ,eks trə 'ɔːd ᵊn ᵊr̯i◄, -ᵊn̯ᵊr-
‖ ɪk 'strɔːrd ᵊn er i ,eks trə 'ɔːrd ᵊn er i◄
extrapo|late ɪk 'stræp ə |leɪt ek-, ək-, ∆-jə-
~lated leɪt ɪd -əd ‖ leɪṭ əd **~lates** leɪts
~lating leɪt ɪŋ ‖ leɪṭ ɪŋ
extrapolation ɪk ,stræp ə 'leɪʃ ᵊn ek-, ək-,
∆-jə- **~s** z
extrapos|e ,eks trə 'pəʊz ‖ -'poʊz **~ed** d **~es**
ɪz əz **~ing** ɪŋ
extraposition ,eks trə pə 'zɪʃ ᵊn **~s** z
extrasensory ,eks trə 'sen̯ts ᵊr̯i ◄
,extra,sensory per'ception
extra-special ,eks trə 'speʃ ᵊl ◄ **~ly** ‿i
extraterrestrial ,eks trə tə 'res tri̯əl ◄ -tɪ'•-,
-te'•-, ∆-'res tʃᵊl
extraterritorial ,eks trə ,ter ɪ 'tɔːr i̯əl
-,•ə- ‖ -'toʊr- **~ly** i
extraterritoriality ,eks trə ,ter ɪ tɔːr i 'æl ət i
-,•ə-, -ɪt i ‖ -əṭ i -toʊr i'•-
extravaganc|e ɪk 'stræv əg ᵊn̯ts ek-, ək- **~es**
ɪz əz
extravagant ɪk 'stræv əg ᵊnt ek-, ək- **~ly** li
~ness nəs nɪs
extravaganza ɪk ,stræv ə 'gænz ə ₍ᵢ₎ek-, ək- **~s**
z
extrava|sate ek 'stræv ə |seɪt ,ek-, ɪk-, ək-
~sated seɪt ɪd -əd ‖ seɪṭ əd **~sates** seɪts
~sating seɪt ɪŋ ‖ seɪṭ ɪŋ
extravasation ek ,stræv ə 'seɪʃ ᵊn ɪk-, ək-,
,eks træv-, -'zeɪʃ- **~s** z
extraversion ,eks trə 'vɜːʃ ᵊn -'vɜːʒ-
‖ -'vɝːʒ ᵊn
extra|vert 'eks trə |vɜːt ‖ -|vɝːt **~verted**
vɜːt ɪd -əd ‖ vɝːṭ əd **~verts** vɜːts ‖ vɝːts
extreme ɪk 'striːm ek-, ək- —*In a stress-*
shifting environment occasionally ,eks triːm, *as*
if underlyingly ,ek 'striːm ◄; ,extreme 'unction
~ly li **~ness** nəs nɪs ‿s
extremism ɪk 'striːm ,ɪz əm ek-, ək-
extremist ɪk 'striːm ɪst ek-, ək-, §‿əst **~s** s
extremit|y ɪk 'strem ət |i ek-, ək-, -ɪt- ‖ -əṭ |i
~ies iz

E

extricable ɪk 'strɪk əb əl ek-, ək-, 'eks trɪk-

extri|cate 'eks trɪ |keɪt -trə- ~cated keɪt ɪd -əd ‖ keɪt̮ əd ~cates keɪts ~cating keɪt ɪŋ ‖ keɪt̮ ɪŋ

extrication ˌeks trɪ 'keɪʃ ən -trə-

extrinsic ⑴eks 'trɪnᵗs ɪk ɪks-, -'trɪnz- ~ally əl_i

extroversion ˌeks trə 'vɜːʃ ən -'vɜːʒ- ‖ -'vɝːʒ ən

extro|vert 'eks trəʊ |vɜːt ‖ -ə |vɝːt ~verted vɜːt ɪd -əd ‖ vɝːt̮ əd ~verts vɜːts ‖ vɝːts

extrud|e ɪk 'struːd ek-, ək- ~ed ɪd əd ~es z ~ing ɪŋ

extrusion ɪk 'struːʒ ən ek-, ək- ~s z

exuberance ɪg 'zjuːb ər_ənts eg-, əg-, ɪk-, ek-, ək-, -'zuːb- ‖ -'zuːb-

exuberant ɪg 'zjuːb ər_ənt eg-, əg-, ɪk-, ek-, ək-, -'zuːb- ‖ -'zuːb- ~ly li

exudation ˌeks ju 'deɪʃ ən ˌegz- ‖ -u-, ˌekʃ u- ~s z

exud|e ɪg 'zjuːd eg-, əg-, ɪk-, ek-, ək-, -'zuːd ‖ -'zuːd ~ed ɪd əd ~es z ~ing ɪŋ

exult ɪg 'zʌlt eg-, əg-, ɪk-, ek-, ək- ~ed ɪd əd ~ing ɪŋ ~s s

exultant ɪg 'zʌlt ənt eg-, əg-, ɪk-, ek-, ək- ~ly li

exultation ˌegz ʌl 'teɪʃ ən ˌeks-, -əl- ~s z

exurb 'eks ɜːb 'egz- ‖ -ɝːb ~s z

exurban ⑴eks 'ɜːb ən ⑴egz- ‖ ek 'sɝːb ən eg 'zɝːb-

exurbanite ⑴eks 'ɜːb ə naɪt ⑴egz- ‖ ek 'sɝːb- eg 'zɝːb- ~s s

exurbia ⑴eks 'ɜːb i_ə ‖ ek 'sɝːb- eg 'zɝːb- ~s z

exuvi|ae ɪg 'zjuːv i_ˌiː eg-, əg-, ɪk-, ek-, ək-, -'zuːv-, -aɪ ‖ -'zuːv- ~al əl

Exxon tdmk 'eks ɒn ‖ -ɑːn

Eyam iːm (!)

Eyck aɪk

eye, Eye aɪ (= I) eyed aɪd eyeing, eying 'aɪ ɪŋ eyes aɪz
'eye ˌcontact; 'eye rhyme; 'eye ˌshadow

eyeball 'aɪ bɔːl ‖ -bɑːl ~ed d ~ing ɪŋ ~s z

eyebath 'aɪ bɑːθ §-bæθ ‖ -bæθ ~s s

eyebright 'aɪ braɪt ~s s

eyebrow 'aɪ braʊ ~s z
'eyebrow ˌpencil

eye-catching 'aɪ ˌkætʃ ɪŋ △-ˌketʃ- ~ly li

eyecup 'aɪ kʌp ~s s

-eyed 'aɪd — brown-eyed ˌbraʊn 'aɪd ◂

eyeful 'aɪ fʊl ~s z

eyeglass 'aɪ glɑːs §-glæs ‖ -glæs ~es ɪz əz

eyelash 'aɪ læʃ ~es ɪz əz

eyelevel 'aɪ ˌlev əl , •'••

eyelet 'aɪ lət -lɪt ~s s

eyelid 'aɪ lɪd ~s z

eyeliner 'aɪ ˌlaɪn ə ‖ -ər ~s z

eye-opener 'aɪ ˌəʊp ən_ə ‖ -ˌoʊp ən_ər ~s z

eyepatch 'aɪ pætʃ ~es ɪz əz

eyepiec|e 'aɪ piːs ~es ɪz əz

eyeshade 'aɪ ʃeɪd ~s z

eyeshot 'aɪ ʃɒt ‖ -ʃɑːt

eyesight 'aɪ saɪt

eyesore 'aɪ sɔː ‖ -sɔːr -soʊr ~s z

eyestalk 'aɪ stɔːk ‖ -stɑːk ~s s

eyestrain 'aɪ streɪn

eyeteeth 'aɪ tiːθ

Eyetie 'aɪ taɪ ~s z

eye|tooth 'aɪ |tuːθ §-tʊθ , •'•• ~teeth tiːθ

eyewash 'aɪ wɒʃ ‖ -wɑːʃ -wɔːʃ

eyewitness 'aɪ ˌwɪt nəs -nɪs , •'••• ~es ɪz əz

eying 'aɪ ɪŋ

Eynon 'aɪn ən —Welsh ['əi non]

Eynsford 'eɪnz fəd ‖ -fərd

Eynsham 'eɪn ʃəm —but locally 'en-

eyot eɪt 'eɪ ət, aɪt eyots eɪts 'eɪ əts, aɪts

Eyre, eyre eə ‖ eər æər

eyr|ie, eyr|y 'ɪər li 'eər-, 'aɪər- ‖ 'er li 'ɪr-, 'aɪər- ~ies iz

Eysenck 'aɪz eŋk

Eyton (i) 'iːt ən, (ii) 'aɪt ən, (iii) 'eɪt ən

Ezekiel ɪ 'ziːk i_əl ə-

Ezra 'ez rə

F f

1 Where the spelling is **f**, the pronunciation is regularly f, as in **fifty** 'fɪft i.

2 Where the spelling is double **ff**, the pronunciation is again f, as in **stiff** stɪf.

3 Exceptionally, the word **of** is pronounced with v: **a piece of wood** ə ˌpiːs əv 'wʊd.

4 f is silent in the old pronunciation of **halfpenny** 'heɪp ni.

5 The sound f is also regularly written **ph**, as in **photograph**, and occasionally **gh**, as in **rough** rʌf.

F, f ef **Fs, fs, F's, f's** efs —*Communications code name:* Foxtrot
fa fɑː
FA ˌef 'eɪ ◄
  ˌFA 'Cup
fab fæb
Faber 'feɪb ə ‖ -ᵊr
Fabergé 'fæb ə ʒeɪ -dʒeɪ ‖ ˌfæb ᵊr 'ʒeɪ
Fabian 'feɪb i_ən ~s z
  'Fabian So,ciety
Fabius 'feɪb i_əs
fable 'feɪb ᵊl ~d d ~s z
fabliau 'fæb li əʊ ‖ -oʊ ~x z —*Fr* [fab li jo]
Fablon *tdmk* 'fæb lɒn -lən ‖ -lɑːn
fabric 'fæb rɪk ~s s
fabri|cate 'fæb rɪ |keɪt -rə- ~cated keɪt ɪd -əd ‖ keɪt̬ əd ~cates keɪts ~cating keɪt ɪŋ ‖ keɪt̬ ɪŋ
fabrication ˌfæb rɪ 'keɪʃ ᵊn -rə- ~s z
fabricator 'fæb rɪ keɪt ə ‖ -ˈrə- ‖ -keɪt̬ ᵊr ~s z
fabulist 'fæb jʊl ɪst -jəl-, §-əst ‖ -jəl- ~s s
fabulous 'fæb jʊl əs -jəl- ‖ -jəl- ~ly li ~ness nəs nɪs
facade, façade fə 'sɑːd fæ-; 'fæs ɑːd ~s z
face feɪs **faced** feɪst **faces** 'feɪs ɪz -əz
  facing/s 'feɪs ɪŋ/z
  'face card; 'face ,flannel; 'face pack; 'face ,powder; ,face 'value, '• ˌ• •
face-ache 'feɪs eɪk ~s s
face-|cloth 'feɪs |klɒθ -klɔːθ ‖ -|klɔːθ -klɑːθ ~cloths klɒθs klɔːθs, klɔːðz ‖ klɔːθs klɔːðz, klɑːθs, klɑːðz
-faced 'feɪst feɪst — **stony-faced** ˌstəʊn i 'feɪst ◄ '• • • ‖ ˌstoʊn-
faceless 'feɪs ləs -lɪs
face-lift 'feɪs lɪft ~s s
face-off 'feɪs ɒf -ɔːf ‖ -ɔːf -ɑːf ~s s
faceplate 'feɪs pleɪt ~s s
facer 'feɪs ə ‖ -ᵊr ~s z

face-sav|er/s 'feɪs ˌseɪv |ə/z ‖ -|ᵊr/z ~ing ɪŋ
facet 'fæs ɪt -ət, -et ~s s
facetiae fə 'siːʃ i_iː
facetious fə 'siːʃ əs ~ly li ~ness nəs nɪs
face-to-face ˌfeɪs tə 'feɪs ◄
facetted 'fæs ɪt ɪd -ət-, -əd ‖ -ət̬-
Fach vɑːk vɑːx —*Welsh* [vaːχ]
facia 'feɪʃ ə 'feɪʃ i_ə ~s z
facial 'feɪʃ ᵊl 'feɪʃ i_əl; 'feɪs i_əl ~ly i ~s z
  'facial nerve
facies 'feɪʃ i iːz 'feɪʃ iːz
facile 'fæs aɪᵊl ‖ -ᵊl ~ly li
facili|tate fə 'sɪl ɪ |teɪt -ɪ- ~tated teɪt ɪd -əd ‖ teɪt̬ əd ~tates teɪts ~tating teɪt ɪŋ ‖ teɪt̬ ɪŋ
facilitation fə ˌsɪl ɪ 'teɪʃ ᵊn -ɪ-
facilitative fə 'sɪl ɪt ət ɪv -ˈ•ɪt-; -ə teɪt ɪv ‖ -ə teɪt̬ ɪv
facilitator fə 'sɪl ə teɪt ə -ˈ•ɪ- ‖ -teɪt̬ ᵊr ~s z
facilit|y fə 'sɪl ət li -ɪt- ‖ -ət̬ li ~ies iz
facing 'feɪs ɪŋ ~s z
Facit *tdmk* 'feɪs ɪt §-ət
facsimile fæk 'sɪm əl i -ɪl- ~d d ~ing ɪŋ ~s z
fact fækt **facts** fækts
fact-finding 'fækt ˌfaɪnd ɪŋ
faction 'fæk ʃᵊn ~s z
factional 'fæk ʃᵊn_əl ~ism ˌɪz əm
factious 'fæk ʃəs ~ly li ~ness nəs nɪs
factitious fæk 'tɪʃ əs ~ly li ~ness nəs nɪs
factitive 'fækt ət ɪv -ɪt- ‖ -ət̬ ɪv ~ly li ~s z
factive 'fækt ɪv ~s z
factoid 'fækt ɔɪd ~s z
factor 'fækt ə ‖ -ᵊr ~ed d **factoring** 'fækt ᵊr_ɪŋ ~s z
factorage 'fækt ᵊr ɪdʒ
factorial fæk 'tɔːr i_əl ‖ -ˈtoʊr- ~ly i ~s z
factoris... —*see* **factoriz...**
factorization ˌfækt ᵊr aɪ 'zeɪʃ ᵊn -ᵊr ɪ- ‖ -ᵊr ə- ~s z

factoriz|e 'fækt ə raız ~**ed** d ~**es** ız əz ~**ing**
ıŋ
factory 'fæk tri 'fækt ər i **factories** 'fæk triz
'fækt ər iz
' **factory farm;** ' **factory ship**
factotum fæk 'təʊt əm ‖ -'toʊt əm ~**s** z
factual 'fæk tʃu_əl -ʃu_əl; 'fækt ju_əl ~**ly** i ~**s**
z
facula 'fæk jʊl ə -jəl- ‖ -jəl ə
facultative 'fæk əlt ət ıv -əl teıt-
‖ 'fæk əl teıt ıv ~**ly** li
facult|y 'fæk əlt li ~**ies** iz
fad fæd **fads** fædz
Fadden 'fæd ən
faddish 'fæd ıʃ ~**ly** li ~**ness** nəs nıs
faddism 'fæd ˌız əm
fade feıd **faded** 'feıd ıd -əd **fades** feıdz
fading 'feıd ıŋ
fadeless 'feıd ləs -lıs ~**ly** li
fadeout 'feıd aʊt ~**s** s
fadge fædʒ **fadges** 'fædʒ ız -əz
fading 'feıd ıŋ ~**s** z
fado 'fɑːd əʊ ‖ -oʊ ~**s** z —*Port* ['fa ðu]
faecal 'fiːk əl
faeces 'fiːs iːz
faerie 'feı ər i 'feər i ‖ 'fer i, 'fær i
Faeroe 'feər əʊ ‖ 'fer oʊ 'fær- *(= pharaoh)* ~**s**
z
Faeroese ˌfeər əʊ 'iːz ◄ ‖ ˌfer oʊ- ˌfær-, -'iːs ◄
faery 'feı ər i 'feər i ‖ 'fer i, 'fær i
faff fæf **faffed** fæft **faffing** 'fæf ıŋ **faffs** fæfs
fag fæg **fagged** fægd **fagging** 'fæg ıŋ **fags**
fægz
ˌfag 'end◄, '••; ˌfagged 'out
Fagan 'feıg ən
fagg|ot 'fæg lət ~**oted** ət ıd -əd ‖ ət əd
~**oting** ət ıŋ ‖ ət ıŋ ~**ots** əts
faggotry 'fæg ətr i
faggotty, faggoty 'fæg ət i ‖ -ət̬ i
Fagin 'feıg ın §-ən
fag|ot 'fæg lət ~**oted** ət ıd -əd ‖ ət əd ~**oting**
ət ıŋ ‖ ət ıŋ ~**ots** əts
fah fɑː
Fahd fɑːd
Fahrenheit 'fær ən haıt 'fɑːr- ‖ 'fer-
Fahy 'fɑː hi -i
faience, faïence faı 'ɒs feı-, -'ɑːn̩s, -'ɒn̩s
‖ feı 'ɑːn̩s faı- —*Fr* [fa jã:s]
fail feıəl **failed** feıəld **failing** 'feıəl ıŋ **fails**
feıəlz
failing n 'feıl ıŋ ~**s** z
fail-safe 'feıəl seıf ˌ•'•
Failsworth 'feıəlz wɜːθ -wəθ ‖ -wərθ
failure 'feıl jə ‖ -jər ~**s** z
fain feın
faineant, feinéant 'feın i_ənt —*Fr* [fɛ ne ã]
fainites 'feın aıts
fains feınz
faint feınt **fainted** 'feınt ıd -əd ‖ 'feın̩t əd
fainter 'feınt ə ‖ 'feın̩t ər **faintest** 'feınt ıst
§-əst ‖ 'feın̩t əst **fainting** 'feınt ıŋ ‖ 'feın̩t ıŋ
faints feın ts

faint-hearted ˌfeınt 'hɑːt ıd ◄ -əd ‖ -'hɑːrt̬ əd ◄
~**ly** li ~**ness** nəs nıs
faintly 'feınt li
faintness 'feınt nəs -nıs
fair feə ‖ feər fæªr **fairer** 'feər ə ‖ 'fer ər
'fær ər **fairest** 'feər ıst §-əst ‖ 'fer əst 'fær-
ˌfair ' copy; ˌfair ' dinkum; ˌfair ' game;' Fair
Isle; ˌfair ' sex, '• •
Fairbairn, Fairbairne 'feə beən ‖ 'fer bern
'fær bærn
Fairbank 'feə bæŋk ‖ 'fer- 'fær-
Fairbanks 'feə bæŋks ‖ 'fer- 'fær-
Fairbourn, Fairbourne 'feə bɔːn ‖ 'fer bɔːrn
'fær-, -boʊrn
Fairbrother 'feə ˌbrʌð ə ‖ 'fer ˌbrʌð ər 'fær-
Fairchild 'feə tʃaıəld ‖ 'fer- 'fær-
Fairclough *(i)* 'feə klʌf ‖ 'fer- 'fær-, *(ii)*
-kləʊ ‖ -kloʊ
Fairfax 'feə fæks ‖ 'fer- 'fær-
Fairfield 'feə fiːəld ‖ 'fer- 'fær-
Fairford 'feə fəd ‖ 'fer fərd 'fær-
fairground 'feə graund ‖ 'fer- 'fær- ~**s** z
fair-haired ˌfeə 'heəd ◄ ‖ ˌfer 'heªrd ◄
ˌfær 'hæªrd
Fairhaven 'feə ˌheıv ən ‖ 'fer- 'fær-
fairi... —*see* **fairy**
fairing 'feər ıŋ ‖ 'fer ıŋ 'fær- ~**s** z
fairish 'feər ıʃ ‖ 'fer ıʃ 'fær-
Fairley, Fairlie 'feə li ‖ 'fer- 'fær-
Fairlight 'feə laıt ‖ 'fer- 'fær-
fairly 'feə li ‖ 'fer- 'fær-
Fairman 'feə mən ‖ 'fer- 'fær-
fair-minded ˌfeə 'maınd ıd ◄ -əd ‖ ˌfer- ˌfær-
~**ness** nəs nıs
Fairmont 'feə mɒnt -mənt ‖ 'fer mɑːnt 'fær-
Fairport 'feə pɔːt ‖ 'fer pɔːrt 'fær-, -poʊrt
fairway 'feə weı ‖ 'fer- 'fær- ~**s** z
fair-weather, Fairweather
'feə ˌweð ə ‖ 'fer ˌweð ər 'fær-
fair|y 'feər li ‖ 'fer li 'fær- ~**ies** iz
'fairy ˌcycle, ˌfairy ' god ˌmother; 'fairy
light; ˌfairy ' ring ‖ '• • •; 'fairy ˌstory
fairyland 'feər i lænd ‖ 'fer- 'fær-
fairy-tale 'feər i teıəl ‖ 'fer- 'fær- ~**s** z
Faisal 'faıs əl
Faisalabad 'faıs əl ə bæd 'faız-, -bɑːd
fait accompli ˌfeıt ə 'kɒmp liː ˌfet-, -'kʌmp-
‖ ˌfeıt ə kɑːm 'pliː —*Fr* [fɛ ta kɔ̃ pli] **faits**
accomplis ˌfeız ə 'kɒmp liː -feıts-, ˌfeıt-,
ˌfez-, -'kʌmp-, -liːz ‖ ˌfeız ə kɑːm 'pliː —*Fr*
[fɛ za kɔ̃ pli]
faites vos jeux ˌfeıt vəʊ 'ʒɜː ˌfet- ‖ -voʊ 'ʒuː
—*Fr* [fɛt vo ʒø]
faith, Faith feıθ **faiths, Faith's** feıθs
'faith ˌhealing
faithful 'feıθ fəl -fʊl ~**ly** _i ~**ness** nəs nıs
Faithful, Faithfull 'feıθ fəl -fʊl
faithless 'feıθ ləs -lıs ~**ly** li ~**ness** nəs nıs
fajita fæ 'hiːt ə fə- ‖ -'hiːt̬ ə fɑː- ~**s** z —*Sp*
[fa 'xi ta ls]
fake feık **faked** feıkt **fakes** feıks **faking**
'feık ıŋ
Fakenham 'feık ən_əm

faker 'feɪk ə ‖ -ᵊr ~s z
fakir 'feɪk ɪə 'fɑːk-, 'fæk-; fə 'kɪə, fæ- ‖ fə 'kɪᵊr
   fɑː-; 'feɪk ᵊr ~s z
Fal fæl
falafel fə 'lɑːf ᵊl
Falange fə 'lændʒ fæ-; 'fæl ændʒ ‖ 'feɪl ændʒ
   —Sp [fa 'laŋ xe]
Falangist fə 'lændʒ ɪst §-əst ~s s
Falasha fə 'læʃ ə ‖ -'lɑːʃ ə ~s z
falcate 'fælk eɪt
falchion 'fɔːltʃ ən 'fɔːlʃ- ‖ 'fɑːltʃ- ~s z
falciform 'fæls ɪ fɔːm -ə- ‖ -fɔːrm

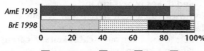

FALCON

| | AmE 'fælk-   'fɔːlk- or 'fɑːlk-   'fɒːk- or 'fɑːk- |
| | BrE 'fɔːlk-   'fælk-   'fɒlk-   'fɔːk- |

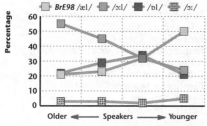

▢ BrE98 /æl/   ▢ /ɔːl/   ■ /ɒl/   ⊞ /ɔː/

Older ⬅ Speakers ➡ Younger

falcon, F~ 'fɔːlk ən 'fælk-, 'fɒlk-, 'fɔːk-
   ‖ 'fælk- 'fɑːlk-, 'fɑːk-, 'fɔːk- —Poll
   panel preferences: AmE 1993, 'fælk- 84%,
   'fɔːlk- or 'fɑːlk- 13%, 'fɔːk- or 'fɑːk- 3%;
   BrE 1998, 'fɔːlk- 38%, 'fælk- 32%, 'fɒlk-
   27%, 'fɔːk- 3%. ~s z
Falconbridge 'fɔːlk ən brɪdʒ 'fælk-, 'fɒlk-,
   'fɔːk-, →-əm- ‖ 'fælk- 'fɔːlk-, 'fɑːlk-
Falconcrest ˌfælk ən 'krest ◂ ˌfɔːlk-, ˌfɒlk-,
   ˌfɒlk-, →ˌ əŋ- ‖ ˌfælk- ˌfɔːlk-, ˌfɑːlk-
falconer, F~ 'fɔːlk ən‿ə 'fælk-, 'fɒlk-, 'fɔːk-
   ‖ 'fælk ᵊn‿ᵊr 'fɔːlk-, 'fɑːlk- ~s z
falconry 'fɔːlk ən ri 'fælk-, 'fɒlk-, 'fɔːk-
   ‖ 'fælk- 'fɔːlk-, 'fɑːlk-
Falder 'fɔːld ə 'fɒld- ‖ 'fɔːld ᵊr 'fɑːld-
falderal 'fæld ə ræl -ɪ- ‖ 'fɑːld ə rɑːl ~s z
Faldo 'fæld əʊ ‖ 'fɑːld oʊ
faldstool 'fɔːld stuːl ‖ 'fɑːld- ~s z
Falernian fə 'lɜːn i ən ‖ -'lɜːn-
Faliscan fə 'lɪsk ən ~s z
Falk fɔːlk fɔːk ‖ fɑːlk
Falkender 'fɔːlk ənd ə ‖ -ᵊr 'fɑːlk-
Falkirk 'fɔːlk ɜːk 'fɒlk-, -ək; §'fæl kɜːk
   ‖ 'fɔːl -kɜ·ːk 'fɑːl-
Falkland 'fɔːlk lənd 'fɔːk-, 'fɒlk- ‖ 'fɔːk-
   'fɑːk- ~s z
   ˌFalkland ˈIslands ‖ ˌ•• ˈ••
Falkner 'fɔːlk nə 'fɔːk-, 'fɒlk-, 'fælk-
   ‖ 'fɔːk nᵊr 'fɑːlk-
Falkus 'fɔːlk əs ‖ 'fɑːlk-
fall, Fall fɔːl ‖ fɑːl **fallen** 'fɔːl ən ‖ 'fɑːl-
   falling 'fɔːl ɪŋ ‖ 'fɑːl- **falls, Falls** fɔːlz ‖ fɑːlz

fell fel
   'fall guy; ˌfalling 'star; 'fall line
Falla 'fæl ə 'fɑːl-, -jə- 'faɪ ə ‖ 'fɑː jə —Sp
   ['fa ʎa, -ja]
fallacious fə 'leɪʃ əs ~ly li ~ness nəs nɪs
fallac|y 'fæl əs |i ~ies iz
fal-lal ˌ fæl 'læl ˌ fæ- ~s z
fallback 'fɔːl bæk ‖ 'fɑːl- ~s s
fallen 'fɔːl ən ‖ 'fɑːl-
Faller 'fæl ə ‖ -ᵊr
fallibility ˌfæl ə 'bɪl ət i ˌ•ɪ-, -ɪt i ‖ -ət̬ i
fallib|le 'fæl əb |ᵊl -ɪb- ~ly li
fall-off 'fɔːl ɒf -ɔːf ‖ -ɔːf 'fɑːl-, -ɑːf ~s s
Fallon 'fæl ən
fallopian, F~ fə 'ləʊp i‿ən ‖ -'loʊp-
   falˌlopian ˈtube
fallout 'fɔːl aʊt ‖ 'fɑːl-
fallow, F~ 'fæl əʊ ‖ -oʊ ~ed d ~ing ɪŋ ~s z
   'fallow deer
Fallowes 'fæl əʊz ‖ -oʊz
Fallowfield 'fæl əʊ fiːᵊld ‖ -oʊ-
Falls fɔːlz ‖ fɑːlz
Falmer 'fælm ə ‖ -ᵊr
Falmouth 'fæl məθ

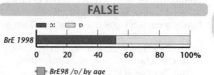

FALSE

| | ■ ɔː   ▢ ɒ |
| BrE 1998 | |

BrE98 /ɒ/ by age

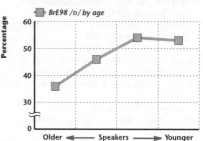

Older ⬅ Speakers ➡ Younger

false fɔːls fɒls ‖ fɔːls fɑːls **falser** 'fɔːls ə
   'fɒls ə ‖ 'fɔːls ᵊr 'fɑːls ᵊr **falsest** 'fɔːls ɪst
   'fɒls-, §-əst ‖ 'fɔːls əst 'fɑːls- —BrE 1998
   poll panel preference: ɔː 52%, ɒ 48%
   ˌfalse aˈlarm; ˌfalse arˈrest; ˌfalse ˈbottom;
   ˌfalse ˈstart; ˌfalse ˈteeth
false-hearted ˌfɔːls 'hɑːt ɪd ◂ ˌfɒls-, -əd
   ‖ ˌfɔːls 'hɑːrt̬ əd ◂ ˌfɑːls-, '•, ••
falsehood 'fɔːls hʊd 'fɒls- ‖ 'fɔːls- 'fɑːls- ~s
   z
falsely 'fɔːls li 'fɒls- ‖ 'fɔːls- 'fɑːls-
falsetto fɔːl 'set əʊ fɒl- ‖ fɔːl 'set̬ oʊ fɑːl- ~s z
falseness 'fɔːls nəs 'fɒls-, -nɪs ‖ 'fɔːls- 'fɑːls-
falsies 'fɔːls iz 'fɒls- ‖ 'fɔːls iz 'fɑːls-
falsifiability ˌfɔːls ɪ faɪˌə 'bɪl ət i ˌfɒls-, ˌ•ə-,
   -ɪt i ‖ ˌfɔːls ə faɪ ə 'bɪl ət̬ i ˌfɑːls-
falsifiab|le 'fɔːls ɪ faɪˌəb ᵊl 'fɒls-, '•ə-,
   ˌ••'••• ‖ 'fɔːls- 'fɑːls- ~ly li
falsification ˌfɔːls ɪf ɪ 'keɪʃ ᵊn ˌfɒls-, ˌ•əf-,
   §-ə'•- ‖ ˌfɔːls- ˌfɑːls- ~s z
falsi|fy 'fɔːls ɪ |faɪ 'fɒls-, -ə- ‖ 'fɔːls- 'fɑːls-

F

~fied faɪd **~fier/s** faɪ‿ə/z ‖ faɪ‿ᵊr/z **~fies**
faɪz **~fying** faɪ ɪŋ
falsit|y 'fɔːls ət |i 'fɒls-, -ɪt- ‖ 'fɔːls ət̬ |i 'fɑːls-
~**ies** iz
Falstaff 'fɔːlst ɑːf 'fɒlst-, §-æf ‖ -æf 'fɑːlst-
Falstaffian ₍ₐ₎fɔːl 'stɑːf i‿ən ₍ₐ₎fɒl-, §-'stæf-
‖ -'stæf- ₍ₐ₎fɑːl-
faltboat 'fælt bəʊt 'fɑːlt-, 'fɔːlt-, 'fɒlt-
‖ 'fɔːlt boʊt 'fɑːlt- ~**s** s
falter 'fɔːlt ə 'fɒlt ə ‖ 'fɔːlt ᵊr 'fɑːlt ᵊr **~ed** d
faltering/ly 'fɔːlt‿ᵊr ɪŋ /li 'fɒlt‿ ‖ 'fɔːlt‿
'fɑːlt‿ ~**s** z
Falwell 'fɔːl wel ‖ 'fɑːl-
Famagusta ˌfæm ə 'ɡʊst ə ◂ ˌfɑːm-
‖ ˌfɑːm ə 'ɡuːst ə
fame feɪm **famed** feɪmd
familial fə 'mɪl i‿əl ‖ fə 'mɪl jəl
familiar fə 'mɪl i‿ə ‖ fə 'mɪl jᵊr **-ly** li
familiaris... —*see* **familiariz...**
familiarit|y fə ˌmɪl i 'ær ət |i -ɪt i
‖ fə ˌmɪl 'jær ət̬ |i -'jer-; -ˌmɪl i 'ær-, -'er-
~**ies** iz
familiarization fə ˌmɪl i‿ər aɪ 'zeɪʃ ᵊn -ɪ'•-
‖ fə ˌmɪl jər ə 'zeɪʃ ᵊn
familiariz|e fə 'mɪl i‿ə raɪz ‖ fə 'mɪl jə raɪz
~**ed** d ~**es** ɪz əz ~**ing** ɪŋ
family 'fæm li 'fæm əl i, -ɪl- **families** 'fæm liz
'fæm əl iz, -ɪl-
,**family al'lowance**; ,**family 'circle**; ,**family
'doctor**; ,**family 'income ,supplement**;
'**family man**; '**family name** '*surname*',
,**family 'name** '*family reputation*'; ,**family
'planning**; ,**family 'tree**
famine 'fæm ɪn §-ən ~**s** z
famish 'fæm ɪʃ ~**ed** t ~**es** ɪz əz ~**ing** ɪŋ
famous 'feɪm əs ~**ly** li ~**ness** nəs nɪs
fan fæn **fanned** fænd **fanning** 'fæn ɪŋ **fans**
fænz
'**fan belt**; '**fan ,heater**
Fan *in names of Welsh mountains* væn —*Welsh*
[van]
Fanagalo ˌfæn ə ɡə 'ləʊ '•••• ‖ ˌfɑːn ə ɡə 'loʊ
fanatic fə 'næt ɪk ‖ -'næt̬ ɪk ~**s** s
fanatical fə 'næt ɪk ᵊl ‖ -'næt̬ ɪk- ~**ly** ‿i
fanaticism fə 'næt ɪ ˌsɪz əm -ə- ‖ -'næt̬ ə-
fancier 'fæn⁀ts i‿ə ‖ ᵊr ~**s** z
fanciful 'fæn⁀ts ɪ fᵊl -ə-, -fʊl ~**ly** ‿i ~**ness** nəs
nɪs
fanc|y, Fanc|y 'fæn⁀ts |i ~**ied** id ~**ier** i‿ə ‖ i‿ᵊr
~**ies** iz ~**iest** i‿ɪst i‿əst ~**ily** ‿i li əl i ~**iness**
i nəs i nɪs ~**ying** i‿ɪŋ
,**fancy 'dress**; '**fancy goods**; '**fancy man**;
'**fancy ,woman**
fancy-free ˌfæn⁀ts i 'friː ◂
fancywork 'fæn⁀ts i wɜːk ‖ -wɜːk
fandango fæn 'dæŋ ɡəʊ ‖ -ɡoʊ ~**s** z
fane, Fane feɪn **fanes** feɪnz
Faneuil 'fæn jəl -ᵊl; 'fæn juˌəl
,**Faneuil 'Hall**
fanfare 'fæn feə ‖ -fer -fær ~**s** z
fanfold 'fæn fəʊld →-fɒʊld ‖ -foʊld
fanfaronade ˌfæn fær ə 'neɪd -fᵊr‿ə-, -'nɑːd
~**s** z

fang fæŋ **fanged** fæŋd **fangs** fæŋz
Fang *African people and language* fæŋ fɑːŋ
fanlight 'fæn laɪt ~**s** s
Fanning 'fæn ɪŋ
fann|y, Fann|y 'fæn |i ~**ies**, ~**y's** iz
fanon 'fæn ən ~**s** z
Fanshawe 'fæn ʃɔː ‖ -ʃɑː
Fant fænt ‖ fɑːnt
Fanta *tdmk* 'fænt ə ‖ 'fænt̬ ə
fantabulous fæn 'tæb jʊl əs -jəl- ‖ -jəl-
fantail 'fæn teɪᵊl ~**ed** d ~**s** z
fan-tan 'fæn tæn
fantasia fæn 'teɪz i‿ə ˌfænt ə 'ziː‿ə, -'siː‿ə
‖ fæn 'teɪʒ ə -'teɪʒ i‿ə; ˌfænt̬ ə 'ziː ə ~**s** z
fantasi... —*see* **fantasy**
fantasis|e, fantasiz|e 'fænt ə saɪz ‖ 'fænt̬ ə-
~**ed** d ~**es** ɪz əz ~**ing** ɪŋ
fantastic ₍ₐ₎fæn 'tæst ɪk fən- ~**al** ᵊl ~**ally** ᵊl‿i
fantasti|cate fæn 'tæst ɪ keɪt -ə- ~**cated**
keɪt ɪd -əd ‖ keɪt̬ əd ~**cates** keɪts ~**cating**
keɪt ɪŋ ‖ keɪt̬ ɪŋ
fantas|y 'fænt əs |i -əz- ‖ 'fænt̬- ~**ied** id ~**ies**
iz ~**ying** i ɪŋ
Fante, Fanti 'fænt i ‖ 'fɑːnt i
fantoccini ˌfænt ə 'tʃiːn i ‖ ˌfænt̬- ˌfɑːnt̬- —*It*
[fan tot 'tʃi ni]
Fantom 'fænt əm ‖ 'fænt̬-
Fanthorpe 'fæn θɔːp ‖ -θɔːrp
Fanum 'feɪn əm
fanzine 'fæn ziːn ~**s** z
FAO ˌef eɪ 'əʊ ‖ -'oʊ
FAQ ˌef eɪ 'kjuː **FAQs, FAQ's** ˌef eɪ 'kjuːz
fæks
far fɑː ‖ fɑːr **farther** 'fɑːð ə ‖ 'fɑːrð ᵊr
farthest 'fɑːð ɪst §-əst ‖ 'fɑːrð- **further**
'fɜːð ə ‖ 'fɜːð ᵊr **furthest** 'fɜːð ɪst §-əst
‖ 'fɜːð-
,**Far 'East**; ,**Far 'Eastern**◂
Fara *island in Orkney* 'fær ə
farad 'fær əd -æd ‖ 'fer- ~**s** z
Faraday 'fær ə deɪ -di ‖ 'fer-
faradic fə 'ræd ɪk
farandole 'fær ən dəʊl →-dɒʊl ‖ -doʊl 'fer-
—*Fr* [fa ʁɑ̃ dɔl] ~**s** z
faraway ˌfɑːr ə 'weɪ ◂
,**faraway 'looks**
farce fɑːs ‖ fɑːrs **farces** 'fɑːs ɪz -əs ‖ 'fɑːrs-
farceur ˌfɑː 'sɜː ‖ ˌfɑːr 'sɝː —*Fr* [faʁ sœːʁ] ~**s**
z
farci, farcie ˌfɑː 'siː ‖ ˌfɑːr- —*Fr* [faʁ si]
farcical 'fɑːs ɪk ᵊl -ək- ‖ 'fɑːrs- ~**ly** ‿i ~**ness**
nəs nɪs
farcy 'fɑːs i ‖ 'fɑːrs i
fare feə ‖ feᵊr fæᵊr (= *fair*) **fared** feəd ‖ feᵊrd
fæᵊrd **fares** feəz ‖ feᵊrz fæᵊrz **faring**
'feər ɪŋ ‖ 'fer ɪŋ 'fær-
Fareham 'feər əm ‖ 'fer- 'fær-
farewell ˌfeə 'wel ◂ ‖ ˌfer- -fær-
Farewell *family name* 'feə wel -wᵊl ‖ 'fer- 'fær-
farfalle fɑː 'fæl eɪ ‖ fɑːr- -'fɑːl- —*It* [far
'fal le]
farfetched ˌfɑː 'fetʃt ◂ ‖ ˌfɑːr-
far-flung ˌfɑː 'flʌŋ ◂ ‖ ˌfɑːr-

Fargo 'faːg əʊ ‖ 'faːrg oʊ
far-gone ˌfaː 'gɒn ◂ §-'gɑːn, §-'gɔːn
‖ ˌfaːr 'gɔːn ◂ -'gɑːn
farina fə 'riːn ə -'raɪn ə
farinaceous ˌfær ɪ 'neɪʃ əs ◂ -ə- ‖ ˌfer-
Faringdon 'fær ɪŋ dən ‖ 'fer-
Farjeon 'faːdʒ ən ‖ 'faːrdʒ-
farl faːl ‖ faːrl farls faːlz ‖ faːrlz
Farleigh, Farley 'faːl i ‖ 'faːrl i
farm faːm ‖ faːrm farmed faːmd ‖ faːrmd
farming 'faːm ɪŋ ‖ 'faːrm ɪŋ farms
faːmz ‖ faːrmz
farmer, F~ 'faːm ə ‖ 'faːrm ᵊr ~s z
farmhand 'faːm hænd ‖ 'faːrm- ~s z
farm|house 'faːm |haʊs ‖ 'faːrm- ~houses
haʊz ɪz -əz
Farmington 'faːm ɪŋ tən ‖ 'faːrm-
farmland 'faːm lænd -lənd ‖ 'faːrm-
farmstead 'faːm sted ‖ 'faːrm- ~s z
farmyard 'faːm jaːd ‖ 'faːrm jaːrd ~s z
Farnaby 'faːn ə bi ‖ 'faːrn-
Farnborough 'faːn bər_ə →'faːm-, §-ˌbʌr-
‖ 'faːrn ˌbɝː oʊ
Farncombe 'faːn kəm →'faːŋ- ‖ 'faːrn-
Farne faːn ‖ faːrn
'Farne ˌIslands
Farnham 'faːn əm ‖ 'faːrn-
Farnley 'faːn li ‖ 'faːrn-
Farnworth 'faːn wɜːθ ‖ 'faːrn wɝːθ
faro 'feər əʊ ‖ 'fer oʊ 'fær- (= pharaoh)
Faro place in Portugal 'faːr əʊ 'feər- ‖ -oʊ
—Port ['fa ru]
Faroe 'feər əʊ ‖ 'fer oʊ 'fær- (= pharaoh) ~s z
Faroese ˌfeər əʊ 'iːz ◂ ‖ ˌfer oʊ- ˌfær-, -'iːs◂
far-off ˌfaːr 'ɒf ◂ -'ɔːf ‖ ˌfaːr 'ɔːf ◂ -'aːf
ˌfar-off ˈlands
farouche fə 'ruːʃ fæ- —Fr [fa ʁuʃ]
Farouk fə 'ruːk
far-out ˌfaːr 'aʊt ◂ ‖ ˌfaːr-
Farquhar 'faːk ə -wə ‖ 'faːrk wᵊr -ᵊr, -waːr
Farquharson 'faːk əs ən -wəs- ‖ 'faːrk wᵊrs
ən -ᵊrs-
Farr faː ‖ faːr
farraginous fə 'rædʒ ɪn əs -'reɪdʒ-, -ən-
farrago fə 'raːg əʊ -'reɪg- ‖ -oʊ ~s z
Farrah 'fær ə ‖ 'fer-
Farrakhan 'fær ə kæn
Farrant 'fær ənt ‖ 'fer-
Farrar 'fær ə ‖ -ᵊr 'fer-
far-reaching ˌfaː 'riːtʃ ɪŋ ◂ ‖ ˌfaːr-
ˌfar-ˌreaching ˈconsequences
Farrell 'fær əl ‖ 'fer-
farrier 'fær i_ə ‖ _ᵊr 'fer- ~s z
Farringdon 'fær ɪŋ dən ‖ 'fer-
farrow, F~ 'fær əʊ ‖ -oʊ 'fer- ~ed d ~ing ɪŋ
~s z
far-seeing ˌfaː 'siː ɪŋ ◂ ‖ ˌfaːr-
Farsi 'faːs i ˌfaː 'siː ‖ 'faːrs i
farsighted ˌfaː 'saɪt ɪd ◂-əd ‖ ˌfaːr 'saɪt̬ əd ◂
~ly li ~ness nəs nɪs
fart faːt ‖ faːrt farted 'faːt ɪd -əd ‖ 'faːrt̬ əd
farting 'faːt ɪŋ ‖ 'faːrt̬ ɪŋ farts faːts ‖ faːrts
farth|er 'faːð ə ‖ 'faːrð| ᵊr ~est ɪst -əst

farthing, F~ 'faːð ɪŋ ‖ 'faːrð- ~s z
farthingale 'faːð ɪŋ geɪl ‖ 'faːrð- ~s z
fartlek 'faːt lek ‖ 'faːrt- ~ked t ~king ɪŋ ~s
s —Swedish ['fat̚ lek]
fasces 'fæs iːz
fascia 'feɪʃ ə 'feɪʃ i_ə, 'fæʃ- ‖ 'fæʃ i_ə 'feɪʃ ə
—In BrE 'fæʃ- as a medical term, otherwise
generally 'feɪʃ-; as a term in classical
architecture, also 'feɪs i_ə. In AmE, generally
'fæʃ i_ə, but 'feɪʃ ə in the sense of 'board
above shopfront' ~s z
fasci|ate 'fæʃ i eɪt ~ated eɪt ɪd -əd ‖ eɪt̬ əd
fascicle 'fæs ɪk ᵊl -ək- ~s z
fascicule 'fæs ɪ kjuːl -ə- ~s z
fasciitis ˌfæʃ i 'aɪt ɪs §-əs ‖ -'aɪt̬ əs
fasci|nate 'fæs ɪ |neɪt -ə- ~nated neɪt ɪd -əd
‖ neɪt̬ əd ~nates neɪts ~nating
neɪt ɪŋ ‖ neɪt̬ ɪŋ
fascinating 'fæs ɪ neɪt ɪŋ -ə- ‖ -neɪt̬ ɪŋ ~ly li
fascination ˌfæs ɪ 'neɪʃ ᵊn -ə- ~s z
fascism 'fæʃ ˌɪz əm
fascist 'fæʃ ɪst §-əst ~s s
fascistic fæ 'ʃɪst ɪk fə-
fash fæʃ fashed fæʃt fashes 'fæʃ ɪz -əz
fashing 'fæʃ ɪŋ
Fashanu 'fæʃ ə nuː
fashion 'fæʃ ᵊn ~ed d ~ing ˌɪŋ ~s z
'fashion plate
-fashion ˌfæʃ ᵊn— Chinese-fashion
ˌtʃaɪ 'niːz ˌfæʃ ᵊn
fashionab|le 'fæʃ ᵊn_əb |ᵊl ~leness ᵊl nəs -nɪs
~ly li
Fashoda fə 'ʃəʊd ə fæ- ‖ -'ʃoʊd ə
Faslane fæz 'leɪn fəs-
Fassbinder 'fæs bɪnd ə ‖ 'faːs bɪnd ᵊr 'fæs-
—Ger Faßbinder ['fas bɪn dɐ]
fast faːst §fæst ‖ fæst fasted 'faːst ɪd §'fæst-,
-əd ‖ 'fæst əd faster 'faːst ə §'fæst ə
‖ 'fæst ᵊr fastest 'faːst ɪst §'fæst-, §-əst
‖ 'fæst- fasting 'faːst ɪŋ §'fæst- ‖ 'fæst ɪŋ
fasts faːsts §fæsts ‖ fæsts
'fast day; ˌfast ˈfood, ' • •; ˌfast ˈlane
fastback 'faːst bæk §'fæst- ‖ 'fæst- ~s s
fastball 'faːst bɔːl §'fæst- ‖ 'fæst- -baːl ~er/s ə/
z ‖ -ᵊr/z
fasten 'faːs ᵊn §'fæs- ‖ 'fæs ᵊn ~ed d ~ing
ˌɪŋ ~s z
fastener 'faːs nə §'fæs-, ' •ᵊn ə ‖ 'fæs ᵊn_ᵊr ~s
z
fastening n 'faːs nɪŋ §'fæs-, ' •ᵊn ɪŋ
‖ 'fæs ᵊn_ɪŋ ~s z
fast-forward ˌfaːst 'fɔː wəd §ˌfæst- ‖ ˌfæst
'fɔːr wᵊrd
fastidious fæ 'stɪd i_əs fə- ~ly li ~ness nəs
nɪs
fastigiate fæ 'stɪdʒ i_ət -eɪt
fastness 'faːst nəs §'fæst-, -nɪs ‖ 'fæst- ~es ɪz
əz
Fastnet 'faːst net §'fæst-, -nɪt ‖ 'fæst-
fast-talk ˌfaːst 'tɔːk §ˌfæst- ‖ ˌfæst- -'taːk
~ed t ~er/s ə/z ‖ ᵊr/z ~ing ɪŋ ~s s
fat fæt fatted 'fæt ɪd -əd ‖ 'fæt̬ əd fatter
'fæt ə ‖ 'fæt̬ ᵊr fattest 'fæt ɪst §-əst

‖ 'fæʧ əst **fatting** 'fæt ɪŋ ‖ 'fæʧ ɪŋ
ˌfat 'cat; ˌfat 'hen
fatal 'feɪt ᵊl ‖ 'feɪṯ ᵊl **~ism** ˌɪz əm **~ist/s** ɪst/s
§-əst/s
fatalistic ˌfeɪt ᵊl 'ɪst ɪk ◄ ‖ ˌfeɪṯ- **~ally** ᵊl i
fatalit|y fə 'tæl ət i feɪ-, -ɪt- ‖ feɪ 'tæl əṯ i fə-
~ies iz
fatally 'feɪt ᵊl i ‖ 'feɪṯ ᵊl i
fata morgana
ˌfɑːt ə mɔː 'gɑːn ə ‖ ˌfɑːṯ ə mɔːr-
fate, Fate feɪt **fated** 'feɪt ɪd -əd ‖ 'feɪṯ əd
fates, Fates feɪts
fateful 'feɪt fᵊl -fʊl **~ly** i
fathead 'fæt hed **~s** z
fatheaded ˌfæt 'hed ɪd ◄ -əd, '••• **~ness** nəs
nɪs
fath|er 'fɑːð ə ‖ -ᵊr **~ered** əd ‖ ᵊrd **~ering**
ᵊr_ɪŋ **~ers** əz ‖ ᵊrz
ˌFather 'Christmas; ˌfather ˌfigure;
'Father's Day; ˌFather 'Time
fatherhood 'fɑːð ə hʊd ‖ -ᵊr-
father-in-law 'fɑːð ᵊr_ɪn ˌlɔː →'•ᵊ_, ᵊr_ən-
‖ 'fɑːð ᵊr_ən ˌlɔː: -ᵊr_ᵊn-, -ˌlɑː: **fathers-in-law**
'fɑːð əz ɪn ˌlɔː: §-ᵊn ˌ• ‖ -ᵊrz ən ˌlɔː: -ˌlɑː:
fatherland 'fɑːð ə lænd ‖ -ᵊr- **~s** z
fatherly 'fɑːð ə li -ᵊl i ‖ -ᵊr-
fathers-in-law —see **father-in-law**
fathom 'fæð əm **~ed** d **~ing** ɪŋ **~s** z
fathomless 'fæð əm ləs -lɪs
fatigu|e fə 'tiːg **~ed** d **~es** z **~ing** ɪŋ
Fatima 'fæt ɪm ə -əm- ‖ 'fæṯ-
fatling 'fæt lɪŋ **~s** z
fat|ly 'fæt li **~ness** nəs nɪs
fatshedera ˌfæts 'hed ᵊr ə **~s** z
fatsia 'fæts i_ə **~s** z
fatso, Fatso 'fæts əʊ ‖ -oʊ **~es, ~s** z
fat-soluble ˌfæt 'sɒl jub ᵊl ◄ -jəb-, '•,•-
‖ 'fæt ˌsɑːl jəb ᵊl
fatstock 'fæt stɒk ‖ -stɑːk
fatt... —see **fat**
fatten 'fæt ᵊn **~ed** d **~er/s** _ə/z ‖ ᵊr/z **~ing**
ˌɪŋ **~s** z
fattish 'fæt ɪʃ ‖ 'fæṯ ɪʃ **~ness** nəs nɪs
fatt|y 'fæt li ‖ 'fæṯ li **~ier** i_ə ‖ i_ᵊr **~ies** iz
~iest i_ɪst i_əst **~iness** i nəs i nɪs
ˌfatty 'acid
fatuit|y fə 'tjuː_ət i fæ-, →§-'tʃuː_, ˌɪt-
‖ -'tuː əṯ li -'tjuː-, -'tʃuː- **~ies** iz
fatuous 'fæt ju_əs 'fætʃ u_əs ‖ 'fætʃ u_əs **~ly**
li **~ness** nəs nɪs
fatwa 'fæt wɑː **~s** z —Arabic ['fat wɑː]
faucal 'fɔːk ᵊl ‖ 'fɑːk-
fauces 'fɔːs iːz ‖ 'fɑːs-
faucet 'fɔːs ɪt -ət ‖ 'fɑːs- **~s** s
Faucett, Faucitt 'fɔːs ɪt -ət ‖ 'fɑːs-
faugh fɔː ‖ fɑː: —or non-speech sequences such
as [pɸ, pɸə]
Faulds (i) fəʊldz →fɒʊldz ‖ foʊldz, (ii) fɔːldz
‖ fɑːldz
Faulkner 'fɔːk nə 'fɔːlk- ‖ -nᵊr 'fɑːk-
Faull fɔːl ‖ fɑːl
fault fɔːlt fɒlt ‖ fɔːlt fɑːlt **faulted** 'fɔːlt ɪd
'fɒlt-, -əd ‖ 'fɔːlt əd 'fɑːlt- **faulting** 'fɔːlt ɪŋ

'fɒlt- ‖ 'fɔːlt ɪŋ 'fɑːlt- **faults** fɔːlts fɒlts
‖ fɔːlts fɑːlts
'fault line; 'fault plane
faultfind|er/s 'fɔːlt ˌfaɪnd lə/z 'fɒlt-
‖ 'fɔːlt ˌfaɪnd -ᵊr/z 'fɑːlt- **~ing** ɪŋ
faultless 'fɔːlt ləs 'fɒlt-, -lɪs ‖ 'fɔːlt- 'fɑːlt- **~ly**
li **~ness** nəs nɪs
fault|y 'fɔːlt li 'fɒlt- ‖ 'fɔːlt li 'fɑːlt- **~ier**
i_ə ‖ i_ᵊr **~iest** i_ɪst i_əst **~ily** ɪ li əl i **~iness**
i nəs i nɪs
faun fɔːn ‖ fɑːn (= fawn) **fauns** fɔːnz ‖ fɑːnz
fauna 'fɔːn ə 'faʊn- ‖ 'fɑːn ə **~s** z
Fauntleroy 'fɒnt lə rɔɪ 'fɔːnt- ‖ 'fɔːnt- 'fɑːnt-
'Fauntleroy suit
Faure fɔː ‖ fɔːr —Fr [fɔːʁ]
Fauré 'fɔːr eɪ 'fɒr- ‖ foʊ 'reɪ fɔː- —Fr [fo ʁe]
Faust faʊst —but the place in NY is fɔːst
Faustian 'faʊst i_ən
Faustus 'faʊst əs 'fɔːst- ‖ 'fɔːst-, 'fɑːst-
faute de mieux ˌfəʊt də 'mjɜː ‖ ˌfoʊt də 'mjuː
—Fr [fot də mjø]
Fauve fəʊv ‖ foʊv —Fr [foːv]
Fauvism 'fəʊv ˌɪz əm ‖ 'foʊv-
Fauvist 'fəʊv ɪst §-əst ‖ 'foʊv- **~s** s
Faux name (i) fɔːks ‖ fɑːks, (ii) fəʊ ‖ foʊ
faux fəʊ ‖ foʊ —see also phrases with this word
faux ami ˌfəʊz æ 'mi: ‖ ˌfoʊz- —Fr [fo za mi]
~s z or as sing.
faux-naif, faux-naïf ˌfəʊ naɪ 'iːf ◄ ‖ ˌfoʊ nɑː-
—Fr [fo na if]
faux pas sing. ˌfəʊ 'pɑː: '•• ‖ ˌfoʊ- —Fr [fo pɑ]
faux pas pl ˌfəʊ 'pɑːz -'pɑː, '•• ‖ ˌfoʊ- —Fr
[fo pɑ]
fave feɪv
Favell 'feɪv ᵊl
Faversham 'fæv ə ʃəm ‖ -ᵊr-
favonian, F~ fə 'vəʊn i_ən feɪ- ‖ -'voʊn-
favor 'feɪv ə ‖ -ᵊr **~ed** d **favoring/ly** 'feɪv
ᵊr_ɪŋ /li **~s** z
favorab|le 'feɪv ᵊr_əb ᵊl **~leness** ᵊl nəs -nɪs
~ly li
favorite 'feɪv rət -rɪt; 'feɪv ᵊr ət,
-ɪt ‖ △'feɪv ᵊrt **~s** s
ˌfavorite 'son
favoritism 'feɪv rə ˌtɪz əm -rɪt-; '•ᵊr ə,•-,
-ᵊr ɪ- ‖ △-ᵊr-
favour 'feɪv ə ‖ -ᵊr **~ed** d **favouring/ly** 'feɪv
ᵊr_ɪŋ /li **~s** z
favourab|le 'feɪv ᵊr_əb ᵊl **~leness** ᵊl nəs -nɪs
~ly li
favourite 'feɪv rət -rɪt; 'feɪv ᵊr ət,
-ɪt ‖ △'feɪv ᵊrt **~s** s
ˌfavourite 'son
favouritism 'feɪv rə ˌtɪz əm -rɪt-; '•ᵊr ə,•-,
-ᵊr ɪ- ‖ △-ᵊr-
Fawcett 'fɔːs ɪt -ət ‖ 'fɑːs-
Fawcus 'fɔːk əs ‖ 'fɑːk-
Fawkes fɔːks ‖ fɑːks
Fawley 'fɔːl i ‖ 'fɑːl i
Fawlty 'fɔːlt i 'fɒlt i ‖ 'fɔːlt i 'fɑːlt i
fawn fɔːn ‖ fɑːn **fawned** fɔːnd ‖ fɑːnd
fawner/s 'fɔːn ə/z ‖ -ᵊr/z 'fɑːn- **fawning/ly**
'fɔːn ɪŋ /li ‖ 'fɑːn- **fawns** fɔːnz ‖ fɑːnz

Fawr 'vaʊ_ə ‖ 'vaʊ_ər —*Welsh* [vaur]
fax, Fax fæks faxed fækst faxes 'fæks ɪz -əz
  faxing 'fæks ɪŋ
fay, Fay, Faye feɪ
Fayed 'faɪ ed
Fayette ₍ₗ₎feɪ 'et
Fayetteville 'feɪ et vɪl -ɪt-, -ət- ‖ -ət vªl -vɪl
Faygate 'feɪ geɪt
Fazackerley, Fazakerley fə 'zæk ə li ‖ -ər-
faze feɪz (= *phase, Fay's*) fazed feɪzd fazes
  'feɪz ɪz -əz fazing 'feɪz ɪŋ
Fazeley 'feɪz li
FBI ˌef biː 'aɪ -bi-
feal|ty 'fiːˌəl |ti ~ties tiz
fear fɪər ‖ fɪər feared fɪəd ‖ fɪərz fearer/s
  'fɪər ə/z ‖ 'fɪr ər/z fearing 'fɪər ɪŋ ‖'fɪr ɪŋ
  fears fɪəz ‖ fɪərz
fearful 'fɪəf ªl 'fɪə fʊl ‖ 'fɪrf ªl ~ly _i ~ness
  nəs nɪs
Feargal, Fearghal 'fɜːg ªl ‖ 'fɜ·ːg-
Feargus 'fɜːg əs ‖ 'fɜ·ːg-
fearless 'fɪə ləs -lɪs ‖ 'fɪr- ~ly li ~ness nəs nɪs
Fearn, Fearne (i) fɜːn ‖ fɜ·ːn, (ii) feən ‖ fern
fearsome 'fɪəs əm ‖ 'fɪrs- ~ly li ~ness nəs nɪs
feasibility ˌfiːz ə 'bɪl ət i ˌˌˌ·ɪ-, -ɪt i ‖ -ət̬ i
  ˌfeasi'bility ˌstudy
feasib|le 'fiːz əb |ªl ‖ -ɪb- ~leness ªl nəs -nɪs ~ly
  li
feast fiːst feasted 'fiːst ɪd -əd feaster/s
  'fiːst ə/z ‖ -ər/z feasting 'fiːst ɪŋ feasts
  fiːsts
  'feast day
feat fiːt (= *feet*) feats fiːts
feath|er 'feð |ə ‖ -|ər ~ered əd ‖ ərd ~ering
  ər_ɪŋ ~ers əz ‖ ərz
  ˌfeather 'bed; ˌfeather 'boa; ˌfeather
  'duster; 'feather star
featherbed v 'feð ə bed ˌˌ·'· ‖ -ər- ~ded ɪd
  əd ~ding ɪŋ ~s z
featherbrained 'feð ə breɪnd ˌˌ·'·◀ ‖ -ər-
featheredg|e 'feð ər edʒ ˌˌ·'· ‖ -ər- ~ed d
  ~es ɪz əz
featheriness 'feð ər_i nəs -nɪs
featherstitch 'feð ə stɪtʃ ‖ -ər- ~ed t ~es ɪz
  əz ~ing ɪŋ
Featherstone (i) 'feð əst ən -ə stəʊn
  ‖ -ər stoʊn, (ii) 'fɜːst ən ‖ 'fɜ·ːst-
Featherstonehaugh (i) 'feð əst
  ən hɔː ‖ 'feð ərst- -haː, (ii) 'fæn ʃɔː ‖ -ʃaː,
  (iii) 'fest ən hɔː ‖ -haː, (iv) 'fiːs ən heɪ, (v)
  'fɪəst ən hɔː ‖ 'fɪrst- -haː
featherweight 'feð ə weɪt ‖ -ər- ~s s
feathery 'feð ər_i
feature 'fiːtʃ ə ‖ -ər ~ed d ~es z featuring
  'fiːtʃ ər_ɪŋ
  'feature film
featureless 'fiːtʃ ə ləs -lɪs ‖ -ər-
Feaver 'fiːv ə ‖ -ər
febrifug|e 'feb rɪ fjuːdʒ -rə- ~es ɪz əz
febrile 'fiːb raɪªl 'feb- ‖ 'feb-
February 'feb ru_ər i 'feb juˌ-, 'feb rʊr i,
  -rər-, -jʊr-, -jər- ‖ 'feb ju er i 'feb ru- —*The
  forms with* j, *although sometimes criticized, are*

FEBRUARY

*often heard from educated speakers (esp. AmE)
and preferred by them. Casually also* 'feb ri.
  —*Poll panel preferences: AmE 1993,* -ju- *64%,*
  -ru- *36%; BrE 1998,* -ru- *61%,* -ju- *39%,
with vowel in* -ary *weak 57%, strong* -eri *43%.*

fecal 'fiːk ªl
feces 'fiːs iːz
fecit 'feɪk ɪt 'fiːs-, §-ət
feckless 'fek ləs -lɪs ~ly li ~ness nəs nɪs
fecund 'fek ənd 'fiːk-, -ʌnd; fɪ 'kʌnd, fə-
fecun|date 'fek ən |deɪt 'fiːk-, -ʌn- ~dated
  deɪt ɪd -əd ‖ deɪt̬ əd ~dates deɪts ~dating
  deɪt ɪŋ ‖ deɪt̬ ɪŋ
fecundity fɪ 'kʌnd ət i fə-, fe-, fiː-, -ɪt- ‖ -ət̬ i
fed, Fed fed feds, Feds fedz
  ˌfed 'up◀
fedayeen, F~ fə 'daː jiːn fe-, fɪ-; ˌfed aɪ 'iːn
  ‖ ˌfed aː 'jiːn
federal 'fed_ər əl ~ism ˌɪz əm ~ist/s ɪst/s
  §əst/s ~ly i
  ˌFederal Re'serve
fede|rate v 'fed ə |reɪt ~rated reɪt ɪd -əd
  ‖ reɪt̬ əd ~rates reɪts ~rating
  reɪt ɪŋ ‖ reɪt̬ ɪŋ
federation ˌfed ə 'reɪʃ ªn ~s z
federative 'fed_ər ət ɪv -ə reɪt ɪv
  ‖ 'fed ə reɪt̬ ɪv _ər ət̬ ɪv ~ly li
fedora, F~ fɪ 'dɔːr ə fə- ‖ -'doʊr- ~s z
fee fiː fees fiːz
feeble 'fiːb ªl ~ness nəs nɪs
feebleminded ˌfiːb ªl 'maɪnd ɪd ◀ -əd ‖ '····
  ~ly li ~ness nəs nɪs
feebly 'fiːb li
feed fiːd fed fed feeding 'fiːd ɪŋ feeds fiːdz
  'feeding ˌbottle
feedback 'fiːd bæk →'fiːb-
feedbag 'fiːd bæg →'fiːb- ~s z
feeder 'fiːd ə ‖ -ər ~s z
feedstock 'fiːd stɒk ‖ -staːk ~s s
feel fiːªl feeling 'fiːªl ɪŋ feels fiːªlz felt felt
feeler 'fiːl ə ‖ -ər ~s z
feelgood 'fiːªl gʊd
feeling 'fiːªl ɪŋ ~ly li ~s z
Feeney, Feeny 'fiːn i
fee-paying 'fiː ˌpeɪ ɪŋ
feet fiːt

Feiffer 'faɪf ə ‖ -ᵊr

feign feɪn (= *fane*) **feigned** feɪnd **feigning**
'feɪn ɪŋ **feigns** feɪnz

feigned|ly 'feɪn ɪd ‖li -əd- **~ness** nəs nɪs

Feilding 'fiːᵊld ɪŋ

Feinstein 'faɪn staɪn

feint feɪnt (= *faint*) **feinted** 'feɪnt ɪd -əd
‖ 'feɪnt̬ əd **feinting** 'feɪnt ɪŋ ‖ 'feɪnt̬ ɪŋ
feints feɪnts

Feisal 'faɪs ᵊl

feist|y 'faɪst li —*but the Jamaican word of*
similar meaning, sometimes so spelt, is 'feɪst li
~ier i‿ə ‖ i‿ᵊr **~iest** i‿ɪst i‿əst **~ily** ɪ li əl i
~iness i nəs i nɪs

felafel fə 'læf ᵊl fɪ-, fe-, -'lɑːf- ‖ -'lɑːf-

feldspar 'feld spɑː ‖ -spɑːr **~s** z

feldspathic feld 'spæθ ɪk '•••

Felice fə 'liːs fɪ-

Felicia fə 'lɪs i‿ə fɪ-, -'lɪʃ- ‖ -'lɪʃ ə -'liːʃ ə

felici|tate fə 'lɪs ɪ teɪt fɪ-, fe-, -ə- **~tated**
teɪt ɪd -əd ‖ teɪt̬ əd **~tates** teɪts **~tating**
teɪt ɪŋ ‖ teɪt̬ ɪŋ

felicitation fə ˌlɪs ɪ 'teɪʃ ᵊn fɪ-, fe-, -ə- **~s** z

felicitous fə 'lɪs ɪt əs fɪ-, fe-, -ət- ‖ -ət̬ əs **~ly** li
~ness nəs nɪs

felicit|y, F~ fə 'lɪs ət i fɪ-, fe-, -ɪt- ‖ -ət̬ i **~ies**
iz

Felindre ve 'lɪndr ə və- —*Welsh* [ve 'lɪn dre]

feline 'fiːl aɪn **~ly** li **~ness** nəs nɪs **~s** z

Felix 'fiːl ɪks

Felixstowe 'fiːl ɪk stəʊ ‖ -stoʊ

fell, Fell fel **felled** feld **felling** 'fel ɪŋ **fells**
felz

fella 'fel ə **~s** z

fellah 'fel ə -ɑː; fə 'lɑː **fellaheen, fellahin**
ˌfel ə 'hiːn '•••; fə ˌlɑː 'hiːn

fell|late fe 'leɪt fə-, fɪ- ‖ 'fell eɪt **~lated** leɪt ɪd
-əd ‖ leɪt̬ əd **~later/s** leɪt ə/z ‖ leɪt̬ ᵊr/z
~lates leɪts **~lating** leɪt ɪŋ ‖ leɪt̬ ɪŋ

fellatio fe 'leɪʃ i əʊ fə-, fɪ-, -'lɑːt- ‖ -oʊ

fellation fe 'leɪʃ ᵊn fə-, fɪ- **~s** z

feller 'fel ə ‖ -ᵊr **~s** z

Felling 'fel ɪŋ

Fellini fe 'liːn i fə-, fɪ- —*It* [fel 'liː ni]

felloe 'fel əʊ ‖ -oʊ (= *fellow*) **~s** z

fellow 'fel əʊ ‖ -oʊ **~s** z
ˌfellow 'creature; ˌfellow 'feeling; ˌfellow
'men; ˌfellow 'traveller

Fellowes, Fellows 'fel əʊz ‖ -oʊz

fellowship 'fel əʊ ʃɪp ‖ -oʊ- **~s** s

felo de se ˌfiːl əʊ di: 'siː ˌfel-, -di'•, -'seɪ,
-deɪ 'seɪ ‖ ˌfel oʊ-

felon 'fel ən **~s** z

felonious fə 'ləʊn i‿əs fe-, fɪ- ‖ -'loʊn- **~ly** li
~ness nəs nɪs

felon|y 'fel ən li **~ies** iz

Felpham 'felp əm -həm; 'felf-

felspar 'fel spɑː ‖ -spɑːr **~s** z

Felstead, Felsted 'fel stɪd -sted

felt felt **felted** 'felt ɪd -əd **felting** 'felt ɪŋ
felts felts

Feltham 'felt əm —*as a family name, also* 'felθ-

Felton 'felt ən

felt-tip 'felt tɪp ˌ•'• **~s** s

Feltz felts

felucca fe 'lʌk ə fə-, fɪ- ‖ -'luːk ə -'lʊk ə,
-'lʌk ə **~s** z

felwort 'fel wɜːt §-wɔːt ‖ -wɜ˞ːt -wɔːrt

fem. fem

female 'fiːm eɪᵊl **~ness** nəs nɪs
ˌfemale im'personator

Femidom *tdmk* 'fem ɪ dɒm -ə- ‖ -dɑːm

Feminax *tdmk* 'fem ɪ næks -ə-

feminine 'fem ən ɪn -ɪn-, §-ən **~ly** li **~ness**
nəs nɪs

femininit|y ˌfem ə 'nɪn ət i ˌ•ɪ-, -ɪt i ‖ -ət̬ i
~ies iz

feminis... —*see* **feminiz...**

feminism 'fem ə ˌnɪz əm -ɪ-

feminist 'fem ən ɪst -ɪn-, §-əst **~s** s

feminization ˌfem ən aɪ 'zeɪʃ ᵊn ˌ•ɪn-, -ɪ'•-
‖ -ən ə-

feminiz|e 'fem ə naɪz -ɪ- **~ed** d **~es** ɪz əz
~ing ɪŋ

femme fem —*but as a French word*, fæm —*Fr*
[fam] **femmes** femz

femme fatale ˌfæm fə 'tɑːl ‖ ˌfem fə 'tæl
ˌfæm-, -'tɑːl —*Fr* [fam fa tal] **femmes**
fatales —*same pronunciation*

femora 'fem ᵊr ə 'fiːm-

femoral 'fem ᵊr‿əl 'fiːm-

femto- ˌfemᵖt əʊ ‖ ˌfemᵖt oʊ — **femtogram**
'femᵖt əʊ græm ‖ -oʊ-

femur 'fiːm ə ‖ -ᵊr **~s** z

fen fen **fens** fenz

Fenby 'fen bi →'fem-

fence fents **fenced** fentst **fencer/s** 'fents ə/
z ‖ -ᵊr/z **fences** 'fents ɪz -əz **fencing**
'fents ɪŋ

Fenchurch 'fen tʃɜːtʃ ‖ -tʃɜ˞ːtʃ

fend fend **fended** 'fend ɪd -əd **fending**
'fend ɪŋ **fends** fendz

fender, F~ 'fend ə ‖ -ᵊr **~s** z

Fenella fə 'nel ə fɪ-

fenes|trate fə 'nes |treɪt fɪ-, fe-; 'fen ɪ s|treɪt,
-ə- **~trated** treɪt ɪd -əd ‖ treɪt̬ əd **~trates**
treɪts **~trating** treɪt ɪŋ ‖ treɪt̬ ɪŋ

fenestration ˌfen ɪ 'streɪʃ ᵊn -ə- **~s** z

feng shui ˌfʌŋ 'ʃweɪ ˌfʊŋ-, ˌfeŋ-, ˌ•'ʃuː i —*Chi*
fēng shuǐ [¹fəŋ ³ʂweɪ]

Fenian 'fiːn i‿ən **~s** z

Fenimore 'fen ɪ mɔː -ə- ‖ -mɔːr -moʊr

fenland, F~ 'fen lənd -lænd

Fenn fen

fennec 'fen ek -ɪk **~s** s

fennel 'fen ᵊl

Fennel, Fennell 'fen ᵊl

Fenner 'fen ə ‖ -ᵊr **~'s** z

Fennimore 'fen ɪ mɔː -ə- ‖ -mɔːr -moʊr

fenny 'fen i

Fenoulhet 'fen ə leɪ -ᵊl eɪ

Fenstanton fen 'stænt ən

Fentiman 'fent ɪ mən -ə-

Fenton 'fent ən ‖ -ᵊn

fenugreek 'fen ju griːk -u- ‖ -jə-

F

Fenwick (i) 'fen ɪk (ii) -wɪk —*The place in Northumberland is* (i). *The US family name is* (ii), *the UK one may be either.*
Feodor 'fiː‿ə dɔː ‖ -dɔːr —*Russ* [fʲɪ 'ɔ dər]
feoff fiːf fef **feoffed** fiːft feft **feoffing** 'fiːf ɪŋ 'fef- **feoffs** fiːfs fefs
feoffee fe 'fiː ₍ₒ₎fiː- ~s z
feral 'fer əl 'fɪər- ‖ 'fɪr-
ferbam 'fɜː bæm 'fɜːb əm ‖ 'fɜˑː bæm
fer-de-lanc|e ˌfeə də 'lɑːnts ˌfɜː-, §-'lænts ‖ ˌferd əl 'ænts -'ɑːnts **-es** ɪz əz
Ferdinand 'fɜːd ɪ nænd -ə-, -ᵊn ænd; -ɪn ənd, -ən‿ənd ‖ 'fɜˑːd ᵊn ænd
Ferens 'fer ənz
Fergal 'fɜːg əl ‖ 'fɜˑːg əl
Fergie 'fɜːg i ‖ 'fɜˑːg i
Fergus 'fɜːg əs ‖ 'fɜˑːg-
Ferguson, Fergusson 'fɜːg əs ᵊn ‖ 'fɜˑːg-
ferial 'fɪər i‿əl 'fer- ‖ 'fɪr- 'fer-
Ferlinghetti ˌfɜːl ɪŋ 'get i ‖ ˌfɜˑːl ɪŋ 'geṭ i
Fermanagh fə 'mæn ə fɜː- ‖ fᵊr-
Fermat fə 'mæt fɜː-; 'fɜːm æt, -ɑː ‖ fer 'mɑː —*Fr* [fɛʁ ma]
fer|ment *v* fə |'ment fɜː- ‖ fᵊr- **~mented** 'ment ɪd -əd ‖ 'menṭ əd **~menting** 'ment ɪŋ ‖ 'menṭ ɪŋ **~ments** 'ments
ferment *n* 'fɜː ment ‖ 'fɜˑː- ~s s
fermentation ˌfɜːm en 'teɪʃ ᵊn -ən-, fə ˌmen- ‖ ˌfɜˑːm- ~s z
Fermi 'fɜːm i 'feəm- ‖ 'fɜˑːm i 'ferm i —*It* ['fer mi]
fermion 'fɜːm i ɒn ‖ 'fɜˑːm i ɑːn 'ferm- ~s z
fermium 'fɜːm i‿əm ‖ 'fɜˑːm- 'ferm-
Fermor 'fɜːm ɔː ‖ 'fɜˑːm ɔːr
Fermoy fə 'mɔɪ fɜː-; 'fɜːm ɔɪ ‖ fᵊr-
fern, Fern fɜːn ‖ fɜˑːn **ferns** fɜːnz ‖ fɜˑːnz
Fernandez fə 'nænd ez fɜː-, -ɪz ‖ fᵊr- fer- —*Sp* Fernández [fer 'nan deθ]
Fernando fə 'nænd əʊ ‖ fᵊr 'nænd oʊ fer-, -'nɑːnd- —*Sp* [fer 'nan do], *Port* [fər 'nɐndu] **Fer,nando 'Po**
Ferndale 'fɜːn deɪᵊl ‖ 'fɜˑːn-
Ferndown 'fɜːn daʊn ‖ 'fɜˑːn-
ferner|y 'fɜːn ər i ‖ 'fɜˑːn- **~ies** ɪz
Ferneyhough, Fernihough (i) 'fɜːn i hʌf ‖ 'fɜˑːn-, (ii) -həʊ ‖ -hoʊ
Fernley 'fɜːn li ‖ 'fɜˑːn-
ferny 'fɜːn i ‖ 'fɜˑːn i
Fernyhalgh (i) 'fɜːn i hʌf ‖ 'fɜˑːn-, (ii) -hælʃ
Fernyhough (i) 'fɜːn i hʌf ‖ 'fɜˑːn-, (ii) -həʊ ‖ -hoʊ
ferocious fə 'rəʊʃ əs fɪ- ‖ -'roʊʃ- **~ly** li **~ness** nəs nɪs
ferocit|y fə 'rɒs ət i fɪ-, -ɪt- ‖ -'rɑːs əṭ i **~ies** ɪz
Ferodo *tdmk* fə 'rəʊd əʊ fɪ- ‖ -'roʊd oʊ
-ferous *stress-imposing* fᵊr əs — **ferriferous** fe 'rɪf ᵊr əs
Ferranti fə 'rænt i fɪ-, fe- ‖ -'rænṭ i -'rɑːnṭ i
Ferrar (i) 'fer ə ‖ -ᵊr, (ii) fə 'rɑː ‖ -'rɑːr
Ferrara fə 'rɑːr ə —*It* [fer 'ra: ra]
Ferrari fə 'rɑːr i —*It* [fer 'ra: ri]
Ferraro fə 'rɑːr əʊ ‖ -oʊ

ferrel, F~ 'fer əl ~s, **F~'s** z
Ferrer (i) 'fer ə ‖ -ᵊr, (ii) fə 'reə ‖ -'reᵊr
Ferrero Rocher *tdmk* fə ˌreər əʊ 'rɒʃ eɪ -ɪ‿rɒ 'ʃeɪ ‖ fə ˌrer oʊ roʊ 'ʃeɪ
ferr|et 'fer |ɪt -ət ‖ -|ət **~eted** ɪt ɪd ət-, -əd ‖ əṭ əd **~eting** ɪt ɪŋ ət- ‖ əṭ ɪŋ **~ets** ɪts əts ‖ əts
ferri- *comb. form*
  with stress-neutral suffix ˌfer i -aɪ — **ferricyanide** ˌfer i 'saɪ‿ə naɪd ‚•aɪ-
  with stress-imposing suffix fe 'rɪ+ — **ferriferous** fe 'rɪf ᵊr əs
ferric 'fer ɪk
ferrie... —*see* ferry
Ferrier 'fer i‿ə ‖ -ᵊr
Ferris, f~ 'fer ɪs §-əs
  'Ferris wheel
ferrite 'fer aɪt
ferro- *comb. form* ˌfer əʊ ‖ -oʊ —
  ferrochromium ˌfer əʊ 'krəʊm i‿əm ‖ -oʊ 'kroʊm-
ferroconcrete ˌfer əʊ 'kɒŋ kriːt -'kɒn- ‖ -oʊ 'kɑːn- -•'•
Ferrograph *tdmk* 'fer əʊ grɑːf -græf ‖ -oʊ græf
ferrous 'fer əs
ferruginous fe 'ruːdʒ ɪn əs fə-, fɪ-, -ᵊn-
ferrule 'fer uːl -əl, -juːl ‖ -əl ~s z
ferr|y, Ferry 'fer li **~ied** id **~ies** ɪz **~ying** i‿ɪŋ
ferryboat 'fer i bəʊt ‖ -boʊt ~s s
ferry|man 'fer i |mən -mæn **~men** mən men
fertile 'fɜːt aɪᵊl ‖ 'fɜˑːṭ ᵊl (*) **~ly** li **~ness** nəs nɪs
fertilis... —*see* fertiliz...
fertility fɜː 'tɪl ət i fə-, -ɪt- ‖ fᵊr 'tɪl əṭ i
  fer'tility drug; fer'tility ˌsymbol
fertilization ˌfɜːt əl aɪ 'zeɪʃ ᵊn ‚•ɪl-, -ɪ'•- ‖ ˌfɜˑːṭ ᵊl ə- ~s z
fertiliz|e 'fɜːt ə laɪz -ɪ-, -ᵊl aɪz ‖ 'fɜˑːṭ ᵊl aɪz **~ed** d **~es** ɪz əz **~ing** ɪŋ
fertilizer 'fɜːt ə laɪz ə '•ɪ-, -ᵊl aɪz- ‖ 'fɜˑːṭ ᵊl aɪz ᵊr ~s z
ferule 'fer uːl -əl, -juːl ‖ -əl ~s z
fervenc|y 'fɜːv ᵊnts li ‖ 'fɜˑːv- **~ies** ɪz
fervent 'fɜːv ᵊnt ‖ 'fɜˑːv- **~ly** li **~ness** nəs nɪs
fervid 'fɜːv ɪd §-əd ‖ 'fɜˑːv- **~ly** li **~ness** nəs nɪs
fervor, fervour 'fɜːv ə ‖ 'fɜˑːv ᵊr ~s z
fescue 'fesk juː ~s z
fess, Fess, fesse fes **fesses** 'fes ɪz -əz
festal 'fest ᵊl **~ly** i
Feste 'fest i
fest|er 'fest lə ‖ -|ᵊr **~ered** əd ‖ ᵊrd **~ering** ᵊr_ɪŋ **~ers** əz ‖ ᵊrz
festination ˌfest ɪ 'neɪʃ ᵊn -ə-
Festiniog fe 'stɪn i ɒg ‖ -ɑːg —*Welsh* Ffestiniog [fe 'stɪn jog]
festival 'fest ɪv ᵊl -əv- ~s z
festive 'fest ɪv **~ly** li **~ness** nəs nɪs
festivit|y fe 'stɪv ət i -ɪt- ‖ -əṭ li **~ies** ɪz
festoon ₍ₒ₎fe 'stuːn **~ed** d **~ing** ɪŋ ~s z
festschrift 'fest ʃrɪft →'feʃ- ~s s —*Ger* F~ ['fɛst ʃʁɪft]
Festus 'fest əs

F

feta 'fet ə —*ModGk* ['fɛ ta]
fetal 'fiːt ᵊl ‖ 'fiːt̬ ᵊl
fetch fetʃ **fetched** fetʃt **fetches** 'fetʃ ɪz -əz
  fetcher/s 'fetʃ ə/z ‖ -ᵊr/z **fetching/ly**
  'fetʃ ɪŋ /li
fete, fête feɪt ‖ fet *(usually = fate)* —*Fr* [fɛt]
  feted, fêted 'feɪt ɪd -əd ‖ 'feɪt̬ əd **fetes,**
  fêtes feɪts **feting, fêting** 'feɪt ɪŋ ‖ 'feɪt̬ ɪŋ
  ,**fête cham'pêtre, ,fêtes cham'pêtres**
  ʃɒm 'peɪtr ə • 'peɪtr ‖ ʃɑːm- —*Fr* [ʃɑ̃ pɛtχ]
feticide 'fiːt ɪ saɪd §-ə- ‖ 'fiːt̬- ~**s** z
fetid 'fet ɪd 'fiːt-, §-əd ‖ 'fet̬ əd ~**ly** li ~**ness**
  nəs nɪs
fetish 'fet ɪʃ 'fiːt- ‖ 'fet̬ ɪʃ ~**es** ɪz əz ~**ism** ,ɪz
  əm ~**ist/s** ɪst/s §əst/s
fetishistic ,fet ɪ 'ʃɪst ɪk ◄ ,fiːt- ‖ ,fet̬ ɪ- ~**ally**
  ᵊl_i
fetlock 'fet lɒk ‖ -lɑːk ~**s** s
fetor 'fiːt ə -ɔː ‖ 'fiːt̬ ᵊr 'fiːt ɔːr ~**s** z
fetta 'fet ə —*ModGk* feta ['fɛ ta]
fetter 'fet ə ‖ 'fet̬ ᵊr ~**ed** d **fettering**
  'fet ᵊr ɪŋ ‖ 'fet̬ ᵊr ɪŋ ~**s** z
Fettes 'fet ɪs -ɪz, -əs, -əz ‖ 'fet̬ əs
fettl|e 'fet ᵊl ‖ 'fet̬ ᵊl ~**ed** d ~**er/s** _ə/z ‖ _ᵊr/z
  ~**es** z ~**ing** _ɪŋ
fettuccin|e, ~i fet u 'tʃiːn i ‖ ,fet̬ ə- —*It* ~e
  [fet tut 'tʃiː ne]
fetus 'fiːt əs ‖ 'fiːt̬ əs ~**es** ɪz əz
feu fjuː *(= few)* **feued** fjuːd **feuing** 'fjuː ɪŋ
  feus fjuːz
feud fjuːd **feuded** 'fjuːd ɪd -əd **feuding**
  'fjuːd ɪŋ **feuds** fjuːdz
feudal 'fjuːd ᵊl ~**ly** i
  'feudal ,system
feudalism 'fjuːd ᵊl ,ɪz əm
feudalistic ,fjuːd ᵊl 'ɪst ɪk ◄ -ə 'lɪst- ~**ally** ᵊl_i
feudatory 'fjuːd ə _tᵊr i ‖ -ə tɔːr i -toʊr i
fever 'fiːv ə ‖ -ᵊr ~**ed** d ~**s** z
  'fever ,pitch, ,• • '•
feverfew 'fiːv ə fjuː ‖ -ᵊr-
feverish 'fiːv ᵊr_ɪʃ ~**ly** li ~**ness** nəs nɪs
Feversham 'fev ə ʃəm ‖ -ᵊr-
few fjuː **fewer** 'fjuː_ə ‖ _ᵊr **fewest** 'fjuː_ɪst
  §_əst
Fewkes fjuːks
fewness 'fjuː nəs -nɪs
Fewston 'fjuːst ən
fey, Fey feɪ
Feydeau 'feɪd əʊ ‖ feɪ 'doʊ —*Fr* [fɛ do]
Feynman 'faɪn mən
fez, Fez fez **fezes, fezzes** 'fez ɪz -əz
ff..., Ff... *in family names* —*see* **F...**
Ffestiniog fe 'stɪn i ɒg ‖ -ɑːg —*Welsh*
  [fe 'sdin jog]
Ffion 'fiː ɒn ‖ -ɑːn —*Welsh* ['fi ɔn]
Ffolkes fəʊks ‖ foʊks
Ffoulkes *(i)* fəʊks ‖ foʊks, *(ii)* fuːks
Ffrangcon 'fræŋk ən
Ffynnongroew, Ffynnongroyw
  ,fʌn ən 'grɔɪ uː, ,fɪn-, →-əŋ- —*Welsh*
  [,fə non 'groi u, -'groi-]
-fiable faɪ_əb ᵊl '• • • —*Although this suffix is*
  usually unstressed in RP and GenAm, in some

other varieties it is stressed, and this variant is
occasionally heard in RP too: i'dentifiable *or*
i,denti'fiable

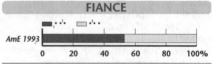
FIANCE

AmE 1993

| 0 | 20 | 40 | 60 | 80 | 100% |

fiance, fiancé, fiancee, fiancée fi 'ɒnˢ eɪ
  -'ɑːnˢ-, -'ɒ̃s- ‖ ,fiː ɑːn 'seɪ fi 'ɑːnˢ eɪ —*Fr*
  [fjɑ̃ se] —*AmE 1993 poll panel preference:*
  ,• •'• 53%, •'• • 47%. ~**s** z
Fianna Fail, Fianna Fáil ,fiː_ən ə 'fɔɪᵊl -'fɔːl;
  ,fiːn ə'• —*Irish* [,fiə nə 'faːlʲ]
fiasco fi 'æsk əʊ ‖ -oʊ **~es, ~s** z
fiat 'fiː æt 'faɪ-, -ət ‖ -ɑːt
Fiat *tdmk* 'fiː_ət -æt ‖ -ɑːt **~s** s
fib fɪb **fibbed** fɪbd **fibbing** 'fɪb ɪŋ **fibs** fɪbz
fibber 'fɪb ə ‖ -ᵊr ~**s** z
fiber 'faɪb ə ‖ -ᵊr ~**s** z
  ,fiber 'optics
fiberboard 'faɪb ə bɔːd ‖ -ᵊr bɔːrd -boʊrd
Fiberglas *tdmk*, **fiberglass** 'faɪb ə glɑːs §-glæs
  ‖ -ᵊr glæs
Fibonacci ,fɪb ə 'nɑːtʃ i ,fiːb- —*It*
  [fi bo 'nat tʃi]
  ,Fibo'nacci ,numbers
fibre 'faɪb ə ‖ -ᵊr ~**s** z
  ,fibre 'optics
fibreboard 'faɪb ə bɔːd ‖ -ᵊr bɔːrd -boʊrd
fibreglass 'faɪb ə glɑːs §-glæs ‖ -ᵊr glæs
fibril 'faɪb rɪl -rᵊl ~**s** z
fibril|late 'fɪb rɪ leɪt 'faɪb-, -rə- ~**lated** leɪt ɪd
  -əd ‖ leɪt̬ əd ~**lates** leɪts ~**lating**
  leɪt ɪŋ ‖ leɪt̬ ɪŋ
fibrillation ,fɪb rɪ 'leɪʃ ᵊn ,faɪb-, -rə- ~**s** z
fibrin 'faɪb rɪn 'fɪb-, §-rən
fibro 'faɪb rəʊ ‖ -roʊ
fibro- *comb. form* ¦faɪb rəʊ ‖ -roʊ —
  fibrocement ,faɪb rəʊ sɪ 'ment -sə'•
  ‖ ,•roʊ-
fibroid 'faɪb rɔɪd ~**s** z
fibrom|a faɪ 'brəʊm ə ‖ -'broʊm ə ~**as** əz
  ~**ata** ət ə ‖ ət̬ ə
fibrosis faɪ 'brəʊs ɪs §-əs ‖ -'broʊs-
fibrositis ,faɪb rə 'saɪt ɪs §-əs ‖ -'saɪt̬ əs
fibrous 'faɪb rəs
fib|ula 'fɪb |jʊl ə ‖ -|jᵊl ə ~**ulae** juː liː jə-
  ‖ jə liː ~**ulas** jʊl əz ‖ jᵊl əz
fiche fiːʃ **fiches** 'fiːʃ ɪz -əz
fichu 'fiːʃ uː 'fɪʃ- ~**s** z
fickle 'fɪk ᵊl ~**ness** nəs nɪs
fiction 'fɪk ʃᵊn ~**s** z
fictional 'fɪk ʃᵊn_ᵊl ~**ly** i
fictionalis... —*see* **fictionaliz...**
fictionalization ,fɪk ʃᵊn_ᵊl aɪ 'zeɪʃ ᵊn _ᵊl ɪ- ‖
  _ᵊl ə- ~**s** z
fictionaliz|e ,fɪk ʃᵊn_ə laɪz ~**ed** d ~**es** ɪz əz
  ~**ing** ɪŋ
fictitious fɪk 'tɪʃ əs ~**ly** li ~**ness** nəs nɪs
fictive 'fɪkt ɪv ~**ness** nəs nɪs
ficus, Ficus 'faɪk əs 'fiːk-
fid fɪd **fids** fɪdz

fiddl|e 'fɪd ᵊl ~**ed** d ~**es** z ~**ing** ɪŋ
fiddleback 'fɪd ᵊl bæk ~**s** s
fiddle-de-dee ˌfɪd ᵊl di 'di:
fiddle-faddle 'fɪd ᵊl ˌfæd ᵊl
fiddler, F~ 'fɪd lə 'fɪd ᵊl_ə ‖ 'fɪd lᵊr 'fɪd ᵊl_ᵊr ~**s**
z
'**fiddler crab**
fiddlestick 'fɪd ᵊl stɪk ~**s** s
fiddlewood 'fɪd ᵊl wʊd
fiddling 'fɪd ᵊl_ɪŋ
fiddl|y 'fɪd ᵊl_i ~**ier** i_ə ‖ i_ᵊr ~**iest** i_ɪst i_əst
Fidel fɪ 'del ₍ₒ₎fi:-, §fə- —*Sp* [fi 'ðel]
Fidelio fɪ 'deɪl i_əʊ fə- ‖ _oʊ
Fidelis fɪ 'deɪl ɪs fə-, §-əs
fidelit|y fɪ 'del ət |i fə-, faɪ-, -ɪt-• ‖ -ət̬ |i ~**ies**
iz
Fidelma fɪ 'delm ə fə-
fidg|et 'fɪdʒ |ɪt -ət ‖ -|ət ~**eted** ɪt ɪd §ət-, -əd
‖ ət̬ əd ~**eting** ɪt ɪŋ §ət- ‖ ət̬ ɪŋ ~**ets** ɪts
§əts ‖ əts
fidget|y 'fɪdʒ ət |i -ɪt- ‖ -ət̬ |i ~**iness** i nəs i nɪs
Fidler *(i)* 'fɪd lə ‖ -lᵊr, *(ii)* 'fi:d-
Fido 'faɪd əʊ ‖ -oʊ
fiducial fɪ 'dju:ʃ i_əl fə-, faɪ-, -'dju:s-,
→§-'dʒu:ʃ-, →§-'dʒu:s-, -'•ᵊl ‖ fə 'du:ʃ ᵊl
-'dju:ʃ- ~**ly** i
fiduciar|y fɪ 'dju:ʃ i_ər li fə-, faɪ-, -'dju:s-,
→§-'dʒu:ʃ-, →§-'dʒu:s-, -'•ᵊr li
‖ fə 'du:ʃ i er li -'dju:ʃ-; -'•ᵊr li ~**ies** iz
fie faɪ
fief fi:f **fiefs** fi:fs
fiefdom 'fi:f dəm ~**s** z
field, Field fi:ᵊld **fielded** 'fi:ᵊld ɪd -əd
fielding 'fi:ᵊld ɪŋ **fields** fi:ᵊldz
'**field day**; '**field e**ˌ**vent**; '**field** ˌ**glasses**;
'**field hand**; '**field** ˌ**hockey**; '**field** '**marshal**◄,
'•ˌ••; '**field** ˌ**mushroom**; '**field test**; '**field**
ˌ**trial**; '**field trip**
fieldcraft 'fi:ᵊld krɑ:ft §-kræft ‖ -kræft
Fielden 'fi:ᵊld ən
fielder, F~ 'fi:ᵊld ə ‖ -ᵊr ~**s** z
fieldfare 'fi:ᵊld feə ‖ -fer -fær ~**s** z
Fielding 'fi:ᵊld ɪŋ
field|mouse 'fi:ᵊld |maʊs ~**mice** maɪs
Fields fi:ᵊldz
fields|man 'fi:ᵊldz |mən ~**men** mən men
field-test 'fi:ᵊld test ~**ed** ɪd əd ~**ing** ɪŋ ~**s** s
fieldwork 'fi:ᵊld wɜ:k ‖ -wɜ·:k
fiend fi:nd **fiends** fi:ndz
fiendish 'fi:nd ɪʃ ~**ly** li ~**ness** nəs nɪs
Fiennes faɪnz
fierce fɪəs ‖ fɪᵊrs **fiercely** 'fɪəs li ‖ 'fɪᵊrs-
fierceness 'fɪəsnɪs -nəs ‖ 'fɪᵊrs- **fiercer**
'fɪəs ə ‖ 'fɪᵊrs ᵊr **fiercest** 'fɪəs ɪst -əst ‖ 'fɪᵊrs-
fier|y 'faɪᵊr |i ~**ier** i_ə ‖ i_ᵊr ~**iest** i_ɪst i_əst
~**ily** əl i i li ~**iness** i nəs i nɪs
fiesta, F~ fi 'est ə ~**s** z
FIFA 'fi:f ə
fife, Fife faɪf **fifed** faɪft **fifes** faɪfs **fifing**
'faɪf ɪŋ
fife-rail 'faɪf reɪᵊl
Fifi 'fi: fi:
Fifield 'faɪ fi:ᵊld

fifteen ˌfɪf 'ti:n ◄ ~**s** z
ˌfifteen '**days**
fifteenth ˌfɪf 'ti:nθ ◄ ~**s** s
fifth fɪfθ fɪftθ, fɪθ **fifths** fɪfθs fɪftθs, fɪfs, fɪθs
ˌFifth A'**mendment**; ˌfifth '**column**
fifth-generation ˌfɪfθ ˌdʒen ə 'reɪʃ ᵊn ◄ ˌfɪftθ-,
ˌfɪθ-
fiftieth 'fɪft i_əθ _ɪθ ~**s** s
fift|y 'fɪft |i ~**ies** iz
fifty-fifty ˌfɪft i 'fɪft i ◄
ˌfifty-ˌfifty '**chance**
fig fɪg **figged** fɪgd **figging** 'fɪg ɪŋ **figs** fɪgz
'**fig leaf**; '**fig tree**
Figaro 'fɪg ə rəʊ ‖ -roʊ
Figg fɪg
Figgis 'fɪg ɪs §-əs
fight faɪt **fighting** 'faɪt ɪŋ ‖ 'faɪt̬ ɪŋ **fights**
faɪts **fought** fɔ:t ‖ fɑ:t
ˌfighting '**chance**
fighter 'faɪt ə ‖ 'faɪt̬ ᵊr ~**s** z
figment 'fɪg mənt ~**s** s
Figueroa ˌfɪg ə 'rəʊ ə ‖ -'roʊ ə
figurative 'fɪg ᵊr_ət ɪv '•jʊr- ‖ -jər ət̬ ɪv ~**ly** li
~**ness** nəs nɪs
fig|ure 'fɪg |ə §-|jə ‖ 'fɪg |jᵊr -jʊr (*) —*The*
pronunciation without j, standard and usual in
BrE, is in AmE generally condemned. ~**ured**
əd §jəd ‖ jᵊrd jʊrd ~**ures** əz §jəz ‖ jᵊrz jʊrz
~**uring** ər ɪŋ §jər- ‖ jər ɪŋ jʊr ɪŋ
ˌfigured '**bass**; **figure of** '**eight**; **figure of**
'**speech**; '**figure** ˌ**skating**
figurehead 'fɪg ə hed ‖ -jᵊr- ~**s** z
figurine ˌfɪg ə ri:n -jʊᵊ-, ˌ•••'• ‖ ˌfɪg jə 'ri:n
-ju- ~**s** z
figwort 'fɪg wɜ:t §-wɔ:t ‖ -wɜ·:t -wɔ:rt ~**s** s
Fiji 'fi: dʒi: ˌ•'•
Fijian fi 'dʒi:_ən ˌfi:- ‖ 'fi: dʒi_ən fɪ 'dʒi: ən ~**s**
z
Fila *tdmk* 'fi:l ɑ: -ə
filament 'fɪl ə mənt ~**s** s
filari|a fɪ 'leᵊr i_|ə fə- ‖ -'ler- -'lær- ~**ae** i:
filariasis ˌfɪl ə 'raɪ_əs ɪs §-əs; fɪ ˌleər i 'eɪs-, fə-
filbert 'fɪlb ət ‖ -ᵊrt ~**s** s
filch fɪltʃ **filched** fɪltʃt **filches** 'fɪltʃ ɪz -əz
filching 'fɪltʃ ɪŋ
file faɪᵊl **filed** faɪᵊld **files** faɪᵊlz **filing** 'faɪᵊl ɪŋ
'**file** ˌ**server**
filename 'faɪᵊl neɪm ~**s** z
filet 'fɪl eɪ -ɪt, §-ət ‖ fɪ 'leɪ ~**s** z
ˌfilet '**mignon** 'mi:n jɒn -'mɪn- ‖ fiˌlet
miˈgnon mɪn 'jɔ:n -'jɑ:n, -'joʊn —*Fr*
[fi le mi njɔ̃]
Filey 'faɪl i
filial 'fɪl i_əl ~**ly** i ~**ness** nəs nɪs
filibeg 'fɪl ɪ beg -ə- ~**s** z
filibuster 'fɪl ɪ bʌst ə '•ə- ‖ -ᵊr ~**ed** d
filibustering 'fɪl ɪ bʌst ər_ɪŋ '•ə- ~**s** z
filigree 'fɪl ɪ gri: -ə- ~**d** d ~**ing** ɪŋ ~**s** z
filing 'faɪᵊl ɪŋ ~**s** z
'**filing** ˌ**cabinet**; '**filing clerk**
Filioque ˌfi:l i 'əʊ kwi ˌfɪl-, ˌfaɪl- ‖ -'oʊ-
the ˌFili'**oque clause**

Filipin|o ˌfɪl ɪ 'piːn| əʊ ◄ -ə- ‖ -oʊ ◄ ~a ə ɑː
  ~**as** əz ɑːz ~**os** əʊz ‖ oʊz
fill fɪl **filled** fɪld **filling** 'fɪl ɪŋ **fills** fɪlz
filler 'fɪl ə ‖ -ᵊr ~**s** z
  '**filler cap**
fill|et 'fɪl| ɪt §-ət ~**eted** ɪt ɪd §ət-, -əd ‖ -ət̬ əd
  ~**eting** ɪt ɪŋ §ət- ‖ ət̬ ɪŋ ~**ets** ɪts §əts
Filleul 'fɪl iˌəl
fill-in 'fɪl ɪn ~**s** z
filling 'fɪl ɪŋ ~**s** z
  '**filling ˌstation**
fillip 'fɪl ɪp §-əp ~**ed** t ~**ing** ɪŋ ~**s** s
Fillmore 'fɪl mɔː ‖ -mɔːr -moʊr
Fillongley 'fɪl ɒŋ li ‖ -ɑːŋ-
fill|y 'fɪl li ~**ies** iz
film fɪlm **filmed** fɪlmd **filming** 'fɪlm ɪŋ **films**
  fɪlmz
  '**film ˌpremière** ‖ '**film preˌmière**; '**film**
  ˌ**setting**; '**film star**; '**film stock**
filmgoer 'fɪlm ˌgəʊ ə ‖ -ˌgoʊ ᵊr ~**s** z
filmic 'fɪlm ɪk
filmstrip 'fɪlm strɪp ~**s** s
film|y 'fɪlm li ~**ier** iˌə ‖ iˌᵊr ~**iest** iˌɪst iˌəst
  ~**ily** ɪ li əli ~**iness** i nəs i nɪs
filo 'fiːl əʊ 'faɪl- ‖ -oʊ —*ModGk* ['fi lo]
Filofax *tdmk* 'faɪl əʊ fæks ‖ -ə- ~**es** ɪz əz
fils '*son*' fiːs —*Fr* [fis]
fils *monetary unit, coin* fɪls
filter 'fɪlt ə ‖ -ᵊr ~**ed** d **filtering** 'fɪlt̬ ᵊr ɪŋ ~**s**
  z
  '**filter bed**; '**filter ˌpaper**; '**filter tip**, ˌ· · '·
filterable 'fɪlt̬ ᵊr əb ᵊl
filter-tipped ˌfɪlt ə 'tɪpt ◄ ‖ -ᵊr-
filth fɪlθ
filth|y 'fɪlθ li ~**ier** iˌə ‖ iˌᵊr ~**iest** iˌɪst iˌəst
  ~**ily** ɪ li əl i ~**iness** i nəs i nɪs
filtrable 'fɪltr əb ᵊl
filtrate *n* 'fɪltr eɪt ~**s** s
filtration fɪl 'treɪʃ ᵊn ~**s** z
fin fɪn —*but as a French word* fæ̃, fæn; *see also*
  phrases with this word **finned** fɪnd **fins** fɪnz
Fina *tdmk* 'fiːn ə 'faɪn-
finable 'faɪn əb ᵊl
finag|le fɪ 'neɪg ᵊl fə- ~**ed** d ~**es** z ~**ing** ˌɪŋ
final 'faɪn ᵊl ~**ly** i ~**s** z
finale fɪ 'nɑːl i fə- ‖ -'næl i -'nɑːl i ~**s** z
finalis... —*see* **finaliz...**
finalist 'faɪn ᵊl ɪst §-əst ~**s** s
finality faɪ 'næl ət i -ɪt- ‖ -ət̬ i
finaliz|e 'faɪn ə laɪz -ᵊl aɪz ~**ed** d ~**es** ɪz əz
  ~**ing** ɪŋ
finally 'faɪn ᵊl i

AmE 1993					
BrE 1998					
0	20	40	60	80	100%

financ|e *n* 'faɪn ænᵗs faɪ 'nænᵗs, fɪ-, fə- —*Poll*
  panel preferences: AmE 1993, '·· *87%,* ·'·
  13%; BrE 1998, '·· *81%,* ·'· *19%.* ~**es** ɪz əz
financ|e *v* faɪ 'nænᵗs fɪ-, fə- ‖ fə- faɪ-;
  'faɪn ænᵗs ~**ed** t ~**es** ɪz əz ~**ing** ɪŋ

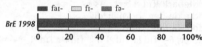

	faɪ-	fɪ-	fə-
BrE 1998			
0	20	40	60	80	100%

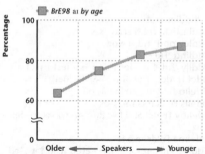

Percentage — BrE98 aɪ *by age* — Older ◄— Speakers —► Younger

financial faɪ 'nænᵗʃ ᵊl fɪ-, fə- ‖ fə- faɪ- —*BrE*
  1998 poll panel preference: faɪ- *79%,* fɪ- *17%,*
  fə- *4%.* ~**ly** i
  fiˌ**nancial 'year**
financier faɪ 'nænᵗs iˌə fɪ-, fə- ‖ ˌfɪn ən 'sɪᵊr
  ˌfaɪn- *(*)* ~**s** z
Finbar 'fɪn bɑː →'fɪm- ‖ -bɑːr
Finborough 'fɪn bᵊr_ə →'fɪm-, §-ˌbʌr ə
  ‖ -ˌbɝː oʊ
finch, Finch fɪntʃ **finches** 'fɪntʃ ɪz -əz
Finchale 'fɪŋk ᵊl
Finchampstead 'fɪntʃ əm sted -əmp-, -stɪd
Finchingfield 'fɪntʃ ɪŋ fiːᵊld
Finchley 'fɪntʃ li
find faɪnd **finding** 'faɪnd ɪŋ **finds** faɪndz
  found faʊnd
finder 'faɪnd ə ‖ -ᵊr ~**s** z
fin de siècle ˌfæ̃ də 'sjek lə ˌfæn-, -si 'eɪk ᵊl
  —*Fr* [fæd sjɛkl]
Findern 'fɪnd ən ‖ -ᵊrn
Findhorn 'fɪnd hɔːn ‖ -hɔːrn
finding 'faɪnd ɪŋ ~**s** z
Findlater 'fɪn lət ə 'fɪnd- ‖ -lət̬ ᵊr
Findlay 'fɪn li 'fɪnd-
Findon 'fɪnd ən
Findus *tdmk* 'fɪnd əs
fine *ordinary senses* faɪn **fined** faɪnd **finer**
  'faɪn ə ‖ -ᵊr **fines** faɪnz **finest** 'faɪn ɪst -əst
  fining 'faɪn ɪŋ
  ˌ**fine 'art**; ˌ**fine 'print**
fine *French word, 'liqueur'* fiːn —*Fr* [fin]
fine *Irish word* 'fɪn ə —*Irish* ['fi nʲə]
  ˌ**Fine 'Gael**
fineable 'faɪn əb ᵊl
fine-drawn ˌfaɪn 'drɔːn ◄ ‖ -'drɑːn ◄
  ˌ**fine-drawn 'features**
finely 'faɪn li
finer|y 'faɪn ᵊr li ~**ies** iz
fines herbes ˌfiːnz 'eəb ˌfiːn-, -'ɜːb ‖ -'eᵊrb
  —*Fr* [fin zɛʁb]
finespun ˌfaɪn 'spʌn ◄ ˌ· ·
finess|e fɪ 'nes fə- ~**ed** t ~**es** ɪz əz ~**ing** ɪŋ
fine-tooth ˌfaɪn 'tuːθ ◄ §-'tʊθ, ˌ· · ~**ed** t
  ˌ**fine-'tooth comb**, ˌ**fine-tooth 'comb**

fine-tun|e ˌfaɪn 'tjuːn →§-'tʃuːn ‖ -'tuːn
  -'tjuːn ~ed d ~es z ~ing ɪŋ
Fingal 'fɪŋ ɡəl
finger 'fɪŋ ɡə ‖ -ɡər fingered 'fɪŋ ɡəd -ɡərd
  fingering 'fɪŋ ɡər_ɪŋ fingers
  'fɪŋ ɡəz ‖ -ɡərz
  'finger bowl
fingerboard 'fɪŋ ɡə bɔːd ‖ -ɡər bɔːrd -bourd
  ~s z
-fingered 'fɪŋ ɡəd ‖ -ɡərd
fingering 'fɪŋ ɡər_ɪŋ ~s z
fingermark 'fɪŋ ɡə mɑːk ‖ -ɡər mɑːrk ~s s
fingernail 'fɪŋ ɡə neɪəl ‖ -ɡər- ~s z
fingerplate 'fɪŋ ɡə pleɪt ‖ -ɡər- ~s s
fingerpost 'fɪŋ ɡə pəʊst ‖ -ɡər poʊst ~s s
finger|print 'fɪŋ ɡə |prɪnt ‖ -ɡər- ~printed
  prɪnt ɪd -əd ‖ prɪnt̬ əd ~printing
  prɪnt ɪŋ ‖ prɪnt̬ ɪŋ ~prints prɪnts
fingerstall 'fɪŋ ɡə stɔːl ‖ -ɡər- -stɑːl ~s z
fingertip 'fɪŋ ɡə tɪp ‖ -ɡər- ~s s
Fingest 'fɪndʒ ɪst §-əst
finial 'fɪn i_əl 'fɪn- ~s z
finical 'fɪn ɪk əl ~ly i ~ness nəs nɪs
finicking 'fɪn ɪk ɪŋ
finickity fɪ 'nɪk ət i fə-, -ɪt- ‖ -ət̬ i
finicky 'fɪn ɪk i
fining 'faɪn ɪŋ ~s z
finis 'fɪn ɪs 'fiːn-, 'faɪn-, §-əs
finish 'fɪn ɪʃ finished 'fɪn ɪʃt finishes
  'fɪn ɪʃ ɪz -əz finishing 'fɪn ɪʃ ɪŋ
  'finishing school; ˌfinishing 'touch
finisher 'fɪn ɪʃ ə ‖ -ər ~s z
Finisterre ˌfɪn ɪ 'steə ◂ -ə- ‖ -'steər
finite 'faɪn aɪt ~ly li ~ness nəs nɪs
finito fɪ 'niːt əʊ fə- ‖ -oʊ —It [fi 'niː to]
fink, Fink, Finke fɪŋk finked fɪŋkt finking
  'fɪŋk ɪŋ finks fɪŋks
Finkelstein 'fɪŋk əl staɪn
Finland 'fɪn lənd
Finlandia fɪn 'lænd i_ə
Finlandi|sation, ~zation ˌfɪn lənd aɪ 'zeɪʃ ən
  -ɪ' • - ‖ -ə 'zeɪʃ-
Finlay 'fɪn li -leɪ
Finlayson 'fɪn lɪs ən
Finn fɪn Finns fɪnz
Finnair tdmk 'fɪn eə ˌ•'• ‖ -er -ær
finnan 'fɪn ən
  ˌfinnan 'haddie 'hæd i
Finnegan 'fɪn ɪɡ ən -əɡ- ~s, ~'s z
  ˌFinnegans 'Wake
Finney 'fɪn i
Finnic 'fɪn ɪk
Finnish 'fɪn ɪʃ
Finno-Ugrian ˌfɪn əʊ 'juːɡ ri_ən ◂ -'uːɡ-
  ‖ ˌ•oʊ-
Finno-Ugric ˌfɪn əʊ 'juːɡ rɪk ◂ -'uːɡ- ‖ -oʊ-
fino 'fiːn əʊ ‖ -oʊ ~s z —Sp ['fi no]
finocchio, finochio fɪ 'nɒk i əʊ fə-
  ‖ -'noʊk i oʊ
Finola fɪ 'nəʊl ə fə- ‖ -'noʊl ə
Finsberg 'fɪnz bɜːɡ ‖ -bɝːɡ
Finsbury 'fɪnz bər_i §-ˌber i ‖ -ˌber i
  ˌFinsbury 'Park

Finucane fɪ 'nuːk ən fə-
Finzi 'fɪnz i
Fiona fi 'əʊn ə ‖ -'oʊn ə
fiord fi 'ɔːd 'fiː ɔːd, fjɔːd ‖ fi 'ɔːrd fjɔːrd ~s z
fipple 'fɪp əl ~s z
fir fɜː ‖ fɝː (= fur) firs fɜːz ‖ fɝːz
Firbank 'fɜː bæŋk ‖ 'fɝː-
fire 'faɪ_ə ‖ 'faɪ_ər ~d d firing
  'faɪ_ər ɪŋ ‖ 'faɪ_ər ɪŋ ~s z
  'fire aˌlarm; 'fire briˌgade; 'fire
  deˌpartment; 'fire drill; 'fire ˌengine; 'fire
  eˌscape; 'fire exˌtinguisher; 'fire ˌfighter;
  'fire ˌfighting; 'fire hose; 'fire ˌhydrant;
  'fire inˌsurance; 'fire ˌirons; 'fire screen;
  'fire ship; 'fire ˌstation; 'fire ˌwarden
fireball 'faɪ_ə bɔːl ‖ 'faɪ_ər- -bɑːl ~s z
firebomb 'faɪ_ə bɒm ‖ 'faɪ_ər bɑːm ~ed d
  ~ing ɪŋ ~s z
firebox 'faɪ_ə bɒks ‖ 'faɪ_ər bɑːks ~es ɪz əz
firebrand 'faɪ_ə brænd ‖ 'faɪ_ər- ~s z
firebrat 'faɪ_ə bræt ‖ 'faɪ_ər- ~s s
firebreak 'faɪ_ə breɪk ‖ 'faɪ_ər- ~s s
firebrick 'faɪ_ə brɪk ‖ 'faɪ_ər- ~s s
firebug 'faɪ_ə bʌɡ ‖ 'faɪ_ər- ~s z
fireclay 'faɪ_ə kleɪ ‖ 'faɪ_ər-
firecracker 'faɪ_ə ˌkræk ə ‖ 'faɪ_ər ˌkræk ər ~s
  z
firecrest 'faɪ_ə krest ‖ 'faɪ_ər- ~s s
firedamp 'faɪ_ə dæmp ‖ 'faɪ_ər-
firedog 'faɪ_ə dɒɡ ‖ 'faɪ_ər dɔːɡ -dɑːɡ ~s z
fire-eater 'faɪ_ər ˌiːt ə ‖ 'faɪ_ər ˌiːt̬ ər ~s z
fire|fly 'faɪ_ə |flaɪ ‖ 'faɪ_ər- ~flies flaɪz
fireguard 'faɪ_ə ɡɑːd ‖ 'faɪ_ər ɡɑːrd ~s z
fire|house 'faɪ_ə |haʊs ‖ 'faɪ_ər- ~houses
  haʊz ɪz -əz
firelight 'faɪ_ə laɪt ‖ 'faɪ_ər-
firelighter 'faɪ_ə ˌlaɪt ə ‖ 'faɪ_ər ˌlaɪt̬ ər ~s z
fire|man 'faɪ_ə |mən ‖ 'faɪ_ər- ~man's mənz
  ~men mən men
fireplac|e 'faɪ_ə pleɪs ‖ 'faɪ_ər- ~es ɪz əz
fireplug 'faɪ_ə plʌɡ ‖ 'faɪ_ər- ~s z
firepower 'faɪ_ə ˌpaʊ_ə ‖ 'faɪ_ər ˌpaʊ_ər
fireproof 'faɪ_ə pruːf §-prʊf ‖ 'faɪ_ər-
fire-rais|er/s 'faɪ_ə ˌreɪz ə/z ‖ 'faɪ_ər ˌreɪz ər/z
  ~ing ɪŋ
fireside 'faɪ_ə saɪd ‖ 'faɪ_ər- ~s z
firestone, F~ 'faɪ_ə stəʊn ‖ 'faɪ_ər stoʊn ~s z
firestorm 'faɪ_ə stɔːm ‖ 'faɪ_ər stɔːrm ~s z
firethorn 'faɪ_ə θɔːn ‖ 'faɪ_ər θɔːrn ~s z
firetrap 'faɪ_ə træp ‖ 'faɪ_ər- ~s s
firewalk|er/s 'faɪ_ə ˌwɔːk ə/
  z ‖ 'faɪ_ər ˌwɔːk ər/z -ˌwɑːk- ~ing ɪŋ
firewall 'faɪ_ə wɔːl ‖ 'faɪ_ər wɔːl -wɑːl ~s z
firewater 'faɪ_ə ˌwɔːt ə ‖ 'faɪ_ər ˌwɔːt̬ ər
  -ˌwɑːt̬ ər
fireweed 'faɪ_ə wiːd ‖ 'faɪ_ər-
firewood 'faɪ_ə wʊd ‖ 'faɪ_ər-
firework 'faɪ_ə wɜːk ‖ 'faɪ_ər wɝːk ~s s
firing 'faɪ_ər ɪŋ ‖ 'faɪ_ər ɪŋ ~s z
  'firing line; 'firing pin; 'firing squad
firkin 'fɜːk ɪn §-ən ‖ 'fɝːk- ~s z
Firle fɜːl ‖ fɝːl

F

firm fɜːm ‖ fɝːm **firmer** 'fɜːm ə ‖ 'fɝːm ᵊr
firmest 'fɜːm ɪst -əst ‖ 'fɝːm- **firms**
fɜːmz ‖ fɝːmz
firmament 'fɜːm ə mənt ‖ 'fɝːm-
firm|ly 'fɜːm |li ‖ 'fɝːm- **~ness** nəs nɪs
firmware 'fɜːm weə ‖ 'fɝːm wer -wær
first fɜːst ‖ fɝːst **firsts** fɜːsts ‖ fɝːsts
ˌfirst 'aid; ˌfirst 'base; ˌfirst 'class◄; ˌfirst
'cousin; ˌfirst-day 'cover; ˌfirst 'floor; ˌfirst
'lady; ˌfirst lieu'tenant◄; ˌfirst 'mate; ˌfirst
'name; ˌfirst 'night; ˌfirst of'fender; ˌfirst
ˌpast the 'post; ˌfirst 'person◄; ˌfirst
re'fusal; ˌfirst 'strike
firstborn 'fɜːst bɔːn ‖ 'fɝːst bɔːrn **~s** z
first-class ˌfɜːst 'klɑːs ◄ §-'klæs ‖ ˌfɝːst 'klæs ◄
ˌfirst-class ho'tel
first-degree ˌfɜːst dɪ 'griː ◄ -də- ‖ ˌfɝːst-
ˌfirst-deˌgree 'murder
firstfruits 'fɜːst fruːts ‖ 'fɝːst-
firsthand ˌfɜːst 'hænd ◄ ‖ ˌfɝːst-
firstly 'fɜːst li ‖ 'fɝːst-
first-nighter ˌfɜːst 'naɪt ə ‖ ˌfɝːst 'naɪt ᵊr **~s** z
first-rate ˌfɜːst 'reɪt ◄ ‖ ˌfɝːst-
first-string ˌfɜːst 'strɪŋ ◄ ‖ ˌfɝːst-
first-time ˌfɜːst 'taɪm ◄ ‖ ˌfɝːst-
ˌfirst-time 'buyer
firth, Firth fɜːθ ‖ fɝːθ **firths** fɜːθs ‖ fɝːθs
firtree 'fɜː triː ‖ 'fɝː- **~s** z
fiscal 'fɪsk ᵊl **~ly** i
ˌfiscal 'year
Fischer 'fɪʃ ə ‖ -ᵊr
fish, Fish fɪʃ **fished** fɪʃt **fishing** 'fɪʃ ɪŋ **fishes**
'fɪʃ ɪz -əz
ˌfish farm; ˌfish 'finger; ˌfishing rod; ˌfish
knife; ˌfish 'n' chips; ˌfish slice; ˌfish stick
Fishbourne 'fɪʃ bɔːn ‖ -bɔːrn -boʊrn
fishbowl 'fɪʃ bəʊl →-bɒʊl ‖ -boʊl **~s** z
fishcake 'fɪʃ keɪk **~s** s
fisher, F~ 'fɪʃ ə ‖ -ᵊr **~s** z
fisher|man 'fɪʃ ə |mən ‖ -ᵊr- **~man's** mənz
~men mən men
fisher|y 'fɪʃ ᵊr |i **~ies** iz
fish-eye 'fɪʃ aɪ
ˌfish-eye 'lens
Fishguard 'fɪʃ ɡɑːd ‖ -ɡɑːrd
fishi... —see **fish, fishy**
Fishley 'fɪʃ li
Fishlock 'fɪʃ lɒk ‖ -lɑːk
fishmonger 'fɪʃ ˌmʌŋ ɡə ‖ -ɡᵊr -ˌmɑːŋ- **~s** z
fishnet 'fɪʃ net **~s** s
fishplate 'fɪʃ pleɪt **~s** s
fishtail 'fɪʃ teɪᵊl **~ed** d **~ing** ɪŋ **~s** z
Fishwick 'fɪʃ wɪk
fish|wife 'fɪʃ |waɪf **~wives** waɪvz
fish|y 'fɪʃ |i **~ier** i_ə ‖ i_ᵊr **~iest** i_ɪst i_əst **~ily**
ɪ li əl i **~iness** i nəs i nɪs
Fisk, Fiske fɪsk
Fison 'faɪs ᵊn
fissile 'fɪs aɪᵊl ‖ -ᵊl (*)
fission 'fɪʃ ᵊn **~s** z
fissionable 'fɪʃ ᵊn_əb ᵊl
fissiparous fɪ 'sɪp ᵊr əs fə-

fissure 'fɪʃ ə -ʊə ‖ -ᵊr **~d** d **fissuring** 'fɪʃ ᵊr ɪŋ
-ʊᵊr- **~s** z
fist fɪst **fisted** 'fɪst ɪd -əd **fisting** 'fɪst ɪŋ **fists**
fɪsts
-fisted 'fɪst ɪd ◄ -əd
fistful 'fɪst fʊl **~s** z
fisticuffs 'fɪst i kʌfs
fistul|a 'fɪst jʊl ə ‖ 'fɪs tʃᵊl ə →'fɪʃ- **~ae** iː
~ar ə ‖ ᵊr **~as** əz **~ous** əs
fit fɪt **fits** fɪts **fitted** 'fɪt ɪd -əd **fitter**
'fɪt ə ‖ 'fɪt̬ ᵊr **fittest** 'fɪt ɪst -əst ‖ 'fɪt̬ əst
fitting 'fɪt ɪŋ ‖ 'fɪt̬ ɪŋ
fitch, Fitch fɪtʃ **fitches** 'fɪtʃ ɪz -əz
fitchew, F~ 'fɪtʃ uː **~s** z
fitful 'fɪt fᵊl -fʊl **~ly** i **~ness** nəs nɪs
fitment 'fɪt mənt **~s** s
fitness 'fɪt nəs -nɪs
fitter, F~ 'fɪt ə ‖ 'fɪt̬ ᵊr **~s** z
fitting 'fɪt ɪŋ ‖ 'fɪt̬ ɪŋ **~ly** li **~ness** nəs nɪs
Fitz fɪts
Fitzgerald, FitzGerald ₍ₜ₎fɪts 'dʒer əld
Fitzgibbon ₍ₜ₎fɪts 'ɡɪb ᵊn
Fitzhardinge ₍ₜ₎fɪts 'hɑːd ɪŋ ‖ -'hɑːrd-
Fitzherbert ₍ₜ₎fɪts 'hɜːb ət ‖ -'hɝːb ᵊrt
Fitzjames ₍ₜ₎fɪts 'dʒeɪmz
Fitzjohn ₍ₜ₎fɪts 'dʒɒn ‖ -'dʒɑːn
Fitzpatrick ₍ₜ₎fɪts 'pætr ɪk
Fitzrovia ₍ₜ₎fɪts 'rəʊv i_ə ‖ -'roʊv-
Fitzroy ₍ₜ₎fɪts 'rɔɪ '• •
Fitzsimmons ₍ₜ₎fɪts 'sɪm ənz
Fitzwalter ₍ₜ₎fɪts 'wɔːlt ə ‖ -'wɔːlt ᵊr -'wɑːlt ᵊr
Fitzwilliam ₍ₜ₎fɪts 'wɪl jəm
five faɪv ——but for clarity in communication
code, fife faɪf **fives** faɪvz
ˌfive-ˌfinger 'exercise; ˌfive o' 'clock◄; ˌfive
o' ˌclock 'shadow; ˌFive-'Year Plan
fivefold 'faɪv fəʊld →-fɒʊld ‖ -foʊld
five-eighth ˌfaɪv 'eɪtθ ◄ §-'eɪθ **~s** s
fivepenc|e 'faɪf pən̩s 'faɪv- **~es** ɪz əz
fivepenn|y 'faɪf pən i 'faɪv- **~ies** iz
fiver 'faɪv ə ‖ -ᵊr **~s** z
five-star ˌfaɪv 'stɑː ◄ ‖ -'stɑːr ◄
ˌfive-star ho'tel
fix fɪks **fixed** fɪkst **fixes** 'fɪks ɪz -əz **fixing**
'fɪks ɪŋ
fixable 'fɪks əb ᵊl
fix|ate fɪk 'seɪt 'fɪks eɪt ‖ 'fɪks eɪt **~ated**
eɪt ɪd -əd ‖ eɪt̬ əd **~ates** eɪts **~ating**
eɪt ɪŋ ‖ eɪt̬ ɪŋ
fixation fɪk 'seɪʃ ᵊn **~s** z
fixative 'fɪks ət ɪv ‖ -ət̬ ɪv **~s** z
fixedly 'fɪks ɪd li -əd-
fixer 'fɪks ə ‖ -ᵊr **~s** z
fixit|y 'fɪks ət i -ɪt- ‖ -ət̬ i **~ies** iz
fixture 'fɪks tʃə ‖ -tʃᵊr **~s** z
fizgig 'fɪz ɡɪɡ **~s** z
fizz fɪz **fizzed** fɪzd **fizzes** 'fɪz ɪz -əz **fizzing**
'fɪz ɪŋ
fizzl|e 'fɪz ᵊl **~ed** d **~es** z **~ing** ᵊ_ɪŋ
fizz|y 'fɪz |i **~ier** i_ə ‖ i_ᵊr **~iest** i_ɪst i_əst
fjord fi 'ɔːd 'fiː ɔːd, fjɔːd ‖ fi 'ɔːrd fjɔːrd **~s** z
flab flæb

flabbergast 'flæb ə gɑːst §-gæst ‖ -ᵊr gæst
~ed ɪd əd ~ing ɪŋ ~s s
flabb|y 'flæb |i ~ier i̯ə ‖ i̯ᵊr ~iest i̯ɪst i̯əst
~ily ɪ li əl i ~iness i nəs i nɪs
flaccid 'flæks ɪd 'flæs-, §-əd ~ly li ~ness nəs
nɪs
flaccidity flæk 'sɪd ət i flæ-, flə-, -ɪt- ‖ -əṭ i
Flack, flack flæk
flag flæg **flagged** flægd **flagging** 'flæg ɪŋ
flags flægz
'**flag day**
flagellant 'flædʒ əl ənt -ɪl-; flə 'dʒel- ~s s
flagel|late v 'flædʒ ə |leɪt -ɪ- ~lated leɪt ɪd -əd
‖ leɪṭ əd ~lates leɪts ~lating leɪt ɪŋ ‖ leɪṭ ɪŋ
flagellate n, adj 'flædʒ əl ət -ɪl-, -ɪt; -ə leɪt ~s s
flagellation ˌflædʒ ə 'leɪʃ ᵊn -ɪ- ~s z
flagell|um flə 'dʒel |əm flæ- ~a ə ~ar ə ‖ ᵊr
~ums əmz
flageolet ˌflædʒ ə 'let -'leɪ ~s s
Flagg flæg
flagon 'flæg ᵊn ~s z
flagpole 'flæg pəʊl →-pɒʊl -poʊl ~s z
flagrancy 'fleɪg rən̩ts i
flagrant 'fleɪg rənt ~ly li
flagrante flə 'grænt i flæ-
flaˌ**grante de**'**licto** dɪ 'lɪkt əʊ də-, deɪ- ‖ -oʊ
flagship 'flæg ʃɪp ~s s
flagstaff, F~ 'flæg stɑːf §-stæf ‖ -stæf ~s s
flagstone 'flæg stəʊn ‖ -stoʊn ~s z
flag-waving 'flæg ˌweɪv ɪŋ
Flaherty 'flɑː hət i 'flæ-, -ət-; 'fleət i ‖ 'flæ ᵊrṭ i
'flɑːrṭ i
flail fleɪᵊl **flailed** fleɪᵊld **flailing** 'fleɪᵊl ɪŋ
flails fleɪᵊlz
flair fleə ‖ fleᵊr flæᵊr **flairs** fleəz ‖ fleᵊrz flæᵊrz
flak flæk
flake fleɪk **flaked** fleɪkt **flakes** fleɪks **flaking**
'fleɪk ɪŋ
flak|y 'fleɪk |i ~ier i̯ə ‖ i̯ᵊr ~iest i̯ɪst i̯əst
~ily ɪ li əl i ~iness i nəs i nɪs
flam flæm **flams** flæmz
flambe, flambé 'flɒm beɪ 'flɑːm-, 'flæm-, -bi
‖ flɑːm 'beɪ —Fr [flɑ̃ be] ~ed d
flambeau 'flæm bəʊ ‖ -boʊ ~x z
flambee, flambée 'flɒm beɪ 'flɑːm-, 'flæm-, -bi
‖ flɑːm 'beɪ —Fr [flɑ̃ be] ~d d
Flamborough 'flæm bər_ə ‖ -ˌbɝː oʊ
ˌFlamborough 'Head
flamboyance flæm 'bɔɪ ən̩ts
flamboyant flæm 'bɔɪ ənt ~ly li ~s s
flame fleɪm **flamed** fleɪmd **flames** fleɪmz
flaming/ly 'fleɪm ɪŋ /li
flamenco flə 'meŋ kəʊ ‖ -koʊ ~s z
flameproof 'fleɪm pruːf §-prʊf ~ed t ~ing
ɪŋ ~s s
flame-thrower 'fleɪm ˌθrəʊ ə ‖ -ˌθroʊ ᵊr ~s z
flaming 'fleɪm ɪŋ
flamingo flə 'mɪŋ gəʊ flæ- ‖ -goʊ ~es, ~s z
Flaminian flə 'mɪn i̯ən flæ-
flammability ˌflæm ə 'bɪl ət i -ɪt i ‖ -əṭ i
flammable 'flæm əb ᵊl
Flamsteed 'flæm stiːd
flan flæn ‖ flɑːn **flans** flænz ‖ flɑːnz

Flanagan 'flæn əg ən
Flanders 'flɑːnd əz §'flænd- ‖ 'flænd ᵊrz
flange flændʒ **flanged** flændʒd **flanges**
'flændʒ ɪz -əz **flanging** 'flændʒ ɪŋ
flank flæŋk **flanked** flæŋkt **flanking** 'flæŋk ɪŋ
flanks flæŋks
flanker 'flæŋk ə ‖ -ᵊr ~s z
flannel 'flæn ᵊl ~ed, ~led d ~ing, ~ling ɪŋ ~s
z
flannelboard 'flæn ᵊl bɔːd ‖ -bɔːrd -boʊrd ~s
z
flannelette ˌflæn ᵊl 'et -ə 'let
flannelgraph 'flæn ᵊl grɑːf -græf ‖ -græf ~s s
flannelly 'flæn ᵊl i
flap flæp **flapped** flæpt **flapping** 'flæp ɪŋ
flaps flæps
flapdoodle 'flæp ˌduːd ᵊl
flapjack 'flæp dʒæk ~s s
flapper 'flæp ə ‖ -ᵊr ~s z
flare fleə ‖ fleᵊr flæᵊr **flared** fleəd ‖ fleᵊrd
flæᵊrd **flares** fleəz ‖ fleᵊrz flæᵊrz **flaring**
'fleər ɪŋ ‖ 'fler ɪŋ 'flær-
'**flare path**
flare-up 'fleər ʌp ‖ 'fler- 'flær- ~s s
flash, Flash flæʃ **flashed** flæʃt **flashes**
'flæʃ ɪz -əz **flashing** 'flæʃ ɪŋ
ˌflash 'flood; 'flash point
flashback 'flæʃ bæk ~s s
flashbulb 'flæʃ bʌlb ~s z
flashcube 'flæʃ kjuːb ~s z
flasher 'flæʃ ə ‖ -ᵊr ~s z
flashgun 'flæʃ gʌn ~s z
flashi... —see **flashy**
flashlight 'flæʃ laɪt ~s s
Flashman 'flæʃ mən
flashover 'flæʃ ˌəʊv ə ‖ -ˌoʊv ᵊr ~s z
flash|y 'flæʃ |i ~ier i̯ə ‖ i̯ᵊr ~iest i̯ɪst i̯əst
~ily ɪ li əl i ~iness i nəs i nɪs
flask, Flask flɑːsk §flæsk ‖ flæsk **flasks** flɑːsks
§flæsks ‖ flæsks
flat flæt **flats** flæts **flatted** 'flæt ɪd -əd
‖ 'flæṭ əd **flatter** 'flæt ə ‖ 'flæṭ ᵊr **flattest**
'flæt ɪst -əst ‖ 'flæṭ əst **flatting**
'flæt ɪŋ ‖ 'flæṭ ɪŋ
ˌflat 'feet; ˌflat ˌracing; ˌflat 'spin
flat-bottomed ˌflæt 'bɒt əmd ◄ ‖ -'bɑːṭ əmd ◄
Flatbush 'flæt bʊʃ
flatcar 'flæt kɑː ‖ -kɑːr ~s z
flat-chested ˌflæt 'tʃest ɪd ◄ -əd
flatfeet —see **flatfoot**
flatfish 'flæt fɪʃ ~es ɪz əz
flat|foot 'flæt |fʊt ~feet fiːt ~foots fʊts
flat-footed ˌflæt 'fʊt ɪd ◄ -əd ‖ -'fʊṭ əd ◄ ~ly li
~ness nəs nɪs
flathead, F~ 'flæt hed ~s z
flatiron 'flæt ˌaɪ_ən ‖ 'flæṭ ˌaɪ_ᵊrn ~s z
Flatland 'flæt lænd
flatlet 'flæt lət -lɪt ~s s
Flatley 'flæt li
flatly 'flæt li
flatmate 'flæt meɪt ~s s
flatness 'flæt nəs -nɪs
flatshare 'flæt ʃeə ‖ -ʃer -ʃær ~s z

F

flatten 'flæt ᵊn ~ed d ~ing _ɪŋ ~s z
flatter 'flæt ə ‖ 'flæţ ᵊr ~ed d flattering/ly
'flæt_ər ɪŋ /li ‖ 'flæţ- ~s z
flatter|y 'flæt ᵊr li ‖ 'flæţ- ~ies iz
flattie 'flæt i ‖ 'flæţ i ~s z
flattish 'flæt ɪʃ ‖ 'flæţ ɪʃ
flattop 'flæt tɒp ‖ -tɑːp ~s s
flatulenc|e 'flæt jʊl ənts 'flætʃ ʊl- ‖ 'flætʃ əl-
~y i
flatulent 'flæt jʊl ənt 'flætʃ ʊl- ‖ 'flætʃ əl-
~ly li
flatus 'fleɪt əs ‖ 'fleɪţ- ~es ɪz əz
flatware 'flæt weə ‖ -wer -wær
flatworm 'flæt wɜːm ‖ -wɝːm ~s z
Flaubert 'fləʊb eə ‖ floʊ 'beᵊr —Fr [flo bɛːʁ]
flaunt flɔːnt ‖ flɑːnt flaunted 'flɔːnt ɪd -əd
‖ 'flɔːnţ əd 'flɑːnţ- flaunting/ly 'flɔːnt ɪŋ /
li ‖ 'flɔːnţ ɪŋ /li 'flɑːnţ- flaunts flɔːnts ‖
flɑːnts
flaunter 'flɔːnt ə ‖ 'flɔːnţ ᵊr 'flɑːnţ- ~s z
flautist 'flɔːt ɪst §-əst ‖ 'flɔːţ- 'flɑːţ-, 'flaʊţ- ~s
s
Flavell (i) 'fleɪv ᵊl, (ii) flə 'vel
Flavia 'fleɪv i_ə
Flavian 'fleɪv i_ən
flavin 'fleɪv ɪn 'flæv-, §-ᵊn ~s z
flavine 'fleɪv iːn 'flæv-, -ɪn
Flavius 'fleɪv i_əs
flavone 'fleɪv əʊn ‖ -oʊn
flavonoid 'fleɪv ə nɔɪd 'flæv- ~s z
flavonol 'fleɪv ə nɒl 'flæv- ‖ -nɔːl -nɑːl, -noʊl
flavor 'fleɪv ə ‖ -ᵊr ~ed d flavoring/s 'fleɪv
ər_ɪŋ/z ~s z
flavor|ful 'fleɪv ə fʊl -fᵊl ‖ -ᵊr- ~less ləs lɪs
~some səm
flavour 'fleɪv ə ‖ -ᵊr ~ed d flavouring/s
'fleɪv ər_ɪŋ/z ~s z
flavour|ful 'fleɪv ə fʊl -fᵊl ‖ -ᵊr- ~less ləs lɪs
~some səm
flaw flɔː ‖ flɑː flawed flɔːd ‖ flɑːd flawing
'flɔːʳ ɪŋ ‖ 'flɔː ɪŋ 'flɑː- flaws flɔːz ‖ flɑːz
flawless 'flɔː ləs -lɪs ‖ 'flɑː- ~ly li ~ness nəs
nɪs
flax flæks
flaxen 'flæks ᵊn
Flaxman 'flæks mən
flay fleɪ flayed fleɪd flaying 'fleɪ ɪŋ flays
fleɪz
flea fliː (= flee) fleas fliːz
'flea ˌmarket
fleabag 'fliː bæg ~s z
fleabane 'fliː beɪn ~s z
fleabite 'fliː baɪt ~s s
flea-bitten 'fliː ˌbɪt ᵊn
fleapit 'fliː pɪt ~s s
fleawort 'fliː wɜːt §-wɔːt ‖ -wɝːt -wɔːrt ~s s
fleche, flèche fleɪʃ fleʃ fleches, flèches
'fleɪʃ ɪz 'fleʃ-, -əz
fleck flek flecked flekt flecking 'flek ɪŋ
flecks fleks (= flex)
Flecker 'flek ə ‖ -ᵊr
flection 'flek ʃᵊn ~s z
flectional 'flek ʃᵊn_ᵊl

flectionless 'flek ʃᵊn ləs -lɪs
fled fled
fledge fledʒ fledged fledʒd fledges 'fledʒ ɪz
-əz fledging 'fledʒ ɪŋ
fledgeling, fledgling 'fledʒ lɪŋ ~s z
flee fliː (= flea) fled fled fleeing 'fliː ɪŋ flees
fliːz
fleece fliːs fleeced fliːst fleeces 'fliːs ɪz -əz
fleecing 'fliːs ɪŋ
fleec|y 'fliːs li ~ier i_ə ‖ i_ᵊr ~iest i_ɪst i_əst
~ily ɪ li əl i ~iness i nəs i nɪs
fleet, Fleet fliːt fleeted 'fliːt ɪd -əd ‖ 'fliːţ əd
fleeter 'fliːt ə ‖ 'fliːţ ᵊr fleetest 'fliːt ɪst -əst
‖ 'fliːţ- fleeting 'fliːt ɪŋ ‖ 'fliːţ ɪŋ
'fleet ˌadmiral; 'Fleet Street
fleeting 'fliːt ɪŋ ‖ 'fliːţ ɪŋ ~ly li ~ness nəs nɪs
Fleetwood 'fliːt wʊd
Fleming 'flem ɪŋ ~s, ~'s z
Flemington 'flem ɪŋ tən
Flemish 'flem ɪʃ
flense flents flenz flensed flent'st flenzd
flenses 'flents ɪz 'flenz-, -əz flensing
'flents ɪŋ 'flenz-
flenser 'flents ə 'flenz- ‖ -ᵊr ~s z
flesh fleʃ fleshed fleʃt fleshes 'fleʃ ɪz -əz
fleshing 'fleʃ ɪŋ
'flesh wound
fleshi... —see fleshy
flesh|ly 'fleʃ |li ~lier li_ə ‖ li_ᵊr ~liest li_ɪst
li_əst ~liness li nəs li nɪs
fleshpot 'fleʃ pɒt ‖ -pɑːt ~s s
flesh|y 'fleʃ |i ~ier i_ə ‖ i_ᵊr ~iest i_ɪst i_əst
~iness i nəs i nɪs
fletcher, F~ 'fletʃ ə ‖ -ᵊr ~s, ~'s z
Fletton, f~ 'flet ᵊn
Fleur flɜː ‖ flɜːː —Fr [flœːʁ]
fleur-de-lis, fleur-de-lys sing. ˌflɜː də 'liː -'liːs
‖ ˌflɜːː- —Fr [flœʁ də lis]
flew, Flew fluː flews fluːz
flex fleks flexed flekst flexes 'fleks ɪz -əz
flexing 'fleks ɪŋ
flexibility ˌfleks ə 'bɪl ət i ˌ•ɪ-, -ɪt i ‖ -əţ i
flexib|le 'fleks əb |ᵊl -ɪb- ~leness ᵊl nəs -nɪs
~ly li
flexion 'flek ʃᵊn
flexional 'flek ʃᵊn_ᵊl
flexionless 'flek ʃᵊn ləs -lɪs
flexitime 'fleks i taɪm
Flexner 'fleks nə ‖ -nᵊr
flexor 'fleks ə -ɔː ‖ -ᵊr -ɔːr ~s z
flextime 'fleks taɪm
flexuous 'fleks ju_əs ‖ 'flek ʃu_əs ~ly li
flexure 'flek ʃə 'fleks jʊə ‖ -ʃᵊr ~s z
flibbertigibbet ˌflɪb ət i 'dʒɪb ɪt -ət ‖ -ᵊrţ i-
'•••,•• ~s s
flick flɪk flicked flɪkt flicking 'flɪk ɪŋ flicks
flɪks
'flick knife
flicker 'flɪk ə ‖ -ᵊr ~ed d flickering 'flɪk ər_ɪŋ
~s z
flier 'flaɪ_ə ‖ 'flaɪ_ᵊr ~s z
flies flaɪz

flight flaɪt **flighted** 'flaɪt ɪd -əd ‖ 'flaɪt̬ əd
  flighting 'flaɪt ɪŋ ‖ 'flaɪt̬ ɪŋ **flights** flaɪts
  'flight deck; ˌflight lieu'tenant◂; 'flight
  ˌnumber; 'flight path; 'flight reˌcorder;
  'flight ˌsergeant
flighti... —see **flighty**
flightless 'flaɪt ləs -lɪs
flight|y 'flaɪt |i ‖ 'flaɪt̬ |i **~ier** i‿ə ‖ i‿ər **~iest**
  i‿ɪst i‿əst **~ily** ɪ li əl i **~iness** i nəs i nɪs
flimflam 'flɪm flæm **~med** d **~ming** ɪŋ **~s** z
flims|y 'flɪmz |i **~ier** i‿ə ‖ i‿ər **~iest** i‿ɪst i‿əst
  ~ily ɪ li əl i **~iness** i nəs i nɪs
flinch 'flɪntʃ **flinched** flɪntʃt **flinches**
  'flɪntʃ ɪz -əz **flinching** 'flɪntʃ ɪŋ
Flinders, f~ 'flɪnd əz ‖ -ərz
fling flɪŋ **flinging** 'flɪŋ ɪŋ **flings** flɪŋz **flung**
  flʌŋ
Flinn flɪn
flint, Flint flɪnt **flints** flɪnts
flintlock 'flɪnt lɒk ‖ -lɑːk **~s** s
Flintshire 'flɪnt ʃə -ʃɪə ‖ -ʃər -ʃɪr
flintstone, F~ 'flɪnt stəʊn ‖ -stoʊn **~s** z
flint|y 'flɪnt |i ‖ 'flɪnt̬ |i **~ier** i‿ə ‖ i‿ər **~iest**
  i‿ɪst i‿əst **~ily** ɪ li əl i **~iness** i nəs i nɪs
flip flɪp **flipped** flɪpt **flipping** 'flɪp ɪŋ **flips**
  flɪps
  'flip side
flip-flop 'flɪp flɒp ‖ -flɑːp **~s** s
flippancy 'flɪp ənts i
flippant 'flɪp ənt **~ly** li
flipper 'flɪp ə ‖ -ər **~s** z
flirt flɜːt ‖ flɜˈːt **flirted** 'flɜːt ɪd -əd ‖ 'flɜˈːt̬ əd
  flirting 'flɜːt ɪŋ ‖ 'flɜˈːt̬ ɪŋ **flirts**
  flɜːts ‖ flɜˈːts
flirtation flɜː 'teɪʃ ən ‖ flɜˈː-
flirtatious flɜː 'teɪʃ əs ‖ flɜˈː- **~ly** li **~ness** nəs
  nɪs
flirty 'flɜːt i ‖ 'flɜˈːt̬ i
flit flɪt **flits** flɪts **flitted** 'flɪt ɪd -əd ‖ 'flɪt̬ əd
  flitting 'flɪt ɪŋ ‖ 'flɪt̬ ɪŋ
flitch flɪtʃ **flitches** 'flɪtʃ ɪz -əz
flitter 'flɪt ə ‖ 'flɪt̬ ər **~ed** d **flittering**
  'flɪt̬ ər ɪŋ ‖ 'flɪt̬ ər ɪŋ **~s** z
Flitton 'flɪt ən
Flitwick 'flɪt ɪk ‖ 'flɪt̬-
flivver 'flɪv ə ‖ -ər **~s** z
Flixton 'flɪkst ən
Flo fləʊ ‖ floʊ
float fləʊt ‖ floʊt **floated** 'fləʊt ɪd -əd
  ‖ 'floʊt̬ əd **floating** 'fləʊt ɪŋ ‖ 'floʊt̬ ɪŋ
  floats fləʊts ‖ floʊts
  ˌfloating 'voter
floatation fləʊ 'teɪʃ ən ‖ floʊ- **~s** z
floating-point ˌfləʊt ɪŋ 'pɔɪnt ‖ ˌfloʊt̬ ɪŋ-
flocculent 'flɒk jʊl ənt ‖ 'flɑːk jəl- **~ly** li
flock flɒk ‖ flɑːk **flocked** flɒkt ‖ flɑːkt
  flocking 'flɒk ɪŋ ‖ 'flɑːk ɪŋ **flocks**
  flɒks ‖ flɑːks
Flodden 'flɒd ən ‖ 'flɑːd-
floe fləʊ ‖ floʊ (= flow) **floes** fləʊz ‖ floʊz
Floella fləʊ 'el ə ‖ floʊ-
flog flɒg ‖ flɑːg **flogged** flɒgd ‖ flɑːgd

flogging/s 'flɒg ɪŋ/z ‖ 'flɑːg ɪŋ/z **flogs**
  flɒgz ‖ flɑːgz
flogger 'flɒg ə ‖ 'flɑːg ər **~s** z
Flo-Jo 'fləʊ dʒəʊ ‖ 'floʊ dʒoʊ
flong flɒŋ ‖ flɔːŋ flɑːŋ **flongs** flɒŋz ‖ flɔːŋz
  flɑːŋz
flood, Flood flʌd **flooded** 'flʌd ɪd -əd
  flooding 'flʌd ɪŋ **floods** flʌdz
  'flood tide
floodgate 'flʌd geɪt →'flʌg- **~s** s
flood|light 'flʌd |laɪt **~lighted** laɪt ɪd -əd
  ‖ laɪt̬ əd **~lighting** laɪt ɪŋ ‖ laɪt̬ ɪŋ **~lights**
  laɪts **~lit** lɪt
Flook flʊk fluːk
floor flɔː ‖ flɔːr floʊr **floored** flɔːd ‖ flɔːrd
  floʊrd **flooring** 'flɔːr ɪŋ ‖ 'floʊr- **floors**
  flɔːz ‖ flɔːrz floʊrz
  'floor cloth; 'floor ˌmanager; 'floor show
floorboard 'flɔː bɔːd ‖ 'flɔːr bɔːrd 'floʊr boʊrd
  ~s z
flooring 'flɔːr ɪŋ ‖ 'floʊr-
floorwalker 'flɔː ˌwɔːk ə ‖ 'flɔːr ˌwɔːk ər
  'floʊr-, -ˌwɑːk ər **~s** z
floos|ie, floos|y, flooz|ie, flooz|y 'fluːz |i **~ies**
  iz
flop flɒp ‖ flɑːp **flopped** flɒpt ‖ flɑːpt
  flopping 'flɒp ɪŋ ‖ 'flɑːp ɪŋ **flops**
  flɒps ‖ flɑːps
flop|house 'flɒp |haʊs ‖ 'flɑːp- **~houses**
  haʊz ɪz -əz
flopp|y 'flɒp |i ‖ 'flɑːp |i **~ier** i‿ə ‖ i‿ər **~ies** iz
  ~iest i‿ɪst i‿əst **~ily** ɪ li əl i **~iness** i nəs i nɪs
  ˌfloppy 'disk
Flopsy, f~ 'flɒps i ‖ 'flɑːps i
flora, Flora 'flɔːr ə ‖ 'floʊr- **~s** z
floral 'flɔːr əl 'flɒr- ‖ 'floʊr- **~ly** i
floreat 'flɒr i æt 'flɔːr- ‖ 'flɔːr-
Florence 'flɒr ənts ‖ 'flɔːr- 'flɑːr- **~'s** ɪz əz
Florentine, f~ 'flɒr ən taɪn -tiːn; flə 'rent aɪn
  ‖ 'flɔːr ən tiːn 'flɑːr- **~s** z
Flores 'flɔːr ɪz -iːz, -ɪs, §-əs ‖ 'floʊr-
  ˌFlores 'Sea
florescence flɔː 'res ənts flɒ-, flə- ‖ floʊ-
floret 'flɒr ət 'flɔːr-, -ɪt ‖ 'flɔːr- 'floʊr- **~s** s
Florey 'flɔːr i 'flɒr- ‖ 'floʊr-
floribunda ˌflɒr ɪ 'bʌnd ə ˌflɔːr-, §-ə- ‖ ˌflɔːr ə-
  ˌfloʊr- **~s** z
floricultural ˌflɔːr ɪ 'kʌltʃ ər‿əl ˌflɒr-,
  ˌ•ə- ‖ ˌfloʊr-
floriculture 'flɔːr ɪ ˌkʌltʃ ə 'flɒr-, -ə- ‖ -ər
  'floʊr-
floriculturist ˌflɔːr ɪ 'kʌltʃ ər‿ɪst ˌflɒr-, ˌ•ə-,
  §-əst ‖ ˌfloʊr- **~s** s
florid 'flɒr ɪd §-əd ‖ 'flɔːr- 'flɑːr- **~ly** li **~ness**
  nəs nɪs
Florida 'flɒr ɪd ə -əd- ‖ 'flɔːr- 'flɑːr-
  ˌFlorida 'Keys
Floridan 'flɒr ɪd ən -əd- ‖ 'flɔːr- 'flɑːr- **~s** z
Floridian flɒ 'rɪd i‿ən flə- ‖ flə- **~s** z
floridity flɒ 'rɪd ət i flɔː-, flə-, -ɪt- ‖ flə 'rɪd ət̬ i
  flɔː-
florin 'flɒr ɪn -ən ‖ 'flɔːr- 'flɑːr- **~s** z
Florio 'flɔːr i əʊ ‖ -oʊ 'floʊr-

florist 'flɒr ɪst 'flɔːr-, §-əst ‖ 'flɔːr- 'flɑːr-, 'floʊr- ~**s** s

floristry 'flɒr ɪs tri 'flɔːr-, -əs- ‖ 'flɔːr- 'flɑːr-, 'floʊr-

Florrie 'flɒr i ‖ 'flɔːr i 'flɑːr i

floruit 'flɒr u ɪt 'flɔːr- ‖ 'flɔːr- 'flɑːr-, 'floʊr-, -ju-

floss, Floss flɒs ‖ flɔːs flɑːs **flossed** flɒst ‖ flɔːst flɑːst **flosses** 'flɒs ɪz -əz ‖ 'flɔːs əz 'flɑːs- **flossing** 'flɒs ɪŋ ‖ 'flɔːs ɪŋ 'flɑːs-

Flossie 'flɒs i ‖ 'flɔːs i 'flɑːs i

floss|y 'flɒs |i ‖ 'flɔːs |i 'flɑːs- ~**ier** i‿ə ‖ i‿ᵊr ~**iest** i‿ɪst i‿əst ~**ily** ɪ li əl i ~**iness** i nəs i nɪs

flotation fləʊ 'teɪʃ ᵊn ‖ floʊ- ~**s** z

flote fləʊt ‖ floʊt

flotilla fləʊ 'tɪl ə ‖ floʊ- ~**s** z

flotsam 'flɒts əm ‖ 'flɑːts-

Flotta 'flɒt ə ‖ 'flɑːt̬ ə

flounce flaʊnts **flounced** flaʊntst **flounces** 'flaʊnts ɪz -əz **flouncing** 'flaʊnts ɪŋ

flounder 'flaʊnd ə ‖ -ᵊr ~**ed** d **floundering** 'flaʊnd_ᵊr ɪŋ ~**s** z

flour 'flaʊ‿ə ‖ 'flaʊ‿ᵊr (= flower) **floured** 'flaʊ‿əd ‖ 'flaʊ‿ᵊrd **flouring** 'flaʊ‿ər ɪŋ ‖ 'flaʊ‿ᵊr ɪŋ **flours** 'flaʊ‿əz ‖ 'flaʊ‿ᵊrz

flourish 'flʌr ɪʃ ‖ 'flɝː- ~**ed** t ~**es** ɪz əz ~**ing** ɪŋ

flourmill 'flaʊ‿ə mɪl ‖ 'flaʊ‿ᵊr- ~**s** z

floury 'flaʊ‿ər i ‖ 'flaʊ‿ᵊr i (= flowery)

flout flaʊt **flouted** 'flaʊt ɪd -əd ‖ 'flaʊt̬ əd **flouting** 'flaʊt ɪŋ ‖ 'flaʊt̬ ɪŋ **flouts** flaʊts

flow fləʊ ‖ floʊ **flowed** fləʊd ‖ floʊd **flowing/ly** 'fləʊ ɪŋ /li ‖ 'floʊ ɪŋ /li **flows** fləʊz ‖ floʊz
'flow ˌdiagram

flow|chart 'fləʊ |tʃɑːt ‖ 'floʊ |tʃɑːrt ~**charted** tʃɑːt ɪd -əd ‖ tʃɑːrt̬ əd ~**charting** tʃɑːt ɪŋ ‖ tʃɑːrt̬ ɪŋ ~**charts** tʃɑːts ‖ tʃɑːrts

flower 'flaʊ‿ə ‖ 'flaʊ‿ᵊr (= flour) **flowered** 'flaʊ‿əd ‖ 'flaʊ‿ᵊrd **flowering/s** 'flaʊ‿ər ɪŋ/z ‖ 'flaʊ‿ᵊr ɪŋ/z **flowers** 'flaʊ‿əz ‖ 'flaʊ‿ᵊrz
'flower girl; ˌflowering 'currant; 'flower ˌpower

flowerbed 'flaʊ‿ə bed ‖ 'flaʊ‿ᵊr- ~**s** z

flowerless 'flaʊ‿ə ləs -lɪs ‖ 'flaʊ‿ᵊr-

flowerpot 'flaʊ‿ə pɒt ‖ 'flaʊ‿ᵊr pɑːt ~**s** s

flower|y 'flaʊ‿ər i ‖ 'flaʊ‿ᵊr i ~**ier** i‿ə ‖ i‿ᵊr ~**iest** i‿ɪst i‿əst ~**ily** əl i ɪ li ~**iness** i nəs i nɪs

flown fləʊn ‖ floʊn

Floyd flɔɪd

flu fluː (= flew, flue)

flub flʌb **flubbed** flʌbd **flubbing** 'flʌb ɪŋ **flubs** flʌbz

Fluck flʌk

fluctu|ate 'flʌk tʃu |eɪt -tju- ~**ated** eɪt ɪd -əd ‖ eɪt̬ əd ~**ates** eɪts ~**ating** eɪt ɪŋ ‖ eɪt̬ ɪŋ

fluctuation ˌflʌk tʃu 'eɪʃ ᵊn -tju- ~**s** z

flue fluː (= flew) **flues** fluːz

fluellen, F~ flu 'el ɪn -ən

fluency 'fluː‿ənts i

fluent 'fluː‿ənt ~**ly** li

fluff flʌf **fluffed** flʌft **fluffing** 'flʌf ɪŋ **fluffs** flʌfs

fluff|y 'flʌf |i ~**ier** i‿ə ‖ i‿ᵊr ~**iest** i‿ɪst i‿əst ~**ily** ɪ li əl i ~**iness** i nəs i nɪs

flugelhorn, flügelhorn 'fluːg ᵊl hɔːn ‖ -hɔːrn ~**s** z

fluid 'fluː‿ɪd ~**ly** li ~**ness** nəs nɪs ~**s** z
ˌfluid 'ounce

fluidity flu 'ɪd ət i -ɪt- ‖ -ət̬ i

fluidis|e, fluidiz|e 'fluː‿ɪ daɪz ~**ed** d ~**es** ɪz əz ~**ing** ɪŋ

fluke fluːk **fluked** fluːkt **flukes** fluːks **fluking** 'fluːk ɪŋ

fluk|ey, fluk|y 'fluːk |i ~**ier** i‿ə ‖ i‿ᵊr ~**iest** i‿ɪst i‿əst

flume fluːm **flumed** fluːmd **flumes** fluːmz **fluming** 'fluːm ɪŋ

flummer|y 'flʌm ᵊr |i ~**ies** iz

flummox 'flʌm əks ~**ed** t ~**es** ɪz əz ~**ing** ɪŋ

flung flʌŋ

flunk flʌŋk **flunked** flʌŋkt **flunking** 'flʌŋk ɪŋ **flunks** flʌŋks

flunk|ey, flunk|y 'flʌŋk |i ~**eys**, ~**ies** iz

Fluon tdmk 'fluː ɒn ‖ -ɑːn

fluor 'fluː ɔː 'fluː‿ə ‖ -ɔːr -ᵊr

fluoresc|e flɔː 'res fluᵊ-, flə-; ˌfluː‿ə 'res ‖ floʊ-; ˌfluː ə 'res ~**ed** t ~**es** ɪz əz ~**ing** ɪŋ

fluoresc|ence flɔː 'res ᵊnts fluᵊ-, flə-; ˌfluː‿ə 'res- ‖ floʊ-; ˌfluː ə 'res- ~**ent** ᵊnt

fluoric flu 'ɒr ɪk ‖ -'ɔːr ɪk -'ɑːr ɪk

fluori|date 'flɔːr ɪ |deɪt -ə-; 'fluː‿ər ɪ deɪt, -ə deɪt ‖ 'flʊr- 'flɔːr-, 'floʊr- ~**dated** deɪt ɪd -əd ‖ deɪt̬ əd ~**dates** deɪts ~**dating** deɪt ɪŋ ‖ deɪt̬ ɪŋ

fluoridation ˌflɔːr ɪ 'deɪʃ ᵊn ˌfluː‿ər ɪ 'deɪʃ-, -ə'•- ‖ ˌflʊr- ˌflɔːr-, ˌfloʊr- ~**s** z

fluoride 'flʊər aɪd 'flɔːr-; 'fluː ə raɪd ‖ 'flʊr- 'flɔːr-, 'floʊr- ~**s** z

fluori|nate 'flɔːr ɪ neɪt 'fluː‿ər ɪ neɪt, -ə neɪt ‖ 'flʊr- 'flɔːr-, 'floʊr- ~**nated** neɪt ɪd -əd ‖ neɪt̬ əd ~**nates** neɪts ~**nating** neɪt ɪŋ ‖ neɪt̬ ɪŋ

fluorination ˌflɔːr ɪ 'neɪʃ ᵊn ˌfluː‿ər ɪ 'neɪʃ-, -ə 'neɪʃ- ‖ ˌflʊr- ˌflɔːr-, ˌfloʊr- ~**s** z

fluorine 'flʊər iːn 'flɔːr-, 'fluː ə riːn ‖ 'flʊr- 'flɔːr-, 'floʊr-

fluorite 'flʊər aɪt 'flɔːr-, 'fluː ə raɪt ‖ 'flʊr- 'flɔːr-, 'floʊr-

fluoro- comb. form
   with stress-neutral suffix ˌflʊər əʊ ˌflɔːr-; ˌfluː ə rəʊ ‖ ˌflʊr oʊ ˌflɔːr-, ˌfloʊr- —
   fluorocarbon ˌflʊər əʊ 'kɑːb ən ˌflɔːr-; ˌfluː ə rəʊ- ‖ ˌflʊr oʊ 'kɑːrb ən ˌflɔːr-, ˌfloʊr-
   with stress-imposing suffix flɔː ˌrɒ+ flʊə-, flə-; ˌfluː‿ə 'rɒ+ ‖ flu ˌrɑː+ flɔː-, floʊ- —
   fluoroscopy flɔː 'rɒsk əp i flʊᵊ-, flə-; ˌfluː‿ə'•- ‖ flu 'rɑːsk əp i flɔː-, floʊ-

fluorosis flɔː 'rəʊs ɪs flʊᵊ-, flə-; ˌfluː‿ə'•-, §-əs ‖ flu 'roʊs əs flɔː-, floʊ-

fluorspar 'flʊə spɑː 'flɔː-; 'fluː ə spɑː ‖ 'flʊr spɑːr 'fluː ᵊr spɑːr, -ɔːr-

fluothane 'fluː‿ə θeɪn

flurr|y, F~ 'flʌr |i ‖ 'flɝː |i ~ied id ~ies iz
    ~ying i_ɪŋ
flush flʌʃ flushed flʌʃt flusher 'flʌʃ ə ‖ -ᵊr
    flushes 'flʌʃ ɪz -əz flushest 'flʌʃ ɪst -əst
    flushing/s 'flʌʃ ɪŋ/z
Flushing 'flʌʃ ɪŋ
fluster 'flʌst ə ‖ -ᵊr ~ed d flustering 'flʌst
    ər_ɪŋ ~s z
flute fluːt fluted 'fluːt ɪd -əd ‖ 'fluːt̬ əd flutes
    fluːts fluting/s 'fluːt ɪŋ/z ‖ 'fluːt̬ ɪŋ/z
flutist 'fluːt ɪst §-əst ‖ 'fluːt̬ əst ~s s
flutter 'flʌt ə ‖ 'flʌt̬ ᵊr ~ed d fluttering
    'flʌt_ər ɪŋ ‖ 'flʌt̬ ᵊr ɪŋ ~s z
fluvial 'fluːv i_əl
flux flʌks fluxed flʌkst fluxes 'flʌks ɪz -əz
    fluxing 'flʌks ɪŋ
fluxion 'flʌk ʃᵊn ~s z
fly flaɪ flew fluː flies flaɪz flown
    fləʊn ‖ floʊn flying 'flaɪ ɪŋ
    ˌfly 'half; ˌflying 'boat; ˌflying 'buttress;
    ˌflying 'colours; ˌflying 'doctor; ˌflying
    'fish; ˌflying 'fox; ˌflying ma,chine; ˌflying
    ˌofficer; ˌflying 'picket; ˌflying 'saucer;
    'flying squad; ˌflying 'start
flyaway 'flaɪ ə ˌweɪ
flyback 'flaɪ bæk
flyblown 'flaɪ bləʊn ‖ -bloʊn
flyby 'flaɪ baɪ ~s z
fly-by-night 'flaɪ baɪ ˌnaɪt §-bɪ-, §-bə-
fly-by-wire ˌflaɪ baɪ 'waɪ_ə ◂ ‖ -'waɪ_ᵊr ◂
flycatcher 'flaɪ ˌkætʃ ə △-ˌketʃ- ‖ -ᵊr ~s z
fly-drive 'flaɪ draɪv ˌ•'• ~s z
flyer 'flaɪ_ə ‖ 'flaɪ_ᵊr ~s z
fly-fish 'flaɪ fɪʃ ~er/s ə/z ‖ ᵊr/z ~ing ɪŋ
fly|leaf 'flaɪ |liːf ~leaves liːvz
Flymo tdmk 'flaɪ məʊ ‖ -moʊ ~s z
Flynn flɪn
flyover 'flaɪ ˌəʊv ə ‖ -ˌoʊv ᵊr ~s z
flypaper 'flaɪ ˌpeɪp ə ‖ -ᵊr ~s z
flypast 'flaɪ pɑːst §-pæst ‖ -pæst ~s s
flypost 'flaɪ pəʊst ‖ -poʊst ~ed ɪd əd ~er/s
    ə/z ‖ ᵊr/z ~ing ɪŋ ~s s
flyscreen 'flaɪ skriːn ~s z
flysheet 'flaɪ ʃiːt ~s s
flyspeck 'flaɪ spek ~ed t ~s s
flyswatter 'flaɪ ˌswɒt ə ‖ -ˌswɑːt̬ ᵊr ~s z
Flyte flaɪt
flytrap 'flaɪ træp ~s s
flyweight 'flaɪ weɪt ~s s
flywheel 'flaɪ wiːᵊl -hwiːᵊl ‖ -hwiːᵊl ~s z
flywhisk 'flaɪ wɪsk -hwɪsk ‖ -hwɪsk ~s s
FM ˌef 'em ◂
    ˌFM 'radio
f-number 'ef ˌnʌm bə ‖ -bᵊr ~s z
FO ˌef 'əʊ ‖ -'oʊ
foal fəʊl →fɒʊl ‖ foʊl foaled fəʊld →fɒʊld
    ‖ foʊld foaling 'fəʊl ɪŋ →'fɒʊl- ‖ 'foʊl ɪŋ
    foals fəʊlz →fɒʊlz ‖ foʊlz
foam fəʊm ‖ foʊm foamed fəʊmd ‖ foʊmd
    foaming/ly 'fəʊm ɪŋ /li ‖ 'foʊm ɪŋ /li foams
    ˌfəʊmz ‖ foʊmz
    ˌfoam 'rubber◂

foam|y 'fəʊm |i ‖ 'foʊm |i ~ier i_ə ‖ i_ᵊr ~iest
    i_ɪst i_əst ~ily ɪ li əl i ~iness i nəs i nɪs
fob fɒb ‖ fɑːb fobbed fɒbd ‖ fɑːbd fobbing
    'fɒb ɪŋ ‖ 'fɑːb ɪŋ fobs fɒbz ‖ fɑːbz
    'fob watch
f.o.b. ˌef əʊ 'biː ‖ -oʊ-
focal 'fəʊk ᵊl ‖ 'foʊk ᵊl ~ly i
    ˌfocal 'length ‖ '•• •; 'focal point
focaccia, foccaccia fəʊ 'kætʃ i_ə ‖ foʊ 'kɑːtʃ-
    —It focaccia [fo 'kat tʃa]
Foch fɒʃ ‖ fɔːʃ fɑːʃ —Fr [fɔʃ]
Fochabers 'fɒk əb əz 'fɒx- ‖ 'fɑːk əb ᵊrz
foci 'fəʊs aɪ 'fəʊk-, -iː ‖ 'foʊs- 'foʊk-
foc's'le 'fəʊks ᵊl ‖ 'foʊks ᵊl ~s z
focus 'fəʊk əs ‖ 'foʊk əs ~ed, ~sed t ~es,
    ~ses ɪz əz ~ing, ~sing ɪŋ
fodder 'fɒd ə ‖ 'fɑːd ᵊr
Foden 'fəʊd ᵊn ‖ 'foʊd-
foe fəʊ ‖ foʊ foes fəʊz ‖ foʊz
foehn, föhn fɜːn ‖ feɪn —Ger [føːn]
foe|man 'fəʊ |mən ‖ 'foʊ- ~men mən men
foetal 'fiːt ᵊl ‖ 'fiːt̬ ᵊl
foetid 'fet ɪd 'fiːt-, §-əd ‖ 'fet̬ əd
foetus 'fiːt əs ‖ 'fiːt̬ əs ~es ɪz əz
fog fɒg ‖ fɑːg fɔːg fogged fɒgd ‖ fɑːgd fɔːgd
    fogging 'fɒg ɪŋ ‖ 'fɑːg ɪŋ 'fɔːg- fogs
    fɒgz ‖ fɑːgz fɔːgz
    'fog lamp, 'fog light
Fogarty 'fəʊg ət i ‖ 'foʊg ᵊrt̬ i
fogbank 'fɒg bæŋk ‖ 'fɑːg- 'fɔːg- ~s s
fogbound 'fɒg baʊnd ‖ 'fɑːg- 'fɔːg-
Fogerty 'fəʊg ət i ‖ 'foʊg ᵊrt̬ i
fogey 'fəʊg i ‖ 'foʊg i ~s z
Fogg fɒg ‖ fɑːg fɔːg
fogg|y 'fɒg |i ‖ 'fɑːg |i 'fɔːg- ~ier i_ə ‖ i_ᵊr
    ~iest i_ɪst i_əst ~ily ɪ li əl i ~iness i nəs i nɪs
    ˌFoggy 'Bottom
foghorn 'fɒg hɔːn ‖ 'fɑːg hɔːrn 'fɔːg- ~s z
fog|y 'fəʊg |i ‖ 'foʊg |i ~ies iz
fohn, föhn fɜːn ‖ feɪn —Ger [føːn]
foible 'fɔɪb ᵊl ~s z
foie gras ˌfwɑː 'grɑː —Fr [fwa ɡʁa]
foil fɔɪᵊl foiled fɔɪᵊld foiling 'fɔɪᵊl ɪŋ foils
    fɔɪᵊlz
foist fɔɪst foisted 'fɔɪst ɪd -əd foisting
    'fɔɪst ɪŋ foists fɔɪsts
Fokker 'fɒk ə ‖ 'fɑːk ᵊr ~s z
fold fəʊld →fɒʊld ‖ foʊld folded 'fəʊld ɪd
    →'fɒʊld-, -əd ‖ 'foʊld əd folding 'fəʊld ɪŋ
    →'fɒʊld- ‖ 'foʊld ɪŋ folds fəʊldz →fɒʊldz
    ‖ foʊldz
foldaway 'fəʊld ə ˌweɪ →'fɒʊld- ‖ 'foʊld-
folder 'fəʊld ə →'fɒʊld- ‖ 'foʊld ᵊr ~s z
folderol 'fɒld ə rɒl -ɪ- ‖ 'fɑːld ə rɑːl ~s z
foldout 'fəʊld aʊt →'fɒʊld- ‖ 'foʊld- ~s s
Foley 'fəʊl i ‖ 'foʊl i
Folger 'fəʊldʒ ə →'fɒʊldʒ- ‖ 'foʊldʒ ᵊr
folia 'fəʊl i_ə ‖ 'foʊl-
foliage 'fəʊl i_ɪdʒ ‖ 'foʊl- ~d d
    'foliage plant
foliar 'fəʊl i_ə ‖ 'foʊl i_ᵊr
foliate adj 'fəʊl i_ət ˌɪt, -eɪt ‖ 'foʊl-

F

foli|ate v 'fəul i ˌeɪt ‖ 'foul- ~ated eɪt ɪd -əd
‖ eɪt̬ əd ~ates eɪts ~ating eɪt ɪŋ ‖ eɪt̬ ɪŋ
foliation ˌfəul i 'eɪʃ ᵊn ‖ ˌfoul- ~s z
folic 'fəul ɪk 'fɒl- ‖ 'foul- 'fɑːl-
ˌfolic 'acid
folie à deux ˌfɒl i æ 'dɜː -i ɑː- ‖ foʊ ˌli: ə 'dʊ
fɑː- —Fr [fɔ li a dø]
folie de grandeur
ˌfɒl i də 'grɒnd ɜː ‖ foʊ ˌli: də grɑːn 'dɜː fɑː-
—Fr [fɔ li də gʁɑ̃ dœːʁ]
Folies Bergere, Folies Bergère ˌfɒl i bɜː 'ʒeə
-bə'•, -beə'• ‖ foʊ ˌli: ber 'ʒeᵊr —Fr
[fɔ li bɛʁ ʒɛːʁ]
folio 'fəul i‿əʊ ‖ 'foul i‿oʊ ~s z
foli|um 'fəul i‿ləm ‖ 'foul- ~a ə
Foljambe 'fʊldʒ əm
folk fəʊk §fəʊlk ‖ foʊk folks fəʊks §fəʊlks
‖ foʊks
'folk dance; 'folk ˌdancer; ˌfolk
ˌety'mology; 'folk ˌmedicine; 'folk ˌsinger;
'folk song
Folkestone 'fəʊkst ən ‖ 'foʊkst-
folklore 'fəʊk lɔː §'fəʊlk- ‖ 'foʊk lɔːr -loʊr
folklorist 'fəʊk lɔːr ɪst §'fəʊlk-, §-əst ‖ 'foʊk-
-loʊr- ~s s
folkloristic ˌfəʊk lɔː 'rɪst ɪk ◀ ‖ ˌfoʊk- -loʊ-
folks|y 'fəʊks li §'fəʊlks- ‖ 'foʊks li ~ier
i‿ə ‖ i‿ᵊr ~iest i‿ɪst i‿əst ~iness i nəs i nɪs
folktale 'fəʊk teɪᵊl §'fəʊlk- ‖ 'foʊk- ~s z
folkway 'fəʊk weɪ §'fəʊlk- ‖ 'foʊk- ~s z
Follett 'fɒl ɪt -ət ‖ 'fɑːl-
Follick 'fɒl ɪk ‖ 'fɑːl-
follicle 'fɒl ɪk ᵊl ‖ 'fɑːl- ~s z
follicular fɒ 'lɪk jʊl ə fə-, -jəl- ‖ fə 'lɪk jəl ᵊr
fɑː-
follie... —see folly
follow 'fɒl əʊ ‖ 'fɑːl oʊ ~ed d following
'fɒl əʊ ɪŋ -u‿ɪŋ ‖ 'fɑːl oʊ ɪŋ ~s z
follower 'fɒl əʊ ə -u‿ə ‖ 'fɑːl oʊ ᵊr ~s z
follow-my-leader ˌfɒl əʊ mə 'liːd ə -mɪ'•-,
-maɪ'• ‖ ˌfɑːl oʊ maɪ 'liːd ᵊr
follow-on ˌfɒl əʊ 'ɒn ‖ ˌfɑːl oʊ 'ɑːn -'ɔːn ~s z
follow-the-leader ˌfɒl əʊ
ðə 'liːd ə ‖ ˌfɑːl oʊ ðə 'liːd ᵊr
follow-through ˌfɒl əʊ 'θruː ‖ ˌfɑːl oʊ- ~s z
follow-up 'fɒl əʊ ʌp ‖ 'fɑːl oʊ- ~s s
foll|y 'fɒl li ‖ 'fɑːl li ~ies iz
Folsom (i) 'fəʊl səm →'fɒʊl- ‖ 'foʊl səm, (ii)
'fɒl- ‖ 'fɑːl- —The places in CA and NM are
(i); the family name may be either.
Fomalhaut 'fɒm ə laʊt 'fəʊm-, -əl hɔːt
‖ 'foʊm əl hɔːt -hɑːt; -ə loʊ
fo|ment fəʊ |'ment ‖ foʊ- '•• ~mented
'ment ɪd -əd ‖ 'ment̬ əd ~menting
'ment ɪŋ ‖ 'ment̬ ɪŋ ~ments 'ments
fomentation ˌfəʊm en 'teɪʃ ᵊn -ən- ‖ ˌfoʊm-
~s z
fond fɒnd ‖ fɑːnd fonder 'fɒnd ə ‖ 'fɑːnd ᵊr
fondest 'fɒnd ɪst -əst ‖ 'fɑːnd-
Fonda 'fɒnd ə ‖ 'fɑːnd ə
fondant 'fɒnd ənt ‖ 'fɑːnd- ~s s
fondl|e 'fɒnd ᵊl ‖ 'fɑːnd- ~ed d ~es z ~ing
‿ɪŋ

fond|ly 'fɒnd |li ‖ 'fɑːnd- ~ness nəs nɪs
fondu, fondue 'fɒnd ju: -u: ‖ fɑːn 'du: -'dju:,
'•• —Fr [fɔ̃ dy] ~s z
font fɒnt ‖ fɑːnt fonts fɒnts ‖ fɑːnts
Fontaine 'fɒnt eɪn ‖ fɑːn 'teɪn
Fontainebleau 'fɒnt ɪn bləʊ →-ɪm-, -ən-
‖ 'fɑːnt ɪn bloʊ △'faʊnt ᵊn blu: —Fr
[fɔ̃ tɛn blo]
Fontana tdmk fɒn 'tɑːn ə ‖ fɑːn 'tæn ə
fontanel, fontanelle ˌfɒnt ə 'nel ‖ ˌfɑːnt ᵊn 'el
'••• ~s z
Fonteyn (i) ˌ(ˌ)fɒn 'teɪn ‖ ˌ(ˌ)fɑːn-, (ii)
'fɒnt eɪn ‖ 'fɑːn teɪn —In AmE usually (i).
Foochow ˌfuː 'tʃaʊ —Chi Fúzhōu [²fu ¹tʂoʊ]
food fuːd §fʊd foods fuːdz §fʊdz
'food chain; 'food ˌpoisoning; 'food
ˌprocessor; 'food stamp
foodie 'fuːd i ~s z
foodstuff 'fuːd stʌf §'fʊd- ~s s
Fookes fuːks
fool fuːl fooled fuːld fooling 'fuːl ɪŋ fools
fuːlz
ˌfool's 'errand; ˌfool's 'paradise
fooler|y 'fuːl ᵊr li ~ies iz
foolhard|y 'fuːl ˌhɑːd li ‖ -ˌhɑːrd li ~ier
i‿ə ‖ i‿ᵊr ~iest i‿ɪst i‿əst ~ily ɪ li əl i ~iness
i nəs i nɪs
foolish 'fuːl ɪʃ ~ly li ~ness nəs nɪs
foolproof 'fuːl pruːf §-prʊf
foolscap 'fuːl skæp 'fuːlz kæp ~s s
Foord fɔːd ‖ fɔːrd foʊrd
foot, Foot fʊt feet fiːt footed 'fʊt ɪd -əd
‖ 'fʊt̬ əd footing 'fʊt ɪŋ ‖ 'fʊt̬ ɪŋ foots fʊts
'foot brake; 'foot fault; 'foot ˌsoldier
footag|e 'fʊt ɪdʒ ‖ 'fʊt̬ ɪdʒ ~es ɪz əz
foot-and-mouth ˌfʊt ᵊn 'maʊθ
ˌfoot-and-'mouth diˌsease
football 'fʊt bɔːl ‖ -bɑːl ~er/s ə/z ‖ ᵊr/z ~s z
'football ˌplayer; 'football pools
foot|bath 'fʊt |bɑːθ §-bæθ ‖ -|bæθ (not 'fʊd-)
~baths bɑːðz §bɑːθs, §bɑːθs, §bæðz ‖ bæðz
bæθs
footboard 'fʊt bɔːd ‖ -bɔːrd -boʊrd (not 'fʊd-)
~s z
footbridg|e 'fʊt brɪdʒ (not 'fʊd-) ~es ɪz əz
Footdee place in Grampian fʊt 'di: —locally
also 'fɪt i
Foote fʊt
-footed 'fʊt ɪd -əd ‖ 'fʊt̬ əd — splay-footed
ˌspleɪ 'fʊt ɪd ◀ -əd ‖ -'fʊt̬ əd ◀
footer n 'football', 'line at end of page'
'fʊt ə ‖ 'fʊt̬ ᵊr ~s z
-footer 'fʊt ə ‖ 'fʊt̬ ᵊr — six-footer
ˌsɪks 'fʊt ə ‖ -'fʊt̬ ᵊr
footfall 'fʊt fɔːl ‖ -fɑːl ~s z
foot-fault v 'fʊt fɔːlt -fɒlt ‖ -fɔːlt -fɑːlt ~ed ɪd
əd ~ing ɪŋ ~s s
foothill 'fʊt hɪl ~s z
foothold 'fʊt həʊld →-hɒʊld ‖ -hoʊld ~s z
footie 'fʊt i ‖ 'fʊt̬ i
footing 'fʊt ɪŋ ‖ 'fʊt̬ ɪŋ ~s z
footl|e 'fuːt ᵊl ‖ 'fuːt̬ ᵊl ~ed d ~es z ~ing ‿ɪŋ
footlight 'fʊt laɪt ~s s

footling 'fuːt lɪŋ
footloose 'fʊt luːs
foot|man 'fʊt |mən ~**men** mən
footmark 'fʊt mɑːk ‖ -mɑːrk ~**s** s
footnote 'fʊt nəʊt ‖ -noʊt ~**s** s
footpad 'fʊt pæd ~**s** z
foot|path 'fʊt |pɑːθ §-pæθ ‖ -|pæθ ~**paths**
  pɑːðz §pæθs, §pɑːθs, §pæðz ‖ pæðz pæθs
footplate 'fʊt pleɪt ~**man** mən mæn ~**men**
  mən men ~**s** s
foot-pound ˌfʊt 'paʊnd '·· ~**s** z
foot-pound-second ˌfʊt ˌpaʊnd 'sek ənd
  →-ŋd ~**s** z
footprint 'fʊt prɪnt ~**s** s
footrac|e 'fʊt reɪs ~**es** ɪz əz
footrest 'fʊt rest ~**s** s
footsie 'fʊts i
footslog 'fʊt slɒg ‖ -slɑːg ~**ged** d ~**ger/s** ə/
  z ‖ ər/z ~**ging** ɪŋ ~**s** z
footsore 'fʊt sɔː ‖ -sɔːr -soʊr ~**ness** nəs nɪs
footstep 'fʊt step ~**s** s
footstool 'fʊt stuːl ~**s** z
footsure 'fʊt ʃɔː -ʃʊə ‖ -ʃʊr -ʃɜ· ~**ness** nəs
  nɪs
footway 'fʊt weɪ ~**s** z
footwear 'fʊt weə ‖ -wer -wær
footwork 'fʊt wɜːk ‖ -wɜ·ːk
footy 'fʊt i ‖ 'fʊt̬ i
foo yong, foo yoong, foo young ˌfuː 'jʌŋ
  -'jɒŋ, -'jʊŋ ‖ -'jʌŋ -'jɔːŋ, -'jɑːŋ, -'jʊŋ
foozl|e 'fuːz əl ~**ed** d ~**er/s** ə/z ‖ ər/z ~**es** z
  ~**ing** ɪŋ
fop fɒp ‖ fɑːp **fops** fɒps ‖ fɑːps
fopper|y 'fɒp ər i ‖ 'fɑːp- ~**ies** iz
foppish 'fɒp ɪʃ ‖ 'fɑːp- ~**ly** li ~**ness** nəs nɪs
for *strong form* fɔː ‖ fɔːr, *weak form* fə ‖ fər —
  In both RP and GenAm ELISION gives rise to
  an occasional prevocalic weak form fr, *used*
  before weak vowels: stay for a week
  ˌsteɪ frə 'wiːk. *There is also a very casual or*
  rapid weak form f. *In RP some speakers also*
  have an occasional prevocalic strong form fɒr,
  used (if at all) only in the phrases for her fɒr ə,
  for him fɒr ɪm, for it fɒr ɪt, for us fɒr əs.
forag|e 'fɒr ɪdʒ ‖ 'fɔːr- 'fɑːr- ~**ed** d ~**er/s** ə/
  z ‖ ər/z ~**es** ɪz əz ~**ing** ɪŋ
  '**forage cap**
foramen fə 'reɪm en fɒ-, -ən ‖ -ən fɔː- ~**s** z
  foramina fə 'ræm ɪn ə fɒ-, -'reɪm-, §-ən-
foraminifer ˌfɒr ə 'mɪn ɪf ə -əf ə
  ‖ ˌfɔːr ə 'mɪn əf ər ˌfɑːr- ~**s** z
foraminif|era fə ˌræm ɪ 'nɪf |ər ə ˌfɒr əm-,
  ˌfɔːr əm-, -ə'·- ~**eral** ər əl ~**erous** ər əs
forasmuch fər ˌəz 'mʌtʃ ˌfɔːrəz 'mʌtʃ, ˌfɒr-
  ‖ ˌfɔːr əz 'mʌtʃ '···
foray v, n 'fɒr eɪ ‖ 'fɔːr eɪ 'fɑːr- ~**ed** d ~**ing** ɪŋ
  ~**s** z
forbad fə 'bæd fɔː- ‖ fər- fɔːr-
forbade fə 'bæd fɔː-, -'beɪd ‖ fər- fɔːr-
for|bear v *'hold oneself back'* fɔː |'beə fə-
  ‖ fɔːr |'beər fər-, -'bæər ~**bearing**
  'beər ɪŋ ‖ 'ber ɪŋ 'bær ɪŋ ~**bears**

'beəz ‖ 'beərz 'bæərz ~**bore** 'bɔː ‖ 'bɔːr
  -'boʊr ~**borne** 'bɔːn ‖ 'bɔːrn -'boʊrn
forbear n *'ancestor'* 'fɔː beə ‖ 'fɔːr ber 'foʊr-,
  -bær ~**s** z
forbearance fɔː 'beər ən's fə- ‖ fɔːr 'ber- fər-,
  -'bær-
Forbes fɔːbz 'fɔːb ɪs, -əs ‖ fɔːrbz —*in Scotland*
  usually as two syllables.
for|bid fə |'bɪd fɔː- ‖ fər- fɔːr- ~**bad** 'bæd
  ~**bade** 'bæd 'beɪd ~**bidden** 'bɪd ən
  ~**bidding** 'bɪd ɪŋ
  for,**bidden 'fruit**
forbidding fə 'bɪd ɪŋ fɔː- ‖ fər- fɔːr- ~**ly** li
  ~**ness** nəs nɪs
forbore fɔː 'bɔː ‖ fɔːr 'bɔːr -'boʊr
forborne fɔː 'bɔːn ‖ fɔːr 'bɔːrn -'boʊrn
Forbush 'fɔː bʊʃ ‖ 'fɔːr-
force fɔːs ‖ fɔːrs foʊrs **forced** fɔːst ‖ fɔːrst
  foʊrst **forces** 'fɔːs ɪz -əz ‖ 'fɔːrs əz 'foʊrs-
forcing 'fɔːs ɪŋ ‖ 'fɔːrs ɪŋ 'foʊrs-
  ,**forced 'march**; ,**force ma'jeure** mæ 'ʒɜː
  mə- ‖ mɑː 'ʒɜ·ː mæ-, mə- —*Fr*
  [fɔʁs ma ʒœːʁ]
force-|feed ˌfɔːs |'fiːd '·· ‖ ˌfɔːrs- ˌfoʊrs-
  ~**fed** 'fed ~**feeding** 'fiːd ɪŋ ~**feeds** 'fiːdz
forceful 'fɔːs fəl -fʊl ‖ 'fɔːrs- 'foʊrs- ~**ly** ˌi
  ~**ness** nəs nɪs
forcemeat 'fɔːs miːt ‖ 'fɔːrs- 'foʊrs-
forceps 'fɔːs eps -ɪps, -əps ‖ 'fɔːrs əps -eps
forcib|le 'fɔːs əb əl -ɪb- ‖ 'fɔːrs- 'foʊrs-
  ~**leness** əl nəs -nɪs ~**ly** li
ford, Ford fɔːd ‖ fɔːrd foʊrd **forded** 'fɔːd ɪd
  -əd ‖ 'fɔːrd əd 'foʊrd- **fording**
  'fɔːd ɪŋ ‖ 'fɔːrd ɪŋ 'foʊrd- **fords, Ford's**
  fɔːdz ‖ fɔːrdz foʊrdz
fordable 'fɔːd əb əl ‖ 'fɔːrd- 'foʊrd-
Forde fɔːd ‖ fɔːrd foʊrd
Fordham 'fɔːd əm ‖ 'fɔːrd- 'foʊrd-
Fordingbridge 'fɔːd ɪŋ brɪdʒ ‖ 'fɔːrd- 'foʊrd-
Fordyce 'fɔːd aɪs fɔː 'daɪs ‖ 'fɔːrd- —*in*
  Scotland ·'·
fore fɔː ‖ fɔːr foʊr (= *four*)
  ,**fore and 'aft**
fore- ˌfɔː ‖ ˌfɔːr- ˌfoʊr-
forearm v *'prepare'* ₍ₒ₎fɔːr 'ɑːm ‖ ₍ₒ₎fɔːr 'ɑːrm
  ₍ₒ₎foʊr- ~**ed** d ~**ing** ɪŋ ~**s** z
forearm n *'limb from elbow to wrist'* 'fɔːr
  ɑːm ‖ 'fɔːr ɑːrm 'foʊr- ~**s** z
forebear n *'ancestor'* 'fɔː beə ‖ 'fɔːr ber 'foʊr-,
  -bær ~**s** z
forebod|e fɔː 'bəʊd fə- ‖ fɔːr 'boʊd foʊr- ~**ed**
  ɪd əd ~**es** z ~**ing** ɪŋ
foreboding fɔː 'bəʊd ɪŋ fə- ‖ fɔːr 'boʊd ɪŋ
  foʊr- ~**ly** li ~**s** z
forebrain 'fɔː breɪn ‖ 'fɔːr- 'foʊr- ~**s** z
forecast v 'fɔː kɑːst §-kæst, ₍ₒ₎·'· ‖ 'fɔːr kæst
  'foʊr- ~**ed** ɪd əd ~**er/s** ə/z ‖ ər/z ~**ing** ɪŋ ~**s**
  s
forecast n 'fɔː kɑːst §-kæst ‖ 'fɔːr kæst 'foʊr-
  ~**s** s
forecastle 'fəʊks əl ‖ 'foʊks- ~**s** z
foreclos|e ₍ₒ₎fɔː 'kləʊz ‖ ₍ₒ₎fɔːr 'kloʊz ₍ₒ₎foʊr-
  ~**ed** d ~**es** ɪz əz ~**ing** ɪŋ

F

foreclosure ₍ₒ₎fɔː ˈkləʊʒ ə ‖ ₍ₒ₎fɔːr ˈkloʊʒ ᵊr
₍ₒ₎foʊr- ~s z
forecourt ˈfɔː kɔːt ‖ ˈfɔːr kɔːrt ˈfoʊr koʊrt ~s
s
foredeck ˈfɔː dek ‖ ˈfɔːr- ˈfoʊr- ~s s
foredoomed ₍ₒ₎fɔː ˈduːmd ‖ ₍ₒ₎fɔːr- ₍ₒ₎foʊr-
forefather ˈfɔː ˌfɑːð ə ‖ ˈfɔːr ˌfɑːð ᵊr ˈfoʊr- ~s
z
forefeet ˈfɔː fiːt ‖ ˈfɔːr- ˈfoʊr-
forefinger ˈfɔː ˌfɪŋ gə ‖ ˈfɔːr ˌfɪŋ gᵊr ˈfoʊr- ~s
z
fore|foot ˈfɔː |fʊt ‖ ˈfɔːr- ˈfoʊr- ~**feet** fiːt
forefront ˈfɔː frʌnt ‖ ˈfɔːr- ˈfoʊr-
fore|go ₍ₒ₎fɔː |ˈgəʊ ‖ ₍ₒ₎fɔːr |ˈgoʊ ₍ₒ₎foʊr- ~**goes**
ˈgəʊz ‖ ˈgoʊz ~**going** ˈgəʊ ɪŋ ‖ ˈgoʊ ɪŋ
~**gone** ˈgɒn §ˈgɔːn, §ˈgɑːn ‖ ˈgɔːn ˈgɑːn
~**went** ˈwent
foregoing adj 'preceding' ˈfɔː ˌgəʊ ɪŋ •ˈ••
‖ ₍ₒ₎fɔːr ˈgoʊ ɪŋ ₍ₒ₎foʊr-
foregoing ptcp 'giving up'
₍ₒ₎fɔː ˈgəʊ ɪŋ ₍ₒ₎fɔːr ˈgoʊ ɪŋ
foregone adj, 'certain' ˈfɔː gɒn §-ˈgɔːn, §-ˈgɑːn
‖ ˈfɔːr gɔːn ˈfoʊr-, -ˈgɑːn
ˌforegone conˈclusion
foregone pp 'given up' ₍ₒ₎fɔː gɒn §-ˈgɔːn,
§-ˈgɑːn ‖ ₍ₒ₎fɔːr ˈgɔːn -ˈgɑːn
foreground ˈfɔː graʊnd ‖ ˈfɔːr- ˈfoʊr- ~**ed** ɪd
əd ~**ing** ɪŋ ~s z
forehand ˈfɔː hænd ‖ ˈfɔːr- ˈfoʊr- ~**ed** ɪd əd
~s z

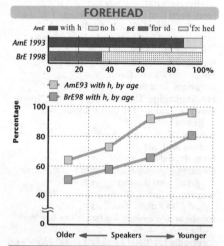

FOREHEAD

forehead ˈfɔː hed ˈfɒr ɪd -əd, -ed ‖ ˈfɔːr hed
ˈfoʊr-, -ed; ˈfɔːr əd, ˈfɑːr- —Poll panel
preferences: AmE 1993, with h 88%, no h 13%;
BrE 1998, ˈfɒr ɪd 35%, ˈfɔː hed 65%. Several
BrE respondents said they would have voted for
ˈfɒr ed, an option not offered. ~s z
foreign ˈfɒr ən -ɪn ‖ ˈfɔːr ən ˈfɑːr- ~**ness** nəs
nɪs
ˌforeign afˈfairs; ˌForeign ˈLegion; ˌforeign
ˈminister; ˈForeign ˌOffice; ˌForeign
ˈSecretary
foreigner ˈfɒr ən ə -ɪn- ‖ ˈfɔːr ən ᵊr ˈfɑːr- ~s z

foreknowledge ₍ₒ₎fɔː ˈnɒl ɪdʒ ‖ ₍ₒ₎fɔːr ˈnɑːl-
₍ₒ₎foʊr-
foreland, F~ ˈfɔː lənd ‖ ˈfɔːr- ˈfoʊr- ~s z
foreleg ˈfɔː leg ‖ ˈfɔːr- ˈfoʊr- ~s z
forelimb ˈfɔː lɪm ‖ ˈfɔːr- ˈfoʊr- ~s z
forelock ˈfɔː lɒk ‖ ˈfɔːr lɑːk ˈfoʊr- ~s s
fore|man, F~ ˈfɔː |mən ‖ ˈfɔːr- ˈfoʊr- ~**men**
mən men
foremast ˈfɔː mɑːst §-mæst, -məst
‖ ˈfɔːr mæst ˈfoʊr-, -məst —naut -məst ~s s
foremost ˈfɔː məʊst ‖ ˈfɔːr moʊst ˈfoʊr-
forename ˈfɔː neɪm ‖ ˈfɔːr- ˈfoʊr- ~s z
forenoon ˈfɔː nuːn §-nʊn ‖ ˈfɔːr- ˈfoʊr- ~s z
forensic fə ˈrenᵗs ɪk fɒ-, -ˈrenz- ~**ally** ᵊl_i
foˌrensic ˈscience
foreordain ˌfɔːr ɔː ˈdeɪn ‖ ˌfɔːr ɔːr- ˌfoʊr-
~**ed** d ~**ing** ɪŋ ~**ment** mənt ~s z
forepart ˈfɔː pɑːt ‖ ˈfɔːr pɑːrt ˈfoʊr- ~s s
forepaw ˈfɔː pɔː ‖ ˈfɔːr- ˈfoʊr-, -pɑː ~s z
foreplay ˈfɔː pleɪ ‖ ˈfɔːr- ˈfoʊr-
forerunner ˈfɔː ˌrʌn ə ‖ ˈfɔːr ˌrʌn ᵊr ˈfoʊr- ~s z
foresail ˈfɔː seɪᵊl -sᵊl ‖ ˈfɔːr- ˈfoʊr- —naut -sᵊl
~s z
fore|see ₍ₒ₎fɔː |ˈsiː fə- ₍ₒ₎fɔːr- ₍ₒ₎foʊr- ~**saw**
ˈsɔː ‖ ˈsɑː ~**seeing** ˈsiː ɪŋ ~**seen** ˈsiːn
foreseeable fɔː ˈsiː_əb ᵊl fə- ‖ ˈfɔːr- foʊr-
foreshadow ₍ₒ₎fɔː ˈʃæd əʊ ‖ ₍ₒ₎fɔːr ˈʃæd oʊ
₍ₒ₎foʊr- ~**ed** d ~**ing** ɪŋ ~s z
foreshore ˈfɔː ʃɔː ‖ ˈfɔːr ʃɔːr ˈfoʊr ʃoʊr ~s z
foreshorten ₍ₒ₎fɔː ˈʃɔːt ən ‖ ₍ₒ₎fɔːr ˈʃɔːrt ən
₍ₒ₎foʊr- ~**ed** d ~**ing** ɪŋ ~s z
foreshow ₍ₒ₎fɔː ˈʃəʊ ‖ ₍ₒ₎fɔːr ˈʃoʊ ~**ed** d ~**ing**
ɪŋ ~n n ~s z
foresight ˈfɔː saɪt ‖ ˈfɔːr- ˈfoʊr-
foreskin ˈfɔː skɪn ‖ ˈfɔːr- ˈfoʊr- ~s z
forest, F~ ˈfɒr ɪst -əst ‖ ˈfɔːr əst ˈfɑːr- ~s s
forestall ₍ₒ₎fɔː ˈstɔːl ‖ ₍ₒ₎fɔːr- ₍ₒ₎foʊr-, -ˈstɑːl
~**ed** d ~**ing** ɪŋ ~s z
forestation ˌfɒr ə ˈsteɪʃ ən -ɪ- ‖ ˌfɔːr- ˌfɑːr-
forester, F~ ˈfɒr ɪst ə -əst- ‖ ˈfɔːr əst ᵊr ˈfɑːr-
~s z
forestry ˈfɒr ɪst ri -əst- ‖ ˈfɔːr- ˈfɑːr-
foretaste n ˈfɔː teɪst ‖ ˈfɔːr- ˈfoʊr- ~s s
foretast|e v ₍ₒ₎fɔː ˈteɪst ‖ ₍ₒ₎fɔːr- ₍ₒ₎foʊr- ~**ed** ɪd
əd ~**es** s ~**ing** ɪŋ
fore|tell ₍ₒ₎fɔː |ˈtel ‖ ₍ₒ₎fɔːr- ₍ₒ₎foʊr- ~**telling**
ˈtel ɪŋ ~**tells** ˈtelz ~**told** ˈtəʊld →ˈtɒʊld
‖ ˈtoʊld
forethought ˈfɔː θɔːt ‖ ˈfɔːr- ˈfoʊr-, -θɑːt
foretold ₍ₒ₎fɔː ˈtəʊld →-ˈtɒʊld ‖ ₍ₒ₎fɔːr ˈtoʊld
₍ₒ₎foʊr-
forever fər ˈev ə ‖ fər ˈev ᵊr
forewarn ₍ₒ₎fɔː ˈwɔːn ‖ ₍ₒ₎fɔːr ˈwɔːrn ₍ₒ₎foʊr-
~**ed** d ~**ing** ɪŋ ~s z
forewent ₍ₒ₎fɔː ˈwent ‖ ₍ₒ₎fɔːr- ₍ₒ₎foʊr-
fore|woman ˈfɔː |ˌwʊm ən ‖ ˈfɔːr- ˈfoʊr-
~**women** ˌwɪm ɪn -ən
foreword ˈfɔː wɜːd ‖ ˈfɔːr wɜːd ˈfoʊr- ~s z
forex ˈfɔr eks ‖ ˈfɔːr- ˈfɑːr-
Forfar ˈfɔːf ə ‖ ˈfɔːrf ᵊr —also spelling
pronunciation ˈfɔː fɑː ‖ ˈfɔːr fɑːr
forf|eit n, v, adj ˈfɔːf |ɪt -ət ‖ ˈfɔːrf |ət ~**eited**

ɪt ɪd §ət-, -əd ‖ əʈ əd **~eiting** ɪt ɪŋ §ət-
‖ əʈ ɪŋ **~eits** ɪts §əts ‖ əts
forfeitable ˈfɔːf ɪt əb əl §ˈ•ət- ‖ ˈfɔːrf əʈ əb əl
forfeiter ˈfɔːf ɪt ə §-ət ə ‖ ˈfɔːrf əʈ ər **~s** z
forfeiture ˈfɔːf ɪtʃ ə §-ətʃ- ‖ ˈfɔːrf ətʃ ər
-ə tʃʊr, -tjʊr **~s** z
forfend fɔː ˈfend ‖ fɔːr- **~ed** ɪd əd **~ing** ɪŋ **~s**
z
forgather fɔː ˈɡæð ə ‖ fɔːr ˈɡæð ər **~ed** d
forgathering fɔː ˈɡæð ər_ɪŋ ‖ fɔːr- **~s** z
forgave fə ˈɡeɪv ‖ fər-
forge fɔːdʒ ‖ fɔːrdʒ foʊrdʒ **forged**
fɔːdʒd ‖ fɔːrdʒd foʊrdʒd **forges** ˈfɔːdʒ ɪz
-əz ‖ ˈfɔːrdʒ əz ˈfoʊrdʒ- **forging**
ˈfɔːdʒ ɪŋ ‖ ˈfɔːrdʒ ɪŋ ˈfoʊrdʒ-
forger ˈfɔːdʒ ə ‖ ˈfɔːrdʒ ər ˈfoʊrdʒ- **~s** z
forgery ˈfɔːdʒ ər_li ‖ ˈfɔːrdʒ- ˈfoʊrdʒ- **~ies** iz
for|get fə |ˈget ‖ fər- —*but in formal style
sometimes* fɔː- ‖ fɔːr- **~gets** ˈgets **~getting**
ˈget ɪŋ ‖ ˈgeʈ ɪŋ **~got** gɒt ‖ ˈgɑːt **~gotten**
ˈgɒt ən ‖ ˈgɑːt ən
forgetful fə ˈget fəl -fʊl ‖ fər- **~ly** i **~ness** nəs
nɪs
forget-me-not fə ˈget mi nɒt ‖ fər ˈget mi nɑːt
~s s
forgettable fə ˈget əb əl ‖ fər ˈgeʈ əb əl
forging ˈfɔːdʒ ɪŋ ‖ ˈfɔːrdʒ ɪŋ ˈfoʊrdʒ- **~s** z
forgivab|le fə ˈgɪv əb əl ‖ fər- fɔːr- **~ly** li
for|give fə |ˈgɪv ‖ fər- —*but in formal style
sometimes* fɔː- ‖ fɔːr- **~gave** ˈgeɪv **~given**
ˈgɪv ən **~gives** ˈgɪvz **~giving** ˈgɪv ɪŋ
forgiveness fə ˈgɪv nəs fɔː-,-nɪs ‖ fər- fɔːr-
forgiving fə ˈgɪv ɪŋ fɔː- ‖ fər- fɔːr- **~ly** li
~ness nəs nɪs
for|go (ˌ)fɔː |ˈgəʊ ‖ (ˌ)fɔːr |ˈgoʊ **~goes**
ˈgəʊz ‖ ˈgoʊz **~going** ˈgəʊ ɪŋ ‖ ˈgoʊ ɪŋ
~gone ˈgɒn §ˈgɔːn, §ˈgɑːn ‖ ˈgɔːn ˈgɑːn
~went ˈwent
forgot fə ˈgɒt ‖ fər ˈgɑːt **~ten** ən
forint ˈfɒr ɪnt §-ənt ‖ ˈfɔːr- —*Hungarian*
[ˈfo rint] **~s** s
fork fɔːk ‖ fɔːrk **forked** fɔːkt ‖ fɔːrkt **forking**
ˈfɔːk ɪŋ ‖ ˈfɔːrk ɪŋ **forks** fɔːks ‖ fɔːrks
ˌforked ˈlightning
forkful ˈfɔːk fʊl ‖ ˈfɔːrk- **~s** z
forklift ˈfɔːk lɪft ˌ•ˈ• ‖ ˈfɔːrk-
ˌfork-ˈlift ˈtruck ˈ• • •
forlorn fə ˈlɔːn (ˌ)fɔː- ‖ fər ˈlɔːrn ˌfɔːr- **~ly** li
~ness nəs nɪs
for ˌlorn ˈhope
form fɔːm ‖ fɔːrm **formed** fɔːmd ‖ fɔːrmd
forming ˈfɔːm ɪŋ ‖ ˈfɔːrm ɪŋ **forms**
fɔːmz ‖ fɔːrmz
formal ˈfɔːm əl ‖ ˈfɔːrm əl
formaldehyde fɔː ˈmæld ɪ haɪd -ə- ‖ fɔːr- fər-
formalin, F~ *tdmk* ˈfɔːm əl ɪn §-ən ‖ ˈfɔːrm-
-ə liːn
formalis... —*see* **formaliz...**
formalism ˈfɔːm ə ˌlɪz əm -əl ˌɪz- ‖ ˈfɔːrm- **~s**
z
formalist ˈfɔːm əl ɪst -əst ‖ ˈfɔːrm- **~s** s
formality fɔː ˈmæl ət li -ɪt- ‖ fɔːr ˈmæl əʈ li
~ies iz

formalization ˌfɔːm əl aɪ ˈzeɪʃ ən -ɪˈ•-
‖ ˌfɔːrm əl ə- **~s** z
formaliz|e ˈfɔːm ə laɪz -əl aɪz ‖ ˈfɔːrm- **~ed** d
~es ɪz əz **~ing** ɪŋ
formally ˈfɔːm əl i ‖ ˈfɔːrm-
formant ˈfɔːm ənt ‖ ˈfɔːrm- **~s** s
ˈformant ˌstructure
form|at *n, v* ˈfɔːm læt ‖ ˈfɔːrm- **~ats** æts
~atted æt ɪd -əd ‖ æʈ əd **~atting**
æt ɪŋ ‖ æʈ ɪŋ
for|mate *v* 'take one's place in a formation'
fɔː |ˈmeɪt ‖ ˈfɔːr|m eɪt **~mated** meɪt ɪd -əd
‖ meɪʈ əd **~mates** meɪts **~mating**
meɪt ɪŋ ‖ meɪʈ ɪŋ
formate *n* 'salt or ester of formic acid'
ˈfɔːm eɪt ‖ ˈfɔːrm- **~s** s
formation fɔː ˈmeɪʃ ən ‖ fɔːr- **~al** _əl **~s** z
formative ˈfɔːm ət ɪv ‖ ˈfɔːrm əʈ ɪv **~ly** li
~ness nɪs **~s** z
formatter ˈfɔːm æt ə ‖ ˈfɔːrm æʈ ər **~s** z
formbook ˈfɔːm bʊk ‖ ˈfɔːrm- **~s** s
Formby ˈfɔːm bi ‖ ˈfɔːrm-
forme fɔːm ‖ fɔːrm (= *form*) **formes**
fɔːmz ‖ fɔːrmz
former ˈfɔːm ə ‖ ˈfɔːrm ər **~s** z
formerly ˈfɔːm ə li -əl i ‖ ˈfɔːrm ər-
formic ˈfɔːm ɪk ‖ ˈfɔːrm-
ˌformic ˈacid
Formica *tdmk*, **f~** fɔː ˈmaɪk ə ‖ fɔːr-

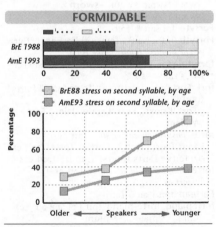

FORMIDABLE

	ˈ• • • •	ˌ• ˈ• •
BrE 1988		
AmE 1993		

0 20 40 60 80 100%

■ BrE88 stress on second syllable, by age
■ AmE93 stress on second syllable, by age

Percentage 100 80 60 40 20 0

Older ◄── Speakers ──► Younger

formidab|le ˈfɔːm ɪd əb əl ˌ• ˈ• • əd-; fə ˈmɪd-, fɔː-
‖ ˈfɔːrm- fər ˈmɪd-, fɔːr- —*Also in an
imitated French form,* ˌfɔːm ɪ ˈdɑːbə_l ‖ ˌfɔːrm-
—*Fr* [fɔʁ mi dabl] —*Poll panel preferences:
BrE 1988,* ˈ• • • • *46%,* ˌ• ˈ• • • *54%; AmE 1993,*
ˈ• • • • *68%,* ˌ• ˈ• • • *32%.* **~ly** li
formless ˈfɔːm ləs -lɪs ‖ ˈfɔːrm- **~ly** li **~ness**
nəs nɪs
Formos|a fɔː ˈməʊs ə -ˈməʊz- ‖ fɔːr ˈmoʊs ə
~an/s ən/z
form|ula ˈfɔːm |jʊl ə -jəl ə ‖ ˈfɔːrm |jəl ə
~ulae ju liː jə-, -laɪ ‖ jə liː **~ulas** jʊl əz
jəl əz ‖ jəl əz
formulaic ˌfɔːm ju ˈleɪ ɪk ◄ -jə- ‖ ˌfɔːrm jə-
~ally əl_i

formular|y ˈfɔːm jʊl ər |i ˈ‿jəl-
‖ ˈfɔːrm jə ler |i ~ies iz
formu|late ˈfɔːm ju |leɪt -jə- ‖ ˈfɔːrm jə-
~lated leɪt ɪd -əd ‖ leɪt̬ əd ~lates leɪts
~lating leɪt ɪŋ ‖ leɪt̬ ɪŋ
formulation ˌfɔːm ju ˈleɪʃ ən -jə- ‖ ˌfɔːrm jə-
~s z
Fornax ˈfɔːn æks ‖ ˈfɔːrn-
Forney ˈfɔːn i ‖ ˈfɔːrn i
forni|cate ˈfɔːn ɪ |keɪt -ə- ‖ ˈfɔːrn- ~cated
keɪt ɪd -əd ‖ keɪt̬ əd ~cates keɪts ~cating
keɪt ɪŋ ‖ keɪt̬ ɪŋ
fornication ˌfɔːn ɪ ˈkeɪʃ ən -ə- ‖ ˌfɔːrn- ~s z
fornicator ˈfɔːn ɪ keɪt ə ˈ‿ə- ‖ ˈfɔːrn ə keɪt̬ ər
~s z
fornix ˈfɔːn ɪks ‖ ˈfɔːrn- fornices ˈfɔːn ɪ siːz
-ə- ‖ ˈfɔːrn-
forrader, forrarder ˈfɒr əd ə ‖ ˈfɔːr əd ər ˈfɑːr-
Forres ˈfɒr ɪs -əs ‖ ˈfɔːr- ˈfɑːr-
Forrest ˈfɒr ɪst -əst ‖ ˈfɔːr- ˈfɑːr-
Forrester ˈfɒr ɪst ə -əst- ‖ ˈfɔːr əst ər ˈfɑːr-
for|sake fə ˈseɪk fɔː- ‖ fər- fɔːr- ~saken ˈseɪk
ən ~sakes ˈseɪks ~saking ˈseɪk ɪŋ ~sook
ˈsʊk
forsooth fə ˈsuːθ fɔː- ‖ fər- fɔːr-
Forster ˈfɔːst ə ˈfɒst- ‖ ˈfɔːrst ər
for|swear ₍ˌ₎fɔː ˈsweə ₍ˌ₎fɔːr ˈsweər -ˈswæər
~swearing ˈsweər ɪŋ ‖ ˈswer ɪŋ ˈswær ɪŋ
~swears ˈsweəz ‖ ˈsweərz ˈswæərz ~swore
ˈswɔː ‖ ˈswɔːr ˈswoʊr ~sworn
ˈswɔːn ‖ ˈswɔːrn ˈswoʊrn
Forsyte ˈfɔː saɪt ‖ ˈfɔːr-
Forsyth (i) fɔː ˈsaɪθ ‖ fɔːr-, (ii) ˈfɔː saɪθ ‖ ˈfɔːr-
—The Scottish family name is (i).
forsythia fɔː ˈsaɪθ i‿ə fə-, -ˈsɪθ- ‖ fɔːr ˈsɪθ i‿ə
fər-, -ˈsaɪθ- ~s z
fort, Fort fɔːt ‖ fɔːrt foʊrt forts fɔːts ‖ fɔːrts
foʊrts
₍ˌ₎Fort ˈKnox; ₍ˌ₎Fort ˈLauderdale; ₍ˌ₎Fort
ˈWilliam
forte 'positive characteristic' ˈfɔːt eɪ -i; fɔːt
‖ fɔːrt foʊrt; ˈfɔːrt̬ i, ˈfɔːrt eɪ fortes ˈfɔːt eɪz
-iz; fɔːts ‖ fɔːrts foʊrts; ˈfɔːrt̬ iz, ˈfɔːrt eɪz
forte loud, Forte family name ˈfɔːt eɪ -i
‖ ˈfɔːrt eɪ ~s z
Fortean ˈfɔːt i‿ən ‖ ˈfɔːrt̬-
fortepiano, forte-piano ˌfɔːt i pi ˈæn əʊ ˌ‿eɪ-,
-ˈɑːn-; ˌ‿‿ˈpjæn-, ˌ‿‿ˈpjɑːn-
‖ ˌfɔːrt̬ i pi ˈɑːn oʊ ˌfɔːrt eɪ- ~s z
fortes —see forte, fortis
Fortescue ˈfɔːt ɪ skjuː -ə- ‖ ˈfɔːrt̬-
forth, Forth fɔːθ ‖ fɔːrθ foʊrθ
forthcoming ₍ˌ₎fɔːθ ˈkʌm ɪŋ ‖ ₍ˌ₎fɔːrθ- ₍ˌ₎foʊrθ-
~ness nəs nɪs
forthright ˈfɔːθ raɪt ˌ‿ˈ‿ ‖ ˈfɔːrθ- ˈfoʊrθ- ~ly
li ~ness nəs nɪs
forthwith ˌfɔːθ ˈwɪθ -ˈwɪð ‖ ˌfɔːrθ- ˌfoʊrθ-
forties, F~ ˈfɔːt iz §-tiz ‖ ˈfɔːrt̬ iz
fortieth ˈfɔːt i‿əθ ‿ɪθ ‖ ˈfɔːrt̬ i‿əθ ~s s
fortifiable ˈfɔːt ɪ faɪˌəb əl ˈ‿ə-, ˌ‿‿ˈ‿‿‿
‖ ˈfɔːrt̬ ə-
fortification ˌfɔːt ɪf ɪ ˈkeɪʃ ən ˌ‿əf-, §-əˈ‿‿
‖ ˌfɔːrt̬ əf- ~s z

forti|fy ˈfɔːt ɪ |faɪ -ə- ‖ ˈfɔːrt̬ ə- ~fied faɪd
~fier/s faɪ‿ə/z ‖ faɪ‿ər/z ~fies faɪz ~fying
faɪ ɪŋ
Fortinbras ˈfɔːt ɪn bræs →-ɪm-, §-ən-
‖ ˈfɔːrt̬ ən-
fortis ˈfɔːt ɪs §-əs ‖ ˈfɔːrt̬ əs fortes ˈfɔːt iːz
-eɪz ‖ ˈfɔːrt̬-
fortissimo fɔː ˈtɪs ɪ məʊ -ə- ‖ fɔːr ˈtɪs ə moʊ
~s z
fortitude ˈfɔːt ɪ tjuːd -ə-, →§-tʃuːd
‖ ˈfɔːrt̬ ə tuːd -tjuːd
fortnight ˈfɔːt naɪt ‖ ˈfɔːrt- ˈfoʊrt- ~s s
fortnight|ly ˈfɔːt naɪt |li ‖ ˈfɔːrt- ˈfoʊrt- ~lies
liz
Fortnum ˈfɔːt nəm ‖ ˈfɔːrt- ~'s z
Fortran, FORTRAN ˈfɔː træn ‖ ˈfɔːr-
fortress ˈfɔːtr əs -ɪs ‖ ˈfɔːrtr əs ~es ɪz əz
fortuitous fɔː ˈtjuː‿ɪt əs →§-ˈtʃuː‿, ət-,
⚠ˌfɔːtʃ u ˈɪʃ əs ◄ ‖ fɔːr ˈtuː‿ət əs fər-, -ˈtjuː-
~ly li ~ness nəs nɪs
fortunate ˈfɔːtʃ ən‿ət‿ɪt ‖ ˈfɔːrtʃ- ~ly li
fortune ˈfɔːtʃ ən -uːn; ˈfɔːt juːn ‖ ˈfɔːrtʃ ən ~s
z
ˈfortune ˌhunter
fortune-tell|er/s ˈfɔːtʃ ən ˌtel ə/z -uːn-;
ˈfɔːt juːn- ‖ ˈfɔːrtʃ ən ˌtel ər/z ~ing ɪŋ
fort|y, Forty ˈfɔːt |i §ˈfɔːt t|i ‖ ˈfɔːrt̬ |i ~ies iz
ˌforty ˈwinks
forty-five ˌfɔːt i ˈfaɪv ◄ §-ti- ‖ ˌfɔːrt̬ i- ~s z
forty-niner ˌfɔːt i ˈnaɪn ə §-ti- ‖ ˌfɔːrt̬ i ˈnaɪn ər
~s z
forum ˈfɔːr əm ‖ ˈfoʊr- ~s z
forward ˈfɔː wəd ‖ ˈfɔːr wərd —but the
adjective and adverb, in BrE nautical use, are
ˈfɒr əd ~ed ɪd əd ~ing ɪŋ ~s z
forward-looking ˌfɔː wəd ˈlʊk ɪŋ ◄ ˌ‿‿ˈ‿‿
‖ ˌfɔːr wərd-
ˌforward-ˌlooking ˈpolicies
forward|ly ˈfɔː wəd |li ‖ ˈfɔːr wərd |li ~ness
nəs nɪs
forwards ˈfɔː wədz ‖ ˈfɔːr wərdz
forwent ₍ˌ₎fɔː ˈwent ‖ ₍ˌ₎fɔːr-
Fosbury ˈfɒz bər i ‖ ˈfɑːz ˌber i
ˌFosbury ˈflop
Fosdick ˈfɒz dɪk ‖ ˈfɑːz-
Fosdyke ˈfɒz daɪk ‖ ˈfɑːz-
foss, Foss fɒs ‖ fɑːs fosses ˈfɒs ɪz -əz
‖ ˈfɑːs əz
foss|a ˈfɒs |ə ‖ ˈfɑːs |ə ~ae iː ~as əz
fosse, Fosse fɒs ‖ fɑːs fosses ˈfɒs ɪz -əz
‖ ˈfɑːs əz
ˌFosse ˈWay
fossick ˈfɒs ɪk ‖ ˈfɑːs- ~ed t ~er/s ə/z ər/z
~ing ɪŋ ~s s
fossil ˈfɒs əl -ɪl ‖ ˈfɑːs əl ~s z
fossilis... —see fossiliz...
fossilization ˌfɒs əl aɪ ˈzeɪʃ ən ˌ‿ɪl-, -ɪˈ‿‿
‖ ˌfɑːs əl ə- ~s z
fossiliz|e ˈfɒs əl aɪz -ɪ laɪz ‖ ˈfɑːs- ~ed d ~es
ɪz əz ~ing ɪŋ
foster, F~ ˈfɒst ə ‖ ˈfɑːst ər ~ed d fostering
ˈfɒst ər‿ɪŋ ‖ ˈfɑːst ər ɪŋ ~s z

foster- 'fɒst ə ‖ 'faːst ᵊr — **foster-brother**
  'fɒst ə ˌbrʌð ə ‖ 'faːst ᵊr ˌbrʌð ᵊr
fosterage 'fɒst ᵊr ɪdʒ ‖ 'faːst-
fosterling 'fɒst ə lɪŋ ‖ 'faːst ᵊr- ~s z
Fothergill 'fɒð ə gɪl ‖ 'faːð ᵊr-
Fotheringay, Fotheringhay 'fɒð
  ᵊr_ɪŋ geɪ ‖ 'faːð- —*but the Northants village
  is nowadays called* -heɪ
Fotheringham 'fɒð ᵊr_ɪŋ əm ‖ 'faːð ᵊr_ɪŋ hæm
Foucault 'fuːk əʊ ₍ᵢ₎fuː 'kəʊ ‖ fuː 'koʊ —*Fr*
  [fu ko]
fouetté 'fuːˌ_ə teɪ ‖ ˌfuː ə 'teɪ —*Fr* [fwɛ te] ~s
  z
fought fɔːt ‖ faːt
foul faʊl (= *fowl*), **fouled** faʊld **fouler**
  'faʊl ə ‖ -ᵊr **foulest** 'faʊl ɪst -əst **fouling**
  'faʊl ɪŋ **foully** 'faʊl li -i **fouls** faʊlz
  ˌfoul 'play
Foula 'fuːl ə
foulard 'fuːl ɑː -aːd; fu 'laː, -'laːd ‖ fu 'laːrd
  ~s z
Foulds fəʊldz →fɒʊldz ‖ foʊldz
Foulkes (i) fəʊks ‖ foʊks, (ii) faʊks
foul-mouthed ˌfaʊl 'maʊðd ◄ ‖ -'maʊθt ◄
foulness 'faʊl nəs -nɪs ~es ɪz əz
Foulness ˌfaʊl 'nes
foul-up 'faʊl ʌp ~s s
found faʊnd **founded** 'faʊnd ɪd -əd
  founding 'faʊnd ɪŋ **founds** faʊndz
  ˌfounding 'father
foundation faʊn 'deɪʃ ᵊn ~s z
  foun'dation course; foun'dation ˌgarment;
  foun'dation stone
foundationer faʊn 'deɪʃ ᵊn_ə ‖ _ᵊr ~s z
founder 'faʊnd ə ‖ -ᵊr ~ed d **foundering**
  'faʊnd_ᵊr ɪŋ ~s z
foundling 'faʊnd lɪŋ ~s z
foundry 'faʊndr |i ~ies iz
fount '*spring, origin*' faʊnt **founts** faʊnts
fount '*set of printing type*' fɒnt faʊnt ‖ faːnt
  faʊnt **founts** fɒnts faʊnts ‖ faːnts faʊnts
fountain 'faʊnt ɪn -ᵊn ‖ 'faʊnt ᵊn ~s z
  'fountain pen; ˌFountains 'Abbey
Fountain, Fountaine 'faʊnt ɪn -ᵊn ‖ 'faʊnt ᵊn
fountainhead 'faʊnt ɪn hed -ᵊn-, ˌ•••
  ‖ 'faʊnt ᵊn- ~s z
four fɔː ‖ fɔːr **four** (= *fore*) **fours** fɔːz ‖ fɔːrz
  fɔʊrz
  'four flush; ˌfour 'hundred◄
Fourcin 'fɔːs ɪn §-ᵊn ‖ 'fɔːrs-
foureyes 'fɔːr aɪz ‖ 'fɔːr- 'foʊr-
fourfold 'fɔː fəʊld →-fɒʊld ‖ 'fɔːr foʊld 'foʊr-
four-footed ˌfɔː 'fʊt ɪd ◄ -əd ‖ ˌfɔːr 'fʊt ᵊd ◄
  ˌfour-
Fourier 'fʊr i_ə 'fʊər-, -eɪ ‖ 'fʊr i eɪ -i_ᵊr —*Fr*
  [fu ʁje]
four-in-hand ˌfɔːr ɪn 'hænd §-ᵊn- ‖ ˌfɔːr ᵊn-
  ˌfour-
four-leaved ˌfɔː 'liːvd ◄ ‖ ˌfɔːr- ˌfour-
  ˌfour-leaved 'clover
four-legged ˌfɔː 'leg ɪd ◄ -əd; -'legd ◄ ‖ ˌfɔːr-
  ˌfour-

four-letter ˌfɔː 'let ə ◄ ‖ ˌfɔːr 'let̬ ᵊr ◄ ˌfour-
  ˌfour-ˌletter 'word
four-o'clock ˌfɔːr ə 'klɒk ◄ ‖ ˌfɔːr ə 'klaːk ◄
  ˌfour-
four-part ˌfɔː 'paːt ◄ ‖ ˌfɔːr 'paːrt ◄ ˌfour-
fourpence 'fɔːp ᵊnts →-mᵖs; 'fɔː pents, ˌ•'•
  ‖ 'fɔːrp- 'foʊrp-
fourpenny 'fɔːp ᵊn_i ‖ 'fɔːr ˌpen i 'foʊr-
four-poster ˌfɔː 'pəʊst ə ◄ ‖ ˌfɔːr 'poʊst ᵊr ◄
  ˌfour- ~s z
  ˌfour-ˌposter 'bed
four-pounder ˌfɔː 'paʊnd ə ‖ ˌfɔːr 'paʊnd ᵊr
  ˌfour- ~s z
fourscore ˌfɔː 'skɔː ◄ ˌ•• ‖ ˌfɔːr 'skɔːr ◄
  ˌfour 'skoʊr
  ˌfourscore and 'ten
foursome 'fɔː səm ‖ 'fɔːr- 'foʊr- ~s z
foursquare ˌfɔː 'skweə ◄ ˌ•• ‖ ˌfɔːr 'skweᵊr ◄
  ˌfour-, -'skwæᵊr
four-star 'fɔː staː ‖ 'fɔːr staːr 'foʊr-
four-stroke 'fɔː strəʊk ‖ 'fɔːr stroʊk 'foʊr-
fourteen ˌfɔː 'tiːn ◄ §ˌfɔːt- ‖ ˌfɔːr- ˌfɔːrt-,
  ˌfour-, ˌfoʊrt- ~s z
fourteenth ˌfɔː 'tiːntθ ◄ §ˌfɔːt- ‖ ˌfɔːr- ˌfɔːrt-,
  ˌfour-, ˌfoʊrt- ~s s
fourth fɔːθ ‖ fɔːrθ foʊrθ (= *forth*) **fourthly**
  'fɔːθ li ‖ 'fɔːrθ li 'foʊrθ- **fourths**
  fɔːθs ‖ fɔːrθs foʊrθs
  ˌfourth di'mension; ˌfourth e'state;
  ˌFourth of Ju'ly
four-wheel ˌfɔː 'wiːᵊl ◄ -'hwiːᵊl ‖ ˌfɔːr 'hwiːᵊl ◄
  ˌfour-
  ˌfour-wheel 'drive
four-wheeler ˌfɔː 'wiːl ə ◄ -'hwiːl-
  ‖ ˌfɔːr 'hwiːl ᵊr ◄ ˌfour- ~s z
fovea 'fəʊv i_ə 'fɒv- ‖ 'foʊv- ~ae iː
Foveaux fə 'vəʊ ‖ -'voʊ
Fowey fɔɪ
Fowke (i) fəʊk ‖ foʊk, (ii) faʊk
Fowkes (i) fəʊks ‖ foʊks, (ii) faʊks
fowl faʊl **fowls** faʊlz
  'fowl pest
fowler, F~ 'faʊl ə ‖ -ᵊr ~s z
Fowles faʊlz
Fowlmere 'faʊl mɪə ‖ -mɪr
fox, Fox fɒks ‖ faːks **foxed** fɒkst ‖ faːkst
  foxes 'fɒks ɪz -əz ‖ 'faːks əz **foxing**
  'fɒks ɪŋ ‖ 'faːks ɪŋ
  'fox ˌterrier
Foxcroft 'fɒks krɒft ‖ 'faːks krɔːft -kraːft
Foxe fɒks ‖ faːks
foxfire 'fɒks ˌfaɪ_ə ‖ 'faːks ˌfaɪ_ᵊr
foxglove 'fɒks glʌv ‖ 'faːks- ~s z
foxhole 'fɒks həʊl →-hɒʊl ‖ 'faːks hoʊl ~s z
foxhound 'fɒks haʊnd ‖ 'faːks- ~s z
foxhunt 'fɒks hʌnt ‖ 'faːks- ~s s
foxhunt|er/s, F~ 'fɒks ˌhʌnt |ə/z ‖ 'faːks ˌhʌnt̬
  |ᵊr/z ~ing ɪŋ
foxi... —*see* **foxy**
foxtail 'fɒks teɪᵊl ‖ 'faːks- ~s z
Foxton 'fɒkst ᵊn ‖ 'faːkst-
foxtrot 'fɒks trɒt ‖ 'faːks traːt ~s s

F

fox|y 'fɒks |i ‖ 'fɑːks |i ~ier i_ə ‖ i_ᵊr ~iest
i_ɪst i_əst ~ily ɪ li əl i ~iness i nəs i nɪs
Foy fɔɪ
foyer 'fɔɪ eɪ -ə; 'fwaɪ eɪ ‖ 'fɔɪ ᵊr -eɪ; 'fwaː jeɪ
—Fr [fwa je] ~s z
Foyle fɔɪᵊl Foyles, Foyle's fɔɪᵊlz
Fra frɑː —It [fra]
frabjous 'fræb dʒəs
fracas sing. 'fræk ɑː ‖ 'freɪk əs 'fræk- (*)
fracas pl 'fræk ɑːz ‖ 'feɪk əs 'fræk- ~es ɪz
əz
fractal 'frækt ᵊl ~s z
fraction 'fræk ʃᵊn ~s z
fractional 'fræk ʃᵊn_əl ~ly i
fractio|nate 'fræk ʃə |neɪt ~nated neɪt ɪd -əd
‖ neɪt̬ əd ~nates neɪts ~nating
neɪt ɪŋ ‖ neɪt̬ ɪŋ
fractionation ˌfræk ʃə 'neɪʃ ᵊn ~s z
fractionator 'fræk ʃə neɪt ə ‖ -neɪt̬ ᵊr ~s z
fractious 'fræk ʃəs ~ly li ~ness nəs nɪs
fracture 'fræk tʃə -ʃə ‖ -tʃᵊr -ʃᵊr ~d d
fracturing 'fræk tʃᵊr_ɪŋ -ʃᵊr_ ~s z
frag fræg fragged frægd fragging 'fræg ɪŋ
frags frægz
fragile 'frædʒ aɪᵊl ‖ -ᵊl (*) ~ly li ~ness nəs nɪs
fragility frə 'dʒɪl ət i fræ-, -ɪt- ‖ -ət̬ i
fragment n 'fræg mənt ~s s
frag|ment v ₍ₒ₎fræg |'ment ‖ '•|• ~mented
'ment ɪd -əd ‖ 'ment̬ əd ~menting
'ment ɪŋ ‖ 'ment̬ ɪŋ ~ments 'ments
fragmental fræg 'ment ᵊl ‖ -'ment̬ ᵊl
fragmentary 'fræg mənt_ər i fræg 'ment-
‖ 'fræg mən ter i
fragmentation ˌfræg mən 'teɪʃ ᵊn -men- ~s z
Fragonard 'fræg ə nɑː -ɒ- ‖ ˌfrɑːg oʊ 'nɑːr
ˌfræg-, -ə- —Fr [fʁa gɔ naːʁ]
fragranc|e 'freɪg rᵊn|ts ~es ɪz əz
fragrant 'freɪg rᵊnt ~ly li ~ness nəs nɪs
frail freɪᵊl frailer 'freɪᵊl ə ‖ -ᵊr frailest
'freɪᵊl ɪst -əst frailly 'freɪᵊl li frailness
'freɪl nəs -nɪs
frail|ty 'freɪᵊl |ti ~ties tiz
Frain freɪn
frame, Frame freɪm framed freɪmd framer/s
'freɪm ə/z ‖ -ᵊr/z frames freɪmz framing
'freɪm ɪŋ
ˌframe of 'mind; ˌframe of 'reference
frame-up 'freɪm ʌp ~s s
framework 'freɪm wɜːk ‖ -wɜːk ~s s
Framingham (i) 'freɪm ɪŋ əm ‖ -hæm, (ii)
'fræm-
Framlingham 'fræm lɪŋ əm ‖ -hæm
Framlington 'fræm lɪŋ tən
Frampton 'fræmpt ən
Fran fræn
franc fræŋk (= frank) —Fr [fʁɑ̃] francs fræŋks
France frɑːnts §fræn̩ts ‖ fræn̩ts France's
'frɑːnts ɪz §'fræn̩ts-, -əz ‖ 'fræn̩ts əz
Frances personal name 'frɑːn̩ts ɪs §'fræn̩ts-, -əs
‖ 'fræn̩ts-
Francesca fræn 'tʃesk ə -'sesk- ‖ frɑːn- fræn-
franchis|e 'fræntʃ aɪz 'frɑːntʃ- ~ed d ~es ɪz
əz ~ing ɪŋ

franchisee ˌfræntʃ aɪ 'ziː ˌfrɑːntʃ- ~s z
franchisement 'fræntʃ ɪz mənt 'frɑːntʃ-, §-əz-
‖ -aɪz- -əz- ~s s
franchisor ˌfræntʃ aɪ 'zɔː ˌfrɑːntʃ-, -ɪ- ‖ -'zɔːr
-ə- ~s z
Francis 'frɑːn̩ts ɪs §'fræn̩ts-, -əs ‖ 'fræn̩ts-
Franciscan fræn 'sɪsk ən ~s z
francium 'fræn̩ts i_əm 'frɑːn̩ts-
Franck composer frɒŋk frɑːŋk ‖ frɑːŋk —Fr
[fʁɑ̃ːk]
Franco 'fræŋk əʊ ‖ -oʊ 'frɑːŋk- —Sp
['fraŋ ko]
Franco- ˌfræŋk əʊ ‖ -oʊ — Franco-British
ˌfræŋk əʊ 'brɪt ɪʃ ◄ ‖ -oʊ 'brɪt̬ ɪʃ ◄
Francois, François 'frɒn̩ts wɑː 'frɑːn̩ts-,
'fræn̩ts-, ˌ•'• ‖ frɑːn 'swɑː —Fr [fʁɑ̃ swa]
Francoise, Françoise 'frɒn̩ts wɑːz 'frɑːn̩ts-,
'fræn̩ts-, ˌ•'• ‖ frɑːn 'swɑːz —Fr [fʁɑ̃ swaːz]
francolin 'fræŋk əʊl ɪn §-ən ‖ -ᵊl_ən ~s z
Franconi|a fræŋ 'kəʊn i_ə ‖ -'koʊn- ~an/s
ən/z
Francophile 'fræŋk əʊ faɪᵊl ‖ -ə- ~s z
francophobe, F~ 'fræŋk əʊ fəʊb ‖ -ə foʊb ~s
z
francophone, F~ 'fræŋk əʊ fəʊn ‖ -ə foʊn ~s
z
frangible 'frændʒ əb ᵊl -ɪb-
frangipani ˌfrændʒ ɪ 'pɑːn i §-ə-, -'pæn-
‖ -'pæn i ~s z
Franglais, f~ 'frɒŋ gleɪ 'frɑːŋ- ‖ frɑːn 'gleɪ
—Fr [fʁɑ̃ glɛ]
frank, Frank fræŋk franked fræŋkt franker
'fræŋk ə ‖ -ᵊr frankest 'fræŋk ɪst -əst
franking 'fræŋk ɪŋ franks fræŋks
Frankau (i) 'fræŋk əʊ ‖ -oʊ, (ii) -aʊ
Frankenstein 'fræŋk ᵊn staɪn -ɪn- —Ger
['fʁaŋk ᵊn ʃtaɪn]
Frankfort places in US 'fræŋk fət ‖ -fᵊrt
Frankfurt 'fræŋk fɜːt -fət ‖ -fᵊrt —Ger
['fʁaŋk fʊʁt]
frankfurter, F~ 'fræŋk fɜːt ə -fət- ‖ -fᵊrt̬ ᵊr ~s
z
Frankie 'fræŋk i
frankincense 'fræŋk ɪn ˌsen̩ts -ən-
Frankish 'fræŋk ɪʃ
Frankland 'fræŋk lənd
franklin, F~ 'fræŋk lɪn -lən ~s, ~'s z
frankly 'fræŋk li
Franklyn 'fræŋk lɪn -lən
frankness 'fræŋk nəs -nɪs
Frant frænt
frantic 'frænt ɪk ‖ 'frænt̬ ɪk ~ally ᵊl_i ~ness
nəs nɪs
Franz frænts frɑːnts ‖ frɑːnts —Ger [fʁants]
—but as an American name also frænz
frap fræp frapped fræpt frapping 'fræp ɪŋ
fraps fræps
frappe, frappé 'fræp eɪ ‖ fræ 'peɪ —Fr
[fʁa pe] ~s z
Frascati fræ 'skɑːt i —It [fra 'ska: ti]
Fraser 'freɪz ə ‖ -ᵊr
Fraserburgh 'freɪz ə bᵊr_ə -ə ˌbʌr ə
‖ -ᵊr ˌbɝː oʊ

frass fræs
frat fræt frats fræts
fratch|y 'frætʃ |i ~iness i nəs i nıs
Frater, f~ 'freıt ə ‖ 'freıt̬ ər
fraternal frə 'tɜn əl ‖ -'tɜːn- ~ism ‚ız əm ~ly i
fraternit|y frə 'tɜːn ət |i -ıt- ‖ -'tɜːn ət̬ |i ~ies
iz
fraternis... —see fraterniz...
fraternization ‚fræt ən aı 'zeıʃ ən -ı'•-
‖ ‚fræt̬ ərn ə-
fraterniz|e 'fræt ə naız -ən aız ‖ -ər- ~ed d
~er/s ə/z ‖ ər/z ~es ız əz ~ing ıŋ
fratricidal ‚frætr ı 'saıd əl ◀ ‚freıtr-, -ə- ~ly i
fratricide 'frætr ı saıd 'freıtr-, -ə- ~s z
Fratton 'fræt ən
Frau frau —Ger [fʁau]
  (i) Frau 'Becker
fraud frɔːd ‖ frɑːd frauds frɔːdz ‖ frɑːdz
fraudster 'frɔːd stə ‖ -stər 'frɑːd- ~s z
fraudulence 'frɔːd jul ənts -jəl-, 'frɔːdʒ əl-
‖ 'frɔːdʒ əl- 'frɑːdʒ-
fraudulent 'frɔːd jul ənt -jəl-, 'frɔːdʒ əl-
‖ 'frɔːdʒ əl- 'frɑːdʒ- ~ly li
fraught frɔːt ‖ frɑːt
fraulein, fräulein 'froı laın 'frau- —Ger
Fräulein ['fʁɔy laın] ~s z
Fraunhofer 'fraun həuf ə ‖ -houf ər —Ger
['fʁaun hoːf ɐ]
  'Fraunhofer lines
fray freı frayed freıd fraying 'freı ıŋ frays
freız
Fray Bentos ‚freı 'bent ɒs ‖ -ous —Sp
[frai 'βen tos]
Frayn, Frayne freın
Frazer 'freız ə ‖ -ər
Frazier 'freız i_ə ‖ 'freız ər -i_ər (*)
frazil 'freız ıl 'fræz-, -əl
frazzl|e 'fræz əl ~ed d ~es z ~ing ‿ıŋ
freak friːk freaked friːkt freaking 'friːk ıŋ
freaks friːks
freakish 'friːk ıʃ ~ly li ~ness nəs nıs
freak-out 'friːk aut ~s s
freak|y 'friːk |i ~ier i_ə ‖ i_ər ~iest i_ıst _əst
~ily ı li əl i ~iness i nəs -nıs
Frean friːn
freckle 'frek əl ~d d ~s z
Fred fred
Freda 'friːd ə
Freddie, Freddy 'fred i
Frederic 'fredr ık 'fred ər ık
Frederica ‚fred ə 'riːk ə fre 'driːk ə
Frederick 'fredr ık 'fred ər ık
Fredericksburg 'fred‿ər ıks bɜːg ‖ -bɜːg
Fredericton 'fredr ık tən 'fred ər ık tən
Fredonia frı 'dəun i_ə frə- ‖ -'doun-
free friː freed friːd freeing 'friː ıŋ freely
'friː li freer 'friː_ə ‖ _ər frees friːz freest
'friː_ıst əst
‚free 'agent; ‚free as‚soci'ation; ‚Free
'Church; ‚free col‚lective 'bargaining; ‚free
'enterprise; ‚free 'gift; ‚free 'hand; ‚free
'house; ‚free 'kick; ‚Free 'Kirk; ‚free 'love;
‚free 'pardon; ‚free 'pass; ‚free 'port; ‚free

'speech; ‚free 'trade, ‚Free Trade 'Hall;
‚free 'verse; ‚free 'will
-free friː —New formations with this suffix tend to
be late-stressed (‚lead-'free), long-established
ones early-stressed ('carefree)
freebas|e 'friː beıs ~ed t ~es ız əz ~ing ıŋ
freebee, freebie 'friːb i ~s z
freeboard 'friː bɔːd ‖ -bɔːrd -bourd
freebooter 'friː ‚buːt ə ‖ -‚buːt̬ ər ~s z
freeborn ‚friː 'bɔːn ◀ '•• ‖ -'bɔːrn ◀
freed friːd
freed|man 'friːd |mən -mæn ~men mən men
freedom 'friːd əm ~s z
  'freedom ‚fighter
freed|woman 'friːd |‚wum ən ~women
‚wım ın -ən
free-fall ‚friː 'fɔːl ◀ '•• ‖ -'fɑːl ~ing ıŋ
free-floating ‚friː 'fləut ıŋ ◀ ‖ -'flout̬ ıŋ ◀
Freefone tdmk 'friː fəun ‖ -foun
free-for-all 'friː fər ‚ɔːl ‚•'•'• ‖ -fər- -‚ɑːl ~s z
freehand 'friː hænd
freehanded ‚friː 'hænd ıd ◀ -əd ~ly li ~ness
nəs nıs
freehold 'friː həuld →-hɒuld ‖ -hould ~s z
freeholder 'friː həuld ə →-hɒuld- ‖ -hould ər
~s z
freelanc|e 'friː lɑːnts §-lænts ‖ -lænts ~ed t
~es ız əz ~ing ıŋ
free-liver ‚friː 'lıv ə ‖ -ər ~s z
free-living ‚friː 'lıv ıŋ ◀
freeload ‚friː 'ləud '•• ‖ -'loud ~ed ıd əd
~er/s ə/z ‖ ər/z ~ing ıŋ ~s z
Freelove 'friː lʌv
freely 'friː li
free|man, F~ 'friː |mən -mæn ~men mən men
freemartin 'friː ‚mɑːt ın §-ən ‖ -‚mɑːrt ən ~s z
freemason, F~ 'friː ‚meıs ən ‚•'• ~s z
freemasonry, F~ 'friː ‚meıs ən ri ‚•'•••
freemen 'friː mən -men
freenet 'friː net ~s s
freephone 'friː fəun ‖ -foun
Freeport 'friː pɔːt ‖ -pɔːrt -pourt
freepost, F~ tdmk 'friː pəust ‖ -poust
freer 'friː_ə ‖ ər ~s z
Freer frıə ‖ frıˑr
free-range ‚friː 'reındʒ ◀
freesheet 'friː ʃiːt ~s s
freesia 'friːz i_ə 'friːʒ ə, 'friːʒ i_ə ‖ 'friːʒ ə ~s z
Freeson 'friːs ən
free-spoken ‚friː 'spəuk ən ◀ ‖ -'spouk- ~ness
nəs nıs
freest 'friː_ıst _əst
free-standing ‚friː 'stænd ıŋ ◀
freestone, F~ 'friː stəun ‖ -stoun
freestyle 'friː staıəl
freethinker ‚friː 'θıŋk ə ‖ -ər ~s z
freethinking ‚friː 'θıŋk ıŋ
Freetown 'friː taun
freeware 'friː weə ‖ -wer -wær
freeway 'friː weı ~s z
freewheel ‚friː 'wiːəl -'hwiːəl, '•• ‖ -'hwiːəl
~ed d ~ing ıŋ ~s z

freewill ˌfriː ˈwɪl ◄
ˌfreewill ˈofferings
freeze friːz (= frees) freezes ˈfriːz ɪz -əz
freezing ˈfriːz ɪŋ froze frəʊz ‖ froʊz
frozen ˈfrəʊz ən ‖ ˈfroʊz ən
ˌfreezing ˈcold; ˈfreezing comˌpartment;
ˈfreezing point
freeze-|dry ˌfriːz |ˈdraɪ ◄ ~dried ˈdraɪd ◄
~dries ˈdraɪz ◄ ~drying ˈdraɪ ɪŋ ◄
freeze-frame ˌfriːz ˈfreɪm ˈ··
freezer ˈfriːz ə ‖ -ər ~s z
freeze-up ˈfriːz ʌp ~s s
Freiburg ˈfraɪ bɜːg -bʊəg ‖ -bɜ̞ːg —Ger
[ˈfʁaɪ bʊʁk]
freight freɪt freighted ˈfreɪt ɪd -əd ‖ ˈfreɪt̬ əd
freighting ˈfreɪt ɪŋ ‖ ˈfreɪt̬ ɪŋ freights freɪts
freighter ˈfreɪt ə ‖ ˈfreɪt̬ ər ~s z
freightliner ˈfreɪt ˌlaɪn ə ‖ -ər ~s z
Fremantle ˈfriː mænt əl ·ˈ·· ‖ -mænt̬ əl
fremitus ˈfrem ɪt əs §-ət- ‖ -ət̬ əs
Fremont ˈfriː mɒnt frɪ ˈmɒnt ‖ -mɑːnt
French, f~ frentʃ
ˌFrench ˈbean; ˌFrench ˈbread; ˌFrench
Caˈnadian; ˈFrench doors; ·ˈ·; ˌFrench
ˈdressing; ˌFrench ˈfries; ˌFrench ˈhorn;
ˌFrench ˈkiss; ˌFrench ˈleave; ˌFrench ˈloaf;
ˌFrench ˈpolish; ˌFrench ˈtoast; ˌFrench
ˈwindows
frenchi|fy, F~ ˈfrentʃ ɪ |faɪ -ə- ~fied faɪd ~fies
faɪz ~fying faɪ ɪŋ
French|man ˈfrentʃ |mən ~men mən
~woman ˌwʊm ən ~women ˌwɪm ɪn §-ən
frenetic frə ˈnet ɪk frɪ-, fre- ‖ -ˈnet̬ ɪk ~ally
əl_i
frenum ˈfriːn əm
frenz|y ˈfrenz |i ~ied/ly id /li ~ies iz
freon, Freon tdmk ˈfriː ɒn ‖ -ɑːn
frequenc|y ˈfriːk wənts |i ~ies iz
ˈfrequency ˌcurve
frequent adj ˈfriːk wənt ~ly li ~ness nəs nɪs
frequent v frɪ ˈkwent frə-, friː-; §ˈfriːk wənt
frequented frɪ ˈkwent ɪd frə-, friː-, -əd;
§ˈfriːk wənt- ‖ -ˈkwent̬ əd frequenting
frɪ ˈkwent ɪŋ frə-, friː-; §ˈfriːk wənt-
‖ -ˈkwent̬ ɪŋ frequents frɪ ˈkwents frə-, friː-;
§ˈfriːk wənts
frequentative frɪ ˈkwent ət ɪv frə-, friː-
‖ -ˈkwent̬ ət̬ ɪv ~s z
Frere (i) frɪə ‖ frɪər, (ii) freə ‖ freər
fresco ˈfresk əʊ ‖ -oʊ ~ed d ~es, ~s z ~ing
ɪŋ
fresh freʃ freshed freʃt fresher ˈfreʃ ə ‖ -ər
freshes ˈfreʃ ɪz -əz freshest ˈfreʃ ɪst -əst
freshing ˈfreʃ ɪŋ
freshen ˈfreʃ ən ~ed d ~ing ˌɪŋ ~s z
fresher ˈfreʃ ə ‖ -ər ~s z
freshet ˈfreʃ ɪt -ət ~s s
freshly ˈfreʃ li
fresh|man ˈfreʃ |mən ~men mən
freshness ˈfreʃ nəs -nɪs
freshwater, F~ ˈfreʃ ˌwɔːt ə ·ˈ·· ‖ -ˌwɔːt̬ ər
-ˌwɑːt̬ ər

Fresnel, f~ ˈfreɪn el ˈfren-, -əl, freɪ ˈnel
‖ freɪ ˈnel —Fr [fʁɛ nɛl]
Fresno ˈfrez nəʊ ‖ -noʊ
fret fret frets frets fretted ˈfret ɪd -əd
‖ ˈfret̬ əd fretting ˈfret ɪŋ ‖ ˈfret̬ ɪŋ
fretful ˈfret fəl -fʊl ~ly i ~ness nəs nɪs
fretsaw ˈfret sɔː ‖ -sɑː ~s z
fretwork ˈfret wɜːk ‖ -wɜ̞ːk
Freud frɔɪd —Ger [fʁɔyt]
Freudian ˈfrɔɪd i_ən ~s z
ˌFreudian ˈslip
Freya ˈfreɪ ə
Freycinet ˈfreɪs ə neɪ —Fr [fʁɛ si nɛ]
friability ˌfraɪ_ə ˈbɪl ət i -ɪt i ‖ -ət̬ i
friable ˈfraɪ_əb əl ~ness nəs nɪs
friar ˈfraɪ_ə ‖ ˈfraɪ_ər ~s z
ˌFriar ˈTuck
friar|y ˈfraɪ_ər |i ~ies iz
fricandeau ˈfrɪk ən dəʊ ‖ -doʊ ˌ··ˈ· ~x z —or
as sing.
fricassee n, v ˈfrɪk ə seɪ -siː, ˌ··ˈ· ‖ ˌfrɪk ə ˈsiː
~d d ~ing ɪŋ ~s z
frication frɪ ˈkeɪʃ ən frə-
fricative ˈfrɪk ət ɪv ‖ -ət̬ ɪv ~s z
friction ˈfrɪk ʃən ~s z
frictional ˈfrɪk ʃən_əl ~ly i ~s z
Friday ˈfraɪ deɪ ˈfraɪd i —see note at -day ~s z
fridge frɪdʒ fridges ˈfrɪdʒ ɪz -əz
fridge-freezer ˌfrɪdʒ ˈfriːz ə ‖ -ər ~s z
fried fraɪd
Friedan friː ˈdæn
Friedman ˈfriːd mən
Friedrich ˈfriːdr ɪk —Ger [ˈfʁiːd ʁɪç]
friend, F~ frend friends frendz
friendless ˈfrend ləs -lɪs ~ness nəs nɪs
friend|ly, F~ ˈfrend |li ~lies liz
ˈfriendly soˌciety
friendship ˈfrend ʃɪp ~s s
frier ˈfraɪ_ə ‖ ˈfraɪ_ər ~s z
Friern ˈfraɪ_ən ˈfriː_ən ‖ ˈfraɪ_ərn
ˌFriern ˈBarnet
fries fraɪz
Fries American family name friːz
Friesian ˈfriːz i_ən ˈfrɪz-; ˈfriːʒ ən, ˈfriːʒ i_ən
‖ ˈfriːʒ ən ~s z
Friesland ˈfriːz lənd -lænd —Dutch [ˈfris lɑnt]
frieze friːz (= frees) friezes ˈfriːz ɪz -əz
frig v 'masturbate; copulate' frɪg frigged frɪgd
frigging ˈfrɪg ɪŋ frigs frɪgz
frig n 'refrigerator' frɪdʒ
frigate ˈfrɪg ət -ɪt ~s s
Frigg frɪg
Frigga ˈfrɪg ə
fright fraɪt frights fraɪts
frighten ˈfraɪt ən ~ed d ~er/s ə/z ‖ ər/z
~ing/ly ˌɪŋ /li ~s z
fright|ful ˈfraɪt |fəl -fʊl ~fully fli fəl i, fʊl i
~fulness fəl nəs fʊl-, -nɪs
frigid ˈfrɪdʒ ɪd §-əd ~ly li ~ness nəs nɪs
Frigidaire tdmk ˌfrɪdʒ ɪ ˈdeə -ə- ‖ -ˈdeər -ˈdæər
~s z
frigidity frɪ ˈdʒɪd ət i -ɪt- ‖ -ət̬ i

frijole frı 'hǝʊl i -eɪ ‖ -'hoʊl i —*Sp* [fri 'xo le]
~s z
frill frıl **frilled** frıld **frilling** 'frıl ıŋ **frills** frılz
frill|y 'frıl |i ~**ier** i‿ǝ ‖ i‿ǝr ~**iest** i‿ıst i‿ǝst
~**iness** i nǝs i nıs
Frimley 'frım li
fringe frınʤ **fringed** frınʤd **fringes**
'frınʤ ız -ǝz **fringing** 'frınʤ ıŋ
'fringe ˌbenefit
Frinton 'frınt ǝn ‖ -ªn
fripper|y 'frıp ǝr |i ~**ies** iz
frisbee, F~ *tdmk* 'frız bi ~**s** z
Frisby 'frız bi
Frisch frıʃ —*Ger* [fʁıʃ]
Frisco 'frısk ǝʊ ‖ -oʊ
frise, frisé, frisee, frisée 'frız eɪ ‖ frı 'zeɪ —*Fr*
[fʁi ze]
Frisian 'frız i‿ǝn 'frıʒ ªn, 'frıʒ i‿ǝn; 'fri:z i‿ǝn;
'fri:ʒ ªn, 'fri:ʒ i‿ǝn ‖ 'frıʒ ªn 'fri:ʒ- ~**s** z
frisk frısk **frisked** frıskt **frisker/s** 'frısk ǝ/
z ‖ -ªr/z **frisking** 'frısk ıŋ **frisks** frısks
frisk|y 'frısk |i ~**ier** i‿ǝ ‖ i‿ªr ~**iest** i‿ıst i‿ǝst
~**ily** ı li ǝl i ~**iness** i nǝs i nıs
frisson 'fri:s ɒn 'frıs-, -õ; fri: 'sõ, frı-
‖ fri: 'soʊn —*Fr* [fʁi sõ] ~**s** z
frit frıt **frits** frıts **fritted** 'frıt ıd -ªd ‖ 'frıt̬ ǝd
fritting 'frıt ıŋ ‖ 'frıt̬ ıŋ
Frith frıθ
fritillar|y frı 'tıl ªr |i frǝ- ‖ 'frıt̬ ªl er |i (*) ~**ies**
iz
Fritos *tdmk* 'fri:t ǝʊz ‖ 'fri:t̬ oʊz
fritter 'frıt ǝ ‖ 'frıt̬ ªr ~**ed** d **frittering**
'frıt‿ǝr ıŋ ‖ 'frıt̬ ǝr ıŋ ~**s** z
Fritz, fritz frıts
Friuli fri 'u:l i —*It* [fri 'u: li]
Friulian fri 'u:l i‿ǝn ~**s** z
frivolit|y frı 'vɒl ǝt |i frǝ-, -ıt- ‖ -'va:l ǝt̬ |i
~**ies** iz
frivolous 'frıv ǝl‿ǝs ~**ly** li ~**ness** nǝs nıs
frizz frız **frizzed** frızd **frizzes** 'frız ız -ǝz
frizzing 'frız ıŋ
frizzl|e 'frız ªl ~**ed** d ~**es** z ~**ing**‿ıŋ
frizz|ly 'frız |li ~**lier** li‿ǝ ‖ li‿ªr ~**liest**
li‿ǝst
frizz|y 'frız |i ~**ier** i‿ǝ ‖ i‿ªr ~**iest** i‿ıst i‿ǝst
~**ily** ı li ǝl i ~**iness** i nǝs i nıs
fro frǝʊ ‖ froʊ
Frobisher 'frǝʊb ıʃ ǝ ‖ 'froʊb ıʃ ªr
ˌFrobisher 'Bay
frock frɒk ‖ fra:k **frocks** frɒks ‖ fra:ks
ˌfrock 'coat ‖ ' ‧
Frodo 'frǝʊd ǝʊ ‖ 'froʊd oʊ
Frodsham 'frɒd ʃǝm ‖ 'fra:d-
Froebel, Fröbel 'frǝʊb ªl 'frɜ:b- ‖ 'freıb-
'frɔıb- —*Ger* ['fʁø: bªl]
frog frɒg ‖ fra:g frɔ:g **frogs** frɒgz ‖ fra:gz
frɔ:gz
frogbit 'frɒg bıt ‖ 'fra:g- 'frɔ:g- ~**s** s
Froggatt 'frɒg ǝt -ıt ‖ 'fra:g-
frogging 'frɒg ıŋ ‖ 'fra:g- 'frɔ:g-
Frogg|ie, frogg|y, F~ 'frɒg |i ‖ 'fra:g |i 'frɔ:g-
~**ies** iz

froghopper 'frɒg ˌhɒp ǝ ‖ 'fra:g ˌha:p ªr
'frɔ:g- ~**s** z
frog|man 'frɒg |mǝn ‖ 'fra:g- 'frɔ:g- ~**men**
mǝn men
frogmarch 'frɒg ma:tʃ ‖ 'fra:g ma:rtʃ 'frɔ:g-
~**ed** t ~**es** ız ǝz ~**ing** ıŋ
Frogmore 'frɒg mɔ: ‖ 'fra:g mɔ:r 'frɔ:g-,
-moʊr
frogspawn 'frɒg spɔ:n ‖ 'fra:g- 'frɔ:g-, -spa:n
frolic 'frɒl ık ‖ 'fra:l- ~**ked** t ~**ker/s** ǝ/z ‖ ªr/z
~**king** ıŋ ~**s** s
frolicsome 'frɒl ık sǝm ‖ 'fra:l-
from *strong form* frɒm ‖ frʌm fra:m, *weak form*
frǝm
fromage frais ˌfrɒm a:ʒ 'freı ‖ frǝ ˌma:ʒ- —*Fr*
[fʁɔ maʒ fʁɛ]
Frome (i) fru:m, (ii) frǝʊm ‖ froʊm —*The*
places and rivers in England and Jamaica are
all (i), although the spelling pronunciation (ii)
can be heard from people not familiar with the
name. Lake F~ in Australia is (ii).
Fromm frɒm ‖ fra:m froʊm
Fron vrɒn ‖ vra:n —*Welsh* [vrɔn]
Froncysyllte ˌvrɒn kǝ 'sʌɬt eɪ →ˌvrɒŋ-
‖ ˌvra:n- —*Welsh* [vrɔn kǝ 'sǝɬ te]
frond frɒnd ‖ fra:nd **fronded** 'frɒnd ıd -ǝd
‖ 'fra:nd ǝd **fronds** frɒndz ‖ fra:ndz
front frʌnt **fronted** 'frʌnt ıd -ǝd ‖ 'frʌnt̬ ǝd
fronter 'frʌnt ǝ ‖ 'frʌnt̬ ªr **frontest**
'frʌnt ıst -ǝst ‖ 'frʌnt̬ ǝst **fronting**
'frʌnt ıŋ ‖ 'frʌnt̬ ıŋ **fronts** frʌnts
ˌfront 'door; ˌfront 'line; 'front man; ˌfront
'page; ˌfront 'room
frontag|e 'frʌnt ıʤ ‖ 'frʌnt̬ ıʤ ~**es** ız ǝz
frontal 'frʌnt ªl ‖ 'frʌnt̬ ªl ~**ly** i
frontbench ˌfrʌnt 'benʧ ◀ '‧‧ ~**er/s** ǝ/z ‖ ªr/z
Frontenac 'frɒnt ǝ næk ‖ 'fra:nt ªn æk —*Fr*
[fʁɔ̃t nak]
frontier 'frʌnt ıǝ 'frɒnt-; frʌn 'tıǝ ‖ frʌn 'tıªr
fra:n- ~**s** z
frontiers|man 'frʌnt ıǝz |mǝn 'frɒnt-;
frʌn 'tıǝz- ‖ frʌn 'tırz- ~**men** mǝn
frontispiec|e 'frʌnt ı spi:s -ǝ- ‖ 'frʌnt̬ ǝ- ~**es**
ız ǝz
front-line ˌfrʌnt 'laın ◀ '‧‧
ˌfront-line 'troops
front-loader ˌfrʌnt 'lǝʊd ǝ ‖ -'loʊd ªr ~**s** z
front-loading ˌfrʌnt 'lǝʊd ıŋ ◀ ‖ -'loʊd ıŋ ◀
front-of-house ˌfrʌnt ǝv 'haʊs ◀ ‖ ˌfrʌnt̬ ǝv-
front-page ˌfrʌnt 'peıʤ ◀'‧‧
front-rank ˌfrʌnt 'ræŋk ◀
front-runner ˌfrʌnt 'rʌn ǝ '‧ˌ‧‧ ‖ -ªr ~**s** z
front-wheel ˌfrʌnt 'wi:ªl ◀-'hwi:ªl ‖ -'*h*wi:ªl ◀
ˌfront-wheel 'drive
frost, Frost frɒst frɔ:st ‖ frɔ:st fra:st **frosted**
'frɒst ıd 'frɔ:st-, -ǝd ‖ 'frɔ:st ǝd 'fra:st-
frosting 'frɒst ıŋ 'frɔ:st- ‖ 'frɔ:st ıŋ 'fra:st-
frosts frɒsts frɔ:sts ‖ frɔ:sts fra:sts
frostbite 'frɒst baıt 'frɔ:st- ‖ 'frɔ:st- 'fra:st-
~**s** s
frostbitten 'frɒst ˌbıt ªn 'frɔ:st- ‖ 'frɔ:st-
'fra:st-

F

frostbound 'frɒst baʊnd 'frɔːst- ‖ 'frɔːst-
'frɑːst-

frostie 'frɒst i 'frɔːst- ‖ 'frɔːst i 'frɑːst-   ~s,
F~s tdmk z

frost|y 'frɒst |i 'frɔːst- ‖ 'frɔːst |i 'frɑːst-   ~ier
i‿ə ‖ i‿ᵊr   ~iest i‿ɪst i‿əst   ~ily ɪ li əl i   ~iness
i nəs i nɪs

froth n frɒθ frɔːθ ‖ frɔːθ frɑːθ   froths frɒθs
frɔːθs ‖ frɔːθs frɑːθs

froth v frɒθ frɔːθ ‖ frɔːθ frɑːθ, frɔːð   frothed
frɒθt frɔːθt ‖ frɔːθt frɑːθt, frɔːðd   frothing
'frɒθ ɪŋ 'frɔːθ- ‖ 'frɔːθ- 'frɑːθ-, 'frɔːð-
froths frɒθs frɔːθs ‖ frɔːθs frɑːθs, frɔːðz

froth|y 'frɒθ |i 'frɔːθ- ‖ 'frɔːθ |i 'frɑːθ-, 'frɔːð-
~ier i‿ə ‖ i‿ᵊr   ~iest i‿ɪst i‿əst   ~ily ɪ li əl i
~iness i nəs i nɪs

frottage 'frɒt ɑːʒ -ɪdʒ; frɒ 'tɑːʒ ‖ frɔː 'tɑːʒ
frɑː-   —Fr [fʁɔ taːʒ]

Froud fraʊd

Froude fruːd

froufrou 'fruː fruː

froward 'frəʊ əd ‖ 'froʊ ᵊrd   ~ly li   ~ness nəs
nɪs

frown fraʊn   frowned fraʊnd   frowner/s
'fraʊn ə/z ‖ -ᵊr/z   frowning/ly 'fraʊn ɪŋ /li
frowns fraʊnz

frowst fraʊst   frowsted 'fraʊst ɪd -əd
frowsting 'fraʊst ɪŋ   frowsts fraʊsts

frowst|y 'fraʊst |i   ~ier i‿ə ‖ i‿ᵊr   ~iest i‿ɪst
i‿əst   ~ily ɪ li əl i   ~iness i nəs i nɪs

frows|y, frowz|y 'fraʊz |i   ~ier i‿ə ‖ i‿ᵊr   ~iest
i‿ɪst i‿əst   ~iness i nəs -nɪs

froze frəʊz ‖ froʊz

frozen 'frəʊz ᵊn ‖ 'froʊz ᵊn   ~ly li   ~ness nəs
nɪs

fructification ˌfrʌkt ɪf ɪ 'keɪʃ ᵊn ˌfrʊkt-, ˌ‿əf-,
§-ə'•-

fructi|fy 'frʌkt ɪ faɪ 'frʊkt-, -ə-   ~fied faɪd
~fies faɪz   ~fying faɪ ɪŋ

fructose 'frʌkt əʊz 'frʊkt-, -əʊs ‖ -oʊs

frugal 'fruːg ᵊl   ~ly i   ~ness nəs nɪs

frugality fruː 'gæl ət i -ɪt- ‖ -ət i

fruit fruːt   fruited 'fruːt ɪd -əd ‖ 'fruːt̬ əd
fruiting 'fruːt ɪŋ ‖ 'fruːt̬ ɪŋ   fruits fruːts
'fruit bat; ˌfruit 'cocktail; 'fruit fly; 'fruit
knife; 'fruit maˌchine; ˌfruit 'salad

fruitarian fruː 'teər i‿ən ‖ -'ter- -'tær-   ~ism
ˌɪz əm   ~s z

fruitcake 'fruːt keɪk   ~s s

fruiterer 'fruːt ᵊr ə ‖ 'fruːt̬ ᵊr ᵊr   ~s z

fruitful 'fruːt fᵊl -fʊl   ~ly i   ~ness nəs nɪs

fruiti... —see fruity

fruition fruː 'ɪʃ ᵊn

fruitless 'fruːt ləs -lɪs   ~ly li   ~ness nəs nɪs

fruit|y 'fruːt |i ‖ 'fruːt̬ |i   ~ier i‿ə ‖ i‿ᵊr   ~iest
i‿ɪst i‿əst   ~iness i nəs i nɪs

frumenty 'fruːm ənt i

frump frʌmp   frumps frʌmps

frumpish 'frʌmp ɪʃ   ~ly li   ~ness nəs nɪs

frump|y 'frʌmp |i   ~ier i‿ə ‖ i‿ᵊr   ~iest i‿ɪst
i‿əst   ~ily ɪ li əl i   ~iness i nəs i nɪs

frus|trate frʌ 's|treɪt 'frʌs |treɪt ‖ 'frʌs |treɪt
~trated treɪt ɪd -əd ‖ treɪt̬ əd   ~trater/s

treɪt ə/z ‖ treɪt̬ ᵊr/z   ~trates treɪts
~trating/ly treɪt ɪŋ /li ‖ treɪt̬ ɪŋ /li

frustration frʌ 'streɪʃ ᵊn   ~s z

frust|um 'frʌst |əm   ~a ə   ~ums əmz

frutesc|ence fruː 'tes |ᵊn¹s   ~ent ᵊnt

fry fraɪ   fried fraɪd   fries fraɪz   frying 'fraɪ ɪŋ
'frying pan

Fry, Frye fraɪ

fryer, frier 'fraɪ‿ə ‖ 'fraɪ‿ᵊr   ~s z

Fryston 'fraɪst ᵊn

fry-up 'fraɪ ʌp   ~s s

f-stop 'ef stɒp ‖ -stɑːp   ~s s

ftp ˌef tiː 'piː -'d d   ~'ing ɪŋ   ~'s z

FTSE, FT-SE 'fʊts i

fubs|y 'fʌbz| i   ~ier i‿ə ‖ i‿ᵊr   ~iest i‿ɪst ‿əst

Fuchs (i) fʊks, (ii) fuːks, (iii) fjuːks —The
explorer was (i). (iii) is AmE only.

fuchsia 'fjuːʃ ə   ~s z

fuchsin 'fuːks ɪn §-ən

fuchsine 'fuːks iːn -ɪn -ɪn ‖ 'fʊks ᵊn 'fjuːks- (*)

fuck fʌk   fucked fʌkt   fucker/s 'fʌk ə/z ‖ -ᵊr/z
fucking 'fʌk ɪŋ   fucks fʌks
ˌfuck 'all, '• •

fucker 'fʌk ə ‖ -ᵊr   ~s z

fuck-up 'fʌk ʌp   ~s s

fucous 'fjuːk əs

fucus 'fjuːk əs

fuddl|e 'fʌd ᵊl   ~ed d   ~es z   ~ing ‿ɪŋ

fuddy-dudd|y 'fʌd i ˌdʌd |i   ~ies iz

fudge, Fudge fʌdʒ   fudged fʌdʒd   fudges
'fʌdʒ ɪz -əz   fudging 'fʌdʒ ɪŋ

Fuegian 'fweɪdʒ ᵊn 'fweɪg i‿ən   ~s z

fuehrer 'fjʊər ə 'fjɔːr- ‖ 'fjʊr ᵊr —Ger Führer
['fyː ʁɐ]   ~s z

fuel 'fjuːʔ əl §fjuːl   ~ed, ~led d   ~ing, ~ling ɪŋ
~s z
'fuel cell; 'fuel oil

fug fʌg   fugs fʌgz

fugacious fjuː 'geɪʃ əs   ~ly li   ~ness nəs nɪs

fugacity fjuː 'gæs ət i -ɪt- ‖ -ət̬ i

fugal 'fjuːg ᵊl   ~ly i

fuggles, F~ 'fʌg ᵊlz

fugg|y 'fʌg| i   ~ier i‿ə ‖ i‿ᵊr   ~iest i‿ɪst ‿əst
~iness i nəs -nɪs

fugitive 'fjuːdʒ ət ɪv -ɪt- ‖ -ət̬ ɪv   ~ly li   ~ness
nəs nɪs

fugu 'fuːg uː —Jp [ɸɯ ɡɯ, -ɡɯ]

fugue fjuːg   fugues fjuːgz

fuhrer, führer 'fjʊər ə 'fjɔːr- ‖ 'fjʊr ᵊr —Ger
Führer ['fyː ʁɐ]   ~s z

Fujairah fu 'dʒaɪᵊr ə

Fuji 'fuːdʒ i —Jp [ɸɯ dʑi]

Fujica tdmk 'fuːdʒ ɪk ə

Fujitsu tdmk fu: 'dʒɪts u: —Jp [ɸɯ 'dʑi tsɯɯ]

Fukuoka ˌfuːk u 'əʊk ə ˌfʊk- ‖ -'oʊk- —Jp
[ɸɯ 'kɯ o ka]

-ful (i) suffix to form adjectives, fᵊl fʊl—
painful 'peɪn fᵊl, -fʊl; (ii) suffix to form nouns
specifying a quantity, fʊl—   spoonful
'spuːn fʊl

Fula 'fuːl ə   ~s z

Fulani fu: 'lɑːn i 'fuːl ɑːn i

Fulbourn 'fʊl bɔːn ‖ -bɔːrn -boʊrn

Fulbright 'fʊl braɪt
Fulbrighter 'fʊl braɪt ə ‖ -braɪt̮ ᵊr ~s z
Fulcher 'fʊltʃ ə ‖ -ᵊr
fulc|rum 'fʌlk |rəm 'fʊlk- ~**ra** rə
ful|fil, ~fill fʊl |'fɪl ~**filled** 'fɪld ~**filler/s**
'fɪl ə/z ‖ 'fɪl ᵊr/z ~**filling** 'fɪl ɪŋ ~**fils, ~fills**
'fɪlz
fulfillment, fulfilment fʊl 'fɪl mənt
Fulford 'fʊl fəd ‖ -fᵊrd
Fulham 'fʊl əm
fuliginous fju 'lɪdʒ ɪn əs §-ən- ~**ly** li
full fʊl **fuller** 'fʊl ə ‖ -ᵊr **fullest** 'fʊl ɪst -əst
,full 'dress; ,full 'house; ,full 'marks; ,full
'moon; ,full 'stop; ,full 'toss
fullback ,fʊl 'bæk '•• ‖ 'fʊl bæk ~**s** s
full-blooded ,fʊl 'blʌd ɪd ◄ -əd ~**ness** nəs nɪs
full-blown ,fʊl 'bləʊn ◄ ‖ -'bloʊn ◄
full-bodied ,fʊl 'bɒd id ◄ ‖ -'bɑːd-
full-dress ,fʊl 'dres ◄
fuller, F~ 'fʊl ə ‖ -ᵊr ~**s, ~'s** z
,fuller's 'earth
Fullerton 'fʊl ət ən ‖ -ᵊrt ᵊn
full-face ,fʊl 'feɪs ◄
full-fashioned ,fʊl 'fæʃ ᵊnd ◄
full-fledged ,fʊl 'fledʒd ◄
full-frontal ,fʊl 'frʌnt ᵊl ◄ ‖ -'frʌnt̮ ᵊl ◄
full-grown ,fʊl 'grəʊn ◄ ‖ -'groʊn ◄
full-hearted ,fʊl 'hɑːt ɪd ◄ -əd ‖ -'hɑːrt̮ əd ◄
full-length ,fʊl 'leŋkθ ◄ -'lenᵗθ
,full-length 'portrait
full-page ,fʊl 'peɪdʒ ◄
full-scale ,fʊl 'skeɪᵊl ◄
,full-scale 'war
full-throated ,fʊl 'θrəʊt ɪd ◄ -əd ‖ -'θroʊt̮ əd ◄
,full-,throated 'roar
full-time ,fʊl 'taɪm ◄
,full-time 'work
fully 'fʊl i
-fully fᵊl_i fʊl i—— **painfully** 'peɪn fᵊl_i -fʊl i
fully-fashioned ,fʊl i 'fæʃ ᵊnd ◄
fully-fledged ,fʊl i 'fledʒd ◄
fully-grown ,fʊl i 'grəʊn ◄ ‖ -'groʊn ◄
fulmar 'fʊlm ə -ɑː ‖ -ᵊr -ɑːr ~**s** z
Fulmer 'fʊlm ə ‖ -ᵊr
fulminant 'fʊlm ɪn ənt 'fʌlm-, -ən-
fulmi|nate 'fʊlm ɪ |neɪt 'fʌlm-, -ə- ~**nated**
neɪt ɪd -əd ‖ neɪt̮ əd ~**nates** neɪts ~**nating**
neɪt ɪŋ ‖ neɪt̮ ɪŋ
fulmination ,fʊlm ɪ 'neɪʃ ᵊn ,fʌlm-, -ə- ~**s** z
fulness 'fʊl nəs -nɪs
fulsome 'fʊls əm ~**ly** li ~**ness** nəs nɪs
Fulton 'fʊlt ən
fulvous 'fʌlv əs 'fʊlv-
Fulwell 'fʊl wel
Fulwood 'fʊl wʊd
Fu Manchu ,fuː mæn 'tʃuː
fumaric fju 'mær ɪk ‖ -'mer-
fumarole 'fjuːm ə rəʊl →-rɒʊl ‖ -roʊl ~**s** z
fumbl|e 'fʌm bᵊl ~**ed** d ~**es** z ~**ing** ɪŋ
fumbler 'fʌm blə ‖ -blᵊr ~**s** z
fume fjuːm **fumed** fjuːmd **fumes** fjuːmz
fuming 'fjuːm ɪŋ
fumigant 'fjuːm ɪg ᵊnt -əg- ~**s** s

fumi|gate 'fjuːm ɪ |geɪt -ə- ~**gated** geɪt ɪd -əd
‖ geɪt̮ əd ~**gates** geɪts ~**gating**
geɪt ɪŋ ‖ geɪt̮ ɪŋ
fumigation ,fjuːm ɪ 'geɪʃ ᵊn -ə- ~**s** z
fumigator 'fjuːm ɪ geɪt ə '•ə- ‖ -geɪt̮ ᵊr ~**s** z
fumitor|y 'fjuːm ɪt_ᵊr li '•ət_ ‖ -ə tɔːr li -toʊr i
~**ies** iz
fun fʌn
'fun fur; 'fun run
funambulist fju 'næm bjʊl ɪst -bjᵊl-, §-əst ~**s**
s
Funchal ,fʊn 'tʃaːl -'ʃaːl —**Port** [fũ 'ʃaɫ]
function 'fʌŋk ʃᵊn ~**ed** d ~**ing** ɪŋ ~**s** z
functional 'fʌŋk ʃᵊn_ᵊl ~**ism** ,ɪz əm ~**ist/s**
ɪst/s §əst/s ~**ly** i
functionar|y 'fʌŋk ʃᵊn_ᵊr li -ʃᵊn ᵊr_li
‖ -ʃə ner li ~**ies** iz
functor 'fʌŋkt ə ‖ -ᵊr ~**s** z
fund fʌnd **funded** 'fʌnd ɪd -əd **funding**
'fʌnd ɪŋ **funds** fʌndz
fundament 'fʌnd ə mənt ~**s** s
fundamental ,fʌnd ə 'ment ᵊl ◄ ‖ -'ment̮ ᵊl ◄
~**ism** ,ɪz əm ~**ist/s** ɪst/s §əst/s ~**ly** i ~**s** z
fund-rais|er/s 'fʌnd reɪz| ə/z ‖ -ᵊr/z ~**ing** ɪŋ
fund|us 'fʌnd| əs ~**i** aɪ
Fundy 'fʌnd i
funeral 'fjuːn ᵊr_ᵊl ~**s** z
'funeral di,rector; 'funeral home; 'funeral
,parlor
funerary 'fjuːn ᵊr_ər i △'fjuːn ər i ‖ -ə rer i
funereal fju 'nɪər i_əl ‖ -'nɪr- ~**ly** i
funfair 'fʌn feə ‖ -fer -fær ~**s** z
fungal 'fʌŋ gᵊl
fungi 'fʌŋ giː -gaɪ; 'fʌndʒ aɪ, -iː
fungible 'fʌndʒ əb ᵊl -ɪb- ~**s** z
fungicidal ,fʌŋ gɪ 'saɪd ᵊl ◄ §-gə-; ,fʌndʒ ɪ-,
§-ə-
fungicide 'fʌŋ gɪ saɪd §-gə-; 'fʌndʒ ɪ-, §-ə- ~**s**
z
fungoid 'fʌŋ gɔɪd
fungous 'fʌŋ gəs (= fungus)
fungus 'fʌŋ gəs **fungi** 'fʌŋ giː -gaɪ; 'fʌndʒ aɪ,
-iː **funguses** 'fʌŋ gəs ɪz -əz
funicular fju 'nɪk jʊl ə fə-, -jᵊl- ‖ -jᵊl ᵊr ~**s** z
fu,nicular 'railway
funk fʌŋk **funked** fʌŋkt **funking** 'fʌŋk ɪŋ
funks fʌŋks
funk|y 'fʌŋk li ~**ier** i_ə ‖ i_ᵊr ~**iest** i_ɪst i_əst
~**ily** i li ᵊl i ~**iness** i nəs i nɪs
fun-loving 'fʌn ,lʌv ɪŋ
funnel 'fʌn ᵊl ~**ed, -led** d ~**ing, -ling** ɪŋ ~**s** z
funn|y 'fʌn li ~**ier** i_ə ‖ i_ᵊr ~**ies** iz ~**iest** i_ɪst
i_əst ~**ily** i li ᵊl i ~**iness** i nəs i nɪs
'funny bone; 'funny ,business; 'funny
farm; ,funny ha'ha hɑː 'hɑː '••; ,funny
'man 'strange man' , 'funny man 'comedian'
Funt fʌnt
fur fɜː ‖ fɜ·ː **furred** fɜːd ‖ fɜ·ːd **furring**
'fɜːr ɪŋ ‖ 'fɜ·ː ɪŋ **furs** fɜːz ‖ fɜ·ːz
'fur seal
furan 'fjʊər æn 'fjɔːr-; fjuᵊ 'ræn ‖ 'fjʊr æn
fjʊ 'ræn

furbelow ˈfɜːb ə ləʊ -ɪ- ‖ ˈfɝːb ə loʊ **~ed** d
~ing ɪŋ **~s** z
furbish ˈfɜːb ɪʃ ‖ ˈfɝːb- **~ed** t **~er/s** ə/z ‖ ᵊr/z
~es ɪz əz **~ing** ɪŋ
Furby tdmk ˈfɜːb i ‖ ˈfɝːb i   **~s** z
Furies, f~ ˈfjʊər iz ˈfjɔːr- ‖ ˈfjʊr iz
furious ˈfjʊər i_əs ˈfjɔːr- ‖ ˈfjʊr- **~ly** li **~ness**
nəs nɪs
furl fɜːl ‖ fɝːl **furled** fɜːld ‖ fɝːld **furling**
ˈfɜːl ɪŋ ‖ ˈfɝːl ɪŋ **furls** fɜːlz ‖ fɝːlz
furlong ˈfɜːl ɒŋ ‖ ˈfɝːl ɔːŋ -ɑːŋ **~s** z
Furlong, Furlonge ˈfɜːl ɒŋ ‖ ˈfɝːl ɔːŋ -ɑːŋ
furlough ˈfɜːl əʊ ‖ ˈfɝːl oʊ **~ed** d **~ing** ɪŋ **~s**
z
furnac|e, F~ ˈfɜːn ɪs -əs ‖ ˈfɝːn- **~es** ɪz əz
Furneaux ˈfɜːn əʊ ‖ ˈfɝː ˈnoʊ
Furnell fɜː ˈnel ‖ fɝː-
Furness ˈfɜːn ɪs -əs; fɜː ˈnes ‖ ˈfɝːn əs
furnish ˈfɜːn ɪʃ ‖ ˈfɝːn- **~ed** t **~er/s** ə/z ‖ ᵊr/z
~es ɪz əz **~ing/s** ɪŋ/z
furniture ˈfɜːn ɪtʃ ə §-ətʃ- ‖ ˈfɝːn ɪtʃ ᵊr
Furnival, Furnivall ˈfɜːn ɪv ᵊl -əv- ‖ ˈfɝːn-
furor ˈfjʊər ɔː ˈfjɔːr- ‖ ˈfjʊr ᵊr -ɔːr, -oʊr **~s** z
furore fjʊ ˈrɔːr i ˈfjʊər ɔː, ˈfjɔːr- ‖ ˈfjʊr ᵊr
-ɔːr, -oʊr **~s** z —This word sounds different
from furor in BrE, but not in AmE.
furph|y, F~ ˈfɜːf i ‖ ˈfɝːf i **~ies** iz
furred fɜːd ‖ fɝːd
furrier ˈfʌr i_ə ‖ ˈfɝː i_ᵊr **~s** z
furrier|y ˈfʌr i_ᵊr| i ‖ ˈfɝː i_ᵊr| i **~ies** iz
furring ˈfɜːr ɪŋ ‖ ˈfɝː ɪŋ
furrow ˈfʌr əʊ ‖ ˈfɝː oʊ **~ed** d **~ing** ɪŋ **~s** z
furr|y ˈfɜːr i ‖ i §ˈfʌr- ‖ ˈfɝː i **~ier** i_ə ‖ i_ᵊr
~iest i_ɪst i_əst **~iness** i nəs i nɪs
further ˈfɜːð ə ‖ ˈfɝːð ᵊr **~ed** d **furthering**
ˈfɜːð ᵊr_ɪŋ ‖ ˈfɝːð ᵊr_ɪŋ **~s** z
ˌfurther ˌeduˈcation
furtherance ˈfɜːð ᵊr_ᵊnᵗs ‖ ˈfɝːð-
furtherer ˈfɜːð ᵊr_ə ‖ ˈfɝːð ᵊr_ᵊr **~s** z
furthermore ˌfɜːð ə ˈmɔː ˈ• • • ‖ ˈfɝːð ᵊr mɔːr
-moʊr
furthermost ˈfɜːð ə məʊst ‖ ˈfɝːð ᵊr moʊst
furthest ˈfɜːð ɪst -əst ‖ ˈfɝːð-
furtive ˈfɜːt ɪv ‖ ˈfɝːṭ ɪv **~ly** li **~ness** nəs nɪs
Furtwängler ˈfʊət veŋ glə ‖ ˈfʊrt weŋ glᵊr
—Ger [ˈfʊʁt veŋ lɐ]
furuncle ˈfjʊər ʌŋk ᵊl ˈfjɔːr- ‖ ˈfjʊr- **~s** z
fur|y, Fur|y ˈfjʊər i ˈfjɔːr- ‖ ˈfjʊr i **~ies** iz
furze fɜːz ‖ fɝːz (= furs)
fusarium fju ˈzeər i_əm ‖ -ˈzer- -ˈzær-
fuˈsarium wilt
fuse n, v fjuːz **fused** fjuːzd **fuses** ˈfjuːz ɪz -əz
fusing ˈfjuːz ɪŋ
ˈfuse box; ˈfuse wire
fusee fju ˈziː **~s** z
fusel ˈfjuːz ᵊl
ˈfusel oil
fuselag|e ˈfjuːz ə lɑːʒ ˈfjuːs-, -ɪ-, -lɪdʒ ‖ ˈfjuːs-
ˈfjuːz- **~es** ɪz əz
Fuseli ˈfjuːz ᵊl i fju ˈzel i

fusibility ˌfjuːz ə ˈbɪl ət i , • ɪ-, -ɪt i ‖ -əṭ i
fusible ˈfjuːz əb ᵊl -ɪb- **~ness** nəs nɪs
fusiform ˈfjuːz ɪ fɔːm -ə- ‖ -fɔːrm
fusilier ˌfjuːz ə ˈlɪə -ɪ- ‖ -ˈlɪᵊr **~s** z
fusillad|e ˌfjuːz ə ˈleɪd -ɪ-, -ˈlɑːd, ˈ• • •
‖ ˈfjuːs ə leɪd ˈfjuːz-, -lɑːd **~ed** ɪd əd **~es** z
~ing ɪŋ
fusilli fu ˈzɪl i fju-, -ˈsɪl-, -ˈsiːl- —It [fu ˈzil li]
fusion ˈfjuːʒ ᵊn **~al** _ᵊl **~ism** ˌɪz əm **~ist/s**
ɪst/s §əst/s **~s** z
ˈfusion bomb
fuss fʌs **fussed** fʌst **fusses** ˈfʌs ɪz -əz
fussing ˈfʌs ɪŋ
fussbudget ˈfʌs ˌbʌdʒ ɪt -ət **~s** s
fussi... —see **fussy**
fusspot ˈfʌs pɒt ‖ -pɑːt **~s** s
fuss|y ˈfʌs |i **~ier** i_ə ‖ i_ᵊr **~iest** i_ɪst i_əst
~ily ɪ li ᵊl i **~iness** i nəs i nɪs
fustanella ˌfʌst ə ˈnel ə **~s** z
fustian ˈfʌst i_ən ‖ ˈfʌs tʃən
fustic ˈfʌst ɪk
fust|y ˈfʌst |i **~ier** i_ə ‖ i_ᵊr **~iest** i_ɪst i_əst
~ily ɪ li ᵊl i **~iness** i nəs i nɪs
futharc, futhark ˈfuː θ ɑːk ‖ -ɑːrk
futile ˈfjuːt aɪᵊl ‖ ˈfjuːṭ ᵊl ˈfjuːt aɪᵊl **~ly** li ‖ i li
~ness nəs nɪs
futilit|y fju ˈtɪl ət i ‖ i -ɪt- ‖ -əṭ |i **~ies** iz
futon ˈfuːt ɒn ˈfjuːt-, ˈfʊt-, -ᵊn; ˌfuː ˈtɒn ‖ -ɑːn
—Jp [ɸɯ̥ ˌton] **~s** z
futtock ˈfʌt ək ‖ ˈfʌṭ ək **~s** s
Futura fju ˈtjʊər ə →§-ˈtʃʊər ə ‖ -ˈtʊr ə -ˈtjʊr ə
future ˈfjuːtʃ ə ‖ -ᵊr **~s** z
ˌfuture ˈperfect
futur|ism ˈfjuːtʃ ᵊr ˌɪz əm **~ist/s** ɪst/s §əst/s
futuristic ˌfjuːtʃ ə ˈrɪst ɪk ◄ **~ally** ᵊl i
futurit|y fju ˈtjʊər ət i ‖ i -ˈtjɔːr-, →§-ˈtʃʊᵊr-,
→§-ˈtʃɔːr-, -ɪt- ‖ i -ˈtʊr əṭ |i **~ies** iz
futurologist ˌfjuːtʃ ə ˈrɒl ədʒ ɪst §-əst ‖ -ˈrɑːl-
~s s
futurology ˌfjuːtʃ ə ˈrɒl ədʒ i ‖ i -ˈrɑːl-
futz fʌts **futzed** fʌtst **futzes** ˈfʌts ɪz -əz
futzing ˈfʌts ɪŋ
fuze fjuːz **fuzed** fjuːzd **fuzes** ˈfjuːz ɪz -əz
fuzing ˈfjuːz ɪŋ
Fuzhou ˌfuː ˈdʒəʊ ‖ -ˈdʒoʊ —Chi Fúzhōu
[²fu ¹tʂou]
fuzz fʌz **fuzzed** fʌzd **fuzzes** ˈfʌz ɪz -əz
fuzzing ˈfʌz ɪŋ
fuzz|y ˈfʌz |i **~ier** i_ə ‖ i_ᵊr **~iest** i_ɪst i_əst
~ily ɪ li ᵊl i **~iness** i nəs i nɪs
fuzzy-wuzz|y ˈfʌz i ˌwʌz |i **~ies** iz
f-word ˈef wɜːd ‖ -wɝːd
-fy faɪ —This suffix imposes antepenultimate
stress (soˈlidify, perˈsonify).
Fybogel tdmk ˈfaɪb əʊ dʒel ‖ -ə-
Fyfe, Fyffe faɪf
Fylde faɪᵊld
Fylingdales ˈfaɪl ɪŋ deɪᵊlz
Fyne faɪn

G g

g   Spelling-to-sound

1 Where the spelling is **g**, the pronunciation is regularly
g, as in **gas** gæs ('hard G').
Less frequently, it is
dʒ, as in **gentle** 'dʒent ᵊl ('soft G').
Occasionally, it is ʒ, as often in **garage** 'gær ɑːʒ ‖ gə 'rɑːʒ.
g also forms part of the digraphs **gh, gu**, and **ng** (see under **n**).

2 Hard G is the usual pronunciation. Soft G and ʒ are found in certain words
where **g** is followed by **e, i, y** — mostly words of French or Latin origin.
Thus on the one hand we have
g in **get** get, **give** gɪv,
but on the other
dʒ in **general** 'dʒen rəl, **ginger** 'dʒɪndʒ ə.

3 Where the spelling is the digraph **dg** before **e, i, y**, the pronunciation is
always dʒ, as in **edge** edʒ, **elegy** 'el ədʒ i.

4 Where the spelling is doubled **gg**, the pronunciation is again regularly g, as
in **egg** eg.
Occasionally, it is dʒ, as in **exaggerate** ɪg 'zædʒ ə reɪt. Note **suggest**, BrE
usually sə 'dʒest but AmE səg 'dʒest.

5 **g** is silent before **m, n**, but only at the beginning or end of a word or stem,
as in **gnat** næt, **sign** saɪn, **phlegm** flem, **foreigner** 'fɒr ən ə ‖ 'fɔːr ən ᵊr.

6 The sound g is also occasionally written **gh**, as in **ghost**, or **gu**, as in **guess**
ges.

gh   Spelling-to-sound

Where the spelling is the occasional digraph **gh**, there are several possible
pronunciations:
g, as in **ghost** gəʊst ‖ goʊst;
f, as in **rough** rʌf; or
silent, after **i** and sometimes other vowel letters, as in **high** haɪ, **eight** eɪt,
daughter 'dɔːt ə ‖ 'dɔːt̬ ᵊr.

gu   Spelling-to-sound

1 Where the spelling is the digraph **gu**, the pronunciation may be
g, as in **guess** ges, **vague** veɪg, or
gw, as in **language** 'læŋ gwɪdʒ.

G

2 Generally speaking, **g** is found at the beginning of a word, and at the end of a word before silent **e**; **gw** is found in the middle of a word.

3 Most instances of **gu** are not digraphs: **gun** gʌn, **regular**, **argue**.

G, g dʒiː **Gs, G's, g's** dʒiːz —*Communications code name:* Golf
gab gæb **gabbed** gæbd **gabbing** 'gæb ɪŋ
  gabs gæbz
Gabalfa gə 'bælv ə -'bælf ə —*Welsh* [ga 'bal va]
gabardine —*see* **gaberdine**
Gabbana gə 'bɑːn ə -'bæn-
Gabbitas 'gæb ɪ tæs §-ə-
gabbl|e 'gæb ᵊl ~**ed** d ~**es** z ~**ing** ɪŋ
gabbro 'gæb rəʊ ‖ -roʊ ~**s** z
gabby, Gabby 'gæb i
gaberdine ˌgæb ə 'diːn ◄ '•••‖ 'gæb ᵊr diːn ~**s** z
gabfest 'gæb fest ~**s** s
Gabi *name (i)* 'gæb i, *(ii)* 'gɑːb i
Gabi *Australian language* 'gʌb i
gabion 'geɪb i_ən ~**s** z
gable, Gable 'geɪb ᵊl ~**d** d ~**s** z
Gabon 'gæb ɒn gæ 'bɒn, gə-, -'bɒ̃ ‖ gə 'boʊn —*Fr* [ga bɔ̃]
Gabonese ˌgæb ə 'niːz ◄ -ɒ-
Gabor *(i)* gə 'bɔː ‖ -'bɔːr, *(ii)* 'gɑːb ɔː ‖ -ɔːr —*Hungarian* Gábor ['ga: bor]
Gaborone ˌgæb ə 'rəʊn i ‖ ˌgɑːb ə 'roʊn i
Gabriel 'geɪb ri_əl
Gabriella ˌgæb ri 'el ə ˌgeɪb-
Gabrielle ˌgæb ri 'el ə ˌgeɪb-, '•••
Gaby *(i)* 'gæb i, *(ii)* 'gɑːb i
gad, Gad gæd **gadded** 'gæd ɪd -əd **gadding** 'gæd ɪŋ **gads** gædz
gadabout 'gæd ə ˌbaʊt ~**s** s
Gadarene ˌgæd ə 'riːn ◄ '•••‖ 'gæd ə riːn ˌGadarene 'swine
Gaddafi gə 'dɑːf i -'dæf- —*Arabic* [ɣæð 'ðɑː fi]
Gaddesden 'gædz dən
gad|fly 'gæd |flaɪ ~**flies** flaɪz
gadget 'gædʒ ɪt -ət ~**s** s
gadgetry 'gædʒ ɪtr i -ətr i
gadolinium ˌgæd ə 'lɪn i_əm -ᵊl 'ɪn-
gadroon gə 'druːn ~**s** z
Gadsby 'gædz bi
Gadsden, Gadsdon 'gædz dən
gadwall 'gæd wɔːl ‖ -wɑːl ~**s** z
gadzooks ˌ₍ᵢ₎gæd 'zuːks
Gaea 'dʒiːˌə
Gael geɪᵊl **Gaels** geɪᵊlz
Gaelic 'geɪl ɪk 'gæl-, 'gɑːl- ˌGaelic 'football
Gaeltacht 'geɪᵊl tæxt -təxt —*Irish* ['geːl təxt]
Gaenor 'geɪn ə 'gaɪn-, -ɔː ‖ -ɔːr —*Welsh* ['gəi nor]
gaff gæf **gaffed** gæft **gaffing** 'gæf ɪŋ **gaffs** gæfs
gaffe gæf **gaffes** gæfs

gaffer 'gæf ə ‖ -ᵊr ~**s** z
gag gæg **gagged** gægd **gagging** 'gæg ɪŋ **gags** gægz
gaga 'gɑː gɑː
Gagarin gə 'gɑːr ɪn §-ən —*Russ* [gʌ 'ga rʲin]
Gagauz ˌgæg ɑː 'uːz
Gagauzi ˌgæg ɑː 'uːz i ◄
gage, Gage geɪdʒ **gages** 'geɪdʒ ɪz -əz
gaggl|e 'gæg ᵊl ~**ed** d ~**es** z ~**ing** ɪŋ
Gaia 'gaɪ ə 'geɪ ə
Gaidhealtachd 'geɪᵊl tək -tæxt —*ScG* ['geːɫ təxk]
gaiet|y 'geɪ ət li -ɪt- ‖ -ət̬ li ~**ies** iz
Gail, Gaile geɪᵊl
gaillardia geɪ 'lɑːd i_ə gə- ‖ -'lɑːrd- ~**s** z
gaily 'geɪ li
gain geɪn **gained** geɪnd **gainer/s** 'geɪn ə/ z ‖ -ᵊr/z **gaining** 'geɪn ɪŋ **gains** geɪnz
gainer 'geɪn ə ‖ -ᵊr ~**s** z
Gaines geɪnz
Gainesville 'geɪnz vɪl -vəl
gainful 'geɪn fᵊl -fʊl ~**ly** _i ~**ness** nəs nɪs
gain|say ˌgeɪn |'seɪ ~**said** 'sed 'seɪd ~**sayer/s** 'seɪ ə/z ‖ -ᵊr/z ~**saying** 'seɪ ɪŋ ~**says** 'seɪz 'sez
Gainsborough 'geɪnz bᵊr_ə ‖ -ˌbɜː oʊ ~**s** z
'gainst genᵊst geɪnᵊst
Gairdner *(i)* 'geəd nə ‖ 'gerd nᵊr, *(ii)* 'gɑːd- ‖ 'gɑːrd-
Gairloch 'geə lɒx -lɒk ‖ 'ger lɑːk
Gaisford 'geɪs fəd ‖ -fᵊrd
gait geɪt (= *gate*)
gaiter 'geɪt ə ‖ 'geɪt̬ ᵊr ~**s** z
Gaitskell, Gaitskill 'geɪt skᵊl -skɪl
Gaius 'gaɪ_əs
gal gæl **gals** gælz
gala 'gɑːl ə 'geɪl ə ‖ 'geɪl ə 'gæl ə ~**s** z
galactagogue gə 'lækt ə gɒg ‖ -gɑːg ~**s** z
galactic gə 'lækt ɪk
Galactica gə 'lækt ɪk ə
galacto- *comb. form*
  with stress-neutral suffix gə ˈlækt əʊ ‖ -ə —
  galactopoietic gə ˌlækt əʊ pɔɪ 'et ɪk ◄ -ə pɔɪ 'et̬ ɪk ◄
  with stress-imposing suffix ˌgæl ək 'tɒ+ -æk- ‖ -'tɑː+ — **galactometer** ˌgæl ək 'tɒm ɪt ə -ˌæk-, -ət ə ‖ -'tɑːm ət̬ ᵊr
galactose gə 'lækt əʊs -əʊz ‖ -oʊs
galah gə 'lɑː ~**s** z
Galahad 'gæl ə hæd
galantine 'gæl ən tiːn ˌ••'• ~**s** z
Galapagos, Galápagos gə 'læp əg əs -ə gɒs ‖ gə 'lɑːp ə goʊs -əg əs —*Sp* [ga 'la pa ɣos]
Galashiels ˌgæl ə 'ʃiːlz
Galatea ˌgæl ə 'tiːˌə

Galatia gə 'leɪʃ ə -'leɪʃ i‿ə
Galatian gə 'leɪʃ ᵊn -'leɪʃ i‿ən ~s z
galax|y 'gæl əks |i ~ies iz
Galba 'gælb ə
galbanum 'gælb ən əm
Galbraith gæl 'breɪθ ‖ 'gælb reɪθ
gale, Gale geɪᵊl gales geɪᵊlz
Galen 'geɪl ən -ɪn
galena, G~ gə 'li:n ə
Galenic, g~ geɪ 'len ɪk gə-
galere, galère gæ 'leə ‖ -'leᵊr —Fr [ga lɛːʁ]
Galicia gə 'lɪs i‿ə -'lɪʃ ə, -'lɪʃ i‿ə ‖ -'lɪʃ ə -'liːʃ-
Galician gə 'lɪs i‿ən -'lɪʃ ᵊn, -'lɪʃ i‿ən ‖ -'lɪʃ ᵊn
    -'liːʃ- ~s z
Galilean ˌgæl ɪ 'liː‿ən ◂ -ə- ~s z
Galilee 'gæl ɪ liː -ə-
Galileo ˌgæl ɪ 'leɪ əʊ -ə-, -'liː- ‖ -oʊ —It
    [ga li 'lɛː o]
galingale 'gæl ɪŋ geɪᵊl ~s z
galipot 'gæl i pɒt ‖ -pɑːt
gall, Gall gɔːl ‖ gɑːl galled gɔːld ‖ gɑːld
    galling 'gɔːl ɪŋ ‖ 'gɑːl- galls gɔːlz ‖ gɑːlz
    'gall ˌbladder; 'gall wasp
Galla 'gæl ə ~s z
Gallacher, Gallaher 'gæl ə hə -əx ə ‖ -ə hᵊr
Gallagher 'gæl ə hə -əx ə, -əg ə ‖ -əg ᵊr
gallant n, adj 'attentive to women' gə 'lænt
    'gæl ənt —ly li ~s s
gallant adj 'brave' 'gæl ənt ~ly li
gallant|ry 'gæl ənt |ri ~ries riz
Gallaudet ˌgæl ə 'det
galleon 'gæl i‿ən ~s z
galleria ˌgæl ə 'riː‿ə ~s z
galler|y 'gæl ᵊr |i ~ies iz
galley, G~ 'gæl i ~s z
    'galley proof; 'galley slave
galliard 'gæl i ɑːd -i‿əd ‖ 'gæl jᵊrd ~s z
Gallic, g~ 'gæl ɪk
gallicism 'gæl ɪ ˌsɪz əm -ə- ~s z
gallimauf|ry ˌgæl ɪ 'mɔːf |ri -ə- ‖ -'mɑːf- ~ries
    riz
gallinaceous ˌgæl ɪ 'neɪʃ əs -ə-
galling 'gɔːl ɪŋ ‖ 'gɑːl- ~ly li
gallinule 'gæl ɪ njuːl -ə- ‖ -nuːl -njuːl ~s z
Gallipoli gə 'lɪp əl i
gallipot 'gæl i pɒt ‖ -pɑːt
gallium 'gæl i‿əm
galli|vant 'gæl ɪ |vænt -ə-, -vɑːnt, ˌ•• '•
    ‖ -ə |vænt ~vanted vænt ɪd vɑːnt-, -əd
    ‖ vænt̬ əd ~vanting vænt ɪŋ vɑːnt- ‖ vænt̬
    ɪŋ ~vants væn/s
Gallo 'gæl əʊ ‖ -oʊ
Gallo- ˌgæl əʊ ‖ -oʊ — Gallo-Romance
    ˌgæl əʊ rəʊ 'mæn/s ◂ ‖ -oʊ roʊ-
gallon 'gæl ən ~s z
galloon gə 'luːn
gallop 'gæl əp ~ed t ~er/s ə/z ‖ ᵊr/z ~ing ɪŋ
    ~s s
Galloway, g~ 'gæl ə weɪ
gallowglass 'gæl əʊ glɑːs §-glæs ‖ -oʊ glæs
    ~es ɪz əz
gallows 'gæl əʊz ‖ -oʊz
    'gallows ˌhumour

gallstone 'gɔːl stəʊn ‖ -stoʊn 'gɑːl- ~s z
Gallup 'gæl əp
    ˌGallup 'poll, '•• • ‖ '•• •
gallus 'gæl əs ~es ɪz əz
galop 'gæl əp gæ 'lɒp ~s s
galore gə 'lɔː ‖ -'lɔːr -'loʊr
galosh gə 'lɒʃ ‖ -'lɑːʃ ~es ɪz əz
Galsworthy (i) 'gɔːlz ˌwɜːð i ‖ -ˌwɜːð i 'gɑːlz-,
    (ii) 'gælz-
Galt gɔːlt gɒlt ‖ gɑːlt
Galton 'gɔːlt ən 'gɒlt- ‖ 'gɑːlt-
galtonia gɔːl 'təʊn i‿ə gɒl- ‖ -'toʊn- gɑːl- ~s
    z
galumph gə 'lʌmᵖf ~ed t ~ing ɪŋ ~s s
galvanic gæl 'væn ɪk ~ally ᵊl_i
galvanis... —see galvaniz...
galvanism 'gælv ə ˌnɪz əm
galvanization ˌgælv ə naɪ 'zeɪʃ ᵊn -ən ɪ-
    ‖ -ən ə-
galvaniz|e 'gælv ə naɪz ~ed d ~er/s ə/z ‖ ᵊr/z
    ~es ɪz əz ~ing ɪŋ
galvano- comb. form
    with stress-neutral suffix ˌgælv ən ə gæl ˌvæn ə
    — galvanoscope 'gælv ən ə skəʊp
    gæl 'væn- ‖ -skoʊp
    with stress-imposing suffix
    ˌgælv ə 'nɒ+ ‖ -'nɑː+ — galvanoscopy
    ˌgælv ə 'nɒsk əp i ‖ -'nɑːsk-
galvanometer ˌgælv ə 'nɒm ɪt ə -ət ə
    ‖ -'nɑːm ət̬ ᵊr ~s z
Galveston, Galvestone 'gælv əst ən -ɪst-
Galway 'gɔːl weɪ ‖ 'gɑːl-
gam gæm gammed gæmd gamming
    'gæm ɪŋ gams gæmz
Gama, gama 'gɑːm ə
Gamage 'gæm ɪdʒ ~'s ɪz əz
Gamaliel gə 'meɪl i‿əl -'mɑːl-
Gambaccini ˌgæm bə 'tʃiːn i
Gambi|a 'gæm bi‿ə ~an/s ən/z
Gambier, g~ 'gæm bi‿ə ‖ ‿ᵊr
gambit 'gæm bɪt §-bət ~s s
gambl|e, G~ 'gæm bᵊl gambled 'gæm bᵊld
    gambler/s 'gæm blə/z ‖ -blᵊr/z gambles
    'gæm bᵊlz gambling 'gæm blɪŋ
gamboge gæm 'bəʊdʒ -'bəʊʒ, -'buːʒ ‖ -'boʊdʒ
gambol 'gæm bᵊl (= gamble) ~ed, ~led d
    ~ing, ~ling ɪŋ ~s z
gambrel 'gæm brəl ~s z
game geɪm gamer 'geɪm ə ‖ ‿ᵊr games
    geɪmz gamest 'geɪm ɪst -əst
    'game plan; 'games ˌmistress
gamecock 'geɪm kɒk ‖ -kɑːk ~s s
gamekeeper 'geɪm ˌkiːp ə ‖ ‿ᵊr ~s z
gamelan 'gæm ə læn -ɪ-
gamesmanship 'geɪmz mən ʃɪp
gamete 'gæm iːt gə 'miːt ~s s
gameto- comb. form
    with stress-neutral suffix gə ˌmiːt əʊ ˌgæm ɪt ə,
    -ət- ‖ gə ˌmiːt̬ ə ˌgæm ət̬ ə — gametocyte
    gə 'miːt əʊ saɪt 'gæm ɪt ə-, -ət- ‖ -'miːt̬ ə-
    'gæm ət̬ ə-
    with stress-imposing suffix ˌgæm ɪ 'tɒ+ §-ə-

‖ -'tɑ:+— **gametogeny** ˌɡæm ɪ 'tɒdʒ ən i ˌ•ə- ‖ -'tɑːdʒ-

gamey 'ɡeɪm i

gamin 'ɡæm ɪn §-ən —*Fr* [ga mæ̃] ~**s** z —*or as sing.*

gamine 'ɡæm iːn ɡæ 'miːn —*Fr* [ga min] ~**s** z

gaming 'ɡeɪm ɪŋ
'gaming ˌtable

Gamlen, Gamlin 'ɡæm lɪn -lən

gamma 'ɡæm ə ~**s** z
ˌgamma 'globulin; ˌgamma ˌradi'ation; 'gamma ray

Gammell 'ɡæm ᵊl

gammer 'ɡæm ə ‖ -ᵊr ~**s** z

gammon, G~ 'ɡæm ən ~**ed** d ~**ing** ɪŋ ~**s** z

gammy 'ɡæm i

-gamous *stress-imposing* ɡəm əs— **bigamous** 'bɪɡ əm əs

gamp, Gamp ɡæmp **gamps** ɡæmps

gamut 'ɡæm ət -ʌt, -ʊt

gam|y 'ɡeɪm |i ~**ier** i‿ə ‖ i‿ᵊr ~**iest** i‿ɪst i‿əst ~**iness** i nəs i nɪs

-gamy *stress-imposing* ɡəm i— **monogamy** mə 'nɒɡ əm i ‖ -'nɑːɡ-

gan ɡæn

Ganda 'ɡænd ə 'ɡɑːnd ə

Gandalf 'ɡænd ælf ‖ -ɑːlf

gander, G~ 'ɡænd ə ‖ -ᵊr ~**s** z

Gandhi 'ɡænd i 'ɡɑːnd i —*Hindi* [ɡɑ̃ː ɖ̤ʱi]

ganef 'ɡɑːn əf ~**s** s

Ganesh ɡə 'neɪʃ -'neʃ —*Hindi* [ɡəne:ʃ]

gang ɡæŋ **ganged** ɡæŋd **ganging** 'ɡæŋ ɪŋ **gangs** ɡæŋz

gang-bang 'ɡæŋ bæŋ ~**ed** d ~**ing** ɪŋ ~**s** z

ganger 'ɡæŋ ə ‖ -ᵊr ~**s** z

Ganges 'ɡændʒ iːz

gangland 'ɡæŋ lænd -lənd

ganglia 'ɡæŋ ɡli‿ə

gangling 'ɡæŋ ɡlɪŋ

gangli|on 'ɡæŋ ɡli‿|ən ~**a** ə ~**ons** ənz

gan|gly 'ɡæŋ |ɡli ~**glier** ɡli‿ə ‖ ɡli‿ᵊr ~**gliest** ɡli‿ɪst ‿əst

gangplank 'ɡæŋ plæŋk ~**s** s

gangren|e 'ɡæŋ ɡriːn ‖ •'• ~**ed** d ~**es** z ~**ing** ɪŋ

gangrenous 'ɡæŋ ɡrɪn əs -ɡrən-

gangsta 'ɡæŋkst ə ~**s** z

gangster 'ɡæŋkst ə ‖ -ᵊr ~**s** z

gangue ɡæŋ (= *gang*)

gangway 'ɡæŋ weɪ ~**s** z

ganister 'ɡæn ɪst ə -əst- ‖ -ᵊr

ganja 'ɡændʒ ə 'ɡɑːndʒ-

gannet 'ɡæn ɪt -ət ~**s** s

Gannex *tdmk* 'ɡæn eks

gansey 'ɡænz i ~**s** z

Gansu ˌɡæn 'suː ‖ ˌɡɑːn- —*Chi* Gānsù [¹kan ⁴su]

gantlet 'ɡænt lət 'ɡɔːnt-, -lɪt ‖ 'ɡɔːnt- 'ɡɑːnt-, 'ɡænt- ~**s** s

gantr|y 'ɡæntr |i ~**ies** iz

Ganymede 'ɡæn ɪ miːd -ə-

gaol dʒeɪᵊl (= *jail*) **gaoled** dʒeɪᵊld **gaoling** 'dʒeɪᵊl ɪŋ **gaols** 'dʒeɪᵊlz

gaolbird 'dʒeɪᵊl bɜːd ‖ -bɝːd ~**s** z

gaoler 'dʒeɪl ə ‖ -ᵊr ~**s** z

gap ɡæp **gaps** ɡæps

gape ɡeɪp **gaped** ɡeɪpt **gaper/s** 'ɡeɪp ə/ z ‖ -ᵊr/z **gapes** ɡeɪps **gaping/ly** 'ɡeɪp ɪŋ /li

gap-toothed ˌɡæp 'tuːθ ◂ -'tuːðd, §-'tʊθt

gar ɡɑː ‖ ɡɑːr

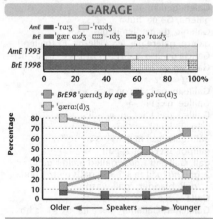

GARAGE

AmE	■■-'rɑːʒ	▢-'rɑːdʒ		
BrE	■■'ɡær ɑːdʒ	▨ -ɪdʒ	▥ɡə 'rɑːdʒ	

	0	20	40	60	80	100%
AmE 1993						
BrE 1998						

BrE98 'ɡærɪdʒ *by age* — ɡə'rɑː(d)ʒ
— 'ɡærɑː(d)ʒ

Percentage (80 70 60 50 40 30 20 10 0)

Older ◀— Speakers —▶ Younger

garag|e *n, v* 'ɡær ɑːʒ -ɑːdʒ, -ɪdʒ; ɡə 'rɑːʒ, -'rɑːdʒ ‖ ɡə 'rɑːʒ -'rɑːdʒ (*) —*Poll panel preferences: AmE 1993,* -'rɑːʒ 52%, -'rɑːdʒ 48%; *BrE 1998,* 'ɡær ɑːdʒ 56% (dʒ 31%, ʒ 25%), -ɪdʒ 38%, ɡə 'rɑːdʒ 5%. ~**ed** d ~**es** ɪz əz ~**ing** ɪŋ
ga'rage ˌsale ‖ ga'rage sale

garam masala ˌɡɑːr əm mə 'sɑːl ə ˌɡʌr-, -mɑː'•- —*Hindi-Urdu* [ɡə rəm mə ʂa: lah]

Garamond 'ɡær ə mɒnd ‖ -mɑːnd

Garand 'ɡær ənd ‖ 'ɡer-; ɡə 'rænd

Garard 'ɡær ɑːd ‖ -ɑːrd 'ɡer-

garb ɡɑːb ‖ ɡɑːrb **garbed** ɡɑːbd ‖ ɡɑːrbd

garbage 'ɡɑːb ɪdʒ ‖ 'ɡɑːrb-
'garbage ˌcan; 'garbage colˌlector; 'garbage truck

garbanzo ɡɑː 'bænz əʊ ‖ ɡɑːr 'bɑːnz oʊ ~**s** z

garbl|e 'ɡɑːb ᵊl ‖ 'ɡɑːrb ᵊl ~**ed** d ~**es** z ~**ing** ɪŋ

Garbo, garbo 'ɡɑːb əʊ ‖ 'ɡɑːrb oʊ ~**s** z

Garcia *English family name (i)* 'ɡɑːs i‿ə ‖ 'ɡɑːrs-, *(ii)* 'ɡɑː ʃ- ‖ 'ɡɑːrʃ-

Garcia *Spanish name* ɡɑː 'siː‿ə ‖ ɡɑːr- —*Sp* García [ɡar 'θi a], *AmSp* [-'si-]

garcon, garçon 'ɡɑːs ɒn -ɒ̃ ‖ ɡɑːr 'soʊn -'sɔ̃ —*Fr* [ɡaʁ sɔ̃]

Garda *lake in Italy* 'ɡɑːd ə ‖ 'ɡɑːrd ə —*It* ['ɡar da]

garda, Garda *Irish policeman* 'ɡɑːd ə ‖ 'ɡɑːrd ə —*Irish* ['ɡar də] **gardai, gardaí, G~** ₍₎ɡɑː 'diː ‖ ₍₎ɡɑːr- —*Irish* ['ɡar diː]
ˌGarda ˌSío'chána ˌʃiː‿ə 'kɔːn ə -'xɔːn- ‖ -'kɑːn-

garden, G~ 'ɡɑːd ᵊn ‖ 'ɡɑːrd ᵊn ~**ed** d ~**ing** ɪŋ ~**s** z
'garden ˌcentre; ˌgarden 'city; 'garden ˌparty; ˌgarden 'suburb

gardener 'ɡɑːd nə ‖ 'ɡɑːrd nᵊr ~**s** z

gardenia gɑː ˈdiːn i‿ə ‖ gɑːr ˈdiːn jə ~**s** z
gardening *n* ˈgɑːd nɪŋ ‖ ˈgɑːrd-
Gardiner ˈgɑːd nə ‖ ˈgɑːrd nᵊr
Gardyne gɑː ˈdaɪn ‖ gɑːr-
Gare du Nord ˌgɑː djuː ˈnɔː ‖ ˌgɑːr duː ˈnɔːr
    —*Fr* [gaʁ dy nɔːʁ]
Garel ˈgær əl ‖ ˈger-
Gareloch ˈgeə lɒx -lɒk ‖ ˈger laːk ˈgær-
Gareth ˈgær əθ -ɪθ, -eθ ‖ ˈger- —*Welsh*
    [ˈga reθ]
Garfield ˈgɑː fiːᵊld ‖ ˈgɑːr-
garfish ˈgɑː fɪʃ ‖ ˈgɑːr-
Garforth ˈgɑː fəθ -fɔːθ ‖ ˈgɑːr fᵊrθ -fɔːrθ,
    -foʊrθ
Garfunkel gɑː ˈfʌŋk ᵊl ˈgɑːf ʌŋk ᵊl ‖ gɑːr-
garganey ˈgɑːg ən i ‖ ˈgɑːrg- ~**s** z
Gargantua gɑː ˈgænt ju‿ə ‖ gɑːr ˈgæntʃ u‿ə
gargantuan gɑː ˈgænt ju‿ən
    ‖ gɑːr ˈgæntʃ u‿ən
gargl|e ˈgɑːg ᵊl ‖ ˈgɑːrg ᵊl ~**ed** d ~**es** z ~**ing**
    ɪŋ
gargoyle ˈgɑː gɔɪᵊl ‖ ˈgɑːr- ~**s** z
Garibaldi, g~ ˌgær ɪ ˈbɔːld i -ə-, -ˈbɒld- ‖ ˌger-,
    -ˈbɑːld i —*It* [ga ri ˈbal di] ~**s** z
garish ˈgeər ɪʃ ˈgɑːr- ‖ ˈger- ˈgær- ~**ly** li
    ~**ness** nəs nɪs
garland, G~ ˈgɑːl ənd ‖ ˈgɑːrl- ~**s** z
garlic, G~, Garlick, Garlicke ˈgɑːl ɪk ‖ ˈgɑːrl-
garlicky ˈgɑːl ɪk i ‖ ˈgɑːrl-
Garman ˈgɑːm ən ‖ ˈgɑːrm-
garment ˈgɑːm ənt ‖ ˈgɑːrm- ~**ed** ɪd əd ~**s** s
Garmisch ˈgɑːm ɪʃ ‖ ˈgɑːrm- —*Ger* [ˈgaʁ mɪʃ]
Garmondsway, Garmonsway
    ˈgɑːm ənz weɪ ‖ ˈgɑːrm-
garn|er, G~ ˈgɑːn ə ‖ ˈgɑːrn ᵊr ~**ered** əd ‖ ᵊrd
    ~**ering** ᵊr ɪŋ ~**ers** əz ‖ ᵊrz
garnet, G~, Garnett ˈgɑːn ɪt -ət ‖ ˈgɑːrn- ~**s** s
garnish ˈgɑːn ɪʃ ‖ ˈgɑːrn- ~**ed** t ~**er/s** ə/
    z ‖ ᵊr/z ~**es** ɪz əz ~**ing** ɪŋ
garnishee ˌgɑːn ɪ ˈʃi: §-ə- ‖ ˌgɑːrn- ~**s** z
garott... —*see* **garrot...**
Garrard ˈgær ɑːd -əd ‖ -ɑːrd ˈger-, -ᵊrd
Garratt ˈgær ət ‖ ˈger-
Garraway ˈgær ə weɪ ‖ ˈger-
garret, G~, Garrett ˈgær ət -ɪt ‖ ˈger- ~**s** s
Garrick ˈgær ɪk ‖ ˈger-
garrison ˈgær ɪs ən -əs- ‖ ˈger- ~**ed** d ~**ing** ɪŋ
    ~**s** z
gar|rote, gar|rotte gə ˈrɒt ‖ -ˈrɑːt -ˈroʊt
    ~**roted, ~rotted** ˈrɒt ɪd -əd ‖ ˈrɑːt̬ əd ˈroʊt̬-
    ~**rotes, ~rottes** ˈrɒts ‖ ˈrɑːts ˈroʊts ~**roting,
    ~rotting** ˈrɒt ɪŋ ‖ ˈrɑːt̬ ɪŋ ˈroʊt̬-
garrulity gə ˈruːl ət i gæ-, -ˈrjuːl-, -ɪt- ‖ -ət̬ i
garrulous ˈgær əl əs -jʊl- ‖ ˈger- ~**ly** li ~**ness**
    nəs nɪs
Garry ˈgær i ‖ ˈger-
garrya ˈgær i‿ə ‖ ˈger- ~**s** z
Garryowen, g~ ˌgær i ˈəʊ ɪn -ən ‖ ˌgær i ˈoʊ ən
    ˌger-
Garscadden gɑː ˈskæd ᵊn ‖ gɑːr-
Garside ˈgɑː saɪd ‖ ˈgɑːr-
Garston ˈgɑːst ən ‖ ˈgɑːrst-
Gartcosh ₍ᵢ₎gɑːt ˈkɒʃ ‖ ₍ᵢ₎gɑːrt ˈkɑːʃ

garter, G~ ˈgɑːt ə ‖ ˈgɑːrt̬ ᵊr ~**ed** d **gartering**
    ˈgɑːt̬‿ᵊr ɪŋ ‖ ˈgɑːrt̬ ᵊr ɪŋ ~**s** z
    ˈgarter snake
garth, Garth gɑːθ ‖ gɑːrθ **garths, Garth's**
    gɑːθs ‖ gɑːrθs
Garton ˈgɑːt ᵊn ‖ ˈgɑːrt ᵊn
Garuda *tdmk* gə ˈruːd ə gæ-
Garvagh ˈgɑːv ə ‖ ˈgɑːrv ə
Garvaghy gɑː ˈvæ hi ‖ gɑːr-
Gary *personal name; place in IN* ˈgær i ‖ ˈger-
Gary *family name* ˈgeər i ‖ ˈger i ˈgær i
gas gæs **gases, gasses** ˈgæs ɪz -əz **gassed**
    gæst **gassing** ˈgæs ɪŋ
    ˈgas ˌchamber; ˌgas ˈfire; ˈgas ˌfitter; ˈgas
    mask; ˈgas ˌpedal; ˈgas ring; ˈgas ˌstation;
    ˌgas ˈturbine ‖ ˈ• , •‿•
gasbag ˈgæs bæg ~**s** z
Gascoigne, Gascoin, Gascoine, Gascoyne
    ˈgæsk ɔɪn
Gascon ˈgæsk ən ~**s** z
Gascony ˈgæsk ən i
gaseous ˈgæs i‿əs ˈgeɪs-, ˈgeɪz- ‖ ˈgæʃ əs
    ~**ness** nəs nɪs
gash, Gash gæʃ **gashed** gæʃt **gashes** ˈgæʃ ɪz
    -əz **gashing** ˈgæʃ ɪŋ
gasholder ˈgæs ˌhəʊld ə ‖ -ˌhoʊld ᵊr ~**s** z
gasifiable ˈgæs ɪ faɪ‿əb əl §ˈ•ə-; ˌ••ˈ•••
gasification ˌgæs ɪf ɪ ˈkeɪʃ ᵊn ˌ•ᵊf-, §-ə'•-
gasi|fy ˈgæs ɪ ˌfaɪ -ə- ~**fied** faɪd ~**fier/s** faɪ‿ə/
    z ‖ faɪ‿ᵊr/z ~**fies** faɪz ~**fying** faɪ ɪŋ
Gaskell ˈgæsk ᵊl
gasket ˈgæsk ɪt -ət ~**s** s
gaskin ˈgæsk ɪn §-ən ~**s** z
gaslamp ˈgæs læmp ~**s** s
gaslight ˈgæs laɪt ~**s** s
gas|man ˈgæs ˌmæn ~**men** men
gasohol ˈgæs ə hɒl ‖ -hɔːl -hɑːl
gasolene, gasoline ˈgæs ə liːn , •‿•ˈ•
gasometer gæ ˈsɒm ɪt ə gə-, -ət ə ‖ -ˈsɑːm ət̬ ᵊr
    ~**s** z
gasp gɑːsp §gæsp ‖ gæsp **gasped** gɑːspt
    §gæspt ‖ gæspt **gasping** ˈgɑːsp ɪŋ §ˈgæsp-
    ‖ ˈgæsp ɪŋ **gasps** gɑːsps §gæsps ‖ gæsps
Gaspar ˈgæsp ə -ɑː ‖ -ᵊr -ɑːr
Gaspé ˈgæsp eɪ ‖ gæ ˈspeɪ —*Fr* [gas pe]
gass|y ˈgæs li ~**ier** i‿ə ‖ i‿ᵊr ~**iest** i ɪst i‿əst
    ~**iness** i nəs i nɪs
gasteropod ˈgæs tᵊr ə pɒd ‖ -pɑːd ~**s** z
gastrectom|y gæ ˈstrekt əm li ~**ies** iz
gastric ˈgæs trɪk
gastritis gæ ˈstraɪt ɪs §-əs ‖ -ˈstraɪt̬ əs
gastro- *comb. form*
    with stress-neutral suffix ˌgæs trəʊ ‖ -troʊ —
    gastroenteric ˌgæs trəʊ en ˈter ɪk ◄ ‖ -troʊ-
    with stress-imposing suffix gæ ˈstrɒ+ ‖ -ˈstrɑː+
    — **gastroscopy** gæ ˈstrɒsk əp i ‖ -ˈstrɑːsk-
gastroenteritis ˌgæs trəʊ ˌent ə ˈraɪt ɪs §-əs
    ‖ -troʊ ˌent̬ ə ˈraɪt̬ əs
gastrointestinal ˌgæs trəʊ ɪn ˈtest ɪn ᵊl ◄ -ᵊn
    əl; ˌ•ɪnt es ˈtaɪn- ‖ -troʊ ɪn ˈtest ᵊn‿əl ◄ ~**ly** i
gastronome ˈgæs trə nəʊm ‖ -noʊm ~**s** z
gastronomic ˌgæs trə ˈnɒm ɪk ◄ ‖ -ˈnɑːm-
    ~**ally** ᵊl‿i

G

gastronomy gæ 'strɒn əm i ‖ -'straːn-
gastropod 'gæs trə pɒd ‖ -paːd ~s z
gasworks 'gæs wɜːks ‖ -wɜːks
gat gæt gats gæts
Gatcomb, Gatcombe 'gæt kəm
gate, Gate geɪt gated 'geɪt ɪd -əd ‖ 'geɪt̮ əd
gates geɪts gating 'geɪt ɪŋ ‖ 'geɪt̮ ɪŋ
'gate ˌmoney
Gateacre 'gæt ək ə ‖ -ər
gateau, gâteau 'gæt əʊ ‖ gæ 'təʊ —Fr [ga to]
~s, ~x z —or as sing.
gatecrash 'geɪt kræʃ ~ed t ~er/s ə/z ‖ ər/z
~es ɪz əz ~ing ɪŋ
gatefold 'geɪt fəʊld →-fɒʊld ‖ -foʊld ~s z
gate|house, G~ 'geɪt |haʊs ~houses haʊz ɪz
-əz
gatekeeper 'geɪt ˌkiːp ə ‖ -ər ~s z
gateleg 'geɪt leg ~s z
gatepost 'geɪt pəʊst ‖ -poʊst ~s s
Gates geɪts
Gateshead 'geɪts hed ˌ•'•
gateway 'geɪt weɪ ~s z
Gath gæθ
gather 'gæð ə §'gaːð- ‖ -ər ~ed d gathering
'gæð ər_ɪŋ §'gaːð- ~s z
Gathercole 'gæð ə kəʊl →-kɒʊl ‖ -ər koʊl
gatherer 'gæð ər_ə §'gaːð- ‖ -ər_ər ~s z
Gathurst 'gæθ ɜːst -əst ‖ -ərst
Gatley 'gæt li
Gatling 'gæt lɪŋ ~s, ~'s z
gator 'geɪt ə ‖ 'geɪt̮ ər ~s z
Gatorade tdmk 'geɪt ə reɪd ˌ•'•• ‖ 'geɪt̮-
Gatsby 'gæts bi
Gatt, GATT gæt
Gatting 'gæt ɪŋ ‖ 'gæt̮ ɪŋ
Gatwick 'gæt wɪk
gauche gəʊʃ ‖ goʊʃ
gauche|ly 'gəʊʃ |li ‖ 'goʊʃ- ~ness nəs nɪs
gaucherie 'gəʊʃ ər i ˌgəʊʃ ə 'riː ‖ ˌgoʊʃ ə 'riː
—Fr [go ʃʁi] ~s z
gaucho 'gaʊtʃ əʊ ‖ -oʊ ~s z
gaudeamus ˌgaʊd i 'aːm ʊs ˌgɔːd-, -'eɪm-, -əs
ˌgaude ˌamus 'igitur
Gaudi, Gaudí gaʊ 'diː 'gaʊd i —Catalan
[gəu 'ði], Sp [gau 'ði]
gaud|y 'gɔːd |i ‖ 'gaːd- ~ier i_ə ‖ i_ər ~iest
i_ɪst i_əst ~ily ɪ li əl i ~iness i nəs i nɪs
gauge geɪdʒ gauged geɪdʒd gauges
'geɪdʒ ɪz -əz gauging 'geɪdʒ ɪŋ
Gauguin 'gəʊg æ -æn ‖ goʊ 'gæn —Fr [go gæ̃]
~s, ~'s z
Gaul gɔːl ‖ gaːl Gauls gɔːlz ‖ gaːlz
gauleiter, G~ 'gaʊ ˌlaɪt ə ‖ -laɪt̮ ər —Ger
['gau lai tɐ] ~s z
Gaulish 'gɔːl ɪʃ ‖ 'gaːl-
Gaullism 'gəʊl ˌɪz əm →'gɒʊl- ‖ 'gɔːl- 'gaːl-,
'goʊl-
Gaullist 'gəʊl ɪst →'gɒʊl-, §-əst ‖ 'gɔːl- 'gaːl-,
'goʊl- ~s s
Gauloise, Gauloises tdmk 'gəʊl waːz ˌ•'•
‖ goʊl 'waːz —Fr [go lwaːz]
gault, Gault gɔːlt gɒlt ‖ gaːlt
Gaumont 'gəʊ mɒnt -mənt ‖ 'goʊ maːnt

gaunt, Gaunt gɔːnt ‖ gaːnt gaunter
'gɔːnt ə ‖ 'gɔːnt̮ ər 'gaːnt̮ ər gauntest
'gɔːnt ɪst -əst ‖ 'gɔːnt̮ əst 'gaːnt̮-
gauntlet 'gɔːnt lət -lɪt ‖ 'gaːnt- ~s s
gaunt|ly 'gɔːnt |li ‖ 'gaːnt- ~ness nəs nɪs
Gausden 'gɔːz dən ‖ 'gaːz-
gauss, Gauss gaʊs
Gaussian 'gaʊs i_ən
Gautama 'gaʊt əm ə 'gaʊt- ‖ 'goʊt-
gauze gɔːz ‖ gaːz gauzes 'gɔːz ɪz -əz ‖ 'gaːz-
gauz|y 'gɔːz |i ‖ 'gaːz- ~ier i_ə ‖ i_ər ~iest
i_ɪst i_əst ~ily ɪ li əl i ~iness i nəs i nɪs
Gavan 'gæv ən
gave geɪv
gavel 'gæv əl ~s z
gavelkind 'gæv əl kaɪnd -kɪnd
Gaveston 'gæv ɪst ən -əst-
gavial 'geɪv i_əl 'gæv- ~s z
Gavin 'gæv ɪn -ən
gavotte gə 'vɒt ‖ -'vaːt ~s s
Gawain 'gaː weɪn 'gæ-, -wɪn; gə 'weɪn
Gawith (i) 'gaʊ_ɪθ, (ii) 'geɪ wɪθ
gawk gɔːk ‖ gaːk gawked gɔːkt ‖ gaːkt
gawking 'gɔːk ɪŋ ‖ 'gaːk- gawks gɔːks ‖
gaːks
gawk|y 'gɔːk |i ‖ 'gaːk- ~ier i_ə ‖ i_ər ~iest
i_ɪst i_əst ~ily ɪ li əl i ~iness i nəs i nɪs
Gawler 'gɔːl ə ‖ -ər 'gaːl-
gawp gɔːp ‖ gaːp gawped gɔːpt ‖ gaːpt
gawping 'gɔːp ɪŋ ‖ 'gaːp- gawps gɔːps
‖ gaːps
gay, Gay geɪ gaily 'geɪ li gayer 'geɪ ə ‖ -ər
gayest 'geɪ ɪst -əst gays geɪz
Gaydon 'geɪd ən
Gaye geɪ
Gayle geɪəl
Gaylord 'geɪ lɔːd ‖ -lɔːrd
Gay-Lussac ˌgeɪ 'luːs æk ‖ -lə 'sæk —Fr
[gɛ ly sak]
gayness 'geɪ nəs -nɪs
Gaynor 'geɪn ə ‖ -ər
Gayton 'geɪt ən
Gaza 'gaːz ə ‖ 'gæz-
ˌGaza 'Strip
gazania gə 'zeɪn i_ə ~s z
Gazdar 'gæz daː ‖ -daːr
gaze geɪz gazed geɪzd gazes 'geɪz ɪz -əz
gazing 'geɪz ɪŋ
gazebo gə 'ziːb əʊ ‖ -'zeɪb oʊ -'ziːb- ~s z
gazelle gə 'zel ~s z
gazer 'geɪz ə ‖ -ər ~s z
ga|zette gə |'zet ~zetted 'zet ɪd -əd ‖ 'zet̮ əd
~zettes 'zets ~zetting 'zet ɪŋ ‖ 'zet̮ ɪŋ
gazetteer ˌgæz ə 'tɪə -ɪ- ‖ -'tɪər ~s z
gazpacho gæz 'pætʃ əʊ gæs-, gəs-, -'paːtʃ-
‖ gə 'spaːtʃ oʊ —Sp [gaθ 'pa tʃo]
gazump gə 'zʌmp ~ed t ~ing ɪŋ ~s s
gazund|er gə 'zʌnd ə ‖ -ər ~ered əd ‖ ərd
~ering ər ɪŋ ~ers əz ‖ ərz
Gazza 'gæz ə
GB ˌdʒiː 'biː
GCE ˌdʒiː siː 'iː ◄ ~s z
GCSE ˌdʒiː siː es 'iː ~s z

Gdansk gə 'dænˑsk ‖ -'dɑːnˑsk —*Polish* Gdańsk [gdajŋsk]

g'day gə 'deɪ

GDP ˌdʒiː diː 'piː

gean giːn **geans** giːnz

gear gɪə ‖ gɪᵊr **geared** gɪəd ‖ gɪᵊrd **gearing** 'gɪər ɪŋ ‖ 'gɪr ɪŋ **gears** gɪəz ‖ gɪᵊrz
ˌgear ˌlever; ˈgear ˌshift; ˈgear ˌstick

gearbox 'gɪə bɒks ‖ 'gɪᵊr bɑːks **~es** ɪz əz

Geary 'gɪər i ‖ 'gɪr i

Gebhard 'geb hɑːd ‖ -hɑːrd

gecko 'gek əʊ ‖ -oʊ **~es, ~s** z

Geddes 'ged ɪs §-əs ‖ -iːz

geddit 'ged ɪt §-ət ‖ 'geţ ət —*This non-standard spelling of* get it *reflects a casual pronunciation with* ţ (= d).

gee, Gee dʒiː **geed** dʒiːd **geeing** 'dʒiː ɪŋ **gees** dʒiːz

gee-gee 'dʒiː dʒiː **~s** z

geek giːk **geeks** giːks

geek|y 'giːk| i **~ier** i ə ‖ i ᵊr **~iest** i ɪst ˌəst

Geelong dʒɪ 'lɒŋ dʒə- ‖ -'lɔːŋ -'lɑːŋ

Geen *(i)* giːn, *(ii)* dʒiːn

geese giːs

Geeson *(i)* 'giːs ᵊn, *(ii)* 'dʒiːs ᵊn

Geevor 'giːv ə ‖ -ᵊr

Ge'ez 'giː ez

geezer 'giːz ə ‖ -ᵊr **~s** z

Geffrye 'dʒef ri

gefilte gə 'fɪlt ə

Gehenna gɪ 'hen ə gə-

Gehrig 'geər ɪg ‖ 'ger-

Geiger 'gaɪg ə ‖ -ᵊr
ˈGeiger ˌcounter

Geikie 'giːk i

geisha 'geɪʃ ə —*Jp* [ge,e ça] **~s** z

Geissler 'gaɪs lə ‖ -lᵊr —*Ger* ['gaɪs lɐ]

gel *'jell, jelly'* dʒel **gelled** dʒeld **gelling** 'dʒel ɪŋ **gels** dʒelz

gel *'girl'* gel **gels** gelz

gelatin 'dʒel ət ɪn §-ən

gelatine 'dʒel ə tiːn ˌ•ˈ•

gelatinous dʒə 'læt ɪn əs dʒɪ-, dʒe-, -ən- ‖ -'læt ᵊn_əs **~ly** li **~ness** nəs nɪs

geld geld **gelded** 'geld ɪd -əd **gelding** 'geld ɪŋ **gelds** geldz **gelt** gelt

Geldart 'geld ɑːt ‖ -ɑːrt

gelding 'geld ɪŋ **~s** z

Geldof 'geld ɒf -ɔːf ‖ -ɔːf -ɑːf

gelid 'dʒel ɪd -əd

gelignite 'dʒel ɪg naɪt -əg-

Gell *(i)* dʒel, *(ii)* gel

Geller 'gel ə ‖ -ᵊr

Gelligaer ˌgeθ li 'geə ˌgeł i-, -'gaɪ_ə ‖ -'geᵊr -'gaɪᵊr —*Welsh* [ˌge łi 'gair, -'gair]

gelt gelt

gem dʒem **gems** dʒemz

Gemara gə 'mɑːr ə ge-

gemeinschaft gə 'maɪn ʃɑːft -ʃæft —*Ger* [gə 'maɪn ʃaft]

gemi|nate v 'dʒem ɪ |neɪt -ə- **~nated** neɪt ɪd -əd ‖ neɪţ əd **~nates** neɪts **~nating** neɪt ɪŋ ‖ neɪţ ɪŋ

geminate n, adj 'dʒem ɪn ət -ən-, -ɪt; -ɪ neɪt, -ə- **~s** s

gemination ˌdʒem ɪ 'neɪʃ ᵊn -ə- **~s** z

Gemini 'dʒem ɪ naɪ -ə-, -niː **~s** z

Geminian ˌdʒem ɪ 'naɪ_ən -ə-, -'niː_ **~s** z

Gemm|a, gemm|a 'dʒem ə **~ae** iː **~as, ~a's** əz

Gemmell, Gemmill 'gem ᵊl

gemmology, gemology dʒe 'mɒl ədʒ i ‖ -'mɑːl-

gemot, gemote gɪ 'məʊt gə- ‖ -'moʊt **~s** s

gemsbok 'gemz bɒk -bʌk ‖ -bɑːk **~s** s

gemstone 'dʒem stəʊn ‖ -stoʊn **~s** z

gen dʒen **genned** dʒend **genning** 'dʒen ɪŋ **gens** dʒenz

-gen dʒᵊn, dʒen — **glycogen** 'glaɪk ədʒ ən -əʊdʒen

gendarme 'ʒɒnd ɑːm 'ʒɒ̃d- ‖ 'ʒɑːnd ɑːrm —*Fr* [ʒɑ̃ daʁm] **~s** z

gender 'dʒend ə ‖ -ᵊr **~s** z

gender-bender 'dʒend ə ˌbend ə ‖ -ᵊr ˌbend ᵊr **~s** z

gene, Gene dʒiːn **genes, Gene's** dʒiːnz
ˈgene ˌpool

genealogical ˌdʒiːn i_ə 'lɒdʒ ɪk ᵊl ◀ ‖ -'lɑːdʒ- **~ly** _i

genealogist ˌdʒiːn i 'æl ədʒ ɪst △-'ɒl-, §-əst ‖ -'ɑːl- **~s** s

genealog|y ˌdʒiːn i 'æl ədʒ |i △-'ɒl- ‖ -'ɑːl- **~ies** iz

genera 'dʒen ər ə

general 'dʒen ᵊr_əl **~s** z
ˌgeneral deˈlivery; ˌgeneral eˈlection; ˌgeneral ˈknowledge; ˌgeneral pracˈtitioner; ˌgeneral ˈstaff; ˌgeneral ˈstrike

generalis... —*see* **generaliz...**

generalissimo ˌdʒen ᵊr_ə 'lɪs ɪ məʊ -'•ə- ‖ -moʊ **~s** z

generalist 'dʒen ᵊr_əl ɪst §-əst **~s** s

generalit|y ˌdʒen ə 'ræl ət |i -ɪt i ‖ -əţ |i **~ies** iz

generalization ˌdʒen ᵊr_əl aɪ 'zeɪʃ ᵊn _əl ɪ- ‖ _əl ə- **~s** z

generaliz|e 'dʒen ᵊr_ə laɪz **~ed** d **~es** ɪz əz **~ing** ɪŋ

generally 'dʒen ᵊr_əl i

generalship 'dʒen ᵊr_əl ʃɪp **~s** s

gene|rate 'dʒen ə |reɪt **~rated** reɪt ɪd -əd ‖ reɪţ əd **~rates** reɪts **~rating** reɪt ɪŋ ‖ reɪţ ɪŋ

generation ˌdʒen ə 'reɪʃ ᵊn **~s** z
ˌgeneˈration gap

generational ˌdʒen ə 'reɪʃ ᵊn_əl ◀ **~ly** i

generativ|e 'dʒen ᵊr_ət ɪv ‖ -ᵊr_əţ ɪv -ə reɪt ɪv **~ely** li **~eness** nəs nɪs **~ist/s** ɪst/s §əst/s

generator 'dʒen ə reɪt ə ‖ -reɪţ ᵊr **~s** z

generic dʒə 'ner ɪk dʒɪ- **~ally** ᵊl_i **~s** s

generosity ˌdʒen ə 'rɒs ət i -ɪt i ‖ -'rɑːs əţ i

generous 'dʒen ᵊr_əs **~ly** li **~ness** nəs nɪs

Genese dʒə 'niːs dʒɪ-

Genesee ˌdʒen ə 'siː -ɪ-

genesis, G~ 'dʒen əs ɪs -ɪs-, -ɪz, §-əs

-genesis 'dʒen əs ɪs -ɪs-, §-əs —
  morphogenesis ˌmɔːf əʊ 'dʒen əs ɪs -ɪs ɪs,
  §-əs ‖ ˌmɔːrf oʊ-
genet *animal* 'dʒen ɪt §-ət ~s s
Genet *French writer* ʒə 'neɪ —*Fr* [ʒə nɛ]
genetic dʒə 'net ɪk dʒɪ- ‖ -'neţ ɪk ~**ally** əl_i ~s
  s
  geˌnetic ˈcode; geˌnetic ˌengiˈneering
geneticist dʒə 'net ɪs ɪst dʒɪ-, -əs-, §-əst
  ‖ -'neţ- ~s s
Geneva dʒə 'niːv ə dʒɪ-
  Geˌneva conˈvention
Genevan dʒə 'niːv ən dʒɪ- ~s z
Genevieve 'dʒen ə viːv -ɪ-, ˌ••'• —*Fr*
  Geneviève [ʒən vjɛːv]
Genghis 'dʒeŋ gɪs 'geŋ-, -gɪz, §-gəs, §-gəz
genial *'cheerful'* 'dʒiːn i_əl ‖ 'dʒiːn jəl ~**ly** i
  ~**ness** nəs nɪs
genial *'of the chin'* dʒə 'niː_əl dʒɪ-, -'naɪ_əl
geniality ˌdʒiːn i 'æl ət i -ɪt i ‖ -əţ i
-genic 'dʒen ɪk 'dʒiːn ɪk — **mutagenic**
  ˌmjuːt ə 'dʒen ɪk ◄ ‖ ˌmjuːţ-
genie, Genie 'dʒiːn i **genies, Genie's** 'dʒiːn iz
genii 'dʒiːn i aɪ
genip 'gɪn ep ~s s
genital 'dʒen ɪt əl -ət- ‖ -əţ əl ~**ly** _i ~s z
genitalia ˌdʒen ɪ 'teɪl i_ə ˌ•'ə-
genitival ˌdʒen ə 'taɪv əl ◄ -ɪ- ~**ly** i ~s z
genitive 'dʒen ət ɪv -ɪt- ‖ -əţ- ~s z
genitourinary ˌdʒen ɪ təʊ 'jʊər ɪn ər_i ˌ•ə-,
  -'jɔːr-, -'••ən- ‖ ˌdʒen ə toʊ 'jʊr ə ner i
geni|us 'dʒiːn i_|əs ~**i** aɪ ~**uses** əs ɪz -əz
  ˌgenius ˈloci
genned-up ˌdʒend 'ʌp ◄
Gennesaret, Gennesareth gə 'nez ər ɪt gɪ-,
  ge-, -ət; -ə ret ‖ -'nes-
Genoa 'dʒen əʊ ə dʒə 'nəʊ ə, dʒɪ-, dʒe-
  ‖ -oʊ ə —*It* Genova ['dʒɛː no va]
genocidal ˌdʒen ə 'saɪd əl ◄ -əʊ-
genocide 'dʒen ə saɪd -əʊ-
Genoese ˌdʒen əʊ 'iːz ◄ ‖ -oʊ- -'iːs
genome 'dʒiːn əʊm ‖ -oʊm ~s z
genotype 'dʒen ə taɪp 'dʒiːn- ~s s
-genous *stress-imposing* dʒən əs —
  androgenous æn 'drɒdʒ ən əs ‖ -'drɑːdʒ-
genre 'ʒɒn rə 'ʒɑːn-, 'ʒō-, 'dʒɒn- ‖ 'ʒɑːn-
  —*Fr* [ʒɑ̃ːʁ]
gent, Gent dʒent **gents** dʒenⱦs
genteel dʒen 'tiːəl dʒən- ~**ly** li ~**ness** nəs nɪs
gentian 'dʒenʧ ən 'dʒenʧ i_ən ~s z
gentile, G~ 'dʒen aɪəl ~s z
gentility dʒen 'tɪl ət i -ɪt- ‖ -əţ i
gentle, G~ 'dʒent əl ‖ 'dʒenⱦ əl **gentler**
  'dʒent lə ‖ -l_ər **gentlest** 'dʒent lɪst -ləst
gentlefolk 'dʒent əl fəʊk ‖ 'dʒenⱦ əl foʊk ~s s
gentle|man, G~ 'dʒent əl |mən ‖ 'dʒenⱦ-
  ~**men** mən men —*in rapid casual AmE also*
  'dʒen əm ən
  ˌgentleman ˈfarmer; ˌgentleman's
  aˈgreement; ˌgentleman's ˈgentleman
gentle|man-at-arms
  ˌdʒent əl |mən ət 'ɑːmz ‖ ˌdʒenⱦ
  əl |mən əţ 'ɑːrmz ~**men-at-arms** mən- men-

gentlemanly 'dʒent əl mən li ‖ 'dʒenⱦ-
gentleness 'dʒent əl nəs -nɪs ‖ 'dʒenⱦ-
gentle|woman 'dʒent əl |ˌwʊm ən ‖ 'dʒenⱦ-
  ~**women** ˌwɪm ɪn -ən
gently 'dʒent li
Gentoo, g~ 'dʒent uː dʒen 'tuː- ~s z
gentrification ˌdʒentr ɪf ɪ 'keɪʃ ən ˌ•əf-, §-ə'•-
  ~s z
gentri|fy 'dʒentr ɪ |faɪ -ə- ~**fied** faɪd ~**fier/s**
  faɪ_ə/z ‖ faɪ_ər/z ~**fies** faɪz ~**fying** faɪ ɪŋ
gentry, G~ 'dʒentr i
genuflect 'dʒen ju flekt -jə- ‖ -jə- ~**ed** ɪd əd
  ~**ing** ɪŋ ~s s
genuflection, genuflexion ˌdʒen ju 'flek ʃən
  -jə- ‖ -jə- ~s z
genuine 'dʒen ju_ɪn §_ən, △-aɪn ~**ly** li ~**ness**
  nəs nɪs
genus 'dʒiːn əs 'dʒen- **genera** 'dʒen ər ə
-geny *stress-imposing* dʒən i — **phylogeny**
  faɪ 'lɒdʒ ən i ‖ -'lɑːdʒ-
geo- *comb. form*
  with stress-neutral suffix ˌdʒiː əʊ ‖ ˌdʒiː oʊ —
  geothermal ˌdʒiː əʊ 'θɜːm əl ◄ ‖ -oʊ 'θɜːm-
  with stress-imposing suffix dʒi 'ɒ+ ‖ dʒi 'ɑː+
  — **geophagy** dʒi 'ɒf ədʒ i ‖ -'ɑːf-
geocentric ˌdʒiː əʊ 'sentr ɪk ◄ ‖ -oʊ- ~**ally** əl_i
GeoCities *tdmk* ˌdʒiː əʊ 'sɪt ɪz ‖ -oʊ 'sɪţ-
geode 'dʒiː əʊd ‖ -oʊd ~s z
geodesic ˌdʒiː əʊ 'diːs ɪk ◄ -'des-; dʒɪə 'diːs ɪk
  ‖ -ə 'des- -'diːs-
  ˌgeoˌdesic ˈdome
geodesist/s dʒi 'ɒd əs ɪst/s -ɪs-, -əz-, -ɪz-,
  §-əst/s ‖ -'ɑːd- ~**y** i
geodetic ˌdʒiː əʊ 'det ɪk ◄ dʒɪə 'det-
  ‖ ˌdʒiː ə 'deţ ɪk ◄ ~**ally** əl_i
Geoff dʒef **Geoff's** dʒefs
Geoffrey 'dʒef ri
Geoghegan (i) 'geɪg ən, (ii) gɪ 'heɪg ən
geographer dʒi 'ɒg rəf ə ‖ -'ɑːg rəf ər ~s z
geographic ˌdʒiː_ə 'græf ɪk dʒɪə 'græf- ~**al** əl
  ~**ally** əl_i
geograph|y dʒi 'ɒg rəf li 'dʒɒg- ‖ -'ɑːg- ~**ies**
  iz
geologic ˌdʒiː_ə 'lɒdʒ ɪk ◄ dʒɪə 'lɒdʒ-
  ‖ -'lɑːdʒ- ~**al** əl ~**ally** əl_i
geologist dʒi 'ɒl ədʒ ɪst §-əst ‖ -'ɑːl- ~s s
geolog|y dʒi 'ɒl ədʒ li i ‖ -'ɑːl- ~**ies** iz
geomatic ˌdʒiː_ə 'mæt ɪk ◄ -əʊ- ‖ -'mæţ ɪk◄
  ~s s
geometer dʒi 'ɒm ɪt ə -ət- ‖ -'ɑːm əţ ər ~s z
geometric ˌdʒiː_ə 'metr ɪk ◄ -əʊ-; dʒɪə 'metr-
  ~**al** əl ~**ally** əl_i
  ˌgeoˌmetric proˈgression
geometrician ˌdʒiː_ə me 'trɪʃ ən -mə'••-;
  dʒi ˌɒm ə- ‖ dʒi ˌɑːm ə- ~s z
geometr|y dʒi 'ɒm ətr li 'dʒɒm-, -ɪtr- ‖ -'ɑːm-
  ~**ies** iz
geophysical ˌdʒiː əʊ 'fɪz ɪk əl ◄ ‖ ˌ•ə- ~**ly** _i
geophysicist ˌdʒiː əʊ 'fɪz ɪs ɪst -əs ɪst, §-əst
  ‖ ˌ•ə- ~s s
geophysics ˌdʒiː əʊ 'fɪz ɪks ‖ -ə-
geopolitical ˌdʒiː əʊ pə 'lɪt ɪk əl ◄ ‖ -ə pə 'lɪţ-
  ~**ly** _i

geopolitics ˌdʒiː əʊ 'pɒl ə tɪks -'•ɪ- ‖ -ə 'pɑːl-
Geordie 'dʒɔːd i ‖ 'dʒɔːrd i ~s z
George dʒɔːdʒ ‖ dʒɔːrdʒ **George's** 'dʒɔːdʒ ɪz
-əz ‖ 'dʒɔːrdʒ əz
ˌGeorge 'Cross
Georges ʒɔːʒ dʒɔːdʒ ‖ ʒɔːrʒ dʒɔːrdʒ —*Fr*
[ʒɔʁʒ]
Georgetown 'dʒɔːdʒ taʊn ‖ 'dʒɔːrdʒ- —*in
Guyana locally* -tʌŋ
georgette, G~ ₍ˌ₎dʒɔː 'dʒet ‖ ₍ˌ₎dʒɔːr- ~s s
Georgia 'dʒɔːdʒ ə 'dʒɔːdʒ i ə ‖ 'dʒɔːrdʒ ə
Georgian 'dʒɔːdʒ ən 'dʒɔːdʒ i ən ‖ 'dʒɔːrdʒ ən
~s z
georgic 'dʒɔːdʒ ɪk ‖ 'dʒɔːrdʒ- ~s s
Georgie 'dʒɔːdʒ i ‖ 'dʒɔːrdʒ i
Georgina dʒɔː 'dʒiːn ə ‖ dʒɔːr-
geostationary ˌdʒiː əʊ 'steɪʃ ən ər_i ◄ -ən_ər-
‖ -oʊ 'steɪʃ ə ner i◄
geosynchronous ˌdʒiː əʊ
'sɪŋk rən əs ◄ ‖ ˌdʒiː oʊ-
Gephardt 'gep hɑːt ‖ -hɑːrt
Geraint 'ger aɪnt •'• —*Welsh* ['ge raint]
Gerald 'dʒer əld
Geraldine 'dʒer əl diːn —*but* -daɪn *in Coleridge*
Geraldo dʒə 'ræld əʊ ‖ hə 'rɑːld oʊ —*Sp*
[xe 'ral do]
Geraldton 'dʒer əld tən
geranium dʒə 'reɪn i_əm dʒɪ- ~s z
Gerard 'dʒer ɑːd -əd; dʒe 'rɑːd, dʒə-
‖ dʒə 'rɑːrd
Gerber *(i)* 'dʒɜːb ə ‖ 'dʒɜ˞ːb ər, *(ii)*
'gɜːb ə ‖ 'gɜ˞ːb ər —*The tdmk for baby food is
usually (ii).*
gerbera 'dʒɜːb ər ə 'gɜːb- ‖ 'dʒɜˑːb- 'gɜˑːb-
~s z
gerbil 'dʒɜːb əl -ɪl ‖ 'dʒɜˑːb- ~s z
Gerda 'gɜːd ə ‖ 'gɜ˞ːd ə
Gerhardi, Gerhardie dʒə 'hɑːd i ‖ dʒ˞r 'hɑːrd i
geriatric ˌdʒer i 'ætr ɪk ◄ ‖ ˌdʒɪr- ~s s
geriatrician ˌdʒer i_ə 'trɪʃ ən ‖ ˌdʒɪr- ~s z
Gericault, Géricault 'ʒer ɪ kəʊ -ə-, ˌ•'•
‖ ˌʒeɪ rɪ 'koʊ —*Fr* [ʒe ʁi ko]
Geritol *tdmk* 'dʒer ɪ tɒl -ə- ‖ -tɑːl
germ dʒɜːm ‖ dʒɜˑːm **germs**
dʒɜːmz ‖ dʒɜˑːmz
ˌgerm 'cell; ˌgerm 'warfare
Germaine dʒə 'meɪn ₍ˌ₎dʒɜː- ‖ dʒ˞r-
German, g~ 'dʒɜːm ən ‖ 'dʒɜˑːm- ~s z
ˌGerman 'measles; ˌGerman 'shepherd
germander dʒɜː 'mænd ə dʒə-
‖ dʒ˞r 'mænd ər ~s z
germane dʒə 'meɪn '•• ‖ dʒ˞r- ~ly li ~ness
nəs nɪs
Germanic, g~ dʒɜː 'mæn ɪk dʒə- ‖ dʒ˞r-
Germanicus dʒɜː 'mæn ɪk əs dʒə- ‖ dʒ˞r-
germanium dʒɜː 'meɪn i_əm dʒə- ‖ dʒ˞r-
German|y 'dʒɜːm ən i ‖ 'dʒɜˑːm- ~ies, ~ys,
~y's z
germicidal ˌdʒɜːm ɪ 'saɪd əl ◄ -ə- ‖ ˌdʒɜˑːm-
germicide 'dʒɜːm ɪ saɪd -ə- ‖ 'dʒɜˑːm- ~s z
germinal 'dʒɜːm ɪn əl -ən- ‖ 'dʒɜˑːm-
germi|nate 'dʒɜːm ɪ |neɪt -ə- ‖ 'dʒɜˑːm-

~**nated** neɪt ɪd -əd ‖ neɪt̬ əd ~**nates** neɪts
~**nating** neɪt ɪŋ ‖ neɪt̬ ɪŋ
germination ˌdʒɜːm ɪ 'neɪʃ ən -ə- ‖ ˌdʒɜˑːm-
~s z
Germiston 'dʒɜːm ɪst ən §-əst- ‖ 'dʒɜˑːm-
Germolene *tdmk* 'dʒɜːm ə liːn ‖ 'dʒɜˑːm-
Geronimo dʒə 'rɒn ɪ məʊ dʒɪ-, dʒe-, -ə-
‖ -'rɑːn ə moʊ
Gerontius gə 'rɒnt i_əs dʒɪ-, dʒə-, -'rɒntʃ-
‖ -'rɑːnt-
gerontocrac|y ˌdʒer ɒn 'tɒk rəs |i ˌ•ən-
‖ -ən 'tɑːk- ~**ies** iz
gerontocratic dʒə ˌrɒnt ə 'kræt ɪk ◄
ˌdʒer ɒnt-, ˌ•ənt- ‖ dʒə ˌrɑːnt̬ ə 'kræt̬ ɪk ◄
gerontological dʒə ˌrɒnt ə 'lɒdʒ ɪk əl ◄
ˌdʒer ɒnt-, ˌ•ənt- ‖ dʒə ˌrɑːnt̬ ə 'lɑːdʒ-
gerontologist ˌdʒer ɒn 'tɒl ədʒ ɪst ˌ•ən-, §-əst
‖ -ən 'tɑːl- ~s s
gerontology ˌdʒer ɒn 'tɒl ədʒ i ˌ•ən-
‖ -ən 'tɑːl-
-gerous *stress-imposing* dʒ˞r əs —
dentigerous dʒen 'tɪdʒ ər əs
Gerrard 'dʒer ɑːd -əd; dʒe 'rɑːd, dʒə-
‖ dʒə 'rɑːrd
Gerry 'dʒer i
gerrymander 'dʒer i mænd ə ˌ•'•|'•• ‖ -ər ~**ed**
d **gerrymandering** 'dʒer i mænd_ər ɪŋ
ˌ•'•'••• ~s z
Gershwin 'gɜːʃ wɪn §-wən ‖ 'gɜˑːʃ-
Gertie 'gɜːt i ‖ 'gɜˑːt̬ i
Gertrude 'gɜːtr uːd ‖ 'gɜˑːtr- -ʊd
Gerty 'gɜːt i ‖ 'gɜˑːt̬ i
gerund 'dʒer ənd -ʌnd ~s z
gerundival ˌdʒer ən 'daɪv əl ◄ -ʌn-
gerundive dʒə 'rʌnd ɪv dʒɪ-, dʒe- ~s z
Gervaise, Gervase 'dʒɜːv eɪz -ɪz, -əs;
dʒɜː 'veɪz, -'veɪs ‖ 'dʒɜˑːv-
Geryon 'ger i_ən
gesellschaft gə 'zel ʃɑːft -ʃæft —*Ger* G~
[gə 'zɛl ʃaft]
gesso 'dʒes əʊ ‖ -oʊ
gestalt gə 'ʃtælt -'ʃtɑːlt; 'dʒest ælt ‖ gə 'ʃtɑːlt
—*Ger* G~ [gə 'ʃtalt] ~**en** ən ~s s
gestapo, G~ ge 'stɑːp əʊ ‖ gə 'stɑːp oʊ —*Ger*
G~ [ge 'sta: po, -'ʃta:-]
gest|ate dʒe 'st|eɪt 'dʒest |eɪt ‖ 'dʒest |eɪt
~**ated** eɪt ɪd -əd ‖ eɪt̬ əd ~**ates** eɪts ~**ating**
eɪt ɪŋ ‖ eɪt̬ ɪŋ
gestation dʒe 'steɪʃ ən ~s z
ge'station ˌperiod
gestatorial ˌdʒest ə 'tɔːr i_əl ◄ ‖ -'toʊr-
gestatory dʒe 'steɪt ər i 'dʒest ə ˌtær i
‖ 'dʒest ə tɔːr i -toʊr i
Gestetner *tdmk* ge 'stet nə gɪ-, gə- ‖ -n˞r
gesticu|late dʒe 'stɪk jʊ |leɪt -jə- ‖ -jə-
~**lated** leɪt ɪd -əd ‖ leɪt̬ əd ~**lates** leɪts
~**lating** leɪt ɪŋ ‖ leɪt̬ ɪŋ
gesticulation dʒe ˌstɪk jʊ 'leɪʃ ən -jə- ‖ -jə-
~s z
ges|ture 'dʒes |tʃə →'dʒeʃ- ‖ -|tʃ˞r ~**tured**
tʃəd ‖ tʃ˞rd ~**tures** tʃəz ‖ tʃ˞rz ~**turing**
tʃər ɪŋ

G

gesundheit gə 'zund haıt —*Ger* G~
  [gə 'zʊnt hait]
get get **gets** gets **getting** 'get ıŋ ‖ 'geṭ ıŋ
  got gɒt ‖ gɑːt **gotten** 'gɒt ᵊn ‖ 'gɑːt ᵊn
get-at-able get 'æt əb ᵊl ‖ geṭ 'æṭ-
getaway 'get ə ˌweɪ ‖ 'geṭ- ~s z
Gethin 'geθ ın
Gething 'geθ ıŋ
Gethsemane geθ 'sem ən i
getout 'get aut ‖ 'geṭ- ~s s
get-together 'get tə ˌgeð ə ‖ -ᵊr ~s z
Getty 'get i ‖ 'geṭ i
Gettysburg 'get ız bɜːg ‖ 'geṭ ız bɝːg
  ˌGettysburg Ad'dress
getup 'get ʌp ‖ 'geṭ- ~s s
get-up-and-go ˌget ʌp ən 'gəʊ →-ᵊŋ' •, →-m' •
  ‖ ˌgeṭ ʌp ən 'goʊ
geum 'dʒiː əm ~s z
gewgaw 'gjuː gɔː 'guː- ‖ -gɑː ~s z
Gewurztraminer, Gewürztraminer
  gə 'vʊəts trə ˌmiːn ə ‖ -'vɝːts trə ˌmiːn ᵊr
  —*Ger* [gə 'vʏʁts tʁa ˌmiːn ɐ]
geyser 'giːz ə 'gaız ə ‖ 'gaız ᵊr (*) —*In BrE*,
  'gaız ə *(if at all) particularly for the meaning
  'hot spring'; the water heater is always* 'giːz-
  ~z z
Ghan *in Australia* gæn
Ghana 'gɑːn ə
Ghanaian gɑː 'neɪ ən gə- ‖ -'naɪ- ~s z
gharry 'gær i ‖ 'ger-
ghast|ly 'gɑːst |li §'gæst- ‖ 'gæst- ~lier
  li ə ‖ li ᵊr ~liest li ˌıst ˌəst ~liness li nəs
  -nıs
ghat, ghaut gɑːt gɔːt, gʌt ‖ gɔːt **ghats,
  Ghats, ghauts** gɑːts gɔːts, gʌts ‖ gɔːts
ghee giː
Ghent gent —*Flemish* Gent [ɣɛnt]
gherkin 'gɜːk ın §-ᵊn ‖ 'gɝːk- ~s z
ghetto 'get əʊ ‖ 'geṭ oʊ ~s z
  'ghetto ˌblaster
ghi giː
Ghia 'giː ə —*It* ['giː a]
Ghibelline 'gıb ə liːn -laın ‖ -ᵊl ən
ghillie 'gıl i ~s z
Ghosh gəʊʃ ‖ goʊʃ
ghost gəʊst ‖ goʊst **ghosted** 'gəʊst ıd -əd
  ‖ 'goʊst əd **ghosting** 'gəʊst ıŋ ‖ 'goʊst ıŋ
  ghosts gəʊsts ‖ goʊsts
  'ghost town
ghost|ly 'gəʊst |li ‖ 'goʊst |li ~lier li ə ‖ li ᵊr
  ~liest li ˌıst ˌəst ~liness li nəs -nıs
ghostwriter 'gəʊst ˌraıt ə ‖ 'goʊst ˌraıṭ ᵊr ~s z
ghoul guːl **ghouls** guːlz
ghoulish 'guːl ıʃ ~ly li ~ness nəs nıs
GHQ ˌdʒiː eıtʃ 'kjuː §-heıtʃ-
ghyll gıl **ghylls** gılz
GI ˌdʒiː 'aı ◄ ~s, ~'s z
Gianni dʒi 'ɑːn i 'dʒɑːn i —*It* ['dʒan ni]
giant 'dʒaı ənt ~s, ~'s s
  ˌGiant's 'Causeway; 'giant ˌkiller; ˌgiant
  'panda
giantess 'dʒaı ənt es -ıs, -əs; ˌdʒaı ən 'tes
  ‖ 'dʒaı ənṭ əs ~es ız əz

giantism 'dʒaı ənt ˌız əm
giaour, G~ 'dʒaʊ ə ‖ 'dʒaʊ ᵊr **giaours, G~**
  'dʒaʊ əz ‖ 'dʒaʊ ᵊrz
giardiasis ˌdʒiː ɑː 'daı əs ıs §-əs ‖ ˌ•ɑːr-
Gib *'Gibraltar'* dʒıb
Gibb gıb
gibber *'speak incoherently'* 'dʒıb ə ‖ -ᵊr ~ed d
  gibbering 'dʒıb ᵊr ıŋ ~s z
Gibberd 'gıb əd ‖ -ᵊrd
gibberelic ˌdʒıb ə 'rel ık ◄

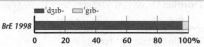

GIBBERISH

	■ 'dʒıb- ▢ 'gıb-	
BrE 1998		
	0 20 40 60 80 100%	

gibberish 'dʒıb ᵊr ıʃ 'gıb- —*BrE 1998 poll
  panel preference:* 'dʒıb- 96%, 'gıb- 4%.
Gibbes gıbz
gibbet 'dʒıb ıt -ət ~s s
gibbon, G~ 'gıb ən ~s z
Gibbons 'gıb ənz
gibbosit|y gı 'bɒs ət i -ıt- ‖ -'bɑːs əṭ i ~ies ız
gibbous 'gıb əs ~ly li ~ness nəs nıs
Gibbs gıbz
gibe dʒaıb *(= jibe)* **gibed** dʒaıbd **gibes**
  dʒaıbz **gibing/ly** 'dʒaıb ıŋ /li
Gibeon 'gıb i ən
Gibeonite 'gıb i ə naıt ~s s
giblets 'dʒıb ləts -lıts
Gibraltar dʒı 'brɔːl t ə dʒə-, -'brɒlt- ‖ -ᵊr
  -'brɑːlt-
Gibraltarian ˌdʒıb rɔːl 'teər i ən ◄ , •rɒl-;
  dʒı ˌbrɔːl-, dʒə-, -ˌbrɒl- ‖ -'ter- , •rɑːl-,
  -'tær- ~s z
Gibson 'gıb sᵊn
gid gıd
Giddens 'gıd ᵊnz
Gidding 'gıd ıŋ
gidd|y, Giddy 'gıd |i ~ied id ~ier i ə ‖ i ᵊr
  ~ies ız ~iest i ˌıst ˌəst ~ily ı li əl i ~iness
  i nəs i nıs ~ying i ˌıŋ
Gide ʒiːd —*Fr* [ʒid]
Gidea 'gıd i ə
Gideon 'gıd i ən ~s z
Gielgud 'giː ᵊl gʊd
GIF, gif gıf dʒıf **GIFs, gifs** gıfs dʒıfs
Giffard, Gifford *(i)* 'dʒıf əd ‖ -ᵊrd, *(ii)* 'gıf-
gift gıft **gifted** 'gıft ıd -əd **gifting** 'gıft ıŋ
  gifts gıfts
  'gift horse; 'gift ˌtoken
gifted 'gıft ıd -əd ~ly li ~ness nəs nıs
giftwrap 'gıft ræp ~ped t ~ping ıŋ ~s s
gig gıg **gigs** gıgz

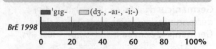

GIGA

	■ 'gıg- ▢ (dʒ-, -aı-, -iː-)	
BrE 1998		
	0 20 40 60 80 100%	

giga- ˌgıg ə — **gigabyte** 'gıg ə baıt —*BrE
  1998 poll panel preference:* 'gıg- 84%, *others
  (*dʒ-, -aı-, -iː-*) 16%.
gigantic dʒaı 'gænt ık ‖ -'gænṭ ık ~ally ᵊl_i

giggl|e 'gɪg əl ~**ed** d ~**er/s** _ə/z ‖ _ər/z ~**es** z
  ~**ing/ly** _ɪŋ /li
Giggleswick 'gɪg əlz wɪk
giggl|y 'gɪg əl_i ‖ i ~**ier** i_ə ‖ i_ər ~**iest** i_ɪst i_əst
  ~**iness** i nəs i nɪs
Gigha 'giː_ə
Gigi 'ʒiː ʒiː
Gigli 'dʒiːl jiː -iː —*It* ['dʒiːʎ ʎi]
gigolo 'dʒɪg ə ləʊ 'ʒɪg- ‖ -loʊ ~**s** z
gigot 'dʒɪg ət 'ʒɪg-, -əʊ ‖ ʒiː 'goʊ —*Fr* [ʒi go]
gigue ʒiːg —*Fr* [ʒig] **gigues** ʒiːgz
Gila 'hiːl ə —*but in BrE a spelling pronunciation*
  'giːl ə *is also heard.*
Gilbert, g~ 'gɪlb ət ‖ -ərt ~**s**, ~**'s** s
Gilbertian gɪl 'bɜːt i_ən -'bɜːʃ ən ‖ -'bɜːt̬- ~**s** z
Gilbey 'gɪlb i
Gilchrist 'gɪl krɪst
gild gɪld (= *guild*) **gilded** 'gɪld ɪd -əd **gilding**
  'gɪld ɪŋ **gilds** gɪldz **gilt** gɪlt
Gildersleeve 'gɪld ə sliːv ‖ -ər-
Gilead 'gɪl i æd ‖ _əd
Giles dʒaɪəlz
gilgai 'gɪlg aɪ
Gilgamesh 'gɪlg ə meʃ
Gilhooley gɪl 'huːl i
Gilkes, Gilks dʒɪlks
gill *'liquid measure'* dʒɪl **gills** dʒɪlz
gill *'organ of breathing'*, *'wattle'*, *'ravine'*,
  'stream' gɪl **gills** gɪlz
Gill *name (i)* gɪl, *(ii)* dʒɪl
Gillespie gɪ 'lesp i gə-
Gillette dʒɪ 'let dʒə-
Gillian 'dʒɪl i_ən
Gilliat, Gilliatt 'gɪl i_ət
Gillick 'gɪl ɪk
gillie, G~ 'gɪl i ~**s** z
Gillies 'gɪl iz
gilliflower 'dʒɪl i ˌflaʊ_ə ‖ -ˌflaʊ_ər ~**s** z
Gilligan 'gɪl ɪg ən
Gillingham *(i)* 'dʒɪl ɪŋ əm, *(ii)* 'gɪl- —*The place
  in Kent is (i); those in Dorset and Norfolk are
  (ii). The family name may be either.*
Gillow 'gɪl əʊ ‖ -oʊ
Gillray 'gɪl reɪ
gilly 'gɪl i
gillyflower 'dʒɪl i ˌflaʊ_ə ‖ -ˌflaʊ_ər ~**s** z
Gilman 'gɪl mən
Gilmore, Gilmour 'gɪl mɔː -mə ‖ -mɔːr -moʊr
Gilpin 'gɪlp ɪn §-ən
Gilroy 'gɪl rɔɪ
gilt gɪlt (= *guilt*) **gilts** gɪlts
gilt-edged ˌgɪlt 'edʒd ◄
Gilwell 'gɪl wəl -wel
gimbals 'dʒɪm bəlz 'gɪm-
gimcrack 'dʒɪm kræk
gimlet 'gɪm lət -lɪt ~**s** s
gimme 'gɪm i
gimmick 'gɪm ɪk ~**s** s
gimmickry 'gɪm ɪk ri
gimmicky 'gɪm ɪk i
gimp gɪmp **gimped** gɪmpt **gimping** 'gɪmp ɪŋ
  gimps gɪmps

Gimson *(i)* 'gɪmps ən, *(ii)* 'dʒɪmps- —*The late
  Prof. A.C.Gimson, phonetician, was (i).*
gin dʒɪn **ginned** dʒɪnd **ginning** 'dʒɪn ɪŋ **gins**
  dʒɪnz
  ˌgin 'rummy; ˌgin 'sling; 'gin trap
Gina 'dʒiːn ə
Gingell 'gɪndʒ əl
ginger, G~ 'dʒɪndʒ ə ‖ -ər ~**ed** d **gingering**
  'dʒɪndʒ ər_ɪŋ ~**s** z
  ˌginger 'ale; ˌginger 'beer; 'ginger group;
  'ginger nut
gingerbread 'dʒɪndʒ ə bred ‖ -ər-
ginger|ly 'dʒɪndʒ ə |li ‖ -ər- ~**liness** li nəs -nɪs
gingersnap 'dʒɪndʒ ə snæp ‖ -ər- ~**s** s
gingery 'dʒɪndʒ ər_i
gingham 'gɪŋ əm ~**s** z
gingival dʒɪn 'dʒaɪv əl 'dʒɪndʒ ɪv-
gingivitis ˌdʒɪndʒ ɪ 'vaɪt ɪs -ə- ‖ -'vaɪt̬ əs
Gingold 'gɪŋ gəʊld →-gɒʊld ‖ -goʊld
Gingrich 'gɪŋ grɪtʃ
ginkgo 'gɪŋk əʊ -gəʊ ‖ -oʊ ~**es** z
Ginn gɪn
ginner|y 'dʒɪn ər| i ~**ies** iz
Ginnie, Ginny 'dʒɪn i
Gino 'dʒiːn əʊ ‖ -oʊ
ginormous dʒaɪ 'nɔːm əs ‖ -'nɔːrm əs
Ginsberg, Ginsburg 'gɪnz bɜːg ‖ -bɜːg
ginseng 'dʒɪn seŋ
Gioconda ˌdʒiː_ə 'kɒnd ə ‖ -'kɑːnd- —*It*
  [dʒo 'kon da]
Giotto 'dʒɒt əʊ 'ʒɒt-; dʒi 'ɒt- ‖ 'dʒɑːt̬ oʊ
  'dʒɔːt̬- —*It* ['dʒɔt to]
Giovanni dʒəʊ 'vɑːn i ˌdʒiː_ə'•-, -'væn-
  ‖ dʒoʊ- dʒə- —*It* [dʒo 'van ni]
gip *'cheat'* dʒɪp **gipped** dʒɪpt **gipping**
  'dʒɪp ɪŋ **gips** dʒɪps
gippo 'dʒɪp əʊ ‖ -oʊ ~**s** z
Gippsland 'gɪps lænd -lənd
gippy 'dʒɪp i
  ˌgippy 'tummy
gips|y, Gips|y 'dʒɪps |i ~**ies**, ~**y's** iz
giraffe dʒə 'rɑːf dʒɪ-, §-'ræf ‖ -'ræf ~**s** s
Giraldus dʒɪ 'ræld əs dʒə-
  Giˌraldus Camˈbrensis kæm 'brenʦ ɪs §-əs
gird gɜːd ‖ gɜːd **girded** 'gɜːd ɪd -əd
  ‖ 'gɜːd əd **girding** 'gɜːd ɪŋ ‖ 'gɜːd ɪŋ **girds**
  gɜːdz ‖ gɜːdz **girt** gɜːt ‖ gɜːt
girder 'gɜːd ə ‖ 'gɜːd ər ~**s** z
girdl|e 'gɜːd əl ‖ 'gɜːd əl ~**ed** d ~**es** z ~**ing**
  _ɪŋ
  'girdle cake
girl gɜːl ‖ gɜːl **girls** gɜːlz ‖ gɜːlz
  ˌgirl 'Friday; ˌgirl 'guide; ˌgirl 'scout ‖ '• •
girlfriend 'gɜːl frend ‖ 'gɜːl- ~**s** z
girlhood 'gɜːl hʊd ‖ 'gɜːl-
girlie 'gɜːl i ‖ 'gɜːl i
girlish 'gɜːl ɪʃ ‖ 'gɜːl- ~**ly** li ~**ness** nəs nɪs
girly 'gɜːl i ‖ 'gɜːl i
girn gɜːn ‖ gɜːn **girned** gɜːnd ‖ gɜːnd
  girning 'gɜːn ɪŋ ‖ 'gɜːn ɪŋ **girns**
  gɜːnz ‖ gɜːnz
giro, Giro 'dʒaɪər əʊ ‖ -oʊ ~**s** z
Girobank *tdmk* 'dʒaɪər əʊ bæŋk ‖ -oʊ-

G

girt gɜːt ‖ gɝːt
girth gɜːθ ‖ gɝːθ **girthed** gɜːθt ‖ gɝːθt
  girthing ˈgɜːθ ɪŋ ‖ ˈgɝːθ ɪŋ **girths**
  gɜːθs ‖ gɝːθs
Girton ˈgɜːt ᵊn ‖ ˈgɝːt ᵊn
Girtonian gɜː ˈtəʊn i_ən ‖ gɝr ˈtoʊn- ~**s** z
Girvan ˈgɜːv ᵊn ‖ ˈgɝːv ᵊn
Gisborne, Gisbourne ˈgɪz bən -bɔːn ‖ -bɔːrn
  -boʊrn
Giselle ʒɪ ˈzel dʒɪ-, dʒə- —*Fr* [ʒi zɛl]
Gish gɪʃ
gismo ˈgɪz məʊ ‖ -moʊ ~**s** z
gissa *nonstd 'give us a'* ˈgɪs ə
Gissing ˈgɪs ɪŋ
gist dʒɪst
git gɪt **gits** gɪts
Gitane *tdmk* ʒɪ ˈtɑːn ‖ -ˈtæn ~**s** z —*Fr* [ʒi tan]
gite, gîte ʒiːt —*Fr* [ʒit] **gites, gîtes** ʒiːts
Gittins ˈgɪt ɪnz §-ᵊnz ‖ ˈgɪt ᵊnz
Giulietta ˌdʒuːl i ˈet ə ‖ -ˈet̮ ə —*It* [dʒu ˈljet ta]
Giuseppe dʒu ˈsep i —*It* [dʒu ˈzɛp pe]
give gɪv **gave** geɪv **given** ˈgɪv ᵊn **gives** gɪvz
  giving ˈgɪv ɪŋ —*The phrase* give me *also has a*
  non-standard casual form ˈgɪm i, *sometimes*
  written gimme; *similarly* give us a, *see* gissa
give-and-take ˌgɪv ᵊn ˈteɪk
giveaway ˈgɪv ə ˌweɪ ~**s** z
given ˈgɪv ᵊn
  ˈgiven name
Givenchy *tdmk* ʒiː ˈvɒntʃ i ‖ ˈʒiːv ɑːn ʃiː; ˌ•ˈ•ˈ•
giver ˈgɪv ə ‖ -ᵊr ~**s** z
Giza ˈgiːz ə
gizmo ˈgɪz məʊ ‖ -moʊ ~**s** z
gizzard ˈgɪz əd ‖ -ᵊrd ~**s** z
glabell|a glə ˈbel |ə ~**ae** iː
glabrous ˈgleɪb rəs
glace, glacé ˈglæs eɪ ˈglɑːs-, -i ‖ glæ ˈseɪ ~**ed**
  d ~**ing** ɪŋ ~**s** z
glacial ˈgleɪʃ ᵊl ˈgleɪʃ i_əl, ˈgleɪs i_əl ~**ly** i
glaci|ate ˈgleɪs i eɪt ˈgleɪʃ- ‖ ˈgleɪʃ i eɪt
  ~**ated** eɪt ɪd -əd ‖ eɪt̮ əd ~**ates** eɪts ~**ating**
  eɪt ɪŋ ‖ eɪt̮ ɪŋ
glaciation ˌgleɪs i ˈeɪʃ ᵊn ˌgleɪʃ- ‖ ˌgleɪʃ- ~**s** z
glacier ˈglæs i_ə ˈgleɪs- ‖ ˈgleɪʃ ᵊr (*) ~**s** z
glacis ˈglæs i -ɪs, -əs ‖ glæ ˈsiː; ~ *pl* z
glaciology ˌgleɪs i ˈɒl ədʒ i ‖ ˌgleɪʃ i ˈɑːl-
glad glæd **gladder** ˈglæd ə ‖ -ᵊr **gladdest**
  ˈglæd ɪst -əst **glads** glædz
  ˌglad ˈeye, ˈ• •; ˌglad ˈhand, ˈ• •; ˈglad
  rags
gladden ˈglæd ᵊn ~**ed** d ~**ing** _ɪŋ ~**s** z
glade gleɪd **glades** gleɪdz
glad-hand ˌglæd ˈhænd ˈ• • ~**ed** ɪd əd ~**er/s**
  ə/z ‖ ᵊr/z ~**ing** ɪŋ ~**s** z
gladiator ˈglæd i eɪt ə ‖ -eɪt̮ ᵊr ~**s** z
gladiatorial ˌglæd i_ə ˈtɔːr i_əl ◄ ‖ -ˈtoʊr-
gladiol|us ˌglæd i ˈəʊl |əs ‖ -ˈoʊl- ~**i** aɪ ~**uses**
  əs ɪz -əz
glad|ly ˈglæd |li ~**ness** nəs nɪs
gladsome ˈglæd səm ~**ly** li ~**ness** nəs nɪs
Gladstone ˈglæd stən ‖ -stoʊn -stən
  ˌGladstone ˈbag ‖ ˈ• • •
Gladwin ˈglæd wɪn §-wən

Gladys ˈglæd ɪs §-əs
Glagolitic, g~ ˌglæg əʊ ˈlɪt ɪk ◄ ‖ -ə ˈlɪt̮ ɪk ◄
glair gleə ‖ gleᵊr glæᵊr
glair|y ˈgleər |i ‖ ˈgler |i ˈglær- ~**iness** i nəs
  i nɪs
Glaisher ˈgleɪʃ ə ‖ -ᵊr
Glaister ˈgleɪst ə ‖ -ᵊr
glam, Glam glæm
Glamis glɑːmz (*!*)
glamor ˈglæm ə ‖ -ᵊr
Glamorgan glə ˈmɔːg ᵊn ‖ -ˈmɔːrg-
glamoris... —*see* **glamoriz...**
glamorization ˌglæm ər aɪ ˈzeɪʃ ᵊn -ər ɪ-
  ‖ -ᵊr ə-
glamoriz|e ˈglæm ə raɪz ~**ed** d ~**es** ɪz əz
  ~**ing** ɪŋ
glamorous ˈglæm ᵊr_əs ~**ly** li ~**ness** nəs nɪs
glamour ˈglæm ə ‖ -ᵊr
glance glɑːn⁀ts §glæn⁀ts ‖ glæn⁀ts **glanced**
  glɑːn⁀tst §glæn⁀tst ‖ glæn⁀tst **glances**
  ˈglɑːn⁀ts ɪz §ˈglæn⁀ts-, -əz ‖ ˈglæn⁀ts əz
  glancing ˈglɑːn⁀ts ɪŋ §ˈglæn⁀ts- ‖ ˈglæn⁀ts-
gland glænd **glands** glændz
glanders ˈglænd əz ˈglɑːnd- ‖ -ᵊrz
glandular ˈglænd jʊl ə ˈglænd⁀ʒ əl ə ‖ ˈglænd⁀ʒ
  əl ᵊr
  ˌglandular ˈfever
glans glænz **glandes** ˈglænd iːz
Glanvill, Glanville ˈglæn vɪl -vᵊl
Glanyrafon, Glan-yr-Afon ˌglæn ər ˈæv ᵊn
  —*Welsh* [glan ər ˈa von]
Glaramara ˌglær ə ˈmɑːr ə ‖ ˌgler-
glare gleə ‖ gleᵊr glæᵊr **glared** gleəd ‖ gleᵊrd
  glæᵊrd **glares** gleəz ‖ gleᵊrz glæᵊrz
  glaring/ly ˈgleər ɪŋ /li ‖ ˈgler ɪŋ /li ˈglær-
Glaser ˈgleɪz ə ‖ -ᵊr

GLASGOW

	z	s	
BrE 1988			
	0 20 40 60 80 100%		

Glasgow ˈglɑːz gəʊ ˈglæz-, ˈglɑːs-, ˈglæs-;
  ˈglɑːsk əʊ, ˈglæsk- ‖ ˈglæs goʊ ˈglæz- —*BrE*
  1988 poll panel preference: z *forms* 85%, s
  forms 15%.
Glaslyn ˈglæs lɪn
glasnost ˈglæs nɒst ˈglæz- ‖ ˈglɑːs noʊst
  —*Russ* [ˈgɫas nəsʲtʲ]
glass, Glass glɑːs §glæs ‖ glæs **glassed** glɑːst
  §glæst ‖ glæst **glasses** ˈglɑːs ɪz §ˈglæs-, -əz
  ‖ ˈglæs əz
  ˌglass ˈeye, ˌglass ˈfibre ◄
glassblower ˈglɑːs ˌbləʊ ə §ˈglæs-
  ‖ ˈglæs ˌbloʊ ᵊr ~**s** z
glasscutter ˈglɑːs ˌkʌt ə §ˈglæs- ‖ ˈglæs ˌkʌt̮ ᵊr
  ~**s** z
glassful ˈglɑːs fʊl §ˈglæs- ‖ ˈglæs- ~**s** z
glass|house ˈglɑːs |haʊs §ˈglæs- ‖ ˈglæs-
  ~**houses** haʊz ɪz -əz
glassine glæ ˈsiːn ‖ glæs- glæ ˈsiːn
glasspaper ˈglɑːs ˌpeɪp ə §ˈglæs-
  ‖ ˈglæs ˌpeɪp ᵊr
glassware ˈglɑːs weə §ˈglæs- ‖ ˈglæs wer -wær

glassworks 'glɑːs wɜːks §'glæs- ‖ 'glæs wɜːks
glasswort 'glɑːs wɜːt §'glæs-, §-wɔːt
‖ 'glæs wɜːt -wɔːrt ~s s
glass|y 'glɑːs |i §'glæs- ‖ 'glæs |i ~ier i‿ə ‖ i‿ər
~iest i‿ɪst i‿əst ~ily ɪ li əl i ~iness i nəs i nɪs
Glastonbury 'glæst ən bər‿i 'glɑːst-, →'•əm-,
§-ˌber i ‖ -ˌber i
Glaswegian glɑːz 'wiːdʒ ən glæz-, glɑːs-,
glæs-, ˌ•- ‖ glæs- ~s z
Glauber 'glaub ə 'gləub ə, 'glɔːb ə ‖ -ər ~'s z
glaucoma glɔː 'kəum ə glau- ‖ glau 'koum ə
glɔː-, glɑː-
glaucomatous glɔː 'kəum ət əs glau-, -'kɒm-
‖ glau 'koum əţ əs glɔː-, glɑː-, -'kɑːm-
glaucous 'glɔːk əs ‖ 'glɑːk-
Glaxo tdmk 'glæks əu ‖ -ou
glaze gleɪz glazed gleɪzd glazes 'gleɪz ɪz -əz
glazing 'gleɪz ɪŋ
Glazebrook 'gleɪz bruk
glazier, G~ 'gleɪz i‿ə 'gleɪʒ ə, 'gleɪʒ i‿ə
‖ 'gleɪʒ ər ~s z
Glazunof, Glazunov 'glæz u nɒf ‖ -ə nouf
-ə nɑːf, -ə nɔːf —Russian [ɡɫə zu 'nɔf]
GLC ˌdʒiː el 'siː
gleam gliːm gleamed gliːmd gleaming
'gliːm ɪŋ gleams gliːmz
glean gliːn gleaned gliːnd gleaner/s
'gliːn ə/z ‖ -ər/z gleaning 'gliːn ɪŋ gleans
gliːnz
Gleason 'gliːs ən
Gleave gliːv
glebe gliːb glebes gliːbz
glee gliː
'glee club
gleeful 'gliː fəl -ful ~ly i ~ness nəs nɪs
gleet gliːt
glen, Glen glen glens, Glen's glenz
Glencoe ₍ₗ₎glen 'kəu →₍ₗ₎gleŋ- ‖ -'kou
Glenda 'glend ə
Glendale 'glen deɪəl
Glendaruel ˌglen də 'ruːⅬ əl
Glendenning glen 'den ɪŋ
Glendinning glen 'dɪn ɪŋ
Glendower glen 'dau‿ə ‖ -'dau‿ər
Gleneagles glen 'iːg əlz
Glenelg glen 'elg
Glenfiddich glen 'fɪd ɪk -ɪx
glengarr|y, G~ glen 'gær |i →gleŋ- ‖ -'ger-,
'••• ~ies iz
Glengormley glen 'gɔːm li →gleŋ- ‖ -'gɔːrm-
Glenice glen ɪs §-əs
Glenlivet glen 'lɪv ɪt -ət
Glenmorangie ˌglen mə 'rændʒ i →ˌglem-;
ˌ•'mɒr əndʒ i
Glenn glen
Glenrothes glen 'rɒθ ɪs §-əs ‖ -'rɑːθ əs
Glenville 'glen vɪl
Glenys 'glen ɪs §-əs
gley gleɪ gleys gleɪz
glia 'gliːⅬ‿ə 'glaɪⅬ
glial 'gliːⅬ‿əl 'glaɪⅬ
glib glɪb glibber 'glɪb ə ‖ -ər glibbest

'glɪb ɪst -əst glibly 'glɪb li glibness
'glɪb nəs -nɪs
glide glaɪd glided 'glaɪd ɪd -əd glides glaɪdz
gliding 'glaɪd ɪŋ
'glide path
glider 'glaɪd ə ‖ -ər ~s z
glimmer 'glɪm ə ‖ -ər ~ed d glimmering
'glɪm ər‿ɪŋ ~s z
glimmering 'glɪm ər‿ɪŋ ~ly li ~s z
glimpse glɪmps glimpsed glɪmpst glimpses
'glɪmps ɪz -əz glimpsing 'glɪmps ɪŋ
Glinka 'glɪŋk ə —Russian ['glʲin kə]
glint glɪnt glinted 'glɪnt ɪd -əd ‖ 'glɪnţ əd
glinting 'glɪnt ɪŋ ‖ 'glɪnţ ɪŋ glints glɪnʦ
glioma glaɪ 'əum ə ‖ -'oum ə ~s z
glissad|e n, v glɪ 'saːd -'seɪd ~ed ɪd əd ~es z
~ing ɪŋ
glissand|o glɪ 'sænd |əu ‖ -'saːnd |ou ~i iː ~os
əuz ‖ ouz
glisten 'glɪs ən ~ed d ~ing ɪŋ ~s z
glister 'glɪst ə ‖ -ər ~ed d glistering 'glɪst
ər‿ɪŋ ~s z
glitch glɪtʃ glitches 'glɪtʃ ɪz -əz
glitter 'glɪt ə ‖ 'glɪţ ər ~ed d glittering
'glɪţ‿ər ɪŋ ‖ 'glɪţ ər ɪŋ ~s z
glitterati ˌglɪt ə 'rɑːt iː -i ‖ ˌglɪţ ə 'rɑːţ i
glitz glɪʦ glitzed glɪʦt glitzes 'glɪʦ ɪz -əz
glitzing 'glɪʦ ɪŋ
glitz|y 'glɪʦ |i ~ier i‿ə ‖ i‿ər ~iest i‿ɪst i‿əst
~iness i nəs i nɪs
Gloag gləug ‖ gloug
gloaming 'gləum ɪŋ ‖ 'gloum ɪŋ
gloat gləut ‖ glout gloated 'gləut ɪd -əd
‖ 'glouţ əd gloating/ly 'gləut ɪŋ /
li ‖ 'glouţ ɪŋ /li gloats gləuʦ ‖ glouʦ
glob glɒb ‖ glɑːb globs glɒbz ‖ glɑːbz
global 'gləub əl ‖ 'gloub əl ~ism ˌɪz əm ~ist/s
ɪst/s §əst/s ~ly i
globalisation, globalization
ˌgləub əl aɪ 'zeɪʃ ən -ɪ'•- ‖ ˌgloub əl ə-
globe gləub ‖ gloub globes gləubz ‖ gloubz
ˌglobe 'artichoke
globefish 'gləub fɪʃ ‖ 'gloub- ~es ɪz əz
globeflower 'gləub ˌflau‿ə ‖ 'gloub ˌflau‿ər ~s
z
globetrott|er/s 'gləub ˌtrɒt ə/
z ‖ 'gloub ˌtrɑːţ ər/z ~ing ɪŋ
globose 'gləub əus gləu 'bəus ‖ 'gloub ous ~ly
li ~ness nəs nɪs
globosity gləu 'bɒs ət i -ɪt- ‖ glou 'bɑːs əţ i
globular 'glɒb jul ə -jəl- ‖ 'glɑːb jəl ər ~ly li
~ness nəs nɪs
globule 'glɒb juːl ‖ 'glɑːb- ~s z
globulin 'glɒb jul ɪn -jəl-, §-ən ‖ 'glɑːb jəl ən
~s z
glockenspiel 'glɒk ən spiːⅬ →-ŋ-, -ʃpiːⅬ
‖ 'glɑːk- —Ger ['glɔk ən ʃpiːl] ~s z
glom glɒm ‖ glɑːm glommed
glɒmd ‖ glɑːmd glomming
'glɒm ɪŋ ‖ 'glɑːm ɪŋ gloms glɒmz ‖ glɑːmz
gloom gluːm
gloom|y 'gluːm |i ~ier i‿ə ‖ i‿ər ~iest i‿ɪst
i‿əst ~ily ɪ li əl i ~iness i nəs i nɪs

gloop gluːp
glop glɒp ‖ glɑːp
Gloria, g~ 'glɔːr i‿ə ‖ 'gloʊr- ~**s** z
  ˌgloria in ex'celsis ek 'sels ɪs ɪk-; eks 'tʃels-,
  ek 'ʃels-, -iːs; ˌGloria 'Patri 'pɑːtr iː 'pætr-, -i
Gloriana ˌglɔːr i 'ɑːn ə ‖ ˌgloʊr-, -'æn-
glorie... —*see* **glory**
glorification ˌglɔːr ɪf ɪ 'keɪʃ ᵊn ‚•əf-,
  §-ə'•- ‖ ˌgloʊr- ~**s** z
glori|fy 'glɔːr ɪ |faɪ -ə- ‖ 'gloʊr- ~**fied** faɪd
  ~**fier/s** faɪ‿ə/z ‖ faɪ‿ᵊr/z ~**fies** faɪz ~**fying**
  faɪ ɪŋ
glorious 'glɔːr i‿əs ‖ 'gloʊr- ~**ly** li ~**ness** nəs
  nɪs
glor|y 'glɔːr |i ‖ 'gloʊr- ~**ied** id ~**ies** iz ~**ying**
  i‿ɪŋ
  'glory hole
gloss glɒs ‖ glɑːs glɔːs **glossed** glɒst ‖ glɑːst
  glɔːst **glosses** 'glɒs ɪz -əz ‖ 'glɑːs əz 'glɔːs-
  glossing 'glɒs ɪŋ ‖ 'glɑːs ɪŋ 'glɔːs-
glossal 'glɒs ᵊl ‖ 'glɑːs ᵊl 'glɔːs-
glossar|y 'glɒs ər‿|i ‖ 'glɑːs- 'glɔːs- ~**ies** iz
glossectomy glɒ 'sekt əm i ‖ glɑː- glɔː-
glossematic ˌglɒs ɪ 'mæt ɪk ◀ -ə-
  ‖ ˌglɑːs ə 'mæt̬ ɪk ◀ glɔːs- ~**s** s
glossi... —*see* **glossy**
glossolalia ˌglɒs əʊ 'leɪl i‿ə ‖ ˌglɑːs ə- ˌglɔːs-
Glossop 'glɒs əp ‖ 'glɑːs-
glossopharyngeal ˌglɒs əʊ ˌfær ɪn 'dʒiːˌ əl
  -fə 'rɪndʒ iˌ əl ‖ ˌglɑːs oʊ ˌfær ən 'dʒiː əl
  ˌglɔːs-, -ˌfer-
gloss|y 'glɒs |i ‖ 'glɑːs |i 'glɔːs- ~**ier** i‿ə ‖ i‿ᵊr
  ~**iest** i‿ɪst i‿əst ~**ily** ɪ li əl i ~**iness** i nəs i nɪs
Gloster 'glɒst ə 'glɔːst- ‖ 'glɑːst ᵊr 'glɔːst-
glottal 'glɒt ᵊl ‖ 'glɑːt̬ ᵊl ~**ly** i ~**s** z
  ˌglottal 'stop
glottalic glɒ 'tæl ɪk ‖ glɑː-
glottalis... —*see* **glottaliz...**
glottalization ˌglɒt ᵊl aɪ 'zeɪʃ ᵊn -ɪ'•-
  ‖ ˌglɑːt̬ ᵊl ə- ~**s** z
glottaliz|e 'glɒt ᵊl aɪz -ə laɪz ‖ 'glɑːt̬ ᵊl aɪz ~**ed**
  d ~**es** ɪz əz ~**ing** ɪŋ
glottis 'glɒt ɪs §-əs ‖ 'glɑːt̬ əs ~**es** ɪz əz
glottochronology ˌglɒt əʊ krə 'nɒl ədʒ i
  ‖ ˌglɑːt̬ oʊ krə 'nɑːl-
Gloucester 'glɒst ə 'glɔːst- ‖ 'glɑːst ᵊr 'glɔːst-
  ~**s** z ~**shire** ʃə ʃɪə ‖ ʃᵊr ʃɪr
glove glʌv **gloved** glʌvd **gloves** glʌvz
  gloving 'glʌv ɪŋ
  'glove com,partment; 'glove ,puppet
glover, G~ 'glʌv ə ‖ -ᵊr ~**s** z
glow gləʊ ‖ gloʊ **glowed** gləʊd ‖ gloʊd
  glowing/ly 'gləʊ ɪŋ /li ‖ 'gloʊ ɪŋ /li **glows**
  gləʊz ‖ gloʊz
glower 'glaʊ‿ə ‖ 'glaʊ‿ᵊr ~**ed** d **glowering/ly**
  'glaʊ‿ər ɪŋ /li ‖ 'glaʊ‿ᵊr ɪŋ /li ~**s** z
glow-worm 'gləʊ wɜːm ‖ 'gloʊ wɜ˞ːm ~**s** z
gloxinia glɒk 'sɪn i‿ə ‖ glɑːk- ~**s** z
Gloy *tdmk* glɔɪ
gloze gləʊz ‖ gloʊz **glozed** gləʊzd ‖ gloʊzd
  glozes 'gləʊz ɪz -əz ‖ 'gloʊz əz **glozing**
  'gləʊz ɪŋ ‖ 'gloʊz ɪŋ
Glubb glʌb

Gluck glʊk —*Ger* [glʊk]
gluco- *comb. form*
  with stress-neutral suffix ˌgluːk əʊ ‖ -oʊ —
  glucocorticoid ˌgluːk əʊ 'kɔːt ɪ kɔɪd -'•ə-
  ‖ -oʊ 'kɔːrt̬-
glucose 'gluːk əʊz -əʊs ‖ -oʊs -oʊz
glucoside 'gluːk əʊ saɪd ‖ -ə- ~**s** z
glue gluː **glued** gluːd **glues** gluːz **gluing**
  'gluːˌ ɪŋ
gluer 'gluːˌ ə ‖ -ᵊr ~**s** z
glue-sniff|er/s 'gluː ˌsnɪf ə/z ‖ -ᵊr/z ~**ing** ɪŋ
gluey 'gluːˌ i
gluhwein, glühwein 'gluː vaɪn —*Ger*
  ['glyː vaɪn]
gluing 'gluːˌ ɪŋ
glum glʌm **glummer** 'glʌm ə ‖ -ᵊr **glummest**
  'glʌm ɪst -əst
glume gluːm (= *gloom*) ~**s** z
glum|ly 'glʌm |li ~**ness** nəs nɪs
gluon 'gluː ɒn ‖ -ɑːn ~**s** z
glut glʌt **gluts** glʌts **glutted** 'glʌt ɪd -əd
  ‖ 'glʌt̬ əd **glutting** 'glʌt ɪŋ ‖ 'glʌt̬ ɪŋ
glutamate 'gluːt ə meɪt ‖ 'gluːt̬- ~**s** s
glutamic gluː 'tæm ɪk
glutamine 'gluːt ə miːn -mɪn ‖ 'gluːt̬-
gluteal 'gluːt i‿əl ‖ 'gluːt̬-
gluten 'gluːt ᵊn -ɪn
gluteus 'gluːt i‿əs ‖ 'gluːt̬-
  ˌgluteus 'maximus
glutinous 'gluːt ɪn əs -ᵊn- ‖ 'gluːt̬ ᵊn əs ~**ly** li
  ~**ness** nəs nɪs
glutton 'glʌt ᵊn ~**s** z
gluttonous 'glʌt ᵊn əs ~**ly** li
gluttony 'glʌt ᵊn i
glyceride 'glɪs ə raɪd ~**s** z
glycerin, glycerine 'glɪs ər‿ɪn §-ᵊr‿ən; -ə riːn,
  ˌglɪs ə 'riːn
glycerol 'glɪs ə rɒl ‖ -roʊl -rɑːl, -rɔːl
glycine 'glaɪs iːn
glyco- *comb. form*
  with stress-neutral suffix ˌglaɪk əʊ ‖ -oʊ —
  glycopeptide ˌglaɪk əʊ 'pept aɪd ‖ -oʊ-
  with stress-imposing suffix
  glaɪ 'kɒ+ ‖ glaɪ 'kɑː+ — **glycogeny**
  glaɪ 'kɒdʒ ən i ‖ -'kɑːdʒ-
glycogen 'glaɪk ədʒ ᵊn -əʊdʒen ‖ -oʊ dʒen
glycol 'glaɪk ɒl ‖ -oʊl -ɑːl, -ɔːl
glycoside 'glaɪk əʊ saɪd ‖ -ə- ~**s** z
Glyder 'glɪd ə ‖ -ᵊr —*Welsh* ['glə der] ~**s** z
Glyn glɪn
Glynde glaɪnd
Glyndebourne 'glaɪnd bɔːn →'glaɪm- ‖ -bɔːrn
  -boʊrn
Glynis 'glɪn ɪs §-əs
Glynn, Glynne glɪn
Glynwed *tdmk* 'glɪn wed
glyph glɪf **glyphs** glɪfs
glyptodont 'glɪpt əʊ dɒnt ‖ -ə dɑːnt ~**s** s
G-man 'dʒiː mæn **G-men** 'dʒiː men
GMT ˌdʒiː em 'tiː
gnarled nɑːld ‖ nɑːrld
gnash næʃ **gnashed** næʃt **gnasher/s** 'næʃ ə/

Glottal stop

A **glottal stop**, symbolized ʔ, is a PLOSIVE made at the glottis (= made by the vocal folds). In English it is sometimes used as a kind of t-sound, and sometimes has other functions.

1 In certain positions ʔ may be used as an allophone of the phoneme t, as when **pointless** ˈpɔɪnt ləs is pronounced ˈpɔɪnʔ ləs. This is known as **glottalling** or **glottal replacement** of t. It is condemned by some people; nevertheless, it is increasingly heard, especially in BrE. Sometimes the glottal articulation accompanies a simultaneous alveolar articulation.

2 ʔ is found as an allophone of t only
- at the **end** of a syllable, and
- if the preceding sound is a vowel or SONORANT.

Provided these conditions are satisfied, it is widely used in both BrE and AmE where the following sound is an obstruent
    football ˈfʊt bɔːl → ˈfʊʔ bɔːl
    outside ˌaʊt ˈsaɪd → ˌaʊʔ ˈsaɪd
    that faint buzz ˌðæt ˌfeɪnt ˈbʌz → ˌðæʔ ˌfeɪnʔ ˈbʌz
– or a nasal
    atmospheric ˌæt məs ˈfer ɪk → ˌæʔ məs ˈfer ɪk
    button ˈbʌt ᵊn → ˈbʌʔ n
    that name ˌðæt ˈneɪm → ˌðæʔ ˈneɪm
– or a semivowel or non-syllabic l
    Gatwick ˈgæt wɪk → ˈgæʔ wɪk
    quite well ˌkwaɪt ˈwel → ˌkwaɪʔ ˈwel
    brightly ˈbraɪt li → ˈbraɪʔ li

Some speakers of BrE also use it at the end of a word under other circumstances as well:
    not only this ˌnɒʔ əʊn li ˈðɪs
    but also that bəʔ ˌɔːl səʊ ˈðæʔ.

Compare AmE ˌnɑːt̬ oʊn li ˈðɪs, bət̬ ˌɔːl soʊ ˈðæt; in this position t̬ is also heard in casual BrE.

3 ʔ is also optionally used as a way of adding emphasis to a syllable that begins with a vowel sound (see HARD ATTACK). It can be used to separate adjacent vowel sounds in successive syllables (= to avoid **hiatus**). In BrE this can be a way of avoiding r (see R LIAISON), as in one pronunciation of **underexpose** ˌʌnd ə ɪk ˈspəʊz (-ə ʔɪk-).

4 ʔ also forms an essential part of certain interjections, e.g. AmE **uh-uh** ˌʔʌʔ ˈʌʔ.

5 A glottal stop is sometimes used, especially in BrE, to strengthen tʃ or tr at the end of a syllable, and also p, t, k if followed by a consonant or at the end of a word. This is known as **glottal reinforcement**.
    teaching ˈtiːtʃ ɪŋ → ˈtiːʔtʃ ɪŋ
    April ˈeɪp rəl → ˈeɪʔp rəl
    right! raɪt → raɪʔt

▶ *Glottal stop*

Learners of English should be careful not to apply glottal reinforcement (as opposed to glottal replacement) in words such as **pretty** ˈprɪt i and **jumping** ˈdʒʌmp ɪŋ.

z ‖ -ᵊr/z **gnashes** ˈnæʃ ɪz -əz **gnashing** ˈnæʃ ɪŋ

gnat næt **gnats** næts

gnaw nɔː ‖ nɑː **gnawed** nɔːd ‖ nɑːd **gnawing** ˈnɔːʳ ɪŋ ‖ ˈnɔː ɪŋ ˈnɑː- **gnawn** nɔːn ‖ nɑːn **gnaws** nɔːz ‖ nɑːz

gneiss naɪs gə ˈnaɪs —*Ger* Gneis [gnaɪs]

gnocchi ˈnɒk i ˈnjɒk i, gə ˈnɒk i ‖ ˈnɑːk i ˈnjɑːk i, ˈnoʊk i —*It* [ˈɲɔk ki]

gnome nəʊm ‖ noʊm **gnomes** nəʊmz ‖ noʊmz

gnomic ˈnəʊm ɪk ‖ ˈnoʊm- **-ally** ᵊl‿i

gnomish ˈnəʊm ɪʃ ‖ ˈnoʊm-

gnomon ˈnəʊm ɒn -ən ‖ ˈnoʊm ɑːn ~**s** z

Gnosall ˈnəʊs ᵊl ‖ ˈnoʊs-

gnostic, G~ ˈnɒst ɪk ‖ ˈnɑːst- ~**s** s

gnosticism, G~ ˈnɒst ɪ ˌsɪz əm -ə- ‖ ˈnɑːst-

-gnosy *stress-imposing* gnəs i —
     pharmacognosy
     ˌfɑːm ə ˈkɒg nəs i ‖ ˌfɑːrm ə ˈkɑːg-

GNP ˌdʒiː en ˈpiː

gnu nuː njuː; gə ˈnuː, -ˈnjuː —*The forms with gə- are jocular, as generally is the entire word. In serious discourse this animal is called a wildebeeste.* **gnus** nuːz njuːz; gə ˈnuːz, -ˈnjuːz

go gəʊ ‖ goʊ —*There are nonstandard weak forms* §gə, §gu **goes** gəʊz ‖ goʊz —*There are nonstandard weak forms* gəz, gʊz **going** ˈgəʊ ɪŋ ‖ ˈgoʊ ɪŋ —*The phrase* **going to**, *when used as a modal (showing the future), has a casual weak form* (ˈ)gən ə, *also* (ˈ)gəʊ ɪn ə, (ˈ)gənt ə, (ˈ)gəʊ ɪnt ə ‖ (ˈ)goʊ‿ən ə, ‿ənt̬ ə. *In RP these are used, if at all, only before words beginning with a consonant sound, being replaced before a vowel sound by* (ˈ)gən u *or other forms with final* u *rather than* ə. *See* gonna. **gone** gɒn §gɔːn, §gɑːn ‖ gɔːn gɑːn **went** went

Goa, goa ˈgəʊ ə ‖ ˈgoʊ ə ~**s** z

goad gəʊd ‖ goʊd **goaded** ˈgəʊd ɪd -əd ‖ ˈgoʊd əd **goading** ˈgəʊd ɪŋ ‖ ˈgoʊd ɪŋ **goads** gəʊdz ‖ goʊdz

go-ahead *n* ˈgəʊ ə ˌhed ‖ ˈgoʊ-

go-ahead *adj* ˈgəʊ ə ˌhed, ˌ•ˈ•ˈ◂ ‖ ˈgoʊ-

goal gəʊl →gɒʊl ‖ goʊl **goals** gəʊlz →gɒʊlz ‖ goʊlz
     goal line

goalie ˈgəʊl i →ˈgɒʊl- ‖ ˈgoʊl i ~**s** z

goalkeeper ˈgəʊl ˌkiːp ə →ˈgɒʊl- ‖ ˈgoʊl ˌkiːp ᵊr ~**s** z

goalmouth ˈgəʊl maʊθ →ˈgɒʊl- ‖ ˈgoʊl-

goalpost ˈgəʊl pəʊst →ˈgɒʊl- ‖ ˈgoʊl poʊst ~**s** s

Goan ˈgəʊ ən ‖ ˈgoʊ ən ~**s** z

Goanese ˌgəʊ ə ˈniːz ◂ ‖ ˌgoʊ- -ˈniːs

goanna gəʊ ˈæn ə ‖ goʊ- ~**s** z

go-as-you-please ˌgəʊ əz ju ˈpliːz→, •ˈəʒ- ‖ ˌgoʊ-

goat gəʊt ‖ goʊt **goats** gəʊts ‖ goʊts

goatee ˌgəʊ ˈtiː ◂ ‖ ˌgoʊ- ~**s** z

goatherd ˈgəʊt hɜːd ‖ ˈgoʊt hɝːd ~**s** z

Goathland ˈgəʊθ lənd ‖ ˈgoʊθ-

goatsbeard ˈgəʊts bɪəd ‖ ˈgoʊts bɪrd ~**s** z

goatskin ˈgəʊt skɪn ‖ ˈgoʊt- ~**s** z

goatsucker ˈgəʊt ˌsʌk ə ‖ ˈgoʊt ˌsʌk ᵊr ~**s** z

gob gɒb ‖ gɑːb **gobbed** gɒbd ‖ gɑːbd **gobbing** ˈgɒb ɪŋ ‖ ˈgɑːb ɪŋ **gobs** gɒbz ‖ gɑːbz

gobbet ˈgɒb ɪt §-ət ‖ ˈgɑːb- ~**s** s

gobbl|e ˈgɒb ᵊl ‖ ˈgɑːb ᵊl ~**ed** d ~**es** z ~**ing** _ɪŋ

gobbledegook, gobbledygook ˈgɒb ᵊl di guːk -gʊk ‖ ˈgɑːb-

gobbler ˈgɒb lə ‖ ˈgɑːb lᵊr ~**s** z

Gobelin ˈgəʊb ᵊl ɪn ˈgɒb-, §-ən ‖ ˈgoʊb- —*Fr* [ɡɔb lɛ̃] ~**s** z

go-between ˈgəʊ bɪ ˌtwiːn -bə-, §-biː- ‖ ˈgoʊ- ~**s** z

Gobi ˈgəʊb i ‖ ˈgoʊb i

gobie... —*see* **goby**

goblet ˈgɒb lət -lɪt ‖ ˈgɑːb- ~**s** s

goblin ˈgɒb lɪn -lən ‖ ˈgɑːb- ~**s** z

gobo ˈgəʊb əʊ ‖ ˈgoʊb oʊ ~**s** z

Gobowen gɒ ˈbəʊ ɪn -ən ‖ gɑː ˈboʊ-

gobsmack ˈgɒb smæk ‖ ˈgɑːb- ~**ed** t ~**ing** ɪŋ ~**s** s

gobstopper ˈgɒb ˌstɒp ə ‖ ˈgɑːb ˌstɑːp ᵊr ~**s** z

go-by 'snub' ˈgəʊ baɪ ‖ ˈgoʊ-

gob|y 'fish' ˈgəʊb |i ‖ ˈgoʊb |i ~**ies** iz

go-cart ˈgəʊ kɑːt ‖ ˈgoʊ kɑːrt ~**s** s

god, God gɒd ‖ gɑːd **gods, God's** gɒdz ‖ gɑːdz

Godalming ˈgɒd ᵊl mɪŋ ‖ ˈgɑːd-

god-awful ˌgɒd ˈɔːf ᵊl ◂ ‖ ˌgɑːd- -ˈɑːf-

Godber ˈgɒd bə→ˈgɒb- ‖ ˈgɑːd bᵊr

god|child ˈgɒd |tʃaɪᵊld ‖ ˈgɑːd- ~**children** ˌtʃɪldr ən ˌtʃʊldr-

goddam, goddamn ˈgɒd æm ‖ ˌgɑːd ˈdæm ◂ ~**ed** d

Goddard ˈgɒd ɑːd -əd ‖ ˈgɑːd ᵊrd -ɑːrd

goddaughter ˈgɒd ˌdɔːt ə ‖ ˈgɑːd ˌdɔːt̬ ᵊr -ˌdɑːt̬- ~**s** z

goddess ˈgɒd es -ɪs, -əs ‖ ˈgɑːd əs ~**es** ɪz əz

Godel, Gödel ˈgɜːd ᵊl ˈgəʊd- ‖ ˈgoʊd- —*Ger* [ˈɡøː dᵊl]

godet ˈgəʊd eɪ -et; gəʊ ˈdet ‖ goʊ ˈdeɪ -ˈdet

godetia gəʊ ˈdiːʃ ə -ˈdiːʃ i‿ə ‖ gə- ~**s** z

godfather 'gɒd ˌfɑːð ə ‖ 'gɑːd ˌfɑːð ər ~s z
god-fearing 'gɒd ˌfɪər ɪŋ ‖ 'gɑːd ˌfɪr ɪŋ
godforsaken 'gɒd fə ˌseɪk ən ˌ•••••
   ‖ 'gɑːd fər-
Godfrey 'gɒd fri ‖ 'gɑːd-
godhead, G~ 'gɒd hed ‖ 'gɑːd-
Godiva gə 'daɪv ə
godless 'gɒd ləs -lɪs ‖ 'gɑːd- ~**ness** nəs nɪs
Godley 'gɒd li ‖ 'gɑːd-
godlike 'gɒd laɪk ‖ 'gɑːd-
god‖ly 'gɒd ‖li ‖ 'gɑːd- ~**liness** li nəs -nɪs
Godmanchester 'gɒd mən ˌtʃest ə ˌ•••••
   ‖ 'gɑːd mən ˌtʃest ər
godmother 'gɒd ˌmʌð ə →'gɒb-
   ‖ 'gɑːd ˌmʌð ər ~s z
Godolphin gə 'dɒlf ɪn §-ən ‖ gə 'dɑːlf-
Godot 'gɒd əʊ ‖ gɑː 'dəʊ gə- —Fr [go do]
godown 'gəʊ daʊn ‖ 'gəʊ- ~s z
godparent 'gɒd ˌpeər ənt →'gɒb-
   ‖ 'gɑːd ˌper- -ˌpær- ~s s
godsend 'gɒd send ‖ 'gɑːd- ~s z
godson 'gɒd sʌn ‖ 'gɑːd- ~s z
godspeed, G~ ˌgɒd 'spiːd ‖ ˌgɑːd-
Godthaab, Godthab 'gɒt hɑːb -hɔːb
   ‖ 'gɑːt hɑːb 'gəʊt- —Danish ['gɔd hoːˀb]
Godunov 'gɒd ə nɒf 'gʊd-, -u- ‖ 'gʊd ə nɔːf
   -nɑːf —Russ [gə du 'nɔf]
Godwin 'gɒd wɪn §-wən ‖ 'gɑːd-
godwit 'gɒd wɪt ‖ 'gɑːd- ~s s
Godzilla gɒd 'zɪl ə ‖ gɑːd-
Goebbels 'gɜːb əlz -əls ‖ 'gʊb- 'gɜːb- —Ger
   ['gœb əls]
goer 'gəʊ ə ‖ 'gəʊ ər ~s z
-goer ˌgəʊ ə ‖ ˌgəʊ ər — **party-goer**
   'pɑːt i ˌgəʊ ə ‖ 'pɑːrt i ˌgəʊ ər
Goering 'gɜːr ɪŋ ‖ 'ger- 'gɜː- —Ger ['gøː ʁɪŋ]
goes gəʊz ‖ gəʊz —There are nonstandard weak
   forms §gəz, §gʊz
Goethals 'gəʊθ əlz ‖ 'gəʊθ-
Goethe 'gɜːt ə ‖ 'geɪt ə 'gɜːt-, -i —Ger
   ['gøː tə]
gofer 'gəʊf ə ‖ 'gəʊf ər ~s z
Goff, Goffe gɒf ‖ gɑːf
goffer 'gəʊf ə ‖ 'gɑːf ər (*) ~**ed** d **goffering**
   'gəʊf ər ˌɪŋ ‖ 'gɑːf ər ɪŋ ~s z
Gog gɒg ‖ gɑːg
Gogarty 'gəʊg ət i ‖ 'gəʊg ərt̬ i
go-getter 'gəʊ ˌget ə ˌ•••• ‖ 'gəʊ ˌget̬ ər ~s z
gogg‖le 'gɒg əl ‖ 'gɑːg əl ~**ed** d ~**es** z ~**ing**
   ɪŋ
   '**goggle box**
goggle-eyed ˌgɒg əl 'aɪd ◄ '••• ‖ ˌgɑːg-
Gogmagog ˌgɒg mə 'gɒg ◄ ‖ ˌgɑːg mə 'gɑːg ◄
   ˌGogmagog 'Hills
go-go 'gəʊ gəʊ ‖ 'gəʊ gəʊ
   '**go-go ˌdancer**
Gogol 'gəʊg ɒl ‖ 'gəʊg ɑːl -əl —Russ ['gɔ gəlʲ]
Goidel 'gɔɪd əl
Goidelic, Goidhelic gɔɪ 'del ɪk
going 'gəʊ ɪŋ ‖ 'gəʊ ɪŋ ~s z —see note at go
-going ˌgəʊ ɪŋ ‖ ˌgəʊ ɪŋ — **party-going**
   'pɑːt i ˌgəʊ ɪŋ ‖ 'pɑːr t̬ i ˌgəʊ ɪŋ

going-over ˌgəʊ ɪŋ 'əʊv ə '•••, ••
   ‖ ˌgəʊ ɪŋ 'əʊv ər
goings-on ˌgəʊ ɪŋz 'ɒn ‖ ˌgəʊ ɪŋz 'ɑːn -'ɔːn
goiter, goitre 'gɔɪt ə ‖ 'gɔɪt̬ ər ~s z
goitrous 'gɔɪtr əs
go-kart 'gəʊ kɑːt ‖ 'gəʊ kɑːrt ~s s
Golan 'gəʊl æn -ɑːn; gəʊ 'lɑːn ‖ 'gəʊl ɑːn
   ˌGolan 'heights
Golborne 'gəʊl bɔːn →'gɒʊl- ‖ 'gəʊl bɔːrn
   -bəʊrn
Golconda gɒl 'kɒnd ə ‖ gɑːl 'kɑːnd ə
gold gəʊld →gɒʊld ‖ gəʊld **golds** gəʊldz
   →gɒʊldz ‖ gəʊldz
   '**Gold Coast**; '**gold ˌdigger**; '**gold dust**;
   ˌgold 'leaf; ˌgold 'medal; ˌgold 'plate;
   '**gold reˌserve**; '**gold rush**; '**gold ˌstandard**
Golda 'gəʊld ə →'gɒʊld- ‖ 'gəʊld ə
Goldberg 'gəʊld bɜːg →'gɒʊld- ‖ 'gəʊld bɜːg
goldbeater 'gəʊld ˌbiːt ə →'gɒʊld- ‖ 'gəʊld
   ˌbiːt̬ ər ~s z
goldbrick 'gəʊld brɪk →'gɒʊld- ‖ 'gəʊld- ~**ed**
   t ~**ing** ɪŋ ~s s
goldcrest 'gəʊld krest →'gɒʊld- ‖ 'gəʊld- ~s
   s
golden 'gəʊld ən →'gɒʊld- ‖ 'gəʊld- ~**ly** li
   ~**ness** nəs nɪs
   '**golden age**, ˌ•• '•; ˌgolden 'eagle;
   ˌGolden 'Fleece; ˌGolden 'Gate◄, ˌGolden
   Gate 'Bridge; ˌgolden 'handshake; ˌgolden
   'jubilee; ˌgolden 'mean; ˌgolden 'oldie;
   ˌgolden 'rule; ˌgolden 'syrup; ˌgolden
   'wedding
goldeneye 'gəʊld ən aɪ →'gɒʊld- ‖ 'gəʊld- ~s
   z
goldenrod 'gəʊld ən rɒd →'gɒʊld-, ˌ•••'•
   ‖ 'gəʊld ən rɑːd
goldfield 'gəʊld fiːəld →'gɒʊld- ‖ 'gəʊld- ~s z
goldfinch 'gəʊld fɪntʃ →'gɒʊld- ‖ 'gəʊld- ~**es**
   ɪz əz
goldfish 'gəʊld fɪʃ →'gɒʊld- ‖ 'gəʊld- ~**es** ɪz
   əz
   '**goldfish bowl**
Goldie 'gəʊld i →'gɒʊld- ‖ 'gəʊld i
Goldilocks, g~ 'gəʊld i lɒks →'gɒʊld-
   ‖ 'gəʊld i lɑːks
Golding 'gəʊld ɪŋ →'gɒʊld- ‖ 'gəʊld-
goldmine 'gəʊld maɪn →'gɒʊld- ‖ 'gəʊld- ~s
   z
gold-plated ˌgəʊld 'pleɪt ɪd ◄ →ˌgɒʊld-, -əd
   ‖ ˌgəʊld 'pleɪt̬ əd ◄
Goldschmidt 'gəʊld ʃmɪt →'gɒʊld- ‖ 'gəʊld-
goldsmith, G~ 'gəʊld smɪθ →'gɒʊld- ‖ 'gəʊld-
   ~s s
Goldwater 'gəʊld ˌwɔːt ə →'gɒʊld-
   ‖ 'gəʊld ˌwɔːt̬ ər -ˌwɑːt̬ ər
Goldwyn 'gəʊld wɪn →'gɒʊld- ‖ 'gəʊld-
golf gɒlf gɒf, gɔːf, §gəʊlf ‖ gɑːlf gɔːlf
   '**golf ball**; '**golf club**; '**golf course**; '**golf
   links**
golfer 'gɒlf ə 'gɒf-, 'gɔːf-, §'gəʊlf- ‖ 'gɑːlf ər
   'gɔːlf- ~s z
golfing 'gɒlf ɪŋ 'gɒf-, 'gɔːf-, §'gəʊlf-
   ‖ 'gɑːlf ɪŋ 'gɔːlf-

G

Golgi 'gɒldʒ i ‖ 'gɔːldʒ i 'gɑːldʒ i —*It* ['gɔl dʒi]
Golgotha 'gɒlg əθ ə ‖ 'gɑːlg-
Goliath, g~ gə 'laɪ̯_əθ gəʊ- ~**s**, ~'**s** s
Golightly gəʊ 'laɪt li ‖ goʊ-
Gollancz 'gɒl æŋks -ənts; gə 'lænts, -'læŋks
‖ gə 'lænts
golliwog, golliwogg 'gɒl i wɒg ‖ 'gɑːl i wɑːg
~**s** z
golly 'gɒl i ‖ 'gɑːl i
gollywog 'gɒl i wɒg ‖ 'gɑːl i wɑːg ~**s** z
Gomer 'gəʊm ə ‖ 'goʊm ᵊr
Gomes 'gəʊm ez ‖ 'goʊm- —*Port* ['go mɪʃ],
BrPort ['go mis]
Gomez 'gəʊm ez ‖ 'goʊm- —*Sp* Gómez
['go meθ, -mes]
Gomm, Gomme gɒm ‖ gɑːm
Gomorrah gə 'mɒr ə ‖ -'mɔːr ə -'mɑːr-
Gompers 'gɒmp əz ‖ 'gɑːmp ᵊrz
Gomperts, Gompertz 'gɒmp əts ‖ 'gɑːmp ᵊrts
Gomshall 'gɒm ʃᵊl 'gʌm- ‖ 'gɑːm-
-gon gən gɒn ‖ gɑːn — **hexagon** 'heks əg ən
-ə gɒn ‖ -ə gɑːn
gonad 'gəʊn æd 'gɒn- ‖ 'goʊn- ~**s** z
gonadotrophin ,gəʊn əd əʊ 'trəʊf ɪn ,gɒn-,
-'trɒf-, -ᵊn ‖ ,goʊn əd ə 'troʊf- ~**s** z
-gonal *stress-imposing* gᵊn əl — **isogonal**
aɪ 'sɒg ᵊn əl ‖ -'saːg-
Goncourt ,gɒn 'kʊə '•• ‖ ,goʊn 'kʊᵊr —*Fr*
[gɔ̃ kuːʁ]
Gond gɒnd ‖ gɑːnd **Gonds** gɒndz ‖ gɑːndz
Gondi 'gɒnd i ‖ 'gɑːnd i
gondola 'gɒnd əl ə ‖ 'gɑːnd- ~**s** z
gondolier ,gɒnd ə 'lɪə -ᵊl 'ɪə ‖ ,gɑːnd ə 'lɪᵊr ~**s**
z
Gondwana gɒn 'dwɑːn ə ‖ gɑːn- ~**land** lænd

GONE

■ gɔːn ▢ gɑːn

AmE 1993

0   20   40   60   80   100%

gone gɒn §gɔːn, §gɑːn ‖ gɔːn gɑːn —*AmE*
1993 poll panel preference: gɔːn 76%, gɑːn
24% *(of those who distinguish these two*
vowels).
goner 'gɒn ə ‖ 'gɔːn ᵊr 'gɑːn- ~**s** z
Goneril 'gɒn ᵊr ɪl -əl ‖ 'gɑːn-
gonfalon 'gɒn fᵊl ən ‖ 'gɑːn- ~**s** z
gong gɒŋ ‖ gɔːŋ gɑːŋ **gongs** gɒŋz ‖ gɔːŋz
gɑːŋz
goniometer ,gəʊn i 'ɒm ɪt ə -ət ə
‖ ,goʊn i 'ɑːm ət ᵊr ~**s** z
goniometric ,gəʊn i_ə 'metr ɪk ◄ ‖ ,goʊn- ~**al**
ᵊl ~**ally** ᵊl_i
gonk gɒŋk ‖ gɑːŋk **gonks** gɒŋks ‖ gɑːŋks
gonna *contracted weak form before a consonant*
(')gən ə —*There is no real RP strong form for*
this informal contraction of going to, *although*
spelling pronunciations 'gɒn ə, 'gʌn ə *are*
sometimes used in reading. There is an AmE
strong form 'gɔːn ə, 'gɑːn ə. —*Before a vowel*
sound, the contracted weak form (')gən u *is*
sometimes used (see discussion at to)

gonococ|cus ,gɒn əʊ
'kɒk |əs ‖ ,gɑːn ə 'kɑːk |əs ~**ci** saɪ siː, aɪ
gonorrhea, gonorrhoea
,gɒn ə 'rɪə ‖ ,gɑːn ə 'riː ə
Gonville 'gɒn vɪl -vᵊl ‖ 'gɑːn-
-gony *stress-imposing* gən i — **cosmogony**
kɒz 'mɒg ən i ‖ kɑːz 'mɑːg-
Gonzales, Gonzalez gɒn 'zɑːl ɪz gən-, -ez, -əz
‖ gən 'zɑːl əs gɑːn-, gɔːn-, -'saːl-, -es —*Sp*
González [gon 'θa leθ, -'sa les]
gonzo 'gɒnz əʊ ‖ 'gɑːnz oʊ ~**s** z
goo guː
goober 'guːb ə ‖ -ᵊr ~**s** z
Gooch guːtʃ
good, Good gʊd **better** 'bet ə ‖ 'beṱ ᵊr **best**
best **goods** gʊdz —*In the phrase* a good deal
('quite a lot') a d *is often lost in RP (providing*
deal *is unstressed), thus* a good deal better
ə ,gʊd iːᵊl 'bet ə
good ,after'noon, ,• ,••'•; ,good 'book;
(ₗ)good 'day; (ₗ)good 'evening; ,Good
'Friday; ,good 'looker; ,good 'looks;
(ₗ)good 'morning; ,good 'offices; ,good
Sa'maritan
Goodall 'gʊd ɔːl ‖ -aːl
Goodbody 'gʊd ,bɒd i →'gʊb- ‖ -,baːd i
good-by, good-bye, goodbye ,gʊd 'baɪ ◄
→,gʊb- ~**s** z
Goodchild 'gʊd tʃaɪᵊld
Goode gʊd
Goodenough 'gʊd ɪ ,nʌf -ə-, -ᵊn ,ʌf
Goodfellow 'gʊd ,fel əʊ ‖ -oʊ
good-for-nothing ,gʊd fə 'nʌθ ɪŋ ◄ '•• ,••
‖ -fᵊr-
Goodge guːdʒ gʊdʒ
Goodhart 'gʊd haːt ‖ -haːrt
good-humored, good-humoured
,gʊd 'hjuːm əd ◄ ‖ -ᵊrd ◄ -'juːm- ~**ly** li
~**ness** nəs nɪs
goodie 'gʊd i ~**s** z
goodish 'gʊd ɪʃ
Goodison 'gʊd ɪs ən -əs-
goodli... —*see* **goodly**
Goodliffe 'gʊd lɪf
good-looking ,gʊd 'lʊk ɪŋ ◄
good|ly 'gʊd |li ~**lier** li_ə ‖ li_ᵊr ~**liest** li_ɪst
_əst ~**liness** li nəs -nɪs
Goodman 'gʊd mən →'gʊb-
good-natured ,gʊd 'neɪtʃ əd ◄ ‖ -ᵊrd ~**ly** li
~**ness** nəs nɪs
goodness 'gʊd nəs -nɪs
goodnight (ₗ)gʊd 'naɪt ◄ gə- ~**s** s
good-o, good-oh ,gʊd 'əʊ ‖ -'oʊ
Goodrich 'gʊd rɪtʃ
goods gʊdz
good-tempered ,gʊd 'temp əd ◄ ‖ -ᵊrd ◄ ~**ly** li
~**ness** nəs nɪs
good|wife 'gʊd |waɪf ~**wives** waɪvz
goodwill ,gʊd 'wɪl ◄
,goodwill 'visit
Goodwin 'gʊd wɪn §-wən
Goodwood 'gʊd wʊd
Goodwright 'gʊd raɪt

good|y 'gʊd li ~ies iz
Goodyear 'gʊd jə -jɪə, -jɔː ‖ -jᵊr -jɪr; 'gʊdʒ ɪr
goody-good|y 'gʊd i ˌgʊd li ˌ•• '•• ~ies iz
goody-two-shoes ˌgʊd i 'tuː ʃuːz
goo|ey 'guː_li ~ier i ə ‖ i ᵊr ~iest i ɪst i əst
~iness i nəs i nɪs
goof guːf **goofed** guːft **goofing** 'guːf ɪŋ
goofs guːfs
goofball 'guːf bɔːl ‖ -bɑːl ~s z
goof|y 'guːf li ~ier i_ə ‖ i_ᵊr ~iest i_ɪst i_əst
~ily ɪ li əl i ~iness i nəs i nɪs
Googie 'guːg i
googl|e 'guːg l|i ~lies liz
googol 'guːg ɒl -ᵊl ‖ -ɔːl -ɑːl, -ᵊl ~s z
googolplex 'guːg ɒl pleks -ᵊl- ‖ -ɔːl- -ɑːl-, -ᵊl-
gooi... —see **gooey**
gook 'sludge' gʊk guːk
gook 'SE Asian' guːk **gooks** guːks
Goole guːl
goolies 'guːl iz
goon guːn **goons** guːnz
gooner|y 'guːn ᵊr li ~ies iz
Goonhilly gʊn 'hɪl i ˌguːn-, '•, ••
goop guːp
goosander guː 'sænd ə ‖ -ᵊr ~s z
goose guːs **geese** giːs **goosed** guːst **gooses,**
goose's 'guːs ɪz -əz **goosing** 'guːs ɪŋ
'goose egg; 'goose ˌpimples
gooseberr|y 'gʊz bᵊr_li §'gʊs-, §'guːs-, §'guːz-
‖ 'guːs ˌber li 'guːz-, -bᵊr_li ~ies iz
goosebumps 'guːs bʌmps
gooseflesh 'guːs fleʃ
goosefoot 'guːs fʊt ~s s
goosegog 'gʊz gɒg ‖ -gɑːg ~s z
gooseneck 'guːs nek ~s s
goosestep 'guːs step ~ped t ~ping ɪŋ ~s s
Goosnargh 'guːs nə ‖ -nᵊr
Goossens 'guːs ᵊnz
GOP ˌdʒiː əʊ 'piː ‖ -oʊ-
gopher 'gəʊf ə ‖ 'goʊf ᵊr ~s z
Gorazde gə 'ræʒ deɪ gɔː-, -də
Gorbachev, Gorbachov 'gɔːb ə tʃɒf -tʃɒv,
ˌ•'•• ‖ 'gɔːrb ə tʃɔːf -tʃɑːf —Russ
[gər bʌ 'tʃɔf]
Gorbals 'gɔːb ᵊlz ‖ 'gɔːrb-
gorblimey ₍ₒ₎gɔː 'blaɪm i ‖ —
Gordian 'gɔːd i_ən ‖ 'gɔːrd-
ˌGordian 'knot
Gordimer 'gɔːd ɪm ə §-əm ə ‖ 'gɔːrd əm ᵊr
Gordon 'gɔːd ᵊn ‖ 'gɔːrd ᵊn
Gordonstoun 'gɔːd ᵊnz tən -ᵊnˈst ᵊn ‖ 'gɔːrd-
gore, Gore gɔː ‖ gɔːr goʊr **gored** gɔːd ‖ gɔːrd
goʊrd **gores** gɔːz ‖ gɔːrz goʊrz **goring**
'gɔːr ɪŋ ‖ 'goʊr-
Gorecki, Górecki gɔː 'ret ski gə- —Polish
[gu 'rets ki]
Gore-Tex tdmk 'gɔː teks ‖ 'gɔːr-
gorge gɔːdʒ ‖ gɔːrdʒ **gorged**
gɔːdʒd ‖ gɔːrdʒd **gorges** 'gɔːdʒ ɪz -əz
‖ 'gɔːrdʒ əz **gorging** 'gɔːdʒ ɪŋ ‖ 'gɔːrdʒ ɪŋ
gorgeous 'gɔːdʒ əs ‖ 'gɔːrdʒ- ~ly li ~ness nəs
nɪs
gorget 'gɔːdʒ ɪt -ət ‖ 'gɔːrdʒ- ~s s

Gorgias 'gɔːdʒ i_əs -æs ‖ 'gɔːrdʒ-
gorgon, G~ 'gɔːg ən ‖ 'gɔːrg- ~s, ~'s z
Gorgonzola ˌgɔːg ən 'zəʊl ə ◄ →-ŋ- ‖ ˌgɔːrg
ən 'zoʊl ə —It [gor gon 'dzɔː la]
Gorham 'gɔːr əm
gori... —see **gory**
gorilla gə 'rɪl ə ~s z
Goring 'gɔːr ɪŋ
Gorki, Gorky 'gɔːk i ‖ 'gɔːrk i —Russ
['gɔrʲ kʲij]
Gorleston 'gɔːlst ən ‖ 'gɔːrlst-
Gorman 'gɔːm ən ‖ 'gɔːrm-
gormandis|e, gormandiz|e
'gɔːm ən daɪz ‖ 'gɔːrm- ~ed d ~er/s ə/
z ‖ ᵊr/z ~es ɪz əz ~ing ɪŋ
Gormanston 'gɔːm ənˈst ən ‖ 'gɔːrm-
gormless 'gɔːm ləs -lɪs ‖ 'gɔːrm- ~ly li ~ness
nəs nɪs
Gormley 'gɔːm li ‖ 'gɔːrm-
Goronwy gə 'rɒn wi gɒ- ‖ -'rɑːn- —Welsh
[gɔ 'rɔ nui, -nwi]
Gorran 'gɒr ən ‖ 'gɔːr-
Gor-Ray tdmk 'gɔː reɪ ‖ 'gɔːr-
Gorringe 'gɒr ɪndʒ -ᵊndʒ ‖ 'gɔːr- 'gɑːr-
gorse gɔːs ‖ gɔːrs
Gorsedd 'gɔːs eð ‖ 'gɔːrs- —Welsh ['gor seð]
Gorseinon gɔː 'saɪn ən ‖ gɔːr- —Welsh
[gor 'səi non]
Gorst gɔːst ‖ gɔːrst
Gorton 'gɔːt ᵊn ‖ 'gɔːrt ᵊn
gor|y 'gɔːr li ‖ 'goʊr- ~ier i_ə ‖ i_ᵊr ~iest i_ɪst
i_əst ~ily ᵊl i ɪ li ~iness i nəs i nɪs
Gosforth 'gɒs fəθ -fɔːθ ‖ 'gɑːs fɔːrθ -foʊrθ
gosh gɒʃ ‖ gɑːʃ
goshawk 'gɒs hɔːk ‖ 'gɑːs- -hɑːk ~s s
Goshen 'gəʊʃ ᵊn ‖ 'goʊʃ ᵊn
gosling, G~ 'gɒz lɪŋ ‖ 'gɑːz- ~s z
go-slow ˌgəʊ 'sləʊ ◄ '•• ‖ ˌgoʊ sloʊ ~s z
gospel, G~ 'gɒsp ᵊl ‖ 'gɑːsp ᵊl ~s z
'gospel ˌmusic; ˌgospel 'truth
gospeler, gospeller 'gɒsp ᵊl ə ‖ 'gɑːsp ᵊl ᵊr ~s
z
Gosport, g~ 'gɒs pɔːt ‖ 'gɑːs pɔːrt -poʊrt ~s s
Goss gɒs ‖ gɔːs gɑːs
Gossage 'gɒs ɪdʒ ‖ 'gɑːs-
gossamer 'gɒs əm ə ‖ 'gɑːs əm ᵊr 'gɑːz- ~ed d
Gosse gɒs ‖ gɔːs gɑːs
gossip 'gɒs ɪp §-əp ‖ 'gɑːs əp ~ed t ~er/s ə/
z ‖ ᵊr/z ~ing ɪŋ ~s s
gossipmonger 'gɒs ɪp ˌmʌŋ gə §-əp-
‖ 'gɑːs əp ˌmʌŋ gᵊr -ˌmɑːŋ- ~s z
gossipy 'gɒs ɪp i §-əp- ‖ 'gɑːs-
gossypol 'gɒs i pɒl ‖ 'gɑːs ə poʊl -pɑːl, -pɔːl
got gɒt ‖ gɑːt
Goth gɒθ ‖ gɑːθ **Goths** gɒθs ‖ gɑːθs
Gotha 'gəʊθ ə 'gəʊt- ‖ 'goʊt ə —Ger ['goː ta]
Gotham place in Notts 'gəʊt əm 'gɒt- ‖ 'goʊt-
'gɑːt̬-
Gotham nickname for NYC 'gɒθ əm 'gəʊθ- ‖
'gɑːθ-
Gothard 'gɒθ ɑːd ‖ 'gɑːθ ɑːrd
Gothenburg 'gɒθ ᵊn bɜːg 'gɒt-

G

|| 'gɑːθ ən bɜːɡ 'gɑːt- —*Swedish* Göteborg
[ˌjœt ə 'bɔrj]
Gothic 'gɒθ ɪk || 'gɑːθ ɪk **~ally** əl_i
Gothicism 'gɒθ ɪ ˌsɪz əm -ə- || 'gɑːθ-
gotta 'gɒt ə || 'gɑːt̬ ə —*Although this spelling is
nonstandard, particularly in BrE, the
pronunciation given is quite usual not only in
GenAm but also in informal RP for* got to
('*must*') *before a word beginning with a
consonant sound. Before a vowel, the
corresponding pronunciation is usually*
'gɒt u || 'gɑːt̬ ə —*see discussion at* to
gotten 'gɒt ən || 'gɑːt ən
gotterdammerung ˌgɒt ə 'dæm ə rʊŋ ˌgɑːt-,
-'dem-, -rʌŋ || ˌgɑːt̬ ər- —*Ger*
Götterdämmerung [ˌgœt ɐ 'dɛm ɐʁ ʊŋ]
Gottfried 'gɒt friːd || 'gɑːt- —*Ger* ['gɔt fʁiːt]
Gotti 'gɒt i || 'gɑːt̬ i
Gottingen, Göttingen 'gɜːt ɪŋ ən 'gɒt- || 'get̬-
'gʊt̬-, 'gɜːt̬- —*Ger* ['gœt ɪŋ ən]
gouach|e gu 'ɑːʃ gwɑːʃ —*Fr* [gwaʃ] **~es** ɪz əz
Gouda 'gaʊd ə || 'guːd ə —*Dutch* ['xɔu daː]
Goudge guːdʒ gʊdʒ
Goudhurst 'gaʊd hɜːst || -hɜːst
gouge gaʊdʒ **gouged** gaʊdʒd **gouges**
'gaʊdʒ ɪz -əz **gouging** 'gaʊdʒ ɪŋ
Gough gɒf || gɑːf
goujon 'guːdʒ ən 'guːʒ-, -ɒn, -ɒ̃ || gu 'ʒoʊn
—*Fr* [gu ʒɔ̃] **~s** z
goulash 'guːl æʃ || -ɑːʃ -æʃ **~es** ɪz əz
Gould guːld gəʊld
Gounod 'guːn əʊ || -oʊ —*Fr* [gu no]
gourami, gouramy gʊ 'rɑːm i 'gʊər əm i **~s** z
gourd, gourde gʊəd gɔːd || gɔːrd gʊrd, gʊərd
gourds, gourdes gʊədz gɔːdz || gɔːrdz
gʊrdz, gʊərdz
Gourlay, Gourley 'gʊəl i || 'gʊrl i
gourmand 'gʊəm ənd 'gɔː- || 'gʊrm ɑːnd
-ənd; gʊr 'mɑːnd —*Fr* [guʁ mɑ̃] **~s** z
gourmet 'gʊəm eɪ 'gɔː- || 'gʊrm eɪ gʊr 'meɪ
—*Fr* [guʁ mɛ] **~s** z
Gourock 'gʊər ək || 'gʊr-
gout gaʊt **gouts** gaʊts
goutweed 'gaʊt wiːd
gout|y 'gaʊt li || 'gaʊt̬ li **~ier** i_ə || i_ər **~iest**
i_ɪst i_əst **~ily** ɪ li əl i **~iness** i nəs i nɪs
Govan 'gʌv ən
gov|ern 'gʌv |ən || -|ərn **~erned** ənd || ərnd
~erning ən_ɪŋ || ərn ɪŋ **~erns** ənz || ərnz
governance 'gʌv ən_ən*s || -ərn ən*s
governess 'gʌv ən_əs -ɪs, -es || -ərn əs **~es** ɪz
əz
government 'gʌv ən mənt →-əm-, -ə- || -ərn-
—*There are also casual forms* 'gʌb m mənt,
'gʌm mənt **~s** s
governmental ˌgʌv ən 'ment əl ◄ →-əm-, -ə-
|| ˌgʌv ərn 'ment̬ əl ◄ **~ly** i
governor 'gʌv ən_ə || 'gʌv ən_ər -ərn ər **~s** z
governor-general ˌgʌv ən_ə 'dʒen rəl -'dʒen
ər əl || -ən_ər- **governors-general**
ˌgʌv ən_əz- || -ən_ərz-
governorship 'gʌv ən_ə ʃɪp || -ən_ər- -ərn ər-
~s s

Govett 'gʌv ɪt -ət
Gow gaʊ
Gowan, gowan 'gaʊ_ən **~s** z
Gower (i) 'gaʊ_ə || 'gaʊ_ər, (ii) gɔː || gɔːr —*The
peninsula in Wales, and the London street, are
(i). The family name is sometimes (ii).*
Gowing 'gaʊ_ɪŋ **~s** z
gown gaʊn **gowned** gaʊnd **gowning**
'gaʊn ɪŋ **gowns** gaʊnz
Gowrie 'gaʊər i
goy gɔɪ **goyim** 'gɔɪ ɪm -jɪm, §-əm **goys** gɔɪz
Goya 'gɔɪ ə —*Sp* ['go ja] **~s**, **~'s** z
Goyt gɔɪt
Gozo 'gəʊz əʊ || 'goʊz oʊ
GP ˌdʒiː 'piː **~s**, **~'s** z
G-Plan *tdmk* 'dʒiː plæn
GPO ˌdʒiː piː 'əʊ ◄ || -'oʊ ◄
Graafian 'grɑːf i_ən 'græf-
grab græb **grabbed** græbd **grabbing**
'græb ɪŋ **grabs** græbz
'grab bag
grabber 'græb ə || -ər **~s** z
graben 'grɑːb ən **~s** z
Gracch|us 'græk ləs **~i** iː aɪ
grace, Grace greɪs **graced** greɪst **graces,
Graces, Grace's** 'greɪs ɪz -əz **gracing**
'greɪs ɪŋ
'grace note
grace-and-favour ˌgreɪs ən 'feɪv ə ◄ -ənd- || -ər
Gracechurch 'greɪs tʃɜːtʃ || -tʃɜːtʃ
graceful 'greɪs fəl -fʊl **~ly** _i **~ness** nəs nɪs
Graceland 'greɪs lænd -lənd
graceless 'greɪs ləs -lɪs **~ly** li **~ness** nəs nɪs
Gracey, Gracie 'greɪs i
gracious 'greɪʃ əs **~ly** li **~ness** nəs nɪs
grackle 'græk əl **~s** z
grad græd **grads** grædz
gradability ˌgreɪd ə 'bɪl ət i -ɪt i || -ət̬ i
gradable 'greɪd əb əl
gradate grə 'deɪt || 'greɪd eɪt **~ated** eɪt ɪd
-əd || eɪt̬ əd **~ates** eɪts **~ating** eɪt ɪŋ || eɪt̬ ɪŋ
gradation grə 'deɪʃ ən greɪ-, græ- **~al** _əl **~s** z
grade, Grade greɪd **graded** 'greɪd ɪd -əd
grades greɪdz **grading** 'greɪd ɪŋ
'grade ˌcrossing; 'grade school
Gradgrind 'græd graɪnd →'græg-
gradience 'greɪd i_ən*s
gradient 'greɪd i_ənt **~s** s
gradual 'grædʒ u_əl 'græd ju_əl; 'grædʒ əl **~ly**
i **~ness** nəs nɪs —*BrE 1998 poll panel
preference* (gradually): dʒ *51%,* dj *49%; born
since 1973,* dʒ *70%,* dj *30%*
graduate *adj, n* 'grædʒ u_ət 'græd ju_, _ɪt, -eɪt
~s s
gradu|ate *v* 'grædʒ u eɪt 'græd ju- **~ated**
eɪt ɪd -əd || eɪt̬ əd **~ates** eɪts **~ating**
eɪt ɪŋ || eɪt̬ ɪŋ
graduation ˌgrædʒ u 'eɪʃ ən ˌgræd ju- **~s** z
gradus 'græd əs 'greɪd- **~es** ɪz əz
Grady 'greɪd i
Graeco- 'griːk əʊ || -oʊ— **Graeco-Roman**
ˌgriːk əʊ 'rəʊm ən ◄ || -oʊ 'roʊm-
Graeme 'greɪ əm greɪm

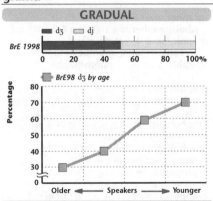

GRADUAL

■ dʒ ▢ dj

BrE 1998

0 20 40 60 80 100%

▶ BrE98 dʒ by age

Percentage

80
70
60
50
40
30
0

Older ◄——— Speakers ———► Younger

graffit|i grə 'fiːt li græ- ‖ -'fiːt̬ li ~o əʊ ‖ oʊ
Grafham, Graffham 'græf əm —but Grafham
  in Cambridgeshire is 'grɑːf-
graft grɑːft §græft ‖ græft **grafted** 'grɑːft ɪd
  §'græft-, -əd ‖ 'græft əd **grafting** 'grɑːft ɪŋ
  §'græft- ‖ 'græft ɪŋ **grafts** grɑːfts §græfts
  ‖ græfts
grafter 'grɑːft ə §'græft- ‖ 'græft ᵊr ~s z
Grafton 'grɑːft ən §'græft- ‖ 'græft-
Graham, g~, Grahame 'greɪ əm
Grahamstown 'greɪ əmz taʊn
Graig graɪg —Welsh [graig]
Grail, grail greɪᵊl **grails** greɪᵊlz
grain greɪn **grained** greɪnd **graining**
  'greɪn ɪŋ **grains** greɪnz
  'grain ˌelevator
Grainger 'greɪndʒ ə ‖ -ᵊr
Grainne, Gráinne 'grɔːn jə ‖ 'grɑːn-
grain|y 'greɪn li ~ier i_ə ‖ i_ᵊr ~iest i_ɪst i_əst
  ~iness i nəs i nɪs
gram, Gram græm **grams** græmz
-gram græm — **gorillagram** gə 'rɪl ə græm
gramercy, G~ grə 'mɜːs i ‖ -'mɜːs i —but in
  NYC G~ Park is 'græm əs i ‖ -ᵊrs i
graminaceous ˌgræm ɪ 'neɪʃ əs ◄ -ə-
grammalogue 'græm ə lɒg ‖ -lɔːg -lɑːg ~s z
grammar 'græm ə ‖ -ᵊr ~s z
  'grammar ˌschool
grammarian grə 'meər i_ən ‖ -'mer- -'mær-
  ~s z
grammatical grə 'mæt ɪk ᵊl ‖ -'mæt̬- ~ly i
grammaticality grə ˌmæt ɪ 'kæl ət i §-ˌ•ə-, -ɪt i
  ‖ -ˌmæt̬ ə 'kæl ət̬ i
gramme græm **grammes** græmz
Gramm|y 'græm li ~ies, ~ys iz
Gram-negative ˌgræm 'neg ət ɪv ◄ ‖ -ət̬-
gramophone 'græm ə fəʊn ‖ -foʊn ~s z
  'gramophone ˌrecord
Grampian 'græmp i_ən ~s z
Gram-positive ˌgræm 'pɒz ət ɪv ◄ -ət-
  ‖ -'pɑːz ət̬-
grampus 'græmp əs ~es ɪz əz
gran, Gran græn —See also phrases with this
  word **grans, Gran's** grænz
Granada grə 'nɑːd ə —Sp [gra 'na ða]
granadilla ˌgræn ə 'dɪl ə ‖ -'diː ə ~s z

Granados grə 'nɑːd ɒs ‖ -oʊs —Sp
  [gra 'na ðos]
granar|y 'græn ər li ‖ 'greɪn- ~ies iz
Granby 'græn bi →'græm-
Gran Canaria ˌgræn kə 'neər i_ə →ˌgræŋ-,
  -'nɑːr- ‖ ˌgrɑːn kə 'nɑːr i_ə -'nær-, -'ner-
  —Sp [ˌgraŋ ka 'na ria]
grand, Grand grænd —but in French
  expressions grɒn, grɒ̃ ‖ grɑːn —Fr [grɑ̃] —See
  also phrases with this word **grander**
  'grænd ə ‖ -ᵊr **grandest** 'grænd ɪst -əst
  grands grændz
  ˌGrand 'Canyon; ˌgrand 'jury; ˌgrand
  'opera; ˌgrand pi̇ ano; ˌGrand 'Rapids;
  ˌgrand 'slam
grandad, G~ 'græn dæd ~s, ~'s z
grandadd|y 'græn ˌdæd li ~ies, ~y's iz
grandchild 'græn tʃaɪᵊld 'grænd- ~'s z
grandchildren 'græn ˌtʃɪldr ən 'grænd-,
  -ˌtʃʊldr- ~'s z
Grand Coulee ˌgrænd 'kuːl i
granddaughter 'græn ˌdɔːt ə 'grænd-
  ‖ -ˌdɔːt̬ ᵊr -ˌdɑːt̬- ~s z
grandduke ˌgrænd 'djuːk ◄ →§-'dʒuːk ‖ -'duːk
  -'djuːk ~s s
grandee græn 'diː ~s z
grandeur 'grændʒ ə 'græn djʊə, 'grɒ̃-, -djə
  ‖ -ᵊr -ʊr
grandfather, G~ 'grænd ˌfɑːð ə ‖ -ᵊr ~s, ~'s z
  ˌgrand ˌfather 'clock
Grand Guignol ˌgrɒn 'giːn jɒl ˌgrɒ̃-
  ‖ ˌgrɑːn giːn 'joʊl -'jɔːl, -'jɑːl —Fr [-gi njɔl]
grandiloquence græn 'dɪl ək wənts
grandiloquent græn 'dɪl ək wənt ~ly li
grandiose 'grænd i əʊs -əʊz ‖ -oʊs, ˌ•'•◄ ~ly li
  ~ness nəs nɪs
grandiosity ˌgrænd i 'ɒs ət i -ɪt i ‖ -'ɑːs ət̬ i
Grandison 'grænd ɪs ən -əs-
grandly 'grænd li
grandma, G~ 'græn mɑː 'grænd-,
  →'græm- ‖ -mɔː ~s, ~'s z
grand mal ˌgrɒn 'mæl ˌgrɒ̃- ‖ ˌgræn 'mɑːl
  ˌgrɑːn-, -'mæl, '•• —Fr [-mal]
grandmama, grandmamma 'grænd mə ˌmɑː
  →'græm- ~s, ~'s z
Grand Marnier tdmk ˌgrɒn 'mɑːn i eɪ
  ˌgrɒ̃- ‖ ˌgrɑːn mɑːrn 'jeɪ —Fr [-maʁ nje]
grandmaster 'grænd ˌmɑːst ə →'græm-,
  §-ˌmæst-, ˌ•'•• ‖ -ˌmæst ᵊr ~s z
grandmother, G~ 'græn ˌmʌð ə 'grænd-,
  →'græm- ‖ -ᵊr ~s, ~'s z
grandness 'grænd nəs -nɪs
grandpa, G~ 'græn pɑː →'græm- ‖ -pɔː ~s,
  ~'s z
grandparent 'grænd ˌpeər ənt →'græm-
  ‖ -ˌper- -ˌpær- ~s s
grand prix ˌgrɒn 'priː ˌgrɒ̃-, ˌgrɑːn-, ˌgrɔːn-,
  →ˌgrɒm-, ˌgrɑːm-, -'mæl, '•• ‖ ˌgrɑːn-
  —Fr [gʁɑ̃ pʁi] **grands prix** —as sing. or with
  added z
grandsire 'grænd ˌsaɪ_ə ‖ -ˌsaɪ_ᵊr ~s z
grandson 'græn sʌn 'grænd- ~s z

G

grands prix ˌgrɒn ˈpriː, ˌgrɒ̃-, ˌgrɑːn-, ˌgrɔːn-,
→ˌgrɒm-, →ˌgrɑːm-, →ˌgrɔːm-, -ˈpriːz
‖ ˌgrɑːn- —*Fr* [ɡʁɑ̃ pʁi]
grandstand ˈgrænd stænd ~s z
grange, G~ greɪndʒ **granges** ˈgreɪndʒ ɪz -əz
Grangemouth ˈgreɪndʒ maʊθ -məθ
Grange-over-Sands
ˌgreɪndʒ əʊv ə ˈsændz ‖ -oʊv ər-
Granger ˈgreɪndʒ ə ‖ -ər
granite ˈgræn ɪt -ət ~s s
granitic grə ˈnɪt ɪk græ- ‖ -ˈnɪt̬ ɪk
grannie, granny, G~ ˈgræn i ~s, ~'s z
   ˈgranny flat; ˈgranny knot; ˌGranny ˈSmith
granola grə ˈnəʊl ə greɪ- ‖ -ˈnoʊl ə
granolithic ˌgræn ə ˈlɪθ ɪk ◄
grant, Grant grɑːnt §grænt ‖ grænt **granted**
   ˈgrɑːnt ɪd §ˈgrænt-, -əd ‖ ˈgrænt̬ əd
   granting ˈgrɑːnt ɪŋ §ˈgrænt- ‖ ˈgrænt̬ ɪŋ
   grants grɑːnts §grænts ‖ grænts
Granta ˈgrɑːnt ə ˈgrænt- ‖ ˈgrænt̬ ə
Grantchester ˈgrɑːn tʃɪst ə ˈgræn-, -tʃəst-,
   §-ˌtʃest- ‖ ˈgræn ˌtʃest ər
grantee ˌ‿grɑːn ˈtiː §ˌ‿græn- ‖ ˌ‿græn- ~s s
Granth grʌnt —*Hindi* [grəntʰ]
Grantham ˈgrænt̬θ əm
Grantley, Grantly ˈgrɑːnt li §ˈgrænt- ‖ ˈgrænt-
grantor ˌ‿grɑːn ˈtɔː §ˌ‿græn-; ˈgrɑːnt ə,
   §ˈgrænt- ‖ ˌ‿græn ˈtɔːr ˈgrænt̬ ər ~s z
Grantown-on-Spey ˌgræn taʊn ɒn ˈspeɪ
   ˌgrænt ən- ‖ -ɑːn ˈspeɪ -ɔːn' •
gran turismo ˌgræn tʊə ˈriːz məʊ -tuə-
   ‖ ˌgrɑːn tʊ ˈriːz moʊ -ˈriːz- —*It*
   [gran tu ˈriz mo]
granular ˈgræn jʊl ə -jəl- ‖ -jəl ər
granularity ˌgræn jʊ ˈlær ət i ,•jə-, -ɪt i
   ‖ -jə ˈlær ət̬ i -ˈler-
granu|late ˈgræn jʊ |leɪt -jə- ‖ -jə- **~lated**
   leɪt ɪd -əd ‖ leɪt̬ əd **~lates** leɪts **~lating**
   leɪt ɪŋ ‖ leɪt̬ ɪŋ
granulation ˌgræn jʊ ˈleɪʃ ən -jə- ‖ -jə- ~s z
granule ˈgræn juːl ~s z
Granville ˈgræn vɪl -vəl
grape greɪp **grapes** greɪps
grapefruit ˈgreɪp fruːt ~s s
Grapelli grə ˈpel i
grapeshot ˈgreɪp ʃɒt ‖ -ʃɑːt
grapevine ˈgreɪp vaɪn ~s z

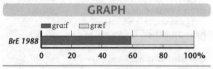

GRAPH

■ grɑːf	□ græf	

BrE 1988

0   20   40   60   80   100%

graph grɑːf græf ‖ græf —*BrE 1988 poll panel*
   preference: grɑːf *59% (southerners 77%),* græf
   41% (southerners 23%). **graphed** grɑːft
   græft ‖ græft **graphing** ˈgrɑːf ɪŋ ˈgræf-
   ‖ ˈgræf ɪŋ **graphs** grɑːfs græfs ‖ græfs
   ˈgraph ˌpaper
-graph grɑːf græf ‖ græf — **photograph**
   ˈfəʊt ə grɑːf -græf ‖ ˈfoʊt̬ ə græf
grapheme ˈgræf iːm ~s z
graphemic græ ˈfiːm ɪk grə- ~ally əl_i

-grapher *stress-imposing* grəf ə ‖ -ər —
   photographer fəʊ ˈtɒg rəf ə ‖ fə ˈtɑːg rəf ər
graphic ˈgræf ɪk ~al əl ~ally əl_i ~s s
   ˌgraphic deˈsign; ˌgraphic deˈsigner
-graphic ˈgræf ɪk — **photographic**
   ˌfəʊt ə ˈgræf ɪk ◄ ‖ ˌfoʊt̬-
graphite ˈgræf aɪt
graphological ˌgræf ə ˈlɒdʒ ɪk əl ◄ ‖ -ˈlɑːdʒ-
   ~ly _i
graphologist græ ˈfɒl ədʒ ɪst grə-, §-əst
   ‖ -ˈfɑːl- ~s s
graphology græ ˈfɒl ədʒ i grə- ‖ -ˈfɑːl-
-graphy *stress-imposing* grəf i —
   photography fəʊ ˈtɒg rəf i ‖ fə ˈtɑːg-
grapnel ˈgræp nəl ~s z
grappa ˈgræp ə ‖ ˈgrɑːp ə —*It* [ˈgrap pa]
Grappelli grə ˈpel i —*Fr* [gra pɛ li]
grappl|e ˈgræp əl ~ed d ~es z ~ing _ɪŋ
   ˈgrappling hook; ˈgrappling ˌiron
graptolite ˈgræpt əʊ laɪt ‖ -ə- ~s s
Grasmere ˈgrɑːs mɪə §ˈgræs- ‖ ˈgræs mɪr
grasp grɑːsp §græsp ‖ græsp **grasped** grɑːspt
   §græspt ‖ græspt **grasping/ly** ˈgrɑːsp ɪŋ /li
   §ˈgræsp- ‖ ˈgræsp ɪŋ /li
grass grɑːs §græs ‖ græs **grassed** grɑːst
   §græst ‖ græst **grasses** ˈgrɑːs ɪz §ˈgræs-, -əz
   ‖ ˈgræs əz **grassing** ˈgrɑːs ɪŋ §ˈgræs-
   ‖ ˈgræs ɪŋ
   ˌgrass ˈroots; ˌgrass ˈwidow; ˌgrass
   ˈwidower
grasshopper ˈgrɑːs ˌhɒp ə §ˈgræs-
   ‖ ˈgræs ˌhɑːp ər ~s z
Grassington ˈgrɑːs ɪŋ tən §ˈgræs- ‖ ˈgræs-
grassland ˈgrɑːs lænd §ˈgræs-, -lənd ‖ ˈgræs-
   ~s z
grass|y ˈgrɑːs li §ˈgræs- ‖ ˈgræs li ~ier
   i_ə ‖ i_ər ~iest i_ɪst i_əst ~iness i nəs i nɪs
grate greɪt **grated** ˈgreɪt ɪd -əd ‖ ˈgreɪt̬ əd
   grates greɪts **grating** ˈgreɪt ɪŋ ‖ ˈgreɪt̬ ɪŋ
grateful ˈgreɪt fəl -fʊl ~ly _i ~ness nəs nɪs
grater ˈgreɪt ə ‖ ˈgreɪt̬ ər
Gratiano ˌgræʃ i ˈɑːn əʊ ˌgrɑːʃ-
   ‖ ˌgrɑːʃ ˈjɑːn oʊ
graticule ˈgræt ɪ kjuːl -ə- ‖ ˈgræt̬ ə- ~s z
gratification ˌgræt ɪf ɪ ˈkeɪʃ ən ,•əf-, §-əˈ•-
   ‖ ˌgræt̬- ~s z
grati|fy ˈgræt ɪ |faɪ -ə- ‖ ˈgræt̬- **~fied** faɪd
   ~fier/s faɪ_ə/z ‖ faɪ_ər/z **~fies** faɪz **~fying/**
   ly faɪ ɪŋ /li
grating ˈgreɪt ɪŋ ‖ ˈgreɪt̬ ɪŋ ~ly li ~s z
gratis ˈgræt ɪs ˈgreɪt-, ˈgrɑːt-, -əs ‖ ˈgræt̬ əs
gratitude ˈgræt ɪ tjuːd -ə-, →§-tʃuːd
   ‖ ˈgræt̬ ə tuːd -tjuːd
Grattan, Gratton ˈgræt ən
gratuitous grə ˈtjuː_ɪt əs →-ˈtʃuː_;
   ⚠ˌgrætʃ u ˈ_ɪʃ əs ‖ -ˈtuː_ ət əs -ˈtjuː- ~ly li
   ~ness nəs nɪs
gratuit|y grə ˈtjuː_ət li →§-ˈtʃuː_, _ɪt-
   ‖ -ˈtuː_ ət li -ˈtjuː- ~ies iz
graupel ˈgraʊp əl
gravadlax ˈgræv əd læks ‖ ˈgrɑːv əd lɑːks
gravamen grə ˈveɪm en -ˈvɑːm-, -ən;
   ˈgræv əm- ‖ -ən

grave n 'burial place'; adj 'serious'; v greɪv
   graved greɪvd **graver** 'greɪv ə ‖ -ᵊr **graves**
   greɪvz **gravest** 'greɪv ɪst -əst **graving**
   'greɪv ɪŋ
   'graving dock
grave accent mark grɑːv ‖ greɪv grɑːv **graves**
   grɑːvz ‖ greɪvz grɑːvz
grave mus 'grɑːv eɪ —It ['gra: ve]
gravedigger 'greɪv ˌdɪg ə ‖ -ᵊr ~s z
gravel 'græv ᵊl ~ed, ~led d ~ing, ~ling ɪŋ ~s
   z
Graveley 'greɪv li
gravelly, G~ 'græv ᵊl i
gravely 'greɪv li
graven 'greɪv ᵊn
graveness 'greɪv nəs -nɪs
Graveney 'greɪv ni
graver 'greɪv ə ‖ -ᵊr ~s z
graves pl 'burial places' greɪvz
graves pl 'accent marks' grɑːvz ‖ greɪvz grɑːvz
Graves family name greɪvz
Graves wine grɑːv —Fr [gʁɑːv]
Gravesend ˌgreɪvz 'end ◂
graveside 'greɪv saɪd
gravestone 'greɪv stəʊn ‖ -stoʊn ~s z
graveyard 'greɪv jɑːd ‖ -jɑːrd ~s z
gravid 'græv ɪd §-əd ~ly li ~ness nəs nɪs
gravie... —see **gravy**
gravitas 'græv ɪ tæs -ə-, -tɑːs
gravi|tate 'græv ɪ |teɪt -ə- ~tated teɪt ɪd -əd
   ‖ teɪt̬ əd ~tates teɪts ~tating
   teɪt ɪŋ ‖ teɪt̬ ɪŋ
gravitation ˌgræv ɪ 'teɪʃ ᵊn -ə- ~al ᵊl ~ally
   ᵊl i
gravitative 'græv ɪ teɪt ɪv '•ə- ‖ -teɪt̬ ɪv
gravit|y 'græv ət li -ɪt- ‖ -ət̬ li ~ies iz
gravlaks 'græv læks ‖ 'grɑːv lɑːks 'græv-
   —Swedish ['grav laks]
gravure grə 'vjʊə -'vjɔː ‖ -'vjʊᵊr
grav|y 'greɪv li ~ies iz
   'gravy boat, 'gravy train
gray, Gray greɪ **grayed** greɪd **grayer**
   'greɪ ə ‖ -ᵊr **grayest** 'greɪ ɪst -əst **graying**
   'greɪ ɪŋ **grays, Grays, Gray's** greɪz
   ˌgray 'area; 'gray ˌmatter; ˌGray's 'Inn
graybeard 'greɪ bɪəd ‖ -bɪrd ~s z
grayhound 'greɪ haʊnd ~s z
grayish 'greɪ ɪʃ
graylag 'greɪ læg ~s z
grayling 'greɪl ɪŋ ~s z
gray|ly 'greɪ |li ~ness nəs nɪs
Grayson 'greɪs ᵊn
graywacke 'greɪ ˌwæk ə
Graz grɑːts —Ger [gʁaːts]
graze greɪz **grazed** greɪzd **grazes** 'greɪz ɪz
   -əz **grazing** 'greɪz ɪŋ
grazer 'greɪz ə ‖ -ᵊr ~s z
grazier 'greɪz i_ə ‖ 'greɪʒ ə, 'greɪʒ i_ə ‖ 'greɪʒ ᵊr
   (*) ~s z
Grealey 'griːl i
grease n griːs
   'grease gun

grease v griːs griːz **greased** griːst griːzd
   greases 'griːs ɪz 'griːz-, -əz **greasing**
   'griːs ɪŋ 'griːz-
   ˌgreased 'lightning
greasepaint 'griːs peɪnt
greaseproof 'griːs pruːf §-prʊf
greaser v 'griːs ə 'griːz- ‖ -ᵊr ~s z

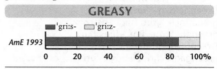

GREASY

■ 'griːs-   □ 'griːz-

AmE 1993					
0	20	40	60	80	100%

greas|y 'griːs li 'griːz- —AmE 1993 poll panel
   preference: 'griːs- 86%, 'griːz- 14%. ~ier
   i_ə ‖ i_ᵊr ~iest i_ɪst i_əst ~ily ɪ li əl i ~iness
   i nəs i nɪs
   ˌgreasy 'spoon
great greɪt (= grate) **greater**
   'greɪt ə ‖ 'greɪt̬ ᵊr **greatest** 'greɪt ɪst -əst
   ‖ 'greɪt̬ əst **greats** greɪts
   ˌGreat 'Barrier Reef; ˌGreat 'Bear; ˌGreat
   'Britain; ˌgreat 'circle; ˌGreat 'Dane;
   ˌGreater 'London◂, ˌGreater ˌLondon
   'Council; ˌGreat 'Lakes; ˌGreat 'Plains
great- ˌgreɪt —Compounds in great- are usually
   late-stressed: ˌgreat-'grand,daughter. However
   great-aunt and great-uncle, which are regularly
   subject to stress-shifting in names (ˌgreat-'aunt◂,
   ˌGreat-Aunt 'Mary), are by some people always
   given early stress.
great-aunt ˌgreɪt 'ɑːnt ◂ §-'ænt, '••
   ‖ ˌgreɪt̬ 'ænt ◂ -'ɑːnt ~s s
greatcoat 'greɪt kəʊt ‖ -koʊt ~s s
great|ly 'greɪt |li ~ness nəs nɪs
Greatorex 'greɪt ə reks ‖ 'greɪt̬-
great-uncle ˌgreɪt 'ʌŋk ᵊl '•ˌ•• ‖ ˌgreɪt̬- ~s z
greave, G~ griːv (= grieve) **greaves** griːvz
Greaves (i) greɪvz, (ii) griːvz
grebe griːb **grebes** griːbz
Grecian 'griːʃ ᵊn ~s z
Greco- ˌgriːk əʊ ˌgrek- ‖ -oʊ — **Greco-
Roman** ˌgriːk əʊ 'rəʊm ən ◂ ˌgrek-
   ‖ -oʊ 'roʊm-
Greece griːs
greed griːd
greed|y 'griːd li ~ier i_ə ‖ i_ᵊr ~iest i_ɪst i_əst
   ~ily ɪ li əl i ~iness i nəs i nɪs
greedy-guts 'griːd i gʌts
Greek, greek griːk **greeked** 'griːk ɪŋ
   greeking 'griːk ɪŋ **Greeks, greeks** griːks
   ˌGreek 'Orthodox
Greeley, Greely 'griːl i
green, Green griːn **greened** griːnd **greener**
   'griːn ə ‖ -ᵊr **greenest** 'griːn ɪst -əst
   greening 'griːn ɪŋ **greens, G~** griːnz
   ˌgreen 'bean; 'green belt; ˌgreen 'fingers;
   ˌgreen 'light; ˌGreen 'Paper; ˌgreen
   'pepper; ˌgreen 'tea; ˌgreen 'thumb
Greenaway 'griːn ə weɪ
greenback 'griːn bæk →'griːm- ~s s
Greenbaum (i) 'griːn baʊm →'griːm-, (ii)
   -bɔːm ‖ -bɑːm, (iii) -bəʊm ‖ -boʊm —The late
   Prof. Sidney G~, grammarian, claimed not to

G

care which variant people used for his name; he
was generally known as (i)

Greenberg 'griːn bɜːg →'griːm- ‖ -bɜːg
Greene griːn
greener|y 'griːn ər |i **~ies** iz
green-eyed ˌgriːn 'aɪd ◂ ‖ '· ·
  ˌgreen-eyed 'monster
Greenfield, g~ 'griːn fiːəld
greenfinch 'griːn fɪntʃ **~es** ɪz əz
green|fly 'griːn |flaɪ **~flies** flaɪz
Greenford 'griːn fəd ‖ -fərd
greengag|e 'griːn geɪdʒ →'griːŋ- **~es** ɪz əz
greengrocer 'griːn ˌgrəʊs ə →'griːŋ-
  ‖ -ˌgrəʊs ər **~s** z
greengrocer|y 'griːn ˌgrəʊs ər_|i →'griːŋ-
  ‖ -ˌgrəʊs- **~ies** iz
Greengross 'griːn grɒs →'griːŋ- ‖ -grɑːs
Greenhalgh 'griːn hælʃ -hɔːlʃ, -hɒlʃ, -hældʒ,
  -hɔːl
Greenham 'griːn əm
Greenhill 'griːn hɪl
greenhorn 'griːn hɔːn ‖ -hɔːrn **~s** z
Greenhough 'griːn ɒf -hɒf, -həʊ, -haʊ, -hʌf
  ‖ -həʊ
green|house 'griːn |haʊs **~houses** haʊz ɪz -əz
  'greenhouse ef ˌfect
greenish 'griːn ɪʃ
Greenland 'griːn lənd -lænd
Greenlandic ˌ₍ˌ₎griːn 'lænd ɪk
green|ly 'griːn |li **~ness** nəs nɪs
Greenock 'griːn ək
Greenough 'griːn əʊ ‖ -oʊ
Greenpeace 'griːn piːs →'griːm-, ˌ·'·
greenroom 'griːn ruːm -rʊm **~s** z
greensand 'griːn sænd **~s** z
greenshank 'griːn ʃæŋk **~s** s
Greenslade 'griːn sleɪd
Greensleeves 'griːn sliːvz
greenstick 'griːn stɪk
greenstone 'griːn stəʊn ‖ -stoʊn
Greenstreet 'griːn striːt
greenstuff 'griːn stʌf
greensward 'griːn swɔːd ‖ -swɔːrd **~s** z
Greenville 'griːn vɪl -vəl
Greenwell 'griːn wəl -wel
Greenwich 'gren ɪtʃ 'grɪn-, -ɪdʒ —*This applies*
  both to the London borough, location of the
  meridian, and to G~ Village in NYC; also to the
  town in CT, though this is sometimes
  'griːn wɪtʃ
  ˌGreenwich 'Mean Time, ˌ· · ˌ· '·;
  ˌGreenwich 'Village
greenwood, G~ 'griːn wʊd **~s** z
Greer grɪə ‖ grɪ°r
greet, Greet griːt **greeted** 'griːt ɪd -əd
  ‖ 'griːt̬ əd **greeting** 'griːt ɪŋ ‖ 'griːt̬ ɪŋ
  greets griːts
greeter 'griːt ə ‖ 'griːt̬ ər **~s** z
Greg greg
gregarious grɪ 'geər i_əs grə- ‖ -'ger- -'gær-
  ~ly li **~ness** nəs nɪs
Gregg greg
Gregor 'greg ə ‖ -ər

Gregorian grɪ 'gɔːr i_ən grə-, gre- ‖ -'goʊr- **~s**
  z
Gregory 'greg ər i
Gregson 'greg sən
Gregynog grɪ 'gʌn ɒg grə-, gre- ‖ -ɑːg
  —*Welsh* [gre 'gə nog]
Greig (i) greg, (ii) griːg
gremlin 'grem lɪn §-lən **~s** z
Grenada grɪ 'neɪd ə grə-, gre-
grenade grɪ 'neɪd grə- **~s** z
Grenadian grɪ 'neɪd i_ən grə-, gre- **~s** z
grenadier ˌgren ə 'dɪə ◂ ‖ -'dɪ°r ◂ **~s** z
grenadilla ˌgren ə 'dɪl ə **~s** z
grenadine, G~ 'gren ə diːn ˌ· ·'· **~s** z
Grendel 'grend ³l
Grendon 'grend ən
Grenfell 'gren f³l -fel
Grenoble grɪ 'nəʊb ³l grə- ‖ -'noʊb- —*Fr*
  [gʁə nɔbl]
Grenville 'gren vɪl -v³l
Gresham 'greʃ əm 'gres-
Gresley 'grez li
Greta (i) 'griːt ə ‖ 'griːt̬ ə, (ii) 'gret ə ‖ 'gret̬ ə
Gretchen 'gretʃ ən —*Ger* ['gʁɛːt çən]
Gretel 'gret ³l ‖ 'gret̬ ³l —*Ger* ['gʁeː t³l]
Gretna 'gret nə
  ˌGretna 'Green
Greville 'grev ɪl -³l
grew, Grew gruː
grey, Grey greɪ **greyed** greɪd **greyer**
  'greɪ ə ‖ -°r **greyest** 'greɪ ɪst -əst **greying**
  'greɪ ɪŋ **greys** greɪz
  ˌgrey 'area; 'grey ˌmatter
greybeard 'greɪ bɪəd ‖ -bɪrd **~s** z
greyhound 'greɪ haʊnd **~s** z
greyish 'greɪ ɪʃ
greylag 'greɪ læg **~s** z
grey|ly 'greɪ |li **~ness** nəs nɪs
Greystoke 'greɪ stəʊk ‖ -stoʊk
greywacke 'greɪ ˌwæk ə
Gribble, g~ 'grɪb ³l
Grice graɪs
Gricean 'graɪs i_ən
gricer 'graɪs ə ‖ -°r **~s** z
grid grɪd **grids** grɪdz
griddl|e 'grɪd ³l **~ed** d **~es** z **~ing** _ɪŋ
gridiron 'grɪd ˌaɪ_ən ‖ -ˌaɪ_°rn **~ed** d **~ing** ɪŋ
  ~s z
Gridley 'grɪd li
gridlock 'grɪd lɒk ‖ -lɑːk **~ed** t **~s** s
grief griːf
Grieg griːg —*Norw* [griːg]
Grierson 'grɪəs ən ‖ 'grɪ°rs ən
grievanc|e 'griːv ³nts §-i_ənts **~es** ɪz əz
grieve, G~ griːv **grieved** griːvd **grieves**
  griːvz **grieving/ly** 'griːv ɪŋ /li
grievous 'griːv əs △'griːv i_əs **~ly** li **~ness**
  nəs nɪs
  ˌgrievous ˌbodily 'harm
griff, griffe grɪf **griffes, griffs** grɪfs
griffin, G~ 'grɪf ɪn -³n **~s** z
Griffith 'grɪf ɪθ §-əθ
Griffiths 'grɪf ɪθs §-əθs

griffon 'grɪf ᵊn ~s z
grift grɪft **grifted** 'grɪft ɪd -əd **grifting**
'grɪft ɪŋ **grifts** grɪfts
grifter 'grɪft ə ‖ -ᵊr ~s z
grig, Grig, Grigg grɪg **grigs, Griggs, Grigg's** grɪgz
Grignard 'gri:n jɑ: ‖ gri:n 'jɑ:rd —Fr
[gʁi njaːʁ]
Grigson 'grɪg sᵊn
grike graɪk **grikes** graɪks
grill grɪl **grilled** grɪld **grilling** 'grɪl ɪŋ **grills**
grɪlz
grille grɪl (= grill) **grilles** grɪlz
grillroom 'grɪl ru:m -rom ~s z
grilse grɪls
grim grɪm **grimmer** 'grɪm ə ‖ -ᵊr **grimmest**
'grɪm ɪst -əst
    ˌgrim ' reaper
grimac|e v, n grɪ 'meɪs grə-; 'grɪm əs ~ed t
    ~es ɪz əz ~ing ɪŋ
Grimaldi grɪ 'mɔːld i grə-, -'mɒld- ‖ -'mɑːld-
grimalkin grɪ 'mælk ɪn grə-, -'mɔːlk-,
    §-ᵊn ‖ -'mɔːlk- ~s z
grime graɪm **grimed** graɪmd **grimes** graɪmz
griming 'graɪm ɪŋ
Grimes graɪmz
Grimethorpe 'graɪm θɔːp ‖ -θɔːrp
grimi... —see **grimy**
grimly 'grɪm li
Grimm grɪm **Grimm's** grɪmz
grimness 'grɪm nəs -nɪs
Grimond 'grɪm ənd
Grimsargh 'grɪmz ə ‖ -ᵊr
Grimsby 'grɪmz bi
Grimshaw 'grɪm ʃɔ: ‖ -ʃɑ:
Grimston 'grɪm'st ən
grim|y 'graɪm li ~ier i_ə ‖ i_ᵊr ~iest i_ɪst i_əst
    ~ily ɪ li əl i ~iness i nəs i nɪs
grin grɪn **grinned** grɪnd **grinning** 'grɪn ɪŋ
grins grɪnz
grind graɪnd **grinding** 'graɪnd ɪŋ **grinds**
graɪndz **ground** graʊnd
    ' grinding wheel
Grindelwald 'grɪnd ᵊl vɑːld -væld, -wɔːld
    —Ger ['grɪn dᵊl valt]
grinder 'graɪnd ə ‖ -ᵊr ~s z
Grindon 'grɪnd ən
grindstone 'graɪnd stəʊn ‖ -stoʊn ~s z
gringo 'grɪŋ gəʊ ‖ -goʊ ~s z
Grinstead, Grinsted 'grɪn stɪd -sted
Grinton 'grɪnt ən
grip grɪp **gripped** grɪpt **gripping/ly**
    'grɪp ɪŋ /li **grips** grɪps
gripe graɪp **griped** graɪpt **gripes** graɪps
griping/ly 'graɪp ɪŋ /li
griper 'graɪp ə ‖ -ᵊr ~s z
grippe grɪp gri:p
gripp... —see **grip**
Griqua 'gri:k wə 'grɪk- ~land lænd
grisaille grɪ 'zeɪ.əl grə-, gri:-, -'zaɪ, -'zaɪᵊl ‖ -'zaɪ
    -'zeɪᵊl —Fr [gʁi zaj]
Griselda grɪ 'zeld ə grə-
griseofulvin ˌgrɪz i əʊ 'fʊlv ɪn ˌgrɪs-, -'fʌlv-,
    §-ᵊn ‖ -i_ə-

grisette grɪ 'zet ~s s
Grisewood 'graɪz wʊd
gris|ly 'grɪz li (= grizzly) ~lier li_ə ‖ li_ᵊr
    ~liest li_ɪst li_əst
grison 'graɪs ᵊn 'grɪz- ~s z
grist, Grist grɪst
gristle 'grɪs ᵊl
grist|ly 'grɪs ᵊl_i ~liness ᵊl i nəs -nɪs
Griswold 'grɪz wᵊld -wəʊld, -ə-wʊʊld ‖ -woʊld
grit grɪt **grits** grɪts **gritted** 'grɪt ɪd -əd
    ‖ 'grɪt̮ əd **gritting** 'grɪt ɪŋ ‖ 'grɪt̮ ɪŋ
gritter 'grɪt ə ‖ 'grɪt̮ ᵊr ~s z
gritt|y 'grɪt li ‖ 'grɪt̮ li ~ier i_ə ‖ i_ᵊr ~iest
    i_əst ~ily ɪ li əl i ~iness i nəs i nɪs
Grizedale 'graɪz deɪᵊl
grizzl|e 'grɪz ᵊl ~ed d ~es z ~ing ɪŋ
grizz|ly 'grɪz li ~lier li_ə ‖ li_ᵊr ~lies liz
    ~liest li_ɪst li_əst
    ˌgrizzly ' bear ‖ ' • • •
groan grəʊn ‖ groʊn **groaned**
    grəʊnd ‖ groʊnd **groaning**
    'grəʊn ɪŋ ‖ 'groʊn ɪŋ **groans**
    grəʊnz ‖ groʊnz
groaner 'grəʊn ə ‖ 'groʊn ᵊr ~s z
groaning 'grəʊn ɪŋ ‖ 'groʊn ɪŋ ~ly li ~s z
groat grəʊt ‖ groʊt **groats** grəʊts ‖ groʊts
grocer 'grəʊs ə ‖ 'groʊs ᵊr ~s z
grocer|y 'grəʊs ᵊr i ‖ 'groʊs- ~ies iz
grockle 'grɒk ᵊl ‖ 'grɑːk- ~s z
Grocott 'grəʊ kɒt ‖ 'groʊ kɑːt
grog grɒg ‖ grɑːg
Grogan 'grəʊg ᵊn ‖ 'groʊg-
grogg|y 'grɒg li ‖ 'grɑːg li ~ier i_ə ‖ i_ᵊr ~iest
    i_ɪst i_əst ~ily ɪ li əl i ~iness i nəs i nɪs
grogram 'grɒg rəm ‖ 'grɑːg-
groin grɔɪn **groining** 'grɔɪn ɪŋ **groins** grɔɪnz
Grolier 'grəʊl i_ə ‖ 'groʊl i_ᵊr —Fr [gʁɔ lje]
grommet 'grɒm ɪt 'grʌm-, -ət ‖ 'grɑːm- ~s s
gromwell 'grɒm wᵊl -wel ‖ 'grɑːm- ~s z
Gromyko grə 'mi:k əʊ ‖ -oʊ —Russ [grʌ 'mi
    kə]
Groningen 'grəʊn ɪŋ ən 'grɒn- ‖ 'groʊn-
    —Dutch ['xroː nɪŋ ən]
groom, Groom gru:m grʊm **grooms** gru:mz
    grʊmz
Groombridge 'gru:m brɪdʒ
grooms|man 'gru:mz |mən 'grʊmz- ~men
    mən men
Groote Eylandt ˌgru:t ˌaɪl ənd ‖ 'gru:t̮-
groove gru:v **grooved** gru:vd **groover/s**
    'gru:v ə/z ‖ -ᵊr/z **grooves** gru:vz **grooving**
    'gru:v ɪŋ
groov|y 'gru:v li ~ier i_ə ‖ i_ᵊr ~iest i_ɪst i_əst
grope grəʊp ‖ groʊp **groped** grəʊpt ‖ groʊpt
    gropes grəʊps ‖ groʊps **groping/ly**
    'grəʊp ɪŋ /li ‖ 'groʊp-
groper 'grəʊp ə ‖ 'groʊp ᵊr ~s z
Gropius 'grəʊp i_əs ‖ 'groʊp-
grosbeak 'grəʊs bi:k 'grɒs- ‖ 'groʊs- ~s s
groschen 'grɒʃ ᵊn 'grəʊʃ- ‖ 'groʊʃ- —Ger
    ['gʁɔʃ ᵊn]
grosgrain 'grəʊ greɪn ‖ 'groʊ-

G

Grosmont (i) 'grəʊ mənt -mɒnt ‖ 'groʊ mɑːnt,
(ii) 'grəʊs- ‖ 'groʊs-, (iii) 'grɒs- ‖ 'grɑːs-
—The place in North Yks is (i) or (ii), that in
Gwent (iii)

gros point ˌgrəʊ 'pɔɪnt ‖ 'groʊ pɔɪnt

gross grəʊs ‖ groʊs grossed grəʊst ‖ groʊst
grosser 'grəʊs ə ‖ 'groʊs ᵊr (= grocer)
grosses 'grəʊs ɪz -əz ‖ 'groʊs əz grossest
'grəʊs ɪst -əst ‖ 'groʊs əst grossing
'grəʊs ɪŋ ‖ 'groʊs ɪŋ

Gross (i) grəʊs ‖ groʊs, (ii) grɒs ‖ grɑːs

Grosseteste 'grəʊs teɪt -test ‖ 'groʊs-

Grossmith 'grəʊs mɪθ ‖ 'groʊs-

Grosvenor 'grəʊv nə 'grəʊv ən ə; §'grɒv-
‖ 'groʊv nᵊr

Grosz grəʊs ‖ groʊs

grosz grɒʃ ‖ grɑːʃ —Polish [grɔʃ] groszy
'grɒʃ i ‖ 'grɑːʃ i —Polish ['grɔ ʃɨ]

grot grɒt ‖ grɑːt grots grɒts ‖ grɑːts

Grote grəʊt ‖ groʊt

grotesque grəʊ 'tesk ‖ groʊ- ~ly li ~ness nəs
nɪs ~s s

grotesquer|ie, grotesquer|y grəʊ 'tesk
ər i ‖ groʊ- ~ies iz

Grotius 'grəʊt i_əs ‖ 'groʊʃ-

grotto 'grɒt əʊ ‖ 'grɑːt oʊ ~es, ~s z

grott|y 'grɒt i ‖ 'grɑːt i ~ier i_ə ‖ i_ᵊr ~iest
i_ɪst i_əst ~iness i nəs i nɪs

grouch graʊtʃ grouched graʊtʃt grouches
'graʊtʃ ɪz -əz grouching 'graʊtʃ ɪŋ

Groucho 'graʊtʃ əʊ ‖ -oʊ

grouch|y 'graʊtʃ i ~ier i_ə ‖ i_ᵊr ~iest i_ɪst
i_əst ~ily ɪ li əl i ~iness i nəs i nɪs

ground graʊnd grounded 'graʊnd ɪd -əd
grounding/s 'graʊnd ɪŋ/z grounds
graʊndz
'ground bait; 'ground conˌtrol; 'ground
crew; ˌground 'floor ◂; ground 'glass ◂;
'ground plan; 'ground rent; 'ground rule;
'ground speed; 'ground staff; 'ground
stroke

groundhog 'graʊnd hɒg ‖ -hɑːg -hɔːg ~s z

groundless 'graʊnd ləs -lɪs ~ly li ~ness nəs
nɪs

groundling 'graʊnd lɪŋ ~s z

groundnut 'graʊnd nʌt ~s s

groundsel 'graʊnd sᵊl ~s z

groundsheet 'graʊnd ʃiːt ~s s

grounds|man 'graʊndz |mən -mæn ~men
mən men

groundswell 'graʊnd swel ~s z

groundwork 'graʊnd wɜːk ‖ -wɜːk

group gruːp grouped gruːpt grouping
'gruːp ɪŋ groups gruːps
ˌgroup 'captain ◂; ˌgroup 'practice; ˌgroup
'therapy

grouper 'gruːp ə ‖ -ᵊr ~s z

groupie 'gruːp i ~s z

grouse graʊs groused graʊst grouses
'graʊs ɪz -əz grousing 'graʊs ɪŋ

grout graʊt grouted 'graʊt ɪd -əd ‖ 'graʊt̬ əd
grouting 'graʊt ɪŋ ‖ 'graʊt̬ ɪŋ grouts graʊts

grove, Grove grəʊv ‖ groʊv groves
grəʊvz ‖ groʊvz

grovel 'grɒv ᵊl 'grʌv- ‖ 'grʌv- 'grɑːv- ~ed,
~led d ~ing, ~ling ˍɪŋ ~s z

Grover 'grəʊv ə ‖ 'groʊv ᵊr

Groves grəʊvz ‖ groʊvz

grow grəʊ ‖ groʊ grew gruː growing
'grəʊ ɪŋ ‖ 'groʊ ɪŋ grown grəʊn §'grəʊ ən
‖ groʊn grows grəʊz ‖ groʊz
'growing pains; 'growing ˌseason

growbag 'grəʊ bæg ‖ 'groʊ- ~s z

grower 'grəʊ ə ‖ 'groʊ ᵊr ~s z

growl graʊl growled graʊld growling
'graʊl ɪŋ growls graʊlz

growler 'graʊl ə ‖ -ᵊr ~s z

grown grəʊn §'grəʊ ən ‖ groʊn

grown-up adj ˌgrəʊn 'ʌp ◂ ‖ ˌgroʊn-
ˌgrown-up 'sons

grown-up n 'grəʊn ʌp ˌ•'• ‖ 'groʊn- ~s s

growth grəʊθ ‖ groʊθ growths
grəʊθs ‖ groʊθs
'growth ˌhormone

groyne grɔɪn (= groin) groynes grɔɪnz

Grozny 'grɒz ni ‖ 'groʊz- —Also, misguidedly,
'grɒz- ‖ 'groʊz- —Russ ['grɔz nij]

grub grʌb grubbed grʌbd grubbing 'grʌb ɪŋ
grubs grʌbz

grubber 'grʌb ə ‖ -ᵊr ~s z

grubb|y 'grʌb i ~ier i_ə ‖ i_ᵊr ~iest i_ɪst i_əst
~ily ɪ li əl i ~iness i nəs i nɪs

grubstak|e 'grʌb steɪk ~ed t ~es s ~ing ɪŋ

grudge grʌdʒ grudged grʌdʒd grudges
'grʌdʒ ɪz -əz grudging/ly 'grʌdʒ ɪŋ /li

gruel 'gruː_əl §gruːl ~ing, ~ling ɪŋ

gruesome 'gruːs əm ~ly li ~ness nəs nɪs

gruff grʌf gruffer 'grʌf ə ‖ -ᵊr gruffest
'grʌf ɪst -əst gruffly 'grʌf li gruffness
'grʌf nəs -nɪs

Gruffydd 'grɪf ɪð —Welsh ['gri fið, 'gri fɪð]

Gruinard 'grɪn jəd ‖ -jᵊrd —There is also a
spelling pronunciation 'gruːˍɪ nɑːd ‖ -nɑːrd

grumbl|e 'grʌm bᵊl ~ed d ~es z
grumbling/ly 'grʌm blɪŋ /li

grumbler 'grʌm blə ‖ -blᵊr ~s z

grummet 'grʌm ɪt -ət ~s s

grump grʌmp grumps grʌmps

grump|y 'grʌmp i ~ier i_ə ‖ i_ᵊr ~iest i_ɪst
i_əst ~ily ɪ li əl i ~iness i nəs i nɪs

Grundig tdmk 'grʌnd ɪg 'grʊnd-

Grundy 'grʌnd i

Grundyism 'grʌnd i ˌɪz əm

grunge grʌndʒ

grunt grʌnt grunted 'grʌnt ɪd -əd ‖ 'grʌnt̬ əd
grunting 'grʌnt ɪŋ ‖ 'grʌnt̬ ɪŋ grunts grʌnts

Grunwell 'grʌn wel

Gruyere, Gruyère 'gruː jeə -jə; gruː 'jeə
‖ gruː 'jeᵊr grɪ- —Fr [gʁy jɛːʁ]

gryphon 'grɪf ᵊn ~s z

g-spot 'dʒiː spɒt ‖ -spɑːt ~s s

Gstaad gə 'ʃtɑːd -'stɑːd —Ger [kʃtaːt]

G-string 'dʒiː strɪŋ ~s z

GTI ˌdʒiː tiː 'aɪ ~s, ~'s z

G

guacamole ˌgwɑːk ə 'məʊl i ‖ -'moʊl i —*Sp*
[gwa ka 'mo le]
Guadalajara ˌgwɑːd ³l ə 'hɑːr ə —*Sp*
[gwa ða la 'xa ɾa]
Guadalcanal ˌgwɑːd ³l kə 'næl —*Sp*
[gwa ðal ka 'nal]
Guadalquivir ˌgwɑːd ³l kwɪ 'vɪə -'kwɪv ə
‖ -'kwɪv ³r -kiː 'vɪ³r —*Sp* [gwa ðal ki 'βiɾ]
Guadeloupe ˌgwɑːd ə 'luːp -³l 'uːp, ' • • • —*Fr*
[gwad lup]
guaiacol 'gwaɪ‿ə kɒl ‖ -koʊl -kɔːl, -kɑːl
guaiacum 'gwaɪ‿ək əm ~s z
Guam gwɑːm
guanabana gwə 'nɑːb ən ə ˌgwɑːn ə 'bɑːn ə
—*Sp* guanábana [gwa 'na βa na]
guanaco gwə 'nɑːk əʊ gwɑː- ‖ -oʊ ~s z
Guangdong ˌgwæŋ 'dʊŋ ‖ ˌgwɑːŋ- —*Chi*
Guǎngdōng [³kwaŋ ¹tʊŋ]
Guangxi ˌgwæŋ 'ʃiː —*Chi* Guǎngxī [³kwaŋ ¹ɕi]
Guangzhou ˌgwæŋ 'dʒəʊ ‖ ˌgwɑːŋ 'dʒoʊ
—*Chi* Guǎngzhōu [³kwaŋ ¹tʂou]
guanidine 'gwɑːn ɪ diːn -ə-, -dɪn; §-ɪd ən, -əd-
guanine 'gwɑːn iːn 'guː‿ə niːn
guano 'gwɑːn əʊ ‖ -oʊ
guanosine 'gwɑːn əʊ siːn -ziːn, -sɪn, §-s³n ‖ -ə-
Guantanamo gwæn 'tɑːn ə məʊ gwɑːn-
‖ gwɑːn 'tɑːn ə moʊ —*Sp* Guantánamo
[gwan 'ta na mo]
guar 'guː ɑː gwɑː ‖ gwɑːr —*In India*, gwɑː(r)
Guarani, Guaraní, g~ ˌgwɑːr ə 'niː 'gwɑːr ən i
—*Sp* [gwa ra 'ni] ~s z
guarantee ˌgær ən 'tiː ◀ ‖ ˌger-, ˌgɑːr- —**d** d
~ing ɪŋ ~s z
guarantor ˌgær ən 'tɔː ‖ -'tɔːr ˌger-, ˌgɑːr- ~s
z
guar|anty 'gær |ən tiː -|ənt i ‖ 'ger-, 'gɑːr-
~anties ən tiːz ənt iz
guard, Guard gɑːd ‖ gɑːrd **guarded** 'gɑːd ɪd
-əd ‖ 'gɑːrd əd **guarding**
'gɑːd ɪŋ ‖ 'gɑːrd ɪŋ **guards** gɑːdz ‖ gɑːrdz
'guard's van
guarded 'gɑːd ɪd -əd ‖ 'gɑːrd əd **~ly** li **~ness**
nəs nɪs
guard|house 'gɑːd |haʊs ‖ 'gɑːrd- **~houses**
haʊz ɪz əz
guardian, G~ 'gɑːd i‿ən ‖ 'gɑːrd- ~s z **~ship**
ʃɪp
ˌguardian 'angel
guardrail 'gɑːd reɪ³l ‖ 'gɑːrd- ~s z
guardroom 'gɑːd ruːm -rʊm ‖ 'gɑːrd- ~s z
guards|man 'gɑːdz |mən -mæn ‖ 'gɑːrdz-
~men mən men
Guatemal|a ˌgwɑːt ə 'mɑːl lə ˌgwæt-, ˌgwʌt-,
-ɪ- ‖ ˌgwɑːt̬ ə- **~an/s** ən/z
guava 'gwɑːv ə 'gwɔːv- ~s z
Guayaquil ˌgwaɪ‿ə 'kiː³l -'kɪl —*Sp* [gwa ja 'kil]
Gubba 'gʌb ə
Gubbins, g~ 'gʌb ɪnz §-ənz
gubernatorial ˌguːb ən‿ə 'tɔːr i‿əl ◀ ˌgjuːb-
‖ ˌguːb ³rn ə- -'toʊr-
Gucci *tdmk* 'guːtʃ i
guck gʌk gʊk

gudgeon 'gʌdʒ ən ~s z
'gudgeon pin
Gudgin 'gʌdʒ ɪn -ən
Gudrun 'gʊdr uːn
Gue gjuː
guelder-ros|e 'geld ə rəʊz ˌ• •'• ‖ -roʊz ~es ɪz
əz
Guelf, Guelph gwelf **Guelfs, Guelphs** gwelfs
guenon 'gwen ən -ɒn; gə 'nɒn, -'nõ; 'giːn ən
‖ gə 'noʊn -'nɑːn ~s z
guerdon 'gɜːd ən ‖ 'gɜːd ən ~s z
guerilla gə 'rɪl ə ge- —*Normally* = gorilla. *The*
ge- *pronunciation aims explicitly to avoid this*
homophony. —*Sp* guerrilla [ge 'rri ʎa, -ja]
Guerin 'geər ɪn §-ən ‖ 'ger-
Guernica 'gɜːn ɪk ə 'gwɜːn-, gɜː 'niːk ə
‖ 'gwern- —*Sp* [geɾ 'ni ka]
Guernsey, g~ 'gɜːnz i ‖ 'gɜː·nz i ~s z
guerrilla gə 'rɪl ə ge- —*see* guerilla
guess ges **guessed** gest (*= guest*) **guesses**
'ges ɪz -əz **guessing** 'ges ɪŋ
guesser 'ges ə ‖ -³r ~s z
guessti|mate *v* 'gest ɪ |meɪt -ə- **~mated**
meɪt ɪd -əd ‖ meɪt̬ əd **~mates** meɪts
~mating meɪt ɪŋ ‖ meɪt̬ ɪŋ
guesstimate *n* 'gest ɪm ət -əm-, -ɪt, -eɪt ~s s
guesswork 'ges wɜːk ‖ -wɜ·ːk
guest, Guest gest **guested** 'gest ɪd -əd
guesting 'gest ɪŋ **guests** gests
'guest ˌworker
guest|house 'gest |haʊs **~houses** haʊz ɪz -əz
guestroom 'gest ruːm -rʊm ~s z
Guevara gə 'vɑːr ə gɪ-, ge- —*Sp* [ge 'βa ɾa]
guff gʌf
guffaw gʌ 'fɔː gə- ‖ -'fɑː; 'gʌf ɔː, -ɑː **~ed** d
guffawing gʌ 'fɔːʳ ɪŋ gə- ‖ -'fɔː ɪŋ -'fɑː ɪŋ;
'gʌf ɔː ɪŋ, -ɑː- ~s z
Guggenheim 'gʊg ən haɪm 'guːg-
Guiana gi 'ɑːn ə gaɪ-, -'æn- ‖ -'æn ə -'ɑːn ə ~s
z —*This is appropriate for the name of the*
general region. Compare **Guyana**, *formerly*
British Guiana.
Guianese ˌgaɪ‿ə 'niːz ◀ ˌgiː‿ ‖ -'niːs
guid gɪd —*or, in Scots dialect pronunciation*
(perhaps simulated), [gyd, gɪd]
guidance 'gaɪd ənts
guide, Guide gaɪd **guided** 'gaɪd ɪd -əd
guides gaɪdz **guiding** 'gaɪd ɪŋ
ˌguided 'missile
guidebook 'gaɪd bʊk →'gaɪb-, §-buːk ~s s
guideline 'gaɪd laɪn ~s z
guider, G~ 'gaɪd ə ‖ -³r ~s z
Guido 'gwiːd əʊ 'giːd- ‖ -oʊ —*It* ['gwi do]
guidon 'gaɪd ən ~s z
guild gɪld (*= gild*) **guilds** gɪldz
Guildenstern 'gɪld ən stɜːn ‖ -stɜ·ːn
guilder 'gɪld ə ‖ -³r ~s z
Guildford 'gɪl fəd ‖ -fərd
guildhall, G~ 'gɪld hɔːl ◀ ˌ•'• ‖ -hɔːl -hɑːl ~s z
guile gaɪ³l
guileful 'gaɪ³l f³l -fʊl **~ly** i **~ness** nəs nɪs
guileless 'gaɪ³l ləs -lɪs **~ly** li **~ness** nəs nɪs
Guilford 'gɪl fəd ‖ -fərd

G

Guilin ˌgweɪ ˈlɪn —*Chi* Guìlín [⁴kweɪ ²lɪn]
Guillaume ˈgiː əʊm ‖ giː ˈjoʊm —*Fr* [gi joːm]
guillemot ˈgɪl ɪ mɒt -ə- ‖ -maːt ~s s
guillotin|e ˈgɪl ə tiːn ˈgiː-, -jə-, ˌ•• ˈ• ~ed d
~es z ~ing ɪŋ
guilt gɪlt
guiltless ˈgɪlt ləs -lɪs ~ly li ~ness nəs nɪs
guilt|y ˈgɪlt |i ~ier i‿ə ‖ i‿ᵊr ~iest i‿ɪst i‿əst
~ily ɪ li əl i ~iness i nəs i nɪs
guinea, G~ ˈgɪn i ~s z
'guinea fowl; 'guinea pig; 'guinea worm
Guinea-Bissau ˌgɪn i bɪ ˈsaʊ
Guinean ˈgɪn i‿ən ~s z
Guinevere ˈgwɪn ɪ vɪə ˈgɪn-, -ə- ‖ -vɪr
Guinness ˈgɪn ɪs -əs; gɪ ˈnes ~es ɪz əz
guipure gɪ ˈpjʊə §gə- ‖ -ˈpjʊᵊr -ˈpʊᵊr
Guisborough ˈgɪz bər‿ə ‖ -ˌbɝː oʊ
guise, Guise gaɪz *(= guys)* —*but the French
name is* giːz guises ˈgaɪz ɪz -əz
Guiseley ˈgaɪz li
guitar gɪ ˈtaː gə- ‖ -ˈtaːr ~s z
Guizhou ˌgweɪ ˈdʒəʊ ‖ -ˈdʒoʊ —*Chi* Guìzhōu
[⁴kweɪ ¹tʂou]
Gujarat, Gujerat ˌgʊdʒ ə ˈraːt ˌguːdʒ- —*Hindi*
[gʊdʒ raːʈ]
Gujarati, Gujerati ˌgʊdʒ ə ˈraːt i ◂ ˌguːdʒ-
—*Hindi* [gʊdʒ ra: ʈi]
Gulag ˈguːl æg -aːg ‖ -aːg
gular ˈgjuːl ə ˈguːl- ‖ -ᵊr
Gulbenkian gʊl ˈbeŋk i‿ən
gulch gʌltʃ gulches ˈgʌltʃ ɪz -əz
gulden ˈgʊld ən ~s z
gules gjuːlz
gulf, Gulf gʌlf gulfs gʌlfs
'Gulf Stream
gull gʌl gulled gʌld gulling ˈgʌl ɪŋ gulls
gʌlz
Gullah ˈgʌl ə ~s z
Gullane *(i)* ˈgɪl ən, *(ii)* ˈgʌlən
gullet ˈgʌl ɪt -ət ~s s
Gullett ˈgʌl ɪt -ət
gulley ˈgʌl i ~s z
gullibility ˌgʌl ə ˈbɪl ət i ˌ-ɪ-, -ɪt i ‖ -əṭ i
gullib|le ˈgʌl əb |ᵊl -ɪb- ~ly li
Gulliford ˈgʌl i fəd ‖ -fᵊrd
Gullit ˈhʊl ɪt ˈhuːl-, §-ət —*Dutch* [ˈxʏl ɪt]
Gulliver ˈgʌl ɪv ə -əv- ‖ -ᵊr
gull|y, Gully ˈgʌl |i ~ies iz
gulp gʌlp gulped gʌlpt gulping ˈgʌlp ɪŋ
gulps gʌlps
gum gʌm gummed gʌmd gumming ˈgʌm ɪŋ
gums gʌmz
ˌgum ˈarabic; 'gum tree
gumbo, Gumbo ˈgʌm bəʊ ‖ -boʊ ~s z
gumboil ˈgʌm bɔɪᵊl ~s z
gumboot ˈgʌm buːt ~s s
Gumbs gʌmz
gumdrop ˈgʌm drɒp ‖ -draːp ~s s
gumma ˈgʌm ə ~s z
Gummer ˈgʌm ə ‖ -ᵊr
Gummidge ˈgʌm ɪdʒ
gumm|y ˈgʌm |i ~ier i‿ə ‖ i‿ᵊr ~ies iz ~iest
i‿ɪst i‿əst

gumption ˈgʌmp ʃən
gumshield ˈgʌm ʃiːᵊld ~s z
gumshoe ˈgʌm ʃuː ~s z
gun gʌn gunned gʌnd gunning ˈgʌn ɪŋ
guns gʌnz
'gun ˌcarriage; 'gun ˌcotton
gunboat ˈgʌn bəʊt →ˈgʌm- ‖ -boʊt ~s s
gundog ˈgʌn dɒg ‖ -dɔːg -daːg ~s z
gundy, Gundy ˈgʌnd i
gunfight ˈgʌn faɪt ~s s
gunfighter ˈgʌn ˌfaɪt ə ‖ -ˌfaɪṭ ᵊr ~s z
gunfire ˈgʌn ˌfaɪ‿ə ‖ -ˌfaɪ‿ᵊr
Gunga Din ˌgʌŋ gə ˈdɪn
gunge gʌndʒ
gung-ho ˌgʌŋ ˈhəʊ ◂ ‖ -ˈhoʊ◂
gungy ˈgʌndʒ i
gunk gʌŋk
gun|man ˈgʌn |mən →ˈgʌm-, -mæn ~men
mən men
gunmetal ˈgʌn ˌmet ᵊl →ˈgʌm- ‖ -ˌmeṭ ᵊl
Gunn gʌn
gunnel ˈgʌn ᵊl ~s z
gunner ˈgʌn ə ‖ -ᵊr ~s z
gunnera ˈgʌn ər ə ~s z
Gunnersbury ˈgʌn əz bər‿i ‖ -ᵊrz ˌber i
gunnery ˈgʌn ər i
Gunnison ˈgʌn ɪs ən
gunny ˈgʌn i
gunnysack ˈgʌn i sæk
gunpoint ˈgʌn pɔɪnt →ˈgʌm-
gunpowder ˈgʌn ˌpaʊd ə →ˈgʌm- ‖ -ᵊr
gunrunn|er/s ˈgʌn ˌrʌn |ə/z ‖ -|ᵊr/z ~ing ɪŋ
gunship ˈgʌn ʃɪp ~s s
gunshot ˈgʌn ʃɒt ‖ -ʃaːt
gunshy ˈgʌn ʃaɪ
gunslinger ˈgʌn ˌslɪŋ ə ‖ -ᵊr ~s z
gunsmith ˈgʌn smɪθ ~s s
Gunter ˈgʌnt ə ‖ -ᵊr —*but as a German name,*
ˈgʊnt ə ‖ -ᵊr —*Ger* Gunter [ˈgʊn tɐ], Günter
[ˈgʏn tɐ]
Gunther ˈgʌntᵊθ ə ‖ -ᵊr —*but as a German name,*
ˈgʊnt ə ‖ -ᵊr —*Ger* Gunther [ˈgʊn tɐ], Günther
[ˈgʏn tɐ]
gunwale ˈgʌn ᵊl ~s z
gunyah ˈgʌn jə ~s z
guoyu ˌgwɔɪ ˈuː -ˈjuː —*Chi* guóyǔ [²kwɔ ³jy]
gupp|y, Guppy ˈgʌp |i ~ies iz
Gupta ˈgʊpt ə ˈgʌpt- —*Hindi* [gʊp ṭaː]
Gur gʊə ‖ gʊᵊr
gurdwara gɜː ˈdwaːr ə gʊə-, ˌ•••;
ˌgʊr ə ˈdwaːr ə ‖ gɝː- ~s z
gurgl|e ˈgɜːg ᵊl ‖ ˈgɝːg ᵊl ~ed d ~es z ~ing
ɪŋ
Gurkha ˈgɜːk ə ˈgʊək- ‖ ˈgɝːk ə ~s z
Gurkhali ₍₎gɜː ˈkaːl i ₍₎gʊə- ‖ ₍₎gɝː-
Gurmukhi ˈgʊə mʊk i ‖ ˈgʊr-
gurnard ˈgɜːn əd ‖ ˈgɝːn ᵊrd ~s z
gurnet ˈgɜːn ɪt §-ət ‖ ˈgɝːn- ~s s
Gurney, g~ ˈgɜːn i ‖ ˈgɝːn i ~'s, ~s z
guru ˈgʊr uː ˈgʊər-; ˈguː ruː ‖ ˈguː ruː —*Hindi*
[gʊ ruː] ~s z
Gus gʌs

gush gʌʃ **gushed** gʌʃt **gushes** 'gʌʃ ɪz -əz
  gushing/ly 'gʌʃ ɪŋ /li
gusher 'gʌʃ ə ‖ -ᵊr ~s z
gush|y 'gʌʃ |i ~ier i‿ə ‖ i‿ᵊr ~iest i‿ɪst i‿əst
  ~ily ɪ li əl i ~iness i nəs i nɪs
guss|et 'gʌs |ɪt §-ət ‖ -ət ~eted ɪt ɪd §ət-, -əd
  ‖ əţ əd ~eting ɪt ɪŋ §ət- ‖ əţ ɪŋ ~ets ɪts
  §əts ‖ əts
Gussie, Gussy, gussy 'gʌs i **gussied** 'gʌs id
gust gʌst **gusted** 'gʌst ɪd -əd **gusting**
  'gʌst ɪŋ **gusts** gʌsts
gustation gʌ 'steɪʃ ᵊn
gustatory 'gʌst ət‿ər i gʌs 'teɪt ər i ‖ -ə tɔːr i
  -toʊr i
Gustav, Gustave 'gʊst ɑːv 'gʌst- ‖ 'gʌst-
Gustavus gʊ 'stɑːv əs gʌ-, gə-
gusto 'gʌst əʊ ‖ -oʊ
gust|y 'gʌst |i ~ier i‿ə ‖ i‿ᵊr ~iest i‿ɪst i‿əst
  ~ily ɪ li əl i ~iness i nəs i nɪs
gut gʌt **guts** gʌts **gutted** 'gʌt ɪd -əd
  ‖ 'gʌţ əd **gutting** 'gʌt ɪŋ ‖ 'gʌţ ɪŋ
gutta 'gʌt ə 'gʊt- ‖ 'gʌţ ə 'gʊţ- **guttae** 'gʌt iː
  'gʊt-
gutta-percha ˌgʌt ə 'pɜːtʃ ə ‖ ˌgʌţ ə 'pɝːtʃ ə
gutter 'gʌt ə ‖ 'gʌţ ᵊr ~ed d **guttering**
  'gʌt‿ər ɪŋ ‖ 'gʌţ ər ɪŋ ~s z
  ˈgutter ˌpress, ˌ•• '•
Gutteridge 'gʌt‿ər ɪdʒ ‖ 'gʌţ ᵊr-
guttersnipe 'gʌt ə snaɪp ‖ 'gʌţ ᵊr- ~s s
guttural 'gʌt‿ər əl ‖ 'gʌţ ər əl →'gʌtr əl ~ism
  ˌɪz əm ~ly i ~ness nəs nɪs ~s z
gutturality ˌgʌt ə 'ræl ət i -ɪt i ‖ ˌgʌţ ə 'ræl əţ i
guv, Guv gʌv
guvnor, guv'nor, G~ 'gʌv nə ‖ -nᵊr ~s z
guy, Guy gaɪ —See also phrases with this word
  guyed gaɪd **guying** 'gaɪ ɪŋ **guys** gaɪz
  ˈguy line; ˈguy rope
Guyana gaɪ 'æn ə -'ɑːn-
Guyanese ˌgaɪ‿ə 'niːz ◄
Guy Fawkes ˌgaɪ 'fɔːks ◄ '•• ‖ -'fɑːks
  ˌGuy ˈFawkes night, '• ••
Guyler 'gaɪl ə ‖ -ᵊr
guzzl|e 'gʌz ᵊl ~ed d ~es z ~ing‿ɪŋ
Gwalia 'gwɑːl i ə
Gwalior 'gwɑːl i ɔː ‖ -ɔːr —Hindi [gʊɑːl jər]
Gwatkin 'gwɒt kɪn ‖ 'gwɑːt-
Gwaun-cae-Gurwen ˌgwaɪn kə 'gɜː wən
  →ˌgwaɪŋ- ‖ -'gɝː- —Welsh
  [gwain kai 'gir wen]
Gwbert 'gʊb ət ‖ -ᵊrt
Gwen gwen
Gwenda 'gwend ə
Gwendolin, Gwendoline, Gwendolyn
  'gwend ə lɪn -ᵊl ɪn, §-ən ‖ -ᵊl ɪn -ən
Gwendraeth 'gwen draɪθ
Gwenllian 'gwen ɬi‿ən —Welsh ['gwen ɬjan]
Gwent gwent

Gwilym 'gwɪl ɪm
Gwydir, Gwydyr (i) 'gwɪd ə -ɪə ‖ -ɪr, (ii)
  'gwaɪd-
Gwyn gwɪn
Gwynant 'gwɪn ænt
Gwynedd 'gwɪn əð -ɪð, -eð —Welsh ['gwi neð]
Gwyneth 'gwɪn əθ -ɪθ, -eθ
Gwynfor 'gwɪn və -vɔː ‖ -vᵊr -vɔːr —Welsh
  ['gwɪn vor]
gwyniad 'gwɪn i æd ~s z
Gwynn, Gwynne gwɪn
Gwynneth 'gwɪn əθ -ɪθ, -eθ
Gwyther (i) 'gwaɪð ə ‖ -ᵊr, (ii) 'gwɪð ə ‖ -ᵊr
gybe dʒaɪb **gybed** dʒaɪbd **gybes** dʒaɪbz
  gybing 'dʒaɪb ɪŋ
Gyle gaɪᵊl
Gyles dʒaɪᵊlz
gym dʒɪm **gyms** dʒɪmz
  ˈgym shoe
gymkhana dʒɪm 'kɑːn ə ~s z
gymnasi|um 'hall for gymnastics'
  dʒɪm 'neɪz i‿|əm ~a ə ~ums əmz
gymnasium 'secondary school' gɪm 'nɑːz i‿əm
  -ʊm —Ger G~ [gʏm 'naː zjʊm] ~s z
gymnast 'dʒɪm næst ‖ -nəst ~s s
gymnastic dʒɪm 'næst ɪk ~ally ᵊl‿i ~s s
gymnosophist dʒɪm 'nɒs əf ɪst §-əst ‖ -'nɑːs-
  ~s s
gymnosperm 'dʒɪm nəʊ spɜːm ‖ -nə spɝːm
  ~s z
gymslip 'dʒɪm slɪp ~s s
gynaec... —see gynec...
gynecological ˌgaɪn ɪk ə 'lɒdʒ ɪk ᵊl ◄ , •ək-
  ‖ -'lɑːdʒ- ˌdʒaɪn- ~ly i
gynecologist ˌgaɪn ɪ 'kɒl ədʒ ɪst , •ə-, §-əst
  ‖ -'kɑːl- ˌdʒaɪn- ~s s
gynecology ˌgaɪn ɪ 'kɒl ədʒ i , •ə- ‖ -'kɑːl-
  ˌdʒaɪn-
gyneciu|um, gynoeci|um gaɪ 'niːs i‿|əm dʒaɪ-
  ~a ə
Gyngell 'gɪndʒ ᵊl
-gynous stress-imposing dʒɪn əs dʒən əs —
  androgynous æn 'drɒdʒ ɪn əs -ən-
  ‖ -'drɑːdʒ-
gyp dʒɪp **gypped** dʒɪpt **gypping** 'dʒɪp ɪŋ
  gyps dʒɪps
gypsophila dʒɪp 'sɒf ɪl ə -əl-, ⚠ˌdʒɪps ə 'fɪl i‿ə
  ‖ -'sɑːf-
gypsum 'dʒɪps əm
gyps|y, Gyps|y 'dʒɪps |i ~ies iz
gyr|ate v dʒaɪ⁼ 'reɪt dʒɪ-, dʒə-; 'dʒaɪᵊr eɪt
  ‖ 'dʒaɪᵊr eɪt ~ated eɪt ɪd -əd ‖ eɪţ əd ~ates
  eɪts ~ating eɪt ɪŋ ‖ eɪţ ɪŋ
gyration dʒaɪᵊ 'reɪʃ ᵊn dʒɪ-, dʒə- ~s z
gyratory dʒaɪᵊ 'reɪt ᵊr i dʒə-; 'dʒaɪᵊr ət‿ər i
  ‖ 'dʒaɪᵊr ə tɔːr i -toʊr i
gyre 'dʒaɪ‿ə ‖ 'dʒaɪ‿ᵊr **gyred**
  'dʒaɪ‿əd ‖ 'dʒaɪ‿ᵊrd **gyres**
  'dʒaɪ‿əz ‖ 'dʒaɪ‿ᵊrz **gyring**
  'dʒaɪ‿ər ɪŋ ‖ 'dʒaɪ‿ᵊr ɪŋ
gyrfalcon 'dʒɜː ˌfɔːlk ən 'dʒɪə-, -ˌfɒːk-, -ˌfælk-
  ‖ 'dʒɝː ˌfælk ən -ˌfɔːlk-, -ˌfɑːlk- ~s z
gyri 'dʒaɪᵊr aɪ

gyro *'gyroscope, gyrocompass'* 'dʒaɪᵊr əʊ ‖ -oʊ
~**s** z

gyro *'meat sandwich'* 'ʒɪər əʊ 'gɪər-
‖ 'dʒaɪᵊr oʊ ~**s** z—*ModGk* ['ji ro]

gyro- *comb. form*
with stress-neutral suffix ˌdʒaɪᵊr əʊ ‖ -ə—
gyrostatic ˌdʒaɪᵊr əʊ
'stæt ɪk ◄ ‖ -ə 'stæt̬ ɪk ◄

gyrocompass 'dʒaɪᵊr əʊ ˌkʌmp əs ‖ -oʊ-
-ˌkɑːmp- ~**es** ɪz əz

gyromagnetic ˌdʒaɪᵊr əʊ mæg 'net ɪk ◄
-məg'•- ‖ -oʊ mæg 'net̬-

gyroscope 'dʒaɪᵊr ə skəʊp ‖ -skoʊp ~**s** s

gyroscopic ˌdʒaɪᵊr ə 'skɒp ɪk ◄ ‖ -'skɑːp- ~**ally**
ᵊl_i

gyr|us 'dʒaɪᵊr |əs ~**i** aɪ

Gytha 'gɪθ ə

gyve dʒaɪv **gyved** dʒaɪvd **gyves** dʒaɪvz
gyving 'dʒaɪv ɪŋ

G

H h

1 Where the spelling is **h**, the pronunciation is regularly h, as in **house** haʊs. The letter **h** may also form part of one of the digraphs **ch, gh, ph, rh, sh, th, wh** (see under **c, g, p, r, s, t, w**, respectively).

2 h is silent in a number of cases:
- at the beginning of the exceptional words **heir, honest, hono(u)r, hour** and their derivatives; also, in AmE only, in **herb**;
- at the end of a word after a vowel letter, as in **oh, hurrah**;
- in most cases where it is at the beginning of a weak-vowelled syllable, as in the WEAK FORMS of **he, her, him, his, has, have**; in words such as **annihilate, vehicle**; and sometimes also in words such as **hotel, historic**.

3 The sound h is also occasionally written **wh**, as in **who** huː.

H, h eɪtʃ §heɪtʃ —*The form* heɪtʃ *is standard in Irish English, but not BrE or AmE.* **H's, h's** 'eɪtʃ ɪz §'heɪtʃ-, -əz —*Communications code name:* Hotel

H₂O ,eɪtʃ tuː 'əʊ §,heɪtʃ- ‖ -'oʊ

ha *interjection* haː

ha *measure —see* **hectare**

Haagen-Dazs, Häagen-Dazs *tdmk* ,haːg ən 'daːz -'daːs, '• • • ‖ 'haːg ən dæs

Haakon 'hɔːk ɒn 'haːk-, -ən ‖ -aːn 'haːk-, -ən —*Norwegian* ['hoː kɔn]

Haarlem 'haːl əm -em ‖ 'haːrl- —*Dutch* ['haːr ləm]

Habakkuk 'hæb ək ək -ə kʌk; hə 'bæk-

habeas corpus ,heɪb i_əs 'kɔːp əs -i æs- ‖ -'kɔːrp-

haberdasher 'hæb ə dæʃ ə ‖ -ər dæʃ ər ~s z

haberdasher|y 'hæb ə dæʃ ər_li ‖ 'hæb ər- ~ies iz

Habgood 'hæb gʊd

Habibie hæ 'biːb i hə- ‖ haː-

habiliment hə 'bɪl ɪ mənt hæ-, -ə- ~s s

habili|tate hə 'bɪl ɪ |teɪt hæ-, -ə- ~tated teɪt ɪd -əd ‖ teɪt̬ əd ~tates teɪts ~tating teɪt ɪŋ ‖ teɪt̬ ɪŋ

habilitation hə ,bɪl ɪ 'teɪʃ ᵊn hæ-, -ə-

habit 'hæb ɪt §-ət ~s s

habitability ,hæb ɪt ə 'bɪl ət i -ɪt i ‖ -ət̬ ə 'bɪl ət̬ i

habitab|le 'hæb ɪt əb |ᵊl -ət əb- ‖ -ət̬ əb- ~ly li

habitant *French settler or descendant* ,æb i 'tɒ̃ ,hæb- ‖ -'taːn ~s z

habitat, H~ *tdmk* 'hæb ɪ tæt -ə- ~s s

habitation ,hæb ɪ 'teɪʃ ᵊn -ə- ~s z

habit-forming 'hæb ɪt ,fɔːm ɪŋ §-ət- ‖ -,fɔːrm-

habitual hə 'bɪtʃ u_əl hæ-, -'bɪt ju_ ~ly i ~ness nəs nɪs

habitu|ate hə 'bɪtʃ u |eɪt hæ-, -'bɪt ju- ~ated eɪt ɪd -əd ‖ eɪt̬ əd ~ates eɪts ~ating eɪt ɪŋ ‖ eɪt̬ ɪŋ

habituation hə ,bɪtʃ u 'eɪʃ ᵊn hæ-, -,bɪt ju-

habitue, habitué hə 'bɪtʃ u eɪ ə-, hæ-, -'bɪt ju- ‖ •,•• '• —*Fr* [a bi tɥe] ~s z

Habsburg 'hæps bɜːg ‖ -bɜ˞ːg —*Ger* ['haːps bʊʁk] ~s z

hacek, háček 'haːtʃ ek ~s s

hachure hæ 'ʃʊə -'ʃjʊə ‖ -'ʃʊ˞r ~s z

hacienda ,hæs i 'end ə ‖ ,haːs- ,aːs- —*AmSp* [a 'sjen da] ~s z

hack, Hack, hacked hækt **hacking** 'hæk ɪŋ **hacks** hæks
  ,hacking 'cough; 'hacking ,jacket

hackamore 'hæk ə mɔː ‖ -mɔːr -moʊr ~s z

hackberr|y 'hæk bər_li -,ber li ‖ -,ber li ~ies iz

hacker, H~ 'hæk ə ‖ -ᵊr ~s z

Hackett 'hæk ɪt §-ət

hackette ,hæk 'et ~s s

hackle 'hæk ᵊl ~s z

Hackman 'hæk mən

hackney, H~ 'hæk ni ~ed d ~ing ɪŋ ~s z
  ,hackney 'carriage, '• • , • •

hacksaw 'hæk sɔː ‖ -saː ~s z

hackwork 'hæk wɜːk ‖ -wɜ˞ːk

had *strong form* hæd, *weak forms* həd, əd, d —*The contracted weak form* d *is used mainly after a vowel (and is often written* 'd*); at the beginning of a sentence the usual weak form is* həd, *or in rapid speech* d.

Haddington 'hæd ɪŋ tən

haddock 'hæd ək ~s s

Haddon 'hæd ən
hade heɪd haded 'heɪd ɪd -əd hades heɪdz
  hading 'heɪd ɪŋ
Haden 'heɪd ən
Hades 'god of underworld'; 'hell' 'heɪd iːz
Hadfield 'hæd fiːəld
Hadith hə 'diːθ hæ- ‖ haː- —Arabic [ħa 'diːθ]
hadj hædʒ haːdʒ
hadji 'hædʒ i 'haːdʒ-, -iː ~s z
Hadlee, Hadley 'hæd li
hadn't 'hæd ənt
Hadrian 'heɪdr i‿ən ~'s z
  ,Hadrian's 'Wall
hadron 'hædr ɒn ‖ -aːn ~s z
hadrosaur 'hædr əʊ sɔː ‖ -ə sɔːr ~s z
hadst strong form hædst, weak forms hədst, ədst
hae heɪ
haecceity hek 'siː‿ət i hiːk-, haɪk-, -ɪt- ‖ -əṭ i
haem hiːm
haematite 'hiːm ə taɪt
haematologist ,hiːm ə 'tɒl ədʒ ɪst §-əst
  ‖ -'taːl- ~s s
haematology ,hiːm ə 'tɒl ədʒ i ‖ -'taːl-
haematom|a ,hiːm ə 'təʊm| ə ‖ -'toʊm| ə ~as
  əz ~ata ət ə ‖ əṭ ə
haemo- comb. form
  with stress-neutral suffix |hiːm əʊ ‖ -oʊ —
  haemodialysis ,hiːm əʊ daɪ 'æl əs ɪs -ɪs ɪs,
  §-əs ‖ ,•oʊ-
  with stress-imposing suffix hiː 'mɒ+ hɪ-
  ‖ -'maː+ — haemolysis hiː 'mɒl əs ɪs hɪ-,
  -ɪs-, §-əs ‖ -'maːl-
haemoglobin ,hiːm ə 'gləʊb ɪn §-ən, '••••
  ‖ 'hiːm ə gloʊb ən
haemophilia ,hiːm ə 'fɪl i‿ə -'fiːl-
haemophiliac ,hiːm ə 'fɪl i æk ◄ -'fiːl- ~s s
haemorrhag|e 'hem ər‿ɪdʒ ~ed d ~es ɪz əz
  ~ing ɪŋ
haemorrhoid 'hem ə rɔɪd ~s z
haemorrhoidal ,hem ə 'rɔɪd əl ◄
Haffner, Hafner 'hæf nə ‖ -nər
hafiz 'haːf ɪz
hafnium 'hæf ni‿əm
Hafod 'hæv ɒd ‖ -aːd —Welsh ['ha vod]
haft haːft §hæft ‖ hæft hafted 'haːft ɪd
  §'hæft-, -əd ‖ 'hæft əd hafting 'haːft ɪŋ
  §'hæft- ‖ 'hæft ɪŋ hafts haːfts §hæfts
  ‖ hæfts
hag hæg hags hægz
HAG, Hag tdmk haːg
Hagan 'heɪg ən
Hagar 'heɪg aː -ə ‖ -aːr -ər
Hagerstown 'heɪg əz taʊn ‖ -ərz-
hagfish 'hæg fɪʃ
Haggai 'hæg aɪ 'hæg i aɪ, -eɪ-
haggard, H~ 'hæg əd ‖ -ərd ~ly li ~ness nəs
  nɪs
Haggerston 'hæg əst ən ‖ -ərst-
haggis 'hæg ɪs §-əs ~es ɪz əz
haggl|e 'hæg əl ~ed d ~es z ~ing ‿ɪŋ
hagio- comb. form
  with stress-neutral suffix |hæg i‿ə |heɪdʒ i‿ə —
  hagioscope 'hæg i‿ə skəʊp 'heɪdʒ- ‖ -skoʊp

  with stress-imposing suffix ,hæg i 'ɒ+ ,heɪdʒ-
  ‖ -'aː+ — hagiolatry ,hæg i 'ɒl ətr i ,heɪdʒ-
  ‖ -'aːl-
hagiograph|y ,hæg i 'ɒg rəf |i ,heɪdʒ- ‖ -'aːg-
  ~ies iz
Hagman 'hæg mən
hag-ridden 'hæg ,rɪd ən
Hague heɪg —Dutch Haag [haːx]
ha-ha interj (,)haː 'haː hʌ-
ha-ha n 'haː haː ~s z
Hahn haːn
hahnium 'haːn i‿əm
Haida 'haɪd ə
Haifa 'haɪf ə
Haig heɪg
Haigh placename heɪ
Haigh family name heɪg
Haight (i) haɪt, (ii) heɪt
Haight-Ashbury ,heɪt 'æʃ bər‿i ‖ -,ber i
Hai Karate tdmk ,haɪ kə 'raːt i ‖ -'raːṭ i
haiku 'haɪk uː —Jp [ha,i kɯ] ~s z
hail heɪəl hailed heɪəld hailing 'heɪəl ɪŋ hails
  heɪəlz
  ,Hail 'Mary
Haile Selassie ,haɪl i sə 'læs i -sɪ'•-
hailer 'heɪəl ə ‖ -ər ~s z
Hailes 'heɪəlz
Hailey 'heɪl i
Haileybury 'heɪl i bər‿i ‖ -,ber i
hail-fellow-well-met ,heɪəl ,fel əʊ
  ,wel 'met ‖ -oʊ- -ə-
Hailsham 'heɪəl ʃəm
hailstone 'heɪəl stəʊn ‖ -stoʊn ~s z
hailstorm 'heɪəl stɔːm ‖ -stɔːrm ~s z
Hailwood 'heɪəl wʊd
Hain heɪn
Hainan ,haɪ 'næn ‖ -'naːn —Chi Hǎinán
  [3haɪ 2nan]
Hainault 'heɪn ɔːt -ɒlt, -ɒlt ‖ -ɔːlt -aːlt
Haines heɪnz
Haiphong ,haɪ 'fɒŋ ‖ -'fɔːŋ -'faːŋ —Vietnamese
  [4haɪ 3fɔŋ]
hair heə ‖ heər hæər hairs heəz ‖ heərz hæərz
  'hair's breadth; ,hair 'shirt; 'hair slide;
  ,hair 'trigger◄
hairball 'heə bɔːl ‖ 'her- 'hæər-, -baːl ~s z
hairbreadth 'heə bredθ -bretθ ‖ 'her- 'hæər-
hairbrush 'heə brʌʃ ‖ 'her- 'hæər- ~es ɪz əz
haircut 'heə kʌt ‖ 'her- 'hæər- ~s s
hairdo 'heə duː ‖ 'her- 'hæər- ~s z
hairdresser 'heə ,dres ə ‖ 'her ,dres ər 'hæər-
  ~s, ~'s z
hairdressing 'heə ,dres ɪŋ ‖ 'her- 'hæər-
hairdryer 'heə ,draɪ‿ə ‖ 'her ,draɪ‿ər ~s z
-haired 'heəd ‖ heərd hæərd — fair-haired
  ,feə 'heəd ◄ ‖ 'fer heərd 'fær hæərd
hairgrip 'heə grɪp ‖ 'her- 'hæər- ~s s
hairi... —see hairy
hairless 'heə ləs -lɪs ‖ 'her- 'hæər- ~ness nəs
  nɪs
hairline 'heə laɪn ‖ 'her- 'hæər- ~s z
hairnet 'heə net ‖ 'her- 'hæər- ~s s
hairpiec|e 'heə piːs ‖ 'her- 'hæər- ~es ɪz əz

hairpin 'heə pɪn ‖ 'her- 'hær- ~s z
  ,hairpin 'bend
hair-raising 'heə ˌreɪz ɪŋ ‖ 'her- 'hær-
hair-restorer 'heə rɪ ˌstɔːr ə -rə-, §-riː-
  ‖ 'her rɪ ˌstɔːr ər 'hær-, -ˌstoʊr- ~s z
hair-splitting 'heə ˌsplɪt ɪŋ ‖ 'her ˌsplɪt̬ ɪŋ 'hær-
hairspring 'heə sprɪŋ ‖ 'her- 'hær- ~s z
hairstreak 'heə striːk ‖ 'her- 'hær- ~s s
hairstyle 'heə staɪəl ‖ 'her- 'hær- ~s z
hairstylist 'heə ˌstaɪəl ɪst §-əst ‖ 'her- 'hær-
  ~s s
hair|y 'heər |i ‖ 'her |i 'hær- ~ier i_ə ‖ i_ər
  ~iest i_ɪst i_əst ~iness i nəs i nɪs
Haiti 'heɪt i 'haɪt-; haɪ 'iːt i, hɑː- ‖ 'heɪt̬ i
Haitian 'heɪʃ ən 'haɪʃ-, '•i_ən; 'heɪt i_ən;
  haɪ 'iːʃ ən, hɑː-, -'iːʃ i_ən ~s z
Haitink 'haɪt ɪŋk —Dutch ['haːi tɪŋk]
haj, hajj hædʒ hɑːdʒ
haji, hajji 'hædʒ i 'hɑːdʒ-, -iː ~s z
haka 'hɑːk ə ~s z
hake heɪk **hakes** heɪks
hakim *'physician'* hə 'kiːm hæ-, hɑː- ~s z
hakim *'judge, ruler'* 'hɑːk ɪm hɑː 'kiːm ~s z
Hakluyt 'hæk luːt 'hæk əl wɪt
Hal hæl
halal hə 'lɑːl 'hæl æl, hæ 'læl —Arabic [ħa 'laːl]
halation hə 'leɪʃ ən ~s z
halberd 'hæl bəd 'hɔːl-, -bɜːd ‖ -bərd ~s z
halberdier ˌhæl bə 'dɪə ˌhɔːl- ‖ -bər 'dɪər ~s z
halcyon 'hæls i_ən ~s z
  ,halcyon 'days
Halcyone hæl 'saɪ_ən i
Haldane 'hɔːld eɪn 'hɒld- ‖ 'hɑːld-
hale, Hale heɪəl (= hail) **haler** 'heɪəl ə ‖ -ər
  halest 'heɪəl ɪst -əst
Haleakala ˌhɑːl i ɑːk ə 'lɑː
haleness 'heɪəl nəs -nɪs
Hales heɪəlz
Halesowen ˌ₍ₕ₎eɪəlz 'əʊ ɪn -ən ‖ -'oʊ-
Halesworth 'heɪəlz wɜːθ ‖ -wərθ
Halex *tdmk* 'heɪl eks
Halewood ˌheɪəl 'wʊd ◂
Haley 'heɪl i
half hɑːf §hæf ‖ hæf —See also phrases with this
  word **halves** hɑːvz §hævz ‖ hævz
  ,half a 'crown; ,half 'board; ,half 'cock;
  ,half 'crown; ,half 'moon; ,half note; ,half
  'term; ,half 'volley
half- ˌhɑːf §ˌhæf ‖ ˌhæf
half-a-dozen ˌhɑːf ə 'dʌz ən ◂ §ˌhæf- ‖ ˌhæf-
half-and-half ˌhɑːf ən 'hɑːf ◂ §ˌhæf ən 'hæf ◂
  ‖ ˌhæf ən 'hæf ◂
half-assed ˌhɑːf 'ɑːst ◂ §ˌhæf-, -'æst
  ‖ ˌhæf 'æst ◂
halfback 'hɑːf bæk §'hæf- ‖ 'hæf- ~s z
half-baked ˌhɑːf 'beɪkt ◂ §ˌhæf- ‖ ˌhæf-
half-breed 'hɑːf briːd §'hæf- ‖ 'hæf- ~s z
half-brother 'hɑːf ˌbrʌð ə §'hæf-
  ‖ 'hæf ˌbrʌð ər ~s z
half-caste 'hɑːf kɑːst §'hæf-, §-kæst
  ‖ 'hæf kæst ~s s
half-close ˌhɑːf 'kləʊs ◂ §ˌhæf- ‖ ˌhæf 'kloʊs ◂

half-hardy ˌhɑːf 'hɑːd i ◂ §ˌhæf-
  ‖ ˌhæf 'hɑːrd i ◂
half-hearted ˌhɑːf 'hɑːt ɪd ◂ §ˌhæf-, -əd
  ‖ ˌhæf 'hɑːrt̬ əd ◂ ~ly li ~ness nəs nɪs
half-holiday ˌhɑːf 'hɒl ə deɪ §ˌhæf-, -ɪ-, -di
  ‖ ˌhæf 'hɑːl- ~s z
half-hour ˌhɑːf 'aʊ_ə ◂ §ˌhæf- ‖ ˌhæf 'aʊ_ər ◂
  ~ly li ~s z
half-length ˌhɑːf 'leŋkθ ◂ §ˌhæf-, §-'lenˡθ
  ‖ ˌhæf-
half-|life 'hɑːf |laɪf §'hæf- ‖ 'hæf- ~lives laɪvz
half-light 'hɑːf laɪt §'hæf- ‖ 'hæf-
half-marathon ˌhɑːf 'mær əθ ən §ˌhæf-, -ə θɒn
  ‖ ˌhæf 'mær ə θɑːn -'mer- ~s z
half-mast ˌhɑːf 'mɑːst §ˌhæf-, §-'mæst
  ‖ ˌhæf 'mæst
half-measures 'hɑːf ˌmeʒ əz §'hæf-, ˌ•'••
  ‖ 'hæf ˌmeʒ ərz -ˌmeɪʒ-
half-nelson ˌhɑːf 'nels ən §ˌhæf- ‖ ˌhæf- '•ˌ••
  ~s z
half-open ˌhɑːf 'əʊp ən ◂ §ˌhæf- ‖ ˌhæf 'oʊp
  ən
Halford 'hæl fəd 'hɔːl-, 'hɒl- ‖ -fərd ~'s z
half past *in expressions of time* ˌhɑːf 'pɑːst ◂
  ˌhɑː:-, ˌhʌ-, §ˌhæf-, §-'pæst ‖ ˌhæf 'pæst ◂
  ,half past 'ten
halfpence 'heɪp ənˡs →m'ˡs
halfpenn|y *n* 'heɪp n|i 'heɪp ən |i —For the
  British coin in use 1971-85, also ˌhɑːf 'pen |i ◂,
  §ˌhæf-, ‖ ˌhæf- ~ies iz
Halfpenny *surname* 'hɑːf pən i §'hæf- ‖ 'hæf-
halfpennyworth 'heɪp ni wɜːθ -wəθ; 'heɪp əθ;
  ˌhɑːf 'pen əθ, §ˌhæf- ‖ 'heɪp ən i wɜːθ —See
  hap'orth
half-price ˌhɑːf 'praɪs ◂ §ˌhæf- ‖ ˌhæf-
half-sister 'hɑːf ˌsɪst ə §'hæf- ‖ 'hæf ˌsɪst ər
  ~s z
half-size ˌhɑːf 'saɪz ◂ §ˌhæf- ‖ ˌhæf-
half-timbered ˌhɑːf 'tɪm bəd ◂ §ˌhæf-
  ‖ ˌhæf 'tɪm bərd ◂
half time ˌhɑːf 'taɪm ◂ §ˌhæf- ‖ 'hæf taɪm
  ,half-time 'score
halftone ˌhɑːf 'təʊn §ˌhæf-, '•• ‖ 'hæf toʊn ~s
  z
half-track *adj* ˌhɑːf 'træk ◂ §ˌhæf- ‖ ˌhæf-
half-track *n* 'hɑːf træk §'hæf- ‖ 'hæf- ~ed t
  ~s s
half-|truth 'hɑːf |truːθ §'hæf-, ˌ•'• ‖ 'hæf-
  ~truths truːðz truːθs
halfway ˌhɑːf 'weɪ ◂ §ˌhæf- ‖ ˌhæf-
  ,halfway 'house
half-wit 'hɑːf wɪt §'hæf- ‖ 'hæf- ~s s
half-witted ˌhɑːf 'wɪt ɪd ◂ §ˌhæf-, -əd
  ‖ ˌhæf 'wɪt̬ əd ◂ ~ly li ~ness nəs nɪs
halibut 'hæl ɪb ət -əb- ~s s
Halicarnassus ˌhæl ɪ kɑː 'næs əs ˌ•ə-
  ‖ -kɑːrˡ•-
halide 'heɪl aɪd 'hæl- ~s z
Halifax 'hæl ɪ fæks -ə-
halitosis ˌhæl ɪ 'təʊs ɪs -ə-, §-əs ‖ -'toʊs-
hall, Hall hɔːl ‖ hɑːl (= haul) **halls** hɔːlz ‖ hɑːlz
  ,hall of 'residence; ,hall 'porter
Hallam 'hæl əm

H

Halle, Hallé 'hæl eɪ -i ‖ 'hɑːl ə
halleluja, hallelujah ˌhæl ɪ 'luː jə -ə- ~s z
Halley (i) 'hæl i; (ii) 'hɔːl i ‖ 'hɑːl i —The
　astronomer and the comet named after him are
　usually (i) in educated speech, although some
　claim that only (ii) is correct. In AmE there is
　also a popular pronunciation 'heɪl i.
halliard 'hæl jəd ‖ -jərd ~s z
Halliday 'hæl ɪ deɪ -ə-
Halliwell 'hæl i wel
hallmark 'hɔːl mɑːk ‖ -mɑːrk 'hɑːl- ~ed t
　~ing ɪŋ ~s s
hallo hə 'ləʊ ˌhæ-, ˌhe-, ˌhʌ- ‖ -'loʊ ~es z
halloo hə 'luː ~ed d ~ing ɪŋ ~s z
Halloran 'hæl ər ən
hallow 'hæl əʊ ‖ -oʊ ~ed d —but in the Lord's
　Prayer also sometimes ed, ɪd, əd ~ing ɪŋ ~s z
Hallowe'en ˌhæl əʊ 'iːn ◄ ‖ -oʊ- ˌhɑːl-
Hallowes, Hallows 'hæl əʊz ‖ -oʊz
hallstand 'hɔːl stænd ‖ 'hɑːl- ~s z
halluci|nate hə 'luːs ɪ |neɪt -'ljuːs-, -ə- ~nated
　neɪt ɪd -əd ‖ neɪt̬ əd ~nates neɪts ~nating
　neɪt ɪŋ ‖ neɪt̬ ɪŋ
hallucination hə ˌluːs ɪ 'neɪʃ ən -ˌljuːs-, -ə- ~s
　z
hallucinatory hə 'luːs ɪn ət_ər i -'ljuːs-, -'•ən_;
　•ˌ•ɪ 'neɪt ər i ◄, •ˌ•ə-, •ˈ•••• ‖ -ən_ə tɔːr i
　-tour i
hallucinogen ˌhæl uː 'sɪn ədʒ ən -ə dʒen;
　hə 'luːs ɪn-, -'•ən- ~s z
hallucinogenic hə ˌluːs ɪn ə 'dʒen ɪk ◄ -ˌljuːs-,
　-ˌ•ən_
hallux 'hæl əks ~es ɪz əz
hallway 'hɔːl weɪ ‖ 'hɑːl- ~s z
halma 'hælm ə
Halmahera ˌhælm ə 'hɪər ə -'hɜːr- ‖ -'hɝː ə
　ˌhɑːlm ə-
halo 'heɪl əʊ ‖ -oʊ ~ed d ~es, ~s z ~ing ɪŋ
halo- comb. form
　with stress-neutral suffix ˈhæl əʊ ‖ -ə —
　halophyte 'hæl əʊ faɪt ‖ -ə-
　with stress-imposing suffix hæ 'lɒ+ ‖ -'lɑː+ —
　halogenous hæ 'lɒdʒ ən əs ‖ -'lɑːdʒ-
halogen 'hæl ə dʒen 'heɪl-, -ədʒ ən ~s z
haloperidol ˌhæl əʊ 'per ɪ dɒl ˌheɪl-, -ə•
　‖ ˌhæl oʊ 'per ə dɔːl -dɑːl, -doʊl
halophyte 'hæl ə faɪt 'heɪl- ~s s
halothane 'hæl əʊ θeɪn 'heɪl- ‖ -ə-
Halpern 'hælp ən ‖ -ərn
Hals hæls hælz ‖ hɑːls hɑːlz —Dutch [hɑls]
Halsbury 'hɔːlz bər_i 'hɒlz- ‖ 'hɔːlz ˌber i
　'hɑːlz-
Halse hæls hɔːls, hɒls ‖ hɑːls, hɔːls
Halstead, Halsted (i) 'hæl sted -stɪd, (ii) 'hɔːl-
　'hɒl- ‖ 'hɑːl-
halt hɔːlt hɒlt ‖ hɑːlt halted 'hɔːlt ɪd 'hɒlt-,
　-əd ‖ 'hɑːlt- halting/ly 'hɔːlt ɪŋ /li
　'hɒlt- ‖ 'hɑːlt- halts hɔːlts hɒlts ‖ hɑːlts
　—BrE 1998 poll panel preference: hɒlt 52%,
　hɔːlt 48%
Haltemprice 'hɔːlt əm praɪs 'hɒlt- ‖ 'hɑːlt-
halter 'hɔːlt ə 'hɒlt- ‖ -ər 'hɑːlt- ~s z

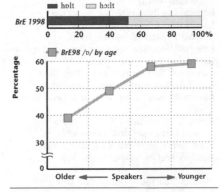

HALT

hɒlt ■　hɔːlt ▨

BrE 1998

0　20　40　60　80　100%

BrE98 /ɒ/ by age

Percentage

Older ◄—— Speakers ——► Younger

haltere 'hælt ɪə 'hɔːlt-, 'hɒlt- ‖ -ɪr 'hɔːlt-,
　'hɑːlt- ~s z
halterneck 'hɔːlt ə nek 'hɒlt- ‖ -ər- 'hɑːlt- ~s
　s
Halton 'hɔːlt ən 'hɒlt- ‖ 'hɑːlt-
halva, halvah 'hælv ə -ɑː ‖ hɑːl 'vɑː '••
halve hɑːv ‖ hæv halved hɑːvd ‖ hævd
　halves hɑːvz ‖ hævz halving
　'hɑːv ɪŋ ‖ 'hæv ɪŋ
halves from half, halve hɑːvz ‖ hævz
halyard 'hæl jəd ‖ -jərd ~s z
ham, Ham hæm hammed hæmd hamming
　'hæm ɪŋ hams hæmz
hamadryad ˌhæm ə 'draɪ əd -æd ~s z
hamadryas ˌhæm ə 'draɪ_əs -æs ~es ɪz əz
Haman 'heɪm ən -æn
Hamas 'hæm æs hæ 'mæs
Hamble 'hæm bəl
Hambledon 'hæm bəl dən
Hambletonian ˌhæm bəl 'təʊn i_ən ‖ -'toʊn-
　~s z
Hambro 'hæm brəʊ -brə ‖ -broʊ 'hɑːm-
Hamburg 'hæm bɜːg ‖ -bɝːg —Ger
　['ham bʊʁk, -bʊɐ̯ç]
hamburger, H~ 'hæm ˌbɜːg ə ‖ -ˌbɝːg ər ~s z
Hamelin 'hæm lɪn 'hæm əl ɪn, -ɪl- —Ger
　Hameln ['haː məln]
Hamersley 'hæm əz li ‖ -ərz-
ham-fisted ˌhæm 'fɪst ɪd ◄ -əd ~ly li ~ness
　nəs nɪs
ham-handed ˌhæm 'hænd ɪd ◄ -əd ~ly li
　~ness nəs nɪs
Hamilcar hæ 'mɪl kɑː hə-; 'hæm əl-, -ɪl- ‖ -kɑːr
Hamill 'hæm əl -ɪl
Hamilton 'hæm əl tən -ɪl-
Hamiltonian ˌhæm əl 'təʊn i_ən ◄ -ɪl- ‖ -'toʊn-
　~s z
Hamish 'heɪm ɪʃ
Hamite 'hæm aɪt ~s s
Hamitic hæ 'mɪt ɪk hə- ‖ -'mɪt̬ ɪk
Hamito-Semitic ˌhæm ɪ təʊ sə 'mɪt ɪk ◄ -ˌ•ə-,
　-sɪ'•- ‖ ˌhæm ə toʊ sə 'mɪt̬ ɪk ◄
hamlet, H~ 'hæm lət -lɪt ~s s
Hamley 'hæm li
Hamlin, Hamlyn 'hæm lɪn §-lən

Hammarskjold 'hæm ə ʃəʊld →-ʃʊʊld
 ‖ -ʳr ʃʊʊld 'hɑːm- —Swedish Hammarskjöld
 ['ˈha mar ɧœld]
hammer, H~ 'hæm ə ‖ -ʳr ~ed d hammering
 'hæm ər‿ɪŋ ~s z
 'hammer drill
hammerbeam 'hæm ə biːm ‖ -ʳr- ~s z
Hammerfest 'hæm ə fest ‖ -ʳr- 'hɑːm-
 —Norw ['ˈham ər fɛst]
hammerhead 'hæm ə hed ‖ -ʳr- ~s z
Hammersley 'hæm əz li ‖ -ʳrz-
Hammersmith 'hæm ə smɪθ ‖ -ʳr-
Hammerstein (i) 'hæm ə staɪn ‖ -ʳr-, (ii) -stiːn
Hammett 'hæm ɪt §-ət
hammock 'hæm ək ~s s
Hammond 'hæm ənd
Hammurabi ,hæm u 'rɑːb i
Hampden 'hæm dən 'hæmp-
hamper 'hæmp ə ‖ -ʳr ~ed d hampering
 'hæmp ər‿ɪŋ ~s z
Hampshire 'hæmp ʃə -ʃɪə ‖ -ʃʳr -ʃɪr
Hampstead 'hæmp stɪd -sted, §-stəd
 ,Hampstead 'Heath
Hampton 'hæmp tən
 ,Hampton 'Court
hamster 'hæmᵖst ə ‖ -ʳr ~s z
hamstring 'hæm strɪŋ ~ing ɪŋ ~s z
 hamstrung 'hæm strʌŋ
Hamtramck hæm 'træm ɪk (!)
hamza, hamzah 'hæmz ə ~s z
Han hæn ‖ hɑːn —Chi hàn [⁴xan]
Hanbury 'hæn bər‿i →'hæm-
Hancock 'hæn kɒk →'hæŋ- ‖ -kɑːk
hand hænd handed 'hænd ɪd -əd handing
 'hænd ɪŋ hands hændz
 'hand ,baggage; 'hand gre,nade; 'hand
 ,luggage; ,hands 'off; ,hands 'up
handbag 'hænd bæg →'hæm- ~s z
handball 'hænd bɔːl →'hæm- ‖ -bɑːl ~s z
handbarrow 'hænd ,bær əʊ →'hæm- ‖ -oʊ
 -,ber- ~s z
handbasin 'hænd ,beɪs ən →'hæm- ~s z
handbell 'hænd bel →'hæm- ~s z
handbill 'hænd bɪl →'hæm- ~s z
handbook 'hænd bʊk →'hæm-, §-buːk ~s s
handbrake 'hænd breɪk →'hæm- ~s s
handcart 'hænd kɑːt →'hæŋ- ‖ -kɑːrt ~s s
handclap 'hænd klæp →'hæŋ- ~s s
handcuff 'hænd kʌf →'hæŋ- ~ed t ~ing ɪŋ
 ~s s
-handed 'hænd ɪd ◂ -əd
handedness 'hænd ɪd nəs -əd-, -nɪs
Handel 'hænd ᵊl —Ger Händel ['hɛn dᵊl]
Handelian hæn 'diːl i‿ən ~s z
handful 'hænd fʊl ~s z
handgun 'hænd gʌn →'hæŋ- ~s z
handhold 'hænd həʊld →-hɒʊld ‖ -hoʊld ~s z
handicap 'hænd i kæp ~ped t ~ping ɪŋ ~s s
handicraft 'hænd i krɑːft §-kræft ‖ -kræft ~s
 s
handie... —see handy
handily 'hænd ɪ li -ᵊl i
handiwork 'hænd i wɜːk ‖ -wɜːk

handker|chief 'hæŋk ə |tʃɪf -tʃəf, -tʃiːf ‖ -ʳr-
 ~chiefs tʃɪfs tʃəfs, tʃiːfs, tʃiːvz ~chieves
 tʃiːvz
handle 'hænd ᵊl ~d d ~s z handling
 'hænd lɪŋ 'hænd ᵊl‿ɪŋ
handlebar 'hænd ᵊl bɑː ‖ -bɑːr ~s z
handler 'hænd lə 'hænd ᵊl‿ə ‖ -lʳr -ᵊl‿ʳr ~s z
Handley 'hænd li
handloom 'hænd luːm ~s z
handmade ,hænd 'meɪd ◂ →,hæm-
handmaid 'hænd meɪd →'hæm- ~s z
handmaiden 'hænd ,meɪd ᵊn →'hæm- ~s z
hand-me-down 'hænd mi daʊn →'hæm- ~s z
handout 'hænd aʊt ~s s
handover 'hænd ,əʊv ə ‖ -,oʊv ʳr ~s z
handpick v ,hænd 'pɪk ◂ →,hæm- ~ed t ~ing
 ɪŋ ~s s
handrail 'hænd reɪᵊl ~s z
handsaw 'hænd sɔː ‖ -sɑː ~s z
handset 'hænd set ~s s
handshake 'hænd ʃeɪk ~s s
hands-off ,hændz 'ɒf ◂ -'ɔːf ◂ ‖ -'ɔːf ◂ -'ɑːf ◂
handsome 'hæn⁺s əm ~ly li ~ness nəs nɪs
hands-on ,hændz 'ɒn ◂ ‖ -'ɑːn ◂ -'ɔːn ◂
handspring 'hænd sprɪŋ ~s z
handstand 'hænd stænd ~s z
hand-to-hand ,hænd tə 'hænd ◂
hand-to-mouth ,hænd tə 'maʊθ ◂
handwork 'hænd wɜːk ‖ -wɜːk
handwriting 'hænd ,raɪt ɪŋ ‖ -,raɪt̬ ɪŋ
handwritten ,hænd 'rɪt ᵊn ◂
hand|y, Handy 'hænd |i ~ier i‿ə ‖ i‿ʳr ~iest
 i‿ɪst i‿əst
handy|man 'hænd i |mæn ~men men
hang hæŋ hanged hæŋd hanging/s
 'hæŋ ɪŋ/z hangs hæŋz hung hʌŋ
 ,Hang 'Seng (,index) seŋ —Cantonese [⁴hɐŋ
 ¹sɐŋ]
hangar 'hæŋ ə -gə ‖ -ʳr -gʳr (usually = hanger)
 ~s z
Hangchow ,hæŋ 'tʃaʊ —Chi Hángzhōu
 [²xaŋ ¹tʂou]
hangdog 'hæŋ dɒg ‖ -dɔːg -dɑːg ~s z
hanger 'hæŋ ə ‖ -ʳr s z
hang|er-on ,hæŋ |ər 'ɒn ‖ -|ʳr 'ɑːn -'ɔːn ~ers-
 on əz 'ɒn ‖ ʳrz 'ɑːn -'ɔːn
hang-glider 'hæŋ ,glaɪd ə ‖ -ʳr ~s z
hang-gliding 'hæŋ ,glaɪd ɪŋ
hang|man 'hæŋ |mən ~men mən
hangnail 'hæŋ neɪᵊl ~s z
hangout 'hæŋ aʊt ~s s
hangover 'hæŋ ,əʊv ə ‖ -,oʊv ʳr ~s z
hangul, H~ 'hæŋ gʊl ‖ 'hɑːn- —Korean hangŭl
 [han gʊl]
hang-up 'hæŋ ʌp ~s s
Hangzhou ,hæŋ 'dʒəʊ ‖ -'dʒoʊ —Chi
 Hángzhōu [²xaŋ ¹tʂou]
Hanif hə 'nɪf
hank, Hank hæŋk hanks hæŋks
hanker 'hæŋk ə ‖ -ʳr ~ed d hankering 'hæŋk
 ər‿ɪŋ ~s z
hankie 'hæŋk i ~s z
Hanks hæŋks

H

hank|y 'hæŋk |i ~ies iz
hanky-panky ˌhæŋk i 'pæŋk i
Hanley 'hæn li
Hann hæn
Hanna, Hannah 'hæn ə
Hannay 'hæn eɪ
Hannibal 'hæn ɪb əl -əb-
Hannington 'hæn ɪŋ tən
Hanoi ₍ᵢ₎hæ 'nɔɪ hə- ‖ hɑː- —*Vietnamese* Ha Nôi [³ha ⁶noi]
Hanover 'hæn əʊv ə ‖ -oʊv ər —*Ger* Hannover [ha 'noː fɐ]
Hanoverian ˌhæn əʊ 'vɪər i‿ən ◄ -'veər- ‖ -ə 'vɪr- -'ver- ~s z
Hanrahan 'hæn rə hən -hæn
Hanratty hæn 'ræt i ‖ -'ræt̬ i '•••
Hans hænᵗs hænz —*Ger* [hans]
Hansa 'hænᵗs ə 'hænz- —*Ger* ['han za]
Hansard 'hænᵗs ɑːd -əd ‖ -ᵊrd
Hanseatic, h~ ˌhænᵗs i 'æt ɪk ◄ ˌhænz- ‖ -'æt̬ ɪk ◄
Hansel, Hänsel 'hænᵗs ᵊl —*Ger* ['han zᵊl, 'hɛn-]
Hansen 'hænᵗs ᵊn
hansom, H~ 'hænᵗs əm (= *handsome*) ~s z
Hanson 'hænᵗs ᵊn
Hants hænts —*or as* Hampshire
Hanukah, Hanukkah 'hɑːn ək ə 'hɒn-, 'hæn-, -ʊk-, -uːk-, -ɑː —*Hebrew* [xa nu 'ka]
hanuman, H~ ˌhʌn u 'mɑːn ˌhɑːn- ~s z —*Hindi* [hə ɳʊ mɑːn̪]
Hanway 'hæn weɪ
Hanwell 'hæn wᵊl -wel
hap hæp happed hæpt happing 'hæp ɪŋ haps hæps
hapax 'hæp æks ˌhapax le'gomenon lɪ 'gɒm ɪn ən lə-, le-, -ən ən, -ə nɒn ‖ -'gɑːm ə nɑːn
ha'penny 'heɪp ni 'heɪp ᵊn i ha'pennies 'heɪp niz 'heɪp ᵊn iz
haphazard ₍ᵢ₎hæp 'hæz əd ◄ ‖ -ᵊrd ◄ ~ly li ~ness nəs nɪs
hapless 'hæp ləs -lɪs
haplography ₍ᵢ₎hæp 'lɒg rəf i ‖ -'lɑːg-
haploid 'hæp lɔɪd ~y i
haplolog|y ₍ᵢ₎hæp 'lɒl ədʒ |i ‖ -'lɑːl- ~ies iz
haply 'hæp li
hap'orth, ha'p'orth 'heɪp əθ ‖ -ᵊrθ ~s s
happen 'hæp ᵊn happened 'hæp ᵊnd →-md happening/s 'hæp ᵊn_ɪŋ/z happens 'hæp ᵊnz →-mz
happenstance 'hæp ᵊn stænᵗs →-m-, -stɑːnᵗs
happie... —*see* happy
happily 'hæp ɪ li -ᵊl i
happiness 'hæp i nəs -nɪs
Happisburgh 'heɪz bᵊr_ə (!)
happ|y, Happy 'hæp |i ~ier i‿ə ‖ i‿ᵊr ~iest i‿ɪst i‿əst
ˌhappy e'vent; ˌhappy ˌhour; ˌhappy 'hunting ˌground; ˌhappy 'medium
happy-go-lucky ˌhæp i gəʊ 'lʌk i ◄ ‖ -goʊ'•-
Hapsburg 'hæps bɜːg ‖ -bɝːg —*Ger* Habsburg ['haːps bʊʁk] ~s z
haptic 'hæpt ɪk

hara-kiri ˌhær ə 'kɪr i -'kɪər-, △-i 'kær i, △-i 'kɑːr i ‖ ˌhɑːr- —*Jp* [ha ˌra ki 'ri]
harangu|e hə 'ræŋ ~ed d ~es z ~ing ɪŋ
Harare hə 'rɑːr i hɑː-, -eɪ

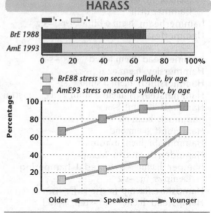

HARASS

	0	20	40	60	80	100%
BrE 1988						
AmE 1993						

■-'•• ▢-•'•

□ BrE88 stress on second syllable, by age
□ AmE93 stress on second syllable, by age

Percentage: 100, 80, 60, 40, 20, 0

Older ◄—— Speakers ——► Younger

harass 'hær əs hə 'ræs ‖ hə 'ræs 'hær əs, 'her- —*The traditional RP form is* 'hær əs. *The pronunciation* hə 'ræs, *which originated in the US, was seemingly first heard in Britain in the 1970's. In time it may predominate in BrE, as it already does in AmE. Meanwhile, it evokes strong negative feelings among those who use the traditional form. Poll panel preferences: BrE 1988,* '•• 68%, •'• 32%; *AmE 1993,* •'• 87%, '•• 13%. ~ed t ~es ɪz əz ~ing ɪŋ ~ment mənt
Harben 'hɑːb ᵊn
Harbin 'hɑː bɪn ˌhɑː 'bɪn ‖ 'hɑːrb ᵊn ˌhɑːr 'bɪn —*Chi* Hā'erbīn [¹xa‿ɚ ¹pɪn]
harbinger 'hɑːb ɪndʒ ə §-əndʒ- ‖ -ᵊr ~s z
harbor 'hɑːb ə ‖ 'hɑːrb ᵊr ~ed d harboring 'hɑːb ᵊr_ɪŋ ‖ 'hɑːrb- ~s z
harbormaster 'hɑːb ə ˌmɑːst ə §-ˌmæst- ‖ 'hɑːrb ᵊr ˌmæst ᵊr ~s z
Harborough 'hɑːb ᵊr_ə ‖ 'hɑːr ˌbɝː oʊ
harbour 'hɑːb ə ‖ 'hɑːrb ᵊr ~ed d harbouring 'hɑːb ᵊr_ɪŋ ‖ 'hɑːrb- ~s z
harbourmaster 'hɑːb ə ˌmɑːst ə §-ˌmæst- ‖ 'hɑːrb ᵊr ˌmæst ᵊr ~s z
Harcourt 'hɑː kɔːt 'hɑːk ət ‖ 'hɑːr kɔːrt -koʊrt; 'hɑːrk ᵊrt
hard hɑːd ‖ hɑːrd harder 'hɑːd ə ‖ 'hɑːrd ᵊr hardest 'hɑːd ɪst -əst ‖ 'hɑːrd- ˌhard 'by◄; ˌhard 'cash; ˌhard 'cider; ˌhard 'copy, '• ,•••; ˌhard 'core *nucleus* , 'hard core *'broken stones'* ; ˌhard 'currency; ˌhard 'disk; ˌhard 'drink; ˌhard 'drugs; ˌhard 'feelings; ˌhard 'labour; ˌhard 'line; ˌhard 'liquor; ˌhard 'luck; ˌhard 'luck ˌstory, ˌ• • '•••; ˌhard of 'hearing; ˌhard 'palate; ˌhard 'rock; ˌhard 'sell; ˌhard 'shoulder; ˌhard 'up◄
hard-and-fast ˌhɑːd ᵊn 'fɑːst ◄ §-'fæst ‖ ˌhɑːrd ᵊn 'fæst ◄
hardback 'hɑːd bæk →'hɑːb- ‖ 'hɑːrd- ~s s
hardball 'hɑːd bɔːl →'hɑːb- ‖ 'hɑːrd- -bɑːl

Hard attack

When a word of syllable begins with a vowel sound, it is possible to start the vowel from a position where the vocal folds are first held closed, then burst open for the vowel: that is, to precede the vowel by a GLOTTAL STOP. This way of starting a vowel is called **hard attack**.

In English, hard attack is not customary. But it is sometimes used for special effect, as a way of emphasizing the importance of a word.

When hard attack is used, and the word in question is preceded by **to**, then the weak form appropriate before a consonant is often used, namely tə. Thus **to eat** is usually tu 'iːt but sometimes tə 'ʔiːt.

---

hard-bitten ˌhɑːd 'bɪt ən ◄ →ˌhɑːb- ‖ ˌhɑːrd-
hardboard 'hɑːd bɔːd →'hɑːb- ‖ 'hɑːrd bɔːrd -boʊrd
hard-boiled ˌhɑːd 'bɔɪəld ◄ →ˌhɑːb- ‖ ˌhɑːrd-
  ˌhard-boiled 'egg
hardbound 'hɑːd baʊnd →'hɑːb- ‖ 'hɑːrd-
Hardcastle 'hɑːd ˌkɑːs əl →'hɑːg-, §-ˌkæs- ‖ 'hɑːrd ˌkæs əl
hard-core ˌhɑːd 'kɔː ◄ →ˌhɑːg-, '•• ‖ ˌhɑːrd 'kɔːr ◄ -'koʊr
  ˌhard-core 'porn
hardcover 'hɑːd ˌkʌv ə →'hɑːg- ‖ 'hɑːrd ˌkʌv ər
hard-done-by ˌhɑːd 'dʌn baɪ →-'dʌm-
hard-earned ˌhɑːd 'ɜːnd ◄ ‖ ˌhɑːrd 'ɜːnd ◄
harden 'hɑːd ən ‖ 'hɑːrd ən -ed d ~ing ɪŋ ~s z
hard-hat 'hɑːd hæt ‖ 'hɑːrd- ~s s
hardheaded ˌhɑːd 'hed ɪd ◄ -əd ‖ ˌhɑːrd- ~ly li ~ness nəs nɪs
hardhearted ˌhɑːd 'hɑːt ɪd ◄ -əd ‖ ˌhɑːrd 'hɑːrt̬ əd ◄ ~ly li ~ness nəs nɪs
hard-hitting ˌhɑːd 'hɪt ɪŋ ◄ ‖ ˌhɑːrd 'hɪt̬ ɪŋ ◄
Hardicanute 'hɑːd ɪ kə ˌnjuːt '•ə-, ˌ•••'• ‖ ˌhɑːrd ə kə 'nuːt -'njuːt
Hardie 'hɑːd i ‖ 'hɑːrd i
hardihood 'hɑːd i hʊd ‖ 'hɑːrd-
hardily 'hɑːd ɪ li -əl i ‖ 'hɑːrd-
hardiness 'hɑːd i nəs -nɪs ‖ 'hɑːrd-
Harding 'hɑːd ɪŋ ‖ 'hɑːrd-
Hardinge (i) 'hɑːd ɪŋ ‖ 'hɑːrd-, (ii) -ɪndʒ
hard-line ˌhɑːd 'laɪn ◄ ‖ ˌhɑːrd-
hard-liner ˌhɑːd 'laɪn ə ◄ '••• ‖ ˌhɑːrd 'laɪn ər ◄ ~s z
hard|ly 'hɑːd |li ‖ 'hɑːrd- ~ness nəs nɪs
hard-nosed ˌhɑːd 'nəʊzd ◄ ‖ ˌhɑːrd 'noʊzd ◄
hard-on 'hɑːd ɒn ‖ 'hɑːrd ɑːn -ɔːn ~s z
hardpan 'hɑːd pæn →'hɑːb- ‖ 'hɑːrd-
hard-pressed ˌhɑːd 'prest ◄ →ˌhɑːb- ‖ ˌhɑːrd-
hard-shell 'hɑːd ʃel ‖ 'hɑːrd- ~s z
hardship 'hɑːd ʃɪp ‖ 'hɑːrd- ~s s
hardtack 'hɑːd tæk ‖ 'hɑːrd-
hardtop 'hɑːd tɒp ‖ 'hɑːrd tɑːp ~s s
hardware 'hɑːd weə ‖ 'hɑːrd wer -wær ~s z

hardwearing ˌhɑːd 'weər ɪŋ ◄ ‖ ˌhɑːrd 'wer ɪŋ ◄ -'wær- ˌhard-ˌwearing 'fabric
Hardwick, Hardwicke 'hɑːd wɪk ‖ 'hɑːrd-
hard-wired ˌhɑːd 'waɪ‿əd ◄ ‖ ˌhɑːrd 'waɪ‿ərd ◄
hardwood 'hɑːd wʊd ‖ 'hɑːrd- ~s z
hard-working ˌhɑːd 'wɜːk ɪŋ ◄ ‖ ˌhɑːrd 'wɜːk ɪŋ ◄
hard|ly, Hard|ly 'hɑːd li ‖ 'hɑːrd li ~ier i‿ə ‖ i‿ər ~ies, ~y's iz ~iest i‿ɪst i‿əst
hare, Hare heə ‖ heər hæær (= hair) **hared** heəd ‖ heərd hæærd **hares** heəz ‖ heərz hæ²rz **haring** 'heər ɪŋ ‖ 'her ɪŋ 'hær- —see also phrases with this word
  'hare ˌcoursing
harebell 'heə bel ‖ 'her- 'hær- ~s z
harebrained 'heə breɪnd ‖ 'her- 'hær-
Harefield 'heə fiːəld ‖ 'her-
Hare Krishna ˌhær i 'krɪʃ nə ˌhɑːr- ‖ ˌhɑːr-, ˌhær-, ˌher-
harelip ˌheə 'lɪp '•• ‖ 'her lɪp 'hær- ~ped t ◄ ~s s
harem 'hɑːr iːm 'heər-, -əm, ₍ₒ₎hɑː 'riːm ‖ 'hær əm 'her- ~s z
Harewood 'heə wʊd ‖ 'her- 'hær- —but 'hɑː- ‖ 'hɑːr- for the Earl of H~, and for H~ House
Harford 'hɑː fəd ‖ 'hɑːr fərd
Hargraves 'hɑː greɪvz ‖ 'hɑːr-
Hargreaves (i) 'hɑː griːvz ‖ 'hɑːr-, (ii) -greɪvz
haricot 'hær ɪ kəʊ -ə- ‖ -koʊ 'her- ~s z
  ˌharicot 'bean, '••••
Harijan 'hʌr ɪdʒ ən 'hɑːr-, §-ədʒ-; -ɪ dʒɑːn, -ə- ‖ 'hɑːr ɪ dʒɑːn 'hær-, 'her-, -dʒæn ~s z
Haringey 'hær ɪŋ geɪ -gi ‖ 'her-
hark hɑːk ‖ hɑːrk **harked** hɑːkt ‖ hɑːrkt **harking** 'hɑːk ɪŋ ‖ 'hɑːrk ɪŋ **harks** hɑːks ‖ hɑːrks
harken 'hɑːk ən ‖ 'hɑːrk- ~ed d ~ing ɪŋ ~s z
Harkness 'hɑːk nəs -nɪs ‖ 'hɑːrk-
Harlan 'hɑːl ən ‖ 'hɑːrl-
Harland 'hɑːl ənd ‖ 'hɑːrl-
Harlech 'hɑːl ək -əx, -ek, -ex ‖ 'hɑːrl- —Welsh ['har lex]

H

Harlem 'hɑːl əm ‖ 'hɑːrl-
Harlemite 'hɑːl ə maɪt ‖ 'hɑːrl- ~s s
harlequin 'hɑːl ə kwɪn -ɪ-, -kɪn ‖ 'hɑːrl- ~s z
harlequinade ˌhɑːl ə kwɪ 'neɪd ‚•ɪ-, -kwə'•,
  -kɪ'• ‖ ˌhɑːrl- ~s z
Harlesden 'hɑːlz dən ‖ 'hɑːrlz-
Harley 'hɑːl i ‖ 'hɑːrl i
  'Harley Street
harlot 'hɑːl ət ‖ 'hɑːrl- ~s s
harlot|ry 'hɑːl ət |ri ‖ 'hɑːrl- ~ries riz
Harlow, Harlowe 'hɑːl əʊ ‖ 'hɑːrl oʊ
harm hɑːm ‖ hɑːrm **harmed** hɑːmd ‖ hɑːrmd
  harming 'hɑːm ɪŋ ‖ 'hɑːrm ɪŋ **harms**
  hɑːmz ‖ hɑːrmz
Harman 'hɑːm ən ‖ 'hɑːrm-
harmattan hɑː 'mæt ᵊn ‖ hɑːr- ˌhɑːrm ə 'tɑːn
  ~s z
Harmer 'hɑːm ə ‖ 'hɑːrm ᵊr
harmful 'hɑːm fᵊl -fʊl ‖ 'hɑːrm- ~ly ‿i ~ness
  nəs nɪs
harmless 'hɑːm ləs -lɪs ‖ 'hɑːrm- ~ly li ~ness
  nəs nɪs
Harmon 'hɑː mən ‖ 'hɑːr-
Harmondsworth
  'hɑːm əndz wɜːθ ‖ 'hɑːrm əndz wᵊrθ
harmonic hɑː 'mɒn ɪk ‖ hɑːr 'mɑːn ɪk ~ally
  ᵊl‿i ~s s
harmonica hɑː 'mɒn ɪk ə ‖ hɑːr 'mɑːn- ~s z
harmonie... —see **harmony**
harmonious hɑː 'məʊn i‿əs ‖ hɑːr 'moʊn- ~ly
  li ~ness nəs nɪs
harmonis... —see **harmoniz...**
harmonist 'hɑːm ən ɪst §-əst ‖ 'hɑːrm- ~s s
harmonium hɑː 'məʊn i‿əm ‖ hɑːr 'moʊn- ~s
  z
harmonization ˌhɑːm ən aɪ 'zeɪʃ ᵊn -ən ɪ-
  ‖ ˌhɑːrm ən ə- ~s z
harmoniz|e 'hɑːm ə naɪz ‖ 'hɑːrm- ~ed d ~es
  ɪz əz ~ing ɪŋ
harmon|y 'hɑːm ən |i ‖ 'hɑːrm- ~ies iz
Harmsworth 'hɑːmz wɜːθ -wəθ ‖ 'hɑːrmz wᵊrθ
harness 'hɑːn ɪs -əs ‖ 'hɑːrn- ~ed t ~es ɪz əz
  ~ing ɪŋ
Harold 'hær əld ‖ 'her-
harp hɑːp ‖ hɑːrp **harped** hɑːpt ‖ hɑːrpt
  harping 'hɑːp ɪŋ ‖ 'hɑːrp ɪŋ **harps**
  hɑːps ‖ hɑːrps
Harpenden 'hɑːp ənd ən →ᵊ-md-
Harper, h~ 'hɑːp ə ‖ 'hɑːrp ᵊr ~s z
  ˌHarpers 'Ferry
Harpic tdmk 'hɑːp ɪk ‖ 'hɑːrp-
harpie... —see **harpy**
harpist 'hɑːp ɪst §-əst ‖ 'hɑːrp- ~s s
harpoon ₍ₒ₎hɑː 'puːn ◀ ‖ ₍ₒ₎hɑːr- ~ed d ~ing ɪŋ
  ~s z
harpsichord 'hɑːps ɪ kɔːd -ə- ‖ 'hɑːrps ɪ kɔːrd
  ~s z
harp|y 'hɑːp |i ‖ 'hɑːrp |i ~ies iz
harquebus 'hɑːk wɪb əs -wəb- ‖ 'hɑːrk- ~es
  ɪz əz
Harrap 'hær əp ‖ 'her-
harridan 'hær ɪd ən -əd- ‖ 'her- ~s z
harrie... —see **harry**

harrier 'hær i‿ə ‖ ᵊr 'her- ~s z
Harries 'hær ɪs -iz ‖ 'her-
Harriet 'hær i‿ət ‖ 'her-
Harrietsham 'hær i‿ət ʃəm ‖ 'her-
Harriman 'hær ɪ mən -ə- ‖ 'her-
Harrington 'hær ɪŋ tən ‖ 'her-
Harriot, Harriott 'hær i‿ət ‖ 'her-
Harris 'hær ɪs §-əs ‖ 'her-
  ˌHarris 'Tweed
Harrisburg 'hær ɪs bɜːɡ -əs- ‖ -bɝːɡ 'her-
Harrison 'hær ɪs ən -əs- ‖ 'her-
Harrod 'hær əd ‖ 'her- ~s, ~'s z
Harrogate 'hær əɡ ət -əʊɡ-, -ɪt; -əʊɡeɪt
  ‖ -oʊ ɡeɪt 'her-
Harrold 'hær əld ‖ 'her-
Harrovian hə 'rəʊv i‿ən hæ- ‖ -'roʊv- ~s z
harrow, H~ 'hær əʊ ‖ -oʊ 'her- ~ed d ~ing/ly
  ɪŋ /li ~s z
harrumph hə 'rʌmpf ~ed t ~ing ɪŋ ~s s
harr|y 'hær |i ‖ 'her- ~ied id ~ies iz ~ying
  i‿ɪŋ
Harry 'hær i ‖ 'her- ~'s z
harsh hɑːʃ ‖ hɑːrʃ **harsher** 'hɑːʃ ə ‖ 'hɑːrʃ ᵊr
  harshest 'hɑːʃ ɪst -əst ‖ 'hɑːrʃ- **harshly**
  'hɑːʃ li ‖ 'hɑːrʃ- **harshness** 'hɑːʃ nəs -nɪs
  ‖ 'hɑːrʃ-
hart, Hart hɑːt ‖ hɑːrt **harts** hɑːts ‖ hɑːrts
hartal 'hɑːt hɜː-; 'hɑːt ɑːl ‖ hɑːr- ~s z
Harte hɑːt ‖ hɑːrt
hartebeest 'hɑːt ɪ biːst -ə-, -bɪəst ‖ 'hɑːrt̬ ə-
  'hɑːrt biːst ~s s
Hartfield 'hɑːt fiːᵊld ‖ 'hɑːrt-
Hartford 'hɑːt fəd ‖ 'hɑːrt fᵊrd
Hartland 'hɑːt lənd ‖ 'hɑːrt-
Hartlepool 'hɑːt lɪ puːl -lə- ‖ 'hɑːrt-
Hartley 'hɑːt li ‖ 'hɑːrt-
Hartnell 'hɑːt nəl ‖ 'hɑːrt-
Hartree, h~ 'hɑː triː ‖ 'hɑːr- ~s z
hartshorn, H~, Hartshorne
  'hɑːts hɔːn ‖ 'hɑːrts hɔːrn
hart's-tongue 'hɑːts tʌŋ §-tɒŋ ‖ 'hɑːrts- ~s z
harum-scarum
  ˌheər əm 'skeər əm ‖ ˌher əm 'sker əm
  ˌhær əm 'skær əm
Harun al-Rashid hæ ˌruːn æl ræ 'ʃiːd hɑː-
  ‖ hɑː ˌruːn ɑːl rɑː 'ʃiːd
haruspex hə 'rʌsp eks hæ-; 'hær ə speks
Harvard 'hɑːv əd ‖ 'hɑːrv ᵊrd
harvest 'hɑːv ɪst -əst ‖ 'hɑːrv- ~ed ɪd əd
  ~er/s ə/z ‖ ᵊr/z ~ing ɪŋ ~s s
  ˌharvest 'festival; ˌharvest 'home; 'harvest
  mite; ˌharvest 'moon; 'harvest mouse
harvest|man 'hɑːv ɪst |mən -əst-, -mæn
  ‖ 'hɑːrv- ~men mən men
Harvey, Harvie 'hɑːv i ‖ 'hɑːrv i
Harwell 'hɑː wəl -wel ‖ 'hɑːr-
Harwich 'hær ɪdʒ -ɪtʃ ‖ 'her-
Harwood 'hɑː wʊd ‖ 'hɑːr-
Haryana ˌhær i 'ɑːn ə ˌhʌr- ‖ ˌhɑːr- —*Hindi*
  [hər 'jɑː nə]
Harz hɑːts ‖ hɑːrts —*Ger* [haːʁts]
has *strong form* hæz, *weak forms* həz, əz, z, s
  —*Of the weak forms,* əz *is not used clause-*

initially, and s, z *are used in that position only in very fast speech; in other environments* həz, əz *are more formal than the contracted forms* s, z. *The most usual weak forms are* əz *after a word ending in* s, z, ʃ, ʒ, tʃ, dʒ; s *after one ending in* p, t, k, f, θ; *and* z *otherwise. The latter two are sometimes shown in writing as the contraction* 's. *See note at* have *concerning the choice between strong and weak form.*

has-been 'hæz biːn -bɪn ‖ -bɪn ~**s** z
Hasdrubal 'hæz drʊb əl -druːb-; -dru bæl
Haseldine 'heɪz əl daɪn
hash hæʃ **hashed** hæʃt **hashes** 'hæʃ ɪz -əz **hashing** 'hæʃ ɪŋ
　,hash 'browns; 'hash mark
Hashemite 'hæʃ ɪ maɪt -ə- ~**s** s
Hashimoto ,hæʃ i 'məʊt əʊ ‖ -'moʊt oʊ
hashish 'hæʃ ɪʃ -iːʃ; hæ 'ʃiːʃ
Hasidic hæ 'sɪd ɪk haː-
Hasidism hæ 'sɪd ,ɪz əm
Haslam 'hæz ləm
Haslemere 'heɪz əl mɪə ‖ -mɪr
haslet 'heɪz lət 'hæz-, -lɪt
Haslett (i) 'heɪz lət -lɪt, (ii) 'hæz-
Haslingden 'hæz lɪŋ dən
hasn't 'hæz ənt
hasp haːsp hæsp ‖ hæsp **hasped** haːspt hæspt ‖ hæspt **hasping** 'haːsp ɪŋ 'hæsp- ‖ 'hæsp ɪŋ **hasps** haːsps hæsps ‖ hæsps
Hassan hə 'saːn hæ-; 'hæs ən ‖ 'haːs aːn
Hasselblad tdmk 'hæs əl blæd ‖ 'haːs əl blaːd
hassle 'hæs əl ~**ed** d ~**es** z ~**ing** ɪŋ
hassock 'hæs ək ~**s** s
hast strong form hæst, weak forms həst, əst, st
hasta la vista ,æst ə lə 'vɪst ə -læ' • -, -laː' • - ‖ ,aːst ə lə 'viːst ə —Sp [,as ta la 'βis ta]
hasta mañana ,æst ə mə 'njaːn ə -mæ' • - ‖ ,aːst ə maː- —Sp [,as ta ma 'ɲa na]
haste heɪst
hasten 'heɪs ən ~**ed** d ~**ing** ɪŋ ~**s** z
hasti... —see **hasty**
Hastings 'heɪst ɪŋz
hast|y 'heɪst |i ~**ier** i‿ə ‖ i‿ər ~**iest** i‿ɪst i‿əst ~**ily** ɪ li əl i ~**iness** i nəs i nɪs
hat hæt **hats** hæts **hatted** 'hæt ɪd -əd ‖ 'hæt̬ əd **hatting** 'hæt ɪŋ ‖ 'hæt̬ ɪŋ
　'hat trick
hatband 'hæt bænd ~**s** z
hatbox 'hæt bɒks ‖ -baːks
hatch, Hatch hætʃ **hatched** hætʃt **hatches** 'hætʃ ɪz -əz **hatching** 'hætʃ ɪŋ
hatchback 'hætʃ bæk ~**s** s
Hatcher 'hætʃ ə ‖ -ər
hatcher|y 'hætʃ ər |i ~**ies** iz
hatchet 'hætʃ ɪt §-ət ~**s** s
　'hatchet job; 'hatchet man
hatchet-faced ,hætʃ ɪt 'feɪst ◂ §-ət-, ' • • •
hatchling 'hætʃ lɪŋ ~**s** z
hatchment 'hætʃ mənt ~**s** s
hatchway 'hætʃ weɪ ~**s** z
hate heɪt **hated** 'heɪt ɪd -əd ‖ 'heɪt̬ əd **hates** heɪts **hating** 'heɪt ɪŋ ‖ 'heɪt̬ ɪŋ
hateful 'heɪt fəl -fʊl ~**ly** i ~**ness** nəs nɪs

hater 'heɪt ə ‖ 'heɪt̬ ər ~**s** z
Hatfield 'hæt fiːəld
hath strong form hæθ, weak forms həθ, əθ
hatha 'hæθ ə 'hʌt- —Hindi [hə t̪ʰə]
Hathaway 'hæθ ə weɪ
Hatherleigh 'hæð ə li -liː ‖ -ər-
Hatherley 'hæð ə li ‖ -ər-
Hathern 'hæð ən ‖ -ərn
Hathersage 'hæð ə seɪdʒ -sɪdʒ, -sedʒ ‖ -ər-
Hathor 'hæθ ɔː ‖ -ɔːr
hatpin 'hæt pɪn ~**s** z
hatred 'heɪt rɪd -rəd ~**s** z
Hatshepsut hæt 'ʃep suːt
hatter 'hæt ə ‖ 'hæt̬ ər ~**s** z
Hatteras 'hæt ər əs ‖ 'hæt̬-
Hattersley 'hæt əz li ‖ 'hæt̬ ərz-
Hattie 'hæt i ‖ 'hæt̬ i
Hatton 'hæt ən
hauberk 'hɔː bɜːk ‖ -bɝːk 'haː- ~**s** s
Haugh (i) hɔː ‖ haː, (ii) hɔːf ‖ haːf, (iii) haːx
Haughey 'hɔː hi 'hɒ- ‖ 'hɔːk i 'haːk-
haughti... —see **haughty**
Haughton 'hɔːt ən ‖ 'haːt-
haught|y 'hɔːt li ‖ 'hɔːt̬ li 'haːt̬- ~**ier** i‿ə ‖ i‿ər ~**iest** i‿ɪst i‿əst ~**ily** ɪ li əl i ~**iness** i nəs i nɪs
haul hɔːl ‖ haːl **hauled** hɔːld ‖ haːld **hauling** 'hɔːl ɪŋ ‖ 'haːl- **hauls** hɔːlz ‖ haːlz
haulage 'hɔːl ɪdʒ ‖ 'haːl-
　'haulage con,tractor
haulier 'hɔːl i‿ə ‖ -ər 'haːl- ~**s** z
haulm hɔːm ‖ haːm **haulms** hɔːmz ‖ haːmz
haunch hɔːntʃ ‖ haːntʃ **haunches** 'hɔːntʃ ɪz -əz ‖ 'haːntʃ-
haunt hɔːnt ‖ haːnt **haunted** 'hɔːnt ɪd -əd ‖ 'hɔːnt̬ əd 'haːnt̬- **haunting/ly** 'hɔːnt ɪŋ /li ‖ 'hɔːnt̬ ɪŋ /li 'haːnt̬- **haunts** hɔːnts ‖ haːnts
Hausa 'haʊs ə 'haʊz ə
hausfrau, H~ 'haʊs fraʊ —Ger ['haʊs fʀaʊ] ~**en** ən ~**s** z
haut|bois sing. 'əʊ |bɔɪ 'həʊ-, 'hɔːt- ‖ 'hoʊ- 'oʊ- ~**bois** pl bɔɪz ~**boy** bɔɪ ~**boys** bɔɪz
haute əʊt ‖ oʊt —Fr [oːt]
　,haute cou'ture; ,haute cui'sine
hauteur əʊ 'tɜː ‖ hoʊ 'tɝː hɔː-, haː- —Fr [o tœːʀ]
Havana hə 'væn ə -'vaːn ə —Sp Habana [a 'βa na]
Havant 'hæv ənt
have strong form hæv, weak forms həv, əv, v
　—The weak form v is used only after a vowel (when it is often written as the contraction 've), or in very fast speech at the beginning of a sentence; əv is not used at the beginning of a sentence. Weak forms of have, has, had are used only when the word functions as the perfective auxiliary, or is the equivalent of have got and is used with an object that is not a pronoun, or in the constructions had better/best/rather. **had** hæd (see) **hadn't** 'hæd ənt **has** hæz (see) **hasn't** 'hæz ənt **haven't** 'hæv ənt **haves** hævz **having** 'hæv ɪŋ
Havel 'haːv əl —Czech ['ha vel]

H

Havelock, h~ 'hæv lɒk ‖ -lɑːk
haven 'heɪv ᵊn ~s z
have-not 'hæv nɒt ˌ•'• ‖ -nɑːt —*contrastively*
always ˌ•'• ~s s
haven't 'hæv ᵊnt
haver 'heɪv ə ‖ -ᵊr ~ed d havering 'heɪv ər_ɪŋ
~s z
Haverfordwest ˌhæv ə fəd 'west
ˌhɑː fəd 'west ‖ ˌhæv ᵊr fᵊrd-
Havergal 'hæv əg ᵊl ‖ -ᵊrg-
Haverhill 'heɪv ər_ɪl -ᵊr_əl, 'heɪv ə hɪl
Havering 'heɪv ər_ɪŋ
Havers 'heɪv əz ‖ -ᵊrz
haversack 'hæv ə sæk ‖ -ᵊr- ~s s
Haversian, h~ hə 'vɜːʃ ᵊn hæ-, -'vɜːʒ-
‖ -'vɜˑʒ ᵊn
haversine 'hæv ə saɪn ‖ -ᵊr- ~s z
Haverstock 'hæv ə stɒk ‖ -ᵊr stɑːk
haves hævz
Haviland 'hæv ɪ lənd -ə-
Havisham 'hæv ɪʃ əm -əʃ-
havoc 'hæv ək
Havre *place in France* 'ɑːv rə —*Fr* Le Havre
[lə aːvʁ]
Havre *place in MT* 'hæv ə ‖ -ᵊr
Havre de Grace *place in MD* ˌhæv ə də 'græs
-'greɪs ‖ ˌ•ᵊr-
haw, Haw hɔː ‖ hɑː hawed hɔːd ‖ hɑːd
hawing 'hɔːʳ ɪŋ ‖ 'hɔː ɪŋ 'hɑː- haws hɔːz
‖ hɑːz
Hawaii hə 'waɪ i hɑː-, -iː ‖ -'wɑː- —*sometimes*
with ʔ *between the last two syllables*
Hawaiian hə 'waɪ_ən -'waɪ i_ən ‖ -'wɑː jən ~s
z
Hawarden (i) 'hɑːd ᵊn ‖ 'hɑːrd ᵊn ; (ii)
'heɪ ˌwɔːd ᵊn ‖ -ˌwɔːrd- —*The place in Clwyd*
is (i); Viscount H~ *and the place in Iowa are*
(ii)
Hawes hɔːz ‖ hɑːz
hawfinch 'hɔː fɪntʃ ‖ 'hɑː- ~es ɪz əz
haw-haw, H~ 'hɔː hɔː ‖ 'hɑː hɑː
Hawick 'hɔː ɪk hɔɪk ‖ 'hɑː-
hawk hɔːk ‖ hɑːk hawked hɔːkt ‖ hɑːkt
hawking 'hɔːk ɪŋ ‖ 'hɑːk- hawks hɔːks
‖ hɑːks
'hawk moth
hawkbit 'hɔːk bɪt ‖ 'hɑːk- ~s s
Hawke hɔːk ‖ hɑːk
hawker 'hɔːk ə ‖ -ᵊr 'hɑːk- ~s z
Hawker-Siddeley *tdmk* ˌhɔːk ə 'sɪd ᵊl_i ‖ -ᵊr-
ˌhɑːk-
Hawkes hɔːks ‖ hɑːks
hawk-eye 'hɔːk aɪ ‖ 'hɑːk- ~d d
Hawking 'hɔːk ɪŋ ‖ 'hɑːk-
Hawkinge 'hɔːk ɪndʒ ‖ 'hɑːk-
Hawkins 'hɔːk ɪnz ‖ 'hɑːk-
hawkish 'hɔːk ɪʃ ‖ 'hɑːk- ~ness nəs nɪs
Hawks hɔːks ‖ hɑːks
hawk's-beard 'hɔːks bɪəd ‖ -bɪrd 'hɑːks- ~s z
hawksbill 'hɔːks bɪl ‖ 'hɑːks- ~s z
Hawksmoor 'hɔːks mʊə -mɔː ‖ -mʊr 'hɑːks-
hawkweed 'hɔːk wiːd ‖ 'hɑːk- ~s z
Hawley 'hɔːl i ‖ 'hɑːl i

Hawn hɔːn ‖ hɑːn
Haworth 'haʊ_əθ 'hɔː- ‖ 'hɔː wᵊrθ 'hɑː-
hawse, Hawse hɔːz ‖ hɑːz hawses 'hɔːz ɪz
-əz ‖ 'hɑːz-
hawser 'hɔːz ə ‖ -ᵊr 'hɑːz- ~s z
hawthorn, H~, Hawthorne 'hɔː θɔːn ‖ -θɔːrn
'hɑː- ~s z
Hawthornden 'hɔː θɔːn dən ‖ -θɔːrn- 'hɑː-
Hawthorne 'hɔː θɔːn ‖ -θɔːrn 'hɑː-
Hawtrey 'hɔːtr i ‖ 'hɑːtr i
Haxey 'hæks i
hay, Hay heɪ hayed heɪd haying 'heɪ ɪŋ
hays heɪz
'hay ˌfever, ˌ• '• •
Hayakawa ˌhaɪ ə 'kɑː wə ‖ ˌhɑː jə-
haycock, H~ 'heɪ kɒk ‖ -kɑːk ~s s
Hayden 'heɪd ᵊn
Haydn *Austrian composer* 'haɪd ᵊn —*Ger*
['haɪ dᵊn] ~'s z
Haydn *English or Welsh name* 'heɪd ᵊn
Haydock 'heɪ dɒk ‖ -dɑːk
Haydon 'heɪd ᵊn
Hayek 'haɪ ek 'hɑː jek
Hayes heɪz
hayfork 'heɪ fɔːk ‖ -fɔːrk ~s s
Hayle heɪᵊl
Hayley 'heɪl i
Hayling 'heɪl ɪŋ
hayloft 'heɪ lɒft -lɔːft ‖ -lɔːft -lɑːft ~s s
haymak|er/s 'heɪ ˌmeɪk |ə/z ‖ -|ᵊr/z ~ing ɪŋ
Hayman 'heɪ mən
Haymarket 'heɪ ˌmɑːk ɪt §-ət ‖ -ˌmɑːrk-
Haynes heɪnz
hayrick 'heɪ rɪk ~s s
Hays heɪz
hayseed 'heɪ siːd ~s z
haystack 'heɪ stæk ~s s
Hayter 'heɪt ə ‖ 'heɪt̬ ᵊr
Hayward 'heɪ wəd ‖ -wᵊrd
haywire 'heɪ ˌwaɪ_ə ‖ -ˌwaɪ_ᵊr
Haywood 'heɪ wʊd
Hayworth 'heɪ wəθ -wɜːθ ‖ -wᵊrθ
Hazan hə 'zæn
hazard 'hæz əd ‖ -ᵊrd ~ed ɪd əd ~ing ɪŋ ~s z
hazardous 'hæz əd əs ‖ -ᵊrd- ~ly li ~ness nəs
nɪs
Hazchem 'hæz kem
haze heɪz hazed heɪzd hazes 'heɪz ɪz -əz
hazing 'heɪz ɪŋ
hazel, Hazel, Hazell 'heɪz ᵊl ~s z
hazelnut 'heɪz ᵊl nʌt ~s s
hazi... —*see* hazy
Hazlerigg 'heɪz ᵊl rɪg
Hazlett, Hazlitt 'hæz lɪt 'heɪz-, -lət
haz|y 'heɪz |i ~ier_ə ‖ i_ᵊr ~iest i_ɪst i_əst
~ily ɪ li ᵊl i ~iness i nəs i nɪs
Hazzard 'hæz əd ‖ -ᵊrd
H-bomb 'eɪtʃ bɒm ‖ -bɑːm ~s z
he *pronoun strong form* hiː; *weak forms* hi, i
—*The form* i *is not used at the beginning of a*
sentence or clause.
he *n* hiː
he- 'hiː — he-goat 'hiː gəʊt ‖ -goʊt

Heacham 'hetʃ əm 'hi:tʃ-
head, Head hed headed 'hed ɪd -əd heading
  'hed ɪŋ heads hedz
  ˌhead ' start; ˌhead ' waiter
headache 'hed eɪk ~s s
headachy 'hed eɪk i
headband 'hed bænd →'heb- ~s z
headbang|er/s 'hed ˌbæŋ| ə/z →'heb- ‖ -ᵊr/z
  ~ing ɪŋ
headboard hed bɔːd →'heb- ‖ -bɔːrd -boʊrd
  ~s z
headcheese 'hed tʃiːz
headdress 'hed dres ~es ɪz əz
-headed 'hed ɪd -əd — bullet-headed
  ˌbʊl ɪt 'hed ɪd ◄ -ət-, -əd
header 'hed ə ‖ -ᵊr ~s z
headfirst ˌhed 'fɜːst ◄ ‖ -'fɜ·ːst ◄
headgear 'hed gɪə →'heg- ‖ -gɪr
head|hunt 'hed |hʌnt ~hunted hʌnt ɪd -əd
  ‖ hʌnt̬ əd ~hunting hʌnt ɪŋ ‖ hʌnt̬ ɪŋ
  ~hunts hʌnts
headhunter 'hed ˌhʌnt ə ‖ -ˌhʌnt̬ ᵊr
headi... —see heady
heading 'hed ɪŋ ~s z
Headingley 'hed ɪŋ li
Headlam 'hed ləm
headlamp 'hed læmp ~s s
headland 'hed lənd -lænd ~s z
headless 'hed ləs -lɪs
Headley 'hed li
headlight 'hed laɪt ~s s
headlin|e 'hed laɪn ~ed d ~es z ~ing ɪŋ
headlock 'hed lɒk ‖ -laːk
headlong 'hed lɒŋ ˌ•'• ‖ -lɔːŋ -laːŋ
head|man 'hed |mən →'heb-, -mæn ~men
  mən men
headmaster ˌhed 'maːst ə ◄ →ˌheb-, §-'mæst-,
  '•ˌ•• ‖ -'mæst ᵊr ◄ ~s z
headmistress ˌhed 'mɪs trəs ◄ →ˌheb-, -trɪs,
  '•ˌ•• ~es ɪz əz
head-on ˌhed 'ɒn ◄ ‖ -'aːn ◄ -'ɔːn
headphone 'hed fəʊn ‖ -foʊn ~s z
headpiec|e 'hed piːs →'heb- ~es ɪz əz
headquarter ˌhed 'kwɔːt ə ◄ →ˌheg-, '•ˌ••
  ‖ 'hed ˌkwɔːrt̬ ᵊr -ˌkwɔːt̬- ~ed d ~s z
headrest 'hed rest ~s s
headroom 'hed ruːm -rʊm
head|scarf 'hed |skaːf ‖ -|skaːrf ~scarves
  skaːvz ‖ skaːrvz
headset 'hed set ~s s
headship 'hed ʃɪp ~s s
headshrinker 'hed ˌʃrɪŋk ə ‖ -ᵊr ~s z
headstall 'hed stɔːl ‖ -staːl ~s z
headstand 'hed stænd ~s z
headstone, H~ 'hed stəʊn ‖ -stoʊn ~s z
headstrong 'hed strɒŋ ‖ -strɔːŋ -straːŋ
head-up adj, adv ˌhed 'ʌp ◄
headwaters 'hed ˌwɔːt əz ‖ -ˌwɔːt̬ ᵊrz -ˌwaːt̬-
headway 'hed weɪ
headwind 'hed wɪnd ~s z
headword 'hed wɜːd ‖ -wɜ·ːd ~s z
head|y 'hed li ~ier i ə ‖ i ᵊr ~iest i ɪst i əst
  ~ily ɪ li əl i ~iness i nəs i nɪs

heal, Heal hiːᵊl healed hiːᵊld healing 'hiːᵊl ɪŋ
  heals, Heal's hiːᵊlz
Healaugh 'hiːl ə
Healdsburg 'hiːᵊldz bɜːg ‖ -bɜ·ːg
healer 'hiːᵊl ə ‖ -ᵊr ~s z
Healey 'hiːl i
health helθ
  ' health ˌcare; ' health ˌcentre; ' health farm;
  ' health food; ˌhealth ' maintenance
  ˌorganiˈzation; ' health ˌvisitor
healthful 'helθ fᵊl -fʊl ~ly i ~ness nəs nɪs
health|y 'helθ li ~ier i ə ‖ i ᵊr ~iest i ɪst i əst
  ~ily ɪ li əl i ~iness i nəs i nɪs
Healy 'hiːl i
Heaney 'hiːn i
Heanor 'hiːn ə 'heɪn ə ‖ -ᵊr
heap hiːp heaped hiːpt heaping 'hiːp ɪŋ
  heaps hiːps
hear hɪə ‖ hɪᵊr (= here) heard hɜːd ‖ hɜ·ːd (!)
  hearing 'hɪər ɪŋ ‖ 'hɪr ɪŋ hears hɪəz ‖ hɪᵊrz
heard, Heard hɜːd ‖ hɜ·ːd (= herd)
hearer 'hɪər ə ‖ 'hɪr ᵊr ~s z
hearing 'hɪər ɪŋ ‖ 'hɪr ɪŋ ~s z
  ' hearing aid
hearken 'haːk ən ‖ 'haːrk ᵊn ~ed d ~ing ɪŋ
  ~s z
Hearn, Hearne hɜːn ‖ hɜ·ːn
hearsay 'hɪə seɪ ˌ•'• ‖ 'hɪr-
hearse hɜːs ‖ hɜ·ːs hearses 'hɜːs ɪz -əz
  ‖ 'hɜ·ːs əz
Hearst hɜːst ‖ hɜ·ːst
heart haːt ‖ haːrt (= hart) hearted 'haːt ɪd
  -əd ‖ 'haːrt̬ əd hearting 'haːt ɪŋ ‖ 'haːrt̬ ɪŋ
  hearts haːts ‖ haːrts
  ' heart atˌtack; ' heart diˌsease; ' heart
  ˌfailure
heartache 'haːt eɪk ‖ 'haːrt̬- ~s s
heartbeat 'haːt biːt ‖ 'haːrt- ~s s
heartbreak 'haːt breɪk ‖ 'haːrt- ~s s
heartbreaking 'haːt ˌbreɪk ɪŋ ‖ 'haːrt- ~ly li
heartbroken 'haːt ˌbrəʊk ən ‖ 'haːrt ˌbroʊk ən
  ~ly li ~ness nəs nɪs
heartburn 'haːt bɜːn ‖ 'haːrt bɜ·ːn
-hearted 'haːt ɪd ◄ -əd ‖ 'haːrt̬ əd — tenderhearted ˌtend ə 'haːt ɪd ◄ -əd
  ‖ -ᵊr 'haːrt̬ əd ◄
hearten 'haːt ən ‖ 'haːrt ᵊn ~ed d ~ing/ly
  ˌɪŋ /li ~s z
heartfelt 'haːt felt ‖ 'haːrt-
hearth haːθ ‖ haːrθ hearths haːθs haːðz
  ‖ haːrθs
hearthrug 'haːθ rʌg ‖ 'haːrθ- ~s z
hearti... —see hearty
heartland 'haːt lænd ‖ 'haːrt- ~s z
heartless 'haːt ləs -lɪs ~ly li ~ness nəs nɪs
heartrending 'haːt ˌrend ɪŋ ‖ 'haːrt- ~ly li
heart-searching
  'haːt ˌsɜːtʃ ɪŋ ‖ 'haːrt ˌsɜ·ːtʃ ɪŋ ~s z
heartsease 'haːts iːz ‖ 'haːrts-
heart-shaped 'haːt ʃeɪpt ‖ 'haːrt-
heartsick 'haːt sɪk ‖ 'haːrt- ~ness nəs nɪs
heartstrings 'haːt strɪŋz ‖ 'haːrt-
heartthrob 'haːt θrɒb ‖ 'haːrt θraːb ~s z

H

heart-to-heart ˌhɑːt tə 'hɑːt ◄ -tu-
‖ ˌhɑːrt tə 'hɑːrt ◄
ˌheart-to-heart 'chat
heartwarming
'hɑːt ˌwɔːm ɪŋ ‖ 'hɑːrt ˌwɔːrm ɪŋ ~**ly** li
heartwood 'hɑːt wʊd ‖ 'hɑːrt-
heart|y 'hɑːt |i ‖ 'hɑːrt̬ |i ~**ier** i‿ə ‖ i‿ər ~**iest**
i‿ɪst i‿əst ~**ily** ɪ li əl i ~**iness** i nəs i nɪs
heat hiːt **heated/ly** 'hiːt ɪd /li -əd /li
‖ 'hiːt̬ əd /li **heating** 'hiːt ɪŋ ‖ 'hiːt̬ ɪŋ **heats**
hiːts
'heat ex,changer; 'heat ex,haustion; 'heat
pump; 'heat rash; 'heat shield; 'heat wave
heater 'hiːt ə ‖ 'hiːt̬ ər ~**s** z
heath, Heath hiːθ **heaths** hiːθs
ˌHeath 'Robinson
Heathcliff, Heathcliffe 'hiːθ klɪf
Heathcoat, Heathcote (i) 'heθ kət, (ii) 'hiːθ-
heathen 'hiːð ən ~**dom** dəm ~**ish** ɪʃ ~**ism** ˌɪz
əm
heather, H~ 'heð ə ‖ -ər —*but the place in Leics
is* 'hiːð- ~**s** z
heather-mixture 'heð ə ˌmɪks tʃə ˌ•‿•'•‿•
‖ -ər ˌmɪks tʃər
heathery 'heð ər i
Heathfield 'hiːθ fiːld
Heathrow ˌhiːθ 'rəʊ ◄ '•‿• ‖ 'hiːθ roʊ
ˌHeathrow 'Airport
Heaton 'hiːt ən
heat-seeking 'hiːt ˌsiːk ɪŋ
heatstroke 'hiːt strəʊk ‖ -stroʊk
heave hiːv **heaved** hiːvd **heaves** hiːvz
heaving 'hiːv ɪŋ **hove** həʊv ‖ hoʊv
heave-ho ˌhiːv 'həʊ ‖ -'hoʊ
heaven, H~ 'hev ən ~**s** z
heavenly 'hev ən li
heaven-sent ˌhev ən 'sent ◄ '•‿•‿•
heavenward 'hev ən wəd ‖ -wərd ~**s** z
heavi... —*see* **heavy**
Heaviside 'hev i saɪd
heav|y 'hev |i ~**ier** i‿ə ‖ i‿ər ~**iest** i‿ɪst i‿əst
~**ily** ɪ li əl i ~**iness** i nəs i nɪs
ˌheavy 'hydrogen; ˌheavy 'industry; ˌheavy
'metal; ˌheavy 'petting; ˌheavy 'water
heavy-duty ˌhev i 'djuːt i ◄ →§-'dʒuːt i
‖ -'duːt̬ i -'djuːt̬ i ◄
heavy-handed ˌhev i 'hænd ɪd ◄ -əd ~**ly** li
~**ness** nəs nɪs
heavy-hearted ˌhev i 'hɑːt ɪd ◄ -əd
‖ -'hɑːrt̬ əd ◄
heavy-laden ˌhev i 'leɪd ən ◄
heavy-set ˌhev i 'set ◄
heavyweight 'hev i weɪt ~**s** s
Hebburn 'heb ɜːn -ən ‖ -ərn
Hebden 'heb dən
hebdomadal heb 'dɒm əd əl ‖ -'dɑːm- ~**ly** i
Hebe 'hiːb i
Hebei ˌhɜː 'beɪ ‖ -hʌ- —*Chi* Héběi [²xx ³pei]
hebephrenia ˌhiːb ɪ 'friːn i‿ə ˌheb-, ˌ•ə-
Heber 'hiːb ə ‖ -ər
Hebraic hɪ 'breɪ ɪk hə-, hiː-
Hebraist 'hiːb reɪ ɪst -ri-, §-əst ~**s** s
Hebrew 'hiːb ruː ~**s** z

Hebridean ˌheb rə 'diː‿ən ◄ -rɪ- ~**s** z
Hebrides 'heb rə diːz -rɪ-
Hebron 'heb rɒn 'hiːb-, -rən ‖ -rən
Hecate 'hek ət i ‖ -ət̬ i —*in Shakespeare also*
'hek ət
hecatomb 'hek ə tuːm -təʊm ‖ -toʊm ~**s** z
Hecht hekt
heck, Heck hek
heckelphone 'hek əl fəʊn ‖ -foʊn ~**s** z
heckl|e 'hek əl ~**ed** d ~**er/s** ‿ə/z ‖ ‿ər/z ~**es** z
~**ing** ‿ɪŋ
Heckmondwike 'hek mənd waɪk
hectare 'hekt eə -ə, -ɑː: ‖ -er -ær ~**s** z
hectic 'hekt ɪk ~**ally** əl‿i
hecto- ˌhekt ə -əʊ — **hectogram**
'hekt ə græm
hectograph 'hekt ə grɑːf -əʊ-, -græf ‖ -græf
~**s** s
hector, H~ 'hekt ə ‖ -ər ~**ed** d **hectoring**
'hekt ər ɪŋ ~**s** z
Hecuba 'hek jʊb ə
he'd *strong form* hiːd, *weak forms* hɪd, ɪd —*The
weak form* ɪd *is not used at the beginning of a
sentence or clause.*
heddle, H~ 'hed əl ~**s** z
Hedex *tdmk* 'hed eks
hedge hedʒ **hedged** hedʒd **hedges** 'hedʒ ɪz
-əz **hedging** 'hedʒ ɪŋ
'hedge ˌsparrow
hedgehog 'hedʒ hɒg -ɒg ‖ -hɔːg -hɑːg ~**s** z
hedgehop 'hedʒ hɒp ‖ -hɑːp ~**ped** t ~**per/s**
ə/z ‖ ər/z ~**ping** ɪŋ ~**s** s
Hedgerley 'hedʒ ə li ‖ -ər-
hedgerow 'hedʒ rəʊ ‖ -roʊ ~**s** z
Hedges 'hedʒ ɪz -əz
Hedley 'hed li
hedonic hiː 'dɒn ɪk hɪ- ‖ -'dɑːn ɪk ~**s** s
hedonism 'hiːd ən ˌɪz əm 'hed-
hedonist 'hiːd ən ɪst 'hed-, §-əst ~**s** s
hedonistic ˌhiːd ə 'nɪst ɪk ◄ ˌhed-, -ən 'ɪst-
~**ally** əl‿i
Hedy 'hed i
heebie-jeebies ˌhiːb i 'dʒiːb iz
heed hiːd **heeded** 'hiːd ɪd -əd **heeding**
'hiːd ɪŋ **heeds** hiːdz
heedful 'hiːd fəl -fʊl ~**ly** i ~**ness** nəs nɪs
heedless 'hiːd ləs -lɪs ~**ly** li ~**ness** nəs nɪs
hee-haw 'hiː hɔː ˌ•'• ‖ -hɑː ~**s** z
heel hiː‿əl **heeled** hiː‿əld **heeling** 'hiː‿əl ɪŋ
heels hiː‿əlz
heelball 'hiː‿əl bɔːl ‖ -bɑːl ~**s** z
heelbar 'hiː‿əl bɑː ‖ -bɑːr ~**s** z
Heenan 'hiːn ən
Heep hiːp
HEFCE 'hef si -ki, -kə
Heffer 'hef ə ‖ -ər
Hefner 'hef nə ‖ -nər
heft heft **hefted** 'heft ɪd -əd **hefting** 'heft ɪŋ
hefts hefts
heft|y 'heft |i ~**ier** i‿ə ‖ i‿ər ~**iest** i‿ɪst i‿əst
~**ily** ɪ li əl i ~**iness** i nəs i nɪs
Hegarty 'heg ət i ‖ -ərt̬ i
Hegel 'heɪg əl —*Ger* ['heː gəl]

Hegelian hɪ 'geɪl i‿ən heɪ-, -'giːl- ~**s** z
hegemonic ˌheg ə 'mɒn ɪk ◄ ˌhiːg-, ˌhedʒ-, -ɪ-
‖ -'mɑːn ɪk ◄
hegemon|y hɪ 'gem ən |i hiː-, -'dʒem-;
'heg ɪm-, 'hedʒ-, '•əm- ‖ hə 'dʒem ən |i hɪ-,
-'gem-; 'hedʒ ə moʊn |i ~**ies** iz
hegira, H~ 'hedʒ ɪr ə -ər-; hɪ 'dʒaɪər ə, he- ~**s**
z
Heidegger 'haɪd eg ə -ɪg- ‖ -ər —*Ger*
['hai dɛg ɐ]
Heidelberg 'haɪd əl bɜːg ‖ -bɝːg —*Ger*
['hai dəl bɛʁk]
Heidi 'haɪd i
heifer 'hef ə ‖ -ər ~**s** z
heigh-ho ˌheɪ 'həʊ '•• ‖ -'hoʊ —*Usually said
with a low-rise nuclear tone.*
height haɪt △haɪtθ **heights** haɪts △haɪtθs
heighten 'haɪt ən ~**ed** d ~**ing** ˌɪŋ ~**s** z
Heighway (i) 'haɪ weɪ, (ii) 'heɪ-
Heilbron, Heilbronn 'haɪəl brɒn ‖ -brɑːn
—*Ger* ['hail bʁɔn]
Heilongjiang ˌheɪ lɒŋ 'dʒæŋ -lʊŋ-, -dʒi 'æŋ
‖ -lʊŋ dʒi 'ɑːŋ —*Chi* Hēilóngjiāng
[¹xei ²lʊŋ ¹tɕjaŋ]
Heimlich 'haɪm lɪk -lɪx —*Ger* ['haɪm lɪç]
'**Heimlich ma**ˌ**noeuvre/ma**ˌ**neuver**
Heine 'haɪn ə —*Ger* ['hai nə]
Heineken *tdmk* 'haɪn ɪk ən -ək-
Heinemann 'haɪn ə mən
Heiney 'haɪn i
Heinkel 'haɪŋk əl
Heinlein 'haɪn laɪn
heinous 'heɪn əs §'hiːn-, △'•i‿əs ~**ly** li ~**ness**
nəs nɪs
Heinz *tdmk* haɪnz haɪnts
heir eə ‖ eər æər (= *air*) **heirs** eəz ‖ eərz æərz
ˌheir ap'parent; ˌheir pre'sumptive
heiress 'eər es -ɪs, -əs; ˌeər 'es ‖ 'er əs 'ær-
~**es** ɪz əz
heirless 'eə ləs -lɪs ‖ 'er- 'ær- ~**ness** nəs nɪs
heirloom 'eə luːm ‖ 'er- 'ær- ~**s** z
heirship 'eə ʃɪp ‖ 'er- 'ær- (= *airship*) ~**s** s
Heisenberg 'haɪz ən bɜːg ‖ -bɝːg —*Ger*
['hai zən bɛʁk]
heist haɪst **heisted** 'haɪst ɪd -əd **heisting**
'haɪst ɪŋ **heists** haɪsts
hejira, H~ 'hedʒ ɪr ə -ər-; hɪ 'dʒaɪər ə, he- ~**s** z
Hekla 'hek lə —*Icelandic* ['hɛhk la]
held held
Helen 'hel ən -ɪn
Helena (i) 'hel ən ə -ɪn-, (ii) hə 'liːn ə hɪ- —*The
place in Montana is* (i); *the personal name was
formerly* (ii) *but is now usually* (i). *See also St
H~.*
Helene he 'leɪn hə-, hɪ- ‖ -'liːn (*)
helenium hə 'liːn i‿əm hɪ-
Helensburgh 'hel ənz bər‿ə '•ɪnz-, §-ˌbʌr ə
‖ 'hel ənz bɝːg
Helfgott 'helf gɒt ‖ -gɑːt
Helga 'helg ə
helianthus ˌhiːl i 'æntθ əs ˌhel- ~**es** ɪz əz
helical 'hel ɪk əl 'hiːl- ~**ly** ˌi
helices 'hel ɪ siːz 'hiːl-, -ə-

helicoid 'hel ɪ kɔɪd -ə- ~**s** z
Helicon, h~ 'hel ɪk ən -ək-; -ɪ kɒn, -ə-
‖ -ə kɑːn -ɪk ən ~**s** z
helicopter 'hel ɪ kɒpt ə '•ə-, '•i-; ˌ•'••
‖ -ə kɑːpt ər 'hiːl- ~**s** z
helideck 'hel i dek ~**s** s
Helier 'hel i‿ə ‖ -ər
Heligoland 'hel ɪ gəʊ lænd '•ə-, -ɪg ə- ‖ -goʊ-
helio- *comb. form*
with stress-neutral suffix ˌhiːl i əʊ ‖ -oʊ —
heliocentric ˌhiːl i əʊ 'sentr ɪk ◄ ‖ -i oʊ-
with stress-imposing suffix ˌhiːl i 'ɒ+ ‖ -'ɑː+ —
heliometer ˌhiːl i 'ɒm ɪt ə -ət ə ‖ -'ɑːm ət ər
Heliogabalus ˌhiːl i‿ə 'gæb əl əs -i əʊ- ‖ -i oʊ-
heliograph 'hiːl i‿ə grɑːf -græf ‖ -græf ~**ed** t
~**ing** ɪŋ ~**s** s
Heliopolis ˌhiːl i 'ɒp əl ɪs §-əs ‖ -'ɑːp-
Helios 'hiːl i ɒs ‖ -ɑːs
heliotrope 'hiːl i‿ə trəʊp 'hel- ‖ -troʊp ~**s** s
heliotropic ˌhiːl i‿ə 'trɒp ɪk ◄ ‖ -'trɑːp ɪk ◄
~**ally** əl‿i
heliotropism ˌhiːl i 'ɒtr ə ˌpɪz əm
'hiːl i‿ə trəʊp ˌɪz-, '•••, •••, ˌ•••'•••
‖ -'ɑːtr-
helipad 'hel i pæd §-ə- ‖ 'hiːl- ~**s** z
heliport 'hel i pɔːt §-ə- ‖ -pɔːrt 'hiːl-, -poʊrt
~**s** s
helium 'hiːl i‿əm
helix 'hiːl ɪks **helices** 'hel ɪ siːz 'hiːl-, -ə- ~**es**
ɪz əz
hell, Hell hel **hells, Hell's** helz
ˌHell's 'Angel
he'll *strong form* hiːl, *weak forms* hiəl, i‿əl —*The
weak form* i‿əl *is not used at the beginning of a
sentence or clause.*
hellacious he 'leɪʃ əs ~**ly** li
Helladic he 'læd ɪk
Hellas 'hel æs
hell-bent ˌhel 'bent ◄
hellcat 'hel kæt ~**s** s
hellebore 'hel ɪ bɔː -ə- ‖ -bɔːr -boʊr ~**s** z
helleborine 'hel ɪ bə raɪn '•ə-, -riːn;
ˌ•• 'bɔːr iːn ~**s** z
Hellene 'hel iːn ~**s** z
Hellenic he 'len ɪk hɪ-, hə-, -'liːn-
Hellenism 'hel ɪn ˌɪz əm -ən- ~**s** z
Hellenistic ˌhel ɪ 'nɪst ɪk ◄ -ə-
Heller 'hel ə ‖ -ər
Hellespont 'hel ɪ spɒnt -ə- ‖ -spɑːnt
hellfire ˌhel 'faɪ‿ə '•• ‖ 'hel ˌfaɪ‿ər
Hellicar 'hel ɪ kɑː -ə- ‖ -kɑːr
hellion 'hel jən ~**s** z
hellish 'hel ɪʃ ~**ly** li ~**ness** nəs nɪs
Hellman 'hel mən
hello hə 'ləʊ he- ‖ -'loʊ ~**ed** d ~**es** z ~**ing** ɪŋ
helluva 'hel əv ə
helm helm **helms** helmz
helm|et 'helm |ɪt -ət ‖ -ət ~**eted** ɪt ɪd ət-, -əd
‖ ət əd ~**ets** ɪts əts ‖ əts
Helmholtz 'helm həʊlts →-hɒʊlts ‖ -hoʊlts
—*Ger* ['hɛlm hɔlts]
helminth 'helm ɪntθ ~**s** s
helminthiasis ˌhelm ɪn 'θaɪ‿əs ɪs §ˌ•ən-, §-əs

helminthological ˌhelm ɪnᵗθ ə 'lɒdʒ ɪk ᵊl ◄
§ˌˌ•ᵊnᵗθ- ‖ -'lɑːdʒ- **~ly** _i
helmintholog|ist/s ˌhelm ɪn 'θɒl ədʒ ǀɪst/s
§ˌˌ•ən-, §-əst/s ‖ -'θɑːl- **~y** i
Helmsdale 'helmz deɪᵊl
Helmsley 'helmz li 'hemz-
helms|man 'helmz ǀmən **~men** mən men
Heloise, Héloïse 'el əʊ iːz ˌˌ•'• ‖ 'hel oʊ iːz
'el- —*Fr* [e lo iːz]
helot 'hel ət **~s** s
helotry 'hel ət ri
help help **helped** helpt **helping/s** 'help ɪŋ/z
helps helps
ˌhelping 'hand
helpful 'help fᵊl -fʊl **~ly** i **~ness** nəs nɪs
Helpmann 'help mən
helpmate 'help meɪt **~s** s
helpmeet 'help miːt **~s** s
Helsinki hel 'sɪŋk i 'hels ɪŋk i —*Finnish*
['hel siŋ ki]
Helston 'helst ən
helter-skelter ˌhelt ə 'skelt ə ‖ -ᵊr 'skelt ᵊr **~s**
z
helve helv **helves** helvz
Helvellyn hel 'vel ɪn -ən
Helvetia hel 'viːʃ ə -'viːʃ i‿ə
Helvetic hel 'vet ɪk ‖ -'veţ ɪk
hem hem **hemmed** hemd **hemming** 'hem ɪŋ
hems hemz
hemal 'hiːm ᵊl
he-|man 'hiː ǀmæn **~men** men
hematite 'hiːm ə taɪt 'hem-
hemato- *comb. form*
  with stress-neutral suffix ǀhiːm ə təʊ ǀhem-
  ‖ -əţ ə — **hematogenesis**
  ˌhiːm ət əʊ 'dʒen əs ɪs ˌhem-, -ɪs ɪs, §-əs
  ‖ -əţ ə-
  with stress-imposing suffix ˌhiːm ə 'tɒ+ ˌhem-
  ‖ -'tɑː+ — **hematogenous** ˌhiːm ə 'tɒdʒ
  ən əs ˌhem- ‖ -'tɑːdʒ-
hematologist ˌhiːm ə 'tɒl ədʒ ɪst §-əst ‖ -'tɑːl-
  ~s s
hematology ˌhiːm ə 'tɒl ədʒ i ‖ -'tɑːl-
hematoma ˌhiːm ə 'təʊm ə ‖ -'toʊm ə **~s** z
heme hiːm
Hemel Hempstead ˌhem ᵊl 'hemp stɪd -stəd,
  -sted
he-men 'hiː men
hemi- ǀhem i — **hemihydrate**
  ˌhem i 'haɪdr eɪt
hemidemisemiquaver
  ˌhem i ˌdem i 'sem i ˌkweɪv ə ‖ -ᵊr **~s** z
Heming 'hem ɪŋ
Hemingway 'hem ɪŋ weɪ
hemiplegia ˌhem i 'pliːdʒ i‿ə -'pliːdʒ ə
hemiplegic ˌhem i 'pliːdʒ ɪk ◄ **~s** s
hemipterous hɪ 'mɪpt ər əs he-, hə-
hemisphere 'hem i sfɪə -ə- ‖ -sfɪr **~s** z
hemispheric ˌhem i 'sfer ɪk ◄ ‖ -'sfɪr- **~al** ᵊl
  ~ally ᵊl‿i
hemistich 'hem i stɪk **~s** s
hemline 'hem laɪn **~s** z
Hemmings 'hem ɪŋz

hemlock 'hem lɒk ‖ -lɑːk **~s** s
hemo- *comb. form*
  with stress-neutral suffix ǀhiːm əʊ ‖ -oʊ —
  hemodialysis ˌhiːm əʊ daɪ 'æl əs ɪs -ɪs ɪs,
  §-əs ‖ ˌˌ•oʊ-
  with stress-imposing suffix hiː 'mɒ+ hɪ-
  ‖ -'mɑː:+ — **hemolysis** hiː 'mɒl əs ɪs hɪ-,
  -ɪs-, §-əs ‖ -'mɑːl-
hemoglobin ˌhiːm ə 'gləʊb ɪn §-ən, '••••
  ‖ 'hiːm ə gloʊb ən
hemophilia ˌhiːm ə 'fɪl i‿ə -'fiːl-
hemophiliac ˌhiːm ə 'fɪl i æk ◄ -'fiːl- **~s** s
hemorrhag|e 'hem ᵊr‿ɪdʒ **~ed** d **~es** ɪz əz
  ~ing ɪŋ
hemorrhoid 'hem ə rɔɪd **~s** z
hemorrhoidal ˌhem ə 'rɔɪd ᵊl ◄
hemp hemp
  'hemp ˌnettle
Hempel 'hemp ᵊl
hempen 'hemp ən
Hempstead 'hempst ed -ɪd, §-əd
hemstitch 'hem stɪtʃ **~ed** t **~es** ɪz əz **~ing** ɪŋ
hen hen **hens** henz
  'hen ˌhouse; 'hen ˌparty
henbane 'hen beɪn →'hem-
henbit 'hen bɪt →'hem-
hence hents
henceforth ˌhenᵗs 'fɔːθ '•• ‖ -'fɔːrθ -'foʊrθ
henceforward ˌhenᵗs 'fɔː wəd ‖ -'fɔːr wᵊrd
hench|man 'henʧ ǀmən **~men** mən
hendeca- *comb. form* ǀhen dek ə •ǀ•• —
  hendecasyllabic ˌhen dek ə sɪ 'læb ɪk ◄ •ˌ•ˌ•-,
  -sə'•-
hendecagon ˌhen 'dek əg ən ‖ -ə gɑːn **~s** z
Henderson 'hend əs ən ‖ -ᵊrs-
hendiadys hen 'daɪ‿əd ɪs §-əs
Hendon 'hend ən
Hendricks, Hendrix 'hendr ɪks
Hendry 'hendr i
Heneage 'hen ɪdʒ
Heneghan 'hen ɪg ən
henge henʤ **henges** 'henʤ ɪz -əz
Hengist 'heŋ gɪst -gəst; -dʒɪst
Henley 'hen li
Henman 'hen mən →'hem-
henna 'hen ə **hennaed** 'hen əd **hennaing**
  'hen ᵊr ɪŋ ‖ -ə ɪŋ **hennas** 'hen əz
Hennessey, Hennessy 'hen əs i -ɪs-
Henning 'hen ɪŋ
henpecked 'hen pekt →'hem-
Henri 'ɒn ri 'ɒ̃-, -riː, ˌˌ•'• ‖ ɑːn 'riː —*Fr* [ɑ̃ ʁi]
  —*but as an American family name,* 'hen ri
henries —*see* **henry**
Henrietta ˌhen ri 'et ə ◄ ‖ -'eţ ə ◄
Henriques hen 'riːk ɪz §-əz
Hen|ry, hen|ry 'hen ǀri **~ries, ~rys, ~ry's** riz
Henryson 'hen rɪs ən -rəs-
Henslow, Henslowe 'henz ləʊ ‖ -loʊ
Henson 'henᵗs ən
Henton 'hent ən ‖ -ᵊn
Henty 'hent i ‖ 'henţ i
hep hep
heparin 'hep ᵊr ɪn §-ən

hepatic hɪ 'pæt ɪk he-, hə- ‖ -'pæt̬ ɪk ~s s
hepatica hɪ 'pæt ɪk ə he-, hə- ‖ -'pæt̬- ~s z
hepatitis ˌhep ə 'taɪt ɪs ◂ -əs ‖ -'taɪt̬ əs ◂
  ˌhepaˌtitis 'B
Hepburn (i) 'hep bɜːn ‖ -bɝːn; (ii) 'heb ɜːn -ən
  ‖ -ɚn
Hephaestus hɪ 'fiːst əs he-, hə- ‖ -'fest- (*)
Hephzibah 'hefs ɪ bɑː 'heps-, -ə- ‖ -əb ə
Heppenstall 'hep ən stɔːl →-m- ‖ -stɑːl
Hepplewhite 'hep əl waɪt -hwaɪt ‖ -ʰwaɪt
hepta- comb. form
  with stress-neutral suffix ˌhept ə —
    heptastich 'hept ə stɪk
  with stress-imposing suffix hep 'tæ+ —
    heptamerous hep 'tæm ər əs
heptagon 'hept əg ən -ə gɒn ‖ -ə gɑːn ~s z
heptagonal hep 'tæg ən əl -**ly** i
heptane 'hept eɪn
heptarch|y 'hept ɑːk li ‖ -ɑːrk li ~**ies** iz
Heptateuch 'hept ə tjuːk →§-tʃuːk ‖ -tuːk
  -tjuːk
heptathlete hep 'tæθ liːt ~s s
heptathlon hep 'tæθ lən -lɒn ‖ -lɑːn ~s z
Hepworth 'hep wɜːθ -wəθ ‖ -wɚθ
her strong form hɜː ‖ hɝː, weak forms
  hə, ɜː, ə ‖ hɚ, ɝː, ɚ —The weak forms
  ɜː, ə ‖ ɝː, ɚ are not used at the beginning of a
  sentence or clause.
Hera 'hɪər ə ‖ 'hɪr ə
Heraclean ˌher ə 'kliː_ən ◂
Heracles 'her ə kliːz
Heraclitus ˌher ə 'klaɪt əs ˌhɪər- ‖ -'klaɪt̬ əs
Heraklion he 'ræk li_ən hɪ-, hə- —ModGk
  [i 'rak ljon]
herald 'her əld ~**ed** ɪd əd ~**ing** ɪŋ ~s z
heraldic hə 'ræld ɪk he-, hɪ- ~**ally** əl_i
herald|ry 'her əld |ri ~**ries** riz

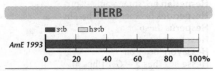

HERB

	■ ɝːb □ hɝːb				
AmE 1993					
0	20	40	60	80	100%

herb hɜːb ‖ ɝːb hɝːb —AmE 1993 poll panel
  preference: ɝːb 90%, hɝːb 10%. **herbs**
  hɜːbz ‖ ɝːbz hɝːbz
  ˌherb 'bennet; ˌherb 'Paris; ˌherb 'Robert
Herb personal name hɜːb ‖ hɝːb
herbaceous hə 'beɪʃ əs hɜː- ‖ hɝː- ɝː-
  herˌbaceous 'border
herbage, H~ 'hɜːb ɪdʒ ‖ 'ɝːb- 'hɝːb-
herbal 'hɜːb əl ‖ 'ɝːb əl 'hɝːb- ~s z
herbalist 'hɜːb əl ɪst §-əst ‖ 'ɝːb- 'hɝːb- ~s s
herbari|um hɜː 'beər i_|əm ‖ hɝː 'ber- ɝː-,
  -'bær- ~**a** ə ~**ums** əmz
Herbert 'hɜːb ət ‖ 'hɝːb ərt
herbicide 'hɜːb ɪ saɪd -ə- ‖ 'hɝːb- 'ɝːb- ~s z
Herbie 'hɜːb i ‖ 'hɝːb i
herbivore 'hɜːb ɪ vɔː -ə- ‖ 'hɝːb ə vɔːr 'ɝːb-,
  -voʊr ~s z
herbivorous hɜː 'bɪv ər_əs hə- ‖ hɝː- ɝː- ~**ly**
  li
Herculaneum ˌhɜːk ju 'leɪn i_əm ‖ ˌhɝːk jə-

Herculean ˌhɜːk ju 'liː_ən ◂ -jə-; hɜː 'kjuːl i_ən
  ‖ ˌhɝːk jə-
Hercules 'hɜːk ju liːz -jə- ‖ 'hɝːk jə-
herd, Herd hɜːd ‖ hɝːd **herded** 'hɜːd ɪd -əd
  ‖ 'hɝːd əd **herding** 'hɜːd ɪŋ ‖ 'hɝːd ɪŋ
  herds hɜːdz ‖ hɝːdz
herds|man 'hɜːdz |mən ‖ 'hɝːdz- ~**men** mən
Herdwick 'hɜːd wɪk ‖ 'hɝːd-
here hɪə ‖ hɪʳr (= hear) **here's** hɪəz ‖ hɪʳrz
hereabout ˌhɪər ə 'baʊt '• • • ‖ 'hɪr ə ˌbaʊt ~s
  s
hereafter ˌhɪər 'ɑːft ə §-'æft- ‖ hɪr 'æft ʳr
hereby ˌhɪə 'baɪ ◂ '• • ‖ ˌhɪr 'baɪ ◂
hereditability hɪ ˌred ɪt ə 'bɪl ət i hə-, he-, -ɪt i
  ‖ -ət ə 'bɪl ət̬ i
hereditab|le hɪ 'red ɪt əb |əl hə-, he-, -'• ət-
  ‖ -'red ət̬- ~**ly** li
hereditament ˌher ɪ 'dɪt ə mənt ˌ•ə- ‖ -'dɪt̬-
  ~s s
hereditarily hə 'red ət_ʳr əl i hɪ-, he-, -'•ɪt_,
  -ɪ li; •, •ə 'ter-, -ɪ 'ter- ‖ hə ˌred ə 'ter əl i
hereditar|y hə 'red ət_ʳr li hɪ-, he-, -'•ɪt_
  ‖ -ə ter li ~**iness** i nəs i nɪs
heredit|y hə 'red ət li hɪ-, he-, -ɪt- ‖ -ət̬ li ~**ies**
  iz
Hereford (i) 'her ɪ fəd -ə- ‖ -fʳrd, (ii)
  'hɜː fəd ‖ 'hɝː fʳrd —The city and former
  county in England are (i); the town in TX is (ii).
  For the breed of cattle or pigs, and for street
  names, etc., (i) in BrE, usually (ii) in AmE.
herein ˌhɪər 'ɪn ◂ ‖ hɪr-
hereinafter ˌhɪər ɪn 'ɑːft ə ◂ §-ən-, §-'æft-
  ‖ ˌhɪr ən 'æft ʳr ◂
Heren 'her ən
hereof ˌhɪəʳr 'ɒv ◂ ‖ hɪr 'ʌv -'ɑːv
Herero hə 'reər oʊ -'rɪər-; 'hɪər ə roʊ, 'heər-
  ‖ -'rer oʊ ~s z
here's hɪəz ‖ hɪʳrz
heresiarch hə 'riːz i ɑːk hɪ-, he-; 'her əs-
  ‖ -ɑːrk ~s s
heres|y 'her əs li -ɪs- ~**ies** iz
heretic 'her ə tɪk -ɪ- ~s s
heretical hə 'ret ɪk əl hɪ-, he- ‖ -'ret̬- ~**ly** _i
hereto ˌhɪə 'tuː ◂ ‖ hɪr-
heretofore ˌhɪə tu 'fɔː ◂ -tə-, -tuː-
  ‖ 'hɪrt ə fɔːr -four, ˌ• •'•
hereunder ˌhɪəʳr 'ʌnd ə ◂ ‖ hɪr 'ʌnd ʳr
hereupon ˌhɪəʳr ə 'pɒn ◂ ‖ 'hɪr ə pɑːn -pɔːn,
  ˌ• •'•
Hereward 'her ɪ wəd -ə- ‖ -wʳrd
herewith ˌhɪə 'wɪð ◂ -'wɪθ ‖ hɪr-
Herford 'hɜː fəd ‖ 'hɝː fʳrd
heriot, H~, Heriott 'her i_ət ~s, ~'s s
Heriot-Watt ˌher i_ət 'wɒt ‖ -'wɑːt
heritable 'her ɪt əb əl '• ət- ‖ 'her ət̬-
heritag|e 'her ɪt ɪdʒ -ət- ‖ -ət̬- ~**es** ɪz əz
herm hɜːm ‖ hɝːm **herms** hɜːmz ‖ hɝːmz
Herman 'hɜːm ən ‖ 'hɝːm-
Hermann 'hɜːm ən ‖ 'hɝːm- —Ger ['hɛʁ man]
hermaphrodite hɜː 'mæf rə daɪt hə- ‖ hʳr- ~s
  s
hermaphroditic hɜː ˌmæf rə 'dɪt ɪk ◂ hə-
  ‖ hʳr ˌmæf rə 'dɪt̬ ɪk ◂ ~**ally** əl_i

H

hermeneutic ˌhɜːm ə 'njuːt ɪk ◀ -ɪ-
‖ ˌhɝːm ə 'nuːṭ ɪk ◀ -'njuːṭ- **~al** ᵊl **~ally** ᵊl_i
~s s
Hermes 'hɜːm iːz ‖ 'hɝːm-
Hermesetas *tdmk* ˌhɜːm ɪ 'siːt əs -ə-, , -əz, -æs
‖ ˌhɝːm ə 'siːṭ əs -əz
hermetic hɜː 'met ɪk hə- ‖ hɝr 'meṭ ɪk **~ally**
ᵊl_i
Hermia 'hɜːm i_ə ‖ 'hɝːm-
Hermione hɜː 'maɪ_ən i hə- ‖ hɝr-
hermit 'hɜːm ɪt §-ət ‖ 'hɝːm- **~s** s
   'hermit crab
hermitag|e 'hɜːm ɪt ɪdʒ -ət- ‖ 'hɝːm əṭ ɪdʒ
—*but the H~ in Leningrad is usually*
ˌeəm ɪ 'tɑːʒ, -ə- ‖ ˌerm- **~es** ɪz əz
Hermon 'hɜːm ən ‖ 'hɝːm-
hern, Hern, Herne hɜːn ‖ hɝːn
hernia 'hɜːn i_ə ‖ 'hɝːn- **~s** z

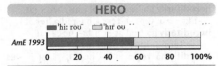

HERO

'hiː roʊ   'hɪr oʊ

AmE 1993

0   20   40   60   80   100%

hero, Hero 'hɪər əʊ ‖ 'hiː roʊ 'hɪr oʊ —*AmE
1993 poll panel preference:* 'hiː roʊ *57%,*
'hɪr oʊ *43%.* **~es** z
   'hero ˌworship
Herod 'her əd
Herodias hə 'rəʊd i æs hɪ-, he-, -əs ‖ -'roʊd-
Herodotus hə 'rɒd ət əs hɪ-, he- ‖ -'rɑːd əṭ əs
heroic hə 'rəʊ ɪk hɪ-, he- ‖ -'roʊ ɪk **~al** ᵊl
~ally ᵊl_i **~s** s
   heˌroic 'couplet
heroin 'her əʊ ɪn §-ən ‖ -oʊ ən
heroine 'her əʊ ɪn 'hɪər-, -iːn, §-ən ‖ -oʊ ən
(usually = heroin) **~s** z
heroism 'her əʊ ˌɪz əm ‖ -oʊ-
heron, Heron 'her ən **~s** z
heron|ry 'her ən |ri **~ries** riz
hero-worship *n, v* 'hɪər əʊ ˌwɜːʃ ɪp §-əp
‖ 'hiː roʊ ˌwɝːʃ əp 'hɪr oʊ- **~ed, ~ped** t
~ing, ~ping ɪŋ **~s** s
herpes 'hɜːp iːz ‖ 'hɝːp-
herpetological ˌhɜːp ɪt ə 'lɒdʒ ɪk ᵊl ◀ , • ət-
‖ ˌhɝːp əṭ ə 'lɑːdʒ- **~ly** _i
herpetologist ˌhɜːp ɪ 'tɒl ədʒ ɪst , • ə-, §-əst
‖ ˌhɝːp ə 'tɑːl- **~s** s
herpetology ˌhɜːp ɪ 'tɒl ədʒ i , • ə-
‖ ˌhɝːp ə 'tɑːl-
Herr heə ‖ heᴙr hæᴙr —*Ger* [heᴙ]
herrenvolk, H~ 'her ən fəʊk -fɒlk ‖ -foʊk
-fɔːlk, -fɑːlk —*Ger* ['heᴙ ᵊn fɔlk]
Herrick 'her ɪk
Herries 'her ɪs -ɪz, §-əs, §-əz
herring, H~ 'her ɪŋ **~s** z
   'herring gull
herringbone 'her ɪŋ bəʊn ‖ -boʊn **~s** z
Herriot 'her i_ət
hers hɜːz ‖ hɝːz
Herschel, Herschell 'hɜːʃ ᵊl ‖ 'hɝːʃ-
herself *strong form* hɜː 'self ‖ hɝː-, *weak forms*
hə-, ɜː-, hə- ‖ ᵊr-, ɝr- —*The forms* ɜː-, ə- ‖ ᵊr-

*are not used at the beginning of a sentence or
clause.*
Hersham 'hɜːʃ əm ‖ 'hɝːʃ-
Hershey 'hɜːʃ i ‖ 'hɝːʃ i
   'Hershey bar
Herstmonceux ˌhɜːsт mən 'sjuː ◀ -'suː
‖ ˌhɝːsт-
Herter 'hɜːt ə ‖ 'hɝːṭ ᵊr
Hertford *(i)* 'hɑː fəd ‖ 'hɑːr fᵊrd, *(ii)*
'hɑːt- ‖ 'hɑːrt-, *(iii)* 'hɜːt- ‖ 'hɝːt- —*The
traditional pronunciation for the English county
town and the Oxford college,* (i), *has been
largely superseded by the spelling pronunciation*
(ii). *As an American name,* (iii). **~shire** ʃə ʃɪə
‖ ʃᵊr ʃɪr
Herts hɑːts ‖ hɑːrts
hertz, Hertz hɜːts ‖ hɝːts —*Ger* [hɛʁts]
Hertzian 'hɜːts i_ən 'heəts- ‖ 'hɝːts- 'herts-
Hertzog 'hɜːts ɒg ‖ 'hɝːts ɑːg
Hervey *(i)* 'hɑːv i ‖ 'hɑːrv i, *(ii)* 'hɜːv i ‖ 'hɝːv i
Herzegovina ˌhɜːts ə 'gɒv ɪn ə ˌheəts-, , • ɪ-,
-ən ə; -gəʊ 'viːn ə ‖ ˌherts ə 'goʊv- —*Serbo-
Croat* Hercegovina ['her tsɛ gɔ vi na]
he's *strong form* hiːz, *weak forms* hiz, ɪz, iz
—*At the beginning of a sentence or clause, only
the forms with* h *are used.*
Heseltine 'hes ᵊl taɪn 'hez-
Hesiod 'hiːs i_əd 'hes-, -ɒd
hesitance 'hez ɪt ᵊnts -ət- ‖ -ᵊnts
hesitanc|y 'hez ɪt ᵊnts li ' • ət- ‖ -ᵊnts li **~ies** iz
hesitant 'hez ɪt ᵊnt -ət- ‖ -ᵊnt **~ly** li
hesi|tate 'hez ɪ |teɪt -ə- **~tated** teɪt ɪd -əd
‖ teɪṭ əd **~tates** teɪts **~tating**
teɪt ɪŋ ‖ teɪṭ ɪŋ
hesitation ˌhez ɪ 'teɪʃ ᵊn -ə- **~s** z
Hesketh 'hesk əθ -ɪθ
Hesperia he 'spɪər i_ə ‖ -'spɪr-
Hesperian he 'spɪər i_ən ‖ -'spɪr-
Hesperides hɪ 'sper ɪ diːz he-, hə-, -ə-
Hesperus 'hesp ᵊr əs
Hess hes
Hessayon 'hes i_ən
Hesse hes 'hes ə —*Ger* ['hɛs ə]
hessian, H~ 'hes i_ən ‖ 'heʃ ᵊn (*) **~s** z
Hessle *place in Humberside* 'hez ᵊl
Hester 'hest ə ‖ -ᵊr
Heston 'hest ən
Heswall 'hez wəl ‖ -wɔːl -wɑːl
het het **hets** hets
   ˌhet 'up
hetaer|a, hetair|a hɪ 'taɪᵊr ə he- ‖ -'tɪr ə **~ae**
iː aɪ **~ai** aɪ **~as** əz
heterarch|y 'het ə rɑːk |i ‖ 'heṭ ə rɑːrk i **~ies**
iz
hetero 'het_ᵊr əʊ ‖ 'heṭ ə roʊ **~s** z
hetero- *comb. form*
   with stress-neutral suffix ˌhet_ᵊr əʊ ‖ ˌheṭ ə roʊ
   — **heterographic**
   ˌhet_ᵊr əʊ 'græf ɪk ◀ ‖ ˌheṭ ə roʊ-
   with stress-imposing suffix
   ˌhet ə 'rɒ+ ‖ ˌheṭ ə 'rɑː+ — **heterography**
   ˌhet ə 'rɒg rəf i ‖ ˌheṭ ə 'rɑːg-
heteroclite 'het_ᵊr əʊ klaɪt ‖ 'heṭ ᵊr ə- **~s** s

heterocyclic ˌhet ər əʊ 'saɪk lɪk ◀ -'sɪk-
  ‖ ˌheṭ ə roʊ-
heterodox 'het ər əʊ dɒks ‖ 'heṭ ər ə dɑːks
  →'hetr ə dɑːks
heterodox|y 'het ər əʊ dɒks li ‖ 'heṭ
  ər ə dɑːks li →'hetr ə dɑːks li **~ies** iz
heterodyne 'het ər əʊ daɪn ‖ 'heṭ ər ə-
  →'hetr ə daɪn
heterogeneity ˌhet ər əʊ dʒə 'niː ət i
  ˌhet ə ˌrɒdʒ ə-, -dʒɪ'•-, -'neɪ-, -ɪt i
  ‖ ˌheṭ ə roʊ dʒə 'niː əṭ i →ˌhetr oʊ dʒə'•-
heterogeneous ˌhet ər əʊ
  'dʒiːn i_əs ◀ ‖ ˌheṭ ə roʊ- →ˌhetr oʊ'•-, -ə'•-
  ~ly li **~ness** nəs nɪs
heteronym 'het ər əʊ nɪm ‖ 'heṭ ə roʊ-
  →'hetr oʊ nɪm, -ə nɪm **~s** z
heteronymous ˌhet ə 'rɒn ɪm əs ◀ -əm əs
  ‖ ˌheṭ ə 'rɑːn-
heterorganic ˌhet ər ɔː 'gæn ɪk ◀ ‖ ˌheṭ ər ɔːr-
heterosexism ˌhet ər əʊ 'seks ˌɪz
  əm ‖ ˌheṭ ə roʊ-
heterosexist ˌhet ər əʊ 'seks ɪst ◀ §-əst
  ‖ ˌheṭ ə roʊ- **~s** s
heterosexual ˌhet ər əʊ 'sek ʃu_əl ◀
  -'seks ju_əl, -'sekʃ əl ‖ ˌheṭ ə roʊ- -ər ə- **~ly**
  i **~s** z
heterosexuality ˌhet ər əʊ ˌsek ʃu 'æl ət i
  -ˌseks ju- ‖ ˌheṭ ə roʊ ˌsekʃ u 'æl əṭ i -ər ə-
heterozyg|ote/s ˌhet ər əʊ 'zaɪg| əʊt/s
  ‖ ˌheṭ ə roʊ 'zaɪg| oʊt/s **~ous** əs
Hetherington 'heð ər_ɪŋ tən
Hettie 'het i ‖ 'heṭ i
Hetton-le-Hole ˌhet ən lɪ 'həʊl -lə'•, →-'hɒʊl
  ‖ -'hoʊl
Hetty 'het i ‖ 'heṭ i
Heugh *family name* hjuː
Heugh *village in Northumberland* hjuːf
Heulwen 'haɪl wen —*Welsh* ['həil wen, 'həil-]
heuristic hjuə 'rɪst ɪk **~ally** əl_i **~s** s
Hever 'hiːv ə ‖ -ər
hew, Hew hjuː ‖ juː **hewed** hjuːd ‖ juːd
  hewing 'hjuː_ɪŋ ‖ 'juː_ **hewn** hjuːn ‖ juːn
  hews hjuːz ‖ juːz
hewer 'hjuː_ə ‖ -ər 'juː_ **~s** z
Hewett, Hewitt 'hjuː_ɪt §_ət ‖ 'juː-
Hewlett 'hjuːl ɪt §-ət ‖ 'juːl-
hewn hjuːn ‖ juːn
Hewson 'hjuːs ən ‖ 'juːs-
hex heks **hexed** hekst **hexes** 'heks ɪz -əz
  hexing 'heks ɪŋ
hexa- *comb. form*
  with stress-neutral suffix ˌheks ə — **hexapod**
  'heks ə pɒd ‖ -pɑːd
  with stress-imposing suffix hek 'sæ+ —
  hexapody hek 'sæp əd i
hexachlorophene ˌheks ə 'klɔːr ə fiːn
  -'klɒr- ‖ -'kloʊr-
hexad 'heks æd **~s** z
hexadecimal ˌheks ə 'des ɪm əl ◀ -əm əl **~ly** i
  ~s z
hexagon 'heks əg ən ‖ -ə gɑːn **~s** z
hexagonal hek 'sæg ən əl **~ly** i
hexagram 'heks ə græm **~s** z

hexahedron ˌheks ə 'hiːdr ən -'hedr- **~s** z
hexameter hek 'sæm ɪt ə -ət- ‖ -əṭ ər **~s** z
hexamine 'heks ə miːn
hexane 'heks eɪn
Hexham 'heks əm
hey heɪ *(= hay)*
heyday 'heɪ deɪ
Heyer 'heɪ ə ‖ -ər
Heyerdahl 'heɪ ə dɑːl 'haɪ_ ‖ 'haɪ_ər-
  —*Norwegian* ['hɛi ər dɑːl]
Heyes heɪz
Heyford 'heɪ fəd ‖ -fərd
Heyhoe 'heɪ həʊ ‖ -hoʊ
Heys heɪz
Heysham 'hiːʃ əm —*Often* 'heɪʃ- *by those not*
  familiar with the name.
Heythrop 'hiːθ rəp -rɒp ‖ -rɑːp
Heywood 'heɪ wʊd
Hezbollah ˌhez bɒ 'lɑː ˌhɪz- ‖ -bə-
Hezekiah ˌhez ɪ 'kaɪ_ə -ə-
hi haɪ *(= high)*
Hialeah ˌhaɪ_ə 'liː_ə
hiatus haɪ 'eɪt əs hi- ‖ -'eɪṭ- **~es** ɪz əz
  hiˌatus 'hernia
Hiawatha ˌhaɪ_ə 'wɒθ ə ‖ -'wɔːθ ə ˌhiː-, -'wɑː-θ-
hibachi hɪ 'bɑːtʃ i —*Jp* ['çi ba tɕi] **~s** z
Hibberd 'hɪb əd ‖ -ərd
Hibbert 'hɪb ət ‖ -ərt
hibernacul|um ˌhaɪb ə 'næk jʊl |əm -jəl əm
  ‖ -ər 'næk jəl- **~a** ə
hiber|nate 'haɪb ə |neɪt ‖ -ər- **~nated** neɪt ɪd
  -əd ‖ neɪṭ əd **~nates** neɪts **~nating**
  neɪt ɪŋ ‖ neɪṭ ɪŋ
hibernation ˌhaɪb ə 'neɪʃ ən ‖ -ər- **~s** z
Hibernia haɪ 'bɜːn i_ə hɪ- ‖ -'bɜːn-
Hibernian haɪ 'bɜːn i_ən hɪ- ‖ -'bɜːn- —*The*
  football team is hɪ- **~s** z
Hibernicism haɪ 'bɜːn ɪ ˌsɪz əm -ə- ‖ -'bɜːn-
  ~s z
hibiscus haɪ 'bɪsk əs hɪ-, hə- **~es** ɪz əz
Hibs hɪbz
hic hɪk
  ˌhic 'jacet◀ 'jæk et 'dʒeɪs-
hiccough, hiccup 'hɪk ʌp -əp **~ed** t **~ing** ɪŋ
  ~s s
hick, Hick hɪk **hicks** hɪks
Hickey, h~ 'hɪk i **~s** z
Hickok 'hɪk ɒk ‖ -ɑːk
hickor|y 'hɪk ər_i **~ies** iz
Hicks hɪks
Hickson 'hɪks ən
hid hɪd
hidalgo hɪ 'dælg əʊ ‖ -oʊ —*Sp* [i 'ðal ɣo] **~s** z
Hidcote 'hɪd kət →'hɪg-
hidden 'hɪd ən
hide haɪd **hidden** 'hɪd ən **hides** haɪdz **hiding**
  'haɪd ɪŋ
hide-and-seek ˌhaɪd ən 'siːk
hideaway 'haɪd ə ˌweɪ **~s** z
hidebound 'haɪd baʊnd →'haɪb-
hi-de-hi ˌhaɪ dɪ 'haɪ -diː-
hideous 'hɪd i_əs **~ly** li **~ness** nəs nɪs
hideout 'haɪd aʊt **~s** s

hidey-hole 'haɪd i həʊl →-hɒʊl ‖ -hoʊl ~s z
hiding 'haɪd ɪŋ ~s z
hie haɪ (= *high*) **hied** haɪd **hieing, hying**
'haɪ ɪŋ **hies** haɪz
hierarch 'haɪᵊr ɑːk ‖ -ɑːrk ~s s
hierarchic ₍ₕ₎haɪᵊ 'rɑːk ɪk ‖ -'rɑːrk- ~al ᵊl ~ally
ᵊl_i
hierarch|y 'haɪᵊr ɑːk |i ‖ -ɑːrk |i ~ies iz
hieratic ₍ₕ₎haɪᵊ 'ræt ɪk ‖ -'ræt̬ ɪk ~al ᵊl ~ally
ᵊl_i
hierocratic ˌhaɪᵊr əʊ 'kræt ɪk ◂ ‖ -ə 'kræt̬ ɪk ◂
~al ᵊl ~ally ᵊl_i
hieroglyph 'haɪᵊr ə glɪf ~s s
hieroglyphic ˌhaɪᵊr ə 'glɪf ɪk ◂ ~al ᵊl ~ally ᵊl_i
~s s
Hieronymus ˌhaɪᵊ 'rɒn ɪm əs ˌhɪᵊ- ‖ -'rɑːn-
hierophant 'haɪᵊr əʊ fænt ‖ -ə- haɪ 'er ə fænt
~s s
hifalutin, hifalutin' ˌhaɪ fə 'luːt ɪn ◂ -ᵊn ‖ -ᵊn
hi-fi 'haɪ faɪ ˌ•'• ~s z
Higginbotham (i) 'hɪg ɪn ˌbɒt əm -ᵊn-, →-ɪm-
‖ -ˌbɑːt̬ əm, (ii) -ˌbɒθ əm ‖ -ˌbɑːθ əm
Higginbottom 'hɪg ɪn ˌbɒt əm -ᵊn-, →-ɪm-
‖ -ˌbɑːt̬ əm
Higgins 'hɪg ɪnz §-ᵊnz
higgl|e 'hɪg ᵊl ~ed d ~es z ~ing _ɪŋ
higgledy-piggledy ˌhɪg ᵊld i 'pɪg ᵊld i ◂
higgler 'hɪg ᵊl_ə ‖ -ᵊr ~s z
Higgs hɪgz
high haɪ **higher** 'haɪ_ə ‖ 'haɪ_ᵊr **highest**
'haɪ_ɪst -əst **highs** haɪz
ˌhigh 'chair, '•• ‖ '• •; ˌHigh 'Church;
ˌHigh Com'mission; ˌHigh Com'missioner,
ˌHigh 'Court◂; ˌhigh ex'plosive; ˌhigh
fi'delity; ˌHigh 'German; ˌhigh 'horse;
ˌhigh 'jinks, '••; ˌhigh 'jump; ˌhigh 'jumper;
'high life; ˌhigh 'mass; 'high point; ˌhigh
'priest; ˌhigh 'priestess; ˌhigh 'profile;
ˌhigh re'lief; 'high road; 'high school;
ˌhigh 'seas; ˌhigh 'season; ˌHigh 'Sheriff;
'high spot; 'high street; ˌhigh 'table; ˌhigh
'tea; ˌhigh tech'nology; ˌhigh 'tide; ˌhigh
'time; ˌhigh 'treason; ˌhigh 'water; ˌhigh
'water mark; ˌHigh 'Wycombe
-high 'haɪ haɪ — **knee-high** ˌniː 'haɪ ◂ '••
Higham 'haɪ_əm —*but the place in S.Yorks. is
locally also* 'hɪk-
high-and-mighty ˌhaɪ_ən 'maɪt i ◂ →-əm-
‖ -'maɪt̬ i
highball 'haɪ bɔːl ‖ -bɑːl ~s z
highborn 'haɪ bɔːn ˌ•'• ‖ -bɔːrn
highboy 'haɪ bɔɪ ~s z
highbrow 'haɪ braʊ ~s z
Highbury 'haɪ bᵊr_i ‖ -ˌber i
high-class ˌhaɪ 'klɑːs ◂ §-'klæs ‖ -'klæs ◂
Highclere 'haɪ klɪə ‖ -klɪr
Highcliffe 'haɪ klɪf
high-density ˌhaɪ 'den̩ts ət i ◂ -ɪt- ‖ -ət̬ i ◂
higher 'haɪ_ə ‖ 'haɪ_ᵊr
ˌhigher ˌedu'cation
higher-up ˌhaɪ_ər 'ʌp ◂ ‖ ˌhaɪ_ᵊr-
highest 'haɪ_ɪst _əst

highfalutin, highfalutin' ˌhaɪ fə 'luːt ɪn ◂ -ᵊn
‖ -ᵊn
highfaluting ˌhaɪ fə 'luːt ɪŋ ◂
high-flier, high-flyer ˌhaɪ 'flaɪ_ə ‖ -'flaɪ_ᵊr ~s
z
high-flown ˌhaɪ 'fləʊn ◂ ‖ -'floʊn ◂
ˌhigh-flown 'language
high-flying ˌhaɪ 'flaɪ ɪŋ ◂
Highgate 'haɪ geɪt -gɪt, -gət
high-grade ˌhaɪ 'greɪd ◂
Highgrove 'haɪ grəʊv ‖ -groʊv
high-handed ˌhaɪ 'hænd ɪd ◂ -əd ~ly li ~ness
nəs nɪs
high-|hat ˌhaɪ |hæt ~hats hæts ~hatted
hæt ɪd -əd ‖ hæt̬ əd ~hatting
hæt ɪŋ ‖ hæt̬ ɪŋ
high-heeled ˌhaɪ 'hiːᵊld ◂
high-keyed ˌhaɪ 'kiːd ◂
highland, H~ 'haɪl ənd ~s z
ˌHighland 'fling
highlander, H~ 'haɪl ənd ə ‖ -ᵊr ~s z
high-level ˌhaɪ 'lev ᵊl ◂
high|light 'haɪ |laɪt ~lighted laɪt ɪd -əd
‖ laɪt̬ əd ~lighting laɪt ɪŋ ‖ laɪt̬ ɪŋ ~lights
laɪts
highlighter 'haɪ laɪt ə ‖ -laɪt̬ ᵊr ~s z
highly 'haɪ li
highly-strung ˌhaɪ li 'strʌŋ ◂
high-minded ˌhaɪ 'maɪnd ɪd ◂ -əd ~ly li
~ness nəs nɪs
Highness *title* 'haɪn əs -ɪs ~es ɪz əz
highness *'quality of being high'* 'haɪ nəs -nɪs
high-octane ˌhaɪ 'ɒkt eɪn ◂ ‖ -'ɑːkt-
high-pass ˌhaɪ 'pɑːs ◂ §-'pæs ‖ -'pæs ◂
high-pitched ˌhaɪ 'pɪtʃt ◂
high-powered ˌhaɪ 'paʊ_əd ◂ ‖ -'paʊ_ᵊrd
high-pressure ˌhaɪ 'preʃ ə ◂ ‖ -ᵊr ◂
high-principled ˌhaɪ 'prɪn̩ts ɪp ᵊld ◂ -əp-
high-profile ˌhaɪ 'prəʊf aɪᵊl ◂ ‖ -'proʊf-
high-ranking ˌhaɪ 'ræŋk ɪŋ ◂
high-res ˌhaɪ 'rez ◂
high-ris|e 'haɪ raɪz ˌ•'•◂ ~es ɪz əz
high-risk ˌhaɪ 'rɪsk ◂
high-sounding ˌhaɪ 'saʊnd ɪŋ ◂
high-speed ˌhaɪ 'spiːd ◂
ˌhigh-speed 'train
high-spirited ˌhaɪ 'spɪr ɪt ɪd §-ət-, -əd
‖ -ət̬ əd ~ly li ~ness nəs nɪs
high-strung ˌhaɪ 'strʌŋ ◂
hightail 'haɪ teɪᵊl ~ed d ~ing ɪŋ ~s z
high-tech ˌhaɪ 'tek ◂
high-tension ˌhaɪ 'ten̩tʃ ᵊn ◂
high-toned ˌhaɪ 'təʊnd ◂ ‖ -'toʊnd ◂
high-up *n* 'haɪ ʌp ~s s
highway 'haɪ weɪ ~s z
ˌHighway 'Code
highway|man 'haɪ weɪ |mən ~men mən
hijack 'haɪ dʒæk ~ed t ~er/s ə/z ‖ ᵊr/z ~ing
ɪŋ ~s s
hike haɪk **hiked** haɪkt **hikes** haɪks **hiking**
'haɪk ɪŋ
hiker 'haɪk ə ‖ -ᵊr ~s z
hila 'haɪl ə

Hilaire hɪ 'leə 'hɪl eə ‖ -'leər —*Fr* [i lɛːʁ]
hilar 'haɪl ə ‖ -ər
hilarious hɪ 'leər i‿əs hə- ‖ -'ler- haɪ-, -'lær-
  ~ly li ~ness nəs nɪs
hilarity hɪ 'lær ət i hə-, -ɪt- ‖ -ət i -'ler-
Hilary 'hɪl ər i
Hilbert 'hɪlb ət ‖ -ərt —*Ger* ['hɪl bɐt], *Czech*
  ['hil bert]
Hilbre 'hɪlb ri
Hilda 'hɪld ə
Hildebrand 'hɪld ə brænd
Hildegarde 'hɪld ə gɑːd ‖ -gɑːrd
Hildenborough 'hɪld ən ˌbʌr ə -bər‿ə
  ‖ -ˌbɝː oʊ
Hilfiger *tdmk* 'hɪlf ɪg ə ‖ -ər
hill, Hill hɪl hills hɪlz
Hillary 'hɪl ər i
hillbill|y 'hɪl ˌbɪl i ~ies iz
Hillel 'hɪl el -əl; hɪ 'leɪəl
Hiller 'hɪl ə ‖ -ər
Hillery 'hɪl ər i
Hillhead ˌhɪl 'hed
Hilliard 'hɪl i‿əd -ɑːd ‖ ‿ərd -ɑːrd
Hillingdon 'hɪl ɪŋ dən
Hillman 'hɪl mən
hillock 'hɪl ək ~s s
Hills hɪlz
Hillsboro, Hillsborough 'hɪlz bər‿ə §-ˌbʌr ə
  ‖ -ˌbɝː oʊ
hillside 'hɪl saɪd ˌ•'• ~s z
hilltop 'hɪl tɒp ‖ -tɑːp ~s s
hilly 'hɪl i
Hilo *place in Hawaii* 'hiːl əʊ ‖ -oʊ
hilt hɪlt hilted 'hɪlt ɪd -əd hilts hɪlts
Hilton 'hɪlt ən
hil|um 'haɪl |əm ~a ə ~i aɪ ~us əs
Hilversum 'hɪlv ə səm -sʊm ‖ -ər- —*Dutch*
  ['hɪl vər sʏm]
him *strong form* hɪm, *weak forms* hɪm, ɪm §həm,
  §əm —*In the rare instances where this word
  occurs after a pause or at the beginning of a
  clause, it is always* hɪm
Himalaya ˌhɪm ə 'leɪ ə hɪ 'mɑːl i‿ə —*Hindi*
  [hɪ maː ləj] ~s z
Himalayan ˌhɪm ə 'leɪ ən ◂ hɪ 'mɑːl i‿ən
Himmler 'hɪm lə ‖ -lər —*Ger* ['hɪm lɐ]
himself *strong form* hɪm 'self §həm-, *weak form*
  ɪm- §əm- —*The weak form is not used at the
  beginning of a sentence or clause.*
Himyaritic ˌhɪm jə 'rɪt ɪk ◂ ‖ -'rɪt̬-
Hinayana ˌhiːn ə 'jɑːn ə ˌhɪn-, -ɪ-
Hinchcliffe 'hɪntʃ klɪf
Hinchingbrooke 'hɪntʃ ɪŋ brʊk
Hinchinbrook 'hɪntʃ ɪn brʊk →-ɪm-; -ən-,
  →-əm-
Hinchliffe 'hɪntʃ lɪf
Hinchley 'hɪntʃ li
Hinckley 'hɪŋk li
hind haɪnd hinds haɪndz
Hind (i) haɪnd, (ii) hɪnd
hindbrain 'haɪnd breɪn →'haɪm- ~s z
Hinde haɪnd

Hindemith 'hɪnd ə mɪt -mɪθ, §-məθ —*Ger*
  ['hɪn də mɪt]
Hindenburg 'hɪnd ən bɜːg →-əm- ‖ -bɝːg
  —*Ger* ['hɪn dn̩ bʊʁk]
hinder *v* 'hɪnd ə ‖ -ər ~ed d hindering
  'hɪnd_ər ɪŋ ~s z
hinder *adj* 'haɪnd ə ‖ -ər ~most
  məʊst ‖ moʊst
hinderer 'hɪnd_ər ə ‖ -ər ~s z
Hindhead 'haɪnd hed
Hindi 'hɪnd i -iː
Hindle 'hɪnd əl
Hindley (i) 'hɪnd li, (ii) 'haɪnd li —*The town in
  Greater Manchester is* (i). *Otherwise,* (ii) *is
  more usual.*
Hindmarsh 'haɪnd mɑːʃ →'haɪm- ‖ -mɑːrʃ
hindmost 'haɪnd məʊst →'haɪm- ‖ -moʊst
hindquarter ˌhaɪnd 'kwɔːt ə →ˌhaɪŋ-, -'kɔːt-,
  '•ˌ•• ‖ 'haɪnd ˌkwɔːrt̬ ər -ˌkwɔːt̬ ər ~s z
hindranc|e 'hɪndr ənts ~es ɪz əz
hindsight 'haɪnd saɪt
Hindu ˌhɪn 'duː ◂ '•• ‖ 'hɪn duː ~s z
  ˌHindu 'Kush kʊʃ kuːʃ
Hinduism 'hɪn du ˌɪz əm ˌ•'duː-
Hindustani ˌhɪn du 'stɑːn i ◂ ‖ -'stæn i ◂
  -'stɑːn i
Hine haɪn
Hines haɪnz
hinge hɪndʒ hinged hɪndʒd hinges 'hɪndʒ ɪz
  -əz hinging 'hɪndʒ ɪŋ
hinn|y 'hɪn li ~ied id ~ies iz ~ying i‿ɪŋ
Hinshelwood 'hɪntʃ əl wʊd
hint hɪnt hinted 'hɪnt ɪd -əd ‖ 'hɪnt̬ əd
  hinting 'hɪnt ɪŋ ‖ 'hɪnt̬ ɪŋ hints hɪnts
hinterland 'hɪnt ə lænd -lənd ‖ 'hɪnt̬ ər-
Hinton 'hɪnt ən
hip hɪp hipped hɪpt hipper 'hɪp ə ‖ -ər
  hippest 'hɪp ɪst -əst
  'hip flask; 'hip joint; ˌhip 'pocket
hip|bath 'hɪp |bɑːθ §-bæθ ‖ -bæθ ~baths
  bɑːðz §bɑːθs, §bæðs, §bæðz ‖ bæðz bæθs
hipbone 'hɪp bəʊn ‖ -boʊn ~s z
hip-hop 'hɪp hɒp ‖ -hɑːp
hiphuggers 'hɪp ˌhʌg əz ‖ -ərz
hipness 'hɪp nəs -nɪs
Hipparchus hɪ 'pɑːk əs ‖ -'pɑːrk-
hippeastrum ˌhɪp i 'æs trəm ~s z
hipped hɪpt
Hippias 'hɪp i æs -i‿əs
hippie 'hɪp i ~s z
hippo, Hippo 'hɪp əʊ ‖ -oʊ ~s z
hippocamp|us ˌhɪp ə 'kæmp |əs ~i aɪ
Hippocrates hɪ 'pɒk rə tiːz ‖ -'pɑːk-
Hippocratic ˌhɪp əʊ 'kræt ɪk ◂ ‖ -ə 'kræt̬ ɪk ◂
  ˌHippoˌcratic 'oath
Hippocrene 'hɪp əʊ kriːn ˌ•'kriːn iː, -i ‖ -ə-
Hippodrome, h~ 'hɪp ə drəʊm ‖ -droʊm ~s z
Hippolyta hɪ 'pɒl ɪt ə -ət- ‖ -'pɑːl ət̬ ə
Hippolyte hɪ 'pɒl ɪ tiː -ə- ‖ -'pɑːl-
Hippolytus hɪ 'pɒl ɪt əs -ət- ‖ -'pɑːl ət̬ əs
hippopot|amus ˌhɪp ə 'pɒt əm əs ‖ -'pɑːt̬-
  ~ami ə maɪ ~amuses əm əs ɪz -əz
hipp|y 'hɪp li ~ies iz

H

hipster 'hɪpst ə ‖ -ᵊr ~s z
hiragana ˌhɪər ə 'gɑːn ə ˌhɪr- ‖ ˌhiː rə- —*Jp*
[çi ˌra 'ŋa na, -'ga-]
Hiram 'haɪᵊr əm
hircine 'hɜːs aɪn -ɪn, §-ᵊn ‖ 'hɜˑːs-
Hird hɜːd ‖ hɜˑːd
hire 'haɪ‿ə ‖ 'haɪ‿ᵊr hired 'haɪ‿əd ‖ 'haɪ‿ᵊrd
hires 'haɪ‿əz ‖ 'haɪ‿ᵊrz hiring/s 'haɪ‿ər ɪŋ/
z ‖ 'haɪ‿ᵊr ɪŋ/z
ˌhire 'purchase
hireling 'haɪ‿ə lɪŋ ‖ 'haɪ‿ᵊr- ~s z
Hirnant 'hɜː nænt ‖ 'hɜˑː- —*Welsh* ['hir nant]
Hirohito ˌhɪr əʊ 'hiːt əʊ ‖ -oʊ 'hiːt oʊ —*Jp*
[çi 'ro çi̥ to]
Hiroshima hɪ 'rɒʃ ɪm ə hə-, -əm-; ˌhɪr ə 'ʃiːm ə,
-ɒ- ‖ ˌhɪr oʊ 'ʃiːm ə hə 'roʊʃ əm ə —*Jp*
[çi ˌro çi ma]
Hirst hɜːst ‖ hɜˑːst
hirsute 'hɜːs juːt -uːt; hɜː 'sjuːt, -'suːt
‖ 'hɜˑːs uːt ~ness nəs nɪs
hirundine hɪ 'rʌnd aɪn -ɪn, §-ᵊn
Hirwain, Hirwaun 'hɪə waɪn ‖ 'hɪr- —*locally
also* 'hɜː wɪn —*Welsh* ['hir wain]
his *strong form* hɪz, *weak forms* hɪz, ɪz §həz, §əz
—*The forms* ɪz, §əz *are not used at the
beginning of a sentence or clause.*
Hiscock *(i)* 'hɪs kɒk ‖ -kɑːk, *(ii)* -kəʊ ‖ -koʊ
Hislop 'hɪz ləp -lɒp ‖ -lɑːp
his'n'hers ˌhɪz ᵊn 'hɜːz ‖ -'hɜˑːz
Hispanic, h~ hɪ 'spæn ɪk ~s s
Hispanicism hɪ 'spæn ɪ ˌsɪz əm -ə- ~s z
Hispaniola ˌhɪsp æn i 'əʊl ə
hɪ ˌspæn-; ˌhɪsp æn 'jəʊl ə ‖ ˌhɪsp ən 'joʊl ə
Hispano- hɪ 'spæn əʊ -'spɑːn-; 'hɪsp ən- ‖ -oʊ
Hispano-Suiza *tdmk* hɪ ˌspæn əʊ 'swiːz ə ‖ -oʊ-
hispid 'hɪsp ɪd §-əd
hiss hɪs hissed hɪst hisser/s 'hɪs ə/z ‖ -ᵊr/z
hisses 'hɪs ɪz -əz hissing 'hɪs ɪŋ
hist hɪst —*or e.g.* [sːt]
histamine 'hɪst ə miːn -mɪn
histo- *comb. form*
with stress-neutral suffix ˌhɪst əʊ ‖ -oʊ —
histocompatible ˌhɪst əʊ kəm 'pæt əb ᵊl ◄
-ɪb ᵊl ‖ -oʊ kəm 'pæt̬-
with stress-imposing suffix hɪ 'stɒ+ ‖ -'stɑː+ —
histolysis hɪ 'stɒl əs ɪs -ɪs-, §-əs ‖ -'stɑːl-
histogram 'hɪst ə græm ~s z
histological ˌhɪst ə 'lɒdʒ ɪk ᵊl ‖ -'lɑːdʒ- ~ly ̩i
histology hɪ 'stɒl ədʒ i ‖ -'stɑːl-
Histon 'hɪst ən
historian hɪ 'stɔːr i‿ən ‖ -'stoʊr- —*sometimes
without h when after the indefinite article an* ~s
z

■with h □without h

BrE 1998

0   20   40   60   80   100%

historic hɪ 'stɒr ɪk ‖ -'stɔːr ɪk -'stɑːr-
—*sometimes without h when after the indefinite
article an* —*BrE 1998 poll panel preference:
with h 94%, without h 6%*

historical hɪ 'stɒr ɪk ᵊl ‖ -'stɔːr- -'stɑːr-
—*sometimes without h when after the indefinite
article an* ~**ly** ̩i
historicism hɪ 'stɒr ɪ ˌsɪz əm -ə- ‖ -'stɔːr-
-'stɑːr-
historicity ˌhɪst ə 'rɪs ət i, •ɒ-, -ɪt i ‖ -ət̬ i
historie... —*see* history
historiographer hɪ ˌstɒr i 'ɒgr əf ə -ˌstɔːr-;
ˌhɪst ɔːr-, •ɒr- ‖ -ˌstɔːr i 'ɑːg rəf ᵊr ~s z
historiography hɪ ˌstɒr i 'ɒgr əf i -ˌstɔːr-;
ˌhɪst ɔːr-, •ɒr- ‖ -ˌstɔːr i 'ɑːg-
his|tory 'hɪs |tri •|tər i ~tories triz tər iz
histrionic ˌhɪs tri 'ɒn ɪk ◄ ‖ -'ɑːn ɪk ◄ ~al ᵊl
~ally ᵊl̩i ~s s
hit hɪt hits hɪts hitting 'hɪt ɪŋ ‖ 'hɪt̬ ɪŋ
'hit list; 'hit man; 'hit pa̩rade
Hitachi *tdmk* hɪ 'tɑːtʃ i -'tætʃ i —*Jp* ['çi ta tçi]
hit-and-miss ˌhɪt ᵊn 'mɪs ◄ -ᵊnd-
hit-and-run ˌhɪt ᵊn 'rʌn ◄ -ᵊnd-
hitch, Hitch hɪtʃ hitched hɪtʃt hitches
'hɪtʃ ɪz -əz hitching 'hɪtʃ ɪŋ
'hitching post
Hitchcock 'hɪtʃ kɒk ‖ -kɑːk
Hitchens 'hɪtʃ ɪnz -ᵊnz
hitchhik|e 'hɪtʃ haɪk ~ed t ~er/s ə/z ‖ ᵊr/z
~es s ~ing ɪŋ
Hitchin 'hɪtʃ ɪn §-ᵊn
Hite haɪt
hitech, hi-tech ˌhaɪ 'tek ◄
hither, H~ 'hɪð ə ‖ -ᵊr
ˌHither 'Green
hitherto ˌhɪð ə 'tuː ◄ ‖ -ᵊr-
Hitler 'hɪt lə ‖ -lᵊr —*Ger* ['hɪt lɐ]
Hitlerian hɪt 'lɪər i‿ən ‖ -'lɪr-
Hitlerism 'hɪt lər ˌɪz əm ‖ 'hɪt lᵊr-
hit-or-miss ˌhɪt ɔː 'mɪs ◄ ‖ -ˌhɪt̬ ᵊr-
hitt... —*see* hit
hitter 'hɪt ə ‖ 'hɪt̬ ᵊr ~s z
Hittite 'hɪt aɪt ~s s
HIV ˌeɪtʃ aɪ 'viː §ˌheɪtʃ-
ˌHIˌV in'fection; ˌHIˌV 'positive
hive haɪv hived haɪvd hives haɪvz hiving
'haɪv ɪŋ
hiway 'haɪ weɪ ~s z
Hixon 'hɪks ᵊn
hiya 'haɪ jə
Hizbollah ˌhɪz bɒ 'lɑː ‖ -bə- ˌhez-
Hluhluwe ʃlu 'ʃluː weɪ ɬu 'ɬuː- —*Zulu*
[ɬu 'ɬuː wɛ]
h'm m, hm —*or e.g.* [m̩m̩m̩]
HMO ˌeɪtʃ em 'əʊ ‖ -'oʊ ~s z
HMS ˌeɪtʃ em 'es ◄ △ˌheɪtʃ-
ˌHMS 'Hood
ho həʊ ‖ hoʊ
Ho Chi Minh ˌhəʊ tʃiː 'mɪn ◄ ‖ ˌhoʊ-
ˌHo Chi ˌMinh 'City
Hoad həʊd ‖ hoʊd
Hoadley, Hoadly 'həʊd li ‖ 'hoʊd-
hoag|lie, hoag|ly 'həʊg li ‖ 'hoʊg li ~ies iz
hoar, Hoar hɔː ‖ hɔːr hour
hoard hɔːd ‖ hɔːrd hourd hoarded 'hɔːd ɪd
-əd ‖ 'hɔːrd əd 'hourd- hoarding

'hɔːd ɪŋ ‖ 'hɔːrd ɪŋ 'hoʊrd- **hoards**
hɔːdz ‖ 'hɔːrdz hoʊrdz
hoarder 'hɔːd ə ‖ 'hɔːrd ər 'hoʊrd- ~s z
hoarding 'hɔːd ɪŋ ‖ 'hɔːrd ɪŋ 'hoʊrd- ~s z
Hoare hɔː ‖ hɔːr hoʊr
hoar-frost ˌhɔː 'frɒst -'frɔːst, '•• ‖ 'hɔːr frɔːst
'hoʊr-, -frɑːst
hoarse hɔːs ‖ hɔːrs hoʊrs **hoarsely**
'hɔːs li ‖ 'hɔːrs li 'hoʊrs- **hoarseness**
'hɔːs nəs -nɪs ‖ 'hɔːrs- 'hoʊrs- **hoarser**
'hɔːs ə ‖ 'hɔːrs ər 'hoʊrs- **hoarsest** 'hɔːs ɪst
-əst ‖ 'hɔːrs əst 'hoʊrs-
hoar|ly 'hɔːr li ‖ 'hoʊr- ~ier i‿ə ‖ i‿ər ~iest
i‿ɪst i‿əst ~iness i nəs i nɪs
hoatzin həʊ 'æts ɪn ˌwɑːt 'siːn ‖ hoʊ- ~s z
hoax həʊks ‖ hoʊks **hoaxed** həʊkst ‖ hoʊkst
hoaxer/s 'həʊks ə/z ‖ 'hoʊks ər/z **hoaxes**
'həʊks ɪz -əz ‖ 'hoʊks əz **hoaxing**
'həʊks ɪŋ ‖ 'hoʊks ɪŋ
hob hɒb ‖ hɑːb **hobs** hɒbz ‖ hɑːbz
Hobart (i) 'həʊb aːt ‖ 'hoʊb aːrt, (ii) -ət ‖ -ərt,
(iii) 'hʌb ət ‖ -ərt —*The place in Tasmania is
(i), that in IN (ii); the 17th-century judge Sir
Henry H~ is believed to have been (iii).*
Hobbes hɒbz ‖ hɑːbz
hobbit 'hɒb ɪt §-ət ‖ 'hɑːb- ~s s
hobbl|e 'hɒb əl ‖ 'hɑːb- ~ed d ~es z ~ing ɪŋ
hobbledehoy ˌhɒb əl di 'hɔɪ '••••
‖ 'hɑːb əl di hɔɪ ~s z
Hobbs hɒbz ‖ hɑːbz
hobb|y 'hɒb li ‖ 'hɑːb li ~ies iz
hobbyhors|e 'hɒb i hɔːs ‖ 'hɑːb i hɔːrs ~es ɪz
əz
hobbyist 'hɒb i ɪst §-əst ‖ 'hɑːb- ~s s
Hobday, h~ 'hɒb deɪ ‖ 'hɑːb-
hobgoblin ˌ₍ᵢ₎hɒb 'gɒb lɪn §-lən, '•, ••
‖ 'hɑːb ˌgɑːb- ~s z
Hobley 'həʊb li ‖ 'hoʊb-
hobnail 'hɒb neɪəl ‖ 'hɑːb- ~ed d ~s z
hobnob 'hɒb nɒb ₍ᵢ₎'•' ‖ 'hɑːb nɑːb ~bed d
~bing ɪŋ ~s z
hobo 'həʊb əʊ ‖ 'hoʊb oʊ ~es, ~s z
Hoboken 'həʊ bəʊk ən ‖ 'hoʊ boʊk- —*Dutch*
['hoː boː kən]
Hobsbawm 'hɒbz bɔːm ‖ 'hɑːbz- -baːm
Hobson 'hɒb sən ‖ 'hɑːb- ~'s z
ˌHobson's 'choice
Hobson-Jobson
ˌhɒb sən 'dʒɒb sən ‖ ˌhɑːb sən 'dʒɑːb sən
Ho Chi Minh ˌhəʊ ˌtʃiː 'mɪn ◄ ‖ ˌhoʊ-
—*Vietnamese* [³ho ²tʃi ¹miɲ]
ˌHo Chi ˌMinh 'City
hock hɒk ‖ hɑːk **hocked** hɒkt ‖ hɑːkt
hocking 'hɒk ɪŋ ‖ 'hɑːk ɪŋ **hocks**
hɒks ‖ hɑːks
hockey 'hɒk i ‖ 'hɑːk i
'hockey ˌstick
Hockney 'hɒk ni ‖ 'hɑːk- ~s, ~'s z
hocus-pocus
ˌhəʊk əs 'pəʊk əs ‖ ˌhoʊk əs 'poʊk əs
hod hɒd ‖ hɑːd **hods** hɒdz ‖ hɑːdz
Hodder 'hɒd ə ‖ 'hɑːd ər
Hoddesdon 'hɒdz dən ‖ 'hɑːdz-

Hoddinott 'hɒd ɪ nɒt -ə- ‖ 'hɑːd ən ɑːt
Hoddle 'hɒd əl ‖ 'hɑːd-
Hodge hɒdʒ ‖ hɑːdʒ
hodge-podge 'hɒdʒ pɒdʒ ‖ 'hɑːdʒ pɑːdʒ
Hodges 'hɒdʒ ɪz -əz ‖ 'hɑːdʒ-
Hodgkin 'hɒdʒ kɪn §-kən ‖ 'hɑːdʒ- ~'s z
'Hodgkin's di,sease
Hodgkinson 'hɒdʒ kɪn sən §-kən- ‖ 'hɑːdʒ-
Hodgson 'hɒdʒ sən ‖ 'hɑːdʒ-
hodometer hɒ 'dɒm ɪt ə -ət- ‖ hoʊ 'dɑːm ət̬ ər
Hodson 'hɒd sən ‖ 'hɑːd-
hoe, Hoe həʊ ‖ hoʊ **hoed** həʊd ‖ hoʊd
hoeing 'həʊ ɪŋ ‖ 'hoʊ ɪŋ **hoes** həʊz ‖ hoʊz
Hoechst hɜːkst ‖ hoʊkst —*Ger* Höchst [høːçst]
hoedown 'həʊ daʊn ‖ 'hoʊ- ~s z
hoer 'həʊ ə ‖ 'hoʊ ər ~s z
Hoey 'həʊ i ‖ 'hoʊ i
Hoffman, Hoffmann 'hɒf mən ‖ 'hɑːf-
Hoffnung 'hɒf nʊŋ ‖ 'hɑːf-
Hofmannsthal 'hɒf mənz taːl ‖ 'hoʊf- —*Ger*
['hoːf mans taːl]
Hofmeister 'hɒf ˌmaɪst ə ‖ 'hɑːf ˌmaɪst ər
—*Ger* ['hoːf ˌmaɪ stɐ]
hog hɒg ‖ hɔːg hɑːg **hogged** hɒgd ‖ hɔːgd
hɑːgd **hogging** 'hɒg ɪŋ ‖ 'hɔːg ɪŋ 'hɑːg ɪŋ
hogs hɒgz ‖ hɔːgz hɑːgz
Hogan, hogan 'həʊg ən ‖ 'hoʊg- ~s z
Hogarth (i) 'həʊ gaːθ ‖ 'hoʊ gaːrθ, (ii)
'hɒg ət ‖ 'hɑːg ərt
Hogarthian həʊ 'gaːθ i‿ən ‖ hoʊ 'gaːrθ- ~s z
Hogben 'hɒg bən ‖ 'hɔːg- 'hɑːg-
Hogg, hogg hɒg ‖ hɔːg hɑːg
hogg... —*see* **hog**
Hoggart 'hɒg ət ‖ 'hɔːg ərt 'hɑːg-
hogget 'hɒg ɪt §-ət ‖ 'hɔːg- 'hɑːg- ~s s
hoggish 'hɒg ɪʃ ‖ 'hɔːg- 'hɑːg- ~ly li ~ness
nəs nɪs
Hogmanay 'hɒg mə neɪ ˌ•• '• ‖ 'hɑːg-
hogshead 'hɒgz hed ‖ 'hɔːgz- 'hɑːgz- ~s z
hog|tie 'hɒg ǀtaɪ ‖ 'hɔːg- 'hɑːg- ~tied taɪd
~tieing, ~tying taɪ ɪŋ ~ties taɪz
hogwash 'hɒg wɒʃ ‖ 'hɔːg waːʃ 'hɑːg-, -wɔːʃ
hogweed 'hɒg wiːd ‖ 'hɔːg- 'hɑːg- ~s z
Hohenlinden ˌhəʊ ən 'lɪnd ən ‖ ˌhoʊ- '••,••
—*Ger* [hoː ən 'lɪn dən]
Hohenzollern ˌhəʊ ən 'zɒl ən ‖
'hoʊ ʊn ˌzaːl ərn —*Ger* [hoː ən 'tsɔl ɐn] ~s z
Hohner *tdmk* 'həʊn ə ‖ 'hoʊn ər —*Ger* ['hoː nɐ]
ho-ho ˌhəʊ 'həʊ ‖ ˌhoʊ 'hoʊ
ho-hum ˌhəʊ 'hʌm ‖ ˌhoʊ-
hoick, hoik hɔɪk **hoicked, hoiked** hɔɪkt
hoicking, hoiking 'hɔɪk ɪŋ **hoicks, hoiks**
hɔɪks
hoi polloi ˌhɔɪ pə 'lɔɪ -pɒ-, -'pɒl ɔɪ
hoist hɔɪst **hoisted** 'hɔɪst ɪd -əd **hoisting**
'hɔɪst ɪŋ **hoists** hɔɪsts
hoity-toity ˌhɔɪt i 'tɔɪt i ‖ ˌhɔɪt̬ i 'tɔɪt̬ i
hok|ey 'həʊk li ‖ 'hoʊk li ~ier i‿ə ‖ i‿ər ~iest
i‿ɪst i‿əst ~eyness, ~iness i nəs i nɪs
ˌhokey 'cokey 'kəʊk i ‖ 'koʊk i
Hokkaido hɒ 'kaɪd əʊ ‖ hoʊ 'kaɪd oʊ haː- —*Jp*
[hok 'kai doo]
Hokonui, h~ ˌhəʊk ə 'nuː i ‖ ˌhoʊk-

hokum 'həʊk əm ‖ 'hoʊk-
Hokusai 'hɒk u saɪ ‖ 'hoʊk- —*Jp* ['ho kᵢu saɪ]
Holbeach, Holbech, Holbeche 'hɒl biːtʃ
  'həʊl- ‖ 'hoʊl-
Holbeck 'hɒl bek 'həʊl- ‖ 'hoʊl-
Holbein 'hɒl baɪn ‖ 'hoʊl- —*Ger* ['hɔl baɪn] ~s
  z
Holborn, Holborne 'həʊb ən 'həʊlb-
  ‖ 'hoʊl bɔːrn —*as a family name, also* 'hɒlb-;
  the place in Scotland is
  həʊl 'bɔːn ‖ hoʊl 'bɔːrn
Holbrook, Holbrooke 'həʊl brʊk →'hɒʊl-
  ‖ 'hoʊl-
Holcomb, Holcombe 'həʊl kəm →'hɒʊl-;
  'hɒl-, 'həʊ- ‖ 'hoʊl-
hold həʊld →hɒʊld ‖ hoʊld **held** held
  holding 'həʊld ɪŋ →'hɒʊld- ‖ 'hoʊld ɪŋ
  holds həʊldz →hɒʊldz ‖ hoʊldz
  'holding ˌcompany; 'holding opeˌration;
  'holding ˌpattern
holdall 'həʊld ɔːl →'hɒʊld- ‖ 'hoʊld- -aːl ~s z
Holden, h~ 'həʊld ən →'hɒʊld- ‖ 'hoʊld-
holder, H~ 'həʊld ə →'hɒʊld- ‖ 'hoʊld ᵊr ~s z
-holder ˌhəʊld ə →ˌhɒʊld- ‖ ˌhoʊld ᵊr —
  kettle-holder 'ket ᵊl ˌhəʊld ə →-ˌhɒʊld-
  ‖ 'ket̬ ᵊl ˌhoʊld ᵊr
Holderness 'həʊld ə nəs →'hɒʊld-, -nɪs
  ‖ 'hoʊld ᵊr-
holdfast 'həʊld faːst →'hɒʊld-, §-fæst
  ‖ 'hoʊld fæst ~s s
holding 'həʊld ɪŋ →'hɒʊld- ‖ 'hoʊld ɪŋ ~s z
holdover 'həʊld ˌəʊv ə →'hɒʊld-
  ‖ 'hoʊld ˌoʊv ᵊr ~s z
holdup 'həʊld ʌp →'hɒʊld- ‖ 'hoʊld- ~s s
hole həʊl →hɒʊl ‖ hoʊl **holed** həʊld →hɒʊld
  ‖ hoʊld *(= hold)* **holes** həʊlz →hɒʊlz ‖ hoʊlz
  holing 'həʊl ɪŋ →'hɒʊl- ‖ 'hoʊl ɪŋ
  ˌhole in 'one
hole-and-corner ˌhəʊl ən 'kɔːn ə →ˌhɒʊl-,
  -ənd-, →-əŋ- ‖ ˌhoʊl ən 'kɔːrn ᵊr
holey 'həʊl i →'hɒʊl- ‖ 'hoʊl i
Holford 'həʊl fəd →'hɒʊl-, 'hɒl- ‖ 'hoʊl fᵊrd
holiday, H~ 'hɒl ə deɪ -ɪ-, -di ‖ 'haːl- ~ed d
  ~ing ɪŋ ~s z
  'holiday camp
holidaymaker 'hɒl ə deɪ ˌmeɪk ə '•ɪ-, '••di-
  ‖ 'haːl ə deɪ ˌmeɪk ᵊr ~s z
holi... —*see* holy
holier-than-thou
  ˌhəʊl iˌə ðən 'ðaʊ ◂ ‖ ˌhoʊl iˌᵊr-
holiness, H~ 'həʊl i nəs -nɪs ‖ 'hoʊl-
Holinshed 'hɒl ɪn ʃed ‖ 'haːl- —*This is the
  usual pronunciation for the 16th-c. chronicler,
  though he may well actually have been*
  -ɪnz hed.
holism 'həʊl ˌɪz əm →'hɒʊl-, 'hɒl- ‖ 'hoʊl-
holistic həʊ 'lɪst ɪk hɒ- ‖ hoʊ- ~ally ᵊl_i
Holland, h~ 'hɒl ənd ‖ 'haːl- —*Dutch*
  ['hɔl ɑnt]
hollandaise ˌhɒl ən 'deɪz ◂ ‖ ˌhaːl- '•••
  ˌhollandaise 'sauce, ‖ ˌ•• '••, '••••
holl|er 'hɒl |ə ‖ 'haːl |ᵊr ~ered əd ‖ ᵊrd ~ering
  ᵊr ɪŋ ~ers əz ‖ ᵊrz

Holles 'hɒl ɪs §-əs ‖ 'haːl-
Holliday 'hɒl ə deɪ -ɪ-, -di ‖ 'haːl-
Hollie 'hɒl i ‖ 'haːl i
Hollinghurst 'hɒl ɪŋ hɜːst ‖ 'haːl ɪŋ hɝːst
Hollingsworth 'hɒl ɪŋz wɜːθ -wəθ
  ‖ 'haːl ɪŋz wɝːθ
Hollins 'hɒl ɪnz §-ənz ‖ 'haːl-
Hollis 'hɒl ɪs §-əs ‖ 'haːl-
hollow 'hɒl əʊ ‖ 'haːl oʊ ~ed d ~ing ɪŋ ~ly li
  ~ness nəs nɪs ~s z
Holloway 'hɒl ə weɪ ‖ 'haːl-
hollowware 'hɒl əʊ weə ‖ 'haːl oʊ wer -wær
holl|y, Holly 'hɒl |i ‖ 'haːl |i ~ies iz
hollyhock 'hɒl i hɒk ‖ 'haːl i haːk -hɔːk ~s s
Hollywood 'hɒl i wʊd ‖ 'haːl-
  ˌHollywood 'stars
holm həʊm ‖ hoʊm *(= home)* **holms**
  həʊmz ‖ hoʊmz
Holm həʊm §həʊlm ‖ hoʊm hoʊlm
Holman 'həʊl mən →'hɒʊl- ‖ 'hoʊl-
Holme həʊm §həʊlm ‖ hoʊm hoʊlm
Holmes həʊmz §həʊlmz ‖ hoʊmz hoʊlmz
Holmesdale 'həʊmz deɪᵊl ‖ 'hoʊmz-
Holmfirth ˌhəʊm 'fɜːθ ˌhoʊm 'fɝːθ
holmium 'həʊlm iˌəm →'hɒʊlm-, 'hɒlm-
  ‖ 'hoʊlm-
holm-oak ˌhəʊm əʊk ˌ•'• ‖ ˌhoʊm oʊk ~s s
Holmwood 'həʊm wʊd ‖ 'hoʊm-
Holness 'həʊl nəs →'hɒʊl-, -nɪs, -nes ‖ 'hoʊl-
holo- *comb. form*
  with stress-neutral suffix ˌhɒl əʊ ‖ ˌhoʊl ə
    ˌhaːl ə — **holoblastic** ˌhɒl əʊ
    'blæst ɪk ◂ ‖ ˌhoʊl ə- ˌhaːl-
  with stress-imposing suffix hɒ 'lɒ+ həʊ-
    ‖ hoʊ 'laː+ hə- — **holopathy** hɒ 'lɒp əθ i
    həʊ- ‖ hoʊ 'laːp-
holocaust 'hɒl ə kɔːst 'həʊl- ‖ 'hoʊl- 'haːl-,
  -kaːst ~s s
Holocene 'hɒl əʊ siːn ‖ 'hoʊl ə- 'haːl-
Holofernes ˌhɒl ə 'fɜːn iːz hə 'lɒf ə niːz
  ‖ ˌhaːl ə 'fɝːn iːz ˌhoʊl-
hologram 'hɒl ə græm ‖ 'hoʊl- 'haːl- ~s z
holograph 'hɒl ə graːf -græf ‖ 'hoʊl ə græf
  'haːl- ~s s
holography hɒ 'lɒg rəf i həʊ- ‖ hoʊ 'laːg rəf i
holophras|e 'hɒl əʊ freɪz ‖ 'hoʊl ə- 'haːl ə-
  ~es ɪz əz
holophrastic ˌhɒl əʊ 'fræst ɪk ◂ ‖ ˌhoʊl ə-
  ˌhaːl ə-
holothurian ˌhɒl əʊ 'θjʊər iˌən -'θɔːr-, -'θʊər-
  ‖ ˌhoʊl ə 'θʊr- ˌhaːl-, -'θjʊr- ~s z
holp həʊlp →hɒʊlp ‖ hoʊlp
holpen 'həʊlp ən →'hɒʊlp- ‖ 'hoʊlp-
Holroyd 'hɒl rɔɪd 'həʊl- ‖ 'haːl- 'hoʊl-
hols *'holidays'* hɒlz ‖ haːlz
Holst həʊlst →hɒʊlst ‖ hoʊlst
Holstein, h~ 'hɒl staɪn 'həʊl- ‖ 'hoʊl stiːn
  -staɪn —*Ger* ['hɔl ʃtaɪn] ~s z
holster 'həʊlst ə →'hɒʊlst- ‖ 'hoʊlst ᵊr ~ed d
  ~s z
Holt həʊlt →hɒʊlt ‖ hoʊlt
Holtby 'həʊlt bi →'hɒʊlt- ‖ 'hoʊlt-

holus-bolus
ˌhəʊl əs ˈbəʊl əs ‖ ˌhoʊl əs ˈboʊl əs

holly ˈhɒʊl i i ‖ ˈhoʊl i i **~ier** i‿ə ‖ i‿ər **~iest** i‿ɪst
i‿əst **~ily** əl i ɪ li **~iness** i nəs i nɪs
ˌHoly ˈBible; ˌHoly Comˈmunion; ˌHoly
ˈFamily; ˌHoly ˈGhost; ˌHoly ˈGrail; the
ˈHoly Land; holy of ˈholies; ˌholy ˈorders;
ˌHoly ˌRoman ˈEmpire; ˌHoly ˈScripture;
ˌHoly ˈSee; ˌHoly ˈSpirit; ˈholy ˌwater,
ˌ·· ˈ··; ˈHoly Week; ˌHoly ˈWrit

Holyhead place in Gwynedd ˌhɒl i ˈhed ◄ ˈ···
‖ ˈhɑːl i hed

Holyoak, Holyoake, Holyoke
ˈhɒʊl i əʊk ‖ ˈhoʊl i oʊk —but Holyoke, MA, is
usually ˈhoʊl joʊk

Holyport place in Berks ˈhɒl i pɔːt ‖ ˈhɑːl i pɔːrt
-poʊrt

Holyrood ˈhɒl i ruːd ‖ ˈhoʊl-

holyston|e ˈhɒʊl i stəʊn ‖ ˈhoʊl i stoʊn **~ed** d
~es z **~ing** ɪŋ

Holywell ˈhɒl i wel -wəl ‖ ˈhɑːl-

homage ˈhɒm ɪdʒ ‖ ˈhɑːm-

hombre ˈɒm breɪ -bri ‖ ˈɑːm bri ˈʌm-, -breɪ
—Sp [ˈom bre] **~s** z

homburg, H~ ˈhɒm bɜːg ‖ ˈhɑːm bɝːg —Ger
[ˈhɔm bʊʁk] **~s** z

home həʊm ‖ hoʊm **homed** həʊmd ‖ hoʊmd
homes həʊmz ‖ hoʊmz **homing**
ˈhəʊm ɪŋ ‖ ˈhoʊm ɪŋ —The phrase at home
formerly had an RP variant ə ˈtəʊm, now
obsolete.
ˌhome ˈbrew; ˌHome ˈCounties; ˌhome
ˌecoˈnomics; ˌhome ˈfront; ˌHome ˈGuard;
ˌhome ˈhelp; ˌhome ˈmovie; ˈHome
ˌOffice; ˌhome ˈrule; ˌhome ˈrun; ˌHome
ˈSecretary; ˌhome ˈstraight; ˌhome
ˈstretch; ˌhome ˈtruth

Home family name (i) həʊm ‖ hoʊm, (ii) hjuːm
—The Earls of Home are (ii).

home-baked ˌhəʊm ˈbeɪkt ◄ ‖ ˌhoʊm-

homebod|y ˈhəʊm ˌbɒd i ‖ ˈhoʊm ˌbɑːd i
~ies iz

homeboy ˈhəʊm bɔɪ ‖ ˈhoʊm- **~s** z

home-brewed ˌhəʊm ˈbruːd ◄ ‖ ˌhoʊm-
ˌhome-brewed ˈbeer

homecoming ˈhəʊm ˌkʌm ɪŋ ‖ ˈhoʊm- **~s** z

homegrown ˌhəʊm ˈgrəʊn ◄ ‖ ˌhoʊm ˈgroʊn ◄
ˌhomegrown ˈcucumbers

homeland ˈhəʊm lænd -lənd ‖ ˈhoʊm- **~s** z

homeless ˈhəʊm ləs -lɪs ‖ ˈhoʊm- **~ness** nəs
nɪs

homelike ˈhəʊm laɪk ‖ ˈhoʊm-

home|ly ˈhəʊm |li ‖ ˈhoʊm- **-lier** li‿ə ‖ li‿ər
~liest li‿ɪst li‿əst **~liness** li nəs li nɪs

homemade ˌhəʊm ˈmeɪd ◄ ‖ ˈhoʊm meɪd -eɪd

homemaker ˈhəʊm ˌmeɪk ə ‖ ˈhoʊm ˌmeɪk ər
~s z

homeo- comb. form
with stress-neutral suffix ˌhəʊm i əʊ ˌhɒm-
‖ ˌhoʊm i‿ə — **homeomorphism** ˌhəʊm i əʊ
ˈmɔːf ˌɪz əm ˌhɒm- ‖ ˌhoʊm i‿ə ˈmɔːrf-
with stress-imposing suffix ˌhəʊm i ˈɒ+ ˌhɒm-

‖ ˌhoʊm i ˈɑː+ — **homeology**
ˌhəʊm i ˈɒl ədʒ i ˌhɒm- ‖ ˌhoʊm i ˈɑːl-

homeopath ˈhəʊm i‿ə pæθ ˈhɒm- ‖ ˈhoʊm- **~s**
s

homeopathic ˌhəʊm i‿ə ˈpæθ ɪk ◄ ˌhɒm-
‖ ˌhoʊm- **~ally** əl_i

homeopathist ˌhəʊm i ˈɒp əθ ɪst ˌhɒm-, §-əst
‖ ˌhoʊm i ˈɑːp- **~s** s

homeopathy ˌhəʊm i ˈɒp əθ i ˌhɒm-
‖ ˌhoʊm i ˈɑːp- ˌhɑːm-

homeostasis ˌhəʊm i əʊ ˈsteɪs ɪs §-əs;
ˌhəʊm i ˈɒst əs ɪs, -əs ‖ ˌhoʊm i oʊ-

homeostatic
ˌhəʊm i əʊ ˈstæt ɪk ◄ ‖ ˌhoʊm i oʊ ˈstæt̬ ɪk ◄
~ally əl_i

homeotic ˌhəʊm i ˈɒt ɪk ◄ ˌhɒm-
‖ ˌhoʊm i ˈɑːt̬ ɪk ◄

homeowner ˈhəʊm ˌəʊn ə ‖ ˈhoʊm ˌoʊn ər **~s**
z

Homer, homer ˈhəʊm ə ‖ ˈhoʊm ər **~s, ~'s** z

Homeric həʊ ˈmer ɪk ‖ hoʊ- **~ally** əl_i

Homerton ˈhɒm ət ən ‖ ˈhɑːm ərt ən

homesick ˈhəʊm sɪk ‖ ˈhoʊm- **~ness** nəs nɪs

homespun ˈhəʊm spʌn ‖ ˈhoʊm-

homestay ˈhəʊm steɪ ‖ ˈhoʊm- **~s** z

homestead n ˈhəʊm sted -stɪd, -stəd ‖ ˈhoʊm-
~s z

homestead v ˈhəʊm sted ‖ ˈhoʊm- **~ed** ɪd əd
~er/s ə/z ‖ ər/z **~ing** ɪŋ **~s** z

hometown ˌhəʊm ˈtaʊn ◄ ‖ ˌhoʊm-

homeward ˈhəʊm wəd ‖ ˈhoʊm wərd **~s** z

homework ˈhəʊm wɜːk ‖ ˈhoʊm wɝːk

hom|ey ˈhəʊm |i ‖ ˈhoʊm |i **-ier** i‿ə ‖ i‿ər
~iest i‿ɪst i‿əst

homicidal ˌhɒm ɪ ˈsaɪd əl ◄ -ə- ‖ ˌhɑːm-
ˌhoʊm- **~ly** i

homicide ˈhɒm ɪ saɪd -ə- ‖ ˈhɑːm- ˈhoʊm- **~s**
z

homiletic ˌhɒm ɪ ˈlet ɪk ◄ -ə-, △-ˈlekt-
‖ ˌhɑːm ə ˈlet̬ ɪk ◄ **~ally** əl_i **~s** s

homil|y ˈhɒm əl |i -ɪl- ‖ ˈhɑːm- **~ies** iz

homing ˈhəʊm ɪŋ ‖ ˈhoʊm ɪŋ
ˈhoming ˌpigeon

hominid ˈhɒm ə nɪd -ɪ-; §-ən əd ‖ ˈhɑːm- **~s** z

hominoid ˈhɒm ə nɔɪd -ɪ- ‖ ˈhɑːm- **~s** z

hominy ˈhɒm ən i -ɪn- ‖ ˈhɑːm-

homo, Homo ˈhəʊm əʊ ‖ ˈhoʊm oʊ **~s** z
ˌHomo ˈsapiens ˈsæp i enz ˈseɪp-, -i‿ənz

homo- comb. form
with stress-neutral suffix ˌhəʊm əʊ ˌhɒm-
‖ ˌhoʊm ə — **homotaxis** ˌhəʊm əʊ ˈtæks ɪs
ˌhɒm-, §-əs ‖ ˌhoʊm ə-
with stress-imposing suffix hə ˈmɒ+ hɒ-
‖ hə ˈmɑː+ hoʊ- — **homogonous** hə ˈmɒg
ən əs hɒ- ‖ hə ˈmɑːg- hoʊ-

homoeo... —see homeo...

homoerotic ˌhəʊm əʊ ɪ ˈrɒt ɪk ◄ ˌhɒm-, -ə'·-
‖ ˌhoʊm oʊ ɪ ˈrɑːt̬ ɪk ◄

homoeroticism ˌhəʊm əʊ ɪ ˈrɒt ɪ ˌsɪz əm
ˌhɒm-, -ə'·-, -'·ə- ‖ ˌhoʊm oʊ ɪ ˈrɑːt̬ ə-

homogeneity ˌhəʊm əʊ dʒə ˈniː_ət i ˌhɒm-,
-dʒɪ'·-, -ˈneɪ-, -ɪt i ‖ ˌhoʊm ə dʒə ˈniː ət̬ i
-ˈneɪ-

H

homogeneous ˌhəʊm əʊ ˈdʒiːn i‿əs ◂ ˌhɒm-
‖ ˌhoʊm ə- **~ly** li **~ness** nəs nɪs
homogenis... —see **homogeniz...**
homogenization hə ˌmɒdʒ ən aɪ ˈzeɪʃ ən hɒ-,
-ˈ•ɪn-, -ɪˈ•- ‖ -ˌmaːdʒ ən ə- hoʊ-
homogeniz|e hə ˈmɒdʒ ə naɪz hɒ-, -ɪ-
‖ -ˈmaːdʒ- hoʊ- **~ed** d **~es** ɪz əz **~ing** ɪŋ
homogenous hə ˈmɒdʒ ən əs hɒ-, -ɪn-
‖ hoʊ ˈmaːdʒ-
homograph ˈhɒm ə graːf ˈhəʊm-, -græf
‖ ˈhaːm ə græf ˈhoʊm- **~s** k
homographic ˌhɒm ə ˈgræf ɪk ◂ ‖ ˌhaːm-
ˌhoʊm-
homolog ˈhɒm ə lɒg ‖ ˈhoʊm ə lɔːg ˈhaːm-,
-laːg **~s** z
homologous hə ˈmɒl əg əs hɒ- ‖ hoʊ ˈmaːl-
hə-
homologue ˈhɒm ə lɒg ‖ ˈhoʊm ə lɔːg ˈhaːm-,
-laːg **~s** z
homolog|y hə ˈmɒl ədʒ i hɒ- ‖ hoʊ ˈmaːl- hə-
~ies iz
homonym ˈhɒm ə nɪm ˈhəʊm- ‖ ˈhaːm-
ˈhoʊm- **~s** z
homonymous hə ˈmɒn ɪm əs hɒ-, -əm-
‖ hoʊ ˈmaːn- hə- **~ly** li
homonymy hə ˈmɒn ɪm i hɒ-, -əm-
‖ hoʊ ˈmaːn- hə-
homophile ˈhəʊm əʊ faɪəl ˈhɒm- ‖ ˈhoʊm ə-
~s z
homophobe ˈhəʊm əʊ fəʊb ˈhɒm-
‖ ˈhoʊm ə foʊb **~s** z
homophobia ˌhəʊm əʊ ˈfəʊb i‿ə ˌhɒm-
‖ ˌhoʊm ə ˈfoʊb-
homophobic ˌhəʊm əʊ ˈfəʊb ɪk ◂ ˌhɒm-
‖ ˌhoʊm ə ˈfoʊb-
homophone ˈhɒm ə fəʊn ˈhəʊm-
‖ ˈhaːm ə foʊn ˈhoʊm- **~s** z
homophonic ˌhɒm ə ˈfɒn ɪk ◂ ˌhəʊm-
‖ ˌhaːm ə ˈfaːn ɪk ◂ ˌhoʊm-, -ˈfoʊn-
homophonous hə ˈmɒf ən əs hɒ- ‖ hoʊ ˈmaːf-
hə-
homophony hə ˈmɒf ən i hɒ- ‖ hoʊ ˈmaːf-
hə-
homorganic ˌhɒm ɔː ˈgæn ɪk ◂ ˌhəʊm-
‖ ˌhoʊm ɔːr- ˌhaːm-

HOMOSEXUAL

	■ ˌhəʊm-	▢ ˌhɒm-
BrE 1988		
0	20 40 60 80	100%

homosexual ˌhəʊm əʊ ˈsek ʃu‿əl ◂ ˌhɒm-,
-ˈseks ju‿əl, -ˈsek ʃəl ‖ ˌhoʊm ə ˈsekʃ u‿əl ◂
-ˈ•əl —*BrE 1988 poll panel preference:* ˌhəʊm-
59%, ˌhɒm- *41%.*
homosexuality ˌhəʊm əʊ ˌsekʃ u ˈæl ət i
ˌhɒm-, -ˌseks ju-, -ɪt i
‖ ˌhoʊm ə ˌsekʃ u ˈæl ət̬ i
homozygous ˌhɒm ə ˈzaɪg əs ◂ ˌhəʊm-
‖ ˌhoʊm- ˌhaːm-
homunc|ulus hɒ ˈmʌŋk |jʊl əs hə-
‖ hoʊ ˈmʌŋk |jəl əs **~uli** jʊ laɪ ‖ jə laɪ
hom|y ˈhəʊm |i ‖ ˈhoʊm li **~ier** i‿ə ‖ i‿ər **~iest**
i‿ɪst i‿əst

Hon. *'Honourable'; 'Honorary'* ɒn ‖ aːn **Hons**
ɒnz ‖ aːnz
Hon *'Honey'* hʌn
honcho ˈhɒntʃ əʊ ‖ ˈhaːntʃ oʊ **~s** z
Honda *tdmk* ˈhɒnd ə ‖ ˈhaːnd ə —*Jp* [ho‚n da]
~s z
Honddu ˈhɒn ði ‖ ˈhaːn-
Hondur|an/s hɒn ˈdjʊər |ən/z -ˈdʊər-,
→§-ˈdʒʊər- ‖ haːn ˈdʊr- -ˈdjʊr- **~as** əs æs
hone, Hone həʊn ‖ hoʊn **honed**
həʊnd ‖ hoʊnd **hones** həʊnz ‖ hoʊnz
honing ˈhəʊn ɪŋ ‖ ˈhoʊn ɪŋ
Honecker ˈhɒn ek ə -ɪk- ‖ ˈhaːn ɪk ər —*Ger*
[ˈhoːn ɛk ɐ]
Honegger ˈhɒn ɪg ə -eg- ‖ ˈhaːn ɪg ər —*Fr*
[ɔ nɛ gɛːʁ]
honest ˈɒn ɪst -əst ‖ ˈaːn əst **~ly** li
honest-to-goodness ˌɒn ɪst tə ˈgʊd nəs ◂
ˌ•əst-, -tuˈ•-, -nɪs ‖ ˌaːn əst-
honesty ˈɒn əst i -ɪst- ‖ ˈaːn-
honey, Honey ˈhʌn i **~ed** d **~s** z
honeybee ˈhʌn i biː **~s** z
honeybun ˈhʌn i bʌn **~s** z
honeybunch ˈhʌn i bʌntʃ **~es** ɪz əz
honeycomb ˈhʌn i kəʊm ‖ -koʊm **~ed** d **~ing**
ɪŋ **~s** z
Honeycomb, Honeycombe
ˈhʌn i kəʊm ‖ -koʊm
honeydew ˈhʌn i djuː →§-dʒuː: -duː: -djuː:
ˌhoneydew ˈmelon
honeyed ˈhʌn id
honeymoon ˈhʌn i muːn **~ed** d **~er/s** ə/
z ‖ ər/z **~ing** ɪŋ **~s** z
ˈhoneymoon ˌcouple
honeysuckle ˈhʌn i ˌsʌk əl **~s** z
Hong Kong ˌhɒŋ ˈkɒŋ ◂ ‖ ˈhaːŋ kaːŋ ˈhɔːŋ-,
-kɔːŋ, ˌ•ˈ• —*Chi* Xiānggǎng [¹çaŋ ³kaŋ],
Cantonese [¹hœːŋ ²kɔːŋ]
Honiara ˌhəʊn i ˈaːr ə ˌhɒn- ‖ ˌhoʊn-
honied ˈhʌn id
honi soit qui mal y pense ˌɒn i ˌswaː
kiː ˌmæl i ˈpɒs ‖ ˌaːn i ˌswaː kiː
ˌmaːl iː ˈpaːns ˌɔːn-, ˌoʊn- —*Fr*
[ɔ ni swa ki ma li pɑ̃ːs]
Honiton ˈhʌn ɪt ən ˈhɒn-, -ət-
honk hɒŋk ‖ haːŋk hɔːŋk **honked**
hɒŋkt ‖ haːŋkt hɔːŋkt **honking**
ˈhɒŋk ɪŋ ‖ ˈhaːŋk ɪŋ ˈhɔːŋk- **honks**
hɒŋks ‖ haːŋks hɔːŋks
honk|ie, honk|y ˈhɒŋk |i ‖ ˈhaːŋk |i ˈhɔːŋk-
~ies iz
honky-tonk ˈhɒŋk i tɒŋk ˌ•ˈ•ˈ• ‖ ˈhaːŋk i taːŋk
ˈhɔːŋk i tɔːŋk **~s** s
Honolulu ˌhɒn ə ˈluːl uː -əl ˈuːl- ‖ ˌhaːn-
honor, Honor ˈɒn ə ‖ ˈaːn ər **~ed** d **honoring**
ˈɒn ər‿ɪŋ ‖ ˈaːn ər‿ɪŋ **~s** z
ˈhonor ˌroll
honorab|le, H~ ˈɒn ər‿əb |əl ‖ ˈaːn- ˈ•ərb |əl
~leness əl nəs -nɪs **~ly** li
ˌhonorable ˈmention
honorari|um ˌɒn ə ˈreər i‿əm -ˈraːr-
‖ ˌaːn ə ˈrer- **~a** ə **~ums** əmz
honorary ˈɒn ər‿ər i ⚠ ˈɒn ər‿i ‖ ˈaːn ə rer i

honorific ˌɒn ə ˈrɪf ɪk ◄ ‖ ˌɑːn- **~ally** ᵊl_i **~s** s
honoris causa hɒ ˌnɔːr ɪs ˈkauz ɑː ɒ-, -ˈkaʊs-,
-ə ‖ oʊ ˌnɔːr əs ˈkaʊs ɑː ɑː-, -, -noʊr-, -ə
honour, H~ ˈɒn ə ‖ ˈɑːn ᵊr **~ed** d **honouring**
ˈɒn ᵊr_ɪŋ ‖ ˈɑːn ᵊr_ɪŋ **~s** z
'honours list
honourab|le, H~ ˈɒn ᵊr_əb |ᵊl ‖ ˈɑːn- ˈ•ᵊrb |ᵊl
~leness ᵊl nəs -nɪs **~ly** li
ˌhonourable 'mention
Honshu ˈhɒn ʃuː ‖ ˈhɑːn- —*Jp* [ˈhon ɕɯɯɯ]
Hoo huː
hooch huːtʃ
hood hʊd **hooded** ˈhʊd ɪd -əd **hooding**
ˈhʊd ɪŋ **hoods** hʊdz
-hood hʊd — **fatherhood** ˈfɑːð ə hʊd ‖ -ᵊr-
hoodlum ˈhuːd ləm ‖ ˈhʊd- ˈhuːd- **~s** z
hoodoo ˈhuː duː **~ed** d **~ing** ɪŋ **~s** z
hood|wink ˈhʊd |wɪŋk **~winked** wɪŋkt
~winking wɪŋk ɪŋ **~winks** wɪŋks
hooey ˈhuː_i
hoof huːf hʊf **hoofed** huːft hʊft **hoofing**
ˈhuːf ɪŋ ˈhʊf- **hoofs** huːfs hʊfs **hooves**
huːvz hʊvz
hoofer ˈhuːf ə ˈhʊf- ‖ -ᵊr **~s** z
Hoogly, Hooghly ˈhuːg li
hoo-ha ˈhuː hɑː **~s** z
hook, Hook hʊk §huːk **hooked** hʊkt §huːkt
hooking ˈhʊk ɪŋ §ˈhuːk- **hooks** hʊks §huːks
hooka, hookah ˈhʊk ə **~s** z
Hooke hʊk §huːk
hooker, H~ ˈhʊk ə §ˈhuːk- ‖ -ᵊr **~s** z
hookey ˈhʊk i
hook-nosed ˌhʊk ˈnəʊzd ◄ §ˌhuːk-, ˈ••
‖ ˈhʊk noʊzd
hookup ˈhʊk ʌp §ˈhuːk- **~s** s
hookworm ˈhʊk wɜːm §ˈhuːk- ‖ -wɜːm **~s** z
hooky ˈhʊk i
Hooley ˈhuːl i
hooligan ˈhuːl ɪg ən -əg- **~s** z
hooliganism ˈhuːl ɪg ən ˌɪz əm ˈ•əg-
Hoon huːn
hoop huːp §hʊp **hooped** huːpt §hʊpt
hooping ˈhuːp ɪŋ §ˈhʊp- **hoops** huːps
§hʊps
Hooper ˈhuːp ə §ˈhʊp- ‖ -ᵊr
hoop-la ˈhuːp lɑː ˈhʊp-
hoopoe ˈhuːp uː -əʊ **~s** z
hooray hu ˈreɪ hə-, ˌhuː- **~ed** d **~ing** ɪŋ **~s** z
hooˌray 'Henry, ˌ•• ˈ••
hoosegow ˈhuːs gaʊ **~s** z
Hoosier, h~ ˈhuːʒ ə ‖ -ᵊr **~s** z
Hooson ˈhuːs ən
hoot huːt **hooted** ˈhuːt ɪd -əd ‖ ˈhuːt̬ əd
hooting ˈhuːt ɪŋ ‖ ˈhuːt̬ ɪŋ **hoots** huːts
hootch, H~ *tdmk* huːtʃ
hootenann|y ˈhuːt ən æn |i **~ies** iz
hooter ˈhuːt ə ‖ ˈhuːt̬ ᵊr **~s** z
Hooton ˈhuːt ən
hoover, H~ ˈhuːv ə ‖ -ᵊr **~ed** d **hoovering**
ˈhuːv ᵊr_ɪŋ **~s** z
hooves huːvz §hʊvz
hop hɒp ‖ hɑːp **hopped** hɒpt ‖ hɑːpt

hopping ˈhɒp ɪŋ ‖ ˈhɑːp ɪŋ **hops**
hɒps ‖ hɑːps
Hopcraft ˈhɒp krɑːft §-kræft ‖ ˈhɑːp kræft
Hopcroft ˈhɒp krɒft -krɔːft ‖ ˈhɑːp krɔːft
-krɑːft
hope, Hope həʊp ‖ hoʊp **hoped**
həʊpt ‖ hoʊpt **hopes** həʊps ‖ hoʊps
hoping ˈhəʊp ɪŋ ‖ ˈhoʊp ɪŋ
'hope chest
hopeful ˈhəʊp fᵊl -fʊl ‖ ˈhoʊp- **~ly** _i **~ness**
nəs nɪs **~s** z
hopeless ˈhəʊp ləs -lɪs ‖ ˈhoʊp- **~ly** li **~ness**
nəs nɪs
Hopi ˈhəʊ piː ˈhəʊp i ‖ ˈhoʊ piː **~s** z
Hopkin ˈhɒp kɪn ‖ ˈhɑːp-
Hopkins ˈhɒp kɪnz ‖ ˈhɑːp-
Hopkinson ˈhɒp kɪn sən ‖ ˈhɑːp-
hoplite ˈhɒp laɪt ‖ ˈhɑːp- **~s** s
hopp... —*see* hop
hopped-up ˌhɒpt ˈʌp ◄ ‖ ˌhɑːpt-
hopper, H~ ˈhɒp ə ‖ ˈhɑːp ᵊr **~s** z
hop-picker ˈhɒp ˌpɪk ə ‖ ˈhɑːp ˌpɪk ᵊr **~s** z
Hoppus ˈhɒp əs ‖ ˈhɑːp-
hopsack ˈhɒp sæk ‖ ˈhɑːp- **~ing** ɪŋ
hopscotch ˈhɒp skɒtʃ ‖ ˈhɑːp skɑːtʃ
Hopton ˈhɒpt ən ‖ ˈhɑːpt-
Hopwood ˈhɒp wʊd ‖ ˈhɑːp-
hora ˈhɔːr ə ‖ ˈhoʊr- **~s** z
Horabin ˈhɒr ə bɪn ‖ ˈhɔːr-
Horace ˈhɒr əs -ɪs ‖ ˈhɔːr- ˈhɑːr-
Horatian hə ˈreɪʃ ᵊn hɒ-, -ˈreɪʃ i_ən
Horatio hə ˈreɪʃ i_əʊ hɒ- ‖ _oʊ -ˈreɪʃ oʊ
Horatius hə ˈreɪʃ i_əs hɒ-, -ˈreɪʃ əs
Horbury ˈhɔː bər_i ‖ ˈhɔːr ˌber i
horde hɔːd ‖ hɔːrd hourd (= *hoard*) **hordes**
hɔːdz ‖ hɔːrdz hourdz
Hordern ˈhɔːd ᵊn ‖ ˈhɔːrd ᵊrn
Hore hɔː ‖ hɔːr hour
Horeb ˈhɔːr eb ‖ ˈhour-
horehound ˈhɔː haʊnd ‖ ˈhɔːr-
horizon hə ˈraɪz ᵊn —*sometimes* ə- *after the*
indefinite article an **~s** z
horizontal ˌhɒr ɪ ˈzɒnt ᵊl ◄ -ə- ‖ ˌhɔːr ə ˈzɑːnt̬
ᵊl ◄ ˌhɑːr- **~ly** i **~s** z
Horley ˈhɔːl i ‖ ˈhɔːrl i
Horlick ˈhɔːl ɪk ‖ ˈhɔːrl-
Horlicks *tdmk* ˈhɔːl ɪks ‖ ˈhɔːrl-
hormonal ₍ₕ₎hɔː ˈməʊn ᵊl ‖ hɔːr ˈmoʊn ᵊl
hormone ˈhɔːm əʊn ‖ ˈhɔːrm oʊn **~s** z
Hormuz ˌhɔː ˈmuːz ˈhɔːm əz ‖ ˌhɔːr- ˈhɔːrm əz
horn, Horn hɔːn ‖ hɔːrn **horned**
hɔːnd ‖ hɔːrnd **horning** ˈhɔːn ɪŋ ‖ ˈhɔːrn ɪŋ
horns hɔːnz ‖ hɔːrnz
hornbeam ˈhɔːn biːm →ˈhɔːm- ‖ ˈhɔːrn- **~s** z
hornbill ˈhɔːn bɪl →ˈhɔːm- ‖ ˈhɔːrn- **~s** z
hornblende ˈhɔːn blend →ˈhɔːm- ‖ ˈhɔːrn- **~s**
z
Hornblower ˈhɔːn ˌbləʊ ə →ˈhɔːm-
‖ ˈhɔːrn ˌbloʊ ᵊr
Hornby ˈhɔːn bi →ˈhɔːm- ‖ ˈhɔːrn-
Horncastle ˈhɔːn ˌkɑːs ᵊl →ˈhɔːŋ-, §-, kæs-
‖ ˈhɔːrn ˌkæs ᵊl
Hornchurch ˈhɔːn tʃɜːtʃ ‖ ˈhɔːrn tʃɜːtʃ

Horne hɔːn ‖ hɔːrn
horned *adj* hɔːnd 'hɔːn ɪd, -əd ‖ hɔːrnd
  'hɔːrn əd
Horner 'hɔːn ə ‖ 'hɔːrn ər
hornet 'hɔːn ɪt -ət ‖ 'hɔːrn- ~s s
  'hornet's nest
Horney 'hɔːn i ‖ 'hɔːrn i
horni... —*see* horny
Horniman 'hɔːn ɪ mən -ə- ‖ 'hɔːrn-
hornpipe 'hɔːn paɪp →'hɔːm- ‖ 'hɔːrn- ~s s
horn-rimmed ˌhɔːn 'rɪmd ◂ ˌhɔːrn-
Hornsby 'hɔːnz bi ‖ 'hɔːrnz-
Hornsea 'hɔːn siː ‖ 'hɔːrn-
Hornsey 'hɔːnz i ‖ 'hɔːrnz i
hornswoggl|e 'hɔːn ˌswɒg əl ‖ 'hɔːrn ˌswɑːg əl
  ~ed d ~es z ~ing ɪŋ
horn|y 'hɔːn i i ‖ 'hɔːrn i i ~ier i‿ə ‖ i‿ər ~iest
  i‿ɪst i‿əst ~ily ɪ li əl i ~iness i nəs i nɪs
horologist hə 'rɒl ədʒ ɪst hɒ-, hɔː-, §-əst
  ‖ hə 'rɑːl- ~s s
horologium, H~ ˌhɒr ə 'ləʊdʒ i‿əm ˌhɔːr-
  ‖ hɔːr ə 'loʊdʒ-
horology hə 'rɒl ədʒ i hɒ-, hɔː- ‖ hə 'rɑːl-
horoscope 'hɒr ə skəʊp ‖ 'hɔːr ə skoʊp 'hɑːr-
  ~s s
Horowitz 'hɒr ə wɪts -vɪts ‖ 'hɔːr- 'hɑːr-
horrendous hɒ 'rend əs hə- ‖ hɔː- hɑː- ~ly li
  ~ness nəs nɪs
horrib|le 'hɒr əb əl -ɪb- ‖ 'hɔːr- 'hɑːr-
  ~leness əl nəs -nɪs ~ly li
horrid 'hɒr ɪd §-əd ‖ 'hɔːr əd 'hɑːr- ~ly li
  ~ness nəs nɪs
horrific hɒ 'rɪf ɪk hə- ‖ hɔː- hɑː- ~ally əl‿i
horri|fy 'hɒr ɪ ˌfaɪ -ə- ‖ 'hɔːr- 'hɑːr- ~fied/ly
  faɪd /li ~fies faɪz ~fying/ly faɪ ɪŋ /li
horripilation hɒ ˌrɪp ɪ 'leɪʃ ən -ə-; ˌhɒr ɪp-,
  ˌ•əp- ‖ hɔː- hɑː-
Horrocks 'hɒr əks ‖ 'hɔːr- 'hɑːr-
horror 'hɒr ə ‖ 'hɔːr ər 'hɑːr- ~s z
  'horror film; 'horror ˌmovie; 'horror ˌstory
horror-stricken 'hɒr ə ˌstrɪk ən ‖ 'hɔːr ər-
  'hɑːr-
horror-struck 'hɒr ə strʌk ‖ 'hɔːr ər- 'hɑːr-
hors de combat ˌɔː də 'kɒm bɑː -'kɔ̃-, -bæt
  ‖ ˌɔːr də koʊm 'bɑː —*Fr* [ɔʁ də kɔ̃ ba]
Horsa 'hɔːs ə ‖ 'hɔːrs ə
Horsbrugh 'hɔːs brə 'hɔːz- ‖ 'hɔːrz-
hors-d'oeuvre, ~s ˌɔː 'dɜːv ‖ ˌɔːr 'dɝːv —*Fr*
  [ɔʁ dœːvʁ]
horse hɔːs ‖ hɔːrs horsed hɔːst ‖ hɔːrst
  horses 'hɔːs ɪz -əz ‖ 'hɔːrs əz horsing
  'hɔːs ɪŋ ‖ 'hɔːrs ɪŋ
  'horse brass; ˌhorse 'chestnut ‖ '• ˌ••;
  'horse ˌopera; 'horse sense
horse-and-buggy ˌhɔːs ən 'bʌg i -ᵊnd-, →-ᵊm-,
  ‖ ˌhɔːrs-
horse-and-cart ˌhɔːs ən 'kɑːt -ᵊnd-, →-ᵊŋ-
  ‖ ˌhɔːrs ən 'kɑːrt
horseback 'hɔːs bæk ‖ 'hɔːrs-
horsebox 'hɔːs bɒks ‖ 'hɔːrs bɑːks ~es ɪz əz
Horseferry 'hɔːs ˌfer i -fər‿i ‖ 'hɔːrs-
horseflesh 'hɔːs fleʃ ‖ 'hɔːrs-
horse|fly 'hɔːs |flaɪ ‖ 'hɔːrs- ~flies flaɪz

Horseguard 'hɔːs gɑːd ‖ 'hɔːrs gɑːrd ~s z
horsehair 'hɔːs heə ‖ 'hɔːrs her -hær
horselaugh 'hɔːs lɑːf §-læf ‖ 'hɔːrs læf ~s s
horse|man 'hɔːs |mən ‖ 'hɔːrs- ~manship
  mən ʃɪp ~men mən men
horsemastership 'hɔːs ˌmɑːst ə ʃɪp §-ˌmæst-
  ‖ 'hɔːrs ˌmæst ər-
horseplay 'hɔːs pleɪ ‖ 'hɔːrs-
horsepower 'hɔːs ˌpaʊ‿ə ‖ 'hɔːrs ˌpaʊ‿ər
horseracing 'hɔːs ˌreɪs ɪŋ ‖ 'hɔːrs-
horseradish 'hɔːs ˌræd ɪʃ ‖ 'hɔːrs- ~es ɪz əz
horseshit 'hɔːs ʃɪt →'hɔːʃ- ‖ 'hɔːrs- →'hɔːrʃ-,
  'hɔːr-
horseshoe 'hɔːs ʃuː →'hɔːʃ- ‖ 'hɔːrs-
  →'hɔːrʃ-, 'hɔːr- ~s z
horsetail 'hɔːs teɪᵊl ‖ 'hɔːrs- ~s z
horse-trading 'hɔːs ˌtreɪd ɪŋ ‖ 'hɔːrs-
horsewhip 'hɔːs wɪp -hwɪp ‖ 'hɔːrs hwɪp
  ~ped t ~ping ɪŋ ~s s
horse|woman 'hɔːs ˌwʊm ən ‖ 'hɔːrs-
  ~women ˌwɪm ɪn §-ən
hors|ey, H~ 'hɔːs li ‖ 'hɔːrs li ~ier i‿ə ‖ i‿ər
  ~iest i‿ɪst i‿əst
Horsfall 'hɒs fɔːl ‖ 'hɔːrs faːl -fɔːl
Horsforth 'hɔːs fəθ ‖ 'hɔːrs fərθ
Horsham 'hɔːʃ əm ‖ 'hɔːrʃ-
horsi... —*see* horsey, horsy
Horsley 'hɔːz li ‖ 'hɔːrz-
Horsmonden ˌhɔːz mən 'den ‖ ˌhɔːrz-
Horsted Keynes ˌhɔːst ɪd 'keɪnz -əd- ‖ ˌhɔːrst-
hors|y 'hɔːs li ‖ 'hɔːrs li ~ier i‿ə ‖ i‿ər ~iest
  i‿ɪst i‿əst
hortative 'hɔːt ət ɪv hɔː 'teɪt- ‖ 'hɔːrt ət ɪv
  ~ly li
hortatory 'hɔːt ət‿ər i hɔː 'teɪt ər i ‖ 'hɔːrt
  ə tɔːr i -toʊr i
Hortensia, h~ hɔː 'tents i‿ə -'tentʃ-
  ‖ hɔːr 'tentʃ- ~s z
horticultural ˌhɔːt ɪ 'kʌltʃ ᵊr‿əl ◂ ˌ•ə-
  ‖ ˌhɔːrt ə- ~ly i
horticulture 'hɔːt ɪ ˌkʌltʃ ə -ə-; §, ••'••
  ‖ 'hɔːrt ə ˌkʌltʃ ər
horticulturist ˌhɔːt ɪ 'kʌltʃ ər ɪst ˌ•ə-, §-əst
  ‖ ˌhɔːrt ə- ~s s
Horton 'hɔːt ən ‖ 'hɔːrt ən
Horus 'hɔːr əs ‖ 'hoʊr-
Horwich 'hɒr ɪtʃ -ɪdʒ ‖ 'hɔːr-
Horwood 'hɔː wʊd ‖ 'hɔːr-
hosanna həʊ 'zæn ə ‖ hoʊ- ~s z
hose, Hose həʊz ‖ hoʊz hosed həʊzd ‖ hoʊzd
  hoses 'həʊz ɪz -əz ‖ 'hoʊz əz hosing
  'həʊz ɪŋ ‖ 'hoʊz ɪŋ
Hosea həʊ 'zɪə ‖ hoʊ 'ziː ə
Hoseason (i) həʊ 'siːz ən '•, •• ‖ hoʊ-, (ii)
  ˌhəʊs i 'eɪs ən -'æs- ‖ ˌhoʊs-
hosel 'həʊz əl ‖ 'hoʊz əl ~s z
hosepipe 'həʊz paɪp ‖ 'hoʊz- ~s s
Hosey 'həʊz i ‖ 'hoʊz i
hosier, H~ 'həʊz i‿ə 'həʊʒ ə, -ə ‖ 'hoʊʒ ər ~s
  z
hosiery 'həʊz i‿ər i 'həʊʒ ər i, -ər i ‖ 'hoʊʒ ər i
Hoskins, Hoskyns 'hɒsk ɪnz §-ənz ‖ 'hɑːsk-
hospic|e 'hɒsp ɪs §-əs ‖ 'hɑːsp- ~es ɪz əz

HOSPITABLE

BrE 1988

| 0 | 20 | 40 | 60 | 80 | 100% |

hospitab|le hɒ 'spɪt əb ᵊl hə-; 'hɒsp ɪt-, '•ət-
∥ 'haːsp əṭ- haː 'spɪṭ- —*BrE 1988 poll panel
preference:* •'••• 81%, '•••• 19%. **~ly** li
hospital 'hɒsp ɪt ᵊl ∥ 'haːsp ɪṭ ᵊl **~s** z
hospitalis... —*see* **hospitaliz...**
hospitalit|y ˌhɒsp ɪ 'tæl ət li ˌ•ə-, -ɪt i
∥ ˌhaːsp ə 'tæl əṭ li **~ies** iz
hospitalization ˌhɒsp ɪt ᵊl aɪ 'zeɪʃ ᵊn ˌ•ət-,
-ɪ'•- ∥ ˌhaːsp ɪṭ ᵊl ə-
hospitaliz|e 'hɒsp ɪt ᵊl aɪz '•ət-, -ə laɪz
∥ 'haːsp ɪṭ- **-ed** d **-es** ɪz əz **~ing** ɪŋ
host, Host həʊst ∥ hoʊst **hosted** 'həʊst ɪd -əd
∥ 'hoʊst əd **hosting** 'həʊst ɪŋ ∥ 'hoʊst ɪŋ
hosts həʊsts ∥ hoʊsts
hosta 'hɒst ə 'həʊst- ∥ 'hoʊst ə 'haːst- **~s** z
hostag|e 'hɒst ɪdʒ ∥ 'haːst- **~es** ɪz əz
hostel 'hɒst ᵊl ∥ 'haːst- **~ing, ~ling** ɪŋ **~s** z
hosteler, hosteller 'hɒst ᵊl ə ∥ 'haːst ᵊl ᵊr **~s**
z
hostel|ry 'hɒst ᵊl |ri ∥ 'haːst- **~ries** riz
hostess 'həʊst ɪs -əs, -es; ˌhəʊs 'tes ∥ 'hoʊst əs
~es ɪz əz
hostile 'hɒst aɪᵊl ∥ 'haːst ᵊl -aɪᵊl **~ly** li
hostilit|y hɒ 'stɪl ət li §hə-, -ɪt- ∥ haː 'stɪl əṭ li
~ies iz
hostler 'ɒs lə 'hɒs- ∥ 'aːs lᵊr 'haːs- **~s** z
hot hɒt ∥ haːt **hots** hɒts ∥ haːts **hotted**
'hɒt ɪd -əd ∥ 'haːṭ əd **hotting**
'hɒt ɪŋ ∥ 'haːṭ ɪŋ
ˌhot 'air; ˌhot 'air balˌloon; ˌhot cross 'bun;
ˌhot 'dog *'frankfurter roll'* ∥ '• •; ˌhot 'flash,
ˌhot 'flush; ˌhot po'tato; 'hot rod; 'hot
seat; 'hot spot; ˌhot 'stuff; ˌhot 'water
hotbed 'hɒt bed ∥ 'haːt- **~s** z
hot-blooded ˌhɒt 'blʌd ɪd ◂ -əd ∥ ˌhaːt- **~ness**
nəs nɪs
Hotbot *tdmk* 'hɒt bɒt ∥ 'haːt baːt
Hotchkiss 'hɒtʃ kɪs ∥ 'haːtʃ-
hotchpot 'hɒtʃ pɒt ∥ 'haːtʃ paːt **~s** s
hotchpotch 'hɒtʃ pɒtʃ ∥ 'haːtʃ paːtʃ **~es** ɪz əz
hot-dog v 'hɒt dɒg ∥ 'haːt dɔːg -daːg **-ged** d
~ging ɪŋ **~s** z
hotel ˌhəʊ 'tel ◂ həʊ-, əʊ- ∥ ˌhoʊ- **~s** z
hotelier həʊ 'tel i eɪ əʊ-, -i̯ə ∥ ˌoʊt ᵊl 'jeɪ
hoʊ 'tel jᵊr, ˌhoʊṭ ᵊl 'ɪᵊr **~s** z
hot|foot ˌhɒt |fʊt ◂ '•• ∥ 'haːt |fʊt **~footed**
fʊt ɪd -əd ∥ fʊṭ əd **~footing** fʊt ɪŋ ∥ fʊṭ ɪŋ
~foots fʊts
hot-gospel|er/s, hot-gospell|er/s ˌhɒt 'gɒsp
ᵊl |ə/z ∥ ˌhaːt 'gaːsp ᵊl |ᵊr/z **~ing** ɪŋ
Hotham *(i)* 'hʌð əm, *(ii)* 'hɒθ əm ∥ 'haːð-, *(iii)*
'hɒt əm ∥ 'haːṭ əm
hothead 'hɒt hed ∥ 'haːt- **~s** z
hotheaded ˌhɒt 'hed ɪd ◂ -əd ∥ ˌhaːt- **~ly** li
~ness nəs nɪs
hot|house 'hɒt |haʊs ∥ 'haːt- **~houses** haʊz ɪz
-əz
hotline 'hɒt laɪn ∥ 'haːt- **~s** z

hotlink 'hɒt lɪŋk ∥ 'haːt- **~s** s
hotly 'hɒt li ∥ 'haːt-
Hotmail *tdmk* 'hɒt meɪᵊl ∥ 'haːt-
hotplate 'hɒt pleɪt ∥ 'haːt- **~s** s
Hotpoint *tdmk* 'hɒt pɔɪnt ∥ 'haːt-
hotpot 'hɒt pɒt ∥ 'haːt paːt **~s** s
hotrod 'hɒt rɒd ∥ 'haːt raːd **~ded** ɪd əd
~der/s ə/z ∥ -ᵊr/z **~ding** ɪŋ **~s** z
hotshot 'hɒt ʃɒt ∥ 'haːt ʃaːt **~s** s
hotspur, H~ 'hɒt spɜː -spə ∥ 'haːt spɜː ~ **~s** z
hott... —*see* **hot**
hot-tempered
ˌhɒt 'temp əd ◂ ∥ ˌhaːt 'temp ᵊrd ◂
Hottentot 'hɒt ᵊn tɒt ∥ 'haːt ᵊn taːt **~s** s
hot-water bottle
ˌhɒt 'wɔːt ə ˌbɒt ᵊl ∥ ˌhaːt 'wɔːṭ ᵊr ˌbaːṭ ᵊl
-'waːṭ- **~s** z
hot-wire v ˌhɒt 'waɪ̯ə ∥ ˌhaːt 'waɪ̯ᵊr **-d** d **~s**
z **hot-wiring**
ˌhɒt 'waɪ̯ᵊr ɪŋ ∥ ˌhaːt 'waɪ̯ᵊr ɪŋ
Houdini huː 'diːn i
hough hɒk ∥ haːk **houghed** hɒkt ∥ haːkt
houghing 'hɒk ɪŋ ∥ 'haːk ɪŋ **houghs**
hɒks ∥ haːks
Hough *(i)* hʌf, *(ii)* hɒf ∥ hɔːf haːf, *(iii)* haʊ
Houghall 'hɒf ᵊl ∥ 'haːf ᵊl
Hougham 'hʌf əm
Houghton *(i)* 'hɔːt ᵊn ∥ 'haːt-, *(ii)* 'haʊt ᵊn, *(iii)*
'həʊt ᵊn ∥ 'hoʊt-
Houghton-le-Spring ˌhaʊt ᵊn li 'sprɪŋ -lə'•
∥ ˌhoʊt-
Houlihan 'huːl i hən -ə-
houmous 'hʊm ʊs 'huːm-, -əs
hound haʊnd **hounded** haʊnd ɪd -əd
hounding 'haʊnd ɪŋ **hounds** haʊndz
Houndsditch 'haʊndz dɪtʃ
hound's-tooth 'haʊndz tuːθ §-tʊθ, ˌ•'•
Hounslow 'haʊnz ləʊ ∥ -loʊ
hour 'aʊ̯ə ∥ 'aʊ̯ᵊr *(= our)* **hours**
'aʊ̯əz ∥ 'aʊ̯ᵊrz
'hour hand
hourglass 'aʊ̯ə glaːs §-glæs ∥ 'aʊ̯ᵊr glæs **~es**
ɪz əz
houri 'hʊər i ∥ 'hʊr i **~s** z
hourly 'aʊ̯ə li ∥ 'aʊ̯ᵊr li
Housatonic ˌhuːs ə 'tɒn ɪk ◂ ˌhuːz- ∥ -'taːn-
house n, adj haʊs **houses** 'haʊz ɪz -əz *(!)*
'house ˌagent; 'house arˌrest, ˌ• •'•;
'house ˌhusband; 'house lights; 'house
ˌmartin; ˌHouse of 'Commons; 'House of
'Lords; ˌHouse of ˌRepre'sentatives; 'house
ˌparty; ˌHouses of 'Parliament; 'house
ˌsparrow
house v haʊz **housed** haʊzd **houses** 'haʊz ɪz
-əz **housing** 'haʊz ɪŋ
House *family name* haʊs
houseboat 'haʊs bəʊt ∥ -boʊt **~s** s
housebound 'haʊs baʊnd
houseboy 'haʊs bɔɪ **~s** z
housebreak|er/s 'haʊs ˌbreɪk |ə/z ∥ |ᵊr/z **~ing**
ɪŋ
housebroken 'haʊs ˌbrəʊk ᵊn ∥ -ˌbroʊk ᵊn

housebuy|er/s 'haʊs ˌbaɪ‿|ə/z ‖ -ˌbaɪ‿|ər/z
　~ing ɪŋ
housecoat 'haʊs kəʊt ‖ -koʊt **~s** s
housecraft 'haʊs krɑːft §-kræft ‖ -kræft
housedog 'haʊs dɒg ‖ -dɔːg -dɑːg **~z** z
housefather 'haʊs ˌfɑːð ə ‖ -ər **~s** z
house|fly 'haʊs |flaɪ **—flies** flaɪz
houseful 'haʊs fʊl **~s** z
Housego 'haʊs gəʊ ‖ -goʊ
household 'haʊs həʊld →-hɒʊld, -əʊld
　‖ -hoʊld **~s** z
　ˌhousehold ˈname
householder, H~ 'haʊs həʊld ə →-hɒʊld-,
　-əʊld- ‖ -hoʊld ər **~s** z
housekeeper 'haʊs ˌkiːp ə ‖ -ər **~s** z
housekeeping 'haʊs ˌkiːp ɪŋ
houseleek 'haʊs liːk **~s** s
housemaid 'haʊs meɪd **~s** z
　ˌhousemaid's ˈknee
house|man 'haʊs |mən -mæn **~men** mən men
housemaster 'haʊs ˌmɑːst ə §-ˌmæst-
　‖ -ˌmæst ər **~ship/s** ʃɪp/s **~s** z
housemistress 'haʊs ˌmɪs trəs -trɪs **~es** ɪz əz
housemother 'haʊs ˌmʌð ə ‖ -ər **~s** z
houseparent 'haʊs ˌpeər ənt ‖ -ˌper- -ˌpær-
　~s s
houseplant 'haʊs plɑːnt §-plænt ‖ -plænt **~s** s
house-proud 'haʊs praʊd
houseroom 'haʊs ruːm -rʊm
houses *from* **house** *n, v* 'haʊz ɪz -əz (!)
house-to-house ˌhaʊs tə 'haʊs ◂ -tu-
housetops 'haʊs tɒps ‖ -tɑːps
house-train 'haʊs treɪn **~ed** d **~ing** ɪŋ **~s** z
housewarming 'haʊs ˌwɔːm ɪŋ ‖ -ˌwɔːrm ɪŋ
　~s z
house|wife 'haʊs |waɪf **—**formerly also 'hʌz ɪf
　~wifely waɪf li **~wives** waɪvz
housewifery 'haʊs wɪf ər‿i ‖ 'haʊs waɪf ər i (*)
　—formerly also 'hʌz ɪf ri, -əf-
housework 'haʊs wɜːk ‖ -wɝːk
housey-housey, housie-housie ˌhaʊz i 'haʊz i
housing 'haʊz ɪŋ **~s** z
　ˈhousing assoˌciation; ˈhousing eˌstate;
　ˈhousing ˌproject
Housman 'haʊs mən
Houston *(i)* 'huːst ən, *(ii)* 'hjuːst ən §'juːst-,
　(iii) 'haʊst ən **—**The Scottish name is (i), the
　Texan (ii), the NYC street and GA county (iii).
Houtman Abrolhos
　ˌhaʊt mən ə 'brɒl əs ‖ -'brɑːl- -'broʊl-
Houyhnhnm 'huːˌɪn əm hu 'ɪn- ‖ 'hwɪn əm
　hu 'ɪn əm
hove, Hove həʊv ‖ hoʊv
hovel 'hɒv əl 'hʌv- ‖ 'hʌv əl 'hɑːv- **~s** z
hov|er 'hɒv |ə 'hʌv- ‖ 'hʌv |ər 'hɑːv- **~ered**
　əd ‖ ərd **~ering** ər‿ɪŋ **~ers** əz ‖ ərz
　ˈhover fly
hovercraft 'hɒv ə krɑːft 'hʌv-, §-kræft
　‖ 'hʌv ər kræft 'hɑːv- **~s** s
hover|fly 'hɒv ə |flaɪ 'hʌv- ‖ 'hʌv ər- 'hɑːv-
　~flies flaɪz
Hoveringham 'hɒv ər‿ɪŋ əm ‖ 'hʌv- 'hɑːv-

hoverport 'hɒv ə pɔːt 'hʌv- ‖ 'hʌv ər pɔːrt
　'hɑːv-, -poʊrt **~s** s
hovertrain 'hɒv ə treɪn 'hʌv- ‖ 'hʌv ər- 'hɑːv-
　~s z
Hovis *tdmk* 'həʊv ɪs §-əs ‖ 'hoʊv-
how haʊ
　ˌHow ˈare you? *(greeting)*, (ˈFine.) ˌHow are
　ˈyou? *(reply)*; ˌHow do you ˈdo?
Howard 'haʊ‿əd ‖ 'haʊ‿ərd **~s**, **~'s** z
howdah 'haʊd ə **~s** z
Howden 'haʊd ən
how-do-you-do *n* ˌhaʊ dju 'duː -djə-, -dʒu-,
　-dʒə-, -di-, -də ju-; ˈ••• **~s** z
howdy 'haʊd i
how-d'ye-do *n* ˌhaʊ djə 'duː -dʒə-, -di-; ˈ•••
　~s z
Howe, howe haʊ
howe'er haʊ 'eə ‖ -'eər
Howell 'haʊ‿əl haʊl ‖ 'haʊ‿əl
Howells 'haʊ‿əlz haʊlz ‖ 'haʊ‿əlz
Howerd 'haʊ‿əd ‖ 'haʊ‿ərd
however haʊ 'ev ə ˌ•ˈ• ‖ -ər
Howie 'haʊ i
Howitt 'haʊ ɪt §-ət
howitzer 'haʊ‿ɪts ə §‿əts- ‖ -ər **~s** z
howl haʊl **howled** haʊld **howling** 'haʊl ɪŋ
　howls haʊlz
Howland 'haʊ lənd
howler 'haʊl ə ‖ -ər **~s** z
howsoever ˌhaʊ səʊ 'ev ə ◂ ‖ -soʊ 'ev ər ◂
Howth *place in Co. Dublin* həʊθ ‖ hoʊθ
howzat ⑴haʊ 'zæt
Hoxha 'hɒdʒ ə ‖ 'hoʊdʒ ɑː 'hɑːdʒ-,-ə
　—Albanian ['ho dʒa]
Hoxton 'hɒkst ən ‖ 'hɑːkst-
hoy, Hoy hɔɪ **hoys** hɔɪz
hoya 'hɔɪ ə **~s** z
hoyden 'hɔɪd ən **~s** z
hoydenish 'hɔɪd ən ɪʃ
Hoylake 'hɔɪ leɪk
Hoyle hɔɪ‿əl
HP ˌeɪtʃ 'piː ◂ §ˌheɪtʃ-
HQ ˌeɪtʃ 'kjuː §ˌheɪtʃ-
HRH ˌeɪtʃ ɑːr 'eɪtʃ §ˌheɪtʃ ɑː 'heɪtʃ ‖ -ɑːr-
HRT ˌeɪtʃ ɑː 'tiː §ˌheɪtʃ- ‖ -ɑːr-
HTML ˌeɪtʃ tiː em 'el §ˌheɪtʃ-
hub hʌb **hubs** hʌbz
Hubbard 'hʌb əd ‖ -ərd
hubbi... **—**see **hubby**
Hubble 'hʌb əl
hubble-bubble 'hʌb əl ˌbʌb əl **~s** z
hubbub 'hʌb ʌb **~s** z
hubb|y 'hʌb |i **~ies** iz
hubcap 'hʌb kæp **~s** s
Hubei ˌhuː 'beɪ **—**Chi Húběi [²xu ³bei]
Hubert 'hjuːb ət ‖ -ərt
hubris 'hjuːb rɪs 'huːb-, §-rəs
hubristic hju 'brɪst ɪk hu- **~ally** əl‿i
Huck hʌk
huckaback 'hʌk ə bæk
huckleberr|y, H~ 'hʌk əl bər‿|i -ˌber |i ‖ -ˌber |i
　~ies iz
Hucknall 'hʌk nəl

huckster 'hʌkst ə ‖ -ər **huckstering** 'hʌkst
ər ɪŋ **~s** z
Huckvale 'hʌk veɪəl
Hudd hʌd
Huddersfield 'hʌd əz fiːəld ‖ -ərz-
huddl|e 'hʌd əl **~ed** d **~es** z **~ing** ɪŋ
Huddleston 'hʌd əl stən
Hudibras 'hjuːd ɪ bræs -ə-
hudibrastic, H~ ˌhjuːd ɪ 'bræst ɪk ◄ -ə-
Hudnott 'hʌd nɒt ‖ -naːt
Hudson 'hʌd sən
  ˌHudson ' Bay; ˌHudson ' River
hue hjuː (= *hew, Hugh*) **hued** hjuːd **hues**
hjuːz
  ˌhue and ' cry
huevos rancheros
  ˌweɪv ɒs ræn 'tʃeər ɒs ‖ -oʊs ræn 'tʃer oʊs
  —*Sp* [ˌwe βos ran 'tʃe ros, -βor-]
Huey 'hjuː i
huff, Huff hʌf **huffed** hʌft **huffing** 'hʌf ɪŋ
huffs hʌfs
huffish 'hʌf ɪʃ **~ly** li **~ness** nəs nɪs
huff|y 'hʌf li **~ier** i ə ‖ i ər **~iest** i ɪst i əst
~ily ɪ li əl i **~iness** i nəs i nɪs
hug hʌg **hugged** hʌgd **hugging** 'hʌg ɪŋ
hugs hʌgz
huge hjuːdʒ §juːdʒ **huger** 'hjuːdʒ ə §'juːdʒ-
‖ -ər **hugest** 'hjuːdʒ ɪst §'juːdʒ-, -əst
huge|ly 'hjuːdʒ li §'juːdʒ- **~ness** nəs nɪs
huggable 'hʌg əb əl
hugger 'hʌg əl -ər **~s** z
hugger-mugger 'hʌg ə ˌmʌg ə ‖ -ər ˌmʌg ər
Huggins 'hʌg ɪnz §-ənz
Hugh hjuː
Hughenden 'hjuːˌ ən dən
Hughes hjuːz
Hughey, Hughie 'hjuːˌ i
Hugo 'hjuːg əʊ ‖ -oʊ
Hugon 'hjuːg ən -ɒn ‖ -aːn
Hugue|not, h~ 'hjuːg ə |nəʊ 'huːg-, -nɒt
‖ -|naːt (*) **~nots** nəʊz nɒts ‖ naːts
huh hʌ hʌh
Huish 'hjuːˌ ɪʃ
hula 'huːl ə **~s** z
hula-hoop, Hula-Hoop *tdmk* 'huːl ə huːp **~s** s
hula-hula ˌhuːl ə 'huːl ə **~s** z
Hulbert 'hʌl bət ‖ -bərt
hulk hʌlk **hulked** hʌlkt **hulking** 'hʌlk ɪŋ
hulks hʌlks
hull, Hull hʌl **hulled** hʌld **hulling** 'hʌl ɪŋ
hulls hʌlz
hullabaloo ˌhʌl ə bə 'luː '•••• **~s** z
hullo hə 'ləʊ ₍ₒ₎hʌ- ‖ -'loʊ **~s** z
Hulme (*i*) hjuːm, (*ii*) hʌlm —*In Britain (i), in the
US (ii).*
Hulot 'uːl əʊ ‖ uː 'loʊ —*Fr* [y lo]
Hulse hʌls
Hulsean hʌl 'siːˌ ən
hum hʌm **hummed** hʌmd **humming** 'hʌm ɪŋ
hums hʌmz
human 'hjuːm ən §'juːm- **~ly** li **~ness** nəs nɪs
~s z

ˌhuman ' being; ˌhuman ' race; ˌhuman
' rights
Humana hjuː 'maːn ə
humane hjuː 'meɪn ˌhjuː:- **~ly** li **~ness** nəs nɪs
humanis... —*see* humaniz...
humanism 'hjuːm ə ˌnɪz əm §'juːm-
humanist 'hjuːm ən ɪst §'juːm-, §-əst **~s** s
humanistic ˌhjuːm ə 'nɪst ɪk ◄ §ˌjuːm- **~ally**
əlˌ i
humanitarian hjuː ˌmæn ɪ 'teər iˌ ən §juː-,
ˌhjum æn-, -ə'•- ‖ -'ter- **~ism** ˌɪz əm
humanit|y hjuː 'mæn ət li §juː-, -ɪt i ‖ -əʈ li **~ies**
iz
humanization ˌhjuːm ən aɪ 'zeɪʃ ən §ˌjuːm-,
-ən ɪ- ‖ -ən ə-
humaniz|e 'hjuːm ə naɪz §'juːm- **~ed** d **~es**
ɪz əz **~ing** ɪŋ
humankind ˌhjuːm ən 'kaɪnd §ˌjuːm-, →-əŋ-
humanly 'hjuːm ən li §'juːm-
humanoid 'hjuːm ə nɔɪd §'juːm- **~s** z
Humber 'hʌm bə ‖ -bər
Humberside 'hʌm bə saɪd ‖ -bər-
Humbert 'hʌm bət ‖ -bərt
humble 'hʌm bəl **humbled** 'hʌm bəld
humbler 'hʌm blə ‖ -blər **humbles**
'hʌm bəlz **humblest** 'hʌm blɪst -bləst
humbling 'hʌm bəl ɪŋ
  ˌhumble ' pie
humbleness 'hʌm bəl nəs -nɪs
humbly 'hʌm bli
Humboldt 'hʌm bəʊlt 'hʊm-, →-bɒʊlt ‖ -boʊlt
  —*Ger* ['hʊm bɔlt]
humbug 'hʌm bʌg **~ged** d **~ging** ɪŋ **~s** z
humbuggery 'hʌm bʌg ər i
humdinger ˌhʌm 'dɪŋ ə ‖ -ər **~s** z
humdrum 'hʌm drʌm
Hume hjuːm
humectant hjuː 'mekt ənt **~s** s
humeral 'hjuːm ər əl **~s** z
hum|erus 'hjuːm |ər əs (= *humorous*) **~eri** ə raɪ
humic 'hjuːm ɪk
humid 'hjuːm ɪd §'juːm-, §-əd
humidification hjuː ˌmɪd ɪf ɪ 'keɪʃ ən §ju-,
•, •'əf-, §-ə'••
humidifier hjuː 'mɪd ɪ faɪˌə §juː- ‖ _ər **~s** z
humidi|fy hjuː 'mɪd ɪ |faɪ §juː-, -ə- **~fied** faɪd
~fies faɪz **~fying** faɪ ɪŋ
humidity hjuː 'mɪd ət i §juː-, -ɪt- ‖ -əʈ i
humid|ly 'hjuːm ɪd |li §'juːm-, §-əd- **~ness** nəs
nɪs
humidor 'hjuːm ɪ dɔː §'juːm-, -ə- ‖ -dɔːr **~s** z
humili|ate hjuː 'mɪl i |eɪt §juː- **~ated** eɪt ɪd -əd
‖ eɪʈ əd **~ates** eɪts **~ating/ly** eɪt ɪŋ /
li ‖ eɪʈ ɪŋ /li
humiliation hjuː ˌmɪl i 'eɪʃ ən ˌhjuːm ɪl-; §juː-
~s z
humility hjuː 'mɪl ət i §juː-, -ɪt- ‖ -əʈ i
humm... —*see* hum
hummingbird 'hʌm ɪŋ bɜːd ‖ -bɝːd **~s** z
hummock 'hʌm ək **~s** s
hummus 'hʊm ʊs 'hʌm-, -əs
humongous hjuː 'mʌŋ gəs

humor 'hju:m ə §'ju:m- ‖ -ºr ~ed d
  humoring hju:m ər_ɪŋ §'ju:m- ~s z
humoral 'hju:m ər əl
humoresque ,hju:m ə 'resk ~s s
humorist 'hju:m ər ɪst §'ju:m-, §-əst ~s s
humoristic ,hju:m ə 'rɪst ɪk ◄ §,ju:m- ~al əl
humorless 'hju:m ə ləs §'ju:m-, -lɪs ‖ -ºr- ~ly
  li ~ness nəs nɪs
humorous 'hju:m ər əs §'ju:m- ~ly li ~ness
  nəs nɪs
humour 'hju:m ə §'ju:m- ‖ -ºr ~ed d
  humouring 'hju:m ər_ɪŋ §'ju:m- ~s z
humourless 'hju:m ə ləs §'ju:m-, -lɪs ‖ -ºr-
  ~ly li ~ness nəs nɪs
hump hʌmp humped hʌmpt humping
  'hʌmp ɪŋ humps hʌmps
humpback 'hʌmp bæk ~ed t
  ,humpbacked 'bridge
Humperdinck German composer 'hʊmp ə dɪŋk
  'hʌmp- ‖ -ºr- —Ger ['hʊm pɐ dɪŋk]
Humperdinck British pop singer
  'hʌmp ə dɪŋk ‖ -ºr-
humph hʌmpf —or e.g. [m̩m, m̩m̩m̩, həmm̩]
  with falling pitch
Humphrey 'hʌmpf ri
Humphreys, Humphries, Humphrys
  'hʌmpf riz
humpt|y 'hʌmpt li ~ies iz
  ,Humpty 'Dumpty 'dʌmpt i
hump|y 'hʌmp li ~ier i_ə ‖ i_ºr ~ies iz ~iest
  i_ɪst _əst
humungous hju 'mʌŋ gəs
humus 'hju:m əs §'ju:m-
Hun hʌn Huns hʌnz
Hunan ,hu: 'næn ‖ -'nɑ:n -'næn —Chi Húnán
  [²xu ²nan]
hunch hʌntʃ hunched hʌntʃt hunches
  'hʌntʃ ɪz -əz hunching 'hʌntʃ ɪŋ
hunchback 'hʌntʃ bæk ~ed t ~s s
hundred 'hʌndr əd -ɪd ‖ 'hʌnd ºrd ~s z
  ,hundreds and 'thousands
hundredfold 'hʌndr əd fəʊld -ɪd-, →-fʊʊld
  ‖ -foʊld 'hʌnd ºrd-
hundredth 'hʌndr ədθ -ɪdθ, -ətθ,
  -ɪtθ ‖ 'hʌnd ºrdθ ~s s
hundredweight 'hʌndr əd weɪt
  -ɪd- ‖ 'hʌnd ºrd- ~s s
hung hʌŋ
Hungarian hʌŋ 'geər i_ən ‖ -'ger- -'gær- ~s z
Hungary 'hʌŋ gər i
hunger 'hʌŋ gə ‖ -gºr ~ed d hungering
  'hʌŋ gər ɪŋ ~s z
  'hunger march; 'hunger ,marcher;
  'hunger strike; 'hunger ,striker
Hungerford 'hʌŋ gə fəd -fɔːd ‖ -gºr fºrd
hun|gry 'hʌŋ |gri ~grier gri_ə ‖ gri_ºr ~griest
  gri_ɪst _əst ~grily grəl i grɪ li
hunk hʌŋk hunks hʌŋks
hunker, H~ 'hʌŋk ə ‖ -ºr ~ed d hunkering
  'hʌŋk ər_ɪŋ ~s z
hunk|y 'hʌŋk |i ~ier i_ə ‖ i_ºr ~iest i_ɪst _əst
hunky-dory ,hʌŋk i 'dɔːr i ‖ -'doʊr-
Hunniford 'hʌn i fəd §-fɔːd ‖ -fºrd

Hunnish, h~ 'hʌn ɪʃ ~ness nəs nɪs
Hunslet 'hʌnz lət -lɪt
Hunstanton hʌn 'stænt ən —locally also
  'hʌnt st ən
hunt hʌnt hunted 'hʌnt ɪd -əd ‖ 'hʌn̪t̬ əd
  hunting 'hʌnt ɪŋ ‖ 'hʌn̪t̬ ɪŋ hunts hʌnts
  'hunting ground
Hunt, Hunte hʌnt
hunter, H~ 'hʌnt ə ‖ 'hʌn̪t̬ ºr ~s z
hunter-gatherer ,hʌnt ə 'gæð ər_ə ‖ ,hʌn̪t̬
  ºr 'gæð ºr_ər ~s z
hunter-killer ,hʌnt ə 'kɪl ə ‖ ,hʌn̪t̬ ºr 'kɪl ºr ~s
  z
Huntingdon 'hʌnt ɪŋ dən ‖ 'hʌn̪t̬- ~shire ʃə
  ʃɪə ‖ ʃºr ʃɪr
Huntingford 'hʌnt ɪŋ fəd ‖ 'hʌn̪t̬ ɪŋ fºrd
Huntington 'hʌnt ɪŋ tən ‖ 'hʌn̪t̬- ~'s z
  ,Huntington 'Beach; ,Huntington's
  cho'rea
Huntley, Huntly 'hʌnt li
huntress 'hʌntr əs -ɪs, -es ~es ɪz əz
hunts|man 'hʌnts |mən ~men mən men
Huntsville 'hʌnts vɪl
Huon 'hju: ɒn ‖ -ɑ:n
Hurd hɜ:d ‖ hɜ:d
hurd|le 'hɜ:d ºl ‖ 'hɜ:d ºl ~ed d ~es z ~ing
  _ɪŋ
hurdler 'hɜ:d lə ‖ 'hɜ:d lºr ~s z
hurdy-gurd|y 'hɜ:d i ,gɜ:d |i, •'••
  ‖ 'hɜ:d i ,gɜ:d i ~ies iz
Hurford 'hɜ: fəd ‖ 'hɜ: fºrd
hurl hɜ:l ‖ hɜ:l hurled hɜ:ld ‖ hɜ:ld hurling
  'hɜ:l ɪŋ ‖ 'hɜ:l ɪŋ hurls hɜ:lz ‖ hɜ:lz
hurley, H~ 'hɜ:l i ‖ 'hɜ:l i ~s z
Hurlingham 'hɜ:l ɪŋ əm ‖ 'hɜ:l-
hurly-burl|y 'hɜ:l i ,bɜ:l |i, •'••
  ‖ ,hɜ:l i 'bɜ:l |i •'••, •• ~ies iz
Hurn hɜ:n ‖ hɜ:n
Huron 'hjʊər ən §'jʊər-, §'hju:r-, -ɒn ‖ 'hjʊr
  ən 'jʊr-, -ɑ:n
hurrah hə 'rɑ: hʊ- ‖ -'rɔ: ~s z
hurray hə 'reɪ hʊ- ~s z
Hurrell (i) 'hʌr əl ‖ 'hɜ:_, (ii) 'hʊər əl ‖ 'hʊr-
hurricane 'hʌr ɪk ən -ək-; -ɪ keɪn, -ə-
  ‖ 'hɜ: ə keɪn ~s z
  'hurricane lamp
hurr|y 'hʌr |i ‖ 'hɜ: |i ~ied/ly id /li ~ies iz
  ~ying i ɪŋ
Hurst hɜ:st ‖ hɜ:st
Hurstmonceux ,hɜ:st mən 'sju: -'su:, -'zu:
  ‖ ,hɜ:st mən 'su:
Hurstpierpoint ,hɜ:st pɪə 'pɔɪnt ‖ ,hɜ:st pɪr-
hurt, Hurt hɜ:t ‖ hɜ:t hurting
  'hɜ:t ɪŋ ‖ 'hɜ:t̬ ɪŋ hurts hɜ:ts ‖ hɜ:ts
hurtful 'hɜ:t fºl -fʊl ‖ 'hɜ:t- ~ly _i
hurt|le 'hɜ:t ºl ‖ 'hɜ:t̬ ºl ~ed d ~es z ~ing _ɪŋ
husband 'hʌz bənd ~ed ɪd əd ~ing ɪŋ ~s z
husband|man 'hʌz bənd |mən →-bəm- ~men
  mən men
husbandry 'hʌz bənd ri
hush hʌʃ hushed hʌʃt hushes 'hʌʃ ɪz -əz
  hushing 'hʌʃ ɪŋ
  'hush ,money; 'Hush ,Puppies tdmk

hushaby, hushabye 'hʌʃ ə baɪ
hush-hush ˌhʌʃ 'hʌʃ ◄ '•• ‖ 'hʌʃ hʌʃ
hush-up n 'hʌʃ ʌp
husk hʌsk husked hʌskt husking 'hʌsk ɪŋ
 husks hʌsks
huski... —see husky
Huskisson 'hʌsk ɪs ən -əs-
husk|y 'hʌsk |i ~ier i_ə ‖ i_ər ~ies iz ~iest
 i_ɪst i_əst ~ily ɪ li əl i ~iness i nəs i nɪs
huss hʌs
Huss hʌs hʊs —German, Czech [hʊs]
Hussain hu 'seɪn
hussar hu 'zɑː hə- ‖ -'zɑːr ~s z
Hussein hu 'seɪn
Hussey 'hʌs i
Hussite 'hʌs aɪt 'hʊs- ~s s
huss|y, Hussy 'hʌs |i 'hʌz- ~ies iz
hustings 'hʌst ɪŋz
hustl|e 'hʌs əl ~ed d ~es z ~ing ɪŋ
hustler 'hʌs lə 'hʌs əl_ə ‖ -lər ~s z
Huston 'hjuːst ən
hut hʌt hutted 'hʌt ɪd -əd ‖ 'hʌt̬ əd hutting
 'hʌt ɪŋ ‖ 'hʌt̬ ɪŋ huts hʌts
hutch, Hutch hʌtʃ hutches 'hʌtʃ ɪz -əz
Hutchence 'hʌtʃ ənts
Hutcheson 'hʌtʃ ɪs ən -əs-
Hutchings 'hʌtʃ ɪŋz
Hutchins 'hʌtʃ ɪnz
Hutchinson 'hʌtʃ ɪn sən -ən-
Hutchison 'hʌtʃ ɪs ən -əs-
hutment 'hʌt mənt ~s s
Hutterite 'hʌt ə raɪt 'hʊt-, 'huːt- ‖ 'hʌt̬-, 'hʊt̬-,
 'huːt̬- ~s s
Hutton 'hʌt ən
Hutu 'huːt uː ~s z
Huxley 'hʌks li
Huxtable 'hʌkst əb əl
Huw hju: —Welsh [hiu, hɪu]
Huygens 'haɪg ənz —Dutch ['hœy xəns]
Huyton 'haɪt ən (= heighten)
huzza, huzzah hu 'zɑ: hʌ-, hə- ~s z
Hwang-Ho ˌhwæŋ 'həʊ ‖ -'hoʊ —Chi Huáng Hé
 [²xwaŋ ²xɤ]
hwyl 'huː_ɪl əl —Welsh [huil, huɪl]
Hy haɪ
hyacinth, H~ 'haɪ_ə sɪntθ ~s s
hyacinthine ˌhaɪ_ə 'sɪntθ aɪn -iːn
Hyacinthus ˌhaɪ_ə 'sɪntθ əs
Hyades 'haɪ_ə diːz
hyaena haɪ 'iːn ə ~s z
hyalin 'haɪ_ə lɪn
hyaline 'haɪ_ə lɪn -liːn, -laɪn
hyalo- comb. form
 with stress-neutral suffix ˈhaɪ_əl əʊ haɪ ˈæl ə
 ‖ -oʊ haɪ ˈæl ə — hyaloplasm 'haɪ_əl əʊ
 ˌplæz əm haɪ 'æl ə- ‖ -oʊˌ•-
 with stress-imposing suffix ˌhaɪ_ə 'lɒ+ ‖ -'lɑː+
 — hyalophagy ˌhaɪ_ə 'lɒf ədʒ i ‖ -'lɑːf-
hyaloid 'haɪ_ə lɔɪd
Hyannis haɪ 'æn ɪs §-əs
Hyatt 'haɪ_ət
hybrid 'haɪb rɪd §-rəd ~s z
 ˌhybrid 'vigour

hybridis... —see hybridiz...
hybridism 'haɪb rɪ ˌdɪz əm ‖ -rə-
hybridity haɪ 'brɪd ət i -ɪt i ‖ -ət̬ i
hybridization ˌhaɪb rɪd aɪ 'zeɪʃ ən ˌ•rəd-, -ɪ'•-
 ‖ -rəd ə- ~s z
hybridiz|e 'haɪb rɪ daɪz -rə- ~ed d ~es ɪz əz
 ~ing ɪŋ
hydatid 'haɪd ət ɪd haɪ 'dæt-, §-əd ‖ -ət̬ əd ~s
 z
Hyde haɪd
 ˌHyde 'Park◄, ˌHyde ˌPark 'Corner
Hyder tdmk 'haɪd ə ‖ -ər —Welsh ['hə der]
Hyderabad 'haɪd ər_ə bæd -bɑːd, ˌ•••'•
hydr|a, Hydra 'haɪdr |ə ~ae iː ~as əz
hydrangea haɪ 'dreɪndʒ ə
 -'dreɪndʒ i_ə ‖ -'drændʒ ə ~s z
hydrant 'haɪdr ənt ~s s
hydrate n 'haɪdr eɪt ~s s
hydr|ate v haɪ 'dr|eɪt 'haɪdr |eɪt ‖ 'haɪdr |eɪt
 ~ated eɪt ɪd -əd ‖ eɪt̬ əd ~ates eɪts ~ating
 eɪt ɪŋ ‖ eɪt̬ ɪŋ
hydration haɪ 'dreɪʃ ən
hydraulic haɪ 'drɔːl ɪk -'drɒl- ‖ -'drɑːl- ~ally
 əl_i ~s s
hydrazine 'haɪdr ə ziːn -zɪn, -zaɪn
hydric 'haɪdr ɪk
hydride 'haɪdr aɪd ~s z
hydro 'haɪdr əʊ ‖ -oʊ ~s z
hydro- comb. form
 with stress-neutral suffix ˈhaɪdr əʊ ‖ -ə —
 hydrotaxis ˌhaɪdr əʊ 'tæks ɪs §-əs ‖ -ə-
 with stress-imposing suffix haɪ 'drɒ+ ‖ -'drɑː+
 — hydrophanous haɪ 'drɒf ən əs ‖ -'drɑːf-
hydrocarbon ˌhaɪdr əʊ 'kɑːb ən ‖ -ə 'kɑːrb-
 ~s z
hydrocele 'haɪdr əʊ siːəl ‖ -ə- ~s z
hydrocephalus ˌhaɪdr əʊ 'kef əl əs -'sef-
 ‖ -oʊ 'sef-
hydrochloric ˌhaɪdr əʊ 'klɒr ɪk ◄ -'klɔːr-
 ‖ -ə 'klɔːr- -'kloʊr-
 ˌhydro chloric 'acid
hydrochloride ˌhaɪdr əʊ 'klɔːr aɪd ‖ -ə-
 -'kloʊr- ~s z
hydrocortisone ˌhaɪdr əʊ 'kɔːt ɪ zəʊn -'•ə-
 ‖ -ə 'kɔːrt̬ ə zoʊn -soʊn
hydrodynamic ˌhaɪdr əʊ daɪ 'næm ɪk ◄ -dɪ'•-
 ‖ ˌhaɪdr oʊ- ~ally əl_i ~s s
hydroelectric ˌhaɪdr əʊ ɪ 'lek trɪk ◄ -ə'•-
 ‖ ˌhaɪdr oʊ- ~ally əl_i
hydrofoil 'haɪdr əʊ fɔɪəl ‖ -ə- ~s z
hydrogen 'haɪdr ədʒ ən -ɪdʒ-, -ɪn
 ˌhydrogen bomb; ˌhydrogen per oxide;
 ˌhydrogen 'sulphide
hydroge|nate 'haɪdr ədʒ ə ˌneɪt -ədʒ ɪ-;
 haɪ 'drɒdʒ- ‖ haɪ 'drɑːdʒ- 'haɪdr ədʒ-
 ~nated neɪt ɪd -əd ‖ neɪt̬ əd ~nates neɪts
 ~nating neɪt ɪŋ ‖ neɪt̬ ɪŋ
hydrographer haɪ 'drɒg rəf ə ‖ -'drɑːg rəf ər
 ~s z
hydrographic ˌhaɪdr əʊ 'græf ɪk ◄ ‖ -ə- ~ally
 əl_i
hydrography haɪ 'drɒg rəf i ‖ -'drɑːg-
hydroid 'haɪdr ɔɪd ~s z

H

hydrologic ˌhaɪdr ə ˈlɒdʒ ɪk ◀ ‖ -ˈlɑːdʒ- **~al** əl
~ally əl_i
hydrologist haɪ ˈdrɒl ədʒ ɪst §-əst ‖ -ˈdrɑːl- **~s**
s
hydrology haɪ ˈdrɒl ədʒ i ‖ -ˈdrɑːl-
hydrolys|e ˈhaɪdr ə laɪz **~ed** d **~es** ɪz əz **~ing**
ɪŋ
hydrolysis haɪ ˈdrɒl əs ɪs -ɪs-, §-əs ‖ -ˈdrɑːl-
hydrolytic ˌhaɪdr ə ˈlɪt ɪk ◀ ‖ -ˈlɪt̬ ɪk ◀ **~ally** əl_i
hydrolyz|e ˈhaɪdr ə laɪz **~ed** d **~es** ɪz əz **~ing**
ɪŋ
hydrometer haɪ ˈdrɒm ɪt ə -ət- ‖ -ˈdrɑːm ət̬ ər
~s z
hydropathy haɪ ˈdrɒp əθ i ‖ -ˈdrɑːp-
hydrophilic ˌhaɪdr əʊ ˈfɪl ɪk ◀ ‖ -ə-
hydrophob|ia ˌhaɪdr əʊ ˈfəʊb i_ə ‖ -ə ˈfoʊb|-
~ic ɪk ◀
hydrophone ˈhaɪdr ə fəʊn ‖ -foʊn **~s** z
hydrophyte ˈhaɪdr ə faɪt **~s** s
hydroplane ˈhaɪdr əʊ pleɪn ‖ -ə- **~s** z
hydroponic ˌhaɪdr əʊ ˈpɒn ɪk ◀ ‖ -ə ˈpɑːn- **~s** s
hydrostatic ˌhaɪdr əʊ ˈstæt ɪk ◀ ‖ -ə ˈstæt̬ ɪk ◀
~ally əl_i **~s** s
hydrotherapy ˌhaɪdr əʊ ˈθer əp i ‖ ˌhaɪdr ə-
hydrotropic ˌhaɪdr əʊ ˈtrɒp ɪk ◀ ‖ -ə ˈtrɑːp ɪk ◀
-ˈtroʊp-
hydrotropism haɪ ˈdrɒtr ə ˌpɪz əm ‖ -ˈdrɑːtr-
hydrous ˈhaɪdr əs
hydroxide haɪ ˈdrɒks aɪd ‖ -ˈdrɑːks- **~s** z
hydroxy haɪ ˈdrɒks i ‖ -ˈdrɑːks i
hydroxyl haɪ ˈdrɒks ɪl -əl ‖ -ˈdrɑːks-
hydrozoan ˌhaɪdr əʊ ˈzəʊ ən ‖ -ə ˈzoʊ- **~s** z
Hydrus ˈhaɪdr əs
hyena haɪ ˈiːn ə **~s** z
hyetograph ˈhaɪ_ət əʊ grɑːf ' ◦ ɪt-, -græf;
haɪ ˈet- ‖ -ət̬ ə græf haɪ ˈet̬- **~s** s
Hygeia haɪ ˈdʒiː_ə
Hygena *tdmk* haɪ ˈdʒiːn ə
hygiene ˈhaɪdʒ iːn
hygienic haɪ ˈdʒiːn ɪk ‖ ˌhaɪdʒ i ˈen ɪk ◀
haɪ ˈdʒen ɪk *(*)* **~ally** əl_i
hygienist ˈhaɪdʒ iːn ɪst haɪ ˈdʒiːn-, §-əst
‖ haɪ ˈdʒiːn əst -ˈdʒen-; ˈhaɪdʒ iːn əst **~s** s
hygrometer haɪ ˈgrɒm ɪt ə -ət- ‖ -ˈgrɑːm ət̬ ər
~s z
hygroscopic ˌhaɪg rə ˈskɒp ɪk ◀ ‖ -ˈskɑːp-
Hylas ˈhaɪl əs -æs
Hylda ˈhɪld ə
Hylton ˈhɪlt ən
Hyman ˈhaɪm ən
hymen, Hymen ˈhaɪm en ‖ -ən **~s** z
hymeneal ˌhaɪm e ˈniː_əl ◀ -ɪ-, -ə- ‖ -ə-
hymenopterous ˌhaɪm ə ˈnɒpt ər əs ◀, • ɪ-,
, • e- ‖ -ˈnɑːpt-
Hymettus haɪ ˈmet əs ‖ -ˈmet̬ əs
Hymie ˈhaɪm i
hymn hɪm (= *him*) **hymned** hɪmd **hymning**
ˈhɪm ɪŋ **hymns** hɪmz
ˈhymn book
hymnal ˈhɪm nəl **~s** z
hymnodist ˈhɪm nəd ɪst §-əst **~s** s
hymnod|y ˈhɪm nəd |i **~ies** iz
hymnology hɪm ˈnɒl ədʒ i ‖ -ˈnɑːl-

Hynd haɪnd
hyoid ˈhaɪ ɔɪd
hyoscine ˈhaɪ əʊ siːn ‖ -ə-
hyoscyamine ˌhaɪ əʊ ˈsaɪ_ə miːn -mɪn, §-mən
‖ ˌhaɪ ə-
hypallage haɪ ˈpæl ədʒ i -əg-, -iː **~s** z
Hypatia haɪ ˈpeɪʃ ə -ˈpeɪʃ i_ə
hype haɪp **hyped** haɪpt **hypes** haɪps **hyping**
ˈhaɪp ɪŋ
ˌhyped ˈup
hyper- *comb. form*
with stress-neutral suffix ˌhaɪp ə ‖ ˌhaɪp ər
—but before a vowel sound, -ər‖ -ər —
hyperpyrexia
ˌhaɪp ə paɪ ˈreks i_ə ‖ ˌhaɪp ər-—
hyperacidity ˌhaɪp ər ə ˈsɪd ət i -æ' • -, -ɪt i
‖ -ər ə ˈsɪd ət̬ i
with stress-imposing suffix
haɪ ˈpɜː+ ‖ haɪ ˈpɝː+— hypergamy
haɪ ˈpɜːɡ əm i ‖ -ˈpɝːɡ-
hyperactive ˌhaɪp ər ˈækt ɪv ◀ ‖ -ər- **~ly** li
hyperactivity ˌhaɪp ər æk ˈtɪv ət i -ɪt i
‖ -ər æk ˈtɪv ət̬ i
hyperbaric ˌhaɪp ə ˈbær ɪk ◀ ‖ -ər- -ˈber-
hyperbaton haɪ ˈpɜːb ə tɒn ‖ -ˈpɝːb ə tɑːn
hyperb|ola haɪ ˈpɜːb |əl ə ‖ -ˈpɝːb|- **~olae** ə liː
~olas əl əz
hyperbole haɪ ˈpɜːb əl i ⚠ ˈhaɪp ə bəʊl
‖ -ˈpɝːb- **~s** z
hyperbolic ˌhaɪp ə ˈbɒl ɪk ◀ ‖ -ər ˈbɑːl ɪk ◀
~ally əl_i
ˌhyperˌbolic ˈfunction
hyperboloid haɪ ˈpɜːb ə lɔɪd ‖ -ˈpɝːb- **~s** z
hyperborean, H~ ˌhaɪp ə ˈbɔːr i_ən-bɔː ˈriː_ən,
-bɒ' • - ‖ ˌhaɪp ər- -ˈbour- **~s** z
hypercorrect ˌhaɪp ə kə ˈrekt ◀ ‖ ˌhaɪp ər- **~ly**
li **~ness** nəs nɪs
hypercorrection ˌhaɪp ə kə ˈrek ʃən ‖ ˌhaɪp ər-
~s z
hypercritical
ˌhaɪp ə ˈkrɪt ɪk əl ◀ ‖ ˌhaɪp ər ˈkrɪt̬- **~ly** _i
hypercube ˈhaɪp ə kjuːb ‖ -ər- **~s** z
hyperglycaemia, hyperglycemia
ˌhaɪp ə glaɪ ˈsiːm i_ə ‖ ˌhaɪp ər-
hypericum haɪ ˈper ɪk əm **~s** z
Hyperides haɪ ˈper ə diːz-ə-; ˌhaɪp ə ˈraɪd iːz
hyperinflation ˌhaɪp ər ɪn ˈfleɪʃ ən
Hyperion haɪ ˈpɪər i_ən-ˈper- ‖ -ˈpɪr-
hyperlink ˈhaɪp ə lɪŋk ‖ -ər- **~s** z
hypermarket ˈhaɪp ə ˌmɑːk ɪt §-ət ‖ -ər ˌmɑːrk-
~s s
hyperpituitarism ˌhaɪp ə pɪ ˈtjuː_ɪt ə ˌrɪz əm
-pə' • -, §→-ˈtʃuː_, §-' • _ət- ‖ -ər pə ˈtuː ət̬-
-ˈtjuː-
hypersensitive ˌhaɪp ə ˈsen‿s ət ɪv ◀-ɪt ɪv
‖ -ər ˈsen‿s ət̬ ɪv ◀ **~ness** nəs nɪs
hypersensitivity ˌhaɪp ə ˌsen‿s ə ˈtɪv ət i -‿• ɪ-,
-ɪt i ‖ -ər ˌsen‿s ə ˈtɪv ət̬ i
hypersonic ˌhaɪp ə ˈsɒn ɪk ◀ ‖ -ər ˈsɑːn ɪk ◀ **~s**
s
hyperspace ˈhaɪp ə speɪs, • • ' • ‖ -ər-
hypertension ˌhaɪp ə ˈtenʃ ən ‖ -ər-
hypertensive ˌhaɪp ə ˈten‿s ɪv ‖ -ər-

hypertext 'haɪp ə tekst ‖ -ᵊr-
hyperthyroid ˌhaɪp ə 'θaɪᵊr ɔɪd ◂ ‖ -ᵊr- **~ism**
ˌɪz əm
hypertroph|y haɪ 'pɜːtr əf |i ‖ -'pɜːtr- **~ied** ɪd
~ies iz **~ying** i ɪŋ
hyperventi|late ˌhaɪp ə 'vent ɪ |leɪt -ə leɪt,
-ᵊl eɪt ‖ -ᵊr 'venţ ᵊl eɪt **~lated** leɪt ɪd -əd
‖ leɪţ əd **~lates** leɪts **~lating** leɪt ɪŋ ‖ leɪţ ɪŋ
hyperventilation ˌhaɪp ə ˌvent ɪ 'leɪʃ ᵊn -ə'•-,
-ᵊl 'eɪʃ- ‖ -ᵊr ˌvenţ ᵊl 'eɪʃ ᵊn
hyph|a 'haɪf |ə **~ae** iː
hyphen 'haɪf ᵊn **~s** z
hyphe|nate 'haɪf ə |neɪt **~nated** neɪt ɪd -əd
‖ neɪţ əd **~nates** neɪts **~nating**
neɪt ɪŋ ‖ neɪţ ɪŋ
hyphenation ˌhaɪf ə 'neɪʃ ᵊn **~s** z
hypnagogic, hypnogogic ˌhɪp nə 'gɒdʒ ɪk ◂
-'gəʊdʒ- ‖ -'gɑːdʒ ɪk ◂ -'goʊdʒ- **~s** s
hypno- *comb. form*
   with stress-neutral suffix ¦hɪp nəʊ ‖ -noʊ —
   hypnotherapy ˌhɪp nəʊ 'θer əp i ‖ ˌhɪp noʊ-
   with stress-imposing suffix hɪp 'nɒ+ ‖ -'nɑː+ —
   hypnology hɪp 'nɒl ədʒ i ‖ -'nɑːl-
Hypnos 'hɪp nɒs -nɑːs -noʊs, -nʊs
hypnos|is hɪp 'nəʊs |ɪs §-əs ‖ -'noʊs- **~es** iːz
hypnotic hɪp 'nɒt ɪk ‖ -'nɑːţ ɪk **~ally** ᵊl_i **~s** s
hypnotis... *—see* **hypnotiz...**
hypnotism 'hɪp nə ˌtɪz əm
hypnotist 'hɪp nət ɪst §-əst ‖ -nəţ- **~s** s
hypnotiz|e 'hɪp nə taɪz **~ed** d **~es** ɪz əz **~ing**
ɪŋ
hypo 'haɪp əʊ ‖ -oʊ
hypo- *comb. form*
   with stress-neutral suffix ¦haɪp əʊ ‖ -ə —*but*
   before a vowel ¦haɪp əʊ ‖ -oʊ —
   hypochlorous ˌhaɪp əʊ 'klɔːr əs ◂ ‖ -ə-
   -'kloʊr- **hypoallergenic**
   ˌhaɪp əʊ ˌæl ə 'dʒen ɪk -ɜː'•- ‖ -oʊ ˌæl ᵊr-
   —The fact that RP ¦haɪp ə *is ambiguous as*
   between hypo- *and* hyper- *means that for clarity*
   one ought preferably to avoid reducing the
   second syllable and ought therefore to say
   ¦haɪp əʊ
   with stress-imposing suffix haɪ 'pɒ+ ‖ -'pɑː+ —
   hypogynous haɪ 'pɒdʒ ɪn əs -ən- ‖ -'pɑːdʒ-
hypocaust 'haɪp əʊ kɔːst ‖ -ə- -kɑːst **~s** s
hypocenter, hypocentre 'haɪp əʊ
   ˌsent ə ‖ -ə ˌsenţ ᵊr **~s** z
hypochondria ˌhaɪp əʊ 'kɒndr i_ə ‖ -ə 'kɑːndr-
hypochondriac ˌhaɪp əʊ
   'kɒndr i æk ‖ -ə 'kɑːndr- **~s** s
hypochondriacal ˌhaɪp əʊ kɒn 'draɪ_ək ᵊl ◂
-kən'•- ‖ -oʊ kɑːn-
hypocorism haɪ 'pɒk ə ˌrɪz əm ˌhaɪp ə 'kɔːr ɪz
əm ‖ -'pɑːk-
hypercoristic ˌhaɪp ə kɔː 'rɪst ɪk ◂-kɒ'•-,
-kə'•- ‖ -ᵊr kə- **~ally** ᵊl_i **~s** s
hypocris|y hɪ 'pɒk rəs |i §haɪ-, -rɪs- ‖ -'pɑːk-
~ies iz
hypocrite 'hɪp ə krɪt **~s** s
hypocritical ˌhɪp ə 'krɪt ɪk ᵊl ◂ ‖ -'krɪţ- **~ly** _i
hypodermic ˌhaɪp əʊ
   'dɜːm ɪk ◂ -ə 'dɝːm ɪk ◂ **~ally** ᵊl_i **~s** s
   ˌhypoˌdermic 'needle

hypodermis ˌhaɪp əʊ 'dɜːm ɪs §-əs
   ‖ -ə 'dɝːm əs
hypogeal ˌhaɪp əʊ 'dʒiː_əl ◂ ‖ -oʊ-
hypoglossal ˌhaɪp əʊ 'glɒs ᵊl ◂ ‖ -ə 'glɑːs ᵊl ◂
hypoglycaem|ia, hypoglycem|ia ˌhaɪp əʊ
   glaɪ 'siːm| i_ə ‖ ˌhaɪp oʊ- **~ic** ɪk ◂
hypoid 'haɪp ɔɪd **~s** z
hyponym 'haɪp əʊ nɪm ‖ -ə- **~s** z
hypostasis haɪ 'pɒst əs ɪs §-əs ‖ -'paːst-
hypostatis... *—see* **hypostatiz...**
hypostatic ˌhaɪp ə 'stæt ɪk ◂ ‖ -'stæţ ɪk ◂
   ˌhypoˌstatic 'union
hypostatization haɪ ˌpɒst ət aɪ 'zeɪʃ ᵊn -ət ɪ-
   ‖ -ˌpɑːst əţ ə-
hypostatiz|e haɪ 'pɒst ə taɪz ‖ -'pɑːst- **~ed** d
~es ɪz əz **~ing** ɪŋ
hypostyle 'haɪp əʊ staɪᵊl ‖ -oʊ-
hyposulfite, hyposulphite ˌhaɪp əʊ
   'sʌlf aɪt ‖ -oʊ-
hypotactic ˌhaɪp əʊ 'tækt ɪk ◂ ‖ -ə- -oʊ-
   ~ally ᵊl_i
hypotaxis ˌhaɪp əʊ 'tæks ɪs §-əs ‖ -ə- -oʊ-
hypotenuse haɪ 'pɒt ə njuːz -ɪ-, -ᵊn juːz
   ‖ -'paːţ ᵊn uːs -juːs *(*)*
hypothalamic ˌhaɪp əʊ θə 'læm ɪk ◂ ‖ ˌhaɪp oʊ-
hypothalamus ˌhaɪp əʊ 'θæl əm əs ‖ ˌhaɪp oʊ-
hypothe|cate haɪ 'pɒθ ə |keɪt -ɪ- ‖ -'pɑːθ- hɪ-
   ~cated keɪt ɪd -əd ‖ keɪţ əd **~cates** keɪts
   ~cating keɪt ɪŋ ‖ keɪţ ɪŋ
hypothecation haɪ ˌpɒθ ə 'keɪʃ ᵊn -ɪ- ‖ -ˌpɑːθ-
   hɪ- **~s** z
hypothermia ˌhaɪp əʊ 'θɜːm i_ə ‖ -oʊ 'θɝːm-
hypoth|esis haɪ 'pɒθ |əs ɪs -ɪs-, §-əs **~eses**
   ə siːz ɪ-
hypothesis|e, hypothesiz|e
   haɪ 'pɒθ ə saɪz ‖ -'pɑːθ- **~ed** d **~es** ɪz əz
   ~ing ɪŋ
hypothetical ˌhaɪp ə 'θet ɪk ᵊl ◂ ‖ -'θeţ- **~ly** _i
hypothyroid ˌhaɪp əʊ 'θaɪᵊr ɔɪd ◂ ‖ -oʊ- **~ism**
   ˌɪz əm
hypoxia haɪ 'pɒks i_ə ‖ -'pɑːks-
hypsometer hɪp 'sɒm ɪt ə -ət- ‖ -'saːm əţ ᵊr
   ~s z
hypsometry hɪp 'sɒm ətr i -ɪtr- ‖ -'saːm-
hyrax 'haɪᵊr æks **~es** ɪz əz
Hyrcania hɜː 'keɪn i_ə ‖ hɝ-
Hyslop 'hɪz ləp
hyssop 'hɪs əp
hysterectom|y ˌhɪst ə 'rekt əm |i **~ies** iz
hysteresis ˌhɪst ə 'riːs ɪs §-əs
hysteria hɪ 'stɪər i_ə ‖ -'stɪr- -'ster- **~s** z
hysteric hɪ 'ster ɪk **~s** s
hysterical hɪ 'ster ɪk ᵊl **~ly** _i
hysteron proteron ˌhɪst ə rɒn 'prɒt ə rɒn
   →-rɒm'•- ‖ ˌhɪst ə raːn 'praːţ ə raːn
Hythe haɪð
Hyundai *tdmk* 'hjʊnd aɪ -eɪ; hɪ 'ʊnd-, -'ʌnd-;
   'haɪ ʌn daɪ, -ən- ‖ 'hʌnd eɪ —*Korean*
   [hjəːn dɛ] —*TV advertising has used different*
   anglicizations at different times.
Hywel 'haʊ_əl —*Welsh* ['hə wel]
Hz hɜːts ‖ hɝːts

I i

i — Spelling-to-sound

1 Where the spelling is **i**, the pronunciation differs according to whether the vowel is short or long, followed or not by **r**, and strong or weak.

2 The 'strong' pronunciation is regularly
ɪ, as in **bit** bɪt ('short I'), or
aɪ, as in **time** taɪm ('long I').

3 Where **i** is followed by **r**, the 'strong' pronunciation is
ɜː ‖ ɝː, as in **firm** fɜːm ‖ fɝːm,
aɪ(ə), as in **fire** faɪə ‖ ˈfaɪ_ᵊr, **virus** ˈvaɪᵊr əs,
or indeed the regular 'short' pronunciation ɪ, as in **miracle** ˈmɪr ək ᵊl.

4 Less frequently, the 'strong' pronunciation is
iː, as in **machine** mə ˈʃiːn.

5 The 'weak' pronunciation is
ɪ, as in **rabbit** ˈræb ɪt (although some speakers, especially of AmE, use ə instead, thus ˈræb ət), or
ə, as in **admiral** ˈæd mᵊr əl.
Where the following sound is a vowel, the 'weak' pronunciation is
i, as in **medium** ˈmiːd i_əm (see COMPRESSION),
or the **i** is silent, serving only to indicate the pronunciation of the consonant, as in **special** ˈspeʃ ᵊl (see **c, s, t**).

6 In the rare cases where **i** is found at the end of a word, the pronunciation is either
strong aɪ, as in **hi** haɪ, or
weak i, as in **spaghetti** spə ˈget i ‖ spə ˈget̬ i.

7 **i** also forms part of the digraphs **ai, ei, ie, oi, ui**.

ie — Spelling-to-sound

1 Where the spelling is the digraph **ie**, the pronunciation is regularly
iː, as in **piece** piːs (especially in the middle of a word), or
aɪ, as in **tie** taɪ (especially at the end of a word), or
ɪə ‖ ɪ, as in **fierce** fɪəs ‖ fɪrs (before **r**).

2 The 'weak' pronunciation in **-ied, -ies** is usually
i, as in **buried** ˈber id.
Thus the spelling change from **y** to **ie** in inflected forms of words written with **y** at the end does not imply any change in pronunciation.

3 Note the exceptional **friend** frend and **sieve** sɪv; also the usual pronunciation of **handkerchief**, -tʃɪf.

4 ie is not a digraph in **science, pliers, society, acquiesce, Viennese, happiest.**

I, i *name of letter* aɪ *(= eye)* **I's, i's** aɪz
—*Communications code name:* India

I *pronoun* aɪ —*This word has no true weak form in RP, though in rapid casual speech it may become monophthongal* [a]. *In GenAm it is sometimes weakened to* ə.

I-5 ˌaɪ ˈfaɪv —*and similarly for the names of other US interstate highways*

Iago i ˈɑːg əʊ ‖ -oʊ —*but as a Welsh personal name,* ˈjɑːg əʊ ‖ -oʊ, —*Welsh* [ˈja go]

Iain ˈiː ən

-ial *stress-imposing* i əl —*This suffix sometimes causes a change in the stressed vowel:* ˌmanaˈgerial -ˈdʒɪər i əl ‖ -ˈdʒɪr-

iamb ˈaɪ æm -æmb **~s** z

iambic aɪ ˈæm bɪk **~s** s

iam|bus aɪ ˈæm |bəs **~bi** baɪ **~buses** bəs ɪz -əz

Ian ˈiː ən —*In AmE sometimes* ˈaɪ ən

-ian *stress-imposing* i ən —*This suffix sometimes causes a change in the stressed vowel:* ₍ᵢ₎Peckˈsniffian -ˈsnɪf i ən, ₍ᵢ₎Chauˈcerian -ˈsɪər i ən ‖ -ˈsɪr i ən

Ianthe aɪ ˈæntᶿ i

Iapetus aɪ ˈæp ɪt əs -ət- ‖ -ət̬ əs

IATA i ˈɑːt ə aɪ-

IATEFL ˌaɪˌə ˈtef əl

iatrogenic aɪ ˌætr əʊ ˈdʒen ɪk ◄, • • • ‖ -ə-

Ibadan ɪ ˈbæd ən ‖ iː ˈbɑːd ən -ɑːn —*Yoruba* [i ba dõ]

Ibbotson ˈɪb əts ən

Ibcol *tdmk* ˈɪb kɒl ‖ -koʊl -kɔːl, -kɑːl

Iberi|a aɪ ˈbɪər i ə ‖ -ˈbɪr- **~an/s** ən/z

ibex ˈaɪb eks **~es** ɪz əz

Ibibio ɪ ˈbɪb i əʊ -ˈbiːb- ‖ -oʊ **~s** z

ibid ˈɪb ɪd §-əd

ibidem ˈɪb ɪ dem -ə-; ɪ ˈbaɪd em

-ibility ə ˈbɪl ət i ɪ-, -ɪt- ‖ -ət̬ i— **visibility** ˌvɪz ə ˈbɪl ət i -ɪˈ• •-, -ɪt i ‖ -ət̬ i

ibis ˈaɪb ɪs §-əs **~es** ɪz əz

Ibiza ɪ ˈbiːθ ə aɪ-, iː-, -ˈbiːz-, -ˈbiːts- —*Sp* [i ˈβi θa], *Catalan* [i ˈβi sa, əi-]

-ible əb əl ɪb əl— **visible** ˈvɪz əb əl -ɪb-

IBM *tdmk* ˌaɪ biː ˈem

ibn, Ibn *in Arabic names* ˈɪb ən

Ibo ˈiːb əʊ ‖ -oʊ —*Ibo* [i gbo] **~s** z

Ibrahim ˈɪb rə hiːm -hɪm, • • • • —*Arabic* [i bra ˈhiːm]

Ibrox ˈaɪb rɒks ‖ -rɑːks

Ibsen ˈɪb sən —*Norwegian* [ˈip sən]

Ibstock ˈɪb stɒk ‖ -stɑːk

ibuprofen ˌaɪb juː ˈprəʊf en -ən; aɪ ˈbjuːp rəʊfen ‖ -ˈproʊf ən

-ic *stress-imposing* ɪk — **periodic** ˌpɪər i ˈɒd ɪk ◄ ‖ ˌpɪr i ˈɑːd ɪk ◄

IC ˌaɪ ˈsiː **ICs** ˌaɪ ˈsiːz

-ical *stress-imposing* ɪk əl — **periodical** ˌpɪər i ˈɒd ɪk əl ◄ ‖ ˌpɪr i ˈɑːd ɪk əl ◄

-ically *stress-imposing* ɪk li ɪk əl i — **periodically** ˌpɪər i ˈɒd ɪk li -ˈɒd ɪk əl i ‖ ˌpɪr i ˈɑːd- —*shown in entries simply as* ɪk əl̩i

Icaria ɪ ˈkeər i ə aɪ- ‖ -ˈker-

Icarus ˈɪk ər əs ˈaɪk-

ICBM ˌaɪ siː biː ˈem **~s** z

ICE CREAM

BrE 1988
0   20   40   60   80   100%

---

ice aɪs **iced** aɪst **ices** ˈaɪs ɪz -əz **icing** ˈaɪs ɪŋ
ˈice age; ˈice axe; ˈice ˌbucket; ˌice ˈcream ◄, ˈ• • ‖ ˈ• • —*BrE 1988 poll panel preference* ˌ• ˈ• 66%, ˈ• • 34%; ˈice-cream ˌsoda; ˈice field; ˈice floe; ˈice ˌhockey; ˌice ˈlolly, ˈ• ˌ••; ˈice pack; ˈice pick; ˈice rink; ˈice sheet; ˈice ˌwater

iceball ˈaɪs bɔːl ‖ -bɑːl

iceberg ˈaɪs bɜːg ‖ -bɝːg **~s** z
ˌiceberg ˈlettuce, ˈ• • ˌ• •

icebound ˈaɪs baʊnd

icebox ˈaɪs bɒks ‖ -bɑːks **~es** ɪz əz

icebreaker ˈaɪs ˌbreɪk ə ‖ -ᵊr **~s** z

icecap ˈaɪs kæp **~s** s

ice-cold ˌaɪs ˈkəʊld ◄→-ˈkɒʊld ‖ -ˈkoʊld ◄

icefall ˈaɪs fɔːl ‖ -fɑːl **~s** z

ice|house ˈaɪs |haʊs **~houses** haʊz ɪz -əz

Iceland ˈaɪs lənd §-lænd

Icelander ˈaɪs lənd ə -lænd- ‖ -ᵊr **~s** z

Icelandic aɪs ˈlænd ɪk

icemaker ˈaɪs ˌmeɪk ə ‖ -ᵊr **~s** z

ice|man ˈaɪs |mæn -mən **~men** men mən

Iceni aɪ ˈsiːn aɪ -i

ice-|skate ˈaɪs |skeɪt ˈaɪˈs keɪt **~skated** skeɪt ɪd-əd ‖ skeɪt̬ əd **~skater/s** skeɪt ə/z ‖ skeɪt̬ ᵊr/z **~skates** skeɪts **~skating** skeɪt ɪŋ ‖ skeɪt̬ ɪŋ

Ice-T ˌaɪs ˈtiː

ice-tray ˈaɪs treɪ **~s** z

Ichabod ˈɪk ə bɒd ˈɪx- ‖ -bɑːd

I Ching ˌiː ˈtʃɪŋ ˌaɪ-, -ˈdʒɪŋ —*Chi yì jīng* [⁴i ¹tɕiŋ]

ich dien ˌɪx ˈdiːn ˌɪk- —*Ger* [ʔɪç ˈdiːn]; *Welsh* eich dyn [əx ˈdiːn, əix-, -ˈdiːn]

ich-laut ˈɪx laʊt ˈɪk- —*Ger* Ich-Laut [ˈʔɪç laʊt] **~s** s

I

ichneumon ɪk 'njuːm ən ‖ -'nuːm- -'njuːm-
~s z
ich'neumon fly
ichor 'aɪk ɔː ‖ -ɔːr
ichthyo- *comb. form*
with stress-neutral suffix ˌɪkθ i‿ə -əʊ ‖ -oʊ —
ichthyophobia ˌɪkθ i‿ə 'fəʊb i‿ə -i əʊ-
‖ -'foʊb- -i oʊ-
with stress-imposing suffix ˌɪkθ i 'ɒ+ ‖ -'ɑː+ —
ichthyophagous ˌɪkθ i 'ɒf əg əs ◄ ‖ -'ɑːf-
ichthyological ˌɪkθ i‿ə 'lɒdʒ ɪk ᵊl ◄ -i əʊ-
‖ -'lɑːdʒ- -i oʊ- ~**ly** ‿i
ichthyolog|ist/s ˌɪkθ i 'ɒl ədʒ ǀɪst/s -§əst/s
‖ -'ɑːl- ~**y** i
ichthyosaurus ˌɪkθ i‿ə 'sɔːr əs ~**es** ɪz əz
ichthyosis ˌɪkθ i 'əʊs ɪs §-əs ‖ -'oʊs-
ICI *tdmk* ˌaɪ siː 'aɪ
-ician 'ɪʃ ᵊn — **musician** mju 'zɪʃ ᵊn
icicle 'aɪs ɪk ᵊl ~**s** z
ici... —*see* **icy**
icing 'aɪs ɪŋ ~**s** z
'**icing** ˌsugar
Icke (i) aɪk, (ii) ɪk
Icknield 'ɪk niːᵊld
ˌIcknield 'Way
ick|y 'ɪk |i ~**ier** i‿ə ‖ i‿ᵊr ~**iest** i‿ɪst i‿əst
~**iness** i nəs -nɪs
icon 'aɪk ɒn -ᵊn ‖ -ɑːn ~**s** z
iconic aɪ 'kɒn ɪk ‖ -'kɑːn-
Iconium aɪ 'kəʊn i‿əm ‖ -'koʊn-
icono- *comb. form*
with stress-neutral suffix aɪ ǀkɒn ə ǀaɪk ɒn ə
‖ aɪ ǀkɑːn ə ǀaɪk ɑːn ə — **iconographic**
aɪ ˌkɒn ə 'græf ɪk ◄ ˌaɪk ɒn- ‖ aɪ ˌkɑːn-
ˌaɪk ɑːn-
with stress-imposing suffix ˌaɪk ə 'nɒ+ -ɒ-
‖ -'nɑː+ — **iconology** ˌaɪk ə 'nɒl ədʒ i ˌ•ɒ-
‖ -'nɑːl-
iconoclasm aɪ 'kɒn ə ˌklæz əm ‖ -'kɑːn-
iconoclast aɪ 'kɒn ə klæst -klɑːst ‖ -'kɑːn- ~**s**
s
iconoclastic aɪ ˌkɒn ə 'klæst ɪk ◄ ˌaɪk ɒn-
‖ aɪ ˌkɑːn- ˌaɪk ɑːn- ~**ally** ᵊl‿i
iconograph|y ˌaɪk ə 'nɒg rəf li ‖ -'nɑːg- ~**ies**
iz
iconost|asis ˌaɪk ə 'nɒst ləs ɪs ˌ•ɒ-, §-əs
‖ -'nɑːst- ~**ases** ə siːz
icosahedr|on ˌaɪk əs ə 'hiːdr |ən ˌ•ɒs-, aɪ ˌkɒs-,
-'hedr- ‖ aɪ ˌkoʊs- -ˌkɑːs-; ˌaɪk oʊs-, ˌ•ɑːs-
~**a** ə ~**ons** ənz
ictal 'ɪkt ᵊl
icteric ɪk 'ter ɪk
icterus 'ɪkt ər əs
ictus 'ɪkt əs ~**es** ɪz əz
icy 'aɪs i **icier** 'aɪs i‿ə ‖ ‿ᵊr **iciest** 'aɪs i‿ɪst ‿əst
icily 'aɪs ɪ li -ᵊli **iciness** 'aɪs i nəs -nɪs
I'd aɪd
id *in psychology* ɪd **ids** ɪdz
ID, id *'(proof of) identity'* ˌaɪ 'diː ˙
ˌI 'D card
-id ɪd §əd — **acarid** 'æk ər ɪd §-əd **arachnid**
ə 'ræk nɪd §-nəd
Ida 'aɪd ə

Idaho 'aɪd ə həʊ ‖ -hoʊ
Idahoan ˌaɪd ə həʊ ən ◄ ˌ••'•• ‖ -hoʊ ən ~**s** z
Idd *Moslem festival* iːd
Iddesleigh 'ɪdz li
-ide aɪd — **lanthanide** 'lænᵗθ ə naɪd

IDEA

AmE 1993

| 0 | 20 | 40 | 60 | 80 | 100% |

idea aɪ 'dɪə ˌaɪ-, §-'diː‿ə ⒤aɪ 'diː ə '•••
—*AmE 1993 poll panel preference:* •'••• 86%,
'•••• 14%. ~**s** z
ideal ⒤aɪ 'dɪəl -'diːˌ‿əl ‖ ⒤aɪ 'diːˌəl ~**ly** i li ~**s** z
idealis... —*see* **idealiz...**
idealism aɪ 'dɪəl ˌɪz əm ˌaɪ-, -'diːˌ‿ə ˌlɪz-;
'aɪd i‿ə ˌlɪz ᵊm ‖ aɪ 'diː‿ə ˌlɪz əm ~**s** z
idealist aɪ 'dɪəl ɪst ˌaɪ-, -'diːˌəl-, 'aɪd iˌ‿əl-, §-əst
‖ aɪ 'diː əl əst ~**s** s
idealistic aɪ ˌdɪə 'lɪst ɪk ◄ ˌaɪd i‿ə 'lɪst ɪk◄,
aɪ ˌdiːˌ‿ə- ‖ aɪ ˌdiː ə 'lɪst ɪk ◄ ˌaɪd i‿ə- ~**ally**
ᵊl‿i
idealization aɪ ˌdɪəl aɪ 'zeɪʃ ᵊn ˌaɪ ˌdɪəl-,
aɪ ˌdiːˌ‿əl aɪ'•-, §ˌaɪd iˌ‿əl-, -ɪ'•-
‖ aɪ ˌdiː əl ə 'zeɪʃ ᵊn ~**s** z
idealiz|e aɪ 'dɪəl aɪz ˌaɪ-; -'diːˌ‿ə laɪz, §'aɪd iˌ‿ə-
‖ aɪ 'diː ə laɪz ~**ed** d ~**es** ɪz əz ~**ing** ɪŋ
ideally ⒤aɪ 'dɪəl i -'diːˌ‿əl i, -li ‖ ⒤aɪ 'diːˌəl i -li
ideate 'aɪd i leɪt ~**ated** eɪt ɪd -əd ‖ eɪt̬ əd
~**ates** eɪts ~**ating** eɪt ɪŋ ‖ eɪt̬ ɪŋ
ideation ˌaɪd i 'eɪʃ ᵊn ~**al** ᵊl ~**ally** ᵊl i
idee, idée 'iːd eɪ iː 'deɪ —*Fr* [i de] **idees,**
idées *as sing., or* z
ˌidee 'fixe, ˌidée 'fixe fɪks fiːks —*Fr* [fiks];
ˌidee re'cu, ˌidée re'çu rə 'suː —*Fr* [ʁə sy]
idem 'ɪd em ˌaɪd-, 'iːd-
identical aɪ 'dent ɪk ᵊl ɪ-, ə- ‖ -'dent̬- ~**ly** i
iˌdentical 'twin
identifiab|le aɪ 'dent i faɪˌəb |ᵊl -'•ə-,
§•, ••'•••• ‖ -'dent̬ ə- ~**ly** li
identification aɪ ˌdent ɪf ɪ 'keɪʃ ᵊn ɪ-, ə-, -ˌ•əf-,
§-ə'•- ‖ -ˌdent̬- ~**s** z
identi|fy aɪ 'dent ɪ |faɪ ɪ-, ə-, -ə- ‖ -'dent̬ ə |faɪ
~**fied** faɪd ~**fier/s** faɪ‿ə/z ‖ faɪ‿ᵊr/z ~**fies**
faɪz ~**fying** faɪ ɪŋ
identikit, I~ *tdmk* aɪ 'dent i kɪt ɪ-, ə- ‖ -'dent̬-
identit|y aɪ 'dent ət li ɪ-, ə-, -ɪt- ‖ -'dent̬ ət̬ li
~**ies** iz
i'dentity card; i'dentity ˌcrisis
ideogram 'ɪd i‿ə græm 'aɪd-, -i əʊ- ~**s** z
ideograph 'ɪd i‿ə grɑːf 'aɪd-, -i əʊ-, -græf
‖ -græf ~**s** s
ideographic ˌɪd i‿ə 'græf ɪk ◄ ˌaɪd-, -i əʊ-
~**ally** ᵊl i
ideography ˌɪd i 'ɒgr əf i ˌaɪd- ‖ -'ɑːg-
ideological ˌaɪd i‿ə 'lɒdʒ ɪk ᵊl ◄ ˌɪd- ‖ -'lɑːdʒ-
~**ly** ‿i
ideologist ˌaɪd i 'ɒl ədʒ ɪst ˌɪd-, §-əst ‖ -'ɑːl-
~**s** s
ideologue 'aɪd i‿ə lɒg ‖ -lɔːg -lɑːg ~**s** z
ideolog|y ˌaɪd i 'ɒl ədʒ li ˌɪd- ‖ -'ɑːl- —*Poll*
panel preferences: AmE 1993, ˌaɪd- 64%, ˌɪd-

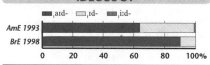

IDEOLOGY

■ ‚aɪd- ▫‚ɪd- ■‚iːd-

AmE 1993

BrE 1998

0 20 40 60 80 100%

*35%, ‚iːd- 1%; BrE 1998, ‚aɪd- 90%, ‚ɪd-
10%.* **~ies** ɪz
ideophone 'ɪd i‿ə fəʊn 'aɪd-, -i əʊ- ‖ -foʊn **~s**
z
ides, Ides aɪdz
idio- *comb. form*
   with stress-neutral suffix ¦ɪd i əʊ ‖ -ə —
   idioglossia ‚ɪd i əʊ 'glɒs i‿ə ‖ -ə 'glɑːs-
   -'gloʊs-
   with stress-imposing suffix ‚ɪd i 'ɒ+ ‖ -'ɑː+ —
   idiopathy ‚ɪd i 'ɒp əθ i ‖ -'ɑːp-
idioc|y 'ɪd i‿əs li **~ies** ɪz
idiolect 'ɪd i‿ə lekt -i əʊ- **~s** s
idiolectal ‚ɪd i‿ə 'lekt ᵊl ◄ -i əʊ- **~ly** i
idiom 'ɪd i‿əm **~s** z
idiomatic ‚ɪd i‿ə 'mæt ɪk ◄ -i əʊ- ‖ -'mæt̬-
~ally ᵊl i
idiosyncras|y ‚ɪd i‿əʊ 'sɪŋk rəs li ‖ -i‿ə- **~ies** ɪz
idiosyncratic ‚ɪd i‿əʊ sɪŋ 'kræt ɪk -sɪn'• -
‖ ‿ə sɪn 'kræt̬ ɪk **~ally** ᵊl i
idiot 'ɪd i‿ət **~s** s
   idiot savant ‚iːd i əʊ sæ 'võ ‚ɪd i‿ət 'sæv ᵊnt
   ‖ ‚iːd joʊ sɑː 'vɑːn -sæ'• —*Fr* [i djo sa vã]
idiotic ‚ɪd i 'ɒt ɪk ◄ ‖ -'ɑːt̬ ɪk **~ally** ᵊl i
Idist 'iːd ɪst §-əst **~s** s
Iditarod *place in AK* aɪ 'dɪt ə rɒd ‖ aɪ 'dɪt̬ ə rɑːd
idle, Idle 'aɪd ᵊl **idleness** 'aɪd ᵊl nəs -nɪs
   idler/s 'aɪd lə/z ‖ -lᵊr/z **idlest** 'aɪd lɪst -ləst
idly 'aɪd li
Ido 'iːd əʊ ‖ -oʊ
idol 'aɪd ᵊl *(= idle)* **~s** z
idolater, idolator aɪ 'dɒl ət ə ‖ -'dɑːl ət̬ ᵊr **~s** z
idolatrous aɪ 'dɒl ətr əs ‖ -'dɑːl- **~ly** li **~ness**
nəs nɪs
idolatr|y aɪ 'dɒl ətr li ‖ -'dɑːl- **~ies** ɪz
idolis... —*see* **idoliz...**
idolization ‚aɪd ᵊl aɪ 'zeɪʃ ᵊn -ᵊl ɪ-, -ə laɪ-
‖ -ᵊl ə-
idoliz|e 'aɪd ᵊl aɪz -ə laɪz **~ed** d **~er/s** ə/
z ‖ ᵊr/z **~es** ɪz əz **~ing** ɪŋ
Idomeneo ɪ ‚dɒm ə 'neɪ əʊ ‖ ‚iːd oʊm ə 'neɪ oʊ
Idomeneus aɪ 'dɒm ɪ njuːs ɪ-, -ə-
‖ -'dɑːm ə nuːs -njuːs
Idris 'ɪdr ɪs 'aɪdr-, §-əs
Idwal 'ɪd wəl
idyl, idyll 'ɪd ᵊl 'aɪd-, -ɪl ‖ 'aɪd ᵊl **~s** z
idyllic ɪ 'dɪl ɪk aɪ- ‖ aɪ- **~ally** ᵊl i
-ie i — **sweetie** 'swiːt i ‖ 'swiːt̬ i
i.e. ‚aɪ 'iː
iechyd da ‚jæk i 'dɑː —*Welsh* [‚je χɪd 'dɑː,
-χɪd-]
-ier *comparative of* **-y** i‿ə ‖ i‿ᵊr — **dirtier**
'dɜːt i‿ə ‖ 'dɜːt̬ i‿ᵊr
-ier *suffix forming nouns* 'ɪə ‖ 'ɪᵊr — **brigadier**
‚brɪg ə 'dɪə ‖ -'dɪᵊr
-ies *pl of* **-y** ɪz — **doggies** 'dɒg ɪz ‖ 'dɔːg ɪz
'dɑːg-

-iest *superlative of* **-y** i‿ɪst ‿əst — **dirtiest**
'dɜːt i‿ɪst ‿əst ‖ 'dɜːt̬ i‿əst
Iestyn 'jest ɪn —*Welsh* ['je sdɪn, -sdɪn]
Ieuan 'jaɪ‿ən -æn —*Welsh* ['jə jan]
if ɪf §ɪv —*In RP this word has no separate weak
form; but in some other varieties, including
GenAm, it may have a weak form* əf **ifs** ɪfs
Ife *family name* aɪf
Ife *place in Nigeria* 'iː feɪ —*Yoruba* [i fe]
-iferous 'ɪf ᵊr əs — **carboniferous** ‚kɑːb ə 'nɪf
ᵊr əs ‖ ‚kɑːrb-
iff ɪf —*Since* iff *is pronounced identically with
plain* if, *its use ('if and only if) is in practice
restricted to writing.*
iff|y 'ɪf li **~iness** nəs i nɪs
Ifield 'aɪ fiːᵊld
Ifor 'aɪv ə 'aɪf-; 'iː vɔː ‖ -ᵊr —*Welsh* ['i vor]
-iform ɪ fɔːm ə- ‖ -fɔːrm — **cruciform**
'kruːs ɪ fɔːm -ə- ‖ -fɔːrm
-ify *stress-imposing* ɪ faɪ ə- — **solidify**
sə 'lɪd ɪ faɪ sɒ-, -ə-
Igbo 'iːb əʊ ‖ -oʊ —*Ibo* [i gbo] **~s** z
Iggy 'ɪg i
Ightham 'aɪt əm ‖ 'aɪt̬-
igitur 'ɪg ɪ tʊə 'ɪdʒ-, §-ə-; -ɪt ə, §-ət ə ‖ -tʊr
igloo 'ɪg luː **~s** z
Ignatian ɪg 'neɪʃ i‿ən -'neɪʃ ᵊn **~s** z
Ignatieff ɪg 'næt i ef ‖ -'næt̬-
Ignatius ɪg 'neɪʃ əs -'neɪʃ i‿əs
igneous 'ɪg ni‿əs
ignimbrite 'ɪg nɪm braɪt §-nəm-
ignis fatuus ‚ɪg nɪs 'fæt juːəs §‚•nəs-,
-'fætʃ u‿ ‖ -'fætʃ u‿əs **ignes fatui**
‚ɪg neɪz 'fæt ju iː, §‚•niːz-, -'fætʃ u-, -aɪ
‖ -niːz 'fætʃ u aɪ
ig|nite ɪg |'naɪt **~nited** 'naɪt ɪd -əd ‖ 'naɪt̬ əd
~nites 'naɪts **~niting** 'naɪt ɪŋ ‖ 'naɪt̬ ɪŋ
ignition ɪg 'nɪʃ ᵊn **~s** z
ignitron ɪg 'naɪtr ɒn 'ɪg nɪ trɒn, -nə- ‖ -ɑːn **~s**
z
ignob|le ɪg 'nəʊb ᵊl ‚ɪg- ‖ -'noʊb- **~ly** li
ignominious ‚ɪg nə 'mɪn i‿əs ◄ ‚•nəʊ- **~ly** li
~ness nəs nɪs
ignomin|y 'ɪg nəm ɪn li -ən i **~ies** ɪz
ignoramus ‚ɪg nə 'reɪm əs **~es** ɪz əz
ignorance 'ɪg nᵊr ᵊnts
ignorant 'ɪg nᵊr ᵊnt **~ly** li
ignore ɪg 'nɔː ‖ -'nɔːr -'noʊr **~d** d **~s** z
   ignoring ɪg 'nɔːr ɪŋ ‖ -'noʊr-
ignotum per ignotius ɪg ‚nəʊt əm ‚pɜːr
ɪg 'nəʊt i‿əs -, •• pər•'•-, -ʊs
‖ ɪg ‚noʊt̬ əm ‚pɜː· ɪg 'noʊt̬-
Igoe 'aɪg əʊ ‖ -oʊ
Igor 'iːg ɔː ‖ -ɔːr —*Russ* ['i gərʲ]
Igorot ‚ɪg ə 'rəʊt ‚ɪg- ‖ -'roʊt **~s** s
iguana ɪ 'gwɑːn ə ‚ɪg ju 'ɑːn ə **~s** z
iguanodon ɪ 'gwɑːn ə dɒn ‚ɪg ju 'ɑːn-, -əd ᵊn
‖ -dɑːn **~s** z
IKBS ‚aɪ keɪ biː 'es
Ike aɪk
IKEA *tdmk* aɪ 'kiː‿ə ɪ 'keɪ ə
ikebana ‚iːk eɪ 'bɑːn ə ‚ɪk-, -i- —*Jp*
[i 'ke ba na]

ikon 'aɪk ɒn -ən ‖ -ɑːn ~s z
il- ₍ᵢ₎ɪ, ˌɪl — **illiberal** ɪ 'lɪb ªr_əl ˌɪ-, ˌɪl-
Ilchester 'ɪl tʃɪst ə ‖ -ˌtʃest ªr
-ile aɪªl ‖ əl *(*) —This BrE-AmE difference is a general tendency; there are several exceptions.*
— **agile** 'ædʒ aɪªl ‖ 'ædʒ əl ◄
ILEA 'ɪl i_ə ˌaɪ el i 'eɪ ◄
ileac (= *iliac*) 'ɪl i æk
Ile de France ˌiːˑl də 'frɒs ‖ -'frɑːnᵗs —*Fr* Île-de-France [il də fʁɑ̃ːs]
ileostom|y ˌɪl i 'ɒst əm ‖i ‖ -'ɑːst- ~ies iz
Iles aɪªlz
ileum 'ɪl i_əm (= *ilium*)
ileus 'ɪl i_əs
ilex 'aɪl eks ~es ɪz əz
Ilford 'ɪl fəd ‖ -fªrd
Ilfracombe 'ɪlf rə kuːm
ilia 'ɪl i_ə
iliac 'ɪl i æk
Iliad 'ɪl i_əd -i æd
Iliffe 'aɪl ɪf
ili|um 'ɪl i_ləm ~a ə
Ilium '*Troy*' 'aɪl i_əm 'ɪl- ‖ 'ɪl-
ilk ɪlk
Ilkeston 'ɪlk ɪst ən -əst-
Ilkley 'ɪlk li
ill ɪl **ills** ɪlz **worse** wɜːs ‖ wɝːs **worst** wɜːst ‖ wɝːst
  ˌill at 'ease; ˌill 'feeling; ˌill 'will
I'll aɪªl
ill-ad|vised ˌɪl əd l'vaɪzd ◄ §-æd- ~visedly 'vaɪz ɪd li -əd-
ill-assorted ˌɪl ə 'sɔːt ɪd ◄ -əd ‖ -'sɔːrt̬ əd ◄
illative ɪ 'leɪt ɪv 'ɪl ət- ‖ 'ɪl ət̬ ɪv ɪ 'leɪt̬-
Illawarra ˌɪl ə 'wɒr ə ‖ -'wɔːr ə
ill-bred ˌɪl 'bred ◄
illegal ɪ 'liːg ªl ˌɪ-, ˌɪl- ~ly i
illegalit|y ˌɪl iː 'gæl ət li , •ɪ-, , •liː-, -ɪt i ‖ -ət̬ i ~ies iz
illegibility ɪ ˌledʒ ə 'bɪl ət i ˌɪ-, ˌɪl-, -ɪ'•-, -ɪt i ‖ -ət̬ i
illegib|le ɪ 'ledʒ əb |ªl ˌɪ-, ˌɪl-, -ɪb- ~ly li
illegitimac|y ˌɪl ə 'dʒɪt əm əs li , •ɪ-, -'•ɪm- ‖ -'dʒɪt̬ əm- ~ies iz
illegitimate ˌɪl ə 'dʒɪt əm ət ◄ , •ɪ-, -ɪm ət, -ɪt ‖ -'dʒɪt̬ əm- ~ly li
ill-equipped ˌɪl ɪ 'kwɪpt ◄ -ə-
ill-fated ˌɪl 'feɪt ɪd ◄ -əd ‖ -'feɪt̬ əd ◄
ill-favored, ill-favoured ˌɪl 'feɪv əd ◄ ‖ -ªrd ◄
ill-founded ˌɪl 'faʊnd ɪd ◄ -əd
ill-gotten ˌɪl 'gɒt ªn ◄ ‖ -'gɑːt ªn ◄
  ˌill-ˌgotten 'gains
illiberal ɪ 'lɪb ªr_əl ˌɪ-, ˌɪl- ~ly i
illicit ɪ 'lɪs ɪt ˌɪ-, ˌɪl-, §-ət ~ly li ~ness nəs nɪs
illimitab|le ɪ 'lɪm ɪt əb |ªl ˌɪ-, ˌɪl-, §-ət əb- ‖ -ət̬ əb- ~ly li
Illingworth 'ɪl ɪŋ wɜːθ -wəθ ‖ -wɝːθ
illinium ɪ 'lɪn i_əm
Illinois ˌɪl ə 'nɔɪ -ɪ-, -'nɔɪz
Illinoisan ˌɪl ə 'nɔɪ ən ◄ -ɪ-, -'nɔɪz ªn ~s z
illterac|y ɪ 'lɪt_ªr əs li ˌɪ-, ˌɪl- ‖ -'lɪt̬ ªr əs li →-'lɪtr əs i ~ies iz

illiterate ɪ 'lɪt_ªr ət ˌɪ-, ˌɪl-, -ɪt ‖ -'lɪt̬ ªr ət →-'lɪtr ət ~ly li ~ness nəs nɪs ~s s
ill-mannered ˌɪl 'mæn əd ◄ ‖ -ªrd ◄ ~ly li
ill-natured ˌɪl 'neɪtʃ əd ◄ ‖ -ªrd◄ ~ly li ~ness nəs nɪs
illness 'ɪl nəs -nɪs ~es ɪz əz
illocution ˌɪl ə 'kjuːʃ ªn ~s z
illocutionary ˌɪl ə 'kjuːʃ ªn ªr_i ◄ -ªn_ªr i ‖ -ə ner i
illogical ɪ 'lɒdʒ ɪk ªl ˌɪ-, ˌɪl- ‖ -'lɑːdʒ- ~ly _i ~ness nəs nɪs
illogicality ɪ ˌlɒdʒ ɪ 'kæl ət i ˌɪ, •ɪ'•-, ˌɪl-; -ə'•-, -ɪt i ‖ ɪ ˌlɑːdʒ ə 'kæl ət̬ i
ill-omened ˌɪl 'əʊm end ◄ -ənd ‖ -'oʊm-
ill-starred ˌɪl 'stɑːd ◄ ‖ -'stɑːrd ◄
ill-tempered ˌɪl 'temp əd ◄ ‖ -ªrd ◄ ~ly li
ill-timed ˌɪl 'taɪmd ◄
ill-|treat ₍ᵢ₎ɪl |'triːt ~treated 'triːt ɪd -əd ‖ 'triːt̬ əd ~treating 'triːt ɪŋ ‖ 'triːt̬ ɪŋ ~treatment 'triːt mənt ~treats 'triːts
Illtud 'ɪlt ɪd —*Welsh* ['ɪɬ tɪd]
illumin|ance ɪ 'luːm ɪn |ənᵗs -'ljuːm-, -ən- ~ant ənt
illumi|nate ɪ 'luːm ɪ |neɪt -'ljuːm-, -ə- ~nated neɪt ɪd -əd ‖ neɪt̬ əd ~nates neɪts ~nating neɪt ɪŋ ‖ neɪt̬ ɪŋ
Illuminati, i~ ɪ ˌluːm ɪ 'nɑːt iː -ə-
illumination ɪ ˌluːm ɪ 'neɪʃ ªn -ˌljuːm-, -ə- ~s z
ill-us|e *v* ˌɪl 'juːz ~ed d ~es ɪz əz ~ing ɪŋ
ill-use *n* ˌɪl 'juːs
illusion ɪ 'luːʒ ªn -'ljuːʒ- ~s z
illusionist ɪ 'luːʒ ªn ɪst -'ljuːʒ-, -ªn_, §-əst ~s s
illusive ɪ 'luːs ɪv -'ljuːs-, §-'luːz- ~ly li ~ness nəs nɪs
illusory ɪ 'luːs ªr_i -'ljuːs-, -'luːz-, -'ljuːz-

ILLUSTRATE

AmE 1993

0   20   40   60   80   100%

illu|strate 'ɪl ə |streɪt -ju- ‖ ɪ 'lʌs treɪt —*AmE 1993 poll panel preference:* '••• 92%, •'•• 8%. ~strated streɪt ɪd -əd ‖ streɪt̬ əd ~strates streɪts ~strating streɪt ɪŋ ‖ streɪt̬ ɪŋ
illustration ˌɪl ə 'streɪʃ ªn ~s z
illustrative 'ɪl ə strət ɪv -streɪt-; ɪ 'lʌs trət ɪv ‖ ɪ 'lʌstr ət̬ ɪv 'ɪl ə streɪt̬ ɪv ~ly li
illustrator 'ɪl ə streɪt ə ‖ -streɪt̬ ªr ~s z
illustrious ɪ 'lʌs tri_əs ~ly li ~ness nəs nɪs
Illyria ɪ 'lɪr i_ə -'lɪªr-
Illyrian ɪ 'lɪr i_ən -'lɪªr- ~s z
Illyricum ɪ 'lɪr ɪk əm -'lɪªr-
ilmenite 'ɪl mə naɪt -mɪ-
Ilminster 'ɪl mɪnst ə ‖ -ªr
Ilocano, Ilokano ˌiːl əʊ 'kɑːn əʊ ‖ -oʊ 'kɑːn oʊ ~s z
Ilona ɪ 'ləʊn ə ‖ -'loʊn ə
Ilson 'ɪls ən
Ilyushin ɪl 'juːʃ ɪn -ªn —*Russ* [ɪlʲ 'ju ʃɨn]
I'm aɪm —*In casual speech the phrase* I'm going to *before a verb is also* aɪŋ ən ə, aɪm ən ə

im- ɪm —*but before* m *usually* ɪ; *generally stressed only for emphasis or if the following syllable is unstressed:* im'possible, ˌimme'morial

image 'ɪm ɪdʒ **imaged** 'ɪm ɪdʒd **images** 'ɪm ɪdʒ ɪz -əz **imaging** 'ɪm ɪdʒ ɪŋ

imager 'ɪm ɪdʒ ə -ədʒ- ‖ -ᵊr ~s z

imager|y 'ɪm ɪdʒ ər‿li ~**ies** iz

imaginab|le ɪ 'mædʒ ɪn əb ᵊl -ən‿əb- ~**ly** li

imaginar|y ɪ 'mædʒ ɪn ər‿li -ən‿ər li ‖ -ə ner li ~**ies** iz ~**ily** əl i ɪ li ~**iness** i nəs i nɪs

imagination ɪ ˌmædʒ ɪ 'neɪʃ ᵊn -ə- ~s z

imaginative ɪ 'mædʒ ɪn ət ɪv -ən‿ət- ‖ -ən‿ət ɪv -ə neɪt ɪv ~**ly** li ~**ness** nəs nɪs

imagin|e ɪ 'mædʒ ɪn -ən ~**ed** d ~**es** z ~**ing** ɪŋ

imagines *from* **imagine** ɪ 'mædʒ ɪnz -ənz

imagines *n pl of* **imago** ɪ 'meɪdʒ ɪ niːz -'mædʒ-, -'maːg-, -ə-

imaging 'ɪm ɪdʒ ɪŋ

imago ɪ 'meɪg əʊ -'maːg- -oʊ ~**es** z

imam ɪ 'maːm 'iː maːm ~s z

imbalanc|e ₍ˌ₎ɪm 'bæl ᵊn⁵s ~**es** ɪz əz

imbecile 'ɪm bə siːᵊl -bɪ-, -saɪᵊl ‖ -bəs ᵊl -ɪl (*) ~s z

imbecilic ˌɪm bə 'sɪl ɪk ◄ -bɪ-

imbecilit|y ˌɪm bə 'sɪl ət li i ˌ•bɪ-, -ɪt i ‖ -əṭ li ~**ies** iz

imbed ɪm 'bed ~**ded** ɪd əd ~**ding** ɪŋ ~s z

Imbert 'ɪm bət ‖ -bᵊrt

imbib|e ɪm 'baɪb ~**ed** d ~**es** z ~**ing** ɪŋ

Imbrium 'ɪm bri‿əm

imbroglio ɪm 'brəʊl i‿əʊ ‖ -'broʊl joʊ ~s z

Imbros 'ɪm brɒs ‖ -braːs

imbru|e ɪm 'bruː ~**ed** d ~**es** z ~**ing** ɪŋ

imbu|e ɪm 'bjuː ~**ed** d ~**es** z ~**ing** ɪŋ

Imelda ɪ 'meld ə

IMF ˌaɪ em 'ef

Imhof 'ɪm həʊf ‖ -hoʊf

imide 'ɪm aɪd ~s z

imine 'ɪm iːn ɪ 'miːn ~s z

imi|tate 'ɪm ɪ ｜teɪt -ə- ~**tated** teɪt ɪd -əd ‖ teɪṭ əd ~**tates** teɪts ~**tating** teɪt ɪŋ ‖ teɪṭ ɪŋ

imitation ˌɪm ɪ 'teɪʃ ᵊn -ə- ~s z

imitative 'ɪm ɪt ət ɪv '•ət-; -ɪ teɪt-, -ə teɪt- ‖ -ə teɪṭ ɪv ~**ly** li ~**ness** nəs nɪs

imitator 'ɪm ɪ teɪt ə '•ə- ‖ -teɪṭ ᵊr ~s z

immaculate ɪ 'mæk jʊl ət ə-, -jəl-, -ɪt ‖ -jəl- ~**ly** li ~**ness** nəs nɪs

　　Im,maculate Con'ception

immanenc|e 'ɪm ən ən⁵s ~**y** i

immanent 'ɪm ən ənt ~**ly** li

Immanuel ɪ 'mæn ju‿əl ə-

immaterial ˌɪm ə 'tɪər i‿əl ◄ ‖ -'tɪr- ~**ly** i ~**ness** nəs nɪs

immature ˌɪm ə 'tjʊə ◄ -'tʃʊə, -'tjɔː, -'tʃɔː ‖ -'tʊᵊr ◄ -'tʃʊᵊr, -'tjʊᵊr ~**ly** li ~**ness** nəs nɪs

immaturity ˌɪm ə 'tjʊər ət i -'tʃʊər-, -'tjɔːr-, -'tʃɔːr-, -ɪt i ‖ -'tʊr əṭ i -'tʃʊr-, -'tjʊr-

immeasurab|le ɪ 'meʒ ər‿əb ᵊl ˌɪ-, ˌɪm- ~**ly** li

immediac|y ɪ 'miːd i‿əs li ə-, -'miːdʒ əs li ~**ies** iz

immediate ɪ 'miːd i‿ət ə-, -'miːdʒ ət, -ɪt ~**ly** li ~**ness** nəs nɪs

Immelmann 'ɪm ᵊl mæn -mən ‖ -mən -maːn —*Ger* ['ʔɪm ᵊl man]

immemorial ˌɪm ə 'mɔːr i‿əl ◄ , •ɪ- ‖ -'moʊr- ~**ly** i

immense ɪ 'men⁵s ə- ~**ly** li ~**ness** nəs nɪs

immensit|y ɪ 'men⁵s ət li ə-, -ɪt- ‖ -əṭ li ~**ies** iz

immers|e ɪ 'mɜːs ə- ‖ ɪ 'mɜ⁓s ~**ed** t ~**es** ɪz əz ~**ing** ɪŋ

immersion ɪ 'mɜːʃ ᵊn ə-, -'mɜːʒ- ‖ ɪ ɪ 'mɜ⁓ʒ ᵊn -'mɜ⁓ʃ- ~s z

　　im'mersion ,heater

immigrant 'ɪm ɪg rənt -əg- ~s s

immi|grate 'ɪm ɪ ｜greɪt -ə- ~**grated** greɪt ɪd -əd ‖ greɪṭ əd ~**grates** greɪts ~**grating** greɪt ɪŋ ‖ greɪṭ ɪŋ

immigration ˌɪm ɪ 'greɪʃ ᵊn -ə- ~s z

imminenc|e 'ɪm ɪn ən⁵s -ən- ~**y** i

imminent 'ɪm ɪn ənt -ən- ~**ly** li

Immingham 'ɪm ɪŋ əm §-həm

immiscib|le ɪ 'mɪs əb ᵊl -ɪb- ~**ly** li

immobile ɪ 'məʊb aɪᵊl ‖ ɪ 'moʊb ᵊl -iːl (*)

immobilis... —*see* **immobiliz...**

immobility ˌɪm əʊ 'bɪl ət i -ɪt i ‖ -oʊ 'bɪl əṭ i

immobilization ɪ ˌməʊb əl aɪ 'zeɪʃ ᵊn -, •ɪl-, -ɪ'•- ‖ ɪ ˌmoʊb əl ə- ~s z

immobiliz|e ɪ 'məʊb ə laɪz -ɪ-, -ᵊl aɪz ‖ ɪ 'moʊb- ~**ed** d ~**er/s** ə/z ‖ ᵊr/z ~**es** ɪz əz ~**ing** ɪŋ

immoderate ɪ 'mɒd ᵊr ət ˌɪ-, ˌɪm-, -ɪt ‖ ɪ 'maːd‿ ~**ly** li ~**ness** nəs nɪs

immodest ɪ 'mɒd ɪst ˌɪ-, ˌɪm-, -əst ‖ ɪ 'maːd- ~**ly** li

immodest|y ɪ 'mɒd əst i ˌɪ-, ˌɪm-, -ɪst- ‖ ɪ 'maːd-

immo|late 'ɪm əʊ ｜leɪt -ə- ~**lated** leɪt ɪd -əd ‖ leɪṭ əd ~**lates** leɪts ~**lating** leɪt ɪŋ ‖ leɪṭ ɪŋ

immolation ˌɪm əʊ 'leɪʃ ᵊn ‖ -ə- ~s z

immoral ɪ 'mɒr əl ə-, ˌɪ-, ˌɪm- ‖ ɪ 'mɔːr əl ɪ 'maːr- ~**ly** i

immoralit|y ˌɪm ə 'ræl ət li i ˌ•ɒ-, ˌ•ɔː-, -ɪt i ‖ -əṭ li ~**ies** iz

immortal ɪ 'mɔːt ᵊl ə-, ˌɪ-, ˌɪm- ‖ ɪ 'mɔːrṭ ᵊl ~**ly** i ~s z

immortalis... —*see* **immortaliz...**

immortality ˌɪm ɔː 'tæl ət i -ɪt i ‖ -ɔːr 'tæl əṭ i

immortaliz|e ɪ 'mɔːt ᵊl aɪz ‖ ɪ 'mɔːrṭ ᵊl aɪz ~**ed** d ~**es** ɪz əz ~**ing** ɪŋ

immortelle ˌɪm ɔː 'tel ‖ -ɔːr- ~s z

immovab|le ɪ 'muːv əb ᵊl ə-, ˌɪ-, ˌɪm- ~**ly** li

immune ɪ 'mjuːn ə-, ˌɪ-

　　im'mune re,sponse; im'mune ,system

immunis... —*see* **immuniz...**

immunit|y ɪ 'mjuːn ət i ə-, -ɪt- ‖ -əṭ li ~**ies** iz

immunization ˌɪm ju naɪ 'zeɪʃ ᵊn , •jə-, -ɪ'•- ‖ ˌɪm jən ə- ɪ ˌmjuːn ə- ~s z

immuniz|e 'ɪm ju naɪz -jə- ‖ -jə- ~**ed** d ~**es** ɪz əz ~**ing** ɪŋ

immuno- *comb. form*

　　with stress-neutral suffix ｜ɪm ju nəʊ ɪ ｜mjuːn əʊ ‖ ｜ɪm jə noʊ ɪ ｜mjuːn oʊ —
　　immunodeficiency ˌɪm ju nəʊ dɪ 'fɪʃ ᵊn⁵s i ɪ ˌmjuːn əʊ-, -də'•- ‖ ˌɪm jə noʊ-

immunological ˌɪm jʊn ə 'lɒdʒ ɪk ᵊl ◂ ɪ ˌmjuːn-
‖ ˌɪm jən ə 'lɑːdʒ- **~ly** ⁀i
immunologist ˌɪm ju 'nɒl ədʒ ɪst §-əst
‖ ˌɪm jə 'nɑːl- **~s** s
immunology ˌɪm ju 'nɒl ədʒ i ‖ ˌɪm jə 'nɑːl-
immunosuppression ˌɪm ju nəʊ sə 'preʃ ᵊn
ɪ ˌmjuːn- ‖ ˌɪm jə noʊ-
immunosuppressive ˌɪm ju nəʊ sə 'pres ɪv
ɪ ˌmjuːn- ‖ ˌɪm jə noʊ- **~s** z
immure ɪ 'mjʊə -'mjɔː ‖ ɪ 'mjʊᵊr **~d** d **~s** z
immuring ɪ 'mjʊər ɪŋ -'mjɔːr- ‖ ɪ 'mjʊr ɪŋ
immutability ɪ ˌmjuːt ə 'bɪl ət i ˌɪ,ˈ•-, ˌɪm,ˈ•-,
-ɪt i ‖ -ˌmjuːt̬ ə 'bɪl ət̬ i
immutab|le ɪ 'mjuːt əb ᵊl -ɪ-, ˌɪm- ‖ -'mjuːt̬-
~ly li
Imogen 'ɪm ədʒ ᵊn -ɪn, -ə dʒen ‖ -ə dʒen -ədʒ
ᵊn
Imogene 'ɪm ə dʒiːn
imp ɪmp **imps** ɪmps
impact n 'ɪm pækt **~s** s
impact v ɪm 'pækt '•• **~ed** ɪd əd **~ing** ɪŋ **~s**
s
impair ɪm 'peə ‖ -'peᵊr -'pæᵊr **~ed** d
impairing ɪm 'peər ɪŋ ‖ -'per ɪŋ -'pær ɪŋ **~s**
z
impairment ɪm 'peə mənt ‖ -'per- -'pær- **~s** s
impala ɪm 'pɑːl ə ‖ -'pæl ə —Zulu [i 'mpʼaː la]
~s z
impal|e ɪm 'peɪᵊl **~ed** d **~es** z **~ing** ɪŋ
impalement ɪm 'peɪᵊl mənt **~s** s
impalpab|le ɪm 'pælp əb ᵊl ˌɪm- **~ly** li
impanel ɪm 'pæn ᵊl **~ed**, **~led** d **~ing**, **~ling**
ɪŋ **~s** z
imparisyllabic ˌɪm ˌpær ɪ sɪ 'læb ɪk -ˌˈ•ə-,
-sə'•- ‖ -ˌper-
imparit|y ɪm 'pær ət i ˌɪm-, -ɪt- ‖ -ət̬ i -'per-
~ies iz
im|part ɪm ɪ'pɑːt ‖ -ɪ'pɑːrt **~parted** 'pɑːt ɪd
-əd ‖ 'pɑːrt̬ əd **~parting** 'pɑːt ɪŋ ‖ 'pɑːrt̬ ɪŋ
~parts 'pɑːts ‖ 'pɑːrts
impartial ɪm 'pɑːʃ ᵊl ˌɪm- ‖ -'pɑːrʃ ᵊl **~ly** i
impartiality ˌɪm ˌpɑːʃ i 'æl ət i •,ˈ••'•-, -ɪt i
‖ ɪm ˌpɑːrʃ i 'æl ət̬ i ˌ•,ˈ••'•-
impassab|le ɪm 'pɑːs əb ᵊl ˌɪm-, §-'pæs-
‖ -'pæs- **~leness** ᵊl nəs -nɪs **~ly** li
impasse æm 'pɑːs ɪm-, ɒm-, -'pæs, '••
‖ 'ɪm pæs •'• —Fr [æ̃ pas] **~es** ɪz əz
impassibility ɪm ˌpæs ə 'bɪl ət i -,ˈ•ɪ-, -ɪt i ‖ -ət̬ i
impassib|le ɪm 'pæs əb ᵊl ˌɪm-, -ɪb• **~ly** li
impassion ɪm 'pæʃ ᵊn **~ed** d **~ing** ɪŋ **~s** z
impassive ɪm 'pæs ɪv **~ly** li **~ness** nəs nɪs
impassivity ˌɪm pæ 'sɪv ət i -ɪt i ‖ -ət̬ i
impasto ɪm 'pæst əʊ -'pɑːst- ‖ -oʊ
impatience ɪm 'peɪʃ ᵊnts
impatiens ɪm 'peɪʃ i enz -'pæt- ‖ -'peɪʃ ᵊnz
-ᵊnts
impatient ɪm 'peɪʃ ᵊnt **~ly** li
impeach ɪm 'piːtʃ **~ed** t **~es** ɪz əz **~ing** ɪŋ
impeccab|le ɪm 'pek əb ᵊl **~ly** li
impecuniosity ˌɪm pɪ ˌkjuːn i 'ɒs ət i -ɪt i
‖ -'ɑːs ət̬ i
impecunious ˌɪm pɪ 'kjuːn i‿əs ◂, •ˈpə- **~ly** li
~ness nəs nɪs

impedance ɪm 'piːd ᵊnts **~es** ɪz əz
imped|e ɪm 'piːd **~ed** ɪd əd **~es** z **~ing** ɪŋ
impediment ɪm 'ped ɪ mənt -ə- **~s** s
impedimenta ɪm ˌped ɪ 'ment ə -ə- ‖ -'ment̬ ə
impel ɪm 'pel **~led** d **~ling** ɪŋ **~s** z
impeller ɪm 'pel ə ‖ -ᵊr **~s** z
impend ɪm 'pend **~ed** ɪd əd **~ing** ɪŋ **~s** z
impenetrability ɪm ˌpen ɪtr ə 'bɪl ət i
ˌ•,ˈ•••'•-, -ətr•'•-, -ɪt i ‖ -ət̬ i
impenetrab|le ɪm 'pen ɪtr əb ᵊl ˌɪm-, -'•ətr-
~ly li
impenitence ɪm 'pen ɪt ᵊnts ˌɪm-, -ət- ‖ -ᵊnts
impenitent ɪm 'pen ɪt ᵊnt ˌɪm-, -ət- ‖ -ᵊnt **~ly**
li **~s** s
imperatival ɪm ˌper ə 'taɪv ᵊl ◂ **~ly** i
imperative ɪm 'per ət ɪv ‖ -ət̬ ɪv **~ly** li **~ness**
nəs nɪs **~s** z
imperator ˌɪmp ə 'rɑːt ɔː -'reɪt- ‖ -ɔːr -'rɑːt̬ ᵊr
imperceptibility ˌɪm pə ˌsept ə 'bɪl ət i -,ˈ•ɪ-,
-ɪt i ‖ ˌɪm pᵊr ˌsept ə 'bɪl ət̬ i
imperceptib|le ˌɪm pə 'sept əb ᵊl -ɪb ᵊl
‖ ˌɪm pᵊr- **~ly** li
imperfect ɪm 'pɜːf ɪkt ˌɪm-, -əkt, -ekt ‖ -'pɝːf-
~ly li **~ness** nəs nɪs **~s** s
imperfection ˌɪm pə 'fek ʃᵊn ‖ ˌɪm pᵊr- **~s** z
imperfective ˌɪm pə 'fekt ɪv ‖ ˌɪm pᵊr- **~ly** li
~s z
imperforate ɪm 'pɜːf ᵊr ət ˌɪm-, ‿ɪt, -ə reɪt
‖ -'pɝːf- **~s** s
imperial ɪm 'pɪər i‿əl ‖ -'pɪr- **~s** z
imperialism ɪm 'pɪər i‿ə ˌlɪz əm ‖ -'pɪr- **~s** z
imperialist ɪm 'pɪər i‿əl ɪst §-əst ‖ -'pɪr- **~s** s
imperialistic ɪm ˌpɪər i‿əl 'ɪst ɪk ◂ ‖ -ˌpɪr- **~ally**
ᵊl‿i
imperially ɪm 'pɪər i‿əl i ‖ -'pɪr-
imperil ɪm 'per ᵊl -ɪl **~ed**, **~led** d **~ing**, **~ling**
ɪŋ **~s** z
imperious ɪm 'pɪər i‿əs ‖ -'pɪr- **~ly** li **~ness**
nəs nɪs
imperishab|le ɪm 'per ɪʃ əb ᵊl **~ly** li
imperium ɪm 'pɪər i‿əm ‖ -'pɪr-
impermanenc|e ɪm 'pɜːm ən ᵊnts ˌɪm-
‖ -'pɝːm- **~y** i
impermanent ɪm 'pɜːm ən ənt ˌɪm- ‖ -'pɝːm-
~ly li
impermeability ɪm ˌpɜːm i‿ə 'bɪl ət i ˌ•,ˈ•-
‖ -ˌpɝːm i‿ə 'bɪl ət̬ i
impermeab|le ɪm 'pɜːm i‿əb ᵊl ˌɪm- ‖ -'pɝːm-
~leness ᵊl nəs -nɪs **~ly** li
impermissibility ˌɪm pə ˌmɪs ə 'bɪl ət i -ɪ'•-,
-ɪt i ‖ -pᵊr ˌmɪs ə 'bɪl ət̬ i
impermissib|le ˌɪm pə 'mɪs əb ᵊl ◂ -ɪb ᵊl
‖ ˌɪm pᵊr- **~ly** li
impersonal ɪm 'pɜːs ᵊn‿ᵊl ˌɪm- ‖ -'pɝːs- **~ly** i
~s z
imperso|nate ɪm 'pɜːs ə ˌneɪt ‖ -'pɝːs-
~nated neɪt ɪd -əd ‖ neɪt̬ əd **~nates** neɪts
~nating neɪt ɪŋ ‖ neɪt̬ ɪŋ
impersonation ɪm ˌpɜːs ə 'neɪʃ ᵊn ‖ -ˌpɝːs- **~s**
z
impersonator
ɪm 'pɜːs ə neɪt ə ‖ -'pɝːs ə neɪt̬ ᵊr **~s** z

impertinenc|e ɪm 'pɜːt ɪn ənts -ən‿
‖ -'pɝːt ən_ənts **~es** ɪz əz **~y** i
impertinent ɪm 'pɜːt ɪn ənt -ən‿
‖ -'pɝːt ən_ənt **~ly** li
imperturbability ˌɪm pə ˌtɜːb ə 'bɪl ət i -ɪt i
‖ -pər ˌtɝːb ə 'bɪl ət̬ i
imperturbab|le
ˌɪm pə 'tɜːb əb |əl ◄ ‖ ˌɪm pər 'tɝːb- **~ly** li
impervious ɪm 'pɜːv i‿əs ˌɪm- ‖ -'pɝːv- **~ly** li
~ness nəs nɪs
impetigo ˌɪm pɪ 'taɪg əʊ -pə-, -pe- ‖ -oʊ
impetuosit|y ɪm ˌpet ju 'ɒs ət |i -ˌpetʃ u-
‖ -ˌpetʃ u 'ɑːs ət̬ |i **~ies** iz
impetuous ɪm 'petʃ u‿əs -'pet ju‿ **~ly** li
~ness nəs nɪs
impetus 'ɪmp ɪt əs -ət- ‖ -ət̬- **~es** ɪz əz
Impex 'ɪmp eks
impi 'ɪmp i —*Zulu* ['iː mp'i] **~s** z
impiet|y ɪm 'paɪ_ət |i ˌɪm-, -ɪt- ‖ -ət̬ |i **~ies** iz
imping|e ɪm 'pɪndʒ **~ed** d **~es** ɪz əz **~ing** ɪŋ
impious 'ɪmp i‿əs ₍ˌ₎ɪm 'paɪ_əs —*The*
traditional, irregular pronunciation 'ɪmp i‿əs
has recently been rapidly losing ground in
favour of ₍ˌ₎ɪm 'paɪ_əs **~ly** li **~ness** nəs nɪs
impish 'ɪmp ɪʃ **~ly** li **~ness** nəs nɪs
implacab|le ɪm 'plæk əb |əl **~leness** əl nəs -nɪs
~ly li
im|plant *v* ɪm ˈplɑːnt §-ˈplænt, ˈ•• ‖ -ˈplænt
~planted 'plɑːnt ɪd §ˈplænt-, -əd ‖ 'plænt̬ əd
~planting 'plɑːnt ɪŋ §ˈplænt- ‖ 'plænt̬ ɪŋ
~plants 'plɑːnts §ˈplænts ‖ 'plænts
implant *n* 'ɪm plɑːnt §-plænt ‖ -plænt **~s** s
implantation ˌɪm plɑːn 'teɪʃ ən -plæn-
‖ -plæn- **~s** z
implausibilit|y ɪm ˌplɔːz ə 'bɪl ət i ˌ•ˌ••ˈ•-,
-ɪt i ‖ -ət̬ i -ˌplɑːz-, ˌ•ˌ••ˈ•-
implausib|le ɪm 'plɔːz əb |əl ˌɪm-, -ɪb- ‖ -'plɑːz-
~ly li
implement *n* 'ɪmp lɪ mənt -lə- **~s** s
imple|ment *v* 'ɪmp lɪ |ment -lə-, -mənt,
§ˌ•ˈ•|ment —*See note at* -ment **~mented**
ment ɪd mənt-, -əd ‖ ment̬ əd **~menting**
ment ɪŋ mənt- ‖ ment̬ ɪŋ **~ments** ments
mənts
implementation ˌɪmp lɪ men 'teɪʃ ən ˌ•ˈlə-,
-mən'•- **~s** z
impli|cate 'ɪmp lɪ |keɪt -lə- **~cated** keɪt ɪd -əd
‖ keɪt̬ əd **~cates** keɪts **~cating**
keɪt ɪŋ ‖ keɪt̬ ɪŋ
implication ˌɪmp lɪ 'keɪʃ ən -lə- **~s** z
implicative ɪm 'plɪk ət ɪv 'ɪmp lɪ keɪt-, ˈ•lə-
‖ 'ɪmp lə keɪt̬ ɪv ɪm 'plɪk ət̬- **~ly** li
implicature ɪm 'plɪk ətʃ ə -ə tjʊə ‖ -ər **~s** z
implicit ɪm 'plɪs ɪt §-ət **~ly** li **~ness** nəs nɪs
implie... —*see* **imply**
implod|e ɪm 'pləʊd ‖ -'ploʊd **~ed** ɪd əd **~es** z
~ing ɪŋ
implore ɪm 'plɔː ‖ -'plɔːr -'plour **~d** d **~s** z
imploring/ly ɪm 'plɔːr ɪŋ /li ‖ -'plour-
implosion ɪm 'pləʊʒ ən ‖ -'ploʊʒ- **~s** z
implosive ɪm 'pləʊs ɪv ˌɪm-, -'pləʊz- ‖ -'ploʊs-
-'plouz- **~ly** li **~s** z

im|ply ɪm |'plaɪ **~plied** 'plaɪd **~plies** 'plaɪz
~plying 'plaɪ ɪŋ
impolite ˌɪm pə 'laɪt ◄ **~ly** li **~ness** nəs nɪs
impolitic ɪm 'pɒl ə tɪk ˌɪm-, -ɪ- ‖ -'pɑːl- **~ly** li
~ness nəs nɪs
imponderab|le ɪm 'pɒnd_ər əb |əl ˌɪm-
‖ -'pɑːnd_ **~leness** əl nəs -nɪs **~les** əlz **~ly** li
im|port *v* ɪm |'pɔːt, ˌ•-, ˈ•• ‖ -|'pɔːrt -'pourt
~ported 'pɔːt ɪd -əd ‖ 'pɔːrt̬ əd 'pourt̬-
~porting 'pɔːt ɪŋ ‖ 'pɔːrt̬ ɪŋ -'pourt̬- **~ports**
'pɔːts ‖ 'pɔːrts 'pourts
import *n* 'ɪm pɔːt ‖ -pɔːrt -pourt **~s** s
importance ɪm 'pɔːt ənts ‖ -'pɔːrt-
important ɪm 'pɔːt ənt ‖ -'pɔːrt- **~ly** li
importation ˌɪm pɔː 'teɪʃ ən ‖ -pɔːr- -pour- **~s**
z
importer ɪm 'pɔːt ə ˌ•-, ˈ••• ‖ -'pɔːrt̬ ər
-'pourt̬- **~s** z
import-export
ˌɪm pɔːt 'eks pɔːt ‖ -'pɔːrt̬ 'eks pɔːrt
-pourt̬ 'eks pourt
importunate ɪm 'pɔːt jun ət -'pɔːtʃ ən‿, -ɪt
‖ -'pɔːrtʃ ən_ət **~ly** li **~ness** nəs nɪs
importun|e ˌɪmp ə 'tjuːn ˌɪm pɔː-, →§-'tʃuːn;
ɪm 'pɔːt juːn, -'pɔːtʃ uːn ‖ ˌɪmp ər 'tuːn
-'tjuːn; ɪm 'pɔːrtʃ ən **~ed** d **~es** z **~ing** ɪŋ
importunit|y ˌɪmp ə 'tjuːn ət |i ˌɪm pɔː-,
→§-'tʃuːn-, -ɪt i ‖ ˌɪmp ər 'tuːn ət̬ |i ˌɪm pɔːr-,
-'tjuːn- **~ies** iz
impos|e ɪm 'pəʊz ‖ -'poʊz **~ed** d **~es** ɪz əz
~ing ɪŋ
imposing ɪm 'pəʊz ɪŋ ‖ -'poʊz ɪŋ **~ly** li **~ness**
nəs nɪs
imposition ˌɪm pə 'zɪʃ ən **~s** z
impossibilit|y ɪm ˌpɒs ə 'bɪl ət i ˌ•ˌ••ˈ•-, -ɪt i
‖ -ˌpɑːs ə 'bɪl ət̬ i **~ies** iz
impossible ɪm 'pɒs əb əl ˌɪm-, -ɪb- ‖ -'pɑːs-
impossibly ɪm 'pɒs əb li -ɪb- ‖ -'pɑːs-
impost 'ɪm pəʊst -pɒst ‖ -poʊst **~s** s
imposter, impostor ɪm 'pɒst ə ‖ -'pɑːst ər **~s**
z
imposture ɪm 'pɒs tʃə ‖ -'pɑːs tʃər **~s** z
impotenc|e 'ɪmp ət ənts ‖ -ənts **~y** i
impotent 'ɪmp ət ənt ‖ -ənt **~ly** li
impound ɪm 'paʊnd **~ed** ɪd əd **~ing** ɪŋ **~s** z
impoverish ɪm 'pɒv ər_ɪʃ ‖ -'pɑːv- **~ed** t **~es**
ɪz əz **~ing** ɪŋ
impoverishment ɪm 'pɒv ər_ɪʃ mənt ‖ -'pɑːv-
~s s
impracticability ɪm ˌprækt ɪk ə 'bɪl ət i
ˌɪm,•••ˈ•-, -ɪt i ‖ -ət̬ i
impracticab|le ɪm 'prækt ɪk əb |əl ˌɪm-
~leness əl nəs -nɪs **~ly** li
impractical ɪm 'prækt ɪk əl ˌɪm- **~ness** nəs nɪs
impracticality ɪm ˌprækt ɪ 'kæl ət i ˌɪm,••ˈ•-,
-ɪt i ‖ -ət̬ i
imprecation ˌɪmp rɪ 'keɪʃ ən -rə-, ˌɪm pre- **~s** z
imprecatory 'ɪmp rɪ keɪt ər i ˈ•rə-, ˌ••ˈ•-;
ɪm 'prek ət_ər i ‖ 'ɪmp rɪk ə tɔːr i ɪm 'prek-,
-tour i
imprecise ˌɪmp rɪ 'saɪs ◄ -prə- **~ly** li
imprecision ˌɪm prɪ 'sɪʒ ən -prə-

impregnability ɪm ˌpreg nə 'bɪl ət i ˌɪm, •'•-,
-ɪt i ‖ -ət̬ i
impregnab|le ɪm 'preg nəb |əl ˌɪm- ~**ly** li
impreg|nate v 'ɪm preg |neɪt •'••
 ‖ ɪm 'preg |neɪt '••• ~**nated** neɪt ɪd -əd
 ‖ neɪt̬ əd ~**nates** neɪts ~**nating**
neɪt ɪŋ ‖ neɪt̬ ɪŋ
impregnation ˌɪm preg 'neɪʃ ən ‖ •,•'•• ~**s** z
impresario ˌɪmp rə 'sɑːr i əʊ ˌ•rɪ-, ˌɪm pre-
 ‖ -oʊ -'ser-, -'sær- ~**s** z
impress v ɪm 'pres ~**ed** t ~**es** ɪz əz ~**ing** ɪŋ
impress n 'ɪm pres ~**es** ɪz əz
impression ɪm 'preʃ ən ~**s** z
impressionability ɪm ˌpreʃ ən ə 'bɪl ət i -ɪt i
 ‖ -ət̬ i
impressionable ɪm 'preʃ ən əb əl ~**ness** nəs
nɪs
impressionism ɪm 'preʃ ən ˌɪz əm -ə ˌnɪz-
impressionist ɪm 'preʃ ən ɪst §ˌəst ~**s** s
impressionistic ɪm ˌpreʃ ə 'nɪst ɪk ◂ ~**ally** əl i
impressive ɪm 'pres ɪv ~**ly** li ~**ness** nəs nɪs
imprest 'ɪm prest •'• ~**s** s
imprimatur ˌɪm prɪ 'mɑːt ə -prə-, -praɪ-,
-'meɪt- ‖ -ur -ər ~**s** z
im|print v ɪm |'prɪnt '•• ~**printed** 'prɪnt ɪd
-əd ‖ 'prɪnt̬ əd ~**printing** 'prɪnt ɪŋ ‖ 'prɪnt̬ ɪŋ
~**prints** 'prɪnts
imprint n 'ɪm prɪnt ~**s** s
imprison ɪm 'prɪz ən ~**ed** d ~**ing** ɪŋ ~**s** z
imprisonment ɪm 'prɪz ən mənt →-'•əm-
improbabilit|y ɪm ˌprɒb ə 'bɪl ət i ˌ•,•'••-,
-ɪt i ˌ-ˌprɑːb ə 'bɪl ət̬ i ~**ies** iz
improbab|le ɪm 'prɒb əb |əl ˌɪm- ‖ -'prɑːb-
~**leness** əl nəs -nɪs ~**ly** li
impromptu ɪm 'prɒmpt juː -'prɒmpt ʃuː
 ‖ -'prɑːmpt uː -juː ~**s** z
improper ɪm 'prɒp ə ˌɪm- ‖ -'prɑːp ər ~**ly** li
~**ness** nəs nɪs
im,proper 'fraction, ˌim,proper 'fraction
impropriet|y ˌɪm prə 'praɪ‿ət i ⚠, •pə-, -ɪt i
 ‖ -ət̬ i ~**ies** iz
improvability ɪm ˌpruːv ə 'bɪl ət i -ɪt i ‖ -ət̬ i
improvable ɪm 'pruːv əb əl
improv|e ɪm 'pruːv ˌɪm- ~**ed** d ~**es** z ~**ing** ɪŋ
improvement ɪm 'pruːv mənt ~**s** s
improver ɪm 'pruːv ə ‖ -ər ~**s** z
improvidence ɪm 'prɒv ɪd ənts ˌɪm-, -əd-
 ‖ -'prɑːv- -ə dents
improvident ɪm 'prɒv ɪd ənt ˌɪm-, -əd-
 ‖ -'prɑːv- -ə dent ~**ly** li
improvisation ˌɪm prə vaɪ 'zeɪʃ ən -prə vɪ-,
-prɒv ɪ- ‖ ɪm ˌprɑːv ə- ˌ•••-, ˌɪm prəv- ~**al**
əl ~**s** z
improvisatory ˌɪm prə 'vaɪz ət‿ər i ◂ -'vɪz-;
-vaɪ 'zeɪt ər i ‖ -ə tɔːr i -tour i
improvis|e 'ɪm prə vaɪz ‖ •'•'• ~**ed** d ~**es** ɪz
əz ~**ing** ɪŋ
imprudence ɪm 'pruːd ənts ˌɪm-
imprudent ɪm 'pruːd ənt ˌɪm- ~**ly** li
impudenc|e 'ɪmp jud ənts ‖ -jəd- ~**y** i
impudent 'ɪmp jud ənt ‖ -jəd- ~**ly** li
impugn ɪm 'pjuːn ~**ed** d ~**ing** ɪŋ ~**s** z

impuls|e 'ɪm pʌls ~**es** ɪz əz
'impulse ˌbuying
impulsion ɪm 'pʌl ʃən ~**s** z
impulsive ɪm 'pʌls ɪv ~**ly** li ~**ness** nəs nɪs
impunit|y ɪm 'pjuːn ət i -ɪt- ‖ -ət̬ i ~**ies** iz
impure ˌɪm 'pjʊə ◂ ɪm-, -'pjɔː: ‖ -'pjʊər ◂ ~**ly** li
~**ness** nəs nɪs
impurit|y ɪm 'pjʊər ət i ˌɪm-, -ɪt- ‖ -'pjʊr ət̬ i
~**ies** iz
imputation ˌɪm pju 'teɪʃ ən ‖ -pjə- -pju- ~**s** z
imputable ɪm 'pjuːt əb əl ‖ -'pjuːt̬-
imputation ˌɪm pju 'teɪʃ ən ‖ -pjə- ~**s** z
im|pute ɪm |'pjuːt ~**puted** 'pjuːt ɪd -əd
 ‖ 'pjuːt̬ əd ~**putes** 'pjuːts ~**puting**
'pjuːt ɪŋ ‖ 'pjuːt̬ ɪŋ
Imran 'ɪm ræn -rɑːn ‖ -rɑːn
in ɪn *There is no separate weak form in RP. In
some other accents, including GenAm, there is a
weak form* §ən
in- ɪn —*but before* n *usually* ɪ; *before* k *or* g
assimilates to ɪŋ; *generally stressed only* (i) *if
meaning 'in' rather than 'not'*; *or* (ii) *for
emphasis*; *or* (iii) *if the following syllable is
unstressed:* in'credible, ˌin'side, ˌinat'tentive
-in ɪn —*but in scientific senses also* §ən —
tannin 'tæn ɪn §-ən ‖ -ən — **teach-in**
'tiːtʃ ɪn
-in' *nonstandard form of* **-ing** ɪŋ ən —*but after* t
or d *usually* ən — **likin'** 'laɪk ɪn -ən — **eatin'**
'iːt ən -ɪn
Ina 'iːn ə 'aɪn ə
inability ˌɪn ə 'bɪl ət i -ɪt i ‖ -ət̬ i
in absentia ˌɪn əb 'sent i‿ə -'sentʃ-, -i ɑː
 ‖ -'sentʃ ə
inaccessibility ˌɪn ək ˌses ə 'bɪl ət i, •æk-,
ˌ•ɪk-, -, •ɪ-, -ɪt i ‖ -ət̬ i
inaccessib|le ˌɪn ək 'ses əb |əl ◂ , •æk-, ˌ•ɪk-,
-ɪb əl ~**ly** li
inaccurac|y ɪn 'æk jər əs |i ˌɪn-, -' • jʊr-, -ɪs i
~**ies** iz
inaccurate ɪn 'æk jər ət ˌɪn-, -jʊr-, -ɪt ~**ly** li
~**ness** nəs nɪs
inaction ɪn 'æk ʃən ˌɪn-
inacti|vate ɪn 'ækt ɪ |veɪt -ə- ~**vated** veɪt ɪd
-əd ‖ veɪt̬ əd ~**vates** veɪts ~**vating**
veɪt ɪŋ ‖ veɪt̬ ɪŋ
inactivation ɪn ˌækt ɪ 'veɪʃ ən ˌ•,••'••-, -ə'••-
~**s** z
inactive ɪn 'ækt ɪv ˌɪn- ~**ly** li ~**ness** nəs nɪs
inactivity ˌɪn æk 'tɪv ət i -ɪt i ‖ -ət̬ i
inadequac|y ɪn 'æd ɪk wəs |i ˌɪn-, -'•ək- ~**ies**
iz
inadequate ɪn 'æd ɪk wət ˌɪn-, -ək-, -wɪt ~**ly** li
inadmissibility ˌɪn əd ˌmɪs ə 'bɪl ət i, •æd-,
-,•ɪ-, -ɪt i ‖ -ət̬ i
inadmissib|le ˌɪn əd 'mɪs əb |əl ◂ , •æd-, -ɪb əl
~**ly** li
inadvertenc|e ˌɪn əd 'vɜːt ənts §-æd- ‖ -'vɜːt̬-
~**es** ɪz əz ~**ies** iz ~**y** i
inadvertent ˌɪn əd 'vɜːt ənt ◂ §-æd- ‖ -'vɜːt̬-
~**ly** li
inadvisability ˌɪn əd ˌvaɪz ə 'bɪl ət i §, •æd-,
-ɪt i ‖ -ət̬ i

inadvisable ˌɪn əd 'vaɪz əb ᵊl ◄ §, • æd-
inalienability ɪn ˌeɪl i‿ən ə 'bɪl ət i ˌɪn, • • • • ' • -,
-ɪt i ‖ -əţ i
inalienab|le ɪn 'eɪl i‿ən əb ᵊl ˌɪn- ~ly li
inamorata ɪn ˌæm ə 'rɑːt ə , • • • ' • - ‖ -'rɑːţ ə
~s z
inamorato ɪn ˌæm ə 'rɑːt əʊ , • • • ' • -
‖ -'rɑːt oʊ ~s z
inane ɪ 'neɪn ~ly li
inanimate ɪn 'æn ɪm ət -əm- ~ly li ~ness nəs
nɪs
inanition ˌɪn ə 'nɪʃ ᵊn
inanit|y ɪ 'næn ət i -ɪt- ‖ -əţ li ~ies iz
inapplicability ˌɪn ə ˌplɪk ə 'bɪl ət i -ɪt i;
ˌ • ˌæp lɪk-, • , • - ‖ ɪn ˌæp lɪk ə 'bɪl əţ i , • , • -
inapplicab|le ɪn ə 'plɪk əb ᵊl ᵊl ₍ᵢ₎ɪn 'æp lɪk-
‖ ɪn 'æp lɪk- ˌɪn- ~ly li
inappropriate ˌɪn ə 'prəʊp ri‿ət ‿ɪt ‖ -'proʊpr-
~ly li ~ness nəs nɪs
inapt ɪn 'æpt ˌɪn-
inaptitude ɪn 'æpt ɪ tjuːd ˌɪn-, -ə-, →§-tʃuːd
‖ -ə tuːd -tjuːd
inarticulac|y ˌɪn ɑː 'tɪk jʊl əs li -' • jəl-
‖ -ɑːr 'tɪk jəl- ~ies iz
inarticulate ˌɪn ɑː 'tɪk jʊl ət ◄ -jəl ət, -ɪt
‖ -ɑːr 'tɪk jəl- ~ly li ~ness nəs nɪs
inartistic ˌɪn ɑː 'tɪst ɪk ◄ ‖ -ɑːr- ~ally ᵊl‿i
inasmuch ˌɪn əz 'mʌtʃ
inattention ˌɪn ə 'tentʃ ᵊn ~s z
inattentive ˌɪn ə 'tent ɪv ◄ ‖ -'tenţ ɪv ◄ ~ly li
~ness nəs nɪs
inaudibility ɪn ˌɔːd ə 'bɪl ət i ˌɪn, • • ' • -, -ɪ ' • -,
-ɪt i ‖ -əţ i -ˌɑːd-
inaudib|le ɪn 'ɔːd əb ᵊl ˌɪn-, -ɪb- ‖ -'ɑːd- ~ly li
inaugural ɪ 'nɔːg jʊr ᵊl -jər-, -ᵊr‿ᵊl ‖ -jər ᵊl
ɪ 'nɑːg-, -ᵊr‿ᵊl ~s z
inaugu|rate ɪ 'nɔːg jə |reɪt -juə-, -ə- ‖ ɪ 'nɑːg-
~rated reɪt ɪd -əd ‖ reɪţ əd ~rates reɪts
~rating reɪt ɪŋ ‖ reɪţ ɪŋ
inauguration ɪ ˌnɔːg jə 'reɪʃ ᵊn ˌɪn ɔːg-, -juə-,
-ə- ‖ ɪ ˌnɑːg- ~s z
inauspicious ˌɪn ɔː 'spɪʃ əs ◄ -ɒ- ‖ -ɑː- ~ly li
~ness nəs nɪs
in-between ˌɪn bɪ 'twiːn ◄ →ˌɪm-, -bə-, §-biː-
~s z
inboard 'ɪn bɔːd →'ɪm- ‖ -bɔːrd -boʊrd
inborn ˌɪn 'bɔːn ◄ →ˌɪm- ‖ -'bɔːrn ◄
ˌinborn a'bility
inbound 'ɪn baʊnd →'ɪm-
inbred ˌɪn 'bred ◄ →ˌɪm-
ˌinbred 'courtesy
inbreeding 'ɪn ˌbriːd ɪŋ →'ɪm-
in-built ˌɪn 'bɪlt ◄ →ˌɪm-, ' • •
Inc ɪŋk —see also Incorporated
Inca 'ɪŋk ə ~s z
incalculab|le ɪn 'kælk jʊl əb ᵊl ˌɪn-, →₍ᵢ₎ɪŋ-,
-' • jəl ‖ -'kælk jəl- ~ly li
incandesc|e ˌɪn kæn 'des →ˌɪŋ-, -kən- ‖ -kən-
~ed t ~es ɪz əz ~ing ɪŋ
incandesc|ence ˌɪn kæn 'des |ᵊnts →ˌɪŋ-, -kən-
‖ -kən- ~ent/ly ᵊnt /li
incantation ˌɪn kæn 'teɪʃ ᵊn →ˌɪŋ- ~s z

incantatory ˌɪn kæn 'teɪt ər i →ˌɪŋ-;
ɪn 'kænt ət‿ər i ‖ ɪn 'kænţ ə tɔːr i -toʊri
incapability ɪn ˌkeɪp ə 'bɪl ət i →ɪŋ-, ˌ • , • • ' • -,
-ɪt i ‖ -əţ i
incapab|le ɪn 'keɪp əb ᵊl →ɪŋ-, ˌ • - ~leness
ᵊl nəs -nɪs ~ly li
incapaci|tate ˌɪn kə 'pæs ɪ |teɪt →ˌɪŋ-, -' • ə-
~tated teɪt ɪd -əd ‖ teɪţ əd ~tates teɪts
~tating teɪt ɪŋ ‖ teɪţ ɪŋ
incapacitation ˌɪn kə ˌpæs ɪ 'teɪʃ ᵊn →ˌɪŋ-,
-ə ' • -
incapacit|y ˌɪn kə 'pæs ət li →ˌɪŋ-, -ɪt i ‖ -əţ li
~ies iz
incapsul... —see encapsul...
in-car ˌɪn 'kɑː ◄ →ˌɪŋ- ‖ -'kɑːr ◄
incarce|rate ɪn 'kɑːs ə |reɪt →ɪŋ- ‖ -'kɑːrs-
~rated reɪt ɪd -əd ‖ reɪţ əd ~rates reɪts
~rating reɪt ɪŋ ‖ reɪţ ɪŋ
incarceration ɪn ˌkɑːs ə 'reɪʃ ᵊn →ɪŋ-,
ˌɪn, • • ' • -, ‖ -ˌkɑːrs- ~s z
incarnadin|e ɪn 'kɑːn ə daɪn →ɪŋ-, -diːn
‖ -'kɑːrn- ~ed d ~es z ~ing ɪŋ
incarnate adj ɪn 'kɑːn ət →ɪŋ-, -ɪt, -eɪt
‖ -'kɑːrn-
incarn|ate v ˌɪn kɑːn |eɪt →'ɪŋ-, • ' • • ‖ -kɑːrn-
~ated eɪt ɪd -əd ‖ eɪţ əd ~ates eɪts ~ating
eɪt ɪŋ ‖ eɪţ ɪŋ
incarnation ˌɪn kɑː 'neɪʃ ᵊn →ˌɪŋ- ‖ -kɑːr- ~s
z
incautious ɪn 'kɔːʃ əs ˌɪn-, →₍ᵢ₎ɪŋ- ‖ -'kɑːʃ- ~ly
li ~ness nəs nɪs
Ince ɪnts
incendiarism ɪn 'send i‿ə ˌrɪz əm
§-'sendʒ ə ˌrɪz əm
incendiar|y ɪn 'send i‿ər li §-'sendʒ ər i
‖ -'send i er li ~ies iz
incense n 'ɪn sents
incens|e v 'enrage' ɪn 'sents ~ed t ~es ɪz əz
~ing ɪŋ
incentive ɪn 'sent ɪv ‖ -'senţ ɪv ~s z
inception ɪn 'sep ʃᵊn ~s z
inceptive ɪn 'sept ɪv ~s z
incertitude ɪn 'sɜːt ɪ tjuːd ˌɪn-, -ə-, →§-tʃuːd
‖ -'sɜːţ ə tuːd -tjuːd ~s z
incessant ɪn 'ses ᵊnt ~ly li ~ness nəs nɪs
incest 'ɪn sest
incestuous ɪn 'sest ju‿əs ‖ -'ses tʃu- ~ly li
~ness nəs nɪs
inch ɪntʃ inched ɪntʃt inches 'ɪntʃ ɪz -əz
inching 'ɪntʃ ɪŋ
Inchcape 'ɪntʃ keɪp ₍ᵢ₎• ' •
inchoate adj ɪn 'kəʊ ət →ɪŋ-, -ɪt, -eɪt; 'ɪŋ kəʊ-
‖ -'koʊ- ~ly li
inchoative ɪn 'kəʊ ət ɪv →ɪŋ- ‖ -'koʊ əţ- ~s z
Inchon ˌɪn 'tʃɒn ◄ ‖ -'tʃɑːn ' • • —Korean
Inchŏn [in tʃʰɔn]
inchworm 'ɪntʃ wɜːm ‖ -wɜːrm ~s z
incidenc|e 'ɪnts ɪd ᵊnts -əd- ‖ -ə dents ~es ɪz
əz
incident 'ɪnts ɪd ᵊnt -əd- ‖ -ə dent ~s s
incidental ˌɪnts ɪ 'dent ᵊl ◄ -ə- ‖ -'denţ ᵊl ◄ ~ly
‿i ~s z
ˌinciˌdental 'comments

incidential ˌɪntˢ ɪ 'denᵗʃ ᵊl ◄ -ə-
incine|rate ɪn 'sɪn ə |reɪt ~rated reɪt ɪd -əd
‖ reɪt̬ əd ~rates reɪts ~rating
reɪt ɪŋ ‖ reɪt̬ ɪŋ
incineration ɪn ˌsɪn ə 'reɪʃ ᵊn ~s z
incinerator ɪn 'sɪn ə reɪt ə ‖ -reɪt̬ ᵊr ~s z
incipienc|e ɪn 'sɪp i_ənts ~y i
incipient ɪn 'sɪp i_ənt ~ly li
incis|e ɪn 'saɪz ~ed d ~es ɪz əz ~ing ɪŋ
incision ɪn 'sɪʒ ᵊn ~s z
incisive ɪn 'saɪs ɪv §-'saɪz- ~ly li ~ness nəs nɪs
incisor ɪn 'saɪz ə ‖ -ᵊr ~s z
in|cite ɪn 'saɪt ~cited 'saɪt ɪd -əd ‖ 'saɪt̬ əd
~cites 'saɪts ~citing 'saɪt ɪŋ ‖ 'saɪt̬ ɪŋ
incitement ɪn 'saɪt mənt ~s s
incivilit|y ˌɪn sə 'vɪl ət li ‚•sɪ-, -ɪt i ‖ -ət̬ li ~ies
iz
inclemency ɪn 'klem ənts i ‚ɪn-, →₍₁₎ɪŋ-
inclement ɪn 'klem ənt ‚ɪn-, →₍₁₎ɪŋ-,
⚠'ɪŋk ᵊl mənt ~ly li
inclination ˌɪn klɪ 'neɪʃ ᵊn →ˌɪŋ-, -klə- ~s z
inclin|e v ɪn 'klaɪn →ɪŋ- ~ed d ~es z ~ing ɪŋ
incline n ɪn klaɪn →'ɪŋ- ~s z
inclinometer ˌɪn klɪ 'nɒm ɪt ə →ˌɪŋ-, ‚•klə-
‖ -'nɑːm ət̬ ᵊr ~s z
inclos|e ɪn 'kləʊz →ɪŋ- ‖ -'kloʊz ~ed d ~es ɪz
əz ~ing ɪŋ
inclosure ɪn 'kləʊʒ ə →ɪŋ- ‖ -'kloʊʒ ᵊr ~s z
includ|e ɪn 'kluːd →ɪŋ- ~ed ɪd əd ~es z ~ing
ɪŋ
inclusion ɪn 'kluːʒ ᵊn →ɪŋ- ~s z
inclusive ɪn 'kluːs ɪv →ɪŋ-, §-'kluːz- ~ly li
~ness nəs nɪs
incognito ˌɪn kɒg 'niːt əʊ ◄ →ˌɪŋ-;
ɪn 'kɒg nɪ təʊ, →ɪŋ-, -nə- ‖ ˌɪn kɑːg 'niːt oʊ
ɪn 'kɑːg nə toʊ
incogniz|ance ɪn 'kɒg nɪz ᵊnts §-'•nəz-
‖ -'kɑːg- ~ant ənt
incoherenc|e ˌɪn kəʊ 'hɪər ᵊnts →ˌɪŋ-
‖ -koʊ 'hɪr- -'her- ~y i
incoherent ˌɪn kəʊ 'hɪər ənt ◄ →ˌɪŋ-
‖ -koʊ 'hɪr- -'her- ~ly li ~ness nəs nɪs
incombustib|le ˌɪn kəm 'bʌst əb ᵊl ◄ →ˌɪŋ-,
§‚•kɒm-, -ɪb ᵊl ~ly li
income 'ɪn kʌm →'ɪŋ-, -kəm ~s z
'income tax
incomer 'ɪn ˌkʌm ə ‖ -ᵊr ~s z
incoming 'ɪn ˌkʌm ɪŋ →'ɪŋ-
incommensurab|le ˌɪn kə 'menᵗʃ ᵊr_əb ᵊl ◄
→ˌɪŋ-, -'menᵗs-, -'•jər- ~ly li
incommensurate ˌɪn kə 'menᵗʃ ᵊr_ət ◄ →ˌɪŋ-,
-'menᵗs-, -'•jər-, ‚ɪt ~ly li ~ness nəs nɪs
incommod|e ˌɪn kə 'məʊd →ˌɪŋ- ‖ -'moʊd
~ed ɪd əd ~es z ~ing ɪŋ
incommodious ˌɪn kə 'məʊd i_əs ◄ →ˌɪŋ-
‖ -'moʊd- ~ly li ~ness nəs nɪs
incommunicab|le ˌɪn kə 'mjuːn ɪk əb ᵊl ◄
→ˌɪŋ- ~ly li
incommunicado ˌɪn kə ˌmjuːn ɪ 'kɑːd əʊ
→ˌɪŋ-, -‚•ə- ‖ -oʊ
incommunicative ˌɪn kə 'mjuːn ɪ kət ɪv ◄
-'•ə-, -keɪt ɪv ‖ -ə keɪt̬ ɪv -ɪk ət̬- ~ly li ~ness
nəs nɪs

incomparability ɪn ˌkɒmp ər_ə 'bɪl ət i →ɪŋ-,
‚•‚•‚•-, -ɪt i; ˌɪn kəm ˌpær ə-, →‚ɪŋ-, §-‚peər-
‖ ɪn ˌkɑːmp ər_ə 'bɪl ət̬ i ‚•‚•‚•-; ˌɪn kəm ˌpær-,
-‚per-

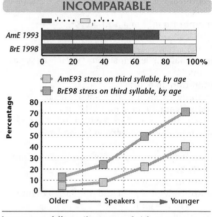

INCOMPARABLE

AmE 1993
BrE 1998

0   20   40   60   80   100%

🔲 AmE93 stress on third syllable, by age
🔲 BrE98 stress on third syllable, by age

Percentage
80
70
60
50
40
30
20
10
0

Older ◄— Speakers —► Younger

incomparab|le ɪn 'kɒmp ər_əb ᵊl →ɪŋ-, ‚•-;
ˌɪn kəm 'pær-, →‚ɪŋ-, §-kɒm-, §-'peər-
‖ ɪn 'kɑːmp ər_əb ᵊl ‚ɪn-; ˌɪn kəm 'per-,
-'pær- —Poll panel preferences: AmE 1993,
‚•'•‚•‚• 76%, ‚•‚•'•‚• 24%; BrE 1998,
‚•'•‚•‚• 59%, ‚•‚•'•‚• 41% ~leness ᵊl nəs
-nɪs ~ly li
incompatibilit|y ˌɪn kəm ˌpæt ə 'bɪl ət li →ˌɪŋ-,
§‚•kɒm-, -‚•ɪ-, -ɪt i ‖ -ˌpæt̬ ə 'bɪl ət̬ li ~ies iz
incompatib|le ˌɪn kəm 'pæt əb ᵊl ◄ →ˌɪŋ-,
§‚•kɒm-, -ɪb ᵊl ‖ -'pæt̬- ~les ᵊlz ~ly li
incompetenc|e ɪn 'kɒmp ɪt ᵊnts →ɪŋ-, ‚•‚•-, -ət-
‖ -'kɑːmp ət ᵊnts ~y i
incompetent ɪn 'kɒmp ɪt ənt →ɪŋ-, ‚•‚•-, -ət-
‖ -'kɑːmp ət ᵊnt ~ly li ~s s
incomplete ˌɪn kəm 'pliːt ◄ →ˌɪŋ-, §-kɒm- ~ly
li ~ness nəs nɪs
incomprehensibility
ɪn ˌkɒmp rɪ ˌhenᵗs ə 'bɪl ət i →ɪŋ-, ‚•‚•‚•-,
-rə‚•- -‚•ɪ-, -ɪt i
‖ ɪn ˌkɑːmp rɪ ˌhenᵗs ə 'bɪl ət̬ i ‚•‚•‚•-
incomprehensib|le ɪn ˌkɒmp rɪ 'henᵗs əb ᵊl ◄
→ɪŋ-, ‚•‚•‚•-, -rə'•-, -ɪb ᵊl ‖ ɪn ˌkɑːmp- ‚•‚•‚•-
~ly li
incomprehension ɪn ˌkɒmp rɪ 'henᵗʃ ᵊn →ɪŋ-,
‚•‚•‚•-, -rə'•- ‖ ɪn ˌkɑːmp- ‚•‚•‚•-
inconceivability ˌɪn kən ˌsiːv ə 'bɪl ət i →ˌɪŋ-,
§‚•kɒn-, -ɪt i ‖ -ət̬ i
inconceivab|le ˌɪn kən 'siːv əb ᵊl ◄ →ˌɪŋ-,
§‚•kɒn- ~leness ᵊl nəs -nɪs ~ly li
inconclusive ˌɪn kən 'kluːs ɪv ◄ →ˌɪŋ-, →-kəŋ-,
§-kɒn-, §-'kluːz- ~ly li ~ness nəs nɪs
incongruit|y ˌɪn kən 'gruː_ət li →ˌɪŋ-,
→ˌ•kəŋ-, ‚•kɒn-, →ˌ•kɒŋ-, ‚ɪt i ‖ -ət̬ li ~ies
iz
incongruous ɪn 'kɒŋ gru_əs →ɪŋ- ‖ -'kɑːŋ-
~ly li ~ness nəs nɪs
inconsequence ɪn 'kɒnts ɪk wənts →ɪŋ-, ‚•-,
-ək-; §-ə kwents ‖ -'kɑːnts-
inconsequent ɪn 'kɒnts ɪk wənt →ɪŋ-, ‚ɪn-,
-ək-; §-ə kwent ‖ -'kɑːnts- ~ly li

inconsequential ɪn ˌkɒnˈs ɪ ˈkwentʃ ᵊl ◂ →ɪŋ-,
ˌɪn, •-, -ə¹ • - ‖ -ˌkɑːnˈts- ~**ly** i ~**ness** nəs nɪs
inconsequentiality
ɪn ˌkɒnts ɪ ˌkwentʃ i ˈæl ət i →ɪŋ-, ˌ•ˌ•-,
-əˌ•-, -ɪt i ‖ -ˌkɑːnts i ˌkwentʃ i ˈæl ət̬ i
inconsiderab|le ˌɪn kən ˈsɪd‿ər əb |ᵊl ◂ →ˌɪŋ-,
§ˌ•kɒn- ~**ly** li
inconsiderate ˌɪn kən ˈsɪd‿ər ət ◂ →ˌɪŋ-,
§ˌ•kɒn-, -ɪt ~**ly** li ~**ness** nəs nɪs
inconsideration ˌɪn kən ˌsɪd ə ˈreɪʃ ᵊn →ˌɪŋ-,
§ˌ•kɒn-
inconsistenc|y ˌɪn kən ˈsɪst ᵊnts li →ˌɪŋ-,
§ˌ•kɒn- ~**ies** iz
inconsistent ˌɪn kən ˈsɪst ᵊnt ◂ →ˌɪŋ-, §-kɒn-
~**ly** li
inconsolab|le ˌɪn kən ˈsəʊl əb |ᵊl ◂ →ˌɪŋ-,
§ˌ•kɒn- ‖ -ˈsoʊl- ~**leness** ᵊl nəs -nɪs ~**ly** li
inconspicuous ˌɪn kən ˈspɪk ju‿əs ◂ →ˌɪŋ-,
§ˌ•kɒn- ~**ly** li ~**ness** nəs nɪs
inconstanc|y ɪn ˈkɒnˈtst ᵊnts li →ɪŋ-, ˌ•-
‖ -ˈkɑːnˈtst- ~**ies** iz
inconstant ɪn ˈkɒnˈtst ᵊnt →ɪŋ-, ˌ•- ‖ -ˈkɑːnˈtst-
~**ly** li
incontestability ˌɪn kən ˌtest ə ˈbɪl ət i →ɪŋ-,
§ˌ•kɒn-, -ɪt i ‖ -ət̬ i
incontestab|le ˌɪn kən ˈtest əb |ᵊl ◂ →ˌɪŋ-,
§ˌ•kɒn- ~**ly** li
incontinence ɪn ˈkɒnt ɪn ənts →ɪŋ-, ˌ•-, -ən‿
‖ -ˈkɑːnt ᵊn‿ənts
incontinent ɪn ˈkɒnt ɪn ənt →ɪŋ-, ˌ•-, -ən‿
‖ -ˈkɑːnt ᵊn‿ənt ~**ly** li
incontrovertib|le ˌɪn ˌkɒntr ə ˈvɜːt əb |ᵊl
→ˌɪŋ-, •ˌ•- ‖ ˌɪn ˌkɑːntr ə ˈvɜːt̬- ~**leness**
ᵊl nəs -nɪs ~**ly** li
inconvenienc|e ˌɪn kən ˈviːn i‿ənts →ˌɪŋ-,
§ˌ•kɒn- ~**ed** t ~**es** ɪz əz ~**ing** ɪŋ
inconvenient ˌɪn kən ˈviːn i‿ənt ◂ →ˌɪŋ-,
§ˌ•kɒn- ~**ly** li
incorpo|rate v ɪn ˈkɔːp ə |reɪt →ɪŋ- ‖ -ˈkɔːrp-
~**rated** reɪt ɪd -əd ‖ reɪt̬ əd ~**rates** reɪts
~**rating** reɪt ɪŋ ‖ reɪt̬ ɪŋ
incorporate adj ɪn ˈkɔːp ər‿ət →ɪŋ-, ‿ɪt, -ə reɪt
‖ -ˈkɔːrp-
incorporation ɪn ˌkɔːp ə ˈreɪʃ ᵊn →ɪŋ-
‖ -ˌkɔːrp- ~**s** z
incorporeal ˌɪn kɔː ˈpɔːr i‿əl ◂ →ˌɪŋ- ‖ ˌɪn kɔːr- -ˈpoʊr- ~**ly** li
incorrect ˌɪn kə ˈrekt ◂ →ˌɪŋ- ~**ly** li ~**ness** nəs
nɪs
incorrigibility ɪn ˌkɒr ɪdʒ ə ˈbɪl ət i →ɪŋ-, ˌ•ˌ•-,
-ədʒ ə-, -ɪt i ‖ ɪn ˌkɔːr ədʒ ə ˈbɪl ət̬ i •ˌkɑːr-,
ˌ•ˌ•-
incorrigib|le ɪn ˈkɒr ɪdʒ əb |ᵊl →ˌɪŋ-, ˌ•-,
-ˈ•ədʒ- ‖ -ˈkɔːr- -ˈkɑːr- ~**les** ᵊlz ~**ly** li
incorrupt ˌɪn kə ˈrʌpt →ˌɪŋ- ~**ly** li ~**ness** nəs
nɪs
incorruptibility ˌɪn kə ˌrʌpt ə ˈbɪl ət i →ˌɪŋ-,
-, -ˌ•ɪ-, -ɪt i ‖ -ət̬ i
incorruptib|le ˌɪn kə ˈrʌpt əb |ᵊl ◂ →ˌɪŋ-, -ɪb ᵊl
~**les** ᵊlz ~**ly** li
incorruption ˌɪn kə ˈrʌp ʃᵊn →ˌɪŋ-
increas|e v ɪn ˈkriːs →ˌɪŋ-, ˌ•-, ˈ•• (not -ˈkriːz)
~**ed** t ~**es** ɪz əz ~**ing/ly** ɪŋ /li

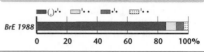
INCREASE

BrE 1988

increas|e n ɪ ˈɪŋ kriːs ˈɪn-, ₍ᵢ₎•ˈ• —*The stress
distinction between verb* •ˈ• *and noun* ˈ•• *is
not always made consistently. Nevertheless,
85% of the BrE 1988 poll panel preferred to
make this distinction (as against 7% preferring*
ˈ•• *for both verb and noun, 5%* •ˈ• *for both,
and 3%* ˈ•• *for the verb,* •ˈ• *for the noun).*
~**es** ɪz əz
incredibility ɪn ˌkred ə ˈbɪl ət i →ˌɪŋ-, ˌ•ˌ•-,
-ɪˈ•-, -ɪt i ‖ -ət̬ i
incredib|le ɪn ˈkred əb |ᵊl →ˌɪŋ-, ˌ•-, -ɪb- ~**ly** li
incredulity ˌɪn krə ˈdjuːl ət i →ˌɪŋ-, ˌ•krɪ-,
ˌ•kre-, ə →§-ˈdʒuːl-, -ɪt i ‖ -ˈduːl ət̬ i -ˈdjuːl-
incredulous ɪn ˈkred jʊl əs →ˌɪŋ-, -jəl-
‖ -ˈkredʒ ᵊl əs ~**ly** li ~**ness** nəs nɪs
increment n ˈɪŋ krɪ mənt ˈɪn-, -krə- ~**s** s
incre|ment v ˈɪŋ krɪ |ment ˈɪn-, -krə- —*See
note at* -ment ~**mented** ment ɪd -əd ‖ ment̬
əd ~**menting** ment ɪŋ ‖ ment̬ ɪŋ ~**ments**
ments
incremental ˌɪŋ krɪ ˈment ᵊl ◂ ˌɪn-, -krə-
‖ -ˈment̬ ᵊl ◂ ~**ly** i
incrimi|nate ɪn ˈkrɪm ɪ |neɪt →ˌɪŋ-, -ə- ~**nated**
neɪt ɪd -əd ‖ neɪt̬ əd ~**nates** neɪts ~**nating**
neɪt ɪŋ ‖ neɪt̬ ɪŋ
incrimination ɪn ˌkrɪm ɪ ˈneɪʃ ᵊn →ˌɪŋ-, -ə-
incriminatory ɪn ˈkrɪm ɪn ət‿ər i →ˌɪŋ-, -ˈ•ən-;
-ˈkrɪm ɪ neɪt ər i, -ˈ•ə-, ˌ•ˌ•ˈ•• ˈ••• ‖ -ə tɔːr i
-toʊr i
incrust ɪn ˈkrʌst →ɪŋ- ~**ed** ɪd əd ~**ing** ɪŋ ~**s** s
incrustation ˌɪn krʌ ˈsteɪʃ ᵊn →ˌɪŋ- ~**s** z
incu|bate ˈɪŋ kju |beɪt ˈɪn- -kjə- ~**bated**
beɪt ɪd -əd ‖ beɪt̬ əd ~**bates** beɪts ~**bating**
beɪt ɪŋ ‖ beɪt̬ ɪŋ
incubation ˌɪŋ kju ˈbeɪʃ ᵊn ˌɪn- ‖ -kjə- ~**s** z
incubator ˈɪŋ kju beɪt ə ˈɪn- ‖ -kjə beɪt̬ ᵊr ~**s** z
in|cubus ˈɪŋ |kjʊb əs ˈɪn- ~**cubi** kju baɪ
~**cubuses** kjʊb əs ɪz -əz
inculc|ate ɪn ˈkʌlk |eɪt →ˈɪŋ-, -kᵊl kleɪt;
ɪn ˈkʌlk-, →ɪŋ- ‖ ɪn ˈkʌlk eɪt ˈ••• ~**ated**
eɪt ɪd -əd ‖ eɪt̬ əd ~**ates** eɪts ~**ating**
eɪt ɪŋ ‖ eɪt̬ ɪŋ
inculcation ˌɪn kʌl ˈkeɪʃ ᵊn →ˌɪŋ-, -kᵊl- ~**s** z
inculp|ate ˈɪn kʌlp |eɪt →ˈɪŋ-; ˈ•••
‖ ɪn ˈkʌlp eɪt ˈ••• ~**ated** eɪt ɪd -əd ‖ eɪt̬ əd
~**ates** eɪts ~**ating** eɪt ɪŋ ‖ eɪt̬ ɪŋ
inculpation ˌɪn kʌl ˈpeɪʃ ᵊn →ˌɪŋ- ~**s** z
inculpatory ɪn ˈkʌlp ət‿ər i →ˌɪŋ-; ˈɪn kʌlp eɪt
ər i, →ˈɪŋ-; ˌɪn kʌl ˈpeɪt-, →ˌɪŋ-
‖ -ˈkʌlp ə tɔːr i -toʊr i
incumbenc|y ɪn ˈkʌm bᵊn¹s li →ɪŋ- ~**ies** iz
incumbent ɪn ˈkʌm bᵊnt →ɪŋ- ~**ly** li ~**s** s
incunabul|um ˌɪn kju ˈnæb jʊl əm →ˌɪŋ- ~**a** ə
~**ar** ə ‖ ᵊr
in|cur ɪn ˈ|kɜː →ɪŋ- ‖ -ˈ|kɜː- ~**curred**
ˈkɜːd ‖ ˈkɜːd ~**curring** ˈkɜːr ɪŋ ‖ ˈkɜː ɪŋ
~**curs** ˈkɜːz ‖ ˈkɜːz

incurability ın ˌkjʊər ə ˈbɪl ət i →ıŋ-, -ˌkjɔːr-, ˌˌˈˌˈ-, -ıt i ‖ ın ˌkjʊr ə ˈbɪl ət̬ i ˌˈˌˈ-

incurab|le ın ˈkjʊər əb |əl →ıŋ-, ˌˈˌ-, -ˈkjɔːr- ‖ -ˈkjʊr- ~leness əl nəs -nıs ~les əlz ~ly li

incurious ın ˈkjʊər i_əs →ıŋ-, ˌˈˌ-, -ˈkjɔːr- ‖ -ˈkjʊr- ~ly li ~ness nəs nıs

incursion ın ˈkɜːʃ ən →ıŋ-, -ˈkɜːʒ- ‖ -ˈkɝːʒ ən ~s z

incurvate adj ın ˈkɜːv eıt →ıŋ-, -ət, -ıt ‖ -ˈkɝːv- ˈˌ, ˌ̈ˈ

incurv|ate v ın kɜːv |eıt →ˈıŋ- ‖ -kɝːv- ˌ̈ˈ ~ated eıt ıd -əd ‖ eıt̬ əd ~ates eıts ~ating eıt ıŋ ‖ eıt̬ ıŋ

incurv|e ˌın ˈkɜːv ◄ →ˌıŋ- ‖ -ˈkɝːv ◄ ~ed d ~es z ~ing ıŋ

incus ˈıŋk əs

incus|e ın ˈkjuːz →ıŋ- ~ed d ~es ız əz ~ing ıŋ

Ind ınd aınd
  Ind Coope tdmk kuːp

indaba ın ˈdɑːb ə —Zulu [i ˈnda: ɓa] ~s z

indebted ın ˈdet ıd -əd ‖ -ˈdet̬ əd ~ness nəs nıs

indecenc|y ın ˈdiːs ənts li ˌın- ~ies ız

indecent ın ˈdiːs ənt ˌın- ~ly li
  inˌdecent asˈsault, ˌˌˈˌ ˌˈˌ ˌˈˌˈ; inˌdecent exˈposure

indecipherability ˌın dı ˌsaıf ər_ə ˈbıl ət i ˌˌˈdə-, §ˌˌˈdiː-, -ıt i ‖ -ət̬ i

indecipherab|le ˌın dı ˈsaıf ər_əb |əl ◄ ˌˌˈdə-, §ˌˌˈdiː- ~leness əl nəs -nıs ~ly li

indecision ˌın dı ˈsıʒ ən -də-, §-diː-, -ˈzıʃ-

indecisive ˌın dı ˈsaıs ıv ◄ -də-, §-diː-, -ˈsaız- ~ly li ~ness nəs nıs

indeclinab|le ˌın dı ˈklaın əb |əl ◄ ˌˌˈdə-, §ˌˌˈdiː- ~leness əl nəs -nıs ~ly li

indecorous ın ˈdek ər əs ˌın-, §ˌın dı ˈkɔːr əs ◄, -də- ‖ ˌın dı ˈkɔːr əs, -ˈkoʊr- ~ly li ~ness nəs nıs

indecorum ˌın dı ˈkɔːr əm -də-, §-diː- ‖ -ˈkoʊr-

indeed ın ˈdiːd ˌın-

indefatigab|le ˌın dı ˈfæt ıg əb |əl ◄ ˌˌˈdə-, §ˌˌˈdiː- ‖ -ˈfæt̬- ~leness əl nəs -nıs ~ly li

indefeasibility ˌın dı ˌfiːz ə ˈbıl ət i ˌˌˈdə- ‖ -ət̬ i

indefeasib|le ˌın dı ˈfiːz əb |əl ◄ ˌˌˈdə-, -ıb ˌ ~ly li

indefensib|le ˌın dı ˈfents əb |əl ◄ ˌˌˈdə-, §ˌˌˈdiː-, -ıb ˌ ~leness əl nəs -nıs ~ly li

indefinab|le ˌın dı ˈfaın əb |əl ◄ ˌˌˈdə-, §ˌˌˈdiː- ~leness əl nəs -nıs ~ly li

indefinite ın ˈdef ən_ət ˌın-, -ın-, ˌˌıt ~ly li ~ness nəs nıs
  inˌdefinite ˈarticle, ˌˌˈˌ, ˌˈˌˈ ˈˌˌˈ

indelib|le ın ˈdel əb |əl ◄ ˌın-, -ıb- ~leness əl nəs -nıs ~ly li

indelicac|y ın ˈdel ık əs li ˌın-, -ˌˈək- ~ies ız

indelicate ın ˈdel ık ət ˌın-, -ək-, -ıt ~ly li ~ness nəs nıs

indemnification ın ˌdem nıf ı ˈkeıʃ ən -ˌˈnəf-, §-əˌˈˌ- ~s z

indemni|fy ın ˈdem nı |faı -nə- ~fied faıd

~fier/s faı_ə/z ‖ faı_ər/z ~fies faız ~fying faı ıŋ

indemnit|y ın ˈdem nət li -nıt- ‖ -nət̬ li ~ies ız

indene ˈınd iːn

in|dent v ın ˈdent ˌˈ◄ˌ◄ ~dented ˈdent ıd -əd ‖ ˈdent̬ əd ~denting ˈdent ıŋ ‖ ˈdent̬ ıŋ ~dents ˈdents

indent n ˈın dent ˌˈˌ ~s s

indentation ˌın den ˈteıʃ ən ~s z

indent|ure n, v ın ˈdentʃ |ə ‖ -ˌˈər ~ured əd ‖ ˌərd ~ures əz ‖ ˌərz ~uring ər_ıŋ

independence ˌın dı ˈpend ənts ◄ -də-, §-diː-
  ˌIndeˈpendence Day;, ˌIndeˌpendence ˈHall

independent, I~ ˌın dı ˈpend ənt ◄ -də-, §-diː- ~ly li ~s s
  ˌindeˌpendent ˈclause

in-depth ˌın ˈdepθ ◄

indescribability ˌın dı ˌskraıb ə ˈbıl ət i ˌˌˈdə-, §ˌˌˈdiː-, -ıt i ‖ -ət̬ i

indescribab|le ˌın dı ˈskraıb əb |əl ◄ ˌˌˈdə-, §ˌˌˈdiː- ~leness əl nəs -nıs ~ly li

Indesit tdmk ˈınd ı sıt -ə-, -e-

indestructibility ˌın dı ˌstrʌkt ə ˈbıl ət i ˌˌˈdə-, §ˌˌˈdiː-, -ˌˌˈı-, -ıt i ‖ -ət̬ i

indestructib|le ˌın dı ˈstrʌkt əb |əl ◄ ˌˌˈdə-, §ˌˌˈdiː-, -ıb əl ~leness əl nəs -nıs ~ly li

indeterminab|le ˌın dı ˈtɜːm ın əb |əl ◄ ˌˌˈdə-, §ˌˌˈdiː-, -ˌˈən_əb- ‖ -ˈtɝː- ~ly li

indeterminac|y ˌın dı ˈtɜːm ın əs li ˌˌˈdə-, §ˌˌˈdiː-, -ˌˈən_əs- ‖ -ˈtɝː- ~ies ız

indeterminate ˌın dı ˈtɜːm ın ət ◄ ˌˌˈdə-, §ˌˌˈdiː-, -ˌˈən_, -ıt ‖ -ˈtɝː- ~ly li ~ness nəs nıs

index n, v ˈınd eks ~ed t ~es ız əz ~ing ıŋ
  indices ˈınd ı siːz -ə-
  ˈindex ˌfinger; ˈindex ˌnumber

indexation ˌınd ek ˈseıʃ ən ~s z

indexer ˈınd eks ə ‖ -ˌər ~s z

indexical ın ˈdeks ık əl ~ly _i

index-|linked ˌınd eks |ˈlıŋkt ◄ ~linking ˈlıŋk ıŋ

India, india ˈınd i_ə
  ˌindia ˈrubber◄, ˌindia-ˌrubber ˈball

Indian ˈınd i_ən ~s z
  ˌIndian ˈcorn; ˌIndian ˈink; ˌIndian ˈOcean; ˌIndian ˈsummer

Indiana ˌınd i ˈæn ə -ˈɑːn-

Indianan ˌınd i ˈæn ən ◄ -ˈɑːn- ~s z

Indianapolis ˌınd i_ə ˈnæp əl ıs §-əs

Indianian ˌınd i ˈæn i_ən ◄ -ˈɑːn- ~s z

Indic ˈınd ık

indi|cate ˈınd ı |keıt -ə- ~cated keıt ıd -əd ‖ keıt̬ əd ~cates keıts ~cating keıt ıŋ ‖ keıt̬ ıŋ

indication ˌınd ı ˈkeıʃ ən -də- ~s z

indicative ın ˈdık ət ıv ‖ -ət̬ ıv ~ly li ~s z

indicator ˈınd ı keıt ə ˌˈˌə- ‖ -keıt̬ ər ~s z
  ˈindicator board

indices ˈınd ı siːz -ə-

in|dict ın ˈdaıt (! = indite) ~dicted ˈdaıt ıd -əd ‖ ˈdaıt̬ əd ~dicting ˈdaıt ıŋ ‖ ˈdaıt̬ ıŋ ~dicts ˈdaıts

indictable ın ˈdaıt əb əl ‖ -ˈdaıt̬-

indiction ɪn ˈdɪk ʃ°n ~s z
indictment ɪn ˈdaɪt mənt ~s s
indie ˈɪnd i ~s z
Indies ˈɪnd iz
indifference ɪn ˈdɪf r°nts -ˈdɪf ər °nts
indifferent ɪn ˈdɪf r°nt -ˈdɪf ər ənt ~ly li
indigence ˈɪnd ɪdʒ °nts
indigene ˈɪnd ɪ dʒiːn §-ə- ~s z
indigenous ɪn ˈdɪdʒ ən_əs -ɪn- ~ly li ~ness
 nəs nɪs
indigent ˈɪnd ɪdʒ ənt ~ly li ~s s
indigestibility ˌɪn dɪ ˌdʒest ə ˈbɪl ət i ˌ•də-,
 ˌ•daɪ-, -ˌ•ɪ-, -ɪt i ‖ -ət̮ i
indigestib|le ˌɪn dɪ ˈdʒest əb |°l ◄ ˌ•də-, ˌ•daɪ-,
 -ɪb °l ~ly li
indigestion ˌɪn dɪ ˈdʒes tʃən -də-, →-ˈdʒeʃ-
indignant ɪn ˈdɪg nənt ~ly li
indignation ˌɪn dɪg ˈneɪʃ °n
indignit|y ɪn ˈdɪg nət i -nɪt- ‖ -nət̮ i ~ies iz
indigo ˈɪnd ɪ gəʊ ‖ -goʊ ~es, ~s z
Indio ˈɪnd i əʊ ‖ -oʊ
Indira ˈɪnd ɪr ə -ər-; ɪn ˈdɪər ə ‖ -ˈdɪr-
indirect ˌɪn də ˈrekt ◄ -dɪ-, -daɪ- ~ly li ~ness
 nəs nɪs
 ˌindiˌrect ˈobject; ˌindiˌrect ˈspeech
indirection ˌɪn də ˈrek ʃ°n -dɪ-, -daɪ-
indiscernib|le ˌɪn dɪ ˈsɜːn əb |°l ◄ ˌ•də-, -ˈzɜːn-,
 -ɪb °l ‖ -ˈsɝːn- -ˈzɝːn- ~ly li
indiscipline ɪn ˈdɪs əp lɪn ˌɪn-, -ˈ•ɪp-, -lən;
 §ˌɪn dɪ ˈsɪp-
indiscreet ˌɪn dɪ ˈskriːt ◄ -də- ~ly li ~ness nəs
 nɪs
indiscretion ˌɪn dɪ ˈskreʃ °n -də- ~s z
indiscriminate ˌɪn dɪ ˈskrɪm ɪn ət ◄ ˌ•də-,
 -ˈ•ən_, -ɪt ~ly li ~ness nəs nɪs
indispensability ˌɪn dɪ ˌspents ə ˈbɪl ət i ˌ•də-,
 -ɪt i ‖ -ət̮ i
indispensab|le ˌɪn dɪ ˈspents əb |°l ◄ ˌ•də-
 ~les °lz ~ly li
indisposed ˌɪn dɪ ˈspəʊzd ◄ -də- ‖ -ˈspoʊzd ◄
indisposition ˌɪn ˌdɪsp ə ˈzɪʃ °n ˌ•ˌ••ˈ•• ~s z
indisputability ˌɪn dɪ ˌspjuːt ə ˈbɪl ət i -ɪt i;
 ɪn ˌdɪs pjuːt-, ˌ•ˌ•••- ‖ -ˌspjuːt̮ ə ˈbɪl ət̮ i
indisputab|le ˌɪn dɪ ˈspjuːt əb |°l ◄ ˌ•də-;
 ₍ₐ₎ɪn ˈdɪs pjuːt- ‖ -ˈspjuːt̮- ~ly li
indissolubility ˌɪn dɪ ˌsɒl jʊ ˈbɪl ət i ˌ•də-,
 -ˌ•jə-, -ɪt i ‖ -ˌsɑːl jə ˈbɪl ət̮ i
indissolub|le ˌɪn dɪ ˈsɒl jʊb |°l ◄ ˌ•də-, -jəb °l
 ‖ -ˈsɑːl jəb |°l ~leness °l nəs -nɪs ~ly li
indistinct ˌɪn dɪ ˈstɪŋkt ◄ -də- ~ly li ~ness nəs
 nɪs
indistinguishab|le ˌɪn dɪ ˈstɪŋ gwɪʃ əb |°l ◄
 ˌ•də- ~ly li
in|dite ɪn |ˈdaɪt ~dited ˈdaɪt ɪd -əd ‖ ˈdaɪt̮ əd
 ~dites ˈdaɪts ~diting ˈdaɪt ɪŋ ‖ ˈdaɪt̮ ɪŋ
indium ˈɪnd i_əm
individual ˌɪnd ɪ ˈvɪdʒ u_əl ◄ ˌ•ə-, -ˈvɪd ju_ ~ly
 i ~s z
individualis... —see individualiz...
individualism ˌɪnd ɪ ˈvɪdʒ u_ə ˌlɪz əm ˌ•ə-,
 -ˈvɪd ju_; -ˈvɪdʒ u ˌlɪz əm ~s z
individualist ˌɪnd ɪ ˈvɪdʒ u_əl ɪst ˌ•ə-, -ˈvɪd ju_,
 §-əst; -ˈvɪdʒ ʊl ɪst, -əst ~s s

individualistic ˌɪnd ɪ ˌvɪdʒ u_ə ˈlɪst ɪk ˌ•ə-,
 -ˌvɪd ju-, -ˌvɪdʒ uˈ•- ~ally °l_i
individualit|y ˌɪnd ɪ ˌvɪdʒ u ˈæl ət i ˌ•ə-,
 -ˌvɪd ju-, -ɪt i ‖ -ət̮ i ~ies iz
individualization ˌɪnd ɪ ˌvɪdʒ u_əl aɪ ˈzeɪʃ °n
 ˌ•ə-, -ˌvɪd ju-, -ɪˈ•- ‖ -əˈ•- ~s z
individualiz|e ˌɪnd ɪ ˈvɪdʒ u_ə laɪz ˌ•ə-,
 -ˈvɪd ju_; -ˈvɪdʒ u laɪz ~ed d ~es ɪz əz
 ~ing ɪŋ
individu|ate ˌɪnd ɪ ˈvɪdʒ u eɪt ˌ•ə-, -ˈvɪd ju-
 ~ated eɪt ɪd -əd ‖ eɪt̮ əd ~ates eɪts ~ating
 eɪt ɪŋ ‖ eɪt̮ ɪŋ
individuation ˌɪnd ɪ ˌvɪdʒ u ˈeɪʃ °n ˌ•ə-,
 -ˌvɪd ju- ~s z
indivisibility ˌɪn dɪ ˌvɪz ə ˈbɪl ət i ˌ•də-, -ˌ•ɪ-,
 -ɪt i ‖ -ət̮ i
indivisib|le ˌɪn dɪ ˈvɪz əb |°l ◄ ˌ•də-, -ɪb °l
 ~leness °l nəs -nɪs ~ly li
Indo- ˈɪnd əʊ ‖ -oʊ — Indo-Pacific
 ˌɪnd əʊ pə ˈsɪf ɪk ◄ ‖ ˌ•oʊ-
Indo-Aryan ˌɪnd əʊ ˈeər i_ən ◄ ‖ -oʊ ˈer- -ˈær-
Indo-China ˌɪnd əʊ ˈtʃaɪn ə ◄ ‖ -oʊ-
Indo-Chinese ˌɪnd əʊ ˌtʃaɪ ˈniːz ‖ -oʊ-
indoctri|nate ɪn ˈdɒk trɪ |neɪt -trə- ‖ -ˈdɑːk-
 ~nated neɪt ɪd -əd ‖ neɪt̮ əd ~nates neɪts
 ~nating neɪt ɪŋ ‖ neɪt̮ ɪŋ
indoctrination ɪn ˌdɒk trɪ ˈneɪʃ °n ˌ•ˌ•-, -trəˈ•-
 ‖ -ˌdɑːk- ~s z
Indo-European ˌɪnd əʊ ˌjʊər ə ˈpiː_ən ◄ -ˌjɔːr-
 ‖ -oʊ ˌjʊr- ~ist/s ɪst/s əst/s
 ˌIndo-Euroˌpean ˈlanguages
Indo-Iranian ˌɪnd əʊ ɪ ˈreɪn i_ən ◄ ‖ ˌ•oʊ-
indole ˈɪnd əʊl →-ɒʊl ‖ -oʊl
indolence ˈɪnd əl ənts
indolent ˈɪnd əl ənt ~ly li
indomitab|le ɪn ˈdɒm ɪt əb |°l -ˈ•ət-
 ‖ -ˈdɑːm ət̮- ~ly li
Indonesia ˌɪnd əʊ ˈniːʒ ə -ˈniːz i_ə, -ˈniːs-;
 -ˈniːʃ ə
Indonesian ˌɪnd əʊ ˈniːʒ °n ◄ -ˈniːz i_ən, -ˈniːs-;
 -ˈniːʃ °n ~s z
indoor ˌɪn ˈdɔː ◄ ‖ -ˈdɔːr ◄ -ˈdoʊr ~s z
 ˌindoor ˈgames
Indore ₍ₐ₎ɪn ˈdɔː ‖ -ˈdɔːr —Hindi Indaur
 [ɪn ̪d̪əʊr]
indors|e ɪn ˈdɔːs ən- ‖ -ˈdɔːrs ~ed t ~es ɪz əz
 ~ement/s mənt/s ~ing ɪŋ
Indra ˈɪndr ə
indrawn ˌɪn ˈdrɔːn ◄ ‖ -ˈdrɑːn
 ˌindrawn ˈbreath
indri ˈɪndr i ~s z
indubitab|le ɪn ˈdjuːb ɪt əb |°l ˌɪn-, →§-ˈdʒuːb-,
 -ˈ•ət- ‖ -ˈduːb ət̮- -ˈdjuːb- ~ly li
induc|e ɪn ˈdjuːs →§-ˈdʒuːs ‖ -ˈduːs -ˈdjuːs
 ~ed t ~es ɪz əz ~ing ɪŋ
inducement ɪn ˈdjuːs mənt →§-ˈdʒuːs-
 ‖ -ˈduːs- -ˈdjuːs- ~s s
induct ɪn ˈdʌkt ~ed ɪd əd ~ing ɪŋ ~s s
inductanc|e ɪn ˈdʌkt °nts ~es ɪz əz
inductee ˌɪn dʌk ˈtiː ~s z
induction ɪn ˈdʌk ʃ°n ~s z
 inˈduction coil
inductive ɪn ˈdʌkt ɪv ~ly li ~ness nəs nɪs

indu|e ɪn 'djuː ən-, →§-'dʒuː ‖ -'duː -'djuː **~ed** d **~es** z **~ing** ɪŋ

indulg|e ɪn 'dʌldʒ **~ed** d **~es** ɪz əz **~ing** ɪŋ

indulgenc|e ɪn 'dʌldʒ ənts **~es** ɪz əz

indulgent ɪn 'dʌldʒ ənt **~ly** li

indu|rate v 'ɪn djuə ‖reɪt §-dʒuə- ‖ -də- -djə- **~rated** reɪt ɪd -əd ‖ reɪt̮ əd **~rates** reɪts **~rating** reɪt ɪŋ ‖ reɪt̮ ɪŋ

indurate adj 'ɪn djuər ət §-dʒuər-, -ɪt, -eɪt ‖ -dər- -djər-

induration ˌɪn djuə 'reɪʃ ən →§-dʒuə- ‖ ˌɪn də- -djə-

Indus 'ɪnd əs

industrial ɪn 'dʌs tri‿əl **~ly** i **~s** z
in‚dustrial 'action; in‚dustrial ‚archae'ology; in‚dustrial de'sign; in‚dustrial e'state; in‚dustrial ‚revo'lution

industrialis... —see **industrializ...**

industrialist ɪn 'dʌs tri‿əl ɪst §-əst **~s** s

industrialization ɪn ˌdʌs tri‿əl aɪ 'zeɪʃ ən -ɪ'‧- ‖ -ə'‧- **~s** z

industrializ|e ɪn 'dʌs tri‿ə laɪz **~ed** d **~es** ɪz əz **~ing** ɪŋ

industrial-strength ɪn 'dʌs tri‿əl streŋkθ §-strenᵗθ

industrious ɪn 'dʌs tri‿əs **~ly** li **~ness** nəs nɪs

indus|try 'ɪnd əs ‖tri §-ʌs- **~tries** triz

in|dwell ₍ₗ₎ɪn l'dwel **~dwelling** 'dwel ɪŋ **~dwells** 'dwelz **~dwelt** 'dwelt

-ine aɪn, iːn, ɪn §ən —As a suffix, iːn in chemical senses ('bromine, 'caffeine), otherwise usually aɪn ('bovine, 'crystalline). When not felt as a suffix, often ɪn §ən ('discipline, 'famine), sometimes stressed iːn (rou'tine).

inebri|ate v ɪ 'niːb ri ‖eɪt **~ated** eɪt ɪd -əd ‖ eɪt̮ əd **~ates** eɪts **~ating** eɪt ɪŋ ‖ eɪt̮ ɪŋ

inebriate adj, n ɪ 'niːb ri‿ət -ɪt, -eɪt **~s** s

inebriation ɪ ˌniːb ri 'eɪʃ ən

inebriety ˌɪn iː 'braɪ‿ət i ‚'ɪ-, §‚'ə-, ‚ɪt i ‖ -ət̮ i

inedibility ɪn ˌed ə 'bɪl ət i ˌɪn,‧-, -ɪ'‧-, -ɪt i ‖ -ət̮ i

inedible ɪn 'ed əb əl ˌɪn-, -ɪb əl

ineducable ɪn 'ed juk əb əl ˌɪn-, -ɪ'‧juːk-; -'edʒ ʊk-, -ɪ'‧ək- ‖ -'edʒ ək-

ineffability ɪn ˌef ə 'bɪl ət i -ɪt i ‖ -ət̮ i

ineffab|le ɪn 'ef əb əl **~leness** əl nəs -nɪs **~ly** li

ineffaceab|le ˌɪn ɪ 'feɪs əb əl ◂ -'e-, ‚-ə- **~ly** li

ineffective ˌɪn ɪ 'fekt ɪv ◂ -ə- **~ly** li **~ness** nəs nɪs

ineffectual ˌɪn ɪ 'fek tʃu‿əl ◂ -ə-, -tju‿əl, -ʃu‿əl **~ly** i **~ness** nəs nɪs

inefficienc|y ˌɪn ɪ 'fɪʃ ənts li -ə- **~ies** ɪz

inefficient ˌɪn ɪ 'fɪʃ ənt ◂ -ə- **~ly** li

inelastic ˌɪn ɪ 'læst ɪk ◂ -ə-, -'lɑːst-

inelasticity ˌɪn ɪ læ 'stɪs ət i ‚-ə-, -lɑː'‧-; ˌɪn ˌiːl æ'‧-, ˌɪn ˌel æ'‧-, -ɑː'‧-, -ɪt i ‖ -ət̮ i

inelegance ɪn 'el ɪg ənts ˌɪn-, -əg-

inelegant ɪn 'el ɪg ənt ˌɪn-, -əg- **~ly** li

ineligibility ɪn ˌel ɪdʒ ə 'bɪl ət i -, ‚-ədʒ-, ‚ˌ‧,‧-, -ɪ'‧-, -ɪt i ‖ -ət̮ i

ineligib|le ɪn 'el ɪdʒ əb əl ˌɪn-, -ɪ'‧ədʒ-, -ɪb əl **~ly** li

ineluctab|le ˌɪn ɪ 'lʌkt əb əl ◂ ‚-ə- **~ly** li

inept ɪ 'nept ˌɪn 'ept ◂ **~ly** li **~ness** nəs nɪs

ineptitude ɪ 'nept ɪ tjuːd -ə-, →§-tʃuːd ‖ -tuːd -tjuːd

inequalit|y ˌɪn ɪ 'kwɒl ət li ‚-iː-, ‚-ə-, -ɪt i ‖ -'kwɑːl ət̮ li **~ies** ɪz

inequitab|le ɪn 'ek wɪt əb əl ˌɪn-, -ɪ'‧wət- ‖ -'ek wət̮- **~leness** əl nəs -nɪs **~ly** li

inequit|y ɪn 'ek wət li ˌɪn-, -ɪt- -wət̮ li **~ies** ɪz

ineradicab|le ˌɪn ɪ 'ræd ɪk əb əl ◂ ‚-ə- **~leness** əl nəs -nɪs **~ly** li

inert ɪ 'nɜːt ‖ ɪ 'nɜːt **~ly** li **~ness** nəs nɪs

inertance ɪ 'nɜːt ənts ‖ -'nɜːt-

inertia ɪ 'nɜːʃ ə -'nɜːʃ i‿ə ‖ ɪ 'nɜːʃ ə i'nertia reel; i‚nertia 'selling, ‧'‧‧ ‚‧‧

inertial ɪ 'nɜːʃ əl -'nɜːʃ i‿əl ‖ ɪ 'nɜːʃ əl

inescapab|le ˌɪn ɪ 'skeɪp əb əl ◂ ‚-ə- **~ly** li

inessential ˌɪn ɪ 'sentʃ əl ◂ -ə- **~s** z

inessive ɪn 'es ɪv ˌɪn- **~s** z

inestimab|le ɪn 'est ɪm əb əl ˌɪn-, -ɪ'‧əm- **~ly** li

inevitability ɪn ˌev ɪt ə 'bɪl ət i ‚‧,‧-, -ət ə-, -ɪt i ‖ -ət̮ ə 'bɪl ət̮ i

inevitab|le ɪn 'ev ɪt əb əl ‚‧,‧-, -ɪ'‧ət- ‖ -'ev ət̮- **~leness** əl nəs -nɪs **~ly** li

inexact ˌɪn ɪg 'zækt ◂ -eg-, -əg-, -ɪk-, -ek-, -ək- **~ly** li **~ness** nəs nɪs

inexactitude ˌɪn ɪg 'zækt ɪ tjuːd ‚-eg-, ‚-əg-, ‚‧ɪk-, ‚-ek-, ‚-ək-, -ə-, →-tʃuːd ‖ -ə tuːd -tjuːd **~s** z

inexcusab|le ˌɪn ɪk 'skjuːz əb əl ◂ ‚-ek-, ‚-ək- **~leness** əl nəs -nɪs **~ly** li

inexhaustib|le ˌɪn ɪg 'zɔːst əb əl ◂ ‚-eg-, ‚-əg-, ‚‧ɪk-, ‚-ek-, ‚-ək-, -ɪb əl ‖ -'zɑːst- **~leness** əl nəs -nɪs **~ly** li

inexorability ɪn ˌeks ər‿ə 'bɪl ət i §-ˌegz-, -ɪt i ‖ -ət̮ i

inexorab|le ɪn 'eks ər‿əb əl §-'egz- **~leness** əl nəs -nɪs **~ly** li

inexpedienc|e ˌɪn ɪk 'spiːd i‿ənts ‚-ek-, ‚-ək- **~y** i

inexpedient ˌɪn ɪk 'spiːd i‿ənt ◂ ‚-ek-, ‚-ək- **~ly** li

inexpensive ˌɪn ɪk 'spents ɪv ◂ -ek-, -ək- **~ly** li **~ness** nəs nɪs

inexperience ˌɪn ɪk 'spɪər i‿ənts ‚-ek-, ‚-ək- ‖ -'spɪr- **~d** t

inexpert ɪn 'eks pɜːt ˌɪn-; ˌɪn ek 'spɜːt ◂, -ɪk-, -ək- ‖ ɪn 'eks pɝːt ˌɪn-; ˌɪn ɪk 'spɝːt ◂ **~ly** li **~ness** nəs nɪs

inexpiab|le ɪn 'eks pi‿əb əl ˌɪn- **~leness** əl nəs -nɪs **~ly** li

inexplicability ˌɪn ɪk ˌsplɪk ə 'bɪl ət i ‚-ek-, ‚‧ək-, -ɪt i; ɪn ˌeks plɪk-, ‚‧,‧-, ‚‧- ‖ -ət̮ i

inexplicab|le ˌɪn ɪk 'splɪk əb əl ◂ ‚-ek-, ‚-ək-; ₍ₗ₎ɪn 'eks plɪk- **~leness** əl nəs -nɪs **~ly** li

inexplicit ˌɪn ɪk 'splɪs ɪt -ek-, -ək-, §-ət **~ly** li **~ness** nəs nɪs

inexpressib|le ˌɪn ɪk 'spres əb əl ◂ ‚-ek-, ‚-ək-, -ɪb əl **~leness** əl nəs -nɪs **~ly** li

inexpressive ˌɪn ɪk 'spres ɪv ◂ -ek-, -ək- **~ly** li **~ness** nəs nɪs

inextinguishab|le ˌɪn ɪk 'stɪŋ gwɪʃ əb əl ◂

ˌ•ek-, ˌ•ək-, -ˈ•wɪʃ- **~leness** ᵊl nəs -nɪs **~ly**
li

in extremis ˌɪn ɪk ˈstriːm ɪs -ek-, -ək-, §-əs

inextricability ˌɪn ɪk ˌstrɪk ə ˈbɪl ət i ˌ•ek-,
ˌ•ək-, -ɪt i; ɪn ˌeks trɪk-, ˌ•, ˌ•- ‖ -ət̬ i

inextricab|le ˌɪn ɪk ˈstrɪk əb |ᵊl ◄ ˌ•ek-, ˌ•ək-;
₍ᵢ₎ɪn ˈeks trɪk- **~leness** ᵊl nəs -nɪs **~ly** li

Inez ˈiːn ez ˈaɪn- ‖ ˈaɪn ez aɪ ˈnez, ˈiːn ez;
iː ˈnez, ɪ- —*Sp* [ˈi neθ]

infallibility ɪn ˌfæl ə ˈbɪl ət i ˌ•, ˌ•-, -ɪˈ•-, -ɪt i
‖ -ət̬ i

infallib|le ɪn ˈfæl əb |ᵊl ˌɪn-, -ɪb- **~leness** ᵊl nəs
-nɪs **~ly** li

infamous ˈɪn fəm əs *(!)* **~ly** li **~ness** nəs nɪs

infam|y ˈɪn fəm |i **~ies** iz

infanc|y ˈɪnᵗf ənᵗs |i **~ies** iz

infant ˈɪnᵗf ənt **~s** s

ˌinfant ˈprodigy; ˈinfant school

infanta ɪn ˈfænt ə —*Sp* [in ˈfan ta] **~s** z

infante ɪn ˈfænt i —*Sp* [in ˈfan te] **~s** z

infanticidal ɪn ˌfænt ɪ ˈsaɪd ᵊl ◄ -ə- ‖ -ˌfænt̬ ə-

infanticide ɪn ˈfænt ɪ saɪd -ə- ‖ -ˈfænt̬ ə- **~s** z

infantile ˈɪnᵗf ən taɪᵊl ‖ -tᵊl

ˌinfantile paˈralysis

infantilism ɪn ˈfænt ɪ ˌlɪz əm -ˈ•ə- ‖ -ˈfænt̬ ə-

infantr|y ˈɪnᵗf əntr |i **~ies** iz

infantry|man ˈɪnᵗf əntr i |mən -mæn **~men**
mən men

infarct ˈɪn fɑːkt •ˈ• ‖ -fɑːrkt **~s** s

infarction ɪn ˈfɑːk ʃᵊn ‖ -ˈfɑːrk- **~s** z

infatu|ate ɪn ˈfæt ju eɪt -ˈfætʃ u- ‖ ɪn ˈfæt̬ʃ u-
~ated eɪt ɪd -əd ‖ eɪt̬ əd **~ates** eɪts **~ating**
eɪt ɪŋ ‖ eɪt̬ ɪŋ

infatuation ɪn ˌfæt ju ˈeɪʃ ᵊn -ˌfætʃ u-
‖ ɪn ˌfæt̬ʃ u- **~s** z

infect ɪn ˈfekt **~ed** ɪd əd **~ing** ɪŋ **~s** s

infection ɪn ˈfek ʃᵊn **~s** z

infectious ɪn ˈfek ʃəs **~ly** li **~ness** nəs nɪs

infective ɪn ˈfekt ɪv **~ness** nəs nɪs

infectivity ˌɪn fek ˈtɪv ət i -ɪt i ‖ -ət̬ i

infelicitous ˌɪn fə ˈlɪs ɪt əs ◄ ˌ•fɪ-, ˌ•fe-, -ət əs
‖ -ət̬ əs ◄ **~ly** li

infelicit|y ˌɪn fə ˈlɪs ət |i ˌ•fɪ-, ˌ•fe-, -ɪt i ‖ -ət̬ |i
~ies iz

infer ɪn ˈfɜː ‖ -ˈfɝː **~red** d **inferring**
ɪn ˈfɜːr ɪŋ ‖ ɪn ˈfɝː ɪŋ **~s** z

inferab|le ɪn ˈfɜːr əb |ᵊl ˈɪnf ər‿əb |ᵊl ‖ -ˈfɝː-
~ly li

inferenc|e ˈɪnᵗf ᵊr ənᵗs **~es** ɪz əz

inferential ˌɪnᵗf ə ˈrenᵗʃ ᵊl ◄ **~ly** i

inferior ɪn ˈfɪər i‿ə ˌɪn- ‖ -ˈfɪr i‿ᵊr **~s** z

inferiorit|y ɪn ˌfɪər i ˈɒr ət |i ˌ•, ˌ•-, -ɪt i
‖ ɪn ˌfɪr i ˈɔːr ət̬ |i -ˈɑːr- **~ies** iz

ɪn ˌferiˈority ˌcomplex

infernal ɪn ˈfɜːn ᵊl ‖ -ˈfɝːn- **~ly** li

inferno, I- ɪn ˈfɜːn əʊ ‖ -ˈfɝːn oʊ **~s** z

inferrab|le ɪn ˈfɜːr əb |ᵊl ˈɪnf ər‿əb |ᵊl ‖ -ˈfɝː-
~ly li

infertile ɪn ˈfɜːt aɪᵊl ˌɪn- ‖ -ˈfɝːt̬ ᵊl *(*)*

infertility ˌɪn fə ˈtɪl ət i ˌ•fɜː-, -ɪt i ‖ -fᵊr ˈtɪl ət̬ i

infest ɪn ˈfest **~ed** ɪd əd **~ing** ɪŋ **~s** s

infestation ˌɪn fe ˈsteɪʃ ᵊn **~s** z

infibu|late ɪn ˈfɪb ju |leɪt -jə- ‖ -jə- **~lated**
leɪt ɪd -əd ‖ leɪt̬ əd **~lates** leɪts **~lating**
leɪt ɪŋ ‖ leɪt̬ ɪŋ

infibulation ɪn ˌfɪb ju ˈleɪʃ ᵊn -jə- ‖ -jə- **~s** z

infidel ˈɪn fɪd ᵊl -fəd-; -fɪ del, -fə- **~s** z

infidelit|y ˌɪn fɪ ˈdel ət i ˌ•fə-, -ɪt i ‖ -ət̬ li **~ies**
iz

infield ˈɪn fiːᵊld **~s** z

infielder ˈɪn ˌfiːᵊld ə ‖ -ᵊr **~s** z

infight|er/s ˈɪn ˌfaɪt ə/z ‖ -ˌfaɪt̬ ᵊr/z **~ing** ɪŋ

infill ˈɪn fɪl **~ed** d **~ing** ɪŋ **~s** z

infil|trate ˈɪn fɪl |treɪt -fᵊl- ‖ ɪn ˈfɪl|tr eɪt
ˈɪn fᵊl |treɪt *(*)* **~trated** treɪt ɪd -əd
‖ treɪt̬ əd **~trates** treɪts **~trating**
treɪt ɪŋ ‖ treɪt̬ ɪŋ

infiltration ˌɪn fɪl ˈtreɪʃ ᵊn -fᵊl- **~s** z

infiltrator ˈɪn fɪl treɪt ə ˈ•fᵊl- ‖ ɪn ˈfɪltr eɪt̬ ᵊr
ˈɪn fᵊl treɪt- **~s** z

infinite ˈɪn fɪn ət -ɪt; ˈɪnf ən‿ət, ‿ɪt —*but in
church music usually* ˈɪn fɪ naɪt, -fə-, -faɪ- **~ly**
li **~ness** nəs nɪs

infinitesimal ˌɪn fɪn ɪ ˈtes ɪm ᵊl ◄ -əˈ•-, -əm ᵊl;
ˌɪnf ən‿, -ˈtez- **~ly** i

infiniti... —*see* **infinity**

infinitival ɪn ˌfɪn ɪ ˈtaɪv ᵊl ◄ ˌ•, ˌ•-, -əˈ•-

infinitive ɪn ˈfɪn ət ɪv -ɪt- ‖ -ət̬ ɪv **~s** z

infinitude ɪn ˈfɪn ɪ tjuːd -ə-, →§-tʃuːd ‖ -tuːd
-tjuːd **~s** z

infinit|y ɪn ˈfɪn ət |i -ɪt- ‖ -ət̬ |i **~ies** iz

infirm ɪn ˈfɜːm ˌɪn- ‖ -ˈfɝːm **~ly** li **~ness** nəs
nɪs

infirmar|y ɪn ˈfɜːm ᵊr |i ‖ -ˈfɝːm- **~ies** iz

infirmit|y ɪn ˈfɜːm ət |i -ɪt- ‖ -ˈfɝːm ət̬ |i **~ies**
iz

infix *n* ˈɪn fɪks **~es** ɪz əz

infix *v* ˈɪn fɪks ₍ᵢ₎•ˈ• **~ed** t **~es** ɪz əz **~ing** ɪŋ

in flagrante ˌɪn flə ˈgrænt i -eɪ ‖ -ˈgrɑːnt-

in flaˌgrante deˈlicto dɪ ˈlɪkt əʊ də-, diː-,
deɪ- ‖ -oʊ

inflam|e ɪn ˈfleɪm **~ed** d **~es** z **~ing** ɪŋ

inflammab|le ɪn ˈflæm əb |ᵊl **~leness** ᵊl nəs
-nɪs **~ly** li

inflammation ɪn flə ˈmeɪʃ ᵊn **~s** z

inflammatory ɪn ˈflæm ət ᵊr i ‖ -ə tɔːr i -toʊr i

inflatable ɪn ˈfleɪt əb ᵊl ‖ -ˈfleɪt̬- **~s** z

in|flate ɪn |ˈfleɪt **~flated** ˈfleɪt ɪd -əd ‖ ˈfleɪt̬ əd
~flates ˈfleɪts **~flating** ˈfleɪt ɪŋ ‖ ˈfleɪt̬ ɪŋ

inflation ɪn ˈfleɪʃ ᵊn **~ism** ˌɪz əm **~s** z

inflationary ɪn ˈfleɪʃ ᵊn ᵊr i -ᵊn‿ᵊr- ‖ -ə ner i

inˌflationary ˈspiral

inflator ɪn ˈfleɪt ə ‖ ɪn ˈfleɪt̬ ᵊr **~s** z

inflect ɪn ˈflekt **~ed** ɪd əd **~ing** ɪŋ **~s** s

inflection ɪn ˈflek ʃᵊn **~al** ᵊl **~s** z

inflexibility ɪn ˌfleks ə ˈbɪl ət i ˌ•, ˌ•-, -ɪˈ•-, -ɪt i
‖ -ət̬ i

inflexib|le ɪn ˈfleks əb |ᵊl ˌɪn-, -ɪb- **~leness**
ᵊl nəs -nɪs **~ly** li

inflexion ɪn ˈflek ʃᵊn **~al** ᵊl **~s** z

inflict ɪn ˈflɪkt **~ed** ɪd əd **~ing** ɪŋ **~s** s

infliction ɪn ˈflɪk ʃᵊn

in-flight ˌɪn ˈflaɪt ◄

ˌin-flight ˈmovies

inflorescenc|e ˌɪn flə 'res ᵊnᵗs -flɔ:-, -flɒ- ‖ -flɔ:-, -floʊ- **~es** ɪz əz
inflow 'ɪn fləʊ ‖ -floʊ **~s** z
influenc|e 'ɪnᵗf lu_ᵊnᵗs **~es** ɪz əz
influential ˌɪnᵗf lu 'enᵗʃ ᵊl ◄ **-ly** i
influenza ˌɪnᵗf lu 'enz ə
influx 'ɪn flʌks **~es** ɪz əz
info 'ɪnᵗf əʊ ‖ -oʊ
infobahn 'ɪnᵗf əʊ bɑːn ‖ -oʊ-
infomercial ˌɪn fəʊ 'mɜːʃ ᵊl ‖ 'ɪn foʊ mɜːʃ ᵊl '•fə- **~s** z
inform ɪn 'fɔːm ‖ -'fɔːrm **~ed** d **~ing** ɪŋ **~s** z
informal ɪn 'fɔːm ᵊl ˌɪn- ‖ -'fɔːrm- **~ly** i
informalit|y ˌɪn fɔː 'mæl ət Ii -ɪt i ‖ -fɔːr 'mæl əţ Ii ˌ•fᵊr- **~ies** iz
informant ɪn 'fɔːm ənt ‖ -'fɔːrm- **~s** s
informatics ˌɪnᵗf ə 'mæt ɪks -ɔː- ‖ -ᵊr 'mæţ-
information ˌɪnᵗf ə 'meɪʃ ᵊn ‖ -ᵊr- ˌinfor'mation reˌtrieval; ˌinfor'mation techˌnology, ˌ••,•• •'•••
informative ɪn 'fɔːm ət ɪv ‖ -'fɔːrm əţ ɪv **~ly** li **~ness** nəs nɪs
informer ɪn 'fɔːm ə ‖ -'fɔːrm ᵊr **~s** z
Infoseek *tdmk* 'ɪnᵗf əʊ siːk ‖ -oʊ-
infotainment ˌɪnᵗf əʊ 'teɪn mənt ‖ -oʊ- '••••
infra 'ɪnᵗf rə
    ˌinfra 'dig
infra- ˌɪnᵗf rə — **infrasonic** ˌɪnᵗf rə 'sɒn ɪk ◄ ‖ -'sɑːn-
infraction ɪn 'fræk ʃᵊn **~s** z
infralapsarian ˌɪnᵗf rə læp 'seər i_ən ◄ ‖ -'ser- -'sær- **~ism** ˌɪz əm **~s** z
infrared ˌɪnᵗf rə 'red ◄
infrastructure 'ɪnᵗf rə ˌstrʌk tʃə ‖ -tʃᵊr **~s** z
infrequency ɪn 'friːk wənᵗs i ˌɪn-
infrequent ɪn 'friːk wənt ˌɪn- **~ly** li
infring|e ɪn 'frɪndʒ **~ed** d **~er/s** ə/z ‖ ᵊr/z **~es** ɪz əz **~ing** ɪŋ
infringement ɪn 'frɪndʒ mənt **~s** s
infundibul|um ˌɪn fʌn 'dɪb jʊl əm -jəl əm ‖ -jəl əm **~a** ə **~ar** ə ‖ ᵊr
infuri|ate ɪn 'fjʊər i eɪt -'fjɔːr- ‖ -'fjʊr- **~ated** eɪt ɪd -əd ‖ eɪţ əd **~ates** eɪts **~ating/ly** eɪt ɪŋ /li ‖ eɪţ-
infus|e ɪn 'fjuːz **~ed** d **~er/s** ə/z ‖ ᵊr/z **~es** ɪz əz **~ing** ɪŋ
infusion ɪn 'fjuːʒ ᵊn **~s** z
infusori|a ˌɪn fju 'zɔːr i_ə ◄ -'sɔːr- ‖ -'zoʊr-, -'soʊr- **~al** əl **~an/s** ən/z
-ing ɪŋ —*For* △ɪn, △ən, *see at* '-in'. —*Note the typical late/early stress difference between phrases, such as a* ˌsinging ca'nary, *where the -ing word is a participial adjective, and compounds, such as a* 'singing ˌlesson, *where the -ing word is a verbal noun (gerund).*
Inga *(i)* 'ɪŋ ə, *(ii)* 'ɪŋ gə
Ingamells 'ɪŋ gə melz
Ingatestone 'ɪŋ gət stəʊn -geɪt- ‖ -stoʊn
ingathering 'ɪn ˌgæð ᵊr_ɪŋ →'ɪŋ-
Inge *family name (i)* ɪŋ, *(ii)* ɪndʒ —*In Britain usually (i), in the US usually (ii).*
Inge *personal name, (i)* 'ɪŋ ə, *(ii)* 'ɪŋ gə

ingenious ɪn 'dʒiːn i_əs ˌɪn- **~ly** li **~ness** nəs nɪs
ingenue, ingénue 'ænʒ ə njuː 'ɒnʒ-, -e-, -eɪ-, -nuː, ˌ•••' ‖ 'ændʒ ə nuː 'ɑːndʒ-, -njuː —*Fr* [æ̃ ʒe ny] **~s** z
ingenuit|y ˌɪndʒ ə 'njuː_ət Ii ˌ•ɪ-, §-'nuː_, ɪt i ‖ -'nuː əţ Ii -'njuː- **~ies** iz
ingenuous ɪn 'dʒen ju_əs **~ly** li **~ness** nəs nɪs
Ingersoll *tdmk* 'ɪŋ gə sɒl ‖ -gᵊr sɔːl -sɑːl, -sᵊl
ingest ɪn 'dʒest ˌɪn- **~ed** ɪd əd **~ing** ɪŋ **~s** s
ingestion ɪn 'dʒes tʃən ˌɪn-, →-'dʒeʃ- **~s** z
Ingham 'ɪŋ əm
ingle, Ingle 'ɪŋ gᵊl **~s** z
Ingleborough 'ɪŋ gᵊl bᵊr_ə §-ˌbʌr ə ‖ -ˌbɜː oʊ
inglenook 'ɪŋ gᵊl nʊk §-nuːk **~s** s
Ingleton 'ɪŋ gᵊl tən
Inglewood 'ɪŋ gᵊl wʊd
Inglis 'ɪŋ glɪs -gᵊlz —*in Scotland,* -gᵊlz
inglorious ɪn 'glɔːr i_əs →ɪŋ-, ˌ•- ‖ -'gloʊr- **~ly** li **~ness** nəs nɪs
Ingmar 'ɪŋ mɑː ‖ -mɑːr
ingoing 'ɪn ˌgəʊ ɪŋ →'ɪŋ- ‖ -ˌgoʊ- **~s** z
Ingold 'ɪŋ gəʊld →-goʊld ‖ -goʊld
Ingoldsby 'ɪŋ gᵊldz bi
ingot 'ɪŋ gət -gɒt **~s** s
ingraft ɪn 'grɑːft ən-, →ɪŋ-, →əŋ-, §-'græft ‖ -'græft **~ed** ɪd əd **~ing** ɪŋ **~s** s
ingrained ɪn 'greɪnd →ɪŋ-, ˌ•-
Ingram 'ɪŋ grəm
Ingrams 'ɪŋ grəmz
ingrate 'ɪn greɪt →'ɪŋ-, •'• **~s** s
ingrati|ate ɪn 'greɪʃ i eɪt →ɪŋ- **~ated** eɪt ɪd -əd ‖ eɪţ əd **~ates** eɪts **~ating/ly** eɪt ɪŋ /li ‖ eɪţ ɪŋ /li
ingratitude ɪn 'græt ɪ tjuːd →ɪŋ-, ˌ•-, -'•ə-, →§-tʃuːd ‖ -'græţ ə tuːd -tjuːd
Ingrebourne 'ɪŋ grɪ bɔːn -grə- ‖ -bɔːrn -boʊrn
ingredient ɪn 'griːd i_ənt →ɪŋ- **~s** s
Ingres 'æŋgr 'æŋ grə —*Fr* [æ̃:gʁ]
ingress 'ɪn gres →'ɪŋ- **~es** ɪz əz
ingressive ɪn 'gres ɪv →ɪŋ-, ˌ•- **~ly** li **~s** z
Ingrid 'ɪŋ grɪd -grəd
in-group *n* 'ɪn gruːp →'ɪŋ- **~s** s
ingrowing ˌɪn 'grəʊ ɪŋ ◄ →ˌɪŋ-, '•, •• ‖ 'ɪn ˌgroʊ ɪŋ
ingrown ˌɪn 'grəʊn ◄ →ˌɪŋ- ‖ -'groʊn ◄
inguinal 'ɪŋ gwɪn ᵊl §-gwən-
Ingush 'ɪŋ gʊʃ
Ingushetia ˌɪŋ gʊ 'ʃet i_ə -'ʃiːʃ ə
Ingvar 'ɪŋ vɑː ‖ -vɑːr
inhab|it ɪn 'hæb ɪt §-ət ‖ -ət **~ited** ɪt ɪd §ət-, -əd ‖ əţ əd **~iting** ɪt ɪŋ §ət- ‖ əţ ɪŋ **~its** ɪts §əts ‖ əts
inhabitable ɪn 'hæb ɪt əb ᵊl §-ət əb- ‖ -əţ əb-
inhabitant ɪn 'hæb ɪt ənt §-ət- ‖ -əţ ᵊnt **~s** s
inhalant ɪn 'heɪl ənt **~s** s
inhalation ˌɪn hə 'leɪʃ ᵊn -ə- **~s** z
inhalator 'ɪn hə leɪt ə ‖ -leɪţ ᵊr 'ɪn ᵊl eɪţ- **~s** z
inhal|e ɪn 'heɪᵊl ˌɪn- **~ed** d **~er/s** ə/z ‖ ᵊr/z **~es** z **~ing** ɪŋ
inharmonious ˌɪn hɑː 'məʊn i_əs ◄ ‖ -hɑːr 'moʊn- **~ly** li **~ness** nəs nɪs

inhere ɪn ˈhɪə ‖ -ˈhɪʳr ~d d ~s z inhering
ɪn ˈhɪər ɪŋ ‖ -ˈhɪr ɪŋ

INHERENT

BrE 1988
■-ˈher- □-ˈhɪər-
0   20   40   60   80   100%

inherent ɪn ˈher ənt -ˈhɪər- ‖ -ˈhɪr- —BrE
1988 poll panel preference: -ˈher- 66%, -ˈhɪər-
34%. ~ly li
inher|it ɪn ˈher ɪt -ət ‖ -lət ~ited ɪt ɪd ət-, -əd
‖ əţ əd ~iting ɪt ɪŋ ət- ‖ əţ ɪŋ ~its ɪts əts
‖ əts
inheritability ɪn ˌher ɪt ə ˈbɪl ət i -ət ə-, -ɪt i
‖ -əţ ə ˈbɪl əţ i
inheritable ɪn ˈher ɪt əb əl -ət •• ‖ -əţ əb əl
inheritanc|e ɪn ˈher ɪt ənts -ət- ‖ -əţ ənts ~es
ɪz əz
inhib|it ɪn ˈhɪb ɪt §-ət -lət ~ited/ly ɪt ɪd /li
§ət-, -əd /li ‖ əţ əd /li ~iting ɪt ɪŋ §ət- ‖ əţ ɪŋ
~its ɪts §əts ‖ əts
inhibition ˌɪn hɪ ˈbɪʃ ən -ɪ-, -ə- ~s z
inhibitor ɪn ˈhɪb ɪt ə §-ət- ‖ -əţ ʳr ~s z
inhibitory ɪn ˈhɪb ɪt ʳr i -ˈ•əţ ‖ -ə tɔːr i -tour i
inhospitab|le ˌɪn hɒ ˈspɪt əb əl ◄ ₍ˌ₎ɪn ˈhɒsp ɪt-,
-ˈ•ət- ‖ ˌɪn hɑː ˈspɪt- ₍ˌ₎ɪn ˈhɑːsp əţ- ~leness
əl nəs -nɪs ~ly li
in-house ˌɪn ˈhaʊs ◄
inhuman ɪn ˈhjuːm ən ˌɪn-, §-ˈjuːm- ~ly li
~ness nəs nɪs
inhumane ˌɪn hju ˈmeɪn ◄ §-ju- ~ly li
inhumanit|y ˌɪn hju ˈmæn ət li §,•ju-, -ɪt i
‖ -əţ li ~ies iz
Inigo ˈɪn ɪ gəʊ -ə- ‖ -goʊ
inimical ɪ ˈnɪm ɪk əl
inimitab|le ɪ ˈnɪm ɪt əb əl -ət əb- ‖ -əţ əb- ~ly
li
iniquitous ɪ ˈnɪk wɪt əs -wət- ‖ -wəţ əs ~ly li
~ness nəs nɪs
iniquit|y ɪ ˈnɪk wət li -wɪt- ‖ -wəţ li ~ies iz
initial ɪ ˈnɪʃ əl ~ed, ~led d ~ing, ~ling ɪŋ ~ly
i ~s z
initialis... —see initializ...
initialization ɪ ˌnɪʃ əl ˌaɪ ˈzeɪʃ ən -əl ˌɪ- ‖ -əl ə-
~s z
initializ|e ɪ ˈnɪʃ ə laɪz -əl aɪz ~ed d ~es ɪz əz
~ing ɪŋ
initi|ate v ɪ ˈnɪʃ i leɪt ~ated eɪt ɪd -əd ‖ eɪţ əd
~ates eɪts ~ating eɪt ɪŋ ‖ eɪţ ɪŋ
initiate n ɪ ˈnɪʃ i‿ət ‿ɪt, -eɪt ~s s
initiation ɪ ˌnɪʃ i ˈeɪʃ ən ~s z
initiative ɪ ˈnɪʃ ət ɪv -ˈnɪʃ i‿ət ɪv ‖ -əţ ɪv ~s z
initiator ɪ ˈnɪʃ i eɪt ə ‖ -eɪţ ʳr ~s z
inject ɪn ˈdʒekt ~ed ɪd əd ~ing ɪŋ ~s s
injection ɪn ˈdʒek ʃən ~s z
injector ɪn ˈdʒekt ə ‖ -ʳr ~s z
in-joke ˈɪn dʒəʊk ‖ -dʒoʊk ~s s
injudicious ˌɪn dʒu ˈdɪʃ əs ◄ ~ly li ~ness nəs
nɪs
Injun ˈɪndʒ ən ~s z
injunct v ɪn ˈdʒʌŋkt ~ed ɪd əd ~ing ɪŋ ~s s
injunction ɪn ˈdʒʌŋk ʃən ~s z

injure ˈɪndʒ ə ‖ -ʳr ~d d ~s z injuring ˈɪndʒ
ʳr‿ɪŋ
injurious ɪn ˈdʒʊər i‿əs △ɪn ˈdʒʊr ʳr əs ‖ ɪn ˈdʒʊr-
~ly li ~ness nəs nɪs
injur|y ˈɪndʒ ʳr li ~ies iz
ˈinjury ˌtime
injustic|e ɪn ˈdʒʌst ɪs ˌɪn-, -əs ~es ɪz əz
ink ɪŋk inked ɪŋkt inking ˈɪŋk ɪŋ inks ɪŋks
Inkatha ɪn ˈkɑːt ə →ɪŋ- —Zulu [iŋ kˈaː tha]
inkblot ˈɪŋk blɒt ‖ -blɑːt ~s s
inkbottle ˈɪŋk ˌbɒt əl ‖ -ˌbɑːţ əl ~s z
ink-cap ˈɪŋk kæp ~s s
Inkerman ˈɪŋk ə mən ‖ -ʳr- -mɑːn —Russ
[ɪn kjɪr ˈman]
inkhorn ˈɪŋk hɔːn ‖ -hɔːrn ~s s
inkjet ˈɪŋk dʒet
inkling ˈɪŋk lɪŋ ~s z
inkpad ˈɪŋk pæd ~s z
Inkpen ˈɪŋk pen
inkpot ˈɪŋk pɒt ‖ -pɑːt ~s s
inkstand ˈɪŋk stænd ~s z
inkwell ˈɪŋk wel ~s z
ink|y ˈɪŋk li ~ier i‿ə ‖ i‿ʳr ~iest i‿ɪst i‿əst
~iness i nəs i nɪs
INLA ˌaɪ en el ˈeɪ
inlaid ˌɪn ˈleɪd ◄
inland adj ˈɪn lənd -lænd
ˌInland ˈRevenue
inland adv ₍ˌ₎ɪn ˈlænd ˈ••
in-laws ˈɪn lɔːz ‖ -lɑːz
inlay n ˈɪn leɪ ~s z
in|lay v ˌɪn ˈleɪ ˈ•• ~laid ˈleɪd ◄ ~laying
ˈleɪ ɪŋ ~lays ˈleɪz
inlet ˈɪn lət -lɪt, -let ~s s
in-line ˌɪn ˈlaɪn ◄
ˌin-line ˈskates
in loco parentis ɪn ˌləʊk əʊ pə ˈrent ɪs §-əs
‖ ɪn ˌloʊk oʊ pə ˈrenţ əs
inly ˈɪn li
Inman ˈɪn mən →ˈɪm-
inmate ˈɪn meɪt →ˈɪm- ~s s
in medias res ɪn ˌmiːd i æs ˈreɪz →ɪm-
-ˌmeɪd-, -ˌmed-, -ɑːs ˈ••, ˌˌəsˈ••, -ˈreɪs
in memoriam ˌɪn mɪ ˈmɔːr i‿əm →ˌɪm-, ˌ•mə-,
-æm ‖ -ˈmoʊr-
in-migrant ˈɪn ˌmaɪg rənt →ˈɪm- ~s s
inmost ˈɪn məʊst →ˈɪm-, -məst ‖ -moʊst
inn ɪn (= in) inns ɪnz
ˌInns of ˈCourt
innards ˈɪn ədz ‖ ʳrdz
innate ˌɪ ˈneɪt ◄ ˌɪ-, ˌɪn- ~ly li ~ness nəs nɪs
ˌinnate ˈknowledge, •ˌ• ˈ••
inner ˈɪn ə ‖ -ʳr ~s z
ˌinner ˈcity; ˌInner ˈHebrides; ˌinner ˈman;
ˈinner ˌtube, ˌ•ˈ• ˈ•
inner-city ˌɪn ə ˈsɪt i ◄ ‖ ˌɪn ʳr ˈsɪt i ◄
innermost ˈɪn ə məʊst ‖ -ʳr moʊst
innerv|ate ˈɪn ɜːv leɪt -ə vleɪt ‖ ɪ ˈnɜːv leɪt
ˈɪn ʳr veɪt ~ated eɪt ɪd -əd ‖ eɪţ əd ~ates
eɪts ~ating eɪt ɪŋ ‖ eɪţ ɪŋ
innervation ˌɪn ɜː ˈveɪʃ ən -ə- ‖ ˌɪn ʳr- ~s z
Innes ˈɪn ɪs -ɪz, -əs, -əz
inning ˈɪn ɪŋ ~s z ~ses zɪz zəz

Innisfail ˌɪn ɪs ˈfeɪᵊl -əs-
Innisfree ˌɪn ɪs ˈfriː -əs-
innit *nonstd form of* **isn't it** ˈɪn ɪt -ət
innkeeper ˈɪn ˌkiːp ə →ˈɪŋ- ‖ -ᵊr ~s z
innocence ˈɪn əs ənᵗs -ʊs-
innocent, I~ ˈɪn əs ənt -ʊs- ~ly li ~s s
innocuous ɪ ˈnɒk ju‿əs ə- ‖ ɪ ˈnɑːk- ~ly li
  ~ness nəs nɪs
innominate ɪ ˈnɒm ɪn ət ə-, -ən-, -ɪt; -ɪ neɪt, -ə-
  ‖ ɪ ˈnɑːm-
inno|vate ˈɪn əʊ |veɪt ‖ -ə- ~vated veɪt ɪd -əd
  ‖ veɪt̬ əd ~vates veɪts ~vating
  veɪt ɪŋ ‖ veɪt̬ ɪŋ
innovation ˌɪn əʊ ˈveɪʃ ᵊn ‖ -ə- ~al ᵊl ◄ ~s z

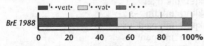

INNOVATIVE

■ ¦ •veɪt•	□ ¦ •vət•	▩ ¦ •¦ ••

BrE 1988

0   20   40   60   80   100%

innovative ˈɪn əʊ veɪt ɪv -vət ɪv; ɪ ˈnəʊv ət ɪv
  ‖ ˈɪn ə veɪt̬ ɪv —*BrE 1988 poll panel*
  preference: ' • •veɪt• 52%, ' • •vət• 42%,
  •¦ '•• 6%. ~ly li ~ness nəs nɪs
innovator ˈɪn ə veɪt ə ‖ -veɪt̬ ᵊr ~s z
innovatory ˈɪn ə veɪt ᵊr i -vət͵ᵊr i
  ‖ ˈɪn əv ə tɔːr i -tour i
Innoxa *tdmk* ɪ ˈnɒks ə ‖ ɪ ˈnɑːks ə
Innsbruck ˈɪnz brʊk —*Ger* [ˈʔɪn̩s bʁʊk]
innuendo ˌɪn ju ˈend əʊ ‖ -oʊ ~es z
innumerab|le ɪ ˈnjuːm ᵊr‿əb |ᵊl ə-, §ɪ ˈnuːm-
  ‖ ɪ ˈnuːm- ɪ ˈnjuːm- ~leness ᵊl nəs-nɪs ~ly
  li
innumeracy ɪ ˈnjuːm ᵊr‿əs i §ɪ ˈnuːm-
  ‖ ɪ ˈnuːm- ɪ ˈnjuːm-
innumerate ɪ ˈnjuːm ᵊr‿ət §ɪ ˈnuːm-, ‿ɪt
  ‖ ɪ ˈnuːm- ɪ ˈnjuːm- ~s s
inocu|late ɪ ˈnɒk ju |leɪt ə-, -jə- ‖ ɪ ˈnɑːk jə-
  ~lated leɪt ɪd -əd ‖ leɪt̬ əd ~lates leɪts
  ~lating leɪt ɪŋ ‖ leɪt̬ ɪŋ
inoculation ɪ ˌnɒk ju ˈleɪʃ ᵊn ə-, -jə-
  ‖ ɪ ˌnɑːk jə- ~s z
inoculator ɪ ˈnɒk ju leɪt ə ə-, -jə-
  ‖ ɪ ˈnɑːk jə leɪt̬ ᵊr ~s z
inoffensive ˌɪn ə ˈfenᵗs ɪv ◄ ~ly li ~ness nəs
  nɪs
inoperab|le ɪn ˈɒp ᵊr‿əb |ᵊl ͵ɪn- ‖ ɪn ˈɑːp- ~ly
  li
inoperative ɪn ˈɒp ᵊr‿ət ɪv ͵ɪn-, -ə reɪt ɪv
  ‖ ɪn ˈɑːp ᵊr‿ət̬ ɪv -ə reɪt̬ ɪv ~ness nəs nɪs
inopportune ɪn ˈɒp ə tjuːn ͵ɪn-, →§-tʃuːn;
  -,•¦•'• ‖ ɪn ˌɑːp ᵊr ˈtuːn ◄ -ˈtjuːn ~ly li
  ~ness nəs nɪs
inordinate ɪn ˈɔːd ɪn ət ən-, -ᵊn‿•, -ɪt
  ‖ -ˈɔːrd ᵊn‿ət ~ly li ~ness nəs nɪs
inorganic ˌɪn ɔː ˈgæn ɪk ◄ ‖ -ɔːr- ~ally ᵊl‿i
  ͵inor͵ganic ˈchemistry
Inouye ɪ ˈnuː eɪ
in-patient ˈɪn ͵peɪʃ ᵊnt →ˈɪm- ~s s
in|put *v, n* ˈɪn |pʊt →ˈɪm- ~puts pʊts ~putted
  pʊt ɪd -əd ‖ pʊt̬ əd ~putting pʊt ɪŋ ‖ pʊt̬ ɪŋ
input/output, input-output ͵ɪn pʊt ˈaʊt pʊt
  →, ͵ɪm- ‖ -pʊt̬-
inquest ˈɪŋ kwest ˈɪn- ~s s

inquietude ɪn ˈkwaɪ‿ə tjuːd →ɪŋ-, ͵‿ɪ tjuːd,
  →§-tʃuːd ‖ -tuːd -tjuːd
inquire ɪn ˈkwaɪ‿ə →ɪŋ-, ən- ‖ -ˈkwaɪ‿ᵊr ~d d
  ~s z inquiring/ly ɪn ˈkwaɪ‿ᵊr ɪŋ /li →ɪŋ-, ən-
  ‖ -ˈkwaɪ‿ᵊr ɪŋ /li

INQUIRY

■ ¦ •• •	□ ¦ •¦ ••	

AmE 1993

0   20   40   60   80   100%

inquir|y ɪn ˈkwaɪ‿ᵊr li →ɪŋ-, ən- ‖ ˈɪn kwər li,
  →ˈɪŋ-, -kwaɪ‿ᵊr-; ɪn ˈkwaɪ‿ᵊr i, →ɪŋ- —*AmE
  1993 poll panel preference:* ' • •• 74%, •¦ '••
  26%. ~ies iz
inquisition, I~ ͵ɪŋ kwɪ ˈzɪʃ ᵊn ͵ɪn-, -kwə- ~s z
inquisitive ɪn ˈkwɪz ət ɪv →ɪŋ-, -ɪt- ‖ -ət̬ ɪv
  ~ly li ~ness nəs nɪs
inquisitor ɪn ˈkwɪz ɪt ə →ɪŋ-, -ət- ‖ -ət̬ ᵊr ~s z
inquisitorial ɪn ͵kwɪz ə ˈtɔːr i‿əl ◄→ɪŋ-, ͵•͵•͵•-,
  -ɪ'•- ‖ -ˈtour- ~ly i
inquorate ͵ɪn ˈkwɔːr eɪt ◄→, ͵ɪŋ-, -ət,
  -ɪt ‖ -ˈkwour-
in re (ᵢ)ɪn ˈriː- ˈreɪ
in-residence (ᵢ)ɪn ˈrez ɪd ənᵗs -əd-
inroad ˈɪn rəʊd ‖ -roʊd ~s z
inrush ˈɪn rʌʃ ~es ɪz əz
insalubrious ͵ɪn sə ˈluːb ri‿əs ◄ -ˈljuːb- ~ly li
  ~ness nəs nɪs
ins and outs ͵ɪnz ᵊn ˈaʊts -ᵊnd-
insane ɪn ˈseɪn ͵ɪn- ~ly li
insanitar|y ɪn ˈsæn ə͵tᵊr li ͵ɪn-, -ʳ•͵ɪ͵ ‖ -ə ter li
  ~iness i nəs i nɪs
insanit|y ɪn ˈsæn ət li ͵ɪn-, -ɪt i ‖ -ət̬ li ~ies iz
insatiab|le ɪn ˈseɪʃ əb |ᵊl -ˈseɪʃ i‿əb |ᵊl ~leness
  ᵊl nəs -nɪs ~ly li
insatiate ɪn ˈseɪʃ i‿ət ͵‿ɪt, -eɪt ~ly li ~ness nəs
  nɪs
inscape ˈɪn skeɪp ~d t ~s s
inscrib|e ɪn ˈskraɪb ~ed d ~es z ~ing ɪŋ
inscription ɪn ˈskrɪp ʃᵊn ~s z
inscrutability ɪn ͵skruːt ə ˈbɪl ət i ͵•͵•͵•-, -ɪt i
  ‖ ɪn ͵skruːt̬ ə ˈbɪl ət̬ i
inscrutab|le ɪn ˈskruːt əb |ᵊl ͵ɪn- ‖ -ˈskruːt̬-
  ~leness ᵊl nəs -nɪs ~ly li
insect ˈɪn sekt ~s s
insecticidal ɪn ͵sekt ɪ ˈsaɪd ᵊl ◄ -ə-
insecticide ɪn ˈsekt ɪ saɪd -ə- ~s z
insectivore ɪn ˈsekt ɪ vɔː -ə- ‖ -vɔːr -voʊr ~s z
insectivorous ͵ɪn sek ˈtɪv ᵊr‿əs ◄
insecure ͵ɪn sɪ ˈkjʊə ◄ -sə-, -ˈkjɔː- ‖ -ˈkjʊᵊr ◄
  ~ly li ~ness nəs nɪs
insecurit|y ͵ɪn sɪ ˈkjʊər ət i ͵•͵•sə-, -ˈkjɔːr-, -ɪt i
  ‖ -ˈkjʊr ət̬ li ~ies iz
insemi|nate ɪn ˈsem ɪ |neɪt -ə- ~nated neɪt ɪd
  -əd ‖ neɪt̬ əd ~nates neɪts ~nating
  neɪt ɪŋ ‖ neɪt̬ ɪŋ
insemination ɪn ͵sem ɪ ˈneɪʃ ᵊn ͵ɪn-, -ə- ~s z
inseminator ɪn ˈsem ɪ neɪt ə -ə -'•ə- ‖ -ə neɪt̬ ᵊr
  ~s z
insensate ɪn ˈsenᵗs eɪt ͵ɪn-, -ət, -ɪt ~ly li
insensibility ɪn ͵senᵗs ə ˈbɪl ət i ͵•͵•͵•'•-, -ɪ'••-,
  -ɪt i ‖ -ət̬ i
insensib|le ɪn ˈsenᵗs əb |ᵊl ͵ɪn-, -ɪb- ~ly li

insensitive ɪn 'sen⁀s ət ɪv ˌɪn-, -ɪt- ‖ -ət̬ ɪv **~ly**
li **~ness** nəs nɪs
insensitivity ɪn ˌsen⁀s ə 'tɪv ət i ˌˌ•ˌ•••'••-, -ɪ'••-,
-ɪt i ‖ -ət̬ i
insenti|ence ɪn 'sen⁀tʃ lən⁀ts -'sen⁀tʃ i‿lən⁀ts **~ent**
ənt
inseparability ɪn ˌsep ər‿ə 'bɪl ət i ˌ•ˌ•ˌ•-, -ɪt i
‖ -ət̬ i
inseparab|le ɪn 'sep ər‿əb ləl ˌɪn- **~leness**
əl nəs -nɪs **~ly** li
in|sert v ɪn |'sɜːt -'zɜːt ‖ -ɪ'sɜ˞ːt **~serted**
'sɜːt ɪd 'zɜːt-, -əd ‖ 'sɜ˞ːt̬ əd **~serting**
'sɜːt ɪŋ 'zɜːt- ‖ 'sɜ˞ːt̬ ɪŋ **~serts** 'sɜːts 'zɜːts
‖ 'sɜ˞ːts
insert n 'ɪn sɜːt -zɜːt ‖ -sɜ˞ːt **~s** s
insertion ɪn 'sɜːʃ ən -'zɜːʃ- ‖ -'sɜ˞ːʃ- **~s** z
in-service ˌɪn 'sɜːv ɪs ◂ -əs ‖ -'sɜ˞ːv-
ˌin-ˌservice 'training
inset n 'ɪn set **~s** s
in|set v ɪn |'set '•• **~sets** 'sets **~setting**
'set ɪŋ ‖ 'set̬ ɪŋ
inshore ˌɪn 'ʃɔː ◂ ‖ -'ʃɔːr ◂ -'ʃoʊr
ˌinshore 'fishing
inside ˌɪn 'saɪd ◂ —but '•• when contrasted with
outside **~s** z
ˌinside 'job, '•• •; ˌinside 'left; ˌinside 'out;
ˌinside 'track
insider ˌɪn 'saɪd ə ◂ ‖ -ᵊr **~s** z
inˌsider 'trading,, •,'•• '••
insidious ɪn 'sɪd i‿əs **~ly** li **~ness** nəs nɪs
insight 'ɪn saɪt **~s** s
insightful 'ɪn saɪt fʊl •'•• **~ly** i
insignia ɪn 'sɪg ni‿ə **~s** z
insignificanc|e ˌɪn sɪg 'nɪf ɪk ən⁀ts **~y** i
insignificant ˌɪn sɪg 'nɪf ɪk ənt ◂ **~ly** li
insincere ˌɪn sɪn 'sɪə ◂ -sᵊn- ‖ -'sɪᵊr ◂ **~ly** li
insincerity ˌɪn sɪn 'ser ət i ˌ•sᵊn-, -ɪt i ‖ -ət̬ i
insinu|ate ɪn 'sɪn ju leɪt **~ated** eɪt ɪd -əd
‖ eɪt̬ əd **~ates** eɪts **~ating** eɪt ɪŋ ‖ eɪt̬ ɪŋ
insinuation ɪn ˌsɪn ju 'eɪʃ ən ˌ•,•- **~s** z
insipid ɪn 'sɪp ɪd §-əd **~ly** li **~ness** nəs nɪs
insipidity ˌɪn sɪ 'pɪd ət i §,•sə-, -ɪt i ‖ -ət̬ i
insist ɪn 'sɪst **~ed** ɪd əd **~ing** ɪŋ **~s** s
insistenc|e ɪn 'sɪst ən⁀ts **~y** i
insistent ɪn 'sɪst ənt **~ly** li
in situ ₍ᵢ₎ɪn 'sɪt juː -'sɪtʃ uː, -'saɪt juː, -'saɪtʃ uː
‖ -'saɪt uː -'siːt-, -'sɪt-, -juː
insobriety ˌɪn səʊ 'braɪ‿ət i -ɪt i
‖ ˌɪn sə 'braɪ ət̬ i
insofar ˌɪn səʊ 'fɑː ◂ ‖ -sə 'fɑːr
insolation ˌɪn səʊ 'leɪʃ ⁿn -soʊ-
insole 'ɪn səʊl →-sɒʊl ‖ -soʊl **~s** z
insolence 'ɪn⁀ts əl ən⁀ts
insolent 'ɪn⁀ts əl ənt **~ly** li
insolubility ɪn ˌsɒl ju 'bɪl ət i ˌ•ˌ•ˌ•-, -ɪt i
‖ ˌɪn ˌsɑːl jə 'bɪl ət̬ i ˌ•ˌ•-
insolub|le ɪn 'sɒl jʊb ləl ˌɪn- ‖ -'sɑːl jəb ləl
~leness əl nəs -nɪs **~ly** li
insolvab|le ɪn 'sɒlv əb ləl ˌɪn-, §-'səʊlv-
‖ -'sɑːlv- **~ly** li
insolvenc|y ɪn 'sɒlv ən⁀ts li ˌɪn- ‖ -'sɑːlv- **~ies**
iz
insolvent ɪn 'sɒlv ənt ˌɪn- ‖ -'sɑːlv- **~s** s

insomnia ɪn 'sɒm ni‿ə ‖ -'sɑːm-
insomniac ɪn 'sɒm ni æk ‖ -'sɑːm- **~s** s
insomuch ˌɪn səʊ 'mʌtʃ ◂ ‖ -sə-
insouciance ɪn 'suːs i‿ən⁀ts -ɒ̃s —Fr
[ɛ̃ su sjɑ̃:s]
insouciant ɪn 'suːs i‿ənt -ɒ̃ —Fr [ɛ̃ su sjɑ̃] **~ly**
li
inspan 'ɪn spæn •'• **~ned** d **~ning** ɪŋ **~s** z
inspect ɪn 'spekt **~ed** ɪd əd **~ing** ɪŋ **~s** s
inspection ɪn 'spek ʃᵊn **~s** z
inspector ɪn 'spekt ə ‖ -ᵊr **~s** z
inspectorate ɪn 'spekt ər‿ət ‿ɪt **~s** s
inspectorship ɪn 'spekt ə ʃɪp ‖ -ᵊr- **~s** s
inspiration ˌɪn spə 'reɪʃ ᵊn -spɪ-, -spaɪᵊ- **~s** z
inspirational ˌɪn spə 'reɪʃ ᵊn‿əl ◂ ˌ•spɪ-,
ˌˌ•spaɪᵊ- **~ly** i
inspiratory ɪn 'spaɪᵊr ət‿ər i -'spɪr- ‖ -ə tɔːr i
-toʊri
inspire ɪn 'spaɪ‿ə ‖ -'spaɪ‿ᵊr **~d** d **~s** z
inspiring/ly ɪn 'spaɪ‿ər ɪŋ /li ‖ -'spaɪ‿ᵊr ɪŋ /li
inspirer ɪn 'spaɪ‿ər ə ‖ -'spaɪ‿ᵊr ᵊr **~s** z
inspir|it ɪn 'spɪr |ɪt -ət ‖ -|ət **~ited** ɪt ɪd ət-, -əd
‖ ət̬ əd **~iting** ɪt ɪŋ ət- ‖ ət̬ ɪŋ **~its** ɪts əts
‖ əts
inspiss|ate ɪn 'spɪs |eɪt '•• **~ated** eɪt ɪd -əd
‖ eɪt̬ əd **~ates** eɪts **~ating** eɪt ɪŋ ‖ eɪt̬ ɪŋ
inst ɪn⁀tst or as **instant, institute**
instabilit|y ˌɪn stə 'bɪl ət i li -ɪt i ‖ -ət̬ li **~ies** iz
instal, install|l ɪn 'stɔːl ‖ -'stɑːl **~led** d **~ling**
ɪŋ **instals, installs** ɪn 'stɔːlz ‖ -'stɑːlz
installation ˌɪn⁀tst ə 'leɪʃ ᵊn **~s** z
installer ɪn 'stɔːl ə ‖ -ᵊr -'stɑːl- **~s** z
instalment, installment ɪn 'stɔːl mənt
‖ -'stɑːl- **~s** s
inˈstallment plan
Instamatic tdmk ˌɪn⁀tst ə 'mæt ɪk ◂ ‖ -'mæt̬ ɪk ◂
~s s
instanc|e 'ɪn⁀tst ən⁀ts **~ed** t **~es** ɪz əz **~ing** ɪŋ
instant 'ɪn⁀tst ənt **~ly** li
instantaneous ˌɪn⁀tst ən 'teɪn i‿əs ◂ **~ly** li
~ness nəs nɪs
instanter ɪn 'stænt ə ‖ -'stænt̬ ᵊr
instanti|ate ɪn 'stæn⁀tʃ i leɪt **~ated** eɪt ɪd -əd
‖ eɪt̬ əd **~ates** eɪts **~ating** eɪt ɪŋ ‖ eɪt̬ ɪŋ
instantiation ɪn ˌstæn⁀tʃ i 'eɪʃ ᵊn **~s** z
instead ɪn 'sted
instep 'ɪn step **~s** s
insti|gate 'ɪn⁀tst ɪ |geɪt -ə- **~gated** geɪt ɪd -əd
‖ geɪt̬ əd **~gates** geɪts **~gating**
geɪt ɪŋ ‖ geɪt̬ ɪŋ
instigation ˌɪn⁀tst ɪ 'geɪʃ ᵊn -ə- **~s** z
instigator 'ɪn⁀tst ɪ geɪt ə '•ə- ‖ -geɪt̬ ᵊr **~s** z
instil, instill|l ɪn 'stɪl **~led** d **~ling** ɪŋ **instils,**
instills ɪn 'stɪlz
instillation ˌɪn⁀tst ɪ 'leɪʃ ᵊn -ə-
instiller ɪn 'stɪl ə ‖ -ᵊr **~s** z
instilment, instillment ɪn 'stɪl mənt
instinct 'ɪn stɪŋ⁀kt **~s** s
instinctive ɪn 'stɪŋ⁀kt ɪv **~ly** li **~ness** nəs nɪs
instinctual ɪn 'stɪŋ⁀kt ju‿əl -'stɪŋ⁀ktʃu‿əl
‖ -'stɪŋ⁀k tʃu‿əl **~ly** i
insti|tute 'ɪn⁀tst ɪ |tjuːt -ə-, →§-tʃuːt ‖ -|tuːt
-tjuːt **~tuted** tjuːt ɪd §→tʃuːt-, -əd ‖ tuːt̬ əd

tjuːʈ ~**tutes** tjuːts →§tʃuːts ‖ tuːts tjuːts
~**tuting** tjuːt ɪŋ →§tʃuːt- ‖ tuːʈ ɪŋ tjuːʈ-
institution ˌɪntˢt ɪ 'tjuːʃ ᵊn -ə-, →§-'tʃuːʃ-
‖ -'tuːʃ ᵊn -'tjuːʃ- ~**al** ᵊl ~**ally** ᵊl i ~**s** z
institutionalis... —*see* **institutionaliz...**
institutionalization
ˌɪntˢt ɪ ˌtjuːʃ ᵊn_ᵊl aɪ 'zeɪʃ ᵊn ˌ•ə-,
→§-ˌtʃuːʃ-, -ɪ'•- ‖ -,tuːʃ ᵊn_ᵊl ə- -ˌt'juːʃ-
institutionaliz|e ˌɪntˢt ɪ 'tjuːʃ ᵊn_ə laɪz ˌ•ə-,
→§-'tʃuːʃ-, -ᵊl aɪz ‖ -'tuːʃ- -'tjuːʃ- ~**ed** d
~**es** ɪz əz ~**ing** ɪŋ
in-store ˌɪn 'stɔː ◄ ‖ -'stɔːr ◄ -'stoʊr
ˌin-store 'banking
Instow 'ɪn stəʊ ‖ -stoʊ
instruct ɪn 'strʌkt ~**ed** ɪd əd ~**ing** ɪŋ ~**s** s
instruction ɪn 'strʌk ʃᵊn ~**s** z
instructional ɪn 'strʌk ʃᵊn_ᵊl ~**ly** i
instructive ɪn 'strʌkt ɪv ~**ly** li ~**ness** nəs nɪs
instructor ɪn 'strʌkt ə ‖ -ᵊr ~**s** z ~**ship/s** ʃɪp/s
instructress ɪn 'strʌk trəs -trɪs, -tres ~**es** ɪz əz
instrument *n* 'ɪntˢ trə mənt -tru- ~**s** s
'instrument ˌpanel
instrument *v* 'ɪntˢ trə ˌment -tru-, ˌ•'•• —*see
note at* -ment ~**mented** ment ɪd -əd ‖ menʈ
əd ~**menting** ment ɪŋ ‖ menʈ ɪŋ ~**ments**
menʈs
instrumental ˌɪntˢ trə 'ment ᵊl ◄ -tru- ‖ -'menʈ
ᵊl ~**ly** i ~**s** z
instrumentalist ˌɪntˢ trə 'ment ᵊl ɪst ˌ•tru-,
§-əst ‖ -'menʈ- ~**s** s
instrumentalit|y ˌɪntˢ trə men 'tæl ət li ˌ•tru-,
-mən'•-, -ɪt i ‖ -əʈ li ~**ies** ɪz
instrumentation ˌɪntˢ trə men 'teɪʃ ᵊn ˌ•tru-,
-mən'•-
insubordinate ˌɪn sə 'bɔːd ɪn ət ◄ -ᵊn_•, -ɪt
‖ -'bɔːrd ᵊn_ət ~**ly** li ~**s** s
insubordination ˌɪn sə ˌbɔːd ə 'neɪʃ ᵊn -ˌ•ɪ-
‖ -ˌbɔːrd ᵊn 'eɪʃ ᵊn
insubstantial ˌɪn səb 'stæntˢ ᵊl ◄ §-sʌb-,
-'stɑːntˢ- ~**ly** i
insufferab|le ɪn 'sʌf ᵊr_əb ᵊl ~**leness** ᵊl nəs
-nɪs ~**ly** li
insufficienc|y ˌɪn sə 'fɪʃ ᵊntˢ li ~**ies** ɪz
insufficient ˌɪn sə 'fɪʃ ᵊnt ◄ ~**ly** li
insuf|flate 'ɪn sə ˌfleɪt ɪn 'sʌf leɪt, '•••
~**flated** fleɪt ɪd -əd ‖ fleɪʈ əd ~**flates** fleɪts
~**flating** fleɪt ɪŋ ‖ fleɪʈ ɪŋ
insufflation ˌɪn sə 'fleɪʃ ᵊn -sʌ- ~**s** z
insular 'ɪntˢ jʊl ə -jəl-; §'ɪntˢ ʊl ə, §-əl- ‖ 'ɪntˢ
əl ᵊr -jəl-; 'ɪntˢ- ~**ly** li
insularism 'ɪntˢ jʊl ə ˌrɪz əm '•jəl-; §'ɪntˢ ʊl-,
§'•əl- ‖ 'ɪntˢ əl- '•jəl-; 'ɪntˢ-
insularity ˌɪntˢ jʊ 'lær ət i ˌ•jə-, -ɪt i; §ˌɪntˢ u-
‖ ˌɪntˢ ə 'lær əʈ i ˌ•jə-, -'ler-; ˌɪntˢ-
insu|late 'ɪntˢ jʊ ˌleɪt -jə-; §'ɪntˢ u- ‖ -ə- *(*)*
~**lated** leɪt ɪd -əd ‖ leɪʈ əd ~**lates** leɪts
~**lating** leɪt ɪŋ ‖ leɪʈ ɪŋ
'insulating ˌtape
insulation ˌɪntˢ jʊ 'leɪʃ ᵊn -jə-; §ˌɪntˢ u- ‖ -ə-
insulator 'ɪntˢ jʊ leɪt ə '•jə-; §'ɪntˢ u-
‖ -ə leɪʈ ᵊr ~**s** z
insulin 'ɪntˢ jʊl ɪn -jəl-, §-ən; §'ɪntˢ ʊl-, -əl-
‖ -əl_ən

insult *v* ɪn 'sʌlt ~**ed** ɪd əd ~**ing** ɪŋ ~**s** s
insult *n* 'ɪn sʌlt ~**s** s
insuperability ɪn ˌsuːp ᵊr_ə 'bɪl ət i -ˌsjuːp-,
ˌ•ˌ•,•-, -ɪt i ‖ -əʈ i
insuperab|le ɪn 'suːp ᵊr_əb ᵊl ˌɪn-, -'sjuːp-
~**leness** ᵊl nəs -nɪs ~**ly** li
insupportab|le ˌɪn sə 'pɔːt əb ᵊl ◄ ‖ -'pɔːrʈ-
-'poʊrʈ- ~**leness** ᵊl nəs -nɪs ~**ly** li
insurable ɪn 'ʃʊər əb ᵊl -'ʃɔːr- ‖ -'ʃʊr- -'ʃɝː-

insuranc|e ɪn 'ʃʊər ᵊntˢ -'ʃɔːr- ‖ -'ʃʊr- -'ʃɝː-;
'ɪn ʃʊr- —*AmE 1993 poll panel preference:*
•'•• *88%,* '••• *12%.* ~**es** ɪz əz
in'surance ˌpolicy
insure ɪn 'ʃʊə -'ʃɔː ‖ -'ʃʊᵊr -'ʃɝː ~**d** d ~**s** z
insuring ɪn 'ʃʊər ɪŋ -'ʃɔːr- ‖ -'ʃʊr ɪŋ -'ʃɝː-
insurer ɪn 'ʃʊər ə -'ʃɔːr ə ‖ -'ʃʊr ᵊr -'ʃɝː- ~**s** z
insurgenc|e ɪn 'sɜːdʒ ᵊntˢ ‖ -'sɜːdʒ- ~**y** i
insurgent ɪn 'sɜːdʒ ᵊnt ‖ -'sɜːdʒ- ~**s** s
insurmountab|le
ˌɪn sə 'maʊnt əb ᵊl ◄ ˌɪn sᵊr 'maʊnʈ- ~**ly** li
insurrection ˌɪn sə 'rek ʃᵊn ~**s** z
insurrectionar|y ˌɪn sə 'rek ʃᵊn_ᵊr li -ʃᵊn ᵊr_li
‖ -ʃə ner li ~**ies** ɪz
inswing 'ɪn swɪŋ ~**s** z
inswinger 'ɪn ˌswɪŋ ə ‖ -ᵊr ~**s** z
intact ɪn 'tækt ˌɪn- ~**ness** nəs nɪs
intaglio ɪn 'tɑːl iˌəʊ -'tæl- ‖ ɪn 'tæl joʊ -'tɑːl-
—*It* [in 'taʎ ʎo] ~**s** z
intake, I- 'ɪn teɪk ~**s** s
intangibility ɪn ˌtændʒ ə 'bɪl ət i ˌ•ˌ•,•-, -ɪ'•-,
-ɪt i ‖ -əʈ i
intangib|le ɪn 'tændʒ əb ᵊl ◄ ˌɪn-, -ɪb- ~**leness**
ᵊl nəs -nɪs ~**ly** li
Intasun *tdmk* 'ɪnt ə sʌn
integer 'ɪnt ɪdʒ ə -ədʒ- ‖ -ᵊr ~**s** z
integral 'ɪnt ɪg rᵊl -əg-; ɪn 'teg-; ⚠'ɪntr ɪg ᵊl,
-əg- ‖ 'ɪnʈ ɪg rᵊl ɪn 'teg- ~**ly** i ~**s** z
ˌintegral 'calculus
inte|grate 'ɪnt ɪ ˌgreɪt -ə- ‖ 'ɪnʈ ə- ~**grated**
greɪt ɪd -əd ‖ greɪʈ əd ~**grates** greɪts
~**grating** greɪt ɪŋ ‖ greɪʈ ɪŋ
ˌintegrated 'circuit
integration ˌɪnt ɪ 'greɪʃ ᵊn -ə- ‖ ˌɪnʈ ə- ~**s** z
integrative 'ɪnt ɪ greɪt ɪv '•ə-, -grət- ‖ 'ɪnʈ
ə greɪʈ ɪv
integrator 'ɪnt ɪ greɪt ə '•ə- ‖ 'ɪnʈ ə greɪʈ ᵊr
~**s** z
integrity ɪn 'teg rət i -rɪt- ‖ -rəʈ i
integument ɪn 'teg ju mənt ‖ -jə- ~**s** s
Intel *tdmk* 'ɪn tel
intellect 'ɪnt ə lekt -ɪ-, -ᵊl ekt ‖ 'ɪnʈ ᵊl ekt ~**s** s
intellectual ˌɪnt ə 'lek tʃuˌᵊl ◄ ˌ•ɪ-, -ᵊl 'ek-,
-tjuˌ•-, -ʃuˌ• ‖ ˌɪnʈ ᵊl 'ek- ~**ly** i ~**s** z
intelligenc|e ɪn 'tel ɪdʒ ᵊntˢ -ədʒ- ~**es** ɪz əz
in'telligence ˌofficer; in'telligence
ˌquotient; in'telligence test
intelligent ɪn 'tel ɪdʒ ᵊnt -ədʒ- ~**ly** li

intelligentsia ɪn ˌtel ɪ 'dʒent si_ə ˌˈˌ•ˌ•-, -'gent-
~s z

intelligibility ɪn ˌtel ɪdʒ ə 'bɪl ət i -ˌ•ədʒ-, -ɪ'•-,
-ɪt i ‖ -ət̬ i

intelligib|le ɪn 'tel ɪdʒ əb |ᵊl -ˌ•ədʒ-, -ɪb ᵊl **~ly**
li

Intelsat 'ɪn tel sæt

intemperance ɪn 'temp ᵊr_ənᵗs ˌɪn-

intemperate ɪn 'temp ᵊr_ət ˌɪn-, ˌɪt **~ly** li
~ness nəs nɪs

intend ɪn 'tend **~ed** ɪd əd **~ing** ɪŋ **~s** z

intendant ɪn 'tend ᵊnt **~s** s

intens|e ɪn 'tenᵗs **~ely** li **~eness** nəs nɪs **~er**
ə ‖ᵊr **~est** ɪst əst

intensification ɪn ˌtenᵗs ɪf ɪ 'keɪʃ ᵊn -ˌ•əf-,
§-əˈ•- **~s** z

intensifier ɪn 'tenᵗs ɪ faɪ_ə -ˈ•ə- ‖ -faɪ_ᵊr **~s** z

intensi|fy ɪn 'tenᵗs ɪ |faɪ -ə- **~fied** faɪd **~fies**
faɪz **~fying** faɪ ɪŋ

intension ɪn 'tenᵗʃ ᵊn (= intention) **~s** z

intensional ɪn 'tenᵗʃ ᵊn_əl (= intentional)

intensit|y ɪn 'tenᵗs ət i -ɪt- ‖ -ət̬ i **~ies** iz

intensive ɪn 'tenᵗs ɪv **~ly** li **~ness** nəs nɪs **~s**
z

   in ˌtensive 'care

intent n, adj ɪn 'tent **~ly** li **~ness** nəs nɪs **~s** s

intention ɪn 'tenᵗʃ ᵊn **~s** z

intentional ɪn 'tenᵗʃ ᵊn_əl **~ly** i

inter v 'bury' ɪn 'tɜː ‖ -'tɜ·ː **~red** d **interring**
ɪn 'tɜːr ɪŋ ‖ -'tɜ·ː ɪŋ **~s** z

inter prep, Lat 'ɪnt ə ‖ 'ɪnt̬ ᵊr

inter- ˌɪnt ə ‖ ˌɪnt̬ ᵊr, but before a vowel sound
ˌɪnt ᵊr ‖ ˌɪnt̬ ᵊr — **intermesh** v
ˌɪnt ə 'meʃ ‖ ˌɪnt̬ ᵊr- — **interurban** ˌɪnt ər
'ɜːb ən ◂ ‖ ˌɪnt̬ ər 'ɜ·ːb-

interact v ˌɪnt ər 'ækt ‖ ˌɪnt̬ ər- **~ed** ɪd əd
~ing ɪŋ **~s** s

interaction ˌɪnt ər 'æk ʃ°n ‖ ˌɪnt̬ ər- **~s** z

interactive ˌɪnt ər 'ækt ɪv ◂ ‖ ˌɪnt̬ ər- **~ly** li

inter alia ˌɪnt ər 'eɪl i_ə -'ɑːl-, -'æl- ‖ ˌɪnt̬ ər-

inter|breed v ˌɪnt ə 'briːd ‖ ˌɪnt̬ ᵊr- **~bred**
'bred **~breeding** 'briːd ɪŋ **~breeds** 'briːdz

intercalary ɪn 'tɜːk ᵊl_ər i ˌɪnt ə 'kæl ər i◂,
-'keɪl- ‖ ɪn 'tɜ·ːk ə ler i ˌɪnt̬ ᵊr 'kæl ər i ◂

interca|late ɪn 'tɜːk ə |leɪt -ᵊl eɪt;
ˌɪnt ə kə 'lleɪt ‖ ɪn 'tɜ·ːk ə |leɪt ˌɪnt̬ ᵊr kə 'lleɪt
~lated leɪt ɪd -əd ‖ leɪt̬ əd **~lates** leɪts
~lating leɪt ɪŋ ‖ leɪt̬ ɪŋ

intercalation ɪn ˌtɜːk ə 'leɪʃ ᵊn ˌɪnt ə kə-
‖ ɪn ˌtɜ·ːk ə- ˌɪnt̬ ᵊr kə- **~s** z

interced|e ˌɪnt ə 'siːd ‖ ˌɪnt̬ ᵊr- **~ed** ɪd əd
~er/s ə/z ‖ ᵊr/z **~es** z **~ing** ɪŋ

intercept v ˌɪnt ə 'sept 'ˌˌ• ‖ ˌɪnt̬ ᵊr- **~ed** ɪd
əd **~ing** ɪŋ **~s** s

intercept n 'ɪnt ə sept ‖ 'ɪnt̬ ᵊr- **~s** s

interception ˌɪnt ə 'sep ʃ°n ‖ ˌɪnt̬ ᵊr- **~s** z

interceptor ˌɪnt ə 'sept ə ‖ ˌɪnt̬ ᵊr 'sept ᵊr **~s** z

intercession ˌɪnt ə 'seʃ ᵊn ‖ ˌɪnt̬ ᵊr- **~al** _əl ◂
~s z

intercessor ˌɪnt ə 'ses ə 'ˌˌˌˌ ‖ ˌɪnt̬ ᵊr 'ses ᵊr
~s z

intercessory ˌɪnt ə 'ses ər_i ◂ ‖ ˌɪnt̬ ᵊr-

interchang|e v ˌɪnt ə 'tʃeɪndʒ ◂ ‖ ˌɪnt̬ ᵊr- **~ed** d
~es ɪz əz **~ing** ɪŋ

interchang|e n 'ɪnt ə tʃeɪndʒ ‖ 'ɪnt̬ ᵊr- **~es** ɪz
əz

interchangeability ˌɪnt ə ˌtʃeɪndʒ ə 'bɪl ət i
-ɪt i ‖ ˌɪnt̬ ᵊr ˌtʃeɪndʒ ə 'bɪl ət̬ i

interchangeab|le ˌɪnt ə 'tʃeɪndʒ əb |ᵊl ◂ ‖ ˌɪnt̬
ᵊr- **~leness** ᵊl nəs -nɪs **~ly** li

inter-city, intercity ˌɪnt ə 'sɪt i ◂ ‖ ˌɪnt̬ ᵊr 'sɪt̬ i ◂

intercollegiate ˌɪnt ə kə 'liːdʒ ət ◂ -ɪt,
-'liːdʒ i_ət, ˌɪt ‖ ˌɪnt̬ ᵊr-

intercom 'ɪnt ə kɒm ‖ 'ɪnt̬ ᵊr kɑːm **~s** z

intercommuni|cate ˌɪnt ə kə 'mjuːn ɪ |keɪt
-'•ə- ‖ ˌɪnt̬ ᵊr- **~cated** keɪt ɪd -əd ‖ keɪt̬ əd
~cates keɪts **~cating** keɪt ɪŋ ‖ keɪt̬ ɪŋ

intercommunication
ˌɪnt ə kə ˌmjuːn ɪ 'keɪʃ ᵊn -ˌ•ə- ‖ ˌɪnt̬ ᵊr- **~s**
z

intercommunion ˌɪnt ə kə 'mjuːn i_ən ‖ ˌɪnt̬
ᵊr-

interconnect ˌɪnt ə kə 'nekt ◂ ‖ ˌɪnt̬ ᵊr- **~ed** ɪd
əd **~ing** ɪŋ **~s** s

intercontinental ˌɪnt ə ˌkɒnt ɪ 'nent ᵊl ◂ -ˌ•ə-
‖ ˌɪnt̬ ᵊr ˌkɑːnt ᵊn 'ent̬ ᵊl ◂

   ˌinterconti ˌnental ˌbal ˌlistic 'missile

intercostal ˌɪnt ə 'kɒst ᵊl ◂ ‖ ˌɪnt̬ ᵊr 'kɑːst ᵊl ◂

intercourse 'ɪnt ə kɔːs ‖ 'ɪnt̬ ᵊr kɔːrs -koʊrs

intercurrent ˌɪnt ə 'kʌr ənt ◂ ‖ ˌɪnt̬ ᵊr 'kɜ·ː- **~ly**
li

inter|cut v ˌɪnt ə |'kʌt ‖ ˌɪnt̬ ᵊr- **~cuts** 'kʌts
~cutting 'kʌt ɪŋ ‖ 'kʌt̬ ɪŋ

interdenominational
ˌɪnt ə dɪ ˌnɒm ɪ 'neɪʃ ᵊn_əl ◂ -də,ˌ•-, -,ˌ•ə-
‖ ˌɪnt̬ ᵊr dɪ ˌnɑːm ə- **~ism** ˌɪz əm

interdental ˌɪnt ə 'dent ᵊl ◂ ‖ ˌɪnt̬ ᵊr 'dent̬ ᵊl ◂
~ly i **~s** z

interdepartmental ˌɪnt ə ˌdiː pɑːt 'ment ᵊl ◂
ˌˌ•ˌdɪ,ˌ•ˌˌ, ˌ•ˌdə,ˌˌ•ˌˌ ‖ ˌɪnt̬
ᵊr ˌdiː pɑːrt 'ment̬ ᵊl ◂ ˌˌ•ˌdɪ,ˌ•ˌˌ **~ly** i
   ˌinterdepart ˌmental 'rivalry

interdependence ˌɪnt ə dɪ 'pend ᵊnᵗs -dəˈ•-,
§-diːˈ•- ‖ ˌɪnt̬ ᵊr-

interdependent ˌɪnt ə dɪ 'pend ənt ◂ -dəˈ•-,
§-diːˈ•- ‖ ˌɪnt̬ ᵊr- **~ly** li

interdict v ˌɪnt ə 'dɪkt -'daɪt ‖ ˌɪnt̬ ᵊr- **~ed** ɪd
əd **~ing** ɪŋ **~s** s

interdict n 'ɪnt ə dɪkt -daɪt ‖ 'ɪnt̬ ᵊr- **~s** s

interdiction ˌɪnt ə 'dɪk ʃ°n ‖ ˌɪnt̬ ᵊr- **~s** z

interdisciplinarity ˌɪnt ə ˌdɪs ə plɪ 'nær ət i
-,ˌ•ɪ-, -ɪt i ‖ ˌɪnt̬ ᵊr ˌdɪs ə plə 'nær ət̬ i -'ner-

interdisciplinary ˌɪnt ə 'dɪs ə plɪn ər_i ◂ -ˈ•ɪ-,
-plən,ˌ•, ˌˌ•,ˌ•ˈ•ˌˌ ‖ ˌɪnt̬ ᵊr
'dɪs ə plə ner i ◂

interest 'ɪntr əst -ɪst, -est; 'ɪnt ə rest ‖ 'ɪnt̬
ə rest **~ed** ɪd əd **~ing** ɪŋ **~s** s
   'interest group

interested 'ɪntr əst ɪd -ɪst-, 'ɪnt ə rest ɪd,
-əd ‖ 'ɪnt̬ ə rest əd **~ly** li **~ness** nəs nɪs

interesting 'ɪntr əst ɪŋ -ɪst-, -est-;
'ɪnt ə rest ɪŋ ‖ 'ɪnt̬ ə rest ɪŋ **~ly** li

interfac|e n 'ɪnt ə feɪs ‖ 'ɪnt̬ ᵊr- **~es** ɪz əz

interfac|e v 'ɪnt ə feɪs ˌˌ•ˈ•ˌˌ ‖ 'ɪnt̬ ᵊr- **~ed** t
~es ɪz əz **~ing** ɪŋ

inter|fere ˌɪnt ə ˈfɪə ‖ ˌɪnt̬ ər ˈfɪʳr -ə- ~fered
ˈfɪəd ‖ ˈfɪʳrd ~feres ˈfɪəz ‖ ˈfɪʳrz ~fering
ˈfɪər ɪŋ ◀ ‖ ˈfɪr ɪŋ ◀
interference ˌɪnt ə ˈfɪər ən¦s ‖ ˌɪnt̬ ər ˈfɪr- -ə-
interferometer ˌɪnt ə fə ˈrɒm ɪt ə -ət ə
‖ ˌɪnt̬ ər fə ˈrɑːm ət̬ ər ˌ•ə-, -fɪˈ•- ~s z
interferometric ˌɪnt ə ˌfer əʊ ˈmetr ɪk ◀ -ˌfɪər-
‖ ˌɪnt̬ ər ˌfɪr ə- ˌ•ə- ~ally ᵊl i
interferon ˌɪnt ə ˈfɪər ɒn ‖ ˌɪnt̬ ər ˈfɪr ɑːn -ə-
Interflora tdmk ˌɪnt ə ˈflɔːr ə ‖ ˌɪnt̬ ər- -ˈflour-
intergalactic ˌɪnt ə gə ˈlækt ɪk ◀ ‖ ˌɪnt̬ ər-
interglacial ˌɪnt ə ˈgleɪs i_əl ◀ -ˈgleɪʃ-, -ˈgleɪʃ ᵊl
‖ ˌɪnt̬ ər ˈgleɪʃ ᵊl ◀
interim ˈɪnt ər ɪm §-əm ‖ ˈɪnt̬-
interior ɪn ˈtɪər i_ə ‖ -ˈtɪr i_ᵊr ~ly li ~s z
in,terior 'decorator
interioris|e, interioriz|e ɪn ˈtɪər i_ə raɪz ‖ -ˈtɪr-
~ed d ~es ɪz əz ~ing ɪŋ
interject ˌɪnt ə ˈdʒekt ‖ ˌɪnt̬ ər- ~ed ɪd əd
~ing ɪŋ ~s s
interjection ˌɪnt ə ˈdʒek ʃᵊn ‖ ˌɪnt̬ ər- ~s z
interlac|e ˌɪnt ə ˈleɪs ‖ ˌɪnt̬ ər- ~ed t ~es ɪz əz
~ing ɪŋ
Interlaken ˈɪnt ə ˌlɑːk ən ˌ•• ‖ ˈɪnt̬ ər-
—Ger [ˈʔɪn tɐ lak ᵊn]
interlanguag|e ˈɪnt ə ˌlæŋ gwɪdʒ -wɪdʒ ‖ ˈɪnt̬
ər- ~es ɪz əz
interlard ˌɪnt ə ˈlɑːd ‖ ˌɪnt̬ ər ˈlɑːrd ~ed ɪd əd
~ing ɪŋ ~s z
inter|leaf n ˈɪnt ə ‖liːf ‖ ˈɪnt̬ ər- ~leaves liːvz
interleav|e v ˌɪnt ə ˈliːv ‖ ˌɪnt̬ ər- ~ed d ~es z
~ing ɪŋ
interleaves n pl ˈɪnt ə liːvz ‖ ˈɪnt̬ ər-
interleaves from v ˌɪnt ə ˈliːvz ‖ ˌɪnt̬ ər-
interlin|e v ˌɪnt ə ˈlaɪn ‖ ˌɪnt̬ ər- ~ed d ~es z
~ing ɪŋ
interlinear ˌɪnt ə ˈlɪn i_ə ◀ ‖ ˌɪnt̬ ər ˈlɪn i_ᵊr
Interlingua, i~ ˌɪnt ə ˈlɪŋ gwə ˈ••, ˌ•• ‖ ˌɪnt̬ ər-
Interlingue ˌɪnt ə ˈlɪŋ gweɪ ‖ ˌɪnt̬ ər-
interlink v ˌɪnt ə ˈlɪŋk ‖ ˌɪnt̬ ər- ~ed t ~ing ɪŋ
~s s
interlock v ˌɪnt ə ˈlɒk ‖ ˌɪnt̬ ər ˈlɑːk ~ed t ~ing
ɪŋ ~s s
interlock n ˈɪnt ə lɒk ‖ ˈɪnt̬ ər lɑːk ~s s
interlocutor ˌɪnt ə ˈlɒk jut ə -jət ə ‖ ˌɪnt̬
ər ˈlɑːk jət̬ ər ~s z
interlocutor|y ˌɪnt ə ˈlɒk jut̬ ͜ər li -ˈ•jət-, ‖ ˌɪnt̬
ər ˈlɑːk jə tɔːr li -tour i ~ies iz
interloper ˈɪnt ə ləʊp ə ˌ••ˈ•• ‖ ˈɪnt̬ ər loup ᵊr
ˌ••ˈ•• ~s z
interlude ˈɪnt ə luːd -ljuːd; -ᵊl uːd, -juːd ‖ ˈɪnt̬
ər- ~s z
intermarriage ˌɪnt ə ˈmær ɪdʒ ‖ ˌɪnt̬ ər- -ˈmer-
intermarr|y ˌɪnt ə ˈmær i ‖ ˌɪnt̬ ər- -ˈmer-
~ied id ~ies iz ~ying i_ɪŋ
intermediar|y ˌɪnt ə ˈmiːd i_ər li ◀ ‖ ˌɪnt̬
ər ˈmiːd i er li ~ies iz
intermediate ˌɪnt ə ˈmiːd i_ət ◀ -ɪt ‖ ˌɪnt̬ ər-
~ly li ~ness nəs nɪs ~s s
interment ɪn ˈtɜː mənt ‖ -ˈtɜː- ~s s
intermezz|o ˌɪnt ə ˈmets ləʊ -ˈmedz- ‖ ˌɪnt̬
ər ˈmets lou ~i i iː ~os əʊz ‖ ouz

interminab|le ɪn ˈtɜːm ɪn əb |ᵊl ˌɪn-, -ᵊn_əb-
‖ -ˈtɜːm- ~ly li
intermingl|e ˌɪnt ə ˈmɪŋ gᵊl ‖ ˌɪnt̬ ər- ~ed d
~es z ~ing ɪŋ
intermission ˌɪnt ə ˈmɪʃ ᵊn ‖ ˌɪnt̬ ər- ~s z
inter|mit ˌɪnt ə ˈmɪt ‖ ˌɪnt̬ ər- ~mits
ˈmɪts~mitted ˈmɪt ɪd -əd ‖ ˈmɪt̬ əd
~mitting ˈmɪt ɪŋ ‖ ˈmɪt̬ ɪŋ
intermittent ˌɪnt ə ˈmɪt ᵊnt ◀ ‖ ˌɪnt̬ ər- ~ly li
intern v 'confine' ɪn ˈtɜːn ‖ -ˈtɜːn ˈ•• ~ed d
~ing ɪŋ ~s z
intern v 'act as an intern(e)' ˈɪn tɜːn ‖ -tɜːn
~ed d ~ing ɪŋ ~s z
intern n ˈɪn tɜːn ‖ -tɜːn ~s z
internal ɪn ˈtɜːn ᵊl ˌɪn- ‖ -ˈtɜːn- ~ly i ~s z
in,ternal com'bustion; In,ternal 'Revenue
,Service
internalis... —see internaliz...
internalization ɪn ˌtɜːn əl aɪ ˈzeɪʃ ᵊn ˌ•ˌ•-,
-ɪˈ•- ‖ ɪn ˌtɜːn ᵊl_ə- ~s z
internaliz|e ɪn ˈtɜːn ə laɪz -ᵊl aɪz ‖ -ˈtɜːn ᵊl aɪz
~ed d ~es ɪz əz ~ing ɪŋ
international, I~ ˌɪnt ə ˈnæʃ ᵊn_əl ◀ ‖ ˌɪnt̬ ər-
~ly i ~s z
,inter,national 'date line; ,inter,national
'law
Internationale ˌɪnt ə ˌnæʃ ə ˈnɑːl
-ˌnæʃ i_ə ˈnɑːl ‖ ˌɪnt̬ ər-
internationalis... —see internationaliz...
international|ism ˌɪnt ə ˈnæʃ ᵊn_əl ˌ•ɪz
əm ‖ ˌɪnt̬ ər- ~ist/s ɪst/s §əst/s
internationalization ˌɪnt ə ˌnæʃ ᵊn_əl
aɪ ˈzeɪʃ ᵊn -ɪˈ•- ‖ ˌɪnt̬ ər ˌnæʃ ᵊn_əl ə-
internationaliz|e ˌɪnt ə ˈnæʃ ᵊn_ə laɪz ‖ ˌɪnt̬ ər-
~ed d ~es ɪz əz ~ing ɪŋ
interne ˈɪn tɜːn ‖ -tɜːn ~s z
internecine ˌɪnt ə ˈniːs aɪn ◀ ‖ ˌɪnt̬ ər ˈniːs ᵊn ◀
-ˈnes-, -iːn, -aɪn
internee ˌɪn tɜː ˈniː ‖ -tɜːˈ- ~s z
Internet, i~ ˈɪnt ə net ‖ ˈɪnt̬ ər-
internist ˈɪn tɜːn ɪst §-əst; •ˈ•• ‖ -ˈtɜːn- ~s s
internment ɪn ˈtɜːn mənt →-ˈtɜːm- ‖ -ˈtɜːn-
~s s
internship ˈɪn tɜːn ʃɪp •ˈ•• ‖ -tɜːn- ~s s
interpel|late ˈɪn tɜːp ə |leɪt -e-; ˌɪnt ə ˈpel eɪt
‖ ˌɪnt̬ ər ˈpel eɪt ɪn ˈtɜːp ə ‖leɪt ~lated
leɪt ɪd -əd ‖ leɪt̬ əd ~lates leɪts ~lating
leɪt ɪŋ ‖ leɪt̬ ɪŋ
interpellation ɪn ˌtɜːp ə ˈleɪʃ ᵊn -e-; ˌɪnt ə pə-,
-pe'•- ‖ ˌɪnt̬ ər pə- ɪn ˌtɜːp ə- ~s z
interpene|trate ˌɪnt ə ˈpen ɪ ‖treɪt -ˈ•ə- ‖ ˌɪnt̬
ər- ~trated treɪt ɪd -əd ‖ treɪt̬ əd ~trates
treɪts ~trating treɪt ɪŋ ‖ treɪt̬ ɪŋ
interpenetration ˌɪnt ə ˌpen ɪ ˈtreɪʃ ᵊn -ˌ•ə-
‖ ˌɪnt̬ ər- ~s z
interpersonal ˌɪnt ə ˈpɜːs ᵊn_əl ◀ ‖ ˌɪnt̬
ər ˈpɜːs-
interplanetary ˌɪnt ə ˈplæn ɪt_ər i ◀-ˈ•ət_ ‖ ˌɪnt̬
ər ˈplæn ə ter i
interplay ˈɪnt ə pleɪ ‖ ˈɪnt̬ ər-
Interpol ˈɪnt ə pɒl ‖ ˈɪnt̬ ər poul (*)
interpo|late ɪn ˈtɜːp ə ‖leɪt ‖ -ˈtɜːp- ~lated

leɪt ɪd -əd ‖ leɪt̬ əd ~lates leɪts ~lating
leɪt ɪŋ ‖ leɪt̬ ɪŋ
interpolation ɪn ˌtɜːp ə ˈleɪʃ ⁿn ‖ -ˌtɜːp- ~s z
interpos|e ˌɪnt ə ˈpəʊz ‖ ˌɪnt̬ ʳr ˈpoʊz ~ed d
~es ɪz əz ~ing ɪŋ
interposition ˌɪnt ə pə ˈzɪʃ ⁿn ɪn ˌtɜːp ə- ‖ ˌɪnt̬
ʳr-
interp|ret ɪn ˈtɜːp |rɪt -rət ‖ -ˈtɜːp |rət ~reted
rɪt ɪd rət-, -əd ‖ rət̬ əd ~reting rɪt ɪŋ rət-
‖ rət̬ ɪŋ ~rets rɪts rəts ‖ rəts
interpretation ɪn ˌtɜːp rɪ ˈteɪʃ ⁿn -rə- ‖ -ˌtɜːp-
~s z
interpretative ɪn ˈtɜːp rɪt ət ɪv -ˈ•rət-;
-rɪ teɪt-, -rə teɪt- ‖ -ˈtɜːp rə teɪt̬ ɪv -rət̬ ət̬-
~ly li
interpreter ɪn ˈtɜːp rɪt ə -rət- ‖ -ˈtɜːp rət̬ ʳr
~s z
interpretive ɪn ˈtɜːp rɪt ɪv -rət- ‖ -ˈtɜːp rət̬ ɪv
~ly li
interquartile ˌɪnt ə ˈkwɔːt aɪəl ◄ ‖ ˌɪnt̬
ʳr ˈkwɔːrt- -ˈkwɔːrt̬ əl ◄ ~s z
interracial ˌɪnt ə ˈreɪʃ əl ◄ ‖ ˌɪnt̬ ʳr- ~ly i
interreg|num ˌɪnt ə ˈreg |nəm ‖ ˌɪnt̬ ʳr- ~na nə
~nums nəmz
interre|late ˌɪnt ə rɪ |ˈleɪt -rəˈ•, §-riːˈ• ‖ ˌɪnt̬ ʳr-
~lated ˈleɪt ɪd -əd ‖ ˈleɪt̬ əd ~lates ˈleɪts
~lating ˈleɪt ɪŋ ‖ ˈleɪt̬ ɪŋ
interrelation ˌɪnt ə rɪ ˈleɪʃ ⁿn -rəˈ•-, §-riːˈ•-
‖ ˌɪnt̬ ʳr- ~s z ~ship/s ʃɪp/s
interro|gate ɪn ˈter ə |geɪt ~gated geɪt ɪd -əd
‖ geɪt̬ əd ~gates geɪts ~gating
geɪt ɪŋ ‖ geɪt̬ ɪŋ
interrogation ɪn ˌter ə ˈgeɪʃ ⁿn ~s z
inˌterroˈgation mark
interrogative ˌɪnt ə ˈrɒg ət ɪv ◄ ‖ ˌɪnt̬
ə ˈrɑːg ət̬ ɪv ◄ ~ly li ~s z
interrogator ɪn ˈter ə geɪt ə ‖ -geɪt̬ ʳr ~s z
interrogator|y ˌɪnt ə ˈrɒg ət̬ ʳr li ◄ ‖ ˌɪnt̬
ə ˈrɑːg ə tɔːr li -toʊr i ~ies iz
interrupt v ˌɪnt ə ˈrʌpt ‖ ˌɪnt̬ ə- ~ed ɪd əd
~ing ɪŋ ~s s
interrupt n ˈɪnt ə rʌpt ˌ•ˈ•ˈ• ‖ ˈɪnt̬ ə- ~s s
interruption ˌɪnt ə ˈrʌp ʃⁿn ‖ ˌɪnt̬ ə- ~s z
inter se ˌɪnt ə ˈseɪ -ˈsiː ‖ ˌɪnt̬ ʳr-
intersect ˌɪnt ə ˈsekt ‖ ˌɪnt̬ ʳr- ~ed ɪd əd ~ing
ɪŋ ~s s
intersection ˌɪnt ə ˈsek ʃⁿn ˈ•ˌ•• ‖ ˈɪnt̬
ʳr ˌsek ʃⁿn ˌ•ˈ•ˈ• ~s z
intersex ˈɪnt ə seks ‖ ˈɪnt̬ ʳr- ~es ɪz əz
interspac|e v ˌɪnt ə ˈspeɪs ˈ•ˈ•ˈ• ‖ ˌɪnt̬ ʳr- ~ed t
~es ɪz əz ~ing ɪŋ
interspac|e n ˈɪnt ə speɪs ˌ•ˈ•ˈ• ‖ ˈɪnt̬ ʳr- ~es ɪz
əz
interspers|e ˌɪnt ə ˈspɜːs ‖ ˌɪnt̬ ʳr ˈspɜːs ~ed t
~es ɪz əz ~ing ɪŋ
interspersion ˌɪnt ə ˈspɜːʃ ⁿn §-ˈspɜːʒ- ‖ ˌɪnt̬
ʳr ˈspɜːʒ ⁿn
interstate adj ˌɪnt ə ˈsteɪt ◄ ˈ•ˈ•ˈ• ‖ ˌɪnt̬ ʳr-
ˌinterstate ˈhighway
interstate n ˈɪnt ə steɪt ‖ ˈɪnt̬ ʳr- ~s s
interstellar ˌɪnt ə ˈstel ə ◄ ‖ ˌɪnt̬ ʳr ˈstel ʳr
ˌinterˌstellar ˈdust
interstic|e ɪn ˈtɜːst ɪs -əs ‖ -ˈtɜːst- ~es ɪz əz

interstitial ˌɪnt ə ˈstɪʃ əl ◄ ‖ ˌɪnt̬ ʳr- ~ly i ~s z
intertextuality ˌɪnt ə ˌteks tʃu ˈæl ət i -tʃuˈ•-,
-ɪt i ‖ ˌɪnt̬ ʳr ˌteks tʃu ˈæl ət̬ i
intertribal ˌɪnt ə ˈtraɪb əl ◄ ‖ ˌɪnt̬ ʳr-
intertwin|e ˌɪnt ə ˈtwaɪn ‖ ˌɪnt̬ ʳr- ~ed d ~es z
~ing ɪŋ
interurban ˌɪnt ʳr ˈɜːb ən ◄ ‖ ˌɪnt̬ ʳr ˈɜːb-
interval ˈɪnt əv əl ‖ ˈɪnt̬ ʳrv əl ~s z
interven|e ˌɪnt ə ˈviːn ‖ ˌɪnt̬ ʳr- ~ed d ~es z
~ing ɪŋ
intervention ˌɪnt ə ˈvenʧ ⁿn ‖ ˌɪnt̬ ʳr- ~ism ɪz
əm ~ist/s ɪst/s §əst/s ‖ əst/s ~s z
inter|view n, v ˈɪnt ə |vjuː ‖ ˈɪnt̬ ʳr- ~viewed
vjuːd ~viewing vjuːˌɪŋ ~views vjuːz
interviewee ˌɪnt ə vju ˈiː ‖ ˌɪnt̬ ʳr- ~s z
interviewer ˈɪnt ə vjuːˌə ‖ ˈɪnt̬ ʳr vjuː ʳr ~s z
intervocalic ˌɪnt ə vəʊ ˈkæl ɪk ◄ ‖ ˌɪnt̬ ʳr voʊ-
~ally əl‿i
inter|weave ˌɪnt ə |ˈwiːv ‖ ˌɪnt̬ ʳr- ~weaves
ˈwiːvz ~weaving ˈwiːv ɪŋ ~wove
ˈwəʊv ‖ ˈwoʊv ~woven
ˈwəʊv ⁿn ◄ ‖ ˈwoʊv ⁿn ◄
intestacy ɪn ˈtest əs i
intestate ɪn ˈtest eɪt -ət, -ɪt ~s s
intestinal ɪn ˈtest ɪn əl -ən‿əl; ˌɪnt e ˈstaɪn əl ◄
intestine ɪn ˈtest ɪn -iːn, -ən ~s z
intifada ˌɪnt ɪ ˈfɑːd ə —Arabic [in ti ˈfɑː ða]
intimac|y ˈɪnt ɪm əs li ˈ•əm- ‖ ˈɪnt̬ əm- ~ies iz
intimate adj, n ˈɪnt ɪm ət -əm-, -ɪt ‖ ˈɪnt̬ əm ət
~ly li ~ness nəs nɪs
inti|mate v ˈɪnt ɪ |meɪt -ə- ‖ ˈɪnt̬ ə- ~mated
meɪt ɪd -əd ‖ meɪt̬ əd ~mates meɪts
~mating meɪt ɪŋ ‖ meɪt̬ ɪŋ
intimation ˌɪnt ɪ ˈmeɪʃ ⁿn -ə- ‖ ˌɪnt̬ ə- ~s z
intimi|date ɪn ˈtɪm ɪ |deɪt ˌɪn-, -ə- ~dated
deɪt ɪd -əd ‖ deɪt̬ əd ~dates deɪts ~dating
deɪt ɪŋ ‖ deɪt̬ ɪŋ
intimidation ɪn ˌtɪm ɪ ˈdeɪʃ ⁿn ˌ•ˌ•-, -əˈ•-
intimidatory ɪn ˌtɪm ɪ ˈdeɪt ʳr i ◄ -ˌ•ə-;
•ˈ•ˈ•ˈ•ˈ• ‖ ɪn ˈtɪm əd ə tɔːr i -toʊr i
into strong form ˈɪn tuː -tu, weak forms (ˈ)ɪnt ə
(especially before a consonant), (ˈ)ɪnt u
(especially before a vowel).
intolerab|le ɪn ˈtɒl ʳr‿əb |əl ‖ -ˈtɑːl- ~leness
əl nəs -nɪs ~ly li
intoleranc|e ɪn ˈtɒl ʳr ənts ˌɪn- ‖ -ˈtɑːl- ~es ɪz
əz
intolerant ɪn ˈtɒl ʳr ənt ˌɪn- ‖ -ˈtɑːl- ~ly li
into|nate ˈɪn təʊ |neɪt ‖ -tə- ~nated neɪt ɪd
-əd ‖ neɪt̬ əd ~nates neɪts ~nating
neɪt ɪŋ ‖ neɪt̬ ɪŋ
intonation ˌɪn tə ˈneɪʃ ⁿn -təʊ- ~s z
ˌintoˈnation ˌpatterns
intonational ˌɪn tə ˈneɪʃ ⁿn‿əl ˌ•təʊ-
intonative ˈɪn təʊ neɪt ɪv ‖ -tə neɪt̬ ɪv
inton|e ɪn ˈtəʊn ‖ -ˈtoʊn ~ed d ~es z ~ing ɪŋ
in toto ɪn ˈtəʊt əʊ ‖ -ˈtoʊt̬ oʊ
Intourist tdmk ˈɪn ˌtʊər ɪst -ˌtɔːr-, §-əst ‖ -ˌtʊr-
intoxicant ɪn ˈtɒks ɪk ənt -ək- ‖ -ˈtɑːks- ~s s
intoxi|cate ɪn ˈtɒks ɪ |keɪt -ə- ‖ -ˈtɑːks-
~cated keɪt ɪd -əd ‖ keɪt̬ əd ~cates keɪts
~cating keɪt ɪŋ ‖ keɪt̬ ɪŋ

intoxication ɪn ˌtɒks ɪ ˈkeɪʃ ən -ə- ‖ -ˌtɑːks-
~s z

intra- ˌɪntr ə — intracardiac
ˌɪntr ə ˈkɑːd i æk ◂ ‖ -ˈkɑːrd-

intractability ɪn ˌtrækt ə ˈbɪl ət i ˌ•ˌ•ˌ•-, -ɪt i
‖ -ət̬ i

intractab|le ɪn ˈtrækt əb |əl ˌɪn- ~leness əl nəs
-nɪs ~ly li

intrados ɪn ˈtreɪd ɒs ‖ ˈɪntr ə dɑːs -doʊ

intramural ˌɪntr ə ˈmjʊər əl ◂ -ˈmjɔːr-
‖ -ˈmjʊr- ~ly i

intramuscular ˌɪntr ə ˈmʌsk jʊl ə ◂ -jəl ə
‖ -jəl ər ◂

intranet ˈɪntr ə net ~s s

intransigenc|e ɪn ˈtræn� ɪdʒ ənts -ˈtrænz-,
-ˈtrɑːnts-, -ˈtrɑːnz-, -ədʒ- ~y i

intransigent ɪn ˈtrænts ɪdʒ ənt -ˈtrænz-,
-ˈtrɑːnts-, -ˈtrɑːnz-, -ədʒ- ~ly li ~s s

intransitive ɪn ˈtrænts ət ɪv ˌɪn-, -ˈtrænz-,
-ˈtrɑːnts-, -ˈtrɑːnz-, -ɪt- ‖ -ət̬ ɪv ~ly li ~ness
nəs nɪs ~s z

intransitivity ɪn ˌtrænts ə ˈtɪv ət i -ˌtrænz-,
-ˌtrɑːnts-, -ˌtrɑːnz-, ˌ•ˌ•ˌ•-, -ɪˈ•-, -ɪt i ‖ -ət̬ i

intrapersonal ˌɪntr ə ˈpɜːs ən əl ◂ ‖ -ˈpɜːs-

intrauterine ˌɪntr ə ˈjuːt ə raɪn ◂ ‖ -ˈjuːt̬ ər ən
-ə raɪn
ˌintra,uterine de'vice

intrava|sate ɪn ˈtræv ə |seɪt ˌ•- ~sated seɪt ɪd
-əd ‖ seɪt̬ əd ~sates seɪts ~sating
seɪt ɪŋ ‖ seɪt̬ ɪŋ

intravasation ɪn ˌtræv ə ˈseɪʃ ən ˌ•ˌ•ˌ•- ~s z

intravenous ˌɪntr ə ˈviːn əs ◂ ⚠-ˈvɪn i‿əs ~es
ɪz əz ~ly li

in-tray ˈɪn treɪ ~s z

intrench ɪn ˈtrentʃ ən- ~ed t ~es ɪz əz ~ing
ɪŋ ~ment/s mənt/s

intrepid ɪn ˈtrep ɪd §-əd ~ly li ~ness nəs nɪs

intrepidity ˌɪn trə ˈpɪd ət i ˌ•trɪ-, ˌ•tre-, -ɪt i
‖ -ət̬ i

intricac|y ˈɪntr ɪk əs li ˈ•ˌ•ək- ~ies iz

intricate ˈɪntr ɪk ət -ək-, -ɪt ~ly li ~ness nəs
nɪs

intrigu|e v ɪn ˈtriːg ~ed d ~es z ~ing ɪŋ

intrigue n ˈɪn triːg ˌ•ˈ• ~s z

intrinsic ɪn ˈtrɪnts ɪk ˌɪn-, -ˈtrɪnz- ~ally əl_i

intro ˈɪntr əʊ ‖ -oʊ ~s z

intro- ˌɪntr əʊ ‖ -ə — introgression ˌɪntr əʊ
ˈgreʃ ən ‖ -ə-

introduc|e ˌɪntr ə ˈdjuːs →§-ˈdʒuːs ‖ -ˈduːs
-ˈdjuːs ~ed t ~es ɪz əz ~ing ɪŋ

introduction ˌɪntr ə ˈdʌk ʃən ~s z

introductor|y ˌɪntr ə ˈdʌkt_ər li ◂ ~ily əl i ɪ li
ˌintro,ductory 'offer

introit ˈɪn trɔɪt ɪn ˈtrəʊ ɪt, §-ət ‖ ɪn ˈtroʊ ət,
ˈ•ˌ• ~s s

introject ˌɪntr əʊ ˈdʒekt ‖ -ə- ~ed ɪd əd ~ing
ɪŋ ~s s

introjection ˌɪntr əʊ ˈdʒek ʃən ‖ -ə-

intromission ˌɪntr əʊ ˈmɪʃ ən ‖ -ə- ~s z

intro|mit ˌɪntr əʊ |ˈmɪt ‖ -ə- ~mits ˈmɪts
~mitted ˈmɪt ɪd -əd ‖ ˈmɪt̬ əd ~mitting
ˈmɪt ɪŋ ‖ ˈmɪt̬ ɪŋ

introspect ˌɪntr əʊ ˈspekt ‖ -ə- ~ed ɪd əd
~ing ɪŋ ~s s

introspection ˌɪntr əʊ ˈspek ʃən ‖ -ə- ~s z

introspective ˌɪntr əʊ ˈspekt ɪv ◂ ‖ -ə- ~ly li
~ness nəs nɪs

introversion ˌɪntr əʊ ˈvɜːʃ ən -ˈvɜːʒ-
‖ -ə ˈvɜːʒ ən

introvert n ˈɪntr əʊ vɜːt ‖ -ə ˈvɜːt ~s s

introvert v ˌɪntr əʊ ˈvɜːt ‖ -ə ˈvɜːt ~verted
ˈvɜːt ɪd -əd ‖ ˈvɜːt̬ əd ~verting
ˈvɜːt ɪŋ ‖ ˈvɜːt̬ ɪŋ ~verts ˈvɜːts ‖ ˈvɜːts

intrud|e ɪn ˈtruːd ~ed ɪd əd ~es z ~ing ɪŋ

intrusion ɪn ˈtruːʒ ən ~s z

intrusive ɪn ˈtruːs ɪv §-ˈtruːz- ~ly li ~ness nəs
nɪs

intrust ɪn ˈtrʌst ən- ~ed ɪd əd ~ing ɪŋ ~s s

intu|bate ˈɪn tju |beɪt →→-tʃu- ‖ -tu- -tju-
~bated beɪt ɪd -əd ‖ beɪt̬ əd ~bates beɪts
~bating beɪt ɪŋ ‖ beɪt̬ ɪŋ

intu|it ɪn ˈtjuː_|ɪt §→→-ˈtʃuː_, §_ət ‖ -ˈtuː_ ət
-ˈtjuː- ~ited ɪt ɪd §ət-, -əd ‖ ət̬ əd ~iting
ɪt ɪŋ §ət- ‖ ət̬ ɪŋ ~its ɪts §əts ‖ əts

intuition ˌɪn tju ˈɪʃ ən →§-tʃu- ‖ -tu- -tju- ~s
z

intuitive ɪn ˈtjuː_ət ɪv →§-ˈtʃuː_, _ɪt ɪv
‖ -ˈtuː_ ət̬ ɪv -ˈtjuː- ~ly li ~ness nəs nɪs

intumesc|e ˌɪn tju ˈmes →§-tʃu- ‖ -tu- -tju-
~ed t ~es ɪz əz ~ing ɪŋ

intumesc|ence ˌɪn tju ˈmes |ənts §§-tʃu- ‖ -tu-
-tju- ~ent ənt

intussuscept ˌɪnt ə sə ˈsept -əs sə- ‖ ˌɪnt̬- ~ed
ɪd əd ~ing ɪŋ ~s s

intussusception ˌɪnt ə sə ˈsep ʃən -əs sə-
‖ ˌɪnt̬-

Inuit ˈɪn u ɪt -juː-, §-ət ~s s

inun|date ˈɪn ʌn |deɪt -ən- ~dated deɪt ɪd -əd
‖ deɪt̬ əd ~dates deɪts ~dating
deɪt ɪŋ ‖ deɪt̬ ɪŋ

inundation ˌɪn ʌn ˈdeɪʃ ən -ən- ~s z

Inupiaq ɪ ˈnuːp i æk

inure ɪ ˈnjʊə ə-, -ˈnjɔː ‖ ɪn ˈjʊər ɪ ˈnʊər ~d d
~s z inuring ɪ ˈnjʊər ɪŋ ə-, -ˈnjɔːr-
‖ ɪn ˈjʊr ɪŋ ɪ ˈnʊr-

in utero ˈɪn ˈjuːt ə rəʊ ‖ ɪn ˈjuːt̬ ə roʊ

in vacuo ɪn ˈvæk ju əʊ ‖ -oʊ

invad|e ɪn ˈveɪd ~ed ɪd əd ~er/s ə/z ‖ ər/z
~es z ~ing ɪŋ

invalid adj 'not valid' ɪn ˈvæl ɪd ˌɪn-, §-əd ~ly li

invalid n, v, adj 'ill, infirm' ˈɪn və liːd -lɪd
‖ -vəl əd ~ed ɪd əd ~ing ɪŋ ~s z

invali|date ɪn ˈvæl ɪ |deɪt ˌɪn-, -ə- ~dated
deɪt ɪd -əd ‖ deɪt̬ əd ~dates deɪts ~dating
deɪt ɪŋ ‖ deɪt̬ ɪŋ

invalidation ɪn ˌvæl ɪ ˈdeɪʃ ən -ə-, ˌ•ˌ•ˌ•-

invalidity ˌɪn və ˈlɪd ət i -ɪt i ‖ -ət̬ i

invaluab|le ɪn ˈvæl ju_əb |əl -ˈvæl jʊb |əl ~ly li

Invar tdmk ɪn ˈvɑː ˈ•• ; ˈɪn və ‖ -ˈvɑːr ˈ••

invariability ɪn ˌveər i_ə ˈbɪl ət i ˌ•ˌ•ˌ•-, -ɪt i
‖ ɪn ˌver i_ə ˈbɪl ət̬ i -ˌvær-

invariab|le ɪn ˈveər i_əb |əl ˌɪn- ‖ -ˈver- -ˈvær-
~leness əl nəs -nɪs ~ly li

invariance ɪn ˈveər i_ənts ˌɪn- ‖ -ˈver- -ˈvær-

invariant ɪn ˈveər iˌənt ˌɪn- ‖ -ˈver- -ˈvær- ~s s

invasion ɪn ˈveɪʒ ᵊn ~s z

invasive ɪn ˈveɪs ɪv §-ˈveɪz- ~ly li

invective ɪn ˈvekt ɪv ~ly li ~ness nəs nɪs

inveigh ɪn ˈveɪ ~ed d ~ing ɪŋ ~s z

inveigl|e ɪn ˈveɪg ᵊl -ˈviːg- ~ed d ~ement mənt ~es z ~ing ɪŋ

in|vent ɪn ˈvent ~vented ˈvent ɪd -əd ‖ ˈvent̬ əd ~venting ˈvent ɪŋ ‖ ˈvent̬ ɪŋ ~vents ˈvents

invention ɪn ˈventʃ ᵊn ~s z

inventive ɪn ˈvent ɪv ‖ -ˈvent̬ ɪv ~ly li ~ness nəs nɪs

inventor ɪn ˈvent ə ‖ ˈvent̬ ᵊr ~s z

inventor|y n, v ˈɪn vənt̬ˌᵊr i li ɪn ˈvent ᵊr li ‖ ˈɪn vən tɔːr li -toʊr i ~ies iz

Inver ˈɪn və ‖ -vᵊr

Inveraray ˌɪn vər ˈeər i -ə ‖ -ˈer i -ˈær i

Invercargill ˌɪn və ˈkɑːg ɪl -ᵊl; -kɑː ˈgɪl ‖ -vᵊr ˈkɑːrg ᵊl

Invergarry ˌɪn və ˈgær i ‖ -vᵊr- -ˈger-

Invergordon ˌɪn və ˈgɔːd ᵊn ‖ -vᵊr ˈgɔːrd ᵊn

Inverkeithing ˌɪn və ˈkiːð ɪŋ ‖ -vᵊr-

Invermoriston ˌɪn və ˈmɒr ɪst ᵊn -ˈᵊst- ‖ -vᵊr ˈmɔːr- -ˈmɑːr-

Inverness ˌɪn və ˈnes ◂ ‖ -vᵊr- ˌInverness ˈTerrace

invers|e adj, n ˌɪn ˈvɜːs ◂ ɪn- ‖ -ˈvɜːs ˈ•• ~ely li ~es ɪz əz ˌinverse proˈportion

inversion ɪn ˈvɜːʃ ᵊn §-ˈvɜːʒ- ‖ -ˈvɜːʒ ᵊn ~s z

in|vert v ɪn ˈvɜːt ˌɪn- ‖ -ˈvɜːt ~verted ˈvɜːt ɪd -əd ‖ ˈvɜːt̬ əd ~verting ˈvɜːt ɪŋ ‖ ˈvɜːt̬ ɪŋ ~verts ˈvɜːts ‖ ˈvɜːts inˌverted ˈcomma; inˌverted ˈsnob

invert adj, n ˈɪn vɜːt ‖ -vɜːt ~s s

invertebrate ɪn ˈvɜːt ɪb rət -əb-, ˌɪn-, -əb-, -rɪt; -ɪ breɪt, -ə- ‖ -ˈvɜːt̬- ~s s

Inverurie ˌɪn vər ˈʊər i ‖ -ˈʊr i

invest ɪn ˈvest ~ed ɪd əd ~ing ɪŋ ~s s

investi|gate ɪn ˈvest ɪ geɪt -ə- ~gated geɪt ɪd -əd ‖ geɪt̬ əd ~gates geɪts ~gating geɪt ɪŋ ‖ geɪt̬ ɪŋ

investigation ɪn ˌvest ɪ ˈgeɪʃ ᵊn -ˌ•ə- ~s z

investigative ɪn ˈvest ɪg ət ɪv -ˈ•əg-; -ɪ geɪt ɪv, -ə•• ‖ -ə geɪt̬ ɪv

investigator ɪn ˈvest ɪ geɪt ə -ˈ•ə- ‖ -geɪt̬ ᵊr ~s z

investigatory ɪn ˈvest ɪg ət̬ˌᵊr i ɪnˌvest ɪ ˈgeɪt ᵊr i ◂ -ˌ•ə-; •ˈ•••• ‖ ɪn ˈvest ɪg ə tɔːr i -toʊr i

investiture ɪn ˈvest ɪtʃ ə -ətʃ ə; -ɪ tjʊə, -ə- ‖ -ətʃ ᵊr -ə tʃʊr ~s z

investment ɪn ˈvest mənt ~s s

investor ɪn ˈvest ə ‖ -ᵊr ~s z

inveterate ɪn ˈvet ᵊr ət -ɪt ‖ -ˈvet̬ ᵊr ət →-ˈvetr ət -ˈly li ~ness nəs nɪs

invidious ɪn ˈvɪd iˌəs ~ly li ~ness nəs nɪs

invigi|late ɪn ˈvɪdʒ ə |leɪt -ɪ- ~lated leɪt ɪd -əd ‖ leɪt̬ əd ~lates leɪts ~lating leɪt ɪŋ ‖ leɪt̬ ɪŋ

invigilation ɪn ˌvɪdʒ ə ˈleɪʃ ᵊn -ɪ- ~s z

invigilator ɪn ˈvɪdʒ ə leɪt ə -ˈ•ɪ- ‖ -leɪt̬ ᵊr ~s z

invigo|rate ɪn ˈvɪg ə |reɪt ~rated reɪt ɪd -əd ‖ reɪt̬ əd ~rates reɪts ~rating reɪt ɪŋ ‖ reɪt̬ ɪŋ

invigoration ɪn ˌvɪg ə ˈreɪʃ ᵊn

invincibility ɪn ˌvɪnˈts ə ˈbɪl ət i ˌ•ˌ•ˌ•-, -ɪˈ•ˌ•-, -ɪt i ‖ -ət̬ i

invincib|le ɪn ˈvɪnˈts əb |ᵊl ˌɪn-, -ɪb- ~leness ᵊl nəs -nɪs ~ly li

inviolability ɪn ˌvaɪˌᵊl ə ˈbɪl ət i ˌ•ˌ•ˌ•-, -ɪt i ‖ -ət̬ i

inviolab|le ɪn ˈvaɪˌᵊl əb |ᵊl ˌɪn- ~leness ᵊl nəs -nɪs ~ly li

inviolate ɪn ˈvaɪˌᵊl ət -ɪt, -ə leɪt ~ly li ~ness nəs nɪs

invisibility ɪn ˌvɪz ə ˈbɪl ət i ˌ•ˌ•ˌ•-, -ɪˈ•ˌ•-, -ɪt i ‖ -ət̬ i

invisib|le ɪn ˈvɪz əb |ᵊl ˌɪn-, -ɪb- ~leness ᵊl nəs -nɪs ~ly li

invitation ˌɪn vɪ ˈteɪʃ ᵊn -və- ~s z

in|vite v ɪn ˈvaɪt ~vited ˈvaɪt ɪd -əd ‖ ˈvaɪt̬ əd ~vites ˈvaɪts ~viting/ly ˈvaɪt ɪŋ /li ‖ ˈvaɪt̬-

invite n ˈɪn vaɪt ~s s

invitee ˌɪn vaɪ ˈtiː -vɪ- ‖ -və- ~s z

in vitro ɪn ˈviːtr əʊ -ˈvɪtr- ‖ -oʊ

in vivo ɪn ˈviːv əʊ -ˈvaɪv- ‖ -oʊ

invocation ˌɪn vəʊ ˈkeɪʃ ᵊn -və- ~s z

invoic|e n, v ˈɪn vɔɪs ~ed t ~es ɪz əz ~ing ɪŋ

invok|e ɪn ˈvəʊk ‖ -ˈvoʊk ~ed t ~es s ~ing ɪŋ

involucre ˈɪn və luːk ə -ljuːk ə, ˌ•ˈ••• ◂ ‖ -ᵊr ~s z

involuntar|ily ɪn ˈvɒl ən tᵊr ᵊl i ˌɪn-, -ən ter ᵊl i, -ɪ li; ˌ•ˌ•ˈ•ter ᵊl i, -ˈtær-, -ɪ li ‖ ɪn ˌvɑːl ən ˈter ᵊl i ˌ•ˌ•ˌ•-, -ˈtær- ~iness i nəs i nɪs

involuntar|y ɪn ˈvɒl ənt̬ˌᵊr li ˌɪn-, §-ən ter i ‖ -ˈvɑːl ən ter li

involute ˈɪn və luːt -ljuːt, ˌ•ˈ•ˈ• ~s s

involution ˌɪn və ˈluːʃ ᵊn -ˈljuːʃ- ~s z

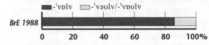

INVOLVE

	■ -ˈvɒlv	▭ -ˈvəʊlv/-ˈvɒʊlv
BrE 1988		
0	20 40 60 80	100%

involv|e ɪn ˈvɒlv §-ˈvəʊlv, →§-ˈvɒʊlv ‖ -ˈvɑːlv —BrE 1988 poll panel preference: -ˈvɒlv 86%, -ˈvəʊlv/-ˈvɒʊlv 14%. ~ed d ~ement/s mənt/s ~es z ~ing ɪŋ

invulnerability ɪn ˌvʌln ᵊr ə ˈbɪl ət i -ˌvʌn-, ˌ•ˌ•ˌ•-, -ɪt i ‖ -ət̬ i

invulnerab|le ɪn ˈvʌln ᵊr əb |ᵊl ˌɪn-, -ˈvʌn- ~leness ᵊl nəs -nɪs ~ly li

inward, I~ ˈɪn wəd ‖ -wᵊrd ~ly li ~ness nəs nɪs ~s z

Inwood ˈɪn wʊd

inwrought ˌɪn ˈrɔːt ◂ ‖ -ˈrɑːt

INXS ɪn ˈeks es

Io ˈaɪ əʊ ‖ -oʊ

I/O ˌaɪ ˈəʊ ◂ ‖ -ˈoʊ ◂ or as input/output

Ioan ˈjəʊ ən ‖ ˈjoʊ- —Welsh [ˈjo an]

iodate ˈaɪˌə deɪt -əʊ- ~s s

iodic aɪ ˈɒd ɪk ‖ -ˈɑːd ɪk

iodide ˈaɪˌə daɪd -əʊ- ~s z

iodin ˈaɪˌəd ɪn -əʊd-, §-ən

iodine 'aɪ‿ə diːn -əʊ-, -daɪn ‖ -daɪn ‿əd ən
iodis... —*see* **iodiz...**
iodization ˌaɪ‿ə daɪ 'zeɪʃ ən ‿əd ɪ- ‖ -əd ə-
iodiz|e 'aɪ‿ə daɪz -əʊ- **~ed** d **~es** ɪz əz **~ing** ɪŋ
iodoform aɪ 'ɒd ə fɔːm ‖ aɪ 'oʊd ə fɔːrm -'ɑːd- (*)
iodopsin ˌaɪ əʊ 'dɒps ɪn §-ən ‖ -ə 'dɑːps-
iodous aɪ 'ɒd əs 'aɪ‿əd- ‖ aɪ 'oʊd- -'ɑːd-, 'aɪ əd-
Iolanthe ˌaɪ‿ə 'lænᵗθ i -əʊ-
Iolo 'jəʊl əʊ ‖ 'joʊl oʊ —*Welsh* ['jo lo]
ion 'aɪ‿ən —*Also occasionally* 'aɪ ɒn ‖ -aːn, *in RP mainly to avoid confusion with iron* **~s** z
-ion *stress-imposing* jən, ən, ‿ən, ‿ᵊn —*often with changes to a stem-final consonant:* in'jection ɪn 'dʒek ʃən
Iona aɪ 'əʊn ə ‖ -'oʊn ə
Ione aɪ 'əʊn i ‖ -'oʊn i
Ionesco ˌiː‿ə 'nesk əʊ -ɒ-; jɒ 'nesk- ‖ -oʊ —*Fr* [jɔ nɛs ko]
Ionia aɪ 'əʊn i‿ə ‖ -'oʊn-
Ionian aɪ 'əʊn i‿ən ‖ -'oʊn- **~s** z
Ionic aɪ 'ɒn ɪk ‖ -'ɑːn- **~s** s
ionis... —*see* **ioniz...**
ionization ˌaɪ‿ən aɪ 'zeɪʃ ən -ɪ'•- ‖ -ə 'zeɪʃ- **~s** z
ioniz|e 'aɪ‿ə naɪz **~ed** d **~er/s** ə/z ‖ ᵊr/z **~es** ɪz əz **~ing** ɪŋ
ionosphere aɪ 'ɒn ə sfɪə ‖ -'ɑːn ə sfɪr
Iorwerth 'jɔː wɜːθ -weəθ ‖ 'jɔːr wᵊrθ —*Welsh* ['jor werθ]
iota aɪ 'əʊt ə ‖ -'oʊt̬ ə **~s** z
IOU ˌaɪ əʊ 'juː ‖ -oʊ- **~s, ~'s** z
Iowa 'aɪ əʊ ə 'aɪ‿ə wə ‖ 'aɪ ə wə
Iowan 'aɪ əʊ ən 'aɪ‿ə wən ‖ 'aɪ ə wən **~s** z
IPA ˌaɪ piː 'eɪ
ipecac 'ɪp ɪ kæk -ə-
ipecacuanha ˌɪp ɪ kæk ju 'æn ə ˌ•ə-, -'ɑːn-
Iphigenia ˌaɪf ɪdʒ ɪ 'naɪ‿ə ˌɪf-, ɪ ˌfɪdʒ-, -ə'•‿
Ipoh 'iːp əʊ ‖ -oʊ
ipomoea ˌɪp ə 'miː‿ə ˌaɪp- **~s** z
ipse dixit ˌɪps i 'dɪks ɪt -eɪ-, §-ət
ipsilateral ˌɪps ɪ 'læt‿ᵊr əl ◄ ‖ -'læt̬ ər əl →-'lætr əl
ipso facto ˌɪps əʊ 'fækt əʊ ◄ ‖ -oʊ 'fækt oʊ ◄
Ipsus 'ɪps əs
Ipswich 'ɪps wɪtʃ
IQ ˌaɪ 'kjuː **~s, ~'s** z
  I'Q test
Iqbal 'ɪk bæl 'ɪg-, -baːl —*Arabic* [ɪq 'baːl]
ir- ɪ —*generally stressed only for emphasis or if the following syllable is unstressed:* ˌɪrre'spective
Ira 'aɪᵊr ə
IRA ˌaɪ ɑːr 'eɪ ◄ -ᵊr-
Irak ɪ 'rɑːk -'ræk
Iraki ɪ 'rɑːk i -'ræk- **~s** z
Iran ɪ 'rɑːn -'ræn
Iranian ɪ 'reɪn i‿ən aɪᵊ-, -'rɑːn- **~s** z
Iraq ɪ 'rɑːk -'ræk ‖ aɪ- —*Arabic* [ʕi 'rɑːq]
Iraqi ɪ 'rɑːk i -'ræk- ‖ aɪ- **~s** z
irascibility ɪ ˌræs ə 'bɪl ət i -ɪ-, ˌ•ɪ-, -ɪt i ‖ -ət̬ i

irascib|le ɪ 'ræs əb ǀᵊl ǀ -ɪb- **~leness** ᵊl nəs -nɪs **~ly** li
irate aɪᵊ 'reɪt ˌ•'• ◄ **~ly** li
ire 'aɪ‿ə ‖ 'aɪ‿ᵊr
ireful 'aɪ‿ə fᵊl -fʊl ‖ 'aɪ‿ᵊr- **~ly** ‿i **~ness** nəs nɪs
Ireland 'aɪ‿ə lənd ‖ 'aɪ‿ᵊr-
Iremonger 'aɪ‿ə ˌmʌŋ gə ‖ 'aɪ‿ᵊr ˌmʌŋ gᵊr -ˌmɑːŋ-
Irene 'aɪᵊ riːn aɪᵊ 'riːn i ‖ aɪ 'riːn i, ˌ•- —*but the name of the Greek goddess is always* -'riːn i
irenic aɪᵊ 'riːn ɪk -'ren- **~ally** ᵊl_i
Ireton 'aɪ‿ə tən ‖ 'aɪ‿ᵊrt ən
Irian *'New Guinea'* ɪr i‿ən 'ɪᵊr-, -aːn
  ˌIrian ˌJaya 'dʒaɪ‿ə 'dʒɑː jə
iridaceous ˌɪr ɪ 'deɪʃ əs ◄ ˌaɪᵊr-, -ə-
iridesc|ence ˌɪr ɪ 'des ǀᵊnts -ə- **~ent** ᵊnt
iridium ɪ 'rɪd i‿əm aɪᵊ-
iridolog|ist/s ˌɪr ɪ 'dɒl ədʒ ǀɪst/s ˌ•ə-, §-əst/s ‖ -'dɑːl- **~y** i
irie 'aɪᵊr i
iris, Iris 'aɪᵊr ɪs §-əs **irises, Iris's** 'aɪᵊr ɪz §-əs-, -əz
Irish 'aɪᵊr ɪʃ **~ism** ˌɪz əm
  ˌIrish 'coffee; ˌIrish 'Sea; ˌIrish 'stew
Irish|man 'aɪᵊr ɪʃ ǀmən **~men** mən men **~ness** nəs nɪs **~ry** ri **~woman** ˌwʊm ən **~women** ˌwɪm ɪn §-ən
iritis aɪᵊ 'raɪt ɪs §-əs ‖ -'raɪt̬ əs
irk ɜːk ‖ ɝːk **irked** ɜːkt ‖ ɝːkt **irking** 'ɜːk ɪŋ ‖ 'ɝːk ɪŋ **irks** ɜːks ‖ ɝːks
irksome 'ɜːk səm ‖ 'ɝːk- **~ly** li **~ness** nəs nɪs
Irkutsk ɜː 'kʊtsk ɪə- ‖ ɪr- —*Russ* [ɪr 'kutsk]
Irlam 'ɜːl əm ‖ 'ɝːl-
Irma 'ɜːm ə ‖ 'ɝːm ə
Irnbru *tdmk* ˌaɪ‿ən bruː →‿əm- ‖ 'aɪ‿ᵊrn-
iron 'aɪ‿ən ‖ 'aɪ‿ᵊrn **ironed** 'aɪ‿ənd ‖ 'aɪ‿ᵊrnd **ironing** 'aɪ‿ən ɪŋ ‖ 'aɪ‿ᵊrn ɪŋ **irons** 'aɪ‿ənz ‖ 'aɪ‿ᵊrnz
  'Iron Age; ˌIron 'Curtain; 'ironing board; 'iron mold, 'iron mould; ˌiron 'rations
Ironbridge 'aɪ‿ən brɪdʒ →‿əm- ‖ 'aɪ‿ᵊrn-
ironclad 'aɪ‿ən klæd →‿əŋ- ‖ 'aɪ‿ᵊrn- **~s** z
iron-gray, iron-grey ˌaɪ‿ən 'greɪ ◄ →‿əŋ- ‖ ˌaɪ‿ᵊrn-
ironic aɪᵊ 'rɒn ɪk ‖ -'rɑːn- **~al** ᵊl **~ally** ᵊl_i
ironie... —*see* **irony**
ironist *'user of irony'* 'aɪᵊr ən ɪst §-əst **~s** s
ironmaster 'aɪ‿ən ˌmaːst ə →‿əm-, §-ˌmæst- ‖ 'aɪ‿ᵊrn ˌmæst ᵊr **~s** z
ironmonger 'aɪ‿ən ˌmʌŋ gə →‿əm- ‖ 'aɪ‿ᵊrn ˌmʌŋ gᵊr -ˌmɑːŋ- **~s** z
ironmonger|y 'aɪ‿ən ˌmʌŋ gᵊr ǀi →'•əm- ‖ 'aɪ‿ᵊrn- ˌmɑːŋ- **~ies** iz
Ironside 'aɪ‿ən saɪd ‖ 'aɪ‿ᵊrn- **~s** z
ironstone 'aɪ‿ən stəʊn ‖ 'aɪ‿ᵊrn stoʊn
ironware 'aɪ‿ən weə ‖ 'aɪ‿ᵊrn wer -wær
ironwood 'aɪ‿ən wʊd ‖ 'aɪ‿ᵊrn-
ironwork 'aɪ‿ən wɜːk ‖ 'aɪ‿ᵊrn wɝːk **~s** s
iron|y *n* 'aɪᵊr ən ǀi **~ies** iz
irony *adj 'like iron'* 'aɪ‿ən i ‖ 'aɪ‿ᵊrn i
Iroquoian ˌɪr ə 'kwɔɪ ən ◄ **~s** z

Iro|quois *sing.* 'ɪr ə |kwɔɪ -kwɔɪz **~quois** *pl* kwɔɪz kwɔɪ

irradi|ateɪ 'reɪd i |eɪt   **~ated**eɪt ɪd -əd‖ eɪt̬ əd   **~ates**eɪts   **~ating**eɪt ɪŋ ‖ eɪt̬ ɪŋ

irradiationɪ ˌreɪd i 'eɪʃ ən   **~s**z

irrationalɪ 'ræʃ ən̯əl ˌɪ- ‖ ˌɪr-   **~ly**i

irrationalit|yɪ ˌræʃ ə 'næl ət li ˌɪ,•-, -ɪt i‖ -ət̬ li ˌɪr,•-   **~ies**iz

Irrawaddy ˌɪr ə 'wɒd i ‖ -'wɑːd i

irrealis ˌɪr i 'ɑːl ɪs §-əs

irreconcilabilityɪ ˌrek ən ˌsaɪl ə 'bɪl ət i ˌɪ,•-, →-ŋ,•-, -ɪt i‖ -ət̬ i

irreconcilab|leɪ ˌrek ən 'saɪl əb |əl ◂ ˌɪ,•-, •'••••, →-ŋ'•-   **~ly**li

irrecoverab|le ˌɪr ɪ 'kʌv ər_əb |əl ◂ ,•ə-, §,•iː-   **~leness**əl nəs -nɪs **~ly**li

irredeemability ˌɪr ɪ ˌdiːm ə 'bɪl ət i ,•ə-, §,•iː-, -ɪt i‖ -ət̬ i

irredeemab|le ˌɪr ɪ 'diːm əb |əl ◂ ,•ə-, §,•iː-   **~les**əlz **~ly**li

irredentism, I~ ˌɪr ɪ 'dent ˌɪz əm ,•ə-

irredentist, I~ ˌɪr ɪ 'dent ɪst ◂ -ə-, §-əst ‖ -'dent̬ əst **~s**s

irreducibility ˌɪr ɪ ˌdjuːs ə 'bɪl ət i ,•ə-, →§-,dʒuːs-, -ɪt i‖ ,duːs ə 'bɪl ət̬ i -,djuːs-

irreducib|le ˌɪr ɪ 'djuːs əb |əl ◂ ,•ə-, §,•iː-, →§-'dʒuːs- ‖ -'duːs- -'djuːs- **~leness**əl nəs -nɪs **~ly**li

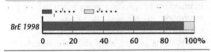

IRREFUTABLE

BrE 1998

0   20   40   60   80   100%

irrefutab|le ˌɪr ɪ 'fjuːt əb |əl ,•ə-, §,•iː-; ɪ 'ref jʊt-, -'•jət- ‖ ˌɪr ɪ 'fjuːt̬ əb |əl ɪ 'ref jət̬-, ˌɪ-, ˌɪr- —*BrE 1998 poll panel preference:* ,••'••• 93%, •'•••• 7%. **~ly** li

irregular ɪ 'reg jʊl ə ˌɪ-, -jəl-, §-əl- ‖ -jəl ᵊr ˌɪr- **~ly** li **~s** z

irregularit|y ɪ ˌreg jʊ 'lær ət li ,ɪr eg-, -jə'•-, -ɪt i‖ ɪ ˌreg jə 'lær ət̬ li ,ɪr,•-, -'ler- **~ies** iz

irrelevanc|e ɪ 'rel əv ən̩ts ,ɪ-, -'•ɪv- ‖ ,ɪr- **~ies** iz **~y** i

irrelevant ɪ 'rel əv ənt ,ɪ-, -ɪv- ‖ ,ɪr- **~ly** li

irreligion ,ɪr ɪ 'lɪdʒ ən ◂ -ə-, §-iː-

irreligious ,ɪr ɪ 'lɪdʒ əs ◂ -ə-, §-iː- **~ly** li **~ness** nəs nɪs

irremediab|le ,ɪr ɪ 'miːd i_əb |əl ◂ ,•ə-, §,•iː- **~ly** li

irremovab|le ,ɪr ɪ 'muːv əb |əl ◂ ,•ə-, §,•iː- **~ly** li

irreparab|le ɪ 'rep ər_əb |əl §,ɪr ɪ 'peər əb |əl ◂, §,•ə-, §,•iː- ‖ ,ɪr-; ,ɪr ɪ 'per-, -'pær- **~leness** əl nəs -nɪs **~ly** li

irreplaceable ,ɪr ɪ 'pleɪs əb əl ◂ ,•ə-, §,•iː-

irrepressib|le ,ɪr ɪ 'pres əb |əl ◂ ,•ə-, §,•iː-, -ɪb əl **~leness** əl nəs -nɪs **~ly** li

irreproachab|le ,ɪr ɪ 'prəʊtʃ əb |əl ◂ ,•ə-, §,•iː- ‖ -'prəʊtʃ- **~leness** əl nəs -nɪs **~ly** li

irresistibility ,ɪr ɪ ,zɪst ə 'bɪl ət i ,•ə-, §,•iː-, -ɪt i‖ -ət̬ i

irresistib|le ,ɪr ɪ 'zɪst əb |əl ◂ ,•ə-, §,•iː-, -ɪb əl **~leness** əl nəs -nɪs **~ly** li

irresoluteɪ 'rez ə luːt ,ɪ-, -ljuːt ‖ -əl ət **~ly**li **~ness**nəs nɪs

irresolutionɪ ˌrez ə 'luːʃ ᵊn ,ɪ,rez ə'•-, -'ljuːʃ-

irrespective,ɪr ɪ 'spekt ɪv ◂ -ə-, §-iː- **~ly**li

irresponsibility,ɪr ɪ ,spɒn̩ts ə 'bɪl ət i ,•ə-, §,•iː-, -ɪ'•-, -ɪt i‖ -,spɑːn̩ts ə 'bɪl ət̬ i

irresponsib|le,ɪr ɪ 'spɒn̩ts əb |əl ◂, •ə-, §,•iː-, -ɪb əl‖ -'spɑːn̩ts- **~leness**əl nəs -nɪs **~ly**li

irretrievab|le,ɪr ɪ 'triːv əb |əl ◂, •ə-, §,•iː- **~leness**əl nəs -nɪs **~ly**li

irreverenceɪ 'rev ᵊr_ən̩ts ,ɪ- ‖ ,ɪr-

irreverentɪ 'rev ᵊr_ənt ,ɪ- ‖ ,ɪr- **~ly**li

irreversibility,ɪr ɪ ,vɜːs ə 'bɪl ət i ,•ə-, §,•iː-, -ɪ'•-, -ɪt i‖ -,vɜːs ə 'bɪl ət̬ i

irreversib|le,ɪr ɪ 'vɜːs əb |əl ◂, •ə-, §,•iː-, -ɪb əl ‖ -'vɜːs- **~leness**əl nəs -nɪs **~ly**li

irrevocabilityɪ ,rev ək ə 'bɪl ət i ,ɪr ɪ ,vəʊk-, -ɪt i‖ -ət̬ i ,ɪr ,rev ək ə'•-

irrevocab|leɪ 'rev ək əb |əl ,ɪr ɪ 'vəʊk-, ,•ə-, §,•iː- ‖ ,ɪr-; ,ɪr ɪ 'vəʊk- **~leness** əl nəs -nɪs **~ly** li

irrigable 'ɪr ɪg əb ᵊl '•əg-

irri|gate 'ɪr ɪ |geɪt -ə- **~gated**geɪt ɪd -əd ‖ geɪt̬ əd **~gates**geɪts **~gating** geɪt ɪŋ ‖ geɪt̬ ɪŋ

irrigation ,ɪr ɪ 'geɪʃ ᵊn -ə- **~al**_əl ◂

irritability ,ɪr ɪt ə 'bɪl ət i ,•ət-, -ɪt i ‖ ,ɪr ət̬ ə 'bɪl ət̬ i

irritab|le 'ɪr ɪt əb |əl -ət əb- ‖ -ət̬ əb- **~leness** əl nəs -nɪs **~ly** li

irritant 'ɪr ɪt ənt -ət- ‖ -ət ᵊnt **~s** s

irri|tate 'ɪr ɪ |teɪt -ə- **~tated**teɪt ɪd -əd ‖ teɪt̬ əd **~tates**teɪts **~tating** teɪt ɪŋ ‖ teɪt̬ ɪŋ

irritation ,ɪr ɪ 'teɪʃ ᵊn -ə- **~s** z

irrupt ɪ 'rʌpt ,ɪ- ‖ ,ɪr- *(usually = erupt)* **~ed** ɪd əd **~ing** ɪŋ **~s** s

irruption ɪ 'rʌp ʃᵊn ,ɪ- ‖ ,ɪr- **~s** z

irruptive ɪ 'rʌpt ɪv ,ɪ- ‖ ,ɪr-

Irvine *(i)* 'ɜːv ɪn §-ᵊn ‖ 'ɜːv-, *(ii)* -aɪn —*The place in Strathclyde is (i), that in CA (ii). As a personal name, usually (i).*

Irving 'ɜːv ɪŋ ‖ 'ɜːv-

Irwell 'ɜː wel ‖ 'ɜː-

Irwin 'ɜː wɪn §-wən ‖ 'ɜː-

is strong form ɪz, weak forms z, s —*After a word ending in* s, z, ʃ, ʒ, tʃ, dʒ *there is no distinct weak form in RP, though in some varieties* §əz *is used. Otherwise, the contracted form* s *may be used after a word ending in* p, t, k, f, θ, *while* z *may be used after one ending in a vowel sound or* b, d, g, v, ð, m, n, ŋ, l *and AmE* r; s *and* z *may be shown in orthography as* 's. *No contraction is possible when this word is stranded:* is *is always strong and uncontracted in* Tell me what that is.

ISA 'aɪs ə **ISAs, ISA's** 'aɪs əz

Isaac 'aɪz ək

Isaacs 'aɪz əks

Isabel 'ɪz ə bel

Isabella ,ɪz ə 'bel ə

Isador, Isadore 'ɪz ə dɔː ‖ -dɔːr -dəʊr

Isadora ,ɪz ə 'dɔːr ə ‖ -'dəʊr-

isagogic ˌaɪs ə 'gɒdʒ ɪk ◄ ‖ -'gɑːdʒ- ~s s
Isaiah aɪ 'zaɪ ə §-'zeɪ ə ‖ aɪ 'zeɪ ə (*)
Isambard 'ɪz əm bɑːd ‖ -bɑːrd
-**isation** aɪ 'zeɪʃ ᵊn ɪ- ‖ ə 'zeɪʃ ᵊn (*) —
  canonisation ˌkæn ən aɪ 'zeɪʃ ᵊn -ən ɪ-
  ‖ -ən ə-
Isbister (i) 'aɪz bɪst ə ‖ -ᵊr, (ii) 'ɪz-
ISBN ˌaɪ es biː 'en
Iscariot ɪ 'skær iˌə 'skariˌə- ‖ ɪ 'sker-
ischaem|ia, ischem|ia ɪ 'skiːm iˌə ~**ic** ɪk
ischi|um 'ɪsk iˌəm ~**a** ə ~**al** əl
ISDN ˌaɪ es diː 'en
-**ise** aɪz —see also -**ize**
isenthalpic ˌaɪs en 'θælp ɪk ◄ ˌaɪz-, -ɪn-, -ᵊn-
isentropic ˌaɪs en 'trɒp ɪk ◄ ˌaɪz-, -ɪn-, -ᵊn-
  ‖ -'traɪp ɪk -'troʊp-
Iseult iː 'zuːlt -'suːlt
-**ish** ɪʃ — **boyish** 'bɔɪ ɪʃ —also informally as a
  separate word, 'to a certain extent' **ish** ɪʃ
Isham 'aɪʃ əm
Isherwood 'ɪʃ ə wʊd ‖ -ᵊr-
Ishmael 'ɪʃ meɪᵊl -mi_əl
Ishmaelite 'ɪʃ miˌə laɪt 'ɪʃ meɪᵊl aɪt;
  'ɪʃ mə laɪt, -mɪ- ~**s** s
Ishtar 'ɪʃt ɑː ‖ -ɑːr
Isidor, Isidore 'ɪz ə dɔː -ɪ- ‖ -dɔːr -doʊr
isinglass 'aɪz ɪŋ glɑːs §-glæs ‖ -ən glæs -ɪŋ-
Isis 'aɪs ɪs §-əs
Isla 'aɪl ə
Islam 'ɪz lɑːm 'ɪs-, -læm, •'• —Arabic [ɪs 'lɑːm]
Islamabad ɪz 'lɑːm ə bæd ɪs-, -'læm-, -bɑːd
Islamic ɪz 'læm ɪk ɪs-, -'lɑːm-
island 'aɪl ənd ~**ed** ɪd əd ~**ing** ɪŋ ~**s** z
islander 'aɪl ənd ə ‖ ᵊr ~**s** z
Islay 'aɪl ə -eɪ
isle aɪᵊl **isles** aɪᵊlz
  Isle of 'Man; Isle of 'Wight
islet 'aɪl ət -ɪt ~**s** s
Isleworth 'aɪz ᵊl wɜːθ -wəθ ‖ -wᵊrθ
Islington 'ɪz lɪŋ tən
Islip (i) 'aɪs lɪp, (ii) 'ɪz- —The places in England
  and NY are (i); the family name is usually (ii)
Islwyn 'ɪs lu ɪn ɪz 'luː_, ɪs- —Welsh ['ɪs lʊɪn,
  -lʊɪn]
ism 'ɪz əm **isms** 'ɪz əmz
-**ism** ˌɪz əm — **Darwinism** 'dɑː wɪ ˌnɪz əm
  -wə- ‖ 'dɑːr-
Ismaili, Isma'ili ˌɪz mɑː 'iːl i ◄ ɪz 'maɪl i
  ‖ ˌɪs meɪ 'ɪl i ˌɪz- —Arabic [ɪs mɑː ʕiː liː] ~**s**
  z
Ismailia, Ismailiya ˌɪz maɪ 'liː_ə ˌɪs-
  ‖ ˌɪz meɪ ə 'liː ə
Ismay 'ɪz meɪ
isn't contracted form 'ɪz ᵊnt
ISO ˌaɪ es 'əʊ ‖ -'oʊ
iso- comb. form
  with stress-neutral suffix ˌaɪs əʊ ‖ -oʊ -ə —
  isoseismal ˌaɪs əʊ 'saɪz mᵊl ◄ ‖ -oʊ-
  with stress-imposing suffix aɪ 'sɒ+ ‖ aɪ 'sɑː+ —
  isogonal aɪ 'sɒg ən əl ‖ -'sɑːg-
isobar 'aɪs əʊ bɑː ‖ -ə bɑːr ~**s** z
isobaric ˌaɪs əʊ 'bær ɪk ◄ ‖ -ə- -'ber-
isobath 'aɪs əʊ bæθ -bɑːθ ‖ -ə bæθ ~**s** s

Isobel 'ɪz ə bel
isochromatic ˌaɪs əʊ krəʊ
  'mæt ɪk ◄ ‖ ˌaɪs ə kroʊ 'mæt̬ ɪk ◄
isochronal aɪ 'sɒk rən əl ‖ -'sɑːk- ~**ly** i
isochronicit|y aɪ ˌsɒk rə 'nɪs ət i ˌaɪs əʊ krə-,
  -ɪt i ‖ aɪ ˌsɑːk rə 'nɪs ət̬ i ~**ies** iz
isochronis|e, isochroniz|e
  aɪ 'sɒk rə naɪz ‖ -'sɑːk- ~**ed** d ~**es** ɪz əz
  ~**ing** ɪŋ
isochronous aɪ 'sɒk rən əs ‖ -'sɑːk- ~**ly** li
isochron|y aɪ 'sɒk rən li ‖ -'sɑːk- ~**ies** iz
isoclinal ˌaɪs əʊ 'klaɪn əl ◄ ‖ -ə-
isocline 'aɪs əʊ klaɪn ‖ -ə- ~**s** z
isoclinic ˌaɪs əʊ 'klɪn ɪk ◄ ‖ -ə-
Isocrates aɪ 'sɒk rə tiːz ‖ -'sɑːk-
isogloss 'aɪs əʊ glɒs ‖ -ə glɑːs -glɔːs ~**es** ɪz əz
isohyet ˌaɪs əʊ 'haɪˌət -ɪt ‖ -oʊ- ~**s** s
iso|late v 'aɪs ə ‖leɪt ◄ 'ɪs- ~**lated** leɪt ɪd -əd
  ‖ leɪt̬ əd ~**lates** leɪts ~**lating** leɪt ɪŋ ‖ leɪt̬ ɪŋ
isolate n, adj 'aɪs əl ət -ɪt; -ə leɪt ‖ 'ɪs- ~**s** s
isolation ˌaɪs ə 'leɪʃ ᵊn ‖ ˌɪs- ~**ism** ɪz əm
  ~**ist/s** ɪst/s §əst/s
isolative 'aɪs ə lˌə ət ɪv -ə leɪt- ‖ 'aɪs ə leɪt̬ ɪv 'ɪs-
  ~**ly** li
Isolda ɪ 'zɒld ə ‖ ɪ 'soʊld ə -'zoʊld ə
Isolde ɪ 'zɒld ə ‖ ɪ 'soʊld •'•ə —Ger
  [ʔi 'zɔl də]
isomer 'aɪs əm ə ‖ -ᵊr ~**s** z
isomeric ˌaɪs əʊ 'mer ɪk ◄ ‖ -ə-
isomerism aɪ 'sɒm ə ˌrɪz əm ‖ -'sɑːm- ~**s** z
isometric ˌaɪs əʊ 'met rɪk ◄ ‖ -ə- ~**s** s
isomorph 'aɪs əʊ mɔːf ‖ -ə mɔːrf ~**s** s
isomorphic ˌaɪs əʊ 'mɔːf ɪk ◄ ‖ -ə 'mɔːrf-
  ~**ally** ᵊl_i
isomorphism ˌaɪs əʊ 'mɔːf ˌɪz əm ‖ -ᵊ 'mɔːrf-
  ~**s** z
Ison 'aɪs ᵊn
isophone 'aɪs əʊ fəʊn ‖ -ə foʊn ~**s** z
isopleth 'aɪs əʊ pleθ ‖ -ə- ~**s** s
isoprene 'aɪs əʊ priːn ‖ -ə-
isopropyl ˌaɪs əʊ 'prəʊp ɪl ◄ -ᵊl ‖ -ə 'proʊp ᵊl ◄
isosceles aɪ 'sɒs ə liːz -ɪ- ‖ -'saɪs-
isospora aɪ 'sɒsp ᵊr ə ‖ -'sɑːsp- ~**s** z
isotherm 'aɪs əʊ θɜːm ‖ -ə θɜːm ~**s** z
isotonic ˌaɪs əʊ 'tɒn ɪk ◄ ‖ -ə 'tɑːn-
isotope 'aɪs ə təʊp -əʊ- ‖ -ə toʊp ~**s** s
isotopic ˌaɪs əʊ 'tɒp ɪk ◄ ‖ -ə 'tɑːp- ~**ally** ᵊl_i
ISP ˌaɪ es 'piː ~**s** z
I-Spy, I-spy ˌaɪ 'spaɪ
Israel 'ɪz reɪᵊl 'ɪz riˌəl ‖ 'ɪz riˌəl —in singing
  usually 'ɪz reɪ el
Israeli ɪz 'reɪl i ~**s** z
Israelite 'ɪz riˌə laɪt 'ɪz reɪᵊl aɪt; 'ɪz rə laɪt, -rɪ-
  ~**s** s
Issigonis ˌɪs ɪ 'gəʊn ɪs -ə-, §-əs ‖ -'goʊn-
issuable 'ɪʃ u_əb ᵊl 'ɪs ju_, 'ɪʃ ju_
issuance 'ɪʃ u_ən¹s 'ɪs ju_, 'ɪʃ ju_
issue 'ɪʃ uː 'ɪs juː, 'ɪʃ juː —BrE 1988 poll panel
  preference: 'ɪʃ uː 49%, 'ɪs juː 30%, 'ɪʃ juː
  21%. In AmE always 'ɪʃ uː. **issued** 'ɪʃ uːd
  'ɪs juːd, 'ɪʃ- **issues** 'ɪʃ uːz 'ɪs juːz, 'ɪʃ-
  issuing 'ɪʃ uː ɪŋ 'ɪs juː ɪŋ, 'ɪʃ-
issuer 'ɪʃ uːˌə 'ɪs juːˌə, 'ɪʃ- ‖ ᵊr ~**s** z

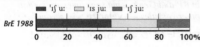

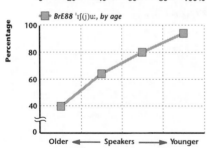

Older ◄——— Speakers ———► Younger

Issus 'ɪs əs
Issy 'ɪs i
-ist ɪst §-əst ‖ əst — **machinist** mə 'ʃiːn ɪst
  §-əst ‖ -əst
Istanbul ˌɪst æn 'bʊl ◄ -ɑːn-, →-æm-,
  -'buːl ‖ '•••—Turkish stanbul [is 'tɑn bʊl]
Isthmian 'ɪsθ mi‿ən ‖ 'ɪs-, 'ɪst-
isthmus 'ɪs məs 'ɪsθ-, 'ɪst- **~es** ɪz əz
-istic 'ɪst ɪk — **impressionistic**
  ɪm ˌpreʃ ə 'nɪst ɪk ◄
istle 'ɪst li
Istria 'ɪs tri‿ə
Isuzu tdmk iː 'suːz uː ɪ-, aɪ- —Jp [i ˌsɯ dzɯ]
it strong form ɪt —There is no distinct weak form
  in RP, but in some other varieties, including
  most GenAm, there is a weak form §ət. —The
  phrases it is, it isn't are often syllabified
  irregularly, as ɪ 'tɪz, ɪ 'tɪz ᵊnt.
IT 'information technology' ˌaɪ 'tiː
ITA, i.t.a. ˌaɪ tiː 'eɪ ◄
Italian ɪ 'tæl jən ə- **~s** z
italianate, I~ ɪ 'tæl jə neɪt ə-
italic, I~ ɪ 'tæl ɪk ə-, aɪ- **~s** s
italicis... —see **italiciz...**
italicization ɪ ˌtæl ɪ saɪ 'zeɪʃ ᵊn ə-, aɪ-, -ˌ•ə-,
  -sɪ'•- ‖ -ə sə- **~s** z
italiciz|e ɪ 'tæl ɪ saɪz ə-, aɪ-, -ə- **~ed** d **~es** ɪz
  əz **~ing** ɪŋ
Italo- ɪ ˈtæl əʊ ə-; ˌɪt əl əʊ ‖ ɪ ˈtæl oʊ ˌɪt ᵊl oʊ
  — **Italo-German** ɪ ˌtæl əʊ 'dʒɜːm ən ◄ ˌɪt
  əl əʊ- ‖ -oʊ 'dʒɝːm ən ◄ ˌɪt ᵊl oʊ-
Italy 'ɪt əl i ‖ 'ɪt ᵊl i
Itasca lake in MN aɪ 'tæsk ə
itch ɪtʃ **itched** ɪtʃt **itches** 'ɪtʃ ɪz -əz **itching**
  'ɪtʃ ɪŋ
Itchen 'ɪtʃ ɪn -ən
itch|y 'ɪtʃ |i **~ier** i‿ə ‖ i‿ᵊr **~iest** i‿ɪst i‿əst
  ~iness i nəs i nɪs
  ˌitchy 'feet; ˌitchy 'palm
it'd 'it would', 'it had' ɪt əd ‖ ɪṭ əd
-ite aɪt — **Luddite** 'lʌd aɪt
item 'aɪt əm -ɪm, -em ‖ 'aɪṭ əm **~s** z
itemis|e, itemiz|e 'aɪt ə maɪz -ɪ- ‖ 'aɪṭ- **~ed** d
  ~es ɪz əz **~ing** ɪŋ
ite|rate 'ɪt ə |reɪt ‖ 'ɪṭ- **~rated** reɪt ɪd -əd

‖ reɪṭ əd **~rates** reɪts **~rating**
  reɪt ɪŋ ‖ reɪṭ ɪŋ
iteration ˌɪt ə 'reɪʃ ᵊn ‖ ˌɪṭ- **~s** z
iterative 'ɪt_ᵊr ət ɪv 'ɪt ə reɪt- ‖ 'ɪṭ ə reɪṭ ɪv
  -ᵊr əṭ- **~ly** li **~ness** nəs nɪs
iterativity ˌɪt_ᵊr ə 'tɪv ət i -ɪt i ‖ ˌɪṭ ᵊr ə 'tɪv əṭ i
Ithaca 'ɪθ ək ə
Ithon 'aɪθ ɒn ‖ -ɑːn —Welsh ['əj θon]
ithyphallic ˌɪθ i 'fæl ɪk ◄ ˌaɪθ- **~s** s
-itides pl of **-itis** 'ɪt ɪ diːz -ə- ‖ -'ɪṭ ə diːz —
  meningitides ˌmen ɪn 'dʒɪt ɪ diːz §ˌ•ən-,
  §-'•ə- ‖ -'dʒɪṭ ə diːz
itinerancy aɪ 'tɪn ər ənts i ɪ-
itinerant aɪ 'tɪn ər ənt ɪ- **~s** s
itinerar|y aɪ 'tɪn ᵊr_ər |i △-'tɪn ər‿li ‖ -ə rer li
  ~ies iz
-ition 'ɪʃ ᵊn — **opposition** ˌɒp ə 'zɪʃ ᵊn ‖ ˌɑːp-
-itious 'ɪʃ əs — **adventitious** ˌæd vən 'tɪʃ əs ◄
  -ven-
-itis aɪt ɪs §-əs ‖ 'aɪṭ əs — **enteritis**
  ˌent ə 'raɪt ɪs §-əs ‖ ˌenṭ ə 'raɪṭ əs
-itive stress-imposing ət ɪv ɪt- ‖ əṭ ɪv —
  competitive kəm 'pet ət ɪv -ɪt- ‖ -'peṭ əṭ ɪv
it'll 'it will' (')ɪt ᵊl ‖ (')ɪṭ ᵊl
Itma 'ɪt mɑː
ITN ˌaɪ tiː 'en
-itory stress-imposing ət_ᵊr i ɪt_ᵊr i ‖ ə tɔːr i
  ə tʊr i (*) — **territory** 'ter ət_ᵊr i '•ɪt_
  ‖ 'ter ə tɔːr i -tʊr i
its ɪts —non-RP weak form əts
it's 'it is'; 'it has' ɪts —non-RP weak form əts
itself ɪt 'self §ət-
itsy-bitsy ˌɪts i 'bɪts i ◄
itty-bitty ˌɪt i 'bɪt i ◄ ‖ ˌɪṭ i 'bɪṭ i ◄
ITV ˌaɪ tiː 'viː ◄
-ity stress-imposing ət i ɪt i ‖ əṭ i — **modernity**
  mɒ 'dɜːn ət i mə-, -ɪt i ‖ mɑː 'dɝːn əṭ i
IUD ˌaɪ juː 'diː **~s, ~'s** z
Ivan 'aɪv ən —but as a foreign name also
  ˌiː 'væn ◄, ɪ-, -'vɑːn
Ivana ɪ 'vɑːn ə -'væn-
Ivanhoe 'aɪv ən həʊ ‖ -hoʊ
-ive ɪv — **prohibitive** prəʊ 'hɪb ɪt ɪv -ət-
  ‖ proʊ 'hɪb əṭ ɪv
I've 'I have' aɪv
Iveagh 'aɪv ə -eɪ
Iveco tdmk ɪ 'veɪk əʊ aɪ 'viːk- ‖ -oʊ
Ivens 'aɪv ᵊnz
Iver 'aɪv ə ‖ -ᵊr
Ives aɪvz
ivi... —see **ivy**
ivied 'aɪv id
Ivor 'aɪv ə ‖ -ᵊr
Ivorian aɪ 'vɔːr i‿ən ɪ- **~s** z
ivor|y, Ivor|y 'aɪv ᵊr_|i **~ies, ~y's** iz
  ˌIvory 'Coast; ˌivory 'tower
ivy, Ivy 'aɪv i **ivied** 'aɪv id **ivies** 'aɪv iz
  'Ivy ˌLeague
Iwan 'juː_ən —Welsh ['i wan]
Iwo 'iː wəʊ ‖ -woʊ -wə
  ˌIwo 'Jima 'dʒiːm ə —Jp [i ˌoo dzi ma]
ixia 'ɪks i‿ə **~s** z
Ixion ɪk 'saɪ‿ən

I

Izaak ˈaɪz ək
Izal *tdmk* ˈaɪz əl
izard, Izard ˈɪz əd ‖ -ᵊrd ~**s** z
-ization ˌaɪ ˈzeɪʃ ᵊn ɪ- ‖ ə ˈzeɪʃ ᵊn (*) —
  velarization ˌviːl ər aɪ ˈzeɪʃ ᵊn -ᵊr-ˈ- ‖ -ə ˈzeɪʃ ᵊn ‖

-ize aɪz —*This suffix is unstressed (though strong) in RP and GenAm, but sometimes stressed in other varieties* — **velarize** ˈviːl ə raɪz §, • • ˈ•

Izzard, i~ *(i)* ˈɪz əd ‖ -ᵊrd, *(ii)* -ɑːd ‖ -ɑːrd

Izzy ˈɪz i

J j

j Spelling-to-sound

1 Where the spelling is **j**, the pronunciation is regularly dʒ, as in **jump** dʒʌmp.

2 Occasionally, in words of foreign origin, it is ʒ, as in **jabot** 'ʒæb əʊ ‖ ʒæ 'bovʊ, or j, as in **hallelujah** ˌhæl ɪ 'luː jə.

3 The sound dʒ is also regularly written **dg** or **g**, as in **hedge** hedʒ, **large** lɑːdʒ ‖ lɑːrdʒ.

J, j dʒeɪ **Js, J's, j's** dʒeɪz —*Communications code name:* Juliet

jab dʒæb **jabbed** dʒæbd **jabbing** 'dʒæb ɪŋ **jabs** dʒæbz

jabber 'dʒæb ə ‖ -ᵊr ~**ed** d **jabbering** 'dʒæb ər_ɪŋ ~**s** z

jabberer 'dʒæb ər ə ‖ -ᵊr ~**s** z

Jabberwock, j~ 'dʒæb ə wɒk ‖ -ᵊr wɑːk ~**y** i

Jabez 'dʒeɪb ez -ɪz

jabiru ˌdʒæb ə 'ruː: -ɪ-, '••• ~**s** z

jaborandi ˌdʒæb ə 'rænd i ˌʒæb-, -ræn 'diː ~**s** z

jabot 'ʒæb əʊ ‖ ʒæ 'bovʊ —*Fr* [ʒa bo] ~**s** z

jacamar 'dʒæk ə mɑː: 'ʒæk- ‖ -mɑːr ~**s** z

jacana dʒə 'kɑːn ə 'dʒæk ən ə; ˌdʒæs ə 'nɑː, ˌʒæs- —*Port* jaçanã [ʒɐ sɐ 'nɐ̃] ~**s** z

jacaranda ˌdʒæk ə 'rænd ə ~**s** z

Jacinta dʒə 'sɪnt ə —*but as a foreign name also* hæ- —*Sp* [xa 'θin ta, -'sin-]

jacinth, J~ 'dʒæs ɪntθ 'dʒeɪs-, §-ᵊntθ ‖ 'dʒeɪs- 'dʒæs- ~**s** s

Jacintha dʒə 'sɪntθ ə dʒæ-

jack, Jack dʒæk **jacked** dʒækt **jacking** 'dʒæk ɪŋ **jacks, Jack's** dʒæks ˌJack 'Frost; 'jack knife; 'jack plug; ˌJack 'Robinson; ˌJack 'Russell; ˌjack 'tar; ˌJack the 'Lad

jackal 'dʒæk ɔːl -əl ‖ -əl -ɔːl, -ɑːl ~**s** z

jackanapes 'dʒæk ə neɪps

jackaroo ˌdʒæk ə 'ruː: ~**ed** d ~**ing** ɪŋ ~**s** z

jackass 'dʒæk æs -ɑːs ~**es** ɪz əz

jackboot 'dʒæk buːt ~**s** s

jackdaw 'dʒæk dɔː ‖ -dɑː ~**s** z

jackeroo ˌdʒæk ə 'ruː: ~**ed** d ~**ing** ɪŋ ~**s** z

jacket 'dʒæk ɪt §-ət ~**s** s

jackfruit 'dʒæk fruːt ~**s** s

jackhammer 'dʒæk ˌhæm ə ‖ -ᵊr ~**s** z

Jackie 'dʒæk i

jack-in-office 'dʒæk ɪn ˌɒf ɪs §-ᵊn-, §-əs ‖ -ˌɑːf əs -ˌɔːf-

jack-in-the-box 'dʒæk ɪn ðə ˌbɒks §'•ᵊn- ‖ -ˌbɑːks ~**es** ɪz əz

jack|knife *n, v* 'dʒæk |naɪf ~**knifed** naɪft ~**knifes** naɪfs ~**knifing** naɪf ɪŋ

Jacklin 'dʒæk lɪn §-lən

Jackman 'dʒæk mən

jack-of-all-trades ˌdʒæk əv 'ɔːl treɪdz ˌ•• ,•'• ‖ -'ɑːl-

jack-o'-lantern ˌdʒæk ə 'lænt ən '•• ,•• ‖ -ᵊrn ~**s** z

jackpot 'dʒæk pɒt ‖ -pɑːt ~**s** s

jackrabbit 'dʒæk ˌræb ɪt §-ət ~**s** s

jacksnipe 'dʒæk snaɪp ~**s** s

Jackson 'dʒæks ən

Jacksonian dʒæk 'səʊn i_ən ‖ -'soʊn- ~**s** z

Jacksonville 'dʒæks ən vɪl

jack-the-lad ˌdʒæk ðə 'læd ~**s** z

Jacky 'dʒæk i

Jacob 'dʒeɪk əb -ʌb ~**'s** z

Jacobean ˌdʒæk əʊ 'biː_ən ◄ ‖ -ə- ~**s** z

Jacobethan ˌdʒæk əʊ 'biːθ ᵊn ◄ ‖ -ə-

Jacobi (i) 'dʒæk əb i, (ii) dʒə 'kəʊb i ‖ -'koʊb-

jacobian, J~ dʒə 'kəʊb i_ən ‖ -'koʊb- ~**s** z

Jacobin 'dʒæk əb ɪn §-ən ~**ism** ˌɪz əm ~**s** z

Jacobite 'dʒæk ə baɪt ~**s** s

Jacobs 'dʒeɪk əbz -ʌbz

Jacobson 'dʒeɪk əb sən

jacobus, J~ dʒə 'kəʊb əs ‖ -'koʊb- ~**es** ɪz əz

Jacoby (i) dʒə 'kəʊb i ‖ -'koʊb-, (ii) 'dʒæk əb i

Jacquard 'dʒæk ɑːd dʒə 'kɑːd ‖ -ɑːrd —*Fr* [ʒa kaːʁ] ~**s** z

Jacqueline 'dʒæk ə liːn -lɪn; 'dʒæk liːn, 'ʒæk-, -lɪn

Jacquelyn 'dʒæk əl_ɪn §-ən

Jacques dʒeɪks dʒæks, ʒæk ‖ ʒɑːk —*Fr* [ʒak]

Jacqui 'dʒæk i

jacuzzi, J~ *tdmk* dʒə 'kuːz i dʒæ- ~**s** z

jade, Jade 'dʒeɪd **jaded** 'dʒeɪd ɪd -əd **jades** dʒeɪdz **jading** 'dʒeɪd ɪŋ

jadeite 'dʒeɪd aɪt ~**s** s

j'adoube ʒæ 'duːb ʒə-, ʒɑː-

jaeger, J~ *tdmk* 'jeɪg ə 'dʒeɪg- ‖ -ᵊr ~**s** z

Jael 'dʒeɪ_əl -el

Jaffa, jaffa 'dʒæf ə jaffas 'dʒæf əz
,Jaffa 'orange
jaffle 'dʒæf əl ~s z
Jaffna 'dʒæf nə
jag, Jag dʒæg jagged v dʒægd jagging
'dʒæg ɪŋ jags, Jags dʒægz
Jagan 'dʒeɪg ən
jagged adj 'dʒæg ɪd -əd ~ly li ~ness nəs nɪs
Jagger 'dʒæg ə ‖ -ər
jagg|y 'dʒæg |i ~ier i_ə ‖ i_ər ~iest i_ɪst i_əst
Jago 'dʒeɪg əʊ ‖ -oʊ
jaguar, J~ 'dʒæg ju_ə §-ɑː ‖ 'dʒæg wɑːr
'dʒæg ju ɑːr ~s z
jaguarondi ,dʒæg wə 'rɒnd i ,ʒæg- ‖ -'rɑːnd i
,dʒɑːg-, ,ʒɑːg- ~s z
jaguarundi ,dʒæg wə 'rʌnd i ,ʒæg- ‖ ,dʒɑːg-,
,ʒɑːg- ~s z
Jah dʒɑː
jai dʒaɪ —Hindi [dʒæ]
jai alai ,haɪ ə 'laɪ '•••; ,haɪ 'laɪ, '•• ‖ 'haɪ laɪ
,haɪ ə 'laɪ
jail dʒeɪəl jailed dʒeɪəld jailing 'dʒeɪəl ɪŋ jails
dʒeɪəlz
jailbird 'dʒeɪəl bɜːd ‖ -bɝːd ~s z
jailbreak 'dʒeɪəl breɪk ~er/s ə/z ‖ ər/z ~s s
jailer, jailor 'dʒeɪl ə ‖ -ər ~s z
jailhouse 'dʒeɪəl haʊs
Jaime 'dʒeɪm i —but as a Spanish name, 'haɪm i
—Sp ['xai me]
Jain dʒaɪn dʒeɪn ~ism ,ɪz əm ~s z
Jaipur ,dʒaɪ 'pʊə -'pɔː ‖ 'dʒaɪ pʊr —Hindi
[dʒəɪ pʊr]
Jairus 'dʒaɪər əs dʒeɪ 'aɪər əs
Jakarta dʒə 'kɑːt ə ‖ -'kɑːrt ə
Jake, jake dʒeɪk Jake's, jakes, Jakes dʒeɪks
Jakobson 'jɑːk əb sən
Jalalabad dʒə 'lɑːl ə bɑːd -'læl-, -bæd, •, •••
—Hindi [dʒə lɑː lɑː bɑːd̪]
jalap 'dʒæl əp 'dʒɒl- ‖ 'dʒɑːl-
jalapeno, jalapeño
,hæl ə 'peɪn jəʊ ‖ ,hɑːl ə 'peɪn joʊ ,hæl-
—Sp [xa la 'pe ɲo] ~s z
jalop|y dʒə 'lɒp |i ‖ -'lɑːp |i ~ies iz
jalousie 'ʒæl u ziː, •••; §dʒə 'luːs i
‖ 'dʒæl əs i (*) ~s z
jam dʒæm jammed dʒæmd jamming
'dʒæm ɪŋ jams dʒæmz
'jam ,session
Jamaica dʒə 'meɪk ə
Jamaican dʒə 'meɪk ən ~s z
Jamal dʒə 'mɑːl
jamb dʒæm dʒæmb (usually = jam) jambs
dʒæmz dʒæmbz
jambalaya ,dʒæm bə 'laɪ_ə ,dʒʌm- ~s z
jamboree ,dʒæm bə 'riː ◄ ~s z
James dʒeɪmz James', James's 'dʒeɪmz ɪz -əz;
dʒeɪmz
Jamesian 'dʒeɪm zi_ən ~s z
Jameson 'dʒeɪm sən 'dʒem ɪs ən, 'dʒɪm-,
'dʒæm-, 'dʒeɪm-, -əs-
Jamestown 'dʒeɪmz taʊn
Jamie 'dʒeɪm i
Jamieson 'dʒeɪm ɪs ən 'dʒem-, 'dʒɪm-, 'dʒæm-

Jamiroquai dʒə 'mɪr ə kwaɪ
jamm... —see jam
jammer 'dʒæm ə ‖ -ər ~s z
Jammu 'dʒæm uː 'dʒʌm-
jamm|y 'dʒæm |i ~ier i_ə ‖ i_ər ~iest i_ɪst
i_əst
jam-packed ,dʒæm 'pækt ◄
Jamshid, Jamshyd ,dʒæm 'ʃiːd '••, -ʃɪd
Jan dʒæn —but as a male name also jæn ‖ jɑːn
(Polish, Czech, Swedish, Norwegian [jan],
Dutch [jɑn]), and by confusion also ʒɒ̃, ʒæn
Jan. dʒæn —see also January
Janacek, Janáček 'jæn ə tʃek -ɑː- —Czech
['ja na: tʃek]
Jancis 'dʒænts ɪs §-əs
Jane dʒeɪn
Janet 'dʒæn ɪt -ət
Janette dʒə 'net dʒæ-
jangl|e 'dʒæŋ gəl ~ed d ~es z ~ing ɪŋ
Janice 'dʒæn ɪs -əs
Janie 'dʒeɪn i
Janine dʒə 'niːn
Janis 'dʒæn ɪs -əs
janissar|y 'dʒæn ɪs ər_li '•əs- ‖ -ə ser li ~ies iz
janitor 'dʒæn ɪt ə -ət- ‖ -ət̬ ər ~s z
janitorial ,dʒæn ɪ 'tɔːr i_əl ◄, •ə- ‖ -'toʊr-
janizar|y 'dʒæn ɪz ər_li '•əz- ‖ -ə zer li ~ies iz
Jansen 'dʒænts ən ~ism ,ɪz əm ~ist/s ɪst/s
§əst/s
Jansky, j~ 'dʒænts ki
Janson 'dʒænts ən
Jantzen tdmk 'dʒænts ən 'jænts-
January tdmk 'dʒæn ju_ər i 'dʒæn jʊr i,
§'dʒæn ju er i ‖ -ju er i
Janus 'dʒeɪn əs
Janvrin 'dʒæn vrɪn -vrən
Jap dʒæp Japs dʒæps
Japan, japan dʒə 'pæn ~ned d ~ning ɪŋ ~s,
~'s z
Japanese ,dʒæp ə 'niːz ◄ ‖-'niːs
,Japanese 'lantern; ,Japanese 'maple;
,Japanese 'people
jape dʒeɪp japes dʒeɪps
Japhet 'dʒeɪf et -ɪt, §-ət
Japheth 'dʒeɪf eθ -ɪθ, §-əθ
Japhetic dʒeɪ 'fet ɪk dʒə- ‖ -'fet̬ ɪk
japonica dʒə 'pɒn ɪk ə ‖ -'pɑːn- ~s z
Jaques (i) dʒeɪks, (ii) dʒæks —but in
Shakespeare 'dʒeɪk wɪz
jar dʒɑː ‖ dʒɑːr jarred dʒɑːd ‖ dʒɑːrd jarring
'dʒɑːr ɪŋ jars dʒɑːz ‖ dʒɑːrz
Jardine 'dʒɑːd iːn ‖ dʒɑːr 'diːn
jardiniere, jardinière ,ʒɑːd ɪn i 'eə
,ʒɑːd ɪn 'jeə ‖ ,dʒɑːrd ən 'ɪər ,ʒɑːrd-, -'jeər
—Fr [ʒaʁ di njɛːʁ] ~s z
Jared 'dʒær əd ‖ 'dʒer-
jargon 'dʒɑːg ən ‖ 'dʒɑːrg- -ɑːn ~s z
jargonistic ,dʒɑːg ə 'nɪst ɪk ◄ ‖ ,dʒɑːrg-
Jarlsberg tdmk 'jɑːlz bɜːg ‖ 'jɑːrlz bɝːg
Jarman 'dʒɑːm ən ‖ 'dʒɑːrm-
Jarndyce 'dʒɑːnd aɪs ‖ 'dʒɑːrnd-
Jarrad 'dʒær əd ‖ 'dʒer-
jarrah 'dʒær ə ‖ 'dʒer- ~s z

Jarratt, Jarrett 'dʒær ət -ɪt ‖ 'dʒer-
Jarrold 'dʒær əld ‖ 'dʒer-
Jarrow 'dʒær əʊ ‖ -oʊ 'dʒer-
Jaruzelski ˌjær u 'zel ski ‖ ˌjɑːr- —Polish
[ja ru 'zel ski]
Jarvik 'dʒɑːv ɪk ‖ 'dʒɑːrv-
Jarvis 'dʒɑːv ɪs §-əs ‖ 'dʒɑːrv-
Jas. dʒæs —see also James
jasmine, J~ 'dʒæz mɪn 'dʒæs-, §-mən ~s, ~'s z
Jason 'dʒeɪs ᵊn
jasper, J~ 'dʒæsp ə ‖ -ᵊr ~s, ~'s z
jaundice 'dʒɔːnd ɪs §-əs ‖ 'dʒɑːnd- ~d t
jaunt dʒɔːnt ‖ dʒɑːnt jaunted 'dʒɔːnt ɪd -əd
‖ 'dʒɔːnt̬ əd 'dʒɑːnt̬- jaunting
'dʒɔːnt ɪŋ ‖ 'dʒɔːnt̬ ɪŋ 'dʒɑːnt̬- jaunts
dʒɔːnts ‖ dʒɑːnts
'jaunting car
jaunt|y 'dʒɔːnt li ‖ 'dʒɔːnt̬ li 'dʒɑːnt̬- ~ier
i‿ə ‖ i‿ᵊr ~iest i‿ɪst i‿əst ~ily i li əl i ~iness
i nəs i nɪs
Java 'dʒɑːv ə ‖ 'dʒæv ə —in AmE the computer
language is 'dʒɑːv ə, and this is also the most
usual pronunciation for the island; but coffee is
often 'dʒæv ə, while the places in NY are
'dʒeɪv ə
Javan 'dʒɑːv ᵊn ‖ 'dʒæv- ~s z
Javanese ˌdʒɑːv ə 'niːz ◄ ‖ ˌdʒæv- ˌdʒɑːv-,
-'niːs
JavaScript 'dʒɑːv ə skrɪpt
javelin 'dʒæv əl ɪn §_ən ~s z
Javits 'dʒæv ɪts §-əts
jaw dʒɔː ‖ dʒɑː jawed dʒɔːd ‖ dʒɑːd jawing
'dʒɔːʳ ɪŋ ‖ 'dʒɔː ɪŋ 'dʒɑː-
jawbone 'dʒɔː bəʊn ‖ -boʊn 'dʒɑː- ~s z
jawbreaker 'dʒɔː ˌbreɪk ə ‖ -ᵊr 'dʒɑː- ~s z
jay, Jay dʒeɪ jays, Jay's dʒeɪz
Jaycee ˌdʒeɪ 'siː
Jayne dʒeɪn
jaywalk 'dʒeɪ wɔːk ‖ -wɑːk ~ed t ~er/s ə/
z ‖ ᵊr/z ~ing ɪŋ ~s s
Jaywick 'dʒeɪ wɪk
jazz dʒæz jazzed dʒæzd jazzes 'dʒæz ɪz -əz
jazzing 'dʒæz ɪŋ
jazz|y 'dʒæz li ~ier i‿ə ‖ i‿ᵊr ~iest i‿ɪst i‿əst
~ily ɪ li əl i ~iness i nəs i nɪs
JCB tdmk ˌdʒeɪ siː 'biː ~s, ~'s z
jealous 'dʒel əs ~ly li ~ness nəs nɪs
jealous|y 'dʒel əs li ~ies iz
Jean female name dʒiːn
Jean male name, French ʒɒ̃ ‖ ʒɑːn —Fr [ʒɑ̃]
Jeanette dʒɪ 'net dʒə-
Jeanie, Jeannie 'dʒiːn i
Jeannine dʒɪ 'niːn dʒə-
jeans, Jeans dʒiːnz
Jeavons 'dʒev ᵊnz
Jeb, Jebb dʒeb
Jebusite 'dʒeb ju zaɪt ‖ -jə saɪt ~s s
Jed dʒed
Jedburgh 'dʒed bər‿ə →'dʒeb-
Jedda, Jeddah 'dʒed ə —Arabic ['dʒed da]
Jedediah ˌdʒed ɪ 'daɪ‿ə ◄ -ə-
Jedi 'dʒed aɪ
jeep, Jeep tdmk dʒiːp jeeps dʒiːps

jeepers 'dʒiːp əz ‖ -ᵊrz
jeepney 'dʒiːp ni ~s z
Jeeps dʒiːps
jeer dʒɪə ‖ dʒɪᵊr jeered dʒɪəd ‖ dʒɪᵊrd
jeering 'dʒɪər ɪŋ ‖ 'dʒɪr ɪŋ jeers
dʒɪəz ‖ dʒɪᵊrz
Jeeves dʒiːvz
jeez dʒiːz
Jeff dʒef
Jefferies 'dʒef riz
Jeffers 'dʒef əz ‖ -ᵊrz
Jefferson 'dʒef əs ən ‖ -ᵊrs-
Jeffersonian ˌdʒef ə 'səʊn i_ən ◄ ‖ -ᵊr 'soʊn-
~s z
Jeffery, Jeffrey 'dʒef ri
Jeffreys, Jeffries 'dʒef riz
Jeger 'dʒeɪg ə ‖ -ᵊr
Jehoshaphat dʒɪ 'hɒʃ ə fæt dʒə-, -'hɒs-
‖ -'hɑːs-
Jehovah dʒɪ 'həʊv ə dʒə- ‖ -'hoʊv ə ~'s z
Je,hovah's 'Witness
Jehu 'dʒiː hju: ‖ -hu:
jejune dʒɪ 'dʒuːn dʒə- ~ly li ~ness nəs nɪs
jejunum dʒɪ 'dʒuːn əm dʒə- ~s z
Jekyll (i) 'dʒek ᵊl -ɪl, (ii) 'dʒiːk-
jell dʒel jelled dʒeld jelling 'dʒel ɪŋ jells
dʒelz
jellaba, jellabah 'dʒel əb ə dʒə 'lɑːb ə ~s z
Jellicoe 'dʒel ɪ kəʊ -ə- ‖ -koʊ
jellie... —see jelly
jello, Jello, Jell-O tdmk 'dʒel əʊ ‖ -oʊ ~s z
jell|y 'dʒel li ~ied id ~ies iz ~ying i‿ɪŋ
ˌjellied 'eels; 'jelly ˌbaby; 'jelly bean; 'jelly
roll
jellyfish 'dʒel i fɪʃ ~es ɪz əz
Jemima dʒɪ 'maɪm ə dʒə-
jemm|y, Jemmy 'dʒem li ~ied id ~ies iz
~ying i‿ɪŋ
Jena 'jeɪn ə —Ger ['jeː na]
je ne sais quoi ˌʒə nə seɪ 'kwɑː —Fr
[ʒən sɛ kwa]
Jenifer 'dʒen ɪf ə -əf- ‖ -ᵊr
Jenkin 'dʒeŋk ɪn §-ən
Jenkins 'dʒeŋk ɪnz §-ənz
Jenkinson 'dʒeŋk ɪn sən §-ən-
Jenks dʒeŋks
Jenner 'dʒen ə ‖ -ᵊr
jennet 'dʒen ɪt §-ət ~s s
Jennie 'dʒen i
jennie... —see jenny
Jennifer 'dʒen ɪf ə -əf- ‖ -ᵊr
Jennings 'dʒen ɪŋz
jenny, Jenny 'dʒen i jennies, Jenny's 'dʒen iz
Jensen 'dʒen⁺s ən —but as a non-English name
also 'jen⁺s- —Danish ['jɛn sən], German
['jɛn zᵊn]
jeopardis|e, jeopardiz|e 'dʒep ə daɪz ‖ -ᵊr-
~ed d ~es ɪz əz ~ing ɪŋ
jeopardy 'dʒep əd i ‖ -ᵊrd i
Jephthah 'dʒefθ ə
jequirity dʒɪ 'kwɪr ət i dʒə-, -ɪt- ‖ -ət̬ i
je'quirity bean
jerboa dʒɜː 'bəʊ ə dʒə- ‖ dʒɜʳ 'boʊ ə ~s z

J

jeremiad ˌdʒer ɪ ˈmaɪˌəd -ə-, -æd **~s** z
Jeremiah ˌdʒer ɪ ˈmaɪˌə ◀ -ə- **~s, ~'s** z
Jeremy ˈdʒer əm ɪ -ɪm-
Jerez hə ˈrez he-, -ˈreθ, -ˈres —*Sp* [xe ˈreθ]
Jericho ˈdʒer ɪ kəʊ ‖ -koʊ
jerk dʒɜːk ‖ dʒɜˠːk **jerked** dʒɜːkt ‖ dʒɜˠːkt
jerking ˈdʒɜːk ɪŋ ‖ ˈdʒɜˠːk ɪŋ **jerks**
dʒɜːks ‖ dʒɜˠːks
jerkin ˈdʒɜːk ɪn §-ən ‖ ˈdʒɜˠːk- **~s** z
jerk|y ˈdʒɜːk |i ‖ ˈdʒɜˠːk |i **~ier** i ə ‖ i ˠr **~iest**
i ɪst i əst **~ily** ɪ li əl i **~iness** i nəs i nɪs
Jermaine dʒə ˈmeɪn ‖ dʒɜˠr-
Jermyn ˈdʒɜːm ɪn §-ən ‖ ˈdʒɜˠːm-
jeroboam, J~ ˌdʒer ə ˈbəʊ əm ‖ -ˈboʊ- **~s** z
Jerome dʒə ˈrəʊm dʒɪ-, dʒe- ‖ -ˈroʊm
Jerrold ˈdʒer əld
jerr|y, Jerr|y ˈdʒer |i **~ies, ~y's** iz
ˈjerry can
jerry-|build ˈdʒer i |bɪld **~builder/s** bɪld ə/
z ‖ -ˠrz **~building** bɪld ɪŋ **~builds** bɪldz
~built bɪlt
jersey, J~ ˈdʒɜːz |i ‖ ˈdʒɜˠːz |i **~s** z
ˌJersey ˈCity
Jerusalem dʒə ˈruːs əl əm dʒɪ-, dʒe- ‖ -ˈruːz-
Je,rusalem ˈartichoke
Jervaulx ˈdʒɜːv əʊ ‖ ˈdʒɜˠːv əʊ —*but as a family
name* -ɪs, -əs
Jervis ˈdʒɜːv ɪs ˈdʒɑːv-, §-əs ‖ ˈdʒɜˠːv-
Jerwood ˈdʒɜː wʊd ‖ ˈdʒɜˠː-
Jespersen ˈjesp əs ən ˈdʒesp- ‖ -ˠrs- —*Dan*
[ˈjes bɐ sən]
Jess, jess dʒes **jessed** dʒest (= *jest*) **jesses**
ˈdʒes ɪz -əz **jessing** ˈdʒes ɪŋ
jessamine, J~ ˈdʒes əm ɪn §-ən
Jesse ˈdʒes i —*sometimes also* dʒes
Jessel ˈdʒes əl
Jessica ˈdʒes ɪk ə
Jessie ˈdʒes i
Jessop ˈdʒes əp
jest dʒest **jested** ˈdʒest ɪd -əd **jesting**
ˈdʒest ɪŋ **jests** dʒests
jester ˈdʒest ə ‖ -ˠr **~s** z
Jesu ˈdʒiːz ju: ‖ -u: —*in singing also* ˈjeɪz u:,
ˈjeɪs- **~'s** z
Jesuit ˈdʒez ju ɪt ˈdʒez-, -u-, §ˌət ‖ ˈdʒez u ət
ˈdʒez- **~s** s
jesuitic, J~ ˌdʒez ju ˈɪt ɪk ◀ ˌdʒez-, -u-
‖ ˌdʒez u ˈɪt ɪk ◀ ˌdʒez- **~al** əl **~ally** əl_i
Jesus ˈdʒiːz əs ‖ -əz **Jesus'** ˈdʒiːz əs ‖ -əz
ˌJesus ˈChrist
jet dʒet **jets** dʒets **jetted** ˈdʒet ɪd -əd
‖ ˈdʒet̬ əd **jetting** ˈdʒet ɪŋ ‖ ˈdʒet̬ ɪŋ
ˈjet ˌengine; ˈjet lag; ˌjet proˈpulsion; ˈjet
set; ˈjet stream
jet-black ˌdʒet ˈblæk ◀
jete, jeté ʒə ˈteɪ —*Fr* [ʒə te, ʃte] **~s** z
jetfoil ˈdʒet fɔɪəl **~s** z
Jethro ˈdʒeθ rəʊ ‖ -roʊ
jet-lagged ˈdʒet lægd
jetliner ˈdʒet ˌlaɪn ə ‖ -ˠr **~s** z
jet-propelled ˌdʒet prə ˈpeld ◀
jetsam ˈdʒet səm -sæm
jet-setter ˈdʒet set ə ‖ -set̬ ˠr

jet-ski ˈdʒet ski: **~ed** d **~es** z **~ing** ɪŋ **~s** z
jettison ˈdʒet ɪs ən -ɪz-, -əs-, -əz- ‖ ˈdʒet̬- **~ed**
d **~ing** ɪŋ **~s** z
jett|y ˈdʒet |i ‖ ˈdʒet̬ |i **~ies** iz
jeu d'esprit, jeux d'esprit ˌʒɜ: de ˈspri: ‖ ˌʒu:-
—*Fr* [ʒø dɛs pʁi]
Jeuda ˈdʒu:d ə
jeunesse dor|ee, -ée ˌʒɜːn es ˈdɔːr eɪ
ʒɜː ˌnes dɔː ˈreɪ ‖ ʒu: ˌnes dɔː ˈreɪ —*Fr*
[ʒœ nɛs dɔ ʁe, -nɛz-]
Jevons ˈdʒev ənz
Jew dʒu: **Jews** dʒu:z
jewel ˈdʒu:ˌəl dʒu:l **~s** z
Jewel, Jewell ˈdʒu:ˌəl dʒu:l
jeweller ˈdʒu:ˌəl ə ˈdʒu:l ə ‖ -ˠr **~s** z
jewellery, jewelry ˈdʒu:ˌəl ri ˈdʒu:l ri; §ˈdʒu:l
ər i
Jewess ˈdʒu: es -ɪs, -əs, ˌdʒu: ˈes ‖ -əs **~es** ɪz
əz
Jewett ˈdʒu:ˌɪt § ət
Jewish ˈdʒu:ˌɪʃ **~ness** nəs nɪs
Jewry ˈdʒʊər i §ˈdʒu: ri ‖ ˈdʒu: ri
jew's-harp ˌdʒu:z ˈhɑːp ‖ ˈdʒu:z hɑːrp ˈdʒu:s-
Jewson ˈdʒu:s ən
Jeyes dʒeɪz
Jezebel ˈdʒez ə bel -ɪ-, -bəl
Jezreel ˈdʒez ri_əl dʒez ˈri:əl
Jiang Qing ˌdʒæŋ ˈtʃɪŋ dʒiˈæŋ- ‖ dʒi ˌɑːŋ-
—*Chi* Jiāng Qīng [¹tɕjaŋ ¹tɕiŋ]
Jiangsu ˌdʒæŋ ˈsu: dʒiˌæŋ- ‖ dʒi ˌɑːŋ- —*Chi*
Jiāngsū [¹tɕjaŋ ¹su]
Jiangxi ˌdʒæŋ ˈʃi: dʒiˌæŋ- ‖ dʒi ˌɑːŋ- —*Chi*
Jiāngxī [¹tɕjaŋ ¹ɕi]
Jiang Zemin ˌdʒæŋ zə ˈmɪn dʒi ˌæŋ-, -zi-
‖ ˌdʒɑː-ŋ, ˌʒɑː-ŋ, dʒi ˌɑː-ŋ- —*Chi* Jiāng Zémín
[¹tɕjaŋ ²tsɤ ²mɪn]
jib dʒɪb **jibbed** dʒɪbd **jibbing** ˈdʒɪb ɪŋ **jibs**
dʒɪbz
jibe dʒaɪb **jibed** dʒaɪbd **jibes** dʒaɪbz **jibing**
ˈdʒaɪb ɪŋ
jicama ˈhi:k əm ə ˈhɪk-
JICTAR ˈdʒɪkt ɑː ‖ -ɑːr
Jif *tdmk* dʒɪf
jiff dʒɪf **jiffs** dʒɪfs
Jiffi *tdmk* ˈdʒɪf i
jiff|y ˈdʒɪf i **jiffies** ˈdʒɪf iz
jig dʒɪg **jigged** dʒɪgd **jigging** ˈdʒɪg ɪŋ **jigs**
dʒɪgz
jigger ˈdʒɪg ə ‖ -ˠr **~ed** d **~s** z
jiggery-pokery ˌdʒɪg ər i ˈpəʊk ər i ‖ -ˈpoʊk-
jiggl|e ˈdʒɪg əl **~ed** d **~es** z **~ing** ɪŋ
jiggly ˈdʒɪg əl_i
jigsaw ˈdʒɪg sɔ: ‖ -sɑ: **~s** z
ˈjigsaw ˌpuzzle
jihad dʒɪ ˈhæd dʒə-, -ˈhɑːd ‖ -ˈhɑːd —*Arabic*
[dʒi ˈhɑːd] **~s** z
Jilin ˌdʒi: ˈlɪn ˈdʒɪl ɪn —*Chi* Jílín [²tɕi ²lin]
Jill dʒɪl
jilt dʒɪlt **jilted** ˈdʒɪlt ɪd -əd **jilting** ˈdʒɪlt ɪŋ
jilts dʒɪlts
Jim dʒɪm
ˌjim ˈcrow, ˌJim ˈCrow law
jiminy ˈdʒɪm ən i -ɪn-

jimjams 'dʒɪm dʒæmz
Jimmi, Jimmie, Jimmy, jimm|y 'dʒɪm |i ~**ies** iz
jimson weed 'dʒɪm's ən wiːd ~**s** z
Jin *dynasty* dʒɪn —*Chi* Jín [³tɕɪn]
Jinan ˌdʒiː 'næn ‖ -'nɑːn —*Chi* Jínán [⁴tɕi ²nan]
Jindiworobak ˌdʒɪnd i 'wɒr ə bæk ‖ -'wɔːr- ~**s**
   s
jingl|e 'dʒɪŋ gəl ~**ed** d ~**es** z ~**ing** ɪŋ
jingo 'dʒɪŋ gəʊ ‖ -goʊ ~**es** z ~**ism** ˌɪz əm
   ~**ist/s** ɪst/s §əst/s ‖ əst/s
jingoistic ˌdʒɪŋ gəʊ 'ɪst ɪk ◂ ‖ -goʊ- ~**ally** əl_i
jinks dʒɪŋks
jinn dʒɪn
Jinnah 'dʒɪn ə
jinni 'dʒɪn i dʒɪ 'niː
Jinnie, Jinny 'dʒɪn i
jinricksha, jinrikisha dʒɪn 'rɪk ʃə ˌ•-, -ʃɔː ‖ -ʃɔː
   -ʃɑː —*Jp* [dʑi,n ri 'ki ça, -'ri ki-] ~**s** z
jinx dʒɪŋks **jinxed** dʒɪŋkst **jinxes** 'dʒɪŋks ɪz
   -əz **jinxing** 'dʒɪŋks ɪŋ
jipijapa ˌhɪp i 'hɑːp ə ~**s** z
jitney 'dʒɪt ni ~**s** z
jitter 'dʒɪt ə ‖ 'dʒɪt̮ ər ~**ed** d **jittering** 'dʒɪt
   ər ɪŋ ‖ 'dʒɪt̮ ər ɪŋ ~**s** z
jitterbug 'dʒɪt ə bʌg ‖ 'dʒɪt̮ ər- ~**ged** d ~**ging**
   ɪŋ ~**s** z
jittery 'dʒɪt ər i ‖ 'dʒɪt̮-
jiujitsu ˌdʒuː 'dʒɪts uː —*Jp* ['dʑɯɯ dʑɯ tsɯ]
jive dʒaɪv **jived** dʒaɪvd **jives** dʒaɪvz **jiving**
   'dʒaɪv ɪŋ
jizz dʒɪz
Jnr —*see* **Junior**
Jo, jo dʒəʊ ‖ dʒoʊ
Joab 'dʒəʊ æb ‖ 'dʒoʊ-
Joachim 'jəʊ ə kɪm ‖ 'joʊ- —*Ger* ['joː ax ɪm]
Joad dʒəʊd ‖ dʒoʊd
Joan dʒəʊn ‖ dʒoʊn
Joanna dʒəʊ 'æn ə ‖ dʒoʊ-
Joanne ₍ᵢ₎dʒəʊ 'æn n ₍ᵢ₎dʒoʊ-
job *'employment, task'* dʒɒb ‖ dʒɑːb **jobbed**
   dʒɒbd ‖ dʒɑːbd **jobbing**
   'dʒɒb ɪŋ ‖ 'dʒɑːb ɪŋ **jobs** dʒɒbz ‖ dʒɑːbz
   ˌjob 'lot, '• •; 'job share
Job *name* dʒəʊb ‖ dʒoʊb **Job's**
   dʒəʊbz ‖ dʒoʊbz
   ˌJob's 'comforter; ˌJob's 'tears
jobber 'dʒɒb ə ‖ 'dʒɑːb ər ~**s** z
jobbery 'dʒɒb ər i ‖ 'dʒɑːb-
Jobcentre 'dʒɒb ˌsent ə ‖ 'dʒɑːb ˌsent̮ ər ~**s** z
jobholder 'dʒɒb ˌhəʊld ə →-ˌhoʊld-
   ‖ 'dʒɑːb ˌhoʊld ər ~**s** z
jobless 'dʒɒb ləs -lɪs ‖ 'dʒɑːb- ~**ness** nəs nɪs
job-sharing 'dʒɒb ˌʃeər ɪŋ ‖ 'dʒɑːb ˌʃer ɪŋ
   -ˌʃær-
Jobson 'dʒɒb sən ‖ 'dʒɑːb-
jobsworth 'dʒɒbz wɜːθ ‖ 'dʒɑːbz wɝːθ ~**s** s
Jo'burg 'dʒəʊ bɜːg ‖ 'dʒoʊ bɝːg
Jocasta dʒəʊ 'kæst ə ‖ dʒoʊ-
Jocelyn 'dʒɒs lɪn -lən; 'dʒɒs əl ɪn, -ən ‖ 'dʒɑːs-
Jock, jock dʒɒk ‖ dʒɑːk **Jock's, jocks**
   dʒɒks ‖ dʒɑːks
jockey 'dʒɒk i ‖ 'dʒɑːk i ~**ed** d ~**ing** ɪŋ ~**s** z
jockstrap 'dʒɒk stræp ‖ 'dʒɑːk- ~**s** s

jocose dʒəʊ 'kəʊs ‖ dʒoʊ 'koʊs dʒə- ~**ly** li
jocosity dʒəʊ 'kɒs ət i -ɪt- ‖ dʒoʊ 'kɑːs ət̮ i
   dʒə-
jocular 'dʒɒk jʊl ə -jəl- ‖ 'dʒɑːk jəl ər ~**ly** li
jocularity ˌdʒɒk jʊ 'lær ət i ˌ•jə-, -ɪt i
   ‖ ˌdʒɑːk jə 'lær ət̮ i -'ler-
jocund 'dʒɒk ənd 'dʒəʊk-, -ʌnd ‖ 'dʒɑːk-
   'dʒoʊk- ~**ly** li
jocundity dʒə 'kʌnd ət i dʒɒ-, dʒəʊ-, -ɪt-
   ‖ dʒoʊ 'kʌnd ət̮ i dʒə-
jod jɒd ‖ jɑːd jɔːd, jʊd **jods** jɒdz ‖ jɑːdz
   jɔːdz, jʊdz
jodhpurs 'dʒɒd pəz ‖ 'dʒɑːd pərz
Jodi, Jodie 'dʒəʊd i ‖ 'dʒoʊd i
Jodrell 'dʒɒdr əl ‖ 'dʒɑːdr-
   ˌJodrell 'Bank
Jody 'dʒəʊd i ‖ 'dʒoʊd i
Joe, joe dʒəʊ ‖ dʒoʊ
   ˌJoe 'Bloggs; ˌJoe 'public
Joel 'dʒəʊ_əl -el ‖ 'dʒoʊ-
Joey, joey 'dʒəʊ i ‖ 'dʒoʊ i ~**s**, ~'**s** z
jog dʒɒg ‖ dʒɑːg **jogged** dʒɒgd ‖ dʒɑːgd
   jogging 'dʒɒg ɪŋ ‖ 'dʒɑːg ɪŋ **jogs**
   dʒɒgz ‖ dʒɑːgz
   'jog trot
jogger 'dʒɒg ə ‖ 'dʒɑːg ər ~**s** z
joggl|e 'dʒɒg əl ‖ 'dʒɑːg- ~**ed** d ~**es** z ~**ing**
   ɪŋ
Johannesburg dʒəʊ 'hæn ɪs bɜːg §-'hɒn-, -ɪz-
   ‖ dʒoʊ 'hæn əs bɝːg
Johannine dʒəʊ 'hæn aɪn ‖ -ən
John, john dʒɒn ‖ dʒɑːn **John's, johns**
   dʒɒnz ‖ dʒɑːnz
   ˌJohn 'Bull; ˌJohn 'Doe
Johnian 'dʒəʊn i_ən ‖ 'dʒoʊn- ~**s** z
Johnnie 'dʒɒn i ‖ 'dʒɑːn i
johnn|y, J~ 'dʒɒn |i ‖ 'dʒɑːn |i ~**ies** iz
johnnycake 'dʒɒn i keɪk ‖ 'dʒɑːn- ~**s** s
johnny-come-late|ly
   ˌdʒɒn i kʌm 'leɪt |li ‖ ˌdʒɑːn- ~**lies** liz
John o'Groats
   ˌdʒɒn ə 'grəʊts ‖ ˌdʒɑːn ə 'groʊts
Johns dʒɒnz ‖ dʒɑːnz
Johnson 'dʒɒnʦ ən ‖ 'dʒɑːnʦ-
Johnsonian dʒɒn 'səʊn i_ən ‖ dʒɑːn 'soʊn-
Johnston *(i)* 'dʒɒnʦt ən ‖ 'dʒɑːnʦt-, *(ii)*
   'dʒɒnʦ ən ‖ 'dʒɑːnʦ-
Johnstone *(i)* 'dʒɒnʦt ən ‖ 'dʒɑːnʦt-, *(ii)*
   'dʒɒnʦ ən ‖ 'dʒɑːnʦ-, *(iii)*
   'dʒɒn stəʊn ‖ 'dʒɑːn stoʊn
Johor, Johore dʒəʊ 'hɔː ‖ dʒə 'hɔːr -'hoʊr
joie de vivre ˌʒwɑː də 'viːv rə -'viːv —*Fr*
   [ʒwad viːvʁ]
join dʒɔɪn **joined** dʒɔɪnd **joining** 'dʒɔɪn ɪŋ
   joins dʒɔɪnz
joiner 'dʒɔɪn ə ‖ -ər ~**s** z
joinery 'dʒɔɪn ər i
joint dʒɔɪnt **jointed** 'dʒɔɪnt ɪd -əd ‖ 'dʒɔɪnt̮ əd
   jointing 'dʒɔɪnt ɪŋ ‖ 'dʒɔɪnt̮ ɪŋ **jointly**
   'dʒɔɪnt li
joint-stock ˌdʒɔɪnt 'stɒk '• • ‖ -'stɑːk
   ˌjoint-'stock ˌcompany
joist dʒɔɪst **joists** dʒɔɪsts

Jojo, jo-jo 'dʒəʊ dʒəʊ ‖ 'dʒoʊ dʒoʊ
jojoba həʊ 'həʊb ə ‖ hoʊ 'hoʊb ə —*Sp*
  [xo 'xo βa]
joke dʒəʊk ‖ dʒoʊk **joked** dʒəʊkt ‖ dʒoʊkt
  jokes dʒəʊks ‖ dʒoʊks **joking/ly**
  'dʒəʊk ɪŋ /li ‖ 'dʒoʊk ɪŋ /li
joker 'dʒəʊk ə ‖ 'dʒoʊk ər ~s z
jok|y 'dʒəʊk |i ‖ 'dʒoʊk |i ~ily ɪ li əl i ~iness
  i nəs i nɪs
Joliet *place in IL* ,dʒəʊl i 'et ' • • • ‖ ,dʒoʊl-
Jolley, Jollie 'dʒɒl i ‖ 'dʒɑːl i
jolli... —*see* jolly
Jolliffe 'dʒɒl ɪf §-əf ‖ 'dʒɑːl-
jollification ,dʒɒl ɪf ɪ 'keɪʃ ən , • əf-, §-ə' • -
  ‖ ,dʒɑːl- ~s z
jollity 'dʒɒl ət i -ɪt- ‖ 'dʒɑːl əţ i
joll|y, Jolly 'dʒɒl |i ‖ 'dʒɑːl |i ~ied id ~ier
  i‿ə ‖ i‿ər ~ies iz ~iest i‿ɪst i‿əst ~ily ɪ li əl i
  ~iness i nəs i nɪs ~ying i‿ɪŋ
  ,Jolly 'Roger
jollyboat 'dʒɒl i bəʊt ‖ 'dʒɑːl i boʊt ~s s
Jolson 'dʒəʊl sən →'dʒɒʊl-; 'dʒɒl- ‖ 'dʒoʊl-
jolt dʒəʊlt →dʒɒʊlt ‖ dʒoʊlt **jolted** 'dʒəʊlt ɪd
  →'dʒɒʊlt-, -əd ‖ 'dʒoʊlt əd **jolting**
  'dʒəʊlt ɪŋ →'dʒɒʊlt- ‖ 'dʒoʊlt ɪŋ
jolty 'dʒəʊlt i →'dʒɒʊlt- ‖ 'dʒoʊlt i
Jolyon 'dʒəʊl i‿ən 'dʒɒl- ‖ 'dʒoʊl jən
Jon dʒɒn ‖ dʒɑːn
Jonah, jonah 'dʒəʊn ə ‖ 'dʒoʊn ə
Jonas 'dʒəʊn əs ‖ 'dʒoʊn-
Jonathan 'dʒɒn əθ ən ‖ 'dʒɑːn-
Jones dʒəʊnz ‖ dʒoʊnz **Joneses** 'dʒəʊnz ɪz -əz
  ‖ 'dʒoʊnz əz
Jonesian 'dʒəʊnz i‿ən ‖ 'dʒoʊnz- ~s z
Jonestown 'dʒəʊnz taʊn ‖ 'dʒoʊnz-
Jong jɒŋ ‖ jɑːŋ
jongleur ,ʒɒŋ 'glɜː ,dʒɒŋ- ‖ 'dʒɑːŋ glər ~s z
  or as sing. —*Fr* [ʒɔ̃ glœːʁ]
Joni 'dʒəʊn i ‖ 'dʒoʊn i
jonquil 'dʒɒŋk wɪl -wəl ‖ 'dʒɑːŋk- 'dʒɑːn kwəl
  ~s z
Jonson 'dʒɒnˑts ən ‖ 'dʒɑːnˑts-
Jools dʒuːlz
Joplin 'dʒɒp lɪn §-lən ‖ 'dʒɑːp-
Jopling 'dʒɒp lɪŋ ‖ 'dʒɑːp-
Joppa 'dʒɒp ə ‖ 'dʒɑːp ə
Jopson 'dʒɒps ən ‖ 'dʒɑːps-
Jordan 'dʒɔːd ən ‖ 'dʒɔːrd-
Jordanian dʒɔː 'deɪn i‿ən ‖ dʒɔːr- ~s z
Jordanhill ,dʒɔːd ən 'hɪl ◂ ‖ ,dʒɔːrd-
Jorge 'hɔː heɪ ‖ 'hɔːr- —*Sp* ['xor xe]
jorum 'dʒɔːr əm ‖ 'dʒoʊr- ~s z
Jose, José həʊ 'zeɪ -'seɪ ‖ hoʊ- —*Sp* [xo 'se]
Joseph 'dʒəʊz ɪf §'dʒəʊs-, -əf ‖ 'dʒoʊz əf
  'dʒoʊs-
Josephine 'dʒəʊz ɪ fiːn §'dʒəʊs-, -ə-
  ‖ 'dʒoʊz ə- 'dʒoʊs-
Josephson 'dʒəʊz ɪf sən 'dʒəʊs-, -əf-
  ‖ 'dʒoʊz- 'dʒoʊs-
Josephus dʒəʊ 'siːf əs ‖ dʒoʊ-
josh, Josh dʒɒʃ ‖ dʒɑːʃ **joshed** dʒɒʃt ‖ dʒɑːʃt
  joshes 'dʒɒʃ ɪz -əz ‖ 'dʒɑːʃ əz **joshing**
  'dʒɒʃ ɪŋ ‖ 'dʒɑːʃ ɪŋ

Joshua 'dʒɒʃ ju‿ə -u‿ə ‖ 'dʒɑːʃ u‿ə
  'Joshua tree
Josiah dʒəʊ 'saɪ‿ə -'zaɪ‿ə ‖ dʒoʊ-
joss, Joss dʒɒs ‖ dʒɑːs
  'joss stick
Jost van Dyke ,jəʊst væn 'daɪk ‖ ,joʊst-
jostl|e 'dʒɒs əl ‖ 'dʒɑːs- ~ed d ~es z ~ing ‿ɪŋ
jot dʒɒt ‖ dʒɑːt **jots** dʒɒts ‖ dʒɑːts **jotted**
  'dʒɒt ɪd -əd ‖ 'dʒɑːţ əd **jotting**
  'dʒɒt ɪŋ ‖ 'dʒɑːţ ɪŋ
jotter 'dʒɒt ə ‖ 'dʒɑːţ ər ~s z
jotting 'dʒɒt ɪŋ ‖ 'dʒɑːţ ɪŋ ~s z
joule, Joule dʒuːl dʒaʊl, dʒəʊl ~s, ~'s z
jounce dʒaʊnˑts **jounced** dʒaʊnˑtst **jounces**
  'dʒaʊnˑts ɪz -əz **jouncing** 'dʒaʊnˑts ɪŋ
journal 'dʒɜːn əl ‖ 'dʒɝːn- ~s z
journalese ,dʒɜːn ə 'liːz -əl 'iːz ‖ ,dʒɝːn əl 'iːz
  -'iːs
journalism 'dʒɜːn ə ,lɪz əm -əl ,ɪz- ‖ 'dʒɝːn-
journalist 'dʒɜːn əl ɪst §-əst ‖ 'dʒɝːn- ~s s
journalistic ,dʒɜːn ə 'lɪst ɪk ◂ -əl 'ɪst-
  ‖ ,dʒɝːn əl 'ɪst ɪk ◂ ~ally əl_i
journey 'dʒɜːn i ‖ 'dʒɝːn i ~ed d ~ing/s ɪŋ/z
  ~s z
journey|man 'dʒɜːn i |mən ‖ 'dʒɝːn- ~men
  mən men
journo 'dʒɜːn əʊ ‖ 'dʒɝːn oʊ ~s z
joust dʒaʊst **jousted** 'dʒaʊst ɪd -əd **jousting**
  'dʒaʊst ɪŋ **jousts** dʒaʊsts
Jove dʒəʊv ‖ dʒoʊv
jovial 'dʒəʊv i‿əl ‖ 'dʒoʊv- ~ly i
joviality ,dʒəʊv i 'æl ət i -ɪt i ‖ ,dʒoʊv i 'æl əţ i
Jovian 'dʒəʊv i‿ən ‖ 'dʒoʊv-
Jowett, Jowitt (*i*) 'dʒaʊ ɪt -ət, (*ii*)
  'dʒəʊ- ‖ 'dʒoʊ-
jowl dʒaʊl **jowls** dʒaʊlz
-jowled 'dʒaʊld
joy, Joy dʒɔɪ **joys** dʒɔɪz
Joyce dʒɔɪs
joyful 'dʒɔɪf əl 'dʒɔɪ fʊl ~ly ‿i ~ness nəs nɪs
joyless 'dʒɔɪ ləs -lɪs ~ly li ~ness nəs nɪs
Joynson 'dʒɔɪnˑts ən
joyous 'dʒɔɪ əs ~ly li ~ness nəs nɪs
joyrid|e 'dʒɔɪ raɪd ~er/s ə/z ‖ ər/z ~ing ɪŋ ~s
  z
joystick 'dʒɔɪ stɪk ~s s
JP ,dʒeɪ 'piː ~s, ~'s z
jpeg, jpg 'dʒeɪ peg ~s, ~'s z
Jr —*see* Junior
Juan waːn hwaːn, 'dʒuːˑ ən ‖ hwaːn —*Sp*
  [xwan]
Juanita wə 'niːt ə xwə-; ,dʒuːˑ ə 'niːt ə
  ‖ waː 'niːţ ə —*Sp* [xwa 'ni ta]
jubilant 'dʒuːb ɪl ənt -əl- ~ly li
Jubilate ,dʒuːb ɪ 'laːt i ,juːb-, -ə-, -eɪ ‖ -'leɪţ i
  ~s z
jubilation ,dʒuːb ɪ 'leɪʃ ən -ə- ~s z
jubilee 'dʒuːb ɪ liː -ə-, , • • ' • ~s z
Judaea dʒu 'dɪə -'diːˑ ə ‖ dʒu 'diː ə
Judaean dʒu 'dɪən -'diːˑ ən ‖ dʒu 'diː ən ~s z
Judaeo- dʒu ˌdiː əʊ -ˌdeɪ- ‖ -oʊ — Judaeo-
  Spanish dʒu ,diː əʊ 'spæn ɪʃ ◂ -,deɪ- ‖ -oʊ-
Judah 'dʒuːd ə

J

Judaic dʒu 'deɪ ɪk ~**a** ə ~**ally** ᵊl_i
judais... —*see* **judaiz...**
Judaism 'dʒuːd eɪ ˌɪz əm -i-; 'dʒuːd ˌɪz əm ‖ -ə-
judaiz|e 'dʒuːd eɪ aɪz ~**ed** d ~**es** ɪz əz ~**er/
s** ə/z ‖ -ᵊr/z ~**ing** ɪŋ
Judas, judas 'dʒuːd əs ~**es, 's** ɪz əz
 'Judas tree
Judd dʒʌd
judder 'dʒʌd ə ‖ -ᵊr ~**ed** d **juddering** 'dʒʌd
 ər ɪŋ ~**s** z
Jude dʒuːd **Jude's** dʒuːdz
Judea dʒu 'dɪə -'diːˌə ‖ dʒu 'diː ə
Judean dʒu 'dɪən -'diːˌən ‖ dʒu 'diː ən ~**s** z
Judeo- dʒu ˌdiː əʊ -ˌdeɪ- ‖ -oʊ— **Judeo-
 Spanish** dʒu ˌdiː əʊ 'spæn ɪʃ ◂ -ˌdeɪ- ‖ -oʊ-
judge dʒʌdʒ **judged** dʒʌdʒd **judges**
 'dʒʌdʒ ɪz -əz **judging** 'dʒʌdʒ ɪŋ
judgement 'dʒʌdʒ mənt ~**s** s
judgemental dʒʌdʒ 'ment ᵊl ‖ -'menṯ ᵊl ~**ly** i
judgeship 'dʒʌdʒ ʃɪp ~**s** s
judgment 'dʒʌdʒ mənt ~**s** s
 'judgment day
judgmental dʒʌdʒ 'ment ᵊl ‖ -'menṯ ᵊl ~**ly** i
Judi 'dʒuːd i
judicative 'dʒuːd ɪk ət ɪv '•ək- ‖ -ɪ keɪṯ ɪv
judicature 'dʒuːd ɪk ə tʃə -tjʊə; dʒu 'dɪk-
 ‖ -ɪ keɪtʃ ᵊr -ɪk ə tʃʊr ~**s** z
judicial dʒu 'dɪʃ ᵊl ~**ly** i
judiciar|y dʒu 'dɪʃ ər li -'dɪʃ iˌər li ‖ -'dɪʃ i er li
 ~**ies** iz
judicious dʒu 'dɪʃ əs ~**ly** li ~**ness** nəs nɪs
Judith 'dʒuːd ɪθ -əθ
judo 'dʒuːd əʊ ‖ -oʊ —*Jp* ['dʑɯɯ doo]
Jud|y, jud|y 'dʒuːd li ~**y's, ~ies** iz
jug dʒʌg **jugged** dʒʌgd **jugging** 'dʒʌg ɪŋ
 jugs dʒʌgz
jugful 'dʒʌg fʊl ~**s** z
juggernaut, J~ 'dʒʌg ə nɔːt ‖ -ᵊr- -nɑːt ~**s** s
juggins 'dʒʌg ɪnz §-ənz
juggl|e 'dʒʌg ᵊl ~**ed** d ~**es** z ~**ing** ɪŋ
juggler 'dʒʌg lə 'dʒʌg ᵊl_ə ‖ 'dʒʌg lᵊr -ᵊlˌər ~**s**
 z
jugglery 'dʒʌg lᵊr i
Jugoslav 'juːg əʊ slɑːv ˌ•'•ˈ• ‖ -oʊ slɑːv -slæv
 ~**s** z
Jugoslavi|a ˌjuːg əʊ 'slɑːv iˌ_ə ‖ ˌ•oʊ- ~**an/s**
 ən/z
jugular 'dʒʌg jʊl ə -jəl- ‖ -jəl ᵊr ~**s** z
 ˌjugular 'vein
Jugurtha dʒu 'gɜːθ ə ju- ‖ -'gɜːθ ə
juice dʒuːs **juiced** dʒuːst **juices** 'dʒuːs ɪz -əz
 juicing 'dʒuːs ɪŋ
juic|y 'dʒuːs li ~**ier** iˌ_ə ‖ iˌ_ᵊr ~**iest** iˌɪst iˌ_əst
 ~**ily** ɪ li əl i ~**iness** i nəs i nɪs
jujitsu dʒu 'dʒɪts uː ˌdʒuː- —*Jp* ['dʑɯɯ
 dʑi tsɯ]
juju 'dʒuːdʒ uː ~**ism** ˌɪz əm ~**s** z
jujube 'dʒuːdʒ uːb ‖ '•ʊb i ~**s** z
jukebox 'dʒuːk bɒks ‖ -bɑːks ~**es** ɪz əz
Jukes dʒuːks
julep 'dʒuːl ɪp -ep, -əp ~**s** s
Jules dʒuːlz —*Fr* [ʒyl]
Julia 'dʒuːl iˌ_ə ‖ 'dʒuːl jə

Julian 'dʒuːl iˌən ‖ 'dʒuːl jən
Juliana ˌdʒuːl i 'ɑːn ə ‖ -'æn ə
Julie 'dʒuːl i
Julien 'dʒuːl iˌən ‖ 'dʒuːl jən
julienne ˌdʒuːl i 'en ◂ ˌʒuːl- —*Fr* [ʒy ljɛn]
Juliet *(i)* 'dʒuːl iˌət ‖ 'dʒuːl jət, *(ii)* ˌdʒuːl i 'et
 '••• —*In Shakespeare, traditionally (i)*
Julius 'dʒuːl iˌəs ‖ 'dʒuːl jəs
July dʒu 'laɪ dʒə-, ˌdʒuː- ~**s** z
jumbl|e 'dʒʌm bᵊl ~**ed** d ~**es** z ~**ing** _ɪŋ
 'jumble sale
jum|bly 'dʒʌm |bli ~**blies** bli z
jumbo, Jumbo 'dʒʌm bəʊ ‖ -boʊ ~**s** z
 'jumbo jet, ˌ•'•
jumbo-sized 'dʒʌm bəʊ saɪzd ‖ -boʊ-
jumbuck 'dʒʌm bʌk ~**s** s

JUMP

jump dʒʌmp **jumped** dʒʌmpt —*BrE 1998 poll
 panel preference:* dʒʌmpt 76%, dʒʌmt 24%.
 jumping 'dʒʌmp ɪŋ **jumps** dʒʌmps
 'jump jet; 'jump leads; 'jump seat
jumped-up ˌdʒʌmpt 'ʌp ◂
jumper 'dʒʌmp ə ‖ -ᵊr ~**s** z
jumping-off ˌdʒʌmp ɪŋ 'ɒf -'ɔːf ‖ -'ɔːf -'ɑːf
 ˌjumping-'off place
jump-off 'dʒʌmp ɒf -ɔːf ‖ -ɔːf -ɑːf ~**s** s
jump-|start 'dʒʌmp| stɑːt ˌ•'•‖ -stɑːrt
 ~**started** stɑːt ɪd -əd ‖ stɑːrṯ əd ~**starting**
 stɑːt ɪŋ ‖ stɑːrṯ ɪŋ ~**starts** stɑːts ‖ stɑːrts
jumpsuit 'dʒʌmp suːt -sjuːt ~**s** s
jump-up 'dʒʌmp ʌp ~**s** s
jump|y 'dʒʌmp li ~**ier** iˌ_ə ‖ iˌ_ᵊr ~**iest** iˌɪst
 iˌ_əst ~**ily** ɪ li əl i ~**iness** i nəs i nɪs
junction 'dʒʌŋk ʃən ~**s** z
 'junction box
juncture 'dʒʌŋk tʃə -ʃə ‖ -tʃᵊr ~**s** z
June dʒuːn **Junes, June's** dʒuːnz
Juneau 'dʒuːn əʊ dʒu 'nəʊ ‖ -oʊ
Jung jʊŋ —*Ger* [jʊŋ]
Jungfrau 'jʊŋ frau —*Ger* ['jʊŋ fʁau]
Jungian 'jʊŋ iˌən ~**s** z
jungle 'dʒʌŋ gᵊl ~**s** z
 'jungle gym
Juninho dʒu 'niːn jəʊ ‖ -joʊ —*Port* [ʒu 'ni ɲu]
junior, J~ 'dʒuːn iˌə ‖ 'dʒuːn jᵊr ~**s** z
 ˌJunior 'College; 'junior school
juniper 'dʒuːn ɪp ə -əp- ‖ -ᵊr ~**s** z
Junipero hu 'niːp ə rəʊ ‖ -roʊ —*Sp* Junípero
 [xu 'ni pe ɾo]
Junius 'dʒuːn iˌəs ‖ 'dʒuːn jəs
junk dʒʌŋk **junked** dʒʌŋkt **junking** 'dʒʌŋk ɪŋ
 junks dʒʌŋks
 **'junk bond; 'junk food; 'junk mail; 'junk
 shop**
Junker 'jʊŋk ə ‖ -ᵊr —*Ger* ['jʊŋ kɐ] ~**s** z
junk|et 'dʒʌŋk |ɪt §-ət ‖ -|ət ~**eted** ɪt ɪd §ət-,
 -əd ‖ əṯ əd ~**eting** ɪt ɪŋ §ət- əṯ ɪŋ ~**ets** ɪts
 §əts ‖ əts
junkie 'dʒʌŋk i ~**s** z

Junkin 'dʒʌŋk ɪn §-ən
junk|y 'dʒʌŋk |i ~ies iz
junkyard 'dʒʌŋk jɑːd ‖ -jɑːrd ~s z
Juno 'dʒuːn əʊ ‖ -oʊ
Junoesque ˌdʒuːn əʊ 'esk ◂ ‖ -oʊ-
Junor 'dʒuːn ə ‖ -ʳr
junta 'dʒʌnt ə 'hʊnt-, 'dʒʊnt- ‖ 'hʊnt ə —Sp
  ['xun ta] ~s z
Jupiter 'dʒuːp ɪt ə -ət- ‖ -ət̬ ʳr
Jura, jura 'dʒʊər ə ‖ 'dʒʊr ə —Fr [ʒy ʁa]
Jurassic dʒʊə 'ræs ɪk
Jurgen, Jürgen 'jɜːg ən 'jʊəg- ‖ 'jɜːg ən
  —Ger ['jʏʁ ɡən]
juridical dʒʊə 'rɪd ɪk ᵊl ~ly ˌi
jurie... —see jury
jurisdiction ˌdʒʊər ɪs 'dɪk ʃᵊn 'dʒɜːr-, 'dʒɔːr-,
  -əs-, -ɪz-, -əz- ‖ ˌdʒʊr- ~s z
jurisprudence ˌdʒʊər ɪs 'pruːd ᵊnᵗs 'dʒɜːr-,
  'dʒɔːr-, -əs-, '•••,•• ‖ ˌdʒʊr-
jurist 'dʒʊər ɪst 'dʒɜːr-, 'dʒɔːr-, §-əst ‖ 'dʒʊr-
  ~s s
juror 'dʒʊər ə 'dʒɜːr-, 'dʒɔːr- ‖ 'dʒʊr ʳr ~s z

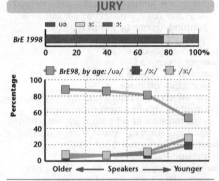

JURY

BrE 1998

| ʊə | ɜː | ɔː |
| 0 | 20 | 40 | 60 | 80 | 100% |

BrE98, by age: /ʊə/ /ɔː/ /ɜː/

Percentage: 100 80 60 40 20 0

Older ← Speakers → Younger

jur|y, Jury 'dʒʊər |i 'dʒɜːr-, 'dʒɔːr- ‖ 'dʒʊr |i
  —BrE 1998 poll preference: ʊə 77%, ɜː 13%,
  ɔː 10%. ~ies iz
jury|man 'dʒʊər i |mən 'dʒɜːr-, 'dʒɔːr- ‖ 'dʒʊr-
  ~men mən men
jurymast 'dʒʊər i mɑːst 'dʒɜːr-, 'dʒɔːr-, -məst,
  §-mæst ‖ 'dʒʊr i mæst —naut -məst
jury|men 'dʒʊər i |mən 'dʒɜːr-, 'dʒɔːr-, -men
  ‖ 'dʒʊr- ~woman ˌwʊm ən ~women
  ˌwɪm ɪn -ən
jus 'law' dʒʌs juːs
jussive 'dʒʌs ɪv ~s z
just adj dʒʌst
just adv strong form dʒʌst dʒəst, dʒest, weak
  form dʒəst §dʒɪst

justic|e, J~ 'dʒʌst ɪs §-əs ~es ɪz əz
  ˌJustice of the 'Peace
justiciable dʒʌ 'stɪʃ i̯əb ᵊl -'stɪʃ əb ᵊl
justiciar|y dʒʌ 'stɪʃ i̯ər li -'stɪʃ ʳr li -i er li
  ~ies iz
justifiability ˌdʒʌst ɪ faɪ̯ə 'bɪl ət i -ɪt i ‖ -ət̬ i

JUSTIFIABLE

■■,•ˑ••• ▭'•••••		
AmE 1993		
BrE 1998		
0	20	40	60	80	100%

justifiab|le ˌdʒʌst ɪ 'faɪ̯əb |ᵊl ,•ə-, '•••••
  —Poll panel preferences: AmE 1993, ˌ•••'•••
  82%, '••••• 18%; BrE 1998, ˌ•••'••• 75%,
  '••••• 25%. ~ly li
justification ˌdʒʌst ɪf ɪ 'keɪʃ ᵊn ˌ•əf-, §-ə'•- ~s
  z
justificatory 'dʒʌst ɪf ɪ keɪt ər i '•əf-, §'••ə-,
  ˌ•••'•••, '••ɪk ət̬ ʳr i ‖ dʒʌ 'stɪf ɪk ə tɔːr i
  -tour i; 'dʒʌst əf ə keɪt̬ ʳr i
justi|fy 'dʒʌst ɪ |faɪ -ə- ~fied faɪd ~fier/s
  faɪ̯ə/z ‖ faɪ̯ʳr/z ~fies faɪz ~fying faɪ ɪŋ
Justin 'dʒʌst ɪn §-ən
Justine 'dʒʌst iːn dʒʌ 'stiːn ‖ dʒʌ 'stiːn —Fr
  [ʒy stin]
Justinian dʒʌ 'stɪn i̯ən
just-in-time ˌdʒʌst ɪn 'taɪm ◂ §-ən-
just|ly 'dʒʌst |li ~ness nəs nɪs
jut dʒʌt juts dʒʌts jutted 'dʒʌt ɪd -əd
  ‖ 'dʒʌt̬ əd jutting 'dʒʌt ɪŋ ‖ 'dʒʌt̬ ɪŋ
jute, Jute dʒuːt jutes, Jutes dʒuːts
Jutland 'dʒʌt lənd —Danish Jylland ['jyl an?]
Juvenal 'dʒuːv ᵊn ᵊl -ɪn-

JUVENILE

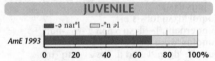

■-ə naɪᵊl ▭-ᵊn əl		
AmE 1993		
0	20	40	60	80	100%

juvenile 'dʒuːv ə naɪᵊl -ɪ- ‖ -ᵊn ᵊl —AmE 1993
  poll panel preference: -ə naɪᵊl 70%, -ᵊn ᵊl
  30%. ~s z
  ˌjuvenile de'linquent
juvenil|ia ˌdʒuːv ə 'nɪl i̯ə ˌ•ɪ- ~ity ət i ɪt i
  ‖ ət̬ i
Juventus ju 'vent əs
juxtapos|e ˌdʒʌkst ə 'pəʊz '•••
  ‖ 'dʒʌkst ə poʊz ~ed d ~es ɪz əz ~ing ɪŋ
juxtaposition ˌdʒʌkst ə pə 'zɪʃ ᵊn ~s z
JVC tdmk ˌdʒeɪ viː 'siː

K k

k   Spelling-to-sound

1 Where the spelling is **k**, the pronunciation is regularly k, as in **kind** kaɪnd. In the digraph **ck**, the pronunciation is again k, as in **back** bæk.

2 **k** is silent at the beginning of a word when followed by **n**, as in **knee** niː.

3 The sound k is also regularly written **c**, as in **cat**, and **ck**, as in **back**. It is sometimes also written **cc**, as in **account**, **qu**, as in **queue**, and in various other ways.

K, k keɪ **k's, Ks, K's** keɪz —*Communications code name:* Kilo
Kaaba 'kɑːb ə 'kɑː əb ə
Kabaka kə 'bɑːk ə
kabala kæ 'bɑːl ə kə-
Kabardian kə 'bɑːd i̯ ən ‖ -'bɑːrd-
kabbala, Kabbalah kæ 'bɑːl ə kə-
kabob kə 'bɒb ‖ -'bɑːb ~s z
kabuki kə 'buːk i kæ- —*Jp* [ka ˌbɯ ki]
Kabul 'kɑːb ʊl 'kɔːb-, -əl; kə 'bʊl
Kabyle kə 'baɪəl
Kaddish, k~ 'kæd ɪʃ ‖ 'kɑːd-
Kadett *tdmk* kə 'det
Kaffir 'kæf ə ‖ -ər ~s z
Kaffraria kæ 'freər i̯ə kə- ‖ -'frer-
Kafir 'kæf ə ‖ -ər ~s z
Kafka 'kæf kə ‖ 'kɑːf- —*Czech, Ger* ['kaf ka]
Kafkaesque ˌkæf kər 'esk ◀ ‖ ˌkɑːf kə-
kaftan 'kæft æn -aːn ‖ -ən kæf 'tæn ~s z
Kagan 'keɪg ən
kagoul, kagoule kə 'guːl ~s z
Kahan kə 'hɑːn
Kahlua, Kahlúa *tdmk* kə 'luː ə kaː-
Kahn kɑːn
Kai kaɪ
  ˌKai 'Tak tæk ‖ taːk —*Cantonese* [²kʰej ¹tɐk]
kail keɪəl
kailyard 'keɪəl jaːd ‖ -jaːrd
kainite 'kaɪn aɪt 'keɪn-
Kaiser 'kaɪz ə ‖ -ər —*Ger* ['kai zɐ] ~s z
Kaiserslautern ˌkaɪz əz 'laʊt ɜːn -ən, '••••
  ‖ -ərz 'laʊt ərn —*Ger* [kai zɐs 'lau tɐn]
kaka 'kɑːk ɑː -ə ~s z
Kakadu ˌkæk ə 'duː ◀ '•••
kakapo 'kɑːk ə pəʊ ‖ -poʊ ~s z
kakemono ˌkæk ɪ 'məʊn əʊ ‖ ˌkɑːk ə 'moʊn oʊ —*Jp* [ka 'ke mo no]
kala-azar ˌkæl ər ə 'zɑː ˌkɑːl- ‖ ˌkɑːl ə ə 'zɑːr ˌkæl-
Kalahari ˌkæl ə 'hɑːr i ◀ ‖ ˌkɑːl-
Kalamazoo, k~ ˌkæl əm ə 'zuː ◀

kalanchoe ˌkæl ən 'kəʊ i →-ən- ‖ -'koʊ i kə 'læŋk u i ~s z
Kalashnikov *tdmk* kə 'læʃ nɪ kɒf -nə- ‖ -'laːʃ nɪ kaːf ~s s
kale keɪəl
kaleidoscope kə 'laɪd ə skəʊp ‖ -skoʊp ~s s
kaleidoscopic kə ˌlaɪd ə 'skɒp ɪk ◀ ‖ -'skaːp- ~ally əl i
kalends 'kæl endz -ɪndz, -əndz
Kalevala ˌkɑːl ɪ 'vɑːl ə ˌkæl-, -ə-, -ɑː, '•••• —*Finnish* ['kɑ le vɑ lɑ]
Kalgoorlie kæl 'gʊəl i ‖ -'gʊrl i
kali *plant* 'keɪl aɪ 'kæl i
Kali *Hindu goddess of destruction* 'kɑːl i —*Skt* ['kɑː li]
Kalimantan ˌkæl ɪ 'mænt ən -æn,-? ‖ ˌkɑːl i 'mɑːnt ən
Kalispel, Kalispell 'kæl ə spel -ɪ-, ˌ•'•
kalmia 'kælm i̯ə ~s z
Kalmuck 'kæl mʌk -mək ~s s
Kalmyk 'kæl mɪk ~s s
Kama 'kɑːm ə
Kamasutra ˌkɑːm ə 'suːtr ə
Kamchatka kæm 'tʃæt kə ‖ kaːm-, -'tʃaːt- —*Russ* [kʌm 'tʃat kə]
Kamen 'keɪm ən
kamikaze ˌkæm ɪ 'kaːz i ◀ -ə- ‖ ˌkaːm- —*Jp* [ka 'mi ka dze] ~s z
Kampala kæm 'paːl ə ‖ kaːm-
kampong, K~ 'kæm pɒŋ ,•'• ‖ 'kaːm pɔːŋ -paːŋ
Kampuche|a ˌkæmp u 'tʃiː ˌ|ə ~an/s ən/z
kana 'kɑːn ə —*Jp* [ka ˌna]
Kanak kə 'naːk -'næk ~s s
kanaka, K~ kə 'næk ə -'naːk ə; 'kæn ək ə ~s z
Kanarese ˌkæn ə 'riːz ◀ -'riːs
Kanchenjunga ˌkæntʃ ən 'dʒʊŋ gə -'dʒʌŋ- ‖ ˌkaːntʃ-
Kandahar ˌkænd ə 'haː ‖ -'haːr '•••
Kandinsky kæn 'dɪntsk i —*Russ* [kʌn 'dÛin skÛij]
Kandy 'kænd i ‖ 'kaːnd i

Kane keɪn
Kanga, kanga 'kæŋ gə
kangaroo ˌkæŋ gə 'ruː ◂ ~s z
  ˌkangaroo 'court, ˌ•••'• •
kanji 'kændʒ i 'kɑːndʒ i ‖ 'kɑːndʒ i —Jp [ka,n
  dʑi] ~s z
Kannada 'kɑːn əd ə 'kæn-
Kano 'kɑːn əʊ ‖ -oʊ
Kansan 'kænz ən ~s z
Kansas 'kænz əs 'kænᵗs-
  ˌKansas 'City ◂, ˌKansas ˌCity 'steak
Kant kænt ‖ kɑːnt —Ger [kant]
Kantian 'kænt i ̯ən ‖ 'kɑːnt- 'kænt- ~s z
Kaohsiung ˌkaʊ 'ʃʊŋ -ʃi 'ʊŋ —Chi Gāoxióng
  [¹gəu ²çjʊŋ]
kaolin 'keɪ əl ɪn §-ən
kaon 'keɪ ɒn ‖ -ɑːn ~s z
kapellmeister kə 'pel ˌmaɪst ə kæ- ‖ -ᵊr ~s z
Kaplan 'kæp lən
kapok 'keɪp ɒk ‖ -ɑːk
Kaposi kə 'pəʊz i kæ-, kɑː-, -'pəʊs-; 'kɑːp əʃ i,
  'kæp- ‖ kə 'poʊs i 'kæp əs i —Hungarian
  ['kɒ po ʃi]
kappa 'kæp ə ~s z
kaput kə 'pʊt kæ- ‖ kɑː-, -'puːt
kara 'kʌr ə —Punjabi [kə raː]
karabiner ˌkær ə 'biːn ə ‖ -ᵊr ˌker- ~s z
Karachi kə 'rɑːtʃ i
Karadzic 'kær ə dʒɪtʃ ‖ 'kɑːr- —Serbian
  Karadžić ['ka ra dʒitɕ]
Karajan 'kær ə jɑːn ‖ 'kɑːr- -jən —Ger
  ['ka: ʁa jan, 'ka-]
Karakoram, Karakorum
  ˌkær ə 'kɔːr əm ‖ ˌkɑːr- -'koʊr-
karakul 'kær ək ᵊl -ə kʊl ‖ 'ker- ~s z
karaoke ˌkær i 'əʊk i -eɪ-, -ə- ‖ -'oʊk- ˌker-
  —Jp [ka ˌra o ke]
karat 'kær ət ‖ 'ker- (= carrot) ~s s
karate kə 'rɑːt i ‖ -'rɑːṭ i —Jp [ka ˌra te]
Kardomah tdmk kɑː 'dəʊm ə ‖ kɑːr 'doʊm ə
karela kə 'rel ə ~s z
Kareli|a kə 'riːl i ̯|ə ~an/s ən/z
Karen female name (i) 'kær ən ‖ 'ker-, (ii) 'kɑːr
  ən
Karen Myanmar people kə 'ren ˌkæ- ~s z
Karenina kə 'ren ɪn ə §-ən- —Russ
  [kʌ 'rʲe nʲɪ nə]
Kariba kə 'riːb ə kæ-
Karin (i) 'kær ɪn -ən ‖ 'ker-, (ii) 'kɑːr-
Karl kɑːl ‖ kɑːrl
Karla 'kɑːl ə ‖ 'kɑːrl ə
Karloff 'kɑːl ɒf ‖ 'kɑːrl ɔːf -ɑːf
Karlsruhe 'kɑːlz ru: ə ‖ 'kɑːrlz- —Ger
  ['kaʁls ʁu: ə]
karma 'kɑːm ə 'kɜːm- ‖ 'kɑːrm ə —Hindi
  [kərm]
Karnataka kə 'nɑːt ək ə ‖ kɑːr 'nɑːṭ-
Karno 'kɑːn əʊ ‖ 'kɑːrn oʊ
Karol 'kær əl ‖ 'ker-
Karoo kə 'ru:
Karpeles 'kɑːp ə liːz -ɪ- ‖ 'kɑːrp-
Karpov 'kɑːp ɒf -ɒv ‖ 'kɑːrp ɑːf —Russ ['kar
  pəf]

karst kɑːst ‖ kɑːrst
kart kɑːt ‖ kɑːrt karting 'kɑːt ɪŋ ‖ 'kɑːrṭ ɪŋ
  karts kɑːts ‖ kɑːrts
karyo- comb. form
  with stress-neutral suffix ˈkær i əʊ ‖ -ə ˌker- —
  karyotype 'kær i ̯əʊ taɪp ‖ -i ̯ə- 'ker-
  with stress-imposing suffix ˌkær i 'ɒ+ ‖ -'ɑː+
  ˌker- — karyogamy ˌkær i 'ɒg əm i ‖ -'ɑːg-
  ˌker-
kasbah 'kæz bɑː -bə ‖ 'kɑːz-
kasha 'kæʃ ə 'kɑːʃ- ‖ 'kɑːʃ ə
Kashmir ˌkæʃ 'mɪə ◂ -'mɪᵊr ˌkæʒ-; '• •
Kashmiri kæʃ 'mɪər i -'mɪr i ˌkæʒ- ~s z
Kasparov kæ 'spɑːr ɒf -ɒv; 'kæsp ə rɒf ‖ -ɑːf
  -ɔːf —Russ [kʌ 'spa rəf]
kat kæt kɑːt ‖ kɑːt
kata... —see cata...
katabatic ˌkæt ə 'bæt ɪk ◂ ˌkæṭ ə 'bæṭ ɪk ◂ ~s
  s
katakana ˌkæt ə 'kɑːn ə ‖ ˌkɑːṭ- —Jp
  [ka ˌta 'ka na, -'ta ka-]
Katanga kə 'tæŋ gə ‖ -'tɑːŋ-
Katarina ˌkæt ə 'riːn ə ‖ ˌkæṭ-
Kate keɪt
Katerina ˌkæt ə 'riːn ə ‖ ˌkæṭ-
Kath kæθ
Katharevousa, Katharevusa, k~
  ˌkæθ ə 'rev us ə -əs ə ‖ ˌkɑːθ- —ModGk
  [ka θa 're vu sa]
Katharine, Katherine 'kæθ ᵊr ɪn §-ᵊr ən —but
  the river and town in N.Terr., Australia, are
  -ə raɪn
Kathie 'kæθ i
Kathleen 'kæθ liːn ‖ ˌ•'• —formerly ˌ•'• in RP
  too
Kathmandu ˌkæt mæn 'duː ◂ ˌkɑːt-, -mən-,
  -mɑːn-
Kathryn 'kæθ rɪn -rən
Kathy 'kæθ i
Katie 'keɪt i ‖ 'keɪṭ i
Katin 'keɪt ɪn §-ᵊn ‖ -ᵊn
Katmai 'kæt maɪ
Katmandu ˌkæt mæn 'duː ◂ ˌkɑːt-, -mən-,
  -mɑːn-
Katowice ˌkæt əʊ 'viːts ə -'vɪts-, -eɪ ‖ -oʊ- -ə-
  —Polish [ka to 'vi tse]
Katrina kə 'triːn ə
Katrine name of loch 'kætr ɪn §-ən
Katy 'keɪt i ‖ 'keɪṭ i
katydid 'keɪt i dɪd ‖ 'keɪṭ- ~s z
Katyn 'kæt ɪn ‖ kɑː 'tiːn kə- —Russ [kʌ 'tɨnʲ]
Katyusha kə 'tjuːʃ ə kæ-
Katz kæts
Kaufman 'kɔːf mən 'kaʊf- ‖ 'kɑːf-
Kaunas 'kaʊn əs —Lith [''kau nas]
Kaur 'kaʊ ə ‖ -ᵊr
kauri 'kaʊᵊr i ~s z
kava 'kɑːv ə
Kavanagh (i) 'kæv ən ə, (ii) kə 'væn ə, (iii)
  'kæv ə nɑː
Kawasaki, k~ ˌkaʊ ə 'sɑːk i ˌkɑː wə- —Jp
  [ka ˌɰa sa ki]
Kay keɪ

kayak 'kaɪ æk ~er/s ə/z ‖ ʰr/z ~s s
Kaye keɪ
kayo ˌkeɪ 'əʊ ‖ -'oʊ ~ed d ~ing ɪŋ ~s z
Kayser Bondor tdmk
  ˌkeɪz ə 'bɒnd ə ‖ -ʰr 'bɑːnd ʰr
Kazakh kə 'zæk -'zɑːk, 'kæz æk ‖ kə 'zɑːk ~s
  s
Kazakhstan ˌkæz æk 'stɑːn ˌkɑːz-, -ɑːk-,
  kə ˌzɑːk-, -'stæn
Kazan kə 'zæn -'zɑːn —Russ [kʌ 'zanʲ]
kazi 'kɑːz i ~s z
kazoo kə 'zuː ~s z
kbyte 'kɪl əʊ baɪt ‖ -ə- ~s s
KC ˌkeɪ 'siː ~s z
kea 'kiːˌə 'keɪ- ~s z
Keady 'kiːd i
Kean, Keane (i) kiːn, (ii) keɪn
Keanu ki 'ɑːn uː
Kearney, Kearny (i) 'kɑːn i ‖ 'kɑːrn i, (ii)
  'kɜːn i ‖ 'kɝːn i —The places in NB and NJ
  are (i); the places in Co. Down and CA are (ii);
  as family names, both pronunciations are found.
Keating 'kiːt ɪŋ ‖ 'kiːt̬ ɪŋ ~'s z
Keaton 'kiːt ʰn
Keats kiːts
Keatsian 'kiːts i ˌən ~s z
Keays kiːz
kebab kɪ 'bæb kə- ‖ -'bɑːb ~s z
Keble 'kiːb ʰl
kebob kɪ 'bɒb kə- ‖ -'bɑːb ~s z
ked ked **keds** kedz
kedge kedʒ **kedged** kedʒd **kedges** 'kedʒ ɪz
  -əz **kedging** 'kedʒ ɪŋ
kedgeree ˌkedʒ ə 'riː '••• ‖ 'kedʒ ə riː ~s z
Kedleston 'ked ʰlst ən —locally also -ləst-
Kedron 'kedr ɒn 'kiːdr-, -ən ‖ 'kiːdr ən
Keds tdmk kedz
Keeble 'kiːb ʰl
Keeffe kiːf
Keegan 'kiːg ən
keel kiːʰl **keeled** kiːʰld **keeling** 'kiːʰl ɪŋ **keels**
  kiːʰlz
Keele kiːʰl
Keeler 'kiːl ə ‖ -ʰr
Keeley 'kiːl i
keelhaul 'kiːʰl hɔːl ‖ -hɑːl ~ed d ~ing ɪŋ ~s z
Keeling 'kiːl ɪŋ
keelson 'kel sʰn 'kiːʰl- ~s z
keen, Keen kiːn **keened** kiːnd **keener**
  'kiːn ə ‖ -ʰr **keenest** 'kiːn ɪst -əst **keening**
  'kiːn ɪŋ **keens** kiːnz
Keenan 'kiːn ən
Keene kiːn
keenly 'kiːn li **keenness** 'kiːn nəs -nɪs
keep kiːp **keeping** 'kiːp ɪŋ **keeps** kiːps **kept**
  kept
keeper 'kiːp ə ‖ -ʰr ~s z
keepnet 'kiːp net ~s s
keepsake 'kiːp seɪk ~s s
keeshond 'keɪs hɒnd ‖ -hɑːnd   ~s z
Keewatin kiː 'weɪt ɪn §-ʰn
kef kef keɪf
keffiya ke 'fiːˌə

Keflavik 'kef lə vɪk —Icelandic Keflavík
  ['cɛp la viːk]
keg keg **kegs** kegz
Kegan 'kiːg ən
kegler 'keg lə ‖ -lʰr ~s z
Keig kiːg
Keighley (i) 'kiːθ li, (ii) 'kiː li —The place in
  WYks is (i); the family or personal name may be
  either (i) or (ii)
Keigwin 'keg wɪn
Keiller, Keillor 'kiːl ə ‖ -ʰr
Keir kɪə ‖ kɪʰr
Keith kiːθ
Kekule, Kekulé 'kek ju leɪ -jə- ‖ 'keɪk ə-
  —Ger ['keː ku le]
Kekwick 'kek wɪk
Keller, k~ 'kel ə ‖ -ʰr ~s z
Kellett 'kel ɪt §-ət
Kelley, Kellie 'kel i
Kellogg 'kel ɒg ‖ -ɔːg -ɑːg ~'s tdmk z
Kelly 'kel i
Kells kelz
keloid 'kiːl ɔɪd ~s z
kelp kelp
kelper 'kelp ə ‖ -ʰr ~s z
kelp|ie, kelp|y 'kelp |i ~ies iz
Kelsey 'kels i
Kelso 'kels əʊ ‖ -oʊ
Kelton 'kelt ən
Kelvin, k~ 'kelv ɪn §-ʰn
Kelvinator tdmk 'kelv ɪ neɪt ə '•ə- ‖ -ə neɪt̬ ʰr
Kelvinside ˌkelv ɪn 'saɪd -ʰn-
Kemble 'kem bʰl
Kemp, kemp kemp
  Kemp Town
Kempis 'kemp ɪs §-əs
Kempson 'kemps ən
kempt kempt
Kemsley 'kemz li
ken, Ken ken
Kenco tdmk 'ken kəʊ →'keŋ- ‖ -koʊ
Kendal, Kendall 'kend ʰl
kendo 'kend əʊ ‖ -oʊ —Jp ['ken doo]
Kendrick 'kendr ɪk
Keneally kɪ 'niːl i kə-, ke-
Kenelm 'ken elm
Kenilworth 'ken ʰl wɜːθ -ɪl-, -wəθ ‖ -wɝːθ
Kenmare ken 'meə ‖ -'meʰr
Kennebunkport ˌken ə 'bʌŋk pɔːt ‖ -pɔːrt
  -poʊrt
Kennedy 'ken əd i -ɪd- ~s, ~'s z
kennel 'ken ʰl ~ed, ~led d ~ing, ~ling ɪŋ ~s
  z
Kennelly 'ken ʰl i
Kennet 'ken ɪt -ət
Kenneth 'ken ɪθ -əθ
kenning, K~ 'ken ɪŋ ~s z
Kennington 'ken ɪŋ tən
Kenny 'ken i
keno 'kiːn əʊ ‖ -oʊ
Kenosha kɪ 'nəʊʃ ə kə- ‖ kə 'noʊʃ ə
kenosis ke 'nəʊs ɪs kɪ-, §-əs ‖ -'noʊs-
Kenrick 'ken rɪk

K

Kensal 'kens əl
Kenshole (i) 'ken ʃəʊl →-ʃʊul ‖ -ʃoʊl, (ii) 'kenz həʊl →-hʊul ‖ -hoʊl
Kensington 'kenz ɪŋ tən
Kensit 'kenz ɪt 'ken^ts-, §-ət
Kensitas tdmk 'kenz ɪ tæs
Kent kent
kentia 'kent i‿ə ~s z
Kentigern 'kent ɪg ən -ɪ gɜːn ‖ 'kenţ ɪ gɝːrn
Kentish 'kent ɪʃ ‖ 'kenţ-
Kenton 'kent ən ‖ -ən
Kentucky ken 'tʌk i ‚•- ‖ kən- (*)
Kenwood 'ken wʊd
Kenworthy 'ken ‚wɜːð i ‖ -‚wɝːð i
Kenya 'ken jə 'kiːn- —Mostly 'kiːn- before independence, 'ken- since.
Kenyan 'ken jən 'kiːn- ~s z
Kenyatta ken 'jæt ə ‖ -'jɑːt ə
Kenyon 'ken jən
Keogh, Keough 'kiː əʊ kjəʊ ‖ 'kiː oʊ
Keown 'kiː əʊn kjəʊn, ki 'əʊn ‖ ki 'oʊn kjoʊn, 'kiː oʊn
kepi 'keɪp i —Fr képi [ke pi] ~s z
Kepler 'kep lə ‖ -lᵊr —Ger ['kɛp lɐ]
Keppel 'kep əl
kept kept
Ker (i) kɜː ‖ kɝː, (ii) kɑː ‖ kɑːr, (iii) keə ‖ keᵊr —In the US, (i); in Scotland, kɛːr (= iii)
Kerala 'ker əl ə kə 'rɑːl ə
keratin 'ker ət ɪn §-ən ‖ -ən
keratitis ‚ker ə 'taɪt ɪs §-əs ‖ -'taɪţ əs
kerato- comb. form
   with stress-neutral suffix 'ker ət əʊ ‖ -əţ oʊ —
   keratoplasty 'ker ət əʊ ‚plæst i ‖ -əţ oʊ-
   with stress-imposing suffix ‚ker ə 'tɒ+ ‖ -'tɑː+
   — keratogenous ‚ker ə 'tɒdʒ ən əs ◄ ‖ -'tɑːdʒ-
keratosis ‚ker ə 'təʊs ɪs §-əs ‖ -'toʊs əs
kerb kɜːb ‖ kɝːb kerbed kɜːbd ‖ kɝːbd
   kerbing 'kɜːb ɪŋ ‖ 'kɝːb ɪŋ kerbs kɜːbz ‖ kɝːbz
'kerb ‚crawler, 'kerb ‚crawling
kerbstone 'kɜːb stəʊn ‖ 'kɝːb stoʊn ~s z
kerchief 'kɜː tʃɪf -tʃəf, -tʃiːf ‖ 'kɝː- ~s s
Kerenski, Kerensky kə 'rent sk i —Russ ['kʲe rʲɪn skʲɪj]
kerf kɜːf ‖ kɝːf kerfs kɜːfs ‖ kɝːfs
kerfuffle kə 'fʌf əl ‖ kᵊr-
Kerguelen 'kɜːg əl ɪn -ɪl-, -ən ‖ 'kɝːg-
Kermadec 'kɜːm ə dek ‖ 'kɝːm-
kermes 'kɜːm iːz -ɪz ‖ 'kɝːm-
kermess 'kɜːm es ‖ 'kɝːm əs kᵊr 'mes
kermis 'kɜːm ɪs §-əs ‖ 'kɝːm-
Kermit 'kɜːm ɪt §-ət ‖ 'kɝːm-
Kermode (i) 'kɜːm əʊd ‖ 'kɝːm oʊd, (ii) kɜː 'məʊd ‖ kɝː 'moʊd
kern, Kern kɜːn ‖ kɝːn kerned kɜːnd ‖ kɝːnd
   kerning 'kɜːn ɪŋ ‖ 'kɝːn ɪŋ kerns kɜːnz ‖ kɝːnz
kernel 'kɜːn əl ‖ 'kɝːn əl ~s z
kerosene, kerosine 'ker ə siːn ‚• •'•
Kerouac 'ker u æk

Kerr (i) kɜː ‖ kɝː, (ii) kɑː ‖ kɑːr, (iii) keə ‖ keᵊr —In the US, (i).
kerria 'ker i‿ə ~s z
Kerrigan 'ker ɪg ən §-əg-
Kerrin 'ker ɪn §-ən
Kerry 'ker i
kersey, K~ 'kɜːz i ‖ 'kɝːz i ~s z
Kershaw 'kɜː ʃɔː ‖ 'kɝː- -ʃɑː
kerygma kə 'rɪg mə
Kes kes
kesh 'Sikh beard and hair' keɪʃ
Kesh keʃ
Kesteven ke 'stiːv ən kɪ-; 'kest ɪv ən, -əv-
Keston 'kest ən
kestrel 'kes trəl ~s z
Keswick place in Cumbria 'kez ɪk
Keswick family name (i) 'kez ɪk, (ii) -wɪk
ketch, Ketch ketʃ ketches 'ketʃ ɪz -əz
Ketchikan 'ketʃ ɪ kæn -ə-
ketchup 'ketʃ əp -ʌp ~s s
ketone 'kiːt əʊn ‖ -oʊn ~s z
ketonuria ‚kiːt əʊ 'njʊər i‿ə ‖ -oʊ 'nʊr- -'njʊr-
ketosis 'kiːt əʊs ɪs kɪ-, §-əs ‖ -'toʊs əs
Kettering 'ket_ər ɪŋ ‖ 'keţ ər ɪŋ
kettle, K~ 'ket əl ‖ 'keţ əl ~s z
kettledrum 'ket əl drʌm ‖ 'keţ- ~s z
Kettley 'ket li
Ketton 'ket ən
Kev kev
Kevin 'kev ɪn §-ən
kevlar, K~ tdmk 'kev lɑː ‖ -lɑːr
Kevorkian kə 'vɔːk i‿ən ‖ -'vɔːrk-
Kew kjuː
‚Kew 'Gardens
kewpie, K~ tdmk 'kjuːp i
kex keks
key, Key kiː keyed kiːd keying 'kiː ɪŋ keys kiːz
‚keyed 'up ◄; 'key ‚money; 'key ring; 'key ‚signature; ‚Key 'West
keyboard 'kiː bɔːd ‖ -bɔːrd -boʊrd ~ed ɪd əd ~er/s ə/z ‖ ᵊr/z ~ing ɪŋ ~s z
Keyes kiːz
keyhole 'kiː həʊl →-hʊul ‖ -hoʊl ~s z
Keynes (i) keɪnz, (ii) kiːnz —as a family name, and for the economist, usually (i); in the placename Horsted K~, (i), but in Milton K~, (ii).
Keynesian 'keɪnz i‿ən ~ism ‚ɪz əm ~s z
keynote 'kiː nəʊt ‖ -noʊt ~s s
Keynsham 'keɪn ʃəm
Keyonna ki 'ɒn ə ‖ -'ɑːn ə
keypad 'kiː pæd ~s z
keypunch 'kiː pʌntʃ ~ed t ~es ɪz əz ~ing ɪŋ
Keyser (i) 'kiːz ə ‖ -ᵊr, (ii) 'kaɪz-
keystone 'kiː stəʊn ‖ -stoʊn ~s z
keystroke 'kiː strəʊk ‖ -stroʊk ~s s
keyword 'kiː wɜːd ‖ -wɝːd ~s z
kg sing. 'kɪl ə græm ~ pl z
Khachaturian ‚kætʃ ə 'tʊər i‿ən ‚kɑːtʃ-, -'tjʊər- ‖ ‚kɑːtʃ ə 'tʊr- —Russ [xə tʃɪ tu 'rʲan]
khaki 'kɑːk i ‖ 'kæk i ~s z

khalif 'keɪl ɪf 'kæl-, §-əf; kæ 'liːf ~s s
khalifate 'kæl ɪ feɪt 'keɪl-, -ə- ~s s
khan, Khan kɑːn khans kɑːnz
khanate 'kɑːn eɪt ~s s
Khartoum, Khartum ˌkɑː 'tuːm kɑː- ‖ ₍ₒ₎kɑːr-
—Arabic [xɑr 'tˤuːm]
khazi 'kɑːz i ~s z
Khayyam kaɪ 'æm -'ɑːm ‖ -'jɑːm
khedive, K~ kɪ 'diːv kə-, ke- ~s z
Khmer kmeə kə 'meə ‖ kə 'meər Khmers
kmeəz kə 'meəz ‖ kə 'meərz
Khomeini kɒ 'meɪn i kəʊ-, həʊ- ‖ koʊ- kə-
Khoisan ˌkɔɪ 'sɑːn -'sæn
Khrushchev 'krʊs tʃɒf 'krʊʃ-, •'• ‖ 'kruːs tʃef
-tʃɔːf, -tʃɑːf, •'• —Russ [xru 'ɕtɕɔf]
Khyber 'kaɪb ə ‖ -ər
ˌKhyber 'Pass
kHz 'kɪl əʊ hɜːts ‖ -ə hɜːts
kiang ki 'æŋ 'kiː æŋ ‖ -'ɑːŋ 'kiː æŋ, -ɑːŋ ~s z
Kia-Ora tdmk ˌkiːˌə 'ɔːr ə
kibbl|e 'kɪb əl ~ed d ~es z ~ing ɪŋ
kibbutz kɪ 'bʊts kibbutzim ˌkɪb ʊt 'siːm
kibitz 'kɪb ɪts ~ed t ~er/s ə/z ‖ ər/z ~es ɪz əz
~ing ɪŋ
kibosh 'kaɪ bɒʃ ‖ -bɑːʃ
kick kɪk kicked kɪkt kicking/s 'kɪk ɪŋ/z kicks
kɪks
kickabout 'kɪk ə ˌbaʊt ~s s
Kickapoo 'kɪk ə puː ~s z
kickback 'kɪk bæk ~s s
kickdown 'kɪk daʊn
kicker 'kɪk ə ‖ -ər ~s z
kick-off 'kɪk ɒf -ɔːf ‖ -ɔːf -ɑːf ~s s
kickshaw 'kɪk ʃɔː ‖ -ʃɑː ~s z
kickstand 'kɪk stænd ~s z
kick-|start 'kɪk |stɑːt ˌ•'• ‖ -|stɑːrt ~started
stɑːt ɪd -əd ‖ stɑːrt̬ əd ~starting
stɑːt ɪŋ ‖ stɑːrt̬ ɪŋ ~starts stɑːts ‖ stɑːrts
kid kɪd kidded 'kɪd ɪd -əd kidding 'kɪd ɪŋ
kids kɪdz
ˌkid 'gloves
Kidd kɪd
Kidderminster 'kɪd ə ˌmɪnst ə ‖ -ər ˌmɪntst ər
kiddie 'kɪd i ~s z
kiddo 'kɪd əʊ ‖ -oʊ
kidd|y 'kɪd li ~ies iz
kid-glove ˌkɪd 'glʌv ◄→, kɪg-
Kidlington 'kɪd lɪŋ tən
kidnap 'kɪd næp ~ed, ~ped t ~er/s, ~per/s
ə/z ‖ ər/z ~ing, ~ping ɪŋ ~s s
kidney 'kɪd ni ~s z
ˈkidney bean; ˈkidney maˌchine; ˈkidney
stone
Kidsgrove 'kɪdz grəʊv ‖ -groʊv
Kidwelly kɪd 'wel i
Kiel kiːəl —Ger [kiːl]
kielbasa kiːəl 'bɑːs ə kɪl-, -'bæs- —Polish
kiełbasa [kʲew 'ba sa]
Kielder 'kiːəld ə ‖ -ər
Kieran, Kieron 'kɪər ən ‖ 'kɪr-
Kierkegaard 'kɪək ə gɑːd ‖ 'kɪrk ə gɑːrd -ɪ-
—Dan ['kʰiɐ gə gɔːʔʁ]
kieselguhr 'kiːz əl gʊə ‖ -gʊr

Kiev 'kiː ef -ev, •'• —Russ ['kʲi jɪf], Ukrainian
Kyiv ['kɨ jɪf]
Kigali kɪ 'gɑːl i kə-
kike kaɪk kikes kaɪks
Kikuyu kɪ 'kuː juː ~s z
Kilauea ˌkɪl ə 'weɪ ə ˌkiːl aʊ 'eɪ ə
Kilbracken kɪl 'bræk ən
Kilbride kɪl 'braɪd
Kilburn 'kɪlb ən 'kɪl bɜːn ‖ -ərn
Kildare kɪl 'deə ‖ -'deər -'dæər
kilderkin 'kɪld ək ɪn §-ən ‖ -ərk- ~s z
Kilfedder kɪl 'fed ə ‖ -ər
Kilian 'kɪl iˌən
kilim, K~ kɪ 'liːm
Kilimanjaro ˌkɪl ɪm ən 'dʒɑːr əʊ, •ə-, -ɪ mæn-,
-ə mæn- ‖ -oʊ
Kilkenny kɪl 'ken i
kill kɪl killed kɪld killing 'kɪl ɪŋ kills kɪlz
Killamarsh 'kɪl ə mɑːʃ ‖ -mɑːrʃ
Killanin kɪ 'læn ɪn kə-, §-ən
Killarney kɪ 'lɑːn i kə- ‖ -'lɑːrn i
killer 'kɪl ə ‖ -ər ~s z
ˌkiller 'whale, '•••
Killiecrankie ˌkɪl i 'kræŋk i
Killin kɪ 'lɪn kə-
Killiney kɪ 'laɪn i kə-
killing 'kɪl ɪŋ ~ly li ~s z
killjoy 'kɪl dʒɔɪ ~s z
Kilmainham kɪl 'meɪn əm
Kilmarnock kɪl 'mɑːn ək -ɒk ‖ -'mɑːrn ək
Kilmuir kɪl 'mjʊə ‖ -'mjʊər
kiln kɪln kɪl kilns kɪlnz kɪlz
Kilner, k~ 'kɪl nə ‖ -nər
Kilnsey 'kɪlnz i
kilo 'kiːl əʊ ‖ -oʊ 'kɪl- ~s z
kilo- 'kɪl əʊ- ‖ 'kɪl ə 'kiːl ə — kilocalorie
'kɪl əʊ ˌkæl ər i ‖ '•ə- 'kiːl-
kilobyte 'kɪl əʊ baɪt ‖ -ə- ~s s
kilocycle 'kɪl əʊ ˌsaɪk əl ‖ -ə- ~s z
kilogram, kilogramme 'kɪl ə græm 'kiːl- ~s z
kilohertz 'kɪl əʊ hɜːts ‖ -ə hɜːts
kiloliter, kilolitre 'kɪl əʊ ˌliːt ə ‖ -ə ˌliːt̬ ər ~s z

KILOMETER

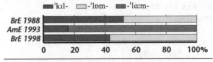

	'kɪl-	-'lɒm-	-'lɑːm-
BrE 1988			
AmE 1993			
BrE 1998			

0   20   40   60   80   100%

kilometer, kilometre 'kɪl ə ˌmiːt ə kɪ 'lɒm ɪt ə,
kə-, -ət- ‖ kə 'lɑːm ət̬ ər kɪ-; 'kɪl ə ˌmiːt̬ ər
—On the analogy of 'centi,metre, 'milli,metre, it
is clear that the stressing 'kilo,metre is logical
and might be expected to predominate.
Nevertheless, many people (particularly in the
US, but also elsewhere) say kɪ'lɒm-. Poll panel
preferences: BrE 1988, 'kɪl- 52%, -'lɒm- 48%;
AmE 1993, -'lɑːm- 84%, 'kɪl- 16%; BrE 1998,
-'lɒm- 57%, -'kɪl- 43%. ~s z
kiloton 'kɪl əʊ tʌn ‖ -ə- ~s z
kilovolt 'kɪl əʊ vəʊlt →-vɒʊlt ‖ -ə voʊlt ~s s
kilowatt 'kɪl ə wɒt ‖ -ə wɑːt ~s s
kilowatt-hour ˌkɪl ə wɒt 'aʊ ə
‖ ˌkɪl ə wɑːt̬ 'aʊ ər ~s z

K

Kilpatrick kɪl 'pætr ɪk
Kilroy ₍ₐ₎kɪl 'rɔɪ '••
Kilsby 'kɪlz bi
kilt kɪlt kilted 'kɪlt ɪd -əd kilts kɪlts
kilter 'kɪlt ə ǁ -ᵊr
Kim kɪm
Kimball 'kɪm bᵊl
Kimber 'kɪm bə ǁ -bᵊr
Kimberley 'kɪm bə li ǁ -bᵊr-
kimberlite 'kɪm bə laɪt ǁ -bᵊr-
Kimberly 'kɪm bə li ǁ -bᵊr-
Kimbolton kɪm 'bəʊlt ᵊn →-'bɒʊlt-
  ǁ -'boʊlt ᵊn
Kimmeridge 'kɪm ə rɪdʒ
kimono kɪ 'məʊn əʊ kə-; §'kɪm ə nəʊ
  ǁ -'moʊn ə -oʊ —Jp [ki ˌmo no]
kin kɪn
-kin kɪn §kən — lambkin 'læm kɪn §-kən
kina 'kiːn ə
Kinabalu ˌkɪn ə 'baːl uː -bə 'luː
kinaesthesia ˌkɪn iːs 'θiːz i‿ə ˌkaɪn-, ˌ•ɪs-, ˌ•əs-
  ǁ ˌkɪn əs 'θiːʒ ə
kinaesthetic ˌkɪn iːs 'θet ɪk ◄ ˌkaɪn-, -ɪs-, -əs-
  ǁ -əs 'θeṭ- ~ally ᵊl‿i
Kincaid kɪn 'keɪd →kɪŋ-
Kincardine kɪn 'kaːd ɪn →kɪŋ-, -ᵊn ǁ -'kaːrd ᵊn
Kincora kɪn 'kɔːr ə →kɪŋ-
kind kaɪnd kinds kaɪndz
kinda 'kaɪnd ə
Kinder 'kɪnd ə ǁ -ᵊr
kindergarten 'kɪnd ə ˌgaːt ᵊn ǁ -ᵊr ˌgaːrt ᵊn ~s
  z
kind-hearted ˌkaɪnd 'haːt ɪd ◄ -əd
  ǁ -'haːrṭ əd ◄ ~ly li ~ness nəs nɪs
kindl|e 'kɪnd ᵊl ~ed d ~es z ~ing ‿ɪŋ
kindling n 'kɪnd lɪŋ
kind|ly 'kaɪnd |li ~lier li‿ə ǁ li‿ᵊr ~liest li‿ɪst
  ‿əst ~liness li nəs -nɪs
kindness 'kaɪnd nəs -nɪs ~es ɪz əz
kindred 'kɪndr əd -ɪd ~ness nəs nɪs
kine kaɪn
kinematic ˌkɪn ɪ 'mæt ɪk ◄ ˌkaɪn-, -ə- ǁ -'mæṭ-
  ~s s
kinesics kaɪ 'niːs ɪks kɪ-, -'niːz-
kinesthesia ˌkɪn iːs 'θiːz i‿ə ˌkaɪn-, ˌ•ɪs-, ˌ•əs-
  ǁ ˌkɪn əs 'θiːʒ ə
kinesthetic ˌkɪn iːs 'θet ɪk ◄ ˌkaɪn-, -ɪs-, -əs-
  ǁ -əs 'θeṭ- ~ally ᵊl‿i
kinetic kaɪ 'net ɪk kɪ-, kə- ǁ kə 'neṭ ɪk kɪ-, kaɪ-
  ~ally ᵊl‿i ~s s
  ki,netic 'energy
kinfolk 'kɪn fəʊk ǁ -foʊk ~s s
king, King kɪŋ kings, King's kɪŋz
  ₍ₐ₎King 'George; King ˌJames 'version,
  ₍ₐ₎•˙'•, ˌ•˙•; ₍ₐ₎King 'Lear; ˌKing's 'Bench,
  ˌKing's 'Bench Di,vision; ˌKing's 'Counsel;
  ˌKings 'Cross◄; ˌKing's 'English; ˌking's
  'evidence; ˌking's 'evil; ˌKing's 'Lynn
kingcup 'kɪŋ kʌp ~s s
kingdom 'kɪŋ dəm ~s z
Kingdon 'kɪŋ dən
kingfisher 'kɪŋ ˌfɪʃ ə ǁ -ᵊr ~s z
Kingham 'kɪŋ əm

kinglet 'kɪŋ lət -lɪt ~s s
king|ly 'kɪŋ |li ~lier li‿ə ǁ li‿ᵊr ~liest li‿ɪst ‿əst
  ~liness li nəs -nɪs
kingmaker 'kɪŋ ˌmeɪk ə ǁ -ᵊr ~s z
kingpin 'kɪŋ pɪn ˌ•'• ~s z
Kingsbridge 'kɪŋz brɪdʒ
Kingsbury 'kɪŋz bər‿i ǁ -ˌber i
Kingsford 'kɪŋz fəd ǁ -fᵊrd
kingship 'kɪŋ ʃɪp ~s s
king-size 'kɪŋ saɪz ~d d
Kingsley 'kɪŋz li
Kingston 'kɪŋkst ᵊn 'kɪŋz tən
  ˌKingston upon 'Thames
Kingstown 'kɪŋz taʊn
Kingsway 'kɪŋz weɪ
Kingswear 'kɪŋz wɪə ǁ -wɪr
Kingswinford kɪŋ 'swɪn fəd ǁ -fᵊrd
Kingswood 'kɪŋz wʊd
Kington 'kɪŋ tən
Kingussie kɪŋ 'juːs i (!)
kink kɪŋk kinked kɪŋkt kinking 'kɪŋk ɪŋ
  kinks kɪŋks
kinkajou 'kɪŋk ə dʒuː ~s z
kink|y 'kɪŋk |i ~ier i‿ə ǁ i‿ᵊr ~iest i‿ɪst i‿əst
  ~ily ɪ li əl i ~iness i nəs i nɪs
Kinloch ₍ₐ₎kɪn 'lɒk -'lɒx ǁ -'laːk
Kinloss ₍ₐ₎kɪn 'lɒs ǁ -'lɔːs -'laːs
Kinnear kɪ 'nɪə -'neə ǁ -'nɪᵊr
Kinnock 'kɪn ək
Kinross ₍ₐ₎kɪn 'rɒs ǁ -'rɔːs -'raːs
Kinsale ₍ₐ₎kɪn 'seɪᵊl
Kinsella (i) ₍ₐ₎kɪn 'sel ə, (ii) 'kɪnˢ əl ə
Kinsey 'kɪnz i
kinsfolk 'kɪnz fəʊk ǁ -foʊk
Kinshasa kɪn 'ʃaːs ə -'ʃæs-, -'ʃɑːz-
kinship 'kɪn ʃɪp
kins|man 'kɪnz |mən ~men mən men
  ~woman ˌwʊm ən ~women ˌwɪm ɪn §-ən
Kintyre ₍ₐ₎kɪn 'taɪ‿ə ǁ kɪn 'taɪ‿ᵊr
kiosk 'kiː ɒsk §'kaɪ- ǁ 'kiː aːsk ki 'aːsk ~s s
Kiowa 'kiː‿ə waː -wə, -weɪ ~s z
kip kɪp kipped kɪpt kipping 'kɪp ɪŋ kips
  kɪps
Kipling 'kɪp lɪŋ
Kiplingesque ˌkɪp lɪŋ 'esk ◄
Kipp kɪp
Kippax 'kɪp æks -æks
kipper 'kɪp ə ǁ -ᵊr ~ed d kippering 'kɪp ᵊr ɪŋ
  ~s z
Kipps kɪps
kir kɪə ǁ kɪᵊr —Fr [kiːʁ]
Kirbigrip tdmk 'kɜːb i grɪp ǁ 'kɜːb- ~s s
Kirby 'kɜːb i ǁ 'kɜːb i
Kirchhoff 'kɜːk ɒf -hɒf ǁ 'kɪrk hɔːf 'kɜːk-,
  -haːf —Ger ['kɪʁç hɔf]
Kirghiz, Kirgiz 'kɜː gɪz 'kɪə- ǁ kɪr 'giːz
Kirghizia kɜː 'gɪz i‿ə kɪə- ǁ kɪr 'giːʒ ə -i‿ə
Kiribati ˌkɪr ɪ 'baːt i ˌkɪᵊr-, -ə-, -'bæt i; ˌ•˙•'bæs,
  '••• —The pronunciation recommended by all
  reference books is -bæs, -'bæs; but the
  influence of orthography is such that this form
  has not established itself in the face of spelling
  pronunciations.

Kiri Te Kanawa ˌkɪr i ti 'kɑːn ə wə ˌkɪər-, -'kæn-

kirk, Kirk kɜːk ‖ kɝːk kirks, Kirk's kɜːks ‖ kɝːks

Kirkbride ₍ₒ₎kɜːk 'braɪd ‖ ₍ₒ₎kɝːk-

Kirkby (i) 'kɜːk bi ‖ 'kɝːk-, (ii) 'kɜːb i ‖ 'kɝːb i —The place in Merseyside is (ii) (!), as are other places in the north of England; places in the Midlands of England are (i); the family name may be either.

Kirkcaldy kə 'kɒd i kɜː-, -'kɔːd- ‖ kɚ 'kɑːd i -'kɔːd-, -'kɑːld-, -'kɔːld- (!)

Kirkcudbright kə 'kuːb ri kɜː- ‖ kɚ- (!)

Kirkdale 'kɜːk deɪəl ‖ 'kɝːk-

Kirkgate streets in Leeds, Bradford 'kɜːg ət 'kɜː geɪt ‖ 'kɝːk geɪt

Kirkham 'kɜːk əm ‖ 'kɝːk-

Kirkland 'kɜːk lənd ‖ 'kɝːk-

Kirklees ₍ₒ₎kɜːk 'liːz ‖ ₍ₒ₎kɝːk-

Kirkpatrick ₍ₒ₎kɜːk 'pætr ɪk ‖ ₍ₒ₎kɝːk-

Kirkstall place in W Yks 'kɜːk stɔːl -stəl ‖ 'kɝːk- -stɑːl

Kirkstone 'kɜːk stən -stəʊn ‖ 'kɝːk stoʊn

Kirkup 'kɜːk əp -ʌp ‖ 'kɝːk-

Kirkwall 'kɜːk wɔːl ‖ 'kɝːk- -wɑːl

Kirov 'kɪər ɒv -ɒf ‖ 'kɪr ɔːf -ɑːf —Russ ['kʲi rəf]

kirpan kɪə 'pɑːn kɜː- ‖ kɪr- —Punjabi [kɪr pɑːn] ~s z

Kirriemuir ˌkɪr i 'mjʊə ‖ -'mjʊər

kirsch kɪəʃ kɜːʃ ‖ kɪrʃ —Ger [kɪʁʃ]

Kirsten 'kɜːst ən -ən ‖ 'kɝːst- —but as a foreign name also 'kɪəst- ‖ 'kɪrst-

Kirstie, Kirsty 'kɜːst i ‖ 'kɝːst i

kirtle 'kɜːt əl ‖ 'kɝːt əl ~s z

Kirton 'kɜːt ən ‖ 'kɝːt-

Kisangani ˌkɪs æŋ 'gɑːn i i ˌkiːs ɑːn-

kish, Kish kɪʃ

kishke 'kɪʃ kə ~s z

kismet 'kɪz met 'kɪs-, -mɪt, -mət

kiss kɪs kissed kɪst kisses 'kɪs ɪz -əz kissing 'kɪs ɪŋ
  'kissing bug; 'kissing gate; ˌkiss of 'death; ˌkiss of 'life

kissable 'kɪs əb əl

kissagram 'kɪs ə græm ~s z

kisser 'kɪs ə ‖ -ər ~s z

Kissimmee kɪ 'sɪm i

Kissinger 'kɪs ɪndʒ ə -əndʒ-; '•ɪŋ ə ‖ -ər

kissogram 'kɪs ə græm ~s z

kit, Kit kɪt kits kɪts kitted 'kɪt ɪd -əd ‖ 'kɪt̬ əd kitting 'kɪt ɪŋ ‖ 'kɪt̬ ɪŋ

Kitaj kɪ 'taɪ

kitbag 'kɪt bæg ~s z

Kit-Cat, kit-cat 'kɪt kæt ~s s

kitchen, K~ 'kɪtʃ ən -ɪn ~s z
  ˌkitchen 'garden

Kitchener 'kɪtʃ ən ə -ɪn- ‖ -ən ər

kitchenette ˌkɪtʃ ə 'net -ɪ- ~s s

kitchen-sink ˌkɪtʃ ən 'sɪŋk ◄ -ɪn-

kitchenware 'kɪtʃ ən weə -ɪn- ‖ -wer

kite, Kite kaɪt kites kaɪts

Kit-E-Kat tdmk 'kɪt i kæt ‖ 'kɪt̬-

Kitemark 'kaɪt mɑːk ‖ -mɑːrk

kith kɪθ
  ˌkith and 'kin

Kit-Kat tdmk 'kɪt kæt ~s s

kitsch kɪtʃ

Kitson 'kɪts ən

Kitt kɪt

kitten 'kɪt ən ~ed d ~ing ɪŋ ~s z

kittenish 'kɪt ən ɪʃ ~ly li ~ness nəs nɪs

Kittitian kɪ 'tɪʃ ən ~s z

kittiwake 'kɪt i weɪk ‖ 'kɪt̬- ~s s

Kitto 'kɪt əʊ ‖ 'kɪt̬ oʊ

Kitts kɪts

kitt|y, Kitt|y 'kɪt li ‖ 'kɪt̬ li ~ies, ~y's iz
  'Kitty Hawk

Kitzbuehel, Kitzbuhel, Kitzbühel 'kɪts bjuː əl -buː əl; '•bjuːl, -buːl —Ger ['kɪts byː əl]

Kiveton place in SYks 'kɪv ɪt ən -ət-

Kiwanian kɪ 'wɑːn i ən §kə- ~s z

Kiwanis kɪ 'wɑːn ɪs §kə-, §-əs

kiwi, Kiwi 'kiː wiː ~s z
  'kiwi fruit

Kizzy 'kɪz i

Klamath 'klæm əθ ~s s
  ˌKlamath 'Falls; 'Klamath weed

klan, Klan klæn

Klans|man 'klænz |mən ~men mən men

Klatt klæt

Klaus klaʊs —Ger [klaʊs]

klavier klæ 'vɪə klə- ‖ -'vɪər ~s z

klaxon, K~ tdmk 'klæks ən ~s z

Klebs-Loffler, Klebs-Löffler ˌklebz 'lʌf lə -'lɜːf- ‖ -'lef lər —Ger [ˌkleːps 'lœf lɐ]

Klee kleɪ —Ger [kleː]

Kleenex tdmk 'kliːn eks ~es ɪz əz

Klein klaɪn

Kleinwort 'klaɪn wɔːt ‖ -wɔːrt

Klemperer 'klemp ər ə ‖ -ər ər —Ger ['klɛmp əʁ ɐ]

klepht kleft (= cleft) klephts klefts

kleptomania ˌklept əʊ 'meɪn i ə ‖ -ə-, '•ə-

kleptomaniac ˌklept əʊ 'meɪn i æk ◄ ‖ -ə-, '•ə- ~s s

klieg kliːg
  'klieg light

Klim tdmk klɪm

Kline klaɪn

klipspringer 'klɪp ˌsprɪŋ ə ‖ -ər ~s z

Klondike 'klɒnd aɪk ‖ 'klɑːnd-

kloof kluːf kloofs kluːfs

Klosters 'kləʊst əz 'klɒst- ‖ 'kloʊst ərz —Ger ['kloː stɐs]

kludge kluːdʒ klʌdʒ kludged kluːdʒd klʌdʒd kludging 'kluːdʒ ɪŋ 'klʌdʒ- kludges 'kluːdʒ ɪz 'klʌdʒ-, -əz

kludgey, kludgy 'kluːdʒ i 'klʌdʒ i

klutz klʌts klutzes 'klʌts ɪz -əz

klutz|y 'klʌts li ~ier i ə ‖ i ər ~iest i ɪst i əst ~iness i nəs i nɪs

klystron, K~ tdmk 'klaɪs trɒn 'klɪs- ‖ -trɑːn ~s z

km —see kilometre

K-Mart tdmk 'keɪ mɑːt ‖ -mɑːrt

knack næk knacks næks

knacker 'næk ə ‖ -ᵊr ~ed d knackering 'næk
ər ɪŋ ~s z
'knacker's yard
knackwurst 'næk vʊəst ‖ 'nɑːk wɜːst -wʊrst
—Ger ['knak vʊʁst]
knap næp (= nap) knapped næpt knapping
'næp ɪŋ knaps næps
Knapp næp
knapsack 'næp sæk ~s s
knapweed 'næp wiːd ~s z
Knaresborough 'neəz bər ə ‖ 'nerz ,bɜːʳ oʊ
Knatchbull 'nætʃ bʊl
knave neɪv (= nave) knaves neɪvz
knaver|ly 'neɪv ər li ~ies iz
knavish 'neɪv ɪʃ ~ly li ~ness nəs nɪs
knawel nɔːl 'nɔː əl ‖ nɑːl
knead niːd (= need) kneaded 'niːd ɪd -əd
kneading 'niːd ɪŋ kneads niːdz
Knebworth 'neb wəθ -wɜːθ ‖ -wᵊrθ
knee niː kneed niːd (= need) kneeing 'niː ɪŋ
knees niːz
'knee ,breeches
Kneebone 'niː bəʊn ‖ -boʊn
kneecap 'niː kæp ~ped t ~ping ɪŋ ~s s
knee-deep ,niː 'diːp ◄
knee-high ,niː 'haɪ ◄
kneehole 'niː həʊl →-hɒʊl ‖ -hoʊl ~s z
knee-jerk 'niː dʒɜːk ‖ -dʒɜːk
kneel niːᵊl kneeled niːᵊld kneeling 'niːᵊl ɪŋ
kneels niːᵊlz knelt nelt
knee-length 'niː leŋᵏθ -lenᵗθ
kneeler 'niːᵊl ə ‖ -ᵊr ~s z
knees-up 'niːz ʌp
knell nel knells nelz
Kneller 'nel ə ‖ -ᵊr
knelt nelt
Knesset 'knes et -ɪt, -ət; kə 'nes•
knew njuː ‖ nuː njuː (= new)
K'nex tdmk kə 'neks
knicker 'nɪk ə ‖ -ᵊr ~s z
knickerbocker, K~ 'nɪk ə bɒk ə ‖ -ᵊr bɑːk ᵊr ~s
z
,knickerbocker 'glory
knick-knack 'nɪk næk ~s s
Knieval kə 'niːv ᵊl
knife naɪf knifed naɪft knifes naɪfs knifing
'naɪf ɪŋ knives naɪvz
knife-edge 'naɪf edʒ
knife-point 'naɪf pɔɪnt
knight, K~ naɪt (= night) knighted 'naɪt ɪd -əd
‖ 'naɪt əd knighting 'naɪt ɪŋ ‖ 'naɪt ɪŋ
knights, Knight's naɪts
knight-errant ,naɪt 'er ənt ‖ ,naɪt- knights-
errant ,naɪts 'er ənt
knighthood 'naɪt hʊd ~s z
knight|ly 'naɪt |li (= nightly) ~liness li nəs -nɪs
Knighton 'naɪt ᵊn
Knightsbridge 'naɪts brɪdʒ
kniphofia nɪ 'fəʊf i_ə naɪ- ‖ -'foʊf- ~s z
knish kə 'nɪʃ knɪʃ knishes kə 'nɪʃ ɪz -əz;
'knɪʃ•
knit nɪt (= nit) knits nɪts knitted 'nɪt ɪd -əd
‖ 'nɪt əd knitter 'nɪt ə ‖ 'nɪt ᵊr ~s z

knitting 'nɪt ɪŋ ‖ 'nɪt ɪŋ
'knitting ,needle
knitwear 'nɪt weə ‖ -wer
knives naɪvz
knob nɒb ‖ nɑːb knobbed nɒbd ‖ nɑːbd
knobs nɒbz ‖ nɑːbz
knobbly 'nɒb ᵊl_i ‖ 'nɑːb-
knobby 'nɒb i ‖ 'nɑːb i
knobkerrie 'nɒb ,ker i -kər- ‖ 'nɑːb- ~s z
knock, Knock nɒk ‖ nɑːk knocked
nɒkt ‖ nɑːkt knocking 'nɒk ɪŋ ‖ 'nɑːk ɪŋ
knocks nɒks ‖ nɑːks
knockabout 'nɒk ə ,baʊt ‖ 'nɑːk- ~s s
knockdown 'nɒk daʊn ‖ 'nɑːk- ~s z
knocker 'nɒk ə ‖ 'nɑːk ᵊr ~s z
knock|er-up ,nɒk |ər 'ʌp ‖ ,nɑːk ᵊr- ~ers-up
əz 'ʌp ‖ ᵊrz 'ʌp
knock-for-knock
,nɒk fə 'nɒk ◄ ‖ ,nɑːk fᵊr 'nɑːk ◄
knock-forward ,nɒk 'fɔː wəd ‖ ,nɑːk 'fɔːr wᵊrd
~s z
Knockholt 'nɒk həʊlt →-hɒʊlt ‖ 'nɑːk hoʊlt
knock-knee ,nɒk 'niː ‖ ,nɑːk- ~d d ◄
knock-on ,nɒk 'ɒn ‖ ,nɑːk 'ɑːn -'ɔːn
,knock-'on ef,fect, ,knock-on ef'fect
knockout 'nɒk aʊt ‖ 'nɑːk- ~s s
knock-up 'nɒk ʌp ‖ 'nɑːk- ~s s
knockwurst 'nɒk wɜːst ‖ 'nɑːk wɜːst -vʊrst
Knole nəʊl →nɒʊl ‖ noʊl
knoll, Knoll nəʊl →nɒʊl ‖ noʊl knolls nəʊlz
→nɒʊlz ‖ noʊlz
Knollys nəʊlz →nɒʊlz ‖ noʊlz
Knopf knɒpf ‖ knɑːpf
Knorr nɔː ‖ nɔːr
Knossos 'knɒs ɒs 'nɒs-, -əs ‖ 'nɑːs əs
knot nɒt ‖ nɑːt (= not) knots nɒts‖ nɑːts
knotted 'nɒt ɪd -əd ‖ 'nɑːt əd knotting
'nɒt ɪŋ ‖ 'nɑːt ɪŋ
knotgrass 'nɒt grɑːs §-græs ‖ 'nɑːt græs
knothole 'nɒt həʊl→-hɒʊl ‖ 'nɑːt hoʊl ~s z
Knott nɒt ‖ nɑːt
knott... —see knot
Knottingley 'nɒt ɪŋ li ‖ 'nɑːt-
knott|y 'nɒt li ‖ 'nɑːt li ~ier i_ə ‖ i_ᵊr ~iest
i_ɪst i_əst ~iness i nəs i nɪs
knout naʊt knouts naʊts
know nəʊ ‖ noʊ (= no) knew njuː ‖ nuː njuː
knowing 'nəʊ ɪŋ ‖ 'noʊ ɪŋ known nəʊn
§'nəʊ ən ‖ noʊn knows nəʊz ‖ noʊz
knowable 'nəʊ əb ᵊl ‖ 'noʊ-
know-all 'nəʊ ɔːl ‖ 'noʊ- -ɑːl ~s z
know-how 'nəʊ haʊ ‖ 'noʊ-
knowing 'nəʊ ɪŋ ‖ 'noʊ ɪŋ ~ly li ~ness nəs nɪs
know-it-all 'nəʊ ɪt ɔːl §-ət- ‖ 'noʊ ət- -ɑːl ~s
z
Knowle nəʊl →nɒʊl ‖ noʊl
knowledge 'nɒl ɪdʒ ‖ 'nɑːl- (!)
knowledgeab|le 'nɒl ɪdʒ əb |ᵊl ‖ 'nɑːl- ~ly li
Knowles nəʊlz →nɒʊlz ‖ noʊlz
known nəʊn §'nəʊ ən ‖ noʊn
know-nothing 'nəʊ ,nʌθ ɪŋ ‖ 'noʊ- ~s z
Knowsley 'nəʊz li ‖ 'noʊz-
Knox nɒks ‖ nɑːks

Knoxville 'nɒks vɪl ‖ 'nɑːks-
Knoydart 'nɔɪd ɑːt -ət ‖ -ɑːrt
knuckl|e 'nʌk ᵊl ~ed d ~es z ~ing _ɪŋ
knucklebone 'nʌk ᵊl bəʊn ‖ -boʊn ~s z
knuckle-duster 'nʌk ᵊl ˌdʌst ə ‖ -ᵊr ~s z
knurl nɜːl ‖ nɜːl knurled nɜːld ‖ nɜːld knurls
    nɜːlz ‖ nɜːlz
Knuston 'nʌst ən
Knutsford 'nʌts fəd ‖ -fᵊrd
KO, k.o. ˌkeɪ 'əʊ ‖ -'oʊ ~'d d ~'ing ɪŋ ~'s z
koa 'kəʊ ə ‖ 'koʊ ə ~s z
koala kəʊ 'ɑːl ə ‖ koʊ- ~s z
koan 'kəʊ æn -ən, -ɑːn ‖ 'koʊ ɑːn —Jp
    [ko,o aN] ~s z
Kobe 'kəʊb eɪ -i ‖ 'koʊb- —Jp ['koo be]
Koblenz kəʊ 'blenʦ ‖ 'koʊ blenʦ —Ger
    ['koː blɛnts]
Koch (i) kəʊk ‖ koʊk, (ii) kɒtʃ ‖ kɑːtʃ, (iii)
    kɒx ‖ kɔːx kɑːx —Ger [kɔx]
Kochel, Köchel 'kɜːk ᵊl 'kɜːx- ‖ 'kɜ·ːʃ ᵊl 'kɜ·ːk-
    —Ger ['kœç ᵊl]
    'Köchel ˌnumber
Kodachrome tdmk
    'kəʊd ə krəʊm ‖ 'koʊd ə kroʊm
Kodak, kodak tdmk 'kəʊd æk ‖ 'koʊd- ~s, ~'s s
Kodaly, Kodály 'kəʊd aɪ ‖ koʊ 'daɪ —Hung
    ['ko daːj]
Kodiak 'kəʊd i æk ‖ 'koʊd-
Koestler 'kɜːsʈ lə ‖ 'kesʈ lᵊr
Kofi 'kəʊf i ‖ 'koʊf i
Koh-i-noor ˌkəʊ i 'nʊə ◄ -'nɔː, '• • •
    ‖ 'koʊ ə nʊr
kohl, Kohl kəʊl →kɒʊl ‖ koʊl —Ger [koːl]
kohlrabi ˌkəʊl 'rɑːb i →ˌkɒʊl- ‖ ˌkoʊl-
koine, koiné 'kɔɪn eɪ -iː, -i ~s z
Kojak 'kəʊdʒ æk ‖ 'koʊdʒ-
Kokomo 'kəʊk ə məʊ ‖ 'koʊk ə moʊ
Kokoschka kəʊ 'kɒʃ kə ‖ kə 'kɑːʃ- -'kɔːʃ-
    —Ger [ko 'kɔʃ ka, 'kɔ kɔʃ ka]
kola, Kola 'kəʊl ə ‖ 'koʊl ə
kolkhoz ˌkɒl 'kɒz -'kɔːz, -'hɔːz ‖ kɑːl 'kɑːz
    -'kɔːz —Russ [kʌɫ 'xɔs] ~es ɪz əz
Kolynos tdmk 'kɒl ɪ nɒs -ə- ‖ 'kɑːl ə nɑːs
Komi 'kəʊm i ‖ 'koʊm i ~s z
Komodo kə 'məʊd əʊ ‖ -'moʊd oʊ
    Ko,modo 'dragon
Komsomol 'kɒm sə mɒl ,• • • • ‖ 'kɑːm sə mɑːl
    -mɔːl, ,• • • • —Russ [kəm sʌ 'moɫ]
Kongo 'kɒŋ gəʊ ‖ 'kɑːŋ goʊ
Konica tdmk 'kɒn ɪk ə 'kəʊn- ‖ 'kɑːn- 'koʊn-
    —Jp ['ko ɲi ka]
Konigsberg, Königsberg 'kɜːn ɪgz bɜːg
    'kəʊn-, -beəg ‖ 'keɪn ɪgz bɜ·ːg 'kʊn- —Ger
    ['køː nɪçs bɛʁk]
Konrad 'kɒn ræd ‖ 'kɑːn-
Kon-Tiki ˌkɒn 'tiːk i -'tɪk- ‖ ˌkɑːn-
Koo kuː
kook kuːk kooks kuːks
kookaburra 'kʊk ə bʌr ə ‖ -bɜ·ː ə ~s z
Kookai, Kookaï tdmk 'kuː kaɪ
kook|y 'kuːk |i ~ier i_ə ‖ i_ᵊr ~iest i_ɪst i_əst
    ~iness i nəs i nɪs
Kool tdmk kuːl

Kool-Aid tdmk 'kuːl eɪd
Kootenay 'kuːt ə neɪ -ᵊn eɪ ‖ -ᵊn eɪ
kop, Kop kɒp ‖ kɑːp (= cop) kops
    kɒps ‖ kɑːps
kopeck, kopek 'kəʊp ek 'kɒp- ‖ 'koʊp- ~s s
kopje 'kɒp i ‖ 'kɑːp i ~s z
koppa 'kɒp ə ‖ 'kɑːp ə ~s z
koppie 'kɒp i ‖ 'kɑːp i ~s z
Koran kɔː 'rɑːn kɒ-, kə- ‖ kə- —Arabic
    [qur 'ʔaːn]
Koranic kɔː 'ræn ɪk kɒ-, kə- ‖ kə-
Kordofan ˌkɔːd əʊ 'fæn -'fɑːn ‖ ˌkɔːrd oʊ 'fɑːn
Kordofanian ˌkɔːd əʊ 'feɪn i_ən ◄ -'fɑːn-
    ‖ ˌkɔːrd oʊ 'fæn-
Korea kə 'rɪə kɒ-, §-'riː_ə ‖ kə 'riː ə
Korean kə 'rɪən kɒ-, §-'riː_ən ‖ kə 'riː ən ~s z
korfball 'kɔːf bɔːl ‖ 'kɔːrf- -bɑːl
korma 'kɔːm ə ‖ 'kɔːrm ə ~s z
Korsakoff, Korsakov, Korsakow
    'kɔːs ə kɒf ‖ 'kɔːrs ə kɑːf -kɔːf —Russ
    ['kɔr sə kəf]
Kos Greek island kɒs ‖ kɑːs kɔːs, koʊs
kos Indian measure of distance kəʊs ‖ koʊs
Kosciusko name of mountain ˌkɒs i 'ʌsk əʊ
    -'ʊsk- ‖ ˌkɑːs i 'ʌsk oʊ ˌkɑːsk- —Polish
    Kościuszko [kɔɕ 'tɕuʃ kɔ]
kosher 'kəʊʃ ə ‖ 'koʊʃ ᵊr
Kosovar 'kɒs ə vɑː ‖ 'koʊs ə vɑːr 'kɑːs-, 'kɔːs-
    ~s z
Kosovo 'kɒs ə vəʊ ‖ 'koʊs ə voʊ 'kɑːs-, 'kɔːs-
    —SCr ['kɔ sɔ vɔ], Albanian Kosova [kɔ 'sɔ va]
Kosset tdmk 'kɒs ɪt §-ət ‖ 'kɑːs-
Kossoff 'kɒs ɒf ‖ 'kɑːs ɔːf -ɑːf
Kotex tdmk 'kəʊt eks ‖ 'koʊt-
kotow ˌkəʊ 'taʊ ‖ koʊ 'toʊ '• • ~ed d ~ing ɪŋ
    ~s z
koumis, koumiss 'kuːm ɪs -əs
Kowloon ˌkaʊ 'luːn ◄ —Cantonese [²kɐw ⁴lɔŋ]
kowtow ˌkaʊ 'taʊ ‖ '• • ~ed d ~ing ɪŋ ~s z
kraal krɑːl §krɔːl kraals krɑːlz §krɔːlz —in
    South African English, krɔːl
Kraft tdmk krɑːft §kræft ‖ kræft
krait kraɪt kraits kraɪts
Krakatoa ˌkræk ə 'təʊ ə ‖ ˌkrɑːk- ‖ -'toʊ ə
kraken 'krɑːk ən 'kreɪk-, 'kræk- ~s z
Krakow 'kræk aʊ -əʊ, -ɒf ‖ 'krɑːk aʊ —Polish
    Kraków ['kra kuf]
Kramer 'kreɪm ə ‖ -ᵊr
kraut, Kraut kraʊt krauts krauts
Kray kreɪ
Krebs krebz
Kremlin, k~ 'krem lɪn §-lən
Kreutzer 'krɔɪts ə ‖ -ᵊr —Ger ['kʁɔy tsɐ]
krill krɪl
krimmer 'krɪm ə ‖ -ᵊr
Krio 'kriː əʊ ‖ -oʊ ~s z
kris 'knife' kriːs krɪs
Kris personal name krɪs
Krishna 'krɪʃ nə
Krishnamurti ˌkrɪʃ nə 'mʊət i -'mɜːt-
    ‖ -'mʊrʈ i
Krispie 'krɪsp i ~s z
Krista 'krɪst ə

Kristen 'krɪst ən
Kristi, Kristie 'krɪst i
Kristle 'krɪst ᵊl
Kristy 'krɪst i
Krona *tdmk*, krona 'krəʊn ə ‖ 'kroʊn ə
—*Swedish* ['kru na] kronor 'krəʊn ɔː
‖ 'kroʊn ɔːr —*Swedish* ['kru nur]
krone 'krəʊn ə ‖ 'kroʊn ə —*Danish* ['kʁo nə]
kroner 'krəʊn ə ‖ 'kroʊn ᵊr —*Danish*
['kʁo nɒ]
Kru kruː Krus kruːz
Kruger 'kruːg ə ‖ -ᵊr —*Afrikaans* ['kry xər]
Krugerrand, k~ 'kruːg ə rænd ~s z
Krupp krʊp krʌp —*Ger* [kʁʊp] Krupp's krʊps
krʌps
Kruschen *tdmk* 'krʊʃ ən 'krʌʃ-
Krushchev 'krʊs tʃɒf 'krʊʃ-, •'• ‖ 'kruːs tʃef
-tʃɔːf, -tʃaːf, •'• —*Russ* [xru 'ɕtɕof]
krypton 'krɪpt ɒn -ən ‖ -aːn
kryptonite 'krɪpt ə naɪt
Kshatriya 'kʃætr i‿ə
Kuala Lumpur ˌkwaːl ə 'lʊmp ʊə ˌkwɒl-,
-'lʌmp-, -ə ‖ -lʊm 'pʊᵊr
Kubla Khan ˌkuːb lə 'kaːn ˌkʊb-
Kublai 'kuːb lə 'kʊb-, -laɪ
Kubrick 'kjuːb rɪk
kuccha 'kʌtʃ ə —*Punjabi* [kət tʃə]
kudos 'kjuːd ɒs ‖ -oʊz 'kuːd-, -oʊs, -aːs
kudu 'kuːd u: 'kʊd- ~s z
kudzu 'kʊd zuː —*Jp* ['kɯ dzɯ]
Kufic 'kuːf ɪk 'kjuːf-
Kuhn kuːn
Kuhnian 'kuːn i‿ən
Ku Klux Klan ˌkuː klʌks 'klæn ˌkjuː:-, △ˌkluː:-
kukri 'kʊk ri ~s z
kulak 'kuːl æk ‖ ku 'laːk -'læk; 'kuːl aːk, -æk
—*Russ* [ku 'ɬak] ~s s
Kultur kʊl 'tʊə ‖ -'tʊᵊr —*Ger* [kʊl 'tuːʁ]
kumis, kumiss 'kuːm ɪs §-əs
kummel, kümmel 'kʊm ᵊl ‖ 'kɪm- *(*) —*Ger*
['kʏm ᵊl]
kumquat 'kʌm kwɒt ‖ -kwaːt ~s s
!Kung, !xũ kʊŋ —*In the language so named, the
exclamation mark denotes a post-alveolar
('palatal') click. This accompanies a voiceless
velar affricate* [kx]. *The vowel is a nasalized*
[ũ]. *The syllable is said on a low rising tone.*
kung fu ˌkʌŋ 'fuː ˌkʊŋ- —*Chi* gōngfū
[¹kʊŋ ¹fu]
Kunming ˌkʊn 'mɪŋ —*Chi* Kūnmíng
[¹kʰwən ²miŋ]
Kuomintang ˌkwəʊ mɪn 'tæŋ ˌgwəʊ mɪn 'dæŋ
‖ ˌkwoʊ mɪn 'taːŋ ˌgwoʊ-, -'tæŋ —*Chi*
Guómíndǎng [²kwɔ ²mɪn ³taŋ]
Kuoni *tdmk* ku 'əʊn i ‖ -'oʊn i
Kurath 'kjʊər æθ ‖ 'kjʊr-
Kurd kɜːd kʊəd ‖ kɝːd kʊᵊrd Kurds kɜːdz
kʊədz ‖ kɝːdz kʊᵊrdz
Kurdish 'kɜːd ɪʃ ‖ 'kɝːd-

Kurdistan ˌkɜːd ɪ 'staːn -ə-, -'stæn
‖ 'kɝːd ə stæn
Kureishi ku 'reʃ i -'reɪʃ-
Kuril, Kurile kʊ 'riːᵊl kju- ‖ 'kʊr ɪl 'kjʊr-
Kurosawa ˌkʊər əʊ 'saː wə ‖ ˌkʊr oʊ- —*Jp*
[ku ˌro sa wa]
kursaal 'kɜːz ᵊl 'kɜːs-; 'kɜː saːl, 'kʊə-, -sᵊl, -zaːl
‖ 'kʊr saːl
Kurt kɜːt kʊət ‖ kɝːt —*Ger* [kʊʁt]
kurtosis kɜː 'təʊs ɪs kə-, §-əs ‖ kɝː 'toʊs əs
kurus kʊ 'rʊʃ -'ruːʃ
Kurzweil 'kɜːz waɪᵊl 'kɜːts-, -vaɪᵊl ‖ 'kɝːz-
Kutch kʌtʃ
Kuwait ku 'weɪt kju-, kə- —*Arabic* [ku 'weːt]
Kuwaiti ku 'weɪt i kju-, kə- ‖ -'weɪt̬ i ~s z
Kvaerner kə 'vɜːn ə -'vaːn- ‖ -'vɝːn ᵊr
—*Norwegian* ["kvæːɳər]
kvas, kvass kvaːs kvæs ‖ kwaːs
kvetch kvetʃ kvetched kvetʃt kvetches
'kvetʃ ɪz -əz kvetching 'kvetʃ ɪŋ
Kwa kwaː
Kwajalein 'kwaːdʒ ə leɪn -ᵊl ən
Kwakiutl ˌkwaːk i 'uːt ᵊl ◄ ‖ -'uːt̬-
Kwandebele, KwaNdebele ˌkwɒnd ɪ 'bel i
ˌkwaːnd-, -'beɪl-, -eɪ ‖ ˌkwaːnd-
Kwanza, Kwanzaa 'kwaːnz ə 'kwænz-, -aː
kwashiorkor kwɒʃ i 'ɔːk ɔː ˌkwæʃ-, -ə
‖ ˌkwaːʃ i 'ɔːrk ᵊr -ɔːr
kwatcha 'kwaːtʃ ə
KwaZulu kwaː 'zuːl uː
kwela 'kweɪl ə
Kwells *tdmk* kwelz
KWIC kwɪk
Kwik-Fit *tdmk* 'kwɪk fɪt
Kwiksave *tdmk* 'kwɪk seɪv
Kyd kɪd
Kyle, kyle kaɪᵊl
Kyleakin ₍ₗ₎kaɪᵊl 'æk ɪn
Kylie 'kaɪl i
kymograph 'kaɪm əʊ graːf -græf ‖ -ə græf ~s
s
kymographic ˌkaɪm əʊ 'græf ɪk ◄ ‖ -ə- ~ally
ᵊl‿i
kymogram 'kaɪm əʊ græm ‖ -ə- ~s z
Kynance 'kaɪn ænᵗs
Kynaston 'kɪn əst ən
Kyocera *tdmk* ˌkaɪ‿ə 'sɪər ə ‖ -'sɪr ə —*Jp*
[kjo ˌo se ɾa]
Kyoto ki 'əʊt əʊ ‖ -'oʊt oʊ —*Jp* ['kjoo to]
kyphosis kaɪ 'fəʊs ɪs §-əs ‖ -'foʊs-
kyphotic kaɪ 'fɒt ɪk ‖ -'faːt̬-
Kyrgystan ˌkɜːg ɪ 'staːn -'stæn ‖ ˌkɪrg- • • •
kyrie 'kɪr i eɪ 'kɪər-, -iː
kyrie e'leison ɪ 'leɪs ɒn e-, -ᵊn; -'leɪ ə sɒn
‖ -aːn
Kyushu ki 'uːʃ uː 'kjuːʃ uː —*Jp* ['kjɯɯ ɕɯɯ]
Kyzyl Kum kə ˌzɪl 'kuːm -'kʊm —*Russ* [kɨ ˌzɨɬ
'kum]

L l

Spelling-to-sound

1 Where the spelling is **l**, the pronunciation is regularly l, as in **little** 'lɪt ᵊl.

2 Where the spelling is double **ll**, the pronunciation is again regularly l, as in **silly** 'sɪl i.

3 **l** is silent in a fair number of words, expecially when it stands between
a and **f**, as in **half** hɑːf ‖ hæf,
a and **k**, as in **talk** tɔːk, or
a and **m**, as in **salmon** 'sæm ən.
Note also **could** kʊd, **should** ʃʊd, **would** wʊd.

L, l el (= **ell**) **Ls, l's, L's** elz —*Communications code name:* Lima 'liːm ə

la lɑː —*but in French, Italian, and Spanish expressions also* lə, læ — *Fr, It, Sp* [la]; *in family names usually* lə —*See also phrases with this word*

LA ˌel 'eɪ ◂ —*see also* Los Angeles
ˌLA 'Law

laager 'lɑːg ə ‖ -ᵊr (= *lager*) ~**ed** d ~**s** z

Laa-Laa 'lɑː lɑː

lab læb **labs** læbz

Laban (i) 'leɪb ən -æn, (ii) 'lɑːb-, (iii) lə 'bæn —*The biblical figure is* (i), *the dance notation system and its inventor* (ii).

label 'leɪb ᵊl ~**ed, ~led** d ~**ing, ~ling** ɪŋ ~**s** z

labia 'leɪb i‿ə
ˌlabia ma'jora mə 'dʒɔːr ə ‖ -'dʒoʊr-; ˌlabia mi'nora mɪ 'nɔːr ə mə- ‖ -'noʊr-

labial 'leɪb i‿əl ~**ly** i ~**s** z

labialis... —*see* **labializ...**

labiality ˌleɪb i 'æl ət i -ɪt i ‖ -əṭ i

labialization ˌleɪb i‿əl aɪ 'zeɪʃ ᵊn -ɪ'•- ‖ -ə 'zeɪʃ- ~**s** z

labializ|e 'leɪb i‿ə laɪz ~**ed** d ~**es** ɪz əz ~**ing** ɪŋ

labial-velar ˌleɪb i‿əl 'viːl ə ◂ ‖ -ᵊr ◂ ~**s** z

labiate 'leɪb i eɪt -ət, -ɪt ~**s** s

labile 'leɪb aɪᵊl ‖ -ᵊl

lability leɪ 'bɪl ət i lə-, -ɪt i ‖ -əṭ i

labiodental ˌleɪb i əʊ 'dent ᵊl ◂ ‖ -oʊ 'denṭ ᵊl ◂ ~**ly** i ~**s** z

labiopalatal ˌleɪb i əʊ 'pæl ət ᵊl ◂ ‖ -oʊ 'pæl əṭ ᵊl ◂ ~**ly** i ~**s** z

labiovelar ˌleɪb i əʊ 'viːl ə ◂ ‖ -oʊ 'viːl ᵊr ◂ ~**s** z

labiovelaris... —*see* **labiovelariz...**

labiovelarization ˌleɪb i əʊ ˌviːl ər aɪ 'zeɪʃ ᵊn -ɪ'•- ‖ -i oʊ ˌviːl ər ə- ~**s** z

labiovelariz|e ˌleɪb i əʊ 'viːl ə raɪz ‖ -i oʊ- ~**ed** d ~**es** ɪz əz ~**ing** ɪŋ

labi|um 'leɪb i‿əm ~**a** ə

La Boheme, La Bohème ˌlɑː bəʊ 'em ˌlæ-, -'eɪm ‖ -boʊ- —*Fr* [la bo ɛm]

labor 'leɪb ə ‖ -ᵊr ~**ed** d **laboring** 'leɪb ᵊr‿ɪŋ ~**s** z
'labor camp; 'Labor Day; 'labor ex,change; 'labor ,market; ,labor of 'love; 'Labor ,Party; 'labor ,union

laborator|y lə 'bɒr ət‿ᵊr i li ‖ 'læb ᵊr‿ə tɔːr li -toʊr i (*) —*In BrE formerly also* 'læb ᵊr‿ət‿ᵊr i ~**ies** iz

laborer 'leɪb ᵊr‿ə ‖ -ᵊr‿ᵊr ~**s** z

labor-intensive ˌleɪb ᵊr ɪn 'tenˢ ɪv ◂ ‖ ˌ•ᵊr-

laborious lə 'bɔːr i‿əs ‖ -'boʊr- ~**ly** li ~**ness** nəs nɪs

Laborite 'leɪb ə raɪt ~**s** s

labor-saving 'leɪb ə ˌseɪv ɪŋ ‖ -ᵊr-

Labouchere ˌlæb uː 'ʃeə '••• ‖ -'ʃeᵊr

labour 'leɪb ə ‖ -ᵊr ~**ed** d **labouring** 'leɪb ᵊr‿ɪŋ ~**s** z
'labour camp; 'Labour Day; 'labour ex,change; 'labour ,market; ,labour of 'love; 'Labour ,Party; 'labour ,union

labourer 'leɪb ᵊr‿ə ‖ -ᵊr‿ᵊr ~**s** z

labour-intensive ˌleɪb ᵊr ɪn 'tenˢ ɪv ◂ ‖ ˌ•ᵊr-

Labourite 'leɪb ə raɪt ~**s** s

labour-saving 'leɪb ə ˌseɪv ɪŋ ‖ -ᵊr-

Labov lə 'bɒv -'bəʊv ‖ -'boʊv

Labovian lə 'bəʊv i‿ən ‖ -'boʊv-

Labrador 'læb rə dɔː ‖ -dɔːr ~**s** z
ˌLabrador re'triever

Labuan lə 'buː‿ən ‖ ˌlɑːb u 'ɑːn

laburnum lə 'bɜːn əm ‖ -'bɜ·ːn- ~**s** z

labyrinth 'læb ə rɪntθ -ɪ- ~**s** s

labyrinthine ˌlæb ə 'rɪntᵗθ aɪn ◂ -ɪ- ‖ -ən -iːn, -aɪn

L

labyrinthitis ˌlæb ər_ɪn 'θaɪt ɪs -ər_ən-, §-əs
‖ -'θaɪt əs
lac *'resin'* læk (= *lack*) **lacs** læks
lac *'100 000'* laːk læk **lacs** laːks læks
Lacan læ 'kɒ̃ -'kaːn ‖ lə 'kaːn —*Fr* [la kɑ̃]
Laccadive 'læk əd ɪv 'laːk-, ə diːv, -daɪv
lace leɪs **laced** leɪst **laces** 'leɪs ɪz -əz **lacing**
'leɪs ɪŋ
Lacedaemon ˌlæs ə 'diːm ən -ɪ-
Lacedaemonian ˌlæs ə dɪ 'məʊn i_ən ◄, •ɪ-,
-də'•- ‖ -'moʊn- **~s** z
lace|rate v 'læs ə |reɪt **~rated** reɪt ɪd -əd
‖ reɪt̬ əd **~rates** reɪts **~rating**
reɪt ɪŋ ‖ reɪt̬ ɪŋ
laceration ˌlæs ə 'reɪʃ ən **~s** z
Lacert|a lə 'sɜːt lə ‖ -'sɝːt̬ lə **~ae** iː
lacewing 'leɪs wɪŋ **~s** z
Lacey 'leɪs i
laches 'lætʃ ɪz 'leɪtʃ-, -əz
Lachesis 'læk ɪs ɪs △'lætʃ-, -əs-, §-əs
Lachlan 'lɒk lən 'læk- ‖ 'laːk-
lachryma Christi ˌlæk rɪm ə 'krɪst i, •rəm-
lachrymal 'læk rɪm əl -rəm- **~s** z
lachrymator 'læk rɪ meɪt ə '•rə- ‖ -meɪt̬ ər **~s**
z
lachrymator|y ˌlæk rɪ 'meɪt ər |i ◄, •rə-, '••••-,
'••mət_ər |i ‖ 'læk rəm ə tɔːr |i -tour i **~ies**
iz
lachrymose 'læk rɪ məʊs -rə-, -məʊz ‖ -moʊs
~ly li
La Cienega ˌlaː si 'en əg ə
lack læk **lacked** lækt **lacking** 'læk ɪŋ **lacks**
læks
lackadaisical ˌlæk ə 'deɪz ɪk əl ◄ **~ly** _i **~ness**
nəs nɪs
Lackawanna ˌlæk ə 'wɒn ə ‖ -'waːn ə
lackey 'læk i **~s** z
lackluster, lacklustre 'læk ˌlʌst ə, •'•• ‖ -ər
Lacock 'leɪk ɒk ‖ -aːk
Laconia lə 'kəʊn i_ə ‖ -'koʊn-
laconic lə 'kɒn ɪk ‖ -'kaːn- **~ally** əl_i
lacquer 'læk ə ‖ -ər **~ed** d **lacquering** 'læk
ər ɪŋ **~s** z
lacrim... —*see* **lachrym...**
lacrosse lə 'krɒs ‖ -'krɔːs -'kraːs
lacrymal 'læk rɪm əl -rəm- **~s** z
lact|ate v ₍ₗ₎læk 't|eɪt 'lækt |eɪt ‖ 'lækt̬ |eɪt
~ated eɪt ɪd -əd ‖ eɪt̬ əd **~ates** eɪts **~ating**
eɪt ɪŋ ‖ eɪt̬ ɪŋ
lactate n 'lækt eɪt **~s** s
lactation ₍ₗ₎læk 'teɪʃ ən **~s** z
lacteal 'lækt i_əl **~s** z
lactic 'lækt ɪk
ˌlactic 'acid
lactobacill|us ˌlækt əʊ bə 'sɪl ləs ‖, •oʊ- **~i** aɪ
lactose 'lækt əʊs -əʊz ‖ -oʊs -oʊz
lacun|a lə 'kjuːn lə læ-, -'kuːn- **~ae** iː aɪ
lac|y, Lacy 'leɪs |i **~ier** i_ə ‖ i_ər **~iest** i_ɪst
i_əst **~iness** i nəs i nɪs
lad læd **lads** lædz
Lada *tdmk* 'laːd ə **~s** z
Ladakh lə 'daːk -'dɔːk

Ladbroke 'læd brʊk →'læb-, -brəʊk ‖ -broʊk
~'s s
Ladd læd
ladder 'læd ə ‖ -ər **~ed** d **laddering** 'læd ər ɪŋ
~s z
ladd|ie, ladd|y 'læd |i **~ies** iz
lade leɪd (= *laid*) **laded** 'leɪd ɪd -əd **laden**
'leɪd ən **lades** leɪdz **lading** 'leɪd ɪŋ
Ladefoged 'læd ɪ fəʊg ɪd '•ə-, -əd ‖ -foʊg-
laden 'leɪd ən
Ladhar Bheinn ˌlaː 'ven ‖ ˌlaːr- —*ScG*
[ˌɫaar 'vjeɲ]
la-di-da ˌlaː di 'daː ◄
ladies 'leɪd iz
ladies-in-waiting ˌleɪd iz ɪn 'weɪt ɪŋ §-ən'•-
‖ -ən 'weɪt̬ ɪŋ
ladieswear 'leɪd iz weə ‖ -wer -wær
Ladin læ 'diːn lə-
lading 'leɪd ɪŋ
Ladino, l~ lə 'diːn əʊ læ- ‖ -oʊ
ladl|e 'leɪd əl **~ed** d **~es** z **~ing** _ɪŋ
lad|y, Lad|y 'leɪd |i **~ies, ~ies', ~y's** iz
'ladies' man; 'ladies' room; ˌLady ˌChapel;
'Lady Day; 'lady's ˌfingers, •••
ladybird 'leɪd i bɜːd ‖ -bɝːd **~s** z
ladybug 'leɪd i bʌg **~s** z
ladyfinger 'leɪd i ˌfɪŋ gə ‖ -gər **~s** z
lady|-in-waiting ˌleɪd i|_ɪn 'weɪt ɪŋ §-ən'•-
‖ -ən 'weɪt̬ ɪŋ **ladies~** ˌleɪd iz-
lady-killer 'leɪd i ˌkɪl ə ‖ -ər **~s** z
ladylike 'leɪd i laɪk
ladyship 'leɪd i ʃɪp **~s** s
Ladysmith 'leɪd i smɪθ
lady's-slipper ˌleɪd iz 'slɪp ə ‖ -ər **~s** z
Lae 'leɪ 'leɪ i, 'laː eɪ
Laertes leɪ 'ɜːt iːz ‖ -'ɝːt̬ iːz
Laetitia lɪ 'tɪʃ ə lə-, liː-, -'tɪʃ i_ə
laetrile, L~ *tdmk* 'leɪ ə traɪəl -trɪl; -ətr əl ‖ -ətr
əl -ə trɪl
laevo- ˌliːv əʊ ‖ -ə — **laevorotation** ˌliːv əʊ
rəʊ 'teɪʃ ən ‖ -ə roʊ-
laevulose 'liːv ju ləʊz 'lev-, -jə-, -ləʊs
‖ -jə loʊs -loʊz
Lafayette ˌlaː faɪ 'et -feɪ- ‖ ˌlæf i- ˌlaːf-, -eɪ-
—*Fr* [la fa jɛt]
Lafcadio læf 'kaːd i əʊ ‖ laːf 'kaːd i oʊ
Laffan lə 'fæn
Laffer 'læf ə ‖ -ər
'Laffer curve
Lafford 'læf əd ‖ -ərd
LaFontaine ˌlæf ɒn 'ten ˌlɑ: fɒn-, -'teɪn
‖ ˌlaː fɔːn 'ten -foʊn- —*Fr* [la fɔ̃ tɛn]
lag læg **lagged** lægd **lagging** 'læg ɪŋ **lags**
lægz
Lagan, lagan 'læg ən
lager 'laːg ə ‖ -ər 'lɔːg- **~s** z
Lagerfeld 'laːg ə felt ‖ -ər-
Lagonda *tdmk* lə 'gɒnd ə ‖ -'gaːnd ə **~s** z
lagoon lə 'guːn **~s** z

Lagos 'leɪɡ ɒs ‖ -ɑːs —*Americans not familiar with Nigeria also sometimes say* 'lɑːɡ oʊs

Lagrange lə 'ɡrɑ̃ʒ læ-, lɑː-, -'ɡrɑːnʒ, -'ɡreɪndʒ ‖ -'ɡrɑːndʒ —*Fr* [la ɡʁɑ̃ːʒ]

La Guardia lə 'ɡwɑːd i̯ə ‖ -'ɡwɑːrd-

Laguna *tdmk* lə 'ɡuːn ə

La‚guna 'Beach

lahar 'lɑː hɑː ‖ -hɑːr ~s z

lah-di-dah ‚lɑː di 'dɑː ◂

Lahnda 'lɑːnd ə

Lahore lə 'hɔː ‖ -'hɔːr -'hoʊr —*Urdu* [lɑː hoːr]

laic 'leɪ ɪk ~al əl ~ally əl_i ~s s

laicis... —*see* **laiciz...**

laicization ‚leɪ ɪs aɪ 'zeɪʃ ən ‚•əs-, -ɪ'•- ‖ -əs ə- ~s z

laiciz|e 'leɪ ɪ saɪz -ə- ~**ed** d ~**es** ɪz əz ~**ing** ɪŋ

laid leɪd

laid-back ‚leɪd 'bæk ◂ →‚leɪb-

Laidlaw 'leɪd lɔː ‖ -lɑː

lain leɪn (= *lane*)

Laindon 'leɪnd ən

Laing (i) læŋ, (ii) leɪŋ

Laingian 'læŋ i_ən ~s z

lair leə ‖ leᵊr læᵊr **lairs** leəz ‖ leᵊrz læᵊrz

laird, Laird leəd ‖ leᵊrd læᵊrd **lairds** leədz ‖ leᵊrdz læᵊrdz

Lairg leəɡ ‖ leᵊrɡ læᵊrɡ

laisser-faire, laissez-faire ‚leɪs eɪ 'feə ‚les- ‖ -'feᵊr -'fæᵊr —*Fr* [lɛ se fɛːʁ]

lait|y 'leɪ ət li -ɪt- ‖ -əţ li ~**ies** iz

Laius 'leɪ i_əs 'laɪ‿əs, 'leɪ- ‖ 'leɪ əs 'leɪ i‿əs

La Jolla lə 'hɔɪ ə

lake, Lake leɪk **lakes** leɪks

Lake 'Charles; 'Lake ‚District; 'Lake ‚Poets; ‚Lake Suc'cess

lakeland, L~ 'leɪk lənd -lænd ~s z

Lakenheath 'leɪk ən hiːθ

Laker 'leɪk ə ‖ -ᵊr

Lakesha lə 'keʃ ə

lakeside, L~ 'leɪk saɪd

lakh lɑːk læk —*Hindi* [lɑːkh] **lakhs** lɑːks læks

Lakme, Lakmé 'læk meɪ -mi

Lakshadweep læk 'ʃæd wiːp

Lalage 'læl əɡ i -ədʒ-

Laleham 'leɪl əm

-lalia 'leɪl i_ə — **coprolalia** ‚kɒp rəʊ 'leɪl i_ə ‖ ‚kɑːp rə-

Lalique *tdmk* læ 'liːk lə- ‖ lɑː- —*Fr* [la lik]

Lallans 'læl ənz

lallation læ 'leɪʃ ən ~s z

lalling 'læl ɪŋ

Lalo 'lɑːl əʊ ‖ -oʊ —*Fr* [la lo]

lam læm **lammed** læmd **lamming** 'læm ɪŋ **lams** læmz

lama 'lɑːm ə ~s z

Lamaism 'lɑːm ər‚ɪz əm ‖ -ə-

Lamarck lə 'mɑːk læ-, lɑː- ‖ -'mɑːrk —*Fr* [la maʁk]

Lamarckian lə 'mɑːk i_ən læ-, lɑː- ‖ -'mɑːrk- ~s z

Lamarr lə 'mɑː ‖ -'mɑːr

lamaser|y 'lɑːm əs ər li ‖ -ə ser li ~**ies** iz

lamb, Lamb læm (= *lam*) **lambed** læmd **lambing** 'læm ɪŋ **lambs, Lamb's** læmz

lambad|a læm 'bɑːd| ə ‖ lɑːm- ~**aed** əd ~**aing** əⁱ ɪŋ ‖ ə ɪŋ ~**as** əz

Lambarene ‚læm bə 'riːn i ‖ ‚lɑːm- —*Fr* Lambaréné [lɑ̃ ba ʁe ne]

lambast læm 'bæst -'bɑːst ~**ed** ɪd əd ~**ing** ɪŋ ~**s** s

lambast|e læm 'beɪst ~**ed** ɪd əd ~**ing** ɪŋ ~**es** s

lambda 'læmd ə ~**s** z

lambdacism 'læmd ə ‚sɪz əm ~**s** z

Lambeg, l~ læm 'beɡ ~**s** z

lambent 'læm bənt ~**ly** li

Lambert, l~ 'læm bət ‖ -bᵊrt ~**s**, ~**'s** s

Lambeth 'læm bəθ

‚Lambeth 'Conference; ‚Lambeth 'Palace; ‚Lambeth 'Walk

lambkin 'læm kɪn §-kən ~**s** z

lamblike 'læm laɪk

Lamborghini *tdmk* ‚læm bɔː 'ɡiːn i -bə- ‖ ‚lɑːm bɔːr- -bᵊr- —*It* [lam bor 'ɡi ni] ~**s** z

Lamborn, Lambourne 'læm bɔːn ‖ -bɔːrn -boʊrn

Lambretta *tdmk* læm 'bret ə ‖ -'breţ ə ~**s** z

Lambrusco, l~ læm 'brʊsk əʊ ‖ -'bruːsk oʊ —*It* [lam 'brus ko]

lambskin 'læm skɪn ~**s** z

Lambton 'læm't ən

LAMDA 'læmd ə

lame leɪm **lamed** leɪmd **lamer** 'leɪm ə ‖ -ᵊr **lames** leɪmz **lamest** 'leɪm ɪst -əst **laming** 'leɪm ɪŋ

‚lame 'duck

lamé 'lɑːm eɪ 'læm- ‖ lɑː 'meɪ læ-

lamell|a lə 'mel |ə -ae iː ‖ -əs əz

lamellibranch lə 'mel ɪ bræŋk §-'•ə-

lame|ly 'leɪm |li ~**ness** nəs nɪs

lament v, n lə 'ment **lamented** lə 'ment ɪd -əd ‖ lə 'menţ əd **lamenting** lə 'ment ɪŋ ‖ lə 'menţ ɪŋ **laments** lə 'ments

lamentab|le 'læm ənt əb |əl '•ɪnt-; lə 'ment- ‖ lə 'menţ- 'læm ənţ- ~**ly** li

lamentation ‚læm ən 'teɪʃ ən -ɪn-, -en- ~**s**, L~**s** z

La Mesa *place in CA* lə 'meɪs ə

lamin|a 'læm ɪn lə -ən- ~**ae** iː ~**as** əz

laminal 'læm ɪn əl -ən- ~**s** z

laminar 'læm ɪn ə -ən- ‖ -ᵊr

‚laminar 'flow

laminaria ‚læm ɪ 'neər i_ə ‚•ə- ‖ -'ner- -'nær-

lami|nate v 'læm ɪ |neɪt -ə- ~**nated** neɪt ɪd -əd ‖ neɪţ əd ~**nates** neɪts ~**nating** neɪt ɪŋ ‖ neɪţ ɪŋ

laminate n, adj 'læm ɪ neɪt -ə-; -ən ət, -ɪt ~**s** s

lamination ‚læm ɪ 'neɪʃ ən -ə- ~**s** z

laminator 'læm ɪ neɪt ə '•ə- ‖ -neɪţ ᵊr ~**s** z

Laming (i) 'leɪm ɪŋ, (ii) 'læm-

Lamington, l~ 'læm ɪŋ tən ~**s** z

Lammas 'læm əs

lammergeier, lammergeyer 'læm ə ɡaɪ‿ə ‖ -ᵊr ɡaɪ‿ᵊr ~**s** z

Lammermoor 'læm ə muə -mɔː, ˌ•••• ‖ -mʊr
-mɔːr, -moʊr
Lammermuir 'læm ə mjuə -mjɔː ‖ -ᵊr mjʊr
ˌLammermuir 'Hills
Lamond 'læm ənd
Lamont (i) 'læm ənt, (ii) lə 'mɒnt ‖ -'maːnt
—In AmE, (ii).
Lamorna lə 'mɔːn ə ‖ -'mɔːrn ə
lamp læmp lamps læmps
lamp-black 'læmp blæk
Lampedusa ˌlæmp ɪ 'djuːz ə -ə-, →-'dʒuːz-,
-'duːz- ‖ -ə 'duːz ə -'duːs- —It
[lam pe 'du: za]
lampern 'læmp ən ‖ -ᵊrn ~s z
Lampeter 'læmp ɪt ə -ət- ‖ -ət̮ ᵊr
lamplight 'læmp laɪt
lamplighter 'læmp ˌlaɪt ə ‖ -ˌlaɪt̮ ᵊr ~s z
Lamplugh 'læmp luː -lə
lampoon ₍ᵢ₎læm 'puːn ~ed d ~ing ɪŋ ~s z
lamp-post 'læmp pəʊst ‖ -poʊst ~s s
lamprey 'læmp ri ~s z
lampshade 'læmp ʃeɪd ~s z
LAN læn or as local area network
Lana 'laːn ə ‖ 'læn ə
Lanagan 'læn əg ən
Lanai, lanai lə 'naɪ laː-, -'naː i ~s z
Lanark 'læn ək ‖ -ᵊrk
Lancashire 'læŋk ə ʃə -ʃɪə ‖ -ʃɪr -ʃᵊr
Lancaster 'læŋk əst ə 'læŋ kaːst ə, -kæst- ‖ -ᵊr
'læŋ kæst ᵊr
Lancastrian læŋ 'kæs tri‿ən ~s z
lance, Lance laːnˢts §læn ts ‖ læn ts lanced
laːnᵗst §læn ts t ‖ læn ts t lances, Lance's
'laːnᵗs ɪz §'læn ts-, -əz ‖ 'læn ts əz lancing
'laːnᵗs ɪŋ §'læn ts- ‖ 'læn ts ɪŋ
ˌlance 'corporal ◂
lancelet 'laːn ts lət §'læn ts-, -lɪt ‖ 'læn ts- ~s s
Lancelot 'laːn ts ə lɒt §'læn ts-, -əl ət
‖ 'læn ts ə laːt -əl ət
lanceolate 'laːn ts i‿ə leɪt §'læn ts-, -lət, -lɪt
‖ 'læn ts-
lancer 'laːn ts ə §'læn ts- ‖ 'læn ts ᵊr ~s z
lancet 'laːn ts ɪt §'læn ts-, -ət ‖ 'læn ts ət ~s s
Lanchester 'laːn tʃ ɪst ə 'læn tʃ-, -əst-,
§'læn ˌtʃest ə ‖ 'læn ˌtʃest ᵊr
Lancia tdmk 'laːn ts i‿ə §'læn ts- —It ['lan tʃa]
~s z
lanci|nate 'læn ts ɪ ˌneɪt 'laːn ts-, -ə- ~nated
neɪt ɪd -əd ‖ neɪt̮ əd ~nates neɪts ~nating
neɪt ɪŋ ‖ neɪt̮ ɪŋ
Lancing 'laːn ts ɪŋ §'læn ts- ‖ 'læn ts ɪŋ
Lancome, Lancôme tdmk
'lɒŋ kəʊm ‖ laːŋ 'koʊm lɔːŋ-
Lancs. læŋks
land, Land lænd landed 'lænd ɪd -əd landing
'lænd ɪŋ lands lændz
'land ˌagent; 'land crab; ˌlanded 'gentry;
ˌLand's 'End
landau, L~ 'lænd ɔː -aʊ ‖ -aʊ -ɔː, -aː ~s z
landaulet, landaulette ˌlænd ɔː 'let ‖ -aː- ~s s
lander, L~ 'lænd ə ‖ -ᵊr ~s z
Landers 'lænd əz ‖ -ᵊrz
landfall 'lænd fɔːl ‖ -faːl ~s z

landfill 'lænd fɪl ~s z
landing 'lænd ɪŋ ~s z
'landing craft; 'landing field; 'landing
gear; 'landing net; 'landing stage;
'landing strip
Landis 'lænd ɪs §-əs
landlad|y 'lænd leɪd |i ~ies iz
landlocked 'lænd lɒkt ‖ -laːkt
landlord 'lænd lɔːd ‖ -lɔːrd ~ism ˌɪz əm ~s z
landlubber 'lænd ˌlʌb ə ‖ -ᵊr ~ly li ~s z
landmark 'lænd maːk →'læm- ‖ -maːrk ~s s
landmass 'lænd mæs →'læm- ~es ɪz əz
landmine 'lænd maɪn →'læm- ~s z
Landor 'lænd ɔː -ə ‖ -ɔːr -ᵊr
landowner 'lænd ˌəʊn ə ‖ -ˌoʊn ᵊr ~s z
landrail 'lænd reɪᵊl ~s z
land rover, Land-Rover tdmk
'lænd ˌrəʊv ə ‖ -ˌroʊv ᵊr ~s z
Landsat 'lænd sæt
landscap|e 'lænd skeɪp ~ed t ~es s ~ing ɪŋ
ˌlandscape 'gardening; 'landscape mode
Landseer 'lænd sɪə ‖ -sɪr
landslide 'lænd slaɪd ~s z
landslip 'lænd slɪp ~s s
landward 'lænd wəd ‖ -wᵊrd ~s z
Landy 'lænd i
lane, Lane leɪn lanes leɪnz
Lanfranc 'læn fræŋk
Lang læŋ
Langan 'læŋ ən
Langbaurgh 'læŋ baːf -baː: ‖ -baːrf -baːr
Langdale 'læŋ deɪᵊl
Lange (i) læŋ (ii) 'lɒŋ i ‖ 'laːŋ i —The NZ
politician is (ii)
Langer 'læŋ ə ‖ -ᵊr
Langerhans 'læŋ ə hænz -hænˢts
‖ 'laːŋ ᵊr haːnz -haːnˢts —Ger ['laŋ ɐ hanˢts]
Langford 'læŋ fəd ‖ -fᵊrd
Langham 'læŋ əm
Langholm place in Dumfries & Galloway
'læŋ əm —often called -həʊm ‖ -hoʊm by
those not familiar with the name
Langland 'læŋ lənd
langlauf 'læŋ laʊf ‖ 'laːŋ- ~er/s ə/z ‖ ᵊr/z
Langley 'læŋ li
Langmuir 'læŋ mjʊə ‖ -mjʊr
Langobardic ˌlæŋ gəʊ 'baːd ɪk ◂ ‖ -ə 'baːrd-
langouste ˌlɒŋ 'guːst '•• ‖ ˌlaːŋ- —Fr
[lɑ̃ gust] ~s s
langoustine ˌlɒŋ gu 'stiːn ‖ ˌlaːŋ- —Fr
[lɑ̃ gu stin] ~s z
langsyne, lang syne ₍ᵢ₎læŋ 'saɪn
Langton 'læŋᵏt ən
Langtry 'læŋ tri
language 'læŋ gwɪdʒ §-wɪdʒ ~es ɪz əz
'language laˌboratory ‖ -ˌlaboratory;
'language ˌteaching
langue lɒŋ laːŋ, laːŋ, lɒ̃g ‖ laːŋ —Fr [lɑ̃ːg]
ˌlangue de 'chat də 'ʃa: —Fr [də ʃa]
Languedoc ˌlɒŋ gə 'dɒk ˌlaːŋ-, '•••
‖ ˌlaːŋ gə 'daːk -'dɔːk, -'doʊk —Fr [lɑ̃g dɔk]
languid 'læŋ gwɪd §-gwəd ~ly li ~ness nəs
nɪs

languish, L~ 'læŋ gwɪʃ ~ed t ~es ɪz əz
~ing/ly ɪŋ/li ~ment mənt
languor 'læŋ gə ‖ -gər
languorous 'læŋ gər əs ~ly li ~ness nəs nɪs
langur læŋ 'gʊə lʌŋ-; 'læŋ gə ‖ -'gʊər ~s z
Lanigan 'læn ɪg ən -əg-
La Niña lə 'niːn jə lɑː-, læ- ‖ lɑː- —Sp
[la 'ni ɲa]
lank læŋk
Lankester 'læŋk ɪst ə -əst- ‖ -ər
lank|ly 'læŋk |li ~ness nəs nɪs
lank|y 'læŋk |i ~ier i‿ə ‖ i‿ər ~iest i‿ɪst i‿əst
~ily ɪ li əl i ~iness i nəs i nɪs
lanner 'læn ə ‖ -ər ~s z
lanolin 'læn əl ɪn §-ən
lanoline 'læn ə liːn -lɪn
Lansbury 'lænz bər‿i ‖ -ˌber i
Lansdown, Lansdowne 'lænz daʊn
Lansing 'lɑːnˈts ɪŋ §'lænˈts- ‖ 'lænˈts ɪŋ
lansker, L~ 'læn skə ‖ -skər
lantern 'lænt ən ‖ -ərn ~s z
lantern-jawed ˌlænt ən 'dʒɔːd ◄ ‖ -ərn- -'dʒɑːd
lanternslide 'lænt ən slaɪd ‖ -ərn- ~s z
lanthanide 'lænᵗθ ə naɪd ~s z
lanthanum 'lænᵗθ ən əm
lanyard 'læn jəd -jɑːd ‖ -jərd ~s z
Lanza 'lænz ə ‖ 'lɑːnz ə
Lanzarote ˌlænz ə 'rɒt i ‖ ˌlɑːnˈts ə 'roʊt̬ i —Sp
[lan θa 'ro te, -sa-]
Lao laʊ
Laocoon, Laocoön leɪ 'ɒk əʊ ɒn -ən
‖ -'ɑːk əʊ ɑːn
Laodamia ˌleɪ əʊ də 'maɪ‿ə ‖ leɪ ˌɑːd ə-
Laodice|a ˌleɪ əʊ dɪ 'siː‿|ə -əd ə- ‖ -əd ə-
leɪ ˌɑːd ə- ~an/s ən/z
Laoighis, Laois liːʃ —Irish [ɫiːʃ]
Laomedon leɪ 'ɒm ɪd ən -əd- ‖ -'ɑːm ə dɑːn
Laos laʊs laʊz; 'lɑː ɒs ‖ 'lɑː oʊs laʊs; 'leɪ ɑːs
Laotian 'laʊʃ ən 'laʊʃ i‿ən; leɪ 'əʊʃ ən,
-'əʊʃ i‿ən ‖ leɪ 'oʊʃ ən 'laʊʃ ən ~s z
Lao-tse, Lao-tsze, Lao-tzu ˌlaʊ 'tseɪ -'tsi:,
-'tsu: —Chi Lǎo Zǐ [³lɐu ³tsɿ]
lap læp lapped læpt lapping 'læp ɪŋ laps
læps
laparoscope 'læp ər‿ə skəʊp ‖ -skoʊp ~s s
laparoscop|y ˌlæp ə 'rɒsk əp |i ‖ -'rɑːsk- ~ies
iz
laparotom|y ˌlæp ə 'rɒt əm |i ‖ -'rɑːt̬ əm |i
~ies iz
lapdog 'læp dɒg ‖ -dɔːg -dɑːg ~s z
lapel lə 'pel læ- ~s z
lap-held 'læp held
Laphroaig lə 'frɔɪg lɑː-, læ-
lapidar|y 'læp ɪd ər i ‖ '•əd‿ ‖ -ə der i ~ies iz
lapilli lə 'pɪl aɪ
lapis lazuli ˌlæp ɪs 'læz jʊl i §,•əs-, -jəl i, -aɪ
‖ -ə liː -'læʒ-
Lapith 'læp ɪθ ~s s
Laplace lə 'plɑːs læ-, lɑː-, -'plæs —Fr [la plas]
Lapland 'læp lænd -lənd
Laplander 'læp lænd ə -lənd- ‖ -ər ~s z
Lapotaire ˌlæp ɒ 'teə -ə- ‖ -oʊ 'teər -'tæər
Lapp læp

lappet 'læp ɪt §-ət ~s s
Lappin 'læp ɪn §-ən
Lappish 'læp ɪʃ
Lapsang Souchong 'læp sæŋ su: 'ʃɒŋ -'tʃɒŋ
‖ ˌlɑːp sɑːŋ 'su: ʃɑːŋ
lapse læps (= laps) lapsed læpst lapses
'læps ɪz -əz lapsing 'læps ɪŋ
lapsus linguae ˌlæps əs 'lɪŋ gwaɪ -gwiː
laptop 'læp tɒp ‖ -tɑːp ~s s
Laputa lə 'pjuːt ə ‖ -'pjuːt̬ ə
Laputan lə 'pjuːt ən ~s z
lapwing 'læp wɪŋ ~s z
Lar, lar lɑː ‖ lɑːr lares 'lɑːr eɪz 'leər iːz
‖ 'lær iːz 'ler- lars lɑːz ‖ lɑːrz
Lara 'lɑːr ə
Laramie 'lær əm i ‖ 'ler-
Larbert 'lɑːb ət ‖ 'lɑːrb ərt
larboard 'lɑːb əd 'lɑː bɔːd ‖ 'lɑːrb ərd
larcenous 'lɑːs ən əs -ɪn- ‖ 'lɑːrs- ~ly li
larcen|y 'lɑːs ən |i -ɪn- ‖ 'lɑːrs- ~ies iz
larch lɑːtʃ ‖ lɑːrtʃ larches 'lɑːtʃ ɪz -əz
‖ 'lɑːrtʃ əz
lard lɑːd ‖ lɑːrd larded 'lɑːd ɪd -əd ‖ 'lɑːrd əd
larding 'lɑːd ɪŋ ‖ 'lɑːrd ɪŋ lards
lɑːdz ‖ lɑːrdz
larder 'lɑːd ə ‖ 'lɑːrd ər ~s z
Lardner 'lɑːd nə ‖ 'lɑːrd nər
lardy 'lɑːd i ‖ 'lɑːrd i
'lardy cake
Laredo lə 'reɪd əʊ ‖ -oʊ
lares 'lɑːr eɪz 'leər iːz ‖ 'lær iːz 'ler-
Largactil, l~ tdmk lɑː 'gækt ɪl -əl ‖ lɑːr-
large, Large lɑːdʒ ‖ lɑːrdʒ larger
'lɑːdʒ ə ‖ 'lɑːrdʒ ər largest 'lɑːdʒ ɪst -əst
‖ 'lɑːrdʒ-
large-hearted ˌlɑːdʒ 'hɑːt ɪd ◄ -əd
‖ ˌlɑːrdʒ 'hɑːrt̬ əd ◄ ~ness nəs nɪs
largely 'lɑːdʒ li ‖ 'lɑːrdʒ li
large-minded ˌlɑːdʒ 'maɪnd ɪd ◄ -əd ‖ ˌlɑːrdʒ-
~ness nəs nɪs
largeness 'lɑːdʒ nəs -nɪs ‖ 'lɑːrdʒ-
large-scale ˌlɑːdʒ 'skeɪəl ◄ ‖ ˌlɑːrdʒ-
largess, largesse ₍ₗ₎lɑː 'dʒes -'ʒes; 'lɑːdʒ es
‖ ₍ₗ₎lɑːr-
larghetto lɑː 'get əʊ ‖ lɑːr 'get̬ oʊ ~s z
largish 'lɑːdʒ ɪʃ ‖ 'lɑːrdʒ-
largo 'lɑːg əʊ ‖ 'lɑːrg oʊ ~s z
Largs lɑːgz ‖ lɑːrgz
lariat 'lær i‿ət ‖ 'ler- ~s s
Larium, l~ 'leər i‿əm ‖ 'ler- 'lær-
Larisa, Larissa lə 'rɪs ə
lark, Lark lɑːk ‖ lɑːrk larked lɑːkt ‖ lɑːrkt
larking 'lɑːk ɪŋ ‖ 'lɑːrk ɪŋ larks
lɑːks ‖ lɑːrks
Larkhall 'lɑːk hɔːl ‖ 'lɑːrk- -hɑːl
Larkin 'lɑːk ɪn §-ən ‖ 'lɑːrk-
larkspur 'lɑːk spɜː ‖ 'lɑːrk spɝː ~s z
larky 'lɑːk i ‖ 'lɑːrk i
Larmor 'lɑːm ə -ɔː: ‖ 'lɑːrm ər -ɔːr
larn lɑːn ‖ lɑːrn larned lɑːnd ‖ lɑːrnd larning
'lɑːn ɪŋ ‖ 'lɑːrn ɪŋ larns lɑːnz ‖ lɑːrns —This
is a non-standard variant of learn, sometimes
used humorously.

L

Larnaca 'lɑːn ək ə ‖ 'lɑːrn-
Larne lɑːn ‖ lɑːrn
Larousse læ 'ruːs ‖ lɑː- —*Fr* [la ʁus]
larrikin 'lær ɪk ɪn -ək-, §-ən ‖ 'ler- ~s z
larrup 'lær əp ‖ 'ler- ~ed t ~ing ɪŋ ~s s
Larry 'lær i ‖ 'ler-
Lars lɑːz ‖ lɑːrz lɑːrs —*Swedish* [lɑːʂ]
,Lars 'Porsena 'pɔːs ɪn ə -ən- ‖ 'pɔːrs-
LARSP lɑːsp ‖ lɑːrsp
larv|a 'lɑːv lə ‖ 'lɑːrv lə ~ae iː eɪ ~al ᵊl
Larwood 'lɑː wʊd ‖ 'lɑːr-
laryngal lə 'rɪŋ gᵊl læ- ~s z
laryngeal lə 'rɪndʒ əl læ-, -'rɪndʒ i‿əl;
  ,lær ɪn 'dʒiː‿əl ◂, -ən- ‖ ,lær ən 'dʒiː əl, ,ler-
  ~s z
laryngealis... —*see* laryngealiz...
laryngealization lə ,rɪndʒ əl aɪ 'zeɪʃ ᵊn læ-,
  -əl ɪ- ‖ -əl ə-
laryngealiz|e lə 'rɪndʒ ə laɪz læ- ~ed d ~es ɪz
  əz ~ing ɪŋ
laryngectomee ,lær ɪn 'dʒekt ə miː ,•ən-,
  ,••,••'• ‖ ,ler- ~s z
laryngectom|y ,lær ɪn 'dʒekt əm li ,•ən- ‖ ,ler-
  ~ies iz
larynges læ 'rɪndʒ iːz lə-
laryngitis ,lær ɪn 'dʒaɪt ɪs -ən-, §-əs ‖ -'dʒaɪt̬ əs
  ,ler-
laryngo- *comb. form*
  with stress-neutral suffix lə ˈrɪŋ gəʊ ‖ -goʊ —
    laryngophantom
    lə ,rɪŋ gəʊ 'fænt əm ‖ -goʊ 'fænt̬-
  with stress-imposing suffix ,lær ɪŋ 'gɒ+ ‖ ,lær
    ən 'gɑː+ ,ler-, →,•ɪŋ- — laryngopathy
    ,lær ɪŋ 'gɒp əθ i ‖ -ən 'gɑːp əθ i ,ler-, →,•ɪŋ-
laryngograph, L~ *tdmk* lə 'rɪŋ gəʊ grɑːf læ-,
  -græf ‖ -gə græf ~s s
laryngographic lə ,rɪŋ gəʊ 'græf ɪk ◂ læ-
  ‖ -gə- ~ally ᵊl_i
laryngography ,lær ɪŋ 'gɒg rəf i ‖ ,lær
  ən 'gɑːg- ,ler-, →,•ɪŋ-
laryngological lə ,rɪŋ gə 'lɒdʒ ɪk ᵊl ◂ læ-
  ‖ -'lɑːdʒ- ~ly _i
laryngolog|ist/s ,lær ɪŋ 'gɒl ədʒ ɪst/s §-əst/s
  ‖ ,lær ən 'gɑːl- ,ler-, →,•ɪŋ- ~y i
laryngoscope lə 'rɪŋ gə skəʊp læ- ‖ -skoʊp
  ~s s
laryngoscopic lə ,rɪŋ gə 'skɒp ɪk ◂ læ-
  ‖ -'skɑːp ɪk ◂ ~ally ᵊl_i
laryngoscop|y ,lær ɪŋ 'gɒsk əp li ‖ ,lær
  ən 'gɑːsk- ,ler-, →,•ɪŋ- ~ies iz
larynx 'lær ɪŋks ‖ 'ler- ~es ɪz əz larynges
  læ 'rɪndʒ iːz lə-
Las *Spanish article* læs ‖ lɑːs —*usually
  unstressed.* —*See also phrases with this word*
  —*Sp* [las]
lasagn|a lə 'zæn |jə -'sæn-, -'zɑːn-, -'sɑːn-
  ‖ -'zɑːn- —*It* [la 'saɲ ɲa] ~e jə jeɪ —*It*
  [-ɲe]
lascar, L~ 'læsk ə ‖ -ᵊr ~s z
Lascaux 'læsk əʊ læ 'skəʊ ‖ lɑː 'skoʊ læ- —*Fr*
  [la sko]
Lascelles 'læs ᵊlz lə 'selz
lascivious lə 'sɪv i‿əs ~ly li ~ness nəs nɪs

Lasdun 'læzd ən
laser 'leɪz ə ‖ -ᵊr ~s z
  'laser ,printer
laserjet 'leɪz ə dʒet ‖ -ᵊr- ~s s
lash læʃ lashed læʃt lashes 'læʃ ɪz -əz
  lashing/s 'læʃ ɪŋ/z
Lasham 'læʃ əm —*locally also* 'læs-
lash-up 'læʃ ʌp ~s s
Laski 'læsk i
Las Palmas læs 'pæl məs ,•-, -'pɑːl-
  ‖ lɑːs 'pɑːlm əs —*Sp* [las 'pal mas]
lass, Lass læs lasses 'læs ɪz -əz
Lassa 'læs ə 'lɑːs-
  ,Lassa 'fever
Lassen 'læs ᵊn
lassi 'læs i 'lʌs- ‖ lɑː 'siː —*Hindi* [lə si]
lassie, L~ 'læs i ~s z
lassitude 'læs ɪ tjuːd -ə-, →§-tʃuːd ‖ -tuːd
  -tjuːd
lasso lə 'suː læ-; 'læs əʊ ‖ 'læs oʊ læ 'suː *(*)
  ~ed d ~ing ɪŋ ~es, ~s z
last, Last lɑːst §læst ‖ læst lasted 'lɑːst ɪd
  §'læst-, -əd ‖ 'læst əd lasting 'lɑːst ɪŋ
  §'læst- ‖ 'læst ɪŋ lasts lɑːsts §læsts ‖ læsts
  ,last 'judgment; ,last 'minute; ,last 'name,
    '• '•; ,last 'night; ,last 'post; ,last 'straw;
  ,last 'week; ,last 'word
last-ditch ,lɑːst 'dɪtʃ ◂ §,læst- ‖ ,læst-
lasting 'lɑːst ɪŋ §'læst- ‖ 'læst ɪŋ ~ly li ~ness
  nəs nɪs
lastly 'lɑːst li §'læst- ‖ 'læst li
last-minute ,lɑːst 'mɪn ɪt ◂ §-ət ‖ ,læst-
Las Vegas læs 'veɪg əs ,•- ‖ lɑːs-
lat læt lats læts
Latakia ,læt ə 'kiː‿ə ‖ ,læt̬- ,lɑːt̬-
Latasha lə 'tæʃ ə
latch lætʃ latched lætʃt latches 'lætʃ ɪz -əz
  latching 'lætʃ ɪŋ
latchet 'lætʃ ɪt -ət ~s s
latchkey 'lætʃ kiː ~s z
  'latchkey child
late leɪt later 'leɪt ə ‖ 'leɪt̬ ᵊr latest 'leɪt ɪst
  -əst ‖ 'leɪt̬ əst
latecomer 'leɪt ,kʌm ə ‖ -ᵊr ~s z
lateen lə 'tiːn ~s z
lately 'leɪt li
latenc|y 'leɪt ᵊnᵗs li ~ies iz
lateness 'leɪt nəs -nɪs ~es ɪz əz
latent 'leɪt ᵊnt ~ly li
  ,latent 'heat
later 'leɪt ə ‖ 'leɪt̬ ᵊr
lateral 'læt_ᵊr_ə ‖ 'læt̬ ᵊr əl →'læt̬r əl ~s z
  ,lateral 'fricative; ,lateral 'thinking
laterality ,læt ə 'ræl ət i -ɪt i ‖ ,læt̬ ə 'ræl ət̬ i
Lateran 'læt ᵊr ən ‖ 'læt̬-
laterite 'læt ə raɪt ‖ 'læt̬-
latest 'leɪt ɪst -əst ‖ 'leɪt̬-
latex 'leɪt eks ~es ɪz əz
LaTeX, LaTEX *computing* 'leɪ tek
lath lɑːθ læθ ‖ læθ laths lɑːθs lɑːðz; læθs,
  læðz ‖ lædz læθs
Latham *(i)* 'leɪð əm, *(ii)* 'leɪθ-
lathe leɪð lathes leɪðz

LATHER

■'lɑːð- ▢'læð-

BrE 1988

0   20   40   60   80   100%

lath|er 'lɑːð lə 'læð- ‖ 'læð |ər —*BrE 1988 poll panel preference:* 'lɑːð- 72% *(southerners 88%),* 'læð- 28% *(southerners 12%).* **~ered** əd ‖ ʰrd **~ering** ər_ɪŋ **~ers** əz ‖ ʰrz
lathery 'lɑːð ər i 'læð- ‖ 'læð-
lathi 'lɑːt i —*Hindi* [laː ţʰi] **~s** z
Lathom *(i)* 'leɪð əm, *(ii)* 'leɪθ-
Latimer 'læt ɪm ə -əm- ‖ 'læt̬ əm ʰr
Latin 'læt ɪn §-ʰn ‖ 'læt ʰn **~s** z
  ˌLatin A'merican◄
Latinate 'læt ɪ neɪt §-ə- ‖-ʰn eɪt
latinis... —*see* **latiniz...**
latin|ism 'læt ɪn ɪˌɪz əm §-ʰn- ‖ 'læt ʰn- **~ist/s** ɪst/s §əst/s ‖ əst/s
latinization ˌlæt ɪn aɪ 'zeɪʃ ʰn §,•ʰn-, -ɪ'•- ‖ ˌlæt ʰn ə-
latiniz|e 'læt ɪ naɪz §-ʰn aɪz ‖ -ʰn aɪz **~ed** d **~es** ɪz əz **~ing** ɪŋ
Latino læ 'tiːn əʊ lə- ‖ -oʊ **~s** z
latish 'leɪt ɪʃ ‖ 'leɪt̬ ɪʃ
latitude 'læt ɪ tjuːd -ə-, →-tʃuːd ‖ 'læt̬ ə tuːd -tjuːd **~s** z
latitudinal ˌlæt ɪ 'tjuːd ɪn ʰl ◄ , •ə-, →§-'tʃuːd-, -ʰn_əl ‖ ˌlæt̬ ə 'tuːd ʰn_əl ◄ -'tjuːd-
latitudinarian ˌlæt ɪ ˌtjuːd ɪ 'neər i_ən , •ə-, →§-ˌtʃuːd-, -, •ə- ‖ ˌlæt̬ ə ˌtuːd ʰn 'er i_ən -ˌtjuːd- **~s** z
Latium 'leɪʃ i_əm
latke 'lɑːt kə **~s** z
Latona lə 'təʊn ə ‖ -'toʊn ə
Latoya lə 'tɔɪ ə
latria lə 'traɪ_ə
latrine lə 'triːn **~s** z
Latrobe, La Trobe lə 'trəʊb ‖ -'troʊb
-latry *stress-imposing* lətr i — **hagiolatry** ˌhæg i 'ɒl ətr i ,heɪdʒ- ‖ -'ɑːl-
latte 'læt eɪ 'lɑːt- ‖ 'lɑːt eɪ **~s** z —*It* ['lat te]
latter 'læt ə ‖ 'læt̬ ʰr
latter-day ˌlæt ə 'deɪ ◄ ‖ ˌlæt̬ ʰr-
  ˌlatter-day 'hero
latterly 'læt ə li -ʰl i ‖ 'læt̬ ʰr li
lattic|e 'læt ɪs -əs ‖ 'læt̬ əs **~ed** t **~es** ɪz əz **~ing** ɪŋ
Lattimore 'læt ɪ mɔː -ə- ‖ 'læt̬ ə mɔːr -moʊr
Latvi|a 'læt vi_ə ‖ 'lɑːt- **~an/s** ən/z
laud, Laud lɔːd ‖ lɑːd **lauded** 'lɔːd ɪd -əd ‖ 'lɑːd- **lauding** 'lɔːd ɪŋ ‖ 'lɑːd- **lauds, Lauds** lɔːdz ‖ lɑːdz
Lauda 'laʊd ə —*Ger* ['lau da]
laudability ˌlɔːd ə 'bɪl ət i -ɪt i ‖ -ət̬ i ˌlɑːd-
laudab|le 'lɔːd əb ‖ʰl ‖ 'lɑːd- **~ly** li
laudanum 'lɔːd ʰn_əm 'lɒd- ‖ 'lɑːd-
laudatory 'lɔːd ət_ər i ‖ -ə tɔːr i 'lɑːd-, -toʊri
Lauder 'lɔːd ə ‖ -ʰr 'lɑːd-
Lauderdale 'lɔːd ə deɪʰl ‖ -ʰr- 'lɑːd-
laugh lɑːf §læf ‖ læf **laughed** lɑːft §læft ‖ læft **laughing** 'lɑːf ɪŋ §'læf- ‖ 'læf ɪŋ

laughs lɑːfs §læfs ‖ læfs
  'laughing gas; ˌlaughing 'jackass
laughab|le 'lɑːf əb ‖ʰl §'læf- ‖ 'læf- **~ly** li
Laugharne lɑːn ‖ lɑːrn
laughingly 'lɑːf ɪŋ li §'læf- ‖ 'læf ɪŋ li
laughingstock 'lɑːf ɪŋ stɒk §'læf- ‖ 'læf ɪŋ stɑːk
laughter 'lɑːft ə §'læft- ‖ 'læft ʰr
Laughton 'lɔːt ʰn ‖ 'lɑːt-
Launceston 'lɔːn'st ən 'lɑːn'st-; 'lɑːn'ts ʰn, 'lɔːn'ts- ‖ 'lɔːn'ts əst ən 'lɑːn'ts- —*but in Tasmania,* 'lɒn'ts əst ən ‖ 'lɑːn'ts-
launch lɔːn'tʃ ‖ lɑːn'tʃ —*In RP formerly also* 'lɑːn'tʃ. **launched** lɔːn'tʃt ‖ lɑːn'tʃt **launcher/s** 'lɔːn'tʃ ə/z ‖ -ʰr/z 'lɑːn'tʃ- **launches** 'lɔːn'tʃ ɪz -əz ‖ 'lɑːn'tʃ- **launching** 'lɔːn'tʃ ɪŋ ‖ 'lɑːn'tʃ-
  'launching pad, 'launch pad; 'launch ˌvehicle
laund|er 'lɔːnd ə ‖ -ʰr 'lɑːnd|- **~ered** əd ‖ ʰrd **~ering** ˌər ɪŋ **~ers** əz ‖ ʰrz
launderette, L~ *tdmk* ˌlɔːnd ə 'ret ˌlɔːn 'dret ‖ ˌlɑːnd- **~s** s
laundress 'lɔːndr es -əs, -ɪs ‖ 'lɑːndr- **~es** ɪz əz
laundrette ˌlɔːn 'dret ‖ ˌlɑːn- **~s** s
laundromat, L~ *tdmk* 'lɔːndr ə mæt ‖ 'lɑːndr- **~s** s
laundr|y 'lɔːndr li ‖ 'lɑːndr- **~ies** iz
  'laundry ˌbasket
Lauper 'laʊp ə ‖ -ʰr
Laura 'lɔːr ə
lauraceous lɒ 'reɪʃ əs lɔː- ‖ lɔː- lɑː-
Laurasia lɔː 'reɪʃ ə -'reɪʒ-, -'reɪʒ i_ə ‖ lɔː 'reɪʒ ə lɑː-, -'reɪʃ-
Laurasian lɔː 'reɪʃ ʰn -'reɪʒ-, -'reɪʒ i_ən ‖ lɔː 'reɪʒ ʰn lɑː-, -'reɪʃ-
laureate 'lɔːr i_ət 'lɒr-, -ɪt ‖ 'lɑːr- **~s** s **~ship** ʃɪp
laurel, L~ 'lɒr əl ‖ 'lɔːr- 'lɑːr- **~s** z
Lauren 'lɔːr ən 'lɒr- ‖ 'lɑːr-
Laurence 'lɒr ən'ts ‖ 'lɔːr- 'lɑːr-
Laurentian lɒ 'ren'tʃ ʰn lɔː- ‖ lɑː- **~s** z
Lauretta lə 'ret ə lɔː- ‖ -'ret̬ ə
lauric 'lɔːr ɪk 'lɒr- ‖ 'lɑːr-
Laurie 'lɒr i ‖ 'lɔːr i
Laurier 'lɒr i ə -eɪ ‖ 'lɔːr i_ʰr ˌlɔːr i 'eɪ
Lauriston 'lɒr ɪst ən -əst- ‖ 'lɔːr- 'lɑːr-
laurustinus ˌlɒr ə 'staɪn əs ˌlɔːr- ‖ ˌlɔːr-
lauryl 'lɒr ɪl 'lɔːr-, -əl ‖ 'lɔːr əl 'lɑːr-
Lausanne ləʊ 'zæn ‖ loʊ- —*Fr* [lo zan, lɔ-]
lav læv **lavs** lævz
lava 'lɑːv ə
lavabo lə 'vɑːb əʊ -'veɪb- ‖ -oʊ **~es** z
lavage 'læv ɪdʒ -ɑːʒ; læ 'vɑːʒ ‖ lə 'vɑːʒ 'læv ɪdʒ
Laval lə 'væl læ- —*Fr* [la val]
lavaliere lə ˌvæl i 'eə ‖ ˌlæv ə 'lɪʰr ˌlɑːv- **~s** z
lavatorial ˌlæv ə 'tɔːr i_əl ◄ ‖ -'toʊr-
lavator|y 'læv ət_ər li ‖ -ə tɔːr li -toʊr i **~ies** iz
lave leɪv **laved** leɪvd **laves** leɪvz **laving** 'leɪv ɪŋ
lavender, L~ 'læv ənd ə -ɪnd- ‖ -ʰr **~s** z
Lavengro lə 'veŋ grəʊ ‖ -groʊ

L

Lavenham 'læv ən_əm
laver *'basin'* 'leɪv ə ‖ -ər ~s z
laver *'seaweed'* 'lɑːv ə ‖ -ər 'leɪv-
Laver *family name* 'leɪv ə ‖ -ər
Lavern, Laverne lə 'vɜːn ‖ -'vɜ˞ːn
Lavers 'leɪv əz ‖ -ərz
Lavinia lə 'vɪn i_ə
lavish 'læv ɪʃ ~ed t ~es ɪz əz ~ing ɪŋ ~ly li
~ness nəs nɪs
Lavoisier lə 'vwɑːz i eɪ læ-, -'vwæz-
‖ ˌlæv wɑː 'zjeɪ —*Fr* [la vwa zje]
lavv|y 'læv |i ~ies iz
law, Law lɔː ‖ lɑː laws lɔːz ‖ lɑːz
law-abiding 'lɔːr ə ˌbaɪd ɪŋ ‖ 'lɔː- 'lɑː-
law-breaker 'lɔː ˌbreɪk ə ‖ -ər 'lɑː- ~s z
Lawes lɔːz ‖ lɑːz
Lawford 'lɔː fəd ‖ -fərd 'lɑː-
lawful 'lɔː fəl -fʊl ‖ 'lɑː- ~ly i ~ness nəs nɪs
Lawler 'lɔːl ə ‖ -ər 'lɑːl-
lawless, L~ 'lɔː ləs -lɪs ‖ 'lɑː- ~ly li ~ness nəs
nɪs
Lawley 'lɔː li ‖ 'lɑː-
lawmaker 'lɔː ˌmeɪk ə ‖ -ər 'lɑː- ~s z
lawn lɔːn ‖ lɑːn lawns lɔːnz ‖ lɑːnz
ˈlawn ˌparty; ˌlawn ˈtennis ‖ˈ•ˌ• ˌ•ˈ••
lawnmower 'lɔːn ˌməʊ ə ‖ -ˌmoʊ ər 'lɑːn- ~s z
Lawrance, Lawrence 'lɒr ənts ‖ 'lɔːr- 'lɑːr-
lawrencium lə 'rents i_əm lɒː-, lɒ- ‖ lɔː- lɑː-
Lawrentian lɒ 'rentʃ ən lɔː-, -'rentʃ i_ən ‖ lɔː-
lɑː- ~s z
Lawrie, Lawry 'lɒr i ‖ 'lɔːr i 'lɑːr i
Lawson 'lɔːs ən ‖ 'lɑːs-
lawsuit 'lɔː suːt -sjuːt ‖ 'lɑː- ~s s
Lawton 'lɔːt ən ‖ 'lɑːt-
lawyer 'lɔː jə 'lɔɪ ə ‖ -jər 'lɑː-; 'lɔɪ ər ~s z
lax læks laxed lækst laxer 'læks ə ‖ -ər laxes
'læks ɪz -əz laxest 'læks ɪst -əst laxing
'læks ɪŋ
Laxalt 'læks ɔːlt ‖ -ɑːlt
laxative 'læks ət ɪv ‖ -ət̬ ɪv ~s z
Laxey 'læks i
laxity 'læks ət i -ɪt- ‖ -ət̬ i
lax|ly 'læks |li ~ness nəs nɪs
lay leɪ laid leɪd laying 'leɪ ɪŋ lays leɪz
ˌlay ˈbrother; ˌlay ˈfigure ‖ˈ• ˌ••; ˌlay
ˈreader; ˌlay ˈsister
layabout 'leɪ ə ˌbaʊt ~s s
layaway 'leɪ əˌweɪ
lay-by 'leɪ baɪ ~s z
Laycock 'leɪ kɒk ‖ -kɑːk
layer 'leɪ ə leə ‖ -ər leʳər ~ed d layering
'leɪ ər ɪŋ 'leər ɪŋ ‖ 'leʳr ɪŋ ~s z
ˈlayer cake
layette leɪ 'et ~s s
lay|man 'leɪ |mən ~men mən
lay-off 'leɪ ɒf -ɔːf ‖ -ɔːf -ɑːf ~s s
layout 'leɪ aʊt ~s s
layover 'leɪ ˌəʊv ə ‖ -ˌoʊv ər ~s z
layperson 'leɪ ˌpɜːs ən ‖ -ˌpɜ˞ːs- ~s z
layshaft 'leɪ ʃɑːft §-ʃæft ‖ -ʃæft ~s s
Layton 'leɪt ən
lay|woman 'leɪ ˌwʊm ən ~women ˌwɪm ɪn
§-ən

Lazard 'læz ɑːd ‖ lə 'zɑːrd ~s z
lazaretto ˌlæz ə 'ret əʊ ‖ -'ret̬ oʊ ~s z
Lazarus 'læz ər_əs
laze leɪz (= *lays*) lazed leɪzd lazes 'leɪz ɪz -əz
lazing 'leɪz ɪŋ
Lazenby 'leɪz ən bi →-əm-
lazi... —*see* lazy
Lazio 'læts i əʊ ‖ 'lɑːts i oʊ —*It* ['lat tsjo]
Lazonby 'leɪz ən bi →-əm-
lazulite 'læz ju laɪt 'læʒ-, -jə- ‖ -'læʒ ə- (*)
laz|y 'leɪz |i ~ier i_ə ‖ i_ər ~iest i_ɪst i_əst ~ily
ɪ li əl i ~iness i nəs i nɪs
lazybones 'leɪz i bəʊnz ‖ -boʊnz
lb *sing.* paʊnd lb *pl* paʊndz lbs paʊndz
lbw ˌel biː 'dʌb əl ju
LCD ˌel siː 'diː ~s, ~'s z
LCM ˌel siː 'em ~s, ~'s z
LDC ˌel diː 'siː ~s, ~'s z
L-dopa, L-Dopa ˌel 'dəʊp ə ‖ -'doʊp ə
L-driver 'el ˌdraɪv ə ‖ -ər ~s z
Le, le *in family names* lə —*See also phrases with
this word* —*and note occasional exceptions, e.g.*
Le Fanu
-le- *in place names* li lə — Stanford-le-Hope
ˌstæn fəd li 'həʊp ‖ -fərd li 'hoʊp
lea, Lea liː (= *lee*) leas liːz
LEA ˌel i iː 'eɪ ~s, ~'s z
leach, Leach liːtʃ (= *leech*) leached liːtʃt
leaches 'liːtʃ ɪz -əz leaching 'liːtʃ ɪŋ
Leacock 'liː kɒk 'leɪ- ‖ -kɑːk
lead *v; n 'guiding, first place/act/actor, leash,
cord, flex'* liːd leading 'liːd ɪŋ leads liːdz
led led
lead *n 'metal'* led leaded 'led ɪd -əd leading
'led ɪŋ leads ledz
Leadbetter 'led ˌbet ə →'leb-; ˌ•'•• ‖ -ˌbet̬ ər
Leadbitter 'led ˌbɪt ə →'leb- ‖ -ˌbɪt̬ ər
leaded 'led ɪd -əd
leaden 'led ən ~ly li ~ness nəs nɪs
Leadenhall 'led ən hɔːl ‖ -hɑːl
leader 'liːd ə ‖ -ər ~s z
leadership 'liːd ə ʃɪp ‖ -ər- ~s s
lead-in 'liːd ɪn ˌ•'• ~s z
leading *adj 'main', 'guiding'* 'liːd ɪŋ ~ly li
ˌleading 'article; ˌleading 'edge; ˌleading
'lady; ˌleading 'light; ˌleading 'question
leading *n 'metal', 'space between rows of type'*
'led ɪŋ
lead poisoning ˌled 'pɔɪz ən ɪŋ
lead time 'liːd taɪm ~s z
leaf liːf leafed liːft leafing 'liːf ɪŋ leafs liːfs
leaves liːvz
'leaf mould
leafage 'liːf ɪdʒ
leafi... —*see* leafy
leafless 'liːf ləs -lɪs ~ness nəs nɪs
leaf|let 'liːf |lət -lɪt ~leted, ~letted lət ɪd lɪt-,
-əd ‖ lət̬ əd ~leting, ~letting lət ɪŋ lɪt-
‖ lət̬ ɪŋ ~lets ləts lɪts ‖ ləts
leaf|y 'liːf |i ~ier i_ə ‖ i_ər ~iest i_ɪst i_əst
~iness i nəs i nɪs
Leagrave 'liː greɪv

league liːg —*In AmE there is also a non-standard pronunciation* lɪg. **leagued** liːgd
　leagues liːgz **leaguing** 'liːg ɪŋ
Leah 'liː‿ə
Leahy 'liː hi 'leɪ-, -i
leak liːk (= *leek*) **leaked** liːkt **leaking** 'liːk ɪŋ
　leaks liːks
leakag|e 'liːk ɪdʒ ~**es** ɪz əz
Leakey 'liːk i
leak|y 'liːk li ~**ier** i‿ə ‖ i‿ər ~**iest** i‿ɪst i‿əst
　~**iness** i nəs i nɪs
Leamington (*i*) 'lem ɪŋ tən, (*ii*) 'liːm- —*The place in England is* (*i*)*; that in Canada,* (*ii*).
　,Leamington 'Spa
lean, Lean liːn **leaned** liːnd lent **leaning**
　'liːn ɪŋ **leans** liːnz **leant** lent
Leander li 'ænd ə ‖ -ər
Leane liːn
leaned liːnd lent
LeAnn, Leanne li 'æn
leanness 'liːn nəs -nɪs
leant lent (= *lent*)
lean-to 'liːn tuː ˌ•'• ~**s** z
leap liːp **leaped** lept liːpt ‖ liːpt **leaping**
　'liːp ɪŋ **leaps** liːps **leapt** lept
　'leap year
leaped lept liːpt ‖ liːpt
leapfrog 'liːp frɒg ‖ -frɔːg -frɑːg ~**ged** d
　~**ging** ɪŋ ~**s** z
leapt lept
Lear lɪə ‖ lɪər
learn lɜːn ‖ lɝːn **learned** lɜːnd lɜːnt ‖ lɝːnd
　learning 'lɜːn ɪŋ ‖ 'lɝːn ɪŋ **learns**
　lɜːnz ‖ lɝːnz **learnt** lɜːnt ‖ lɝːnt
learned *past & pp of* learn; *adj 'acquired by experience'* lɜːnd lɜːnt ‖ lɝːnd
learned *adj 'scholarly', 'well-informed'* 'lɜːn ɪd
　-əd ‖ 'lɝːn əd ~**ly** li ~**ness** nəs nɪs
learner 'lɜːn ə ‖ 'lɝːn ər ~**s** z
　,learner 'driver
learnt lɜːnt ‖ lɝːnt
Leary 'lɪər i ‖ 'lɪr i
lease liːs **leased** liːst **leases** 'liːs ɪz -əz
　leasing 'liːs ɪŋ
leaseback 'liːs bæk ~**s** s
leasehold 'liːs həʊld →-hɒʊld ‖ -hoʊld ~**er/s**
　ə/z ‖ ər/z ~**s** z
leash liːʃ **leashed** liːʃt **leashes** 'liːʃ ɪz -əz
　leashing 'liːʃ ɪŋ
Leason 'liːs ən
least liːst
leastways 'liːst weɪz
leastwise 'liːst waɪz
leat liːt **leats** liːts
Leatham (*i*) 'liːθ əm, (*ii*) 'liːð-
leather, L~ 'leð ə ‖ -ər ~**ed** d **leathering** 'leð
　ər‿ɪŋ ~**s** z
leatherback 'leð ə bæk ‖ -ər- ~**s** s
leatherette, L~ *tdmk* ,leð ə 'ret ◄
Leatherhead 'leð ə hed ‖ -ər-
leatherjacket 'leð ə ,dʒæk ɪt §-ət ‖ -ər- ~**s** s
leather|y 'leð ər‿li ~**iness** i nəs i nɪs

leave liːv **leaves** liːvz **leaving** 'liːv ɪŋ **left**
　left
　'leave ,taking
leaved liːvd
leaven 'lev ən ~**ed** d ~**ing** _ɪŋ ~**s** z
Leavenworth 'lev ən wɜːθ -wəθ ‖ -wɝːθ
leaves liːvz
leave-taking 'liːv ,teɪk ɪŋ
leaving 'liːv ɪŋ ~**s** z
Leavis 'liːv ɪs -əs
Leavisite 'liːv ɪ saɪt -ə- ~**s** s
Leavitt 'lev ɪt §-ət
Lebanese ,leb ə 'niːz ◄ ‖ -'niːs ◄
Lebanon 'leb ən ən -ə nɒn ‖ -ə nɑːn
lebensraum, L~ 'leɪb ənz raʊm →-mz-, -ənˈts-
　—*Ger* ['leː bəns ʁaʊm, -bms-]
Lebon 'liːb ən
Le Bon lə 'bɒn ‖ -'bɑːn -'bɔːn
Lebowa lə 'bəʊ ə ‖ -'boʊ ə
Lec *tdmk* lek
Le Carré lə 'kær eɪ ‖ lə kɑː 'reɪ
lech letʃ **leched** letʃt **leches** 'letʃ ɪz -əz
　leching 'letʃ ɪŋ
lecher 'letʃ ə ‖ -ər ~**s** z
lecherous 'letʃ ər‿əs ~**ly** li ~**ness** nəs nɪs
lecher|y 'letʃ ər li ~**ies** iz
Lechlade 'letʃ leɪd
Lechmere 'letʃ mɪə 'leʃ- ‖ -mɪr
lecithin 'les ɪθ ɪn -ə-, -ən
Leckhampton 'lek ,hæm't ən
Lecky 'lek i
Leconfield 'lek ən fiː‿əld
Le Corbusier lə kɔː 'buːz i eɪ -'bjuːz-
　‖ lə ,kɔːrb uːz 'jeɪ -uːs- —*Fr* [lə kɔʁ by zje]
lect lekt **lects** lekts
lectal 'lekt ᵊl
lectern 'lekt ən -ɜːn ‖ -ᵊrn ~**s** z
lectionar|y 'lek ʃᵊn ər‿li -ʃᵊn‿ər li ‖ -ʃə ner li
　~**ies** iz
lector 'lekt ɔː ‖ -ɔːr -ər ~**s** z
lecture 'lek tʃ ə -ʃə ‖ -tʃᵊr -ʃᵊr ~**d** d ~**s** z
　lecturing 'lek tʃᵊr‿ɪŋ -ʃᵊr‿ɪŋ
lecturer 'lek tʃᵊr‿ə -ʃᵊr‿ə ‖ -tʃᵊr ər -ʃᵊr‿ər ~**s** z
lectureship 'lek tʃə ʃɪp -ʃə- ‖ -tʃᵊr- -ʃᵊr- ~**s** s
led led
LED ,el iː 'diː ~**s**, ~'s z
Leda 'liːd ə 'leɪd ə
Ledbury 'led bᵊr‿i →'leb- ‖ -,ber i
lederhosen 'leɪd ə ,həʊz ən ‖ -ᵊr ,hoʊz ən
　—*Ger* ['leː dɐ ,hoːz ᵊn]
Ledgard 'ledʒ ɑːd ‖ -ɑːrd
ledge ledʒ **ledged** ledʒd **ledges** 'ledʒ ɪz -əz
ledger, L~ 'ledʒ ə ‖ -ər ~**s** z
lee, Lee liː **lees, Lee's** liːz
　,lee 'shore ‖ '• •; ,lee 'tide ‖ '• •
leech, Leech liːtʃ **leeched** liːtʃt **leeches**
　'liːtʃ ɪz -əz **leeching** 'liːtʃ ɪŋ
Leeds liːdz
leek, Leek liːk **leeks** liːks
Leeming 'liːm ɪŋ
leer lɪə ‖ lɪər **leered** lɪəd ‖ lɪərd **leering**
　'lɪər ɪŋ ‖ 'lɪr ɪŋ **leers** lɪəz ‖ lɪərz

L

leer|y 'lɪər |i ‖ 'lɪr |i **~ier** i‿ə ‖ i‿ər **~iest** i‿ɪst
  i‿əst **~ily** əl i ɪ li **~iness** i nəs i nɪs
lees, Lees liːz
Leeson 'liːs ən
leet liːt **leets** liːts
leeward, L~ 'liː wəd ‖ -wərd —*also nautical*
  'luː‿əd, 'ljuː‿ ‖ ‿ərd **~s** z
  'Leeward ˌIslands ‖ ˌ•• '••
leeway 'liː weɪ
Lefanu, Le Fanu *(i)* 'lef ə njuː -nuː ‖ -nuː -njuː,
  (ii) lə 'fɑːn uː
Lefevre 'fiːv ə ‖ -ər —*but as a French name,*
  lə 'fev —*Fr* Lefebvre, Lefèvre [lə fɛːvʁ]
left left
  ˌleft 'luggage ˌoffice; ˌleft 'wing ◄
left-hand ˌleft 'hænd ◄
  ˌleft-hand 'side
left-handed ˌleft 'hænd ɪd ◄ -əd **~ly** li **~ness**
  nəs nɪs
left-hander ˌleft 'hænd ə ‖ -ər **~s** z
leftie... —*see* **lefty**
leftist 'left ɪst §-əst **~s** s
leftover 'left ˌəʊv ə ‖ -ˌoʊv ər **~s** z
leftward 'left wəd ‖ -wərd **~s** z
left-winger ˌleft 'wɪŋ ə ‖ -ər **~s** z
left|y 'left |i **~ies** iz
leg leg **legged** legd **legging** 'leg ɪŋ **legs** legz
  ˌleg 'side
legac|y 'leg əs |i **~ies** iz
legal 'liːg əl **~ly** i
  ˌlegal 'aid; ˌlegal 'tender
legalese ˌliːg ə 'liːz -əl 'iːz ‖ -'liːs
legalis... —*see* **legaliz...**
legalism 'liːg ə ˌlɪz əm -əl ˌɪz-
legalistic ˌliːg ə 'lɪst ɪk ◄ -əl 'ɪst- **~ally** əl_i
legalit|y lɪ 'gæl ət |i liː-, -ɪt- ‖ -ət̬ |i **~ies** iz
legalization ˌliːg əl aɪ 'zeɪʃ ən -əl ɪ- ‖ -əl ə- **~s**
  z
legaliz|e 'liːg ə laɪz -əl aɪz **~ed** d **~es** ɪz əz
  ~ing ɪŋ
Legard 'ledʒ əd ‖ -ərd
legate *n* 'leg ət -ɪt, -eɪt **~s** s
legatee ˌleg ə 'tiː **~s** z
legation lɪ 'geɪʃ ən lə- **~s** z
legato lɪ 'gɑːt əʊ lə-, le- ‖ -oʊ **~s** z
LegCo 'ledʒ kəʊ ‖ -koʊ
legend 'ledʒ ənd -ɪnd **~s** z
legendary 'ledʒ ənd_ər i '• ɪnd- ‖ -ən der i
leger, Leger 'ledʒ ə ‖ -ər **~s** z
  'leger line
legerdemain ˌledʒ ə də 'meɪn ‖ ˌ•ər-
Leggatt 'leg ət
Legg, Legge leg
legged *adj* 'leg ɪd -əd; legd
leggings 'leg ɪŋz
legg|y 'leg |i **~ier** i‿ə ‖ i‿ər **~iest** i‿ɪst i‿əst
  ~iness i nəs i nɪs
Legh liː
Leghorn *place: old name for Livorno* 'leg hɔːn
  ˌ•'• ‖ -hɔːrn
leghorn *'straw; hat; breed of fowl'* le 'gɔːn
  ˌleg 'hɔːn, '•• ‖ 'leg hɔːrn -ərn
legibility ˌledʒ ə 'bɪl ət i ˌ•ɪ-, -ɪt i ‖ -ət̬ i

legib|le 'ledʒ əb |əl -ɪb- **~ly** li
legion 'liːdʒ ən **~s** z
legionar|y 'liːdʒ ən ər_li ‖ -ə ner li **~ies** iz
legionell|a ˌliːdʒ ə 'nel |ə **~ae** iː **~as** əz
legionnaire ˌliːdʒ ə 'neə ‖ -'neər -'næər **~s** z
  ˌlegion'naires' diˌsease
legi|slate 'ledʒ ɪ |sleɪt -ə- **~slated** sleɪt ɪd -əd
  ‖ sleɪt̬ əd **~slates** sleɪts **~slating**
  sleɪt ɪŋ ‖ sleɪt̬ ɪŋ
legislation ˌledʒ ɪ 'sleɪʃ ən -ə-
legislative 'ledʒ ɪs lət ɪv '•əs-; -ɪ sleɪt-,
  -ə sleɪt- ‖ -ə sleɪt̬ ɪv -əs lət̬ ɪv **~ly** li **~s** z
legislator 'ledʒ ɪ sleɪt ə '•ə- ‖ -ə sleɪt̬ ər **~s** z
legislature 'ledʒ ɪs lətʃ ə '•əs-; -lə tʃʊə;
  -ɪ sleɪtʃ ə, -ə•• ‖ -ə sleɪtʃ ər, ˌ••'•• **~s** z
legit lɪ 'dʒɪt lə-
legitimacy lɪ 'dʒɪt əm əs i lə-, -'•ɪm- ‖ -'dʒɪt̬-
legitimate *adj* lɪ 'dʒɪt əm ət lə-, -ɪm-, -ɪt
  ‖ -'dʒɪt̬- **~ly** li
legiti|mate *v* lɪ 'dʒɪt ə |meɪt lə-, -ɪ- ‖ -'dʒɪt̬-
  ~mated meɪt ɪd -əd ‖ meɪt̬ əd **~mates** meɪts
  ~mating meɪt ɪŋ ‖ meɪt̬ ɪŋ
legitimation lɪ ˌdʒɪt ə 'meɪʃ ən lə-, -ɪ- ‖ -ˌdʒɪt̬-
legitimatis... —*see* **legitimatiz...**
legitimatization lɪ ˌdʒɪt əm ət aɪ 'zeɪʃ ən lə-,
  -, •ɪm-, -ɪ'•- ‖ -ˌdʒɪt̬ əm ət̬ ə-
legitimatiz|e lɪ 'dʒɪt əm ə taɪz lə-, -'•ɪm-
  ‖ -'dʒɪt̬- **~ed** d **~es** ɪz əz **~ing** ɪŋ
legitimis... —*see* **legitimiz...**
legitimization lɪ ˌdʒɪt əm aɪ 'zeɪʃ ən lə-,
  -, •ɪm-, -ɪ'•- ‖ -ˌdʒɪt̬ əm ə-
legitimiz|e lɪ 'dʒɪt ə maɪz lə-, -ɪ- ‖ -'dʒɪt̬- **~ed**
  d **~es** ɪz əz **~ing** ɪŋ
legless 'leg ləs -lɪs
Lego *tdmk* 'leg əʊ ‖ -oʊ —*Danish* ['le: go]
leg-over 'leg ˌəʊv ə ‖ -ˌoʊv ər
leg-pull 'leg pʊl **~s** z
Legree lɪ 'griː lə-
legroom 'leg ruːm -rʊm
legume 'leg juːm lɪ 'gjuːm, lə- **~s** z
leguminous lɪ 'gjuːm ɪn əs lə-, le-, -ən-
leg-warmer 'leg ˌwɔːm ə ‖ -ˌwɔːrm ər
legwork 'leg wɜːk ‖ -wɜːk
Lehar, Lehár leɪ 'hɑː lɪ-, lə-, 'leɪ hɑː ‖ 'leɪ hɑːr
  —*Hungarian* ['lɛ hɑːr]
Le Havre lə 'ɑːv rə -'hɑːv-, -ə ‖ -ər —*Fr*
  [lə aːvʁ]
Lehigh 'liː haɪ
Lehmann *(i)* 'leɪ mən, *(ii)* 'liː- —*Usually (i).*
Lehrer 'leər ə 'lɪər- ‖ 'lɪr ər
lei leɪ 'leɪ i **leis** leɪz 'leɪ iz
Leibnitz, Leibniz 'laɪb nɪts 'liːb- —*Ger*
  ['laɪb nɪts]
Leica *tdmk* 'laɪk ə —*Ger* ['laɪ ka] **~s** z
Leicester 'lest ə ‖ -ər (!) —*Sometimes called*
  'laɪ sest ər *by those not familiar with the name.*
Leicestershire, Leics, Leics. 'lest ə ʃə -ʃɪə
  ‖ -ər ʃər -ʃɪr
Leiden 'laɪd ən 'leɪd- —*Dutch* ['lɛi dən]
Leif liːf
Leigh *(i)* liː, *(ii)* laɪ —*Usually (i); but some places*
  in the south of England are (ii).
Leighton 'leɪt ən

Leila 'liːl ə 'leɪl ə
Leinster 'lent⁵st ə ‖ -ᵊr —*but the Duke of L~ is*
  'lɪnt⁵st-
Leintwardine 'lent wə daɪn -diːn; 'lænt ə diːn
  ‖ -wᵊr-
Leipzig 'laɪp sɪg -sɪk —*Ger* ['laɪp tsɪç]
Leishman 'liːʃ mən 'lɪʃ-
leishmania ₍ₗ₎liːʃ 'meɪn i_ə
leishmaniasis ˌliːʃ mə 'naɪ_əs ɪs §-əs
Leister *name* 'lest ə ‖ -ᵊr
leister *'spear'* 'liːst ə ‖ -ᵊr
leisure 'leʒ ə ‖ 'liːʒ ᵊr 'leʒ-, 'leɪʒ- ~**d** d ~**liness**
  li nəs -nɪs ~**ly** li
leisurewear 'leʒ ə weə ‖ 'liːʒ ᵊr wer 'leʒ-,
  'leɪʒ-, -wær
Leith liːθ
leitmotif, leitmotiv, leitmotive 'laɪt məʊ ˌtiːf
  '•ˌməʊt ɪv ‖ -moʊ- —*Ger* ['laɪt mo ˌtiːf]
Leitrim 'liːtr ɪm §-əm
Leix liːʃ
lek lek **lekked** lekt **lekking** 'lek ɪŋ **leks** leks
lekker 'lek ə ‖ -ᵊr
Leland 'liːl ənd
Lely 'liːl i
leman 'lem ən 'liːm- ~**s** z
Leman *surname; street name in London* 'lem ən
  'liːm-
Le Mans lə 'mɒ̃ ‖ -'mɑːn —*Fr* [lə mɑ̃]
Lemesurier lə 'meʒ ər_ə ‖ -ᵊr_ər lə ˌmeʒ ər_i 'eɪ
lemm|a 'lem |ə ~**as** əz ~**ata** ət ə ‖ əţ ə
lemmatis... —*see* **lemmatiz...**
lemmatization ˌlem ət aɪ 'zeɪʃ ᵊn -ət ɪ- ‖ -ət ə-
  ~**s** z
lemmatiz|e 'lem ə taɪz ~**ed** d ~**es** ɪz əz ~**ing**
  ɪŋ
lemme 'lem i —*This is a non-standard or casual*
  form of let me
lemming 'lem ɪŋ ~**s** z
lemming-like 'lem ɪŋ laɪk
Lemmon 'lem ən
lem|niscus lem 'nɪsk əs ~**nisci** 'nɪs aɪ 'nɪsk-,
  -iː
Lemnos 'lem nɒs ‖ -nɑːs -noʊs
lemon, Lemon 'lem ən ~**s** z
  ˌlemon 'curd; 'lemon grass; ˌlemon
  meˌringue 'pie; ˌlemon 'sole; ˌlemon
  'squash; ˌlemon 'yellow◄
lemonade ˌlem ə 'neɪd ◄ ~**s** z
Le Monde lə 'mɒnd ‖ -'mɔːnd -'mɑːnd —*Fr*
  [lə mɔ̃ːd]
lemony 'lem ən i
Lempert 'lemp ət ‖ -ᵊrt
Lempriere ˌlemp ri eə ‖ ˌlemp ri 'eᵊr
Lemsip *tdmk* 'lem sɪp
Lemuel 'lem ju_əl
lemur 'liːm ə -jʊə ‖ -ᵊr ~**s** z
Len len
Lena *personal name* 'liːn ə
Lena *river* 'leɪn ə 'liːn- —*Russ* ['lʲe nə]
lend lend **lending** 'lend ɪŋ **lends** lendz **lent**
  lent
  'lending ˌlibrary
lender 'lend ə ‖ -ᵊr ~**s** z

lenes 'liːn iːz 'leɪn-, -eɪz

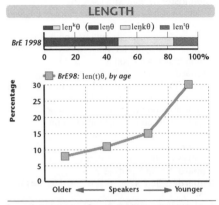

LENGTH

	leŋᵏθ	(▪leŋθ)	leŋkθ	len̩θ

BrE 1998

0   20   40   60   80   100%

BrE98: len(t)θ, *by age*

Percentage — Older ◄— Speakers —► Younger

length leŋᵏθ §lenᵗθ —*BrE 1998 poll panel*
  preference: leŋᵏθ 84% (leŋθ 48%, leŋkθ 36%),
  lenᵗθ 16%. **lengths** leŋᵏθs §lenᵗθs
lengthen 'leŋᵏθ ən §'lenᵗθ- ~**ed** d ~**ing** ɪŋ ~**s**
  z
length|ways 'leŋᵏθ |weɪz §'lenᵗθ- ~**wise** waɪz
length|y 'leŋᵏθ |i §'lenᵗθ- ~**ier** i_ə ‖ i_ᵊr ~**iest**
  i_ɪst i_əst ~**ily** ɪ li əl i ~**iness** i nəs i nɪs
lenienc|e 'liːn i_ənts ~**y** i
lenient 'liːn i_ənt ~**ly** li
Lenihan 'len ə hən
Lenin 'len ɪn §-ən —*Russ* ['lʲe nʲɪn]
Leningrad 'len ɪn græd →-ɪŋ-, §-ən- —*Russ*
  [lʲɪ nʲɪn 'grat]
Lenin|ism 'len ɪn ɪˌɪz əm §-ən- ~**ist/s** ɪst/s
  §əst/s ‖ əst/s
lenis 'liːn ɪs 'leɪn-, §-əs **lenes** 'liːn iːz 'leɪn-,
  -eɪz
le|nite lɪ |'naɪt lə- ~**nited** 'naɪt ɪd -əd
  ‖ 'naɪţ əd ~**nites** 'naɪts ~**niting**
  'naɪt ɪŋ ‖ 'naɪţ ɪŋ
lenition lɪ 'nɪʃ ᵊn lə- ~**s** z
lenity 'len ət i 'liːn-, -ɪt- ‖ -əţ i
Lennie 'len i
Lennon 'len ən
Lennox 'len əks
Lenny 'len i
leno 'liːn əʊ ‖ -oʊ ~**s** z
Leno *(i)* 'liːn əʊ ‖ -oʊ, *(ii)* 'len- —*Jay Leno, TV*
  personality, is (ii)
Lenor *tdmk* lɪ 'nɔː lə- ‖ -'nɔːr
Lenore lɪ 'nɔː lə- ‖ -'nɔːr -'noʊr
Lenox 'len əks
lens lenz **lenses** 'lenz ɪz -əz
lent, Lent lent
lenten 'lent ən ‖ -ᵊn
Lentheric, Lenthéric *tdmk* 'lɒnᵗθ ər ɪk 'lɒ̃θ-
  ‖ 'lɑːnᵗθ-
lenticel 'lent ɪ sel §-ə- ‖ 'lenţ ə- ~**s** z
lenticular len 'tɪk jʊl ə -jəl- ‖ -jəl ᵊr
lentigo len 'taɪg əʊ ‖ -oʊ
lentil 'lent ɪl -ᵊl ‖ 'lenţ ᵊl ~**s** z
lentivirus 'lent i ˌvaɪ_ᵊr əs ‖ 'lenţ- ~**es** ɪz əz
lento 'lent əʊ ‖ -oʊ ~**s** z
Leo 'liː_əʊ ‖ 'liː oʊ

L

Leofric 'lef rɪk 'leɪ əf rɪk ‖ li 'ɑːf rɪk

Leominster *(i)* 'lemᵖst ə ‖ -ᵊr, *(ii)* 'lem ɪnᵗst ə ‖ -ənᵗst ᵊr —*The place in England is (i), that in MA (ii).*

Leon *personal name* 'liː_ən 'leɪ-, -ɒn ‖ -ɑːn

León *place in Spain* leɪ 'ɒn ‖ -'oʊn —*Sp* [le 'on]

Leona li 'əʊn ə ‖ -'oʊn ə

Leonard 'len əd ‖ -ᵊrd

Leonardo ˌliː_əʊ 'nɑːd əʊ ˌleɪ- ‖ ˌliː ə 'nɑːrd oʊ

Leonid 'liː_əʊn ɪd 'leɪ-, §-əd ‖ -ən-

Leonidas li 'ɒn ɪ dæs -ə- ‖ -'ɑːn əd əs

Leonie *(i)* 'liː_ən i, *(ii)* li 'əʊn i ‖ -'oʊn i

leonine, L~ 'liː_əʊ naɪn ‖ -ə-

Leonora ˌliː_ə 'nɔːr ə ‖ -'noʊr-

Leontes li 'ɒnt iːz leɪ- ‖ -'ɑːnt-

leopard 'lep əd ‖ -ᵊrd **~s** z

leopardess 'lep əd es -ɪs, -əs ‖ -ᵊrd əs **~es** ɪz əz

Leopold 'liː_ə pəʊld →-pɒʊld ‖ -poʊld —*but as a foreign name also* 'leɪ-

leotard 'liː_ə tɑːd 'leɪ-, -əʊ- ‖ -tɑːrd **~s** z

Lepanto lɪ 'pænt əʊ lə- ‖ -oʊ —*It* ['lɛː pan to]

leper 'lep ə ‖ -ᵊr **~s** z

lepidopter|a, L~ ˌlep ɪ 'dɒpt ər ə ˌ•ə- ‖ -'dɑːpt- **~ist/s** ɪst/s §əst/s ‖ əst/s **~ous** əs

Lepidus 'lep ɪd əs -əd-

Lepontine lə 'pɒnt aɪn lɪ- ‖ -'pɑːnt-

Leppard 'lep ɑːd ‖ -ɑːrd

leprechaun 'lep rə kɔːn -rɪ-, -hɔːn ‖ -kɑːn **~s** z

leprosari|um ˌlep rə 'seər i_ləm ‖ -'ser- **~a** ə **~ums** əmz

leprosy 'lep rəs i

leprous 'lep rəs **~ly** li **~ness** nəs nɪs

Lepsius 'leps i_əs

leptokurtic ˌlept əʊ 'kɜːt ɪk ◄ ‖ -ə 'kɝːt̬ ɪk ◄

lepton 'lept ɒn ‖ -ɑːn **~s** z

leptospirosis ˌlept əʊ spaɪᵊ 'rəʊs ɪs §-əs ‖ -ə spaɪ 'roʊs əs

Lepus 'liːp əs 'lep-

Lermontov 'leə mɒnt ɒf ‖ 'ler mɑːnt ɔːf —*Russ* ['lʲer mən təf]

Lerner 'lɜːn ə ‖ 'lɝːn ᵊr

Leroy *(i)* 'liː rɔɪ, *(ii)* lə 'rɔɪ —*As a family name, (ii).*

Lerwick 'lɜː wɪk ‖ 'lɝː-

Les *personal name (i) short for* **Leslie** lez, *(ii) short for* **Lester** les

les *French plural 'the'* leɪ —*but before a vowel sound* leɪz —*See also phrases with this word* —*Fr* [le, lez]

Le Saux lə 'səʊ ‖ -'soʊ

Lesbia 'lez bi_ə

lesbian, L~ 'lez bi_ən **~ism** ˌɪz əm **~s** z

Lesbos 'lez bɒs ‖ -bɑːs -boʊs

lèse-majesté ˌleɪz 'mædʒ ə steɪ ˌliːz-, -'mæʒ-, -ɪ-, -e- ‖ ˌliːz 'mædʒ əst i —*Fr* [lɛz ma ʒɛs te]

lese-majesty ˌliːz 'mædʒ əst i ˌleɪz-, -ɪst-

lesion 'liːʒ ᵊn **~s** z

Lesley, Leslie 'lez li ‖ 'les-

Lesmahagow ˌles mə 'heɪg əʊ ‖ -oʊ

Lesney *tdmk* 'lez ni

Lesotho lə 'suːt uː lɪ-, leɪ-, -'səʊt əʊ ‖ -'soʊt oʊ —*Sotho* [lɪ 'suː tʰʊ]

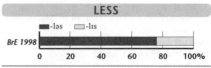

LESS

BrE 1998 ■-ləs ▢-lɪs

0 20 40 60 80 100%

less les

-less ləs lɪs —*In singing, a strong-vowelled form* les *is usual.* —*BrE 1998 poll panel preference (for the word* careless, *disregarding votes for* -les): -ləs 76%, -lɪs 24% — **faithless** 'feɪθ ləs -lɪs, *in singing* -les

lessee ₍ₗₑ'siː **~s** z

lessen 'les ᵊn *(= lesson)* **~ed** d **~ing** _ɪŋ **~s** z

Lesseps 'les əps -eps —*Fr* [lɛ sɛps]

lesser, L~ 'les ə ‖ -ᵊr

Lessing 'les ɪŋ

lesson 'les ᵊn **~s** z

lessor ₍ₗₑ'sɔː 'les ɔː ‖ ₍ₗₑ'sɔːr 'les ɔːr **~s** z

lest lest

Lester 'lest ə ‖ -ᵊr

Lestrange, L'Estrange lɪ 'streɪndʒ lə-

let let —*The phrase* let me *has a non-standard casual form* 'lem i, *sometimes written* lemme **lets, let's** lets **letting** 'let ɪŋ ‖ 'let̬ ɪŋ

-let lət lɪt — **leaflet** 'liːf lət -lɪt

letch letʃ **letched** letʃt **letches** 'letʃ ɪz -əz **letching** 'letʃ ɪŋ

Letchworth 'letʃ wəθ -wɜːθ ‖ -wɝːθ

letdown 'let daʊn **~s** z

lethal 'liːθ ᵊl

lethality liː 'θæl ət i -ɪt- ‖ -ət̬ i

lethally 'liːθ ᵊl i

lethargic lə 'θɑːdʒ ɪk lɪ-, le- ‖ -'θɑːrdʒ- **~ally** ᵊl_i

lethargy 'leθ ədʒ i ‖ -ᵊrdʒ i

Lethbridge 'leθ brɪdʒ

Lethe 'liːθ i -iː

Le Tissier lə 'tɪs i eɪ

Letitia lə 'tɪʃ ə lɪ-, -'tɪʃ i_ə ‖ -'tiːʃ ə

Letraset *tdmk* 'letr ə set

let's *contracted form* lets

Lett let **Letts, Lett's** lets

letter 'let ə ‖ 'let̬ ᵊr **~ed** d **lettering** 'let ᵊr ɪŋ ‖ 'let̬ ᵊr ɪŋ **~s** z 'letter bomb; ˌletter of 'credit; 'letter ˌopener

letterbox 'let ə bɒks ‖ 'let̬ ᵊr bɑːks **~es** ɪz əz

letterhead 'let ə hed ‖ 'let̬ ᵊr- **~s** z

Letterman 'let ə mən ‖ 'let̬ ᵊr-

letter-perfect ˌlet ə 'pɜːf ɪkt ◄ -ekt, §-əkt ‖ ˌlet̬ ᵊr 'pɝːf ɪkt ◄

letterpress 'let ə pres ‖ 'let̬ ᵊr-

Lettice 'let ɪs §-əs ‖ 'let̬ əs

Lettish 'let ɪʃ ‖ 'let̬ ɪʃ

lettuc|e, L~ 'let ɪs -əs ‖ 'let̬ əs **~es** ɪz əz

letup 'let ʌp ‖ 'let̬- **~s** s

Leuchars *family name* 'luːk əs ‖ -ᵊrs

Leuchars *place in Fife* 'luːk əz 'luːx- ‖ -ᵊrz

leucin 'luːs ɪn 'ljuːs-, §-ən

leucine 'luːs iːn 'ljuːs-

leucite 'luːs aɪt 'ljuːs-

leuco- *comb. form*
  with stress-neutral suffix ˌluːk əʊ ˌljuːk əʊ
  ‖ ˌluːk ə — **leucoderma** ˌluːk əʊ ˈdɜːm ə
  ˌljuːk- ‖ -ə ˈdɝːm ə
  with stress-imposing suffix lu ˈkɒ+ lju-
  ‖ lu ˈkɑː+ — **leucopathy** lu ˈkɒp əθ i lju-
  ‖ -ˈkɑːp-
leucocyte ˈluːk əʊ saɪt ˈljuːk- ‖ -ə- ~**s** s
leucopenia ˌluːk əʊ ˈpiːn i ə ˌljuːk- ‖ ˌ•ə-
leucotomis|e, leucotomiz|e lu ˈkɒt ə maɪz lju-
  ‖ lu ˈkɑːt̬- ~**ed** d ~**es** ɪz əz ~**ing** ɪŋ
leucotom|y lu ˈkɒt əm i lju- ‖ lu ˈkɑːt̬- ~**ies** iz
leukaemia, leukemia lu ˈkiːm i ə lju- ~**s** z
leuko... —*see* **leuco...**
le|vant, L~ lə ˈvænt lɪ- ~**vanted** ˈvænt ɪd -əd
  ‖ ˈvænt̬ əd ~**vanting** ˈvænt ɪŋ ‖ ˈvænt̬ ɪŋ
  ~**vants** ˈvænts
Levantine ˈlev ən taɪn -tiːn ‖ lə ˈvænt ən, -aɪn
  ~**s** z
levator lə ˈveɪt ə lɪ-, -ɔː ‖ -ˈveɪt̬ ər ~**s** z
levee ˈlev i -eɪ ~**s** z
level ˈlev əl ~**ed, ~led** d ~**ing, ~ling** ɪŋ ~**s** z
  ˌlevel ˈcrossing
leveler, L~ ˈlev əl ə ‖ -ər ~**s** z
level-headed ˌlev əl ˈhed ɪd ◄ ‖ ˈ••,•• ~**ly** li
  ~**ness** nəs nɪs
leveller, L~ ˈlev əl ə ‖ -ər ~**s** z
level-pegging ˌlev əl ˈpeg ɪŋ
Leven (i) ˈlev ən, (ii) ˈliːv ən —*Most rivers of this
  name, and the Loch, are (ii), but the river in
  Cumbria is (i). The family name may be either.*
Levens ˈlev ənz
lev|er ˈliːv ə ‖ ˈlev ər ˈliːv- ~**ered** əd ‖ ərd
  ~**ering** ər_ɪŋ ~**ers** əz ‖ ərz
Lever ˈliːv ə ‖ -ər
leverag|e ˈliːv ər_ɪdʒ ˈlev- ‖ ˈlev- ~**ed** d ~**es**
  ɪz əz ~**ing** ɪŋ
leveret ˈlev ər_ət -ɪt ~**s** s
Leverhulme ˈliːv ə hjuːm ‖ -ər-
Levett ˈlev ɪt -ət
Levi *biblical name* ˈliːv aɪ
Levi *personal or family name*, (i) ˈlev i, (ii) ˈliːv i
leviathan, L~ lə ˈvaɪ_əθ ən lɪ- ~**s** z
levi... —*see* **levy**
Levin, levin ˈlev ɪn §-ən ~**s** z
Levine lə ˈviːn
levirate ˈliːv ər ət ˈlev-, -ɪr-, -ɪt; -ə reɪt
Levi's *tdmk*, **Levis** '*jeans*' ˈliːv aɪz
Levi-Strauss, Lévi-Strauss ˌlev i ˈstraʊs ˌleɪv-
  —*Fr* [lə vi strɔːs]
levi|tate ˈlev ɪ teɪt -ə- ~**tated** teɪt ɪd -əd
  ‖ teɪt̬ əd ~**tates** teɪts ~**tating**
  teɪt ɪŋ ‖ teɪt̬ ɪŋ
levitation ˌlev ɪ ˈteɪʃ ən -ə- ~**s** z
Levite ˈliːv aɪt ~**s** s
Levitic|us lə ˈvɪt ɪk ləs lɪ- ‖ -ˈvɪt̬- ~**al** əl
Levittown ˈlev ɪt taʊn -ət-
levit|ly ˈlev ət li -ɪt- ‖ -ət̬ li ~**ies** iz
levodopa ˌliːv əʊ ˈdəʊp ə ˌlev- ‖ -ə ˈdoʊp ə
  ˈ••,••
lev|y *v, n* ˈlev li ~**ied** id ~**ies** iz ~**ying** i_ɪŋ
Levy *name*, (i) ˈliːv i, (ii) ˈlev i

lewd luːd ljuːd **lewder** ˈluːd ə ˈljuːd- ‖ -ər
  lewdest ˈluːd ɪst ˈljuːd-, -əst
lewd|ly ˈluːd lli ˈljuːd- ~**ness** nəs nɪs
Lewes ˈluː_ɪs §-əs
Lewin ˈluː_ɪn §-ən
Lewinsky lə ˈwɪn ski
Lewis, lewis ˈluː_ɪs §-əs
Lewisham ˈluː_ɪʃ əm
lewisite ˈluː_ɪ saɪt §-ə-
Lex, lex leks
lexeme ˈleks iːm ~**s** z
lexemic lek ˈsiːm ɪk
lexical ˈleks ɪk əl ~**ly** _i
lexico- *comb. form*
  with stress-neutral suffix ˌleks ɪ kəʊ ‖ -koʊ —
  lexicostatistics
  ˌleks ɪ kəʊ stə ˈtɪst ɪks ‖ ,••koʊ-
  with stress-imposing suffix ˌleks ɪ ˈkɒ+ -ə-
  ‖ -ˈkɑː+ — **lexicology** ˌleks ɪ ˈkɒl ədʒ i ˌ•ə-
  ‖ -ˈkɑːl-
lexicographer ˌleks ɪ ˈkɒg rəf ə ˌ•ə-
  ‖ -ˈkɑːg rəf ər ~**s** z
lexicographic ˌleks ɪk ə ˈgræf ɪk ◄ ˌ•ək- ~**ally**
  əl_i
lexicography ˌleks ɪ ˈkɒg rəf i ˌ•ə- ‖ -ˈkɑːg-
lexicological ˌleks ɪk ə ˈlɒdʒ ɪk əl ◄ ˌ•ək-
  ‖ -ˈlɑːdʒ- ~**ly** _i
lexicologist ˌleks ɪ ˈkɒl ədʒ ɪst ˌ•ə-, §-əst
  ‖ -ˈkɑːl- ~**s** s
lexicology ˌleks ɪ ˈkɒl ədʒ i ˌ•ə- ‖ -ˈkɑːl-
lexicon ˈleks ɪk ən -ɒk-; -ɪ kɒn, -ə- ‖ -ə kɑːn
  ~**s** z
Lexington ˈleks ɪŋ tən
lexis ˈleks ɪs §-əs
Lexus *tdmk* ˈleks əs
ley leɪ li
Ley (i) liː, (ii) leɪ
Leyburn ˈleɪ bɜːn ‖ -bɝːn
Leyden ˈlaɪd ən
Leyland ˈleɪ lənd
leylandii leɪ ˈlænd i aɪ •ˈ•• aɪ
Leys liːz
Leysdown ˈleɪz daʊn
Leyton ˈleɪt ən
Leystonstone ˈleɪt ən stəʊn ‖ -stoʊn
lezzie ˈlez i ~**s** z
Lhasa ˈlɑːs ə ˈlæs- —*Chi* Lāsà [¹la ⁴sa]
  ˌLhasa ˈapso ˈæps əʊ ‖ ˈɑːps oʊ
li liː
LI ˌel ˈaɪ —*see also* Long Island
liabilit|y ˌlaɪ_ə ˈbɪl ət i li -ɪt i ‖ -ət̬ li ~**ies** iz
liable ˈlaɪ_əb əl
liais|e li ˈeɪz laɪ- ~**ed** d ~**es** ɪz əz ~**ing** ɪŋ
liaison li ˈeɪz ən laɪ-, -ɒn, -õ ‖ ˈliː ə zɑːn, ,••ˈ•;
  △ˈleɪ-; li ˈeɪz ɑːn —*Fr* [ljɛ zɔ̃] ~**s** z
Liam ˈliː_əm
liana li ˈɑːn ə -ˈæn- ~**s** z
liane li ˈɑːn -ˈæn ~**s** z
Lianne li ˈæn
Liao *dynasty* li ˈaʊ —*Chi* Liáo [²ljɐu]
Liaoning li ˌaʊ ˈnɪŋ —*Chi* Liáoníng [²ljɐu ²niŋ]
liar ˈlaɪ_ə ‖ ˈlaɪ_ər ~**s** z
Lias, lias ˈlaɪ_əs

L

liassic, L~ laɪ ˈæs ɪk
LIAT *airline* ˈliː æt ˈliː‿ət
lib, Lib lɪb
　ˌLib ˈDem/s dem/z
Libanus ˈlɪb ən əs
libation laɪ ˈbeɪʃ ən lɪ- ~s z
libber ˈlɪb ə ‖ -ər ~s z
Libbie, Libby ˈlɪb i
Lib-Dem, Libdem ˌlɪb ˈdem ◂ ~s z
libel ˈlaɪb əl ~ed, ~led d ~ing, ~ling ɪŋ ~s z
libellous, libelous ˈlaɪb əl əs ~ly li
Liberace ˌlɪb ə ˈrɑːtʃ i
liberal, L~ ˈlɪb ər‿əl ~ly i ~s z
　ˌliberal ˈarts; ˌLiberal ˈDemocrat; ˈLiberal
　ˌParty; ˌliberal ˈstudies
liberalis... —*see* **liberaliz...**
liberalism ˈlɪb ər‿əl ˌɪz əm
liberalit|y ˌlɪb ə ˈræl ət i -ɪt i ‖ -əṭ li ~ies iz
liberalization ˌlɪb ər‿əl aɪ ˈzeɪʃ ən -ɪ'•- ‖ -ə'•-
　~s z
liberaliz|e ˈlɪb ər‿ə laɪz ~ed d ~es ɪz əz ~ing
　ɪŋ
liberally ˈlɪb ər‿əl i
libe|rate ˈlɪb ə ˌreɪt ~rated reɪt ɪd -əd ‖ reɪṭ əd
　~rates reɪts ~rating reɪt ɪŋ ‖ reɪṭ ɪŋ
liberation ˌlɪb ə ˈreɪʃ ən ◂ ~ist/s ˌɪst/s §‿əst/s
　‖ ‿əst/s
　ˌlibeˌration theˈology, ˌ•••'•• •ˌ•••
liberator ˈlɪb ə reɪt ə ‖ -reɪṭ ər ~s z
Liberi|a laɪ ˈbɪər i‿ə ‖ -ˈbɪr- ~an/s ən/z
libertarian ˌlɪb ə ˈteər i‿ən ◂ -ər ˈter- ~s z
liberti... —*see* **liberty**
libertine ˈlɪb ə tiːn -taɪn ‖ -ər- ~s z
Liberton ˈlɪb ət ən ‖ -ərt ən
libert|y, L~ ˈlɪb ət li ‖ ərṭ li ~ies iz
libidinal lɪ ˈbɪd ɪn əl lə-, -ən‿əl ‖ -ən‿əl
libidinous lɪ ˈbɪd ɪn əs lə-, -ən‿əs ‖ -ən‿əs
libido lɪ ˈbiːd əʊ lə- ‖ -oʊ ˈlɪb ə doʊ ~s z
Libra ˈliːb rə ˈlɪb-, ˈlaɪb-
Libran ˈliːb rən ˈlɪb-, ˈlaɪb- ~s z
librarian laɪ ˈbreər i‿ən lɪ-, lə- ‖ -ˈbrer- ~s z
　~ship ʃɪp
librar|y ˈlaɪb rər li ˈlaɪb ər‿i ‖ ˈlaɪb rer li -rər i,
　△-er i, -ər‿i ~ies iz —*The awkwardness of
　two r's in the same unstressed syllable makes
　people tend to drop the first of them. While
　perhaps condemned by the speech-conscious,
　such reduced pronunciations are nevertheless
　often heard from educated speakers. Where in
　AmE the second syllable has a strong vowel, the
　reduction is more noticeable, hence less
　frequently heard and more strongly disapproved
　of.*
librate laɪ ˈb|reɪt ˈlaɪb |reɪt ‖ ˈlaɪb |reɪt ~rated
　reɪt ɪd -əd ‖ reɪṭ əd ~rates reɪts ~rating
　reɪt ɪŋ ‖ reɪṭ ɪŋ
libration laɪ ˈbreɪʃ ən ~s z
librettist lɪ ˈbret ɪst lə-, §-əst ‖ -ˈbreṭ əst ~s s
librett|o lɪ ˈbret ləʊ lə- ‖ -ˈbreṭ loʊ ~i iː ~os
　əʊz ‖ oʊz
Libreville ˈliːb rə vɪl -viːl
Librium *tdmk* ˈlɪb ri‿əm
Liby|a ˈlɪb i‿ə ~an/s ən/z

lice laɪs
licenc|e, licens|e ˈlaɪs ən‿ts ~ed t ~es ɪz əz
　~ing ɪŋ
　ˌlicensed ˈpremises; ˌlicensed ˌpractical
　ˈnurse; ˌlicensed ˈvictualler; ˈlicense plate;
　ˈlicensing laws
licensee ˌlaɪs ən ˈsiː ~s z
licenser, licensor ˈlaɪs ən‿ts ə ‖ -ər ~s z
licentiate laɪ ˈsentʃ i‿ət lɪ-, -ˈsen‿ts-, -ɪt ~s s
licentious laɪ ˈsentʃ əs ~ly li ~ness nəs nɪs
lichee ˌlaɪ ˈtʃiː ˈlɪtʃ iː, ˈliːtʃ-, -i ‖ ˈliːtʃ i ˈlaɪtʃ i
　~s z
lichen ˈlaɪk ən ˈlɪtʃ ən, -ɪn ~s z
Lichfield ˈlɪtʃ fiːəld
licit ˈlɪs ɪt §-ət ~ly li ~ness nəs nɪs
lick lɪk **licked** lɪkt **licking** ˈlɪk ɪŋ **licks** lɪks
lickerish ˈlɪk ər ɪʃ
lickety-split ˌlɪk ət i ˈsplɪt -ɪt i- ‖ -əṭ i-
lickspittle ˈlɪk ˌspɪt əl ‖ -ˌspɪṭ əl ~s z
licorice ˈlɪk ər‿ɪs ‿ɪʃ, §‿əs
lictor ˈlɪkt ə -ɔː ‖ -ər ~s z
lid lɪd **lidded** ˈlɪd ɪd -əd **lids** lɪdz
Liddle ˈlɪd əl
Liddell *(i)* ˈlɪd əl, *(ii)* lɪ ˈdel
Liddon ˈlɪd ən
lido ˈliːd əʊ ‖ -oʊ ~s z
lie laɪ **lain** leɪn **lay** leɪ **lied** laɪd **lies** laɪz
　lying ˈlaɪ ɪŋ
　ˈlie deˌtector
Liebfraumilch, l~ ˈliːb fraʊ mɪlk -mɪlx, -mɪlʃ
　—*Ger* [ˈliːp fʁaʊ mɪlç]
Liebig ˈliːb ɪg —*Ger* [ˈliː bɪç]
Liechtenstein ˈlɪkt ən staɪn ˈlɪxt- —*Ger*
　[ˈlɪçt ən ʃtaɪn]
lied *past and pp of* **lie** laɪd
lied *'musical setting'* liːd —*Ger* [liːt] **lieder**
　ˈliːd ə ‖ -ər —*Ger* [ˈliː dɐ]
lie-down ˌlaɪ ˈdaʊn '•• ~s z
lief liːf *(= leaf)*
liege liːdʒ liːʒ **lieges** ˈliːdʒ ɪz ˈliːʒ-, -əz
　ˌliege ˈlord; ˈliege man
Liege, Liège li ˈeɪʒ -ˈeʒ —*Fr* [ljɛːʒ]
lie-in ˌlaɪ ˈɪn '•• ~s z
lien ˈliː‿ən liːn **liens** ˈliː‿ənz liːnz
lieu luː ljuː
lieutenanc|y lef ˈten ən‿ts li ləf- ‖ luː- *(*)* ~ies
　iz
lieutenant lef ˈten ənt ləf- ‖ luː- *(*)* ~s s
life laɪf **life's** laɪfs **lives** laɪvz
　ˈlife belt; ˈlife ˌcycle; ˈlife exˈpectancy,
　'• •ˌ•••; ˌlife imˈprisonment; ˈlife
　inˌsurance; ˈlife ˌjacket; ˈlife ˌpeer, ˌlife
　ˈpeeress; ˈlife preˌserver; ˈlife ˌraft; ˈlife
　ˈsavings; ˈlife ˌstory; ˌlife ˈwork, ˌlife's
　ˈwork
life-and-death ˌlaɪf ən ˈdeθ ◂
lifeblood ˈlaɪf blʌd
lifeboat ˈlaɪf bəʊt ‖ -boʊt ~s s
lifebuoy ˈlaɪf bɔɪ ~s z
life-giving ˈlaɪf ˌgɪv ɪŋ
lifeguard ˈlaɪf gɑːd ‖ -gɑːrd ~s z
lifeless ˈlaɪf ləs -lɪs ~ly li ~ness nəs nɪs
lifelike ˈlaɪf laɪk

L

lifeline 'laɪf laɪn ~s z
lifelong 'laɪf lɒŋ ‚•'•◄ ‖ -lɔːŋ -lɑːŋ
lifer 'laɪf ə ‖ -ᵊr ~s z
life-saver 'laɪf ‚seɪv ə ‖ -ᵊr ~s z
life-size 'laɪf saɪz ‚•'•◄ -d d
lifespan 'laɪf spæn ~s z
lifestyle 'laɪf staɪᵊl ~s z
life-support 'laɪf sə ‚pɔːt ‚• •'• ‖ -‚pɔːrt
   -‚poʊrt
lifetime 'laɪf taɪm ~s z
Liffey 'lɪf i
Lifford 'lɪf əd ‖ -ᵊrd
lift lɪft lifted 'lɪft ɪd -əd lifting 'lɪft ɪŋ lifts
   lɪfts
liftboy 'lɪft bɔɪ ~s z
lift|man 'lɪft |mæn ~men men
liftoff 'lɪft ɒf -ɔːf ‖ -ɔːf -ɑːf ~s s
ligament 'lɪg ə mənt ~s s
ligamental ‚lɪg ə 'ment ᵊl ◄ ‖ -'menṯ ᵊl ◄
ligand 'lɪg ænd 'laɪg- ~s z
lig|ate 'laɪg |eɪt ~ated eɪt ɪd -əd ‖ eɪṯ əd
   ~ates eɪts ~ating eɪt ɪŋ ‖ eɪṯ ɪŋ
ligature 'lɪg ətʃ ə -ə tjʊə, -ə tʃʊə ‖ -ə tʃʊr
   -ətʃ ᵊr, -ə tʊr ~s z
liger 'laɪg ə ‖ -ᵊr ~s z
ligger 'lɪg ə ‖ -ᵊr ~s z
light laɪt lighted 'laɪt ɪd -əd ‖ 'laɪṯ əd lighter
   'laɪt ə ‖ 'laɪṯ ᵊr lightest 'laɪt ɪst -əst
   ‖ 'laɪṯ əst lighting 'laɪt ɪŋ ‖ 'laɪṯ ɪŋ lights
   laɪts lit lɪt
   ‚light 'aircraft; ‚light 'ale; ‚light 'bulb; ‚light
   'heavyweight; ‚lighting-'up time; 'light
   ‚meter; 'light pen; 'light year
lighten 'laɪt ᵊn ~ed d ~ing ‚ɪŋ ~s z
lighter 'laɪt ə ‖ 'laɪṯ ᵊr ~s z
lighterage 'laɪt ᵊr ɪdʒ ‖ 'laɪṯ-
lighter|man 'laɪt ə mən ‖ 'laɪṯ ᵊr- ~men mən
   men
lightface 'laɪt feɪs
light-fingered ‚laɪt 'fɪŋ gəd ◄ ‖ -gᵊrd ◄ ~ness
   nəs nɪs
Lightfoot 'laɪt fʊt
light-headed ‚laɪt 'hed ɪd ◄ -əd ~ly li ~ness
   nəs nɪs
light-hearted ‚laɪt 'hɑːt ɪd ◄ -əd ‖ -'hɑːrṯ əd ◄
   ~ly li ~ness nəs nɪs
light|house 'laɪt |haʊs ~houses haʊz ɪz -əz
lightly 'laɪt li
light-minded ‚laɪt 'maɪnd ɪd ◄ -əd ~ly li
   ~ness nəs nɪs
lightness 'laɪt nəs -nɪs ~es ɪz əz
lightning 'laɪt nɪŋ
   'lightning bug; 'lightning con‚ductor;
   ‚lightning 'strike 'sudden stoppage',
   'lightning strike 'atmospheric discharge'
lightship 'laɪt ʃɪp ~s s
lights-out ‚laɪts 'aʊt '• •
lightweight 'laɪt weɪt ~s s
ligneous 'lɪg ni‚əs
lignification ‚lɪg nɪf ɪ 'keɪʃ ᵊn ‚• nəf-, §-ə'• -
ligni|fy 'lɪg nɪ |faɪ -nə- ~fied faɪd ~fies faɪz
   ~fying faɪ ɪŋ
lignin 'lɪg nɪn §-nən

lignite 'lɪg naɪt
lignocaine 'lɪg nəʊ keɪn ‖ -ə-
lignum vitae ‚lɪg nəm 'vaɪt i -'viːt aɪ ‖ -'vaɪṯ i
   -ə
Liguri|a lɪ 'gjʊər i‚ə ‖ -'gjʊr- ~an/s ən/z
likable 'laɪk əb ᵊl ~ness nəs nɪs
like laɪk liked laɪkt likes laɪks liking 'laɪk ɪŋ
-like laɪk — springlike 'sprɪŋ laɪk
likeable 'laɪk əb ᵊl ~ness nəs nɪs
likelihood 'laɪk li hʊd ~s z
likely 'laɪk li
like-minded ‚laɪk 'maɪnd ɪd ◄ -əd ~ly li ~ness
   nəs nɪs
liken 'laɪk ᵊn ~ed d ~ing ‚ɪŋ ~s z
likeness 'laɪk nəs -nɪs ~es ɪz əz
likewise 'laɪk waɪz
liking 'laɪk ɪŋ ~s z
Likud lɪ 'kʊd -'kuːd ‖ -'kuːd
lilac, Lilac 'laɪl ək ‖ -ɑːk, -æk ~s s
Lilburne 'lɪl bɜːn ‖ -bɜːn
Lilian 'lɪl i‚ən
Lilias 'lɪl i‚əs
Liliburlero ‚lɪl i bə 'leər əʊ ‖ -bᵊr 'ler oʊ
lilie... —see lily
Lilith 'lɪl ɪθ -əθ
Lille liːᵊl —Fr [lil]
Lillee 'lɪl i
Lillehammer 'lɪl ɪ hæm ə ‖ -ə hɑːm ᵊr -hæm •
   —Norw ["lɪl lə ha mər]
Lil-lets tdmk lɪ 'lets
Lilley 'lɪl i
Lillian 'lɪl i‚ən
Lillibullero ‚lɪl i bə 'leər əʊ ‖ -'ler oʊ
Lillie 'lɪl i
Lilliput 'lɪl ɪ pʌt -ə-, -pʊt; -ɪp ət, -əp-
lilliputian, L~ ‚lɪl ɪ 'pjuːʃ ᵊn ◄ -ə-, -'pjuːʃ i‚ən
   ~s z
Lilly 'lɪl i
Lillywhite 'lɪl i waɪt -hwaɪt ‖ -hwaɪt
lilo, li-lo, Lilo, Li-lo tdmk 'laɪ ləʊ ‖ -loʊ ~s z
Lilongwe lɪ 'lɒŋ weɪ ‖ -'lɔːŋ- -'lɑːŋ-
lilt, Lilt tdmk lɪlt lilted 'lɪlt ɪd -əd lilting
   'lɪlt ɪŋ lilts lɪlts
lilting 'lɪlt ɪŋ ~ly li ~ness nəs nɪs
lil|y, Lill|y 'lɪl |i ~ies, ~y's iz
   ‚lily of the 'valley
lily-livered ‚lɪl i 'lɪv əd ◄ ‖ -ᵊrd ◄
lily-white ‚lɪl i 'waɪt ◄ -'hwaɪt ‖ -'hwaɪt ◄
Lima, lima (i) 'liːm ə, (ii) 'laɪm ə —The place in
   Peru —Sp ['li ma] —and the communications
   code name for the letter L are (i); the place in
   Ohio is (ii); the bean is (ii) in AmE, either in
   BrE.
   'lima bean
limacon, limaçon 'lɪm ə sɒn ‖ -sɑːn
   ‚liːm ə 'soʊn —Fr [li ma sɔ̃] ~s z
Limassol 'lɪm ə sɒl ‖ -sɔːl -sɑːl, -soʊl, ‚• •'•
Limavady ‚lɪm ə 'væd i
limb lɪm limbs lɪmz
limber 'lɪm bə ‖ -bᵊr ~ed d limbering
   'lɪm bᵊr‚ɪŋ ~s z
limbic 'lɪm bɪk
limbless 'lɪm ləs -lɪs

L

limbo, Limbo 'lɪm bəʊ ‖ -boʊ ~s z
Limburger 'lɪm bɜːg ə ‖ -bɜ·ːg ʳr
lim|bus 'lɪm |bəs ~bi baɪ
lime laɪm limed laɪmd limes laɪmz liming
'laɪm ɪŋ
,lime 'green◄; 'lime tree
limeade ˌlaɪm 'eɪd ~s z
Limehouse 'laɪm haʊs
limejuic|e 'laɪm dʒuːs ~es ɪz əz
limekiln 'laɪm kɪln -kɪl ~s z
limelight 'laɪm laɪt ~s s
limen 'laɪm en -ən ~s z limina 'lɪm ɪn ə §-ən ə
limerick, L~ 'lɪm ər_ɪk ~s s
limestone 'laɪm stəʊn -stoʊn
limey, Limey 'laɪm i ~s z
limin|a 'lɪm ɪn |ə §-ən- ~al ᵊl
lim|it 'lɪm |ɪt §-ət ‖ -lət ~ited ɪt ɪd §ət-, -əd
‖ əʈ əd ~iting ɪt ɪŋ §ət- ‖ əʈ ɪŋ ~its ɪts §əts
‖ əts
,limited ,lia'bility
limitation ˌlɪm ɪ 'teɪʃ ᵊn -ə- ~s z
limitless 'lɪm ɪt ləs §-ət-, -lɪs ~ly li ~ness nəs
nɪs
limn lɪm (= limb) limned lɪmd limning
'lɪm ɪŋ -nɪŋ limns lɪmz
limo 'lɪm əʊ ‖ -oʊ ~s z
Limoges lɪ 'məʊʒ ‖ -'moʊʒ —Fr [li mɔːʒ]
Limousin ˌlɪm u 'zæn -'zæ̃ —Fr [li mu zæ̃]
limousine ˌlɪm ə 'ziːn '••• ‖ 'lɪm ə ziːn ,••'•
~s z
limp lɪmp limped lɪmpt limping 'lɪmp ɪŋ
limps lɪmps
limpet 'lɪmp ɪt §-ət ~s s
limpid 'lɪmp ɪd §-əd ~ly li ~ness nəs nɪs
limpidity lɪm 'pɪd ət i -ɪt- ‖ -əʈ i
limp|ly 'lɪmp |li ~ness nəs nɪs
Limpopo lɪm 'pəʊp əʊ ‖ -'poʊp oʊ
limp-wristed ˌlɪmp 'rɪst ɪd ◄ -əd ◄
lim|y 'laɪm |i ~ier i_ə ‖ i_ʳr ~iest i_ɪst i_əst
Linacre 'lɪn ək ə ‖ -ʳr
linage 'laɪn ɪdʒ
Lin Biao ˌlɪn bi 'aʊ —Chi Lín Biāo [²lɪn ¹pjɐu]
Linch lɪntʃ
linchpin 'lɪntʃ pɪn ~s z
Lincoln 'lɪŋk ən ~'s z ~shire ʃə ʃɪə ‖ ʃʳr ʃɪr
,Lincoln's 'Inn
Lincs, Lincs. lɪŋks
linctus 'lɪŋkt əs ~es ɪz əz
Lind lɪnd
Linda 'lɪnd ə
lindane 'lɪnd eɪn
Lindbergh 'lɪnd bɜːg ‖ -bɜ·ːg
linden, L~ 'lɪnd ən ~s z
Lindisfarne 'lɪnd ɪs faːn -əs- ‖ -faːrn
Lindley 'lɪnd li
Lindo 'lɪnd əʊ ‖ -oʊ
Lindon 'lɪnd ən
Lindsay, Lindsey 'lɪndz i
Lindwall 'lɪnd wɔːl ‖ -waːl
Lindy 'lɪnd i
line, Line laɪn lined laɪnd lines laɪnz lining
'laɪn ɪŋ
'line ˌdrawing; 'line ˌprinter

lineag|e 'descent' 'lɪn i_ɪdʒ ~es ɪz əz
lineage 'number of lines' 'laɪn ɪdʒ
lineal 'lɪn i_əl ~ly i
lineament 'lɪn i_ə mənt ~s s
linear 'lɪn i_ə ‖ ʳr ~ly li
,Linear 'B; ,linear 'programming
linearit|y ˌlɪn i 'ær ət i ˌli -ɪt i ‖ -əʈ i -'er- ~ies iz
lineation ˌlɪn i 'eɪʃ ᵊn ~s z
linebacker 'laɪn ˌbæk ə ‖ -ʳr ~s z
Lineker 'lɪn ɪk ə -ək- ‖ -ʳr
line|man 'laɪn |mən ~men mən
linen 'lɪn ɪn §-ən ~s z
'linen ˌbasket
lineout 'laɪn aʊt ~s s
liner 'laɪn ə ‖ -ʳr ~s z
linertrain 'laɪn ə treɪn ‖ -ʳr- ~s z
lineshoot|er/s 'laɪn ˌʃuːt |ə/z ‖ -ˌʃuːʈ |ʳr/z ~ing
ɪŋ
lines|man 'laɪnz |mən ~men mən men
lineup 'laɪn ʌp ~s s
Linford 'lɪn fəd ‖ -fʳrd
ling, Ling lɪŋ lings lɪŋz
-ling lɪŋ — underling 'ʌnd ə lɪŋ ‖ -ʳr-
Lingala lɪŋ 'gaːl ə
lingam 'lɪŋ gəm ~s z
linger 'lɪŋ gə ‖ -gʳr ~ed d lingering/ly
'lɪŋ gər_ɪŋ /li ~s z
lingerie 'lændʒ ər i 'lɒndʒ-; -ə reɪ
‖ ˌlaːndʒ ə 'reɪ -'riː, '••• —Fr [lɛ̃ʒ ʁi]
Lingfield 'lɪŋ fiːᵊld
lingo 'lɪŋ gəʊ ‖ -goʊ ~es z
lingua 'lɪŋ gwə
,lingua 'franca 'fræŋk ə
lingual 'lɪŋ gwəl §-gju_əl ~s z
Linguaphone tdmk 'lɪŋ gwə fəʊn ‖ -foʊn
Linguarama tdmk ˌlɪŋ gwə 'raːm ə ‖ -'ræm-
-'raːm-
linguine, linguini lɪŋ 'gwiːn i —It [liŋ 'gwiː ne]
linguist 'lɪŋ gwɪst §-gwəst ~s s
linguistic lɪŋ 'gwɪst ɪk ~ally ᵊl_i ~s s
liniment 'lɪn ə mənt -ɪ- ~s s
lining 'laɪn ɪŋ ~s z
link, Link lɪŋk linked lɪŋkt linking 'lɪŋk ɪŋ
links lɪŋks
linkag|e 'lɪŋk ɪdʒ ~es ɪz əz
Linklater (i) 'lɪŋk ˌleɪt ə ‖ -leɪʈ ʳr, (ii)
-lət ə ‖ -ləʈ ʳr —The author Eric L~ prefers (ii).
link|man 'lɪŋk |mæn —but in the obsolete sense
'torchbearer' was usually -mən ~men men
linkup 'lɪŋk ʌp ~s s
Linley 'lɪn li
Linlithgow lɪn 'lɪθ gəʊ ‖ -goʊ
Linnae|us, Linne|us lɪ 'niː_|əs -'neɪ |əs ~an/s
ən/z
linnet 'lɪn ɪt §-ət ~s s
Linnhe 'lɪn i
lino 'laɪn əʊ ‖ -oʊ ~s z
linocut 'laɪn əʊ kʌt ‖ -oʊ- ~s s
linoleic ˌlɪn əʊ 'liː_ɪk ◄ -'leɪ- ‖ -ə-
linoleum lɪ 'nəʊl i_əm lə- ‖ -'noʊl- ~s z
Linotype tdmk 'laɪn əʊ taɪp ‖ -ə-
linseed 'lɪn siːd
'linseed oil, ˌ•• '•

linsey-woolsey ˌlɪnz i 'wʊlz i ~s z
lint lɪnt
lintel 'lɪnt ᵊl ~s z
Linton 'lɪnt ən ‖ -ᵊn
Lintott 'lɪn tɒt ‖ -tɑːt
Linus 'laɪn əs
Linux 'lɪn əks 'laɪn-
Linwood 'lɪn wʊd
Linz lɪnᵗs —Ger [lɪnts]
lion 'laɪ_ən ~s z
Lionel 'laɪ_ən ᵊl
lioness 'laɪ_ən es -ɪs, -əs; ˌlaɪ_ə 'nes ‖ -əs ~es
ɪz əz
Lionheart 'laɪ_ən hɑːt ‖ -hɑːrt
lion-hearted ˌlaɪ_ən 'hɑːt ɪd ◂ -əd, '•• ˌ••
‖ -'hɑːrt̬ əd ◂
lionis... —see **lioniz...**
lionization ˌlaɪ_ən aɪ 'zeɪʃ ᵊn ˌ•ən ɪ- ‖ -ən ə-
lioniz|e 'laɪ_ə naɪz ~ed d ~er/s ə/z ‖ ᵊr/z ~es
ɪz əz ~ing ɪŋ
lip lɪp **lipped** lɪpt **lipping** 'lɪp ɪŋ **lips** lɪps
'lip gloss; 'lip ˌservice
Lipari 'lɪp ər i —It ['liː pa ɾi]
lipase 'laɪp eɪs 'lɪp-, -eɪz
lipid 'lɪp ɪd §-əd ~s z
Lipman, Lipmann 'lɪp mən
lipo- comb. form
with stress-neutral suffix ˈlɪp əʊ ˌlaɪp- ‖ -ə —
lipochrome 'lɪp əʊ krəʊm 'laɪp- ‖ -ə kroʊm
with stress-imposing suffix lɪ 'pɒ+ laɪ- ‖ -'pɑː+
— **lipolysis** lɪ 'pɒl əs ɪs -ɪs-, §-əs ‖ -'pɑːl-
lipoid 'lɪp ɔɪd 'laɪp- ~s z
lipom|a lɪ 'pəʊm ə lə-, laɪ- ‖ -'poʊm ə ~as əz
~ata ət ə ‖ ət̬ ə
liposome 'lɪp əʊ səʊm 'laɪp- ‖ -ə soʊm ~s z
liposuction 'lɪp əʊ ˌsʌk ʃ ᵊn 'laɪp- ‖ -oʊ- -ə-
Lippizaner ˌlɪp ɪt 'sɑːn ə ◂ -ət- ‖ -ᵊr ◂ ~s z
Lippmann 'lɪp mən
lipp|y 'lɪp li ~ier i_ə ‖ i_ᵊr ~iest i_ɪst i_əst
lip-|read present 'lɪp |riːd ~read past, pp red
~reader/s riːd ə/z ‖ -ᵊr/z ~reading riːd ɪŋ
~reads riːdz
lipstick 'lɪp stɪk ~s s
lip-sync, lip-synch 'lɪp sɪŋk
Lipton 'lɪpt ən
liquefaction ˌlɪk wɪ 'fæk ʃ ᵊn -wə-
lique|fy 'lɪk wɪ |faɪ -wə- ~fied faɪd ~fier/s
faɪ_ə/z ‖ faɪ_ᵊr/z ~fies faɪz ~fying faɪ ɪŋ
liquescenc|e lɪ 'kwes ᵊnᵗs ~y i
liquescent lɪ 'kwes ᵊnt
liqueur lɪ 'kjʊə lə-, -'kjɔː, -'kjɜː ‖ -'kɜˑ -'kjʊr
—Fr [li kœːʁ] ~s z
liquid 'lɪk wɪd §-wəd ~ly li ~s z
ˌliquid 'crystal; ˌliquid 'oxygen
liquidambar ˌlɪk wɪd 'æm bə §-wəd-, '••••
‖ -bᵊr ~s z
liqui|date 'lɪk wɪ |deɪt -wə- ~dated deɪt ɪd -əd
‖ deɪt̬ əd ~dates deɪts ~dating
deɪt ɪŋ ‖ deɪt̬ ɪŋ
liquidation ˌlɪk wɪ 'deɪʃ ᵊn -wə- ~s z
liquidator 'lɪk wɪ deɪt ə ‖ '•wə- ‖ -deɪt̬ ᵊr ~s z
liquidity lɪ 'kwɪd ət i lə-, -ɪt- ‖ -ət̬ i

liquidis|e, liquidiz|e 'lɪk wɪ daɪz -wə- ~ed d
~er/s ə/z ‖ ᵊr/z ~es ɪz əz ~ing ɪŋ
liquor 'lɪk ə ‖ -ᵊr —also (med, pharm) 'laɪk-,
-wɔː ‖ -wɔːr ~ed d **liquoring** 'lɪk ər ɪŋ ~s z
liquorice 'lɪk ər ɪs ˌɪʃ, §_əs
ˌliquorice 'allsorts
lira 'lɪər ə ‖ 'lɪr ə —It ['liː ɾa] **lire** 'lɪər ə -eɪ, -i
‖ 'lɪr eɪ —It ['liː ɾe]
liriodendron ˌlɪr i_əʊ 'dendr ən ‖ -i_ə- ~s z
liripipe 'lɪr i paɪp -ə- ~s s
Lisa (i) 'liːs ə, (ii) 'liːz ə, (iii) 'laɪz ə
Lisbet 'lɪz bət -bet, -bɪt
Lisbeth 'lɪz bəθ -beθ, -bɪθ
Lisbon 'lɪz bən —Port Lisboa [liʒ 'βoɐ]
Lisburn 'lɪz bɜːn ‖ -bᵊrn
Liskeard lɪ 'skɑːd ‖ -'skɑːrd
lisle, Lisle laɪᵊl —but as a French name, liːᵊl
—Fr [lil]
lisp, LISP lɪsp **lisped** lɪspt **lisping** 'lɪsp ɪŋ
lisps lɪsps
lisper 'lɪsp ə ‖ -ᵊr ~s z
Lissajous ˌliːs ə ʒuː 'lɪs-; ˌ••'•• —Fr [li sa ʒu]
lissom, lissome 'lɪs əm ~ly li ~ness nəs nɪs
Lisson 'lɪs ᵊn
list lɪst **listed** 'lɪst ɪd -əd **listing** 'lɪst ɪŋ **lists**
lɪsts
'list price
listel 'lɪst ᵊl ~s z
listen 'lɪs ᵊn ~ed d ~ing ˌɪŋ ~s z
listenable 'lɪs ᵊn_əb ᵊl
listener 'lɪs ᵊn_ə ‖ ᵊ_r ~s z
Lister, l~ 'lɪst ə ‖ -ᵊr ~s, ~'s z
listeria lɪ 'stɪər i_ə ‖ -'stɪr- ~s z
Listerine tdmk 'lɪst ə riːn
listeriosis lɪ ˌstɪər i 'əʊs ɪs -əs; ˌlɪst ɪər•'••
‖ lɪ ˌstɪr i 'oʊs əs
listing 'lɪst ɪŋ ~s z
'listing ˌpaper
listless 'lɪst ləs -lɪs ~ly li ~ness nəs nɪs
Liston 'lɪst ən
Listowel lɪ 'stəʊ əl ‖ -'stoʊ-
Liszt lɪst —Hung [list]
lit lɪt
Lita 'liːt ə ‖ 'liːt̬ ə
Li Tai Po ˌliː ˌtaɪ 'pəʊ ‖ -'poʊ —Chi Lǐ Dài Bái
[³li ⁴tai ²pai]
litan|y 'lɪt ᵊn li ‖ -ᵊn i ~ies iz
Litchfield 'lɪtʃ fiːᵊld
litchi ˌlaɪ 'tʃiː 'lɪtʃ iː, 'liːtʃ-, -i ‖ 'liːtʃ i 'laɪtʃ i
~s z
lit crit ˌlɪt 'krɪt
lite laɪt
-lite laɪt — **chrysolite** 'krɪs ə laɪt
liter 'liːt ə ‖ 'liːt̬ ᵊr ~s z
literacy 'lɪt_ᵊr əs i ‖ 'lɪt̬ ᵊr- →'lɪtr əs i
literal 'lɪt_ᵊr əl ‖ 'lɪt̬ ᵊr əl →'lɪtr əl ~ism ˌɪz əm
~ist/s ɪst/s §əst/s ‖ əst/s ~ly i ~ness nəs nɪs
~s z
literar|ly 'lɪt_ᵊr ər li △'lɪtr li ‖ 'lɪt̬ ə rer li ~ily
əl i ɪ li ~iness i nəs -nɪs
literate 'lɪt_ᵊr ət -ɪt ‖ 'lɪt̬ ᵊr ət →'lɪtr ət ~s s
literati ˌlɪt ə 'rɑːt iː ‖ ˌlɪt̬ ə 'rɑːt̬ i

literatim ˌlɪt ə ˈrɑːt ɪm -ˈreɪt-, §-əm ‖ -ˈreɪt̬ əm -ˈrɑːt̬-
literature ˈlɪtr ətʃ ə -ɪtʃ-; -ə tʃʊə, -ɪ-; ˈlɪt ər • • ‖ ˈlɪt̬ ər ətʃ ər -ə tʃʊr, →ˈlɪtr • • ~s z
-lith lɪθ — **megalith** ˈmeg ə lɪθ
litharge ˈlɪθ ɑːdʒ ‖ -ɑːrdʒ lɪ ˈθɑːrdʒ
lithe laɪð ‖ laɪθ
lithe|ly ˈlaɪð |li ‖ ˈlaɪθ- ~**ness** nəs nɪs
lithesome ˈlaɪð səm ‖ ˈlaɪθ-
Lithgow ˈlɪθ gəʊ ‖ -goʊ
lithia ˈlɪθ i‿ə
lithic ˈlɪθ ɪk
-lithic ˈlɪθ ɪk — **megalithic** ˌmeg ə ˈlɪθ ɪk ◂
lithium ˈlɪθ i‿əm
litho ˈlaɪθ əʊ ‖ -oʊ
litho- comb. form
  with stress-neutral suffix ¦lɪθ əʊ ‖ -ə —
  lithosphere ˈlɪθ əʊ sfɪə ‖ -ə sfɪr
  with stress-imposing suffix lɪ ˈθɒ+ ‖ -ˈθɑː+ —
  lithotomy lɪ ˈθɒt əm i ‖ -ˈθɑːt̬-
lithograph ˈlɪθ əʊ grɑːf ˈlaɪθ-, -græf ‖ -ə græf ~**s** s
lithographer lɪ ˈθɒg rəf ə laɪ- ‖ -ˈθɑːg rəf ər ~**s** z
lithographic ˌlɪθ əʊ ˈgræf ɪk ◂ ˌlaɪθ- ‖ -ə- ~**ally** ᵊl‿i
lithography lɪ ˈθɒg rəf i laɪ- ‖ -ˈθɑːg-
Lithuania ˌlɪθ ju ˈeɪn i‿ə ‚•u- ‖ ˌlɪθ u-
Lithuanian ˌlɪθ ju ˈeɪn i‿ən ◂ ‚•u- ‖ ˌlɪθ u- ~**s** z
litigant ˈlɪt ɪg ənt -əg- ‖ ˈlɪt̬ ɪg- ~**s** s
liti|gate ˈlɪt ɪ |geɪt -ə- ‖ ˈlɪt̬ ə- ~**gated** geɪt ɪd -əd ‖ geɪt̬ əd ~**gates** geɪts ~**gating** geɪt ɪŋ ‖ geɪt̬ ɪŋ
litigation ˌlɪt ɪ ˈgeɪʃ ᵊn -ə- ‖ ˌlɪt̬- ~**s** z
litigious lɪ ˈtɪdʒ əs lə- ~**ly** li ~**ness** nəs nɪs
litmus ˈlɪt məs
  ˈlitmus ˌpaper; ˈlitmus test
litotes ˈlaɪt əʊ tiːz laɪ ˈtəʊt iːz ‖ ˈlaɪt̬ ə tiːz ˈlɪt̬-; laɪ ˈtoʊt iːz
litre ˈliːt ə ‖ ˈliːt̬ ər ~**s** z
litter ˈlɪt ə ‖ ˈlɪt̬ ər ~**ed** d **littering** ˈlɪt ər ɪŋ ‖ ˈlɪt̬ ər ɪŋ ~**s** z
litterateur, littérateur ˌlɪt‿ᵊr ə ˈtɜː ‖ ˌlɪt̬ ər ə ˈtɜː -ˈtʊᵊr; →ˌlɪtr ə' • • —Fr [li te ʁa tœːʁ] ~**s** z
litterbag ˈlɪt ə bæg ‖ ˈlɪt̬ ər- ~**s** z
litterbin ˈlɪt ə bɪn ‖ ˈlɪt̬ ər- ~**s** z
litterbug ˈlɪt ə bʌg ‖ ˈlɪt̬ ər- ~**s** z
litterlout ˈlɪt ə laʊt ‖ ˈlɪt̬ ər- ~**s** s
little, L~ ˈlɪt ᵊl ‖ ˈlɪt̬ ᵊl **least** liːst **less** les **littler** ˈlɪt ᵊl‿ə ‖ -ᵊr
  ˌlittle ˈfinger; ˌlittle ˌpeople; ˈLittle Rock place in AR; ˌlittle ˈwoman
Littlehampton ˌlɪt ᵊl ˈhæmp tən ◂ ' • •, • • ‖ ˌlɪt̬-
Littlejohn ˈlɪt ᵊl dʒɒn ‖ ˈlɪt̬ ᵊl dʒɑːn
Littler ˈlɪt lə ‖ -lᵊr
Littlestone ˈlɪt ᵊl stən -stəʊn ‖ ˈlɪt̬ ᵊl stoʊn
Littleton ˈlɪt ᵊl tən ‖ ˈlɪt̬-
Litton ˈlɪt ᵊn
littoral ˈlɪt ᵊr ᵊl ‖ ˈlɪt̬-, ˌlɪt̬ ə ˈræl, -ˈrɑːl ~**s** z
liturgic lɪ ˈtɜːdʒ ɪk lə- ‖ -ˈtɜːdʒ- ~**al** ᵊl ~**ally** ᵊl‿i ~**s** s

liturgist ˈlɪt ədʒ ɪst §-əst ‖ ˈlɪt̬ ᵊrdʒ- ~**s** s
liturg|y ˈlɪt ədʒ |li ‖ ˈlɪt̬ ᵊrdʒ |i ~**ies** iz
livable ˈlɪv əb ᵊl
live v lɪv **lived** lɪvd **lives** lɪvz **living** ˈlɪv ɪŋ
live adj, adv laɪv
  ˌlive perˈformance; ˌlive ˈwire
liveable ˈlɪv əb ᵊl
lived-in ˈlɪvd ɪn
live-in ˌlɪv ˈɪn ◂
  ˌlive-in ˈlover
livelihood ˈlaɪv li hʊd ~**s** z
livelong ˈlɪv lɒŋ ˈlaɪv- ‖ -lɔːŋ -lɑːŋ
live|ly, L~ ˈlaɪv |li ~**lier** li‿ə ‖ li‿ᵊr ~**liest** li‿ɪst li‿əst ~**liness** li nəs -nɪs
liven ˈlaɪv ᵊn ~**ed** d ~**ing** ‿ɪŋ ~**s** z
Livens ˈlɪv ᵊnz
liver ˈlɪv ə ‖ -ᵊr ~**s** z
  ˈliver salts; ˈliver ˌsausage; ˈliver spot
Liver Building, bird, symbol of Liverpool ˈlaɪv ə ‖ -ᵊr
liverie... —see **livery**
liverish ˈlɪv ᵊr ɪʃ ~**ness** nəs nɪs
Livermore ˈlɪv ə mɔː ‖ -ᵊr mɔːr -moʊr
Liverpool ˈlɪv ə puːl ‖ -ᵊr-
Liverpudlian ˌlɪv ə ˈpʌd li‿ən ◂ ‖ ‚•ᵊr- ~**s** z
Liversedge ˈlɪv ə sedʒ ‖ -ᵊr-
liverwort ˈlɪv ə wɜːt §-wɔːt ‖ -ᵊr wɜːt -wɔːrt ~**s** s
liverwurst ˈlɪv ə wɜːst ‖ -ᵊr wɜːst -wɔːrst, -wʊʃt
liver|y ˈlɪv ᵊr |i ~**ied** id ~**ies** iz
  ˈlivery ˌcompany; ˈlivery ˌstable
livery|man ˈlɪv ᵊr‿i |mən ~**men** mən men
lives pl of **life** laɪvz
lives 3 sing. of **live** lɪvz
Livesey (i) ˈlɪv si, (ii) -zi
livestock ˈlaɪv stɒk ‖ -stɑːk
Livia ˈlɪv i‿ə
livid ˈlɪv ɪd §-əd ~**ly** li ~**ness** nəs nɪs
living ˈlɪv ɪŋ ~**s** z
  ˌliving ˈfossil; ˌliving ˈmemory; ˈliving room; ˌliving ˈstandard; ˌliving ˈwage
Livings ˈlɪv ɪŋz
Livingston ˈlɪv ɪŋ stən
Livingstone ˈlɪv ɪŋ stən -stəʊn ‖ -stoʊn
Livoni|a lɪ ˈvəʊn i‿ə ‖ -ˈvoʊn- ~**an/s** ən/z
Livy ˈlɪv i
lixivi|ate lɪk ˈsɪv i |eɪt ~**ated** eɪt ɪd -əd ‖ eɪt̬ əd ~**ates** eɪts ~**ating** eɪt ɪŋ ‖ eɪt̬ ɪŋ
Liz lɪz
Liza (i) ˈlaɪz ə (ii) ˈliːz ə
lizard, L~ ˈlɪz əd ‖ -ᵊrd ~**s** z
Lizzie ˈlɪz i
Ljubljana ˌlʊb li ˈɑːn ə ‖ ˌluːb- —Slovene [lʲu ˈblʲa: na]
'll ᵊl, əl —Following a word other than a pronoun this contracted form is pronounced as a separate syllable, thus Jim'll do it ˈdʒɪm ᵊl ˌduː ɪt, Lucy'll do it ˈluːs i‿əl ˌduː ɪt. See, however, the entries **I'll, he'll, she'll, there'll, they'll, we'll, you'll**
llama ˈlɑːm ə ~**s** z

Liquids

The English **liquids** are l and r. Both are usually voiced APPROXIMANTS. The difference between them is that

- l is ALVEOLAR and **lateral** (= the air escapes over one or both sides of the tongue, passing round the tongue tip);
- r is POST-ALVEOLAR and **median** (= the air escapes over the tongue tip, while the sides of the tongue are pressed firmly against the roof of the mouth).

In both cases there is some ALLOPHONIC variation:

(i) Both may be voiceless because of the ASPIRATION of a preceding plosive, e.g. **play** pleɪ, **pray** preɪ.

(ii) In RP l is clear (= has e-resonance) before a vowel sound or j, but **dark** (= has ʊ-resonance; allophonic symbol ɫ) elsewhere. Hence **like** laɪk, **value** 'væl juː (clear), **milk** mɪlk (= mɪɫk), **fall** fɔːl (= fɔːɫ). In AmE, l may be fairly dark everywhere.

(iii) In a consonant cluster after t or d, r is made FRICATIVE instead of approximant. The result is that tr and dr form AFFRICATES, e.g. **train** treɪn, **drain** dreɪn.

Llan *prefix in Welsh names* læn θlæn, ɫæn —*In Welsh this is* ɫan, *usually anglicized as* læn *or, when unstressed,* lən. *The Welsh sound (a voiceless alveolar lateral fricative) is however sometimes imitated by the non-Welsh as the cluster* θl, *or even as* xl. *No AmE forms are given for the Welsh names that follow.*

Llanberis læn 'ber ɪs θlæn- —*Welsh* [ɫan 'be ris]

Llandaff 'lænd əf 'ɫæn dæf, 'θlæn-, ‚ ‚•'• —*Welsh* Llandaf [ɫan 'da:v]

Llandeilo læn 'daɪl əʊ 'θlæn- —*Welsh* [ɫan 'dəi lo]

Llandovery læn 'dʌv ər‿i θlæn- —*Welsh* Llanymddyfri [‚ɫan əm 'ðəv ri]

Llandrindod læn 'drɪn dɒd θlæn- —*Welsh* [ɫan 'drin dod]

Llandudno læn 'dɪd nəʊ θlæn-, -'dʌd- —*Welsh* [ɫan 'dïd no, -'did-]

Llanelli lə 'neθ li ɫə-, læ-, θlæ-, θlə- —*Welsh* [ɫan 'eɫ i]

Llanfairfechan ‚læn feə 'fek ən ‚θlæn-, -fə-, ‚•'•,vaɪ‿ə'•• —*Welsh* [‚ɫan vair 've χan]

Llanfairpwll ‚læn feə 'puːɫ -,vaɪ‿ə-, -'pʊɫ *Also* **Llanfairpwllgwyngyll** ‚læn vaɪ‿ə puːɫ 'gwɪn gɪɫ →-'gwɪŋ- —*usually called* **Llanfair P.G.** ‚læn feə ‚pi: 'dʒi: ‚θlæn-, ‚•'•,vaɪ‿ə,•'• —*The full form, famous for its length, is* Llanfairpwllgwyngyllgogerychwyrn-drobwll-llandysiliogogogoch —*Welsh* [‚ɫan vair puɫ ‚gwïn gïɫ go ‚ger ə ‚χwərn ‚dro buɫ ‚ɫan də ‚sil jo ‚go go 'go:χ] *(or with* [ɪ] *for* [ï], [pʊɫ, buɫ] *for* [puɫ, buɫ])

Llangollen læn 'gɒθ lən θlæn-, →læŋ- —*Welsh* [ɫan 'go ɫen]

Llangranog læn 'græn ɒg θlæn-, →læŋ-, -əg —*Welsh* [ɫan 'gra nog]

Llangurig læn 'gɪr ɪg θlæn-, →læŋ- —*Welsh* [ɫan 'gɨ rɪg, -'gi-]

Llanrwst læn 'ruːst θlæn- —*Welsh* [ɫan 'ru:st]

Llantrisant læn 'trɪs ənt

Llanuwchllyn læn 'juːk lɪn θlæn-, lən-, θlən-, -'juːx- —*Welsh* [ɫan 'iuχ ɫïn, -'iuχ ɫin]

Llanwrtyd læn 'ʊət ɪd θlæn- —*Welsh* [ɫan 'ʊr tɪd, -tïd]

Llareggub lə 'reg əb læ-, θlə-, θlæ-, -ʌb —*not a real Welsh name*

Llewelyn lə 'wel ɪn θlə-; lu 'el-, θlu- —*Welsh* ['ɫwe lin; ɫe 'we lin, -lin]

Lleyn liːn θliːn, leɪn, θleɪn —*Welsh* Llŷn [ɫïːn, ɫiːn]

Lloret lə 'ret —*Sp* [ʎo 'ret, jo-], *Catalan* [ʎu 'ret ʃ

Lloyd lɔɪd

Llywelyn lə 'wel ɪn θlə-, §-ən; lu 'el-, θlu- —*Welsh* [ɫə 'we lin, -lin]

lo ləʊ ‖ loʊ
  ‚lo and be'hold

loach, Loach ləʊtʃ ‖ loʊtʃ **loaches** 'ləʊtʃ ɪz -əz ‖ 'loʊtʃ əz

load ləʊd ‖ loʊd **loaded** 'ləʊd ɪd -əd ‖ 'loʊd əd
  loading 'ləʊd ɪŋ ‖ 'loʊd ɪŋ **loads** ləʊdz ‖ loʊdz
  'load ‚factor

loadsamoney ‚ləʊdz ə ‚mʌn i ‖ 'loʊdz-
loadstar 'ləʊd stɑː ‖ 'loʊd stɑːr ~s z

loaf ləʊf ‖ loʊf **loafed** ləʊft ‖ loʊft **loafing** 'ləʊf ɪŋ ‖ 'loʊf ɪŋ **loafs** ləʊfs ‖ loʊfs **loaves** ləʊvz ‖ loʊvz

loafer 'ləʊf ə ‖ 'loʊf ər ~s z
loafsugar 'ləʊf ‚ʃʊg ə ‖ 'loʊf ‚ʃʊg ər

L

loam ləʊm ‖ loʊm
loamy 'ləʊm i ‖ 'loʊm i
loan ləʊn ‖ loʊn **loaned** ləʊnd ‖ loʊnd
  loaning 'ləʊn ɪŋ ‖ 'loʊn ɪŋ **loans**
  ləʊnz ‖ loʊnz
loanword 'ləʊn wɜːd ‖ 'loʊn wɝːd ~s z
loath ləʊθ △ləʊð ‖ loʊθ loʊð
loathe ləʊð ‖ loʊð **loathed** ləʊðd ‖ loʊðd
  loather/s 'ləʊð ə/z ‖ 'loʊð ər/z **loathes**
  ləʊðz ‖ loʊðz **loathing/ly** 'ləʊð ɪŋ /
  li ‖ 'loʊð ɪŋ /li
loathsome 'ləʊð səm 'ləʊθ- ‖ 'loʊð- 'loʊθ-
  ~**ly** li ~**ness** nəs nɪs
loaves ləʊvz ‖ loʊvz
lob lɒb ‖ lɑːb **lobbed** lɒbd ‖ lɑːbd **lobbing**
  'lɒb ɪŋ ‖ 'lɑːb ɪŋ **lobs** lɒbz ‖ lɑːbz
lobate 'ləʊb eɪt ‖ 'loʊb-
lobb|y 'lɒb |i ‖ 'lɑːb |i ~**ied** id ~**ies** iz ~**ying**
  i_ɪŋ
lobbyist 'lɒb i ɪst -əst ‖ 'lɑːb- ~s s
lobe ləʊb ‖ loʊb **lobed** ləʊbd ‖ loʊbd **lobes**
  ləʊbz ‖ loʊbz
lobelia ləʊ 'biːl i_ə ‖ loʊ- ~s z
lobeline 'ləʊb ə liːn ‖ 'loʊb-
lobloll|y 'lɒb ˌlɒl |i ‖ 'lɑːb ˌlɑːl |i ~**ies** iz
lobotomis|e, lobotomiz|e ləʊ
  'bɒt ə maɪz ‖ loʊ 'bɑːt̬- lə- ~**ed** d ~**es** ɪz əz
  ~**ing** ɪŋ
lobotom|y ləʊ 'bɒt əm |i ‖ loʊ 'bɑːt̬- lə- ~**ies**
  iz
lobscouse 'lɒb skaʊs ‖ 'lɑːb-
lobster 'lɒb stə ‖ 'lɑːb stər ~s z
lobsterpot 'lɒb stə pɒt ‖ 'lɑːb stər pɑːt ~s s
lobular 'lɒb jʊl ə ‖ 'lɑːb jəl ər
lobule 'lɒb juːl ‖ 'lɑːb- ~s z
local, Local 'ləʊk ᵊl ‖ 'loʊk ᵊl ~**ly** i ~s z
  ˌlocal ˌarea 'network; ˌlocal au'thority;
  ˌlocal 'colour; ˌlocal 'derby; ˌlocal 'option;
  'local time, · • '·
lo-cal '*low-calorie*' ˌləʊ 'kæl ◄ ‖ ˌloʊ-
locale ləʊ 'kɑːl ‖ loʊ 'kæl ~s z
localis... —*see* **localiz...**
localism 'ləʊk ᵊl ˌɪz əm ‖ 'loʊk- ~s z
localit|y ləʊ 'kæl ət i -ɪt- ‖ loʊ 'kæl ət̬ i ~**ies**
  iz
localization ˌləʊk ᵊl aɪ 'zeɪʃ ᵊn -ᵊl ɪ- ‖ ˌloʊk
  ᵊl ə- ~s z
localiz|e 'ləʊk ə laɪz -ᵊl aɪz ‖ 'loʊk- ~**ed** d ~**es**
  ɪz əz ~**ing** ɪŋ
locally 'ləʊk ᵊl i ‖ 'loʊk-
Locarno ləʊ 'kɑːn əʊ lɒ- ‖ loʊ 'kɑːrn oʊ —*It*
  [lo 'kar no]
loc|ate ləʊ 'k|eɪt ‖ 'loʊk eɪt loʊ 'k|eɪt ~**ated**
  eɪt ɪd -əd ‖ eɪt̬ əd ~**ates** eɪts ~**ating**
  eɪt ɪŋ ‖ eɪt̬ ɪŋ
location ləʊ 'keɪʃ ᵊn ‖ loʊ- ~s z
locative 'lɒk ət ɪv ‖ 'lɑːk ət̬ ɪv ~s z
loch lɒx lɒk ‖ lɑːk lɑːx **lochs** lɒxs lɒks ‖ lɑːks
  lɑːxs
Lochearnhead lɒx ˌɜːn 'hed lɒk- ‖ lɑːk ˌɝːn-
  lɑːx-
Lochgilphead lɒx 'gɪlp hed lɒk- ‖ lɑːk- lɑːx-
Lochinvar ˌlɒx ɪn 'vɑː ˌlɒk- ‖ ˌlɑːk ən 'vɑːr

Lochinver lɒ 'xɪn və -'kɪn- ‖ lɑː 'kɪn vər
loci 'ləʊs aɪ 'ləʊk-, 'lɒk-, -iː ‖ 'loʊs aɪ 'loʊk-, -iː
lock, Lock lɒk ‖ lɑːk **locked** lɒkt ‖ lɑːkt
  locking 'lɒk ɪŋ ‖ 'lɑːk ɪŋ **locks** lɒks ‖ lɑːks
  'lock ˌkeeper
Locke lɒk ‖ lɑːk
locker 'lɒk ə ‖ 'lɑːk ər ~s z
  'locker room
Lockerbie 'lɒk əb i ‖ 'lɑːk ərb i
locker-room 'lɒk ə ruːm -rʊm ‖ 'lɑːk ər-
locket 'lɒk ɪt §-ət ‖ 'lɑːk- ~s s
Lockhart *(i)* 'lɒk ət ‖ 'lɑːk ᵊrt, *(ii)* -hɑːt ‖ -hɑːrt
Lockheed 'lɒk hiːd ‖ 'lɑːk-
lockjaw 'lɒk dʒɔː ‖ 'lɑːk- -dʒɑː
locknut 'lɒk nʌt ‖ 'lɑːk- ~s s
lockout 'lɒk aʊt ‖ 'lɑːk- ~s s
Locksley 'lɒks li ‖ 'lɑːks-
locksmith 'lɒk smɪθ ‖ 'lɑːk- ~s s
lockstitch 'lɒk stɪtʃ ‖ 'lɑːk- ~**ed** t ~**es** ɪz əz
  ~**ing** ɪŋ
lockup 'lɒk ʌp ‖ 'lɑːk- ~s s
Lockwood 'lɒk wʊd ‖ 'lɑːk-
Lockyer 'lɒk jə ‖ 'lɑːk jər
loco 'ləʊk əʊ ‖ 'loʊk oʊ ~s z
locomotion
  ˌləʊk ə 'məʊʃ ᵊn ‖ ˌloʊk ə 'moʊʃ ᵊn
locomotive ˌləʊk ə 'məʊt ɪv ◄ '·· ··
  ‖ ˌloʊk ə 'moʊt̬ ɪv ◄ ~s z
locomotor ˌləʊk əʊ
  'məʊt ə ◄ ‖ ˌloʊk ə 'moʊt̬ ər ◄
  ˌloco̩motor a'taxia
locoweed 'ləʊk əʊ wiːd ‖ 'loʊk oʊ-
Locris 'ləʊk rɪs 'lɒk-, -rəs ‖ 'loʊk-
locum 'ləʊk əm 'lɒk- ‖ 'loʊk- ~s z
  ˌlocum 'tenens 'ten enz 'tiːn- ‖ -ənz
locus 'ləʊk əs 'lɒk- ‖ 'loʊk-
  ˌlocus 'classicus 'klæs ɪk əs; ˌlocus 'standi
  'stænd aɪ
locust 'ləʊk əst ‖ 'loʊk- ~s s
locution ləʊ 'kjuːʃ ᵊn lɒ- ‖ loʊ- ~s z
locutionary ləʊ 'kjuːʃ ᵊn ər_i -ᵊn_ər i
  ‖ loʊ 'kjuːʃ ə ner i
Lod lɒd ‖ loʊd
lode, Lode ləʊd ‖ loʊd *(= load)* **lodes**
  ləʊdz ‖ loʊdz
loden 'ləʊd ᵊn ‖ 'loʊd ᵊn
lodestar 'ləʊd stɑː ‖ 'loʊd stɑːr ~s z
lodestone 'ləʊd stəʊn ‖ 'loʊd stoʊn ~s z
lodge, Lodge lɒdʒ ‖ lɑːdʒ **lodged**
  lɒdʒd ‖ lɑːdʒd **lodges** 'lɒdʒ ɪz -əz ‖ 'lɑːdʒ-
  lodging 'lɒdʒ ɪŋ ‖ 'lɑːdʒ ɪŋ
lodger 'lɒdʒ ə ‖ 'lɑːdʒ ər ~s z
lodging 'lɒdʒ ɪŋ ‖ 'lɑːdʒ ɪŋ ~s z
  'lodging house
lodgment 'lɒdʒ mənt ‖ 'lɑːdʒ- ~s s
Lodi *places in US* 'ləʊd aɪ ‖ 'loʊd-
Lodore ləʊ 'dɔː ‖ loʊ 'dɔːr
Lodz wʊdʒ wuːtʃ ‖ loʊdz lɑːdz, wuːdʒ —*Polish*
  Łódź [wutɕ]
Loeb ləʊb lɜːb ‖ loʊb —*Ger* [løːp]
loess, löss 'ləʊ es -ɪs, -əs; lɜːs ‖ les lʌs, 'loʊ əs,
  lɝːs —*Ger* [lœs, løːs]
Loewe 'ləʊ i ‖ loʊ

Lofoten ləʊ ˈfəʊt ən ˈ•,•• ‖ ˈloʊ foʊt ən
—Norw [ˈluː fut ən]
loft lɒft ‖ lɔːft lɑːft **lofts** lɒfts ‖ lɔːfts lɑːfts
Lofthouse ˈlɒft haʊs -əs ‖ ˈlɔːft- ˈlɑːft-
Lofting ˈlɒft ɪŋ ‖ ˈlɔːft ɪŋ ˈlɑːft-
Loftus ˈlɒft əs ‖ ˈlɔːft- ˈlɑːft-
loft|y ˈlɒft li ‖ ˈlɔːft li ˈlɑːft- **~ier** i‿ə ‖ i‿ər
~iest i‿ɪst i‿əst **~ily** ɪ li əl i **~iness** i nəs i nɪs
log lɒg ‖ lɔːg lɑːg **logged** lɒgd ‖ lɔːgd lɑːgd
logging ˈlɒg ɪŋ ‖ ˈlɔːg ɪŋ ˈlɑːg-
ˌlog ˈcabin
-log lɒg ‖ lɔːg lɑːg — **catalog** ˈkæt ə lɒg -əl ɒg
‖ ˈkæt̬ əl ɔːg -ɑːg
Logan ˈləʊg ən ‖ ˈloʊg-
loganberr|y ˈləʊg ən bər‿li →ˈ•ŋ-, →ˈ•əm-,
-ˌber li ‖ ˈloʊg ən ˌber li **~ies** iz
logarithm ˈlɒg ə rɪð əm -rɪθ əm ‖ ˈlɔːg- ˈlɑːg-
~s z
logarithmic ˌlɒg ə ˈrɪð mɪk ◄ -ˈrɪθ- ‖ ˌlɔːg-
ˌlɑːg- **~al** əl **~ally** əl‿i
logbook ˈlɒg bʊk §-buːk ‖ ˈlɔːg- ˈlɑːg- **~s** s
loge ləʊʒ ‖ loʊʒ **loges** ˈləʊʒ ɪz -əz ‖ ˈloʊʒ-
logg... —see log
logger ˈlɒg ə ‖ ˈlɔːg ər ˈlɑːg- **~s** z
loggerhead ˈlɒg ə hed ‖ ˈlɔːg ər- ˈlɑːg- **~s** z
loggia ˈlɒdʒ i‿ə ˈləʊdʒ- ‖ ˈloʊdʒ ə ˈloʊdʒ i‿ə
~s z
logic ˈlɒdʒ ɪk ‖ ˈlɑːdʒ- **~s** s
Logica tdmk ˈlɒdʒ ɪk ə ‖ ˈlɑːdʒ-
logical ˈlɒdʒ ɪk əl ‖ ˈlɑːdʒ- **~ly** ˍi **~ness** nəs
nɪs
-logical ˈlɒdʒ ɪk əl ‖ ˈlɑːdʒ- — **cytological**
ˌsaɪt əʊ ˈlɒdʒ ɪk əl ◄ ˌsaɪt̬ ə ˈlɑːdʒ-
logicality ˌlɒdʒ ɪ ˈkæl ət i §,•ə-, -ɪt i
‖ ˌlɑːdʒ ə ˈkæl ət̬ i
logician ləʊ ˈdʒɪʃ ən lɒ- ‖ loʊ- **~s** z
Logie ˈləʊg i ‖ ˈloʊg i
logi... —see logy
-logist stress-imposing lədʒ ɪst §-əst —
physiologist ˌfɪz i ˈɒl ədʒ ɪst §-əst ‖ -ˈɑːl-
logistic ləʊ ˈdʒɪst ɪk lɒ- ‖ loʊ- **~al** əl **~ally** əl‿i
~s s
logjam ˈlɒg dʒæm ‖ ˈlɔːg- ˈlɑːg- **~s** z
loglog ˌlɒg ˈlɒg ‖ ˌlɔːg ˈlɔːg ˌlɑːg ˈlɑːg
logo, Logo, LOGO ˈləʊg əʊ ˈlɒg- ‖ ˈloʊg oʊ
~s z
logo- comb. form
with stress-neutral suffix ˌlɒg əʊ ‖ ˌlɔːg ə
ˌlɑːg ə — **logographic** ˌlɒg əʊ
ˈgræf ɪk ◄ ‖ ˌlɔːg ə- ˌlɑːg-
with stress-imposing suffix lɒ ˈgɒ+ ‖ loʊ ˈgɑː+
— **logography** lɒ ˈgɒg rəf i ‖ loʊ ˈgɑːg-
logogram ˈlɒg ə græm ‖ ˈlɔːg- ˈlɑːg- **~s** z
logon ˌlɒg ˈɒn ‖ ˌlɔːg ˈɑːn ˌlɑːg-, -ˈɔːn **~s** z
logopaed|ic, logoped|ic
ˌlɒg ə ˈpiːd| ɪk ◄ ‖ ˌlɔːg-, ˌlɑːg- **~ics** ɪks
~ist/s ɪst/s əst/s
logorrhea, logorrhoea ˌlɒg ə ˈriː‿ə ‖ ˌlɔːg-
ˌlɑːg-
Logos, logos ˈlɒg ɒs ˈləʊg- ‖ ˈloʊg ɑːs -ɔːs,
-oʊs
logotype ˈlɒg əʊ taɪp ‖ ˈlɔːg ə- ˈlɑːg- **~s** s

logroll|er/s ˈlɒg ˌrəʊl lə/z →-ˌrɒʊl-
‖ ˈlɔːg ˌroʊl lər/z ˈlɑːg- **~ing** ɪŋ
Logue ləʊg ‖ loʊg
-logue lɒg ‖ lɔːg lɑːg — **monologue**
ˈmɒn ə lɒg ‖ ˈmɑːn ə lɔːg -lɑːg
logwood ˈlɒg wʊd ‖ ˈlɔːg- ˈlɑːg-
log|y ˈləʊg li ‖ ˈloʊg li **~ier** i‿ə ‖ i‿ər **~iest** i‿ɪst
i‿əst **~ily** ɪ li əl i **~iness** i nəs i nɪs
-logy stress-imposing lədʒ i — **analogy**
ə ˈnæl ədʒ i
Lohengrin ˈləʊ ən grɪn -ɪn-, →-əŋ- ‖ ˈloʊ-
—Ger [ˈloː ən gʁiːn]
loin lɔɪn **loins** lɔɪnz
loin|cloth ˈlɔɪn |klɒθ →ˈlɔɪŋ-, -klɔːθ ‖ -|klɔːθ
-klɑːθ **~cloths** klɒθs klɒðz, klɔːðz, klɔːθs
‖ klɔːðz klɔːθs, klɑːðz, klɑːθs
Loire lwɑː ‖ lwɑːr —Fr [lwaːʁ]
Lois ˈləʊ ɪs §-əs ‖ ˈloʊ-
loiter ˈlɔɪt ə ‖ ˈlɔɪt̬ ər **~ed** d **loitering**
ˈlɔɪt‿ər ɪŋ ‖ ˈlɔɪt̬ ər ɪŋ **~s** z
Lola ˈləʊl ə ‖ ˈloʊl ə
Lolita lɒ ˈliːt ə ləʊ- ‖ loʊ ˈliːt̬ ə **~s** z
loll lɒl ‖ lɑːl **lolled** lɒld ‖ lɑːld **lolling**
ˈlɒl ɪŋ ‖ ˈlɑːl ɪŋ **lolls** lɒlz ‖ lɑːlz
Lollard ˈlɒl əd -ɑːd ‖ ˈlɑːl ərd **~s** z
lollie... —see lolly
lollipop ˈlɒl i pɒp ‖ ˈlɑːl i pɑːp **~s** s
ˈlollipop man, ˈlollipop ˌwoman
lollo rosso ˌlɒl əʊ ˈrɒs əʊ ‖ ˌlɑːl oʊ ˈrɑːs oʊ
ˌloʊl-, -ˈrous- —It [ˌlɒl lo ˈros so]
lollop ˈlɒl əp ‖ ˈlɑːl- **~ed** t **~ing** ɪŋ **~s** s
loll|y ˈlɒl li ‖ ˈlɑːl li **~ies** iz
Loma Prieta ˌləʊm ə pri ˈet ə
‖ ˌloʊm ə pri ˈeɪt̬ ə- -ˈet̬-
Lomas ˈləʊm əs -æs ‖ ˈloʊm æs
Lomax ˈləʊm æks -əks ‖ ˈloʊm-
Lombard ˈlɒm bəd ˈlʌm-, -bɑːd ‖ ˈlɑːm bərd
-bɑːrd **~s** z
ˈLombard Street
Lombardo lɒm ˈbɑːd əʊ ‖ lɑːm ˈbɑːrd oʊ —It
[lom ˈbar do]
Lombardy ˈlɒm bəd i ˈlʌm- ‖ -bərd i -bɑːrd i
ˌLombardy ˈpoplar
Lombok ˈlɒm bɒk ‖ ˈlɑːm bɑːk •ˈ•
Lombrosian lɒm ˈbrəʊz i‿ən ‖ lɑːm ˈbroʊz-
-ˈbroʊʒ ən **~s** z
Lombroso lɒm ˈbrəʊz əʊ ‖ lɑːm ˈbroʊz oʊ —It
[lom ˈbro so]
Lome, Lomé ˈləʊ meɪ ‖ loʊ ˈmeɪ —Fr [lɔ me]
Lomu ˈləʊm uː ‖ ˈloʊm-
Lomond ˈləʊm ənd ‖ ˈloʊm-
London ˈlʌnd ən (!)
ˌLondon ˈAirport; ˌLondon ˈBridge;
ˌLondon ˈpride
Londonderry ˈlʌnd ən ˌder i -ənd‿ər i;
ˌlʌnd ən ˈder i◄ —Lord L~ is ˈlʌnd ənd‿ər i
Londoner ˈlʌnd ən ə ‖ -ər **~s** z
lone ləʊn ‖ loʊn
ˌLone ˈRanger; ˌlone ˈwolf
lone|ly ˈləʊn |li ‖ ˈloʊn- **~lier** li‿ə ‖ li‿ər **~liest**
li‿ɪst li‿əst **~liness** li nəs li nɪs
ˌlonely ˈhearts, ˈ•••
loner ˈləʊn ə ‖ ˈloʊn ər **~s** z

lonesome 'ləʊn səm ‖ 'loʊn- **~ly** li **~ness** nəs nɪs

long, Long lɒŋ ‖ lɔːŋ laːŋ **longed** lɒŋd ‖ lɔːŋd laːŋd **longer** 'lɒŋ gə ‖ 'lɔːŋ gᵊr 'laːŋ- **longest** 'lɒŋ gɪst -gəst ‖ 'lɔːŋ gəst 'laːŋ- **longing** 'lɒŋ ɪŋ ‖ 'lɔːŋ ɪŋ 'laːŋ- **longs** lɒŋz ‖ lɔːŋz laːŋz
'Long Beach; ˌlong di'vision; ˌlong 'haul; ₍ₗ₎Long 'Island, Long ˌIsland 'Sound, ˌ•ˌ••'•; 'long johns; 'long jump, 'long ˌjumper; 'long shot; ˌlong 'suit; ˌlong 'ton; ˌlong 'vac, ˌlong va'cation; ˌlong 'wave, '••

Longannet lɒŋ 'æn ɪt -ət ‖ lɔːŋ- laːŋ-
longboat 'lɒŋ bəʊt ‖ 'lɔːŋ boʊt 'laːŋ- **~s** s
longbow 'lɒŋ bəʊ ‖ 'lɔːŋ boʊ 'laːŋ- **~s** z
Longbridge 'lɒŋ brɪdʒ ‖ 'lɔːŋ- 'laːŋ-
long-distance ˌlɒŋ 'dɪst ᵊnts ◄ ‖ ˌlɔːŋ- ˌlaːŋ-
long-drawn-out ˌlɒŋ drɔːn 'aʊt ◄ ‖ ˌlɔːŋ- ˌlaːŋ drɑːn-
longer comparative adj 'lɒŋ gə ‖ 'lɔːŋ gᵊr 'laːŋ- —But the agent noun longer 'one that longs', if ever used, is pronounced without g, as -ə ‖ -ᵊr
longeron 'lɒndʒ ər ən ‖ 'laːndʒ ə rɑːn **~s** z
longest 'lɒŋ gɪst -gəst ‖ 'lɔːŋ- 'laːŋ-
longevity lɒn 'dʒev ət i lɒŋ-, -ɪt- ‖ laːn 'dʒev əṭ i lɔːn-
Longfellow 'lɒŋ ˌfel əʊ ‖ 'lɔːŋ ˌfel oʊ 'laːŋ-
Longford 'lɒŋ fəd ‖ 'lɔːŋ fᵊrd 'laːŋ-
long-haired ˌlɒŋ 'heəd ◄ ‖ ˌlɔːŋ 'heᵊrd ◄ ˌlaːŋ-
longhand 'lɒŋ hænd ‖ 'lɔːŋ- 'laːŋ-
long-haul ˌlɒŋ 'hɔːl ◄ '•• ‖ ˌlɔːŋ- ˌlaːŋ 'haːl ◄
long-headed ˌlɒŋ 'hed ɪd ◄ -əd ‖ ˌlɔːŋ- ˌlaːŋ-
longhop 'lɒŋ hɒp ‖ 'lɔːŋ haːp 'laːŋ- **~s** s
longhorn 'lɒŋ hɔːn ‖ 'lɔːŋ hɔːrn 'laːŋ- **~s** z
Longhurst 'lɒŋ hɜːst ‖ 'lɔːŋ hɜːst 'laːŋ-
Longines tdmk 'lɒndʒ iːn ‖ laːn 'dʒiːn
longing 'lɒŋ ɪŋ ‖ 'lɔːŋ ɪŋ 'laːŋ- **~ly** li **~s** z
Longinus lɒn 'dʒaɪn əs lɒŋ 'giːn- ‖ laːn-
longish 'lɒŋ ɪʃ 'lɔːŋ- ‖ 'lɔːŋ- 'laːŋ-

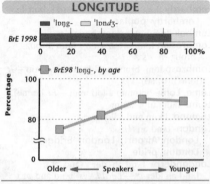

LONGITUDE

■ 'lɒŋg- □ 'lɒndʒ-

BrE 1998

0 20 40 60 80 100%

■ BrE98 'lɒŋg-, by age

Percentage
100
80
0
Older ◄── Speakers ──► Younger

longitude 'lɒŋ gɪ tjuːd -gə-, -dɪ-, -tɪ-, →§-tʃuːd; 'lɒndʒ ɪ-, -ə- ‖ 'laːndʒ ə tuːd -tjuːd —BrE 1998 poll panel preference 'lɒŋg- 85%, 'lɒndʒ- 15%. Several respondents spontaneously mentioned 'lɒŋ dɪ-, which was not given as an option in the questionnaire. **~s** z

longitudinal ˌlɒŋ gɪ 'tjuːd ɪn ᵊl ◄ ˌ•gə-, ˌlɒndʒ ɪ-, ˌ•ə-, →§-'tʃuːd-, -ᵊn_ᵊl ‖ ˌlaːndʒ ə 'tuːd ᵊn_ᵊl ◄ -'tjuːd- **~ly** i
Longland 'lɒŋ lənd ‖ 'lɔːŋ- 'laːŋ-
Longleat 'lɒŋ liːt ‖ 'lɔːŋ- 'laːŋ-
long-lived ˌlɒŋ 'lɪvd ◄ ‖ ˌlɔːŋ 'laɪvd ◄ ˌlaːŋ-, -'lɪvd ◄ (*)
Longman 'lɒŋ mən ‖ 'lɔːŋ- 'laːŋ-
Longobardi ˌlɒŋ gəʊ 'baːd i -iː ‖ ˌlɔːŋ gə 'baːrd i ˌlaːŋ-, -aɪ
long-playing ˌlɒŋ 'pleɪ ɪŋ ◄ ‖ ˌlɔːŋ- ˌlaːŋ- ˌlong-ˌplaying 'record
long-range ˌlɒŋ 'reɪndʒ ◄ ‖ ˌlɔːŋ- ˌlaːŋ- ˌlong-range 'missiles
Longridge 'lɒŋ grɪdʒ -rɪdʒ ‖ 'lɔːŋ- 'laːŋ-
longship 'lɒŋ ʃɪp ‖ 'lɔːŋ- 'laːŋ- **~s** s
longshore|man 'lɒŋ ʃɔː |mən ‖ 'lɔːŋ ʃɔːr- 'laːŋ-, -ʃoʊr- **~men** mən men
longsighted ˌlɒŋ 'saɪt ɪd ◄ -əd ‖ ˌlɔːŋ 'saɪṭ əd ◄ ˌlaːŋ- **~ness** nəs nɪs
longstanding ˌlɒŋ 'stænd ɪŋ ◄ ‖ ˌlɔːŋ- ˌlaːŋ-
longstop 'lɒŋ stɒp ‖ 'lɔːŋ staːp 'laːŋ- **~s** s
longsuffering ˌlɒŋ 'sʌf ər_ɪŋ ◄ ‖ ˌlɔːŋ- ˌlaːŋ- **~ly** li
long-term ˌlɒŋ 'tɜːm ◄ ‖ ˌlɔːŋ 'tɜːm ◄ ˌlaːŋ-
Longton 'lɒŋ tən ‖ 'lɔːŋ- 'laːŋ-
Longtown 'lɒŋ taʊn ‖ 'lɔːŋ- 'laːŋ-
longueur ₍ₗ₎lɒŋ 'gɜː ‖ loʊn 'gɜː: —Fr [lɔ̃ gœːʁ] **~s** z
Longus 'lɒŋ gəs ‖ 'lɔːŋ- 'laːŋ-
longways 'lɒŋ weɪz ‖ 'lɔːŋ- 'laːŋ-
longwearing ˌlɒŋ 'weər ɪŋ ◄ ‖ ˌlɔːŋ 'wer ɪŋ ◄ ˌlaːŋ-
longwinded ˌlɒŋ 'wɪnd ɪd ◄ -əd ‖ ˌlɔːŋ- ˌlaːŋ- **~ly** li **~ness** nəs nɪs
longwise 'lɒŋ waɪz ‖ 'lɔːŋ- 'laːŋ-
Longyearbyen 'lɒŋ jɪə ˌbjuː ən '•jɜː, -ˌbuː• ‖ 'lɔːŋ jɪr- 'laːŋ- —Norw ['lɔŋ jiːr byː ən]
lonicera lɒ 'nɪs ər_ə lə- ‖ loʊ-
Lonnie 'lɒn i ‖ 'laːn i
Lonrho tdmk 'lɒn rəʊ 'lʌn- ‖ 'laːn roʊ
Lonsdale 'lɒnz deɪᵊl ‖ 'laːnz-
loo luː **loos** luːz
Looe luː
loofa, loofah 'luːf ə **~s** z
look lʊk §luːk **looked** lʊkt §luːkt **looking** 'lʊk ɪŋ §'luːk- **looks** lʊks §luːks 'looking glass
look-alike 'lʊk ə ˌlaɪk §'luːk- **~s** s
looker 'lʊk ə §'luːk- ‖ -ᵊr **~s** z
looker-on ˌlʊk ər 'ɒn §ˌluːk- ‖ -ᵊr 'aːn -'ɔːn **lookers-on** ˌlʊk əz 'ɒn §ˌluːk- ‖ -ᵊrz 'aːn -'ɔːn
look-in 'lʊk ɪn §'luːk-
lookout 'lʊk aʊt §'luːk- **~s** s
look-over 'lʊk ˌəʊv ə §'luːk- ‖ -ˌoʊv ᵊr
look-see ˌlʊk 'siː §ˌluːk-, '••
lookup 'lʊk ʌp §'luːk- **~s** s
loom luːm **loomed** luːmd **looming** 'luːm ɪŋ **looms** luːmz
loon luːn **loons** luːnz
loon|ey, loon|y 'luːn |i **~ier** i_ə ‖ i_ᵊr **~ies,**

~**eys** ɪz ~**iest** i_ɪst i_əst
  '**loony bin**
loop luːp **looped** luːpt **looper/s** 'luːp ə/
  z ‖ -ªr/z **looping** 'luːp ɪŋ **loops** luːps
loophole 'luːp həʊl →-hɒʊl ‖ -hoʊl ~**s** z
loopy 'luːp i
loose luːs **loosed** luːst **looser** 'luːs ə ‖ -ªr
  looses 'luːs ɪz -əz **loosest** 'luːs ɪst -əst
  loosing 'luːs ɪŋ
  ˌloose 'change; ˌloose 'end
loosebox 'luːs bɒks ‖ -bɑːks ~**es** ɪz əz
loose-leaf ˌluːs 'liːf ◄
loose-limbed ˌluːs 'lɪmd ◄
loosely 'luːs li
loosen 'luːs ªn ~**ed** d ~**ing** _ɪŋ ~**s** z
looseness 'luːs nəs -nɪs
loosestrife 'luːs straɪf -traɪf ~**s** s
loot luːt **looted** 'luːt ɪd -əd ‖ 'luːt̬ əd **looting**
  'luːt ɪŋ ‖ 'luːt̬ ɪŋ **loots** luːts
looter 'luːt ə ‖ 'luːt̬ ªr ~**s** z
lop lɒp ‖ lɑːp **lopped** lɒpt ‖ lɑːpt **lopping**
  'lɒp ɪŋ ‖ 'lɑːp ɪŋ **lops** lɒps ‖ lɑːps
lope ləʊp ‖ loʊp **loped** ləʊpt ‖ loʊpt **lopes**
  ləʊps ‖ loʊps **loping** 'ləʊp ɪŋ ‖ 'loʊp ɪŋ
lop-eared ˌlɒp 'ɪəd ◄ ‖ ˌlɑːp 'ɪªrd ◄
Lopez, López 'ləʊp ez ‖ 'loʊp- —*Sp* ['lo peθ,
  -pes]
Lop Nur ˌlɒp 'nʊə ‖ ˌlɔːp 'nʊªr ˌlɑːp-, ˌloʊp-
  —*Chi* Luóbùbó [²lwɔ ⁴pu ²pɔ]
lop-sided ˌlɒp 'saɪd ɪd ◄ -əd ‖ ˌlɑːp- ~**ly** li
  ~**ness** nəs nɪs
loquacious ləʊ 'kweɪʃ əs lɒ- ‖ loʊ- ~**ly** li
  ~**ness** nəs nɪs
loquacity ləʊ 'kwæs ət i lɒ-, -ɪt-
  ‖ loʊ 'kwæs ət̬ i
loquat 'ləʊ kwɒt -kwət ‖ 'loʊ kwɑːt ~**s** s
lor lɔː ‖ lɔːr
Lora 'lɔːr ə
Loraine lə 'reɪn lɒ-
Loram 'lɔːr əm
loran 'lɔːr ən ~**s** z
Lorca 'lɔːk ə ‖ 'lɔːrk ə —*Sp* ['lor ka]
Lorcan 'lɔːk ən ‖ 'lɔːrk-
lord, Lord lɔːd ‖ lɔːrd —*but as a vocative in a*
  court of law, my lord *is also* mɪ 'lʌd, mə-
  lorded 'lɔːd ɪd -əd ‖ 'lɔːrd əd **lording**
  'lɔːd ɪŋ ‖ 'lɔːrd ɪŋ **lords, Lords, Lord's**
  lɔːdz ‖ lɔːrdz
  ˌLord 'Chancellor; ˌLord Chief 'Justice;
  ⸜Lord 'Mayor; ˌLord's 'Prayer
lordling 'lɔːd lɪŋ ‖ 'lɔːrd- ~**s** z
lord|ly 'lɔːd |li ‖ 'lɔːrd- ~**lier** li_ə ‖ li_ªr ~**liest**
  li_ɪst li_əst ~**liness** li nəs li nɪs
lordosis lɔː 'dəʊs ɪs §-əs ‖ lɔːr 'doʊs əs
lordship, L~ 'lɔːd ʃɪp ‖ 'lɔːrd- ~**s** s
lordy 'lɔːd i ‖ 'lɔːrd i
lore lɔː ‖ lɔːr loʊr
L'Oréal *tdmk* ˌlɒr i 'æl '••• ‖ ˌlɔːr i 'æl -'ɑːl
Lorelei 'lɒr ə laɪ 'lɔːr- ‖ 'lɔːr- —*Ger*
  ['lo: ʁə laɪ]
Loren 'lɔːr en -ən; lɔː 'ren, lə- ‖ 'lɔːr ən —*It*
  ['lɔː ren]

Lorentz 'lɒr ənts 'lɔːr- ‖ 'lɔːr- 'loʊr- —*Dutch*
  ['lo: rənts]
Lorenz 'lɒr ənz 'lɔːr- 'loʊr- —*but as a*
  German name, 'lɔːr ənts, 'lɒr- —*Ger*
  ['lo: ʁɛnts]
Lorenzo lə 'renz əʊ lɒ- ‖ -oʊ lɔː-
Loretta lə 'ret ə lɒ-, lɔː- ‖ lə 'ret̬ ə lɔː-
Loretto lə 'ret əʊ lɔː- ‖ lə 'ret̬ oʊ lɔː-
lorgnette ₍₎lɔːn 'jet ‖ lɔːrn- —*Fr* [lɔʁ njɛt] ~**s**
  s
Lorie 'lɒr i ‖ 'lɔːr i
lorie... —*see* **lory**
lorikeet 'lɒr ɪ kiːt -ə-, ˌ••'• ‖ 'lɔːr- 'lɑːr- ~**s** s
lorimer, L~ 'lɒr ɪm ə -əm- ‖ 'lɔːr əm ªr ~**s** z
loris, Loris 'lɔːr ɪs §-əs ‖ 'loʊr- ~**es** ɪz əz
lorn lɔːn ‖ lɔːrn
Lorna 'lɔːn ə ‖ 'lɔːrn ə
Lorne lɔːn ‖ lɔːrn
Lorraine lə 'reɪn lɒ-, lɔː- —*Fr* [lɔ ʁɛn]
lorr|y 'lɒr |i §'lʌr- ‖ 'lɔːr |i 'lɑːr- ~**ies** iz
  'lorry park
lor|y 'lɔːr |i ‖ 'loʊr- ~**ies** iz
Los Alamos lɒs 'æl ə mɒs ‖ lɔːs 'æl ə moʊs
  lɑːs-
Los Angeles lɒs 'ændʒ ə liːz -ɪ-, -lɪs, -ləs
  ‖ lɔːs 'ændʒ əl əs lɑːs-, -'æŋ gəl-, -ə liːz
lose luːz **loses** 'luːz ɪz -əz **losing** 'luːz ɪŋ **lost**
  lɒst lɔːst ‖ lɔːst lɑːst
Loseley 'ləʊz li ‖ 'loʊz-
loser 'luːz ə ‖ -ªr ~**s** z
Losey 'ləʊz i ‖ 'loʊz i
Los Gatos lɒs 'gæt əʊs ‖ lɔːs 'gɑːt̬ oʊs lɑːs-,
  loʊs-
loss lɒs lɔːs ‖ lɔːs lɑːs **losses** 'lɒs ɪz 'lɔːs-, -əz
  ‖ 'lɔːs əz 'lɑːs-
  'loss adˌjuster; 'loss ˌleader
Lossiemouth ˌlɒs i 'maʊθ ‖ ˌlɔːs- ˌlɑːs-
lossy 'lɒs i ‖ 'lɔːs i 'lɑːs-
lost lɒst lɔːst ‖ lɔːst lɑːst
  ˌlost 'cause; ˌlost 'property
Lostwithiel lɒst 'wɪθ i_əl ‖ lɔːst- lɑːst-
lot, Lot lɒt ‖ lɑːt **lots** lɒts ‖ lɑːts
loth ləʊθ ‖ loʊθ
Lothario ləʊ 'θɑːr i əʊ lɒ-, -'θeər-
  ‖ loʊ 'θer i oʊ oʊ -'θær-
Lothbury 'ləʊθ bər_i 'lɒθ- ‖ 'loʊθ ˌber i
Lothian 'ləʊð i_ən ‖ 'loʊð- ~**s** z
lotic 'ləʊt ɪk ‖ 'loʊt̬ ɪk
lotion 'ləʊʃ ªn ‖ 'loʊʃ- ~**s** z
lotsa '*lots of* 'lɒts ə ‖ 'lɑːts ə
lotta '*lot of* 'lɒt ə ‖ 'lɑːt̬ ə
lotter|y 'lɒt_ər i ‖ 'lɑːt̬ ər i →'lɑːtr i ~**ies** iz
Lottie 'lɒt i ‖ 'lɑːt̬ i
lotto, Lotto 'lɒt əʊ ‖ 'lɑːt̬ oʊ
lotus 'ləʊt əs ‖ 'loʊt̬ əs ~**es** ɪz əz
lotus-eater 'ləʊt əs ˌiːt ə ‖ 'loʊt̬ əs ˌiːt̬ ªr ~**s** z
Lou luː
louche luːʃ
loud laʊd **louder** 'laʊd ə ‖ -ªr **loudest**
  'laʊd ɪst -əst
Loudan, Loudon, Loudoun 'laʊd ªn
louden 'laʊd ªn ~**ed** d ~**ing** _ɪŋ ~**s** z
loudhailer ˌlaʊd 'heɪl ə ‖ -ªr ~**s** z

L

loudly 'laʊd li

loud|mouth 'laʊd |maʊθ **~mouths** maʊðz
maʊθs

loudmouthed ˌlaʊd 'maʊðd ◄ -'maʊθt, '• •

loudness 'laʊd nəs -nɪs **~es** ɪz əz

loudspeaker ˌlaʊd 'spiːk ə '•ˌ•• ‖ -ᵊr **~s** z

Loudwater 'laʊd ˌwɔːt ə ‖ -ˌwɔːt ᵊr -ˌwɑːt̬-

Louella lu 'el ə

lough, Lough lɒx lɒk ‖ lɑːk lɑːx —*but as a
family name also* lʌf, ləʊ ‖ loʊ **loughs** lɒxs
lɒks ‖ lɑːks lɑːxs

Loughboro', Loughborough 'lʌf bər_ə §-,bʌr-
‖ -,bɝː oʊ

Loughlin 'lɒx lɪn 'lɒk-, -lən ‖ 'lɑːk-

Loughton 'laʊt ᵊn

Loughor 'lʌx ə ‖ 'lʌk ᵊr

Louie 'luːˌi

Louis (i) 'luːˌi, (ii) ˌɪs §ˌəs —*Fr* [lwi, lu i]
ˌLouis Qua'torze kə 'tɔːz kæ- ‖ -'tɔːrz —*Fr*
[ka tɔrz]; ˌLouis 'Quinze kænz —*Fr* [kæ̃ːz];
ˌLouis 'Seize sez seɪz —*Fr* [sɛːz]; ˌLouis
'Treize trez treɪz —*Fr* [tʁɛːz]

Louisa lu 'iːz ə

Louisburg 'luːˌɪs bɜːg §ˌəs- ‖ -bɝːg

louis d'or ˌluːˌi 'dɔː ‖ -'dɔːr **~s** z

Louise lu 'iːz

Louisiana lu ˌiːz i 'æn ə ˌluːˌɪz-, -'ɑːn-

Louisville 'luːˌi vɪl §ˌə-

lounge laʊndʒ **lounged** laʊndʒd **lounges**
'laʊndʒ ɪz -əz **lounging** 'laʊndʒ ɪŋ
'lounge bar, ˌ• '•; 'lounge suit

lounger 'laʊndʒ ə ‖ -ᵊr **~s** z

Lounsbury 'laʊnz bər_i ‖ -ˌber i

loupe luːp (= *loop*) **loupes** luːps

lour 'laʊ_ə ‖ 'laʊ_ᵊr **~ed** d **louring**
'laʊ_ər ɪŋ ‖ 'laʊ_ᵊr ɪŋ **~s** z

Lourdes lʊəd lʊədz, lɔːdz ‖ lʊᵊrd —*Fr* [luʁd]

louse *n* laʊs **lice** laɪs

louse *v* laʊz laʊs **loused** laʊzd laʊst **louses**
'laʊz ɪz 'laʊs-, -əz **lousing** 'laʊz ɪŋ 'laʊs-

lous|y 'laʊz li **~ier** i_ə ‖ i_ᵊr **~iest** i_ɪst i_əst
~ily ɪ li əl i **~iness** i nəs i nɪs

lout laʊt **louts** laʊts

Louth (i) laʊθ, (ii) laʊð —*The place in England
is* (i), *the place in Ireland* (ii)

loutish 'laʊt ɪʃ ‖ 'laʊt̬ ɪʃ **~ly** li **~ness** nəs nɪs

Louvain lu 'væn -'væ̃; 'luːv æn, -æ̃ —*Fr* [lu vɛ̃]

louv|er, louv|re 'luːv lə ‖ -lᵊr **~ered, ~red**
əd ‖ ᵊrd **~ers, ~res** əz ‖ ᵊrz

Louvre *museum* 'luːvˌrə luːv ‖ 'luːv ᵊr —*Fr*
[luːvʁ]

lovab|le 'lʌv əb |əl **~leness** əl nəs -nɪs **~ly** li

lovage 'lʌv ɪdʒ

lovat, Lovat 'lʌv ət

love, Love lʌv **loved** lʌvd **loves** lʌvz **loving**
'lʌv ɪŋ
'love afˌfair; 'love match; 'love nest; 'love
ˌstory

loveab|le 'lʌv əb |əl **~leness** əl nəs -nɪs **~ly** li

lovebird 'lʌv bɜːd ‖ -bɝːd **~s** z

lovebite 'lʌv baɪt **~s** s

love|child 'lʌv |tʃaɪᵊld **~children** ˌtʃɪldr ᵊn

Loveday 'lʌv deɪ

love-hate ˌlʌv 'heɪt
ˌlove-'hate reˌlationship

love-in-a-mist ˌlʌv ɪn ə 'mɪst §ˌ•ᵊn-

Lovejoy 'lʌv dʒɔɪ

Lovelace 'lʌv leɪs

loveless 'lʌv ləs -lɪs **~ly** li **~ness** nəs nɪs

loveli... —*see* **lovely**

love-lies-bleeding ˌlʌv laɪz 'bliːd ɪŋ

Lovell 'lʌv ᵊl

lovelock, L~ 'lʌv lɒk ‖ -lɑːk **~s** s

lovelorn 'lʌv lɔːn ‖ -lɔːrn

love|ly 'lʌv |li **~lier** li_ə ‖ li_ᵊr **~lies** liz **~liest**
li_ɪst li_əst **~liness** li nəs -nɪs

lovemaking 'lʌv ˌmeɪk ɪŋ

lover 'lʌv ə ‖ -ᵊr **~ly** li **~s** z

Loveridge 'lʌv rɪdʒ

lovesick 'lʌv sɪk **~ness** nəs nɪs

lovey 'lʌv i **~s** z

lovey-dovey ˌlʌv i 'dʌv i ◄ '••, ••

Lovibond 'lʌv i bɒnd ‖ -bɑːnd

loving 'lʌv ɪŋ **~ly** li
'loving cup; ˌloving 'kindness

low, Low ləʊ ‖ loʊ (= *lo*) **lowed** ləʊd ‖ loʊd
lower 'ləʊ ə ‖ 'loʊ ᵊr **lowest** 'ləʊ ɪst -əst
‖ 'loʊ əst **lowing** 'ləʊ ɪŋ ‖ 'loʊ ɪŋ **lows**
ləʊz ‖ loʊz
ˌLow 'Church; ˌLow 'German; 'low life;
ˌlow 'profile; ˌlow ˌseason; ˌlow 'tide; ˌlow
'water, ˌlow 'water mark

lowborn ˌləʊ 'bɔːn ◄ ‖ 'loʊ bɔːrn

lowboy 'ləʊ bɔɪ ‖ 'loʊ-

lowbred ˌləʊ 'bred ◄ ‖ ˌloʊ- '••

lowbrow 'ləʊ braʊ ‖ 'loʊ- **~s** z

lowdown *n* 'ləʊ daʊn ‖ 'loʊ-

low-down *adj* ˌləʊ 'daʊn ◄ ‖ ˌloʊ-

Lowe ləʊ ‖ loʊ

Lowell 'ləʊ əl ‖ 'loʊ əl

Lowenbrau, Löwenbräu *tdmk*
'ləʊ ən braʊ ‖ 'loʊ- —*Ger* ['løː vᵊn bʁɔy]

lower *v* 'threaten' 'laʊ_ə ‖ 'laʊ_ᵊr **~ed** d
lowering 'laʊ_ər ɪŋ ‖ 'laʊ_ᵊr ɪŋ **~s** z

lower *v* 'bring down' 'ləʊ ə ‖ 'loʊ ᵊr **~ed** d
lowering 'ləʊ ər ɪŋ ‖ 'loʊ ᵊr ɪŋ **~s** z

lower *adj, comp of* **low** 'ləʊ ə ‖ 'loʊ ᵊr
ˌlower 'case◄; ˌlower 'class◄; ˌLower (ˌ)East
'Side; ˌLower 'House

lowermost 'ləʊ ə məʊst ‖ 'loʊ ᵊr moʊst

Lowestoft 'ləʊst ɒft 'ləʊ ɪst ɒft, -əst-; -əft, -əf
‖ 'loʊst ɔːft -ɑːft, -əf

low-key ˌləʊ 'kiː ◄ ‖ ˌloʊ-

lowland, L~ 'ləʊ lənd ‖ 'loʊ- **~s** z

lowlander 'ləʊ lənd ə ‖ 'loʊ lənd ᵊr **~s** z

low-life 'ləʊ laɪf ‖ 'loʊ- **~s** s

low-loader ˌləʊ 'ləʊd ə ‖ ˌloʊ 'loʊd ᵊr **~s** z

low|ly 'ləʊ |li ‖ 'loʊ |li **~lier** li_ə ‖ li_ᵊr **~liest**
li_ɪst li_əst **~liness** li nəs li nɪs

low-lying ˌləʊ 'laɪ ɪŋ ◄ ‖ ˌloʊ-

Lowman 'ləʊ mən ‖ 'loʊ-

low-minded ˌləʊ 'maɪnd ɪd ◄ -əd ‖ ˌloʊ- **~ly** li
~ness nəs nɪs

Lowndes laʊndz

low-necked ˌləʊ 'nekt ◄ ‖ ˌloʊ-

lowness 'ləʊ nəs -nɪs ‖ 'loʊ-

low-pass ˌləʊ ˈpɑːs ◂ §-ˈpæs ‖ ˌloʊ ˈpæs ◂
low-pitched ˌləʊ ˈpɪt ʃt ◂ ‖ ˌloʊ-
low-profile ˌləʊ ˈprəʊf aɪəl ◂ ‖ ˌloʊ ˈproʊf-
Lowrie, Lowry ˈlaʊər i
low-rise ˌləʊ ˈraɪz ◂ ‖ ˌloʊ-
low-spirited ˌləʊ ˈspɪr ɪt ɪd ◂ -ət-, -əd
  ‖ ˌloʊ ˈspɪr əţ əd ◂
Lowther ˈlaʊð ə ‖ -ər —*but as a family name*
  sometimes ˈləʊð- ‖ ˈloʊð-
Lowton ˈləʊt ᵊn ‖ ˈloʊt ᵊn
lox lɒks ‖ lɑːks
Loxene *tdmk* ˈlɒks iːn ‖ ˈlɑːks-
Loxley ˈlɒks li ‖ ˈlɑːks-
loxodromic
  ˌlɒks ə ˈdrɒm ɪk ◂ ‖ ˌlɑːks ə ˈdrɑːm ɪk ◂
  ~ally ᵊl i
Loy lɔɪ
loyal ˈlɔɪ əl
loyalism ˈlɔɪ ə ˌlɪz əm
loyalist, L~ ˈlɔɪ əl ɪst §-əst
loyally ˈlɔɪ əl i
loyal|ty ˈlɔɪ əl |ti **~ties** tiz
Loyd lɔɪd
Loyola ˈlɔɪ əl ə lɔɪ ˈəʊl- ‖ lɔɪ ˈoʊl ə —*Sp*
  [lo ˈjo la]
lozeng|e ˈlɒz ɪndʒ -əndʒ ‖ ˈlɑːz- **~es** ɪz əz
LP ˌel ˈpiː ~**s**, ~**'s** z
LPC ˌel piː ˈsiː
LPG ˌel piː ˈdʒiː
L-plate ˈel pleɪt ~**s** s
LSD ˌel es ˈdiː
LSE ˌel es ˈiː
Ltd —*see* **Limited**
Luanda lu ˈænd ə ‖ -ˈɑːnd- —*Port* [ˈlwɐn dɐ]
Luba ˈluːb ə
Lubavitcher ˈluːb ə vɪtʃ ə ‖ -ər ~**s** z
lubber ˈlʌb ə ‖ -ər ~**s** z
Lubbock ˈlʌb ək
lube luːb **lubed** luːbd **lubes** luːbz **lubing**
  ˈluːb ɪŋ
Lubeck, Lübeck ˈluː bek ˈljuː- —*Ger* [ˈlyː bɛk]
lubricant ˈluːb rɪk ənt ˈljuː-, -rək- ~**s** s
lubri|cate ˈluːb rɪ |keɪt ˈljuː-, -rə- **~cated**
  keɪt ɪd -əd ‖ keɪţ əd **~cates** keɪts **~cating**
  keɪt ɪŋ ‖ keɪţ ɪŋ
lubrication ˌluːb rɪ ˈkeɪʃ ᵊn ˌljuːb-, -rə- ~**s** z
lubricator ˈluːb rɪ keɪt ə ˈljuː-, ˈ•rə- ‖ -keɪţ ər
  ~**s** z
lubricious lu ˈbrɪʃ əs ljuː- ~**ly** li ~**ness** nəs
  nɪs
lubricity lu ˈbrɪs ət i ljuː-, -ɪt- ‖ -əţ i
Lucan ˈluːk ən
Lucas ˈluːk əs
Luce luːs
Lucent *tdmk* ˈluːs ᵊnt
lucerne, L~ lu ˈsɜːn ‖ -ˈsɝːn —*Fr* [ly sɛʀn]
Lucia ˈluːs i‿ə ˈluːʃ-, ˈluːʃ ə —*but as an Italian*
  name lu ˈtʃiː‿ə, *It* [lu ˈtʃiː a] —*see also* St
  Lucia
Lucian ˈluːs i‿ən ˈluːʃ- ‖ ˈluːʃ ᵊn
lucid ˈluːs ɪd ˈljuːs-, §-əd ~**ly** li ~**ness** nəs nɪs
lucidity luː ˈsɪd ət i ljuː-, -ɪt- ‖ -əţ i
Lucie ˈluːs i

Lucifer, l~ ˈluːs ɪf ə -əf- ‖ -ər ~**s** z
luciferin luː ˈsɪf ər ɪn §-ən
Lucille lu ˈsiːᵊl
Lucinda luː ˈsɪnd ə
Lucite *tdmk* ˈluːs aɪt
Lucius ˈluːs i‿əs ˈluːʃ- ‖ ˈluːʃ əs
luck, Luck lʌk **lucked** lʌkt **lucking** ˈlʌk ɪŋ
  lucks lʌks
luckless ˈlʌk ləs -lɪs ~**ly** li ~**ness** nəs nɪs
Lucknow ˈlʌk naʊ ˌ•ˈ• —*Hindi* [ləkʰ nəw]
luck|y, Lucky ˈlʌk |i ~**ier** i‿ə ‖ i‿ər ~**iest** i‿ɪst
  i‿əst ~**ily** ɪ li əl i ~**iness** i nəs i nɪs
  ˌlucky ˈdip
Lucozade *tdmk* ˈluːk əʊ zeɪd ‖ -ə-
lucrative ˈluːk rət ɪv ˈljuːk- ‖ -rəţ ɪv
lucre ˈluːk ə ˈljuːk- ‖ -ər
Lucrece lu ˈkriːs ljuː-
Lucretia lu ˈkriːʃ ə ljuː-, -ˈkriːʃ i‿ə
Lucretius lu ˈkriːʃ əs ljuː-, -ˈkriːʃ i‿əs
lucu|brate ˈluːk ju |breɪt ˈljuː k- ‖ -jə-
  ~brated breɪt ɪd -əd ‖ breɪţ əd **~brates**
  breɪts **~brating** breɪt ɪŋ ‖ breɪţ ɪŋ
lucubration ˌluːk ju ˈbreɪʃ ᵊn ‖ -jə- ~**s** z
Lucull|us lu ˈkʌl əs ljuː- **~an** ən
Lucy ˈluːs i
Lud, lud lʌd
Luddite, l~ ˈlʌd aɪt ~**s** s
lude luːd **ludes** luːdz
Ludgate ˈlʌd gət -gɪt, -geɪt
ludic ˈluːd ɪk ˈljuːd-
ludicrous ˈluːd ɪk rəs ˈljuːd-, -ək- ~**ly** li ~**ness**
  nəs nɪs
Ludlow ˈlʌd ləʊ ‖ -loʊ
Ludlum ˈlʌd ləm
Ludmila, Ludmilla lʊd ˈmɪl ə
ludo, Ludo ˈluːd əʊ ‖ -oʊ
Ludovic ˈluːd ə vɪk
Ludwig ˈlʊd vɪg ˈluːd- ‖ ˈlʌd wɪg ˈlʊd-, -vɪg
  —*Ger* [ˈluːt vɪç]
luff lʌf **luffed** lʌft **luffing** ˈlʌf ɪŋ **luffs** lʌfs
Lufthansa *tdmk* ˈlʊft ˌhænz ə -ˌhænᵗs-
  ‖ -ˌhɑːnz ə —*Ger* [ˈlʊft ˌhan za]
Luftwaffe ˈlʊft ˌwæf ə -ˌvæf-, -ˌwɑːf-, -ˌvɑːf-
  ‖ -ˌvɑːf ə —*Ger* [ˈlʊft ˌvaf ə]
lug lʌg **lugged** lʌgd **lugging** ˈlʌg ɪŋ **lugs**
  lʌgz
Luganda lu ˈgænd ə -ˈgɑːnd- ‖ -ˈgɑːnd ə
Lugano lu ˈgɑːn əʊ lə- ‖ -oʊ —*It* [lu ˈgaː no]
Lugard ˈluː gɑːd ˌ•ˈ• ‖ -gɑːrd
luge luːʒ luːdʒ **luged** luːʒd luːdʒd **luges**
  ˈluːʒ ɪz ˈluːdʒ-, -əz **luging** ˈluːʒ ɪŋ ˈluːdʒ-
Luger *tdmk* ˈluːg ə ‖ -ər —*Ger* [ˈluː gɐ] ~**s** z
luggage ˈlʌg ɪdʒ
  ˈluggage ˌlabel; ˈluggage rack; ˈluggage
  van
lugg... —*see* **lug**
lugger ˈlʌg ə ‖ -ər ~**s** z
lughole ˈlʌg həʊl →-hɒʊl ‖ -hoʊl —*humorously*
  also BrE -əʊl ~**s** z
Lugosi lu ˈgəʊs i ‖ -ˈgoʊs-
lugsail ˈlʌg seɪᵊl —*naut* -sᵊl ~**s** z
lugubrious lə ˈguːb ri‿əs lu-, -ˈgjuːb- ~**ly** li
  ~**ness** nəs nɪs

L

lugworm 'lʌg wɜːm ‖ -wɝːm ~s z
Luigi lu 'iːdʒ i
Lukacs, Lukács 'luːk ætʃ ‖ -ɑːtʃ —*Hungarian* ['lu kaːtʃ]
Luke luːk
lukewarm ˌluːk 'wɔːm ◄ ' • • ‖ -'wɔːrm **~ly** li **~ness** nəs nɪs
lull lʌl **lulled** lʌld **lulling** 'lʌl ɪŋ **lulls** lʌlz
lulla|by 'lʌl ə |baɪ **~bied** baɪd **~bies** baɪz **~bying** baɪ ɪŋ
Lulworth 'lʌl wəθ -wɜːθ ‖ -wɝːθ
Lulu, lulu 'luːl uː ~**s**, ~'**s** z
lum lʌm **lumz** lʌmz
lumbago lʌm 'beɪg əʊ ‖ -oʊ
lumbar 'lʌm bə -baː ‖ -bᵊr -baːr
lumber 'lʌm bə ‖ -bᵊr **~ed** d **lumbering** 'lʌm bər_ɪŋ ~**s** z
lumberjack 'lʌm bə dʒæk ‖ -bᵊr- ~**s** s
lumber|man 'lʌm bə |mən -mæn ‖ -bᵊr- ~**men** mən men
lumber-room 'lʌm bə ruːm -rʊm ‖ -bᵊr- ~**s** z
lumberyard 'lʌm bə jaːd ‖ -bᵊr jaːrd ~**s** z
lumen 'luːm ɪn -ən, -en ‖ -ən ~**s** z
lumiere, lumière, L~ 'luːm i eə , • • ' • ‖ ˌluːm i 'eᵊr —*Fr* [ly mjɛːʁ]
luminanc|e 'luːm ɪn ənts 'ljuːm-, -ən- ~**es** ɪz əz
luminar|y 'lum ɪn ər_li 'ljuːm-, ' • ən- ‖ -ə ner li ~**ies** iz
luminesc|e ˌluːm ɪ 'nes ˌljuːm-, -ə- ~**ed** t ~**es** ɪz əz ~**ing** ɪŋ
luminescence ˌluːm ɪ 'nes ᵊnts ˌljuːm-, -ə-
luminescent ˌluːm ɪ 'nes ᵊnt ◄ ˌljuːm-, -ə-
luminosit|y ˌluːm ɪ 'nɒs ət li ˌljuːm-, ˌ • ə-, -ɪt i ‖ -'naːs əţ li ~**ies** iz
luminous 'luːm ɪn əs 'ljuːm-, -ən- ~**ly** li ~**ness** nəs nɪs
Lumley 'lʌm li
lumme 'lʌm i
lummox 'lʌm əks ~**es** ɪz əz
lummy 'lʌm i
lump lʌmp **lumped** lʌmpt **lumping** 'lʌmp ɪŋ **lumps** lʌmps ˌlump 'sum
lumpectom|y ˌlʌmp 'ekt əm li ~**ies** iz
lumpen 'lʌmp ən 'lʊmp-
lumpenproletariat ˌlʌmp ən ˌprəʊl ə 'teər i_ət ˌlʊmp-, →-, ' • əm-, -, • ɪ-, -æt ‖ -ˌprəʊl ə 'ter-
lumpfish 'lʌmp fɪʃ ~**es** ɪz əz
lumpish 'lʌmp ɪʃ ~**ly** li ~**ness** nəs nɪs
Lumpkin 'lʌmp kɪn §-kən
lump|y 'lʌmp li ~**ier** i_ə ‖ i_ᵊr ~**iest** i_ɪst i_əst
Lumsden 'lʌmz dən
Luna, luna 'luːn ə 'ljuːn- ˈluna moth
lunac|y 'luːn əs li ~**ies** iz
lunar 'luːn ə ‖ -ᵊr
lunate 'luːn eɪt -ət, -ɪt
lunatic 'luːn ə tɪk ~**s** s ˈlunatic aˌsylum; ˈlunatic ˈfringe
lunation lu 'neɪʃ ən ~**s** z
lunch lʌntʃ **lunched** lʌntʃt **lunches** 'lʌntʃ ɪz -əz **lunching** 'lʌntʃ ɪŋ

lunchbox 'lʌntʃ bɒks ‖ -baːks ~**es** ɪz əz
luncheon 'lʌntʃ ən ~**s** z ˈluncheon ˌmeat; ˈluncheon ˌvoucher
luncheonette ˌlʌntʃ ə 'net ~**s** s
lunchtime 'lʌntʃ taɪm ~**s** z
Lund *place in Sweden* lʊnd —*Swedish* [lɵnd], *Danish* [lɔnʔ]
Lund *family name* lʌnd
Lundy 'lʌnd i
lune, Lune luːn ljuːn **lunes** luːnz ljuːnz
Luneburg 'luːn ə bɜːg ‖ -bɝːg —*Ger* Lüneburg ['lyː nə bʊʁk]
lunette (ˌ)luː 'net (ˌ)lju:- ~**s** s
lung lʌŋ **lunged** lʌŋd **lungs** lʌŋz
lunge lʌndʒ **lunged** lʌndʒd **lunges** 'lʌndʒ ɪz -əz **lunging** 'lʌndʒ ɪŋ
lunged '*having lungs*' lʌŋd
lunged *past & pp of* **lunge** lʌndʒd
lungfish 'lʌŋ fɪʃ ~**es** ɪz əz
lungi 'lʊŋ gi ~**s** z
lungpower 'lʌŋ ˌpaʊ_ə ‖ -ˌpaʊ_ᵊr
Lunn lʌn
Lunt lʌnt
Luo 'luː əʊ ‖ -oʊ
lupanar lu 'peɪn ə -'paːn-, -aː ‖ -ᵊr ~**s** z
Lupercal 'luːp ə kæl 'ljuːp-, -3ː- ‖ -ᵊr-
Lupercalia ˌluːp ə 'keɪl i_ə ˌljuːp-, , • 3ː- ‖ , • ᵊr-
lupin, lupine *n, flower* 'luːp ɪn §-ən ~**s** z
lupine *adj* 'luːp aɪn 'ljuːp-
lupus, Lupus 'luːp əs 'ljuːp-
lur lʊə lɜː ‖ lʊᵊr **lurs** lʊəz lɜːz ‖ lʊᵊrz
lurch lɜːtʃ ‖ lɝːtʃ **lurched** lɜːtʃt ‖ lɝːtʃt **lurches** 'lɜːtʃ ɪz -əz ‖ 'lɝːtʃ əz **lurching** 'lɜːtʃ ɪŋ ‖ 'lɝːtʃ ɪŋ
lurcher 'lɜːtʃ ə ‖ 'lɝːtʃ ᵊr ~**s** z

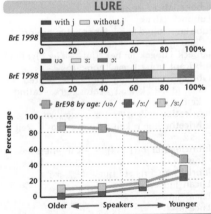

LURE

BrE 1998

with j / without j

0 20 40 60 80 100%

BrE 1998

ʊə / 3ː / ɔː

0 20 40 60 80 100%

BrE98 by age: /ʊə/ /ɔː/ /3ː/

Percentage 100 / 80 / 60 / 40 / 20 / 0

Older ◄— Speakers —► Younger

lure ljʊə lʊə, lj3ː, ljɔː ‖ lʊᵊr —*BrE 1998 poll panel preference: with j 58%, without j 42%; ʊə 72%, 3ː 17%, ɔː 10%.* **lured** ljʊəd lʊəd, lj3ːd, ljɔːd ‖ lʊᵊrd **lures** ljʊəz lʊəz, lj3ːz, ljɔːz ‖ lʊᵊrz **luring** 'ljʊər ɪŋ 'lʊər-, 'lj3ːr-, 'ljɔːr- ‖ 'lʊr ɪŋ
Lurex *tdmk* 'ljʊər eks 'lʊər-, 'lj3ːr-, 'ljɔːr- ‖ 'lʊr-
Lurgan 'lɜːg ən ‖ 'lɝːg-

lurgy 'lɜːg i ‖ 'lɝːg i
lurid 'ljʊər ɪd 'lʊər-, 'ljɜːr-, 'ljɔːr-, §-əd
   ‖ 'lʊr əd **~ly** li **~ness** nəs nɪs
lurk lɜːk ‖ lɝːk **lurked** lɜːkt ‖ lɝːkt **lurking**
   'lɜːk ɪŋ ‖ 'lɝːk ɪŋ **lurks** lɜːks ‖ lɝːks
lurker 'lɜːk ə ‖ 'lɝːk ᵊr **~s** z
Lurpak *tdmk* 'lɜː pæk ‖ 'lɝː-
Lusaka lu 'sɑːk ə lʊ-, -'zɑːk-
Lusatia lu 'seɪʃ ə -'seɪʃ i‿ə
Lusatian lu 'seɪʃ ᵊn -'seɪʃ i‿ən **~s** z
luscious 'lʌʃ əs **~ly** li **~ness** nəs nɪs
lush, Lush lʌʃ **lusher** 'lʌʃ ə ‖ -ᵊr **lushes** 'lʌʃ ɪz
   -əz **lushest** 'lʌʃ ɪst -əst
Lushington 'lʌʃ ɪŋ tən
lush‖ly 'lʌʃ ‖li **~ness** nəs nɪs
Lusiad 'luːs i æd 'ljuːs- **~s** z
Lusitani‖a ˌluːs ɪ 'teɪn i‿ə ˌ•ə- **~an/s** ən/z
lust lʌst **lusted** 'lʌst ɪd -əd **lusting** 'lʌst ɪŋ
   lusts lʌsts
luster 'lʌst ə ‖ -ᵊr **~s** z
lustful 'lʌst fᵊl -fʊl **~ly** i **~ness** nəs ˌnɪs
lusti... —*see* **lusty**
lustral 'lʌs trəl
lus‖trate lʌ 's‖treɪt 'lʌs ‖treɪt ‖ 'lʌs ‖treɪt
   ~trated treɪt ɪd -əd ‖ treɪt̬ əd **~trates** treɪts
   ~trating treɪt ɪŋ ‖ treɪt̬ ɪŋ
lustration lʌ 'streɪʃ ᵊn **~s** z
lustre 'lʌst ə ‖ -ᵊr **~s** z
lustrous 'lʌs trəs **~ly** li **~ness** nəs nɪs
lus‖trum 'lʌs ‖trəm **~tra** trə **~trums** trəmz
lust‖y 'lʌst ‖i **~ier** i‿ə ‖ i‿ᵊr **~iest** i‿ɪst i‿əst
   ~ily ɪ li əl i **~iness** i nəs i nɪs
lutanist 'luːt ᵊn ɪst 'ljuːt-, §-əst ‖ -ᵊn‿əst **~s** s
lute luːt ljuːt **lutes** luːts ljuːts
luteal 'luːt i‿əl 'ljuːt- ‖ 'luːt̬-
luteinis‖e, luteiniz‖e 'luːt i‿ɪ naɪz 'ljuːt-, -i‿ə-;
   '•ɪ naɪz, -ə-, -iː-, -ᵊn aɪz ‖ 'luːt̬- **~ed** d **~es** ɪz
   əz **~ing** ɪŋ
lutenist 'luːt ᵊn ɪst 'ljuːt-, §-əst ‖ -ᵊn‿əst **~s** s
lutetium lu 'tiːʃ əm -'tiːʃ i‿əm
Luther 'luːθ ə ‖ -ᵊr —*Ger* ['lʊt ɐ]
Lutheran 'luːθ ᵊr‿ən **~ism** ˌɪz əm **~s** z
Lutine ˌluː 'tiːn ◂
Luton 'luːt ᵊn
Lutterworth 'lʌt ə wəθ -wɜːθ ‖ 'lʌt̬ ᵊr wɝːθ
Lutyens 'lʌt jənz 'lʌtʃ ᵊnz
lutz, Lutz lʊts luːts **lutzes** 'lʊts ɪz 'luːts-, -əz
luv lʌv **luvs** lʌvz
luvv‖ie, luvv‖y 'lʌv‖i **~ies** iz
lux, Lux *tdmk* lʌks
lux‖ate lʌk 's‖eɪt 'lʌks ‖eɪt ‖ 'lʌks ‖eɪt **~ated**
   eɪt ɪd -əd ‖ eɪt̬ əd **~ates** eɪts **~ating**
   eɪt ɪŋ ‖ eɪt̬ ɪŋ
luxation lʌk 'seɪʃ ᵊn **~s** z
luxe lʌks lʊks, luːks ‖ lʊks lʌks, luːks —*Fr*
   [lyks]
Luxemburg 'lʌks əm bɜːg ‖ -bɝːg —*Ger*
   ['lʊks əm bʊʁk], *Fr* Luxembourg [lyk sɑ̃ buːʁ]
Luxor 'lʌks ɔː ‖ -ɔːr
luxuri‖ance lʌg 'zjʊər i‿ᵊnᵗs ləg-, lʌk-, -'zʊər-;
   lʌk 'sjʊər- -'ʃʊər- ‖ lʌg 'ʒʊr- lʌk 'ʃʊr-
   ~ant/ly ənt /li

luxuri‖ate lʌg 'zjʊər i ‖eɪt ləg-, lʌk-, -'ʒʊər-;
   lʌk 'sjʊər-, -'ʃʊər- ‖ lʌg 'ʒʊr- lʌk 'ʃʊr-
   ~ated eɪt ɪd -əd ‖ eɪt̬ əd **~ates** eɪts **~ating**
   eɪt ɪŋ ‖ eɪt̬ ɪŋ

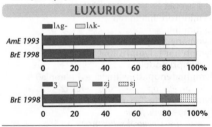

LUXURIOUS

luxurious lʌk 'ʒʊər i‿əs lək-, lʌg-, ləg-, -'ʃʊər-,
   -'zjʊər-, -'sjʊər- ‖ lʌg 'ʒʊr- lʌk 'ʃʊr- —*Poll
panel preferences: AmE 1993,* lʌg- *79%,* lʌk-
21%. BrE 1998: lʌk- *67%,* lʌg- *33%;* ʒ *50%,*
ʃ *26%,* zj *13%,* sj *11%.* **~ly** li **~ness** nəs nɪs

LUXURY

	'lʌk-		'lʌg-		

BrE 1988

AmE 1993

| 0 | 20 | 40 | 60 | 80 | 100% |

luxur‖y 'lʌk ʃᵊr‿li §'lʌg ʒᵊr‿li ‖ 'lʌg ʒᵊr‿li
   'lʌk ʃᵊr‿li —*Poll panel preferences: BrE 1988,*
   'lʌk- *96%,* 'lʌg- *4%; AmE 1993,* 'lʌk- *48%,*
   'lʌg- *52%.* **~ies** iz
Luzon ˌlu: 'zɒn ‖ -'zɑːn
Lvov lə 'vɒf ‖ -'vɑːf -'vɔːf —*Ukrainian* Lwiw
   [lʲiwʲifʲ], *Polish* Lwów [lvuf], *Russian* [lʲvof]
-ly li —*After a stem ending in* l, *one* l *is usually
lost, together with any* ə, *thus* fully 'fʊl i, *gently*
   'dʒent li.
Lyall 'laɪ‿əl
Lybrand 'laɪ brænd
lycanthrope 'laɪk ᵊn θrəʊp laɪ 'kænᵗθ rəʊp
   ‖ -θroʊp **~s** s
lycanthropy laɪ 'kænᵗθ rəp i
lycee, lycée 'liːs eɪ ‖ liː 'seɪ —*Fr* [li se] **~s** z
Lyceum laɪ 'siː‿əm
lychee ˌlaɪ 'tʃiː '••; 'lɪtʃ i ‖ 'liːtʃ i **~s** z
lychgate 'lɪtʃ geɪt **~s** s
lychnis 'lɪk nɪs §-nəs
Lyci‖a 'lɪs i‿ə ‖ 'lɪʃ- **~an/s** ən/z
Lycidas 'lɪs ɪ dæs -ə-
lycopodium ˌlaɪk ə 'pəʊd i‿əm ‖ -'poʊd-
Lycos *tdmk* 'laɪk ɒs ‖ -ɑːs
Lycra *tdmk* 'laɪk rə
Lycurgus laɪ 'kɜːg əs ‖ -'kɝːg-
Lydd lɪd
lyddite 'lɪd aɪt
Lydgate 'lɪd geɪt →'lɪg-, -gɪt —*but in Sheffield,*
   'lɪdʒ ɪt
Lydi‖a 'lɪd i‿ə **~an/s** ən/z
lye laɪ *(= lie)*
Lyell 'laɪ‿əl
Lygon 'laɪg ən
lying 'laɪ‿ɪŋ
lying-in ˌlaɪ‿ɪŋ 'ɪn **lyings-in** ˌlaɪ‿ɪŋz 'ɪn
Lyle laɪᵊl

L

Lyly 'lɪl i
Lyme laɪm
lyme-grass 'laɪm grɑːs §-græs ‖ -græs
Lymeswold *tdmk* 'laɪmz wəʊld →-wʊld
  ‖ -woʊld
Lymington 'lɪm ɪŋ tən
Lymm lɪm
Lympany 'lɪmp ən i
lymph lɪmpf **lymphs** lɪmpfs
  'lymph node
lymphadenopath|y ˌlɪmpf ˌæd ɪ 'nɒp əθ |i
  -ˌˈə-, -ən 'ɒp- ‖ -ən 'ɑːp- **~ies** iz
lymphatic lɪm 'fæt ɪk ‖ -'fæt̬- **~s** s
lympho- *comb. form*
  with stress-neutral suffix ˈlɪmpf əʊ ‖ -ə —
  lymphocyte 'lɪmpf əʊ saɪt ‖ -ə-
  with stress-imposing suffix lɪm 'fɒ+ ‖ -'fɑː+ —
  lymphopathy lɪm 'fɒp əθ i ‖ -'fɑːp-
lymphoma lɪm 'fəʊm ə ‖ -'foʊm ə **~s** z
Lympne lɪm
Lynam 'laɪn əm
lynch, Lynch lɪntʃ **lynched** lɪntʃt **lynches**
  'lɪntʃ ɪz -əz **lynching** 'lɪntʃ ɪŋ
  'lynch law; 'lynch mob
Lynchburg 'lɪntʃ bɜːg ‖ -bɝːg
Lyndhurst 'lɪnd hɜːst ‖ -hɝːst
Lyndon 'lɪnd ən
Lyneham 'laɪn əm
Lynette lɪ 'net
Lynmouth 'lɪn məθ →'lɪm-
Lynn, Lynne lɪn
Lynton 'lɪnt ən ‖ -ən
lynx, Lynx lɪŋks **lynxes** 'lɪŋks ɪz -əz
lynx-eyed ˌlɪŋks 'aɪd ◄ '··
lyo- *comb. form*
  with stress-neutral suffix ˈlaɪ əʊ ‖ -ə —
  lyophilic ˌlaɪ əʊ 'fɪl ɪk ◄ ‖ -ə-
  with stress-imposing suffix laɪ 'ɒ+ ‖ -'ɑː+ —
  lyophilize laɪ 'ɒf ɪ laɪz -ə- ‖ -'ɑːf ə-
Lyon *surname* 'laɪ_ən

Lyonesse ˌlaɪ_ə 'nes
lyonnaise ˌliː_ə 'neɪz ◄ ˌlaɪ_ —*Fr* [ljɔ nɛːz]
Lyonnesse ˌlaɪ_ə 'nes
Lyons *family name* 'laɪ_ənz
Lyons *place in France* 'liː ɒ̃ -ɒn; 'laɪ_ənz
  ‖ liː 'ɑːn -'ɔːn —*Fr* Lyon [ljɔ̃]
Lyra 'laɪ°r ə
lyre 'laɪ_ə ‖ 'laɪ_°r *(= liar)* **lyres**
  'laɪ_əz ‖ 'laɪ_°rz
lyrebird 'laɪ_ə bɜːd ‖ 'laɪ_°r bɝːd **~s** z
lyric 'lɪr ɪk **~al** °l **~ally** °l_i **~s** s
lyricism 'lɪr ɪ ˌsɪz əm -ə-
lyricist 'lɪr ɪs ɪst -əs-, §-əst **~s** s
lyrist *'lyric poet'* 'lɪr ɪst §-əst **~s** s
lyrist *'lyre player'* 'laɪ_ər ɪst 'lɪr ɪst; §-əst **~s** s
Lysander laɪ 'sænd ə ‖ -°r
-lyse laɪz — **paralyse** 'pær ə laɪz ‖ 'per-
Lysenko lɪ 'seŋk əʊ lə- ‖ -oʊ —*Russian*
  [ɫɪ 'sʲen kə]
lysergic laɪ 'sɜːdʒ ɪk lɪ-, lə- ‖ -'sɝːdʒ-
  ly ˌsergic 'acid
Lysias 'lɪs i æs ‖ -əs
lysis 'laɪs ɪs §-əs
-lysis *stress-imposing* ləs ɪs lɪs-, §-əs —
  paralysis pə 'ræl əs ɪs -ɪs-, §-əs
Lysistrata laɪ 'sɪs trət ə ˌlɪs ɪ 'strɑːt ə, ˌlɪz-
  ‖ ˌlɪs ə 'strɑːt ə laɪ 'sɪs trət̬ ə
lysol, Lysol *tdmk* 'laɪs ɒl ‖ -ɔːl -ɑːl, -oʊl
lysosome 'laɪs əʊ səʊm ‖ -ə soʊm **~s** z
lysozyme 'laɪz əʊ zaɪm ‖ -ə zaɪm
Lystra 'lɪs trə
lystrosaur 'lɪs trəʊ sɔː ‖ -trə sɔːr
-lyte laɪt — **electrolyte** ɪ 'lek trəʊ laɪt ə-
  ‖-trə-
Lytham 'lɪð əm
-lytic 'lɪt ɪk ‖ 'lɪt̬ ɪk — **electrolytic** ɪ ˌlek trəʊ
  'lɪt ɪk ◄ ‖ -trə 'lɪt̬ ɪk ◄
Lyttelton 'lɪt °l tən ‖ 'lɪt̬-
Lytton 'lɪt °n

M m

1 Where the spelling is **m**, the pronunciation is regularly m, as in **medium** 'miːd i‿əm.

2 Where the spelling is double **mm**, the pronunciation is again regularly m, as in **hammer** 'hæm ə ‖ 'hæm ᵊr.

M, m em   M's, m's, Ms emz —*Communications code name:* Mike

'm m —*see* I'm

M'..., M'...*in this dictionary listed alphabetically as if written* Mac...

M1 ˌem 'wʌn §-'wɒn   M25 ˌem ˌtwent i 'faɪv △-ˌtwen i- ‖ -ˌtwenṭ i-   M40 ˌem 'fɔːt i ‖ -'fɔːrṭ i —*and similarly for other British motorway numbers*

ma, Ma mɑː   mas, Ma's mɑːz

MA *'master of arts'* ˌem 'eɪ

MA —*see* Massachusetts

Maalox *tdmk* 'meɪ lɒks ‖ -lɑːks

ma'am *strong form* mæm mɑːm, *weak form* məm —*After* yes *there is also a weak form* əm.

Maas mɑːs —*Dutch* [maːs]

Maastricht 'mɑːs trɪkt -trɪxt —*Dutch* [ma: 'strɪxt]

Mab, Mabb mæb

Mabel 'meɪb ᵊl

Mabinogion ˌmæb ɪ 'nɒg i ɒn ˌ•ə-, -i‿ən ‖ -'noʊg i ɑːn —*Welsh* [ma bi 'nog jon]

Mablethorpe 'meɪb ᵊl θɔːp ‖ -θɔːrp

Mableton 'meɪb ᵊl tən

Mabley (i) 'meɪb li, (ii) 'mæb li

Mabon (i) 'meɪb ən, (ii) 'mæb ən

Mac, mac mæk

Mac-, Mc- *prefix in names: (i) usually, unstressed* mək, *or sometimes* mæk (*perhaps depending on degree of formality*): Mc'Donald, Mac'Donald, Mac'donald; *but (ii)* ˌmæk *before an unstressed syllable:* 'McEnroe, ˌMacEnroe; (iii) mə *before* k, g: Mc'Gill, Mac'Gill, Mac'gill, Mac 'Gill. *This prefix is spelt sometimes* Mac, *sometimes* Mc, *sometimes* M' *or* M', *and the stem which follows may be spelt with a capital letter or with a small one. Particularly in Ireland, the prefix is sometimes written as a separate word. To save repetition, many entries below are shown only in the* Mc- *form, with a capital letter for the stem, all written as one word.* Mc- *is in any case listed here alphabetically as if it were* Mac-.

macabre mə 'kɑːb_rə -ə ‖ -ᵊr -ly li

macadam, McAdam mə 'kæd əm

macadamia ˌmæk ə 'deɪm i‿ə ~s z ˌmaca'damia nut

macadamis|e, macadamiz|e mə 'kæd ə maɪz ~ed d ~es ɪz əz ~ing ɪŋ

Macafee, McAfee (i) ˌmæk ə 'fiː '•••, (ii) mə 'kæf i -'kɑːf-

McAleese ˌmæk ə 'liːs

McAlery ˌmæk ə 'lɪər i ‖ -'lɪr i

McAlinden, McAlindon ˌmæk ə 'lɪnd ən

McAlister, McAllister mə 'kæl ɪst ə -əst- ‖ -ᵊr

McAloon ˌmæk ə 'luːn

McAlpine mə 'kælp aɪn -ɪn, §-ən

McAnally ˌmæk ə 'næl i

McAnespie ˌmæk ə 'nesp i

McAnulty ˌmæk ə 'nʌlt i

Macao mə 'kaʊ —*Port* Macáu [mɐ 'kau], *Chi* Ào Mén [⁴ɐu ²mən]

macaque mə 'kɑːk -'kæk; 'mæk æk ~s s

McArdle mə 'kɑːd ᵊl ‖ -'kɑːrd-

macarena ˌmæk ə 'reɪn ə ‖ ˌmɑːk- —*Sp* macareña [ma ka 're ɲa]

macaroni ˌmæk ə 'rəʊn i ◀ ‖ -'roʊn i ◀ ~es, ~s z ˌmaca,roni 'cheese

macaronic ˌmæk ə 'rɒn ɪk ◀ ‖ -'rɑːn ɪk ◀ ~s s

macaroon ˌmæk ə 'ruːn ~s z

McArthur mə 'kɑːθ ə ‖ -'kɑːrθ ᵊr

Macassar, m~ mə 'kæs ə ‖ -ᵊr Ma'cassar oil

McAteer ˌmæk ə 'tɪə '••• ‖ -'tɪᵊr

Macau, Macáu mə 'kaʊ —*Port* [mɐ 'kau], *Chi* Ào Mén [⁴ɐu ²mən]

Macaulay, McAulay, McAuley mə 'kɔːl i ‖ -'kɑːl-

McAuliffe mə 'kɔːl ɪf §-əf ‖ -'kɑːl-

Macavity mə 'kæv ət i -ɪt- ‖ -əṭ i

McAvoy 'mæk ə vɔɪ

macaw mə 'kɔː ‖ -'kɑː ~s z

McBain mək 'beɪn §mæk-

Macbeth, McBeth mək 'beθ mæk-

McBrain, McBrayne mək 'breɪn §mæk-

McBrearty mək 'brɪət i §mæk- ‖ -'brɪrṭ i

McBride mək 'braɪd §mæk-

McCabe mə 'keɪb

M

Maccabae|an, Maccabe|an ˌmæk ə ˈbiː_lən ◄
-ˈbeɪ- ~us əs
Maccabees ˈmæk ə biːz
Maccabeus ˌmæk ə ˈbiː_əs ◄ -ˈbeɪ-
McCaffray, McCaffrey mə ˈkæf ri
McCain mə ˈkeɪn
McCall mə ˈkɔːl ‖ -ˈkɑːl
McCallum mə ˈkæl əm
McCambridge mə ˈkeɪm brɪdʒ
McCanlis mə ˈkæn lɪs -ləs
McCann mə ˈkæn
McCarran mə ˈkær ən ‖ -ˈker-
McCarthy mə ˈkɑːθ i ‖ -ˈkɑːrθ i ~ism ˌɪz əm
McCarthyite mə ˈkɑːθ i aɪt ‖ -ˈkɑːrθ- ~s s
McCartney mə ˈkɑːt ni ‖ -ˈkɑːrt-
McCaskill mə ˈkæsk əl -ɪl
McCavish mə ˈkæv ɪʃ
macchiato ˌmæk i ˈɑːt əʊ ‖ ˌmɑːk i ˈɑːt̬ oʊ —It
[mak ˈkja: to]
McCleary, McCleery mə ˈklɪər i ‖ -ˈklɪr i
McClellan mə ˈklel ən
McClelland mə ˈklel ənd
Macclesfield ˈmæk əlz fiːəld
McClintock mə ˈklɪnt ɒk -ək ‖ -ɑːk
McCloskey mə ˈklɒsk i ‖ -ˈklɑːsk i
McClure mə ˈkluə ‖ -ˈkluər
McCluskie mə ˈklʌsk i
Maccoby ˈmæk əb i
McColl mə ˈkɒl ‖ -ˈkɑːl
McConachie, McConachy, McConaghy,
McConochie mə ˈkɒn ək i -əx i, -ə hi
‖ -ˈkɑːn-
McCool mə ˈkuːl
McCormack mə ˈkɔːm ək -æk ‖ -ˈkɔːrm-
McCormick mə ˈkɔːm ɪk §-ək ‖ -ˈkɔːrm-
McCorquodale mə ˈkɔːk ə deɪəl ‖ -ˈkɔːrk-
McCowan mə ˈkaʊ_ən
McCoy mə ˈkɔɪ
McCrae, McCrea mə ˈkreɪ
McCreadie, McCready (i) mə ˈkriːd i, (ii)
mə ˈkred i
McCrindell, McCrindle mə ˈkrɪn dəl
McCrum mə ˈkrʌm
McCullers mə ˈkʌl əz ‖ -ərz
McCulloch, McCullough mə ˈkʌl ək -əx
McCurtain, McCurtin mə ˈkɜːt ɪn -ən
‖ -ˈkɜːt ən
McCusker mə ˈkʌsk ə ‖ -ər
McDade mək ˈdeɪd
McDermot, McDermott
mək ˈdɜːm ət ‖ -ˈdɜːm-
McDiarmid mək ˈdɜːm ɪd §mæk-, -ˈdeəm-,
§-əd ‖ -ˈdɜːm-
McDonagh mək ˈdɒn ə ‖ -ˈdɑːn ə
McDonald, Macdonald mək ˈdɒn əld mæk-
‖ -ˈdɑːn- ~'s tdmk z
McDonnell (i) ˌmæk də ˈnel, (ii) mək ˈdɒn əl
§mæk- ‖ -ˈdɑːn-
McDougal, McDougall mək ˈduːg əl mæk-
McDowall, McDowell (i)
mək ˈdaʊ_əl ‖ -ˈdaʊ_əl, (ii) -ˈdəʊ- ‖ -ˈdoʊ-
McDuff, Macduff mək ˈdʌf mæk-

mace, Mace meɪs Maced meɪst maces,
Maces ˈmeɪs ɪz -əz Macing ˈmeɪs ɪŋ
mace-bearer ˈmeɪs ˌbeər ə ‖ -ˌber ər -ˌbær- ~s
z
macedoine, macédoine ˌmæs ɪ ˈdwɑːn -ə-,
ˈ••• ~s z
Macedon ˈmæs ɪd ən -əd- ‖ -ə dɑːn
Macedoni|a ˌmæs ɪ ˈdəʊn i_ə ˌ•ə- ‖ -ˈdoʊn-
~an/s ən/z
McElderry, McEldery ˈmæk əl ˌder i ˌ••ˈ••
McElhone ˈmæk əl həʊn ‖ -hoʊn
McElligott mə ˈkel ɪg ət -əg-
McElroy ˈmæk əl rɔɪ —but in AmE also mə ˈkel-
McElwain (i) ˈmæk əl weɪn, (ii) mə ˈkel weɪn
mæk-
McEnroe ˈmæk ɪn rəʊ -ən- ‖ -roʊ
mace|rate ˈmæs ə |reɪt ~rated reɪt ɪd -əd
‖ reɪt̬ əd ~rates reɪts ~rating
reɪt ɪŋ ‖ reɪt̬ ɪŋ
maceration ˌmæs ə ˈreɪʃ ən ~s z
macerator ˈmæs ə reɪt ə ‖ -reɪt̬ ər ~s z
McEvoy ˈmæk ɪ vɔɪ -ə-
McEwan, McEwen mə ˈkjuː_ən
McFadden mək ˈfæd ən
McFadyean, McFadyen, McFadzean
mək ˈfæd jən §mæk-
McFarland mək ˈfɑːl ənd ‖ -ˈfɑːrl-
McFarlane mək ˈfɑːl ɪn §mæk-, -ən ‖ -ˈfɑːrl-
McFee, McFie mək ˈfiː mæk-
McGahey mə ˈgɑː hi -ˈgæ-, -ˈgæx i
McGee mə ˈgiː
McGill mə ˈgɪl
McGillicuddy (i) ˈmæg lɪ ˌkʌd i, (ii)
mə ˈgɪl i ˌkʌd i
McGilligan mə ˈgɪl ɪg ən -əg-
McGillivray mə ˈgɪl ɪv ri -əv-, -reɪ
McGillycuddy (i) ˈmæg lɪ ˌkʌd i, (ii)
mə ˈgɪl i ˌkʌd i
ˌMacgilly ˌcuddy's ˈReeks
McGinn mə ˈgɪn
McGinty mə ˈgɪnt i ‖ -ˈgɪnt̬ i
McGlashan mə ˈglæʃ ən
McGoldrick mə ˈgəʊld rɪk →-ˈgɒʊld-
‖ -ˈgoʊld-
McGonagall mə ˈgɒn əg əl ‖ -ˈgɑːn-
McGoohan mə ˈguː_ən -hən
McGough mə ˈgɒf ‖ -ˈgɑːf -ˈgɔːf
McGovern mə ˈgʌv ən ‖ -ərn
McGowan mə ˈgaʊ_ən
McGrady mə ˈgreɪd i (!)
McGrath mə ˈgrɑːθ -ˈgræθ, -ˈgrɑː ‖ -ˈgræθ —In
Ireland also -ˈgræh
McGraw mə ˈgrɔː ‖ -ˈgrɑː
McGregor mə ˈgreg ə ‖ -ər
McGuffey mə ˈgʌf i
McGuffin mə ˈgʌf ɪn §-ən
McGuigan mə ˈgwiːg ən -ˈgwɪg-
McGuinness mə ˈgɪn ɪs §-əs
McGuire mə ˈgwaɪ_ə ‖ -ˈgwaɪ_ər
McGurk mə ˈgɜːk ‖ -ˈgɜːrk
McGwire mə ˈgwaɪ_ə ‖ -ˈgwaɪ_ər
Mach, mach mɑːk mæk, mɒk —Ger [max]
McHale mək ˈheɪəl

M

Macheath mək ˈhiːθ mæk-
Machen (i) ˈmeɪtʃ ɪn -ən, (ii) ˈmæk-, (iii) ˈmæx-
—The place in Gwent is (iii)
McHenry mək ˈhen ri
machete mə ˈʃet i -ˈtʃet-, -ˈtʃeɪt-; mə ˈʃet
‖ mə ˈʃet̬ i -ˈtʃet̬-; mə ˈʃet machetes
mə ˈʃet iz -ˈtʃet-, -ˈtʃeɪt-; mə ˈʃets
‖ mə ˈʃet̬ iz -ˈtʃet̬-; mə ˈʃets
Machiavelli ˌmæk i‿ə ˈvel i —It [ma kja ˈvɛl li]
Machiavellian ˌmæk i‿ə ˈvel i‿ən ◂ ~ism ˌɪz
əm ~s z
machico|late mə ˈtʃɪk əʊ ‖leɪt mæ- ‖ -ə-
~lated leɪt ɪd -əd ‖ leɪt̬ əd ~lates leɪts
~lating leɪt ɪŋ ‖ leɪt̬ ɪŋ
machicolation mə ˌtʃɪk əʊ ˈleɪʃ ᵊn mæ- ‖ -ə-
~s z
Machin ˈmeɪtʃ ɪn §-ən
machi|nate ˈmæk ɪ ‖neɪt ˈmæʃ-, -ə- ~nated
neɪt ɪd -əd ‖ neɪt̬ əd ~nates neɪts ~nating
neɪt ɪŋ ‖ neɪt̬ ɪŋ
machination ˌmæk ɪ ˈneɪʃ ᵊn ˌmæʃ-, -ə- ~s z
machine mə ˈʃiːn machined mə ˈʃiːnd
machines mə ˈʃiːnz machining mə ˈʃiːn ɪŋ
maˈchine code; maˈchine ˌgunner;
maˈchine tool
machinegun mə ˈʃiːn gʌn →-ˈʃiːŋ- ~ned d
~ning ɪŋ ~s z
machine-readable mə ˌʃiːn ˈriːd əb ᵊl ◂
machiner|y mə ˈʃiːn ər‿li ~ies iz
machine-wash mə ˌʃiːn ˈwɒʃ ‖ -ˈwɔːʃ -ˈwɑːʃ
~ed t ~es ɪz əz ~ing ɪŋ
machine-washable
mə ˌʃiːn ˈwɒʃ əb ᵊl ‖ -ˈwɔːʃ- -ˈwɑːʃ-
machinist mə ˈʃiːn ɪst -əst ~s s
machismo mə ˈtʃɪz məʊ mæ-, △-ˈkɪz-
‖ mɑː ˈtʃiːz moʊ mə-, -ˈtʃɪz- —Sp
[ma ˈtʃiz mo]
macho ˈmætʃ əʊ ˈmɑːtʃ- ‖ ˈmɑːtʃ oʊ △ˈmɑːk-
~s z
Machrihanish ˌmæk rɪ ˈhæn ɪʃ ˌmæx-, -rə-
Machu Picchu ˌmætʃ uː ˈpɪk tʃuː ˌmɑːtʃ-,
-ˈpiːk- ‖ ˌmɑːtʃ uː ˈpiːk tʃu —Sp
[ˈma tʃu ˈpik tʃu]
Machynlleth mə ˈkʌn ɬəθ —Welsh
[ma ˈχən ɬeθ]
McIlroy ˈmæk ɪl rɔɪ -ᵊl-, ˌˌˈˌ•ˈˌ•
McIlvaney ˌmæk ᵊl ˈveɪn i -ɪl-
McIlvenny ˌmæk ᵊl ˈven i -ɪl-
McIlwain ˈmæk ᵊl weɪn -ɪl-
McIlwraith ˈmæk ᵊl reɪθ -ɪl-
McIndoe ˈmæk ɪn dəʊ -ən- ‖ -doʊ
McInnes, McInnis mə ˈkɪn ɪs §-əs
McIntosh, macintosh ˈmæk ɪn tɒʃ §-ən-
‖ -tɑːʃ ~es ɪz əz
McIntyre ˈmæk ɪn taɪ‿ə §ˈ•ən- ‖ -taɪ‿ər
McIver, McIvor (i) mə ˈkaɪv ə ‖ -ᵊr, (ii)
mə ˈkiːv ə ‖ -ᵊr
MacJob (ˌ)mək ˈdʒɒb ‖ -ˈdʒɑːb —also ˈ••, when
in contrast to (real) job ~s z
mack, Mack mæk macks mæks
Mackay, McKay (i) mə ˈkaɪ, (ii) mə ˈkeɪ —In
BrE usually (i).
McKechnie mə ˈkex ni -ˈkek-

McKee mə ˈkiː
McKellar mə ˈkel ə ‖ -ᵊr
McKellen mə ˈkel ən
McKendrick mə ˈkendr ɪk
McKenna mə ˈken ə
Mackenzie, McKenzie mə ˈkenz i
McKeown mə ˈkjəʊn ‖ -ˈkjoʊn
mackerel ˈmæk rəl ˈmæk ər əl ~s z
McKern mə ˈkɜːn ‖ -ˈkɜːn
McKerras mə ˈker əs
Mackeson ˈmæk ɪs ən -əs-
Mackie ˈmæk i
McKie (i) mə ˈkaɪ, (ii) mə ˈkiː
Mackin ˈmæk ɪn §-ən
Mackinac, Mackinaw, m~ˈmæk ɪ nɔː -ə- ‖ -nɑː
~s z
McKinlay, McKinley mə ˈkɪn li
McKinnon mə ˈkɪn ən
mackintosh, M~ ˈmæk ɪn tɒʃ §-ən- ‖ -tɑːʃ
~es ɪz əz
McKittrick mə ˈkɪtr ɪk
McLachlan mə ˈklɒx lən -ˈklɒk- ‖ -ˈklɑːk-
MacLaine mə ˈkleɪn
Maclaren, McLaren mə ˈklær ən ‖ -ˈkler-
McLaughlin mə ˈklɒx lɪn -ˈklɒk-, -ˈglɒx-, §-lən
‖ -ˈklɑːk-
McLaurin mə ˈklɔːr ɪn -ˈklɒr-, §-ən
McLean, Maclean (i) mə ˈkleɪn, (ii) mə ˈkliːn
Macleans tdmk mə ˈkliːnz
McLehose ˈmæk ᵊl həʊz -lɪ-, -lə- ‖ -hoʊz
McLeish, MacLeish mə ˈkliːʃ mæk ˈliːʃ
McLennan mə ˈklen ən
Macleod, McLeod mə ˈklaʊd (!)
McLiammoir mə ˈkliːəm ɔː ‖ -ˈkliː ə mɔːr
McLintock mə ˈklɪnt ɒk -ək ‖ -ɑːk
McLoughlin mə ˈklɒx lɪn -ˈklɒk-, -ˈglɒk-, §-lən
‖ -ˈklɑːk-
McLuhan mə ˈkluː‿ən
McLysaght mə ˈklaɪs ət -ə, -əkt
McMahon mək ˈmɑːn §mæk-, -ˈmɑː ən,
-ˈmæ hən ‖ -ˈmæn
McManaman mək ˈmæn əm ən
McManus mək ˈmæn əs §mæk-, -ˈmɑːn-,
-ˈmeɪn-
McMartin mək ˈmɑːt ɪn mæk-, §-ᵊn
‖ -ˈmɑːrt ᵊn
McMaster mək ˈmɑːst ə mæk-, §-ˈmæst-
‖ -ˈmæst ᵊr
McMenemey, McMenemy mək ˈmen əm i
McMichael mək ˈmaɪk ᵊl
Macmillan, McMillan mək ˈmɪl ən mæk-
McMullan, McMullen mək ˈmʌl ən
McMurdo mək ˈmɜːd əʊ ‖ -ˈmɜːd oʊ
McMurray mək ˈmʌr i ‖ -ˈmɜː i
McMurtry mək ˈmɜːtr i ‖ -ˈmɜːtr i
McNab mək ˈnæb §mæk-
McNaghten, McNaghton mək ˈnɔːt ᵊn
mæk- ‖ -ˈnɑːt-
McNair mək ˈneə ‖ -ˈneᵊr
McNally mək ˈnæl i
Macnamara, McNamara
ˌmæk nə ˈmɑːr ə ‖ ˈmæk nə ˌmær ə -ˌmer ə
McNamee ˌmæk nə ˈmiː

M

McNaughten, McNaughton mək 'nɔːt ən
mæk- ‖ -'nɑːt-
McNeice mək 'niːs
McNeil mək 'niːəl
McNeilage mək 'niːl ɪdʒ
McNeill mək 'niːəl
McNestry mək 'nes tri
MacNugget *tdmk* mək 'nʌg ɪt mæk-, §-ət ~s s
Macon *place in Georgia* 'meɪk ən
Macon *place in France; wine* 'mɑːk ɒ̃ 'mæk-,
-ɒn ‖ mɑː 'koʊn —*Fr* Mâcon [ma kɔ̃]
Maconachie mə 'kɒn ək i -əx i, -ə hi ‖ -'kɑːn-
Maconchy mə 'kɒŋk i ‖ -'kɑːŋk i
Maconochie mə 'kɒn ək i -əx- ‖ -'kɑːn-
McPhail mək 'feɪəl
McPhee mək 'fiː
McPherson mək 'fɜːs ən mæk-, -'fɪəs-
‖ -'fɜːs ən
McQuade mə 'kweɪd
Macquarie, McQuarrie mə 'kwɒr i ‖ -'kwɔːr i
-'kwɑːr i
McQueen mə 'kwiːn
McRae mə 'kreɪ
macrame, macramé mə 'krɑːm i -eɪ
‖ 'mæk rə meɪ (*)
Macready, McReady mə 'kriːd i
macro 'mæk rəʊ ‖ -roʊ ~s z
macro- *comb. form*
with stress-neutral suffix ¦mæk rəʊ ‖ -roʊ
— macroclimatic ˌmæk rəʊ klaɪ 'mæt ɪk ◄
‖ ˌmæk roʊ klaɪ 'mæt̬ ɪk ◄
with stress-imposing suffix
mæ 'krɒ+ ‖ mæ 'krɑː+ — macropterous
mæ 'krɒpt ər əs ‖ -'krɑːpt-
macrobiotic ˌmæk rəʊ baɪ 'ɒt ɪk ◄ -bi'•-
‖ -rə baɪ 'ɑːt̬ ɪk ◄ ~ally əl_i ~s s
macrocarpa ˌmæk rəʊ 'kɑːp ə ‖ -roʊ 'kɑːrp ə
macrocosm 'mæk‿r əʊ ˌkɒz əm ‖ -ə ˌkɑːz əm
macroeconomic ˌmæk rəʊ ˌiːk ə 'nɒm ɪk ◄
-ˌek- ‖ -roʊ ˌek ə 'nɑːm-, -ˌiːk- ~s s
macron 'mæk rɒn 'meɪk-, -rən ‖ -rɑːn ~s z
macrophag|e 'mæk rəʊ feɪdʒ ‖ -rə- ~es ɪz əz
Macrossan mə 'krɒs ən ‖ -'krɔːs- -'krɑːs-
McShea mək 'ʃeɪ §mæk-
McSorley mək 'sɔːl i ‖ -'sɔːrl i
McSwiney mək 'swɪn i mæk-, -'swɪn-
McTaggart mək 'tæg ət mæk- ‖ -ərt
McTavish mək 'tæv ɪʃ mæk-
McTeague mək 'tiːg mæk-
McTeer mək 'tɪə mæk-, mə- ‖ -'tɪər
mac|ula 'mæk ¦jʊl ə -jəl- ‖ -jəl ə ~ulae ju liː
jə• ‖ jə liː
ˌmacula 'lutea 'luːt i_ə ‖ 'luːt̬-
McVay, McVeagh, McVeigh, McVey mək 'veɪ
McVicar mək 'vɪk ə ‖ -ər
McVitie, McVittie mək 'vɪt i mæk- ‖ -'vɪt̬ i
McWhirter mək 'wɜːt ə mæk-, -'hwɜːt-
‖ -'hwɜːt̬ ər
McWilliams mək 'wɪl jəmz mæk-
Macy 'meɪs i Macy's *tdmk* 'meɪs ɪz
mad, Mad mæd madder 'mæd ə ‖ -ər
maddest 'mæd ɪst -əst
Madagascan ˌmæd ə 'gæsk ən ◄ ~s z

Madagascar ˌmæd ə 'gæsk ə ‖ -ər
madam, Madam 'mæd əm ~s, ~'s z
Madame, m~ 'mæd əm ‖ mə 'dɑːm, -'dæm
—*Fr* [ma dam] ~s, ~'s z
Madang mə 'dæŋ ‖ mɑː 'dɑːŋ
madcap 'mæd kæp →'mæg- ~s s
madden, M~ 'mæd ən ~ed d ~ing/ly ɪŋ /li
~s z
madder 'mæd ə ‖ -ər
Maddie 'mæd i
madding 'mæd ɪŋ
Maddison 'mæd ɪs ən -əs-
Maddock 'mæd ək
Maddocks, Maddox 'mæd əks
made meɪd
Madeira mə 'dɪər ə ‖ -'dɪr ə —*Port* [mɐ 'ðɐi ɾɐ,
ma 'dei ɾa]
Ma'deira cake
Madejski mə 'deɪsk i
Madeleine, m~ 'mæd əl ɪn §-ən; -ə leɪn, -əl eɪn
~s z
Madeley 'meɪd li
Madeline 'mæd əl ɪn §_ən —*formerly also*
-ə laɪn
mademoiselle, M~ ˌmæd əm wə 'zel ◄ -ə'•;
ˌmæm wə 'zel —*Fr* [mad mwa zɛl, man-] ~s
z
made-to-measure ˌmeɪd tə 'meʒ ə ◄ ‖ -ər ◄
made-up ˌmeɪd 'ʌp ◄
ˌmade-up 'story
Madge mædʒ
mad|house 'mæd ¦haʊs ~houses haʊz ɪz -əz
Madingley 'mæd ɪŋ li
Madison 'mæd ɪs ən -əs-
ˌMadison 'Avenue
Madley 'mæd li
madly 'mæd li
mad|man 'mæd ¦mən →'mæb- ~men mən
men
madness 'mæd nəs -nɪs ~es ɪz əz
madonna, M~ mə 'dɒn ə ‖ -'dɑːn ə —*It*
[ma 'dɔn na] ~s, ~'s z
Madras mə 'drɑːs -'dræs —*but the place in OR
is* 'mædr əs
madras *'cotton'* 'mædr əs mə 'drɑːs -'dræs
madrepore 'mædr ɪ pɔː -ə-, ˌ••'• ‖ -pɔːr -poʊr
~s z
Madrid mə 'drɪd —*Sp* [ma 'ðrið]
madrigal 'mædr ɪg əl -əg- ~s z
madrilene, madrilène ˌmædr ɪ 'len -ə-, -'leɪn,
'••• —*Fr* [ma dʀi lɛn] ~s z
madrona, madrone mə 'drəʊn ə ‖ -'droʊn ə
~s z
mad|woman 'mæd ¦ˌwʊm ən ~women
ˌwɪm ɪn -ən
Mae meɪ
ˌMae 'West
Maecenas maɪ 'siːn æs miː-, -əs ‖ -əs
Maelor 'maɪl ɔː ‖ -ɔːr —*Welsh* ['məɪ lor, 'məɪ-]
maelstrom, M~ 'meɪəl strɒm -strəm, -strəʊm
‖ -strəm -strɑːm ~s z
maenad 'miːn æd ~s z
Maendy 'meɪnd i 'maɪnd- —*Welsh* ['məɪn di]

Maentwrog maɪn ˈtʊər ɒg ‖ -ˈtʊr ɑːg —*Welsh* [məin ˈtu rog, məin-]

Maerdy ˈmɑːd i ‖ ˈmɑːrd i —*but some places of this name have an alternative pronunciation* ˈmeɪ əd i ‖ -ᵊrd i *or* ˈmaɪˌəd i ‖ ˈmaɪᵊrd i

Maesteg ˌmaɪs ˈteɪg —*Welsh* [mais ˈteːg, maːs-]

maestoso maɪ ˈstəʊs əʊ -ˈstəʊz- ‖ -ˈstoʊs oʊ -ˈstoʊz- —*It* [ma e ˈstoː so]

maestro ˈmaɪs trəʊ ‖ -troʊ —*It* [ma ˈɛs tro] ~**s** z

Maeterlinck ˈmeɪt ə lɪŋk ‖ ˈmeɪt̬ ᵊr- —*Fr* [mɛ tɛʁ læ̃ːk]

Maev, Maeve meɪv

Mafeking ˈmæf ɪk ɪŋ -ək-

maffia, mafia, Mafia ˈmæf iˌə ˈmɑːf- ‖ ˈmɑːf- ˈmæf-

mafios|o ˌmæf i ˈəʊs ˌəʊ ˌmɑːf-, -ˈəʊz- ‖ ˌmɑːf i ˈoʊs ˌoʊ ˌmæf-, -ˈoʊz- ~**i** iː

mag mæg **mags** mægz

Magarshack ˈmæg ə ʃæk ‖ -ᵊr-

magazine ˌmæg ə ˈziːn ˈ•••‖ ˈmæg ə ziːn ˌˈ•• ‹ ~**s** z

Magda ˈmægd ə

Magdala ˈmægd əl ə mæg ˈdɑːl ə

Magdalen ˈmægd əl ɪn -ən —*but the Oxford college is* ˈmɔːd lɪn, -lən ‖ ˈmɔːd-, ˈmɑːd-

Magdalene ˌmægd ə ˈliːn i ˈmægd ə liːn, -lɪn —*but the Cambridge college is* ˈmɔːd lɪn, -lən ‖ ˈmɔːd-, ˈmɑːd-

Magdalenian ˌmægd ə ˈliːn iˌən ◂

mage meɪdʒ **mages** ˈmeɪdʒ ɪz -əz

Magee mə ˈgiː

Magellan mə ˈgel ən -ˈdʒel- ‖ -ˈdʒel ən

Magellanic ˌmæg ɪ ˈlæn ɪk ◂ ˌmædʒ-, -ə- ‖ ˌmædʒ-

    ˌMagelˌlanic ˈcloud

magenta, M~ mə ˈdʒent ə ‖ -ˈdʒent̬ ə

Maggie, m~ ˈmæg i

maggot ˈmæg ət ~**s** s

maggoty ˈmæg ət i ‖ -ət̬ i

Maggs mægz

Maghera ˌmæk ə ˈrɑː ˌmæ hə-

Magherafelt ˌmæk ᵊrˌə ˈfelt ˌmæ hᵊr_

Maghreb ˈmɑːg reb ˈmæg-, ˈmʌg-, -rɪb, -rəb; mɑː ˈgreb, mə-

Maghull mə ˈgʌl

magi, Magi ˈmeɪdʒ aɪ ˈmeɪg-

magic ˈmædʒ ɪk ~**ked** t ~**king** ɪŋ ~**s** s

    ˌmagic ˈcarpet; ˌmagic ˈeye; ˌmagic ˈlantern; ˌMagic ˈMarker *tdmk*; ˌmagic ˈsquare; ˌmagic ˈwand

magical ˈmædʒ ɪk ᵊl ~**ly** _i

magician mə ˈdʒɪʃ ᵊn ~**s** z

Magilligan mə ˈgɪl ɪg ən

Maginnis mə ˈgɪn ɪs §-əs

Maginot ˈmæʒ ɪ nəʊ ˈmædʒ-, -ə- ‖ -noʊ —*Fr* [ma ʒi no]

    ˈMaginot Line

magisteri|al ˌmædʒ ɪ ˈstɪər iˌəl ◂ ˌˈ•ə- ‖ -ˈstɪr- ~**ally** ᵊl_i ~**um** əm

magistrac|y ˈmædʒ ɪs trəs |i ˈ•əs- ~**ies** iz

magistral ˈmædʒ ɪs trəl -əs-; mə ˈdʒɪs-, mæ-

magistrate ˈmædʒ ɪ streɪt -ə-; -əs trət, -trɪt ~**s** s

maglev, M~ ˈmæg lev

mag|ma ˈmæg |mə ~**mas** məz ~**mata** mət ə ‖ mət̬ ə

Magna, magna ˈmæg nə

    ˌMagna ˈCarta, ˌMagna ˈCharta ˈkɑːt ə ‖ -ˈkɑːrt̬ ə

magna cum laude ˌmæg nə kʊm ˈlaʊd eɪ ˌ•nɑː-

magnanimity ˌmæg nə ˈnɪm ət i -ɪt i ‖ -ət̬ i

magnanimous mæg ˈnæn ɪm əs məg-, -əm- ~**ly** li ~**ness** nəs nɪs

magnate ˈmæg neɪt -nət, -nɪt ~**s** s

magnesia, M~ mæg ˈniːʃ ə məg-, -ˈniːs iˌə, -ˈniːʒ ə, -ˈniːz iˌə

magnesite ˈmæg nɪ saɪt -nə-

magnesium mæg ˈniːz iˌəm məg-, -ˈniːʒ əm, -ˈniːs iˌəm, -ˈniːʃ əm

    magˌnesium hyˈdroxide

magnet ˈmæg nɪt -nət ~**s** s

magnetic mæg ˈnet ɪk məg- ‖ -ˈnet̬ ɪk ~**ally** ᵊl_i

    magˌnetic ˈfield; magˌnetic ˈnorth; magˌnetic ˈpole; magˌnetic ˈtape

magnetis... —*see* **magnetiz...**

magnetism ˈmæg nə ˌtɪz əm -nɪ-

magnetite ˈmæg nə taɪt -nɪ-

magnetization ˌmæg nət aɪ ˈzeɪʃ ᵊn ˌ•nɪt-, -ɪ'•• ‖ -nət ə- ~**s** z

magnetiz|e ˈmæg nə taɪz -nɪ- ~**ed** d ~**es** ɪz əz ~**ing** ɪŋ

magneto mæg ˈniːt əʊ məg- ‖ -ˈniːt̬ oʊ ~**s** z

magneto- *comb. form*
    with stress-neutral suffix mæg ˈniːt əʊ ‖ -ˈniːt̬ ə — **magnetosphere** mæg ˈniːt əʊ sfɪə ‖ -ˈniːt̬ ə sfɪr
    with stress-imposing suffix ˌmæg nə ˈtɒ+ -nɪ- ‖ -ˈtɑː+ — **magnetometer** ˌmæg nə ˈtɒm ɪt ə ˌ•nɪ-, -ət ə ‖ -ˈtɑːm ət̬ ᵊr

magnetron ˈmæg nə trɒn -nɪ- ‖ -trɑːn ~**s** z

Magnificat mæg ˈnɪf ɪ kæt məg-, -ə- ~**s** s

magnification ˌmæg nɪf ɪ ˈkeɪʃ ᵊn ˌ•nəf-, §-əˈ•• ~**s** z

magnificence mæg ˈnɪf ɪs ᵊn¹s məg-, -əs-

magnificent mæg ˈnɪf ɪs ᵊnt məg-, -əs- ~**ly** li

magnifico mæg ˈnɪf ɪ kəʊ §-ə- ‖ -koʊ ~**s** z

magnifier ˈmæg nɪ faɪˌə ˈ•nə- ‖ -faɪ ᵊr ~**s** z

magni|fy ˈmæg nɪ |faɪ -nə- ~**fied** faɪd ~**fies** faɪz ~**fying** faɪ ɪŋ

    ˈmagnifying glass

magniloquence mæg ˈnɪl ək wən¹s

magniloquent mæg ˈnɪl ək wənt ~**ly** li

magnitude ˈmæg nɪ tjuːd -nə-, →§-tʃuːd ‖ -tuːd -tjuːd ~**s** z

magnolia, M~ mæg ˈnəʊl iˌə məg- ‖ -ˈnoʊl- ~**s** z

Magnox, m~ ˈmæg nɒks ‖ -nɑːks

magnum ˈmæg nəm ~**s** z

    ˌmagnum ˈopus

Magnus ˈmæg nəs

    ˈMagnus hitch

Magnusson ˈmæg nəs ən

M

Magog 'meɪ gɒg ‖ -gɑːg
Magoo mə 'guː
magpie 'mæg paɪ ~s z
Magrath mə 'grɑː- -'grɑːθ, -'græθ
Magraw mə 'grɔː ‖ -'grɑː
Magri 'mæg ri
Magritte mæ 'griːt mə- ‖ mɑː- —*Fr* [ma gʁit]
Magruder mə 'gruːd ə ‖ -ᵊr
maguey mə 'geɪ 'mæg weɪ
Maguire mə 'gwaɪ̯ə ‖ -'gwaɪ̯ᵊr
magus, Magus 'meɪg əs **magi, Magi**
  'meɪdʒ aɪ 'meɪg-
Magwitch 'mæg wɪtʃ
Magyar 'mæg jɑː ‖ -jɑːr ~s z —*Hung*
  ['mɒ djɒr]
Mahabharata mə ˌhɑː 'bɑːr ət ə ˌmɑː hə-,
  ˌmæ hə-,-'bær- —*Hindi* [mə ha: bha: rət̪]
Mahaffy mə 'hæf i
Mahalia mə 'heɪl i̯ə
maharaja, maharajah ˌmɑː hə 'rɑːdʒ ə -ə-
  —*Hindi* [mə ha: ra: dʒa:, ma:-] ~s z
maharanee, maharani ˌmɑː hə 'rɑːn i -ə-
  —*Hindi* [mə ha: ra: ni, ma:-] ~s z
Maharashtra ˌmɑː hə 'ræʃ trə -ə-, -'rɑːʃ-
  —*Hindi* [mə ha: raʃtr]
Maharishi ˌmɑː hə 'rɪʃ i -ə- —*Hindi*
  [mə hər ʃi]
Mahathir ˌmæ hə 'tɪə ˌmɑː- ‖ ˌmɑː hə 'tɪᵊr
mahatma, M~ mə 'hɑːt mə -'hæt- —*Hindi*
  [mə ha:t̪ ma:] ~s s
Mahayana ˌmɑː hə 'jɑːn ə mə ˌhɑː'•• —*Hindi*
  [mə ha: jən]
Mahdi 'mɑːd i -iː
Mahé 'mɑː eɪ -heɪ —*Fr* [ma e]
Maher *(i)* mɑː ‖ mɑːr, *(ii)* 'meɪ ə ‖ _ᵊr
mah-jong, mah-jongg ˌmɑː 'dʒɒŋ ‖ -'ʒɑːŋ
  -'dʒɑːŋ, -'ʒɔːŋ, -'dʒɔːŋ; '••
Mahler 'mɑːl ə ‖ -ᵊr —*Ger* ['ma: lɐ]
mahlstick 'mɔːl stɪk ‖ 'mɑːl- 'mɔːl- ~s s
Mahmud mɑː 'muːd
mahoe 'mɑː həʊ i ‖ mə 'hoʊ 'mɑː hoʊ
mahogany mə 'hɒg ən i ‖ i -'hɑːg- ~ies iz
Mahomet mə 'hɒm ɪt -et, §-ət ‖ -'hɑːm-
Mahommed mə 'hɒm ɪd -ed, §-ət ‖ -'hɑːm-
Mahommedan mə 'hɒm ɪd ən -əd- ‖ -'hɑːm-
  ~s z
Mahon *family name* mɑːn 'mæ hən ‖ mæn
mahonia mə 'həʊn i̯ə ‖ -'hoʊn- ~s z
Mahoney, Mahony *(i)* 'mɑː ən i, *(ii)*
  mə 'həʊn i ‖ -'hoʊn i
Mahood mə 'hʊd
mahout mə 'haʊt mɑː-, -'huːt ~s s
Mai *(i)* meɪ, *(ii)* maɪ
Maia 'maɪ̯ə 'meɪ ə
maid meɪd *(= made)* **maids** meɪdz
  ˌMaid 'Marian; ˌmaid of 'honour
Maida 'meɪd ə
maidan maɪ 'dɑːn mæ- ~s z
maiden, M~ 'meɪd ən ~s z
  'maiden name; ˌmaiden 'over
maidenhair 'meɪd ən heə ‖ -her -hær
maidenhead, M~ 'meɪd ən hed ~s z
maidenhood 'meɪd ən hʊd

maiden|ly 'meɪd ən |li ~**liness** li nəs -nɪs
Maidment 'meɪd mənt →'meɪb-
maidservant 'meɪd ˌsɜːv ᵊnt ‖ -ˌsɜːv- ~s s
Maidstone 'meɪd stən -stəʊn ‖ -stoʊn
maieutic meɪ 'juːt ɪk maɪ- ‖ -'juːt̬-
maigre 'meɪg ə ‖ -ᵊr
Maigret 'meɪg reɪ ‖ ˌmeɪ 'greɪ —*Fr* [mɛ ɡʁɛ]
mail meɪᵊl *(= male)* **mailed** meɪᵊld **mailing**
  'meɪᵊl ɪŋ **mails** meɪᵊlz
  'mailing list; ˌmail 'order◄; 'mail train
mailbag 'meɪᵊl bæg ~s z
mailbox 'meɪᵊl bɒks ‖ -bɑːks ~es ɪz əz
Mailer 'meɪl ə ‖ -ᵊr
Mailgram *tdmk* 'meɪᵊl græm ~s z
mail|man 'meɪᵊl |mæn ~**men** men
mailshot 'meɪᵊl ʃɒt ‖ -ʃɑːt ~s s
maim meɪm **maimed** meɪmd **maiming**
  'meɪm ɪŋ **maims** meɪmz
Maimonides maɪ 'mɒn ɪ diːz -ə- ‖ -'mɑːn-
main meɪn **mains** meɪnz
  ˌmain 'chance; ˌmain 'clause; ˌmain 'drag;
  ˌmain 'line◄; 'Main Street; ˌmain 'verb
Main *river in Germany* maɪn meɪn —*Ger* [main]
Maine meɪn
mainframe 'meɪn freɪm ~s s
Maingay 'meɪn geɪ →'meɪŋ-
mainland 'meɪn lənd -lænd
mainlin|e 'meɪn laɪn ,•'• ~**ed** d ~**er/s** ə/
  z ‖ ᵊr/z ~**es** z ~**ing** ɪŋ
mainly 'meɪn li
mainmast 'meɪn mɑːst →'meɪm-, §-mæst,
  -məst ‖ -mæst —*naut* -məst ~s s
mainsail 'meɪn seɪᵊl -sᵊl —*naut* -sᵊl ~s z
mainspring 'meɪn sprɪŋ ~s z
mainstay 'meɪn steɪ ~s z
mainstream 'meɪn striːm

MAINTAIN

	(ˌ)meɪn-		men-		mən-
BrE 1988					
0	20	40	60	80	100%

---

maintain (ˌ)meɪn 'teɪn men-, mən- —*BrE 1988*
  poll panel preference: (ˌ)meɪn- *90%,* men- *6%,*
  mən- *4%.* ~**ed** d ~**ing** ɪŋ ~**s** z
maintenance 'meɪnt ən_ən¹s -ɪn-;
  ⚠(ˌ)meɪn 'teɪn- ‖ -ᵊn_
  'maintenance ˌorder
Mainwaring *(i)* 'mæn ər ɪŋ, *(ii)* 'meɪn ˌweər ɪŋ
  -wər-; ˌ•'•• ‖ -ˌwer-
Mainz maɪnts —*Ger* [maints]
Mair 'maɪ̯ə ‖ 'maɪ̯ᵊr —*Welsh* [mair] —*but as a
  family name,* meə ‖ meᵊr
Maire 'mær i ‖ 'mer- —*but as a family name,*
  meə ‖ meᵊr
Mairead mə 'reɪd
Maisie 'meɪz i
maisonette, maisonnette ˌmeɪz ə 'net ˌmeɪs-,
  -ən 'et ~s s
Maitland 'meɪt lənd
maitre d', maître d' ˌmeɪtr ə 'diː
  ˌmetr- ‖ ˌmeɪt̬ ᵊr- ~s z
maitre d'hotel, maître d'hôtel
  ˌmeɪtr ə dəʊ 'tel ◄ ˌmetr- ‖ -doʊ 'tel

,meɪt̬ ər-   —Fr [mɛ tʀə do tɛl] **maitres**
d'hotel, maîtres d'hôtel ,meɪtr əz-
,metr əz- ‖ ,meɪt̬ ərz-
maize meɪz (= *maze*)
majestic, M~ mə 'dʒest ɪk ~**al** əl ~**ally** əl̩ i
majest|ly, M~'mædʒ əst li -ɪst- ~**ies** iz
majolica mə 'dʒɒl ɪk ə -'jɒl- ‖ -'dʒɑːl-
major, Major 'meɪdʒ ə ‖ -ər ~**ed** d **majoring**
'meɪdʒ ər_ɪŋ ~**s** z
,major 'general◂; ,major 'key; ,major
'league◂; ,major 'suit
Majorc|a mə 'jɔːk |ə maɪ 'ɔːk-, mə 'dʒɔːk-
‖ -'jɔːrk |ə -'dʒɔːrk ə —*Sp* Mallorca
[ma 'ʎor ka, -'jor-] ~**an/s** ən/z
majordomo ,meɪdʒ ə 'dəʊm əʊ ‖ -ər 'doʊm oʊ
~**s** z
majorette ,meɪdʒ ə 'ret ~**s** s
majoritarian mə ,dʒɒr ɪ 'teər i_ən ◂ -,•ə-
‖ -,dʒɔːr ə 'ter- -,dʒɑːr- ~**s** z
majorit|y mə 'dʒɒr ət li -ɪt- ‖ -'dʒɔːr ət̬ li
-'dʒɑːr- ~**ies** iz
ma'jority ,leader
majuscule 'mædʒ ə skjuːl ‖ mə 'dʒʌsk juːl ~**s**
z
Makarios mə 'kɑːr i ɒs -'kær- ‖ -oʊs -ɑːs, _əs
make meɪk **made** meɪd **makes** meɪks
making 'meɪk ɪŋ
make-believe 'meɪk bɪ ,liːv -bə-, -§biː-, ,•••'•
makeover 'meɪk ,əʊv ə ‖ -,oʊv ər ~**s** z
Makepeace 'meɪk piːs
maker, Maker 'meɪk ə ‖ -ər ~**s** z
Makerere mə 'ker ər i
makeshift 'meɪk ʃɪft
make-up 'meɪk ʌp ~**s** s
makeweight 'meɪk weɪt ~**s** s
making 'meɪk ɪŋ ~**s** z
-making ,meɪk ɪŋ — **sick-making**
'sɪk ,meɪk ɪŋ
Makins 'meɪk ɪnz §-ənz
mako 'mɑːk əʊ 'meɪk- ‖ -oʊ ~**s** z
mal- mæl — **maladaptive** ,mæl ə 'dæpt ɪv ◂
Malabar 'mæl ə bɑː ,••'•◂ ‖ -bɑːr
malacca, M~ mə 'læk ə ‖ -'lɑːk ə ~**s** z
Malachi 'mæl ə kaɪ
malachite 'mæl ə kaɪt
Malachy 'mæl ək i
maladi... —*see* **malady**
maladjust|ed ,mæl ə 'dʒʌst ɪd ◂ -əd ~**ment**
mənt
maladministration ,mæl əd ,mɪn ɪ 'streɪʃ ən
,•æd-, -ə'•-
maladroit ,mæl ə 'drɔɪt ◂ ~**ly** li ~**ness** nəs nɪs
malad|y 'mæl əd li ~**ies** iz
Malaga 'mæl əg ə —*Sp* Málaga ['ma la ɣa]
Malagasy ,mæl ə 'gæs i ◂ -'gɑːz i
Malahide 'mæl ə haɪd
malaise mə 'leɪz mæ-
Malamud 'mæl ə mʊd
malamute 'mæl ə mjuːt -muːt ~**s** s
Malaprop, m~ 'mæl ə prɒp ‖ -prɑːp
malapropism 'mæl ə prɒp ,ɪz əm ‖ '•• prɑːp-
~**s** z
malapropos ,mæl ,æp rə 'pəʊ ,•'••• ‖ -'poʊ

malar 'meɪl ə ‖ -ər
malaria mə 'leər i_ə ‖ -'ler-
malari|al mə 'leər i_|əl ‖ -'ler- ~**ous** əs
malarkey, malarky mə 'lɑːk i ‖ -'lɑːrk i
Malathion *tdmk* ,mæl ə 'θaɪ_ən
Malawi, Malaŵi mə 'lɑː wi ~**an/s** ən/z
Malay mə 'leɪ ‖ 'meɪ leɪ mə 'leɪ ~**s** z
Malaya mə 'leɪ ə
Malayalam ,mæl eɪ 'ɑːl əm ◂ -i-, -ə 'jɑːl-
Malayan mə 'leɪ ən ~**s** z
Malayo-Polynesian mə ,leɪ əʊ ,pɒl i 'niːz i_ən
-'niːʒ-, -'niːʒ ən ‖ -oʊ ,paːl ə 'niːʒ ən -'niːʃ ən
Malaysia mə 'leɪz i_ə -'leɪʒ-, -'leɪʒ ə
‖ mə 'leɪʒ ə -'leɪʃ ə
Malaysian mə 'leɪz i_ən -'leɪʒ-, -'leɪʒ ən
‖ mə 'leɪʒ ən -'leɪʃ ən ~**s** z
Malcolm 'mælk əm —*rarely also* 'mɔːlk-
malcontent 'mæl kən ,tent §-kɒn-
‖ ,mæl kən 'tent ~**s** s
malcontented ,mæl kən 'tent ɪd ◂ §-kɒn-, -əd
‖ -'tent̬ əd ◂
mal de mer ,mæl də 'meə ‖ -'meər —*Fr*
[mal də mɛːʀ]
Malden 'mɔːld ən 'mɒld- ‖ 'mɑːld-
Maldive 'mɔːld iːv 'mɒld-, 'mɑːld-, -ɪv,
-aɪv ‖ 'mɑːld-, 'mæld- ~**s** z
Maldivian mɔːl 'dɪv i_ən mɒl-, mɑː- ‖ mɑːl-,
mæl- ~**s** z
Maldon 'mɔːld ən 'mɒld- ‖ 'mɑːld-
Maldwyn (*i*) 'mæld wɪn, (*ii*) 'mɔːld-
'mɒld- ‖ 'mɑːld-
male, Male meɪəl **males** meɪəlz
,male 'chauvinist◂, ,male ,chauvinist 'pig
malediction ,mæl ɪ 'dɪk ʃən -ə- ~**s** z
malefactor 'mæl ɪ fækt ə '••ə- ‖ -ər ~**s** z
malefic mə 'lef ɪk
malefic|ence mə 'lef ɪs |ən̩ts mæ-, §-əs- ~**ent**
ənt
maleic mə 'leɪ ɪk -'liː-
maleness 'meɪəl nəs -nɪs
Malet 'mæl ɪt -ət
malevolence mə 'lev əl ən̩ts mæ-
malevolent mə 'lev əl ənt mæ- ~**ly** li
malfeasance ₍ᵢ₎mæl 'fiːz ən̩ts
Malfi 'mælf i
malformation ,mæl fɔː 'meɪʃ ən -fə- ‖ -fɔːr-
-fər- ~**s** z
malformed ,mæl 'fɔːmd ◂ ‖ -'fɔːrmd ◂
malfunction ,mæl 'fʌŋk ʃən ~**ed** d ~**ing** ɪŋ
~**s** z
Malham 'mæl əm
Malhotra məl 'həʊtr ə ‖ -'hoʊtr-
Mali 'mɑːl i
Malian 'mɑːl i_ən ~**s** z
Malibu 'mæl ɪ buː -ə-
malic 'mæl ɪk 'meɪl-
malice 'mæl ɪs §-əs
malicious mə 'lɪʃ əs ~**ly** li ~**ness** nəs nɪs
malign mə 'laɪn ~**ed** d ~**ing** ɪŋ ~**ly** li ~**s** z
malignanc|y mə 'lɪg nən̩ts li ~**ies** iz
malignant mə 'lɪg nənt ~**ly** li
maligner mə 'laɪn ə ‖ -ər ~**s** z
malignit|y mə 'lɪg nət li -nɪt- ‖ -nət̬ li ~**ies** iz

M

Malin 'mæl ɪn §-ən
malinger mə 'lɪŋ gə ‖ -gᵊr ~ed d
  malingering mə 'lɪŋ gᵊr_ɪŋ ~s z
malingerer mə 'lɪŋ gᵊr ə ‖ -gᵊr ᵊr
Malinowski ˌmæl ɪ 'nɒf ski -ə- ‖ -'nɑːf- -'nɔːf-
malkin, M~ 'mɔːk ɪn 'mɔːlk- 'mɒlk-,
  §-ən ‖ 'mɑːk-, 'mælk- ~s z

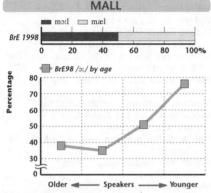

MALL

■ mɔːl ☐ mæl

BrE 1998

0   20   40   60   80   100%

Percentage

■ BrE98 /ɔː/ by age

80
70
60
50
40
30
0

Older ◄━━━ Speakers ━━━► Younger

mall, Mall mɔːl mæl, mɒl ‖ mɑːl —BrE 1998
  poll panel preference, in the sense 'shopping
  centre': mɔːl 50% (born since 1973: 76%), mæl
  50%. Several respondents voted for mɒl, not an
  option offered. Always mæl in the London
  place-names The Mall, Chiswick Mall, Pall
  Mall. malls mɔːlz mælz, mɒlz ‖ mɑːlz
Mallaig 'mæl eɪg
Mallalieu 'mæl ə lju: -ljɜː, -lu: ‖ -lu:
Mallam 'mæl əm
mallard 'mæl ɑːd -əd ‖ -ᵊrd ~s z
Mallarmé 'mæl ɑː meɪ ‖ ˌmæl ɑːr 'meɪ —Fr
  [ma laʁ me]
malleability ˌmæl i_ə 'bɪl ət i -ɪt i ‖ -əṭ i
malleab|le 'mæl i_əb |ᵊl ~leness ᵊl nəs -nɪs
  ~ly li
mallee 'mæl i ~s z
mallei 'mæl i aɪ
malle|olus mə 'li:_ᵊl əs ~oli ə laɪ
Malleson 'mæl ɪs ən -əs-
mallet 'mæl ɪt -ət ~s s
Mallet, Mallett 'mæl ɪt -ət
malle|us 'mæl i_əs ~i aɪ
Malling places in Kent 'mɔːl ɪŋ ‖ 'mɑːl-
  —Occasionally also, inappropriately, 'mæl-
Mallinson 'mæl ɪn sən -ən-
Mallorca mə 'jɔːk ə məl- ‖ -'jɔːrk ə
Mallory 'mæl ər i
mallow, M~ 'mæl əʊ ‖ -oʊ ~s z
Malmesbury 'mɑːmz bər_i §'mɒlmz- ‖ -ˌber i
Malmo, Malmö, Malmoe 'mælm əʊ ‖ -oʊ
  —Swed Malmö ['ˈmalm øː]
malmsey 'mɑːmz i §'mɒlmz-
malnourished ˌmæl 'nʌr ɪʃt ◄ ‖ -'nɜ·:-
malnutrition ˌmæl nju 'trɪʃ ən ‖ -nu- -nju-
malodorous mæl 'əʊd ər əs ‖ -'oʊd- ~ly li
  ~ness nəs nɪs
Malone mə 'ləʊn ‖ -'loʊn
Malory 'mæl ər i

Malpas (i) 'mɔːlp əs 'mɔːp- ‖ 'mɑːlp-, (ii)
  'məʊp əs ‖ 'moʊp-, (iii) 'mælp əs —The place
  in Cheshire is (i) or (iii), that in Cornwall (ii),
  that in Gwent (iii); the family name is usually
  (iii).
Malpighi mæl 'piːg i —It [mal 'pi: gi]
Malpighian mæl 'pɪg i_ən -'piːg-
Malplaquet 'mæl plə keɪ ˌ•·'• —Fr
  [mal pla kɛ]

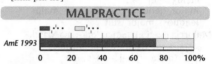

MALPRACTICE

■ ˌ•ˈ•• ☐ ˈ•ˌ••

AmE 1993

0   20   40   60   80   100%

malpractice ˌmæl 'prækt ɪs §-əs, '•ˌ•• —AmE
  1993 poll panel preference: ˌ•ˈ••• 75%, '•ˌ••
  25%.
  ˌmal'practice inˌsurance
malt mɔːlt mɒlt ‖ mɑːlt malted 'mɔːlt ɪd
  'mɒlt, -əd ‖ 'mɑːlt- malting/s 'mɔːlt ɪŋ/z
  'mɒlt- ‖ 'mɑːlt- malts mɔːlts mɒlts ‖ mɑːlts
  ˌmalted 'milk
Malta 'mɔːlt ə 'mɒlt- ‖ 'mɑːlt-
Maltby 'mɔːlt bi 'mɒlt- ‖ 'mɑːlt-
Maltese ˌmɔːl 'tiːz ◄ ˌmɒl- ‖ ˌmɑːl-, -'tiːs ◄
  ˌMaltese 'cross
Malteser tdmk mɔːl 'tiːz ə mɒl- ‖ -ᵊr mɑːl- ~s
  z
Malthus 'mælθ əs
Malthusian mæl 'θjuːz i_ən mɔːl-, mɒl-, -'θuːz-
  ‖ -'θuːʒ ən mɔːl-, mɑːl- ~s z
Malton 'mɔːlt ən 'mɒlt- ‖ 'mɑːlt-
Maltravers mæl 'træv əz ‖ -ᵊrz
mal|treat ˌmæl |'triːt ~treated 'triːt ɪd -əd
  ‖ 'triːṭ əd ~treating 'triːt ɪŋ ‖ 'triːṭ ɪŋ
  ~treatment 'triːt mənt ~treats 'triːts
maltster 'mɔːlt stə 'mɒlt- ‖ -stᵊr 'mɑːlt- ~s z
Malvern (i) 'mɔːlv ən 'mɔːv-, 'mɒlv- ‖ -ᵊrn
  'mɑːlv-, (ii) 'mælv ən ‖ -ᵊrn —In England (i),
  in the US (ii).
malversation ˌmæl vɜː 'seɪʃ ən -və- ‖ -vᵊr-
Malvinas mæl 'viːn əz mɔːl-, mɒl- —AmSp
  [mal 'βi nas, -nah]
Malvolio mæl 'vəʊl i_əʊ ‖ -'voʊl i_oʊ
Malyon 'mæl jən
mam, Mam mæm mams, Mam's mæmz
mama, Mama mə 'mɑː 'mæm ə ‖ 'mɑːm ə (*)
  ~s, ~'s z
  'Mama's boy
Mamaroneck mə 'mær ə nek ‖ -'mer-
mamba 'mæm bə ‖ 'mɑːm- 'mæm-, -bɑː ~s z
mambo 'mæm bəʊ ‖ 'mɑːm boʊ ~ed d ~es,
  ~s z ~ing ɪŋ
Mameluke 'mæm ɪ luːk -ə-, -ljuːk
Mamet 'mæm ɪt -ət
Mamie 'meɪm i
mamma, Mamma 'mother' mə 'mɑː ‖ 'mɑːm ə
  ~s, ~'s z
mamm|a 'breast' 'mæm |ə ~ae iː
mammal 'mæm ᵊl ~s z
mammalian mə 'meɪl i_ən mæ- ~s z
mammar|y 'mæm ər li ~ies iz
  'mammary gland

M

mammee mæ ˈmiː -ˈmeɪ ‖ mɑː-
mammogram ˈmæm ə græm ~s z
mammography mæ ˈmɒg rəf i ‖ -ˈmɑːg-
mammon, M~ ˈmæm ən
mammoth ˈmæm əθ ~s s
mamm|y, Mammy ˈmæm |i ~ies iz
man, Man mæn **manned** mænd **manning** ˈmæn ɪŋ **man's** mænz **men** men **men's** menz
 ˌman ˈFriday; ˌman in the ˈmoon; ˌman in the ˈstreet; ˌman ˈjack; ˌman of ˈletters; ˌman of ˈstraw
-man mən, mæn —*This suffix may be weak or strong. (i) In most well-established formations, written as one word, it is weak,* mən: policeman pə ˈliːs mən. *(ii) Where written hyphenated or as two words, and in new formations, it is usually strong,* mæn: spaceman ˈspeɪs mæn. *Note* batman *'army servant'* ˈbæt mən, *but* Batman *(cartoon character)* ˈbæt mæn
mana ˈmɑːn ə
man-about-town ˌmæn ə ˌbaʊt ˈtaʊn **men-about-town** ˌmen-
manacl|e ˈmæn ək əl -ed d ~es z ~ing _ɪŋ
manag|e ˈmæn ɪdʒ -ədʒ ~ed d ~es ɪz əz ~ing ɪŋ
manageability ˌmæn ɪdʒ ə ˈbɪl ət i ˌ•ədʒ-, -ɪt i ‖ -ət̬ i
manageab|le ˈmæn ɪdʒ əb |əl ˈ•ədʒ- ~ly li
management ˈmæn ɪdʒ mənt -ədʒ- ~s s
manager ˈmæn ɪdʒ ə -ədʒ- ‖ -ər ~s z
manageress ˌmæn ɪdʒ ə ˈres ˌ•ədʒ-, ˈ•••• ‖ ˈmæn ɪdʒ ər əs (*) ~es ɪz əz
managerial ˌmæn ə ˈdʒɪər i_əl ◄ ‖ -ˈdʒɪr- ~ly i
managership ˈmæn ɪdʒ ə ʃɪp ˈ•ədʒ- ‖ -ər• ~s s
Managua mə ˈnæg wə -ˈnɑːg- ‖ -ˈnɑːg- —*Sp* [ma ˈna ɣwa]
manana, mañana mæn ˈjɑːn ə mən- ‖ mən- mɑːn- —*Sp* [ma ˈɲa na]
Manasseh mə ˈnæs i -ə ‖ -ə
man-at-arms ˌmæn ət ˈɑːmz ‖ -ət̬ ˈɑːrmz **men-at-arms** ˌmen-
manatee ˌmæn ə ˈtiː ‖ ˈmæn ə tiː ~s z
-mancer ˌmæn|s ə ‖ -ər — **necromancer** ˈnek rə ˌmæn|s ə ‖ -ər
Manchester ˈmæntʃ ɪst ə -əst-; ˈmæn ˌtʃest- ‖ -ər
manchineel ˌmæntʃ ɪ ˈniːəl -ə- ~s z
Manchu ˌmæn ˈtʃuː ◄ —*Chi* Mǎn Zhōu [³man ¹tʂou]
Manchukuo ˌmæn tʃuː ˈkwəʊ ‖ -ˈkwoʊ —*Chi* Mǎn Zhōu Guó [³man ¹tʂou ²kwɔ]
Manchuri|a mæn ˈtʃʊər i_ə ‖ -ˈtʃʊr- ~an/s ən/z
manciple ˈmænᵗs ɪp əl -əp- ~s z
mancozeb ˈmæŋk əʊ zeb ‖ -ə-
Mancunian mæn ˈkjuːn i_ən →mæŋ- ~s z
-mancy ˌmænᵗs i — **necromancy** ˈnek rə ˌmænᵗs i
Manda ˈmænd ə
mandala ˈmænd əl ə ˈmʌnd-; mæn ˈdɑːl ə ~s z
Mandalay ˌmænd ə ˈleɪ ◄ -əl ˈeɪ; ˈ•••

mandamus mæn ˈdeɪm əs ~es ɪz əz
mandarin, M~ ˈmænd ər ɪn §-ən, ˌmænd ə ˈrɪn ~s z
 ˌmandarin ˈduck; ˌmandarin ˈorange
mandarinate ˈmænd_ər ɪ neɪt ˌ•ər ə- ~s s
mandatar|y ˈmænd ət_ər li ˈ•ɪt_, mæn ˈdeɪt ər li -ə ter li ~ies iz
mandate *n* ˈmænd eɪt -ɪt, -ət ~s s
mand|ate *v* ˌmæn ˈd|eɪt ˈmænd |eɪt ‖ ˈmænd eɪt ~ated eɪt ɪd -əd ‖ eɪt̬ əd ~ates eɪts ~ating eɪt ɪŋ ‖ eɪt̬ ɪŋ
mandator|y ˈmænd ət_ər li ˈ•ɪt_, mæn ˈdeɪt ər li -ə tɔːr li -tour i ~ies iz
man-day ˈmæn deɪ ˌ•ˈ• ~s z
Mande ˈmænd eɪ ˈmɑːnd- ‖ ˈmɑːnd eɪ mɑːn ˈdeɪ ~s z
Mandela mæn ˈdel ə -ˈdeɪl- —*Xhosa* [ma ˈndɛː la]
Mandelbaum ˈmænd əl baʊm
Mandelbrot ˈmænd əl brəʊt ‖ ˈmɑːnd əl broʊt ˈmænd-
Mandelson ˈmænd əl sən
Mandelstam ˈmænd əl stæm -stəm
Mandeville ˈmænd ə vɪl -ɪ-
mandible ˈmænd ɪb əl -əb- ~s z
Mandingo mæn ˈdɪŋ gəʊ ‖ -goʊ ~s z
mandolin, mandoline ˌmænd ə ˈlɪn -əl ˈɪn; ˈmænd əl ɪn, §-ən ~s z
mandorla mæn ˈdɔːl ə ‖ -ˈdɔːrl ə ~s z
mandragora mæn ˈdræg ər ə
mandrake ˈmændr eɪk ~s s
mandrax, M~ *tdmk* ˈmændr æks ~es ɪz əz
mandrel, mandril ˈmændr əl -ɪl ~s z
mandrill ˈmændr ɪl -əl ~s z
Mandy ˈmænd i
mane meɪn (= *main*) **maned** meɪnd **manes** meɪnz
Manea ˈmeɪn i
man-eat|er/s ˈmæn ˌiːt |ə/z ‖ -ˌiːt̬ |ər/z ~ing ɪŋ
maneb ˈmæn eb
maneg|e, manèg|e mæ ˈneɪʒ -ˈneʒ —*Fr* [ma nɛːʒ] ~es ɪz əz
manes, Manes *'shades of the dead'* ˈmɑːn eɪz -eɪs; ˈmeɪn iːz
Manet ˈmæn eɪ ‖ mæ ˈneɪ mə- —*Fr* [ma nɛ] ~s, ~'s z
maneuvrability mə ˌnuːv ər_ə ˈbɪl ət i -ɪt i ‖ -ət̬ i
maneuvrable mə ˈnuːv ər_əb əl
maneuv|re, maneuv|er mə ˈnuːv lə ‖ -lər ~ered, ~red əd ‖ ərd ~ering, ~ring ər_ɪŋ ~ers, ~res əz ‖ ərz
Manfred ˈmæn frɪd -frəd, -fred
manful ˈmæn fəl -fʊl ~ly i ~ness nəs nɪs
manga ˈmæŋ gə ‖ ˈmɑːŋ- —*Jp* [ma,ŋ ŋa]
mangabey ˈmæŋ gə beɪ -biː ~s z
manganate ˈmæŋ gə neɪt ~s s
manganese ˈmæŋ gə niːz ˌ•ˈ•◄ ‖ -niːs
manganic mæn ˈgæn ɪk →mæŋ-
manganous ˈmæŋ gən əs mæn ˈgæn əs, →mæŋ-
mange meɪndʒ

M

mangel-wurzel 'mæŋ gəl ˌwɜːz əl ‖ -ˌwɜːz- **~s** z

manger 'meɪndʒ ə ‖ -ər **~s** z

mangetout ˌmɒndʒ 'tuː ˌmɑːndʒ-, ˌmɒ̃ʒ-; '• • ‖ ˌmɑːndʒ- —Fr [mɑ̃ʃ tu]

mangl|e 'mæŋ gəl **~ed** d **~es** z **~ing** ˌɪŋ

mango 'mæŋ gəʊ ‖ -goʊ **~es**, **~s** z

mangold, M~ 'mæn gəʊld →-gɒʊld ‖ -goʊld **~s** z

mangosteen 'mæŋ gəʊ stiːn **~s** z

Mangotsfield 'mæŋ gəts fiːəld

mangrove 'mæŋ grəʊv 'mæn- ‖ -groʊv **~s** z 'mangrove swamp

mangl|y 'meɪndʒ li **~ier** i ə ‖ i ər **~iest** i ɪst i əst **~ily** ɪ li əl i **~iness** i nəs i nɪs

manhandl|e 'mæn ˌhænd əl ˌ•'• • **~ed** d **~es** z **~ing** ˌɪŋ

Manhattan, m~ mæn 'hæt ən mən- **~s**, **~'s** z

manhole 'mæn həʊl →-hɒʊl ‖ -hoʊl **~s** z 'manhole ˌcover

manhood 'mæn hʊd

manhour 'mæn ˌaʊ ə ‖ -ˌaʊ ər **~s** z

manhunt 'mæn hʌnt **~s** s

mania 'meɪn i ə **~s** z

-mania 'meɪn i ə — pyromania ˌpaɪər ə 'meɪn i ə

maniac 'meɪn i æk **~s** s

-maniac 'meɪn i æk — pyromaniac ˌpaɪər ə 'meɪn i æk

maniacal mə 'naɪ ək əl **~ly** i

manic 'mæn ɪk **~s** s

manic-depressive ˌmæn ɪk dɪ 'pres ɪv ◄ -də'• •, §-diː'• • **~s** z

Manichaean, Manichean ˌmæn ɪ 'kiː ən ◄ -ə- **~s** z

Manichaeism, Manicheism ˌmæn ɪ 'kiː ˌɪz əm -ə-

manicure 'mæn ɪ kjʊə -ə-, -kjɔː ‖ -kjʊr -kjɜː **~d** d **~s** z **manicuring** 'mæn ɪ kjʊər ɪŋ '•ə-, -kjɔːr ɪŋ ‖ -kjʊr ɪŋ -kjɜː ɪŋ

manicurist 'mæn ɪ kjʊər ɪst '•ə-, -kjɔːr ɪst, §-əst ‖ -kjʊr əst **~s** s

manifest adj, n, v 'mæn ɪ fest -ə- **~ed** ɪd əd **~ing** ɪŋ **~s** s

manifestation ˌmæn ɪ fe 'steɪʃ ən ˌ•ə-, -fə'• • **~s** z

manifestly 'mæn ɪ fest li '•ə-

manifesto ˌmæn ɪ 'fest əʊ -ə- ‖ -oʊ **~es**, **~s** z

manifold, M~ 'mæn ɪ fəʊld -ə-, →-fɒʊld ‖ -foʊld **~ed** ɪd əd **~ing** ɪŋ **~ly** li **~ness** nəs nɪs **~s** z

manikin 'mæn ɪk ɪn -ək-, §-ən **~s** z

manila, M~, manilla mə 'nɪl ə **~s** z Maˌnila 'hemp

Manilow 'mæn ɪ ləʊ -əl əʊ ‖ -loʊ

manioc 'mæn i ɒk ‖ -aːk

maniple 'mæn ɪp əl -əp- **~s** z

manipulability mə ˌnɪp jʊl ə 'bɪl ət i -ˌ•jəl-, -ɪt i ‖ -jəl ə 'bɪl ət i

manipulab|le mə 'nɪp jʊl əb |əl -jəl əb- ‖ -jəl əb- **~ly** li

manipu|late mə 'nɪp ju leɪt -jə- ‖ -jə- **~lated**

leɪt ɪd -əd ‖ leɪt əd **~lates** leɪts **~lating** leɪt ɪŋ ‖ leɪt ɪŋ

manipulation mə ˌnɪp ju 'leɪʃ ən -jə- ‖ -jə- **~s** z

manipulative mə 'nɪp jʊl ət ɪv -jəl ət-; -ju leɪt-, -jə leɪt- ‖ -jə leɪt ɪv -jə lət- **~ly** li **~ness** nəs nɪs

Manitoba ˌmæn ɪ 'təʊb ə -ə- ‖ -'toʊb ə

manitou 'mæn ɪ tuː §-ə-

Manitoulin ˌmæn ɪ 'tuːl ɪn -ə-, §-ən

mankind mæn 'kaɪnd →mæŋ-, ˌ•• —but in the rare sense 'men as distinct from women', '• •

mank|y 'mæŋk |i **~ier** i ə ‖ i ər **~iest** i ɪst i əst

Manley, Manly 'mæn li

man|ly 'mæn |li **~lier** li ə ‖ li ər **~liest** li ɪst li əst **~liness** li nəs -nɪs

man-made ˌmæn 'meɪd ◄ →ˌmæm- ˌman-made 'fibres

Mann mæn

manna 'mæn ə

mannequin 'mæn ɪk ɪn -ək-, §-ən **~s** z

manner 'mæn ə ‖ -ər **~ed** d **~s** z

mannerism 'mæn ər ˌɪz əm **~s** z

manner|ly 'mæn ə |li ‖ -ər- **~liness** li nəs -nɪs

Manners 'mæn əz ‖ -ərz

Mannheim 'mæn haɪm —Ger ['man haɪm]

mannikin 'mæn ɪk ɪn -ək-, §-ən **~s** z

Manning 'mæn ɪŋ

Manningham 'mæn ɪŋ əm

mannish 'mæn ɪʃ **~ly** li **~ness** nəs nɪs

mannitol 'mæn ɪ tɒl §-ə- ‖ -toʊl -taːl, -tɔːl

Manny 'mæn i

manoeuvrability mə ˌnuːv ər ə 'bɪl ət i -ɪt i ‖ -əț i

manoeuvrable mə 'nuːv ər əb əl

manoeuv|re, maneuv|er mə 'nuːv |ə ‖ -|ər **~ered**, **~red** əd ‖ ərd **~ering**, **~ring** ər ˌɪŋ **~ers**, **~res** əz ‖ ərz

man-of-war ˌmæn əv 'wɔː -ə- ‖ -'wɔːr **men-of-war** ˌmen-

manometer mə 'nɒm ɪt ə mæ-, §-ət- ‖ -'naːm əț ər **~s** z

manometric ˌmæn əʊ 'metr ɪk ◄ -ə- **~al** əl **~ally** əl‿i

manor 'mæn ə ‖ -ər (= manner) **~s** z 'manor house

Manorbier ˌmæn ə 'bɪə ‖ -ər 'bɪər

manorial mə 'nɔːr i əl mæ- ‖ -'noʊr-

man-o'-war ˌmæn ə 'wɔː ‖ -'wɔːr **men-o'-war** ˌmen-

manpower 'mæn ˌpaʊ ə →'mæm- ‖ -ˌpaʊ ər

manque, manqué 'mɒŋk eɪ 'mɑːŋk- ‖ mɑː 'ŋ keɪ —Fr [mɑ̃ ke]

Manresa mæn 'reɪs ə -'reɪz- ‖ mɑːn- mæn- —Sp [man 'rre sa]

mansard 'mæns ɑːd -əd ‖ -ɑːrd -ərd **~s** z

manse mænʦ **manses** 'mænʦ ɪz -əz

Mansel, Mansell 'mænʦ əl

manservant 'mæn ˌsɜːv ənt ‖ -ˌsɜːv- **~s** s

Mansfield 'mænʦ fiːəld

-manship mən ʃɪp — gamesmanship 'geɪmz mən ʃɪp

mansion 'mæn^tʃ ən ~s z
  ,Mansion 'House, · · ·
man-size 'mæn saɪz ~d d
manslaughter 'mæn ,slɔːt ə ‖ -,slɔːt̬ ər -,slɑːt̬-
Manson 'mæn^ts ən
Manston 'mæn^tst ən
manta, Manta 'mænt ə ‖ 'mænt̬ ə ~s z
mantel 'mænt əl ‖ 'mænt̬ əl (= mantle) ~s z
mantelpiec|e 'mænt əl piːs ‖ 'mænt̬- ~es ɪz əz
mantel|shelf 'mænt əl |ʃelf ‖ 'mænt̬ əl-
  ~shelves ʃelvz
mantic 'mænt ɪk ‖ 'mænt̬ ɪk
mantilla mæn 'tɪl ə ‖ -'tiː ə —Sp [man 'ti ʎa,
  -ja] ~s z
Mantinea ,mænt ɪ 'niː ə -ə-, -'neɪ-
mantis 'mænt ɪs §-əs ‖ 'mænt̬ əs ~es ɪz əz
mantissa mæn 'tɪs ə ~s z
mantl|e 'mænt əl ‖ 'mænt̬ əl ~ed d ~es z ~ing
  ɪŋ
man-to-man ,mæn tə 'mæn ◀
Mantovani ,mænt ə 'vɑːn i
mantra 'mæntr ə 'mʌntr- ~s z
mantrap 'mæn træp ~s s
Mantu|a, m~ 'mænt ju_ə -u_; 'mænt̬ʃ u_ə
  ‖ 'mænt̬ʃ u_ə ~an/s ən/z
manual 'mæn ju_əl ~ly i ~s z
Manuel family name 'mæn ju_əl -el
Manuel forename ,mæn 'wel· ·; 'mæn ju_əl
  ‖ mæn 'wel —Sp [ma 'nwel]
manufac|ture ,mæn ju 'fæk |tʃə -jə-, -ə-, -ʃə
  ‖ -jə 'fæk |tʃ^ər -ʃ^ər ~tured tʃəd ‖ tʃ^ərd
  ~tures tʃəz ‖ tʃ^ərz ~turing tʃ^ər ɪŋ
manufacturer ,mæn ju 'fæk tʃ^ər_ə, ·jə-, ,·ə-,
  -ʃ^ər_ə ‖ -jə 'fæk tʃ^ər_^ər -ʃ^ər_^ər ~s z
manumission ,mæn ju 'mɪʃ ən -jə- ‖ -jə- ~s z
manu|mit ,mæn ju |'mɪt -jə- ‖ -jə- ~mits
  'mɪts ~mitted 'mɪt ɪd -əd ‖ 'mɪt̬ əd
  ~mitting 'mɪt ɪŋ ‖ 'mɪt̬ ɪŋ
manure mə 'njʊə -'njɔː; ‖ -'nʊ^ər -'njʊ^ər ~d d
  manuring mə 'njʊər ɪŋ -'njɔː- ‖ -'nʊr ɪŋ
  -'njʊr- ~s z
manuscript 'mæn ju skrɪpt -jə- ‖ -jə- ~s s
Manwaring 'mæn ər ɪŋ ‖ -wɔːr-
Manx mæŋ_ks
  ,Manx 'cat
Manx|man 'mæŋ_ks |mən -mæn ~men mən
  men
many 'men i —There are occasional weak forms
  mən i, mni (esp. in how many); in AmE also
  'mɪn i. —In Ireland often 'mæn i **more**
  mɔː ‖ mɔːr mʊər **most** məʊst ‖ moʊst
many-sided ,men i 'saɪd ɪd ◀ -əd ~ness nəs
  nɪs
manzanilla, M~ ,mænz ə 'nɪl ə ‖ -'niː ə —Sp
  [man θa 'ni ʎa, -ja] ~s z
Mao maʊ
  Mao Tsetung ,maʊt sɪ 'tʊŋ -tseɪ-; **Mao**
  Zedong ,maʊd zə 'dʊŋ —both Chi Máo
  Zédōng [²mɐu ²tsɤ ¹tʊŋ]
Maoism 'maʊ ,ɪz əm
Maoist 'maʊ ɪst §-əst ~s s
Maori 'maʊ^ər i —Maori ['ma o ri] ~s z

map mæp **mapped** mæpt **mapping/s**
  'mæp ɪŋ/z **maps** mæps
maple 'meɪp əl ~s z
  'maple leaf; ,maple 'syrup
Maplin 'mæp lɪn -lən
Mapp mæp
Mappin 'mæp ɪn §-ən
Mapplethorpe 'meɪp əl θɔːp 'mæp- ‖ -θɔːrp
map-read|er/s 'mæp ,riːd |ə/z ‖ -|^ər/z ~ing ɪŋ
Maputo mə 'puːt əʊ ‖ -oʊ
maquette mæ 'ket ~s s
maquillage ,mæk i ˌɑːʒ -'jɑːʒ —Fr [ma ki jaːʒ]
maquis mæ 'kiː mɑː-; 'mæk iː, 'mɑːk- —Fr
  [ma ki]
mar, Mar mɑː ‖ mɑːr **marred** mɑːd ‖ mɑːrd
  marring 'mɑːr ɪŋ **mars** mɑːz ‖ mɑːrz
Mar. —see **March**
marabou, marabout 'mær ə buː ‖ 'mer- ~s z
maraca mə 'ræk ə ‖ -'rɑːk ə -'ræk- ~s z
Maradona ,mær ə 'dɒn ə ‖ -'dɑːn- ,mer- —Sp
  [ma ra 'ðo na]
maraschino, M~ ,mær ə 'skiːn əʊ ◀ -'ʃiːn-
  ‖ -oʊ ◀ ,mer-, -'ʃiːn- ~s z
maras|mus mə 'ræz |məs ~mic mɪk
Marat 'mær ɑː ‖ mə 'rɑː —Fr [ma ʁa]
Marathi mə 'rɑːt i ‖ -'rɑːt̬ i —Hindi [mə ra: t̬ʰi]
  ~s z
marathon, M~ 'mær əθ ən -ə θɒn ‖ -ə θɑːn
  'mer- ~er/s ə/z ‖ -^ər/z ~s z
maraud mə 'rɔːd ‖ -'rɑːd ~ed əd ~er/s ə/
  z ‖ ^ər/z ~ing ɪŋ ~s z
Marazion ,mær ə 'zaɪ_ən ‖ ,mer-
Marbella place in Spain mɑː 'beɪ ə -jə ‖ mɑːr-
  —There is also a spelling pronunciation
  ⚠-'bel ə —Sp [mar 'βe ʎa, -ja]
marbl|e 'mɑːb əl ‖ 'mɑːrb- ~ed d ~es z ~ing
  ɪŋ
Marblehead 'mɑːb əl hed ,· ·'· ‖ 'mɑːrb-
Marburg 'mɑː bɜːg ‖ 'mɑːr bɜːg —Ger
  ['mɑːʁ bʊʁk]
marc, Marc mɑːk ‖ mɑːrk (= mark)
Marcan 'mɑːk ən ‖ 'mɑːrk- ·
marcasite 'mɑːk ə saɪt ‖ 'mɑːrk-
Marceau ,mɑː 'səʊ ‖ ,mɑːr 'soʊ —Fr [maʁ so]
Marcel, m~ ₍ₒ₎mɑː 'sel ‖ ₍ₒ₎mɑːr- ~led d ~ling
  ɪŋ ~s z
Marcella ₍ₒ₎mɑː 'sel ə ‖ ₍ₒ₎mɑːr-
Marcelle ₍ₒ₎mɑː 'sel ‖ ₍ₒ₎mɑːr-
Marcellus mɑː 'sel əs ‖ mɑːr-
march, March mɑːtʃ ‖ mɑːrtʃ **marched**
  mɑːtʃt ‖ mɑːrtʃt **marches, March's**
  'mɑːtʃ ɪz -əz ‖ 'mɑːrtʃ əz **marching**
  'mɑːtʃ ɪŋ ‖ 'mɑːrtʃ ɪŋ
  'marching ,orders
Marchant 'mɑːtʃ ənt ‖ 'mɑːrtʃ-
marcher 'mɑːtʃ ə ‖ 'mɑːrtʃ ^ər ~s z
marchioness ,mɑːʃ ə 'nes 'mɑːʃ ən_ɪs, _əs
  ‖ 'mɑːrʃ ən_əs ~es ɪz əz
Marchmont 'mɑːtʃ mənt ‖ 'mɑːrtʃ-
march-past 'mɑːtʃ pɑːst §-pæst ‖ 'mɑːrtʃ pæst
  ~s s
Marcia 'mɑːs i_ə 'mɑːʃ ə ‖ 'mɑːrʃ ə
Marciano ,mɑːs i 'ɑːn əʊ ‖ ,mɑːrs i 'æn oʊ

Marco 'mɑːk əʊ ‖ 'mɑːrk oʊ
Marconi mɑː 'kəʊn i ‖ mɑːr 'koʊn i —It
[mar 'koː ni]
Marcos 'mɑːk ɒs ‖ 'mɑːrk oʊs
Marcus 'mɑːk əs ‖ 'mɑːrk-
Marcuse mɑː 'kuːz ə ‖ mɑːr-
Marden 'mɑːd ᵊn ‖ 'mɑːrd- —The place in Kent
is sometimes ₍ᵢ₎mɑː 'den ‖ ₍ᵢ₎mɑːr-
Mardi Gras ˌmɑːd i 'grɑː ‖ 'mɑːrd i grɑː -grɔː;
ˌ•ᵊ•
mardy 'mɑːd i ‖ 'mɑːrd i
mare 'she-horse' meə ‖ meᵊr mæᵊr mares,
mare's meəz ‖ meᵊrz mæᵊrz
'mare's nest
mare 'lunar plain', 'sea' 'mɑːr eɪ 'mær-, -i
maria 'mɑːr i‿ə 'mær-
Maree mə 'riː
Marengo mə 'reŋ gəʊ ‖ -goʊ —It [ma 'reŋ go]
mare's-tail 'meəz teɪᵊl ‖ 'merz- 'mærz- ~s z
marg mɑːdʒ ‖ mɑːrdʒ
Margach 'mɑːg ə ‖ 'mɑːrg ə
Margam 'mɑːg əm ‖ 'mɑːrg-
Margaret 'mɑːg rət -rɪt; 'mɑːg ər ət, -ɪt
‖ 'mɑːrg-
Margaretting ˌmɑːg ə 'ret ɪŋ ‖ ˌmɑːrg ə 'reṭ ɪŋ
margarine ˌmɑːdʒ ə 'riːn ˌmɑːg-, '•••
‖ 'mɑːrdʒ ᵊr‿ən -ə riːn (*)
Margarita, m~ ˌmɑːg ə 'riːt ə ‖ ˌmɑːrg ə 'riːṭ ə
~s, ~'s z
margarite 'mɑːg ə raɪt ‖ 'mɑːrg-
Margary 'mɑːg ər i ‖ 'mɑːrg-
Margate 'mɑː geɪt -gɪt, -gət ‖ 'mɑːr-
margay 'mɑːg eɪ ‖ 'mɑːrg- mɑːr 'geɪ ~s z
marge mɑːdʒ ‖ mɑːrdʒ
Margerison (i) 'mɑːdʒ ᵊr‿ɪs ən‿əs ən
‖ 'mɑːrdʒ-, (ii) mɑː 'dʒer- ‖ mɑːr-
margin 'mɑːdʒ ɪn §-ᵊn ‖ 'mɑːrdʒ- ~s z
marginal 'mɑːdʒ ɪn ᵊl -ᵊn‿ᵊl ‖ 'mɑːrdʒ- ~ly i
marginalia ˌmɑːdʒ ɪ 'neɪl i‿ə,•ə- ‖ ˌmɑːrdʒ-
marginalis... —see marginaliz...
marginality ˌmɑːdʒ ɪ 'næl ət i,•ə-, -ɪt i
‖ ˌmɑːrdʒ ə 'næl əṭ i
marginalization ˌmɑːdʒ ɪn ᵊl aɪ 'zeɪʃ ᵊn
ˌ•ᵊn‿ᵊl-, -ɪ'•- ‖ ˌmɑːrdʒ ᵊn‿ᵊl ə-
marginaliz|e 'mɑːdʒ ɪn ə laɪz -ᵊn‿ə-, -ᵊl aɪz
~ed d ~es ɪz əz ~ing ɪŋ
Margo 'mɑːg əʊ ‖ 'mɑːrg oʊ
Margolis mɑː 'gəʊl ɪs §-əs ‖ mɑːr 'goʊl-
Margot 'mɑːg əʊ -ət ‖ 'mɑːrg oʊ
margrave 'mɑː greɪv ‖ 'mɑːr- ~s z
marguerite, M~ ˌmɑːg ə 'riːt ‖ ˌmɑːrg- ~s, ~'s
s
Marham (i) 'mær əm ‖ 'mer-, (ii) 'mɑːr əm
—Both (i) and (ii) are heard for the place in
Norfolk.
Mari 'mɑːr i ~s z
Maria personal name (i) mə 'riː‿ə, (ii) mə 'raɪ‿ə
—Always (ii) in the phrase Black Maria
maria, Maria Latin pl of mare 'mɑːr i‿ə 'mær-
mariachi ˌmær i 'ɑːtʃ i ‖ ˌmɑːr- ˌmær- —Sp
[ma 'rja tʃi]
Marian forename 'mær i‿ən §-æn ‖ 'mer-
Marian adj, n 'meər i‿ən ‖ 'mer-

Mariana ˌmær i 'ɑːn ə ◀ ˌmeər-, -'æn-
‖ -'æn ə ◀ ˌmer-; ˌmɑːr i 'ɑːn ə ~s z
ˌMariana 'Trench
Marianne ˌmær i 'æn ‖ ˌmer- —Fr [ma ʁi jan]
Marie (i) mə 'riː, (ii) 'mɑːr i, (iii) 'mær i —In
AmE (i).
ˌMarie ˌAntoi'nette ‖ Maˌrie-
Marienbad 'mær i‿ən bæd mə 'riː‿ən-,
→ˌ•əm• ‖ 'mer- —Ger [ma 'ʁiː ən baːt]
Marietta ˌmær i 'et ə ‖ -'eṭ ə ˌmer-
marigold, M~ 'mær i gəʊld §-ə-, →ˌ-gɒʊld
‖ -ə goʊld 'mer- ~s z
marihuana, marijuana ˌmær ɪ 'wɑːn ə -ə-,
-'hwɑːn-; ˌmær i ju 'ɑːn ə ‖ ˌmer-
Marilyn 'mær əl ɪn -ɪl-, -ən ‖ 'mer-
marimba mə 'rɪm bə ~s z
Marin (i) 'mɑːr ɪn §-ən, (ii) 'mær- ‖ 'mer-, (iii)
mə 'rɪn —The county in CA is (iii).
marina, M~ mə 'riːn ə ~s z
marinad|e ˌmær ɪ 'neɪd -ə-, '••• ‖ ˌmer- ~ed
ɪd əd ~es z ~ing ɪŋ
marinara ˌmær ɪ 'nɑːr ə -ə- ‖ -'ner ə ˌmer-,
ˌmɑːr-, -'nɑːr-, -'nær- —It [ma ri 'naː ra]
mari|nate 'mær ɪ neɪt -ə- ‖ 'mer- ~nated
neɪt ɪd -əd ‖ neɪṭ əd ~nates neɪts ~nating
neɪt ɪŋ ‖ neɪṭ ɪŋ
marine mə 'riːn ~s z
Maˌrine 'Corps
mariner, M~ 'mær ɪn ə -ən- ‖ -ᵊn ᵊr 'mer- ~s
z
mariniere ˌmær ɪn 'jeə ‖ ˌmɑːr ᵊn 'jeᵊr ˌmær-,
ˌmer- —Fr marinière [ma ʁi njɛːʁ]
Marino mə 'riːn əʊ ‖ -oʊ
Mario 'mær i əʊ 'mɑːr- ‖ 'mɑːr i oʊ 'mær-,
'mer-
mariolatry, M~ ˌmeər i 'ɒl ətr i ˌmær-
‖ ˌmer i 'ɑːl- ˌmær-
Mariology, M~ ˌmeər i 'ɒl ədʒ i ˌmær- ‖ ˌmer i 'ɑːl-
ˌmær-
Marion 'mær i‿ən 'meər- ‖ 'mer-
marionette ˌmær i‿ə 'net ‖ ˌmer- ~s s
mariposa ˌmær ɪ 'pəʊz ə ‖ -'poʊz ə ˌmer-,
-'pous-
ˌmari'posa ˌlily
Marischal 'mɑːʃ ᵊl ‖ 'mɑːrʃ-
Marist 'meər ɪst §-əst ‖ 'mer- 'mær- ~s s
marital 'mær ɪt ᵊl -ət- ‖ -əṭ ᵊl 'mer- —In BrE
formerly also mə 'raɪt- ~ly i
maritime, M~ 'mær ɪ taɪm -ə- ‖ 'mer- ~s z
Marius 'mær i‿əs 'mɑːr-, 'meər- ‖ 'mer-, 'mɑːr-
marjoram, M~ 'mɑːdʒ ᵊr‿əm ‖ 'mɑːrdʒ-
Marjoribanks 'mɑːtʃ bæŋks ‖ 'mɑːrtʃ-
Marjorie, Marjory 'mɑːdʒ ᵊr‿i ‖ 'mɑːrdʒ-
mark, Mark mɑːk ‖ mɑːrk marked
mɑːkt ‖ mɑːrkt marking
'mɑːk ɪŋ ‖ 'mɑːrk ɪŋ marks mɑːks ‖ mɑːrks
₍ᵢ₎Mark 'Antony
markdown 'mɑːk daʊn ‖ 'mɑːrk- ~s z
marked|ly 'mɑːk ɪd |li -əd- ‖ 'mɑːrk- ~ness
nəs nɪs
marker, M~ 'mɑːk ə ‖ 'mɑːrk ᵊr ~s z
mark|et 'mɑːk |ɪt §-ət ‖ 'mɑːrk |ət ~eted ɪt ɪd
§ət-, -əd ‖ əṭ əd ~eting ɪt ɪŋ §ət- ‖ əṭ ɪŋ

~ets ɪts §əts ‖ əts
,market 'forces; ,market 'garden ‖ '•• ,••,
~er/s, ~ing; ,market 'price ‖ '•• •; ,market
re'search, -'research ‖ '•• •, •, ‖ -, •• ;
'market town; ,market 'value, '•• ,••
marketability ,mɑːk ɪt ə 'bɪl ət i §, • ət-, -ɪt i
‖ ,mɑːrk ət̬ ə 'bɪl ət̬ i
marketable 'mɑːk ɪt əb əl §'• ət- ‖ 'mɑːrk ət̬-
marketeer ,mɑːk ɪ 'tɪə -ə- ‖ ,mɑːrk ə 'tɪər ~s
z
marketplac|e 'mɑːk ɪt pleɪs §-ət- ‖ 'mɑːrk-
~es ɪz əz
Market Rasen ,mɑːk ɪt 'reɪz ən §-ət- ‖ ,mɑːrk-
Markey 'mɑːk i ‖ 'mɑːrk i
Markham 'mɑːk əm ‖ 'mɑːrk-
marking 'mɑːk ɪŋ ‖ 'mɑːrk ɪŋ ~s z
'marking ink
Markov 'mɑːk ɒv -ɒf ‖ 'mɑːrk ɑːf -ɔːf —Russ
['mar kəf]
,Markov 'process ‖ '•• ,••
Markova mɑː 'kəʊv ə ‖ mɑːr 'koʊv ə —Russ
['mar kə və]
Marks mɑːks ‖ mɑːrks
,Marks and 'Spencer tdmk
marks|man 'mɑːks |mən ‖ 'mɑːrks- ~manship
mən ʃɪp ~men mən men ~woman ,wʊm ən
~women ,wɪm ɪn §-ən
markup 'mɑːk ʌp ‖ 'mɑːrk- ~s s
marl mɑːl ‖ mɑːrl
Marlboro tdmk 'mɑːl bər̯ə 'mɔːl- ‖ 'mɑːrl-
Marlboro, Marlborough place name, family
name 'mɔːl bər̯ə 'mɑːl- ‖ 'mɑːrl ,bɝ: ə
'mɔːrl-, -oʊ
Marlene (i) 'mɑːl iːn ,mɑː 'liːn ‖ mɑːr 'liːn, (ii)
mɑː 'leɪn ə ‖ mɑːr- —As an English name, (i);
as a German name, (ii). —Ger [maʁ 'leː nə]
Marler 'mɑːl ə ‖ 'mɑːrl ər
Marley 'mɑːl i ‖ 'mɑːrl i
marlin, marline 'mɑːl ɪn §-ən ‖ 'mɑːrl- ~s z
marlinespike, marlinspike 'mɑːl ɪn spaɪk -ən-
‖ 'mɑːrl- ~s s
Marlon 'mɑːl ən -ɒn ‖ 'mɑːrl-
Marlow, Marlowe 'mɑːl əʊ ‖ 'mɑːrl oʊ
Marmaduke 'mɑːm ə djuːk →§-dʒuːk
‖ 'mɑːrm ə duːk -djuːk
marmalade 'mɑːm ə leɪd ‖ 'mɑːrm- ~s z
,marmalade 'cat
Marmara 'mɑːm ər ə ‖ 'mɑːrm-
Marmion 'mɑːm i‿ən ‖ 'mɑːrm-
marmite, M~ tdmk 'mɑːm aɪt ‖ 'mɑːrm-
Marmora 'mɑːm ər ə ‖ 'mɑːrm-
marmoreal mɑː 'mɔːr i‿əl ‖ mɑːr- -'moʊr-
marmoset 'mɑːm ə zet -set, ,••'• ‖ 'mɑːrm-
~s s
marmot 'mɑːm ət ‖ 'mɑːrm- ~s s
Marn, Marne mɑːn ‖ mɑːrn
Marner 'mɑːn ə ‖ 'mɑːrn ər
Marnie 'mɑːn i ‖ 'mɑːrn i
marocain 'mær ə keɪn ,••'• ‖ 'mer-
Maronite 'mær ə naɪt ‖ 'mer- ~s s
maroon mə 'ruːn ~ed d ~ing ɪŋ ~s z
Marplan tdmk 'mɑː plæn ‖ 'mɑːr-
Marple 'mɑːp əl ‖ 'mɑːrp əl

Marprelate 'mɑː ,prel ət -ɪt ‖ 'mɑːr-
Marquand 'mɑːk wənd ‖ ,mɑːr 'kwɑːnd
marque mɑːk ‖ mɑːrk (= mark) marques
mɑːks ‖ mɑːrks
marquee (,)mɑː 'kiː ‖ (,)mɑːr- ~s z
Marquesan mɑː 'keɪz ən -'keɪs- ‖ mɑːr- ~s z
Marquesas mɑː 'keɪz əz -'keɪs əs, -æs ‖ mɑːr-
marquess 'mɑːk wɪs -wəs ‖ 'mɑːrk- ~es ɪz əz
marquetry 'mɑːk ɪtr i -ətr- ‖ 'mɑːrk-
marquis, M~ 'mɑːk wɪs -wəs; (,)mɑː 'kiː
‖ 'mɑːrk wəs (,)mɑːr 'kiː ~es ɪz əz
marquis|e (,)mɑː 'kiːz ‖ (,)mɑːr- ~es ɪz əz
Marr mɑː ‖ mɑːr
Marrakech, Marrakesh ,mær ə 'keʃ
mə 'ræk eʃ ‖ ,mer-
marram 'mær əm ‖ 'mer-
'marram grass
marriag|e 'mær ɪdʒ ‖ 'mer- ~es ɪz əz
'marriage ,broker; ,marriage 'guidance;
'marriage lines
marriageability ,mær ɪdʒ ə 'bɪl ət i ,• əˈdʒ-, -ɪt i
‖ -ət̬ i ,mer-
marriageable 'mær ɪdʒ əb əl '• ədʒ- ‖ 'mer-
~ness nəs nɪs
married 'mær id ‖ 'mer- ~s z
Marriott 'mær i‿ət ‖ 'mer-, -ɑːt
marron 'mær ən -ɒ̃ ‖ 'mer-; mə 'roʊn, mæ-
—Fr [ma ʁɔ̃] ~s z —or as sing.
marrow 'mær əʊ ‖ -oʊ 'mer- ~s z
marrowbone 'mær əʊ bəʊn ‖ -ə boʊn 'mer-,
-oʊ- ~s z
marrowfat 'mær əʊ fæt ‖ -oʊ- 'mer-, -ə-
,marrowfat 'pea

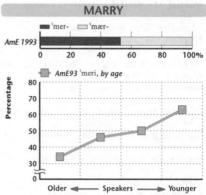

MARRY

■ 'mer- ☐ 'mær-

AmE 1993

0   20   40   60   80   100%

AmE93 'meri, by age

Percentage 80 / 70 / 60 / 50 / 40 / 30 / 0

Older ◀— Speakers —▶ Younger

marr|y 'mær |i ‖ 'mer- —AmE 1993 poll panel
preference: 'mer- 53%, 'mær- 47%. ~ied id
~ies iz ~ying i‿ɪŋ
Marryat 'mær i‿ət ‖ 'mer-
Mars mɑːz ‖ mɑːrz
Marsala, m~ mɑː 'sɑːl ə ‖ mɑːr- —It
[mar 'sa: la]
Marsden 'mɑːz dən ‖ 'mɑːrz-
Marseillaise ,mɑːs eɪ 'eɪz -'jeɪz, -'ez; -əl-;
-ə 'leɪz, -'lez ‖ ,mɑːrs- —Fr [maʁ sɛ jɛːz]
Marseilles (,)mɑː 'seɪ -'seɪlz ‖ (,)mɑːr- —Fr
Marseille [maʁ sɛj]

M

marsh, Marsh mɑːʃ ‖ mɑːrʃ **marshes** 'mɑːʃ ɪz
-əz ‖ 'mɑːrʃ əz
'marsh gas; ˌmarsh 'marigold
Marsha 'mɑːʃ ə ‖ 'mɑːrʃ ə
marshal 'mɑːʃ əl ‖ 'mɑːrʃ əl ~ed, ~led d ~ing,
~ling ˌɪŋ ~s z
'marshalling yard; ˌmarshal of the ˌRoyal
'Air Force
Marshall 'mɑːʃ əl ‖ 'mɑːrʃ əl
'Marshall Plan
Marshalsea 'mɑːʃ əl siː -siː ‖ 'mɑːrʃ-
Marsham 'mɑːʃ əm ‖ 'mɑːrʃ-
marshiness 'mɑːʃ i nəs -nɪs ‖ 'mɑːrʃ-
marshland 'mɑːʃ lænd -lənd ‖ 'mɑːrʃ- ~s z
marshmallow ˌ(ˌ)mɑːʃ 'mæl əʊ ‖ 'mɑːrʃ ˌmel oʊ
-ˌmæl-, -ə (*) ~s z
marshy 'mɑːʃ i ‖ 'mɑːrʃ i
Marsilius mɑː 'sɪl i̯əs ‖ mɑːr-
Marson 'mɑːs ən ‖ 'mɑːrs ən
Marston 'mɑːst ən ‖ 'mɑːrst ən
ˌMarston 'Moor
marsupial mɑː 'suːp i̯əl -'sjuːp- ‖ mɑːr- ~s z
marsupi|um mɑː 'suːp i̯ləm -'sjuːp- ‖ mɑːr-
~a ə
mart mɑːt ‖ mɑːrt **marts** mɑːts ‖ mɑːrts
martagon 'mɑːt əg ən ‖ 'mɑːrt̬- ~s z
Martel, Martell mɑː 'tel ‖ mɑːr-
martello, M~ mɑː 'tel əʊ ‖ mɑːr 'tel oʊ ~s z
Marˌtello 'tower
marten 'mɑːt ɪn -ən ‖ 'mɑːrt ən ~s z
Martens (i) 'mɑːt ɪnz -ənz ‖ 'mɑːrt ənz, (ii)
mɑː 'tenz ‖ mɑːr-
Martha 'mɑːθ ə ‖ 'mɑːrθ ə
Marti 'mɑːt i ‖ 'mɑːrt̬ i
martial, M~ 'mɑːʃ əl ‖ 'mɑːrʃ əl (= marshal)
~ly i
ˌmartial 'arts; ˌmartial 'law
Martian, m~ 'mɑːʃ ən 'mɑːʃ i̯ən ‖ 'mɑːrʃ- ~s
z
Martin, m~ 'mɑːt ɪn §-ən ‖ 'mɑːrt ən ~s, ~'s z
Martina mɑː 'tiːn ə ‖ mɑːr-
Martineau 'mɑːt ɪ nəʊ -ə-, -ən əʊ
‖ 'mɑːrt ən oʊ
martinet ˌmɑːt ɪ 'net -ə-, -ən 'et ‖ ˌmɑːrt ən 'et
~s s
Martinez mɑː 'tiːn ez ‖ mɑːr 'tiːn es -əs —Sp
Martínez [mar 'ti neθ, -nes]
martingale 'mɑːt ɪn geɪ°l →-ɪŋ-, §-°n-
‖ 'mɑːrt ən- ~s z
martini, M~ tdmk mɑː 'tiːn i ‖ mɑːr- ~s z
Martinique ˌmɑːt ɪ 'niːk -ə-, -ən 'iːk
‖ ˌmɑːrt ən 'iːk
Martinmas 'mɑːt ɪn məs →-ɪm-, §-°n-, -mæs
‖ 'mɑːrt ən-
Martinu 'mɑːt ɪ nuː §-ə- ‖ 'mɑːrt-ˌ —Czech
Martinů ['mar ci nuː]
Martland 'mɑːt lənd ‖ 'mɑːrt-
martlet 'mɑːt lət -lɪt ‖ 'mɑːrt- ~s s
Marty 'mɑːt i ‖ 'mɑːrt̬ i
Martyn 'mɑːt ɪn §-ən ‖ 'mɑːrt ən
martyr 'mɑːt ə ‖ 'mɑːrt̬ ər ~ed d **martyring**
'mɑːt ər ɪŋ ‖ 'mɑːrt̬ ər ɪŋ ~s z
martyrdom ˌ'mɑːt ə dəm ‖ 'mɑːrt̬ ər- ~s z

martyrolog|y ˌmɑːt ə 'rɒl ədʒ |i ‖ ˌmɑːrt̬ ə 'rɑːl- ~ies iz
marvel 'mɑːv əl ‖ 'mɑːrv əl ~ed, ~led d ~ing,
~ling ɪŋ ~s z
Marvell 'mɑːv əl ‖ 'mɑːrv əl
marvellous, marvelous 'mɑːv ləs 'mɑːv əl əs
‖ 'mɑːrv- ~ly li ~ness nəs nɪs
Marvin 'mɑːv ɪn §-ən ‖ 'mɑːrv ən
Marwick 'mɑː wɪk ‖ 'mɑːr-
Marx mɑːks ‖ mɑːrks **Marx's** 'mɑːks ɪz -əz
‖ 'mɑːrks əz
'Marx ˌBrothers
Marxian 'mɑːks i̯ən ‖ 'mɑːrks-
Marxism 'mɑːks ˌɪz əm ‖ 'mɑːrks-
Marxism-Leninism ˌmɑːks ˌɪz əm 'len ɪn ˌɪz
əm §-'•ən- ‖ ˌmɑːrks-
Marxist 'mɑːks ɪst §-əst ‖ 'mɑːrks- ~s s
Marxist-Leninist ˌmɑːks ɪst 'len ɪn ɪst
§-əst 'len ɪn əst, §-ən• ‖ ˌmɑːrks- ~s s
Mary 'meər i ‖ 'mer i 'mær i
ˌMary ˌQueen of 'Scots
Maryland 'meər ɪ lənd 'mer-, -ə-, -lænd ‖ 'mer
əl ənd 'mær-
Marylebone 'mær əl ə bən '•ɪ-, -lɪ•, -bəʊn;
'mær ɪb ən, 'mɑːl-, -əb- ‖ 'mer əl ə boʊn
'mær-
Maryport 'meər i pɔːt ‖ 'mer i pɔːrt -poʊrt
marzipan 'mɑːz ɪ pæn -ə-, ˌ•'•'• ‖ 'mɑːrz-
'mɑːrts-, -pɑːn
Masada mə 'sɑːd ə
Masai 'mɑː saɪ ˌ•'•, mə 'saɪ
masala mə 'sɑːl ə
Mascagni mæ 'skæn ji -'skɑːn- ‖ mɑː 'skɑːn ji
mæ- —It [ma 'skaɲ ɲi]
Mascall 'mæsk əl
mascara mæ 'skɑːr ə mə- ‖ -'skær ə -'sker-
(*) ~'d, ~ed d ~s z
Mascarene, m~ ˌmæsk ə 'riːn ◂ ~s z
mascarpone ˌmæsk ɑː 'pəʊn i -ə-, -eɪ; -'pəʊn
‖ ˌmɑːsk ɑːr 'poʊn eɪ —It [ma skar 'po: ne]
mascot 'mæsk ət -ɒt ‖ -ɑːt -ət ~s s
masculine 'mæsk jʊl ɪn 'mɑːsk-, -jəl-, §-ən,
§-ju laɪn, -jə- ‖ -jəl ən ~ly li ~ness nəs nɪs
~s z
masculinis... —see masculiniz...
masculinity ˌmæsk ju 'lɪn ət i ˌmɑːsk-, ˌ•jə-,
-ɪt i ‖ -jə 'lɪn ət̬ i
masculinization ˌmæsk jʊl ɪn aɪ 'zeɪʃ ən
ˌmɑːsk-, ˌ•jəl-, ˌ•'•ən-, -ɪ'•-
‖ ˌmæsk jəl ən ə-
masculiniz|e 'mæsk ʊl ɪ naɪz 'mɑːsk-, '•jəl-,
§-ə• ‖ 'mæsk jəl ən ə- ~ed d ~es ɪz əz ~ing ɪŋ
Masefield 'meɪs fiː°ld 'meɪz-
maser 'meɪz ə ‖ -ər ~s z
Maserati tdmk ˌmæz ə 'rɑːt i ‖ ˌmɑːs ə 'rɑːt̬ i
ˌmæz ə- ~s z
Maseru mə 'sɪər uː -'seər- ‖ 'mæz ə ruː 'mɑːs-
mash mæʃ **mashed** mæʃt **mashes** 'mæʃ ɪz
-əz **mashing** 'mæʃ ɪŋ
Masham (i) 'mæs əm, (ii) 'mæʃ əm —The place
in N.Yorks. is (i), the breed of sheep and the
family name either (i) or (ii).
masher 'mæʃ ə ‖ -ər ~s z

mashie 'mæʃ i ~s z
Mashonaland mə 'ʃɒn ə lænd -'ʃəʊn- ‖ -'ʃɑːn-
-'ʃoʊn-
mask mɑːsk §mæsk ‖ mæsk **masked** mɑːskt
§mæskt ‖ mæskt **masking** 'mɑːsk ɪŋ
§'mæsk- ‖ 'mæsk ɪŋ **masks** mɑːsks §mæsks
‖ mæsks
'**masking tape**
Maskall, Maskell 'mæsk əl
masochism 'mæs ə ˌkɪz əm 'mæz-
masochist 'mæs ək ɪst 'mæz-, §-əst ~s s
masochistic ˌmæs ə 'kɪst ɪk ◄ ˌmæz- ~ally əl_i
mason, Mason 'meɪs ən ~s z
'**Mason jar**
Mason-Dixon ˌmeɪs ən 'dɪks ən
ˌMason-'Dixon line
masonic, M~ mə 'sɒn ɪk -'zɒn- ‖ -'sɑːn-
Masonite tdmk 'meɪs ə naɪt
mason|ry 'meɪs ən |ri ~ries riz
Masora, Masorah mə 'sɔːr ə ‖ -'soʊr-
Masorete 'mæs ə riːt ~s s
Masoretic ˌmæs ə 'ret ɪk ◄ ‖ -'ret̬-
masque mɑːsk mæsk ‖ mæsk (= mask)
masques mɑːsks mæsks ‖ mæsks

MASQUERADE

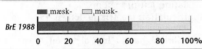

masquerad|e n, v ˌmæsk ə 'reɪd ˌmɑːsk- —BrE
1988 poll panel preference: ˌmæsk- 62%
(southerners 48%), ˌmɑːsk- 39% (southerners
52%). In AmE always ˌmæsk-. ~ed ɪd əd
~er/s ə/z ‖ ər/z ~es z ~ing ɪŋ
mass common n, v, adj mæs **massed** mæst
masses 'mæs ɪz -əz **massing** 'mæs ɪŋ
ˌmass 'media; ˌmass pro'duction
Mass 'eucharist', 'music for the Mass' mæs mɑːs
Masses 'mæs ɪz 'mɑːs-, -əz
Mass. 'Massachusetts' mæs —or as
Massachusetts

MASSACHUSETTS

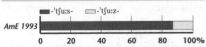

Massachusetts ˌmæs ə 'tʃuːs ɪts -'tʃuːz-, -əts
—AmE 1993 poll panel preference: -'tʃuːs-
87%, -'tʃuːz- 13%.
massacre 'mæs ək ə -ɪk- ‖ -ər ~d d ~s z
massacring 'mæs ək ər_ɪŋ
massag|e 'mæs ɑːʒ -ɑːdʒ ‖ mə 'sɑːʒ -'sɑːdʒ (*)
~ed d ~es ɪz əz ~ing ɪŋ
'**massage** ˌparlour ‖ mas'sage ˌparlor
Massapequa ˌmæs ə 'piːk wə ◄
ˌMassaˌpequa 'Park
massasauga ˌmæs ə 'sɔːɡ ə ‖ -'sɑːɡ- ~s z
Masscomp tdmk 'mæs kɒmp ‖ -kɑːmp ~s s
massé 'mæs i ‖ mæ 'seɪ ~s z
Massenet 'mæs ə neɪ ‖ ˌmæs ə 'neɪ —Fr
[ma nɛ]
Massereene 'mæs ə riːn

masseter mæ 'siːt ə mə-; 'mæs ɪt ə, -ət-
‖ -'siːt̬ ər ~s z
masseur mæ 'sɜː mə- ‖ -'sʊ²r ~s z
masseus|e mæ 'sɜːz mə- ‖ -'suːz -'suːs, -'sʊz
~es ɪz əz
Massey, Massie 'mæs i
massif 'mæs iːf mæ 'siːf ‖ mæ 'siːf —Fr
[ma sif] ~s s
massiness 'mæs i nəs -nɪs
Massinger 'mæs ɪndʒ ə -əndʒ- ‖ -ər
massive 'mæs ɪv ~ly li ~ness nəs nɪs
massless 'mæs ləs -lɪs ~ness nəs nɪs
Masson 'mæs ən
mass-produc|e ˌmæs prə 'djuːs ◄ →§-'dʒuːs
‖ -'duːs ◄ -'djuːs ~ed t ~es ɪz əz ~ing ɪŋ
massy 'mæs i
mast mɑːst §mæst ‖ mæst **masts** mɑːsts
§mæsts ‖ mæsts
mastectom|y mæ 'stekt əm |i mə- ~ies iz
master, M~ 'mɑːst ə §'mæst- ‖ 'mæst ər ~ed
d **mastering** 'mɑːst ər ɪŋ →'mɑːs trɪŋ;
§'mæst ər ɪŋ, →§'mæs trɪŋ ‖ 'mæst ər ɪŋ
→'mæs trɪŋ ~s, ~'s z
'**master card**; '**master key**, ˌ·· '·; ˌMaster
of 'Arts; ˌmaster of 'ceremonies; ˌMaster
of 'Science; '**master race**; '**master's**
deˌgree; ˌmaster 'sergeant◄
master-at-arms ˌmɑːst ər ət 'ɑːmz §ˌmæst-
‖ ˌmæst ər ət̬ 'ɑːrmz **masters-at-arms**
-əz ət- ‖ -ərz ət̬-
MasterCard tdmk 'mɑːst ə kɑːd §'mæst-
‖ 'mæst ər kɑːrd ~s z
masterful 'mɑːst ə fəl §'mæst-, -fʊl ‖ 'mæst ər-
~ly _i ~ness nəs nɪs
master|ly 'mɑːst ə |li §'mæst-, -əl i ‖ 'mæst ər-
~liness li nəs li nɪs
Masterman 'mɑːst ə mən §'mæst- ‖ 'mæst ər-
mastermind n, v 'mɑːst ə maɪnd §'mæst-,
ˌ··'· ‖ 'mæst ər- ~ed ɪd əd ~ing ɪŋ ~s z
masterpiec|e 'mɑːst ə piːs §'mæst-
‖ 'mæst ər- ~es ɪz əz
Masters 'mɑːst əz §'mæst- ‖ 'mæst ərz
masterstroke 'mɑːst ə strəʊk §'mæst-
‖ 'mæst ər stroʊk ~s s
masterwork 'mɑːst ə wɜːk §'mæst-
‖ 'mæst ər wɜˑk ~s s
mastery 'mɑːst ər |i →'mɑːs trli; §'mæst ər li,
→§'mæs trli ‖ 'mæst ər li →'mæs trli ~ies iz
masthead 'mɑːst hed §'mæst- ‖ 'mæst- ~s z
mastic 'mæst ɪk
masti|cate 'mæst ɪ |keɪt §-ə- ~cated keɪt ɪd
-əd ‖ keɪt̬ əd ~cates keɪts ~cating
keɪt ɪŋ ‖ keɪt̬ ɪŋ
mastication ˌmæst ɪ 'keɪʃ ən §-ə- ~s z
masticator|y 'mæst ɪ kət ər li -keɪt ər li,
ˌ··'keɪt ər li ‖ -kə tɔːr li -toʊr i ~ies iz
mastiff 'mæst ɪf 'mɑːst-, §-əf ~s s
mastitis mæ 'staɪt ɪs mə-, §-əs ‖ -'staɪt̬ əs
mastodon 'mæst ə dɒn -əd ən ‖ -dɑːn ~s z
mastoid 'mæst ɔɪd ~s z
mastoiditis ˌmæst ɔɪ 'daɪt ɪs §-əs ‖ -'daɪt̬ əs
Mastroianni ˌmæs trəʊ 'jɑːn i ˌmɑːs-,
-'jæn- ‖ -troʊ- —It [mas tro 'jan ni]

M

mastur|bate 'mæst ə |beɪt 'mɑːst- ‖ -ᵊr-
~bated beɪt ɪd -əd ‖ beɪt̬ əd ~bates beɪts
~bating beɪt ɪŋ ‖ beɪt̬ ɪŋ
masturbation ,mæst ə 'beɪʃ ᵊn ,mɑːst- ‖ -ᵊr-
~s z
masturbatory ,mæst ə 'beɪt ər i ◄ ,mɑːst-,
'• • • • ‖ 'mæst ᵊrb ə tɔːr i -tour i
mat mæt mats mæts matted 'mæt ɪd -əd
‖ 'mæt̬ əd matting 'mæt ɪŋ ‖ 'mæt̬ ɪŋ
Mata Hari ,mɑːt ə 'hɑːr i ‖ ,mɑːt̬-
Matabele ,mæt ə 'biːl i ◄ -'bel- ‖ ,mæt̬- ~land
lænd ~s z
matador 'mæt ə dɔː ‖ 'mæt̬ ə dɔːr ~s z
Matapan 'mæt ə pæn ,• • '• ‖ 'mæt̬-
match mætʃ matched mætʃt matches
'mætʃ ɪz -əz matching 'mætʃ ɪŋ
,match 'point ‖ '• •
matchboard 'mætʃ bɔːd ‖ -bɔːrd -bourd
matchbook 'mætʃ bʊk §-buːk ~s s
matchbox 'mætʃ bɒks ‖ -bɑːks ~es ɪz əz
matchless 'mætʃ ləs -lɪs ~ly li ~ness nəs nɪs
matchlock 'mætʃ lɒk ‖ -lɑːk ~s s
matchmak|er/s 'mætʃ ,meɪk |ə/z ‖ -|ᵊr/z ~ing
ɪŋ
matchplay 'mætʃ pleɪ
matchstick 'mætʃ stɪk ~s s
matchwood 'mætʃ wʊd
mate meɪt mated 'meɪt ɪd -əd ‖ 'meɪt̬ əd
mates meɪts mating 'meɪt ɪŋ ‖ 'meɪt̬ ɪŋ
maté 'mæt eɪ 'mɑːt- ‖ 'mɑːt eɪ mɑː 'teɪ
matelot 'mæt ləʊ 'mæt əl əʊ ‖ -loʊ ~s z
mater, Mater 'meɪt ə 'mɑːt- ‖ 'meɪt̬ ᵊr 'mɑːt̬-
~s, ~'s z
,Mater ,Dolo'rosa ,dɒl ə 'rəʊs ə -'rəʊz-
‖ ,doʊl ə 'roʊs ə -ɑː
materia mə 'tɪər i ə ‖ -'tɪr-
ma,teria 'medica 'med ɪk ə
material mə 'tɪər i əl ‖ -'tɪr- ~s z
materialis... —see materializ...
materialism mə 'tɪər i ə ,lɪz əm ‖ -'tɪr-
materialist mə 'tɪər i əl ɪst §-əst ‖ -'tɪr- ~s s
materialistic mə ,tɪər i ə 'lɪst ɪk ◄ ‖ -,tɪr- ~ally
əl i
materialization mə ,tɪər i əl aɪ 'zeɪʃ ᵊn -ɪ' • -
‖ mə ,tɪr i əl ə- ~s z
materializ|e mə 'tɪər i ə laɪz ‖ -'tɪr- ~ed d
~es ɪz əz ~ing ɪŋ
material|ly mə 'tɪər i əl li ‖ -'tɪr- ~ness nəs
nɪs
materiel, matériel mə ,tɪər i 'el -'tɪər i əl
‖ -,tɪr- —Fr [ma te ʁjɛl]
maternal mə 'tɜːn ᵊl ‖ -'tɜːn ᵊl ~ly i
maternity mə 'tɜːn ət i -ɪt- ‖ -'tɜːn ət̬ i
mateship 'meɪt ʃɪp
matey 'meɪt i ‖ 'meɪt̬ i ~ness nəs nɪs
math mæθ
mathematical ,mæθ ə 'mæt ɪk ᵊl ◄ ,• ɪ-;
mæθ 'mæt- ‖ -'mæt̬- ~ly ̩i
mathematician ,mæθ əm ə 'tɪʃ ᵊn ,• ɪm- ~s z
mathematics ,mæθ ə 'mæt ɪks -ɪ-; mæθ 'mæt-
‖ -'mæt̬ ɪks
Mather (i) 'meɪð ə ‖ -ᵊr, (ii) 'mæð-, (iii) 'meɪθ-
Matheson 'mæθ ɪs ᵊn -əs-

Mathew 'mæθ juː
Mathias mə 'θaɪ_əs
Mathis 'mæθ ɪs §-əs
maths mæθs
Matilda mə 'tɪld ə
matinee, matinée 'mæt ɪ neɪ §-ə-, §-ᵊn eɪ
‖ ,mæt ᵊn 'eɪ (*) ~s z
'matinee ,idol ‖ ,mati'nee ,idol
matins 'mæt ɪnz §-ᵊnz ‖ -ᵊnz
Matisse mæ 'tiːs —Fr [ma tis]
Matlock 'mæt lɒk ‖ -lɑːk
Mato Grosso ,mæt əʊ 'grɒs əʊ ,mɑːt-
‖ ,mæt ə 'groʊs oʊ —Port [,ma tu 'gro su]
matriarch 'meɪtr i ɑːk 'mætr- ‖ -ɑːrk ~s s
matriarch|al ,meɪtr i 'ɑːk |ᵊl ◄ ,mætr-, '• • • •
‖ -'ɑːrk |ᵊl ◄ ~ic ɪk ◄
matriarch|y 'meɪtr i ɑːk |i 'mætr- ‖ -ɑːrk |i
~ies ɪz
matric mə 'trɪk
matrices 'meɪtr ɪ siːz 'mætr-, -ə-
matricide 'meɪtr ɪ saɪd 'mætr-, -ə- ‖ 'mætr-
'meɪtr- ~s z
matriculant mə 'trɪk jʊl ənt -jəl- ‖ -jəl- ~s s
matricu|late mə 'trɪk jʊ |leɪt -jə- ‖ -jə-
~lated leɪt ɪd -əd ‖ leɪt̬ əd ~lates leɪts
~lating leɪt ɪŋ ‖ leɪt̬ ɪŋ
matriculation mə ,trɪk jʊ 'leɪʃ ᵊn -jə- ‖ -jə-
~s z
matrilineal ,mætr ɪ 'lɪn i_əl ◄ ,meɪtr-, ,• ə- ~ly
i
matrilocal ,mætr ɪ 'ləʊk ᵊl ◄ ,meɪtr-, -ə-,
'• •, • • ‖ -ə 'loʊk ᵊl ◄ ~ly i
matrimonial ,mætr ɪ 'məʊn i_əl ◄, • ə-
‖ -'moʊn- ~ly i
matrimon|y 'mætr ɪm ən li '• əm- ‖ -ə moʊn li
(*) ~ies ɪz
matrix 'meɪtr ɪks —in printing also 'mætr- ~es
ɪz əz
matron, M~ 'meɪtr ᵊn ~liness li nəs -nɪs ~ly
li ~s z
Matsu ,mæt 'suː ‖ ,mɑːt- —Chi Mǎzǔ
[¹ma ³tsu]
Matsui tdmk mæt 'suː i —Jp [ma ,tsɯ i]
Matsushita tdmk ,mæt su 'ʃiːt ə ‖ ,mɑːt- —Jp
[ma ,tsɯ 'çi ta]
matt mæt matts mæts
Mattachine ,mæt ə 'ʃiːn ‖ ,mæt̬-
matte mæt mattes mæts
matted 'mæt ɪd -əd ‖ 'mæt̬ əd ~ly li ~ness
nəs nɪs
matter 'mæt ə ‖ 'mæt̬ ᵊr ~ed d ~s z
Matterhorn 'mæt ə hɔːn ‖ 'mæt̬ ᵊr hɔːrn
matter-of-course ,mæt_ər əv 'kɔːs ◄ ‖ ,mæt̬
ᵊr əv 'kɔːrs ◄ -'kours
matter-of-fact ,mæt_ər əv 'fækt ◄ -ə' • ‖ ,mæt̬
ᵊr- ~ly li ~ness nəs nɪs
Matthäus mə 'teɪ əs —Ger [ma 'tɛː ʊs]
Matthean mæ 'θiː_ən mə-
Matthes 'mæθ ɪz -əz, -əs
Matthew 'mæθ juː
Matthews 'mæθ juːz
Matthey 'mæθ i 'mæt- ‖ 'mæt̬-
Matthias mə 'θaɪ_əs

Matthiessen 'mæθ ɪs ən §-əs-
Mattie 'mæt i ‖ 'mæṭ i
matting 'mæt ɪŋ ‖ 'mæṭ ɪŋ
mattins 'mæt ɪnz §-ᵊnz ‖ -ᵊnz
mattock 'mæt ək ‖ 'mæṭ- ~s s
mattress 'mætr əs -ɪs ~es ɪz əz
matu|rate 'mætʃ u ǀreɪt -ə-; 'mæt juᵊ-, -jə-
　‖ -ə- ~rated reɪt ɪd -əd ‖ reɪṭ əd ~rates
　reɪts ~rating reɪt ɪŋ ‖ reɪṭ ɪŋ
maturation ˌmætʃ u 'reɪʃ ᵊn -ə-; ˌmæt juᵊ-, -jə-
　‖ -ə- ~s z
mature adj, v mə 'tʃuə -'tjuə, -'tjɔː, -'tʃɔː
　‖ -'tuᵊr -'tʃuᵊr, -'tjuᵊr ~d d ~ly li ~ness nəs
　nɪs　maturer mə 'tʃuər ə -'tjuər-, -'tjɔːr-,
　-'tʃɔːr- ‖ -'tur ᵊr -'tʃur-, -'tjur- ~s z
　maturest mə 'tʃuər ɪst -'tjuər-, -'tjɔːr-,
　-'tʃɔːr-, -əst ‖ -'tur əst -'tʃur-, -'tjur-
　maturing mə 'tʃuər ɪŋ -'tjuər-, -'tjɔːr-,
　-'tʃɔːr- ‖ -'tur ɪŋ -'tʃur-, -'tjur-
　maˌture 'student
maturit|y mə 'tʃuər ət i -ɪ -'tjuər-, -'tjɔːr-,
　-'tʃɔːr-, -ɪt- ‖ -'tur əṭ i -'tʃur-, -'tjur- ~ies iz
matutinal ˌmæt ju 'taɪn ᵊl ◂ ˌmætʃ u-, §-ə-;
　mə 'tjuːt ɪn-, -ᵊnəl ‖ ˌmætʃ u- mə 'tuːt ᵊn_əl,
　-'tjuːt- ~ly i
matza, matzah 'mɒts ə 'mɑːts-, 'mæts-
　‖ 'mɑːts ə ~s z
matzo, matzoh 'mɒts ə 'mɑːts-, 'mæts-, -əʊ
　‖ 'mɑːts ə -oʊ ~s z
mauby 'mɔːb i ‖ 'mɑːb-
Maud, maud, Maude mɔːd ‖ mɑːd mauds,
　Maud's mɔːdz ‖ mɑːdz
maudlin 'mɔːd lɪn §-lən ‖ 'mɑːd- ~ly li
Maudling 'mɔːd lɪŋ ‖ 'mɑːd-
Maudsley 'mɔːdz li ‖ 'mɑːdz-
Maufe mɔːf ‖ mɑːf
Mauger 'meɪdʒ ə ‖ -ᵊr
Maugham mɔːm ‖ mɑːm (!) —occasionally also
　'mɒf əm ‖ 'mɔːf-, 'mɑːf-
Maughan mɔːn ‖ mɑːn
Maui 'maʊ i
maul mɔːl ‖ mɑːl mauled mɔːld ‖ mɑːld
　mauling 'mɔːl ɪŋ ‖ 'mɑːl-
Mauleverer mə 'lev ᵊr ə mɔː- ‖ -ᵊr ᵊr
maulstick 'mɔːl stɪk ‖ 'mɑːl- ~s s
Mau Mau 'maʊ maʊ ˌ•'• ~s z
Maumee mɔː 'miː '•• ‖ mɑː-
Mauna Kea ˌmaʊn ə 'keɪ ə
Mauna Loa ˌmaʊn ə 'ləʊ ə ‖ -'loʊ ə
maunder, M~ 'mɔːnd ə ‖ -ᵊr 'mɑːnd- ~ed d
　maundering 'mɔːnd ᵊr ɪŋ ‖ 'mɑːnd ‿ ~s z
Maundy, m~ 'mɔːnd i ‖ 'mɑːnd-
　'Maundy ˌmoney; ˌMaundy 'Thursday
Maupassant 'məʊp ə sɒ̃ -æ- ‖ 'moʊp ə sɑːnt
　ˌ••'• —Fr [mo pa sɑ̃]
Maureen 'mɔːr iːn mɔː 'riːn ‖ mɔː 'riːn mɑː-
Mauretani|a ˌmɒr ɪ 'teɪn i_ə ˌmɔːr-, ˌ•ə-
　‖ ˌmɔːr ə- ~an/s ən/z
Mauriac 'mɔːr i æk 'məʊ ri- ‖ ˌmɔːr i 'ɑːk —Fr
　[mɔ ʁjak]
Maurice (i) 'mɒr ɪs §-əs ‖ 'mɔːr əs 'mɑːr-, (ii)
　mɒ 'riːs mə- ‖ mɔː- mɑː-

Maurit|ian/s mə 'rɪʃ |ᵊn/z mɒ-, mɔː- ‖ mɔː-
　mɑː-, -'rɪʃ li_ən/z ~ius əs ‖ i_əs
Mauser 'maʊz ə ‖ -ᵊr —Ger ['mau zɐ] ~s z
mausoleum ˌmɔːs ə 'liː_əm ˌmɔːz-, ˌmaʊz-,
　-'leɪ- ‖ ˌmɑːs-, ˌmɔːz-, ˌmɑːz- ~s z
mauve məʊv ‖ moʊv mɔːv, mɑːv (!)
maven 'meɪv ᵊn ~s z
maverick 'mæv ᵊr_ɪk ~s s
Mavis, mavis 'meɪv ɪs §-əs ~es, ~'s ɪz əz
Mavor 'meɪv ə ‖ -ᵊr
maw, Maw mɔː ‖ mɑː maws mɔːz ‖ mɑːz
Mawddach 'maʊð əx -ək —Welsh ['mau ðaχ]
Mawdesley, Mawdsley 'mɔːdz li ‖ 'mɑːdz-
Mawer mɔː 'mɔː ‿ 'mɔːr ᵊr 'mɑː‿
Mawgan 'mɔːg ᵊn ‖ 'mɑːg-
Mawhinny mə 'wɪn i -'hwɪn- ‖ -'hwɪn-
mawkish 'mɔːk ɪʃ ‖ 'mɑːk- ~ly li ~ness nəs
　nɪs
Mawson 'mɔːs ᵊn ‖ 'mɑːs-
Max, max mæks　Max's 'mæks ɪz -əz
　ˌMax 'Factor tdmk
Maxell tdmk 'mæks el mæk 'sel
maxi 'mæks i ~s, ~'s z
maxill|a mæk 'sɪl |ə ~ae iː
maxillary mæk 'sɪl ᵊr i ‖ 'mæks ə ler i (*)
maxim, Maxim 'mæks ɪm §-əm ~s z
maxima 'mæks ɪm ə -əm-
maximal 'mæks ɪm ᵊl -ᵊm_ᵊl ~ly i
maximalist 'mæks ɪm ᵊl ɪst '•ᵊm-, §-əst ~s s
Maximilian ˌmæks ɪ 'mɪl i_ən ˌ•ə-
　‖ ˌmæks ə 'mɪl jən
maximin 'mæks i mɪn ˌ••'• ‖ -ə-
maximis... —see maximiz...
maximization ˌmæks ɪm aɪ 'zeɪʃ ᵊn ˌ•əm-,
　-ɪ'•- ‖ -əm ə- ~s z
maximiz|e 'mæks ɪ maɪz -ə- ~ed d ~es ɪz əz
　~ing ɪŋ
maxim|um 'mæks ɪm |əm -əm- ~a ə ~ums
　əmz
Maximus, m~ 'mæks ɪm əs -əm-
Maxine ˌmæks 'iːn '••
Maxton 'mækst ᵊn
Maxwell, m~ 'mæks wel -wəl ~s z
may, May meɪ
　'May Day
Maya Central American people 'maɪ‿ə 'mɑː jə
　~s z
Maya personal name (i) 'meɪ ə, (ii) 'maɪ‿ə
Maya Hindu deity, maya 'illusion' 'maɪ‿ə
　'mɑː jə
Mayall 'meɪ ɔːl ᵊl ‖ -ɑːl
Mayan 'maɪ‿ən ~s z
maybe 'meɪb i 'meɪ biː, ₍ᵢ₎•'• —There is also a
　casual form 'meb i. The stress pattern ₍ᵢ₎•'• is
　usual only when the word is at the end of a
　clause or sentence, with a concessive meaning:
　They will try, ₍ᵢ₎may'be; but they will not
　succeed.
maybeetle 'meɪ ˌbiːt ᵊl ‖ -ˌbiːṭ- ~s z
Maybelline tdmk 'meɪb ə liːn -e-, ˌ••'•
maybug 'meɪ bʌg ~s z
mayday, M~ 'meɪ deɪ

Mayer *(i)* 'meɪ ə meə ‖ -ᵊr, *(ii)* 'maɪ‿ə ‖ -ᵊr *(i) is an English form, (ii) a German form —Ger* ['mai ɐ]

mayest 'meɪ ɪst -əst; meɪst

Mayfair 'meɪ feə ‖ -fer -fær

Mayfield 'meɪ fiːᵊld

Mayflower, m~ 'meɪ ˌflaʊ‿ə ‖ -ˌflaʊ‿ᵊr **~s** z

may|fly 'meɪ |flaɪ **~flies** flaɪz

mayhem 'meɪ hem

Mayhew 'meɪ hjuː

Maynard 'meɪn əd -ɑːd ‖ -ᵊrd -ɑːrd

Mayne meɪn

Maynooth mə 'nuːθ meɪ-

mayn't meɪnt 'meɪ ənt

Mayo, mayo 'meɪ əʊ ‖ -oʊ —*in Irish English the placename is also* •'•

mayonnaise ˌmeɪ ə 'neɪz ◀ ‖ 'meɪ ə neɪz ˌ•'•; 'mæn eɪz

mayor, Mayor meə ‖ 'meɪ‿ᵊr meᵊr **mayors, Mayor's** meəz ‖ 'meɪ‿ᵊrz meᵊrz

mayoral 'meər əl meɪ 'ɔːr əl ‖ 'meɪ‿ᵊr əl

mayoralty 'meər əl ti ‖ 'meɪ‿ᵊr əl ti 'mer əl ti

mayoress ˌmeər 'es '••; 'meər ɪs, -əs ‖ 'meɪ‿ᵊr əs 'mer əs

mayorship 'meə ʃɪp ‖ 'meɪ‿ᵊr ʃɪp 'meᵊr• **~s** s

Mayotte maɪ 'ɒt -'jɒt ‖ -'jɑːt —*Fr* [ma jɔt]

maypole 'meɪ pəʊl →-pɒʊl ‖ -poʊl **~s** z

mayst meɪst

mayweed 'meɪ wiːd **~s** z

mazard 'mæz əd -ᵊrd **~s** z

Mazarin 'mæz ə rɪn -ræn —*Fr* [ma za ʁæ̃]

mazarine ˌmæz ə riːn ˌ••'• ◀

Mazawattee *tdmk* ˌmæz ə 'wɒt i ‖ -'wɑːt̬ i

Mazda *tdmk* 'mæz də

Mazdaism 'mæz dər ˌɪz əm ‖ -də-

maze meɪz **mazes** 'meɪz ɪz -əz

Mazeppa mə 'zep ə

mazuma mə 'zuːm ə

mazurka mə 'zɜːk ə ‖ -'zɝːk ə -'zʊrk- —*Polish* [ma 'zur ka] **~s** z

maz|y 'meɪz |i **~ier** i‿ə ‖ i‿ᵊr **~iest** i‿ɪst i‿əst **~ily** ɪ li əl i **~iness** i nəs i nɪs

MBA ˌem biː 'eɪ

MBE ˌem biː 'iː

Mbeki əm 'bek i —*Xhosa* [mbe: ki]

mbyte, Mbyte 'meg ə baɪt **~s** s

MC ˌem 'siː **~'d** d **~'ing** ɪŋ **~'s** z

Mc... —*see* **Mac...** —*Names beginning* Mc- *are listed in this dictionary under the spelling* Mac-

MCC ˌem si: 'si:

MCP ˌem si: 'pi: **~s**, **~'s** z

MD ˌem 'di:

me mi:, *weak form* mi
'me ˌgene·ˌration

ME *medical condition* ˌem 'i:

mea culpa ˌmeɪ ə 'kʊlp ə -ɑː 'kʊlp ɑː

Meacham 'mi:tʃ əm

Meacher 'mi:tʃ ə ‖ -ᵊr

mead mi:d

Mead, Meade mi:d

meadow 'med əʊ ‖ -oʊ **~s** z

Meadowcroft 'med əʊ krɒft ‖ -oʊ krɔ:ft -krɑ:ft

meadowlark 'med əʊ lɑ:k ‖ -oʊ lɑ:rk **~s** s

Meadows 'med əʊz ‖ -oʊz

meadowsweet 'med əʊ swi:t ‖ -oʊ- -ə- **~s** s

meager, M~, meagre 'mi:g ə ‖ -ᵊr **~ly** li **~ness** nəs nɪs

Meagher mɑ: ‖ mɑ:r

Meaker 'mi:k ə ‖ -ᵊr

Meakin 'mi:k ɪn §-ən

meal mi:ᵊl **meals** mi:ᵊlz
'meal ˌticket

mealie 'mi:l i **~s** z

mealtime 'mi:ᵊl taɪm **~s** z

mealworm 'mi:ᵊl wɜ:m ‖ -wɝ:m **~s** z

meal|y 'mi:l |i **~ier** i‿ə ‖ i‿ᵊr **~iest** i‿ɪst i‿əst **~iness** i nəs i nɪs

mealybug 'mi:l i bʌg **~s** z

mealy-mouthed ˌmi:l i 'maʊðd ◀ ‖ -'maʊθt ◀

mean mi:n **meaner** 'mi:n ə ‖ -ᵊr **meanest** 'mi:n ɪst -əst **meaning** 'mi:n ɪŋ **means** mi:nz **meant** ment *(!)*
'means test; ˌmean 'time

meander, M~ mi 'ænd ə ‖ -ᵊr **~ed** d **meandering/ly** mi 'ænd‿ᵊr ɪŋ /li **~s** z

meanie 'mi:n i **~s** z

meaning 'mi:n ɪŋ **~s** z

meaningful 'mi:n ɪŋ fᵊl -fʊl **~ly** li **~ness** nəs nɪs

meaningless 'mi:n ɪŋ ləs -lɪs **~ly** li **~ness** nəs nɪs

mean|ly 'mi:n |li **~ness** nəs nɪs

meant ment *(!)*

meantime 'mi:n taɪm ˌ•'•

meanwhile 'mi:n waɪᵊl -hwaɪᵊl, ˌ•'• ‖ -hwaɪᵊl

mean|y 'mi:n|i **~ies** iz

Meara *(i)* 'mɪər ə, *(ii)* 'mɑ:r ə

Mearns *place in Grampian* meənz ‖ meᵊrnz

Mears mɪəz ‖ mɪᵊrz

Measham 'mi:ʃ əm

measles 'mi:z ᵊlz

meas|ly 'mi:z |li 'mi:z ᵊl i **~liness** li nəs -nɪs

measurable 'meʒ ᵊr‿əb ᵊl ‖ 'meɪʒ-

MEASURE

	◼ 'meʒ-	▢ 'meɪʒ-			
AmE 1993					
0	20	40	60	80	100%

---

meas|ure 'meʒ |ə ‖ -|ᵊr 'meɪʒ- —*AmE 1993 poll panel preference:* 'meʒ- 95%, 'meɪʒ- 5%. **~ured** əd ‖ ᵊrd **~uring** ᵊr‿ɪŋ **~ures** əz ‖ ᵊrz
'measuring jug

measureless 'meʒ ə ləs -lɪs ‖ -ᵊr- 'meɪʒ- **~ly** li

measurement 'meʒ ə mənt ‖ -ᵊr- 'meɪʒ- **~s** s

measurer 'meʒ ᵊr ə ‖ -ᵊr 'meɪʒ- **~s** z

meat mi:t *(= meet)* **meats** mi:ts
ˌmeat 'loaf '• •

meat-ax, meat-ax|e 'mi:t æks ‖ 'mi:t̬- **~ed** t **~es** ɪz əz **~ing** ɪŋ

meatball 'mi:t bɔ:l ‖ -bɑ:l **~s** z

Meath *county in Ireland* mi:ð —*but by outsiders often called* mi:θ

meati... —*see* **meaty**

meatless 'mi:t ləs -lɪs

meatus mi 'eɪt əs ‖ -'eɪt̬- **~es** ɪz əz

M

meat|y 'mi:t |i ‖ 'mi:ṭ li **~ier** i_ə ‖ i_ər **~iest**
i_ıst i_əst **~ily** ı li əl i **~iness** i nəs i nıs
Mebyon Kernow
ˌmeb i_ən 'kɜ:n əʊ ‖ -'kɝ:n oʊ
Mecca, mecca 'mek ə —Arabic ['mak ka]
meccano, M~ tdmk mı 'kɑ:n əʊ mə-, me- ‖ -oʊ
Mecham 'mi:k əm
mechanic mı 'kæn ık mə- **~s** s
mechanical mı 'kæn ık əl mə- **~ly** _i **~ness**
nəs nıs **~s** z
me ˌchanical ˌengi'neering
mechanis... —see **mechaniz...**
mechanism 'mek ə ˌnız əm **~s** z
mechanist 'mek ən ıst §-əst **~s** s
mechanistic ˌmek ə 'nıst ık ◄ **~ally** əl_i
mechanization ˌmek ən aı 'zeıʃ ən -ən ı-
‖ -ən ə-
mechaniz|e 'mek ə naız **~ed** d **~es** ız əz
~ing ıŋ
Mechlin 'mek lın §-lən —Dutch Mechelen
['mɛ xə lən], French Malines [ma lin]
Mecklenburg 'mek lən bɜ:g -lın-, →-ləm-
‖ -bɝ:g —Ger ['me: klən bʊʁk]
meconium mı 'kəʊn i_əm mə- ‖ -'koʊn-
Med med
MEd ˌem 'ed
medal 'med əl **~s** z
medalist 'med əl ıst §-əst **~s** s
medallion mə 'dæl i_ən mı- ‖ -'dæl jən **~s** z
medallist 'med əl ıst §-əst **~s** s
Medan 'meıd æn -ɑ:n ‖ meı 'dɑ:n
Medau 'med aʊ
Medawar 'med ə wə ‖ -wər
meddl|e 'med əl (= medal) **~ed** d **~er/s** _ə/z ‖
ər/z **~es** z **~ing** ıŋ
meddlesome 'med əl səm **~ly** li **~ness** nəs nıs
Mede mi:d **Medes** mi:dz
Medea mə 'dıə mı-, -'di:_ə ‖ mə 'di: ə
Medevac 'med ı ˌvæk -ə-
medfly 'med flaı
media pl of **medium**; 'means of communication'
'mi:d i_ə
media other senses; Latin adj 'mi:d i_ə 'med-
Media 'country of the Medes' 'mi:d i_ə
mediaeval ˌmed i 'i:v əl ◄ me 'di:v əl ‖ ˌmi:d-
ˌmed-, ˌmıd-; mı 'di:v əl (*) **~ism** ˌız əm
~ist/s ıst/s §əst/s ‖ əst/s **~ly** i
medial 'mi:d i_əl **~ly** i
median 'mi:d i_ən **~ly** li **~s** z
mediant 'mi:d i_ənt **~s** s
mediastin|um ˌmi:d i_ə 'staın əm **~a** ə **~al**
əl ◄
medi|ate v 'mi:d i eıt **~ated** eıt ıd -əd ‖ eıṭ əd
~ates eıts **~ating** eıt ıŋ ‖ eıṭ ıŋ
mediation ˌmi:d i 'eıʃ ən **~s** z
mediator 'mi:d i eıt ə ‖ -eıṭ ər **~s** z
medic 'med ık **~s** s
Medicaid, m~ 'med ı keıd
medical 'med ık əl **~ly** _i **~s** z
'medical card; 'medical cer,tificate
medicament mə 'dık ə mənt mı-, me-;
'med ık- **~s** s
Medicare, m~ 'med ı keə ‖ -ker -kær

medi|cate 'med ı ˌkeıt §-ə- **~cated** keıt ıd -əd
‖ keıṭ əd **~cates** keıts **~cating**
keıt ıŋ ‖ keıṭ ıŋ
medication ˌmed ı 'keıʃ ən §-ə- **~s** z
Medici 'med ı tʃi: §-ə-; me 'di:tʃ i, mə-, mı-
—It ['me: di tʃi]
medicinal mə 'dıs ən_əl mı-, me-, -ın-
—formerly also ˌmed ı 'saın əl, 'med sən_əl
~ly i
medicine 'med sən -sın, 'med ıs ən, -əs-, -ın
~s z
'medicine chest; 'medicine man
medick 'med ık **~s** s
medico 'med ı kəʊ ‖ -koʊ **~s** z
medieval ˌmed i 'i:v əl ◄ me 'di:v əl ‖ ˌmi:d-
ˌmed-, ˌmıd-; mı 'di:v əl (*) **~ism** ˌız əm
~ist/s ıst/s §əst/s ‖ əst/s **~ly** i
Medina, m~ (i) me 'di:n ə mə-, mı-, (ii)
-'daın ə —the place in Saudi Arabia is (i)
—Arabic [me 'di: na]; that in OH, (ii).
mediocre ˌmi:d i 'əʊk ə ◄ ˌmed-, '•••◄
‖ -'oʊk ər ◄
mediocrit|y ˌmi:d i 'ɒk rət li ˌmed-, -ıt i
‖ -'ɑːkr əṭ li **~ies** iz
medi|tate 'med ı ˌteıt -ə- **~tated** teıt ıd -əd
‖ teıṭ əd **~tates** teıts **~tating**
teıt ıŋ ‖ teıṭ ıŋ
meditation ˌmed ı 'teıʃ ən -ə- **~s** z
meditative 'med ıt ət ıv -ət ət-; -ı teıt-,
-ə teıt- ‖ -ə teıṭ ıv **~ly** li **~ness** nəs nıs
Mediterranean ˌmed ı tə 'reın i_ən ◄, '•ə- **~s** z
ˌMediter,ranean 'Sea
medi|um 'mi:d i_əm **~a** ə **~ums** əmz
ˌmedium 'wave◄
medlar 'med lə ‖ -lər **~s** z
medley 'med li **~s** z
Medlicott 'med lı kɒt ‖ -kɑ:t
Medlock 'med lɒk ‖ -lɑ:k
Medoc, Médoc 'med ɒk meı 'dɒk ‖ meı 'dɑ:k
—Fr [me dɔk]
Medresco me 'dresk əʊ mə-, mı- ‖ -oʊ
medulla me 'dʌl ə mə-, mı-
me ˌdulla ˌoblon'gata
ˌɒb lɒŋ 'gɑ:t ə ‖ ˌɑ:b lɔ:ŋ 'gɑ:ṭ ə -lɑ:ŋ-
medullary me 'dʌl ər i mə-, mı- ‖ 'med əl er i
'medʒ-; mə 'dʌl ər i (*)
Medusa, m~ mə 'dju:z ə me-, mı-, -'dju:s-,
→§-'dʒu:z- ‖ -'du:s ə -'dju:s-, -'du:z-,
-'dju:z- **~s**, **~'s** z
Medway 'med weı
Medwin 'med wın
Mee mi:
meed mi:d **meeds** mi:dz
Meehan 'mi:_ən
meek, Meek mi:k
meek|ly 'mi:k |li **~ness** nəs nıs
meerkat 'mıə kæt ‖ 'mır- **~s** s
meerschaum 'mıəʃ əm 'mıə ʃaʊm ‖ 'mırʃ əm
'mır ʃɔ:m, -ʃɑ:m
Meerut 'mıər ət —Hindi [me: rət[h]]
meet mi:t **meeting** 'mi:t ıŋ ‖ 'mi:ṭ ıŋ **meets**
mi:ts **met** met

M

meeting 'miːt ɪŋ ‖ 'miːt̬ ɪŋ ~s z
'meeting point

meeting|house 'miːt ɪŋ |haʊs ‖ 'miːt̬- ~houses
haʊz ɪz -əz

meg, Meg meg megs megz

mega 'meg ə

mega- comb. form ¦meg ə — megastar
'meg ə staː ‖ -staːr

megabuck 'meg ə bʌk ~s s

megabyte 'meg ə baɪt ~s s

megacycle 'meg ə ˌsaɪk əl ~s z

megadeath 'meg ə deθ ~s s

megahertz 'meg ə hɜːts ‖ -hɝːts

megalith 'meg ə lɪθ ~s s

megalithic ˌmeg ə 'lɪθ ɪk ◄

megalo- comb. form
with stress-neutral suffix ¦meg ə ləʊ -əl əʊ
‖ -loʊ — megaloblastic
ˌmeg ə ləʊ 'blæst ɪk ◄ -əl əʊ- ‖ -ə loʊ-
with stress-imposing suffix ˌmeg ə 'lɒ+ ‖ -'laː+
— megalopolis, M~ ˌmeg ə 'lɒp əl ɪs §-əs
‖ -'laːp-

megalomania ˌmeg əl əʊ 'meɪn i_ə ‖ -əl ə-

megalomaniac ˌmeg əl əʊ 'meɪn i æk ‖ -əl ə-
~s s

megalosaur 'meg əl əʊ sɔː ‖ -ə sɔːr ~s z

Megan (i) 'meg ən, (ii) 'miːg-, (iii) 'meɪg- —In
BrE always (i).

Megane, Mégane mə 'gæn me- ‖ -'gaːn —Fr
[me gan]

megaphone 'meg ə fəʊn ‖ -foʊn ~s z

Megara, m~ 'meg ər ə

megaron 'meg ə rɒn ‖ -raːn

megastar 'meg ə staː ‖ -staːr ~s z

megastore 'meg ə stɔː ‖ -stɔːr ~s z

megatheri|um ˌmeg ə 'θɪər i_ləm ‖ -'θɪr- ~a ə

megaton 'meg ə tʌn ~s z

megawatt 'meg ə wɒt ‖ -waːt ~s s

Megger tdmk 'meg ə ‖ -ər

Meggeson 'meg ɪs ən -əs-

Meggezones tdmk 'meg ɪ zəʊnz -ə- ‖ -zoʊnz

Meggison 'meg ɪs ən -əs-

Megillah, m~ mə 'gɪl ə ~s z

megilp mə 'gɪlp

megohm 'meg əʊm ‖ -oʊm ~s z

megrim 'miːg rɪm -rəm ~s z

Mehmet 'mem et —Turkish [mɛh 'mɛt]

Mehta 'meɪt ə

Meier 'maɪ_ə ‖ 'maɪ_ər

Meikle 'miːk əl

Meiklejohn (i) 'miːk əl dʒɒn ‖ -dʒaːn, (ii) 'mɪk-

meios|is maɪ 'əʊs ɪs meɪ-, §-əs ‖ -'oʊs- ~es iːz

Meir mɪə ‖ mɪər —but as an Israeli name,
meɪ 'ɪə ‖ -'ɪər

Meirion 'maɪ_r i ɒn ‖ -aːn —Welsh ['məir jon]

Meirionnydd ˌmer i 'ɒn ɪð -ɪθ, -əθ ‖ -'aːn-
—Welsh [məir 'jɔn ɪð, -ɪð]

Meissen 'maɪs ən —Ger ['mai sən]
'Meissen ware

Meistersinger 'maɪst ə ˌsɪŋ ə ‖ -ər ˌsɪŋ ər —Ger
['mai stɐ ˌzɪŋ ɐ] ~s z

Mekka 'mek ə

Mekong ˌmiː 'kɒŋ ◄ ˌmeɪ- ‖ ˌmeɪ 'kɔːŋ ◄
-'kaːŋ
ˌMekong 'Delta

Mel, mel mel mels, Mel's melz

melamine 'mel ə miːn -mɪn, -maɪn

melancholia ˌmel ən 'kəʊl i_ə →ˌ•əŋ- ‖ -'koʊl-

melancholic ˌmel ən 'kɒl ɪk ◄ →-əŋ- ‖ -'kaːl-
~ally əl_i

melancholy 'mel ən kəl i →ˌ•əŋ-, -kɒl i
‖ -kaːl i

Melanchthon mə 'læŋk θən mɪ-, me-,
-θɒn ‖ -θaːn —Ger [me 'lanç tɔn]

Mela|nesia ˌmel əl 'niːz i_ə -'niːʒ ə, -'niːs i_ə,
-'niːʃ ə ‖ -'niːʒ ə -'niːʃ ə ~nesian/s
'niːz i_ən/z ◄ 'niːʒ ən/z, 'niːs i_ən/z, 'niːʃ ən/z
‖ -'niːʒ ən/z ◄ 'niːʃ ən/z

melang|e, mélang|e meɪ 'laːnʒ me-, -'lɒ̃ʒ —Fr
[me lɑ̃ːʒ] ~es ɪz əz

Melanie 'mel ən i

melanin 'mel ən ɪn §-ən

melanism 'mel ə ˌnɪz əm

melano- comb. form ¦mel ə nəʊ ‖ -ə noʊ -ən ə
— melanocyte 'mel ə nəʊ saɪt ‖ -ə noʊ-
-ə nə-

melanoma ˌmel ə 'nəʊm ə ‖ -'noʊm ə ~s z

melanuria ˌmel ə 'njʊər i_ə ‖ -'nʊr- -'njʊr-

Melba 'melb ə

Melbourne (i) 'mel bɔːn ‖ -bɔːrn -boʊrn, (ii)
'melb ən ‖ -ərn —The places in
Cambridgeshire and Derbyshire are (i). The
place in Australia is (ii) locally, but is often
called (i) by non-Australians.

Melchers 'meltʃ əz ‖ -ərz

Melchett 'meltʃ ɪt -ət

Melchior 'melk i ɔː ‖ -ɔːr

Melchizedek mel 'kɪz ə dek

meld meld melded 'meld ɪd -əd melding
'meld ɪŋ melds meldz

Meldrum 'meldr əm

Meleager ˌmel i 'eɪg ə ‖ -'eɪdʒ ər

melee, mêlée 'mel eɪ me 'leɪ ‖ 'meɪl eɪ meɪ 'leɪ
(*) ~s z

Melhuish (i) 'mel ɪʃ, (ii) 'mel hjuː ɪʃ -juː-, -uː-,
(iii) mel 'hjuːˌ_ɪʃ

Melia 'miːl i_ə

melic 'mel ɪk

melilot 'mel ɪ lɒt -ə- ‖ -laːt ~s s

Melina mə 'liːn ə me-, mɪ-

melinite 'mel ɪ naɪt -əˌ•

melio|rate 'miːl i_ə |reɪt ~rated reɪt ɪd -əd
‖ reɪt̬ əd ~rates reɪts ~rating
reɪt ɪŋ ‖ reɪt̬ ɪŋ

melioration ˌmiːl i_ə 'reɪʃ ən ~s z

meliorative 'miːl i_ər ət ɪv _ə reɪt- ‖ _ə reɪt̬ ɪv

meliorism 'miːl i_ə ˌrɪz əm

meliorist 'miːl i_ər ɪst §-əst ~s s

melisma mə 'lɪz mə mɪ-, me- ~s z

melismatic ˌmel ɪz 'mæt ɪk ◄ §, •əz-
‖ -'mæt̬ ɪk ◄

Melissa mə 'lɪs ə mɪ-, me-

Melksham 'melk ʃəm

mellifflu|ence mə 'lɪf lu_|ənˀs mɪ-, me- ~ent
ənt

mellifluous mə 'lɪf lu‿əs mɪ-, me- **~ly** li **~ness** nəs nɪs

Mellish 'mel ɪʃ

Mellony 'mel ən i

Mellor 'mel ə ‖ -ᵊr

Mellors 'mel əz ‖ -ᵊrz

mellow 'mel əʊ ‖ -oʊ **~ed** d **~er** ə ‖ ᵊr **~est** ɪst əst **~ing** ɪŋ **~ly** li **~ness** nəs nɪs **~s** z

Melly 'mel i

melodeon mə 'ləʊd i‿ən mɪ-, me- ‖ -'loʊd- **~s** z

melodic mə 'lɒd ɪk mɪ-, me- ‖ -'lɑːd- **~ally** ᵊl‿i

melodica mə 'lɒd ɪk ə mɪ-, me- ‖ -'lɑːd- **~s** z

melodie... —*see* **melody**

melodion mə 'ləʊd i‿ən mɪ-, me- ‖ -'loʊd- **~s** z

melodious mə 'ləʊd i‿əs mɪ-, me- ‖ -'loʊd- **~ly** li **~ness** nəs nɪs

melodis... —*see* **melodize**

melodist 'mel əd ɪst §-əst **~s** s

melodiz|e 'mel ə daɪz **~ed** d **~es** ɪz əz **~ing** ɪŋ

melodrama 'mel ə ˌdrɑːm ə -əʊ- ‖ -ˌdræm- **~s** z

melodramatic ˌmel ə drə 'mæt ɪk ◂ , ·əʊ- ‖ -'mæt̬ ɪk ◂ **~ally** ᵊl‿i **~s** s

melod|y, M~ 'mel əd li —*Occasionally, and particularly in singing, also* -əʊd- ‖ -oʊd- **~ies** iz

Meloids *tdmk* 'mel ɔɪdz

melon 'mel ən **~s** z

Melos 'miːl ɒs 'mel- ‖ -ɑːs

Melpomene mel 'pɒm ən i -ɪn i, -iː ‖ -'pɑːm-

Melrose 'mel rəʊz ‖ -roʊz

melt melt **melted** 'melt ɪd -əd **melting/ly** 'melt ɪŋ /li **melts** melts

'melting point; 'melting pot

meltag|e 'melt ɪdʒ **~es** ɪz əz

meltdown 'melt daʊn **~s** z

Melton, m~ 'melt ən

ˌMelton 'Mowbray

Meltonian *tdmk* mel 'təʊn i‿ən ‖ -'toʊn-

meltwater 'melt ˌwɔːt ə ‖ -,wɔːt̬ ᵊr -,wɑːt̬- **~s** z

Melville 'mel vɪl

Melvin, Melvyn 'melv ɪn §-ən

member 'mem bə ‖ -bᵊr **~s** z

ˌMember of 'Parliament

membership 'mem bə ʃɪp ‖ -bᵊr- **~s** s

membrane 'mem breɪn **~s** z

membranous 'mem brən əs mem 'breɪn-

meme miːm **memes** miːmz

memento mə 'ment əʊ mɪ-, me-, ⚠məʊ- ‖ -'ment̬ oʊ **~es, ~s** z

me,mento 'mori 'mɒr iː 'mɔːr-, -i, -aɪ ‖ 'mɔːr-

Memnon 'mem nɒn -nən ‖ -nɑːn

memo 'mem əʊ 'miːm- ‖ -oʊ **~s** z

'memo pad

memoir 'mem wɑː ‖ -wɑːr -wɔːr **~s** z

memorabilia ˌmem ᵊr‿ə ˌbɪl i‿ə -'biːl-

memorab|le 'mem ᵊr‿əb |ᵊl **~leness** ᵊl nəs -nɪs **~ly** li

memorand|um ˌmem ə 'rænd |əm **~a** ə **~ums** əmz

memorial mə 'mɔːr i‿əl mɪ-, me- ‖ -'moʊr- **~ly** i **~s** z

memorialis|e, memorializ|e mə 'mɔːr i‿ə laɪz mɪ-, me- ‖ -'moʊr- **~ed** d **~es** ɪz əz **~ing** ɪŋ

memorie... —*see* **memory**

memoris... —*see* **memoriz...**

memorization ˌmem ər aɪ 'zeɪʃ ᵊn -ə' · • - ‖ -ə' · •-

memoriz|e 'mem ə raɪz **~ed** d **~es** ɪz əz **~ing** ɪŋ

memor|ly 'mem ᵊr‿li **~ies** iz

'memory span

Memphis 'mempf ɪs §-əs

memsahib 'mem sɑːb 'mem ˌsɑː ɪb, -hɪb **~s** z

men men **men's** menz

'men's room

-men mən, men —*See note at* **-man.** *The pronunciation* men *is used for the plural rather more widely than* mæn *is for the singular.*

menac|e 'men əs -ɪs **~ed** t **~er/s** ə/z ‖ ᵊr/z **~es** ɪz əz **~ing/ly** ɪŋ /li

menag|e, ménag|e ⁽ᵢ⁾me 'nɑːʒ ⁽ᵢ⁾meɪ-, mə-, mɪ-, -'næʒ; 'meɪn ɑːʒ ‖ meɪ 'nɑːʒ mə- —*Fr* [me nɑːʒ] **~es** ɪz əz

mé,nage à 'trois, ˌ · · • '· ‖ ɑː 'trwɑː —*Fr* [a tʁwa]

menagerie mə 'nædʒ ər‿i mɪ-, me-, -'næʒ-, -'nɑːʒ- **~s** z

Menai 'men aɪ —*Welsh* ['me naɪ, -ne]

ˌMenai 'Bridge; ˌMenai 'Strait

Menander mə 'nænd ə mɪ-, me- ‖ -ᵊr

menarche me 'nɑːk i mɪ-, mə-; 'men ɑːk ‖ -'nɑːrk i

Mencap 'men kæp →'meŋ-

Mencken 'meŋk ən

mend mend **mended** 'mend ɪd -əd **mending** 'mend ɪŋ **mends** mendz

mendacious men 'deɪʃ əs **~ly** li **~ness** nəs nɪs

mendacity men 'dæs ət i -ɪt- ‖ -ət̬ i

Mende 'mend eɪ

Mendel 'mend ᵊl

Mendeleev ˌmend ə 'leɪ ev , · ɪ-, -ef; -ᵊl 'eɪ- —*Russ* [mjɪnjɪ djɪ 'ljejɪf]

mendelevium ˌmend ə 'liːv i‿əm , · ɪ-; -ᵊl 'iːv-

Mendeleyev ˌmend ə 'leɪ ev , · ɪ-, -ef, -əf; -ᵊl 'eɪ- —*Russ* [mjɪnjɪ djɪ 'ljejɪf]

Mendelian men 'diːl i‿ən

Mendelism 'mend ᵊl ˌɪz əm -ə ˌlɪz-

Mendelssohn 'mend ᵊl sᵊn —*Ger* ['men dᵊl zoːn]

mender 'mend ə ‖ -ᵊr **~s** z

Mendez, Méndez 'mend ez ‖ men 'dez —*Sp* ['men deθ, -des]

mendicant 'mend ɪk ᵊnt §-ək- **~s** s

Mendip 'mend ɪp **~s** s

ˌMendip 'Hills

Mendocino ˌmend ə 'siːn əʊ ‖ -oʊ

Mendoza men 'dəʊz ə ‖ -'doʊz ə —*AmSp* [men 'do sa]

Menelaus ˌmen ɪ 'leɪ əs -ə-, -ᵊl 'eɪ-

mene mene tekel upharsin

M

ˌmiːn i 'miːn i ˌtek ᵊl ju 'fɑːs ɪn §-ᵊn ‖ -'fɑːrs-
-ˌtiːk-, -'fers-

Menevia mɪ 'niːv i_ə mə-

menfolk 'men fəʊk ‖ -foʊk

Mengistu meŋ 'gɪst uː men-

menhaden men 'heɪd ᵊn mən- ~s z

menhir 'men hɪə ‖ -hɪr ~s z

menial 'miːn i_əl ~ly i ~s z

Meniere, Ménière 'men i eə 'meɪn-, ˌ•••
‖ mən 'jeᵊr ˌmeɪn-; 'men jᵊr —Fr [me njɛːʁ]
'**Ménière's di**ˌ**sease** ‖ **Mén'ière's-**

meningeal me 'nɪndʒ i_əl mə-, mɪ-;
ˌmen ɪn 'dʒiː_əl ◂, -ən-

meninges me 'nɪndʒ iːz mə-, mɪ-

meningitis ˌmen ɪn 'dʒaɪt ɪs -ən-, §-əs
‖ -'dʒaɪt̬ əs

meningococc|al mə ˌnɪndʒ əʊ 'kɒk ᵊl ◂
-ˌnɪŋ gəʊ- ‖ -ə 'kɑːk ᵊl ◂ **~us** əs

meninx 'men ɪŋks **meninges** me 'nɪndʒ iːz
mə-, mɪ-

me|niscus mə l'nɪsk əs mɪ-, me- **~nisci** 'nɪs aɪ
'nɪsk-, -iː

Menlo 'men ləʊ ‖ -loʊ

Mennonite 'men ə naɪt ~s s

men-at-arms ˌmen ət 'ɑːmz ‖ -ət̬ 'ɑːrmz

men-of-war ˌmen əv 'wɔː -ə- ‖ -'wɔːr

Menominee, Menomini, Menomonee,
Menomonie mə 'nɒm ən i mɪ-, me-
‖ -'nɑːm- ~s z

menopausal ˌmen əʊ 'pɔːz ᵊl ◂ ˌmiːn- ‖ -ə-
-'pɑːz-

menopause 'men əʊ pɔːz 'miːn- ‖ -ə- -pɑːz

menorah mə 'nɔːr ə mɪ- ‖ -'noʊr- ~s z

menorrhagia ˌmen ə 'reɪdʒ i_ə ˌmiːn-; -'reɪdʒ ə

menorrhoea ˌmen ə 'riː_ə ˌmiːn-

Menotti mə 'nɒt i mɪ-, me- ‖ -'nɑːt̬ i —It
[me 'nɔt ti]

mens menz
ˌmens 'rea 'riː_ə 'reɪ ə; ˌmens 'sana 'sɑːn ə
'sæn- (in ˌcorpore 'sano ɪn ˌkɔːp
ər i 'sɑːn əʊ →ɪŋ-, -, •ə reɪ-, -'sæn-
‖ ɪn ˌkɔːrp ər i 'sɑːn oʊ)

Mensa 'men⁺s ə

mensch men⁺ʃ **menschen** 'men⁺ʃ ən
mensches 'men⁺ʃ ɪz -əz

menses 'men⁺s iːz

Menshevik 'men⁺ʃ ə vɪk -ɪ-, -viːk ~s s

Menshevism 'men⁺ʃ ə ˌvɪz əm -ɪ-

Menston 'men⁺st ən

menstrual 'men⁺s tru_əl
ˌmenstrual 'period

menstru|ate 'men⁺s tru leɪt ‖ 'men strleɪt
~ated eɪt ɪd -əd ‖ eɪt̬ əd **~ates** eɪts **~ating**
eɪt ɪŋ ‖ eɪt̬ ɪŋ

menstruation ˌmen⁺s tru 'eɪʃ ᵊn ‖ men 'streɪʃ-
~s z

mensurability ˌmen⁺ʃ ər_ə 'bɪl ət i ˌmen⁺s-,
ˌ•jər-, -ɪt i ‖ -ət̬ i

mensurable 'men⁺ʃ ər_əb ᵊl 'men⁺s-, '•jər-

mensural 'men⁺ʃ ər əl 'men⁺s-, -jər-

mensuration ˌmen⁺ʃ ə 'reɪʒ ᵊn ˌmen⁺s-, -jə-

menswear 'menz weə ‖ -wer -wær

-ment noun ending mənt, verb ending ment —
ornament n 'ɔːn ə mənt ‖ 'ɔːrn-, v
'ɔːn ə ment ‖ 'ɔːrn- —This ending is usually
weak in nouns, strong in verbs (although this
standard distinction is not always observed by
native speakers). In most cases -ment is
unstressed and has no effect on stress. In two-
syllable verbs, however, it is stressed: compare
the noun 'segment and the verb to seg'ment.
There are various exceptions, including
'comment v., n., la'ment v., n., torment, ferment
(in these latter two the ending is always strong,
unstressed in the noun but stressed in the verb).

Mentadent tdmk 'ment ə dent ‖ 'ment̬-

mental 'ment ᵊl ‖ 'ment̬ ᵊl **~ly** i
ˌmental 'age◂, a ˌmental age of 'ten;
ˌmental de'fective; ˌmental 'health;
'mental ˌhospital; ˌmental 'note

-mental 'ment ᵊl ‖ 'ment̬ ᵊl — **ornamental**
ˌɔːn ə 'ment ᵊl ◂ ‖ ˌɔːrn ə 'ment̬ ᵊl ◂

mentalism 'ment ᵊl ˌɪz əm -ə ˌlɪz- ‖ 'ment̬-

mentalist 'ment ᵊl ɪst §-əst; -ə lɪst, §-ləst
‖ 'ment̬- ~s s

mentalistic ˌment ə 'lɪst ɪk ◂ ˌment ᵊl 'ɪst-
‖ ˌment̬ ᵊl 'ɪst ɪk ◂ **~ally** ᵊl_i

mentalit|y men 'tæl ət i li -ɪt- ‖ -ət̬ i li **~ies** iz

menthol 'menθ ɒl ‖ -ɔːl -ɑːl

mentholated 'menθ ə leɪt ɪd -əd ‖ -leɪt̬ əd

mention 'men⁺ʃ ᵊn **~ed** d **~ing** ɪŋ ~s z

mentor, M~ 'ment ɔː -ə ‖ 'ment ɔːr 'ment̬ ᵊr
~ed d **mentoring** 'ment ər ɪŋ -ɔːr- ‖ 'ment̬
ᵊr ɪŋ 'ment ɔːr- ~s z

menu 'men ju ‖ 'meɪn- ~s z

menu-driven 'men ju ˌdrɪv ᵊn ˌ•••• ‖ 'meɪn-

Menuhin 'men ju_ɪn §_ən

Menzies 'menz iz —but in Scotland usually
'mɪŋ ɪs, -ɪz

Meols (i) miː_ᵊlz, (ii) melz —Places near
Southport, Merseyside (formerly Lancs.), are (i);
that near Hoylake, Merseyside (formerly
Cheshire), is (ii).

Meon place in Hampshire 'miː_ən

Meopham place in Kent 'mep əm

meow mi 'aʊ **~ed** d **~ing** ɪŋ ~s z

MEP ˌem iː 'piː ~s z

mepacrine 'mep ə krɪn -kriːn

Mephisto mə 'fɪst əʊ mɪ-, me- ‖ -oʊ

Mephisto phelean, m~ ˌmef ɪst ə 'fiːl i_ən ◂
ˌ•əst-; mə ˌfɪst-, mɪ-, me-;
ˌmef ɪ ˌstɒf ə 'liː_ən ‖ -ə ˌstɑːf ə 'liː ən

Mephistopheles ˌmef ɪ 'stɒf ə liːz ˌ•ə-, -'•ɪ-
‖ -'stɑːf-

mephitic mɪ 'fɪt ɪk mə-, me- ‖ -'fɪt̬-

meprobamate ˌmep rəʊ 'bæm eɪt
me 'prəʊb ə meɪt, mɪ-, mə- ‖ ˌmep roʊ-

-mer mə ‖ mᵊr — **monomer**
'mɒn əʊm ə ‖ 'mɑːn əm ᵊr

Merc mɜːk ‖ mɝːk

mercantile 'mɜːk ᵊn taɪᵊl →ᵊ-ŋ- ‖ 'mɝːk
ᵊn tiːᵊl -taɪᵊl, -t̬ᵊl

mercantilism 'mɜːk ᵊnt ɪ ˌlɪz əm →'•ŋt-, -ə ˌ•-,
-ᵊl ˌɪz-, -ᵊn taɪ ˌlɪz- ‖ 'mɝːk ᵊn tiː ˌlɪz əm
-taɪ ˌ•-

M

mercantilist 'mɜːk ənt ɪl ɪst →'•ŋt-, -əl ɪst,
-aɪl ɪst, §-əst; mɜː 'kænt əl- ‖ 'mɝːk
ən tiːl əst -taɪl əst ~s s

mercaptan mɜː 'kæpt æn ‖ mᵊr-

Mercator mɜː 'keɪt ə mə-, -ɔː ‖ mᵊr 'keɪt̬ ᵊr ~'s
z

**Mer,cator pro'jection, Mer,cator's
pro'jection**

Merced place in CA mɜː 'sed ‖ mᵊr-

Mercedes mə 'seɪd ɪz mɜː-, -iːz ‖ mᵊr- —The
pl of the tdmk is pronounced the same as the
sing., or with -iːz.

mercenar|y 'mɜːs ᵊn ᵊr_|i '•ɪn- ‖ 'mɝːs ᵊn er |i
~ies iz

mercer, M~ 'mɜːs ə ‖ 'mɝːs ᵊr ~s z

merceris|e, merceriz|e 'mɜːs ə raɪz ‖ 'mɝːs-
~ed d ~es ɪz əz ~ing ɪŋ

merchandise n 'mɜːtʃ ᵊn daɪz -daɪs ‖ 'mɝːtʃ-

merchandis|e, merchandiz|e v 'mɜːtʃ
ᵊn daɪz ‖ 'mɝːtʃ- ~ed d ~er/s ə/z ‖ ᵊr/z
~es ɪz əz ~ing ɪŋ

merchant, M~'mɜːtʃ ᵊnt ‖ 'mɝːtʃ- ~s s
,merchant 'bank, ~er, ~ing; ,merchant
ma'rine; ,merchant 'navy; ,merchant
'seaman

merchantable 'mɜːtʃ ᵊnt əb ᵊl ‖ 'mɝːtʃ ᵊnt̬-

merchant|man 'mɜːtʃ ᵊnt |mən ‖ 'mɝːtʃ-
~men mən men

Mercia 'mɜːs i_ə 'mɜːʃ-, 'mɜːʃ ə ‖ 'mɝːʃ i_ə
'mɝːʃ ə

Mercian 'mɜːs i_ən 'mɜːʃ-, 'mɜːʃ ᵊn
‖ 'mɝːʃ i_ən 'mɝːʃ ᵊn ~s z

mercie... —see **mercy**

merciful 'mɜːs ɪ fᵊl -ə-, -fʊl ‖ 'mɝːs- ~ly _i
~ness nəs nɪs

merciless 'mɜːs ɪ ləs -ə- ‖ 'mɝːs- ~ly li ~ness
nəs nɪs

Merck mɜːk ‖ mɝːk

mercurial mɜː 'kjʊər i_əl ‖ mᵊr 'kjʊr- ~ly i ~s
z

mercuric mɜː 'kjʊər ɪk ‖ mᵊr 'kjʊr-

Mercurochrome tdmk
mɜː 'kjʊər ə krəʊm ‖ mᵊr 'kjʊr ə kroʊm

mercurous 'mɜːk jʊᵊr əs -jər- ‖ 'mɝːk jər-

mercur|y, M~ 'mɜːk jʊᵊr |i -jər- ‖'mɝːk jər |i
~ies, ~y's iz

Mercutio mɜː 'kjuːʃ i əʊ ‖ mᵊr 'kjuːʃ i oʊ

merc|y, Merc|y 'mɜːs |i ‖ 'mɝːs li ~ies, ~y's iz
'mercy ,killing

mere mɪə ‖ mɪᵊr **meres** mɪəz ‖ mɪᵊrz **merest**
'mɪər ɪst -əst ‖ 'mɪr əst

Meredith 'mer əd ɪθ -ɪd-, §-əθ —In Wales
me 'red ɪθ

Meredydd mə 'red ɪð -ɪθ —Welsh [me 're dið]

merely 'mɪə li ‖ 'mɪr-

merest 'mɪər ɪst -əst ‖ 'mɪr-

meretricious ,mer ə 'trɪʃ əs ◂ -ɪ- ~ly li ~ness
nəs nɪs

Merfyn 'mɜːv ɪn ‖ 'mɝːv- —Welsh ['mer vin,
-vɪn]

merganser mɜː 'gænᵗs ə -'gænz-
‖ mᵊr 'gænᵗs ᵊr ~s z

merge mɜːdʒ ‖ mɝːdʒ **merged**
mɜːdʒd ‖ mɝːdʒd **merges** 'mɜːdʒ ɪz -əz
‖ 'mɝːdʒ əz **merging** 'mɜːdʒ ɪŋ ‖ 'mɝːdʒ ɪŋ

merger 'mɜːdʒ ə ‖ 'mɝːdʒ ᵊr ~s z

Merida 'mer ɪd ə -əd- —Sp Mérida ['me ri ða]

Meriden 'mer ɪd ᵊn -əd-

meridian mə 'rɪd i_ən mɪ- ~s z

meridional mə 'rɪd i_ən ᵊl mɪ- ~s z

meringue mə 'ræŋ ~s z

merino mə 'riːn əʊ ‖ -oʊ ~s z

Merioneth ,mer ɪ 'ɒn əθ -ɪθ, -eθ ‖ -'ɑːn-
—Welsh Meirionnydd [,mair 'jɒn ïð, -ɪð]

meristem 'mer ɪ stem -ə- ~s z

mer|it 'mer |ɪt -ət ‖ -|ət ~ited ɪt ɪd ət-, -əd
‖ ət̬ əd ~iting ɪt ɪŋ ət- ‖ ət̬ ɪŋ ~its ɪts əts
‖ əts

meritocrac|y ,mer ɪ 'tɒk rəs ‖ ,•ə- ‖ -'tɑːk-
~ies iz

meritocrat 'mer ɪt əʊ kræt §'•ət- ‖ -ət̬ ə- ~s s

meritocratic ,mer ɪt əʊ 'kræt ɪk ◂ §,•ət-
‖ -ət̬ ə 'kræt̬- ~ally ᵊl_i

meritorious ,mer ɪ 'tɔːr i_əs ◂ ,•ə- ‖ -'toʊr-
~ly li ~ness nəs nɪs

merkin 'mɜːk ɪn §-ᵊn ‖ 'mɝːk- ~s z

Merle, merle mɜːl ‖ mɝːl **merles, Merle's**
mɜːlz ‖ mɝːlz

merlin, M~ 'mɜːl ɪn §-ᵊn ‖ 'mɝːl- ~s, ~'s z

merlot, M~ 'mɜːl əʊ 'meəl- ‖ mᵊr 'loʊ mer-
—Fr [mɛʁ lo]

mermaid 'mɜː meɪd ‖ 'mɝː- ~s z

mer|man 'mɜː |mæn ‖ 'mɝː- ~men men

-merous stress-imposing mᵊr əs —
polymerous pə 'lɪm ᵊr əs

Merovingian ,mer əʊ 'vɪndʒ i_ən ◂ ‖ ,•ə- ~s z

Merrick 'mer ɪk

merri... —see **merry**

Merrilies 'mer əl iz -ɪl-

Merrill 'mer əl -ɪl

Merrimac, Merrimack 'mer ɪ mæk -ə-

Merriman 'mer i mən

merriment 'mer i mənt

Merrion 'mer i_ən

merr|y, Merry 'mer li ~ier i_ə ‖ i_ᵊr ~iest i_ɪst
i_əst ~ily ɪ li əl i ~iness i nəs i nɪs

Merrydown tdmk 'mer i daʊn

merry-go-round 'mer i gəʊ ,raʊnd ‖ -i goʊ-
-ɪ gə- ~s z

merrymak|er/s 'mer i ,meɪk |ə/z ‖ -|ᵊr/z ~ing
ɪŋ

merrythought 'mer i θɔːt ‖ -θɑːt ~s s

Merryweather 'mer i ,weð ə ‖ -ᵊr

Mersey 'mɜːz i ‖ 'mɝːz i

Merseyside 'mɜːz i saɪd ‖ 'mɝːz-

Merstham 'mɜːst əm ‖ 'mɝːst-

Merthyr 'mɜːθ ə ‖ 'mɝː:θ ᵊr —Welsh ['mer θɪr,
-θir]
,Merthyr 'Tydfil 'tɪd vɪl —Welsh ,Merthyr
'Tudful ['tɪd vɪl]

Merton 'mɜːt ᵊn ‖ 'mɝːt ᵊn

Mervin, Mervyn 'mɜːv ɪn §-ᵊn ‖ 'mɝːv-

Meryl 'mer əl -ɪl

mesa, Mesa 'meɪs ə ~s z

M

mesallianc|e, mésallianc|e me 'zæl i‿ən¹s
meɪ-, -ɒs ‖ meɪ- ˌmeɪz ə 'laɪ ən¹s —Fr
[me za ljɑːs] ~es ɪz əz
mescal 'mesk æl me 'skæl
mescalin, mescaline 'mesk əl ɪn §-ən, -ə liːn
Mesdames, m~ 'meɪ dæm -dæmz ‖ meɪ 'dɑːm
—Fr [me dam]
mesdemoiselles ˌmeɪd əm‿wə 'zel—Fr
[med mwa zel]
meseemed mɪ 'siːmd meseems mɪ 'siːmz
mesembryanthemum
mə ˌzem bri 'æn¹θ ɪm əm mɪ-, -əm‿əm ~s z
mesencephalon ˌmes en 'kef ə lɒn ˌmez-,
→ˌ•eŋ-; -'sef- ‖ -'sef ə lɑːn
mesenchyme 'mes eŋ kaɪm 'mez-
mesh meʃ meshed meʃt meshes 'meʃ ɪz -əz
meshing 'meʃ ɪŋ
Meshach 'miːʃ æk
meshuga, meshugga mə 'ʃʊg ə
mesial 'miːz i‿əl 'miːs-
mesmeric mez 'mer ɪk
mesmeris... —see mesmeriz...
mesmerism 'mez mə ˌrɪz əm
mesmerist 'mez mər ɪst §-əst ~s s
mesmeriz|e 'mez mə raɪz ~ed d ~er/s ə/z
‖ ər/z ~es ɪz əz ~ing ɪŋ
mesne miːn (= mean)
meso- comb. form
with stress-neutral suffix ˈmes əʊ ˈmez-, ˈmiːs-,
ˈmiːz- ‖ -ə— mesophyte 'mes əʊ faɪt
'mez-, 'miːs-, 'miːz- ‖ -ə-
mesolect 'mes əʊ lekt 'mez-, 'miːs-, 'miːz-
‖ -ə- ~s s
mesolectal ˌmes əʊ 'lekt əl ◄ ˌmez-, ˌmiːs-,
ˌmiːz- ‖ -ə- ~ly i
Mesolithic, m~ ˌmes əʊ 'lɪθ ɪk ◄ ˌmez-, ˌmiːs-,
ˌmiːz- ‖ -ə-
mesomorph 'mes əʊ mɔːf 'mez-, 'miːs-, 'miːz-
‖ -oʊ mɔːrf -ə- ~s s
mesomorphic ˌmes əʊ 'mɔːf ɪk ◄ ˌmez-, ˌmiːs-,
ˌmiːz- ‖ -oʊ 'mɔːrf- -ə'•-
meson 'miːz ɒn 'miːs-, 'mez-, 'mes-, 'meɪz-
‖ -ɑːn
Mesopotamia ˌmes ə pə 'teɪm i‿ə ˌmesp ə'•-
mesothelioma ˌmes əʊ ˌθiːl i 'əʊm ə ˌmez-,
ˌmiːs-, ˌmiːz- ‖ -ə ˌθiːl i 'oʊm ə -~s z
mesothelium ˌmes əʊ 'θiːl i‿əm ˌmez-, ˌmiːs-,
ˌmiːz- ‖ ˌ•ə-
mesozoic ˌmes əʊ 'zəʊ ɪk ◄ ˌmez-, ˌmiːs-,
ˌmiːz- ‖ -ə 'zoʊ-
mesquite, M~ me 'skiːt mə-, mɪ-; 'mesk iːt
mess mes messed mest messes 'mes ɪz -əz
messing 'mes ɪŋ
'mess ˌjacket; 'mess kit
messag|e 'mes ɪdʒ ~es ɪz əz
Messalina ˌmes ə 'liːn ə -'laɪn-
messenger, M~ 'mes ᵊndʒ ə -ɪndʒ- ‖ -ᵊr ~s z
Messer 'mes ə ‖ -ᵊr
Messerschmidt tdmk 'mes ə ʃmɪt ‖ -ᵊr- —Ger
['mɛs ɐ ʃmɪt]
Messiaen 'mes jɒ̃ -jɑːn ‖ mes 'jɑːn —Fr
[mɛ sjɑ̃, -sjæ̃]
messiah, M~ mə 'saɪ‿ə mɪ-, me- ~s z

messianic, M~ ˌmes i 'æn ɪk ◄ ~ally ᵊl‿i
messi... —see messy
Messieurs, m~ meɪ 'sjɜːz me-; 'mes əz
‖ meɪs 'jɜːz məs-, -'juː: —Fr [me sjø]
Messina me 'siːn ə mə-, mɪ- —It [mes 'siː na]
messmate 'mes meɪt ~s s
Messrs 'mes əz ‖ -ᵊrz
messuag|e 'mes wɪdʒ 'mes ju‿ɪdʒ ~es ɪz əz
mess|y 'mes li ~ier i‿ə ‖ i‿ᵊr ~iest i‿ɪst i‿əst
~ily ɪ li əl i ~iness i nəs i nɪs
mestizo me 'stiːz əʊ mɪ-, mə- ‖ -oʊ -'stiːs- ~s
z
met, Met met
'Met ˌOffice
meta fuel 'miːt ə ‖ —
meta in Roman circus 'miːt ə 'meɪt- ‖ 'miːt̬ ə
Meta forename 'miːt ə ‖ 'miːt̬ ə
Meta river in Colombia 'meɪt ə ‖ 'meɪt̬ ə —Sp
['me ta]
meta- comb. form
with stress-neutral suffix ˈmet ə ‖ ˈmet̬ ə —
metastatic
ˌmet ə 'stæt ɪk ◄ ‖ ˌmet̬ ə 'stæt̬ ɪk ◄
with stress-imposing suffix mə 'tæ+ mɪ-, me-
— metastasis mə 'tæst əs ɪs mɪ-, me-, §-əs
metabolic ˌmet ə 'bɒl ɪk ◄ ‖ ˌmet̬ ə 'bɑːl ɪk ◄
~ally ᵊl‿i
metabolis... —see metaboliz...
metabolism mə 'tæb ə ˌlɪz əm mɪ-, me- ~s z
metabolite mə 'tæb ə laɪt mɪ-, me- ~s s
metaboliz|e mə 'tæb ə laɪz mɪ-, me- ~ed d
~es ɪz əz ~ing ɪŋ
metacarpal
ˌmet ə 'kɑːp əl ◄ ‖ ˌmet̬ ə 'kɑːrp əl ◄ ~s z
metacarpus ˌmet ə 'kɑːp əs ‖ ˌmet̬ ə 'kɑːrp əs
metacenter, metacentre
'met ə ˌsent ə ‖ 'met̬ ə ˌsent̬ ᵊr ~s z
metal 'met əl ‖ 'met̬ əl ~ed, ~led d ~ing,
~ling ɪŋ ~s z
metalanguag|e 'met ə ˌlæŋ gwɪdʒ §-wɪdʒ
‖ 'met̬- ~es ɪz əz
metaldehyde me 'tæld ɪ haɪd mə-, mɪ-, -ə-
metalinguistic ˌmet ə lɪŋ 'gwɪst ɪk ◄ ‖ ˌmet̬-
~ally ᵊl‿i ~s s
metallic me 'tæl ɪk mə-, mɪ- ~ally ᵊl‿i
Metallica me 'tæl ɪk ə mə-, mɪ-
metalliferous ˌmet ə 'lɪf ᵊr əs ◄ -əl 'ɪf-
‖ ˌmet̬ əl 'ɪf-
metalloid 'met ə lɔɪd -əl ɔɪd ‖ 'met̬ əl ɔɪd ~s z
metallurgical ˌmet ə 'lɜːdʒ ɪk əl ◄ -əl 'ɜːdʒ-
‖ ˌmet̬ əl 'ɜːdʒ- ~ally ᵊl‿i
metallurgist me 'tæl ədʒ ɪst mə-, mɪ-, §-əst;
'met əl ɜːdʒ- ‖ 'met̬ əl 'ɜːdʒ əst ~s s
metallurgy me 'tæl ədʒ i mə-, mɪ-;
'met əl ɜːdʒ- ‖ 'met̬ əl 'ɜːdʒ i
metalwork 'met əl wɜːk ‖ 'met̬ əl wɜːrk
metalwork|er/s 'met əl ˌwɜːk ə/
z ‖ 'met̬ əl ˌwɜːrk ᵊr/z ~ing ɪŋ
metamere 'met ə mɪə ‖ 'met̬ ə mɪr ~s z
metamerism me 'tæm ə ˌrɪz əm mɪ-, mə-
metamorphic
ˌmet ə 'mɔːf ɪk ◄ ‖ ˌmet̬ ə 'mɔːrf ɪk ◄

M

metamorphism ˌmet ə 'mɔːf ˌɪz
əm ‖ ˌmeţ ə 'mɔːrf- ~s z
metamorphos|e
ˌmet ə 'mɔːf əʊz ‖ ˌmeţ ə 'mɔːrf oʊz -oʊs
~**ed** d ~**es** ɪz əz ~**ing** ɪŋ
metamorphoses *from v* ˌmet ə 'mɔːf əʊz ɪz -əz
‖ ˌmeţ ə 'mɔːrf oʊz əz -'•oʊs-
metamorphoses *n pl* ˌmet ə 'mɔːf ə siːz
-mɔː 'fəʊs iːz ‖ ˌmeţ ə 'mɔːrf-
metamorphos|is ˌmet ə 'mɔːf əs ‖ɪs
-mɔː 'fəʊs-, §-əs ‖ ˌmeţ ə 'mɔːrf- ~**es** iːz
metaphor 'met əf ə -ə fɔː ‖ 'meţ ə fɔːr -əf ər
~s z
metaphorical ˌmet ə 'fɒr ɪk əl ◀ ‖ ˌmeţ ə 'fɔːr-
-'faːr- ~**ly** _i
metaphras|e 'met ə freɪz ‖ 'meţ- ~**ed** d ~**es**
ɪz əz ~**ing** ɪŋ
metaphysical, M~ ˌmet ə 'fɪz ɪk əl ◀ ˌmeţ-
~**ly** _i ~s z
metaphysics ˌmet ə 'fɪz ɪks ‖ ˌmeţ-
metastable ˌmet ə 'steɪb əl ◀ ‖ ˌmeţ-
metast|asis me 'tæst |əs ɪs mɪ-, mə-, §-əs
~**ases** ə siːz
metastasis|e, metastasiz|e me 'tæst ə saɪz
mɪ-, mə- ~**ed** d ~**es** ɪz əz ~**ing** ɪŋ
metastatic ˌmet ə 'stæt ɪk ◀ ‖ ˌmeţ ə 'stæţ ɪk ◀
metatarsal ˌmet ə 'taːs əl ◀ ‖ ˌmeţ ə 'taːrs əl ◀
~s z
metatars|us ˌmet ə 'taːs |əs ‖ ˌmeţ ə 'taːrs |əs
~**i** aɪ
metath|esis me 'tæθ |əs ɪs mɪ-, mə-, §-əs
~**eses** ə siːz
metathesis|e, metathesiz|e me 'tæθ ə saɪz
mɪ-, mə- ~**ed** d ~**es** ɪz əz ~**ing** ɪŋ
Metaxa *tdmk* me 'tæks ə mɪ-, mə-
Metcalf, Metcalfe 'met kaːf §-kæf, -kəf ‖ -kæf
mete miːt *(= meet)* **meted** 'miːt ɪd -əd
‖ 'miːţ əd **metes** miːts **meting**
'miːt ɪŋ ‖ 'miːţ ɪŋ
metempsychosis ˌmet emp saɪ 'kəʊs ɪs ˌ•əm-,
§-əs ‖ ˌmeţ əm saɪ 'koʊs əs ˌmə ˌtemps ə-
meteor 'miːt i ə -ɔː ‖ 'miːţ i ər -ɔːr ~s z
'meteor ˌshower
meteoric ˌmiːt i 'ɒr ɪk ◀ ‖ ˌmiːţ i 'ɔːr ɪk ◀ -'aːr-
~**ally** əl_i
meteorite 'miːt i ə raɪt ‖ 'miːţ- ~s s
meteoroid 'miːt i ə rɔɪd ‖ 'miːţ- ~s z
meteorological ˌmiːt i ˌər ə 'lɒdʒ ɪk əl ◀
⚠ˌmiːt ˌɔr ə'•- ‖ ˌmiːţ i ˌər ə 'laːdʒ- ~**ly** _i
meteorologist ˌmiːt i ə 'rɒl ədʒ ɪst
⚠ˌmiːt ə'•-, §-əst ‖ ˌmiːţ i ə 'raːl- ~s s
meteorology ˌmiːt i ə 'rɒl ədʒ i ⚠ˌmiːt ə'•-
‖ ˌmiːţ i ə 'raːl-
meter 'miːt ə ‖ 'miːţ ər ~**ed** d **metering** 'miːt
ər ɪŋ ‖ 'miːţ ər ɪŋ ~s z
-meter *(i)* ˌmiːt ə ‖ ˌmiːţ ər, *(ii)* mɪt ə -mət ə
‖ məţ ər —*Pronunciation (i) is used (a) in units
of length (also spelt* -metre*):* 'centi,meter/
'centi,metre, *and sometimes (b) in the meaning
'measuring device':*'volt,meter. *The stress-
imposing pronunciation (ii) is used (c) with
reference to versification:* pen'tameter, *and
sometimes (d) for 'measuring device':*

ba'rometer. *(Hence the different pronunciations
of the two senses of* micrometer.*) In the words*
altimeter *and* kilometer/kilometre *the two types
have been confused, giving rise to competing
pronunciations with different stressings.*
meth- *comb. form before vowel* meθ—*or, in BrE
only,* mi:θ —*see following*
methacrylate meθ 'æk rɪ leɪt -'•rə-
methadone 'meθ ə dəʊn ‖ -doʊn
methane 'miːθ eɪn ‖ 'meθ- *(*)*
methanoic ˌmeθ ə 'nəʊ ɪk ◀ ‖ -'noʊ-
methanol 'meθ ə nɒl 'miːθ- ‖ -nɔːl -naːl, -noʊl
metheglin 'θeg lɪn mɪ-, mə-, §-lən
methinks mi 'θɪŋks
method 'meθ əd ~s z
methodical mə 'θɒd ɪk əl mɪ-, me- ‖ -'θaːd-
~**ly** _i ~**ness** nəs nɪs
methodics mə 'θɒd ɪks mɪ-, me- ‖ -'θaːd-
Methodism 'meθ ə ˌdɪz əm
Methodist 'meθ əd ɪst §-əst ~s s
Methodius me 'θəʊd i_əs mɪ-, mə- ‖ -'θoʊd-
methodological
ˌmeθ əd ə 'lɒdʒ ɪk əl ◀ -'laːdʒ- ~**ly** _i
methodologist ˌmeθ ə 'dɒl ədʒ ɪst §-əst
‖ -'daːl- ~s s
methodolog|y ˌmeθ ə 'dɒl ədʒ |i ‖ -'daːl- ~**ies**
iz
methought mi 'θɔːt ‖ -'θaːt
meths meθs
Methuen *(i)* 'meθ ju_ən -u_, ˌ_ɪn, *(ii)*
mə 'θjuː_ən mɪ-, me-, -'θuː_, ɪn —*The English
family name is (i); the place in MA is (ii).*
Methuselah, m~ mə 'θjuːz əl ə mɪ-, -'θuːz-
‖ -'θuːz- ~**s, ~'s** z
Methven 'meθ vən
methyl 'meθ əl -ɪl —*in BrE technical usage also*
'miːθ aɪəl
,methyl 'alcohol
methylamine me 'θaɪl ə miːn mɪ:-, mɪ-, mə-;
ˌmeθ ɪl 'æm iːn, -əl- ‖ ˌmeθ əl ə 'miːn
-'æm ən; mə 'θɪl ə miːn
methy|late *n, v* 'meθ ə |leɪt -ɪ- ~**lated** leɪt ɪd
-əd ‖ leɪţ əd ~**lates** leɪts ~**lating**
leɪt ɪŋ ‖ leɪţ ɪŋ
,methylated 'spirits
methylene 'meθ ə liːn -ɪ-
metic 'met ɪk ‖ 'meţ- ~s s
meticulous mə 'tɪk jʊl əs mɪ-, me-, -jəl- ‖ -jəl-
~**ly** li ~**ness** nəs nɪs
metier, métier 'met i eɪ 'meɪt- ‖ 'meɪt jeɪ •'•
—*Fr* [me tje] ~s z
metis, métis *sing.* meɪ 'tiː -'tiːs, *pl* -'tiː -'tiːs,
-'tiːz
Metonic me 'tɒn ɪk mɪ-, mə- ‖ -'taːn-
Me,tonic 'cycle
metonym 'met ə nɪm ‖ 'meţ- ~s z
metonym|y me 'tɒn əm |i mə-, mɪ-, -ɪm-
‖ -'taːn- ~**ies** iz
me-too ˌmiː 'tuː ~**ism** ˌɪz əm
met|ope 'met |əʊp -|əp i ‖ 'meţ |əp i ~**opes**
əʊps əp iz ‖ əp iz
metre 'miːt ə ‖ 'miːţ ər ~s z
-metre ˌmiːt ə ‖ ˌmiːţ ər —*see note at* -meter

M

metric 'metr ɪk ~s s
  ,metric 'ton
-metric 'metr ɪk — **parametric** ,pær ə 'metr ɪk ◄ ‖ ,per-
metrical 'metr ɪk ᵊl ~ly _i
-metrical 'metr ɪk ᵊl — **parametrical** ,pær ə 'metr ɪk ᵊl ◄ ‖ ,per-
metricality ,metr ɪ 'kæl ət i ,•ə-, -ɪt i ‖ -əţ i
metri|cate 'metr ɪ |keɪt -ə- ~**cated** keɪt ɪd -əd ‖ keɪţ əd ~**cates** keɪts ~**cating** keɪt ɪŋ ‖ keɪţ ɪŋ
metrication ,metr ɪ 'keɪʃ ᵊn -ə-
metricis|e, metriciz|e 'metr ɪ saɪz -ə- ~**ed** d ~**es** ɪz əz ~**ing** ɪŋ
metro, Metro 'metr əʊ ‖ -oʊ me 'troʊ ~**s** z
metro- *comb. form*
  with stress-neutral suffix (i) ˌmetr əʊ ‖ -ə, (ii) ˌmiːtr əʊ ‖ -ə —(i) *particularly in the senses* '*measurement', 'mother'*; (ii) *particularly in the sense 'uterus'* — **metronymic** ,metr əʊ 'nɪm ɪk ◄ ‖ -ə-
  with stress-imposing suffix mɪ 'trɒ+ mə-, me- ‖ -'trɑː+ — **metrolog|y** mɪ 'trɒl ədʒ li mə-, me- ‖ -'trɑːl- ~**ies** iz
Metro-Goldwin-Mayer ,metr əʊ ,gəʊld wɪn 'meɪ ə →-,gɒʊld-, →-wɪm' • • ‖ -oʊ ,goʊld wɪn 'meɪ ᵊr
Metroland 'metr əʊ lænd ‖ -oʊ-
metronidazole ,metr əʊ 'naɪd ə zəʊl -ɒn 'aɪd-, →-zɒʊl ‖ -ə 'naɪd ə zoʊl
metronome 'metr ə nəʊm ‖ -noʊm ~**s** z
Metropole 'metr ə pəʊl →-pɒʊl ‖ -poʊl ~**s** z
metropolis, M~ mə 'trɒp əl ɪs mɪ-, me-, §-əs ‖ -'trɑːp- ~**es** ɪz əz
metropolitan, M~ ,metr ə 'pɒl ɪt ᵊn ◄ -'•ət- ‖ -'pɑːl ət ᵊn ◄ ~**s** z
metrorrhagia ,miːtr əʊ 'reɪdʒ i_ə ,metr-, ,•ɔː-, -'reɪdʒ ə ‖ ,•ə-
-metry *stress-imposing* mətr i mɪtr i — **chronometry** krə 'nɒm ətr i -ɪtr- ‖ -'nɑːm-
Metternich 'met ə nɪk -nɪx ‖ 'meţ ᵊr- —*Ger* ['mɛt ɐ nɪç]
mettle 'met ᵊl ‖ 'meţ ᵊl (= *metal*)
mettlesome 'met ᵊl səm ‖ 'meţ-
Mettoy *tdmk* 'met ɔɪ
Metuchen mɪ 'tʌtʃ ᵊn mə-
Metz mets —*Fr* [mɛs]
meuniere, meunière ,mɜːn i 'eə '• • • ‖ mʌn 'jeᵊr —*Fr* [mø njɛːʁ]
Meurig 'maɪᵊr ɪg —*Welsh* ['məi rig, 'məi-]
Meuse mɜːz ‖ mjuːz mʊz —*Fr* [møːz]
Meux (i) mjuːks, (ii) mjuːz, (iii) mjuː
Mevagissey ,mev ə 'gɪs i -'gɪz-
mew mjuː **mewed** mjuːd **mewing** 'mjuː ɪŋ **mews** mjuːz (= *muse*)
Mewes (i) 'mev ɪs §-əs, (ii) 'mjuː_ɪs §_əs
mewl mjuːl (= *mule*) **mewled** mjuːld **mewling** 'mjuːl ɪŋ **mewls** mjuːlz
mews mjuːz
Mexboro', Mexborough 'meks bᵊr_ə ‖ -,bɜː oʊ
Mexicali ,meks ɪ 'kæl i -'kɑːl- —*Sp* [me xi 'ka li]

Mexican 'meks ɪk ən ~**s** z
Mexico 'meks ɪk əʊ ‖ -oʊ —*Sp* México, Méjico ['me xi ko]
  ,Mexico 'City
Mey meɪ
Meyer (i) 'maɪ_ə ‖ 'maɪ_ᵊr, (ii) 'meɪ ə ‖ -ᵊr, (iii) meə ‖ meᵊr, (iv) mɪə ‖ mɪᵊr
Meynell (i) 'men ᵊl, (ii) meɪ 'nel
Meyrick 'mer ɪk
mezereon mə 'zɪər i_ən mɪ-, me- ‖ -'zɪr- ~**s** z
mezuzah mə 'zʊz ə -'zuːz- ~**s** z
mezzanine 'mets ə niːn 'mez- ‖ 'mez- ~**s** z
mezzo 'mets əʊ 'medz- ‖ -oʊ ~**s** z
mezzo-soprano ,mets əʊ sə 'prɑːn əʊ ,medz- ‖ -oʊ sə 'præn oʊ -'prɑːn- ~**s** z
mezzo|tint 'mets əʊ |tɪnt 'medz- ‖ -oʊ- ~**tinted** tɪnt ɪd -əd ‖ tɪnţ əd ~**tinting** tɪnt ɪŋ ‖ tɪnţ ɪŋ ~**tints** tɪnts
mg —*see* milligram(s)
MGM *tdmk* ,em dʒiː 'em
mho məʊ ‖ moʊ **mhos** məʊz ‖ moʊz
MHz —*see* megahertz
mi miː
MI5 ,em aɪ 'faɪv
MI6 ,em aɪ 'sɪks
Mia 'miː_ə
Miami maɪ 'æm i
miaow mi 'aʊ ,miː- ~**ed** d ~**ing** ɪŋ ~**s** z
miasma mi 'æz mə maɪ- ~**s** z
mica 'maɪk ə
micaceous maɪ 'keɪʃ əs
Micah 'maɪk ə
Micawber, m~ mə 'kɔːb ə mɪ- ‖ -ᵊr -'kɑːb-
micawberish mə 'kɔːb ᵊr ɪʃ mɪ- ‖ -'kɑːb-
mice maɪs
Michael 'maɪk ᵊl
Michaela (i) mɪ 'keɪl ə mə-, (ii) maɪ-
Michaelis (i) mɪ 'keɪl ɪs mə-, §-əs, (ii) -'kaɪl-
Michaelmas 'mɪk ᵊl məs
  ,Michaelmas 'daisy
Michel mɪ 'ʃel miː- —*Fr* [mi ʃɛl]
Michelangelo ,maɪk ᵊl 'ændʒ ə ləʊ ,mɪk-, -'•ɪ- ‖ -loʊ —*It* [mi ke 'lan dʒe lo]
Micheldever 'mɪtʃ ᵊl dev ə ‖ -ᵊr
Michele, Michèle mɪ 'ʃel miː- —*Fr* [mi ʃɛl]
Michelin *tdmk* 'mɪtʃ ᵊl_ɪn 'mɪʃ- —*Fr* [mi ʃlæ̃] —*In BrE the* M~ *Guide is usually pronounced as if French.*
Michelle mɪ 'ʃel miː-
Michelmore 'mɪtʃ ᵊl mɔː ‖ -mɔːr -moʊr
Michelob *tdmk* 'mɪk ə ləʊb -ᵊl əʊb ‖ -ᵊl oʊb
Michelson (i) 'maɪk ᵊl sᵊn, (ii) 'mɪtʃ- —*The physicist A A M~ was* (i).
Michener (i) 'mɪʃ nə ‖ -nᵊr, (ii) 'mɪtʃ ən_ə ‖ -ᵊn_ᵊr —*The novelist James M~ is* (ii).
Michie 'mɪk i 'mɪx-, 'miː x-
Michigan 'mɪʃ ɪg ən △'mɪtʃ-
Michigander ,mɪʃ ɪ 'gænd ə ‖ -ᵊr ~**s** z
Mick, mick mɪk **micks, Mick's** mɪks
Mickey, mickey, Mickie 'mɪk i
  ,mickey 'finn; ,Mickey 'Mouse
mickle 'mɪk ᵊl
Mickleham 'mɪk ᵊl əm

M

Mickleover 'mɪk əl ˌəʊv ə ‖ -ˌoʊv ər
Micklethwaite 'mɪk əl θweɪt
Micklewhite 'mɪk əl waɪt -hwaɪt ‖ -hwaɪt
Micky, micky 'mɪk i
Micmac 'mɪk mæk ~s s
micra, Micra tdmk 'maɪk rə
micro 'maɪk rəʊ ‖ -roʊ ~s z
micro- comb. form
   with stress-neutral suffix ˈmaɪk rəʊ ‖ -roʊ —
   microfossil ˌmaɪk rəʊ 'fɒs əl ‖ -roʊ 'faːs-
   with stress-imposing suffix maɪ 'krɒ+ ‖ -'kraː+
   — micrography maɪ 'krɒg rəf i ‖ -'kraːg-
microbe 'maɪk rəʊb ‖ -roʊb ~s z
microbial maɪ 'krəʊb i_əl ‖ -'kroʊb-
microbiological
   ˌmaɪk rəʊ ˌbaɪ_ə 'lɒdʒ ɪk əl ‖ -roʊ ˌbaɪ ə 'laːdʒ-
   ~ly _i
microbiologist ˌmaɪk rəʊ baɪ 'ɒl ədʒ ɪst §-əst
   ‖ -roʊ baɪ 'aːl- ~s s
microbiology
   ˌmaɪk rəʊ baɪ 'ɒl ədʒ i ‖ -roʊ baɪ 'aːl-
microchip 'maɪk rəʊ tʃɪp ‖ -roʊ- ~s s
microclimate 'maɪk rəʊ ˌklaɪm ət -ɪt ‖ -roʊ-
   ~s s
microcline 'maɪk rəʊ klaɪn ‖ -roʊ- ~s z
microcomputer 'maɪk rəʊ kəm ˌpjuːt ə
   §-kɒm, ˌ•- ‖ -roʊ kəm ˌpjuːt ər ~s z
microcosm 'maɪk rəʊ ˌkɒz əm ‖ -rə ˌkaːz- ~s z
microdot 'maɪk rəʊ dɒt ‖ -rə daːt -roʊ- ~s s
microelectronic ˌmaɪk rəʊ ɪ ˌlek 'trɒn ɪk ˌ•·ə-,
   -ˌel ek'•-, -ˌɪl ek'•-, -ˌiːl ek'•-
   ‖ -roʊ ɪ ˌlek 'traːn- ~s s
microfarad 'maɪk rəʊ ˌfær əd -æd ‖ -roʊ-
   -ˌfer- ~s z
microfich|e 'maɪk rəʊ fiːʃ -fɪʃ ‖ -rə- ~es ɪz əz
microfilm 'maɪk rəʊ fɪlm ‖ -rə- ~ed d ~ing ɪŋ
   ~s z
microgroove 'maɪk rəʊ gruːv ‖ -rə- -roʊ- ~s z
microlight 'maɪk rəʊ laɪt ‖ -rə- -roʊ- ~s s
micromesh 'maɪk rəʊ meʃ ‖ -roʊ-
micrometer 'instrument' maɪ 'krɒm ɪt ə -ət-
   ‖ -'kraːm ət ər ~s z
micrometer, micrometre 'micron'
   'maɪk rəʊ ˌmiːt ə maɪ 'krɒm ɪt ə, -ət ə
   ‖ -roʊ ˌmiːt ər ~s z
microminiaturis... —see microminiaturiz...
microminiaturization ˌmaɪk rəʊ ˌmɪn ətʃ
   ər aɪ 'zeɪʃ ən -, •ɪtʃ-, -, •i_ətʃ•••-, -ɪ'••
   ‖ -roʊ ˌmɪn i_ətʃ ər ə-, -, •ətʃ•••-
microminiaturiz|e ˌmaɪk rəʊ 'mɪn ətʃ ə raɪz
   -ɪ'•ɪtʃ-, -ɪ'•i_ətʃ•• ‖ -roʊ 'mɪn i_ətʃ- -ɪ'•ətʃ-
   ~ed d ~es ɪz əz ~ing ɪŋ
micron 'maɪk rɒn -rən ‖ -raːn ~s z
Micronesia ˌmaɪk rəʊ 'niːz i_ə -'niːʒ ə,
   -'niːs i_ə, -'niːʃ ə ‖ -rə 'niːʒ ə -'niːʃ-
Micronesian ˌmaɪk rəʊ 'niːz i_ən ◀ -'niːʒ n,
   -'niːs i_ən, -'niːʃ ən ‖ -rə 'niːʒ ən -'niːʃ- ~s z
microorganism ˌmaɪk rəʊ 'ɔːg ə ˌnɪz əm
   ˈ•• ‖ -roʊ 'ɔːrg- ~s z
Micropal 'maɪk rəʊ pæl ‖ -roʊ-
microphone 'maɪk rə fəʊn ‖ -foʊn ~s z
microprocessor 'maɪk rəʊ ˌprəʊs es ə -ɪs ə,
   §-əs ə; ˌ••'••• ‖ -rə ˌpraːs es ər -əs ər ~s z

microscope 'maɪk rə skəʊp ‖ -skoʊp ~s s
microscopic ˌmaɪk rə 'skɒp ɪk ◀ ‖ -'skaːp ɪk ◀
   ~ally əl_i
microscopy maɪ 'krɒsk əp i ‖ -'kraːsk-
microsecond 'maɪk rəʊ ˌsek ənd , ••'•• ‖ -rə-
   -roʊ-, ⚠-ənt ~s z
Microsoft tdmk 'maɪk rəʊ sɒft ‖ -rə sɔːft -saːft
microtome 'maɪk rəʊ təʊm ‖ -rə toʊm ~s z
microwav|e 'maɪk rə weɪv -rəʊ- ‖ -rə- -roʊ-
   ~able əb əl ~ed d ~es z ~ing ɪŋ
mictu|rate 'mɪk tju ˌreɪt -tʃə- ‖ -tʃə- -tə-
   ~rated reɪt ɪd -əd ‖ reɪt əd ~rates reɪts
   ~rating reɪt ɪŋ ‖ reɪt ɪŋ
micturation ˌmɪk tju 'reɪʃ ən -tʃə- ‖ -tʃə- -tə-
   ~s z
micturition ˌmɪk tju 'rɪʃ ən -tʃə- ‖ -tʃə- -tə-
   ~s z
mid mɪd
   ˌMid Gla'morgan
mid- ˌmɪd — mid-Atlantic
   ˌmɪd ət 'lænt ɪk ◀ ‖ -'lænt̬-
midair ˌmɪd 'eə ◀ ‖ -'eər ◀ -'æər
Midas 'maɪd əs -æs
midcourse ˌmɪd 'kɔːs ◀ →ˌmɪg- ‖ -'kɔːrs ◀
   -'koʊrs
midday ˌmɪd 'deɪ ◀ '••
midden 'mɪd ən ~s z
middie... —see middy
middle 'mɪd əl ~s z
   ˌmiddle 'age; ˌMiddle 'Ages; ˌmiddle 'C;
   ˌmiddle 'class◀; ˌmiddle 'course, '•• •;
   ˌmiddle 'distance; ˌmiddle 'ear; ˌMiddle
   'East; ˌMiddle 'Eastern◀; ˌMiddle 'English;
   ˌmiddle 'finger; ˌmiddle 'management;
   ˌmiddle 'name; ˌmiddle of 'nowhere;
   'middle school; ˌMiddle 'West
middle-aged ˌmɪd əl 'eɪdʒd ◀
   ˌmiddle-aged 'spread
middlebrow 'mɪd əl braʊ ~s z
Middlebury place in VT 'mɪd əl ˌber i
middle-class ˌmɪd əl 'klɑːs ◀ §-'klæs ‖ -'klæs ◀
middle-distance ˌmɪd əl 'dɪst ənts ◀
Middleham 'mɪd əl əm
middle|man 'mɪd əl ˌmæn ~men men
Middlemarch 'mɪd əl mɑːtʃ ‖ -mɑːrtʃ
Middlemast 'mɪd əl mɑːst §-mæst ‖ -mæst
middlemen 'mɪd əl men
middle-of-the-road ˌmɪd əl_əv ðə 'rəʊd ◀
   -əl_ə ðə- ‖ -'roʊd ◀
Middlesboro, Middlesborough place in KY
   'mɪd lz bər_ə ‖ -ˌbɜː ə
Middlesbrough place in England 'mɪd lz brə
Middlesex 'mɪd əl seks
middle-sized ˌmɪd əl 'saɪzd ◀
Middleton 'mɪd əl tən
Middletown 'mɪd əl taʊn
middleweight 'mɪd əl weɪt ~s s
Middlewich 'mɪd əl wɪtʃ
middling 'mɪd əl_ɪŋ ~ly li
Middx —see Middlesex
midd|y 'mɪd li ~ies iz
midfield 'mɪd fiːəld ˌ•'• ~er/s ə/z ‖ ər/z
midge mɪdʒ midges 'mɪdʒ ɪz -əz

M

midget 'mɪdʒ ɪt §-ət **~s** s
Midgley 'mɪdʒ li
midgut 'mɪd gʌt →'mɪg- **~s** s
Midhurst 'mɪd hɜːst ‖ -hɝːst
midi *'mid-length (garment)'* 'mɪd i **~s** z
Midi *'south of France'* mi 'diː miː- —*Fr* [mi di]
MIDI, Midi *computer interface* 'mɪd i **~s** z
Midian 'mɪd i‿ən
Midianite 'mɪd i‿ə naɪt **~s** s
midinette ˌmɪd i 'net —*Fr* [mi di nɛt] **~s** s
midiron 'mɪd ˌaɪ‿ən ‖ -ˌaɪ‿ərn **~s** z
midland, M~ 'mɪd lənd **~s** z
Midler 'mɪd lə ‖ -lər
mid-life ˌmɪd 'laɪf ◄
  ˌmid-life 'crisis
Midlothian mɪd 'ləʊð i‿ən ‖ -'loʊð-
midmost 'mɪd məʊst →'mɪb- ‖ -moʊst
midnight 'mɪd naɪt
  ˌmidnight 'sun
mid-off ˌmɪd 'ɒf -'ɔːf ‖ -'ɔːf -'ɑːf **~s** s
mid-on ˌmɪd 'ɒn ‖ -'ɑːn -'ɔːn **~s** z
midpoint 'mɪd pɔɪnt →'mɪb- **~s** s
midriff 'mɪd rɪf **~s** s
midship 'mɪd ʃɪp **~s** s
midship|man 'mɪd ʃɪp |mən **~men** mən
midst mɪdst mɪtst
midstream ˌmɪd 'striːm ◄
midsummer ˌmɪd 'sʌm ə ◄ '•ˌ•• ‖ -ᵊr ◄ **~s, ~'s**
  z
  ˌMid,summer 'Day; ˌmid,summer
  'madness
midterm ˌmɪd 'tɜːm ◄ ‖ -'tɝːm ◄ —*but in the
  sense '~ examination' usually* '•• —
  midterms ˌmɪd tɜːmz ‖ -tɝːmz
midtown 'mɪd taʊn
midway *adj, adv* ˌmɪd 'weɪ ◄
midway *n, M~* 'mɪd weɪ
midweek ˌmɪd 'wiːk ◄
Midwest ˌmɪd 'west
Midwestern ˌmɪd 'west ən ◄ ‖ -ᵊrn ◄
Midwesterner ˌmɪd 'west ən ə ‖ -ᵊrn ər **~s** z
midwicket ˌmɪd 'wɪk ɪt §-ət
mid|wife 'mɪd |waɪf **~wives** waɪvz
midwifery ˌmɪd 'wɪf ər‿i '•••• ‖ 'mɪd waɪf-
midwinter ˌmɪd 'wɪnt ə ◄ ‖ -'wɪnt̬ ər ◄
midwives 'mɪd waɪvz
Miele *tdmk* 'miːl ə
mien miːn (= *mean*) **miens** miːnz
Miers 'maɪ‿əz ‖ 'maɪ‿ᵊrz
Mies van der Rohe ˌmiːz væn də 'rəʊ ə ˌmiːs-
  ‖ -dᵊr 'roʊ ə ˌ•vɑːn-; ˌ•'••ˌ••
miff mɪf **miffed** mɪft **miffing** 'mɪf ɪŋ **miffs**
  mɪfs
MiG mɪg **MiGs, MiG's** mɪgz
might maɪt
might-have-beens 'maɪt əv biːnz -ə-, -bɪnz
  ‖ 'maɪt̬ əv bɪnz
mighti... —*see* **mighty**
mightily 'maɪt ɪ li -ᵊl i ‖ 'maɪt̬ ᵊl i
mightn't 'maɪt ᵊnt
might|y 'maɪt |i ‖ 'maɪt̬ |i **~ier** i‿ə ‖ i‿ᵊr **~iest**
  i‿ɪst i‿əst **~iness** i nəs i nɪs

mignon 'mɪn jɒn ˌ•'• ‖ miːn 'joʊn -'jɑːn,
  -'jɔːn —*Fr* [mi njɔ̃]
mignonette, M~ ˌmiːn jə 'net **~s** s

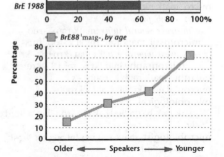

MIGRAINE

■ 'miːg- ■ 'maɪg-

BrE 1988					
0	20	40	60	80	100%

■ BrE88 'maɪg-, by age

Percentage — Older ◄— Speakers —► Younger
(80, 70, 60, 50, 40, 30, 20, 10, 0)

migraine 'miːg reɪn 'maɪg-, 'mɪg- ‖ 'maɪg-
  —*BrE 1988 poll panel preference:* 'miːg- *61%,*
  'maɪg- *39%.* **~s** z
migrant 'maɪg rənt **~s** s
mig|rate ₍ᵢ₎maɪ 'g|reɪt 'maɪg |reɪt ‖ 'maɪg |reɪt
  ~rated reɪt ɪd -əd ‖ reɪt̬ əd **~rates** reɪts
  ~rating reɪt ɪŋ ‖ reɪt̬ ɪŋ
migration ₍ᵢ₎maɪ 'greɪʃ ᵊn **~al** ᵊl **~s** z
migratory 'maɪg rət‿ər i ₍ᵢ₎maɪ 'greɪt ər i
  ‖ 'maɪg rə tɔːr i -toʊr i
Miguel mi: 'gel mɪ- —*Sp, Port* [mi 'ɣel]
mikado, M~ mɪ 'kɑːd əʊ mə- ‖ -oʊ —*Jp*
  [mi ˌka do] **~s** z
Mikardo mɪ 'kɑːd əʊ mə- ‖ -'kɑːrd oʊ
mike, Mike maɪk **mikes, Mike's** maɪks
Mikey 'maɪk i
Mikhail mɪ 'kaɪᵊl -'xaɪᵊl —*Russ* [mjɪ xʌ 'ił]
mil mɪl (= *mill*) **mils** mɪlz
milad|y mɪ 'leɪd |i mə- **~ies** iz
milag|e 'maɪl ɪdʒ 'maɪᵊl- **~es** ɪz əz
Milan mɪ 'læn mə-, -'lɑːn —*formerly* 'mɪl ən;
  but the place in IN is 'maɪl æn —*It* Milano
  [mi 'la: no]
Milanese ˌmɪl ə 'niːz ◄ -'neɪz ‖ -'niːs —*but as a
  cookery term also* ˌ••'neɪz eɪ
milch mɪltʃ
  'milch cow
mild maɪᵊld **milder** 'maɪᵊld ə ‖ -ᵊr **mildest**
  'maɪᵊld ɪst -əst
milden 'maɪᵊld ᵊn **~ed** d **~ing** ɪŋ **~s** z
Mildenhall 'mɪld ᵊn hɔːl ‖ -hɑːl
mildew 'mɪl djuː →§-dʒuː ‖ -duː -djuː **~ed** d
  ~ing ɪŋ **~s** z
mildewy 'mɪl djuː‿i →§-dʒuː‿ ‖ -duː‿i -djuː-
mildly 'maɪᵊld li
Mildmay 'maɪᵊld meɪ
mildness 'maɪᵊld nəs -nɪs
Mildred 'mɪldr əd -ɪd
mile maɪᵊl **miles** maɪᵊlz
mileag|e 'maɪl ɪdʒ 'maɪᵊl- **~es** ɪz əz
mileometer maɪ 'lɒm ɪt ə ˌmaɪᵊl 'ɒm-, -ət-
  ‖ -'lɑːm ət̬ ᵊr **~s** z
milepost 'maɪᵊl pəʊst ‖ -poʊst **~s** s
miler 'maɪl ə 'maɪᵊl- ‖ -ᵊr **~s** z

M

miles *pl of* **mile** maɪᵊlz
miles *Latin, 'soldier'* 'miːl eɪz -eɪs ‖ -eɪs
  ˌmiles ˌgloriˈosus ˌglɔːr i ˈəʊs əs -ʊs ‖ -ˈoʊs-
  ˌgloʊr-
Miles *name* maɪᵊlz
Milesian maɪ 'liːz i_ən mɪ-, -'liːʒ-, -'liːʒ ᵊn
  ‖ -'liːʒ ᵊn -'liːʃ- ~s z
milestone 'maɪᵊl stəʊn ‖ -stoʊn ~s z
Miletus maɪ 'liːt əs mɪ-, mə- ‖ -'liːt̬-
milfoil 'mɪl fɔɪᵊl ~s z
Milford 'mɪl fəd ‖ -fᵊrd
  ˌMilford 'Haven
Milhaud 'miː əʊ -jəʊ ‖ miː 'oʊ -'joʊ —*Fr*
  [mi jo, -lo]
miliaria ˌmɪl i 'eər i_ə ‖ -'er- -'ær-
miliary 'mɪl i_ər i ‖ -i er i
milieu 'miːl jɜː ₍ᵢ₎•'• ‖ miːl 'juː mɪl- —*Fr*
  [mi ljø] ~s z ~x z *or as sing.*
militancy 'mɪl ɪt ᵊnᵗs i '•ət-
militant 'mɪl ɪt ᵊnt -ət- ~ly li ~s s
militaria ˌmɪl ɪ 'teər i_ə ˌ•ə- ‖ -'ter- -'tær-
militarily 'mɪl ɪt_ᵊr əl i -ɪ li; ˌmɪl ɪ 'ter-, ˌ•ə-
  ‖ ˌmɪl ə 'ter-
militaris... —*see* **militariz...**
militarism 'mɪl ɪt ə ˌrɪz əm '•ət-
militarist 'mɪl ɪt ᵊr ɪst '•ət-, §-əst ~s s
militaristic ˌmɪl ɪt ə 'rɪst ɪk ◂ ˌ•ət- ~ally ᵊl_i
militarization ˌmɪl ɪt ᵊr aɪ 'zeɪʃ ᵊn ˌ•ət-, -ɪ'•
  ‖ -ə'•- ~s z
militariz|e 'mɪl ɪt ə raɪz '•ət- ~ed d ~es ɪz əz
  ~ing ɪŋ
military 'mɪl ɪ_tᵊr i '•ə_ ‖ -ə ter i
  ˌmilitary poˈlice
mili|tate 'mɪl ɪ |teɪt -ə- ~tated teɪt ɪd -əd
  ‖ teɪt̬ əd ~tates teɪts ~tating
  teɪt ɪŋ ‖ teɪt̬ ɪŋ
militia mə 'lɪʃ ə mɪ- ~man mən ~men mən
  men ~s z
milk mɪlk **milked** mɪlkt **milking** 'mɪlk ɪŋ
  milks mɪlks
  ˌmilk 'chocolate; 'milk float; 'milking
  maˌchine; 'milking stool; ˌmilk 'pudding;
  'milk run; ˌmilk 'shake, ‖ '• •; 'milk tooth
milki... —*see* **milky**
milkmaid 'mɪlk meɪd ~s z
milk|man 'mɪlk |mən ~men mən men
milksop 'mɪlk sɒp ‖ -saːp ~s s
milkweed 'mɪlk wiːd ~s z
milkwort 'mɪlk wɜːt §-wɔːt ‖ -wɜ˞ːt -wɔːrt ~s
  s
milk|y 'mɪlk |i ~ier i_ə ‖ i_ᵊr ~iest i_ɪst i_əst
  ~iness i nəs i nɪs
  ˌMilky 'Way
mill, Mill mɪl **milled** mɪld **milling** 'mɪl ɪŋ
  mills mɪlz
Millais 'mɪl eɪ mɪ 'leɪ ‖ mɪ 'leɪ
Millan 'mɪl ən
Millar 'mɪl ə ‖ -ᵊr
Millard 'mɪl aːd ‖ -ᵊrd
Millbank 'mɪl bæŋk
millboard 'mɪl bɔːd ‖ -bɔːrd -boʊrd
milldam 'mɪl dæm ~s z

millefeuille ˌmiː ᵊl 'fɔɪ ˌmɪl-, -'fɜː jə —*Fr*
  [mil fœj]
millefiori ˌmɪl i fi 'ɔːr i ˌmɪl i 'fjɔːr i
millenarian ˌmɪl ə 'neər i_ən ◂ ˌ•ɪ- ‖ -'ner-
  -'nær- ~ism ˌɪz əm ~s z
millenni|um mɪ 'len i_|əm mə- ~a ə ~al əl
  ~ums əmz
millepede 'mɪl ɪ piːd -ə- ~s z
millepore 'mɪl ɪ pɔː -ə- ‖ -pɔːr -poʊr ~s z
miller, M~ 'mɪl ə ‖ -ᵊr ~s z
millet 'mɪl ɪt §-ət ~s s
Millet *French name* 'miː eɪ -jeɪ ‖ miː 'jeɪ —*Fr*
  [mi jɛ, -lɛ]
Millett 'mɪl ɪt §-ət
milli- ˌmɪl i -ə — **millisecond** 'mɪl ɪ ˌsek ənd
  §-ə-, →-ŋd ‖ ⚠-ənt
milliard 'mɪl i aːd 'mɪl jaːd ‖ -aːrd ~s z
Milliband 'mɪl ɪ bænd §-ə-
millibar 'mɪl i baː ‖ -baːr ~s z
Millicent 'mɪl ɪs ənt -əs-
Millie 'mɪl i
Milligan 'mɪl ɪg ən
milligram, milligramme 'mɪl i græm -ə- ~s z
Millikan 'mɪl ɪk ən
milliliter, millilitre 'mɪl i ˌliːt ə -ə- ‖ -ə ˌliːt̬ ᵊr
  ~s z
millimeter, millimetre 'mɪl i ˌmiːt ə -ə-
  ‖ -ə ˌmiːt̬ ᵊr ~s z
milliner 'mɪl ɪn ə -ən- ‖ -ᵊr ~s z
millinery 'mɪl ɪn ᵊr_i '•ən- ‖ -ə ner i
Millington 'mɪl ɪŋ tən
million 'mɪl jən 'mɪl i_ən ~s z
millionaire ˌmɪl jə 'neə ◂ -i_ə- ‖ -'neᵊr -'næᵊr;
  '••• ~s z
millionairess ˌmɪl jə 'neər ɪs -əs, -es; -neə 'res
  ‖ -'ner əs -'nær- ~es ɪz əz
millionth 'mɪl jᵊntθ 'mɪl i_ᵊntθ ~s s
millipede 'mɪl ɪ piːd -ə- ~s z
millisec|ond 'mɪl ɪ ˌsek |ənd -ə-, →-ŋd ‖ ⚠-ənt
  ~onds əndz →ŋdz ‖ ⚠ənts
Millom 'mɪl əm
millpond 'mɪl pɒnd ‖ -paːnd ~s z
millrace 'mɪl reɪs
Mills mɪlz
millstone 'mɪl stəʊn ‖ -stoʊn ~s z
Millwall 'mɪl wɔːl -wəl, ˌmɪl 'wɔːl ‖ -waːl
millwheel 'mɪl wiːᵊl -hwiːᵊl ‖ -hwiːᵊl ~s z
millwright 'mɪl raɪt ~s s
Milman 'mɪl mən
Milne mɪln mɪl
Milner 'mɪln ə ‖ -ᵊr
Milnes mɪlnz mɪlz
Milngavie mɪl 'gaɪ mʌl- *(!)*
Milo, milo 'maɪl əʊ 'miːl- ‖ -oʊ
milometer maɪ 'lɒm ɪt ə -ət- ‖ -'laːm ət̬ ᵊr ~s
  z
milord mɪ 'lɔːd mə- ‖ -'lɔːrd ~s z
Milos 'miːl ɒs ‖ -aːs -oʊs
Milosevic mɪ 'lɒʃ ə vɪtʃ -'lɒs- ‖ -'loʊs- -'laːs-
  —*Serbian* Milošević [mi 'lo ʃe vitç]
Milport 'mɪl pɔːt ‖ -pɔːrt -poʊrt
milquetoast, M~ 'mɪlk təʊst ‖ -toʊst ~s s

M

milt, Milt mɪlt **milted** 'mɪlt ɪd -əd **milting**
'mɪlt ɪŋ **milts** mɪlts
Miltiades mɪl 'taɪ‿ə diːz
Milton 'mɪlt ən
,Milton 'Keynes kiːnz
Miltonic mɪl 'tɒn ɪk ‖ -'tɑːn-
Milwaukee mɪl 'wɔːk i -iː ‖ -'wɑːk-
Mimas 'maɪm əs -æs
mime maɪm **mimed** maɪmd **mimes** maɪmz
miming 'maɪm ɪŋ
mimeo 'mɪm i əʊ ‖ -oʊ ~**ed** d ~**ing** ɪŋ ~**s** z
mimeograph, M~ 'mɪm i‿ə grɑːf -græf ‖ -græf
~**ed** t ~**ing** ɪŋ ~**s** s
mimesis mɪ 'miːs ɪs mə-, maɪ-, §-əs
mimetic mɪ 'met ɪk mə-, maɪ- ‖ -'met̬- ~**ally**
əl‿i
Mimi 'miːm i 'miː miː
mimic 'mɪm ɪk ~**ked** t ~**king** ɪŋ ~**s** s
mimic|ry 'mɪm ɪk |ri -ək- ~**ries** riz
mimosa mɪ 'məʊz ə §mə-, -'məʊs- ‖ -'moʊs ə
-'moʊz- ~**s** z
mims|y 'mɪmz| i ~**ier** i‿ə ‖ i‿ər ~**iest** i‿ɪst
‿əst ~**ily** ɪ li əl i ~**iness** i nəs -nɪs
mimulus 'mɪm jʊl əs -jəl- ‖ -jəl-
min. —*see (i)* **minimum** *(ii)* **minute/s**
Min *river* mɪn —*Chi* Mín [²mɪn]
min|a 'maɪn |ə ~**ae** iː ~**as** əz
minaret ,mɪn ə 'ret '•••• ~**s** s
minator|y 'mɪn ət‿ər li 'maɪn- ‖ -ə tɔːr li
-toʊr i ~**ily** əl i ɪ li
mince mɪnᵗs **minced** mɪnᵗst **minces** 'mɪnᵗs ɪz
-əz **mincing/ly** 'mɪnᵗs ɪŋ /li
,mince 'pie; 'mincing ma,chine
mincemeat 'mɪnᵗs miːt
mincer 'mɪnᵗs ə ‖ -ər ~**s** z
Minch mɪntʃ **Minches** 'mɪntʃ ɪz -əz
mind maɪnd **minded** 'maɪnd ɪd -əd **minding**
'maɪnd ɪŋ **minds** maɪndz
'mind ,reader, 'mind ,reading; ,mind's
'eye
Mindanao ,mɪnd ə 'naʊ ‖ -'nɑː oʊ
mind-bending 'maɪnd ,bend ɪŋ →'maɪm- ~**ly**
li
mind-blowing 'maɪnd ,bləʊ ɪŋ →'maɪm-
‖ -,bloʊ-
mind-boggling 'maɪnd ,bɒg əl‿ɪŋ →'maɪm-
‖ -,bɑːg- ~**ly** li
minder 'maɪnd ə ‖ -ər ~**s** z
mind-expanding 'maɪnd ɪk ,spænd ɪŋ -ek-,
-ək-
mindful 'maɪnd fəl -fʊl ~**ly** ‿i ~**ness** nəs nɪs
mindless 'maɪnd ləs -lɪs ~**ly** li ~**ness** nəs nɪs
mindset 'maɪnd set ~**s** s
Mindy 'maɪnd i
mine maɪn **mined** maɪnd *(= mind)* **mines**
maɪnz **mining** 'maɪn ɪŋ
'mine de,tector
minefield 'maɪn fiːəld ~**s** z
Minehead 'maɪn hed ,•'•
minelayer 'maɪn ,leɪ ə ‖ -ər ~**s** z
minelaying 'maɪn ,leɪ ɪŋ
Minelli mɪ 'nel i mə-
miner 'maɪn ə ‖ -ər ~**s** z

mineral 'mɪn ªr‿əl ~**s** z
'mineral oil; 'mineral ,water
mineralogical ,mɪn ªr‿ə 'lɒdʒ ɪk ªl ◄ -'lɑːdʒ-
~**ly** ‿i
mineralogist ,mɪn ə 'ræl ədʒ ɪst △-'rɒl-,
§-əst ‖ -'rɑːl- ~**s** s
mineralogy ,mɪn ə 'ræl ədʒ i △-'rɒl- ‖ -'rɑːl-
Minerva mɪ 'nɜːv ə mə- ‖ -'nɝːv-
minestrone ,mɪn ə 'strəʊn i -ɪ- ‖ -'stroʊn i
△-'stroʊn
minesweeper 'maɪn ,swiːp ə ‖ -ər ~**s** z
minesweeping 'maɪn ,swiːp ɪŋ
Ming *dynasty* mɪŋ —*Chi* Míng [²mɪŋ]
minge mɪndʒ
mingl|e 'mɪŋ gªl ~**ed** d ~**er/s** ə/z ‖ ªr/z ~**es** z
~**ing** ‿ɪŋ
mingogram 'mɪŋ gəʊ græm ‖ -gə- ~**s** z
mingograph, M~ 'mɪŋ gəʊ grɑːf -græf
‖ -gə græf ~**s** s
Mingrelian mɪŋ 'griːl i‿ən →mɪŋ-
Mingulay 'mɪŋ gʊ leɪ
Mingus 'mɪŋ gəs
mingl|y 'mɪndʒ |i ~**ier** i‿ə ‖ i‿ªr ~**iest** i‿ɪst i‿əst
mini, Mini 'mɪn i ~**s, ~'s** z
mini- |mɪn i— **minilecture** 'mɪn i ,lek tʃə -ʃə
‖ -tʃªr -ʃªr
miniature 'mɪn ətʃ ə -ɪtʃ-, -i‿ətʃ ə
‖ 'mɪn i‿ªtʃ ªr‿ə tʃʊr; 'mɪn ɪ tʃʊr ~**s** z
miniaturis... —*see* **miniaturiz...**
miniaturist 'mɪn ətʃ ªr ɪst '•ɪtʃ-, '•i‿ətʃ•‿•,
§-əst ‖ 'mɪn i ,ətʃ ªr əst -ə tʃʊr əst;
'mɪn ɪ tʃʊr əst ~**s** s
miniaturization ,mɪn ətʃ ªr aɪ 'zeɪʃ ªn
,mɪn ɪtʃ-, -i‿ətʃ ªr aɪ-, -ɪ'•- ‖ ,mɪn i ,ətʃ
ªr ə 'zeɪʃ ªn ,mɪn ətʃ ªr ə'•- ~**s** z
miniaturiz|e 'mɪn ətʃ ə raɪz '•ɪtʃ-, -i‿ətʃ ə-
‖ 'mɪn i ,ətʃ ə raɪz 'mɪn ətʃ ə raɪz ~**ed** d ~**es**
ɪz əz ~**ing** ɪŋ
minibus 'mɪn i bʌs ~**ed**, ~**sed** t ~**es**, ~**ses** ɪz
əz ~**ing**, ~**sing** ɪŋ
minicab 'mɪn i kæb ~**s** z
minicomputer 'mɪn i kəm ,pjuːt ə §-kɒm,•-,
,•••'•• ‖ -,pjuːt̬ ªr ~**s** z
minim 'mɪn ɪm §-əm ~**s** z
minima 'mɪn ɪm ə -əm-
minimal 'mɪn ɪm ªl -əm- ~**ly** i
,minimal 'pair
minimalism 'mɪn ɪm ªl ,ɪz əm '•əm-
minimalist 'mɪn ɪm ªl ɪst '•əm-, §-əst ~**s** s
minimax 'mɪn ɪ mæks -ə-
minimis... —*see* **minimiz...**
minimization ,mɪn ɪ maɪ 'zeɪʃ ªn ,•ə- ‖ -əm ə-
minimiz|e 'mɪn ɪ maɪz -ə- ~**ed** d ~**es** ɪz əz
~**ing** ɪŋ
minim|um 'mɪn ɪm |əm -əm- ~**a** ə ~**ums** əmz
,minimum 'wage
minimus 'mɪn ɪm əs -əm-
mining 'maɪn ɪŋ
minion 'mɪn jən 'mɪn i‿ən ~**s** z
miniscule, minuscule 'mɪn ə skjuːl -ɪ- ~**s** z
miniseries 'mɪn i ,sɪər iːz -ɪz ‖ -,sɪr-
mini|skirt 'mɪn i |skɜːt ‖ -|skɝːt ~**skirted**

skɜːt ɪd -əd ‖ skɜ·ːt̬ əd **~skirts**
　skɜːts ‖ skɜ·ːts
minister 'mɪn ɪst ə -əst- ‖ -ər **~ed** d
　ministering 'mɪn ɪst ər ɪŋ 'ˌ•əst-;
　→'mɪn ɪ strɪŋ, -ə- **~s** z
　ˌministering 'angel
ministerial ˌmɪn ɪ 'stɪər i‿əl ◂ ˌ•ə- ‖ -'stɪr- **~ly**
　i
ministrant 'mɪn ɪs trənt -əs- **~s** s
ministration ˌmɪn ɪ 'streɪʃ ᵊn -ə- **~s** z
minis|try 'mɪn ɪs |tri -əs- **~tries** triz
minium 'mɪn i‿əm
miniver, M~ 'mɪn ɪv ə -əv- ‖ -ər
mink mɪŋk **minks** mɪŋks
minke 'mɪŋk i -ə ‖ -ə **~s** z
Minkowski mɪŋ 'kɒf ski ‖ -'kɑːf- -'kɔːf-
Minna 'mɪn ə
Minneapolis ˌmɪn i 'æp əl ɪs §-əs
Minnehaha ˌmɪn i 'hɑː hɑː
Minnelli mɪ 'nel i mə-
minneola ˌmɪn i 'əʊl ə ‖ -'oʊl ə **~s** z
minnesinger 'mɪn ɪ ˌsɪŋ ə -ə- ‖ -ər **~s** z
Minnesota ˌmɪn ɪ 'səʊt̬ ə -ə- ‖ -'soʊt̬ ə
Minnesotan ˌmɪn ɪ 'səʊt̬ ᵊn ◂ -ə- ‖ -'soʊt̬ ᵊn ◂
　~s z
Minnie 'mɪn i
minnow 'mɪn əʊ ‖ -oʊ **~s** z
Minoan mɪ 'nəʊ ən mə-, maɪ- ‖ -'noʊ ən **~s** z
Minogue mɪ 'nəʊg mə- ‖ -'noʊg
Minolta *tdmk* mɪ 'nɒlt ə mə-, -'nəʊlt-
　‖ -'nɑːlt ə -'noʊlt- —*Jp* [mi ˌno ɾɯ ta]
minor, Minor 'maɪn ə ‖ -ər (= *miner*) **~ed** d
　minoring 'maɪn ər ɪŋ **~s** z
　ˌminor 'planet; ˌminor 'suit
Minorca mɪ 'nɔːk ə mə- ‖ -'nɔːrk ə —*Sp*
　Menorca [me 'noɾ ka]
Minories 'mɪn ər iz
minorit|y maɪ 'nɒr ət |i mɪ-, mə, -ɪt-
　‖ mə 'nɔːr ət̬ |i maɪ-, -'nɑːr- **~ies** iz
Minos 'maɪn ɒs ‖ -əs -ɑːs
Minotaur 'maɪn ə tɔː ‖ 'mɪn ə tɔːr 'maɪn- **~s** z
Minsk mɪnᵗsk
minster, M~ 'mɪnᵗst ə ‖ -ər **~s** z
minstrel 'mɪnᵗs trəl **~s** z
minstrel|sy 'mɪnᵗs trəl |si **~sies** siz
mint mɪnt **minted** 'mɪnt ɪd -əd ‖ 'mɪnt̬ əd
　minting 'mɪnt ɪŋ ‖ 'mɪnt̬ ɪŋ **mints** mɪnts
　ˌmint 'julep; ˌmint 'sauce ‖ '• •
mintag|e 'mɪnt ɪdʒ ‖ 'mɪnt̬- **~es** ɪz əz
Minter 'mɪnt ə ‖ 'mɪnt̬ ər
Minto 'mɪnt əʊ ‖ -oʊ
Minton 'mɪnt ən ‖ -ᵊn
minty, Minty 'mɪnt i ‖ 'mɪnt̬ i
minuend 'mɪn ju end **~s** z
minuet ˌmɪn ju 'et **~s** s
minus 'maɪn əs **~es** ɪz əz
　ˌminus 'one; 'minus ˌsign
minuscule 'mɪn ə skjuːl -ɪ- ‖ mɪ 'nʌsk juːl **~s**
　z
min|ute *n, v* 'mɪn |ɪt §-ət ‖ -|ət **~uted** ɪt ɪd
　§ət-, -əd ‖ ət̬ əd **~utes** ɪts §əts ‖ əts **~uting**
　ɪt ɪŋ §ət- ‖ ət̬ ɪŋ
　'minute ˌhand; 'minute ˌsteak

minute *adj 'tiny'* maɪ 'njuːt ˌ•'• ‖ -'nuːt -'njuːt
　~ly li
minute|man, M~ 'mɪn ɪt |mæn §-ət- **~men**
　men
minuteness maɪ 'njuːt nəs ˌ•-, -nɪs ‖ -'nuːt-
　-'njuːt-
minuti|a maɪ 'njuːʃ i‿ə mɪ-, mə-, -'nuːʃ-,
　-'njuːt-, -'nuːt- ‖ -'nuːʃ- -'njuːʃ- **~ae** iː aɪ
minx mɪŋks **minxes** 'mɪŋks ɪz -əz
Miocene 'maɪ‿ə siːn
MIPS, mips mɪps
Miquelon 'miːk ə lɒn ‖ -lɑːn -lɔːn —*Fr* [mi klɔ̃]
Mir mɪə ‖ mɪᵊr —*Russ* [mʲiɾ]
Mira 'maɪᵊr ə ‖ 'mɪr-
Mirabeau 'mɪr ə bəʊ ‖ -boʊ —*Fr* [mi ʁa bo]
Mirabel 'mɪr ə bel
miracle 'mɪr ək ᵊl -ɪk- **~s** z
　'miracle ˌdrug; 'miracle ˌplay
miraculous mə 'ræk jʊl əs mɪ-, -jəl- ‖ -jəl-
　~ly li **~ness** nəs nɪs
mirag|e, M~ 'mɪr ɑːʒ mə 'rɑːʒ, mɪ- ‖ mə 'rɑːʒ
　~es ɪz əz
Miranda mə 'rænd ə mɪ-
MIRAS 'maɪᵊr əs -æs
mire 'maɪ‿ə ‖ 'maɪ‿ᵊr **mired**
　'maɪ‿əd ‖ 'maɪ‿ᵊrd **mires** 'maɪ‿əz ‖ 'maɪ‿ᵊrz
　miring 'maɪ‿ər ɪŋ ‖ 'maɪ‿ᵊr ɪŋ
mirepoix ˌmɪə 'pwɑː ‖ ˌmɪr- —*Fr* [miʁ pwa]
Mirfield 'mɜː fiːᵊld ‖ 'mɜ·ː-
Mirfin 'mɜːf ɪn §-ᵊn ‖ 'mɜ·ːf-
Miriam 'mɪr i‿əm
mirk mɜːk ‖ mɜ·ːk
mirk|y 'mɜːk |i ‖ 'mɜ·ːk |i **~ier** i‿ə ‖ i‿ᵊr **~iest**
　i‿ɪst i‿əst **~ily** ɪ li əl i **~iness** i nəs i nɪs
Miró mɪ 'rəʊ ‖ -'roʊ —*Sp, Catalan* [mi 'ro]
Mirren 'mɪr ᵊn
Mirro *tdmk* 'mɪr əʊ ‖ -oʊ
mirror 'mɪr ə ‖ -ər **~ed** d **mirroring** 'mɪr ər ɪŋ
　~s z
　ˌmirror 'image, '•• ˌ••; 'mirror ˌwriting
mirth mɜːθ ‖ mɜ·ːθ
mirthful 'mɜːθ fᵊl -fʊl ‖ 'mɜ·ːθ-
mirthless 'mɜːθ ləs -lɪs ‖ 'mɜ·ːθ-
MIRV mɜːv ‖ mɜ·ːv **~ed** d **~ing** ɪŋ **~s** z
mir|ly 'maɪᵊr |li **~ier** i‿ə ‖ i‿ᵊr **~iest** i‿ɪst i‿əst
　~iness i nəs i nɪs
mis- ˌmɪs
misadventure ˌmɪs əd 'ventʃ ə §-æd- ‖ -ər **~s**
　z
misadvis|e ˌmɪs əd 'vaɪz §-æd- **~ed** d **~es** ɪz
　əz **~ing** ɪŋ
misalign ˌmɪs ə 'laɪn **~ed** d **~ing** ɪŋ
　~ment/s mənt/s **~s** z
misallianc|e ˌmɪs ə 'laɪ ᵊnts **~es** ɪz əz
misandry mɪs 'ændr i 'mɪs ᵊndr i
misanthrope 'mɪs ᵊn θrəʊp 'mɪz-, -æn-
　‖ -θroʊp **~s** s
misanthropic ˌmɪs ᵊn 'θrɒp ɪk ◂ ˌmɪz-, -æn-
　‖ -'θrɑːp- **~ally** ᵊl i
misanthropist mɪs 'ænθ rəp ɪst mɪz-, §-əst **~s**
　s
misanthropy mɪs 'ænθ rəp i mɪz-
misapplication ˌmɪs ˌæp lɪ 'keɪʃ ᵊn -lə'•- **~s** z

misap|ply ˌmɪs ə lˈplaɪ ~**plied** ˈplaɪd ~**plies** ˈplaɪz ~**plying** ˈplaɪ ɪŋ

misapprehend ˌmɪs ˌæp rɪ ˈhend -rə- ~**ed** ɪd əd ~**ing** ɪŋ ~**s** z

misapprehension ˌmɪs ˌæp rɪ ˈhenᵗʃ ən -rə- ~**s** z

misappropri|ate ˌmɪs ə ˈprəʊp ri leɪt ‖ -ˈproʊp- ~**ated** eɪt ɪd -əd ‖ eɪt̬ əd ~**ates** eɪts ~**ating** eɪt ɪŋ ‖ eɪt̬ ɪŋ

misappropriation ˌmɪs ə ˌprəʊp ri ˈeɪʃ ən ‖ -ˌproʊp- ~**s** z

misbegotten ˌmɪs bɪ ˈɡɒt ən ◂ -bə-, §-biː- ‖ -ˈɡɑːt ən ◂

misbehav|e ˌmɪs bɪ ˈheɪv -bə-, §-biː- ~**es** z ~**ing** ɪŋ

misbehavior, misbehaviour ˌmɪs bɪ ˈheɪv jə -bə-, §-biː- ‖ -jᵊr ~**s** z

misc. —*see* **miscellaneous**

miscalcu|late ˌmɪs ˈkælk ju lleɪt -jə- ‖ -jə- ~**lated** leɪt ɪd -əd ‖ leɪt̬ əd ~**lates** leɪts ~**lating** leɪt ɪŋ ‖ leɪt̬ ɪŋ

miscalculation ˌmɪs ˌkælk ju ˈleɪʃ ən -jə- ‖ -jə- ~**s** z

miscall ˌmɪs ˈkɔːl ‖ -ˈkɑːl ~**ed** d ~**ing** ɪŋ ~**s** z

Miscampbell mɪ ˈskæm bᵊl

miscarriag|e ₍ᵢ₎mɪs ˈkær ɪdʒ ◂ ˈ•,•• ‖ ˈ•,•• -ˌker- ~**es** ɪz əz **mis,carriage of 'justice** ‖ ,•,•-

miscarr|y ₍ᵢ₎mɪs ˈkær li ˈ•,•• ‖ -ˈker- ~**ied** id ~**ies** iz ~**ying** i ɪŋ

miscast ˌmɪs ˈkɑːst §-ˈkæst ‖ -ˈkæst ~**ing** ɪŋ ~**s** s

miscegenation ˌmɪs ɪdʒ ə ˈneɪʃ ən ,•ədʒ-, -ɪˈ•-; mɪ ˌsedʒ-, mə-

miscellanea ˌmɪs ə ˈleɪn i‿ə

miscellaneous ˌmɪs ə ˈleɪn i‿əs ◂ ~**ly** li ~**ness** nəs nɪs

miscellanist mɪ ˈsel ən ɪst mə-, §-əst; ˈmɪs ə leɪn- ‖ ˈmɪs ə leɪn- ~**s** s

miscellan|y mɪ ˈsel ən li mə-, ˈmɪs ə leɪn li ‖ ˈmɪs ə leɪn li (*) ~**ies** iz

mischance ˌmɪs ˈtʃɑːnᵗs →§,mɪʃ-, §-ˈtʃænᵗs, ˈ•• ‖ -ˈtʃænᵗs

mischief ˈmɪs tʃɪf →§ˈmɪʃ-, §-tʃəf, §-tʃiːf ~**s** s

mischief-mak|er/s ˈmɪs tʃɪf ˌmeɪk| ə/z →§ˈmɪʃ-, §-tʃəf-, §-tʃiːf- ‖ -ᵊr/z ~**ing** ɪŋ

mischievous ˈmɪs tʃɪv əs →§ˈmɪʃ-, -tʃəv-; △mɪs ˈtʃiːv-, △-iˌəs —*Poll panel preferences:* *AmE 1993,* ˈmɪs- 67%, -ˈtʃiːv- *33%; BrE* *1998,* ˈmɪs- 73%, -ˈtʃiːv- 27%. ~**ly** li ~**ness** nəs nɪs

miscible ˈmɪs əb ᵊl -ɪb-

misconceiv|e ˌmɪs kən ˈsiːv §-kɒn- ~**ed** d ~**es** z ~**ing** ɪŋ

misconception ˌmɪs kən ˈsep ʃᵊn §-kɒn- ~**s** z

misconduct *n* ˌmɪs ˈkɒn dʌkt ‖ -ˈkɑːn-

misconduct *v* ˌmɪs kən ˈdʌkt §-kɒn- ~**ed** ɪd əd ~**ing** ɪŋ ~**s** s

misconstruction ˌmɪs kən ˈstrʌk ʃᵊn §-kɒn- ~**s** z

misconstru|e ˌmɪs kən ˈstruː §-kɒn- ~**ed** d ~**es** z ~**ing** ɪŋ

MISCHIEVOUS

ˈmɪs- / -ˈtʃiːv-

AmE 1993

BrE 1998

0 20 40 60 80 100%

AmE93 stress on second syllable, by age

BrE98 stress on second syllable, by age

Percentage

Older ← Speakers → Younger

mis|count *v* ˌmɪs ˈkaʊnt ~**counted** ˈkaʊnt ɪd -əd ‖ ˈkaʊnt̬ əd ~**counting** ˈkaʊnt ɪŋ ‖ ˈkaʊnt̬ ɪŋ ~**counts** ˈkaʊn/s

miscount *n* ˈmɪs kaʊnt ,•ˈ• ~**s** s

miscreant ˈmɪs kri‿ənt ~**s** s

miscu|e *v, n* ˌmɪs ˈkjuː ~**ed** d ~**es** z ~**ing** ɪŋ

mis|date *v* ˌmɪs lˈdeɪt ~**dated** ˈdeɪt ɪd -əd ‖ ˈdeɪt̬ əd ~**dates** ˈdeɪts ~**dating** ˈdeɪt ɪŋ ‖ ˈdeɪt̬ ɪŋ

misdeal *n* ˌmɪs ˈdiːᵊl ˈ•• ~**s** z

misdeal *v* ˌmɪs ˈdiːᵊl ~**ing** ɪŋ ~**s** z **misdealt** ˌmɪs ˈdelt

misdeed ˌmɪs ˈdiːd ˈ•• ~**s** z

misdemeanor, misdemeanour ˌmɪs dɪ ˈmiːn ə -də-, §-diː- ‖ -ᵊr ~**s** z

misdirect ˌmɪs də ˈrekt -dɪ-, -daɪᵊ- ~**ed** ɪd əd ~**ing** ɪŋ ~**s** s

misdirection ˌmɪs də ˈrek ʃᵊn -dɪ-, -daɪᵊ- ~**s** z

misdoing ˌmɪs ˈduːˌɪŋ ˈ•,•• ~**s** z

mise-en-scene, mise-en-scène ˌmiːz ɒn ˈseɪn -ˈsen ‖ -ɑːn- —*Fr* [mi zɑ̃ sɛn]

miser ˈmaɪz ə ‖ -ᵊr ~**s** z

miserab|le ˈmɪz ᵊrˌəb ᵊl →ˈmɪʒ rəb ᵊl ‖ ˈmɪz ᵊrb ᵊl ~**leness** ᵊl nəs -nɪs ~**ly** li

misere, misère mɪ ˈzeə §mə- ‖ -ˈzeᵊr

miserere, M~ ˌmɪz ə ˈreər i -ˈrɪər-, -eɪ ‖ -ˈrer- -ˈrɪr-

misericord mɪ ˈzer ɪ kɔːd mə-, -ə- ‖ -kɔːrd ~**s** z

miserie... —*see* **misery**

miser|ly ˈmaɪz ə lli -ᵊl i ‖ -ᵊr- ~**liness** li nəs li nɪs

miser|y ˈmɪz ᵊrˌli →ˈmɪʒ rli ~**ies** iz

misfeasanc|e ₍ᵢ₎mɪs ˈfiːz ᵊnᵗs ~**es** ɪz əz

misfire *v* ˌmɪs ˈfaɪ‿ə ‖ -ˈfaɪ‿ᵊr ~**d** d ~**s** z **misfiring** ˌmɪs ˈfaɪ‿ər ɪŋ ‖ -ˈfaɪ‿ᵊr ɪŋ

misfire *n* ˌmɪs ˈfaɪ‿ə ˈ•,•• ‖ -ˈfaɪ‿ᵊr ˈ•,•• ~**s** z

misfit ˈmɪs fɪt ,•ˈ• ~**s** s

misfortune mɪs ˈfɔːtʃ ən -uːn ‖ -ˈfɔːrtʃ- ~**s** z

misgiving ₍ᵢ₎mɪs ˈɡɪv ɪŋ ~**s** z

misgovern ˌmɪs ˈɡʌv ən ‖ -ᵊrn ~**ed** d ~**ing** ɪŋ ~**s** z

misguided ₍ᵢ₎mɪs ˈɡaɪd ɪd -əd ~**ly** li

M

mishandl|e ˌmɪs 'hænd əl ~**ed** d ~**es** z ~**ing**
_ɪŋ
mishap 'mɪs hæp ₍ᵢ₎•'• ~**s** s
Mishcon 'mɪʃ kɒn ‖ -kɑːn
ˌMishcon de 'Reya də 'reɪ ə
mis|hear ˌmɪs ˈhɪə ‖ -ˈhɪʳr ~**heard**
'hɜːd ◀ ‖ 'hɜːd ◀ ~**hearing** 'hɪər ɪŋ ‖ 'hɪr ɪŋ
~**hears** 'hɪəz ‖ 'hɪʳrz
mis|hit _v_ ˌmɪs ˈhɪt ~**hits** 'hɪts ~**hitting**
'hɪt ɪŋ ‖ 'hɪt̬ ɪŋ
mishit _n_ 'mɪs hɪt ˌ•'• ~**s** s
mishmash 'mɪʃ mæʃ ‖ -mɑːʃ -mæʃ _(*)_
Mishna, Mishnah 'mɪʃ nə
misinform ˌmɪs ɪn ˈfɔːm §-ən- ‖ -ˈfɔːrm ~**ed** d
~**ing** ɪŋ ~**s** z
misinformation ˌmɪs ɪn fə ˈmeɪʃ ən §ˌ•ən-
‖ -ɪn fəʳr-
misinterp|ret ˌmɪs ɪn ˈtɜːp |rɪt §-ən-, -rət
‖ -ˈtɜːp |rət -ət ~**reted** rɪt ɪd §rət-, -əd
‖ rət̬ əd ət̬- ~**reting** rɪt ɪŋ §rət- ‖ rət̬ ɪŋ ət̬-
~**rets** rɪts §rəts ‖ rəts əts
misinterpretation ˌmɪs ɪn ˌtɜːp rɪ ˈteɪʃ ən
§ˌ•ən-, -rəˈ•- ‖ -ˌtɜːp rə- -ˌtɜːp ə- ~**s** z
misjudg|e ˌmɪs ˈdʒʌdʒ ~**ed** d ~**es** ɪz əz ~**ing**
ɪŋ
misjudgement, misjudgment
₍ᵢ₎mɪs ˈdʒʌdʒ mənt ~**s** s
Miskin 'mɪsk ɪn §-ən
mis|lay ₍ᵢ₎mɪs ˈleɪ ~**laid** 'leɪd ~**laying** 'leɪ ɪŋ
~**lays** 'leɪz
mis|lead ₍ᵢ₎mɪs ˈliːd ~**leading/ly** 'liːd ɪŋ /li
~**leads** 'liːdz ~**led** 'led
mismanag|e ˌmɪs ˈmæn ɪdʒ ~**ed** d ~**es** ɪz əz
~**ing** ɪŋ
mismanagement ˌmɪs ˈmæn ɪdʒ mənt
mismatch _v_ ˌmɪs ˈmætʃ ~**ed** t ~**es** ɪz əz ~**ing**
ɪŋ
mismatch _n_ 'mɪs mætʃ ˌ•'• ~**es** ɪz əz
mismeasure ˌmɪs ˈmeʒ ə ‖ -əʳr -ˈmeɪʒ- ~**ment**
mənt
misnam|e ˌmɪs ˈneɪm ~**ed** d ~**es** z ~**ing** ɪŋ
misnomer ˌmɪs ˈnəʊm ə ‖ -ˈnoʊm əʳr ~**s** z
miso 'miːs əʊ ‖ -oʊ —_Jp_ ['mi so]
misogynist mɪ ˈsɒdʒ ən ɪst maɪ-, mə-, -ɪn-,
§-əst ‖ -ˈsɑːdʒ- ~**s** s
misogynistic mɪ ˌsɒdʒ ə ˈnɪst ɪk ◀ maɪ-, mə-,
-ɪn-, §-əst ‖ -ˌsɑːdʒ-
misogyny mɪ ˈsɒdʒ ən i maɪ-, mə-, -ɪn-
‖ -ˈsɑːdʒ-
misplac|e ˌmɪs ˈpleɪs ~**ed** t ◀ ~**es** ɪz əz ~**ing**
ɪŋ
misplacement ˌmɪs ˈpleɪs mənt
mis|print _v_ ˌmɪs ˈprɪnt ~**printed** 'prɪnt ɪd -əd
‖ 'prɪnt̬ əd ~**printing** 'prɪnt ɪŋ ‖ 'prɪnt̬ ɪŋ
~**prints** 'prɪnts
misprint _n_ 'mɪs prɪnt ~**s** s
misprision ˌmɪs ˈprɪʒ ən
mispronounc|e ˌmɪs prə ˈnaʊnts ~**ed** t ~**es** ɪz
əz ~**ing** ɪŋ
mispronunciation ˌmɪs prə ˌnʌnts i ˈeɪʃ ən
⚠-ˌnaʊnts- ~**s** z
misquotation ˌmɪs kwəʊ ˈteɪʃ ən ‖ -kwoʊ- ~**s**
z

mis|quote ˌmɪs ˈkwəʊt ‖ -ˈkwoʊt ~**quoted**
'kwəʊt ɪd -əd ‖ 'kwoʊt̬ əd ~**quotes**
'kwəʊts ‖ 'kwoʊts ~**quoting**
'kwəʊt ɪŋ ‖ 'kwoʊt̬ ɪŋ
mis|read _v pres_ ˌmɪs ˈriːd ~**read** _v past & pp_
'red ~**reading** 'riːd ɪŋ ~**reads** 'riːdz
misre|port ˌmɪs rɪ ˈpɔːt -rə-, §-riː- ‖ -ˈpɔːrt
-ˈpoʊrt ~**ported** 'pɔːt ɪd -əd ‖ 'pɔːrt̬ əd
'poʊrt̬- ~**porting** 'pɔːt ɪŋ ‖ 'pɔːrt̬ ɪŋ 'poʊrt̬-
~**ports** 'pɔːts ‖ 'pɔːrts 'poʊrts
misrepre|sent ˌmɪs ˌrep rɪ ˈzent -rə-,
§-riː- ‖ ˌ•, •- ~**sented** 'zent ɪd -əd ‖ 'zent̬ əd
~**senting** 'zent ɪŋ ‖ 'zent̬ ɪŋ ~**sents** 'zents
misrepresentation ˌmɪs ˌrep rɪ zen ˈteɪʃ ən
-, •rə-, §-, •riː-, -zən'• - ‖ ˌ•, •- ~**s** z
misrul|e _v, n_ ˌmɪs ˈruːl ~**ed** d ~**es** z ~**ing** ɪŋ
miss, Miss mɪs —_For the noun, when used with a_
name, there is also an occasional weak form
§məs **missed** mɪst **misses** 'mɪs ɪz -əz
missing 'mɪs ɪŋ
₍ᵢ₎Miss 'Abbott; ˌmissing 'link
missal 'mɪs əl ~**s** z
missel 'mɪs əl 'mɪz-
Missenden 'mɪs ənd ən
misshap|e _v_ ˌmɪs ˈʃeɪp →ˌmɪʃ- ~**ed** t ~**en** ən
~**es** s ~**ing** ɪŋ
misshape _n_ 'mɪs ʃeɪp →'mɪʃ- ~**s** s
missile 'mɪs aɪəl -əl ‖ -əl ~**s** z
mission 'mɪʃ ən ~**s** z
missionar|y 'mɪʃ ən ər_li -ən_əʳr- ‖ -ə ner li
~**ies** iz
'missionary poˌsition
missioner 'mɪʃ ən_ə ‖ _əʳr ~**s** z
missis 'mɪs ɪz §-əz
Mississauga ˌmɪs ɪ ˈsɔːg ə -ə- ‖ -ˈsɑːg-
Mississippi ˌmɪs ɪ ˈsɪp i -ə-
ˌMissisˌsippi 'Delta
Mississippian ˌmɪs ɪ ˈsɪp i_ən ◀ ˌ•ə- ~**s** z
missive 'mɪs ɪv ~**s** z
Missolonghi ˌmɪs ə ˈlɒŋ gi ‖ -ˈlɔːŋ- -ˈlɑːŋ-
Missoula mɪ ˈzuːl ə mə-
Missouri mɪ ˈzʊər i mə-, -ˈsʊər- ‖ -ˈzʊr i -ˈzɜː-,
-ə
Missourian mɪ ˈzʊər i_ən mə-, -ˈsʊər- ‖ -ˈzʊr-
-ˈzɜː- ~**s** z
misspell ˌmɪs ˈspel ~**ed** d ~**ing** ɪŋ ~**s** z
misspelt ˌmɪs ˈspelt ◀
misspend ˌmɪs ˈspend ~**ing** ɪŋ ~**s** z **misspent**
ˌmɪs ˈspent ◀
ˌmisspent 'youth
mis|state ˌmɪs ˈsteɪt ~**stated** 'steɪt ɪd -əd
‖ 'steɪt̬ əd ~**states** 'steɪts ~**stating**
'steɪt ɪŋ ‖ 'steɪt̬ ɪŋ
misstatement ˌmɪs ˈsteɪt mənt ~**s** s
missus 'mɪs ɪz §-əz ‖ 'mɪs əz 'mɪz-, -əs
miss|y, Missy 'mɪs li ~**ies** iz
mist mɪst **misted** 'mɪst ɪd -əd **misting**
'mɪst ɪŋ **mists** mɪsts
mistak|e _v, n_ mɪ ˈsteɪk mə- ~**en** ən ~**es** s
~**ing** ɪŋ **mistook** mɪ ˈstʊk mə-, §-ˈstuːk
mistaken mɪ ˈsteɪk ən mə- ~**ly** li ~**ness** nəs
nɪs

M

mister, M~ 'mɪst ə ‖ -ªr ~s z
  ₍ᵢ₎**Mister 'Jones**
misti... —*see* **misty**
mistim|e ˌmɪs 'taɪm ~**ed** d ~**es** z ~**ing** ɪŋ
mistle 'mɪs ªl 'mɪz-
  '**mistle thrush**
mistletoe 'mɪs ªl təʊ 'mɪz- ‖ -toʊ
mistook mɪ 'stʊk mə-, §-'stuːk
mistral 'mɪs trəl -trɑːl; mɪ 'strɑːl, mə- —*Fr*
  [mi stʁal]
mistrans|late ˌmɪs trænz 'leɪt -trɑːnz-,
  -trænʦ-, -trɑːnʦ-, -trənz-, -trənʦ- ‖ -'•|•
  ~**lated** leɪt ɪd -əd ‖ leɪt̬ əd ~**lates** leɪts
  ~**lating** leɪt ɪŋ ‖ leɪt̬ ɪŋ
mistranslation ˌmɪs trænz 'leɪʃ ªn -trɑːnz-,
  -trænʦ-, -trɑːnʦ-, -trənz-, -trənʦ- ~**s** z
mis|treat ˌmɪs ǀ'triːt ~**treated** 'triːt ɪd -əd
  ‖ 'triːt̬ əd ~**treating** 'triːt ɪŋ ‖ 'triːt̬ ɪŋ
  ~**treats** 'triːts
mistreatment ˌmɪs 'triːt mənt ~**s** s
mistress, M~ 'mɪs trəs -trɪs ~**es** ɪz əz
mistrial ˌmɪs 'traɪ_əl '•ˌ•• ~**s** z
mistrust *v, n* ˌmɪs 'trʌst ~**ed** ɪd əd ~**ing/ly**
  ɪŋ /li ~**s** s
mistrustful ˌmɪs 'trʌst fªl -fʊl ~**ly** ᵢ ~**ness** nəs
  nɪs
mist|y 'mɪst |i ~**ier** i_ə ‖ i_ªr ~**iest** i_ɪst i_əst
  ~**ily** ɪ li əl i ~**iness** i nəs i nɪs
misunder|stand ˌmɪs ˌʌnd ə ǀ'stænd ‖ -ªr- •ˌ•-
  ~**standing/s** 'stænd ɪŋ/z ~**stands** 'stændz
  ~**stood** 'stʊd
misus|e *v* ˌmɪs 'juːz →§ˌmɪʃ- ~**ed** d ~**es** ɪz əz
  ~**ing** ɪŋ
misus|e *n* ˌmɪs 'juːs →§ˌmɪʃ- ~**es** ɪz əz
MIT ˌem aɪ 'tiː ◄
Mita 'miːt ə
Mitch, mitch mɪtʃ
Mitcham 'mɪtʃ əm
Mitchel, Mitchell 'mɪtʃ ªl
Mitchison 'mɪtʃ ɪs ªn -əs-
Mitchum 'mɪtʃ əm
mite maɪt (*= might*) **mites** maɪts
miter 'maɪt ə ‖ 'maɪt̬ ªr ~**ed** d **mitering** 'maɪt
  ªr ɪŋ ‖ 'maɪt̬ ªr ɪŋ ~**s** z
Mitford 'mɪt fəd ‖ -fªrd
Mithraic mɪ 'θreɪ ɪk
Mithraism 'mɪθ reɪ ˌɪz əm -rə-; mɪθ 'reɪ, ••
Mithraist 'mɪθ reɪ ɪst -rə-, §-əst; mɪθ 'reɪ- ~**s** s
Mithras 'mɪθ ræs -rəs
Mithridates ˌmɪθ rə 'deɪt iːz -rɪ-
miti|gate 'mɪt ɪ ǀgeɪt §-ə- ‖ 'mɪt̬ ə- ~**gated**
  geɪt ɪd -əd ‖ geɪt̬ əd ~**gates** geɪts ~**gating**
  geɪt ɪŋ ‖ geɪt̬ ɪŋ
mitigation ˌmɪt ɪ 'geɪʃ ªn §-ə- ‖ ˌmɪt̬ ə-
mitochondri|on ˌmaɪt əʊ
  'kɒndr i_ǀən ‖ ˌmaɪt̬ ə 'kɑːndr- ~**a** ə ~**al** əl
mitosis ₍ᵢ₎maɪ 'təʊs ɪs §-əs ‖ -'toʊs əs
mitrailleuse ˌmɪtr aɪ 'ɜːz ‖ -ə 'jɜːz —*Fr*
  [mi tʁa jøːz]
mitral 'maɪtr əl
mitr|e 'maɪt ə ‖ 'maɪt̬ ªr ~**ed** d ~**es** z **mitring**
  'maɪt̬ ªr ɪŋ ‖ 'maɪt̬ ªr ɪŋ
  '**mitre joint**

Mitsubishi *tdmk* ˌmɪts u 'bɪʃ i ‖ ˌmiːts uː 'biːʃ iː
  —*Jp* [mi ˌtsɯ 'bi çi]
mitt mɪt **mitts** mɪts
mitten 'mɪt ªn ~**s** z
Mitterand 'miːt ə rɒ̃ 'mɪt- ‖ -rɑːn —*Fr*
  [mi tɛ ʁɑ̃]
Mitton 'mɪt ªn
Mitty 'mɪt i ‖ 'mɪt̬ i ~**ish** ɪʃ
Mitylene ˌmɪt ə 'liːn i -ɪ-, →-ªl 'iːn- ‖ ˌmɪt̬-
Mitzi 'mɪts i
mitzvah 'mɪts və
Miwok 'miː wɒk ‖ -wɑːk ~**s** s
mix mɪks **mixed** mɪkst **mixes** 'mɪks ɪz -əz
  mixing 'mɪks ɪŋ
  ˌmixed 'bag; ˌmixed 'blessing; ˌmixed
  'doubles; ˌmixed e'conomy; ˌmixed
  'farming; ˌmixed 'grill; ˌmixed 'marriage;
  ˌmixed 'metaphor
mix-and-match ˌmɪks ªn 'mætʃ ◄ -ªnd-, →-ªm-
mixed-ability ˌmɪkst ə 'bɪl ət i -ɪt i ‖ -ət̬ i
mixed up, mixed-up ˌmɪkst 'ʌp ◄
  ˌmixed-up 'kid
mixer 'mɪks ə ‖ -ªr ~**s** z
Mixtec 'miːs tek ~**s** s
mixture 'mɪks tʃə ‖ -tʃªr ~**s** z
mix-up 'mɪks ʌp ~**s** s
mizen, mizzen 'mɪz ªn ~**s** z
mizzenmast 'mɪz ªn mɑːst →-ªm-, §-mæst
  ‖ -mæst ~**s** s
mizzl|e 'mɪz ªl ~**ed** d ~**es** z ~**ing** ˌɪŋ
ml *sing.* 'mɪl i ˌliːt ə -ə- ‖ -ə ˌliːt̬ ªr *pl* z
mm *sing.* 'mɪl i ˌmiːt ə -ə- ‖ -ə ˌmiːt̬ ªr *pl* z
mnemonic nɪ 'mɒn ɪk nə-, niː-, mnɪ- ‖ -'mɑːn-
  ~**ally** ªl_i ~**s** s
Mnemosyne nɪ 'mɒz ɪn i nə-, niː-, mnɪ-,
  -'mɒs-, -ªn- ‖ -'mɑːs ªn i -'mɑːz-
mo, Mo məʊ ‖ moʊ
MO ˌem 'əʊ ‖ -'oʊ —*also see* Missouri
-mo məʊ ‖ moʊ — **twelvemo**
  'twelv məʊ ‖ -moʊ
moa 'məʊ ə ‖ 'moʊ ə ~**s** z
Moab 'məʊ æb ‖ 'moʊ-
Moabite 'məʊ ə baɪt ‖ 'moʊ- ~**s** s
moan məʊn ‖ moʊn **moaned** məʊnd ‖ moʊnd
  moaning 'məʊn ɪŋ ‖ 'moʊn ɪŋ **moans**
  məʊnz ‖ moʊnz
moat, Moat məʊt ‖ moʊt **moated** 'məʊt ɪd
  -əd ‖ 'moʊt̬ əd **moating** 'məʊt ɪŋ ‖ 'moʊt̬ ɪŋ
  moats məʊts ‖ moʊts
mob mɒb ‖ mɑːb **mobbed** mɒbd ‖ mɑːbd
  mobbing 'mɒb ɪŋ ‖ 'mɑːb ɪŋ **mobs**
  mɒbz ‖ mɑːbz
Mobberley 'mɒb ə li ‖ 'mɑːb ªr-
mobcap 'mɒb kæp ‖ 'mɑːb- ~**s** s
Moberly 'məʊb ə li ‖ 'moʊb ªr-
Mobil *tdmk* 'məʊb ªl -ɪl ‖ 'moʊb-
mobile 'məʊb aɪªl ‖ 'moʊb ªl -iːªl, -aɪªl ~**s** z
  ˌmobile 'home ‖ '••• ; ˌmobile 'library;
  ˌmobile 'phone
Mobile *place in AL* məʊ 'biːªl 'məʊb iːªl
  ‖ moʊ 'biːªl 'moʊb iːªl
mobilis... —*see* **mobiliz...**
mobility məʊ 'bɪl ət i -ɪt i ‖ moʊ 'bɪl ət̬ i

mobilization ˌməʊb əl aɪ 'zeɪʃ ən ˌ•ɪl-, -ɪ'•- ‖ ˌmoʊb əl ə- ~s z

mobiliz|e 'məʊb ə laɪz -ɪ-, -əl aɪz ‖ 'moʊb- ~**ed** d ~**es** ɪz əz ~**ing** ɪŋ

Mobius, Möbius, m~ 'mɜːb i‿əs 'məʊb- ‖ 'moʊb- 'meɪb- —*Ger* ['møː bi ʊs] ˌMobius 'strip ‖ '• • • •

mobster 'mɒb stə ‖ 'mɑːb stᵊr ~s z

Mobutu məʊ 'buːt uː ‖ moʊ-

Moby 'məʊb i ‖ 'moʊb i ˌMoby 'Dick

Mocatta məʊ 'kæt ə ‖ moʊ 'kæt̬ ə

moccasin 'mɒk əs ɪn §-ᵊn ‖ 'mɑːk- ~s z

mocha, Mocha 'mɒk ə 'məʊk- ‖ 'moʊk ə

mock mɒk ‖ mɑːk mɔːk **mocked** mɒkt ‖ mɑːkt mɔːkt **mocking/ly** 'mɒk ɪŋ /li ‖ 'mɑːk ɪŋ /li 'mɔːk- **mocks** mɒks ‖ mɑːks mɔːks ˌmock ˌturtle 'soup

mocker 'mɒk ə ‖ 'mɑːk ᵊr 'mɔːk- ~s z

mocker|y 'mɒk ᵊr i ‖ 'mɑːk- 'mɔːk- ~**ies** iz

mock-heroic ˌmɒk hə 'rəʊ ɪk ◄ -hɪ-, -he- ‖ ˌmɑːk hɪ 'roʊ ɪk ◄ ˌmɔːk- ~**ally** ᵊl‿i ~s s

mockingbird 'mɒk ɪŋ bɜːd ‖ 'mɑːk ɪŋ bɜːd 'mɔːk- ~s z

mock-up 'mɒk ʌp ‖ 'mɑːk- 'mɔːk- ~s s

mod, Mod *'modern; (adherent of, pertaining to) fashion style'* mɒd ‖ mɑːd **mods** mɒdz ‖ mɑːdz ˌmod 'con

mod, Mod *'Gaelic meeting'* mɒd məʊd ‖ moʊd —*ScG* Mòd [mɔːd]

MoD *'Ministry of Defence'* ˌem əʊ 'diː ◄ -oʊ-

modacrylic ˌmɒd ə 'krɪl ɪk ◄ ‖ ˌmɑːd- ˌmodaˌcrylic 'fibre

modal 'məʊd ᵊl ‖ 'moʊd ᵊl ~s z ˌmodal au'xiliary

modalit|y məʊ 'dæl ət i -ɪt- ‖ moʊ 'dæl ət̬ i ~**ies** iz

modally 'məʊd ᵊl i ‖ 'moʊd ᵊl i

mode məʊd ‖ moʊd **modes** məʊdz ‖ moʊdz

model 'mɒd ᵊl ‖ 'mɑːd ᵊl ~**ed, -led** d ~**er/s, -ler/s** ˌə/z ‖ ˌᵊr/z ~**ing, -ling** ˌɪŋ ~s z

modem 'məʊd em -əm ‖ 'moʊd- ~s z

Modena 'mɒd ɪn ə -ᵊn ə; mɒ 'deɪn ə, mə- ‖ 'moʊd ᵊn ə 'mɔːd-, 'mɑːd-, -ɑː: —*It* ['mɔː de na]

moderate *adj, n* 'mɒd‿ᵊr ət -ɪt ‖ 'mɑːd‿ ~**ly** li ~**ness** nəs nɪs ~s s

mode|rate *v* 'mɒd ə ˌreɪt ‖ 'mɑːd- ~**rated** reɪt ɪd -əd ‖ reɪt̬ əd ~**rates** reɪts ~**rating** reɪt ɪŋ ‖ reɪt̬ ɪŋ

moderation ˌmɒd ə 'reɪʃ ən ‖ ˌmɑːd- ~s z

moderato ˌmɒd ə 'rɑːt əʊ ‖ ˌmɑːd ə 'rɑːt̬ oʊ ~s z

moderator 'mɒd ə reɪt ə ‖ 'mɑːd ə reɪt̬ ᵊr ~s z

modern 'mɒd ᵊn ‖ 'mɑːd ᵊrn ~**ly** li ~**ness** nəs nɪs ~s z ˌModern 'English◄, ˌModern ˌEnglish 'Language; ˌModern 'Greek; ˌmodern 'jazz; ˌmodern pen'tathlon

modernis... —*see* **moderniz...**

modernism 'mɒd ə ˌnɪz əm -ᵊn ˌɪz- ‖ 'mɑːd ᵊr-

modernist 'mɒd ᵊn ɪst §-əst ‖ 'mɑːd ᵊrn- ~s s

modernistic ˌmɒd ə 'nɪst ɪk ◄ -ᵊn 'ɪst- ‖ ˌmɑːd ᵊr- ~**ally** ᵊl‿i

modernit|y mɒ 'dɜːn ət i li mə-, -ɪt- ‖ mɑː 'dɜːn ət̬ i li moʊ-, mə- ~**ies** iz

modernization ˌmɒd ə naɪ 'zeɪʃ ən -nɪ'•-; -ᵊn‿aɪ-, -ᵊn‿ɪ- ‖ ˌmɑːd ᵊrn ə- ~s z

moderniz|e 'mɒd ə naɪz -ᵊn aɪz ‖ 'mɑːd ᵊr- ~**ed** d ~**es** ɪz əz ~**ing** ɪŋ

modest 'mɒd ɪst §-əst ‖ 'mɑːd əst ~**ly** li

Modestine ˌmɒd ɪ stiːn -ə-, ˌ•• '•‖ 'mɑːd-

Modesto mə 'dest əʊ ‖ -oʊ

modest|y, M~ 'mɒd əst i li -ɪst- ‖ 'mɑːd- ~**ies** iz

modicum 'mɒd ɪk əm -ək- ‖ 'mɑːd- 'moʊd- ~s z

modification ˌmɒd ɪf ɪ 'keɪʃ ən ˌ•əf-, §-ə'•- ‖ ˌmɑːd- ~s z

modi|fy 'mɒd ɪ ˌfaɪ -ə- ‖ 'mɑːd- ~**fied** faɪd ~**fier/s** faɪ‿ə/z ‖ faɪ‿ᵊr/z ~**fies** faɪz ~**fying** faɪ ɪŋ

Modigliani ˌmɒd ɪl 'jɑːn i ‖ ˌmoʊd iːl- moʊ ˌdiːl i 'ɑːn i —*It* [mo diʎ 'ʎaː ni]

modiolus məʊ 'diː‿əl əs -'daɪ‿ ‖ moʊ 'daɪ əl əs mə-

modish 'məʊd ɪʃ ‖ 'moʊd- ~**ly** li ~**ness** nəs nɪs

modiste məʊ 'diːst ‖ moʊ- ~s s

modular 'mɒd jʊl ə -jəl-; →'mɒdʒ ʊl ə, -əl- ‖ 'mɑːdʒ ᵊl ᵊr

modularis... —*see* **modulariz...**

modularity ˌmɒd ju 'lær ət i →ˌmɒdʒ u-, -ɪt i ‖ ˌmɑːdʒ ə 'lær ət̬ i -'ler-

modularization ˌmɒd jʊl ᵊr aɪ 'zeɪʃ ᵊn ˌ•jəl-, -ɪ'•-; →ˌmɒdʒ ʊl-, ˌ•əl- ‖ ˌmɑːdʒ əl ᵊr ə-

modulariz|e 'mɒd jʊl ə raɪz '•jəl-; →'mɒdʒ ʊl-, '•əl- ‖ 'mɑːdʒ əl ə raɪz ~**ed** d ~**es** ɪz əz ~**ing** ɪŋ

modu|late 'mɒd ju ˌleɪt →'mɒdʒ u-, -ə- ‖ 'mɑːdʒ ə- ~**lated** leɪt ɪd -əd ‖ leɪt̬ əd ~**lates** leɪts ~**lating** leɪt ɪŋ ‖ leɪt̬ ɪŋ

modulation ˌmɒd ju 'leɪʃ ən →ˌmɒdʒ u-, ˌ•ə- ‖ ˌmɑːdʒ ə- ~s z

module 'mɒd juːl →'mɒdʒ uːl ‖ 'mɑːdʒ uːᵊl ~s z

modulo 'mɒd ju ləʊ -jə-‖ 'mɑːdʒ ə loʊ

modulus 'mɒd jʊl əs -jəl- ‖ 'mɑːdʒ əl əs **moduli** 'mɒd ju laɪ -liː ‖ 'mɑːdʒ ə laɪ

modus 'məʊd əs 'mɒd- ‖ 'moʊd əs ˌmodus ˌope'randi ˌɒp ə 'rænd iː -aɪ ‖ ˌɑːp-; ˌmodus vi'vendi vɪ 'vend iː §və-, -aɪ

Moesia 'miːs i‿ə 'miːz-; 'miːʃ ə, 'miːʒ ə ‖ 'miːʃ-

Moffat, Moffatt 'mɒf ət ‖ 'mɑːf-

mog, Mog mɒg ‖ mɑːg **mogs** mɒgz ‖ mɑːgz

Mogadishu ˌmɒg ə 'dɪʃ uː ‖ ˌmɑːg- ˌmɔːg-, -'diːʃ-

Mogadon *tdmk* 'mɒg ə dɒn ‖ 'mɑːg ə dɑːn

Mogador ˌmɒg ə 'dɔː '• • • ‖ ˌmɑːg ə 'dɔːr -'doʊr

Mogford 'mɒg fəd ‖ 'mɑːg fᵊrd

Mogg mɒg ‖ mɑːg

Moggach 'mɒg əx -ək ‖ 'mɑːg ək

mogg|ie, mogg|y 'mɒg li ‖ 'mɑːg li ~**ies** iz

M

Mogollon ˌməʊg ə 'jɒʊn ‖ ˌmoʊg ə 'joʊn
mogul, Mogul 'məʊg əl -ʊl, -ʌl ‖ 'moʊg-
mʊʊ 'gʌl ~s z
mohair 'məʊ heə ‖ 'moʊ her -hær
Mohamma... —see Mohamme...
Mohammed məʊ 'hæm ɪd -əd, -ed ‖ moʊ-
—Arabic [mu 'ħam mad]
Mohammedan məʊ 'hæm ɪd ən -əd- ‖ moʊ-
~ism ˌɪz əm ~s z
Mohan 'məʊ hæn -hən, -ən ‖ 'moʊ-
Mohave məʊ 'haːv i ‖ mə- moʊ- ~s z
Mohawk, m~ 'məʊ hɔːk ‖ 'moʊ- -haːk ~s s
Mohican, m~ məʊ 'hiːk ən 'məʊ ɪk- ‖ moʊ-
mə- ~s z
Moho 'məʊ həʊ ‖ 'moʊ hoʊ
Mohole 'məʊ həʊl →-hɒʊl ‖ 'moʊ hoʊl
Mohorovicic ˌməʊ hə 'rəʊv ɪ tʃɪtʃ -'•ə-
‖ ˌmoʊ hə 'roʊv- —Serbo-Croat Mohorovičić
[mɔ xɔ 'rɔ vi tʃitɕ]
Mohs məʊz ‖ moʊz —Ger [moːs]
Mohun (i) 'məʊ ən -hən ‖ 'moʊ hən; (ii) muːn
moi mwaː —Fr [mwa]
Moi African name mɔɪ
moidore ˌmɔɪ 'dɔː 'mɔɪd ɔː ‖ 'mɔɪd ɔːr -oʊr ~s
z
moietˌly 'mɔɪ ət li -ɪ- ‖ -əṭ li ~ies iz
Moir 'mɔɪ ə ‖ mɔɪᵊr
Moira 'mɔɪᵊr ə
moire mwaː ‖ mwaːr mɔːr, moʊr
moiré 'mwaːr eɪ ‖ mwaː 'reɪ 'mɔːr eɪ, 'moʊr-
Moiseivich, Moiseiwitsch mɔɪ 'zeɪ ɪ vɪtʃ -'seɪ-
moist mɔɪst moister 'mɔɪst ə ‖ -ᵊr moistest
'mɔɪst ɪst -əst
moisten 'mɔɪs ən
moistˌly 'mɔɪst ˌli ~ness nəs nɪs
moisture 'mɔɪs tʃə ‖ -tʃᵊr
moisturisˌe, moisturizˌe 'mɔɪs tʃə raɪz ~er/s
ə/z ‖ ᵊr/z
moither 'mɔɪð ə ‖ -ᵊr ~ed d moithering
'mɔɪð ᵊr ɪŋ ~s z
Mojave məʊ 'haːv i ‖ mə- moʊ-
Moˌjave 'Desert
moke məʊk ‖ moʊk mokes məʊks ‖ moʊks
molal 'məʊl əl →'mɒʊl- ‖ 'moʊl-
molar 'məʊl ə ‖ 'moʊl ᵊr ~s z
molasses məʊ 'læs ɪz -əz ‖ mə-
mold, Mold məʊld →mɒʊld ‖ moʊld molded
'məʊld ɪd →'mɒʊld-, -əd ‖ 'moʊld əd
molding/s 'məʊld ɪŋ/z →'mɒʊld-
‖ 'moʊld ɪŋ/z molds məʊldz →mɒʊldz
‖ moʊldz
Moldaviˌa mɒl 'deɪv iˌə ‖ maːl- ~an/s ən/z
moldˌer 'məʊld ə →'mɒʊld- ‖ 'moʊld ᵊr
~ered əd ‖ ᵊrd ~ering ᵊr ɪŋ ~ers əz ‖ ᵊrz
Moldova mɒl 'dəʊv ə ‖ maːl 'doʊv ə
moldˌy 'məʊld li →'mɒʊld- ‖ 'moʊld li ~ier
iˌə ‖ iˌᵊr ~iest iˌɪst iˌəst ~iness i nəs i nɪs
mole, Mole məʊl →mɒʊl ‖ moʊl moles məʊlz
→mɒʊlz ‖ moʊlz
Molech 'məʊl ek ‖ 'moʊl-
molecular mə 'lek jʊl ə məʊ-, mɒ-, -jəl-
‖ -jəl ᵊr
molecule 'mɒl ɪ kjuːl 'məʊl-, -ə- ‖ 'maːl- ~s z

molehill 'məʊl hɪl →'mɒʊl- ‖ 'moʊl- ~s z
Molesey 'məʊlz i →'mɒʊlz- ‖ 'moʊlz i
moleskin 'məʊl skɪn →'mɒʊl- ‖ 'moʊl- ~s z
molest mə 'lest məʊ- ~ed ɪd əd ~ing ɪŋ ~s s
molestation ˌməʊl e 'steɪʃ ən ‖ ˌmoʊl- ~s z
molester mə 'lest ə məʊ- ‖ -ᵊr ~s z
Molesworth 'məʊlz wɜːθ →'mɒʊlz-, -wəθ
‖ 'moʊlz wᵊrθ
Moliere, Molière 'mɒl i eə 'məʊl- ‖ moʊl 'jeᵊr
—Fr [mɔ ljɛːʁ]
Molina məʊ 'liːn ə ‖ moʊ- mə-
Moline məʊ 'liːn ‖ moʊ-
moll, Moll mɒl ‖ maːl molls mɒlz ‖ maːlz
Mollie, mollie 'mɒl i ‖ 'maːl i ~s, ~'s z
mollifiable 'mɒl ɪ faɪˌəb əl §ˌ•'•ˌ•'•• ‖ 'maːl-
mollification ˌmɒl ɪf ɪ 'keɪʃ ən ˌ•əf-, §-ə'•-
‖ ˌmaːl-
molliˌfy 'mɒl ɪ |faɪ -ə- ‖ 'maːl- ~fied faɪd
~fier/s faɪˌə/z ‖ faɪˌᵊr/z ~fies faɪz ~fying/
ly faɪ ɪŋ /li
Molloy mə 'lɔɪ
mollusc, mollusk 'mɒl əsk -ʌsk ‖ 'maːl- ~s s
Mollweide 'mɒl vaɪd ə ‖ 'mɔːl- 'maːl- —Ger
['mɔl vaɪ də]
Mollˌy, mollˌy 'mɒl li ‖ 'maːl li ~ies, ~y's iz
mollycoddlˌe 'mɒl i ˌkɒd əl ‖ 'maːl i ˌkaːd əl
~ed d ~es z ~ing ˌɪŋ
Moloch, m~ 'məʊl ɒk ‖ 'moʊl aːk 'maːl ək ~s
s
Moloney, Molony mə 'ləʊn i ‖ -'loʊn i
Molotov 'mɒl ə tɒf ‖ 'maːl ə tɔːf 'moʊl-,
'mɔːl-, -taːf —Russ ['mɔ łə təf]
ˌMolotov 'cocktail
molt məʊlt →mɒʊlt ‖ moʊlt molted 'məʊlt ɪd
→'mɒʊlt-, -əd ‖ 'moʊlt əd molting
'məʊlt ɪŋ →'mɒʊlt- ‖ 'moʊlt ɪŋ molts
məʊlts →mɒʊlts ‖ moʊlts
molten 'məʊlt ən →'mɒʊlt- ‖ 'moʊlt-
molto 'mɒlt əʊ ‖ 'moʊlt oʊ —It ['mɔl to]
Molton 'məʊlt ən →'mɒʊlt- ‖ 'moʊlt-
Moluccˌa məʊ 'lʌk lə ‖ mə- ~an/s ən/z ~as əz
moly 'məʊl i ‖ 'moʊl i
molybdate mə 'lɪbd eɪt mɒ-, məʊ- ~s s
molybdenum mə 'lɪbd ən əm mɒ-, məʊ-
molybdic mə 'lɪbd ɪk mɒ-, məʊ-
Molyneaux 'mɒl ɪ nəʊ -ə- ‖ 'maːl ə noʊ
Molyneux (i) 'mɒl ɪ njuː -ə- ‖ 'maːl-, (ii) 'mʌl-,
(iii) -njuːks
mom, Mom mɒm ‖ maːm moms, Mom's
mɒmz ‖ maːmz
Mombasa mɒm 'bæs ə -'baːs- ‖ maːm 'baːs ə
-'bæs- —Swahili [mo 'mba sa]
moment 'məʊm ənt ‖ 'moʊm- ~ly li ~s s
momenta məʊ 'ment ə ‖ moʊ 'menṭ ə
momentarily 'məʊm ənt_ᵊr əl i -ɪ li;
ˌməʊm ən 'ter əl i, -ɪ li ˌmoʊm ən 'ter əl i
momentarˌly 'məʊm ənt_ᵊr li ‖ 'moʊm ən ter li
~iness i nəs i nɪs
momentous məʊ 'ment əs ‖ moʊ 'menṭ əs mə-
~ly li ~ness nəs nɪs
momentˌum məʊ 'ment əm ‖ moʊ 'menṭ əm
mə- ~a ə
momma, Momma 'mɒm ə ‖ 'maːm ə ~s, ~'s z

momm|ie, momm|y, M~ 'mɒm |i ‖ 'mɑːm |i
~ies, ~y's iz
Momus 'məʊm əs ‖ 'moʊm-
Mon *name of language or people* məʊn mɒn
‖ moʊn
Mon. —*see* Monday
Mona, mona 'məʊn ə ‖ 'moʊn ə ~s, ~'s z
,Mona 'Lisa
Monaco 'mɒn ə kəʊ mə 'nɑːk əʊ ‖ 'mɑːn ə koʊ
mə 'nɑːk oʊ —*Fr* [mɔ na ko], *It* ['mɔː na ko]
monad 'mɒn æd 'məʊn- ‖ 'moʊn- ~s z
Monadhliadh ,məʊn ə 'liː‿ə ‖ ,moʊn-
monadic mɒ 'næd ɪk məʊ‿ ‖ moʊ- mə-
monadism 'mɒn ə ,dɪz əm 'məʊn-, -æd ,ɪz-
‖ 'moʊn æd ,ɪz-
monadnock, M~ mə 'næd nɒk ‖ -nɑːk ~s s
Monaghan, Monahan 'mɒn ə hən ‖ 'mɑːn-
-hæn
monandrous mɒ 'nændr əs mə- ‖ mə-
monarch 'mɒn ək §-ɑːk ‖ 'mɑːn ᵊrk -ɑːrk ~s s
monarchal mə 'nɑːk ᵊl mɒ- ‖ mə 'nɑːrk- mɑː-
~ly i
monarchic mə 'nɑːk ɪk mɒ- ‖ mə 'nɑːrk- mɑː-
~ally ᵊl‿i
monarchism 'mɒn ə ,kɪz əm ‖ 'mɑːn ᵊr- -ɑːr-
monarchist 'mɒn ək ɪst §-əst ‖ 'mɑːn ᵊrk-
-ɑːrk- ~s s
monarch|y 'mɒn ək |i ‖ 'mɑːn ᵊrk |i -ɑːrk- ~ies
iz
Monash 'mɒn æʃ ‖ 'mɑːn-
monasterial ,mɒn ə 'stɪᵊr i‿əl ◂ ‖ ,mɑːn ə 'stɪr-
monastery 'mɒn əs tᵊr_i ‖ 'mɑːn ə ster i
monastic mə 'næst ɪk mɒ- ~ally ᵊl‿i ~s s
monasticism mə 'næst ɪ ,sɪz əm mɒ-, -ə-
Monastir ,mɒn ə 'stɪə ‖ ,mɑːn ə 'stɪᵊr
monatomic ,mɒn ə 'tɒm ɪk ◂ ‖ ,mɑːn ə 'tɑːm-
monaural mɒn 'ɔːr əl ◂ ‖ ,mɑːn- ~ly i
Monchen-Gladbach, Mönchen-Gladbach
,mʌntʃ ən 'glæd bæk →-əŋ- —*Ger*
[,mœn çᵊn 'glat bax]
Monck mʌŋk
Monckton 'mʌŋkt ən
Moncreiff, Moncreiffe, Moncrieff,
Moncrieffe mən 'kriːf →-məŋ-, mɒn- ‖ mɑːn-
Mond mɒnd ‖ mɑːnd —*Ger* [mɔnt]
Mondale 'mɒn deɪᵊl ‖ 'mɑːn-
Monday 'mʌnd eɪ -i —*See note at* -day ~s, ~'s
z
,Monday 'morning, that ,Monday
'morning ,feeling; 'Monday Club
Mondeo *tdmk* ₍ᵢ₎mɒn 'deɪ əʊ ‖ ,mɑːn 'deɪ oʊ
~s z
mondo, Mondo 'mɒnd əʊ ‖ 'mɑːnd oʊ
Mondrian 'mɒndr i ɑːn ,•‿•‿• ‖ 'mɔːndr-
'mɑːndr- —*Dutch* ['mɔn driː aːn]
monecious mɒ 'niːʃ əs mə- ‖ mɑː-
Monegasque, Monégasque ,mɒn ɪ 'gæsk ◂
-ə- ‖ ,mɑːn- ~s s —*Fr* [mɔ ne gask]
moneme 'mɒn iːm 'məʊn- ‖ 'moʊn- ~s z
monera, M~ 'nɪᵊr ə mɒ-, məʊ- ‖ mə 'nɪr ə
mɑː-, moʊ-
Monet 'mɒn eɪ ‖ moʊ 'neɪ —*Fr* [mɔ nɛ]

monetarism 'mʌn ɪt ə ,rɪz əm 'mɒn-, '•ət-
‖ 'mɑːn ə tə- 'mʌn-
monetarist 'mʌn ɪt‿ər ɪst 'mɒn-, '•ət‿, §-əst
‖ 'mɑːn ə tər əst 'mʌn- ~s s
monetary 'mʌn ɪt‿ər i 'mɒn-, '•ət‿
‖ 'mɑːn ə ter i 'mʌn-
money, Money 'mʌn i moneyed, monied
'mʌn id moneys, monies 'mʌn iz
'money ,market; 'money ,order; 'money
,spider; 'money sup,ply
moneybags 'mʌn i bægz
moneybox 'mʌn i bɒks ‖ -bɑːks ~es ɪz əz
moneychanger 'mʌn i ,tʃeɪndʒ ə ‖ -ᵊr ~s z
moneygrub|ber/s 'mʌn i ,grʌb |ə/z ‖ -|ᵊr/z
~bing ɪŋ
moneylend|er/s 'mʌn i ,lend |ə/z ‖ -|ᵊr/z ~ing
ɪŋ
moneymak|er/s 'mʌn i ,meɪk |ə/z ‖ -|ᵊr/z ~ing
ɪŋ
Moneypenny 'mʌn i ,pen i 'mɒn- ‖ 'mɑːn-
moneyspinner 'mʌn i ,spɪn ə ‖ -ᵊr ~s z
moneywort 'mʌn i wɜːt §-wɔːt ‖ -wɝːt -wɔːrt
monger 'mʌŋ gə ‖ 'mɑːŋ gᵊr 'mʌŋ- ~s z
Mongol, m~ 'mɒŋ gᵊl -gɒl ‖ 'mɑːŋ-
'mɑːn goʊl, →'mɑːŋ- ~s z
Mongoli|a mɒŋ 'gəʊl i‿ə ‖ mɑːŋ 'goʊl- mɑːn-
~an/s ən/z
Mongolic mɒŋ 'gɒl ɪk ‖ mɑːn 'gɑːl ɪk →mɑːŋ-
mongolism 'mɒŋ gə ,lɪz əm -gɒ- ‖ 'mɑːn-
→'mɑːŋ-
Mongoloid, m~ 'mɒŋ gə lɔɪd ‖ 'mɑːn-
→'mɑːŋ- ~s z
mongoos|e 'mɒŋ guːs 'mʌŋ- ‖ 'mɑːn-
→'mɑːŋ- ~es ɪz əz
mongrel 'mʌŋ grəl ‖ 'mɑːŋ- ~ism ,ɪz əm ~s z
mongrelis... —*see* mongreliz...
mongrelization ,mʌŋ grəl aɪ 'zeɪʃ ᵊn -ɪ'•-
‖ -ə'•- ,mɑːŋ-
mongreliz|e 'mʌŋ grə laɪz ‖ 'mɑːŋ- ~ed d
~es ɪz əz ~ing ɪŋ
Monica 'mɒn ɪk ə §-ək- ‖ 'mɑːn-
monicker 'mɒn ɪk ə ‖ 'mɑːn ɪk ᵊr ~s z
monie... —*see* money
Monifieth ,mɒn ɪ 'fiːθ
moniker 'mɒn ɪk ə ‖ 'mɑːn ɪk ᵊr ~s z
monilia mɒ 'nɪl i‿ə mə- ‖ moʊ-
moniliform mɒ 'nɪl ɪ fɔːm mə-, -ə-
‖ moʊ 'nɪl ə fɔːrm
Monique mɒ 'niːk ‖ moʊ- mə- —*Fr* [mɔ nik]
monism 'mɒn ,ɪz əm ‖ 'moʊn- 'mɑːn-
monist 'mɒn ɪst §-əst ‖ 'moʊn- 'mɑːn- ~s s
monistic mɒ 'nɪst ɪk mə- ‖ moʊ- mɑː- ~ally
ᵊl‿i
monitor 'mɒn ɪt ə -ət- ‖ 'mɑːn ət ᵊr ~ed d
monitoring 'mɒn ɪt‿ər ɪŋ '•ət‿ ‖ 'mɑːn ət
ᵊr ɪŋ →'mɑːn ətr ɪŋ ~s z
monk, Monk mʌŋk monks mʌŋks
monkey 'mʌŋk i ~ed d ~ing ɪŋ ~s z
'monkey ,business; 'monkey nut; 'monkey
wrench
monkey-puzzle 'mʌŋk i ,pʌz ᵊl ~s z
monkfish 'mʌŋk fɪʃ

M

Mon-Khmer ˌməʊn ˈkmeə ◄ ˌməʊn kə ˈmeə
‖ ˌmoʊn ˈkmeᵊr ˌmoʊn kə ˈmeᵊr
monkhood ˈmʌŋk hʊd
Monkhouse ˈmʌŋk haʊs
monkish ˈmʌŋk ɪʃ **~ly** li **~ness** nəs nɪs
Monkton ˈmʌŋk tən
Monmouth ˈmɒn məθ ˈmʌn-, →ˈmɒm-
‖ ˈmɑːn-
Monmouthshire ˈmɒn məθ ʃə ˈmʌn-,
→ˈmɒm-, -ʃɪə ‖ ˈmɑːn məθ ʃᵊr -ʃɪr
Monnow ˈmɒn əʊ ˈmʌn- ‖ ˈmɑːn oʊ
mono ˈmɒn əʊ ‖ ˈmɑːn oʊ
Mono *lake in CA* ˈməʊn əʊ ‖ ˈmoʊn oʊ
mono- *comb. form*
  with stress-neutral suffix ˌmɒn əʊ ‖ ˌmɑːn ə
  -oʊ, *but before a vowel always* -əʊ ‖ -oʊ —
  monochord ˈmɒn əʊ kɔːd ‖ ˈmɑːn ə kɔːrd —
  monoacidic ˌmɒn əʊ ə ˈsɪd ɪk ◄ -æˈ• -
  ‖ ˌmɑːn oʊ-
  with stress-imposing suffix mə ˈnɒ+ mɒ-
  ‖ mə ˈnɑː+ mɑː- — **monology** mə ˈnɒl ədʒ i
  mɒ- ‖ mə ˈnɑːl- mɑː-
Monoceros mə ˈnɒs ər əs ‖ -ˈnɑːs-
monochrome ˈmɒn ə krəʊm -əʊ-
‖ ˈmɑːn ə kroʊm
monocle ˈmɒn ək ᵊl ‖ ˈmɑːn ɪk- **~d** d **~s** z
monoclonal ˌmɒn əʊ
  ˈkləʊn ᵊl ◄ ‖ ˌmɑːn ə ˈkloʊn ᵊl ◄ -oʊ-
monocoque ˈmɒn əʊ kɒk ‖ ˈmɑːn ə koʊk
  -kɑːk **~s** s
monocot ˈmɒn əʊ kɒt ‖ ˈmɑːn ə kɑːt **~s** s
monocotyledon ˌmɒn əʊ ˌkɒt ə ˈliːd ᵊn -ɪˈ• -,
  -ᵊl ˈiːd- ‖ ˌmɑːn ə ˌkɑːt ᵊl ˈiːd ᵊn **~s** z
monocular mɒ ˈnɒk jʊl ə mə-, -jəl-
‖ mɑː ˈnɑːk jəl ᵊr
monoculture ˈmɒn əʊ ˌkʌltʃ ə
‖ ˈmɑːn ə ˌkʌltʃ ᵊr
monod|y ˈmɒn əd |i ‖ ˈmɑːn- **~ies** iz
monoecious mɒ ˈniːʃ əs mə- ‖ mɑː- **~ly** li
monofil ˈmɒn əʊ fɪl ‖ ˈmɑːn ə-
monogamist mə ˈnɒg əm ɪst mɒ-, §-əst
‖ -ˈnɑːg- **~s** s
monogamous mə ˈnɒg əm əs mɒ- ‖ -ˈnɑːg-
  ~ly li
monogamy mə ˈnɒg əm i mɒ- ‖ -ˈnɑːg-
monogenetic ˌmɒn əʊ dʒə ˈnet ɪk ◄ -dʒɪˈ• -
‖ ˌmɑːn ə dʒə ˈnet ɪk ◄
monoglot ˈmɒn əʊ glɒt ‖ ˈmɑːn ə glɑːt **~s** s
monogram ˈmɒn ə græm ‖ ˈmɑːn- **~med** d **~s**
  z
monograph ˈmɒn ə grɑːf -græf ‖ ˈmɑːn ə græf
  ~s s
monogyny mə ˈnɒdʒ ən i mɒ-, -ɪn- ‖ -ˈnɑːdʒ-
monolingual ˌmɒn əʊ ˈlɪŋ gwəl ◄
  ˌ• • ˈlɪŋ gjuː_əl ‖ ˌmɑːn ə- ˌmoʊn- **~s** z
monolith ˈmɒn ə lɪθ -ᵊl ɪθ ‖ ˈmɑːn- **~s** s
monolithic ˌmɒn ə ˈlɪθ ɪk ◄ -ᵊl ˈɪθ- ‖ ˌmɑːn-
  ~ally ᵊl_i
monolog, monologue ˈmɒn ə lɒg -ᵊl ɒg
‖ ˈmɑːn ᵊl ɔːg -ɑːg **~s** z
monologuist ˈmɒn ə lɒg ɪst -ᵊl ɒg-, §-əst
‖ ˈmɑːn ᵊl ɔːg əst -ɑːg- **~s** s
monomania ˌmɒn əʊ ˈmeɪn i_ə ‖ ˌmɑːn ə-

monomaniac ˌmɒn əʊ ˈmeɪn i æk ‖ ˌmɑːn ə-
  ~s s
monomark, M~ *tdmk* ˈmɒn əʊ
  mɑːk ‖ ˈmɑːn ə mɑːrk **~s** s
monomer ˈmɒn əm ə ‖ ˈmɑːn əm ᵊr **~s** z
monomeric ˌmɒn ə ˈmer ɪk ◄ ‖ ˌmɑːn-
monomial mɒ ˈnəʊm i_əl mə- ‖ mɑː ˈnoʊm-
  ~s z
monomorphemic ˌmɒn əʊ
  mɔː ˈfiːm ɪk ◄ ‖ ˌmɑːn ə mɔːr-
Monongahela mə ˌnɒŋ gə ˈhiːl ə ◄ ‖ -nɑːŋ-
  Mo ˌnonga ˌhela ˈRiver
mononucleosis ˌmɒn əʊ ˌnjuːk li ˈəʊs ɪs
  §-ˌnuːk-, §-əs ‖ ˌmɑːn oʊ ˌnuːk li ˈoʊs əs
  -ˌnjuːk-
monophonic ˌmɒn əʊ ˈfɒn ɪk ◄
‖ ˌmɑːn ə ˈfɑːn ɪk ◄ -ˈfoʊn- **~ally** ᵊl_i
monophthong ˈmɒn əf θɒŋ -əp-, -ə-
‖ ˈmɑːn əf θɔːŋ -ə-, -θɑːŋ **~ing** ɪŋ **~s** z
monophthongal ˌmɒn əf ˈθɒŋ gᵊl ◄ -əp-, -ə-
‖ ˌmɑːn əf ˈθɔːŋ gᵊl ◄ -ə-, -ˈθɑːŋ- **~ly** li
monophthongis... —*see* **monophthongiz...**
monophthongization
  ˌmɒn əf θɒŋ gaɪ ˈzeɪʃ ᵊn, ˌ• əp-, ˌ• ə-, -aɪ ˈ• -,
  -gɪ ˈ• -, -ɪ ˈ• - ‖ ˌmɑːn əf θɔːŋ gə- ˌ• • θɑːŋ-,
  -ə ˈ• - **~s** z
monophthongiz|e ˈmɒn əf θɒŋ gaɪz ˈ• əp-,
  -aɪz ‖ ˈmɑːn əf θɔːŋ gaɪz ˈ• ə-, -θɑːŋ • , -aɪz
  ~ed d **~es** ɪz əz **~ing** ɪŋ
Monophysite mə ˈnɒf ɪ saɪt -ə- ‖ mə ˈnɑːf ə-
  ~s s
monoplane ˈmɒn ə pleɪn ‖ ˈmɑːn- **~s** z
Monopole, m~ ˈmɒn ə pəʊl →-pɒʊl
‖ ˈmɑːn ə poʊl **~s** z
monopolie... —*see* **monopoly**
monopolis... —*see* **monopoliz...**
monopolist mə ˈnɒp ᵊl ɪst §-əst ‖ -ˈnɑːp- **~s** s
monopolistic mə ˌnɒp ə ˈlɪst ɪk ◄ ‖ -ˌnɑːp-
  ~ally ᵊl_i
monopolization mə ˌnɒp ə laɪ ˈzeɪʃ ᵊn -ɪ ˈ• -
‖ -ˌnɑːp ᵊl ə- **~s** z
monopoliz|e mə ˈnɒp ə laɪz ‖ -ˈnɑːp- **~ed** d
  ~es ɪz əz **~ing** ɪŋ
monopol|y, M~ *tdmk* mə ˈnɒp ᵊl |i ‖ -ˈnɑːp-
  ~ies iz
monopson|y mə ˈnɒps ən |i ‖ -ˈnɑːps- **~ies** iz
monorail ˈmɒn əʊ reɪᵊl ‖ ˈmɑːn ə- **~s** z
monosodium ˌmɒn əʊ
  ˈsəʊd i_əm ◄ ‖ ˌmɑːn ə ˈsoʊd-
  ˌmono ˌsodium ˈglutamate
monospac|e ˈmɒn əʊ speɪs ‖ ˈmɑːn oʊ- **~ed** t
  ~es ɪz əz **~ing** ɪŋ
monosyllabic ˌmɒn əʊ sɪ ˈlæb ɪk ◄ -səˈ• -
‖ ˌmɑːn ə sə- **~ally** ᵊl_i
monosyllable ˈmɒn əʊ ˌsɪl əb ᵊl, ˌ• • ˈ• • •
‖ ˈmɑːn ə- **~s** z
monotheism ˈmɒn əʊ θi ˌɪz əm ˈ• • • ˌθiː ɪz əm;
  mə ˈnɒθ i ˌɪz əm ‖ ˈmɑːn ə-
monotheist ˈmɒn əʊ θi ɪst -ˌθiː ɪst, §-əst;
  mə ˈnɒθ i • ‖ ˈmɑːn ə- **~s** s
monotheistic ˌmɒn əʊ θi ˈɪst ɪk ◄ , ˌ• • ˌθiː ˈ• • ;
  mə ˌnɒθ i ˈ• - ‖ ˌmɑːn ə-
monotone ˈmɒn ə təʊn ‖ ˈmɑːn ə toʊn **~s** z

monotonous mə 'nɒt ən əs ‖ -'naːt ᵊn‿əs **~ly**
  li **~ness** nəs nɪs
monotony mə 'nɒt ən i ‖ -'naːt ᵊn i
monotreme 'mɒn əʊ triːm ‖ 'maːn ə- **~s** z
monotype, M~ tdmk 'mɒn əʊ taɪp ‖ 'maːn ə-
  ~s s
monoxide mə 'nɒks aɪd mɒ- ‖ mə 'naːks-
  maː- **~s** z
Monro, Monroe mən 'rəʊ ˌmʌn-, ˌmɒn-
  ‖ -'roʊ
Monrovia mən 'rəʊv i‿ə mɒn- ‖ -'roʊv-
mons, Mons mɒnz ‖ maːnz —Fr [mɔ̃ːs]
  mons 'veneris 'ven ər ɪs §-əs
Monsanto tdmk mɒn 'sænt əʊ ‖ maːn 'sænt oʊ
Monsarrat 'mɒn sə ræt ˌ•'•' ‖ ˌmaːn sə 'raːt
  -'ræt
Monsieur, m~ mə 'sjɜː; 'mʊs jɜː, -jə ‖ məs 'juː
  →məʃ-, -'jɜˑ; mə 'sɪᵊr —There is an
  occasional weak form mə sjə —Fr [mə sjø]
Monsignor, m~ mɒn 'siːn jə ‖ maːn 'siːn jᵊr
  —It [mon siɲ 'ɲoːr]
monsoon ˌmɒn 'suːn ◂ mɒn-, mən- ‖ ˌmaːn-
  ~s z
  ˌmonsoon 'low
monster 'mɒnˡst ə ‖ 'maːnˡst ᵊr **~s** z
monstera mɒn 'stɪər ə 'mɒnˡst ᵊr ə ‖ 'maːnˡst
  ᵊr ə **~s** z
monstranc|e 'mɒnˡts trənˡts ‖ 'maːnˡts- **~es** ɪz
  əz
monstrosit|y mɒn 'strɒs ət i mən-, -ɪt-
  ‖ maːn 'straːs ət̬ i **~ies** iz
monstrous 'mɒnˡs trəs ‖ 'maːnˡts- **~ly** li **~ness**
  nəs nɪs
Mont mɒnt ‖ maːnt —but in names of
  mountains mɒ̃, mɒn ‖ mɔːn, maːn, moʊn —Fr
  [mɔ̃]
  ˌMont 'Blanc blɒ̃ blɒŋ ‖ blaːŋ —Fr [blɑ̃]
montag|e mɒn 'taːʒ mɒ̃-, '•• ‖ maːn- moʊn-
  —Fr [mɔ̃ taːʒ] **~es** ɪz əz
Montagu, Montague 'mɒnt ə gjuː ‖ 'maːnt̬-
  ~s, ~'s z
Montaigne mɒn 'teɪn ‖ maːn- moʊn- —Fr
  [mɔ̃ tɛnj]
montan 'mɒnt ən -æn ‖ 'maːnt ᵊn
Montan|a mɒn 'tæn ə -'taːn- ‖ maːn- **~an/s**
  ən/z
montane 'mɒnt eɪn ‖ ˌmaːn 'teɪn '••
montbretia mɒn 'briːʃ ə →mɒm- ‖ maːn- **~s**
  z
Monte, monte 'mɒnt i ‖ 'maːnt̬ i —It
  ['mon te]
  ˌMonte 'Carlo —Fr [mɔ̃ te kaʁ lo]
Montebello ˌmɒnt ɪ 'bel əʊ -ə- ‖ ˌmaːnt̬
  ə 'bel oʊ
Montefiore ˌmɒnt ɪ fi 'ɔːr i -ə-, -eɪ ‖ ˌmaːnt̬-
Montego mɒn 'tiːg əʊ ‖ maːn 'tiːg oʊ
  Monˌtego 'Bay
Monteith, m~ mɒn 'tiːθ ‖ maːn- **~s** s
Montel ˌmɒn 'tel ◂ ‖ ˌmaːn-
Montenegrin ˌmɒnt ɪ 'niːg rɪn ◂ -ə-, -'neɪg-,
  -'neg-, §-rən ‖ ˌmaːnt̬ ə- **~s** z
Montenegro ˌmɒnt ɪ 'niːg rəʊ -ə-, -'neɪg-,
  -'neg- ‖ ˌmaːnt̬ ə 'niːg roʊ -'neg-

Monterey place in CA, **Monterrey** place in
  Mexico ˌmɒnt ə 'reɪ -ɪ- ‖ ˌmaːnt̬- —Sp
  [mon te 'rrei]
Montesquieu ˌmɒnt e 'skjɜː -'skjuː, '•••
  ‖ ˌmaːnt̬ ə 'skjuː ˌmoʊnt̬- —Fr [mɔ̃ tɛs kjø]
Montessori ˌmɒnt ə 'sɔːr i -e-, -ɪ- ‖ ˌmaːnt̬-
  -'soʊr- —It [mon tes 'sɔː ri]
Monteux mɒn 'tɜː ‖ moʊn 'tʌ —Fr [mɔ̃ tø]
Monteverdi ˌmɒnt ɪ 'veəd i -ə-, -'vɜːd-
  ‖ ˌmaːnt̬ ə 'verd i ˌmɔːnt̬-, -'vɜːɪd- —It
  [mon te 'ver di]
Montevideo ˌmɒnt ɪ vɪ 'deɪ əʊ ˌ•ə-, §-və'•-,
  ˌ•••'vɪd i əʊ ‖ ˌmaːnt̬ ə və 'deɪ oʊ
  ˌ•••'vɪd i oʊ
Montezuma ˌmɒnt ɪ 'zuːm ə -ə-, -'zjuːm-
  ‖ ˌmaːnt̬-
Montfort 'mɒnt fət -fɔːt ‖ 'maːnt fᵊrt —Fr
  [mɔ̃ fɔːʁ]
Montgolfier, m~ mɒnt 'gɒlf i‿ə →mɒŋk-, -eɪ
  ‖ maːnt 'gaːlf i‿ᵊr •,•i 'eɪ —Fr [mɔ̃ gɔl fje]
  ~s z
Montgomerie, Montgomery (i) mənt 'gʌm
  ər‿i mən-, mɒnt-, mɒn- ‖ maːnt-, (ii)
  -'gɒm- ‖ -'gaːm-
month mʌntᵗθ **months** mʌntᵗθs →mʌnᵗs
month|ly 'mʌntᵗθ ‖li **~lies** liz
Monticello ˌmɒnt ɪ 'tʃel əʊ -'sel- ‖ ˌmaːnt̬
  ɪ 'tʃel oʊ -'sel-
Montmartre mɒn 'maːtr →mɒm-, -'maːtr ə
  ‖ moʊn 'maːr trə mɔːn- —Fr [mɔ̃ maʁtχ]
Montmorency ˌmɒnt mə 'ren ᵗs i ‖ ˌmaːnt-
Montpelier, Montpellier mɒnt 'pel i‿ə mɒm-,
  -eɪ ‖ maːn pel 'jeɪ ˌmɔːn-, ˌmaːn- —but the
  place in VT is -'piːl i‿ə ‖ maːnt 'piːl i‿ᵊr —Fr
  [mɔ̃ pə lje, -pɛ-]
Montreal ˌmɒntr i 'ɔːl ◂ ‖ ˌmaːntr- ˌmʌntr-,
  -'aːl —Fr Montréal [mɔ̃ ʁe al]
Montreux mɒn 'trɜː -'trəʊ ‖ moʊn 'trʊ -'truː
  —Fr [mɔ̃ tʁø]
Montrose mɒn 'trəʊz mən- ‖ maːn 'troʊz
Mont-Saint-Michel ˌmɒnt ˌsæn mɪ 'ʃel ˌmɒ̃-,
  →-ˌsæm-, -miː- ‖ ˌmoʊn- ˌmɔːn-, ˌmaːn-
  —Fr [mɔ̃ sæ̃ mi ʃel]
Montserrat ˌmɒnts ə 'ræt -se-, '••• ‖ ˌmaːnts-
  -'raːt —In the West Indies, locally usually '•••
  —Catalan [munt sə 'rrat]
Montserratian ˌmɒnts ə 'reɪʃ ᵊn ◂ -se-
  ‖ ˌmaːnts- **~s** z
Monty 'mɒnt i ‖ 'maːnt i
monument, M~ 'mɒn ju mənt -jə ‖ 'maːn jə-
  ~s s
monumental ˌmɒn ju 'ment ᵊl ◂ -jə-
  ‖ ˌmaːn jə 'ment̬ ᵊl ◂ **~ly** i
Monymusk ˌmɒn i 'mʌsk ‖ ˌmaːn-
Monza 'mɒnz ə ‖ 'maːnz ə —It ['mon tsa]
Monzie mɒ 'niː mə- ‖ maː-
moo muː **mooed** muːd (= mood) **mooing**
  'muː ɪŋ **moos** muːz
mooch muːtʃ **mooched** muːtʃt **mooches**
  'muːtʃ ɪz -əz **mooching** 'muːtʃ ɪŋ
moocow 'muː kaʊ **~s** z
mood muːd **moods** muːdz
Moodey, Moodie 'muːd i

M

mood|y, Moody 'mu:d |i ~ier i_ə ‖ i_ər ~iest
i_ɪst i_əst ~ily ɪ li əl i ~iness i nəs i nɪs
Moog tdmk məʊg mu:g ‖ moʊg
‚Moog 'synthesizer
moola, moolah 'mu:l ə
mooli 'mu:l i
moon, Moon mu:n mooned mu:nd
mooning 'mu:n ɪŋ moons mu:nz
'moon shot
moonbeam 'mu:n bi:m →'mu:m- ~s z
moon|calf 'mu:n |ka:f →'mu:ŋ-, §-kæf ‖ -|kæf
~calves ka:vz §kævz ‖ kævz
Moonee, Mooney, Moonie 'mu:n i ~s z
mooni... —see moony
moon|light 'mu:n |laɪt ~lighter/s laɪt ə/z
‖ laɪt̬ ər/z ~lighting laɪt ɪŋ ‖ laɪt̬ ɪŋ
‚moonlight 'flit
moonlit 'mu:n lɪt
moonscape 'mu:n skeɪp ~s s
moonshine 'mu:n ʃaɪn
moonshiner 'mu:n ʃaɪn ə ‖ -ər ~s z
moonstone 'mu:n stəʊn ‖ -stoʊn ~s z
moonstruck 'mu:n strʌk
moon|y 'mu:n |i ~ier i_ə ‖ i_ər ~iest i_ɪst i_əst
~ily ɪ li əl i
moor, Moor mʊə mɔ: ‖ mʊər moored mʊəd
mɔ:d ‖ mʊərd mooring 'mʊər ɪŋ 'mɔ:r-
‖ 'mʊər ɪŋ
moorcock, M~ 'mʊə kɒk 'mɔ:- ‖ 'mʊr ka:k
Moorcroft 'mʊə krɒft 'mɔ:- ‖ 'mʊr krɔ:ft
-kra:ft
Moore mʊə mɔ: ‖ mʊər mɔ:r, moʊr
Moorgate 'mʊə geɪt 'mɔ:- ‖ 'mʊr-
Moorhead 'mʊə hed 'mɔ:- ‖ 'mʊr-
moorhen 'mʊə hen 'mɔ:- ‖ 'mʊr- ~s z
Moorhouse 'mʊə haʊs 'mɔ:- ‖ 'mʊr-
moorings 'mʊər ɪŋz 'mɔ:r- ‖ 'mʊr ɪŋz
Moorish 'mʊər ɪʃ 'mɔ:r- ‖ 'mʊr ɪʃ
moorland, M~ 'mʊə lənd 'mɔ:-, -lænd ‖ 'mʊr-
~s z
moose mu:s
moot mu:t mooted 'mu:t ɪd -əd ‖ 'mu:t̬ əd
mooting 'mu:t ɪŋ ‖ 'mu:t̬ ɪŋ moots mu:ts
‚moot 'point; ‚moot 'question
Moots mu:ts
mop mɒp ‖ ma:p mopped mɒpt ‖ ma:pt
mopping 'mɒp ɪŋ ‖ 'ma:p ɪŋ mops
mɒps ‖ ma:ps
mope məʊp ‖ moʊp moped məʊpt ‖ moʊpt
mopes məʊps ‖ moʊps moping
'məʊp ɪŋ ‖ 'moʊp ɪŋ
moped n 'məʊ ped ‖ 'moʊ- ~s z
mopoke 'məʊp əʊk ‖ 'moʊp oʊk ~s s
mopp... —see mop
moppet 'mɒp ɪt §-ət ‖ 'ma:p- ~s s
Mopsy 'mɒps i ‖ 'ma:ps i
mop-up 'mɒp ʌp ‖ 'ma:p- ~s s
moquette mɒ 'ket məʊ- ‖ moʊ-
mor|a 'mɔ:r |ə ‖ 'moʊr- ~ae i: ~as əz
Morag 'mɔ:r æg ‖ 'moʊr-
moraic mɔ: 'reɪ ɪk ‖ moʊ-
moraine mə 'reɪn mɒ- ~s z

moral 'mɒr əl ‖ 'mɔ:r əl 'ma:r- ~s z
‚Moral Ma'jority; ‚Moral Re'armament
morale mə 'ra:l mɒ- ‖ mə 'ræl (*)
moralis... —see moraliz...
moralist 'mɒr əl ɪst §-əst ‖ 'mɔ:r- 'ma:r- ~s s
moralistic ‚mɒr ə 'lɪst ɪk ◀ ‖ ‚mɔ:r- ‚ma:r-
~ally əl_i
moralit|y mə 'ræl ət i mɒ-, -ɪt- ‖ mə 'ræl ət̬ i
mɔ:- ~ies iz
mo'rality play
moraliz|e 'mɒr ə laɪz ‖ 'mɔ:r- 'ma:r- ~ed d
~er/s ə/z ‖ ər/z ~es ɪz əz ~ing ɪŋ
morally 'mɒr əl i ‖ 'mɔ:r- 'ma:r-
Moran (i) 'mɔ:r ən 'mɒr-, (ii) mə 'ræn
mɒ- ‖ mɑ:-
Morant mə 'rænt mɒ- ‖ mɔ:-
morass mə 'ræs mɒ- ‖ mɔ:- ~es ɪz əz
moratori|um ‚mɒr ə 'tɔ:r i_|əm ‖ ‚mɔ:r-
‚ma:r-, -'toʊr- ~a ə ~ums əmz
Moravi|a mə 'reɪv i_|ə mɒ- ~an/s ən/z
moray 'kind of eel' 'mɒr eɪ 'mɔ:r-; mə 'reɪ, mɒ-
‖ 'mɔ:r eɪ 'moʊr-; mə 'reɪ ~s z
Moray 'mʌr i △'mɒr-, -eɪ ‖ 'mɜ:ˈ i (= Murray)
morbid 'mɔ:b ɪd §-əd ‖ 'mɔ:rb- ~ly li ~ness
nəs nɪs
morbidezza ‚mɔ:b ɪ 'dets ə §-ə- ‖ ‚mɔ:rb- —It
[mor bi 'det tsa]
morbidit|y mɔ: 'bɪd ət i -ɪt- ‖ mɔ:r 'bɪd ət̬ i
~ies iz
mordancy 'mɔ:d ənts i ‖ 'mɔ:rd-
mordant 'mɔ:d ənt ‖ 'mɔ:rd- ~ly li ~s s
Mordecai 'mɔ:d ɪ kaɪ -ə-; • • 'keɪ aɪ, • • 'kaɪ i
‖ 'mɔ:rd-
Morden 'mɔ:d ən ‖ 'mɔ:rd-
mordent 'mɔ:d ənt ‖ 'mɔ:rd- ~s s
Mordor 'mɔ:d ɔ: ‖ 'mɔ:rd ɔ:r
Mordvin 'mɔ:d vɪn ‖ 'mɔ:rd-
more, More mɔ: ‖ mɔ:r moʊr
Morea mɔ: 'riə mɒ-, mə- ‖ mɔ: 'ri: ə moʊ-
Morecambe, Morecombe 'mɔ:k əm ‖ 'mɔ:rk-
moreish 'mɔ:r ɪʃ ‖ 'moʊr-
morel mə 'rel mɒ- ‖ mɔ:- ~s z
morello mə 'rel əʊ mɒ- ‖ -oʊ ~s z
moreover mɔ:r 'əʊv ə mər- ‖ -'oʊv ər moʊr-;
' • • •
mores 'mɔ:r eɪz -i:z ‖ 'moʊr-
Moresby 'mɔ:z bi ‖ 'mɔ:rz- 'moʊrz- —but the
place in Cumbria is 'mɒr ɪs bi
Moresque (i)mɔ: 'resk mə-
Moreton 'mɔ:t ən ‖ 'mɔ:rt- 'moʊrt-
Moretonhampstead ‚mɔ:t ən 'hæmp stɪd
-sted ‖ ‚mɔ:rt- ‚moʊrt-
Morfa 'mɔ:v ə ‖ 'mɔ:rv ə —Welsh ['mɔr va]
Morfudd, Morfydd 'mɔ:v ɪð ‖ 'mɔ:rv-
—Welsh ['mor vɪð, -vɪð]
Morgan 'mɔ:g ən ‖ 'mɔ:rg-
morganatic ‚mɔ:g ə 'næt ɪk ◀
‖ ‚mɔ:rg ə 'næt̬ ɪk ◀ ~ally əl_i
morgen 'mɔ:g ən ‖ 'mɔ:rg- ~s z
Morgenthau 'mɔ:g ən θɔ: ‖ 'mɔ:rg- -θa:
morgue mɔ:g ‖ mɔ:rg morgues
mɔ:gz ‖ mɔ:rgz
MORI 'mɔ:r i 'mɒr-

Moriarty ˌmɒr i 'ɑːt i ‖ ˌmɔːr i 'ɑːrt̬ i
moribund 'mɒr ɪ bʌnd -ə-; -ɪb ənd, -əb-
  ‖ 'mɔːr- 'mɑːr- ~ly li
Morison 'mɒr ɪs ən -əs- ‖ 'mɔːr- 'mɑːr-
Morland 'mɔː lənd ‖ 'mɔːr-
Morley 'mɔːl i ‖ 'mɔːrl i
Mormon 'mɔːm ən ‖ 'mɔːrm- ~ism ˌɪz əm ~s
  z
morn mɔːn ‖ mɔːrn morns mɔːnz ‖ mɔːrnz
Morna 'mɔːn ə ‖ 'mɔːrn ə
mornay, M~ 'mɔːn eɪ ‖ mɔːr 'neɪ —Fr
  [mɔʁ nɛ]
morning 'mɔːn ɪŋ ‖ 'mɔːrn ɪŋ ~s z
  'morning coat; 'morning dress, ˌ• • '•;
  ˌmorning 'glory ‖ '• • ˌ• •'; ˌMorning
  'Prayer; 'morning ˌsickness; ˌmorning 'star
morning-after ˌmɔːn ɪŋ 'ɑːft ə ◂ §-'æft-
  ‖ ˌmɔːrn ɪŋ 'æft ər ◂
  ˌmorning-'after pill
Mornington 'mɔːn ɪŋ tən ‖ 'mɔːrn-
  ˌMornington 'Crescent
Moroccan mə 'rɒk ən ‖ -'rɑːk- ~s z
Morocco, m~ mə 'rɒk əʊ ‖ -'rɑːk oʊ
moron 'mɔːr ɒn ‖ 'mɔːr ɑːn 'moʊr- ~s z
Moroni mə 'rəʊn i ‖ -'roʊn i mɔː-
moronic mə 'rɒn ɪk mɒ-, mɔː- ‖ -'rɑːn ɪk
  ~ally ᵊl_i
morose mə 'rəʊs mɒ- ‖ -'roʊs mɔː- ~ly li
  ~ness nəs nɪs
Morpeth 'mɔːp əθ ‖ 'mɔːrp-
morph mɔːf ‖ mɔːrf morphed mɔːft ‖ mɔːrft
  morphing 'mɔːf ɪŋ ‖ 'mɔːrf ɪŋ morphs
  mɔːfs ‖ mɔːrfs
morph- comb. form before vowel
  with unstressed suffix 'mɔːf ‖ 'mɔːrf —
morphon 'mɔːf ɒn ‖ 'mɔːrf ɑːn
  with stressed suffix mɔːf ‖ mɔːrf —
  morphosis mɔː 'fəʊs ɪs §-əs ‖ mɔːr 'foʊs-
-morph mɔːf ‖ mɔːrf — isomorph 'aɪs əʊ
  mɔːf ‖ -ə mɔːrf
morpheme 'mɔːf iːm ‖ 'mɔːrf- ~s z
morphemic mɔː 'fiːm ɪk ‖ mɔːr- ~ally ᵊl_i ~s
  s
Morphett 'mɔːf ɪt §-ət ‖ 'mɔːrf ət
Morpheus 'mɔːf juːs 'mɔːf i_əs ‖ 'mɔːrf-
morphia 'mɔːf i_ə ‖ 'mɔːrf-
-morphic 'mɔːf ɪk ‖ 'mɔːrf ɪk — isomorphic
  ˌaɪs əʊ 'mɔːf ɪk ◂ ‖ -ə 'mɔːrf-
morphine 'mɔːf iːn ‖ 'mɔːrf-
morpho- comb. form before cons
  with stress-neutral suffix ˈmɔːf əʊ ‖ 'mɔːrf oʊ
    — morphotectonics
  ˌmɔːf əʊ tek 'tɒn ɪks ‖ ˌmɔːrf oʊ tek 'tɑːn-
  with stress-imposing suffix
  mɔː 'fɒ+ ‖ mɔːr 'fɑː+ — morphometry
  mɔː 'fɒm ətr i -ɪtr- ‖ mɔːr 'fɑːm-
morphological
  ˌmɔːf ə 'lɒdʒ ɪk ᵊl ◂ ‖ ˌmɔːrf ə 'lɑːdʒ- ~ly _i
morpholog|y mɔː 'fɒl ədʒ |i ‖ mɔːr 'fɑːl- ~ies
  iz
morphophoneme ˌmɔːf əʊ
  'fəʊn iːm ‖ ˌmɔːrf oʊ 'foʊn- ~s z

morphophonemic ˌmɔːf əʊ fəʊ
  'niːm ɪk ◂ ‖ ˌmɔːrf oʊ fə- ~ally ᵊl_i ~s s
morphophonology ˌmɔːf əʊ fəʊ
  'nɒl ədʒ i ‖ ˌmɔːrf oʊ fə 'nɑːl-
morphosyntactic
  ˌmɔːf əʊ sɪn 'tækt ɪk ◂ ‖ ˌmɔːrf oʊ-
-morphous 'mɔːf əs ‖ 'mɔːrf əs —
  isomorphous ˌaɪs əʊ 'mɔːf əs ◂ ‖ -ə 'mɔːrf-
Morphy 'mɔːf i ‖ 'mɔːrf i
-morphy mɔːf i ‖ mɔːrf i — isomorphy
  'aɪs əʊ mɔːf i ‖ -ə mɔːrf i
Morrell (i) mə 'rel mɒ-, (ii) 'mʌr əl ‖ 'mɝ-
Morrill 'mɒr ɪl -əl ‖ 'mɔːr- 'mɑːr-
Morris, m~ 'mɒr ɪs §-əs ‖ 'mɔːr- 'mɑːr-
  'morris dance; 'morris ˌdancer; 'morris
  men
Morrison 'mɒr ɪs ən §-əs- ‖ 'mɔːr- 'mɑːr-
Morrissey 'mɒr ɪs i -əs- ‖ 'mɔːr- 'mɑːr-
Morristown 'mɒr ɪs taʊn §-əs- ‖ 'mɔːr- 'mɑːr-
morrow, M~ 'mɒr əʊ ‖ 'mɔːr oʊ 'mɑːr- ~s z
Morse, morse mɔːs ‖ mɔːrs morses, Morse's
  'mɔːs ɪz -əz ‖ 'mɔːrs əz
  ˌMorse 'code
morsel 'mɔːs ᵊl ‖ 'mɔːrs- ~s z
Mort, mort mɔːt ‖ mɔːrt morts, Mort's
  mɔːts ‖ mɔːrts
mortadella ˌmɔːt ə 'del ə ‖ ˌmɔːrt̬ ə- ~s z
mortal 'mɔːt ᵊl ‖ 'mɔːrt̬ ᵊl ~s z
  ˌmortal 'sin
mortalit|y mɔː 'tæl ət |i -ɪt- ‖ mɔːr 'tæl ət̬ |i
  ~ies iz
mortally 'mɔːt əl i ‖ 'mɔːrt̬ ᵊl i
mortar 'mɔːt ə ‖ 'mɔːrt̬ ər ~ed d mortaring
  'mɔːt ər ɪŋ ‖ 'mɔːrt̬ ər ɪŋ ~s z
mortarboard 'mɔːt ə bɔːd ‖ 'mɔːrt̬ ər bɔːrd
  -boʊrd ~s z
Morte d'Arthur ˌmɔːt 'dɑːθ ə ‖ ˌmɔːrt 'dɑːrθ ər
Mortehoe 'mɔːt həʊ ‖ 'mɔːrt hoʊ
mortgag|e 'mɔːg ɪdʒ ‖ 'mɔːrg- ~ed d ~es ɪz
  əz ~ing ɪŋ
mortgagee ˌmɔːg ɪ 'dʒiː -ə- ‖ ˌmɔːrg- ~s z
mortgagor ˌmɔːg ɪ 'dʒɔː -ə-; 'mɔːg ɪdʒ ə, -ədʒ-
  ‖ ˌmɔːrg ə 'dʒɔːr 'mɔːrg ədʒ ər ~s z
mortic|e 'mɔːt ɪs §-əs ‖ 'mɔːrt̬ əs ~ed t ~es ɪz
  əz ~ing ɪŋ
mortician mɔː 'tɪʃ ən ‖ mɔːr- ~s z
mortification ˌmɔːt ɪf ɪ 'keɪʃ ən ˌ•əf-, §-ə'•-
  ‖ ˌmɔːrt̬ əf- ~s z
morti|fy 'mɔːt ɪ |faɪ -ə- ‖ 'mɔːrt̬ ə- ~fied faɪd
  ~fies faɪz ~fying/ly faɪ ɪŋ /li
Mortimer 'mɔːt ɪm ə -əm- ‖ 'mɔːrt̬ əm ər
mortis|e 'mɔːt ɪs §-əs ‖ 'mɔːrt̬ əs ~ed t ~es ɪz
  əz ~ing ɪŋ
  'mortise lock
Mortlake 'mɔːt leɪk ‖ 'mɔːrt-
mortmain 'mɔːt meɪn ‖ 'mɔːrt-
Morton 'mɔːt ən ‖ 'mɔːrt ən
mortuar|y 'mɔːtʃ u_ər i ‖ 'mɔːtʃ ər li;
  'mɔːt ju_ər i, 'mɔːt jʊr li ‖ 'mɔːrtʃ u er li
  ~ies iz
mosaic, M~ məʊ 'zeɪ ɪk ‖ moʊ- ~s s
moschatel ˌmɒsk ə 'tel ‖ ˌmɑːsk- ˌ• • • ~s z
Moscow 'mɒsk əʊ ‖ 'mɑːsk aʊ -oʊ

M

Moseley 'məʊz li ‖ 'moʊz-
Moselle məʊ 'zel ‖ moʊ- —*Fr* [mo zɛl], *Ger*
  Mosel ['moː zᵊl]
Moses 'məʊz ɪz -əz ‖ 'moʊz-
mosey 'məʊz i ‖ 'moʊz i **~ed** d **~ing** ɪŋ **~s** z
mosh mɒʃ ‖ mɑːʃ **moshed** mɒʃt ‖ mɑːʃt
  moshes 'mɒʃ ɪz -əz ‖ 'mɑːʃ əz **moshing**
  'mɒʃ ɪŋ ‖ 'mɑːʃ ɪŋ
Moskva 'mɒsk və ‖ mɑːsk 'vɑː —*Russ*
  [mʌ 'skva]
Moskvich *tdmk* 'mɒsk vɪtʃ ‖ 'mɑːsk- —*Russ*
  [mʌ 'skv·itʃ] **~es** ɪz əz
Moslem 'mɒz ləm 'mʊz-, -lɪm, -lem ‖ 'mɑːz-
  'mɑːs- **~s** z
Mosley *family name (i)* 'məʊz li ‖ 'moʊz-, *(ii)*
  'mɒz- ‖ 'mɑːz-
mosque mɒsk ‖ mɑːsk **mosques**
  mɒsks ‖ mɑːsks
mosquito mə 'skiːt əʊ mɒ- ‖ -'skiːt̬ oʊ **~es**, **~s**
  z
  mo'squito net
moss, Moss mɒs ‖ mɔːs mɑːs **mosses** 'mɒs ɪz
  -əz ‖ 'mɔːs əz 'mɑːs-
Mossad 'mɒs æd ‖ mə 'sɑːd mɑː-, moʊ-
Mossbauer, Mössbauer 'mɒs ˌbaʊ ə
  ‖ 'mɔːs ˌbaʊ ᵊr 'mɑːs- —*Ger* ['mœs bau ɐ]
  'Mössbauer efˌfect
moss-grown 'mɒs grəʊn ‖ 'mɔːs groʊn 'mɑːs-
Mossi 'mɒs i ‖ 'mɑːs i
Mossman 'mɒs mən ‖ 'mɔːs- 'mɑːs-
Mossop 'mɒs əp ‖ 'mɔːs- 'mɑːs-
moss|y 'mɒs li ‖ 'mɔːs li 'mɑːs- **~ier** i_ə ‖ i_ᵊr
  ~iest i_ɪst i_əst **~iness** i nəs i nɪs
most məʊst ‖ moʊst **mostly** 'məʊst
  li ‖ 'moʊst-
  ˌmost of 'all
-most məʊst ‖ moʊst — **innermost**
  'ɪn ə məʊst ‖ -ᵊr moʊst
Mostar 'mɒst ɑː ‖ 'mɑːst ɑːr 'moʊst-
  —*Croatian* [''mɔ staːr]
Mostyn 'mɒst ɪn §-ən ‖ 'mɑːst-
mot məʊ ‖ moʊ —*Fr* [mo] **mots** məʊz ‖ moʊz
  ˌmot 'juste ʒuːst —*Fr* [ʒyst]
M.o.T., MOT ˌem əʊ 'tiː ‖ -oʊ- **~'d** d **~'ing** ɪŋ
  ~s, ~'s z
mote məʊt ‖ moʊt (= *moat*) **motes**
  məʊts ‖ moʊts
motel ₍ᵢ₎məʊ 'tel ‖ ₍ᵢ₎moʊ- **~s** z
motet ₍ᵢ₎məʊ 'tet ‖ ₍ᵢ₎moʊ- **~s** s
moth mɒθ ‖ mɔːθ mɑːθ **moths** mɒθs ‖ mɔːðz
  mɑːðz, mɔːθs, mɑːθs
Mothaks *tdmk* 'mɒθ æks ‖ 'mɔːθ- 'mɑːθ-
mothball 'mɒθ bɔːl ‖ 'mɔːθ- 'mɑːθ bɑːl **~ed** d
  ~ing ɪŋ **~s** z
moth-eaten 'mɒθ ˌiːt ᵊn ‖ 'mɔːθ- 'mɑːθ-
mother, M~ 'mʌð ə ‖ -ᵊr **~ed** d **mothering**
  'mʌð ᵊr_ɪŋ **~s** z
  'mother ˌcountry; ˌMother 'Goose,
  ˌMother 'Goose rhyme; ˌmother 'hen;
  'Mothering ˌSunday; ˌMother 'Nature;
  'mother's boy; 'Mother's Day; ˌmother's
  'ruin; ˌmother su'perior; ˌmother 'tongue,
  '...

motherboard 'mʌð ə bɔːd ‖ -ᵊr bɔːrd -boʊrd
  ~s z
Mothercare *tdmk* 'mʌð ə keə ‖ -ᵊr ker
mothercraft 'mʌð ə krɑːft §-kræft ‖ -ᵊr kræft
motherese ˌmʌð ə 'riːz
motherfuck|er/s 'mʌð ə ˌfʌk| ə/z ‖ -ᵊr ˌfʌk| ᵊr/
  z **~ing** ɪŋ
motherhood 'mʌð ə hʊd ‖ -ᵊr-
mother-in-law 'mʌð ᵊr_ɪn ˌlɔː: '•ə-, -ᵊr_ən-
  ‖ -ᵊr_ən- -ˌlɑː: **~s, ~'s** z **mothers-in-law**
  'mʌð əz ɪn ˌlɔː: §-ən, • ‖ -ᵊrz ən- -ˌlɑː:
motherless 'mʌð ə ləs -lɪs ‖ -ᵊr- **~ness** nəs nɪs
mother|ly 'mʌð ə |li ‖ -ᵊr- **~liness** li nəs -nɪs
mother-of-pearl ˌmʌð ᵊr_əv 'pɜːl ◂ ‖ -'pɜːl ◂
mother-of-thousands ˌmʌð ᵊr_əv 'θaʊz ᵊndz
mothers- —*see* **mother-**
mother-to-be ˌmʌð ə tə 'biː ‖ , •ᵊr- **mothers-**
  to-be ˌmʌð əz tə 'biː ‖ , •ᵊrz-
Motherwell 'mʌð ə wəl -wel ‖ -ᵊr-
mothproof 'mɒθ pruːf §-prʊf ‖ 'mɔːθ- 'mɑːθ-
  ~ed t ~ing ɪŋ ~s s
moth|y 'mɒθ |i ‖ 'mɔːθ |i 'mɑːθ- **~ier** i_ə ‖ i_ᵊr
  ~iest i_ɪst i_əst
motif ₍ᵢ₎məʊ 'tiːf mɒ- ‖ moʊ- **~s** s
motile 'məʊt aɪᵊl ‖ 'moʊt̬ ᵊl 'moʊt aɪᵊl (*)
motility məʊ 'tɪl ət i -ɪt- ‖ moʊ 'tɪl ət̬ i
motion, M~ 'məʊʃ ᵊn ‖ 'moʊʃ ᵊn **~ed** d **~ing**
  ɪŋ **~s** z
  ˌmotion 'picture◂; 'motion ˌsickness
motionless 'məʊʃ ᵊn ləs -lɪs ‖ 'moʊʃ- **~ly** li
  ~ness nəs nɪs
moti|vate 'məʊt ɪ |veɪt -ə- ‖ 'moʊt̬ ə- **~vated**
  veɪt ɪd -əd ‖ veɪt̬ əd **~vates** veɪts **~vating**
  veɪt ɪŋ ‖ veɪt̬ ɪŋ
motivation ˌməʊt ɪ 'veɪʃ ᵊn -ə- ‖ ˌmoʊt̬ ə- **~s**
  z
motivational ˌməʊt ɪ 'veɪʃ ᵊn_ᵊl ◂, • ə-
  ‖ ˌmoʊt̬ ə- **~ly** i
motive 'məʊt ɪv ‖ 'moʊt̬ ɪv **~s** z
motley, M~ 'mɒt li ‖ 'mɑːt-
motmot 'mɒt mɒt ‖ 'mɑːt mɑːt **~s** s
motocross 'məʊt əʊ krɒs -krɔːs
  ‖ 'moʊt̬ oʊ krɔːs -krɑːs
motor 'məʊt ə ‖ 'moʊt̬ ᵊr **~ed** d **motoring**
  'məʊt ᵊr ɪŋ ‖ 'moʊt̬ ᵊr ɪŋ **~s** z
  'motor lodge; 'motor ˌscooter; ˌmotor
  'vehicle
motorbike 'məʊt ə baɪk ‖ 'moʊt̬ ᵊr- **~s** s
motorboat 'məʊt ə bəʊt ‖ 'moʊt̬ ᵊr boʊt **~s** s
motorcade 'məʊt ə keɪd ‖ 'moʊt̬ ᵊr- **~s** z
motorcar 'məʊt ə kɑː ‖ 'moʊt̬ ᵊr kɑːr **~s** z
motorcoach 'məʊt ə kəʊtʃ ‖ 'moʊt̬ ᵊr koʊtʃ
  ~es ɪz əz
motorcycle 'məʊt ə ˌsaɪk ᵊl ‖ 'moʊt̬ ᵊr- **~s** z
motorcyclist 'məʊt ə ˌsaɪk lɪst §-ləst
  ‖ 'moʊt̬ ᵊr- **~s** s
motoris... —*see* **motoriz...**
motorist 'məʊt ᵊr ɪst §-əst ‖ 'moʊt̬ ᵊr- **~s** s
motoriz|e 'məʊt ə raɪz ‖ 'moʊt̬ ə- **~ed** d **~es**
  ɪz əz **~ing** ɪŋ
motor|man 'məʊt ə |mən -mæn ‖ 'moʊt̬ ᵊr-
  ~men mən men

motor|mouth 'məʊt ə ˌmaʊθ ‖ 'moʊt̬ ər-
~**mouths** maʊðz

motorway 'məʊt ə weɪ ‖ 'moʊt̬ ər- ~**s** z

Motown 'məʊ taʊn ‖ 'moʊ-

Mott mɒt ‖ mɑːt

motte mɒt ‖ mɑːt **mottes** mɒts ‖ mɑːts

mottl|e 'mɒt əl ‖ 'mɑːt̬ əl ~**ed** d ~**es** z ~**ing**
ɪŋ

motto 'mɒt əʊ ‖ 'mɑːt̬ oʊ ~**es**, ~**s** z

Mottram 'mɒtr əm ‖ 'mɑːtr-

Motu 'məʊt uː ‖ 'moʊt-

motu proprio ˌməʊt uː 'prɒp ri əʊ -'prəʊp-
‖ ˌmoʊt uː 'proʊp ri oʊ

moue muː (= *moo*) —*Fr* [mu] **moues** muːz

moufflon, mouflon 'muːf lɒn ‖ -lɑːn ~**s** z

mouille, mouillé 'mwiː eɪ 'muː jeɪ ‖ muː 'jeɪ
—*Fr* [mu je]

mould, Mould məʊld →mɒʊld ‖ moʊld
moulded 'məʊld ɪd →'mɒʊld-, -əd
‖ 'moʊld əd **moulding/s** 'məʊld ɪŋ/z
→'mɒʊld- ‖ 'moʊld ɪŋ/z **moulds** məʊldz
→mɒʊldz ‖ moʊldz

mould|er 'məʊld |ə →'mɒʊld- ‖ 'moʊld |ər
~**ered** əd ‖ ərd ~**ering** ər ɪŋ ~**ers** əz ‖ ərz

mould|y 'məʊld |i →'mɒʊld- ‖ 'moʊld |i ~**ier**
i ə ‖ i ər ~**iest** i ɪst i əst ~**iness** i nəs i nɪs

Moulinex *tdmk* 'muːl ɪ neks -ə-

Moulin Rouge ˌmuːl æn 'ruːʒ —*Fr*
[mu lɛ̃ ʁuːʒ]

moult, Moult məʊlt →mɒʊlt ‖ moʊlt
moulted 'məʊlt ɪd →'mɒʊlt-, -əd
‖ 'moʊlt əd **moulting** 'məʊlt ɪŋ →'mɒʊlt-
‖ 'moʊlt ɪŋ **moults** məʊlts →mɒʊlts
‖ moʊlts

Moulton 'məʊlt ən →'mɒʊlt- ‖ 'moʊlt-

mound maʊnd **mounds** maʊndz

mount, Mount maʊnt **mounted** 'maʊnt ɪd
-əd ‖ 'maʊnt̬ əd **mounting**
'maʊnt ɪŋ ‖ 'maʊnt̬ ɪŋ **mounts** maʊnts
ˌMount 'Everest; ˌMount 'Pleasant;
ˌMount 'Rushmore; ˌMount 'Vernon

mountain 'maʊnt ɪn -ən ‖ -ən —*In singing
sometimes* -eɪn ~**s** z
'mountain ˌlion; 'mountain range;
ˌMountain 'Standard Time, 'Mountain
Time

mountaineer ˌmaʊnt ɪ 'nɪə -ə- ‖ -ən 'ɪər ~**ed** d
mountaineering ˌmaʊnt ɪ 'nɪər ɪŋ ˌ•ə-
‖ -ən 'ɪr ɪŋ ~**s** z

mountainous 'maʊnt ɪn əs -ən- ‖ -ən-

mountainside 'maʊnt ɪn saɪd -ən- ‖ -ən- ~**s** z

mountaintop 'maʊnt ɪn tɒp -ən- ‖ -ən tɑːp ~**s**
s

Mountbatten maʊnt 'bæt ən ‖ '•ˌ•• ••

mountebank 'maʊnt ɪ bæŋk -ə- ‖ 'maʊnt̬- ~**s**
s

Mountford 'maʊnt fəd ‖ -fərd

Mountie 'maʊnt i ‖ 'maʊnt̬ i ~**s** z

Mountjoy maʊnt 'dʒɔɪ '•••

Mountsorrel ˌmaʊnt 'sɒr əl ‖ -'sɔːr- -'sɑːr-

Mount|y 'maʊnt |i ‖ 'maʊnt̬ |i ~**ies** iz

Moureen 'mɔːr iːn mɔː 'riːn

mourn mɔːn mʊən ‖ mɔːrn mourn **mourned**
mɔːnd mʊənd ‖ mɔːrnd mournd **mourning**
'mɔːn ɪŋ 'mʊən- ‖ 'mɔːrn ɪŋ 'moʊrn-
mourns mɔːnz mʊənz ‖ mɔːrnz moʊrnz

Mourne mɔːn ‖ mɔːrn moʊrn

mourner 'mɔːn ə 'mʊən- ‖ 'mɔːrn ər 'moʊrn-
~**s** z

mournful 'mɔːn fəl 'mʊən-, -fʊl ‖ 'mɔːrn-
'moʊrn- ~**ly** _i ~**ness** nəs nɪs

mourning 'mɔːn ɪŋ 'mʊən- ‖ 'mɔːrn ɪŋ
'moʊrn-

Mousa *place in Shetland* 'muːz ə

mouse *n* maʊs **mice** maɪs **mice's** 'maɪs ɪz -əz
mouse's 'maʊs ɪz -əz

mouse *v* maʊz maʊs **moused** maʊzd maʊst
mouses 'maʊz ɪz 'maʊs-, -əz **mousing**
'maʊz ɪŋ 'maʊs-

mousehole 'maʊs həʊl →-hɒʊl ‖ -hoʊl ~**s** z

Mousehole *place in Cornwall* 'maʊz əl

mouser 'maʊz ə 'maʊs- ‖ -ər ~**s** z

mouselike 'maʊs laɪk

mousetrap 'maʊs træp ~**s** s

mous|ey 'maʊs |i ~**ier** i ə ‖ i ər ~**iest** i ɪst
i əst ~**iness** i nəs i nɪs

moussaka mu 'saːk ə —*ModGk* [mu sa 'ka] ~**s**
z

mousse muːs (= *moose*) **mousses** 'muːs ɪz -əz

Moussec *tdmk* ˌmuː 'sek

Moussorgsky mu 'sɔːg ski mə-, -'zɔːg-
‖ -'sɔːrg- -'zɔːrg- —*Russ* ['mu sərk skʲɪj]

moustach|e mə 'staːʃ mu-, §-'stæʃ, §-'stɒʃ
‖ 'mʌst æʃ mə 'stæʃ (*) ~**ed** t ~**es** ɪz əz

mous|y 'maʊs |i ~**ier** i ə ‖ i ər ~**iest** i ɪst i əst
~**iness** i nəs i nɪs

mouth *n* maʊθ **mouths** maʊðz §maʊθs

mouth *v* maʊð **mouthed** maʊðd maʊθt **mouths**
maʊðz **mouthing** 'maʊð ɪŋ

-**mouthed** 'maʊðd 'maʊθt — **foul-mouthed**
ˌfaʊl 'maʊðd ◀ -'maʊθt

mouthful 'maʊθ fʊl ~**s** z

mouthorgan 'maʊθ ˌɔːg ən ‖ -ˌɔːrg- ~**s** z

mouthpart 'maʊθ paːt ‖ -paːrt ~**s** s

mouthpiec|e 'maʊθ piːs ~**es** ɪz əz

mouth-to-mouth ˌmaʊθ tə 'maʊθ ◀ -tu-
ˌmouth-to-ˌmouth reˌsusci'tation

mouthwash 'maʊθ wɒʃ ‖ -wɔːʃ -waːʃ ~**es** ɪz
əz

mouthwatering 'maʊθ ˌwɔːt_ər ɪŋ ‖ -ˌwɔːt̬
ər ɪŋ -ˌwaːt̬-

mouth|y 'maʊð| i 'maʊθ| i ~**ier** i ə ‖ i ər
~**iest** i ɪst ˌ_əst

movable 'muːv əb əl
ˌmovable 'feast

move muːv (!) **moved** muːvd **moves** muːvz
moving 'muːv ɪŋ
ˌmoving 'picture; ˌmoving 'staircase;
'moving van '*removal van*'

moveable 'muːv əb əl

movement 'muːv mənt ~**s** s

mover 'muːv ə ‖ -ər ~**s** z

movie 'muːv i ~**s** z
'movie star

moviego|er/s 'muːv i ˌɡəʊ ə/z ‖ -ˌɡoʊ ər/z
~ing ɪŋ
moviemak|er/s 'muːv i ˌmeɪk ə/z ‖ -ər/z ~ing
ɪŋ
Movietone tdmk 'muːv i təʊn ‖ -toʊn
moving 'muːv ɪŋ ~ly li
mow 'cut down' məʊ ‖ moʊ (= mo) mowed
məʊd ‖ moʊd mowing 'məʊ ɪŋ ‖ 'moʊ ɪŋ
mown məʊn ‖ moʊn mows məʊz ‖ moʊz
'mowing maˌchine
mow 'stack', v 'store hay' maʊ mowed maʊd
mowing 'maʊ ɪŋ mows maʊz —but usually
məʊ ‖ moʊ in the inn name,Barley 'Mow
mow 'grimace' maʊ mowed maʊd mowing
'maʊ ɪŋ mows maʊz
Mowat, Mowatt (i) 'məʊ ət ‖ 'moʊ-, (ii) 'maʊ-
Mowbray 'məʊb ri -reɪ ‖ 'moʊb-
mower, Mower 'məʊ ə ‖ 'moʊ ər ~s z
Mowgli 'maʊɡ li
Mowlam, Mowlem 'məʊl əm ‖ 'moʊl-
mown məʊn ‖ moʊn (= moan)
moxa 'mɒks ə ‖ 'maːks ə
moxibustion ˌmɒks ɪ 'bʌs tʃən -ə- ‖ ˌmaːks-
moxie 'mɒks i ‖ 'maːks i
Moy mɔɪ
Moya 'mɔɪ ə
Moygashel mɔɪ 'ɡæʃ əl 'mɔɪɡ əʃ-
Moynahan 'mɔɪn ə hən -hæn
Moyne mɔɪn
Moynihan 'mɔɪn i ˌən -ɪ hæn, -ə-
Moyra 'mɔɪər ə
Mozambican, Mozambiquan ˌməʊz əm 'biːk
ən ◄ -æm- ‖ ˌmoʊz- ~s z
Mozambique ˌməʊz əm 'biːk -æm- ‖ ˌmoʊz-
Mozarab məʊ 'zær əb ‖ moʊ- -'zer- ~s z
Mozarabic məʊ 'zær əb ɪk ‖ moʊ- -'zer-
Mozart 'məʊts aːt ‖ 'moʊts aːrt —Ger
['moː tsaʁt]
Mozartian ˌməʊt 'saːt i ˌən ◄ ‖ moʊt 'saːrṭ i ˌən
~s z
mozzarella ˌmɒts ə 'rel ə ◄ ‖ ˌmaːts- ˌmoʊts-
—It [mot tsa 'rɛl la]
MP ˌem 'piː MPs, MP's ˌem 'piːz
mph ˌem piː: 'eɪtʃ §-'heɪtʃ —or as miles per
hour, miles an hour
MPhil ˌem 'fɪl
Mr 'mɪst ə ‖ -ər
Mrs 'mɪs ɪz §-əz ‖ 'mɪz-
Ms mɪz məz, məs —As a self-designation, mɪz
seems to be preferred. Those who say məz, məs
may use it in stressed as well as unstressed
position. Some claim the word is
unpronounceable.
ms —see manuscript
MS 'multiple sclerosis' ˌem 'es
MSc ˌem es 'siː
MS-DOS tdmk ˌem es 'dɒs ‖ -'dɔːs -'daːs
mss —see manuscripts
Mt —see Mount
MTV ˌem tiː 'viː
mu mjuː (= mew)
Mubarak mu 'baːr æk -'bær-, -ək —Arabic
[mu 'ba: rak]

much, Much mʌtʃ more mɔː ‖ mɔːr moʊr
most məʊst ‖ moʊst muchness 'mʌtʃ nəs
-nɪs
mucic 'mjuːs ɪk
Mucilage 'mjuːs ɪl ɪdʒ -əl- ~es ɪz əz
mucilaginous ˌmjuːs ɪ 'lædʒ ɪn əs ◄ ˌ•ə-,
-ən əs
mucin 'mjuːs ɪn §-ən ~s z
muck, Muck mʌk mucked mʌkt mucking
'mʌk ɪŋ mucks mʌks
mucker 'mʌk ə ‖ -ər ~s z
muckheap 'mʌk hiːp ~s s
muckle 'mʌk əl
ˌMuckle 'Flugga 'flʌɡ ə
muckrak|er/s 'mʌk reɪk |ə/z ‖ -|ər/z ~ing ɪŋ
muck|y 'mʌk li ~ier i ə ‖ i ər ~iest i ɪst i əst
muco- comb. form
with stress-neutral suffix ˌmjuːk əʊ ‖ -oʊ —
mucofibrous ˌmjuːk əʊ 'faɪb rəs ◄ -oʊ-
with stress-imposing suffix mju 'kɒ+ ‖ -'kaː+
— mucoclasis mju 'kɒk ləs ɪs §-əs ‖ -'kaːk-
mucous 'mjuːk əs (= mucus)
ˌmucous 'membrane
Mu-cron tdmk 'mjuː krɒn ‖ -kraːn
mucus 'mjuːk əs
mud mʌd muds mʌdz
'mud bath; ˌmud 'pie; ˌmud ˌpuppy
mudbank 'mʌd bæŋk →'mʌb- ~s s
mud|bath 'mʌd| baːθ →'mʌb-, §-bæθ ‖ -bæθ
~baths baːðz §baːθs, §bæθs, §bæðz ‖ bæðz
bæθs
Mudd mʌd
muddi... —see muddy
muddl|e 'mʌd əl ~ed d ~es z ~ing ɪŋ
muddle-headed ˌmʌd əl 'hed ɪd ◄ -əd ~ly li
~ness nəs nɪs
mudd|y 'mʌd li ~ied id ~ier i ə ‖ i ər ~ies iz
~iest i ɪst i əst ~ily ɪ li əl i ~iness i nəs i nɪs
~ying i ɪŋ
Mudeford 'mʌd i fəd ‖ -fərd (!)
mudfish 'mʌd fɪʃ ~es ɪz əz
mudflap 'mʌd flæp ~s s
mudflat 'mʌd flæt ~s s
Mudge mʌdʒ
mudguard 'mʌd ɡaːd →'mʌg- ‖ -ɡaːrd ~s z
Mudie 'mjuːd i
mudlark 'mʌd laːk ‖ -laːrk ~s s
mudpack 'mʌd pæk →'mʌb- ~s s
mudskipper 'mʌd ˌskɪp ə ‖ -ər ~s z
mudslide 'mʌd slaɪd ~s z
mudsling|er/s 'mʌd ˌslɪŋ |ə/z ‖ -|ər/z ~ing ɪŋ
muesli 'mjuːz li 'muːz- ‖ 'mjuːs- ~s z
muezzin mu 'ez ɪn mjuː-, §-ən ~s z
muff mʌf muffed mʌft muffing 'mʌf ɪŋ
muffs mʌfs
muffin 'mʌf ɪn §-ən ~s z
muffl|e 'mʌf əl ~ed d ~es z ~ing ɪŋ
muffler 'mʌf lə ‖ -lər ~s z
Muffy 'mʌf i
mufti, Mufti 'mʌft i ~s z
mug mʌg mugged mʌgd mugging/s
'mʌg ɪŋ/z mugs mʌgz
'mug's game

Mugabe mu 'gɑːb i -eɪ
mugful 'mʌg fʊl ~s z
mugger 'mʌg ə ‖ -ᵊr ~s z
Muggeridge 'mʌg ər_ɪdʒ
muggins, M~ 'mʌg ɪnz §-ənz
Muggleton 'mʌg ᵊl tən
Muggletonian ˌmʌg ᵊl 'təʊn i_ən ‖ -'toʊn- ~s z
mugg|ly 'mʌg li ~ier i_ə ‖ i_ᵊr ~iest i_ɪst i_əst
~ily ɪ li əl i ~iness i nəs i nɪs
mugho 'mjuːg əʊ 'muːg- ‖ -oʊ ~s z
mugshot 'mʌg ʃɒt ‖ -ʃɑːt ~s s
mugwort 'mʌg wɜːt -wɔːt ‖ -wɜ˞ːt -wɔːrt ~s s
mugwump 'mʌg wʌmp ~s s
Muhammed mu 'hæm ɪd -əd, -ed —*Arabic*
[mu 'hħam mad]
Muhammedan mu 'hæm ɪd ən -əd- ~ism ˌɪz
əm ~s z
Muir mjʊə mjɔː ‖ mjʊᵊr
Muirhead 'mjʊə hed 'mjɔː- ‖ 'mjʊr-
mujaheddin, mujahedeen ˌmuːdʒ ə he 'diːn
ˌmʊdʒ-, ˌmuːʒ-, ˌ•ɑː-, -hə'• —*Arabic*
[mu dʒa: hi 'diːn]
Mukden 'mʊk dən
mukluk 'mʌk lʌk ~s s
mulatto mju 'læt əʊ mu-, mə- ‖ -'læt oʊ -'lɑːt̬-
~s z
mulberr|y 'mʌl bər_li ‖ -ˌber li ~ies iz
Mulcaghey mʌl 'kæx i -'kæ hi
Mulcahy mʌl 'kæ hi
mulch mʌltʃ **mulched** mʌltʃt **mulches**
'mʌltʃ ɪz -əz **mulching** 'mʌltʃ ɪŋ
mulct mʌlkt **mulcted** 'mʌlkt ɪd -əd **mulcting**
'mʌlkt ɪŋ **mulcts** mʌlkts
Muldoon mʌl 'duːn
mule mjuːl **mules** mjuːlz
Mules mjuːlz
muleteer ˌmjuːl ə 'tɪə -ɪ- ‖ -'tɪᵊr ~s z
mulga 'mʌlg ə ~s z
Mulhearn mʌl 'hɜːn ‖ -'hɜ˞ːn
Mulholland mʌl 'hɒl ənd ‖ -'hɑːl-
mulish 'mjuːl ɪʃ ~ly li ~ness nəs nɪs
mull, Mull mʌl **mulled** mʌld **mulling** 'mʌl ɪŋ
mulls mʌlz
mulla, mullah 'mʌl ə 'mʊl- ~s z
Mullan 'mʌl ən
mullein 'mʌl ɪn -eɪn, -ən ~s z
Muller 'mʌl ə ‖ -ᵊr —*but as a German name*
'mʊl-, 'muːl-, 'mjuːl- —*Ger* Müller ['mʏl ɐ]
mullet 'mʌl ɪt -ət ~s s
Mulley 'mʌl i
Mulligan, m~ 'mʌl ɪg ən -əg- ~s z
mulligatawny ˌmʌl ɪg ə 'tɔːn i ◄ ˌ•əg- ‖ -'tɑːn-
Mulliken 'mʌl ɪk ən
mullion 'mʌl i_ən ‖ 'mʌl jən ~ed d ~s z
Mulroney mʌl 'rəʊn i ‖ -'roʊn i
multi- *comb. form*
with stress-neutral suffix ˌmʌlt i ‖ -aɪ
multiethnic ˌmʌlt i 'eθ nɪk ◄ ‖ -aɪ-
with stress-imposing suffix mʌl 'tɪ+ —
multiparous mʌl 'tɪp ər əs
multicolored, multicoloured 'mʌlt i ˌkʌl əd
ˌ•'•• ‖ -ᵊrd -aɪ-

multicultural ˌmʌlt i 'kʌltʃ ᵊr_əl ◄ ‖ ˌ•aɪ- ~ly i
multifarious ˌmʌlt ɪ 'feər i_əs ◄ ˌ•ə- ‖ -'fer-
-'fær- ~ly li ~ness nəs nɪs
multiform 'mʌlt i fɔːm -ə- ‖ -fɔːrm
multiformity ˌmʌlt i 'fɔːm ət i ˌ•ə-, -ɪt i
‖ -'fɔːrm ət̬ i
multigrav|ida ˌmʌlt i 'græv |ɪd ə -əd ə ~idae
ɪ diː ə-
multilateral ˌmʌlt i 'læt_ᵊr əl ◄ ‖ -'læt̬ ər əl ◄
→-'lætr əl ~ly i
ˌmulti,lateral 'trade
multilingual ˌmʌlt i 'lɪŋ gwəl ◄
-'lɪŋ gju_əl ‖ ˌ•aɪ- ~ly i
ˌmulti,lingual 'secretary
multimedia ˌmʌlt i 'miːd i_ə ‖ ˌ•aɪ-
multimillionaire ˌmʌlt i ˌmɪl jə 'neə ‖ -'neᵊr
ˌ•aɪ-, -'næᵊr; ˌ••'••• ~s z
multinational ˌmʌlt i 'næʃ ᵊn_əl ◄ ‖ ˌ•aɪ- ~s z
multip|ara mʌl 'tɪp |ər ə ~arae ə riː ~arous
ər əs
multiple 'mʌlt ɪp ᵊl -əp- ~s z
ˌmultiple scle'rosis
multiple-choice ˌmʌlt ɪp ᵊl 'tʃɔɪs ˌ•əp-
ˌmultiple-'choice ˌquestion
multiplex 'mʌlt ɪ pleks -ə-, -i- ~ed t ~es ɪz əz
~ing ɪŋ
multiplexer, multiplexor 'mʌlt ɪ pleks ə '•ə-
‖ -ᵊr ~s z
multiplicand ˌmʌlt ɪ plɪ 'kænd ˌ•ə-, §-plə'• ~s
z
multiplication ˌmʌlt ɪ plɪ 'keɪʃ ᵊn ˌ•ə-, §-plə'•-
~s z
ˌmultipli'cation sign; ˌmultipli'cation
ˌtable
multiplicative ˌmʌlt ɪ 'plɪk ət ɪv ˌ•ə-;
'••plɪ keɪt ɪv, -plə•• ‖ -'plɪk ət̬ ɪv
'••plə keɪt̬ ɪv ~ly li
multiplicit|y ˌmʌlt ɪ 'plɪs ət li ˌ•ə-, -ɪt i ‖ -ət̬ li
~ies iz
multi|ply *v* 'mʌlt ɪ |plaɪ -ə- ~plied plaɪd
~plier/s plaɪ_ə/z ‖ plaɪ_ᵊr/z ~plies plaɪz
~plying plaɪ ɪŋ
multiply *adv* 'mʌlt əp li -ɪp-
multipurpose ˌmʌlt i 'pɜːp əs ◄ ‖ -'pɜ˞ːp əs ◄
-aɪ-
multiraci|al ˌmʌlt i 'reɪʃ |ᵊl ◄ ‖ -aɪ- ~alism
ə ˌlɪz əm ~ally əl i
multistage 'mʌlt i steɪdʒ
multistorey, multistory ˌmʌlt i 'stɔːr i ◄ ‖ -aɪ-,
-'stoʊr-
ˌmulti,storey 'carpark
multitasking ˌmʌlt i 'tɑːsk ɪŋ §-'tæsk-
‖ -'tæsk-
multitude 'mʌlt ɪ tjuːd -ə-, →§tʃuːd ‖ -tuːd
-tjuːd ~s z
multitudinous ˌmʌlt ɪ 'tjuːd ɪn əs ◄ ˌ•ə-,
→§'tʃuːd-, -ᵊn_əs ‖ -'tuːd ᵊn_əs -'tjuːd- ~ly
li
multum in parvo ˌmʊlt ʊm ɪn 'pɑːv əʊ ˌmʌlt-,
ˌ•əm-, →-ɪm'•-, §-ən'•- ‖ -'pɑːrv oʊ
-'pɑːr woʊ
mum, Mum mʌm **mums, Mum's** mʌmz
Mumbai ˌmʊm 'baɪ

M

mumbl|e 'mʌm bᵊl ~ed d ~es z ~ing _ɪŋ
Mumbles 'mʌm bᵊlz
mumbling 'mʌm bᵊl_ɪŋ ~ly li
mumbo jumbo
  ˌmʌm bəʊ 'dʒʌm bəʊ ‖ -boʊ 'dʒʌm boʊ
Mumford 'mʌm fəd ‖ -fᵊrd
Mumm mʌm mʊm
mummer 'mʌm ə ‖ -ᵊr ~s z
Mummerset, m~ 'mʌm ə set ‖ -ᵊr-
mummer|y 'mʌm ər li ~ies iz
mummie... —see mummy
mummification ˌmʌm ɪf ɪ 'keɪʃ ᵊn ˌ•əf-, §-ə'•-
mummi|fy 'mʌm ɪ Ifaɪ -ə- ~fied faɪd ~fies
  faɪz ~fying faɪ ɪŋ
mumming 'mʌm ɪŋ
mumm|y, M~ 'mʌm li ~ies, ~y's iz
mumpish 'mʌmp ɪʃ ~ly li ~ness nəs nɪs
mumps mʌmps
mumsy, Mumsy 'mʌmz i
Muncaster 'mʌŋk əst ə §'mʌŋ ˌkɑːst ə,
  §-ˌkæst- ‖ 'mʌn ˌkæst ᵊr
munch mʌntʃ munched mʌntʃt munches
  'mʌntʃ ɪz -əz munching 'mʌntʃ ɪŋ
Munch mʊŋk —Norwegian [mʉ ŋk]
Munchausen, Munchhausen, Münchhausen
  'mʌntʃ aʊz ᵊn 'mʊntʃ-, -haʊz-; mʌn 'tʃɔːz ᵊn
  —Ger ['mʏnç haʊ zᵊn]
munchies, M~ tdmk 'mʌntʃ iz
munchkin, M~ 'mʌntʃ kɪn ~s z
Muncie 'mʌnᵗs i
Munda 'mʊnd ə
mundane ˌʊmʌn 'deɪn '•• ~ly li ~ness nəs
  nɪs
Munday 'mʌn deɪ
Mundesley 'mʌnz li
mung mʌŋ
Mungo, mungo 'mʌŋ gəʊ ‖ -goʊ
Munich 'mjuːn ɪk -ɪx —Ger München
  ['mʏn çən]
municipal mju 'nɪs ɪp ᵊl -əp-; §ˌmjuːn ɪ 'sɪp-,
  -ə- ~ly i
municipalis... —see municipaliz...
municipalit|y mju ˌnɪs ɪ 'pæl ət li ˌmjuːn ɪs-,
  -ə'••, -ət i ‖ -ət̬ li ~ies iz
municipalization mju ˌnɪs ɪp ᵊl aɪ 'zeɪʃ ᵊn
  -ˌ•əp-, -ɪ'•• ; §ˌmjuːn ɪ 'sɪp-, -ə- ‖ -ə'•- ~s z
municipaliz|e mju 'nɪs ɪp ə laɪz -'•əp-;
  §ˌmjuːn ɪ 'sɪp-, -ə- ~ed d ~es ɪz əz ~ing ɪŋ
munificence mju 'nɪf ɪs ᵊnᵗs -əs-
munificent mju 'nɪf ɪs ᵊnt -əs- ~ly li
muniment 'mjuːn ɪ mənt -ə- ~s s
munition mju 'nɪʃ ᵊn ~s z
Munn mʌn
Munro, Munroe, Munrow mən 'rəʊ mʌn-
  ‖ -'roʊ
Munsell 'mʌnᵗs ᵊl
Munster province of Ireland 'mʌnᵗst ə ‖ -ᵊr
Munster, Münster place in Germany
  'mʊnᵗst ə ‖ -ᵊr —Ger ['mʏn stɐ]
munt mʊnt munts mʊnᵗs
muntjac, muntjak 'mʌnt dʒæk 'mʌntʃ æk ~s s
Muntz mʌnᵗs
muon 'mjuː ɒn ‖ -ɑːn ~s z

muppet, M~ 'mʌp ɪt §-ət ~s s
muraena mjuᵊ 'riːn ə ~s z
mural 'mjʊər əl 'mjɔːr- ‖ 'mjʊr əl ~s z
Murchison (i) 'mɜːtʃ ɪs ᵊn §-əs- ‖ 'mɜːtʃ-, (ii)
  'mɜːk- ‖ 'mɜːk-
murder 'mɜːd ə ‖ 'mɜːd ᵊr ~ed d murdering
  'mɜːd ᵊr ɪŋ ‖ 'mɜːd ᵊr ɪŋ ~s z
murderer 'mɜːd ᵊr ə ‖ 'mɜːd ər ᵊr ~s z
murderess 'mɜːd ə res -ᵊr ɪs, -ᵊr əs;
  ˌmɜːd ə 'res ‖ 'mɜːd ᵊr əs ~es ɪz əz
murderous 'mɜːd ᵊr əs ‖ 'mɜːd_ ~ly li ~ness
  nəs nɪs
Murdo 'mɜːd əʊ ‖ 'mɜːd oʊ
Murdoch 'mɜːd ɒk -əx ‖ 'mɜːd ɑːk
Murdock 'mɜːd ɒk ‖ 'mɜːd ɑːk
murex 'mjʊər eks 'mjɔːr- ‖ 'mjʊr- ~es ɪz əz
Murfin 'mɜːf ɪn §-ᵊn ‖ 'mɜːf-
Murfreesboro
  'mɜːf riz ˌbʌr ə ‖ 'mɜːf riz ˌbɝː oʊ -ɪz-, -ə
Murgatroyd 'mɜːg ə trɔɪd ‖ 'mɜːg-
Muriel 'mjʊər i_əl 'mjɔːr- ‖ 'mjʊr-
Murillo mjuᵊ 'rɪl əʊ -jəʊ ‖ -oʊ —Sp [mu 'ri ʎo,
  -jo]
murine 'mjʊər aɪn -ɪn, §-ᵊn ‖ 'mjʊr-
murk mɜːk ‖ mɜːk
murk|y 'mɜːk li ‖'mɜːk li ~ier i_ə ‖ i_ᵊr ~iest
  i_ɪst i_əst ~ily ɪ li əl i ~iness i nəs i nɪs
Murmansk mɜː 'mænᵗsk mə- ‖ mʊr 'mɑːnᵗsk
  '•• —Russ ['mur mənsk]
murmur 'mɜːm ə ‖ 'mɜːm ᵊr ~ed d
  murmuring/ly 'mɜːm ᵊr_ɪŋ /li ‖ 'mɜːm
  ᵊr ɪŋ /li ~s z
Murph|y, murph|y 'mɜːf li ‖ 'mɜːf li ~ies,
  ~y's iz
  'Murphy's Law, ˌ••'•
murrain 'mʌr ɪn -ᵊn, -eɪn ‖ 'mɜː ᵊn ~s z
Murray 'mʌr i -eɪ ‖ 'mɜː i
Murrayfield 'mʌr i fiːᵊld ‖ 'mɜː-
murre mɜː ‖ mɜː (= myrrh) murres
  mɜːz ‖ mɜːz
Murrell (i) 'mʌr əl ‖ 'mɜː_əl, (ii) mʌ 'rel mə-
Murrow 'mʌr əʊ ‖ 'mɜː oʊ
Murrumbidgee ˌmʌr əm 'bɪdʒ i ‖ ˌmɜː əm-
Mururoa ˌmʊr ə 'rəʊ ə ‖ ˌmu ru 'rou ə
musaceous mju 'zeɪʃ əs
Muscadet, m~ 'mʌsk ə deɪ ˌ••'• —Fr
  [my ska de] ~s z
muscadine 'mʌsk ə daɪn -əd ɪn, -əd ᵊn ~s z
muscae volitantes ˌmʌsk i ˌvɒl ɪ 'tænt iːz
  ˌmʊsk-, ˌmʌs-, ˌ•aɪ-, -ə'•-, -eɪz ‖ -ˌvɑːl-
muscat 'mʌsk ət -æt ~s s
Muscat 'mʌsk æt mʌ 'skæt —Arabic
  ['mas qatˤ]
muscatel ˌmʌsk ə 'tel ~s z
muscl|e 'mʌs ᵊl (= mussel) ~ed d ~es ɪz əz ~ing
  _ɪŋ
muscle-bound 'mʌs ᵊl baʊnd
muscle|man 'mʌs ᵊl Imæn ~men men
muscly 'mʌs ᵊl_i
muscovado ˌmʌsk ə 'vɑːd əʊ -'veɪd- ‖ -oʊ
Muscovite, m~ 'mʌsk ə vaɪt ~s s
Muscovy 'mʌsk əv i

muscular 'mʌsk jʊl ə -jəl- ‖ -jəl ər ~ly li
  ‚muscular ' dystrophy
muscularity ‚mʌsk ju 'lær ət i -ɪt i
  ‖ -jə 'lær ət̬ i -'ler-
musculature 'mʌsk jʊl ətʃ ə '•jəl-, -ə tjʊə
  ‖ -jəl ə tʃʊr -ətʃ ər ~s z
muse, Muse mju:z mused mju:zd muses,
  Muses 'mju:z ɪz -əz musing/ly 'mju:z ɪŋ /li
musette mju 'zet —Fr [my zɛt] ~s s
museum mju 'zi:_əm ‚mju:- —Occasionally
  also -'zeɪ- ~s z
  mu'seum piece
Museveni mu 'sev ən i ‚mu:s ə 'veɪn i
Musgrave 'mʌz greɪv
Musgrove 'mʌz grəʊv ‖ -groʊv
mush 'soft mass, porridge' mʌʃ ‖ mʊʃ
mush 'face; fellow' mʊʃ
mush 'travel by dog team'; interj mʌʃ mushed
  mʌʃt mushes 'mʌʃ ɪz -əz mushing 'mʌʃ ɪŋ
mushroom 'mʌʃ rʊm -ru:m ‖ -ru:m -rʊm,
  -ru:n, 'mʌʃ ə- ~ed d ~ing ɪŋ ~s z
mush|y 'mʌʃ |i ‖ 'mʊʃ- ~ier i_ə ‖ i_ər ~iest
  i_ɪst i_əst ~ily ɪ li əl i ~iness i nəs i nɪs
music 'mju:z ɪk
  'music box; 'music ‚center, 'music ‚centre;
  'music hall; 'music stand
musical 'mju:z ɪk əl ~ly _i ~s z
  'musical box; ‚musical 'chairs; ‚musical
  'instrument
musicale ‚mju:z ɪ 'ka:l -'kæl ‖ -'kæl ~s z
musically 'mju:z ɪk əl_i
musicassette ‚mju:z ɪ kə 'set -kæ'• ~s s
musician mju 'zɪʃ ən ~s z ~ship ʃɪp
musicological ‚mju:z ɪk ə 'lɒdʒ ɪk əl ◂ ‚•ək-
  ‖ -'la:dʒ- ~ly _i
musicolog|ist/s ‚mju:z ɪ 'kɒl ədʒ |ɪst/s ‚•ə-,
  §-əst/s ‖ -'ka:l- ~y i
musique concrète
  mju ‚zi:k kɒŋ 'kret ‖ -koʊŋ- -kɔ:ŋ-, -ka:ŋ-
  —Fr [my zik kɔ̃ kʁɛt]
musk mʌsk
  'musk deer
muskeg 'mʌsk eg -eɪg
muskellung|e 'mʌsk ə lʌndʒ ~es ɪz əz
musket 'mʌsk ɪt -ət ~s s
musketeer ‚mʌsk ə 'tɪə -ɪ- ‖ -'tɪər ~s z
musketry 'mʌsk ɪtr i -ətr-
Muskie 'mʌsk i
muskmelon 'mʌsk ‚mel ən ~s z
Muskogean mʌ 'skəʊg i_ən ‖ -'skoʊg-
Muskogee mʌ 'skəʊg i ‖ -'skoʊg i ~s z
muskrat 'mʌsk ræt ~s s
musk|y 'mʌsk |i ~ier i_ə ‖ i_ər ~iest i_ɪst i_əst
  ~iness i nəs i nɪs
Muslim 'mʊz lɪm 'mʌz-, 'mʊs-, -ləm ‖ 'mu:z-,
  'mu:s-, 'mʌs- —BrE 1998 poll panel
  preference: 'mʊ- 70%, 'mʌ- 30%, -z- 89%,
  -s- 11%, -lɪm 91%, -ləm 9%. ~s z
muslin 'mʌz lɪn -ləm ~s z
musquash 'mʌsk wɒʃ ‖ -wɑ:ʃ -wɔ:ʃ ~es ɪz əz
muss mʌs mussed mʌst (= must) musses
  'mʌs ɪz -əz mussing 'mʌs ɪŋ
mussel 'mʌs əl ~s z

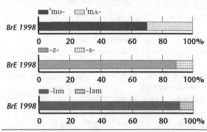

Musselburgh 'mʌs əl bər_ə -‚bʌr ə ‖ -‚bɝ: oʊ
Mussolini ‚mʊs ə 'li:n i ‚mʌs- ‖ ‚mu:s- —It
  [mus so 'li: ni]
Mussorgsky mu 'sɔ:g ski mə-, -'zɔ:g-
  ‖ -'sɔ:rg- -'zɔ:rg- —Russ ['mu sərk skɪj]
must strong form mʌst, weak forms məst, məs
mustach|e mə 'sta:ʃ mʊ-, §-'stæʃ, §-'stɒʃ
  ‖ 'mʌst æʃ mə 'stæʃ ~ed t ~es ɪz əz
mustachio mə 'sta:ʃ i əʊ -'stæʃ- ‖ -i oʊ -'•oʊ
  ~s z
Mustafa 'mʊst əf ə 'mʌst-, -ə fa:; mu 'sta:f ə,
  mə-
mustang 'mʌst æŋ ~s z
Mustapha 'mʊst əf ə 'mʌst-, -ə fa:;
  mu 'sta:f ə, mə-
mustard 'mʌst əd ‖ -ərd ~s z
  'mustard gas; 'mustard ‚plaster
muster 'mʌst ə ‖ -ər ~ed d mustering 'mʌst
  ər ɪŋ →'mʌs trɪŋ ~s z
musth mʌst
musti... —see musty
Mustique mu 'sti:k
mustn't 'mʌs ənt →-ən
must|y 'mʌst li ~ier i_ə ‖ i_ər ~iest i_ɪst i_əst
  ~ily ɪ li əl i ~iness i nəs i nɪs
mutability ‚mju:t ə 'bɪl ət i -ɪt i
  ‖ ‚mju:t̬ ə 'bɪl ət̬ i
mutab|le 'mju:t əb |əl ‖ 'mju:t̬- ~leness əl nəs
  -nɪs ~ly li
mutagen 'mju:t ədʒ ən -ə dʒen ‖ 'mju:t̬- ~s z
mutagenic ‚mju:t ə 'dʒen ɪk ◂ ‚mju:t̬- ~ally
  əl_i
mutagenicity ‚mju:t ə dʒe 'nɪs ət i -ɪt i
  ‖ ‚mju:t̬ ədʒ ə 'nɪs ət̬ i
mutant 'mju:t ənt ~s s
mutate mju 'teɪt ‖ 'mju:t eɪt ~tated teɪt ɪd
  -əd ‖ teɪt̬ əd ~tates teɪts ~tating
  teɪt ɪŋ ‖ teɪt̬ ɪŋ
mutation mju 'teɪʃ ən ~s z
mutatis mutandis mu ‚ta:t ɪs mu 'tænd ɪs
  mju-, -‚teɪt-, -‚i:s-, -mju'•-, -i:s ‖ -'ta:nd-
Mutch, mutch mʌtʃ mutches 'mʌtʃ ɪz -əz
mute mju:t muted 'mju:t ɪd -əd ‖ 'mju:t̬ əd
  mutely 'mju:t li muteness 'mju:t nəs -nɪs
  muter 'mju:t ə ‖ 'mju:t̬ ər mutes mju:ts
  mutest 'mju:t ɪst -əst ‖ 'mju:t̬ əst muting
  'mju:t ɪŋ ‖ 'mju:t̬ ɪŋ
muti|late 'mju:t ɪ |leɪt -ə-, -əl eɪt
  ‖ 'mju:t̬ əl eɪt ~lated leɪt ɪd -əd ‖ leɪt̬ əd
  ~lates leɪts ~lating leɪt ɪŋ ‖ leɪt̬ ɪŋ

M

mutilation ˌmjuːt ɪ 'leɪʃ ᵊn -ə-, -ᵊl 'eɪʃ- ‖ ˌmjuːt ᵊl 'eɪʃ ᵊn ~s z

mutineer ˌmjuːt ɪ 'nɪə -ə-, -ᵊn 'ɪə ‖ ˌmjuːt ᵊn 'ɪᵊr ~s z

mutini... —see mutiny

mutinous 'mjuːt ɪn əs -ᵊn- ‖ -ᵊn_əs ~ly li ~ness nəs nɪs

mutin|y 'mjuːt ᵊn |i -ɪn- ‖ -ᵊn |i ~ied id ~ies iz ~ying i ɪŋ

mutism 'mjuːt ,ɪz əm ‖ 'mjuːt̬-

mutt mʌt mutts mʌts

mutter, M~ 'mʌt ə ‖ 'mʌt̬ ᵊr ~ed d
muttering/ly 'mʌt_ᵊr ɪŋ /li ‖ 'mʌt̬ ᵊr ɪŋ /li
→'mʌtr ɪŋ /li ~s z

mutterer 'mʌt ᵊr ə ‖ 'mʌt̬ ᵊr ᵊr ~s z

mutton 'mʌt ᵊn

muttonchop ˌmʌt ᵊn 'tʃɒp ◄ ‖ 'mʌt ᵊn tʃɑːp ~s s
ˌmuttonchop 'whiskers

muttonhead 'mʌt ᵊn hed ~s z

mutual 'mjuːtʃ u_əl 'mjuːt ju_; 'mjuːtʃ əl ~ly i ~s z
'mutual fund

mutuality ˌmjuːtʃ u 'æl ət i ˌmjuːt ju-, -ɪt i ‖ -ət̬ i

muu-muu 'muː muː ~s z

Muxworthy 'mʌks ˌwɜːð i ‖ -ˌwɜ˞ːð i

Muybridge 'maɪ brɪdʒ

muzak, Muzak tdmk 'mjuːz æk

muzz mʌz muzzed mʌzd muzzes 'mʌz ɪz -əz muzzing 'mʌz ɪŋ

muzzl|e 'mʌz ᵊl ~ed d ~es z ~ing_ɪŋ

muzzle-loader 'mʌz ᵊl ˌləʊd ə ‖ -ˌloʊd ᵊr ~s z

muzz|y 'mʌz li ~ier i_ə ‖ i_ᵊr ~iest i_ɪst i_əst ~ily ɪ li əl i ~iness i nəs i nɪs

mwah mwɑː mwʌ

my maɪ —There are also weak forms mi, mə, found mainly in British regional (non-RP) speech (where it may be shown in spelling as me), but also sometimes, mainly in set phrases, in casual RP. Otherwise, there is no distinct weak form.

myalgia maɪ 'ældʒ ə -i_ə

myalgic maɪ 'ældʒ ɪk

myall, Myall 'maɪ ɔːl ‖ -ɑːl ~s z

Myanmar 'miː_ᵊn mɑː →_ᵊm-; mi 'æn mɑː ‖ -mɑːr mi ˌɑːn 'mɑːr

myasthenia ˌmaɪ_əs 'θiːn i_ə

myasthenic ˌmaɪ_əs 'θen ɪk ◄

myceli|um maɪ 'siːl i_|əm ~a ə

mycella maɪ 'sel ə

Mycenae maɪ 'siːn i -iː

Mycenaean ˌmaɪs ə 'niː_ᵊn ◄ -ɪ-, -iː- ~s z

myco- comb. form
with stress-neutral suffix ˌmaɪk əʊ ‖ -ə —
mycotoxin ˌmaɪk əʊ 'tɒks ɪn §-ᵊn ‖ -ə 'tɑːks ᵊn
with stress-imposing suffix maɪ 'kɒ+ ‖ -'kɑː+ —
mycologist maɪ 'kɒl ədʒ ɪst §-əst ‖ -'kɑːl-

mycology maɪ 'kɒl ədʒ i ‖ -'kɑːl-

mycosis maɪ 'kəʊs ɪs §-əs ‖ -'koʊs əs

mydriasis maɪ 'draɪ_əs ɪs mɪ-, §-əs

myelin 'maɪ_əl ɪn -ɪl-, §-ən
ˌmyelin 'sheath

myelitis ˌmaɪ_ə 'laɪt ɪs -ɪ-, §-əs ‖ -'laɪt̬ əs

myelo- comb. form
with stress-neutral suffix ˌmaɪ_əl əʊ maɪ ˌel əʊ ‖ ˌmaɪ əl ə — myelogram 'maɪ_əl əʊ græm maɪ 'el- ‖ 'maɪ əl ə-
with stress-imposing suffix ˌmaɪ_ə 'lɒ+ ‖ -'lɑː+ — myelography ˌmaɪ_ə 'lɒg rəf i ‖ -'lɑːg-

myeloid 'maɪ_ə lɔɪd

myelom|a ˌmaɪ_ə 'ləʊm |ə ‖ -'loʊm |ə ~as əz ~ata ət ə ‖ ət̬ ə

Myer 'maɪ_ə ‖ 'maɪ_ᵊr

Myers 'maɪ_əz ‖ 'maɪ_ᵊrz

Myfanwy mə 'væn wi mɪ-, -'fæn- —Welsh [mə 'van wi, -'va nui]

Mykonos 'miːk ə nɒs 'mɪk- ‖ -nɑːs -noʊs, -nɔːs —ModGk ['mi kɔ nɔs]

mylar, Mylar tdmk 'maɪl ɑː ‖ -ɑːr

Myles maɪᵊlz

mylonite 'maɪl ə naɪt 'mɪl-

myna, mynah 'maɪn ə ~s z
'mynah bird

Mynd mɪnd

Mynett, Mynott 'maɪn ət

myo- comb. form
with stress-neutral suffix ˌmaɪ əʊ ‖ -ə —
myocardial ˌmaɪ əʊ 'kɑːd i_əl ◄ ‖ -ə 'kɑːrd-
with stress-imposing suffix maɪ 'ɒ+ ‖ -'ɑː+ —
myopathy maɪ 'ɒp əθ i ‖ -'ɑːp-

myocardiogram ˌmaɪ əʊ 'kɑːd i_ə græm ‖ -ə 'kɑːrd- ~s z

myoclonic ˌmaɪ əʊ 'klɒn ɪk ◄ ‖ -ə 'klɑːn ɪk ◄
ˌmyo,clonic 'spasm

myoelastic ˌmaɪ əʊ ɪ 'læst ɪk ◄ -ə'•-, -'lɑːst- ‖ ˌmaɪ oʊ-

myope 'maɪ əʊp ‖ -oʊp ~s s

myopia maɪ 'əʊp i_ə ‖ -'oʊp-

myopic maɪ 'ɒp ɪk -'əʊp- ‖ -'ɑːp ɪk -'oʊp- ~ally ᵊl_i

myosin 'maɪ əʊ sɪn -əs ᵊn ‖ -əs ᵊn

myosotis ˌmaɪ_ə 'səʊt ɪs §-əs ‖ -'soʊt̬ əs

Myra 'maɪᵊr ə

myriad 'mɪr i_əd ~s z

myriapod 'mɪr i_ə pɒd ‖ -pɑːd ~s z

myrmecophagous ˌmɜːm i 'kɒf əg əs ◄ ˌ•ə- ‖ ˌmɜ˞ːm ə 'kɑːf-

Myrmidon, m~ 'mɜːm ɪd ᵊn -əd-; -ɪ dɒn, -ə- ‖ 'mɜ˞ːm ə dɑːn -əd ᵊn ~s z

Myrna 'mɜːn ə ‖ 'mɜ˞ːn ə

myrobalan maɪᵊ 'rɒb əl ən mɪ-, mə- ‖ -'rɑːb- ~s z

Myron 'maɪᵊr ᵊn

myrrh mɜː ‖ mɜ˞ː

myrtle, M~ 'mɜːt ᵊl ‖ 'mɜ˞ːt̬ ᵊl ~s, ~'s z

myself maɪ 'self mɪ-, mə- —In BrE the forms mɪ-, mə- are on the whole restricted to very casual or non-standard speech.

Mysore ₍ᵢ₎maɪ 'sɔː ‖ -'sɔːr -'soʊr

mystagogue 'mɪst ə gɒg ‖ -gɑːg -gɔːg

mysterious mɪ 'stɪər i_əs mə- ‖ -'stɪr- ~ly li ~ness nəs nɪs

M

myster|y 'mɪs tr│i 'mɪst ər │i **~ies** iz
  'mystery play; 'mystery tour
mystic, M~ 'mɪst ɪk **~s** s
mystical 'mɪst ɪk əl **~ly** _i **~ness** nəs nɪs
mysticism 'mɪst ɪ ˌsɪz əm -ə-
mystification ˌmɪst ɪf ɪ 'keɪʃ ən ˌ•əf-, §-ə'•-
  ~s z
mysti|fy 'mɪst ɪ │faɪ -ə- **~fied** faɪd **~fier/s**
  faɪ_ə/z ‖ faɪ_ər/z **~fies** faɪz **~fying** faɪ ɪŋ
mystique mɪ 'stiːk ˌmɪs 'tiːk **~s** s
myth mɪθ **myths** mɪθs
mythic 'mɪθ ɪk **~al** əl **~ally** əl_i
mytho- comb. form
  with stress-neutral suffix ˌmɪθ əʊ ‖ -ə —
  mythopoeic ˌmɪθ əʊ 'piː ɪk ◂ ‖ -ə-
  with stress-imposing suffix mɪ 'θɒ+ mə-, maɪ-
  ‖ -'θɑː+ — **mythography** mɪ 'θɒg rəf i mə-,
  maɪ- ‖ -'θɑːg-
Mytholmroyd ˌmaɪð əm 'rɔɪd

mythological ˌmɪθ ə 'lɒdʒ ɪk əl ◂ ˌmaɪθ-
  ‖ -'lɑːdʒ- **~ly** _i
mythologist mɪ 'θɒl ədʒ ɪst mə-, maɪ-, §-əst
  ‖ -'θɑːl- **~s** s
mytholog|y mɪ 'θɒl ədʒ │i mə-, maɪ- ‖ -'θɑːl-
  ~ies iz
mytho|poeia ˌmɪθ əʊ │'piːˌə ‖ -ə- **~poeic**
  'piː ɪk ◂
Mytilene ˌmɪt ɪ 'liːn i -ə-, -əl 'iːn-, -iː
  ‖ ˌmɪt əl 'iːn i
Mytton 'mɪt ən
myxedema, myxoedema ˌmɪks ɪ 'diːm ə -iː-,
  §-ə-
myxomatosis ˌmɪks əm ə 'təʊs ɪs §-əs
  ‖ -'toʊs əs
myxomycete ˌmɪks əʊ maɪ 'siːt ˌ••'•• ‖ ˌ•oʊ-
  ~s s
myxovirus 'mɪks əʊ ˌvaɪər əs ˌ••'•• ‖ -ə- **~es**
  ɪz əz

M

Nn

---

n	Spelling-to-sound

1 Where the spelling is **n**, the pronunciation is regularly n, as in **nation** 'neɪʃ ᵊn, or ŋ, as in **think** θɪŋk. **n** also forms part of the digraph **ng**.

2 The pronunciation is n everywhere EXCEPT
  • before the sound k (written **c, g, k, q, x**), and
  • where the spelling is the digraph **ng** (see **ng** 2, 3 below),
  in which cases the pronunciation is regularly ŋ.
  Examples:
  n in **net, fan, unit, enter**;
  ŋ in **uncle, anger, thanks, conquer, anxious, wing**.

3 Where the spelling is doubled **nn**, the pronunciation is again regularly n, as in **funny** 'fʌn i.

4 **n** is silent when it follows **m** at the end of a word, and in the corresponding inflected forms, as in **column** 'kɒl əm ‖ 'kɑːl əm, **condemned** kən 'demd (but **hymnal** 'hɪmnəl).

---

ng	Spelling-to-sound

1 Where the spelling is the digraph **ng**, the pronunciation is regularly
  ŋ, as in **singing** 'sɪŋ ɪŋ,
  ŋg, as in **angle** 'æŋ gəl, or
  ndʒ, as in **strange** streɪndʒ.

2 The pronunciation is ŋ when **ng** is at the end of a word or stem. Examples: **hang** hæŋ, **singer** 'sɪŋ ə ‖ 'sɪŋ ᵊr, **strongly** 'strɒŋ li ‖ 'strɔːŋ li. (Although in this position plain [ŋ] is standard in RP and GenAm, some speakers use [ŋg].)

3 The pronunciation is usually ŋg when **ng** is in the middle of a word (and not at the end of a stem). Examples: **hungry** 'hʌŋ gri, **finger** 'fɪŋ gə ‖ 'fɪŋ gᵊr, **single** 'sɪŋ gəl.

4 The pronunciation is ndʒ
  where the spelling is **nge** at the end of a word, as in **challenge** 'tʃæl ɪndʒ,
  and sometimes before **e, i, y** in the middle of a word, as in **danger** 'deɪndʒ ə ‖ 'deɪndʒ ᵊr.

5 The three pronunciations corresponding to the spelling **ng** are illustrated in the same context in the sets
  singer 'sɪŋ ə ‖ -ᵊr,
  finger 'fɪŋ gə ‖ -gᵊr,

ginger 'dʒɪn*dʒ* ə ‖ -ᵊr;
hanger 'hæŋ ə ‖ -ᵊr,
anger 'æŋ gə ‖ -gᵊr,
danger 'deɪn*dʒ* ə ‖ -ᵊr.

6 Where **n** belongs to a prefix and **g** to a stem, they do not form a digraph. Consequently, the pronunciation is usually n, as in **ingenious** ɪn 'dʒiːn i‿əs. However, where the **g** is hard, then the n may become ŋ by ASSIMILATION. This is regular where the syllable containing the nasal is stressed, as in **congress** 'kɒŋ gres ‖ 'kaːŋ grəs, and otherwise optional, as in **conclusion** kən 'kluːʒ ᵊn →kəŋ-. (The assimilation seems to be usually made in BrE but rarely in AmE).

N, n en **N's, n's, Ns** enz *Communications code name:* November
N —*see* North, Northerly, Northern
'n, 'n' *conventional spelling for the weak form of* and ən, ᵊn, ⁿ
 ˌfish 'n' 'chips
Naafi, NAAFI 'næf i
naan naːn næn
Naas *place in Co. Kildare* neɪs
nab næb **nabbed** næbd **nabbing** 'næb ɪŋ **nabs** næbz
Nabarro nə 'baːr əʊ ‖ -oʊ
Nabataean, Nabatean ˌnæb ə 'tiː‿ən ◄ ~s z
nabb... —*see* nab
Nabbs næbz
Nabisco *tdmk* nə 'bɪsk əʊ næ- ‖ -oʊ
Nablus 'naːb ləs 'næb-, -lʊs
nabob 'neɪb ɒb ‖ -aːb ~s z
Nabokov nə 'bəʊk ɒf 'næb ə kɒf ‖ -'bɔːk əf -'baːk-; 'næb ə kaːf, 'naːb-, -kɔːf
Naboth 'neɪb ɒθ ‖ -aːθ -oʊθ
nacelle nə 'sel næ- ~s z
nacho 'naːtʃ əʊ ‖ -oʊ ~s z
Nacogdoches *place in TX* ˌnæk ə 'dəʊtʃ ɪz -əz ‖ -'doʊtʃ əz
nacre 'neɪk ə ‖ -ᵊr
nacreous 'neɪk ri‿əs
NACRO 'næk rəʊ ‖ -roʊ
Na-Dene, Na-Déné ˌnaː 'deɪn i -'den-, -eɪ; -də 'neɪ; nə 'diːn
Nader 'neɪd ə ‖ -ᵊr
Nadi *place in Fiji* 'nænd ɪ 'naːnd i
Nadia *(i)* 'neɪd i‿ə, *(ii)* 'naːd i‿ə
Nadine neɪ 'diːn nə-
nadir 'neɪd ɪə 'næd- ‖ -ɪr -ᵊr ~s z
Nadir næ 'dɪə ‖ -'dɪᵊr
nae neɪ
naev|us 'niːv |əs ~i aɪ
naff næf **naffer** 'næf ə ‖ -ᵊr **naffest** 'næf ɪst -əst
 ˌnaff 'off
NAFTA 'næft ə
nag næg **nagged** nægd **nagger/s** 'næg ə/ z ‖ -ᵊr/z **nagging** 'næg ɪŋ **nags** nægz
Naga 'naːg ə ‖ -aː ~s z

Nagaland 'naːg ə lænd
nagana nə 'gaːn ə
Nagano ˌnæg ə nəʊ 'naːg- ‖ -noʊ nə 'gaːn oʊ —*Jp* ['na ŋa no, -ga-]
Nagari 'naːg ər i
Nagasaki ˌnæg ə 'saːk i ˌnaːg- ‖ -'sæk- —*Jp* [na 'ŋa sa ki, -'ga-]
nagg... —*see* nag
Nagorno-Karabakh nə ˌgɔːn əʊ ˌkær ə 'bæk -'baːk ‖ nə ˌgɔːrn oʊ ˌkaːr ə 'baːk —*Russ* [nə ˌgor nə kə rə 'bax]
Nagoya nə 'gɔɪ ə —*Jp* ['na ŋo ja, -go-]
Nagpur ˌnæg 'pʊə ˌnaːg-, -'pɔː ‖ ˌnaːg 'pʊᵊr
Nagy nɒdʒ ‖ naːdʒ —*Hung* [nɒdʲ]
nah *informal, 'no'* næː nʌː ‖ naː
Nahuatl 'naː waːt ᵊl • ‖ • • **~an** ˌən ~s z
Nahum 'neɪ həm -hʌm, -əm
naiad 'naɪ æd 'naɪ‿əd **naiades** 'naɪ‿ə diːz ~s z
naif, naïf naɪ 'iːf naː-
nail neɪᵊl **nailed** neɪᵊld **nailing** 'neɪᵊl ɪŋ **nails** neɪᵊlz
 'nail ˌfile; 'nail ˌpolish; 'nail ˌscissors; 'nail ˌvarnish
nail-bit|er/s 'neɪᵊl ˌbaɪt |ə/z ‖ -ˌbaɪt̮ |ᵊr/z **~ing/ly** ɪŋ /li
nailbrush 'neɪᵊl brʌʃ **~es** ɪz əz
nailclipper 'neɪᵊl ˌklɪp ə ‖ -ᵊr ~s z
Nailsea 'neɪᵊl siː
Nailsworth 'neɪᵊlz wəθ -wɜːθ ‖ -wᵊrθ -wɜːθ
Naipaul 'naɪ pɔːl
naira 'naɪᵊr ə
Nairn neən ‖ neᵊrn næᵊrn
Nairobi naɪᵊ 'rəʊb i ‖ -'roʊb i
Naish *(i)* neɪʃ, *(ii)* næʃ
Naismith 'neɪ smɪθ
naive, naïve naɪ 'iːv naː- **~ly** li **~ness** nəs nɪs
naiveté, naïveté naɪ 'iːv ə teɪ naː-; -'iːv teɪ —*Fr* [na if te]
naivet|y, naïvet|y naɪ 'iːv ət |i naː-, -ɪt-; -'iːv t|i ‖ -ət̮ |i **~ies** iz
naked 'neɪk ɪd -əd *(!)* **~ly** li **~ness** nəs nɪs
naker 'neɪk ə 'næk- ‖ -ᵊr ~s z
Nakhichevan ˌnaːk ɪ tʃ i 'vaːn ˌnæk-, ˌ•ə-, -tʃ ə • •, -'væn —*Russ* [nə xʲi tʃi 'vanʲ]
NALGO 'nælg əʊ ‖ -oʊ

N

Nam, 'Nam *'Vietnam'* næm nɑːm
Nama 'nɑːm ə ‖ -ɑː ~s z
Namaland 'nɑːm ə lænd
Namaqualand nə 'mɑːk wə lænd
namby-pam|by ˌnæm bi 'pæm |bi ◂ ~bies biz
name neɪm named neɪmd names neɪmz
  naming 'neɪm ɪŋ
  'name day
namedrop 'neɪm drɒp ‖ -drɑːp ~ped t ~per/
  s ə/z ‖ ᵊr/z ~ping ɪŋ ~s s
nameless 'neɪm ləs -lɪs ~ly li ~ness nəs nɪs
namely 'neɪm li
nameplate 'neɪm pleɪt ~s s
namesake 'neɪm seɪk ~s s
nametag 'neɪm tæg ~s z
Namibi|a nə 'mɪb i‿ə ~an/s ən/z
Namier 'neɪm ɪə 'neɪm i‿ə ‖ -ɪr
Namur næ 'mjʊə -'mʊə ‖ nə 'mjʊᵊr -'mʊᵊr
  —*Fr* [na my:ʁ]
nan *'bread'* nɑːn næn
nan *'grandmother'*, Nan *personal name* næn
  nans, Nan's nænz
Nanaimo nə 'naɪm əʊ næ- ‖ -oʊ
Nanak 'nɑːn ək
Nancarrow næn 'kær əʊ →næŋ- ‖ -oʊ -'ker-
Nance, nance nænᵗs
Nanchang ˌnæn 'tʃæŋ ◂ ‖ ˌnɑːn 'tʃɑːŋ —*Chi*
  Nánchāng [²nan ¹tṣʰaŋ]
Nanci, Nancie, Nancy *personal name*, n~
  'nænᵗs i
Nancy *place in France* ˌnɒ̃ 'siː ˌnɑːn-, ' • • —*Fr*
  [nɑ̃ si]
NAND nænd
  'NAND gate
Nandi *place in Fiji* 'nænd ɪ 'nɑːnd i
nandina næn 'diːn ə ~s z
Nanette næ 'net nə-
Nanga Parbat ˌnʌŋ gə 'pɜːb ət ˌnæŋ-, -'pɑːb-,
  -æt ‖ -'pɝːrb- -'pɑːrb-
Nanjing ˌnæn 'dʒɪŋ ‖ ˌnɑːn- —*Chi* Nánjīng
  [²nan ¹dʒiŋ]
nankeen ₍ˌ₎næn 'kiːn ◂ →næŋ-
  ˌnankeen 'kestrel
Nanking ˌnæn |'kɪŋ ◂ →ˌnæŋ- ‖ ˌnɑːn- —*Chi*
  Nánjīing [²nan ¹dʒiŋ]
Nannie 'næn i
Nanning ˌnæn 'nɪŋ ◂ ‖ ˌnɑːn- —*Chi* Nánníng
  [²nan ²niŋ]
nann|y, Nann|y 'næn li ~ies, ~y's iz
  'nanny goat
nannygai 'næn i gaɪ ~s z
nano- ¦næn əʊ ‖ -ə -oʊ — nanosecond
  'næn əʊ ˌsek ənd →-ŋd ‖ -ə-
  nanotechnology ˌnæn əʊ
  tek 'nɒl ədʒ i ‖ -oʊ tek 'nɑːl-
Nanook 'næn uːk -ʊk
Nansen 'nænᵗs ən ‖ 'nɑːnᵗs-
Nant *in Welsh placenames* nænt —*Welsh* [nant]
Nantes *in* næn/s, nɒnt —*Fr* [nɑ̃ːt]
Nantffrancon nænt 'fræŋk ən —*Welsh*
  [nant 'fraŋ kon]
Nantgarw nænt 'gær u: —*Welsh* [nant 'ga ru]
Nantucket næn 'tʌk ɪt -ət

Nantwich 'nænt wɪtʃ
Naoise 'niːʃ ə -i
Naomi *(i)* 'neɪ əm i ‖ -aɪ, *(ii)*
  neɪ 'əʊm i ‖ -'oʊm i -aɪ
nap næp napped næpt napping 'næp ɪŋ
  naps næps
Napa 'næp ə
  ˌNapa 'Valley◂
napalm 'neɪp ɑːm 'næp-, §-ɑːlm ~ed d ~ing
  ɪŋ ~s z
nape neɪp napes neɪps
Naphtali 'næft ə laɪ
naphtha 'næfθ ə 'næpθ-
naphthalene 'næfθ ə liːn 'næpθ-
naphthol 'næfθ ɒl 'næpθ- ‖ -ɔːl -ɑːl, -oʊl
Napier 'neɪp i‿ə ‖ -ᵊr —*but a few people with this*
  surname call it nə 'pɪə ‖ -'pɪᵊr
Napierian nə 'pɪər i‿ən neɪ- ‖ -'pɪr-
napkin 'næp kɪn §-kən ~s z
  'napkin ring
Naples 'neɪp ᵊlz
Napoleon, n~ nə 'pəʊl i‿ən ‖ -'poʊl- ~s, ~'s z
Napoleonic nə ˌpəʊl i 'ɒn ɪk ◂
  ‖ nə ˌpoʊl i 'ɑːn ɪk ◂
napolitaine, N~ næ ˌpɒl i 'teɪn nə-, -ə-
  ‖ -ˌpɑːl- —*Fr* [na pɔ li tɛn]
nappe næp
napp|y 'næp li ~ies iz
  'nappy rash; 'nappy ˌliner
Nara 'nɑːr ə —*Jp* ['na ra]
Narayan nə 'raɪ‿ən
Narbonne ₍ₒ₎nɑː 'bɒn ‖ ₍ₒ₎nɑːr 'bɔːn -'bɑːn,
  -'bʌn —*Fr* [naʁ bɔn]
narc nɑːk ‖ nɑːrk narcs nɑːks ‖ nɑːrks
narciss|i nɑː 'sɪs aɪ -iː ‖ nɑːr- ~ism ˌɪz əm
  ~ist ɪst §əst
narcissistic ˌnɑːs ɪ 'sɪst ɪk ◂ -ə- ‖ ˌnɑːrs- ~ally
  ᵊl‿i
narciss|us, N~ nɑː 'sɪs əs ‖ nɑːr- ~i aɪ
narcolepsy 'nɑːk əʊ leps i ‖ 'nɑːrk ə-
narcoleptic ˌnɑːk əʊ 'lept ɪk ◂ ‖ -ə-
narcos|is nɑː 'kəʊs ɪs §-əs ‖ nɑːr 'koʊs ləs
  ~es iːz
narcotic nɑː 'kɒt ɪk ‖ nɑːr 'kɑːt̬ ɪk ~ally ᵊl‿i
  ~s s
narcotis... —*see* narcotiz...
narcotism 'nɑːk ə ˌtɪz əm ‖ 'nɑːrk-
narcotiz|e 'nɑːk ə taɪz ‖ 'nɑːrk- ~ed d ~es ɪz
  əz ~ing ɪŋ
nard nɑːd ‖ nɑːrd
nardoo ˌnɑː 'duː ‖ ˌnɑːr-
nareal 'neər i‿əl ‖ 'ner- 'nær-
Narelle nə 'rel
nares 'neər iːz ‖ 'ner- 'nær-
narghile, nargile, nargileh 'nɑːg ə leɪ -ɪ-, -li
  ‖ 'nɑːrg- ~s z
narial 'neər i‿əl ‖ 'ner- 'nær-
Narita 'nær ɪt ə -ət-; nə 'riːt ə —*Jp* ['na ri ta]
nark nɑːk ‖ nɑːrk narked nɑːkt ‖ nɑːrkt
  narking 'nɑːk ɪŋ ‖ 'nɑːrk ɪŋ narks
  nɑːks ‖ nɑːrks
nark|y 'nɑːk li ‖ 'nɑːrk li ~ier i‿ə ‖ i‿ᵊr ~iest
  i‿ɪst i‿əst

Narnia 'nɑːn i_ə ‖ 'nɑːrn-
Narraganset, Narrangansett
,nær ə 'gæn¹s ɪt ◀ -ət ‖ ,ner-
,Narra,gansett 'Bay
Narrandera *place in NSW* nə 'rænd ər ə
narrate nə 'reɪt næ- ‖ 'nær eɪt 'ner-; næ 'reɪt
  narrated nə 'reɪt ɪd næ-, -əd ‖ 'nær eɪt əd
  'ner-; næ 'reɪt- narrates nə 'reɪts næ-
  ‖ 'nær eɪts 'ner-; næ 'reɪts narrating
  nə 'reɪt ɪŋ næ- ‖ 'nær eɪt ɪŋ 'ner-; næ 'reɪt-
narration nə 'reɪʃ ᵊn næ- ‖ næ- ~s z
narrative 'nær ət ɪv ‖ -ət̬ ɪv 'ner- ~ly li ~s z
narrator nə 'reɪt ə næ-; 'nær ət ə ‖ 'nær eɪt̬ ᵊr
  'ner-, -ət̬-; næ 'reɪt̬-, nə- *(*)* ~s z
narrow 'nær əʊ ‖ -oʊ 'ner- ~ed d ~er ə ‖ ᵊr
  ~est ɪst əst ~ing ɪŋ ~ly li ~ness nəs nɪs ~s
  z
  'narrow boat; ,narrow 'gauge◀, '·· ·;
  ,narrow 'squeak
narrowcast 'nær əʊ kɑːst §-kæst ‖ -oʊ kæst
  'ner- ~er/s ə/z ‖ ᵊr/z ~ing ɪŋ
narrow-minded ,nær əʊ 'maɪnd ɪd ◀ -əd ‖ -oʊ-
  ,ner- ~ly li ~ness nəs nɪs
narthex 'nɑːθ eks ‖ 'nɑːrθ- ~es ɪz əz
narwhal 'nɑː wəl ‖ 'nɑːr *h*wɑːl ~s z
nary 'neər i ‖ 'ner i 'nær-
n-ary 'en ər i
NASA 'næs ə 'nɑːs-
nasal 'neɪz ᵊl ~s z
nasalis... —*see* nasaliz...
nasality neɪ 'zæl ət i -ɪt- ‖ -ət̬ i
nasalization ,neɪz ᵊl aɪ 'zeɪʃ ᵊn -əl ɪ- ‖ -əl ə-
  ~s z
nasaliz|e 'neɪz ə laɪz -ᵊl aɪz ~ed d ~es ɪz əz
  ~ing ɪŋ
nasally 'neɪz ᵊl i
nascent 'næs ᵊnt ‖ 'neɪs-
naseberr|y 'neɪz ,ber li ~ies iz
Naseby 'neɪz bi
Nash, Nashe næʃ
Nashua 'næʃ u_ə
Nashville 'næʃ vɪl -vᵊl
nasi goreng ,nɑːs i gə 'reŋ ,næs-, ,nɑːz-,
  -'gɒr eŋ, -'gɔːr eŋ —*Bahasa Ind*
  [,na si 'go reŋ]
nasion 'neɪz i_ən -ɒn ‖ -ɑːn ~s z
Nasmyth *(i)* 'neɪs mɪθ *(ii)* 'neɪz- *(iii)* 'næs-
nasofrontal ,neɪz əʊ 'frʌnt ᵊl ◀ ‖ -oʊ 'frʌnt̬ ᵊl ◀
nasopharyngeal ,neɪz əʊ ,fær ɪn 'dʒɪ_əl
  -,·ən-; -fə 'rɪndʒ i_əl, -fæ'·- ‖ ,·oʊ- -,fer-
nasopharynx ,neɪz əʊ ,fær ɪŋks , · · ‖ · · · ‖ -oʊ-
  -,fer- *(*)* ~es ɪz əz
Nassau *places in Bahamas and USA* 'næs ɔː ‖ -ɑː
Nassau *region of Germany* 'næs aʊ ‖ 'nɑːs-
  —*Ger* ['na saʊ]
Nassau *princely family* 'næs ɔː -aʊ ‖ 'nɑːs aʊ
Nasser 'næs ə 'nɑːs- ‖ -ᵊr —*Arabic* ['na: sˤ ɪr]
Nastase nə 'stɑːz i næ-, -eɪ
nastic 'næst ɪk
nast|y 'nɑːst li §'næst- ‖ 'næst li *(*)* ~ier
  i_ə ‖ i_ᵊr ~ies iz ~iest i_ɪst i_əst ~ily ɪ li əl i
  ~iness i nəs i nɪs

Nat næt Nats, Nat's næts
natal 'neɪt ᵊl ‖ 'neɪt̬ ᵊl
Natal *province of South Africa* nə 'tæl -'tɑːl
Natalie 'næt əl i ‖ 'næt̬ ᵊl i
natalit|y neɪ 'tæl ət i nə-, -ɪt- ‖ -ət̬ li ~ies iz
Natasha nə 'tæʃ ə ‖ -'tɑːʃ ə
natch nætʃ
Natchez 'nætʃ ɪz -əz
Natchitoches *place in Louisiana* 'næk ə tɒʃ
  -ət əʃ ‖ -ə tɑːʃ -ət̬ əʃ
nates 'neɪt iːz
NATFHE 'næt fi -fiː
Nathan 'neɪθ ᵊn
Nathanael, Nathaniel nə 'θæn i_əl
Natick 'neɪt ɪk
nation 'neɪʃ ᵊn ~s z
  ,nation 'state, '·· ·
national 'næʃ ᵊn_əl ~s z
  ,national 'anthem; ,national 'debt;
  ,National 'Front; ,national 'government;
  ,National 'Health ,Service; ,National
  In'surance; ,national 'park; ,national
  'service; ,National 'Trust
nationalis... —*see* nationaliz...
nationalism 'næʃ ᵊn_əl ,ɪz əm ~s z
nationalist 'næʃ ᵊn_əl ɪst §-əst ~s s
nationalistic ,næʃ ᵊn_ə 'lɪst ɪk ◀ _əl 'ɪst- ~ally
  ᵊl_i
nationalit|y ,næʃ ə 'næl ət li ,næʃ '···, -ɪt i
  ‖ -ət̬ li ~ies iz
nationalization ,næʃ ᵊn_əl aɪ 'zeɪʃ ᵊn -ɪ'·-
  ‖ -ə 'zeɪʃ- ~s z
nationaliz|e 'næʃ ᵊn_ə laɪz _əl aɪz ~ed d ~es
  ɪz əz ~ing ɪŋ
nationally 'næʃ ᵊn_əl i
nationhood 'neɪʃ ᵊn hʊd
nation-state ,neɪʃ ᵊn 'steɪt ‖ '···
nationwide, N~ ,neɪʃ ᵊn 'waɪd ◀ '···
  ,nationwide 'broadcast
native 'neɪt ɪv ‖ 'neɪt̬ ɪv ~s z
  ,Native 'American; ,native 'speaker
native-born ,neɪt ɪv 'bɔːn ◀ '···
  ‖ ,neɪt̬ ɪv 'bɔːrn ◀
native|ly 'neɪt ɪv |li ‖ 'neɪt̬ ɪv- ~ness nəs nɪs
nativit|y, N~ nə 'tɪv ət li -ɪt- ‖ -ət̬ li neɪ- ~ies
  iz
  na'tivity play
NATO, Nato 'neɪt əʊ ‖ 'neɪt̬ oʊ 'neɪ toʊ
natron 'neɪtr ən -ɒn ‖ -ɑːn
NATSOPA næt 'səʊp ə ‖ -'soʊp ə
natter 'næt ə ‖ 'næt̬ ᵊr ~ed d nattering
  'næt ᵊr ɪŋ ‖ 'næt̬ ᵊr ɪŋ ~s z
natterjack 'næt ə dʒæk ‖ 'næt̬ ᵊr- ~s s
natt|y 'næt li ‖ 'næt̬ li ~ier i_ə ‖ i_ᵊr ~iest i_ɪst
  i_əst ~ily ɪ li əl i ~iness i nəs i nɪs
natural 'nætʃ ᵊr_əl ~s z
  ,natural 'gas; ,natural 'history; ,natural
  phi'losophy; ,natural 'science; ,natural
  se'lection
naturalis... —*see* naturaliz...
naturalism 'nætʃ ᵊr_ə ,lɪz əm
naturalist 'nætʃ ᵊr_əl ɪst §-əst ~s s
naturalistic ,nætʃ ᵊr_ə 'lɪst ɪk ◀ ~ally ᵊl_i

N

naturalization ˌnætʃ ər_ə laɪ 'zeɪʃ ən -ər_əl aɪ-,
-ər_əl ɪ- ‖ -ər_əl ə- ~s z
naturaliz|e 'nætʃ ər_ə laɪz _əl aɪz ~ed d ~es
ɪz əz ~ing ɪŋ
natural|ly 'nætʃ ər_əl i ~ness nəs nɪs
nature 'neɪtʃ ə ‖ -ər ~d d ~s z
   'nature re,serve; 'nature ,study
naturism 'neɪtʃ ər ˌɪz əm
naturist 'neɪtʃ ər ɪst §-əst ~s s
naturopath 'neɪtʃ ər əʊ pæθ 'nætʃ- ‖ -ər ə-
   ~s s
naturopathic ˌneɪtʃ ər əʊ 'pæθ ɪk ◄ ˌnætʃ-
   ‖ -ər ə- ~ally əl_i
naturopathy ˌneɪtʃ ə 'rɒp əθ i ˌnætʃ- ‖ -'rɑːp-
NatWest tdmk ˌnæt 'west ◄
Naucratis 'nɔːk rət ɪs §-əs ‖ -rət̬-
Naugahyde tdmk 'nɔːg ə haɪd ‖ 'nɑːg-
naught nɔːt ‖ nɑːt naughts nɔːts ‖ nɑːts
Naughtie 'nɒxt i ‖ 'nɔːkt i
naught|y 'nɔːt li ‖ 'nɔːt̬ li 'nɑːt̬- ~ier i_ə ‖ i_ər
   ~iest i_ɪst i_əst ~ily ɪ li əl i ~iness i nəs i nɪs
Naunton 'nɔːnt ən ‖ 'nɔːnt ən 'nɑːnt-
naupli|us 'nɔːp li_əs ‖ 'nɑːp- ~i aɪ i:
Nauru nə 'ruː naʊ-, nɑː-, '•• ; nɑː 'uː ruː ~an/s
   ən/z
nausea 'nɔːs i_ə 'nɔːz- ‖ 'nɔːz- 'nɑːz-, 'nɔːs-,
   'nɑːs-; 'nɔːʃ ə, 'nɑː.ʃ-, 'nɔːʒ-, 'nɑːʒ-
nause|ate 'nɔːs i eɪt 'nɔːz- ‖ 'nɔːz- 'nɑːz-,
   'nɔːs-, 'nɑːs-, 'nɔːʃ-, 'nɑːʃ-, 'nɔːʒ-, 'nɑːʒ-
   ~ated eɪt ɪd -əd ‖ eɪt̬ əd ~ates eɪts
   ~ating/ly eɪt ɪŋ /li ‖ eɪt̬ ɪŋ /li
nauseous 'nɔːs i_əs 'nɔːz- ‖ 'nɔːʃ əs 'nɑːʃ-;
   'nɔːz i_əs, 'nɑːz- ~ly li ~ness nəs nɪs
Nausicaa, Nausicaä nɔː 'sɪk i_ə -eɪ ə ‖ nɑː-
nautch nɔːtʃ ‖ nɑːtʃ nautches 'nɔːtʃ ɪz
   -əz ‖ 'nɑːtʃ-
nautical 'nɔːt ɪk əl ‖ 'nɔːt̬ ɪk əl 'nɑːt̬- ~ly_i
   ,nautical 'mile
naut|ilus, N~ tdmk 'nɔːt |ɪl əs -əl- ‖ 'nɔːt̬ |əl əs
   'nɑːt̬- ~ili ɪ laɪ əl aɪ, ɪ liː, əl iː ‖ əl aɪ əl iː
   ~iluses ɪl əs ɪz əl-, -əz ‖ əl əs əz
Navaho, Navajo 'næv ə hɑʊ ‖ -hoʊ 'nɑːv- ~s z
naval 'neɪv əl
navarin 'næv ər_ɪn §-ər_ən —Fr [na va ʁæ̃] ~s
   z
Navarino ˌnæv ə 'riːn əʊ ‖ -oʊ
Navarone 'næv ə rəʊn ,••'• ‖ -roʊn
Navarre nə 'vɑː ‖ -'vɑːr —Fr [na vaːʁ]
nave neɪv naves neɪvz
navel 'neɪv əl (= naval) ~s z
   'navel ,orange
navicular nə 'vɪk jʊl ə -jəl- ‖ -jəl ər
navie... —see navy
navigability ˌnæv ɪg ə 'bɪl ət i -ɪt i ‖ -ət̬ i
navigab|le 'næv ɪg əb |əl ~leness əl nəs -nɪs
   ~ly li
navi|gate 'næv ɪ |geɪt -ə- ~gated geɪt ɪd -əd
   ‖ geɪt̬ əd ~gates geɪts ~gating
   geɪt ɪŋ ‖ geɪt̬ ɪŋ
navigation ˌnæv ɪ 'geɪʃ ən -ə-
navigational ˌnæv ɪ 'geɪʃ ən_əl ◄ ,•ə- ~ly i
navigator 'næv ɪ geɪt ə '•ə- ‖ -geɪt̬ ər ~s z

Navratilova næv ˌræt ɪ 'ləʊv ə nəv-, ˌnæv rət-
   ‖ ˌnæv rət tɪ 'loʊv ə , •ræ- —Czech
   Navratilová ['na vra ci lo vaː]
navv|y 'næv li ~ies iz
nav|y 'neɪv li ~ies iz
   ,navy 'blue ◄
nawab nə 'wɑːb -'wɔːb ‖ -'wɔːb ~s z
Naxalite 'næks ə laɪt 'nʌks- ~s z
Naxos 'næks ɒs ‖ -ɑːs 'nɑːks-, -oʊs, -əs
nay neɪ nays neɪz
Nayland 'neɪl ənd
Nayler, Naylor 'neɪl ə ‖ -ər
naysayer 'neɪ ˌseɪ ə ‖ -ər ~s z
Nazarene ˌnæz ə 'riːn '••• ~s z
Nazareth 'næz ər əθ -ɪθ
Nazarite 'næz ə raɪt -ər aɪt ~s z
Nazca 'næz kə ‖ 'nɑːsk ə —AmSp ['nas ka]
Naze neɪz
Nazeing 'neɪz ɪŋ
Nazi, nazi 'nɑːts i 'næts-, 'nɑːz- ~s z
Naziism 'nɑːts i ,ɪz əm 'næts-, 'nɑːz-
Nazism 'nɑːts ,ɪz əm 'næts-, 'nɑːz-
NB ,en 'biː —see also nota bene, Nebraska, New
   Brunswick
NBA ,en biː 'eɪ→,em-
NBC ,en biː 'siː→,em-
NCO ,en si 'əʊ ‖ -'oʊ ~s, ~'s z
NCP ,en siː 'piː
Ndebele ən dɪ 'bel i ,en-, -də-, -deɪ-, -'beɪl-,
   -'biːl-, -eɪ ~s z
N'Djamena ən dʒæ 'meɪn ə ‖ -dʒɑː-
Ndola ən 'dəʊl ə ‖ -'doʊl-
NE —see northeast, northeastern
Neagh neɪ
Neagle 'niːg əl
Neal, Neale, Neall niː_əl
Neanderthal ni 'ænd ə tɑːl neɪ-, -θɔːl; -ət əl
   ‖ -ər θɔːl -'ɑːnd-, -tɔːl, -tɑːl —Ger
   [ne 'an dɐ taːl] ~s z
   Ne'anderthal ,man, •,••• '•
neap niːp neaps niːps
   'neap ,tide
Neapolis ni 'æp əl ɪs §-əs
neapolitan, N~ nɪə 'pɒl ɪt ən ,niː_ə'•••◄, -ət
   ən ‖ ,niː ə 'pɑːl ət ən ◄ ~s z
near nɪə ‖ nɪər neared nɪəd ‖ nɪərd nearer
   'nɪər ə ‖ 'nɪr ər nearest 'nɪər ɪst -əst
   ‖ 'nɪr əst nearing 'nɪər ɪŋ ‖ 'nɪr ɪŋ nears
   nɪəz ‖ nɪərz
   ,Near 'East, ,Near 'Eastern; ,nearest and
   'dearest; ,near 'miss; ,near 'thing
nearby adj, adv ,nɪə 'baɪ ◄ ‖ ,nɪr-
   a ,nearby 'restaurant
Nearctic ,ni: 'ɑːkt ɪk ◄ -'ɑːrkt- -'ɑːrt̬-
near|ly 'nɪə |li ‖ 'nɪr |li ~ness nəs nɪs
nearside 'nɪə saɪd ,•'• ‖ 'nɪr-
nearsighted ,nɪə 'saɪt ɪd ◄ -əd, '•,••
   ‖ ,nɪr 'saɪt̬ əd ◄ ~ly li ~ness nəs nɪs
Neasden 'niːzd ən
neat niːt neater 'niːt ə ‖ 'niːt̬ ər neatest
   'niːt ɪst -əst ‖ 'niːt̬ əst
neaten 'niːt ən ~ed d ~ing _ɪŋ ~s z
neath, 'neath niːθ

Neath niːθ
neat|ly 'niːt |li ~**ness** nəs nɪs
Neave niːv
neb neb **nebs** nebz
nebbich, nebbish 'neb ɪʃ ~**es** ɪz əz
Nebo *mountain in Jordan* 'niːb əʊ ‖ -oʊ
Nebo *places in Wales* 'neb əʊ ‖ -oʊ
Nebrask|a nə 'bræsk |ə nɪ- ~**an/s** ən/z
Nebuchadnezzar, n~ ˌneb jʊk əd 'nez ə ˌ•jək-
   ‖ ˌneb ək əd 'nez ər ˌ•jək- ~**s** z
neb|ula 'neb |jʊl ə -jəl- ‖ -|jəl ə ~**ulae** ju liː
   jə- ‖ jə liː ~**ular** jʊl ə jəl- ‖ jəl ər ~**ulas**
   jʊl əz jəl- ‖ jəl əz
nebuliser, nebulizer 'neb ju laɪz ə ‖ -jə laɪz ər
   ~**s** z
nebulosit|y ˌneb ju 'lɒs ət i ˌ•jə-, -ɪt i
   ‖ -'lɑːs əṭ li ~**ies** ɪz
nebulous 'neb jʊl əs -jəl- ‖ -jəl əs ~**ly** li
   ~**ness** nəs nɪs
NEC ˌen iː 'siː
necessarily ˌnes ə 'ser əl i ˌ•ɪ-; 'nes əs ər̩əl i,
   '•ɪs-, ˌɪ li —*BrE 1998 poll panel preference:*
   ˌ•'••• 72%, '•••• 28%

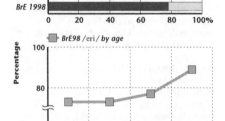

NECESSARY

	■ -seri	□ -səri
BrE 1998		
0	20 40 60 80	100%

BrE98 /erɪ/ by age

Percentage — 100, 80, 0
Older ◄——— Speakers ———► Younger

necessar|y 'nes ə ser li '•ɪ-; 'nes əs ər̩li, '•ɪs-
   —*BrE 1998 poll panel preference:* -seri 78%,
   -səri 22%. ~**ies** ɪz
   ˌnecessary 'evil
necessi|tate nə 'ses ɪ |teɪt nɪ-, ne-, -ə- ~**tated**
   teɪt ɪd -əd ‖ teɪṭ əd ~**tates** teɪts ~**tating**
   teɪt ɪŋ ‖ teɪṭ ɪŋ
necessitous nə 'ses ɪt əs nɪ-, ne-, -ət- ‖ -əṭ əs
   ~**ly** li ~**ness** nəs nɪs
necessit|y nə 'ses ɪt li nɪ-, ne-, -ət- ‖ -əṭ li ~**ies**
   ɪz
neck nek **necked** nekt **necking** 'nek ɪŋ
   necks neks
neck-and-neck ˌnek ən 'nek ◄
Neckar 'nek ə -ɑː ‖ -ər —*Ger* ['nɛk aʁ]
neckband 'nek bænd ~**s** z
-necked 'nekt — **long-necked**
   ˌlɒŋ 'nekt ◄ ‖ ˌlɔːŋ- ˌlɑːŋ-
Necker 'nek ə ‖ -ər —*Fr* [nɛ kɛʁ]
neckerchief 'nek ə tʃɪf -tʃiːf ‖ -ər- -tʃəf ~**s** s
necklac|e 'nek ləs -lɪs ~**ed** t ~**es** ɪz əz ~**ing**
   ɪŋ
necklet 'nek lət -lɪt ~**s** s
neckline 'nek laɪn ~**s** z
necktie 'nek taɪ ~**s** z

neckwear 'nek weə ‖ -wer -wær
necro- *comb. form*
   with stress-neutral suffix ˌnek rəʊ ‖ -roʊ —
   necrobiosis ˌnek rəʊ baɪ 'əʊs ɪs §-əs
   ‖ -roʊ baɪ 'oʊs-
   with stress-imposing suffix ne 'krɒ+ nɪ-, nə-
   ‖ -'krɑː+ — **necrolog|y** ne 'krɒl ədʒ li nɪ-,
   nə- ‖ -'krɑːl- ~**ies** iz
necromancer 'nek rəʊ mænts ə ‖ -rə mænts ər
   ~**s** z
necromancy 'nek rəʊ mænts i ‖ -rə mænts i
necrophilia ˌnek rəʊ 'fɪl i ə -'fiːl- ‖ ˌ•rə-
necrophiliac ˌnek rəʊ 'fɪl i æk -'fiːl- ‖ ˌ•rə- ~**s**
   s
necrophilism ne 'krɒf ɪ ˌlɪz əm nə-, nɪ-, -'•ə-
   ‖ -'krɑːf-
necropolis ne 'krɒp əl ɪs nə-, nɪ-, §-əs
   ‖ -'krɑːp- ~**es** ɪz əz
necrops|y 'nek rɒps li ‖ -rɑːps- ~**ies** ɪz
necrosis ne 'krəʊs ɪs nə-, nɪ-, §-əs ‖ -'kroʊs-
necrotic ne 'krɒt ɪk nə-, nɪ- ‖ -'krɑːṭ ɪk
nectar 'nekt ə ‖ -ər ~**s** z
nectarine 'nekt ə riːn -ər ɪn, §-ər ən ~**s** z
nectar|y 'nekt ər li ~**ies** ɪz
Ned ned
Neddie, Neddy 'ned i ~**s**, ~'**s** z
nee, née neɪ △niː *(= nay)*
need niːd **needed** 'niːd ɪd -əd **needing**
   'niːd ɪŋ **needs** niːdz
needful 'niːd fəl -fʊl ~**ly** i ~**ness** nəs nɪs
Needham 'niːd əm
needl|e, N~ 'niːd əl ~**ed** d ~**es** z ~**ing** ˌɪŋ
needlecord 'niːd əl kɔːd ‖ -kɔːrd ~**s** z
needlecraft 'niːd əl krɑːft §-kræft ‖ -kræft
needlefish 'niːd əl fɪʃ
needlepoint 'niːd əl pɔɪnt
needless 'niːd ləs -lɪs ~**ly** li ~**ness** nəs nɪs
needle|woman 'niːd əl ˌwʊm ən ~**women**
   ˌwɪm ɪn -ən
needlework 'niːd əl wɜːk ‖ -wɜːːk
needn't 'niːd ənt →-ᵊn
need|y 'niːd li ~**ier** i ə ‖ i ər ~**iest** i ɪst i əst
   ~**ily** ɪ li əl i ~**iness** i nəs i nɪs
neem niːm
neep niːp **neeps** niːps
ne'er neə ‖ neᵊr næᵊr
ne'er-do-well ˌneə du ˌwel ‖ ˌner- ˌnær- ~**s** z
nefarious nɪ 'feər i ˌəs nə-, ne- ‖ -'fer- -'fær-
   ~**ly** li ~**ness** nəs nɪs
Nefertiti ˌnef ə 'tiːt i ‖ -ər 'tiːṭ i
Neff nef
Nefyn 'nev ɪn
NEG, neg. neg
negate nɪ |'geɪt nə-, ne- ~**gated** 'geɪt ɪd -əd
   ‖ 'geɪṭ əd ~**gates** 'geɪts ~**gating**
   'geɪt ɪŋ ‖ 'geɪṭ ɪŋ
negation nɪ 'geɪʃ ən nə-, ne- ~**s** z
negativ|e 'neg ət ɪv ‖ -əṭ ɪv ~**ed** d ~**ely** li
   ~**eness** nəs nɪs ~**es** z ~**ing** ɪŋ
negativism 'neg ət ɪv ˌɪz əm -ət əv- ‖ -əṭ ɪv-
negativistic ˌneg ət ɪ 'vɪst ɪk ◄ -ət ə- ‖ -əṭ ɪ-
   ~**ally** əl_i
negativity ˌneg ə 'tɪv ət i -ɪt i ‖ -əṭ i

N

negator nɪ 'geɪt ə nə-, ne- ‖ -'geɪʈ ᵊr ~s z
Negeb 'neg eb
Negev 'neg ev nɪ 'gev, nə-
neglect v, n nɪ 'glekt nə-, §₍ᵢ₎ne- ~ed ɪd əd
~ing ɪŋ ~s s
neglectful nɪ 'glekt fᵊl nə-, §₍ᵢ₎ne-, -fʊl ~ly i
~ness nəs nɪs
negligee, négligée 'neg lɪ ʒeɪ -lə-, -liː-
‖ ˌneg lə 'ʒeɪ '•• —Fr négligée [ne gli ʒe]
~s z
negligenc|e 'neg lɪdʒ ᵊnᵗs -lədʒ- ~es ɪz əz
negligent 'neg lɪdʒ ᵊnt -lədʒ- ~ly li
negligib|le 'neg lɪdʒ əb |ᵊl '•lədʒ-, -ɪb ᵊl
~leness ᵊl nəs -nɪs ~ly li
negotiable nɪ 'gəʊʃ i̯_əb ᵊl nə-, -'gəʊʃ əb ᵊl
‖ -'goʊʃ- -'•əb ᵊl
negotiability nɪ ˌgəʊʃ i̯_ə 'bɪl ət i nə-, -ɪt i;
-ˌgəʊʃ ə 'bɪl- ‖ nɪ ˌgoʊʃ i̯_ə 'bɪl əʈ i
-ˌgoʊʃ ə 'bɪl-
negoti|ate nɪ 'gəʊʃ i |eɪt nə-, -'gəʊs- ‖ -'goʊʃ-
~ated eɪt ɪd -əd ‖ eɪʈ əd ~ates eɪts ~ating
eɪt ɪŋ ‖ eɪʈ ɪŋ
negotiation nɪ ˌgəʊʃ i 'eɪʃ ᵊn nə-, -ˌgəʊs-
‖ -ˌgoʊʃ- -ˌgoʊs- ~s z
negotiator nɪ 'gəʊʃ i eɪt ə nə-, -'gəʊs-
‖ -'goʊʃ i eɪʈ ᵊr ~s z
negress, Negress 'niːg res -rəs, -rɪs ~es ɪz əz
Negri 'neg ri
Negrillo nɪ 'grɪl əʊ nə-, ne- ‖ -oʊ -'griː-, -joʊ
~s z
negritude 'neg rɪ tjuːd 'niːg-, -rə-, →§-tʃuːd
‖ -tuːd -tjuːd
negro, Negro person 'niːg rəʊ ‖ -roʊ ~es z
Negro name of river 'neɪg rəʊ 'neg- ‖ -roʊ
negroid, N~ 'niːg rɔɪd ~s z
negroni, N~ nɪ 'grəʊn i ne-, nə- ‖ -'groʊn i
~s z
negus, Negus 'niːg əs ~es ɪz əz
Nehemiah ˌniː_ə 'maɪ_ə ˌneɪ-, -hə-, -ɪ-, -hɪ-
Nehru 'neər u: ‖ 'neɪ ru: 'ner u: —Hindi
[n̪eh ruː]
neigh neɪ (= nay) neighed neɪd neighing
'neɪ ɪŋ neighs neɪz
neighbo... —see neighbou...
neighbour 'neɪb ə ‖ -ᵊr ~s z
neighbourhood 'neɪb ə hʊd ‖ -ᵊr- ~s z
ˌneighbourhood 'watch
neighbouring 'neɪb ᵊr_ɪŋ
neighbour|ly 'neɪb ə |li ‖ -ᵊr- ~liness li nəs
-nɪs
Neil, Neill niːᵊl
Neilson 'niːl sᵊn
Neisse 'naɪs ə —Ger Neisse, Neiße ['nai sə]
neither 'naɪð ə 'niːð- ‖ 'niːð ᵊr 'naɪð- —See
preference poll figures at either
Nejd neʒd
Nekrasov ne 'krɑːs ɒv nɪ- ‖ -oʊv —Russ
[nʲɪ 'kra səf]
nekton 'nekt ɒn -ᵊn ‖-ɑːn
Nell nel
Nellie 'nel i
Nellis 'nel ɪs §-əs
nelly, N~ 'nel i

Nelson, n~ 'nels ᵊn ~s, ~'s z
nematic nɪ 'mæt ɪk nə-, ne- ‖ -'mæʈ- ~s s
nematocyst 'nem ət əʊ sɪst nɪ 'mæt-, nə-, ne-
‖ 'nem əʈ ə- nɪ 'mæʈ ə- ~s s
nematode 'nem ə təʊd ‖ -toʊd ~s z
nembutal, N~ tdmk 'nem bju tæl -bjə-, -tɒl,
-taːl ‖ -bjə tɔːl -taːl, -tæl ~s z
nem con, nem. con. ˌnem 'kɒn ‖ -'kɑːn
Nemea nɪ 'miː_ə nə-, ne-; 'nem i_ə, 'niːm-
Nemean nɪ 'miː_ən nə-, ne-; 'nem i_ən, 'niːm-
~s z
nem|esis, N~ 'nem |əs ɪs -ɪs-, §-əs ~eses ə siːz
ɪ-
Nemo 'niːm əʊ ‖ -oʊ
nemophila nɪ 'mɒf ɪl ə nə-, -əl- ‖ -'mɑːf- ~s z
Nene name of river niːn nen —The river in the
English midlands is known as the nen upstream
(e.g. at Northampton) but as the niːn
downstream (e.g. at Peterborough and
Wisbech).
nene kind of bird 'neɪn eɪ ~s z
Nennius 'nen i_əs
neo- comb. form
with stress-neutral suffix ˈniː əʊ ‖ -ə -oʊ —
neophilia ˌniː əʊ 'fɪl i_ə ‖ -ᵊ-
with stress-imposing suffix ni 'ɒ+ ‖ -'ɑː+ —
neophilism ni 'ɒf ɪ ˌlɪz əm -'•ə- ‖ -'ɑːf-
Neocene, n~ 'niː əʊ siːn ‖ -ə-
neoclassic ˌniː əʊ 'klæs ɪk ◀ ‖ ˌ•oʊ- ~al ᵊl ◀
neoclassicism ˌniː əʊ 'klæs ɪ ˌsɪz əm -'•ə-
‖ ˌ•oʊ-
neoclassicist ˌniː əʊ 'klæs ɪs ɪst -əs ɪst, §-əst
‖ ˌ•oʊ- ~s s
neocolonialism ˌniː əʊ kə 'ləʊn i_ə ˌlɪz
əm ‖ ˌniː oʊ kə 'loʊn jə ˌlɪz əm
neocolonialist ˌniː əʊ kə 'ləʊn i_əl ɪst ◀ §-əst
‖ ˌniː oʊ kə 'loʊn jəl əst ◀ ~s s
neocortex ˌniː əʊ 'kɔːt eks ‖ -oʊ 'kɔːrt-
neodymium ˌniː əʊ 'dɪm i_əm ‖ ˌ•oʊ-
Neogaea ˌniː əʊ 'dʒiː_ə ‖ -ə-
neoimpressionism ˌniː əʊ ɪm 'preʃ ᵊn ˌɪz əm
-ə ˌnɪz- ‖ ˌ•oʊ-
neoimpressionist ˌniː əʊ ɪm 'preʃ ᵊn_ɪst §_əst
‖ ˌ•oʊ- ~s s
Neo-Latin ˌniː əʊ 'læt ɪn ◀ §-ᵊn ‖ -oʊ 'læt ᵊn◀
neolithic, N~ ˌniː əʊ 'lɪθ ɪk ◀ ‖ -ə-
neologism ni 'ɒl ə ˌdʒɪz əm 'niː_əl- ‖ -'ɑːl- ~s
z
neologis|e, neologiz|e ni 'ɒl ə dʒaɪz ‖ -'ɑːl-
~ed d ~es ɪz əz ~ing ɪŋ
Neo-Melanesian ˌniː əʊ ˌmel ə 'niːz i_ən ◀
-'niːʒ ᵊn, -'niːs i_ən, -'niːʃ ᵊn
‖ ˌniː oʊ ˌmel ə 'niːʒ ᵊn ◀ -'niːʃ-
neomycin ˌniː əʊ 'maɪs ɪn §-ᵊn ‖ -oʊ- -ə-
neon 'niː ɒn -ᵊn ‖ -ɑːn
ˈneon light
neonatal ˌniː əʊ 'neɪt ᵊl ◀ ‖ -oʊ 'neɪʈ- ~ly i
neonate 'niː əʊ neɪt ‖ -ə- ~s s
neophyte 'niː əʊ faɪt ‖ -ə- ~s s
neoplasm 'niː əʊ ˌplæz əm ‖ -ə- ~s z
neoprene 'niː əʊ priːn ‖ -ə-
Neoptolemus ˌniː ɒp 'tɒl əm əs əs -ɪm əs
‖ -ɑːp 'tɑːl-

neotame 'niː əʊ teɪm ‖ -ə-

neotenous ni 'ɒt ən əs ‖ -'aːt ᵊn əs

neoteny ni 'ɒt ən i ‖ -'aːt ᵊn i

neoteric ˌniː əʊ 'ter ɪk ◄ ‖ -ə- ~s s

Neozoic ˌniː əʊ 'zəʊ ɪk ◄ ‖ -oʊ 'zoʊ-

Nepal nɪ 'pɔːl nə-, ne-, -'paːl ‖ nə 'pɔːl -'paːl, -'pæl

Nepalese ˌnep ə 'liːz ◄ -ɔː-, -aː-; -ᵊl 'iːz

Nepali nɪ 'pɔːl i nə-, ne-, -'paːl- ‖ nə 'pɔːl i -'paːl-, -'pæl- ~s z

Nepean nɪ 'piː_ən nə-

nepenthe nɪ 'penᵗθ i ne-, nə-

NEPHEW

■ 'nef- □ 'nev-

BrE 1988

| 0 | 20 | 40 | 60 | 80 | 100% |

■ BrE88 /f/ by age

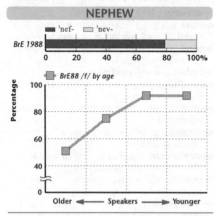

Older ◄━━━ Speakers ━━━► Younger

---

nephew 'nef juː 'nev- —BrE 1988 poll panel preference: 'nef- 79%, 'nev- 21%. It is evident that the traditional RP form with v has been largely displaced by the spelling pronunciation, as has long been the case in AmE. ~s z

nephrite 'nef raɪt

nephritic nɪ 'frɪt ɪk nə-, ne- ‖ -'frɪt̬ ɪk

nephritis nɪ 'fraɪt ɪs nə-, ne-, §-əs ‖ -'fraɪt̬ əs

nephro- comb. form
    with stress-neutral suffix ˌnef rəʊ ‖ -rə — nephrolith 'nef rəʊ lɪθ ‖ -rə-
    with stress-imposing suffix ne 'frɒ+ nɪ-, nə- ‖ nɪ 'fraː+ — nephrotomy ne 'frɒt əm i nɪ-, nə- ‖ nɪ 'fraːt̬ əm i

ne plus ultra ˌneɪ plʊs 'ʊltr aː ˌniː-, -plʌs-, -'ʌltr-, -ə

nepotism 'nep ə ˌtɪz əm

nepotistic ˌnep ə 'tɪst ɪk ◄ ~al ᵊl ◄

Neptune, n~ 'nep tjuːn -tʃuːn ‖ -tuːn -tjuːn ~s, ~'s z

Neptunian, n~ nep 'tjuːn i_ən →§-'tʃuːn- ‖ -'tuːn- -'tjuːn-

neptunium nep 'tjuːn i_əm →§-'tʃuːn- ‖ -'tuːn- -'tjuːn-

nerd nɜːd ‖ nɜ˞ːd nerds nɜːdz ‖ nɜ˞ːdz

Nereid, n~ 'nɪər i ɪd ‖ 'nɪr- ~s z

Nereus 'nɪər i uːs ˌ_əs ‖ 'nɪr-

Nero 'nɪər əʊ ‖ 'niː roʊ 'nɪr oʊ

Nerurkar nɪ 'rɜːk ə nə- ‖ -'rɜ˞ːk ᵊr

Nerva 'nɜːv ə ‖ 'nɜ˞ːv ə

nerve nɜːv ‖ nɜ˞ːv nerved nɜːvd ‖ nɜ˞ːvd nerves nɜːvz ‖ nɜ˞ːvz nerving 'nɜːv ɪŋ ‖ 'nɜ˞ːv ɪŋ

'nerve cell; 'nerve ˌcentre; 'nerve gas; 'nerve ˌimpulse

nerveless 'nɜːv ləs -lɪs ‖ 'nɜ˞ːv- ~ly li ~ness nəs nɪs

nerve-racking, nerve-wracking 'nɜːv ˌræk ɪŋ ‖ 'nɜ˞ːv-

nervine 'nɜːv iːn -aɪn ‖ 'nɜ˞ːv-

nervous 'nɜːv əs ‖ 'nɜ˞ːv əs ~ly li ~ness nəs nɪs
    ˌnervous 'breakdown; 'nervous ˌsystem

nervure 'nɜːv jʊə -jə ‖ 'nɜ˞ːv jʊr -jᵊr ~s z

nerv|y 'nɜːv li ‖ 'nɜ˞ːv li ~ier i_ə ‖ i_ᵊr ~iest i_ɪst i_əst ~ily ɪ li əl i ~iness i nəs i nɪs

Nerys 'ner ɪs §-əs

Nesbit, Nesbitt 'nez bɪt

Nescafe, Nescafé tdmk 'nes kæ ˌfeɪ -ˌkæf i, -eɪ; 'nes kæf ‖ ˌ•ˈ•ˈ•

nescience 'nes i_ənᵗs ‖ 'neʃ ᵊnᵗs 'neʃ i_ənᵗs

nescient 'nes i_ənt ‖ 'neʃ ᵊnt 'neʃ i_ənt ~s s

nesh neʃ

Nesquik tdmk 'nes kwɪk

ness, Ness nes nesses, Ness's 'nes ɪz -əz

-ness nəs nɪs —The noun-forming suffix has no effect upon word stress: 'careless, 'carelessness. —In singing, a strong-vowelled form nes is customary.

-ness in place names 'nes — Sheerness ˌʃɪə 'nes ◄ ‖ ˌʃɪr-

Nesselrode, n~ 'nes ᵊl rəʊd ‖ -roʊd —Russ [nⁱi sɪɫ 'rɔ də]

Nessie 'nes i

Nessler 'nes lə ‖ -lᵊr —Ger ['nɛs lɐ]

Nessun dorma ˌnes uːn 'dɔːm ə ‖ -'dɔːrm ə —It [ˌsun 'dɔr ma]

Nessus 'nes əs

nest, Nest nest nested 'nest ɪd -əd nesting 'nest ɪŋ nests nests
    'nest egg

Nesta 'nest ə

nestl|e 'nes ᵊl ~ed d ~es z ~ing ˌɪŋ

Nestlé tdmk 'nes leɪ -li, -ᵊl

nestling n 'young bird' 'nest lɪŋ ~s s

nestling ptcp of nestle 'nes ᵊl_ɪŋ

Neston 'nest ən

Nestor 'nest ɔː -ə ‖ -ᵊr -ɔːr

Nestorian ne 'stɔːr i_ən ‖ -'stoʊr- ~ism ˌɪz əm ~s z

Nestorius ne 'stɔːr i_əs ‖ -'stoʊr-

net net nets nets netted 'net ɪd -əd ‖ 'net̬ əd netting 'net ɪŋ ‖ 'net̬ ɪŋ

Netanyahu ˌnet ən 'jɑː huː -æn-

netball 'net bɔːl ‖ -bɑːl

nether 'neð ə ‖ -ᵊr

Netherlander 'neð ᵊl ənd ə -ə -ə lænd ə ‖ -ᵊr lənd ᵊr -lænd- ~s z

Netherlands 'neð ᵊl əndz ‖ -ᵊr ləndz
    ˌNetherlands An'tilles

nethermost 'neð ə məʊst ‖ -ᵊr moʊst

Netherton 'neð ət ən ‖-ᵊrt ᵊn

netherworld 'neð ə wɜːld ‖ -ᵊr wɜ˞ːld

netiquette 'net ɪ ket -ɪk ət, ˌnet ɪ 'ket ‖ 'net̬ ɪk ət -ɪ ket

Netley 'net li

N

Netscape *tdmk* 'net skeɪp
netsuke 'net ski -skeɪ; 'nets ʊk i, -eɪ —*Jp*
[ne ˌtsu̥ke] ~s z
nett net
nett... —*see* **net**
Nettie 'net i ‖ 'net̬ i
netting 'net ɪŋ ‖ 'net̬ ɪŋ
nettl|e 'net ᵊl ‖ 'net̬ ᵊl ~**ed** d ~**es** z ~**ing** ɪŋ
  'nettle rash
Nettlefold 'net ᵊl fəʊld →-fɒʊld ‖ 'net̬ ᵊl foʊld
Nettleship 'net ᵊl ʃɪp ‖ 'net̬-
network 'net wɜːk ‖ -wɝːk ~**ed** t ~**er/s** ə/z
  ‖ ᵊr/z ~**ing** ɪŋ ~**s** s
Neubrandenburg
  ˌnɔɪ 'brænd ən bɜːg ‖ -'brɑːnd ən bɝːg —*Ger*
  [nɔy 'bran dᵊn bʊrk]
Neuchâtel, Neufchâtel ˌnɜː ʃæ 'tel ◂ -ʃə-
  ‖ ˌnuː- ˌnʊ- —*Fr* [nø ʃa tɛl]
neum, neume njuːm §nuːm ‖ nuːm njuːm
  neums, neumes njuːmz §nuːmz ‖ nuːmz
  njuːmz
Neumann 'njuː mən §'nuː- ‖ 'nuː- 'njuː —*but*
  as a German name, 'nɔɪ- —*Ger* ['nɔy man]
neural 'njʊər ᵊl 'njɔːr- §'nʊər- ‖ 'nʊr ᵊl 'njʊr-,
  'nɝː-
neuralgia njʊə 'rældʒ ə njɔː-, §nuᵊ- ‖ nu- nju-
neuralgic njʊə 'rældʒ ɪk njɔː-, §nuᵊ- ‖ nu-
  nju-
neurasthenia ˌnjʊər əs 'θiːn i ə ˌnjɔːr-,
  §ˌnʊər-, -ˌæs- ‖ ˌnʊr- ˌnjʊr-
neurasthenic ˌnjʊər əs 'θen ɪk ◂ ˌnjɔːr-,
  §ˌnʊər-, -æs- ‖ ˌnʊr- ˌnjʊr- ~**ally** ᵊl_i
neuritis njʊə 'raɪt ɪs njɔː-, §nuᵊ-, §-əs
  ‖ nu 'raɪt̬ əs nju-
neuro- *comb. form*
  with stress-neutral suffix ˌnjʊər əʊ ˌnjɔːr-,
  §ˌnʊər- ‖ ˌnʊr oʊ ˌnjʊr- — **neurobiology**
  ˌnjʊər əʊ baɪ 'ɒl ədʒ i ˌnjɔːr-, §ˌnʊər-
  ‖ ˌnʊr oʊ baɪ 'ɑːl- ˌnjʊr-
  with stress-imposing suffix njʊə 'rɒ+ njɔː-,
  §nuᵊ- ‖ nu 'rɑː+ nju- — **neuropathy**
  njʊə 'rɒp əθ i §nuᵊ- ‖ nu 'rɑːp- nju-
neurological ˌnjʊər ə 'lɒdʒ ɪk ᵊl ◂, njɔːr-,
  §ˌnʊər- ‖ ˌnʊr ə 'lɑːdʒ- ˌnjʊr- ~**ly** _i
neurologist njʊə 'rɒl ədʒ ɪst njɔː-, §nuᵊ-, §-əst
  ‖ nu 'rɑːl- nju- ~**s** s
neurology njʊə 'rɒl ədʒ i njɔː-, §nuᵊ-
  ‖ nu 'rɑːl- nju-
neuroma njʊə 'rəʊm ə ‖ -'roʊm ə ~**s** z
neuron 'njʊər ɒn 'njɔːr-, §'nʊər- ‖ 'nʊr ɑːn
  'njʊr-; 'njuː rɑːn ~**s** z
neurone 'njʊər əʊn 'njɔːr-, §'nʊər- ‖ 'nʊr oʊn
  'njʊr-; 'njuː roʊn ~**s** z
neuropath|y njʊə 'rɒp əθ i njɔː-, §nuᵊ-
  ‖ nu 'rɑːp- nju- ~**ies** iz
neurosci|ence ˌnjʊər əʊ 'saɪ_ᵊnts ˌnjɔːr-,
  §ˌnʊər-, '•• ,•• ‖ ˌnʊr oʊ- ˌnjʊr- ~**ences**
  ᵊnts ɪz -əz ~**entist/s** ᵊnt ɪst/s§-əst/s ‖ ᵊnt̬
  əst/s
neuros|is njʊə 'rəʊs ɪs njɔː-, §nuᵊ-, §-əs
  ‖ nu 'roʊs- nju- ~**es** iːz
neurosurgeon ˌnjʊər əʊ 'sɜːdʒ ən ˌnjɔː-,

§ˌnʊər-, '••,•• ‖ ˌnʊr oʊ 'sɝːdʒ ən ˌnjʊr- ~**s**
  z
neurosurgery ˌnjʊər əʊ 'sɜːdʒ ər_i ˌnjɔː-,
  §ˌnʊər-, '••,••• ‖ ˌnʊr oʊ 'sɝːdʒ-
neurosurgical ˌnjʊər əʊ 'sɜːdʒ ɪk ᵊl ◂ ˌnjɔː-,
  §ˌnʊər-, '••,••• ‖ ˌnʊr oʊ 'sɝːdʒ- ~**ly** _i
neurotic njʊə 'rɒt ɪk njɔː-, §nuᵊ- ‖ nu 'rɑːt̬ ɪk
  nju- ~**ally** ᵊl_i ~**s** s
neuroticism njuᵊ 'rɒt ɪ ˌsɪz əm njɔː-, §nuᵊ-,
  -'•ə- ‖ nu 'rɑːt̬ ə- nju-
neurotransmitter ˌnjʊər əʊ trænz 'mɪt ə
  ˌnjɔːr-, §ˌnʊər-, -trɑːnz'••, -trænts'••,
  -trɑːnts'•• ‖ ˌnʊr oʊ trænts 'mɪt̬ ər
  -trænz'••, '•••,••
neut|er 'njuːt ə §'nuːt- ‖ 'nuːt̬ ᵊr 'njuːt̬-
  ~**ered** əd ‖ ᵊrd ~**ering** ər ɪŋ ~**ers** əz ‖ ᵊrz
neutral 'njuːtr ᵊl §'nuːtr- ‖ 'nuːtr ᵊl 'njuːtr-
  ~**s** z
neutralis... —*see* **neutraliz...**
neutralism 'njuːtr ə ˌlɪz əm §'nuːtr-, -ᵊl ˌɪz-
  ‖ 'nuːtr- 'njuːtr-
neutralist 'njuːtr ᵊl ɪst §'nuːtr-, §-əst ‖ 'nuːtr-
  'njuːtr- ~**s** s
neutrality nju 'træl ət i §nu-, -ɪt-
  ‖ nu 'træl ət̬ i nju-
neutralization ˌnjuːtr ᵊl aɪ 'zeɪʃ ᵊn §ˌnuːtr-,
  -ɪ'•- ‖ ˌnuːtr əl ə-, ˌnjuːtr- ~**s** z
neutraliz|e 'njuːtr ə laɪz §'nuːtr- ‖ 'nuːtr-
  'njuːtr- ~**ed** d ~**es** ɪz əz ~**ing** ɪŋ
neutrally 'njuːtr ᵊl i §'nuːtr- ‖ 'nuːtr- 'njuːtr-
neutrino nju 'triːn əʊ §nu- ‖ nu 'triːn oʊ nju-
  ~**s** z
neutron 'njuːtr ɒn §'nuːtr- ‖ 'nuːtr ɑːn
  'njuːtr- ~**s** z
  'neutron bomb; 'neutron star
neutropenia ˌnjuːtr əʊ 'piːn i ə §ˌnuːtr-
  ‖ ˌnuːtr oʊ 'piːn jə ˌnjuːtr-
neutrophil 'njuːtr əʊ fɪl §'nuːtr- ‖ 'nuːtr ə-
  'njuːtr-
Neva *river in USSR* 'neɪv ə 'niːv- —*Russ*
  [nⁱ 'va]
Nevad|a nɪ 'vɑːd ə nə-, ne- ‖ nɪ 'væd ə
  -'vɑːd- —*but places in AR, IA, MO are also*
  -'veɪd- ~**an/s** ᵊn/z
Nevard nə 'vɑːd nɪ- ‖ -'vɑːrd
Neve niːv
névé 'nev eɪ ‖ neɪ 'veɪ —*Fr* [ne ve]
never 'nev ə ‖ -ᵊr
never-ending ˌnev ᵊr 'end ɪŋ ◂ -ə-
nevermore ˌnev ə 'mɔː ‖ -ᵊr 'mɔːr -'moʊr
never-never ˌnev ə 'nev ə ‖ -ᵊr 'nev ᵊr
  ˌnever-'never land
nevertheless ˌnev ə ðə 'les ‖ ˌnev ᵊr-
Nevil, Nevill, Neville 'nev ᵊl -ɪl
Nevin 'nev ɪn -ᵊn
Nevinson 'nev ɪnts ᵊn -ᵊnts-
Nevis *mountain and loch in Scotland* 'nev ɪs §-əs
Nevis *island in West Indies* 'niːv ɪs §-əs
nev|us 'niːv əs ~**i** aɪ ~**uses** əs ɪz -əz
new njuː §nuː ‖ nuː nju: —*AmE 1993 poll panel
  preference:* nu: 86%, nju: 14%. —*See also
  phrases with this word* **newer** 'njuː_ə §'nuː-
  ‖ 'nuː ᵊr 'njuː- **newest** 'njuː_ɪst §'nuː_, _əst

Neutralization

1 Two PHONEMES may, in certain phonetic environments, not be distinguishable. We say the **opposition** between them is **neutralized**.

2 In most environments English p and b are in opposition: that is, they carry a potential difference in meaning. This can be seen in pairs such as **pin** pɪn and **bin** bɪn, **cup** kʌp and **cub** kʌb. After s, however, the opposition is neutralized (since p here has no ASPIRATION). Conventionally, we write **spin** phonemically as spɪn; but since there is no possible difference between p and b here we could just as well write sbɪn.

3 One type of neutralization is symbolized explicitly in LPD by the use of the symbols i and u. The opposition between iː and ɪ operates in most environments, as seen in **green** griːn and **grin** grɪn, **leap** liːp and **lip** lɪp. But there are two environments in which it is neutralized:

- when the vowel is in a WEAK syllable at the end of a word (or at the end of part of a compound word or of a stem), as in **happy** ˈhæp i, **valley** ˈvæl i, **babies** ˈbeɪb iz.
- when the vowel is in a weak syllable before another vowel, as in **radiation** ˌreɪd i ˈeɪʃ ᵊn, **glorious** ˈɡlɔːr i ₐəs.

In these positions the vowel is traditionally identified with ɪ. But in fact some speakers use ɪ, some use iː, some use something intermediate or indeterminate, and some fluctuate between the two possibilities. Modern pronunciation dictionaries use the symbol i, which reflects this.

Similarly, the LPD symbol u represents the neutralization of the opposition between uː and ʊ. This neutralization is found not only in i environments, but also in certain others, for example, in one pronunciation of **stimulate** ˈstɪm ju leɪt.

Do not confuse neutralization with the term **neutral vowel**, a name sometimes used for ə.

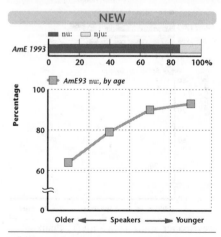

NEW

AmE 1993 — ■ nuː □ njuː

0 20 40 60 80 100%

AmE93 nuː, by age

Percentage: 100 / 80 / 60 / 0

Older ◀— Speakers —▶ Younger

‖ ˈnuː əst ˈnjuː-
ˌNew ˈAge◂, ˌNew Age ˈtraveller; ˌnew ˈblood; ˌnew ˈbroom; ₍ᵢ₎New ˈBrunswick;

ˌNew ˌCaleˈdonia; ˌnew ˈdeal, ˌNew ˈDeal; ₍ᵢ₎New ˈDelhi; ₍ᵢ₎New ˈEngland; ˌNew ˈForest◂, ˌNew ˌForest ˈpony; ₍ᵢ₎New ˈGuinea; ₍ᵢ₎New ˈHampshire; New ˈHaven *place in CN*; ₍ᵢ₎New ˈJersey; ₍ᵢ₎New ˈMexico; ˌnew ˈmoon; New ˈOrleans, ˌNew Orˈleans; ˌNew ˈQuay *place in Dyfed*; ˌNew ˈRight; ˌNew ˌScotland ˈYard; ˌNew South ˈWales; ˌNew ˈTestament; ˈnew town, ˌˌ· ˈ·; ˌNew ˈWave◂, New Wave ˈmusic; ˌNew ˈWorld; ˌnew ˈyear◂, ˌNew Yearʼs ˈDay, ˌNew Yearʼs ˈEve; ₍ᵢ₎New ˈYork, ˌNew York ˈCity, ₍ᵢ₎New ˈYorker, ˌNew York ˈState

Newark ˈnjuːɹ_ək §ˈnuː- ‖ ˈnuː ᵊrk ˈnjuː- —*but the place in DE is* -ɑːk ‖ -ɑːrk

Newbiggin ˈnjuː ˌbɪg ɪn §ˈnuː-, §-ən ‖ ˈnuː- ˈnjuː-

Newbold ˈnjuː bəʊld §ˈnuː-, →-bɒʊld ‖ ˈnuː boʊld ˈnjuː-

N

Newbolt 'nju: bəʊlt §'nu:-, →-bɒʊlt
‖ 'nu: boʊlt 'nju:-
newborn 'nju: bɔːn §'nu:-; ‚•'•◄ ‖ 'nu: bɔːrn
'nju:-
Newbridge 'nju: brɪdʒ §'nu:- ‖ 'nu:- 'nju:-
Newbrough 'nju: brʌf §'nu:- ‖ 'nu:- 'nju:-
Newburg, n~ 'nju: bɜːg §'nu:- ‖ 'nu: bɜ˞g
'nju:-
Newburgh 'nju: bər‿ə §'nu:- ‖ 'nu: bɜ˞g
'nju:-
Newbury 'nju: bər‿i §'nu:- ‖ 'nu: ‚ber i 'nju:-,
-bər‿i
Newby 'nju:b i §'nu:b- ‖ 'nu:b i 'nju:b-
Newcastle 'nju: ‚kɑːs əl §'nu:-, §-‚kæs-, §•'••
‖ 'nu: ‚kæs əl 'nju:- —In Tyne & Wear, locally
nju: 'kæs əl
‚Newcastle-on-'Tyne, ‚Newcastle-u‚pon-
'Tyne, locally New‚castle-; ‚Newcastle-
‚under-'Lyme
Newcomb, Newcombe, Newcome 'nju:k əm
§'nu:k- ‖ 'nu:k- 'nju:k-
newcomer 'nju: ‚kʌm ə §'nu:- ‖ 'nu: ‚kʌm ə˞r
'nju:- ~s z
Newdigate 'nju:d ɪ geɪt §'nu:d-, -ə-, -gɪt, -gət
‖ 'nu:d- 'nju:d-
Newe nju: §nu: ‖ nu: nju:
newel 'nju:‿əl §'nu:‿ ‖ 'nu: əl 'nju:- ~s z
New Englander nju: 'ɪŋ glənd ə §nu-, -lənd ə
‖ nu 'ɪŋ glənd ə˞r nju- ~s z
newfangled ‚nju: 'fæŋ gəld ◄ §‚nu:- ‖ ‚nu:-
‚nju:-; ‚•'•◄
Newfie 'nju:f i §'nu:f- ‖ 'nu:f i 'nju:f- ~s z
new-found ‚nju: 'faʊnd ◄§‚nu:- ‖ ‚nu:- ‚nju:-
Newfoundland 'nju:f ənd lənd §'nu:f-, -lænd,
‚•'••; nju 'faʊnd-, §nu- ‖ 'nu:f ənd lənd
'nju:f-, -lænd; nu 'faʊnd-, nju- —Locally
‚•'•. The breed of dog is usually •'••. ~s,
~'s z
Newfoundlander ‚nju:f ənd 'lænd ə §‚nu:f-;
'••••, -lənd ə; nju 'faʊndləndə, §nu-
‖ 'nu:f ənd lənd ə˞r 'nju:f-, -lænd ə˞r ~s z
Newgate 'nju: geɪt §'nu:-, -gɪt, -gət ‖ 'nu:-
'nju:-
Newham 'nju:‿əm §'nu:‿, -hæm; ‚•'hæm ◄
‖ 'nu:- 'nju:-
Newhaven place in Sussex 'nju: ‚heɪv ən §'nu:-,
‚•'•• ‖ 'nu:- 'nju:-
Newington 'nju:‿ɪŋ tən §'nu:‿ ‖ 'nu:- 'nju:-
newish 'nju:‿ɪʃ §'nu:‿ ‖ 'nu:- 'nju:-
new-laid ‚nju: 'leɪd ◄ §‚nu:- ‖ ‚nu:- ‚nju:-
‚new-laid 'eggs
Newlands 'nju: ləndz §'nu:- ‖ 'nu:- 'nju:-
newly 'nju: li §'nu:- ‖ 'nu:- 'nju:-
Newlyn 'nju: lɪn §'nu:- ‖ 'nu:- 'nju:-
newlywed 'nju: li wed §'nu:-, ‚••'•◄ ‖ 'nu:-
'nju:- ~s z
Newman 'nju: mən §'nu:- ‖ 'nu:- 'nju:-
Newmark 'nju: mɑːk §'nu:- ‖ 'nu: mɑːrk
'nju:-
Newmarket, n~ 'nju: ‚mɑːk ɪt §'nu:-, §-ət
‖ 'nu: ‚mɑːrk ət 'nju:-
new-mown ‚nju: 'məʊn ◄ §‚nu:-

‖ ‚nu: 'moʊn ◄ ‚nju:-
‚new-mown 'hay
Newnes nju:nz §nu:nz ‖ nu:nz nju:nz
newness 'nju: nəs §'nu:-, -nɪs ‖ 'nu:- 'nju:-
Newnham 'nju:n əm §'nu:n- ‖ 'nu:n- 'nju:n-
New Orleans ‚nju: 'ɔːl i_ənz §‚nu:-, -'ɔːl ənz,
-ɔː 'li:nz ‖ ‚nu: 'ɔːrl ənz ‚nju:-; ‚nu: ɔːr 'li:nz,
‚nju:-
Newport 'nju: pɔːt §'nu:- ‖ 'nu: pɔːrt 'nju:-,
-poʊrt —but in ‚Newport'News, place in VA,
sometimes -pət ‖ -pə˞rt
Newquay place in Cornwall 'nju: ki: §'nu:-
‖ 'nu:- 'nju:-
Newry 'njʊər i §'nʊə˞- ‖ 'nu: ri 'nju:-
news nju:z §nu:z ‖ nu:z nju:z
'news ‚agency; 'news ‚conference
newsagent 'nju:z ‚eɪdʒ ənt §'nu:z- ‖ 'nu:z-
'nju:z- ~s s
newsboy 'nju:z bɔɪ §'nu:z- ‖ 'nu:z- 'nju:z-
~s z
newscast 'nju:z kɑːst §'nu:z-, §-kæst
‖ 'nu:z kæst 'nju:z- ~er/s ə/z ‖ ə˞r/z ~ing ɪŋ
~s s
newsflash 'nju:z flæʃ §'nu:z- ‖ 'nu:z- 'nju:z-
~es ɪz əz
newshawk 'nju:z hɔːk §'nu:z- ‖ 'nu:z-
'nju:z-, -hɑːk ~s s
newshound 'nju:z haʊnd §'nu:z- ‖ 'nu:z-
'nju:z- ~s z
newsletter 'nju:z ‚let ə §'nu:z- ‖ 'nu:z ‚leṱ ə˞r
'nju:z- ~s z
news|man 'nju:z| mæn §'nu:z-, -mən ‖ 'nu:z-
'nju:z- ~men men mən
newsmonger 'nju:z ‚mʌŋ gə §'nu:z-
‖ 'nu:z ‚mʌŋ gə˞r 'nju:z-, -‚mɑːŋ- ~s z
Newsom, Newsome family name 'nju:s əm
§'nu:s- ‖ 'nu:s- 'nju:s-
Newsome place in West Yorks. 'nju:z əm
§'nu:z- ‖ 'nu:z- 'nju:z-

NEWSPAPER

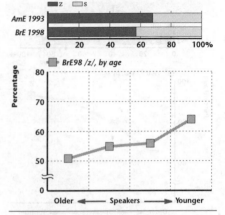

	z	s
AmE 1993		
BrE 1998		

0   20   40   60   80   100%

BrE98 /z/, by age

Percentage: 80, 70, 60, 50, 0

Older ◄— Speakers —► Younger

---

newspaper 'nju:z ‚peɪp ə 'nju:s-, §'nu:z-,
§'nu:s- ‖ 'nu:z ‚peɪp ə˞r 'nju:z-, 'nu:s-, 'nju:s-
—Poll panel preferences: AmE 1993, z 68%, s
32%; BrE 1998, z 57%, s 43%. ~s z

news|person 'njuːz ˌpɜːs ᵊn §'nuːz-
‖ 'nuːz ˌpɝːs ᵊn 'njuːz- ~people ˌpiːp ᵊl
newspeak, N~ 'njuː spiːk §'nuː- ‖ 'nuː- 'njuː-
newsprint 'njuːz prɪnt §'nuːz- ‖ 'nuːz- 'njuːz-
newsreader 'njuːz ˌriːd ə §'nuːz-
‖ 'nuːz ˌriːd ᵊr 'njuːz- ~s z
newsreel 'njuːz riːᵊl §'nuːz- ‖ 'nuːz- 'njuːz-
~s z
newsroom 'njuːz ruːm §'nuːz-, -rʊm ‖ 'nuːz-
'njuːz- ~s z
newssheet 'njuːz ʃiːt §'nuːz-, →'njuːʒ-
‖ 'nuːz- 'njuːz- ~s s
newsstand 'njuːz stænd §'nuːz- ‖ 'nuːz-
'njuːz- ~s z
Newstead 'njuːst ɪd -ed ‖ 'nuːst- 'njuːst-
newsvendor 'njuːz ˌvend ə §'nuːz-
‖ 'nuːz ˌvend ᵊr 'njuːz- ~s z
newsworthy 'njuːz ˌwɜːð i §'nuːz-
‖ 'nuːz ˌwɝːð i 'njuːz-
news|y 'njuːz li §'nuːz- ‖ 'nuːz li 'njuːz- ~ier
i ə ‖ i ᵊr ~ies iz ~iest i ɪst i ᵊst ~iness
i nəs i nɪs
newt njuːt §nuːt ‖ nuːt njuːt newts njuːts
§nuːts ‖ nuːts njuːts
Newton, n~ 'njuːt ᵊn §'nuːt- ‖ 'nuːt ᵊn 'njuːt-
~s, ~'s z
Newtonian nju 'təʊn i_ən §nu- ‖ nu 'toʊn-
nju-
Newton-le-Willows ˌnjuːt ᵊn li 'wɪl əʊz §ˌnuːt-
‖ ˌnuːt ᵊn li 'wɪl oʊz ˌnjuːt-
Newtonmore ˌnjuːt ᵊn 'mɔː §ˌnuːt-
‖ ˌnuːt ᵊn 'mɔːr ˌnjuː-, -'moʊr
Newtown 'njuː taʊn §'nuː- ‖ 'nuː- 'njuː-
—but in Irish compound place-names, ˌnjuːt ᵊn,
§'njuːt- ‖ 'nuːt ᵊn, ˌnjuːt- —
Newtownabbey ˌnjuːt ᵊn 'æb i §ˌnuːt-
‖ ˌnuːt- ˌnjuːt-, Newtownards
ˌnjuːt ᵊn 'ɑːdz §ˌnuːt- ‖ ˌnuːt ᵊn 'ɑːrdz
ˌnjuːt-
New York ˌnjuː 'jɔːk◄ §ˌnuː- ‖ ₍ᵢ₎nuː 'jɔːrk ◄
₍ᵢ₎njuː- ~er/s ə/z ‖ ᵊr/z
ˌNew York 'City
New Zealand nju 'ziːl ənd ˌnjuː-, §nu-, §ˌnuː-
‖ nu- nju-, ˌnuː-, ˌnjuː- —locally sometimes
-'zɪl-
New ˌZealand 'flax
New Zealander nju 'ziːl ənd ə ˌnjuː-, §nu-,
§ˌnuː- ‖ nu 'ziːl ənd ᵊr nju-, ˌnuː-, ˌnjuː- ~s
z
next nekst
next-door ˌnekst 'dɔː ◄ ‖ -'dɔːr ◄ -'doʊr
ˌnext-door 'neighbour
nexus 'neks əs ~es ɪz əz
Ney neɪ —Fr [nɛ]
Nez Perce, Nez Percé ˌnez 'pɜːs ˌnes-, -'peəs,
-'peəs eɪ ‖ -'pɝːs —Fr [ne pɛʁ se]
Ng ɪŋ eŋ —Cantonese [⁴ŋ, ⁴m]
Ngaio, ngaio 'naɪ əʊ ‖ -oʊ —Maori ['ŋai o] ~s,
~'s z
Ngiyambaa, Ngiyampaa Australian language
'ŋeəm bɑː
Nguni ᵊŋ 'guːn i
NHS ˌen eɪtʃ 'es §-heɪtʃ-

Nhulunbuy place in Australia 'nuːl ən bɔɪ
→-əm-
Ni 'nickel' ˌen 'aɪ
Ni, Ní in Irish names niː —Irish [ɲiː]
niacin 'naɪ_əs ɪn §-ᵊn
Niagara naɪ 'æg ər_ə ni-
Ni,agara 'Falls
Niall (i) niːᵊl, (ii) 'naɪ_əl
Niamey ni 'ɑːm eɪ ˌniə 'meɪ ‖ ˌniː ə 'meɪ —Fr
[nja mɛ]
nib nɪb nibs nɪbz
nibbl|e 'nɪb ᵊl ~ed d ~es z ~ing ɪŋ
Nibelung 'niːb ə lʊŋ —Ger ['niː bə lʊŋ]
Nibelungenlied 'niːb ə lʊŋ ən liːd -liːt —Ger
['niː bə lʊŋ ən liːt]
niblick 'nɪb lɪk ~s s
NiCad, NiCd 'naɪ kæd
Nicaea naɪ 'siː_ə
NiCam tdmk 'naɪ kæm
Nicaragua ˌnɪk ə 'ræg ju_ə -'rɑːg-, -'•wə
‖ -'rɑːg wə —Sp [ni ka 'ra ɣwa]
Nicaraguan ˌnɪk ə 'ræg ju_ən◄ -'rɑːg-, -'•wən
‖ -'rɑːg wən ◄ ~s z
nice naɪs nicer 'naɪs ə ‖ -ᵊr nicest 'naɪs ɪst
-əst
Nice place in France niːs —Fr [nis]
nicely 'naɪs li
Nicene ˌnaɪ 'siːn ◄
ˌNicene 'Creed
niceness 'naɪs nəs -nɪs
nicet|y 'naɪs ət i -ɪt- ‖ -əṭ i ~ies iz

	■niːʃ	▭nɪtʃ			
BrE 1998					
	0 20	40	60	80	100%

niche niːʃ nɪtʃ ‖ nɪtʃ —BrE 1998 poll panel
preference: niːʃ 95%, nɪtʃ 5%. AmE only nɪtʃ.
niches 'niːʃ ɪz 'nɪtʃ-, 'nɪʃ-, -əz ‖ 'nɪtʃ əz
Nichol 'nɪk ᵊl
Nichola 'nɪk əl ə
Nicholas 'nɪk əl_əs
Nicholls, Nichols 'nɪk ᵊlz
Nicholson 'nɪk ᵊl sən
Nicias 'nɪs i_əs
nick, Nick nɪk nicked nɪkt nicking 'nɪk ɪŋ
nicks, Nick's nɪks
nickel 'nɪk ᵊl ~s z
ˌnickel 'silver
nickel-and-dime ˌnɪk ᵊl ən 'daɪm
nickelodeon ˌnɪk ə 'ləʊd i_ən ‖ -'loʊd- ~s z
nickel-|plate ˌnɪk ᵊl 'pleɪt ◄ ~plated 'pleɪt ɪd
-əd ‖ 'pleɪṭ əd ~plates 'pleɪts ~plating
'pleɪt ɪŋ ‖ 'pleɪṭ ɪŋ
nicker 'nɪk ə ‖ -ᵊr ~ed d nickering 'nɪk ər ɪŋ
~s z
Nicki 'nɪk i
Nickleby 'nɪk ᵊl bi
nicknack 'nɪk næk ~s s
nicknam|e 'nɪk neɪm ~ed d ~es z ~ing ɪŋ
Nicky 'nɪk i
Nicobar 'nɪk əʊ bɑː ‖ - bɑːr
Nicodemus ˌnɪk ə 'diːm əs

N

nicoise, niçoise (ˌ)niː 'swɑːz nɪ- —*Fr*
  [ni swaːz]
Nicol 'nɪk ᵊl
Nicola 'nɪk ᵊl ə
Nicole nɪ 'kəʊl →-'kɒʊl ‖ -'koʊl
Nicolette ˌnɪk ə 'let
Nicoll 'nɪk ᵊl
Nicolson 'nɪk ᵊl sən
Nicomachean naɪ ˌkɒm ə 'kiː_ən ◄ ,•••'••
  ‖ -ˌkɑːm-
Nicomachus (ˌ)naɪ 'kɒm ək əs ‖ -'kɑːm-
Nicosia ˌnɪk ə 'siː_ə
nicotinamide ˌnɪk ə 'tɪn ə maɪd -'tiːn- ‖ -mɪd
nicotine 'nɪk ə tiːn ˌ•'•
nic|tate nɪk 'teɪt 'nɪk|t eɪt ~tated teɪt ɪd -əd
  ‖ teɪt̬ əd ~tates teɪts ~tating
  teɪt ɪŋ ‖ teɪt̬ ɪŋ
nicti|tate 'nɪkt ɪ |teɪt -ə- ~tated teɪt ɪd -əd
  ‖ teɪt̬ əd ~tates teɪts ~tating
  teɪt ɪŋ ‖ teɪt̬ ɪŋ
Niddrie, Niddry 'nɪdr i
nidicolous nɪ 'dɪk ᵊl əs
nidifugous nɪ 'dɪf jʊg əs -jəg-
nid|us 'naɪd ləs ~i aɪ ~uses əs ɪz -əz
Niebuhr 'niː bʊə ‖ -bʊr —*Ger* ['niː buːɐ]
niece niːs nieces 'niːs ɪz -əz
Niedersachsen 'niːd ə ˌsæks ᵊn ‖ -ᵊr ˌsɑːks-
  —*Ger* ['niː dɐ ˌzak sᵊn]
niello ni 'el əʊ ‖ -oʊ ~ed d ~ing ɪŋ ~s z
Nielsen 'niːᵊls ᵊn
Niemann 'niːm ən
Niemeyer 'niː maɪ_ə ‖ -maɪ_ᵊr
Niersteiner 'nɪə staɪn ə -ʃtaɪn- ‖ 'nɪr staɪn ᵊr
  —*Ger* ['niːɐ ʃtaɪn ɐ]
Nietzsche 'niːtʃ ə ‖ -i —*Ger* ['niː tʃə, 'niːts ʃə]
niff nɪf niffed nɪft niffing 'nɪf ɪŋ niffs nɪfs
niffy 'nɪf i
nift|y 'nɪft li ~ier i_ə ‖ i_ᵊr ~ies iz ~iest i_ɪst
  i_əst ~ily ɪ li əl i
Nige naɪdʒ
Nigel 'naɪdʒ ᵊl
nigella, N~ naɪ 'dʒel ə
Niger *river* 'naɪdʒ ə ‖ -ᵊr
Niger *country* niː 'ʒeə 'naɪdʒ ə ‖ 'naɪdʒ ᵊr —*Fr*
  [ni ʒɛːʁ]
Niger-Congo ˌnaɪdʒ ə 'kɒŋ gəʊ ◄
  ‖ -ᵊr 'kɑːŋ goʊ ◄
Nigeria naɪ 'dʒɪər i_ə ‖ -'dʒɪr-
Nigerian naɪ 'dʒɪər i_ən ə ‖ -'dʒɪr- ~s z
niggard 'nɪg əd ‖ -ᵊrd ~s z
niggard|ly 'nɪg əd |li ‖ -ᵊrd- ~liness li nəs -nɪs
nigger 'nɪg ə ‖ -ᵊr ~s z
niggl|e 'nɪg ᵊl ~ed d ~es z ~ing _ɪŋ
niggler 'nɪg lə ‖ -lᵊr ~s z
niggl|ly 'nɪg |li ~liness li nəs -nɪs
nigh naɪ
night naɪt nights naɪts
  'night ˌblindness, ˌ• '••; 'night owl; 'night
  school; 'night shift; 'night soil; 'night
  watch, ˌ• '••; ˌnight 'watchman
nightcap 'naɪt kæp ~s s
nightclothes 'naɪt kləʊðz -kləʊz ‖ -klouz
  -kloʊðz

nightclub 'naɪt klʌb ~bed d ~ber/s ə/z ‖ ᵊr/z
  ~bing ɪŋ ~s z
nightdress 'naɪt dres ~es ɪz əz
nightfall 'naɪt fɔːl ‖ -fɑːl
nightgown 'naɪt gaʊn ~s z
nighthawk 'naɪt hɔːk ‖ -hɑːk ~s s
nightie 'naɪt i ‖ 'naɪt̬ i ~s z
nightingale, N~ 'naɪt ɪŋ geɪᵊl ‖ 'naɪt ᵊn-
  'naɪt̬ ɪŋ- ~s z
nightjar 'naɪt dʒɑː ‖ -dʒɑːr ~s z
nightlife 'naɪt laɪf
nightlight 'naɪt laɪt ~s s
nightline 'naɪt laɪn ~s z
nightlong ˌnaɪt 'lɒŋ ◄ '•• ‖ -'lɔːŋ ◄ -'lɑːŋ
nightly 'naɪt li
nightmare 'naɪt meə ‖ -mer -mær ~s z
nightmarish 'naɪt meər ɪʃ ‖ -mer- -mær- ~ly
  li ~ness nəs nɪs
night-night ˌnaɪt 'naɪt
nightrider 'naɪt raɪd ə ‖ -ᵊr ~s z
nightshade 'naɪt ʃeɪd ~s z
nightshirt 'naɪt ʃɜːt ‖ -ʃɝːt ~s s
nightsoil 'naɪt sɔɪl
nightspot 'naɪt spɒt ‖ -spɑːt ~s s
nightstick 'naɪt stɪk ~s s
nighttime 'naɪt taɪm
nightwear 'naɪt weə ‖ -wer
nig-nog 'nɪg nɒg ‖ -nɑːg ~s z
nihil 'naɪ hɪl 'niː-, 'nɪ-, -həl
nihilism 'naɪ ɪ ˌlɪz əm 'niː-, -hɪ-, -ə-, -hə-;
  'nɪ hɪ-, -hə-
nihilist 'naɪ ɪl ɪst 'niː-, -hɪl-, -əl-, -həl-, §-əst;
  'nɪ hɪl-, -həl- ~s s
nihilistic ˌnaɪ ɪ 'lɪst ɪk ◄ ˌniː-, -hɪ-, -ə-, -hə-;
  ˌnɪ hɪ-, -hə-
nihil obstat ˌnaɪ hɪl 'ɒb stæt ˌniː-, ˌnɪ-, -həl-
  ‖ -'ɑːb-
Nijinsky nɪ 'dʒɪn¦sk i nə-, -'ʒɪn¦sk- —*Russ*
  [nʲɪ 'ʒɪn skʲɪj]
Nijmegen 'naɪ meɪg ᵊn •'•• —*Dutch*
  ['nɛi meː xən]
-nik nɪk —*refusenik* rɪ 'fjuːz nɪk rə-, §riː-
Nike 'naɪk i -iː; naɪk
Nikita nɪ 'kiːt ə nə- ‖ -'kiːt̬ ə —*Russ* [nʲɪ 'kʲi tə]
Nikkei nɪ 'keɪ —*Jp* [ɲik ˌkei, -ˌkee]
Nikki 'nɪk i
Nikon *tdmk* 'nɪk ɒn ‖ 'naɪk ɑːn 'niːk- —*Jp*
  ['ɲi koɴ]
nil nɪl
  ˌnil ˌdespeˈrandum ˌdesp ə 'rænd əm
Nile naɪᵊl
nilgai 'nɪlg aɪ ~s z
Nilo-Saharan ˌnaɪl əʊ sə 'hɑːr
  ən ◄ ‖ ˌnaɪl oʊ sə 'hær ən ◄ -'her-, -'hɑːr-
Nilotic naɪ 'lɒt ɪk ‖ -'lɑːt̬ ɪk
Nilsen, Nilsson 'niːᵊls ᵊn 'nɪls-
nim nɪm
nimbi 'nɪm baɪ
nim|ble 'nɪm |bᵊl ~bler blə ‖ blᵊr ~blest blɪst
  bləst ~bleness bᵊl nəs -nɪs ~bly bli
nimbostratus ˌnɪm bəʊ 'streɪt əs ‖ -boʊ 'streɪt̬-
  -'stræt̬-
nim|bus 'nɪm |bəs ~bi baɪ ~buses bəs ɪz -əz

nim|by, NIM|BY 'nɪm| bi ~bies biz ~byism
  bi ˌɪz əm
Nîmes niːm —Fr [nim]
nimini-piminy, niminy-piminy
  ˌnɪm ən i 'pɪm ən i ◄ -ɪn i 'pɪm ɪn-
Nimitz 'nɪm ɪts §-əts
Nimmo 'nɪm əʊ ‖ -oʊ
Nimrod, n~ 'nɪm rɒd ‖ -rɑːd ~s, ~'s z
Nin nɪn niːn
Nina 'niːn ə
nincompoop 'nɪŋk əm puːp 'nɪn kəm- ~s s
nine naɪn —but for clarity in communication
  code, niner 'naɪn ə ‖ -ər nines naɪnz
  ˌnine days' 'wonder
ninefold 'naɪn fəʊld →-fɒʊld ‖ -foʊld
ninepin 'naɪn pɪn →'naɪm- ~s z
nineteen ˌnaɪn 'tiːn ◄ —occasionally, when
  stress-shifted, also 'naɪn tən ~s z
  ˌnineteen 'people; ˌnineteen ˌninety-'nine
nineteenth ˌnaɪn 'tiːntθ ◄ ~s s
  ˌnineteenth 'hole
ninetieth 'naɪnt i əθ -ɪθ ‖ 'naɪnt̬ i əθ ~s s
Ninette nɪ 'net niː-
ninet|y 'naɪnt i ‖ 'naɪnt̬ i ~ies iz
ninety-nine ˌnaɪnt i 'naɪn ◄ ‖ ˌnaɪnt̬-
ninety-ninth ˌnaɪnt i 'naɪntθ ◄ ‖ ˌnaɪnt̬-
Nineveh 'nɪn ɪv ə -əv-
Ningbo ˌnɪŋ 'bəʊ ‖ -'boʊ —Chi Níngbō
  [2 nin 1 bo]
Ningxia ˌnɪŋ ʃi 'ɑː —Chi Níngxià [2niŋ 4çja]
Ninian 'nɪn i_ən
ninish 'naɪn ɪʃ
ninja 'nɪndʒ ə ~s z
ninn|y 'nɪn li ~ies iz
Nintendo tdmk nɪn 'tend əʊ ‖ -oʊ
ninth naɪntθ ninthly 'naɪntθ li ninths naɪntθs
niobate 'naɪ əʊ beɪt ‖ -ə-
Niobe 'naɪ_əb i -əʊb i ‖ -ə biː
niobic naɪ 'əʊb ɪk ‖ -'oʊb-
niobium naɪ 'əʊb i_əm ‖ -'oʊb-
nip, Nip nɪp nipped nɪpt nipping/ly
  'nɪp ɪŋ /li nips nɪps
nipper 'nɪp ə ‖ -ər ~s z
nippi... —see nippy
nipple 'nɪp əl ~s z
nipplewort 'nɪp əl wɜːt §-wɔːt ‖ -wɝːt -wɔːrt
  ~s s
Nippon 'nɪp ɒn ‖ -ɑːn nɪ 'pɑːn —Jp [ɲip 'poɴ]
Nipponese ˌnɪp ə 'niːz ◄ ‖ -'niːs ◄
nipp|ly 'nɪp li ~ier i_ə ‖ i_ər ~iest i_ɪst i_əst
  ~ily ɪ li əl i ~iness i nəs i nɪs
NIREX, Nirex tdmk 'naɪər eks
nirvana, N~ nɪə 'vɑːn ə nɜː- ‖ nɪr- -'væn-
  —Hindi [ɳɪr vaːɳ]
Nis, Niš nɪʃ niːʃ
Nisan 'naɪs æn 'nɪs-, -ɑːn ‖ 'nɪːs ɑːn 'nɪs ən
Nisbet, Nisbett 'nɪz bət -bɪt
nisi 'naɪs aɪ 'niːs i
  ˌnisi 'prius 'praɪ_əs 'priː_əs
Nissan tdmk 'nɪs æn ‖ -ɑːn 'niːs- —Jp
  [ɲis ˌsaɴ]
Nissen 'nɪs ən
  'Nissen hut

nit nɪt nits nɪts
Nita 'niːt ə ‖ 'niːt̬ ə
nite naɪt
niter 'naɪt ə ‖ 'naɪt̬ ər
niterie 'naɪt ər i ‖ 'naɪt̬- ~s z
nitpick|er/s 'nɪt ˌpɪk |ə/z ‖ -|ər/z ~ing ɪŋ
nitrate 'naɪtr eɪt -ət, -ɪt ~s s
nitrazepam naɪ 'træz ɪ pæm -'treɪz-, -ə-
nitre 'naɪt ə ‖ 'naɪt̬ ər
nitric 'naɪtr ɪk
  ˌnitric 'acid
nitride 'naɪtr aɪd ~s z
nitrile 'naɪtr aɪ‿l -ɪl, §-əl ~s z
nitrite 'naɪtr aɪt ~s s
nitro 'naɪtr əʊ ‖ -oʊ
nitro- comb. form
  with stress-neutral suffix ˌnaɪtr əʊ ‖ -oʊ —
  nitrobenzene ˌnaɪtr əʊ 'benz iːn ‖ -oʊ-
  -ben 'ziːn
  with stress-imposing suffix naɪ 'trɒ+ ‖ -'trɑː+
  — nitrometer naɪ 'trɒm ɪt ə -ət-
  ‖ -'trɑːm ət̬ ər
nitrocellulose ˌnaɪtr əʊ 'sel ju ləʊs -'•jə-, -ləʊz
  ‖ -oʊ 'sel jə loʊs -loʊz
nitrochalk, Nitro-chalk tdmk
  'naɪtr əʊ tʃɔːk ‖ -oʊ- -tʃɑːk
nitrogen 'naɪtr ədʒ ən
nitrogenous naɪ 'trɒdʒ ən əs -ɪn- ‖ -'trɑːdʒ-
nitroglycerin, nitroglycerine ˌnaɪtr əʊ 'glɪs
  ər ɪn -ˌ•ə-, -iːn, §-ən ‖ -ˌ•ə-
nitrosamine naɪ 'trəʊz ə miːn -'trəʊs-;
  ˌnaɪtr əʊs ə 'miːn, -'æm iːn, '••••‖ -'troʊs-
nitrous 'naɪtr əs
nitty 'nɪt i ‖ 'nɪt̬ i
nitty-gritty ˌnɪt i 'grɪt i ‖ ˌnɪt̬ i 'grɪt̬ i
nitwit 'nɪt wɪt ~s s
Niu Gini ˌ(ˌ)nju: 'gɪn i
Niue 'nju: eɪ ni 'u: eɪ ‖ ni 'u: eɪ
Nivea tdmk 'nɪv i_ə-eɪ
Niven 'nɪv ən
nix nɪks nixed nɪkst nixes 'nɪks ɪz -əz
  nixing 'nɪks ɪŋ
Nixdorf tdmk 'nɪks dɔːf ‖ -dɔːrf
nixie 'nɪks i ~s z
Nixon 'nɪks ən
Nixonian nɪk 'səʊn i_ən ‖ -'soʊn-
Nizam, nizam nɪ 'zɑːm naɪ-, -'zæm ~s s
Nizhni Novgorod ˌnɪʒ ni 'nɒv gə rɒd
  ‖ -'nɑːv gə rɑːd —Russ [ˌɲiʒ nʲi 'nov gə rət]
Nkomo ən 'kəʊm əʊ →ˑŋ- ‖ -'koʊm oʊ
  —Ndebele [ŋk'ɔː mɔ]
Nkrumah ən 'kruːm ə →ˑŋ-
no nəʊ ‖ noʊ —There is also an occasional weak
  form nə noes nəʊz ‖ noʊz
  'no ball; ˌno 'way
no., No. —see number; North nos. —see
  numbers
no-account ˌnəʊ ə 'kaʊnt ◄ ‖ ˌnoʊ-
Noachian nəʊ 'eɪk i_ən ‖ noʊ-
Noah 'nəʊ ə ‖ 'noʊ ə
  ˌNoah's 'ark
Noakes nəʊks ‖ noʊks
Noam 'nəʊ əm nəʊm ‖ 'noʊ əm noʊm

N

nob nɒb ‖ nɑːb **nobs** nɒbz ‖ nɑːbz
no-ball ˌnəʊ ˈbɔːl ‖ ˌnoʊ- -ˈbɑːl **~ed** d **~ing**
ɪŋ **~s** z
nobbl|e ˈnɒb əl ‖ ˈnɑːb əl **~ed** d **~es** z **~ing**
_ɪŋ
nobbut ˈnɒb ət ‖ ˈnɑːb-
nobby, Nobby ˈnɒb i ‖ ˈnɑːb i
Nobel ₍ˌ₎nəʊ ˈbel ‖ ₍ˌ₎noʊ- —*Swedish* [nɔ ˈbɛl]
No,bel ˈprize, ˌNobel ˈprize
nobelium nəʊ ˈbiːl i̯ əm ‖ noʊ- -ˈbel-
nobiliary nəʊ ˈbɪl i̯ ər i ‖ noʊ ˈbɪl i er i
-ˈbɪl jər i
nobilit|y nəʊ ˈbɪl ət |i -ɪt- ‖ noʊ ˈbɪl ət̬ |i **~ies**
iz
noble, Noble ˈnəʊb əl ‖ ˈnoʊb əl **nobler**
ˈnəʊb lə ‖ ˈnoʊb lər **nobles**
ˈnəʊb əlz ‖ ˈnoʊb əlz **noblest** ˈnəʊb lɪst -ləst
‖ ˈnoʊb ləst
noble|man ˈnəʊb əl |mən ‖ ˈnoʊb- **~men** mən
noble-minded ˌnəʊb əl ˈmaɪnd ɪd ◄ -əd
‖ ˌnoʊb-
nobleness ˈnəʊb əl nəs -nɪs ‖ ˈnoʊb-
noblesse oblige nəʊ ˌbles əʊ ˈbliːʒ , • • ' •
‖ noʊ ˌbles oʊ- —*Fr* [nɔ blɛs ɔ bliːʒ]
noble|woman ˈnəʊb əl |ˌwʊm ən ‖ ˈnoʊb-
~women ˌwɪm ɪn §-ən
nobly ˈnəʊb li ‖ ˈnoʊb li
nobod|y ˈnəʊb əd |i ˈnəʊ ˌbɒd |i ‖ ˈnoʊb əd |i
ˈnoʊ ˌbɑːd |i, -bʌd i **~ies, ~y's** iz
nock nɒk ‖ nɑːk (= *knock*) **nocked**
nɒkt ‖ nɑːkt **nocking** ˈnɒk ɪŋ ‖ ˈnɑːk ɪŋ
nocks nɒks ‖ nɑːks
no-claim ˌnəʊ ˈkleɪm ‖ ˌnoʊ- **~s** z
ˌno-claim(s) ˈbonus, , • ' • , • •
noctilucent ˌnɒkt ɪ ˈluːs ənt §-ə-, -ˈljuːs-
‖ ˌnɑːkt ə-
noctuid ˈnɒkt ju̯ ɪd ˈnɒk tʃu̯, §_əd
‖ ˈnɑːk tʃu əd -tu- **~s** z
nocturn ˈnɒkt ɜːn ˌnɒk ˈtɜːn ‖ ˈnɑːkt ɝːn **~s** z
nocturnal nɒk ˈtɜːn əl ‖ nɑːk ˈtɜːn əl **~ly** i
nocturne ˈnɒkt ɜːn ˌnɒk ˈtɜːn ‖ ˈnɑːkt ɝːn **~s**
z
nod nɒd ‖ nɑːd **nodded** ˈnɒd ɪd -əd ‖ ˈnɑːd əd
nodding ˈnɒd ɪŋ ‖ ˈnɑːd ɪŋ **nods**
nɒdz ‖ nɑːdz
ˌnodding acˈquaintance
nodal ˈnəʊd əl ‖ ˈnoʊd əl
nodality nəʊ ˈdæl ət i -ɪt- ‖ noʊ ˈdæl ət̬ i
nodd... —*see* nod
noddle ˈnɒd əl ‖ ˈnɑːd əl **~s** z
Nodd|y, nodd|y ˈnɒd |i ‖ ˈnɑːd |i **~ies, ~y's** iz
node nəʊd ‖ noʊd **nodes** nəʊdz ‖ noʊdz
nodular ˈnɒd jʊl ə -jəl- ‖ ˈnɑːdʒ əl ər
nodule ˈnɒd juːl ‖ ˈnɑːdʒ uːl **~s** z
Noel, Noël *personal name* ˈnəʊ̯_əl -el ‖ ˈnoʊ-
Noel, Noël ˈ*Christmas*' nəʊ ˈel ‖ noʊ-
Noele ˌnəʊ ˈel◄ ‖ ˌnoʊ-
noes *pl of* no nəʊz ‖ noʊz (= *nose*)
noesis nəʊ ˈiːs ɪs §-əs ‖ noʊ-
noetic nəʊ ˈet ɪk ‖ noʊ ˈet̬ ɪk
no-fault ˌnəʊ ˈfɔːlt ◄-ˈfɒlt ‖ ˌnoʊ ˈfɔːlt ◄
-ˈfɑːlt

no-fly ˌnəʊ ˈflaɪ ◄ ‖ ˌnoʊ-
ˌno-ˈfly ˌzone, , • • ' •
no-frills ˌnəʊ ˈfrɪlz ◄ ‖ ˌnoʊ-
nog nɒg ‖ nɑːg **nogs** nɒgz ‖ nɑːgz
noggin ˈnɒg ɪn §-ən ‖ ˈnɑːg- **~s** z
no-go ˌnəʊ ˈgəʊ ◄ ‖ ˌnoʊ ˈgoʊ ◄
ˌno-ˈgo ˌarea, , • • ' • • •
no-good ˌnəʊ ˈgʊd ◄ ‖ ˌnoʊ-
Noh nəʊ ‖ noʊ —*Jp* [no,o]
no-holds-barred ˌnəʊ həʊldz ˈbɑːd ◄
→-hʊʊldz- ‖ ˌnoʊ hoʊldz ˈbɑːrd ◄
no-hope ˌnəʊ ˈhəʊp ◄ ‖ ˌnoʊ ˈhoʊp ◄
no-hoper ˌnəʊ ˈhəʊp ə ‖ ˌnoʊ ˈhoʊp ər **~s** z
nohow ˈnəʊ haʊ ‖ ˈnoʊ-
noir nwɑː ‖ nwɑːr —*Fr* [nwaːʁ]
noise nɔɪz **noised** nɔɪzd **noises** ˈnɔɪz ɪz -əz
noising ˈnɔɪz ɪŋ
noiseless ˈnɔɪz ləs -lɪs **~ness** nəs nɪs
noise-maker ˈnɔɪz ˌmeɪk ə ‖ -ər **~s** z
noisette nwɑː ˈzet nwæ- —*Fr* [nwa zɛt] **~s** s
—*or as singular*
noisi... —*see* noisy
noisome ˈnɔɪs əm **~ly** li **~ness** nəs nɪs
nois|y ˈnɔɪz |i **~ier** i̯ ə ‖ i̯ ər **~iest** i̯ ɪst i̯ əst
~ily ɪ li əl i **~iness** i nəs i nɪs
Nokia *tdmk* ˈnɒk i̯ ə ‖ ˈnoʊk i̯ ə
Nola ˈnəʊl ə ‖ ˈnoʊl ə
Nolan ˈnəʊl ən ‖ ˈnoʊl ən
nolens volens
ˌnəʊl enz ˈvəʊl enz ‖ ˌnoʊl enz ˈvoʊl-
noli-me-tangere, noli me tangere
ˌnəʊl i ˌmeɪ ˈtæŋ gər i -ˌmiː-, -ˈtændʒ ər-,
-gə reɪ ‖ ˌnoʊl-
nolle prosequi ˌnɒl i ˈprɒs ɪ kwaɪ -ˈ• ə-, -kwiː
‖ ˌnɑːl i ˈprɑːs-
nolo contendere ˌnəʊl əʊ kən ˈtend ər i
-kɒn ˈ• -, -ə reɪ ‖ ˌnoʊl oʊ-
nomad ˈnəʊm æd ‖ ˈnoʊm- **~s** z
nomadic nəʊ ˈmæd ɪk ‖ noʊ- **~ally** əl_i
nomadism ˈnəʊm æd ˌɪz əm ‖ ˈnoʊm-
no-man's-land ˈnəʊ mænz lænd ‖ ˈnoʊ-
nom de guerre ˌnɒm də ˈgeə ˌnɒ̃-
‖ ˌnɑːm də ˈgeər -dɪ- —*Fr* [nɔ̃d gɛːʁ] **noms
de guerre** *same pronunciation*
nom de plume ˌnɒm də ˈpluːm ˌnɒ̃-; ' • • •
‖ ˌnɑːm- —*Fr* [nɔ̃d plym] **noms de plume**
same pronunciation
Nome nəʊm ‖ noʊm
nomenclature nəʊ ˈmeŋk lətʃ ə ;
ˈnəʊm ən kleɪtʃ ə, ˈnɒm-, →-əŋ-, ' • en-,
→-eŋ- ‖ ˈnoʊm ən kleɪtʃ ər
noʊ ˈmen klə tʃʊr, →-ˈmeŋ-, -klətʃ ər **~s** z
nominal ˈnɒm ɪn əl -ən-, -ᵊn_əl ‖ ˈnɑːm ən əl
-ᵊn_əl **~s** z
nominally ˈnɒm ɪn əl i -ᵊn_əl i ‖ ˈnɑːm ən əl i
-ᵊn_əl-
nomi|nate ˈnɒm ɪ |neɪt -ə- ‖ ˈnɑːm- **~nated**
neɪt ɪd -əd ‖ neɪt̬ əd **~nates** neɪts **~nating**
neɪt ɪŋ ‖ neɪt̬ ɪŋ
nomination ˌnɒm ɪ ˈneɪʃ ᵊn -ə- ‖ ˌnɑːm- **~s** z
nominative ˈnɒm ən ət ɪv ' • ɪn- ‖ ˈnɑːm
ən ət̬ ɪv **~s** z
nominator ˈnɒm ɪ neɪt ə -ə- ‖ -neɪt̬ ər **~s** z

nominee ˌnɒm ɪ ˈniː ◂ -ə- ‖ ˌnɑːm- ~s z
nomo- *comb. form*
  with stress-neutral suffix ˈnɒm ə ˈnəʊm-
  ‖ ˈnɑːm ə ˈnoʊm- — **nomogram**
  ˈnɒm ə græm ˈnəʊm- ‖ ˈnɑːm- ˈnoʊm-
  with stress-imposing suffix nɒ ˈmɒ+ nəʊ-
  ‖ noʊ ˈmɑː+ — **nomology** nɒ ˈmɒl ədʒ i
  nəʊ- ‖ noʊ ˈmɑːl-
Nomura nəʊ ˈmjʊər ə -ˈmʊər- ‖ noʊ ˈmjʊr ə
  —*Jp* [no ˌmɯ ɾa]
-nomy *stress-imposing* nəm i — **taxonomy**
  tæk ˈsɒn əm i ‖ -ˈsɑːn-
non nɒn nəʊn ‖ nɑːn noʊn —*See also phrases*
  with this word
non- ˈnɒn ‖ ˈnɑːn —*Also occasionally* ˈnʌn —
  nonacademic ˌnɒn ˌæk ə ˈdem ɪk ˌnʌn-
  ‖ ˌnɑːn-
nonage ˈnəʊn ɪdʒ ˈnɒn- ‖ ˈnoʊn- ˈnɑːn-
nonagenarian ˌnəʊn ə dʒə ˈneər i ̩ən ◂ ˌnɒn-,
  -dʒɪ ◂- ‖ ˌnoʊn ə dʒə ˈner- ˌnɑːn- ~s z
nonagon ˈnɒn əg ən ˈnəʊn-, -ə gɒn
  ‖ ˈnɑːn ə gɑːn ˈnoʊn- ~s z
nonaggression ˌnɒn ə ˈgreʃ ən ‖ ˌnɑːn-
nonalcoholic
  ˌnɒn ˌælk ə ˈhɒl ɪk ◂ ˌnɑːn ˌælk ə ˈhɔːl ɪk ◂
  -ˈhɑːl-
  ˌnonalcoˌholic ˈbeverage
nonaligned ˌnɒn ə ˈlaɪnd ◂ -əl ˈaɪnd ◂ ‖ ˌnɑːn-
nonalignment ˌnɒn ə ˈlaɪn mənt →-laɪm-;
  -əl ˈaɪn- ‖ ˌnɑːn-
nonappearanc|e
  ˌnɒn ə ˈpɪər ənts ‖ ˌnɑːn ə ˈpɪr- ~es ɪz əz
nonary ˈnəʊn ər i ˈnɒn- ‖ ˈnoʊn- ˈnɑːn-
nonassertive
  ˌnɒn ə ˈsɜːt ɪv ◂ ‖ ˌnɑːn ə ˈsɝːt̬ ɪv ◂
nonbeliever ˌnɒn bɪ ˈliːv ə -bə-
  ‖ ˌnɑːn bɪ ˈliːv ər ~s z
nonce nɒnts ‖ nɑːnts **nonces** ˈnɒnts ɪz -əz
  ‖ ˈnɑːnts əz
  ˈnonce word
nonchalance ˈnɒntʃ əl ənts ‖ ˌnɑːn ʃə ˈlɑːnts
  ◂ ••• (*)
nonchalant ˈnɒntʃ əl ənt ‖ ˌnɑːn ʃə ˈlɑːnt ◂
  ◂ ••• ~ly li
noncombatant ˌnɒn ˈkɒm bət ənt →ˌnɒŋ-,
  -ˈkʌm-; ˌ•kəm ˈbæt ənt, §-kɒm-
  ‖ ˌnɑːn kəm ˈbæt ənt ˌ•ˈkɑːm bət ənt ~s s
noncommissioned ˌnɒn kə ˈmɪʃ ənd ◂ →ˌnɒŋ-
  ‖ ˌnɑːn-
  ˌnoncomˌmissioned ˈofficer
noncommittal ˌnɒn kə ˈmɪt əl ◂ →ˌnɒŋ-
  ‖ ˌnɑːn kə ˈmɪt̬ əl ◂ ~ly i
non compos mentis ˌnɒn ˌkɒmp əs ˈment ɪs
  →ˌnɒŋ-, ˌnəʊn-, -, •ɒs-
  ‖ nɑːn ˌkɑːmp əs ˈment̬ əs noʊn-, ˌ•ˌ•ˈ•••
nonconductor ˌnɒn kən ˈdʌkt ə →ˌnɒŋ-,
  §-kɒn- ‖ ˌnɑːn kən ˈdʌkt ər ~s z
nonconformism ˌnɒn kən ˈfɔːm ˌɪz əm
  →ˌnɒŋ-, §,•kɒn- ‖ ˌnɑːn kən ˈfɔːrm-
nonconformist, N~ ˌnɒn kən ˈfɔːm ɪst ◂
  →ˌnɒŋ-, §-kɒn-, §-əst
  ‖ ˌnɑːn kən ˈfɔːrm əst ◂ ~s s

nonconformity, N~ ˌnɒn kən ˈfɔːm ət i
  →ˌnɒŋ-, §,•kɒn-, -ɪt i ‖ ˌnɑːn kən ˈfɔːrm ət̬ i
noncontributory ˌnɒn kən ˈtrɪb jʊt̬ ər i ◂
  →ˌnɒŋ-, §,•kɒn-; ˌ•ˌkɒn trɪ ˈbjuːt ər i,
  -trəˈ••- ‖ ˌnɑːn kən ˈtrɪb jə tɔːr i ◂ -toʊr i
noncooperation, non-co-operation
  ˌnɒn kəʊ ˌɒp ə ˈreɪʃ ən ˌnɒŋ-
  ‖ ˌnɑːn koʊ ˌɑːp-
nondescript ˈnɒn dɪ skrɪpt -də-, §-diː-
  ‖ ˌnɑːn dɪ ˈskrɪpt ◂ ~s s
nondrip ˌnɒn ˈdrɪp ◂ ‖ ˌnɑːn-
none nʌn §nɒn (= nun)
nonentit|y nɒ ˈnent ət i nə-, -ɪt- ‖ nɑː ˈnent̬
  ət̬ li ~ies iz
nones nəʊnz ‖ noʊnz
nonesuch ˈnʌn sʌtʃ §ˈnɒn-
nonet (ˌ)nəʊ ˈnet nɒ- ‖ noʊ- ~s s
nonetheless ˌnʌn ðə ˈles §ˌnɒn-
non-event ˌnɒn ɪ ˈvent -ə-, §-iː-; ˈ••• ‖ ˌnɑːn-
  ~s s
nonexistent ˌnɒn ɪg ˈzɪst ənt ◂ -eg-, -əg-, -ɪk-,
  -ek-, -ək- ‖ ˌnɑːn-
nonfat ˌnɒn ˈfæt ◂ ‖ ˌnɑːn-
non-feasance ˌnɒn ˈfiːz ənts ‖ ˌnɑːn-
nonfiction ˌnɒn ˈfɪk ʃən ‖ ˌnɑːn-
non-finite ˌnɒn ˈfaɪn aɪt ◂ ‖ ˌnɑːn-
nonflammable ˌnɒn ˈflæm əb əl ◂ ‖ ˌnɑːn-
noninterference ˌnɒn ˌɪnt ə ˈfɪər
  ənts ‖ ˌnɑːn ˌɪnt̬ ər ˈfɪr ənts
nonintervention
  ˌnɒn ˌɪnt ə ˈventʃ ən ‖ ˌnɑːn ˌɪnt̬ ər- ~ist/s
  ɪst/s §əst/s
non-iron ˌnɒn ˈaɪ ̩ən ◂ ‖ ˌnɑːn ˈaɪ ̩ərn ◂
nonjuror ˌnɒn ˈdʒʊər ə ‖ ˌnɑːn ˈdʒʊr ər ~s z
nonlinear ˌnɒn ˈlɪn i ̩ə ◂ ‖ ˌnɑːn ˈlɪn i ̩ər ◂
no-no ˈnəʊ nəʊ ‖ ˈnoʊ noʊ ~s z
nonobservance ˌnɒn əb ˈzɜːv ənts §-ɒb-
  ‖ ˌnɑːn əb ˈzɝːv-
no-nonsense ˌnəʊ ˈnɒnts
  ənts ◂ ‖ ˌnoʊ ˈnɑːn sents ◂ -ˈnɑːnts ənts
nonoxynol nəʊ ˈnɒks ɪ nɒl -ə-
  ‖ noʊ ˈnɑːks ə nɑːl -nɔːl, -noʊl
nonpareil ˌnɒn pə ˈreɪəl →ˌnɒm-; ˈnɒn pər ̩əl,
  →ˈnɒm- ‖ ˌnɑːn pə ˈrel ◂
nonpayment ˌnɒn ˈpeɪ mənt ◂ →ˌnɒm-
  ‖ ˌnɑːn-
non-playing nɒn ˈpleɪ ɪŋ ◂ →ˌnɒm- ‖ ˌnɑːn-
  ˌnon-ˌplaying ˈcaptain
nonplus ˌnɒn ˈplʌs →ˌnɒm-, ˈ•• ‖ ˌnɑːn- ~sed
  t ~ses ɪz əz ~sing ɪŋ
non-profit ˌnɒn ˈprɒf ɪt →ˌnɒm-, §-ət
  ‖ ˌnɑːn ˈprɑːf-
non-profit-making ˌnɒn ˈprɒf ɪt ˌmeɪk ɪŋ
  →ˌnɒm-, §-ˈ•ət- ‖ ˌnɑːn ˈprɑːf-
nonproliferation ˌnɒn prəʊ ˌlɪf ə ˈreɪʃ ən
  →ˌnɒm- ‖ ˌnɑːn prə-
nonresident ˌnɒn ˈrez ɪd ənt ◂ -əd- ‖ ˌnɑːn-
  ~s s
nonrestrictive ˌnɒn rɪ ˈstrɪkt ɪv ◂ -rə-, §-riː-
  ‖ ˌnɑːn-
nonreturnable ˌnɒn rɪ ˈtɜːn əb əl ◂ ˌ•rə-,
  §ˌ•riː- ‖ ˌnɑːn rɪ ˈtɝːn-
nonrhotic ˌnɒn ˈrəʊt ɪk ◂ ‖ ˌnɑːn ˈroʊt̬ ɪk ◂

N

nonrhoticity ˌnɒn rəʊ 'tɪs ət i -ɪt i
‖ ˌnɑːn roʊ 'tɪs ət̬ i
nonsense 'nɒnᵗs ənᵗs ‖ 'nɑːn senᵗs 'nɑːnᵗs ənᵗs
nonsensical nɒn 'senᵗs ɪk ᵊl ‖ ˌnɑːn- **~ly** ˌi
non sequitur ˌnɒn 'sek wɪt ə ˌnəʊn-, -wət-
‖ ˌnɑːn 'sek wət̬ ᵊr -wə tʊr **~s** z
nonskid ˌnɒn 'skɪd ◄ ‖ ˌnɑːn-
non-slip ˌnɒn 'slɪp ◄ ‖ ˌnɑːn-
nonsmoker ˌnɒn 'sməʊk ə ‖ ˌnɑːn 'smoʊk ᵊr
~s z
non-specific ˌnɒn spə 'sɪf ɪk ◄ -spɪ- ‖ ˌnɑːn-
ˌnon-speˌcific ˌureˈthritis
nonstandard
ˌnɒn 'stænd əd ◄ ‖ ˌnɑːn 'stænd ᵊrd
nonstarter ˌnɒn 'stɑːt ə ‖ ˌnɑːn 'stɑːrt̬ ᵊr **~s** z
nonstick ˌnɒn 'stɪk ◄ ‖ ˌnɑːn-
ˌnon-stick ˈfrying-pan
nonstop ˌnɒn 'stɒp ◄ ‖ ˌnɑːn 'stɑːp ◄
Nonsuch 'nɒn sʌtʃ 'nʌn- ‖ 'nɑːn- 'nʌn-
non-swimmer ˌnɒn 'swɪm ə ‖ ˌnɑːn 'swɪm ᵊr
~s z
non troppo ˌnɒn 'trɒp əʊ ˌnəʊn-
‖ ˌnɑːn 'trɑːp oʊ ˌnoʊn-, -'troʊp- —*It*
[non 'trɔp po]
non-U ˌnɒn 'juː ◄ ‖ ˌnɑːn-
nonunion ˌnɒn 'juːn i̯ ən ◄ ‖ ˌnɑːn-
nonverbal ˌnɒn 'vɜːb ᵊl ◄ ‖ ˌnɑːn 'vɝːb ᵊl ◄
nonviolence ˌnɒn 'vaɪ̯ əl ənᵗs ‖ ˌnɑːn-
nonviolent ˌnɒn 'vaɪ̯ əl ənt ◄ ‖ ˌnɑːn- **~ly** li
nonwhite, non-White ˌnɒn 'waɪt ◄ -'hwaɪt
‖ ˌnɑːn 'hwaɪt ◄ **~s** s
noodle 'nuːd ᵊl **~s** z
nook nʊk §nuːk **nooks** nʊks §nuːks
nookie, nooky 'nʊk i
noon nuːn **noons** nuːnz
Noonan 'nuːn ən
noonday 'nuːn deɪ
no one *pronoun*, **no-one** 'nəʊ wʌn §-wɒn **no
one's, no-one's** 'nəʊ wʌnz §-wɒnz
noontide 'nuːn taɪd
noose nuːs **noosed** nuːst **nooses** 'nuːs ɪz -əz
noosing 'nuːs ɪŋ
Nootka 'nʊt kə 'nuːt-
nopal 'nəʊp ᵊl ‖ 'noʊp ᵊl **~s** z
nope nəʊp ‖ noʊp —*usually said with the p
unreleased*
noplace 'nəʊ pleɪs ‖ 'noʊ-
nor nɔː ‖ nɔːr —*There is also an occasional weak
form* nə ‖ nᵊr
NOR nɔː ‖ nɔːr
nor-, nor'- nɔː ‖ nɔːr —*but in RP before a vowel,*
nɔːr— **nor'-east** ˌnɔːr 'iːst ◄ ‖ ˌnɔːr-
Nora 'nɔːr ə
noradrenalin, noradrenaline ˌnɔːr ə 'dren
əl ɪn -iːn, §-ən
Norah 'nɔːr ə
Noraid 'nɔːr eɪd
Norbert 'nɔːb ət ‖ -ᵊrt
Norden 'nɔːd ᵊn ‖ 'nɔːrd ᵊn
Nordic, n~ 'nɔːd ɪk ‖ 'nɔːrd ɪk **~s** s
Nordrhein-Westfalen ˌnɔːd raɪn vest
'faːl ən ‖ ˌnɔːrd- —*Ger*
[ˌnɔʁt raɪn vɛst 'faːl ən]

Nordstrom *tdmk* 'nɔːd strɒm -strəm
‖ 'nɔːrd strəm -stroʊm
Nore nɔː ‖ nɔːr
Noreen 'nɔːr iːn nɔː 'riːn ‖ nɔː 'riːn
Norfolk *place in England* 'nɔːf ək ‖ 'nɔːrf- —*but
places in the US are also* -ɔːk, -ɑːk. *The island
off Australia is locally* 'nɔː fəʊk.
ˌNorfolk ˈBroads, ˌNorfolk ˈjacket; ˌNorfolk
ˈterrier
nori 'nɔːr i 'nɒr- —*Jp* [no 'ri]
noria 'nɔːr i̯ ə ‖ 'noʊr- **~s** z
Noricum 'nɒr ɪk əm ‖ 'nɔːr- 'nɑːr-
Noriega ˌnɒr i 'eɪg ə ‖ ˌnɔːr- —*Sp* [no 'rje ɣa]
Norland, n~ 'nɔː lənd ‖ 'nɔːr-
norm, Norm nɔːm ‖ nɔːrm **norms, Norm's**
nɔːmz ‖ nɔːrmz
Norma 'nɔːm ə ‖ 'nɔːrm ə
normal, N~ 'nɔːm ᵊl ‖ 'nɔːrm ᵊl **~s** z
normalcy 'nɔːm ᵊl si ‖ 'nɔːrm-
normalis... —*see* **normaliz...**
normality nɔː 'mæl ət i -ɪt- ‖ nɔːr 'mæl ət̬ i
normalization ˌnɔːm ᵊl aɪ 'zeɪʃ ᵊn -ᵊl ɪ-
‖ ˌnɔːrm ᵊl ə- **~s** z
normaliz|e 'nɔːm ə laɪz ‖ 'nɔːrm- **~ed** d **~es**
ɪz əz **~ing** ɪŋ
normally 'nɔːm ᵊl i ‖ 'nɔːrm-
Norman 'nɔːm ən ‖ 'nɔːrm ən
ˌNorman ˈConquest
Normanby 'nɔːm ən bi →-ᵊm- ‖ 'nɔːrm-
Normand 'nɔːm ænd -ənd ‖ 'nɔːrm-
Normandy 'nɔːm ənd i ‖ 'nɔːrm-
Normanton 'nɔːm ən tən ‖ 'nɔːrm-
normative 'nɔːm ət ɪv ‖ 'nɔːrm ət̬ ɪv **~ly** li
~ness nəs nɪs
Norn nɔːn ‖ nɔːrn
Norrie 'nɒr i ‖ 'nɔːr i 'nɑːr-
Norris 'nɒr ɪs §-əs ‖ 'nɔːr əs 'nɑːr-
Norrköping 'nɔː tʃɜːp ɪŋ ‖ 'nɔːr tʃoʊp-
—*Swed* ['nɔr ɕøː piŋ]
Norroy 'nɒr ɔɪ ‖ 'nɔːr- 'nɑːr-
Norse nɔːs ‖ nɔːrs
Norse|man 'nɔːs |mən ‖ 'nɔːrs- **~men** mən
men
north, North nɔːθ ‖ nɔːrθ
ˌNorth ˌCaroˈlina; ˌNorth Daˈkota; ˌNorth
Koˈrea; ˌNorth ˈPole; ˌNorth ˈSea; ˌNorth
ˈStar; ˌNorth ˈYorkshire
Northallerton nɔːθ 'æl ət ən nɔːð-
‖ nɔːrθ 'æl ᵊrt ᵊn
Northampton nɔː 'θæmpt ən nə-,
nɔːθ 'hæmpt- ‖ nɔːr- **~shire** ʃə ʃɪə ‖ ʃᵊr ʃɪr
Northanger nɔː 'θæŋ gə 'nɔːθ ˌæŋ gə, -ˌhæŋ-,
-ə ‖ nɔːr 'θæŋ gᵊr ˌæŋ-, -ˌhæŋ-
Northants 'nɔːθ ænts nɔː 'θænts ‖ 'nɔːrθ-
northbound 'nɔːθ baʊnd ‖ 'nɔːrθ-
Northbrook 'nɔːθ brʊk ‖ 'nɔːrθ-
Northcliffe 'nɔːθ klɪf ‖ 'nɔːrθ-
Northcote 'nɔːθ kət -kɒt, -kəʊt ‖ 'nɔːrθ koʊt
northcountry|man ˌnɔːθ 'kʌntr i |mən -mæn
‖ ˌnɔːrθ- **~men** mən men
northeast, N~ ˌnɔːθ 'iːst ◄ ‖ ˌnɔːrθ- —*also
naut* ˌnɔːr- **~er/s** ə/z ‖ ᵊr/z **~erlies**
əl iz ‖ ᵊr liz **~erly** əl i ‖ ᵊr li **~ern** ən ‖ ᵊrn

N

~erner/s ən ə/z ‖ ᵊrn ᵊr/z **~ward/s** wəd/
z ‖ wᵊrd/z
Northenden 'nɔːð ᵊnd ən ‖ 'nɔːrð-
norther|ly 'nɔːð ə |li -əl i ‖ 'nɔːrð ᵊr |li **~lies**
liz
northern, N~ 'nɔːð ᵊn ‖ 'nɔːrð ᵊrn
ˌNorthern 'Ireland; ˌnorthern 'lights;
ˌNorthern 'Territory
northerner, N~ 'nɔːð ən ə ‖ 'nɔːrð ᵊrn ᵊr -ᵊn-
~s z
northernmost 'nɔːð ᵊn məʊst →-ᵊm-
‖ -ᵊrn moʊst
Northfield 'nɔːθ fiːᵊld ‖ 'nɔːrθ- **~s** z
Northfleet 'nɔːθ fliːt ‖ 'nɔːrθ-
Northiam 'nɔːð i_əm ‖ 'nɔːrð-
northing 'nɔːð ɪŋ 'nɔːθ- ‖'nɔːrθ ɪŋ 'nɔːrð- **~s**
z
North|man 'nɔːθ mən ‖ 'nɔːrθ- **~men** mən
men
Northolt 'nɔːθ əʊlt →-ɒlt ‖ 'nɔːrθ oʊlt
Northrop, Northrup 'nɔːθ rəp ‖ 'nɔːrθ-
Northumberland nɔː 'θʌm bə lənd nə-
‖ nɔːr 'θʌm bᵊr-
Northumbri|a nɔː 'θʌm bri_ə ‖ nɔːr- **~an/s**
ən/z
northward 'nɔːθ wəd ‖ 'nɔːrθ wᵊrd **~s** z
northwest, N~ ˌnɔːθ 'west ◄ ‖ˌnɔːrθ- —also
naut ˌnɔː- ‖ ˌnɔːr- **~er/s** ə/z ‖ ᵊr/z **~erlies**
əl iz ‖ ᵊr liz **~erly** əl i ‖ ᵊr li **~ern** ən ‖ ᵊrn
~ward/s wəd/z ‖ wᵊrd/z
ˌNorthwest 'Territories
Northwich 'nɔːθ wɪtʃ ‖ 'nɔːrθ-
Northwood 'nɔːθ wʊd ‖ 'nɔːrθ-
Norton 'nɔːt ᵊn ‖ 'nɔːrt ᵊn
Norvic tdmk 'nɔː vɪk ‖ 'nɔːr-
Norwalk 'nɔː wɔːk ‖ 'nɔːr- -wɑːk
Norway 'nɔː weɪ ‖ 'nɔːr weɪ
ˌNorway 'spruce
Norwegian nɔː 'wiːdʒ ᵊn ‖ nɔːr- **~s** z
Norwich place in England 'nɒr ɪdʒ -ɪtʃ ‖ 'nɔːr-
'nɑːr-
Norwich place in CT 'nɔː wɪtʃ ‖ 'nɔːr-
Norwood 'nɔː wʊd ‖ 'nɔːr-
nos, nos., Nos. 'nʌm bəz ‖ -bᵊrz
nose nəʊz ‖ noʊz **nosed** nəʊzd ‖ noʊzd
noses 'nəʊz ɪz -əz ‖ 'noʊz əz **nosing**
'nəʊz ɪŋ ‖ 'noʊz ɪŋ
nosebag 'nəʊz bæg ‖ 'noʊz- **~s** z
nosebleed 'nəʊz bliːd ‖ 'noʊz- **~s** z
nosecone 'nəʊz kəʊn ‖ 'noʊz koʊn **~s** z
nose|dive 'nəʊz |daɪv ‖ 'noʊz- **~dived** daɪvd
~dives daɪvz **~diving** daɪv ɪŋ **~dove**
dəʊv ‖ doʊv
no-see-um ˌnəʊ 'siː əm ‖ ˌnoʊ- **~s** z
nosegay 'nəʊz geɪ ‖ 'noʊz- **~s** z
nosey —see **nosy**
Nosferatu ˌnɒs fə 'rɑːt uː -fe- ‖ ˌnɑːs-
nosh nɒʃ ‖ nɑːʃ **noshed** nɒʃt ‖ nɑːʃt **noshes**
'nɒʃ ɪz -əz ‖ 'nɑːʃ əz **noshing**
'nɒʃ ɪŋ ‖ 'nɑːʃ ɪŋ
nosher|y 'nɒʃ ᵊr i ‖ 'nɑːʃ- **~ies** iz
no-show 'nəʊ ʃəʊ ‖ 'noʊ ʃoʊ **~s** z
nosh-up 'nɒʃ ʌp ‖ 'nɑːʃ- **~s** s

no-side ˌnəʊ 'saɪd ‖ ˌnoʊ-
noso- comb. form
with stress-neutral suffix ¦nɒs əʊ ‖ ¦noʊs ə
¦nɑːs oʊ — **nosographic** ˌnɒs əʊ
'græf ɪk ◄ ‖ ˌnoʊs ə- ˌnɑːs oʊ-
with stress-imposing suffix nɒ 'sɒ+ ‖ noʊ 'sɑː+
— **nosology** nɒ 'sɒl ədʒ i ‖ noʊ 'sɑːl-
no-smoking ˌnəʊ 'sməʊk ɪŋ ‖ ˌnoʊ 'smoʊk ɪŋ
ˌno-'smoking sign
nostalgia nɒ 'stældʒ ə -'stældʒ i_ə ‖ nɑː- nə-
nostalgic nɒ 'stældʒ ɪk ‖ nɑː- nə- **~ally** ᵊl_i
Nostradamus ˌnɒs trə 'dɑːm əs -'deɪm-
‖ ˌnɑːs- ˌnoʊs-
nostril 'nɒs trəl -trɪl ‖ 'nɑːs- **~s** z
nostrum 'nɒs trəm ‖ 'nɑːs- **~s** z
nos|y 'nəʊz |i ‖ 'noʊz |i **~ier** i_ə ‖ i_ᵊr **~iest**
i_ɪst i_əst **~ily** ɪ li əl i **~iness** i nəs i nɪs
ˌnosy 'parker
not nɒt ‖ nɑːt —There is no weak form other
than the contracted n't used with certain
modals.
nota bene ˌnəʊt ə 'ben i -ɑː-, -'biːn-, -eɪ
‖ ˌnoʊt̬ ə- -'beɪn eɪ
notabilit|y ˌnəʊt ə 'bɪl ət li -ɪt i
‖ ˌnoʊt̬ ə 'bɪl ət̬ li **~ies** iz
notab|le 'nəʊt əb |ᵊl ‖ 'noʊt̬- **~les** ᵊlz **~ly** li
notarie... —see **notary**
notaris... —see **notariz...**
notarization ˌnəʊt ᵊr aɪ 'zeɪʃ ᵊn -ᵊr ɪ- ‖ ˌnoʊt̬
ᵊr ə-
notariz|e 'nəʊt ə raɪz ‖ 'noʊt̬- **~ed** d **~es** ɪz əz
~ing ɪŋ
notar|y 'nəʊt ᵊr |i ‖ 'noʊt̬- **~ies** iz
no|tate nəʊ 'teɪt ‖ 'noʊ|t eɪt **~tated** teɪt ɪd
-əd ‖ teɪt̬ əd **~tates** teɪts **~tating**
teɪt ɪŋ ‖ teɪt̬ ɪŋ
notation nəʊ 'teɪʃ ᵊn ‖ noʊ- **~s** z
notch nɒtʃ ‖ nɑːtʃ **notched** nɒtʃt ‖ nɑːtʃt
notches 'nɒtʃ ɪz -əz ‖ 'nɑːtʃ əz **notching**
'nɒtʃ ɪŋ ‖ 'nɑːtʃ ɪŋ
note nəʊt ‖ noʊt **noted** 'nəʊt ɪd -əd ‖ 'noʊt̬ əd
notes nəʊts ‖ noʊts **noting**
'nəʊt ɪŋ ‖ 'noʊt̬ ɪŋ
notebook 'nəʊt bʊk §-buːk ‖ 'noʊt- **~s** s
notecas|e 'nəʊt keɪs ‖ 'noʊt- **~es** ɪz əz
noted 'nəʊt ɪd -əd ‖ 'noʊt̬ əd **~ly** li **~ness** nəs
nɪs
notelet 'nəʊt lət -lɪt ‖ 'noʊt- **~s** s
notepad 'nəʊt pæd ‖ 'noʊt- **~s** z
notepaper 'nəʊt ˌpeɪp ə ‖ 'noʊt̬ ˌpeɪp ᵊr
noteworth|y 'nəʊt ˌwɜːð |i ‖ 'noʊt̬ ˌwɜːð li
~ily ɪ li əl i **~iness** i nəs i nɪs
nothing 'nʌθ ɪŋ §'nɒθ- **~ness** nəs nɪs
ˌnothing 'doing; (there's) ˌnothing 'for it;
(there's) ˌnothing 'to it
notic|e 'nəʊt ɪs §-əs ‖ 'noʊt̬ əs **~ed** t **~es** ɪz əz
~ing ɪŋ
'notice board
noticeab|le 'nəʊt ɪs əb |ᵊl '•ᵊs- ‖ 'noʊt̬ əs- **~ly**
li
notifiable 'nəʊt ɪ faɪˌəb ᵊl '•ə-, ˌ••'•••
‖ 'noʊt̬-

N

notification ,nəʊt ɪf ɪ 'keɪʃ ᵊn , • əf-, §-ə' • -
‖ ,noʊt̮- ~s z
noti|fy 'nəʊt ɪ |faɪ -ə- ‖ 'noʊt̮ ə- ~**fied** faɪd
~**fier/s** faɪ ̮ə/z ‖ faɪ ̮ᵊr/z ~**fies** faɪz ~**fying**
faɪ ɪŋ
notion 'nəʊʃ ᵊn ‖ 'noʊʃ ᵊn ~s z
notional 'nəʊʃ ᵊn ̮əl ‖ 'noʊʃ- ~**ly** i
notoriety ,nəʊt ə 'raɪ ̮ət i ‖ ,noʊt̮ ə 'raɪ ̮ət̮ i
notorious nəʊ 'tɔːr i ̮əs ‖ noʊ- nə-, -'toʊr- ~**ly**
li ~**ness** nəs nɪs
Notre Dame (i) ,nəʊtr ə 'dɑːm ◀ ,nɒtr-
‖ ,noʊt̮ ᵊr 'dɑːm 'noʊtr ə- (ii) -'deɪm —for the
Paris cathedral, and for the religious order in
France and Britain, (i); in the United States (ii).
—Fr [nɔ tʁə dam]
no-trump ,nəʊ 'trʌmp ◀ ‖ ,noʊ- ~s s
Nott nɒt ‖ nɑːt
Notting Hill ,nɒt ɪŋ 'hɪl ◀ ‖ ,nɑːt̮-
Nottingham 'nɒt ɪŋ əm §-həm ‖ 'nɑːt̮- -hæm
~**shire** ʃə ʃɪə ‖ ʃᵊr ʃɪr
Notts nɒts ‖ nɑːts
Notus 'nəʊt əs ‖ 'noʊt̮ əs
notwithstanding ,nɒt wɪð 'stænd ɪŋ ◀ -wɪθ-
‖ ,nɑːt̮-
Nouakchott ,nuː æk 'ʃɒt ‖ -ɑːk 'ʃɑːt —Fr
[nwak ʃɔt]
nougat 'nuːg ɑː §'nʌg ət ‖ 'nuːg ət (*)
nought nɔːt ‖ nɑːt **noughts** nɔːts ‖ nɑːts
,**noughts and 'crosses**
Noumea, Nouméa nuː 'miː ̮ə -'meɪ ̮ə —Fr
[nu me a]
noumenon 'nuːm ən ən 'naʊm-, -ɪn-; -ə nɒn,
-ɪ- ‖ -ə nɑːn
noun naʊn **nouns** naʊnz
nourish 'nʌr ɪʃ ‖ 'nɝː ɪʃ ~**ed** t ~**es** ɪz əz
~**ing/ly** ɪŋ/li ~**ment** mənt
nous naʊs
nouveau, ~x 'nuːv əʊ ‖ ,nuː 'voʊ —Fr [nu vo]
,**nouveau(x) 'riche(s)** riːʃ ə —Fr [ʁiʃ]
nouvelle cuisine ,nuːv el kwɪ 'ziːn nu ,vel • ' • ,
-kwiː' • —Fr [nu vɛl kɥi zin]
nouvelle vague ,nuːv el 'vɑːg —Fr
[nu vɛl vag]
Nov —see **November**
nov|a, Nov|a 'nəʊv |ə ‖ 'noʊv |ə ~**ae** iː ~**as** əz
,**Nova 'Scotia** 'skəʊʃ ə ‖ 'skoʊʃ ə
Novartis tdmk nəʊ 'vɑːt ɪs §-əs ‖ noʊ 'vɑːrt̮ əs
Novaya Zemlya ,nəʊv ə jə 'zem li ̮ə ,nɒv-,
, • ɑː- ‖ ,noʊv- —Russ [,nɔ və jə zʲɪm 'lʲa]
novel 'nɒv ᵊl §'nʌv- ‖ 'nɑːv ᵊl ~s z
novelette ,nɒv ə 'let -ᵊl 'et ‖ ,nɑːv- ~s s
novelettish ,nɒv ə 'let ɪʃ ◀ -ᵊl 'et-
‖ ,nɑːv ə 'let̮ ɪʃ ◀ -ᵊl 'et̮-
novelist 'nɒv ᵊl ɪst §-əst ‖ 'nɑːv- ~s s
novelistic ,nɒv ə 'lɪst ɪk ◀ -ᵊl 'ɪst- ‖ ,nɑːv-
novell|a nəʊ 'vel |ə ‖ noʊ- ~**as** əz ~**e** iː eɪ
Novello nə 'vel əʊ ‖ -oʊ
novelt|y 'nɒv ᵊlt |i ‖ 'nɑːv- ~**ies** iz
November nəʊ 'vem bə ‖ noʊ 'vem bᵊr nə- ~s
z
novena nəʊ 'viːn ə ‖ noʊ- ~s z
Novgorod 'nɒv gə rɒd ‖ 'nɑːv gə rɑːd —Russ
['nɔv gə rət]

Novial 'nəʊv i ̮əl ‖ 'noʊv-
novic|e 'nɒv ɪs §-əs ‖ 'nɑːv əs ~**es** ɪz əz
noviciate, novitiate nəʊ 'vɪʃ i ̮ət -ɪt, -eɪt
‖ noʊ 'vɪʃ ət nə-, -'vɪʃ i ̮ət, -i eɪt ~s s
novocain, novocaine, N~ tdmk 'nəʊv əʊ keɪn
'nɒv- ‖ 'noʊv ə-
Novosibirsk ,nəʊv əʊ sɪ 'bɪəsk -sə' •
‖ ,noʊv ə sə 'bɪᵊrsk —Russ [nə və sʲɪ 'bʲirsk]
Novotel tdmk 'nəʊv əʊ ,tel ‖ 'noʊv oʊ- -ə-
now naʊ
nowadays 'naʊ ̮ə deɪz
Nowell personal name 'nəʊ ᵊl -el ‖ 'noʊ-
Nowell 'Christmas' nəʊ 'el ‖ noʊ-
nowhere 'nəʊ weə -hweə ‖ 'noʊ hwer -hwær
—Occasionally also -wə ‖ -hwᵊr
no-win ,nəʊ 'wɪn ◀ ‖ ,noʊ-
,**no-'win situ,ation,** • • , • • ' • •
nowise 'nəʊ waɪz ‖ 'noʊ-
nowt naʊt nəʊt
noxious 'nɒk ʃəs ‖ 'nɑːk- ~**ly** li ~**ness** nəs nɪs
Noyes family name nɔɪz
Noyes Fludde ,nɔɪ əz 'flʊd
nozzle 'nɒz ᵊl ‖ 'nɑːz ᵊl ~s z
NPR ,en piː 'ɑː ‖ -'ɑːr
nr see **near**
NSPCC ,en es ,piː siː 'siː
NSU ,en es 'juː
-n't ᵊnt —This contraction of **not** does not
receive stress, even for contrast: either you DID
or you DIDN'T 'dɪd ᵊnt .
nth enᵗθ
n-tuple 'en tjʊp ᵊl ,en 'tjuːp ᵊl, →§-'tʃuːp-
‖ 'en tʊp ᵊl -tjʊp ᵊl, ,en 'tuːp ᵊl, -'tjuːp- ~s z
n-type 'en taɪp
nu name of Greek letter njuː §nuː ‖ nuː njuː
Nuala 'nʊəl ə ‖ 'nuː əl ə
nuanc|e 'njuː ɑːnᵗs 'nuː-, -ɒnᵗs, -ɒ̃s, , • ' • ‖ 'nuː-
'njuː- —Fr [nɥɑ̃ːs] ~**es** ɪz əz
nub nʌb **nubs** nʌbz
Nuba 'njuːb ə §'nuːb- ‖ 'nuːb ə 'njuːb-
nubbin 'nʌb ɪn §-ən ~s z
nubble 'nʌb ᵊl ~s z
nubbly 'nʌb ᵊl ̮i
nubby 'nʌb i
Nubi|a 'njuːb i ̮ə §'nuːb- ‖ 'nuːb- 'njuːb-
~**an/s** ən/z
,**Nubian 'Desert**
nubile 'njuːb aɪᵊl §'nuːb- ‖ 'nuːb ᵊl 'njuːb-,
-aɪᵊl

NUCLEAR

	-li̯_ə	-jələ
BrE 1998		

0 20 40 60 80 100%

nuclear 'njuːk li ̮ə §'nuːk-, △-jəl ə ‖ 'nuːk li ̮ᵊr
'njuːk-, △-jəl ᵊr —BrE 1998 poll panel
preference: -li ̮ə 94%, -jələ 6%.
,**nuclear 'energy;** ,**nuclear re'actor;**
,**nuclear 'tone;** ,**nuclear 'winter**
nuclear-free ,njuːk li ̮ə 'friː ◀ §,nuːk-, △, • jəl-
‖ ,nuːk li ̮ᵊr- ,njuːk-, △, • jəl-
nuclei 'njuːk li aɪ §'nuːk-, -iː ‖ 'nuːk- 'njuːk-

nucleic nju 'kli: ɪk §nu-, -'kleɪ- ‖ nu- nju-
nu₁cleic 'acid
nucleo- *comb. form*
  with stress-neutral suffix ˌnju:k li əʊ §ˌnu:k-
  ‖ ˌnu:k li ə ˌnju:k- — **nucleoplasm**
  'nju:k li əʊ ˌplæz əm §'nu:k- ‖ 'nu:k li ə-
  'njʌk-
  with stress-imposing suffix ˌnju:k li 'ɒ+ ˌnu:k-
  ‖ ˌnu:k li 'ɑ:+ ˌnju:k- — **nucleofugal**
  ˌnju:k li 'ɒf jʊg əl ◄ §ˌnu:k-
  ‖ ˌnu:k li 'ɑ:f jəg əl ◄ ˌnju:k-
nucleol|us nju 'kli:ˌəl ləs §nu-;
  ˌnju:k li 'əʊl ləs, §ˌnu:k- ‖ nu- nju- ~i aɪ
nucleon 'nju:k li ɒn §'nu:k- ‖ 'nu:k li ɑ:n
  'nju:k- ~s s
nucleonic ˌnju:k li 'ɒn ɪk ◄ §ˌnu:k-
  ‖ ˌnu:k li 'ɑ:n ɪk ◄ ˌnju:k- ~s s
nucleoside 'nju:k liˌə saɪd §'nu:k- ‖ 'nu:k-
  'nju:k- ~s z
nucleotide 'nju:k liˌə taɪd §'nu:k- ‖ 'nu:k-
  'nju:k- ~s z
nucle|us 'nju:k liˌləs §'nu:k-, ⚠-jəl- ‖ 'nu:k-
  'nju:k-, , ⚠-jəl- ~i aɪ i:
nuclide 'nju:k laɪd §'nu:k- ‖ 'nu:k- 'nju:k- ~s
  z
nuddy 'nʌd i
nude nju:d §nu:d ‖ nu:d nju:d **nudes** nju:dz
  §nu:dz ‖ nu:dz nju:dz
nudge nʌdʒ **nudged** nʌdʒd **nudges** 'nʌdʒ ɪz
  -əz **nudging** 'nʌdʒ ɪŋ
nudibranch 'nju:d ɪ bræŋk §'nu:d-, §-ə-
  ‖ 'nu:d- 'nju:d- ~s s
nudism 'nju:d ˌɪz əm §'nu:d- ‖ 'nu:d- 'nju:d-
nudist 'nju:d ɪst §'nu:d-, §-əst ‖ 'nu:d əst
  'nju:d- ~s s
nudit|y 'nju:d ət li §'nu:d-, -ɪt- ‖ 'nu:d əṭ li
  'nju:d- ~ies iz
nudnik 'nʊd nɪk ~s s
Nuffield 'nʌf i:ᵊld
nugatory 'nju:g ətˌər i §'nu:g-; nju: 'geɪt ər i
  ‖ 'nu:g ə tɔ:r i 'nju:g-, -toʊr-
Nugent 'nju:dʒ ənt §'nu:dʒ- ‖ 'nu:dʒ-
  'nju:dʒ-
nugget 'nʌg ɪt §-ət ~s s
nuisanc|e 'nju:s ᵊnts §'nu:s- ‖ 'nu:s- 'nju:s-
  ~es ɪz əz
  'nuisance ˌvalue
Nuits-Saint-George ˌnwi: sæn 'ʒɔ:ʒ -'dʒɔ:dʒ
  ‖ -'ʒɔ:rʒ —*Fr* [nɥi sæ̃ ʒɔʁʒ]
NUJ ˌen ju: 'dʒeɪ
nuke nju:k §nu:k ‖ nu:k nju:k **nuked** nju:kt
  §nu:kt ‖ nu:kt nju:kt **nukes** nju:ks §nu:ks
  ‖ nu:ks nju:ks **nuking** 'nju:k ɪŋ §'nu:k-
  ‖ 'nu:k ɪŋ 'nju:k-
null nʌl
  ˌnull and 'void
nullah 'nʌl ə -ɑ: ~s z
nulla-nulla 'nʌl ə ˌnʌl ə ~s z
Nullarbor 'nʌl ə bɔ: ‖ -bɔ:r
  ˌNullarbor 'Plain
nullification ˌnʌl ɪf ɪ 'keɪʃ ᵊn ˌ•əf-, §-ə'•-
nulli|fy 'nʌl ɪ faɪ -ə- ~fied faɪd ~fier/s faɪ‿ə/
  z ‖ faɪ‿ᵊr/z ~fies faɪz ~fying faɪ ɪŋ

nullip|ara nʌ 'lɪp ᵊr ə ~arae ə ri:
nullit|y 'nʌl ət li -ɪt- ‖ -əṭ li ~ies iz
nul points ˌnʊl 'pwæl -'pwæŋ —*Fr* [nyl pwæ̃]
NUM ˌen ju 'em
Numa 'nju:m ə 'nu:m- ‖ 'nu:m ə 'nju:m-
numb nʌm **numbed** nʌmd **number**
  'nʌm ə ‖ -ᵊr **numbest** 'nʌm ɪst -əst
  numbing/ly 'nʌm ɪŋ /li **numbs** nʌmz
numbat 'nʌm bæt ~s s
number *n, v* 'nʌm bə ‖ -bᵊr ~ed d
  numbering 'nʌm bᵊr‿ɪŋ ~s z
  ˌnumber 'one◄; ˌNumber 'Ten◄, ˌNumber
  Ten 'Downing Street
number *adj* '*more numb*' 'nʌm ə ‖ -ᵊr
number-crunch|er/s 'nʌm bə ˌkrʌntʃ |ə/z
  ‖ -bᵊr ˌkrʌntʃ |ᵊr/z ~ing ɪŋ
numberless 'nʌm bə ləs -lɪs ‖ -bᵊr-
numberplate 'nʌm bə pleɪt ‖ -bᵊr- ~s s
Numbers 'nʌm bəz ‖ -bᵊrz
numbly 'nʌm li
numbskull 'nʌm skʌl ~s z
numerable 'nju:m ᵊr‿əb ᵊl §'nu:m- ‖ 'nu:m-
  'nju:m-
numeracy 'nju:m ᵊr‿əs i §'nu:m- ‖ 'nu:m-
  'nju:m-
numeral 'nju:m ᵊr‿əl §'nu:m- ‖ 'nu:m-
  'nju:m- ~s z
numerate *adj* 'nju:m ᵊr‿ət §'nu:m-, -ɪt, -ə reɪt
  ‖ 'nu:m- 'nju:m-
numeration ˌnju:m ə 'reɪʃ ᵊn §ˌnu:m- ‖ ˌnu:m-
  ˌnju:m-
numerator 'nju:m ə reɪt ə §'nu:m-
  ‖ 'nu:m ə reɪṭ ᵊr 'nju:m- ~s z
numeric nju 'mer ɪk §nu- ‖ nu- nju- ~al ᵊl
  ~ally ᵊl‿i ~s s
numero uno ˌnu:m ə rəʊ 'u:n əʊ ˌnju:-
  ‖ ˌnu:m ə roʊ 'u:n oʊ ˌnju:m-
numerological ˌnju:m ᵊr‿ə 'lɒdʒ ɪk ᵊl ◄
  §ˌnu:m- ‖ ˌnu:m ᵊr‿ə 'lɑ:dʒ- ˌnju:m- ~ly‿i
numerology ˌnju:m ə 'rɒl ədʒ i §ˌnu:m-
  ‖ ˌnu:m ə 'rɑ:l- ˌnju:m-
numerous 'nju:m ᵊr‿əs §'nu:m- ‖ 'nu:m-
  'nju:m- ~ly li ~ness nəs nɪs
Numidi|a nju 'mɪd iˌə §nu- ‖ nu- nju- ~an/s
  ən/z
numinous 'nju:m ɪn əs §'nu:m-, -ən- ‖ 'nu:m-
  'nju:m-
numismatic ˌnju:m ɪz 'mæt ɪk ◄ §ˌnu:m-
  ‖ ˌnu:m əz 'mæṭ ɪk ◄ ˌnju:m-, ˌ•əs- ~s s
numismatist nju: 'mɪz mət ɪst §nu:-, §-əst
  ‖ nu: 'mɪz məṭ əst nju:-, -'mɪs- ~s s
nummary 'nʌm ᵊr i ◄
nummular 'nʌm jʊl ə -jəl- ‖ -jəl ᵊr
numskull 'nʌm skʌl ~s z
nun nʌn **nuns** nʌnz
nunatak 'nʌn ə tæk ~s s
Nunavut 'nu:n ə vu:t
Nunawading 'nʌn ə wɒd ɪŋ ‖ -wɑ:d •
Nunc Dimittis ˌnʌŋk dɪ 'mɪt ɪs ˌnʊŋk-, -daɪ-,
  -də-, §-əs ‖ -'mɪṭ əs
nunciature 'nʌnts iˌə tjʊə ˌəᵊtʃ ə‖ˌə tjʊr
  ˌəᵊtʃ ᵊr ~s z

N

nuncio 'nʌnts i əʊ 'nʌntʃ-, 'nʊnts-, 'nʊntʃ-
‖ -oʊ ~s z
Nuneaton nʌn 'iːt ᵊn
Nunn nʌn
nunner|y 'nʌn ər |i ~ies iz
Nupe *African language and people* 'nuːp eɪ
NUPE *trade union* 'njuːp i 'nuːp-
nuptial 'nʌp ʃᵊl -tʃᵊl; △'nʌp ʃu‿əl, △-tʃu‿əl
~ly i ~s z
Nuremberg 'njʊər əm bɜːg 'njɔːr-
‖ 'nʊr əm bɜːg 'njʊr- —*Ger* Nürnberg
['nʏʁn bɛʁk]
Nureyev 'njʊər i ef njuᵊ 'reɪ-, -ev ‖ nu 'reɪ-
—*Russ* [nu 'rʲɪe jɪf]
Nuristan ˌnʊər ɪ 'staːn -'stæn ‖ ˌnʊr ɪ 'stæn
-'staːn
Nurofen *tdmk* 'njʊər əʊ fen §'nʊər- ‖ 'nʊr ə-
'njʊr-
nurse, Nurse nɜːs ‖ nɜˑs nursed nɜːst ‖ nɜˑst
nurses 'nɜːs ɪz -əz ‖ 'nɜˑs əz nursing
'nɜːs ɪŋ ‖ 'nɜˑs ɪŋ
nurseling 'nɜːs lɪŋ ‖ 'nɜˑs- ~s z
nursemaid 'nɜːs meɪd ‖ 'nɜˑs- ~s z
nurser|y 'nɜːs ər‿|i ‖ 'nɜˑs ər‿|i ~ies iz
'nursery rhyme; 'nursery school
nurserymaid 'nɜːs ər‿i meɪd ‖ 'nɜˑs- ~s z
nursery|man 'nɜːs ər‿i |mən ‖ 'nɜˑs- ~men
mən
nursing 'nɜːs ɪŋ ‖ 'nɜˑs ɪŋ
'nursing home; ˌnursing 'mother
nursling 'nɜːs lɪŋ ‖ 'nɜˑs- ~s z
nurture 'nɜːtʃ ə ‖ 'nɜˑtʃ ər ~ed d ~s z
nurturing 'nɜːtʃ ər ɪŋ ‖ 'nɜˑtʃ ər ɪŋ
NUS ˌen ju 'es
Nussbaum 'nʊs baʊm
nut nʌt nuts nʌts nutted 'nʌt ɪd -əd
‖ 'nʌt̬ əd nutting 'nʌt ɪŋ ‖ 'nʌt̬ ɪŋ
NUT *trades union* ˌen ju: 'ti:
nutation nju: 'teɪʃ ᵊn §nu:- ‖ nu:- nju:- ~s z
nut-brown ˌnʌt 'braʊn ◂
ˌnut-brown 'hair
nutcas|e 'nʌt keɪs ~es ɪz əz
nutcracker 'nʌt ˌkræk ə ‖ -ᵊr ~s z
nuthatch 'nʌt hætʃ ~es ɪz əz
nut|house 'nʌt |haʊs ~houses haʊz ɪz -əz
Nutkin 'nʌt kɪn
Nutley 'nʌt li
nutmeg 'nʌt meg
Nutrasweet, NutraSweet *tdmk* 'nju:tr ə swi:t
§'nu:tr- ‖ 'nu:tr- 'nju:tr-

nutria 'nju:tr i‿ə §'nu:tr- ‖ 'nu:tr- 'nju:tr- ~s
z
nutrient 'nju:tr i‿ənt §'nu:tr- ‖ 'nu:tr-
'nju:tr- ~s s
nutriment 'nju:tr ɪ mənt §'nu:tr-, -ə- ‖ 'nu:tr-
'nju:tr- ~s s
nutrition nju 'trɪʃ ᵊn §nu- ‖ nu- nju- ~al ‿əl
~ally ‿əl i
nutritionist nju 'trɪʃ ᵊn‿ɪst §nu-, §‿əst ‖ nu-
nju- ~s s
nutritious nju 'trɪʃ əs §nu- ‖ nu- nju- ~ly li
~ness nəs nɪs
nutritive 'nju:tr ət ɪv §'nu:tr-, -ət-
‖ 'nu:tr ət̬ ɪv 'nju:tr- ~ly li ~s z
nuts nʌts
nutshell 'nʌt ʃel ~s z
Nutt nʌt
Nuttall 'nʌt ɔːl ‖ -ɑːl
nutt... *see* nut
nutter, N~ 'nʌt ə ‖ 'nʌt̬ ər ~s z
Nutting, n~ 'nʌt ɪŋ ‖ 'nʌt̬ ɪŋ
Nutton 'nʌt ᵊn
nutt|y 'nʌt li ‖ 'nʌt̬ li ~ier i‿ə ‖ i‿ᵊr ~iest i‿ɪst
i‿əst ~ily ɪ li əl i ~iness i nəs i nɪs
nux vomica ˌnʌks 'vɒm ɪk ə ‖ -'vɑːm-
Nuyts nɔɪts
nuzzl|e 'nʌz ᵊl ~ed d ~es z ~ing ‿ɪŋ
NVQ ˌen vi: 'kju: ~s z
NY —*see* New York
Nyack 'naɪ æk
Nyanja ni 'ændʒ ə
nyanza, N~ ni 'ænz ə naɪ-
Nyasaland naɪ 'æs ə lænd ni-
NYC —*see* New York City
Nye, nye naɪ nyes, Nye's naɪz
Nyerere njə 'reər i nɪ-, nɪə-, -'rer- ‖ -'rer-
nylon 'naɪl ɒn ‖ -ɑːn ~s z
nymph nɪmᵖf nymphs nɪmᵖfs
nymphet 'nɪmᵖf ɪt -ət, -et; nɪm 'fet ~s s
nympho 'nɪmᵖf əʊ ‖ -oʊ ~s z
nymphomania ˌnɪmᵖf ə 'meɪn i‿ə
nymphomaniac ˌnɪmᵖf ə 'meɪn i æk ~s s
Nynorsk 'ni: nɔːsk ‖ -nɔːrsk —*Norw*
['ny: nɔʂk]
Nyree 'naɪᵊr i:
nystagmus nɪ 'stæg məs
nystatin 'nɪst ə tɪn §-ət ᵊn
NZ ˌen 'zed ◂ ‖ -'zi: ◂ —*see* New Zealand

O o

o — Spelling-to-sound

1 Where the spelling is **o**, the pronunciation differs according to whether the vowel is
  - short or long,
  - followed or not by **r**, and
  - strong or weak.

2 The 'strong' pronunciation is regularly
  ɒ ‖ ɑː, as in **lot** lɒt ‖ lɑːt ('short O')
  əʊ ‖ oʊ, as in **nose** nəʊz ‖ noʊz ('long O').

3 Less frequently, it is
  ʌ, as in **come** kʌm (especially before **m, n, v, th**),
  uː, as in **move** muːv,
  ʊ, as in **woman** 'wʊm ən (note also ɪ in **women**), or
  ɒ ‖ ɔː, as in **cross** krɒs ‖ krɔːs (but some speakers of AmE use ɑː instead, thus krɑːs)
  Note also the exceptional **gone** gɒn ‖ gɔːn.

4 Where the spelling is **or**, the 'strong' pronunciation is
  ɔː, as in **north** nɔːθ ‖ nɔːrθ,
  or indeed, especially in BrE, the regular 'short' pronunciation
  ɒ ‖ ɑː, as in **moral** 'mɒr əl (AmE 'mɔːr əl, 'mɑːr əl).

5 Less frequently, it is
  ɜː ‖ ɜ˞ː, as in **work** wɜːk ' wɜ˞ːk (especially after **w**), or
  ʌ ‖ ɜ˞ː, as in **worry** 'wʌr i ‖ 'wɜ˞ː i.

6 The 'weak' pronunciation is
  ə, as in **method** 'meθ əd, **Oxford** 'ɒks fəd ‖ 'ɑːks fə˞rd.
  In unstressed syllables there are often two possibilities, ə or əʊ ‖ oʊ, the second being associated with careful speech or unfamiliar words, thus **phonetics** fəʊ 'net ɪks ‖ foʊ 'neṭ ɪks as a little-used word, but fə 'net ɪks ‖ -'neṭ- as an everyday word.

7 **o** also forms part of the digraphs **oa, oe, oi, oo, ou, ow, oy** (see below).

oa — Spelling-to-sound

1 Where the spelling is the digraph **oa**, the pronunciation is regularly
  əʊ ‖ oʊ, as in **road** rəʊd ‖ roʊd, or
  ɔː, as in **board** bɔːd ‖ bɔːrd (before **r**).

2 Note the exceptional words **broad** brɔːd (and derivatives **abroad, broaden**), **cupboard** 'kʌb əd ‖ 'kʌb ᵊrd.

3 **oa** is not a digraph in **oasis, Noah, coalescence, protozoa**.

O

oe   Spelling-to-sound

1 Where the spelling is the digraph **oe**, the pronunciation is regularly əʊ ‖ oʊ, as in **toe** təʊ ‖ toʊ.

2 Exceptionally, it is
uː in **shoe** ʃuː, **canoe**,
ʌ in **does** (from **do**) dʌz,
iː in **phoenix** 'fiːn ɪks and other words of Greek origin.

3 **oe** is not a digraph in **poem, poetic, coerce, Noel**.

oi, oy   Spelling-to-sound

1 Where the spelling is one of the digraphs **oi** and **oy**, the pronunciation is regularly
ɔɪ, as in **noise** nɔɪz, **boy** bɔɪ.

2 In words of French origin, the pronunciation is often
wɑː, as in **patois** 'pæt wɑː.

3 Occasionally **oi** is weak, as in the usual pronunciation of **tortoise** 'tɔːt əs ‖ 'tɔːrt̬ əs.

4 Note the exceptional words **choir** 'kwaɪə ‖ 'kwaɪ ᵊr, **buoy** bɔɪ (AmE also 'buː i).

5 **oi** is not a digraph in **coincidence, soloist**.

oo   Spelling-to-sound

1 Where the spelling is the digraph **oo**, the pronunciation is regularly either
uː, as in **food** fuːd, or
ʊ, as in **good** gʊd.
There is no rule, although ʊ is commoner before **k** (**book** bʊk). In some words both pronunciations are in use, as **room**.

2 Less frequently, the pronunciation is
ʌ, as in **blood** blʌd, **flood**.

3 Where the spelling is **oor**, the pronunciation is
ɔː, as in **door** dɔː ‖ dɔːr, or
ʊə ‖ ʊ as in **moor** mʊə ‖ mʊr (but BrE now often mɔː).

4 Note the exceptional word **brooch** brəʊtʃ ‖ broʊtʃ (AmE also bruːtʃ).

5 **oo** is not a digraph in **zoology, cooperate**.

ou, ow   Spelling-to-sound

1 Where the spelling is one of the digraphs **ou** and **ow**, the pronunciation is regularly
     aʊ, as in **round** raʊnd, **cow** kaʊ.

2 Less frequently, it is
     əʊ ‖ oʊ, as in **soul** səʊl ‖ soʊl, **own** əʊn ‖ oʊn,
     ʌ, as in **touch** tʌtʃ, or
     uː, as in **group** gruːp.

3 Note also the exceptional **could** kʊd, **should, would**.

4 Where the spelling is the notorious **ough**, the pronunciation may be any of the following:
     ɔː, as in **thought** θɔːt,
     uː, as in **through** θruː,
     aʊ, as in **bough** baʊ,
     əʊ ‖ oʊ, as in **though** ðəʊ ‖ ðoʊ,
     ʌf, as in **rough** rʌf,
     ɒf ‖ ɔːf, as in **cough** kɒf ‖ kɔːf,
     ə ‖ oʊ, as in **thorough** 'θʌr ə ‖ 'θɝː oʊ;
     there are also other possibilities in **lough, hiccough** (more usually written **loch, hiccup**).

5 Where the spelling is **our**, the pronunciation may be
     aʊ ə, as in **flour** 'flaʊ_ə ‖ 'flaʊ_ər,
     ɔː, as in **four** fɔː ‖ fɔːr,
     ɜː ‖ ɝː, as in **journey** 'dʒɜːn i ‖ 'dʒɝːn i,
     ʌ ‖ ɝː, as in **courage** 'kʌr ɪdʒ ‖ 'kɝː ɪdʒ, or
     ʊə ‖ ʊ, as in **tourist** 'tʊər ɪst ‖ 'tʊr əst (BrE also ɔː); also
     ʊ in the exceptional **courier**, usually 'kʊr i ə ‖ 'kʊr i_ər.

O, o əʊ ‖ oʊ **O's, o's, Os** əʊz ‖ oʊz
—*Communications code name:* Oscar
   'O ˌlevel; ˌO'V ˌlanguage
O, O' *in family names* əʊ ‖ oʊ —*This prefix is unstressed; it is occasionally reduced to* ə
o' ə —*weak form only; see* of
Oadby 'əʊd bi →'əʊb- ‖ 'oʊd-
oaf əʊf ‖ oʊf **oafs** əʊfs ‖ oʊfs
oafish 'əʊf ɪʃ ‖ 'oʊf ɪʃ **~ly** li **~ness** nəs nɪs
Oahu əʊ 'ɑː huː ‖ oʊ 'ɑː huː ə 'wɑː-
oak əʊk ‖ oʊk **oaks** əʊks ‖ oʊks
   ˌOak 'Ridge; 'oak tree
oak-apple 'əʊk ˌæp əl ‖ 'oʊk-
oaken 'əʊk ən ‖ 'oʊk ən
Oakengates 'əʊk ən geɪts →-ŋ- ‖ 'oʊk-
Oakes əʊks ‖ oʊks
Oakham 'əʊk əm ‖ 'oʊk-

Oakhampton ˌəʊk 'hæmp tən ◂ ‖ 'oʊk ˌ••
Oakland 'əʊk lənd ‖ 'oʊk-
Oakleigh, Oakley 'əʊk li ‖ 'oʊk-
Oaks əʊks ‖ oʊks
Oaksey 'əʊks i ‖ 'oʊks i
oakum 'əʊk əm ‖ 'oʊk-
Oakville 'əʊk vɪl ‖ 'oʊk-
Oamaru 'ɒm ə ruː ‖ 'ɑːm-
OAP ˌəʊ eɪ 'piː ‖ ˌoʊ- **~s, ~'s** z
oar ɔː ‖ ɔːr oʊr (*= ore*) **oared** ɔːd ‖ ɔːrd oʊrd
   oaring 'ɔːr ɪŋ ‖ 'oʊr- **oars** ɔːz ‖ ɔːrz oʊrz
oarfish 'ɔː fɪʃ ‖ 'ɔːr 'oʊr-
oarlock 'ɔː lɒk ‖ 'ɔːr lɑːk 'oʊr- **~s** s
oars|man 'ɔːz |mən ‖ 'ɔːrz- 'oʊrz- **~manship** mən ʃɪp **~men** mən **~woman** ˌwʊm ən **~women** ˌwɪm ɪn §-ən
oarweed 'ɔː wiːd ‖ 'ɔːr- 'oʊr-

OAS ˌəʊ eɪ 'es ‖ ˌoʊ-
oas|is, O~ əʊ 'eɪs ‖ɪs §-əs ‖ oʊ- ~es iːz
oast əʊst ‖ oʊst
  'oast house
oat əʊt ‖ oʊt oats əʊts ‖ oʊts
oatcake 'əʊt keɪk ‖ 'oʊt- ~s s
oaten 'əʊt ᵊn ‖ 'oʊt ᵊn
Oates əʊts ‖ oʊts
oath əʊθ ‖ᵗ oʊθ oaths əʊðz əʊθs ‖ oʊðz oʊθs
oatmeal 'əʊt miːᵊl ‖ 'oʊt-
oats əʊts ‖ oʊts
OAU ˌəʊ eɪ 'juː ‖ ˌoʊ-
Oaxaca wə 'hɑːk ə wɑː- —Sp [wa 'xa ka]
Ob river in USSR ɒb ‖ oʊb ɑːb, ɔːb —Russ [opʲ]
Obadiah ˌəʊb ə 'daɪ‿ə ‖ ˌoʊb-
Oban 'əʊb ᵊn ‖ 'oʊb-
obbligat|o ˌɒb lɪ 'gɑːt ‖əʊ -lə-
  ‖ ˌɑːb lə 'gɑːt ‖oʊ ~i iː ~os əʊz ‖ oʊz
obcordate ɒb 'kɔːd eɪt ‖ ɑːb 'kɔːrd-
obduracy 'ɒb djʊr əs i ‖•'djɔːr- ‖ 'ɑːb dʊr əs i
  ‖•'djʊr-, ‖•'dɜr-, ‖•'djɔːr-
obdurate 'ɒb djʊr ət -djɔːr-, -ɪt ‖ 'ɑːb dʊr ət
  -djʊr-, -dɜr-, -djɔːr- ~ly li ~ness nəs nɪs
OBE ˌəʊ biː 'iː ‖ ˌoʊ- ~s, ~'s z
obeah 'əʊb i‿ə ‖ 'oʊb-
obedience ə 'biːd i‿ᵊnᵗs əʊ- ‖ oʊ- ə-
obedient ə 'biːd i‿ᵊnt əʊ- ‖ oʊ- ə- ~ly li
obeisanc|e əʊ 'beɪs ᵊnᵗs -'biːs- ‖ oʊ- ə- ~es ɪz
  əz
obelisk 'ɒb ᵊl ɪsk §-əsk ‖ 'ɑːb ə lɪsk 'oʊb- ~s s
ob|elus 'ɒb ᵊl əs -ɪl- ‖ 'ɑːb- ~eli ə laɪ ɪ-
Oberammergau ˌəʊb ər 'æm ə gaʊ ‖ ˌoʊb
  ər 'ɑːm ᵊr gaʊ —Ger [ˌʔoː bɐ 'ʔam ɐ gaʊ]
Oberland 'əʊb ə lænd ‖ 'oʊb ᵊr- —Ger
  ['ʔoː bɐ lant]
Oberlin 'əʊb ə lɪn ‖ 'oʊb ᵊr- —Fr [o bɛʁ lɛ̃]
Oberon 'əʊb ᵊr‿ᵊn -ə rɒn ‖ 'oʊb ə rɑːn
obese əʊ 'biːs ‖ oʊ- ~ness nəs nɪs
obesity əʊ 'biːs ət i -ɪt- ‖ oʊ 'biːs ət̬ i
obey ə 'beɪ əʊ- ‖ oʊ- ~ed d ~ing ɪŋ ~s z
obfusc|ate 'ɒb fʌsk eɪt -fə skeɪt ‖ 'ɑːb- ‖•'•••
  ~ated eɪt ɪd -əd ‖ eɪt̬ əd ~ates eɪts ~ating
  eɪt ɪŋ ‖ eɪt̬ ɪŋ
obfuscation ˌɒb fʌ 'skeɪʃ ᵊn -fə- ‖ ˌɑːb- ~s z
obi 'witchcraft' 'əʊb i ‖ 'oʊb i
obi 'sash' 'əʊb i ‖ 'oʊb i —Jp ['o bi] ~s z
obit 'əʊb ɪt 'ɒb-, §-ət ‖ 'oʊb- —as a shortening
  of obituary, also əʊ 'bɪt ‖ oʊ- ~s s
obiter 'ɒb ɪt ə 'əʊb-, -ət- ‖ 'oʊb ət̬ ᵊr 'ɑːb-
  ˌobiter 'dictum
obituarist ə 'bɪtʃ u‿ər ɪst əʊ-, ɒ-, -'bɪt ju‿,
  §-əst; -'bɪtʃ ᵊr‿ɪst ‖ -u er əst ~s s
obituaris|e, obituariz|e ə 'bɪtʃ u‿ə raɪz əʊ-, ɒ-,
  -'bɪt ju‿, -'bɪtʃ ə raɪz ~ed d ~es ɪz əz ~ing
  ɪŋ
obituar|y ə 'bɪtʃ u‿ər li əʊ-, ɒ-, -'bɪt ju‿; -'bɪtʃ
  ər‿li ‖ -u er li ~ies ɪz
object n 'ɒb dʒekt -dʒɪkt ‖ 'ɑːb- ~s s
  'object ˌlesson
object v əb 'dʒekt §ₒ₍ᵢ₎ɒb- ‖ ₍ᵢ₎ɑːb- ~ed ɪd əd
  ~ing ɪŋ ~s s
objecti|fy v əb 'dʒekt ɪ |faɪ §ₒ₍ᵢ₎ɒb-, -ə- ‖ ₍ᵢ₎ɑːb-
  ~fied faɪd ~fies faɪz ~fying faɪ ɪŋ

objection əb 'dʒek ʃᵊn §ₒ₍ᵢ₎ɒb- ‖ ₍ᵢ₎ɑːb- ~s z
objectionab|le əb 'dʒek ʃᵊn_əb ‖ᵊl
  §ₒ₍ᵢ₎ɒb- ‖ ₍ᵢ₎ɑːb- ~ly li
objectival ˌɒb dʒɪk 'taɪv ᵊl ◄ -dʒek- ‖ ˌɑːb-
objective əb 'dʒekt ɪv ₍ᵢ₎ɒb- ‖ ₍ᵢ₎ɑːb- —When
  contrastively stressed, as opposed to subjective,
  usually 'ɒb•• ‖ 'ɑːb•• ~ly li ~ness nəs nɪs
  ~s z
objectivity ˌɒb dʒek 'tɪv ət i ˌ•dʒɪk-, -ɪt i
  ‖ ˌɑːb dʒek 'tɪv ət̬ i
objector əb 'dʒekt ə §ₒ₍ᵢ₎ɒb- ‖ -ᵊr ₍ᵢ₎ɑːb- ~s z
objet, objets 'ɒb ʒeɪ ‖ ˌɔːb 'ʒeɪ ◄ ˌɑːb- —Fr
  [ɔb ʒɛ]
  ˌobjet(s) 'd'art dɑː ‖ dɑːr —Fr [dɑːʁ];
  ˌobjet(s) 'trouvé(s) -trou'vé(s)
  'truːv eɪ ‖ truː 'veɪ —Fr [tʁu ve]
objur|gate 'ɒb dʒə |geɪt -dʒɜː- ‖ 'ɑːb dʒ‿ɜr-
  ~gated geɪt ɪd -əd ‖ geɪt̬ əd ~gates geɪts
  ~gating geɪt ɪŋ ‖ geɪt̬ ɪŋ
objurgation ˌɒb dʒə 'geɪʃ ᵊn -dʒɜː-
  ‖ ˌɑːb dʒᵊr- ~s z
objurgatory ɒb 'dʒɜːg ət‿ᵊr i əb-; ˌɒb dʒə geɪt
  ᵊr i, '•dʒɜː-, ˌ••'•••• ‖ əb 'dʒɜːg ə tɔːr i
  -toʊr i
oblast 'ɒb lɑːst -læst, -ləst ‖ 'ɑːb- 'ɔːb- ~s s
  —Russ ['ɔ bləsʲtʲ]
oblate n, adj 'ɒb leɪt əʊ'bleɪt, ɒ- ‖ 'ɑːb leɪt
  ɑː 'bleɪt, oʊ- ~ly li ~ness nəs nɪs ~s s
  ˌoblate 'sphere
oblation ə 'bleɪʃ ᵊn əʊ-, ɒ- ‖ oʊ- ~s z
obli|gate 'ɒb lɪ |geɪt -lə- ‖ 'ɑːb- ~gated
  geɪt ɪd -əd ‖ geɪt̬ əd ~gates geɪts ~gating
  geɪt ɪŋ ‖ geɪt̬ ɪŋ
obligation ˌɒb lɪ 'geɪʃ ᵊn -lə- ‖ ˌɑːb- ~s z
obligator|y ə 'blɪg ət‿ᵊr li ɒ- ‖ ə 'blɪg ə tɔːr li
  ɑː-, -toʊr i; 'ɑːb lɪg- ~ily əl ɪ ɪ li
oblig|e ə 'blaɪdʒ əʊ- ~ed d ~es ɪz əz ~ing ɪŋ
obligee ˌɒb lɪ 'dʒiː -lə- ‖ ˌɑːb- ~s z
obliging ə 'blaɪdʒ ɪŋ əʊ- ~ly li ~ness nəs nɪs
obligor ˌɒb lɪ 'gɔː -lə- ‖ ˌɑːb lə 'gɔːr '••• ~s z
oblique ə 'bliːk əʊ-, ɒ- ‖ oʊ-, -'blaɪk —The AmE
  pronunciation -'blaɪk is esp. military. ~ly li
  ~ness nəs nɪs ~s s
  o,blique 'angle
obliquit|y ə 'blɪk wət li əʊ-, ɒ-, -ɪt- ‖ -wət̬ li
  oʊ- ~ies ɪz
oblite|rate ə 'blɪt ə |reɪt ɒ- ‖ ə 'blɪt̬- oʊ-
  ~rated reɪt ɪd -əd ‖ reɪt̬ əd ~rates reɪts
  ~rating reɪt ɪŋ ‖ reɪt̬ ɪŋ
obliteration ə ˌblɪt ə 'reɪʃ ᵊn ɒ- ‖ ə ˌblɪt̬- oʊ-
  ~s z
oblivion ə 'blɪv i‿ᵊn ɒ-, əʊ- ‖ oʊ-, ɑː-
oblivious ə 'blɪv i‿əs ɒ-, əʊ- ‖ oʊ-, ɑː- ~ly li
  ~ness nəs nɪs
oblong 'ɒb lɒŋ ‖ 'ɑːb lɔːŋ -lɑːŋ ~s z
obloqu|y 'ɒb lək |wi ‖ 'ɑːb- ~uies wiz
obnoxious əb 'nɒk ʃəs ɒb- ‖ ɑːb 'nɑːk- əb-
  ~ly li ~ness nəs nɪs
oboe 'əʊb əʊ ‖ 'oʊb oʊ ~s z
  ˌoboe d'a'more də 'mɔːr i dɑː-, -eɪ
oboist 'əʊb əʊ ɪst §-əst ‖ 'oʊb oʊ- ~s s
obol 'ɒb ɒl -ᵊl ‖ 'ɑːb ᵊl 'oʊb- ~s s
ob|olus 'ɒb ᵊl əs ‖ 'ɑːb- ~oli ə laɪ

Obote əʊ ˈbəʊt eɪ -i ‖ oʊ ˈboʊt-
O'Boyle əʊ ˈbɔɪəl ‖ oʊ-
O'Brady (i) əʊ ˈbreɪd i ‖ oʊ-, (ii) əʊ
  ˈbrɔːd i ‖ oʊ- -ˈbrɑːd- —In AmE, (i).
O'Brien, O'Bryan əʊ ˈbraɪˌən ‖ oʊ-
obscene əb ˈsiːn ₍ᵢ₎ɒb- ‖ ₍ᵢ₎ɑːb- ~ly li
obscenit|y əb ˈsen ət |i ɒb-, -ˈsiːn-, -ɪt- ‖ -əţ |i
  ɑːb- ~ies iz
obscurantism ˌɒb skjuə ˈrænt ˌɪz əm, •ˈskjə-
  ‖ əb ˈskjʊr ən ˌtɪz əm ɑːb-; ˌɑːb skju ˈræn-
  (*)
obscurantist ˌɒb skjuə ˈrænt ɪst ◄ -skjə-, §-əst
  ‖ əb ˈskjʊr ənt əst ɑːb-; ˌɑːb skju ˈrænt- (*)
  ~s s
obscure adj, v əb ˈskjʊə ɒb-, -ˈskjɔː ‖ -ˈskjʊər
  ɑːb- ~d d ~ly li ~ness nəs nɪs obscurer
  əb ˈskjʊər ə ɒb-, -ˈskjɔːr- ‖ -ˈskjʊr ər ɑːb-
  obscures əb ˈskjʊəz ɒb-, -ˈskjɔːz ‖ -ˈskjʊərz
  ɑːb- obscurest əb ˈskjʊər ɪst ɒb-, -ˈskjɔːr-,
  -əst ‖ -ˈskjʊr əst ɑːb- obscuring
  əb ˈskjʊər ɪŋ ɒb-, -ˈskjɔːr- ‖ -ˈskjʊr ɪŋ ɑːb-
obscurit|y əb ˈskjʊər ət |i ɒb-, -ˈskjɔːr-, -ɪt-
  ‖ -ˈskjʊr əţ |i ɑːb- ~ies iz
obse|crate ˈɒb sɪ |kreɪt -sə- ‖ ˈɑːb- ~crated
  kreɪt ɪd -əd ‖ kreɪţ əd ~crates kreɪts
  ~crating kreɪt ɪŋ ‖ kreɪţ ɪŋ
obsecration ˌɒb sɪ ˈkreɪʃ ən -sə- ‖ ˌɑːb- ~s z
obsequies ˈɒb sək wiz -sɪk-; ɒb ˈsiːk- ‖ ˈɑːb-
obsequious əb ˈsiːk wi‿əs ɒb-, △-ju‿əs ‖ ɑːb-
  ~ly li ~ness nəs nɪs
observab|le əb ˈzɜːv əb |əl §₍ᵢ₎ɒb- ‖ -ˈzɝːv-
  ~les əlz ~ly li
observanc|e əb ˈzɜːv ənᵗs §₍ᵢ₎ɒb- ‖ -ˈzɝːv- ~es
  ɪz əz
observant əb ˈzɜːv ənt §₍ᵢ₎ɒb- ‖ -ˈzɝːv- ~ly li
observation ˌɒbz ə ˈveɪʃ ən ˌɒb sə- ‖ ˌɑːbz ər-
  ˌɑːb sər- ~al ᵊl ~ally ᵊl i ~s z
  ˌobserˈvation car; ˌobserˈvation post
observator|y əb ˈzɜːv ətr |i §₍ᵢ₎ɒb-, -ˈzɜːv ət
  ər |i ‖ -ˈzɝːv ə tɔːr |i -toʊr i ~ies iz
observ|e əb ˈzɜːv §₍ᵢ₎ɒb- ‖ -ˈzɝːv ~ed d ~es z
  ~ing/ly ɪŋ /li
observer, O~ əb ˈzɜːv ə §₍ᵢ₎ɒb- ‖ -ˈzɝːv ər ~s
  z
obsess əb ˈses ɒb- ‖ ɑːb- ~ed t ~es ɪz əz
  ~ing ɪŋ
obsession əb ˈseʃ ən ɒb- ‖ ɑːb- ~al ᵊl ~s z
obsessive əb ˈses ɪv ɒb- ‖ ɑːb- ~ly li ~ness
  nəs nɪs ~s z
obsidian əb ˈsɪd i‿ən ɒb-
obsolescence ˌɒb sə ˈles ənᵗs ‖ ˌɑːb-
obsolescent ˌɒb sə ˈles ənt ◄ ‖ ˌɑːb- ~ly li
obsolete ˈɒb sə liːt ˌ•••‖ ˌɑːb sə ˈliːt ◄ ˈ•••
  ~ly li ~ness nəs nɪs
obstacle ˈɒb stək əl -stɪk- ‖ ˈɑːb- ~s z
  ˈobstacle course; ˈobstacle race
obstetric əb ˈstetr ɪk ɒb- ‖ ɑːb- ~al ᵊl ~ally
  ᵊl‿i ~s s
obstetrician ˌɒb stə ˈtrɪʃ ən -stɪ-, -ste- ‖ ˌɑːb-
  ~s z
obstinacy ˈɒb stɪn əs i ˈ•stən- ‖ ˈɑːb-
obstinate ˈɒb stɪn ət -stən-, -ɪt ‖ ˈɑːb- ~ly li
  ~ness nəs nɪs

obstipation ˌɒb stɪ ˈpeɪʃ ən -stə- ‖ ˌɑːb-
obstreperous əb ˈstrep ər əs ɒb- ‖ ɑːb- ~ly li
  ~ness nəs nɪs
obstruct əb ˈstrʌkt §₍ᵢ₎ɒb- ‖ ₍ᵢ₎ɑːb- ~ed ɪd əd
  ~ing ɪŋ ~s s
obstruction əb ˈstrʌk ʃən §₍ᵢ₎ɒb- ‖ ₍ᵢ₎ɑːb- ~ism
  ˌɪz əm ~ist/s ˌɪst/s §ˌəst/s ‖ əst/s ~s z
obstructive əb ˈstrʌkt ɪv §₍ᵢ₎ɒb- ‖ ₍ᵢ₎ɑːb- ~ly li
  ~ness nəs nɪs
obstruent ˈɒb stru‿ənt ‖ ˈɑːb- ~s s
obtain əb ˈteɪn §₍ᵢ₎ɒb- ‖ ₍ᵢ₎ɑːb- ~ed d ~er/s ə/
  z ‖ ər/z ~ing ɪŋ ~s z
obtainable əb ˈteɪn əb əl §₍ᵢ₎ɒb- ‖ ₍ᵢ₎ɑːb-
obtrud|e əb ˈtruːd ɒb- ‖ ɑːb- ~ed ɪd əd ~es z
  ~ing ɪŋ
obtrusive əb ˈtruːs ɪv ɒb-, §-ˈtruːz- ‖ ɑːb- ~ly
  li ~ness nəs nɪs
obtrusion əb ˈtruːʒ ən ɒb- ‖ ɑːb- ~s z
obtu|rate ˈɒb tjuə |reɪt -tʃə- ‖ ˈɑːb tə |reɪt
  -tjə- ~rated reɪt ɪd -əd ‖ reɪţ əd ~rates
  reɪts ~rating reɪt ɪŋ ‖ reɪţ ɪŋ
obturation ˌɒb tjuə ˈreɪʃ ən ‖ ˌɑːb tə- -tjə- ~s
  z
obturator ˈɒb tjuə reɪt ə ‖ ˈɑːb tə reɪţ ər ˈ•tjə-
  ~s z
obtuse əb ˈtjuːs ɒb- ‖ əb ˈtuːs ɑːb-, -ˈtjuːs ~ly
  li ~ness nəs nɪs
obvers|e ˈɒb vɜːs ‖ ˈɑːb vɝːs ˌ•ˈ•, əbˈ• ~es ɪz
  əz ~ely li
ob|vert ɒb |ˈvɜːt ɑːb |ˈvɝːt ~verted ˈvɜːt ɪd
  -əd ‖ ˈvɝːţ əd ~verting ˈvɜːt ɪŋ ‖ ˈvɝːţ ɪŋ
  ~verts ˈvɜːts ‖ ˈvɝːts
obvi|ate ˈɒb vi |eɪt ‖ ˈɑːb- ~ated eɪt ɪd -əd
  ‖ eɪţ əd ~ates eɪts ~ating eɪt ɪŋ ‖ eɪţ ɪŋ
obviative ˈɒb vi‿ət ɪv ‖ ˈɑːb vi eɪţ ɪv
obvious ˈɒb vi‿əs ‖ ˈɑːb- ~ly li ~ness nəs nɪs
obvolute ˈɒb və luːt -ljuːt, ˌ•••‖ ˈɑːb-
obvolution ˌɒb və ˈluːʃ ən -ˈljuːʃ- ‖ ˌɑːb-
O'Byrne əʊ ˈbɜːn ‖ oʊ ˈbɝːn
O'Callaghan əʊ ˈkæl ə hən -gən, -hæn ‖ oʊ-
ocarina ˌɒk ə ˈriːn ə ‖ ˌɑːk- ~s z
O'Casey əʊ ˈkeɪs i ‖ oʊ-
Occam ˈɒk əm ‖ ˈɑːk- ~s s
  ˌOccam's ˈrazor
occasion ə ˈkeɪʒ ən §əʊ- ~ed d ~ing ˌɪŋ ~s z
occasional ə ˈkeɪʒ ənˌəl §əʊ- ~ly li
Occident, o- ˈɒks ɪd ənt -əd- ‖ ˈɑːks- -ə dent
occidental, O- ˌɒks ɪ ˈdent ᵊl ◄ -ə-
  ‖ ˌɑːks ə ˈdenţ ᵊl ◄ ~s z
occipital ɒk ˈsɪp ɪt ᵊl -ət- ‖ ɑːk ˈsɪp əţ ᵊl ~s z
occiput ˈɒks ɪ pʌt -ə-, -pət ‖ ˈɑːks- ~s s
occlud|e ə ˈkluːd ɒ- ‖ ɑː- ~ed ɪd əd ~es z
  ~ing ɪŋ
occlusal ə ˈkluːz ᵊl ɒ-, -ˈkluːs- ‖ ɑː-
occlusion ə ˈkluːʒ ən ɒ- ‖ ɑː- ~s z
occlusive ə ˈkluːs ɪv ɒ-, §-ˈkluːz- ‖ ɑː- ~s z
occult adj, n ˈɒk ʌlt ɒ ˈkʌlt, ə- ‖ ə ˈkʌlt ɑː-,
  oʊ-; ˈɑːk ʌlt
occult v ə ˈkʌlt ɒ- ‖ ɑː- ~ed ɪd əd ~ing ɪŋ ~s
  s
occultation ˌɒk ʌl ˈteɪʃ ən -ᵊl- ‖ ˌɑːk- ~s z
occultism ˈɒk ʌl ˌtɪz əm -ᵊl-; ɒ ˈkʌl-, ə-
  ‖ ə ˈkʌl- ɑː-; ˈɑːk ᵊl-

occultist 'ɒk ʌlt ɪst -ᵊlt-, §-əst; ɒ 'kʌlt-, ə-
‖ ə 'kʌlt əst ɑː-; 'ɑːk ᵊlt- ~s s

occupanc|y 'ɒk jup ən¹s |i '•jəp- ‖ 'ɑːk jəp-
~ies iz

occupant 'ɒk jup ᵊnt -jəp- ‖ 'ɑːk jəp- ~s s

occupation ˌɒk ju 'peɪʃ ᵊn -jə- ‖ ˌɑːk jə- ~s z

occupational ˌɒk ju 'peɪʃ ᵊn_ᵊl ◂, •jə-
‖ ˌɑːk jə- ~ly i
ˌoccuˌpational 'therapy

occu|py 'ɒk ju |paɪ -jə- ‖ 'ɑːk jə |paɪ ~pied
paɪd ~pier/s paɪ_ə/z ‖ paɪ_ᵊr/z ~pies paɪz
~pying paɪ ɪŋ

oc|cur ə |'kɜː §ɒ- ‖ ə |'kɜː ~curred
'kɜːd ‖ 'kɜːd ~curring 'kɜːr ɪŋ ‖ 'kɜː ɪŋ
~curs 'kɜːz ‖ 'kɜːz

occurrenc|e ə 'kʌr ᵊn¹s §ɒʊ-, §-'kɜːr- ‖ ə 'kɜː
ᵊn¹s ~es ɪz əz

ocean 'əʊʃ ᵊn ‖ 'oʊʃ ᵊn ~s z

oceanari|um ˌəʊʃ ə 'neər i_ləm ‖ ˌoʊʃ ə 'ner-
-'nær- ~a ə ~ums əmz

oceangoing 'əʊʃ ᵊn ˌɡəʊ ɪŋ ‖ 'oʊʃ ᵊn ˌɡoʊ ɪŋ

Oceani|a ˌəʊs i 'ɑːn i_|ə ˌəʊʃ-, -'eɪn-
‖ ˌoʊʃ i 'æn i_|ə -'ɑːn- ~an/s ən/z ◂

oceanic, O~ ˌəʊʃ i 'æn ɪk ◂ ˌəʊs- ‖ ˌoʊʃ-

Oceanid, o~ əʊ 'siː_ən ɪd -'ʃiː, §-əd ‖ oʊ- ~s z

oceanographer ˌəʊʃ ə 'nɒɡ rəf ə ˌəʊʃ i_ə'•-
‖ ˌoʊʃ ə 'nɑːɡ rəf ᵊr ~s z

oceanographic ˌəʊʃ ən_ə 'ɡræf ɪk ◂, • i_ən-
‖ ˌoʊʃ-

oceanography ˌəʊʃ ə 'nɒɡ rəf i ˌəʊʃ i_ə'•-
‖ ˌoʊʃ ə 'nɑːɡ rəf i

Oceanside 'əʊʃ ᵊn saɪd ‖ 'oʊʃ-

Oceanus əʊ 'siː_ən əs -'ʃiː_ ‖ oʊ-

ocell|us əʊ 'sel ləs ‖ oʊ- ~i aɪ iː

ocelot 'ɒs ə lɒt 'əʊs-, -ɪ- ‖ 'ɑːs ə lɑːt 'oʊs- ~s
s

och ɒx ‖ ɑːk

oche 'ɒk i ‖ 'ɑːk i ~s z

ocher 'əʊk ə ‖ 'oʊk ᵊr ~s z

ocherous 'əʊk ər_əs ‖ 'oʊk-

Ochil 'əʊk ᵊl 'əʊx- ‖ 'oʊk-

Ochiltree 'ɒk ᵊl triː 'ɒx-, 'əʊk-, 'əʊx-, -ɪl-, -tri
‖ 'ɑːk- 'oʊk-

ochlocracy ɒ 'klɒk rəs i ‖ ɑː 'klɑːk-

ochone ɒx 'əʊn ‖ —

ochre 'əʊk ə ‖ 'oʊk ᵊr ~s z

ochreous 'əʊk ri_əs -ər- ‖ 'oʊk ər_əs -ri_əs

ochry 'əʊk ər_i ‖ 'oʊk-

ocker, Ocker 'ɒk ə ‖ 'ɑːk ᵊr ~dom dəm ~s z

Ockham 'ɒk əm ‖ 'ɑːk-

Ockley 'ɒk li ‖ 'ɑːk-

o'clock ə 'klɒk §ɒʊ- ‖ ə 'klɑːk

O'Connell əʊ 'kɒn ᵊl ‖ oʊ 'kɑːn ᵊl

O'Conner, O'Connor əʊ 'kɒn ə ‖ oʊ 'kɑːn ᵊr

ocotillo ˌɒk ə 'tiːl jəʊ -'tiː-, -'tiː əʊ
‖ ˌoʊk ə 'tiːl joʊ -'tiː oʊ ~s z

OCR ˌəʊ siː 'ɑː ‖ ˌoʊ siː 'ɑːr

Ocracoke 'əʊk rə kəʊk ‖ 'oʊk rə koʊk

oct- comb. form before vowel |ɒkt ‖ |ɑːkt —
octad 'ɒkt æd ‖ 'ɑːkt-

octa- comb. form
with stress-neutral suffix |ɒkt ə ‖ |ɑːkt ə —
octachord 'ɒkt ə kɔːd ‖ 'ɑːkt ə kɔːrd

with stress-imposing suffix ɒk 'tæ+ ‖ ɑːk 'tæ+
— octameter ɒk 'tæm ɪt ə -ət-
‖ ɑːk 'tæm ət ᵊr

octad 'ɒkt æd ‖ 'ɑːkt- ~s z

octagon 'ɒkt əɡ ən ‖ 'ɑːkt ə ɡɑːn (*) ~s z

octagonal ɒk 'tæɡ ᵊn ᵊl ‖ ɑːk- ~ly i

octahedral ˌɒkt ə 'hiːdr ᵊl ◂ -'hedr- ‖ ˌɑːkt-

octahedr|on ˌɒkt ə 'hiːdr |ən -'hedr- ‖ ˌɑːkt-
~a ə ~ons ᵊnz

octal 'ɒkt ᵊl ‖ 'ɑːkt ᵊl

octane 'ɒkt eɪn ‖ 'ɑːkt-

Octans 'ɒkt ænz ‖ 'ɑːkt-

octant 'ɒkt ᵊnt ‖ 'ɑːkt- ~s s

Octateuch 'ɒkt ə tjuːk §-tʃuːk ‖ 'ɑːkt ə tuːk
-tjuːk

octave 'ɒkt ɪv §-əv, -eɪv ‖ 'ɑːkt- —Generally
-ɪv, §-əv as a musical or literary term, but -eɪv
in the sense 'period of eight days' ~s z

Octavia ɒk 'teɪv i_ə -'tɑːv- ‖ ɑːk-

Octavian ɒk 'teɪv i_ən -'tɑːv- ‖ ɑːk-

Octavius ɒk 'teɪv i_əs -'tɑːv- ‖ ɑːk-

octavo ɒk 'teɪv əʊ -'tɑːv- ‖ ɑːk 'teɪv oʊ -'tɑːv-
~s z

octennial ɒk 'ten i_əl ‖ ɑːk-

octet ɒk 'tet ‖ ɑːk- ~s s

octo- comb. form
with stress-neutral suffix |ɒkt əʊ ‖ |ɑːkt ə—
octosyllable 'ɒkt əʊ ˌsɪl əb ᵊl, •• '•••
‖ 'ɑːkt ə-

October ɒk 'təʊb ə ‖ ɑːk 'toʊb ᵊr ~s z

octodecimo ˌɒkt əʊ 'des ɪ məʊ -ə•
‖ ˌɑːkt oʊ 'des ə moʊ

octogenarian ˌɒkt əʊ dʒə 'neər i_ən ◂, ••dʒɪ-
‖ ˌɑːkt ə dʒə 'ner- ~s z

octopod 'ɒkt ə pɒd ‖ 'ɑːkt ə pɑːd ~s z

oct|opus 'ɒkt |əp əs -ə pʊs ‖ 'ɑːkt- ~opi ə paɪ
~opuses əp əs ɪz -pʊs-, -əz

octoroon ˌɒkt ə 'ruːn ‖ ˌɑːkt- ~s z

octosyllabic ˌɒkt əʊ sɪ 'læb ɪk ◂ -sə'•-
‖ ˌɑːkt ə-

octosyllable 'ɒkt əʊ ˌsɪl əb ᵊl, •• '•••
‖ 'ɑːkt oʊ-

octuple 'ɒkt jʊp ᵊl -jəp-, §-əp-; ɒk 'tjuːp ᵊl
‖ 'ɑːkt ʊp ᵊl -jʊp-; ɑːk 'tuːp-, -'tjuːp- ~s z

ocular 'ɒk jʊl ə -jəl- ‖ 'ɑːk jᵊl ᵊr ~ly li ~s z

oculist 'ɒk jʊl ɪst -jᵊl-, §-əst ‖ 'ɑːk jᵊl əst ~s s

oculogyric ˌɒk ju ləʊ 'dʒɪr ɪk ◂, •jə-
‖ ˌɑːk jə loʊ-

oculomotor ˌɒk ju ləʊ 'məʊt ə ◂, •jə-
‖ ˌɑːk jə loʊ 'moʊt̬ ᵊr ◂

OD ˌəʊ 'diː ‖ ˌoʊ- ~'d, ~ed, ~d ~ing, ~'ing ɪŋ
~s, ~'s z

odalisk, odalisque 'əʊd ə lɪsk 'ɒd-, →-ᵊl ɪsk
‖ 'oʊd ᵊl ɪsk ~s s

O'Daly əʊ 'deɪl i ‖ oʊ-

odd ɒd ‖ ɑːd odder 'ɒd ə ‖ 'ɑːd ᵊr oddest
'ɒd ɪst -əst ‖ 'ɑːd əst odds ɒdz ‖ ɑːdz
'odd bod; ˌodd man 'out; ˌodds and 'ends

oddball 'ɒd bɔːl →'ɒb- ‖ 'ɑːd- -bɑːl ~s z

Oddbins tdmk 'ɒd bɪnz →'ɒb- ‖ 'ɑːd-

Oddfellow 'ɒd ˌfel əʊ ‖ 'ɑːd ˌfel oʊ ~s z

Oddie 'ɒd i ‖ 'ɑːd i

oddish 'ɒd ɪʃ ‖ 'ɑːd ɪʃ

oddit|y 'ɒd ət |i -ɪt- ‖ 'ɑːd əṭ |i **~ies** iz
odd-job |man ˌɒd 'dʒɒb |mæn ‖ ˌɑːd 'dʒɑːb-
  ~men men
oddly 'ɒd li ‖ 'ɑːd li
oddment 'ɒd mənt →'ɒb- ‖ 'ɑːd-
oddness 'ɒd nəs -nɪs ‖ 'ɑːd nəs **~es** ɪz əz
odds-on ˌɒdz 'ɒn ◄ ‖ ˌɑːdz 'ɑːn ◄ -'ɔːn
ode əʊd ‖ oʊd **odes** əʊdz ‖ oʊdz
-ode əʊd ‖ oʊd — **pentode** 'pent əʊd ‖ -oʊd
O'Dea (i) əʊ 'deɪ ‖ oʊ-, (ii) əʊ 'diː ‖ oʊ-
Odell (i) 'əʊd əl ‖ 'oʊd əl, (ii) əʊ 'del ‖ oʊ-
Odense 'əʊd ənts ə ‖ 'oʊd- —Danish
  ['oːʔ ðᵊn sə]
Odeon 'əʊd i_ən ‖ 'oʊd- **~s** z
Oder 'əʊd ə ‖ 'oʊd ᵊr —Ger ['ʔoː dɐ]
Oder-Neisse Line ˌəʊd ə 'naɪs ə laɪn ‖ ˌoʊd ᵊr-
Odessa əʊ 'des ə ‖ oʊ- —Russ [ʌ 'dʲɛ sə]
Odets əʊ 'dets ‖ oʊ-
Odette əʊ 'det ‖ oʊ- —Fr [o dɛt]
Odeum, odeum əʊ 'diː_əm 'əʊd i_əm
  ‖ oʊ 'diː əm 'oʊd i_əm
Odgers 'ɒdʒ əz ‖ 'ɑːdʒ ᵊrz
Odham 'ɒd əm ‖ 'ɑːd-
Odiham 'əʊd i_əm -həm ‖ 'oʊd-
Odile əʊ 'diːᵊl ‖ oʊ-
Odin 'əʊd ɪn §-ᵊn ‖ 'oʊd-
odious 'əʊd i_əs ‖ 'oʊd- **~ly** li **~ness** nəs nɪs
odium 'əʊd i_əm ‖ 'oʊd-
Odo 'əʊd əʊ ‖ 'oʊd oʊ
Odoacer ˌɒd əʊ 'eɪs ə ˌəʊd- ‖ ˌoʊd oʊ 'eɪs ᵊr
O'Doherty əʊ 'dɒx ət i -'dəʊ-, -'dɒ hət-
  ‖ oʊ 'dɑː hᵊrṭ i -'dɔːrṭ i
odometer əʊ 'dɒm ɪt ə ɒ-, -ət-
  ‖ oʊ 'dɑːm əṭ ᵊr **~s** z
O'Donnell əʊ 'dɒn ᵊl ‖ oʊ 'dɑːn ᵊl
O'Donovan əʊ 'dʌn əv ən ən -'dɒn- ‖ oʊ 'dɑːn-
odontolog|ist/s ˌɒd ɒn 'tɒl ədʒ ɪst/s ˌəʊd-,
  §-əst/s ‖ ˌoʊd ɑːn 'tɑːl- ˌɑːd- **-y** i
odor 'əʊd ə ‖ 'oʊd ᵊr **~ed** d **~s** z
odorless 'əʊd ə ləs -lɪs; -ᵊl əs, -ɪs ‖ 'oʊd ᵊr-
odoriferous ˌəʊd ə 'rɪf ᵊr əs ◄ ‖ ˌoʊd- **~ly** li
  ~ness nəs nɪs
Odo-Ro-No tdmk ˌəʊd əʊ
  'rəʊn əʊ ‖ ˌoʊd ə 'roʊn oʊ
odorous 'əʊd ᵊr əs ‖ 'oʊd- **~ly** li **~ness** nəs
  nɪs
odour 'əʊd ə ‖ 'oʊd ᵊr **~ed** d **~s** z
odourless 'əʊd ə ləs -lɪs; -ᵊl əs, -ɪs ‖ 'oʊd ᵊr-
O'Dowd əʊ 'daʊd ‖ oʊ-
O'Dwyer əʊ 'dwaɪ_ə ‖ oʊ 'dwaɪ_ᵊr
Odysseus ə 'dɪs juːs ɒ-, əʊ-, -'dɪs i_əs
  ‖ oʊ 'dɪs i_əs -'dɪʃ-, ə 'dɪs juːs
Odyssey, o~ 'ɒd əs i -ɪs- ‖ 'ɑːd- **~s** z
oec... —see **ec...**
OECD ˌəʊ iː siː 'diː ‖ ˌoʊ-
oecumenic ˌiːk juː 'men ɪk ◄ ˌek- ‖ ˌek jə-
  ~al/ly ᵊl /_i
OED ˌəʊ iː 'diː ‖ ˌoʊ-
oedem|a ɪ 'diːm ə i:- **~as** əz **~ata** ət ə ‖ əṭ ə
oedematous ɪ 'diːm ət əs i:- ‖ -əṭ əs
Oedipal, o~ 'iːd ɪp ᵊl -əp- ‖ 'ed əp ᵊl 'iːd- (*)
Oedipus 'iːd ɪp əs -əp- ‖ 'ed əp əs 'iːd-
  'Oedipus ˌcomplex

oeil-de-boeuf ˌɜː i də 'bɜːf ˌ-jə- ‖ ˌʌd ə 'bʌf
  —Fr [œj də bœf]
oenology iː 'nɒl ədʒ i ‖ -'nɑːl-
Oenone iː 'nəʊn i ‖ -'noʊn i
oenophile 'iːn əʊ faɪᵊl ‖ 'iːn ə- **~s** z
o'er ɔː 'əʊ ə ‖ ɔːr oʊr
oersted 'ɜːst ɪd -ed, -əd ‖ 'ɜːst əd —Danish
  Ørsted ['œʁ sdeð] **~s** z
oesophageal iː ˌsɒf ə 'dʒiː_əl ◄ ɪ-, ə-,
  ˌiːs ɒf ə'•- ‖ ɪ ˌsɑːf- ˌiːs ə 'fædʒ i_əl ◄
oesoph|agus iː 'sɒf ləg əs ɪ-, ə- ‖ ɪ 'sɑːf- **~agi**
  ə gaɪ -dʒaɪ **~aguses** əg əs ɪz -əz
oestradiol ˌiːs trə 'daɪ ɒl ˌes-, -əl; iː 'stræd i ɒl
  ‖ ˌes trə 'daɪ ɔːl -ɑːl, -oʊl
oestrogen 'iːs trədʒ ᵊn 'es-, -trə dʒen ‖ 'es- **~s**
  z
oestrous, oestrus 'iːs trəs 'es- ‖ 'es- (*)
oeuvre 'ɜːv rə 'ɜːv ə ‖ 'ʊv rə 'ʊv ᵊr —Fr [œːvʁ]
of strong form ɒv ‖ ʌv, ɑːv (*), weak form əv
  —There is also an informal rapid-speech or
  nonstandard weak form, used before consonants
  only, ə. It is sometimes written o'.
O'Faolain, O'Faoláin əʊ 'feɪl ən -'fæl-, -ɔɪn
  ‖ oʊ-
off ɒf ɔːf ‖ ɔːf ɑːf
  'off ˌchance; ˌoff 'colour◄; ˌoff 'line◄
off- ˌɒf ˌɔːf ‖ ˌɔːf ˌɑːf — **off-air**
  ˌɒf 'eə ◄ ‖ ˌɔːf 'eᵊr ◄, ɑːf-, -'æᵊr
Offa 'ɒf ə ‖ 'ɔːf ə 'ɑːf-
offal 'ɒf ᵊl ‖ 'ɔːf ᵊl 'ɑːf-
Offaly 'ɒf ᵊl i ‖ 'ɔːf- 'ɑːf-
offbeat adj ˌɒf 'biːt ◄ ˌɔːf-, '•• ‖ ˌɔːf- ˌɑːf-
offbeat n 'ɒf biːt 'ɔːf- ‖ 'ɔːf- 'ɑːf- **~s** s
off-chance 'ɒf tʃɑːnts 'ɔːf-, §-tʃænts
  ‖ 'ɔːf tʃænts 'ɑːf-
off-color, off-colour ˌɒf 'kʌl ə ◄ ˌɔːf-
  ‖ ˌɔːf 'kʌl ᵊr ◄ ˌɑːf-
offcut 'ɒf kʌt 'ɔːf- ‖ 'ɔːf- 'ɑːf- **~s** s
Offenbach 'ɒf ᵊn bɑːk ‖ 'ɔːf- 'ɑːf- —Fr
  [ɔ fɛn bak], Ger ['ʔɔf ᵊn bax]
offenc|e ə 'fents §əʊ- **~eless** ləs lɪs **~es** ɪz əz
offend ə 'fend §əʊ- **~ed** ɪd əd **~er/s** ə/z ᵊr/z
  ~ing ɪŋ **~s** z
offens|e ə 'fents §əʊ- —but in AmE in the
  sporting meaning 'attack, attacking side' often
  'ɑːf ents, 'ɔːf- **~eless** ləs lɪs **~es** ɪz əz
offensive ə 'fents ɪv —but in the sense
  'relating to attack' also 'ɒf ents ɪv ‖ 'ɔːf-, 'ɑːf-
  ~ly li **~ness** nəs nɪs **~s** z
offer 'ɒf ə ‖ 'ɔːf ᵊr 'ɑːf- **~ed** d **offering/s** 'ɒf
  ᵊr_ɪŋ/z ‖ 'ɔːf ᵊr_ɪŋ/z 'ɑːf- **~s** z
offertor|y 'ɒf ət_ᵊr i ‖ 'ɔːf ᵊr tɔːr i 'ɑːf-,
  -toʊr i **~ies** iz
off-glide 'ɒf glaɪd 'ɔːf- ‖ 'ɔːf- 'ɑːf- **~s** z
offhand ˌɒf 'hænd ◄ ˌɔːf- ‖ ˌɔːf- ˌɑːf-
offhanded ˌɒf 'hænd ɪd ˌɔːf-, -əd ‖ ˌɔːf- ˌɑːf-
  ~ly li **~ness** nəs nɪs
offic|e 'ɒf ɪs §-əs ‖ 'ɑːf əs 'ɔːf- **~es** ɪz əz
  'office ˌblock; 'office ˌboy, 'office ˌgirl;
  'office ˌhours, ˌ•• '•
office-bearer 'ɒf ɪs ˌbeər ə §-əs-
  ‖ 'ɑːf əs ˌber ᵊr **~s** z

officeholder 'ɒf ɪs ˌhəʊld ə §-əs-
‖ 'ɑːf əs ˌhoʊld ᵊr 'ɔːf- ~s z
officer 'ɒf ɪs ə §-əs- ‖ 'ɑːf əs ᵊr 'ɔːf- ~ed d ~s
z
official ə 'fɪʃ ᵊl §əʊ- ~dom dəm ~s z
officialese ə ˌfɪʃ ə 'liːz §əʊ-, •'•• ‖ -'liːs
officialis|e, officializ|e ə 'fɪʃ ə laɪz §əʊ- ~ed d
~es ɪz əz ~ing ɪŋ
officially ə 'fɪʃ ᵊl i §əʊ-
officiant ə 'fɪʃ i‿ənt §əʊ- ~s s
offici|ate ə 'fɪʃ i |eɪt §əʊ- ~ated eɪt ɪd -əd
‖ eɪt̬ əd ~ates eɪts ~ating eɪt ɪŋ ‖ eɪt̬ ɪŋ
officiation ə ˌfɪʃ i 'eɪʃ ᵊn §əʊ-
officious ə 'fɪʃ əs §əʊ- ~ly li ~ness nəs nɪs
offing 'ɒf ɪŋ 'ɔːf- ‖ 'ɔːf ɪŋ 'ɑːf-
offish 'ɒf ɪʃ 'ɔːf- ‖ 'ɔːf ɪʃ 'ɑːf- ~ly li ~ness
nəs nɪs
off-key ˌɒf 'kiː ◄ ˌɔːf- ‖ ˌɔːf-, ˌɑːf-
off-licenc|e 'ɒf ˌlaɪs ᵊnts 'ɔːf-, •'•• ‖ 'ɔːf-
'ɑːf- ~es ɪz əz
off-load ˌɒf 'ləʊd ˌɔːf- ‖ ˌɔːf 'loʊd ˌɑːf- ~ed ɪd
əd ~ing ɪŋ ~s z
off-peak ˌɒf 'piːk ◄ ˌɔːf- ‖ ˌɔːf-, ˌɑːf-
off-piste ˌɒf 'piːst ◄ ˌɔːf- ‖ ˌɔːf-, ˌɑːf-
offprint 'ɒf prɪnt 'ɔːf- ‖ 'ɔːf- 'ɑːf- ~s s
off-putting 'ɒf ˌpʊt ɪŋ 'ɔːf-, •'•• ‖ 'ɔːf ˌpʊt̬ ɪŋ
'ɑːf-
off-ramp 'ɒf ræmp 'ɔːf- ‖ 'ɔːf- 'ɑːf- ~s s
off-road ˌɒf 'rəʊd ◄ ˌɔːf- ‖ ˌɔːf 'roʊd ◄ ˌɑːf-
offscouring 'ɒf skaʊᵊr ɪŋ 'ɔːf- ‖ 'ɔːf- 'ɑːf- ~s
z
off-screen ˌɒf 'skriːn ◄ ˌɔːf- ‖ ˌɔːf-, ˌɑːf-
offset n 'ɒf set 'ɔːf- ‖ 'ɔːf- 'ɑːf- ~s s
off|set v ˌɒf |'set ˌɔːf-, '•• ‖ ˌɔːf-, ˌɑːf- ~sets
'sets ~setting 'set ɪŋ ‖ 'set̬ ɪŋ
offshoot 'ɒf ʃuːt 'ɔːf- ‖ 'ɔːf- 'ɑːf- ~s s
offshore ˌɒf 'ʃɔː ◄ ˌɔːf- ‖ ˌɔːf 'ʃɔːr ◄ ˌɑːf-,
-'ʃoʊr
offsid|e ˌɒf 'saɪd ◄ ˌɔːf- ‖ ˌɔːf-, ˌɑːf- ~er/s ə/
z ‖ ᵊr/z ~es z
offspring 'ɒf sprɪŋ 'ɔːf- ‖ 'ɔːf- 'ɑːf-
offstage ˌɒf 'steɪdʒ ◄ ˌɔːf- ‖ ˌɔːf- ˌɑːf-
off-street ˌɒf 'striːt ◄ ˌɔːf- ‖ ˌɔːf- ˌɑːf-
ˌoff-street 'parking
off-the-cuff ˌɒf ðə 'kʌf ◄ ‖ ˌɔːf- ˌɑːf-
off-the-peg ˌɒf ðə 'peg ◄ ‖ ˌɔːf- ˌɑːf-
off-the-record ˌɒf ðə 'rek ɔːd ◄ ˌɔːf-, §-əd
‖ ˌɔːf ðə 'rek ᵊrd ◄ ˌɑːf-
off-the-shelf ˌɒf ðə 'ʃelf ◄ ‖ ˌɔːf- ˌɑːf-
off-the-shoulder ˌɒf ðə 'ʃəʊld ə ◄ ˌɔːf-,
→-'ʃɒʊld- ‖ ˌɔːf ðə 'ʃoʊld ᵊr ◄ ˌɑːf-
off-the-wall ˌɒf ðə 'wɔːl ◄ ˌɔːf- ‖ ˌɔːf- ˌɑːf-,
-'wɑːl
off-white ˌɒf 'waɪt ◄ ˌɔːf-, -'hwaɪt
‖ ˌɔːf 'hwaɪt ◄ ˌɑːf-
Ofgas 'ɒf gæs 'ɔːf- ‖ 'ɔːf- 'ɑːf-
O'Fiaich əʊ 'fiː ‖ oʊ- —Irish [oː 'fiə]
oflag 'ɒf læg -lɑːg ‖ 'ɑːf- 'ɔːf- —Ger
['ʔɔf laːk]
O'Flaherty əʊ 'flɑː hət i -'flæ-, -ət-; -'fleət i
‖ oʊ 'flæ‿ᵊrt̬ i -'flert̬ i
O'Flynn əʊ 'flɪn ‖ oʊ-
Ofsted 'ɒf sted ‖ 'ɑːf- 'ɔːf-

oft ɒft ɔːft ‖ ɔːft ɑːft
Oftel 'ɒf tel ‖ 'ɑːf- 'ɔːf-

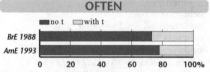

OFTEN

	no t	with t
BrE 1988		
AmE 1993		

0 20 40 60 80 100%

often 'ɒf ᵊn 'ɒft ən, 'ɔːf ᵊn, 'ɔːft ən ‖ 'ɔːf ᵊn
'ɑːf-; 'ɔːft ən, 'ɑːft- —Many speakers use both
the form without t and the form with it. Poll
panel preferences: BrE 1988, no t 73%, with t
27%; with ɒ 99%, with ɔː 1%; AmE 1993, no t
78%, with t 22%. ~er ə ‖ ᵊr ~est ɪst ˌəst
~times taɪmz
ofttimes 'ɒft taɪmz 'ɔːft- ‖ 'ɔːft- 'ɑːft-
Og ɒg ‖ ɔːg ɑːg
Ogaden ˌɒg ə 'den ‖ ˌɑːg- ˌoʊg-
ogam 'ɒg əm 'əʊg-; ɔːm ‖ 'ɑːg- 'ɔːg-, 'oʊg-
Ogbomosho
ˌɒg bə 'məʊʃ əʊ ‖ ˌɑːg bə 'moʊʃ oʊ
Ogden, Ogdon 'ɒgd ən ‖ 'ɔːgd- 'ɑːgd-
ogee 'əʊdʒ iː ‖ 'oʊdʒ iː oʊ 'dʒiː ~s z
Ogen 'əʊg en ‖ 'oʊg-
Ogg ɒg ‖ ɔːg ɑːg
ogham 'ɒg əm 'əʊg-; ɔːm ‖ 'ɑːg- 'ɔːg-, 'oʊg-
Ogilvie, Ogilvy 'əʊg ᵊlv i ‖ 'oʊg-
ogival əʊ 'dʒaɪv ᵊl ‖ oʊ-
ogive 'əʊdʒ aɪv ‖ 'oʊdʒ- ~s z

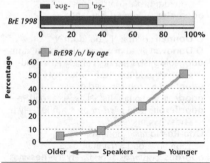

OGLE

	'əʊg-	'ɒg-
BrE 1998		

0 20 40 60 80 100%

BrE98 /ɒ/ by age

Percentage
60
50
40
30
20
10
0

Older ← Speakers → Younger

og|le 'əʊg |ᵊl 'ɒg- ‖ 'oʊg |ᵊl 'ɑːg- —BrE 1998
poll panel preference: 'əʊg- 76%, 'ɒg- 24%.
~led ᵊld ~les ᵊlz ~ling ᵊl‿ɪŋ
Oglethorpe 'əʊg ᵊl θɔːp ‖ 'oʊg ᵊl θɔːrp
Ogmore 'ɒg mɔː ‖ 'ɔːg mɔːr 'ɑːg-, -moʊr
Ogoni əʊ 'gəʊn i ‖ oʊ 'goʊn i ~land lænd
O'Grady əʊ 'greɪd i ‖ oʊ-
ogre 'əʊg ə ‖ 'oʊg ᵊr ~s z
ogreish 'əʊg ᵊr ɪʃ ‖ 'oʊg-
ogress 'əʊg rɪs -rəs, -res ‖ 'oʊg ᵊr‿əs ~es ɪz əz
Ogwen 'ɒg wen ‖ 'ɔːg- 'ɑːg-
Ogwr 'ɒg ʊə ‖ 'ɔːg ʊr 'ɑːg- —Welsh ['ɔ gur]
oh əʊ ‖ oʊ (= O) oh's, ohs əʊz ‖ oʊz
OH —see Ohio
O'Hagan əʊ 'heɪg ən ‖ oʊ-
O'Halloran əʊ 'hæl ər ən ‖ oʊ-
O'Hanlon əʊ 'hæn lən ‖ oʊ-
O'Hara əʊ 'hɑːr ə ‖ oʊ 'hær ə -'her-

O'Hare əʊ 'heə ‖ oʊ 'heᵊr -'hæᵊr
O'Higgins əʊ 'hɪg ɪnz §-ənz ‖ oʊ-
Ohio əʊ 'haɪ əʊ ‖ oʊ 'haɪ oʊ ~an/s ən/z
ohmic 'əʊm ɪk ‖ 'oʊm-
ohm, Ohm əʊm ‖ oʊm —Ger [ʔoːm] ohms
əʊmz ‖ oʊmz
OHMS ˌəʊ eɪtʃ em 'es §,• heɪtʃ- ‖ ˌoʊ-
oho əʊ 'həʊ ‖ oʊ 'hoʊ
OHP ˌəʊ eɪtʃ 'piː ‖ ˌoʊ- ~s z
oi ɔɪ
oick ɔɪk oicks ɔɪks
-oid ɔɪd — planetoid 'plæn ə tɔɪd -ɪ-
oidi|um əʊ 'ɪd i‿ləm ‖ oʊ- ~a ə
oik ɔɪk oiks ɔɪks
oil ɔɪᵊl oiled ɔɪᵊld oiling 'ɔɪᵊl ɪŋ oils ɔɪᵊlz
'oil drum; 'oil paint; 'oil ˌpainting; 'oil
slick; 'oil ˌtanker; 'oil well
oil-bearing 'ɔɪᵊl ˌbeər ɪŋ ‖ -ˌber- -ˌbær-
oilbird 'ɔɪᵊl bɜːd ‖ -bɜ·ːd ~s z
oilcake 'ɔɪᵊl keɪk
oilcan 'ɔɪᵊl kæn ~s z
oilcloth 'ɔɪᵊl klɒθ -klɔːθ ‖ -klɔːθ -klɑːθ
oiler 'ɔɪᵊl ə ‖ -ᵊr ~s z
oilfield 'ɔɪᵊl fiːᵊld ~s z
oil-fired 'ɔɪᵊl ˌfaɪ‿əd ˌ•'•• ‖ -ˌfaɪ‿ᵊrd
oili... —see oily
oil|man 'ɔɪᵊl |mæn -mən ~men men mən
oilrig 'ɔɪᵊl rɪg ~s z
oilseed 'ɔɪᵊl siːd
oilskin 'ɔɪᵊl skɪn ~s z
oil|y 'ɔɪl li ~ier i‿ə ‖ i‿ᵊr ~iest i‿ɪst i‿əst
~iness i nəs i nɪs
oink ɔɪŋk oinks ɔɪŋks
ointment 'ɔɪnt mənt ~s s
Oireachtas 'er əkθ əs 'eər-, -əkt- —Irish
['ɛ rəx təs]
Oise waːz —Fr [waːz]
Oistrakh 'ɔɪs trɑːk -trɑːx —Russ ['ɔj strəx]
Ojibwa, Ojibway əʊ 'dʒɪb weɪ -wə ‖ oʊ- ~s z
OK, O.K. ₍ᵢ₎əʊ 'keɪ ‖ ₍ᵢ₎oʊ- ~'d d ~'ing ɪŋ ~'s z
okapi əʊ 'kɑːp i ‖ oʊ- ~s z
Okavango
ˌɒk ə 'væŋ gəʊ ◄ ‖ ˌoʊk ə 'væŋ goʊ ◄ -'vɑːŋ-
ˌOkaˌvango 'Swamp
okay ₍ᵢ₎əʊ 'keɪ ‖ ₍ᵢ₎oʊ- ~ed d ~ing ɪŋ ~s z
Okayama ˌəʊk ə 'jɑːm ə ˌɒk- ‖ ˌoʊk- —Jp
[o 'ka ja ma]
Okazaki ˌəʊk ə 'zɑːk i ‖ ˌoʊk- —Jp [o ˌka
dza ki]
Okeechobee ˌəʊk ɪ 'tʃəʊb i ‖ ˌoʊk ə 'tʃoʊb i
O'Keefe, O'Keeffe əʊ 'kiːf ‖ oʊ-
Okefenokee ˌəʊk ɪf ɪ 'nəʊk i ◄ ,•əf-, -ə'•-
‖ ˌoʊk əf ə 'noʊk i
ˌOkefeˌnokee 'Swamp
Okehampton ˌəʊk 'hæmpt ən ‖ 'oʊk i ,••
okey-doke ˌəʊk i 'dəʊk ‖ ˌoʊk i 'doʊk
okey-dokey ˌəʊk i 'dəʊk i ‖ ˌoʊk i 'doʊk i
Okhotsk əʊ 'kɒtsk ɒ-, '•• oʊ 'kɑːtsk —Russ
[ʌ 'xɔtsk]
Okie 'əʊk i ‖ 'oʊk i ~s z
Okina|wa ˌɒk i 'nɑː |wə ˌəʊk-, -ə- ‖ ˌoʊk ə-
-'naʊ ə —Jp [o ˌki na wa] ~wan/s wən/z ◄

Oklahom|a ˌəʊk lə 'həʊm |ə ◄
‖ ˌoʊk lə 'hoʊm |ə ◄ ~an/s ən/z
ˌOklaˌhoma 'City
okra 'əʊk rə 'ɒk- ‖ 'oʊk rə
Okri 'ɒk ri ‖ 'ɑːk-
-ol ɒl ‖ ɔːl ɑːl, oʊl — glycerol 'glɪs ə rɒl ‖ -rɔːl
-rɑːl, -roʊl
ol' elided form of old əʊl →ɒʊl ‖ oʊl
Olaf 'əʊl əf -æf, -ɑːf ‖ 'oʊl- —Norw ['ˈuː laf]
Olav 'əʊl æv -əv ‖ 'oʊl-
Olave 'ɒl əv -ɪv, -eɪv ‖ 'ɑːl-
Olbers 'ɒlb əz ‖ 'oʊlb ᵊrz —Ger ['ʔɔl bɐs]
Olbia 'ɒlb i‿ə ‖ 'ɑːlb- —It ['ɔl bja]
old əʊld →ɒʊld ‖ oʊld older 'əʊld ə →'ɒʊld-
‖ 'oʊld ᵊr oldest 'əʊld ɪst →'ɒʊld-, -əst
‖ 'oʊld əst
ˌold 'age◄, ˌold age 'pension, ˌold age
'pensioner; ˌOld 'Bailey; 'old boy 'former
pupil' , ˌold 'boy 'old chap' ; ˌold-'boy
ˌnetwork, '•• ,••; ˌOld 'Catholic; ˌOld
Church Sla'vonic; ˌOld 'English ◄; ˌold
'flame; ˌold girl ' former pupil'; ˌold 'guard,
'• •; ˌold 'hand; ˌold 'hat; ˌold 'lady; ˌold
'lag; ˌold 'maid; ˌold 'man; ˌold 'master;
ˌOld 'Nick; ˌold 'people's home; 'old
school ' conservative attitudes', ˌold 'school ◄
'former place of learning' , ˌold school 'tie;
ˌOld 'Testament ◄; ˌold 'wives' tale; ˌold
'woman; ˌOld 'World ◄
Oldbury 'əʊld bər‿i →'ɒʊld- ‖ 'oʊld ˌber i
Oldcastle 'əʊld ˌkɑːs ᵊl →'ɒʊld-, §-ˌkæs-
‖ 'oʊld ˌkæs ᵊl
olden 'əʊld ən →'ɒʊld- ‖ 'oʊld ən
Oldenburg 'əʊld ən bɜːg →'ɒʊld-, →-əm-
‖ 'oʊld ən bɜ·ːg —Ger ['ʔɔl dᵊn bʊʁk, -bʊʁç]
olde worlde ˌəʊld i 'wɜːld i ◄ →ˌɒʊld-
‖ ˌoʊld i 'wɜ·ːld i
old-fashioned ˌəʊld 'fæʃ ᵊnd ◄ →ˌɒʊld-
‖ ˌoʊld-
Oldfield 'əʊld fiːᵊld →'ɒʊld- ‖ 'oʊld-
old-fogeyish, old-fogyish ˌəʊld 'fəʊg i ɪʃ
→ˌɒʊld- ‖ ˌoʊld 'foʊg-
Oldham 'əʊld əm →'ɒʊld- ‖ 'oʊld-
oldie 'əʊld i →'ɒʊld- ‖ 'oʊld i ~s z
oldish 'əʊld ɪʃ →'ɒʊld- ‖ 'oʊld-
old-line ˌəʊld 'laɪn ◄ →ˌɒʊld- ‖ ˌoʊld-
old-maidish ˌəʊld 'meɪd ɪʃ ◄ →ˌɒʊld- ‖ ˌoʊld-
Oldrey 'əʊldr i ‖ 'ɒʊldr- ‖ 'oʊldr i
Oldsmobile tdmk 'əʊldz məʊ ˌbiːᵊl →'ɒʊldz-
‖ 'oʊldz mə ˌbiːᵊl ~s z
old-stager ˌəʊld 'steɪdʒ ə →ˌɒʊld- ‖ ˌoʊld-
'steɪdʒ ᵊr ~s z
oldster 'əʊld stə →'ɒʊld- ‖ 'oʊld stᵊr ~s z
old-tim|e ˌəʊld 'taɪm ◄ →ˌɒʊld-, '•• ‖ ˌoʊld-
~er/s ə/z ‖ ᵊr/z
ˌold-time 'dancing
Olduvai 'ɒld ə vaɪ 'əʊld-, -u-, -ju- ‖ 'ɔːld-
'ɑːld-, 'oʊld-
ˌOlduvai 'Gorge
old-womanish ˌəʊld 'wʊm ən ɪʃ ◄ →ˌɒʊld-
‖ ˌoʊld-
old-world ˌəʊld 'wɜːld ◄ →ˌɒʊld- ‖ ˌoʊld
'wɜ·ːld ◄

O

olé əʊ 'leɪ ‖ oʊ-
-ole əʊl→ʊʊl ‖ oʊl— **benzole** 'benz əʊl
→-ʊʊl ‖ -oʊl —*but note also words such as*
hyperbole, systole *with* əl i
oleaginous ˌəʊl i 'ædʒ ɪn əs -ən- ‖ ˌoʊl- ~**ly** li
~**ness** nəs nɪs
oleander ˌəʊl i 'ænd ə ‖ 'oʊl i ænd ər, •ˌ•'•ˌ•
~**s** z
olearia ˌɒl i 'eər i‿ə ˌəʊl- ‖ ˌoʊl i 'er- -'ær- ~**s**
z
O'Leary əʊ 'lɪər i ‖ oʊ 'lɪr i
oleaster ˌəʊl i 'æst ə ‖ 'oʊl i æst ər, •ˌ•'•ˌ• ~**s** z
oleate 'əʊl i eɪt ‖ 'oʊl- ~**s** s
olecranon əʊ 'lek rə nɒn ˌəʊl ɪ 'kreɪn ən, -ə-
‖ oʊ 'lek rə nɑːn
olefin 'əʊl ɪ fɪn -ə-, -fiːn, -fən ‖ 'oʊl- ~**s** z
olefine 'əʊl ɪ fiːn -ə-, -fɪn ‖ 'oʊl- ~**s** z
Oleg 'əʊl eg 'ɒl- ‖ 'oʊl- —*Russ* [ʌ 'lʲek]
oleic əʊ 'liː ɪk -'leɪ- ‖ oʊ-
oleo 'əʊl i əʊ ‖ 'oʊl i oʊ
oleo- *comb. form* ˈəʊl i əʊ ‖ ˈoʊl i oʊ—
oleoresin ˌəʊl i əʊ 'rez ɪn §-ən
‖ ˌoʊl i oʊ 'rezən
oleograph 'əʊl i‿ə grɑːf -græf ‖ 'oʊl i‿ə græf
~**s** s
olfaction ɒl 'fæk ʃən ‖ ɑːl- oʊl-
olfactory ɒl 'fækt ər‿i ‖ ɑːl- oʊl-
Olga 'ɒlg ə ‖ 'oʊlg ə —*Russ* ['ɔlʲgə]
Olifant 'ɒl ɪf ənt -əf- ‖ 'ɑːl-
oligarch 'ɒl ɪ gɑːk -ə- ‖ 'ɑːl ə gɑːrk 'oʊl- ~**s** s
oligarchic ˌɒl ɪ 'gɑːk ɪk ◂-ə-
‖ ˌɑːl ə 'gɑːrk ɪk ◂ˌoʊl-
oligarch|y 'ɒl ɪ gɑːk |i ◂•'•- ‖ 'ɑːl ə gɑːrk |i
'oʊl- ~**ies** iz
oligo- *comb. form*
with stress-neutral suffix ˌɒl ɪ gəʊ-ə-
‖ ˌɑːl ɪ goʊ ˌoʊl- — oligosaccharide
ˌɒl ɪ gəʊ 'sæk ə raɪd ˌ•ˌ•- ‖ ˌɑːl ɪ goʊ- ˌoʊl-,
-ər əd
with stress-imposing suffix ˌɒl ɪ 'gɒ+ -ə-
‖ ˌɑːl ə 'gɑː+ ˌoʊl- — oligopsony ˌɒl ɪ 'gɒps
ən i, •ˌ•- ‖ ˌɑːl ə 'gɑːps- ˌoʊl-
Oligocene 'ɒl ɪ gəʊ siːn ɒ 'lɪg əʊ- ‖ 'ɑːl ɪ goʊ-
'oʊl-; ə 'lɪg ə-
oligomer 'ɒl ɪ 'gəʊm ə ɒ 'lɪg əm ə, ə-;
'ɒl ɪg əm ə, '•əg- ‖ ə 'lɪg əm ər ~**s** z
oligopol|y ˌɒl ɪ 'gɒp əl |i, •ˌ•- ‖ ˌɑːl ə 'gɑːp-
~**ies** iz
olio 'əʊl i əʊ ‖ 'oʊl i oʊ ~**s** z
Oliphant 'ɒl ɪf ənt -əf- ‖ 'ɑːl-
olivaceous ˌɒl ɪ 'veɪʃ əs ◂-ə- ‖ ˌɑːl-
olivary 'ɒl ɪv ər i '•əv- ‖ 'ɑːl ə ver i
olive, Olive 'ɒl ɪv §-əv ‖ 'ɑːl ɪv -əv ~**s**, ~**'s** z
'olive branch; ˌolive 'drab; ˌolive 'oil,
'•ˌ• ‖ '•ˌ•
olivenite ɒ 'lɪv ə naɪt əʊ-, 'ɒl ɪv- ‖ oʊ-
Oliver 'ɒl ɪv ə -əv- ‖ 'ɑːl əv ər
Olivet 'ɒl ɪ vet -ə-; -ɪv ət, -ɪt ‖ 'ɑːl-
Olivetti *tdmk* ˌɒl ɪ 'vet i -ə- ‖ ˌɑːl ə 'veţ i —*It*
[o li 'vet ti]
Olivia ə 'lɪv i‿ə ɒ-, əʊ- ‖ oʊ-
Olivier ə 'lɪv i eɪ ɒ-, -ə ‖ oʊ-
olivine 'ɒl ɪ viːn -ə-, ˌ•'•

olla podrida ˌɒl ə pə 'driːd ə, •ˌ jə-, -pɒ '•-
‖ ˌɑːl- ˌɔː- —*Sp* [ˌo ʎa po 'ðri ða, ˌo ja-]
Ollerenshaw (i) 'ɒl ər ən ʃɔː ‖ 'ɑːl- -ʃɑː, (ii)
ˌɒl ə 'ren- ‖ ˌɑːl-
Ollerton 'ɒl ət ən ‖ 'ɑːl ərt ən
Ollie 'ɒl i ‖ 'ɑːl i
olm əʊlm→ʊʊlm, ɒlm ‖ oʊlm
Olney 'əʊln i→'ʊʊln- ‖ 'oʊln i
olog|y 'ɒl ədʒ |i ‖ 'ɑːl- ~**ies** iz —*see also* -logy
Olomouc 'ɒl ə maʊts -ɒ- ‖ 'oʊl oʊ- —*Czech*
['o lo moʊts]
oloroso ˌɒl ə 'rəʊs əʊ ˌoʊl-, -'rəʊz-
‖ ˌoʊl ə 'roʊs oʊ ~**s** z —*Sp* [o lo 'ro so]
Olsen, Olson 'əʊls ən→'ʊʊls- ‖ 'oʊls-
Olwen 'ɒl wen -wɪn, §-wən ‖ 'ɑːl- —*Welsh*
['ɔl wen]
Olwyn 'ɒl wɪn §-wən ‖ 'ɑːl-
Olympia ə 'lɪmp i‿ə əʊ- ‖ oʊ-
Olympiad ə 'lɪmp i æd əʊ- ‖ oʊ- ~**s** z
Olympian ə 'lɪmp i‿ən əʊ- ‖ oʊ- ~**s** z
Olympic ə 'lɪmp ɪk əʊ- ‖ oʊ- ~**s** s
Oˌlympic 'Games
Olympus ə 'lɪmp əs əʊ- ‖ oʊ-
Olynthus əʊ 'lɪntᵗθ əs ‖ oʊ- ə-
om, Om əʊm ɒm ‖ oʊm ɔːm, ɑːm —*Skt* [oːm]
-oma 'əʊm ə ‖ 'oʊm ə— melanoma
ˌmel ə 'nəʊm ə ‖ -'noʊm ə
Omagh 'əʊm ə -ɑː ‖ 'oʊm-
Omaha 'əʊm ə hɑː ‖ 'oʊm- -hɔː
O'Mahoney əʊ 'mɑː ən i ‖ oʊ- ˌoʊ mə 'hoʊn i
O'Malley (i) əʊ 'mæl i ‖ oʊ-, (ii) -'meɪl i
Oman *name of country* əʊ 'mɑːn ‖ oʊ- —*Arabic*
[ʕu 'mɑːn]
Oman *family name* 'əʊm ən ‖ 'oʊm-
Omani əʊ 'mɑːn i ‖ oʊ- ~**s** z
Omar 'əʊm ɑː ‖ 'oʊm ɑːr -ər
ˌOmar Khay'yam, ˌOmar Khay'yám
kaɪ 'æm -'ɑːm ‖ kaɪ 'jɑːm -'jæm
O'Mara əʊ 'mɑːr ə ‖ oʊ-
omas|um əʊ 'meɪs |əm ‖ oʊ- ~**a** ə
ombuds|man 'ɒm bʊdz |mən -bʌdz-, -mæn
‖ 'ɑːm- ~**men** mən men
Omdurman ˌɒm dɜː 'mɑːn -də-, -'mæn;
'ɒm də mən ‖ ˌɑːm dər 'mɑːn -dʊr- —*Arabic*
[um dur 'mɑːn]
-ome əʊm ‖ oʊm— phyllome 'fɪl əʊm ‖ -oʊm
O'Meara (i) əʊ 'mɑːr ə ‖ oʊ-, (ii)
-'meər ə ‖ -'mer ə -'mær-, (iii)
-'mɪər ə ‖ -'mɪr ə
omega, Omega 'əʊm ɪg ə -əg- ‖ oʊ 'meɪg ə
-'meg-, -'miːg- (*) ~**s** z
omelet, omelette 'ɒm lət -lɪt, -let ‖ 'ɑːm-
'ɑːm əl ət ~**s** s
omen 'əʊm en -ən ‖ 'oʊm ən ~**s** z
oment|um əʊ 'ment əm ‖ oʊ 'menţ əm ~**a** ə
omer, Omer 'əʊm ə ‖ 'oʊm ər ~**s** z
omerta, omertà əʊ 'mɜːt ə -'meət-;
ˌoʊm ə 'tɑː ‖ oʊ 'mert ə ˌoʊm ər 'tɑː —*It*
[o mer 'ta]
omicron əʊ 'maɪk rɒn -rən; 'ɒm ɪk-
‖ 'ɑːm ə krɑːn 'oʊm- (*) ~**s** z
ominous 'ɒm ɪn əs 'əʊm-, -ən- ‖ 'ɑːm- —*BrE*

OMINOUS

	■ 'ɒm-	▢ 'əʊm-
BrE 1998		

0 20 40 60 80 100%

1998 poll panel preference: 'ɒm- *98%,* 'əʊm-
2%. **~ly** li **~ness** nəs nɪs
omissible əʊ 'mɪs əb ᵊl -ɪb- ‖ oʊ-
omission əʊ 'mɪʃ ᵊn ‖ oʊ- ə- **~s** z
o|mit əʊ |'mɪt ‖ oʊ- ə- **~mits** 'mɪts **~mitted**
'mɪt ɪd -əd ‖ 'mɪt̬ əd **~mitting**
'mɪt ɪŋ ‖ 'mɪt̬ ɪŋ
ommatidi|um ˌɒm ə 'tɪd i‿ləm ‖ ˌɑːm- **~a** ə
~al əl
omni- *comb. form*
  with stress-neutral suffix 'ɒm nɪ -nə ‖ ˈɑːm- —
  omnicompetent ˌɒm nɪ 'kɒmp ɪt ənt ◄
  §, •nə-, -'•ət- ‖ ˌɑːm nɪ 'kɑːmp ət ənt ◄ , •nə-
  with stress-imposing suffix ɒm 'nɪ+ ‖ ɑːm- —
  omnivorous ɒm 'nɪv ər_əs ‖ ɑːm-
omnibus 'ɒm nɪb əs -nəb-; -nɪ bʌs, -nə-
  ‖ 'ɑːm- **~es** ɪz əz
omnifarious ˌɒm nɪ 'feər i‿əs ◄ , •nə-
  ‖ ˌɑːm nə 'fer- -'fær-
omnipotence ɒm 'nɪp ət ᵊnts
  ‖ ɑːm 'nɪp ət ᵊnts
omnipotent ɒm 'nɪp ət ənt ‖ ɑːm 'nɪp ət ᵊnt
  ~ly li
omnipresence ˌɒm nɪ 'prez ᵊnts -nə- ‖ ˌɑːm-
omnipresent ˌɒm nɪ 'prez ᵊnt ◄ -nə- ‖ ˌɑːm-
omniscience ɒm 'nɪs i‿ənts -'nɪʃ-, -'nɪʃ ᵊnts
  ‖ ɑːm 'nɪʃ ᵊnts
omniscient ɒm 'nɪs i‿ənt -'nɪʃ-, -'nɪʃ ᵊnt
  ‖ ɑːm 'nɪʃ ᵊnt **~ly** li
omnium, O~ 'ɒm ni‿əm ‖ 'ɑːm-
omnium-gatherum ˌɒm ni‿əm 'gæð
  ər əm ‖ ˌɑːm-
omnivore 'ɒm nɪ vɔː -nə- ‖ 'ɑːm nɪ vɔːr -voʊr
  ~s z
omnivorous ɒm 'nɪv ər_əs ‖ ɑːm- **~ly** li **~ness**
  nəs nɪs
Omo *tdmk* 'əʊm əʊ ‖ 'oʊm oʊ
Omotic əʊ 'mɒt ɪk ‖ oʊ 'mɑːt̬ ɪk
omph|alos 'ɒmᵖf ə lɒs ‖ 'ɑːmᵖf əl əs **~ali**
  ə laɪ
Omsk ɒmᵖsk ‖ ɔːmᵖsk ɑːmᵖsk —*Russ* [ɒmsk]
on ɒn ‖ ɑːn ɔːn
  'on side *'leg side'*
on- ¦ɒn ‖ ¦ɑːn ¦ɔːn — **on-going**
  ˌɒn 'gəʊ ɪŋ ◄ ‖ ˌɑːn ˌgoʊ ɪŋ 'ɔːn-
-on ɒn, ən ‖ ɑːn, ən —*When this is a true suffix*
  (e'lectron), *it is usually strong. When it is a*
  mere ending ('common) *it is usually weak, but*
  there are a number of exceptions ('coupon) *and*
  words where speakers disagree ('lexicon). *In*
  many cases BrE prefers a weak vowel, AmE a
  strong vowel ('Amazon).
on-again off-again ˌɒn ə ˌgen 'ɒf ə ˌgen ◄
  -ˌgeɪn'•, ˌgeɪn, -'ɒːf•, • ‖ ˌɑːn•, •'ɔːf•, •
  -'ɑːf•, •; ˌɔːn•, •'ɔːf-
onager 'ɒn ədʒ ə -əg- ‖ 'ɑːn ɪdʒ ᵊr **~s** z
  onagri 'ɒn ə graɪ ‖ 'ɑːn-
on-air ˌɒn 'eə ◄ ‖ ˌɑːn 'eᵊr ◄ ˌɔːn-, -'æᵊr

Onan 'əʊn æn -ən ‖ 'oʊn-
onanism 'əʊn ə ˌnɪz əm -æ- ‖ 'oʊn-
Onassis əʊ 'næs ɪs §-əs ‖ oʊ- -'nɑːs-
on-board 'ɒn bɔːd ‖ 'ɑːn bɔːrd 'ɔːn-, -boʊrd
ONC ˌəʊ en 'siː ‖ ˌoʊ- **~s, ~'s** z
once wʌnts §wɒnts
once-over 'wʌnts ˌəʊv ə §'wɒnts-, ˌ•'•‿•
  ‖ -ˌoʊv ᵊr
oncer 'wʌnts ə §'wɒnts- ‖ -ᵊr **~s** z
onchocerciasis ˌɒŋk əʊ sɜː 'kaɪ_əs ɪs , • •sə-,
  -'saɪ-, §-əs ‖ ˌɑːŋk oʊ sɜː-
onco- *comb. form*
  with stress-neutral suffix ˌɒŋk əʊ ‖ ˈɑːŋk oʊ -ə
  — **oncocyte** 'ɒŋk əʊ saɪt ‖ 'ɑːŋk oʊ- -ə-
  with stress-imposing suffix ɒŋ 'kɒ+ ‖ ɑːn 'kɑː+
  →ɑːŋ- — **oncology** ɒŋ 'kɒl ədʒ i ‖ ɑːn 'kɑːl-
  →ɑːŋ-
oncogene 'ɒŋk əʊ dʒiːn ‖ 'ɑːŋk oʊ- -ə- **~s** z
oncoming 'ɒn ˌkʌm ɪŋ →'ɒŋ- ‖ 'ɑːn- 'ɔːn-
oncost 'ɒn kɒst →'ɒŋ-, -kɔːst ‖ 'ɑːn kɔːst
  'ɔːn-, -'kɑːst **~s** s
OND ˌəʊ en 'diː ‖ ˌoʊ- **~s, ~'s** z
Ondaatje ɒn 'dɑːtʃ ə ‖ ɑːn-

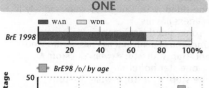

ONE

	■ wʌn	▢ wɒn
BrE 1998		

0 20 40 60 80 100%

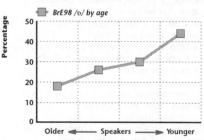

BrE98 /ɒ/ by age

Percentage (y-axis: 0, 10, 20, 30, 40, 50)

Older ◄—— Speakers ——► Younger

one wʌn §wɒn —*BrE 1998 poll panel*
  preference: wʌn *70%,* wɒn *30%. —In standard*
  speech this word has no weak form. See,
  however, '**un. ones, one's** wʌnz §wɒnz
  ˌone a'nother
one- ¦wʌn §¦wɒn — **one-tailed** ˌwʌn 'teɪᵊld ◄
  §ˌwɒn-
one-acter ˌwʌn 'ækt ə §ˌwɒn- ‖ -ᵊr **~s** z
O'Neal əʊ 'niːᵊl ‖ oʊ-
one-armed ˌwʌn 'ɑːmd ◄ §ˌwɒn- ‖ -'ɑːrmd ◄
  ˌone-armed 'bandit
one-eyed ˌwʌn 'aɪd ◄ §ˌwɒn-
Onega ɒ 'neɪg ə -'neg- ‖ oʊ 'neg ə -'niːg-;
  oʊn 'jeɪg ə —*Russ* [ʌ 'nʲɛ gə]
Onegin ɒ 'neɪg ɪn əʊ-, ɒn 'jeɪg-, -ən ‖ oʊ- ɑː-
one-horse ˌwʌn 'hɔːs ◄ §ˌwɒn- ‖ -'hɔːrs ◄
  ˌone-horse 'town
Oneida əʊ 'naɪd ə ‖ oʊ- **~s** z
O'Neil, O'Neill əʊ 'niːᵊl ‖ oʊ-
oneiromancy əʊ 'naɪᵊr ə mænts i ‖ oʊ-
one-legged ˌwʌn 'leg ɪd ◄ §ˌwɒn-, -əd, ˌ•'legd
one-liner ˌwʌn 'laɪn ə §ˌwɒn- ‖ -ᵊr **~s** z

O

one-man ˌwʌn 'mæn ◄ →,wʌm-, §,wɒn-
　ˌone-man 'band
oneness 'wʌn nəs §'wɒn-, -nɪs
one-night ˌwʌn 'naɪt ◄ §,wɒn-
　ˌone-night 'stand
one-off ˌwʌn 'ɒf ◄ §,wɒn-, -'ɔːf ‖ -'ɔːf ◄ -'ɑːf
　~s s
one-on-one ˌwʌn ɒn 'wʌn §,wɒn • 'wɒn ‖ -ɑːn-
　-ɔːn-
Oneonta ˌəʊn i 'ɒnt ə ‖ ˌoʊn i 'ɑːnt̬ ə
one-parent ˌwʌn 'peər ənt ◄ →,wʌm-, §,wɒn-
　‖ -'per- -'pær-
　ˌone-ˌparent 'family
one-piece ˌwʌn 'piːs ◄ →,wʌm-, §,wɒn-
　ˌone-piece 'snowsuit

ONEROUS

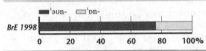

onerous 'əʊn ər əs 'ɒn- ‖ 'oʊn- 'ɑːn- —*BrE
1998 poll panel preference:* 'əʊn- 76%, 'ɒn-
24%. ~ly li ~ness nəs nɪs
oneself wʌn 'self wʌnz-, §wɒn-
one-sided ˌwʌn 'saɪd ɪd ◄ §,wɒn-, -əd ~ly li
　~ness nəs nɪs
　ˌone-ˌsided 'argument
Onesimus əʊ 'niːs ɪm əs -'nes-, -əm- ‖ oʊ-
one-star ˌwʌn 'stɑː ◄ ,wɒn- ‖ -'stɑːr ◄
　ˌone-star ho'tel
one-stop 'wʌn stɒp §'wɒn- ‖ -stɑːp
onetime 'wʌn taɪm §'wɒn-
one-to-one ˌwʌn tə 'wʌn ◄ §,wɒn • 'wɒn, -tu-
one-track ˌwʌn 'træk ◄ §,wɒn-
　ˌone-track 'mind
one-two ˌwʌn 'tuː §,wɒn-
one-upmanship ₍ᵢ₎wʌn 'ʌp mən ʃɪp §₍ᵢ₎wɒn-
one-way ˌwʌn 'weɪ ◄ §,wɒn-
　ˌone-way 'traffic
on-glide 'ɒn glaɪd →'ɒŋ- ‖ 'ɑːn- 'ɔːn- ~s z
ongoing 'ɒn ˌgəʊ ɪŋ →'ɒŋ-, ˌ•'••
　‖ 'ɑːn ˌgoʊ ɪŋ 'ɔːn-
onion 'ʌn jən ~s z
Onions (i) 'ʌn jənz, (ii) əʊ 'naɪ_ənz ‖ oʊ-
　—*The lexicographer C.T.Onions was (i).*
onionskin 'ʌn jən skɪn
onium 'əʊn i_əm ‖ 'oʊn-
onkaparinga, O~ ,ɒŋk ə pə 'rɪŋ gə ‖ ,ɑːŋk-
online, on-line ,ɒn 'laɪn ◄ ‖ ,ɑːn- ,ɔːn-
　ˌonline 'help
onlooker 'ɒn ˌlʊk ə ‖ 'ɑːn ˌlʊk ᵊr 'ɔːn- ~s z
only 'əʊn li §-i ‖ 'oʊn li (*!*)
o.n.o. —*see* or near offer
Ono 'əʊn əʊ ‖ 'oʊn oʊ —*Jp* [o ˌno]
onomastic ,ɒn əʊ 'mæst ɪk ◄ ‖ ,ɑːn oʊ- -ə- ~s
　s
onomatopoeia ,ɒn əʊ mæt ə 'piː_ə
　‖ ,ɑːn ə mæt̬ ə 'piː ə, ˌ••'maːt̬-
onomatopoeic ,ɒn əʊ mæt ə 'piː ɪk ◄
　‖ ,ɑːn ə mæt̬- ,••'maːt̬- ~ally ᵊl_i
Onondaga ,ɒn ən 'dɑːg ə ◄ -'dɔːg- ‖ ,ɑːn-
　-'dɔːg- ~s z
on-ramp 'ɒn ræmp ‖ 'ɑːn- 'ɔːn- ~s s

onrush 'ɒn rʌʃ ‖ 'ɑːn- 'ɔːn- ~es ɪz əz
onrushing 'ɒn ˌrʌʃ ɪŋ ‖ 'ɑːn- 'ɔːn-
on-screen ,ɒn 'skriːn ◄ ‖ ,ɑːn- ,ɔːn-
onset 'ɒn set ‖ 'ɑːn- 'ɔːn- ~s s
onshore ,ɒn 'ʃɔː ◄ ‖ ,ɑːn 'ʃɔːr ◄ ,ɔːn-, -'ʃoʊr
onside ,ɒn 'saɪd ◄ ‖ ,ɑːn- ,ɔːn-
onslaught 'ɒn slɔːt ‖ 'ɑːn- 'ɔːn-; -slɑːt ~s s
Onslow 'ɒnz ləʊ ‖ 'ɑːnz loʊ
onstream ,ɒn 'striːm ◄ ‖ ,ɑːn- ,ɔːn-
Ontario ɒn 'teər i əʊ ‖ ɑːn 'ter i oʊ -'tær-
onto *before a consonant* 'ɒn tə ‖ 'ɑːn tə 'ɔːn-,
　elsewhere 'ɒn tu -tuː ‖ 'ɑːn tu 'ɔːn-, -tə
ontogenesis ,ɒnt əʊ 'dʒen əs ɪs -ɪs •, §-əs
　‖ ,ɑːnt̬ oʊ-
ontogenetic ,ɒnt əʊ dʒə 'net ɪk ◄ -dʒɪ'• •
　‖ ,ɑːnt̬ oʊ dʒə 'net̬ ɪk ◄ ~ally ᵊl_i
ontogen|y ɒn 'tɒdʒ ən |i -ɪn- ‖ ɑːn 'tɑːdʒ-
　~ies iz
ontological ,ɒnt ə 'lɒdʒ ɪk ᵊl ◄ ,ɒnt ᵊl 'ɒdʒ-
　‖ ,ɑːnt̬ ᵊl 'ɑːdʒ- ~ly ˌi
ontology ɒn 'tɒl ədʒ i ‖ ɑːn 'tɑːl-
onus 'əʊn əs ‖ 'oʊn əs ~es ɪz əz
onward 'ɒn wəd ‖ 'ɑːn wərd 'ɔːn- ~s z
-onym *stress-imposing* ən ɪm §-əm ‖ ə nɪm —
　acronym 'æk rən ɪm §-əm ‖ -ə nɪm
onyx 'ɒn ɪks 'əʊn- ‖ 'ɑːn ɪks
oo-, oö- *comb. form*
　with stress-neutral suffix ¦əʊ ə ‖ ¦oʊ ə —
　oocyte, oöcyte 'əʊ ə saɪt ‖ 'oʊ-
　with stress-imposing suffix əʊ 'ɒ+ ‖ oʊ 'ɑː+ —
　oogamy, oögamy əʊ 'ɒg əm i ‖ oʊ 'ɑːg-
oodles 'uːd ᵊlz
oof uːf
ooh uː oohed uːd oohing 'uː ɪŋ oohs uːz
ooh-la-la, oo-la-la ,uː lɑː 'lɑː
oolite 'əʊ ə laɪt ‖ 'oʊ- ~s s
oolith 'əʊ ə lɪθ 'uː_ ‖ 'oʊ- ~s s
oolitic ,əʊ ə 'lɪt ɪk ◄ ,oʊ ə 'lɪt̬ ɪk ◄
oological ,əʊ ə 'lɒdʒ ɪk ᵊl ◄ ‖ ,oʊ ə 'lɑːdʒ-
oolog|y əʊ 'ɒl ədʒ |i ‖ oʊ 'ɑːl- ~ist/s ɪst/s
　§əst/s
oolong, O~ 'uː ˌlɒŋ ,•'• ‖ -lɔːŋ -lɑːŋ
oompah 'uːm pɑː 'ʊm- ~s s
oomph ʊmᵖf uːmᵖf
Oona, Oonagh 'uːn ə
oops ʊps wʊps, uːps
oops-a-daisy ,ʊps ə 'deɪz i ,wʊps-, ,uːps-,
　'••,•• ‖ '••,••
Oort ɔːt ‖ ɔːrt oʊrt —*Dutch* [oːrt]
Oosterhuis 'əʊst ə haʊs ‖ 'oʊst ᵊr- —*Dutch*
　['oː stər hœys]
ooze uːz oozed uːzd oozes 'uːz ɪz -əz
　oozing 'uːz ɪŋ
ooz|y 'uːz |i ~ier i_ə ‖ i_ᵊr ~iest i_ɪst i_əst
　~ily ɪ li ᵊl i ~iness i nəs i nɪs
op ɒp ‖ ɑːp
　'op art
Op —*see* Opus
opacit|y əʊ 'pæs ət |i -ɪt- ‖ oʊ 'pæs ət̬ |i ~ies
　iz
opal 'əʊp ᵊl ‖ 'oʊp ᵊl ~s z
opalescence ,əʊp ə 'les ᵊn¦s ,ɒp-, →,•'ᵊl 'es-
　‖ ,oʊp-

opalescent ˌəʊp ə 'les ᵊnt ◄ ˌɒp-, →-, •ᵊl 'es-
‖ ˌoʊp-
opaline 'əʊp ə laɪn -liːn, →-ᵊl aɪn, →-ᵊl iːn
‖ 'oʊp-
opaque əʊ 'peɪk ‖ oʊ- **~ly** li **~ness** nəs nɪs
op. cit. ˌɒp 'sɪt ‖ ˌɑːp-
ope əʊp ‖ oʊp **oped** əʊpt ‖ oʊpt **opes**
əʊps ‖ oʊps **oping** 'əʊp ɪŋ ‖ 'oʊp ɪŋ
OPEC 'əʊp ek ‖ 'oʊp-
Opel _tdmk_ 'əʊp ᵊl ‖ 'oʊp ᵊl —_Ger_ ['ʔoː pᵊl] **~s** z
op|en 'əʊp |ᵊn ‖ 'oʊp |ᵊn **~ened** ᵊnd →md
~ener ᵊn‿ə ‖ ᵊn‿ᵊr **~enest** ᵊn‿ɪst ‿əst
~ening ᵊn‿ɪŋ **~ens** ᵊnz →mz
'open day; ˌopen 'house; ˌopen 'letter;
ˌopen 'sandwich; ˌopen 'season; ˌopen
'secret; ˌopen 'sesame; ˌOpen ˌUni'versity;
ˌopen 'verdict
open-air ˌəʊp ᵊn 'eə ◄ ‖ ˌoʊp ᵊn 'eᵊr ◄ -'æᵊr
open-and-shut ˌəʊp ᵊn‿ᵊn 'ʃʌt ◄ -ᵊn‿ᵊnd-
‖ ˌoʊp-
opencast 'əʊp ᵊn kɑːst →-m-, →-ᵊŋ-, §-kæst
‖ 'oʊp ᵊn kæst
open-door ˌəʊp ᵊn 'dɔː ◄→-m- ‖ ˌoʊp
ᵊn 'dɔːr ◄ -'doʊr
open-ended ˌəʊp ᵊn 'end ɪd ◄ -əd ‖ ˌoʊp-
~ness nəs nɪs
opener 'əʊp ᵊn‿ə ‖ 'oʊp ᵊn‿ᵊr **~s** z
open-eyed ˌəʊp ᵊn 'aɪd ◄ ‖ ˌoʊp-
open-handed ˌəʊp ᵊn 'hænd ɪd ◄ -əd ‖ ˌoʊp-
'• • , • • **~ly** li **~ness** nəs nɪs
open-heart ˌəʊp ᵊn 'hɑːt ◄ ‖ ˌoʊp ᵊn 'hɑːrt ◄
ˌopen-ˌheart 'surgery
open-hearted ˌəʊp ᵊn 'hɑːt ɪd ◄ -əd ‖ ˌoʊp
ᵊn 'hɑːrt̬ əd ◄ ' • • , • •
open-hearth ˌəʊp ᵊn 'hɑːθ ◄ ‖ ˌoʊp ᵊn 'hɑːrθ ◄
opening 'əʊp ᵊn‿ɪŋ ‖ 'oʊp ᵊn‿ɪŋ **~s** z
'opening time
openly 'əʊp ᵊn li →-m- ‖ 'oʊp-
open-minded ˌəʊp ᵊn 'maɪnd ɪd ◄→-m-, -əd
‖ ˌoʊp- ' • • , • • **~ly** li **~ness** nəs nɪs
open-mouthed ˌəʊp ᵊn 'maʊðd ◄→-m-,
§-'maʊθt ‖ ˌoʊp- ' • • •
openness 'əʊp ᵊn nəs →-m-, -nɪs ‖ 'oʊp-
open-plan ˌəʊp ᵊn 'plæn ◄→-m- ‖ ˌoʊp-
Openshaw 'əʊp ᵊn ʃɔː →-m- ‖ 'oʊp- -ʃɑː
openwork 'əʊp ᵊn wɜːk →-m- ‖ 'oʊp ᵊn wɜ˞ːk
opera 'ɒp ᵊr‿ə ‖ 'ɑːp ᵊr‿ə ⚠ i —_also as an_
Italian word, It ['o pe ra] —_or as a French_
word, Fr opéra [ɔ pe ʁa] —_but as the plural of_
opus, _sometimes_ 'əʊp- ‖ 'oʊp- **~s** z
ˌopéra 'bouffe buːf —_Fr_ [buf]; ˌopera
'buffa 'buːf ə —_It_ ['buf fa]; ˌopéra
co'mique kɒ 'miːk ‖ kɑː-; 'opera ˌglasses;
'opera house; ˌopera 'seria 'sɪər i‿ə ‖ 'sɪr-
—_It_ ['sɛː rja]
operability ˌɒp ᵊr‿ə 'bɪl ət i -ɪt i ‖ ˌɑːp
ᵊr‿ə 'bɪl ət̬ i
operable 'ɒp ᵊr‿əb ᵊl ‖ 'ɑːp-
operand 'ɒp ə rænd -ər ᵊnd ‖ 'ɑːp- **~s** z
operant 'ɒp ᵊr ᵊnt ‖ 'ɑːp- **~s** s
ope|rate 'ɒp ə |reɪt ‖ 'ɑːp- **~rated** reɪt ɪd -əd
‖ reɪt̬ əd **~rates** reɪts **~rating**
reɪt ɪŋ ‖ reɪt̬ ɪŋ

'operating ˌsystem; 'operating ˌtable;
'operating ˌtheatre
operatic ˌɒp ə 'ræt ɪk ◄ ‖ ˌɑːp ə 'ræt̬ ɪk ◄ **~ally**
ᵊl‿i **~s** s
operation ˌɒp ə 'reɪʃ ᵊn ‖ ˌɑːp- **~s** z
ˌope'rations re ˌsearch, - ˌresearch;
ˌope'rations room
operational ˌɒp ə 'reɪʃ ᵊn‿ᵊl ◄ ‖ ˌɑːp- **~ly** i
ˌopeˌrational re'search, - 'research
operative 'ɒp ᵊr‿ət ɪv -ə reɪt- ‖ 'ɑːp ᵊr‿ət̬ ɪv
-ə reɪt̬- —_The pronunciation_ -reɪt ɪv ‖ -reɪt̬ ɪv
is heard more often for the noun than for the
adj. **~s** z
operator 'ɒp ə reɪt ə ‖ 'ɑːp ə reɪt̬ ᵊr **~s** z
opercul|um əʊ 'pɜːk jʊl |əm ɒ-, -jəl-
‖ oʊ 'pɜ˞ːk jəl |əm **~a** ə
operetta ˌɒp ə 'ret ə ‖ ˌɑːp ə 'ret̬ ə **~s** z
operettist ˌɒp ə 'ret ɪst §-əst ‖ ˌɑːp ə 'ret̬ əst
~s s
Ophelia ə 'fiːl i‿ə əʊ-, ɒ- ‖ oʊ-
ophicleide 'ɒf ɪ klaɪd §-ə- ‖ 'ɑːf- **~s** z
ophidian ɒ 'fɪd i‿ən əʊ- ‖ oʊ- **~s** z
Ophir 'əʊf ə ‖ 'oʊf ᵊr
Ophiuchus ɒ 'fjuːk əs ˌɒf i 'uːk əs
‖ ˌɑːf i 'juːk əs ˌoʊf-
ophthalmia ɒf 'θælm i‿ə ɒp- ‖ ɑːf- ɑːp-
ophthalmic ɒf 'θælm ɪk ɒp- ‖ ɑːf- ɑːp-
ophthalmo- _comb. form_
with stress-neutral suffix ɒf ˈθælm əʊ ɒp-
‖ ɑːf ˈθælm ə ɑːp- — **ophthalmoscopic**
ɒf ˌθælm əʊ 'skɒp ɪk ◄ ɒp-
‖ ɑːf ˌθælm ə 'skɑːp ɪk ◄ ɑːp-
with stress-imposing suffix ˌɒfθ æl 'mɒ+ ˌɒpθ-
‖ ˌɑːfθ æl 'mɑː+ ˌɑːpθ- — **ophthalmoscopy**
ˌɒfθ æl 'mɒsk əp i ˌɒpθ- ‖ ˌɑːfθ æl 'mɑːsk-
ˌɑːpθ-
ophthalmolog|ist/s ˌɒfθ æl 'mɒl ədʒ |ɪst/s
ˌɒpθ-, §-əst/s ‖ ˌɑːfθ æl 'mɑːl- ˌɑːpθ- **~y** i
ophthalmoscope ɒf 'θælm ə skəʊp ɒp-
‖ ɑːf 'θælm ə skoʊp ɑːp- **~s** s
Ophüls 'əʊf ᵊlz ‖ oʊ 'fʊlz —_Ger_ ['ɔ fʏls]
-opia 'əʊp i‿ə ‖ 'oʊp i‿ə — **diplopia**
dɪ 'pləʊp i‿ə ‖ -'ploʊp-
opiate 'əʊp i‿ət -ɪt, -eɪt ‖ 'oʊp- **~s** s
Opie 'əʊp i ‖ 'oʊp i
opin|e əʊ 'paɪn ‖ oʊ- **~ed** d **~es** z **~ing** ɪŋ
opinion ə 'pɪn jən §əʊ- **~s** z
o'pinion poll
opinionated ə 'pɪn jə neɪt ɪd §əʊ-, -əd
‖ -neɪt̬ əd
opioid 'əʊp i ɔɪd ‖ 'oʊp- **~s** z
opisthobranch əʊ 'pɪs θə bræŋk ə- oʊ- **~s** z
opium 'əʊp i‿əm ‖ 'oʊp-
'opium den; 'opium ˌpoppy
Oporto əʊ 'pɔːt əʊ ‖ oʊ 'pɔːrt̬ oʊ -'poʊrt̬-
—_Port_ [u 'por tu]
opossum ə 'pɒs əm ‖ ə 'pɑːs əm 'pɑːs əm **~s**
z
Oppenheim 'ɒp ᵊn haɪm ‖ 'ɑːp-
Oppenheimer 'ɒp ᵊn haɪm ə ‖ 'ɑːp ᵊn haɪm ᵊr
oppidan 'ɒp ɪd ᵊn §-ᵊd- ‖ 'ɑːp- **~s** z
opponent ə 'pəʊn ᵊnt ‖ ə 'poʊn ᵊnt **~s** s

opportune 'ɒp ə tjuːn →-tʃuːn, ˌ•••
‖ ˌɑːp ər 'tuːn ◄ -'tjuːn (*) ~ly li ~ness nəs
nɪs

opportun|ism ˌɒp ə 'tjuːn ˌɪz əm →-'tʃuːn-,
'••••• ‖ ˌɑːp ər 'tuːn- -'tjuːn- ~ist/s ɪst/
s ◄ §əst/s

opportunistic ˌɒp ə tju 'nɪst ɪk ◄→-tʃuː'•-
‖ ˌɑːp ər tuː- -tjuː'•- ~ally əl_i

opportunit|y ˌɒp ə 'tjuːn ət li →-'tʃuːn-, -ɪt i
‖ ˌɑːp ər 'tuːn əţ li -'tjuːn- ~ies iz

opposable ə 'pəʊz əb əl ‖ ə 'pouz-

oppos|e ə 'pəʊz ‖ ə 'pouz ~ed d ~es ɪz əz
~ing ɪŋ

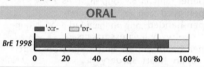

OPPOSITE

	-əz-	-əs-
BrE 1988		
0 20 40 60 80 100%

opposite 'ɒp əz ɪt -əs-, §-ət ‖ 'ɑːp- —BrE 1988
poll panel preference: -əz- 67%, -əs- 33%. ~ly
li ~ness nəs nɪs ~s s
ˌopposite 'number; ˌopposite 'sex

opposition ˌɒp ə 'zɪʃ ən ‖ ˌɑːp- ~al əl ◄ ~s z

oppress ə 'pres §əʊ- ~ed t ~es ɪz əz ~ing ɪŋ

oppression ə 'preʃ ən §əʊ- ~s z

oppressive ə 'pres ɪv §əʊ- ~ly li ~ness nəs
nɪs

oppressor ə 'pres ə §əʊ- ‖ -ər ~s z

opprobrious ə 'prəʊb ri_əs ‖ ə 'proub- ~ly li
~ness nəs nɪs

opprobrium ə 'prəʊb ri_əm ‖ ə 'proub-

oppugn ə 'pjuːn ~ed d ~er/s ə/z ‖ ər/z
~ing ɪŋ ~s z

Oprah 'əʊp rə ‖ 'oup rə

Opren tdmk 'əʊp rən -ren ‖ 'ɑːp- 'oup-

opsonic ɒp 'sɒn ɪk ‖ ɑːp 'sɑːn ɪk

opsonin 'ɒps ən ɪn §-ən ‖ 'ɑːps-

opt ɒpt ‖ ɑːpt opted 'ɒpt ɪd -əd ‖ 'ɑːpt əd
opting 'ɒpt ɪŋ ‖ 'ɑːpt ɪŋ opts ɒpts ‖ ɑːpts

Optacon tdmk 'ɒpt ək ən ‖ 'ɑːpt ə kɑːn

optative 'ɒpt ət ɪv ɒp 'teɪt ɪv ‖ 'ɑːpt əţ ɪv ~s z

optic 'ɒpt ɪk ‖ 'ɑːpt ɪk ~s s

optical 'ɒpt ɪk əl ‖ 'ɑːpt- ~ly _i
ˌoptical 'character recogˌnition; ˌoptical
'fibre; ˌoptical il'lusion

optician ɒp 'tɪʃ ən ‖ ɑːp- ~s z

optim|a 'ɒpt ɪm ə -əm- ‖ 'ɑːpt- ~al/ly əl /i

optimality ˌɒpt ɪ 'mæl ət i ˌ•ə-, -ɪt i
‖ ˌɑːpt ə 'mæl əţ i

optimis... —see optimiz...

optimism 'ɒpt ɪ ˌmɪz əm -ə- ‖ 'ɑːpt-

optimist 'ɒpt ɪm ɪst -əm-, §-əst ‖ 'ɑːpt- ~s s

optimistic ˌɒpt ɪ 'mɪst ɪk ◄ -ə- ‖ ˌɑːpt- ~ally
əl_i

optimization ˌɒpt ɪm aɪ 'zeɪʃ ən ˌ•əm-, -ɪ'•-
‖ ˌɑːpt əm ə- ~s z

optimiz|e 'ɒpt ɪ maɪz -ə- ‖ 'ɑːpt- ~ed d ~es
ɪz əz ~ing ɪŋ

optim|um 'ɒpt ɪm əm -əm- ‖ 'ɑːpt- ~a ə
~ums əmz

option 'ɒp ʃən ‖ 'ɑːp ʃən ~s z

optional 'ɒp ʃən_əl ‖ 'ɑːp- ~ly i

optoelectronic ˌɒpt əʊ ɪ ˌlek 'trɒn ɪk -ə-,ˌ•-;
ˌ••,el ek-, -ˌel ɪk-, -ˌɪl ek-, -ˌiːl ek-
‖ ˌɑːpt oʊ ɪ ˌlek 'trɑːn ɪk ~s s

optometr|ist/s ɒp 'tɒm ətr ɪst/s -ɪtr-, §-əst/s
‖ ɑːp 'tɑːm- ~y i

Optrex tdmk 'ɒp treks ‖ 'ɑːp-

opul|ence 'ɒp jʊl ən°s -jəl- ‖ 'ɑːp jəl- ~ent/
ly ənt /li

opuntia əʊ 'pʌn°tʃ i_ə ɒ- ‖ oʊ- -'pʌn°tʃ ə ~s z

opus 'əʊp əs 'ɒp- ‖ 'oup əs opera 'əʊp ər ə
'ɒp- ‖ 'oup- 'ɑːp- ~es ɪz əz

or ɔː 'ɔːr —In AmE ɔː is a strong form, paired
with a weak form ər. In BrE, however, ɔː
normally has no weak form: there is only an
occasional weak form ə, used chiefly in set
phrases.

-or ə ‖ ər —also occasionally for emphasis
ɔː ‖ ɔːr — generator 'dʒen ə reɪt ə ‖ -reɪţ ər

ora, Ora 'ɔːr ə ‖ 'our-

orach, orach|e 'ɒr ɪtʃ -ətʃ ‖ 'ɔːr ɪtʃ 'ɑːr- ~es
ɪz əz

oracle 'ɒr ək əl -ɪk- ‖ 'ɔːr- 'ɑːr- ~s z

oracular ɒ 'ræk jʊl ə ə-, ɔː-, -jəl-
‖ ɔː 'ræk jəl ər oʊ-, ə- ~ly li

oracy 'ɔːr əs i 'ɒr- ‖ 'our-

Oradea ɒ 'rɑːd i_ə ɔː- ‖ ɔː- —Romanian
[o 'ra dea]

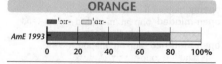

ORAL

	'ɔːr-	'ɒr-
BrE 1998		
0 20 40 60 80 100%

oral 'ɔːr əl §'ɒr- ‖ 'our- —BrE 1998 poll panel
preference: 'ɔːr- 87%, 'ɒr- 13%. ~ly i ~s z

Oran ə 'ræn ɔː-, -'rɑːn ‖ ɔː-, oʊ- —Fr [ɔ ʁɑ̃]

Orana ə 'rɑːn ə

ORANGE

	'ɔːr-	'ɑːr-
AmE 1993		
0 20 40 60 80 100%

orang|e, O~ 'ɒr ɪndʒ -əndʒ ‖ 'ɔːr- 'ɑːr- —AmE
1993 poll panel preference: 'ɔːr- 80%, 'ɑːr-
20%. ~es ɪz əz
'orange ˌblossom; ˌOrange Free 'State,
ˌ•• '•

orangeade ˌɒr ɪndʒ 'eɪd -əndʒ- ‖ ˌɔːr-ˌɑːr- ~s
z

Orange|man 'ɒr ɪndʒ ˌmən -əndʒ-, -mæn ‖ 'ɔːr-
'ɑːr- ~men mən men

oranger|y 'ɒr ɪndʒ ər_li '•əndʒ- ‖ 'ɔːr- 'ɑːr-
~ies iz

orangoutan, orangoutang, orangutan,
orangutang ɔː 'ræŋ ə tæn ɒ-, ə-, -u-, -tæŋ,
ˌ•,••'•; ˌ••'uː tæn, -'juː-, -tɑːn ‖ ə- ~s z

o|rate ɔː 'reɪt ɒ-, ə- ‖ oʊ- ~rated 'reɪt ɪd -əd
‖ 'reɪţ əd ~rates 'reɪts ~rating
'reɪt ɪŋ ‖ 'reɪţ ɪŋ

oration ə 'reɪʃ ən ɔː-, ɒ- ‖ oʊ- ~s z

orator 'ɒr ət ə ‖ 'ɔːr əţ ər 'ɑːr- ~s z

oratorical ˌɒr ə 'tɒr ɪk əl ◄ ‖ ˌɔːr ə 'tɔːr-
ˌɑːr ə 'tɑːr- ~ly _i

Optional sounds

1 **Optional** sounds are sounds that are pronounced by some speakers or on some occasions, but are omitted by other speakers or on other occasions. In LPD they are indicated in two ways: by **italics** and by **raised** letters.

2 Sounds shown in **italics** are sounds which the foreign learner is recommended to include (although native speakers sometimes omit them). They denote sounds that may optionally be **elided**.

lunch lʌnt*ʃ*   Some say lʌntʃ, others say lʌnʃ. LPD recommends lʌntʃ.

bacon 'beɪk *ə*n   Some say 'beɪk ən, others say 'beɪk n. LPD recommends 'beɪk ən.

3 Sounds shown with **raised letters** are sounds which the foreign learner is recommended to ignore (although native speakers sometimes include them). They denote sounds that may optionally be **inserted**.

fence fen^ts   Some say fens, others say fents. LPD recommends fens.

sadden 'sæd ^ən   Some say 'sæd n, others say 'sæd ən. LPD recommends 'sæd n

---

oratorio ˌɒr ə 'tɔːr i əʊ ‖ ˌɔːr ə 'tɔːr i oʊ ˌɑːr-, -'toʊr- ~s z

oratory, O~ 'ɒr ət ̯ər i ‖ 'ɔːr ə tɔːr i 'ɑːr-, -toʊr i

orb ɔːb ‖ ɔːrb **orbs** ɔːbz ‖ ɔːrbz

Orbach 'ɔː bæk ‖ 'ɔːr bɑːk

orbed ɔːbd ‖ ɔːrbd —*in poetry also* 'ɔːb ɪd, -əd ‖ 'ɔːrb-

orbicular ɔː 'bɪk jʊl ə -jəl- ‖ ɔːr 'bɪk jəl ər

Orbison 'ɔːb ɪs ən -əs- ‖ 'ɔːrb-

orb|it 'ɔːb |ɪt §-ət ‖ 'ɔːrb |ət **~ited** ɪt ɪd §ət-, -əd ‖ ət ̯əd **~iting** ɪt ɪŋ §ət- ‖ ət ̯ɪŋ **~its** ɪts §əts ‖ əts

orbital 'ɔːb ɪt əl §-ət- ‖ 'ɔːrb ət ̯əl **~ly** i

orbitale ˌɔːb ɪ 'tɑːl i -ə-, -'teɪl- ‖ ˌɔːrb-

orbiter 'ɔːb ɪt ə §-ət- ‖ 'ɔːrb ət ̯ər ~s z

orc ɔːk ‖ ɔːrk **orcs** ɔːks ‖ ɔːrks

Orcadian ɔː 'keɪd i‿ən ‖ ɔːr- ~s z

orchard, O~ 'ɔːtʃ əd ‖ 'ɔːrtʃ ərd ~s z

orchestra 'ɔːk ɪs trə -əs-, -es- ‖ 'ɔːrk- ~s z 'orchestra ˌpit

orchestral ɔː 'kes trəl ‖ ɔːr- **~ly** i

orche|strate 'ɔːk ɪ |streɪt -ə-, -e- ‖ 'ɔːrk- **~strated** streɪt ɪd -əd ‖ streɪt ̯əd **~strates** streɪts **~strating** streɪt ɪŋ ‖ streɪt ̯ɪŋ

orchestration ˌɔːk ɪ 'streɪʃ ən -ə-, -e- ‖ ˌɔːrk- ~s z

orchestrina ˌɔːk ɪ 'striːn ə -ə- ‖ ˌɔːrk- ~s z

orchestrion ɔː 'kes tri‿ən ‖ ɔːr- -ɑːn ~s z

orchid 'ɔːk ɪd §-əd ‖ 'ɔːrk əd ~s z

orchidaceous ˌɔːk ɪ 'deɪʃ əs §-ə- ‖ ˌɔːrk-

orchidectom|y ˌɔːk ɪ 'dekt əm |i -ə- ‖ ˌɔːrk- **~ies** iz

orchil 'ɔːk ɪl 'ɔːtʃ-, §-əl ‖ 'ɔːrk- 'ɔːrtʃ-

orchis 'ɔːk ɪs §-əs ‖ 'ɔːrk-

orchitis ɔː 'kaɪt ɪs §-əs ‖ ɔːr 'kaɪt ̯əs

Orcus 'ɔːk əs ‖ 'ɔːrk əs

Orczy 'ɔːts i 'ɔːks i, 'ɔːk zi ‖ 'ɔːrts i

Ord ɔːd ‖ ɔːrd

ordain ₍₎ɔː 'deɪn ‖ ɔːr- **~ed** d **~ing** ɪŋ ~s z

Orde ɔːd ‖ ɔːrd

ordeal ɔː 'diːəl 'ɔːd iːəl ‖ ɔːr- ~s z

order 'ɔːd ə ‖ 'ɔːrd ər **~ed** d **ordering** 'ɔːd_ər ɪŋ ‖ 'ɔːrd_ər ɪŋ ~s z 'order ˌpaper

order|ly 'ɔːd əl i ‖ 'ɔːrd ər |li **~lies** liz

ordinaire ˌɔːd ɪ 'neə -ə-, -ən 'eə ‖ ˌɔːrd ən 'eər -'æər —*Fr* [ɔʁ di nɛːʁ]

ordinal 'ɔːd ɪn əl -ən_əl ‖ 'ɔːrd ən_əl ~s z

ordinanc|e 'ɔːd ɪn ənts -ən_ənts ‖ 'ɔːrd ən_ənts **~es** ɪz əz

ordinand 'ɔːd ɪ nænd -ə-, -ən ænd, ˌ•• '• ‖ 'ɔːrd ən ænd ˌ•• '• ~s z

ordinarily 'ɔːd ən ər_əl i '•ɪn-, '•ən_ər əl i, -ɪ li; ˌ••'er əl i, -ɪ li ‖ ˌɔːrd ən 'er əl i

ordinar|y 'ɔːd ən ər_li '•ɪn-, -ən_ər i; -er i ‖ 'ɔːrd ən er i —*1998 BrE poll panel preference*: -ri 34%, -əri 32%, -eri 34%. **~ies** iz 'ordinary ˌlevel; ˌordinary 'seaman

ordinate 'ɔːd ən_ət -ɪn-, ‿ɪt, -eɪt ‖ 'ɔːrd- ~s s

ordination ˌɔːd ɪ 'neɪʃ ən -ə-, -ən 'eɪʃ- ‖ ˌɔːrd ən 'eɪʃ ən ~s z

ordines 'ɔːd ɪ niːz -ə- ‖ 'ɔːrd-

ordnance 'ɔːd nənts ‖ 'ɔːrd- ˌOrdnance 'Survey

ordo 'ɔːd əʊ ‖ 'ɔːrd oʊ **ordines** 'ɔːd ɪ niːz -ə- ‖ 'ɔːrd-

O

ORDINARY

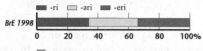

BrE 1998

| -ri | -əri | -eri |

0   20   40   60   80   100%

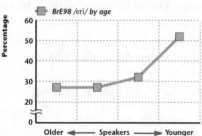

BrE98 /eri/ by age

Older ◄——— Speakers ———► Younger

Ordovician ˌɔːd əʊ 'vɪʃ i‿ən ◄ -'vɪs-, -'vɪʃ ən
‖ ˌɔːrd ə 'vɪʃ ən ◄
ordure 'ɔːd jʊə ‖ 'ɔːrdʒ ʊr 'ɔːrd jʊr
Ordzhonikidze ˌɔːdʒ ɒn i 'kɪdz i ˌ•ən-
‖ ˌɔːrdʒ ɑːn- —*Russ* [ar dʒə nji 'ki dzji]
ore, Ore ɔː ‖ ɔːr ʊʊr **ores** ɔːz ‖ ɔːrz ʊʊrz
öre 'ɜːr ə ‖ 'ɝː ə —*Swedish* ['øː rə]
oread 'ɔːr i æd ~s z
Örebro 'ɜːr ə bruː ‖ 'ɝː- —*Swedish*
[œ: rə 'bruː]
orectic ɒ 'rekt ɪk ə- ‖ ɔː-
oregano ˌɒr ɪ 'gɑːn əʊ -ə- ‖ ə 'reg ə noʊ ɔː-
(*)
Oregon 'ɒr ɪg ən -əg- ‖ 'ɔːr- 'ɑːr-, -ə gɑːn
ˌOregon 'grape; ˌOregon 'Trail
Oregonian ˌɒr ɪ 'gəʊn i‿ən ◄ ˌ•ə-
‖ ˌɔːr ə 'goʊn- ˌɑːr- ~s z
O'Reilly əʊ 'raɪl i ‖ oʊ-
Oreo *tdmk*, **oreo** 'ɔːr i əʊ ‖ -oʊ 'oʊr- ~s z
Oresteia ˌɒr ɪ 'staɪ‿ə ˌɔːr-, -ə-, -'steɪ ə, -'stiː‿ə
‖ ˌɔːr-, ˌoʊr-
Orestes ɒ 'rest iːz ɔː-, ə- ‖ ə-
orfe ɔːf ‖ ɔːrf **orfes** ɔːfs ‖ ɔːrfs
Orfeo ɔː 'feɪ əʊ 'ɔːf i əʊ ‖ ɔːr 'feɪ oʊ 'ɔːrf i oʊ
—*It* [or 'fɛː o]
Orff ɔːf ‖ ɔːrf —*Ger* [ʔɒʁf]
Orford 'ɔːf əd ‖ 'ɔːrf ʔrd
org *WWW and e-mail* ɔːg ‖ ɔːrg
organ 'ɔːg ən ‖ 'ɔːrg ən ~s z
'organ ˌgrinder; 'organ pipe
organa 'ɔːg ən ə ‖ 'ɔːrg-
organdie, organdy 'ɔːg ənd i i ‖ 'ɔːrg- ~ies iz
organelle ˌɔːg ə 'nel ‖ ˌɔːrg- ~s z
organic ɔː 'gæn ɪk ‖ ɔːr- ~ally ʔl‿i
organis... —*see* **organiz...**
organism 'ɔːg ə ˌnɪz əm -ən ˌɪz- ‖ 'ɔːrg- ~s z
organist 'ɔːg ən ɪst §-əst ‖ 'ɔːrg- ~s s
organization ˌɔːg ən aɪ 'zeɪʃ ʔn -ɪ'•- ‖ ˌɔːrg
ən‿ə- ~s z
organizational ˌɔːg ən aɪ 'zeɪʒ ʔn‿ʔl ◄ -ɪ'•-
‖ ˌɔːrg ən‿ə- ~ly i
organiz|e 'ɔːg ə naɪz -ən aɪz ‖ 'ɔːrg- ~ed d
~er/s ə/z ‖ ʔr/z ~es ɪz əz ~ing ɪŋ
ˌorganized 'crime
organo- *comb. form*
with stress-neutral suffix ɔː ˌgæn əʊ ˌɔːg ən əʊ

‖ ɔːr ˌgæn ə ˌɔːrg ən ə— **organochlorine**
ɔː ˌgæn əʊ 'klɔːr iːn ˌɒg ən- ‖ ɔːr ˌgæn ə-
ˌɔːrg ən-, -'kloʊr-, -ən
with stress-imposing suffix
ˌɔːg ə 'nɒ+ ‖ ˌɔːrg ə 'nɑː+ —
organography
ˌɔːg ə 'nɒg rəf i ‖ ˌɔːrg ə 'nɑːg-
organon 'ɔːg ə nɒn ‖ 'ɔːrg ə nɑːn ~s z
organa 'ɔːg ən ə ‖ 'ɔːrg-
organ|um 'ɔːg ən |əm ‖ 'ɔːrg- ~a ə
organza ɔː 'gænz ə ‖ ɔːr-
orgasm 'ɔːg æz əm ‖ 'ɔːrg- ~ed d ~ing ɪŋ
~s z
orgasmic ɔː 'gæz mɪk ‖ ɔːr- ~ally ʔl‿i
orgeat 'ɔːʒ ɑː ‖ 'ɔːrʒ- —*Fr* [ɔʁ ʒa]
orgiastic ˌɔːdʒ i 'æst ɪk ◄ ‖ ˌɔːrdʒ- ~ally ʔl‿i
orgi... —*see* **orgy...**
orgone 'ɔːg əʊn ‖ 'ɔːrg oʊn
Orgreave 'ɔː griːv ‖ 'ɔːr-
org|y 'ɔːdʒ |i ‖ 'ɔːrdʒ li ~ies iz
Oriana ˌɔːr i 'ɑːn ə ˌɒr-
oriel, Oriel 'ɔːr i‿əl ‖ 'oʊr- ~s z
ˌoriel 'window, '•••, ••
orient, O~ *adj, n* 'ɔːr i‿ənt 'ɒr- ‖ 'oʊr-
ˌOrient Ex'press
ori|ent *v* 'ɔːr i |ent 'ɒr- ‖ 'oʊr- ~ented ent ɪd
-əd ‖ enţ əd ~enting ent ɪŋ ‖ enţ ɪŋ ~ents
ents
oriental, O~ ˌɔːr i 'ent ʔl ◄ ˌɒr- ‖ -'enţ ʔl ◄ ˌoʊr-
~ism ˌɪz əm ~ist/s ɪst/s §əst/s ‖ əst/s ~s z
orien|tate 'ɔːr i‿ən |teɪt 'ɒr-, -i en- ‖ 'oʊr-
~tated teɪt ɪd -əd ‖ teɪţ əd ~tates teɪts
~tating teɪt ɪŋ ‖ teɪţ ɪŋ
orientation ˌɔːr i‿ən 'teɪʃ ʔn ˌɒr-, -i en- ‖ ˌoʊr-
~s z
orien|teer ˌɔːr i‿ən |'tɪə ˌɒr-, -i en|- ‖ -'tɪr ˌoʊr-
~teering 'tɪər ɪŋ ‖ 'tɪr ɪŋ ~teered
'tɪəd ‖ 'tɪrd ~teers 'tɪəz ‖ 'tɪrd
orific|e 'ɒr əf ɪs -ɪf-, §-əs ‖ 'ɔːr əf əs 'ɑːr- ~es
ɪz əz
oriflamme 'ɒr i flæm -ə- ‖ 'ɔːr ə- 'ɑːr- ~s z
origami ˌɒr ɪ 'gɑːm i ˌɔːr-, -ə- ‖ ˌɔːr ə- —*Jp*
[o 'ri ŋa mi, -ga-]
origanum ə 'rɪg ən əm ɒ-; ˌɒr ɪ 'gɑːn-, -ə-
Origen 'ɒr ɪ dʒen -ə- ‖ 'ɔːr- 'ɑːr-
origin 'ɒr ɪdʒ ɪn -ədʒ-, -ən ‖ 'ɔːr- 'ɑːr- ~s z
original ə 'rɪdʒ ʔn‿ʔl ɒ-, -ɪn- ~s z
o,riginal 'sin
originalit|y ə ˌrɪdʒ ə 'næl ət i ɒ-, -, •ɪ-, -ɪt i
‖ -əţ li ~ies iz
originally ə 'rɪdʒ ʔn‿ʔl i ɒ-, -'•ɪn-
origi|nate ə 'rɪdʒ ə |neɪt ɒ-, -ɪ- ~nated neɪt ɪd
-əd ‖ neɪţ əd ~nates neɪts ~nating
neɪt ɪŋ ‖ neɪţ ɪŋ
origination ə ˌrɪdʒ ə 'neɪʃ ʔn ɒ-, -ɪ-
originative ə 'rɪdʒ ə neɪt ɪv ɒ-, -ɪ•, -ən‿ət ɪv,
-ɪn ət ɪv ‖ -neɪţ ɪv ~ly li
originator ə 'rɪdʒ ə neɪt ə ɒ-, -'•ɪ- ‖ -neɪţ ʔr
~s z
O-ring 'əʊ rɪŋ ‖ 'oʊ- ~s z
Orinoco ˌɒr ɪ 'nəʊk əʊ -ə- ‖ ˌɔːr ə 'noʊk oʊ
ˌoʊr- —*Sp* [o ri 'no ko]
Orinthia ə 'rɪntθ i‿ə ɒ-

oriole 'ɔːr i əʊl →-ɒʊl, -əl ‖ -oʊl 'oʊr- **~s** z
Orion ə 'raɪ_ən ɒ-, ɔː- ‖ oʊ-   **Orionis**
  ,ɔːr i 'əʊn ɪs §-əs ‖ -'oʊn-
O'Riordan (i) əʊ 'rɪəd ᵊn ‖ oʊ 'rɪrd ᵊn, (ii) əʊ
  'raɪ_əd ᵊn ‖ oʊ 'raɪ_ᵊrd ᵊn
orison 'ɒr ɪz ᵊn -əz- ‖ 'ɔːr əs- 'aːr-, -əz- **~s** z
Orissa ɒ 'rɪs ə ɔː-, ə- ‖ oʊ-
Oriya ɒ 'riː_ə ɔː-, ə- ‖ ɔː-
ork ɔːk ‖ ɔːrk **orks** ɔːks ‖ ɔːrks
Orkney 'ɔːk ni ‖ 'ɔːrk- **~s** z
  '**Orkney ,Islands** ‖ , • • ◄
Orlando ɔː 'lænd əʊ ‖ ɔːr 'lænd oʊ
orle ɔːl ‖ ɔːrl   **orles** ɔːlz ‖ ɔːrlz
Orleans, Orléans ɔː 'liː_ənz 'ɔːl i_, ,ɔːl eɪ 'ɒ̃
  ‖ 'ɔːrl i_ənz ɔːr 'liːnz —Fr [ɔʁ le ɑ̃]
Orlon, orlon tdmk 'ɔːl ɒn ‖ 'ɔːrl aːn
orlop 'ɔː lɒp ‖ 'ɔːr laːp **~s** s
Orly 'ɔːl i ‖ 'ɔːrl i ɔːr 'liː —Fr [ɔʁ li]
Orm, Orme ɔːm ‖ ɔːrm
Ormandy 'ɔːm ənd i ‖ 'ɔːrm-
Ormeau 'ɔːm əʊ • ' • ‖ 'ɔːrm oʊ
ormer 'ɔːm ə ‖ 'ɔːrm ᵊr **~s** z
Ormerod 'ɔːm ᵊr_ɒd ‖ 'ɔːrm ᵊr_aːd
Ormesby 'ɔːmz bi ‖ 'ɔːrmz-
ormolu 'ɔːm ə luː -lju: ‖ 'ɔːrm-
Ormond, Ormonde 'ɔːm ənd ‖ 'ɔːrm-
Ormrod 'ɔːm rɒd ‖ 'ɔːrm raːd
Ormsby 'ɔːmz bi ‖ 'ɔːrmz-
Ormskirk 'ɔːmz kɜːk 'ɔːmᵖs- ‖ 'ɔːrmz kɜːːk
Ormulum 'ɔːm jʊl əm -jəl- ‖ 'ɔːrm-
ornament n 'ɔːn ə mənt ‖ 'ɔːrn- **~s** s
orna|ment v 'ɔːn ə |ment ‖ 'ɔːrn- —See note at
  -ment **~mented** ment ɪd -əd ‖ ment̬ əd
  ~menting ment ɪŋ ‖ ment̬ ɪŋ **~ments** ments
ornamental ,ɔːn ə 'ment ᵊl ◄ ‖ ,ɔːrn ə 'ment̬
  ᵊl ◄ **~ly** i
ornamentation ,ɔːn ə men 'teɪʃ ᵊn -əm ən-
  ‖ ,ɔːrn- **~s** z
ornate ⁽ᵢ⁾ɔː 'neɪt ⁽ᵢ⁾ɔːr- **~ly** li **~ness** nəs nɪs
orner|y 'ɔːn ᵊr_li ‖ 'ɔːrn- 'aːn- **~ier** i_ə ‖ i_ᵊr
  ~iest i_ɪst i_əst **~iness** i nəs i nɪs
ornitho- comb. form
  with stress-neutral suffix ¦ɔːn ɪθ əʊ -əθ-
  ‖ ¦ɔːrn əθ ə — **ornithomancy** 'ɔːn ɪθ əʊ
  ,mænᵗs i ‖ 'ɔːrn əθ ə-
  with stress-imposing suffix ,ɔːn ɪ 'θɒ+ -ə-
  ‖ ,ɔːrn ə 'θɑ:+ — **ornithoscopy**
  ,ɔːn ɪ 'θɒsk əp i , • ə- ‖ ,ɔːrn ə 'θɑːsk-
ornithological ,ɔːn ɪθ ə 'lɒdʒ ɪk ᵊl ◄ , • əθ-
  ‖ ,ɔːrn əθ ə 'laːdʒ- **~ly** _i
ornitholog|ist/s ,ɔːn ɪ 'θɒl ədʒ ɪst/s , • ə-,
  §-əst/s ‖ ,ɔːrn ə 'θɑːl- **~y** i
ornithopter 'ɔːn ɪ θɒpt ə ' • ə-
  ‖ 'ɔːrn ə θɑːpt ᵊr **~s** z
ornithosis ,ɔːn ɪ 'θəʊs ɪs -ə-, §-əs
  ‖ ,ɔːrn ə 'θoʊs əs
oro- comb. form
  with stress-neutral suffix ¦ɒr əʊ ¦ɔːr- ‖ ¦ɔːr ə
  ¦aːr-, ¦oʊr- — **orographic** ,ɒr əʊ 'græf ɪk ◄
  ,ɔːr- ‖ ,ɔːr ə-, ,aːr-, ,oʊr-
  with stress-imposing suffix ɒ 'rɒ+ ɔː-
  ‖ ɔː 'raː+ aː-, oʊ- — **orology** ɒ 'rɒl ədʒ i ɔː-
  ‖ ɔː 'raːl ədʒ i aː-, oʊ-

oronasal ,ɔːr əʊ 'neɪz ᵊl ◄ ‖ -oʊ- ,oʊr-
Oronsay 'ɒr ᵊn seɪ -zeɪ ‖ 'ɔːr-
Orontes ə 'rɒnt iːz ɒ- ‖ ɔː 'raːnt iːz aː-, oʊ-
oropharynx 'ɔːr əʊ ,fær ɪŋks , • • ' • •
  ‖ 'ɔːr oʊ ,fær- 'oʊr-, -ə-, -,fer-
orotund 'ɒr əʊ tʌnd 'ɔːr- ‖ 'ɔːr ə- 'aːr-, 'oʊr-
orotundity ,ɒr əʊ 'tʌnd ət i ,ɔːr-, -ɪt i
  ‖ ,ɔːr ə 'tʌnd ət̬ i ,aːr-, ,oʊr-
O'Rourke əʊ 'rɔːk -'rʊək ‖ oʊ 'rɔːrk
orphan 'ɔːf ᵊn ‖ 'ɔːrf ᵊn **~ed** d **~ing** ɪŋ **~s** z
orphanag|e 'ɔːf ᵊn ɪdʒ ‖ 'ɔːrf- **~es** ɪz əz
orphanhood 'ɔːf ᵊn hʊd ‖ 'ɔːrf-
Orphean ɔː 'fiː_ən 'ɔːf i_ən ‖ ɔːr 'fiː ən 'ɔːrf i_
  ~s z
Orpheus 'ɔːf juːs 'ɔːf i_əs ‖ 'ɔːrf-
Orphic 'ɔːf ɪk ‖ 'ɔːrf-
Orphism 'ɔːf ,ɪz əm ‖ 'ɔːrf-
orphrey 'ɔːf ri ‖ 'ɔːrf- **~s** z
orpiment 'ɔːp ɪ mənt §-ə- ‖ 'ɔːrp-
orpin 'ɔːp ɪn §-ᵊn ‖ 'ɔːrp- **~s** z
orpine 'ɔːp aɪn -ɪn, §-ᵊn ‖ 'ɔːrp ᵊn **~s** z
Orpington 'ɔːp ɪŋ tən ‖ 'ɔːrp- **~s** z
Orr ɔː ‖ ɔːr
Orrell 'ɒr əl ‖ 'ɔːr- 'aːr-
orrer|y 'ɒr ᵊr li ‖ 'ɔːr- 'aːr- **~ies** iz
orris 'ɒr ɪs §-əs ‖ 'ɔːr- 'aːr-
Orsini ɔː 'siːn i ‖ ɔːr- —It [or 'siː ni]
Orsino ɔː 'siːn əʊ ‖ ɔːr 'siːn oʊ
Orson 'ɔːs ᵊn ‖ 'ɔːrs ᵊn
ortanique ,ɔːt ə 'niːk -ᵊn 'iːk ‖ ,ɔːrt ᵊn 'iːk **~s** s
Ortega ɔː 'teɪg ə ‖ ɔːr- —Sp [or 'te ɣa]
orthicon 'ɔːθ ɪ kɒn -ə- ‖ 'ɔːrθ ɪ kaːn **~s** z
ortho- comb. form
  with stress-neutral suffix ¦ɔːθ əʊ ‖ ¦ɔːrθ ə -oʊ
  — **orthotone** 'ɔːθ əʊ təʊn ‖ 'ɔːrθ ə toʊn
  -oʊ-
  with stress-imposing suffix ɔː 'θɒ+ ‖ ɔːr 'θaː+
  — **orthotropous** ɔː 'θɒtr əp əs ‖ ɔːr 'θɑːtr-
orthocenter, orthocentre
  'ɔːθ əʊ ,sent ə ‖ 'ɔːrθ ə ,sent̬ ᵊr -oʊ- **~s** z
orthochromatic ,ɔːθ əʊ krəʊ
  'mæt ɪk ◄ ‖ ,ɔːrθ ə kroʊ 'mæt̬ ɪk **~ally** ᵊl_i
orthoclase 'ɔːθ əʊ kleɪz -kleɪs ‖ 'ɔːrθ ə- -oʊ-
orthodontic ,ɔːθ əʊ 'dɒnt ɪk ◄ ‖ ,ɔːrθ ə 'daːnt̬
  ɪk ◄ **~s** s
orthodontist ,ɔːθ əʊ 'dɒnt ɪst §-əst
  ‖ ,ɔːrθ ə 'daːnt̬ əst **~s** s
orthodox, O~ 'ɔːθ ə dɒks ‖ 'ɔːrθ ə daːks
  ,**Orthodox 'Church**
orthodox|y 'ɔːθ ə dɒks li ‖ 'ɔːrθ ə daːks li **~ies**
  iz
orthoepic ,ɔːθ əʊ 'ep ɪk ‖ ,ɔːrθ oʊ-
orthoep|ist/s 'ɔːθ əʊ ,ep ɪst/s §-əst/s, , • • ' • •;
  ɔː 'θəʊ ɪp-, -' • əp- ‖ 'ɔːrθ oʊ- **~y** i
orthogonal ɔː 'θɒg ᵊn ᵊl ‖ ɔːr 'θaːg- **~ly** i
orthographer ɔː 'θɒg rəf ə ‖ ɔːr 'θaːg rəf ᵊr
  ~s z
orthographic ,ɔːθ ə 'græf ɪk ◄ ‖ ,ɔːrθ- **~ally**
  ᵊl_i
orthograph|y ɔː 'θɒg rəf li ‖ ɔːr 'θaːg- **~ies** iz
orthopaed|ic, orthoped|ic ,ɔːθ ə 'piːd ɪk ◄
  ‖ ,ɔːrθ- **~ics** ɪks **~ist/s** ɪst/s §əst/s ‖ əst/s
  ~y i

orthopter|a ɔː ˈθɒpt ər ǀə ǁ ɔːr ˈθɑːpt- **~an** ən
~ous əs
orthoptic ɔː ˈθɒpt ɪk ǁ ɔːr ˈθɑːpt ɪk **~s** s
orthostich|ous ɔː ˈθɒst ɪk ǀəs -ək- ǁ ɔːr ˈθɑːst-
~y i
orthotic ɔː ˈθɒt ɪk ǁ ɔːr ˈθɑːt ɪk **~s** s
ortolan ˈɔːt əl ən -ə læn ǁ ˈɔːrt̬ əl ən **~s** z
Orton ˈɔːt ən ǁ ˈɔːrt ən
Ortonesque ˌɔːt ə ˈnesk ◄—►-ən ˈesk
ǁ ˌɔːrt ən ˈesk ◄
orts ɔːts ǁ ɔːrts
Orville ˈɔː vɪl ˈɔːv əl ǁ ˈɔːrv əl
Orwell ˈɔː wel -wəl ǁ ˈɔːr-
Orwellian ɔː ˈwel i‿ən ǁ ɔːr-
-ory ər i ǁ ər i, ɔːr i ʊʊr i —This suffix is usually
stress-neutral when attached to a free stem
(diˈrectory, ˈpromissory); otherwise it imposes
stress on one of the two preceding syllables
(perˈfunctory, ˈrepertory). It has a strong vowel
in AmE (-ɔːr i) if the preceding vowel is weak
(ˈdormitory); otherwise, and always in BrE, it
has a weak vowel.
oryx ˈɒr ɪks ǁ ˈɔːr- ˈɑːr-, ˈoʊr- **~es** ɪz əz
os *'bone'; 'mouth'* ɒs ǁ ɑːs
Osag|e ˌoʊ ˈseɪdʒ ˈ•• ǁ ˌoʊ- **~es** ɪz əz
Osaka əʊ ˈsɑːk ə ˈ•••, ˈɔːs ək ə ǁ oʊ- —Jp
[o,o sa ka]
Osama bin Laden əʊ ˌsɑːm ə bɪn ˈlɑːd ən -en
ǁ oʊ- —Arabic [u ˈsaː ma bin ˈlaː dan]
Osbert ˈɒz bət -bɜːt ǁ ˈɑːz bərt
Osborn, Osborne, Osbourne ˈɒz bɔːn -bən
ǁ ˈɑːz bɔːrn
Oscan ˈɒsk ən ǁ ˈɑːsk-
Oscar, oscar ˈɒsk ə ǁ ˈɑːsk ər
oscil|late ˈɒs ɪ ǀleɪt -ə-, -əl eɪt ǁ ˈɑːs- **~lated**
leɪt ɪd -əd ǁ leɪt̬ əd **~lates** leɪts **~lating**
leɪt ɪŋ ǁ leɪt̬ ɪŋ
oscillation ˌɒs ɪ ˈleɪʃ ən -ə-, -əl ˈeɪʃ- ǁ ˌɑːs- **~s**
z
oscillator ˈɒs ɪ leɪt ə ˈ•ə-, -əl eɪt- ǁ ˈɑːs ə leɪt̬ ər
~s z
oscillatory ˈɒs ɪl ət ər i ˈ•əl-; ˌɒs ɪ ˈleɪt ər i,
ˌ•ə-, ˈ••••• ǁ ˈɑːs əl ə tɔːr i -toʊr i
oscillo- *comb. form*
with stress-neutral suffix ə ¦sɪl əʊ ɒ- ǁ ə ¦sɪl ə
— **oscillographic** ə ˌsɪl əʊ ˈgræf ɪk ◄ ɒ-
ǁ ə ˌsɪl ə-
with stress-imposing suffix ˌɒs ɪ ˈlɒ+ -ə-
ǁ ˌɑːs ə ˈlɑː+ — **oscillography**
ˌɒs ɪ ˈlɒg rəf i -ə- ǁ ˌɑːs ə ˈlɑːg-
oscillogram ə ˈsɪl ə græm ɒ- ǁ ɑː- **~s** z
oscillograph ə ˈsɪl ə grɑːf ɒ-, -græf ǁ -græf ɑː-
~s s
oscilloscope ə ˈsɪl ə skəʊp ɒ- ǁ -skoʊp ɑː- **~s**
s
Osco-Umbrian ˌɒsk əʊ ˈʌm bri‿ən ◄ ǁ ˌɑːsk oʊ-
osculant ˈɒsk jʊl ənt -jəl- ǁ ˈɑːsk jəl-
oscular ˈɒsk jʊl ə -jəl- ǁ ˈɑːsk jə lər
oscu|late ˈɒsk jʊ ǀleɪt ǁ ˈɑːsk jə- **~lated** leɪt ɪd
-əd ǁ leɪt̬ əd **~lates** leɪts **~lating**
leɪt ɪŋ ǁ leɪt̬ ɪŋ
osculation ˌɒsk jʊ ˈleɪʃ ən -jə- ǁ ˌɑːsk jə- **~s** z

osculatory ˈɒsk jʊl ət ˌər i ˈ•ˌjəl-,
ˌɒsk ju ˈleɪt ˌər i ǁ ˈɑːsk jəl ə tɔːr i -toʊr i
oscul|um ˈɒsk jʊl ǀəm -jəl- ǁ ˈɑːsk jəl- **~a** ə
-oses ˈəʊs iːz ǁ ˈoʊs iːz — **fibroses**
faɪ ˈbrəʊs iːz ǁ -ˈbroʊs-
Osgood ˈɒz gʊd ǁ ˈɑːz-
O'Shaughnessy əʊ ˈʃɔːn əs i -ɪs- ǁ oʊ- -ˈʃɑːn-
O'Shea *(i)* əʊ ˈʃeɪ ǁ oʊ-, *(ii)* -ˈʃiː
Oshkosh ˈɒʃ kɒʃ ǁ ˈɑːʃ kɑːʃ
osier ˈəʊz i‿ə ˈəʊʒ ə, ˈəʊʒ i‿ə ǁ ˈoʊʒ ər ˈoʊz i‿ər
~s z
Osijek ˈɒs i ek ǁ ˈoʊs- —Croatian [ˈɔ si jɛk]
Osiris əʊ ˈsaɪər ɪs ɒ-, §-əs ǁ oʊ-
-osis ˈəʊs ɪs §-əs ǁ ˈoʊs əs — **ornithosis**
ˌɔːn ɪ ˈθəʊs ɪs -ə-, §-əs ǁ ˌɔːr nə ˈθoʊs əs
-osity ˈɒs ət i -ɪt i ǁ ˈɑːs ət̬ i— **verbosity**
vɜː ˈbɒs ət i -ɪt i ǁ vɜːˈ ˈbɑːs ət̬ i
Oslo ˈɒz ləʊ ˈɒs- ǁ ˈɑːz loʊ ˈɑːs- —Norw
[ˈˈus lu]
Osman ɒz ˈmɑːn ɒs-; ˈɒz mən ǁ ˈɑːz mən ˈɑːs-
Osmanli ɒz ˈmæn li ɒs-, -ˈmɑːn- ǁ ɑːz- ɑːs- **~s**
z
Osmiroid *tdmk* ˈɒz mə rɔɪd -mi- ǁ ˈɑːz-
osmium ˈɒz mi‿əm ǁ ˈɑːz-
Osmond ˈɒz mənd ǁ ˈɑːz- **~s** z
osmosis ɒz ˈməʊs ɪs ɒs-, §-əs ǁ ɑːs ˈmoʊs əs
ɑːz-
Osmotherley, Osmotherly
ɒz ˈmʌð ə li ǁ ɑːz ˈmʌð ər-
osmotic ɒz ˈmɒt ɪk ɒs- ǁ ɑːz ˈmɑːt̬ ɪk ɑːs-
~ally əl_i
Osmund, o~ ˈɒz mənd ǁ ˈɑːz- ˈɑːs-
osmunda ɒz ˈmʌnd ə ǁ ɑːz- ɑːs-
Osnabruck, Osnabrück ˈɒz nə brʊk ǁ ˈɑːz-
—Ger [ˈʔɔs na ˈbʁʏk]
Osnaburg, Osnaburgh, o~ ˈɒz nə bɜːg
ǁ ˈɑːz nə bɜːˈg
osprey ˈɒsp ri -reɪ ǁ ˈɑːsp- **~s** z
Ossa ˈɒs ə ǁ ˈɑːs ə
osseous ˈɒs i‿əs ǁ ˈɑːs- **~ly** li
Osset ˈɒs ɪt §-ət ǁ ˈɑːs- **~s** s
Ossetia ɒ ˈset i‿ə ɒ ˈsiːʃ ə ǁ ɑː ˈset̬ i‿ə ɑː ˈsiːʃ ə
Ossetian ɒ ˈset i‿ən ɒ ˈsiːʃ ən ǁ ɑː ˈset̬ i‿ən
ɑː ˈsiːʃ ən **~s** z
Ossetic ɒ ˈset ɪk ǁ ɑː ˈset̬ ɪk
Ossett ˈɒs ɪt §-ət ǁ ˈɑːs-
Ossian ˈɒs i‿ən ǁ ˈɑːʃ ən ˈɑːs i‿ən
Ossianic ˌɒs i ˈæn ɪk ◄ ǁ ˌɑːs- ˌɑːʃ-
ossicle ˈɒs ɪk əl ǁ ˈɑːs- **~s** z
ossification ˌɒs ɪf i ˈkeɪʃ ən, ˈ•əf-, §-əˈ•- ǁ ˌɑːs-
ossifrag|e ˈɒs ɪf rɪdʒ -ə-, -ɪ freɪdʒ, -ə- ǁ ˈɑːs-
~es ɪz əz
ossi|fy ˈɒs ɪ ǀfaɪ -ə- ǁ ˈɑːs- **~fied** faɪd **~fies**
faɪz **~fying** faɪ ɪŋ
Ossining ˈɒs ən ɪŋ -ɪn- ǁ ˈɑːs-
osso bucco, osso buco ˌɒs əʊ ˈbʊk əʊ-ˈbuːk-
ǁ ˌoʊs oʊ ˈbuːk oʊ ɑːs- —It [ˌɔs so ˈbu ko]
ossuar|y ˈɒs ju‿ər li ǁ ˈɑːs ju er li **~ies** iz
osteitis ˌɒst i ˈaɪt ɪs §-əs ǁ ˌɑːst i ˈaɪt̬ əs
Ostend ˌɒst ˈend ǁ ˌɑːst- —Dutch Oostende
[oːst ˈen də], —Fr Ostende [ɔs ˈtɑ̃ːd]
ostensib|le ɒ ˈstenˈs əb ǀəl -ɪb- ǁ ɑː- ə- **~ly** li
ostensive ɒ ˈstenˈs ɪv ǁ ɑː- **~ly** li

ostentation ˌɒst en 'teɪʃ ⁿn -ən- ‖ ˌɑːst-
ostentatious ˌɒst en 'teɪʃ əs ◂ -ən- ‖ ˌɑːst-
~ly li ~ness nəs nɪs
osteo- comb. form
  with stress-neutral suffix ˈɒst i‿əʊ ‖ ˈɑːst i‿ə
  — osteoclast 'ɒst i‿əʊ klæst ‖ 'ɑːst i‿ə-
  with stress-imposing suffix
  ˌɒst i 'ɒ+ ‖ ˌɑːst i 'ɑː+ — osteology
  ˌɒst i 'ɒl ədʒ i ‖ ˌɑːst i 'ɑːl-
osteoarthritis ˌɒst i‿əʊ ɑː ˈθraɪt ɪs §-əs
  ‖ ˌɑːst i‿ʊ ɑːr 'θraɪt̬ əs
osteomalacia ˌɒst i‿əʊ mə 'leɪʃ i‿ə -'leɪʃ ə
  ‖ ˌɑːst i‿ʊ-
osteomyelitis ˌɒst i‿əʊ ˌmaɪ‿ə 'laɪt ɪs §-əs
  ‖ ˌɑːst i‿ʊ ˌmaɪ ə 'laɪt̬ əs
osteopath 'ɒst i‿əʊ pæθ ‖ 'ɑːst i‿ə- ~s s
osteopathic ˌɒst i‿əʊ 'pæθ ɪk ◂ ‖ ˌɑːst i‿ə-
  ~ally ᵊl‿i
osteopathy ˌɒst i 'ɒp əθ i ‖ ˌɑːst i 'ɑːp-
osteoporosis ˌɒst i‿əʊ pɔː 'rəʊs ɪs §-əs
  ‖ ˌɑːst i‿ʊ pə 'roʊs əs
Osterley 'ɒst ə li →-ᵊl i ‖ 'ɑːst ᵊr-
Ostermilk tdmk 'ɒst ə mɪlk ‖ 'ɑːst ᵊr-
Ostia 'ɒst i‿ə ‖ 'ɑːst-
ostiar|y 'ɒst i‿ər i ‖ ‖ 'ɑːst i er li ~ies iz
ostinato ˌɒst ɪ 'nɑːt əʊ -ə- ‖ ˌɑːst ə 'nɑːt̬ oʊ
  ˌɔːst- ~s z
osti|um 'ɒst i‿ləm ‖ 'ɑːst- ~a ə
ostler, O~ 'ɒs lə ‖ 'ɑːs lᵊr ~s z
ostom|y 'ɒst əm| i ‖ 'ɑːst- ~ies iz —see also
  -stomy
ostracis... —see ostraciz...
ostracism 'ɒs trə ˌsɪz əm ‖ 'ɑːs- ~s z
ostraciz|e 'ɒs trə saɪz ‖ 'ɑːs- ~ed d ~es ɪz əz
  ~ing ɪŋ
Ostrava 'ɒs trəv ə ‖ 'ɔːs- 'ɑːs-, 'oʊs- —Czech
  ['ɔ stra va]
ostrich 'ɒs trɪtʃ -trɪdʒ ‖ 'ɑːs- 'ɔːs- ~es ɪz əz
  'ostrich egg; 'ostrich ˌfeather
Ostrogoth 'ɒs trəʊ gɒθ ‖ 'ɑːs trə gɑːθ ~s s
Ostrogothic ˌɒs trəʊ
  'gɒθ ɪk ◂ ‖ ˌɑːs trə 'gɑːθ ɪk ◂
Ostwald 'ɒst vælt ‖ 'ɑːst- —Ger ['ɔst valt]
Ostyak 'ɒst jæk 'ɒst i æk ‖ 'ɑːst jɑːk -i ɑːk,
  -æk ~s s
O'Sullivan əʊ 'sʌl ɪv ən -əv- ‖ oʊ-
Oswald 'ɒz wəld ‖ 'ɑːz-
Oswaldtwistle 'ɒz wəld ˌtwɪs ᵊl -ᵊl- ‖ 'ɑːz-
Oswego ɒ 'swiːg əʊ -'zwiːg- ‖ ɑː 'swiːg oʊ
Oswestry 'ɒz wəs tri -wɪs- ‖ 'ɑːz-
Osyth 'əʊz ɪθ 'əʊs- ‖ 'oʊz-
Otago əʊ 'tɑːg əʊ ɒ- ‖ oʊ 'tɑːg oʊ
Otaheite ˌəʊt ə 'hiːt i -'heɪt- ‖ ˌoʊt̬ ə 'hiːt̬ i
otarine 'əʊt ə raɪn ‖ 'oʊt̬-
otar|y 'əʊt ər| i ‖ 'oʊt̬- ~ies iz
O tempora! O mores ₍ᵢ₎əʊ 'temp
  ər ə ₍ᵢ₎əʊ 'mɔːr iːz -eɪz, -eɪs ‖ ₍ᵢ₎oʊ 'temp
  ər ə ₍ᵢ₎oʊ- -'mour-
Otford 'ɒt fəd ‖ 'ɑːt fᵊrd
Othello əʊ 'θel əʊ ɒ- ‖ ə 'θel oʊ oʊ-
other 'ʌð ə ‖ 'ʌð ᵊr others 'ʌð əz ‖ -ᵊrz
otherwise 'ʌð ə waɪz ‖ -ᵊr-

otherworld|ly ˌʌð ə 'wɜːld |li ◂ ‖ -ᵊr- 'wɜːld-
  ~liness li nəs -nɪs
Othman ɒθ 'mɑːn ‖ ɑːθ-
Otho 'əʊθ əʊ ‖ 'oʊθ oʊ
otic 'əʊt ɪk 'ɒt- ‖ 'oʊt̬ ɪk 'ɑːt̬-
-otic 'ɒt ɪk ‖ 'ɑːt̬ ɪk —but 'əʊt ɪk ‖ 'oʊt̬ ɪk when
  not related to a noun in -osis — symbiotic
  ˌsɪm baɪ 'ɒt ɪk ◂ ‖ -'ɑːt̬ ɪk ◂ — periotic
  ˌper i 'ɒt ɪk ◂ ‖ -'oʊt̬ ɪk ◂
otiose 'əʊt i‿əʊs 'əʊʃ-, -əʊz; 'əʊʃ i‿əs
  ‖ 'oʊʃ i oʊs 'oʊt̬- ~ly li
otiosity ˌəʊt i 'ɒs ət i ˌəʊʃ-, -ɪt i ‖ ˌoʊʃ i 'ɑːs ət̬ i
  ˌoʊt̬-
Otis 'əʊt ɪs §-əs ‖ 'oʊt̬ əs
otitis əʊ 'taɪt ɪs §-əs ‖ oʊ 'taɪt̬ əs
Otley 'ɒt li ‖ 'ɑːt-
oto- comb. form
  with stress-neutral suffix ˈəʊt əʊ ‖ ˈoʊt̬ ə —
  otocyst 'əʊt əʊ sɪst ‖ 'oʊt̬ ə-
  with stress-imposing suffix əʊ 'tɒ+ ‖ oʊ 'tɑː+
  — otology əʊ 'tɒl ədʒ i ‖ oʊ 'tɑːl-
otolaryngolog|ist/s ˌəʊt əʊ
  ˌlær ɪŋ 'gɒl ədʒ |ɪst/s §-əst/s
  ‖ ˌoʊt̬ oʊ ˌlær ɪŋ 'gɑːl- -ˌler- ~y i
O'Toole əʊ 'tuːl ‖ oʊ-
Otranto ɒ 'trænt əʊ 'ɒtr ən təʊ ‖ oʊ 'trɑːnt oʊ
  —It ['ɔː tran to]
OTT ˌəʊ tiː 'tiː ‖ ˌoʊ-
ottar 'ɒt ə ‖ 'ɑːt̬ ᵊr
ottava əʊ 'tɑːv ə ɒ- ‖ oʊ-
  otˌtava 'rima 'riːm ə
Ottawa 'ɒt ə wə ‖ 'ɑːt̬ ə wə -waː, -wɔː
otter 'ɒt ə ‖ 'ɑːt̬ ᵊr ~s z
Otterburn 'ɒt ə bɜːn ‖ 'ɑːt̬ ᵊr bɜːrn
Ottery 'ɒt ər i ‖ 'ɑːt̬-
ottfur hook 'ɒt fə hʊk §-huːk ‖ 'ɑːt fᵊr- ~s s
Otto, otto 'ɒt əʊ ‖ 'ɑːt̬ oʊ
Ottoline 'ɒt ə lɪn -ᵊl ɪn ‖ 'ɑːt̬-
ottoman, O~ 'ɒt ə mən -əʊ- ‖ 'ɑːt̬- ~s z
Otway 'ɒt weɪ ‖ 'ɑːt-
ouabain ˌwaː 'beɪ ɪn -'baː-, '•••
Ouachita 'wɒʃ ə tɔː ‖ 'waːʃ- -taː ~s z
Ouagadougou ˌwaːg ə 'duːg uː ˌwæg-
oubliette ˌuːb li 'et ~s s
ouch aʊtʃ
oud uːd ouds uːdz
Oudenaarde, Oudenarde 'uːd ə nɑːd -ᵊn ɑːd
  ‖ -nɑːrd —Dutch ['ɔu də naːr də]
Oudh aʊd
ought ɔːt ‖ ɑːt —The combination ought to is
  often pronounced with a single t, as
  'ɔːt ə ‖ 'ɔːt̬ ə (esp. before a consonant sound;
  also, esp. BrE, 'ɔːt u before a vowel sound).
Oughtershaw 'aʊt ə ʃɔː ‖ 'aʊt̬ ᵊr- -ʃaː
Oughterside 'aʊt ə saɪd ‖ 'aʊt̬ ᵊr-
oughtn't 'ɔːt ənt →-ən ‖ 'ɑːt-
Oughton (i) 'aʊt ən, (ii) 'ɔːt ən ‖ 'ɑːt-
Ouida 'wiːd ə
ouija, O~ tdmk 'wiːdʒ ə -aː, -i
  'ouija board
ould dialectal form of old aʊld
Ould family name (i) əʊld →ɒʊld ‖ oʊld, (ii)
  uːld

Oulton 'əʊlt ən→'ɒʊlt- ‖ 'oʊlt ən
ounce aʊnts **ounces** 'aʊnts ɪz -əz
Oundle 'aʊnd əl
our 'aʊ‿ə ɑː ‖ 'aʊ‿ər ɑːr —*Some speakers use* ɑː ‖ ɑːr *as the weak form,* 'aʊ‿ə ‖ 'aʊ‿ər *as the strong; others use only one or only the other. In RP the latter form in any case readily undergoes smoothing (see* COMPRESSION*) to* [aː, ɑː]*.*
　,Our 'Father; ₍ᵢ₎Our 'Lady; ₍ᵢ₎Our 'Lord
-our ə ‖ ər — **armour** 'ɑːm ə ‖ 'ɑːrm ər
ours 'aʊ‿əz ɑːz ‖ 'aʊ‿ərz ɑːrz
our|self ₍ᵢ₎aʊ‿ə ‖'self ɑː ‖'self ‖ ₍ᵢ₎aʊ‿ər ‖'self ɑːr ‖'self **~selves** 'selvz
-ous əs — **hazardous** 'hæz əd əs ‖ -ərd-
　carnivorous kɑː 'nɪv ər‿əs ‖ kɑːr-
Ouse uːz
ousel 'uːz əl **~s** z
Ouseley, Ousley 'uːz li
Ouspensky u 'spentsk i —*Russ* [u 'sp̡ienj si̯ku̯ij]
oust aʊst **ousted** 'aʊst ɪd -əd **ousting** 'aʊst ɪŋ **ousts** aʊsts
ouster 'aʊst ə ‖ -ər **~s** z
out aʊt **outed** 'aʊt ɪd -əd ‖ 'aʊt̬ əd **outing** 'aʊt ɪŋ ‖ 'aʊt̬ ɪŋ **outs** aʊts
out- ˌaʊt
outag|e 'aʊt ɪdʒ ‖ 'aʊt̬- **~es** ɪz əz
out-and-out ˌaʊt ən 'aʊt ◂ -ənd-
　ˌout-and-ˌout 'failure
outback, O~ 'aʊt bæk
outbalanc|e ˌaʊt 'bæl ənts **~ed** t **~es** ɪz əz
　~ing ɪŋ
outbid ˌaʊt 'bɪd **~ding** ɪŋ **~s** z
outboard 'aʊt bɔːd ‖ -bɔːrd -boʊrd **~s** z
　ˌoutboard 'motor
outbound 'aʊt baʊnd
outbrav|e ˌaʊt 'breɪv **~ed** d **~es** z **~ing** ɪŋ
outbreak 'aʊt breɪk **~s** s
outbuilding 'aʊt ˌbɪld ɪŋ **~s** z
outburst 'aʊt bɜːst ‖ -bɜːːst **~s** s
outcast, outcaste 'aʊt kɑːst §-kæst ‖ -kæst **~s** s
outclass ˌaʊt 'klɑːs §-'klæs ‖ -'klæs **~ed** t **~es** ɪz əz **~ing** ɪŋ
outcome 'aʊt kʌm **~s** z
outcrop 'aʊt krɒp ‖ -krɑːp **~ped** t **~ping** ɪŋ **~s** s
out|cry 'aʊt ˌkraɪ **~cries** kraɪz
out|date ˌaʊt ‖'deɪt **~dated** 'deɪt ɪd ◂ -əd ‖ 'deɪt̬ əd ◂ **~dates** 'deɪts **~dating** 'deɪt ɪŋ ‖ 'deɪt̬ ɪŋ
outdid ˌaʊt 'dɪd
outdistanc|e ˌaʊt 'dɪst ənts **~ed** t **~es** ɪz əz **~ing** ɪŋ
out|do ˌaʊt ‖'duː **~did** 'dɪd **~does** 'dʌz **~done** 'dʌn
outdoor ˌaʊt 'dɔː ◂ ‖ -'dɔːr ◂ -'doʊr **~s** z
　ˌoutdoor 'shoes
outer 'aʊt ə ‖ 'aʊt̬ ər
　ˌOuter 'Hebrides
outermost 'aʊt ə məʊst ‖ 'aʊt̬ ər moʊst
outerwear 'aʊt ə weə ‖ 'aʊt̬ ər wer -wær
outfac|e ˌaʊt 'feɪs **~ed** t **~es** ɪz əz **~ing** ɪŋ
outfall 'aʊt fɔːl ‖ -fɑːl **~s** z

outfield 'aʊt fiːəld
outfielder 'aʊt fiːəld ə ‖ -ər **~s** z
out|fight ˌaʊt ‖'faɪt **~fighting** 'faɪt ɪŋ ‖ 'faɪt̬ ɪŋ **~fights** 'faɪts **~fought** 'fɔːt ‖ 'fɑːt
out|fit 'aʊt ‖fɪt **~fits** fɪts **~fitted** fɪt ɪd -əd ‖ fɪt̬ əd **~fitting** fɪt ɪŋ ‖ fɪt̬ ɪŋ
outfitter 'aʊt fɪt ə ‖ -fɪt̬ ər **~s** z
outflank ˌaʊt 'flæŋk **~ed** t **~ing** ɪŋ **~s** s
outflow *n* 'aʊt fləʊ ‖ -floʊ **~s** z
outflow *v* ˌaʊt 'fləʊ ‖ -'floʊ **~ed** d **~ing** ɪŋ **~s** z
outfought ˌaʊt 'fɔːt ‖ -'fɑːt
outfox ˌaʊt 'fɒks ‖ -'fɑːks **~ed** t **~es** ɪz əz **~ing** ɪŋ
outgeneral ˌaʊt 'dʒen ər‿əl **~ed**, **~led** d **~ing**, **~ling** ɪŋ **~s** z
outgo *n* 'aʊt gəʊ ‖ -goʊ **~es** z
outgoing *n* 'aʊt gəʊ ɪŋ ‖ -goʊ- **~s** z
outgoing *adj* ˌaʊt 'gəʊ ɪŋ ◂ '•• ‖ -'goʊ-
outgrew ˌaʊt 'gruː
out-group *n* 'aʊt gruːp **~s** s
out|grow ˌaʊt ‖'grəʊ ‖ -‖'groʊ **~grew** 'gruː **~growing** 'grəʊ ɪŋ ‖ 'groʊ ɪŋ **~grown** 'grəʊn ‖ 'groʊn **~grows** 'grəʊz ‖ 'groʊz
outgrowth 'aʊt grəʊθ ‖ -groʊθ **~s** s
outguess ˌaʊt 'ges **~ed** t **~es** ɪz əz **~ing** ɪŋ
outgun ˌaʊt 'gʌn **~ned** d **~ning** ɪŋ **~s** z
out-Herod ˌaʊt 'her əd **~ed** ɪd əd **~ing** ɪŋ **~s** z
out|house 'aʊt ‖haʊs **~houses** haʊz ɪz -əz
Outhwaite *(i)* 'aʊθ weɪt, *(ii)* 'əʊθ- ‖ 'oʊθ-, *(iii)* 'uːθ-
outing 'aʊt ɪŋ ‖ 'aʊt̬ ɪŋ **~s** z
outlaid ˌaʊt 'leɪd '••
outlander, O~ 'aʊt lænd ə ‖ -ər **~s** z
outlandish ₍ᵢ₎aʊt 'lænd ɪʃ **~ly** li **~ness** nəs nɪs
outlast ˌaʊt 'lɑːst §-'læst ‖ -'læst **~ed** ɪd əd **~ing** ɪŋ **~s** s
outlaw *n, v* 'aʊt lɔː ‖ -lɑː **~ed** d **outlawing** 'aʊt lɔːr ɪŋ ‖ -lɔː- ɪŋ -lɑː- **~s** z
outlaw|ry 'aʊt lɔː ‖ri -lɑː- **~ries** riz
outlay *n* 'aʊt leɪ **~s** z
out|lay *v* ˌaʊt ‖'leɪ '•• **~laid** 'leɪd **~laying** 'leɪ ɪŋ **~lays** 'leɪz
outlet 'aʊt let -lət, -lɪt **~s** s
outlier 'aʊt ˌlaɪ‿ə ‖ -ˌlaɪ‿ər **~s** z
outline *n* 'aʊt laɪn **~s** z
outlin|e *v* 'aʊt laɪn, •'• **~ed** d **~es** z **~ing** ɪŋ
outliv|e ˌaʊt 'lɪv **~ed** d **~es** z **~ing** ɪŋ
outlook 'aʊt lʊk §-luːk **~s** s
outlying 'aʊt ˌlaɪ ɪŋ, •'••
outmaneuve|r, outmanoeuv|re ˌaʊt mə 'nuːv ə ‖ -ər -'njuːv- **~red** əd ‖ ərd **~res** əz ‖ ərz **~ring** ər‿ɪŋ ‖ ər‿ɪŋ
outmarch ˌaʊt 'mɑːtʃ ‖ -'mɑːrtʃ **~ed** t **~es** ɪz əz **~ing** ɪŋ
outmatch ˌaʊt 'mætʃ **~ed** t **~es** ɪz əz **~ing** ɪŋ
outmoded ˌaʊt 'məʊd ɪd ◂ -əd ‖ -'moʊd- **~ly** li **~ness** nəs nɪs
outmost 'aʊt məʊst ‖ -moʊst
outnumber ˌaʊt 'nʌm bə ‖ -bər **~ed** d **outnumbering** ˌaʊt 'nʌm bər‿ɪŋ **~s** z
out-of-date ˌaʊt əv 'deɪt ◂ ‖ ˌaʊt̬-

out-of-door ˌaʊt əv ˈdɔː ◂ ‖ ˌaʊt̮ əv ˈdɔːr ◂ -ˈdoʊr

out-of-pocket ˌaʊt əv ˈpɒk ɪt ◂ §-ət ‖ ˌaʊt̮ əv ˈpɑːk-
   ˌout-of-ˌpocket exˈpenses

out-of-state ˌaʊt əv ˈsteɪt ◂ ‖ ˌaʊt̮-

out-of-the-way ˌaʊt əv ðə ˈweɪ ◂ -ə ðə- ‖ ˌaʊt̮-
   ˌout-of-the-ˌway ˈplaces

outpac|e ˌaʊt ˈpeɪs ~**ed** t ~**es** ɪz əz ~**ing** ɪŋ

outpatient ˈaʊt ˌpeɪʃ ᵊnt ~**s** s

outperform ˌaʊt pə ˈfɔːm ‖ -pᵊr ˈfɔːrm ~**ed** d ~**ing** ɪŋ ~**s** z

outplacement ˈaʊt ˌpleɪs mənt ~**s** s

outplay ˌaʊt ˈpleɪ ~**ed** d ~**ing** ɪŋ ~**s** z

out|point ˌaʊt ˈpɔɪnt ~**pointed** ˈpɔɪnt ɪd -əd ‖ ˈpɔɪnt̮ əd ~**pointing** ˈpɔɪnt ɪŋ ‖ ˈpɔɪnt̮ ɪŋ ~**points** ˈpɔɪnts

outport ˈaʊt pɔːt ‖ -pɔːrt -poʊrt ~**s** s

outpost ˈaʊt pəʊst ‖ -poʊst ~**s** s

outpour n ˈaʊt pɔː ‖ -pɔːr -poʊr ~**s** z

outpour v ˌaʊt ˈpɔː ‖ -ˈpɔːr -ˈpoʊr ~**ed** d
   outpouring ˈaʊt ˌpɔːr ɪŋ ‖ -ˈpoʊr- ~**s** z

outpouring n ˈaʊt ˌpɔːr ɪŋ ˌ•ˈ•• ‖ -ˌpoʊr- ~**s** z

out|put n, v ˈaʊt ˌpʊt ~**puts** pʊts ~**putted** pʊt ɪd -əd ‖ ˈpʊt̮ əd ~**putting** pʊt ɪŋ ‖ ˈpʊt̮ ɪŋ

outrag|e v ˈaʊt reɪdʒ ˌ•ˈ• ~**ed** d ~**es** ɪz əz ~**ing** ɪŋ

outrag|e n ˈaʊt reɪdʒ ~**es** ɪz əz

outrageous ˌaʊt ˈreɪdʒ əs ~**ly** li ~**ness** nəs nɪs

Outram (i) ˈuːtr əm, (ii) ˈaʊtr əm

outran ˌaʊt ˈræn

outrang|e ˌaʊt ˈreɪndʒ ~**ed** d ~**es** ɪz əz ~**ing** ɪŋ

out|rank ˌaʊt ˈræŋk ~**ranked** ˈræŋkt ~**ranking** ˈræŋk ɪŋ ~**ranks** ˈræŋks

outre, outré ˈuːtr eɪ ‖ uː ˈtreɪ —Fr [u tʁe]

outreach v ˌaʊt ˈriːtʃ ~**ed** t ~**es** ɪz əz ~**ing** ɪŋ

outreach n ˈaʊt riːtʃ ~**es** ɪz əz

out|ride ˌaʊt ˈraɪd ~**ridden** ˈrɪd ᵊn ~**rides** ˈraɪdz ~**rode** ˈrəʊd ‖ ˈroʊd

outrider ˈaʊt ˌraɪd ə ‖ -ᵊr ~**s** z

outrigger ˈaʊt ˌrɪg ə ‖ -ᵊr ~**s** z

outright adj ˈaʊt raɪt

outright adv ˌaʊt ˈraɪt ˈ••

outrival ˌaʊt ˈraɪv ᵊl ~**ed**, ~**led** d ~**ing**, ~**ling** ɪŋ ~**s** z

outrode ˌaʊt ˈrəʊd ‖ -ˈroʊd

out|run ˌaʊt ˈrʌn ~**ran** ˈræn ~**running** ˈrʌn ɪŋ ~**runs** ˈrʌnz

outrush ˈaʊt rʌʃ ~**es** ɪz əz

out|sell ˌaʊt ˈsel ~**selling** ˈsel ɪŋ ~**sells** ˈselz ~**sold** ˈsəʊld →ˈsɒʊld ‖ ˈsoʊld

outset ˈaʊt set

out|shine ˌaʊt ˈʃaɪn ~**shines** ˈʃaɪnz ~**shining** ˈʃaɪn ɪŋ ~**shone** ˈʃɒn ‖ ˈʃoʊn (*)

outside ˌaʊt ˈsaɪd ◂ —stressed ˈ•• whenever contrasted with inside ~**s** z
   ˌoutside ˈbroadcast; ˌoutside ˈworld

outsider ˌaʊt ˈsaɪd ə ‖ -ᵊr ~**s** z

outsize ˌaʊt ˈsaɪz ◂ ˈ•• ~**d** d

outskirts ˈaʊt skɜːts ‖ -skɜːrts

out|smart ˌaʊt ˈsmaːt ‖ -ˈsmaːrt ~**smarted** ˈsmaːt ɪd -əd ‖ ˈsmaːrt̮ əd ~**smarting** ˈsmaːt ɪŋ ‖ ˈsmaːrt̮ ɪŋ ~**smarts** ˈsmaːts ‖ ˈsmaːrts

outsourc|e ˈaʊt sɔːs ‖ -sɔːrs -soʊrs ~**ed** t ~**es** ɪz əz ~**ing** ɪŋ

outspan, O~ n ˈaʊt spæn ~**s** z

outspan v ˌaʊt ˈspæn ~**ned** d ~**ning** ɪŋ ~**s** z

outspend ˌaʊt ˈspend ~**ing** ɪŋ ~**s** z
   outspent ˌaʊt ˈspent

outspoken ⍀ˌaʊt ˈspəʊk ᵊn ‖ -ˈspoʊk- ~**ly** li ~**ness** nəs nɪs

outspread v, adj ˌaʊt ˈspred ◂ ~**ing** ɪŋ ~**s** z

outspread n ˈaʊt spred

outstanding ⍀ˌaʊt ˈstænd ɪŋ ~**ly** li

outstar|e ⍀ˌaʊt ˈsteə ‖ -ˈsteᵊr -ˈstæᵊr ~**d** d ~**s** z
   outstaring ˌaʊt ˈsteər ɪŋ ‖ -ˈster ɪŋ -ˈstær-

outstation ˈaʊt ˌsteɪʃ ᵊn ~**ed** d ~**s** z

outstay ˌaʊt ˈsteɪ ~**ed** d ~**ing** ɪŋ ~**s** z

outstretched ˌaʊt ˈstretʃt

outstrip ˌaʊt ˈstrɪp ~**ped** t ~**ping** ɪŋ ~**s** s

outswing ˈaʊt swɪŋ ~**er/s** ə/z ‖ ᵊr/z ~**s** z

outta 'out of' ˈaʊt ə ‖ ˈaʊt̮ ə

out-take ˈaʊt teɪk ~**s** s

outtalk ˌaʊt ˈtɔːk ‖ -ˈtɑːk ~**ed** t ~**ing** ɪŋ ~**s** s

out-tray ˈaʊt treɪ ~**s** z

outturn ˈaʊt tɜːn ‖ -tɜːn ~**s** z

out|vote ˌaʊt ˈvəʊt ‖ -ˈvoʊt ~**voted** ˈvəʊt ɪd -əd ‖ ˈvoʊt̮ əd ~**votes** ˈvəʊts ‖ ˈvoʊts ~**voting** ˈvəʊt ɪŋ ‖ ˈvoʊt̮ ɪŋ

outward ˈaʊt wəd ‖ -wᵊrd ~**ly** li ~**ness** nəs nɪs ~**s** z
   ˌOutward ˈBound

out|wear ˌaʊt ˈweə ‖ -ˈweᵊr -ˈwæᵊr ~**wearing** ˈweər ɪŋ ‖ ˈwer ɪŋ ˈwær- ~**wears** ˈweəz ‖ ˈweᵊrz ˈwæᵊrz ~**worn** ˈwɔːn ◂ ‖ ˈwɔːrn ◂ ˈwoʊrn

outweigh ˌaʊt ˈweɪ ~**ed** d ~**ing** ɪŋ ~**s** z

out|wit ˌaʊt ˈwɪt ~**wits** ˈwɪts ~**witted** ˈwɪt ɪd -əd ‖ ˈwɪt̮ əd ~**witting** ˈwɪt ɪŋ ‖ ˈwɪt̮ ɪŋ

outwith ˌaʊt ˈwɪθ ◂ -ˈwɪð —Since this is mainly a Scottish word, it tends to be said with the θ of Scottish with

outwore ˌaʊt ˈwɔː ‖ -ˈwɔːr -ˈwoʊr

outwork n ˈaʊt wɜːk ‖ -wɜːrk ~**er/s** ə/z ‖ ᵊr/z

out|worn ˌaʊt ˈwɔːn ◂ ‖ -ˈwɔːrn ◂ -ˈwoʊrn

ouzel ˈuːz ᵊl ~**s** z

ouzo ˈuːz əʊ ‖ -oʊ —Gk [ˈu zɔ]

ova ˈəʊv ə ‖ ˈoʊv ə

oval, Oval ˈəʊv ᵊl ‖ ˈoʊv- ~**ly** i ~**ness** nəs nɪs ~**s** z
   ˌOval ˈOffice, ˈ•• ˌ••

Ovaltine tdmk ˈəʊv ᵊl tiːn ‖ ˈoʊv-

Ovambo əʊ ˈvæm bəʊ ‖ oʊ ˈvɑːm boʊ

ovarian əʊ ˈveər i‿ən ‖ oʊ ˈver- -ˈvær-

ovar|y ˈəʊv ᵊr i ‖ ˈoʊv- ~**ies** iz

ovate Welsh title ˈɒv ət -ɪt; ˈəʊv eɪt ‖ ˈɑːv- ~**s** s

ovate 'egg-shaped' ˈəʊv eɪt -ət, -ɪt ‖ ˈoʊv- ~**ly** li

ovation əʊ ˈveɪʃ ᵊn ‖ oʊ- ~**s** z

Ove Arup ˌəʊv ˈær əp ‖ ˌoʊv- -ˈer-

oven ˈʌv ᵊn ~**s** z

ovenbird ˈʌv ᵊn bɜːd →-ᵊm- ‖ -bɜːrd ~**s** z

O

Ovenden *(i)* 'ɒv ᵊn dən ‖ 'ɑːv-, *(ii)*
ˈəʊv- ‖ 'oʊv-

ovenproof 'ʌv ᵊn pruːf →-ᵊm-, §-pruf

oven-ready ˌʌv ᵊn 'red i ◄
ˌoven-ˌready 'turkey

Ovens 'ʌv ᵊnz

ovenware 'ʌv ᵊn weə ‖ -wer -wær

over, Over 'əʊv ə ‖ 'oʊv ᵊr ~s z
ˌover and 'done with

over- ¦əʊv ə ‖ ¦oʊv ᵊr —*but before a vowel
sound,* ¦əʊv ᵊr‖ ¦oʊv ᵊr

overabundance ˌəʊv ᵊr ə 'bʌnd ᵊnᵗs ˌ•'rə'••
‖ ˌoʊv ᵊr

overachiever ˌəʊv ᵊr ə 'tʃiːv ə ˌ•'rə'•• ‖ ˌoʊv
ᵊr ə 'tʃiːv ᵊr ~s z

overact ˌəʊv ᵊr 'ækt ‖ ˌoʊv ᵊr- ~ed ɪd əd
~ing ɪŋ ~s s

overactive ˌəʊv ᵊr 'ækt ɪv ◄ ‖ ˌoʊv ᵊr-

overactivity ˌəʊv ᵊr æk 'tɪv ət i -ɪt i ‖ ˌoʊv
ᵊr æk 'tɪv ət̬ i

overage *adj* 'too old', ˌəʊv ᵊr 'eɪdʒ ◄ ‖ ˌoʊv ᵊr-

overage *n* 'surplus' 'əʊv ᵊr ɪdʒ ‖ 'oʊv-

overall *adj, adv* ˌəʊv ᵊr 'ɔːl ◄ ‖ ˌoʊv ᵊr- -'ɑːl

overall *n* 'əʊv ᵊr ɔːl ‖ 'oʊv ᵊr- -ɑːl ~s z

overambitious ˌəʊv ᵊr æm 'bɪʃ əs ◄ ‖ ˌoʊv ᵊr-
~ly li

overanxiety ˌəʊv ᵊr æŋ 'zaɪ ət i ˌ•'•æŋg-ˌ_ɪt i
‖ ˌoʊv ᵊr æŋ 'zaɪ ət̬ i

overanxious ˌəʊv ᵊr 'æŋk ʃəs ◄ ‖ ˌoʊv ᵊr- -ly
li ~ness nəs nɪs

overarch ˌəʊv ᵊr 'ɑːtʃ ‖ ˌoʊv ᵊr 'ɑːrtʃ ~ed t
~es ɪz əz ~ing ɪŋ

overarm 'əʊv ᵊr ɑːm ‖ 'oʊv ᵊr ɑːrm

overawe ˌəʊv ᵊr 'ɔː ‖ ˌoʊv ᵊr- -'ɑː ~awed
ɔːd ‖ ɑːd ~awes ɔːz ‖ 'ɑːz ~awing
'ɔːʳ ɪŋ ‖ 'ɔː ɪŋ 'ɑː-

overbalanc|e ˌəʊv ə 'bæl ᵊnᵗs ‖ ˌoʊv ᵊr- ~ed t
~es ɪz əz ~ing ɪŋ

over|bear ˌəʊv ə ¦'beə ‖ ˌoʊv ᵊr ¦'beᵊr -'bæᵊr
~bearing/ly 'beər ɪŋ /li ‖ 'ber ɪŋ /li 'bær-
~bore 'bɔː ‖ 'bɔːr 'boʊr ~borne
'bɔːn ‖ 'bɔːrn 'boʊrn

overbid *v* ˌəʊv ə 'bɪd ‖ ˌoʊv ᵊr- ~ding ɪŋ ~s z

overbid *n* 'əʊv ə bɪd ‖ 'oʊv ᵊr- ~s z

overbite 'əʊv ə baɪt ‖ 'oʊv ᵊr-

over|blow *v* ˌəʊv ə ¦'bləʊ ‖ ˌoʊv ᵊr ¦'bloʊ '•••
~blew 'bluː ~blowing 'bləʊ ɪŋ ‖ 'bloʊ ɪŋ
~blown 'bləʊn ‖ 'bloʊn ~blows
'bləʊz ‖ 'bloʊz

overboard 'əʊv ə bɔːd ˌ••'• ‖ 'oʊv ᵊr bɔːrd
-boʊrd

overbook ˌəʊv ə 'bʊk §-'buːk ‖ ˌoʊv ᵊr- ~ed t
~ing ɪŋ ~s s

overbor... —*see* overbear

overbridg|e 'əʊv ə brɪdʒ ‖ 'oʊv ᵊr- ~es ɪz əz

over|burden *v* ˌəʊv ə 'bɜːd ᵊn ‖ ˌoʊv ᵊr 'bɜːd ᵊn
~ed d ~ing ˌ_ɪŋ ~s z

overburden *n*
'əʊv ə ˌbɜːd ᵊn ‖ 'oʊv ᵊr ˌbɜːd ᵊn ~s z

overcall *v* ˌəʊv ə 'kɔːl ‖ ˌoʊv ᵊr- -'kɑːl ~ed d
~ing ɪŋ ~s z

overcall *n* 'əʊv ə kɔːl ‖ 'oʊv ᵊr- -kɑːl ~s z

overcame ˌəʊv ə 'keɪm ‖ ˌoʊv ᵊr-

overcapacity ˌəʊv ə kə 'pæs ət i -ɪt i
‖ ˌoʊv ᵊr kə 'pæs ət̬ i

overcast *adj* ˌəʊv ə 'kɑːst ◄ §-'kæst, '•••
‖ ˌoʊv ᵊr 'kæst ◄

overcast *n* 'əʊv ə kɑːst §-kæst ‖ 'oʊv ᵊr kæst

overcharg|e *v* ˌəʊv ə 'tʃɑːdʒ ‖ ˌoʊv ᵊr 'tʃɑːrdʒ
~ed d ~es ɪz əz ~ing ɪŋ

overcharg|e *n* ˌəʊv ə tʃɑːdʒ ‖ 'oʊv ᵊr tʃɑːrdʒ
~es ɪz əz

overcloud ˌəʊv ə 'klaʊd ‖ ˌoʊv ᵊr- ~ed ɪd əd
~ing ɪŋ ~s z

overcoat 'əʊv ə kəʊt ‖ 'oʊv ᵊr koʊt ~s s

over|come ˌəʊv ə ¦'kʌm ‖ ˌoʊv ᵊr- ~came
'keɪm ~comes 'kʌmz ~coming 'kʌm ɪŋ

overcom|mit ˌəʊv ə kə ¦'mɪt ‖ ˌoʊv ᵊr- ~mits
'mɪts ~mitted 'mɪt ɪd -əd ‖ 'mɪt̬ əd
~mitting 'mɪt ɪŋ ‖ 'mɪt̬ ɪŋ

overcompen|sate ˌəʊv ə 'kɒmp ən ˌseɪt -en-
‖ ˌoʊv ᵊr 'kɑːmp- ~sated seɪt ɪd -əd ‖ seɪt̬ əd
~sates seɪts ~sating seɪt ɪŋ ‖ seɪt̬ ɪŋ

overcompensation ˌəʊv ə ˌkɒmp ən 'seɪʃ ᵊn
-ˌen- ‖ ˌoʊv ᵊr ˌkɑːmp- ~s z

overconfid|ence ˌəʊv ə 'kɒn fɪd ᵊnᵗs -fəd-
‖ ˌoʊv ᵊr 'kɑːn- ~ent/ly ᵊnt /li

overcook ˌəʊv ə 'kʊk ◄ §-'kuːk ‖ ˌoʊv ᵊr- ~ed
t ~ing ɪŋ ~s s

overcrop ˌəʊv ə 'krɒp ‖ ˌoʊv ᵊr 'krɑːp ~ped t
~ping ɪŋ ~s s

overcrowd ˌəʊv ə 'kraʊd ‖ ˌoʊv ᵊr- ~ed ɪd əd
~ing ɪŋ ~s z

overdevelop ˌəʊv ə dɪ 'vel əp -ə də-, §-ə diː-
‖ ˌoʊv ᵊr- ~ed t ~ing ɪŋ ~ment mənt ~s s

over|do ˌəʊv ə ¦'duː ‖ ˌoʊv ᵊr- ~did 'dɪd
~does 'dʌz ~done 'dʌn ◄ ~doing 'duːʳ ɪŋ

overdos|e *n* 'əʊv ə dəʊs §-dəʊz ‖ 'oʊv ᵊr doʊs
~es ɪz əz

overdos|e *v* ˌəʊv ə 'dəʊs §-'dəʊz
‖ ˌoʊv ᵊr 'doʊs ~ed t ~es ɪz əz ~ing ɪŋ

overdraft 'əʊv ə drɑːft §-dræft ‖ 'oʊv ᵊr dræft
~s s

over|draw ˌəʊv ə‖ 'drɔː ‖ ˌoʊv ᵊr‖- -'drɑː, '•••
~drawing 'drɔːʳ ɪŋ ‖ 'drɔː ɪŋ 'drɑː- ~drawn
'drɔːn ◄ ‖ 'drɑːn ~draws 'drɔːz ‖ 'drɑːz
~drew 'druː

overdress *v* ˌəʊv ə 'dres ‖ ˌoʊv ᵊr- ~ed t ◄ ~es
ɪz əz ~ing ɪŋ

overdress *n* 'əʊv ə dres ‖ 'oʊv ᵊr- ~es ɪz əz

overdrew ˌəʊv ə 'druː ‖ ˌoʊv ᵊr- '•••

overdrive *n* 'əʊv ə draɪv ‖ 'oʊv ᵊr-

overdue ˌəʊv ə 'djuː ◄ →§-'dʒuː
‖ ˌoʊv ᵊr 'duː ◄ -'djuː
ˌoverdue 'bills

over|eat ˌəʊv ᵊr/ 'iːt ‖ ˌoʊv ᵊr‖ 'iːt ~ate 'et
'eɪt ‖ 'eɪt ~eaten 'iːt ᵊn ~eating
'iːt ɪŋ ‖ 'iːt̬ ɪŋ ~eats 'iːts

overesti|mate *v* ˌəʊv ᵊr 'est ɪ ˌmeɪt -'•ə-
‖ ˌoʊv ᵊr- ~mated meɪt ɪd -əd ‖ meɪt̬ əd
~mates meɪts ~mating meɪt ɪŋ ‖ meɪt̬ ɪŋ

overestimate *n* ˌəʊv ᵊr 'est ɪm ət -'•əm-, -ɪt;
-ɪ meɪt, -ə meɪt ‖ ˌoʊv ᵊr- ~s s

overex|cite ˌəʊv ᵊr ɪk ¦'saɪt -ek'•, -ək'•,
ˌ•rɪk'•, ˌ•rək'• ‖ ˌoʊv ᵊr- ~cited 'saɪt ɪd

-əd ‖ ˈsaɪt̬ əd **~citement** ˈsaɪt mənt **~cites**
ˈsaɪts **~citing** ˈsaɪt ɪŋ ‖ ˈsaɪt̬ ɪŋ

overe|xert ˌəʊv ər ɪg ˈˌzɜːt -eg'•, -əg'•, -ɪk'•,
-ek'•, -ək'•, ˌ•rɪg'•, ˌ•rəg'• ‖ ˌoʊv
ər ɪg ˈzɜːt **~xerted** ˈzɜːt ɪd -əd ‖ ˈzɜːt̬ əd
~xerting ˈzɜːt ɪŋ ‖ ˈzɜːt̬ ɪŋ **~xerts**
ˈzɜːts ‖ ˈzɜːts

overexertion ˌəʊv ər ɪg ˈzɜːʃ ᵊn -eg'•, -əg'•,
-ɪk'•, -ek'•, -ək'•, ˌ•rɪg'•, ˌ•rəg'• ‖ ˌoʊv
ər ɪg ˈzɜːʃ ᵊn **~s** z

overexpos|e ˌəʊv ər ɪk ˈspəʊz -ek'•, -ək'•,
ˌ•rɪk'•, ˌ•rək'• ‖ ˌoʊv ər ɪk ˈspoʊz **~ed** d
~es ɪz əz **~ing** ɪŋ

overexposure ˌəʊv ər ɪk ˈspəʊʒ ə -ek'••,
-ək'••, ˌ•rɪk'•, ˌ•rək'• ‖ ˌoʊv ər ɪk ˈspoʊʒ ər
~s z

overextend ˌəʊv ər ɪk ˈstend -ek'•, -ək'•,
ˌ•rɪk'•, ˌ•rək'• ‖ ˌoʊv ər_ **~ed** ɪd ◄ əd
~ing ɪŋ **~s** z

over|feed ˌəʊv ə ‖ ˈfiːd ‖ ˌoʊv ər- **~fed** ˈfed
~feeding ˈfiːd ɪŋ **~feeds** ˈfiːdz

over|flew ˌəʊv ə ‖ ˈfluː ‖ ˌoʊv ər- **~flies** ˈflaɪz

overflight ˈəʊv ə flaɪt ‖ ˈoʊv ər- **~s** s

overflow v ˌəʊv ə ‖ ˈfləʊ ‖ ˌoʊv ər ˈfloʊ **~ed** d
~ing ɪŋ **~s** z

overflow n ˈəʊv ə fləʊ ‖ ˈoʊv ər floʊ **~s** z

over|fly ˌəʊv ə ‖ ˈflaɪ ◄ ‖ ˌoʊv ər- **~flew** ˈfluː
~flies ˈflaɪz **~flown** ˈfləʊn ‖ ˈfloʊn **~flying**
ˈflaɪ ɪŋ

overfond ˌəʊv ə ‖ ˈfɒnd ◄ ‖ ˌoʊv ər ˈfɑːnd ◄

overgarment
ˈəʊv ə ˌgɑːm ənt ‖ ˈoʊv ər ˌgɑːrm ənt **~s** s

overgeneralis... —*see* **overgeneraliz...**

overgeneralization
ˌəʊv ə ˌdʒen ᵊr_əl aɪ ˈzeɪʃ ᵊn _əl ɪ-
‖ ˌoʊv ər ˌdʒen ᵊr_əl ə ˈzeɪʃ ᵊn

overgeneraliz|e ˌəʊv ə ˈdʒen ᵊr_ə
laɪz ‖ ˌoʊv ər- **~ed** d **~es** ɪz əz **~ing** ɪŋ

overgraz|e ˌəʊv ə ˈgreɪz ‖ ˌoʊv ər- **~ed** d **~es**
ɪz əz **~ing** ɪŋ

overgrown ˌəʊv ə ˈgrəʊn ◄ ‖ ˌoʊv ər ˈgroʊn ◄
ˌovergrown ˈgarden

overgrowth ˈəʊv ə grəʊθ ‖ ˈoʊv ər groʊθ

overhand ˈəʊv ə hænd ‖ ˈoʊv ər-

over|hang v ˌəʊv ə ‖ ˈhæŋ ‖ ˌoʊv ər- **~hanging**
ˈhæŋ ɪŋ ◄ **~hangs** ˈhæŋz **~hung** ˈhʌŋ ◄

overhang n ˈəʊv ə hæŋ ‖ ˈoʊv ər- **~s** z

overhast|y ˌəʊv ə ˈheɪst li ‖ ˌoʊv ər- **~ily** ɪ li
əl i **~iness** i nəs i nɪs

overhaul v ˌəʊv ə ˈhɔːl ‖ ˌoʊv ər- -ˈhɑːl **~ed** d
~ing ɪŋ **~s** z

overhaul n ˈəʊv ə hɔːl ‖ ˈoʊv ər- -hɑːl **~s** z

overhead adj, adv ˌəʊv ə ˈhed ◄ ‖ ˌoʊv ər-
ˌoverhead ˈcamshaft; ˌoverhead proˈjector

overhead n ˈəʊv ə hed ‖ ˈoʊv ər- **~s** z

over|hear ˌəʊv ə ‖ ˈhɪə ‖ ˌoʊv ər ˈhɪʳr **~heard**
ˈhɜːd ◄ ‖ ˈhɜːd ◄ (!) **~hearing**
ˈhɪər ɪŋ ‖ ˈhɪr ɪŋ **~hears** ˈhɪəz ‖ ˈhɪʳrz

over|heat ˌəʊv ə ‖ ˈhiːt ‖ ˌoʊv ər- **~heated**
ˈhiːt ɪd -əd ‖ ˈhiːt̬ əd **~heating**
ˈhiːt ɪŋ ‖ ˈhiːt̬ ɪŋ **~heats** ˈhiːts

overhung ˌəʊv ə ˈhʌŋ ◄ ‖ ˌoʊv ər-

overindulg|e ˌəʊv ər ɪn ˈdʌldʒ ‖ ˌoʊv ər- **~ed**
d **~ence** ᵊnts **~ent/ly** ᵊnt /li **~es** ɪz əz
~ing ɪŋ

overjoyed ˌəʊv ə ˈdʒɔɪd ◄ ‖ ˌoʊv ər-

overkill ˈəʊv ə kɪl ‖ ˈoʊv ər-

overladen ˌəʊv ə ˈleɪd ᵊn ◄ ‖ ˌoʊv ər-

overlaid ˌəʊv ə ˈleɪd ◄ ‖ ˌoʊv ər-

overland ˈəʊv ə lænd ˌ••'•◄ ‖ ˈoʊv ər- **~er/s**
ə/z ‖ ᵊr/z

overlap v ˌəʊv ə ˈlæp ‖ ˌoʊv ər- **~ped** t **~ping**
ɪŋ **~s** s

overlap n ˈəʊv ə læp ‖ ˈoʊv ər- **~s** s

over|lay v ˌəʊv ə ‖ˈleɪ ‖ ˌoʊv ər- **~laid** ˈleɪd
~laying ˈleɪ ɪŋ **~lays** ˈleɪz

overlay n ˈəʊv ə leɪ ‖ ˈoʊv ər- **~s** z

overleaf ˌəʊv ə ˈliːf '•••◄ ‖ ˈoʊv ər liːf

over|leap ˌəʊv ə ‖ˈliːp ‖ ˌoʊv ər- **~leaped** ˈlept
ˈliːpt ‖ ˈliːpt **~leaping** ˈliːp ɪŋ **~leaps** ˈliːps
~leapt ˈlept

over|lie ˌəʊv ə ‖ˈlaɪ ‖ ˌoʊv ər- **~lain** ˈleɪn **~lay**
ˈleɪ **~lies** ˈlaɪz **~lying** ˈlaɪ ɪŋ

overload v ˌəʊv ə ˈləʊd ‖ ˌoʊv ər ˈloʊd **~ed** ɪd
əd **~ing** ɪŋ **~s** z

overload n ˈəʊv ə ləʊd ‖ ˈoʊv ər loʊd **~s** z

overlong ˌəʊv ə ˈlɒŋ ◄ ‖ ˌoʊv ər ˈlɔːŋ ◄ -ˈlɑːŋ

overlook v ˌəʊv ə ˈlʊk §-ˈluːk ‖ ˌoʊv ər- **~ed** t
~ing ɪŋ **~s** s

overlook n ˈəʊv ə lʊk §-luːk ‖ ˈoʊv ər- **~s** s

overlord ˈəʊv ə lɔːd ‖ ˈoʊv ər lɔːrd **~s** z **~ship**
ʃɪp

overly ˈəʊv ə li ‖ ˈoʊv ər-

overlying ˌəʊv ə ˈlaɪ ɪŋ ◄ ‖ ˌoʊv ər-

overman v ˌəʊv ə ˈmæn ‖ ˌoʊv ər- **~ned** d
~ning nɪŋ **~s** z

overmast|er ˌəʊv ə ˈmɑːst ə §-ˈmæst-
‖ ˌoʊv ər ˈmæst ᵊr **~ered** əd ‖ ᵊrd **~ering**
ᵊr_ɪŋ **~ers** əz ‖ ᵊrz

overmuch ˌəʊv ə ˈmʌtʃ ◄ ‖ ˌoʊv ər-

overnight adj, adv ˌəʊv ə ˈnaɪt ◄ ‖ ˌoʊv ər-
ˌovernight ˈbag

overoptimistic ˌəʊv ər ˌɒpt ɪ ˈmɪst ɪk ◄ -ˌ•ə-
‖ ˌoʊv ər ˌɑːpt- **~ally** ᵊl_i

overpaid ˌəʊv ə ˈpeɪd ◄ ‖ ˌoʊv ər-

overpass ˈəʊv ə pɑːs §-pæs ‖ ˈoʊv ər pæs **~es**
ɪz əz

over|pay v ˌəʊv ə ‖ˈpeɪ ‖ ˌoʊv ər- **~paid** ˈpeɪd ◄
~paying ˈpeɪ ɪŋ **~pays** ˈpeɪz

overplay ˌəʊv ə ˈpleɪ ‖ ˌoʊv ər- **~ed** d **~ing** ɪŋ
~s z

overplus ˈəʊv ə plʌs ‖ ˈoʊv ər-

overpopu|late ˌəʊv ə ˈpɒp ju leɪt -'•jə-
‖ ˌoʊv ər ˈpɑːp jə- **~lated** leɪt ɪd -əd ‖ leɪt̬ əd
~lates leɪts **~lating** leɪt ɪŋ ‖ leɪt̬ ɪŋ

overpopulation ˌəʊv ə ˌpɒp ju ˈleɪʃ ᵊn -jə'••-
‖ ˌoʊv ər ˌpɑːp jə-

overpower ˌəʊv ə ˈpaʊ_ə ‖ ˌoʊv ər ˈpaʊ_ᵊr **~ed**
d **overpowering/ly** ˌəʊv ə ˈpaʊ_ər ɪŋ /
li ‖ ˌoʊv ər ˈpaʊ_ᵊr ɪŋ /li **~s** z

overpressure ˈəʊv ə ˌpreʃ ə ‖ ˈoʊv ər ˌpreʃ ᵊr

overpriced ˌəʊv ə ˈpraɪst ◄ ‖ ˌoʊv ər-

over|print v ˌəʊv ə ‖ˈprɪnt ‖ ˌoʊv ər- **~printed**
ˈprɪnt ɪd -əd ‖ ˈprɪnt̬ əd **~printing**
ˈprɪnt ɪŋ ‖ ˈprɪnt̬ ɪŋ **~prints** ˈprɪn/s

overprint *n* ˈəʊv ə prɪnt ‖ ˈoʊv ᵊr- ~s s
overproduc|e ˌəʊv ə prə ˈdjuːs
§-ˈduːs §→ˈdʒuːs ‖ ˌoʊv ᵊr prə ˈduːs -ˈdjuːs
~ed t ~es ɪz əz ~ing ɪŋ
overproduction ˌəʊv ə prə ˈdʌk ʃᵊn ‖ ˌoʊv ᵊr-
overproof ˌəʊv ə ˈpruːf ‖ ˌoʊv ᵊr-
overprotect ˌəʊv ə prəʊ ˈtekt ‖ ˌoʊv ᵊr prə-
~ed ɪd əd ~ing ɪŋ ~s s
overprotective ˌəʊv ə prəʊ
ˈtekt ɪv ◄ ‖ ˌoʊv ᵊr prə-
overqualified ˌəʊv ə ˈkwɒl ɪ faɪd ◄ -ˈ•ə-
‖ ˌoʊv ᵊr ˈkwɑːl-
overran ˌəʊv ə ˈræn ‖ ˌoʊv ᵊr-
over|rate ˌəʊv ə |ˈreɪt ‖ ˌoʊv ᵊr- ~rated
ˈreɪt ɪd ◄ -əd ‖ ˈreɪt̬ əd ◄ ~rates ˈreɪts
~rating ˈreɪt ɪŋ ‖ ˈreɪt̬ ɪŋ
overreach ˌəʊv ə ˈriːtʃ ‖ ˌoʊv ᵊr- ~ed t ~es ɪz
əz ~ing ɪŋ
overreact ˌəʊv ə ri ˈækt ‖ ˌoʊv ᵊr- ~ed ɪd əd
~ing ɪŋ ~s s
overreaction ˌəʊv ə ri ˈæk ʃᵊn ‖ ˌoʊv ᵊr- ~s z
over|ride *v* ˌəʊv ə |ˈraɪd ‖ ˌoʊv ᵊr- ~ridden
ˈrɪd ᵊn ~rides ˈraɪdz ~riding/ly ˈraɪd ɪŋ /li
~rode ˈrəʊd ‖ ˈroʊd
override *n* ˈəʊv ə raɪd ‖ ˈoʊv ᵊr- ~s z
overrider ˈəʊv ə raɪd ə ‖ ˈoʊv ᵊr raɪd ᵊr- ~s z
overripe ˌəʊv ə ˈraɪp ‖ ˌoʊv ᵊr- ~ness nəs nɪs
overrul|e ˌəʊv ə ˈruːl ‖ ˌoʊv ᵊr- ~ed d ~es z
~ing ɪŋ
over|run *v* ˌəʊv ə |ˈrʌn ‖ ˌoʊv ᵊr- ~ran ˈræn
~running ˈrʌn ɪŋ ~runs ˈrʌnz
overrun *n* ˈəʊv ə rʌn ‖ ˈoʊv ᵊr- ~s z
oversaw ˌəʊv ə ˈsɔː ‖ ˌoʊv ᵊr- -ˈsɑː
oversea ˌəʊv ə ˈsiː ◄ ‖ ˌoʊv ᵊr- ~s z
ˌoverseas ˈposting
over|see ˌəʊv ə |ˈsiː ‖ ˌoʊv ᵊr- ~saw ˈsɔː ‖ ˈsɑː
~seeing ˈsiː ɪŋ ~seen ˈsiːn ~sees ˈsiːz
overseer ˈəʊv ə sɪə ˈ•• ˌsiː ə ‖ ˈoʊv ᵊr sɪr
ˈ•• ˌsiː ᵊr ~s z
over|sell ˌəʊv ə |ˈsel ‖ ˌoʊv ᵊr- ~selling ˈsel ɪŋ
~sells ˈselz ~sold ˈsəʊld →ˈsɒʊld ‖ ˈsoʊld
oversensitive ˌəʊv ə ˈsen̩ts ət ɪv -ɪt ɪv
‖ ˌoʊv ᵊr ˈsen̩ts ət̬ ɪv
oversensitivity ˌəʊv ə ˌsen̩ts ə ˈtɪv ət i -ɪˈ•-,
-ɪt i ‖ ˌoʊv ᵊr ˌsen̩ts ə ˈtɪv ət̬ i
oversew ˈəʊv ə səʊ ˌ•ˈ• ‖ ˈoʊv ᵊr soʊ ~ed d
~ing ɪŋ ~n n ~s z
oversexed ˌəʊv ə ˈsekst ◄ ‖ ˌoʊv ᵊr-
overshadow ˌəʊv ə ˈʃæd əʊ ‖ ˌoʊv ᵊr ˈʃæd oʊ
~ed d ~ing ɪŋ ~s z
overshoe ˈəʊv ə ʃuː ‖ ˈoʊv ᵊr- ~s z
overshoot *n* ˈəʊv ə ʃuːt ‖ ˈoʊv ᵊr- ~s s
over|shoot *v* ˌəʊv ə |ˈʃuːt ‖ ˌoʊv ᵊr- ~shooting
ˈʃuːt ɪŋ ‖ ˈʃuːt̬ ɪŋ ~shoots ˈʃuːts ~shot
ˈʃɒt ‖ ˈʃɑːt ◄
overside ˈəʊv ə saɪd ‖ ˈoʊv ᵊr-
oversight ˈəʊv ə saɪt ‖ ˈoʊv ᵊr- ~s s
oversimplification ˌəʊv ə ˌsɪmp lɪf ɪ ˈkeɪʃ ᵊn
-ˌ•ləf-, §-əˈ•• ‖ ˌoʊv ᵊr- ~s z
oversimpli|fy ˌəʊv ə ˈsɪmp lɪ |faɪ -ˈ•lə-
‖ ˌoʊv ᵊr- ~fied faɪd ~fies faɪz ~fying
faɪ ɪŋ

oversize *adj* ˌəʊv ə ˈsaɪz ◄ ‖ ˌoʊv ᵊr- ~d d
ˌoversize ˈboots
over|sleep *v* ˌəʊv ə |ˈsliːp ‖ ˌoʊv ᵊr- ~sleeping
ˈsliːp ɪŋ ~sleeps ˈsliːps ~slept ˈslept
oversold ˌəʊv ə ˈsəʊld →-ˈsɒʊld
‖ ˌoʊv ᵊr ˈsoʊld
overspend *n* ˈəʊv ə spend ‖ ˈoʊv ᵊr- ~s z
over|spend *v* ˌəʊv ə |ˈspend ‖ ˌoʊv ᵊr-
~spending ˈspend ɪŋ ~spends ˈspendz
~spent ˈspent
overspill *n* ˈəʊv ə spɪl ‖ ˈoʊv ᵊr- ~s z
overstaff ˌəʊv ə ˈstɑːf §-ˈstæf ‖ ˌoʊv ᵊr ˈstæf
~ed t ~ing ɪŋ ~s s
over|state ˌəʊv ə |ˈsteɪt ‖ ˌoʊv ᵊr- ~stated
ˈsteɪt ɪd -əd ‖ ˈsteɪt̬ əd ~states ˈsteɪts
~stating ˈsteɪt ɪŋ ‖ ˈsteɪt̬ ɪŋ
overstatement ˌəʊv ə ˈsteɪt mənt ˈ••ˌ••
‖ ˈoʊv ᵊr ˌsteɪt- ~s s
overstay ˌəʊv ə ˈsteɪ ‖ ˌoʊv ᵊr- ~ed d ~er/s
ə/z ‖ ᵊr/z ~ing ɪŋ ~s z
oversteer *v* ˌəʊv ə ˈstɪə ‖ ˌoʊv ᵊr ˈstɪᵊr ~ed d
oversteering
ˌəʊv ə ˈstɪər ɪŋ ‖ ˌoʊv ᵊr ˈstɪr ɪŋ ~s z
oversteer *n* ˈəʊv ə stɪə ‖ ˈoʊv ᵊr stɪr
overstep *v* ˌəʊv ə ˈstep ‖ ˌoʊv ᵊr- ~ped t
~ping ɪŋ ~s s
overstock *v* ˌəʊv ə ˈstɒk ‖ ˌoʊv ᵊr ˈstɑːk ~ed t
~ing ɪŋ ~s s
overstrain *n* ˈəʊv ə streɪn ˌ••ˈ• ‖ ˈoʊv ᵊr-
overstrain *v* ˌəʊv ə ˈstreɪn ‖ ˌoʊv ᵊr- ~ed d
~ing ɪŋ ~s z
overstretch ˌəʊv ə ˈstretʃ ‖ ˌoʊv ᵊr- ~ed t
~es ɪz əz ~ing ɪŋ
overstrung ˌəʊv ə ˈstrʌŋ ◄ ˈ••• ‖ ˌoʊv ᵊr-
overstuffed ˌəʊv ə ˈstʌft ◄ ‖ ˌoʊv ᵊr-
oversubscrib|e ˌəʊv ə səb ˈskraɪb §-sʌb ˈ•
‖ ˌoʊv ᵊr- ~ed d ~es z ~ing ɪŋ
oversup|ply *v* ˌəʊv ə sə |ˈplaɪ ‖ ˌoʊv ᵊr- ~plied
ˈplaɪd ~plies ˈplaɪz ~plying ˈplaɪ ɪŋ
oversupply *n* ˌəʊv ə sə ˈplaɪ ˈ•••ˌ•
‖ ˈoʊv ᵊr sə ˌplaɪ
overt əʊ ˈvɜːt ˈəʊv ɜːt ‖ oʊ ˈvɜːt ˈoʊv ɜːt ~ly
li
overtake ˌəʊv ə ˈteɪk ‖ ˌoʊv ᵊr- ~taken ˈteɪk
ᵊn ◄ ~takes ˈteɪks ~taking ˈteɪk ɪŋ ~took
ˈtʊk §ˈtuːk
overtax *v* ˌəʊv ə ˈtæks ‖ ˌoʊv ᵊr- ~ed t ~es ɪz
əz ~ing ɪŋ
over-the-counter
ˌəʊv ə ðə ˈkaʊnt ə ◄ ‖ ˌoʊv ᵊr ðə ˈkaʊnt̬ ᵊr ◄
over-the-top
ˌəʊv ə ðə ˈtɒp ◄ ‖ ˌoʊv ᵊr ðə ˈtɑːp ◄
over|throw *v* ˌəʊv ə |ˈθrəʊ ◄ ‖ ˌoʊv ᵊr |ˈθroʊ
~threw ˈθruː ~throwing ˈθrəʊ ɪŋ ‖ ˈθroʊ ɪŋ
~thrown ˈθrəʊn ◄ §ˈθrəʊ ᵊn ‖ ˈθroʊn ◄
~throws ˈθrəʊz ‖ ˈθroʊz
overthrow *n* ˈəʊv ə θrəʊ ‖ ˈoʊv ᵊr θroʊ ~s z
overthrust ˈəʊv ə θrʌst ‖ ˈoʊv ᵊr- ~s s
overtime *n, adv* ˈəʊv ə taɪm ‖ ˈoʊv ᵊr-
ˈovertime ˌban
overtire ˌəʊv ə ˈtaɪ_ə ◄ ‖ ˌoʊv ᵊr ˈtaɪ_ᵊr ◄ ~d d
overtiring ˌəʊv ə ˈtaɪ_ər ɪŋ
‖ ˌoʊv ᵊr ˈtaɪ_ᵊr ɪŋ ~s z

Overton 'əʊv ət ən ‖ 'oʊv ərt ən
overtone 'əʊv ə təʊn ‖ 'oʊv ər toʊn **~s** z
overtook ,əʊv ə 'tʊk §-'tu:k ‖ ,oʊv ər-
overtop ,əʊv ə 'tɒp ‖ ,oʊv ər 'ta:p **~ped** t
  ~ping ɪŋ **~s** s
overtrick 'əʊv ə trɪk ‖ 'oʊv ər- **~s** s
overtrump ,əʊv ə 'trʌmp ‖ ,oʊv ər- **~ed** t
  ~ing ɪŋ **~s** s
overture 'əʊv ə tjʊə -tʃʊə, -tʃə ‖ 'oʊv ər tʃʊr
  -tʃər, -tjʊr **~s** z
overturn v ,əʊv ə 'tɜːn ‖ ,oʊv ər 'tɜ·ːn **~ed** d
  ~ing ɪŋ **~s** z
overus|e v ,əʊv ə 'juːz ‖ ,oʊv ər- **~ed** d **~es** ɪz
  əz **~ing** ɪŋ
overuse n ,əʊv ə 'juːs ‖ ,oʊv ər-
overvalu|e ,əʊv ə 'væl juː ‖ ,oʊv ər- **~ed** d
  ~es z **~ing** ɪŋ
overview 'əʊv ə vjuː ‖ 'oʊv ər- **~s** z
overweening ,əʊv ə 'wiːn ɪŋ ◀ ‖ ,oʊv ər- **~ly** li
over|weight v, adj ,əʊv ə 'weɪt ◀ ‖ ,oʊv ər-
  ~weighted 'weɪt ɪd -əd ‖ 'weɪt̬ əd
  ~weighting 'weɪt ɪŋ ‖ 'weɪt̬ ɪŋ **~weights**
  'weɪts
overweight n 'əʊv ə weɪt ‖ 'oʊv ər-
overwhelm ,əʊv ə 'welm -'hwelm
  ‖ ,oʊv ər 'hwelm **~ed** d **~ing/ly** ɪŋ /li **~s** z
over|wind ,əʊv ə 'waɪnd ‖ ,oʊv ər- **~winding**
  'waɪnd ɪŋ **~winds** 'waɪndz **~wound**
  'waʊnd
overwint|er ,əʊv ə 'wɪnt ə ‖ ,oʊv ər 'wɪnt̬ ər
  ~ered əd ‖ ərd **~ering** _ər ɪŋ ‖ ər ɪŋ **~ers**
  əz ‖ ərz
overwork v ,əʊv ə 'wɜːk ‖ ,oʊv ər 'wɜ·ːk **~ed** t
  ~ing ɪŋ **~s** s
overwork n ,əʊv ə 'wɜːk '•• ‖ ,oʊv ər 'wɜ·ːk
overwound ,əʊv ə 'waʊnd ◀ ‖ ,oʊv ər-
over|write ,əʊv ə |'raɪt ‖ ,oʊv ər- **~writes**
  'raɪts **~writing** 'raɪt ɪŋ ‖ 'raɪt̬ ɪŋ **~written**
  'rɪt ən **~wrote** 'rəʊt ‖ 'roʊt
overwrought ,əʊv ə 'rɔːt ◀ ‖ ,oʊv ər- -'raːt
overzealous ,əʊv ə 'zel əs ◀ ‖ ,oʊv ər- **~ly** li
  ~ness nəs nɪs
Ovett 'əʊv et əʊ 'vet ‖ 'oʊv et oʊ 'vet
Ovid (i) 'ɒv ɪd §-əd ‖ 'aːv-; (ii) 'əʊv ɪd §-əd
  ‖ 'oʊv- —The Latin poet is known as (i); the
  American place name and personal name is (ii).
Ovidian ɒ 'vɪd i_ən əʊ- ‖ oʊ- aː-
Oviedo ,ɒv i 'eɪd əʊ ,əʊv- ‖ ,oʊv i 'eɪd oʊ —Sp
  [o 'βje ðo]
oviduct 'əʊv i dʌkt §-ə- ‖ 'oʊv ə- **~s** s
oviform 'əʊv i fɔːm §-ə- ‖ 'oʊv ə fɔːrm
ovine 'əʊv aɪn ‖ 'oʊv-
Oving 'əʊv ɪŋ ‖ 'oʊv-
Ovingdean 'əʊv ɪŋ diːn 'ɒv- ‖ 'oʊv-
oviparous əʊ 'vɪp ər əs ‖ oʊ- **~ly** li
ovipositor ,əʊv i 'pɒz ɪt ə §,•ə-, §-ət ə
  ‖ ,oʊv ə 'paːz ət̬ ər '•••,••• **~s** z
ovoid 'əʊv ɔɪd ‖ 'oʊv- **~s** z
ovo|lo 'əʊv ə |ləʊ ‖ 'oʊv ə |loʊ **~li** liː
ovoviviparity ,əʊv əʊ ,vɪv ɪ 'pær ət i -ə'•-, -ət i
  ‖ ,oʊv oʊ ,vɪv ə 'pær ət̬ i
ovoviviparous ,əʊv əʊ vɪ 'vɪp ər əs ◀ -və'•-,
  -vaɪ'•- ‖ ,oʊv oʊ vaɪ-

ovular 'ɒv jʊl ə 'əʊv-, -jəl- ‖ 'aːv jəl ər 'oʊv-
ovu|late v 'ɒv ju |leɪt 'əʊv-, -jə- ‖ 'aːv jə-
  'oʊv- **~lated** leɪt ɪd -əd ‖ leɪt̬ əd **~lates** leɪts
  ~lating leɪt ɪŋ ‖ leɪt̬ ɪŋ
ovulation ,ɒv ju 'leɪʃ ən ,əʊv-, -jə- ‖ ,aːv jə-
  ,oʊv- **~s** z
ovule 'ɒv juːl 'əʊv- ‖ 'aːv- 'oʊv- **~s** z
ov|um 'əʊv əm ‖ 'oʊv əm **~a** ə
ow aʊ
Owain 'əʊ aɪn ‖ 'oʊ- —Welsh ['ə waɪn, 'o-]
Owbridge 'əʊ brɪdʒ ‖ 'oʊ-
owe əʊ ‖ oʊ (= oh, O) **owed** əʊd ‖ oʊd **owes**
  əʊz ‖ oʊz **owing** 'əʊ ɪŋ ‖ 'oʊ ɪŋ
Owen 'əʊ ɪn -ən ‖ 'oʊ ən
Owens 'əʊ ɪnz -ənz ‖ 'oʊ ənz
Ower (i) 'aʊ_ə ‖ 'aʊ_ər, (ii) 'əʊ ə ‖ 'oʊ ər
  —Usually (i). **~s** z
owing 'əʊ ɪŋ ‖ 'oʊ ɪŋ
owl aʊl **owls** aʊlz
owlet 'aʊl ət -ɪt, -et **~s** s
owlish 'aʊl ɪʃ **~ly** li **~ness** nəs nɪs
owl-like 'aʊl laɪk
own əʊn ‖ oʊn **owned** əʊnd ‖ oʊnd **owning**
  'əʊn ɪŋ ‖ 'oʊn ɪŋ **owns** əʊnz ‖ oʊnz
  ,on your 'own; ,own 'goal
own-brand ,əʊn 'brænd ◀ →,əʊm-ˌ '•• ‖ ,oʊn-
  ~s z
owner 'əʊn ə ‖ 'oʊn ər **~s** z
owner-driver ,əʊn ə 'draɪv ə ‖ ,oʊn ər 'draɪv ər
  ~s z
owner-occu|pied ,əʊn ər 'ɒk ju |paɪd ◀ -'•jə-
  ‖ ,oʊn ər 'aːk jə- **~pier/s** paɪ_ə/z ‖ paɪ_ər/z
ownership 'əʊn ə ʃɪp ‖ 'oʊn ər-
own-label ,əʊn 'leɪb əl ◀ ‖ ,oʊn-
owt aʊt əʊt —This is a non-standard variant of
  aught
ox ɒks ‖ aːks **oxen** 'ɒks ən ‖ 'aːks ən **ox's**
  'ɒks ɪz -əz ‖ 'aːks əz
oxalate 'ɒks ə leɪt →-əl eɪt ‖ 'aːks-
oxalic (ˌ)ɒk 'sæl ɪk ‖ (ˌ)aːk-
oxalis ɒk 'sæl ɪs -'saːl-, 'ɒks əl-, §-əs
  ‖ aːk 'sæl əs 'aːks əl-
oxbow 'ɒks bəʊ ‖ 'aːks boʊ **~s** z
Oxbridge 'ɒks brɪdʒ ‖ 'aːks-
oxcart 'ɒks kaːt ‖ 'aːks kaːrt **~s** s
oxen 'ɒks ən ‖ 'aːks ən
Oxenden 'ɒks ənd ən ‖ 'aːks-
Oxenford 'ɒks ən fɔːd -fəd ‖ 'aːks ən fɔːrd
  -fərd
Oxenham 'ɒks ən_əm ‖ 'aːks-
Oxenholme 'ɒks ən həʊm ‖ 'aːks ən hoʊm
oxer 'ɒks ə ‖ 'aːks ər **~s** z
oxeye 'ɒks aɪ ‖ 'aːks- **~s** z
  ,oxeye 'daisy
Oxfam 'ɒks fæm ‖ 'aːks-
Oxford, o~ 'ɒks fəd ‖ 'aːks fərd **~shire** ʃə ʃɪə
  ‖ ʃər ʃɪr **~s, ~'s** z
  ,Oxford 'Circus; ,Oxford 'English; 'Oxford
  ,movement; 'Oxford Street
Oxhey 'ɒks i -heɪ ‖ 'aːks-
oxhide 'ɒks haɪd ‖ 'aːks-
oxidant 'ɒks ɪd ənt -əd- ‖ 'aːks- (usually =
  occident) **~s** s

oxidas|e 'ɒks ɪ deɪz -ə-, -deɪs ‖ 'ɑːks- ~es ɪz
əz
oxidation ,ɒks ɪ 'deɪʃ ən -ə- ‖ ,ɑːks- ~s z
oxidative 'ɒks ɪ deɪt ɪv '•ə- ‖ 'ɑːks ə deɪt̬ ɪv
oxide 'ɒks aɪd ‖ 'ɑːks- ~s z
oxidis... —see oxidiz...
oxidization ,ɒks ɪd aɪ 'zeɪʃ ən ,•əd-, -ɪ'•-
‖ ,ɑːks əd ə- ~s z
oxidiz|e 'ɒks ɪ daɪz -ə- ‖ 'ɑːks ə- ~ed d ~es
ɪz əz ~ing ɪŋ
oxime 'ɒks iːm -aɪm ‖ 'ɑːks- ~s z
Oxley 'ɒks li ‖ 'ɑːks-
oxlip 'ɒks lɪp ‖ 'ɑːks- ~s s
Oxnard (i) 'ɒks nəd ‖ 'ɑːks nərd, (ii)
-nɑːd ‖ -nɑːrd —The place in CA is (ii).
Oxo tdmk 'ɒks əʊ ‖ 'ɑːks oʊ
Oxon 'ɒks ɒn -ən, ɒk 'sɒn ‖ 'ɑːks ɑːn
Oxonian ɒk 'səʊn i ən ‖ ɑːk 'soʊn- ~s z
oxonium ɒk 'səʊn i əm ‖ ɑːk 'soʊn-
oxpecker 'ɒks ,pek ə ‖ 'ɑːks ,pek ər ~s z
Oxshott 'ɒk ʃɒt 'ɒks- ‖ 'ɑːk ʃɑːt
oxtail 'ɒks teɪəl ‖ 'ɑːks- ~s z
Oxted 'ɒkst ɪd -əd, -ed ‖ 'ɑːkst əd
Oxton 'ɒkst ən ‖ 'ɑːkst-
oxtongue 'ɒks tʌŋ §-tɒŋ ‖ 'ɑːks- ~s z
Oxus 'ɒks əs ‖ 'ɑːks əs
oxy- comb. form
with stress-neutral suffix |ɒks i ‖ |ɑːks i —
oxychloride
,ɒks i 'klɔːr aɪd ‖ ,ɑːks i 'klɔːr aɪd -'kloʊr-
with stress-imposing suffix ɒk 'sɪ+ ‖ ɑːk 'sɪ+
— oxypathy ɒk 'sɪp əθ i ‖ ɑːk-
oxyacetylene ,ɒks i_ə 'set ə liːn ◂ -'•ɪ-, -lɪn;
-əl iːn, -ɪn ‖ ,ɑːks i ə 'set̬ əl iːn ◂ -ən
Oxydol tdmk 'ɒks ɪ dɒl ‖ 'ɑːks ə dɔːl -dɑːl
oxygen 'ɒks ɪdʒ ən -ədʒ- ‖ 'ɑːks-
'oxygen mask; 'oxygen tent
oxyge|nate 'ɒks ɪdʒ ə |neɪt '•ədʒ-; ɒk 'sɪdʒ-
‖ 'ɑːks- ~nated neɪt ɪd -əd ‖ neɪt̬ əd ~nates
neɪts ~nating neɪt ɪŋ ‖ neɪt̬ ɪŋ
oxygenation ,ɒks ɪdʒ ə 'neɪʃ ən ɒk ,sɪdʒ ə-
‖ ,ɑːks- ~s z
oxygenis|e, oxygeniz|e 'ɒks ɪdʒ ə naɪz '•ədʒ-
‖ 'ɑːks- ~ed d ~es ɪz əz ~ing ɪŋ
oxymor|on ,ɒks i 'mɔːr |ɒn -ən
‖ ,ɑːks i 'mɔːr |ɑːn -'moʊr- ~a ə ~ons ɒnz
ənz ‖ ɑːnz
Oxyrhynchus ,ɒks i 'rɪŋk əs ‖ ,ɑːks-
oxytocic ,ɒks i 'təʊs ɪk ◂ ‖ ,ɑːks i 'toʊs ɪk ◂ ~s
s
oxytocin ,ɒks i 'təʊs ɪn §-ən ‖ ,ɑːks i 'toʊs ən
oxytone 'ɒks i təʊn ‖ 'ɑːks i toʊn ~s z
oyer 'ɔɪ ə ‖ 'ɔɪ ər
oyes, oyez əʊ 'jez -'jes, -'jeɪ, '•• ‖ oʊ-
oyster 'ɔɪst ə ‖ -ər ~s z
'oyster bed
oyster-catcher 'ɔɪst ə ,kætʃ ə §-,ketʃ-
‖ -ər ,kætʃ ər ~s z
Oystermouth 'ɔɪst ə maʊθ ‖ -ər-
oz, oz. sing. aʊnts, pl 'aʊnts ɪz -əz
Oz ɒz ‖ ɑːz
Ozalid tdmk 'ɒz əl ɪd 'əʊz- ‖ 'ɑːz-
Ozanne əʊ 'zæn ‖ oʊ-
Ozark 'əʊz ɑːk ‖ 'oʊz ɑːrk ~s s
ozocerite əʊ 'zəʊk ə raɪt -'zəʊs-;
,əʊz əʊ 'sɪər aɪt ‖ oʊ 'zoʊk- -'zoʊs-;
,oʊz oʊ 'sɪr aɪt
ozokerite əʊ 'zəʊk ə raɪt ,əʊz əʊ 'kɪər aɪt
‖ oʊ 'zoʊk- ,oʊz oʊ 'kɪr aɪt
ozone 'əʊz əʊn əʊ 'zəʊn ‖ 'oʊz oʊn oʊ 'zoʊn
'ozone ,layer, •'• , ••
ozonic əʊ 'zɒn ɪk ‖ oʊ 'zɑːn ɪk
ozoniferous ,əʊz əʊ 'nɪf ər əs ‖ ,oʊz ə-
ozonosphere əʊ 'zəʊn ə sfɪə -'zɒn-
‖ oʊ 'zoʊn ə sfɪr -'zɑːn-
ozs, ozs. 'aʊnts ɪz -əz
Ozymandias ,ɒz i 'mænd i_əs ,•ə-, -æs ‖ ,ɑːz-
Ozzie 'ɒz i ‖ 'ɑːz i

P p

p — Spelling-to-sound

1 Where the spelling is **p**, the pronunciation is regularly p, as in **pipe** paɪp. **p** also forms part of the digraph **ph**.

2 Where the spelling is double **pp**, the pronunciation is regularly p, as in **happy** ˈhæp i.

3 **p** is normally silent at the beginning of a word before **n, s, t**, as in **pneumonia, psychiatrist, ptomaine**.

ph — Spelling-to-sound

1 Where the spelling is the digraph **ph**, the pronunciation is regularly f, as in **photograph** ˈfəʊt ə grɑːf ‖ ˈfoʊt̬ ə græf.

2 Exceptionally, it is
p, as in **shepherd** ˈʃep əd ‖ ˈʃep ᵊrd, **Clapham** ˈklæp əm (in these words the **h** was originally part of a suffix, and hence silent);
v, as in **Stephen** ˈstiːv ᵊn and the older pronunciation of **nephew** ˈnev juː (now usually ˈnef-).

P, p piː P's, p's, Ps piːz —*Communications code name:* Papa
p *'penny, pence'* piː —*See note at* pence
pa, Pa pɑː ‖ pɔː pas, Pa's pɑːz ‖ pɔːz
PA ˌpiː ˈeɪ —*but see also* Pennsylvania
pa'anga pɑː ˈæŋ ə -gə ‖ -ˈɑːŋ-
Pablo ˈpæb ləʊ ‖ ˈpɑːb loʊ —*Sp* [ˈpa βlo]
pabulum ˈpæb jʊl əm -jəl- ‖ -jəl-
PABX ˌpiː eɪ biː ˈeks
paca ˈpɑːk ə ˈpæk ə ~s z
pace *n, v* peɪs paced peɪst paces ˈpeɪs ɪz -əz
  pacing ˈpeɪs ɪŋ
  ˈpace ˌbowler
pace *prep* 'with due deference to' ˈpeɪs i ˈpɑːtʃ eɪ, ˈpɑːk-
Pace *family name* peɪs
pacemaker ˈpeɪs ˌmeɪk ə ‖ -ᵊr ~s z
pacer ˈpeɪs ə ‖ -ᵊr ~s z
pacesetter ˈpeɪs ˌset ə ‖ -ˌset̬ ᵊr ~s z
pac|ey ˈpeɪs li ~ier i_ə ‖ i_ᵊr ~iest i_ɪst i_əst ~ily ɪ li əl i
pachisi pə ˈtʃiːz i pæ-, -ˈtʃiːs-
Pachuco pə ˈtʃuːk əʊ ‖ -oʊ ~s z —*Sp* [pa ˈtʃu ko]
pachyderm ˈpæk ɪ dɜːm ‖ -dɝːm ~s z
pachydermatous
  ˌpæk i ˈdɜːm ət əs ◄ ‖ -ˈdɝːm ət̬ əs ◄

pacific, P~ pə ˈsɪf ɪk ~ally ᵊl̩i
  Pa̱cific ˌNorthˈwest; Paˌcific ˈOcean; Paˌcific ˈrim
pacification ˌpæs ɪf ɪ ˈkeɪʃ ᵊn ˌ•əf-, §-əˈ•- ~s z
pacificatory ˌpæs ɪf ɪ ˈkeɪt ər i ◄ ˌ•əf-, -əˈ•-, pə ˈsɪf ɪk ət̬ᵊr i ‖ pə ˈsɪf ɪk ə tɔːr i -tour i
pacificist pə ˈsɪf ɪs ɪst pæ-, -əs-, §-əst ~s s
pacifier ˈpæs ɪ faɪ_ə ˈ•ə- ‖ -faɪ_ᵊr ~s z
pacifism ˈpæs ɪ ˌfɪz əm -ə-
pacifist ˈpæs ɪf ɪst -əf-, §-əst ~s s
paci|fy ˈpæs ɪ lfaɪ -ə- ~fied faɪd ~fies faɪz ~fying faɪ ɪŋ
Pacino pə ˈtʃiːn əʊ ‖ -oʊ
pack pæk packed pækt *(= pact)* packing ˈpæk ɪŋ packs pæks
  ˈpack ˌanimal; ˈpack ice; ˈpacking case
package ˈpæk ɪdʒ ~ed d ~es ɪz əz ~ing ɪŋ
  ˈpackage deal; ˌpackage ˈholiday; ˈpackage store; ˈpackage tour, ˌ•• ˈ•
Packard ˈpæk ɑːd -ᵊrd ‖ -ᵊrd
packed-out ˌpækt ˈaʊt ◄
packer, P~ ˈpæk ə ‖ -ᵊr ~s z
pack|et ˈpæk lɪt §-ət ‖ -lət ~eted ɪt ɪd §ət-, -əd ‖ ət̬ əd ~eting ɪt ɪŋ §ət- ‖ ət̬ ɪŋ ~ets ɪts §əts ‖ əts
packhors|e ˈpæk hɔːs ‖ -hɔːrs ~es ɪz əz
pack|man ˈpæk| mən -mæn ~men mən men

P

packsaddle 'pæk ˌsæd əl ~s z
Pac-man *tdmk* 'pæk mæn
pact pækt **pacts** pækts
pac|y 'peɪs |i ~ier i_ə ‖ i_ər ~iest i_ɪst i_əst
~ily ɪ li əl i
pad pæd **padded** 'pæd ɪd -əd **padding**
'pæd ɪŋ **pads** pædz
Padang 'pɑː dæŋ -dɑːŋ
Padarn 'pæd ən -aːn ‖ -ərn -aːrn —*Welsh*
['pa darn]
padauk pə 'daʊk
Padbury 'pæd bər_i →'pæb- ‖ -ˌber i
padd... —*see* **pad**
Paddick 'pæd ɪk
paddie... —*see* **paddy**
Paddington 'pæd ɪŋ tən
paddl|e 'pæd əl ~ed d ~es z ~ing ˌɪŋ
'paddle boat; 'paddle ˌsteamer; 'paddling
pool; 'paddle wheel
paddock, P~ 'pæd ək ~s s
paddy, Paddy 'pæd li ~ies, ~y's iz
'paddy field; 'paddy ˌwagon
paddymelon 'pæd i ˌmel ən ~s z
paddywhack 'pæd i wæk -hwæk ‖ -hwæk ~s s
pademelon 'pæd i ˌmel ən ~s z
Paderborn ˌpɑːd ə 'bɔːn '•••‖ -'bɔːrn —*Ger*
[paː dɐ 'bɔʁn]
Paderewski ˌpæd ə 'ref ski -'rev- ‖ ˌpɑːd-
—*Polish* [pa dɛ 'rɛf ski]
Padfield 'pæd fiːəld
Padiham 'pæd i_əm
padlock 'pæd lɒk ‖ -laːk ~ed t ~ing ɪŋ ~s s
Padmore 'pæd mɔː →'pæb- ‖ -mɔːr -moʊr
Padraic 'pɑːdr ɪk -ɪg
Padraig 'pɑːdr ɪg —*Irish* ['pa rɪg]
padre 'pɑːdr i -eɪ ~s z
padron|e pə 'drəʊn li pæ-, -eɪ ‖ -'droʊn li ~es
iz ~i iː
padsaw 'pæd sɔː ‖ -saː ~s z
Padstow 'pæd stəʊ ‖ -stoʊ
Padu|a 'pæd ju_lə ‖ 'pædʒ u_lə —*It* Padova
['pa do va] ~an/s ən/z
Paducah pə 'duːk ə -'djuːk-
paean 'piː_ən ~s z
paederast 'ped ə ræst 'piːd- ~s s
paederastic ˌped ə 'ræst ɪk ◄ ˌpiːd- ~ally əl_i
paederasty 'ped ə ræst i 'piːd-
paediatric ˌpiːd i 'ætr ɪk ◄ ~ally əl_i ~s s
paediatrician ˌpiːd i_ə 'trɪʃ ən ~s z
paedophile 'piːd əʊ faɪəl ‖ 'ped ə- 'piːd- ~s z
paedophilia ˌpiːd əʊ 'fɪl i_ə ‖ ˌped ə- ˌpiːd-
paedophiliac ˌpiːd əʊ 'fɪl i æk ‖ ˌped ə- ˌpiːd-
~s s
paella paɪ 'el ə ‖ pɑː- -'eɪl jə, -'eɪ- —*Sp*
[pa 'e ʎa, -ja] ~s z
paeon 'piː_ən -aːn ~s z
paeon|y 'piː_ən li ~ies iz
pagan 'peɪg ən ~dom dəm ~s z
Paganini ˌpæg ə 'niːn i ‖ ˌpɑːg- —*It*
[pa ga 'ni: ni]
paganism 'peɪg ən ˌɪz əm
page, Page peɪdʒ **paged** peɪdʒd **pages,**

Page's 'peɪdʒ ɪz -əz **paging** 'peɪdʒ ɪŋ
'page boy
pageant 'pædʒ ənt ~s s
pageantr|y 'pædʒ əntr li ~ies iz
pager 'peɪdʒ ə ‖ -ər ~s z
Paget 'pædʒ ɪt -ət ~'s s
'Paget's di,sease
Pagham 'pæg əm
paginate 'pædʒ ɪ |neɪt -ə- ~nated neɪt ɪd -əd
‖ neɪt̬ əd ~nates neɪts ~nating
neɪt ɪŋ ‖ neɪt̬ ɪŋ
pagination ˌpædʒ ɪ 'neɪʃ ən -ə- ~s z
Paglia 'paːl jə 'pæg li_ə
Pagliacci ˌpæl i 'aːtʃ i il ‖ ˌpaːl 'jaːtʃ i —*It*
[pa 'ʎat tʃi]
Pagnell 'pæg nəl
Pagnol pæn 'jɒl ‖ -'joʊl —*Fr* [pa 'njɔl]
pagoda pə 'gəʊd ə ‖ -'goʊd ə ~s z
pa'goda tree
Pago Pago ˌpaːg əʊ 'paːg əʊ
ˌpæŋ gəʊ 'pæŋ gəʊ, ˌpeɪg əʊ 'peɪg əʊ
‖ ˌpaːŋ goʊ 'paːŋ goʊ ˌpaːg oʊ 'paːg oʊ
pah paː
Pahang pə 'hʌŋ -'hæŋ ‖ -'haːŋ
Pahari pə 'haːr i
Pahlavi 'paːl əv i
paid peɪd
paid-up ˌpeɪd 'ʌp ◄
ˌpaid-up 'members
Paige peɪdʒ
paigle 'peɪg əl ~s z
Paignton 'peɪnt ən ‖ -ən
pail peɪəl **pails** peɪəlz
pailful 'peɪl fʊl ~s z
paillass|e 'pæl i æs ,•••‖ pæl 'jæs ~es ɪz əz
paillette ₍ₗₗ₎pæl 'jet ˌpæl i 'et ‖ paɪ 'jet —*Fr*
[pa jɛt] ~s s
pain, Pain peɪn **pained** peɪnd **paining**
'peɪn ɪŋ **pains** peɪnz
pain au chocolat ˌpæn əʊ 'ʃɒk ə laː
‖ -oʊ ˌʃaːk ə 'laː —*Fr* [pɛ̃ o ʃɔ kɔ la]
Paine peɪn
painful 'peɪn fəl -fʊl ~ly_i ~ness nəs nɪs
painkiller 'peɪn ˌkɪl ə →'peɪŋ- ‖ -ər ~s z
painless 'peɪn ləs -lɪs ~ly li ~ness nəs nɪs
painstaking 'peɪnz ˌteɪk ɪŋ ~ly li
Painswick 'peɪnz wɪk
paint peɪnt **painted** 'peɪnt ɪd -əd ‖ 'peɪnt̬ əd
painting/s 'peɪnt ɪŋ/z ‖ 'peɪnt̬ ɪŋ/z **paints**
peɪnts
paintball 'peɪnt bɔːl ‖ -baːl ~er/s ə/z ‖ ər/z
~ing ɪŋ
paintbox 'peɪnt bɒks ‖ -baːks ~es ɪz əz
paintbrush 'peɪnt brʌʃ ~es ɪz əz
painter, P~ 'peɪnt ə ‖ 'peɪnt̬ ər ~s z
painterly 'peɪnt ə li →-əl i ‖ 'peɪnt̬ ər li
paintwork 'peɪnt wɜːk ‖ -wɜːk
pair peə ‖ peər pæər **paired** peəd ‖ peərd
pæərd **pairing** 'peər ɪŋ ‖ 'per ɪŋ 'pær- **pairs**
peəz ‖ peərz pæərz
pais|a 'paɪs ɑː ~as ɑːz ~e eɪ
Paish peɪʃ
Paisley, p~ 'peɪz li ~s, ~'s z

Paiute ˌpaɪ 'uːt -'juːt, '•• ~s s
pajama pə 'dʒɑːm ə △bə- ‖ -'dʒæm ə ~ed d
~s z
pakapoo ˌpæk ə 'puː ◄ ~s z
ˌpakapoo 'ticket, ˌ••'• ˌ••
pak-choi ˌpæk 'tʃɔɪ ˌpɑːk- ˌbɒk- ‖ ˌpɑːk-
ˌbɑːk-
pakeha, P~ 'pɑːk i hɑː -ə-, ˌ••'• ~s z
Pakenham family name 'pæk ən‿əm
Pakenham place in Suffolk 'peɪk ən‿əm
Paki 'pæk i 'pɑːk i ~s z
Paki-bashing 'pæk i ˌbæʃ ɪŋ 'pɑːk-
Pakistan ˌpɑːk ɪ 'stɑːn ˌpæk-, -ə- ‖ 'pæk ɪ stæn
'pɑːk ɪ stɑːn, ˌ••'• (*)
Pakistani ˌpɑːk ɪ 'stɑːn i ◄ -ə-, -'stæn-
‖ ˌpæk ɪ 'stæn i ◄ ˌpɑːk ɪ 'stɑːn i ~s z
pakora pə 'kɔːr ə ‖ -'koʊr-
pal, Pal, PAL pæl palled pæld palling 'pæl ɪŋ
pals pælz
palac|e 'pæl əs -ɪs ~es ɪz əz
ˌpalace ˌrevo'lution
paladin 'pæl əd ɪn §-ən ~s z
Palaearctic ˌpæl i 'ɑːkt ɪk ◄ ˌpeɪl-
‖ ˌpeɪl i 'ɑːrkt ɪk ◄ -'ɑːrt̬-
palaeo- comb. form
    with stress-neutral suffix ¦pæl i əʊ ¦peɪl-
    ‖ ¦peɪl i oʊ — palaeomagnetism
    ˌpæl i əʊ 'mæg nə ˌtɪz əm ˌpeɪl-, -'•nɪ-
    ‖ ˌpeɪl i oʊ-
    with stress-imposing suffix ˌpæl i 'ɒ+ ˌpeɪl-
    ‖ ˌpeɪl i 'ɑː+ — palaeographer
    ˌpæl i 'ɒg rəf ə ˌpeɪl- ‖ ˌpeɪl i 'ɑːg rəf ər ~s z
palaeobotany ˌpæl i əʊ 'bɒt ən i ˌpeɪl-
‖ ˌpeɪl i oʊ 'bɑːt ən‿i
Palaeocene, p~ 'pæl i əʊ siːn 'peɪl- ‖ 'peɪl i ə-
palaeographic ˌpæl i əʊ 'græf ɪk ◄ ˌpeɪl-
‖ ˌpeɪl i ə-
palaeography ˌpæl i 'ɒg rəf i ˌpeɪl-
‖ ˌpeɪl i 'ɑːg-
Palaeolithic, p~ ˌpæl i əʊ 'lɪθ ɪk ◄ ˌpeɪl-
‖ ˌpeɪl i ə-
palaeontological ˌpæl i ˌɒnt ə 'lɒdʒ ɪk əl ˌpeɪl-
‖ ˌpeɪl i ˌɑːnt̬ əl 'ɑːdʒ ɪk əl
palaeontolog|ist/s ˌpæl i ɒn 'tɒl ədʒ ɪst/s
ˌpeɪl-, §-əst/s ‖ ˌpeɪl i ɑːn 'tɑːl ədʒ ləst/s ~y i
Palaeozoic, p~ ˌpæl i əʊ 'zəʊ ɪk ◄ ˌpeɪl-
‖ ˌpeɪl i ə 'zoʊ ɪk ◄
palaes|tra pə 'laɪs |trə -'liːs-, -'les- ‖ -'les-
~trae triː traɪ ~tras trəz
palais sing. 'pæl eɪ -i ‖ pæ 'leɪ palais pl
'pæl eɪz ‖ pæ 'leɪz
ˌpalais de 'danse ‖ •,•- də 'dɑːnts -'dɒ̃s,
§-'dænts ‖ də 'dænts
palankeen, palanquin ˌpæl ən 'kiːn →-əŋ- ~s
z
palatability ˌpæl ət ə 'bɪl ət i ˌ•ɪt-, -ɪt i
‖ ˌpæl ət̬ ə 'bɪl ət̬ i
palatab|le 'pæl ət əb |əl -ɪt əb- ‖ -ət̬ əb-
~leness əl nəs -nɪs ~ly li
palatal 'pæl ət əl pə 'leɪt əl ‖ -ət̬ əl —In
    phonetics '•••, in anatomy (BrE) sometimes
    •'•• ~ly i ~s z
palatalis... —see palataliz...

palatalization ˌpæl ət əl aɪ 'zeɪʃ ən pə ˌleɪt-,
-ɪ'•- ‖ -ət̬ əl ə- ~s z
palataliz|e 'pæl ət ə laɪz pə 'leɪt-, →-əl aɪz
‖ -ət̬ əl- ~ed d ~es ɪz əz ~ing ɪŋ
palate 'pæl ət -ɪt ~s s
palatial pə 'leɪʃ əl -'leɪʃ i‿əl ~ly i
palatinate, P~ pə 'læt ɪn ət -ən-, -ɪt ‖ -ən ət ~s
s
palatine, P~ 'pæl ə taɪn ~s z
palatogram 'pæl ət əʊ græm ‖ -ət̬ ə- ~s z
palatographic ˌpæl ət əʊ 'græf ɪk ◄ ‖ -ət̬ ə-
~ally əl i
palatography ˌpæl ə 'tɒg rəf i ‖ -'tɑːg-
Palau pə 'laʊ pɑː-
palaver pə 'lɑːv ə ‖ -ər -'læv- ~s z
Palawan pə 'lɑː wən
palazz|o pə 'læts ləʊ ‖ -'lɑːts loʊ ~i iː ~os
əʊz ‖ oʊz —It [pa 'lat tso]
pale peɪəl (= pail) paler 'peɪəl ə ‖ -ər palest
'peɪəl ɪst -əst
ˌpale 'ale
Pale in eastern Ireland peɪəl
Pale place in Bosnia 'pɑːl eɪ —Serbian ['pa le]
Palearctic ˌpæl i 'ɑːkt ɪk ◄ ˌpeɪl-
‖ ˌpeɪl i 'ɑːrkt ɪk ◄ -'ɑːrt̬-
palefac|e 'peɪəl feɪs ~es ɪz əz
pale|ly 'peɪəl |li ~ness nəs nɪs
paleo-, palaeo- comb. form
    with stress-neutral suffix ¦pæl i əʊ ¦peɪl-
    ‖ ¦peɪl i oʊ — paleomagnetism
    ˌpæl i əʊ 'mæg nə ˌtɪz əm ˌpeɪl-, -'•nɪ-
    ‖ ˌpeɪl i oʊ-
    with stress-imposing suffix ˌpæl i 'ɒ+ ˌpeɪl-
    ‖ ˌpeɪl i 'ɑː+ — paleographer
    ˌpæl i 'ɒg rəf ə ˌpeɪl- ‖ ˌpeɪl i 'ɑːg rəf ər ~s z
paleobotany ˌpæl i əʊ 'bɒt ən i ˌpeɪl-
‖ ˌpeɪl i oʊ 'bɑːt ən‿i
Paleocene, p~ 'pæl i əʊ siːn 'peɪl- ‖ 'peɪl i ə-
paleographic ˌpæl i əʊ 'græf ɪk ◄ ˌpeɪl-
‖ ˌpeɪl i ə-
paleography ˌpæl i 'ɒg rəf i ˌpeɪl-
‖ ˌpeɪl i 'ɑːg-
Paleolithic, p~ ˌpæl i əʊ 'lɪθ ɪk ◄ ˌpeɪl-
‖ ˌpeɪl i ə-
paleontological ˌpæl i ˌɒnt ə 'lɒdʒ ɪk əl ˌpeɪl-
‖ ˌpeɪl i ˌɑːnt̬ əl 'ɑːdʒ ɪk əl
paleontolog|ist/s ˌpæl i ɒn 'tɒl ədʒ ɪst/s
ˌpeɪl-, §-əst/s ‖ ˌpeɪl i ɑːn 'tɑːl ədʒ ləst/s ~y i
paleotype 'pæl i əʊ taɪp 'peɪl- ‖ 'peɪl i oʊ-
Paleozoic, p~ ˌpæl i əʊ 'zəʊ ɪk ◄ ˌpeɪl-
‖ ˌpeɪl i ə 'zoʊ ɪk ◄
Palermo pə 'leəm əʊ -'lɜːm- ‖ -'lerm oʊ
-'lɜːm- —It [pa 'lɛr mo]
Palestine 'pæl ə staɪn -ɪ-
Palestinian ˌpæl ə 'stɪn i‿ən ◄ ˌ•ɪ- ~s z
pales|tra pə 'les |trə -'liːs- ~trae triː traɪ, treɪ
~tras trəz
Palestrina ˌpæl ə 'striːn ə -ɪ-, -e- —It
[pa le 'stri na]
Palethorp, Palethorpe 'peɪəl θɔːp ‖ -θɔːrp
palette 'pæl ət -ɪt, -et ~s s
ˌpalette knife
Paley 'peɪl i

P

palfrey, P~ 'pɔːlf ri 'pɒlf- ‖ 'pɑːlf- ~s z
Palfreyman 'pɔːlf ri mən 'pɒlf- ‖ 'pɑːlf-
Palgrave 'pæl greɪv 'pɔːl- ‖ 'pɔːl-, 'pɑːl-
Pali 'pɑːl i
palimony 'pæl ɪm ən i '•ə- ‖ -ə moʊn i (*)
palimpsest 'pæl ɪmp sest -əmp- ~s s
Palin 'peɪl ɪn §-ən
palindrome 'pæl ɪn drəʊm -ən- ‖ -droʊm ~s z
palindromic ˌpæl ɪn 'drɒm ɪk ◄ -ən-
   ‖ -'droʊm ɪk ◄ -'drɑːm-
paling, P~ 'peɪl ɪŋ ~s z
palingenesis ˌpæl ɪn 'dʒen əs ɪs ,•ən-, -ɪs ɪs,
   §-əs
palinode 'pæl ɪ nəʊd -ə- ‖ -noʊd ~s z
palisad|e ˌpæl ɪ 'seɪd -ə- ~ed ɪd əd ~es z
   ~ing ɪŋ
palish 'peɪl ɪʃ
Palitoy tdmk 'pæl ɪ tɔɪ -ə-
Palk pɔːk pɔːlk ‖ pɑːk, pɔːlk, pɑːlk
pall pɔːl ‖ pɑːl palled pɔːld ‖ pɑːld palling
   'pɔːl ɪŋ ‖ 'pɑːl- palls pɔːlz ‖ pɑːlz
Palladian pə 'leɪd i_ən -'lɑːd-
palladic pə 'læd ɪk -'leɪd-
Palladio pə 'læd i əʊ -'lɑːd- ‖ -'lɑːd i oʊ —It
   [pal 'laː dio]
palladium, P~ pə 'leɪd i_əm
palladous pə 'leɪd əs 'pæl əd-
Pallas 'pæl əs -æs
   ˌPallas A'thene
pallbearer 'pɔːl ˌbeər ə ‖ -ˌber ər 'pɑːl-, -ˌbær-
   ~s z
pallet 'pæl ət -ɪt ~s s
palletis... —see palletiz...
palletization ˌpæl ət aɪ 'zeɪʃ ən ,•ɪt-, -ɪ'•-
   ‖ -ət ə-
palletiz|e 'pæl ə taɪz -ɪ- ~ed d ~es ɪz əz ~ing
   ɪŋ
palliass|e 'pæl i æs ,•'• ‖ pæl 'jæs ~es ɪz əz
palli|ate 'pæl i eɪt ~ated eɪt ɪd -əd ‖ eɪt̬ əd
   ~ates eɪts ~ating eɪt ɪŋ ‖ eɪt̬ ɪŋ
palliation ˌpæl i 'eɪʃ ən ~s z
palliative 'pæl i_ət ɪv ‖ -i eɪt̬ ɪv -i_ət̬ ɪv ~s z
pallid 'pæl ɪd §-əd ~ly li ~ness nəs nɪs
Palliser 'pæl ɪs ə -əs- ‖ -ər
palli|um 'pæl i_əm ~a ə ~ums əmz
Pall Mall ˌpæl 'mæl ◄ —Formerly also
   ˌpel 'mel ◄
pallor 'pæl ə ‖ -ər
pally 'pæl i

PALM

	no l	with l
AmE 1993		
BrE 1998		

0   20   40   60   80   100%

palm pɑːm §pɑːlm, §pælm, §pɒlm ‖ pɑːlm
pɑːm, pɔːlm, pɔːm —Poll panel preferences:
AmE 1993, no l 47%, with l 53%; BrE 1998 no l
85%, with l 15%. palmed pɑːmd §pɑːlmd,
§pælmd, §pɒlmd ‖ pɑːlmd pɑːmd, pɔːlmd,
pɔːmd palming 'pɑːm ɪŋ §'pɑːlm-, §'pælm-,
§'pɒlm- ‖ 'pɑːlm ɪŋ 'pɑːm-, 'pɔːlm-, 'pɔːm-
palms pɑːmz §pɑːlmz, §pælmz, §pɒlmz

‖ pɑːlmz pɑːmz, pɔːlmz, pɔːmz
ˌPalm 'Beach; 'palm oil; ˌPalm 'Springs;
   ˌPalm 'Sunday; ˌpalm 'wine
Palma 'pælm ə 'pɑːm-, 'pɑːlm-, §'pɒlm-
   ‖ 'pɑːlm ə -ɑː: —Sp ['pal ma]
palmar 'pælm ə §'pɑːlm-, §'pɒlm-, -ɑː: ‖ -ər
palmate 'pælm eɪt 'pɑːm-, §'pɑːlm-, §'pɒlm-,
   -ət, -ɪt ~ly li
palmcorder 'pɑːm ˌkɔːd ə §'pɑːlm-, §'pælm-,
   §'pɒlm-; ,•'•• ‖ 'pɑːlm ˌkɔːrd ər 'pɑːm-,
   'pɔːlm-, 'pɔːm- ~s z
Palme 'pɑːlm ə —Swedish ['pal mə]
palmer, P~ 'pɑːm ə §'pɑːlm-, §'pælm-, §'pɒlm-
   ‖ 'pɑːlm ər 'pɑːm-, 'pɔːlm-, 'pɔːm- ~s, ~'s z
Palmerston 'pɑːm əst ən §'pɑːlm-, §'pælm-,
   §'pɒlm- ‖ 'pɑːlm ərst- 'pɑːm-, 'pɔːlm-,
   'pɔːm-
   ˌPalmerston 'North
palmetto pæl 'met əʊ pɑː-, §pɑːl-, §pɒl-
   ‖ -'met̬ oʊ ~s z
palmist 'pɑːm ɪst §'pɑːlm-, §'pælm-, §'pɒlm-,
   §-əst ‖ 'pɑːlm ɪst 'pɑːm-, 'pɔːlm-, 'pɔːm- ~s s
palmistry 'pɑːm ɪs tri §'pɑːlm-, §'pælm-,
   §'pɒlm-, -əs- ‖ 'pɑːlm əs tri 'pɑːm-, 'pɔːlm-,
   'pɔːm-
palmitate 'pælm ɪ teɪt 'pɑːm-, §'pɑːlm-,
   §'pɒlm-, -ə- ~s s
palmitic pælm 'ɪt ɪk pɑː-, §pɑːl-, §pɒl-
   ‖ -'ɪt̬ ɪk
palmitin 'pælm ɪt ɪn 'pɑːm-, §'pɑːlm-, §'pɒlm-,
   -ət-, §-ən ‖ -ət ən
Palmolive tdmk ˌpɑːm 'ɒl ɪv §ˌpɑːlm-, §ˌpælm-,
   §ˌpɒlm-, §-əv ‖ ˌpɑːlm 'ɑːl ɪv ˌpɑːm-, ˌpɔːlm-,
   ˌpɔːm-
palmtop 'pɑːm tɒp §'pɑːlm-, §'pælm-, §'pɒlm-
   ‖ 'pɑːlm tɑːp 'pɑːm-, 'pɔːlm-, 'pɔːm- ~s s
palm|y 'pɑːm li §'pɑːlm-, §'pælm-,
   §'pɒlm- ‖ 'pɑːlm li 'pɑːm-, 'pɔːlm-, 'pɔːm-
   ~ier i_ə ‖ i_ər ~iest i_ɪst i_əst
Palmyra, p~ ₍ₗ₎pæl 'maɪ³r ə ~s z
Palo Alto ˌpæl əʊ 'ælt əʊ ‖ ˌpæl oʊ 'ælt̬ oʊ
palolo pə 'ləʊl əʊ ‖ -'loʊl oʊ
Palomar 'pæl əʊ mɑː ‖ -ə mɑːr ,•'•
palomino, P~ ˌpæl ə 'miːn əʊ ‖ -oʊ ~s z
palooka pə 'luːk ə ~s z
Palouse pə 'luːs
palp pælp palps pælps
palpability ˌpælp ə 'bɪl ət i -ɪt i ‖ -ət̬ i
palpab|le 'pælp əb |ᵊl ~ly li
palp|ate v pæl 'pleɪt 'pælp leɪt ‖ 'pælp leɪt
   ~ated eɪt ɪd -əd ‖ eɪt̬ əd ~ates eɪts ~ating
   eɪt ɪŋ ‖ eɪt̬ ɪŋ
palpate adj 'pælp eɪt
palpation pæl 'peɪʃ ən
palpebral 'pælp ɪb rəl -əb-; pæl 'piːb-, -'peb-
palpi 'pælp aɪ -iː
palpi|tate 'pælp ɪ |teɪt -ə- ~tated teɪt ɪd -əd
   ‖ teɪt̬ əd ~tates teɪts ~tating
   teɪt ɪŋ ‖ teɪt̬ ɪŋ
palpitation ˌpælp ɪ 'teɪʃ ən -ə- ~s z
palsgrave, P~ 'pɔːlz greɪv ‖ 'pɑːlz-
pals|y 'pɔːlz li 'pɒlz- ‖ 'pɑːlz- ~ied id ~ies iz
   ~ying i ɪŋ

palsy-walsy ˌpælz i ˈwælz i ◂
palt|er ˈpɔːlt lə ˈpɒlt- ‖ -|ˀr ˈpɑːlt- ~ered
əd ‖ ˀrd ~ering ˌˀr ıŋ ~ers əz ‖ ˀrz
Paltrow ˈpæltr əʊ ‖ -oʊ
paltr|y ˈpɔːltr li ˈpɒltr- ‖ ˈpɑːltr- ~ier i̯ə ‖ i̯ˀr
~iest i̯ıst i̯əst ~ily ı li əl i ~iness i nəs i nıs
paludal pə ˈluːd əl -ˈljuːd-; ˈpæl jʊd-, -jəd-
Paludrine, p~ ˈpæl ju drın -u-, -jə-, -driːn
palynolog|ist/s ˌpæl ı ˈnɒl ədʒ |ıst/s ˌ•ə-,
§-əst/s ‖ -ˈnɑːl- ~y i
Pam pæm
Pama-Nyungan ˌpɑːm ə ˈnjʊŋ ən ◂ -gən
Pamela ˈpæm əl̯ə -ıl ə
Pamir pə ˈmıə ‖ -ˈmıˀr ~s z
Pamlico ˈpæm lı kəʊ -lə- ‖ -koʊ
ˌPamlico ˈSound
pampa, Pampa ˈpæmp ə —Sp [ˈpam pa]
pampas ˈpæmp əs -əz
ˈpampas grass
pamper ˈpæmp ə ‖ -ˀr ~ed d ~pampering
ˈpæmp ˀr̯ıŋ ~s z
Pampers tdmk ˈpæmp əz ‖ -ˀrz
pamphlet ˈpæmpf lət -lıt ~s s
pamphle|teer ˌpæmpf lə |ˈtıə -lı- ‖ -|ˈtıˀr
~teered ˈtıəd ‖ ˈtıˀrd ~teering
ˈtıər ıŋ ‖ ˈtır ıŋ ~teers ˈtıəz ‖ ˈtıˀrz
Pamphyli|a pæm ˈfıl i̯ə ~an/s ən/z
Pamplona pæm ˈpləʊn ə ‖ -ˈploʊn ə — Sp
[pam ˈplo na]
pan, Pan pæn —but in the sense 'betel leaf',
pɑːn panned pænd panning ˈpæn ıŋ pans
pænz
ˌPan ˈAm tdmk
pan- ˌpæn — Pan-African ˌpæn ˈæf rık ən ◂
panacea ˌpæn ə ˈsıə -ˈsiː̯ə ‖ -ˈsiː ə ~s z
panache pə ˈnæʃ pæ-, -ˈnɑːʃ
panada pə ˈnɑːd ə ~s z
Panadol tdmk ˈpæn ə dɒl ‖ -dɑːl ~s z
Panama, p~ ˈpæn ə mɑː ˌ•ˈ•ˈ• ‖ -mɔː — Sp
Panamá [pa na ˈma] ~s, ~'s z
ˌPanama Caˈnal; ˌPanama ˈhat
Panamanian ˌpæn ə ˈmeın i̯ən ◂ ~s z
Panasonic tdmk ˌpæn ə ˈsɒn ık ‖ -ˈsɑːn ık
panatela, panatella ˌpæn ə ˈtel ə ~s z
Panathenaea ˌpæn ˌæθ ı ˈniː̯ə •, ˌ•ˈ•ˈ••, -əˈ•-
pancak|e ˈpæn keık ˈpæŋk eık ~ed t ~es s
~ing ıŋ
ˈPancake Day; ˌpancake ˈlanding; ˌpancake
ˈroll; ˌPancake ˈTuesday
panchax ˈpæn tʃæks ~es ız əz
panchromatic ˌpæn krəʊ ˈmæt ık ◂→ˌpæŋ-
‖ -kroʊ ˈmæt̬ ık ◂ -krə-
Pancras ˈpæŋk rəs
pancreas ˈpæŋk ri̯əs -æs ‖ ˈpæn kri- ~es ız əz
pancreatic ˌpæŋk ri ˈæt ık ◂ ‖ -ˈæt̬ ık ◂
ˌpæn kri-
pancreatin ˈpæŋk ri̯ət ın pæn ˈkriː̯, →ˌpæŋ-,
§-ən ‖ -ən
pancreatitis ˌpæŋk ri̯ə ˈtaıt ıs §-əs ‖ -ˈtaıt̬ əs
panda ˈpænd ə ~s z
ˈpanda car; ˌpanda ˈcrossing
pandanus pæn ˈdeın əs -ˈdæn- ~es ız əz
Pandarus ˈpænd ˀr əs

pandect ˈpæn dekt ~s s
pandemic ˌ(ı)pæn ˈdem ık ~s s
pandemonium ˌpænd ə ˈməʊn i̯əm ˌ•ı-
‖ -ˈmoʊn-
pander ˈpænd ə ‖ -ˀr ~ed d pandering
ˈpænd ˀr ıŋ ~s z
pandialectal ˌpæn ˌdaı̯ə ˈlekt əl ◂
pandit, P~ ˈpænd ıt ˈpʌnd-, §-ət —Hindi
[pən ˌɖıt̪] ~s s
Pandora, p~ ˌ(ı)pæn ˈdɔːr ə ‖ -ˈdoʊr- ~s, ~'s z
Panˌdora's ˈbox
pandowd|y pæn ˈdaʊd.li ~ies iz
pane, Pane peın (= pain) paned peınd panes
peınz
panegyric ˌpæn ə ˈdʒır ık -ı- ‖ -ˈdʒaır- ~s s
panegyrist ˌpæn ə ˈdʒır ıst -ı-, §-əst,
ˈ••••‖ -ˈdʒaır- ~s s
panegyris|e, panegyriz|e ˈpæn ədʒ ə raız
ˈ•ıdʒ-, -ı• ~ed d ~es ız əz ~ing ıŋ
panel ˈpæn əl ~ed, ~led d ~ing, ~ling ıŋ ~s z
ˈpanel ˌbeater; ˈpanel saw
panelist, panellist ˈpæn əl ıst §-əst ~s z
panetton|e ˌpæn ə ˈtəʊn li -ı- ‖ -ˈtoʊn li ˌpɑːn-
—It [pa netˈ ˈtoː ne] ~es ız ~i iː
pan-|fry ˈpæn |fraı ~fried fraıd ~fries fraız
~frying fraı ıŋ
panful ˈpæn fʊl ~s z
pang pæŋ pangs pæŋz
panga ˈpæŋ gə ‖ ˈpɑːŋ gə ~s z
Pangaea pæn ˈdʒiː̯ə
Pangbourne ˈpæŋ bɔːn ‖ -bɔːrn -boʊrn
Pangloss ˈpæn glɒs →ˈpæŋ- ‖ -glɑːs -glɔːs
Panglossian, p~ ˌ(ı)pæn ˈglɒs i̯ən →ˌ(ı)pæŋ-
‖ -ˈglɑːs- -ˈglɔːs-
pangolin pæŋ ˈgəʊl ın §-ən; ˈpæŋg əʊ lın, §-lən
‖ ˈpæŋ gəl ən ˈpæn-, •ˈgoʊl- ~s z
panhandl|e ˈpæn ˌhænd əl ~ed d ~er/s ˌə/
z ‖ ˌˀr/z ~es z ~ing ˌıŋ
panhellenic ˌpæn hı ˈlen ık ◂ -he-, -hə-, -ı-, -ə-,
-ˈliːn-
panhellenism ˌpæn ˈhel ın ˌız əm -ən-
panic ˈpæn ık ~ked t ~king ıŋ ~s s
ˈpanic ˌbutton; ˈpanic ˌstations
panicky ˈpæn ık i
panicle ˈpæn ık əl ~s z
panic-|stricken ˈpæn ık ˌstrık ən ~struck
strʌk
panicle ˈpæn ık əl ~s z
Panini Italian name pə ˈniːn i —It [pa ˈniː ni]
Panini Sanskrit name ˈpɑːn ı niː -ni —Skt
[ˈpɑː ɳı ɳi]
Panjab ˌpʌn ˈdʒɑːb ˈ••
Panjabi ˌ(ı)pʌn ˈdʒɑːb i pən-, -iː ~s z
panjandrum pæn ˈdʒændr əm pən- ~s z
Pankhurst ˈpæŋk hɜːst ‖ -hɜ˞ːst
panlectal ˌpæn ˈlekt əl ◂
Panmunjom ˌpæn mʊn ˈdʒɒm
‖ ˌpɑːn mʊn ˈdʒɑːm —Korean
[pʰan mun dʒɔm]
pannage ˈpæn ıdʒ
Pannal, Pannell ˈpæn əl
panne pæn (= pan)
pannier ˈpæn i̯ə ‖ ˌˀr ~ed d ~s z

P

pannikin 'pæn ɪ kɪn -ə-, §-kən ~s z
Pannonia pə 'nəʊn i‿ə pæ- ‖ -'noʊn-
panoch|a pə 'nəʊtʃ |ə ‖ -'noʊtʃ- ~e i
panop|ly 'pæn əp |li ~lied lid ~lies liz
panoptic ₍ᵢ₎pæn 'ɒpt ɪk ‖ -'ɑːpt- ~al əl
panopticon ₍ᵢ₎pæn 'ɒpt ɪk ən §-ək-
 ‖ -'ɑːpt ə kɑːn ~s z
panorama, P~ ˌpæn ə 'rɑːm ə ‖ -'ræm ə -'rɑːm-
 ~s z
panoramic ˌpæn ə 'ræm ɪk ◄ -'rɑːm- ~ally əl‿i
panpipes 'pæn paɪps →'pæm-
Pan-Slavism ˌpæn 'slɑːv ˌɪz əm -'slæv-
pans|y, Pans|y 'pænz li ~ies, ~y's iz
pant pænt panted 'pænt ɪd -əd ‖ 'pænt̬ əd
 panting/ly 'pænt ɪŋ /li ‖ 'pænt̬ ɪŋ /li pants
 pænts
Pantagruel ˌpænt ə gru 'el '•‿gru‿əl
 ‖ pæn 'tæg ru el ˌpænt̬ ə 'gruː‿əl —Fr
 [pɑ̃ ta gʁy ɛl]
Pantagruelian ˌpænt ə gru el i‿ən ◄
 ˌpænt ə 'gruːl i‿ən ‖ ˌpænt̬ ə-
pantalette ˌpænt ə 'let -əl 'et ‖ ˌpænt̬ əl 'et ~s
 s
pantaloon, P~ ˌpænt ə 'luːn →-əl 'uːn, '•••
 ‖ ˌpænt̬ əl 'uːn ~s z
pantechnicon pæn 'tek nɪk ən ~s z
Pantelleria ˌpæn tel ə 'riː‿ə •ˌ•- —It
 [pan tel le 'riː a]
Pantene tdmk ˌpæn 'ten
pantheism 'pæntᵗθ i ˌɪz əm
pantheist 'pæntᵗθ i ɪst §-əst ~s s
pantheistic ˌpæntᵗθ i 'ɪst ɪk ◄ ~al əl ~ally əl‿i
pantheon 'pæntᵗθ i‿ən pæn 'θiː‿, -ɒn ‖ -ɑːn ~s
 z
panther 'pæntᵗθ ə ‖ -ᵊr ~s z
pantie girdle 'pænt i ˌgɜːd əl ‖ 'pænt̬ i ˌgɝːd əl
 ~s z
panties 'pænt iz ‖ 'pænt̬ iz
pantihose 'pænt i həʊz ‖ 'pænt̬ i hoʊz
pantile 'pæn taɪəl ~s z
panto 'pænt əʊ ‖ -oʊ ~s z
pantograph 'pænt əʊ grɑːf -græf ‖ 'pænt̬
 ə græf ~s s
pantomime 'pænt ə maɪm ‖ 'pænt̬- ~s z
pantomimic ˌpænt ə 'mɪm ɪk ◄ ‖ ˌpænt̬-
pantomimist 'pænt ə maɪm ɪst §-əst, ˌ•••••
 ‖ 'pænt̬- ~s s
Panton 'pænt ən ‖ -ᵊn
pantothenic ˌpænt ə 'θen ɪk ◄ ‖ ˌpænt̬-
pantr|y 'pæntr li ~ies iz
pants pænts
pantsuit 'pænt suːt -sjuːt
pant|y 'pænt li ‖ 'pænt̬ li ~ies iz
 'panty hose; 'panty raid
Pantycelyn ˌpænt ə 'kel ɪn —Welsh
 [ˌpant ə 'ke lin]
pantywaist 'pænt i weɪst ‖ 'pænt̬- ~s s
Pan Yan tdmk ˌpæn 'jæn ◄
Panza 'pænz ə —Sp ['pan θa]
panzer 'pænz ə ‖ -ᵊr —Ger ['pan tsɐ] ~s z
pap, Pap pæp paps pæps
papa, Papa pə 'pɑː ‖ 'pɑːp ə —but as code

name for the letter P, usually 'pɑːp ə even in
 BrE ~s z
papabile pɑː 'pɑːb ɪ leɪ —It [pa 'paː bi le]
papac|y 'peɪp əs li ~ies iz
Papadopoulos ˌpæp ə 'dɒp əl əs
 ‖ ˌpɑːp ə 'dɑːp- —Greek [pa pa 'ðo pu los]
papadum 'pæp əd əm 'pʌp-, 'pɒp-, -ə dʌm ~s
 z
papain pə 'peɪ ɪn -'paɪ-, §-ən
papal 'peɪp əl ~ly i
Papandreou ˌpæp æn 'dreɪ uː ‖ ˌpɑːp ɑːn-
 —Greek [pa pan 'dre u]
paparazz|o ˌpæp ə 'ræts |əʊ -'rɑːts-
 ‖ ˌpɑːp ə 'rɑːts |oʊ -'rɑːz- ~i i -iː —It
 [pa pa 'rat tso]
papaverine pə 'pæv ə riːn -'peɪv-, -rɪn, -rən
papaw 'pɔːp ɔː pə 'pɔː ‖ 'pɔːp ɔː 'pɑːp-; -ɑː ~s
 z
papaya pə 'paɪ‿ə ~s z
Papeete ˌpɑːp i 'eɪt i -ə-, -'iːt-; pə 'piːt i
 ‖ -'eɪt eɪ pə 'piːt̬ i
paper 'peɪp ə ‖ -ᵊr ~ed d papering 'peɪp
 ᵊr‿ɪŋ ~s z
 ˌpaper 'bag (bag made of paper), 'paper bag
 (bag for newspapers); 'paper chase; 'paper
 clip; 'paper knife; 'paper ˌmoney; ˌpaper
 'tiger; 'paper trail
paperback 'peɪp ə bæk ‖ -ᵊr- ~s s
paperboy 'peɪp ə bɔɪ ‖ -ᵊr- ~s z
paperclip 'peɪp ə klɪp ‖ -ᵊr- ~s s
paperhanger 'peɪp ə ˌhæŋ ə ‖ -ᵊr ˌhæŋ ᵊr ~s z
paperless 'peɪp ə ləs -lɪs ‖ -ᵊr-
paperweight 'peɪp ə weɪt ‖ -ᵊr- ~s s
paperwork 'peɪp ə wɜːk ‖ -ᵊr wɝːk
papery 'peɪp ᵊr i
Paphlagoni|a ˌpæf lə 'gəʊn i‿ə ‖ -'goʊn-
 ~an/s ən/z
Paphos 'pæf ɒs 'peɪf- ‖ -oʊs 'pɑːf- —Greek
 ['pa fos]
Papiament|o ˌpæp i‿ə 'ment əʊ ˌpɑːp-
 ‖ ˌpɑːp jə 'ment oʊ ~u uː
papier-mache, papier-mâché
 ˌpæp i eɪ 'mæʃ eɪ ◄ ˌpeɪp ə 'mæʃ-
 ‖ ˌpeɪp ᵊr mə 'ʃeɪ ◄ -mæ'• (*) —Fr
 [pa pje ma ʃe]
papill|a pə 'pɪl ə ~ae iː
papillary pə 'pɪl ᵊr i ‖ 'pæp ə ler i
papillate 'pæp ɪ leɪt -ə-, →-əl eɪt, pə 'pɪl eɪt
papillom|a ˌpæp ɪ 'ləʊm lə -ə- ‖ -'loʊm lə ~as
 əz ~ata ət ə ‖ ət̬ ə
papillon, P~ 'pæp ɪ lɒn -ə- ‖ -lɑːn 'pɑːp- —Fr
 [pa pi jɔ̃] ~s z
papillote 'pæp ɪ lɒt -ə-, -ləʊt ‖ ˌpæp ɪ 'joʊt
 ˌpɑːp- —Fr [pa pi jɔt] ~s s
papist 'peɪp ɪst §-əst ~s s
papistic peɪ 'pɪst ɪk pə- ~al əl
papistry 'peɪp ɪs tri -əs-
papoos|e pə 'puːs ‖ pæ- pə- ~es ɪz əz
papp|ous, ~us 'pæp |əs ~i aɪ
papp|y 'pæp li ~ier i‿ə ‖ i‿ᵊr ~iest i‿ɪst i‿əst
 ~ies iz
paprika 'pæp rɪk ə; pə 'priːk ə, pæ-
 ‖ pə 'priːk ə pæ- (*)

Papu|a 'pæp u_|ə 'pɑːp-, -ju- **~an/s** ən/z
 ˌPapua New 'Guinea
papule 'pæp juːl **~s** z
Papworth 'pæp wɜːθ -wəθ ‖ -wᵊrθ
papyr|us pə 'paɪᵊr |əs **~i** aɪ **~uses** əs ɪz -əz
par, Par pɑː ‖ pɑːr
 ˌpar 'value
para *'paratrooper', 'paragraph'* 'pær ə ‖ 'per ə
 ~s z
para *monetary unit* 'pɑːr ə **~s** z
Pará *river in Brazil* pə 'rɑː— —*Port* [pɐ 'ra]
para- *comb. form*
 with stress-neutral suffix ˌpær ə ‖ ˌper ə —
 parapraxis ˌpær ə 'præks ɪs §-əs ‖ ˌper-
 with stress-imposing suffix pə 'ræ+ —
 parabasis pə 'ræb əs ɪs §-əs
parable 'pær əb ᵊl ‖ 'per- **~s** z
parabola pə 'ræb əl ə **~s** z
parabolic ˌpær ə 'bɒl ɪk ◄ ‖ ˌpær ə 'bɑːl ɪk ◄
 ˌper- **~al** ᵊl **~ally** ᵊl_i
paraboloid pə 'ræb ə lɔɪd **~s** z
Paraburdoo ˌpær ə bə 'duː ‖ -bᵊr'• ˌper-
Paracelsus ˌpær ə 'sels əs ‖ ˌper-
paracetamol ˌpær ə 'siːt ə mɒl -'set-
 ‖ -'siːt ə mɑːl ˌper-, -'set-, -mɔːl, -moʊl **~s** z
para|chute 'pær ə |ʃuːt ‖ 'per- **~chuted**
 ʃuːt ɪd -əd ‖ 'ʃuːt̬ əd **~chutes** ʃuːts
 ~chuting ʃuːt ɪŋ ‖ ʃuːt̬ ɪŋ
parachutist 'pær ə ʃuːt ɪst §-əst, ˌ••'••
 ‖ -ʃuːt̬ əst 'per- **~s** s
Paraclete, p~ 'pær ə kliːt ‖ 'per-
parad|e pə 'reɪd **~ed** ɪd əd **~es** z **~ing** ɪŋ
 pa'rade ground
paradichlorobenzene ˌpær ə ˌdaɪ klɔːr əʊ
 'benz iːn ˌ•••ˌ•- ‖ -oʊ'•• ˌper-, -kloʊr•'•••,
 -ben 'ziːn
paradigm 'pær ə daɪm ‖ 'per-, -dɪm **~s** z
paradigmatic ˌpær ə dɪg 'mæt ɪk ◄ ‖ -'mæt̬ ɪk ◄
 ˌper- **~ally** ᵊl_i
paradisal ˌpær ə 'daɪs ᵊl ◄ -'daɪz- ‖ ˌper-
paradise, P~ 'pær ə daɪs ‖ 'per-, -daɪz
paradisiac ˌpær ə 'dɪz i æk ◄ ; -'dɪs-;
 -dɪ 'saɪ_æk, -də'•- ‖ ˌper-
paradisiacal ˌpær ə dɪ 'saɪ_ək ᵊl ◄ -də'•- ‖ ˌper-
parador 'pær ə dɔː ‖ ˌpɑːr ɑː 'dɔːr —*Sp*
 [pa ra 'ðor] **~s** z
parados 'pær ə dɒs ‖ -dɑːs 'per- **~es** ɪz əz
paradox 'pær ə dɒks ‖ -dɑːks 'per- **~es** ɪz əz
paradoxical ˌpær ə 'dɒks ɪk ᵊl ◄ ‖ -'dɑːks-
 ˌper- **~ly** _i **~ness** nəs nɪs
paraffin 'pær ə fɪn -fiːn, ˌ••'••; §'pær əf
 ən ‖ 'per-
 'paraffin wax, ˌ••• '•
paraglid|er 'pær ə ˌglaɪd ə ‖ -ᵊr 'per- **~ers**
 əz ‖ ᵊrz **~ing** ɪŋ
paragoge ˌpær ə 'gəʊdʒ i ‖ -'goʊdʒ i ˌper-
paragogic ˌpær ə 'gɒdʒ ɪk ◄ ‖ -'gɑːdʒ- ˌper-
paragon 'pær əg ən ‖ -ə gɑːn 'per-, -əg ən *(*)*
 ~s z
paragraph 'pær ə grɑːf -græf ‖ -græf 'per-
 ~ed t **~ing** ɪŋ **~s** s
paragraphia ˌpær ə 'græf i_ə -'grɑːf- ‖ ˌper-

Paraguay 'pær ə gwaɪ ˌ••'• ‖ 'per-, -gweɪ —*Sp*
 [pa ra 'ɣwai]
Paraguayan ˌpær ə 'gwaɪ_ən ◄ ‖ ˌper-, -'gweɪ-
 ~s z
parakeet 'pær ə kiːt ˌ••'• ‖ 'per- **~s** s
paralanguage 'pær ə ˌlæŋ gwɪdʒ -wɪdʒ ‖ 'per-
paraldehyde pə 'ræld ɪ haɪd -'•ə-
paralegal ˌpær ə 'liːg ᵊl ◄ ‖ ˌper- **~s** z
paralinguistic ˌpær ə lɪŋ 'gwɪst ɪk ◄ ‖ ˌper-
 ~ally ᵊl_i **~s** s
parallactic ˌpær ə 'lækt ɪk ◄ ‖ ˌper- **~ally** ᵊl_i
parallax 'pær ə læks ‖ 'per- **~es** ɪz əz
parallel 'pær ə lel -ᵊl əl ‖ 'per- **~ed, ~led** d
 ~ing, ~ling ɪŋ **~s** z
 ˌparallel 'bars
parallelepiped ˌpær ə lel ə 'paɪp ed
 ˌ•••'ep ɪ ped, -ə• ‖ ˌper- **~s** z
parallelism 'pær ə lel ˌɪz əm -ləl,•-;
 △'pær ə ˌlɪz əm ‖ 'per- **~s** z
parallelogram ˌpær ə 'lel ə græm ‖ ˌper- **~s** z
paralogism pə 'ræl ə ˌdʒɪz əm **~s** z
Paralympics ˌpær ə 'lɪmp ɪks ‖ ˌper-
paralysation ˌpær ə laɪ 'zeɪʃ ᵊn ‖ -lə'•- ˌper-
paralys|e 'pær ə laɪz ‖ 'per- **~ed** d **~es** ɪz əz
 ~ing/ly ɪŋ/ li
paralyses *from v* 'pær ə laɪz ɪz -əz ‖ 'per-
paralyses *n pl* pə 'ræl ə siːz -ɪ-
paral|ysis pə 'ræl |əs ɪs -ɪs-, §-əs **~yses** ə siːz ɪ-
paralytic ˌpær ə 'lɪt ɪk ◄ ‖ -'lɪt̬ ɪk ◄ ˌper- **~ally**
 ᵊl_i **~s** s
paralyzation ˌpær ə laɪ 'zeɪʃ ᵊn ‖ -lə'•- ˌper-
paralyz|e 'pær ə laɪz ‖ 'per- **~ed** d **~es** ɪz əz
 ~ing ɪŋ
paramagnetic ˌpær ə mæg 'net ɪk ◄ -məg'•-
 ‖ -'net̬ ɪk ◄ ˌper-
paramagnetism ˌpær ə 'mæg nə ˌtɪz əm
 -'•nɪ- ‖ ˌper-
Paramaribo ˌpær ə 'mær ɪ bəʊ §-'•ə- ‖ -boʊ
 ˌper- —*Dutch* [pa: ra: 'ma: ri bo:]
paramatta ˌpær ə 'mæt ə ‖ -'mæt̬ ə ˌper-
parameci|um ˌpær ə 'miːs i_|əm ‖ ˌper-, -'miːʃ-
 ~a ə **~ums** əmz
paramedic ˌpær ə 'med ɪk ‖ ˌper- **~al** ᵊl ◄ **~s** s
parameter pə 'ræm ɪt ə -ət- ‖ -ət̬ ᵊr **~s** z
parameteris... —*see* **parameteriz...**
parameterization pə ˌræm ɪt_ᵊr aɪ 'zeɪʃ ᵊn
 -ˌ•ət_, -ɪ'•- ‖ -ət̬ ᵊr ə- →-ˌ•ətr ə'••
parameteriz|e pə 'ræm ɪt ə raɪz -'•ət-;
 →•'•ɪ traɪz, -ə- **~ed** d **~es** ɪz əz **~ing** ɪŋ
parametric ˌpær ə 'metr ɪk ◄ ‖ ˌper- **~ally** ᵊl_i
parametris... —*see* **parametriz...**
parametrization pə ˌræm ətr aɪ 'zeɪʃ ᵊn -ˌ•ɪtr-,
 -ɪ'•- ‖ -ə'•-
parametriz|e pə 'ræm ə traɪz -ɪ- **~ed** d **~es** ɪz
 əz **~ing** ɪŋ
paramilitar|y ˌpær ə 'mɪl ɪt_ᵊr li ◄ -'•ət_
 ‖ -ə ter li ˌper- **~ies** iz
paramnesia ˌpær æm 'niːz i_ə -'niːʒ ə ‖ -'niːʒ ə
 ˌper-
paramount 'pær ə maʊnt ‖ 'per- **~cy** si **~ly** li
paramour, P~ 'pær ə mʊə -mɔː ‖ 'pær ə mɔːr
 'per- **~s** z
Paramus pə 'ræm əs

Paraná ˌpær ə 'nɑː ‖ ˌper-, ˌpɑːr- —*Port*
[pɐ rɐ 'na], *Sp* [pa ra 'na]

parang 'pɑːr æŋ ~**s** z

paranoi|a ˌpær ə 'nɔɪ |ə ‖ ˌper- ~**ac** æk ◀ ɪk
~**acally** æk ᵊl_i ɪk-

paranoid 'pær ə nɔɪd ‖ 'per- ~**s** z

paranormal ˌpær ə 'nɔːm ᵊl ◀ -'nɔːrm ᵊl ◀
ˌper- ~**ly** i

parapet 'pær əp ɪt -ət, -ə pet ‖ 'per- ~**s** s

paraph 'pær æf -əf ‖ 'per-; pə 'ræf ~**s** s

paraphernalia ˌpær ə fə 'neɪl i_ə ‖ -ə fᵊr- ˌper-

paraphilia ˌpær ə 'fɪl i_ə ‖ ˌper- ~**s** z

paraphras|e *n, v* 'pær ə freɪz ‖ 'per- ~**ed** d
~**es** ɪz əz ~**ing** ɪŋ

paraphrastic ˌpær ə 'fræst ɪk ◀ ‖ ˌper- ~**ally**
ᵊl_i

paraplegia ˌpær ə 'pliːdʒ ə -'pliːdʒ i_ə ‖ ˌper-

paraplegic ˌpær ə 'pliːdʒ ɪk ◀ ‖ ˌper- ~**s** s

paraprax|is ˌpær ə 'præks |ɪs ˌper- ~**es** iːz

parapsychologic ˌpær ə ˌsaɪk ə 'lɒdʒ ɪk
-ˌpsaɪk- ‖ -'lɑːdʒ- ˌper- ~**al/ly** ᵊl/_i

parapsycholog|ist/s ˌpær ə saɪ 'kɒl ədʒ |ɪst/s
-psaɪ'•-, §-əst/s ‖ -'kɑːl- ˌper- ~**y** i

paraquat, P~ *tdmk* 'pær ə kwɒt -kwæt ‖ -kwɑːt
'per-

paras 'pær əz ‖ 'per-

parasailing 'pær ə ˌseɪᵊl ɪŋ ‖ 'per-

parasang 'pær ə sæŋ ‖ 'per- ~**s** z

parascend|ing 'pær ə ˌsend| ɪŋ ‖ 'per- ~**er/s**
ə/z ‖ ᵊr/z

para|shah, P~ 'pær ə |ʃɑː ‖ 'pɑːr- ~**shoth**
ʃəʊt ‖ ʃoʊt

parasite 'pær ə saɪt ‖ 'per- ~**s** s

parasitic ˌpær ə 'sɪt ɪk ◀ ‖ -'sɪt̮ ɪk ◀ ˌper- ~**al** ᵊl
~**ally** ᵊl_i

parasitism 'pær ə saɪt ˌɪz əm -sɪ ˌtɪz- ‖ -ə saɪt̮-
'per-, -sə ˌtɪz-

parasitology ˌpær ə saɪt 'ɒl ədʒ i -sɪ 'tɒl-
‖ -saɪt̮ 'ɑːl- ˌper-, -sə 'tɑːl-

parasol 'pær ə sɒl ˌ•••' ‖ -sɔːl 'per-, -sɑːl ~**s** z

parasympathetic
ˌpær ə ˌsɪmp ə 'θet ɪk ◀ ‖ -'θet̮ ɪk ◀ ˌper-

parasynthesis ˌpær ə 'sɪntᵊθ əs ɪs -ɪs ɪs, §-əs
‖ ˌper-

parasynthetic ˌpær ə sɪn 'θet ɪk ◀ ‖ -'θet̮ ɪk ◀
ˌper- ~**ally** ᵊl_i

paratactic ˌpær ə 'tækt ɪk ◀ ‖ ˌper- ~**ally** ᵊl_i

parataxis ˌpær ə 'tæks ɪs §-əs, '••••‖ ˌper-

parathion ˌpær ə 'θaɪ ɒn -'θaɪˌɒn ‖ -ɑːn ˌper-

parathyroid ˌpær ə 'θaɪᵊr ɔɪd ◀ ‖ ˌper- ~**s** z
ˌpara'thyroid gland, ••,••'•

paratroop 'pær ə truːp ‖ 'per- ~**er/s** ə/z ‖ ᵊr/z
~**s** s

paratyphoid ˌpær ə 'taɪf ɔɪd ‖ ˌper-

paravane 'pær ə veɪn ‖ 'per- ~**s** z

parboil 'pɑː bɔɪᵊl ‖ 'pɑːr- ~**ed** d ~**ing** ɪŋ ~**s** z

parbuckle 'pɑː bʌk ᵊl ‖ 'pɑːr- ~**s** z

parcel 'pɑːs ᵊl ‖ 'pɑːrs ᵊl ~**ed**, ~**led** d ~**ing**,
~**ling** ˌɪŋ ~**s** z
'parcel post

parch pɑːtʃ ‖ pɑːrtʃ **parched** pɑːtʃt ‖ pɑːrtʃt
parches 'pɑːtʃ ɪz -əz ‖ 'pɑːrtʃ əz **parching**
'pɑːtʃ ɪŋ ‖ 'pɑːrtʃ ɪŋ

parchedness 'pɑːtʃt nəs -nɪs ‖ 'pɑːrtʃt-

parcheesi, parchesi pɑː 'tʃiːz i -'tʃiːs i ‖ pɑːr-

parchment 'pɑːtʃ mənt ‖ 'pɑːrtʃ- ~**s** s

pard pɑːd ‖ pɑːrd **pards** pɑːdz ‖ pɑːrdz

pardalote 'pɑːd ə ləʊt →-ᵊl əʊt ‖ 'pɑːrd ᵊl oʊt
~**s** s

pardner, P~ 'pɑːd nə ‖ 'pɑːrd nᵊr ~**s** z

Pardoe 'pɑːd əʊ ‖ 'pɑːrd oʊ

pardon 'pɑːd ᵊn ‖ 'pɑːrd ᵊn ~**ed** d ~**ing** ˌɪŋ
~**s** z

pardonab|le 'pɑːd ᵊn_əb |ᵊl ‖ 'pɑːrd- ~**ly** li

pardoner 'pɑːd ᵊn_ə ‖ 'pɑːrd ᵊn_ᵊr ~**s** z

pare peə ‖ peᵊr pæᵊr (= *pair*) **pared**
peəd ‖ peᵊrd pæᵊrd **pares** peəz ‖ peᵊrz
pæᵊrz **paring** 'peər ɪŋ ‖ 'per ɪŋ 'pær-

paregoric ˌpær ə 'gɒr ɪk ◀ -ɪ- ‖ -'gɔːr ɪk ◀
ˌper-, -'gɑːr-

parenchyma pə 'reŋk ɪm ə §-əm-

par|ent *n, v* 'peər |ənt ‖ 'per |ənt 'pær- ~**ented**
ənt ɪd -əd ‖ ənt̮ əd ~**enting** ənt ɪŋ ‖ ənt̮ ɪŋ
~**ents** ənts
'parent ˌcompany,, ••' •••

parentag|e 'peər ənt ɪdʒ ‖ 'per ənt̮ ɪdʒ 'pær-
~**es** ɪz əz

parental pə 'rent ᵊl ‖ -'rent̮ ᵊl ~**ly** i

parenteral pæ 'rent ər əl pə- ‖ -'rent̮-

parenth|esis pə 'rentᵊθ |əs ɪs -ɪs-, §-əs ~**eses**
ə siːz ɪ-

parenthesis|e, parenthesiz|e pə 'rentᵊθ ə saɪz
~**ed** d ~**es** ɪz əz ~**ing** ɪŋ

parenthetic ˌpær ən 'θet ɪk ◀ -en- ‖ -'θet̮ ɪk ◀
ˌper- ~**al** ᵊl ~**ally** ᵊl_i

parenthood 'peər ənt hʊd ‖ 'per- 'pær-

parentless 'peər ənt ləs -lɪs ‖ 'per- 'pær-

parent-teacher ˌpeər ənt 'tiːtʃ ə ‖ ˌper
ənt 'tiːtʃ ᵊr ˌpær-
ˌparent-'teacher associˌation

pareo 'pɑːr eɪ əʊ pɑː 'reɪ- ‖ -oʊ ~**s** z

parer 'peər ə ‖ 'per ᵊr 'pær- ~**s** z

parerg|on pə 'rɜːg |ɒn -'eəg-, -|ən ‖ -'rɜːg ɑːn
-'rerg- ~**a** ə

paresis pə 'riːs ɪs §-əs; 'pær əs-, -ɪs-

paretic pə 'ret ɪk ‖ -'ret̮-

pareu 'pɑːr eɪ uː pɑː 'reɪ- ~**s** z

par excellence ₍ₗ₎pɑːr 'eks ə lɑːⁿs -lõs,
-əl ˌənts ‖ ˌpɑːr ˌeks ə 'lɑːⁿts —*Fr*
[pa ʁɛk sɛ lɑ̃ːs]

parfait ˌpɑː 'feɪ '•• ‖ ˌpɑːr- ~**s** z

Parfitt 'pɑːf ɪt §-ət ‖ 'pɑːrf-

parfum pɑː 'fã̃ -'fʌm ‖ pɑːr- —*Fr* [paʁ fœ̃]

parg|et 'pɑːdʒ |ɪt §-ət ‖ 'pɑːrdʒ |ət ~**eted** ɪt ɪd
§ət-, -əd ‖ ət̮ əd ~**eting** ɪt ɪŋ §ət- ‖ ət̮ ɪŋ
~**ets** ɪts §əts ‖ əts

Pargiter 'pɑːdʒ ɪt ə §-ət- ‖ 'pɑːrdʒ ət̮ ᵊr

Parham 'pær əm

parhelia pɑː 'hiːl i_ə ‖ pɑːr-

parheliacal ˌpɑː hɪ 'laɪ_ək ᵊl ◀ §-hə- ‖ ˌpɑːr-

parhelic ₍ₗ₎pɑː 'hiːl ɪk ‖ ₍ₗ₎pɑːr-

parheli|on pɑː 'hiːl i_ən -ɒn ‖ pɑːr- ~**a** ə

pariah pə 'raɪ_ə 'pær i_ə ~**s** z

Parian 'peər i_ən ‖ 'per- 'pær- ~**s** z

parietal pə 'raɪ_ət ᵊl -ɪt- ‖ -ət̮ ᵊl ~**s** z

pari-mutuel ˌpær i 'mjuːtʃ u‿əl -'mjuːt juˌəl,
-'mjuːtʃ əl ‖ ˌper- ~s z
paring 'peər ɪŋ ‖ 'per- 'pær- (= pairing)
pari passu ˌpær i 'pæs uː ˌpɑːr-,
-juː ‖ ˌpɑːr i 'pɑːs uː
paripinnate ˌpær ɪ 'pɪn eɪt ◄ -ə- ‖ ˌper-
Paris 'pær ɪs §-əs ‖ 'per- —Fr [pa ʁi]
parish, P~ 'pær ɪʃ ‖ 'per- ~es ɪz əz
ˌparish 'clerk; ˌparish 'priest; ˌparish
'register
parishioner pə 'rɪʃ ᵊn‿ə ‖ ˌ‿ər ~s z
parish-pump ˌpær ɪʃ 'pʌmp ‖ ˌper-
Parisian pə 'rɪz iˌən ‖ pə 'rɪʒ ᵊn -'riːʒ- (*) ~s z
parisyllabic ˌpær ɪ sɪ 'læb ɪk ◄ ˌ•ə-,
-sə'•- ‖ ˌper-
parit|y 'pær ət li -ɪt- ‖ -əṭ li 'per- ~ies iz
park, Park pɑːk ‖ pɑːrk **parked** pɑːkt ‖ pɑːrkt
parking 'pɑːk ɪŋ ‖ 'pɑːrk ɪŋ **parks**
pɑːks ‖ pɑːrks
ˌPark 'Avenue
parka 'pɑːk ə ‖ 'pɑːrk ə ~s z
park-and-ride ˌpɑːk ənd 'raɪd ‖ ˌpɑːrk-
Parke pɑːk ‖ pɑːrk
Parker 'pɑːk ə ‖ 'pɑːrk ər
Parkes pɑːks ‖ pɑːrks
Parkeston, Parkestone 'pɑːkst ən ‖ 'pɑːrkst-
Parkgate (i) 'pɑːk geɪt ‖ 'pɑːrk-, (ii), •' • —In
Co. Antrim, (i); in Cheshire, (ii).
Parkhouse 'pɑːk haʊs ‖ 'pɑːrk-
Parkhurst 'pɑːk hɜːst ‖ 'pɑːrk hɜːst
parkin, P~ 'pɑːk ɪn §-ən ‖ 'pɑːrk-
parking 'pɑːk ɪŋ ‖ 'pɑːrk ɪŋ
'parking ˌgarage ‖ '•• •,•; 'parking light;
'parking lot; 'parking ˌmeter; 'parking
space; 'parking ˌticket; park ˌkeeper
Parkinson 'pɑːk ɪn sən §-ən- ‖ 'pɑːrk- ~'s z
'Parkinson's diˌsease; 'Parkinson's law
parkinsonian ˌpɑːk ɪn 'səʊn iˌən ◄ ‖ ˌpɑːrk
ən 'soʊn-
parkinsonism 'pɑːk ɪn sə ˌnɪz əm §'•ən-,
-sən ˌɪz- ‖ 'pɑːrk-
parkland 'pɑːk lænd ‖ 'pɑːrk- ~s z
Parkray tdmk 'pɑːk reɪ ‖ 'pɑːrk-
Parks pɑːks ‖ pɑːrks
Parkstone 'pɑːkst ən ‖ 'pɑːrk stoʊn
parkway 'pɑːk weɪ ‖ 'pɑːrk- ~s z
park|y 'pɑːk li ‖ 'pɑːrk li ~ier iˌə ‖ iˌər ~iest
iˌɪst iˌəst
parlance 'pɑːl ənᵗs ‖ 'pɑːrl-
parlando pɑː 'lænd əʊ ‖ pɑːr 'lɑːnd oʊ —It
[par 'lan do]
parlay 'pɑːl i ‖ 'pɑːrl eɪ -i ~ed d ~ing ɪŋ ~s z
parley 'pɑːl i ‖ 'pɑːrl i ~ed d ~ing ɪŋ ~s z
parleyvoo ˌpɑːl i 'vuː ‖ ˌpɑːrl-
parliament, P~ 'pɑːl ə mənt -ɪ-, -jə- ‖ 'pɑːrl-
~s s
parliamentarian ˌpɑːl ə men 'teər iˌən ˌ•ɪ-,
ˌ•jə-, -mən'•- ‖ ˌpɑːrl ə men 'ter- -mən'•-
~ism ˌɪz əm ~s z
parliamentary ˌpɑːl ə 'ment ᵊr i ◄ ˌ•ɪ-, ˌ•jə-
‖ ˌpɑːrl ə 'menṭ-
Parlophone tdmk 'pɑːl ə fəʊn ‖ 'pɑːrl ə foʊn

parlor, parlour 'pɑːl ə ‖ 'pɑːrl ər ~s z
'parlor car; 'parlour game; 'parlour maid
parlous 'pɑːl əs ‖ 'pɑːrl əs ~ly li ~ness nəs
nɪs
parlyaree ˌpɑːl i 'ɑːr i ‖ ˌpɑːrl-
Parma 'pɑːm ə ‖ 'pɑːrm ə —It ['par ma]
Parmenides pɑː 'men i diːz -ə- ‖ pɑːr-
Parmenter 'pɑːm ɪnt ə -ənt- ‖ 'pɑːrm ənt ər
Parmentier pɑː 'ment iˌə -'mɒnt i eɪ;
'pɑːm ənt jeɪ ‖ ˌpɑːrm ən 'tjeɪ —Fr
[paʁ mã tje] (*)
Parmesan ˌpɑːm ɪ 'zæn ◄ -ə- ‖ 'pɑːrm ə zɑːn
-ʒɑːn, -zæn; -əz ən (*)
ˌParmesan 'cheese
parmigiana ˌpɑːm ɪ 'dʒɑːn ə -'ʒɑːn- ‖ ˌpɑːrm-
—It [par mi 'dʒa na]
Parminter 'pɑːm ɪnt ə -ənt- ‖ 'pɑːrm ənt ər
Parmiter 'pɑːm ɪt ə -ət- ‖ 'pɑːrm əṭ ər
Parnassian pɑː 'næs iˌən ‖ pɑːr- ~s z
Parnassus pɑː 'næs əs ‖ pɑːr- —ModGk
Parnossos [par na 'sɔs]
Parnell (i) pɑː 'nel ‖ pɑːr-, (ii)
'pɑːn ᵊl ‖ 'pɑːrn ᵊl
Parnes pɑːnz ‖ pɑːrnz
parochial pə 'rəʊk iˌəl ‖ -'roʊk- ~ism ˌɪz əm
~ly i
parodist 'pær əd ɪst §-əst ‖ 'per- ~s s
parod|y 'pær əd li ‖ 'per- ~ied id ~ies iz
~ying i ɪŋ
paroecious pə 'riːʃ əs
parol 'pær ᵊl pə 'rəʊl, →-'roʊl ‖ 'per-
parol|e pə 'rəʊl →-'roʊl ‖ -'roʊl ~ed d ~es z
~ing ɪŋ
parolee pə ˌrəʊ 'liː ‖ -ˌroʊ- pə 'roʊl iː ~s z
paronomasia ˌpær ən ə 'meɪz iˌə -ə nəʊ-,
-'meɪs- ‖ ˌpær ə noʊ 'meɪʒ ə ˌper-, -'meɪʒ iˌə
paronychia ˌpær ə 'nɪk iˌə ‖ ˌper-
paronym 'pær ə nɪm ‖ 'per- ~s z
paronym|ous pə 'rɒn ɪm ləs pæ-, -əm-
‖ -'rɑːn- ~ously əs li ~y i
Paroo 'pɑːr uː
Paros 'peər ɒs 'pær-, 'pɑːr- ‖ 'per ɑːs 'pær-
parotid pə 'rɒt ɪd §-əd ‖ -'rɑːṭ əd
parotitis ˌpær ə 'taɪt ɪs §-əs ‖ -'taɪṭ əs ˌper-
-parous stress-imposing pər əs — **oviparous**
əʊ 'vɪp ər əs ‖ oʊ-
parousia, P~ pə 'ruːz iˌə -'ruːs-
paroxysm 'pær ək ˌsɪz əm -ɒk-;
pə 'rɒks ˌɪz- ‖ 'per-; pə 'rɑːks ˌɪz- ~s z
paroxysmal ˌpær ək 'sɪz məl ◄ -ɒk- ‖ ˌper- ~ly
i
paroxytone pə 'rɒks ɪ təʊn pæ-, -ə-
‖ -'rɑːks ə toʊn ~s z
Parozone tdmk 'pær ə zəʊn ‖ -zoʊn ˌper-
parquet 'pɑːk eɪ -i ‖ pɑːr 'keɪ (*) ~ed d ~ing
ɪŋ ~s z
parquetr|y 'pɑːk ɪtr li -ətr- ‖ 'pɑːrk- ~ies iz
parr, Parr pɑː ‖ pɑːr (= par) **parrs, Parr's**
pɑːz ‖ pɑːrz
Parracombe 'pær ə kuːm ‖ 'per-
Parramatta, p~ ˌpær ə 'mæt ə ‖ -'mæṭ ə ˌper-
parrel 'pær ᵊl ‖ 'per- ~s z
Parret, Parrett 'pær ɪt §-ət ‖ 'per-

parricidal ˌpær ɪ 'saɪd ᵊl ◂ -ə- ‖ ˌper-
parricide 'pær ɪ saɪd -ə- ‖ 'per- ~s z
Parrish 'pær ɪʃ ‖ 'per-
parr|ot, P~ 'pær |ət ‖ 'per- ~oted ət ɪd -əd
  ‖ ət̬ əd ~oting ət ɪŋ ‖ ət̬ ɪŋ ~ots əts
parrot-fashion 'pær ət ˌfæʃ ᵊn ‖ 'per-
parrotfish 'pær ət fɪʃ ‖ 'per- ~es ɪz əz
Parrott 'pær ət ‖ 'per-
parr|y, Parry 'pær |i ‖ 'per- ~ied id ~ies iz
  ~ying i ɪŋ
parsable 'paːz əb ᵊl ‖ 'paːrs-
parse paːz ‖ paːrs (*) parsed paːzd ‖ paːrst
  parses 'paːz ɪz -əz ‖ 'paːrs əz parsing
  'paːz ɪŋ ‖ 'paːrs ɪŋ
parsec 'paː sek ‖ 'paːr- ~s s
Parsee 'paːs iː ˌpaː 'siː ‖ 'paːrs iː ˌpaːr 'siː —In
  India, ˌ•'• ~s z
parser 'paːz ə ‖ 'paːrs ᵊr ~s z
Parsi —see Parsee
Parsifal 'paːs ɪf ᵊl -əf-; -ɪ faːl, -ə-, -fæl ‖ 'paːrs-
  —Ger ['paʁ zi fal]
parsimonious ˌpaːs ɪ 'məʊn i̯əs ◂ ˌ•ə-
  ‖ ˌpaːrs ə 'moʊn- ~ly li ~ness nəs nɪs
parsimony 'paːs ɪm ən i ˈ•əm-
  ‖ 'paːrs ə moʊn i (*)
Parsippany pə 'sɪp ən i ‖ pᵊr-
parsley 'paːs li ‖ 'paːrs li
Parsley family name 'paːz li ‖ 'paːrz-
Parslow 'paːz ləʊ ‖ 'paːrz loʊ 'paːrs-
parsnip 'paːs nɪp §-nəp ‖ 'paːrs- ~s s
parson 'paːs ᵊn ‖ 'paːrs ᵊn ~s z
  ˌparson's 'nose
parsonag|e 'paːs ᵊn ˌɪdʒ ‖ 'paːrs- ~es ɪz əz
parsonic paː 'sɒn ɪk ‖ paːr 'saːn ɪk ~al ᵊl
Parsons 'paːs ᵊnz ‖ 'paːrs-
part paːt ‖ paːrt parted 'paːt ɪd -əd
  ‖ 'paːrt̬ əd parting 'paːt ɪŋ ‖ 'paːrt̬ ɪŋ parts
  paːts ‖ paːrts
  ˌpart ex'change; ˌpart of 'speech; 'part
  work
par|take paː |'teɪk ‖ paːr- pᵊr- ~taken 'teɪk
  ᵊn ~taker/s 'teɪk ə/z ‖ 'teɪk ᵊr/z ~takes
  'teɪks ~taking 'teɪk ɪŋ ~took 'tʊk §'tuːk
parterre paː 'teə ‖ paːr 'teᵊr —Fr [paʁ tɛːʁ]
  ~s z
Parthenia paː 'θiːn i̯ə ‖ paːr-
parthenium paː 'θiːn i̯əm ‖ paːr- ~s z
parthenogenesis ˌpaːθ ə nəʊ 'dʒen əs ɪs ˌ•ɪ-,
  -ɪs ɪs, §-əs ‖ ˌpaːrθ ə noʊ-
Parthenon 'paːθ ᵊn ən -ɪn-; -ə nɒn, -ɪ-
  ‖ 'paːrθ ə naːn
Parthenope paː 'θen əp i ‖ paːr-
Parthi|a 'paːθ i̯ə ‖ 'paːrθ- ~an/s ən/z
partial 'paːʃ ᵊl ‖ 'paːrʃ ᵊl ~ness nəs nɪs ~s z
partialit|y ˌpaːʃ i 'æl ət i -ɪt i ‖ ˌpaːrʃ i 'æl ət̬ i
  ~ies iz
partially 'paːʃ ᵊl̯i ‖ 'paːrʃ-
participant paː 'tɪs ɪp ᵊnt -əp- ‖ pᵊr- paːr- ~s
  s
partici|pate paː 'tɪs ɪ peɪt -ə- ‖ paːr- pᵊr-
  ~pated peɪt ɪd -əd ‖ peɪt̬ əd ~pates peɪts
  ~pating peɪt ɪŋ ‖ peɪt̬ ɪŋ

participation paː ˌtɪs ɪ 'peɪʃ ᵊn ˌpaːt ɪs-, -ə'•-
  ‖ paːr- pᵊr-
participator paː 'tɪs ɪ peɪt ə -ə-
  ‖ paːr 'tɪs ə peɪt̬ ᵊr pᵊr- ~s z
participatory paː ˌtɪs ɪ 'peɪt ᵊr i ◂ ˌpaːt ɪs-,
  -ə'•-; paː 'tɪs ɪ pət̬_ᵊr i, -'•ə-
  ‖ paːr 'tɪs əp ə tɔːr i pᵊr-, -toʊr i
participial ˌpaːt ɪ 'sɪp i̯əl ◂ ˌ•ə- ‖ ˌpaːrt̬ ə- ~ly
  i
participle 'paːt ɪs ɪp ᵊl '•əs-, -əp•; paː 'tɪs-;
  'paːts ɪp ᵊl, -əp- ‖ 'paːrt̬ ə sɪp ᵊl ~s z
Partick 'paːt ɪk ‖ 'paːrt̬ ɪk
particle 'paːt ɪk ᵊl ‖ 'paːrt̬- ~s z
parti-colored, parti-coloured ˌpaːt i 'kʌl əd ◂
  ˈ•ˌ•ˌ•, ‖ ˌpaːrt̬ i 'kʌl ᵊrd ◂
particular pə 'tɪk jʊl ə -jəl-; ⚠-'tɪk lə
  ‖ pᵊr 'tɪk jəl ᵊr pə- ~s z
particularis... —see particulariz...
particularism pə 'tɪk jʊl ə_ˌrɪz əm -'•jəl-
  ‖ pᵊr 'tɪk jəl- pə-, paːr-
particularit|y pə ˌtɪk ju 'lær ət i -ˌ•jə-, -ɪt i
  ‖ pᵊr ˌtɪk jə 'lær ət̬ i pə-, paːr ˌtɪkˌ•'•-, -'ler-
  ~ies iz
particularization pə ˌtɪk jʊl ər aɪ 'zeɪʃ ᵊn
  -ˌ•jəl-, -ɪ'•- ‖ pᵊr ˌtɪk jəl ᵊr ə- pə-, paːr-
particulariz|e pə 'tɪk jʊl ə raɪz -'•jəl-
  ‖ pᵊr 'tɪk jəl- pə-, paːr- ~ed d ~es ɪz əz
  ~ing ɪŋ
particularly pə 'tɪk jʊl ə li -'•jəl-
  ‖ pᵊr 'tɪk jəl ᵊr- pə- —in casual speech
  sometimes also -'tɪk jəl̯i
particulate paː 'tɪk jʊl ət pə-, -ɪt, -ju leɪt
  ‖ paːr 'tɪk jəl ət pᵊr-, -jə leɪt
parting 'paːt ɪŋ ‖ 'paːrt̬ ɪŋ ~s z
  ˌparting 'shot
Partington 'paːt ɪŋ tən ‖ 'paːrt̬-
parti pris ˌpaːt i 'priː ‖ ˌpaːrt̬- —Fr [paʁ ti pʁi]
partisan ˌpaːt i 'zæn ◂ -ə-, '•ˌ•ˌ• ‖ 'paːrt̬ əz ᵊn
  -əs-; -ə zæn (*) ~s z ~ship ʃɪp
partita paː 'tiːt ə ‖ paːr 'tiːt̬ ə
-partite 'paːt aɪt ‖ 'paːrt- — tripartite
  ˌ(ˌ)traɪ 'paːt aɪt ‖ -'paːrt-
partition paː 'tɪʃ ᵊn pə- ‖ paːr- pᵊr- ~ed d
  ~ing ˌɪŋ ~s z
partitive 'paːt ət ɪv -ɪt- ‖ 'paːrt̬ ət̬ ɪv ~ly li ~s
  z
partiz... —see partis...
partly 'paːt li ‖ 'paːrt-
partner 'paːt nə ‖ 'paːrt nᵊr ~ed d
  partnering 'paːt nər ɪŋ ‖ 'paːrt nᵊr ɪŋ ~less
  ləs lɪs ~s z ~ship/s ʃɪp/s ə
Parton 'paːt ᵊn ‖ 'paːrt ᵊn
partook paː 'tʊk §-'tuːk ‖ paːr-
partridg|e, P~ 'paːtr ɪdʒ ‖ 'paːrtr ɪdʒ ~es ɪz
  əz
part-singing 'paːt ˌsɪŋ ɪŋ ‖ 'paːrt-
part-song 'paːt sɒŋ ‖ 'paːrt sɔːŋ -saːŋ ~s z
part-time ˌpaːt 'taɪm ◂ ‖ ˌpaːrt-
  ˌpart-time 'job
part-timer ˌpaːt 'taɪm ə ‖ ˌpaːrt 'taɪm ᵊr ~s z
parturient paː 'tjʊər i̯ənt ‖ paːr 'tʊr- -'tjʊr-
parturition ˌpaːt jʊ 'rɪʃ ᵊn -jə-, ˌpaːtʃ ə-
  ‖ ˌpaːrt̬ ə- ˌpaːrtʃ ə-, ˌpaːrt ju-

partway ˌpɑːt ˈweɪ ◀ ' •• ‖ ˌpɑːrt-
part|y ˈpɑːt li ‖ ˈpɑːrt̬ li ~ied id ~ies iz ~ying
i ɪŋ
  ˌparty ˈline '*political view*' , ˈparty line
  '*shared phone line*' ; ˈparty piece; ˌparty
  ˈpolitics; ˈparty ˌpooper; ˌparty ˈwall
party-col... —*see* parti-col...
partygoer ˈpɑːt i ˌgəʊ ə ‖ ˈpɑːrt̬ i ˌgoʊ ər ~s z
parvenu, parvenue ˈpɑːv ə njuː -nuː
  ‖ ˈpɑːrv ə nuː -njuː —*Fr* [paʁ və ny] ~s z
parvo ˈpɑːv əʊ ‖ ˈpɑːrv oʊ ~s z
parvovirus ˈpɑːv əʊ ˌvaɪər əs ‖ ˈpɑːrv oʊ- ~es
iz əz
Parzival ˈpɑːts ɪ fɑːl -ə- ‖ ˈpɑːrts- —*Ger*
['par tsi fal]
pas pɑː —*Fr* [pa] —*see also phrases with this
word*
Pasadena ˌpæs ə ˈdiːn ə
Pasargadae pə ˈsɑːg ə di: ‖ -ˈsɑːrg-
pascal *unit of pressure* ˈpæsk əl
  ₍ᵢ₎pæ ˈskæl ‖ ₍ᵢ₎pɑː ˈskɑːl ~s z
Pascal *proper name; computer language*
  ₍ᵢ₎pæ ˈskæl -ˈskɑːl; ˈpæsk æl, -ɑːl, -əl —*Fr*
[pa skal]
Pascale ₍ᵢ₎pæ ˈskɑːl -ˈskæl
paschal ˈpæsk əl ˈpɑːsk-
Pasco, Pascoe ˈpæsk əʊ ‖ -oʊ
pas de basque ˌpɑː də ˈbɑː -ˈbɑːsk ‖ -ˈbæsk
  —*Fr* [pad bask]
pas de deux ˌpɑː də ˈdɜː ‖ -ˈduː -ˈdɜː· —*Fr*
[pad dø]
pash pæʃ pashes ˈpæʃ ɪz -əz
pasha, Pasha ˈpɑːʃ ə ˈpæʃ-, pə ˈʃɑː ~s z
Pashto ˈpʌʃt əʊ ˈpæʃt- ‖ -oʊ
pasigraph|y pə ˈsɪg rəf li ~ies iz
Pasiphae, Pasiphaë pə ˈsɪf i iː -eɪ- ‖ -ə-
Pasmore ˈpɑːs mɔː ˈpæs- ‖ ˈpæs mɔːr -moʊr
paso doble ˌpæs əʊ ˈdəʊb leɪ ‖ ˌpɑːs oʊ ˈdoʊb-
  —*Sp* [ˌpa so ˈðoβ le]
Pasolini ˌpæs əʊ ˈliːn i ‖ -oʊ- —*It* [pa zo ˈli: ni]
pasqueflower ˈpæsk ˌflaʊ‿ə ˈpɑːsk- ‖ -ˌflaʊ‿ər
~s z
pasquinad|e ˈpæsk wɪ ˈneɪd -wə- ~ed ɪd əd
~es z ~ing ɪŋ
pass pɑːs §pæs ‖ pæs passed pɑːst §pæst
  ‖ pæst passes ˈpɑːs ɪz §ˈpæs- -əz ‖ ˈpæs əz
passing ˈpɑːs ɪŋ §ˈpæs- ‖ ˈpæs ɪŋ
  ˈpass deˌgree; ˌpass ˈout *v*; ˈpass out *n*
passab|le ˈpɑːs əb |əl §ˈpæs- ‖ ˈpæs- ~leness
əl nəs -nɪs ~ly li
passacaglia ˌpæs ə ˈkɑːl i‿ə ‖ ˌpɑːs- -ˈkæl-
  —*Not actually an Italian word.*
passade pæ ˈseɪd pə-
passag|e ˈpæs ɪdʒ —*but as a move in dressage,
also* pæ ˈsɑːʒ ~es ɪz əz
passageway ˈpæs ɪdʒ weɪ ~s z
Passaic pə ˈseɪ ɪk
Passamaquoddy ˌpæs əm ə ˈkwɒd i ‖ -ˈkwɑːd i
passant ˈpæs ənt ˈpɑːs-, -ɒt —*Fr* [pa sɑ̃]
Passat *tdmk* pæ ˈsæt -ˈsɑːt
passbook ˈpɑːs bʊk §ˈpæs-, §-buːk ‖ ˈpæs- ~s
s
Passchendaele ˈpæʃ ən deɪəl

passe, passé, passée ˈpɑːs eɪ ˈpæs- ‖ pæ ˈseɪ
  —*Fr* [pa se] *(*)*
passenger, P~ ˈpæs ɪndʒ ə -əndʒ- ‖ -ər ~s z
passe-partout ˌpæs pɑː ˈtuː ˌpɑːs-, -pə-, ' •••
  ‖ -pɑːr ˈtuː -pər- —*Fr* [pas paʁ tu]
pass|erby ˌpɑːs lə ˈbaɪ §ˌpæs- ‖ ˌpæs |ər ˈbaɪ
  ' ••• ~ersby əz ˈbaɪ ‖ ərz ˈbaɪ
passerine ˈpæs ə raɪn -riːn
Passfield ˈpɑːs fiːəld ˈpæs- ‖ ˈpæs-
passible '*capable of feeling*' ˈpæs ɪb əl -əb-
passim ˈpæs ɪm §-əm
passing ˈpɑːs ɪŋ §ˈpæs- ‖ ˈpæs ɪŋ
  ˈpassing note; ˌpassing ˈoff; ˌpassing ˈout;
  ˈpassing shot
passion, P~ ˈpæʃ ən ~s z
  ˈpassion play; ˌPassion ˈSunday; ˌPassion
  ˈweek
passionate ˈpæʃ ən ət ~ly li
passionflower ˈpæʃ ən ˌflaʊ‿ə ‖ -ˌflaʊ‿ər ~s z
passionfruit ˈpæʃ ən fruːt ~s s
passionless ˈpæʃ ən ləs -lɪs ~ly li ~ness nəs
nɪs
Passiontide ˈpæʃ ən taɪd
passive ˈpæs ɪv §-əv ~ly li ~ness nəs nɪs ~s z
passivity pæ ˈsɪv ət i pə-, -ɪt- ‖ -ət̬ i
passivis... —*see* passiviz...
passivization ˌpæs ɪv aɪ ˈzeɪʃ ən ˌ•əv-, -ɪˈ•-
  ‖ -ɪv ə-
passiviz|e ˈpæs ɪ vaɪz -ə- ~ed d ~es ɪz əz
~ing ɪŋ
passkey ˈpɑːs kiː §ˈpæs- ‖ ˈpæs- ~s z
Passmore ˈpɑːs mɔː ˈpæs- ‖ ˈpæs mɔːr -moʊr
passover, P~ ˈpɑːs ˌəʊv ə §ˈpæs-
  ‖ ˈpæs ˌoʊv ər ~s z
passport ˈpɑːs pɔːt §ˈpæs- ‖ ˈpæs pɔːrt -poʊrt
~s s
password ˈpɑːs wɜːd §ˈpæs- ‖ ˈpæs wɜːd ~s z
Passy pæ ˈsiː ‖ pɑː- —*Fr* [pa si]
past pɑːst §pæst ‖ pæst
  ˌpast ˈmaster; ˌpast ˈparticiple, -·' •••;
  ˌpast ˈperfect; ˌpast ˈtense
pasta ˈpæst ə ‖ ˈpɑːst ə *(*)*
past|e peɪst ~ed ɪd əd ~es s ~ing ɪŋ
pasteboard ˈpeɪst bɔːd ‖ -bɔːrd -boʊrd
pastel ˈpæst əl ₍ᵢ₎pæ ˈstel ‖ pæ ˈstel ~s z
pastelist, pastellist ˈpæst əl ɪst §-əst
  ‖ pæ ˈstel- ~s s
pastern ˈpæst ən -ɜːn ‖ -ərn ~s z
Pasternak ˈpæst ə næk ‖ -ər- —*Russ* [pə sitʲɪr
ˈnak]
paste-up ˈpeɪst ʌp ~s s
Pasteur ₍ᵢ₎pæ ˈstɜː ˌpɑː- ‖ -ˈstɜː· —*Fr*
[pa stœːʁ]
pasteuris... —*see* pasteuriz...
pasteurization ˌpɑːs tʃər aɪ ˈzeɪʃ ən ˌpæs-;
  ˌpɑːst ər-, ˌpæst-, ˌ•jʊr-; -ɪˈ•- ‖ ˌpæs tʃər ə-
  ˌ•tər-
pasteuriz|e ˈpɑːs tʃə raɪz ˈpæs-; ˈpɑːst ə-,
  ˈpæst-, -juə-, -jə- ‖ ˈpæs tʃə raɪz -tə- ~ed d
~es ɪz əz ~ing ɪŋ
pastich|e pæ ˈstiːʃ ˈpæst iːʃ ‖ pɑː- ~es ɪz əz
pastil, pastille ˈpæst əl -ɪl; ₍ᵢ₎pæ ˈstiːəl ~s z
pastime ˈpɑːs taɪm §ˈpæs- ‖ ˈpæs- ˌ~s z

pasting 'peɪst ɪŋ ~s z
pastis pæ 'stiːs -'stɪs —Fr [pa stis]
past-master 'pɑːst ˌmɑːst ə §-ˌmæst-, ˌ•'•• ‖ 'pæsɪ ˌmæst ʰr
Paston 'pæst ən
pastor 'pɑːst ə §'pæst- ‖ 'pæst ʰr ~s z
pastoral 'pɑːst ʰr_əl 'pæst-; §pɑː 'stɔːr əl, §pæ- ‖ 'pæst- —but as a noun, sometimes ˌ•ə 'rɑːl ~s z
pastorale ˌpæst ə 'rɑːl ˌpɑːst-, -'ræl; -'•i ~s z
pastoral|ism 'pɑːst ʰr_əl ‖ˌɪz əm 'pæst- ‖ 'pæst- ~ist/s ɪst/s §əst/s ‖ əst/s ~ly i
pastorate 'pɑːst ʰr ət §'pæst-, -ɪt ~s s
pastrami pə 'strɑːm i pæ-
pas|try 'peɪs |tri ~tries triz
pastrycook 'peɪs tri kʊk §-kuːk ~s s
pasturage 'pɑːs tʃʰr ɪdʒ §'pæs-, -tjʊr-, -tjər- ‖ 'pæs-
pasture n, v 'pɑːs tʃə §'pæs-, -tjə, -tjʊə ‖ 'pæs tʃʰr ~d d ~s z pasturing 'pɑːs tʃʰr ɪŋ §'pæs-, -tjər-, -tjʊr- ‖ 'pæs tʃʰr ɪŋ
pastureland 'pɑːs tʃə lænd §'pæs- ‖ 'pæs tʃʰr- ~s z
past|ly n 'pie' 'pæst |i 'pɑːst- ~ies iz
past|ly adj 'paste-like' 'peɪst |i ~ier i_ə ‖ i_ʰr ~iest i_ɪst i_əst ~iness i nəs i nɪs
pasty-faced 'peɪst i feɪst ˌ••'•
pat, Pat pæt pats, Pat's pæts patted 'pæt ɪd -əd ‖ 'pæt̬ əd patting 'pæt ɪŋ ‖ 'pæt̬ ɪŋ
pat-a-cake 'pæt ə keɪk ‖ 'pæt̬-
patagi|um pə 'teɪdʒ i_əm ˌpæt ə 'dʒaɪ_ləm ‖ ˌpæt̬- ~a ə
Patagoni|a ˌpæt ə 'gəʊn i_ə ‖ ˌpæt̬ ə 'goʊn- ~an/s ən/z ◄
pataka 'Maori storehouse' 'pɑːt ə kɑː ‖ 'pɑːt̬- ~s z
Pataki pə 'tæk i
pat-ball 'pæt bɔːl ‖ -bɑːl
patch, Patch pætʃ patched pætʃt patches, Patch's 'pætʃ ɪz -əz patching 'pætʃ ɪŋ ˌpatch 'pocket
patchouli 'pætʃ ʊl i -əl-; pə 'tʃuːl-, -iː
patchwork 'pætʃ wɜːk ‖ -wɜːk ~s s
patch|y 'pætʃ |i ~ier i_ə ‖ i_ʰr ~iest i_ɪst i_əst ~ily ɪ li əl i ~iness i nəs i nɪs
Pate peɪt
pate 'top of the head' peɪt pates peɪts
pate, paté, pâté 'meat spread' 'pæt eɪ -i ‖ pɑː 'teɪ pæ- —Fr [pa te] (*) pates, patés, pâtés 'pæt eɪz -iz ‖ pɑː 'teɪz pæ- —see also phrases with this word
pâte 'paste for porcelain' pɑːt —Fr [pat]
pâté de foie ˌpæt eɪ də 'fwɑː ˌ•i- ‖ pɑː ˌteɪ pæ- —Fr [pa ted fwa] ˌpâté de ˌfoie 'gras grɑː —Fr [gʁa]
Patel (i) pə 'tel, (ii) pə 'teɪ_əl
Pateley 'peɪt li
patell|a pə 'tel ə ~ae iː ~ar ə ‖ ʰr ~as əz
paten 'pæt ən ~s z
patency 'peɪt ənts i
pat|ent n, adj, v 'peɪt |ənt 'pæt- ‖ 'pæt |ənt 'peɪt- (*) —In BrE the pronunciation 'pæt- is

mainly restricted to technical use; in AmE the pronunciation 'peɪt- is used only in the sense 'open, obvious'. ~ented ənt ɪd -əd ‖ ənt̬ əd ~enting ənt ɪŋ ‖ ənt̬ ɪŋ ~ents ən/s ˌpatent 'leather◄; ˌpatent 'medicine; 'Patent ˌOffice
patentable 'peɪt ənt əb əl 'pæt- ‖ 'pæt ənt̬-
patentee ˌpeɪt ən 'tiː ˌpæt- ‖ ˌpæt̬- ~s z
patently 'peɪt ənt li
Pater, pater 'father' peɪt ə ‖ 'peɪt̬ ʰr ~s, ~'s z
pater 'prayer' 'pæt ə 'pɑːt- ‖ 'pɑːt er 'pɑːt̬ ʰr ~s z
paterfamilias ˌpeɪt ə fə 'mɪl i æs ˌpæt-, -əs ‖ ˌpɑːt̬ ʰr fə 'miːl i_əs ˌpeɪt̬-, ˌpæt̬- ~es ɪz əz
paternal pə 'tɜːn əl ‖ -'tɜːn-
paternalism pə 'tɜːn əl ˌɪz əm -ə ˌlɪz- ‖ -'tɜːn-
paternalistic pə ˌtɜːn ə 'lɪst ɪk ◄ -əl 'ɪst- ‖ pə ˌtɜːn əl 'ɪst ɪk ◄ ~ally əl_i
paternally pə 'tɜːn əl i ‖ -'tɜːn-
paternity pə 'tɜːn ət i -ɪt- ‖ -'tɜːn ət̬ i —In contrast with maternity, sometimes 'pə,••• paˈternity test
paternoster, P~ ˌpæt ə 'nɒst ə ◄ ‖ ˌpɑːt̬ ʰr 'nɑːst ʰr ◄ ˌpæt̬-, -'nɔːst-, '••,•• ~s z ˌPaternoster 'Row
Paterson 'pæt əs ən ‖ 'pæt̬ ʰrs ən
path 'way' pɑːθ §pæθ ‖ pæθ (*) paths pɑːðz §pæðz, §pɑːθs, §pæθs ‖ pæðz pæθs
path 'pathology' pæθ 'path lab
PATH NY-NJ subway system pæθ
-path pæθ — osteopath 'ɒst i əʊ pæθ ‖ 'ɑːst i ə pæθ
Pathan pə 'tɑːn —Hindi [pə t̪ʰaːn] ~s z
Pathé 'pæθ eɪ
pathetic pə 'θet ɪk ‖ -'θet̬ ɪk ~ally əl_i
pathfinder 'pɑːθ ˌfaɪnd ə §'pæθ- ‖ 'pæθ ˌfaɪnd ʰr ~s z
pathic 'pæθ ɪk ~s s
-pathic pæθ ɪk — psychopathic ˌsaɪk əʊ 'pæθ ɪk ◄ -ə-
pathless 'pɑːθ ləs §'pæθ-, -lɪs ‖ 'pæθ- ~ness nəs nɪs
Pathmark tdmk 'pæθ mɑːk ‖ -mɑːrk
patho- comb. form with stress-neutral suffix ˌpæθ əʊ ‖ -oʊ — pathopsychology ˌpæθ əʊ saɪ 'kɒl ədʒ i ‖ -oʊ saɪ 'kɑːl- with stress-imposing suffix pə 'θɒ+ ‖ -'θɑː+ — patholysis pə 'θɒl əs ɪs -ɪs ɪs, §-əs ‖ -'θɑːl-
pathogen 'pæθ ədʒ ən -ə dʒen ~s z
pathogenic ˌpæθ ə 'dʒen ɪk ◄ ~ally əl_i
pathognomy pə 'θɒg nəm i ‖ -'θɑːg-
pathognomical ˌpæθ ə 'lɒdʒ ɪk əl ◄ ‖ -'lɑːdʒ- ~ly _i
pathologist pə 'θɒl ədʒ ɪst §-əst ‖ -'θɑːl- ~s s
patholog|y pə 'θɒl ədʒ |i ‖ -'θɑːl- ~ies iz
pathos 'peɪθ ɒs ‖ -ɑːs -ɔːs, -oʊs
pathway 'pɑːθ weɪ §'pæθ- ‖ 'pæθ- ~s z
-pathy stress-imposing pəθ i — telepathy tə 'lep əθ i tɪ-, te-
Patiala ˌpʌt i 'ɑːl ə ‖ ˌpʌt̬-

patience, P~ 'peɪʃ ənᵗs
patient 'peɪʃ ənt ~s s
patina 'pæt ɪn ə -ən-, pə 'tiːn ə ‖ pə 'tiːn ə (*)
  ~s z
patio 'pæt i əʊ ‖ 'pæt i oʊ 'paːt- ~s z
patisserie, pâtisserie pə 'tiːs ər_i pæ-, -'tɪs-
  —Fr [pa tis ʁi] ~s z
Patmore 'pæt mɔː ‖ -mɔːr -moʊr
Patmos 'pæt mɒs ‖ -məs -maːs, -moʊs
Patna 'pæt nə 'pʌt-   —Hindi [pət n̩aː]
pat|ois sing. 'pæt |waː ‖ 'paːt-   —Fr [pa twa]
  ~ois pl waːz —Fr [pa twa]
Paton 'peɪt ən
Patras 'pætr æs -əs; pə 'træs —Gk ['pa tras]
patrial 'peɪtr i_əl 'pætr- ~s z
patriality ˌpeɪtr i 'æl ət i ˌpætr- ‖ -ət̬ i
patriarch 'peɪtr i aːk 'pætr- ‖ -aːrk ~s s
patriarchal ˌpeɪtr i 'aːk əl ◄ ˌpætr- ‖ -'aːrk əl ◄
  ~ism ˌɪz əm ~ly i
patriarchate 'peɪtr i aːk ət 'pætr-, -ɪt, -eɪt
  ‖ -aːrk- ~s s
patriarch|y 'peɪtr i aːk |i 'pætr- ‖ -aːrk |i ~ies
  iz
Patrice pə 'triːs
Patricia pə 'trɪʃ ə -'trɪʃ i_ə ‖ -'triːʃ-
patrician pə 'trɪʃ ən ~s z
patriciate pə 'trɪʃ i_ət -eɪt
patricide 'pætr ɪ saɪd 'peɪtr-, -ə- ~s z
Patrick 'pætr ɪk
patriclinous pə 'trɪk lɪn əs -lən-;
  ˌpætr ɪ 'klaɪn əs ◄, -ə-
Patricroft 'pætr ɪ krɒft -ə-‖ -krɔːft -kraːft
patrilineal ˌpætr ə 'lɪn i_əl ◄, •ɪ-
patrilocal ˌpætr ɪ 'ləʊk əl ◄, •ə-, •••, ••
  ‖ -'loʊk əl ◄
patrimonial ˌpætr ɪ 'məʊn i_əl ◄ ‖ -'moʊn- ~ly
  i
patrimon|y 'pætr ɪm ən |i '•əm- ‖ -ə moʊn li
  (*) ~ies iz
patriot 'pætr i_ət 'peɪtr- ‖ 'peɪtr- ~s s

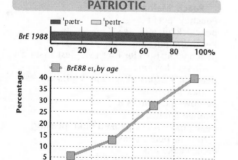

PATRIOTIC

	'pætr-	'peɪtr-
BrE 1988		
0	20	40	60	80	100%

BrE88 eɪ, by age

Percentage	
40	
35	
30	
25	
20	
15	
10	
5	
0	

Older ◄—— Speakers ——► Younger

patriotic ˌpætr i 'ɒt ɪk ◄ ˌpeɪtr-
  ‖ ˌpeɪtr i 'aːt̬ ɪk ◄ —BrE 1988 poll panel
  preference 'pætr- 79%, 'peɪtr- 21%. ~ally əl_i
patriotism 'pætr i_ə ˌtɪz əm 'peɪtr- ‖ 'peɪtr-
patristic pə 'trɪst ɪk pæ- ~s s
Patroclus pə 'trɒk ləs ‖ -'troʊk-

patrol pə 'trəʊl →-'trɒʊl ‖ -'troʊl ~led d
  ~ling ɪŋ ~s z
  pa'trol car; pa'trol ˌwagon
patrol|man pə 'trəʊl |mən →-'trɒʊl-, -mæn
  ‖ -'troʊl- ~men mən men
patrology pə 'trɒl ədʒ i pæ- ‖ -'traːl-
patron 'peɪtr ən ~s z
  ˌpatron 'saint
patronage 'pætr ən ɪdʒ
patronal pə 'trəʊn əl pæ- ‖ 'peɪtr ən_əl (*)
patroness ˌpeɪtr ə 'nes '•••; -ən əs, -ɪs 'peɪtr
  ən əs ~es ɪz əz

PATRONISE

	'peɪtr-	'pætr-
AmE 1993		
BrE 1998		
0	20	40	60	80	100%

patronis|e, patroniz|e 'pætr ə naɪz ‖ 'peɪtr-
  'pætr- —Poll panel preferences: AmE 1993,
  'peɪtr- 64%, 'pætr- 36%; BrE 1998, 'pætr-
  97%, 'peɪtr- 3%. ~ed d ~es ɪz əz ~ing ɪŋ
patronymic ˌpætr ə 'nɪm ɪk ◄ ~ally əl_i ~s s
pats|y, Pats|y 'pæts li ~ies, ~y's iz
patten, P~ 'pæt ən ~s z
patter 'pæt ə ‖ 'pæt̬ ər ~ed d pattering 'pæt
  ər ɪŋ ‖ 'pæt̬ ər ɪŋ ~s z
Patterdale 'pæt ə deɪəl ‖ 'pæt̬ ər-
pattern 'pæt ən ‖ 'pæt̬ ərn ~ed d ~ing ˌɪŋ ‖ ɪŋ
  ~s z
Patterson 'pæt əs ən ‖ 'pæt̬ ərs ən
Patti, Pattie 'pæt i ‖ 'pæt̬ i
Pattison 'pæt ɪs ən -əs- ‖ 'pæt̬-
Patton 'pæt ən
patt|y, Patt|y 'pæt li ‖ 'pæt̬ li ~ies, ~y's iz
patulous 'pæt jʊl əs -jəl- ‖ 'pæt̬ʃ əl əs ~ly li
  ~ness nəs nɪs
patzer 'paːts ə 'pæts- ‖ -ər ~s z
paua 'paʊ_ə ~s z
paucal 'pɔːk əl ‖ 'paːk-
paucity 'pɔːs ət i -ɪt- ‖ -ət̬ i 'paːs-
Paul pɔːl ‖ paːl   Paul's pɔːlz ‖ paːlz
Paula 'pɔːl ə ‖ 'paːl-
Paulette ˌ(ˌ)pɔː 'let ‖ ˌ(ˌ)paː-
Pauli (i) 'paʊl i, (ii) 'pɔːl i ‖ 'paːl-
Pauline forename 'pɔːl iːn ‖ ˌ(ˌ)pɔː 'liːn ˌ(ˌ)paː- (*)
Pauline adj 'relating to St Paul'; n 'pupil of St
  Paul's School' 'pɔːl aɪn ‖ 'paːl- ~s z
Pauling 'pɔːl ɪŋ ‖ 'paːl-
Paulinus pɔː 'laɪn əs ‖ paː-
Paull pɔːl ‖ paːl
paulownia pɔː 'ləʊn i_ə ‖ -'loʊn- paː- ~s z
Pauncefote 'pɔːnᵗs fət -fʊt ‖ 'paːnᵗs-
paunch pɔːnᵗʃ ‖ paːnᵗʃ paunches 'pɔːnᵗʃ ɪz
  -əz ‖ 'paːnᵗʃ-
paunch|y 'pɔːnᵗʃ li ‖ 'paːnᵗʃ- ~iness i nəs i nɪs
pauper 'pɔːp ə ‖ -ər 'paːp- ~s z
pauperis... —see pauperiz...
pauperism 'pɔːp ər ˌɪz əm ‖ 'paːp-
pauperization ˌpɔːp ər aɪ 'zeɪʃ ən -ɪ'•- ‖ -ər ə-
  ˌpaːp-
pauperiz|e 'pɔːp ə raɪz ‖ 'paːp- ~ed d ~es ɪz
  əz ~ing ɪŋ

paupiette ˌpəʊp i 'et ‖ ˌpoʊp- ~s s *or as*
  singular —*Fr* [po pjɛt]
Pausanias pɔː 'seɪn i æs -əs ‖ paː-
pause pɔːz ‖ paːz **paused** pɔːzd ‖ paːzd
  pauses 'pɔːz ɪz -əz ‖ 'paːz- **pausing** 'pɔːz ɪŋ
  ‖ 'paːz-
pavan, pavane pə 'væn -'vaːn, 'pæv ən
  ‖ pə 'vaːn -'væn ~s z
Pavarotti ˌpæv ə 'rɒt i ‖ -'raːt̮ i —*It*
  [pa va 'rɔt ti]
pave peɪv **paved** peɪvd **paves** peɪvz **paving**
  'peɪv ɪŋ
pavé 'pæv eɪ ‖ pæ 'veɪ —*Fr* [pa ve]
pavement 'peɪv mənt ~s s
  'pavement ˌartist
Pavey 'peɪv i
pavilion pə 'vɪl i ən ‖ pə 'vɪl jən ~ed d ~ing
  ɪŋ ~s z
paving 'peɪv ɪŋ
  'paving stone
pavior, paviour, P~ 'peɪv jə ‖ -jər ~s z
Pavitt 'pæv ɪt §-ət
Pavlov 'pæv lɒv ‖ -laːv 'paːv- —*Russ*
  ['pav ɫəf]
Pavlova, p~ pæv 'ləʊv ə 'pæv ləv ə
  ‖ paːv 'loʊv ə pæv- —*Russ* ['pav ɫə və] ~s z
Pavlovian ˌpæv 'ləʊv i ən ‖ -'loʊv- ˌpaːv-
Pavlow 'pæv ləʊ ‖ -loʊ
Pavo 'paːv əʊ ‖ -oʊ
Pavonia pə 'vəʊn i ə ‖ -'voʊn-
pavonine 'pæv əʊ naɪn ‖ -ə-
paw pɔː ‖ paː **pawed** pɔːd ‖ paːd **pawing**
  'pɔː ɪŋ ‖ 'paː- **paws** pɔːz ‖ paːz
pawk|y 'pɔːk li i ‖ 'paːk- ~ier i ə ‖ i ər ~iest
  i ɪst i əst ~ily ɪ li əl i ~iness i nəs i nɪs
pawl pɔːl ‖ paːl (= *pall, Paul*) **pawls** pɔːlz
  ‖ paːlz
pawn pɔːn ‖ paːn **pawned** pɔːnd ‖ paːnd
  pawning 'pɔːn ɪŋ ‖ 'paːn- **pawns** pɔːnz
  ‖ paːnz
pawnbrok|er/s 'pɔːn ˌbrəʊk |ə/z ‖ -ˌbroʊk |ər/z
  'paːn- ~ing ɪŋ
Pawnee pɔː 'niː ‖ paː- ~s z
pawnshop 'pɔːn ʃɒp ‖ -ʃaːp 'paːn- ~s s
pawpaw, paw-paw 'pɔː pɔː ‖ 'paː paː ~s z
Pawtucket pɔː 'tʌk ɪt pə-, §-ət ‖ pə- pɔː-, paː-
pax, Pax pæks ‖ paːks
  ˌPax 'Christi 'krɪst i; ˌPax Ro'mana rəʊ
  'maːn ə ‖ roʊ-; ˌpax vo'biscum vəʊ 'bɪsk əm
  -ʊm ‖ voʊ-
Paxo *tdmk* 'pæks əʊ ‖ -oʊ
Paxos 'pæks ɒs ‖ -oʊs —*Gk* [pa 'ksos]
Paxton 'pækst ən
pay peɪ **paid** peɪd **paying** 'peɪ ɪŋ **pays** peɪz
  'pay claim; 'pay dirt; 'pay ˌenvelope;
  ˌpaying 'guest; 'pay ˌpacket; 'pay phone;
  'pay ˌstation; 'pay train
payable 'peɪ əb əl
payback 'peɪ bæk
paybed 'peɪ bed ~s z
paycheck, paycheque 'peɪ tʃek ~s s
payday 'peɪ deɪ ~s z
PAYE ˌpiː eɪ waɪ 'iː

payee ˌpeɪ 'iː ~s z
payer 'peɪ ə ‖ -ər ~s z
paying-in slip ˌpeɪ ɪŋ 'ɪn slɪp ~s s
payload 'peɪ ləʊd ‖ -loʊd ~s z
paymaster 'peɪ ˌmaːst ə §-ˌmæst- ‖ -ˌmæst ər
  ~s z
  ˌpaymaster 'general
payment 'peɪm ənt ~s s
Payn, Payne peɪn
paynim, P~ 'peɪn ɪm
Paynter 'peɪnt ə ‖ 'peɪnt̮ ər
payoff 'peɪ ɒf -ɔːf ‖ -ɔːf -aːf ~s s
payola peɪ 'əʊl ə ‖ -'oʊl ə
payout 'peɪ aʊt ~s s
payphone 'peɪ fəʊn ‖ -foʊn ~s z
payroll 'peɪ rəʊl →-rɒʊl ‖ -roʊl ~s z
payslip 'peɪ slɪp ~s s
Payton 'peɪt ən
pay-TV ˌpeɪ tiː 'viː: '••,•
pazazz pə 'zæz
PBS ˌpiː biː 'es
PC, P.C. ˌpiː 'siː ◄ ~s, ~'s z
PCB ˌpiː siː 'biː ~s z
PE ˌpiː 'iː
pea piː **peas** piːz
  ˌpea 'green◄; 'pea ˌjacket; ˌpea 'souper
Peabody 'piː ˌbɒd i 'peɪ-; 'piːb əd i ‖ -ˌbaːd i
peace, Peace piːs
  'Peace Corps; 'peace ˌoffering; 'peace
  pipe
peaceab|le 'piːs əb |əl ~leness əl nəs -nɪs ~ly
  li
peaceful 'piːs fəl -fʊl ~ly ˌi ~ness nəs nɪs
Peacehaven 'piːs ˌheɪv ən
peacekeep|er 'piːs ˌkiːp |ə ‖ -ər ~ers əz ‖ -ərz
  ~ing ɪŋ
peacemak|er 'piːs ˌmeɪk |ə ‖ -ər ~ers əz ‖ -ərz
  ~ing ɪŋ
peacenik 'piːs nɪk ~s s
peacetime 'piːs taɪm
peach, Peach piːtʃ **peaches** 'piːtʃ ɪz -əz
  ˌPeach 'Melba
Peachey 'piːtʃ i
peachick 'piː tʃɪk ~s s
Peachum 'piːtʃ əm
peach|y 'piːtʃ li ~ier i ə ‖ i ər ~iest i ɪst i əst
  ~iness i nəs i nɪs
peacock, P~ 'piːk ɒk 'piː kɒk ‖ 'piː kaːk ~s s
  ˌpeacock 'blue◄
peafowl 'piː faʊl ~s z
peahen 'piː hen ~s z
peak piːk (= *peek*) **peaked** piːkt **peaking**
  'piːk ɪŋ **peaks** piːks
Peak, Peake piːk
  'Peak ˌDistrict; ˌpeak 'time◄
peaked *adj* 'having a peak'; *past and pp of*
  peak piːkt
peaked *adj* 'peaky, pale' — ‖ 'piːk əd
Peaker 'piːk ə ‖ -ər
peaky 'piːk i
peal piːəl (= *peel*) **pealed** piːəld **pealing**
  'piːəl ɪŋ **peals** piːəlz
Peano pi 'aːn əʊ ‖ -oʊ —*It* [pe 'aː no]

peanut 'piː nʌt ~s s
,peanut 'butter ◄ ‖ '·· ,··; ,peanut ,butter 'sandwich
pear peə ‖ peᵊr pæᵊr *(= pair)* **pears** peəz ‖ peᵊrz pæᵊrz
Pear *family name* pɪə ‖ peᵊr
Pearce pɪəs ‖ pɪᵊrs
pearl, Pearl pɜːl ‖ pɜˑl **pearled** pɜːld ‖ pɜˑld
pearling 'pɜːl ɪŋ ‖ 'pɜˑl ɪŋ **pearls** pɜːlz ‖ pɜˑlz
'pearl ,diver; ,Pearl 'Harbor
pearlite 'pɜːl aɪt ‖ 'pɜˑl-
pearlwort 'pɜːl wɜːt -wɔːt ‖ 'pɜˑl wɜˑt -wɔːrt
pearl|y 'pɜːl li i ‖ 'pɜˑl li ~ier iˌə ‖ iˌᵊr ~ies iz
~iest iˌɪst iˌəst ~iness i nəs i nɪs
,pearly 'gates
pearmain, P~ 'peə meɪn 'pɜː- ‖ 'per- ~s z
Pearn pɜːn ‖ pɜˑn
Pears *family name (i)* pɪəz ‖ pɪᵊrz, *(ii)*
peəz ‖ peᵊrz pæᵊrz —*The singer* Sir Peter
Pears *was (i), but the brand of soap is (ii)*
Pearsall 'pɪəs ᵊl -ɔːl ‖ 'pɪrs ɔːl -aːl
Pearse pɪəs ‖ pɪᵊrs
pear-shaped 'peə ʃeɪpt ‖ 'per- 'pær-
Pearson 'pɪəs ᵊn ‖ 'pɪrs ᵊn
Peart pɪət ‖ pɪᵊrt
Peary 'pɪər i ‖ 'pɪr i
peasant 'pez ᵊnt ~s s
,Peasants' Re'volt
peasantry 'pez ᵊntr i
pease, Pease piːz
,pease 'pudding
Peaseblossom 'piːz ,blɒs əm ‖ -,blɑːs əm
peasecod 'piːz kɒd ‖ -kaːd ~s z
peashooter 'piː ,ʃuːt ə ‖ -,ʃuːt ᵊr ~s z
pea-souper ,piː 'suːp ə ‖ -ᵊr ~s z
peat, Peat, Peate piːt
'peat bog
peat|y 'piːt li i ‖ 'piːt li ~ier iˌə ‖ iˌᵊr ~iest
iˌɪst ˌəst ~iness i nəs -nɪs
Peaudouce *tdmk* ,pəʊ 'duːs ‖ ,poʊ-
peav|ey, peav|y, P~ 'piːv li ~eys, ~ies iz
pebbl|e 'peb ᵊl ~ed d ~es z ~ing ɪŋ
pebble-dash 'peb ᵊl dæʃ ~ed t ~es ɪz əz
~ing ɪŋ
pebbly 'peb ᵊl i
pec pek **pecs** peks
pecan pɪ 'kæn 'piːk æn, -ᵊn ‖ pɪ 'kaːn -'kæn;
'piːk æn ~s z
peccadillo ,pek ə 'dɪl əʊ ‖ -oʊ ~s z
peccar|y 'pek ᵊr i ~ies iz
peccavi pe 'kaːv iː —*Formerly* -'keɪv aɪ
peck, Peck pek **pecked** pekt **pecking** 'pek ɪŋ
pecks peks
'pecking ,order
pecker 'pek ə ‖ -ᵊr ~s z
Peckham 'pek əm
Peckinpah 'pek ɪn paː -ᵊn-
peckish 'pek ɪʃ ~ly li ~ness nəs nɪs
Peckitt 'pek ɪt §-ət
Pecksniff 'pek snɪf
Pecksniffian ₍ᵢ₎pek 'snɪf iˌən
Peconic pɪ 'kɒn ɪk ‖ -'kaːn-

pecorino ,pek ə 'riːn əʊ ‖ -oʊ —*It*
[pe ko 'ri: no]
Pecos 'peɪk əs -ɒs ‖ -oʊs
Pécs petʃ ‖ peɪtʃ —*Hungarian* [peːtʃ]
pecten 'pekt ɪn -en, §-ᵊn
pectic 'pekt ɪk
pectin 'pekt ɪn §-ᵊn
pecti|nate 'pekt ɪ |neɪt -ə- ~nated neɪt ɪd -əd
‖ neɪt̬ əd ~nately neɪt li
pectoral 'pekt ᵊrˌəl ~s z
,pectoral 'cross; ,pectoral 'fin
pecu|late 'pek ju |leɪt -jə- ‖ -jə- ~lated leɪt ɪd
-əd ‖ leɪt̬ əd ~lates leɪts ~lating
leɪt ɪŋ ‖ leɪt̬ ɪŋ
peculation ,pek ju 'leɪʃ ᵊn -jə- ‖ -jə- ~s z
peculator 'pek ju leɪt ə '·jə- ‖ -jə leɪt̬ ᵊr ~s z
peculiar pɪ 'kjuːl iˌə pə-, △bə- ‖ -'kjuːl jᵊr ~s
z
peculiarit|y pɪ ,kjuːl i 'ær ət li pə-, △bə-, -ɪt i
‖ -ət̬ li -'er-; ·,·'jær-, -'jer- ~ies iz
peculiarly pɪ 'kjuːl iˌə li pə-, △bə-
‖ -'kjuːl jᵊr li
pecuniar|y pɪ 'kjuːn iˌər li pə-, -'kjuːn ᵊr li
‖ -i er li ~ily ᵊl i ɪ li
-ped ped — **biped** 'baɪ ped
pedagogic ,ped ə 'gɒdʒ ɪk ◄ -'gəʊdʒ-, -'gɒg-
‖ -'gaːdʒ ɪk -'goʊdʒ- ~ally ᵊlˌi
pedagogue 'ped ə gɒg ‖ -gaːg ~s z
pedagogy 'ped ə gɒdʒ i -gəʊdʒ-, -gɒg-
‖ -goʊdʒ i -gaːdʒ-
pedal *n, v* 'ped ᵊl *(= peddle)* ~ed, ~led d ~ing,
~ling ˌɪŋ ~s z
pedal *adj* 'piːd ᵊl 'ped-
pedalo 'ped ə ləʊ →-ᵊl əʊ ‖ -ᵊl oʊ ~s s
pedant 'ped ᵊnt ~s s
pedantic pɪ 'dænt ɪk pə-, pe- ‖ -'dænt̬ ɪk ~ally
ᵊlˌi
pedantr|y 'ped ᵊntr li ~ies iz
Pedder 'ped ə ‖ -ᵊr
peddl|e 'ped ᵊl ~ed d ~es z ~ing ɪŋ
peddler 'ped lə ‖ -lᵊr ~s z
-pede piːd — **millipede** 'mɪl ɪ piːd -ə-
Peden 'piːd ᵊn
pederast 'ped ə ræst 'piːd- ~s s
pederastic ,ped ə 'ræst ɪk ◄ ,piːd- ~ally ᵊlˌi
pederasty 'ped ə ræst i 'piːd-
pedestal 'ped ɪst ᵊl -əst- ~s z
pedestrian pə 'des tri ən pɪ- ~s z
pe,destrian 'crossing
pedestrianis... —*see* pedestrianiz...
pedestrianization pə ,des tri ən aɪ 'zeɪʃ ᵊn pɪ-,
-ɪ'·- ‖ -ə'·-
pedestrianiz|e pə 'des triˌə naɪz pɪ- ~ed d
~es ɪz əz ~ing ɪŋ
Pedi 'ped i
pediatric ,piːd i 'ætr ɪk ◄ ~ally ᵊlˌi ~s s
pediatrician ,piːd iˌə 'trɪʃ ᵊn ~s z
pedicab 'ped i kæb ~s z
pedicel 'ped ɪ sel -ə- ~s z
pedicle 'ped ɪk ᵊl ~s z
pedicular pɪ 'dɪk jʊl ə pe-, pə-, -jəl- ‖ -jəl ᵊr
pedicure 'ped ɪ kjʊə -ə-, -kjɔː ‖ -kjʊr ~s z

P

pedicurist 'ped ɪ kjuər ɪst '•ə-, ˌ-ə kjɔːr-, §-əst ‖ -kjʊr əst ~s s
pediform 'ped ɪ fɔːm ‖ -fɔːrm
pedigree 'ped ɪ griː -ə- ~d d ~s z
pediment 'ped ɪ mənt -ə- ~s s
pedimented 'ped ɪ ment ɪd '•ə-, -mənt-, -əd ‖ -menṯ əd
pedipalp 'ped ɪ pælp ~s s
pedlar 'ped lə ‖ -lᵊr ~s z
pedogenesis ˌped əʊ 'dʒen əs ɪs ˌpiːd-, -ɪs ɪs, §-əs ‖ ˌ•ᵊ-
pedometer pɪ 'dɒm ɪt ə pə-, pe-, -ət- ‖ -'dɑːm əṯ ᵊr ~s z
pedophile 'piːd əʊ faɪᵊl '-ə- 'ped- ~s z
pedophilia ˌpiːd əʊ 'fɪl i‿ə ‖ ˌ•ᵊ- ˌped-
pedophiliac ˌpiːd əʊ 'fɪl i æk ‖ ˌ•ᵊ- ˌped- ~s s
Pedro, p~ 'pedr əʊ 'peɪdr-, 'piːdr- ‖ 'peɪdr oʊ —Sp ['pe ðro]
Peds tdmk pedz
peduncle pɪ 'dʌŋk ᵊl pə-, pe- ‖ 'piːd ʌŋk ᵊl ~s z
peduncular pɪ 'dʌŋk jʊl ə pə-, pe-, -jəl- ‖ -jəl ᵊr
pedunculate pɪ 'dʌŋk ju leɪt pə-, pe-, -jə-, -lət, -lɪt ‖ -jə-
pee piː **peed** piːd **peeing** 'piː ɪŋ **pees** piːz
Peeb|les 'piːb |ᵊlz **~lesshire** ᵊlz ʃə→ᵊlʒ-, -ʃɪə, §-ˌʃaɪ‿ə ‖ -ʃᵊr-ʃɪr, ˌʃaɪᵊr
Pee Dee ˌpiː 'diː ◂ ˌPee Dee 'River
peek, Peek piːk **peeked** piːkt **peeking** 'piːk ɪŋ **peeks** piːks
peekaboo ˌpiːk ə 'buː '•••
peel, Peel, Peele piːᵊl **peeled** piːᵊld **peeling** 'piːᵊl ɪŋ **peels** piːᵊlz
peeler 'piːl ə ‖ -ᵊr ~s z
peen piːn
peep piːp **peeped** piːpt **peeping** 'piːp ɪŋ **peeps** piːps ˌpeeping 'Tom
peepbo 'piːp bəʊ -əʊ, ˌ•'• ‖ -boʊ
peeper 'piːp ə ‖ -ᵊr ~s z
peephole 'piːp həʊl→-hɒʊl ‖ -hoʊl ~s z
peepshow 'piːp ʃəʊ ‖ -ʃoʊ ~s z
peep-toe 'piːp təʊ ‖ -toʊ
peepul 'piːp ᵊl (= people) ~s z
peer pɪə ‖ pɪᵊr **peered** pɪəd ‖ pɪᵊrd **peering** 'pɪər ɪŋ ‖ 'pɪr ɪŋ **peers** pɪəz ‖ pɪᵊrz ˌpeer group; ˌpeer re'view
peerag|e 'pɪər ɪdʒ ‖ 'pɪr- ~es ɪz əz
peeress ˌpɪər 'es '••, -əs, -ɪs ‖ 'pɪr əs ~es ɪz əz
peerie 'pɪər i ‖ 'pɪr i
peerless 'pɪə ləs -lɪs ‖ 'pɪr- ~ly li ~ness nəs nɪs
peeve piːv **peeved** piːvd **peeving** 'piːv ɪŋ **peeves** piːvz
peevish 'piːv ɪʃ ~ly li ~ness nəs nɪs
peewee, P~ 'piː wiː ~s z
peewit 'piː wɪt ~s s
peg, Peg, Pegg peg **pegged** pegd **pegging** 'peg ɪŋ **pegs** pegz ˌpeg 'leg ‖ '• •

Pegasus 'peg əs əs
pegboard 'peg bɔːd ‖ -bɔːrd -boʊrd ~s z
Peggie 'peg i
Peggotty 'peg ət i ‖ -əṯ i
Peggy 'peg i
Pegler 'peg lə ‖ -lᵊr
pegmatite 'peg mə taɪt
peignoir 'peɪn wɑː ‖ peɪn 'wɑːr —Fr [pɛn waːʁ, pɛnj-] ~s z
Peiping ˌpeɪ 'pɪŋ
Peirce pɪəs ‖ pɪᵊrs
pejoration ˌpiːdʒ ə 'reɪʃ ᵊn ˌpedʒ-
pejorative pɪ 'dʒɒr ət ɪv pə-, -'dʒɔːr-; 'piːdʒ ər‿ət- ‖ -'dʒɔːr əṯ ɪv -'dʒɑːr-; 'pedʒ ə reɪṯ ɪv ~ly li ~s z
peke piːk (= peak) **pekes** piːks
Pekin ˌpiː 'kɪn ◂
Pekines|e ˌpiːk ɪ 'niːz ◂-ə- ‖ -'niːs -**es** ɪz əz
Peking ˌpiː 'kɪŋ ◂—see also Beijing
Pekingese ˌpiːk ɪ 'niːz ◂-ɪŋ 'iːz ◂, -ə- ‖ -'niːs, -ɪŋ 'iːs, •••
pekoe 'piːk əʊ ‖ -oʊ
pelag|e 'pel ɪdʒ ~es ɪz əz
pelagian, P~ pɪ 'leɪdʒ i‿ən pə-, pe-, -'leɪdʒ ən ~ism ˌɪz əm ~s z
pelagic pə 'lædʒ ɪk pɪ-, pe-
Pelagius pɪ 'leɪdʒ i‿əs pə-, pe-
pelargonium ˌpel ə 'gəʊn i‿əm ˌ•ɑː- ‖ -ɑːr 'goʊn- ~s z
Pelasgian pe 'læz dʒi‿ən pɪ-, pə-, -gi‿ən; -'læz dʒən ~s z
Pele, Pelé, Pelee, Pelée 'pel eɪ pə 'leɪ ‖ pə 'leɪ 'peɪ leɪ —Fr [pə le]
pelerine 'pel ə riːn -rɪn ~s z
Peleus 'piːl juːs 'piːl i‿əs, 'pel-
pelf pelf
Pelham, p~ 'pel əm ~s, ~'s z
Pelias 'piːl i æs -əs
pelican, P~ 'pel ɪk ən ~s z ˌpelican 'crossing
Pelion 'piːl i‿ən -ɒn
peliss|e pə 'liːs pe-, pɪ- ~es ɪz əz
Pella 'pel ə
pellagra pə 'læg rə pɪ-, pe-, -'leɪg-, -'lɑːg-
Pelleas, Pelléas 'pel eɪ æs -i- —Fr [pɛ le ɑːs]
Pelles 'pel iːz
pell|et 'pel |ɪt §-ət ‖ -ət -**eted** ɪt ɪd §ət-, -əd ‖ əṯ əd -**eting** ɪt ɪŋ §ət- ‖ əṯ ɪŋ -**ets** ɪts §əts ‖ əts
Pelletier 'pel ət i eɪ ‖ ˌpel ə 'tɪᵊr—Fr [pɛl 'tje]
pellicle 'pel ɪk ᵊl ~s z
pellicular pə 'lɪk jʊl ə pe-, pɪ-, -jəl- ‖ -jəl ᵊr
pellitor|y 'pel ɪt ᵊr i ‖ •ət‿ ‖ -ə tɔːr i -toʊr i ~ies iz
pell-mell ˌpel 'mel ◂
pellucid pɪ 'luːs ɪd pə-, pe-, -'ljuːs-, §-əd ~ly li ~ness nəs nɪs
Pelman 'pel mən ~ism ˌɪz əm
pelmet 'pelm ɪt -ət ~s s
Peloponnese 'pel əp ə niːs ˌ•••'• ‖ ˌpel əp ə 'niːz -'niːs —ModGk Peloponnesos [pe lo 'po ni sos]

Peloponnesian ˌpel əp ə ˈniːʃ ᵊn ◄
-ˈniːʃ i_ən ‖ -ˈniːʒ- ~s z
ˌPelopon‿nesian ˈWar
Peloponnesus ˌpel əp ə ˈniːs əs
Pelops ˈpiːl ɒps ˈpel- ‖ -ɑːps
pelorus pə ˈlɔːr əs pɪ- ‖ -ˈloʊr ~es ɪz əz
pelota pə ˈlɒt ə pɪ-, pe-, -ˈloʊt- ‖ -ˈloʊt̬ ə —Sp
[pe ˈlo ta]
pelt pelt **pelted** ˈpelt ɪd -əd **pelting** ˈpelt ɪŋ
pelts pelts
peltast ˈpelt æst ~s s
peltate ˈpelt eɪt —ly li
Peltier ˈpelt i eɪ —Fr [pɛl tje]
Pelton ˈpelt ən
pelvic ˈpelv ɪk
pelv|is ˈpelv |ɪs §-əs ~es iːz ~ises ɪs ɪz §əs ɪz,
-əz
Pemba ˈpem bə
Pemberton ˈpem bət ən ‖ -bᵊrt ᵊn
Pembrey ₍ᵢ₎pem ˈbreɪ ˈpem bri
Pembridge ˈpem brɪdʒ
Pembroke ˈpem brʊk -brək, -brəʊk ‖ -brʊk
-brʊk ~shire ʃə ʃɪə ‖ ʃᵊr ʃɪr
Pembury ˈpem bᵊr_i
pemican, pemmican ˈpem ɪk ən
pemphigus ˈpempf ɪg əs §-əg-; pem ˈfaɪg-
pen pen **penned** pend pend (= pend) **penning**
ˈpen ɪŋ **pens** penz
ˈpen friend; ˈpen name; ˈpen pal; ˈpen
ˌpusher
penal ˈpiːn ᵊl
ˈpenal ˌcolony
penalis... —see **penaliz...**
penalization ˌpiːn ᵊl aɪ ˈzeɪʃ ᵊn -ɪˈ•- ‖ -ᵊl ə-
ˌpen- ~s z
penaliz|e ˈpiːn ə laɪz -ᵊl aɪz ‖ ˈpiːn ᵊl aɪz ˈpen-
~ed d ~es ɪz əz ~ing ɪŋ
penally ˈpiːn ᵊl i
penalt|y ˈpen ᵊlt |i ~ies iz
ˈpenalty ˌarea; ˈpenalty box; ˈpenalty goal;
ˈpenalty kick
penanc|e ˈpen ənts ~es ɪz əz
pen-and-ink ˌpen ən ˈɪŋk ◄ -ənd-
Penang pɪ ˈnæŋ pə-, pe-
Penarth pe ˈnɑːθ pə- ‖ -ˈnɑːrθ —Welsh
[pe ˈnarθ]
penates pe ˈnɑːt eɪz pɪ-, pə-, -iːz, -ˈneɪt iːz
‖ ˈneɪt̬- -ˈnɑːt-
pence penᵗs —There is a BrE weak form pənᵗs,
but it is now fairly rare. Prices are usually
quoted with the strong form penᵗs or with **p** piː,
usually stressed: **15p**
ˌfɪf ˈtiːn ˈpenᵗs ,, ˌfɪf ˈtiːn ˈpiː, less commonly
ˌfɪf ˈtiːn pənᵗs
penchant ˈpɒ̃ ʃɒ̃ ˈpɒn ʃɒn, ˈpɒŋ ʃɒŋ ‖ ˈpenʧ
ənt (*) —Fr [pɑ̃ ʃɑ̃] ~s z ‖ s
pencil ˈpenᵗs ᵊl -ɪl ~ed, ~led d ~ing, ~ling ɪŋ
~s z
ˈpencil ˌcase; ˈpencil ˌsharpener
Pencoed ₍ᵢ₎pen ˈkɔɪd →ₒₓ peŋ-
pend pend **pending** ˈpend ɪŋ
pendant ˈpend ənt ~s s
Pendennis pen ˈden ɪs §-əs

pendent ˈpend ənt ~ly li ~s s
pendente lite pen ˌdent i ˈlaɪt iː -i
pendentive pen ˈdent ɪv ‖ -ˈden̪t̬ ɪv ~s z
Pender ˈpend ə ‖ -ᵊr
Penderecki ˌpend ə ˈret ski —Polish
[pen de ˈrets ki]
Pendergast ˈpend ə gɑːst §-gæst ‖ -ᵊr gæst
Pendine ₍ᵢ₎pen ˈdaɪn
pending ˈpend ɪŋ
Pendle ˈpend ᵊl
Pendlebury ˈped ᵊl bər_i ‖ -ˌber i
Pendleton ˈpend ᵊl tən
pendragon, P~ pen ˈdræg ən ~s z
pendulous ˈpend jʊl əs -jəl- ‖ ˈpendʒ əl əs
~ly li ~ness nəs nɪs
pendulum ˈpend jʊl əm -jəl- ‖ ˈpendʒ əl əm
~s z
Penelope pə ˈnel əp i pɪ-
peneplain, peneplane ˈpiːn ɪ pleɪn ˈpen-, -ə-,
ˌ••ˈ• ~s z
penetrability ˌpen ətr ə ˈbɪl ət i ,•ɪtr-, -ɪt i
‖ -ət̬ i
penetrab|le ˈpen ətr əb |ᵊl ˈ•ɪtr- ~ly li
penetralia ˌpen ə ˈtreɪl i_ə ,•ɪ-
penetrance ˈpen ətr ənᵗs -ɪtr-
pene|trate ˈpen ə |treɪt -ɪ- ~**trated** treɪt ɪd -əd
‖ treɪt̬ əd ~**trates** treɪts ~**trating/ly**
treɪt ɪŋ /li ‖ treɪt̬ ɪŋ /li
penetration ˌpen ə ˈtreɪʃ ᵊn -ɪ- ~s z
penetrative ˈpen ətr ət ɪv ˈ•ɪtr-; -ə treɪt-,
-ɪ treɪt- ‖ -ə treɪt̬ ɪv ~ly li ~ness nəs nɪs
Penfold ˈpen fəʊld →-fɒʊld ‖ -foʊld
penfriend ˈpen frend ~s z
Pengam ˈpeŋ gəm
Penge pendʒ
Pengelly pen ˈgel i →peŋ-
penguin, P~ ˈpeŋ gwɪn §-gwən ~s z
Penhaligon pen ˈhæl ɪg ən
penicillin ˌpen ə ˈsɪl ɪn -ɪ-, §-ən
penicillium ˌpen ə ˈsɪl i_əm ,•ɪ-
Penicuik ˈpen i kʊk
penile ˈpiːn aɪᵊl ‖ -ᵊl
penillion pe ˈnɪθ li_ən pɪ-, pə-, -ˈnɪl i_ —Welsh
[pe ˈnɪɬ jon]
peninsula pə ˈnɪnᵗs jʊl ə pɪ-, pe-, -ˈnɪnᵗʃ ʊl ə
‖ -ᵊl ə ~s z
peninsular pə ˈnɪnᵗs jʊl ə pɪ-, pe-, -ˈnɪnᵗʃ ʊl ə
‖ -ᵊl ᵊr
penis ˈpiːn ɪs §-əs ~es ɪz əz
Penistone ˈpen ɪst ən
penitence ˈpen ɪt ənᵗs -ət- ‖ -ət ənᵗs
penitent ˈpen ɪt ənt -ət- ‖ -ət ᵊnt ~ly li ~s s
penitential ˌpen ɪ ˈtenʧ ᵊl ◄ -ə- ~ly i
penitentiar|y ˌpen ɪ ˈtenʧ ᵊr |i ,•ə- ~ies iz
Penk peŋk
Penkhull ˈpeŋk ᵊl -hʌl
pen|knife ˈpen |naɪf ~**knives** naɪvz
Penkridge ˈpeŋk rɪdʒ
Penlee ₍ᵢ₎pen ˈliː
Penmaenmawr, Penmaen-mawr
ˌpen mən ˈmaʊ_ə →ˌpem-, →,•məm-,
,•maɪn-; ,••ˈmɔː ‖ -ˈmaʊ_ᵊr —Welsh
[ˌpɛn maɪn ˈmaur, -mən-]

pen|man 'pen mən →'pem- ~manship
mən ʃɪp ~men mən men
Penn pen
Penn. pen *or as* Pennsylvania
penn|a 'pen |ə ~ae iː
pennant, P~ 'pen ənt ~s s
penne pen eɪ -i —*It* [pen ne]
Penney, Pennie 'pen i
penni... —*see* penny
penniless 'pen ɪ ləs -ə-, -lɪs; -əl əs, -ɪs ~ly li
~ness nəs nɪs
Pennine 'pen aɪn ~s z
Pennine Way
Pennington 'pen ɪŋ tən
pennon 'pen ən ~ed d ~s z
pennorth, penn'orth 'pen əθ ǁ -ərθ
Pennsylvania ˌpenᵗs əl 'veɪn i‿ə ◂, •ɪl-
ǁ ˌ••'•jə ◂
Pennsylvania Dutch
Pennsylvanian ˌpenᵗs əl 'veɪn i‿ən ◂, •ɪl-
ǁ ˌ••'•jən ◂ ~s z
penn|y, Penn|y 'pen |i ~ies, ~y's iz
penny black; penny dreadful; penny
whistle
-penny *adj-forming suffix* pən i, ˌpen i —
tenpenny 'ten pən i 'temp ən‿i, 'ten ˌpen i
—*The post-decimalization equivalent is*
pence, p, *thus* a 10p packet
ə ˌten pi: 'pæk ɪt : *see note at* pence
penny-ante ˌpen i 'ænt i ◂ ǁ -'ænt̬ i ◂
pennycress 'pen i kres
Pennycuick (i) 'pen i kʊk, (ii) -kwɪk, (iii) -kjuːk
penny-farthing ˌpen i 'fɑːð ɪŋ ǁ -'fɑːrð- ~s z
Pennyfeather 'pen i ˌfeð ə ǁ -ᵊr
penny-halfpen|ny ˌpen i 'heɪp |ni ~nies niz
penny-pinch|er/s 'pen i ˌpɪntʃ| ə/z ǁ ᵊr/z
~ing ɪŋ
pennyroyal ˌpen i 'rɔɪ‿əl ~s z
pennyweight 'pen i weɪt ~s s
penny-wise ˌpen i 'waɪz ◂
pennywort 'pen i wɜːt §-wɔːt ǁ -wɝːt -wɔːrt
pennyworth 'pen əθ 'pen i wɜːθ, -wəθ
ǁ 'pen i wɝːθ ~s s
Penobscot pə 'nɒb skɒt pe-, pɪ- ǁ -'nɑːb skɑːt
penological ˌpiːn ə 'lɒdʒ ɪk əl ǁ -'lɑːdʒ- ~ly ‿i
penology ₍ᵢ₎pi: 'nɒl ədʒ i pɪ- ǁ -'nɑːl-
Penrhos *place in Gwynedd* 'pen rəʊs -rɒs
ǁ -roʊs —*Welsh* ['pen hroːs]
Pen-rhos *places in Gwynedd, Gwent, Powys*
ˌpen 'rəʊs ◂ ǁ -'roʊs —*Welsh* [ˌpɛn 'hroːs]
Penrhyn 'pen rɪn —*Welsh* ['pɛn hrin, -hrin]
Penrhyndeudraeth ˌpen rɪn 'daɪdr əθ -aɪθ
—*Welsh* [ˌpɛn hrin 'dəɪ draɪθ]
Penrith *place in Cumbria* 'pen rɪθ, •'• —*locally
also* 'pɪər ɪθ
Penrith *place in NSW* 'pen rɪθ -rəθ —*locally*
-rəθ
Penrose 'pen rəʊz ₍ᵢ₎•'• ǁ -roʊz
Penry 'pen ri
Penryn ₍ᵢ₎pen 'rɪn
Pensacola ˌpenᵗs ə 'kəʊl ə ǁ -'koʊl ə
Pensarn *place in Dyfed* 'pen sɑːn ǁ -sɑːrn

Pen-sarn *places in Clwyd and Gwynedd*
pen 'sɑːn ǁ -'sɑːrn
penseroso ˌpenᵗs ə 'rəʊz əʊ -'rəʊs- ǁ -'roʊs oʊ
Penshurst 'penz hɜːst ǁ -hɝːst
pensile 'penᵗs aɪᵊl ǁ -ᵊl
pension *'payment'* 'penᵗʃ ᵊn ~ed d ~ing ‿ɪŋ
~s z
pension fund
pension *'boarding-house'* 'põs jõ ǁ pɑːns 'joʊn
—*Fr* [pɑ̃ sjɔ̃] ~s z
pensionable 'penᵗʃ ᵊn_əb əl
pensioner 'penᵗʃ ᵊn_ə ǁ _ər ~s z
pensive 'penᵗs ɪv ~ly li ~ness nəs nɪs
penstemon pen 'stiːm ən 'penᵗst ɪm-, -əm- ~s
z
penstock 'pen stɒk ǁ -stɑːk ~s s
pent pent
pent up ◂
pent- *comb. form* ˌpent — pentoxide
ˌpent 'ɒks aɪd ǁ -'ɑːks-
penta- *comb. form*
with stress-neutral suffix ˌpent ə ǁ ˌpent̬ ə —
pentaprism 'pent ə ˌprɪz əm ǁ 'pent̬ ə-
with stress-imposing suffix pen 'tæ+ —
pentamerous pen 'tæm ər əs
pentacle 'pent ək əl ǁ 'pent̬- ~s z
pentad 'pent æd ~s z
pentagon, P~ 'pent əg ən-ə gɒn ǁ 'pent̬
ə gɑːn ~s z
pentagonal pen 'tæg ən əl
pentagram 'pent ə græm ǁ 'pent̬- ~s z
pentahedr|on ˌpent ə 'hiːdr |ən -'hedr-
ǁ ˌpent̬- ~a ə ~al əl ~ons ənz
pentamerous pen 'tæm ər əs
pentameter pen 'tæm ɪt ə -ət- ǁ -ət̬ ᵊr ~s z
pentane 'pent eɪn
pentangle 'pent ˌæŋ gᵊl ~s z
Pentateuch 'pent ə tjuːk →§-tʃuːk ǁ 'pent̬
ə tuːk -tjuːk
pentathlete pen 'tæθ liːt ~s s
pentathlon pen 'tæθ lən -lɒn ǁ -lɑːn
pentatonic ˌpent ə 'tɒn ɪk ◂ ǁ ˌpent̬ ə 'tɑːn ɪk ◂
Pentax *tdmk* 'pent æks
Pentecost 'pent ɪ kɒst -ə- ǁ 'pent̬ ɪ kɔːst
-kɑːst
pentecostal ˌpent ɪ 'kɒst ᵊl ◂-ə- ǁ ˌpent̬
ɪ 'kɔːst ᵊl ◂ -'kɑːst- ~ism ˌɪz əm
Pentel *tdmk* 'pen tel
Pentelicus pen 'tel ɪk əs
Pentelikon pen 'tel ɪk ᵊn -ɪ kɒn ǁ -ɪ kɑːn
Penthesilea ˌpenᵗθ es ɪ 'leɪ ə, •ᵊs-, -ə'•-, -'liː‿ə
Pentheus 'penᵗθ juːs 'penᵗθ i‿əs
pent|house 'pent |haʊs ~houses haʊz ɪz -əz
pentiment|o ˌpent ɪ 'ment əʊ-ə- ǁ ˌpent̬
ə 'ment oʊ ~i iː —*It* [pen ti 'men tlo, -i]
Pentire pen 'taɪ‿ə ǁ -'taɪ‿ᵊr
Pentium *tdmk* 'pent i‿əm ǁ 'pent̬-
Pentland 'pent lənd
Pentland Firth
pentobarbitone ˌpent əʊ 'bɑːb ɪ təʊn -'•ə-
ǁ ˌpent̬ ə 'bɑːrb ə toʊn
pentode 'pent əʊd ǁ -oʊd ~s z
Penton 'pent ən ǁ -ᵊn

Pentonville 'pent ən vɪl ˌ••'• ‖ -ən-
pentose 'pent əʊz -əʊs ‖ -oʊs -oʊz
Pentothal *tdmk* 'pent ə θæl -θɒl, -θɔːl ‖ 'penţ
ə θɔːl -θɑːl
Pentre 'pentr ə 'pen treɪ —*Welsh* ['pen tre]
Pentreath pen 'triːθ
pentstemon pent 'stiːm ən pen-, -'stem-;
'penɪst ɪm-, -əm- ~s z
pent-up ˌpent 'ʌp ◄ ‖ ˌpenţ-
ˌpent-up e'motions
penuche pə 'nuːtʃ i
penult pə 'nʌlt pɪ-, pe- ‖ 'piːn ʌlt (*)
penultimate pə 'nʌlt ɪm ət pɪ-, pe-, -əm ət, -ɪt
~ly li ~s s
penum|bra pə 'nʌm |brə pɪ-, pe- ~brae briː
~bral brəl ~bras brəz
penurious pə 'njʊər i_əs pɪ-, pe- ‖ -'nʊr-
-'njʊr- ~ly li ~ness nəs nɪs
penury 'pen jər i -jʊr-
Penutian pɪ 'njuːt i_ən pe-, pə-, -'nuːt-;
-'njuːʃ ən, -'nuːʃ- ‖ -'nuːʃ-
Penwith ₍ₕ₎pen 'wɪθ
Penwortham 'pen wəð əm ‖ -wərð-
Penybont, Pen-y-bont ˌpen ə 'bɒnt -i- ‖ —
—*Welsh* [ˌpen ə 'bɔnt]
Penyghent ˌpen i 'gent '•••
Pen-y-groes ˌpen ə 'grɔɪs -i-, -'grəʊs —*Welsh*
[ˌpen ə 'grɔis]
Penzance pen 'zænᵗs pən-, -'zɑːnᵗs
peon 'piː_ən -ɒn ‖ -aːn —*formerly, and in India,*
pjuːn ~s z
peonage 'piː_ən ɪdʒ
peon|y 'piː_ən |i ~ies iz
peopl|e 'piːp ᵊl ~ed d ~es z ~ing _ɪŋ
Peoria pi 'ɔːr i_ə ‖ -'oʊr-
Peover 'piːv ə ‖ -ᵊr
pep, PEP pep pepped pept pepping 'pep ɪŋ
peps peps
'pep pill; 'pep talk
Pepe 'pep eɪ —*Sp* ['pe pe]
peperomia ˌpep ə 'rəʊm i_ə ‖ -'roʊm- ~s z
peperoni ˌpep ə 'rəʊn i ‖ -'roʊn i
Pepin 'pep ɪn §-ən
Pepita pe 'piːt ə pə- ‖ -'piːţ ə —*Sp* [pe 'pi ta]
peplum 'pep ləm ~s z
Peppard 'pep aːd ‖ -aːrd
pepp... —*see* pep
pepper, P~ 'pep ə ‖ -ᵊr ~ed d peppering
'pep ᵊr_ɪŋ ~s z
'pepper mill; 'pepper pot
pepper-and-salt ˌpep ᵊr_ən 'sɒlt ◄ ˌ•ə-, -ənd'•,
-'sɔːlt ‖ -'sɔːlt -'saːlt
pepperbox 'pep ə bɒks ‖ -ᵊr baːks ~es ɪz əz
peppercorn 'pep ə kɔːn ‖ -ᵊr kɔːrn ~s z
ˌpeppercorn 'rent
peppermint 'pep ə mɪnt ‖ -ᵊr- ~s s
pepperoni ˌpep ə 'rəʊn i ‖ -'roʊn i
pepper|y 'pep ᵊr li ~iness i nəs i nɪs
Peppiatt 'pep i_ət
pepp|y 'pep li ~iness i nəs i nɪs
Pepsi *tdmk* 'peps i ~s z
Pepsi-Cola *tdmk* ˌpeps i 'kəʊl ə ‖ -'koʊl ə
pepsin 'peps ɪn §-ən ~s z

Pepsodent *tdmk* 'peps əʊ dent -əd ənt ‖ -əd
ənt
peptic 'pept ɪk
ˌpeptic 'ulcer
peptide 'pept aɪd ~s z
Pepto-Bismol *tdmk* ˌpept əʊ
'bɪz mɒl ‖ -toʊ 'bɪz maːl
peptone 'pept əʊn ‖ -oʊn ~s z
Pepys (i) piːps, (ii) 'pep ɪs, (iii) peps —*the
diarist is* (i)
Pequot 'piː kwɒt ‖ -kwaːt ~s s
per pɜː ‖ pɜːː, *weak form* pə ‖ pᵊr —*see also
phrases with this word*
per- pə ‖ pᵊr (*but before a vowel* pər), *or*
ˌpɜː ‖ ˌpɜːː (*but in RP before a vowel* ˌpɜːr)
peradventure ˌpɜːr əd 'ventʃ ə ˌper-, pər_,
§-æd- ‖ 'pɜːː əd ˌventʃ ᵊr 'per-; ˌ•••
Perahia pə 'raɪ_ə
Perak 'peər ə 'pɪər ə ‖ 'per ə —*There are also
spelling pronunciations* pə 'ræk, pe-,
pɪ- ‖ -'raːk, 'peɪ ræk —*Malay* [pe ɾaʔ]
perambu|late pə 'ræm bju |leɪt -bjə- ‖ -bjə-
~lated leɪt ɪd -əd ‖ leɪţ əd ~lates leɪts
~lating leɪt ɪŋ ‖ leɪţ ɪŋ
perambulation pə ˌræm bju 'leɪʃ ən -bjə-
‖ -bjə- ~s z
perambulator pə 'ræm bju leɪt ə -'•bjə-
‖ -bjə leɪţ ᵊr ~s z
per annum pər 'æn əm ‖ pᵊr-
perborate pə 'bɔːr eɪt pɜː-; 'pɜːb ə reɪt ‖ pᵊr-
-'boʊr- ~s s
percale pə 'keɪ_ᵊl -'kaːl ‖ pᵊr-
per capita pə 'kæp ɪt ə ˌ•ˌpɜː-, §-ət-
‖ pᵊr 'kæp əţ ə
perceivab|le pə 'siːv əb |ᵊl ‖ pᵊr- ~ly li
perceiv|e pə 'siːv ‖ pᵊr- ~ed d ~es z ~ing ɪŋ
percent, per cent pə 'sent ‖ pᵊr-
percentag|e pə 'sent ɪdʒ ‖ pᵊr 'senţ ɪdʒ ~es ɪz
əz
percentile pə 'sent aɪ_ᵊl ‖ pᵊr- -'senţ ᵊl ~s z
percept 'pɜː sept ‖ 'pɜːː- ~s s
perceptibility pə ˌsept ə 'bɪl ət i -ˌ•ɪ-, -ɪt i
‖ pᵊr ˌsept ə 'bɪl əţ i
perceptib|le pə 'sept əb |ᵊl -'•ɪb- ‖ pᵊr- ~ly li
perception pə 'sep ʃən ‖ pᵊr- ~s z
perceptive pə 'sept ɪv ‖ pᵊr- ~ly li ~ness nəs
nɪs
perceptivity ˌpɜː sep 'tɪv ət i pə ˌsep-, -ɪt i
‖ ˌpɜːː sep 'tɪv əţ i
perceptual pə 'sep tʃu_əl -ʃu_; -'sept ju_ ‖ pᵊr-
~ly i
Perceval 'pɜːs ɪv ᵊl -əv- ‖ 'pɜːːs-
perch pɜːtʃ ‖ pɜːːtʃ perched pɜːtʃt ‖ pɜːːtʃt
perches 'pɜːtʃ ɪz -əz ‖ 'pɜːːtʃ əz perching
'pɜːtʃ ɪŋ ‖ 'pɜːːtʃ ɪŋ
perchance pə 'tʃaːnᵗs ˌpɜː-, §-'tʃænᵗs
‖ pᵊr 'tʃænᵗs
Percheron 'pɜːʃ ə rɒn ‖ 'pɜːːtʃ ə raːn 'pɜːːʃ-
—*Fr* [pɛʁ ʃə ʁɔ̃] ~s z
percipience pə 'sɪp i_ənᵗs ‖ pᵊr-
percipient pə 'sɪp i_ənt ‖ pᵊr- ~ly li ~s s
Percival 'pɜːs ɪv ᵊl -əv- ‖ 'pɜːːs-

perco||late 'pɜːk ə |leɪt △-ju-, △-jə- ‖ 'pɜːk-
~**lated** leɪt ɪd -əd ‖ leɪt̬ əd ~**lates** leɪts
~**lating** leɪt ɪŋ ‖ leɪt̬ ɪŋ

percolation ˌpɜːk ə 'leɪʃ ᵊn △-ju-, △-jə-
‖ ˌpɜːk- ~**s** z

percolator 'pɜːk ə leɪt ə △'•ju-, △'•jə-
‖ 'pɜːk ə leɪt̬ ᵊr ~**s** z

per contra ˌpɜː 'kɒntr ə pə- ‖ ˌpɜː 'kɑːntr ə

percuss pə 'kʌs ‖ pᵊr- ~**ed** t ~**es** ɪz əz ~**ing**
ɪŋ

percussion pə 'kʌʃ ᵊn ‖ pᵊr- ~**s** z
per'cussion cap

percussionist pə 'kʌʃ ᵊn‿ɪst §‿əst ‖ pᵊr- ~**s** s

percussive pə 'kʌs ɪv ‖ pᵊr- ~**ly** li ~**ness** nəs
nɪs

percutaneous ˌpɜː kju 'teɪn i‿əs ‖ ˌpɜː- ~**ly** li

Percy 'pɜːs i ‖ 'pɜːs i

per diem ˌpɜː 'diː em pə-, -'daɪ-, -əm ‖ pᵊr-
ˌpɜː-

Perdita 'pɜːd ɪt ə §-ət- ‖ 'pɜːd ət̬ ə pᵊr 'diːt̬ ə

perdition pə 'dɪʃ ᵊn pɜː- ‖ pᵊr-

Perdue, p~ 'pɜːd juː ‖ pᵊr 'duː -'djuː

pere, père, Père peə ‖ peᵊr —*Fr* [pɛːʁ]

peregri||nate 'per əg rɪ |neɪt '•ɪg-, -rə•
~**nated** neɪt ɪd -əd ‖ neɪt̬ əd ~**nates** neɪts
~**nating** neɪt ɪŋ ‖ neɪt̬ ɪŋ

peregrination ˌper əg rɪ 'neɪʃ ᵊn ˌ•ɪg-, -rə'•-
~**s** z

peregrine, P~ 'per əg rɪn -ɪg-, §-rən; -ɪ griːn,
-ə- ~**s** z
ˌperegrine 'falcon

pereira, P~ pə 'reər ə -'rɪər- ‖ -'rer ə
pe'reira bark

Perelman (i) 'per əl mən, (ii) 'pɜːl mən ‖ 'pɜːl-
—*Usually* (i).

peremptor||y pə 'rempt ᵊr‿li pɪ-; 'per əmpt-
—*Both stressings are in use among English
lawyers.* ~**ily** əl i ɪ li ~**iness** i nəs i nɪs

perennial pə 'ren i‿əl ~**ly** i ~**s** z

perentie pə 'rent i ‖ -'rent̬ i ~**s** z

Peres pə 'rez

perestroika ˌper ə 'strɔɪk ə -ɪ- — *Russ* [pʲɪ
rʲɪ 'stroj kə]

Pérez de Cuéllar ˌper əz də 'kweɪl jɑː ˌ•ɪz-,
ˌ•ez- -'kweɪ- ‖ -jɑːr —*AmSp*
[ˌpe res de 'kwe jɑr, ˌ•reh-]

perfect *adj, n* 'pɜːf ɪkt -ekt, §-əkt ‖ 'pɜːf- ~**s** s
ˌperfect 'tense; ˌperfect 'participle

perfect *v* pə 'fekt pɜː- ‖ pᵊr- ~**ed** ɪd əd ~**ing**
ɪŋ ~**s** s

perfectibility pə ˌfekt ə 'bɪl ət i pɜː-, -, •ɪ-, -ɪt i
‖ pᵊr ˌfekt ə 'bɪl ət̬ i

perfectib||le pə 'fekt əb ᵊl pɜː-, -'•ɪb- ‖ pᵊr-
~**ly** li

perfection pə 'fek ʃᵊn ‖ pᵊr- ~**s** z

perfectionism pə 'fek ʃᵊn ˌɪz əm ‖ pᵊr-

perfectionist pə 'fek ʃᵊn‿ɪst §‿əst ‖ pᵊr- ~**s** s

perfective pə 'fekt ɪv ‖ pᵊr- ~**ly** li ~**ness** nəs
nɪs ~**s** z

perfect||ly 'pɜːf ɪkt li -ekt-, §-əkt- ‖ 'pɜːf-
~**ness** nəs nɪs

perfecto pə 'fekt əʊ ‖ pᵊr 'fekt oʊ ~**s** z

perfervid pɜː 'fɜːv ɪd pə-, §-əd ‖ pᵊr 'fɜːv- ~**ly**
li ~**ness** nəs nɪs

perfidious pə 'fɪd i‿əs pɜː- ‖ pᵊr- ~**ly** li ~**ness**
nəs nɪs

perfid||y 'pɜːf əd i -ɪd- ‖ 'pɜːf- ~**ies** iz

perfoliate pə 'fəʊl i‿ət ‿ɪt, -eɪt ‖ pᵊr 'foʊl-

perfo||rate v 'pɜːf ə |reɪt ‖ 'pɜːf- ~**rated**
reɪt ɪd -əd ‖ reɪt̬ əd ~**rates** reɪts ~**rating**
reɪt ɪŋ ‖ reɪt̬ ɪŋ

perforate *adj* 'pɜːf ᵊr‿ət ‿ɪt, -ə reɪt ‖ 'pɜːf-

perforation ˌpɜːf ə 'reɪʃ ᵊn ‖ ˌpɜːf- ~**s** z

perforator 'pɜːf ə reɪt ə ‖ 'pɜːf ə reɪt̬ ᵊr ~**s** z

perforce pə 'fɔːs pɜː- ‖ pᵊr 'fɔːrs -'foʊrs

perform pə 'fɔːm ‖ pᵊr 'fɔːrm ~**ed** d ~**ing** ɪŋ
~**s** z

performanc||e pə 'fɔːm ən̩ts ‖ pᵊr 'fɔːrm- ~**es**
ɪz əz

performative pə 'fɔːm ət ɪv ‖ pᵊr 'fɔːrm ət̬ ɪv
~**s** z

performer pə 'fɔːm ə ‖ pᵊr 'fɔːrm ᵊr ~**s** z

perfume *n* 'pɜː fjuːm ‖ 'pɜː fjuːm pᵊr 'fjuːm
~**s** z

perfum||e *v* 'pɜː fjuːm pə 'fjuːm, pɜː-
‖ pᵊr 'fjuːm 'pɜː fjuːm ~**ed** d ~**es** z ~**ing**
ɪŋ

perfumer pə 'fjuːm ə pɜː-; 'pɜː fjuːm ə
‖ pᵊr 'fjuːm ᵊr 'pɜː fjuːm ᵊr ~**s** z

perfumer||y pə 'fjuːm ᵊr li pɜː- ‖ pᵊr- ~**ies** iz

perfumier pə 'fjuːm i‿ə pɜː-, -eɪ
‖ pᵊr 'fjuːm i‿ᵊr ~**s** z

perfunctor||y pə 'fʌŋkt ᵊr‿li pɜː- ‖ pᵊr- ~**ily** əl i
ɪ li ~**iness** i nəs i nɪs

perfus||e pə 'fjuːz pɜː- ‖ pᵊr- ~**ed** d ~**es** ɪz əz
~**ing** ɪŋ

perfusion pə 'fjuːʒ ᵊn pɜː- ‖ pᵊr- ~**s** z

Pergamon 'pɜːg əm ən ‖ 'pɜːg- -ə mɑːn

Pergamum 'pɜːg əm əm ‖ 'pɜːg-

pergola 'pɜːg əl ə pə 'gəʊl ə ‖ 'pɜːg əl ə
pᵊr 'goʊl ə ~**s** z

Pergolesi ˌpɜːg əʊ 'leɪz i ‖ ˌpɜːg ə- -'leɪs- —*It*
[per go 'le: si]

Perham 'per əm

perhaps pə 'hæps ‖ pᵊr- —*informally also*
pᵊr 'æps, præps

peri 'pɪər i ‖ 'pɪr i ~**s** z

peri- *comb. form*
with stress-neutral suffix ˈper i —*but before a
consonant sound often* ˈper ɪ, §ˈper ə ‖ ˈper ə
— **perinatal**
ˌper i 'neɪt ᵊl ◂ ‖ ˌper ə 'neɪt̬ ᵊl ◂
with stress-imposing suffix pə 'rɪ+ pɪ-, pe- —
pericope pə 'rɪk əp i pɪ-, pe-

perianth 'per i æntθ ~**s** s

pericarditis ˌper i kɑː 'daɪt ɪs §-əs
‖ ˌper ə kɑːr 'daɪt̬ əs

pericardi||um ˌper i 'kɑːd i‿ləm ‖ -ə 'kɑːrd- ~**a**
ə ~**ums** əmz

pericarp 'per i kɑːp -ə- ‖ -ə kɑːrp ~**s** s

Periclean ˌper ɪ 'kliː ən ◂ -ə-

Pericles 'per ɪ kliːz -ə-

pericynthion ˌper i 'sɪntθ i‿ən ‖ -ə 'sɪntθ i aːn

peridot 'per i dɒt ‖ -ə dɑːt -doʊ

perigee 'per ɪ dʒiː -iː-, -ə- ~**s** z

Perigord, Périgord 'per ɪ gɔː -ə- ‖ ˌper ə 'gɔːr
—*Fr* [pe ʁi gɔːʁ]
periheli|on ˌper i 'hiːl i ˌ|ən ‖ ˌ•ə- **~a** ə
peril 'per əl -ɪl **~s** z
perilous 'per əl əs -ɪl- **~ly** li **~ness** nəs nɪs
perilune 'per i luːn -ljuːn ‖ -ə-
perimeter pə 'rɪm ɪt ə pɪ-, pe-, -ət- ‖ -ət̬ ər **~s**
z
perinatal ˌper ɪ 'neɪt əl -ə- ‖ -'neɪt̬-
perineal ˌper ɪ 'niːˌəl -ə-
perine|um ˌper ɪ 'niːˌ|əm -ə- **~a** ə
period 'pɪər iˌəd ‖ 'pɪr- **~s** z
    'period piece
periodate pər 'aɪˌə deɪt ‖ pər- **~s** s
periodic *'recurring at intervals'*
    ˌpɪər i 'ɒd ɪk ◄ ‖ ˌpɪr i 'ɑːd ɪk ◄
    ˌperiˌodic 'table
periodic *'derived by addition of water to* I_2O_7'
    ˌpɜːr aɪ 'ɒd ɪk ◄ ‖ ˌpɜː- aɪ 'ɑːd-
periodical ˌpɪər i 'ɒd ɪk əl ◄ ‖ ˌpɪr i 'ɑːd ɪk əl ◄
    ~ly ˌi **~s** z
periodicity ˌpɪər iˌə 'dɪs ət i ‖ ˌpɪr iˌə 'dɪs ət̬ i
periodont|al ˌper i əʊ
    'dɒnt |əl ◄ ‖ ˌper i oʊ 'dɑːnt̬ |əl ◄ -ə'•- **~ic**
    -ɪk ◄ **~ics** ɪks **~ist/s** ɪst/s §-əst/s
perioste|um ˌper i 'ɒst iˌ|əm ‖ -'ɑːst- **~a** ə **~al**
    əl
periotic ˌper i 'əʊt ɪk ◄ -'ɒt- ‖ -'oʊt̬-
peripatetic, P~ ˌper ɪ pə 'tet ɪk ◄, -ə-, ˌˌ•i-
    ‖ -'tet̬- **~ally** əlˌi **~s** s
peripeteia, peripetia ˌper ɪ pə 'tiːˌə, -ə-, ˌˌ•i-,
    -'taɪˌə **~s** z
peripet|y pə 'rɪp ət i pe-, pɪ- ‖ -ət̬ li **~ies** iz
peripheral pə 'rɪf ər̬əl pɪ-, pe- **~s** z
    peˌripheral 'nervous ˌsystem
peripherality pə ˌrɪf ə 'ræl ət i pɪ-, pe-, -ɪt i
    ‖ -ət̬ i
peripherally pə 'rɪf ər̬əl i pɪ-, pe-
peripher|y pə 'rɪf ər̬li pɪ-, pe- **~ies** iz
periph|rasis pə 'rɪf |rəs ɪs pɪ-, pe-, §-əs **~rases**
    rə siːz
periphrastic ˌper ɪ 'fræst ɪk ◄ -ə-, -i- **~ally** əlˌi
perique pə 'riːk
periscope 'per ɪ skəʊp -ə- ‖ -skoʊp **~s** s
periscopic ˌper ɪ 'skɒp ɪk ◄ -ə- ‖ -'skɑːp ɪk ◄
perish 'per ɪʃ **~ed** t **~es** ɪz əz **~ing/ly** ɪŋ /li
perishability ˌper ɪʃ ə 'bɪl ət i -ɪt i ‖ -ət̬ i
perishable 'per ɪʃ əb əl **~ness** nəs nɪs **~s** z
perisher 'per ɪʃ ə ‖ -ər **~s** z
perispom|enon
    ˌper i 'spəʊm ə nɒn ‖ -'spoʊm ə nɑːn **~ena**
    ən ə
perissodactyl pə ˌrɪs əʊ 'dækt ɪl pɪ-, pe-, §-əl,
    ˌ•'••, ˌ•• ‖ -ə'•- **~s** z
peristalsis ˌper ɪ 'stæls ɪs -ə-, §-əs ‖ -'stɔːls əs
    -'stɑːls-, -'stæls-
peristaltic ˌper ɪ 'stælt ɪk ◄ -ə- ‖ -'stɔːlt ɪk ◄
    -'stɑːlt-, -'stælt-
peristyle 'per ɪ staɪəl -ə-, -i- **~s** z
peritone|um ˌper ɪ təʊ 'niːˌ|əm ˌ•ə-
    ‖ ˌper ət̬ ən 'iː |əm **~a** ə
peritonitis ˌper ɪ təʊ 'naɪt ɪs ˌ•ə-, §-əs
    ‖ ˌper ət̬ ən 'aɪt̬ əs

Perivale 'per ɪ veɪəl -i-, -ə-
periwig 'per i wɪg **~ged** d **~s** z
periwinkle 'per i ˌwɪŋk əl **~s** z
perjure 'pɜːdʒ ə ‖ 'pɜːdʒ ər **~d** d **perjuring**
    'pɜːdʒ ər ɪŋ ‖ 'pɜːdʒ ər ɪŋ **~s** z
perjurer 'pɜːdʒ ər ə ‖ 'pɜːdʒ ər ər **~s** z
perjurious pɜː 'dʒʊər iˌəs pə-, -'dʒɔːr-
    ‖ pɜː 'dʒʊr- pər- **~ly** li **~ness** nəs nɪs
perjur|y 'pɜːdʒ ər |i **~ies** iz
perk pɜːk ‖ pɜːk **perked** pɜːkt ‖ pɜːkt
    perking 'pɜːk ɪŋ ‖ 'pɜːk ɪŋ **perks**
    pɜːks ‖ pɜːks
perki... —*see* **perky**
Perkin 'pɜːk ɪn §-ən ‖ 'pɜːk-
Perkins 'pɜːk ɪnz §-ənz ‖ 'pɜːk-
Perks pɜːks ‖ pɜːks
perk|y, Perky 'pɜːk li ‖ 'pɜːk li **~ier** iˌə ‖ iˌər
    ~iest iˌɪst iˌəst **~ily** ɪ li əl i **~iness** i nəs i nɪs
perlative 'pɜːl ət ɪv ‖ 'pɜːl ət̬-
Perlis 'pɜːl ɪs §-əs —*Malay* ['per lis]
perlite 'pɜːl aɪt ‖ 'pɜːl-
Perlman 'pɜːl mən ‖ 'pɜːl-
perlocution ˌpɜː ləʊ 'kjuːʃ ən -lɒ- ‖ ˌpɜː lə-
perlocutionary ˌpɜː ləʊ 'kjuːʃ ən ər i ◄, ˌ•lɒ-
    ‖ ˌpɜː lə 'kjuːʃ ə ner i ◄
perm pɜːm ‖ pɜːm **permed** pɜːmd ‖ pɜːmd
    perming 'pɜːm ɪŋ ‖ 'pɜːm ɪŋ **perms**
    pɜːmz ‖ pɜːmz
Perm *place in Russia* pɜːm ‖ pɜːm —*Russ*
    [pʲermʲ]
permaculture
    'pɜːm ə ˌkʌltʃ ə ‖ 'pɜːm ə ˌkʌltʃ ər
permafrost 'pɜːm ə frɒst -frɔːst
    ‖ 'pɜːm ə frɔːst -frɑːst
permalloy 'pɜːm ə lɔɪ pɜːm 'æl ɔɪ
    ‖ ˌpɜːm 'æl ɔɪ 'pɜːm ə lɔɪ
permanenc|e 'pɜːm ən ˌənts ‖ 'pɜːm- **~ies** iz
    ~y i
permanent 'pɜːm ən ənt ‖ 'pɜːm- **~ly** li **~s** s
    ˌpermanent 'wave; ˌpermanent 'way
permanganate pə 'mæŋ gə neɪt pɜː-; -gən ɪt,
    -ət ‖ pər- **~s** s
permanganic ˌpɜː mæn 'gæn ɪk ◄ →-mæŋ-
    ‖ ˌpɜː-
permeability ˌpɜːm iˌə 'bɪl ət i -ɪt i
    ‖ ˌpɜːm iˌə 'bɪl ət̬ i
permeab|le 'pɜːm iˌəb əl ‖ 'pɜːm- **~ly** li
permeance 'pɜːm iˌənts ‖ 'pɜːm-
perme|ate 'pɜːm i eɪt ‖ 'pɜːm- **~ated** eɪt ɪd
    -əd ‖ eɪt̬ əd **~ates** eɪts **~ating** eɪt ɪŋ ‖ eɪt̬ ɪŋ
permeation ˌpɜːm i 'eɪʃ ən ‖ ˌpɜːm-
Permian 'pɜːm iˌən ‖ 'pɜːm-
permissib|le pə 'mɪs əb əl -'•ɪb- ‖ pər-
    ~leness əl nəs -nɪs **~ly** li
permission pə 'mɪʃ ən ‖ pər- **~s** z
permissive pə 'mɪs ɪv ‖ pər- **~ly** li **~ness** nəs
    nɪs
per|mit *v* pə |'mɪt ‖ pər- **~mits** 'mɪts **~mitted**
    'mɪt ɪd -əd ‖ 'mɪt̬ əd **~mitting**
    'mɪt ɪŋ ‖ 'mɪt̬ ɪŋ
permit *n* 'pɜːm ɪt ‖ 'pɜː- mɪt pər 'mɪt **~s** s
permittivity ˌpɜːm ɪ 'tɪv ət i, ˌ•ə-
    ‖ ˌpɜːm ɪ 'tɪv ət̬ i

P

permu|tate 'pɜːm ju |teɪt -jə- ‖ 'pɝːm-
pᵊr 'mjuːlt eɪt **~tated** teɪt ɪd -əd ‖ teɪt̬ əd
~tates teɪts **~tating** teɪt ɪŋ ‖ teɪt̬ ɪŋ
permutation ˌpɜːm ju 'teɪʃ ᵊn -jə- ‖ ˌpɝːm-
~al ᵊl **~s** z
per|mute pə |'mjuːt ‖ pᵊr- **~muted** 'mjuːt ɪd
-əd ‖ 'mjuːt̬ əd **~mutes** 'mjuːts **~muting**
'mjuːt ɪŋ ‖ 'mjuːt̬ ɪŋ
Permutit *tdmk* pə 'mjuːt ɪt §-ət; 'pɜːm jʊt-
‖ pᵊr 'mjuːt̬-
Pernambuco ˌpɜːn əm 'buːk əʊ -æm-, -'bjuːk-
‖ ˌpɝːn əm 'buːk oʊ —*Port* [pɐ nɐm 'bu ku]
pernicious pə 'nɪʃ əs pɜː- ‖ pᵊr- **~ly** li **~ness**
nəs nɪs
per̩nicious a'naemia
pernickety pə 'nɪk ət i -ɪt- ‖ pᵊr 'nɪk ət̬ i
Pernod *tdmk* 'pɜːn əʊ 'peən- ‖ per 'noʊ —*Fr*
[pɛʁ no]
Peron, Perón pə 'rɒn pe-, pɪ- ‖ -'roʊn —*Sp*
[pe 'ron]
perone|al ˌper əʊ 'niː_əl ◄ ‖ -oʊ- -ə- **~us** əs
pero|rate 'per ə |reɪt -ɒ-, -ɔː- ‖ 'pɝː- **~rated**
reɪt ɪd -əd ‖ reɪt̬ əd **~rates** reɪts **~rating**
reɪt ɪŋ ‖ reɪt̬ ɪŋ
peroration ˌper ə 'reɪʃ ᵊn ‖ ˌpɝː- **~s** z
Perowne pə 'rəʊn pe- ‖ -'roʊn
peroxide pə 'rɒks aɪd ‖ -'rɑːks- **~s** z
pe̩roxide 'blonde
perpend *n* 'pɜː pend ‖ 'pɝː- **~s** z
perpendicular ˌpɜːp ən 'dɪk jʊl ə ◄ →ˌ•m-,
-jəl ə ‖ ˌpɝːp ən 'dɪk jəl ᵊr **~ly** li **~s** z
perpendicularity ˌpɜːp ən ˌdɪk ju 'lær ət i
→ˌ•m-, -ˌ•jə-, -ɪt i ‖ ˌpɝːp ən ˌdɪk jə 'lær ət̬ i
-'ler-
perpe|trate 'pɜːp ə |treɪt -ɪ- ‖ 'pɝːp- **~trated**
treɪt ɪd -əd ‖ treɪt̬ əd **~trates** treɪts
~trating treɪt ɪŋ ‖ treɪt̬ ɪŋ
perpetration ˌpɜːp ə 'treɪʃ ᵊn -ɪ- ‖ ˌpɝːp- **~s** z
perpetrator 'pɜːp ə treɪt ə '•ɪ-
‖ 'pɝːp ə treɪt̬ ᵊr **~s** z

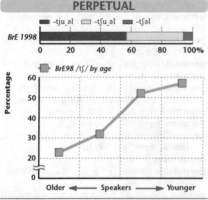

PERPETUAL

	-tju_əl	-tʃu_əl	-tʃəl
BrE 1998			

0 20 40 60 80 100%

BrE98 /tʃ/ by age

Percentage: 60 50 40 30 20 0

Older ◄—— Speakers ——► Younger

perpetual pə 'pet ju_əl -'petʃ u_, -'petʃ əl
‖ pᵊr 'petʃ u_əl —*BrE 1998 poll panel
preference:* -tju_əl *57%,* -tʃu_əl *37%,* -tʃəl *5%.*
~ly i
perpetu|ate pə 'pet ju |eɪt -'petʃ u-

‖ pᵊr 'petʃ u |eɪt **~ated** eɪt ɪd -əd ‖ eɪt̬ əd
~ates eɪts **~ating** eɪt ɪŋ ‖ eɪt̬ ɪŋ
perpetuation pə ˌpet ju 'eɪʃ ᵊn -ˌpetʃ u-
‖ pᵊr ˌpetʃ u-
perpetuit|y ˌpɜːp ə 'tjuː_ət li ˌ•ɪ-, §→-'tʃuː_,
_ɪt i ‖ ˌpɝːp ə 'tuː_ət̬ li -'tjuː- **~ies** iz
perpetuum mobile pə ˌpet ju_əm 'məʊb əl i
pɜː-, -ˌpetʃ u_, -ˌpet u_, -ɪl•, -eɪ
‖ pᵊr ˌpetʃ u əm 'moʊb-
Perpignan 'pɜːp iːn jɒ̃ ‖ ˌpɝːp iːn 'jɑːn —*Fr*
[pɛʁ pi njɑ̃]
perplex pə 'pleks ‖ pᵊr- **~ed** t **~es** ɪz əz **~ing**
ɪŋ
perplexed|ly pə 'pleks ɪd lli -əd-; pə 'plekst lli
‖ pᵊr- **~ness** nəs nɪs
perplexit|y pə 'pleks ət li -ɪt- ‖ pᵊr 'pleks ət̬ li
~ies iz
per pro ˌpɜː 'prəʊ ◄ ‖ ˌpɝː 'proʊ ◄
perquisite 'pɜːk wɪz ɪt -wəz-, §-ət ‖ 'pɝːk- **~s**
s
Perranporth ˌper ən 'pɔːθ →-əm- ‖ -'pɔːrθ
Perrault 'per əʊ ‖ pe 'roʊ —*Fr* [pɛ ʁo]
Perrier *tdmk* 'per i eɪ ˌ••'• —*Fr* [pɛ ʁje] **~s** z
Perrin 'per ɪn §-ᵊn —*but as a French name, also*
-æ̃, *Fr* [pɛ ʁæ̃]
perruquier pə 'ruːk i eɪ —*Fr* [pɛ ʁy kje] **~s** z
perr|y, Perr|y 'per li **~ies, ~y's** iz
Persaud pə 'sɔːd ‖ pᵊr- -'sɑːd
Perse, perse pɜːs ‖ pɝːs
per se ˌpɜː 'seɪ ‖ ˌpɝː- ˌper-, -'siː
perse|cute 'pɜːs ɪ |kjuːt -ə- ‖ 'pɝːs- **~cuted**
kjuːt ɪd -əd ‖ kjuːt̬ əd **~cutes** kjuːts
~cuting kjuːt ɪŋ ‖ kjuːt̬ ɪŋ
persecution ˌpɜːs ɪ 'kjuːʃ ᵊn -ə- ‖ ˌpɝːs- **~s** z
persecutor 'pɜːs ɪ kjuːt ə '•ə-
‖ 'pɝːs ɪ kjuːt̬ ᵊr **~s** z
persecutory ˌpɜːs ɪ 'kjuːt ər i ˌ•ə-, '••••
‖ 'pɝːs ɪ kjuːt̬ ər i -kju tɔːr i, -kju toʊr i
Perseid 'pɜːs i ɪd §'•əd ‖ 'pɝːs- **~s** z
Persephone pɜː 'sef ən i pə- ‖ pᵊr-
Persepolis pɜː 'sep əl ɪs pə-, §-əs ‖ pᵊr-
Perseus 'pɜːs juːs 'pɜːs i_əs ‖ 'pɝːs i_əs
'pɝːs juːs, -uːs
perseverance ˌpɜːs ɪ 'vɪər ᵊnᵗs -ə-
‖ ˌpɝːs ə 'vɪr-
perseve|rate pə 'sev ə |reɪt ‖ pᵊr- **~rated**
reɪt ɪd -əd ‖ reɪt̬ əd **~rates** reɪts **~rating**
reɪt ɪŋ ‖ reɪt̬ ɪŋ
perseveration pə ˌsev ə 'reɪʃ ᵊn pɜː- ‖ pᵊr- **~s**
z
persevere ˌpɜːs ɪ 'vɪə -ə- ‖ ˌpɝːs ə 'vɪʳr **~d** d
~s z **persevering/ly** ˌpɜːs ɪ 'vɪər ɪŋ /li, ˌ•ə-
‖ ˌpɝːs ə 'vɪr ɪŋ /li
Pershing 'pɜːʃ ɪŋ ‖ 'pɝːʃ ɪŋ
Pershore 'pɜː ʃɔː ‖ 'pɝː ʃɔːr -ʃoʊr
Persi|a 'pɜːʃ lə 'pɜːʒ- ‖ 'pɝːʒ lə **~an/s** ᵊn/z
̩Persian 'cat
persienne ˌpɜːs i 'en ‖ ˌpɝːz- —*Fr* [pɛʁ sjɛn]
~s z
persiflage 'pɜːs ɪ flɑːʒ 'peəs-, -ə-, ˌ••'•
‖ 'pɝːs- 'pers- —*Fr* [pɛʁ si flɑːʒ]
Persil *tdmk* 'pɜːs ɪl -ᵊl ‖ 'pɝːs-
persimmon pə 'sɪm ən pɜː- ‖ pᵊr- **~s** z

Persis 'pɜːs ɪs §-əs ‖ 'pɝːs-
persist pə 'sɪst ‖ pər- -'zɪst ~ed ɪd əd ~ing ɪŋ
~s s
persistenc|e pə 'sɪst ənts ‖ pər- -'zɪst- ~y i
persistent pə 'sɪst ənt ‖ pər- -'zɪst- ~ly li
persnickety pə 'snɪk ət i -ɪt- ‖ pər 'snɪk əţ i
person 'pɜːs ən ‖ 'pɝːs ən ~s z
person|a pə 'səʊn ə pɜː- ‖ pər 'soʊn ə -ɑː
~ae iː aɪ ~as əz
ˌpersona 'grata 'grɑːt ə 'greɪt- ‖ 'grɑːţ ə
'græţ-, 'greɪţ-; perˌsona ˌnon 'grata nəʊn
nɒn ‖ nɑːn noʊn
personable 'pɜːs ən_əb əl ‖ 'pɝːs- ~leness
əl nəs -nɪs
personag|e 'pɜːs ən_ɪdʒ ‖ 'pɝːs- ~es ɪz əz
personal 'pɜːs ən_əl ‖ 'pɝːs- ~s z
ˌpersonal as'sistant; 'personal ˌcolumn;
ˌpersonal com'puter; ˌpersonal e'state;
ˌpersonal 'pronoun; ˌpersonal 'property;
ˌpersonal 'stereo
personalis... —see personaliz...
personalit|y ˌpɜːs ə 'næl ət li -ɪt i
‖ ˌpɝːs ə 'næl əţ li ~ies iz
ˌperso'nality cult; ˌperso'nality test
personalization ˌpɜːs ən_əl aɪ 'zeɪʃ ən -ɪ' •-
‖ ˌpɝːs ən_əl ə-
personaliz|e 'pɜːs ən_ə laɪz -əl aɪz ‖ 'pɝːs-
~ed d ~es ɪz əz ~ing ɪŋ
personally 'pɜːs ən_əl i ‖ 'pɝːs-
perso|nate v 'pɜːs ə |neɪt -ə|n eɪt ‖ 'pɝːs-
~nated neɪt ɪd -əd ‖ neɪţ əd ~nates neɪts
~nating neɪt ɪŋ ‖ neɪţ ɪŋ
personation ˌpɜːs ə 'neɪʃ ən ‖ ˌpɝːs- ~s z
personator 'pɜːs ə neɪt ə →-ən eɪt-
‖ 'pɝːs ən eɪţ ər ~s z
personification pə ˌsɒn ɪf ɪ 'keɪʃ ən pɜː-,
-ˌ•əf-, §-ə' •- ‖ pər ˌsɑːn- ~s z
personi|fy pə 'sɒn ɪ |faɪ pɜː-, -ə- ‖ pər 'sɑːn-
~fied faɪd ~fier/s faɪ_ə/z ‖ faɪ_ər/z ~fies
faɪz ~fying faɪ ɪŋ
personnel ˌpɜːs ə 'nel -ən 'el ‖ ˌpɝːs-
ˌperson'nel ˌmanager
person-to-person ˌpɜːs ən tə 'pɜːs ən ◄ -ən tu-
‖ ˌpɝːs ən tə 'pɝːs ən ◄
perspective pə 'spekt ɪv ‖ pər- ~ly li ~s z
perspex, P~ tdmk 'pɜːsp eks ‖ 'pɝːsp-
perspicacious ˌpɜːsp ɪ 'keɪʃ əs ◄ -ə- ‖ ˌpɝːsp-
~ly li ~ness nəs nɪs
perspicacity ˌpɜːsp ɪ 'kæs ət i ˌ•ə-, -ɪt i
‖ ˌpɝːsp ə 'kæs əţ i
perspicuity ˌpɜːsp ɪ 'kjuː_ət i ˌ•ə-, ˌ_ɪt i
‖ ˌpɝːsp ə 'kjuː əţ i
perspicuous pə 'spɪk ju_əs ‖ pər- ~ly li ~ness
nəs nɪs
perspiration ˌpɜːsp ə 'reɪʃ ən ‖ ˌpɝːsp-
perspiratory pə 'spaɪ_ər ət_ər i -'spɪr-; 'pɜːsp
ər• • •, '•ɪr- ‖ pər 'spaɪr ə tɔːr i 'pɝːsp ər_ə-,
-toʊr i
perspire pə 'spaɪ_ə ‖ pər 'spaɪ_ər ~d d ~s z
perspiring pə 'spaɪ_ər ɪŋ ‖ pər 'spaɪ_ər ɪŋ
persuad|e pə 'sweɪd ‖ pər- ~ed ɪd əd ~er/s
ə/z ‖ ər/z ~es z ~ing ɪŋ
persuasion pə 'sweɪʒ ən ‖ pər- ~s z

persuasive pə 'sweɪs ɪv -'sweɪz- ‖ pər- ~ly li
~ness nəs nɪs
pert pɜːt ‖ pɝːt perter 'pɜːt ə ‖ 'pɝːţ ər
pertest 'pɜːt ɪst -əst ‖ 'pɝːţ əst
pertain pə 'teɪn pɜː- ‖ pər- ~ed d ~ing ɪŋ ~s
z
Perth pɜːθ ‖ pɝːθ
Perthite 'pɜːθ aɪt ~s s
Perthshire 'pɜːθ ʃə -ʃɪə, -ˌʃaɪ_ə ‖ 'pɝːθ ʃər -ʃɪr,
-ˌʃaɪ_ər
pertinacious ˌpɜːt ɪ 'neɪʃ əs ◄ -ə-
‖ ˌpɝːt ən 'eɪʃ əs ~ly li ~ness nəs nɪs
pertinacity ˌpɜːt ɪ 'næs ət i ˌ•ə-, -ɪt i
‖ ˌpɝːt ən 'æs əţ i
pertinence 'pɜːt ɪn ənts -ən- ‖ 'pɝːt ən_ənts
pertinent 'pɜːt ɪn ənt -ən- ‖ 'pɝːt ən_ənt ~ly
li
pert|ly 'pɜːt| li ‖ 'pɝːt| li ~ness nəs -nɪs
perturb pə 'tɜːb pɜː- ‖ pər 'tɝːb ~ed d ~ing
ɪŋ ~s z
perturbation ˌpɜːt ə 'beɪʃ ən ˌpɜː tɜː-
‖ ˌpɝːţ ər-, ˌpɝː tɝː-, ~s z
pertussis pə 'tʌs ɪs §-əs ‖ pər-
Pertwee 'pɜːt wiː ‖ 'pɝːt-
Peru pə 'ruː —Sp Perú [pe 'ru] ~'s z
Perugia pə 'ruːdʒ ə pɪ-, pe-, -'ruːdʒ i_ə —It
[pe 'ru: dʒa]
Perugino ˌper u 'dʒiːn əʊ ‖ -oʊ —It
[pe ru 'dʒi: no]
peruke pə 'ruːk pe- ~s s
perusal pə 'ruːz əl pe- ~s z
perus|e pə 'ruːz pe- ~ed d ~es ɪz əz ~ing ɪŋ
Perutz pə 'rʊts -'ruːts —Ger ['peʁ ʊts]
Peruvian pə 'ruːv i_ən pe- ~s z
Peruzzi pə 'ruːts i —It [pe 'rut tsi]
perv, perve pɜːv ‖ pɝːv perved
pɜːvd ‖ pɝːvd perves pɜːvz ‖ pɝːvz
perving 'pɜːv ɪŋ ‖ 'pɝːv ɪŋ
pervad|e pə 'veɪd pɜː- ‖ pər- ~ed ɪd əd ~es z
~ing ɪŋ
pervasion pə 'veɪʒ ən ‖ pər-
pervasive pə 'veɪs ɪv pɜː-, -'veɪz- ‖ pər- ~ly li
~ness nəs nɪs
perverse pə 'vɜːs ‖ pər 'vɝːs ~ly li ~ness nəs
nɪs
perversion pə 'vɜːʃ ən -'vɜːʒ- ‖ pər 'vɝːʒ ən
-'vɝːʃ- ~s z
perversit|y pə 'vɜːs ət li -ɪt- ‖ pər 'vɝːs əţ li
~ies iz
perversive pə 'vɜːs ɪv ‖ pər 'vɝːs ɪv
per|vert v pə 'vɜːt ‖ pər 'vɝːt ~verted
'vɜːt ɪd -əd ‖ 'vɝːţ əd ~verting
'vɜːt ɪŋ ‖ 'vɝːţ ɪŋ ~verts 'vɜːts ‖ 'vɝːts
pervert n 'pɜː vɜːt ‖ 'pɝː vɝːt ~s s
perverter pə 'vɜːt ə ‖ pər 'vɝːţ ər ~s z
pervious 'pɜːv i_əs ‖ 'pɝːv- ~ness nəs nɪs
Pery (i) 'peər i ‖ 'per i 'pær-, (ii) 'pɪər i ‖ 'pɪr i,
(iii) 'per i
Pesach 'peɪs ɑːk -ɑːx
Pescadores ˌpesk ə 'dɔːr iːz ‖ -'doʊr-
peseta pə 'seɪt ə ‖ -'seɪţ ə —Sp [pe 'se ta] ~s z
pesewa pe 'siː wə pɪ-, pə- ~s z
Peshawar pə 'ʃɑː wə pe-, -'ʃɔː- ‖ -wər

pesk|y 'pesk |i **~ier** i‿ə ‖ i‿ᵊr **~iest** i‿ɪst i‿əst
~ily ɪ li əl i **~iness** i nəs i nɪs
peso 'peɪs əʊ ‖ -oʊ —*Sp* ['pe so] **~s** z
pessar|y 'pes ər |i **~ies** iz
pessimism 'pes ə ˌmɪz əm 'pez-, -ɪ-
pessimist 'pes əm ɪst 'pez-, -ɪm-, §-əst **~s** s
pessimistic ˌpes ə 'mɪst ɪk ◂ ˌpez-, -ɪ- **~ally** ᵊl‿i
pest pest **pests** pests
Pest *place in Hungary* pest peʃt —*Hung* [pɛʃt]
Pestalozzi ˌpest ə 'lɒts i ‖ -'lɑːts i —*It*
[pes ta 'lɔt tsi]
pester 'pest ə ‖ -ᵊr **~ed** d **pestering** 'pest
ər‿ɪŋ **~s** z
pesticide 'pest ɪ saɪd -ə- **~s** z
pestiferous pes 'tɪf ər‿əs **~ly** li
pestilenc|e 'pest ɪl |ənᵗs -əl-, △-jʊl- **~es** ɪz əz
pestilent 'pest ɪl ənt -əl-, △-jʊl- **~ly** li
pestilential ˌpest ɪ 'lenᵗʃ ᵊl ◂ -ə-, →-ᵊl 'enᵗʃ-
~ly i
pestl|e 'pes ᵊl 'pest- **~ed** d **~es** z **~ing** ‿ɪŋ
pesto 'pest əʊ ‖ -oʊ —*It* ['pes to]
pet, PET pet **pets** pets **petted** 'pet ɪd -əd
‖ 'peṭ əd **petting** 'pet ɪŋ ‖ 'peṭ ɪŋ
'pet ˌname, ˌ‧ ˈ‧; **'PET ˌscanner**
Peta 'piːt ə ‖ 'piːṭ ə
Pétain 'pet æ ‖ peɪt- ‖ peɪ 'tæ —*Fr* [pe tæ̃]
petal 'pet ᵊl ‖ 'peṭ ᵊl **~ed,** **~led** d **~s** z
petanque, pétanque ˌpeɪ 'tɒŋk ‖ -'tɑːŋk —*Fr*
[pe tɑ̃k]
petard pe 'tɑːd pɪ-, pə-; 'pet ɑːd ‖ -'tɑːrd **~s** z
petasus 'pet əs əs ‖ 'peṭ- **~es** ɪz əz
Pete piːt
petechi|a pe 'tiːk i‿ə pɪ-, pə- **~ae** iː
Peter, peter 'piːt ə ‖ 'piːṭ ᵊr **~ed** d **petering**
'piːt‿ər ɪŋ ‖ 'piːṭ ər ɪŋ **~s, ~'s** z
ˌPeter 'Pan
Peterboro', Peterborough 'piːt ə bər‿ə -ˌbʌr ə
‖ 'piːṭ ᵊr ˌbɜː oʊ
Peterhead ˌpiːtə 'hed ‖ ˌpiːṭ ᵊr-
Peterkin 'piːt ə kɪn ‖ 'piːṭ ᵊr-
Peterlee ˌpiːt ə 'liː ‖ ˈ‧‧‧ ‖ ˌpiːṭ ᵊr-
Peterloo ˌpiːt ə 'luː ◂ ‖ ˌpiːṭ ᵊr-
ˌPeterloo 'massacre
peter|man 'piːt ə |mən -mæn ‖ 'piːṭ ᵊr- **~men**
mən men
Peters 'piːt əz ‖ 'piːṭ ᵊrz
Petersburg 'piːt əz bɜːg ‖ 'piːṭ ᵊrz bɜːg
Petersfield 'piːt əz fiːᵊld ‖ 'piːṭ ᵊrz-
Petersham, p~ 'piːt əʃ əm ‖ 'piːṭ ᵊrʃ- -ᵊr ʃæm
Peterson 'piːt əs ən ‖ 'piːṭ ᵊrs ən
Petherick 'peθ ər‿ɪk
Pethick 'peθ ɪk
pethidine 'peθ ɪ diːn -ə-
petillant, pétillant 'pet ɪ ɒ̃ -ɪl ənt, §-ᵊl-
‖ ˌpeɪt ɪ 'jɑːn —*Fr* [pe ti jɑ̃]
petiole 'pet i əʊl 'piːt-, →-ɒʊl ‖ 'peṭ i oʊl **~s** z
petit 'pet i pə 'tiː ‖ 'peṭ i —*Fr* [pə ti]
ˌpetit 'bourgeois, ˌ‧‧ ‧'‧; ˌpetit
ˌbourgeoi'sie; ˌpetit 'four fʊə fɔː ‖ fɔːr foʊr
—*Fr* [fuʁ]; ˌpetit 'mal mæl ‖ mɑːl mæl —*Fr*
[mal]; ˌpetit 'point; ˌpetit(s) 'pois pwɑː
—*Fr* [pwa]
petite pə 'tiːt —*Fr* [pə tit]

petition pə 'tɪʃ ᵊn pɪ- **~ed** d **~ing** ‿ɪŋ **~s** z
petitioner pə 'tɪʃ ᵊn‿ə pɪ- ‖ ‿ᵊr **~s** z
petitio principii pɪ ˌtɪʃ i əʊ prɪn 'sɪp i aɪ pe-,
pə-, -ˌtɪt-, -'kɪp-, -iː ‖ -ˌ‧ ‧oʊ-
Peto 'piːt əʊ ‖ 'piːṭ oʊ
Petofi, Petöfi 'pet əf i -ɜːf i ‖ 'peṭ əf i —*Hung*
Petöfi ['pɛ tø: fi]
Petra 'petr ə 'piːtr-
Petrarch 'petr ɑːk ‖ -ɑːrk
Petrarchan pe 'trɑːk ən pɪ-, pə- ‖ -'trɑːrk-
petrel 'petr əl (= *petrol*) **~s** z
Petri 'piːtr ɪ 'petr i —*Ger* ['peː tʁi]
Petrie 'piːtr i
petrifaction ˌpetr ɪ 'fæk ʃᵊn -ə-
petri|fy 'petr ɪ |faɪ -ə- **~fied** faɪd **~fies** faɪz
~fying faɪ ɪŋ
Petrine 'piːtr aɪn
petro- *comb. form*
with stress-neutral suffix ¦petr əʊ ‖ -ə —
petrological ˌpetr əʊ 'lɒdʒ ɪk ᵊl ◂ ‖ -ə 'lɑːdʒ-
with stress-imposing suffix pe 'trɒ+ pɪ-, pə-
‖ -'trɑː+ — **petrography** pe 'trɒg rəf i pɪ-,
pə- ‖ -'trɑːg-
Petroc 'petr ɒk ‖ -ɑːk
petrochemical ˌpetr əʊ 'kem ɪk ᵊl ‖ ˌ‧oʊ- **~s**
z
petrodollar 'petr əʊ ˌdɒl ə ‖ -oʊ ˌdɑːl ᵊr **~s** z
Petrofina *tdmk* ˌpetr əʊ 'fiːn ə ‖ -oʊ-
petroglyph 'petr əʊ glɪf -ə- **~s** s
Petrograd 'petr ə græd —*Russ* [pʲɪ trɑ 'grat]
petrol 'petr əl
'petrol ˌstation; 'petrol ˌtank
petrolatum ˌpetr ə 'leɪt əm ‖ -'leɪṭ əm -'lɑːṭ-
petrol-bomb 'petr əl bɒm ‖ -bɑːm **~ed** d
~ing ɪŋ **~s** z
petroleum pə 'trəʊl i‿əm pɪ- ‖ -'troʊl-
pe,troleum 'jelly
petrologist pə 'trɒl ədʒ ɪst pɪ-, pe-, §-əst
‖ -'trɑːl- **~s** s
petrology pə 'trɒl ədʒ i pɪ-, pe- ‖ -'trɑːl-
Petronas pe 'trəʊn æs pɪ-, pə-, -əs ‖ -'troʊn-
-ɑːs
Petronella, p~ ˌpetr ə 'nel ə
Petronius pɪ 'trəʊn i‿əs pə-, pe- ‖ -'troʊn-
Petropavlovsk ˌpetr əʊ 'pæv lɒfsk
‖ -ə 'pæv lɔːfsk -lɑːfsk —*Russ*
[pʲɪ trɑ 'pav ləfsk]
Petruchio pɪ 'truːtʃ i‿əʊ pə-, pe-, -'truːk- ‖ -oʊ
pe-tsai ˌpeɪt 'saɪ
petticoat 'pet i kəʊt ‖ 'peṭ i koʊt **~s** s
ˌPetticoat 'Lane
Pettifer 'pet ɪf ə -əf- ‖ 'peṭ əf ᵊr
pettifog 'pet i fɒg ‖ 'peṭ i fɔːg -fɑːg **~ged** d
~ger/s ə/z ‖ ᵊr/z **~ging** ɪŋ **~s** z
Pettigrew 'pet i gruː ‖ 'peṭ-
pettish 'pet ɪʃ ‖ 'peṭ ɪʃ **~ly** li **~ness** nəs nɪs
Pettit 'pet ɪt §-ət ‖ 'peṭ ət
pettitoes 'pet i təʊz ‖ 'peṭ i toʊz
Pettitt 'pet ɪt §-ət ‖ 'peṭ ət
pett|y, Petty 'pet |i ‖ 'peṭ |i **~ier** i‿ə ‖ i‿ᵊr
~iest i‿ɪst i‿əst **~ily** ɪ li əl i **~iness** i nəs i nɪs
ˌpetty 'bourgeois, ˌ‧‧ ‧'‧; ˌpetty 'cash;
ˌpetty 'larceny; ˌpetty 'officer◂

Petula pə 'tjuːl ə pɪ-, pe-, →§-'tʃuːl- ‖ -'tuːl ə
  -'tjuːl-

petulanc|e 'pet jʊl ən‖s 'petʃ əl- ‖ 'petʃ əl- ~**y**
  i

petulant 'pet jʊl ənt 'petʃ əl- ‖ 'petʃ əl- ~**ly** li

Petulengro ˌpet ju 'leŋ grəʊ -ə-, ˌpetʃ ə-
  ‖ ˌpetʃ ə 'leŋ groʊ

petunia pə 'tjuːn i‿ə pɪ-, pe- ‖ pɪ 'tuːn jə
  -'tjuːn- ~**s** z

petuntse peɪ 'tʊnts ə pɪ-, -'tʌnts-, -i

Petworth 'pet wɜːθ -wəθ ‖ -wʰrθ

Peugeot *tdmk* 'pɜːʒ əʊ 'pjuːʒ-, 'pjuːdʒ-, -ɒt
  ‖ pju: 'ʒoʊ puː-, pɜ·ː- —*Fr* [pø ʒo]

Pevensey 'pev ᵊnz i

Peveril 'pev ᵊr‿əl -ɪl

Pevsner 'pevz nə ‖ -nᵊr

pew pjuː **pews** pjuːz

pewit 'piː wɪt ‖ 'pju: ət ~**s** s

Pewsey 'pjuːz i

pewter 'pjuːt ə ‖ 'pju:ṭ ᵊr

pewterer 'pjuːt ᵊr ə ‖ 'pjuːṭ ᵊr ᵊr ~**s** z

peyote peɪ 'əʊt i pi- ‖ -'oʊṭ i —*Sp* [pe 'jo te]

Peyton 'peɪt ᵊn

pfenn|ig 'fen ˌɪg 'pfen-, -ɪk —*Ger* ['pfɛn ɪç]
  ~**igs** ɪgz ɪks

Pfizer 'faɪz ə ‖ -ᵊr

PG ˌpiː 'dʒiː ~**s**, ~'**s** z

PGA ˌpiː dʒiː 'eɪ

pH ˌpiː 'eɪtʃ §-'heɪtʃ

Phaeacian fi 'eɪʃ ᵊn ~**s** z

Phaedo 'fiːd əʊ -faɪd- ‖ -oʊ 'fed-

Phaedra 'fiːdr ə -faɪdr- ‖ 'fedr ə

Phaedrus 'fiːdr əs -faɪdr- ‖ 'fedr əs

phaen... —*see* **phen...**

Phaethon, Phaëthon 'feɪ əθ ᵊn -ɪθ- ‖ -ə θɑːn

phaeton 'feɪt ᵊn ‖ 'feɪ ət ᵊn ~**s** z

phage feɪdʒ **phages** 'feɪdʒ ɪz -əz

phagocyte 'fæg əʊ saɪt ‖ -ə- ~**s** s

phagocytosis ˌfæg əʊ saɪ 'təʊs ɪs §-əs
  ‖ -oʊ saɪ 'toʊs-

-phagous *stress-imposing* fəg əs —
  saprophagous sæ 'prɒf əg əs ‖ -'prɑːf-

-phagy *stress-imposing* fədʒ i — **geophagy**
  dʒi 'ɒf ədʒ i ‖ -'ɑːf-

Phaidon *tdmk* 'faɪd ᵊn

phalang|e 'fæl ændʒ fə 'lændʒ ‖ 'feɪl- ~**es** ɪz
  əz

phalanger fə 'lændʒ ə ‖ -ᵊr ~**s** z

Phalangist fə 'lændʒ ɪst fæ-, §-əst;
  'fæl əndʒ- ‖ feɪ- ~**s** s

phalanx 'fæl æŋks ‖ 'feɪl- 'fæl- **phalanges**
  fə 'lændʒ iːz fæ- feɪ-

phalaris 'fæl ᵊr ɪs §-əs

phalarope 'fæl ə rəʊp ‖ -roʊp ~**s** s

phalli 'fæl aɪ -iː

phallic 'fæl ɪk

phallocrat 'fæl əʊ kræt ‖ -ə- ~**s** s

phallocratic ˌfæl əʊ 'kræt ɪk ◂ ‖ -ə 'kræṭ-

phall|us 'fæl‖ əs ~**i** aɪ -iː **-uses** əs ɪz -əz

phanerogam 'fæn ᵊr əʊ gæm fə 'ner- ‖ -ᵊr ə-
  ~**s** z

phanerogamic ˌfæn ᵊr əʊ 'gæm ɪk ◂ ‖ -oʊˈ•-

phanerogamous ˌfæn ə 'rɒg əm əs ◂ ‖ -'rɑːg-

phanerozoic, P~ ˌfæn ᵊr əʊ 'zəʊ ɪk ◂ ‖ -ə 'zoʊ-

phantasm 'fæn ˌtæz əm ~**s** z

phantasmagoria ˌfænt æz mə 'gɒr i‿ə
  fæn ˌtæz-, -'gɔːr- ‖ fæn ˌtæz mə 'gɔːr i‿ə
  -'goʊr-

phantasmagoric ˌfænt æz mə 'gɒr ɪk ◂
  fæn ˌtæz- ‖ fæn ˌtæz mə 'gɔːr ɪk ◂ -'gɑːr-
  ~**al** ᵊl

phantasmal fæn 'tæz məl

phantasmic fæn 'tæz mɪk

phantas|y 'fænt əs ‖i i 'fænṭ- ~**ies** iz

phantom 'fænt əm ‖ 'fænṭ əm ~**s** z
  ˌphantom 'limb

-phany *stress-imposing* fən i — **theophany**
  θi 'ɒf ən i ‖ -'ɑːf-

Pharaoh, p~ 'feər əʊ ‖ 'fer oʊ 'fær-; 'feɪ roʊ
  ~**s** z
  'pharaoh ant

Pharaonic ˌfeər eɪ 'ɒn ɪk ◂ feə 'rɒn-
  ‖ ˌfer eɪ 'ɑːn ɪk ◂ ˌfær-

pharisaic, P~ ˌfær ɪ 'seɪ ɪk ◂ -ə- ‖ ˌfer- ~**al** ᵊl
  ~**ally** ᵊl‿i ~**alness** ᵊl nəs -nɪs

Pharisaism 'fær ɪ seɪ ˌɪz əm '•ə- ‖ 'fer-

pharisee, P~ 'fær ɪ siː -ə- ‖ 'fer- ~**s** z

pharmaceutic ˌfɑːm ə 'suːt ɪk ◂ -'sjuːt-,
  -'kjuːt- ‖ ˌfɑːrm ə 'suːṭ ɪk ◂ ~**al** ᵊl ~**ally** ᵊl‿i
  ~**s** s

pharmacist 'fɑːm əs ɪst §-əst ‖ 'fɑːrm- ~**s** s

pharmaco- *comb. form*
  with stress-neutral suffix
  ˌfɑːm ə kəʊ ‖ ˌfɑːrm ə koʊ —
  pharmacodynamic
  ˌfɑːm ə kəʊ daɪ 'næm ɪk ◂ ‖ ˌfɑːrm ə koʊ-
  with stress-imposing suffix
  ˌfɑːm ə 'kɒ+ ‖ ˌfɑːrm ə 'kɑː+ —
  pharmacognosy
  ˌfɑːm ə 'kɒg nəs i ‖ ˌfɑːrm ə 'kɑːg-

pharmacological
  ˌfɑːm ə kə 'lɒdʒ ɪk ᵊl ◂ ‖ ˌfɑːrm ək ə 'lɑːdʒ-
  ~**ly** ‿i

pharmacologist ˌfɑːm ə 'kɒl ədʒ ɪst §-əst
  ‖ ˌfɑːrm ə 'kɑːl- ~**s** s

pharmacology
  ˌfɑːm ə 'kɒl ədʒ i ‖ ˌfɑːrm ə 'kɑːl-

pharmacopoei|a, pharmacopei|a
  ˌfɑːm ə kə 'piː‿ə -kəʊ'•- ‖ ˌfɑːrm- ~**al** əl
  ~**as** əz

pharmac|y 'fɑːm əs ‖i i 'fɑːrm- ~**ies** iz

Pharos 'feər ɒs ‖ 'fer ɑːs 'fær-

Pharsalus fɑː 'seɪl əs ‖ fɑːr-

pharyngal fə 'rɪŋ gᵊl fæ- ~**s** z

pharyngeal ˌfær ən 'dʒiː‿əl ◂ -ɪn-;
  fə 'rɪndʒ i‿əl, fæ- ‖ ˌfer- ~**s** z

pharynges fæ 'rɪndʒ iːz fə-

pharyngitis ˌfær ən 'dʒaɪt ɪs -ɪn-, §-əs
  ‖ -'dʒaɪṭ əs ˌfer-

pharyngo- *comb. form*
  with stress-neutral suffix fə ˌrɪŋ gəʊ ‖ -gə —
  pharyngoscope fə 'rɪŋ gəʊ
  skəʊp ‖ -gə skoʊp
  with stress-imposing suffix
  ˌfær ɪŋ 'gɒ+ ‖ -'gɑː+ ˌfer- —

pharyngotomy ˌfær ɪŋ 'gɒt əm i ‖ -'gɑːt̬-
ˌfer-
pharynx 'fær ɪŋks ‖ 'fer- ~es ɪz əz
pharynges fæ 'rɪndʒ iːz fə-
phase feɪz phased feɪzd phases 'feɪz ɪz -əz
phasing 'feɪz ɪŋ
phase-out 'feɪz aʊt ~s s
phaser 'feɪz ə ‖ -ər ~s z
phasmid 'fæz mɪd §-məd ~s z
phatic 'fæt ɪk ‖ 'fæt̬ ɪk
PhD ˌpiː eɪtʃ 'diː §-heɪtʃ- ~s, ~'s z
pheasant 'fez ᵊnt ~s s
Phebe, p~ 'fiːb i ~s, ~'s z
Phebus 'fiːb əs
Phedo 'fiːd əʊ 'faɪd- ‖ -oʊ
Phedra 'fiːdr ə 'faɪdr-
Phedrus 'fiːdr əs 'faɪdr-
Pheidippides faɪ 'dɪp ɪ diːz -ə-
Phelan (i) 'fiːl ən, (ii) 'feɪl ən
phellem 'fel em -əm
Phelps felps
phenacetin fə 'næs ət ɪn fɪ-, fe-, -ɪt ɪn, §-ən
phenetic fə 'net ɪk fɪ- ‖ -'net̬- ~s s
Phenicia fə 'nɪʃ ə fɪ-; -'nɪʃ i_ə ‖ -'niːʃ-
Phenician fə 'nɪʃ ən fɪ-; -'nɪʃ i_ən ‖ -'niːʃ- ~s z
phenobarbital ˌfiːn əʊ 'bɑːb ɪt ᵊl -ət ᵊl
‖ -oʊ 'bɑːrb ə tɔːl -tɑːl
phenobarbitone ˌfiːn əʊ 'bɑːb ɪ təʊn -'•ə-
‖ -oʊ 'bɑːrb ə toʊn
phenol 'fiːn ɒl ‖ -oʊl -ɔːl, -ɑːl ~s z
phenolic fɪ 'nɒl ɪk §fə- ‖ -'noʊl- -'nɑːl-
phenolphthalein ˌfiːn ɒl 'θeɪl i_ɪn ˌ•ᵊl-, -'θæl-,
-'fθæl-, ˌ•ən, -'•iːn ‖ ˌfiːn ᵊl 'θæl i_ən
phenom fɪ 'nɒm fə- ‖ -'nɑːm ~s z
phenomena fə 'nɒm ɪn ə fɪ-, -ən- ‖ -'nɑːm-
phenomenal fə 'nɒm ɪn ᵊl fɪ-, -ən- ‖ -'nɑːm-
~ly i
phenomenological fə ˌnɒm ɪn ə 'lɒdʒ ɪk ᵊl ◂
fɪ-, -ˌ•ən- ‖ -ˌnɑːm ən ə 'lɑːdʒ- ~ly _i
phenomenology fə ˌnɒm ɪ 'nɒl ədʒ i fɪ-, -ˌ•ə-
‖ -ˌnɑːm ə 'nɑːl-
phenomen|on fə 'nɒm ɪn |ən fɪ-, -ən-
‖ 'nɑːm ə n|ɑːn -ən |ən ~a ə (*)
phenotype 'fiːn əʊ taɪp ‖ -ə- ~s s
phenotypic ˌfiːn əʊ 'tɪp ɪk ◂ ‖ -ə- ~al ᵊl ~ally
ᵊl_i
Phensic tdmk 'fen¹s ɪk 'fenz-
phenyl 'fiːn aɪᵊl 'fen-, -ᵊl, -ɪl ‖ 'fen ᵊl 'fiːn-
phenylalanine ˌfiːn ɪl 'æl ə niːn ˌfen-, ˌ•ᵊl-,
ˌ•aɪᵊl- ‖ ˌfen ᵊl-
phenylketonuria ˌfiːn ɪl ˌkiːt əʊ 'njʊər i_ə
ˌfen-, ˌ•-ᵊl-, ˌ•aɪᵊl- ‖ ˌfen ᵊl ˌkiːt oʊ 'nʊr i_ə
-ˌkiːt ᵊn 'ʊr-, -'jʊr-
pheromonal ˌfer ə 'məʊn ᵊl ◂ ‖ -'moʊn-
pheromone 'fer ə məʊn ‖ -moʊn ~s z
phew fjuː —and non-speech sounds such as [ʍ,
ʍu, ʍʊ, ɸ, pɸ:]
phi faɪ phis faɪz
ˌPhi ˌBeta 'Kappa
phial 'faɪ_ᵊl ~s z
Phibbs fɪbz
Phidias 'fɪd i æs 'faɪd- ‖ -əs
Phidippides faɪ 'dɪp ɪ diːz -ə-

Phil fɪl
phil- comb. form before vowel
  before unstressed syllable ¦fɪl — philatelic
  ˌfɪl ə 'tel ɪk ◂
  before stressed syllable fɪ 'l+ fə- ‖ fə 'l+ —
  philately fɪ 'læt əl i fə- ‖ fə 'læt̬ ᵊl i
-phil fɪl — Francophil 'fræŋk əʊ fɪl ‖ -oʊ- -ə-
Philadelphia ˌfɪl ə 'delf i_ə
Philadelphian ˌfɪl ə 'delf i_ən ◂ ~s z
philadelphus ˌfɪl ə 'delf əs ~es ɪz əz
philander fɪ 'lænd ə fə- ‖ -ər ~ed d
  philandering fɪ 'lænd _ər ɪŋ fə- ~s z
philanderer fɪ 'lænd _ər ə fə- ‖ -ər ~s z
philanthrope 'fɪl ən θrəʊp -æn- ‖ -θroʊp ~s s
philanthropic ˌfɪl ən 'θrɒp ɪk ◂ -æn- ‖ -'θrɑːp-
  ~al ᵊl ~ally ᵊl_i
philanthropist fɪ 'læn¹θ rəp ɪst fə-, §-əst ~s s
philanthrop|y fɪ 'læn¹θ rəp |i fə- ~ies iz
philatelic ˌfɪl ə 'tel ɪk ◂ ~ally ᵊl_i
philatelist fɪ 'læt əl ɪst fə-, §-əst ‖ fə 'læt̬ ᵊl əst
  ~s s
philately fɪ 'læt əl i fə- ‖ fə 'læt̬ ᵊl i
Philbin 'fɪl bɪn
Philby 'fɪl bi
-phile faɪᵊl — Anglophile 'æŋ gləʊ faɪᵊl ‖ -ə-
Phileas 'fɪl i_əs
Philemon fɪ 'liːm ɒn faɪ-, fə-, -mən ‖ -ən
Philharmonia ˌfɪl hɑː 'məʊn i_ə ˌ•ɑː-, ˌ•ə-
  ‖ -hɑːr 'moʊn-
philharmonic ˌfɪl ɑː 'mɒn ɪk ◂ -ə-, -hɑː-
  ‖ -hɑːr 'mɑːn- -ᵊr- ~s s
philhellene ˌfɪl 'hel iːn '•ᵊ, •'•• ~s z
philhellenic ˌfɪl he 'liːn ɪk ◂ -hə-, -'len-
philhellenism ˌfɪl 'hel ə ˌnɪz əm -ɪ-
-philia 'fɪl i_ə — necrophilia ˌnek rəʊ
  'fɪl i_ə ‖ ˌ•ə-
-philiac 'fɪl i æk — coprophiliac ˌkɒp rəʊ
  'fɪl i æk ‖ ˌkɑːp rə-
-philic 'fɪl ɪk — photophilic ˌfəʊt əʊ
  'fɪl ɪk ◂ ‖ ˌfoʊt̬ ə-
Philip 'fɪl ɪp §-əp
Philippa 'fɪl ɪp ə -əp-
Philippe fɪ 'liːp —Fr [fi lip]
Philippi fɪ 'lɪp aɪ fə-; 'fɪl ɪ paɪ, -ə-
Philippian fɪ 'lɪp i_ən fə- ~s z
philippic fɪ 'lɪp ɪk fə- ~s s
Philippine 'fɪl ə piːn -ɪ-; ˌ•'•ᵊ• ~s z
Philips 'fɪl ɪps §-əps
Philipson 'fɪl ɪps ən §-əps-
Philistia fɪ 'lɪst i_ə fə-
philistine, P~ 'fɪl ɪ staɪn -ə- ‖ -stiːn fɪ 'lɪst ən,
  -iːn (*) ~s z
philistinism 'fɪl ɪst ɪ ˌnɪz əm '•əst-, -ə, •-
  ‖ 'fɪl ə stiː-
Phillip, Phillipp 'fɪl ɪp §-əp
Phillips 'fɪl ɪps §-əps
Phillis 'fɪl ɪs §-əs
Phillpot, Phillpott 'fɪl pɒt ‖ -pɑːt
phillumenist fɪ 'luːm ən ɪst fə-, -'ljuːm-, -ɪn-,
  §-əst ~s s
phillumeny fɪ 'luːm ən i fə-, -'ljuːm-, -ɪn-
Philly 'fɪl i
Philo 'faɪl əʊ ‖ -oʊ

P

philo- *comb. form*
  with stress-neutral suffix ˌfɪl əʊ ‖ -ə —
  philosophical ˌfɪl əʊ 'sɒf ɪk ᵊl ◄ ‖ -ə 'saːf-
  with stress-imposing suffix fɪ 'lɒ+ ‖ -'lɑː+ —
  philogyny fɪ 'lɒdʒ ən i fə-, -ɪn- ‖ -'lɑːdʒ-
Philoctetes ˌfɪl ək 'tiːt iːz -ɒk-
philodendron, P~ ˌfɪl ə 'dendr ən ~s z
philological ˌfɪl əʊ 'lɒdʒ ɪk ᵊl ◄ ‖ -ə 'lɑːdʒ- ~**ly**
  ˌi
philologist fɪ 'lɒl ədʒ ɪst fə-, §-əst ‖ -'lɑːl- ~**s** s
philology fɪ 'lɒl ədʒ i fə- ‖ -'lɑːl-
Philomel, p~ 'fɪl əʊ mel ‖ -ə- ~**s** z
Philomela ˌfɪl əʊ 'miːl ə ‖ -ə-
Philomena ˌfɪl əʊ 'miːn ə ‖ -ə-
philoprogenitive ˌfɪl əʊ prəʊ 'dʒen ət ɪv ◄
  -ɪt ɪv ‖ -ə proʊ 'dʒen ət̬ ɪv ~**ly** li ~**ness** nəs
  nɪs
philosopher fə 'lɒs əf ə fɪ- ‖ -'lɑːs əf ᵊr ~**s** z
  phi,losopher's 'stone
philosophic ˌfɪl ə 'sɒf ɪk ◄ -'zɒf- ‖ -'saːf-
  -'zɑːf- ~**al** ᵊl ◄ ~**ally** ᵊl‿i
philosophis|e, philosophiz|e fə 'lɒs ə faɪz fɪ-
  ‖ -'lɑːs- ~**ed** d ~**er/s** ə/z ‖ ᵊr/z ~**es** ɪz əz
  ~**ing** ɪŋ
philosoph|y fə 'lɒs əf |i fɪ- ‖ -'lɑːs- ~**ies** iz
Philostratus fɪ 'lɒs trət əs fə- ‖ -'lɑːs-
-philous *stress-imposing* fɪl əs -fəl- ‖ fəl əs —
  acidophilous ˌæs ɪ 'dɒf ɪl əs ◄ §, •ə-, -əl əs
  ‖ ˌæs ə 'daːf əl əs ◄
Philp fɪlp
Philpot 'fɪl pɒt ‖ -paːt
Philpots 'fɪl pɒts ‖ -paːts
philter, philtre 'fɪlt ə ‖ -ᵊr *(= filter)* ~**s** z
phimosis faɪ 'məʊs ɪs §-əs ‖ -'moʊs əs
Phineas 'fɪn i‿əs -æs
Phipps fɪps
phiz, Phiz fɪz *(= fizz)*
Phizackerley fɪ 'zæk ᵊl ə fə- ‖ -ᵊr li
phizog 'fɪz ɒg ‖ -ɑːg
phlebitic flɪ 'bɪt ɪk flə- ‖ -'bɪt̬-
phlebitis flɪ 'baɪt ɪs flə-, §-əs ‖ -'baɪt̬ əs
phlebotom|y flɪ 'bɒt əm |i flə- ‖ -'baːt̬- ~**ies**
  iz
Phlegethon 'fleg ɪθ ᵊn -əθ-; -ɪ θɒn, -ə-
  ‖ -ə θaːn
phlegm flem
phlegmatic fleg 'mæt ɪk ‖ -'mæt̬ ɪk ~**ally** ᵊl‿i
phlegmy 'flem i
phloem 'fləʊ ɪm -em, §-əm ‖ 'floʊ em
phlogistic flɒ 'dʒɪst ɪk ‖ floʊ-
phlogiston flɒ 'dʒɪst ᵊn -ɒn ‖ floʊ- -ɑːn
phlox flɒks ‖ flaːks *(= flocks)* **phloxes**
  'flɒks ɪz -əz ‖ 'flaːks əz
Phnom Penh ˌnɒm 'pen ˌpnɒm-, pə ˌnɒm 'pen
  ‖ ˌnaːm- —*Khmer* [phnɔm 'piɲ]
-phobe fəʊb ‖ foʊb — **Anglophobe** 'æŋ gləʊ
  fəʊb ‖ -glə foʊb
phobia 'fəʊb i‿ə ‖ 'foʊb i‿ə ~**s** z
-phobia 'fəʊb i‿ə ‖ 'foʊb i‿ə — **Francophobia**
  ˌfræŋ kəʊ 'fəʊb i‿ə ‖ -ə 'foʊb-
phobic 'fəʊb ɪk ‖ 'foʊb ɪk ~**s** s
-phobic 'fəʊb ɪk ‖ 'foʊb ɪk — **Russophobic**
  ˌrʌs əʊ 'fəʊb ɪk ◄ ‖ -ə 'foʊb-

Phobos 'fəʊb ɒs ‖ 'foʊb aːs
Phocaea fəʊ 'siː‿ə ‖ foʊ-
Phocian 'fəʊʃ i‿ən 'fəʊs- ‖ 'foʊʃ- ~**s** z
phocine 'fəʊs aɪn ‖ 'foʊs-
Phocion 'fəʊs i‿ən ‖ 'foʊʃ i‿ən -aːn
Phocis 'fəʊs ɪs §-əs ‖ 'foʊs-
phocomelia ˌfəʊk əʊ 'miːl i‿ə ‖ ˌfoʊk oʊ-
phocomely fəʊ 'kɒm əl i -ɪl- ‖ foʊ 'kaːm-
Phoebe, p~ 'fiːb i ~**s**, ~**'s** z
Phoebus 'fiːb əs
Phoenicia fə 'nɪʃ ə fɪ-; -'nɪʃ i‿ə ‖ -'niːʃ-
  Phoenician fə 'nɪʃ ᵊn fɪ-; -'nɪʃ i‿ən ‖ -'niːʃ-
  ~**s** z
phoenix, P~ 'fiːn ɪks ~**es**, ~**'s** ɪz əz
phon fɒn ‖ faːn **phons** fɒnz ‖ faːnz
phon- *comb. form before vowel*
  before unstressed syllable ˌfəʊn- ˌfɒn- ‖ ˌfoʊn
  — **phoniatric** ˌfəʊn i 'ætr ɪk ◄ ˌfɒn-
  ‖ ˌfoʊn-
  before stressed syllable fəʊ 'n+ ‖ foʊ 'n+ —
  phonendoscope fəʊ
  'nend ə skəʊp ‖ foʊ 'nend ə skoʊp
phonaesthesia ˌfəʊn iːs 'θiːz i‿ə ˌ•ɪs-, ˌ•əs-,
  -'θiːʒ- ‖ ˌfoʊn əs 'θiːʒ ə
phon|ate fəʊ 'n|eɪt ‖ 'foʊn eɪt ~**ated** eɪt ɪd
  -əd ‖ eɪt̬ əd ~**ates** eɪts ~**ating** eɪt ɪŋ ‖ eɪt̬ ɪŋ
phonation fəʊ 'neɪʃ ᵊn ‖ foʊ-
  pho'nation type
phonatory fəʊ 'neɪt ᵊr i 'fəʊn ət‿ᵊr i
  ‖ 'foʊn ə tɔːr i -toʊr i
phone fəʊn ‖ foʊn **phoned** fəʊnd ‖ foʊnd
  phones fəʊnz ‖ foʊnz **phoning**
  'fəʊn ɪŋ ‖ 'foʊn ɪŋ
  'phone book; 'phone box; 'phone call
-phone fəʊn ‖ foʊn — **anglophone** 'æŋ gləʊ
  fəʊn ‖ -ə foʊn
phonecard, P~ 'fəʊn kaːd →'fəʊŋ-
  ‖ 'foʊn kaːrd ~**s** z
phone-in 'fəʊn ɪn ‖ 'foʊn- ~**s** z
phonematic ˌfəʊn ɪ 'mæt ɪk ◄ -iː-, -ə-
  ‖ ˌfoʊn ə 'mæt̬ ɪk ◄
phoneme 'fəʊn iːm ‖ 'foʊn- ~**s** z
phonemic fəʊ 'niːm ɪk ‖ fə- foʊ- ~**ally** ᵊl‿i ~**s**
  s
phonemicis... —*see* **phonemiciz...**
phonemicist fəʊ 'niːm ɪs ɪst -əs-, §-əst ‖ fə-
  foʊ- ~**s** s
phonemicization fəʊ ˌniːm ɪs aɪ 'zeɪʃ ᵊn
  -ˌ•əs-, -ɪ'•- ‖ fə ˌniːm əs ə- foʊ- ~**s** z
phonemiciz|e fəʊ 'niːm ɪ saɪz -ə- ‖ fə- foʊ-
  ~**ed** d ~**es** ɪz əz ~**ing** ɪŋ
phonesthesia ˌfəʊn iːs 'θiːz i‿ə ˌ•ɪs-, ˌ•əs-,
  -'θiːʒ- ‖ ˌfoʊn əs 'θiːʒ ə
phone-tapping 'fəʊn ˌtæp ɪŋ ‖ 'foʊn- ~**s** z
phonetic fə 'net ɪk fəʊ- ‖ -'net̬ ɪk ~**ally** ᵊl‿i
  ~**s** s
  pho,netic 'symbol
Phonetica fəʊ 'net ɪk ə ‖ fə 'net̬-
phonetician ˌfəʊn ɪ 'tɪʃ ᵊn ˌfɒn-, -ə- ‖ ˌfoʊn-
  ˌfaːn- ~**s** z
phoneticis... —*see* **phoneticiz...**
phoneticization fəʊ ˌnet ɪs aɪ 'zeɪʃ ᵊn -ˌ•əs-
  ‖ foʊ ˌnet̬ əs ə- fə-

phoneticiz|e fəʊ 'net ɪ saɪz -ə- ‖ foʊ 'net̬- fə-
~**ed** d ~**es** ɪz əz ~**ing** ɪŋ
phon|ey, phon|y 'fəʊn li ‖ 'foʊn li ~**eyness,**
~**iness** i nəs i nɪs ~**eys, ~ies** ɪz ~**ier** i_ə ‖ i_ər
~**iest** i_ɪst i_əst ~**ily** ɪ li əl i
ˌ**phoney** 'war
phoniatric ˌfəʊn i 'ætr ɪk ◄ ˌfɒn- ‖ ˌfoʊn-
ˌfɑːn- ~**s** s
phonic 'fɒn ɪk 'fəʊn- ‖ 'fɑːn ɪk 'foʊn- ~**s** s
phono- *comb. form*
  with stress-neutral suffix ˌfəʊn əʊ ˌfɒn-
  ‖ ˌfoʊn ə — **phonoscope** 'fəʊn əʊ skəʊp
  'fɒn- ‖ 'foʊn ə skoʊp
  with stress-imposing suffix fəʊ 'nɒ+ ‖ fə 'nɑː+
  foʊ- — **phonometer** fəʊ 'nɒm ɪt ə -ət-
  ‖ fə 'nɑːm ət̬ ər foʊ-
phonogram 'fəʊn ə græm ‖ 'foʊn- ~**s** z
phonograph 'fəʊn ə grɑːf -græf
  ‖ 'foʊn ə græf ~**s** s
phonographic ˌfəʊn ə 'græf ɪk ◄ ‖ ˌfoʊn-
~**ally** əl_i
phonological ˌfəʊn ə 'lɒdʒ ɪk əl ◄ ˌfɒn-,
-əl 'ɒdʒ- ‖ ˌfoʊn əl 'ɑːdʒ- ˌfɑːn- ~**ly** _i
phonologist fəʊ 'nɒl ədʒ ɪst §-əst ‖ fə 'nɑːl-
foʊ- ~**s** s
phonolog|y fəʊ 'nɒl ədʒ li ‖ fə 'nɑːl- foʊ-
~**ies** ɪz
phonotactic ˌfəʊn əʊ 'tækt ɪk ◄ ˌfɒn- ‖ ˌfoʊn-
ˌfɑːn- ~**ally** əl_i ~**s** s
-phonous *stress-imposing* fən əs —
  homophonous hə 'mɒf ən əs hɒ-
  ‖ hə 'mɑːf-
phon|y 'fəʊn li ‖ 'foʊn li ~**iness** i nəs i nɪs
~**ies** ɪz ~**ier** i_ə ‖ i_ər ~**iest** i_ɪst i_əst ~**ily**
ɪ li əl i
-phony *stress-imposing* fən i — **cacophony**
  kæ 'kɒf ən i ‖ -'kɑːf-
phooey 'fuː_i
-phore fɔː ‖ fɔːr foʊr — **anthophore** 'æn[t]θ əʊ
  fɔː ‖ -ə fɔːr -foʊr
-phoresis fə 'riːs ɪs §-əs — **electrophoresis**
  ɪ ˌlek trəʊ fə 'riːs ɪs ə-, §-əs ‖ -,·trə-
phormium 'fɔːm i_əm ‖ 'fɔːrm-
-phorous *stress-imposing* fər əs —
  anthophorous æn 'θɒf ər əs ‖ -'θɑːf-
phosgene 'fɒz dʒiːn 'fɒs- ‖ 'fɑːz-
phosphatas|e 'fɒs fə teɪz -teɪs ‖ 'fɑːs- ~**es** ɪz
əz
phosphate 'fɒs feɪt ‖ 'fɑːs- ~**s** s
phosphatic (ˌ)fɒs 'fæt ɪk ‖ (ˌ)fɑːs 'fæt̬ ɪk -'feɪt̬-
phosphene 'fɒs fiːn ‖ 'fɑːs- ~**s** z
phosphide 'fɒs faɪd ‖ 'fɑːs- ~**s** z
phosphite 'fɒs faɪt ‖ 'fɑːs- ~**s** s
phospho- *comb. form*
  with stress-neutral suffix ˌfɒs fəʊ ‖ ˌfɑːs foʊ —
  phospholipid ˌfɒs fəʊ 'lɪp ɪd §-əd
  ‖ ˌfɑːs foʊ- ~**s** z
phosphor 'fɒs fə ‖ 'fɑːs fər -fɔːr ~**s** z
phosphoresc|e ˌfɒs fə 'res ‖ ˌfɑːs- ~**ed** t ~**es**
ɪz əz ~**ing** ɪŋ
phosphorescence ˌfɒs fə 'res ən[t]s ‖ ˌfɑːs-
phosphorescent ˌfɒs fə 'res ənt ◄ ‖ ˌfɑːs- ~**ly**
li

phosphoric (ˌ)fɒs 'fɒr ɪk ‖ (ˌ)fɑːs 'fɔːr ɪk -'fɑːr-
phosphorous 'fɒs fər_əs ‖ 'fɑːs-
phosphorus, P~ 'fɒs fər_əs ‖ 'fɑːs-
phosphory|late fɒs 'fɒr ə leɪt 'fɒs fər-, -ɪ •
  ‖ fɑːs 'fɔːr- -'fɑːr- ~**lated** leɪt ɪd -əd
  ‖ leɪt̬ əd ~**lates** leɪts ~**lating** leɪt ɪŋ ‖ leɪt̬ ɪŋ
phosphorylation fɒs ˌfɒr ə 'leɪʃ ən ,···'··,
  ,·fər-, -ɪ'·- ‖ fɑːs ˌfɔːr- -ˌfɑːr-, ,···'··
phossy 'fɒs i ‖ 'fɑːs i
photic 'fəʊt ɪk ‖ 'foʊt̬ ɪk
photo 'fəʊt əʊ ‖ 'foʊt̬ oʊ ~**s** z
  'photo call; ˌphoto 'finish; 'photo op,
  'photo oppor,tunity
photo- *comb. form*
  with stress-neutral suffix ˌfəʊt əʊ ‖ ˌfoʊt̬ oʊ —
  photomicrograph ˌfəʊt əʊ 'maɪk rəʊ grɑːf
  -græf ‖ ˌfoʊt̬ oʊ 'maɪk rə græf
  with stress-imposing suffix
  fəʊ 'tɒ+ ‖ foʊ 'tɑː+ — **photometry**
  fəʊ 'tɒm ətr i -ɪtr- ‖ foʊ 'tɑːm-
photocell 'fəʊt əʊ sel ‖ 'foʊt̬ oʊ- ~**s** z
photochemical ˌfəʊt əʊ 'kem ɪk əl ◄ ‖ ˌfoʊt̬ oʊ-
~**ly** _i
photochromic ˌfəʊt əʊ
  'krəʊm ɪk ◄ ‖ ˌfoʊt̬ oʊ 'kroʊm ɪk ◄ ~**s** s
photocomposition
  ˌfəʊt əʊ ˌkɒmp ə 'zɪʃ ən ‖ ˌfoʊt̬ oʊ ˌkɑːmp-
photocopier 'fəʊt əʊ ˌkɒp i_ə ,··'···
  ‖ 'foʊt̬ oʊ ˌkɑːp i_ər '·ə- ~**s** z
photocop|y *n, v* 'fəʊt əʊ ˌkɒp li ,··'···
  ‖ 'foʊt̬ oʊ ˌkɑːp li -ə- ~**ied** id ~**ies** ɪz ~**ying**
i ɪŋ
photoelectric ˌfəʊt əʊ ɪ 'lek trɪk ◄ -ə'·-
  ‖ ˌfoʊt̬ oʊ- ~**ally** əl_i
  ˌphotoe,lectric 'cell
Photofit *tdmk* 'fəʊt əʊ fɪt ‖ 'foʊt̬ oʊ-
photoflood 'fəʊt əʊ flʌd ‖ 'foʊt̬ oʊ- ~**s** z
photogenic ˌfəʊt əʊ 'dʒen ɪk ◄ -'dʒiːn-
  ‖ ˌfoʊt̬ ə- ~**ally** əl_i
photogrammetr|ist/s ˌfəʊt əʊ 'græm ətr ɪst/s
-ɪtr-, §-əst/s ‖ ˌfoʊt̬ oʊ- ~**y** i
photograph *n, v* 'fəʊt ə grɑːf -græf
  ‖ 'foʊt̬ ə græf ~**ed** t ~**ing** ɪŋ ~**s** s
photographer fə 'tɒg rəf ə ‖ -'tɑːg rəf ər ~**s** z
photographic ˌfəʊt ə 'græf ɪk ◄ ‖ ˌfoʊt̬ ə-
~**ally** əl_i
  ˌphoto,graphic 'memory
photography fə 'tɒg rəf i ‖ -'tɑːg-
photogravure ˌfəʊt əʊ
  grə 'vjʊə ‖ ˌfoʊt̬ ə grə 'vjʊər ~**s** z
photolitho ˌfəʊt əʊ 'laɪθ əʊ ‖ ˌfoʊt̬ oʊ 'lɪθ oʊ
photolithography ˌfəʊt əʊ lɪ 'θɒg rəf i -laɪ'·-,
§-lə'·- ‖ ˌfoʊt̬ oʊ lɪ 'θɑːg-
photometer fəʊ 'tɒm ɪt ə §-ət-
  ‖ foʊ 'tɑːm ət̬ ər ~**s** z
photomontag|e ˌfəʊt əʊ
  mɒn 'tɑːʒ ‖ ˌfoʊt̬ oʊ mɑːn- ,·ə- ~**es** ɪz əz
photon 'fəʊt ɒn ‖ 'foʊt ɑːn ~**s** z
photonasty 'fəʊt əʊ ˌnæst i ‖ 'foʊt̬ oʊ-
photophobia ˌfəʊt əʊ 'fəʊb i_ə ‖ ˌfoʊt̬ ə 'foʊb-
photo-reconnaissance ˌfəʊt əʊ rɪ 'kɒn ɪs ən[t]s
-rə'·-, §-riː'·-, -'·əs- ‖ ˌfoʊt̬ oʊ rɪ 'kɑːn əz
ən[t]s -'·əs-

Phoneme and allophone

1 A **phoneme** is one of the basic distinctive units in the phonetics of a language. The actual speech sounds which represent it are its **allophones**. Phonemes have the power of distinguishing words in the language (e.g. p and b, as in **pit** pɪt and **bit** bɪt); allophones, as such, do not (e.g. clear and dark varieties of l).

2 Each language has its own phonemic system and its own rules for determining the allophones appropriate to the phonemes in various phonetic environments. In English, for example, the phoneme p comprises both aspirated and unaspirated allophones (see ASPIRATION). In some other languages, e.g. Hindi, aspirated and unaspirated plosives represent distinct phonemes. English ʃ varies according to its surroundings (see COARTICULATION). The phoneme iː comprises both clipped and unclipped allophones (see CLIPPING).

3 The allophones of a phoneme are phonetically similar to one another. More importantly, their distribution is either **complementary** (= predictable by rule from the context) or else **random** (= in free variation). When it is important to distinguish phonemic transcription from allophonic or impressionistic transcription, it is usual to enclose the former in slants / /, the latter in square brackets [ ].

4 The phonetic notation in LPD is phonemic, with the following minor exceptions:
- The symbols i, u are employed to reflect the NEUTRALIZATION of /iː - ɪ/ and /uː - ʊ/ in certain positions.
- For AmE, the allophone [t̬] of /t/ is symbolized explicitly.
- For BrE, the optional allophones [ɒʊ] of /əʊ/ is symbolized explicitly.
- For some speakers (not of RP), ʌ and ə are not in contrast.
- Italic and raised symbols show the possibility of omission or insertion of a sound.
- The marks ‿, ◄, §, ⚠ are added.

P

---

photosensitis... —*see* photosensitiz...
photosensitive ˌfəʊt əʊ 'sen⸳ts ət ɪv ◄ -ɪt ɪv
‖ ˌfoʊt̬ oʊ 'sen⸳ts ət̬ ɪv ◄
photosensitivity ˌfəʊt əʊ ˌsen⸳ts ə 'tɪv ət i -ɪ'•-,
-ɪt i ‖ ˌfoʊt̬ oʊ ˌsen⸳ts ə 'tɪv ət̬ i
photosensitization
ˌfəʊt əʊ ˌsen⸳ts ət aɪ 'zeɪʃ ᵊn -ˌ•ɪt-, -ɪ'•-
‖ ˌfoʊt̬ oʊ ˌsen⸳ts ət̬ ə-
photosensitiz|e ˌfəʊt əʊ 'sen⸳ts ə taɪz -'•ɪ-
‖ ˌfoʊt̬ oʊ- ~ed d ~es ɪz əz ~ing ɪŋ
photoset 'fəʊt əʊ set ‖ 'foʊt̬ oʊ- ~s s
photosphere 'fəʊt əʊ sfɪə ‖ 'foʊt̬ oʊ sfɪr
photostat, P~ *tdmk* 'fəʊt əʊ stæt ‖ 'foʊt̬ ə-
~ed, ~ted ɪd əd ~ing, ~ting ɪŋ ~s s
photostatic ˌfəʊt əʊ
'stæt ɪk ◄ ‖ ˌfoʊt̬ ə 'stæt̬ ɪk ◄ ~ally ᵊl‿i
photosynthesis ˌfəʊt əʊ 'sɪntθ əs ɪs -ɪs ɪs, §-əs
‖ ˌfoʊt̬ oʊ-

photosynthesis|e, photosynthesiz|e
ˌfəʊt əʊ 'sɪntθ ə saɪz -'•ɪ- ‖ ˌfoʊt̬ oʊ- ~ed d
~es ɪz əz ~ing ɪŋ
photosynthetic ˌfəʊt əʊ sɪn 'θet ɪk ◄
‖ ˌfoʊt̬ oʊ sɪn 'θet̬ ɪk ◄ ~ally ᵊl‿i
phototropic ˌfəʊt əʊ 'trɒp ɪk ◄ -'trəʊp-
‖ ˌfoʊt̬ ə 'traːp ɪk ◄ -'troʊp- ~ally ᵊl‿i
phototropism ˌfəʊt əʊ 'trəʊp ɪz əm
fəʊ 'tɒtr ə ˌpɪz- ‖ foʊ 'taːtr ə ˌpɪz əm
ˌfoʊt̬ oʊ 'troʊp ˌɪz-
phrasal 'freɪz ᵊl ~ly i
ˌphrasal 'verb
phrase freɪz (= *frays*) phrased freɪzd
phrases 'freɪz ɪz -əz phrasing/s 'freɪz ɪŋ/z
'phrase ˌmarker
phrasebook 'freɪz bʊk §-buːk ~s s
phraseological ˌfreɪz i‿ə 'lɒdʒ ɪk ᵊl ◄ ‖ -'laːdʒ-
~ly ‿i

phraseolog|y ˌfreɪz i 'ɒl ədʒ |i ‖ -'ɑːl- **~ies** iz

phrase-structure 'freɪz ˌstrʌk tʃə ˏ•'•• ‖ -tʃʳr

phratr|y 'freɪtr |i **~ies** iz

phreatic fri 'æt ɪk ‖ -'æt̬-

phrenetic frə 'net ɪk frɪ-, fre- ‖ -'net̬ ɪk **~al** ᵊl **~ally** ᵊl_i

phrenic 'fren ɪk

phrenological ˌfren ə 'lɒdʒ ɪk ᵊl ◂ ‖ -'lɑːdʒ-

phrenolog|ist/s frə 'nɒl ədʒ |ɪst/s frɪ-, fre-, §-əst/s ‖ -'nɑːl- **~y** i

Phrygi|a 'frɪdʒ i_ə **~an/s** ən/z

Phryne 'fraɪn i

phthalein 'θeɪl i_ɪn 'θæl-, 'fθæl-, ˏ_ən; '•iːn ‖ 'θæl i_ən 'θeɪl-, '•iːn

phthalic 'θæl ɪk 'fθæl-, 'θeɪl-

phthisis 'θaɪs ɪs 'taɪs-, 'fθaɪs-, §-əs

Phuket ˌpuː 'ket —Thai ['¹phuː ²'ked]

phut, phutt fʌt

phwoar BrE interjection fwɔː or various non-speech vocalizations such as [ɸuɔa]

phyco- comb. form
  with stress-neutral suffix ˌfaɪk əʊ ‖ -oʊ —
  phycomycetous ˌfaɪk əʊ maɪ 'siːt əs ◂ ‖ -oʊ maɪ 'siːt̬-
  with stress-imposing suffix faɪ 'kɒ+ ‖ -'kɑː+ — **phycology** faɪ 'kɒl ədʒ i ‖ -'kɑːl-

Phyfe faɪf

phyla 'faɪl ə

phylacter|y fɪ 'lækt ər |i **~ies** iz

phyletic faɪ 'let ɪk ‖ -'let̬- **~ally** ᵊl_i

Phyllida 'fɪl ɪd ə -əd-

Phyllis 'fɪl ɪs §-əs

phyllo- comb. form with stress-neutral suffix ˌfɪl əʊ ‖ -ə — **phyllotaxis** ˌfɪl əʊ 'tæks ɪs §-əs ‖ -ə-

-phyllous 'fɪl əs — **monophyllous** ˌmɒn əʊ 'fɪl əs ◂ ‖ ˌmɑːn ə-

Phyllosan tdmk 'fɪl əʊ sæn ‖ -oʊ-

phylloxera fɪ 'lɒks ər ə ˌfɪl ɒk 'sɪər ə ‖ ˌfɪl ɑːk 'sɪr ə fɪ 'lɑːks ər ə

phylo- comb. form
  with stress-neutral suffix ˌfaɪl əʊ ‖ -oʊ —
  phylogenetic ˌfaɪl əʊ dʒə 'net ɪk ◂ -dʒɪ'•- ‖ ˌfaɪl oʊ dʒə 'net̬ ɪk ◂
  with stress-imposing suffix faɪ 'lɒ+ ‖ -'lɑː+ — **phylogeny** faɪ 'lɒdʒ ən i -ɪn- ‖ -'lɑːdʒ-

phyl|um 'faɪl |əm **~a** ə

physalis faɪ 'seɪl ɪs §-əs; 'faɪs əl-

physiatrist ˌfɪz i 'ætr ɪst §-əst

physic 'fɪz ɪk **~ked** t **~king** ɪŋ **~s** s

physical 'fɪz ɪk ᵊl **~ly** _i **~s** z
  ˌphysical ˌeduˈcation; ˌphysical ˈjerks; ˌphysical ˈtraining

physicality ˌfɪz ɪ 'kæl ət i ˏ•ə-, -ɪt i ‖ -ət̬ i

physician fɪ 'zɪʃ ᵊn fə- **~s** z

physicist 'fɪz ɪs ɪst -əs-, §-əst **~s** s

physics 'fɪz ɪks

physio 'fɪz i əʊ ‖ -oʊ **~s** z

physio- comb. form
  with stress-neutral suffix ˌfɪz i əʊ ‖ -oʊ -ə —
  physiocrat 'fɪz i əʊ kræt ‖ -i oʊ- -i_ə-
  with stress-imposing suffix ˌfɪz i 'ɒ+ ‖ -'ɑː+ — **physiography** ˌfɪz i 'ɒg rəf i ‖ -'ɑːg-

physiognomic ˌfɪz i_ə 'nɒm ɪk ◂ ‖ -'nɑːm- **~ally** ᵊl_i

physiognom|y ˌfɪz i 'ɒn əm |i -'ɒg nəm- ‖ -'ɑːg nəm |i -'ɑːn əm- **~ies** iz **~ist/s** ɪst/s §-əst/s

physiological ˌfɪz i_ə 'lɒdʒ ɪk ᵊl ◂ ‖ -'lɑːdʒ- **~ly** i

physiologist ˌfɪz i 'ɒl ədʒ ɪst §-əst ‖ -'ɑːl- **~s** s

physiology ˌfɪz i 'ɒl ədʒ i ‖ -'ɑːl-

physiotherapist ˌfɪz i_əʊ 'θer əp ɪst §-əst ‖ ˌ•-oʊ- **~s** s

physiotherapy ˌfɪz i_əʊ 'θer əp i ‖ ˌ••oʊ-

physique fɪ 'ziːk fə- **~s** s

physostigmine ˌfaɪs əʊ 'stɪg miːn ‖ -ə-

-phyte faɪt — **epiphyte** 'ep i faɪt

Phythian 'fɪð i_ən

phyto- comb. form
  with stress-neutral suffix ˌfaɪt əʊ ‖ ˌfaɪt oʊ —
  phytopathology ˌfaɪt əʊ pə 'θɒl ədʒ i -pæ'•- ‖ ˌfaɪt̬ oʊ pə 'θɑːl-
  with stress-imposing suffix faɪ 'tɒ+ ‖ -'tɑː+ — **phytography** faɪ 'tɒg rəf i ‖ -'tɑːg-

pi paɪ **pis** paɪz

Piacenza ˌpiːˏə 'tʃen/s ə —It [pja 'tʃen tsa]

Piaf 'piː æf ‖ piː 'ɑːf —Fr [pjaf]

piaff|e pi 'æf **~ed** t **~ing** ɪŋ **~s** s

piaffer pi 'æf ə ‖ -ʳr **~s** z

Piaget pi 'æʒ eɪ -'ɑːʒ- ‖ ˌpiː ə 'ʒeɪ -ɑː- —Fr [pja ʒɛ]

Piagetian ˌpiːˏə 'ʒet i_ən ◂ ˏ•ɑːː-; -'ʒeɪ ən ‖ -'ʒeɪ ən **~s** z

pia mater ˌpaɪˏə 'meɪt ə ˌpiːˏ ‖ -'meɪt̬ ʳr ˌpiː ə 'mɑːt̬ ʳr, '••,••

pianissimo ˌpiːˏə 'nɪs ɪ məʊ ˏ•ɑː-, -ə• ‖ -moʊ **~s** z

pianist 'piːˏən ɪst 'pjɑːn ɪst, pi 'æn ɪst, §-əst ‖ pi 'æn əst 'piː ən- **~s** s

piano n 'instrument' pi 'æn əʊ -'ɑːn-; 'pjæn əʊ, 'pjɑːn- ‖ -oʊ **~s** z
  piˌano acˈcordion; piˌano duˈet; piˈano ˌwire

piano adv; adj; n '(passage played) softly' 'pjɑːn əʊ pi 'ɑːn əʊ ‖ pi 'ɑːn oʊ **~s** z

pianoforte pi ˌæn əʊ 'fɔːt i -ˌɑːn-, -eɪ; -'fɔːt; ˌpjæn əʊ'•-, ˌpjɑːn- ‖ -oʊ 'fɔːrt eɪ -'foʊrt-, -i; -'•ə fɔːrt, -foʊrt **~s** z

pianola, P~ tdmk ˌpiːˏə 'nəʊl ə -æ-; pɪəˈ•• ‖ -'noʊl- **~s** z

piassava ˌpiːˏə 'sɑːv ə

piaster, piastre pi 'æst ə -'ɑːst- ‖ -ʳr **~s** z

piazza pi 'æts ə -'ɑːts-, -'ædz- ‖ -'ɑːz ə -'æz-
  (*) —It ['pjat tsa] **~s** z

pibroch 'piːb rɒk -rɒx, -rɒʃ ‖ -rɑːk —ScG piobaireachd ['piːb rɔxk] **~s** s

pic pɪk **pics** pɪks

pica 'paɪk ə **~s** z

picador 'pɪk ə dɔː ‖ -dɔːr **~s** z

Picard 'pɪk ɑːd ‖ piː 'kɑːrd —Fr [pi kaːʁ]

Picardy 'pɪk əd i ‖ -ʳrd i —Fr Picardie [pi kaʁ di]

picaresque ˌpɪk ə 'resk ◂

picaroon ˌpɪk ə 'ruːn **~s** z

Picasso pɪ 'kæs əʊ -'kɑːs- ‖ -'kɑːs oʊ —*Sp*
[pi 'ka so]
picayune ˌpɪk ə 'juːn ◂ -eɪ-, -i-, -i 'uːn ~**s** z
Piccadilly ˌpɪk ə 'dɪl i ◂
ˌPicca,dilly 'Circus
piccalilli ˌpɪk ə 'lɪl i '•••
piccaninn|y ˌpɪk ə 'nɪn li '•••• ~**ies** iz
piccolo 'pɪk ə ləʊ ‖ -loʊ ~**s** z
pice paɪs
pichiciago ˌpɪtʃ i si 'eɪg əʊ ˌ•ə-, -'ɑːg- ‖ -oʊ
~**s** z
pichiciego ˌpɪtʃ i si 'eɪg əʊ ˌ•ə- ‖ -oʊ ~**s** z
pick, Pick pɪk **picked** pɪkt **picking** 'pɪk ɪŋ
picks pɪks
pickaback 'pɪk ə bæk
pickan... —*see* piccan...
pickax, pickax|e 'pɪk æks ~**ed** t ~**es** ɪz əz
~**ing** ɪŋ
picker 'pɪk ə ‖ -ᵊr ~**s** z
pickerel 'pɪk ᵊr_əl ~**s** z
Pickering 'pɪk ᵊr_ɪŋ
picker-up ˌpɪk ər ˈʌp ‖ -ᵊr-
pick|et 'pɪk |ɪt §-ət ‖ -|ət ~**eted** ɪt ɪd §ət-, -əd
‖ əṭ əd ~**eting** ɪt ɪŋ §ət- ‖ əṭ ɪŋ ~**ets** ɪts
§əts ‖ əts
'picket line
Pickett 'pɪk ɪt §-ət
Pickford 'pɪk fəd ‖ -fᵊrd
pickings 'pɪk ɪŋz
pickl|e 'pɪk ᵊl ~**ed** d ~**es** z ~**ing** _ɪŋ
Pickles 'pɪk ᵊlz
picklock 'pɪk lɒk ‖ -lɑːk ~**s** s
pick-me-up 'pɪk mi ʌp ~**s** s
pickpocket 'pɪk ˌpɒk ɪt §-ət ‖ -ˌpɑːk ət ~**s** s
Pickthorne 'pɪk θɔːn ‖ -θɔːrn
Pickup *family name* 'pɪk ʌp
pick-up 'pɪk ʌp ~**s** s
Pickwick 'pɪk wɪk
ˌPickwick 'Papers ‖ '•• ˌ••
Pickwickian ₍ₐ₎pɪk 'wɪk i_ən
pick|y 'pɪk li ~**ier** i_ə ‖ i_ᵊr ~**iest** i_ɪst i_əst
~**iness** i nəs i nɪs
picnic 'pɪk nɪk ~**ked** t ~**king** ɪŋ ~**s** s
picnicker 'pɪk nɪk ə ‖ -ᵊr ~**s** z
pico- 'piːk əʊ 'paɪk- ‖ -oʊ — **picofarad**
'piːk əʊ ˌfær əd 'paɪk-, -æd ‖ -oʊ- -ˌfer-
picot 'piːk əʊ pɪ 'kəʊ ‖ -oʊ pi: 'koʊ —*Fr*
[pi ko]
picotee ˌpɪk ə 'tiː ~**s** z
picrate 'pɪk reɪt ~**s** s
picric 'pɪk rɪk
Pict pɪkt **Picts** pɪkts
Pictish 'pɪkt ɪʃ
pictogram 'pɪkt əʊ græm ‖ -ə- ~**s** z
pictograph 'pɪkt əʊ grɑːf -græf ‖ -ə græf ~**s** s
pictographic ˌpɪkt əʊ 'græf ɪk ◂ ‖ -ə- ~**ally** ᵊl_i
pictography pɪk 'tɒg rəf i ‖ -'tɑːg-
Picton 'pɪkt ən
Pictor 'pɪkt ə ‖ -ᵊr
pictorial pɪk 'tɔːr i_əl ‖ -'toʊr- ~**ly** i
Pictoris pɪk 'tɔːr ɪs §-əs ‖ -'toʊr-
pic|ture 'pɪk |tʃə -ʃə; Δ'pɪ|tʃ ə ‖ 'pɪk |tʃᵊr
~**tured** tʃəd ʃəd ‖ tʃᵊrd ~**tures** tʃəz ʃəz

‖ tʃᵊrz ~**turing** tʃᵊr ɪŋ ʃᵊr_ɪŋ
'picture book; 'picture frame; ˌpicture
'postcard; 'picture rail
picturesque ˌpɪk tʃə 'resk ◂ -ʃə- ~**ly** li ~**ness**
nəs nɪs
piddl|e 'pɪd ᵊl ~**ed** d ~**es** z ~**ing** _ɪŋ
piddock 'pɪd ək ~**s** s
Pidgeon 'pɪdʒ ən
pidgin, P~ 'pɪdʒ ɪn -ən ~**s** z
ˌPidgin 'English
pidginis... —*see* pidginiz...
pidginization ˌpɪdʒ ɪn aɪ 'zeɪʃ ᵊn ˌ•ən-, -ɪ'•-
‖ -ən ə-
pidginize 'pɪdʒ ɪ naɪz -ə-
pie paɪ **pies** paɪz
'pie chart
piebald 'paɪ bɔːld ‖ -bɑːld ~**s** z
piece piːs (= *peace*) —*but in Fr phrases also*
pi 'es, pɪəs —*Fr* pièce [pjɛs] **pieced** piːst
pieces 'piːs ɪz -əz **piecing** 'piːs ɪŋ —*see also*
phrases with this word
ˌpiece of 'cake; ˌpieces of 'eight; ˌpiece of
'work; 'piece rate
piece de resistance, pièce de résistance
pi ˌes də re 'zɪst ɒs -rɪ'•-, -rə'•-, -riː'•-;
ˌpɪəs••'•-; -ən's; -ˌrez i 'stɒs
‖ pi ˌes də rɪ ˌzi: 'stɑːn's —*Fr*
[pjɛs də re zis tɑ̃ːs, pjɛz-]
piecemeal 'piːs miːᵊl
piecework 'piːs wɜːk ‖ -wɜːk
piecrust 'paɪ krʌst ~**s** s
pied paɪd
ˌPied 'Piper
pied-a-terre, pied-à-terre pi ˌeɪd ɑː 'teə
ˌpiː ed-, -ə'• ‖ -'teᵊr —*Fr* [pje ta tɛːʁ]
pieds-~ pi ˌeɪd -ˌeɪdz; ˌpiː ed, ˌpiː edz —*Fr*
as in sing.
Piedmont, p~ 'piːd mɒnt ‖ -mɑːnt
Piedmontese ˌpiːd mən 'tiːz ◂ -mɒn- ‖ -mɑːn-
-'tiːs
pie-eyed ˌpaɪ 'aɪd ◂
pie|man 'paɪ |mən ~**men** mən men
pier pɪə ‖ pɪᵊr (= *peer*) **piers** pɪəz ‖ pɪᵊrz
'pier glass
pierce, P~ pɪəs ‖ pɪᵊrs **pierced** pɪəst ‖ pɪᵊrst
pierces pɪəs ɪz -əz ‖ 'pɪrs əz **piercing/ly**
'pɪəs ɪŋ /li ‖ 'pɪrs ɪŋ /li
Piercy 'pɪəs i ‖ 'pɪrs i
Pierian paɪ 'ɪər i_ən pi-, -'er- ‖ -'ɪr-
pieris 'paɪ_ər ɪs paɪ 'ɪər-, §-əs
Pierre *personal name* pi 'eə 'piː eə ‖ -'eᵊr —*Fr*
[pjɛːʁ]
Pierre *place in SD* pɪə ‖ pɪᵊr
pierrot, P~ 'pɪər əʊ ‖ 'piː ə roʊ ˌ••'• —*Fr*
[pjɛ ʁo] ~**s** z
Piers pɪəz ‖ pɪᵊrz
Piesporter 'piːz pɔːt ə ‖ -pɔːrṭ ᵊr —*Ger*
['piːs pɔʁt ɐ]
pieta, pietà ˌpiː e 'tɑː -eɪ-, '••• ‖ -eɪ- —*It*
[pje 'ta]
Pietermaritzburg ˌpiːt ə 'mær ɪts bɜːg §-'•əts-
‖ ˌpiːṭ ᵊr 'mær əts bɜːg -'mer-
pietism, P~ 'paɪ_ə ˌtɪz əm -ɪ-

pietist, P~ 'paɪˌət ɪst -əst ‖ -ət̬- **~s** s
pietistic ˌpaɪˌə 'tɪst ɪk ◄
piet|y 'paɪˌət |i -ɪt- ‖ -ət̬ |i **~ies** iz
piezo- *comb. form*
    with stress-neutral suffix ˌpiːz əʊ paɪ ˌiːz əʊ,
    pi ˌets əʊ, ˌpaɪ ɪ zəʊ ‖ pi ˌeɪz oʊ -ˌeɪts- —
    piezochemistry ˌpiːz əʊ 'kem ɪst ri
    paɪ ˌiːz əʊˈ•-, pi ˌets-, ˌpaɪ ɪ zəʊ-, -ˈ•əst-
    ‖ pi ˌeɪz oʊ- -ˌeɪts-
    with stress-imposing suffix ˌpiːˌə 'zɒ+ ˌpaɪ-, -ɪ-
    ‖ ˌpiː ə 'zɑː+ ˌpaɪ-, -eɪ- — **piezometry**
    ˌpiːˌə 'zɒm ətr i ˌpaɪ-, ˌ•ɪ-, -ɪtr i ‖ -'zɑːm-
    ˌ•eɪ-
piezoelectric ˌpiːz əʊ ɪ 'lek trɪk ◄ ˌpiːts-;
    paɪ ˌiːz əʊ ɪ'•-, pi ˌets-, ˌpaɪ ɪ zəʊ ɪ'•-
    ‖ pi ˌeɪz oʊ- -ˌeɪts-
    ˌpiezoeˌlectric 'crystal ‖ piˌezo-
Pifco *tdmk* 'pɪf kəʊ ‖ -koʊ
piffl|e 'pɪf ᵊl **~ed** d **~es** z **~ing** ɪŋ
pig pigged pɪgd **pigging** 'pɪg ɪŋ **pigs**
    pɪgz
    'pig ˌiron; 'pig ˌLatin
pigeon 'pɪdʒ ən -ɪn **~s** z
pigeon-chested ˌpɪdʒ ən 'tʃest ɪd ◄ -ɪn-,
    -əd ‖ ˈ•ˌ•ˌ•
pigeonhol|e 'pɪdʒ ən həʊl -ɪn-, →-ʰɒʊl ‖ -hoʊl
    ~ed d **~es** z **~ing** ɪŋ
pigeon-toed 'pɪdʒ ən təʊd ˌ•ˈ• ‖ -toʊd
pigger|y 'pɪg ər li **~ies** iz
piggi... —*see* **piggy**
piggish 'pɪg ɪʃ **~ly** li **~ness** nəs nɪs
Piggott 'pɪg ət
piggl|y 'pɪg li **~ier** iˌə ‖ iˌᵊr **~ies** iz **~iest** i ɪst
    iˌəst
piggyback 'pɪg i bæk **~ed** t **~ing** ɪŋ **~s** s
piggybank 'pɪg i bæŋk **~s** s
pigheaded ˌpɪg 'hed ɪd ◄ -əd **~ly** li **~ness** nəs
    nɪs
piglet 'pɪg lət -lɪt **~s** s
pigmeat 'pɪg miːt
pigment *n* 'pɪg mənt **~s** s
pig|ment *v* pɪg ˈ|ment 'pɪg |mənt **~mented**
    ment ɪd mənt-, -əd ‖ ment̬ əd mənt̬-
    ~menting ment ɪŋ mənt- ‖ ment̬ ɪŋ mənt̬-
    ~ments ments
pigmentation ˌpɪg men 'teɪʃ ən -mən- **~s** z
pig|my, Pig|my 'pɪg |mi **~mies** miz
pignut 'pɪg nʌt **~s** s
Pigott 'pɪg ət
pigpen 'pɪg pen **~s** z
pigskin 'pɪg skɪn
pigsticking 'pɪg ˌstɪk ɪŋ
pig|sty 'pɪg |staɪ **~sties** staɪz
pigswill 'pɪg swɪl
pigtail 'pɪg teɪᵊl **~ed** d **~s** z
pigwash 'pɪg wɒʃ ‖ -wɔːʃ -wɑːʃ
pigweed 'pɪg wiːd
pika 'paɪk ə 'piːk- **~s** s
pike, Pike paɪk **piked** paɪkt **pikes, Pike's**
    paɪks **piking** 'paɪk ɪŋ
    ˌPike's 'Peak
pikelet 'paɪk lət -lɪt **~s** s
pike|man 'paɪk |mən **~men** mən men

pikeperch 'paɪk pɜːtʃ ‖ -pɝːtʃ **~es** ɪz əz
piker 'paɪk ə ‖ -ᵊr **~s** z
pikestaff 'paɪk stɑːf §-stæf ‖ -stæf **~s** s
pilaf, pilaff 'piːl æf 'pɪl- ‖ pɪ 'lɑːf 'piːl ɑːf **~s** s
pilaster pɪ 'læst ə pə- ‖ -ᵊr 'paɪl æst- **~ed** d
    ~s z
Pilate 'paɪl ət
Pilatus pɪ 'lɑːt əs pə- —*Ger* [pi 'lɑː tʊs]
pilau 'piːl aʊ 'pɪl-; pɪ 'laʊ, pə- ‖ pɪ 'loʊ -'lɔː,
    -'lɑː, -'laʊ **~s** z
pilchard 'pɪltʃ əd ‖ -ᵊrd **~s** z
pile paɪᵊl **piled** paɪᵊld **piles** paɪᵊlz **piling**
    'paɪᵊl ɪŋ
pilea 'pɪl iˌə 'paɪl- **~s** z
pileated 'paɪl i eɪt ɪd 'pɪl-, -əd ‖ 'pɪl i eɪt̬- 'paɪl
pile-driver 'paɪᵊl ˌdraɪv ə ‖ -ᵊr **~s** z
pile|um 'paɪl iˌəm **~a** ə
pileup 'paɪᵊl ʌp **~s** s
pile|us 'paɪl iˌəs **~i** aɪ iː
pilfer 'pɪlf ə ‖ -ᵊr **~ed** d **pilfering** 'pɪlf ər_ɪŋ
    ~s z
pilferage 'pɪlf ər_ɪdʒ
pilferer 'pɪlf ər ə ‖ -ᵊr ər **~s** z
pilgrim, P~ 'pɪl grɪm -grəm **~s, ~'s** z
    ˌPilgrim 'Fathers
pilgrimag|e 'pɪl grɪm ɪdʒ -grəm- **~es** ɪz əz
Pilipino ˌpɪl ɪ 'piːn əʊ -ə- ‖ -oʊ
Pilkington 'pɪlk ɪŋ tən
pill pɪl **pilled** pɪld **pilling** 'pɪl ɪŋ **pills** pɪlz
pillag|e 'pɪl ɪdʒ **~ed** d **~es** ɪz əz **~ing** ɪŋ
pillager 'pɪl ɪdʒ ə ‖ -ᵊr **~s** z
pillar 'pɪl ə ‖ -ᵊr **~ed** d **~s** z
    'pillar box; ˌpillar box 'red ◄
pillbox 'pɪl bɒks ‖ -bɑːks **~es** ɪz əz
Pilley 'pɪl i
Pilling 'pɪl ɪŋ
pillion 'pɪl jən 'pɪl iˌən **~s** z
pilliwinks 'pɪl ɪ wɪŋks §-ə-
pillock 'pɪl ək **~s** s
pillor|y 'pɪl ər li **~ied** id **~ies** iz **~ying** i ɪŋ
pillow 'pɪl əʊ ‖ -oʊ **~ed** d **~ing** ɪŋ **~s** z
    'pillow slip; 'pillow talk
pillowcas|e 'pɪl əʊ keɪs ‖ -ə- -oʊ- **~es** ɪz əz
Pillsbury 'pɪlz bər_i ‖ -ˌber i
pillwort 'pɪl wɜːt §-wɔːt ‖ -wɝːt -wɔːrt
pilocarpine ˌpaɪl əʊ 'kɑːp iːn -aɪn, -ɪn
    ‖ -oʊ 'kɑːrp-
pilonidal ˌpaɪl əʊ 'naɪd ᵊl ◄ ‖ -ə-
pil|ot 'paɪl |ət **~oted** ət ɪd -əd ‖ ət̬ əd **~oting**
    ət ɪŋ ‖ ət̬ ɪŋ **~ots** əts
    'pilot ˌburner; 'pilot lamp; 'pilot light;
    'pilot ˌofficer
pilotage 'paɪl ət ɪdʒ ‖ -ət̬-
Pilsen 'pɪlz ən 'pɪls- —*Ger* ['pɪl zᵊn], *Czech*
    Plzeň ['pᵊl zeɲ]
pilsener, pilsner, P~ 'pɪlz nə 'pɪls-, ˈ•ᵊn ə
    ‖ -nᵊr **~s** z
Pilsudski pɪl 'sʊd ski—*Polish* Piłsudski
    [piw 'sut ski]
Piltdown 'pɪlt daʊn
Pilton 'pɪlt ən
pilule 'pɪl juːl **~s** z
Pima 'piːm ə **~s** z

Piman 'piːm ən

pimento pɪ 'ment əʊ pə- ‖ -'menṭ oʊ ~s z

pimiento ˌpɪm i 'ent əʊ pɪm 'jent-; pɪ 'ment-, pə- ‖ pəm 'jenṭ oʊ pə 'menṭ- ~s z

Pimlico 'pɪm lɪ kəʊ -lə- ‖ -koʊ

Pimm pɪm Pimm's pɪmz

pimp pɪmp pimped pɪmpt pimping 'pɪmp ɪŋ pimps pɪmps

pimpernel 'pɪmp ə nel -nəl ‖ -ᵊr- ~s z

pimple 'pɪmp ᵊl ~d d ~s z

pimp|ly 'pɪmp |li ~liness li nəs -nɪs

pimpmobile 'pɪmp məʊ ˌbiːl -mə- -moʊ- ~s z

pin, PIN pɪn pinned pɪnd pinning 'pɪn ɪŋ pins pɪnz
'pin ˌmoney; 'PIN ˌnumber; ˌpins and 'needles

pina colada, pińa colada ˌpiːn ə kəʊ 'laːd ə ˌ•jə- ‖ -jə kə- -ə kə- —Sp [ˌpi ɲa ko 'la ða] ~s z

pinafore 'pɪn ə fɔː ‖ -fɔːr -four ~s z

pinata, pińata piːn 'jɑːt ə pɪn- ‖ -'jɑːṭ ə —Sp [pi 'ɲa ta] ~s z

Pinatubo ˌpɪn ə 'tuːb əʊ ‖ ˌpiːn ə 'tuːb oʊ

pinball 'pɪn bɔːl →'pɪm- ‖ -bɑːl ~s z

pince-nez sing. ˌpæn¹s 'neɪ ˌpɪn¹s-, -'nez —Fr [pɛ̃s ne] ~ pl z

pincer 'pɪn¹s ə ‖ -ᵊr ~s z
'pincer ˌmovement

pincerlike 'pɪn¹s ə laɪk ‖ -ᵊr-

pinch pɪnt͡ʃ pinched pɪnt͡ʃt pinches 'pɪnt͡ʃ ɪz -əz pinching 'pɪnt͡ʃ ɪŋ

pinchbeck, P~ 'pɪnt͡ʃ bek

Pincher 'pɪnt͡ʃ ə ‖ -ᵊr

pinch-|hit ˌpɪnt͡ʃ |'hɪt ~hits 'hɪts ~hitter/s 'hɪt ə/z ‖ 'hɪṭ ᵊr/z ~hitting 'hɪt ɪŋ ‖ 'hɪṭ ɪŋ

pinchpenn|y 'pɪnt͡ʃ ˌpen |i ~ies iz

Pinckney 'pɪŋk ni

Pincus 'pɪŋk əs

pincushion 'pɪn ˌkʊʃ ᵊn →'pɪŋ- ~s z

Pindar 'pɪnd ə -aː ‖ -ᵊr -aːr

Pindaric ₍ₒ₎pɪn 'dær ɪk ‖ -'der-

pindown 'pɪn daʊn

Pindus 'pɪnd əs

pine, Pine paɪn pined paɪnd pines paɪnz pining 'paɪn ɪŋ
'pine cone; 'pine ˌkernel; 'pine ˌmarten; 'pine ˌneedle

pineal 'pɪn i‿əl ₍ₒ₎paɪ 'niː‿əl
'pineal gland

pineapple 'paɪn æp ᵊl -ˌ•• ~s z
'pineapple juice

pinene 'paɪn iːn

Pinero pɪ 'nɪər əʊ pə-, -'neər- ‖ -'nɪr oʊ -'ner-

pinetree 'paɪn triː ~s z

pinet|um paɪ 'niːt |əm ‖ -'niːṭ |əm ~a ə

pinewood, P~ 'paɪn wʊd ~s z

piney 'paɪn i

pinfall 'pɪn fɔːl ‖ -fɑːl ~s z

Pinfold 'pɪn fəʊld →-fɒʊld ‖ -foʊld

ping pɪŋ pinged pɪŋd pinging 'pɪŋ ɪŋ pings pɪŋz

pinger 'pɪŋ ə ‖ -ᵊr ~s z

pingo 'pɪŋ gəʊ ‖ -goʊ ~s z

ping-pong, Ping-Pong tdmk 'pɪŋ pɒŋ ‖ -paːŋ -pɔːŋ

Pingtung ˌpɪŋ 'tʌŋ —Chi Píngdōng [²pʰiŋ ¹tʊŋ]

pinguid 'pɪŋ gwɪd §-gwəd

pinhead 'pɪn hed ~s z

pinhole 'pɪn həʊl →-hɒʊl ‖ -hoʊl ~s z

pinion 'pɪn jən ~ed d ~ing ɪŋ ~s z

pink pɪŋk pinked pɪŋkt pinker 'pɪŋk ə ‖ -ᵊr pinkest 'pɪŋk ɪst §-əst pinking 'pɪŋk ɪŋ pinks pɪŋks
ˌpink 'elephant; ˌpink 'gin; 'pinking ˌscissors; 'pinking shears

Pinkerton 'pɪŋk ət ᵊn ‖ -ᵊrt ᵊn

pinkeye 'pɪŋk aɪ

pinkie 'pɪŋk i ~s z

pinkish 'pɪŋk ɪʃ

pinkness 'pɪŋk nəs -nɪs

pinko 'pɪŋk əʊ ‖ -oʊ ~es, ~s z

pink|y 'pɪŋk |i ~ies iz

pinn|a 'pɪn |ə ~ae iː ~as əz

pinnace 'pɪn əs -ɪs ~es ɪz əz

pinnacl|e 'pɪn ək ᵊl -ɪk- ~ed d ~ing ₍ₒ₎ɪŋ ~es z

pinnate 'pɪn eɪt -ət, -ɪt ~ly li

pinnatifid pɪ 'næt ɪ fɪd §-ə- ‖ -'næṭ-

pinn... —see pin

pinner, P~ 'pɪn ə ‖ -ᵊr

Pinney 'pɪn i

Pinnock 'pɪn ək

pinn|y 'pɪn |i ~ies iz

Pinocchio pɪ 'nəʊk i‿əʊ pə-, -'nɒk- ‖ -'noʊk i oʊ —It [pi 'nɔk kjo]

pinochle, pinocle 'piː ˌnʌk ᵊl -ˌnɒk-

pinole pɪ 'nəʊl i pə- ‖ -'noʊl i

Pinot 'piːn əʊ ‖ -oʊ —Fr [pi no]

pin|point 'pɪn |pɔɪnt →'pɪm- ~pointed pɔɪnt ɪd -əd ‖ pɔɪnṭ əd ~pointing pɔɪnt ɪŋ ‖ pɔɪnṭ ɪŋ ~points pɔɪnts

pinprick 'pɪn prɪk →'pɪm- ~ed t ~ing ɪŋ ~s s

pinstripe 'pɪn straɪp ~d t ~s s
ˌpinstripe 'suit

pint paɪnt pints paɪnts

pinta 'tropical disease', P~ 'pɪnt ə 'piːnt- ‖ 'pɪnṭ ə 'pɪnt aː —Sp ['pin ta]

pinta 'pint (of milk)' 'paɪnt ə ‖ 'paɪnṭ ə ~s z

pintable 'pɪn ˌteɪb ᵊl ~s z

pintado pɪn 'taːd əʊ ‖ -oʊ

pintail 'pɪn teɪᵊl ~s z

Pinter 'pɪnt ə ‖ 'pɪnṭ ᵊr

Pinteresque ˌpɪnt ər 'esk ◂ ‖ ˌpɪnṭ ə 'resk ◂

Pinterish 'pɪnt ər ɪʃ ‖ 'pɪnṭ-

pintle 'pɪnt ᵊl ‖ 'pɪnṭ ᵊl ~s z

pinto 'pɪnt əʊ ‖ 'pɪnṭ oʊ ~s z
'pinto bean

pint-size 'paɪnt saɪz ~d d

pinup 'pɪn ʌp ~s s

pinwheel 'pɪn wiːᵊl -hwiːᵊl ‖ -hwiːᵊl ~s z

pinworm 'pɪn wɜːm ‖ -wɝːm ~s z

pinxit 'pɪŋks ɪt §-ət

Pinxton 'pɪŋkst ən

piny 'paɪn i

P

pinyin, P~ ˌpɪn ˈjɪn ◄ —*Chi* pīnyīn [¹pʰɪn ¹jɪn]
piolet ˈpiːˌə leɪ ‖ ˌpiː ə ˈleɪ ~s z
pion ˈpaɪ ɒn -ən ‖ -ɑːn ~s z
pioneer, P~ ˌpaɪˌə ˈnɪə ◄ ‖ -ˈnɪᵊr ~ed d
  pioneering ˌpaɪˌə ˈnɪər ɪŋ ◄ ‖ -ˈnɪr ɪŋ ◄ ~s z
  ˌpioˌneering ˈwork
pious ˈpaɪˌəs ~ly li ~ness nəs nɪs
pip, Pip pɪp **pipped** pɪpt **pipping** ˈpɪp ɪŋ
  pips pɪps
pipal ˈpiːp ᵊl ~s z
pipe paɪp **piped** paɪpt **pipes** paɪps **piping**
  ˈpaɪp ɪŋ
  ˈpipe ˌcleaner; ˌpiped ˈmusic; ˈpipe dream;
  ˈpipe ˌorgan; ˈpipe rack; ˌpiping ˈhot◄
pipeclay ˈpaɪp kleɪ
pipefish ˈpaɪp fɪʃ ~es ɪz əz
pipeful ˈpaɪp fʊl ~s z
pipelin|e ˈpaɪp laɪn ~ed d ~es z ~ing ɪŋ
piper, Piper ˈpaɪp ə ‖ -ᵊr ~s z
piperaceous ˌpɪp ə ˈreɪʃ əs ˌpaɪp-
piperade ˌpɪp ə ˈrɑːd ˌpiːp- ~s z
piperazine pɪ ˈper ə ziːn paɪ-, -zɪn
piperidine pɪ ˈper ɪ diːn paɪ-, -ə-, -dɪn
pipette pɪ ˈpet ‖ paɪ- ~s s
pipewort ˈpaɪp wɜːt §-wɔːt ‖ -wɝːt -wɔːrt
Pipex *tdmk* ˈpaɪp eks
piping ˈpaɪp ɪŋ
pipistrelle ˌpɪp ɪ ˈstrel -ə-, ˈ• • • ~s z
pipit ˈpɪp ɪt §-ət ~s s
pipkin ˈpɪp kɪn §-kən ~s z
Pippa ˈpɪp ə
pipp... —*see* **pip**
pippin ˈpɪp ɪn §-ən ~s z
pipsqueak ˈpɪp skwiːk ~s s
piquancy ˈpiːk ənˣs i
piquant ˈpiːk ənt -ɑːnt ~ly li
pique piːk *(= peak)* **piqued** piːkt **piques** piːks
  piquing ˈpiːk ɪŋ
piqué ˈpiːk eɪ ‖ piː ˈkeɪ —*Fr* [pi ke]
piquet *'card game'* pɪ ˈket -ˈkeɪ
Piquet ˈpiːk eɪ
pirac|y ˈpaɪᵊr əs |i ˈpɪr- ~ies iz
Piraeus ₍ᵢ₎paɪ ˈriːˌəs pɪ ˈreɪ əs, pə- —*ModGk*
  Piraievs [pi rɛ ˈɛfs, -ˈa]
Piran ˈpɪr ən
Pirandello ˌpɪr ən ˈdel əʊ ‖ -oʊ —*It*
  [pi ran ˈdel lo]
piranha, piraña pə ˈrɑːn ə pɪ-, -jə ‖ -ˈræn- ~s
  z
  piˈranha fish
pir|ate ˈpaɪᵊr |ət -ɪt ~ated ət ɪd ɪt-, -əd ‖ əṭ əd
  ~ates əts ɪts ~ating ət ɪŋ ɪt- ‖ əṭ ɪŋ
piratical ₍ᵢ₎paɪ ˈræt ɪk ᵊl pɪ-, pə- ‖ -ˈræṭ- ~ly i
Pirbright ˈpɜː braɪt ‖ ˈpɝː-
Pirelli *tdmk* pə ˈrel i pɪ- —*It* [pi ˈrɛl li]
Pirie ˈpɪr i
Pirithous, Pirithoüs paɪᵊ ˈrɪθ əʊ əs ‖ -oʊ əs
pirog, pirogue pɪ ˈrəʊg pə- ‖ -ˈroʊg ˈpiː roʊg
  ~s z
piroshki pɪ ˈrɒʃ ki pə-; ˌpɪr əʃ ˈkiː ‖ -ˈrɔːʃ-
  -ˈrɑːʃ-, -ˈrʌʃ- —*Russ* [pjɪ rʌ ˈʃkjі]
pirou|ette ˌpɪr u |ˈet ~etted ˈet ɪd -əd ‖ ˈeṭ əd
  ~ettes ˈets ~etting ˈet ɪŋ ‖ ˈeṭ ɪŋ

pirozhki —*see* **piroshki**
Pisa ˈpiːz ə —*It* [ˈpiː sa]
pis aller ˌpiːz ˈæl eɪ ‖ -æ ˈleɪ —*Fr* [pi za le]
Pisan ˈpiːz ᵊn ~s z
piscatorial ˌpɪsk ə ˈtɔːr iˌəl ◄ ‖ -ˈtoʊr- ~ly ̩i
piscatory ˈpɪsk əṭˌᵊr i ‖ -ə tɔːr i -toʊr i
Piscean ˈpaɪs iˌən ˈpɪsk-, ˈpɪs-; paɪ ˈsiːˌ ~s z
Pisces ˈpaɪs iːz ˈpɪsk-, ˈpɪs-
pisci- *comb. form*
  with stress-neutral suffix ˌpɪs ɪ — **pisciculture**
  ˈpɪs ɪ ˌkʌltʃ ə ‖ -ᵊr
  with stress-imposing suffix pɪ ˈsɪ+ §pə- —
  piscivorous pɪ ˈsɪv ᵊr əs §pə-
piscin|a pɪ ˈsiːn |ə §pə-, -ˈʃiːn-, -ˈsaɪn- ~ae iː
  ~as əz
piscine ˈpɪs aɪn ˈpɪsk-, ˈpaɪs-, -iːn ~s z
Pisgah ˈpɪz gɑː: -gə
pish pɪʃ
Pisidia paɪ ˈsɪd iˌə
Pisistratus paɪ ˈsɪs trət əs ‖ -trəṭ-
piss pɪs **pissed** pɪst **pisses** ˈpɪs ɪz -əz **pissing**
  ˈpɪs ɪŋ
pissant ˈpɪs ænt ~ing ɪŋ ~s s
Pissarro pɪ ˈsɑːr əʊ ‖ -ˈoʊ —*Fr* [pi sa ʁo]
pissoir ˈpɪs wɑː ‖ piː ˈswɑːr —*Fr* [pi swaːʁ] ~s
  z
piss-take ˈpɪs teɪk ~s s
piss-up ˈpɪs ʌp ~s s
pistachio pɪ ˈstɑːʃ i əʊ pə-, -ˈstæʃ-, -ˈstætʃ-
  ‖ -ˈstæʃ i oʊ -ˈstɑːʃ- ~s z
piste piːst **pistes** piːsts
pistil ˈpɪst ɪl -ᵊl ~s z
pistol ˈpɪst ᵊl ~s z
  ˈpistol grip
pistole pɪ ˈstəʊl ‖ -ˈstoʊl ~s z
pistol-whip ˈpɪst ᵊl wɪp -hwɪp ‖ -ʍɪp ~ped t
  ~ping ɪŋ ~s s
piston ˈpɪst ən ~s z
  ˈpiston ring; ˈpiston rod
pit pɪt **pits** pɪts **pitted** ˈpɪt ɪd -əd ‖ ˈpɪṭ əd
  pitting ˈpɪt ɪŋ ‖ ˈpɪṭ ɪŋ
  ˈpit bull, ˌpit bull ˈterrier; ˈpit ˌpony; ˈpit
  stop
pita ˈpɪt ə ˈpiːt- ‖ ˈpiːṭ ə
pit-a-pat ˌpɪt ə ˈpæt ˈ• • • ‖ ˌpɪṭ ə pæt -ɪ-
Pitcairn ˈpɪt keən • ˈ• ‖ -kern —*as a family*
  name, usually • ˈ•
pitch pɪtʃ **pitched** pɪtʃt **pitches** ˈpɪtʃ ɪz -əz
  pitching ˈpɪtʃ ɪŋ
  ˈpitch pine; ˈpitch pipe
pitch-and-putt ˌpɪtʃ ən ˈpʌt -ᵊnd-, →ᵊm-
pitch-and-toss ˌpɪtʃ ən ˈtɒs -ᵊnd-, -ˈtɔːs
  ‖ -ˈtɔːs -ˈtɑːs
pitch-black ˌpɪtʃ ˈblæk ◄
pitchblende ˈpɪtʃ blend
pitch-dark ˌpɪtʃ ˈdɑːk ◄ ‖ -ˈdɑːrk ◄
pitcher ˈpɪtʃ ə ‖ -ᵊr ~s z
  ˈpitcher plant
pitchfork ˈpɪtʃ fɔːk ‖ -fɔːrk ~s s
pitch|man ˈpɪtʃ |mən -mæn ~men mən men
pitch|y ˈpɪtʃ |i ~ier iˌə ‖ iˌᵊr ~iest iˌɪst iˌəst
  ~iness i nəs -nɪs
piteous ˈpɪt iˌəs ~ly li ~ness nəs nɪs

P

pitfall 'pɪt fɔːl ‖ -fɑːl ~s z
pith pɪθ pithed pɪθt pithing 'pɪθ ɪŋ piths
pɪθs
  ,pith 'helmet‖ '•,••
pithead 'pɪt hed ~s z
pithecanthropus, P~ ,pɪθ i 'kænᵗθ rəp əs
  -kæn 'θrəʊp- ‖ -kæn 'θroʊp-
pith|y 'pɪθ |i ~ier i‿ə ‖ i‿ʳr ~iest i‿ɪst i‿əst
  ~ily ɪ li əl i ~iness i nəs i nɪs
pitiab|le 'pɪt i‿əb |əl ‖ 'pɪt̬- ~leness əl nəs -nɪs
  ~ly li
pitie... —see pity
pitiful 'pɪt ɪ fəl -ə-, -fʊl ‖ 'pɪt̬- ~ly ‿i ~ness nəs
  nɪs
pitiless 'pɪt ɪ ləs -ə-, -lɪs; -əl əs, -ɪs ‖ 'pɪt̬- ~ly li
  ~ness nəs nɪs
Pitjantjatjara ,pɪtʃ ən tʃə 'tʃær ə
Pitlochry pɪt 'lɒx ri -'lɒk- ‖ -'lɑːk-
pit|man, P~ 'pɪt |mən ~men mən men
Pitney 'pɪt ni
piton 'piːt ɒn -ð ‖ -ɑːn —Fr [pi tɔ̃] ~s z
pitot, Pitot 'piːt əʊ ‖ -oʊ ~s z
  'Pitot tube
Pitsea 'pɪt siː
Pitt pɪt
pitta 'kind of bread' 'pɪt ə 'piːt- ‖ 'piːt̬ ə
  'pitta bread
pitta 'kind of bird' 'pɪt ə ‖ 'pɪt̬ ə ~s z
pittanc|e 'pɪt ᵊn|s ~es ɪz əz
Pittenweem ,pɪt ən 'wiːm
pitter-patter 'pɪt ə ,pæt ə ,••'••
  ‖ 'pɪt̬ ʳr ,pæt̬ ʳr -i-
pittosporum pɪ 'tɒsp ʳr əm ‖ -'tɑːsp-
Pittsburg, Pittsburgh 'pɪts bɜːg ‖ -bɝːg
pituitar|y pɪ 'tjuː‿ɪ‿t̬ər li pə-, →§-'tʃuː‿, ‿ə‿
  ‖ -'tuː ə ter li -'tjuː- ~ies ɪz
  pi'tuitary gland
pituri 'pɪtʃ ʳr i
pity 'pɪt i ‖ 'pɪt̬ i pitied 'pɪt id ‖ 'pɪt̬ id pities
  'pɪt iz ‖ 'pɪt̬ iz pitying/ly 'pɪt i ɪŋ /li ‖ 'pɪt̬ i-
pityriasis ,pɪt ɪ 'raɪ‿əs ɪs ,•ə-, §-əs ‖ ,pɪt̬-
Pius 'paɪ‿əs
piv|ot 'pɪv |ət ~oted ət ɪd -əd ‖ ət̬ əd ~oting
  ət ɪŋ ‖ ət̬ ɪŋ ~ots əts
pivotal 'pɪv ət əl ‖ -ət̬ əl ~ly ‿i
pix pɪks (= picks)
pixel 'pɪks əl -el ~s z
pixelation ,pɪks ə 'leɪʃ ən →-əl 'eɪʃ-
pix|elate 'pɪks| ə leɪt →-əl eɪt ~elated
  ə leɪt ɪd -əd ‖ -əl eɪt̬ əd ~elates ə leɪts
  →əl eɪts ~elating ə leɪt ɪŋ ‖ əl eɪt̬ ɪŋ
pixie 'pɪks i ~s z
pixilated 'pɪks ɪ leɪt ɪd '•ə- ‖ -leɪt̬ əd
pix|y 'pɪks |i ~ies iz
Pizarro pɪ 'zɑːr əʊ ‖ -oʊ —Sp [pi 'θa rro, -'sa-]
pizza 'piːts ə ~s z
pizzazz pə 'zæz pɪ-
pizzeria ,piːts ə 'riː‿ə ,pɪts- ~s z
Pizzey (i) 'pɪts i, (ii) 'pɪz i
pizzicato ,pɪts ɪ 'kɑːt əʊ -ə- ‖ -'kɑːt̬ oʊ ~s z
pizzle 'pɪz əl ~s z
PL/1 ,piː el 'wʌn §-'wɒn
placab|le 'plæk əb |əl ~ly li

placard n 'plæk ɑːd ‖ -ɑːrd -ərd ~s z
placard v 'plæk ɑːd ‖ -ɑːrd -ərd; plə 'kɑːrd,
  plæ- ~ed ɪd əd ~ing ɪŋ ~s z
pla|cate plə 'keɪt ‖ 'pleɪk eɪt (*) ~cated
  keɪt ɪd -əd ‖ keɪt̬ əd ~cates keɪts ~cating
  keɪt ɪŋ ‖ keɪt̬ ɪŋ
placatory plə 'keɪt ər i pleɪ-; 'plæk ət‿ər i
  ‖ 'pleɪk ə tɔːr i 'plæk-, -toʊr i (*)
place pleɪs placed pleɪst places 'pleɪs ɪz -əz
  placing/s 'pleɪs ɪŋ/z
  'place card; 'place mat; 'place name;
  'place ,setting
placebo plə 'siːb əʊ plæ- ‖ -oʊ ~s z
  pla'cebo ef,fect
placekick 'pleɪs kɪk ~ed t ~er/s ə/z ‖ ʳr/z
  ~ing ɪŋ ~s s
place|man 'pleɪs |mən ~men mən
placement 'pleɪs mənt ~s s
pla|centa plə 'sent ə ‖ -'sent̬ ə ~centae
  'sent iː ~cental 'sent əl ‖ 'sent̬ əl ~centas
  'sent əz ‖ 'sent̬ əz
placer ore deposit 'plæs ə ‖ -ʳr
placet 'pleɪs et -ɪt ~s s
placid 'plæs ɪd §-əd ~ly li ~ness nəs nɪs
placidity plə 'sɪd ət i plæ-, -ɪt- ‖ -ət̬ i
placket 'plæk ɪt §-ət ~s s
plagal 'pleɪg əl
plage 'beach' plɑːʒ plages 'plɑːʒ ɪz -əz —Fr
  [plaːʒ]
plage 'bright region on the sun' plɑːʒ pleɪdʒ
  plages 'plɑːʒ ɪz 'pleɪdʒ-, -əz
plagiarism 'pleɪdʒ ə ,rɪz əm -i‿ə- ~s z
plagiaris... —see plagiariz...
plagiarist 'pleɪdʒ ʳr ɪst -i‿ər-, §-əst ~s s
plagiaristic ,pleɪdʒ ə 'rɪst ɪk ◂ -i‿ə-
plagiariz|e 'pleɪdʒ ə raɪz -i‿ə- ~ed d ~es ɪz əz
  ~ing ɪŋ
plagioclas|e 'pleɪdʒ i‿ə kleɪz -kleɪs ~es ɪz əz
plague pleɪg plagued pleɪgd plagues pleɪgz
  plaguing 'pleɪg ɪŋ
plagu|ey, plagu|y 'pleɪg |i ~ily əl i ɪ li
plaice pleɪs (= place)
plaid plæd (!) plaids plædz
Plaid Cymru ,plaɪd 'kʌm ri -'kʊm-, -'kuːm-
  —Welsh [ˌplaɪd 'kəm ri, -rɪ]
plain pleɪn (= plane) plainer 'pleɪn ə ‖ -ʳr
  plainest 'pleɪn ɪst -əst
  ,plain 'chocolate; ,plain 'flour; ,plain
  'sailing
plainchant 'pleɪn tʃɑːnt §-tʃænt ‖ -tʃænt
plain-clothes ,pleɪn 'kləʊðz ◂→ ,pleɪŋ-, -kləʊz
  ‖ -'kloʊz -'kloʊðz
plain|ly 'pleɪn |li ~ness nəs nɪs
plains|man 'pleɪnz |mən ~men mən men
plainsong 'pleɪn sɒŋ ‖ -sɔːŋ -sɑːŋ
plainspoken ,pleɪn 'spəʊk ən ◂ ‖ -'spoʊk ən ◂
  ~ness nəs nɪs
plains|woman 'pleɪnz |,wʊm ən ~women
  ,wɪm ɪn -ən
plaint pleɪnt plaints pleɪnts
plaintiff 'pleɪnt ɪf §-əf ‖ 'pleɪnt̬ əf ~s s
plaintive 'pleɪnt ɪv ‖ 'pleɪnt̬ ɪv ~ly li ~ness
  nəs nɪs

Plaistow *(i)* 'plɑːst əʊ 'plæst- ‖ -oʊ, *(ii)*
'pleɪst əʊ ‖ -oʊ —*The places in Greater
London are (i). The family name may be either
(i) or (ii).*

plait plæt ‖ pleɪt plæt *(!)* **plaited** 'plæt ɪd -əd
‖ 'pleɪt̬ əd 'plæt̬- **plaiting** 'plæt ɪŋ ‖ 'pleɪt̬ ɪŋ
'plæt̬- **plaits** plæts ‖ pleɪts plæts

plan plæn **planned** plænd **planning** 'plæn ɪŋ
plans plænz
'planning per‚mission

planar 'pleɪn ə ‖ -ᵊr *(= plainer)*

planarian plə 'neər i‿ən ‖ -'ner- -'nær- ~**s** z

planchet 'plɑːntʃ ɪt §'plæntʃ-, §-ət ‖ 'plæntʃ ət
~**s** s

planchette plɑːn 'ʃet plɒ̃-, plæn- ‖ plæn— —*Fr*
[plɑ̃ ʃɛt] ~**s** s

Planck plæŋk ‖ plɑːŋk —*Ger* [plaŋk]

plane pleɪn **planned** pleɪnd **planes** pleɪnz
planing 'pleɪn ɪŋ
'plane tree

planer 'pleɪn ə ‖ -ᵊr ~**s** z

planet 'plæn ɪt §-ət ~**s** s

planetari|um ‚plæn ə 'teər i‿|əm ‚•ɪ- ‖ -'ter-
-'tær- ~**a** ə ~**ums** əmz

planetary 'plæn ət‿ᵊr i ‖•ɪt̬‿ ‖ -ə ter i

planetesimal ‚plæn ɪ 'tes ɪm ᵊl ◂ ‚•ə-, -'tez-,
-əm ᵊl

planetoid 'plæn ə tɔɪd -ɪ- ~**s** z

plangency 'plændʒ ᵊntˢ i

plangent 'plændʒ ᵊnt ~**ly** li

plani... —*see* **plane**

planigale 'plæn ɪ geɪᵊl -ə- ~**s** z

planimeter plæ 'nɪm ɪt ə plə-, pleɪ- -ət- ‖ -ət̬ ᵊr
~**s** z

planimetric ‚plæn ɪ 'metr ɪk ◂ -ə- ~**al/ly** ᵊl /‿i

planimetry plæ 'nɪm ətr i plə-, pleɪ-, -ɪtr-

planish 'plæn ɪʃ ~**ed** t ~**es** ɪz əz ~**ing** ɪŋ

plank plæŋk **planked** plæŋkt **planking**
'plæŋk ɪŋ **planks** plæŋks

plankton 'plæŋkt ən -ɒn ‖ -ɑːn

planktonic plæŋk 'tɒn ɪk ‖ -'tɑːn ɪk

plann... —*see* **plan**

planner 'plæn ə ‖ -ᵊr ~**s** z

plano-concave ‚pleɪn əʊ 'kɒn keɪv ◂ →-'kɒŋ-,
‚•••'• ‖ -oʊ 'kɑːn-

plano-convex ‚pleɪn əʊ 'kɒn veks ◂ ‚•••'•
‖ -oʊ 'kɑːn-

plant, Plant plɑːnt §plænt ‖ plænt **planted**
'plɑːnt ɪd §'plænt-, -əd ‖ 'plænt̬ əd
planting/s 'plɑːnt ɪŋ/z §'plænt- ‖ 'plænt̬ ɪŋ/
z

Plantagenet plæn 'tædʒ ən‿ət -'•ɪn-, -ɪt, -et
~**s** s

plantain 'plænt ɪn 'plɑːnt-, -ən ‖ -ᵊn ~**s** z

plantar 'plænt ə -ɑː- ‖ 'plænt̬ ᵊr 'plænt ɑːr

plantation plɑːn 'teɪʃ ᵊn plæn- ‖ plæn- ~**s** z

planter, P~ 'plɑːnt ə §'plænt- ‖ 'plænt̬ ᵊr ~**s** s

plantigrade 'plænt ɪ greɪd 'plɑːnt-, §-ə-
‖ 'plænt̬ ə- ~**s** z

Plantin 'plænt ɪn 'plɑːnt-, -ən ‖ plɑːn 'tæn

plantocrac|y ‚plɑːn 'tɒkr əs li §‚plæn-
‖ plæn 'tɑːk- ~**ies** iz

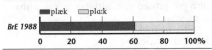

plaque plæk plɑːk, pleɪk —*BrE 1988 poll panel
preference:* plæk 61%, plɑːk 39%. *Some people
distinguish between a* plæk *on a wall and* plɑːk
or pleɪk *on their teeth. In AmE always* plæk.
plaques plæks plɑːks, pleɪks

plash plæʃ **plashed** plæʃt **plashes** 'plæʃ ɪz
-əz **plashing** 'plæʃ ɪŋ

plashy 'plæʃ i

-plasia 'pleɪz i‿ə ‖ 'pleɪʒ i‿ə 'pleɪʒ ə —
hypoplasia ‚haɪp əʊ 'pleɪz i‿ə ‖ -oʊ 'pleɪʒ-
-'•ə

-plasm ‚plæz əm — **protoplasm** 'prəʊt əʊ
‚plæz əm ‖ 'proʊt̬ ə-

plasma 'plæz mə ~**s** z

plasmapheresis ‚plæz mə 'fer əs ɪs -'fɪər-, §-əs

plasmid 'plæz mɪd §-məd ~**s** z

plasmo- *comb. form*
with stress-neutral suffix ¦plæz məʊ ‖ -mə —
plasmosome 'plæz məʊ səʊm ‖ -mə soʊm
with stress-imposing suffix
plæz 'mɒ+ ‖ -'mɑː+ — **plasmolysis**
plæz 'mɒl əs ɪs -ɪs ɪs, §-əs ‖ -'mɑːl-

plasmodi|um plæz 'məʊd i‿|əm ‖ -'moʊd- ~**a**
ə ~**al** ᵊl

Plassey 'plæs i ‖ 'plɑːs-

-plast plæst — **chloroplast** 'klɔːr əʊ
plæst ‖ -ə- 'kloʊr-

plast|er 'plɑːst |ə §'plæst- ‖ 'plæst |ᵊr ~**ered**
əd ‖ ᵊrd ~**ering** ᵊr‿ɪŋ ~**ers** əz ‖ ᵊrz
‚plaster 'cast, '•• •; ‚plaster of 'Paris

plasterboard 'plɑːst ə bɔːd §'plæst-
‖ 'plæst ᵊr bɔːrd -boʊrd

plasterer 'plɑːst ər‿ə §'plæst- ‖ 'plæst ᵊr ᵊr
~**s** z

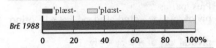

plastic 'plæst ɪk 'plɑːst- —*BrE 1988 poll panel
preference* 'plæst- 92% *(southerners 94%)*,
'plɑːst- 9% *(southerners 6%). In AmE always*
'plæst-. ~**s** s
‚plastic 'art; ‚plastic 'bullet; ‚plastic
ex'plosive; ‚plastic 'surgeon; ‚plastic
'surgery

-plastic 'plæst ɪk — **protoplastic** ‚prəʊt əʊ
'plast ɪk ◂ ‖ ‚proʊt̬ ə-

plasticine, P~ *tdmk* 'plæst ə siːn 'plɑːst-, -ɪ-

plasticity plæ 'stɪs ət i plɑː:-, -ɪt- ‖ -ət̬ i

plasticis... —*see* **plasticiz...**

plasticization ‚plæst ɪs aɪ 'zeɪʃ ᵊn ‚•əs-, -ɪ'•-
‖ -əs ə-

plasticiz|e 'plæst ɪ saɪz -ə- ~**ed** d ~**er/s** ə/
z ‖ ᵊr/z ~**es** ɪz əz ~**ing** ɪŋ

plastid 'plæst ɪd §-əd ~**s** z

plastron 'plæs trən ~**s** z

P

-plasty ˌplæst i — rhinoplasty 'raɪn əʊ
ˌplæst i ‖ -oʊ-
plat plæt plats plæts platted 'plæt ɪd -əd
‖ 'plæt̬ əd platting 'plæt ɪŋ ‖ ' plæt̬ ɪŋ
Plata 'plɑːt ə ‖ 'plɑːt̬ ə —Sp ['pla ta]
Plataea plə 'tiːˌə plæ-
plat du jour ˌplɑː duː 'ʒʊə -djuː-, -də-
‖ -də 'ʒʊᵊr —Fr [pla dy ʒuːʁ] plats du jour
 same pronunciation
plate, Plate pleɪt plated 'pleɪt ɪd -əd
‖ 'pleɪt̬ əd plates pleɪts plating
'pleɪt ɪŋ ‖ 'pleɪt̬ ɪŋ
 ˌplate 'glass◄; 'plate rack; ˌplate tec'tonics
plateau 'plæt əʊ plæ 'təʊ, plə- ‖ plæ 'toʊ ~s,
~x z
plateful 'pleɪt fʊl ~s z
plate-glass ˌpleɪt 'glɑːs ◄ §-'glæs ‖ -'glæs ◄
 ˌplate-glass 'window
platelayer 'pleɪt ˌleɪ ə ‖ -ᵊr ~s z
platelet 'pleɪt lət -lɪt ~s s
platen 'plæt ᵊn ~s z
plater, P~ 'pleɪt ə ‖ 'pleɪt̬ ᵊr ~s z
platform 'plæt fɔːm ‖ -fɔːrm ~s z
Plath plæθ
Platignum tdmk plæ 'tɪg nəm plə-
platino- comb. form
 with stress-neutral suffix ˌplæt ɪn əʊ -ən-
 ‖ -ən oʊ — platinocyanic ˌplæt ɪn əʊ
 saɪ 'æn ɪk ◄ ˌ•ən- ‖ ˌ•ən oʊ-
platinum 'plæt ɪn əm -ᵊn_ ‖ -ᵊn_əm
 ˌplatinum 'blonde
platitude 'plæt ɪ tjuːd -ə-, →§-tʃuːd
 ‖ 'plæt̬ ə tuːd -tjuːd ~s z
platitudinis|e, platitudiniz|e
 ˌplæt ɪ 'tjuːd ɪ naɪz ˌ•ə-, →§-'tʃuːd-, -ᵊn aɪz
 ‖ ˌplæt̬ ə 'tuːd ᵊn aɪz -'tjuːd- ~ed d ~es ɪz
 əz ~ing ɪŋ
platitudinous ˌplæt ɪ 'tjuːd ɪn əs ◄ ˌ•ə-,
 →§-'tʃuːd-, -ᵊn_əs ‖ ˌplæt̬ ə 'tuːd ᵊn_əs ◄
 -'tjuːd- ~ly li
Plato 'pleɪt əʊ ‖ 'pleɪt̬ oʊ
platonic, P~ plə 'tɒn ɪk ‖ -'tɑːn ɪk ~ally ᵊl_i
Platonism 'pleɪt ə ˌnɪz əm -ᵊn ˌɪz-
 ‖ 'pleɪt̬ ᵊn ˌɪz əm
Platonist 'pleɪt ᵊn ɪst §-əst ‖ -ᵊn- ~s s
platoon plə 'tuːn ~s z
Platt plæt
Plattdeutsch 'plæt dɔɪtʃ ‖ 'plɑːt- —Ger
 ['plat dɔytʃ]
Platte plæt
platter 'plæt ə ‖ 'plæt̬ ᵊr ~s z
Platting 'plæt ɪŋ ‖ 'plæt̬ ɪŋ
plat|y 'kind of fish' 'plæt |i ‖ 'plæt̬ |i ~ies, ~ys iz
platyhelminth ˌplæt i 'helm ɪntθ ‖ ˌplæt̬ i- ~s s
platykurtic ˌplæt i 'kɜːt ɪk ◄ ‖ ˌplæt̬ i 'kɜːt̬ ɪk ◄
platypus 'plæt ɪp əs -əp-; -ɪ pʊs ‖ 'plæt̬- ~es ɪz
 əz
platyrrhine 'plæt ɪ raɪn -ə- ‖ 'plæt̬-
plaudit 'plɔːd ɪt §-ət ‖ 'plɑːd- ~s s
plausibility ˌplɔːz ə 'bɪl ət i ˌ•ɪ-, -ɪt i ‖ -ət̬ i
 ˌplɑːz-
plausib|le 'plɔːz əb |ᵊl -ɪb- ‖ 'plɑːz- ~leness
 ᵊl nəs -nɪs ~ly li

Plautus 'plɔːt əs ‖ 'plɔːt̬ əs 'plɑːt̬-
Plaxtol 'plækst ᵊl
play pleɪ played pleɪd playing 'pleɪ ɪŋ plays
 pleɪz
 'play dough; 'playing card; 'playing field
playable 'pleɪ əb ᵊl
play-act 'pleɪ ækt ~ed ɪd əd ~ing ɪŋ ~or/s
 ə/z ‖ ᵊr/z ~s s
playback 'pleɪ bæk ~s s
playbill 'pleɪ bɪl ~s z
playboy 'pleɪ bɔɪ ~s z
Play-Doh tdmk 'pleɪ dəʊ ‖ -doʊ
played-out ˌpleɪd 'aʊt ◄
player, P~ 'pleɪ ə ‖ -ᵊr ~s, ~'s z
 ˌplayer pi'ano
Playfair 'pleɪ feə ‖ -fer -fær
playfellow 'pleɪ ˌfel əʊ ‖ -oʊ ~s z
Playford 'pleɪ fəd ‖ -fᵊrd
playful 'pleɪf ᵊl 'pleɪ fʊl ~ly _i ~ness nəs nɪs
playgoer 'pleɪ ˌgəʊ ə ‖ -ˌgoʊ ᵊr ~s z
playground 'pleɪ graʊnd ~s z
playgroup 'pleɪ gruːp ~s s
play|house 'pleɪ |haʊs ~houses haʊz ɪz -əz
playlet 'pleɪ lət -lɪt ~s s
playlist 'pleɪ lɪst ~s s
playmate 'pleɪ meɪt ~s s
play-off 'pleɪ ɒf -ɔːf ‖ -ɔːf -ɑːf ~s s
playpen 'pleɪ pen ~s z
playroom 'pleɪ ruːm -rʊm ~s z
playschool 'pleɪ skuːl ~s z
PlayStation tdmk 'pleɪ ˌsteɪʃ ᵊn
playsuit 'pleɪ suːt -sjuːt ~s s
Playtex tdmk 'pleɪ teks
plaything 'pleɪ θɪŋ ~s z
playtime 'pleɪ taɪm ~s z
playwright 'pleɪ raɪt ~s s
plaza, Plaza 'plɑːz ə ‖ 'plæz- —Sp ['pla θa,
 -sa] ~s z
plc ˌpiː el 'siː
plea pliː pleas pliːz (= please)
 'plea ˌbargaining
pleach pliːtʃ pleached pliːtʃt pleaches
 'pliːtʃ ɪz -əz pleaching 'pliːtʃ ɪŋ
plead pliːd pleaded 'pliːd ɪd -əd pleading
 'pliːd ɪŋ pleads pliːdz pled pled
pleader 'pliːd ə ‖ -ᵊr ~s z
pleading 'pliːd ɪŋ ~ly li ~s z
 w,
pleasanc|e, P~ 'plez ᵊnts ~es ɪz əz
pleas|ant 'plez| ᵊnt ~anter ᵊnt ə ‖ ᵊnt̬ ᵊr
 ~antest ᵊnt ɪst -əst ‖ ᵊnt̬ əst
pleasant|ly 'plez ᵊnt| li ~ness nəs nɪs
pleasantr|y 'plez ᵊntr |i ~ies iz
please pliːz pleased pliːzd pleases 'pliːz ɪz
 -əz pleasing 'pliːz ɪŋ
Pleasence 'plez ᵊnts
pleasing 'pliːz ɪŋ ~ly li
pleasurab|le 'pleʒ ᵊr_əb |ᵊl ~leness ᵊl nəs -nɪs
 ~ly li
pleas|ure 'pleʒ ə ‖ -|ᵊr 'pleɪʒ- ~ured əd ‖ ᵊrd
 ~ures əz ‖ ᵊrz ~uring ᵊr_ɪŋ
 'pleasure boat; 'pleasure trip

pleat pli:t **pleated** 'pli:t ɪd -əd ‖ 'pli:t̬ əd
  pleating 'pli:t ɪŋ ‖ 'pli:t̬ ɪŋ **pleats** pli:ts
pleb pleb **plebs** plebz
plebby 'pleb i
plebe pli:b **plebes** pli:bz
plebeian plə 'bi:‿ən pli- ~s z
plebiscite 'pleb ɪ saɪt -ə-; -ɪs ɪt, -əs-, -§ət ~s s
plebs plebz
plec|tron 'plek |trən ‖ -|trɑ:n ~**tra** trə
  ~**trum/s** trəm/z
pled pled
pledge pledʒ **pledged** pledʒd **pledges**
  'pledʒ ɪz -əz **pledging** 'pledʒ ɪŋ
pledgee ˌpledʒ 'i: ~s z
pledger, P~ 'pledʒ ə ‖ -ər ~s z
pledget 'pledʒ ɪt §-ət ~s s
pledgor ˌpledʒ 'ɔ: ‖ -'ɔ:r ~s z
-plegia 'pli:dʒ ə 'pli:dʒ i‿ə — **paraplegia**
  ˌpær ə 'pli:dʒ ə -'•i‿ə ‖ ˌper-
-plegic 'pli:dʒ ɪk — **quadriplegic**
  ˌkwɒdr ɪ 'pli:dʒ ɪk ◂ -ə- ‖ ˌkwɑ:dr-
Pleiad, p~ 'plaɪ‿əd ‖ 'pli: əd 'pleɪ-, -æd ~s z
  —Fr Pléiade [ple jad]
Pleiades 'plaɪ‿ə di:z ‖ 'pli:- 'pleɪ-
plein-air ˌpleɪn 'eə ◂ ‖ -'eər ◂ -'æər —Fr
  [ple nɛːʁ]
pleistocene, P~ 'plaɪst əʊ si:n ‖ -ə-
plenar|y 'pli:n ər ‖i 'plen- ~**ies** iz ~**ily** əl i ɪ li
plenipotentiar|y ˌplen ɪ pə 'tenʧ ‿ər ‿li ◂, •ə-,
  -pəʊ'••-, -'•i‿ər ‖i -'tenʧ i er ‖i -'tenʧ ‿i ər ‖i ~**ies** iz
plenitude 'plen ɪ tju:d -ə-, →§-tʃu:d ‖ -ə tu:d
  -tju:d ~s z
plenteous 'plent i‿əs ‖ 'plenʧ- ~**ly** li ~**ness**
  nəs nɪs
plentiful 'plent ɪf əl -əf-, -ʊl ‖ 'plenʧ- ~**ly** ‿i
  ~**ness** nəs nɪs
plenty 'plent i ‖ 'plenʧ i —A casual-speech form
  'plen i is also heard in BrE
plenum 'pli:n əm 'plen-, 'pleɪn- ~s z
pleonasm 'pli:‿ə ˌnæz əm ~s z
pleonastic ˌpli:‿ə 'næst ɪk ◂ ~**ally** əl‿i
plesiosaur 'pli:s i‿ə sɔ: 'pli:z- ‖ 'pli:z i‿ə sɔ:r
  ~s z
plesiosaur|us ˌpli:s i‿ə 'sɔ:r |əs ‖ ˌpli:z- ~**i** aɪ
Plessey 'ples i
plethora 'pleθ ər ə ple 'θɔ:r ə, plə-, plɪ-
plethoric ple 'θɒr ɪk plə-, plɪ- ‖ -'θɔ:r ɪk -'θɑːr-
  ~**ally** əl‿i
plethysmograph plə 'θɪz məʊ grɑːf plɪ-, ple-,
  -'θɪs-, -græf ‖ -ə græf ~s s
pleur|a 'plʊər ə 'plɔ:r- ‖ 'plʊr ə ~**ae** i: ~**al** əl
  (= plural)
pleurisy 'plʊər əs i 'plɔːr-, -ɪs- ‖ 'plʊr-
pleuritic plʊə 'rɪt ɪk ‖ -'rɪt̬ ɪk
pleuropneumonia ˌplʊər əʊ nju 'məʊn i‿ə
  §-nu'••- ‖ ˌplʊr oʊ nu 'moʊn- -nju'•- ~**like**
  laɪk
Plexiglas, p~, plexiglass tdmk 'pleks i glɑːs
  §-glæs ‖ -glæs
plexor 'pleks ə ‖ -ər ~s z
plexus 'pleks əs ~**es** ɪz əz
Pleydell (i) 'pled əl, (ii) pleɪ 'del
pliability ˌplaɪ‿ə 'bɪl ət i -ɪt i ‖ -ət̬ i

pliab|le 'plaɪ‿əb |əl ~**leness** əl nəs -nɪs ~**ly** li
pliancy 'plaɪ‿ən̩ts i
pliant 'plaɪ‿ənt ~**ly** li ~**ness** nəs nɪs
plica 'plaɪk ə **plicae** 'plaɪs i: 'plaɪk-
plié 'pli: eɪ ‖ pli: 'eɪ —Fr [pli e] ~s z
plie... —see **ply**
pliers 'plaɪ‿əz ‖ 'plaɪ‿ərz
plight plaɪt **plighted** 'plaɪt ɪd -əd ‖ 'plaɪt̬ əd
  plighting 'plaɪt ɪŋ ‖ 'plaɪt̬ ɪŋ **plights** plaɪts
plimsole, plimsoll, P~ 'plɪm's əl
  'plɪm səʊl ‖ -soʊl ~s z
  'Plimsoll line, 'Plimsoll mark
pling plɪŋ **plings** plɪŋz
plink plɪŋk **plinked** plɪŋkt **plinking** 'plɪŋk ɪŋ
  plinks plɪŋks
Plinlimmon plɪn 'lɪm ən
plinth plɪntθ **plinths** plɪntθs
Pliny 'plɪn i
pliocene, P~ 'plaɪ əʊ si:n ‖ -ə-
plip plɪp
plisse, plissé 'pli:s eɪ 'plɪs- ‖ plɪ 'seɪ
PLO ˌpi: el 'əʊ ‖ -'oʊ
plod plɒd ‖ plɑ:d **plodded** 'plɒd ɪd -əd
  ‖ 'plɑ:d əd **plodding** 'plɒd ɪŋ ‖ 'plɑ:d ɪŋ
  plods plɒdz ‖ plɑ:dz
Ploesti, Ploiesti plɔɪ 'eʃt i —Romanian Ploieşti
  [plo 'jeʃti]
Plomer family name (i) 'pləʊm ə ‖ 'ploʊm ər, (ii)
  'plu:m ə ‖ -ər —The writer William P~
  inherited the pronunciation (i), but chose to
  change it to (ii).
Plomley 'plʌm li
plonk plɒŋk ‖ plɑ:ŋk **plonked** plɒŋkt
  plonking/ly 'plɒŋk ɪŋ /li ‖ 'plɑ:ŋk ɪŋ /li
  plonks plɒŋks ‖ plɑ:ŋks
plonker 'plɒŋk ə ‖ 'plɑ:ŋk ər ~s z
plop plɒp ‖ plɑ:p **plopped** plɒpt ‖ plɑ:pt
  plopping 'plɒp ɪŋ ‖ 'plɑ:p ɪŋ **plops**
  plɒps ‖ plɑ:ps
plosion 'pləʊʒ ən ‖ 'ploʊʒ ən ~s z
plosive 'pləʊs ɪv 'pləʊz- ‖ 'ploʊs- 'ploʊz- ~s
  z
plot plɒt ‖ plɑ:t **plots** plɒts ‖ plɑ:ts **plotted**
  'plɒt ɪd -əd ‖ 'plɑ:t̬ əd **plotting**
  'plɒt ɪŋ ‖ 'plɑ:t̬ ɪŋ
Plotinus pləʊ 'taɪn əs plɒ- ‖ ploʊ-
plotter 'plɒt ə ‖ 'plɑ:t̬ ər ~s z
plough, Plough plaʊ **ploughed** plaʊd
  ploughing 'plaʊ‿ɪŋ **ploughs** plaʊz
ploughboy 'plaʊ bɔɪ ~s z
ploughland 'plaʊ lænd
plough|man 'plaʊ |mən ~**men** mən men
  ˌploughman's 'lunch
ploughshare 'plaʊ ʃeə ‖ -ʃer -ʃær ~s z
Plouviez 'plu:v i eɪ
Plovdiv 'plɒv dɪv ‖ 'plɑ:v- 'ploʊv- —Bulgarian
  ['plov dif]
plover 'plʌv ə ‖ -ər 'ploʊv- ~s z
plow, Plow plaʊ **plowed** plaʊd **plowing**
  'plaʊ‿ɪŋ **plows** plaʊz
plowboy 'plaʊ bɔɪ ~s z
plowland 'plaʊ lænd
plow|man 'plaʊ |mən ~**men** mən men

plowshare 'plaʊ ʃeə ‖ -ʃer -ʃær ~s z
Plowden 'plaʊd ən
Plowright 'plaʊ raɪt
ploy plɔɪ **ploys** plɔɪz
pluck plʌk **plucked** plʌkt **plucking** 'plʌk ɪŋ
plucks plʌks
pluck|y 'plʌk |i ~**ier** i‿ə ‖ i‿ər ~**iest** i‿ɪst i‿əst
~**ily** ɪ li əl i ~**iness** i nəs i nɪs
plug plʌg **plugged** plʌgd **plugging** 'plʌg ɪŋ
plugs plʌgz
plug-compatible ˌplʌg kəm 'pæt əb əl ◄
§ˌkɒm-, -ɪb əl ‖ -'pæt̬- ~**s** z
plughole 'plʌg həʊl →-hɒʊl ‖ -hoʊl ~s z
plug-in 'plʌg ɪn ~**s** z
plug-ug|ly 'plʌg ˌʌg |li ~**lies** liz
plum plʌm **plums** plʌmz
'plum ˌcake; ˌplum 'duff; ˌplum 'pudding;
'plum ˌtree
plumag|e 'plu:m ɪdʒ ~**es** ɪz əz
plumb plʌm (= plum) **plumbed** plʌmd
plumbing 'plʌm ɪŋ **plumbs** plʌmz
'plumb ˌline
plumbago plʌm 'beɪg əʊ ‖ -oʊ ~**s** z
plumber 'plʌm ə ‖ -ər ~**s** z
ˌplumber's 'friend, ˌplumber's 'helper
plumbic 'plʌm bɪk
plumbing 'plʌm ɪŋ
plumbous 'plʌm bəs
plumbum 'plʌm bəm 'plʊm-
plume plu:m **plumed** plu:md **plumes** plu:mz
pluming 'plu:m ɪŋ
Plummer 'plʌm ə ‖ -ər
plumm|et 'plʌm |ɪt §-ət ‖ -|ət ~**eted** ɪt ɪd §ət-,
-əd ‖ ət̬ əd ~**eting** ɪt ɪŋ §ət- ‖ ət̬ ɪŋ ~**ets** ɪts
§əts ‖ əts
plumm|y 'plʌm |i ~**ier** i‿ə ‖ i‿ər ~**iest** i‿ɪst
i‿əst ~**iness** i nəs i nɪs
plumose 'plu:m əʊs plu: 'məʊs ‖ 'plu:m oʊs
plu: 'moʊs
plump plʌmp **plumped** plʌmpt **plumper**
'plʌmp ə ‖ -ər **plumpest** 'plʌmp ɪst -əst
plumping 'plʌmp ɪŋ **plumply** 'plʌmp li
plumpness 'plʌmp nəs -nɪs **plumps** plʌmps
Plumpton 'plʌmpt ən
Plumptre, Plumtre 'plʌmp tri:
Plumstead 'plʌmpst ɪd -ed
plumule 'plu:m ju:l ~**s** z
plunder 'plʌnd ə ‖ -ər ~**ed** d **plundering**
'plʌnd‿ər ɪŋ ~**s** z
plunderer 'plʌnd‿ər ə ‖ -ər ~**s** z
plunderous 'plʌnd ər əs
plunge plʌndʒ **plunged** plʌndʒd **plunges**
'plʌndʒ ɪz -əz **plunging** 'plʌndʒ ɪŋ
plunger 'plʌndʒ ə ‖ -ər ~**s** z
plunk plʌŋk **plunked** plʌŋkt **plunking**
'plʌŋk ɪŋ **plunks** plʌŋks
Plunket, Plunkett 'plʌŋk ɪt §-ət
pluperfect ˌplu: 'pɜːf ɪkt ◄ -ekt, §-əkt ‖ -'pɜˑf-
'•ˌ•• ~**s** s
plural 'plʊər əl 'plɔːr- ‖ 'plʊr əl ~**s** z
pluralis... —see **pluraliz...**
pluralism 'plʊər ə ˌlɪz əm 'plɔːr-, -əl ˌɪz-
‖ 'plʊr-

pluralist 'plʊər əl ɪst 'plɔːr-, §-əst ‖ 'plʊr- ~**s** s
pluralistic ˌplʊər ə 'lɪst ɪk ◄ ˌplɔːr- ‖ ˌplʊr-
~**ally** əl‿i
pluralit|y plʊə 'ræl ət |i ˌplʊə-, ˌplɔː-, -ɪt-
‖ -ət̬ |i ~**ies** iz
pluralization ˌplʊər əl aɪ 'zeɪʃ ən ˌplɔːr-, -ɪ'•-
‖ ˌplʊr əl ə-
pluraliz|e 'plʊər ə laɪz 'plɔːr- ‖ 'plʊr- ~**ed** d
~**es** ɪz əz ~**ing** ɪŋ
pluri- ˌplʊər i ˌplɔːr i ‖ ˌplʊr i — **plurisyllable**
ˌplʊər i 'sɪl əb əl ˌplɔːr- ‖ ˌplʊr-
plus plʌs **pluses, plusses** 'plʌs ɪz -əz
ˌplus 'fours; 'plus sign
plus ça change ˌplu: sɑ: 'ʃɒnʒ ‖ -'ʃɑːnʒ —Fr
[ply sa ʃɑ̃ːʒ]
plush plʌʃ
plush|y 'plʌʃ |i ~**ier** i‿ə ‖ i‿ər ~**iest** i‿ɪst i‿əst
~**ily** ɪ li əl i ~**iness** i nəs i nɪs
Plutarch 'plu:t ɑːk ‖ -ɑːrk
Pluto 'plu:t əʊ ‖ 'plu:t̬ oʊ
plutocrac|y plu: 'tɒk rəs |i ‖ -'tɑːk- ~**ies** iz
plutocrat 'plu:t əʊ kræt ‖ 'plu:t̬ ə- ~**s** s
plutocratic ˌplu:t əʊ
'kræt ɪk ◄ ‖ ˌplu:t̬ ə 'kræt̬ ɪk ◄ ~**ally** əl‿i
Plutonian plu: 'təʊn i‿ən ‖ -'toʊn-
plutonic plu: 'tɒn ɪk ‖ -'tɑːn ɪk
plutonium plu: 'təʊn i‿əm ‖ -'toʊn-
pluvial 'plu:v i‿əl ~**s** z
pluviometer ˌplu:v i 'ɒm ɪt ə -ət ə ‖ -'ɑːm ət̬ ər
~**s** z
pluvious 'plu:v i‿əs
ply plaɪ **plied** plaɪd **plies** plaɪz **plying** 'plaɪ ɪŋ
Plymouth 'plɪm əθ
ˌPlymouth 'Brethren; ˌPlymouth 'Rock
Plynlimon plɪn 'lɪm ən —Welsh Pumlimon
[pɪm 'lɪm ɔn]
plywood 'plaɪ wʊd ~**s** z
PM, pm ˌpi: 'em ◄
PMT ˌpi: em 'ti:
p-n ˌpi: 'en
pneumatic nju 'mæt ɪk §nu- ‖ nu 'mæt̬ ɪk nju-
~**ally** əl‿i ~**s** s
pneuˌmatic 'drill
pneumatophore 'nju:m ət əʊ fɔ: §'nu:m-;
nju 'mæt-, §nu- ‖ nu 'mæt̬ ə fɔːr nju-, -foʊr;
'nu:m ət̬-,'nju:m- ~**s** z
pneumo- comb. form
with stress-neutral suffix ˌnju:m əʊ §ˌnu:m-
‖ ˌnu:m ə ˌnju:m- — **pneumogastric**
ˌnju:m əʊ 'gæs trɪk ◄ §ˌnu:m- ‖ ˌnu:m ə-
ˌnju:m-
with stress-imposing suffix nju 'mɒ+ §nu-
‖ nu 'mɑː+ nju- — **pneumography**
nju 'mɒg rəf i §nu- ‖ nu 'mɑːg- nju-
pneumoconiosis ˌnju:m əʊ ˌkəʊn i 'əʊs ɪs
§ˌnu:m-, §-əs ‖ ˌnu:m oʊ ˌkoʊn i 'oʊs əs
ˌnju:m-
pneumocystis ˌnju:m əʊ 'sɪst ɪs §-əs
‖ ˌnu:m ə- ˌnju:m-
ˌpneumoˌcystis ca'rinii kə 'raɪn i aɪ kæ-,
-'rɪn-
pneumonia nju 'məʊn i‿ə §nu- ‖ nu 'moʊn-
nju-

P

pneumonic nju 'mɒn ɪk §nu- ‖ nu 'maːn ɪk
nju-
pneumothorax ˌnjuːm əʊ 'θɔːr æks §ˌnuːm-
‖ ˌnuːm ə-ˌnjuːm-, -'θoʊr-
PNG ˌpiː en 'dʒiː
Pnom Penh ˌpnɒm 'pen ˌnɒm-, pə ˌnɒm 'pen
‖ ˌpnaːm- ˌnaːm —*Khmer* [phnɔm 'piɲ]
Pnyx pnɪks nɪks
po pəʊ ‖ poʊ
Po *name of river, name of Teletubby* pəʊ ‖ poʊ
—*It* [pɔ]
Po *'polonium'* ˌpiː 'əʊ ‖ -'oʊ
PO ˌpiː 'əʊ ◀ ‖ -'oʊ ◀ ~**s**, ~'**s** z
poach pəʊtʃ ‖ poʊtʃ **poached** pəʊtʃt ‖ poʊtʃt
poaches 'pəʊtʃ ɪz -əz ‖ 'poʊtʃ əz **poaching**
'pəʊtʃ ɪŋ ‖ 'poʊtʃ ɪŋ
poacher 'pəʊtʃ ə ‖ 'poʊtʃ ər ~**s** z
Pobjoy 'pɒb dʒɔɪ ‖ 'paːb-
Pocahontas ˌpɒk ə 'hɒnt əs -æs
‖ ˌpoʊk ə 'haːnt̬ əs
pochard 'pəʊtʃ əd 'pɒtʃ- ‖ 'poʊtʃ ərd ~**s** z
pochette pɒ 'ʃet ‖ poʊ- ~**s** s
pock pɒk ‖ paːk **pocked** pɒkt ‖ paːkt
pock|et 'pɒk |ɪt §-ət ‖ 'paːk |ət ~**eted** ɪt ɪd
§ət-, -əd ‖ ət̬ əd ~**eting** ɪt ɪŋ §ət- ‖ ət̬ ɪŋ
~**ets** ɪts §əts ‖ əts
'**pocket** ˌmoney
pocketable 'pɒk ɪt əb əl §'•ət- ‖ 'paːk ət̬-
pocketbook 'pɒk ɪt bʊk §-ət-, §-buːk ‖ 'paːk-
~**s** s
pocketful 'pɒk ɪt fʊl §-ət- ‖ 'paːk- ~**s** z
pocket-handker|chief ˌpɒk ɪt 'hæŋk ə |tʃɪf
§,•ət-, -tʃəf, -tʃiːf ‖ ˌpaːk ət 'hæŋk ər-
~**chiefs** tʃɪfs tʃəfs, tʃiːfs, tʃiːvz
pocket|knife 'pɒk ɪt |naɪf §-ət- ‖ 'paːk-
~**knives** naɪvz
Pocklington 'pɒk lɪŋ tən ‖ 'paːk-
pockmark 'pɒk maːk ‖ 'paːk maːrk ~**ed** t
~**ing** ɪŋ ~**s** s
poco 'pəʊk əʊ ‖ 'poʊk oʊ —*It* ['pɔ: ko]
Pocock 'pəʊ kɒk ‖ 'poʊ kaːk
pococurante
ˌpəʊk əʊ kjʊə 'rænt i ‖ ˌpoʊk oʊ kʊ 'rænt̬ i
-kjʊ'•-, -'raːnt̬- ~**s** z
pod pɒd ‖ paːd **podded** 'pɒd ɪd -əd ‖ 'paːd əd
podding 'pɒdɪŋ ‖ 'paːd ɪŋ **pods**
pɒdz ‖ paːdz
-pod pɒd ‖ paːd— **arthropod** 'aːθ rəʊ
pɒd ‖ 'aːrθ rə paːd
podagra pɒ 'dæg rə pəʊ-, 'pɒd əg- ‖ pə-
'paːd əg-
poddly 'pɒd li ‖ 'paːd li ~**ies** iz
Podge, podge pɒdʒ ‖ paːdʒ
podgly 'pɒdʒ li ‖ 'paːdʒ li ~**ier** i_ə i_ər ~**iest**
i_ɪst i_əst ~**ily** ɪ li əl i ~**iness** i nəs i nɪs
Podhoretz pɒd 'hɒr ets ‖ paːd 'hɔːr- -'haːr-
podiatric ˌpəʊd i 'ætr ɪk ◀ ˌpɒd- ‖ ˌpoʊd-
podiatr|ist/s pəʊ 'daɪ_ətr| ɪst/s §-əst/s ‖ pə-
poʊ- ~**y** i
podi|um/s 'pəʊd i_|əm/z ‖ 'poʊd- ~**a** ə
-podous *stress-imposing* pəd əs —
gastropodous gæ 'strɒp əd əs ‖ -'straːp-
Podmore 'pɒd mɔː ‖ 'paːd mɔːr -moʊr

podsol ˌpɒd sɒl ‖ 'paːd saːl -sɔːl ~**s** z
Podunk 'pəʊ dʌŋk ‖ 'poʊ-
podzol 'pɒd zɒl ‖ 'paːd zaːl -zɔːl ~**s** z
Poe pəʊ ‖ poʊ
poem 'pəʊ ɪm -əm, -em; △pəʊm ‖ 'poʊ əm ~**s**
z
poes|y 'pəʊ əz li -ɪz-, -ez- ‖ 'poʊ- -əs- ~**ies** iz
poet 'pəʊ ɪt -ət, -et ‖ 'poʊ ət ~**s** s
ˌpoet 'laureate
poetaster ˌpəʊ ɪ 'tæst ə -ə-, -e-, -'teɪst-, '•••
‖ 'poʊ ə tæst ər ~**s** z
poetess ˌpəʊ ɪ 'tes -ə-, -e-; 'pəʊ ɪt ɪs, -ət-, -et-,
-əs, -es ‖ 'poʊ ət̬ əs ~**es** ɪz əz
poetic pəʊ 'et ɪk ‖ poʊ 'et̬ ɪk ~**al** əl ~**ally** əl_i
~**s** s
poˌetic 'justice; poˌetic 'licence
poetry 'pəʊ ətr i -ɪtr- ‖ 'poʊ-
po-faced ˌpəʊ 'feɪst ◀ '•• ‖ ˌpoʊ-
pogey 'pəʊg i ‖ 'poʊg i ~**s** z
pogley, poglie 'pəʊg li ~**eys**, ~**ies** iz
pogge pɒg ‖ paːg **pogges** pɒgz ‖ paːgz
Poggenpohl *tdmk* 'pɒg ən pəʊl →-əm-, →-ŋ-,
→-pɒʊl ‖ 'paːg ən poʊl —*Ger* ['pɔ gən poːl]
pogo 'pəʊg əʊ ‖ 'poʊg oʊ
'**pogo** stick
pogrom 'pɒg rəm -rɒm ‖ 'poʊg rəm pə 'graːm,
-'grʌm ~**s** z
Pogue pəʊg ‖ poʊg **Pogues** pəʊgz ‖ poʊgz
pogly 'pəʊg li ‖ 'poʊg li ~**ies** iz
-poiesis pɔɪ 'iːs ɪs §-əs — **haemopoiesis**
ˌhiːm əʊ pɔɪ 'iːs ɪs §-əs ‖ ,•ə-
-poietic pɔɪ 'et ɪk ‖ pɔɪ 'et̬ ɪk —
haemopoietic ˌhiːm əʊ
pɔɪ 'et ɪk ◀ -ə 'et̬ ɪk ◀
poignancy 'pɔɪn jən|s i -ənt|s-
poignant 'pɔɪn jənt -ənt ~**ly** li
poikilotherm 'pɔɪk ɪl əʊ θɜːm '•əl-; pɔɪ 'kɪl-
‖ -ə θɜːm -oʊ- ~**s** z
poikilothermic ˌpɔɪk ɪl əʊ 'θɜːm ɪk ◀ ,•əl-
‖ -ə 'θɜːm ɪk ◀ -oʊ-
Poindexter 'pɔɪn ˌdekst ə ‖ -ər
Poincaré 'pwæŋ kæ reɪ ,••'• ‖ ˌpwaːŋ kɑː 'reɪ
—*Fr* [pwæ̃ ka ʁe]
poinciana ˌpɔɪn|s i 'ɑːn ə -'æn- ‖ -'æn ə ~**s** z
poinsettia pɔɪn 'set i_ə ‖ -'set̬- ~**s** z
point pɔɪnt **pointed** 'pɔɪnt ɪd -əd ‖ 'pɔɪnt̬ əd
pointing 'pɔɪnt ɪŋ ‖ 'pɔɪnt̬ ɪŋ **points** pɔɪnts
'point ˌduty; ˌpoint of 'order; ˌpoint of
'view
point-blank ˌpɔɪnt 'blæŋk ◀
ˌpoint-blank re'fusal
point-by-point ˌpɔɪnt baɪ 'pɔɪnt ◀
pointed 'pɔɪnt ɪd -əd ‖ 'pɔɪnt̬ əd ~**ly** li ~**ness**
nəs nɪs
pointer 'pɔɪnt ə ‖ 'pɔɪnt̬ ər ~**s** z
pointillism 'pɔɪnt ɪ ˌlɪz əm 'pwænt-, -ə-, -, -iː-,
-ˌjɪz-; -əl ˌɪz- ‖ 'pɔɪnt̬ əl ˌɪz əm 'pwænt̬- —*Fr*
pointillisme [pwɛ̃ ti jism]
pointillist 'pɔɪnt ɪl ɪst 'pwænt-, -i-, -əl-, §-əst
‖ 'pɔɪnt̬ əl- 'pwæn tiː 'jiːst ~**s** s —*Fr*
pointilliste [pwɛ̃ ti jist]
pointless 'pɔɪnt ləs -lɪs ~**ly** li ~**ness** nəs nɪs
Pointon 'pɔɪnt ən ‖ -ən

points|man ˈpɔɪnts |mən **~men** mən men
point-to-point ˌpɔɪnt tə ˈpɔɪnt -tu-
pointy ˈpɔɪnt i ‖ ˈpɔɪnt̬ i
Poirot ˈpwɑːr əʊ ‖ pwɑː ˈroʊ —Fr [pwa ʁo]
poise pɔɪz **poised** pɔɪzd **poises** ˈpɔɪz ɪz -əz
 poising ˈpɔɪz ɪŋ
poison ˈpɔɪz ən **~ed** d **~ing** ɪŋ **~s** z
 ˌpoison ˈgas,·· ·; ˌpoison ˈivy
poisonous ˈpɔɪz ən_əs **~ly** li **~ness** nəs nɪs
poison-pen ˌpɔɪz ən ˈpen→-ᵊm-
 ˌpoison-ˈpen ˌletter
Poisson ˈpwɑːs ɒn ˈpwæs-, ˈpwʌs-, -ɒ̃, -ᵊn
 ‖ pwɑː ˈsoʊn -ˈsɔːn, -ˈsɑːn —Fr [pwa sɔ̃]
 ˌPoisson ˌdistriˈbution · · , · · ˈ · ·
Poitier ˈpwɒt i eɪ ˈpwɑːt-, ˈpɔɪt- ‖ ˈpwɑːt- -jeɪ
Poitiers ˈpwɑːt i eɪ ˈpwɒt- ‖ ˌpwɑːt̬ i ˈeɪ —Fr
 [pwa tje]
poke pəʊk ‖ poʊk **poked** pəʊkt ‖ poʊkt
 pokes pəʊks ‖ poʊks **poking**
 ˈpəʊk ɪŋ ‖ ˈpoʊk ɪŋ
poker ˈpəʊk ə ‖ ˈpoʊk ᵊr **~s** z
 ˈpoker face
poker-faced ˈpəʊk ə feɪst ˌ··ˈ·◄ ‖ ˈpoʊk ᵊr-
pokerwork ˈpəʊk ə wɜːk ‖ ˈpoʊk ᵊr wɜːk
pokeweed ˈpəʊk wiːd ‖ ˈpoʊk-
pok|ey, pok|ie, pok|y ˈpəʊk |i ‖ ˈpoʊk |i **~eys**
 iz **~ier** i_ə ‖ i_ᵊr **~ies** iz **~iest** i_ɪst i_əst
 ~ily i li əl i **~iness** i nəs i nɪs
pol pɒl ‖ pɑːl **pols** pɒlz ‖ pɑːlz
 ˌPol ˈPot
Polabian pəʊ ˈleɪb i_ən -ˈlɑːb- ‖ poʊ-
Polack, Polak ˈpəʊl æk -ək ‖ ˈpoʊl- **~s** s
Poland ˈpəʊl ənd ‖ ˈpoʊl-
Polanski pə ˈlænˡsk i pɒ- ‖ poʊ-
polar ˈpəʊl ə ‖ ˈpoʊl ᵊr
 ˌpolar ˈbear ‖ ˈ · · ·
Polari pəʊ ˈlɑːr i ‖ pə-
polarimeter ˌpəʊl ə ˈrɪm ɪt ə -ət ə
 ‖ ˌpoʊl ə ˈrɪm ət̬ ᵊr **~s** z
Polaris pəʊ ˈlɑːr ɪs -ˈlær-, -ˈleər-, §-əs
 ‖ pə ˈlær əs poʊ-, -ˈler-, -ˈlɑːr-
polaris... —see **polariz...**
polariscope pəʊ ˈlær ɪ skəʊp -ˈ·ə-
 ‖ poʊ ˈlær ə skoʊp pə-, -ˈler- **~s** s
polarit|y pəʊ ˈlær ət i -ɪt- ‖ poʊ ˈlær ət̬ i pə-,
 -ˈler- **~ies** iz
polarization ˌpəʊl ər aɪ ˈzeɪʃ ᵊn -ɪˈ·- ‖ ˌpoʊl
 ᵊr ə- **~s** z
polariz|e ˈpəʊl ə raɪz ‖ ˈpoʊl- **~ed** d **~es** ɪz əz
 ~ing ɪŋ
Polaroid tdmk ˈpəʊl ə rɔɪd ‖ ˈpoʊl- **~s** z
polder ˈpəʊld ə→ˈpɒʊld-, ˈpɒld- ‖ ˈpoʊld ᵊr
 ~s z
Poldhu ₍ₒ₎pɒl ˈdjuː →§-ˈdʒuː ‖ ₍ₒ₎pɑːl ˈduː -ˈdjuː
pole pəʊl→pɒʊl ‖ poʊl **poled** pəʊld→pɒʊld
 ‖ poʊld **poles** pəʊlz→pɒʊlz ‖ poʊlz **poling**
 ˈpəʊl ɪŋ →ˈpɒʊl- ‖ ˈpoʊl ɪŋ
 ˈpole poˌsition; ˈpole star; ˈpole vault
Pole ˈPolish person' pəʊl→pɒʊl ‖ poʊl **Poles**
 pəʊlz→pɒʊlz ‖ poʊlz
Pole surname (i) pəʊl→pɒʊl ‖ poʊl, (ii) puːl
poleax, poleax|e ˈpəʊl æks→ˈpɒʊl- ‖ ˈpoʊl-
 ~ed t **~es** ɪz əz **~ing** ɪŋ

polecat ˈpəʊl kæt →ˈpɒʊl- ‖ ˈpoʊl- **~s** s
Polegate ˈpəʊl geɪt →ˈpɒʊl- ‖ ˈpoʊl-
polemarch ˈpɒl ɪ mɑːk -ə- ‖ ˈpɑːl ə mɑːrk **~s**
 s
polemic pə ˈlem ɪk pəʊ-, pɒ- **~al** ᵊl **~ally** ᵊl_i
 ~s s
polemicist pə ˈlem ɪs ɪst -əs-, §-əst **~s** s
polenta pəʊ ˈlent ə ‖ poʊ ˈlent̬ ə pə-, -ˈlent ɑː
Polesden ˈpəʊlz dən→ˈpɒʊlz- ‖ ˈpoʊlz-
 ˌPolesden ˈLacey
Polesworth ˈpəʊlz wəθ→ˈpɒʊlz-, -wɜːθ
 ‖ ˈpoʊlz wᵊrθ
pole-vault ˈpəʊl vɔːlt →ˈpɒʊl-, -vɒlt ‖ ˈpoʊl-
 -vɑːlt **~ed** ɪd əd **~er/s** ə/z ‖ ᵊr/z **~ing** ɪŋ **~s**
 s
Poliakoff ˌpɒl i ˈɑːk ɒf ‖ ˌpɑːl i ˈɑːk ɔːf -ɑːf
polic|e pə ˈliːs pʊ-; pliːs; §ˈpəʊl iːs **~ed** t **~es**
 ɪz əz **~ing** ɪŋ
 poˌlice ˈconstable◄; poˈlice dog; poˈlice
 force; poˈlice ˌofficer; poˈlice state; poˈlice
 ˌstation
police|man pə ˈliːs |mən pʊ-; pliːs |mən;
 §ˈpəʊl iːs- **~men** mən men **~woman**
 ˌwʊm ən **~women** ˌwɪm ɪn §-ən
polic|y ˈpɒl əs i -ɪs- ‖ ˈpɑːl- **~ies** iz
policyholder ˈpɒl əs i ˌhəʊld ə ˈ·ɪs-, →-ˌhɒʊld-
 ‖ ˈpɑːl əs i ˌhoʊld ᵊr **~s** z
polio ˈpəʊl i əʊ ‖ ˈpoʊl i oʊ
poliomyelitis ˌpəʊl i_əʊ ˌmaɪ_ə ˈlaɪt ɪs -ɪˈ·-,
 §-əs ‖ ˌpoʊl i oʊ ˌmaɪ ə ˈlaɪt̬ əs
polis ˈpɒl ɪs §-əs ‖ ˈpɑːl əs ˈpoʊl-
-polis stress-imposing pəl ɪs§-əs— **Annapolis**
 ə ˈnæp ᵊl ɪs §-əs
Polisario ˌpɒl ɪ ˈsɑːr i əʊ ,·ˈ·ə-
 ‖ ˌpoʊl ə ˈsɑːr i oʊ ˌpɑːl-
polish v, n ˈpɒl ɪʃ ‖ ˈpɑːl ɪʃ **~ed** t **~es** ɪz əz
 ~ing ɪŋ
Polish adj ˈpəʊl ɪʃ ‖ ˈpoʊl ɪʃ
politburo, P~ ˈpɒl ɪt ˌbjʊər əʊ pə ˈliːt-, pə ˈlɪt-,
 -ˌbjɔːr-, ˈ··bjʊᵊ ˌrəʊ ‖ ˈpɑːl ət ˌbjʊr oʊ
po|lite pə ˈlaɪt **~litely** ˈlaɪt li **~liteness**
 ˈlaɪt nəs -nɪs **~liter** ˈlaɪt ə ‖ ˈlaɪt̬ ᵊr **~litest**
 ˈlaɪt ɪst -əst ‖ ˈlaɪt̬ əst
politesse ˌpɒl ɪ ˈtes -ə- ‖ ˌpɑːl-
politic ˈpɒl ə tɪk -ɪ- ‖ ˈpɑːl- **~ly** li **~s** s
political pə ˈlɪt ɪk ᵊl ‖ -ˈlɪt̬- **~ly** _i
 poˌlitical aˈsylum; poˌlitical geˈography;
 poˌlitical ˈprisoner; poˌlitical ˈscience
politicalis... —see **politicaliz...**
politicalization pə ˌlɪt ɪk ᵊl aɪ ˈzeɪʃ ᵊn -ɪˈ·-
 ‖ -ˌlɪt̬ ɪk ᵊl ə-
politicaliz|e pə ˈlɪt ɪk ə laɪz -ᵊl aɪz ‖ -ˈlɪt̬- **~ed**
 d **~es** ɪz əz **~ing** ɪŋ
politician ˌpɒl ə ˈtɪʃ ᵊn -ɪ- ‖ ˌpɑːl- **~s** z
politicis... —see **politiciz...**
politicization pə ˌlɪt ɪ saɪ ˈzeɪʃ ᵊn -ə-, ˌ·ə-, -sɪˈ·-
 ‖ -ˌlɪt̬ əs ə-
politiciz|e pə ˈlɪt ɪ saɪz -ə- ‖ -ˈlɪt̬- **~ed** d **~es**
 ɪz əz **~ing** ɪŋ
politick|ing ˈpɒl ə tɪk |ɪŋ ˈ·ɪ- ‖ ˈpɑːl- **~ed** t
politico pə ˈlɪt ɪ kəʊ ‖ -ˈlɪt̬ ɪ koʊ **~s** z
politico- comb. form pə ˌlɪt ɪ kəʊ ‖ -ˌlɪt̬ ɪ koʊ—

politicoeconomic pə ˌlɪt ɪk əʊ ˌiːk ə 'nɒm ɪk
-ˌek- ‖ pə ˌlɪt̬ ɪ koʊ ˌek ə 'naːm ɪk
politics 'pɒl ə tɪks -ɪ- ‖ 'paːl-
polit|y 'pɒl ət li -ɪt- ‖ 'paːl ət̬ li **~ies** iz
Polk pəʊk ‖ poʊk
polk|a 'pɒlk |ə 'pəʊlk- ‖ 'poʊlk |ə 'poʊk- —*In*
polka dot, *AmE usually* 'poʊk ə **~aed** əd
~aing əʳ ɪŋ ‖ ə ɪŋ **~as** əz
'polka dot
Polkinghorn, Polkinghorne
'pɒlk ɪŋ hɔːn ‖ 'paːlk ɪŋ hɔːrn
poll *n, v* pəʊl→pɒʊl, §pɒl ‖ poʊl —*but in the*
obsolete senses 'parrot', 'student taking pass
degree' was pɒl ‖ paːl **polled** pəʊld→pɒʊld
‖ poʊld **polling** 'pəʊl ɪŋ→'pɒʊl- ‖ 'poʊl ɪŋ
polls pəʊlz→pɒʊlz ‖ poʊlz
'polling booth; 'polling day; 'polling
ˌstation; 'poll tax
Poll *name* pɒl ‖ paːl
pollack 'pɒl ək ‖ 'paːl- **~s** s
pollan 'pɒl ən ‖ 'paːl- **~s** z
pollard 'pɒl əd -aːd ‖ -ᵊrd **~ed** ɪd əd **~ing** ɪŋ
~s z
Pollard 'pɒl aːd -əd ‖ -aːrd -ᵊrd
pollen, P~ 'pɒl ən ‖ 'paːl-
'pollen count
polli|nate 'pɒl ə |neɪt -ɪ- ‖ 'paːl- **~nated**
neɪt ɪd -əd ‖ neɪt̬ əd **~nates** neɪts **~nating**
neɪt ɪŋ ‖ neɪt̬ ɪŋ
pollination ˌpɒl ə 'neɪʃ ᵊn -ɪ- ‖ ˌpaːl- **~s** z
Pollit, Pollitt 'pɒl ɪt -ət ‖ 'paːl-
polliwog 'pɒl i wɒg ‖ 'paːl i waːg -wɔːg **~s** z
Pollock, p~, Pollok 'pɒl ək ‖ 'paːl- **~s** s
Pollokshields ˌpɒl ək 'ʃiːᵊldz ‖ ˌpaːl-
pollster 'pəʊl stə→'pɒʊl-, §'pɒl- ‖ 'poʊl stᵊr
~s z
pollutant pə 'luːt ᵊnt -'ljuːt- **~s** s
pol|lute pə |'luːt -'ljuːt **~luted** 'luːt ɪd 'ljuːt-,
-əd ‖ 'luːt̬ əd **~lutes** 'luːts 'ljuːts **~luting**
'luːt ɪŋ 'ljuːt- ‖ 'luːt̬ ɪŋ
pollution pə 'luːʃ ᵊn -'ljuːʃ- **~s** z
Pollux 'pɒl əks ‖ 'paːl-
Polly 'pɒl i ‖ 'paːl i
Pollyanna ˌpɒl i 'æn ə ‖ ˌpaːl- **~s**, **~'s** z
Pollyanna|ish
ˌpɒl i 'æn əʳ| ɪʃ ◀ ‖ ˌpaːl i 'æn əl ɪʃ ◀ **~ism** ˌɪz
əm
Polmont 'pəʊl mɒnt→'pɒʊl- ‖ 'poʊl maːnt
—*but in Scotland, locally* -mənt
polo, Polo 'pəʊl əʊ ‖ 'poʊl oʊ
'polo neck
polonais|e ˌpɒl ə 'neɪz ‖ ˌpaːl-, ˌpoʊl- **~es** ɪz
əz
polonium pə 'ləʊn i̯ əm ‖ -'loʊn-
Polonius pə 'ləʊn i̯ əs ‖ -'loʊn-
polony pə 'ləʊn i ‖ -'loʊn i
Polperro pɒl 'per əʊ ‖ paːl 'per oʊ
Polson 'pəʊl sən→'pɒʊl- ‖ 'poʊl-
poltergeist 'pɒlt ə gaɪst 'pəʊlt-, △-dʒaɪst
‖ 'poʊlt ᵊr- **~s** s
poltroon pɒl 'truːn ‖ paːl- **~s** z
poltroonery pɒl 'truːn ᵊr i ‖ paːl-
Polwarth 'pɒl wəθ ‖ 'paːl wᵊrθ

poly 'pɒl i ‖ 'paːl i **~s** z
'poly bag
poly- *comb. form*
with stress-neutral suffix ˌpɒl i ‖ ˌpaːl i —*but in*
certain more familiar words, before a
consonant, also ˌpɒl ə ‖ ˌpaːl ə —
polygenesis ˌpɒl i 'dʒen əs ɪs -ɪs ɪs, §-əs
‖ ˌpaːl-
with stress-imposing suffix pə 'lɪ+ pɒ- —
polyphagous pə 'lɪf əg əs pɒ-
polyamide ˌpɒl i 'æm aɪd -ɪd, §-əd ‖ ˌpaːl- **~s** z
polyandrous ˌpɒl i 'ændr əs ◀ ‖ ˌpaːl-
polyandry ˌpɒl i 'ændr i '••,•• ‖ ˌpaːl-
polyanth|a ˌpɒl i 'ænᵗθ |ə ‖ ˌpaːl- **~as** əz
~us/es əs /ɪz -əz
Polybius pə 'lɪb i̯ əs pɒ-
polycarbonate ˌpɒl i 'kaːb ə neɪt -nət, -nɪt
‖ ˌpaːl i 'kaːrb- **~s** s
Polycarp 'pɒl i kaːp ‖ 'paːl i kaːrp
Polycell *tdmk* 'pɒl i sel ‖ 'paːl-
polychaete 'pɒl i kiːt ‖ 'paːl- **~s** s
polychlorinated ˌpɒl i 'klɔːr ɪ neɪt ɪd ◀-'•ə-,
-əd ‖ ˌpaːl i 'klɔːr ə neɪt̬ əd ◀-'kloʊr-
polychrom|e 'pɒl i krəʊm ‖ 'paːl i kroʊm **~y** i
polyclinic ˌpɒl i 'klɪn ɪk '••,•• ‖ ˌpaːl-
polycotton ˌpɒl i 'kɒt ᵊn ◀ ‖ ˌpaːl i 'kaːt ᵊn ◀
Polycrates pə 'lɪk rə tiːz pɒ-
polydactyl ˌpɒl i 'dækt ɪl ◀-ᵊl ‖ ˌpaːl-
polyester ˌpɒl i 'est ə ◀'••,•• ‖ 'paːl i ˌest ᵊr
~s z
polyethylene ˌpɒl i 'eθ ə liːn ◀-'•ɪ-, -ᵊl iːn
‖ ˌpaːl-
Polyfilla *tdmk* 'pɒl i ˌfɪl ə ‖ 'paːl-
polygamist pə 'lɪg əm ɪst pɒ-, §-əst **~s** s
polygamous pə 'lɪg əm əs pɒ- **~ly** li
polygamy pə 'lɪg əm i pɒ-
polyglot 'pɒl i glɒt ‖ 'paːl i glaːt **~s** s
polygon 'pɒl ɪg ᵊn -əg-; -i gɒn ‖ 'paːl i gaːn
~s z
polygonal pə 'lɪg ᵊn ᵊl pɒ- **~ly** i
polygonum pə 'lɪg ᵊn əm pɒ-
polygraph 'pɒl i graːf -græf ‖ 'paːl i græf **~s** s
Polygrip *tdmk* 'pɒl i grɪp ‖ 'paːl-
polygynous pə 'lɪdʒ ᵊn əs pɒ-, -ɪn-
polygyny pə 'lɪdʒ ᵊn i pɒ-, -ɪn-
polyhedr|on ˌpɒl i 'hiːdr |ən -'hedr- ‖ ˌpaːl-
~a ə **~al** əl **~ons** ᵊnz
Polyhymnia ˌpɒl i 'hɪm ni̯ ə ‖ ˌpaːl-
polylectal ˌpɒl i 'lekt ᵊl ◀ ‖ ˌpaːl-
polymath 'pɒl i mæθ ‖ 'paːl- **~s** s
polymer 'pɒl ɪm ə-əm- ‖ 'paːl əm ᵊr **~s** z
polymeras|e 'pɒl ɪm ə reɪz '•əm-; pə 'lɪm-,
-reɪs ‖ 'paːl əm-
polymeric ˌpɒl i 'mer ɪk ◀ ‖ ˌpaːl ə-
polymeris... —*see* **polymeriz...**
polimerism pə 'lɪm ə ˌrɪz əm pɒ-; 'pɒl ɪm-,
'•əm- ‖ 'paːl əm-
polymerization ˌpɒl ɪm ᵊr aɪ 'zeɪʃ ᵊn,-'•əm-,
-ɪ'•; pə ˌlɪm- ‖ ˌpaːl əm ər ə- pə ˌlɪm-
polymeriz|e 'pɒl ɪm ə raɪz '•əm-; pə 'lɪm-
‖ 'paːl- **~ed** d **~es** ɪz əz **~ing** ɪŋ
polymerous pə 'lɪm ᵊr əs pɒ-

polymorph|ic ˌpɒl i 'mɔːf |ɪk ◄
‖ ˌpɑːl i 'mɔːrf |ɪk ◄ **~ism** ˌɪz əm **~ous** əs ◄

■ -ˈniːziə   ▢ -ˈniːʒə   ■ -ˈniːsiə   ▨ -ˈniːʃə

BrE 1998

0   20   40   60   80   100%

Polynesia ˌpɒl ɪ 'niːz i‿ə ˌ•ə-, -'niːʒ ə, -'niːs i‿ə,
-'niːʃ ə ‖ ˌpɑːl ə 'niːʒ ə -'niːʃ- —*BrE 1998*
poll panel preference: -'niːziə 54%, -'niːʒə
39%, -'niːsiə 4%, -'niːʃə 4%.
Polynesian ˌpɒl ɪ 'niːz i‿ən ˌ•ə-, -'niːʒ ən,
-'niːs i‿ən, -'niːʃ ən ‖ ˌpɑːl ə 'niːʒ ən -'niːʃ-
~s z
Polynices ˌpɒl i 'naɪs iːz ‖ ˌpɑːl-
polynomial ˌpɒl i 'nəʊm i‿əl ◄ ‖ ˌpɑːl ə 'noʊm-
~s z
polyp 'pɒl ɪp -əp ‖ 'pɑːl əp **~s** s
polypeptide ˌpɒl i 'pept aɪd ‖ ˌpɑːl- **~s** z
Polyphemus ˌpɒl ɪ 'fiːm əs -ə- ‖ ˌpɑːl-
polyphonic ˌpɒl i 'fɒn ɪk ◄ ‖ ˌpɑːl i 'fɑːn ɪk ◄
~ally əl‿i
polyphon|y pə 'lɪf ən i pɒ- **~ies** iz
polypi 'pɒl ɪ paɪ -ə- ‖ 'pɑːl-
polyploid 'pɒl i plɔɪd ‖ 'pɑːl- **~s** z
polypod 'pɒl i pɒd ‖ 'pɑːl i pɑːd **~s** z
polypod|y 'pɒl i pəʊd li ‖ 'pɑːl ə poʊd li **~ies**
iz
polypropylene ˌpɒl i 'prəʊp ə liːn ◄ -'•ɪ-
‖ ˌpɑːl i 'proʊp-
polypous 'pɒl ɪp əs -əp- ‖ 'pɑːl-
polypus 'pɒl ɪp əs -əp- ‖ 'pɑːl- **~es** ɪz əz
polysaccharide ˌpɒl i 'sæk ə raɪd ‖ ˌpɑːl **~s** z
polysemous pə 'lɪs ɪm əs pɒ-, -əm-;
ˌpɒl i 'siːm əs ‖ ˌpɑːl i 'siːm əs **~ly** li
polysemy pə 'lɪs ɪm i pɒ-, -əm-; 'pɒl i ˌsiːm i,
ˌ•'•'•• ‖ ˌpɑːl i 'siːm i
polystyrene ˌpɒl i 'staɪər iːn ◄ ‖ ˌpɑːl-
polysyllabic ˌpɒl i sɪ 'læb ɪk ◄ -sə'•- ‖ ˌpɑːl-
~ally əl‿i
polysyllable 'pɒl i ˌsɪl əb əl ˌ••'••• ‖ 'pɑːl- **~s**
z
polysyndeton ˌpɒl i 'sɪnd ət ən -'•ɪt-
‖ ˌpɑːl i 'sɪnd ə taːn
polysynthetic
ˌpɒl i sɪn 'θet ɪk ◄ ‖ ˌpɑːl i sɪn 'θeţ ɪk ◄
polysystemic ˌpɒl i sɪ 'stiːm ɪk ◄ -sə'•-, -'stem-
‖ ˌpɑːl-
polytechnic ˌpɒl i 'tek nɪk -ə- ‖ ˌpɑːl- **~s** s
polytetrafluoroethylene
ˌpɒl i ˌtetr ə ˌfluər əʊ 'eθ ə liːn -ˌflɔːr-
‖ ˌpɑːl i ˌtetr ə ˌflʊr oʊ-
polytheism 'pɒl i θi ˌɪz əm ˌ•'•ˌθiː ɪz əm
‖ 'pɑːl-
polytheist 'pɒl i θi ɪst ˌ•'•ˌθiː ɪst, §-əst ‖ 'pɑːl-
~s s
polytheistic ˌpɒl i θi 'ɪst ɪk ◄ ‖ ˌpɑːl- **~ally** əl‿i
polythene 'pɒl ɪ θiːn -ə- ‖ 'pɑːl-
polyunsaturate ˌpɒl i ʌn 'sætʃ ə reɪt -ʊ•,
-'sæt jʊ- ‖ ˌpɑːl- **~s** s
polyunsatu|rated ˌpɒl i ʌn 'sætʃ ə reɪt ɪd ◄
-'•ʊ-, -'sæt jʊ-, -əd
‖ ˌpɑːl i ʌn 'sætʃ ə reɪţ əd ◄

polyurethane ˌpɒl i 'jʊər ə θeɪn ◄ -'jɔːr-, -'•ɪ-,
△-θiːn ‖ ˌpɑːl i 'jʊr-
polyvalent ˌpɒl i 'veɪl ənt pə 'lɪv əl ənt, pɒ-
‖ ˌpɑːl-
polyvinyl ˌpɒl i 'vaɪn əl ◄ -ɪl ‖ ˌpɑːl-
Polyxena pə 'lɪks ən ə pɒ-, -ɪn-
Polzeath pɒl 'zeθ -'ziːθ ‖ poʊl-
pom, Pom pɒm ‖ pɑːm **poms, Poms**
pɒmz ‖ pɑːmz
poma, Poma 'pɒm ə 'pəʊm ə ‖ 'pɑːm ə
'poʊm ə
pomace 'pʌm ɪs 'pɒm-, §-əs ‖ 'pɑːm-
pomad|e pəʊ 'meɪd pɒ-, -'maːd ‖ poʊ- pɑː-
~ed ɪd əd **~es** z **~ing** ɪŋ
Pomagne *tdmk* pəʊ 'meɪn ‖ poʊ-
pomander pəʊ 'mænd ə ‖ 'poʊm ænd ər
poʊ 'mænd ər **~s** z
pome pəʊm ‖ poʊm **pomes** pəʊmz ‖ poʊmz
pomegranate 'pɒm ɪ græn ət ˌ•'•ə-, -ɪt
‖ 'pɑːm-ˌ•græn ət, 'pʌm- **~s** s
pomelo 'pɒm ə ləʊ -ɪ-; pə 'mel əʊ
‖ 'pɑːm ə loʊ **~s** z
Pomerani|a ˌpɒm ə 'reɪn i‿ə ‖ ˌpɑːm- **~an/s**
ən/z
Pomeroy (i) 'pɒm ə rɔɪ ‖ 'pɑːm-, (ii)
'pəʊm- ‖ 'poʊm-
pomfret *'kind of fish'* 'pɒmpf rət -rɪt
Pomfret, p~ 'pɒmpf rət 'pʌmpf-, -rɪt ‖ 'pɑːmpf-
'**Pomfret cake**
pomiferous pɒ 'mɪf ər əs pə- ‖ poʊ-
pommel *n* 'pɒm əl 'pʌm- ‖ 'pʌm əl 'pɑːm- **~s**
z
pommel *v* 'pʌm əl 'pɒm- **~ed, ~led** d **~ing,**
~ling ɪŋ **~s** z
pomm|ie, pomm|y, Pomm|y 'pɒm li ‖ 'pɑːm li
~ies iz
Pomo 'pəʊm əʊ ‖ 'poʊm oʊ **~s** z
Pomona, p~ pəʊ 'məʊn ə ‖ pə 'moʊn ə
pomp pɒmp ‖ pɑːmp **pomps** pɒmps ‖ pɑːmps
pompadour, P~ 'pɒmp ə dʊə -dɔː
‖ 'pɑːmp ə dɔːr -doʊr, -dʊr —*Fr* [pɔ̃ pa duːʁ]
~s z
pompano, P~ 'pɒmp ə nəʊ 'pʌmp-
‖ 'pɑːmp ə noʊ **~s** z
'**Pompano 'Beach**
Pompeian, Pompeiian pɒm 'peɪ ən -'piː‿
‖ pɑːm- **~s** z
Pompeii pɒm 'peɪ i -iː; pɒm 'peɪ ‖ pɑːm-
Pompey 'pɒmp i ‖ 'pɑːmp i
Pomphrey 'pɒmpf ri ‖ 'pɑːmpf-
Pompidou 'pɒmp ɪ duː -ə- ‖ 'pɑːmp- —*Fr*
[pɔ̃ pi du]
pompom 'pɒm pɒm ‖ 'pɑːm pɑːm **~s** z
pompon 'pɒm pɒn ‖ 'pɑːm pɑːn —*Fr* [pɔ̃ pɔ̃]
~s z
pomposit|y pɒm 'pɒs ət li -ɪt-
‖ pɑːm 'pɑːs əţ li **~ies** iz
pompous 'pɒmp əs ‖ 'pɑːmp əs **~ly** li **~ness**
nəs nɪs
'**pon** pɒn ‖ pɑːn
ponce pɒnᵗs ‖ pɑːnᵗs **ponced** pɒnᵗst ‖ pɑːnᵗst
ponces 'pɒnᵗs ɪz -əz ‖ 'pɑːnᵗs əz **poncing**
'pɒnᵗs ɪŋ ‖ 'pɑːnᵗs ɪŋ

Ponce *Spanish name; place in PR* 'pɒnˡts eɪ
pɒnˡts ‖ 'pɔːnˡts eɪ 'paːnˡts-, 'poʊnˡts- —*AmSp*
['pon se]
poncey 'pɒnˡts i ‖ 'paːnˡts i
poncho 'pɒntʃ əʊ ‖ 'paːntʃ oʊ—*Sp* ['pon tʃo]
~s z
poncy 'pɒnˡts i ‖ 'paːnˡts i
pond, Pond pɒnd ‖ paːnd **ponds**
pɒndz ‖ paːndz
pond|er 'pɒnd |ə ‖ 'paːnd |ᵊr ~**ered** əd ‖ ᵊrd
~**ering/s** _ᵊr ɪŋ/z ~**ers** əz ‖ ᵊrz
ponderosa ˌpɒnd ə 'rəʊz ə -'rəʊs-
‖ ˌpaːnd ə 'roʊs ə -'roʊz- ~s z
ponderous 'pɒnd_ᵊr əs ‖ 'paːnd_ ~**ly** li ~**ness**
nəs nɪs
Ponders 'pɒnd əz ‖ 'paːnd ᵊrz
Pondicherry ˌpɒnd ɪ 'tʃer i §-ə-, -'ʃer-
‖ ˌpaːnd-
Pondo 'pɒnd əʊ ‖ 'paːnd oʊ ~**land** lænd ~s z
pondweed 'pɒnd wiːd ‖ 'paːnd-
pone pəʊn ‖ poʊn—*but in the sense 'player to
right of dealer', also* 'pəʊn i ‖ 'poʊn i ~s z
pong pɒŋ ‖ paːŋ pɔːŋ **ponged** pɒŋd ‖ paːŋd
pɔːŋd **ponging** 'pɒŋ ɪŋ ‖ 'paːŋ ɪŋ 'pɔːŋ-
pongs pɒŋz ‖ paːŋz pɔːŋz
pongee ˌ₍₎pɒn 'dʒiː ' • • ‖ ₍₎paːn-
pongid 'pɒndʒ ɪd §-əd ‖ 'paːndʒ- ~s z
pongo 'pɒŋ gəʊ ‖ 'paːŋ goʊ ~s z
pongy 'pɒŋ i ‖ 'paːŋ i 'pɔːŋ-
poniard 'pɒn jəd -jaːd ‖ 'paːn jᵊrd ~**ed** ɪd əd
~**ing** ɪŋ ~s z
ponie... —*see* **pony**
pons pɒnz ‖ paːnz **pontes**
'pɒnt iːz ‖ 'paːnt iːz
ˌpons ˌasiˈnorum ˌæs ɪ 'nɔːr əm -ə-,
-ʊm ‖ -'noʊr-
Ponson 'pɒnˡts ən ‖ 'paːnˡts-
Ponsonby 'pɒnˡts ən bi →-ᵊm- ‖ 'paːnˡts-
Pont pɒnt ‖ paːnt
Pontardawe ˌpɒnt ə 'daʊ_i -eɪ ‖ ˌpaːnt ᵊr-
—*Welsh* [ˌpɔnt ar 'dau e]
Pontardulais ˌpɒnt ə 'dɪl əs -'dʌl-, -aɪs ‖ ˌpaːnt
ᵊr- —*Welsh* Pontarddulais [ˌpɔnt ar 'ði laɪs]
Pontchartrain 'pɒntʃ ə treɪn ˌ • • ' • ‖ 'paːntʃ ᵊr-
Pontefract 'pɒnt ɪ frækt -ə- ‖ 'paːnt- —*locally
formerly also* 'pʌmpf rət, 'pɒmpf-, -rɪt
Ponteland ˌpɒnt 'iːl ənd ‖ ˌpaːnt-
pontes 'pɒnt iːz ‖ 'paːnt iːz
Pontfaen, Pont-faen ₍₎pɒnt 'vaɪn ‖ ₍₎paːnt-
Ponti 'pɒnt i ‖ 'paːnt̬ i
Pontiac 'pɒnt i æk ‖ 'paːnt̬- ~s s
Pontic 'pɒnt ɪk ‖ 'paːnt̬ ɪk
pontifex, P~ 'pɒnt ɪ feks -ə- ‖ 'paːnt̬ ə-
pontifices, P~ pɒn 'tɪf ə siːz -ɪ- ‖ paːn-
pontiff 'pɒnt ɪf ‖ 'paːnt̬ əf ~s s
pontifical pɒn 'tɪf ɪk ᵊl ‖ paːn- ~**ally** ᵊl_i ~s z
pontificate *n* pɒn 'tɪf ɪk ət -ək ət, -ɪt; -ɪ keɪt,
-ə keɪt ‖ paːn- ~s s
pontifi|cate *v* pɒn 'tɪf ɪ |keɪt -ə- ‖ paːn-
~**cated** keɪt ɪd -əd ‖ keɪt̬ əd ~**cates** keɪts
~**cating** keɪt ɪŋ ‖ keɪt̬ ɪŋ
pontification pɒn ˌtɪf ɪ 'keɪʃ ᵊn ˌpɒnt ɪf-, -ə-
‖ paːn- ~s z

Pontin 'pɒnt ɪn §-ən ‖ 'paːnt ᵊn ~'s z
Pontine, p~ 'pɒnt aɪn ‖ 'paːnt-
ˌPontine 'Marshes
Ponting 'pɒnt ɪŋ ‖ 'paːnt̬-
Pontius 'pɒnt i_əs 'pɒntʃ-, 'pɒntʃ əs
‖ 'paːntʃ əs
ˌPontius 'Pilate
Pont l'Évêque ˌpɒ̃ leɪ 'vek ‖ ˌpaːn- ˌpaːnt-
—*Fr* [pɔ̃ le vɛk]
Pontllan-fraith ˌpɒnt læn 'vraɪθ -θlæn-
‖ ˌpaːnt- —*Welsh* [pɔnt ɬan 'vraiθ]
Ponton 'pɒnt ən ‖ 'paːnt ᵊn
pontoon ₍₎pɒn 'tuːn ‖ ₍₎paːn- ~s z
Pontop 'pɒnt ɒp ‖ 'paːnt aːp
ˌPontop 'Pike
Pontus 'pɒnt əs ‖ 'paːnt̬-
Pont-y-clun ˌpɒnt ə 'kliːn -i- ‖ ˌpaːnt̬- —*Welsh*
[ˌpɔnt ə 'kliːn]
Pontypool ˌpɒnt ə 'puːl -i-, ' • • • ‖ ˌpaːnt̬-
—*Welsh* [ˌpɔnt ə 'puːl]
Pontypridd ˌpɒnt ə 'priːð ˌ • i-, -'prɪd, ' • • •
‖ ˌpaːnt̬- —*Welsh* [ˌpɔnt ə 'priːð]
pon|y 'pəʊn li i ‖ 'poʊn li ~**ies** iz
ˌpony exˈpress
ponytail 'pəʊn i teɪᵊl ‖ 'poʊn- ~s z
pony-trekk|ing 'pəʊn i ˌtrek| ɪŋ ‖ 'poʊn-
~**er/s** ə/z ‖ ᵊr/z
Ponzi 'pɒnz i ‖ 'paːnz i
'Ponzi scheme
poo puː **pooed** puːd **pooing** 'puː ɪŋ **poos**
puːz
pooch puːtʃ **pooches** 'puːtʃ ɪz -əz
poodle 'puːd ᵊl ~s z
poof pʊf puːf ~s s
poofter 'pʊft ə 'puːft- ‖ -ᵊr ~s z
poofy 'pʊf i 'puːf-
pooh, Pooh puː
Pooh-Bah ˌpuː 'baː
pooh-pooh ˌpuː 'puː ~**ed** d ~**ing** ɪŋ ~s z
Pook puːk
pool puːl **pooled** puːld **pooling** 'puːl ɪŋ
pools puːlz
Poole puːl
Poolewe pʊl 'juː ₍₎puːl-
Pooley 'puːl i
poolroom 'puːl ruːm -rʊm ~s z
poolside 'puːl saɪd
poon puːn **poons** puːnz
Poona 'puːn ə
poontang 'puːn tæŋ
poop puːp **pooped** puːpt **pooping** 'puːp ɪŋ
poops puːps
'poop deck
pooper-scooper 'puːp ə ˌskuːp ə ‖ -ᵊr ˌskuːp ᵊr
~s z
poor pɔː pʊə ‖ pʊᵊr pɔːr, poʊr —*Poll panel
preferences: BrE 1988* pɔː *57%,* pʊə *43%; BrE
1998, those born since 1973* pɔː *82%,* pʊə *18%.*
poorer 'pɔːr ə 'pʊər- ‖ 'pʊr ᵊr 'pɔːr-, 'poʊr-
poorest 'pɔːr ɪst 'pʊər-, -əst ‖ 'pʊr əst 'pɔːr-,
'poʊr-
'poor box; 'poor law; ˌpoor reˈlation;
ˌpoor 'white

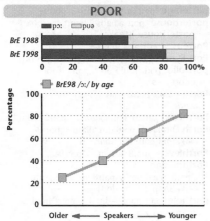

POOR

■ pɔː ☐ puə

BrE 1988
BrE 1998

0 20 40 60 80 100%

▣ BrE98 /ɔː/ by age

Percentage
100
80
60
40
20
0

Older ◀— Speakers —▶ Younger

Poore puə pɔː ǁ puᵊr pɔːr, pʊʊr
poor|house 'pɔː ǀhaʊs 'puə- ǁ 'pʊr- 'pɔːr-, 'pʊʊr- ~**houses** haʊz ɪz -əz
poorly adv 'pɔː li 'puə- ǁ 'pʊr li 'pɔːr-, 'pʊʊr- ,poorly 'off◀
poorly adj 'pɔːl i 'puəl i ǁ 'pʊrl i 'pɔːrl-, 'pʊʊrl-
poorness 'pɔː nəs 'puə-, -nɪs ǁ 'pʊr- 'pɔːr-, 'pʊʊr-
poor-spirited ,pɔː 'spɪr ɪt ɪd ◀ ,puə-, §-ət-, -əd ǁ ,pʊr 'spɪr əṭ əd ◀ ,pɔːr-, ,pʊʊr-
Pooter 'puːt ə ǁ 'puːṭ ᵊr
Pooterish 'puːt ər ɪʃ ǁ 'puːṭ-
poove puːv **pooves** puːvz
pop, Pop pɒp ǁ pɑːp **popped** pɒpt ǁ pɑːpt **popping** 'pɒp ɪŋ ǁ 'pɑːp ɪŋ **pops** pɒpsǁ pɑːps
'pop art, ,◦ '◦◀; 'pop ,concert; 'pop group; 'pop ,music; 'popping crease
popadam, popadom, popadum 'pɒp əd əm ǁ 'pɑːp- ~**s** z
popcorn 'pɒp kɔːn ǁ 'pɑːp kɔːrn
pop-down 'pɒp daʊn ǁ ' pɑːp-
pope, Pope pəʊp ǁ poʊp **popes, Pope's** pəʊps ǁ poʊps
,Pope's 'nose
popery 'pəʊp ər i ǁ 'poʊp-
Popeye 'pɒp aɪ ǁ 'pɑːp-
pop-eyed ,pɒp 'aɪd ◀ '◦◦ ǁ 'pɑːp aɪd
popgun 'pɒp gʌn ǁ 'pɑːp- ~**s** z
Popham 'pɒp əm ǁ 'pɑːp-
popinjay 'pɒp ɪn dʒeɪ §-ən- ǁ 'pɑːp- ~**s** z
popish 'pəʊp ɪʃ ǁ 'poʊp- ~**ly** li ~**ness** nəs nɪs
poplar, P~ 'pɒp lə ǁ 'pɑːp lᵊr ~**s** z
poplin 'pɒp lɪn §-lən ǁ 'pɑːp- ~**s** z
popliteal ,pɒp lɪ 'tiː_əl ◀ -lə-; pɒ 'plɪt i_əl ǁ ,pɑːp-
Popocatepetl ,pɒp əʊ kæt ə 'pet ᵊl -ɪ'◦•-; ,◦•◦'••••ǁ ,poʊp ə kæṭ ə 'peṭ ᵊl ,pɑːp- —Sp Popacatépetl [po po ka 'te petl]
popover 'pɒp ,əʊv ə ǁ 'pɑːp ,oʊv ᵊr ~**s** z
poppa, Poppa 'pɒp ə ǁ 'pɑːp ə ~**s**, ~'**s** z
poppadom, poppadum 'pɒp əd əm ǁ 'pɑːp- ~**s** z
popp... —see pop

Poppaea pɒ 'piː_ə ǁ pɑː-
popper, P~ 'pɒp ə ǁ 'pɑːp ᵊr ~**s** z
Popperian pɒ 'pɪər i_ən ǁ pɑː 'pɪr-
poppet 'pɒp ɪt §-ət ǁ 'pɑːp- ~**s** s
poppi... —see pop, poppy
poppl|e 'pɒp ᵊl ǁ 'pɑːp ᵊl ~**ed** d ~**es** z ~**ing** _ɪŋ
Popplewell 'pɒp ᵊl wel ǁ 'pɑːp-
Poppleton 'pɒp ᵊl tən ǁ 'pɑːp-
popp|y, Poppy 'pɒp li ǁ 'pɑːp li ~**ies** iz
'Poppy Day
poppycock 'pɒp i kɒk ǁ 'pɑːp i kɑːk
popshop 'pɒp ʃɒp ǁ 'pɑːp ʃɑːp ~**s** s
popsicle, P~ tdmk 'pɒps ɪk ᵊl ǁ 'pɑːps- ~**s** z
pops|ie, pops|y 'pɒps li ǁ 'pɑːps li ~**ies** iz
populace 'pɒp jʊl əs -jəl-, -ɪs ǁ 'pɑːp jəl əs
popular 'pɒp jʊl ə -jəl- ǁ 'pɑːp jəl ᵊr
popularis... —see populariz...
popularity ,pɒp jʊ 'lær ət i ,◦jə-, -ɪt i ǁ ,pɑːp jə 'lær əṭ i -'ler-
popularization ,pɒp jʊl ᵊr aɪ 'zeɪʃ ᵊn ,◦jəl-, -ɪ'◦- ǁ ,pɑːp jəl ᵊr ə- ~**s** z
populariz|e 'pɒp jʊl ə raɪz '◦jəl- ǁ 'pɑːp jəl- ~**ed** d ~**es** ɪz əz ~**ing** ɪŋ
popularly 'pɒp jʊl ə li '◦jəl- ǁ 'pɑːp jəl ᵊr li
popu|late 'pɒp jʊ |leɪt -jə- ǁ 'pɑːp jə- ~**lated** leɪt ɪd -əd ǁ leɪṭ əd ~**lates** leɪts ~**lating** leɪt ɪŋ ǁ leɪṭ ɪŋ
population ,pɒp jʊ 'leɪʃ ᵊn -jə- ǁ ,pɑːp jə- ~**s** z
,popu'lation ex,plosion
populism, P~ 'pɒp jʊ ,lɪz əm -jə- ǁ 'pɑːp jə-
populist, P~ 'pɒp jʊl ɪst -jəl-, §-əst ǁ 'pɑːp jəl- ~**s** s
populous 'pɒp jʊl əs -jəl- ǁ 'pɑːp jəl əs ~**ly** li ~**ness** nəs nɪs
pop-up 'pɒp ʌp ǁ 'pɑːp ʌp ~**s** s
porbeagle 'pɔː ,biːg ᵊl ǁ 'pɔːr- ~**s** z
porcelain 'pɔːs ᵊl_ɪn _ən, -eɪn ǁ 'pɔːrs- 'poʊrs- ~**s** z
porch pɔːtʃ ǁ pɔːrtʃ poʊrtʃ **porches** 'pɔːtʃ ɪz -əz ǁ 'pɔːrtʃ əz 'poʊrtʃ-
Porchester 'pɔːtʃ ɪst ə -əst-, §-est- ǁ 'pɔːr ,tʃest ᵊr
porcine 'pɔːs aɪn ǁ 'pɔːrs-
porcin|o pɔː 'tʃiːn| əʊ ǁ pɔːr 'tʃiːn| oʊ ~**i** iː —It [por 'tʃiː no]
porcupine 'pɔːk jʊ paɪn -jə- ǁ 'pɔːrk jə- ~**s** z
pore pɔː ǁ pɔːr poʊr **pored** pɔːd ǁ pɔːrd poʊrd **pores** pɔːz ǁ pɔːrz poʊrz **poring** 'pɔːr ɪŋ ǁ 'poʊr-
porg|y, Porg|y 'pɔːg li ǁ 'pɔːrg li ~**ies**, ~**y's** iz
pork pɔːk ǁ pɔːrk poʊrk
'pork ,barrel; ,pork 'chop ǁ '◦ •; ,pork 'pie
porker 'pɔːk ə ǁ 'pɔːrk ᵊr 'poʊrk- ~**s** z
pork|ie, Pork|ie, pork|y, Pork|y 'pɔːk li ǁ 'pɔːrk li 'poʊrk- ~**ies**, ~**y's** iz ~**iness** i nəs i nɪs
Porlock 'pɔː lɒk ǁ 'pɔːr lɑːk
porn pɔːn ǁ pɔːrn
porno 'pɔːn əʊ ǁ 'pɔːrn oʊ
pornographer pɔː 'nɒg rəf ə pə- ǁ pɔːr 'nɑːg rəf ᵊr ~**s** z

pornographic ˌpɔːn ə 'græf ɪk ◄ ‖ ˌpɔːrn-
~ally ᵊl‿i
pornography pɔː 'nɒg rəf i pə- ‖ pɔːr 'nɑːg-
poromeric ˌpɔːr əʊ 'mer ɪk ◄ ˌpɒr- ‖ -ə-
ˌpoʊr-
porosit|y pɔː 'rɒs ət |i -ɪt- ‖ pə 'rɑːs əṭ |i pɔː-,
poʊ- ~ies iz
porous 'pɔːr əs ‖ 'poʊr- ~ly li ~ness nəs nɪs
porphyria pɔː 'fɪr i‿ə -'faɪᵊr- ‖ pɔːr-
porphyrin 'pɔːf ər ɪn -ɪr-, §-ən ‖ 'pɔːrf- ~s z
porphyr|y 'pɔːf ər li -ɪr- ‖ 'pɔːrf- ~ies iz
porpois|e 'pɔːp əs ‖ 'pɔːrp- —occasionally also
a spelling pronunciation △'pɔː pɔɪs,
-pɔɪz ‖ 'pɔːr- ~es ɪz əz
porridge 'pɒr ɪdʒ ‖ 'pɔːr- 'pɑːr-
porringer 'pɒr ɪndʒ ə -əndʒ- ‖ 'pɔːr əndʒ ər
'pɑːr- ~s z
Porsche tdmk pɔːʃ 'pɔːʃ ə ‖ pɔːrʃ 'pɔːrʃ ə, -i
—Ger ['pɔʁ ʃə] Porsches 'pɔːʃ ɪz -əz
‖ 'pɔːrʃ əz -iz
Porsena 'pɔːs ən ə -ɪn- ‖ 'pɔːrs-
Porson 'pɔːs ᵊn ‖ 'pɔːrs-
port pɔːt ‖ pɔːrt poʊrt ported 'pɔːt ɪd -əd
‖ 'pɔːrṭ əd 'poʊrt- porting 'pɔːt ɪŋ ‖ 'pɔːrṭ ɪŋ
'poʊrt- ports pɔːts ‖ pɔːrts poʊrts —see also
phrases with this word
ˌPort E'lizabeth; ₍ₗ₎Port 'Harcourt; ₍ₗ₎Port
'Hedland; ₍ₗ₎Port 'Jackson; ₍ₗ₎Port 'Lincoln;
₍ₗ₎Port 'Moresby; ˌport of 'call; ˌport of
'entry; Port of 'Spain; ₍ₗ₎Port 'Stanley
portability ˌpɔːt ə 'bɪl ət i -ɪt i ‖ ˌpɔːrṭ ə 'bɪl əṭ i
ˌpoʊrṭ-
portable 'pɔːt əb ᵊl ‖ 'pɔːrṭ- 'poʊrṭ- ~ness nəs
nɪs ~s z
Portacrib tdmk 'pɔːt ə krɪb ‖ 'pɔːrṭ- 'poʊrṭ-
Portadown ˌpɔːt ə 'daʊn ‖ ˌpɔːrṭ- ˌpoʊrṭ-
portage 'pɔːt ɪdʒ ˌpɔː 'tɑːʒ ‖ 'pɔːrṭ ɪdʒ 'poʊrṭ-;
pɔːr 'tɑːʒ
Portage 'pɔːt ɪdʒ ‖ 'pɔːrṭ ɪdʒ 'poʊrṭ-
ˌPortage la 'Prairie
Portakabin tdmk 'pɔːt ə ˌkæb ɪn §-ən ‖ 'pɔːrṭ-
'poʊrṭ- ~s z
portal, P~ 'pɔːt ᵊl ‖ 'pɔːrṭ ᵊl 'poʊrṭ- ~s z
Portaloo, p~ tdmk 'pɔːt ə lu: ‖ 'pɔːrṭ- ~s z
portament|o ˌpɔːt ə 'ment |əʊ
‖ ˌpɔːrṭ ə 'ment |oʊ ˌpoʊrṭ- ~i i:
Port Askaig ₍ₗ₎pɔːt 'æsk eɪg ‖ ₍ₗ₎pɔːrṭ- ₍ₗ₎poʊrṭ-
portative 'pɔːt ət ɪv ‖ 'pɔːrṭ əṭ ɪv 'poʊrṭ-
Port-au-Prince ˌpɔːt əʊ 'prɪnts ‖ ˌpɔːrṭ oʊ
ˌpoʊrṭ- —Fr [pɔʁ to pʁɛ̃s]
Portbury 'pɔːt bər‿i ‖ 'pɔːrt ˌber i 'poʊrt-
portcullis pɔːt 'kʌl ɪs -əs ‖ pɔːrt- poʊrt- ~es
ɪz əz
porte, P~ pɔːt ‖ pɔːrt poʊrt
porte-cochere, porte-cochère
ˌpɔːt kɒ 'ʃeə ‖ ˌpɔːrt koʊ 'ʃeᵊr ˌpoʊrt- ~s z
portend pɔː 'tend ‖ pɔːr- poʊr- ~ed ɪd əd
~ing ɪŋ ~s z
portent 'pɔːt ent ‖ 'pɔːrt- 'poʊrt- ~s s
portentous pɔː 'tent əs △-'tentʃ- ‖ pɔːr 'tenṭ
əs poʊr- ~ly li ~ness nəs nɪs
Porteous 'pɔːt i‿əs ‖ 'pɔːrṭ-
porter, P~ 'pɔːt ə ‖ 'pɔːrṭ ər 'poʊrṭ- ~s z

porterage 'pɔːt ər ɪdʒ ‖ 'pɔːrṭ- 'poʊrṭ-
porterhouse 'pɔːt ə haʊs ‖ 'pɔːrṭ ər- 'poʊrṭ-
ˌporterhouse 'steak
Porteus 'pɔːt i‿əs ‖ 'pɔːrṭ-
Port Eynon ₍ₗ₎pɔːt 'aɪn ən ‖ ₍ₗ₎pɔːrṭ- ₍ₗ₎poʊrṭ-
portfolio ˌpɔːt 'fəʊl i‿əʊ ‖ ˌpɔːrt 'foʊl i oʊ
ˌpoʊrt- ~s z
Porth pɔːθ ‖ pɔːrθ —see also phrases with this
word
Porthcawl ₍ₗ₎pɔːθ 'kɔːl -'kaʊl ‖ ₍ₗ₎pɔːrθ- -'kɑːl
Porth Dinllaen ˌpɔːθ dɪn 'θlaɪn ‖ ˌpɔːrθ-
—Welsh [ˌpɔrθ dɪn 'ɬaɪn, -'ɬiːn]
Porthleven ₍ₗ₎pɔːθ 'lev ᵊn ‖ ₍ₗ₎pɔːrθ-
Porthmadog
₍ₗ₎pɔːθ 'mæd ɒg ‖ ₍ₗ₎pɔːrθ 'mæd ɔːg -ɑːg
—Welsh [pɔrθ 'ma dog]
porthole 'pɔːt həʊl →-hɒʊl ‖ 'pɔːrt hoʊl
'poʊrt- ~s z
Portia 'pɔːʃ ə 'pɔːʃ i‿ə ‖ 'pɔːrʃ ə 'poʊrʃ-
portico 'pɔːt ɪ kəʊ ‖ 'pɔːrṭ ɪ koʊ 'poʊrṭ- ~s z
portiere, portière ˌpɔːt i 'eə ‖ ˌpɔːrṭ i 'eᵊr
ˌpoʊrṭ-; pɔːr 'tɪᵊr, poʊr- —Fr [pɔʁ tjɛːʁ] ~s
z
Portillo pɔː 'tɪl əʊ ‖ pɔːr 'tɪl oʊ
portion 'pɔːʃ ᵊn ‖ 'pɔːrʃ ᵊn 'poʊrʃ- ~ed d
~ing ɪŋ ~less ləs lɪs ~s z
Portishead 'pɔːt ɪs hed §-əs- ‖ 'pɔːrṭ- 'poʊrṭ-
Portland, p~ 'pɔːt lənd ‖ 'pɔːrt- 'poʊrt-
ˌPortland ce'ment; ˌPortland 'stone
Portlaoise ˌpɔːt 'liːʃ ə ‖ ˌpɔːrt- ˌpoʊrt-
port|ly 'pɔːt |li ‖ 'pɔːrt- 'poʊrt- ~liness li nəs
-nɪs
Portmadoc ˌpɔːt 'mæd ək ‖ ˌpɔːrt- ˌpoʊrt-
Portman 'pɔːt mən ‖ 'pɔːrt- 'poʊrt-
portmanteau
₍ₗ₎pɔːt 'mænt əʊ ‖ pɔːrt 'mænt oʊ poʊrt- ~s,
~x z
₍ₗ₎port'manteau word
Portmeirion ₍ₗ₎pɔːt 'mer i‿ən ‖ ₍ₗ₎pɔːrt-
₍ₗ₎poʊrt-
Portnoy 'pɔːt nɔɪ ‖ 'pɔːrt- 'poʊrt-
Porto 'pɔːt əʊ ‖ 'pɔːrṭ oʊ 'poʊrṭ-
Porto Alegre ˌpɔːt əʊ ə 'leg ri ˌ•u- ‖ ˌpɔːrṭ u-
-rə —Port Pôrto Alegre [por tu ɐ 'lɛ gri]
Portobello ˌpɔːt əʊ 'bel əʊ ◄ ‖ ˌpɔːrṭ ə 'bel oʊ ◄
ˌpoʊrṭ-
Portofino ˌpɔːt əʊ 'fiːn əʊ ‖ ˌpɔːrṭ ə 'fiːn oʊ
—It [por to 'fiː no]
Porton 'pɔːt ᵊn ‖ 'pɔːrt ᵊn
Porto Ric|o ˌpɔːt əʊ 'riːk ləʊ ‖ ˌpɔːrṭ ə 'riːk loʊ
ˌpoʊrṭ- ~an/s ən/z
portrait 'pɔːtr ət -ɪt, -eɪt ‖ 'pɔːrtr ət 'poʊrtr-
~s s
portraitist 'pɔːtr ət ɪst -ɪt-, -eɪt-, §-əst
‖ 'pɔːrtr əṭ əst 'poʊrtr- ~s s
portraiture 'pɔːtr ɪtʃ ə -ətʃ-; -ɪ tjʊə, -ə-
‖ 'pɔːrtr ə tʃʊr 'poʊrtr-, -ətʃ ər
portray pɔː 'treɪ ‖ pɔːr- poʊr-, pᵊr- ~ed d
~ing ɪŋ ~s z
portrayal pɔː 'treɪ‿əl ‖ pɔːr- pᵊr- ~s z
portrayer pɔː 'treɪ ə ‖ pɔːr 'treɪ ər pᵊr- ~s z
Portreath pɔː 'triːθ ‖ pɔːr-
Portree pɔː 'triː ‖ pɔːr-

Portrush ₍ˌ₎pɔːt ˈrʌʃ ‖ ₍ˌ₎pɔːrt- ₍ˌ₎poʊrt-
Port Said ˌpɔːt ˈsaɪd -ˈsaː iːd ‖ ˌpɔːrt- ˌpoʊrt-
Port Salut ˌpɔː sæ ˈluː -sə- ‖ ˌpɔːr- ˌpoʊr-
—Fr [pɔʁ sa ly]
Portscatho ₍ˌ₎pɔːt ˈskæθ əʊ ‖ ₍ˌ₎pɔːrt ˈskæθ oʊ
₍ˌ₎poʊrt-
Portsea ˈpɔːts i ˈpɔːt siː ‖ ˈpɔːrt siː ˈpoʊrt-
Portslade ˌpɔːt ˈsleɪd ◂ ‖ ˌpɔːrt- ˌpoʊrt-
Portsmouth ˈpɔːts məθ ‖ ˈpɔːrts- ˈpoʊrts-
Port Talbot ₍ˌ₎pɔːt ˈtɔːlb ət pɔː-, pə-, -ˈtælb-,
-ˈtɒlb- ‖ ₍ˌ₎pɔːrt- ₍ˌ₎poʊrt-, -ˈtɑːlb-
portugaise ˌpɔːtʃ u ˈɡeɪz ◂ ‖ ˌpɔːrtʃ- ˌpoʊrtʃ-
—Fr [pɔʁ ty ɡɛːz]
Portugal ˈpɔːtʃ ʊɡ ᵊl -əɡ-; ˈpɔːt jʊɡ-
‖ ˈpɔːrtʃ əɡ ᵊl ˈpoʊrtʃ-
Portuguese ˌpɔːtʃ u ˈɡiːz ◂ -ə-; ˌpɔːt ju-
‖ ˌpɔːrtʃ- ˌpoʊrtʃ-, -ˈɡiːs, '• • •
ˌPortuˌguese ˈfood; ˌPortuguese ˌman-of-
ˈwar
pose pəʊz ‖ poʊz posed pəʊzd ‖ poʊzd
poses ˈpəʊz ɪz -əz ‖ ˈpoʊz əz posing
ˈpəʊz ɪŋ ‖ ˈpoʊz ɪŋ
Poseidon pə ˈsaɪd ᵊn pɒ- ‖ poʊ-
poser ˈpəʊz ə ‖ ˈpoʊz ᵊr ~s z
poseur ₍ˌ₎pəʊ ˈzɜː ‖ poʊ ˈzɜː ~s z
posey ˈpəʊz i ‖ ˈpoʊz i
posh pɒʃ ‖ paːʃ poshly ˈpɒʃ li ‖ ˈpaːʃ-
poshness ˈpɒʃ nəs -nɪs ‖ ˈpaːʃ-
pos|it ˈpɒz ɪt §-ət ‖ ˈpaːz ət ~ited ɪt ɪd §ət-,
-əd ‖ əţ əd ~iting ɪt ɪŋ §ət- ‖ əţ ɪŋ ~its ɪts
§əts ‖ əts
position pə ˈzɪʃ ᵊn ~ed d ~ing ɪŋ ~s z
positional pə ˈzɪʃ ᵊn_ᵊl ~ly i
positive ˈpɒz ət ɪv -ɪt-; ˈpɒz tɪv ‖ ˈpaːz əţ ɪv
ˈpaːz tɪv ~ly li —but as an interj in AmE,
sometimes ˌpaːz ə ˈtɪv li ~s z
ˌpositive diˌscrimiˈnation; ˌpositive ˈpole
positivism ˈpɒz ət ɪv ˌɪz əm '•ɪt- ‖ ˈpaːz əţ-
positivist ˈpɒz ət ɪv ɪst '•ɪt-, §-əst ‖ ˈpaːz əţ-
~s s
positron ˈpɒz ɪ trɒn -ə- ‖ ˈpaːz ə traːn ~s z
positronium ˌpɒz ɪ ˈtrəʊn i_əm ˌ•ə-
‖ ˌpaːz ə ˈtroʊn- ~s z
Posner ˈpɒz nə ‖ ˈpaːz nᵊr
posological ˌpɒs ə ˈlɒdʒ ɪk ᵊl ◂ ‖ ˌpaːs ə ˈlaːdʒ-
~ly _i
posology pəʊ ˈsɒl ədʒ i ‖ pə ˈsaːl- poʊ-
poss. pɒs ‖ paːs
posse ˈpɒs i ‖ ˈpaːs i ~s z
possess pə ˈzes ~ed t ~es ɪz əz ~ing ɪŋ
possession pə ˈzeʃ ᵊn ~s z
possessive pə ˈzes ɪv ~ly li ~ness nəs nɪs ~s
z
posˌsessive ˈpronoun
possessor pə ˈzes ə ‖ -ᵊr ~s z
possessory pə ˈzes ᵊr i
posset ˈpɒs ɪt §-ət ‖ ˈpaːs ət ~s s
possibilit|y ˌpɒs ə ˈbɪl ət i ‖ ˌ•ɪ-, -ɪt i
‖ ˌpaːs ə ˈbɪl əţ li ~ies iz
possible ˈpɒs əb ᵊl -ɪb- ‖ ˈpaːs- ~s z
possibly ˈpɒs əb li -ɪb- ‖ ˈpaːs-
possum, P~ ˈpɒs əm ‖ ˈpaːs- ~s z

post, Post pəʊst ‖ poʊst posted ˈpəʊst ɪd -əd
‖ ˈpoʊst əd posting ˈpəʊst ɪŋ ‖ ˈpoʊst ɪŋ
posts pəʊsts ‖ poʊsts
ˈpost exˌchange; ˈpost horn; ˈpost house;
ˈpost ˌoffice; ˈpost office box
post- ˌpəʊst ‖ ˌpoʊst —if the following sound is
a consonant (not h), the t can optionally be
elided — post-Victorian ˌpəʊst
vɪk ˈtɔːr i_ən ◂ ˌpoʊst- -ˈtoʊr-
Posta ˈpɒst ə ‖ ˈpoʊst ə
postag|e ˈpəʊst ɪdʒ ‖ ˈpoʊst- ~es ɪz əz
ˈpostage stamp
postal, P~ ˈpəʊst ᵊl ‖ ˈpoʊst- ~ly i
ˌpostal ˈorder, '• • ˌ• •
postbag ˈpəʊst bæg ‖ ˈpoʊst- ~s z
post-bellum ˌpəʊst ˈbel əm ◂ ‖ ˌpoʊst-
postbox ˈpəʊst bɒks ‖ ˈpoʊst baːks ~es ɪz əz
postcard ˈpəʊst kaːd ‖ ˈpoʊst kaːrd ~s z
post-chais|e ˈpəʊst ʃeɪz ‖ ˈpoʊst- ~es ɪz əz
postcode ˈpəʊst kəʊd ‖ ˈpoʊst koʊd ~s z
postconsonantal ˌpəʊst
ˌkɒnts ə ˈnænt ᵊl ◂ ‖ ˌpoʊst ˌkaːnts ə ˈnænţ
ᵊl ◂ ~ly i
post|date ˌpəʊst ǀˈdeɪt ◂ ‖ ˌpoʊst- ~dated
ˈdeɪt ɪd -əd ‖ ˈdeɪţ əd ~dates ˈdeɪts
~dating ˈdeɪt ɪŋ ‖ ˈdeɪţ ɪŋ
postdoc ˌpəʊst ˈdɒk ‖ ˌpoʊst ˈdaːk '• • ~s s
postdoctoral ˌpəʊst ˈdɒkt ər əl ◂ →-ˈdɒk trəl
‖ ˌpoʊst ˈdaːkt-
poster, P~ ˈpəʊst ə ‖ ˈpoʊst ᵊr ~s z
ˈposter ˌcolour; ˈposter paint
poste restante
ˌpəʊst ˈrest ɒnt ‖ ˌpoʊst re ˈstaːnt —Fr
[pɔst ʁɛs tãːt]
posterior pɒ ˈstɪər i_ə ‖ paː ˈstɪr i_ᵊr poʊ- ~ly
li ~s z
posteriority pɒ ˌstɪər i ˈɒr ət i ˌpɒst ɪər-, -ɪt i
‖ paː ˌstɪr i ˈɔːr əţ i -ˈaːr-
posterity pɒ ˈster ət i -ɪt- ‖ paː ˈster əţ i
postern ˈpɒst ən ˈpəʊst- ‖ ˈpoʊst ᵊrn ˈpaːst-
~s z
postfix ˈpəʊst fɪks ‖ ˈpoʊst-
post-free ˌpəʊst ˈfriː ◂ ‖ ˌpoʊst-
Postgate ˈpəʊst geɪt ‖ ˈpoʊst-
postglacial ˌpəʊst ˈgleɪs i_əl ◂ -ˈgleɪʃ i_əl,
-ˈgleɪʃ ᵊl ‖ ˌpoʊst ˈgleɪʃ ᵊl ◂
postgrad ˈpəʊst græd ˌ•ˈ• ‖ˈpoʊst- ~s z
postgraduate ₍ˌ₎pəʊst ˈgræd ju_ət -ˈgrædʒ u_,
ˌ_ɪt ₍ˌ₎poʊst ˈgrædʒ u_ət ~s s
posthaste ˌpəʊst ˈheɪst ‖ ˌpoʊst-
post hoc ˌpəʊst ˈhɒk -ˈhəʊk ‖ ˌpoʊst ˈhaːk
posthumous ˈpɒst jʊm əs -jəm-; ˈpɒs tʃʊm-,
-tʃəm- ‖ ˈpaːs tʃəm əs -tʃʊm- ~ly li ~ness
nəs nɪs
postich|e pɒ ˈstiːʃ ‖ pɔː- paː- ~es ɪz əz
postie ˈpəʊst i ‖ ˈpoʊst i ~s z
postilion, postillion pɒ ˈstɪl i_ən pə-
‖ poʊ ˈstɪl jən pə- ~s z
postimpressionism ˌpəʊst ɪm ˈpreʃ ᵊn ˌɪz əm
-ə ˌnɪz- ‖ ˌpoʊst-
postimpressionist ˌpəʊst ɪm ˈpreʃ ᵊn_ɪst ◂ _əst
‖ ˌpoʊst- ~s s
posting ˈpəʊst ɪŋ ‖ ˈpoʊst ɪŋ ~s z

P

Post-it *tdmk* ˈpəust ɪt §-ət ‖ ˈpoust- **~s** s
Postlethwaite ˈpɒs əl θweɪt ‖ ˈpɑːs-
postlude ˈpəus*t* luːd -ljuːd ‖ ˈpous*t*- **~s** z
post|man ˈpəus*t* |mən ‖ ˈpous*t*- **~men** mən
 ˌpostman's ˈknock
postmark *n, v* ˈpəus*t* mɑːk ‖ ˈpous*t* mɑːrk **~ed** t **~ing** ɪŋ **~s** s
postmaster ˈpəus*t* ˌmɑːst ə §-ˌmæst- ‖ ˈpous*t* ˌmæst ər **~s** z
 ˌPostˌmaster ˈGeneral
postmen ˈpəus*t* mən ‖ ˈpous*t*-
post meridiem ˌpəus*t* mə ˈrɪd i‿əm -em ‖ ˌpous*t*-
postmistress ˈpəus*t* ˌmɪs trəs -trɪs ‖ ˈpous*t*- **~es** ɪz əz
post-modern ˌpəus*t* ˈmɒd ən ‖ ˌpous*t* ˈmɑːd ərn **~ism** ˌɪz *ə*m **~ist/s** ɪst/s §əst/s
postmortem ˌpəus*t* ˈmɔːt əm -em, ˈ•ˌ•• ‖ ˌpous*t* ˈmɔːrt̬ əm **~s** z
postnatal ˌpəus*t* ˈneɪt əl ◂ ‖ ˌpous*t* ˈneɪt̬ əl ◂ **~ly** i
postoperative ˌpəust ˈɒp *ə*r‿ət ɪv ◂ -ə reɪt- ‖ ˌpoust ˈɑːp *ə*r‿ət̬ ɪv ◂ **~ly** li
postpaid ˌpəus*t* ˈpeɪd ◂ ‖ ˌpous*t*-
post-partum ˌpəus*t* ˈpɑːt əm ◂ ‖ ˌpous*t* ˈpɑːrt̬ əm ◂
postpon|e ₍ₗ₎pəus*t* ˈpəun ◂ pəs- ‖₍ₗ₎pous*t* ˈpoun **~ed** d **~es** z **~ing** ɪŋ
postpos|e ˌpəus*t* ˈpəuz ◂ ˈ•• ‖ ˌpous*t* ˈpouz ◂ ˈ•• **~ed** d **~es** ɪz əz **~ing** ɪŋ
postposition ˌpəus*t* pə ˈzɪʃ ən ‖ ˌpous*t*- **~al** ‿*ə*l **~s** z
postpositive ˌpəus*t* ˈpɒz ət ɪv -ɪt- ‖ ˌpous*t* ˈpɑːz ət̬ ɪv **~ly** li **~s** z
postprandial ˌpəus*t* ˈprænd i‿əl ◂ ‖ ˌpous*t*-
postscript, P~ ˈpəus*t* skrɪpt ‖ ˈpous*t*- **~s** s
postulant ˈpɒs tjʊl ənt ‖ ˈpɑːs tʃəl- **~s** s
postu|late *v* ˈpɒs tju |leɪt ‖ ˈpɑːs tʃə- **~lated** leɪt ɪd -əd ‖ leɪt̬ əd **~lates** leɪts **~lating** leɪt ɪŋ ‖ leɪt̬ ɪŋ
postulate *n* ˈpɒs tjʊl ət -ɪt; -tju leɪt ‖ ˈpɑːs tʃəl ət -tʃə leɪt **~s** s
postulation ˌpɒs tju ˈleɪʃ ən ‖ ˌpɑːs tʃə- **~s** z
Postum *tdmk* ˈpɒst əm ˈpəust- ‖ ˈpɑːst-
postural ˈpɒs tʃər *ə*l -tjʊr- ‖ ˈpɑːs-
posture ˈpɒs tʃə -tjʊə ‖ ˈpɑːs tʃər **~d** d
 posturing ˈpɒs tʃər ɪŋ -tjʊər- ‖ ˈpɑːs- **~s** z
postviral ˌpəus*t* ˈvaɪər *ə*l ◂ ‖ ˌpous*t*-
postvocalic ˌpəus*t* vəu ˈkæl ɪk ◂ ‖ ˌpous*t* və- **~ally** əl‿i
postwar ˌpəus*t* ˈwɔː ◂ ‖ ˌpous*t* ˈwɔːr ◂
pos|y, Pos|y ˈpəuz |i ‖ ˈpouz |i **~ies, ~y's** iz
pot pɒt ‖ pɑːt **pots** pɒts ‖ pɑːts **potted** ˈpɒt ɪd -əd ‖ ˈpɑːt̬ əd **potting** ˈpɒt ɪŋ ‖ ˈpɑːt̬ ɪŋ
 ˈpot plant; ˈpotting shed
potability ˌpəut ə ˈbɪl ət i -ɪt i ‖ ˌpout̬ ə ˈbɪl ət̬ i
potable ˈpəut əb əl ‖ ˈpout̬- **~ness** nəs nɪs
potage pɒ ˈtɑːʒ pəu-; ˈpɒt ɑːʒ, ˈpəut- ‖ pou- —*Fr* [pɔ taːʒ]
potash ˈpɒt æʃ ‖ ˈpɑːt̬-
potassic pə ˈtæs ɪk
potassium pə ˈtæs i‿əm
 poˌtassium ˈcyanide
potation pə*u* ˈteɪʃ ən ‖ pou- **~s** z
potato pə ˈteɪt əu ⚠bə- ‖ pə ˈteɪt̬ ou pət̬ ˈeɪt̬-, -ə **~es** z
 poˈtato ˌbeetle; poˈtato cake; poˈtato chip; poˌtato ˈcrisp; poˈtato ˌpeeler
potatory ˈpəut ət‿*ə*r i ‖ ˈpout̬ ə tɔːr i -tour i
pot-au-feu ˌpɒt əu ˈfɜː ‖ ˌpɑːt̬ ou ˈfʌ —*Fr* [po to fø]
Potawatomi ˌpɒt ə ˈwɒt əm i ‖ ˌpɑːt̬ ə ˈwɑːt̬- **~s** z
potbell|ied ˌpɒt ˈbel |id ◂ ˈ•ˌ•• ‖ ˈpɑːt ˌbel |id **~y** i
potboiler ˈpɒt ˌbɔɪl ə ‖ ˈpɑːt ˌbɔɪl ər **~s** z
potbound ˈpɒt baʊnd ‖ ˈpɑːt-
potch pɒtʃ ‖ pɑːtʃ
poteen pə ˈtʃiːn pɒ-, pəu-, -ˈtiːn ‖ pou-
Potemkin pə ˈtemᵖ kɪn §-kən ‖ pou- —*Russ* [pʌ ˈtʲɔm kʲɪn]
 Poˌtemkin ˈvillage
potenc|y ˈpəut əntˢ |i ‖ ˈpout- **~ies** iz
potent ˈpəut ənt ‖ ˈpout- **~ly** li **~ness** nəs nɪs
potentate ˈpəut ən teɪt ‖ ˈpout- **~s** s
potential pə ˈtentʃ əl pəu- **~ly** i **~s** z
potentialit|y pə ˌtentʃ i ˈæl ət |i pəu-, -ɪt i ‖ -ət̬ |i **~ies** iz
potenti|ate pə*u* ˈtentʃ i |eɪt ‖ pə- **~ated** eɪt ɪd -əd ‖ eɪt̬ əd **~ates** eɪts **~ating** eɪt ɪŋ ‖ eɪt̬ ɪŋ
potentiation pə*u* ˌtentʃ i ˈeɪʃ ən ‖ pə- **~s** z
potentilla ˌpəut ən ˈtɪl ə ‖ ˌpout- **~s** z
potentiometer pə ˌtentʃ i ˈɒm ɪt ə pəu-, -ət ə ‖ -ˈɑːm ət̬ ər **~s** z
potful ˈpɒt fʊl ‖ ˈpɑːt- **~s** z
pothead ˈpɒt hed ‖ ˈpɑːt- **~s** z
potheen pə ˈtʃiːn pɒ-, pəu-, -ˈtiːn, -ˈθiːn ‖ pou-
poth|er ˈpɒð |ə ‖ ˈpɑːð |ər **~ered** əd ‖ ərd **~ering** *ə*r‿ɪŋ **~ers** əz ‖ ərz
potherb ˈpɒt hɜːb ‖ ˈpɑːt̬ ɜːb **~s** z
pothol|e ˈpɒt həul →-hɒul ‖ ˈpɑːt houl **~ed** d **~er/s** ə/z ‖ ər/z **~es** z **~ing** ɪŋ
pothook ˈpɒt hʊk §-huːk ‖ ˈpɑːt- **~s** s
pot|house ˈpɒt |haʊs ‖ ˈpɑːt- **~houses** haʊz ɪz -əz
pothunt|er/s ˈpɒt ˌhʌnt |ə/z ‖ ˈpɑːt ˌhʌnt̬ |ər/z **~ing** ɪŋ
potich|e pɒ ˈtiːʃ ‖ pou- —*Fr* [pɔ tiʃ] **~es** ɪz əz
Potidae|a ˌpɒt ɪ ˈdiː‿|ə -ə- ‖ ˌpɑːt̬- **~an/s** ən/z
potion ˈpəuʃ ən ‖ ˈpouʃ ən **~s** z
Potiphar ˈpɒt ɪf ə -əf-; -ɪ fɑː, -ə- ‖ ˈpɑːt̬ əf ər
potlatch ˈpɒt lætʃ ‖ ˈpɑːt- **~es** ɪz əz
potluck ˌpɒt ˈlʌk ‖ ˌpɑːt-
pot|man ˈpɒt |mən ‖ ˈpɑːt- **~men** mən men
Potomac pə ˈtəum æk -ək ‖ -ˈtoum ək -ɪk
potoroo ˌpəut ə ˈruː ˌpɒt- ‖ ˌpout̬- **~s** z
Potosi *(i)* pə ˈtəus i ‖ -ˈtous i *(ii)* ˌpɒt əu ˈsiː ‖ ˌpout̬ ə- —*Places in the US are (i); in Bolivia, (ii)* —*Sp* Potosí [po to ˈsi]
potpourri ˌpəu ˈpʊr i ˌpɒt-, -ˈpʊər-, ˌ• pʊ ˈriː ‖ ˌpou pʊ ˈriː —*Fr* [po pu ʁi]
pot-roast ˈpɒt rəust ‖ ˈpɑːt roust **~ed** ɪd əd **~ing** ɪŋ **~s** s

Potsdam 'pɒts dæm ‖ 'pɑːts- —Ger
['pɔts dam]
potsherd 'pɒt ʃɜːd ‖ 'pɑːt ʃɜ̩ːd ~s z
potshot 'pɒt ʃɒt ‖ 'pɑːt ʃɑːt ~s s
Pott pɒt ‖ pɑːt
pottage 'pɒt ɪdʒ ‖ 'pɑːt̬-
pott... —see pot
potter, P~ 'pɒt ə ‖ 'pɑːt̬ ər ~ed d pottering
'pɒt_ər ɪŋ ‖ 'pɑːt̬ ər ɪŋ ~s, ~'s z
ˌpotter's 'wheel
Potteries 'pɒt ər iz ‖ 'pɑːt̬-
Potterton 'pɒt ət ən ‖ 'pɑːt̬ ərt ən
potter|y 'pɒt_ər li ‖ 'pɑːt̬ ər li ~ies iz
Pottinger 'pɒt ɪndʒ ə -əndʒ- ‖ 'pɑːt əndʒ ər
potto 'pɒt əʊ ‖ 'pɑːt̬ oʊ ~s z
Potts pɒts ‖ pɑːts
pott|y 'pɒt li ‖ 'pɑːt̬ li ~ier i_ə ‖ i_ər ~ies iz
~iest i_ɪst i_əst ~iness i nəs i nɪs
potty-trained 'pɒt i treɪnd ‖ 'pɑːt̬-
pouch paʊtʃ pouched paʊtʃt pouches
'paʊtʃ ɪz -əz pouching 'paʊtʃ ɪŋ
pouf, pouffe 'seat', 'hairstyle', 'padding' puːf
poufs, pouffes puːfs
pouf, pouffe derogatory slang 'homosexual' pʊf
puːf poufs, pouffes pʊfs puːfs, puːvz
Poughill (i) 'pɒf ɪl -əl ‖ 'pɑːf-, (ii) 'pʌf-, (iii)
'paʊ-
Poughkeepsie pə 'kɪps i (!)
Poujad|ism ˌpuː 'ʒɑːd ˌɪz əm '••,•• ~ist/s
ɪst/s əst/s
Poulenc 'puːl æŋk —Fr [pu læk]
Poulsen, Poulson 'pəʊl sən →'pɒʊl- ‖ 'poʊl-
poult 'chick' pəʊlt →pɒʊlt ‖ poʊlt poults
pəʊlts →pɒʊlts ‖ poʊlts
poult 'fabric' puːlt pʊlt poults puːlts pʊlts
Poulteney 'pəʊlt ni →'pɒʊlt- ‖ 'poʊlt-
Poulter 'pəʊlt ə →'pɒʊlt- ‖ 'poʊlt ər
poulterer 'pəʊlt_ər ə →'pɒʊlt_ ‖ 'poʊlt ər ər
~s z
poultic|e 'pəʊlt ɪs →'pɒʊlt-, -əs ‖ 'poʊlt əs
~ed t ~es ɪz əz ~ing ɪŋ
Poultney 'pəʊlt ni →'pɒʊlt- ‖ 'poʊlt-
Poulton 'pəʊlt ən →'pɒʊlt- ‖ 'poʊlt-
Poulton-le-Fylde ˌpəʊlt ən lə 'faɪəld →ˌpɒʊlt-,
-lɪ- ‖ ˌpoʊlt-
poultry 'pəʊltr i →'pɒʊltr- ‖ 'poʊltr i
poultry|man 'pəʊltr i |mən →'pɒʊltr-
‖ 'poʊltr- ~men mən men
pounce paʊnts pounced paʊntst pounces
'paʊnts ɪz -əz pouncing 'paʊnts ɪŋ
pound, Pound paʊnd pounded 'paʊnd ɪd -əd
pounding/s 'paʊnd ɪŋ/z pounds, Pound's
paʊndz
'pound cake; ˌpound 'sterling
poundag|e 'paʊnd ɪdʒ ~es ɪz əz
-pounder 'paʊnd ə ‖ -ər — two-pounder
ˌtuː 'paʊnd ə ‖ -ər
Pountney 'paʊnt ni
Poupart (i) 'puːp ɑːt ‖ puː 'pɑːrt, (ii)
'pəʊp- ‖ poʊ-
pour pɔː ‖ pɔːr pʊər (= pore) poured
pɔːd ‖ pɔːrd pʊərd pouring 'pɔːr ɪŋ ‖ 'pʊər-
pours pɔːz ‖ pɔːrz pʊərz

pourboire pʊə 'bwɑː '•• ‖ pʊr 'bwɑːr ~s z
—Fr [puʁ bwaːʁ]
pourer 'pɔːr ə ‖ 'pɔːr ər 'pʊər- ~s z
pous|sette puː |'set ~setted 'set ɪd -əd
‖ 'set̬ əd ~settes 'sets ~setting
'set ɪŋ ‖ 'set̬ ɪŋ
poussin, P~ 'puːs æn -ɪn, §-ən ‖ puː 'sæn —Fr
[pu sæ̃] ~s, ~'s z
pout paʊt pouted 'paʊt ɪd -əd ‖ 'paʊt̬ əd
pouting 'paʊt ɪŋ ‖ 'paʊt̬ ɪŋ pouts paʊts
pouter 'paʊt ə ‖ 'paʊt̬ ər ~s z
poverty 'pɒv ət i ‖ 'pɑːv ərt̬ i
'poverty trap
poverty-stricken 'pɒv ət i ˌstrɪk ən ‖ 'pɑːv ərt̬-
Povey (i) 'pəʊv i ‖ 'poʊv i, (ii) pə 'veɪ
pow interj paʊ
POW ˌpiː əʊ 'dʌb əl juː ‖ -ˌoʊ- -ə jə ~s, ~'s z
powder 'paʊd ə ‖ -ər ~ed d powdering
'paʊd_ər ɪŋ ~s z
ˌpowder 'blue◄; 'powder keg; 'powder
puff; 'powder room
Powderham 'paʊd_ər əm
powdery 'paʊd_ər i
Powell (i) 'paʊ_əl paʊl, (ii) 'pəʊ əl ‖ 'poʊ-
—The writer Anthony P~ is (ii).
power, Power 'paʊ_ə ‖ 'paʊ_ər powered
'paʊ_əd ‖ 'paʊ_ərd powering
'paʊ_ər ɪŋ ‖ 'paʊ_ər ɪŋ powers
'paʊ_əz ‖ 'paʊ_ərz
'power base; 'power ˌbroker; 'power cut;
'power dive; 'power drill; ˌpower of
at'torney; 'power pack; 'power plant;
'power play; 'power point; ˌpower
'politics; 'power ˌstation; ˌpower 'steering;
'power ˌstructure
powerboat 'paʊ_ə bəʊt ‖ 'paʊ_ər boʊt ~s s
-powered 'paʊ_əd ‖ 'paʊ_ərd — low-powered
ˌləʊ 'paʊ_əd ◄ ‖ ˌloʊ 'paʊ_ərd ◄
powerful 'paʊ_əf əl _ə fʊl ‖ 'paʊ_ərf əl _ər fʊl
~ly _i ~ness nəs nɪs
power|house 'paʊ_ə |haʊs ‖ 'paʊ_ər- ~houses
haʊz ɪz -əz
powerless 'paʊ_ə ləs -lɪs ‖ 'paʊ_ər- ~ly li
~ness nəs nɪs
Powerscourt (i) 'paʊ_əz kɔːt ‖ 'paʊ_ərz kɔːrt
-koʊrt, (ii) 'pɔːz• ‖ 'pɔːrz•
Powhatan 'paʊ_ə tæn ˌ•'•; 'paʊ hæt ən
Powis (i) 'paʊ ɪs §-əs, (ii) 'pəʊ- ‖ 'poʊ-
Pownall 'paʊn əl
powwow n, v 'paʊ waʊ ~ed d ~ing ɪŋ ~s z
Powys (i) 'pəʊ ɪs §-əs ‖ 'poʊ-, (ii) 'paʊ-
—Welsh ['pə wis, 'po-] —The Welsh county is
(ii), but the family name is usually (i).
pox pɒks ‖ pɑːks poxes 'pɒks ɪz -əz
‖ 'pɑːks əz
poxy 'pɒks i ‖ 'pɑːks i
Poynings 'pɔɪn ɪŋz
Poynting 'pɔɪnt ɪŋ ‖ 'pɔɪnt̬-
Pozidriv tdmk 'pɒz ɪ draɪv -ə- ‖ 'pɑːz-
Poznan, Poznań 'pɒz næn ˌ•'• ‖ 'poʊz nɑːn
—Polish ['pɔ znaj̃]
PPS ˌpiː piː 'es
PR ˌpiː 'ɑː ‖ -'ɑːr

P

Praa preɪ
practicability ˌprækt ɪk ə 'bɪl ət i -ɪt i ‖ -ət̬ i
practicab|le 'prækt ɪk əb |ᵊl **~ly** li
practical 'prækt ɪk ᵊl **~s** z
  ˌpractical 'joke
practicalit|y ˌprækt ɪ 'kæl ət |i , • ə-, -ɪt i ‖ -ət̬ |i
  ~ies iz
practically 'prækt ɪk li -ɪk ᵊl_i
practic|e, practis|e 'prækt ɪs §-əs **~ed** t **~es**
  ɪz əz **~ing** ɪŋ
practitioner præk 'tɪʃ ᵊn_ə ‖ _ᵊr **~s** z
Pradesh prə 'deɪʃ -'deʃ —*Hindi* [prə ɖeːʃ]
Prado 'prɑːd əʊ ‖ -oʊ —*Sp* ['pra ðo]
praecox 'priː kɒks 'praɪ- ‖ -kɑːks
Praed preɪd
praedial 'priːd i_əl
praelector ₍ᵢ₎praɪ 'lekt ə ₍ᵢ₎priː-, -ɔː ‖ -ᵊr **~s** z
praemunire ˌpraɪ mju 'nɪər i ˌpriː-, -mjə-,
  -'naɪᵊr- ‖ -'nɪr i
prae|nomen ˌpriː |'nəʊm en ˌpraɪ-
  ‖ -|'noʊm ən **~nomina** 'nɒm ɪn ə 'nəʊm-,
  -ən- ‖ 'nɑːm- 'noʊm-
praepostor prɪ 'pɒst ə ˌpriː- ‖ -'pɑːst ᵊr **~s** z
praesidi|um prɪ 'sɪd i_|əm prə-, praɪ-, -'zɪd- **~a**
  ə
praetor 'priːt ə -ɔː ‖ 'priːt̬ ᵊr **~s** z
praetorian prɪ 'tɔːr i_ən priː-, praɪ- ‖ -'toʊr-
  ~s z
pragmatic præg 'mæt ɪk ‖ -'mæt̬ ɪk **~ally** ᵊl_i
  ~s s
pragmatism 'præg mə ˌtɪz əm
pragmatist 'præg mət ɪst §-əst ‖ -mət̬- **~s** s
Prague prɑːg
prairie 'preər i ‖ 'prer i **~s** z
  'prairie dog; ˌprairie 'rose
praise preɪz (= *prays*) **praised** preɪzd **praises**
  'preɪz ɪz -əz **praising** 'preɪz ɪŋ
praiser 'preɪz ə ‖ -ᵊr **~s** z
praiseworth|y 'preɪz ˌwɜːd |i ‖ -ˌwɜːð |i **~ily**
  ɪ li əl i **~iness** i nəs i nɪs
Prakrit 'prɑː krɪt **~s** s
praline 'prɑːl iːn ‖ 'preɪl- 'prɑːl- **~s** z
pram '*baby carriage*' præm **prams** præmz
pram '*boat*' prɑːm præm **prams** prɑːmz
  præmz
prana 'prɑːn ə
prance prɑːn̪ts §prænᵗs ‖ prænᵗs **pranced**
  prɑːnᵗst §prænᵗst ‖ prænᵗst **prancer/s**
  'prɑːnᵗs ə/z §'prænᵗs- ‖ 'prænᵗs ᵊr/z
prances 'prɑːnᵗs ɪz §'prænᵗs-, -əz
  ‖ 'prænᵗs əz **prancing** 'prɑːnᵗs ɪŋ §'prænᵗs-
  ‖ 'prænᵗs ɪŋ
prancer 'prɑːnᵗs ə §'prænᵗs ə ‖ 'prænᵗs ᵊr **~s** z
prandial 'prænd i_əl **~ly** i
prang præŋ **pranged** præŋd **pranging**
  'præŋ ɪŋ **prangs** præŋz
Prangnell 'præŋ nᵊl
prank præŋk **pranks** præŋks
prank|ish 'præŋk |ɪʃ **~some** səm
prankster 'præŋkst ə ‖ -ᵊr **~s** z
p'raps præps —*see* **perhaps**
prase preɪz

praseodymium ˌpreɪz i_əʊ 'dɪm i_əm ‖ -oʊ' • -
  ˌpreɪs-
prat præt **prats** præts
Pratchett 'prætʃ ɪt §-ət
prate preɪt **prated** 'preɪt ɪd -əd ‖ 'preɪt̬ əd
  prates preɪts **prating** 'preɪt ɪŋ ‖ 'preɪt̬ ɪŋ
prater 'preɪt ə ‖ 'preɪt̬ ᵊr **~s** z
pratfall 'præt fɔːl ‖ -fɑːl **~s** z
pratincole 'præt ɪŋ kəʊl 'preɪt-, →-kɒʊl
  ‖ 'præt̬ ᵊn koʊl **~s** z
pratique 'præt iːk -ɪk; præ 'tiːk ‖ præ 'tiːk
Pratt præt
prattl|e 'præt ᵊl ‖ 'præt̬ ᵊl **~ed** d **~er/s** _ə/z
  ‖ _ᵊr/z **~es** z **~ing** _ɪŋ
Pravda 'prɑːv də —*Russ* ['prav də]
prawn prɔːn ‖ prɑːn **prawns** prɔːnz ‖ prɑːnz
  ˌprawn 'cocktail; ˌprawn 'cracker
praxis 'præks ɪs §-əs
Praxiteles præk 'sɪt ə liːz -ɪ-; -ᵊl iːz ‖ -'sɪt̬ ᵊl iːz
pray preɪ **prayed** preɪd **praying** 'preɪ ɪŋ
  prays preɪz (= *praise*)
  ˌpraying 'mantis
prayer '*act/words of praying*' preə ‖ preᵊr præᵊr
  ~s z
  'prayer book; 'prayer ˌmeeting; 'prayer
  mat; 'prayer rug; 'prayer wheel
prayer '*one that prays*' 'preɪ ə ‖ -ᵊr **~s** z
prayerful 'preə fᵊl ‖ 'prer- 'prær- **~ly** i **~ness**
  nəs nɪs
pre- ˌpriː, prɪ, prə, pri, ˌpre —*Compare* re-. *As*
  a productive prefix meaning 'before' (sometimes
  spelt with a hyphen), ˌpriː (preadapt
  ˌpriː_ə 'dæpt, pre-sleep ˌpriː 'sliːp ◄).
  Otherwise, with a vaguer meaning,
  prɪ, prə, §pri: *before a consonant sound*
  (prepare prɪ 'peə prə-, §prɪː- ‖ -'peᵊr); *but if*
  stressed through the operation of a stressing
  rule usually ˌpre+ (preparation
  ˌprep ə 'reɪʃ ᵊn).
preach priːtʃ **preached** priːtʃt **preaches**
  'priːtʃ ɪz -əz **preaching** 'priːtʃ ɪŋ
preacher, P~ 'priːtʃ ə ‖ -ᵊr **~s** z
preachi|fy 'priːtʃ ɪ |faɪ §-ə- **~fied** faɪd **~fies**
  faɪz **~fying** faɪ ɪŋ
preach|y 'priːtʃ |i **~ier** i_ə ‖ i_ᵊr **~iest** i_ɪst
  _əst **~iness** i nəs -nɪs
preadamic ˌpriː_ə 'dæm ɪk ◄
preadamite ˌpriː 'æd ə maɪt ◄ **~s** s
preamble pri 'æm bᵊl 'priː ˌæm- **~s** z
pre-amp 'priː æmp **~s** s
preamplification ˌpriː ˌæmp lɪf ɪ 'keɪʃ ᵊn
  • ,• • • ʹ• •, -ləf • ʹ• -, §-ə'• -
preampli|fy ₍ᵢ₎priː 'æmp lɪ |faɪ -lə- **~fied** faɪd
  ~fier/s faɪ_ə/z ‖ faɪ_ᵊr/z **~fies** faɪz **~fying**
  faɪ ɪŋ
prearrang|e ˌpriː_ə 'reɪndʒ ◄ **~ed** d **~ement**
  mənt **~es** ɪz əz **~ing** ɪŋ
prebend 'preb ənd **~s** z
prebendar|y 'preb ənd_ᵊr |i ‖ -ᵊn der |i **~ies** iz
precambrian, Pre-Cambrian
  ₍ᵢ₎priː 'kæm bri_ən
precancerous ˌpriː 'kænᵗs ᵊr_əs

precarious prɪ ˈkeər i‿əs prə-, §priː- ‖ -ˈker-
-ˈkær- ~**ly** li ~**ness** nəs nɪs
precast ˌpriː ˈkɑːst ◂ §-ˈkæst ‖ -ˈkæst ◂ ˈ• •
~**ing** ɪŋ ~**s** s
precatory ˈprek ət‿ər i ‖ -ə tɔːr i -tour i
precaution prɪ ˈkɔːʃ ən prə-, §priː- ‖ -ˈkɑːʃ- ~**s**
z
precautionary prɪ ˈkɔːʃ ən ər‿i §priː-, -ən‿ər i
‖ -ə ner i -ˈkɑːʃ-
preced|e prɪ ˈsiːd prə-, ˌpriː- ~**ed** ɪd əd ~**es** z
~**ing** ɪŋ
precedence ˈpres ɪd ənts ˈpriːs-, -əd-;
ˌpriː ˈsiːd ənts, prɪ-, prə-
precedent n ˈpres ɪd ənt ˈpriːs-, -əd- ~**s** s
precedent adj prɪ ˈsiːd ənt ˈpres ɪd ənt, ˈpriːs-,
-əd- ~**ly** li
precedented ˈpres ɪ dent ɪd ˈpriːs-, ˈ•ə-,
-dənt •, -əd ‖ -denṭ əd
precedential ˌpres ɪ ˈdentʃ əl ◂ ˈpriːs-, -ə-
precentor prɪ ˈsent ə prə-, ˌpriː- ‖ -ˈsenṭ ər ~**s**
z
precept ˈpriː sept ~**s** s
preceptor prɪ ˈsept ə prə-, §priː- ‖ -ər
ˈpriː sept ər ~**s** z
precess prɪ ˈses prə-, ˌpriː- ~**ed** t ~**es** ɪz əz
~**ing** ɪŋ
precession prɪ ˈseʃ ən prə-, ˌpriː- ~**s** z
precessional prɪ ˈseʃ ən‿əl prə-, ˌpriː-
precinct ˈpriː sɪŋkt ~**s** s
preciosity ˌpreʃ i ˈɒs ət i ˌpres-, -ɪt i ‖ -ˈɑːs əṭ i
precious ˈpreʃ əs ~**ly** li ~**ness** nəs nɪs
ˌprecious ˈmetal; ˌprecious ˈstone
precipic|e ˈpres əp ɪs -ɪp-, §-əs ~**es** ɪz əz
precipitant prɪ ˈsɪp ɪt ənt prə-, §priː-, -ət- ~**s** s
precipi|tate v prɪ ˈsɪp ɪ |teɪt prə-, §priː-, -ə-
~**tated** teɪt ɪd -əd ‖ teɪṭ əd ~**tates** teɪts
~**tating** teɪt ɪŋ ‖ teɪṭ ɪŋ
precipitate n, adj prɪ ˈsɪp ɪt ət prə-, §priː-, -ət-,
-ɪt; -ɪ teɪt, -ə- ‖ -əṭ ət -ə teɪt ~**ly** li ~**ness**
nəs nɪs ~**s** s
precipitation prɪ ˌsɪp ɪ ˈteɪʃ ən prə-, §priː-, -ə-
~**s** z
precipitous prɪ ˈsɪp ɪt əs prə-, §priː-, -ət-
‖ -əṭ əs ~**ly** li ~**ness** nəs nɪs
precis, précis n sing., v ˈpreɪs iː ‖ preɪ ˈsiː (*)
~**ed** d ~**es** z ~**ing** ɪŋ
precis, précis n pl ˈpreɪs iːz ‖ preɪ ˈsiːz (*)
precise prɪ ˈsaɪs prə-, §priː- ~**ly** li ~**ness** nəs
nɪs
precision prɪ ˈsɪʒ ən prə-, §priː- ~**ist/s** ɪst/s
§əst/s ‖ əst/s
precision-made prɪ ˌsɪʒ ən ˈmeɪd ◂ prə-, §priː-,
→-ˈəm-
preclassical ˌpriː ˈklæs ɪk əl ◂
preclinical ˌpriː ˈklɪn ɪk əl ◂
preclud|e prɪ ˈkluːd prə-, priː- ~**ed** ɪd əd ~**es**
z ~**ing** ɪŋ
preclusion prɪ ˈkluːʒ ən prə-, priː-
preclusive prɪ ˈkluːs ɪv prə-, priː- ‖ -ˈkluːz- ~**ly**
li
precocial prɪ ˈkəʊʃ əl prə-, §priː- ‖ -ˈkoʊʃ-
precocious prɪ ˈkəʊʃ əs prə-, §priː- ‖ -ˈkoʊʃ əs
~**ly** li ~**ness** nəs nɪs

precocity prɪ ˈkɒs ət i prə-, §priː-, -ɪt-
‖ -ˈkɑːs əṭ i
precognition ˌpriː kɒg ˈnɪʃ ən ‖ -kɑːg-
pre-Columbian ˌpriː kə ˈlʌm bi‿ən ◂
ˌpre-Coˌlumbian ˈpottery
preconceiv|e ˌpriː kən ˈsiːv ◂ §-kɒn- ~**ed** d
~**es** z ~**ing** ɪŋ
ˌprecon ˌceived iˈdeas
preconception ˌpriː kən ˈsep ʃən §-kɒn- ~**s** z
precon|cert ˌpriː kən |ˈsɜːt §-kɒn- ‖ -|ˈsɜːt
~**certed** ˈsɜːt ɪd -əd ‖ ˈsɜːṭ əd ~**certing**
ˈsɜːt ɪŋ ‖ ˈsɜːṭ ɪŋ ~**certs** ˈsɜːts ‖ ˈsɜːts
precondition ˌpriː kən ˈdɪʃ ən §-kɒn- ~**s** z
preconis|e, preconiz|e ˈpriːk ə naɪz ~**ed** d
~**es** ɪz əz ~**ing** ɪŋ
preconsonantal
ˌpriː ˌkɒnts ə ˈnænt əl ◂ ‖ -ˌkɑːnts ə ˈnænṭ əl ◂
-ˈnenṭ- ~**ly** i
precook ˌpriː ˈkʊk §-ˈkuːk ~**ed** t ◂ ~**ing** ɪŋ ~**s**
s
precursive prɪ ˈkɜːs ɪv prə-, ˌpriː- ‖ -ˈkɝːs ɪv
~**ly** li
precursor prɪ ˈkɜːs ə prə-, ˌpriː- ‖ -ˈkɝːs ər ~**s**
z
precursor|y prɪ ˈkɜːs ər i prə-, ˌpriː- ‖ -ˈkɝːs-
~**ily** əl i ɪ i li
predaceous, predacious prɪ ˈdeɪʃ əs prə-,
§priː- ~**ness** nəs nɪs
pre|date 'antedate' ₍ˌ₎priː |ˈdeɪt ~**dated** ˈdeɪt ɪd
-əd ‖ ˈdeɪṭ əd ~**dates** ˈdeɪts ~**dating**
ˈdeɪt ɪŋ ‖ ˈdeɪṭ ɪŋ
pre|date 'prey on' prɪ |ˈdeɪt prə-, §priː-
~**dated** ˈdeɪt ɪd -əd ‖ ˈdeɪṭ əd ~**dates** ˈdeɪts
~**dating** ˈdeɪt ɪŋ ‖ ˈdeɪṭ ɪŋ
predation prɪ ˈdeɪʃ ən prə-, §priː- ~**s** z
predator ˈpred ət ə -ɪt- ‖ -əṭ ər -tɔːr ~**s** z
predator|y ˈpred ət‿ər i ‖ -ə tɔːr i -tour i ~**ily**
əl i ɪ i li ~**iness** i nəs i nɪs
predeceas|e ˌpriː dɪ ˈsiːs -də- ~**ed** t ~**es** ɪz əz
~**ing** ɪŋ

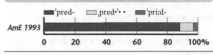
predecessor ˈpriːd ɪ ses ə ˈ• ə-, ˌ• • ˈ• •
‖ ˈpred ə ses ər, ˌ• ˈ• • •; ˈpriːd- —AmE 1993
poll panel preference: ˈpred- 88%, ˌpredˈ• • •
9%, ˈpriːd- 3%. ~**s** z
predefin|e ˌpriː dɪ ˈfaɪn -də- §-diː- ~**ed** d ◂
~**es** z ~**ing** ɪŋ
predesti|nate v ₍ˌ₎priː ˈdest ɪ |neɪt prɪ-, -ə-
~**nated** neɪt ɪd -əd ‖ neɪṭ əd ~**nates** neɪts
~**nating** neɪt ɪŋ ‖ neɪṭ ɪŋ
predestinate adj ₍ˌ₎priː ˈdest ɪn ət prɪ-, -ən-, -ɪt;
-ɪ neɪt, -ə- ~**ly** li
predestination ˌpriː dest ɪ ˈneɪʃ ən prɪ-,
ˌpriː-, • • ˈ• • -, -ə ˈ• -
predestin|e ₍ˌ₎priː ˈdest ɪn prɪ-, -ən ~**ed** d ~**es**
z ~**ing** ɪŋ
predetermination ˌpriː dɪ ˌtɜːm ɪ ˈneɪʃ ən
ˌ• ˈdə-, -, -ˌ• ə- ‖ -ˌtɝːm-

predetermin|e ˌpriː dɪ ˈtɜːm ɪn -də-, -ən
∥ -ˈtɝːm ən ~ed d ◂ ~es z ~ing ɪŋ
predeterminer ˌpriː dɪ ˈtɜːm ɪn ə ˌ•də-, -ən ə
∥ -ˈtɝːm ən ər ~s z
predial ˈpriːd i‿əl
predicability ˌpred ɪk ə ˈbɪl ət i -ɪt i ∥ -əţ i
predicable ˈpred ɪk əb ᵊl ~ness nəs nɪs ~s z
predicament prɪ ˈdɪk ə mənt prə-, §priː- —but
in the sense 'logical category', also ˈpred ɪk-
~s s
predicate n ˈpred ɪk ət ˈpriːd-, -ɪt; -ɪ keɪt ~s s
predi|cate v ˈpred ɪ |keɪt ~cated keɪt ɪd -əd
∥ keɪţ əd ~cates keɪts ~cating
keɪt ɪŋ ∥ keɪţ ɪŋ
predication ˌpred ɪ ˈkeɪʃ ᵊn -ə- ~s z
predicative prɪ ˈdɪk ət ɪv prə-, §priː- -əţ ɪv
ˈpred ɪk-; ˈpred ɪ keɪţ ɪv ~ly li ~ness nəs nɪs
~s z
predicator ˈpred ɪ keɪt ə ˈ•ə- ∥ -keɪţ ər ~s z
predict prɪ ˈdɪkt prə-, §priː- ~ed ɪd əd ~ing
ɪŋ ~s s
predictability prɪ ˌdɪkt ə ˈbɪl ət i prə-, §priː-,
-ɪt i ∥ -əţ i
predictab|le prɪ ˈdɪkt əb ᵊl prə-, §priː- ~ly li
prediction prɪ ˈdɪk ʃᵊn prə-, §priː- ~s z
predictive prɪ ˈdɪkt ɪv prə-, §priː- ~ly li ~ness
nəs nɪs
predictor prɪ ˈdɪkt ə prə-, §priː- ∥ -ᵊr ~s z
predigest ˌpriː daɪ ˈdʒest -dɪ-, -də- ~ed ɪd ◂
əd ~ing ɪŋ ~s s
predilection ˌpriːd ɪ ˈlek ʃᵊn -ə-, -ᵊl ˈek-;
△-ˈlɪk- ∥ ˌpred ᵊl ˈek ʃᵊn ˌpriːd- ~s z
predispos|e ˌpriː dɪ ˈspəʊz -də- ∥ -ˈspoʊz ~ed
d ~es ɪz əz ~ing ɪŋ
predisposition ˌpriː ˌdɪsp ə ˈzɪʃ ᵊn ~s z
prednisolone pred ˈnɪs ə ləʊn ∥ -loʊn
prednisone ˈpred nɪ səʊn -nə-, -zəʊn ∥ -soʊn
-zoʊn
predominanc|e prɪ ˈdɒm ɪn ənts prə-, §priː-,
-ən- ∥ -ˈdɑːm- ~y i
predominant prɪ ˈdɒm ɪn ənt prə-, §priː-, -ən-
∥ -ˈdɑːm- ~ly li
predomi|nate prɪ ˈdɒm ɪ |neɪt prə-, §priː-, -ə-
∥ -ˈdɑːm- ~nated neɪt ɪd -əd ∥ neɪţ əd
~nates neɪts ~nating neɪt ɪŋ ∥ neɪţ ɪŋ
Preece priːs
pre-echo ˌpriː ˈek əʊ ∥ -oʊ ~es z
pre-eclampsia ˌpriː ɪ ˈklæmps i‿ə ˌ•e-, ˌ•ə-
Preedy ˈpriːd i
preeminence pri ˈem ɪn ənts ˌpriː-, -ən-
preeminent pri ˈem ɪn ənt ˌpriː-, -ən- ~ly li
preempt pri ˈempt ˌpriː- ~ed ɪd əd ~ing ɪŋ
~s s
preemption pri ˈemp ʃᵊn ˌpriː- ~s z
preemptive pri ˈempt ɪv ˌpriː- ~ly li
preemptor pri ˈempt ə ˌpriː-, -ɔː ∥ -ᵊr ~s z
preen, Preen priːn preened priːnd preening
ˈpriːn ɪŋ preens priːnz
preexilian ˌpriː ˈzɪl i‿ən ◂ ˌ•eg-, ˌ•əg-, ˌ•ɪk-,
ˌ•ek-, ˌ•ək-
pre-exilic ˌpriː ɪg ˈzɪl ɪk ◂ -eg-, -əg-, -ɪk-, -ek-,
-ək-

preexist ˌpriː ɪg ˈzɪst -eg-, -əg-, -ɪk-, -ek-, -ək-
~ed ɪd əd ~ing ɪŋ ~s s
preexistenc|e ˌpriː ɪg ˈzɪst ᵊnts -eg-, -əg-, -ɪk-,
-ek-, -ək- ~es ɪz əz
preexistent ˌpriː ɪg ˈzɪst ᵊnt ◂ -eg-, -əg-, -ɪk-,
-ek-, -ək- ~ly li
prefab ˈpriː fæb ~s z
prefabri|cate ˌpriː ˈfæb rɪ |keɪt -rə- ~cated
keɪt ɪd -əd ∥ keɪţ əd ~cates keɪts ~cating
keɪt ɪŋ ∥ keɪţ ɪŋ
prefabrication ˌpriː ˌfæb rɪ ˈkeɪʃ ᵊn •ˌ••ˈ•-,
-rə•ˈ•- ~s z
prefac|e n, v ˈpref əs -ɪs ~ed t ~es ɪz əz ~ing
ɪŋ
prefator|y ˈpref ət‿ər i ∥ -ə tɔːr i -toʊr i ~ily
əl i ɪ li
prefect ˈpriː fekt ~s s
prefectorial ˌpriː fek ˈtɔːr i‿əl ◂ ∥ -ˈtoʊr-
prefectural prɪ ˈfek tʃər əl ⑴priː-, -tjʊr-;
ˈpriː fek-
prefecture ˈpriː fek tʃə -tʃʊə; -fekt jʊə ∥ -tʃᵊr
~s z
prefer prɪ ˈfɜː prə-, §priː- ∥ -ˈfɝː ~red d
preferring prɪ ˈfɜːr ɪŋ prə-, §priː- ∥ -ˈfɝː ɪŋ
~s z
pre.ferred 'stock
preferability ˌpref ᵊr‿ə ˈbɪl ət i △prɪ ˌfɜːr ə-,
prə-, priː- ∥ -əţ i △prɪ ˌfɝː ə-
preferab|le ˈpref ᵊr‿əb ᵊl △prɪ ˈfɜːr əb ᵊl,
prə-, priː- ∥ △prɪ ˈfɝː- ~leness ᵊl nəs -nɪs
~ly li
preferenc|e ˈpref ᵊr‿ənts ~es ɪz əz
ˈpreference ˌshares
preferential ˌpref ə ˈrentʃ ᵊl ◂ ~ly i
preferment prɪ ˈfɜː mənt prə-, §priː- ∥ -ˈfɝː-
~s s
prefiguration ˌpriː ˌfɪg ə ˈreɪʃ ᵊn -juᵊ- ∥ -jə-
~s z
prefigure ⑴priː ˈfɪg ə ∥ -jᵊr (*) ~d d ~s z
prefiguring ⑴priː ˈfɪg ər ɪŋ ∥ -jᵊr ɪŋ ~ment
mənt
prefix n ˈpriː fɪks ~es ɪz əz
prefix v ˈpriː fɪks ⑴priː ˈfɪks ~ed t ~es ɪz əz
~ing ɪŋ
prefixal ⑴priː ˈfɪks ᵊl ˈpriː fɪks- ~ly i
preformation ˌpriː fɔː ˈmeɪʃᵊn ∥ -fɔːr-
prefrontal ⑴priː ˈfrʌnt ᵊl ∥ -ˈfrʌnţ ᵊl
preggers ˈpreg əz ∥ -ᵊrz
pregnanc|y ˈpreg nənts i ~ies iz
pregnant ˈpreg nənt ~ly li
prehead ˈpriː hed ~s z
pre|heat ˌpriː |ˈhiːt ~heated ˈhiːt ɪd ◂ -əd
∥ ˈhiːţ əd ◂ ~heating ˈhiːt ɪŋ ∥ ˈhiːţ ɪŋ
~heats ˈhiːts
ˌpre.heated 'oven
prehensile prɪ ˈhents aɪᵊl prə-, §priː- ∥ -ᵊl (*)
prehistoric ˌpriː hɪ ˈstɒr ɪk ◂ -ɪ- ∥ -ˈstɔːr ɪk
-ˈstɑːr- ~ally ᵊl‿i
prehistory ˌpriː ˈhɪs tri -tᵊr i
pre-ignition ˌpriː ɪg ˈnɪʃ ᵊn
prejudg|e ˌpriː ˈdʒʌdʒ ~ed d ~ement, ~ment
mənt ~es ɪz əz ~ing ɪŋ

prejudic|e 'predʒ u dɪs -ə-, §-dəs, §-daɪs
‖ -əd əs ~ed t ~es ɪz əz ~ing ɪŋ
prejudicial ˌpredʒ u 'dɪʃ ᵊl ◄ -ə- ‖ -ə- ~ly i
prelac|y 'prel əs |i ~ies iz
prelapsarian ˌpri: læp 'seər i_ən ◄ ‖ -'ser- ~s z
prelate 'prel ət -ɪt ~s s
prelim 'pri: lɪm prɪ 'lɪm, prə-, ˌpri:- ~s z
preliminar|y prɪ 'lɪm ɪn ᵊr_|i prə-, pri:-,
-ᵊn_ər |i; §-ɪ ner |i, §-ə ner i ‖ -ə ner |i ~ies iz
~ily ᵊl i ɪ li
prelingual ˌpri: 'lɪŋ gwəl ◄ ˌ•'lɪŋ gju_əl ◄ ~ly i
preliterate ₍ᵢ₎pri: 'lɪt_ər ət ◄ -ɪt ‖ -'lɪt_ər-
→ -'lɪtr-
prelude 'prel ju:d ~s z
prelusive prɪ 'lu:s ɪv -'lju:s- ‖ -'lu:z- ~ly li
Prem prem
premarital ₍ᵢ₎pri: 'mær ɪt ᵊl -ət- ‖ -ət ᵊl -'mer-
~ly i

PREMATURE

BrE 1998

◾ '•••	▭ •ˌ•ʼ•				
0	20	40	60	80	100%

premature 'prem ətʃ ə 'pri:m-; -ə tjʊə, -tʃʊə,
-tjɔ:, -tʃɔ:; ˌ•ə 'tʃʊə, -'tʃɔ:, -'tjʊə, -'tjɔ:
‖ ˌpri:m ə 'tʊr ◄ -'tʃʊʳr, -'tjʊʳr; '••• —BrE
1998 poll panel preference: '••• 59%, ••ˈ•
41%. (*) ~ly li ~ness nəs nɪs
prematurity ˌprem ə 'tʃʊər ət i ˌpri:m-,
-'tjʊər-, -'tʃɔ:r-, -ɪt i
‖ ˌpri:m ə 'tʊr ət̬ i -'tʃʊr-, -'tjʊr-
premed ₍ᵢ₎pri: 'med ~s z
premedical ₍ᵢ₎pri: 'med ɪk ᵊl
premedication ˌpri: med ɪ 'keɪʃ ᵊn •ˌ,••ˈ•- ~s
z
premedi|tate ₍ᵢ₎pri: 'med ɪ |teɪt prɪ-, prə-, -ə-
~tated teɪt ɪd -əd ‖ teɪt̬ əd ~tates teɪts
~tating teɪt ɪŋ ‖ teɪt̬ ɪŋ
premeditation pri: ˌmed ɪ 'teɪʃ ᵊn prɪ-, prə-,
-ə-; ˌpri:, ••ˈ•-, -ə'•-
premenstrual ˌpri: 'men̩ts tru_əl ◄
ˌpreˌ menstrual' tension
premier 'prem i_ə 'pri:m- ‖ prɪ 'mɪʳr -'mjɪʳr;
'pri:m i_ər (*) ~s z
premiere, première 'prem i eə -i_ə, ˌ••'eə
‖ prɪ 'mɪʳr pre-, -'mjɪʳr; prɪm 'jeʳr (*) ~s z
Preminger 'prem ɪndʒ ə ‖ -ᵊr
prem|ise n 'prem| ɪs §-əs; ~ises ɪs ɪz əs-, -əz;
ɪ si:z, ə-
premis|e v 'prem ɪs §-əs; prɪ 'maɪz, prə- ~ed t
~es ɪz əz ~ing ɪŋ
premiss 'prem ɪs §-əs ~es ɪz əz
premium 'pri:m i_əm ~s z
'premium bond, ˌ••• ˈ•
premodification ˌpri: ˌmɒd ɪf ɪ 'keɪʃ ᵊn -ˌ•əf-,
§-ə'•• ‖ -ˌmɑ:d-
premodi|fy ˌpri: 'mɒd ɪ |faɪ -ə- ‖ -'mɑ:d-
~fied faɪd ~fier/s faɪ_ə/z ‖ faɪ_ər/z ~fies
faɪz ~fying faɪ ɪŋ
premolar ₍ᵢ₎pri: 'məʊl ə ‖ -'moʊl ər ~s z
premonition ˌprem ə 'nɪʃ ᵊn ˌpri:m- ~s z
premonitor|y prɪ 'mɒn ɪt_ər |i prə-, ₍ᵢ₎pri:-,
-'•ət_ ‖ -'mɑ:n ə tɔ:r |i -toʊr i ~ily ᵊl i ɪ li

prenatal ˌpri: 'neɪt ᵊl ◄ ‖ -'neɪt̬ ᵊl ◄ ~ly i
Prendergast 'prend ə gɑ:st -gæst ‖ -ᵊr gæst
prentice, P~, Prentis, Prentiss 'prent ɪs §-əs
‖ 'prent̬ əs
prenuptial ˌpri: 'nʌp ʃᵊl ◄ -tʃᵊl; ⚠-'nʌp ʃu_əl,
⚠-tʃu_əl ~ly i ~s z —The nonstandard
pronunciations are reflected in a nonstandard
spelling prenuptual
preoccupation pri: ˌɒk ju 'peɪʃ ᵊn ˌpri:, ••ˈ•-,
-jə'•- ‖ -ˌɑ:k jə- ~s z
preoccu|py pri: 'ɒk ju |paɪ ˌpri:-, -jə-
‖ -'ɑ:k jə- ~pied paɪd ~pies paɪz ~pying
paɪ ɪŋ
preordain ˌpri: ɔ: 'deɪn ‖ -ɔ:r- ~ed d ~ing ɪŋ
~s z
preordination pri: ˌɔ:d ɪ 'neɪʃ ᵊn ˌ•, ••ˈ••,
-ə'•-, -ᵊn 'eɪʃ- ‖ -ˌɔ:rd ᵊn 'eɪʃ ᵊn ~s z
prep prep prepped prept prepping 'prep ɪŋ
preps preps
'prep school
prepack ˌpri: 'pæk ~ed t ◄ ~ing ɪŋ ~s s
prepackag|e ˌpri: 'pæk ɪdʒ ~ed d ◄ ~es ɪz əz
~ing ɪŋ
prepaid ˌpri: 'peɪd ◄
preparation ˌprep ə 'reɪʃ ᵊn ~s z
preparative prɪ 'pær ət ɪv prə-, §pri:- ‖ -ət̬ ɪv
-'per- ~ly li ~s z
preparator|y prɪ 'pær ət_ər |i prə-, §pri:-
‖ -ə tɔ:r |i -'per-, -toʊr i; 'prep ᵊr_ə- ~ily ᵊl i
ɪ li
preˈ paratory school
prepare prɪ 'peə prə-, §pri:- ‖ -'peʳr -'pæʳr ~d
d preparing prɪ 'peər ɪŋ prə-, §pri:-
‖ -'per ɪŋ -'pær- ~s z
preparedness prɪ 'peər ɪd nəs prə-, §pri:-,
-əd-, -nɪs; -'peəd nəs, -nɪs ‖ -'per əd- -'pær-;
-'perd nəs, -'pærd-
pre|pay ˌpri: 'peɪ ~paid 'peɪd ◄ ~paying
'peɪ ɪŋ ~payment 'peɪ mənt ~pays 'peɪz
prepense prɪ 'pen̩ts ˌpri:-, prə- ~ly li
preponderanc|e prɪ 'pɒnd_ər ᵊn̩ts prə-, ₍ᵢ₎pri:-
‖ -'pɑ:nd_ ~y i
preponderant prɪ 'pɒnd_ər ᵊnt prə-, ₍ᵢ₎pri:-
‖ -'pɑ:nd_ ~ly li
preponde|rate prɪ 'pɒnd ə |reɪt prə-, ₍ᵢ₎pri:-
‖ -'pɑ:nd- ~rated reɪt ɪd -əd ‖ reɪt̬ əd
~rates reɪts ~rating reɪt ɪŋ ‖ reɪt̬ ɪŋ
prepos|e ˌpri: 'pəʊz ‖ -'poʊz ~ed d ◄ ~es ɪz
əz ~ing ɪŋ
preposition ˌprep ə 'zɪʃ ᵊn ~s z
prepositional ˌprep ə 'zɪʃ ᵊn_əl ◄ ~ly i ~s z
ˌprepoˌsitional' phrase
prepositive ₍ᵢ₎pri: 'pɒz ət ɪv -ɪt- ‖ -'pɑ:z ət̬ ɪv
~ly li ~s z
prepossess ˌpri: pə 'zes ~ed t ~es ɪz əz ~ing
ɪŋ
prepossessing|ly ˌpri: pə 'zes ɪŋ |li ~ness nəs
nɪs
prepossession ˌpri: pə 'zeʃ ᵊn ~s z
preposterous prɪ 'pɒst ᵊr_əs prə-, §pri:-
‖ -'pɑ:st- ~ly li ~ness nəs nɪs
prepotency ₍ᵢ₎pri: 'pəʊt ᵊn̩ts i ‖ -'poʊt-
prepotent ₍ᵢ₎pri: 'pəʊt ᵊnt ‖ -'poʊt- ~ly li

P

prepp|ie, prepp|y 'prep |i ~**ier** i‿ə ‖ i‿ər ~**ies**
iz ~**iest** i‿ɪst ‿əst
preprint 'priː prɪnt ~**s** s
preproduction ˌpriː prə 'dʌk ʃən
prepubescent ˌpriː pju 'bes ənt ◂
prepuc|e 'priːp juːs ~**es** ɪz əz
prequel 'priː kwəl ~**s** z
Pre-Raphaelite ˌ(ˌ)priː 'ræf ə laɪt ˌ(ˌ)•‿ˌ•‿i‿ə•,
ˌ(ˌ)•‿ˌ•ˈeɪ ə• ‖ ˌ(ˌ)•ˈreɪf- ~**s** s
prerecord ˌpriː rɪ 'kɔːd -rə-, §-riː- ‖ -ˈkɔːrd
~**ed** ɪd ◂ əd ~**ing** ɪŋ ~**s** z
prerequisite ˌ(ˌ)priː 'rek wəz ɪt -wɪz-, §-ət ~**s** s
prerogative prɪ 'rɒg ət ɪv prə-, §priː-
‖ -ˈrɑːg ət̬ ɪv ~**s** z
pres|a 'preɪs| ə -ɑː ‖ 'preɪs| ə ~**as** əz ɑːz ~**e** eɪ
—*It* ['pre sa]
presag|e *v, n* 'pres ɪdʒ -ɑːʒ; prɪ 'seɪdʒ, prə-,
ˌ(ˌ)priː- ~**ed** d ~**es** ɪz əz ~**ing** ɪŋ
presbyopia ˌprez bi 'əʊp i‿ə ˌpres-, ˌ•baɪ-
‖ -ˈoʊp-
presbyopic ˌprez bi 'ɒp ɪk ◂ ˌpres-, -baɪ-
‖ -ˈɑːp ɪk ◂
presbyter 'prez bɪt ə 'pres-, -bət- ‖ -bət̬ ər ~**s**
z
Presbyterian, p~ ˌprez bɪ 'tɪər i‿ən ◂ ˌpres-,
ˌ•bə- ‖ -ˈtɪr- ~**ism** ˌɪz əm ~**s** z
presbyter|y 'prez bɪt‿ər li 'pres-, '•bət‿;
§-bɪ ter i, §-bə•• ‖ -bə ter li ~**ies** ɪz
Prescelly, Prescely prɪ 'sel i prə-, pre- —*Welsh*
Preseli [pre 'sɛ li]
preschool *n* 'priː skuːl ~**er/s** ə/z ‖ ər/z ~**s** z
preschool *adj* ˌpriː 'skuːl ◂
ˌpreschool 'playgroup
prescience 'pres i‿ənts 'preʃ- ‖ 'preʃ ənts
'priːʃ-, -i‿ənts
prescient 'pres i‿ənt 'preʃ- ‖ 'preʃ ənt 'priːʃ-,
-i‿ənt ~**ly** li
prescientific ˌpriː ˌsaɪ ən 'tɪf ɪk ◂
prescind prɪ 'sɪnd prə-, ˌpriː- ~**ed** ɪd əd ~**ing**
ɪŋ ~**s** z
Prescot, Prescott 'presk ət -ɒt ‖ -ɑːt
prescrib|e prɪ 'skraɪb prə-, §priː- ~**ed** d ~**er/s**
ə/z ‖ ər/z ~**es** z ~**ing** ɪŋ
prescript *n* 'priː skrɪpt ~**s** s
prescript *adj* prɪ 'skrɪpt prə-, priː-; 'priː skrɪpt
prescription prɪ 'skrɪp ʃən prə-, priː- ~**s** z
preˈscription charge; preˈscription drug
prescriptive prɪ 'skrɪpt ɪv prə-, priː- ~**ly** li
~**ness** nəs nɪs
preˌscriptive 'right
prescriptiv|ism prɪ 'skrɪpt ɪv ˌɪz əm prə-, priː-
~**ist/s** ɪst/s §əst/s ‖ əst/s
presenc|e 'prez ənts ~**es** ɪz əz
ˌpresence of 'mind
present *adj; n 'gift'; n 'time now'* 'prez ənt ~**ly**
li ~**s** s
ˌpresent 'participle; ˌpresent 'perfect;
ˌpresent 'tense
pre|sent *v; n 'military stance'* prɪ |'zent prə-,
§priː- ~**sented** 'zent ɪd -əd ‖ 'zent̬ əd
~**senting** 'zent ɪŋ ‖ 'zent̬ ɪŋ ~**sents** 'zents
presentab|le prɪ 'zent əb |əl prə-, §priː-
‖ -ˈzent̬- ~**leness** əl nəs -nɪs ~**ly** li

presentation ˌprez ən 'teɪʃ ən ˌpriːz-, -en- ~**s** z
ˌpresenˈtation ˌcopy
presentational ˌprez ən 'teɪʃ ən‿əl ◂ ˌpriːz-,
ˌ•en-
present-day ˌprez ənt 'deɪ ◂
presenter prɪ 'zent ə prə-, §priː- ‖ -ˈzent̬ ər ~**s**
z
presentient prɪ 'sentʃ ənt prə-, ˌ(ˌ)priː-, -ˈzentʃ-,
-ˈ•i‿ənt, -ˈsent i‿ənt
presentiment prɪ 'zent ɪ mənt prə-, §priː-,
-ˈsent-, -ə- ‖ -ˈzent̬- ~**s** s
presently 'prez ənt li
presentment prɪ 'zent mənt prə-, §priː-
preservable prɪ 'zɜːv əb əl prə-, §priː-
‖ -ˈzɜːːv-
preservation ˌprez ə 'veɪʃ ən ‖ -ər- ~**s** z
ˌpreserˈvation ˌorder
preservative prɪ 'zɜːv ət ɪv prə-, §priː-
‖ -ˈzɜːv ət̬ ɪv ~**s** z
preserv|e prɪ 'zɜːv prə-, §priː- ‖ -ˈzɜːv ~**ed** d
~**er/s** ə/z ‖ ər/z ~**es** z ~**ing** ɪŋ
pre|set ˌpriː |'set ◂ ~**sets** 'sets ~**setting**
'set ɪŋ ‖ 'set̬ ɪŋ
Preshaw 'preʃ ɔː ‖ -ɑː
preshrunk ˌpriː 'ʃrʌŋk ◂
ˌpreshrunk 'jeans
presid|e prɪ 'zaɪd prə-, §priː- ~**ed** ɪd əd ~**es** z
~**ing** ɪŋ
presidenc|y 'prez ɪd ənts li '•‿əd- ‖ -ə dents li
~**ies** ɪz
president, P~ 'prez ɪd ənt -əd- ‖ -ə dent ~**s** s
president-elect ˌprez ɪd ənt ɪ 'lekt ˌ•əd-, -ə'•
‖ ˌ•‿ənt̬ ˌ•ə dent̬-
presidential ˌprez ɪ 'dentʃ əl ◂ -ə- ~**ly** i
presidio prɪ 'sɪd i əʊ prə-, priː-, -ˈzɪd- ‖ -oʊ
-ˈsiːd- —*Sp* [pre 'si ðjo] ~**s** z
presidi|um prɪ 'sɪd i‿ləm prə-, priː-, -ˈzɪd- ~**a** ə
Presley 'prez li 'pres-
pre-Socratic, Presocratic ˌpriː səʊ
'kræt ɪk ◂ ‖ -sə 'kræt̬- -soʊ- ~**s** s
press, Press pres **pressed** prest **presses**
'pres ɪz -əz **pressing** 'pres ɪŋ
'press ˌagency; 'press ˌagent; 'press
ˌbaron; 'press box; 'press ˌconference;
'press ˌcutting; 'press ˌgallery; 'press
ˌofficer; 'press reˌlease; 'press run; 'press
ˌsecretary
pressgang 'pres gæŋ ~**ed** d ~**ing** ɪŋ ~**s** z
pressie 'prez i ~**s** z
pressing 'pres ɪŋ ~**ly** li ~**s** z
press|man 'pres |mæn -mən ~**men** men -mən
pressmark 'pres mɑːk ‖ -mɑːrk ~**s** s
press-stud 'pres stʌd 'prest ʌd ~**s** z
press-up 'pres ʌp ~**s** s
pressure 'preʃ ə ‖ -ər ~**d** d **pressuring** 'preʃ
ər‿ɪŋ ~**s** z
'pressure ˌcooker; 'pressure gauge;
'pressure group; 'pressure point
pressuris... —*see* pressuriz...
pressurization ˌpreʃ ər aɪ 'zeɪʃ ən -ɪ'•- ‖ -ə'•-
~**s** z
pressuriz|e 'preʃ ə raɪz ~**ed** d ~**es** ɪz əz ~**ing**
ɪŋ

Prestatyn pre 'stæt ɪn prɪ-, -ᵊn —*Welsh*
[pre 'sdat ɪn, -ɪn]
Prestbury 'prest bər_i
Prestcold *tdmk* 'prest kəʊld →-kɒʊld ‖ -koʊld
Presteigne (ˌ)pre 'stiːn
Prestel *tdmk* 'pres tel
Prester 'prest ə ‖ -ᵊr
prestidigitation ˌprest ɪ dɪdʒ ɪ 'teɪʃ ᵊn ˌ•ə-,
-ə'•- ~s z
prestidigitator ˌprest ɪ 'dɪdʒ ɪ teɪt ə ˌ•ə-, -'•ə-
‖ -teɪt ᵊr ~s z
prestige (ˌ)pre 'stiːʒ -'stiːdʒ
Prestige *family name* 'prest ɪdʒ

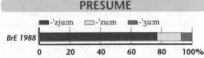
prestigious pre 'stɪdʒ əs prɪ-, prə-, -'stiːdʒ-,
-'•i_əs —*Poll panel preferences: AmE 1993,*
-'stiːdʒ- 64%, -'stɪdʒ- 36%; BrE 1998,
-'stɪdʒ- 91%, -'stiːdʒ- 9%. ~ly li ~ness nəs
nɪs
prestissimo pre 'stɪs ɪ məʊ -ə- ‖ -moʊ ~s z
presto, P~ 'prest əʊ ‖ -oʊ ~s z
Preston 'prest ən
Prestonpans ˌprest ən 'pænz →-əm-
prestressed ˌpriː 'strest ◂
ˌprestressed 'concrete
Prestwich 'prest wɪtʃ
Prestwick 'prest wɪk
presumably prɪ 'zjuːm əb li prə-, §priː-,
-'zuːm-, §-'ʒuːm- ‖ -'zuːm-

PRESUME

■-'zjuːm □-'zuːm ▬-'ʒuːm

BrE 1988

0   20   40   60   80   100%

presum|e prɪ 'zjuːm prə-, §priː-, -'zuːm,
§-'ʒuːm ‖ -'zuːm —*BrE 1988 poll panel*
preference: -'zjuːm 77%, -'zuːm 16%, -'ʒuːm
8%. ~ed d ~es z ~ing ɪŋ
presumedly prɪ 'zjuːm ɪd li prə-, §priː-,
-'zuːm-, -'ʒuːm-, -əd- ‖ -'zum əd li -'zuːmd li
presumption prɪ 'zʌmp ʃᵊn prə-, §priː-, ~s z
presumptive prɪ 'zʌmpt ɪv prə-, §priː- ~ly li
presumptuous prɪ 'zʌmp tʃu_əs prə-, §priː-,
-tju_əs, -ʃu_əs; -'zʌmp tʃəs, -ʃəs ~ly li
~ness nəs nɪs
presuppos|e ˌpriː sə 'pəʊz ‖ -'poʊz ~ed d ~es
ɪz əz ~ing ɪŋ
presupposition ˌpriː ˌsʌp ə 'zɪʃ ᵊn ~s z
prêt-à-porter ˌpret ɑː 'pɔːt eɪ ◂ ‖ -pɔːr 'teɪ
—*Fr* [pʀɛ ta pɔr te]
pretax ˌpriː 'tæks ◂
ˌpretax 'profits
preteen ˌpriː 'tiːn ◂ ~s z
pretenc|e prɪ 'tents prə-, §priː- ‖ 'priː tents (*)
~es ɪz əz
pretend prɪ 'tend prə-, §priː- ~ed ɪd əd ~ing
ɪŋ ~s z

pretender prɪ 'tend ə prə-, §priː- ‖ -ᵊr ~s z
pretens|e prɪ 'tents prə-, §priː- ‖ 'priː tents (*)
~es ɪz əz
pretension prɪ 'tentʃ ᵊn prə-, §priː- ~s z
pretentious prɪ 'tentʃ əs prə-, §priː- ~ly li
~ness nəs nɪs
preterit, preterite 'pret ᵊr ɪt -ət ‖ 'preţ ᵊr ət
~s s
pretermission ˌpriːt ə 'mɪʃ ᵊn ‖ ˌpriːţ ᵊr-
preter|mit ˌpriːt ə 'mɪt ‖ ˌpriːţ ᵊr- ~mits 'mɪts
~mitted 'mɪt ɪd -əd ‖ 'mɪţ əd ~mitting
'mɪt ɪŋ ‖ 'mɪţ ɪŋ
preternatural ˌpriːt ə 'nætʃ ᵊr_əl ◂ ‖ ˌpriːţ ᵊr-
~ism ˌɪz əm ~ly i ~ness nəs nɪs
pretext 'priː tekst ~s s
pretonic ˌpriː 'tɒn ɪk ◂ ‖ -'tɑːn ɪk ◂ ~ally ᵊl_i
pretor 'priːt ə -ɔː ‖ 'priːţ ᵊr ~s z
Pretori|a prɪ 'tɔːr i_ə prə-, priː- ‖ -'toʊr- ~us
əs
pretorian prɪ 'tɔːr i_ən priː-, praɪ- ‖ -'toʊr- ~s
z
pretti... —*see* pretty
prettification ˌprɪt ɪf ɪ 'keɪʃ ᵊn ˌ•əf-, §-ə'•-
‖ ˌprɪţ- ~s z
pretti|fy 'prɪt ɪ faɪ §-ə- ‖ 'prɪţ- ~fied faɪd
~fier/s faɪ_ə/z ‖ faɪ_ᵊr/z ~fies faɪz ~fying
faɪ ɪŋ
prett|y 'prɪt li i 'prɪţ li (!) —*In AmE there are*
also casual forms 'pɜːţ i, 'prʊţ i ~ied id ~ier
i_ə ‖ i_ᵊr ~ies iz ~iest i_ɪst i_əst ~ily i li əl i
~iness i nəs i nɪs ~ying i ɪŋ
ˌpretty 'good; a ˌpretty 'penny
pretty-pretty 'prɪt i ˌprɪt i ‖ 'prɪţ i ˌprɪţ i
pretzel 'prets ᵊl ~s z
prevail prɪ 'veɪᵊl prə-, §priː- ~ed d ~ing/ly
ɪŋ /li ~s z
prevalenc|e 'prev əl ᵊnts ~es ɪz əz
prevalent 'prev əl ənt ~ly li
prevari|cate prɪ 'vær ɪ keɪt prə-, §priː-,
-ə- ‖ -'ver- ~cated keɪt ɪd -əd ‖ keɪţ əd
~cates keɪts ~cating keɪt ɪŋ ‖ keɪţ ɪŋ
prevarication prɪ ˌvær ɪ 'keɪʃ ᵊn prə-, §priː-,
-ə'•- ‖ -ˌver- ~s z
prevaricator prɪ 'vær ɪ keɪt ə prə-, §priː-, -'•ə-
‖ -keɪţ ᵊr -'ver- ~s z
prevenient prɪ 'viːn i_ənt prə-, (ˌ)priː- ~ly li
pre|vent prɪ l'vent prə-, §priː- —*but in the*
obsolete sense 'go before', ˌpriː- ~vented
'vent ɪd -əd 'venţ əd ~venting
'vent ɪŋ ‖ 'venţ ɪŋ ~vents 'vents
preventability, preventibility
prɪ ˌvent ə 'bɪl ət i prə-, §priː-, -ɪt i ‖ -ˌvenţ
ə 'bɪl əţ i
preventab|le, preventib|le prɪ 'vent əb |ᵊl
prə-, §priː- ‖ -'venţ- ~ly li
preventative prɪ 'vent ət ɪv prə-, §priː-
‖ -'venţ əţ ɪv ~ly li ~ness nəs nɪs ~s z
preventer prɪ 'vent ə prə-, §priː- ‖ -'venţ ᵊr
~s z
prevention prɪ 'ventʃ ᵊn prə-, §priː-
preventive prɪ 'vent ɪv prə-, §priː- ‖ -'venţ ɪv
~ly li ~ness nəs nɪs ~s z
preverbal ˌpriː 'vɜːb ᵊl ◂ ‖ -'vɜːb ᵊl ◂

preview 'priː vjuː ~ed d ~ing ɪŋ ~s z
Previn 'prev ɪn §-ən
previous 'priːv i_əs ~ly li ~ness nəs nɪs
prevision ˌpriː 'vɪʒ ən prɪ-, prə-
prevocalic ˌpriː vəʊ 'kæl ɪk ◀ -voʊ- -və-
~ally əl_i
prewar ˌpriː 'wɔː ◀ ‖ -'wɔːr ◀
ˌprewar 'prices
Prewett 'pruː_ɪt §-ət
prey preɪ (= pray) preyed preɪd preying
'preɪ ɪŋ preys preɪz
preyer 'preɪ ə ‖ -ər ~s z
prezzie 'prez i ~s z
Priam 'praɪ_əm -æm
priapic praɪ 'æp ɪk -'eɪp-
priapism 'praɪ_əp ˌɪz əm
Priapus praɪ 'eɪp əs 'praɪ_əp əs
Pribilof 'prɪb ɪ lɒf -ə-, -ləf ‖ -lɑːf -lɔːf
price, Price praɪs priced praɪst prices,
Price's 'praɪs ɪz -əz pricing/s 'praɪs ɪŋ/z
'price conˌtrol; 'price list; 'price tag; 'price
war
priceless 'praɪs ləs -lɪs ~ly li ~ness nəs nɪs
pric|ey 'praɪs |i ~ier i_ə ‖ i_ər ~iest i_ɪst i_əst
~ily ɪ li əl i ~iness i nəs i nɪs
Prichard 'prɪtʃ əd ‖ -ərd
prick prɪk pricked prɪkt pricking/s 'prɪk ɪŋ/z
pricks prɪks
pricker 'prɪk ə ‖ -ər ~s z
pricket 'prɪk ɪt §-ət ~s s
prickl|e 'prɪk əl ~ed d ~es z ~ing _ɪŋ
prick|ly 'prɪk |li -əl_i ~lier li_ə ‖ li_ər ~liest
li_ɪst li_əst ~liness li nəs li nɪs
ˌprickly 'heat; ˌprickly 'pear
pride, Pride praɪd prided 'praɪd ɪd -əd
prides, Pride's praɪdz priding 'praɪd ɪŋ
Prideaux 'prɪd əʊ ‖ -oʊ
prideful 'praɪd fəl -fʊl ~ly _i ~ness nəs nɪs
prie... —see pry
prie-dieu ˌpriː 'djɜː '• • ‖ -'djʊ ~s, ~x z —or
as sing. —Fr [pʁi djø]
priest priːst priests priːsts
priestcraft 'priːsːɹ krɑːft §-kræft ‖ -kræft
priestess ˌpriːst 'es ◀ 'priːst es, -ɪs, -əs
‖ 'priːst əs ~es ɪz əz
priesthood 'priːst hʊd
Priestland 'priːst lənd
Priestley 'priːst li
priest|ly 'priːst |li ~lier li_ə ‖ li_ər ~liest li_ɪst
li_əst ~liness li nəs li nɪs
priest-ridden 'priːst ˌrɪd ən
prig prɪg prigs prɪgz
priggery 'prɪg ər i
priggish 'prɪg ɪʃ ~ly li ~ness nəs nɪs
prim prɪm primmer 'prɪm ə ‖ -ər primmest
'prɪm ɪst -əst
prima ballerina ˌpriːm ə ˌbæl ə 'riːn ə ~s z
primac|y 'praɪm əs |i ~ies iz
prima donna ˌpriːm ə 'dɒn ə ‖ ˌprɪm ə 'dɑːn ə
ˌpriːm- ~s z
primaeval praɪ 'miːv əl ~ly i
prima facie ˌpraɪm ə 'feɪʃ i ◀ -'feɪs-, -iː, -'• i iː,
§-'feɪʃ ə

Primakov 'priːm ə kɒf ˌ• • '• ‖ -kɔːf -kɑːf,
-koʊv —Russ [prʲi mʌ 'kɔf]
primal 'praɪm əl
primaquine 'praɪm ə kwiːn

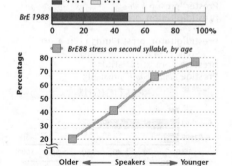

PRIMARILY

primarily praɪ 'mer əl i -'meər-, -ɪ li;
'praɪm ər_əl i ‖ 'praɪm er- —BrE 1988 poll
panel preference: '• • • • 49%, •ˌ• • • 51%.
primar|y 'praɪm ər li ‖ -er li -ər i ~ies iz
ˌprimary 'accent; ˌprimary 'colour;
'primary school; ˌprimary 'stress
primate 'archbishop' 'praɪm ət -ɪt, -eɪt ~s s
~ship/s ʃɪp/s
primate 'higher mammal' 'praɪm eɪt primates
'praɪm eɪts praɪ 'meɪt iːz
primatolog|ist/s ˌpraɪm ə 'tɒl ədʒ ɪst/s §-əst/s
‖ -'tɑːl- ~y i
prime, Prime praɪm —in the phrase prime
minister also ˌ(ˌ)praɪ primed praɪmd primes
praɪmz priming/s 'praɪm ɪŋ/z
ˌprime 'cost; ˌprime me'ridian; ˌprime
'minister; ˌprime 'mover; ˌprime 'number;
'prime rate,ˌ• '•; 'prime time, ˌ• '•
primer 'paint'; 'explosive' 'praɪm ə ‖ -ər ~s z
primer 'introductory book' 'praɪm ə ‖ 'prɪm ər
(*) ~s z
primeval praɪ 'miːv əl ~ly i
primigrav|ida ˌpraɪm ɪ 'græv ɪd ə ˌpriːm-, ˌ•ə-,
-'•əd- ~idae ɪ diː ə- ~idas ɪd əz əd-
priming 'praɪm ɪŋ ~s z
primip|ara praɪ 'mɪp |ər ə ~arae ə riː ~aras
ər əz ~arous ər əs
primitive 'prɪm ət ɪv -ɪt- ‖ -əṯ ɪv ~ly li ~ness
nəs nɪs ~s z
primitiv|ism 'prɪm ət ɪv ˌɪz əm '•ɪt- ‖ '•əṯ-
~ist/s ɪst/s §əst/s
primly 'prɪm li
primm... —see prim
primness 'prɪm nəs -nɪs
primo 'priːm əʊ ‖ -oʊ ~s z
primogenitor ˌpraɪm əʊ 'dʒen ɪt ə ˌpriːm-,
-ət ə ‖ -oʊ 'dʒen əṯ ər ~s z
primogeniture ˌpraɪm əʊ 'dʒen ɪtʃ ə ˌpriːm-,
-ət ʃ ə, -ɪt jʊə ‖ -oʊ 'dʒen ətʃ ər -ə tʃʊr
primordial praɪ 'mɔːd i_əl ‖ -'mɔːrd- ~ly i ~s
z
primp prɪmp primped prɪmpt primping
'prɪmp ɪŋ primps prɪmps

primros|e, P~ 'prɪm rəʊz ‖ -roʊz ~es ɪz əz
  ˌprimrose 'path; ˌprimrose 'yellow◄
primula, P~ 'prɪm jʊl ə -jəl- ‖ -jəl ə ~s z
primum mobile ˌpraɪm əm 'məʊb ɪl i ˌpriːm-,
  ˌʊm-, -əl iː; -ɪ leɪ, -ə • ‖ -'moʊb-
primus *tdmk* 'praɪm əs ~es ɪz əz
  ˌprimus ˌinter 'pares ˌɪnt ə 'pɑːr iːz -'pær-,
  -ɪz -ˌɪnt̬ ər 'pær iːz -'per-; 'primus stove
prince, P~ prɪnts princes, Prince's 'prɪnts ɪz
  -əz
  ₍ₒ₎Prince 'Charming; ˌprince 'consort;
  ₍ₒ₎Prince 'Edward ˌIsland ' • , • • ' • • ;
  ˌPrince of 'Wales; ˌprince 'regent
princedom 'prɪnts dəm ~s z
princeling 'prɪnts lɪŋ ~s z
prince|ly 'prɪnts |li ~lier li_ə ‖ li_ər ~liest li_ɪst
  _əst ~liness li nəs -nɪs
Princes Risborough ˌprɪnts ɪz 'rɪz bər_ə ˌ•əz-
  ‖ -ˌbɜː oʊ

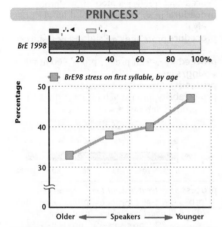

PRINCESS

BrE 1998   ▪ˈ•◄   ▫ˈ•‧

0   20   40   60   80   100%

▨ BrE98 stress on first syllable, by age

Percentage

50

40

30

0

Older ◄— Speakers —► Younger

princess, P~ ˌprɪn 'ses ◄ prɪn-; 'prɪnts es
  ‖ 'prɪnts əs 'prɪn ses ~es ɪz əz —*BrE 1998
  poll panel preference:* ˌ•'•◄ 60%, '•• 40%.
  —*The streets named* Princess St *in Manchester
  and Huddersfield, in the north of England, are
  often pronounced locally as if spelt* Prince's
  Street.
  ˌPrincess 'Di; ˌprincess 'royal
Princeton 'prɪnts tən
Princetown 'prɪnts taʊn
principal 'prɪnts əp əl -ɪp- *(= principle)* ~s z
  ˌprincipal 'boy; ˌprincipal 'parts
principalit|y, P~ ˌprɪnts ə 'pæl ət li ˌ•ɪ-, -ɪt li
  ‖ -ət̬ li ~ies iz
principally 'prɪnts əp əl_i '•ɪp-
principalship 'prɪnts əp əl ʃɪp '•ɪp- ~s s
Principe, Príncipe 'prɪnts ɪ peɪ -ə-; -ɪp i, -əp i,
  -ə —*Port* ['prĩ si pə]
Principia prɪn 'sɪp i_ə
principi|um prɪn 'sɪp i_əm prɪŋ 'kɪp- ~a ə
principle 'prɪnts əp əl -ɪp- ~d d ~s z
Pring prɪŋ
Pringle 'prɪŋ gəl
prink prɪŋk prinked prɪŋkt prinking 'prɪŋk ɪŋ
  prinks prɪŋks

Prinknash 'prɪn ɪdʒ (!)
Prinn prɪn
Prinnie, Prinny 'prɪn i
Prinsep 'prɪnts ep
print prɪnt printed 'prɪnt ɪd -əd ‖ 'prɪnt̬ əd
  printing/s 'prɪnt ɪŋ/z ‖ 'prɪnt̬ ɪŋ/z prints
  prɪnts
  ˌprinted 'circuit; 'printed ˌmatter;
  'printing ink; 'printing maˌchine; 'printing
  press; 'print run; 'print shop
printable 'prɪnt əb əl ‖ 'prɪnt̬-
Printator *tdmk* ₍ₒ₎prɪn 'teɪt ə ‖ -'teɪt̬ ər ~s z
printed-paper ˌprɪnt ɪd 'peɪp ə ◄ -əd-, →-ɪb-
  ‖ ˌprɪnt̬ əd 'peɪp ər ◄
printer 'prɪnt ə ‖ 'prɪnt̬ ər ~s z
printer|y 'prɪnt ər |i ‖ 'prɪnt̬- ~ies iz
printhead 'prɪnt hed ~s z
printmak|er/s 'prɪnt meɪk ə/z ‖ -ər/z ~ing ɪŋ
printout 'prɪnt aʊt ‖ 'prɪnt̬- ~s s
print-through 'prɪnt θruː
printwheel 'prɪnt wiːəl -hwiːəl ‖ -hwiːəl ~s z
prion *bird* 'praɪ ɒn ‖ -ɑːn ~s z
prion *infectious particle* 'priː ɒn 'praɪ- ‖ -ɑːn
  ~s z
prior, Prior 'praɪ_ə ‖ 'praɪ_ər ~s z
prioress ˌpraɪ_ə 'res 'praɪ_ər es, -əs, -ɪs
  ‖ 'praɪ ər əs ~es ɪz əz
priori... —*see* priory
prioritis|e, prioritiz|e praɪ 'ɒr ɪ taɪz -ə- ‖ -'ɔːr-
  -'ɑːr- ~ed d ~es ɪz əz ~ing ɪŋ
priorit|y praɪ 'ɒr ət li -ɪt- ‖ -'ɔːr ət̬ li -'ɑːr-
  ~ies iz
prior|y, P~ 'praɪ_ər |i ~ies iz
Priscian 'prɪʃ i_ən 'prɪʃ ən
Priscilla prɪ 'sɪl ə prə-
prise praɪz *(= prize)* prised praɪzd prises
  'praɪz ɪz -əz prising 'praɪz ɪŋ
prism 'prɪz əm ~s z
prismatic ₍ₒ₎prɪz 'mæt ɪk ‖ -'mæt̬ ɪk ~ally əl_i
prison 'prɪz ən ~s z
  'prison camp; ˌprison 'visitor
prisoner 'prɪz ən_ə ‖ _ər ~s z
  ˌprisoner of 'war
priss|y 'prɪs |i ~ier i_ə ‖ i_ər ~iest i_ɪst i_əst
  ~ily ɪ li əl i ~iness i nəs i nɪs
Pristina prɪ 'stiːn ə -'ʃtiːn-; 'prɪʃt ɪn ə, 'priːʃt-
  —*SCr* Priština ['priː ʃti na]
pristine 'prɪst iːn -aɪn; prɪ 'stiːn
Pritchard 'prɪtʃ əd -ɑːd ‖ -ərd -ɑːrd
Pritchett 'prɪtʃ ɪt -ət
prithee 'prɪð i -iː
Pritt prɪt

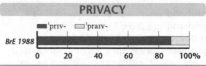

PRIVACY

▬ 'prɪv-   ▫ 'praɪv-

BrE 1988   0   20   40   60   80   100%

privacy 'prɪv əs i 'praɪv- ‖ 'praɪv- —*BrE 1988
poll panel preference:* 'prɪv- 88%, 'praɪv- 12%.
private 'praɪv ət -ɪt ~ly li ~ness nəs nɪs ~s s
  ˌprivate de'tective; ˌprivate 'enterprise;
  ˌprivate 'eye; ˌprivate in'vestigator;
  ˌprivate 'member('s bill); ˌprivate 'parts;

ˌprivate ˈschool; ˌprivate ˈsector◂; ˌprivate ˈsoldier

privateer ˌpraɪv ə ˈtɪə -ɪ- ‖ -ˈtɪʳr ~s z

privation praɪ ˈveɪʃ ən ~s z

privatis... —see privatiz...

privative ˈprɪv ət ɪv praɪ ˈveɪt ɪv ‖ -əṭ ɪv ~ly li

privatization ˌpraɪv ət aɪ ˈzeɪʃ ən ˌ•ɪt-, -ɪ ̍• - ‖ -əṭ ə- ~s z

privatiz|e ˈpraɪv ə taɪz -ɪ- ~ed d ~es ɪz əz ~ing ɪŋ

privet ˈprɪv ɪt §-ət ~s s

privi... —see privy

privilege|e ˈprɪv əl_ɪdʒ -ɪl- ~ed d ~es ɪz əz

privit|ly ˈprɪv ət li -ɪt- ‖ -əṭ li ~ies ɪz

priv|y ˈprɪv li ~ier i_ə ‖ i_ʳr ~ies iz ~iest i_ɪst i_əst ~ily i li əl i

ˌPrivy ˈCouncil; ˌPrivy ˈPurse; ˌPrivy ˈSeal

prix fixe ˌpri: ˈfɪks -ˈfi:ks —Fr [pʁi fiks]

prize praɪz prized praɪzd prizes ˈpraɪz ɪz -əz prizing ˈpraɪz ɪŋ

ˌprize ˈcattle; ˈprize day; ˈprize ˌmoney; ˈprize ring

prize|fight ˈpraɪz |faɪt ~fighter/s faɪt ə/z ‖ faɪt ʳr/z ~fighting faɪt ɪŋ ‖ faɪṭ ɪŋ

prize|man ˈpraɪz |mən ~men mən men

prizewinner ˈpraɪz ˌwɪn ə ‖ -ʳr ~s z

pro prəʊ ‖ proʊ pros prəʊz ‖ proʊz

pro-
ˌprəʊ, prə, prəʊ, ˌprɒ ‖ ˌproʊ, prə, ˌprɑ: —
As a productive prefix meaning 'in favour of'
(sometimes spelt with a hyphen), ˌprəʊ ‖ ˌproʊ
(pro-French ˌprəʊ ˈfrentʃ ◂ ‖ ˌproʊ-).
Otherwise, with a vaguer meaning, prə *(before*
a consonant sound only: proclaim prə ˈkleɪm),
or in less familiar words and slower speech
prəʊ ‖ proʊ; *but if stressed through the*
operation of a stressing rule usually
ˌprɒ+ ‖ ˌprɑ:+ (proclamation
ˌprɒk lə ˈmeɪʃ ən ‖ ˌprɑːk-). *See individual*
entries.

PRO initials ˌpi: ɑːr ˈəʊ ‖ -ɑːr ˈoʊ ~s, ~ʼs z

PRO grammatical term prəʊ ‖ proʊ

proa ˈprəʊ ə ‖ ˈproʊ ə ~s z

proactive ₍ₒ₎prəʊ ˈækt ɪv ‖ ₍ₒ₎proʊ-

pro-am ˌprəʊ ˈæm ◂ ‖ ₍ₒ₎proʊ-

probabilistic ˌprɒb əb ə ˈlɪst ɪk ◂ ˌ•ˈ•ɪ- ‖ ˌprɑːb- ~ally əl_i

probabilit|y ˌprɒb ə ˈbɪl ət li -ɪt i ‖ ˌprɑːb ə ˈbɪl əṭ li ~ies iz

probable ˈprɒb əb əl ‖ ˈprɑːb- ~s z

probably ˈprɒb əb li ‖ ˈprɑːb- —*In casual*
speech sometimes ˈprɒb li ‖ ˈprɑːb-

proband ˈprəʊb ənd -ænd ‖ ˈproʊb- ~s z

probang ˈprəʊb æŋ ‖ ˈproʊb- ~s z

probate n ˈprəʊb eɪt -ət, -ɪt ‖ ˈproʊb-

prob|ate v ˈprəʊb |eɪt ‖ ˈproʊb- ~ated eɪt ɪd -əd ‖ eɪṭ əd ~ates eɪts ~ating eɪt ɪŋ ‖ eɪṭ ɪŋ

probation prə ˈbeɪʃ ən prəʊ- ‖ proʊ- ~s z
proˈbation ofˌficer

probationary prə ˈbeɪʃ ən_ər i prəʊ-, -ən ʳr_i ‖ proʊ ˈbeɪʃ ə ner i

probationer prə ˈbeɪʃ ən_ə prəʊ- ‖ proʊ ˈbeɪʃ ən_ʳr ~s z

probative ˈprəʊb ət ɪv ‖ ˈproʊb əṭ ɪv

probe prəʊb ‖ proʊb probed prəʊbd ‖ proʊbd probes prəʊbz ‖ proʊbz probing ˈprəʊb ɪŋ ‖ ˈproʊb ɪŋ

Probert (i) ˈprəʊb ət ‖ ˈproʊb ʳrt, (ii) ˈprɒb- ‖ ˈprɑːb-

probing ˈprəʊb ɪŋ ‖ ˈproʊb ɪŋ ~ly li ~s z

probity ˈprəʊb ət i -ɪt- ‖ ˈproʊb əṭ i

problem ˈprɒb ləm -lɪm, -lem ‖ ˈprɑːb- —*In*
very casual speech also -ᵊm ~s z
ˈproblem child

problematic ˌprɒb lə ˈmæt ɪk ◂ -lɪ- ‖ ˌprɑːb lə ˈmæṭ ɪk ◂ ~al əl ◂ ~ally əl_i

pro bono ˌprəʊ ˈbəʊn əʊ ‖ ˌproʊ ˈboʊn oʊ

proboscis prəʊ ˈbɒs ɪs -ˈbɒsk-, -ˈbəʊs-, §-əs ‖ prə ˈbɑːs əs -ˈbɑːsk- ~es ɪz əz

Probyn ˈprəʊb ɪn §-ən ‖ ˈproʊb-

procaine ˈprəʊ keɪn ˌ•ˈ• ‖ ˈproʊ-

procathedral ˌprəʊ kə ˈθiːdr əl ‖ ˌproʊ- ~s z

Procea tdmk ˈprəʊs i_ə prəʊ ˈsiː_ə ‖ ˈproʊs-

procedural prəʊ ˈsiːdʒ ʳr_əl -ˈsiːd jʊr əl ‖ prə- ~ly i

procedure prəʊ ˈsiːdʒ ə -ˈsiːd jə ‖ prə ˈsiːdʒ ʳr ~s z

proceed v prə ˈsiːd prəʊ- ‖ proʊ- ~ed ɪd əd ~ing/s ɪŋ/z ~s z

proceeds n ˈprəʊs iːdz ‖ ˈproʊs-

pro-celebrity ˌprəʊ sɪ ˈleb rət i ◂ ˌ•sɪ-, -rɪt i ‖ ˌproʊ sə ˈleb rəṭ i ◂

PROCESS

	'prɑːs es	'prɑːs əs	'proʊs es	'proʊs əs
AmE 1993				

0   20   40   60   80   100%

process n; v ʻtreat, submit to a ~ʼ ˈprəʊs es ˈprɒs-, -ɪs, §-əs ‖ ˈprɑːs es ˈproʊs-, -əs —*AmE*
1993 poll panel preference: ˈprɑːs es 86%;
ˈprɑːs əs 7%; ˈproʊs es 6%, ˈproʊs əs 1%.
~ed t ~es ɪz əz ‖ iːz ~ing ɪŋ
ˌprocessed ˈcheese

process v ʻwalk in processionʼ prəʊ ˈses ‖ prə- ~ed t ~es ɪz əz ~ing ɪŋ

procession prə ˈseʃ ən ~s z

processional prə ˈseʃ ən_əl ~ly i ~s z

processor ˈprəʊs es ə ˈprɒs-, -ɪs-, §-əs- ‖ ˈprɑːs es ʳr ~s z

pro-choice ˌprəʊ ˈtʃɔɪs ◂ ‖ ˌproʊ-

Procktor ˈprɒkt ə ‖ ˈprɑːkt ʳr

proclaim prə ˈkleɪm prəʊ- ‖ proʊ- ~ed d ~er/s ə/z ‖ ʳr/z ~ing ɪŋ ~s z

proclamation ˌprɒk lə ˈmeɪʃ ən ‖ ˌprɑːk- ~s z

proclamatory prəʊ ˈklæm ət_ər i ‖ proʊ ˈklæm ə tɔːr i -toʊr i

proclitic ₍ₒ₎prəʊ ˈklɪt ɪk ‖ ₍ₒ₎proʊ ˈklɪṭ ɪk ~s s

proclivit|y prəʊ ˈklɪv ət li -ɪt- ‖ proʊ ˈklɪv əṭ li ~ies iz

Procne ˈprɒk ni ‖ ˈprɑːk-

proconsul ˌprəʊ ˈkɒnts əl ‖ ˌproʊ ˈkɑːnts əl ~s z

proconsular ˌprəʊ ˈkɒnts jʊl ə -jəl- ‖ ˌproʊ ˈkɑːnts əl_ʳr

proconsulate ˌprəʊ ˈkɒnts jʊl ət -jəl-, -ɪt ‖ ˌproʊ ˈkɑːnts əl_ət ~s s

P

proconsulship
  ,prəʊ 'kɒnts əl ʃɪp ‖ ,prəʊ 'kɑːnts- ~s s

procrasti|nate prəʊ 'kræst ɪ ˌneɪt -ə- ‖ prə- prəʊ-, pə- ~**nated** neɪt ɪd -əd ‖ neɪt̬ əd ~**nates** neɪts ~**nating** neɪt ɪŋ ‖ neɪt̬ ɪŋ

procrastination prəʊ ˌkræst ɪ 'neɪʃ ən ˌprəʊ-, -ə- ‖ prə- prəʊ-, pə- ~s z

procrastinator prəʊ 'kræst ɪ neɪt ə-ˈ•ə- ‖ prə 'kræst ə neɪt̬ ər prəʊ-, pə- ~s z

procre|ate 'prəʊk ri eɪt ,•ˈ•ˈ• ‖ 'prəʊk- ~**ated** eɪt ɪd -əd ‖ eɪt̬ əd ~**ates** eɪts ~**ating** eɪt ɪŋ ‖ eɪt̬ ɪŋ

procreation ˌprəʊk ri 'eɪʃ ən ‖ ˌprəʊk-

procreative 'prəʊk ri eɪt ɪv 'prɒk-, -ri_ət-; ˌ•ˈ•eɪt• ‖ 'prəʊk ri eɪt̬ ɪv

Procrust|ean prəʊ 'krʌst li_ən ‖ prəʊ- prə-, pə- ~**es** iːz

Procter 'prɒkt ə ‖ 'prɑːkt ər

proctitis prɒk 'taɪt ɪs §-əs ‖ prɑːk 'taɪt̬ əs

procto- *comb. form*
  with stress-neutral suffix ˈprɒkt əʊ ‖ ˈprɑːkt ə
  — **proctotome** 'prɒkt əʊ
  təʊm ‖ 'prɑːkt ə toʊm
  with stress-imposing suffix
  prɒk 'tɒ+ ‖ prɑːk 'tɑː+ — **proctology**
  prɒk 'tɒl ədʒ i ‖ prɑːk 'tɑːl-

proctor, P~ 'prɒkt ə ‖ 'prɑːkt ər ~s z

proctorial prɒk 'tɔːr i_əl ‖ prɑːk- -'toʊr-

proctoscope 'prɒkt ə skəʊp ‖ 'prɑːkt ə skoʊp ~s s

procumbent prəʊ 'kʌm bənt ‖ prəʊ-

procuration ˌprɒk ju 'reɪʃ ən -jə- ‖ ˌprɑːk jə- ~s z

procurator 'prɒk ju reɪt ə ˈ•jə- ‖ 'prɑːk jə reɪt̬ ər ~s z
  ,procurator 'fiscal

procurable prə 'kjʊər əb əl prəʊ-, -'kjɔːr- ‖ -'kjʊr- prəʊ-

procure prə 'kjʊə prəʊ-, -'kjɔː ‖ -'kjʊər prəʊ- ~**d** d ~**ment/s** mənt/s ~s z **procuring** prə 'kjʊər ɪŋ prəʊ-, -'kjɔːr- ‖ -'kjʊr ɪŋ prəʊ-

procurer prə 'kjʊər ə prəʊ-, -'kjɔːr- ‖ -'kjʊr ər prəʊ- ~s z

procuress prə 'kjʊər es prəʊ-, -'kjɔːr-, -ɪs, -əs; 'prɒk jʊr-, -jər- ‖ -'kjʊr əs prəʊ- ~**es** ɪz əz

Procyon 'prəʊs i_ən ‖ 'proʊs i ɑːn

prod, Prod prɒd ‖ prɑːd **prodded** 'prɒd ɪd -əd ‖ 'prɑːd əd **prodding** 'prɒd ɪŋ ‖ 'prɑːd ɪŋ **prods, Prods** prɒdz ‖ prɑːdz

Prodd|ie, Prodd|y 'prɒd| i ‖ 'prɑːd| i ~**ies** iz

Prodi 'prəʊd i ‖ 'proʊd i —*It* ['prɔː di]

prodigal 'prɒd ɪg əl ‖ 'prɑːd- ~**ly** _i ~s z
  ,prodigal 'son

prodigalit|y ˌprɒd ɪ 'gæl ət li ,•ə-, -ɪt i ‖ ˌprɑːd ə 'gæl ət̬ li ~**ies** iz

prodigious prə 'dɪdʒ əs ~**ly** li ~**ness** nəs nɪs

prodig|y 'prɒd ədʒ i -ɪdʒ- ‖ 'prɑːd- ~**ies** iz

prodromal ₍ₙ₎prəʊ 'drəʊm əl ‖ ₍ₙ₎proʊ 'droʊm əl

prodrome 'prəʊ drəʊm ‖ 'proʊ droʊm ~s z

produc|e v prə 'djuːs §-'duːs, →§-'dʒuːs ‖ -'duːs -'djuːs ~**ed** t ~**es** ɪz əz ~**ing** ɪŋ

produce n 'prɒd juːs 'prɒdʒ uːs ‖ 'proʊ duːs -djuːs; 'prɑːd uːs, -juːs *(*)*

producer prə 'djuːs ə §-'duːs-, →§-'dʒuːs- ‖ -'duːs ər ~s z

producible prə 'djuːs əb əl §-'duːs-, →§-'dʒuːs- ‖ -'duːs- -'djuːs-

product 'prɒd ʌkt -əkt ‖ 'prɑːd- ~s s
  'product line

production prə 'dʌk ʃən ~s z
  pro'duction line

productive prə 'dʌkt ɪv ~**ly** li ~**ness** nəs nɪs

productivity ˌprɒd ʌk 'tɪv ət i ˌprəʊd-, ˌ•ək-, -ɪt i ‖ ˌprəʊ dʌk 'tɪv ət̬ i proʊ ˌdʌk 'tɪv-, prə-; ˌprɑːd ək 'tɪv-

proem 'prəʊ em ‖ 'proʊ- ~s z

prof prɒf ‖ prɑːf **profs** prɒfs ‖ prɑːfs

Prof. prɒf ‖ prɑːf —*or see* Professor

profanation ˌprɒf ə 'neɪʃ ən ‖ ˌprɑːf-

profan|e v, adj prə 'feɪn prəʊ- ‖ prəʊ- ~**ed** d ~**ely** li ~**er/s** ə/z ‖ ər/z ~**eness** nəs nɪs ~**es** z ~**ing** ɪŋ

profanit|y prə 'fæn ət li prəʊ-, -ɪt- ‖ -ət̬ i prəʊ- ~**ies** iz

profess prə 'fes prəʊ- ‖ prəʊ- ~**ed** t ~**es** ɪz əz ~**ing** ɪŋ

professedly prə 'fes ɪd li prəʊ-, -əd- ‖ prəʊ-

profession prə 'feʃ ən ~s z

professional prə 'feʃ ən_əl ~**ism** ˌɪz əm ~**ly** i

professor prə 'fes ə ‖ -ər ~s z

professorate prə 'fes ər ət -ɪt ~s s

professorial ˌprɒf ə 'sɔːr i_əl ◄, •ɪ-, ,•e- ‖ ˌproʊf-, ˌprɑːf-, -'soʊr- ~**ly** i

professoriate ˌprɒf ə 'sɔːr i_ət ,•ɪ-, ,•e-, -ɪt, -eɪt ‖ ˌproʊf- ˌprɑːf-

professorship prə 'fes ə ʃɪp ‖ -ər- ~s s

proff|er 'prɒf ə ‖ 'prɑːf ər ~**ered** əd ‖ ərd ~**ering** ər_ɪŋ ~**ers** əz ‖ ərz

proficienc|y prə 'fɪʃ ənts li ~**ies** iz

proficient prə 'fɪʃ ənt ~**ly** li

profil|e 'prəʊf aɪ əl ‖ 'proʊf- —*formerly also* -iːəl ~**ed** d ~**es** z ~**ing** ɪŋ

prof|it 'prɒf |ɪt §-ət ‖ 'prɑːf |ət ~**ited** ɪt ɪd §ət-, -əd ‖ ət̬ əd ~**iting** ɪt ɪŋ §ət- ‖ ət̬ ɪŋ ~**its** ɪts §əts ‖ əts
  'profit ˌmargin; 'profit ˌsharing

profitability ˌprɒf ɪt ə 'bɪl ət i ,•ət-, -ɪt i ‖ ˌprɑːf ət̬ ə 'bɪl ət̬ i

profitab|le 'prɒf ɪt əb |əl '•ət- ‖ 'prɑːf ət̬- ~**ly** li

profi|teer ˌprɒf ɪ |'tɪə -ə- ‖ ˌprɑːf ə |'tɪər ~**teered** 'tɪəd ‖ 'tɪərd ~**teering** 'tɪər ɪŋ ‖ 'tɪr ɪŋ ~**teers** 'tɪəz ‖ 'tɪərz

profiterole prə 'fɪt ə rəʊl prɒ-, -'fiːt-, →-rɒʊl; 'prɒf ɪt-, ˌ•ˈ•ˈ• ‖ -'fɪt̬ ə roʊl ~s z

profitless 'prɒf ɪt ləs §-ət-, -lɪs ‖ 'prɑːf-

profligacy 'prɒf lɪg əs i ˈ•ləg- ‖ 'prɑːf-

profligate 'prɒf lɪg ət -ləg-, -ɪt ‖ 'prɑːf- ~**ly** li ~**ness** nəs nɪs

pro-form ₍ₙ₎prəʊ fɔːm ‖ 'proʊ fɔːrm

pro forma ₍ₙ₎prəʊ 'fɔːm ə ◄ ‖ ₍ₙ₎proʊ 'fɔːrm ə

profound prə 'faʊnd prəʊ- ‖ prəʊ- ~**er** ə ‖ ər ~**est** ɪst əst ~**ly** li ~**ness** nəs nɪs

Profumo prə 'fjuːm əʊ prəʊ- ‖ -oʊ

profundit|y prə 'fʌnd ət |i prɒʊ-, -ɪt- ‖ -əṭ |i
~**ies** iz

profuse prə 'fjuːs prəʊ- ‖ proʊ- ~**ly** li ~**ness**
nəs nɪs

profusion prə 'fjuːʒ ᵊn prəʊ- ‖ proʊ- ~**s** z

prog prɒg ‖ praːg **progs** prɒgz ‖ praːgz

progenitor prəʊ 'dʒen ɪt ə §-ət-
‖ proʊ 'dʒen əṭ ᵊr prə- ~**s** z

progen|y 'prɒdʒ ən |i 'prəʊdʒ-, -ɪn- ‖ 'praːdʒ-
~**ies** iz

progesterone prəʊ 'dʒest ə rəʊn
‖ proʊ 'dʒest ə roʊn

progestogen prəʊ 'dʒest ədʒ ən -ɪn, -ə dʒen
‖ proʊ- ~**s** z

proglott|id/s prəʊ 'glɒt |ɪd/z §-əd/z
‖ proʊ 'glaːṭ |əd/z ~**is** ɪs §əs

prognathic prɒg 'næθ ɪk ‖ praːg-

prognathism 'prɒg nə ˌθɪz əm ‖ 'praːg-

prognathous 'prɒg nəθ əs prɒg 'neɪθ-
‖ 'praːg nəθ əs praːg 'neɪθ-

prognos|is prɒg 'nəʊs |ɪs §-əs ‖ praːg 'noʊs |əs
~**es** iːz

prognostic prɒg 'nɒst ɪk ‖ praːg 'naːst ɪk ~**s** s

prognosti|cate prɒg 'nɒst ɪ |keɪt §-ə-
‖ praːg 'naːst- ~**cated** keɪt ɪd -əd ‖ keɪṭ əd
~**cates** keɪts ~**cating** keɪt ɪŋ ‖ keɪṭ ɪŋ

prognostication prɒg ˌnɒst ɪ 'keɪʃ ᵊn prəg-,
ˌprɒg••'•-, §-ə'•- ‖ praːg••'•- ~**s** z

prognosticator prɒg 'nɒst ɪ keɪt ə §-'•ə-
‖ praːg 'naːst ə keɪṭ ᵊr ~**s** z

program 'prəʊ græm §-grəm ‖ 'proʊ- ~**ed**,
~**med** d ~**ing**, ~**ming** ɪŋ ~**s** z
ˌprogrammed 'course; ˌprogrammed
in'struction; ˌprogrammed 'learning;
'programme ˌmusic

programmable prəʊ 'græm əb ᵊl 'prəʊ græm-
‖ 'proʊ græm- •'•••

programmatic
ˌprəʊg rə 'mæt ɪk ◀ ‖ ˌproʊg rə 'mæṭ ɪk ◀
~**ally** ᵊl_i

programm|e 'prəʊ græm §-grəm ‖ 'proʊ- ~**ed**
d ~**es** z ~**ing** ɪŋ

programmer 'prəʊ græm ə §-grəm-
‖ 'proʊ græm ᵊr -grəm- ~**s** z

progress n 'prəʊ gres 'prɒg res ‖ 'praːg rəs
-res
'progress ˌchaser; 'progress re,port

progress v prəʊ 'gres 'prəʊ gres ‖ prə- ~**ed** t
~**es** ɪz əz ~**ing** ɪŋ

progression prəʊ 'greʃ ᵊn ‖ prə- ~**al** ᵊl ~**s** z

progressive prəʊ 'gres ɪv ‖ prə- ~**ly** li ~**ness**
nəs nɪs ~**s** z

progressivism prəʊ 'gres ɪv ˌɪz əm ‖ prə-

prohib|it prəʊ 'hɪb |ɪt §-ət ‖ proʊ 'hɪb ət prə-
~**ited** ɪt ɪd §ət-, -əd ‖ əṭ əd ~**iting** ɪt ɪŋ §ət-
‖ əṭ ɪŋ ~**its** ɪts §əts ‖ əts

prohibition ˌprəʊ ɪ 'bɪʃ ᵊn -hɪ-, -ə-, §-hə-
‖ ˌproʊ ə- ~**ism** ˌɪz əm ~**ist/s** ɪst/s §əst/s
‖ əst/s ~**s** z

prohibitive prəʊ 'hɪb ɪt ɪv -ət-
‖ proʊ 'hɪb əṭ ɪv prə- ~**ly** li

prohibitory prəʊ 'hɪb ɪt ᵊr i -'•ət
‖ proʊ 'hɪb ə tɔːr i prə-, -toʊr i

BrE 1998

■ ɒ   ☐ əʊ

0   20   40   60   80   100%

project v prə 'dʒekt prəʊ-, prɒ- ~**ed** ɪd əd
~**ing** ɪŋ ~**s** s

project n 'prɒdʒ ekt -ɪkt; 'prəʊ dʒekt
‖ 'praːdʒ- —BrE 1998 poll panel preference: ɒ
84%, əʊ 16%. ~**s** s

projectile prəʊ 'dʒekt aɪᵊl 'prɒdʒ ekt-, -ɪkt-
‖ prə 'dʒekt ᵊl ~**s** z

projection prə 'dʒek ʃᵊn prəʊ-, prɒ- ~**s** z

projectionist prə 'dʒek ʃᵊn_ɪst prəʊ-, prɒ-,
§_əst ~**s** s

projective prəʊ 'dʒekt ɪv ‖ prə- ~**ly** li

projector prə 'dʒekt ə prəʊ-, prɒ- ‖ -ᵊr ~**s** z

prokaryote ₍ₗ₎prəʊ 'kær i əʊt -ɒt
‖ ₍ₗ₎proʊ 'kær i oʊt -'ker- ~**s** s

prokaryotic prəʊ ˌkær i 'ɒt ɪk, •, ••'•-
‖ proʊ ˌkær i 'aːṭ ɪk ◀

Prokofiev prə 'kɒf i ef ‖ -'kɔːf i_əf -'koʊf-, -ef
—Russ [prʌ 'kɔfj jɪf]

prolactin prəʊ 'lækt ɪn §-ᵊn ‖ proʊ-

prolaps|e n 'prəʊ læps prəʊ 'læps ‖ proʊ 'læps
'•• ~**es** ɪz əz

prolaps|e v prəʊ 'læps 'prəʊ læps ‖ proʊ- ~**ed**
t ~**es** ɪz əz ~**ing** ɪŋ

prolate 'prəʊl eɪt prəʊ 'leɪt ‖ 'proʊl- ~**ly** li
~**ness** nəs nɪs

prolative prəʊ 'leɪt ɪv 'prəʊl ət- ‖ proʊ 'leɪṭ ɪv

prole prəʊl →prɒʊl ‖ proʊl **proles** prəʊlz
→prɒʊlz ‖ proʊlz

proleg 'prəʊ leg ‖ 'proʊ- ~**s** z

prolegom|enon ˌprəʊl ə 'gɒm |ɪn ən ˌ•ɪ-, ˌ•e-,
-ᵊn ən; -ɪɪ nɒn, -ə• ‖ ˌproʊl ɪ 'gaːm |ə naːn
~**ena** ɪn ə ən-

prolepsis prəʊ 'liːps ɪs -'leps-, §-əs
‖ proʊ 'leps əs

proleptic prəʊ 'lept ɪk ‖ proʊ- ~**ally** ᵊl_i

proletarian ˌprəʊl ə 'teər i_ən ◀, ˌ•ɪ-, ˌ•e-
‖ ˌproʊl ə 'ter- -'tær- ~**s** z

proletariat ˌprəʊl ə 'teər i_ət ˌ•ɪ-, ˌ•e-, -æt
‖ ˌproʊl ə 'ter- -'tær- ~**s** s

pro-life ₍ₗ₎prəʊ 'laɪf ₍ₗ₎proʊ-

prolife|rate prəʊ 'lɪf ə |reɪt ‖ prə- ~**rated**
reɪt ɪd -əd ‖ reɪṭ əd ~**rates** reɪts ~**rating**
reɪt ɪŋ ‖ reɪṭ ɪŋ

proliferation prəʊ ˌlɪf ə 'reɪʃ ᵊn ‖ prə- ~**s** z

prolific prəʊ 'lɪf ɪk ‖ prə- ~**acy** əs i ~**ally** ᵊl_i
~**ness** nəs nɪs

prolix 'prəʊ lɪks ₍ₗ₎•'• ‖ proʊ 'lɪks '•• ~**ly** li

prolixity prəʊ 'lɪks ət i -ɪt i ‖ proʊ 'lɪks əṭ i

prolocutor prəʊ 'lɒk jʊt ə -jət-
‖ proʊ 'laːk jəṭ ᵊr ~**s** z

prolog, PROLOG, prologue
'prəʊ lɒg ‖ 'proʊ lɔːg -laːg ~**s** z

prolong prəʊ 'lɒŋ ‖ prə 'lɔːŋ -'laːŋ ~**ed** d
~**ing** ɪŋ ~**s** z

prolongation ˌprəʊ lɒŋ 'geɪʃ ᵊn ‖ ˌproʊ lɔːŋ-
-laːŋ-; prə,•'•• ~**s** z

P

prom, PROM prɒm ‖ prɑːm **proms, PROMs**
  prɒmz ‖ prɑːmz
promenad|e ˌprɒm ə ˈnɑːd ◄ -ɪ-, ˈ•••
  ‖ ˌprɑːm ə ˈneɪd ◄ -ˈnɑːd (*) —but in square
  dancing, -ˈneɪd ◄ even in BrE ~**ed** ɪd əd
  ~**er/s** ə/z ‖ ər/z ~**es** z ~**ing** ɪŋ
  ˌpromenade ˈconcert,ˌ••ˈ•ˌ••;
  ˌprome'nade deck
Promethean prəʊ ˈmiːθ i‿ən ‖ prə- ~**s** z
Prometheus prəʊ ˈmiːθ juːs -ˈmiːθ i‿əs ‖ prə-
promethium prəʊ ˈmiːθ i‿əm ‖ prə-
prominenc|e ˈprɒm ɪn ənts -ən- ‖ ˈprɑːm- ~**es**
  ɪz əz ~**y** i
prominent ˈprɒm ɪn ənt -ən- ‖ ˈprɑːm- ~**ly** li
promiscuit|y ˌprɒm ɪ ˈskjuːʒ ət li ˌ•ə-, ˌɪt i
  ‖ ˌprɑːm ə ˈskjuː əʒ li ˌproʊm- ~**ies** iz
promiscuous prə ˈmɪsk ju‿əs prɒ- ‖ proʊ- ~**ly**
  li ~**ness** nəs nɪs
promis|e v, n ˈprɒm ɪs §-əs ‖ ˈprɑːm əs ~**ed** t
  ~**es** ɪz əz ~**ing/ly** ɪŋ /li
  ˌPromised ˈLand ‖ ˈ•••
promisee ˌprɒm ɪ ˈsiː §-ə- ‖ ˌprɑːm- ~**s** z
promisor ˌprɒm ɪ ˈsɔː ˈ••• ‖ ˌprɑːm ə ˈsɔːr ~**s**
  z
promissory ˈprɒm ɪs ər‿i prəʊ ˈmɪs-
  ‖ ˈprɑːm ə sɔːr i -soʊr i
prommer ˈprɒm ə ‖ ˈprɑːm ər ~**s** z
promo ˈprəʊm əʊ ‖ ˈproʊm oʊ ~**s** z
promontor|y ˈprɒm ənt‿ər i ‖ ˈprɑːm ən tɔːr li
  -toʊr i ~**ies** iz
pro|mote prə ˈməʊt ‖ -ˈmoʊt ~**moted**
  ˈməʊt ɪd -əd ‖ ˈmoʊt̬ əd ~**motes**
  ˈməʊts ‖ ˈmoʊts ~**moting**
  ˈməʊt ɪŋ ‖ ˈmoʊt̬ ɪŋ
promoter prə ˈməʊt ə ‖ -ˈmoʊt̬ ər ~**s** z
promotion prə ˈməʊʃ ən ‖ -ˈmoʊʃ ən ~**s** z
promotional prə ˈməʊʃ ən‿əl ‖ -ˈmoʊʃ- ~**ly** i
prompt prɒmpt ‖ ˈprɑːmpt **prompted**
  ˈprɒmpt ɪd -əd ‖ ˈprɑːmpt əd **prompter/s**
  ˈprɒmpt ə/z ‖ ˈprɑːmpt ər/z **promptest**
  ˈprɒmpt ɪst -əst ‖ ˈprɑːmpt əst **prompting/
  s** ˈprɒmpt ɪŋ/z ‖ ˈprɑːmpt- **prompts**
  prɒmpts ‖ prɑːmpts
promptitude ˈprɒmpt ɪ tjuːd -ə-, →§-tʃuːd
  ‖ ˈprɑːmpt ə tuːd -tjuːd
prompt|ly ˈprɒmpt |li ‖ ˈprɑːmpt- ~**ness** nəs
  nɪs
promul|gate ˈprɒm əl |geɪt ‖ ˈprɑːm-
  proʊ ˈmʌlg eɪt ~**gated** geɪt ɪd -əd ‖ geɪt̬ əd
  ~**gates** geɪts ~**gating** geɪt ɪŋ ‖ geɪt̬ ɪŋ
promulgation ˌprɒm əl ˈgeɪʃ ən ‖ ˌprɑːm-
  ˌproʊm- ~**s** z
promulgator ˈprɒm əl geɪt ə ‖ ˈprɑːm əl geɪt̬ ər
  ˈproʊm- ~**s** z
pronate prəʊ ˈneɪt ˈprəʊn eɪt ‖ ˈproʊn eɪt
  pronated prəʊ ˈneɪt ɪd -əd; ˈprəʊn eɪt-
  ‖ ˈproʊn eɪt̬ əd **pronates** prəʊ ˈneɪts
  ˈprəʊn eɪts ‖ ˈproʊn eɪts **pronating** prəʊ
  ˈneɪt ɪŋ ˈprəʊn eɪt- ‖ ˈproʊn eɪt̬ ɪŋ
pronation prəʊ ˈneɪʃ ən ‖ ˈproʊn eɪʃ ən
pronator prəʊ ˈneɪt ə ‖ ˈproʊn eɪt̬ ər ~**s** z
prone prəʊn ‖ proʊn
-prone prəʊn ‖ proʊn — **accident-prone**
  ˈæks ɪd ənt prəʊn ˈ••ˌəd- ‖ -proʊn
prone|ly ˈprəʊn |li ‖ ˈproʊn- ~**ness** nəs nɪs
prong prɒŋ ‖ prɔːŋ prɑːŋ **pronged**
  prɒŋd ‖ prɔːŋd prɑːŋd **pronging**
  ˈprɒŋ ɪŋ ‖ ˈprɔːŋ ˈprɑːŋ- **prongs**
  prɒŋz ‖ prɔːŋz prɑːŋz
-pronged ˈprɒŋd ‖ ˈprɔːŋd ˈprɑːŋd — **three-
  pronged** ˌθriː ˈprɒŋd ◄ ‖ -ˈprɔːŋd ◄ -ˈprɑːŋd
pronghorn ˈprɒŋ hɔːn ‖ ˈprɔːŋ hɔːrn ˈprɑːŋ-
  ~**s** z
pronominal prəʊ ˈnɒm ɪn əl -ən‿əl
  ‖ proʊ ˈnɑːm ən‿əl ~**s** z
pronominalis... —see **pronominaliz...**
pronominalization prəʊ ˌnɒm ɪn əl aɪ ˈzeɪʃ ən
  -ˌ•ən‿, -ɪˈ•- ‖ proʊ ˌnɑːm ən‿əl ə- ~**s** z
pronominaliz|e prəʊ ˈnɒm ɪn ə laɪz -ˈ•ən‿,
  -əl aɪz ‖ proʊ ˈnɑːm- ~**ed** d ~**es** ɪz əz ~**ing**
  ɪŋ
pronominally prəʊ ˈnɒm ɪn əl i -ən‿əl-
  ‖ proʊ ˈnɑːm ən‿əl i
pronoun ˈprəʊ naʊn ‖ ˈproʊ- ~**s** z
pronounc|e prə ˈnaʊnts ~**ed** t ~**es** ɪz əz ~**ing**
  ɪŋ
pronounceable prə ˈnaʊnts əb əl
pronouncedly prə ˈnaʊnts ɪd li -əd-
pronouncement prə ˈnaʊnts mənt ~**s** s
pronto ˈprɒnt əʊ ‖ ˈprɑːnt oʊ
pronunciamento prə ˌnʌnts i‿ə ˈment əʊ
  -ˌnʌntʃ- ‖ proʊ ˌnʌnts i‿ə ˈment̬ oʊ —Sp
  [pro nun θja ˈmen to, ••sja-] ~**s** z
pronunciation prə ˌnʌnts i ˈeɪʃ ən △-ˌnaʊnts-
  ~**s** z
proof pruːf §prʊf **proofs** pruːfs §prʊfs
  ˌproof ˈspirit ˈ• ‚••
-proof pruːf §prʊf — **mothproof** ˈmɒθ pruːf
  §-prʊf ‖ ˈmɔːθ- ˈmɑːθ-
proof|read pres ˈpruːf |riːd §ˈprʊf- ~**read** past
  & pp red ~**reader/s** riːd ə/z ‖ riːd ər/z
  ~**reading** riːd ɪŋ ~**reads** riːdz
Proops pruːps
prop prɒp ‖ prɑːp **propped** prɒpt ‖ prɑːpt
  propping ˈprɒp ɪŋ ‖ ˈprɑːp ɪŋ **props**
  prɒps ‖ prɑːps
  ˈprop shaft
propaedeutic ˌprəʊ pi ˈdjuːt ɪk ◄ §-ˈduːt-,
  →§-ˈdʒuːt- ‖ ˌproʊ pi ˈduːt̬ ɪk ◄ -ˈdjuːt̬- ~**al**
  əl ~**s** s
propaganda ˌprɒp ə ˈgænd ə ‖ ˌprɑːp-
propagandis... —see **propagandiz...**
propagandist ˌprɒp ə ˈgænd ɪst §-əst ‖ ˌprɑːp-
  ~**s** s
propagandiz|e ˌprɒp ə ˈgænd aɪz ‖ ˌprɑːp-
  ~**ed** d ~**es** ɪz əz ~**ing** ɪŋ
propa|gate ˈprɒp ə |geɪt ‖ ˈprɑːp- ~**gated**
  geɪt ɪd -əd ‖ geɪt̬ əd ~**gates** geɪts ~**gating**
  geɪt ɪŋ ‖ geɪt̬ ɪŋ
propagation ˌprɒp ə ˈgeɪʃ ən ‖ ˌprɑːp- ~**s** z
propagative ˈprɒp ə geɪt ɪv ‖ ˈprɑːp ə geɪt̬ ɪv
  ~**ly** li
propagator ˈprɒp ə geɪt ə ‖ ˈprɑːp ə geɪt̬ ər ~**s**
  z
propane ˈprəʊp eɪn ‖ ˈproʊp-

P

P

proparoxytone ˌprəʊ pə ˈrɒks ɪ təʊn ◂, •ˈpæ-,
-ˈ•ə- ‖ ˌproʊ pæ ˈrɑːks ɪ toʊn ◂ -pə- **~s** z
propel prə ˈpel **~led** d **~ling** ɪŋ **~s** z
proˈpelling ˌpencil, •,•• ′••
propellant, propellent prə ˈpel ənt **~s** s
propeller prə ˈpel ə ‖ -ər **~s** z
proˈpeller shaft
propene ˈprəʊp iːn ‖ ˈproʊp-
propensit|y prəʊ ˈpen^ts ət li -ɪt-
‖ prə ˈpen^ts ət li **~ies** iz
proper ˈprɒp ə ‖ ˈprɑːp ər
ˌproper ˈfraction; ˌproper ˈname; ˌproper
ˈnoun
properly ˈprɒp əl i ‖ ˈprɑːp ər li —*In RP there is
also a casual form* ˈprɒp li
Propertius prəʊ ˈpɜːʃ əs -ˈpɜːʃ i_əs
‖ proʊ ˈpɝːʃ əs
propert|y ˈprɒp ət li ‖ ˈprɑːp ərt li **~ied** id
~ies iz
ˈproperty boom
prophase ˈprəʊ feɪz ‖ ˈproʊ-
prophec|y *n* ˈprɒf əs li -ɪs- ‖ ˈprɑːf- **~ies** iz
prophe|sy *v* ˈprɒf ə ‖saɪ -ɪ- ‖ ˈprɑːf- **~sied**
saɪd **~sies** saɪz **~sying** saɪ ɪŋ
prophet, P~ ˈprɒf ɪt §-ət ‖ ˈprɑːf ət *(= profit)*
~s s
prophetess ˌprɒf ɪ ˈtes -ə-, ′•••; ˈprɒf ɪt ɪs,
-ət-, -əs ‖ ˈprɑːf ət əs **~es** ɪz əz
prophethood ˈprɒf ɪt hʊd §-ət- ‖ ˈprɑːf ət-
prophetic prəʊ ˈfet ɪk ‖ prə ˈfet̬ ɪk **~al** əl **~ally**
əl_i
prophylactic ˌprɒf ə ˈlækt ɪk ◂ -ɪ- ‖ ˌproʊf-
ˌprɑːf- **~ally** əl_i **~s** s
prophylaxis ˌprɒf ə ˈlæks ɪs -ɪ-, §-əs ‖ ˌproʊf-
ˌprɑːf-
propinquity prəʊ ˈpɪŋk wət i -wɪt-
‖ prə ˈpɪŋk wət̬ i
propionate ˈprəʊp i_ə neɪt ‖ ˈproʊp-
propionic ˌprəʊp i ˈɒn ɪk ◂ ‖ ˌproʊp i ˈɑːn ɪk ◂
propiti|ate prəʊ ˈpɪʃ i eɪt ‖ proʊ- **~ated** eɪt ɪd
-əd ‖ eɪt̬ əd **~ates** eɪts **~ating** eɪt ɪŋ ‖ eɪt̬ ɪŋ
propitiation prəʊ ˌpɪʃ i ˈeɪʃ ən ‖ proʊ- **~s** z
propitiator prəʊ ˈpɪʃ i eɪt ə ‖ proʊ ˈpɪʃ i eɪt̬ ər
~s z
propitiator|y prəʊ ˈpɪʃ i_ə_tər li -eɪt ər li,
•,••ˈeɪt ər li ‖ proʊ ˈpɪʃ i_ə tɔːr li -toʊr i
~ies iz
propitious prə ˈpɪʃ əs **~ly** li **~ness** nəs nɪs
propjet ˈprɒp dʒet ‖ ˈprɑːp- **~s** s
propolis ˈprɒp əl ɪs §-əs ‖ ˈprɑːp-
proponent prə ˈpəʊn ənt ‖ -ˈpoʊn- **~s** s
Propontis prəʊ ˈpɒnt ɪs §-əs ‖ prə ˈpɑːnt̬ əs
proportion prə ˈpɔːʃ ən ‖ -ˈpɔːrʃ ən pə-,
-ˈpoʊrʃ- **~ed** d **~ing** ɪŋ **~s** z
proportionab|le prə ˈpɔːʃ ən_əb |əl ‖ -ˈpɔːrʃ-
pə-, -ˈpoʊrʃ- **~leness** əl nəs -nɪs **~ly** li
proportional prə ˈpɔːʃ ən_əl ‖ -ˈpɔːrʃ- pə-,
-ˈpoʊrʃ- **~s** z
proˌportional ˌrepresenˈtation
proportionality prə ˌpɔːʃ ə ˈnæl ət i -ɪt i
‖ -ˌpɔːrʃ ə ˈnæl ət̬ i pə-, -ˌpoʊrʃ-
proportionally prə ˈpɔːʃ ən_əl i ‖ -ˈpɔːrʃ- pə-,
-ˈpoʊrʃ-

proportionate *adj* prə ˈpɔːʃ ən_ət -ɪt ‖ -ˈpɔːrʃ-
pə-, -ˈpoʊrʃ- **~ly** li **~ness** nəs nɪs
proposal prə ˈpəʊz əl ‖ -ˈpoʊz əl **~s** z
propos|e prə ˈpəʊz ‖ -ˈpoʊz **~ed** d **~er/s** ə/z
‖ -ər/z **~es** ɪz əz **~ing** ɪŋ
proposition ˌprɒp ə ˈzɪʃ ən ‖ ˌprɑːp- **~ed** d
~ing ɪŋ **~s** z
propositional ˌprɒp ə ˈzɪʃ ən_əl ◂ ‖ ˌprɑːp- **~ly**
i
propound prə ˈpaʊnd **~ed** ɪd əd **~ing** ɪŋ **~s** z
propranolol prəʊ ˈpræn ə lɒl
‖ proʊ ˈpræn ə lɑːl -lɔːl, -loʊl
proprietar|y prə ˈpraɪ_ət_ər li ‖ -ə ter li **~ies** iz
~ily əl i -ɪ li
proprietor prə ˈpraɪ_ət ə ‖ -_ət̬ ər **~s** z **~ship**
ʃɪp
proprietorial prə ˌpraɪ_ə ˈtɔːr i_əl ‖ proʊ-,
-ˈtoʊr- **~ly** i
proprietress prə ˈpraɪ_ətr əs -ɪs, -es **~es** ɪz əz
propriet|y prə ˈpraɪ_ət li -ɪt- ‖ -_ət̬ li **~ies** iz
proprioception ˌprəʊp ri_ə ˈsep ʃən ˌprɒp-,
-əʊ′•- ‖ ˌproʊp ri oʊ-
proprioceptive ˌprəʊp ri_ə ˈsept ɪv ◂ ˌprɒp-,
-əʊ′•- ‖ ˌproʊp ri oʊ- **~ly** li
proprioceptor ˌprəʊp ri_ə ˈsept ə ˌprɒp-,
-əʊ′•- ‖ ˌproʊp ri oʊ ˈsept ər **~s** z
proptosis prɒp ˈtəʊs ɪs §-əs ‖ prɑːp ˈtoʊs-
propulsion prə ˈpʌlʃ ən
propulsive prə ˈpʌls ɪv
propyl ˈprəʊp ɪl -əl, -aɪəl ‖ ˈproʊp-
propylae|um ˌprɒp ɪ ˈliː_əm ˌprəʊp-, -ə-
‖ ˌprɑːp- ˌproʊp- **~a** ə
propylene ˈprəʊp ɪ liːn -ə- ‖ ˈproʊp-
pro rata ₍ₒ₎prəʊ ˈrɑːt ə -ˈreɪt- ‖ ₍ₒ₎proʊ ˈreɪt̬ ə
-ˈrɑːt̬-, -ˈræt̬-
pro|rate ˌprəʊ |ˈreɪt ₍ₒ₎proʊ- **~rated** ˈreɪt ɪd
-əd ‖ ˈreɪt̬ əd **~rates** ˈreɪts **~rating**
ˈreɪt ɪŋ ‖ ˈreɪt̬ ɪŋ
prorogation ˌprəʊ rəʊ ˈɡeɪʃ ən ˌprɒr ə-
‖ ˌproʊ rə-, ˌprɔːr ə- **~s** z
prorogu|e prəʊ ˈrəʊɡ ‖ proʊ ˈroʊɡ prə- **~ed** d
~es z **~ing** ɪŋ
prosaic prəʊ ˈzeɪ ɪk ‖ proʊ- **~ally** əl_i **~ness**
nəs nɪs
pros and cons ˌprəʊz ən ˈkɒnz -ənd-, →ᵊŋ-
‖ ˌproʊz ən ˈkɑːnz
prosceni|um prəʊ ˈsiːn i_əm ‖ proʊ- **~a** ə
~ums əmz
prosciutto prəʊ ˈʃuːt əʊ ‖ proʊ ˈʃuːt oʊ —*It*
[pro ˈʃut to]
proscrib|e prəʊ ˈskraɪb ‖ proʊ- **~ed** d **~es** z
~ing ɪŋ
proscription prəʊ ˈskrɪp ʃən ‖ proʊ- **~s** z
proscriptive prəʊ ˈskrɪpt ɪv ‖ proʊ- **~ly** li
~ness nəs nɪs
prose prəʊz ‖ proʊz **prosed** prəʊzd ‖ proʊzd
proses ˈprəʊz ɪz -əz ‖ ˈproʊz əz **prosing**
ˈprəʊz ɪŋ ‖ ˈproʊz ɪŋ
prose|cute ˈprɒs ɪ |kjuːt -ə- ‖ ˈprɑːs- **~cuted**
kjuːt ɪd -əd ‖ kjuːt̬ əd **~cutes** kjuːts
~cuting kjuːt ɪŋ ‖ kjuːt̬ ɪŋ
prosecution ˌprɒs ɪ ˈkjuːʃ ən -ə- ‖ ˌprɑːs- **~s** z

prosecutor 'prɒs ɪ kjuːt ə ˈˌ•ə-
‖ 'prɑːs ɪ kjuːt̬ ər ~s z

prosecutorial ˌprɒs ɪ kju 'tɔːr i‿əl ◂ ˌˌ•ə-
‖ ˌprɑːs- -'tour-

proselyte 'prɒs ə laɪt -ɪ- ‖ 'prɑːs- ~s s

proselytis... —*see* **proselytiz...**

proselytism 'prɒs əl ə ˌtɪz əm 'ˌ•ɪl-, -ɪ, •-
‖ 'prɑːs- 'ˌ•ə laɪ-

proselytiz|e 'prɒs əl ə taɪz 'ˌ•ɪl-, -ɪ• ‖ 'prɑːs-
~ed d ~es ɪz əz ~ing ɪŋ

Proserpina prə 'sɜːp ɪn ə prɒ-, prəʊ-, §-ən-
‖ prə 'sɜːp- prou-

Proserpine 'prɒs ə paɪn ‖ 'prɑːs ər-

prosimian prəʊ 'sɪm i‿ən ‖ prou- ~s z

prosodic prə 'sɒd ɪk prəʊ-, -'zɒd- ‖ -'sɑːd ɪk
~ally əl‿i

prosodist 'prɒs əd ɪst 'prɒz-, 'prəʊz-, §-əst
‖ 'prɑːs- ~s s

prosod|y 'prɒs əd li 'prɒz-, 'prəʊz- ‖ 'prɑːs-
~ies iz

prosopopeia, prosopopoeia ˌprɒs əʊp əʊ
'piːʒ ə prəʊ ˌsəʊp- ‖ ˌprɑːs əp ə-
prou ˌsoup ə-, ˌprous oup ə-

prospect *n* 'prɒsp ekt ‖ 'prɑːsp- ~s s

prospect *v* prə 'spekt prɒ-; 'prɒsp ekt
‖ 'prɑːsp ekt *(*)* ~ed ɪd əd ~ing ɪŋ ~s s

prospective prə 'spekt ɪv prɒ- ‖ prɑː- ~ly li

prospector prə 'spekt ə prɒ-; 'prɒsp ekt ə
‖ 'prɑːsp ekt ər *(*)* ~s z

prospectus prə 'spekt əs prɒ- ‖ prɑː- ~es ɪz
əz

prosp|er 'prɒsp lə ‖ 'prɑːsp lər ~ered əd ‖ ərd
~ering ər_ɪŋ ~ers əz ‖ ərz

prosperit|y prɒ 'sper ət li prə-, -ɪt i
‖ prɑː 'sper ət̬ i ~ies iz

Prospero 'prɒsp ə rəʊ ‖ 'prɑːsp ə rou

prosperous 'prɒsp ər_əs ‖ 'prɑːsp- ~ly li
~ness nəs nɪs

Prosser 'prɒs ə ‖ 'prɑːs ər

Prost prɒst prəʊst ‖ proust

prostaglandin ˌprɒst ə 'glænd ɪn §-ən
‖ ˌprɑːst- ~s z

prostate 'prɒst eɪt ‖ 'prɑːst- ~s s
'prostate gland

prostatectom|y ˌprɒst ə 'tekt əm li ‖ ˌprɑːst-
~ies iz

prostatic prɒ 'stæt ɪk prə- ‖ prɑː 'stæt̬ ɪk

prosthes|is ₍ᵢ₎prɒs 'θiːs lɪs prəs-, §-əs;
'prɒs θəs-, -θɪs- ‖ prɑːs- ~es iːz

prosthetic ₍ᵢ₎prɒs 'θet ɪk prəs- ‖ prɑːs 'θet̬ ɪk
~ally əl‿i ~s s

prosthodont|ics ˌprɒs θəʊ
'dɒnt| ɪks ‖ ˌprɑːs θə 'dɑːnt̬| ɪks ~ist/s ɪst/s
§əst/s

prosti|tute *v, n* 'prɒst ɪ |tjuːt -ə-, →§-tʃuːt
‖ 'prɑːst ə |tuːt -tjuːt ~tuted tjuːt ɪd
→§tʃuːt-, -əd ‖ tuːt̬ əd tjuːt̬- ~tutes tjuːts
→§tʃuːts ‖ tuːts tjuːts ~tuting tjuːt ɪŋ
→§tʃuːt- ‖ tuːt̬ ɪŋ tjuːt̬-

prostitution ˌprɒst ɪ 'tjuːʃ ən -ə-, →§-'tʃuːʃ-
‖ ˌprɑːst ə 'tuːʃ ən -'tjuːʃ-

prostrate *adj* 'prɒs treɪt prɒ 'streɪt, prə-
‖ 'prɑːs-

pro|strate *v* prɒ 'streɪt prə- ‖ 'prɑːs treɪt *(*)*
~strated streɪt ɪd -əd ‖ streɪt̬ əd ~strates
streɪts ~strating streɪt ɪŋ ‖ streɪt̬ ɪŋ

prostration prɒ 'streɪʃ ən prə- ‖ prɑː- ~s z

prostyle 'prəʊ staɪəl ‖ 'prou-

pros|y 'prəʊz li ‖ 'prouz li ~ier i‿ə ‖ i‿ər ~iest
i‿ɪst i‿əst ~ily ɪ li əl i ~iness i nəs i nɪs

prot- *comb. form before vowel* prəʊt ‖ prout —
protoxide prəʊ 'tɒks aɪd ‖ prou 'tɑːks-

protactinium ˌprəʊt æk 'tɪn i‿əm ‖ ˌprout̬-

protagonist prəʊ 'tæg ən ɪst §-əst ‖ prou- ~s
s

Protagoras prəʊ 'tæg ə ræs -ər əs ‖ prou-

protanopia ˌprəʊt ə 'nəʊp i‿ə -ən 'əʊp-
‖ ˌprout̬ ən 'oup-

protanopic ˌprəʊt ə 'nɒp ɪk ◂ -ən 'ɒp-
‖ ˌprout̬ ən 'ɑːp ɪk ◂

prot|asis 'prɒt ləs ɪs §-əs ‖ 'prɑːt̬- ~ases ə siːz

protea 'prəʊt i‿ə ‖ 'prout̬ i‿ə ~s z

protean prəʊ 'tiː‿ən 'prəʊt i‿ən ‖ 'prout̬ i‿ən
prou 'tiː ən

proteas|e 'prəʊt i eɪz -eɪs ‖ 'prout̬- ~es ɪz əz

protect prə 'tekt prəʊ- ‖ prou- ~ed ɪd əd
~ing ɪŋ ~s s

protecting/ly prə 'tekt ɪŋ /li prəʊ- ‖ prou-
~ness nəs nɪs

protection prə 'tek ʃən prəʊ- ‖ prou- ~ism ˌɪz
əm ~ist/s ɪst/s §əst/s ‖ əst/s
pro'tection ˌracket

protective prə 'tekt ɪv prəʊ- ‖ prou- ~ly li
~ness nəs nɪs
pro,tective 'custody

protector, P~ prə 'tekt ə prəʊ- ‖ -ərprou-
~ship/s ʃɪp/s ~s z

protectorate, P~ prə 'tekt ər_ət prəʊ-,
ˌɪt ‖ prou- ~s s

protectress prə 'tek trəs prəʊ-, -trɪs ‖ prou-
~es ɪz əz

protege, protégé, protegee, protégée
'prɒt ə ʒeɪ 'prəʊt-, -ɪ- ‖ 'prout̬- ˌˌ•• —*Fr*
[pʁɔ te ʒe] ~s z

protein 'prəʊt iːn 'prəʊt i‿ɪn ‖ 'prout̬- ~s z

pro tem ˌprəʊ 'tem ‖ ₍ᵢ₎prou-

proterozoic, P~ ˌprəʊt ər_əʊ 'zəʊ ɪk ◂ ˌprɒt̬_
‖ ˌprɑːt̬ ər ə 'zou ɪk ◂ ˌprout̬-

protest *v* prə 'test prəʊ-,
'prəʊt est ‖ 'prout̬ est ~ed ɪd əd ~ing/ly
ɪŋ /li ~s s

protest *n* 'prəʊt est ‖ 'prout̬ est ~s s

protestant, P~ 'prɒt ɪst ənt -əst- ‖ 'prɑːt̬- ~s
s

protestantism, P~ 'prɒt ɪst ənt ˌɪz əm 'ˌ•əst-
‖ 'prɑːt̬ əst ənt̬-

protestation ˌprɒt e 'steɪʃ ən ˌprəʊt-, -ə-, -e-
‖ ˌprɑːt̬ ə- ˌprout̬ ə-, ˌprout e- ~s z

protester prə 'test ə prəʊ-; 'prəʊt est ə
‖ 'prout̬ est ər prə 'test- ~s z

Proteus 'prəʊt juːs 'prəʊt i‿əs ‖ 'prout̬ i‿əs
'prout juːs

prothalami|on ˌprəʊ θə 'leɪm i‿lən ‖ ˌprou-
-i lɑːn ~a ə ~um əm

Prothero, Protheroe 'prɒð ə rəʊ ‖ 'prɑːð ə rou

proth|esis 'prɒθ ləs ɪs-ɪs-, §-əs ‖ 'praːθ- ~eses
ə siːz ɪ-
prothetic prəʊ 'θet ɪk ‖ prə 'θeṭ ɪk praː- ~ally
əl̩ i
prothonotar|y ˌprəʊθ əʊ 'nəʊt ərl i prəʊ
'θɒn ət̬ˌərl i ‖ prəʊ 'θaːn ə tərl i
ˌprəʊθ oʊ 'noʊṭ ərl i ~ies iz
protist 'prəʊt ɪst §-əst ‖ 'proʊṭ- ~s s
protist|a prəʊ 'tɪst lə ‖ proʊ- ~an/s ən/z ~ic
ɪk
protium 'prəʊt iˌəm ‖ 'proʊṭ- 'proʊʃ-
proto- comb. form
with stress-neutral suffix ¦prəʊt əʊ ‖ ¦proʊṭ oʊ
— Proto-Norse
ˌprəʊt əʊ 'nɔːs ◀ ‖ ˌproʊṭ oʊ 'nɔːrs ◀
with stress-imposing suffix
prəʊ 'tɒ+ ‖ proʊ 'taː+— protogynous
prəʊ 'tɒdʒ ɪn əs-ən- ‖ proʊ 'taːdʒ-
protocol 'prəʊt əʊ kɒl ‖ 'proʊṭ ə kaːl-kɔːl,
-koʊl ~s z
Proto-Indo-European ˌprəʊt əʊ ˌɪnd əʊ
jʊər ə 'piːˌən-jɔːr ə'•-
‖ ˌproʊṭ oʊ ˌɪnd oʊ jʊr-
protolanguag|e 'prəʊt əʊ ˌlæŋ gwɪdʒ-wɪdʒ,
ˌ•••'•• ‖ 'proʊṭ oʊ- ~es ɪzəz
proton, P~ 'prəʊt ɒn ‖ 'proʊt aːn ~s z
protonotar|y ˌprəʊt əʊ 'nəʊt ərl i prəʊ
'tɒn ət̬ˌərl i ‖ proʊ 'taːn ə terl i
ˌproʊt oʊ 'noʊṭ ərl i ~ies iz
protoplasm 'prəʊt əʊ ˌplæz əm ‖ 'proʊṭ ə-
protoplast 'prəʊt əʊ plæst-plaːst ‖ 'proʊṭ ə-
~s s
prototherian
ˌprəʊt əʊ 'θɪər iˌən ◀ ‖ ˌproʊṭ ə 'θɪr- ~s z
prototypical ˌprəʊt əʊ 'tɪp ɪk əl ◀ ‖ ˌproʊṭ ə-
~ly ˌi
prototyp|e 'prəʊt əʊ taɪp ‖ 'proʊṭ ə- ~ed t
~es s ~ing ɪŋ
protozo|a ˌprəʊt əʊ
'zəʊ lə ◀ ‖ ˌproʊṭ ə 'zoʊ lə ◀ ~an/s ən/z ~ic
ɪk ◀ ~on ɒnən ‖ aːn
protozoology ˌprəʊt əʊ zəʊ 'ɒl ədʒ i-zuː'•-
‖ ˌproʊṭ ə zoʊ 'aːl-
protract prə 'trækt prəʊ- ‖ proʊ- ~ed ɪdəd
~ing ɪŋ ~s s
protracted/ly prə 'trækt ɪd /liprəʊ-,
-əd- ‖ proʊ- ~ness nəsnɪs
protractile prə 'trækt aɪəlprəʊ- ‖ -əlproʊ-
protraction prə 'træk ʃənprəʊ- ‖ proʊ- ~s z
protractor prə 'trækt əprəʊ- ‖ proʊ 'trækt ər
'••• ~s z
protrud|e prə 'truːd prəʊ- ‖ proʊ- ~ed ɪdəd
~ing ɪŋ ~es z
protrusion prə 'truːʒ ənprəʊ- ‖ proʊ- ~s z
protrusive prə 'truːs ɪvprəʊ-, §-'truːz- ‖ proʊ-
~ly li ~ness nəsnɪs
protuberanc|e prə 'tjuːb ər_ənt sprəʊ-,
→§-'tʃuːb-, ⚠-'truːb- ‖ -'tuːb- -'tjuːb- ~es
ɪzəz
protuberant prə 'tjuːb ər_əntprəʊ-,
→§-'tʃuːb-, ⚠-'truːb- ‖ -'tuːb- -'tjuːb- ~ly
li
Protus 'prəʊt əs ‖ 'proʊṭ əs

proud, Proud praʊd prouder 'praʊd ə ‖ -ər
proudest 'praʊd ɪst-əst
Proudfoot 'praʊd fʊt
Proudhon 'pruːd ɒn ‖ pruː 'dɔːn-'daːn, -'doʊn
—Fr [pʁu dɔ̃]
Proudie 'praʊd i
proudly 'praʊd li
Proulx pruː
Proust pruːst—Fr [pʁust]
Proustian 'pruːst iˌən ~s z
proustite 'pruːst aɪt
Prout praʊt
provab|le 'pruːv əb |əl ~ly li
Provan 'prɒv ənprəʊv- ‖ 'praːv-
prove pruːv(!) proved pruːvd proven
'pruːv ənprəʊv- proves pruːvz proving
'pruːv ɪŋ
proving ground
proven 'pruːv ənprəʊv-
provenance 'prɒv ən ən̩ts-ɪn- ‖ 'praːv-
-ə naːnts
Provencal, Provençal, Provencale,
Provençale ˌprɒv ɒn 'saːl ◀-ð̃-, -ən-
‖ ˌpraːv aːn-, ˌproʊv- —Fr [pʁɔ vã sal]
Provence prɒ 'vɒ̃sprə- ‖ prə 'vaːntsproʊ-
—Fr [pʁɔ vãːs]
provender 'prɒv ɪnd ə-ənd- ‖ 'praːv ənd ər
provenience prə 'viːn iˌən̩tsprəʊ- ‖ proʊ-
proverb, P~ 'prɒv ɜːb ‖ 'praːv ɜːb(! NB not
•'•) —but as a grammatical term, 'kind of
pro-form', 'prəʊ vɜːb ‖ 'proʊ vɜːb ~s z
proverbial prə 'vɜːb iˌəlprɒ-, prəʊ- ‖ -'vɜːb-
~ly i
provid|e prə 'vaɪdprəʊ- ~ed ɪdəd ~ing ɪŋ
~es z
providence, P~ 'prɒv ɪd ən̩ts-əd- ‖ 'praːv-
-ə den̩ts
provident 'prɒv ɪd ənt-əd- ‖ 'praːv- ~ly li
providential ˌprɒv ɪ 'den̩tʃ əl ◀-ə- ‖ ˌpraːv-
~ly i
provider prə 'vaɪd ə§prəʊ- ‖ -ər ~s z
provinc|e, P~ 'prɒv ɪn̩ts§-ən̩ts ‖ 'praːv- ~es ɪz
əz
Provincetown 'prɒv ɪn̩ts taʊn§-ən̩ts- ‖ 'praːv-
provincial prə 'vɪn̩tʃ əl ~ism ˌɪz əm ~s z
provinciality prə ˌvɪn̩tʃ i 'æl ət i-ɪt i ‖ -əṭ i
provision prə 'vɪʒ ən̩prəʊ- ~ed d ~ing ˌɪŋ ~s
z
provisional, P~ prə 'vɪʒ ən̩ˌəlprəʊ- ~ism ˌɪz
əm ~ly i ~s z
proviso prə 'vaɪz əʊprəʊ- ‖ -oʊ ~s, ~es z
provisor prə 'vaɪz əprəʊ- ‖ -ər ~s z
provisory prə 'vaɪz ər i
Provo, p~ 'prəʊv əʊ ‖ 'proʊv oʊ ~s z
provocation ˌprɒv ə 'keɪʃ ən̩-əʊ- ‖ ˌpraːv- ~s
z
provocative prə 'vɒk ət ɪvprəʊ- ‖ -'vaːk əṭ ɪv
~ly li ~ness nəsnɪs
provok|e prə 'vəʊkprəʊ- ‖ -'voʊk ~ed t ~es
s ~ing/ly ɪŋ /li
provolone ˌprəʊv ə 'ləʊn i ‖ ˌproʊv ə 'loʊn i
—It [pro vo 'lo ne]

provost 'prɒv əst 'prəʊv-, -ɒst ‖ 'proʊv oʊst
  'prɑːv əst ~s s ~**ship/s** ʃɪp/s —*but in* p~
  marshal *and other military senses,*
  prə 'vəʊ ‖ 'proʊv oʊ , *with a correspondiong*
  plural ~**s** z
  pro,vost 'marshal ‖ ,provost-
prow praʊ **prows** praʊz
prowess 'praʊ es 'prəʊ-, -ɪs, -əs, •'es
  ‖ 'praʊ əs
prowl praʊl **prowled** praʊld **prowling**
  'praʊl ɪŋ **prowls** praʊlz
  'prowl car
prowler 'praʊl ə ‖ -ᵊr ~s z
Prowse (i) praʊs, (ii) praʊz
prox, prox. prɒks ‖ prɑːks
proxemic prɒk 'siːm ɪk ‖ prɑːk- ~s s
proxie... —*see* **proxy**
Proxima 'prɒks ɪm ə -əm- ‖ 'prɑːks-
proximal 'prɒks ɪm əl -əm- ‖ 'prɑːks- ~**ly** i
proximate 'prɒks ɪm ət -əm-, -ɪt ‖ 'prɑːks- ~**ly**
  li
proxime accessit ,prɒks ɪm i æk 'ses ɪt ,••eɪ-,
  -ək'•-, -ə 'kes-, §-ət ‖ ,prɑːks- ~s s
proximit|y prɒk 'sɪm ət li -ɪt- ‖ prɑːk 'sɪm ət ̬ li
  ~**ies** iz
proximo 'prɒks ɪ məʊ -ə- ‖ 'prɑːks ə moʊ
prox|y 'prɒks li ‖ 'prɑːks li ~**ies** iz
Prozac *tdmk* 'prəʊz æk ‖ 'proʊz-
Pru pruː
prude pruːd **prudes** pruːdz
prudence, P~ 'pruːd ᵊnts
prudent 'pruːd ᵊnt ~**ly** li
prudential, P~ pru 'denᵗʃ ᵊl ~**ly** i
pruder|y 'pruːd ər li ~**ies** iz
Prudhoe (i) 'prʌd əʊ -həʊ ‖ -oʊ, (ii) 'pruːd-
  —*The place in Northumberland is* (i), *locally*
  §'prʊd-; *but* P~ Bay *in AK is* (ii).
  ,Prudhoe 'Bay
Prud'hon pruː 'dɒ̃ ‖ -'dɑːn —*Fr* [pʀy dɔ̃]
prudish 'pruːd ɪʃ ~**ly** li ~**ness** nəs nɪs
Prue pruː
Prufrock 'pruː frɒk ‖ -frɑːk
prune pruːn **pruned** pruːnd **prunes** pruːnz
  pruning 'pruːn ɪŋ
  'pruning hook; 'pruning knife
Prunella, p~ pru 'nel ə
prunus, P~ 'pruːn əs ~**es** ɪz əz
prurienc|e 'prʊər i_ənts ‖ 'prʊr- ~**y** i
prurient 'prʊər i_ənt ‖ 'prʊr- ~**ly** li
pruriginous prʊə 'rɪdʒ ɪn əs -ən-
prurigo prʊə 'raɪg əʊ ‖ -oʊ
pruritus prʊə 'raɪt əs ‖ -'raɪt ̬ əs
  pru,ritus 'ani 'eɪn aɪ
prusik, P~ 'prʌs ɪk ~**ed** t ~**ing** ɪŋ ~**s** s
Prussi|a 'prʌʃ lə ‖ -**an/s** ᵊn/z
  ,Prussian 'blue◄
prussic 'prʌs ɪk
  ,prussic 'acid
pry, Pry praɪ **pried** praɪd (= *pride*) **pries** praɪz
  (= *prize*) **prying/ly** 'praɪ ɪŋ /li
Pryce praɪs
Prynne prɪn
Pryor 'praɪ_ə ‖ 'praɪ_ᵊr

prytaneum ,prɪt ə 'niː_əm -ᵊn 'iː_ ‖ -ᵊn 'iː əm
Przewalski prəʒ ɪ 'væl ski -ə'•; ,pɜːʒ•'••;
  ʃə'••; -'wɔːl-, -'wɒl- ‖ ʃə 'vaɪl ski prɪz-,
  -'waːl- —*Russ* [pʒɨ 'valɨ skɨɪj] ~'**s** z
  Prze,walski's 'horse
PS, P.S. ,piː 'es ~'**s** ɪz əz
ps... *Note: words spelt with* ps... *are*
  occasionally pronounced with initial ps, *as*
  written, rather than with the usual plain s
  sound. Thus psalm *is occasionally pronounced*
  psaːm. *This is not shown in individual entries.*
psalm saːm §saːlm, §sɒlm **psalms** saːmz
  §saːlmz, §sɒlmz
psalmist 'saːm ɪst §'saːlm-, §'sɒlm-, §-əst ~**s** s
psalmodic sæl 'mɒd ɪk saː- ‖ -'maːd-
psalmod|y 'saːm əd li 'sælm-, §'saːlm-, §'sɒlm-
  ~**ies** iz
psalter, P~ 'sɔːlt ə 'sɒlt- ‖ -ᵊr 'saːlt- ~**s** z
psalteri|um sɔːl 'tɪər i_əm sɒl- ‖ -'tɪr- saːl-
  ~**a** ə
psalter|y 'sɔːlt ər li 'sɒlt- ‖ 'saːlt- ~**is** iz
psephological ,siːf ə 'lɒdʒ ɪk ᵊl ◄ ,sef-
  ‖ -'laːdʒ- ~**ly** ͜i
psephologist sɪ 'fɒl ədʒ ɪst sə-, se-, siː-, §-əst
  ‖ -'faːl- ~**s** s
psephology sɪ 'fɒl ədʒ i sə-, se-, siː- ‖ -'faːl-
pseud sjuːd suːd ‖ suːd **pseuds** sjuːdz suːdz
  ‖ suːdz
pseudepigrapha ,sjuːd ɪ 'pɪg rəf ə ,suːd-, •'ə-,
  ,•e- ‖ ,suːd-
pseudo 'sjuːd əʊ 'suːd- ‖ 'suːd oʊ
pseudo- *comb. form*
  with stress-neutral suffix ¦sjuːd əʊ ¦suːd-
  ‖ ¦suːd oʊ— **pseudo-Marxist**
  ,sjuːd əʊ 'maːks ɪst ◄ ,suːd-, §-əst
  ‖ ,suːd oʊ 'maːrks əst ◄
pseudomonas ,sjuːd əʊ 'məʊn əs ,suːd-;
  sjuː 'dɒm ən əs, su- ‖ ,suːd ə 'moʊn əs
  suː 'daːm ən əs
pseudonym 'sjuːd ə nɪm 'suːd-, -ᵊn ɪm
  ‖ 'suːd ᵊn ɪm ~**s** z
pseudonymous sjuː 'dɒn ɪm əs suː-, -əm-
  ‖ suː 'daːn- ~**ly** li
pseudopod 'sjuːd əʊ pɒd 'suːd- ‖ 'suːd ə paːd
  ~**s** z
pseudopodi|um ,sjuːd əʊ 'pəʊd i_əm ,suːd-
  ‖ ,suːd oʊ 'poʊd- -ə- ~**a** ͜ə
pseudy 'sjuːd i 'suːd- ‖ 'suːd i
pshaw pɸə, pɸ, pʃə, ‖ ʃɔː ʃə; —*now obsolete:*
  the spelling may have represented a bilabial
  affricate with 'lip voice' (a 'raspberry', a
  'Bronx cheer').
psi psaɪ saɪ **psis** psaɪz saɪz
psilocybin ,saɪl əʊ 'saɪb ɪn ,sɪl-, §-ən ‖ ,-ə-
Psion *tdmk* 'saɪ ɒn ‖ -aːn
psittacine 'sɪt ə saɪn -sɪn ‖ 'sɪt ̬ ə-
psittacosis ,sɪt ə 'kəʊs ɪs §-əs ‖ ,sɪt ̬ ə 'koʊs əs
psoas 'səʊ æs -əs ‖ 'soʊ-
psoriasis sə 'raɪ_əs ɪs sɒ-, sɔː-, -əs ‖ soʊ-
psoriatic ,sɔːr i 'æt ɪk ◄ sɒː 'raɪ_ət ɪk ‖ -'æt ̬ ɪk ◄
  ,soʊr-
psst ps, pst

P

psych, psyche *v* saɪk **psyched** saɪkt **psyches**
v, **psychs** saɪks **psyching** 'saɪk ɪŋ
psyche *n*, P~ 'saɪk i -iː ~s z
psychedelia ˌsaɪk ə 'diːl i‿ə ˌ•ɪ-
psychedelic ˌsaɪk ə 'del ɪk ◄ -ɪ- ~**ally** əl_i
psychiatric ˌsaɪk i 'ætr ɪk ◄ -aɪ- ~**al** əl ~**ally**
əl_i
psychiatrist saɪ 'kaɪˌətr ɪst sɪ-, sə-, §-əst ~**s** s
psychiatry saɪ 'kaɪˌətr i sɪ-, sə-
psychic 'saɪk ɪk ~**al** əl ~**ally** əl_i ~**s** s
psycho 'saɪk əʊ ‖ -oʊ ~**s** z
psycho- *comb. form*
    with stress-neutral suffix ¦saɪk əʊ ‖ -oʊ —
    psychosocial
    ˌsaɪk əʊ 'səʊʃ əl ◄ ‖ -oʊ 'soʊʃ əl ◄
    with stress-imposing suffix saɪ 'kɒ+ ‖ -'kɑː+ —
    psychometry saɪ 'kɒm ətr i -ɪtr- ‖ -'kɑːm-
psychoacoustic ˌsaɪk əʊ ə 'kuːst ɪk ◄ ‖ ˌ•oʊ-
~**al** əl ~**ally** əl_i ~**s** s
psychoactive ˌsaɪk əʊ 'ækt ɪv ◄ ‖ -oʊ-
psychoanalys|e ˌsaɪk əʊ 'æn ə laɪz -əl aɪz
‖ -oʊ 'æn əl aɪz ~**ed** d ~**es** ɪz əz ~**ing** ɪŋ
psychoanalysis ˌsaɪk əʊ ə 'næl əs ɪs -ɪs ɪs §-əs
‖ ˌ•oʊ-
psychoanalyst ˌsaɪk əʊ 'æn əl ɪst §-əst ‖ ˌ•oʊ-
~**s** s
psychoanalytic ˌsaɪk əʊ ˌæn ə 'lɪt ɪk ◄ -əl 'ɪt-
‖ -oʊ ˌæn əl 'ɪt̬ ɪk ◄ ~**al** əl ~**ally** əl_i
psychoanalyz|e ˌsaɪk əʊ 'æn ə laɪz -əl aɪz
‖ -oʊ 'æn əl aɪz ~**ed** d ~**es** ɪz əz ~**ing** ɪŋ
psychobabble 'saɪk əʊ ˌbæb əl ‖ -oʊ-
psychochemical ˌsaɪk əʊ 'kem ɪk əl ◄ ‖ ˌ•oʊ-
~**s** z
psychodrama 'saɪk əʊ ˌdrɑːm ə ‖ -ə- -ˌdræm-
~**s** z
psychognosis saɪ 'kɒg nəs ɪs §-əs ‖ -'kɑːg-
psychokinesis ˌsaɪk əʊ kaɪ 'niːs ɪs -kɪˈ•-,
§-kəˈ•- ‖ ˌ•oʊ-
psychokinetic ˌsaɪk əʊ kaɪ 'net ɪk ◄ -kɪˈ•-,
§-kəˈ•- ‖ -oʊ kaɪ 'net̬ ɪk ◄
psycholinguist ˌsaɪk əʊ 'lɪŋ gwɪst §-gwəst
‖ -oʊ- ~**s** s
psycholinguistic
ˌsaɪk əʊ lɪŋ 'gwɪst ɪk ◄ ‖ ˌ•oʊ- ~**ally** əl_i ~**s**
s
psychological ˌsaɪk ə 'lɒdʒ ɪk əl ◄ ‖ -'lɑːdʒ-
~**ly** _i
    ˌpsychoˌlogical 'warfare
psychologism saɪ 'kɒl ə ˌdʒɪz əm ‖ -'kɑːl-
psychologist saɪ 'kɒl ədʒ ɪst §-əst ‖ -'kɑːl-
psycholog|y saɪ 'kɒl ədʒ li ‖ -'kɑːl- ~**ies** iz
psychometric ˌsaɪk əʊ 'metr ɪk ◄ -ə- ~**ally**
əl_i ~**s** s
psychometry saɪ 'kɒm ətr i -ɪtr- ‖ -'kɑːm-
psychopath 'saɪk əʊ pæθ ‖ -ə- ~**s** s
psychopathic ˌsaɪk əʊ 'pæθ ɪk ◄ ‖ -ə- ~**ally** əl_i
psychopathological
    ˌsaɪk əʊ ˌpæθ ə 'lɒdʒ ɪk əl ◄ ‖ -oʊ ˌpæθ ə 'lɑːdʒ-
psychopathology ˌsaɪk əʊ pə 'θɒl ədʒ i -pæˈ•-
‖ -oʊ pə 'θɑːl-
psychophysical ˌsaɪk əʊ 'fɪz ɪk əl ◄ ‖ ˌ•oʊ- ~**ly**
_i
psychoses saɪ 'kəʊs iːz ‖ -'koʊs-

psychosexual ˌsaɪk əʊ 'seks ju‿əl ◄ -'sekʃ u‿•,
-'sekʃ əl ‖ -oʊ 'sekʃ u‿əl ◄ -ˈ•əl ~**ly** i
psychos|is saɪ 'kəʊs ‖ɪs §-əs ‖ -'koʊs- ~**es** iːz
psychosocial ˌsaɪk əʊ 'səʊʃ əl ◄ ‖ -oʊ 'soʊʃ-
~**ly** i
psychosomatic ˌsaɪk əʊ səʊ
'mæt ɪk ◄ ‖ -ə sə 'mæt̬ ɪk ◄ ~**ally** əl_i
psychotherapeutic 'saɪk əʊ
    ˌθer ə 'pjuːt ɪk ‖ -oʊ ˌθer ə 'pjuːt̬ ɪk ~**ally** əl_i
    ~**s** s
psychotherapist ˌsaɪk əʊ 'θer əp ɪst §-əst
‖ ˌ•oʊ- ~**s** s
psychotherapy ˌsaɪk əʊ 'θer əp i ‖ ˌ•oʊ-
psychotic saɪ 'kɒt ɪk ‖ -'kɑːt̬ ɪk ~**ally** əl_i ~**s** s
psychotropic ˌsaɪk əʊ 'trɒp ɪk ◄ -'trəʊp-
‖ -ə 'troʊp ɪk ◄ ~**ally** əl_i ~**s** s
psychrometer saɪ 'krɒm ɪt ə -ət-
‖ -'krɑːm ət̬ ər ~**s** z
psyllid 'sɪl ɪd §-əd ~**s** z
PTA ˌpiː tiː 'eɪ
Ptah tɑː ptɑː; pə 'tɑː
ptarmigan 'tɑːm ɪg ən -əg- ‖ 'tɑːrm- ~**s** z
pteridophyte 'ter ɪd ə faɪt ˈ•əd-; tə 'rɪd- ~**s** s
pteridology ˌter ɪ 'dɒl ədʒ i ˌ•ə- ‖ -'dɑːl-
pterygium tə 'rɪdʒ i‿əm
pterodactyl ˌter əʊ 'dækt ɪl -əl ‖ -ə- ~**s** z
pterosaur 'ter ə sɔː ‖ -sɔːr ~**s** z
-pterous *stress-imposing* ptər əs — **dipterous**
'dɪpt ər əs
pterygoid 'ter ɪ gɔɪd -ə-
PTFE ˌpiː tiː ef 'iː
PTO, pto ˌpiː tiː 'əʊ ‖ -'oʊ
Ptolemaeus ˌtɒl ə 'miːˌəs -ɪ-, -'meɪ- ‖ ˌtɑːl-
Ptolemaic ˌtɒl ə 'meɪ ɪk ◄ -ɪ- ‖ ˌtɑːl-
Ptolemy 'tɒl əm i -ɪm- ‖ 'tɑːl-
ptomain, ptomaine 'təʊm eɪn təʊ 'meɪn
‖ 'toʊm- ~**s** z
ptosed təʊzd ‖ toʊzd
ptosis 'təʊs ɪs §-əs ‖ 'toʊs-
ptotic 'təʊt ɪk 'tɒt- ‖ 'toʊt̬-
Pty = proprietary prə 'praɪˌətˌ ər li ‖ -ə ter li
ptyalin 'taɪˌəl ɪn §-ən
p-type 'piː taɪp
pub pʌb **pubbed** pʌbd **pubbing** 'pʌb ɪŋ
pubs pʌbz
pub-crawl 'pʌb krɔːl ‖ -krɑːl ~**ed** d ~**er/s** ə/z
‖ ər/z ~**ing** ɪŋ ~**s** z
pube pjuːb **pubes** pjuːbz
pubertal 'pjuːb ət əl ‖ -ərt̬ əl
puberty 'pjuːb ət i ‖ -ərt̬ i
pubes *'groin; pubic hair'* 'pjuːb iːz —*but as a*
colloquial word, taken as a plural, usually
pjuːbz
pubes *plural of* pubis 'pjuːb iːz
pubescence pju 'bes ənts
pubescent pju 'bes ənt
pubic 'pjuːb ɪk
pub|is 'pjuːb ‖ɪs §-əs ~**es** iːz
public 'pʌb lɪk
    ˌpublic 'bar; ˌpublic 'company; ˌpublic
    conˈvenience; ˌpublic 'enemy; ˌpublic
    'gallery; ˌpublic 'house; ˌPublic 'Lending
    Right; ˌpublic 'library; ˌpublic 'nuisance;

‚public o'pinion; ‚public 'ownership;
‚public 'prosecutor; ‚public re'lations;
‚public 'school,'‧ ‧ ‧; ‚public 'speaking;
‚public 'spirit; ‚public 'works
public-address ‚pʌb lɪk ə 'dres
  ‚public-ad'dress ‚system
publican 'pʌb lɪk ən ~s z
publication ‚pʌb lɪ 'keɪʃ ᵊn -lə- ~s z
publicis|e 'pʌb lɪ saɪz -lə- ~ed d ~es ɪz əz
  ~ing ɪŋ
publicist 'pʌb lɪs ɪst -ləs, §-əst ~s s
publicity pʌb 'lɪs ət i pəb-, -ɪt- ‖ -əţ i
publiciz|e 'pʌb lɪ saɪz -lə- ~ed d ~es ɪz əz
  ~ing ɪŋ
public|ly 'pʌb lɪk ‖li ~ness nəs nɪs
public-spirited ‚pʌb lɪk 'spɪr ɪt ɪd ◄ -ət ɪd, -əd
  ‖ -əţ əd ◄ ~ness nəs nɪs
publish 'pʌb lɪʃ ~ed t ~es ɪz əz ~ing ɪŋ
  'publishing house
publishable 'pʌb lɪʃ əb ᵊl
publisher 'pʌb lɪʃ ə ‖ -ᵊr ~s z
Publius 'pʌb li‿əs
Puccini pu 'tʃiːn i —*It* [put 'tʃiː ni]
puccoon pə 'kuːn pʌ- ~s z
puce pjuːs
puck, Puck pʌk **pucks, Puck'** s pʌks
pucker 'pʌk ə ‖ -ᵊr ~ed d **puckering** 'pʌk
  ər‿ɪŋ ~s z
Puckeridge 'pʌk ər‿ɪdʒ
puckish 'pʌk ɪʃ ~ly li ~ness nəs nɪs
pud pʊd **puds** pʊdz
pudding 'pʊd ɪŋ —*There is also a non-standard*
  form △'pʊd ᵊn, *sometimes written* pudden ~s
  z
puddl|e 'pʌd ᵊl ~ed d ~es z ~ing ‿ɪŋ
Puddletown 'pʌd ᵊl taʊn
puddock 'pʌd ək ~s s
pudend|um pju 'dend ləm ~a ə
pudg|y 'pʌdʒ li ~ier i‿ə ‖ i‿ᵊr ~iest i‿ɪst i‿əst
  ~ily ɪ li əl i ~iness i nəs i nɪs
Pudsey 'pʌd si 'pʌdz i
pudu 'puːd uː ~s z
pueblo, P~ 'pweb ləʊ pu 'eb ləʊ ‖ -loʊ —*Sp*
  ['pwe βlo] ~s z
puerile 'pjʊər aɪᵊl 'pjɔːr-; 'pjuːᵊ raɪᵊl ‖ 'pjʊr
  əl -aɪl ~ly li ~ness nəs nɪs
puerilit|y pjʊᵊ 'rɪl ət li ₍ᵢ₎pjʊə-, ₍ᵢ₎pjɔː-, ‚pjuːᵊ‿ə-,
  -ɪt i ‖ -əţ li ~ies iz
puerperal pju 'ɜːp ᵊr‿əl ‖ -'ɜːp-
puerperium ‚pjuː‿ə 'pɪər i‿əm ‖ -'pɪr-
Puerto 'pwɜːt əʊ 'pweət- ‖ 'pwerţ oʊ —*Sp*
  ['pwer to] —*see also phrases with this word*
Puerto Ric|an/s ‚pwɜːt əʊ 'riːk |ən/z ◄ ‚pweət-,
  ‚pɔːt- ‖ ‚pwerţ ə- ‚pɔːrţ-, ‚poʊrţ- ~o əʊ ‖ oʊ
  —*Sp* ['rri ko]
puff pʌf **puffed** pʌft **puffing** 'pʌf ɪŋ **puffs**
  pʌfs
puffa 'pʌf ə
  'puffa ‚jacket
puffball 'pʌf bɔːl ‖ -bɑːl ~s z
puffer 'pʌf ə ‖ -ᵊr ~s z
puffery 'pʌf ər i
puffi... —*see* **puffy**

puffin 'pʌf ɪn §-ᵊn ~s z
puffin|ry 'pʌf ɪn |ri §-ᵊn- ~ries riz
puff-puff 'pʌf pʌf ~s s
puff|y 'pʌf li ~ier i‿ə ‖ i‿ᵊr ~iest i‿ɪst i‿əst
  ~iness i nəs i nɪs
puftaloon ‚pʌft ə 'luːn ~s z
pug pʌg **pugged** pʌgd **pugging** 'pʌg ɪŋ
  pugs pʌgz
Puget 'pjuːdʒ ɪt §-ət
puggaree 'pʌg ər‿i ~s z
puggree 'pʌg ri ~s z —*Hindi* [pə griː]
Pugh, Pughe pju:
pugilism 'pjuːdʒ ɪ ‚lɪz əm -ə-
pugilist 'pjuːdʒ ɪl ɪst -ᵊl-, §-əst ~s s
pugilistic ‚pjuːdʒ ɪ 'lɪst ɪk ◄ -ə- ~ally ᵊl_i
Pugin 'pjuːdʒ ɪn §-ᵊn
pug-mill 'pʌg mɪl ~s z
pugnacious pʌg 'neɪʃ əs ~ly li ~ness nəs nɪs
pugnacity pʌg 'næs ət i -ɪt- ‖ -əţ i
pug-nose ‚pʌg 'nəʊz '‧ ‧ ‖ 'pʌg noʊz ~d d ◄
Pugwash 'pʌg wɒʃ ‖ -wɔːʃ -wɑːʃ
puisne 'pjuːn i
puissance 'pwiːs ɒ̃s -ɒnts, -ᵊnts, -ænts
  ‖ 'pjuː əs ᵊnts —*In poetic usage also*
  'pjuː‿ɪs ᵊnts, -əs-; pju 'ɪs-; 'pwɪs ᵊnts
puissant 'pwiːs ɒnt 'pjuː‿ɪs ᵊnt, -əs-; pju 'ɪs-;
  'pwɪs ᵊnt ‖ 'pjuː əs ənt ~ly li
puja 'puːdʒ ə -ɑː ~s z —*Hindi* [puː dʒaː]
puke pjuːk **puked** pjuːkt **pukes** pjuːks
  puking 'pjuːk ɪŋ
pukeko 'pʊk ə kəʊ ‖ -koʊ ~s z
pukka 'pʌk ə
pula 'puːl ə 'pjuːl- 'pʊl-
Pulaski pə 'læsk i pju-, pʊ-
Pulborough 'pʊl bər‿ə ‖ -‚bɜː oʊ
pulchritude 'pʌlk rɪ tjuːd -rə-, →§-tʃuːd
  ‖ -tuːd -tjuːd
pulchritudinous ‚pʌlk rɪ 'tjuːd ɪn əs ◄ ‚‧rə-,
  →§-'tʃuːd-, -ən_əs ‖ -'tuːd ən_əs ◄ -'tjuːd-
pule pjuːl **puled** pjuːld **pules** pjuːlz
  puling/ly 'pjuːl ɪŋ /li
Pulham 'pʊl əm
puli 'pjuːl i 'pʊl-, 'puːl- ~s z
Pulitzer 'pʊl ɪts ə 'pjuːl-, §-əts- ‖ -ᵊr
pull-in 'pʊl ɪn ~s z
pull pʊl **pulled** pʊld **pulling** 'pʊl ɪŋ **pulls**
  pʊlz
pullback 'pʊl bæk ~s s
pulldown 'pʊl daʊn
Pullen 'pʊl ɪn -ən
pullet 'pʊl ɪt -ət ~s s
pulley 'pʊl i ~s z
pull-in 'pʊl ɪn ~s z
Pullman, p~ 'pʊl mən ~s z
pull-on 'pʊl ɒn ‖ -ɑːn -ɔːn
pullorum pʊ 'lɔːr əm pə- ‖ -'loʊr-
pull-out 'pʊl aʊt ~s s
pullover 'pʊl ‚əʊv ə ‖ -‚oʊv ᵊr ~s z
pullthrough 'pʊl θruː ~s z
pullu|late 'pʌl ju |leɪt -jə- ‖ -jə- ~lated leɪt ɪd
  -əd ‖ leɪţ əd ~lates leɪts ~lating
  leɪt ɪŋ ‖ leɪţ ɪŋ
pullulation ‚pʌl ju 'leɪʃ ᵊn -jə- ‖ -jə- ~s z
Pullum 'pʊl əm

pull-up 'pʊl ʌp ~s s
Pulman 'pʊl mən
pulmonary 'pʌl mən ər_i 'pʊl- ‖ -mə ner i
pulmonic pʌl 'mɒn ɪk pʊl- ‖ -'mɑːn ɪk ~**ally**
ᵊl_i
pulp pʌlp **pulped** pʌlpt **pulping** 'pʌlp ɪŋ
pulps pʌlps
pulpit 'pʊlp ɪt §'pʌlp-, §-ət ~s s
pulp|y 'pʌlp li ~**ier** i_ə ‖ i_ᵊr ~**iest** i_ɪst i_əst
~**iness** i nəs i nɪs
pulque 'pʊlk i 'puːlk-, -eɪ —Sp ['pul ke]
pulsar 'pʌls ɑː ‖ -ɑːr ~s z
pulsate pʌl 'seɪt ‖ 'pʌls eɪt **pulsated**
pʌl 'seɪt ɪd -əd ‖ 'pʌls eɪt̬ əd **pulsates**
pʌl 'seɪts ‖ 'pʌls eɪts **pulsating**
pʌl 'seɪt ɪŋ ‖ 'pʌls eɪt̬ ɪŋ
pulsatile 'pʌls ə taɪᵊl ‖ -ət̬ ᵊl
pulsation pʌl 'seɪʃ ᵊn ~s z
pulsative 'pʌls ət ɪv ‖ -ət̬-
pulsator 'pʌls eɪt ə ‖ 'pʌls eɪt̬ ᵊr ~s z
pulsatory pʌl 'seɪt ər i 'pʌls eɪt_ᵊr i
‖ 'pʌls ə tɔːr i -toʊr i
pulse pʌls **pulsed** pʌlst **pulses** 'pʌls ɪz -əz
pulsing 'pʌls ɪŋ
pulsimeter pʌl 'sɪm ɪt ə -ət- ‖ -ət̬ ᵊr ~s z
Pulteney (i) 'pʌlt ən_i (ii) 'pʊult- →'pʊʊlt-
‖ 'poʊlt-
pulu 'puːl u:
pulveris... —see **pulveriz...**
pulverization ˌpʌlv ər_aɪ 'zeɪʃ ᵊn ˌpʊlv-, _ɪ'•-
‖ -ᵊr_ə-
pulveriz|e 'pʌlv ə raɪz 'pʊlv- ~**ed** d ~**es** ɪz əz
~**ing** ɪŋ
pulverulent pʌl 'ver ʊl ənt -jʊl-, -ᵊl-
pulvinar pʌl 'vaɪn ə ‖ -ᵊr ~s z
pulvi|nate 'pʌlv ɪ |neɪt -ə- ~**nated** neɪt ɪd -əd
‖ neɪt̬ əd ~**nately** neɪt li
puma 'pjuːm ə ‖ 'puːm- ~s z
pumice 'pʌm ɪs §-əs
pumice stone 'pʌm ɪs stəʊn -i-, §-əs- ‖ -stoʊn
~s z
pummel 'pʌm ᵊl ~**ed**, ~**led** d ~**ing**, ~**ling** ɪŋ
~s z
pump pʌmp **pumped** pʌmpt **pumping**
'pʌmp ɪŋ **pumps** pʌmps
'**pump room**
pumpernickel 'pʌmp ə ˌnɪk ᵊl 'pʊmp- ‖ -ᵊr-
—Ger ['pʊm pɐ nɪkᵊl]
Pumphrey 'pʌmpf ri
pumpkin 'pʌmp kɪn §-kən ‖ △'pʌŋk ən ~s z
pun pʌn **punned** pʌnd **punning/ly** 'pʌn ɪŋ /li
puns pʌnz
punch, Punch pʌntʃ **punched** pʌntʃt
punches, Punch's 'pʌntʃ ɪz -əz **punching**
'pʌntʃ ɪŋ
'**punch ball**; '**punch bowl**; '**punch card**;
ˌ**punched** '**card**; '**punching bag**; '**punch
line**
Punch-and-Judy ˌpʌntʃ ən 'dʒuːd i -ənd-
ˌ**Punch-and-'Judy show**
punchbowl 'pʌntʃ bəʊl →-bɒʊl ‖ -boʊl ~s z
punch-drunk 'pʌntʃ drʌŋk ˌ•'•
puncheon 'pʌntʃ ən ~s z

puncher 'pʌntʃ ə ‖ -ᵊr ~s z
Punchinello, p~ ˌpʌntʃ ɪ 'nel əʊ -ə- ‖ -oʊ ~s,
~**es** z
punchline 'pʌntʃ laɪn ~s z
punch-up 'pʌntʃ ʌp ~s s
punch|y 'pʌntʃ li ~**ier** i_ə ‖ i_ᵊr ~**iest** i_ɪst
i_əst ~**ily** ɪ li əl i ~**iness** i nəs i nɪs
punctate adj 'pʌŋkt eɪt
punctilio pʌŋk 'tɪl i əʊ ‖ -oʊ ~s z
punctilious pʌŋk 'tɪl i_əs ~**ly** li ~**ness** nəs nɪs
punctual 'pʌŋk tʃu_əl -tju_əl
punctuality ˌpʌŋk tʃu 'æl ət i ,•tju-, -ɪt i ‖ -ət̬ i
punctually 'pʌŋk tʃu_əl i -tju_əl-
punctu|ate 'pʌŋk tʃu eɪt -tju- ~**ated** eɪt ɪd
-əd ‖ eɪt̬ əd ~**ates** eɪts ~**ating** eɪt ɪŋ ‖ eɪt̬ ɪŋ
punctuation ˌpʌŋk tʃu 'eɪʃ ᵊn -tju- ~s z
ˌ**punctu'ation mark**

PUNCTURE

■ -ŋktʃ-	▨ -ŋtʃ-	■ -ntʃ-	▩ -ŋkʃ-

BrE 1998

0   20   40   60   80   100%

puncture 'pʌŋk tʃə -ʃə; §'pʌntʃ ə ‖ -tʃᵊr —BrE
1998 poll panel preference: -ŋktʃ- 87%,
-ŋtʃ-6%, -ntʃ- 4%, -ŋkʃ- 3%. ~**d** d
puncturing 'pʌŋk tʃər ɪŋ -ʃər_ɪŋ ~s z
pundit 'pʌnd ɪt §-ət ~s s
pungency 'pʌndʒ ᵊnᵗs i
pungent 'pʌndʒ ᵊnt ~**ly** li
Pune 'puːn ə
puni... —see **puny**
Punic 'pjuːn ɪk
punish 'pʌn ɪʃ ~**ed** t ~**er/s** ə/z ‖ ᵊr/z ~**es** ɪz
əz ~**ing/ly** ɪŋ /li
punishable 'pʌn ɪʃ əb ᵊl
punishment 'pʌn ɪʃ mənt ~s s
punitive 'pjuːn ət ɪv -ɪt- ‖ -ət̬ ɪv ~**ly** li ~**ness**
nəs nɪs
Punjab pʌn 'dʒɑːb pʊn-, '•• —There is no
etymological justification for the pʊn forms.
Punjabi pʌn 'dʒɑːb i pʊn-, -iː ~s z
punji 'pʌndʒ i ~s z
punk pʌŋk **punks** pʌŋks
ˌ**punk 'rock**, ˌ**punk 'rocker**
punka, punkah 'pʌŋk ə ~s z
punk|y 'pʌŋk li ~**ier** i_ə ‖ i_ᵊr ~**iest** i_ɪst i_əst
~**iness** i nəs i nɪs
punnet 'pʌn ɪt §-ət ~s s
punster 'pʌn stə ‖ -stᵊr ~s z
punt 'boat'; 'kick'; 'gamble'; 'hollow at base of
bottle' pʌnt **punted** 'pʌnt ɪd -əd ‖ 'pʌnt̬ əd
punting 'pʌnt ɪŋ ‖ 'pʌnt̬ ɪŋ **punts** pʌnts
punt 'Irish pound' pʊnt **punts** pʊnts
punter 'pʌnt ə ‖ 'pʌnt̬ ᵊr ~s z
punt|y 'pʌnt li ‖ 'pʌnt̬ li ~**ies** iz
pun|y 'pjuːn li ~**ier** i_ə ‖ i_ᵊr ~**iest** i_ɪst i_əst
~**ily** ɪ li əl i ~**iness** i nəs i nɪs
pup pʌp **pupped** pʌpt **pupping** 'pʌp ɪŋ
pups pʌps
pup|a 'pjuːp |ə ~**ae** iː ~**al** ᵊl ~**as** əz
pup|ate pjuː 'peɪt ‖ 'pjuːp eɪt ~**ated** eɪt ɪd
-əd ‖ eɪt̬ əd ~**ates** eɪts ~**ating** eɪt ɪŋ ‖ eɪt̬ ɪŋ
pupation pjuː 'peɪʃ ᵊn

pupil ˈpjuːp ᵊl -ɪl ~s z
pupilage, pupillage ˈpjuːp ᵊl ɪdʒ -ɪl-
pupillary ˈpjuːp ᵊl ᵊr i ˈ•ɪl- ‖ -ə ler i
puppadum ˈpʌp ə dʌm ~s z
puppet ˈpʌp ɪt §-ət ~s s
puppeteer ˌpʌp ɪ ˈtɪə -ə- ‖ -ˈtɪ³r ~s z
puppetry ˈpʌp ɪtr i -ətr-
Puppis ˈpʌp ɪs
puppl|y ˈpʌp |i ~ies iz
 ˈpuppy dog; ˈpuppy fat; ˈpuppy love
Purbeck ˈpɜː bek ‖ ˈpɜˑ-
purblind ˈpɜː blaɪnd ‖ ˈpɜˑ- ~ly li ~ness nəs
 nɪs
Purcell (i) ˈpɜːs ᵊl ‖ ˈpɜˑːs ᵊl, (ii) pɜː ˈsel ‖ pɜˑː-
 —The composer was (i).
purchasable ˈpɜːtʃ əs əb ᵊl ˈ•ɪs- ‖ ˈpɜˑːtʃ-
purchas|e, P~ ˈpɜːtʃ əs -ɪs ‖ ˈpɜˑːtʃ əs ~ed t
 ~er/s ə/z ‖ -ᵊr/z ~es ɪz əz ~ing ɪŋ
 ˈpurchase tax; ˈpurchasing ˌpower
purda, purdah ˈpɜːd ə -ɑː ‖ ˈpɜˑːd ə —Hindi-
 Urdu [pər ɖaː]
Purdie ˈpɜːd i ‖ ˈpɜˑːd i
Purdon ˈpɜːd ᵊn ‖ ˈpɜˑːd ᵊn
Purdue ˈpɜːd juː ‖ pᵊr ˈduː
Purdy ˈpɜːd i ‖ ˈpɜˑːd i
pure pjʊə pjɔː ‖ pjʊᵊr pjɜˑː purer ˈpjʊər ə
 ˈpjɔːr- ‖ ˈpjʊr ᵊr ˈpjɜˑː- purest ˈpjʊər ɪst
 ˈpjɔːr-, -əst ‖ ˈpjʊr əst ˈpjɜˑː-
pureblood ˈpjʊə blʌd ˈpjɔː- ‖ ˈpjʊr- ˈpjɜˑː-
pureblooded ˌpjʊə ˈblʌd ɪd ◂ ˌpjɔː-, -əd
 ‖ ˌpjʊr- ˌpjɜˑː-
purebred ˈpjʊə bred ˈpjɔː- ‖ ˈpjʊr- ˈpjɜˑː- ~s
 z
puree, purée ˈpjʊər eɪ ˈpjɔːr- ‖ pjʊ ˈreɪ -ˈriː
 ~s z
purely ˈpjʊə li ˈpjɔː- ‖ ˈpjʊr- ˈpjɜˑː-
purfl|e ˈpɜːf ᵊl ‖ ˈpɜˑːf ᵊl ~ed d ~es z ~ing/s
 ɪŋ/z
Purfleet ˈpɜː fliːt ‖ ˈpɜˑː-
purgation pɜː ˈɡeɪʃ ᵊn ‖ pɜˑː-
purgative ˈpɜːɡ ət ɪv △ˈpɜːdʒ- ‖ ˈpɜˑːɡ ət̬ ɪv
 ~s z
purgatorial ˌpɜːɡ ə ˈtɔːr i_əl ◂ ‖ ˌpɜˑːɡ- -ˈtoʊr-
purgator|y, P~ ˈpɜːɡ ətr |i ‖ ˈpɜˑːɡ ə tɔːr i
 -toʊr i ~ies iz
purge pɜːdʒ ‖ pɜˑːdʒ purged pɜːdʒd ‖ pɜˑːdʒd
 purges ˈpɜːdʒ ɪz -əz ‖ ˈpɜˑːdʒ əz purging
 ˈpɜːdʒ ɪŋ ‖ ˈpɜˑːdʒ ɪŋ
purification ˌpjʊər ɪf ɪ ˈkeɪʃ ᵊn ˌpjɔːr-, ˌ•əf-,
 §-ə•- ‖ ˌpjʊr- ˌpjɜˑː- ~s z
purificator ˈpjʊər ɪf ɪ keɪt ə ˈpjɔːr-, ˈ•əf-,
 §-ə•• ‖ ˈpjʊr əf ə keɪt̬ ᵊr ˈpjɜˑː- ~s z
purificatory ˌpjʊər ɪf ɪ ˈkeɪt ᵊr i ˌpjɔːr-, ˌ•əf-,
 §, ••ə-, ˈ•••••-, ˈ••fɪk ət̬_ᵊr i
 ‖ pju ˈrɪf ɪk ə tɔːr i pjə-, -toʊr i; ˈpjʊr əf ək-,
 ˈpjɜˑː-
puri|fy ˈpjʊər ɪ |faɪ ˈpjɔːr-, -ə- ‖ ˈpjʊr- ˈpjɜˑː-
 ~fied faɪd ~fier/s faɪ_ə/z ‖ faɪ_ᵊr/z ~fies
 faɪz ~fying faɪ ɪŋ
Purim ˈpʊər ɪm ˈpjʊər-, pʊə ˈriːm ‖ ˈpʊr-
Purina tdmk pjə ˈriːn ə pjʊə-
purine ˈpjʊər iːn ˈpjɔːr-, -aɪn ‖ ˈpjʊr-
purism ˈpjʊər ˌɪz əm ˈpjɔːr- ‖ ˈpjʊr-

purist ˈpjʊər ɪst ˈpjɔːr-, §-əst ‖ ˈpjʊr əst ~s s
puristic pjʊ ˈrɪst ɪk pjɔː- ~al ᵊl ~ally ᵊl_i
Puritan ˈpjʊər ɪt ᵊn ˈpjɔːr-, -ət- ‖ ˈpjʊr ət ᵊn
 ~s z
puritanical ˌpjʊər ɪ ˈtæn ɪk ᵊl ◂ ˌpjɔːr-, ˌ•ə-
 ‖ ˌpjʊr- ~ly i ~ness nəs nɪs
Puritanism ˈpjʊər ɪt ᵊn ˌɪz əm ˈpjɔːr-, ˈ•ət-
 ‖ ˈpjʊr ət ᵊn-
purity ˈpjʊər ət i ˈpjɔːr-, -ɪt- ‖ ˈpjʊr ət̬ i
purl pɜːl ‖ pɜˑːl (= pearl) purled pɜːld ‖ pɜˑːld
 purling ˈpɜːl ɪŋ ‖ ˈpɜˑːl ɪŋ purls
 pɜːlz ‖ pɜˑːlz
purler ˈpɜːl ə ‖ ˈpɜˑːl ᵊr ~s z
Purley ˈpɜːl i ‖ ˈpɜˑːl i
purlieu ˈpɜːl juː §-luː ‖ ˈpɜˑːl uː -juː ~s z
purlin, purline ˈpɜːl ɪn §-ən ‖ ˈpɜˑːl- ~s z
purloin pɜː ˈlɔɪn ˈ•• ‖ pɜˑː- ~ed d ~ing ɪŋ ~s
 z
Purnell pɜː ˈnel ‖ pɜˑː-
purpl|e ˈpɜːp ᵊl ‖ ˈpɜˑːp ᵊl ~ed d ~es z ~ing
 ɪŋ
 ˌpurple ˈheart, ˌPurple ˈHeart; ˌpurple
 ˈpassage, ˌpurple ˈpatch
purplish ˈpɜːp ᵊl_ɪʃ ‖ ˈpɜˑːp-
purport v pə ˈpɔːt pɜː-; ˈpɜːp ət, -ɔːt
 ‖ pᵊr ˈpɔːrt -ˈpoʊrt purported pə ˈpɔːt ɪd
 pɜː-, -əd; ˈpɜːp ət-, -ɔːt- ‖ pᵊr ˈpɔːrt̬ əd
 -ˈpoʊrt- purporting pə ˈpɔːt ɪŋ pɜː-;
 ˈpɜːp ət-, -ɔːt- ‖ pᵊr ˈpɔːrt̬ ɪŋ -ˈpoʊrt- ~s s
purport n ˈpɜː pɔːt ˈpɜːp ət ‖ ˈpɜˑː pɔːrt -poʊrt
 ~s s
purpos|e n, v ˈpɜːp əs ‖ ˈpɜˑːp əs ~ed t ~es ɪz
 əz ~ing ɪŋ
purpose-built ˌpɜːp əs ˈbɪlt ◂ ‖ ˌpɜˑːp-
purposeful ˈpɜːp əs fᵊl -fʊl ‖ ˈpɜˑːp- ~ly _i
 ~ness nəs nɪs
purposeless ˈpɜːpəs ləs -lɪs ‖ ˈpɜˑːp- ~ly li
 ~ness nəs nɪs
purposely ˈpɜːp əs li ‖ ˈpɜˑːp-
purposive ˈpɜːp əs ɪv ‖ ˈpɜˑːp- pᵊr ˈpoʊs- ~ly
 li ~ness nəs nɪs
purpura ˈpɜːp jʊr ə -jᵊr- ‖ ˈpɜˑːp jᵊr ə -ᵊr ə
purr pɜː ‖ pɜˑː purred pɜːd ‖ pɜˑːd purring
 ˈpɜːr ɪŋ ‖ ˈpɜˑː ɪŋ purrs pɜːz ‖ pɜˑːz
purse pɜːs ‖ pɜˑːs pursed pɜːst ‖ pɜˑːst
 purses ˈpɜːs ɪz -əz ‖ ˈpɜˑːs əz pursing
 ˈpɜːs ɪŋ ‖ ˈpɜˑːs ɪŋ
 ˈpurse strings
purser ˈpɜːs ə ‖ ˈpɜˑːs ᵊr ~s z
purse-snatch|er/s ˈpɜːs ˌsnætʃ |ə/z
 ‖ ˈpɜˑːs ˌsnætʃ |ᵊr/z ~ing ɪŋ
purslane ˈpɜːs lən -lɪn, -leɪn ‖ ˈpɜˑːs- ~s z
pursuance pə ˈsjuː_ən̩s -ˈsuː_ ‖ pᵊr ˈsuː-
pursuant pə ˈsjuː_ənt -ˈsuː_ ‖ pᵊr ˈsuː- ~ly li
pur|sue pə |ˈsjuː -ˈsuː ‖ pᵊr |ˈsuː ~sued ˈsjuːd
 ˈsuːd ‖ ˈsuːd ~sues ˈsjuːz ˈsuːz ‖ ˈsuːz
 ~suing ˈsjuː_ɪŋ ˈsuː_ ‖ ˈsuː ɪŋ
pursuer pə ˈsjuː_ə -ˈsuː_ ‖ pᵊr ˈsuː_ᵊr ~s z
pursuit pə ˈsjuːt -ˈsuːt ‖ pᵊr ˈsuːt ~s s
pursuivant ˈpɜːs ɪv ənt -əv-, -wɪv- ‖ ˈpɜˑːs- ~s
 s
purulenc|e ˈpjʊər ʊl ən̩ts -jʊl-, -ᵊl- ‖ ˈpjʊr əl-
 -jəl- ~y i

purulent 'pjʊər ʊl ənt -jʊl-, -əl- ‖ 'pjʊr əl-
-jəl- **~ly** li
Purves 'pɜːv ɪs §-əs ‖ 'pɜːv əs
purvey pə 'veɪ pɜː- ‖ pər 'veɪ 'pɜːv eɪ **~ed** d
~ing ɪŋ **~s** z
purveyance pə 'veɪ ənᵗs pɜː- ‖ pər-
purveyor pə 'veɪ ə pɜː- ‖ pər 'veɪ ᵊr **~s** z
purview 'pɜː vjuː ‖ 'pɜːː- **~s** z
Purvis 'pɜːv ɪs §-əs ‖ 'pɜːv əs
pus pʌs
Pusan ˌpuː 'sæn ‖ -'sɑːn —*Korean* [pu san]
Pusey 'pjuːz i
Puseyite 'pjuːz i aɪt **~s** s
push pʊʃ **pushed** pʊʃt **pushes** 'pʊʃ ɪz -əz
pushing 'pʊʃ ɪŋ
'push ˌbutton
pushbike 'pʊʃ baɪk **~s** s
push-button 'pʊʃ ˌbʌt ᵊn
pushcart 'pʊʃ kɑːt ‖ -kɑːrt **~s** s
push-chain 'pʊʃ tʃeɪn **~s** z
pushchair 'pʊʃ tʃeə ‖ -tʃer **~s** z
pushdown 'pʊʃ daʊn
pusher 'pʊʃ ə ‖ -ᵊr **~s** z
pushful 'pʊʃ fᵊl -fʊl **~ly** _i **~ness** nəs nɪs
Pushkin 'pʊʃ kɪn —*Russ* ['pʊʃ kjɪn]
pushover 'pʊʃ ˌəʊv ə ‖ -ˌoʊv ᵊr **~s** z
pushpin 'pʊʃ pɪn **~s** z
push-pull ˌpʊʃ 'pʊl ◄
pushrod 'pʊʃ rɒd ‖ -rɑːd **~s** z
push-|start 'pʊʃ |stɑːt ˌ•'• ‖ -|stɑːrt **~started**
stɑːt ɪd -əd ‖ stɑːrt̬ əd **~starting**
stɑːt ɪŋ ‖ stɑːrt̬ ɪŋ **~starts** stɑːts ‖ stɑːrts
Push|to 'pʌʃ| təʊ ‖ -toʊ **~tu** tuː
push-up 'pʊʃ ʌp **~s** s
push|y 'pʊʃ li **~ier** i‿ə ‖ i‿ᵊr **~iest** i‿ɪst i‿əst
~ily ɪ li əl i **~iness** i nəs i nɪs
pusillanimity ˌpjuːs ɪl ə 'nɪm ət i ˌpjuːz-, ˌ•əl-,
-æ'•-, -ɪt i ‖ -ət̬ i
pusillanimous ˌpjuːs ɪ 'læn ɪm əs ◄ ˌpjuːz-,
ˌ•ə-, -əm əs **~ly** li
puss pʊs **pusses** 'pʊs ɪz -əz
'puss moth
puss|y *n* 'pʊs li **~ies** iz
ˌpussy 'willow, '•• , ••
pussy *adj, 'purulent'* 'pʌs i
pussycat 'pʊs i kæt **~s** s
pussy|foot 'pʊs i |fʊt **~footed** fʊt ɪd -əd
‖ fʊt̬ əd **~footer/s** fʊt ə/z ‖ fʊt̬ ᵊr/z
~footing fʊt ɪŋ ‖ fʊt̬ ɪŋ **~foots** fʊts
pustular 'pʌst jʊl ə -jəl-; →§'pʌs tʃʊl ə, -tʃəl-
‖ 'pʌs tʃəl ᵊr
pustule 'pʌst juːl →§'pʌs tʃuːl ‖ 'pʌs tʃuːl **~s**
z
put pʊt **puts** pʊts **putting** 'pʊt ɪŋ
putative 'pjuːt ət ɪv ‖ 'pjuːt̬ ət̬ ɪv **~ly** li
put-down 'pʊt daʊn **~s** z
Putnam 'pʌt nəm
Putney 'pʌt ni
put-off 'pʊt ɒf -ɔːf ‖ 'pʊt̬ ɔːf -ɑːf **~s** s
put-on 'pʊt ɒn ‖ 'pʊt̬ ɑːn -ɔːn **~s** z
putonghua ˌpuː tɒŋ 'hwaː ‖ -tɔːŋ- -tɑːŋ-
—*Chinese* pŭtōnghuà [³pʰu ¹tʰʊŋ ⁴xwa]

put-|put 'pʌt |pʌt ˌ•'• **~puts** pʌts **~putted**
pʌt ɪd -əd ‖ pʌt̬ əd **~putting** pʌt ɪŋ ‖ pʌt̬ ɪŋ
putrefaction ˌpjuːtr ɪ 'fæk ʃᵊn -ə-
putrefactive ˌpjuːtr ɪ 'fækt ɪv ◄ -ə-
putre|fy 'pjuːtr ɪ |faɪ -ə- **~fied** faɪd **~fies** faɪz
~fying faɪ ɪŋ
putresc|ence pju: 'tres |ᵊnᵗs **~ent** ᵊnt
putrid 'pjuːtr ɪd §-əd
putridity pju: 'trɪd ət i -ɪt- ‖ -ət̬ i
putrid|ly 'pjuːtr ɪd |li §-əd- **~ness** nəs nɪs
putsch pʊtʃ **putsches** 'pʊtʃ ɪz -əz
putt pʌt **putted** 'pʌt ɪd -əd ‖ 'pʌt̬ əd **putting**
'pʌt ɪŋ ‖ 'pʌt̬ ɪŋ **putts** pʌts
puttee 'pʌt i -iː, pʌ 'tiː ‖ pʌ 'tiː **~s** z
Puttenham 'pʌt ᵊn_əm
putter *n 'one that puts'* 'pʊt ə ‖ 'pʊt̬ ᵊr **~s** z
putter *v; n 'golfer, golf club'* 'pʌt ə ‖ 'pʌt̬ ᵊr
~s z
putti *plural of* putto 'pʊt i -iː ‖ 'puːt̬ iː
puttie... —*see* putty
putting *pres ptcp of* **put** 'pʊt ɪŋ ‖ 'pʊt̬ ɪŋ
putting *pres ptcp of* **putt** 'pʌt ɪŋ ‖ 'pʌt̬ ɪŋ
'putting green
Puttnam 'pʌt nəm
putto 'pʊt əʊ ‖ 'puːt oʊ **putti** 'pʊt i -iː
‖ 'puːt̬ iː
putt|y 'pʌt li ‖ 'pʌt̬ li **~ied** id **~ies** iz **~ying**
i ɪŋ
put-up 'pʊt ʌp ‖ 'pʊt̬ ʌp
put-upon 'pʊt ə ˌpɒn ‖ 'pʊt̬ ə ˌpɑːn -ˌpɔːn
Put-U-Up *tdmk* 'pʊt ju ʌp
putz pʌts pʊts **putzes** 'pʌts ɪz 'pʊts-, -əz
Puy-de-Dôme ˌpwiː də 'dəʊm ‖ -'doʊm —*Fr*
[pɥi̯ də doːm]
puzzl|e 'pʌz ᵊl **~ed** d **~es** z **~ing/ly** _ɪŋ /li
puzzlement 'pʌz ᵊl mənt
puzzler 'pʌz ᵊl_ə ‖ _ᵊr **~s** z
PVC ˌpiː viː 'siː ◄
Pwllheli pə 'θel i pʊ-, -'ɬel-, pʊθ 'lel i —*Welsh*
[puːɬ 'he li, pʊɬ-]
PX ˌpiː 'eks **~s** ɪz əz
pyaemia paɪ 'iːm i‿ə
Pybus 'paɪb əs
Pydna 'pɪd nə
Pye paɪ
Pyecombe 'paɪ kuːm
pye-dog 'paɪ dɒg ‖ -dɔːg -dɑːg **~s** z
pyelo- *comb. form*
with stress-neutral suffix ˌpaɪ‿ə ləʊ ‖ ˌpaɪ ə loʊ
— **pyelogram** 'paɪ‿ə ləʊ græm ‖ 'paɪ ə loʊ-
with stress-imposing suffix ˌpaɪ‿ə 'lɒ+ ‖ -'lɑː+
— **pyelography** ˌpaɪ‿ə 'lɒg rəf i ‖ -'lɑːg-
pyemia paɪ 'iːm i‿ə
pygmaean pɪg 'miː‿ən
Pygmalion pɪg 'meɪl i‿ən
pygmean pɪg 'miː‿ən
pygmy, Pygmy 'pɪg mi **pygmies, P~** 'pɪg miz
pyjama pə 'dʒɑːm ə pɪ-, △bə- ‖ -'dʒæm- **~s** z
Pyke paɪk
pyknic 'pɪk nɪk (= *picnic*)
pylon 'paɪl ən -ɒn ‖ -ɑːn **~s** z
pyloric paɪ 'lɒr ɪk -'lɔːr- ‖ -'lɔːr ɪk -'loʊr-
pylor|us paɪ 'lɔːr |əs ‖ -'loʊr- **~i** aɪ iː

Pylos 'paɪl ɒs ‖ -ɑːs
Pym, Pymm pɪm
Pynchon 'pɪntʃ ən
pyo- *comb. form*
  with stress-neutral suffix ˌpaɪ əʊ ‖ -ə —
  pyogenic ˌpaɪ əʊ 'dʒen ɪk ◄ -'dʒiːn- ‖ -ə-
  with stress-imposing suffix paɪ 'ɒ+ ‖ -'ɑː+ —
  pyogenous paɪ 'ɒdʒ ən əs ‖ -'ɑːdʒ-
pyoid 'paɪ ɔɪd
Pyongyang ˌpjɒŋ 'jæŋ ‖ ˌpjʌŋ 'jɑːŋ ˌpjɑːŋ-
  —*Korean* [pʰjʌŋ jaŋ]
pyorrhea, pyorrhoea ˌpaɪ ə 'rɪə §-'riː ə
  ‖ ˌpaɪ ə 'riː ə
pyosis paɪ 'əʊs ɪs §-əs ‖ -'oʊs əs
pyracantha ˌpaɪər ə 'kæn̩θ ə ~s z
Pyrah 'paɪər ə
pyramid 'pɪr ə mɪd **~ed** ɪd əd **~ing** ɪŋ **~s** z
  'pyramid ˌselling,, ˙ ˙ ˙ ' ˙ ˙
pyramidal pɪ 'ræm ɪd əl pə-, §-əd əl;
  'pɪr ə mɪd əl, ˌ ˙ ˙ ' ˙ ˙ **~ly** i
Pyramus 'pɪr əm əs
pyran 'paɪər æn paɪ 'ræn
pyrargyrite paɪə 'rɑːdʒ ə raɪt -ɪ- ‖ -'rɑːrdʒ-
pyre 'paɪ_ə ‖ 'paɪ_ər **pyres** 'paɪ_əz ‖ 'paɪ_ərz
pyrene 'paɪər iːn —*but in the sense 'nutlet', also*
  paɪə 'riːn **~s** z
Pyrene paɪ 'riːn i
Pyrenean ˌpɪr ə 'niː_ən ◄ -ɪ- **~s** z
Pyrenees ˌpɪr ə 'niːz -ɪ- ‖ 'pɪr ə niːz (*)
pyrethrin paɪə 'riːθ rɪn §-rən ‖ -'reθ-
pyrethrum paɪə 'riːθ rəm ‖ -'reθ-
pyretic paɪə 'ret ɪk ‖ -'reţ ɪk
Pyrex *tdmk* 'paɪər eks
pyrexia paɪə 'reks i_ə
Pyrford 'pɜː fəd ‖ 'pɜ·ː fərd
pyridine 'pɪr ɪ diːn -ə-
pyriform 'pɪr ɪ fɔːm 'paɪər-, -ə- ‖ -fɔːrm
pyrimidine paɪə 'rɪm ɪ diːn -ə- ‖ pə-
pyrite 'paɪər aɪt
pyrites paɪə 'raɪt iːz pɪ-, pə-; 'paɪər aɪts

‖ pə 'raɪţ iz
pyritic paɪə 'rɪt ɪk pɪ-. pə-
pyro- *comb. form*
  with stress-neutral suffix ˌpaɪər əʊ ‖ -ə —
  pyrophosphate ˌpaɪər əʊ 'fɒs feɪt ‖ -ə 'fɑːs-
  with stress-imposing suffix paɪə 'rɒ+ ‖ -'rɑː+ —
  pyrolysis paɪə 'rɒl əs ɪs -ɪs-, §-əs ‖ -'rɑːl-
pyroclastic ˌpaɪər əʊ 'klæst ɪk ◄ ‖ -ə-
  ˌpyroˌclastic 'flow
pyrogallic ˌpaɪər əʊ 'gæl ɪk ◄ ‖ -ə- **~ol** ɒl ‖ ɔːl
  -ɑːl, -oʊl
pyromania ˌpaɪər əʊ 'meɪn i_ə ‖ ˌ˙ə-
pyromaniac ˌpaɪər əʊ 'meɪn i æk ‖ ˌ˙ə- **~s** s
pyrosis paɪə 'rəʊs ɪs §-əs ‖ -'roʊs əs
pyrotechnic ˌpaɪər əʊ 'tek nɪk ◄ ‖ -ə- **~al** əl
  ~ally əl_i **~s** s
pyroxene paɪə 'rɒks iːn ‖ -'rɑːks- pə-
Pyrrha 'pɪr ə
Pyrrhic, p~ 'pɪr ɪk **~s** s
Pyrrho 'pɪr əʊ ‖ -oʊ
Pyrrhus 'pɪr əs
pyrrole 'pɪr əʊl→-ɒʊl; pɪ 'rəʊl, §pə- ‖ 'pɪr oʊl
pyruvic paɪə 'ruːv ɪk
Pytchley 'paɪtʃ li
Pythagoras paɪ 'θæg ər əs -ə ræs ‖ pə- pɪ-
Pythagorean paɪ ˌθæg ə 'riː_ən ◄ ˌpaɪ θæg ə' ˙-
  ‖ pə- pɪ- **~ism** ˌɪz əm **~s** z
Pytheas 'pɪθ i_əs -æs
Pythia 'pɪθ i_ə
Pythian 'pɪθ i_ən
Pythias 'pɪθ i æs -i_əs
python, P~ 'paɪθ ən ‖ -ɑːn -ən **~s** z
Pythonesque ˌpaɪθ ə 'nesk ◄
pythoness 'paɪθ ə nes -ən ɪs, -ən əs ‖ -ən əs
  'pɪθ- **~es** ɪz əz
pythonic paɪ 'θɒn ɪk pɪ- ‖ -'θɑːn-
pyuria paɪ 'jʊər i_ə ‖ -'jʊr-
pyx pɪks (= *picks*) **pyxes** 'pɪks ɪz -əz
pyxie 'pɪks i **~s** z

P

Q q

q Spelling-to-sound

1 Except in occasional words from foreign languages, the letter **q** is always followed by **u**. Where the spelling is the resultant digraph **qu**, the pronunciation is regularly
kw, as in **quite** kwaɪt, or
k, as in **picturesque** ˌpɪk tʃə ˈresk.

2 The pronunciation is generally kw. Examples: **queen** kwiːn, **squeak** skwiːk, **equal** ˈiːk wəl, **liquid** ˈlɪk wɪd.

3 However, in the case of **que** at the end of a word, and in a minority of other words, the pronunciation is k. Examples: **clique** kliːk, **cheque** tʃek (AmE spelling: **check**); **queue** kjuː, **liquor** ˈlɪk ə ‖ ˈlɪk ər.

4 Where the spelling is **cqu**, the pronunciation is again either kw, as in **acquaint** ə ˈkweɪnt, or k, as in **lacquer** ˈlæk ə ‖ ˈlæk ər.

Q, q kjuː: **Q's, q's, Qs, qs** kjuːz
—*Communications code name:* Quebec
ˈQ ˌfever

Qaddafi, Qadhafi gə ˈdɑːf i -ˈdæf- —*Arabic*
[ɣað ˈða fi]

Qantas *tdmk* ˈkwɒnt əs-æs ‖ ˈkwɑːnt-

Qatar ˈkæt ɑː ˈgæt-, -ˈkʌt-, -ˈgʌt-; gæ ˈtɑː, kæ-, kə- ‖ ˈkɑːt ɑːr kə ˈtɑːr —*Arabic* [ˈqɑ tˤɑr]

Qatari kæ ˈtɑːr i gæ-, kə- ~s z

QC, Q.C. ˌkjuː ˈsiː ~s, ~'s z

QED, q.e.d. ˌkjuː iː ˈdiː

Qin *dynasty* tʃɪn —*Chinese* Qín [²tɕʰɪn]

Qing *dynasty* tʃɪŋ —*Chinese* Qīng [¹tɕʰɪŋ]

Qingdao ˌtʃɪŋ ˈdaʊ —*Chinese* Qīngdǎo [¹tɕʰɪŋ ³tau]

Qinghai ˌtʃɪŋ ˈhaɪ
—*Chinese* Qīnghǎi [¹tɕʰɪŋ ³xai]

Qom kʊm kɒm, xʊm —*Persian* [ˈkom]

qoph kɒf kɔːf, kʊf, kəʊf ‖ kɔːf kɑːf, koʊf

qt, q.t. ˌkjuː ˈtiː

Q-Tip *tdmk* ˈkjuː tɪp ~s s

qua kweɪ kwɑː

Quaalude *tdmk* ˈkweɪ luːd ~s z

quack kwæk **quacked** kwækt **quacking**
ˈkwæk ɪŋ **quacks** kwæks

quackery ˈkwæk ər i

quad kwɒd ‖ kwɑːd **quads** kwɒdz ‖ kwɑːdz

Quadragesim|a ˌkwɒdr ə ˈdʒes ɪm |ə -əm ə
‖ ˌkwɑːdr- ~**al** əl

quadrangle ˈkwɒdr æŋ gəl ‖ ˈkwɑːdr- ~s z

quadrangular kwɒ ˈdræŋ gjʊl ə -gjəl-
‖ kwɑː ˈdræŋ gjəl ər

quadrant ˈkwɒdr ənt ‖ ˈkwɑːdr- ~s s

quadrantal kwɒ ˈdrænt əl ‖ kwɑː ˈdrænt̬ əl

quadraphonic ˌkwɒdr ə ˈfɒn ɪk ◄
‖ ˌkwɑːdr ə ˈfɑːn ɪk ◄ ~**ally** əl̬i ~s s

quadraphony kwɒ ˈdrɒf ən i -ˈdræf-;
ˈkwɒdr ə fɒn i ‖ kwɑː ˈdrɑːf-
ˈkwɑːdr ə fɑːn i

quadrasonic ˌkwɒdr ə ˈsɒn ɪk ◄
‖ ˌkwɑːdr ə ˈsɑːn ɪk ◄ ~**ally** əl̬i ~s s

quadrat ˈkwɒdr ət -æt ‖ ˈkwɑːdr- ~s s

quadrate *n, adj* ˈkwɒdr eɪt -ət, -ɪt ‖ ˈkwɑːdr-
~s s

quadr|ate *v* kwɒ ˈdr|eɪt ‖ ˈkwɑːdr eɪt ~**ated**
eɪt ɪd -əd ‖ eɪt̬ əd ~**ates** eɪts ~**ating**
eɪt ɪŋ ‖ eɪt̬ ɪŋ

quadratic kwɒ ˈdræt ɪk ‖ kwɑː ˈdræt̬ ɪk ~s s
qua**dratic e**ˈ**quation**

quadrature ˈkwɒdr ətʃ ə -ɪtʃ-; -ət jʊə, -ɪt-
‖ ˈkwɑːdr ətʃ ər -ə tʃʊr, -ə tʊr ~s z

quadrenni|al kwɒ ˈdren i |əl ‖ kwɑː- ~**a** ə
~**ally** əl̬i ~**um** əm

quadri- *comb. form*
with stress-neutral suffix ˈkwɒdr ɪ -ə
‖ ˈkwɑːdr ə — **quadrilingual**
ˌkwɒdr ɪ ˈlɪŋ gwəl ◄-ə-, §-ˈlɪŋ gju əl
‖ ˌkwɑːdr ə-
with stress-imposing suffix kwɒ ˈdrɪ+ ‖ kwɑː-
— **quadripara** kwɒ ˈdrɪp ər ə ‖ kwɑː-

quadric ˈkwɒdr ɪk ‖ ˈkwɑːdr ɪk

quadriceps ˈkwɒdr ɪ seps -ə- ‖ ˈkwɑːdr- ~**es**
ɪz əz

quadriga kwɒ ˈdriːg ə kwə-, -ˈdraɪg- ‖ kwɑː-
~s z

quadrilateral ˌkwɒdr ɪ ˈlæt ər əl ◄ , • ə-
‖ ˌkwɑːdr ə ˈlæt̬ ər əl ◄ →-ˈlætr əl ~s z

quadrilingual ˌkwɒdr ɪ ˈlɪŋ gwəl ◄ -ə-
‖ ˌkwɑːdr ə- ~**ly** i ~**s** z
quadrille kwə ˈdrɪl kwɒ- ‖ kwɑː- ~**s** z
quadrillion kwɒ ˈdrɪl jən -i‿ən ‖ kwɑː ˈdrɪl jən
~**s** z
quadrinomial ˌkwɒdr ɪ ˈnəʊm i‿əl ◄ ˌ•ə-
‖ ˌkwɑːdr ə ˈnoʊm- ~**s** z
quadripartite ˌkwɒdr ɪ ˈpɑːt aɪt ◄ -ə-
‖ ˌkwɑːdr ə ˈpɑːrt aɪt ◄
quadriplegia ˌkwɒdr ɪ ˈpliːdʒ i‿ə ˌ•ə-,
-ˈpliːdʒ ə ‖ ˌkwɑːdr ə-
quadriplegic ˌkwɒdr ɪ ˈpliːdʒ ɪk ◄ ˌ•ə-
‖ ˌkwɑːdr ə- ~**s** z
quadrivium kwɒ ˈdrɪv i‿əm ‖ kwɑː-
quadroon kwɒ ˈdruːn ‖ kwɑː- ~**s** z
quadrophonic ˌkwɒdr ə ˈfɒn ɪk ◄
‖ ˌkwɑːdr ə ˈfɑːn ɪk ◄ ~**ally** ᵊl‿i ~**s** s
quadrophony kwɒ ˈdrɒf ən i ˈkwɒdr ə fɒn i
‖ kwɑː ˈdrɑːf- ˈkwɑːdr ə fɑːn i
quadrumanous kwɒ ˈdruːm ən əs ‖ kwɑː-
quadruped ˈkwɒdr u ped -ə- ‖ ˈkwɑːdr ə- ~**s**
z
quadrupl|e ˈkwɒdr ʊp ᵊl -əp-; kwɒ ˈdruːp-
‖ kwɑː ˈdruːp ᵊl -ˈdrʌp-; ˈkwɑːdr əp- ~**ed** d
~**es** z ~**ing** ɪŋ
quadruplet ˈkwɒdr ʊp lət -əp-, -lɪt, -let;
kwɒ ˈdruːp-, §-ˈdrʌp- ‖ kwɑː ˈdruːp-
-ˈdrʌp-; ˈkwɑːdr əp- ~**s** s
quadruplex ˈkwɒdr u pleks -ə-;
kwɒ ˈdruːp leks ‖ ˈkwɑːdr ə pleks
kwɑː ˈdruːp leks
quadruplicate adj kwɒ ˈdruːp lɪk ət -lək ət, -ɪt;
-lɪ keɪt, -lə- ‖ kwɑː- ~**s** s
quadrupli|cate v kwɒ ˈdruːp lɪ |keɪt -lə-
‖ kwɑː- ~**cated** keɪt ɪd -əd ‖ keɪt əd ~**cates**
keɪts ~**cating** keɪt ɪŋ ‖ keɪt ɪŋ
quadruply ˈkwɒdr ʊp li -əp-; kwɒ ˈdruːp-
‖ kwɑː- ˈdruːp li -ˈdrʌp-; ˈkwɑːdr əp-
quaestor ˈkwiːst ə ˈkwaɪst-, -ɔː- ‖ ˈkwest ᵊr
ˈkwiːst- ~**s** z
quaff kwɒf kwɑːf ‖ kwɑːf kwæf **quaffed**
kwɒft kwɑːft ‖ kwɑːft kwæft **quaffing**
ˈkwɒf ɪŋ ˈkwɑːf- ‖ ˈkwɑːf ɪŋ ˈkwæf- **quaffs**
kwɒfs kwɑːfs ‖ kwɑːfs kwæfs
quaffer ˈkwɒf ə ˈkwɑːf- ‖ ˈkwɑːf ᵊr ˈkwæf-
~**s** z
quag kwæg kwɒg ‖ kwɑːg **quags** kwægz
kwɒgz ‖ kwɑːgz
quagga ˈkwæg ə ˈkwɒg- ‖ ˈkwɑːg- ~**s** z
quagg|y ˈkwæg li ˈkwɒg- ‖ ˈkwɑːg- ~**ier**
i‿ə ‖ i‿ᵊr ~**iest** i‿ɪst i‿əst ~**iness** i nəs i nɪs
Quaglino's tdmk
kwæg ˈliːn əʊz ‖ kwɑːg ˈliːn oʊz

QUAGMIRE

ˈkwɒg- ‖ ˈkwæg-

BrE 1998

0	20	40	60	80	100%

---

quagmire ˈkwɒg maɪ‿ə ˈkwæg-
‖ ˈkwæg maɪ‿ᵊr ˈkwɑːg- —*BrE 1998 poll
panel preference:* ˈkwɒg- 62%, ˈkwæg- 38%.
~**s** z

quahog ˈkwɑː hɒg ‖ ˈkwɔː hɔːg ˈkwɑː-,
ˈkwoʊ-, ˈkoʊ-, -hɑːg ~**s** z
Quai d'Orsay ˌkeɪ ˈdɔːs eɪ ‖ -dɔːr ˈseɪ —*Fr*
[ke dɔʁ sɛ]
Quaid kweɪd
quail, Quail kweɪᵊl **quailed** kweɪᵊld **quailing**
ˈkweɪᵊl ɪŋ **quails** kweɪᵊlz
Quain kweɪn
quaint kweɪnt **quainter** ˈkweɪnt ə ‖ ˈkweɪnt̬ ᵊr
quaintest ˈkweɪnt ɪst -əst ‖ ˈkweɪnt̬-
quaint|ly ˈkweɪnt |li ~**ness** nəs nɪs
quake kweɪk **quaked** kweɪkt **quakes** kweɪks
quaking ˈkweɪk ɪŋ
Quaker ˈkweɪk ə ‖ -ᵊr ~**ly** li ~**s** z
Quakerism ˈkweɪk ər‿ɪz əm
quak|y ˈkweɪk li ~**ier** i‿ə ‖ i‿ᵊr ~**iest** i‿ɪst i‿əst
~**ily** ɪ li əl i ~**iness** i nəs i nɪs
Qualcast tdmk ˈkwɒl kɑːst -§kæst
‖ ˈkwɑːl kæst
Qualcomm tdmk ˈkwɒl kɒm ‖ ˈkwɑːl kɑːm
qualification ˌkwɒl ɪf ɪ ˈkeɪʃ ᵊn ˌ•əf-, §-ə• ᵊ-
‖ ˌkwɑːl- ~**s** z
qualificative ˈkwɒl ɪf ɪk ət ɪv ˈ•əf-; -ɪ keɪt ɪv,
-ə• • ; ˌ• • ɪ ˈkeɪt ɪv◄, -ə• • •
‖ ˈkwɑːl əf ə keɪt ɪv
qualificatory ˌkwɒl ɪf ɪ ˈkeɪt ər‿i ˌ•əf-, §-ə• • -
‖ ˈkwɑːl əf ɪk ə tɔːri ˈ• ɪf-, -toʊr i
quali|fy ˈkwɒl ɪ |faɪ -ə- ‖ ˈkwɑːl- ~**fied** faɪd
~**fier/s** faɪ‿ə/z ‖ faɪ‿ᵊr/z ~**fies** faɪz ~**fying**
faɪ ɪŋ
qualitative ˈkwɒl ɪt ət ɪv ˈ•ət-; -ɪ teɪt-, -ə teɪt-
‖ ˈkwɑːl ə teɪt̬ ɪv ~**ly** li
qualit|y ˈkwɒl ət li -ɪt- ‖ ˈkwɑːl ət̬ li ~**ies**
iz
qualm kwɑːm kwɔːm, §kwɑːlm ‖ kwɔːm,
kwɑːlm **qualms** kwɑːmz kwɔːmz,
§kwɑːlmz ‖ kwɔːmz, kwɑːlmz
qualmish ˈkwɑːm ɪʃ ˈkwɔːm-,
§ˈkwɑːlm- ‖ ˈkwɔːm-, ˈkwɑːlm- ~**ly** li
~**ness** nəs nɪs
quandar|y ˈkwɒnd_ər li ‖ ˈkwɑːnd_ ~**ies** iz
quandong ˈkwɒnd ɒŋ ‖ ˈkwɑːnd ɑːŋ ~**s** z
quango ˈkwæŋ gəʊ ‖ -goʊ ~**s** z
Quant, quant kwɒnt ‖ kwɑːnt
quant|a ˈkwɒnt ə ‖ ˈkwɑːnt̬ ə ~**al** ᵊl
Quantel tdmk ˌkwɒn ˈtel ˈ• • ‖ ˌkwɑːn-
quantic ˈkwɒnt ɪk ‖ ˈkwɑːnt̬ ɪk
quantifiable ˈkwɒnt ɪ faɪ‿əb ᵊl ˈ•ə-, ˌ• •ˈ• • •
‖ ˈkwɑːnt̬-
quantification ˌkwɒnt ɪf ɪ ˈkeɪʃ ᵊn ˌ•əf-, §-ə• • -
‖ ˌkwɑːnt̬-
quanti|fy ˈkwɒnt ɪ |faɪ -ə- ‖ ˈkwɑːnt̬- ~**fied**
faɪd ~**fier/s** faɪ‿ə/z ‖ faɪ‿ᵊr/z ~**fies** faɪz
~**fying** faɪ ɪŋ
quantile ˈkwɒnt aɪᵊl ‖ ˈkwɑːnt aɪᵊl ˈkwɑːnt̬ ᵊl
~**s** z
quantis... —*see* **quantiz...**
quantitative ˈkwɒnt ɪt ət ɪv ˈ•ət-; -ɪ teɪt-,
-ə teɪt- ‖ ˈkwɑːnt̬ ə teɪt̬ ɪv ~**ly** li
quantit|y ˈkwɒnt ət li -ɪt- ‖ ˈkwɑːnt̬ ət̬ li ~**ies**
iz
ˈquantity surˌveyor, ˌ• • •ˈ• •
quantization ˌkwɒnt aɪ ˈzeɪʃ ᵊn -ɪ- ‖ ˌkwɑːnt̬
ə-

Q

quantiz|e 'kwɒnt aɪz ‖ 'kwɑːnt- **~ed** d **~es** ɪz əz **~ing** ɪŋ
Quantock 'kwɒnt ək -ɒk ‖ 'kwɑːnt ɑːk **~s** s
quant|um 'kwɒnt əm ‖ 'kwɑːnʈ əm **~a** ə ˌquantum 'jump; ˌquantum 'leap; ˌquantum me'chanics; 'quantum ˌtheory
quarantin|e 'kwɒr ən tiːn ‖ 'kwɔːr- 'kwɑːr- **~ed** d **~es** z **~ing** ɪŋ
quark *'elementary particle'* kwɑːk kwɔːk ‖ kwɔːrk kwɑːrk **quarks** kwɑːks kwɔːks kwɔːrks kwɑːrks
quark *'soft cheese'* kwɑːk ‖ kwɑːrk —*Ger* [kvaʁk]
Quarles kwɔːlz kɔːlz ‖ kwɔːrlz
Quarndon 'kwɔːn dən 'kɔːn- ‖ 'kwɔːrn-
quarrel 'kwɒr əl ‖ 'kwɑːr əl 'kwɔːr- **~ed, ~led** d **~ing, ~ling** ɪŋ **~s** z
quarreler, quarreller 'kwɒr əl ə ‖ 'kwɑːr əl ʰr 'kwɔːr- **~s** z
quarrelsome 'kwɒr əl səm ‖ 'kwɑːr- 'kwɔːr- **~ly** li **~ness** nəs nɪs
quarr|y, Q~ 'kwɒr li ‖ 'kwɑːr li 'kwɔːr- **~ied** id **~ies** ɪz **~ying** i ɪŋ
quarry|man 'kwɒr i mən -mæn ‖ 'kwɑːr- 'kwɔːr- **~men** mən men
quart *'two pints'* kwɔːt kɔːt ‖ kwɔːrt **quarts** kwɔːts kɔːts ‖ kwɔːrts
quart *in fencing; at cards* kɑːt ‖ kɑːrt
quartan 'kwɔːt ʰn 'kɔːt- ‖ 'kwɔːrt ʰn **~s** z
quarte kɑːt ‖ kɑːrt —*Fr* [kaʁt]
quart|er 'kwɔːt ə 'kɔːt- ‖ 'kwɔːrʈ ʰr —*AmE also occasionally dissimilated to* 'kwɔːʈ ʰr **~ered** əd ‖ ʰrd **~ering/s** ʰr ɪŋ/z **~ers** əz ‖ ʰrz
'quarter day; 'quarter note; 'quarter ˌsessions
quarterback 'kwɔːt ə bæk 'kɔːt- ‖ 'kwɔːrʈ ʰr- **~s** s
quarterdeck 'kwɔːt ə dek 'kɔːt- ‖ 'kwɔːrʈ ʰr- **~s** s
quarterfinal ˌkwɔːt ə 'faɪn ᵊl ˌkɔːt- ‖ ˌkwɔːrʈ ʰr- **~ist/s** ɪst/s§əst/s **~s** z
quarterlight 'kwɔːt ə laɪt 'kɔːt-, -ᵊl aɪt ‖ 'kwɔːrʈ ʰr- **~s** s
quarter|ly 'kwɔːt əl i 'kɔːt- ‖ 'kwɔːrʈ ʰr lli **~lies** liz
Quartermaine 'kwɔːt ə meɪn 'kɔːt- ‖ 'kwɔːrʈ ʰr-
quartermaster 'kwɔːt ə ˌmɑːst ə 'kɔːt-, §-,mæst- ‖ 'kwɔːrʈ ʰr ˌmæst ʰr **~s** z
ˌquarterˌmaster 'general; ˌquarterˌmaster 'sergeant
quartern 'kwɔːt ʰn 'kɔːt- ‖ 'kwɔːrʈ ʰrn **~s** z
quarter|staff 'kwɔːt ə ˌstɑːf 'kɔːt-, §-stæf ‖ 'kwɔːrʈ ʰr ˌstæf **~staves** steɪvz -stɑːvz
quartet, quartette ₍ₗ₎kwɔː 'tet ₍ₗ₎kɔː- ‖ ₍ₗ₎kwɔːr- **~s** s
quartic 'kwɔːt ɪk 'kɔːt- ‖ 'kwɔːrʈ ɪk **~s** s
quartile 'kwɔːt aɪᵊl 'kɔːt- ‖ 'kwɔːrt aɪᵊl 'kwɔːrʈ ᵊl **~s** z
quarto 'kwɔːt əʊ 'kɔːt- ‖ 'kwɔːrʈ oʊ **~s** z
quartz kwɔːts kɔːts ‖ kwɔːrts (= *quarts*)
quartzite 'kwɔːts aɪt 'kɔːts- ‖ 'kwɔːrts-

quasar 'kweɪz ɑː 'kweɪs- ‖ -ɑːr **~s** z
quash kwɒʃ ‖ kwɑːʃ **quashed** kwɒʃt ‖ kwɑːʃt **quashes** 'kwɒʃ ɪz -əz ‖ 'kwɑːʃ əz **quashing** 'kwɒʃ ɪŋ ‖ 'kwɑːʃ ɪŋ
Quashi, Quashie 'kwɒʃ i 'kwɑːʃ- ‖ 'kwɑːʃ i
quasi 'kweɪz aɪ 'kweɪs-, 'kwɑːz-, 'kwæz-, -i
quasi- ˌkweɪz aɪ ˌkweɪs-, ˌkwɑːz-, ˌkwæz-, -i — ˌquasi-judicial ˌkweɪz aɪ dʒu 'dɪʃ ᵊl ◂ ˌkweɪs-, ˌkwɑːz-, ˌkwæz-, ˌ•i-
Quasimodo ˌkwɑːz ɪ 'məʊd əʊ ˌkwɒz-, ˌkwæz- ‖ -'moʊd oʊ —*Formerly* ˌkweɪs aɪ-. *The Italian poet was* [kwa 'zi: mo do].
quassia 'kwɒʃ ə 'kwɒʃ iˌə ‖ 'kwɑːʃ ə
quatercentenary ˌkwæt ə sen 'tiːn ʰr i ˌkwɒt-, ˌkweɪt-, -'ten- ‖ ˌkwɑːʈ ʰr sen 'ten ʰr i -'sent ʰn er i
Quatermain 'kwɔːt ə meɪn 'kɔːt- ‖ 'kwɑːʈ ʰr-
Quatermass 'kweɪt ə mæs ‖ 'kweɪʈ ʰr-
quaternar|y, Q~ kwə 'tɜːn ʰr li kwɒ- ‖ 'kwɑːʈ ʰr ner li kwə 'tɝːn ʰr li **~ies** ɪz
quaternion kwə 'tɜːn iˌən kwɒ- ‖ kwə 'tɝːn kwɑː- **~s** z
quatrain 'kwɒtr eɪn -ʰn ‖ 'kwɑːtr- **~s** z
quatrefoil 'kætr ə fɔɪᵊl ‖ 'kæʈ ʰr- **~s** z
Quattro 'kwɒtr əʊ 'kwætr- ‖ 'kwɑːtr oʊ
quattrocento ˌkwætr əʊ 'tʃent əʊ ˌkwɒtr- ‖ ˌkwɑːtr oʊ 'tʃent oʊ —*It* [kwat tro 'tʃen to]
quaver 'kweɪv ə ‖ -ʰr **~ed** d **quavering/ly** 'kweɪv ʰr ɪŋ /li **~s** z
quay, Quay kiː ‖ keɪ, kweɪ *(in RP, and in GA mostly, = key)* —*but as a family name, usually* kweɪ **quays** kiːz ‖ keɪz, kweɪz
quayage 'kiː ɪdʒ ‖ 'keɪ-, 'kweɪ-
Quayle kweɪᵊl
quayside 'kiː saɪd ‖ 'keɪ-, 'kweɪ-
quean kwiːn (= *queen*) **queans** kwiːnz
Queanbeyan 'kwiːn bi_ən →'kwiːm-
queas|y 'kwiːz li **~ier** iˌə ‖ iˌʰr **~iest** iˌɪst iˌəst **~ily** ɪ li əl i **~iness** i nəs i nɪs
Quebec, Québec kwɪ 'bek kwə-, kə- —*Fr* [ke bɛk]
Quebecer, Quebecker kwɪ 'bek ə kwə-, kə- ‖ -ʰr **~s** z
Quebecois, Québécois, q~ ˌkeɪb e 'kwɑː ◂ ˌkeb-, -ɪ-, -ə- —*Fr* [ke be kwa]
quebracho keɪ 'brɑːtʃ əʊ kɪ- ‖ -oʊ —*Sp* [ke 'βra tʃo] **~s** z
Quechua 'ketʃ uˌə ‖ ˈ•wɑː **~s** z
queen, Queen kwiːn **queened** kwiːnd **queening** 'kwiːn ɪŋ **queens** kwiːnz ₍ₗ₎Queen 'Anne; 'queen cake; ˌqueen 'consort; ˌQueen E'lizabeth; ˌqueen 'mother; ˌQueen's 'Bench, ˌQueen's 'Bench Diˌvision; ˌQueen's 'Council; ˌQueen's 'English; ˌqueen's 'evidence
Queenborough 'kwiːn bər_ə ‖ -ˌbɝː oʊ
queendom 'kwiːn dəm
Queenie 'kwiːn i
queenlike 'kwiːn laɪk
queen|ly 'kwiːn lli **~liness** li nəs -nɪs
Queens kwiːnz

Queensberry 'kwi:nz bər_i §-,ber i ‖ -,ber i
,Queensberry 'Rules ‖ '• • • •
Queensferry 'kwi:nz ,fer i
queen-size 'kwi:n saiz
Queensland 'kwi:nz lənd -lænd —*In Australia usually* -lænd
Queenstown 'kwi:nz taʊn
Queensway 'kwi:nz wei
queer kwiə ‖ kwiʳr **queerer**
'kwiər ə ‖ 'kwir ʳr **queerest** 'kwiər ist -əst
‖ 'kwir əst
'Queer Street
queerish 'kwiər iʃ ‖ 'kwir-
queer|ly 'kwiə ‖li ‖ 'kwir- ~**ness** nəs nis
quefrency 'kwi:f rənᵗs i
quel kel —*Fr* [kɛl]
quell kwel **quelled** kweld **quelling** 'kwel iŋ
quells kwelz
Quellenforschung 'kwel ən ,fɔːʃ ʊŋ ‖ -,fɔːrʃ-
—*Ger* ['kvɛ lən ,fɔʁ ʃʊŋ]
Quemoy ki 'mɔi ke- —*Chinese* Jīnmén [¹tɕin ²mən]
quench kwentʃ **quenched** kwentʃt
quenches 'kwentʃ iz -əz **quenching**
'kwentʃ iŋ
quencher 'kwentʃ ə ‖ -ʳr ~**s** z
quenda 'kwend ə ~**s** z
quenelle kə 'nel ~**s** z
Quenington 'kwen iŋ tən
Quennell kwi 'nel kwə-; 'kwen ᵊl
Quentin 'kwent in §-ən ‖ -ᵊn
quercitron 'kwɜ: sitr ən ,•'•• ‖ 'kwɜ·:- ~**s** z
queri... —*see* **query**
quern kwɜ:n ‖ kwɜ·:n **querns**
kwɜ:nz ‖ kwɜ·:nz
querulous 'kwer ʊl əs -jʊl-, -əl- ‖ -əl əs ~**ly** li
~**ness** nəs nis
quer|y 'kwiər ‖i ‖ 'kwir ‖i 'kwer- ~**ied** id ~**ies**
iz ~**ying** i iŋ
quesadilla ,keis ə 'di: ə ~**s** z —*Sp*
[ke sa 'ði ʎa, -ja]
quest kwest **quested** 'kwest id -əd **questing**
'kwest iŋ **quests** kwests
Quested 'kwest id -əd
question 'kwes tʃən →'kweʃ-, -tʃən ~**ed** d
~**ing** iŋ ~**s** z
'question ,mark; 'question ,master;
'question ,tag; 'question ,time; 'question word
questionab|le 'kwes tʃən əb ‖əl →'kweʃ-,
'•tʃən- ~**leness** ᵊl nəs -nis ~**ly** li
questionnaire ,kwes tʃə 'neə ,kes-, →,kweʃ-,
,•ti_ə'•, '•••• ‖ -'neʳr -'næʳr —*BrE 1998 poll panel preference:* 'kwe- 94%, 'ke- 6%; *born since 1973,* 'kwe- 100%. ~**s** z
questor 'kwi:st ə 'kwaist-, -ɔ: ‖ 'kwest ʳr
'kwi:st- ~**s** z
Quetta 'kwet ə ‖ 'kweṭ ə
quetzal 'kets ᵊl 'kwets-; ket 'sæl ‖ ket 'saːl
-'sæl ~**s** z
Quetzalcoatl
,kets ᵊl kəʊ 'æt ᵊl ‖ ket 'saːl kwaːṭ ᵊl
•'•koʊ ,aːṭ ᵊl

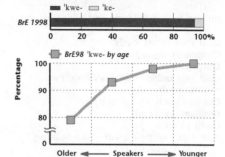

queue kju: *(! = cue)* **queued** kju:d **queues**
kju:z **queuing** 'kju:_iŋ
queue-jump 'kju: dʒʌmp ~**ed** t ~**er/s** ə/z
‖ ʳr/z ~**ing** iŋ ~**s** s
Quex kweks
Quezon 'keiz ɒn 'keis- ‖ -aːn
,Quezon 'City
Qufu ,tʃuː 'fuː —*Chinese* Qūfù [¹tɕʰy ⁴fu]
quibb|le 'kwib ᵊl ~**ed** d ~**er/s** _ə/z ‖ _ʳr/z ~**es**
z ~**ing** _iŋ
quiche kiːʃ **quiches** 'kiːʃ iz -əz
quick, Quick kwik **quicker** 'kwik ə ‖ 'kwik ʳr
quickest 'kwik ist -əst
,quick 'march ‖ '• •
quick-change ,kwik 'tʃeindʒ
quicken 'kwik ən ~**ed** d ~**ing** _iŋ ~**s** z
quick-fire ,kwik 'fai_ə ◄ ‖ -'fai_ʳr ◄
quick-|freeze ,kwik 'friːz **~freezes** 'friːz iz
-əz **~froze** 'frəʊz ‖ 'froʊz **~frozen**
'frəʊz ᵊn ◄ ‖ 'froʊz ᵊn ◄
quickie 'kwik i ~**s** z
quicklime 'kwik laim
quickly, Q~ 'kwik li
quickness 'kwik nəs -nis
quicksand 'kwik sænd ~**s** z
quickset 'kwik set
quicksilver 'kwik ,silv ə ‖ -ʳr
quickstep 'kwik step ~**s** s
quick-tempered ,kwik 'temp əd ◄ ‖ -ʳrd ◄
'•,••
quickthorn 'kwik θɔːn ‖ -θɔːrn
quick-witted ,kwik 'wit id ◄ -əd ‖ -'wiṭ əd ◄
'•,•• ~**ly** li ~**ness** nəs nis
quid kwid **quids** kwidz
,quids 'in
quiddit|y 'kwid ət ‖i -it- ‖ -əṭ ‖i ~**ies** iz
quid pro quo ,kwid prəʊ 'kwəʊ ‖ -proʊ 'kwoʊ
~**s** z
quiescence kwi 'es ᵊnᵗs kwai-
quiescent kwi 'es ᵊnt kwai- ~**ly** li
quiet 'kwai_ət **quieted** 'kwai_ət id -əd
‖ -əṭ əd **quieter** 'kwai_ət ə ‖ -əṭ ʳr **quietest**
'kwai_ət ist -əst ‖ -əṭ əst **quieting**
'kwai_ət iŋ ‖ -əṭ iŋ **quiets** 'kwai_əts
quieten 'kwai_ət ᵊn ~**ed** d ~**ing** _iŋ ~**s** z
quietism 'kwai_ət ,iz əm -it- ‖ -əṭ-
quietist 'kwai_ət ist -it-, §-əst ‖ -əṭ- ~**s** s
quiet|ly 'kwai_ət ‖ li ~**ness** nəs -nis

quietude 'kwaɪ_ə tjuːd ‑ɪ‑, →§‑tʃuːd ‖ ‑tuːd
‑tjuːd

quietus kwaɪ 'iːt əs kwi‑, ‑'eɪt‑ ‖ ‑'iːt̮ əs ~es ɪz
əz

quiff kwɪf **quiffs** kwɪfs

Quiggin 'kwɪg ɪn §‑ən

Quigley 'kwɪg li

quill kwɪl **quilled** kwɪld **quilling** 'kwɪl ɪŋ
quills kwɪlz

Quiller-Couch ˌkwɪl ə 'kuːtʃ ‖ ‑ər‑

Quilliam 'kwɪl i_əm

Quilp kwɪlp

quilt kwɪlt **quilted** 'kwɪlt ɪd‑əd **quilting**
'kwɪlt ɪŋ **quilts** kwɪlts

Quilter, q~ 'kwɪlt ə ‖ ‑ər

quim kwɪm **quims** kwɪmz

quin, Quin kwɪn **quins** kwɪnz

quinary 'kwaɪn ər i

Quinault *family name* 'kwɪn əlt

quince kwɪnts **quinces** 'kwɪnts ɪz‑əz

quincentenar|y ˌkwɪn sen 'tiːn ər li,•sən‑,
‑'ten‑ ‖ ‑'ten ər li,•'sent ən er i **~ies** iz

quincentennial ˌkwɪn sen 'ten i_əl ◂,•sən‑ ~s
z

Quincey 'kwɪnts i

quincuncial kwɪn 'kʌntʃ əl→kwɪŋ‑ **‑ly** i

quincunx 'kwɪn kʌŋks→'kwɪŋ‑; 'kwɪŋk ʌŋks
~es ɪz əz

Quincy 'kwɪnts i

quindecagon ₍ₗ₎kwɪn 'dek əg ən ‖ ‑ə gɑːn ~s z

quindecennial ˌkwɪn dɪ 'sen i_əl ◂,•də‑,,•de‑
~ly i

quinine kwɪ 'niːn kwə‑; 'kwɪn iːn ‖ 'kwaɪn aɪn
'kwɪn‑ *(*)*

Quink *tdmk* kwɪŋk

Quinlan 'kwɪn lən

Quinn kwɪn

quinoline 'kwɪn ə liːn ‑lɪn, §‑lən; ‑əl iːn, ‑ɪn,
§‑ən ‖ ‑əl iːn

quinone kwɪ 'nəʊn 'kwɪn əʊn ‖ ‑'noʊn
'kwaɪn oʊn

quinquagenarian ˌkwɪŋk wə dʒə 'neər i_ən ◂
,•wɪ‑,,••dʒɪ‑ ‖ ‑'ner‑ ‑'nær‑ ~s z

Quinquagesima ˌkwɪŋk wə 'dʒes ɪm ə ◂,•wɪ‑,
‑əm ə

quinque‑ *comb. form*
with stress-neutral suffix ˈkwɪŋk wɪ §‑wə —
quinquepartite ˌkwɪŋk wɪ 'pɑːt aɪt ◂ §‑wə‑
‖ ‑'pɑːrt‑

quinquenni|al kwɪŋ 'kwen i_əl kwɪn‑ **~a** ə
~ally əl_i **~um** əm

quinquevalent ˌkwɪŋk wɪ 'veɪl ənt ◂ §‑wə‑;
kwɪn 'kwev əl‑,→kwɪŋ‑

quinsy 'kwɪnz i

quint kwɪnt kɪnt **quints** kwɪnts kɪnts

quintain 'kwɪnt ən ‑ɪn ‖ ‑ᵊn ~s z

quintal 'kwɪnt əl ~s z

quintan 'kwɪnt ən ‖ ‑ᵊn ~s z

quintessence kwɪn 'tes ənts

quintessential ˌkwɪnt ɪ 'sentʃ əl ◂‑ə‑ ‖ ˌkwɪnt̮
ə‑ **~ly** i

quintet, quintette ₍ₗ₎kwɪn 'tet ~s s

quintic 'kwɪnt ɪk ‖ 'kwɪnt̮ ɪk

quintile 'kwɪnt aɪᵊl ~s z

Quintilian kwɪn 'tɪl i_ən

quintillion kwɪn 'tɪl jən‑i_ən ~s z

Quintin 'kwɪnt ɪn §‑ən ‖ ‑ᵊn

Quinton 'kwɪnt ən ‖ ‑ᵊn

quintupl|e 'kwɪnt jʊp əl‑əp‑; kwɪn 'tjuːp‑
‖ kwɪn 'tuːp əl‑'tjuːp‑, ‑'tʌp‑; 'kwɪnt̮ əp‑
~ed d **~es** z **~ing** _ɪŋ

quintuplet 'kwɪnt jʊp lət ‑əp‑, ‑lɪt, ‑let;
kwɪn 'tjuːp‑, §‑'tʌp‑ ‖ kwɪn 'tʌp lət ‑'tuːp‑,
‑'tjuːp‑; 'kwɪnt̮ əp‑ ~s s

Quintus 'kwɪnt əs ‖ 'kwɪnt̮ əs

quinze kænz—*Fr* [kɛ̃ːz]

quip kwɪp **quipped** kwɪpt **quipping** 'kwɪp ɪŋ
quips kwɪps

quipster 'kwɪps tə ‖ ‑t̮ər ~s z

quipu 'kiːp uː 'kwɪp‑

quire 'kwaɪ_ə ‖ 'kwaɪ_ər *(= choir)* **quires**
'kwaɪ_əz ‖ 'kwaɪ_ərz

Quirinal 'kwɪr ɪn əl‑ən‑

Quirinus kwɪ 'raɪn əs kwə‑

quirk kwɜːk ‖ kwɝːk **quirks** kwɜːks ‖ kwɝːks

Quirk, Quirke kwɜːk ‖ kwɝːk

quirk|y 'kwɜːk li ‖ 'kwɝːk li **~ier** i_ə ‖ i_ᵊr
~iest i_ɪst i_əst **~ily** ɪ li əl i **~iness** i nəs i nɪs

quirt kwɜːt ‖ kwɝːt **quirts** kwɜːts ‖ kwɝːts

quisling 'kwɪz lɪŋ ~s z

quit kwɪt **quits** kwɪts **quitted** 'kwɪt ɪd‑əd
‖ 'kwɪt̮ əd **quitting** 'kwɪt ɪŋ ‖ 'kwɪt̮ ɪŋ

quitch kwɪtʃ

quite kwaɪt

Quito 'kiːt əʊ ‖ ‑oʊ—*Sp* ['ki to]

quitrent 'kwɪt rent

quits kwɪts

quittanc|e 'kwɪt ənts ~es ɪz əz

quitter 'kwɪt ə ‖ 'kwɪt̮ ər ~s z

quittor 'kwɪt ə ‖ 'kwɪt̮ ər

quiver 'kwɪv ə ‖ ‑ər **~ed** d **quivering/ly** 'kwɪv
ər_ɪŋ /li ~s z

quiverful 'kwɪv ə fʊl ‖ ‑ər‑ ~s z

qui vive ˌkiː 'viːv

Quix *tdmk* kwɪks

Quixote 'kwɪks ət ‑əʊt; kɪ 'həʊt i ‖ kiː 'hoʊt̮ i
—*Sp* [ki 'xo te]

quixotic kwɪk 'sɒt ɪk ‖ ‑'sɑːt̮ ɪk **~al** əl **~ally**
əl_i

quixotism 'kwɪks ə ˌtɪz əm

quiz kwɪz **quizzed** kwɪzd **quizzes** 'kwɪz ɪz
‑əz **quizzing** 'kwɪz ɪŋ

quizmaster 'kwɪz ˌmɑːst ə §‑ˌmæst‑
‖ ‑ˌmæst ər ~s z

quizzical 'kwɪz ɪk əl **~ly** _i

quo kwəʊ ‖ kwoʊ
ˌquo 'vadis 'vɑːd ɪs 'wɑːd‑, §‑əs

quod kwɒd ‖ kwɑːd

quodlibet 'kwɒd lɪ bet ‑lə‑ ‖ 'kwɑːd‑ ~s s

quoin kɔɪn kwɔɪn **quoined** kɔɪnd kwɔɪnd
quoining 'kɔɪn ɪŋ 'kwɔɪn‑ **quoins** kɔɪnz
kwɔɪnz

quoit kɔɪt kwɔɪt **quoits** kɔɪts kwɔɪts

quokka 'kwɒk ə ‖ 'kwɑːk ə ~s z

quoll kwɒl ‖ kwɑːl **quolls** kwɒlz ‖ kwɑːlz

quondam 'kwɒnd æm ‑əm ‖ 'kwɑːnd‑

Quonset _tdmk_ 'kwɒnˢɪt -ət, -et ‖ 'kwɑːnˢts ət
'kwɑːnz-
  '**Quonset hut**
quorate 'kwɔːr eɪt -ət, -ɪt ‖ 'kwoʊr-
Quorn kwɔːn ‖ kwɔːrn
quorum 'kwɔːr əm ‖ 'kwoʊr- ~s z
Quosh _tdmk_ 'kwɒʃ ‖ kwɑːʃ
quota 'kwəʊt ə §'kəʊt- ‖ 'kwoʊt̬ ə ~s z
quotability ˌkwəʊt ə 'bɪl ət i §ˌkəʊt-, -ɪt i
  ‖ ˌkwoʊt̬ ə 'bɪl ət̬ i ˌkoʊt̬-
quotab|le 'kwəʊt əb |əl §'kəʊt- ‖ 'kwoʊt̬-
  'koʊt̬- **~ly** li
quotation kwəʊ 'teɪʃ ən kwə-, §kəʊ- ‖ kwoʊ-
  koʊ- **~s** z
  quoˈtation mark
quote kwəʊt §kəʊt ‖ kwoʊt koʊt **quoted**
'kwəʊt ɪd §'kəʊt- ‖ 'kwoʊt̬ əd 'koʊt̬-
quotes kwəʊts §kəʊts ‖ kwoʊts koʊts
quoting 'kwəʊt ɪŋ §'kəʊt- ‖ 'kwoʊt̬ ɪŋ
'koʊt̬-
quoth kwəʊθ §kəʊθ ‖ kwoʊθ
quotha 'kwəʊθ ə §'kəʊθ- ‖ 'kwoʊθ ə
quotidian kwəʊ 'tɪd i‿ən kwɒ-, §kəʊ- ‖ kwoʊ-
quotient 'kwəʊʃ ənt §'kəʊʃ- ‖ 'kwoʊʃ ənt **~s** s
Qur'an, Quran kɔː 'rɑːn kə-, kɒ-, -'ræn
  ‖ kə 'rɑːn -'ræn; kuᵊr 'ɑːn, -'æn —_Arabic_
  [qur 'ʔɑːn]
Quy kwaɪ
Qwaqwa 'kwɑːk wə
q.v. ˌkjuː 'viː
qwerty, QWERTY 'kwɜːt i ‖ 'kwɜ·ːt̬ i 'kwert̬-

R r

r   Spelling-to-sound

1 Where the spelling is **r**, the pronunciation is regularly r, as in **run** rʌn.

2 Where the spelling is double **rr**, the pronunciation is again regularly r, as in **merry** 'mer i.

3 When the spelling is **r** followed by a consonant letter or a silent **e**, or when **r** is at the end of a word, then the pronunciation differs in different varieties of English:
  - In RP, the **r** is silent. The same applies to most varieties of English English, to Australian English, and to the other 'non-rhotic' accents. In connected speech, however, r may be pronounced at the end of a word if the next word begins with a vowel sound (see R-LIAISON).
  - In GenAm, the pronunciation is r. The same applies to Scottish English, to Irish English, and to the other 'rhotic' accents. In GenAm, the r coalesces with a preceding [ɜː] vowel to give ɝː.
  - Examples:

	RP	GenAm
farm	fɑːm	fɑːrm
more	mɔː	mɔːr
stir	stɜː	stɝː
murder	'mɜːd ə	'mɝːd ər

4 In the middle or at the end of a word, **r** frequently affects the preceding vowel. Consequently **ar, er, ir, or, ur, yr** could be regarded as digraphs, and **air, are, ear, eer, eir, ere, eur, ier, ire, oar, oor, ore, our, ure** as trigraphs (see individual entries).

5 The sound r may also appear in non-rhotic accents in certain cases where no corresponding letter **r** is written, as when **thawing** is pronounced 'θɔːr ɪŋ. This is known as 'intrusive r'; see R-LIAISON. Note also the exceptional word **colonel** 'kɜːn əl ‖ 'kɝːn əl.

6 The exceptional word **iron** is pronounced as if written **iorn**, namely 'aɪ ən ‖ 'aɪ ərn.

rh   Spelling-to-sound

Where the spelling is the digraph **rh** or its doubled form **rrh**, the pronunciation is regularly the same as that of the letter **r**:
r, as in **rhythm** 'rɪð əm, **rhapsody** 'ræps əd i; or
silent ‖ r, as in **catarrh** kə 'tɑː ‖ kə 'tɑːr.

R, r ɑː ‖ ɑːr **R's, r's, Rs, rs** ɑːz ‖ ɑːrz
—*Communications code name:* Romeo
RA ˌɑːr 'eɪ ‖ ˌɑːr-
Ra rɑː
Raasay 'rɑːs eɪ
Rab ræb
Raban 'reɪb ən
Rabat rə 'bɑːt rɑː-, -'bæt —*Arabic* [rɑ 'bɑːtˤ],
Fr [ʁa ba]
Rabaul rə 'baʊl
rabb|et 'ræb |ɪt §-ət ‖ -|ət **~eted** ɪt ɪd §ət-, -əd
‖ ət̬ əd **~eting** ɪt ɪŋ §ət- ‖ ət̬ ɪŋ **~ets** ɪts
§əts ‖ əts
rabbi 'ræb aɪ **~s** z
Rabbie 'ræb i
rabbinate 'ræb ɪn ət §-ən-, -ɪt; -ɪ neɪt, -ə- **~s** s
rabbinic, R~ rə 'bɪn ɪk ræ- **~al** əl **~ally** əl̬ i
rabbinistic ˌræb ɪ 'nɪst ɪk ◄ -ə-
rabb|it 'ræb |ɪt §-ət ‖ -|ət **~ited** ɪt ɪd §ət-, -əd
‖ ət̬ əd **~iting** ɪt ɪŋ §ət- ‖ ət̬ ɪŋ **~its** ɪts §əts
‖ əts
  'rabbit ˌhutch; 'rabbit ˌpunch; 'rabbit
  ˌwarren
rabbitfish 'ræb ɪt fɪʃ §-ət-
rabble 'ræb əl **~s** z
rabble-rouser 'ræb əl ˌraʊz ə ‖ -ər **~s** z
rabble-rousing 'ræb əl ˌraʊz ɪŋ
Rabelais 'ræb ə leɪ -əl eɪ ‖ ˌ•• '• —*Fr* [ʁa blɛ]
Rabelaisian ˌræb ə 'leɪz i_ən ◄ -'leɪʒ ən
‖ -'leɪʒ ən ◄
rabid 'ræb ɪd 'reɪb-, §-əd **~ly** li **~ness** nəs nɪs
rabidity rə 'bɪd ət i -ɪt i ‖ -ət̬ i
rabies 'reɪb iːz -ɪz
rabietic ˌreɪb i 'et ɪk ◄ ‖ -'et̬ ɪk ◄
Rabin 'reɪb ɪn §-ən —*but as an Israeli name,*
ræ 'biːn ‖ rɑː-
Rabindranath rə 'bɪndr ə nɑːθ -nɑːt —*Hindi*
[rə ʋɪŋ ɖrə n̪ɑːt̪ʰ], *Bengali* [ro biŋ ɖrɔ nɑt̪ʰ]
Rabinowitz rə 'bɪn ə wɪts ræ-, -vɪts
RAC ˌɑːr eɪ 'siː
Racal *tdmk* 'reɪk ɔːl -əl ‖ -ɑːl
raccoon rə 'kuːn ræ- ‖ ræ- **~s** z
race reɪs **raced** reɪst **races** 'reɪs ɪz -əz **racing**
'reɪs ɪŋ
  'race ˌcard; 'race ˌmeeting; ˌrace re'lations;
  'race ˌriot
racecours|e 'reɪs kɔːs ‖ -kɔːrs -koʊrs **~es** ɪz əz
racegoer 'reɪs ˌgəʊ ə ‖ -ˌgoʊ ər **~s** z
racehors|e 'reɪs hɔːs ‖ -hɔːrs **~es** ɪz əz
raceme 'ræs iːm 'reɪs-; ræ 'siːm, rə- ‖ reɪ 'siːm
rə- **~s** z
racemic rə 'siːm ɪk ræ-, reɪ-, -'sem-
racer 'reɪs ə ‖ -ər **~s** z
racetrack 'reɪs træk **~s** s
raceway 'reɪs weɪ **~s** z
Rachael, Rachel 'reɪtʃ əl —*but as a French*
name, ræ 'ʃel, *Fr* [ʁa ʃɛl]
Rachelle rə 'ʃel 'reɪtʃ əl
rachis 'reɪk ɪs §-əs
rachitis rə 'kaɪt ɪs ræ-, §-əs ‖ -'kaɪt̬ əs
Rachman 'ræk mən
Rachmaninoff, Rachmaninov

ræk 'mæn ɪn ɒf ‖ rɑːk 'mɑːn ə nɔːf -nɑːf
  —*Russ* [rʌx 'ma nʲɪ nəf]
Rachmanism, r~ 'ræk mən ˌɪz əm
racial 'reɪʃ əl 'reɪʃ i_əl, 'reɪs i_əl
racialism 'reɪʃ ə ˌlɪz əm -əl ˌɪz-; 'reɪʃ i_əl ˌɪz
əm, 'reɪs-
racialist 'reɪʃ əl ɪst 'reɪʃ i_əl ɪst, 'reɪs-, §-əst **~s**
s
racially 'reɪʃ əl i 'reɪʃ i_əl i, 'reɪs-
Racine *French writer* ræ 'siːn rə- —*Fr* [ʁa sin]
Racine *place in Wisconsin* rə 'siːn reɪ-
racism 'reɪs ˌɪz əm
racist 'reɪs ɪst 'reɪʃ-, §-əst **~s** s
rack ræk **racked** rækt **racking** 'ræk ɪŋ **racks**
ræks
rack|et 'ræk |ɪt §-ət ‖ -|ət **~eted** ɪt ɪd §ət-, -əd
‖ ət̬ əd **~eting** ɪt ɪŋ §ət- ‖ ət̬ ɪŋ **~ets** ɪts
§əts ‖ əts
racketball 'ræk ɪt bɔːl §-ət- ‖ -bɑːl
racke|teer ˌræk ə |'tɪə -ɪ- ‖ -|'tɪ°r **~teered**
'tɪəd ‖ 'tɪ°rd **~teering** 'tɪər ɪŋ ‖ 'tɪr ɪŋ
~teers 'tɪəz ‖ 'tɪ°rz
rackety 'ræk ət i -ɪt- ‖ -ət̬ i
Rackham 'ræk əm
rack-rail 'ræk reɪəl
rack-|rent 'ræk |rent **~ rented** rent ɪd -əd
‖ rent̬ əd **~renter/s** rent ə/z ‖ rent̬ ər/z
~renting rent ɪŋ ‖ rent̬ ɪŋ **~rents** rents
raclette ræ 'klet —*Fr* [ʁa klɛt]
raconteur ˌræk ɒn 'tɜː ‖ -ɑːn 'tɜ˞ː -ən- —*Fr*
[ʁa kɔ̃ tœːʁ] **~s** z
racoon rə 'kuːn ræ- ‖ ræ- **~s** z
racquet 'ræk ɪt §-ət **~s** s
racquetball 'ræk ɪt bɔːl -ət- ‖ -bɑːl
rac|y 'reɪs |i **~ier** i_ə ‖ i_ər **~iest** i_ɪst i_əst
~ily ɪ li əl i **~iness** i nəs i nɪs
rad ræd **rads** rædz
RADA 'rɑːd ə
radar 'reɪd ɑː ‖ -ɑːr **~s** z
Radbourne 'ræd bɔːn →'ræb- ‖ -bɔːrn -boʊrn
Radburn 'ræd bɜːn →'ræb- ‖ -bɜ˞ːn
Radcliff, Radcliffe, Radclyffe 'ræd klɪf →'ræg-
raddle 'ræd əl **~d** d
Radetzky rə 'det ski ræ- ‖ rɑː- —*Ger*
[ʁa 'dɛts ki]
Radford 'ræd fəd ‖ -fərd
radial 'reɪd i_əl **~ly** i **~s** z
  ˌradial 'tyre
radial-ply ˌreɪd i_əl 'plaɪ ◄ '••••
radian 'reɪd i_ən **~s** z
radiance 'reɪd i_ənts
radiant 'reɪd i_ənt **~ly** li **~s** s
radi|ate 'reɪd i |eɪt **~ated** eɪt ɪd -əd ‖ eɪt̬ əd
~ates eɪts **~ating** eɪt ɪŋ ‖ eɪt̬ ɪŋ
radiation ˌreɪd i 'eɪʃ ən **~s** z
  ˌradi'ation ˌsickness
radiator 'reɪd i eɪt ə ‖ -eɪt̬ ər **~s** z
radical 'ræd ɪk əl **~s** z
radicalis... —*see* **radicaliz...**
radicalism 'ræd ɪk əl ˌɪz əm
radicaliz|e 'ræd ɪk ə laɪz **~ed** d **~es** ɪz əz
~ing ɪŋ
radically 'ræd ɪk əl̬_i

radicchio rə ˈdɪk i əʊ ræ- ‖ rə ˈdiːk i‿əʊ rɑː-
—*It* [ra ˈdik kjo]
Radice rə ˈdiːtʃ i -eɪ
radices ˈreɪd ɪ siːz ˈræd-, §-ə-
radicle ˈræd ɪk ᵊl (= *radical*) ~s z
radii ˈreɪd i aɪ
radio ˈreɪd i əʊ ‖ -oʊ ~ed d ~ing ɪŋ ~s z
ˌradio aˈlarm,ˈ· · · ·,·; ˌradio aˈstronomy,
ˈ· · · ·,· · ·; ˈradio ˌbeacon; ˈradio car;
ˈradio ˌfrequency; ˌradio ˈtelescope; ˈradio
wave
radio- *comb. form*
with stress-neutral suffix ¦reɪd i əʊ ‖ -oʊ —
radionuclide ˌreɪd i əʊ ˈnjuːk laɪd §-ˈnuːk-
‖ -oʊ ˈnuːk- -ˈnjuːk-
with stress-imposing suffix ˌreɪd i ˈɒ+ ‖ -ˈɑː+
— **radioscopy** ˌreɪd i ˈɒsk əp i ‖ -ˈɑːsk-
radioactive ˌreɪd i‿əʊ ˈækt ɪv ◄ ‖ ˌ· ·‿oʊ- ~ly li
ˌradioˌactive deˈcay
radioactivity ˌreɪd i‿əʊ æk ˈtɪv ət i -ɪt i
‖ -oʊ æk ˈtɪv əṭ i
radiocarbon ˌreɪd i əʊ ˈkɑːb ᵊn ◄ ‖ -oʊ ˈkɑːrb
ən ◄
ˌradioˌcarbon ˈdating
radiogram ˈreɪd i‿əʊ græm ‖ -i‿oʊ- ~s z
radiograph ˈreɪd i‿əʊ grɑːf -græf ‖ -oʊ græf
~s s
radiographer ˌreɪd i ˈɒg rəf ə ‖ -ˈɑːg rəf ᵊr ~s
z
radiographic ˌreɪd ɪ‿əʊ ˈgræf ɪk ◄ -i‿ə- ~ally
ᵊl‿i
radiography ˌreɪd i ˈɒg rəf i ‖ -ˈɑːg-
radioisotope ˌreɪd i‿əʊ ˈaɪs əʊ
təʊp ‖ -oʊ ˈaɪs ə toʊp ~s s
radiolarian ˌreɪd i əʊ ˈleər i‿ən ‖ -oʊ ˈler-
-ˈlær- ~s z
radiolocation ˌreɪd i‿əʊ ləʊ
ˈkeɪʃ ᵊn ‖ -i‿oʊ loʊ-
radiological ˌreɪd i‿əʊ ˈlɒdʒ ɪk ᵊl ◄ ‖ -ə ˈlɑːdʒ-
~ly ‿i
radiologist ˌreɪd i ˈɒl ədʒ ɪst §-əst ‖ -ˈɑːl- ~s s
radiology ˌreɪd i ˈɒl ədʒ i ‖ -ˈɑːl-
radionic ˌreɪd i ˈɒn ɪk ◄ ‖ -ˈɑːn- ~s s
radiopag|e ˌreɪd i əʊ ˈpeɪdʒ ‖ -i oʊ- ~ed d
~er/s ə/z ‖ -ᵊr/z ~es ɪz əz ~ing ɪŋ
radiopaque ˌreɪd i əʊ ˈpeɪk ◄ ‖ -i oʊ-
radiophonic ˌreɪd i‿əʊ ˈfɒn ɪk ◄ ‖ -oʊ ˈfɑːn ɪk ◄
radioscopy ˌreɪd i ˈɒsk əp i ‖ -ˈɑːsk-
radiosonde ˈreɪd i əʊ sɒnd ‖ -oʊ sɑːnd ~s z
radiotherapist ˌreɪd i‿əʊ ˈθer əp ɪst §-əst
‖ ˌ· ·‿oʊ- ~s s
radiotherapy ˌreɪd i‿əʊ ˈθer əp i ‖ ˌ· ·‿oʊ-
radish ˈræd ɪʃ ~es ɪz əz
radium ˈreɪd i‿əm
radi|us ˈreɪd i‿əs ~i aɪ ~uses əs ɪz -əz
radix ˈreɪd ɪks **radices** ˈreɪd ɪ siːz ˈræd-, §-ə-
radixes ˈreɪd ɪks ɪz -əz
Radlett ˈræd lət -lɪt
Radley ˈræd li
Radnor ˈræd nə ‖ -nᵊr -nɔːr ~**shire** ʃə ʃɪə ‖ ʃᵊr
ʃɪr
radome ˈreɪd əʊm ‖ -oʊm ~s z
radon ˈreɪd ɒn ‖ -ɑːn

Radovan ˈræd ə væn ‖ ˈrɑːd ə vɑːn —*Serbian*
[ˈra do van]
Radox *tdmk* ˈreɪd ɒks ‖ -ɑːks
radula ˈræd jʊl ə §ˈrædʒ ᵊl- ‖ ˈrædʒ əl ə
radulae ˈræd ju liː §ˈrædʒ ə- ‖ ˈrædʒ ə liː
Rae reɪ
Raeburn ˈreɪ bɜːn ‖ -bɝːn
Rael-Brook *tdmk* ˌreɪᵊl ˈbrʊk
Raelene ˈreɪ liːn
RAF ˌɑːr eɪ ˈef —*also, informally,* ræf
Rafe reɪf
Rafferty, r~ ˈræf ət i ‖ -ᵊrṭ i
raffia ˈræf i‿ə
raffinose ˈræf ɪ nəʊz -ə-, -nəʊs ‖ -noʊs
raffish ˈræf ɪʃ ~**ly** li ~**ness** nəs nɪs
raffl|e ˈræf ᵊl ~**ed** d ~**es** z ~**ing** ‿ɪŋ
Raffles ˈræf ᵊlz
rafflesia ræ ˈfliːz i‿ə -ˈfliːʒ- ‖ rə ˈfliːʒ ə ræ- ~**s**
z
Rafsanjani ˌræf sæn ˈdʒɑːn i -sɑːn- ‖ ˌrɑːf sᵊn-
ˌrʌf-, -sɑːn- —*Farsi* [ræf sæn dʒɑ ˈniː]
raft, Raft rɑːft §ræft ‖ ræft **rafted** ˈrɑːft ɪd
§ˈræft-, -əd ‖ ˈræft əd **rafting** ˈrɑːft ɪŋ
§ˈræft- ‖ ˈræft ɪŋ **rafts** rɑːfts §ræfts ‖ ræfts
rafter ˈrɑːft ə §ˈræft- ‖ ˈræft ᵊr ~**s** z
rafts|man ˈrɑːfs |mən §ˈræfts- ‖ ˈræfts- ~**men**
mən -men
rag ræg **ragged** *past & pp* rægd **ragging**
ˈrægɪŋ **rags** rægz
ˌrag ˈdoll ‖ ˈ· ·; ˈrag trade
raga ˈrɑːg ə rɑːg ~**s** z
ragamuffin ˈræg ə ˌmʌf ɪn §-ᵊn ~**s** z
rag-and-bone |man ˌræg ən ˈbəʊn |mæn -ənd-,
→-əm-, →-ˈbəʊm- ‖ -ˈboʊn- ~**men** men
ragbag ˈræg bæg ~**s** z
rage reɪdʒ **raged** reɪdʒd **rages** ˈreɪdʒ ɪz -əz
raging ˈreɪdʒ ɪŋ
ragg... —*see* rag
ragga ˈræg ə
ragged *adj* ˈræg ɪd -əd ~**ly** li ~**ness** nəs nɪs
ˌragged ˈrobin
raggedy ˈræg əd i -ɪd-
raggle-taggle ˈræg ᵊl ˌtæg ᵊl ◄ ˈ· · ·, · ·
ragi... —*see* rage
raglan, R~ ˈræg lən ~**s** z
Rag|man, r~ ˈræg |mən ~**men** men mən
ragout ræ ˈguː ˈræg uː ~**s** z
ragpicker ˈræg ˌpɪk ə ‖ -ᵊr ~**s** z
ragstone ˈræg stəʊn ‖ -stoʊn
ragtag ˈræg tæg
ragtime ˈræg taɪm
Ragu *tdmk* ræ ˈguː ˈræg uː
ragweed ˈræg wiːd
ragworm ˈræg wɜːm ‖ -wɝːm ~**s** z
ragwort ˈræg wɜːt §-wɔːt ‖ -wɝːt -wɔːrt ~**s** s
rah rɑː
rah-rah ˈrɑː rɑː ‖ ˈrɔː rɔː
Rahway *place in NJ* ˈrɔː weɪ ˈrɑː-
raid reɪd **raided** ˈreɪd ɪd -əd **raiding** ˈreɪd ɪŋ
raids reɪdz
raider ˈreɪd ə ‖ -ᵊr ~**s** z
Raif reɪf
Raikes reɪks

R-liaison

1 In BrE (RP) and other NON-RHOTIC accents, a word in isolation never ends in r. But in connected speech an r may be pronounced in some cases if the next word begins with a vowel sound.

2 This typically happens with a word that ends in one of the vowels ə, ɑː, ɔː, ɜː, ɪə, eə, ʊə.

far fɑː ‖ fɑːr   In isolation, or before a consonant sound, this word is pronounced fɑː. But in a phrase such as **far away, far out** it is usually pronounced fɑːr.

near nɪə ‖ nɪ°r   In isolation, the RP form is nɪə. But in a phrase such as **near enough** it is usually pronounced nɪər.

3 Usually, as in the cases just mentioned, the spelling includes r. The added r-sound is then known as **linking r**. It corresponds to a historical r, now lost before a consonant or pause. (In **rhotic** accents, such as GenAm, this r is still always present, and is therefore not 'linking'.)

4 In RP, however, as in other non-rhotic accents, the sound r is frequently added even if there is no letter **r** in the spelling. This **intrusive r** does not correspond to historical r, and there is no corresponding r in AmE.

comma ˈkɒmə ‖ ˈkɑːm ə   In isolation, the RP form is ˈkɒm ə. But in a phrase such as **put a comma in**, it is often pronounced ˈkɒm ər. (In GenAm it is always ˈkɑːm ə, whatever the environment.)

thaw θɔː   In isolation, RP **thaw** is θɔː. In the phrase **thaw out**, intrusive r may be added, giving ˌθɔːr ˈaʊt. (In GenAm there is no r.)

5 In principle, LPD shows the CITATION pronunciation of words. Therefore it does not indicate places where r-liaison is likely across a word boundary. They can be inferred from the rules given above. However, LPD **does** show r-liaison within a word, both linking and intrusive. Linking r within a word, being obligatory, is shown in ordinary type; intrusive r, being optional (and disapproved of by some) is shown in raised type.

storing ˈstɔːr ɪŋ

thawing ˈθɔːʳ ɪŋ

R

---

rail reɪəl **railed** reɪəld **railing** ˈreɪəl ɪŋ **rails** reɪəlz
 ˈrail ˌticket
railcar ˈreɪəl kɑː ‖ -kɑːr ~s z
railcard ˈreɪəl kɑːd ‖ -kɑːrd ~s z
railhead ˈreɪəl hed ~s z
railing ˈreɪl ɪŋ ~s z
railler|y ˈreɪl ər |i ~ies iz
railroad ˈreɪəl rəʊd ‖ -roʊd ~ed ɪd əd ~ing ɪŋ
 ~s z
Railtrack *tdmk* ˈreɪəl træk
Railton ˈreɪəlt ən

railway ˈreɪəl weɪ ~s z
 ˈrailway ˌstation; ˈrailway train
railway|man ˈreɪəl weɪ |mən -wɪ- ~men mən
 men
raiment ˈreɪm ənt
rain reɪn **rained** reɪnd **raining** ˈreɪn ɪŋ **rains**
 reɪnz
 ˈrain check; ˈrain ˌforest; ˈrain gauge
Raina (*i*) raɪ ˈiːn ə, (*ii*) ˈreɪn ə
rainbird ˈreɪn bɜːd ‖ -bɜːd ~s z
rainbow, R~ ˈreɪn bəʊ →ˈreɪm- ‖ -boʊ ~s z
raincoat ˈreɪn kəʊt →ˈreɪŋ- ‖ -koʊt ~s s
raindrop ˈreɪn drɒp ‖ -drɑːp ~s s

Raine reɪn
rainfall 'reɪn fɔːl ‖ -faːl
Rainford 'reɪn fəd ‖ -fərd
Rainhill ˌreɪn 'hɪl
Rainier *prince of Monaco* 'reɪn i eɪ ‖ rə 'nɪər
reɪ-; ren 'jeɪ —*Fr* [ʀɛ nje]
Rainier *Mount* 'reɪn iˍ‿ə rə 'nɪə, reɪ- ‖ rə 'nɪər
reɪ-; 'reɪn ɪr
rainproof 'reɪn pruːf →'reɪm-, §-prʊf ~ed t
~ing ɪŋ ~s s
rainstorm 'reɪn stɔːm ‖ -stɔːrm ~s z
rainwater 'reɪn ˌwɔːt ə ‖ -ˌwɔːt̬ ər -ˌwaːt̬-
rainwear 'reɪn weə ‖ -wer -wær
rain|y 'reɪn |i ~ier iˍ‿ə ‖ iˍ‿ər ~iest iˍɪst iˍ‿əst
~ily ɪ liˍəl i ~iness i nəs i nɪs
Raisa raɪ 'iːs ə raː:- ‖ raː:- —*Russ* [rʌ 'i sə]
raise reɪz raised reɪzd raises 'reɪz ɪz -əz
raising 'reɪz ɪŋ
raisin 'reɪz ən ~s z
Raison 'reɪz ən
raison d'etre, raison d'être ˌreɪz ɒ̃ 'detr ə -ɒn-
‖ -oʊn- —*Fr* [ʀɛ zɔ̃ dɛtχ]
Raistrick 'reɪs trɪk
raj raːdʒ raːʒ —*There is no justification in Hindi
for the pronunciation* raːʒ *often heard in
English.* —*Hindi* [raːdʒ]
raja, rajah 'raːdʒ ə ~s z
Rajasthan ˌraːdʒ ə 'staːn
Rajasthani ˌraːdʒ ə 'staːn i ◄
Rajneesh ˌraːdʒ 'niːʃ
Rajpoot, Rajput 'raːdʒ pʊt ~s s —*Hindi*
[raːdʒ puːt̪]
Rajputana ˌraːdʒ pʊ 'taːn ə
rake reɪk raked reɪkt rakes reɪks raking
'reɪk ɪŋ
rake-off 'reɪk ɒf ‖ -ɔːf -aːf ~s s
raki 'raːk i 'ræk-; raː 'kiː
rakish 'reɪk ɪʃ ~ly li ~ness nəs nɪs
rale, râle raːl ræl rales, râles raːlz rælz
Ralegh, Raleigh (*i*) 'raːl i, (*ii*) 'rɔːl i ‖ 'raːl i,
(*iii*) 'ræl i —*Sir Walter R~ was probably (ii), as
is the place in NC; R~ bicycles are (ii) in AmE,
(iii) in BrE.*
Ralf (*i*) rælf, (*ii*) reɪf
rallentando ˌræl ən 'tænd əʊ -en-
‖ ˌraːl ən 'taːnd oʊ (*) —*It* [ral len 'tan do]
~s z
rall|y 'ræl |i ~ied id ~ies iz ~ying iˍɪŋ
rallycross 'ræl i krɒs -krɔːs ‖ -krɔːs -kraːs
Ralph (*i*) rælf, (*ii*) reɪf —*In AmE,* (*i*).
Ralston 'rɔːlst ən 'rɒlst- ‖ 'raːlst-
ram, Ram, RAM ræm rammed ræmd
ramming 'ræm ɪŋ rams ræmz
Rama 'raːm ə
Ramachandra ˌraːm ə 'tʃʌndr ə -'tʃændr-
ramada, R~ *tdmk* rə 'maːd ə ~s z
Ramadan ˌræm ə 'daːn ˌraːm-, ˌrʌm-, -'dæn,
'•••
Ramadge, Ramage 'ræm ɪdʒ
Ramakrishna ˌraːm ə 'krɪʃ nə
Raman 'raːm ən
Ramayana rə 'maɪˍən ə -'maː jən- —*Hindi*
[raː maː jən]

Rambert 'rɒm beə 'rɒ̃- ‖ raːm 'beər
rambl|e 'ræm bəl ~ed d ~es z ~ing ˍɪŋ
rambler 'ræm blə ‖ -blər ~s z
rambling *adj* 'ræm blɪŋ ~ly li
Rambo 'ræm bəʊ ‖ -boʊ
Ramboesque ˌræm bəʊ 'esk ◄ ‖ -boʊ-
Rambouillet rɒm 'buː ˌjeɪ ræm-, -leɪ; '•••
‖ ˌraːm bu 'jeɪ ˌræm-, -'leɪ —*Fr* [ʀɑ̃ bu jɛ]
rambunctious ræm 'bʌŋk ʃəs ~ly li ~ness nəs
nɪs
rambutan ræm 'buːt ən ˌræm bu 'tæn, -'taːn
~s z
Rameau 'raːm əʊ 'ræm- ‖ ræ 'moʊ raː:- —*Fr*
[ʀa mo]
ramekin 'ræm ɪ kɪn -ə-, 'ræm kɪn, §-kən ~s z
Ramelson 'ræm əl sən
Rameses 'ræm ɪ siːz -ə-
ramie 'ræm i 'raːm-
ramification ˌræm ɪf ɪ 'keɪʃ ən, ˌ•əf-, §-ə'•- ~s
z
rami|fy 'ræm ɪ |faɪ -ə- ~fied faɪd ~fies faɪz
~fying faɪ ɪŋ
Ramillies 'ræm ɪl ɪz -əl- —*Fr* [ʀa mi ji]
Ramirez rə 'mɪər ez ‖ -'mɪr- —*Sp* [rra 'mi reθ,
-res]
ramjet 'ræm dʒet ~s s
rammer 'ræm ə ‖ -ər ~s z
rammish 'ræm ɪʃ ~ly li ~ness nəs nɪs
Ramon, Ramón rə 'mɒn ræ- ‖ -'moʊn —*Sp*
[ra 'mon]
Ramona rə 'məʊn ə ræ- ‖ -'moʊn ə
Ramos 'raːm ɒs ‖ raː 'moʊs 'reɪm oʊs —*Sp*
['rra mos], *Port* ['rrɐ muʃ, -mus]
ramose 'reɪm əʊs -əʊz; ræ 'məʊs ‖ -oʊs
ramp ræmp ramped ræmpt ramping
'ræmp ɪŋ ramps ræmps
rampag|e *v* ræm 'peɪdʒ 'ræmp eɪdʒ ~ed d
~es ɪz əz ~ing ɪŋ
rampag|e *n* 'ræmp eɪdʒ ræm 'peɪdʒ ~es ɪz əz
rampageous ræm 'peɪdʒ əs ~ly li ~ness nəs
nɪs
rampant 'ræmp ənt ~ly li
rampart 'ræmp aːt -ət ‖ -aːrt -ərt ~s s
rampion 'ræmp iˍən ~s z
Ramprakash 'ræm prə kæʃ
Rampton 'ræmpt ən
ram-raid 'ræm reɪd ~ed ɪd əd ~er/s ə/
z ‖ ər/z ~ing ɪŋ ~s z
ramrod 'ræm rɒd ‖ -raːd ~s z
Ramsaran 'raːmᵖs ər ən
Ramsay 'ræm zi
Ramsbotham 'ræmz ˌbɒθ əm -ˌbɒt- ‖ -ˌbaː:θ-
Ramsbottom 'ræmz ˌbɒt əm ‖ -ˌbaːt̬-
Ramsden 'ræmz dən
Ramses 'ræm siːz
Ramsey 'ræmz i
Ramsgate 'ræmz geɪt -gɪt
ramshackle 'ræm ˌʃæk əl
ramshorn 'ræmz hɔːn ‖ -hɔːrn
ramson 'ræmz ən 'ræmᵖs- ~s z
ram|us 'reɪm |əs ~i aɪ
ran ræn
Ranby 'ræn bi →'ræm-

rance rænᵗs rɑːnᵗs ‖ rænᵗs

ranch rɑːntʃ §ræntʃ ‖ ræntʃ **ranched** rɑːntʃt §ræntʃt ‖ ræntʃt **ranches** 'rɑːntʃ ɪz §'ræntʃ-, -əz ‖ 'ræntʃ əz **ranching** 'rɑːntʃ ɪŋ §'ræntʃ- ‖ 'ræntʃ ɪŋ
'**ranch house**

rancher 'rɑːntʃ ə §'ræntʃ- ‖ 'ræntʃ ᵊr **~s** z

ranchero rɑːn 'tʃeər əʊ ræn- ‖ -'tʃer oʊ **~s** z

rancho, R~ 'rɑːntʃ əʊ §'ræntʃ- ‖ -oʊ **~s** z

rancid 'rænᵗs ɪd §-əd **~ness** nəs nɪs

rancidity ræn 'sɪd ət i -ɪt- ‖ -əṱ i

rancor 'ræŋk ə ‖ -ᵊr

rancorous 'ræŋk ər əs **~ly** li **~ness** nəs nɪs

rancour 'ræŋk ə ‖ -ᵊr *(= ranker)*

rand, Rand rænd rɑːnt, rɒnt *—Afrikaans* [rɑnt]

Randal, Randall 'rænd ᵊl

Randalstown 'rænd ᵊlz taʊn

R and B ˌɑːr ən 'biː →-əm-, -ənd- ‖ ˌɑːr-

R and D ˌɑːr ən 'diː -ənd- ‖ ˌɑːr-

randi... *—see* **randy**

Randolph 'rænd ɒlf -ᵊlf ‖ -ɑːlf

random 'rænd əm

randomis... *—see* **randomiz...**

randomization ˌrænd əm aɪ 'zeɪʃ ᵊn -əm ɪ- ‖ -əm ə- **~s** z

randomiz|e 'rænd ə maɪz §ˌ• •'• **~ed** d **~es** ɪz əz **~ing** ɪŋ

random|ly 'rænd əm |li **~ness** nəs nɪs

rand|y, Randy 'rænd |i **~ier** i‿ə ‖ i‿ᵊr **~iest** i‿ɪst i‿əst **~ily** ɪ li əl i **~iness** i nəs i nɪs

ranee 'rɑːn i ₍ₗ₎rɑː 'niː **~s** z

Ranelagh 'ræn ɪl ə -əl-, -i; -ə lɔː

Ranfurly 'rænf əl i ræn 'fɜːl i ‖ -ᵊrl i

rang ræŋ

range reɪndʒ **ranged** reɪndʒd **ranges** 'reɪndʒ ɪz -əz **ranging** 'reɪndʒ ɪŋ
'**range** ˌ**finder**

ranger, R~ 'reɪndʒ ə ‖ -ᵊr **~s** z

rangi... *—see* **range**

Rangoon ₍ₗ₎ræŋ 'guːn ‖ ₍ₗ₎ræn-

rang|y 'reɪndʒ |i **~ier** i‿ə ‖ i‿ᵊr **~iest** i‿ɪst i‿əst **~iness** i nəs i nɪs

rani 'rɑːn i ₍ₗ₎rɑː 'niː **~s** z

Ranjit 'rʌn dʒɪt 'ræn-

rank, Rank ræŋk *—but as a German name in AmE,* rɑːŋk **ranked** ræŋkt **ranking** 'ræŋk ɪŋ **ranks** ræŋks
ˌ**rank and** '**file**

ranker 'ræŋk ə ‖ -ᵊr **~s** z

Rankin, Rankine 'ræŋk ɪn §-ən

rankl|e 'ræŋk ᵊl **~ed** d **~es** z **~ing** ‿ɪŋ

rank|ly 'ræŋk| li **~ness** nəs nɪs

rankshift 'ræŋk ʃɪft **~ed** ɪd əd **~ing** ɪŋ **~s** s

Rannoch 'ræn ək -əx

ransack 'ræn sæk **~ed** t **~er/s** ə/z ‖ ᵊr/z **~ing** ɪŋ **~s** s

ransom 'rænᵗs əm **~ed** d **~er/s** ə/z ‖ ᵊr/z **~ing** ɪŋ **~s** z

Ransom, Ransome 'rænᵗs əm

rant rænt **ranted** 'rænt ɪd -əd ‖ 'rænṱ əd **ranting/ly** 'rænt ɪŋ /li ‖ 'rænṱ- **rants** rænts

Rantzen 'rænts ᵊn

Ranulph 'ræn ʌlf -ᵊlf

ranunc|ulus rə 'nʌŋk |jʊl əs -jəl- ‖ -|jəl əs **~uli** ju laɪ jə- ‖ jə laɪ **~uluses** jʊl əs ɪz jəl-, -əz ‖ jəl əs əz

Raoul raʊ 'uːl rɑː- *—Fr* [ʁa ul]

rap ræp **rapped** ræpt **rapping** 'ræp ɪŋ **raps** ræps

rapacious rə 'peɪʃ əs **~ly** li **~ness** nəs nɪs

rapacity rə 'pæs ət i -ɪt- ‖ -əṱ i

Rapallo rə 'pæl əʊ ‖ -'pɑːl oʊ *—It* [ra 'pal lo]

rape reɪp **raped** reɪpt **rapes** reɪps **raping** 'reɪp ɪŋ
'**rape oil**

Raper 'reɪp ə ‖ -ᵊr

rapeseed 'reɪp siːd

raphae 'reɪf iː

Raphael 'ræf eɪ əl 'ræf eɪᵊl, 'ræf i‿əl *—These forms may be heard for the angel, the surname, and the artist (It* Raffaello [raf fa 'ɛl lo]*). The angel and surname, though not the artist, are further sometimes pronounced* 'reɪf ᵊl, -jəl. *The artist is sometimes* 'ræf aɪ el ‖ ˌrɑːf aɪ 'el.

raph|e 'reɪf |i -iː **~ae** iː

rapid 'ræp ɪd §-əd **~ly** li **~ness** nəs nɪs **~s** z
ˌ**rapid** '**transit**

Rapidan ˌræp ɪ 'dæn -ə-

rapid-fire ˌræp ɪd 'faɪ‿ə ◂ §-əd- ‖ ˌræp əd 'faɪ‿ᵊr ◂

rapidity rə 'pɪd ət i ræ-, -ɪt- ‖ -əṱ i

rapier 'reɪp i‿ə ‖ ‿ᵊr **~s** z

rapine 'ræp aɪn -ɪn, §-ən

rapist 'reɪp ɪst §-əst **~s** s

Rapoport 'ræp əʊ pɔːt ‖ -ə pɔːrt

Rappahannock ˌræp ə 'hæn ək ◂

rapparee ˌræp ə 'riː **~s** z

rappel ræ 'pel rə- **~ed, ~led** d **~ing, ~ling** ɪŋ **~s** z

rapport ræ 'pɔː rə-; 'ræp ɔː ‖ -'pɔːr -'poʊr *—Fr* [ʁa pɔːʁ]

rapporteur ˌræp ɔː 'tɜː ‖ -ɔːr 'tɝː *—Fr* [ʁa pɔʁ tœːʁ] **~s** z

rapprochement ræ 'prɒʃ mɒ̃ rə-, -'prəʊʃ-, -mɒŋ ‖ ˌræp roʊʃ 'mɑːn *—Fr* [ʁa pʁɔʃ mɑ̃]

rapscallion ræp 'skæl i‿ən **~s** z

rapt ræpt

raptor 'ræpt ə -ɔː ‖ -ᵊr -ɔːr **~s** z

raptorial ræp 'tɔːr i‿əl ‖ -'toʊr-

rapture 'ræp tʃə ‖ -tʃᵊr **~s** z

rapturous 'ræp tʃər‿əs **~ly** li **~ness** nəs nɪs

Rapunzel rə 'pʌnz ᵊl

Raquel ræ 'kel rə- ‖ rɑː- *—Sp* [rra 'kel]

rara avis ˌreər ᵊr 'eɪv ɪs ˌrɑːr ᵊr 'æv-, -'ɑːv-, §-əs; -'ɑː wɪs ‖ ˌrer ə- ˌrær-

rare reə ‖ reᵊr ræᵊr **rarer** 'reər ə ‖ 'rer ᵊr 'rær- **rarest** 'reər ɪst -əst ‖ 'rer əst 'rær-
ˌ**rare** '**earth**, ˌ**rare** '**earth** ˌ**element**

rarebit 'reə bɪt 'ræb ɪt, §-ət ‖ 'rer- 'rær-

rarefaction ˌreər ɪ 'fæk ʃᵊn -ə- ‖ ˌrer- ˌrær-

rare|fy 'reər ɪ |faɪ -ə- ‖ 'rer- 'rær- **~fied** faɪd **~fies** faɪz **~fying** faɪ ɪŋ

rarely 'reə li ‖ 'rer li 'rær-

rareripe 'reə raɪp ‖ 'rer- 'rær-

raring 'reər ɪŋ ‖ 'rer ɪŋ 'rær-

Raritan 'rær ɪt ən -ət- ‖ -ət ᵊn

R

rarit|y ˈreər ət |i -ɪt- ‖ ˈrer ət̬ |i ˈrær- **~ies** iz
Rarotonga ˌreər ə ˈtɒŋ gə -ˈtɒŋ ə
  ‖ ˌrær ə ˈtɑːŋ gə ˌrer-, ˌrɑːr-, -ˈtɔːŋ-
rasbora ræz ˈbɔːr ə ‖ -ˈbour- **~s** z
rascal ˈrɑːsk əl §ˈræsk- ‖ ˈræsk əl **~s** z
rascalit|y rɑː ˈskæl ət |i ræ-, -ɪt- ‖ ræ ˈskæl ət̬ |i
  ~ies iz
rascally ˈrɑːsk əl i §ˈræsk- ‖ ˈræsk-
rash ræʃ **rasher** ˈræʃ ə ‖ -ər **rashes** ˈræʃ ɪz -əz
  rashest ˈræʃ ɪst -əst
rasher ˈræʃ ə ‖ -ər **~s** z
Rashid ræ ˈʃiːd ‖ rɑː-
rash|ly ˈræʃ |li **~ness** nəs nɪs
Rask ræsk —*Danish* [ʀasg]
Rasmus ˈræz məs
rasp rɑːsp §ræsp ‖ ræsp **rasped** rɑːspt §ræspt
  ‖ ræspt **rasping** ˈrɑːsp ɪŋ §ˈræsp- ‖ ˈræsp ɪŋ
  rasps rɑːsps §ræsps ‖ ræsps
raspberr|y, R~ ˈrɑːz bər_|i ˈrɑːs-, §ˈræz-
  ‖ ˈræz ˌber li -bər_li (*) **~ies** iz
Rasputin ræ ˈspjuːt ɪn -ˈspuː-, §-ən ‖ -ən —*Russ*
  [rʌ ˈspu tʲin]
Rasta ˈræst ə ˈrʌst- ‖ ˈrɑːst- **~s** z
Ras Tafari, Rastafari ˌræs tə ˈfɑːr i —*in
  Jamaica also* -fə ˈraɪ
Rastafarian, r~ ˌræst ə ˈfeər i_ən ◂ ˌrʌst-,
  -ˈfɑːr- ‖ -ˈfer- **~ism** ˌɪz əm **~s** z
Rasta|man ˈræst əl mæn ˈrʌst- ‖ ˈrɑːst- **~men**
  men
raster ˈræst ə ‖ -ər **~s** z
rasteris|e, rasteriz|e ˈræst ə raɪz **~ed** d
  ~er/s ə/z ‖ ər/z **~es** ɪz əz **~ing** ɪŋ
Rastrick ˈræs trɪk
Rastus ˈræst əs
rat ræt **rats** ræts **ratted** ˈræt ɪd -əd ‖ ˈræt̬ əd
  ratting ˈræt ɪŋ ‖ ˈræt̬ ɪŋ
  ˈrat race; ˈrat run; ˈrat trap
rata *tree* ˈrɑːt ə ‖ ˈrɑːt̬ ə **~s** z —*see also* **pro
  rata**
ratable ˈreɪt əb əl ‖ ˈreɪt̬-
ratafia ˌræt ə ˈfɪə -ˈfiː_ə ‖ ˌræt̬ ə ˈfiː ə **~s** z
rataplan ˌræt ə ˈplæn ‖ ˌræt̬- **~ned** d **~ning**
  ɪŋ **~s** z
rat-a-tat ˌræt ə ˈtæt ˈ • • • ‖ ˌræt̬-
rat-a-tat-tat ˌræt ə ˌtæt ˈtæt ‖ ˌræt̬-
ratatouille ˌræt ə ˈtwiː -æ-, -ˈtuː_i ‖ ˌræt̬- —*Fr*
  [ʀa ta tuj]
ratbag ˈræt bæg **~s** z
rat-catcher ˈræt ˌkætʃ ə ‖ -ər **~s** z
ratchet ˈrætʃ ɪt §-ət **~s** s
Ratcliff, Ratcliffe ˈræt klɪf
rate reɪt **rated** ˈreɪt ɪd -əd ‖ ˈreɪt̬ əd **rates**
  reɪts **rating** ˈreɪt ɪŋ ‖ ˈreɪt̬ ɪŋ
  ˌrate of exˈchange
rateable ˈreɪt əb əl ‖ ˈreɪt̬-
  ˌrateable ˈvalue
rate-cap ˈreɪt kæp **~ped** t **~ping** ɪŋ **~s** s
ratel ˈreɪt əl ˈrɑːt-, -el ‖ ˈreɪt̬ əl ˈrɑːt̬- **~s** z
ratepayer ˈreɪt ˌpeɪ ə ‖ -ər **~s** z
ratfink ˈræt fɪŋk **~s** s
Rathbone ˈræθ bəʊn ‖ -boʊn
rathe reɪð

rather ˈrɑːð ə §ˈræð- ‖ ˈræð ər —*As a BrE
  interjection, ˈcertainly', also* ˌrɑː ˈðɜː
Rather *family name* ˈræð ə ‖ -ər
Rathfarnham ræθ ˈfɑːn əm ‖ -ˈfɑːrn-
Rathlin ˈræθ lɪn §-lən
Rathgar ræθ ˈgɑː ‖ -ˈgɑːr
Rathmines ræθ ˈmaɪnz
ratification ˌræt ɪf ɪ ˈkeɪʃ ən ˌ•əf-, §-ə-ˈ•-
  ‖ ˌræt̬- **~s** z
rati|fy ˈræt ɪ |faɪ -ə- ‖ ˈræt̬ ə |faɪ **~fied** faɪd
  ~fier/s faɪ_ə/z ‖ faɪ_ər/z **~fies** faɪz **~fying**
  faɪ ɪŋ
rating ˈreɪt ɪŋ ‖ ˈreɪt̬ ɪŋ **~s** z
ratio ˈreɪʃ i_əʊ ‖ -oʊ ˈreɪʃ oʊ **~s** z
ratioci|nate ˌræt i ˈɒs ɪ |neɪt ˌræʃ-, -ˈəʊs-,
  -ə neɪt, -əln eɪt ‖ ˌræt̬ i ˈɑːs əln eɪt ˌræt̬-,
  -ˈoʊs- **~nated** neɪt ɪd -əd ‖ neɪt̬ əd **~nates**
  neɪts **~nating** neɪt ɪŋ ‖ neɪt̬ ɪŋ
ratiocination ˌræt i ˌɒs ɪ ˈneɪʃ ən ˌræʃ-, -ˌəʊs-,
  -ə'•- ‖ ˌræʃ i ˌɑːs- ˌræt̬-, -ˌoʊs- **~s** z
ration ˈræʃ ən ‖ ˈreɪʃ- **~ed** d **~ing** ɪŋ **~s** z
rational ˈræʃ ən_əl
rationale ˌræʃ ə ˈnɑːl -ˈnæl; -ˈnɑːl eɪ ‖ -ˈnæl **~s**
  z
rationalis... —*see* **rationaliz...**
rationalism ˈræʃ ən_ə ˌlɪz əm -ən_əl ˌɪz-
rationalist ˈræʃ ən_əl ɪst §-əst **~s** s
rationalistic ˌræʃ ən_ə ˈlɪst ɪk ◂ **~ally** əl_i
rationalit|y ˌræʃ ə ˈnæl ət |i -ɪt i ‖ -ət̬ li **~ies** iz
rationalization ˌræʃ ən_əl aɪ ˈzeɪʃ ən -əl ɪ-
  ‖ -əl ə- **~s** z
rationaliz|e ˈræʃ ən_ə laɪz -ən_əl aɪz **~ed** d
  ~es ɪz əz **~ing** ɪŋ
rationally ˈræʃ ən_əl i
Ratisbon ˈræt ɪz bɒn -ɪs-, -əz-, -əs-
  ‖ ˈræt̬ əs bɑːn
ratite ˈræt aɪt **~s** s
ratlin, ratline ˈræt lɪn §-lən **~s** z
Ratner ˈræt nə ‖ -nər
ratoon rə ˈtuːn ræ- **~ed** d **~ing** ɪŋ **~s** z
Ratskeller ˈræts ˌkel ə ‖ ˈrɑːts ˌkel ər —*Ger*
  [ˈʀaːts ˌkel ɐ] **~s** z
rat-tail ˈræt teɪəl **~s** z
rattan rə ˈtæn ræ- **~s** z
rat-tat ˌræt ˈtæt
Rattenbury ˈræt ən bər_i ‖ -ˌber i
ratt... —*see* **rat**
ratter ˈræt ə ‖ ˈræt̬ ər **~s** z
Rattigan ˈræt ɪg ən -əg- ‖ ˈræt̬-
rattl|e, R~ ˈræt əl ‖ ˈræt̬ əl **~ed** d **~es** z **~ing**
  ɪŋ
rattle-brained ˈræt əl breɪnd ‖ ˈræt̬-
rattler ˈræt əl_ə ‖ ˈræt̬ lər ˈræt̬ əl ər **~s** z
rattlesnake ˈræt əl sneɪk ‖ ˈræt̬- **~s** s
rattletrap ˈræt əl træp ‖ ˈræt̬- **~s** s
rattling ˈræt əl_ɪŋ ‖ ˈræt̬ lɪŋ ˈræt̬ əl ɪŋ
rattly ˈræt əl_i ‖ ˈræt̬ li ˈræt̬ əl i
rattoon —*see* **ratoon**
rat-trap ˈræt træp **~s** s
Rattray ˈrætr i -eɪ
ratt|ly ˈræt li ‖ ˈræt̬ li **~ier** i_ə ‖ i_ər **~iest** i_ɪst
  i_əst **~ily** ɪ li əl i **~iness** i nəs -nɪs
raucous ˈrɔːk əs ‖ ˈrɑːk- **~ly** li **~ness** nəs nɪs

Raul raʊ 'uːl rɑː- —*Sp* [rra 'ul]
raunch|y 'rɔːntʃ |i ‖ 'rɑːntʃ- ~ier i‿ə ‖ i‿ər
~iest i‿ɪst i‿əst ~ily ɪ li əl i ~iness i nəs i nɪs
Raunds rɔːndz ‖ rɑːndz
Rauschenberg 'raʊʃ ən bɜːg ‖ -bɝːg
rauwolfia rɔː 'wʊlf i‿ə raʊ-, -'wɒlf- ‖ rɑː-
ravag|e 'ræv ɪdʒ ~ed d ~es ɪz əz ~ing ɪŋ
rave reɪv raved reɪvd raves reɪvz raving
'reɪv ɪŋ
ravel 'ræv əl ~ed, ~led d ~ing, ~ling ɪŋ ~s z
Ravel ræ 'vel rə- ‖ rɑː- —*Fr* [ʁa vɛl]
ravelin 'ræv lɪn §-lən ~s z
raven n, adj, Raven 'reɪv ən ~s z
raven v 'ræv ən ~ed d ~ing ‿ɪŋ ~s z
Ravenglass 'reɪv ən glɑːs →-əŋ-, §-glæs ‖ -glæs
raven-haired ˌreɪv ən 'heəd ◄ ‖ -'heərd ◄
-'hæərd
ravening 'ræv ən ɪŋ ~ly li
Ravenna rə 'ven ə —*It* [ra 'ven na]
ravenous 'ræv ən‿əs ~ly li ~ness nəs nɪs
Ravensbourne 'reɪv ənz bɔːn ‖ -bɔːrn -boʊrn
raver 'reɪv ə ‖ -ər ~s z
Raverat 'rɑːv ə rɑː
rave-up 'reɪv ʌp ~s s
ravin 'ræv ɪn §-ən
ravine rə 'viːn ~s z
raving 'reɪv ɪŋ ~ly li ~s z
ravioli ˌræv i 'əʊl i ‖ -'oʊl i ˌrɑːv-
ravish 'ræv ɪʃ ~ed t ~es ɪz əz ~ing/ly ɪŋ /li
raw rɔː ‖ rɑː rawer 'rɔːʳ ə ‖ 'rɔː ʳr 'rɑː-
rawest 'rɔːʳ ɪst -əst ‖ 'rɔː əst 'rɑː-
ˌraw 'deal; ˌraw ma'terials
Rawalpindi ˌrɔːl 'pɪnd i ˌrɑː wəl'•-
‖ ˌrɑː wəl'•-
raw-boned ˌrɔː 'bəʊnd ◄ ‖ -'boʊnd ◄ ˌrɑː-
Rawdon 'rɔːd ən ‖ 'rɑːd-
rawhide 'rɔː haɪd ‖ 'rɑː-
Rawle rɔːl ‖ rɑːl
Rawlings 'rɔːl ɪŋz ‖ 'rɑːl-
Rawlins 'rɔːl ɪnz §-ənz ‖ 'rɑːl-
Rawlinson 'rɔːl ɪnˈts ən §-ənˈts- ‖ 'rɑːl-
Rawlplug, r~ tdmk 'rɔːl plʌg|| 'rɑːl-
raw|ly 'rɔː |li ‖ 'rɑː- ~ness nəs nɪs
Rawmarsh 'rɔː mɑːʃ ‖ -mɑːrʃ 'rɑː-
Rawson 'rɔːs ən ‖ 'rɑːs-
Rawsthorne 'rɔːs θɔːn ‖ -θɔːrn 'rɑːs-, 'rɔːz-,
'rɑːz-
Rawtenstall 'rɒt ən stɔːl 'rɔːt- ‖ 'rɔːt-
'rɑːt ən stɑːl
ray, Ray reɪ rays reɪz
Ray-Bans tdmk 'reɪ bænz
Raybould 'reɪ bəʊld →-bɒʊld ‖ -boʊld
Rayburn 'reɪ bɜːn ‖ -bɝːn
Rayleen 'reɪ liːn
Rayleigh 'reɪl i
rayless 'reɪ ləs -lɪs
Rayment 'reɪm ənt
Raymond 'reɪm ənd
Raynaud 'reɪn əʊ ‖ reɪ 'noʊ —*Fr* [ʁɛ no]
Rayner 'reɪn ə ‖ -ər
Raynes reɪnz
rayon 'reɪ ɒn ‖ -ɑːn ~s z

raze reɪz (= raise) razed reɪzd razes 'reɪz ɪz
-əz razing 'reɪz ɪŋ
razoo rɑː 'zuː rə-
razor 'reɪz ə ‖ -ər ~ed d razoring 'reɪz ər ɪŋ
~s z
'razor blade; ˌrazor 'edge, ˌrazor's 'edge
razorback 'reɪz ə bæk ‖ -ər- ~s s
razorbill 'reɪz ə bɪl ‖ -ər- ~s z
razorshell 'reɪz ə ʃel ‖ -ər- ~s z
razz ræz razzed ræzd razzes 'ræz ɪz -əz
razzing 'ræz ɪŋ
razzamatazz ˌræz əm‿ə 'tæz '•••
razzia 'ræz i‿ə ~s z
razzle 'ræz əl
razzle-dazzle ˌræz əl 'dæz əl '••,••
razzmatazz ˌræz mə 'tæz '•••
RC ˌɑː 'siː ‖ ˌɑːr-
r-colored, r-coloured 'ɑː ˌkʌl əd ‖ 'ɑːr ˌkʌl ərd
Rd —*see* Road
re note in music reɪ
re prep 'regarding' riː reɪ
RE 'religious education' ˌɑːr 'iː ‖ ˌɑːr-
re- ˌriː, rɪ, rə, ri, §riː —(i) As a productive prefix
meaning 'again' (sometimes spelt with a
hyphen), ˌriː (refill v ˌriː 'fɪl, n 'riː fɪl). Any
words in re- not included below may be assumed
to involve this productive prefix. (ii) Otherwise,
with a vaguer meaning, ri before a vowel sound
(react ri 'ækt), and rɪ, rə, §ri: before a
consonant (return rɪ 'tɜːn, rə-, §riː:- ‖ -'tɝːn);
but if stressed through the operation of a
stressing rule usually ˌre+ (recommend
ˌrek ə 'mend)
're ə ‖ -ər → they're, we're, you're
Rea (i) reɪ, (ii) riː
reach riːtʃ reached riːtʃt reaches 'riːtʃ ɪz -əz
reaching 'riːtʃ ɪŋ
reach-me-down 'riːtʃ mi daʊn ~s z
react ri 'ækt ~ed ɪd əd ~ing ɪŋ ~s s
reactance ri 'ækt ənˈts
reactant ri 'ækt ənt ~s s
reaction ri 'æk ʃən ~s z
re'action time
reactionar|y ri 'æk ʃən ər_|i -ʃən_ər li
‖ -ʃə ner li ~ies iz
reacti|vate ri 'ækt ɪ |veɪt ˌriː-, -ə- ~vated
veɪt ɪd -əd ‖ veɪt̬ əd ~vates veɪts ~vating
veɪt ɪŋ ‖ veɪt̬ ɪŋ
reactivation ri ˌækt ɪ 'veɪʃ ən ˌriː, ••'••-, -ə'•-
~s z
reactive ri 'ækt ɪv ~ly li ~ness nəs nɪs
reactor ri 'ækt ə ‖ -ər ~s z
read v pres; n riːd (= reed) read v past, pp red
(= red) reading 'riːd ɪŋ reads riːdz
'reading ˌmatter; 'reading room
Read riːd
readability ˌriːd ə 'bɪl ət i -ɪt i ‖ -ət̬ i
readab|le 'riːd əb |əl ~ly li
readdress ˌriː ə 'dres ~ed t ~es ɪz əz ~ing ɪŋ
Reade riːd
reader, R~ 'riːd ə ‖ -ər ~s z
readership 'riːd ə ʃɪp ‖ -ər- ~s s
readi... —*see* ready

R

reading 'riːd ɪŋ ~s z
Reading *name* 'red ɪŋ
readjust ˌriː ə 'dʒʌst ~ed ɪd əd ~ing ɪŋ
~ment/s mənt/s ~s s
Readman (i) 'red mən, (ii) 'riːd-
readmission ˌriːd əd 'mɪʃ ən →ˌəb-, -æd- ~s z
read|mit ˌriː‿əd |'mɪt →ˌəb-, -æd- ~mits
'mɪts ~mitted 'mɪt ɪd -əd ‖ 'mɪt̬ əd
~mitting 'mɪt ɪŋ ‖ 'mɪt̬ ɪŋ
readmittanc|e ˌriː‿əd 'mɪt ənts→ˌəb-, -æd-
~es ɪz əz
readout 'riːd aʊt ~s s
readthrough 'riːd θruː ~s z
read|y 'red li ~ied id ~ier i‿ə ‖ i‿ər ~ies iz
~iest i‿ɪst i‿əst ~ily ɪ li əl i ~iness i nəs i nɪs
~ying i ɪŋ
ˌready 'cash; ˌready 'money
ready-made ˌred i 'meɪd ◄ ' • • • ~s z
ready-mix ˌred i 'mɪks ◄ ' • • • ~ed t
ready-to-wear ˌred i tə 'weə ◄ -tu- ‖ -'weər
-'wæər
reaffirm ˌriː‿ə 'fɜːm ‖ -'fɝːm ~ed d ~ing ɪŋ
~s z
reaffirmation ˌriː æf ə 'meɪʃ ən • ˌ • • ' • -
‖ -ər ' • - ~s z
reafforest ˌriː‿ə 'fɒr ɪst -əst ‖ -'fɔːr əst -'fɑːr-
~ed ɪd əd ~ing ɪŋ ~s s
reafforestation ˌriː‿ə ˌfɒr ɪ 'steɪʃ ən -ˌ • ə-
‖ -ˌfɔːr- -ˌfɑːr- ~s z
Reagan 'reɪg ən
Reaganomics ˌreɪg ə 'nɒm ɪks ‖ -'nɑːm-
reagent ri 'eɪdʒ ənt ~s s

REAL

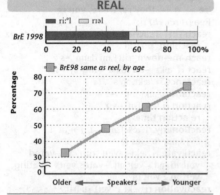

real *adj, adv, n 'reality'* rɪəl riːəl ‖ riːəl 'riː‿əl
—*BrE 1998 poll panel preference:* riːəl (*i.e.
same as reel*) 55%, rɪəl 45%
ˌreal e'state; ˌreal estate ˌagent; ˌreal
'property
real *n 'coin'*, **Real** *name of football team*
ˌreɪ 'ɑːl 'reɪ‿əl —*Sp, Port* [ˌre 'al] ~s z
realgar ri 'ælg ə -ɑː ‖ -ər -ɑːr
realia reɪ 'ɑːl i‿ə ri 'eɪl-
realign ˌriː‿ə 'laɪn ~ed d ~ing ɪŋ ~ment/s
mənt/s ~s z
realis... —*see* **realiz...**
realism 'rɪəl ˌɪz əm 'riːəl- ‖ 'riː ə ˌlɪz əm
realist 'rɪəl ɪst 'riːəl-, §-əst ‖ 'riː əl əst ~s s

realistic ˌrɪə 'lɪst ɪk ◄ ˌriː- ‖ ˌriː ə 'lɪst ɪk ◄
~ally əl_i
realit|y ri 'æl ət li -ɪt i ‖ -ət̬ li ~ies iz
realizable 'rɪəl aɪz əb əl 'riːəl- ‖ 'riː ə laɪz əb əl
realization ˌrɪəl aɪ 'zeɪʃ ən ˌriːəl-, -ɪ' • -
‖ ˌriː əl ə 'zeɪʃ ən ~s z
realiz|e 'rɪəl aɪz 'riːəl- ‖ 'riː ə laɪz ~ed d ~es
ɪz əz ~ing ɪŋ
real-life ˌrɪəl 'laɪf ◄ ˌriːəl- ‖ ˌriːəl-
reallo|cate ˌriː 'æl əʊ |keɪt ‖ -ə |keɪt ~cated
keɪt ɪd -əd ‖ keɪt̬ əd ~cates keɪts ~cating
keɪt ɪŋ ‖ keɪt̬ ɪŋ
reallocation ˌriː ˌæl əʊ 'keɪʃ ən ‖ -ə-

REALLY

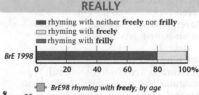

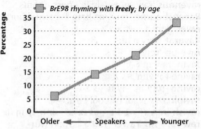

really 'rɪəl i 'riːəl i, 'reəl i ‖ 'riːl i 'riː‿əl i —*BrE
1998 poll panel preference: rhyming with
neither freely nor frilly 80%; rhyming with
freely 19%, rhyming with frilly 1%.*
realm relm **realms** relmz
realpolitik reɪ 'ɑːl pɒl ɪ ˌtiːk -ə, • , • ˌ • • • ' •
‖ -' • poʊl- —*Ger* R~ [ʁe 'aːl po li ˌtiːk]
real-time ˌrɪəl 'taɪm ◄ ˌriːəl- ‖ ˌriːəl-
realtor, R~ *tdmk* 'rɪəl tə 'riːəl-, -tɔː ‖ 'riːəlt ər
-ɔːr ~s z
realty 'rɪəl ti 'riːəl- ‖ 'riː‿əlt i
ream riːm **reamed** riːmd **reaming** 'riːm ɪŋ
reams riːmz
reamer 'riːm ə ‖ -ər ~s z
reani|mate ˌriː 'æn ɪ |meɪt -ə- ~mated
meɪt ɪd -əd ‖ meɪt̬ əd ~mates meɪts
~mating meɪt ɪŋ ‖ meɪt̬ ɪŋ
reap riːp **reaped** riːpt **reaping** 'riːp ɪŋ **reaps**
riːps
reaper 'riːp ə ‖ -ər ~s z
reap|pear ˌriː‿ə |'pɪə ‖ -|'pɪər ~peared
'pɪəd ‖ 'pɪərd ~pearing 'pɪər ɪŋ ‖ 'pɪr ɪŋ
~pears 'pɪəz ‖ 'pɪərz
reappearanc|e ˌriː‿ə 'pɪər ənts ‖ -'pɪr- ~es ɪz
əz
reapplication ˌriː æp lɪ 'keɪʃ ən ri ˌæp- ~s z
reap|ply ˌriː‿ə |'plaɪ ~plied 'plaɪd ~plies
'plaɪd ~plying 'plaɪ ɪŋ
reap|point ˌriː‿ə |'pɔɪnt ~pointment/s
'pɔɪnt mənt/s ~pointed 'pɔɪnt ɪd -əd
‖ 'pɔɪnt̬ əd ~pointing 'pɔɪnt ɪŋ ‖ 'pɔɪnt̬ ɪŋ
~points 'pɔɪnts

R

reappraisal ˌriːə ˈpreɪz əl ~s z
reappraisle ˌriːə ˈpreɪz ~ed d ~es ɪz əz ~ing ɪŋ
rear rɪə ‖ rɪʳr **reared** rɪəd ‖ rɪʳrd **rearing** ˈrɪər ɪŋ ‖ ˈrɪr ɪŋ **rears** rɪəz ‖ rɪʳrz
ˌrear ˈadmiral⁴; ˌrear ˈend
Rearden, Reardon ˈrɪəd ən ‖ ˈrɪrd ən
rear-end ˌrɪər ˈend ‖ ˌrɪr- ~ed ɪd əd ~er/s ə/z ‖ ər/z ~ing ɪŋ ~s z
rearguard ˈrɪə ɡɑːd ‖ ˈrɪr ɡɑːrd ~s z
ˌrearguard ˈaction
rearm ri ˈɑːm ˌriː- ‖ -ˈɑːrm ~ed d ~ing ɪŋ ~s z
rearmament ri ˈɑːm ə mənt ˌriː- ‖ -ˈɑːrm-
rearmost ˈrɪə məʊst ‖ ˈrɪr moʊst
rearrangle ˌriːə ˈreɪndʒ ~ed d ~ement/s mənt/s ~es ɪz əz ~ing ɪŋ
rearview ˈrɪə vjuː ‖ ˈrɪr-
ˌrearview ˈmirror
rearward ˈrɪə wəd ‖ ˈrɪr wəʳrd ~s z
reason, R~ ˈriːz ən ~ed d ~ing/s ɪŋ/z ~s z
reasonable ˈriːz ən_əb |əl ~ly li ~ness nəs nɪs
reasoner ˈriːz ən_ə ‖ _ər ~s z
reasonless ˈriːz ən ləs -lɪs ~ly li ~ness nəs nɪs
reassemble ˌriːə ˈsem bəl ~ed d ~es z ~ing ɪŋ
reas|sert ˌriːə ˈsɜːt ‖ -ˈsɜːt ~serted ˈsɜːt ɪd -əd ‖ ˈsɜːt̬ əd ~serting ˈsɜːt ɪŋ ‖ ˈsɜːt̬ ɪŋ ~serts ˈsɜːts ‖ ˈsɜːts
reassess ˌriːə ˈses ~ed t ~es ɪz əz ~ing ɪŋ ~ment/s mənt/s
reassign ˌriːə ˈsaɪn ~ed d ~ing ɪŋ ~s z
reas|sure ˌriːə |ˈʃɔː -ˈʃʊə, rɪə˖ ‖ -|ˈʃʊər -ˈʃɜː ~sured ˈʃɔːd ˈʃʊəd ‖ ˈʃʊəʳrd ˈʃɜːd ~sures ˈʃɔːz ˈʃʊəz ‖ ˈʃʊəʳrz ˈʃɜːz ~suring/ly ˈʃɔːr ɪŋ /li ˈʃʊər- ‖ ˈʃʊr ɪŋ /li ˈʃɜː-
reassurancle ˌriːə ˈʃʊər ənʦ -ˈʃɔːr- ‖ -ˈʃʊr- -ˈʃɜː- ~es ɪz əz
Reaumur, Réaumur ˈreɪ əʊ mjʊə ‖ ˌreɪ oʊ ˈmjʊəʳr —Fr [ʁe o my:ʁ]
Reave riːv
reawaken ˌriːə ˈweɪk ən ~ed d ~ing ɪŋ ~s z
Reay reɪ
reb, Reb reb **rebs, Rebs** rebz
rebarbative rɪ ˈbɑːb ət ɪv rə-, §riː- ‖ -ˈbɑːrb ət̬ ɪv
rebate n 'deduction' ˈriː beɪt rɪ ˈbeɪt, rə-, §riː- ~s s
rebate n 'groove, joint' ˈriː beɪt ˈræb ɪt, §-ət ~s s
re|bate v 'deduct'; 'form rebate in' rɪ ˈbeɪt rə-, §riː-; ˈriː ˌbeɪt ~bated beɪt ɪd -əd ‖ beɪt̬ əd ~bates beɪts ~bating beɪt ɪŋ ‖ beɪt̬ ɪŋ
rebec, rebeck ˈriːb ek ˈreb- ~s s
Rebecca, Rebekah rɪ ˈbek ə rə-, §riː-
rebel v rɪ ˈbel rə-, §riː- ~led d ~ling ɪŋ ~s z
rebel n, adj ˈreb əl ~s z
rebellion rɪ ˈbel jən rə-, §riː-, -i_ən ~s z
rebellious rɪ ˈbel jəs rə-, §riː-, -i_əs ~ly li ~ness nəs nɪs
rebind ˌriː ˈbaɪnd ~ing ɪŋ ~s z **rebound** ˌriː ˈbaʊnd

rebirth ˌriː ˈbɜːθ ‖ -ˈbɜːθ ~er/s ə/z ‖ -əʳr/z ~ing ɪŋ ~s s
re|boot v ˌriː |ˈbuːt ~booted ˈbuːt ɪd -əd ‖ ˈbuːt̬ əd ~booting ˈbuːt ɪŋ ‖ ˈbuːt̬ ɪŋ ~boots ˈbuːts
reboot n ˈriː buːt ˌ•ˈ• ~s s
rebore v ˌriː ˈbɔː ‖ -ˈbɔːr -ˈboʊr ~d d ~s z **reboring** ˌriː ˈbɔːr ɪŋ ‖ -ˈboʊr-
rebore n ˈriː bɔː ‖ -bɔːr -boʊr ~s z
reborn ˌriː ˈbɔːn ‖ -ˈbɔːrn
rebound v 'bounce back; have unexpected effect' rɪ ˈbaʊnd rə-, §riː- ~ed ɪd əd ~ing ɪŋ ~s z
rebound n ˈriː baʊnd ~s z
rebound adj 'again subjected to binding' ˌriː ˈbaʊnd ◀
rebozo rɪ ˈbəʊz əʊ rə- ‖ -ˈboʊz oʊ -ˈboʊs- —AmSp [rre ˈβo so] ~s z
rebuff v rɪ ˈbʌf rə-, §riː- ~ed t ~ing ɪŋ ~s s
rebuff n rɪ ˈbʌf rə-, §riː-, ˈriː bʌf ~s s
rebuild v ˌriː ˈbɪld ~ing ɪŋ ~s z **rebuilt** ˌriː ˈbɪlt ◀
rebuild n ˌriː ˈbɪld ˈ•• ~s z
rebukle v, n rɪ ˈbjuːk rə-, §riː- ~ed t ~es s ~ing ɪŋ
rebus ˈriːb əs ~es ɪz əz
re|but rɪ |ˈbʌt rə-, §riː- ~buts ˈbʌts ~butted ˈbʌt ɪd -əd ‖ ˈbʌt̬ əd ~butting ˈbʌt ɪŋ ‖ ˈbʌt̬ ɪŋ
rebuttal rɪ ˈbʌt əl rə-, §riː- ‖ -ˈbʌt̬ əl ~s z
rebutter rɪ ˈbʌt ə rə-, §riː- ‖ -ˈbʌt̬ əʳr ~s z
rec rek
recalcitrancle rɪ ˈkæls ɪtr ənts rə-, §riː-, -ətr- ~y i
recalcitrant rɪ ˈkæls ɪtr ənt rə-, §riː-, -ətr- ~ly li ~s s
recall v rɪ ˈkɔːl rə-, §riː- ‖ -ˈkɑːl ~ed d ~ing ɪŋ ~s z
recall n rɪ ˈkɔːl rə-, §riː-, ˈriː kɔːl ‖ -ˈkɑːl ~s z
recallable rɪ ˈkɔːl əb əl rə-, §riː- ‖ -ˈkɑːl-
re|cant rɪ |ˈkænt rə-, §riː- ~canted ˈkænt ɪd -əd ‖ ˈkænt̬ əd ~canting ˈkænt ɪŋ ‖ ˈkænt̬ ɪŋ ~cants ˈkænts
recantation ˌriː kæn ˈteɪʃ ən ~s z
recap v 'recapitulate', n 'recapitulation' ˈriː kæp ˌriː ˈkæp, rɪ-, rə- ~ped t ~ping ɪŋ ~s s
recap v 'retread' ˌriː ˈkæp ~ped t ~ping ɪŋ ~s s
recap n 'retread' ˈriː kæp ~s z
recapitu|late ˌriː kə ˈpɪtʃ u |leɪt -ˈpɪt ju- ‖ -ˈpɪtʃ ə- ~lated leɪt ɪd -əd ‖ leɪt̬ əd ~lates leɪts ~lating leɪt ɪŋ ‖ leɪt̬ ɪŋ
recapitulation ˌriː kə ˌpɪtʃ u ˈleɪʃ ən -ˌpɪt ju- ‖ -ˌpɪtʃ ə- ~s z
recapitulatory ˌriː kə ˈpɪtʃ ʊl ət_ər i -ˈpɪt ʊl-; -ˌpɪtʃ u ˈleɪt ər i, -ˌpɪt ju- ‖ -əl ə tɔːr i -toʊr i
recap|ture ˌriː ˈkæp |tʃ ə -ʃə ‖ -ltʃ əʳr ~tured tʃ əd ʃəd ‖ tʃ əʳrd ~tures tʃ əz ʃəz ‖ tʃ əʳrz ~turing tʃ ər ɪŋ ʃər_ɪŋ
recast ˌriː ˈkɑːst §-ˈkæst ‖ -ˈkæst ~ing ɪŋ ~s s
recce ˈrek i ~d, ~ed d ~ing ɪŋ ~s z
recedle rɪ ˈsiːd rə-, ˌriː- ~ed ɪd əd ~es z ~ing ɪŋ

re|ceipt rɪ ˈsiːt rə-, §riː- (!) ~ceipted ˈsiːt ɪd -əd ‖ ˈsiːt̬ əd ~ceipting ˈsiːt ɪŋ ‖ ˈsiːt̬ ɪŋ ~ceipts ˈsiːts

receivable rɪ ˈsiːv əb ᵊl rə-, §riː- ~s z

receiv|e rɪ ˈsiːv rə-, §riː- ~ed d ~es z ~ing ɪŋ
Re,ceived Pro,nunci'ation; re'ceiving ,order

receiver rɪ ˈsiːv ə rə-, §riː- ‖ -ᵊr ~s z ~ship ʃɪp

recency ˈriːs ᵊn̩ts i

recension rɪ ˈsen̩ʃ ᵊn rə-, §riː- ~s z

recent ˈriːs ᵊnt ~ly li ~ness nəs nɪs

recept ˈriː sept ~s s

receptacle rɪ ˈsept ək ᵊl rə-, §riː-, -ɪk- ~s z

reception rɪ ˈsep ʃᵊn rə-, §riː- ~s z
re'ception room

receptionist rɪ ˈsep ʃᵊn ɪst rə-, §riː-, §_əst ~s s

receptive rɪ ˈsept ɪv rə-, §riː-, ~ly li ~ness nəs nɪs

receptivity ˌriː sep ˈtɪv ət i ˌres ep-, rɪ ˌsep-, -ɪt i ‖ -ət̬ i

receptor rɪ ˈsept ə rə-, §riː- ‖ -ᵊr ~s z

recess n, v rɪ ˈses rə-, §riː-; ˈriː ses ‖ ˈriː ses rɪ ˈses —Some speakers may distinguish the verb •ˈ• from the noun ˈ•• ~ed t ~es ɪz əz ~ing ɪŋ

recession rɪ ˈseʃ ᵊn rə-, §riː- ~s z

recessional rɪ ˈseʃ ᵊn_əl rə-, §riː- ~s z

recessive rɪ ˈses ɪv rə-, §riː- ~ly li ~ness nəs nɪs ~s z

Rechabite ˈrek ə baɪt ~s s

recharg|e v ˌriː ˈtʃɑːdʒ ‖ -ˈtʃɑːrdʒ ~ed d ~es ɪz əz ~ing ɪŋ

recharg|e n ˈriː tʃɑːdʒ ‖ -tʃɑːrdʒ ~es ɪz əz

recherche, recherché rə ˈʃeəʃ eɪ ‖ -ˌʃer ˈʃeɪ —Fr [ʁə ʃɛʁ ʃe]

recidivism rɪ ˈsɪd ɪ ˌvɪz əm rə-, §riː-, -ˈ•ə-

recidivist rɪ ˈsɪd ɪv ɪst rə-, §riː-, -əv-, §-əst ~s s

Recife rə ˈsiːf i re-, -ə —BrPort [ʁɛ ˈsi fi, xe-]

recipe ˈres əp i -ɪp- (!) ~s z

recipient rɪ ˈsɪp i_ənt rə-, §riː- ~s s

reciprocal rɪ ˈsɪp rək ᵊl rə-, §riː- ~ly i ~s z

reciprocality rɪ ˌsɪp rə ˈkæl ət i rə-, §riː-, -ɪt i ‖ -ət̬ i

recipro|cate rɪ ˈsɪp rə ˌkeɪt rə-, §riː- ~cated keɪt ɪd -əd ‖ keɪt̬ əd ~cates keɪts ~cating keɪt ɪŋ ‖ keɪt̬ ɪŋ

reciprocation rɪ ˌsɪp rə ˈkeɪʃ ᵊn rə-, §riː- ~s z

reciprocit|y ˌres ɪ ˈprɒs ət i ˌ•ə-, -ɪt i ‖ -ˈprɑːs ət̬ li ~ies iz

recision rɪ ˈsɪʒ ᵊn rə-, §riː- ~s z

recital rɪ ˈsaɪt ᵊl rə-, §riː- ‖ -ˈsaɪt̬ ᵊl ~ist/s ɪst/s §əst/s ‖ əst/s ~s z

recitation ˌres ɪ ˈteɪʃ ᵊn -ə- ~s z

recitative n ˌres ɪt ə ˈtiːv -ᵊt-, •ˈ•ə- ‖ -ət̬ ə- ~s z

re|cite rɪ ˈsaɪt rə-, §riː- ~cited ˈsaɪt ɪd -əd ‖ ˈsaɪt̬ əd ~cites ˈsaɪts ~citing ˈsaɪt ɪŋ ‖ ˈsaɪt̬ ɪŋ

reck rek recked rekt recking ˈrek ɪŋ recks reks

reckless ˈrek ləs -lɪs ~ly li ~ness nəs nɪs

reckon ˈrek ᵊn ~ed d ~ing/s _ɪŋ/z ~s z

reckoner ˈrek ᵊn_ə ‖ -ᵊn_ᵊr ~s z

reclaim v rɪ ˈkleɪm rə-, ˌriː-, ~ed d ~ing ɪŋ ~s z

reclaim n rɪ ˈkleɪm rə-, ˌriː-, ˈriː kleɪm ~s z

reclamation ˌrek lə ˈmeɪʃ ᵊn ~s z

reclin|e rɪ ˈklaɪn rə-, §riː- ~ed d ~er/s ə/z ‖ ᵊr/z ~es ɪz əz ~ing ɪŋ

reclus|e rɪ ˈkluːs rə-, §riː-; ˈrek luːs ‖ ˈrek luːs rɪ ˈkluːs ~es ɪz əz

reclusive rɪ ˈkluːs ɪv rə-, §riː-, §-ˈkluːz- ~ly li ~ness nəs nɪs

recognis... —see recogniz...

recognition ˌrek əg ˈnɪʃ ᵊn △-ə- ~s z

recognizability ˌrek əg ˌnaɪz ə ˈbɪl ət i △, •ə-, -ɪt i ‖ -ət̬ i

recognizab|le ˈrek əg naɪz əb |ᵊl △ˈ•ə-, ˌ••ˈ•- ~ly li

recognizanc|e rɪ ˈkɒg nɪz ᵊn̩ts rə-, §riː-, -ˈkɒn ɪz- ‖ -ˈkɑːg nɪz ᵊn̩ts -ˈkɑːn ɪz- ~es ɪz əz

recogniz|e ˈrek əg naɪz △-ə naɪz; §ˌ••ˈ• ~ed d ~es ɪz əz ~ing ɪŋ

recoil v rɪ ˈkɔɪᵊl rə-, §riː- ~ed d ~ing ɪŋ ~s z

recoil n ˈriː kɔɪᵊl rɪ ˈkɔɪᵊl, rə-, §riː- ~s z

recoilless rɪ ˈkɔɪᵊl ləs rə-, §riː-, -lɪs ‖ ˈriː••

recollect ˌrek ə ˈlekt ~ed ɪd əd ~ing ɪŋ ~s s

recollection ˌrek ə ˈlek ʃᵊn ~s z

recombinant (ˌ)riː ˈkɒm bɪn ənt rɪ-, rə-, -ˈ•bən- ‖ -ˈkɑːm- ~s s

recombination ˌriː ˌkɒm bɪ ˈneɪʃ ᵊn •ˌ••ˈ••, -bə•- ‖ -ˌkɑːm- ~s z

recommenc|e ˌriː kə ˈmen̩ts ~ed t ~ement mənt ~es ɪz əz ~ing ɪŋ

recommend ˌrek ə ˈmend ~ed ɪd əd ~ing ɪŋ ~s z

recommendation ˌrek ə men ˈdeɪʃ ᵊn -mən•- ~s z

recompens|e v, n ˈrek əm pen̩ts ~ed t ~es ɪz əz ~ing ɪŋ

reconcilab|le ˈrek ᵊn saɪᵊl əb |ᵊl →ˈ•ŋ-, ˌ••ˈ••• ~leness ᵊl nəs -nɪs ~ly li

reconcil|e ˈrek ᵊn saɪᵊl →-ŋ-, ˌ••ˈ• ~ed d ~er/s ə/z ‖ ᵊr/z ~es ɪz əz ~ing ɪŋ

reconciliation ˌrek ᵊn sɪl i ˈeɪʃ ᵊn →, •ŋ- ~s z

reconciliatory ˌrek ᵊn ˈsɪl i_ət_ᵊr i →, •ŋ-, §, •••ˈeɪt ᵊr i ‖ ə tɔːr i -tour i

recondite ˈrek ᵊn daɪt →-ə-ŋ-; rɪ ˈkɒnd aɪt, rə- ‖ rɪ ˈkɑːnd aɪt ~ly li ~ness nəs nɪs

recondition ˌriː kən ˈdɪʃ ᵊn §-kɒn- ~ed d ◀ ~ing _ɪŋ ~s z

reconnaissance rɪ ˈkɒn ɪs ᵊn̩ts rə-, §riː-, -əs- ‖ -ˈkɑːn əs ᵊn̩ts -əs-

recon|noiter, recon|noitre ˌrek ə ‖ˈnɔɪt ə ‖ ˌriːk ə ‖ˈnɔɪt̬ ᵊr ,rek- (*) ~noitered, ~noitred ˈnɔɪt əd ‖ ˈnɔɪt̬ ᵊrd ~noitering, ~noitring ˈnɔɪt_ᵊr ɪŋ ‖ ˈnɔɪt̬ ᵊr ɪŋ →-ˈnɔɪtr ɪŋ ~noiters, ~noitres ˈnɔɪt əz ‖ ˈnɔɪt̬ ᵊrz

reconqu|er rɪ ˈkɒŋk| ə ‖ -ˈkɑːŋk| ᵊr ~ered əd ‖ -ᵊrd ~ering ᵊr ɪŋ ~ers əz ‖ ᵊrz

reconquest ˌriː ˈkɒŋk west ‖ -ˈkɑːn kwest →-ˈkɑːŋ-, -kwəst ~s s

reconsid|er ˌriː kən ˈsɪd |ə §-kɒn- ‖ -|ᵊr ~ered əd ‖ ᵊrd ~ering _ᵊr ɪŋ ~ers əz ‖ ᵊrz

reconsideration ˌriː kən ˌsɪd ə ˈreɪʃ ən §-kɒn-
reconsti|tute ˌriː ˈkɒnˈst ɪ ˌtjuːt -ə-, →§-tʃuːt
  ‖ -ˈkɑːnˈst ə ˌtuːt -tjuːt **~tuted** tjuːt ɪd
  →§tʃuːt-, -əd ‖ tuːt əd tjuːt- **~tutes** tjuːts
  →§tʃuːts ‖ tuːts tjuːts **~tuting** tjuːt ɪŋ
  →§tʃuːt- ‖ tuːt ɪŋ tjuːt-
reconstitution ˌriː ˌkɒnˈst ɪ ˈtjuːʃ ən -ˌˌ•ə-,
  →§-ˈtʃuːʃ- ‖ -ˌkɑːnˈst ə ˈtuːʃ ən -ˈtjuːʃ- **~s** z
reconstruct ˌriː kən ˈstrʌkt §-kɒn- **~ed** ɪd əd
  ~ing ɪŋ **~s** s
reconstruction ˌriː kən ˈstrʌk ʃən §-kɒn- **~s** z
record v rɪ ˈkɔːd rə-, §riː- ‖ -ˈkɔːrd **~ed** ɪd əd
  ~ing/s ɪŋ/z **~s** z
  re͵corded deˈlivery; re͵cording ͵studio
record n, adj ˈrek ɔːd -əd ‖ -ərd **~s** z
  ˈrecord ͵library; ˈrecord ͵player
record-break|er/s ˈrek ɔːd ͵breɪk ə/z §-əd-,
  →ˈˌ•ə:b- ‖ -ərd ͵breɪk ər/z **~ing** ɪŋ
recorder rɪ ˈkɔːd ə rə-, §riː- ‖ -ˈkɔːrd ər **~s** z
  ~ship ʃɪp
recordist rɪ ˈkɔːd ɪst rə-, §riː:-, §-əst ‖ -ˈkɔːrd-
  ~s s
re|count v 'tell' rɪ ‖ˈkaʊnt rə-, §riː:- **~counted**
  ˈkaʊnt ɪd -əd ‖ ˈkaʊnt̬ əd **~counting**
  ˈkaʊnt ɪŋ ‖ ˈkaʊnt̬ ɪŋ **~counts** ˈkaʊnts
re|count v 'count again' ˌriː ‖ˈkaʊnt **~counted**
  ˈkaʊnt ɪd -əd ‖ ˈkaʊnt̬ əd **~counting**
  ˈkaʊnt ɪŋ ‖ ˈkaʊnt̬ ɪŋ **~counts** ˈkaʊnts
recount n ˈriː kaʊnt ˌˈˈ **~s** s
recoup rɪ ˈkuːp rə-, §riː:- **~ed** t **~ing** ɪŋ
  ~ment mənt **~s** s
recourse rɪ ˈkɔːs rə-, §riː:- ‖ ˈriː kɔːrs -koʊrs;
  rɪ ˈˈ (*)
recov|er 'regain; find again; get better' rɪ ˈkʌv ə
  rə-, §riː:- ‖ -ər **~ered** əd ‖ ərd **~ering** ər_ɪŋ
  ~ers əz ‖ ərz
recov|er 'cover again' ˌriː ˈkʌv ə ‖ -ər **~ered**
  əd ‖ ərd **~ering** ər_ɪŋ **~ers** əz ‖ ərz
recoverability rɪ ˌkʌv ər_ə ˈbɪl ət i rə-, §riː:-,
  -ɪt i ‖ -ət̬ i
recoverable rɪ ˈkʌv ər_əb əl rə-, §riː:-
recover|y rɪ ˈkʌv ər_li rə-, §riː:- **~ies** iz
  reˈcovery room
recreant ˈrek ri_ənt **~s** s
recre|ate 'create anew' ˌriː kri ˈeɪt **~ated**
  ˈeɪt ɪd -əd ‖ ˈeɪt̬ əd **~ates** ˈeɪts **~ating**
  ˈeɪt ɪŋ ‖ ˈeɪt̬ ɪŋ
recreation 'amusement' ˌrek ri ˈeɪʃ ən **~s** z
  ͵recreˈation ground; ͵recreˈation room
recreation 'creating anew' ˌriː kri ˈeɪʃ ən
recreational ˌrek ri ˈeɪʃ ən_əl
recrimi|nate rɪ ˈkrɪm ɪ ‖neɪt rə-, §riː:-, -ə-
  ~nated neɪt ɪd -əd ‖ neɪt̬ əd **~nates** neɪts
  ~nating neɪt ɪŋ ‖ neɪt̬ ɪŋ
recrimination rɪ ˌkrɪm ɪ ˈneɪʃ ən rə-, §riː:-, -ə-
  ~s z
recriminatory rɪ ˈkrɪm ɪn ət_ər i rə-, §riː:-,
  -ˈˈ•ən_; •,•ɪ ˈneɪt ər i ◄, -ə'•- ‖ -ən_ə tɔːr i
  -toʊr i
recrudesc|e ˌriː kruː ˈdes ˌrek ruː- **~ed** t **~es**
  ɪz əz **~ing** ɪŋ
recrudescenc|e ˌriː kruː ˈdes ənts ˌrek ruː- **~es**
  ɪz əz

recrudescent ˌriː kruː ˈdes ənt ◄ ˌrek ruː:-
re|cruit v, n rɪ ‖ˈkruːt rə-, §riː:- **~cruited**
  ˈkruːt ɪd -əd ‖ ˈkruːt̬ əd **~cruiting**
  ˈkruːt ɪŋ ‖ ˈkruːt̬ ɪŋ **~cruits** ˈkruːts
recruitment rɪ ˈkruːt mənt rə-, §riː:-
rectal ˈrekt əl **~ly** i
rectangle ˈrek tæŋ ɡəl **~s** z
rectangular rek ˈtæŋ ɡjʊl ə -ɡjəl- ‖ -ɡjəl ər
  ~ly li
rectifiable ˈrekt ɪ faɪ_əb əl,•ə-, ͵••ˈ•••
rectification ˌrekt ɪf ɪ ˈkeɪʃ ən ͵•əf-, §-ə'•- **~s**
  z
recti|fy ˈrekt ɪ ‖faɪ -ə- **~fied** faɪd **~fier/s**
  faɪ_ə/z ‖ faɪ_ər/z **~fies** faɪz **~fying** faɪ ɪŋ
rectilinear ˌrekt ɪ ˈlɪn i_ə ◄ ,•ə- ‖ _ər **~ly** li
rectitude ˈrekt ɪ tjuːd -ə-, →§-tʃuːd ‖ -tuːd
  -tjuːd
recto ˈrekt əʊ ‖ -oʊ **~s** z
rector ˈrekt ə ‖ -ər **~s** z **~ship/s** ʃɪp/s
rectorial rek ˈtɔːr i_əl ‖ -ˈtoʊr-
rector|y ˈrekt ər_li **~ies** iz
rectrix ˈrek trɪks **rectrices** ˈrek trɪ siːz -trə-;
  rek ˈtraɪs iːz
rectum ˈrekt əm **~s** z
Reculver rɪ ˈkʌlv ə rə-, §riː:- ‖ -ər
recumbent rɪ ˈkʌm bənt rə-, §riː:- **~ly** li
recupe|rate rɪ ˈkjuːp ə ‖reɪt rə-, §riː:-, -ˈkuːp-
  ~rated reɪt ɪd -əd ‖ reɪt̬ əd **~rates** reɪts
  ~rating reɪt ɪŋ ‖ reɪt̬ ɪŋ
recuperation rɪ ˌkjuːp ə ˈreɪʃ ən rə-, §riː:-,
  -ˌkuːp-
recuperative rɪ ˈkjuːp ər_ət ɪv rə-, §riː:-,
  -ˈkuːp-, -ə reɪt- ‖ -ə reɪt̬ ɪv -ər_ət̬ ɪv
recur rɪ ˈkɜː rə-, §riː:- ‖ -ˈkɜː: **~red** d
  recurring rɪ ˈkɜːr ɪŋ rə-, §riː:- ‖ -ˈkɜː: ɪŋ **~s** z
recurrenc|e rɪ ˈkʌr ənts rə-, §riː:-, §-ˈkɜːr-
  ‖ -ˈkɜː: ənts **~es** ɪz əz
recurrent rɪ ˈkʌr ənt rə-, §riː:-, §-ˈkɜːr-
  ‖ -ˈkɜː: ənt **~ly** li
recursion rɪ ˈkɜːʃ ən rə, §riː:-, §-ˈkɜːʒ-
  ‖ -ˈkɜː:ʒ ən **~s** z
recursive rɪ ˈkɜːs ɪv rə-, §riː:- ‖ -ˈkɜː:s ɪv **~ly** li
  ~ness nəs nɪs
recurved ˌriː ˈkɜːvd rɪ-, rə- ‖ -ˈkɜː:vd
recusancy ˈrek jʊz ənts i rɪ ˈkjuːz-, rə-, §riː:-
  ‖ -jəz-
recusant ˈrek jʊz ənt rɪ ˈkjuːz-, rə-, §riː:-
  ‖ -jəz- **~s** s
recyclable ˌriː ˈsaɪk əl_əb əl ◄
recycl|e ˌriː ˈsaɪk əl **~ed** d **~es** z **~ing** _ɪŋ
red, Red red **redder** ˈred ə ‖ -ər **reddest**
  ˈred ɪst -əst **reds, Reds** redz
  ͵red ˈadmiral; ͵red aˈlert; ͵red ˈblood cell;
  ͵rectal ˈcarpet; ͵Red ˈCrescent; ͵Red ˈCross;
  ͵red ˈdeer; ͵red ˈdwarf; (͵)Red ˈEnsign; ͵red
  ˈflag; ͵red ˈgiant; ͵red ˈherring; ͵Red
  ˈIndian; ͵red ˈlight; ͵red ˈmeat; ͵red
  ˈpepper; ͵Red ˈSea; ͵red ˈsetter; ͵red ˈtape
redact rɪ ˈdækt rə-, §riː:- **~ed** ɪd əd **~ing** ɪŋ **~s**
  s
redaction rɪ ˈdæk ʃən rə-, §riː:- **~s** z
redan rɪ ˈdæn rə-, §riː:- **~s** z
redback ˈred bæk →ˈreb- **~s** s

R

R

red-blooded ,red 'blʌd ɪd ◄→,reb-, -əd ~**ness**
  nəs nɪs
Redbourn, Redbourne 'red bɔːn →'reb-
  ‖ -bɔːrn -boʊrn
redbreast 'red brest →'reb- ~**s** s
redbrick 'red brɪk →'reb-, ,•'• ~**s** s
Redbridge 'red brɪdʒ →'reb-
redbud 'red bʌd →'reb- ~**s** z
redcap 'red kæp →'reg- ~**s** s
Redcar 'red kɑː →'reg- ‖ -kɑːr
Redcliffe 'red klɪf →'reg-
redcoat 'red kəʊt →'reg- ‖ -koʊt ~**s** s
redcurrant ,red 'kʌr ənt ◄→,reg-, '•,••
  ‖ -'kɝ: ənt ~**s** s
Reddaway 'red ə weɪ
redden 'red ən ~**ed** d ~**ing** _ɪŋ ~**s** z
Redding 'red ɪŋ
reddish, R~ 'red ɪʃ ~**ness** nəs nɪs
Redditch 'red ɪtʃ
redeco|rate ⓤ,riː 'dek ə |reɪt ~**rated** reɪt ɪd -əd
  ‖ reɪt̬ əd ~**rates** reɪts ~**rating**
  reɪt ɪŋ ‖ reɪt̬ ɪŋ
redecoration riː ,dek ə 'reɪʃ ən ,•,••'•• ~**s** z
redeem rɪ 'diːm rə-, §riː- ~**ed** d ~**ing** ɪŋ ~**s** z
redeemable rɪ 'diːm əb əl rə-, §riː-
redeemer, R~ rɪ 'diːm ə rə-, §riː- ‖ -ər ~**s** z
redefin|e ,riː dɪ 'faɪn -də-, §-diː- ~**ed** d ~**es** z
  ~**ing** ɪŋ
redemption rɪ 'demp ʃən rə-, §riː- ~**s** z
redemptive rɪ 'dempt ɪv rə-, §riː- ~**ly** li
Redemptorist rɪ 'dempt ər_ɪst rə-, §riː-, §_ əst
  ~**s** s
redeploy ,riː dɪ 'plɔɪ -də-, §-diː- ~**ed** d ~**ing**
  ɪŋ ~**ment** mənt ~**s** z
Redesdale 'riːdz deɪəl
redevelop ,riː dɪ 'vel əp -də-, §-diː- ~**ed** t
  ~**ing** ɪŋ ~**ment/s** mənt/s ~**s** s
redeye 'red aɪ ~**s** z
red-faced ,red 'feɪst ◄
red-facedly ,red 'feɪs ɪd li -əd-; -'feɪst li
Redfearn, Redfern 'red fɜːn ‖ -fɝːn
redfin 'red fɪn ~**s** z
Redford 'red fəd ‖ -fərd
Redgrave 'red greɪv →'reg-
red-handed ,red 'hænd ɪd ◄ -əd ~**ly** li
redhead, R~ 'red hed ~**s** z
Redheugh (i) 'red hjuːf, (ii) -juːf, (iii) -jəf
Redhill ,red 'hɪl
red-hot ,red 'hɒt ◄ ‖ -'hɑːt ◄
  ,red-hot 'poker
redi|a 'riːd i_|ə ~**ae** iː
redial ,riː 'daɪ_əl ◄ ~**ed**, ~**led** d ~**ing**, ~**ling**
  ɪŋ ~**s** z
redid ,riː 'dɪd
Rediffusion tdmk ,riː dɪ 'fjuːʒ ən -də-
redirect ,riː də 'rekt -dɪ-, -daɪə- ~**ed** ɪd əd
  ~**ing** ɪŋ ~**s** s
redirection ,riː də 'rek ʃən -dɪ-, -daɪə-
redistribute ,riː dɪ 'strɪb juːt -də-;
  ,riː 'dɪs trɪ bjuːt, -trə- ‖ -jət **redistributed**
  ,riː dɪ 'strɪb jʊt ɪd ,•də-, -əd; -'dɪs trɪ bjuːt-,
  -'•trə- ‖ -jət̬ əd **redistributes**
  ,riː dɪ 'strɪb juːts -də-; -'dɪs trɪ bjuːts, -trə-

redistributing ,riː dɪ 'strɪb jʊt ɪŋ ,•də-;
  -'dɪs trɪ bjuːt-, -'•trə- ‖ -jət̬ ɪŋ
redistribution ,riː ,dɪs trɪ 'bjuːʃ ən -trə- ~**s** z
redivivus ,red ɪ 'vaɪv əs -ə-, -'viːv-
red-letter ,red 'let ə ‖ -'let̬ ər
  ,red-'letter day
red-light ,red 'laɪt
  ,red-'light ,district
redly 'red li
Redman 'red mən →'reb-
Redmond 'red mənd →'reb-
redneck 'red nek ~**s** s
redness 'red nəs -nɪs ~**es** ɪz əz
redo ,riː 'duː **redid** ,riː 'dɪd **redoes** ,riː 'dʌz
  redoing ,riː 'duː_ɪŋ **redone** ,riː 'dʌn
redolenc|e 'red əl ən¹s -əʊl- ~**y** i
redolent 'red əl ənt -əʊl- ~**ly** li
redoubl|e ,riː 'dʌb əl rɪ-, rə- ~**ed** d ~**es** z
  ~**ing** _ɪŋ
redoubt rɪ 'daʊt rə-, §riː- ~**s** s
redoubtab|le rɪ 'daʊt əb əl rə-, §riː:- ‖ -'daʊt̬-
  ~**ly** li
redound rɪ 'daʊnd rə-, §riː:- ~**ed** ɪd əd ~**ing** ɪŋ
  ~**s** z
redox 'riːd ɒks 'red- ‖ -ɑːks
Redpath 'red pɑːθ →'reb-, §-pæθ ‖ -pæθ
redpoll 'red pəʊl →'reb-, →-pɒʊl, -pɒl ‖ -poʊl
  ~**s** z
redraft v ,riː 'drɑːft §-'dræft ‖ -'dræft ~**ed** ɪd
  əd ~**ing** ɪŋ ~**s** s
redraft n 'riː drɑːft §-dræft ‖ -dræft ~**s** s
redress v 'put right' rɪ 'dres rə-, §riː:- ~**ed** t
  ~**es** ɪz əz ~**ing** ɪŋ
redress n 'satisfaction' rɪ 'dres rə-, §riː:-;
  'riː dres
Redruth ,red 'ruːθ '••
redshank 'red ʃæŋk ~**s** s
redskin 'red skɪn ~**s** z
redstart 'red stɑːt ‖ -stɑːrt ~**s** s
reduc|e rɪ 'djuːs rə-, §riː:-, →§-'dʒuːs ‖ -'duːs
  -'djuːs ~**ed** t ~**es** ɪz əz ~**ing** ɪŋ
  re,duced 'circumstances
reducer rɪ 'djuːs ə rə-, §riː:-, →-'dʒuːs-
  ‖ -'duːs ər -'djuːs- ~**s** z
reducibility rɪ ,djuːs ə 'bɪl ət i rə-, §riː:-,
  →-,dʒuːs-, -ɪt i ‖ rɪ ,duːs ə 'bɪl ət̬ i -,djuːs-
reducib|le rɪ 'djuːs əb əl rə-, §riː:-, →§-'dʒuːs-,
  -ɪb- ‖ -'duːs- -'djuːs- ~**ly** li
reductase rɪ 'dʌkt eɪz rə-, §riː:-, -eɪs
reductio ad absurdum
  rɪ ,dʌkt i əʊ ,æd əb 'sɜːd əm rə-, §riː:-,
  -,dʌkʃ-, -æb'•- ‖ -oʊ ,æd əb 'sɝ:d əm
reduction rɪ 'dʌk ʃən rə-, §riː:- ~**ism** ,ɪz əm
  ~**ist/s** ɪst/s §əst/s ‖ əst/s ~**s** z
reductive rɪ 'dʌkt ɪv rə-, §riː:-
redundanc|y rɪ 'dʌnd ən¹s li rə-, §riː:- ~**ies** iz
redundant rɪ 'dʌnd ənt rə-, §riː:- ~**ly** li
redupli|cate rɪ 'djuːp lɪ |keɪt rə-, ,riː-,
  →§-'dʒuːp-, -lə- ‖ -'duːp- -'djuːp- ~**cated**
  keɪt ɪd -əd ‖ keɪt̬ əd ~**cates** keɪts ~**cating**
  keɪt ɪŋ ‖ keɪt̬ ɪŋ
reduplication rɪ ,djuːp lɪ 'keɪʃ ən rə-,

→§-,dʒuːp-, ˌriː, • • ' • •, -lə- ‖ -ˌduːp-
-ˌdjuːp- ~s z

reduplicative rɪ 'djuːp lɪk ət ɪv rə-, §riː-,
→-'dʒuːp-, -lək • •; -lɪ keɪt ɪv, -lə • •
‖ rɪ 'duːp lə keɪt ɪv -'djuːp-

Redvers 'red vəz ‖ -vᵊrz

redwing, R~ 'red wɪŋ ~s z

redwood, R~ 'red wʊd ~s z

Ree riː

Rée reɪ

reebok, R~ _tdmk_ 'riː bɒk -bʌk ‖ -baːk ~s s

Reece riːs

reecho ri 'ek əʊ ˌriː- ‖ -oʊ ~ed d ~es z ~ing
ɪŋ

reed, Reed riːd **reeded** 'riːd ɪd -əd **reeding/s**
'riːd ɪŋ/z **reeds** riːdz
   'reed ˌorgan

reedling 'riːd lɪŋ ~s z

reedu|cate ˌriː 'ed ju |keɪt ri' • -, -'edʒ u-,
§-'edʒ ə- ‖ -'edʒ ə- ~**cated** keɪt ɪd -əd
‖ keɪt̬ əd ~**cates** keɪts ~**cating**
keɪt ɪŋ ‖ keɪt̬ ɪŋ

reeducation ˌriː ˌed ju 'keɪʃ ᵊn ri, • -, -ˌedʒ u-,
§-ˌedʒ ə- ‖ -ˌedʒ ə- • , • • ' • •

reed|y 'riːd li ~**ier** i‿ə ‖ i‿ᵊr ~**iest** i‿ɪst i‿əst
~**iness** i nəs i nɪs

reef riːf **reefed** riːft **reefing** 'riːf ɪŋ **reefs**
riːfs
   'reef knot

reefer 'riːf ə ‖ -ᵊr ~s z
   'reefer ˌjacket

reek riːk **reeked** riːkt **reeking** 'riːk ɪŋ **reeks**
riːks

Reekie 'riːk i

reel riːᵊl **reeled** riːᵊld **reeling** 'riːᵊl ɪŋ **reels**
riːᵊlz

reelect ˌriː ɪ 'lekt -ə- ~**ed** ɪd əd ~**ing** ɪŋ ~s s

reelection ˌriː ɪ 'lek ʃᵊn -ə- ~s z

reel-to-reel ˌriːᵊl tə 'riːᵊl ◄

re-enact ˌriː ɪn 'ækt en-, -ən- ~**ed** ɪd əd
~**ing** ɪŋ ~**ment/s** mənt/s ~s s

reenter, re-enter ri 'ent ə ˌriː- ‖ -'ent̬ ᵊr ~**ed**
d **reentering, re-entering** ri 'ent ‿ər ɪŋ ˌriː-
‖ -'ent̬ ‿ər ɪŋ →-'entr ɪŋ

reentrant, re-entrant ri 'entr ənt ~s s

reentr|y, re-entr|y ri 'entr li ˌriː- ~**ies** iz

Reepham 'riːf əm

Rees, Reese riːs _(!)_

reestablish ˌriː ɪ 'stæb lɪʃ -ə- ~**ed** t ~**es** ɪz əz
~**ing** ɪŋ ~**ment** mənt

reeve, Reeve riːv **reeved** riːvd **reeves** riːvz
reeving 'riːv ɪŋ **rove** rəʊv ‖ roʊv

Reeves riːvz

reexamination ˌriː ɪg ˌzæm ɪ 'neɪʃ ᵊn , • eg-,
ˌ • əg-, • ɪk-, • ek-, • ək-, -ə' • - ~s z

reexamin|e ˌriː ɪg 'zæm ɪn -eg-, -əg-, -ɪk-, -ek-,
-ək-, §-ᵊn ~**ed** d ~**es** z ~**ing** ɪŋ

ref ref **refs** refs

refac|e ₍ˌ₎riː 'feɪs ~**ed** t ~**es** ɪz əz ~**ing** ɪŋ

refashion ₍ˌ₎riː 'fæʃ ᵊn ~**ed** d ~**ing** ‿ɪŋ ~s z

refector|y rɪ 'fekt ᵊr‿li rə-, §riː-; 'ref ɪkt-,
'ref əkt- ~**ies** iz

refer rɪ 'fɜː rə-, §riː- ‖ -'fɜː: ~**red** d **referring**
rɪ 'fɜː ɪŋ rə-, §riː- ‖ -'fɜː: ɪŋ ~s z

referable rɪ 'fɜːr əb əl rə-, §riː-; 'ref ᵊr‿əb əl
‖ -'fɜː:-

referee ˌref ə 'riː ~**d** d ~**ing** ɪŋ ~s z

referenc|e 'ref ᵊr‿ᵊnts ~**ed** t ~**es** ɪz əz ~**ing**
ɪŋ
   'reference ˌbook; 'reference ˌlibrary

referend|um ˌref ə 'rend |əm ~**a** ə ~**ums** əmz

referent 'ref ᵊr‿ᵊnt ~s s

referential ˌref ə 'rent ʃ ᵊl ◄ ~**ly** i

referrab... —_see_ **referab...**

referral rɪ 'fɜːr ᵊl rə-, §riː- ‖ -'fɜː: ᵊl ~s z

reffo 'ref əʊ ‖ -oʊ ~s z

refill _v_ ₍ˌ₎riː 'fɪl ~**ed** d ~**ing** ɪŋ ~s z

refill _n_ 'riː fɪl , • ' • ~s z

refin|e rɪ 'faɪn rə-, §riː- ~**ed** d ~**es** z ~**ing** ɪŋ

refinement rɪ 'faɪn mənt rə-, §riː-, →-'faɪm-
~s s

refiner rɪ 'faɪn ə rə-, §riː- ‖ -ᵊr ~s z

refiner|y rɪ 'faɪn ᵊr‿li rə-, §riː- ~**ies** iz

re|fit _v_ ₍ˌ₎riː 'fɪt ~**fits** 'fɪts ~**fitted** 'fɪt ɪd -əd
‖ 'fɪt̬ əd ~**fitting** 'fɪt ɪŋ ‖ 'fɪt̬ ɪŋ

refit _n_ 'riː fɪt , • ' • ~s s

re|flate ₍ˌ₎riː 'fleɪt ~**flated** 'fleɪt ɪd -əd
‖ 'fleɪt̬ əd ~**flates** 'fleɪts ~**flating**
'fleɪt ɪŋ ‖ 'fleɪt̬ ɪŋ

reflation ₍ˌ₎riː 'fleɪʃ ᵊn ~s z

reflationary ₍ˌ₎riː 'fleɪʃ ᵊn ᵊr i -ᵊn‿ər i ‖ -ə ner i

reflect rɪ 'flekt rə-, §riː- ~**ed** ɪd əd ~**ing** ɪŋ ~s
s
   re'flecting ˌtelescope

reflection rɪ 'flek ʃᵊn rə-, §riː- ~s z

reflective rɪ 'flekt ɪv rə-, §riː- ~**ly** li ~**ness** nəs
nɪs

reflectivit|y ˌriː flek 'tɪv ət li rɪ, • ' • • •, rə-,
§riː-; -ɪt i ‖ -ət̬ li ~**ies** iz

reflector rɪ 'flekt ə rə-, §riː- ‖ -ᵊr ~s z

reflet rə 'fleɪ rɪ- ~s z —_Fr_ [ʁə flɛ]

reflex _n, adj_ 'riː fleks ~**es** ɪz əz

reflex _v_ rɪ 'fleks rə-, ˌriː-, 'riː fleks ~**ed** t ~**es**
ɪz əz ~**ing** ɪŋ

reflexion rɪ 'flek ʃᵊn rə-, §riː- ~s z

reflexive rɪ 'fleks ɪv rə-, §riː- ~**ly** li ~**ness** nəs
nɪs ~s z
   re,flexive 'pronoun

reflexivis... —_see_ **reflexiviz...**

reflexivity ˌriː flek 'sɪv ət i rɪ, • ' • • •, rə-, §riː-,
-ɪt i ‖ -ət̬ i

reflexivization rɪ ˌfleks ɪv aɪ 'zeɪʃ ᵊn rə-, §riː-,
-, • əv-, -ɪ ' • - ‖ -ə' • - ~s z

reflexiviz|e rɪ 'fleks ɪ vaɪz rə-, §riː-, -ə- ~**ed** d
~**es** ɪz əz ~**ing** ɪŋ

reflexology ˌriː flek 'sɒl ədʒ i ‖ -'saːl-

re|float ₍ˌ₎riː |'fləʊt ‖ -'floʊt ~**floated** 'fləʊt ɪd
-əd ‖ 'floʊt̬ əd ~**floating** 'fləʊt ɪŋ ‖ 'floʊt̬ ɪŋ
~**floats** 'fləʊts ‖ 'floʊts

refluent 'ref lu‿ənt

reflux _n_ 'riː flʌks ~**es** ɪz əz

reforest ₍ˌ₎riː 'fɒr ɪst -əst ‖ -'fɔːr əst -'faːr-
~**ed** ɪd əd ~**ing** ɪŋ ~s s

reforestation riː ˌfɒr ɪ 'steɪʃ ᵊn , • , • • ' • • •, -ə' • -
‖ -ˌfɔːr- -ˌfaːr- ~s z

R

reform *v* *'improve, rectify'* ; *n* rɪ 'fɔːm rə-, §riː-
‖ -'fɔːrm ~**ed** d ~**ing** ɪŋ ~**s** z
reform, re-form *v* *'form again'*
ˌriː 'fɔːm ‖ -'fɔːrm ~**ed** d ~**ing** ɪŋ ~**s** z
reform|at ˌriː 'fɔːm læt ‖ -'fɔːrm- ~**ats** æts
~**atted** æt ɪd -əd ‖ æt̬ əd ~**atting**
æt ɪŋ ‖ æt̬ ɪŋ
reformation, R~ ˌref ə 'meɪʃ ᵊn -ɔː- ‖ -ᵊr- ~**s** z
reformative rɪ 'fɔːm ət ɪv rə-, §riː-
‖ -'fɔːrm ət̬ ɪv
reformator|y rɪ 'fɔːm ət‿ᵊr_i rə-, §riː-
‖ -'fɔːrm ə tɔːr i -tour i -**tour** i ~**ies** iz
reformism rɪ 'fɔːm ˌɪz əm rə-, §riː- ‖ -'fɔːrm-
reformist rɪ 'fɔːm ɪst rə-, §riː-, §-əst ‖ -'fɔːrm-
~**s** s
refract rɪ 'frækt rə-, §riː- ~**ed** ɪd əd ~**ing** ɪŋ
~**s** s
re'fracting ˌtelescope
refraction rɪ 'fræk ʃᵊn rə-, §riː- ~**s** z
refractive rɪ 'frækt ɪv rə-, §riː- ~**ly** li ~**ness**
nəs nɪs
re ˌfractive 'index
refractivity ˌriː fræk 'tɪv ət i rɪ,•'•••, rə-,
§riː-, -ɪt ‖ -ət̬ i
refractometer ˌriː fræk 'tɒm ɪt ə rɪ,•'•••, rə-,
§riː-, -ət ə ‖ -'tɑːm ət̬ ᵊr ~**s** z
refractor rɪ 'frækt ə rə-, §riː- ‖ -ᵊr ~**s** z
refractor|y rɪ 'frækt ᵊr_li rə-, §riː- ~**ies** iz ~**ily**
əl i ɪ li ~**iness** i nəs i nɪs
refrain *v, n* rɪ 'freɪn rə-, §riː- ~**ed** d ~**ing** ɪŋ
~**s** z
refresh rɪ 'freʃ rə-, §riː- ~**ed** t ~**er/s** ə/z ‖ ᵊr/z
~**es** ɪz əz ~**ing/ly** ɪŋ /li
re'fresher course
refreshment rɪ 'freʃ mənt rə-, §riː- ~**s** s
refried ˌriː 'fraɪd ◄
refrigerant rɪ 'frɪdʒ ᵊr‿ənt rə-, §riː- ~**s** s
refrige|rate rɪ 'frɪdʒ ə |reɪt rə-, §riː- ~**rated**
reɪt ɪd -əd ‖ reɪt̬ əd ~**rates** reɪts ~**rating**
reɪt ɪŋ ‖ reɪt̬ ɪŋ
refrigeration rɪ ˌfrɪdʒ ə 'reɪʃ ᵊn rə-, §riː-
refrigerator rɪ 'frɪdʒ ə reɪt ə rə-, §riː- ‖ -reɪt̬ ᵊr
~**s** z
re ˌfrigerator-'freezer, •'••••,••
reft reft
refuel ˌriː 'fjuː_əl ,•'fjuː|l ~**ed, -led** d ~**ing,**
~**ling** ɪŋ ~**s** z
refug|e 'ref juːdʒ -juːʒ ~**es** ɪz əz
refugee ˌref ju 'dʒiː ~**s** z
refulgence rɪ 'fʌldʒ ᵊn⁀s rə-, §riː-, -'fʊldʒ-
refulgent rɪ 'fʌldʒ ənt rə-, §riː-, -'fʊldʒ- ~**ly** li
refund *v* rɪ 'fʌnd rə-, ₍₎riː-, 'riː fʌnd ~**ed** ɪd əd
~**ing** ɪŋ ~**s** z
refund *n* 'riː fʌnd ~**s** z
refurbish ₍₎riː 'fɜːb ɪʃ ‖ -'fɜːb ɪʃ ~**ed** t ~**es** ɪz
əz ~**ing** ɪŋ ~**ment/s** mənt/s
refusal rɪ 'fjuːz ᵊl rə-, §riː- ~**s** z
refus|e *v* rɪ 'fjuːz rə-, §riː- ~**ed** d ~**es** ɪz əz
~**ing** ɪŋ
refuse *n* 'ref juːs (!)
'refuse dump
refusenik rɪ 'fjuːz nɪk rə-, §riː- ~**s** s

refutable rɪ 'fjuːt əb ᵊl rə-, §riː-; 'ref jʊt-
‖ rɪ 'fjuːt̬- 'ref jət̬-
refutation ˌref ju 'teɪʃ ᵊn ~**s** z
re|fute rɪ |'fjuːt rə-, §riː- ~**futed** 'fjuːt ɪd -əd
‖ 'fjuːt̬ əd ~**futes** 'fjuːts ~**futing**
'fjuːt ɪŋ ‖ 'fjuːt̬ ɪŋ
Reg redʒ (!) **Reg's** 'redʒ ɪz -əz
-reg *BrE stress-neutral suffix relating to age of*
cars redʒ— **S-reg** 'es redʒ
regain rɪ 'geɪn rə-, ˌriː- ~**ed** d ~**ing** ɪŋ ~**s** z
regal 'riːg ᵊl
regal|e rɪ 'geɪᵊl rə-, §riː- ~**ed** d ~**es** z ~**ing** ɪŋ
regalia rɪ 'geɪl i_ə rə-, §riː- ‖ •'•_jə
regalit|y riː 'gæl ət i rɪ-, -ɪt- ‖ -ət̬ li ~**ies** iz
regally 'riːg ᵊl i
Regan 'riːg ən
regard *v, n* rɪ 'gɑːd rə-, §riː- ‖ -'gɑːrd ~**ed** ɪd
əd ~**ing** ɪŋ ~**s** z
regardful rɪ 'gɑːd fᵊl rə-, §riː-, -fʊl ‖ -'gɑːrd-
~**ly** _i ~**ness** nəs nɪs
regardless rɪ 'gɑːd ləs rə-, §riː-, -lɪs ‖ -'gɑːrd-
~**ly** li ~**ness** nəs nɪs
regatta rɪ 'gæt ə rə- ‖ -'gæt̬ ə -'gɑːt̬- ~**s** z
regenc|y, R~ 'riːdʒ ᵊn⁀s li ~**ies** iz
regenerate *adj* rɪ 'dʒen ᵊr‿ət rə-, ˌriː-, -ɪt,
-ə reɪt ~**ness** nəs nɪs
regene|rate *v* rɪ 'dʒen ə |reɪt rə-, ˌriː- ~**rated**
reɪt ɪd -əd ‖ reɪt̬ əd ~**rates** reɪts ~**rating**
reɪt ɪŋ ‖ reɪt̬ ɪŋ
regeneration rɪ ˌdʒen ə 'reɪʃ ᵊn rə-, ˌriː:,••'••
~**s** z
regenerative rɪ 'dʒen ᵊr‿ət ɪv rə-, §riː-,
§-ə reɪt ɪv ‖ -ᵊr‿ət̬ ɪv -ə reɪt̬ ɪv ~**ly** li
Regensburg 'reɪg ᵊnz bɜːg -bʊəg ‖ -bɜːg
—*Ger* ['ʁeː gᵊns bʊʁk]
regent, R~ 'riːdʒ ənt ~**s** -s, ~'**s** s ~**ship/s** ʃɪp/s
ˌRegent's 'Park; 'Regent Street
reggae 'reg eɪ
Reggie 'redʒ i
Reggio 'redʒ i əʊ ‖ -oʊ —*It* ['red dʒo]
regicide 'redʒ ɪ saɪd -ə- ~**s** z
regime, régime reɪ 'ʒiːm re-, rɪ-, rə-, §-'dʒiːm;
'reɪʒ iːm ‖ rə- —*Fr* [ʁe ʒim] ~**s** z
regimen 'redʒ ɪm ən -əm-; -ɪ men, -ə- ~**s** z
regiment *n* 'redʒ ɪ mənt -ə- ~**s** s
regi|ment *v* 'redʒ ɪ |ment -ə-, ,••'|• —*See note*
at -ment ~**mented** ment ɪd -əd ‖ ment̬ əd
~**menting** ment ɪŋ ‖ ment̬ ɪŋ ~**ments** men⁀ts
regimental ˌredʒ ɪ 'ment ᵊl ◄ -ə- ‖ -'ment̬ ᵊl ◄
~**ly** i ~**s** z
regimentation ˌredʒ ɪ men 'teɪʃ ᵊn ,•ə-,
-mən'•-
Regina rɪ 'dʒaɪn ə rə-, §riː- —*but as a personal*
name, sometimes -'dʒiː n-
Reginald 'redʒ ɪn əld -ᵊn_əld
region 'riːdʒ ᵊn ~**s** z
regional 'riːdʒ ᵊn_ᵊl
regionalism 'riːdʒ ᵊn_ə ˌlɪz əm
regionality ˌriːdʒ ə 'næl ət i -ɪt i ‖ -ət̬ i
regionally 'riːdʒ ᵊn_ᵊl i
Regis 'riːdʒ ɪs §-əs
register 'redʒ ɪst ə -əst- ‖ -ᵊr ~**ed** d
registering 'redʒ ɪst ᵊr‿ɪŋ '•əst- ~**s** z

,Registered ,General 'Nurse; ,Registered 'Nurse; ,registered 'mail; ,registered 'post; 'register ,office

registrable 'redʒ ɪs trəb ᵊl '•əs-

registrant 'redʒ ɪs trənt -əs- **~s** s

registrar ,redʒ ɪ 'strɑː -ə-, '•••‖ 'redʒ ə strɑːr **~s** z

registrar|y 'redʒ ɪs trər li '•əs- ‖ -trer li **~ies** iz

registration ,redʒ ɪ 'streɪʃ ᵊn -ə- **~s** z ,regi'stration ,document; ,regi'stration ,number

regis|try 'redʒ ɪs |tri -əs- **~tries** triz 'registry ,office

Regius 'riːdʒ i‿əs 'riːdʒ əs

reglet 'reg lət -lɪt **~s** s

regnal 'reg nᵊl

regnant 'reg nənt

rego 'redʒ əʊ ‖ -oʊ

regress *v* rɪ 'gres rə-, ,riː- **~ed** t **~es** ɪz əz **~ing** ɪŋ

regress *n* 'riː gres

regression rɪ 'greʃ ᵊn rə-, ,riː- **~s** z re'gression a,nalysis

regressive rɪ 'gres ɪv rə-, ,riː- **~ly** li **~ness** nəs nɪs

re|gret *v, n* rɪ ‖'gret rə-, §riː- **~grets** 'grets **~gretted** 'gret ɪd -əd ‖ 'greṭ əd **~gretting** 'gret ɪŋ ‖ 'greṭ ɪŋ

regretful rɪ 'gret fᵊl rə-, §riː-, -fʊl **~ly** _i **~ness** nəs nɪs

regrettab|le rɪ 'gret əb |ᵊl rə-, §riː- ‖ -'greṭ- **~ly** li

regrett... —*see* **regret...**

regroup ,riː 'gruːp **~ed** t **~ing** ɪŋ **~s** s

regular 'reg jʊl ə -jəl-, ⚠-əl‿ə ‖ -jəl ᵊr **~s** z

regularis... —*see* **regulariz...**

regularit|y ,reg ju 'lær ət li ,•jə-, ⚠'•ə-, -ɪt i ‖ -jə 'lær əṭ li -'ler- **~ies** iz

regularization ,reg jʊl ər aɪ 'zeɪʃ ᵊn ,•jəl-, ⚠,•əl‿, -ɪ'•- ‖ -jəl ər ə- **~s** z

regulariz|e 'reg jʊl ə raɪz '•jəl-, ⚠'•əl‿ ‖ '•jəl- **~ed** d **~es** ɪz əz **~ing** ɪŋ

regularly 'reg jʊl ə li '•jəl-, ⚠'•əl‿əl i ‖ -jəl ᵊr li

regu|late 'reg ju |leɪt -jə-, §-ə- ‖ -jə- **~lated** leɪt ɪd -əd ‖ leɪṭ əd **~lates** leɪts **~lating** leɪt ɪŋ ‖ leɪṭ ɪŋ

regulation ,reg ju 'leɪʃ ᵊn -jə-, ⚠-ə- ‖ -jə- **~s** z

regulative 'reg jʊl ət ɪv '•jəl-; -ju leɪt ɪv ‖ -jə leɪṭ ɪv -jəl əṭ-

regulator 'reg ju leɪt ə '•jə-, ⚠'•ə- ‖ -jə leɪṭ ᵊr **~s** z

REGULATORY

BrE 1998					
0	20	40	60	80	100%

■-'leɪt- ▨'•-lət- ■'•-leɪt-•

regulatory ,reg ju 'leɪt ər i ,•jə-, ⚠,•ə-, '••••, '••lət‿ər i ‖ 'reg jəl ə tɔːr i -toʊr i —*BrE 1998 poll panel preference:* -'leɪt- *55%,* '••lət- *33%,* '••leɪt•• *13%.*

regulo 'reg ju ləʊ -jə-, ⚠-ə- ‖ -jə loʊ

regulus, R~ 'reg jʊl əs -jəl-, §-əl- ‖ -jəl-

regurgi|tate rɪ 'gɜːdʒ ɪ teɪt rə-, ,riː-, -ə- ‖ -'gɜːdʒ- **~tated** teɪt ɪd -əd ‖ teɪṭ əd **~tates** teɪts **~tating** teɪt ɪŋ ‖ teɪṭ ɪŋ

regurgitation rɪ ,gɜːdʒ ɪ 'teɪʃ ᵊn rə-, ,riː-, •••'•••, -ə'•- ‖ -,gɜːdʒ- **~s** z

rehab 'riː hæb

rehabili|tate ,riː‿ə 'bɪl ɪ |teɪt ,•hə-, -'•ə- **~tated** teɪt ɪd -əd ‖ teɪṭ əd **~tates** teɪts **~tating** teɪt ɪŋ ‖ teɪṭ ɪŋ

rehabilitation ,riː‿ə ,bɪl ɪ 'teɪʃ ᵊn ,•hə-, -ə'•- **~s** z

rehash *v* ₍ᵢ₎riː 'hæʃ **~ed** t **~es** ɪz əz **~ing** ɪŋ

rehash *n* 'riː hæʃ ,•'• **~es** ɪz əz

re|hear ,riː ‖'hɪə ‖ -'hɪᵊr **~heard** 'hɜːd ‖ 'hɝːd **~hearing** 'hɪər ɪŋ ‖ 'hɪr ɪŋ **~hears** 'hɪəz ‖ 'hɪᵊrz

rehearsal rɪ 'hɜːs ᵊl rə-, §riː- ‖ -'hɝːs ᵊl **~s** z

rehears|e rɪ 'hɜːs rə-, §riː- ‖ -'hɝːs **~ed** t **~es** ɪz əz **~ing** ɪŋ

re|heat *v* ,riː ‖'hiːt **~heated** 'hiːt ɪd -əd ‖ 'hiːṭ əd **~heating** 'hiːt ɪŋ ‖ 'hiːṭ ɪŋ **~heats** 'hiːts

reheat *n* 'riː hiːt **~s** s

Rehnquist 'ren kwɪst →'reŋ-

Rehoboam, r~ ,riː‿ə 'bəʊ əm -hə-, ‖ -'boʊ əm **~s** z

rehous|e ,riː 'haʊz **~ed** d **~es** ɪz əz **~ing** ɪŋ

re|hydrate ,riː haɪ 'dreɪt ‖ -'haɪdr eɪt **~hydrated** haɪ 'dreɪt ɪd əd ‖ 'haɪdr eɪṭ əd **~hydrates** haɪ 'dreɪts ‖ 'haɪdr eɪts **~hydrating** haɪ 'dreɪt ɪŋ ‖ 'haɪdr eɪṭ ɪŋ

rehydration ,riː haɪ 'dreɪʃ ᵊn

Reich raɪk raɪx, raɪʃ —*Ger* [ʁaɪç]

Reichstag 'raɪks tɑːg 'raɪxs-, 'raɪʃ- —*Ger* ['ʁaɪçs tɑːk]

Reid riːd

reification ,reɪ ɪf ɪ 'keɪʃ ᵊn ,riː-, ,•əf-, §-ə'•-

rei|fy 'reɪ ɪ |faɪ 'riː-, -ə- **~fied** faɪd **~fies** faɪz **~fying** faɪ ɪŋ

Reigate 'raɪ geɪt -gɪt

reign reɪn (= *rain*) **reigned** reɪnd **reigning** 'reɪn ɪŋ **reigns** reɪnz ,reign of 'terror

Reilly 'raɪl i

reimburs|e ,riː ɪm 'bɜːs -əm- ‖ -'bɝːs **~ed** t **~ement/s** mənt/s **~es** ɪz əz **~ing** ɪŋ

Reims riːmz —*Fr* [ʁæ̃ːs]

rein reɪn (= *rain*) **reined** reɪnd **reining** 'reɪn ɪŋ **reins** reɪnz

reincarn|ate *v* ,riː ɪn 'kɑːn |eɪt →-ɪŋ-, ,•'•••; -kɑː 'n|eɪt ‖ -'kɑːrn |eɪt **~ated** eɪt ɪd -əd ‖ eɪṭ əd **~ates** eɪts **~ating** eɪt ɪŋ ‖ eɪṭ ɪŋ

reincarnate *adj* ,riː ɪn 'kɑːn ət ◂ →-ɪŋ-, -ɪt, -eɪt ‖ -'kɑːrn ət

reincarnation ,riː ɪn kɑː 'neɪʃ ᵊn →-ɪŋ- ‖ -kɑːr'•- **~s** z

reindeer 'reɪn dɪə ‖ -dɪr

reinforc|e ,riː ɪn 'fɔːs §-ən- ‖ -'fɔːrs -'foʊrs **~ed** t **~ement/s** mənt/s **~es** ɪz əz **~ing** ɪŋ ,reinforced 'concrete

Reinhardt, Reinhart 'raɪn hɑːt ‖ -hɑːrt

R

rein|state ˌriː ɪn |ˈsteɪt **~stated** ˈsteɪt ɪd -əd
‖ ˈsteɪt̬ əd **~statement** ˈsteɪt mənt **~states**
ˈsteɪts **~stating** ˈsteɪt ɪŋ ‖ ˈsteɪt̬ ɪŋ

reinsurance ˌriː ɪn ˈʃʊər ənts -ˈʃɔːr-
‖ -ˈʃʊr ənts -ˈʃɝː-

reinsure ˌriː ɪn ˈʃʊə -ˈʃɔː ‖ -ˈʃʊər -ˈʃɝː **~d** d
reinsuring ˌriː ɪn ˈʃʊər ɪŋ -ˈʃɔːr- ‖ -ˈʃʊr ɪŋ
-ˈʃɝː- **~s** z

reinvigo|rate ˌriː ɪn ˈvɪg ə |reɪt **~rated** reɪt ɪd
-əd ‖ reɪt̬ əd **~rates** reɪts **~rating**
reɪt ɪŋ ‖ reɪt̬ ɪŋ

reinvigoration ˌriː ɪn ˌvɪg ə ˈreɪʃ ən

reissu|e v, n ˌriː ˈɪʃ uː -ˈɪs juː, -ˈɪʃ juː **~ed** d
~es z **~ing** ɪŋ

reite|rate riː ˈɪt ə |reɪt ˌriː- ‖ -ˈɪt̬- **~rated** reɪt ɪd
-əd ‖ reɪt̬ əd **~rates** reɪts **~rating**
reɪt ɪŋ ‖ reɪt̬ ɪŋ

reiteration riː ˌɪt ə ˈreɪʃ ən ˌriː-, •ˈ••• ‖ -ˌɪt̬- **~s** z

Reith riːθ

reject v rɪ ˈdʒekt rə-, §riː- **~ed** ɪd əd **~ing** ɪŋ
~s s

reject n ˈriː dʒekt **~s** s

rejection rɪ ˈdʒek ʃən rə-, §riː- **~s** z

rejig ˌriː ˈdʒɪg **~ged** d **~ging** ɪŋ **~s** z

rejoic|e rɪ ˈdʒɔɪs rə-, §riː- **~ed** t **~es** ɪz əz
~ing/ly ɪŋ /li

rejoin 'reply' rɪ ˈdʒɔɪn rə-, §riː- **~ed** d **~ing** ɪŋ
~s z

rejoin 'join again' , **re-join** ˌriː ˈdʒɔɪn **~ed** d
~ing ɪŋ **~s** z

rejoinder rɪ ˈdʒɔɪnd ə rə-, §riː- ‖ -ᵊr **~s** z

rejuve|nate rɪ ˈdʒuːv ə |neɪt rə-, §riː-, -ɪ-
~nated neɪt ɪd -əd ‖ neɪt̬ əd **~nates** neɪts
~nating neɪt ɪŋ ‖ neɪt̬ ɪŋ

rejuvenation rɪ ˌdʒuːv ə ˈneɪʃ ən rə-,
ˌriː-, •ˈ•••, -ɪ'•- **~s** z

rejuvenesc|ence ˌriː ˌdʒuːv ə ˈnes ᵊnts
rɪ, •ˈ•••, rə-, -ɪ'•- **~ent** ənt

rekindl|e ₍ˌ₎riː ˈkɪnd ᵊl **~ed** d **~es** z **~ing** ˌɪŋ

relaid ˌriː ˈleɪd ◄

relaps|e v rɪ ˈlæps rə-, §riː- **~ed** t **~es** ɪz əz
~ing ɪŋ

relaps|e n rɪ ˈlæps rə-, §riː-; ˈriː læps **~es** ɪz əz

re|late, R~ rɪ |ˈleɪt rə-, §riː- **~lated** ˈleɪt ɪd -əd
‖ ˈleɪt̬ əd **~lates** ˈleɪts **~lating**
ˈleɪt ɪŋ ‖ ˈleɪt̬ ɪŋ

related rɪ ˈleɪt ɪd -əd ‖ -ˈleɪt̬ əd **~ness** nəs nɪs

relation rɪ ˈleɪʃ ən rə-, §riː- **~s** z

relational rɪ ˈleɪʃ ᵊn_əl rə-, §riː-

relationship rɪ ˈleɪʃ ən ʃɪp rə-, §riː- **~s** s

relatival ˌrel ə ˈtaɪv ᵊl ◄

relative ˈrel ət ɪv ‖ -ət̬ ɪv **~ly** li **~ness** nəs nɪs
~s z

ˌrelative ˈclause; ˌrelative ˈpronoun

relativis... —see **relativiz...**

relativism ˈrel ət ɪv ˌɪz əm ‖ ˈrel ət̬-

relativistic ˌrel ət ɪv ˈɪst ɪk ◄ -əv'•• ‖ ˌrel ət̬-
~ally ᵊl_i

relativity, R~ ˌrel ə ˈtɪv ət i -ɪt i ‖ -ət̬ i

relativization ˌrel ət ɪv aɪ ˈzeɪʃ ən -ɪ'•-
‖ ˌrel ət̬ ɪv ə- **~s** z

relativiz|e ˈrel ət ɪv aɪz ‖ ˈrel ət̬- **~ed** d **~es** ɪz
əz **~ing** ɪŋ

relator rɪ ˈleɪt ə rə-, §riː- ‖ -ˈleɪt̬ ᵊr **~s** z

relaunch v ˌriː ˈlɔːntʃ ‖ -ˈlɑːntʃ **~ed** t **~es** ɪz
əz **~ing** ɪŋ

relaunch n ˈriː lɔːntʃ ‖ -lɑːntʃ **~es** ɪz əz

relax rɪ ˈlæks rə-, §riː- **~ed** t **~es** ɪz əz **~ing**
ɪŋ

relaxant rɪ ˈlæks ənt rə-, §riː- **~s** s

relaxation ˌriː læk ˈseɪʃ ən ˌrel ək- **~s** z

relay n ˈriː leɪ **~s** z
ˈrelay ˌrace; ˈrelay ˌstation

relay v 'send by relay' ˈriː leɪ rɪ ˈleɪ, rə-, riː-
~ed d **~ing** ɪŋ **~s** z

re|lay v 'lay again' ˌriː |ˈleɪ **~laid** ˈleɪd **~laying**
ˈleɪ ɪŋ **~lays** ˈleɪz

releas|e v, n rɪ ˈliːs rə-, §riː- **~ed** t **~es** ɪz əz
~ing ɪŋ

rele|gate ˈrel ɪ |geɪt -ə- **~gated** geɪt ɪd -əd
‖ geɪt̬ əd **~gates** geɪts **~gating**
geɪt ɪŋ ‖ geɪt̬ ɪŋ

relegation ˌrel ɪ ˈgeɪʃ ən -ə- **~s** z

re|lent rɪ |ˈlent rə-, §riː- **~lented** ˈlent ɪd -əd
‖ ˈlent̬ əd **~lenting** ˈlent ɪŋ ‖ ˈlent̬ ɪŋ **~lents**
ˈlents

relentless rɪ ˈlent ləs rə-, §riː-, -lɪs **~ly** li
~ness nəs nɪs

relevanc|e ˈrel əv ᵊnts -ɪv-; △ˈrev ᵊl- **~y** i

relevant ˈrel əv ənt -ɪv-; △ˈrev ᵊl- **~ly** li

reliability rɪ ˌlaɪ_ə ˈbɪl ət i rə-, §riː-, -ɪt i ‖ -ət̬ i

reliab|le rɪ ˈlaɪ_əb |ᵊl rə-, §riː- **~ly** li

reliance rɪ ˈlaɪ_ənts rə-, §riː-

reliant rɪ ˈlaɪ_ənt rə-, §riː- **~ly** li

relic ˈrel ɪk **~s** s

relict ˈrel ɪkt **~s** s

relie... —see **rely**

relief rɪ ˈliːf rə-, §riː- **~s** s
reˈlief ˌmap; reˈlief ˌroad

reliev|e rɪ ˈliːv rə-, §riː- **~ed** d **~es** z **~ing** ɪŋ

reliever rɪ ˈliːv ə rə-, §riː- ‖ -ᵊr **~s** z

relievo rɪ ˈliːv əʊ rə-, §riː-; ˌrel i ˈeɪv əʊ ‖ -oʊ
~s z

religion rɪ ˈlɪdʒ ən rə-, §riː- **~s** z

religiose rɪ ˈlɪdʒ i əʊs rə-, §riː-, -əʊz ‖ -oʊs

religiosity rɪ ˌlɪdʒ i ˈɒs ət i rə-, §riː-, -ɪt i;
ˌrel ɪ ˈdʒɒs••, •ˈə- ‖ -ˈɑːs ət̬ i

religious rɪ ˈlɪdʒ əs rə-, §riː- **~ly** li **~ness** nəs
nɪs

relin|e ˌriː ˈlaɪn **~ed** d **~es** z **~ing** ɪŋ

relinquish rɪ ˈlɪŋk wɪʃ rə-, §riː- **~ed** t **~es** ɪz
əz **~ing** ɪŋ **~ment** mənt

reliquar|y ˈrel ɪk wər li '•ək- ‖ -ə kwer li **~ies**
iz

relish n, v ˈrel ɪʃ **~ed** t **~es** ɪz əz **~ing** ɪŋ

reliv|e ˌriː ˈlɪv **~ed** d **~es** z **~ing** ɪŋ

reload ˌriː ˈləʊd ‖ -ˈloʊd **~ed** ɪd əd **~ing** ɪŋ **~s**
z

reloc|ate ˌriː ləʊ ˈkleɪt ‖ ˌriː ˈloʊk leɪt
-loʊ ˈkleɪt **~ated** eɪt ɪd -əd ‖ eɪt̬ əd **~ates**
eɪts **~ating** eɪt ɪŋ ‖ eɪt̬ ɪŋ

relocation ˌriː ləʊ ˈkeɪʃ ən ‖ -loʊ- **~s** z

reluctance rɪ ˈlʌkt ənts rə-, §riː-

reluctant rɪ ˈlʌkt ənt rə-, §riː- **~ly** li

reluctivity ˌrel ʌk ˈtɪv ət i ˌriː lʌk-, rɪ ˌlʌk-,
rə ˌlʌk-, §riː ˌlʌk-, -ɪt i ‖ -ət̬ i

R

re|ly rɪ |ˈlaɪ rə-, §riː- ~lied ˈlaɪd ~lies ˈlaɪz
  ~lying ˈlaɪ ɪŋ
rem rem
REM rem ˌɑːr iː ˈem ‖ ˌɑːr iː ˈem
remade ˌriː ˈmeɪd
remain rɪ ˈmeɪn rə-, §riː- ~ed d ~ing ɪŋ ~s z
remaind|er n, v ˈmeɪnd |ə rə-, §riː- ‖ -|ər
  ~ered əd ‖ ərd ~ering _ər ɪŋ ~ers əz ‖ ərz
re|make v ˌriː |ˈmeɪk ~made ˈmeɪd ~makes
  ˈmeɪks ~making ˈmeɪk ɪŋ
remake n ˈriː meɪk ~s s
remand rɪ ˈmɑːnd rə-, §riː-, §-ˈmænd ‖ -ˈmænd
  ~ed ɪd əd ~ing ɪŋ ~s z
remanence ˈrem ən ənts
remark rɪ ˈmɑːk rə-, §riː- ‖ -ˈmɑːrk ~ed t
  ~ing ɪŋ ~s s
remarkab|le rɪ ˈmɑːk əb |əl rə-, §riː- ‖ -ˈmɑːrk-
  ~ly li
remarque, R~ rɪ ˈmɑːk rə- ‖ -ˈmɑːrk
remarriag|e ˌriː ˈmær ɪdʒ ‖ -ˈmer- ~es ɪz əz
remarr|y ˌriː ˈmær i ‖ -ˈmer- ~ied id ~ies iz
  ~ying i ɪŋ
rematch n ˈriː mætʃ ~es ɪz əz
Rembrandt ˈrem brænt -brɒnt —Dutch
  [ˈrɛm brɑnt] ~s, ~'s s
REME ˈriːm i
remediab|le rɪ ˈmiːd i_əb |əl rə-, §riː- ~leness
  əl nəs -nɪs ~ly li
remedial rɪ ˈmiːd i_əl rə-, §riː- ~ly i
remediation rɪ ˌmiːd i ˈeɪʃ ən rə-, §riː-
remed|y ˈrem əd li -ɪd- ~ied id ~ies iz ~ying
  i ɪŋ
remem|ber rɪ ˈmem |bə rə-, §riː- ‖ -|bər
  ~bered bəd ‖ bərd ~bering bər_ɪŋ ~bers
  bəz ‖ bərz
remembranc|e rɪ ˈmem brənts rə-, §riː-,
  △-ˈmem bər ənts ~er/s ə/z ‖ -ər/z ~es ɪz əz
  Reˈmembrance Day; Reˌmembrance
  ˈSunday
Remick ˈrem ɪk
remilitaris... —see remilitariz...
remilitarization ˌriː ˌmɪl ɪt_ər aɪ ˈzeɪʃ ən -ˌ•ət-,
  •ˌ••••ˈ••, -ɪˈ•- ‖ -əʈ ər ə-
remilitariz|e ⒤riː ˈmɪl ɪt ə raɪz -ˈ•ət-
  ‖ -əʈ ə raɪz ~ed d ~es ɪz əz ~ing ɪŋ
remind rɪ ˈmaɪnd rə-, §riː- ~ed ɪd əd ~ing ɪŋ
  ~s z
reminder rɪ ˈmaɪnd ə rə-, §riː- ‖ -ər ~s z
Remington ˈrem ɪŋ tən
reminisc|e ˌrem ɪ ˈnɪs -ə- ~ed t ~es ɪz əz
  ~ing ɪŋ
reminiscenc|e ˌrem ɪ ˈnɪs ənts -ə- ~es ɪz əz
reminiscent ˌrem ɪ ˈnɪs ənt ◄ -ə- ~ly li
remiss rɪ ˈmɪs rə-, §riː- ~ness nəs nɪs
remission rɪ ˈmɪʃ ən rə-, §riː- ~s z
re|mit v rɪ ˈmɪt rə-, §riː- ~mits ˈmɪts ~mitted
  ˈmɪt ɪd -əd ‖ ˈmɪʈ əd ~mitting
  ˈmɪt ɪŋ ‖ ˈmɪʈ ɪŋ
remit n rɪ mɪt rɪ ˈmɪt, rə-, riː- ~s s
remittanc|e rɪ ˈmɪt ənts rə-, §riː- ~es ɪz əz
remittee rɪ ˌmɪt ˈiː rə-, §riː- ~s s
remittent rɪ ˈmɪt ənt rə-, §riː- ~ly li
remitter rɪ ˈmɪt ə rə-, §riː- ‖ -ˈmɪʈ ər ~s z

remix n ˈriː mɪks ~es ɪz əz
remnant, R~ ˈrem nənt ~s s
remodel ⒤riː ˈmɒd əl ‖ -ˈmɑːd əl ~ed, ~led d
  ~ing, ~ling ɪŋ ~s z
remold v ˌriː ˈməʊld →-ˈmɒʊld ‖ -ˈmoʊld ~ed
  ɪd əd ~ing ɪŋ ~s z
remold n ˈriː məʊld →-mɒʊld ‖ -moʊld ~s z
remonstranc|e rɪ ˈmɒnts trənts rə-, §riː-
  ‖ -ˈmɑːnts- ~es ɪz əz
remonstrant, R~ rɪ ˈmɒnts trənt rə-, §riː-
  ‖ -ˈmɑːnts- ~s s
remons|trate ˈrem ən s|treɪt rɪ ˈmɒn-, rə-, §riː-
  ‖ rɪ ˈmɑːnts |treɪt ~trated treɪt ɪd -əd
  ‖ treɪʈ əd ~trates treɪts ~trating
  treɪt ɪŋ ‖ treɪʈ ɪŋ
remonstration ˌrem ən ˈstreɪʃ ən ‖ rɪ ˌmɑːn-
  ~s z
remonstrative rɪ ˈmɒnts trət ɪv rə-, §riː-
  ‖ -ˈmɑːnts trəʈ ɪv
remontant rɪ ˈmɒnt ənt rə-, §riː- ‖ -ˈmɑːnt ənt
  ~s s
remora ˈrem ər ə rɪ ˈmɔːr ə, rə-, §riː- ~s z
remorse rɪ ˈmɔːs rə-, §riː- ‖ -ˈmɔːrs
remorseful rɪ ˈmɔːs fəl rə-, §riː-, -fʊl ‖ -ˈmɔːrs-
  ~ly _i ~ness nəs nɪs
remorseless rɪ ˈmɔːs ləs rə-, §riː-, -lɪs
  ‖ -ˈmɔːrs- ~ly li ~ness nəs nɪs
re|mote rɪ ˈməʊt rə-, §riː- ‖ -ˈmoʊt ~moter
  ˈməʊt ə ‖ ˈmoʊʈ ər ~motest ˈməʊt ɪst -əst
  ‖ ˈmoʊʈ əst
  reˌmote conˈtrol
remote|ly rɪ ˈməʊt |li rə-, §riː- ‖ -ˈmoʊt-
  ~ness nəs nɪs
remoulade, rémoulade ˌrem ə ˈleɪd -u-, -ˈlɑːd
  ‖ ˌreɪm ə ˈlɑːd -u- ~s z
remould v ˌriː ˈməʊld →-ˈmɒʊld ‖ -ˈmoʊld
  ~ed ɪd əd ~ing ɪŋ ~s z
remould n ˈriː məʊld →-mɒʊld ‖ -moʊld ~s z
re|mount v ˌriː |ˈmaʊnt ~mounted ˈmaʊnt ɪd
  -əd ‖ ˈmaʊnʈ əd ~mounting
  ˈmaʊnt ɪŋ ‖ ˈmaʊnʈ ɪŋ ~mounts ˈmaʊnts
remount n ˈriː maʊnt ˌ•ˈ• ~s s
removability rɪ ˌmuːv ə ˈbɪl ət i rə-, §riː- ‖ -əʈ i
removab|le rɪ ˈmuːv əb |əl rə-, §riː- ~leness
  əl nəs -nɪs ~ly li
removal rɪ ˈmuːv əl rə-, §riː- ~s z
  reˈmoval van
remov|e rɪ ˈmuːv rə-, §riː- ~ed d ~es z ~ing
  ɪŋ
remover rɪ ˈmuːv ə rə-, §riː- ‖ -ər ~s z
-remover rɪ ˌmuːv ə rə-, §riː- ‖ -ər — stain-
  remover ˈsteɪn rɪ ˌmuːv ə -rə-, §-riː- ‖ -ər
Remploy tdmk ˈrem plɔɪ
remune|rate rɪ ˈmjuːn ə |reɪt rə-, §riː- ~rated
  reɪt ɪd -əd ‖ reɪʈ əd ~rates reɪts ~rating
  reɪt ɪŋ ‖ reɪʈ ɪŋ
remuneration rɪ ˌmjuːn ə ˈreɪʃ ən rə-, §riː-,
  △-ˌnjuː m- ~s z
remunerative rɪ ˈmjuːn ər_ət ɪv rə-, §riː-,
  △-ˈnjuː m-, -ə reɪt- ‖ -ər_əʈ ɪv -ə reɪʈ- ~ly li
  ~ness nəs nɪs
Remus ˈriːm əs
Remy, Rémy ˈreɪm i ‖ reɪ ˈmiː —Fr [ʁə mi, ʁe-]

renaissanc|e, R~ rɪ 'neɪs ənts rə-, §riː-, -ɒs;
ˌren eɪ 'sɒ̃s ‖ ˌren ə 'sɑːnts -'zɑːnts, '••• (*)
—Fr [ʁə nɛ sɑ̃s] ~es ɪz əz
renal 'riːn əl
renam|e ₍ᵢ₎riː 'neɪm ~ed d ~es z ~ing ɪŋ
renascenc|e rɪ 'næs ənts rə-, §riː-, -'neɪs- ~es
ɪz əz
renascent rɪ 'næs ənt rə-, §riː-, -'neɪs-
Renata rɪ 'nɑːt ə rə- ‖ -'nɑːt ə
Renault 'ren əʊ ‖ rə 'nɔːlt -'nɑːlt, -'noʊ (*)
—Fr [ʁə no] ~s z
rend rend rending 'rend ɪŋ rends rendz
rent rent
Rendall, Rendell 'rend əl
render 'rend ə ‖ -ər ~ed d rendering/s
'rend_ər ɪŋ/z ~s z
rendezvous v, n sing. 'rɒnd ɪ vuː -ə-, -eɪ-
‖ 'rɑːnd eɪ- —Fr [ʁɑ̃ de vu] ~ n pl; v 3rd
sing. z ~ed d ~ing ɪŋ
rendzina rend 'ziːn ə -s z
rendition ren 'dɪʃ ən ~s z
Rene, René man's name (i) 'ren eɪ 'rən-, -i, (ii)
rə 'neɪ —in AmE (ii)
Renee, Renée woman's name (i) 'ren eɪ 'rən-,
(ii) rə 'neɪ, (iii) 'riːn i —in AmE (ii)
Rene woman's name, short for Irene 'riːn i
renegade 'ren ɪ geɪd -ə- ~s z
reneg|e, renegu|e rɪ 'niːg rə-, §riː-, -'neɪg,
-'neg ‖ -'nɪg -'neg, -'niːg ~ed d ~es z ~ing
ɪŋ
renew rɪ 'njuː rə-, ˌriː-, §-'nuː ‖ -'nuː -'njuː
~ed d ~ing ɪŋ ~s z
renewability rɪ ˌnjuː_ə 'bɪl ət i rə-, §riː-,
§-ˌnuː_, -ɪt i ‖ -ˌnuː ə 'bɪl ət̬ i -ˌnjuː-
renewable rɪ 'njuː_əb əl rə-, ˌriː-, §-'nuː_
‖ -'nuː əb əl -'njuː-
renewal rɪ 'njuː_əl rə-, ˌriː-, -'njuːl, §-'nuː_,
§-'nuːl ‖ -'nuː əl -'njuː- ~s z
renewer rɪ 'njuː_ə rə-, §riː-, §-'nuː_ ‖ -'nuː ər
-'njuː- ~s z
Renfrew 'ren fruː
reniform 'ren ɪ fɔːm 'riːn-, -ə- ‖ -fɔːrm
renin 'riːn ɪn §-ən
Renishaw 'ren ɪ ʃɔː §-ə- ‖ -ʃɑː
renminbi ˌren mɪn 'biː →ˌrem-, →-mɪm —Chi
rénmínbì [²ʐ,ən ²mɪn ⁴pi]
Rennell 'ren əl ‖ rə 'nel
Rennes ren —Fr [ʁɛn]
rennet 'ren ɪt §-ət
Rennie 'ren i ~s tdmk z
rennin 'ren ɪn §-ən
Reno 'riːn əʊ ‖ -oʊ
Renoir 'ren wɑː 'rən-; rə 'nwɑː ‖ rən 'wɑːr
'ren• —Fr [ʁə nwaːʁ] ~s, ~'s z
renounc|e rɪ 'naʊnts rə-, §riː- ~ed t ~es ɪz əz
~ing ɪŋ ~ement mənt
reno|vate 'ren əʊ |veɪt ‖ -ə- ~vated veɪt ɪd
-əd ‖ veɪt̬ əd ~vates veɪts ~vating
veɪt ɪŋ ‖ veɪt̬ ɪŋ
renovation ˌren əʊ 'veɪʃ ən ‖ -ə- ~s z
renown rɪ 'naʊn rə-, §riː- ~ed d
Renshaw 'ren ʃɔː ‖ -ʃɑː
Rensselaer ˌrents ə 'lɪə ‖ -'lɪər

rent rent rented 'rent ɪd -əd ‖ 'rent̬ əd
renting 'rent ɪŋ ‖ 'rent̬ ɪŋ rents rents
'rent boy; 'rent strike
rentable 'rent əb əl ‖ 'rent̬-
rent-a-car 'rent ə kɑː ‖ 'rent̬ ə kɑːr
rent-a-crowd 'rent ə kraʊd ‖ 'rent̬-
rental 'rent əl ‖ 'rent̬ əl ~s z
rent-a-mob 'rent ə mɒb ‖ 'rent̬ ə mɑːb
rent-a-quote 'rent ə kwəʊt ‖ 'rent̬ ə kwoʊt
renter 'rent ə ‖ 'rent̬ ər ~s z
rent-free ˌrent 'friː ◄
rentier 'rɒnt i eɪ 'rɑːnt- ‖ rɑːn 'tjeɪ —Fr
[ʁɑ̃ tje] ~s z
Rentokil tdmk 'rent əʊ kɪl ‖ 'rent̬ ə-
Renton 'rent ən ‖ -ən
renunciation rɪ ˌnʌnts i 'eɪʃ ən rə-, §riː- ~s z
Renwick (i) 'ren ɪk, (ii) -wɪk
reop|en riː 'əʊp |ən ˌriː- ‖ -'oʊp |ən ~ened ənd
→md ~ening ən_ɪŋ ~ens ənz →mz
reorganis... —see reorganiz...
reorganization riː ˌɔːg ən aɪ 'zeɪʃ ən
ˌriː-,•••'••, -ɪ'•- ‖ -ˌɔːrg ən_ə- ~s z
reorganiz|e riː 'ɔːg ə naɪz ˌriː- ‖ -'ɔːrg- ~ed d
~es ɪz əz ~ing ɪŋ
rep rep reps reps
repaid rɪ 'peɪd rə-, ₍ᵢ₎riː-
repair rɪ 'peə rə-, §riː- ‖ -'peər -'pæər ~ed d
repairing rɪ 'peər ɪŋ rə-, §riː- ‖ -'per ɪŋ
-'pæer- ~s z
repairable rɪ 'peər əb əl rə-, §riː- ‖ -'per-
-'pæer-
repairer rɪ 'peər ə rə-, §riː- ‖ -'per ər -'pæer- ~s
z
repair|man rɪ 'peə |mæn rə-, §riː-, -mən
‖ -'per- -'pæer- ~men men mən
reparab|le 'rep ər_əb |əl ~ly li
reparation ˌrep ə 'reɪʃ ən ~s z
reparative rɪ 'pær ət ɪv rə-, §riː-; 'rep ər_
‖ -ət̬ ɪv -'per-
repartee ˌrep ɑː 'tiː ‖ -ɑːr 'teɪ -ər-, -'tiː
repast rɪ 'pɑːst rə-, §riː-, §-'pæst; 'riː pɑːst,
§-pæst ‖ -'pæst ~s s
repatri|ate ˌriː 'pætr i |eɪt riː-, rɪ- ‖ -'peɪtr- (*)
~ated eɪt ɪd -əd ‖ eɪt̬ əd ~ates eɪts ~ating
eɪt ɪŋ ‖ eɪt̬ ɪŋ
repatriation ˌriː ˌpætr i 'eɪʃ ən riː-,•••'••, rɪ-,
rə- ‖ riː ˌpeɪtr- ˌ•ˌ•ˌ•'•• ~s z
re|pay rɪ |'peɪ rə-, ₍ᵢ₎riː- ~paid 'peɪd ~paying
'peɪ ɪŋ ~pays 'peɪz
repayable rɪ 'peɪ əb əl rə-, ₍ᵢ₎riː-
repayment rɪ 'peɪ mənt rə-, ˌriː- ~s s
repeal v, n rɪ 'piːl rə-, §riː- ~ed d ~ing ɪŋ ~s
z
re|peat v, n rɪ |'piːt rə-, §riː- ~peated/ly
'piːt ɪd /li -əd /li ‖ 'piːt̬ əd /li ~peating
'piːt ɪŋ ‖ 'piːt̬ ɪŋ ~peats 'piːts
repeater rɪ 'piːt ə rə-, §riː- ‖ -'piːt̬ ər ~s z
repechage, repêchage 'rep ə ʃɑːʒ -ɪ-, ,••'•
—Fr [ʁə pɛ ʃaːʒ]
repel rɪ 'pel rə-, §riː- ~led d ~ling ɪŋ ~s z
repellant, repellent rɪ 'pel ənt rə-, §riː- ~s s
repellor rɪ 'pel ə rə-, §riː- ‖ -ər ~s z

re|pent rɪ |'pent rə-, §riː- **~pented** 'pent ɪd
-əd ‖ 'penṭ əd **~penting** 'pent ɪŋ ‖ 'penṭ ɪŋ
~pents 'penʦ

repentanc|e rɪ 'pent ənʦ rə-, §riː- ‖ -ənʦ **~es**
ɪz əz

repentant rɪ 'pent ənt rə-, §riː- ‖ -ᵊnt **~ly** li

repercussion ˌriːp ə 'kʌʃ ᵊn ‖ -ᵊr- ˌrep- **~s** z

repertoire 'rep ə twɑː ‖ -ᵊr twɑːr -ə- **~s** z

repertor|y 'rep ət‿ər li ‖ -ᵊr tɔːr li '•ə-, -toʊr i
~ies iz
   'repertory ˌcompany

repetend 'rep ɪ tend -ə-, ˌ•'•ˌ **~s** z

repetiteur, répétiteur rɪ ˌpet ɪ 'tɜː rə-, -,•ə-;
ˌrep ə tiː'• ‖ ˌreɪ peɪt ɪ 'tɜː ˌ•pet- —Fr
[ʁə pe ti tœːʁ] **~s** z

repetition ˌrep ə 'tɪʃ ᵊn -ɪ- **~s** z

repetitious ˌrep ə 'tɪʃ əs ◄ -ɪ- **~ly** li **~ness** nəs
nɪs

repetitive rɪ 'pet ət ɪv rə-, §riː-, -ɪt-
‖ -'peṭ əṭ ɪv **~ly** li **~ness** nəs nɪs

rephras|e ˌriː 'freɪz **~ed** d **~es** ɪz əz **~ing** ɪŋ

repin|e rɪ 'paɪn rə-, §riː- **~ed** d **~es** z **~ing** ɪŋ

replac|e rɪ 'pleɪs rə-, ₍ₒ₎riː- **~ed** t **~es** ɪz əz
~ing ɪŋ

replaceable rɪ 'pleɪs əb ᵊl rə-, ₍ₒ₎riː-

replacement rɪ 'pleɪs mənt rə-, ₍ₒ₎riː- **~s** s

replay v ˌriː 'pleɪ **~ed** d **~ing** ɪŋ **~s** z

replay n 'riː pleɪ **~s** z

replenish rɪ 'plen ɪʃ rə-, §riː- **~ed** t **~es** ɪz əz
~ing ɪŋ **~ment/s** mənt/s

replete rɪ 'pliːt rə-, §riː- **~ness** nəs nɪs

repletion rɪ 'pliːʃ ᵊn rə-, §riː-

replevin rɪ 'plev ɪn rə-, §riː-, §-ᵊn

replev|y rɪ 'plev li rə-, §riː- **~ied** id **~ies** iz
~ying i ɪŋ

replica 'rep lɪk ə **~s** z —formerly also
   rɪ 'pliːk ə, rə-

replicability ˌrep lɪk ə 'bɪl ət i -ɪt i ‖ -əṭ i

replicable 'rep lɪk əb ᵊl

repli|cate v 'rep lɪ |keɪt -lə- **~cated** keɪt ɪd -əd
‖ keɪṭ əd **~cates** keɪts **~cating**
   keɪt ɪŋ ‖ keɪṭ ɪŋ

replication ˌrep lɪ 'keɪʃ ᵊn -lə- **~s** z

re|ply rɪ |'plaɪ rə-, §riː- **~plied** 'plaɪd **~plies**
'plaɪz **~plying** 'plaɪ ɪŋ

reply-paid rɪ ˌplaɪ 'peɪd ◄ rə-, §riː-

repo 'riː pəʊ ‖ -poʊ **~s** z

répondez s'il vous plaît
   rɪ ˌpɒnd eɪ ˌsiː vuː 'pleɪ rə-, reɪ-, -,sɪl-
   ‖ -,pɔːnd- -,pɑːnd- —Fr [ʁə pɔ̃ de sil vu plɛ]

re|port v, n rɪ |'pɔːt rə-, §riː- ‖ -|'pɔːrt -'poʊrt
~ported/ly 'pɔːt ɪd /li -əd- ‖ 'pɔːrṭ- 'poʊrṭ-
~porting 'pɔːt ɪŋ ‖ 'pɔːrṭ ɪŋ 'poʊrṭ- **~ports**
'pɔːts ‖ 'pɔːrts 'poʊrts
   re,ported 'speech

reportage ˌrep ɔː 'tɑːʒ rɪ 'pɔːt ɪdʒ rə-,
§riː-;‖ rɪ 'pɔːrṭ ɪdʒ -'poʊrṭ-; ˌrep ɔːr 'tɑːʒ, -ᵊr-

reporter rɪ 'pɔːt ə rə-, §riː- ‖ -'pɔːrṭ ᵊr -'poʊrṭ-
~s z

reportorial ˌrep ɔː 'tɔːr i_əl ◄ ˌriːp-, ˌ•ə-
   ‖ ˌrep ᵊr- -'toʊr- **~ly** i

repos|e v, n rɪ 'pəʊz rə-, §riː- ‖ -'poʊz **~ed** d
~es ɪz əz **~ing** ɪŋ

reposeful rɪ 'pəʊz fᵊl rə-, §riː-, -fʊl ‖ -'poʊz-
~ly i **~ness** nəs nɪs

repositor|y rɪ 'pɒz ɪt‿ər i rə-, §riː-, -'•ət‿
   ‖ -'pɑːz ə tɔːr li -toʊr i **~ies** iz

repossess ˌriː pə 'zes **~ed** t **~es** ɪz əz **~ing** ɪŋ

repossession ˌriː pə 'zeʃ ᵊn **~s** z

repousse, repoussé rə 'puːs eɪ rɪ- ‖ -ˌpuː 'seɪ
   —Fr [ʁə pu se]

repp rep

reprehend ˌrep rɪ 'hend -rə- **~ed** ɪd əd **~ing**
ɪŋ **~s** z

reprehensibility ˌrep rɪ ˌhenʦ ə 'bɪl ət i ˌ•rə-,
-,•ɪ-, -ɪt i ‖ -əṭ i

reprehensib|le ˌrep rɪ 'henʦ əb ᵊl ◄ ˌ•rə-,
-ɪb ᵊl **~ly** li

reprehension ˌrep rɪ 'henʧ ᵊn -rə-

repre|sent ˌrep rɪ |'zent -rə- **~sented** 'zent ɪd
-əd ‖ 'zenṭ əd **~senting** 'zent ɪŋ ‖ 'zenṭ ɪŋ
~sents 'zenʦ

re-pre|sent ˌriː prɪ |'zent -prə- **~sented**
'zent ɪd -əd ‖ 'zenṭ əd **~senting**
'zent ɪŋ ‖ 'zenṭ ɪŋ **~sents** 'zenʦ

representation ˌrep rɪ zen 'teɪʃ ᵊn, ˌ•rə-,
-zən'•- **~s** z

representational ˌrep rɪ zen 'teɪʃ ᵊn‿əl ◄ ˌ•rə-,
-zən'•- **~ism** ˌɪz əm

representative ˌrep rɪ 'zent ət ɪv ◄ ˌ•rə-
   ‖ -'zenṭ əṭ ɪv ◄ **~ly** li **~ness** nəs nɪs **~s** z

repress rɪ 'pres rə-, §riː- **~ed** t **~es** ɪz əz **~ing**
ɪŋ

repression rɪ 'preʃ ᵊn rə-, §riː- **~s** z

repressive rɪ 'pres ɪv rə-, §riː- **~ly** li **~ness**
nəs nɪs

repressor rɪ 'pres ə rə-, §riː- ‖ -ᵊr **~s** z

repriev|e rɪ 'priːv rə-, §riː- **~ed** d **~es** z **~ing**
ɪŋ

reprimand v 'rep rɪ mɑːnd -rə-, ˌ•'•ˌ ‖ -mænd
~ed ɪd əd **~ing** ɪŋ **~s** z

reprimand n 'rep rɪ mɑːnd -rə- ‖ -mænd **~s** z

re|print v ˌriː |'prɪnt **~printed** 'prɪnt ɪd -əd
   ‖ 'prɪnṭ əd **~printing** 'prɪnt ɪŋ ‖ 'prɪnṭ ɪŋ
~prints 'prɪnʦ

reprint n 'riː prɪnt ˌ•'• **~s** s

reprisal rɪ 'praɪz ᵊl rə-, §riː- **~s** z

repris|e rɪ 'priːz rə-, §riː-, -'praɪz **~ed** d **~es** ɪz
əz **~ing** ɪŋ

repro 'riː prəʊ ‖ -proʊ **~s** z

reproach n, v rɪ 'prəʊʧ rə-, §riː- ‖ -'proʊʧ
~ed t **~es** ɪz əz **~ing** ɪŋ

reproachful rɪ 'prəʊʧ fᵊl rə-, §riː-, -fʊl
   ‖ -'proʊʧ- **~ly** i **~ness** nəs nɪs

repro|bate 'rep rəʊ |beɪt ‖ -rə- **~bated** beɪt ɪd
-əd ‖ beɪṭ əd **~bates** beɪts **~bating**
   beɪt ɪŋ ‖ beɪṭ ɪŋ

reprobation ˌrep rəʊ 'beɪʃ ᵊn ‖ -rə-

reprocess ˌriː 'prəʊs es -'prɒs-, -ɪs, §-əs
   ‖ -'prɑːs- **~ed** t **~es** ɪz əz **~ing** ɪŋ

reproduc|e ˌriːp rə 'djuːs ˌrep-, →§-'dʒuːs
   ‖ -'duːs -'djuːs **~ed** t **~er/s** ə/z ‖ ᵊr/z **~es** ɪz
   əz **~ing** ɪŋ

reproducible ˌriːp rə 'djuːs əb ᵊl ◄ ˌrep-,
   →§-'dʒuːs-, -ɪb ᵊl ‖ -'duːs- -'djuːs-

reproduction ˌriːp rə 'dʌk ʃᵊn ˌrep- **~s** z

reproductive ˌriːp rə 'dʌkt ɪv ◂ ˌrep- **~ly** li
~ness nəs nɪs
reprographer rɪ 'prɒg rəf ə riː- ‖ -'prɑːg rəf ˀr
~s z
reprographic ˌriːp rə 'græf ɪk ◂ ˌrep- **~ally** ᵊl̬_i
~s s
reprography rɪ 'prɒg rəf i riː- ‖ -'prɑːg-
reproof n, 'rebuke' rɪ 'pruːf rə-, §riː-, §-'prʊf
~s s
reproof v, 'proof again' ˌriː 'pruːf §-'prʊf **~ed** t
~ing ɪŋ **~s** s
reprov|e rɪ 'pruːv rə-, §riː- **~ed** d **~es** z
~ing/ly ɪŋ /li
reptile 'rept aɪᵊl ‖ -ᵊl -aɪᵊl **~s** z
reptilian rep 'tɪl i_ən **~s** z
Repton 'rept ən
republic, R~ rɪ 'pʌb lɪk rə-, §riː- **~s** s
republican, R~ rɪ 'pʌb lɪk ən rə-, §riː- **~s** z
republicanism, R~ rɪ 'pʌb lɪk ən ˌɪz əm rə-,
§riː-
repudi|ate rɪ 'pjuːd i eɪt rə-, §riː- **~ated**
eɪt ɪd -əd ‖ eɪt̬ əd **~ates** eɪts **~ating**
eɪt ɪŋ ‖ eɪt̬ ɪŋ **~ator/s** eɪt ə/z ‖ eɪt̬ ˀr/z
repudiation rɪ ˌpjuːd i 'eɪʃ ən rə-, §riː- **~s** z
repugnance rɪ 'pʌg nən¹s rə-, §riː-
repugnant rɪ 'pʌg nənt rə-, §riː- **~ly** li
repuls|e v, n rɪ 'pʌls rə-, §riː- **~ed** t **~es** ɪz əz
~ing ɪŋ
repulsion rɪ 'pʌlʃ ən rə-, §riː- **~s** z
repulsive rɪ 'pʌls ɪv rə-, §riː- **~ly** li **~ness** nəs
nɪs
reputability ˌrep jʊt ə 'bɪl ət i §, • jət-, -ɪt i
‖ -jət̬ ə 'bɪl ət̬ i
reputab|le 'rep jʊt əb ᵊl §'• jət-; rɪ 'pjuːt-,
§rə- ‖ 'rep jət̬- **~ly** li
reputation ˌrep ju 'teɪʃ ən §-jə- ‖ -jə- **~s** z
repute rɪ 'pjuːt rə-, §riː-
reputed rɪ 'pjuːt ɪd rə-, §riː-, -əd ‖ -'pjuːt̬ əd
~ly li
request rɪ 'kwest rə-, §riː- **~ed** ɪd əd **~ing** ɪŋ
~s s
re'quest stop
requiem 'rek wi_əm -em **~s** z
ˌrequiem 'mass
requiescat ˌrek wi 'esk æt ‖ ˌreɪk-, -ɑːt
require rɪ 'kwaɪ_ə rə-, §riː- ‖ -'kwaɪ_ˀr **~d** d
~ment/s mənt/s **~s** z **requiring**
rɪ 'kwaɪ_ər ɪŋ rə-, §riː- ‖ -'kwaɪ_ˀr ɪŋ
requisite 'rek wɪz ɪt -wəz-, §-ət **~s** s
requisition ˌrek wɪ 'zɪʃ ən -wə- **~ed** d **~ing**
ɪŋ **~s** z
requital rɪ 'kwaɪt ᵊl rə-, §riː- ‖ -'kwaɪt̬ ᵊl **~s** z
re|quite rɪ l'kwaɪt rə-, §riː- **~quited** 'kwaɪt ɪd
-əd ‖ 'kwaɪt̬ əd **~quites** 'kwaɪts **~quiting**
'kwaɪt ɪŋ ‖ 'kwaɪt̬ ɪŋ
reran ₍ᵢ₎riː 'ræn
reredos 'rɪə dɒs ‖ 'rɪr dɑːs 'rer ə dɑːs **~es** ɪz
əz
rereleas|e v ˌriː rɪ 'liːs ◂ -rə-, §-riː- **~ed** t **~es**
ɪz əz **~ing** ɪŋ
rereleas|e n 'riː rɪ liːs -rə-, §-riː-, ˌ•'• **~es** ɪz
əz

re|route ˌriːl 'ruːt -'raʊt —see note at route.
~routed 'ruːt ɪd -əd ‖ 'ruːt̬ əd 'raʊt-
~routeing, ~routing 'ruːt ɪŋ ‖ 'ruːt̬ ɪŋ 'raʊt-
~routes 'ruːts 'raʊts
re|run v ₍ᵢ₎riː l'rʌn **~ran** 'ræn **~running**
'rʌn ɪŋ **~runs** 'rʌnz
rerun n 'riː rʌn **~s** z
res reɪz reɪs, riːz ‖ reɪs riːz —see also phrases
with this word
resale 'riː seɪᵊl ˌ•'• **~s** z
reschedul|e ˌriː 'ʃed juːl -'ʃedʒ uːl, -'sked juːl,
-'skedʒ uːl ‖ -'skedʒ ʊl -uːl, -ᵊl **~ed** d **~es** z
~ing ɪŋ
rescind rɪ 'sɪnd rə-, §riː- **~ed** ɪd əd **~ing** ɪŋ
~s z
rescission rɪ 'sɪʒ ən rə-, §riː- **~s** z
rescript 'riː skrɪpt **~s** s
resc|ue 'resk |juː **~ued** juːd **~ues** juːz **~uing**
juː_ɪŋ
rescuer 'resk juː_ə ‖ -ˀr **~s** z

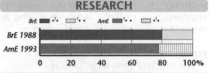

research v, n rɪ 'sɜːtʃ rə-, §riː-, §-'zɜːtʃ;
'riː sɜːtʃ ‖ rɪ 'sɜːtʃ 'riː sɜːtʃ —the
-'sɜːtʃ ‖ -'sɜːtʃ form appears still to
predominate in universities, although
'riː sɜːtʃ ‖ -sɜːtʃ has increasingly displaced it
in general usage both in Britain and in America.
Some speakers may distinguish between the verb
•'• and the noun '••. Poll panel preferences:
BrE 1988, •'• 80%, '•• 20% (university
teachers: •'• 95%, '•• 5%); AmE 1993, n, '••
78%, •'• 22%. **~ed** t **~es** ɪz əz **~ing** ɪŋ
researcher rɪ 'sɜːtʃ ə rə-, §riː-, §-'zɜːtʃ-;
'riː sɜːtʃ ə ‖ rɪ 'sɜːtʃ ˀr 'riː sɜːtʃ ˀr **~s** z
resect rɪ 'sekt rə-, §riː- **~ed** ɪd əd **~ing** ɪŋ **~s**
s
resection rɪ 'sek ʃən rə-, §riː- **~s** z
reseda 'res ɪd ə -əd-; rɪ 'siːd ə, rə- ‖ rɪ 'siːd ə
'reɪz ə dɑː
reseed ˌriː 'siːd **~ed** ɪd əd **~ing** ɪŋ **~s** z
reselect ˌriː sə 'lekt -sɪ- **~ed** ɪd əd **~ing** ɪŋ **~s**
s
reselection ˌriː sə 'lek ʃən -sɪ- **~s** z
resemblanc|e rɪ 'zem blən¹s rə-, §riː- **~es** ɪz
əz
resembl|e rɪ 'zem bᵊl rə-, §riː- **~ed** d **~es** z
~ing ɪŋ
re|sent rɪ l'zent rə-, §riː- **~sented** 'zent ɪd -əd
‖ 'zent̬ əd **~senting** 'zent ɪŋ ‖ 'zent̬ ɪŋ
~sents 'zents
resentful rɪ 'zent fᵊl rə-, §riː-, -fʊl **~ly** _i
~ness nəs nɪs
resentment rɪ 'zent mənt rə-, §riː- **~s** s
reserpine 'res ə piːn -pɪn; rɪ 'sɜːp iːn, rə-, -ɪn,
§-ən ‖ 'res ˀr- rɪ 'sɜːp iːn
reservation ˌrez ə 'veɪʃ ən ‖ -ˀr- **~s** z
reserv|e v, n rɪ 'zɜːv rə-, §riː- ‖ -'zɜːv **~ed** d
~es z **~ing** ɪŋ

R

reservedly rɪ ˈzɜːv ɪd li rə-, §riː-, -əd- ‖ -ˈzɝː-v-
reservist rɪ ˈzɜːv ɪst rə-, §riː-, §-əst ‖ -ˈzɝː-v-
~s s
reservoir ˈrez əv wɑː §-ə vɔː ‖ -ᵊrv wɑːr -əv-,
-wɔːr, -ɔːr ~s z
re|set ˌriː ˈset ~sets ˈsets ~setting/s ˈset ɪŋ/z
‖ ˈset ɪŋ/z
resettl|e ˌ(ˌ)riː ˈset ᵊl ‖ -ˈset̬ ᵊl ~ed d ~es z
~ing ˌɪŋ
resettlement ˌ(ˌ)riː ˈset ᵊl mənt ‖-ˈset̬ ᵊl-
res gestae ˌreɪz ˈgest aɪ ˌreɪs-, ˌriːz- -ˈdʒest-,
-iː ‖ ˌreɪs-, ˌriːz-
reshuffl|e v ˌ(ˌ)riː ˈʃʌf ᵊl ~ed d ~es z ~ing ˌɪŋ
reshuffle n ˈriː ˌʃʌf ᵊl ˌˌ•ˈ•• ~s z
resid|e rɪ ˈzaɪd rə-, §riː- ~ed ɪd əd ~es z ~ing
ɪŋ
residenc|e ˈrez ɪd ənts -əd- ‖ -ə dents ~es ɪz
əz ~ies ɪz ~y i
resident ˈrez ɪd ənt -əd- ‖ -ə dent ~s s
residential ˌrez ɪ ˈdentʃ ᵊl ◂ -ə- ~ly i
residentiar|y ˌrez ɪ ˈdentʃ ər li ˌ•ə-,
-ˈ•i ᵊr li ‖ -ˈ•i er li ~ies ɪz
residual rɪ ˈzɪd ju ᵊl rə-, §riː-, -ˈzɪdʒ u ᵊl
‖ -ˈzɪdʒ u ᵊl -ˈzɪdʒ ᵊl ~ly i ~s z
residuary rɪ ˈzɪd ju ᵊr i rə-, §riː-, -ˈzɪd jʊr i;
-ˈzɪdʒ uᵊr i ‖ -ˈzɪdʒ u er i
residue ˈrez ɪ djuː -ə-, →§-dʒuː ‖ -duː -djuː ~s
z
residu|um rɪ ˈzɪd ju̯ əm rə-, §riː-, -ˈzɪdʒ u̯
‖ -ˈzɪdʒ u̯ əm ~a ə
resign rɪ ˈzaɪn rə-, §riː- ~ed d ~ing ɪŋ ~s z
resignation ˌrez ɪg ˈneɪʃ ᵊn ~s z
resignedly rɪ ˈzaɪn ɪd li rə-, §riː-, -əd-
resil|e rɪ ˈzaɪᵊl rə-, §riː- ~ed d ~es z ~ing ɪŋ
resilienc|e rɪ ˈzɪl i̯ ənts rə-, §riː- ~y i
resilient rɪ ˈzɪl i̯ ənt rə-, §riː- ~ly li
resin ˈrez ɪn §-ᵊn ~s z
resi|nate ˈrez ɪ ˌneɪt §-ə-, -ᵊn eɪt ‖ -ᵊn eɪt
~nated neɪt ɪd -əd ‖ neɪt̬ əd ~nates neɪts
~nating neɪt ɪŋ ‖ neɪt̬ ɪŋ
resinous ˈrez ɪn əs -ᵊn̯əs
res ipsa loquitur ˌreɪz ˌɪps ə ˈlɒk wɪt ə ˌreɪs-,
ˌriːz-, -, •ɑː-, §-wət•, -ʊə
‖ ˌreɪs ˌɪps ə ˈlouk wət̬ ᵊr ˌriːz-
resist rɪ ˈzɪst rə-, §riː- ~ed ɪd əd ~ing ɪŋ ~s s
resistanc|e rɪ ˈzɪst ənts rə-, §riː- ~es ɪz əz
resistant rɪ ˈzɪst ənt rə-, §riː- ~ly li
resistib|le rɪ ˈzɪst əb ᵊl rə-, §riː-, -ɪb- ~ly li
resistive rɪ ˈzɪst ɪv rə-, §riː- ~ly li
resistivity ˌriːz ɪ ˈstɪv ət i ˌrez-, §,•ə-, -ɪt•;
rɪ ˌzɪ ˈstɪv-, rə- ‖ -ət̬ i
resistor rɪ ˈzɪst ə rə-, §riː- ‖ -ᵊr ~s z
re|sit v ˌriː ‖ˈsɪt ~sat ˈsæt ~sits ˈsɪts ~sitting
ˈsɪt ɪŋ ‖ ˈsɪt̬ ɪŋ
resit n ˈriː sɪt ~s s
Resnais rə ˈneɪ re- —Fr [ʁɛ nɛ]
resol|e ˌriː ˈsəʊl →-ˈsɒʊl ‖ -ˈsoʊl ~ed d ~es z
~ing ɪŋ
resoluble rɪ ˈzɒl jʊb ᵊl rə- ‖ -ˈzɑːl jəb ᵊl ~ness
nəs nɪs
resolute ˈrez ə luːt -ljuːt ~ly li ~ness nəs nɪs
resolution ˌrez ə ˈluːʃ ᵊn -ˈljuːʃ- ~s z

resolvability rɪ ˌzɒlv ə ˈbɪl ət i rə-, §riː-,
-,zəʊlv-, -ɪt i ‖ -,zɑːlv ə ˈbɪl ət̬ i
resolvable rɪ ˈzɒlv əb ᵊl rə-, §riː-, -ˈzəʊlv-
‖ rɪ ˈzɑːlv- ~ness nəs nɪs
resolv|e rɪ ˈzɒlv rə-, §riː-, §-ˈzəʊlv ‖ -ˈzɑːlv
~ed d ~es z ~ing ɪŋ
Resolven rɪ ˈzɒlv ən ‖ -ˈzɑːlv-
resolvent rɪ ˈzɒlv ᵊnt rə-, §riː-, §-ˈzəʊlv-
‖ -ˈzɑːlv- ~s s
resonanc|e ˈrez ᵊn_ənts ~es ɪz əz
resonant ˈrez ᵊn_ənt ~ly li ~s s
reso|nate ˈrez ə ˌneɪt ~nated neɪt ɪd -əd
‖ neɪt̬ əd ~nates neɪts ~nating
neɪt ɪŋ ‖ neɪt̬ ɪŋ
resonation ˌrez ə ˈneɪʃ ᵊn
resonator ˈrez ə neɪt ə ‖ -neɪt̬ ᵊr ~s z
resorb rɪ ˈsɔːb rə-, ˌriː-, -ˈzɔːb ‖ -ˈsɔːrb -ˈzɔːrb
~ed d ~ing ɪŋ ~s z
resorcinol rɪ ˈzɔːs ɪ nɒl rə-, re-, -ə-
‖ -ˈzɔːrs ᵊn ɔːl -ɑːl
resorption rɪ ˈsɔːp ʃᵊn rə-, ˌriː-, -ˈzɔːp-
‖ -ˈsɔːrp- -ˈzɔːrp-
resorptive rɪ ˈsɔːpt ɪv rə-, ˌriː-, -ˈzɔːpt-
‖ -ˈsɔːrpt- -ˈzɔːrpt-
re|sort v, n rɪ ‖ˈzɔːt rə-, §riː- ‖ -‖ˈzɔːrt ~sorted
ˈzɔːt ɪd -əd ‖ ˈzɔːrt̬ əd ~sorting
ˈzɔːt ɪŋ ‖ ˈzɔːrt̬ ɪŋ ~sorts ˈzɔːts ‖ ˈzɔːrts
resound rɪ ˈzaʊnd rə-, §riː- ~ed ɪd əd ~ing/ly
ɪŋ /li ~s z

RESOURCE

	■-ˈzɔːs	▢-ˈsɔːs	■ˈ••
BrE 1988			

0   20   40   60   80   100%

resourc|e rɪ ˈzɔːs rə-, §riː-, -ˈsɔːs; ˈriː sɔːs, -zɔːs
‖ ˈriː sɔːrs -soʊrs —BrE 1988 poll panel
preference: -ˈzɔːs 50%, -ˈsɔːs 45%, ˈ•• 6%.
~ed t ~es ɪz əz ~ing ɪŋ
resourceful rɪ ˈzɔːs fᵊl rə-, §riː-, -ˈsɔːs-, -fʊl
‖ rɪ ˈsɔːrs- -ˈsoʊrs-, -ˈzɔːrs-, -ˈzoʊrs- ~ly ‿i
~ness nəs nɪs
respect v, n rɪ ˈspekt rə-, §riː- ~ed ɪd əd ~ing
ɪŋ ~s s
respectability rɪ ˌspekt ə ˈbɪl ət i rə-, §riː-, -ɪt i
‖ -ət̬ i
respectab|le rɪ ˈspekt əb ᵊl rə-, §riː- ~leness
ᵊl nəs -nɪs ~ly li
respecter rɪ ˈspekt ə rə-, §riː- ‖ -ᵊr ~s z
respectful rɪ ˈspekt fᵊl rə-, §riː-, -fʊl ~ly ‿i
~ness nəs nɪs
respective rɪ ˈspekt ɪv rə-, §riː- ~ly li ~ness
nəs nɪs
Respighi re ˈspiːg i rɪ-, rə- —It [re ˈspiː gi]
respiration ˌresp ə ˈreɪʃ ᵊn -ɪ-
respirator ˈresp ə reɪt ə ‖ -reɪt̬ ᵊr ~s z
respiratory rɪ ˈspɪr ət_ᵊr i rə-, re-, §riː-,
-ˈspaɪᵊr-; ˈresp ᵊr_ət̬; ˈresp ə reɪt ᵊr i,
ˌ•ˈ•••• ‖ ˈresp ᵊr_ə tɔːr i rɪ ˈspaɪr ə-, -toʊr i
—Poll panel preferences: AmE 1993, ˈ•••••
95%, •ˈ•••• 5%; BrE 1998, -ˈspɪr- 59%,
ˈresp ᵊrət- 34%, ˈresp ə reɪt- 5%, -ˈspaɪᵊr-
2%.

respire rɪ ˈspaɪ_ə rə-, §ri:- ‖ -ˈspaɪ_ər **~d** d **~s** z **respiring** rɪ ˈspaɪ_ər ɪŋ rə-, §ri:- ‖ -ˈspaɪ_ər ɪŋ

respite ˈresp aɪt -ɪt, §-ət ‖ -ət rɪ ˈspaɪt **~s** s

resplendenc|e rɪ ˈsplend ənᵗs rə-, §ri:- **~y** i

resplendent rɪ ˈsplend ənt rə-, §ri:- **~ly** li

respond rɪ ˈspɒnd rə-, §ri:- ‖ -ˈspɑːnd **~ed** ɪd əd **~ing** ɪŋ **~s** z

respondent rɪ ˈspɒnd ənt rə-, §ri:- ‖ -ˈspɑːnd- **~s** s

respons|e rɪ ˈspɒnᵗs rə-, §ri:- ‖ -ˈspɑːnᵗs **~es** ɪz əz

responsibilit|y rɪ ˌspɒnᵗs ə ˈbɪl ət li rə-, §ri:-, -ˌˈɪ-, -ɪt i ‖ -ˌspɑːnᵗs ə ˈbɪl ət̬ li **~ies** iz

responsib|le rɪ ˈspɒnᵗs əb |əl rə-, §ri:-, -ɪb- ‖ rɪ ˈspɑːnᵗs- **~ly** li

responsive rɪ ˈspɒnᵗs ɪv rə-, §ri:- ‖ -ˈspɑːnᵗs ɪv **~ly** li **~ness** nəs nɪs

responsor|y rɪ ˈspɒnᵗs ər li rə-, §ri:- ‖ rɪ ˈspɑːnᵗs- **~ies** iz

respray v ˌri: ˈspreɪ **~ed** d **~ing** ɪŋ **~s** z

respray n ˈri: spreɪ **~s** z

rest rest **rested** ˈrest ɪd -əd **resting** ˈrest ɪŋ **rests** rests
ˈrest cure; ˈrest home; ˈresting place; ˈrest ˌperiod; ˈrest room

restag|e ˌri: ˈsteɪdʒ **~ed** d **~es** ɪz əz **~ing** ɪŋ

re|state ˌri: |ˈsteɪt **~stated** ˈsteɪt ɪd -əd ‖ ˈsteɪt̬ əd **~statement/s** ˈsteɪt mənt/s **~states** ˈsteɪts **~stating** ˈsteɪt ɪŋ ‖ ˈsteɪt̬ ɪŋ

restau|rant ˈrest ə |rɒnt -rɑːnt, -rɒŋ, -rɒ̃, -rãː, -rɔ̃ː; -əlr ənt; ˈres tlrɒnt, -tlrɑːnt, -tlrɒ̃, -tlrənt ‖ ˈrest əlr ənt -ə lrɑːnt; ˈres tlrənt, -tlrɑːnt —*BrE 1998 poll panel preference:* -rɒnt 39% *(born since 1973: 72%),* -rɑːnt 33%, -r *plus nasalized vowel 18%,* -rɑːnt 6%, -rɒŋ 4%. **~rants** rɒnᵗs rɑːnᵗs, rɒŋz, rɒ̃z, rãːz, rɔ̃ːz, rənᵗs ‖ rənᵗs rɑːnts
ˈrestaurant car

restaurateur ˌrest ər_ə ˈtɜː -ɒr ə-, -ɔːr ə-, ⚠-ə rɒn- ‖ -ˈtɜˑ-ˈtʊər —*Fr* [ʁɛs tɔ ʁa tœːʁ] **~s** z

restful ˈrest fəl -fʊl **~ly** i **~ness** nəs nɪs

restharrow ˈrest ˌhær əʊ ‖ -oʊ -ˌher-

restitution ˌrest ɪ ˈtjuːʃ ᵊn -ə-, →§-ˈtʃuːʃ- ‖ -ˈtuːʃ ᵊn -ˈtjuːʃ- **~s** z

restive ˈrest ɪv **~ly** li **~ness** nəs nɪs

restless ˈrest ləs -lɪs **~ly** li **~ness** nəs nɪs

restock ˌri: ˈstɒk ‖ -ˈstɑːk **~ed** t **~ing** ɪŋ **~s** s

Reston ˈrest ən

restoration, R~ ˌrest ə ˈreɪʃ ᵊn **~s** z

restorative rɪ ˈstɔːr ət ɪv rə-, §ri:-, -ˈstɒr-; ˈrest ə reɪt- ‖ -ət̬ ɪv -ˈstoʊr- **~s** z

restore rɪ ˈstɔː rə-, §ri:- ‖ -ˈstɔːr -ˈstoʊr **~d** d **~s** z **restoring** rɪ ˈstɔːr ɪŋ rə-, §ri:- ‖ -ˈstoʊr-

restorer rɪ ˈstɔːr ə rə-, §ri:- ‖ -ᵊr -ˈstoʊr- **~s** z

restrain rɪ ˈstreɪn rə-, §ri:- ‖ -əⁱr/z **~ing** ɪŋ

restraint rɪ ˈstreɪnt rə-, §ri:- **~s** s

restrict rɪ ˈstrɪkt rə-, §ri:- **~ed** ɪd əd **~ing** ɪŋ **~s** s

restriction rɪ ˈstrɪk ʃᵊn rə-, §ri:- **~s** z

restrictive rɪ ˈstrɪkt ɪv rə-, §ri:- **~ly** li **~ness** nəs nɪs
re,strictive ˈpractice

restructure ˌri: ˈstrʌk tʃə -ʃə ‖ -tʃᵊr **~d** d **~s** z **restructuring** ˌri: ˈstrʌk tʃᵊr ɪŋ -ʃᵊr_ɪŋ

result v, n rɪ ˈzʌlt rə-, §ri:- **~ed** ɪd əd **~ing** ɪŋ **~s** s

resultant rɪ ˈzʌlt ənt rə-, §ri:- ‖ -ᵊnt **~s** s

resultative rɪ ˈzʌlt ət ɪv rə-, §ri:- ‖ -ət̬ ɪv **~s** z

resum|e v rɪ ˈzjuːm rə-, §ri:-, -ˈzuːm, §-ˈʒuːm ‖ -ˈzuːm **~ed** d **~es** z **~ing** ɪŋ

resume, résumé, resumé ˈrez ju meɪ ˈreɪz-, -u-; rɪ ˈzjuːm eɪ, rə-, §ri:-, -ˈzuːm- ‖ ˈrez ə meɪ ˈreɪz-, -u-, ˌˈˈ **~s** z

resumption rɪ ˈzʌmp ʃᵊn rə-, §ri:- **~s** z

resumptive rɪ ˈzʌmpt ɪv rə-, §ri:- **~ly** li **~s** z

resurfac|e ˌri: ˈsɜːf ɪs -əs ‖ -ˈsɜˑːf əs **~ed** t **~es** ɪz əz **~ing** ɪŋ

resurg|e rɪ ˈsɜːdʒ rə-, §ri:- ‖ -ˈsɜˑːdʒ **~ed** d **~es** ɪz əz **~ing** ɪŋ

resurgenc|e rɪ ˈsɜːdʒ ənᵗs rə-, §ri:- ‖ rɪ ˈsɜˑːdʒ- **~es** ɪz əz

resurgent rɪ ˈsɜːdʒ ənt rə-, §ri:- ‖ rɪ ˈsɜˑːdʒ-

resurrect ˌrez ə ˈrekt **~ed** ɪd əd **~ing** ɪŋ **~s** s

resurrection, R~ ˌrez ə ˈrek ʃᵊn **~s** z

resusci|tate rɪ ˈsʌs ɪ |teɪt rə-, ˌri:-, -ə- **~tated** teɪt ɪd -əd ‖ teɪt̬ əd **~tates** teɪts **~tating** teɪt ɪŋ ‖ teɪt̬ ɪŋ

resuscitation rɪ ˌsʌs ɪ ˈteɪʃ ᵊn rə-, ˌri:-, ˌˈˈˈ, -əˈˈ- **~s** z

ret ret **rets** rets **retted** ˈret ɪd -əd ‖ ˈret̬ əd **retting** ˈret ɪŋ ‖ ˈret̬ ɪŋ

retable n rɪ ˈteɪb ᵊl rə-, ri:-; ˈri:, ** **~s** z

retail v ˈsell' ˈri: teɪᵊl ₍ᵢ₎ˈˈ **~ed** d **~ing** ɪŋ **~s** z

retail v ˈpass on, relate' rɪ ˈteɪᵊl rə-, ₍ᵢ₎ri:- **~ed** d **~ing** ɪŋ **~s** z

retail n, adj ˈri: teɪᵊl
ˌretail ˈprice ˌindex

retailer ˈri: teɪᵊl ə ‖ -ᵊr **~s** z

retain rɪ ˈteɪn rə-, §ri:- **~ed** d **~ing** ɪŋ **~s** z

retainer rɪ ˈteɪn ə rə-, §ri:- ‖ -ᵊr **~s** z

re|take v ₍ᵢ₎ri: |ˈteɪk **~taken** ˈteɪk ən **~takes** ˈteɪks **~taking** ˈteɪk ɪŋ **~took** ˈtʊk §ˈtuːk

retake n ˈri: teɪk **~s** s

retali|ate rɪ ˈtæl i |eɪt rə-, §ri:- **~ated** eɪt ɪd -əd ‖ eɪt̬ əd **~ates** eɪts **~ating** eɪt ɪŋ ‖ eɪt̬ ɪŋ

retaliation rɪ ˌtæl i ˈeɪʃ ᵊn rə-, §ri:- **~s** z

retaliatory rɪ ˈtæl i ə_t̬ᵊr i rə-, §ri:-; -eɪt ᵊr i, ˈˈˈˈeɪt- ‖ -ə tɔːr i -tour i

Retallack rɪ ˈtæl ək rə-

retard v; n ˈslowdown' rɪ ˈtɑːd rə-, §ri:- ‖ -ˈtɑːrd **~ed** ɪd əd **~ing** ɪŋ **~s** z

retard n ˈmentally retarded person' ˈri: tɑːd ‖ -tɑːrd **~s** z

retardant rɪ ˈtɑːd ənt rə-, §ri:- ‖ rɪ ˈtɑːrd- **~s** s

retardate rɪ ˈtɑːd eɪt rə-, §ri:- ‖ -ˈtɑːrd- **~s** s

retardation ˌri: tɑː ˈdeɪʃ ᵊn ‖ -tɑːr- rɪ ˌˈˈˈ **~s** z

retch retʃ ri:tʃ **retched** retʃt ri:tʃt **retches** ˈretʃ ɪz ri:tʃ-, -əz **retching** ˈretʃ ɪŋ ˈri:tʃ-

rete ˈri:t i ‖ ˈri:t̬ i ˈreɪt i **retia** ˈri:t i_ə ˈri:ʃ- ‖ ˈri:t̬ i_ə ˈreɪt̬-

re|tell ˌriː |ˈtel ~telling ˈtel ɪŋ ~tells ˈtelz
~told ˈtəʊld →ˈtɒʊld ‖ ˈtoʊld
retention rɪ ˈtentʃ ən rə-, §riː- ~s z
  re'tention fee
retentive rɪ ˈtent ɪv rə-, §riː- ‖ -ˈtenʈ ɪv ~ly li
~ness nəs nɪs
Retford ˈret fəd ‖ -fərd
re|think v ˌriː |ˈθɪŋk ~thinking ˈθɪŋk ɪŋ
~thinks ˈθɪŋks ~thought ˈθɔːt ‖ ˈθɑːt
rethink n ˈriː θɪŋk ˌ•ˈ• ~s s
retiari|us ˌret i ˈeər i‿ləs ˌriːt-, ˌriːʃ-,
-ˈɑːr- ‖ ˌret̬ i ˈer- ~i aɪ iː
reticence ˈret ɪs ənts -əs- ‖ ˈret̬ əs-
reticent ˈret ɪs ənt -əs- ‖ ˈret̬ əs- ~ly li
reticle ˈret ɪk əl ‖ ˈret̬- ~s z
reticular rɪ ˈtɪk jʊl ə rə-, §riː-, -jəl- ‖ -jəl ər
reticu|late v rɪ ˈtɪk ju |leɪt rə-, §riː-, -jə- ‖ -jə-
~lated leɪt ɪd -əd ‖ leɪt̬ əd ~lates leɪts
~lating leɪt ɪŋ ‖ leɪt̬ ɪŋ
reticulate adj rɪ ˈtɪk jʊl ət rə-, §riː-, -jəl-, -ɪt
reticulation rɪ ˌtɪk ju ˈleɪʃ ən rə-, §riː-, -jə-
‖ -jə- ~s z
reticule ˈret ɪ kjuːl -ə- ‖ ˈret̬- ~s z
reticul|um, R~ rɪ ˈtɪk jʊl əm rə-, -jəl- ‖ -jəl-
~a ə
ret|ina ˈret |ɪn ə §-ən‿ə ‖ -ⁱn‿ə ~inae ɪ niː
§ən iː ‖ -ⁱn iː ~inas ɪn əz §ən‿əz ‖ ⁱn‿əz
retinal ˈret ɪn əl §-ən‿əl ‖ ˈret̬ ən‿əl
retinitis ˌret ɪ ˈnaɪt ɪs -ə-, -ən ˈaɪt-, §-əs
‖ ˌret̬ ən ˈaɪt̬ əs
  ˌreti,nitis ˌpigmen'tosa ˌpɪg men ˈtəʊs ə
-ˈtəʊz- ‖ -ˈtoʊs ə
retino- comb. form
  with stress-neutral suffix ˈret ɪn əʊ -ən-
  ‖ ˈret̬ ən ə — retinoscope ˈret ɪn əʊ
  skəʊp ‖ -ən ə skoʊp
  with stress-imposing suffix ˌret ɪ ˈnɒ+ -ə-
  ‖ ˌret̬ ən ˈɑː+ — retinopathy ˌret ɪ ˈnɒp əθ i
  ˌ•ə- ‖ ˌret̬ ən ˈɑːp-
retinol ˈret ɪ nɒl -ə- ‖ ˈret̬ ən ɔːl -ɑːl, -oʊl
retinue ˈret ɪ njuː §-ə-; §-ən juː, -uː ‖ ˈret̬ ən uː
-juː ~s z
retire rɪ ˈtaɪ‿ə rə-, §riː- ‖ -ˈtaɪ‿ər ~d d ~s z
  retiring/ly rɪ ˈtaɪ‿ər ɪŋ /li ‖ -ˈtaɪ‿ər ɪŋ /li
retiree rɪ ˌtaɪ‿ə ˈriː rə-, §riː-, ˌriː•-; •ˈ••
‖ rɪ ˌtaɪə ˈriː ~s z
retirement rɪ ˈtaɪ‿ə mənt rə-, §riː-
‖ -ˈtaɪ‿ər mənt ~s s
  re'tirement age; re'tirement ˌpension
re|tort v, n rɪ |ˈtɔːt rə-, §riː- ‖ -ˈtɔːrt ~torted
ˈtɔːt ɪd -əd ‖ ˈtɔːrt̬ əd ~torting
ˈtɔːt ɪŋ ‖ ˈtɔːrt̬ ɪŋ ~torts ˈtɔːts ‖ ˈtɔːrts
retortion rɪ ˈtɔːʃ ən rə-, §riː- ‖ -ˈtɔːrʃ-
retouch v ˌriː ˈtʌtʃ ~ed t ~es ɪz əz ~ing ɪŋ
retouch n ˈriː tʌtʃ ˌ•ˈ• ~es ɪz əz
retrac|e rɪ ˈtreɪs rə-, ˌriː- ~ed t ~es ɪz əz
~ing ɪŋ
retract rɪ ˈtrækt rə-, §riː- ~ed ɪd əd ~ing ɪŋ
~s z
retractable, retractible rɪ ˈtrækt əb əl rə-, §riː-
retractile rɪ ˈtrækt aɪəl rə-, §riː- ‖ -əl
retraction rɪ ˈtræk ʃən rə-, §riː- ~s z
retractor rɪ ˈtrækt ə rə-, §riː- ‖ -ər ~s z

retread v ˌriː ˈtred ~ed ɪd əd ~ing ɪŋ ~s z
retrod ˌriː ˈtrɒd ‖ -ˈtrɑːd retrodden
ˌriː ˈtrɒd ən ‖ -ˈtrɑːd ən
retread n ˈriː tred ~s z
re|treat v, n rɪ |ˈtriːt rə-, §riː- ~treated ˈtriːt ɪd
-əd ‖ ˈtriːt̬ əd ~treating ˈtriːt ɪŋ ‖ ˈtriːt̬ ɪŋ
~treats ˈtriːts
retrench rɪ ˈtrentʃ rə-, §riː- ~ed t ~es ɪz əz
~ing ɪŋ ~ment/s mənt/s
retrial ˌriː ˈtraɪ‿əl ˈ•‿•• ‖ -ˈtraɪ‿əl ˈ•‿•• ~s z
retribution ˌretr ɪ ˈbjuːʃ ən -ə-
retributive rɪ ˈtrɪb jʊt ɪv rə-, §riː-, -jət-;
§ˈretr ɪ bjuːt-, ˈ•ə- ‖ -jət̬ ɪv ~ly li
retributory rɪ ˈtrɪb jʊt‿ər i rə-, §riː-, -jət‿
‖ -jə tɔːr i -toʊr-
retri... —see retry
retrievability rɪ ˌtriːv ə ˈbɪl ət i rə-, -ɪt i ‖ -ət̬ i
retrievable rɪ ˈtriːv əb əl rə-, §riː-
retrieval rɪ ˈtriːv əl rə-, §riː- ~s z
retriev|e rɪ ˈtriːv rə-, §riː- ~ed d ~es z ~ing
ɪŋ
retriever rɪ ˈtriːv ə rə-, §riː- ‖ -ər ~s z
retro ˈretr əʊ ‖ -oʊ
retro- ˌretr əʊ ‖ -oʊ —formerly also ˈriːtr-
  — retrobronchial ˌretr əʊ
  ˈbrɒŋk i‿əl ◂ ‖ -oʊ ˈbrɑːŋk-
retroactive ˌretr əʊ ˈækt ɪv ◂ ‖ -oʊ- ~ly li
retroced|e ˌretr əʊ ˈsiːd ‖ -oʊ- ~ed ɪd əd ~es
z ~ing ɪŋ
retrocession ˌretr əʊ ˈseʃ ən ‖ -oʊ-
retrochoir ˈretr əʊ ˌkwaɪ‿ə ‖ -oʊ ˌkwaɪ‿ər ~s
z
retroflex adj, n, v ˈretr əʊ fleks ‖ -ə- ~ed t
~es ɪz əz ~ing ɪŋ
retroflexion ˌretr əʊ ˈflek ʃən ‖ -ə- ~s z
retrograd|e ˈretr əʊ greɪd ‖ -ə- ~ed ɪd əd
~ely li ~es z ~ing ɪŋ
retrogress ˌretr əʊ ˈgres ‖ -ə- ~ed t ~es ɪz əz
~ing ɪŋ
retrogression ˌretr əʊ ˈgreʃ ən ‖ -ə- ~s z
retrogressive ˌretr əʊ ˈgres ɪv ◂ ‖ -ə- ~ly li
retrorocket ˈretr əʊ ˌrɒk ɪt §-ət ‖ -oʊ ˌrɑːk ət
~s s
retrospect ˈretr əʊ spekt ‖ -ə-
retrospection ˌretr əʊ ˈspek ʃən ‖ -ə-
retrospective ˌretr əʊ ˈspekt ɪv ◂ ‖ -ə- ~ly li
~ness nəs nɪs ~s z
  ˌretro,spective ˌexhi'bition
retrousse, retroussé rə ˈtruːs eɪ rɪ-, §riː-
‖ rə ˌtruː ˈseɪ ˌretr u- (*) —Fr [ʁə tʁu se]
retroversion ˌretr əʊ ˈvɜːʃ ən -ˈvɜːʒ-
. ‖ -oʊ ˈvɜːʒ ən ~s z
Retrovir tdmk ˈretr əʊ vɪə ‖ -oʊ vɪr
retrovirus ˈretr əʊ ˌvaɪ‿ər əs ˌ••ˈ•• ‖ -ə- ~es ɪz
əz
re|try ˌriː |ˈtraɪ ~tried ˈtraɪd ~tries ˈtraɪz
~trying ˈtraɪ ɪŋ
retsina ret ˈsiːn ə ˈrets ɪn ə, -ən- —ModGk
[rɛ ˈtsi na] ~s z
Rett ret
return v, n rɪ ˈtɜːn rə-, §riː- ‖ -ˈtɜ̩ːn ~ed d
~ing ɪŋ ~s z
  re'turning ,officer

R

returnable rɪ 'tɜːn əb əl rə-, §riː- ‖ -'tɝːn- ~s
z

returnee rɪ ˌtɜː 'niː rə-, §riː-, -'tɜːn iː
‖ rɪ ˌtɝː 'niː ~s z

returner rɪ 'tɜːn ə rə-, §riː- ‖ -'tɝːn ər ~s z

retuse rɪ 'tjuːs rə-, riː-, §-'tuːs, →§'tʃuːs
‖ -'tuːs -'tjuːs ~ness nəs nɪs

Reuben 'ruːb ən -ɪn

reunification ˌriː ˌjuːn ɪf ɪ 'keɪʃ ən •ˌ•••'••,
-əf•'••-, §-ə'•- ~s z

reuni|fy ⑴riː 'juːn ɪ |faɪ -ə- ~fied faɪd ~fies
faɪz ~fying faɪ ɪŋ

reunion ⑴riː 'juːn i_ən ‖ -'juːn jən ~s z

Reunion, Réunion island
⑴riː 'juːn i_ən ‖ -'juːn jən —Fr [ʁe y njɔ̃]

reu|nite ˌriː ju |'naɪt ~nited 'naɪt ɪd -əd
‖ 'naɪt̬ əd ~nites naɪts ~niting
'naɪt ɪŋ ‖ 'naɪt̬ ɪŋ

reusable ⑴riː 'juːz əb əl ◂

reus|e v ˌriː 'juːz ~ed d ~es ɪz əz ~ing ɪŋ

reuse n ˌriː 'juːs

Reuter 'rɔɪt ə ‖ 'rɔɪt̬ ər ~s z

rev rev **revs** revz **revved** revd **revving**
'rev ɪŋ
'rev ˌcounter

Rev rev or as **Reverend**

revaluation ˌriː ˌvæl ju 'eɪʃ ən •ˌ•••'•• ~s z

reval|ue ⑴riː 'væl |juː ~ued juːd ~ues juːz
~uing juː_ɪŋ

revamp v ⑴riː 'væmp ~ed t ~ing ɪŋ ~s s

revamp n 'riː væmp ˌ•'• ~s s

revanch|ism rɪ 'væntʃ |ˌɪz əm rə, §riː-,
-'vɑːntʃ-, -'vɒ̃ʃ- ~ist/s ɪst/s §əst/s ‖ əst/s

Revd —see **Reverend**

reveal v, n rɪ 'viː_əl rə-, §riː- ~ed d ~ing/ly
ɪŋ /li ~s z

reveille rɪ 'væl i rə-, §riː-, -'vel- ‖ 'rev əl i (*)
~s z

revel v, n 'rev əl ~ed, ~led d ~ing, ~ling ɪŋ
~s z

revelation, R~ ˌrev ə 'leɪʃ ən ~s z

reveler, reveller 'rev əl ə ‖ -əl_ər ~s z

Revell 'rev əl

revel|ry 'rev əl |ri ~ries riz

Revelstoke 'rev əl stəʊk ‖ -stoʊk

reven|ant 'rev ən |ənt -ɪn-; -ə n|ænt, -n|ɑ̃ː
~ants ənts ænts, ɑ̃ːz

reveng|e v, n rɪ 'vendʒ rə-, §riː- ~ed d ~es ɪz
əz ~ing ɪŋ

revengeful rɪ 'vendʒ fəl rə-, §riː- ~ly _i
~ness nəs nɪs

revenue 'rev ə njuː: -ɪ-, §-nuː ‖ -nuː —formerly
also rɪ 'ven juː, rə-, §riː- ~s z

reverb 'riː vɜːb rɪ 'vɜːb, rə-, riː- ‖ 'riː vɝːb
rɪ 'vɝːb ~s z

reverberant rɪ 'vɜːb ər_ənt rə-, §riː- ‖ -'vɝːb-
~ly li

reverbe|rate rɪ 'vɜːb ə |reɪt rə-, §riː- ‖ -'vɝːb-
~rated reɪt ɪd -əd ‖ reɪt̬ əd ~rates reɪts
~rating reɪt ɪŋ ‖ reɪt̬ ɪŋ

reverberation rɪ ˌvɜːb ə 'reɪʃ ən rə-, §riː-
‖ -ˌvɝːb- ~s z

reverberator|y rɪ 'vɜːb ər_ət_ər |i -reɪt ər |i
‖ rɪ 'vɝːb ər_ə tɔːr |i -tour i; △•'•ə•• ~ies
iz

revere, R~ rɪ 'vɪə rə-, §riː- ‖ -'vɪ°r ~d d ~s z
revering rɪ 'vɪər ɪŋ rə-, §riː- ‖ -'vɪr ɪŋ

reverenc|e 'rev ər_ənts ~ed t ~es ɪz əz ~ing
ɪŋ

rever|end, R~ 'rev ər_|ənd △ˌənt ~ends əndz
△ənts
ˌReverend 'Mother

reverent 'rev ər_ənt ~ly li

reverential ˌrev ə 'rentʃ əl ◂ ~ly i

reverie 'rev ər i ~s z

revers sing. rɪ 'vɪə rə-, §riː-, -'veə ‖ -'vɪ°r -'ve°r

revers pl rɪ 'vɪəz rə-, §riː-, -'veəz ‖ -'vɪ°rz
-'ve°rz

reversal rɪ 'vɜːs əl rə-, §riː- ‖ -'vɝːs əl ~s z

revers|e adj, n, v rɪ 'vɜːs rə-, §riː- ‖ -'vɝːs ~ed
t ~ely li ~es ɪz əz ~ing ɪŋ
reˌverse diˌscrimi'nation; reˌversing light

reversi rɪ 'vɜːs i rə-, §riː- ‖ -'vɝːs i

reversibility rɪ ˌvɜːs ə 'bɪl ət i rə-, §riː-, -,•ɪ-,
-ɪt i ‖ -ˌvɝːs ə 'bɪl ət̬ i

reversib|le rɪ 'vɜːs əb |əl rə-, §riː-, -ɪb-
‖ -'vɝːs- ~leness əl nəs -nɪs ~ly li

reversion rɪ 'vɜːʃ ən rə-, §riː-, -'vɜːʒ-
‖ -'vɝːʒ ən -'vɝːʃ- ~s z

reversionary rɪ 'vɜːʃ ən_ər i rə-, §riː-, -'vɜːʒ-,
-ən ər_i ‖ rɪ 'vɝːʒ ə ner i -'vɝːʃ-

re|vert rɪ |'vɜːt rə-, §riː- ‖ -|'vɝːt ~verted
'vɜːt ɪd -əd ‖ 'vɝːt̬ əd ~verting
'vɜːt ɪŋ ‖ 'vɝːt̬ ɪŋ ~verts 'vɜːts ‖ 'vɝːts

re|vet rɪ |'vet rə-, §riː- ~ vets 'vets ~vetted
'vet ɪd -əd ‖ 'vet̬ əd ~vetting
'vet ɪŋ ‖ 'vet̬ ɪŋ

revetment rɪ 'vet mənt rə-, §riː- ~s s

Revie 'riːv i

review n, v rɪ 'vjuː rə-, §riː- ~ed d ~ing ɪŋ ~s
z

reviewer rɪ 'vjuː_ə rə-, §riː- ‖ _ər ~s z

revil|e rɪ 'vaɪ°l rə-, §riː- ~ed d ~er/s ə/z ‖ ər/z
~es z ~ing ɪŋ

Revill 'rev əl -ɪl

revis|e rɪ 'vaɪz rə-, §riː- ~ed d ~er/s ə/z ‖ ər/z
~es ɪz əz ~ing ɪŋ
Reˌvised 'Version

revision rɪ 'vɪʒ ən rə-, §riː- ~s z

revisionism rɪ 'vɪʒ ən ˌɪz əm rə-, §riː-

revisionist rɪ 'vɪʒ ən_ɪst rə-, §riː-, §-əst ~s s

revis|it ˌriː 'vɪz |ɪt §-ət ‖ -|ət ~ited ɪt ɪd §ət-,
-əd ‖ ət̬ əd ~iting ɪt ɪŋ §ət- ‖ ət̬ ɪŋ ~its ɪts
§əts ‖ əts

revitalis... —see **revitaliz...**

revitalization ˌriː ˌvaɪt əl aɪ 'zeɪʃ ən •ˌ•••'••
‖ ˌriː ˌvaɪt̬ əl ə 'zeɪʃ ən ˌ•ˌ•••'••

revitaliz|e ⑴riː 'vaɪt ə laɪz -əl aɪz ‖ -'vaɪt̬ əl aɪz
~ed d ~es ɪz əz ~ing ɪŋ

revival rɪ 'vaɪv əl rə-, §riː- ~s z

revivalism rɪ 'vaɪv əl ˌɪz əm rə-, §riː-

revivalist rɪ 'vaɪv əl ɪst rə-, §riː-, §-əst ~s s

reviv|e rɪ 'vaɪv rə-, §riː- ~ed d ~es z ~ing ɪŋ

revivi|fy ⑴riː 'vɪv ɪ |faɪ rɪ-, -ə- ~fied faɪd ~fies
faɪz ~fying faɪ ɪŋ

reviviscence ˌrev ɪ 'vɪs ᵊn⁺s -ə-
Revlon *tdmk* 'rev lɒn ‖ -lɑːn
revocab|le 'rev ək əb |ᵊl rɪ 'vəʊk-, rə-,
  §riː- ‖ rɪ 'voʊk- **~leness** ᵊl nəs -nɪs **~ly** li
revocation ˌrev əʊ 'keɪʃ ᵊn ‖ -ə- **~s** z
revok|e rɪ 'vəʊk rə-, §riː- ‖ -'voʊk **~ed** t **~es**
  s **~ing** ɪŋ
revolt *v, n* rɪ 'vəʊlt rə-, §riː-, →-'vɒʊlt ‖ -'voʊlt
  ~ed ɪd əd **~ing/ly** ɪŋ /li **~s** s
revolution ˌrev ə 'luːʃ ᵊn -'ljuːʃ- **~s** z
revolutionar|y ˌrev ə 'luːʃ ᵊn ᵊr‿li ◄ -'ljuːʃ-,
  -ᵊn‿ər li ‖ -ə ner li **~ies** iz
revolunis|e, revolutioniz|e
  ˌrev ə 'luːʃ ə naɪz -'ljuːʃ- **~ed** d **~es** ɪz əz
  ~ing ɪŋ
revolv|e rɪ 'vɒlv rə-, §riː-, §-'vəʊlv ‖ -'vɑːlv
  ~ed d **~es** z **~ing** ɪŋ
  re ˌvolving 'credit; re ˌvolving 'door
revolver rɪ 'vɒlv ə rə-, §riː-, §-'vəʊlv-
  ‖ -'vɑːlv ᵊr **~s** z
revue rɪ 'vjuː rə- *(= review)* **~s** z
revulsion rɪ 'vʌlʃ ᵊn rə-, §riː- **~s** z
Rew ruː
reward *n, v* rɪ 'wɔːd rə-, §riː- ‖ -'wɔːrd **~ed** ɪd
  əd **~ing/ly** ɪŋ /li **~s** z
rewind *v* ₍ᵢ₎riː 'waɪnd **~ing** ɪŋ **~s** z rewound
  ₍ᵢ₎riː 'waʊnd
rewind *n* 'riː waɪnd ₍ᵢ₎•'• **~s** z
rewire ˌriː 'waɪ‿ə ‖ -'waɪ‿ᵊr **~d** d **~s** z
  rewiring/s ˌriː 'waɪ‿ər ɪŋ/z ‖ -'waɪ‿ᵊr ɪŋ/z
reword ˌriː 'wɜːd ‖ -'wɝːd **~ed** ɪd əd **~ing/s**
  ɪŋ/z **~s** z
rework ˌriː 'wɜːk ‖ -'wɝːk **~ed** t **~ing/s** ɪŋ/z
  ~s s
rewrite *n* 'riː raɪt ˌ•'• **~s** s
re|write *v* ˌriː |'raɪt **~writes** 'raɪts **~written**
  'rɪt ᵊn ◄ **~wrote** 'rəʊt ‖ 'roʊt
Rex, rex reks **Rex's** 'reks ɪz -əz
rexine, R~ *tdmk* 'reks iːn
Rey reɪ
Reye raɪ reɪ **Reye's** raɪz reɪz
  'Reye's ˌsyndrome
Reyes raɪz reɪz
Reykjavik 'reɪk jə vɪk 'rek-, 'raɪk-, -viːk
  —*Icelandic* Reykjavík ['reːɪ ca viːk]
Reynard, r~ 'ren ɑːd 'reɪn-, -əd ‖ -ɑːrd -ᵊrd
Reynold 'ren ᵊld
Reynolds 'ren ᵊldz
Rh ˌɑːr 'eɪtʃ ◄ §ˌɑː 'heɪtʃ ‖ ˌɑːr 'eɪtʃ ◄ —*or as*
  'Rhesus
  ˌR'h ˌfactor; ˌRh 'negative; ˌRh 'positive
rhabdo- *comb. form* |ˌræbd əʊ ‖ -oʊ —
  rhabdovirus 'ræbd əʊ ˌvaɪᵊr əs ‖ -oʊ-
Rhadamanth|us ˌræd ə 'mænᵗθ |əs **~ine**
  aɪn ◄ ‖ ᵊn ◄ aɪn ◄ **~ys** ɪs əs §əs
Rhaet|ia 'riːʃ |ə -li‿ə **~an/s** ᵊn/z i‿ən/z
Rhaetic 'riːt ɪk ‖ 'riːt̬ ɪk
Rhaeto-Romance ˌriːt əʊ rəʊ
  'mænᵗs ◄ ‖ ˌriːt̬ oʊ roʊ-
Rhaeto-Romanic ˌriːt əʊ rəʊ
  'mæn ɪk ◄ ‖ ˌriːt̬ oʊ roʊ-
rhapsodic ræp 'sɒd ɪk ‖ -'sɑːd ɪk **~ally** ᵊl‿i

rhapsodis|e, rhapsodiz|e 'ræps ə daɪz **~ed** d
  ~es ɪz əz **~ing** ɪŋ
rhapsod|y 'ræps əd li **~ies** iz
rhatan|y 'ræt ᵊn li ‖ 'ræt̬ ᵊn li **~ies** iz
Rhayader 'raɪ‿əd ə ‖ -ᵊr
rhea, Rhea rɪə 'riː‿ə ‖ 'riː ə **rheas, Rhea's** rɪəz
  'riː‿əz ‖ 'riː əz
rhebok 'riː bɒk ‖ -bɑːk **~s** s
Rhee riː
Rhees riːs
Rheidol 'raɪd ɒl ‖ -ɑːl -ɔːl, -oʊl —*Welsh*
  ['hrəi dol]
Rheims riːmz —*French* Reims[ʁæːs]
rhematic riː 'mæt ɪk ‖ -'mæt̬-
rheme riːm *(= ream)* **rhemes** riːmz
Rhenish 'ren ɪʃ 'riːn-
rhenium 'riːn i‿əm
rheo- *comb. form*
  with stress-neutral suffix |riː‿ə -əʊ ‖ -oʊ —
  rheoscope 'riː‿ə skəʊp -əʊ- ‖ -skoʊp
  with stress-imposing suffix ri 'ɒ⁺ ‖ ri 'ɑː⁺ —
  rheology ri 'ɒl ədʒ i ‖ ri 'ɑːl-
rheostat 'riː‿ə stæt -əʊ- **~s** s
rhesus, R~ 'riːs əs
  'Rhesus ˌfactor; 'rhesus ˌmonkey; ˌRhesus
  'negative
Rhet... —*see* **Rhaet...**
rhetoric 'ret ə rɪk ‖ 'ret̬- *(!)*
rhetorical rɪ 'tɒr ɪk ᵊl rə- ‖ rɪ 'tɔːr- -'tɑːr- **~ly**
  ‿i
  rhe ˌtorical 'question
rhetorician ˌret ə 'rɪʃ ᵊn ‖ ˌret̬- **~s** z
Rhett ret
rheum ruːm
rheumatic ru 'mæt ɪk ‖ -'mæt̬ ɪk **~s** s
  rheu ˌmatic 'fever
rheumaticky ru 'mæt ɪk i ‖ -'mæt̬-
rheumatism 'ruːm ə tɪz əm
rheumatoid 'ruːm ə tɔɪd
rheumatological
  ˌruːm ət ə 'lɒdʒ ɪk ᵊl ◄ -ət̬ ə 'lɑːdʒ- **~ly** ‿i
rheumatologist ˌruːm ə 'tɒl ədʒ ɪst §-əst
  ‖ -'tɑːl- **~s** s
rheumatology ˌruːm ə 'tɒl ədʒ i ‖ -'tɑːl-
rheumy 'ruːm i
Rhian 'riː‿ən —*Welsh* ['hriː an]
Rhiannon ri 'æn ən —*Welsh* [hri 'an on]
Rhianydd ri 'æn ɪð —*Welsh* [hri 'a nið, -nɪð]
Rhine raɪn —*Ger* Rhein [ʁaɪn]
Rhineland 'raɪn lænd -lənd —*Ger* Rheinland
  ['ʁaɪn lant]
rhinestone 'raɪn stəʊn ‖ -stoʊn **~s** z
rhinitis raɪ 'naɪt ɪs §-əs ‖ -'naɪt̬ əs
Rhinns rɪnz
rhino 'raɪn əʊ ‖ -oʊ **~s** z
rhino- *comb. form*
  with stress-neutral suffix |raɪn əʊ ‖ -oʊ
  — **rhinoplasty** 'raɪn əʊ ˌplæst i ‖ -oʊ-
  with stress-imposing suffix raɪ 'nɒ⁺ ‖ -'nɑː⁺
  — **rhinologist** raɪ 'nɒl ədʒ ɪst §-əst ‖ -'nɑːl-
rhinoceros raɪ 'nɒs ᵊr‿əs ‖ -'nɑːs- **~es** ɪz əz
Rhinog 'riːn ɒg 'rɪn- ‖ -ɑːg —*Welsh* ['hriː nog]
Rhiwbina ru 'baɪn ə —*Welsh* [hrɪu 'bəi na]

R

R

rhizo- *comb. form*
  with stress-neutral suffix ˌraɪz əʊ ‖ -oʊ —
  rhizocarpous ˌraɪz əʊ 'kɑːp əs ◄
  ‖ -oʊ 'kɑːrp-
  with stress-imposing suffix raɪ 'zɒ+ ‖ -'zɑː+ —
  rhizotomy raɪ 'zɒt əm i ‖ -'zɑːt̬-
rhizome 'raɪz əʊm ‖ -oʊm ~s z
rho rəʊ ‖ roʊ (= *roe*) rhos rəʊz ‖ roʊz
Rhoda 'rəʊd ə ‖ 'roʊd ə
rhodamine 'rəʊd ə miːn ‖ 'roʊd-
Rhode Island 'rəʊd ˌaɪl ənd ˌ•'•◄
  ‖ roʊd 'aɪl ənd ˌ•- ~er/s ə/z ‖ ᵊr/z
  ˌRhode ˌIsland 'Red ‖ •ˌ•• '•
Rhodes rəʊdz ‖ roʊdz
  ˌRhodes 'scholar, '• ˌ••
Rhodesi|a rəʊ 'diːʃ ə -ɪ'diːʒ-, -i_ə; -'diːs i_ə,
  -'diːz- ‖ roʊ 'diːʒ ə ~an/s ən/z i_ən/z
Rhodian 'rəʊd i_ən ‖ 'roʊd- ~s z
rhodium 'rəʊd i_əm ‖ 'roʊd-
rhododendron ˌrəʊd ə 'dendr ən -ɪ- ‖ ˌroʊd-
  ~s z
rhodolite 'rɒd ə laɪt 'rəʊd-, -ᵊl aɪt ‖ 'roʊd ᵊl aɪt
  ~s s
Rhodope 'rɒd əp i rɒ 'dəʊp i, rəʊ- ‖ 'rɑːd-
rhodopsin rəʊ 'dɒps ɪn §-ən ‖ roʊ 'dɑːps ən
rhodora rəʊ 'dɔːr ə ‖ roʊ- -'doʊr- ~s z
Rhodri 'rɒdr i ‖ 'rɑːdr i —*Welsh* ['hrod ri]
rhomb rɒm rɒmb ‖ raːm raːmb rhombs rɒmz
  rɒmbz ‖ raːmz raːmbz
rhombohedr|on ˌrɒm bəʊ 'hiːdr |ən -'hedr-
  ‖ ˌraːm boʊ- -bə- ~a ə ~ons ənz
rhomboid 'rɒm bɔɪd ‖ 'raːm- ~s z
rhom|bus 'rɒm |bəs ‖ 'raːm- ~bi baɪ ~buses
  bəs ɪz -əz
Rhona 'rəʊn ə ‖ 'roʊn ə
rhonch|us 'rɒŋk |əs ‖ 'raːŋk- ~i aɪ
Rhonda 'rɒnd ə ‖ 'raːnd ə
Rhondda 'rɒnd ə 'rɒn ðə ‖ 'raːnd ə —*Welsh*
  ['hron ða]
  ˌRhondda 'Valley
Rhone, Rhône rəʊn ‖ roʊn —*French* [ʁoːn]
Rhonwen 'rɒn wɪn -wən, -wen ‖ 'raːn-
  —*Welsh* ['hron wen]
Rhoose ruːs
Rhos rəʊs ‖ roʊs —*Welsh* [hroːs]
Rhosllanerchrugog ˌrəʊs ˌlæn ə 'kriːg ɒg
  ‖ ˌroʊs ˌlæn ᵊr 'kriːg aːg —*Welsh*
  [ˌhroːs ˌɬa nerχ 'ri gog, -'ri-]
Rhosneigr ˌrəʊs 'naɪg ə ‖ ˌroʊs 'naɪg ᵊr
  —*Welsh* [ˌhroːs 'nəigr, -'nəi gir]
Rhossili rɒ 'sɪl i ‖ raː-
rhotacis... —*see* rhotaciz...
rhotacism 'rəʊt ə ˌsɪz əm ‖ 'roʊt̬- ~s z
rhotacization ˌrəʊt əs aɪ 'zeɪʃ ən -ɪ'•-
  ‖ ˌroʊt̬ əs ə- ~s z
rhotaciz|e 'rəʊt ə saɪz ‖ 'roʊt̬- ~ed d ~es ɪz
  əz ~ing ɪŋ
rhotic 'rəʊt ɪk ‖ 'roʊt̬ ɪk ~s s
rhoticity rəʊ 'tɪs ət i -ɪt- ‖ roʊ 'tɪs ət̬ i
rhubarb 'ruːb ɑːb ‖ -ɑːrb
Rhuddlan 'rɪð lən 'rʌd-, -læn —*Welsh*
  ['hrið lan, 'hrɪð-]
Rhum rʌm

rhumb rʌm (= *rum*) rhumbs rʌmz
Rhyd-ddu ˌriːd 'ði: —*Welsh* [ˌhriːd 'ði:,
  ˌhriːd 'ði:]
Rhydderch 'rʌð ək -əx ‖ -ᵊrk —*Welsh*
  ['hrə ðerχ]
Rhydding 'rɪd ɪŋ
Rhyl rɪl —*Welsh* [hrɪl, hrɪl]
rhyme raɪm (= *rime*) rhymed raɪmd rhymes
  raɪmz rhyming 'raɪm ɪŋ
  'rhyming slang, ˌ•• '•
rhymer 'raɪm ə ‖ -ᵊr ~s z
rhymester 'raɪmᵖst ə ‖ -ᵊr ~s z
Rhymney 'rʌm ni
rhyolite 'raɪ_ə laɪt ~s s
rhyolitic ˌraɪ_ə 'lɪt ɪk ◄ ‖ -'lɪt̬ ɪk ◄
Rhys (i) riːs; (ii) raɪs —*Welsh* [hriːs, hriːs]
  —*The writer Jean Rhys is (i).*
rhythm 'rɪð əm ~s z
  ˌrhythm and 'blues; 'rhythm ˌmethod;
  'rhythm ˌsection
rhythmic 'rɪð mɪk ~ally ᵊl_i
ria 'riː_ə ~s z
rial ri 'ɑːl 'riː ɑːl ‖ -'ɔːl —*but as an obsolete*
  English coin, 'raɪ_əl ~s z
Rialto ri 'ælt əʊ ‖ -oʊ —*It* [ri 'al to]
rib rɪb ribbed rɪbd ribbing 'rɪb ɪŋ ribs rɪbz
  'rib cage
ribald 'rɪb ᵊld 'raɪb-, -ɔːld ‖ -ɔːld, -aːld ~ly li
  ~s z
ribaldr|y 'rɪb ᵊldr li 'raɪb-, -ɔːldr- ~ies iz
riband 'rɪb ənd ~s z
Ribbentrop 'rɪb ən trɒp →-m- ‖ -traːp —*Ger*
  ['ʁɪb n tʁɔp]
Ribble 'rɪb ᵊl
ribb|on 'rɪb |ən ~oned ənd →md ~oning
  ən ɪŋ ~ons ənz →mz
  ˌribbon de'velopment
Ribena *tdmk* raɪ 'biːn ə
riboflavin, riboflavine ˌraɪb əʊ 'fleɪv ɪn -iːn,
  §-ən ‖ -oʊ- '••,•••
ribonucleic ˌraɪb əʊ nju 'kliː_ɪk ◄ §-nu'•-,
  -'kleɪ- ‖ -oʊ nu- -nju'•-
ribosomal ˌraɪb əʊ 'səʊm ᵊl ◄ ‖ -ə 'soʊm ᵊl ◄
ribosome 'raɪb əʊ səʊm ‖ -ə soʊm ~s z
Rib|ston 'rɪb stən ~stone stəʊn ‖ stoʊn
ribwort 'rɪb wɜːt §-wɔːt ‖ -wɝːt -wɔːrt ~s s
Ricard|o rɪ 'kɑːd ləʊ ‖ -'kɑːrd loʊ ~ian i_ən
Riccarton 'rɪk ət ən ‖ -ᵊrt ən
Ricci 'riːtʃ i —*It* ['rit tʃi]
rice, Rice raɪs riced raɪst rices 'raɪs ɪz -əz
  ricing 'raɪs ɪŋ
  'rice bowl; ˌRice 'Krispies *tdmk*; 'rice
  ˌpaddy; 'rice ˌpaper; ˌrice'pudding
Rice-a-Roni *tdmk* ˌraɪs ə 'rəʊn i ‖ -'roʊn i
ricer 'raɪs ə ‖ -ᵊr ~s z
rich, Rich rɪtʃ richer 'rɪtʃ ə ‖ -ᵊr richest
  'rɪtʃ ɪst -əst
Richard 'rɪtʃ əd ‖ -ᵊrd
Richards 'rɪtʃ ədz ‖ -ᵊrdz
Richardson 'rɪtʃ əd sən ‖ -ᵊrd-
Richelieu 'riːʃ ljɜː 'rɪʃ-, -lju:; '•ə• ‖ 'rɪʃ lu:
  'riːʃ-, -lju:, ˌ•'•; '•ə•, ˌ•ə'• —*Fr* [ʁi ʃə ljø]
riches, R~ 'rɪtʃ ɪz -əz

Richey, Richie 'rɪt∫ i
Richfield 'rɪt∫ fiː^əld
Richland 'rɪt∫ lənd
richly 'rɪt∫ li
Richmal 'rɪt∫ m^əl
Richmond 'rɪt∫ mənd
  ,Richmond 'Hill; ,Richmond-u_(ı)pon-
  'Thames; ,Richmond, Vir'ginia;
  ,Richmond, 'Yorks
richness 'rɪt∫ nəs -nɪs
Richter 'rɪkt ə 'rɪxt- ‖ -^ər —Ger ['ʁɪç tɐ], Russ
  [' rʲix tʲir] —Charles R~, the seismologist, was
  an American; it is therefore appropriate for the
  'Richter scale he devised to be pronounced in an
  English way, with k. Nevertheless, in BrE it is
  often said with x.
Richthofen 'rɪxt əʊf ^ən 'rɪkt- ‖ 'rɪkt oʊf ^ən
  —Ger ['ʁɪçt hoːf n]
ricin 'raɪs ɪn 'rɪs-, §-^ən
ricinoleate ,raɪs ɪ 'nəʊl i eɪt ,rɪs-, ‚•ə- ‖ -'noʊl-
ricinoleic ,rɪs ɪn əʊ 'liː ɪk ◂ ,raɪs-, ‚•ən-, -'leɪ-;
  -'əʊl i ɪk ‖ -^ən oʊ-
rick, Rick rɪk **ricked** rɪkt **ricking** 'rɪk ɪŋ **ricks**
  rɪks
Rickard 'rɪk ɑːd ‖ -ɑːrd
Rickards 'rɪk ɑːdz ‖ -ɑːrdz
Rickenbacker 'rɪk ən bæk ə ‖ -^ər
rickets 'rɪk ɪts §-əts
Rickett 'rɪk ɪt §-ət
Ricketts 'rɪk ɪts §-əts
rickettsi|a rɪ 'kets i_ə ~**ae** iː ~**al** əl ~**as** əz
rickety 'rɪk ət i -ɪt- ‖ -əṭ i
Rickey, r~, Ricki, Rickie 'rɪk i
rickrack 'rɪk ræk
Rickmansworth 'rɪk mənz wɜːθ -wəθ ‖ -wɝːθ
Rickover 'rɪk əʊv ə ‖ -oʊv ^ər
Ricks rɪks
ricksha, rickshaw 'rɪk ∫ɔː ‖ -∫ɑː ~**s** z
Ricky 'rɪk i
Rico 'riːk əʊ ‖ -oʊ
rico|chet 'rɪk ə |∫eɪ -∫et, ‚•• '|• ~**cheted,**
  ~**chetted** ∫eɪd ∫et ɪd, -əd ~**cheting,**
  ~**chetting** ∫eɪ ɪŋ ∫et ɪŋ ~**chets** ∫eɪz ∫ets
  —The -tt- spellings are used, if at all, only by
  the minority, if it still exists, who pronounce
  -∫et, -'∫et. It is very possible that both this
  spelling and this pronunciation are now
  obsolete.
Ricoh tdmk 'riːk əʊ ‖ -oʊ —Jp [ri ,koo]
ricotta rɪ 'kɒt ə rə- ‖ -'koːṭ ə -'kɑːt- —It
  [ri 'kɔt ta]
rictus 'rɪkt əs ~**es** ɪz əz
rid rɪd **ridded** 'rɪd ɪd -əd **ridding** 'rɪd ɪŋ **rids**
  rɪdz
riddance 'rɪd ^ən^ts
Riddell (i) 'rɪd ^əl (ii) rɪ 'del rə-
ridden 'rɪd ^ən
-ridden ,rɪd ^ən — **damp-ridden** 'dæmp ,rɪd ^ən
Ridding 'rɪd ɪŋ
riddl|e, R~ 'rɪd ^əl ~**ed** d ~**es** z ~**ing** ‿ɪŋ
ride raɪd **ridden** 'rɪd ^ən **rides** raɪdz **riding**
  'raɪd ɪŋ **rode** rəʊd ‖ roʊd
Rideout 'raɪd aʊt

rider, Rider 'raɪd ə ‖ -^ər ~**s** z
riderless 'raɪd ə ləs -lɪs; -^əl əs, -ɪs ‖ -^ər-
ridge, Ridge rɪdʒ **ridged** rɪdʒd **ridges**
  'rɪdʒ ɪz -əz **ridging** 'rɪdʒ ɪŋ
ridgel 'rɪdʒ ^əl ~**s** z
ridgeling 'rɪdʒ lɪŋ ~**s** z
ridgepole 'rɪdʒ pəʊl →-pɒʊl ‖ -poʊl ~**s** z
ridgeway, R~, Ridgway 'rɪdʒ weɪ ~**s** z
ridicul|e n, v 'rɪd ɪ kjuːl -ə- ~**ed** d ~**es** z ~**ing**
  ɪŋ
ridiculous rɪ 'dɪk jʊl əs rə-, -jəl- ‖ -jəl- ~**ly** li
  ~**ness** nəs nɪs
riding, R~ 'raɪd ɪŋ ~**s** z
Ridley 'rɪd li
Ridout (i) 'raɪd aʊt (ii) 'rɪd aʊt
Ridpath 'rɪd pɑːθ →'rɪb-, §-pæθ ‖ -pæθ
Riefenstahl 'riːf ɪn ∫tɑːl -stɑːl —Ger
  ['ʁiːf n ∫taːl]
Riegger 'riːg ə ‖ -^ər
Riemann 'riː mən ‖ -mɑːn —Ger ['ʁiː man]
riesling, R~ 'riːz lɪŋ 'riːs- —Ger ['ʁiːs lɪŋ] ~**s** z
Rieu ri 'uː 'riː u:
Rievaulx 'riːv əʊ -əʊz; 'rɪv əz ‖ -oʊ
rife raɪf **rifer** 'raɪf ə ‖ -^ər **rifest** 'raɪf ɪst -əst
riff, Riff rɪf **riffs** rɪfs
riffl|e 'rɪf ^əl ~**ed** d ~**es** z ~**ing** ‿ɪŋ
riffraff 'rɪf ræf
Rifkind 'rɪf kɪnd
rifl|e 'raɪf ^əl ~**ed** d ~**es** z ~**ing** ‿ɪŋ
  'rifle range
rifle|man 'raɪf ^əl |mən -mæn ~**men** mən men
rift rɪft **rifted** 'rɪft ɪd -əd **rifting** 'rɪft ɪŋ **rifts**
  rɪfts
  'rift ,valley, ‚• '••
rig rɪg **rigged** rɪgd **rigging/s** 'rɪg ɪŋ/z **rigs**
  rɪgz
Riga 'riːg ə —formerly also 'raɪg ə —Latvian
  Rīga ['riː ga]
rigadoon ,rɪg ə 'duːn ~**s** z
rigatoni ,rɪg ə 'təʊn i ‖ -'toʊn i
Rigby 'rɪg bi
Rigel 'raɪg ^əl 'raɪdʒ-
Rigg rɪg
rigger 'rɪg ə ‖ -^ər ~**s** z
rigg... —see **rig**
right raɪt (= rite, write) **righted** 'raɪt ɪd -əd
  ‖ 'raɪṭ əd **righter** 'raɪt ə ‖ 'raɪṭ ^ər **rightest**
  'raɪt ɪst -əst ‖ 'raɪṭ əst **righting**
  'raɪt ɪŋ ‖ 'raɪṭ ɪŋ **rights** raɪts
  'right ,angle,‚• '••; ,right a'way; ,right of
  'way; 'rights ,issue; ,right 'triangle; ,right
  'whale; ,right 'wing◂
right-about 'raɪt ə ,baʊt ‖ 'raɪṭ-
right-angled 'raɪt ,æŋ g^əld ,•'•• ‖ 'raɪṭ-
right-branching 'raɪt ,brɑːn_t∫ ɪŋ §-,bræn_t∫-,
  ‚•'•• ‖ -,bræn_t∫ ɪŋ
righteous 'raɪt∫ əs 'raɪt i_əs ~**ly** li ~**ness** nəs
  nɪs
rightful 'raɪt f^əl -fʊl ~**ly** ‿i ~**ness** nəs nɪs
right-hand ,raɪt 'hænd ◂ ‖ '••
  ,right-hand 'bend; ,right-hand 'man
right-handed ,raɪt 'hænd ɪd ◂ -əd ~**ly** li
  ~**ness** nəs nɪs

right-hander ˌraɪt ˈhænd ə ‖ -ᵊr ~s z
rightism ˈraɪt ˌɪz əm ‖ ˈraɪt̮-
rightist ˈraɪt ɪst §-əst ‖ ˈraɪt̮ əst ~s s
rightly ˈraɪt li
right-minded ˌraɪt ˈmaɪnd ɪd ◂ -əd ~ly li
~ness nəs nɪs
rightness ˈraɪt nəs -nɪs
righto ˌraɪt ˈəʊ ‖ ˌraɪt̮ ˈoʊ
right-on ˌraɪt ˈɒn ◂ ‖ ˌraɪt̮ ˈɑːn ◂ -ˈɔːn
right-thinking ˈraɪt ˌθɪŋk ɪŋ ˌ•ˈ••
rightward ˈraɪt wəd ‖ -wᵊrd ~s z
right-wing ˌraɪt ˈwɪŋ ◂ ~er/s ə/z ‖ ᵊr/z
righty-ho ˌraɪt i ˈhəʊ ‖ ˌraɪt̮ i ˈhoʊ
rigid ˈrɪdʒ ɪd §-əd
rigidit|y rɪ ˈdʒɪd ət li rə-, -ɪt- ‖ -ət̮ li ~ies iz
rigid|ly ˈrɪdʒ ɪd ‖li §-əd- ~ness nəs nɪs
Rigil ˈraɪdʒ ᵊl -ɪl
rigmarole ˈrɪg mə rəʊl →-rɒʊl ‖ -roʊl ~s z
Rigoletto ˌrɪg ə ˈlet əʊ ‖ -ˈlet̮ oʊ —It
[ri go ˈlet to]
rigor ˈrɪg ə ‖ -ᵊr —but as a medical term, also
ˈraɪg ɔː ‖ -ɔːr ~s z
ˌrigor ˈmortis ˈmɔːt ɪs §-əs ‖ ˈmɔːrt̮ əs
rigorous ˈrɪg ᵊr_əs ~ly li ~ness nəs nɪs
rigour ˈrɪg ə ‖ -ᵊr ~s z
rig-out ˈrɪg aʊt ~s s
Rigsby ˈrɪgz bi
Rig-Veda ˌrɪg ˈveɪd ə
Riis riːs
Rijeka ri ˈek ə -ˈeɪk- —Croatian [ri ˈˈɛ ka]
Rikki ˈrɪk i
Rikki-Tiki-Tavi ˌrɪk i tɪk i ˈtɑːv i -ˈteɪv- ‖ -ˈtæv-
rile raɪᵊl riled raɪᵊld riles raɪᵊlz riling ˈraɪᵊl ɪŋ
Riley ˈraɪl i
riliev|o ˌrɪl i ˈeɪv ləʊ ‖ rɪl ˈjeɪv loʊ —It
[ri ˈlje vo] ~i iː
Rilke ˈrɪlk ə —Ger [ˈʁɪl kə]
rill rɪl rills rɪlz
rillettes ₍ᵢ₎riː ˈet —Fr [ʁi jɛt]
rim rɪm rimmed rɪmd rimming ˈrɪm ɪŋ rims
rɪmz
Rimbaud ˈræm bəʊ ‖ ræm ˈboʊ —Fr [ʁæ̃ bo]
Rimbault English family name ˈrɪm bəʊlt
→-bɒʊlt ‖ -boʊlt
rime raɪm rimed raɪmd rimes raɪmz riming
ˈraɪm ɪŋ —see also phrases with this word
rime riche ˌriːm ˈriːʃ rimes riches same
pronunciation
rimester ˈraɪmˈst ə ‖ -ᵊr ~s z
Rimington ˈrɪm ɪŋ tən
Rimini ˈrɪm ən i -ɪn- —It [ˈriː mi ni]
rimless ˈrɪm ləs -lɪs
-rimmed ˈrɪmd — plastic-rimmed
ˌplæst ɪk ˈrɪmd ◂ ˌplɑːst-
Rimmer ˈrɪm ə ‖ -ᵊr
Rimsky-Korsakov ˌrɪmˈ ski ˈkɔːs ə kɒf -kɒv
‖ -ˈkɔːrs ə kɔːf -kɑːf —Russ
[ˌrʲim skʲɪj ˈkor sə kəf]
Rinaldo rɪ ˈnæld əʊ rə- ‖ -ˈnɑːld oʊ -ˈnæld-
rind raɪnd rinds raɪndz
rinderpest ˈrɪnd ə pest ‖ -ᵊr-
ring, Ring rɪŋ rang ræŋ ringed rɪŋd ringing
ˈrɪŋ ɪŋ rings rɪŋz rung rʌŋ

ˈring ˌbinder, ˌ•ˈ••; ˈring ˌfinger; ˈring
main; ˈring road; ˈring ˌspanner
ringbark ˈrɪŋ bɑːk ‖ -bɑːrk ~ed t ~ing ɪŋ ~s
s
ringbolt ˈrɪŋ bəʊlt →-bɒʊlt ‖ -boʊlt ~s s
ringer, R~ ˈrɪŋ ə ‖ -ᵊr ~s z
ring-fenc|e ˌrɪŋ ˈfenᵗs ~ed t ◂ ~es ɪz əz
~ing ɪŋ
ringgit ˈrɪŋ gɪt §-gət ~s s
ringhals ˈrɪŋ hæls -hɑːls
ringleader ˈrɪŋ ˌliːd ə ‖ -ᵊr ~s z
ringlet ˈrɪŋ lət -lɪt ringleted ˈrɪŋ lət ɪd -lɪt-,
-əd ‖ -lət̮ əd ~s s
ringmaster ˈrɪŋ ˌmɑːst ə §-ˌmæst- ‖ -ˌmæst ᵊr
~s z
ringneck ˈrɪŋ nek ~s s
ring-pull ˈrɪŋ pʊl ~s z
ringside ˈrɪŋ saɪd
ring-tailed ˈrɪŋ teɪᵊld
Ringway ˈrɪŋ weɪ
Ringwood ˈrɪŋ wʊd
ringworm ˈrɪŋ wɜːm ‖ -wɝːm
rink rɪŋk rinks rɪŋks
rinkhals ˈrɪŋk hæls -hɑːls
rinky-dink ˈrɪŋk i dɪŋk
rinse rɪnᵗs rinsed rɪnᵗst rinses ˈrɪnᵗs ɪz -əz
rinsing ˈrɪnᵗs ɪŋ
Rintoul rɪn ˈtuːl ˈ••
Rio ˈriː əʊ ‖ -oʊ —Sp [ˈrri o], Port [ˈrri u, ˈxi u]
ˌRio de Ja'neiro də ʒə ˈnɪər əʊ deɪ-, dɪ-,
-dʒə ˈ•-, -ˈneər- ‖ deɪ ʒə ˈner oʊ -ˈnɪr- —Port
[ˌxiu di ʒɐ ˈneɪ ru]; ˌRio ˈGrande grænd
ˈgrænd i —Sp [ˈgran de]; ˌRio ˈTinto
ˈtɪnt əʊ ‖ -oʊ —Sp [ˈtin to]
Rioja ri ˈɒk ə -ˈɒx-, -ˈəʊk-, -ˈəʊx- ‖ -ˈoʊ hɑː
—Sp [ˈrrjo xa]
Riordan ˈrɪəd ᵊn ‖ ˈrɪrd ᵊn
riot ˈraɪ‿ət rioted ˈraɪ‿ət ɪd -əd ‖ -ət̮ əd
rioting ˈraɪ‿ət ɪŋ ‖ -ət̮ ɪŋ riots ˈraɪ‿əts
ˈriot act
rioter ˈraɪ‿ət ə ‖ -ət̮ ᵊr ~s z
riotous ˈraɪ‿ət əs ‖ -ət̮ əs ~ly li ~ness nəs nɪs
rip, Rip rɪp ripped rɪpt ripping ˈrɪp ɪŋ rips
rɪps
ˌRip Van ˈWinkle
RIP ˌɑːr aɪ ˈpiː ‖ ˌɑːr-
riparian raɪ ˈpeər i_ən rɪ- ‖ -ˈper- ~s z
ripcord ˈrɪp kɔːd ‖ -kɔːrd ~s z
ripe raɪp riper ˈraɪp ə ‖ -ᵊr ripest ˈraɪp ɪst
-əst
ripely ˈraɪp li
ripen ˈraɪp ən ~ed d ~ing ‿ɪŋ ~s z
ripeness ˈraɪp nəs -nɪs
ripieno ˌrɪp i ˈeɪn əʊ ‖ -oʊ —It [ri ˈpje: no] ~s
z
Ripley ˈrɪp li
Ripman ˈrɪp mən
rip-off ˈrɪp ɒf -ɔːf ‖ -ɔːf -ɑːf ~s s
Ripon ˈrɪp ən
ripost, ripost|e n, v rɪ ˈpɒst -ˈpəʊst ‖ -ˈpoʊst
~ed ɪd əd ~ing ɪŋ ~es, ~s s
ripp... —see rip
ripper ˈrɪp ə ‖ -ᵊr ~s z

ripping 'rɪp ɪŋ **~ly** li

rippl|e 'rɪp əl **~ed** d **~es** z **~ing/ly** _ɪŋ /li

ripplet 'rɪp lət -lɪt **~s** s

Rippon 'rɪp ən

riprap 'rɪp ræp **~ped** t **~ping** ɪŋ **~s** s

rip-roaring ˌrɪp 'rɔːr ɪŋ ◄ ‖ -'roʊr-

ripsaw 'rɪp sɔː ‖ -sɑː **~s** z

ripsnort|er/s 'rɪp snɔːt lə/z ‖ -snɔːrt̬ lər/z
    ~ing/ly ɪŋ /li

riptide 'rɪp taɪd **~s** z

ripuarian, R~ ˌrɪp ju 'eər i_ən ◄ ‖ -'er- **~s** z

Risborough, Risboro' 'rɪz bər_ə ‖ -ˌbɜː oʊ

RISC, risc rɪsk

Risca 'rɪsk ə

Risdon 'rɪz dən

rise raɪz **risen** 'rɪz ən (!) **rises** 'raɪz ɪz -əz
    rising 'raɪz ɪŋ **rose** rəʊz ‖ roʊz

riser 'raɪz ə ‖ -ər **~s** z

risibility ˌrɪz ə 'bɪl ət i ˌraɪz-, ˌ•ɪ-, -ɪt i ‖ -ət̬ i

risib|le 'rɪz əb |əl 'raɪz-, -ɪb- **~ly** li

rising 'raɪz ɪŋ **~s** z
    ˌrising 'damp

risk rɪsk **risked** rɪskt **risking** 'rɪsk ɪŋ **risks**
    rɪsks

risk|y 'rɪsk |i **~ier** i_ə ‖ i_ər **~iest** i_ɪst i_əst
    ~ily ɪ li əl i **~iness** i nəs i nɪs

Risley 'rɪz li

Risorgimento rɪ ˌsɔːdʒ ɪ 'ment əʊ rə-, riː-,
    -ˌ•ə- ‖ rɪ ˌsɔːrdʒ ɪ 'ment oʊ -ˌzɔːrdʒ-;
    ˌriː•••• —It [ri sor dʒi 'men to]

risotto rɪ 'zɒt əʊ -'sɒt- ‖ -'sɔːt oʊ -'sɑːt̬-,
    -'zɑːt̬- —It [ri 'sɔt to] **~s** z

risque, risqué 'rɪsk eɪ ‖ rɪ 'skeɪ —Fr [ʁis ke]

Riss rɪs

rissole 'rɪs əʊl →-ɒʊl ‖ -oʊl rɪ 'soʊl **~s** z

Rita 'riːt ə ‖ 'riːt̬ ə

Ritalin tdmk 'rɪt əl ɪn ‖ 'rɪt̬-

ritardando ˌrɪt ɑː 'dænd əʊ
    ‖ ˌriː tɑːr 'dɑːnd oʊ rɪ ˌtɑːr- **~s** z

Ritchie 'rɪtʃ i

rite raɪt —but as a French word, riːt —Fr [ʁit]
    rites raɪts

ritenuto ˌrɪt ə 'njuːt əʊ -'nuːt-
    ‖ ˌriːt ə 'nuːt oʊ

ritornell|o ˌrɪt ə 'nel |əʊ -ɔː-; -ən 'el-
    ‖ ˌrɪt̬ ər 'nel |oʊ **~i** iː **~os** əʊz ‖ oʊz

Ritson 'rɪts ən

ritual 'rɪtʃ u_əl 'rɪt ju_əl ‖ 'rɪtʃ əl **~s** z

ritualis... —see **ritualiz...**

ritualism 'rɪtʃ u_əl ˌɪz əm 'rɪt ju_ ‖ 'rɪtʃ əl, •••

ritualist 'rɪtʃ u_əl ɪst 'rɪt ju_, §-əst ‖ 'rɪtʃ əl•
    ~s s

ritualistic ˌrɪtʃ u_ə 'lɪst ɪk ◄ ˌrɪt ju_,
    ˌrɪtʃ u 'lɪst- ‖ ˌrɪtʃ ə 'lɪst- **~ally** əl_i

ritualization ˌrɪtʃ u_əl aɪ 'zeɪʃ ən ˌrɪt ju_, -ɪ'•-
    ‖ -ə'•-, ˌ•əl•'••

ritualiz|e 'rɪtʃ u_ə laɪz 'rɪt ju_,
    'rɪtʃ u• ‖ 'rɪtʃ ə laɪz **~ed** d **~es** ɪz əz **~ing**
    ɪŋ

ritually 'rɪtʃ u_əl i 'rɪt ju_ ‖ 'rɪtʃ əl i

Ritz rɪts

ritz|y 'rɪts |i **~ier** i_ə ‖ i_ər **~iest** i_ɪst i_əst
    ~ily ɪ li əl i **~iness** i nəs i nɪs

rival 'raɪv əl **~ed, ~led** d **~ing, ~ling** ɪŋ **~s** z

rival|ry 'raɪv əl |ri **~ries** riz

rive raɪv **rived** raɪvd **riven** 'rɪv ən (!) **rives**
    raɪvz **riving** 'raɪv ɪŋ

Rivelin 'rɪv əl_ɪn

riven 'rɪv ən

river, River 'rɪv ə ‖ -ər **~s** z
    'river ˌbasin; 'river ˌblindness

Rivera rɪ 'veər ə ‖ -'ver ə —Sp [rri 'βe ɾa]

riverbed 'rɪv ə bed ‖ -ər- **~s** z

riverboat 'rɪv ə bəʊt ‖ -ər boʊt **~s** s

Riverina ˌrɪv ə 'riːn ə

riverine 'rɪv ə raɪn -riːn, -rɪn

Rivers 'rɪv əz ‖ -ərz

riverside, R~ 'rɪv ə saɪd ‖ -ər-

riv|et 'rɪv |ɪt §-ət ‖ -|ət **~eted** ɪt ɪd §ət-, -əd
    ‖ ət̬ əd **~eting** ɪt ɪŋ §ət- ‖ ət̬ ɪŋ **~ets** ɪts
    §əts ‖ əts

riveter 'rɪv ɪt ə -ət- ‖ -ət̬ ər **~s** z

Rivett rɪ 'vet

riviera, R~ ˌrɪv i 'eər ə ‖ -'er ə **~s** z

Rivington 'rɪv ɪŋ tən

rivulet 'rɪv jul ət -ɪt, -ju let ‖ -jəl- **~s** s

Rix rɪks

Riyadh 'riː æd -ɑːd, •'• ‖ riː 'jɑːd —Arabic
    [ri 'jaːðˤ]

riyal ri 'ɑːl -'jɑːl, -'æl, '•• **~s** z

Rizla tdmk 'rɪz lə

RN ˌɑːr 'en

RNA ˌɑːr en eɪ 'eɪ

Roaccutane tdmk rəʊ 'æk ju teɪn ‖ roʊ 'æk jə-

roach, Roach rəʊtʃ ‖ roʊtʃ **roaches, Roach's**
    'rəʊtʃ ɪz -əz ‖ 'roʊtʃ əz

road rəʊd ‖ roʊd **roads** rəʊdz ‖ roʊdz
    'road hog; 'road ˌmanager; 'road
    ˌmender; 'road ˌroller; 'road sense; 'road
    tax; 'road test; 'road works

roadbed 'rəʊd bed →'rəʊb- ‖ 'roʊd-

roadblock 'rəʊd blɒk →'rəʊb- ‖ 'roʊd blɑːk
    ~s s

roadbook 'rəʊd bʊk →'rəʊb-, §-buːk ‖ 'roʊd-
    ~s s

roadholding 'rəʊd ˌhəʊld ɪŋ →-ˌhɒʊld-
    ‖ 'roʊd ˌhoʊld ɪŋ

road|house 'rəʊd |haʊs ‖ 'roʊd- **~houses**
    haʊz ɪz -əz

roadie 'rəʊd i ‖ 'roʊd i **~s** z

road|man 'rəʊd |mən →'rəʊb-, -mæn ‖ 'roʊd-
    ~men mən men

roadrunner 'rəʊd ˌrʌn ə ‖ 'roʊd ˌrʌn ər **~s** z

roadshow 'rəʊd ʃəʊ ‖ 'roʊd ʃoʊ **~s** z

roadside 'rəʊd saɪd ‖ 'roʊd- **~s** z

roadstead 'rəʊd sted ‖ 'roʊd- **~s** z

roadster 'rəʊd stə ‖ 'roʊd stər **~s** z

road-test 'rəʊd test ‖ 'roʊd- **~ed** ɪd əd **~ing**
    ɪŋ **~s** s

roadway 'rəʊd weɪ ‖ 'roʊd- **~s** z

roadwork 'rəʊd wɜːk ‖ 'roʊd wɜːk **~s** s

roadworth|y 'rəʊd ˌwɜːð li ‖ 'roʊd ˌwɜːð li
    ~iness i nəs i nɪs

Roald 'rəʊ əld ‖ 'roʊ- —Norw ['rru al]

roam rəʊm ‖ roʊm **roamed** rəʊmd ‖ roʊmd

roaming 'rəʊm ɪŋ ‖ 'roʊm ɪŋ **roams**
rəʊmz ‖ roʊmz
roamer 'rəʊm ə ‖ 'roʊm ᵊr **~s** z
roan rəʊn ‖ roʊn
Roanoke 'rəʊ ə nəʊk 'rəʊn əʊk ‖ 'roʊ ə noʊk
'roʊn oʊk
roar rɔː ‖ rɔːr roʊr **roared** rɔːd ‖ rɔːrd roʊrd
roaring 'rɔːr ɪŋ ‖ 'roʊr- **roars** rɔːz ‖ rɔːrz
roʊrz
ˌroaring 'forties
roarer 'rɔːr ə ‖ -ᵊr 'roʊr- **~s** z
roast rəʊst ‖ roʊst **roasted** 'rəʊst ɪd -əd
‖ 'roʊst əd **roasting/s** 'rəʊst ɪŋ/z
‖ 'roʊst ɪŋ/z **roasts** rəʊsts ‖ roʊsts
roaster 'rəʊst ə ‖ 'roʊst ᵊr **~s** z
Roath rəʊθ ‖ roʊθ
rob, Rob rɒb ‖ rɑːb **robbed** rɒbd ‖ rɑːbd
robbing 'rɒb ɪŋ ‖ 'rɑːb ɪŋ **robs** rɒbz ‖ rɑːbz
ˌRob 'Roy
robalo rəʊ 'bɑːl əʊ ‖ roʊ 'bɑːl oʊ **~s** z
Robb rɒb ‖ rɑːb
robb... —*see* **rob**
Robbe-Grillet ˌrɒb griː 'eɪ ‖ ˌroʊb- ˌrɑːb- —*Fr*
[ʁɔb gʁi jɛ]
Robben 'rɒb ɪn -ᵊn ‖ 'rɑːb ən
robber 'rɒb ə ‖ 'rɑːb ᵊr **~s** z
ˌrobber 'baron,' ˌ• • , • •
robber|y 'rɒb ᵊr |i ‖ 'rɑːb- **~ies** iz
Robbialac *tdmk* 'rɒb i‿ə læk ‖ 'rɑːb-
Robbie 'rɒb i ‖ 'rɑːb i
Robbin 'rɒb ɪn §-ᵊn ‖ 'rɑːb ən
Robbins 'rɒb ɪnz §-ᵊnz ‖ 'rɑːb ənz
robe, Robe rəʊb ‖ roʊb **robed** rəʊbd ‖ roʊbd
robes rəʊbz ‖ roʊbz **robing**
'rəʊb ɪŋ ‖ 'roʊb ɪŋ
Robens 'rəʊb ɪnz -ənz ‖ 'roʊb ənz
Robert 'rɒb ət ‖ 'rɑːb ᵊrt
Roberta rə 'bɜːt ə rɒ-, rəʊ- ‖ rə 'bɝːt̬ ə roʊ-
Roberto rə 'bɜːt əʊ rɒ-, rəʊ- ‖ rə 'bɝːt̬ oʊ roʊ-
—*It* [ro 'bɛr to], *Sp* [rro 'βer to]
Roberts 'rɒb əts ‖ 'rɑːb ᵊrts
Robertson 'rɒb ət sən ‖ 'rɑːb ᵊrt-
Robeson 'rəʊb sən ‖ 'roʊb-
Robespierre 'rəʊbz pɪə 'rəʊbz pi‿eə
‖ 'roʊbz pɪr 'roʊbz pi er —*Fr* [ʁɔ bɛs pjɛːʁ]
Robey 'rəʊb i ‖ 'roʊb i
robin, Robin 'rɒb ɪn §-ᵊn ‖ 'rɑːb ən **~s** z
ˌRobin 'Hood ‖ ' • •
Robina rɒ 'biːn ə rəʊ- ‖ rə 'biːn ə
robinia, R~ rə 'bɪn i‿ə rɒ-, rəʊ- **~s** z
Robinne 'rɒb ɪn §-ᵊn ‖ 'rɑːb ən
Robins *(i)* 'rɒb ɪnz §-ᵊnz ‖ 'rɑːb ənz, *(ii)*
'rəʊb- ‖ 'roʊb-
Robinson 'rɒb ɪn sən §-ᵊn- ‖ 'rɑːb-
ˌRobinson 'Crusoe
roble 'rəʊb leɪ ‖ 'roʊb- **~s** z
robot 'rəʊb ɒt -ət ‖ 'roʊb ɑːt -ət **~s** s
robotic rəʊ 'bɒt ɪk ‖ roʊ 'bɑːt̬ ɪk **~s** s
Robson 'rɒb sən ‖ 'rɑːb-
robust rəʊ 'bʌst 'rəʊ bʌst ‖ roʊ 'bʌst ' • • **~ly**
li **~ness** nəs nɪs
robusta rəʊ 'bʌst ə ‖ roʊ- **~s** z
Roby 'rəʊb i ‖ 'roʊb i

Robyn 'rɒb ɪn §-ən ‖ 'rɑːb ən
roc rɒk ‖ rɑːk *(= rock)*
rocaille rɒ 'kaɪ rəʊ- ‖ roʊ- rɑː- —*Fr* [ʁɔ kaj]
rocambole 'rɒk əm bəʊl →-bɒʊl
‖ 'rɑːk əm boʊl
Rocco 'rɒk əʊ ‖ 'rɑːk oʊ —*It* ['rɔk ko]
Rocester 'rəʊst ə ‖ 'roʊst ᵊr
Rochdale 'rɒtʃ deɪᵊl ‖ 'rɑːtʃ-
Roche *(i)* rəʊtʃ ‖ roʊtʃ, *(ii)* rəʊʃ ‖ roʊʃ, *(iii)*
rɒʃ ‖ rɑːʃ
Rochelle rɒ 'ʃel rə- ‖ roʊ-
roche moutonnée ˌrɒʃ muː 'tɒn eɪ
-ˌmuːt ɒ 'neɪ ‖ ˌrɔːʃ ˌmuːt ᵊn 'eɪ ˌroʊʃ-
roches moutonnées *same pronunciation, or*
-z
Rochester 'rɒtʃ ɪst ə -əst- ‖ 'rɑːtʃ est ᵊr -əst-
rochet 'rɒtʃ ɪt -ət ‖ 'rɑːtʃ ət **~s** s
Rochford 'rɒtʃ fəd ‖ 'rɑːtʃ fᵊrd
rock, Rock rɒk ‖ rɑːk **rocked** rɒkt ‖ rɑːkt
rocking 'rɒk ɪŋ ‖ 'rɑːk ɪŋ **rocks** rɒks ‖ rɑːks
ˌrock 'bottom◂; 'rock cake; 'rock dash;
'rock dove; 'rock ˌgarden; 'rock ˌhopper;
'rocking chair; 'rocking horse; 'rock
ˌmusic; 'rock muˌsician; 'rock plant; 'rock
ˌsalmon; 'rock salt
rockabilly 'rɒk ə ˌbɪl i ‖ 'rɑːk-
rockbound 'rɒk baʊnd ‖ 'rɑːk-
rock-climb|er/s 'rɒk ˌklaɪm |ə/z
‖ 'rɑːk ˌklaɪm |ᵊr/z **~ing** ɪŋ
Rockefeller 'rɒk ə ˌfel ə -ɪ- ‖ 'rɑːk ə ˌfel ᵊr
'Rockefeller ˌCenter ‖ , • • • • ' • •
rocker 'rɒk ə ‖ 'rɑːk ᵊr **~s** z
rocker|y 'rɒk ᵊr |i ‖ 'rɑːk- **~ies** iz
rock|et 'rɒk |ɪt §-ət ‖ 'rɑːk |ət **~eted** ɪt ɪd §ət-,
-əd ‖ ət̬ əd **~eting** ɪt ɪŋ §ət- ‖ ət̬ ɪŋ **~ets** ɪts
§əts ‖ əts
'rocket ˌengine; 'rocket ˌlauncher; 'rocket
range
rocketry 'rɒk ɪt ri §-ət- ‖ 'rɑːk-
rockfall 'rɒk fɔːl ‖ 'rɑːk- -fɑːl **~s** z
rockfish 'rɒk fɪʃ ‖ 'rɑːk- **~es** ɪz əz
Rockford 'rɒk fəd ‖ 'rɑːk fᵊrd
Rockhampton rɒk 'hæmp tən ‖ rɑːk-
Rockies 'rɒk iz ‖ 'rɑːk iz
Rockingham 'rɒk ɪŋ əm ‖ 'rɑːk-
Rockley 'rɒk li ‖ 'rɑːk li
rockling 'rɒk lɪŋ ‖ 'rɑːk-
rock 'n' roll, rock'n'roll ˌrɒk ən 'rəʊl →-ŋ-,
→-'rɒʊl ‖ ˌrɑːk ən 'roʊl **~er/s** ə/z ‖ ᵊr/z
rockros|e 'rɒk rəʊz ‖ 'rɑːk roʊz **~es** ɪz əz
Rockwell 'rɒk wəl -wel ‖ 'rɑːk-
rock-wool 'rɒk wʊl ‖ 'rɑːk-
rock|y, Rock|y 'rɒk li ‖ 'rɑːk li **~ier** i‿ə ‖ i‿ᵊr
~ies, ~y's iz **~iest** i‿ɪst i‿əst **~iness** i nəs
i nɪs
ˌRocky ˌMountain 'goat; ˌRocky
'Mountains
rococo rə 'kəʊk əʊ rəʊ- ‖ -'koʊk oʊ
ˌroʊk ə 'koʊ
rod rɒd ‖ rɑːd **rods** rɒdz ‖ rɑːdz
Rod, Rodd rɒd ‖ rɑːd
Roddick 'rɒd ɪk ‖ 'rɑːd ɪk
Roddy 'rɒd i ‖ 'rɑːd i

rode rəʊd ‖ roʊd (= *road*)
rodent ˈrəʊd ᵊnt ‖ ˈroʊd ᵊnt ~s s
  ˌrodent ˈulcer
rodeo rəʊ ˈdeɪ əʊ ˈrəʊd i- ‖ roʊ ˈdeɪ oʊ
  ˈroʊd i- ~s z
Roderic, Roderick ˈrɒd ᵊr ɪk ‖ ˈrɑːd-
Rodger ˈrɒdʒ ə ‖ ˈrɑːdʒ ᵊr
Rodgers ˈrɒdʒ əz ‖ ˈrɑːdʒ ᵊrz
Rodin ˈrəʊd æn -ǽ ‖ roʊ ˈdæn —*Fr* [ʁɔ dæ̃]
Roding ˈrəʊd ɪŋ ‖ ˈroʊd ɪŋ —*Locally also* ˈruːð-,
  ˈruːd-
Rodney ˈrɒd ni ‖ ˈrɑːd ni
rodomontad|e ˌrɒd ə mɒn ˈtɑːd ˌrəʊd-, -ˈteɪd
  ‖ ˌrɑːd ə mɑːn ˈteɪd ˌroʊd-, -əm ən-, -ˈtɑːd
  ~ed ɪd əd ~es z ~ing ɪŋ
Rodrigues, Rodriguez *(i)* rɒ ˈdriːgz ‖ rɑː-, *(ii)*
  rɒ ˈdriːg ez ‖ rɑː- —*Port* [ʁu ˈðri ɣɪʃ,
  xo ˈdri ɣeθ, -ɣes], *Span* [rro ˈðri ɣeθ, -ɣes] —*In
  AmE usually (ii)*.
Rodway ˈrɒd weɪ ‖ ˈrɑːd-
roe, Roe rəʊ ‖ roʊ **roes** rəʊz ‖ roʊz (= *rose*)
  ˈroe deer
Roebling ˈrəʊb lɪŋ ‖ ˈroʊb-
roebuck, R~ ˈrəʊ bʌk ‖ ˈroʊ- ~s s
Roedean ˈrəʊ diːn ‖ ˈroʊ-
Roehampton ˌrəʊ ˈhæmp tən ‖ ˌroʊ-
roentgen, R~ ˈrɒnt gən ˈrʌnt-, ˈrɜːnt-, -jən
  ‖ ˈrent gən ˈrʌnt-, ˈrʊnt-, -dʒən —*Ger*
  [ˈʁœnt gᵊn] ~s z
Roethke ˈret kə ˈrɜːθ- ‖ ˈreθ-, -ki
Roff, Roffe rɒf ‖ rɔːf rɑːf
Roffey ˈrɒf i ‖ ˈrɔːf i ˈrɑːf-
rogation, R~ rəʊ ˈgeɪʃ ᵊn ‖ roʊ-
  Roˈgation Days
Roger, roger ˈrɒdʒ ə ‖ ˈrɑːdʒ ᵊr ~ed d
  rogering ˈrɒdʒ ᵊr ɪŋ ~s z
Rogers ˈrɒdʒ əz ‖ ˈrɑːdʒ ᵊrz
Roget ˈrɒʒ eɪ ˈrəʊʒ- ‖ roʊ ˈʒeɪ ˈ•• ~'s z
rogue rəʊg ‖ roʊg **rogued** rəʊgd ‖ roʊgd
  rogues rəʊgz ‖ roʊgz **roguing**
  ˈrəʊg ɪŋ ‖ ˈroʊg ɪŋ
  ˌrogues' ˈgallery
roguer|y ˈrəʊg ᵊr |i ‖ ˈroʊg- ~ies iz
roguish ˈrəʊg ɪʃ ‖ ˈroʊg- ~ly li ~ness nəs nɪs
Rohan ˈrəʊ ən ‖ ˈroʊ-
Rohypnol *tdmk* rəʊ ˈhɪp nɒl ‖ roʊ ˈhɪp nɔːl
  -nɑːl
roil rɔɪᵊl **roiled** rɔɪᵊld **roiling** ˈrɔɪᵊl ɪŋ **roils**
  rɔɪᵊlz
Roisin, Roisín rʌ ˈʃiːn rɒ-
roister ˈrɔɪst ə ‖ -ᵊr ~ed d **roistering**
  ˈrɔɪst ᵊr ɪŋ ~s z
Rokeby ˈrəʊk bi ‖ ˈroʊk-
Roker ˈrəʊk ə ‖ ˈroʊk ᵊr
Roland ˈrəʊl ənd ‖ ˈroʊl-
role, rôle rəʊl →rɒʊl ‖ roʊl (= *roll*) **roles,**
  rôles rəʊlz →rɒʊlz ‖ roʊlz
  ˈrole ˌmodel; ˈrole play, ˈrole ˌplaying
Rolex *tdmk* ˈrəʊl eks ‖ ˈroʊl- ~es ɪz əz
Rolf, rolf rɒlf ‖ rɑːlf rɔːlf **rolfed** rɒlft ‖ rɑːlft
  rɔːlft **rolfing** ˈrɒlf ɪŋ ‖ ˈrɑːlf ɪŋ ˈrɔːlf- **rolfs,**
  Rolf's rɒlfs ‖ rɑːlfs rɔːlfs
Rolfe *(i)* rəʊf ‖ roʊf, *(ii)* rɒlf ‖ rɑːlf rɔːlf

roll rəʊl →rɒʊl ‖ roʊl **rolled** rəʊld →rɒʊld
  ‖ roʊld **rolling** ˈrəʊl ɪŋ →ˈrɒʊl- ‖ ˈroʊl ɪŋ
  ˈroll bar; ˈroll call; ˌrolled ˈgold◂; ˈrolling
  mill; ˈrolling pin; ˈrolling stock; ˌrolling
  ˈstone, ˌRolling ˈStones; ˌroll of ˈhonour
rollaway ˈrəʊl ə ˌweɪ →ˈrɒʊl- ‖ ˈroʊl- ~s z
Rollei *tdmk* ˈrəʊl aɪ ‖ ˈroʊl- —*Ger* [ˈʁɔl aɪ]
roller ˈrəʊl ə →ˈrɒʊl- ‖ ˈroʊl ᵊr ~s z
  ˈroller ˌbearing; ˈroller blind; ˈroller
  ˌcoaster; ˈRoller ˌDerby,ˌ•• ˈ••• *tdmk*; ˈroller
  skate; ˈroller ˌtowel
Rollerblad|e *tdmk*, **r~** ˈrəʊl ə bleɪd →ˈrɒʊl-
  ‖ ˈroʊl ᵊr- ~ed ɪd əd ~er/s ə/z ‖ ᵊr/z ~es z
  ~ing ɪŋ
roller-|skate ˈrəʊl ə |skeɪt →ˈrɒʊl- ‖ ˈroʊl ᵊr-
  ~skated skeɪt ɪd -əd ‖ skeɪt̬ əd ~skater/s
  skeɪt ə/z ‖ skeɪt̬ ᵊr/z ~skates skeɪts
  ~skating skeɪt ɪŋ ‖ skeɪt̬ ɪŋ
Rolleston ˈrəʊlst ᵊn →ˈrɒʊlst- ‖ ˈroʊlst-
rollick ˈrɒl ɪk ‖ ˈrɑːl ɪk ~ed t ~ing/ly ɪŋ /li ~s
  s
Rollins ˈrɒl ɪnz §-ənz ‖ ˈrɑːl-
rollmop ˈrəʊl mɒp →ˈrɒʊl- ‖ ˈroʊl mɑːp ~s s
rollneck ˈrəʊl nek →ˈrɒʊl- ‖ ˈroʊl- ~s s
Rollo ˈrɒl əʊ ‖ ˈrɑːl oʊ
roll-on ˈrəʊl ɒn →ˈrɒʊl- ‖ ˈroʊl ɑːn -ɔːn ~s z
  ˌroll-on ˌroll-ˈoff◂ ˌrəʊl ˈɒf ◂ →ˌrɒʊl-, -ˈɔːf
  ‖ ˌroʊl ˈɔːf ◂ -ˈɑːf; ˌroll-on ˌroll-off ˈcar
  ˌferry
rollover ˈrəʊl ˌəʊv ə →ˈrɒʊl- ‖ ˈroʊl ˌoʊv ᵊr
Rolls rəʊlz →rɒʊlz ‖ roʊlz ~es ɪz əz
Rolls-Royc|e *tdmk* ˌrəʊlz ˈrɔɪs →ˌrɒʊlz-
  ‖ ˌroʊlz- ~es ɪz əz
rolltop ˈrəʊl tɒp →ˈrɒʊl- ‖ ˈroʊl tɑːp ~s s
rollup ˈrəʊl ʌp →ˈrɒʊl- ‖ ˈroʊl- ~s s
Rolo *tdmk* ˈrəʊl əʊ →ˈrɒʊl- ‖ ˈroʊl oʊ ~s z
Rolodex *tdmk* ˈrəʊl ə deks →ˈrɒʊl- ‖ ˈroʊl-
Rolph rɒlf ‖ rɑːlf
Rolston ˈrəʊlst ᵊn →ˈrɒʊlst- ‖ ˈroʊlst-
Rolt rəʊlt →rɒʊlt ‖ roʊlt
roly-pol|y ˌrəʊl i ˈpəʊl li ◂ →ˌrɒʊl i ˈpɒʊl i
  ‖ ˌroʊl i ˈpoʊl li ◂ ~ies iz
  ˌroly-ˌpoly ˈpudding
ROM *'computer memory'* rɒm ‖ rɑːm
Rom *'gypsy'* rɒm rəʊm ‖ roʊm
Romagna rəʊ ˈmɑːn jə ‖ roʊ- —*It*
  [ro ˈmaɲ ɲa]
Romaic rəʊ ˈmeɪ ɪk ‖ roʊ-
Romaine, r~ rəʊ ˈmeɪn ‖ roʊ-
  roˌmaine ˈlettuce
Roman, roman ˈrəʊm ən ‖ ˈroʊm ən —*but as a
  French word,* ˈrəʊm̃ɒ̃l roʊ ˈmɑːn, *Fr* [ʁɔ mɑ̃]
  (see phrases) ~s z
  ˌRoman ˈalphabet; ˌRoman ˈcandle;
  ˌRoman ˈCatholic; ˌRoman Caˈtholiˌcism;
  ˌRoman ˈEmpire; ˌRoman ˈlaw; ˌRoman
  ˈnose; ˌRoman ˈnumeral
roman à clef rəʊ ˌmɒ̃ ɑː ˈkleɪ -ˌmɑːn-
  ‖ roʊ ˌmɑːn- **romans à clef** *same
  pronunciation* —*Fr* [ʁɔ mɑ̃ a kle]
romanc|e, R~ rəʊ ˈmænᵗs ˈrəʊm ænᵗs
  ‖ roʊ ˈmænᵗs ˈroʊm ænᵗs ~ed t ~er/s ə/z
  ‖ ᵊr/z ~es ɪz əz ~ing ɪŋ

Romanes *family name* rəʊ ˈmɑːn ɪz -ɪs, -es
‖ roʊ-
Romanes *language* ˈrɒm ə nes -ən ɪs, §-əs
‖ ˈrɑːm-
Romanesque ˌrəʊm ə ˈnesk ◂ ‖ ˌroʊm-
roman fleuve rəʊ ˌmɒ̃ ˈflɜːv ‖ roʊ ˌmɑːn ˈflʌv
  romans fleuve *same pronunciation* —*Fr*
  [ʁɔ mɑ̃ flœːv]
Romani|a ru ˈmeɪn i‿ə rəʊ- ‖ roʊ- ~**an/s** ən/z
romanic, R~ rəʊ ˈmæn ɪk ‖ roʊ-
romanis... —*see* **romaniz...**
Romanism ˈrəʊm ən ˌɪz əm ‖ ˈroʊm-
Romanist ˈrəʊm ən ɪst §-əst ‖ ˈroʊm- ~**s** s
romanization ˌrəʊm ən aɪ ˈzeɪʃ ən -ɪˈ•-
  ‖ ˌroʊm ən ə- ~**s** z
romaniz|e ˈrəʊm ə naɪz ‖ ˈroʊm- ~**ed** d ~**er/s**
  ə/z ‖ ᵊr/z ~**es** ɪz əz ~**ing** ɪŋ
Romano, r~ rəʊ ˈmɑːn əʊ ‖ roʊ ˈmɑːn oʊ
Romano- rəʊ ˈmɑːn əʊ -ˌmæn- ‖ rə ˌmɑːn oʊ
  — **Romano-British** rəʊ ˌmɑːn əʊ ˈbrɪt ɪʃ ◂
  -ˌmæn- ‖ rə ˌmɑːn oʊ ˈbrɪt ɪʃ ◂
Roma|nov ˈrəʊm ə ˌnɒf -nɒv ‖ ˈroʊm ə ˌnɔːf
  -nɑːf —*Russ* [rʌ ˈma nəf] ~**novs** nɒfs nɒvz
  ‖ nɔːfs nɑːfs
Romansch, Romansh rəʊ ˈmænᵗʃ ru- ‖ roʊ-
  -ˈmɑːnᵗʃ
romantic rəʊ ˈmænt ɪk ‖ roʊ ˈmænt̬ ɪk rə-
  ~**ally** ᵊl‿i ~**s** s
romanticis... —*see* **romanticiz...**
romanticism rəʊ ˈmænt ɪ ˌsɪz əm -ə-
  ‖ roʊ ˈmænt̬ ə- rə-
romanticist rəʊ ˈmænt ɪs ɪst -əs-, §-əst
  ‖ roʊ ˈmænt̬ə- rə-
romanticization rəʊ ˌmænt ɪs aɪ ˈzeɪʃ ən
  -ˌ•əs-, -ɪˈ•- ‖ roʊ ˌmænt̬ əs ə-
romanticiz|e rəʊ ˈmænt ɪ saɪz -ə-
  ‖ roʊ ˈmænt̬ ə- rə- ~**ed** d ~**es** ɪz əz ~**ing** ɪŋ
Roman|y ˈrɒm ən li ˈrəʊm- ‖ ˈrɑːm- ˈroʊm-
  ~**ies** iz
Rombauer ˈrɒm baʊ‿ə ‖ ˈrɑːm baʊ‿ᵊr
Romberg ˈrɒm bɜːɡ ‖ ˈrɑːm bɝːɡ
Rome rəʊm ‖ roʊm —*Formerly also* ruːm
  Rome's rəʊmz ‖ roʊmz —*It* Roma [ˈro ma]
Romeo ˈrəʊm i‿əʊ ‖ ˈroʊm i‿oʊ ~**s**, ~'**s** z
romer ˈrəʊm ə ‖ ˈroʊm ᵊr ~**s** z
Romero rəʊ ˈmeər əʊ ‖ roʊ ˈmer oʊ rə- —*Sp*
  [rro ˈme ro]
Romford ˈrɒm fəd ˈrʌm- ‖ ˈrɑːm fᵊrd
romic, Romic ˈrəʊm ɪk ‖ ˈroʊm-
Romiley, Romilly ˈrɒm əl i -ɪl- ‖ ˈrɑːm-
Romish ˈrəʊm ɪʃ ‖ ˈroʊm ɪʃ
Rommel ˈrɒm əl ‖ ˈrɑːm əl ˈrʌm- —*Ger*
  [ˈʁɔm əl]
Romney ˈrɒm ni ˈrʌm- ‖ ˈrɑːm-
romneya ˈrɒm ni‿ə ‖ ˈrɑːm- ~**s** z
romp rɒmp ‖ rɑːmp **romped** rɒmpt ‖ rɑːmpt
  romping ˈrɒmp ɪŋ ‖ ˈrɑːmp ɪŋ **romps**
  rɒmps ‖ rɑːmps
romper ˈrɒmp ə ‖ ˈrɑːmp ᵊr ~**s** z
  '**romper suit**
Romsey ˈrɒm zi ˈrʌm- ‖ ˈrɑːm zi
Romulus ˈrɒm jʊl əs ‖ ˈrɑːm jəl əs
Ron rɒn ‖ rɑːn

Rona ˈrəʊn ə ‖ ˈroʊn ə
Ronald ˈrɒn əld ‖ ˈrɑːn əld
Ronaldsay ˈrɒn əld seɪ -ʃeɪ ‖ ˈrɑːn-
Ronaldsway ˈrɒn əldz weɪ ‖ ˈrɑːn-
Ronan ˈrəʊn ən ‖ ˈroʊn-
rondavel ˈrɒnd ə vel rɒn ˈdɑːv əl ‖ ˈrɑːnd- ~**s**
  z
rondeau ˈrɒnd əʊ ‖ ˈrɑːnd oʊ rɑːn ˈdoʊ ~**s**, ~**x**
  z —*or as sing.*
rondel ˈrɒnd əl ‖ ˈrɑːnd əl rɑːn ˈdel ~**s** z
rondo ˈrɒnd əʊ ‖ ˈrɑːnd oʊ rɑːn ˈdoʊ ~**s** z
roneo, R~ *tdmk* ˈrəʊn i‿əʊ ‖ ˈroʊn i‿oʊ ~**ed** d
  ~**ing** ɪŋ ~**s** z
Ronnie ˈrɒn i ‖ ˈrɑːn i
Ronsard ˈrɒn sɑː ‖ roʊn ˈsɑːr —*Fr* [ʁɔ̃ saːʁ]
Ronson ˈrɒnᵗs ən ‖ ˈrɑːnᵗs ən
Ronstadt ˈrɒn stæt ‖ ˈrɑːn-
röntgen, R~ ˈrɒnt ɡən ˈrʌnt-, ˈrɜːnt-, -jən
  ‖ ˈrent ɡən ˈrʌnt-, ˈrʊnt-, -dʒən —*Ger*
  [ˈʁœnt ɡ‿ən] ~**s** z
Ronuk *tdmk* ˈrɒn ək ˈrəʊn-, -ʌk ‖ ˈrɑːn-
roo, Roo ruː **roos** ruːz
rood ruːd (= *rude*) **roods** ruːdz
  '**rood loft**; '**rood screen**
roof ruːf rʊf **roofed** ruːft rʊft, ruːvd **roofing**
  ˈruːf ɪŋ ˈrʊf-, ˈruːv- **roofs** ruːfs ruːvz, rʊfs
  '**roof ˌgarden**; '**roof rack**
roofless ˈruːf ləs §ˈrʊf-, -lɪs
rooftop ˈruːf tɒp ˈrʊf- ‖ -tɑːp ~**s** s
rooftree ˈruːf triː ˈrʊf- ~**s** z
rooibos ˈrɔɪ bɒs ‖ -bɔːs -bɑːs
rooinek ˈrɔɪ nek ~**s** s
rook rʊk **rooked** rʊkt §ruːkt **rooking**
  ˈrʊk ɪŋ §ˈruːk- **rooks** rʊks §ruːks
Rook, Rooke rʊk §ruːk
rooker|y ˈrʊk ᵊr li §ˈruːk- ~**ies** iz
rook|ie, rook|y ˈrʊk li ~**ies** iz
room ruːm rʊm —*Poll panel preferences: BrE
  1988,* ruːm 82%, rʊm 19%; *AmE 1993* ruːm
  93%, rʊm 7%. *Some who say* ruːm *for this
  word on its own nevertheless say* rʊm *in
  compounds: see* bedroom. **roomed** ruːmd
  rʊmd **rooming** ˈruːm ɪŋ ˈrʊm- **rooms**
  ruːmz rʊmz
  '**rooming house**; '**room ˌservice**
Room, Roome ruːm
-roomed ˈruːmd ˈrʊmd — **three-roomed**
  ˌθriː ˈruːmd ◂ -ˈrʊmd
roomer ˈruːm ə ˈrʊm- ‖ -ᵊr ~**s** z
roomette ˌruːm ˈet ˌrʊm- ~**s** s
roomful ˈruːm fʊl ˈrʊm- ~**s** z
roommate ˈruːm meɪt ˈrʊm- ~**s** s
room|y ˈruːm li ˈrʊm- ~**ier** i‿ə ‖ i‿ᵊr ~**iest** i‿ɪst
  i‿əst ~**ily** ɪ li əl i ~**iness** i nəs i nɪs
Rooney ˈruːn i
Roope ruːp
Roosevelt ˈrəʊz ə velt ˈrəʊs-, -vᵊlt; ˈruːs-
  ‖ ˈroʊz- ~**s**, ~'**s** s
roost ruːst **roosted** ˈruːst ɪd -əd **roosting**
  ˈruːst ɪŋ **roosts** ruːsts
rooster ˈruːst ə ‖ -ᵊr ~**s** z
root, Root ruːt §rʊt **rooted** ˈruːt ɪd §ˈrʊt-, -əd
  ‖ ˈruːt̬ əd ˈrʊt̬- **rooting** ˈruːt ɪŋ §ˈrʊt-

‖ 'ruːt̮ ɪŋ 'rʊt̮- **roots** ruːts §rʊts
'**root** ˌbeer, ˌ·ˈ ˈ·; '**root** ca͵nal; ˌroot ͵mean
'square; 'root crop; 'root ͵vegetable,
ˌ·ˈ·ˈ··

Rootes ruːts
root|le 'ruːt ᵊl ~**ed** d ~**es** z ~**ing** ɪŋ
rootless 'ruːt ləs §'rʊt-, -lɪs ~**ness** nəs nɪs
rootlet 'ruːt lət §'rʊt-, -lɪt ~**s** s
rootstock 'ruːt stɒk §'rʊt- ‖ -staːk ~**s** s
rope rəʊp ‖ roʊp **roped** rəʊpt ‖ roʊpt **ropes**
rəʊps‖ roʊps **roping** 'rəʊp ɪŋ ‖ 'roʊp ɪŋ
͵rope 'ladder, ˈ· ͵·ˈ·
ropedancer 'rəʊp ͵daːnts ə -͵dænts-
‖ 'roʊp ͵dænts ᵊr ~**s** z
Roper 'rəʊp ə ‖ 'roʊp ᵊr
ropewalk 'rəʊp wɔːk ‖ 'roʊp- -waːk ~**ed** t
~**ing** ɪŋ ~**s** s
ropewalker 'rəʊp ͵wɔːk ə ‖ 'roʊp ͵wɔːk ᵊr
-͵waːk- ~**s** z
ropeway 'rəʊp weɪ ‖ 'roʊp- ~**s** z
rop|ey, rop|y 'rəʊp li ‖ 'roʊp li ~**ier** i͵ə ‖ i͵ᵊr
~**iest** i͵ɪst i͵əst ~**ily** ɪ li əl i ~**iness** i nəs i nɪs
Roquefort, r~ 'rɒk fɔː ‖ 'roʊk fᵊrt —*Fr*
[ʁɔk fɔːʁ]
roquet 'rəʊk i -eɪ ‖ roʊ 'keɪ ~**ed** d ~**ing** ɪŋ ~**s**
z
Rorke rɔːk ‖ rɔːrk roʊrk
ro-ro 'rəʊ rəʊ ‖ 'roʊ roʊ ~**s**, ~'**s** z
rorqual 'rɔːk wəl -ᵊl ‖ 'rɔːrk- ~**s** z
Rorschach 'rɔː ʃaːk -ʃæk ‖ 'rɔːr- 'roʊr- —*Ger*
['ʁɔʁ ʃax]
'Rorschach test
rort rɔːt ‖ rɔːrt **rorts** rɔːts ‖ rɔːrts
Rory 'rɔːr i ‖ 'roʊr-
Ros *short for* **Rosalind** *etc* rɒz ‖ raːz
Ros *family name* rɒs ‖ rɔːs raːs
Rosa 'rəʊz ə ‖ 'roʊz ə
rosaceous rəʊ 'zeɪʃ əs ‖ roʊ-
Rosaleen *(i)* 'rɒz ə liːn ‖ 'raːz-, *(ii)*
'rəʊz- ‖ 'roʊz-
Rosalie *(i)* 'rɒz ə li ‖ 'raːz-, *(ii)* 'rəʊz- ‖ 'roʊz-
Rosalind 'rɒz ə lɪnd ‖ 'raːz-
Rosaline 'rɒz ə lɪn -liːn, -laɪn ‖ 'raːz-
Rosamond, Rosamund 'rɒz ə mənd ‖ 'raːz-
'roʊz-
rosaniline rəʊ 'zæn ə liːn -laɪn; -ᵊl iːn, -aɪn;
-ᵊl ɪn, §-ᵊn ‖ roʊ 'zæn ᵊl ən -aɪn
Rosanna rəʊ 'zæn ə ‖ roʊ-
Rosanne rəʊ 'zæn ‖ roʊ-
Rosario rəʊ 'zaːr i əʊ -'saːr- ‖ roʊ 'saːr i oʊ
-'zaːr- —*Sp* [ɾɾo 'sa ɾjo]
rosari|um rəʊ 'zeər i͵əm ‖ roʊ 'zer- -'zær- ~**a**
ə ~**ums** əmz
rosar|y 'rəʊz ᵊr li ‖ 'roʊz- ~**ies** iz
Roscoe, r~ 'rɒsk əʊ ‖ 'raːsk oʊ ~**s**, ~'**s** z
Roscommon rɒs 'kɒm ən ‖ raːs 'kaːm ən
rose, Rose rəʊz ‖ roʊz **roses** 'rəʊz ɪz -əz
‖ 'roʊz əz
'rose ͵garden; 'rose 'window, ˈ· ͵··
rosé 'rəʊz eɪ rəʊ 'zeɪ ‖ roʊ 'zeɪ ~**s** z
Roseanne *(i)* rəʊ 'zæn ‖ roʊ-, *(ii)*
͵rəʊz i 'æn ‖ ͵roʊz-
roseate 'rəʊz i͵ət -ɪt, -eɪt ‖ 'roʊz- ~**ly** li

Roseau rəʊ 'zəʊ ‖ roʊ 'zoʊ
rosebay ͵rəʊz 'beɪ ˈ·· ‖ 'roʊz beɪ ~**s** z
Roseberry, Rosebery 'rəʊz bər͵i ‖ 'roʊz-
-͵beri
rosebud 'rəʊz bʌd ‖ 'roʊz- ~**s** z
rose-colored, rose-coloured
'rəʊz ͵kʌl əd ‖ 'roʊz ͵kʌl ᵊrd
Rosecrans 'rəʊz kræns 'rəʊz ə kræns ‖ 'roʊz-
Rosedale 'rəʊz deɪᵊl ‖ 'roʊz-
rose hip, rosehip 'rəʊz hɪp ‖ 'roʊz- ~**s** s
rosella rəʊ 'zel ə ‖ roʊ- ~**s** z
roselle, R~ rəʊ 'zel ‖ roʊ- ~**s**, ~'**s** z
Rosemarie ͵rəʊz mə 'riː ‖ ͵roʊz- ˈ···
rosemar|y, R~ 'rəʊz mər͵li ‖ 'roʊz ͵mer li ~**ies**
iz
Rosen 'rəʊz ᵊn ‖ 'roʊz ᵊn
Rosenberg 'rəʊz ᵊn bɜːg ‖ 'roʊz ᵊn bɝːg ~**s** z
Rosencrantz 'rəʊz ᵊn kræn*t*s ‖ 'roʊz-
Rosenthal *(i)* 'rəʊz ᵊn θɔːl ‖ 'roʊz- -θaːl, *(ii)*
-taːl
roseola rəʊ 'ziː͵əl ə ͵rəʊz i 'əʊl ə ‖ roʊ 'ziː əl ə
͵roʊz i 'oʊl ə ~**s** z
roseroot 'rəʊz ruːt §-rʊt ‖ 'roʊz-
Rosetta rəʊ 'zet ə ‖ roʊ 'zet̮ ə
Ro͵setta 'stone ‖ ·ˈ·ˈ·
rosette rəʊ 'zet ‖ roʊ- ~**s** s
Rosewall 'rəʊz wɔːl ‖ 'roʊz- -waːl
Rosewarne 'rəʊz wɔːn ‖ 'roʊz wɔːrn
rosewater 'rəʊz ͵wɔːt ə ‖ 'roʊz ͵wɔːt̮ ᵊr -͵waːt̮-
rosewood 'rəʊz wʊd ‖ 'roʊz-
Rosh Hashana, Rosh Hashanah ͵rɒʃ hə 'ʃaːn ə
-hæ- ‖ ͵roʊʃ haː 'ʃɔːn ə ͵rɔːʃ-, ͵raːʃ-, -hə-,
-'ʃaːn-, -'ʃoʊn-
Rosheen rɒ 'ʃiːn ‖ roʊ-
Rosicrucian ͵rəʊz i 'kruːʃ ᵊn ͵rɒz-, -'kruːʃ i͵ən
‖ ͵roʊz ə- ~**s** z
Rosie 'rəʊz i ‖ 'roʊz i
rosin 'rɒz ɪn §-ᵊn ‖ 'raːz- ~**ed** d ~**ing** ɪŋ ~**s** z
Rosinante ͵rɒz ɪ 'nænt i -ə- ‖ ͵raːz- —*Sp*
[ɾɾo si 'nan te]
Roskilde 'rɒsk ɪld ə ‖ 'raːsk- 'roʊsk- —*Danish*
['ʁɔs ki lə]
Roslea rɒs 'leɪ ‖ rɔːs- raːs-
Roslin, Roslyn 'rɒz lɪn §-lən ‖ 'raːz-
ROSPA, RoSPA 'rɒsp ə ‖ 'raːsp ə
Ross rɒs ‖ rɔːs raːs
͵Ross 'Sea
Rossall 'rɒs ᵊl ‖ 'rɔːs- 'raːs-
Rossendale 'rɒs ᵊn deɪᵊl ‖ 'rɔːs- 'raːs-
Rossetti *(i)* rə 'zet i rɒ- ‖ roʊ 'zet̮ i, *(ii)*
-'set i ‖ -'set̮ i
Rossini rɒ 'siːn i rə- ‖ roʊ- —*It* [ros 'si: ni]
Rossiter 'rɒs ɪt ə -ət- ‖ 'rɔːs ət̮ ᵊr 'raːs-
Rosslare ͵rɒs 'leə ˈ·· ‖ ͵rɔːs 'leᵊr ͵raːs-, -'læᵊr
Rosslyn 'rɒs lɪn §-lən ‖ 'rɔːs- 'raːs-
Ross-on-Wye ͵rɒs ɒn 'waɪ ‖ ͵rɔːs aːn- ͵raːs-,
-ɔːn-
roster 'rɒst ə ‖ 'raːst ᵊr ~**ed** d **rostering** 'rɒst
ᵊr͵ɪŋ ‖ 'raːst ᵊr͵ɪŋ ~**s** z
Rostock 'rɒst ɒk ‖ 'raːst aːk —*Ger* ['ʁɔs tɔk]
Rostov 'rɒst ɒv -ɒf ‖ 'raːst aːv -aːf —*Russ*
[ɾʌs 'tɔf]
͵Rostov-on-'Don

ros|tra 'rɒs |trə ‖ 'rɑːs- **~tral** trəl **~trate**
treɪt
Rostrevor rɒs 'trev ə ‖ rɑːs 'trev ər
Rostropovich ˌrɒs trə 'pəʊv ɪtʃ
‖ ˌrɑːs trə 'poʊv ɪtʃ —*Russ* [rəs trʌ 'pɔ vjɪtʃ]
ros|trum 'rɒs |trəm ‖ 'rɑːs- **~tra** trə **~trums**
trəmz
ros|y 'rəʊz |i ‖ 'roʊz i **~ier** i_ə ‖ i_ər **~iest** i_ɪst
i_əst **~ily** ɪ li əl i **~iness** i nəs i nɪs
Rosyth rə 'saɪθ rɒ-
rot rɒt ‖ rɑːt **rots** rɒts ‖ rɑːts **rotted** 'rɒt ɪd
-əd ‖ 'rɑːt̬ əd **rotting** 'rɒt ɪŋ ‖ 'rɑːt̬ ɪŋ
rota, Rota 'rəʊt ə ‖ 'roʊt̬ ə **~s** z
Rotarian rəʊ 'teər i_ən ‖ roʊ 'ter- **~s** z
rotar|y, R~ 'rəʊt ər |i ‖ 'roʊt̬- **~ies** iz
'Rotary Club; ˌrotary 'tiller
rotatab|le rəʊ 'teɪt əb |əl ‖ 'roʊt eɪt̬- **~ly** li
rotate rəʊ 'teɪt ‖ 'roʊt eɪt **rotated** rəʊ 'teɪt ɪd
-əd ‖ 'roʊt eɪt̬ əd **rotates**
rəʊ 'teɪts ‖ 'roʊt eɪts **rotating**
rəʊ 'teɪt ɪŋ ‖ 'roʊt eɪt̬ ɪŋ
rotation rəʊ 'teɪʃ ən ‖ roʊ- **~s** z
rotative rəʊ 'teɪt ɪv 'rəʊt ət- ‖ 'roʊt̬ ət̬ ɪv **~ly**
li
rotator rəʊ 'teɪt ə ‖ 'roʊt eɪt̬ ər **~s** z
rotatory rəʊ 'teɪt ər i 'rəʊt ət_ər i
‖ 'roʊt̬ ə tɔːr i -toʊr i (*)
Rotavator —*see* **Rotovator**
rotavirus 'rəʊt ə ˌvaɪ_ər əs ‖ 'roʊt̬- **~es** ɪz əz
rote rəʊt ‖ roʊt (= *wrote*)
rotenone 'rəʊt ə nəʊn -ɪ-, -ən əʊn
‖ 'roʊt ən oʊn
rotgut 'rɒt gʌt ‖ 'rɑːt-
Roth (*i*) rɒθ ‖ rɔːθ rɑːθ, (*ii*) rəʊθ ‖ roʊθ
Rothamsted 'rɒθ əm sted ‖ 'rɑː θ-
Rothay 'rɒθ eɪ ‖ 'rɑː θ-
Rothbury 'rɒθ bər_i ‖ 'rɑː θ-
Rothenstein 'rəʊθ ən staɪn 'rəʊt-, 'rɒθ-
‖ 'rɑː θ-
Rother 'rɒð ə ‖ 'rɑːð ər
Rotherfield 'rɒð ə fiːəld ‖ 'rɑːð ər-
Rotherham 'rɒð ər_əm ‖ 'rɑːð-
Rotherhithe 'rɒð ə haɪð ‖ 'rɑːð ər-
Rothermere 'rɒð ə mɪə ‖ 'rɑːð ər mɪr
Rothersthorpe 'rɒð əz θɔːp ‖ 'rɑːð ərz θɔːrp
—*In Northants, locally also* -θrəp
Rotherwick 'rɒð ə wɪk ‖ 'rɑːð ər- —*formerly
also* -ər ɪk
Rothes 'rɒθ ɪz -ɪs, §-əz, §-əs ‖ 'rɑːθ-
Rothesay 'rɒθ si -seɪ ‖ 'rɑːθ-
Rothko 'rɒθ kəʊ ‖ 'rɑːθ koʊ
Rothman 'rɒθ mən ‖ 'rɔːθ- 'rɑːθ-
Rothschild 'rɒθs tʃaɪəld 'rɒθ- ‖ 'rɔːθs- 'rɑːθs-,
'rɔːθ-, 'rɑːθ- **~s**, **~'s** z
roti 'rəʊt i ‖ 'roʊt̬ i **~s** z —*Hindi* [roː ʈi]
rotifer 'rəʊt ɪf ə §-əf- ‖ 'roʊt̬ əf ər **~s** z
rotifer|a rəʊ 'tɪf ər_|ə ‖ roʊ- **~al** əl **~ous** əs
rotisserie rəʊ 'tɪs ər i -'tiːs- ‖ roʊ- **~s** z
roto 'rəʊt əʊ ‖ 'roʊt̬ oʊ **~s** z
Rotodyne 'rəʊt əʊ daɪn ‖ 'roʊt̬ ə-

rotogravure ˌrəʊt əʊ grə 'vjʊə
‖ ˌroʊt̬ ə grə 'vjʊ_ər
rotor 'rəʊt ə ‖ 'roʊt̬ ər **~s** z
Rotorua ˌrəʊt ə 'ruː_ə ‖ ˌroʊt̬-
rototill 'rəʊt ə tɪl ‖ 'roʊt̬- **~ed** d **~ing** ɪŋ **~s** z
rototiller, R~ *tdmk* 'rəʊt ə ˌtɪl ə
‖ 'roʊt̬ ə ˌtɪl ər **~s** z
roto|vate 'rəʊt ə |veɪt ‖ 'roʊt̬- **~vated** veɪt ɪd
-əd ‖ veɪt̬ əd **~vates** veɪts **~vating**
veɪt ɪŋ ‖ veɪt̬ ɪŋ
rotovator, R~ *tdmk* 'rəʊt ə veɪt ə
‖ 'roʊt̬ ə veɪt̬ ər **~s** z
rotten 'rɒt ən ‖ 'rɑːt ən **~er** ə ‖ ər **~est** ɪst əst
~ly li **~ness** nəs nɪs
ˌrotten 'borough
rottenstone 'rɒt ən stəʊn ‖ 'rɑːt ən stoʊn
rotter 'rɒt ə ‖ 'rɑːt̬ ər **~s** z
Rotterdam 'rɒt ə dæm ˌ•••• ‖ 'rɑːt̬ ər-
—*Dutch* [rɔt ər 'dɑm]
Rottingdean 'rɒt ɪŋ diːn ‖ 'rɑːt̬- —*locally also*
ˌ•••
Rottweiler, r~ 'rɒt waɪl ə -vaɪl- ‖ 'rɑːt waɪl ər
~s z
rotund rəʊ 'tʌnd 'rəʊt ʌnd ‖ roʊ 'tʌnd
'roʊt ʌnd
rotunda, R~ rəʊ 'tʌnd ə ‖ roʊ- **~s** z
rotundity rəʊ 'tʌnd ət i -ɪt- ‖ roʊ 'tʌnd ət̬ i
rotund|ly rəʊ 'tʌnd |li 'rəʊt ʌnd- ‖ roʊ 'tʌnd-
'roʊt ʌnd- **~ness** nəs nɪs
rouble 'ruːb əl **~s** z
roué 'ruː eɪ ‖ ru 'eɪ **~s** z
Rouen 'ruː ɒ̃ ‖ ru 'ɑːn —*Fr* [ʁwɑ̃]
rouge ruːʒ **rouged** ruːʒd **rouges** 'ruːʒ ɪz -əz
rouging 'ruːʒ ɪŋ —*Fr* [ʁuʒ]
ˌrouge et 'noir eɪ 'nwɑː ‖ -'nwɑːr —*Fr*
[e nwaːʁ]
rough rʌf (= *ruff*) **roughed** rʌft **rougher**
'rʌf ə ‖ -ər **roughest** 'rʌf ɪst -əst **roughing**
'rʌf ɪŋ **roughs** rʌfs
ˌrough 'diamond; ˌrough 'paper; 'rough
stuff; ˌrough 'trade
Rough rʌf —*but* Rough Tor *in Cornwall is* raʊ
roughage 'rʌf ɪdʒ
rough-and-ready ˌrʌf ən 'red i ◂ -ənd-
rough-and-tumble ˌrʌf ən 'tʌm bəl -ənd-
roughcast 'rʌf kɑːst §-kæst ‖ -kæst **~ing** ɪŋ
~s s
rough-|dry 'rʌf |draɪ ˌ•'• **~dried** draɪd
~dries draɪz **~drying** draɪ ɪŋ
roughen 'rʌf ən **~ed** d **~ing** _ɪŋ **~s** z
rough-|hew ˌrʌf |'hjuː **~hewed** 'hjuːd
~hewing 'hjuː ɪŋ **~hewn** 'hjuːn ◂ **~hews**
'hjuːz
roughhouse *n* 'rʌf haʊs
roughish 'rʌf ɪʃ **~ness** nəs nɪs
roughly 'rʌf li
roughneck 'rʌf nek **~s** s
roughness 'rʌf nəs -nɪs **~es** ɪz əz
roughrider ˌrʌf 'raɪd ə '•ˌ•• ‖ -ər **~s** z
roughshod 'rʌf ʃɒd ‖ -ʃɑːd
Roughton (*i*) 'raʊt ən, (*ii*) 'ruːt ən
roulade ru 'lɑːd **~s** z
rouleau 'ruːl əʊ ‖ ru 'loʊ **~s, ~x** z

roulette ru |'let ~letted 'let ɪd -əd || 'leṭ əd
~lettes 'lets ~letting 'let ɪŋ || 'leṭ ɪŋ
Roumani|a ru 'meɪn i‿ə ~an/s ən/z
round raʊnd rounded 'raʊnd ɪd -əd rounder
'raʊnd ə || -ər roundest 'raʊnd ɪst -əst
rounding 'raʊnd ɪŋ rounds raʊndz
ˌround 'bracket; ˌround 'robin; ˌRound
'Table; ˌround 'trip
roundabout n, adj, prep 'raʊnd ə ˌbaʊt ~s s
round-arm 'raʊnd ɑːm || -ɑːrm
rounded 'raʊnd ɪd -əd ~ly li ~ness nəs nɪs
roundel 'raʊnd əl ~s z
roundelay 'raʊnd ə leɪ -ɪ-, -əl eɪ ~s z
rounders 'raʊnd əz || -ərz
round-eyed ˌraʊnd 'aɪd ◄
roundhand 'raʊnd hænd
Roundhay 'raʊnd eɪ -i —There is also a spelling
pronunciation -heɪ.
Roundhead 'raʊnd hed ~s z
round|house 'raʊnd |haʊs ~houses haʊz ɪz
-əz
roundish 'raʊnd ɪʃ ~ness nəs nɪs
round|ly 'raʊnd |li ~ness nəs nɪs
round-shouldered ˌraʊnd 'ʃəʊld əd ◄
→ˌ-'ʃɒʊld- || -'ʃoʊld ərd ◄
rounds|man 'raʊndz |mən ~men mən -men
round-table ˌraʊnd 'teɪb əl ◄
ˌround-ˌtable diˈscussions
round-the-clock ˌraʊnd ðə 'klɒk ◄ || -'klɑːk ◄
round-trip ˌraʊnd 'trɪp ◄
ˌround-trip 'ticket
roundup 'raʊnd ʌp ~s s
roundwood, R~ 'raʊnd wʊd
roundworm 'raʊnd wɜːm || -wɜ˞ːm ~s z
Rountree 'raʊn triː
roup bird disease ruːp
Rourke rɔːk || rɔːrk roʊrk
Rous raʊs
rouse raʊz roused raʊzd rouses 'raʊz ɪz -əz
rousing/ly 'raʊz ɪŋ /li
Rouse raʊs
Rousseau 'ruːs əʊ || ruː 'soʊ —Fr [ʁu so]
Roussillon ˌruːs iː -ˈõ -'jõ || -'joʊn —Fr
[ʁu si jɔ̃]
roust raʊst rousted 'raʊst ɪd-əd rousting
'raʊst ɪŋ rousts raʊsts
roustabout 'raʊst ə ˌbaʊt ~s s
rout, Rout raʊt routed 'raʊt ɪd -əd || 'raʊṭ əd
routing 'raʊt ɪŋ || 'raʊṭ ɪŋ routs raʊts

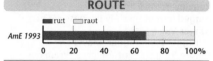

ROUTE

	■ ruːt	☐ raʊt			
AmE 1993					
0	20	40	60	80	100%

route ruːt raʊt —in BrE the form raʊt is
confined to army usage, but in AmE it is more
widespread. —AmE 1993 poll panel preference:
ruːt 68%, raʊt 32%. routed 'ruːt ɪd -əd
|| 'ruːṭ əd 'raʊṭ- routeing/s, routing/s
'ruːt ɪŋ/z || 'ruːṭ ɪŋ/z 'raʊṭ- routes ruːts raʊts
ˈroute march
router 'tool for hollowing' 'raʊt ə || 'raʊṭ ər ~s z
Routh raʊθ

routine ˌruː 'tiːn ◄ ru- ~s z
Routledge 'raʊt lɪdʒ 'rʌt-, -ledʒ
roux sing. ruː (= rue) roux pl ruːz or as sing.
rove rəʊv || roʊv roved rəʊvd || roʊvd roves
rəʊvz || roʊvz roving 'rəʊv ɪŋ || 'roʊv ɪŋ
ˌroving comˈmission; ˌroving 'eye
rover, Rover 'rəʊv ə || 'roʊv ər ~s, ~'s z
row v 'use oars', n 'line', 'trip in rowing boat'
Row name of thoroughfare rəʊ || roʊ (= roe)
rowed rəʊd || roʊd (= road) rowing
'rəʊ ɪŋ || 'roʊ ɪŋ rows rəʊz || roʊz (= rose)
ˈrow house; ˈrowing boat; ˈrowing
maˌchine
row 'quarrel, (make) noise' raʊ rowed raʊd
rowing 'raʊ‿ɪŋ rows raʊz (= rouse)
Rowallan raʊ 'æl ən || roʊ-
rowan, Rowan 'rəʊ ən 'raʊ‿ən || 'roʊ ən ~s z
ˈrowan tree
rowanberr|y 'rəʊ ən ˌber li 'raʊ‿ən-, →-əm-
|| 'roʊ- ~ies iz
Rowant 'raʊ‿ənt
rowboat 'rəʊ bəʊt || 'roʊ boʊt ~s s
Rowbotham, Rowbottom
'rəʊ ˌbɒt əm || 'roʊ ˌbɑːṭ əm
rowd|y 'raʊd li ~ier i‿ə || i‿ər ~ies iz ~iest
i‿ɪst i‿əst ~ily ɪ li əl i ~iness i nəs i nɪs
~yism i ˌɪz əm
Rowe rəʊ || roʊ
rowel 'raʊ‿əl raʊl || 'raʊ‿əl ~ed, ~led d ~ing,
~ling ɪŋ ~s z
Rowena rəʊ 'iːn ə || roʊ-
Rowenta tdmk rəʊ 'ent ə || roʊ 'enṭ ə
rower 'rəʊ ə || 'roʊ ər ~s z
Rowland 'rəʊl ənd || 'roʊl-
Rowlands 'rəʊl əndz || 'roʊl-
Rowlandson 'rəʊl ənd sən || 'roʊl-
Rowley 'rəʊl i || 'roʊl i —but R~ Regis in WMids
is 'raʊl i
rowlock 'rɒl ək 'rʌl- || 'rɑːl- —Also, but not
among sailors, 'rəʊ lɒk || 'roʊ lɑːk ~s s
Rowney (i) 'raʊn i, (ii) 'rəʊn i || 'roʊn i
Rowntree 'raʊn triː
ˌRowntree 'Mackintosh tdmk
Rowridge 'raʊ rɪdʒ
Rowse raʊs
Rowsley 'rəʊz li || 'roʊz-
Rowton 'raʊt ən
Roxana rɒk 'sɑːn ə || rɑːk 'sæn ə
Roxanna rɒk 'sæn ə || rɑːk-
Roxanne, r~ rɒk 'sæn || rɑːk-
Roxburgh 'rɒks bər‿ə || 'rɑːks ˌbɜ˞ː oʊ
Roxy 'rɒks i || 'rɑːks i
Roy rɔɪ
royal 'rɔɪ‿əl ~s z
ˌroyal 'blue ◄; ˌroyal 'flush; ˌRoyal
'Highness; ˌroyal preˈrogative
royale, R~ rɔɪ 'ɑːl -'æl || -'æl
royalism 'rɔɪ‿əl ˌɪz əm
royalist 'rɔɪ‿əl ɪst §-əst ~s s
royally 'rɔɪ‿əl i
royalty 'rɔɪ‿əl ti
Royce rɔɪs
Royden, Roydon 'rɔɪd ən

Royle rɔɪ^əl
Royston 'rɔɪst ən
Royton 'rɔɪt ən
Roz rɒz ‖ rɑːz
rozzer 'rɒz ə ‖ 'rɑːz ər ~s z
RP ˌɑː 'piː ‖ ˌɑːr-
rpm ˌɑː piː 'em ‖ ˌɑːr-
-rrhagia 'reɪdʒ i‿ə 'reɪdʒ ə ‖ 'reɪdʒ ə 'reɪʒ ə —
 menorrhagia ˌmen ə 'reɪdʒ i‿ə , • • ' • ə
 ‖ -'reɪdʒ ə -'reɪʒ-
-rrhaphy *stress-imposing* rəf i —
 colporrhaphy kɒl 'pɒr əf i ‖ kɑːl 'pɔːr-
 -'pɑːr-
-rrhea, -rrhoea 'rɪə 'riː‿ə ‖ 'riː ə —
 blenorrhea, blennorrhoea ˌblen ə 'rɪə
 -'riː‿ə ‖ -'riː ə
RSJ ˌɑːr es 'dʒeɪ ~s z
RSVP ˌɑːr es viː 'piː
Ruabon ru 'æb ən —*Welsh* [riu 'a bon]
Ruanda ru 'ænd ə ‖ -'ɑːnd ə
Ruane ru 'eɪn
Ruaridh 'ruər i 'rɔːr- ‖ 'rur i
rub rʌb **rubbed** rʌbd **rubbing/s** 'rʌb ɪŋ/z
 rubs rʌbz
rub-a-dub 'rʌb ə dʌb
rub-a-dub-dub ˌrʌb ə dʌb 'dʌb
rubaiyat, rubáiyát, R~ 'ruː baɪ æt -jæt, -ɑːt,
 -jɑːt, • ' • • ‖ -jɑːt
rubato ru 'bɑːt əʊ ‖ -oʊ ~s z
rubb... —*see* **rub**
rubber 'rʌb ə ‖ 'rʌb ər ~s z
 ˌrubber 'band; 'rubber boot; ˌrubber
 'dinghy; 'rubber plant; ˌrubber 'stamp;
 'rubber tree
rubberis|e, rubberiz|e 'rʌb ə raɪz ~ed d ~es
 ɪz əz ~ing ɪŋ
rubberneck 'rʌb ə nek ‖ -ər- ~ed t ~er/s ə/z
 ‖ ər/z ~ing ɪŋ ~s s
rubber-stamp ˌrʌb ə 'stæmp ‖ -ər- ~ed t ~ing
 ɪŋ ~s s
rubbery 'rʌb ər i
rubbish 'rʌb ɪʃ ~ed t ~es ɪz əz ~ing ɪŋ
 'rubbish bin
rubbishy 'rʌb ɪʃ i
rubble 'rʌb ^əl
Rubbra 'rʌb rə
rubdown 'rʌb daʊn ~s z
rube, Rube ruːb **rubes, Rube's** ruːbz
rubella ru 'bel ə
Ruben 'ruːb ɪn -ən
Rubens 'ruːb ɪnz -ənz —*Dutch* ['ry: bəns]
rubeola ru 'biː‿əl ə ˌru:b i 'əʊl ə ‖ ˌru:b i 'oʊl ə
Rubery 'ruːb ər i
rubesc|ence ru 'bes ^ən^ts ~ent ənt
Rubicon 'ruːb ɪk ən -ɪ kɒn, §-ə- ‖ -ɪ kɑːn
rubicund 'ruːb ɪk ənd §-ək-, -ɪ kʌnd, §-ə-
rubicundity ˌru:b ɪ 'kʌnd ət i §-ə-, -ɪt i ‖ -ət̬ i
rubidium ru 'bɪd i‿əm
rubie... —*see* **ruby**
Rubik 'ruːb ɪk ~'s s
Rubin 'ruːb ɪn §-ən
Rubinstein 'ruːb ɪn staɪn -ən-
ruble 'ruːb ^əl ~s z

rubric 'ruːb rɪk ~s s
ruby, Ruby 'ruːb i **rubies** 'ruːb iz
RUC ˌɑː juː 'siː ‖ ˌɑːr-
ruche ruːʃ **ruched** ruːʃt **ruches** 'ruːʃ ɪz -əz
 ruching 'ruːʃ ɪŋ
ruck rʌk **rucked** rʌkt **rucking** 'rʌk ɪŋ **rucks**
 rʌks
ruckle 'rʌk ^əl ~s z
rucksack 'rʌk sæk 'rʊk- ~s s
ruckus 'rʌk əs ~es ɪz əz
ruction 'rʌk ʃ^ən ~s z
rudbeckia rʌd 'bek i‿ə →rʌb-, ˌru:d- ~s z
Rudd, rudd rʌd **rudds** rʌdz
rudder 'rʌd ə ‖ -ər ~ed d ~s z
rudderless 'rʌd ə ləs -lɪs, -^əl əs ‖ -ər-
Ruddigore 'rʌd ɪ gɔː: ‖ -gɔːr
ruddl|e 'rʌd ^əl ~ed d ~es z ~ing ɪŋ
Ruddock, r~ 'rʌd ək ~s s
rudd|y 'rʌd li ~ier i‿ə ‖ i‿ər ~iest i‿ɪst i‿əst
 ~ily ɪ li əl i ~iness i nəs i nɪs
rude ruːd **rudely** 'ruːd li **rudeness** 'ruːd nəs
 -nɪs **ruder** 'ruːd ə ‖ -ər **rudest** 'ruːd ɪst -əst
Rudge rʌdʒ
Rudgwick 'rʌdʒ wɪk -ɪk
Rudi 'ruːd i
rudiment 'ruːd ɪ mənt -ə- ~s s
rudi|mentary ˌru:d ɪ 'ment ər i ◂, • ə-
 ~mentarily 'ment ər əl i -ɪ li; ˌmen 'ter əl i
 ~mentariness 'ment ər i nəs -nɪs
Rudolf, Rudolph 'ruːd ɒlf ‖ -ɑːlf
Rudy 'ruːd i
Rudyard 'rʌd jəd -jɑːd; 'rʌdʒ əd ‖ -jərd -jɑːrd
rue ruː **rued** ruːd (= *rude*) **rues** ruːz **ruing**
 'ruː‿ɪŋ
rueful 'ruː f^əl -fʊl ~ly ‿i ~ness nəs nɪs
ruff, Ruff rʌf **ruffed** rʌft **ruffing** 'rʌf ɪŋ **ruffs**
 rʌfs
ruffian 'rʌf i‿ən ~ism ˌɪz əm ~ly li ~s z
ruffl|e 'rʌf ^əl ~ed d ~es z ~ing ‿ɪŋ
Rufflette *tdmk* ˌrʌf 'let ˌrʌf ^əl 'et
Rufford 'rʌf əd ‖ -ərd
rufous 'ruːf əs
Rufus 'ruːf əs
rug rʌg **rugs** rʌgz
Rugbeian rʌg 'biː‿ən ~s z
rugby, Rugby 'rʌg bi
 ˌrugby 'football; ˌRugby 'League; ˌRugby
 'Union
Rugeley 'ruːdʒ li 'ruːʒ-
rugged 'rʌg ɪd §-əd ~ly li ~ness nəs nɪs
rugger 'rʌg ə ‖ -ər
 'rugger ball; 'rugger ˌplayer
rugose 'ruːg əʊs -əʊz; ru 'gəʊs ‖ 'ruːg oʊs ~ly
 li
rugosity ru: 'gɒs ət i -ɪt- ‖ -'gɑːs ət̬ i
Ruhr rʊə ‖ rʊər —*Ger* [ʁuːɐ]
ruin 'ruː‿ɪn §-ən ~ed d ~ing ɪŋ ~s z
ruination ˌruː‿ɪ 'neɪʃ ^ən §-ə-
ruinous 'ruː‿ɪn əs §-ən- ~ly li ~ness nəs nɪs
Ruisdael 'raɪz dɑːl 'riːz-, -deɪ^əl —*Dutch*
 ['rœyz dɑːl]
Ruislip 'raɪs lɪp

rule, Rule ruːl **ruled** ruːld **rules** ruːlz **ruling**
'ruːl ɪŋ
,rule of 'thumb
rulebook 'ruːl bʊk §-buːk ~s s
ruler 'ruːl ə ‖ -ᵊr ~s z
ruling 'ruːl ɪŋ ~s z
,ruling 'class
rum rʌm **rummer** 'rʌm ə ‖ -ᵊr **rummest**
'rʌm ɪst -əst **rums** rʌmz
Rumani|a ru 'meɪn i‿|ə ~an/s ən/z
rumba 'rʌm bə 'rʊm- ‖ 'ruːm- ~ed d
rumbaing 'rʌm bəʳ ɪŋ 'rʊm- ‖ -bə ɪŋ 'ruːm-
~s z
Rumbelow 'rʌm bə ləʊ ‖ -loʊ
rumbl|e 'rʌm bᵊl ~ed d ~es z ~ing ‿ɪŋ
rumbling 'rʌm blɪŋ ~ly li ~s z
Rumbold 'rʌm bəʊld →-bɒʊld ‖ -boʊld
rumbustious rʌm 'bʌs tʃəs -'bʌs ti‿əs,
⚠-'bʌs tʃu‿əs ~ly li ~ness nəs nɪs
Rumelia ru 'miːl i‿ə
rum|en 'ruːm |en -ɪn, -ən ~ens enz ɪnz, ənz
~ina ɪn ə ən ə
Rumford 'rʌm fəd ‖ -fᵊrd
ruminant 'ruːm ɪn ənt -ən- ~s s
rumi|nate 'ruːm ɪ |neɪt -ə- ~nated neɪt ɪd -əd
‖ neɪt̬ əd ~nates neɪts ~nating/ly neɪt ɪŋ /
li ‖ neɪt̬ ɪŋ /li
rumination ,ruːm ɪ 'neɪʃ ᵊn -ə- ~s z
ruminative 'ruːm ɪ nət ɪv '•ə-, -neɪt ɪv
‖ -ə neɪt̬ ɪv ~ly li
rumly 'rʌm li
rummag|e 'rʌm ɪdʒ ~ed d ~er/s ə/z ‖ ᵊr/z
~es ɪz əz ~ing ɪŋ
'rummage sale
rummer 'rʌm ə ‖ -ᵊr ~s z
rumm|y 'rʌm li ~ier i‿ə ‖ i‿ᵊr ~ies iz ~iest
i‿ɪst ‿əst
rumness 'rʌm nəs -nɪs
rumor, rumour 'ruːm ə ‖ -ᵊr ~ed d
rumoring, rumouring 'ruːm əʳ ɪŋ ~s z
rumormonger, rumourmonger
'ruːm ə ,mʌŋ gə §-,mɒŋ- ‖ -ᵊr ,mʌŋ gᵊr
-,mɑːŋ- ~s z
rump rʌmp **rumps** rʌmps
,rump 'steak
Rumpelstiltskin ,rʌmp ᵊl 'stɪlt skɪn
rumpl|e 'rʌmp ᵊl ~ed d ~es z ~ing ‿ɪŋ
Rumpole 'rʌmp əʊl →-ɒʊl ‖ -oʊl
rumpus 'rʌmp əs ~es ɪz əz
'rumpus room
run rʌn **ran** ræn **running** 'rʌn ɪŋ **runs** rʌnz
runabout 'rʌn ə ,baʊt ~s s
runagate 'rʌn ə geɪt ~s s
run-around 'rʌn ə ,raʊnd
runaway 'rʌn ə ,weɪ ~s z
runcible 'rʌnts əb ᵊl -ɪb-
Runcie 'rʌnts i
Runciman 'rʌnts ɪ mən
runcinate 'rʌnts ɪn ət -ən-, -ɪt; -ɪ neɪt, -ə•
Runcorn 'rʌn kɔːn →'rʌŋ- ‖ -kɔːrn
Rundall, Rundell, Rundle 'rʌnd ᵊl
rundown n 'rʌn daʊn ~s z
run-down adj ,rʌn 'daʊn ◂

rune ruːn **runes** ruːnz
rung rʌŋ **rungs** rʌŋz
runic 'ruːn ɪk
run-in n 'rʌn ɪn ~s z
runnel 'rʌn ᵊl ~s z
runner 'rʌn ə ‖ -ᵊr ~s z
'runner bean,, • • '•
runn|er-up ,rʌn |ər 'ʌp ‖ -|ər 'ʌp ~ers-up
əz 'ʌp ‖ ᵊrz 'ʌp
running 'rʌn ɪŋ
'running board; ,running 'jump; 'running
light; ,running 'mate; ,running 'water
runn|y 'rʌn li ~ier i‿ə ‖ i‿ᵊr ~iest i‿ɪst i‿əst
~iness i nəs -nɪs
Runnymede 'rʌn i miːd
runoff, run-off 'rʌn ɒf -ɔːf ‖ -ɔːf -ɑːf ~s s
run-of-the-mill ,rʌn əv ðə 'mɪl ◂ -ə ðə-
run-on 'rʌn ɒn ‖ -ɑːn -ɔːn ~s z
run-out 'rʌn aʊt ~s s
runt rʌnt **runts** rʌnts
run-through 'rʌn θruː ~s z
runtish 'rʌnt ɪʃ ‖ 'rʌnt̬ ɪʃ
runt|y 'rʌnt li ‖ 'rʌnt̬ i ~iness i nəs i nɪs
run-up 'rʌn ʌp ~s s
runway 'rʌn weɪ ~s z
Runyon 'rʌn jən
rupee ,ru: 'pi: ru- ‖ 'ru:p i: ru 'pi: ~s z
Rupert 'ruːp ət ‖ -ᵊrt
rupiah ru 'piː‿ə ~s z
rupture 'rʌp tʃə -ʃə ‖ -tʃᵊr ~d d ~s z
rupturing 'rʌp tʃər ɪŋ -ʃər‿ɪŋ
rural 'rʊər ᵊl ‖ 'rʊr əl
,rural 'dean
rurality rʊᵊ 'ræl ət i -ɪt- ‖ -ət̬ i
rurally 'rʊər əl i ‖ 'rʊr əl i
ruridecanal ,rʊər ɪ dɪ 'keɪn ᵊl ◂ ,•ə-, -də'•-
‖ ,rʊr-
Ruritani|a ,rʊər ɪ 'teɪn i‿|ə ,•ə- ‖ ,rʊr- ~an/s
ən/z
ruse ruːz ‖ ruːs ruːz **ruses** 'ruːz ɪz -əz ‖ 'ruːs-
'ruːz-
rusé 'ruːz eɪ ‖ ruː 'zeɪ —Fr [ʁy ze]
Rusedski ru 'set ski -'sed-, -'zet-
rush, Rush rʌʃ **rushed** rʌʃt **rushes** 'rʌʃ ɪz -əz
rushing/ly 'rʌʃ ɪŋ /li
'rush hour
Rushdie 'rʊʃ di —This is reportedly the writer
Salman R~'s preference, though he is often
referred to as 'rʌʃ di
rusher 'rʌʃ ə ‖ -ᵊr ~s z
rushlight 'rʌʃ laɪt ~s s
Rushmere 'rʌʃ mɪə ‖ -mɪr
Rushmore 'rʌʃ mɔː ‖ -mɔːr -moʊr
Rusholme 'rʌʃ həʊm -əm ‖ -hoʊm
Rushton 'rʌʃt ən
Rushworth 'rʌʃ wɜːθ ‖ -wɜːθ
rush|ly 'rʌʃ li ~ier i‿ə ‖ i‿ᵊr ~iest i‿ɪst i‿əst
~iness i nəs i nɪs
rusk, Rusk rʌsk **rusks** rʌsks
Ruskin 'rʌsk ɪn §-ən
Rusper 'rʌsp ə ‖ -ᵊr
Russ rʌs
russe ruːs

R

Russel, Russell 'rʌs ᵊl
russet 'rʌs ɪt §-ət ~s s
Russia 'rʌʃ ə ~s, ~'s z
Russian 'rʌʃ ᵊn ~s z
Russian rou'lette
Russianis... —*see* **Russianiz...**
Russianization, r~ ˌrʌʃ ᵊn aɪ 'zeɪʃ ᵊn -ɪ' • -
‖ -ə' • -
Russianiz|e, r~ 'rʌʃ ə naɪz -ᵊn aɪz ~ed d ~er/s
ə/z ‖ ᵊr/z ~es ɪz əz ~ing ɪŋ
Russianness 'rʌʃ ᵊn nəs -nɪs
Russification ˌrʌs ɪf ɪ 'keɪʃ ᵊn , • əf-, §-ə' • -
Russi|fy 'rʌs ɪ |faɪ -ə- ~fied faɪd ~fies faɪz
~fying faɪ ɪŋ
Russk|i, Russk|y 'rʌsk i ~ies iz
Russo- ˌrʌs əʊ ‖ -oʊ — **Russo-Japanese**
ˌrʌs əʊ ˌdʒæp ə 'niːz ‖ ˌrʌs oʊ-
rust, Rust rʌst **rusted** 'rʌst ɪd -əd **rusting**
'rʌst ɪŋ **rusts** rʌsts
'rust belt
rustbucket 'rʌst ˌbʌkɪt §-ət ~s s
rustic 'rʌst ɪk ~s s
rusti|cate 'rʌst ɪ |keɪt §-ə- ~cated keɪt ɪd -əd
‖ keɪt̬ əd ~cates keɪts ~cating
keɪt ɪŋ ‖ keɪt̬ ɪŋ
rustication ˌrʌst ɪ 'keɪʃ ᵊn §-ə- ~s z
rusticity rʌ 'stɪs ət i -ɪt i ‖ -ət̬ i
rustl|e 'rʌs ᵊl ~ed d ~es z ~ing ˌɪŋ
rustler 'rʌs lə 'rʌs ᵊl ə ‖ -ᵊl ᵊr ~s z
rustless 'rʌst ləs -lɪs
rustling 'rʌs ᵊl ɪŋ ~ly li
Ruston 'rʌst ən
rustproof 'rʌst pruːf §-prʊf ~ed t ~ing ɪŋ ~s
s
rust|y, Rusty 'rʌst li ~ier i ə ‖ i ᵊr ~iest i ɪst
i əst ~ily ɪ li əl i ~iness i nəs i nɪs
Ruswarp 'rʌs əp ‖ -ᵊrp
rut rʌt **ruts** rʌts **rutted** 'rʌt ɪd -əd ‖ 'rʌt̬ əd
rutting 'rʌt ɪŋ ‖ 'rʌt̬ ɪŋ
rutabaga ˌruːt ə 'beɪg ə ˌrʊt-, ' • • , • • ‖ ˌruːt̬-
~s z
Rutgers 'rʌt gəz ‖ -gᵊrz
Ruth, ruth ruːθ
Rutheni|a ru 'θiːn i ə |ə ~an/s ᵊn/z
ruthenic ru 'θen ɪk -'θiːn-
ruthenium ru 'θiːn i əm
Rutherford, r~ 'rʌð ə fəd ‖ -ᵊr fᵊrd ~s, ~'s z

rutherfordium ˌrʌð ə 'fɔːd i əm ‖ , • ᵊr 'fɔːrd-
-'foʊrd-
Rutherglen 'rʌð ə glen ‖ -ᵊr- —*locally* -glən
Ruthie 'ruːθ i
Ruthin 'rɪθ ɪn —*also, from those unfamiliar with
the name, a spelling pronunciation* 'ruːθ-.
—*Welsh* Rhuthun ['hri θɪn, 'hri θɪn]
ruthless 'ruːθ ləs -lɪs ~ly li ~ness nəs nɪs
Ruthven *(i)* 'rɪv ᵊn, *(ii)* 'ruːθ vən, *(iii)* 'rʌθ vən
—*The place in Tayside, and the Baron, are (i);
the place in Grampian and the loch are (iii).*
rutilant 'ruːt ɪl ənt -əl- ‖ 'ruːt̬ ᵊl-
rutile 'ruːt aɪᵊl ‖ -iːᵊl -aɪᵊl
Rutland 'rʌt lənd
Rutledge 'rʌt lɪdʒ
rutt... —*see* **rut, rutty**
Rutter 'rʌt ə ‖ 'rʌt̬ ᵊr
ruttish 'rʌt ɪʃ ‖ 'rʌt̬ ɪʃ ~ly li ~ness nəs nɪs
rutt|y 'rʌt li ‖ 'rʌt̬ li ~ier i ə ‖ i ᵊr ~iest i ɪst
əst ~iness i nəs -nɪs
Ruud ruːd —*Dutch* [ʁyːt]
Ruwenzori ˌruː ən 'zɔːr i -en- ‖ -'zoʊr-
Ruysdael 'raɪz dɑːl 'riːz-, -deɪᵊl —*Dutch*
['rœyz dɑːl]
Ruyter 'raɪt ə ‖ 'rɔɪt̬ ᵊr —*Dutch* ['rœy tər]
Rwand|a ru 'ænd ə -'ɒnd- ‖ -'ɑːnd- ~an/s
ᵊn/z
-ry ri — **heraldry** 'her əldr i
Ryan 'raɪ ən
Ryanair *tdmk* 'raɪ ən eə , • • ' • ‖ -eᵊr
Rycroft 'raɪ krɒft ‖ -krɔːft -krɑːft
Rydal 'raɪd ᵊl
Ryde raɪd
Ryder 'raɪd ə ‖ -ᵊr
rye, Rye raɪ **ryes** raɪz
rye-grass 'raɪ grɑːs §-græs ‖ -græs ~es ɪz əz
Ryeland, Ryland 'raɪ lənd
Rylands 'raɪ ləndz
Ryle raɪᵊl
Ryman 'raɪm ən
ryot 'raɪ ət *(= riot)* ~s s
Ryton 'raɪt ᵊn
Ryukyu ri 'uː kjuː —*Jp* [rjɯ,ɯ 'kjɯɯ] ~s z
Ryvita *tdmk* ₍ᵢ₎raɪ 'viːt ə ‖ -'viːt̬ ə
Rzeszów 'ʒeʃ uːv —*Polish* ['ʒɛ ʃuf]

S s

Spelling-to-sound

1 Where the spelling is **s**, the pronunciation is regularly
   s, as in **sense** sen^ts ('voiceless S'), or
   z, as in **rises** 'raɪz ɪz ('voiced S').
   Less frequently, it is
   ʒ, as in **pleasure** 'pleʒ ə ‖ 'pleʒ ³r.
   s may also form part of the digraphs **sh** or **si**, and of **sc** or **sch** (see under **c**).

2 At the beginning of a word, the pronunciation is regularly s, as in **say** seɪ,
   sleep sliːp, **stand** stænd. (In this position, with spelling **s**, the pronunciation
   is never z.) This also applies in compounds, for example, **insight** 'ɪn saɪt.
   Exceptionally, the pronunciation is ʃ at the beginning of the words **sure** ʃɔː
   ʃʊə ‖ ʃʊ³r ʃɝː and **sugar** 'ʃʊg ə ‖ 'ʃʊg ³r and their derivatives (for example:
   assurance, sugary).

3 In the middle of a word, we must take account of the letters on either side of
   the **s**.
   - Where **s** is between a vowel letter and a consonant letter, the pronunciation
     is usually s if the following consonant sound is voiceless, z if it is voiced.
     Thus:
     s in **taste** teɪst;
     z in **wisdom** 'wɪz dəm.
     Before silent **t**, however, the pronunciation is s, as in **listen** 'lɪs ³n.
   - Where **s** is between two vowel letters, the pronunciation may be either
     s, as in **basin** 'beɪs ³n, **crisis** 'kraɪs ɪs, or
     z, as in **poison** 'pɔɪz ³n, **easy** 'iːz i.
   There is no rule: each word must be considered separately.
   Where the spelling is **s** between a vowel and **ion, ual, ure**, the pronunciation
   is mostly ʒ, as in **explosion** ɪk 'spləʊʒ ³n ‖ ɪk 'sploʊʒ ³n (silent **i**), **usual**
   'juːʒ ³l, **pleasure** 'pleʒ ə ‖ 'pleʒ ³r.
   Where the spelling is **s** between a vowel and **ia, ian**, speakers vary: some use
   ʃ, some use ʒ, as in **Asia** 'eɪʃ ə or 'eɪʒ ə (silent **i**).
   - Where **s** follows a consonant letter, the pronunciation is usually s in **ls, ns,
     rs**, or if the preceding sound is voiceless, but z otherwise. Thus:
     s in **consider** kən 'sɪd ə ‖ -³r, **cursor** 'kɜːs ə ‖ 'kɝːs ³r, **gipsy** 'dʒɪps i;
     z in **clumsy** 'klʌmz i, **observe** əb 'zɜːv ‖ əb 'zɝːv.
   Compare **insist** ɪn 'sɪst and **resist** rɪ 'zɪst. However, in some words both
   pronunciations are in use, for example **absorb, translate**.
   Where the spelling has **s** between **l, n, r** and **ion, ial, ure**, the pronunciation is
   correspondingly ʃ (with **i** silent), as in **expulsion** ɪk 'spʌlʃ ³n, **tension**
   'tentʃ ³n, **controversial** ˌkɒntr ə 'vɜːʃ ³l ‖ ˌkɑːntr ə 'vɝːʃ ³l. However, in
   -ersion, -ersia(n) AmE has ʒ, as in **Persian** 'pɜːʃ ³n ‖ 'pɝːʒ ³n.

4 Where the spelling has **s** at the end of a word, or before silent **e** at the end of a word, the pronunciation may be either

s, as in **gas** gæs, **loose** luːs, **case** keɪs, or

z, as in **has** hæz, **choose** tʃuːz, **phrase** freɪz.

For **s** in **lse, nse, rse**, we usually get

s, as in **else** els, **immense** ɪ 'menˢs, **horse** hɔːs ‖ hɔːrs.

Beyond this, there is no rule: each word must be considered separately. Sometimes there is a distinction between related parts of speech that are spelled identically, as with **use** (juːs noun, juːz verb) and **close** (kləʊs ‖ kloʊs adjective, kləʊz ‖ kloʊz verb). (But there are also cases with no such distinction, as **promise** and **base**, always with s.) There is a BrE-AmE difference in the word **erase** ɪ 'reɪz ‖ ɪ 'reɪs.

5 The inflectional ending **-s, -es** is discussed in its alphabetic place.

6 Where the spelling has double **ss**, the pronunciation is regularly

s, as in **lesson** 'les ᵊn, **kiss** kɪs.

Exceptionally, it is

z, notably in the words **dessert** dɪ 'zɜːt ‖ dɪ 'zɝːt, **possess** pə 'zes, **scissors** 'sɪz əz ‖ 'sɪz ᵊrz and their derivatives.

In **ssion, ssia, ssian, ssure**, it is

ʃ, as in **mission** 'mɪʃ ᵊn, **pressure** 'preʃ ə ‖ 'preʃ ᵊr.

7 **s** is silent in various words, including **island** 'aɪl ənd and several words of French origin, among them **corps** kɔː ‖ kɔːr, **aisle, debris, précis, viscount, Grosvenor, Illinois**.

8 The sound s is also often written **c, sc** before **e, i, y**.

sh   Spelling-to-sound

1 Where the spelling is the digraph **sh**, the pronunciation is regularly ʃ, as in **sheep** ʃiːp, **fish** fɪʃ.

2 **sh** is not a digraph in words such as **mishap** 'mɪs hæp. The spelling of certain proper names has been reinterpreted in pronunciation so as to make **sh** a digraph: **Lewisham** was once **Lewis** plus **ham**, but is now 'luː ɪʃ əm.

3 ʃ is also written in a number of other ways, including those represented in the examples **ocean, machine, precious, sugar, conscience, compulsion, pressure, mission, creation**.

S, s es   **S's, s's, Ss** 'es ɪz -əz —*Communications code name:* Sierra
   ˌS'I ˌunit; ˌS₍ᵢ₎V'O ˌlanguage

-s, -es *pl ending; 3rd sing. present ending,* **-'s** *possessive sing. ending;* **-s', -es'** *possessive pl ending* s, z, ɪz əz —*There are three regular pronunciations:*
   After a sibilant (s, z, ʃ, ʒ, tʃ, dʒ), *the pronunciation is* ɪz *or, less commonly in BrE but usually in AmE,* əz, *as* faces, 'feɪs ɪz -əz, Mitch's 'mɪtʃ ɪz, -əz. (*In singing, exceptionally, a strong-vowelled variant* ez *is usual if the spelling is* es, *as* 'feɪs ez.)
   Otherwise, after a voiced consonant (b, d, g, v, ð, m, n, ŋ, l, *AmE* r) *or a vowel sound, the pronunciation is* z, *as* names, name's neɪmz; *after a voiceless consonant* (p, t, k, f, θ), *the pronunciation is* s, *as* cats, cat's kæts.

—Certain nouns whose last sound is a voiceless fricative switch it to a voiced fricative before the plural and plural possessive endings. The ending naturally then takes the form z. *The change is shown in spelling in the case of* f — v *(wife* waɪf — *wives, wives'* waɪvz), *but not for* θ — ð, s — z *(mouth* maʊθ — *mouths, mouths'* maʊðz). *In the possessive sing. and with the contracted forms of* is *and* has, *there is no such change (wife's* waɪfs, *mouth's* maʊθs). *—With proper names ending in a sibilant, usage varies. Usually, the possessive is pronounced regularly, though the spelling may vary:* Jones', Jones's 'dʒəʊnz ɪz ‖ 'dʒoʊnz əz. *Less commonly, the possessive ending is unpronounced (*dʒəʊnz ‖ dʒoʊnz); *the corresponding spelling is then* Jones'.

-'s *contracted form of* **is** s, z, ɪz —*The rules are identical to those for the 3rd sing. present ending (except that it is not usually used after a sibilant and that there is no strong-vowelled variant):* the boy's asleep ðə ˌbɔɪz ə 'sliːp

-'s *contracted form of* **has** s, z, əz —*The rules are identical to those for the 3rd sing. present ending:* the boy's begun ðə ˌbɔɪz bɪ 'ɡʌn —*except that on the rare occasions when it is used after a sibilant the pronunciation is* əz: the bus's arrived ðə ˌbʌs əz ə 'raɪvd

Saab *tdmk* saːb   **Saabs** saːbz
Saar saː ‖ saːr —*Ger* [zaːɐ]
Saarbrücken ˌsaː 'brʊk ən '• • • ‖ ˌsaːr- '• • • —*Ger* [zaːɐ 'bʀʏk ən]
Saarland 'saː lænd ‖ 'saːr- —*Ger* ['zaːɐ lant]
Saatchi 'saːtʃ i
Saba *island in the Caribbean* 'seɪb ə —*though some reference books wrongly claim it is* 'saːb ə *or* 'sæb ə
Saba *ancient kingdom in Arabia* 'seɪb ə 'saːb ə
sabadilla ˌsæb ə 'dɪl ə
Sabaean sə 'biː_ən ~s z
Sabah *territory in Malaysia* 'saːb ə -aː
Sabaoth 'sæb eɪ ɒθ -i-; sæ 'beɪ ɒθ, sə-, -əθ ‖ -aːθ -ɔːθ
Sabatier sə 'bæt i eɪ ‖ ˌsaːb aː 'tjeɪ —*Fr* [sa ba tje]
Sabatini ˌsæb ə 'tiːn i
sabbatarian, S~ ˌsæb ə 'teər i_ən ◄ ‖ -'ter- ~s z
Sabbath 'sæb əθ ~s s
sabbatical, S~ sə 'bæt ɪk əl ‖ -'bæt- ~s z   sab,batical 'year
Sabean sə 'biː_ən ~s z
Sabellian sə 'bel i_ən ~s z
Sabena *tdmk* sə 'biːn ə sæ- —*Fr* [sa be na]
saber... —*see* **sabre...**
Sabian 'seɪb i_ən ~s z
Sabin *(i)* 'seɪb ɪn §-ən, *(ii)* 'sæb-
sabin 'seɪb ɪn §-ən ~s z
Sabina sə 'biːn ə
Sabine *ancient people and language* 'sæb aɪn ‖ 'seɪb- ~s z
Sabine *river, lake and pass in USA* sə 'biːn

Sabine *family name (i)* 'sæb aɪn, *(ii)* 'seɪb aɪn -ɪn, §-ən —*Usually (i) in Britain, (ii) in US*
sabir, Sabir sə 'bɪə sæ- ‖ -'bɪ³r
sable 'seɪb ³l ~s z
sabot 'sæb əʊ ‖ -oʊ sæ 'boʊ, sə- —*Fr* [sa bo] ~s z
sabotag|e *n, v* 'sæb ə taːʒ -taːdʒ ~ed d ~es ɪz əz ~ing ɪŋ
saboteur ˌsæb ə 'tɜː '• • • ‖ -'tɜː -'tʊ³r ~s z
sabra, Sabra 'saːb rə ~s z
sab|re, sab|er 'seɪb |ə ‖ -|³r ~red, ~ered əd ‖ ³rd ~res, ~ers əz ‖ ³rz ~ring, ~ering ³r_ɪŋ
sabre-rattling 'seɪb ə ˌræt ³l_ɪŋ ‖ -³r ˌræt-
sabretach|e 'sæb ə tæʃ -taːʃ ~es ɪz əz
sabre-toothed ˌseɪb ə 'tuːθt ◄ §-'tʊθt ‖ -³r- ˌsabre-toothed 'tiger
Sabrina sə 'briːn ə -'braɪn-
sac sæk *(= sack)* **sacs** sæks
Sacajawea ˌsæk ədʒ ə 'wiː_ə
saccade sæ 'kaːd sə-, -'keɪd ~s z
saccharide 'sæk ə raɪd ~s z
saccharin, saccharine *n* 'sæk ³r_ɪn §-³r_ən, -ə riːn ~s z
saccharine *adj* 'sæk ə riːn -raɪn, -³r_ɪn, §-³r_ən ~ly li
Sacco 'sæk əʊ ‖ -oʊ
saccule 'sæk juːl ~s z
sacerdotal ˌsæs ə 'dəʊt ³l ◄ ˌsæk- ‖ -³r 'doʊt ³l ◄ ~ly i
Sacha 'sæʃ ə
sachem 'seɪtʃ əm
sachet 'sæʃ eɪ ‖ sæ 'ʃeɪ (*) ~s z
Sacheverell sə 'ʃev ³r_əl
Sachs sæks —*but as a German name,* zæks ‖ zaːks —*Ger* [zaks]
sack sæk **sacked** sækt **sacking** 'sæk ɪŋ **sacks** sæks 'sack race
sackbut 'sæk bʌt ~s s
sackcloth 'sæk klɒθ -klɔːθ ‖ -klɔːθ -klaːθ
Sacker 'sæk ə ‖ -³r
sackful 'sæk fʊl ~s z **sacksful** 'sæks fʊl
sacking 'sæk ɪŋ ~s z
sackload 'sæk ləʊd ‖ -oʊd ~s z
Sackville 'sæk vɪl -v³l ˌSackville-'West
sacral 'seɪk rəl 'sæk- —*Some speakers (esp. AmE) distinguish between* 'seɪk- '*holy' and* 'sæk- '*of the sacrum'*
sacrament, S~ 'sæk rə mənt ~s s
sacramental ˌsæk rə 'ment ³l ◄ ‖ -'menţ ³l ◄ ~ly i
Sacramento ˌsæk rə 'ment əʊ ‖ -'menţ oʊ
sacred 'seɪk rɪd -rəd ~ly li ~ness nəs nɪs ˌsacred 'cow; ˌSacred 'Heart
sacrific|e *n, v* 'sæk rɪ faɪs -rə- ~ed t ~es ɪz əz ~ing ɪŋ
sacrificial ˌsæk rɪ 'fɪʃ ³l ◄ -rə- ~ly i
sacrilege 'sæk rəl ɪdʒ -rɪl-
sacrilegious ˌsæk rə 'lɪdʒ əs ◄ -rɪ- ~ly li ~ness nəs nɪs
sacring 'seɪk rɪŋ

S

sacristan 'sæk rɪst ən -rəst- ~s z
sacrist|y 'sæk rɪst |i -rəst- ~ies iz
sacroiliac ˌseɪk rəʊ 'ɪl i æk ˌsæk- ‖ ˌ•roʊ-
sacrosanct 'sæk rəʊ sæŋkt ‖ -roʊ- ~ness nəs nɪs
sacrosanctity ˌsæk rəʊ 'sæŋkt ət i -ɪt i ‖ -roʊ 'sæŋkt ət̬ i
sac|rum 'seɪk |rəm 'sæk- ‖ 'sæk- 'seɪk- ~ra rə
sad sæd **sadder** 'sæd ə ‖ -ᵊr **saddest** 'sæd ɪst -əst
Sadat sə 'dæt ‖ -'dɑːt sɑː- —Arabic [sa: da:t]
Saddam sə 'dæm ₍ₐ₎sæ-, -'dɑːm, 'sæd əm —Arabic [sadˤ 'dˤam]
sadden 'sæd ᵊn ~ed d ~ing/ly ɪŋ /li ~s z
saddl|e 'sæd ᵊl ~ed d ~es z ~ing ɪŋ
  'saddle soap; 'saddle stitch
saddleback 'sæd ᵊl bæk ~s s
saddlebag 'sæd ᵊl bæg ~s z
saddlecloth 'sæd ᵊl klɒθ -klɔːθ ‖ -klɔːθ -klɑːθ
saddler, S~ 'sæd lə ‖ -lᵊr ~s z
saddlery 'sæd lər i
saddle-sore 'sæd ᵊl sɔː ‖ -sɔːr -soʊr
saddo 'sæd əʊ ‖ -oʊ ~s z
Sadducee 'sæd jʊ siː ‖ 'sædʒ ə siː 'sæd jə- ~s z
Sade French writer sɑːd —Fr [sad]
Sade singer 'ʃɑː deɪ
sadhu 'sɑːd uː ~s z
Sadie 'seɪd i
  ˌSadie 'Hawkins Day
sadiron 'sæd ˌaɪ ən ‖ -ˌaɪ ᵊrn ~s z
sadism 'seɪd ˌɪz əm ‖ 'sæd-
sadist 'seɪd ɪst §-əst ‖ 'sæd- ~s s
sadistic sə 'dɪst ɪk ~ally ᵊl i
Sadleir, Sadler 'sæd lə ‖ -lᵊr
  ˌSadler's 'Wells
sad|ly 'sæd |li ~ness nəs nɪs
sadomasochism ˌseɪd əʊ 'mæs ə ˌkɪz əm -'mæz- ‖ ˌ•oʊ- ˌsæd-
sadomasochistic ˌseɪd əʊ ˌmæs ə 'kɪst ɪk -ˌmæz- ‖ ˌ•oʊ- ˌsæd-
s.a.e. ˌes eɪ 'iː
safari sə 'fɑːr i ~s z
  sa'fari park; sa'fari suit
safe seɪf **safer** 'seɪf ə ‖ -ᵊr **safes** seɪfs **safest** 'seɪf ɪst -əst
  ˌsafe 'house; ˌsafe ˌperiod; ˌsafe 'sex
safebreaker 'seɪf ˌbreɪk ə ‖ -ᵊr ~s z
safe-conduct ˌseɪf 'kɒn dʌkt -dəkt ‖ -'kɑːn- ~s s
safe-deposit 'seɪf dɪ ˌpɒz ɪt -də-, §-diː-, §-ət, ˌ•• '•• ‖ -ˌpɑːz ət ~s s
  'safe-deˌposit ˌbox
safeguard 'seɪf gɑːd ‖ -gɑːrd ~ed ɪd əd ~ing ɪŋ ~s z
safekeeping ˌseɪf 'kiːp ɪŋ
safely 'seɪf li
safe|ty 'seɪf |ti §'seɪf ət i ~ties tiz
  'safety belt; 'safety catch; 'safety ˌcurtain; 'safety-deˌposit ˌbox; 'safety glass; 'safety ˌhelmet; 'safety ˌisland; 'safety lamp; 'safety match; 'safety net; 'safety pin; 'safety ˌrazor; 'safety valve

safety-first ˌseɪf ti 'fɜːst ◄ ‖ -'fɝːst ◄
Safeway tdmk 'seɪf weɪ ~'s z
safflower 'sæf laʊ ə ‖ -laʊ ᵊr
saffron, S~ 'sæf rən
sag sæg **sagged** sægd **sagging** 'sæg ɪŋ **sags** sægz
saga 'sɑːg ə ~s z
sagacious sə 'geɪʃ əs ~ly li ~ness nəs nɪs
sagacity sə 'gæs ət i -ɪt- ‖ -ət̬ i
sagamore 'sæg ə mɔː ‖ -mɔːr -moʊr ~s z
Sagan British/American family name 'seɪg ən —but the French name is [sa gɑ̃]
Sagar 'seɪg ə ‖ -ᵊr
sage seɪdʒ **sager** 'seɪdʒ ə ‖ -ᵊr **sages** 'seɪdʒ ɪz -əz **sagest** 'seɪdʒ ɪst -əst
  ˌsage 'green◄
sagebrush 'seɪdʒ brʌʃ
sagely 'seɪdʒ li
Sager 'seɪg ə ‖ -ᵊr
saggar, sagger 'sæg ə ‖ -ᵊr ~s z
sagg|y 'sæg |i ~ier i ə ‖ i ᵊr ~iest i ɪst i əst ~iness i nəs i nɪs
Saginaw 'sæg ɪ nɔː -ə- ‖ -nɑː
sagitta, S~ sə 'dʒɪt ə -'gɪt- ‖ -'dʒɪt̬ ə
sagittal 'sædʒ ɪt ᵊl §-ət-; sə 'dʒɪt ᵊl ‖ -ət̬ ᵊl -ly i
Sagittari|us ˌsædʒ ɪ 'teər i ˌləs ˌ•ə- ‖ -'ter- ~an/s ən/z
sago 'seɪg əʊ ‖ -oʊ
saguaro sə 'gwɑːr əʊ -'wɑːr- ‖ -oʊ -ə- ~s z
Saguenay ˌsæg ə 'neɪ ◄
Sahaptin sɑː 'hæpt ɪn sə-, §-ən ~s z
Sahar|a sə 'hɑːr ə ‖ -'hær ə -'her-, -'hɑːr- ~an ən
Sahel sə 'hel sɑː-
sahib sɑːb 'sɑː hɪb, -ɪb, -iːb ~s z
said sed §seɪd (!)
Said place saɪd sɑː 'iːd
saiga 'saɪg ə
Saigon ˌsaɪ 'gɒn ‖ -'gɑːn
sail seɪᵊl **sailed** seɪᵊld **sailing/s** 'seɪᵊl ɪŋ/z **sails** seɪᵊlz
  'sailing boat; 'sailing ship
sailboard 'seɪᵊl bɔːd ‖ -bɔːrd -boʊrd ~s z
sailboat 'seɪᵊl bəʊt ‖ -boʊt ~s s
sailcloth 'seɪᵊl klɒθ -klɔːθ ‖ -klɔːθ -klɑːθ
sailfish 'seɪᵊl fɪʃ
sailor 'seɪl ə 'seɪᵊl- ‖ -ᵊr ~s z
  'sailor suit
sailplane 'seɪᵊl pleɪn ~s z
sainfoin 'sæn fɔɪn 'seɪn-
Sainsbury 'seɪnz bər_i ‖ -ˌber i ~'s z
saint, Saint strong form seɪnt, weak form sᵊnt —but in French names sæ̃ —Fr [sɛ̃]. —For the common noun and family name, only the strong form is used. For the title before a name the weak form is usual in BrE but not in AmE.
  sainted 'seɪnt ɪd -əd ‖ 'seɪnt̬ əd **saints, Saints** seɪnts —For names beginning Saint, see under **St**
  'saint's day
sainthood 'seɪnt hʊd
Saint-Etienne, Saint-Étienne ˌsænt et i 'en ˌ•eɪ- —Fr [sæ̃ te tjɛn]

Saint John *place in New Brunswick*
seınt 'dʒɒn ‖ -'dʒɑːn
saint|ly 'seınt |li ~**lier** li‿ə ‖ li‿ər ~**liest** li‿ıst
‿əst ~**liness** li nəs -nıs
saintpaulia sᵊnt 'pɔːl i‿ə →sᵊm-, ˌseınt-
‖ ˌseınt- -'pɑːl- ~**s** z
Saint-Saens, Saint-Saëns ˌsæ 'sɒ̃s -'sɒ̃
‖ ˌsæn 'sɑːn -'sɑːns —*Fr* [sæ̃ sɑ̃ːs]
Saintsbury 'seınts bər‿i ‖ -ˌber i
Saipan ˌsaı 'pæn
Saisho *tdmk* 'seıʃ əʊ ‖ -oʊ
saith seθ seıθ; 'seı ıθ, -əθ
saithe seıθ seıð
sake *'advantage, purpose'* seık **sakes** seıks
for ˌgoodness 'sake,• '•••
sake *'alcoholic drink'* 'sɑːk i -eı —*Jp* [sa ˌke]
saker 'seık ə ‖ -ər ~**s** z
Sakhalin 'sæk ə liːn 'sɑːk-, -lın, ˌ•••'• —*Russ*
[sə xʌ 'lʲin]
Sakharov 'sæk ə rɒf -rɒv ‖ 'sɑːk ə rɔːf 'sæk-,
-rɑːf —*Russ* ['sa xə rəf, sʌ 'xa rəf] —*The*
physicist Andrei S~ *was* ['sa xə rəf]
saki, Saki 'sɑːk i ~**s** z
sal, Sal sæl
ˌsal amˈmoniac
salaam sə 'lɑːm sæ- ~**ed** d ~**ing** ıŋ ~**s** z
salable 'seıl əb əl
salacious sə 'leıʃ əs ~**ly** li ~**ness** nəs nıs
salacity sə 'læs ət i -ıt- ‖ -ət̬ i
salad 'sæl əd ~**s** z
'salad bar; 'salad cream; 'salad days; ˌsalad
'dressing, '••,••‖'••,••; 'salad oil
Saladin 'sæl əd ın §-ən
Salaman 'sæl ə mæn -mən
Salamanca ˌsæl ə 'mæŋk ə —*Sp* [sa la 'maŋ ka]
salamander 'sæl ə mænd ə ‖ -ᵊr ~**s** z
salami sə 'lɑːm i ~**s** z
Salamis 'sæl əm ıs §-əs
salariat sə 'leər i æt -i‿ət ‖ -'lær- -'ler-
salar|y 'sæl ər‿li ~**ied** id ~**ies** iz
Salazar ˌsæl ə 'zɑː ‖ -'zɑːr —*Port* [sɐ lɐ 'zaɾ]
salbutamol sæl 'bjuːt ə mɒl ‖ -'bjuːt̬ ə mɔːl
-mɑːl, -moʊl
salchow 'sælk əʊ 'sɔːlk-, 'sɒlk- ‖ -oʊ ~**s** z
Salcombe 'sɔːlk əm 'sɒlk- ‖ 'sɑːlk-
sale, Sale seıᵊl *(= sail)* **sales** seıᵊlz
'sales pitch; 'sales repreˌsentative; 'sales
reˌsistance; 'sales slip; 'sales staff; 'sales
talk; 'sales tax
saleable 'seıl əb əl
Salem 'seıl əm -em
Salerno sə 'lɜːn əʊ -'leən- ‖ -'lern oʊ -'lɜːn-
—*It* [sa 'ler no]
saleroom 'seıᵊl ruːm -rʊm ~**s** z
salesclerk 'seıᵊlz klɑːk ‖ -klɜːk ~**s** s
salesgirl 'seıᵊlz gɜːl ‖ -gɜːl ~**s** z
Salesian sə 'liːz i‿ən -'liːʒ- ‖ sə 'liːʒ ən -'liːʃ-
~**s** z
saleslad|y 'seıᵊlz ˌleıd li ~**ies** iz
sales|man 'seıᵊlz |mən ~**manship** mən ʃıp
~**men** mən men ~**people** ˌpiːp ᵊl ~**person/**
s ˌpɜːs ᵊn/z ‖ ˌpɝːs ᵊn/z
salesroom 'seıᵊlz ruːm -rʊm ~**s** z

sales|woman 'seıᵊlz |ˌwʊm ən ~**women**
ˌwım ın §-ən
Salford 'sɔːl fəd 'sɒl- ‖ -fᵊrd 'sɑːl- —*A spelling*
pronunciation 'sæl- *is sometimes heard.*
Salfords 'sæl fədz 'sɔːl-, 'sɒl- ‖ -fᵊrdz
Salian 'seıl i‿ən ~**s** z
Salic, salic 'sæl ık 'seıl-
salicylate sə 'lıs ı leıt -ə-, -ᵊl eıt ~**s** s
salicylic ˌsæl ı 'sıl ık ◄ -ə-
salienc|e 'seıl i‿ənᵊs ~**y** i
salient 'seıl i‿ənt ~**ly** li ~**ness** nəs nıs ~**s** s
Salieri ˌsæl i 'eər i ‖ sə 'jer i sæl- —*It*
[sa 'ljɛː ri]
saliferous sə 'lıf ər‿əs sæ-
sali|fy 'sæl ı |faı §-ə- ~**fied** faıd ~**fies** faız
~**fying** faı ıŋ
Salina *place in KS* sə 'laın ə
Salinas *place in CA* sə 'liːn əs
saline 'seıl aın -iːn ‖ -iːn -aın
Saline *place in Fife* 'sæl ın §-ən
Saline *place in MI* sə 'liːn
Salinger 'sæl ındʒ ə §-əndʒ- ‖ -ᵊr
salinity sə 'lın ət i sæ-, -ıt- ‖ -ət̬ i
salinometer ˌsæl ı 'nɒm ıt ə ˌ•ə-, -ət ə
‖ -'nɑːm ət̬ ᵊr ~**s** z
Salisbury 'sɔːlz bər‿i 'sɒlz- ‖ 'sɑːlz-, -ˌber i *(!)*
ˌSalisbury 'Plain
Salish 'seıl ıʃ ~**an** ən
saliva sə 'laıv ə
salivary 'sæl ıv ər‿i '•əv-; sə 'laıv ər i
‖ 'sæl ə ver i
sali|vate 'sæl ı |veıt -ə- ~**vated** veıt ıd -əd
‖ veıt̬ əd ~**vates** veıts ~**vating**
veıt ıŋ ‖ veıt̬ ıŋ
salivation ˌsæl ı 'veıʃ ᵊn -ə-
Salk sɔːlk sɔːk ‖ sɑːlk, sɔːk, sɑːk
Salkeld 'sɔːlk ᵊld 'sɒlk- ‖ 'sɑːlk- —*locally also*
'sæf ᵊld
sallet 'sæl ıt -ət ~**s** s
Sallis 'sæl ıs §-əs
sallow 'sæl əʊ ‖ -oʊ ~**ed** d ~**ing** ıŋ ~**ly** li
~**ness** nəs nıs ~**s** z ~**y** i
Sallust 'sæl əst
sall|y, Sall|y 'sæl li ~**ied** id ~**ies**, ~**y's** iz ~**ying**
i‿ıŋ
Sally-Ann, Sally-Anne ˌsæl i 'æn
salmagundi ˌsælm ə 'gʌnd i ~**s** z
salmanazar, S~ ˌsælm ə 'neız ə -'næz- ‖ -ᵊr
~**s** z
salmi, salmis 'sælm i -iː
salmon, S~ 'sæm ən ~**s** z
ˌsalmon 'pink◄; 'salmon trout
salmonell|a ˌsælm ə 'nel ə ˌsæm- ~**ae** iː ~**as**
əz
Salome sə 'ləʊm i -eı ‖ -'loʊm-
salon 'sæl ɒn -ɒ̃, §-ɒŋ ‖ sə 'lɑːn 'sæl ɑːn ~**s** z
Salonica, Salonika sə 'lɒn ık ə ˌsæl ə 'naık ə,
-'niːk- ‖ sə 'lɑːn- —*Gk* Thessaloniki
[θε sa lɔ 'ni ci]
saloon sə 'luːn ~**s** z
sa'loon bar
Salop 'sæl əp -ɒp
salopettes ˌsæl ə 'pets

Salopian sə 'ləʊp i ‿ən ‖ -'loʊp- **~s** z
salpingectom|y ˌsælp ɪn 'dʒekt əm |i **~ies** iz
salpingitis ˌsælp ɪn 'dʒaɪt ɪs §-əs ‖ -'dʒaɪt̬ əs
salpingo- *comb. form*
  with stress-neutral suffix sæl ˌpɪŋ gəʊ ‖ -gə —
    salpingogram sæl 'pɪŋ gəʊ græm
    ‖ -gə græm
  with stress-imposing suffix ˌsælp ɪŋ 'gɒ+
    ‖ -'gɑː+ — **salpingoscopy**
    ˌsælp ɪŋ 'gɒsk əp i ‖ -'gɑːsk-
salsa 'sæls ə ‖ 'sɑːls ə 'sɔːls- —*Sp* ['sal sa]
salsify 'sæls əf i 'sɔːls-, 'sɒls-, -ɪf-; -ə faɪ, -ɪ-

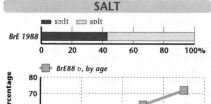

SALT

■ sɔːlt □ sɒlt

BrE 1988

0   20   40   60   80   100%

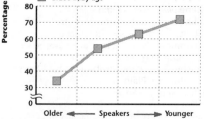

■ BrE88 ɒ, by age

Percentage

80
70
60
50
40
30
0

Older ◄— Speakers —► Younger

salt, Salt, SALT sɔːlt sɒlt ‖ sɔːlt sɑːlt —*BrE
1988 poll panel preference:* sɔːlt *43%*, sɒlt
57%. **salted** 'sɔːlt ɪd 'sɒlt-, -əd ‖ 'sɔːlt əd
'sɑːlt- **salting** 'sɔːlt ɪŋ 'sɒlt- ‖ 'sɔːlt ɪŋ
'sɑːlt- **salts** sɔːlts sɒlts ‖ sɔːlts sɑːlts
**'salt dome; ˌSalt Lake 'City; 'salt marsh;
'salt ˌshaker**
Saltaire ₍ˌ₎sɔːl 'teə ₍ˌ₎sɒl- ‖ ₍ˌ₎sɔːl 'teᵊr ₍ˌ₎sɑːl-,
-'tæᵊr
saltant 'sælt ənt 'sɔːlt-, 'sɒlt- ‖ 'sɔːlt-, 'sɑːlt-
saltarell|o ˌsælt ə 'rel ləʊ ˌsɔːlt-, ˌsɒlt- ‖ -loʊ
ˌsɑːlt- **~i** iː
Saltash 'sɔːlt æʃ 'sɒlt- ‖ 'sɔːlt- 'sɑːlt-
saltation sæl 'teɪʃ ᵊn sɔːl-, sɒl- ‖ sɔːl-, sɑːl- **~s**
z
saltbox, salt-box 'sɔːlt bɒks 'sɒlt-
‖ 'sɔːlt bɑːks 'sɑːlt- **~es** ɪz əz
Saltburn 'sɔːlt bɜːn 'sɒlt- ‖ 'sɔːlt bɜːn 'sɑːlt-
saltbush 'sɔːlt bʊʃ 'sɒlt- ‖ 'sɔːlt- 'sɑːlt-
saltcellar 'sɔːlt ˌsel ə 'sɒlt- ‖ 'sɔːlt ˌsel ᵊr
'sɑːlt- **~s** z
Saltcoats 'sɔːlt kəʊts 'sɒlt- ‖ 'sɔːlt koʊts
'sɑːlt-
Salter, s~ 'sɔːlt ə 'sɒlt- ‖ 'sɔːlt ᵊr 'sɑːlt- **~s,
~'s** z
Salterton 'sɔːlt ət ən 'sɒlt- ‖ 'sɔːlt ᵊrt ᵊn
'sɑːlt-
saltfish 'sɔːlt fɪʃ 'sɒlt- ‖ 'sɔːlt- 'sɑːlt-
Salthouse 'sɔːlt haʊs 'sɒlt- ‖ 'sɔːlt- 'sɑːlt-
saltimbocca ˌsælt ɪm 'bɒk ə ˌsɔːlt-, ˌsɒlt-
‖ ˌsɑːlt ɪm 'boʊk ə ˌsɔːlt-, ˌsɑːlt-, -'bɑːk- —*It*
[sal tim 'bok ka] **~s** z
saltine sɔːl 'tiːn sɒl- ‖ sɔːl- sɑːl- **~s** z

saltire 'sɔːlt aɪ‿ə 'sɒlt- ‖ 'sɔːlt aɪ‿ᵊr 'sɑːlt- **~s**
z
Saltley 'sɔːlt li 'sɒlt- ‖ 'sɔːlt- 'sɑːlt-
saltlick 'sɔːlt lɪk 'sɒlt- ‖ 'sɔːlt- 'sɑːlt- **~s** s
Saltmarsh 'sɔːlt mɑːʃ 'sɒlt- ‖ 'sɔːlt mɑːrʃ
'sɑːlt-
Salton 'sɔːlt ən 'sɒlt- ‖ 'sɔːlt- 'sɑːlt-
ˌSalton 'Sea
Saltoun 'sɔːlt ən 'sælt-, 'sɒlt- ‖ 'sɔːlt- 'sɑːlt-
saltpan 'sɔːlt pæn 'sɒlt- ‖ 'sɔːlt- 'sɑːlt- **~s** z
saltpeter, saltpetre ˌsɔːlt 'piːt ə ˌsɒlt-, '•,•'
‖ ˌsɔːlt 'piːt̬ ᵊr ˌsɑːlt-
saltwater 'sɔːlt ˌwɔːt ə 'sɒlt- ‖ 'sɔːlt ˌwɔːt̬ ᵊr
'sɑːlt-, -ˌwɑːt̬-
saltworks 'sɔːlt wɜːks 'sɒlt- ‖ 'sɔːlt wɜːks
'sɑːlt-
saltwort 'sɔːlt wɜːt 'sɒlt-, §-wɔːt ‖ 'sɔːlt wɜːt
'sɑːlt-, -wɔːrt **~s** s
salt|y 'sɔːlt li 'sɒlt- ‖ 'sɔːlt li 'sɑːlt- **~ier**
i‿ə ‖ i‿ᵊr **~iest** i‿ɪst i‿əst **~ily** ɪ li əl i **~iness**
i nəs ɪ nɪs
salubrious sə 'luːb ri‿əs -'ljuːb- **~ly** li **~ness**
nəs nɪs
salubrity sə 'luːb rət i -'ljuːb-, -rɪt- ‖ -rət̬ i
Saluki, s~ sə 'luːk i **~s** z
salutar|y 'sæl jʊt‿ᵊr li ‖ -jə ter li **~iness** i nəs
i nɪs
salutation ˌsæl ju 'teɪʃ ᵊn ‖ -jə- **~s** z
sa|lute sə |'luːt -'ljuːt **~luted** 'luːt ɪd 'ljuːt-,
-əd ‖ 'luːt̬ əd **~lutes** 'luːts 'ljuːts **~luting**
'luːt ɪŋ 'ljuːt- ‖ 'luːt̬ ɪŋ
Salvador 'sælv ə dɔː ˌ•• '• ‖ -dɔːr —*Sp*
[sal βa 'ðor]
Salvadorean, Salvadorian ˌsælv ə 'dɔːr i‿ən ◄
~s z
salvag|e 'sælv ɪdʒ **~ed** d **~es** ɪz əz **~ing** ɪŋ
salvageable 'sælv ɪdʒ əb ᵊl
salvarsan 'sælv ə sæn -əs ən ‖ -ᵊr-
salvation sæl 'veɪʃ ᵊn, sæl- **~s** z
Sal'vation ˌArmy, ˌ•,•• '••
salvationist, S~ sæl 'veɪʃ ᵊn‿ɪst §-əst **~s** z
salve *n, v 'soothe'* sælv sɑːv ‖ sæv *(*)* **salved**
sælvd sɑːvd ‖ sævd **salves** sælvz sɑːvz
‖ sævz **salving** 'sælv ɪŋ 'sɑːv- ‖ 'sæv ɪŋ
salve *v 'salvage'* sælv **salved** sælvd **salves**
sælvz **salving** 'sælv ɪŋ
salve *Latin interj* 'sælv eɪ -i; 'sæl weɪ ‖ 'sɑːl weɪ
~s z
salver 'sælv ə ‖ -ᵊr **~s** z
Salvesen, Salveson 'sælv ɪs ən -əs-
salvia 'sælv i‿ə **~s** z
salvo 'sælv əʊ ‖ -oʊ **~s, ~es** z
sal volatile ˌsæl və 'læt əl i -vɒ- ‖ -'læt̬ ᵊl i
Salyut sæl 'juːt səl- ‖ sɑːl- —*Russ* [sʌ 'lʲut]
Salzburg 'sælts bɜːg 'sɔːlts-, 'sɒlts-
‖ 'sɔːlz bɜːg 'sɑːlz- —*Ger* ['zalts buʁk]
Sam sæm
SAM sæm ˌes eɪ 'em
Samantha sə 'mænt θ ə
samara 'sæm ᵊr ə sə 'mɑːr ə **~s** z
Samara sə 'mɑːr ə —*Russ* [sʌ 'ma rə]
Samaranch 'sæm ə ræn —*Catalan*
[sə mə 'rank]

Samaria sə 'meər i‿ə ‖ sə 'mer- -'mær-
Samaritan sə 'mær ɪt ən -ət- ‖ -ət ən -'mer-
~s z
samarium sə 'meər i‿əm ‖ sə 'mer- -'mær-
Samarkand ˌsæm ɑː 'kænd -ə-, '•‿•• ‖ -ər-
—Russ [sə mʌr 'kant]
samarskite 'sæm ɑːsk aɪt -ə skaɪt;
sə 'mɑːsk aɪt ‖ 'sæm ɑːrsk- sə 'mɑːrsk-
sam|ba 'sæm |bə ‖ 'sɑːm- ~baed bəd ~baing
bə^r ɪŋ ‖ bə ɪŋ ~bas bəz
sambal 'sæm bəl —Malay ['sam bal]
sambar, sambur 'sæm bə 'sɑːm- ‖ -bər ~s z
sambo, Sambo 'sæm bəʊ ‖ -boʊ ~s, ~'s z
same seɪm
same-day ˌseɪm 'deɪ ◄
sameness 'seɪm nəs -nɪs
samey 'seɪm i
Sami 'sæm i 'sɑːm i ‖ 'sɑːm i
Samian 'seɪm i‿ən ~s z
samisen 'sæm ɪ sen §-ə- ~s z
samite 'sæm aɪt 'seɪm-
samizdat ˌsæm ɪz 'dæt '•‿•• ‖ 'sɑːm iːz dɑːt
—Russ [sə mʲɪ 'zdat]
Samlesbury 'sæmz bər‿i 'sɑːmz- ‖ -ˌber i
Sammie, Sammy 'sæm i
Samnite 'sæm naɪt ~s s
Samnium 'sæm ni‿əm
Samo|a sə 'məʊ |ə sɑː- ‖ -'moʊ |ə ~an/s ən/z
Samos 'seɪm ɒs 'sæm- ‖ -ɑːs 'sæm oʊs
—ModGk ['sa mɔs]
samosa sə 'məʊs ə sæ-, -'məʊz- ‖ -'moʊs ə ~s
z
Samothrace 'sæm əʊ θreɪs ‖ -ə-
samovar 'sæm ə vɑː, ˌ••'• ‖ -vɑːr —Russ
[sə mʌ 'var] ~s z
Samoyed, Samoyede sə 'mɔɪ ed -ɪd;
ˌsæm ɔɪ 'ed, -ə 'jed ~s z
samp sæmp
sampan 'sæm pæn ~s z
samphire 'sæmpf aɪ‿ə ‖ -aɪ‿ər
Sampford 'sæmp fəd ‖ -fərd
sampl|e 'sɑːmp əl §'sæmp- ‖ 'sæmp əl ~ed d
~es z ~ing ɪŋ
sampler 'sɑːmp lə §'sæmp- ‖ 'sæmp lər ~s z
Sampras 'sæmp rəs
Sampson 'sæmps ən
Samson 'sæmps ən
Samsonite tdmk 'sæmps ən aɪt
Samsung tdmk 'sæm sʌŋ —Korean ['sam sʊŋ]
Samuel 'sæm ju‿əl
Samuels 'sæm ju‿əlz
samurai 'sæm u‿ə raɪ -ə-, -ju‿ə- ‖ -ə- —Jp
[sa ˌmɯ ɾai] ~s z
San, san sæn —but in foreign names, AmE sɑːn
—It, Sp [san]
San'a, Sanaa sə 'nɑː sɑː-, 'sɑːn ə —Arabic
[san ˈʕaː]
San Andreas ˌsæn æn 'dreɪ əs ◄
ˌSan Andˌreas 'Fault
San Antonio ˌsæn æn 'təʊn i‿əʊ ‖ -'toʊn i oʊ
sanatari|um ˌsæn ə 'teər i‿|əm ‖ -'ter- -'tær-
~a ə ~ums əmz

Sanatogen tdmk sə 'næt ədʒ ən -ə dʒen
‖ -'næt-
sanatori|um ˌsæn ə 'tɔːr i‿|əm ‖ -'toʊr- ~a ə
~ums əmz
San Bernardino ˌsæn ˌbɜːn ə 'diːn əʊ →ˌsæm-
‖ -ˌbɜːn ər 'diːn oʊ -ˌ•ə-
ˌSan Bernarˌdino 'Mountains
San Carlos (ᵢ)sæn 'kɑːl ɒs →(ᵢ)sæŋ-, -əs
‖ -'kɑːrl əs
Sancerre sɒ̃ 'seə sæn- ‖ sɑːn 'seər —Fr
[sɑ̃ sɛːʁ]
Sanchez 'sænt∫ ez —Sp Sánchez ['san t∫eθ,
-t∫es]
Sancho 'sænt∫ əʊ ‖ 'sɑːnt∫ oʊ —Sp ['san t∫o]
ˌSancho 'Panza 'pænz ə ‖ 'pɑːnz ə —Sp
['pan θa, -sa]
San Clemente ˌsæn klə 'ment i →ˌsæŋ-, -klɪ-
‖ -'ment i
sanctification ˌsæŋkt ɪf ɪ 'keɪ∫ ən ˌ•əf-, §-ə'•-
sancti|fy 'sæŋkt ɪ |faɪ -ə- ~fied faɪd ~fier/s
faɪ‿ə/z ‖ faɪ‿ər/z ~fies faɪz ~fying faɪ ɪŋ
sanctimonious ˌsæŋkt ɪ 'məʊn i‿əs ◄ ˌ•ə-
‖ -'moʊn- ~ly li ~ness nəs nɪs
sanctimony 'sæŋkt ɪ mən i '•ə-, -məʊn i
‖ -moʊn i
sanction 'sæŋk∫ ən ~ed d ~ing ɪŋ ~s z
sanctit|y 'sæŋkt ət |i -ɪt- ‖ -ət |i ~ies iz
sanctuar|y, S~ 'sæŋkt∫ u‿ər li 'sæŋkt ju‿ ‖ -er li
~ies iz
sanct|um 'sæŋkt |əm ~a ə ~ums əmz
ˌsanctum 'sanctorum sæŋk 'tɔːr əm
Sanctus 'sæŋkt əs -ʊs
'Sanctus bell
sand sænd sanded 'sænd ɪd -əd sanding
'sænd ɪŋ sands sændz
'sand ˌdollar; 'sand dune; 'sand fly; 'sand
ˌmartin; 'sand ˌtable; 'sand trap; 'sand
yacht
Sand name of novelist sɒ̃d ‖ sɑːnd —Fr [sɑ̃ːd]
sandal 'sænd əl ~ed, ~led d ~s z
sandalwood 'sænd əl wʊd ~s z
sandarac, sandarach 'sænd ə ræk ~s s
Sanday 'sænd eɪ -i
Sandbach 'sænd bæt∫ →'sæm-
sandbag 'sænd bæg →'sæm- ~ged d ~ger/s
ə/z ‖ -ər/z ~ging ɪŋ ~s z
sandbank 'sænd bæŋk →'sæm- ~s s
sandbar 'sænd bɑː →'sæm- ‖ -bɑːr ~s z
sandblast 'sænd blɑːst →'sæm-, §-blæst
‖ -blæst ~ed ɪd əd ~er/s ə/z ‖ -ər/z ~ing ɪŋ
~s s
sandbox 'sænd bɒks →'sæm- ‖ -bɑːks ~es ɪz
əz
'sandbox tree
sandboy 'sænd bɔɪ →'sæm- ~s z
Sandburg 'sænd bɜːg ‖ -bɝːg
sandcastle 'sænd ˌkɑːs əl →'sæŋ-, §-ˌkæs-
‖ -ˌkæs əl ~s z
Sandell (i) 'sænd əl, (ii) sæn 'del
Sandeman 'sænd ɪ mən -ə-; 'sænd mən
sander 'sænd ə ‖ -ər ~s z
sanderling 'sænd ə lɪŋ -əl ɪŋ ‖ -ər- ~s z
Sanders 'sɑːnd əz §'sænd- ‖ 'sænd ərz

Sanderson 'sɑːnd əs ən §'sænd-
 ‖ 'sænd ər sən
Sanderstead 'sɑːnd ə sted §'sænd-, -stɪd
 ‖ 'sænd ər-
Sandes sændz
sand|fly 'sæn*d* |flaɪ **~flies** flaɪz
Sandford 'sæn*d* fəd -fɔːd ‖ -fərd -fɔːrd, -foʊrd
Sandgate 'sæn*d* geɪt →'sæŋ-, -gɪt
sandglass 'sæn*d* glɑːs →'sæŋ-, §-glæs ‖ -glæs
 ~es ɪz əz
sandhi 'sænd i 'sʌnd-, -hiː —*Hindi* [sən ḍʰi]
 'sandhi phe,nomena
Sandhurst 'sænd hɜːst ‖ -hɜːːst
Sandiacre 'sænd i ,eɪk ə ‖ -ər
Sandie, s~ 'sænd i
San Diego ,sæn di 'eɪg əʊ ‖ -oʊ
Sandinista ,sænd ɪ 'niːst ə ◂ -ə- **~s** z
sandlot 'sæn*d* lɒt ‖ -lɑːt
sandman 'sæn*d* mæn →'sæm-
San Domingo ,sæn də 'mɪŋ gəʊ ‖ -goʊ —*Sp*
 [san do 'miŋ go]
Sandor 'sænd ə ‖ -ər —*but as a Hungarian name
 also* 'ʃɑːnd-, -ɔː ‖ -ɔːr —*Hung* Sándor
 ['ʃɑːn dor]
Sandown 'sænd aʊn
Sandoz *tdmk* 'sænd ɒz ‖ -ɑːz —*Fr* [sã do]
sandpaper 'sæn*d* ,peɪp ə →'sæm- ‖ -ər **~ed** d
 sandpapering 'sæn*d* ,peɪp ər_ɪŋ **~s** z
sandpiper 'sæn*d* ,paɪp ə →'sæm- ‖ -ər **~s** z
sandpit 'sæn*d* pɪt →'sæm- **~s** s
Sandra 'sændr ə 'sɑːndr-
Sandringham 'sændr ɪŋ əm §-həm
Sands sændz
sandshoe 'sæn*d* ʃuː **~s** z
sandstone 'sæn*d* stəʊn ‖ -stoʊn **~s** z
sandstorm 'sæn*d* stɔːm ‖ -stɔːrm **~s** z
Sandusky sæn 'dʌsk i sən-

SANDWICH

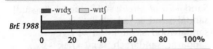

	-wɪdʒ	-wɪtʃ
BrE 1988		

0   20   40   60   80   100%

sandwich, S~ 'sæn wɪdʒ 'sæn*d*-, 'sæm-, -wɪtʃ
 —*BrE 1988 poll panel preference:* -wɪdʒ 54%,
 -wɪtʃ 47%. **sandwiched** 'sæn wɪdʒd 'sæn*d*-,
 'sæm-, -wɪtʃt **~es** ɪz əz **~ing** ɪŋ
 'sandwich board; 'sandwich course;
 'sandwich man
sandwort 'sæn*d* wɜːt §-wɔːt ‖ -wɜːːt -wɔːrt
 ~s s
sand|y, Sand|y 'sænd |i **~ier** i_ə ‖ i_ər **~iest**
 i_ɪst i_əst **~iness** i nəs i nɪs **S~y's** iz
 ,Sandy 'Hook
sandyacht 'sæn*d* jɒt ‖ -jɑːt **~s** s
Sandys sændz
sane seɪn **saner** 'seɪn ə ‖ -ər **sanest** 'seɪn ɪst
 -əst
sane|ly 'seɪn |li **~ness** nəs nɪs
San Fernando ,sæn fə 'nænd əʊ
 ‖ -fər 'nænd oʊ
Sanford 'sæn fəd ‖ -fərd
Sanforis|e, Sanforiz|e *tdmk* 'sæn fə raɪz **~ed** d
 ~es ɪz əz **~ing** ɪŋ

San Francisco ,sæn frən 'sɪsk əʊ -fræn- ‖ -oʊ
 ,San Fran,cisco 'Bay
San Gabriel sæn 'geɪb ri_əl →sæŋ-
sangaree ,sæŋ gə 'riː
Sanger 'sæŋ ə ‖ -ər
sangfroid ,sɒŋ 'frwɑː ,sæŋ-, ,sɑːŋ- ‖ ,sɑːŋ-
 —*Fr* [sã fʁwa]
Sango ,sæŋ gəʊ 'sɑːŋ- ‖ 'sɑːŋ goʊ
Sangre de Cristo
 ,sæŋ gri də 'krɪst əʊ ◂ -oʊ ◂
sangria sæn 'griː_ə →sæŋ-; 'sæŋ gri_ə —*Sp*
 sangría [saŋ 'gri a]
Sangster 'sæŋkst ə ‖ -ər
sanguinary 'sæŋ gwɪn ər_i '·gwən-
 ‖ -gwə ner i
sanguine 'sæŋ gwɪn §-gwən **~ly** li **~ness** nəs
 nɪs
sanguineous sæŋ 'gwɪn i_əs sæn-
sanguinity sæŋ 'gwɪn ət i sæn-, -ɪt- ‖ -əṭ i
Sanhedrin 'sæn ə drɪn -ɪ-, §-ədr ən;
 sæn 'hedr ɪn, -'hiːdr-, §-ən ‖ sæn 'hedr ən
sanicle 'sæn ɪk əl **~s** z
sanitari|um ,sæn ə 'teər i_|əm ,·ɪ- ‖ -'ter-
 -'tær- **~a** ə **~ums** əmz
sanitarily 'sæn ət_ər əl i '·ɪt_, -ɪ li; ,sæn ə 'ter-,
 ,·ɪ- ‖ ,sæn ə 'ter-
sanitary 'sæn ət_ər i '·ɪt_ ‖ -ə ter i
 ,sanitary 'napkin; 'sanitary ,towel
sanitation ,sæn ɪ 'teɪʃ ən -ə-
 ,sani'tation ,worker
sanitis|e, sanitiz|e 'sæn ɪ taɪz -ə- **~ed** d **~es**
 ɪz əz **~ing** ɪŋ
sanitori|um ,sæn ə 'tɔːr i_|əm ,·ɪ- ‖ -'toʊr- **~a**
 ə **~ums** əmz
sanity 'sæn ət i -ɪt- ‖ -əṭ i
San Jacinto (*i*) ,sæn dʒə 'sɪnt əʊ ‖ -'sɪnṭ oʊ
 -'siːnt-, (*ii*) -hə- —*in TX* (*i*), *in CA* (*ii*)
San Joaquin *river and valley in CA*
 ,sæn wɑː 'kiːn ‖ -wɔː-
San Jose *place in CA*, **San José** *place in Costa
 Rica* ,sæn həʊ 'zeɪ -əʊ- ‖ -ə 'zeɪ -hoʊ-, -oʊ-,
 -'seɪ —*Sp* [saŋ xo 'se]
San Juan ,sæn 'wɑːn -'hwɑːn
 ,San ,Juan Capi'strano ,kæp ɪ 'strɑːn əʊ -ə-
 ‖ -oʊ
sank sæŋk
Sankey 'sæŋk i
San Leandro ,sæn li 'ændr əʊ ‖ -oʊ
San Luis Obispo ,sæn ,luː_ɪs ə 'bɪsp əʊ '·,·ə,
 _əs ə-, _i ə- ‖ -oʊ -'biːsp-
San Marcos sæn 'mɑːk əs →sæm-
 ‖ -'mɑːrk əs
San Marino ,sæn mə 'riːn əʊ →,sæm- ‖ -oʊ
San Mateo ,sæn mə 'teɪ əʊ →,sæm- ‖ -oʊ
San Miguel ,sæn mɪ 'gel →,sæm- —*Sp*
 [sam mi 'gel]
San Pedro (*i*) sæn 'pedr əʊ →sæm- ‖ -oʊ, (*ii*)
 sæn 'piːdr əʊ →sæm- ‖ -oʊ —*The suburb of
 Los Angeles CA, and the river in AZ, are usually
 (i); all other places are (ii).* —*Sp* [sam 'pe dro]
San Quentin sæn 'kwent ɪn →sæŋ-, §-ən ‖ -ən
Sanquhar 'sæŋk ə ‖ -ər
San Rafael *place in CA* ,sæn rə 'fel

San Remo ₍ᵢ₎sæn 'reɪm əʊ -'riːm- ‖ -oʊ —*It*
[san 'rɛː mo]
sans sænz —*Fr* [sɑ̃]
San Salvador ₍ᵢ₎sæn 'sælv ə dɔː ‖ -dɔːr
sans-culotte ˌsænz kju 'lɒt -ku- ‖ -'lɑːt —*Fr*
[sɑ̃ ky lɔt] ~**s** s
San Sebastian, San Sebastián
ˌsæn sə 'bæst i‿ən ˌ•sɪ- ‖ -'bæs tʃən —*Sp*
[san se βas 'tjan]
sanserif ˌsæn 'ser ɪf ˌsænz-, -əf
sansevieria ˌsæn sɪ 'vɪər i‿ə ˌ•sə- ‖ -'vɪr- ~**s** z
Sanskrit 'sænˀs krɪt -krət
Sanskritic sæn 'skrɪt ɪk ‖ -'skrɪt̮ ɪk
sans serif, sanserif ˌsæn 'ser ɪf ˌsænz-, -əf
Sansom 'sænˀs əm
Sanson 'sænˀs ən
Santa 'sænt ə 'sɑːnt- ‖ 'sænt̮ ə —*and in AmE,
but only for saints' names treated as Italian or
Spanish (not for place names in the US, not for
Santa Claus), also* 'sɑːnt ə — *It, Sp* ['san ta]
~**s, 's** z
Santa Ana ˌsænt ər 'æn ə ‖ ˌsænt̮ ə-
Santa Barbara ˌsænt ə 'bɑːb ər‿ə ‖ ˌsænt̮
ə 'bɑːrb-
Santa Catalina ˌsænt ə ˌkæt ə 'liːn ə
→ -əl 'iːn ə ‖ ˌsænt̮ ə ˌkæt̮ əl 'iːnə
Santa Claus 'sænt ə klɔːz 'sɑːnt-, ˌ•••
‖ 'sænt̮- -i-, -klɑːz
Santa Cruz *place in CA* ˌsænt ə 'kruːz ‖
'sænt̮ ə kruːz ˌ•• '• —*locally usually* '• • •
Santa Fe, Santa Fé ˌsænt ə 'feɪ '• • •
‖ 'sænt̮ ə feɪ ˌ•• '•
Santali sʌn 'tɑːl i sən-, sæn-
Santa Maria ˌsænt ə mə 'riː‿ə ‖ ˌsænt̮- —*Sp*
[san ta ma 'ri a]
Santa Monica ˌsænt ə 'mɒn ɪk ə §-ək ə
‖ ˌsænt̮ ə 'mɑːn-
Santander ˌsænt ən 'deə ˌsæn tæn-,
⚠sæn 'tænd ə ‖ ˌsɑːn tɑːn 'deᵊr —*Sp*
[san tan 'der]
Santa Rosa ˌsænt ə 'rəʊz ə ‖ ˌsænt̮ ə 'roʊz ə
Santayana ˌsænt ə 'jɑːn ə -aɪ 'ɑːn ə
‖ ˌsænt̮ i 'æn ə -'ɑːn ə
Santee ₍ᵢ₎sæn 'tiː '••
Santer 'sænt ə ‖ 'sænt̮ ᵊr —*Fr* [sɑ̃ tɛːʁ]
santeria, S~ ˌsænt ə 'riː‿ə ‖ ˌsænt̮- ˌsɑːnt̮-
—*Sp* santería [san te 'ri a]
Santiago ˌsænt i 'ɑːg əʊ ‖ ˌsænt̮ i 'ɑːg oʊ
ˌsɑːnt̮- —*Sp* [san 'tja ɣo]
Santo, santo 'sænt əʊ ‖ 'sænt̮ oʊ 'sɑːnt- —*It,
Sp* ['san to] ~**s** z
Santo Domingo ˌsænt əʊ də 'mɪŋ gəʊ
‖ ˌsænt̮ ə də 'mɪŋ goʊ —*Sp*
[san to ðo 'miŋ go]
santolina ˌsænt ə 'liːn ə -əl 'iːn- ‖ ˌsænt̮ əl 'iːn ə
santonica sæn 'tɒn ɪk ə ‖ -'tɑːn-
santonin 'sænt ən ɪn §-ən
Santorini ˌsænt ə 'riːn i ‖ ˌsæn tə-
Santos 'sænt ɒs ‖ 'sænt̮ əs —*Port* ['sʌn tuʃ,
-tus]
Sanyo *tdmk* 'sæn jəʊ ‖ -joʊ —*Jp* [sa,ɴ joo,
sa,ĩ-]
Saoirse 'seəʃ ə ‖ 'serʃ ə —*Irish* ['seːrʲ ʃə]

Saône səʊn ‖ soʊn —*Fr* [soːn]
São Paulo saʊm 'paʊl əʊ saʊ-, -u ‖ -oʊ —*Port*
[sẽum 'paulu]
São Tomé ˌsaʊn tə 'meɪ ˌsaʊ- —*Port*
[sẽun tu 'mɛ]
sap sæp **sapped** sæpt **sapping** 'sæp ɪŋ **saps**
sæps
sapele, S~ sə 'piːl i
saphen|a sə 'fiːn |ə ~**ae** iː
saphenous sə 'fiːn əs 'sæf ɪn əs, -ən-
sapid 'sæp ɪd §-əd
sapience 'seɪp i‿ənˀs 'sæp-
sapiens 'sæp i enz 'seɪp-
sapient 'seɪp i‿ənt 'sæp- ~**ly** li
Sapir sə 'pɪə sə 'pɪə ‖ sə 'pɪᵊr
sapling 'sæp lɪŋ ~**s** z
sapodilla ˌsæp ə 'dɪl ə ~**s** z
saponaceous ˌsæp ə 'neɪʃ əs ◄ ~**ness** nəs nɪs
saponification sə ˌpɒn ɪf ɪ 'keɪʃ ᵊn -,•əf-,
§-ə'•- ‖ sə ˌpɑːn-
saponi|fy sə 'pɒn ɪ |faɪ -ə- ‖ sə 'pɑːn- ~**fied**
faɪd ~**fier/s** faɪ‿ə/z ‖ faɪ‿ᵊr/z ~**fies** faɪz
~**fying** faɪ ɪŋ
saponin 'sæp ən ɪn §-ən ~**s** z
sapp... —*see* **sap**
sapper 'sæp ə ‖ -ᵊr ~**s** z
sapphic, S~ 'sæf ɪk ~**s** s
Sapphira sə 'faɪᵊr ə sæ-
sapphire 'sæf aɪ‿ə ‖ 'sæf aɪ‿ᵊr ~**s** z
sapphism 'sæf ˌɪz əm
Sappho 'sæf əʊ ‖ -oʊ
Sapporo sə 'pɔːr əʊ sæ- ‖ -oʊ —*Jp*
[sap ˌpo ɾo]
sapp|y 'sæp |i ~**ier** i‿ə ‖ i‿ᵊr ~**iest** i‿ɪst i‿əst
~**ily** ɪ li əl i ~**iness** i nəs i nɪs
sapro- *comb. form*
  with stress-neutral suffix ¦sæp rəʊ ‖ -rə —
  saprophyte 'sæp rəʊ faɪt ‖ -rə-
  with stress-imposing suffix
  sæ 'prɒ+ ‖ sæ 'prɑː+ — **saprophagous**
  sæ 'prɒf əg əs ‖ sæ 'prɑːf-
sapwood 'sæp wʊd
Sara *(i)* 'sɑːr ə, *(ii)* 'seər ə ‖ 'ser ə 'sær-
saraband, sarabande ˌsær ə bænd ‖ 'ser- ~**s** z
Saracen 'sær əs ən ‖ 'ser- ~**s** z
Saracenic ˌsær ə 'sen ɪk ◄ ‖ ˌser-
Saragossa ˌsær ə 'gɒs ə ‖ -'gɑːs ə ˌser- —*Sp*
Zaragoza [θa ɾa 'ɣo θa]
Sarah 'seər ə ‖ 'ser ə 'sær-
Sarah-Jane ˌseər ə 'dʒeɪn ‖ ˌser- ˌsær-
Sarajevo ˌsær ə 'jeɪv əʊ ‖ -oʊ ˌser- —*Serbian-
Croatian* [sa ɾa 'je vɔ]
saran, Saran sə 'ræn
Saranac 'sær ə næk ‖ 'ser-
Sarasota ˌsær ə 'səʊt ə ‖ -'soʊt̮ ə ˌser-
Saratoga ˌsær ə 'təʊg ə ‖ -'toʊg ə ˌser-
  ˌSaraˌtoga 'Springs
Saratov sə 'rɑːt ɒv ‖ -ɑːv —*Russ* [sʌ 'ra təf]
Sarawak sə 'rɑː wək -wɑ, -wæk;
  'sær ə- ‖ -wɑːk
sarcasm 'sɑːk ˌæz əm ‖ 'sɑːrk-
sarcastic sɑː 'kæst ɪk ‖ sɑːr- ~**ally** ᵊl‿i
sarcenet 'sɑːs nət -nɪt -net ‖ 'sɑːrs-

S

sarco- *comb. form*
  with stress-neutral suffix ¦saːk əʊ ‖ ¦saːrk ə —
  sarcocele 'saːk əʊ siːʲl ‖ 'saːrk ə-
  with stress-imposing suffix
  saː 'kɒ+ ‖ saːr 'kaː+ — **sarcolysis**
  saː 'kɒl əs ɪs -ɪs-, §-əs ‖ saːr 'kaːl-
sarcoma saː 'kəʊm ə ‖ saːr 'koʊm ə ~**s** z
sarcoph|agus saː 'kɒf ləg əs ‖ saːr 'kaːf- ~**agi**
  ə gaɪ -dʒaɪ
sard saːd ‖ saːrd **sards** saːdz ‖ saːrdz
Sardanapalus ˌsaːd ə 'næp əl əs ˌsaːd ᵊn 'æp-;
  ˌsaːd ᵊn ə 'paːl əs ‖ ˌsaːrd ᵊn 'æp-
sardine *fish* ˌsaː 'diːn ◂ ‖ ˌsaːr- ~**s** z
  ˌsardine 'sandwich
sardine *gemstone* 'saːd aɪn ‖ 'saːrd- ~**s** z
Sardini|a saː 'dɪn i‿ə ‖ saːr- ~**an/s** ən/z
Sardis 'saːd ɪs §-əs ‖ 'saːrd-
sardius 'saːd i‿əs ‖ 'saːrd- ~**es** ɪz əz
sardonic saː 'dɒn ɪk ‖ saːr 'daːn ɪk ~**ally** ᵊl‿i
sardonyx 'saːd ə nɪks -ᵊn ɪks; ˌsaː 'dɒn ɪks
  ‖ saːr 'daːn ɪks 'saːrd ᵊn- ~**es** ɪz əz
saree 'saːr i —*Hindi* ['saː ɽi] ~**s** z
Sargant 'saːdʒ ᵊnt ‖ 'saːrdʒ-
sargasso, S~ saː 'gæs əʊ ‖ saːr 'gæs oʊ ~**s** z
  Sarˌgasso 'Sea
sarge saːdʒ ‖ saːrdʒ
Sargeant, Sargent 'saːdʒ ᵊnt ‖ 'saːrdʒ-
Sargon 'saːg ɒn ‖ 'saːrg aːn
sari 'saːr i —*Hindi* ['saː ɽi] ~**s** z
Sarille *tdmk* sə 'rɪl
sarin 'saːr ɪn ‖ 'sær-, §-ᵊn
Sark, sark saːk ‖ saːrk **Sark's, sarks**
  saːks ‖ saːrks
sarking 'saːk ɪŋ ‖ 'saːrk ɪŋ
sark|y 'saːk li ‖ 'saːrk li ~**ier** i‿ə ‖ i‿ᵊr ~**iest**
  i‿ɪst i‿əst ~**ily** ɪ li ᵊl i ~**iness** i nəs i nɪs
Sarmatia saː 'meɪʃ ə -'meɪʃ i‿ə ‖ saːr-
Sarmatian saː 'meɪʃ ᵊn -'meɪʃ i‿ən ‖ saːr- ~**s** z
Sarnia 'saːn i‿ə ‖ 'saːrn i‿ə
sarnie *'sandwich'* 'saːn i ‖ — ~**s** z
sarong sə 'rɒŋ ‖ -'rɔːŋ -'raːŋ ~**s** z
Saronic, s~ sə 'rɒn ɪk ‖ -'raːn ɪk
saros 'seər ɒs 'seɪ rɒs ‖ 'ser aːs 'sær- ~**es** ɪz əz
Saro-Wiwa ˌsær əʊ 'wiː wə ˌsaːr- ‖ ˌsaːr oʊ-
  ˌsær-
Saroyan sə 'rɔɪ ən
Sarpedon saː 'piːd ᵊn -ɒn ‖ saːr- -aːn
sarracenia ˌsær ə 'siːn i‿ə -'sen- ‖ ˌser- ~**s** z
Sarre saː ‖ saːr
sarsaparilla ˌsaːsp ə 'rɪl ə ◂ ˌsaːs əp ə 'rɪl ə
  ‖ ˌsæsp- ˌsaːrsp-, -'rel-
sarsen 'saːs ᵊn ‖ 'saːrs ᵊn ~**s** z
sarsenet 'saːs nət -nɪt, -net ‖ 'saːrs-
Sarson 'saːs ᵊn ‖ 'saːrs ᵊn
sartor, S~ 'saːt ə -ɔː ‖ 'saːrt̬ ᵊr
sartorial saː 'tɔːr i‿əl ‖ saːr- -'toʊr- ~**ly** i
sartorius saː 'tɔːr i‿əs ‖ saːr- -'toʊr-
Sartre saːtr 'saːtr ə ‖ 'saːrtr ə —*Fr* [saʁtʁ]
Sarum 'seər əm ‖ 'ser əm 'sær-
SAS ˌes eɪ 'es
sash sæʃ **sashed** sæʃt **sashes** 'sæʃ ɪz -əz
  sashing 'sæʃ ɪŋ
  'sash cord; ˌsash 'window,'• ,••

Sasha 'sæʃ ə ‖ 'saːʃ ə
sashay 'sæʃ eɪ sæ 'ʃeɪ ‖ sæ 'ʃeɪ ~**ed** d ~**ing** ɪŋ
  ~**s** z
sashimi sæ 'ʃiːm i sə- ‖ saː- —*Jp* [sa ˌçi 'mi]
Saskatchewan sæ 'skætʃ ə wən sə-, -ɪ-, -wɒn
  ‖ -waːn
Saskatoon, s~ ˌsæsk ə 'tuːn
Saskia 'sæsk i‿ə
Sasquatch, s~ 'sæsk wætʃ -wɒtʃ ‖ -waːtʃ
sass sæs **sassed** sæst **sasses** 'sæs ɪz -əz
  sassing 'sæs ɪŋ
sassab|ly 'sæs əb li ~**ies** iz
sassafras 'sæs ə fræs ~**es** ɪz əz
Sassanid 'sæs ᵊn ɪd §-əd ~**s** z
Sassanidae sə 'sæn ɪ diː -ə-
Sasse sæs
Sassenach 'sæs ə næk -næx; -ᵊn ək, -ᵊn əx
  —*ScG and Ir* ['sa sə nəx] ~**s** s
Sassoon sə 'suːn sæ-
sass|y 'sæs li ~**ier** i‿ə ‖ i‿ᵊr ~**iest** i‿ɪst i‿əst
  ~**ily** ɪ li ᵊl i ~**iness** i nəs i nɪs
sat sæt
Satan 'seɪt ᵊn —*formerly also* 'sæt-
satanic sə 'tæn ɪk ~**al** ᵊl ~**ally** ᵊl‿i
Satanism 'seɪt ᵊn ˌɪz əm
Satanist 'seɪt ᵊn ɪst §-əst ~**s** s
satay 'sæt eɪ 'saːt- ‖ 'saːt-
satchel 'sætʃ ᵊl ~**s** z
sate seɪt **sated** 'seɪt ɪd -əd ‖ 'seɪt̬ əd **sates**
  seɪts **sating** 'seɪt ɪŋ ‖ 'seɪt̬ ɪŋ
saté 'sæt eɪ 'saːt- ‖ 'saːt-
sateen sə 'tiːn sæ- ~**s** z
satellite 'sæt ə laɪt -ɪ-, →-ᵊl aɪt ‖ 'sæt̬ ᵊl aɪt ~**s**
  s
satem 'saːt əm 'sæt-, 'seɪt-, -em
satiab|le 'seɪʃ əb ᵊl 'seɪʃ i‿əb ᵊl ~**leness**
  ᵊl nəs -nɪs ~**ly** li
sati|ate *v* 'seɪʃ i eɪt ~**ated** eɪt ɪd -əd ‖ eɪt̬ əd
  ~**ates** eɪts ~**ating** eɪt ɪŋ ‖ eɪt̬ ɪŋ
satiation ˌseɪʃ i 'eɪʃ ᵊn
Satie 'sæt i 'saːt i ‖ sæ 'tiː saː- —*Fr* [sa ti]
satiety sə 'taɪ‿ət i 'seɪʃ i‿, -ɪt i ‖ -ət̬ i
satin 'sæt ɪn §-ᵊn ‖ -ᵊn ~**s** z
satinet, satinette ˌsæt ɪ 'net §-ə-, -ᵊn 'et
  ‖ -ᵊn 'et
satinwood 'sæt ɪn wʊd §-ᵊn- ‖ -ᵊn-
satiny 'sæt ɪn i §-ᵊn- ‖ -ᵊn i
satire 'sæt aɪ‿ə ‖ 'sæt̬ aɪ‿ᵊr ~**s** z
satiric sə 'tɪr ɪk ~**al** ᵊl ~**ally** ᵊl‿i ~**alness** ᵊl nəs
  -nɪs
satiris... —*see* **satiriz...**
satirist 'sæt ᵊr ɪst -ɪr-, §-əst ‖ 'sæt̬- ~**s** s
satirization ˌsæt ᵊr aɪ 'zeɪʃ ᵊn , • ɪr-, -ɪ • -
  ‖ ˌsæt̬ ᵊr ə-
satiriz|e 'sæt ə raɪz -ɪ- ‖ 'sæt̬- ~**ed** d ~**es** ɪz əz
  ~**ing** ɪŋ
satisfaction ˌsæt ɪs 'fæk ʃᵊn -əs- ‖ ˌsæt̬- ~**s** z
satisfactor|ly ˌsæt ɪs 'fækt ᵊr‿li ◂ , • əs- ‖ ˌsæt̬-
  ~**ily** ᵊl ɪ ɪ li ~**iness** i nəs i nɪs
satis|fy 'sæt ɪs |faɪ -əs- ‖ 'sæt̬- ~**fied** faɪd
  ~**fier/s** faɪ‿ə/z ‖ faɪ‿ᵊr/z ~**fies** faɪz ~**fying/**
  ly faɪ ɪŋ /li
satrap 'sætr æp -əp ‖ 'seɪtr- ~**s** s

satrap|y 'sætr əp |i ‖ 'seɪtr- **~ies** iz
satsuma, S~ sæt 'suːm ə 'sæts əm ə, -u maː
—*Jp* ['sa tsɯ ma] **~s** z
Satterthwaite 'sæt ə θweɪt ‖ 'sæṭ ər-
satu|rate 'sætʃ ə |reɪt -ʊ-; 'sæt jʊ- **~rated**
reɪt ɪd -əd ‖ reɪṭ əd **~rates** reɪts **~rating**
reɪt ɪŋ ‖ reɪṭ ɪŋ
saturation ˌsætʃ ə 'reɪʃ ᵊn -ʊ-; ˌsæt jʊ-
ˌsatu'ration point
Saturday 'sæt ə deɪ -di; △'sæt di ‖ 'sæṭ ᵊr-
—*See note at* -day **~s** z
ˌSaturday 'night
Saturn 'sæt ɜːn -ᵊn ‖ 'sæṭ ᵊrn —'s z
saturnalia, S~ ˌsæt ə 'neɪl i ə , • ɜː- ‖ ˌsæṭ ᵊr-
Saturnian, s~ sæ 'tɜːn i ən sə- ‖ -'tɝːn-
saturnine 'sæt ə naɪn ‖ 'sæṭ ᵊr-
satyagraha, S~ sʌt 'jɑːg rə hə 'sʌt jəg rə hə,
-jə grɑː hə, -hɑː —*Hindi* [sə t̪jə grəh]
satyr 'sæt ə ‖ 'seɪt ᵊr 'sæṭ- **~s** z
satyriasis ˌsæt ə 'raɪˌəs ɪs , • ɪ-, §-əs ‖ ˌseɪṭ-
ˌsæṭ-
satyric sə 'tɪr ɪk ‖ seɪ-
sauce sɔːs ‖ sɑːs **sauced** sɔːst ‖ sɑːst **sauces**
'sɔːs ɪz -əz ‖ 'sɑːs- **saucing** 'sɔːs ɪŋ ‖ 'sɑːs-
saucepan 'sɔːs pən §'sɒs-, §-pæn ‖ -pæn 'sɑːs-
~s z
saucer 'sɔːs ə ‖ -ᵊr 'sɑːs- **~s** z
Sauchiehall ˌsɒk i 'hɔːl ˌsɒːk-, ˌsɒx-, ˌsɔːx-
‖ ˌsɑːk i 'hɔːl ˌsɔːk-, -'hɑːl
Saucony *tdmk* sɔː 'kəʊn i ‖ -'koʊn i sɑː-
sauc|y 'sɔːs |i ‖ 'sɑːs- **~ier** i ə ‖ i ᵊr **~iest** i ˌɪst
i ˌəst **~ily** ɪ li əl i **~iness** i nəs i nɪs
Saud saʊd sɑː 'uːd —*Ar* [sa ʕuːd]
Saudi 'saʊd i 'sɔːd-; sɑː 'uːd i ‖ 'sɔːd-, 'sɑːd-
—*Ar* [sa 'ʕuː diː] **~s** z
ˌSaudi A'rabia
sauerbraten 'saʊ‿ə brɑːt ᵊn ‖ 'saʊ‿ᵊr- —*Ger*
['zaʊ ɐ ˌbʁaː tn̩]
sauerkraut 'saʊ‿ə kraʊt ‖ 'saʊ‿ᵊr- —*Ger*
['zaʊ ɐ kʁaʊt]
sauger 'sɔːg ə ‖ -ᵊr 'sɑːg- **~s** z
Saughall 'sɔːk ᵊl ‖ 'sɑːk-
Saughton 'sɒxt ən ‖ 'sɔːkt ən 'sɑːkt-
Saugus 'sɔːg əs ‖ 'sɑːg-
Sauk sɔːk ‖ sɑːk **Sauks** sɔːks ‖ sɑːks
Saul sɔːl ‖ sɑːl
Sault Sainte Marie, Sault Ste Marie
ˌsuː ˌseɪnt mə 'riː
sauna 'sɔːn ə 'saʊn- ‖ 'sɑːn-, 'saʊn- —*Finnish*
['sau na] **~s** z
Saunders *(i)* 'sɔːnd əz ‖ -ᵊrz, *(ii)* 'sɑːnd-
Saundersfoot 'sɔːnd əz fʊt ‖ -ᵊrz- 'sɑːnd-
Saunderson *(i)* 'sɔːnd əs ən ‖ -ᵊrs-, *(ii)* 'sɑːnd-
saunter 'sɔːnt ə ‖ 'sɔːnṭ ᵊr 'sɑːnṭ- **~ed** d
sauntering 'sɔːnt ᵊr ɪŋ ‖ 'sɔːnṭ ᵊr ɪŋ 'sɑːnṭ-
~s z
Saunton 'sɔːnt ən ‖ 'sɑːnt-
-saur sɔː ‖ sɔːr — **stegosaur** 'steg ə sɔː ‖ -sɔːr
saurian 'sɔːr i ən **~s** z
sauropod 'sɔːr ə ʊ pɒd ‖ -ə pɑːd **~s** z
-saurus 'sɔːr əs — **stegosaurus**
ˌsteg ə 'sɔːr əs

sausag|e 'sɒs ɪdʒ ‖ 'sɔːs ɪdʒ 'sɑːs- *(!)* **~es** ɪz
əz
'sausage dog; 'sausage meat; ˌsausage
'roll
Saussure səʊ 'sjʊə -'sʊə ‖ soʊ 'sʊᵊr -'sjʊᵊr
—*Fr* [so syːʁ]
Saussurean, Saussurian səʊ 'sjʊər iˌən -'sʊᵊr-
‖ soʊ 'sʊr- -'sjʊr- **~s** z
saute, sauté 'səʊt eɪ 'sɔːt-, -i ‖ soʊ 'teɪ sɔː-,
sɑː- **~d, ~ed** d **~ing** ɪŋ **~s** z
Sauterne, Sauternes səʊ 'tɜːn -'teən
‖ soʊ 'tɝːn -'teᵊrn —*Fr* Sauternes [so tɛʁn]
sauve qui peut ˌsəʊv kiː 'pɜː ‖ ˌsoʊv kiː 'pʊ
—*Fr* [sov ki pø]
Sauvignon 'səʊv iːn jɒn -ɪn-, -jɒ̃, • • '•
‖ ˌsoʊv iːn 'joʊn —*Fr* [so vi njɔ̃]
savag|e, S~ 'sæv ɪdʒ **~ed** d **~ely** li **~es** ɪz əz
~ing ɪŋ
savager|y 'sæv ɪdʒ ᵊr_li **~ies** iz
savanna, savannah, S~ sə 'væn ə **~s** z
savant 'sæv ᵊnt ‖ sə 'vɑːnt sæ- *(*)* —*Fr*
[sa vɑ̃] **~s** s
savarin, S~ 'sæv ə ræ̃ -rɪn; -ᵊr ən —*Fr*
[sa va ʁæ̃] **~s** z
save seɪv **saved** seɪvd **saves** seɪvz **saving**
'seɪv ɪŋ
ˌsaving 'grace
saveloy 'sæv ə lɔɪ -ɪ-, , • • '• **~s** z
saver 'seɪv ə ‖ -ᵊr **~s** z
Savernake 'sæv ə næk ‖ -ᵊr- —*There is also a*
spelling pronunciation △-neɪk.
Savile, Savill 'sæv ᵊl -ɪl
savings 'seɪv ɪŋz
'savings acˌcount; ˌsavings and 'loan,
ˌsavings and 'loan associˌation; 'savings
bank
savior, saviour, S~ 'seɪv jə ‖ -jᵊr **~s** z
Savlon *tdmk* 'sæv lɒn ‖ -lɑːn
savoir-faire ˌsæv wɑː 'feə ˌsʌv- ‖ -wɑːr 'feᵊr
-'fæᵊr —*Fr* [sa vwaʁ fɛːʁ]
savoir-vivre ˌsæv wɑː 'viːv rə ˌsʌv- ‖ -wɑːr-
—*Fr* [sa vwaʁ viːvʁ]
Savonarola ˌsæv ᵊn‿ə 'rəʊl ə ‖ -'roʊl ə —*It*
[sa vo na 'rɔː la]
savor, savour 'seɪv ə ‖ -ᵊr **~ed** d **savoring,**
savouring 'seɪv ᵊr_ɪŋ **~s** z
savor|y, savour|y, Savory 'seɪv ᵊr_li **~ies** iz
Savoy, savoy sə 'vɔɪ **~s, ~'s** z
Savoyard sə 'vɔɪ ɑːd ˌsæv ɔɪ 'ɑːd
‖ ˌsæv ɔɪ 'ɑːrd **~s** z
savv|y 'sæv |i **~ied** id **~ies** iz **~ying** iˌɪŋ
saw sɔː ‖ sɑː **sawed** sɔːd ‖ sɑːd **sawing**
'sɔːʳ ɪŋ ‖ 'sɔː ɪŋ 'sɑː- **sawn** sɔːn ‖ sɑːn **saws**
sɔːz ‖ sɑːz
'saw atˌtachment
Saward 'seɪ wəd ‖ -wᵊrd
Sawatch sə 'wɒtʃ ‖ -'wɑːtʃ
sawbones 'sɔː bəʊnz ‖ -boʊnz 'sɑː-
Sawbridgeworth 'sɔː brɪdʒ wɜːθ -wəθ ‖ -wɝːθ
'sɑː- —*Formerly locally also* 'sæps wəθ
sawbuck 'sɔː bʌk ‖ 'sɑː- **~s** s
sawdust 'sɔː dʌst ‖ 'sɑː-

S

sawed-off ˌsɔːd ˈɒf ◂ -ˈɔːf ‖ -ˈɔːf ◂ ˌsɑːd ˈɑːf◂
ˌsawed-off ˈshotgun
sawfish ˈsɔː fɪʃ ‖ ˈsɑː-
saw|fly ˈsɔː |flaɪ ‖ ˈsɑː- **~flies** flaɪz
sawhors|e ˈsɔː hɔːs ‖ -hɔːrs ˈsɑː- **~es** ɪz əz
sawmill ˈsɔː mɪl ‖ ˈsɑː- **~s** z
sawn sɔːn ‖ sɑːn
sawn-off ˌsɔːn ˈɒf ◂ -ˈɔːf ‖ -ˈɔːf ◂ ˌsɑːn ˈɑːf◂
ˌsawn-off ˈshotgun
sawpit ˈsɔː pɪt ‖ ˈsɑː- **~s** s
Sawston ˈsɔːst ən ‖ ˈsɑːst-
sawtooth ˈsɔː tuːθ §-tʊθ ‖ ˈsɑː- **~ed** t
Sawtry ˈsɔːtr i ‖ ˈsɑːtr-
saw-wort ˈsɔː wɜːt §-wɔːt ‖ -wɝːt ˈsɑː-, -wɔːrt
sawyer, S~ ˈsɔː jə ‖ -jᵊr ˈsɑː-; ˈsɔɪ_ᵊr **~s** z
sax sæks **saxes** ˈsæks ɪz -əz
Saxa *tdmk* ˈsæks ə
Saxby ˈsæks bi
saxe, Saxe sæks
ˌsaxe ˈblue◂
Saxe-Coburg-Gotha ˌsæks ˌkəʊ bɜːg ˈgəʊθ ə
-ˈgəʊt- ‖ -ˌkoʊ bɝːg ˈgoʊθ ə
saxhorn ˈsæks hɔːn ‖ -hɔːrn **~s** z
saxifrag|e ˈsæks ɪ freɪdʒ -ə-, -frɪdʒ, -freɪʒ **~es**
ɪz əz
Saxin *tdmk* ˈsæks ɪn §-ən
Saxmundham sæks ˈmʌnd əm
Saxo ˈsæks əʊ ‖ -oʊ
ˌSaxo Gramˈmaticus grə ˈmæt ɪk əs ‖ -ˈmæt̬-
Saxon ˈsæks ən **~s** z
Saxone *tdmk* ˌsæk ˈsəʊn ‖ -ˈsoʊn
Saxony, s~ ˈsæks ən i
saxophone ˈsæks ə fəʊn ‖ -foʊn **~s** z
saxophonist sæk ˈsɒf ən ɪst ˈsæks ə fəʊn-,
§-əst ‖ ˈsæks ə foʊn əst
Saxton ˈsækst ən

sez seɪz
BrE 1998
0 20 40 60 80 100%

say seɪ **said** sed *(!)* **saying/s** ˈseɪ ɪŋ/z **says**
sez §seɪz —*BrE 1998 poll panel preference:*
sez *84%,* seɪz *16%.*
Saybolt ˈseɪ bəʊlt →-bɒʊlt ‖ -boʊlt
Sayce seɪs
Sayer, s~ ˈseɪ ə ‖ -ᵊr
Sayers ˈseɪ əz ‖ -ᵊrz
Sayle seɪᵊl
says sez §seɪz *(!)*
say-so ˈseɪ səʊ ‖ -soʊ **~s** z
sazarac, sazerac, S~ *tdmk* ˈsæz ə ræk **~s** s
S-bend ˈes bend **~s** z
scab skæb **scabbed** skæbd **scabbing**
ˈskæb ɪŋ **scabs** skæbz
scabbard ˈskæb əd ‖ -ᵊrd **~s** z
scabb|y ˈskæb |i **~ier** i_ə ‖ i_ᵊr **~iest** i_ɪst i_əst
~ily ɪ li əl i **~iness** i nəs i nɪs
scabies ˈskeɪb iːz ˈskeɪb i_iːz
scabious ˈskeɪb i_əs **~es** ɪz əz
scabrous ˈskeɪb rəs ˈskæb- ‖ ˈskæb- **~ly** li
~ness nəs nɪs
scad skæd **scads** skædz

Scafell ˌskɔː ˈfel ◂ ˌskɑː-
ˌScafell ˈPike
scaffold ˈskæf əʊld →-ɒʊld, -ᵊld ‖ -ᵊld -oʊld
~ed ɪd əd **~er/s** ə/z ‖ -ᵊr/z **~ing** ɪŋ **~s** z
scag skæg
scagliola skæl ˈjəʊl ə ‖ -ˈjoʊl ə —*It*
[skaʎ ˈʎɔː la]
scala, Scala ˈskɑːl ə —*In anatomy, also* ˈskeɪl ə
scalability ˌskeɪl ᵊl ə ˈbɪl ət i -ɪt i ‖ -ət̬ i
scalable ˈskeɪl əb ᵊl
scalar ˈskeɪl ə -ɑː ‖ -ᵊr -ɑːr **~s** z
scalawag ˈskæl ə wæg -i- **~s** z
scald skɔːld §skɒld ‖ skɑːld **scalded** ˈskɔːld ɪd
§ˈskɒld-, -əd ‖ ˈskɑːld- **scalding/s**
ˈskɔːld ɪŋ/z §ˈskɒld- ‖ ˈskɑːld- **scalds**
skɔːldz §skɒldz ‖ skɑːldz
scale skeɪᵊl **scaled** skeɪᵊld **scales** skeɪᵊlz
scaling ˈskeɪᵊl ɪŋ
scalene ˈskeɪl iːn ˌskeɪ ˈliːn ◂
scalen|us skeɪ ˈliːn |əs skə- **~i** aɪ
scaler ˈskeɪl ə ‖ -ᵊr **~s** z
Scalextric *tdmk* ˌskeɪ ˈleks trɪk
Scaliger ˈskæl ɪdʒ ə -§ədʒ- ‖ -ᵊr
scallion ˈskæl i_ən ‖ ˈskæl jən **~s** z

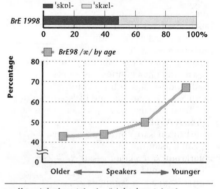

ˈskɒl- ˈskæl-
BrE 1998
0 20 40 60 80 100%

BrE98 /æ/ by age
Older ◄— Speakers —► Younger
Percentage: 40 50 60 70 80

scallop ˈskɒl əp ˈskæl- ‖ ˈskæl əp ˈskɑːl-
—*BrE 1998 poll panel preference:* ˈskɒl- *49%,*
ˈskæl- *51%.* **~ed** t **~ing** ɪŋ **~s** s
scallywag ˈskæl i wæg **~s** z
scaloppin|e ˌskæl ə ˈpiːn li ‖ ˌskɑːl- **~i** i ː i
scalp skælp **scalped** skælpt **scalping**
ˈskælp ɪŋ **scalps** skælps
Scalpay ˈskælp eɪ -i
scalpel ˈskælp ᵊl **~s** z
scalper ˈskælp ə ‖ -ᵊr **~s** z
scal|y ˈskeɪl |i **~ier** i_ə ‖ i_ᵊr **~iest** i_ɪst i_əst
~iness i nəs i nɪs
scam skæm **scammed** skæmd **scamming**
ˈskæm ɪŋ **scams** skæmz
Scammell ˈskæm ᵊl
scammer ˈskæm ə ‖ -ᵊr **~s** z
scammon|y ˈskæm ən li **~ies** iz
scamp skæmp **scamped** skæmpt **scamping**
ˈskæmp ɪŋ **scamps** skæmps
scamper ˈskæmp ə ‖ -ᵊr **~ed** d **scampering/s**
ˈskæmp ᵊr_ɪŋ/z **~s** z
scampi ˈskæmp i

scampish 'skæmp ɪʃ ~**ly** li ~**ness** nəs nɪs
scan skæn **scanned** skænd **scanning**
 'skæn ɪŋ **scans** skænz
scandal 'skænd ᵊl ~**s** z
scandalis|e, scandaliz|e 'skænd ᵊl aɪz -ə laɪz
 ~**ed** d ~**es** ɪz əz ~**ing** ɪŋ
scandalmonger 'skænd ᵊl ˌmʌŋ gə -ˌmɒŋ-
 ‖ -gᵊr -ˌmɑːŋ- ~**s** z
scandalous 'skænd ᵊl əs ~**ly** li ~**ness** nəs nɪs
scandent 'skænd ənt
Scanderbeg 'skænd ə beg ‖ -ᵊr-
Scandi|a, s~ 'skænd i‿ə ~**an** ən
Scandic 'skænd ɪk
Scandinavi|a ˌskænd ɪ 'neɪv i‿ə ˌ•ə- ~**an/s**
 ən/z
scandium 'skænd i‿əm
Scania tdmk 'skæn i‿ə
Scanlan, Scanlon 'skæn lən
scann... —see **scan**
scanner 'skæn ə ‖ -ᵊr ~**s** z
scansion 'skæntʃ ᵊn ~**s** z
scansorial skæn 'sɔːr i‿əl ‖ -'soʊr-
scant skænt **scanter** 'skænt ə ‖ 'skænt̬ ᵊr
 scantest 'skænt ɪst -əst ‖ 'skænt̬ əst
scanti... —see **scanty**
scantling 'skænt lɪŋ ~**s** z
scant|ly 'skænt |li ~**ness** nəs nɪs
scant|y 'skænt |i ‖ 'skænt̬ |i ~**ier** i‿ə ‖ i‿ᵊr ~**ies**
 iz ~**iest** i‿ɪst i‿əst ~**ily** ɪ li əl i ~**iness** nəs
 i nɪs
Scapa 'skɑːp ə 'skæp-
 ˌScapa 'Flow
-scape skeɪp — **seascape** 'siː skeɪp
scape|goat 'skeɪp |gəʊt ‖ -|goʊt ~**goated**
 gəʊt ɪd -əd ‖ goʊt̬ əd ~**goating**
 gəʊt ɪŋ ‖ goʊt̬ ɪŋ ~**goats** gəʊts ‖ goʊts
scapegrac|e 'skeɪp greɪs ~**es** ɪz əz
scaphoid 'skæf ɔɪd ~**s** z
scapolite 'skæp əʊ laɪt ‖ -ə-
scap|ula 'skæp |jʊl ə §-jəl- ‖ -|jəl ə ~**ulae**
 ju liː jə- ‖ jə liː ~**ulas** jʊl əz jəl- ‖ jəl əz
scapular 'skæp jʊl ə §-jəl- ‖ -jəl ᵊr ~**s** z
scar skɑː ‖ skɑːr **scarred** skɑːd ‖ skɑːrd
 scarring 'skɑːr ɪŋ **scars** skɑːz ‖ skɑːrz
 'scar ˌtissue
scarab 'skær əb ‖ 'sker- ~**s** z
scarabae|us ˌskær ə 'biːˌ|əs ‖ ˌsker- ~**i** aɪ
Scaramouch, Scaramouche 'skær ə muːtʃ
 -muːʃ, -maʊtʃ ‖ 'sker-
Scarboro', Scarborough
 'skɑː bᵊr‿ə ‖ 'skɑːr ˌbɝː oʊ
Scarbrough 'skɑː brə ‖ 'skɑːr- -broʊ
scarce skeəs ‖ skeᵊrs skæᵊrs **scarcer**
 'skeəs ə ‖ 'skeᵊrs ᵊr 'skæᵊrs- **scarcest**
 'skeəs ɪst -əst ‖ 'skeᵊrs əst 'skæᵊrs-
scarce|ly 'skeəs |li ‖ 'skeᵊrs |li 'skæᵊrs- ~**ness**
 nəs nɪs
scarcit|y 'skeəs ət |i -ɪt- ‖ 'skers ət̬ |i 'skærs-
 ~**ies** iz
scare skeə ‖ skeᵊr skæᵊr **scared**
 skeəd ‖ skeᵊrd skæᵊrd **scares** skeəz ‖ skeᵊrz
 skæᵊrz **scaring** 'skeər ɪŋ ‖ 'sker ɪŋ 'skær-
scarecrow 'skeə krəʊ ‖ 'sker kroʊ 'skær- ~**s** z

scaredy-cat, scaredy cat 'skeəd i kæt ‖ 'skerd-
 'skærd- ~**s** s
scaremonger 'skeə ˌmʌŋ gə -ˌmɒŋ-
 ‖ 'sker ˌmʌŋ gᵊr 'skær-, -ˌmɑːŋ- ~**s** z
scarer 'skeər ə ‖ 'sker ᵊr 'skær- ~**s** z
scar|ey 'skeər |i ‖ 'sker |i 'skær- ~**ier** i‿ə ‖ i‿ᵊr
 ~**iest** i‿ɪst i‿əst ~**ily** əl i ɪ li ~**iness** i nəs
 i nɪs
scarf skɑːf ‖ skɑːrf **scarfed** skɑːft ‖ skɑːrft
 scarfing 'skɑːf ɪŋ ‖ 'skɑːrf ɪŋ **scarfs**
 skɑːfs ‖ skɑːrfs **scarves** skɑːvz ‖ skɑːrvz
Scarfe skɑːf ‖ skɑːrf
Scargill 'skɑː gɪl 'skɑːg ᵊl ‖ 'skɑːr-
scari... —see **scary**
scarification ˌskær ɪf ɪ 'keɪʃ ᵊn ˌskeər-, ˌ•əf-,
 §-ə'•- ‖ ˌsker- ~**s** z
scarificator 'skær ɪf ɪ keɪt ə 'skeər-, '•əf-,
 §'••ə- ‖ -keɪt̬ ᵊr 'sker- ~**s** z
scari|fy 'skær ɪ faɪ 'skeər-, -ə- ‖ 'sker- ~**fied**
 faɪd ~**fier/s** faɪˌə/z ‖ faɪˌᵊr/z ~**fies** faɪz
 ~**fying** faɪ ɪŋ
Scarisbrick 'skeəz brɪk ‖ 'skerz- 'skærz-
scarlatina ˌskɑːl ə 'tiːn ə ‖ ˌskɑːrl-
Scarlatti skɑː 'læt i ‖ skɑːr 'lɑːt̬ i —It
 [skar 'lat ti]
scarlet 'skɑːl ət -ɪt ‖ 'skɑːrl-
 ˌscarlet 'fever; ˌscarlet 'pimpernel; ˌscarlet
 'runner; ˌscarlet 'woman
Scarlett 'skɑːl ət -ɪt ‖ 'skɑːrl-
Scarman 'skɑː mən ‖ 'skɑːr-
scarp skɑːp ‖ skɑːrp **scarped** skɑːpt ‖ skɑːrpt
 scarping 'skɑːp ɪŋ ‖ 'skɑːrp ɪŋ **scarps**
 skɑːps ‖ skɑːrps
scarper 'skɑːp ə ‖ 'skɑːrp ᵊr ~**ed** d
 scarpering 'skɑːp ᵊr‿ɪŋ ‖ 'skɑːrp- ~**s** z
scarr... —see **scar**
scarves skɑːvz ‖ skɑːrvz
scar|y 'skeər |i ‖ 'sker |i 'skær- ~**ier** i‿ə ‖ i‿ᵊr
 ~**iest** i‿ɪst i‿əst ~**ily** əl i ɪ li ~**iness** i nəs
 i nɪs
Scase skeɪs
scat skæt **scats** skæts **scatted** 'skæt ɪd -əd
 ‖ 'skæt̬ əd **scatting** 'skæt ɪŋ ‖ 'skæt̬ ɪŋ
scathing 'skeɪð ɪŋ ~**ly** li
scatological ˌskæt ə 'lɒdʒ ɪk ᵊl ◀ -ᵊl 'nɒdʒ-
 ‖ ˌskæt̬ ᵊl 'ɑːdʒ- ~**ly** ᵢ
scatology skæ 'tɒl ədʒ i ‖ -'tɑːl-
scatter 'skæt ə ‖ 'skæt̬ ᵊr ~**ed** d **scattering**
 'skæt̬ ᵊr‿ɪŋ ‖ 'skæt̬ ᵊr‿ɪŋ ~**s** z
 'scatter ˌcushion; 'scatter ˌdiagram
scatterbrain 'skæt ə breɪn ‖ 'skæt̬ ᵊr- ~**ed** d
 ~**s** z
Scattergood 'skæt ə gʊd ‖ 'skæt̬ ᵊr-
scatt|y 'skæt |i ‖ 'skæt̬ |i ~**ier** i‿ə ‖ i‿ᵊr ~**iest**
 i‿ɪst i‿əst ~**ily** ɪ li əl i ~**iness** i nəs i nɪs
scaup skɔːp ‖ skɑːp **scaups** skɔːps ‖ skɑːps
scaveng|e 'skæv ɪndʒ -ᵊndʒ ~**ed** d ~**es** ɪz əz
 ~**ing** ɪŋ
scavenger 'skæv ɪndʒ ə -ᵊndʒ- ‖ -ᵊr ~**s** z
scena 'ʃeɪn ə ‖ -ɑː —It ['ʃɛː na]
scenario sə 'nɑːr i‿əʊ sɪ-, se-, -'neər-
 ‖ sə 'nær i oʊ -'ner-, -'nɑːr- ~**s** z

S

scenarist 'si:n ər ɪst sə 'nɑːr-, sɪ-, se-, §-əst
‖ sə 'nær əst -'ner-, -'nɑːr-
scene si:n (= seen) scenes si:nz
scenery 'si:n ər i
sceneshifter 'si:n ˌʃɪft ə ‖ -ər ~s z
scenic 'si:n ɪk 'sen- ~ally əl_i
scenographer si: 'nɒg rəf ə ‖ -'nɑːg rəf ər ~s
z
scenographic ˌsi:n əʊ 'græf ɪk ◄ ‖ -ə- ~ally əl_i
scenography si: 'nɒg rəf i ‖ -'nɑːg-
scent sent (= cent, sent) scented 'sent ɪd -əd
‖ 'senṯ əd scenting 'sent ɪŋ ‖ 'senṯ ɪŋ
scents senṯs
'scent mark
sceptic, S~ 'skept ɪk ~s s
sceptical 'skept ɪk əl ~ly_i ~ness nəs nɪs
scepticism 'skept ɪ ˌsɪz əm -ə-
scepter, sceptre 'sept ə ‖ -ər ~ed d ~s z
schadenfreude 'ʃɑːd ən ˌfrɔɪd ə —Ger S~
['ʃɑːd n ˌfʁɔyd ə]
Schaefer, Schaeffer, Schafer 'ʃeɪf ə ‖ -ər
Schaghticoke 'skæt i kʊk 'ʃæt-, -kəʊk ‖ 'skæṯ-
'ʃæṯ-, -koʊk
Schapiro ʃə 'pɪər əʊ ‖ -'pɪr oʊ

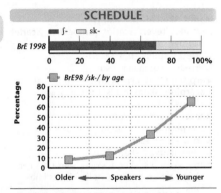

SCHEDULE

schedulle 'ʃed ju:l 'ʃedʒ u:l; 'sked ju:l,
'skedʒ u:l ‖ 'skedʒ u:l -əl —The AmE
pronunciation with sk- is increasingly heard in
BrE. BrE 1998 poll panel preference: ʃ- 70%,
sk- 30% (born since 1973, 65%); -dj- 79%,
-dʒ- 21%. ~ed d ~es z scheduling
'ʃed jʊl ɪŋ 'ʃedʒ ʊl-; 'sked jʊl-, 'skedʒ ʊl-
‖ 'skedʒ u:l ɪŋ -əl-
scheelite 'ʃi:əl aɪt
Scheherazade ʃə ˌher ə 'zɑːd ə ʃɪ-, -,hɪər-,
-'zɑːd
Scheldt ʃelt skelt —Dutch Schelde ['sxɛl də]
schema 'ski:m ə ~s z schemata 'ski:m ət ə
ski: 'mɑːt ə ‖ 'ski:m əṯ ə ski: 'mɑːṯ ə —The
classically correct plural form, with initial
stress, is being displaced by a new form with
penultimate stress.
schematic ski: 'mæt ɪk skɪ- ‖ -'mæṯ ɪk ~ally
əl_i ~s s
schematis... —see schematiz...
schematism 'ski:m ə ˌtɪz əm ~s z
schematization ˌski:m ət aɪ 'zeɪʃ ən -ɪ'•-
‖ -əṯ ə- ~s z

schematiz|e 'ski:m ə taɪz ~ed d ~es z ~ing
ɪŋ
scheme ski:m schemed ski:md schemes
ski:mz scheming 'ski:m ɪŋ
schemer 'ski:m ə ‖ -ər ~s z
Schenectady skɪ 'nekt əd i skə-
Schengen 'ʃeŋ ən —Ger ['ʃɛŋ ən]
scherzando skeət 'sænd əʊ sk3:t-
‖ skert 'sɑːnd oʊ —It [sker 'tsan do] ~s z
scherz|o 'skeəts |əʊ 'sk3:t- ‖ 'skerts |oʊ —It
['sker tso] ~i i: ~os əʊz ‖ oʊz
Scheveningen 'skeɪv ən_ɪŋ ən —Dutch
['sxe: və nɪŋ ən]
Schiaparelli ˌskæp ə 'rel i ˌʃæp- ‖ ˌskjɑːp- —It
[skja pa 'rel li]
Schick ʃɪk
Schiedam 'ski: dæm ˌ•'•, skɪ- —Dutch
[sxi 'dɑm]
Schiller, s~ 'ʃɪl ə ‖ -ər —Ger ['ʃɪl ɐ]
schilling 'ʃɪl ɪŋ ~s z
Schiphol 'skɪp ɒl ‖ -oʊl —Dutch [sxɪp 'hɔl, '••]
schipperke 'ʃɪp ək i 'skɪp- ‖ -ərk i ~s z

SCHISM

schism 'skɪz əm 'sɪz- —The traditional 'sɪz- is
being displaced, except perhaps among the
clergy, by 'skɪz-. BrE 1988 poll panel
preference: 'skɪz- 71%, 'sɪz- 29%. ~s z
schismatic skɪz 'mæt ɪk sɪz- ‖ -'mæṯ ɪk ~ally
əl_i ~s s
schist ʃɪst schists ʃɪsts
schistosome 'ʃɪst əʊ səʊm ‖ -ə soʊm ~s z
schistosomiasis ˌʃɪst əʊ səʊ 'maɪ_əs ɪs §-əs
‖ -ə soʊ-
schizanthus, S~ skɪt 'sænᵗθ əs skɪ 'zænᵗθ- ~es
ɪz əz
schizo 'skɪts əʊ ‖ -oʊ ~s z
schizo- comb. form
with stress-neutral suffix 'skɪts əʊ 'skɪz-,
'skaɪz- — schizocarp 'skɪts əʊ kɑːp 'skɪz-,
'skaɪz- ‖ -ə kɑːrp
with stress-imposing suffix skɪt 'sɒ+ skɪ 'zɒ+,
skaɪ- ‖ -'sɑː+ — schizogony skɪt 'sɒg ən i
skɪ 'zɒg-, skaɪ- ‖ skɪ 'zɑːg- skɪt 'sɑːg-
schizoid 'skɪts ɔɪd 'skɪdz- ~s z
schizont 'skɪts ɒnt 'skaɪz-, 'skɪz- ‖ -ɑːnt ~s s
schizophrenia ˌskɪts əʊ 'fri:n i_ə ‖ ˌ•ə- -'fren-
~s z
schizophrenic ˌskɪts əʊ 'fren ɪk ◄ -'fri:n- ‖ -ə-
~ally əl_i ~s s
Schlegel 'ʃleɪg əl —Ger ['ʃle: gl]
Schleicher 'ʃlaɪk ə 'ʃlaɪx- ‖ -ər —Ger ['ʃlai çɐ]
schlemiel ʃlə 'mi:əl ~s z
schlep, schlepp ʃlep schlepped ʃlept
schlepping 'ʃlep ɪŋ schleps, schlepps ʃleps
Schlesinger 'ʃles ɪndʒ ə -əndʒ- ‖ -ər
Schleswig 'ʃlez vɪg 'ʃles-, -wɪg —Ger
['ʃle:s vɪç]
Schleswig-Holstein ˌʃlez vɪg 'hɒl staɪn ˌʃles-,

-wɪg-, -'həʊl- ‖ -'hoʊl- —*Ger*
[ˌʃleːs vɪç 'hɔl ʃtaɪn]
Schliemann 'ʃliː mən -mæn —*Ger* [ˈʃliː man]
schlieren 'ʃlɪər ən ‖ 'ʃlɪr ən
schlock ʃlɒk ‖ ʃlɑːk
schlock|y 'ʃlɒk |i ‖ 'ʃlɑːk |i ~**ier** i_ə ‖ i_ər ~**iest**
    i_ɪst i_əst
schmaltz, schmalz ʃmɔːlts ʃmɒlts, ʃmælts
    ‖ ʃmɑːlts ʃmɔːlts
schmaltzy, schmalzy 'ʃmɔːlts i 'ʃmɒlts-,
    'ʃmælts- ‖ 'ʃmɑːlts i 'ʃmɔːlts-
Schmidt ʃmɪt
schmo, schmoe ʃməʊ ‖ ʃmoʊ **schmoes**
    ʃməʊz ‖ ʃmoʊz
schmooze ʃmuːz **schmoozed** ʃmuːzd
    schmoozes 'ʃmuːz ɪz -əz **schmoozing**
    'ʃmuːz ɪŋ
schmuck ʃmʌk **schmucks** ʃmʌks
Schnabel 'ʃnɑːb əl
schnapps, schnaps ʃnæps
schnauzer 'ʃnaʊts ə ‖ -ər 'ʃnaʊz- ~**s** z
Schneider, s~ 'ʃnaɪd ə ‖ -ər —*Ger* [ˈʃnai dɐ] ~**s**
    z
schnitzel 'ʃnɪts əl △'snɪtʃ- ~**s** z
Schnitzler 'ʃnɪts lə ‖ -lər —*Ger* [ˈʃnɪts lɐ]
schnook ʃnʊk **schnooks** ʃnʊks
schnorkel —*see* **snorkel**
schnorrer 'ʃnɒr ə 'ʃnɔːr- ‖ 'ʃnɔːr ər 'ʃnoʊr-
    ~**s** z
schnozzle 'ʃnɒz əl 'snɒz- ‖ 'ʃnɑːz əl ~**s** z
Schoenberg, Schönberg
    'ʃɜːn bɜːg ‖ 'ʃoʊn bɝːg 'ʃɜːn- —*Ger*
    [ˈʃøːn bɛʁk]
Schofield 'skəʊ fiːəld ‖ 'skoʊ-
schola cantorum ˌskəʊl ə kæn 'tɔːr əm
    ‖ ˌskoʊl- -'toʊr-
scholar 'skɒl ə ‖ 'skɑːl ər ~**s** z
scholar|ly 'skɒl ə |li ‖ 'skɑːl ər |li ~**liness** li nəs
    -nɪs
scholarship 'skɒl ə ʃɪp ‖ 'skɑːl ər-
    'scholarship boy
scholastic skə 'læst ɪk skɒ- ~**ally** əl_i ~**s** s
scholasticism skə 'læst ɪ ˌsɪz əm skɒ-, -'•ə-
Scholefield 'skəʊl fiːəld →'skɒʊl- ‖ 'skoʊl-
Scholes skəʊlz →skɒʊlz ‖ skoʊlz
Scholey 'skəʊl i ‖ 'skoʊl i
Scholfield (i) 'skəʊ fiːəld ‖ 'skoʊ-, (ii) 'skəʊl-
    →'skɒʊl- ‖ 'skoʊl-
scholiast 'skəʊl i æst əst ‖ 'skoʊl- ~**s** s
scholi|um 'skəʊl i_əm ‖ 'skoʊl- ~**a** ə ~**ums**
    əmz
Scholl (i) ʃɒl ‖ ʃɑːl ʃɔːl, (ii) ʃəʊl →ʃɒʊl ‖ ʃoʊl
Schonfield 'skɒn fiːəld ‖ 'skɑːn-
Schonberg, Schönberg 'ʃɜːn bɜːg -beəg
    ‖ 'ʃoʊn bɝːg 'ʃɜːn- —*Ger* [ˈʃøːn bɛʁk]
school skuːl **schooled** skuːld **schooling**
    'skuːl ɪŋ **schools** skuːlz
    **'school board; ˌschool 'tie; ˌschool
    'uniform; ˌschool 'year**
schoolboy 'skuːl bɔɪ ~**s** z
school|child 'skuːl |tʃaɪəld ~**children** ˌtʃɪldr
    ən ˌtʃʊldr-
schooldays 'skuːl deɪz

schoolfellow 'skuːl ˌfel əʊ ‖ -oʊ ~**s** z
schoolgirl 'skuːl gɜːl ‖ -gɝːl ~**s** z
school|house 'skuːl |haʊs ~**houses** ˌhaʊz ɪz
    -əz
schoolkid 'skuːl kɪd ~**s** z
school-leaver ˌskuːl 'liːv ə '•ˌ•• ‖ -ər ~**s** z
school-leaving ˌskuːl 'liːv ɪŋ '•ˌ••
school|man 'skuːl |mæn -mən ~**men** men mən
schoolmarm 'skuːl mɑːm ‖ -mɑːrm ~**s** z
schoolmast|er 'skuːl ˌmɑːst ə §-ˌmæst-
    ‖ -ˌmæst |ər ~**ering** ər ɪŋ ~**ers** əz ‖ ərz
schoolmate 'skuːl meɪt ~**s** s
schoolmen 'skuːl men -mən
schoolmistress 'skuːl ˌmɪs trəs -trɪs ~**es** ɪz əz
schoolmistressy 'skuːl ˌmɪs trəs i -trɪs-
schoolroom 'skuːl ruːm -rʊm ~**s** z
schoolteacher 'skuːl ˌtiːtʃ ə ‖ -ər ~**s** z
schoolteaching 'skuːl ˌtiːtʃ ɪŋ
schoolwork 'skuːl wɜːk ‖ -wɝːk
schooner ˌskuːn ə ‖ -ər ~**s** z
Schopenhauer 'ʃəʊp ən haʊ_ə 'ʃɒp- ‖ 'ʃoʊp
    ən haʊ_ər —*Ger* [ˈʃoːp n hau ɐ]
schorl ʃɔːl ‖ ʃɔːrl
schottisch|e ʃɒ 'tiːʃ ‖ 'ʃɑːtʃ ɪʃ ~**es** ɪz əz
Schottky 'ʃɒt ki ‖ 'ʃɑːt ki
Schreiber 'ʃraɪb ə ‖ -ər
Schreiner 'ʃraɪn ə ‖ -ər
Schroder 'ʃrəʊd ə ‖ 'ʃroʊd ər
Schröder 'ʃrɜːd ə ‖ 'ʃroʊd ər 'ʃreɪd- —*Ger*
    [ˈʃʁøː dɐ]
Schrodinger, Schrödinger
    'ʃrɜːd ɪŋ ə ‖ 'ʃroʊd ɪŋ ər 'ʃreɪd- —*Ger*
    [ˈʃʁøː dɪŋ ɐ]
Schroeder 'ʃrɜːd ə ‖ 'ʃroʊd ər 'ʃreɪd- —*Ger*
    [ˈʃʁøː dɐ]
schtick ʃtɪk
schtuck ʃtʊk
schtup ʃtʊp **schtupped** ʃtʊpt **schtupping**
    'ʃtʊp ɪŋ **schtups** ʃtʊps
Schubert 'ʃuːb ət -ɜːt ‖ -ərt —*Ger* [ˈʃu bɐt]
Schultz, Schultz ʃʊlts
Schumacher 'ʃuː ˌmæk ə ‖ -ər -ˌmɑːk- —*Ger*
    [ˈʃu ˌmax ɐ]
Schuman 'ʃuːm ən —*Fr* [ʃu man]
Schumann 'ʃuːm ən -æn, -ɑːn ‖ -ɑːn —*Ger*
    [ˈʃu man]
schuss ʃʊs ʃuːs, ʃuːʃ —*Ger* [ʃʊs] **schussed**
    ʃʊst ʃuːst, ʃuːʃt **schusses** 'ʃʊs ɪz 'ʃuːs-,
    'ʃuːʃ-, -əz **schussing** 'ʃʊs ɪŋ 'ʃuːs-, 'ʃuːʃ-
Schuyler 'skaɪl ə ‖ -ər
Schuylerville 'skaɪl ə vɪl ‖ -ər-
Schuylkill *river in PA* 'skuːl kɪl 'skuːk əl
schwa ʃwɑː ʃvɑː **schwas** ʃwɑːz ʃvɑːz
Schwab ʃwɑːb
Schwann ʃwɒn ʃwæn ‖ ʃwɑːn ʃvɑːn —*Ger*
    [ʃvan]
Schwartz ʃwɔːts ‖ ʃwɔːrts —*but as a German
    name,* ʃvɑːts ‖ ʃvɑːrts —*Ger* [ʃvaʁts]
Schwartzenegger
    'ʃwɔːts ə neg ə ‖ 'ʃwɔːrts ə neg ər —*Ger*
    [ˈʃvaʁts ən ɛg ɐ]
Schwartzschild 'ʃwɔːts ʃɪld →'ʃwɔːtʃ-;
    -tʃaɪəld ‖ 'ʃwɔːrts- —*Ger* [ˈʃvaʁts ʃɪlt]

Schwarzkopf 'ʃvɑːts kɒpf 'ʃwɑːts-, 'ʃwɔːts-
‖ 'ʃwɔːrts kaːpf 'ʃvɑːrts- —*Ger*
['ʃvaʁts kɔpf]
Schwarzwald 'ʃvɑːts væld 'ʃwɑːts-, -wæld
‖ 'ʃvɑːrts vaːld —*Ger* ['ʃvaʁts valt]
Schweitzer 'ʃwaɪts ə 'ʃvaɪts- ‖ -ᵊr —*Ger*
['ʃvai tsɐ]
Schweppes *tdmk* ʃweps
sciatic saɪ 'æt ɪk ‖ -'æt̬ ɪk
sciatica saɪ 'æt ɪk ə ‖ -'æt̬-
Scicon *tdmk* 'saɪ kɒn ‖ -kɑːn
science 'saɪ ᵊnᵗs sciences 'saɪ ᵊnᵗs ɪz -əz
ˌscience 'fiction; 'science park
scientific ˌsaɪ ən 'tɪf ɪk ◄ ~ally ᵊl̩ i
ˌscien tific 'method
scientism 'saɪ ən ˌtɪz əm
scientist 'saɪ ᵊnt ɪst §-əst ‖ 'saɪ ənt̬ əst ~s s
scientologist, S~ ˌsaɪ ən 'tɒl ədʒ ɪst §-əst
‖ -'tɑːl- ~s s
Scientology *tdmk* ˌsaɪ ən 'tɒl ədʒ i ‖ -'tɑːl-
sci-fi ˌsaɪ 'faɪ ◄
scilicet 'sɪl ɪ set 'saɪl-, -ə-; 'skiːl ɪ ket
scilla, S~ 'sɪl ə ~s z
Scillies 'sɪl iz
Scillonian sɪ 'ləʊn i̯ən sə- ‖ -'loʊn- ~s z
Scill|y 'sɪl |i ~ies iz
scimitar 'sɪm ɪt ə ə-ət-; -ɪ tɑː, -ə- ‖ -ət̬ ᵊr -ə tɑːr
~s z
scintilla sɪn 'tɪl ə ~s z
scintill|ate 'sɪnt ɪ |leɪt -ə-, -ᵊl |eɪt ‖ 'sɪnt̬ ᵊl |eɪt
~ated eɪt ɪd -əd ‖ eɪt̬ əd ~ates eɪts ~ating
eɪt ɪŋ ‖ eɪt̬ ɪŋ
scintillation ˌsɪnt ɪ 'leɪʃ ᵊn -ə-, -ᵊl 'eɪʃ-
‖ ˌsɪnt̬ ᵊl 'eɪʃ ᵊn ~s z
scintillator 'sɪnt ɪ leɪt ə '•ə-, -ᵊl eɪt ə
‖ 'sɪnt̬ ᵊl eɪt̬ ᵊr ~s z
scintillometer ˌsɪnt ɪ 'lɒm ɪt ə ,•ə-, -ᵊl 'ɒm-,
-ət ə ‖ ˌsɪnt̬ ᵊl 'ɑːm ət̬ ᵊr ~s z
sciolism 'saɪ ə ˌlɪz əm -əʊ-
sciolist 'saɪ əl ɪst -əʊl-, §-əst ~s s
sciolistic ˌsaɪ ə 'lɪst ɪk ◄ -əʊ-
scion 'saɪ ən ~s z
Scioto *river in OH* saɪ 'əʊt əʊ ‖ -'oʊt̬ ə -oʊ
Scipio 'skɪp i əʊ 'sɪp- ‖ -oʊ
scire facias ˌsaɪ ər i 'feɪʃ i æs -əs ‖ ˌsaɪ ᵊr-
scirocco, S~ sɪ 'rɒk əʊ sə-, ʃɪ- ‖ -'rɑːk oʊ —*It*
[ʃi 'rɔk ko] ~s z
scirrh|us 'sɪr |əs 'skɪr- ~i aɪ ~ous əs ~uses
əs ɪz -əz
scission 'sɪʒ ᵊn 'sɪʃ- ~s z
scissor 'sɪz ə ‖ -ᵊr (!) ~ed d scissoring
'sɪz ᵊr ɪŋ ~s z
scissors-and-paste ˌsɪz əz ən 'peɪst →-əm'•-,
-ənd'•- ‖ ˌsɪz ᵊrz-
ˌscissors-and-'paste job
Scituate 'sɪtʃ u eɪt
sclaff sklæf sclaffed sklæft sclaffing
'sklæf ɪŋ sclaffs sklæfs
sclera 'sklɪər ə ‖ 'sklɪr ə 'skler-
sclero- *comb. form*
with stress-neutral suffix ˌsklɪər əʊ ˌskler-
‖ ˌsklɪr ə ˌskler- — scleroderma ˌsklɪər əʊ
'dɜːm ə ˌskler- ‖ ˌsklɪr ə 'dɜːm ə ˌskler-

with stress-imposing suffix sklə 'rɒ+ sklɪ-,
sklɪə-, skle- ‖ sklə 'rɑː+ sklɪ- —
sclerotomy sklə 'rɒt əm i sklɪ-, sklɪə-, skle-
‖ -'rɑːt-
sclerom|a sklə 'rəʊm ə sklɪ-, sklɪə-, skle-
‖ -'roʊm ə ~as əz ~ata ət ə ‖ ət̬ ə
scleros|is sklə 'rəʊs ɪs sklɪ-, sklɪə-, skle-, §-əs
‖ -'roʊs əs ~es iːz
sclerotic sklə 'rɒt ɪk sklɪ-, sklɪə-, skle-
‖ -'rɑːt̬ ɪk
sclerous 'sklɪər əs 'skler- ‖ 'sklɪr əs 'skler-
Scobell ₍ᵤ₎skəʊ 'bel ‖ skoʊ bel
Scobie, Scoby 'skəʊb i ‖ 'skoʊb i
scoff skɒf ‖ skɑːf skɔːf scoffed skɒft ‖ skɑːft
skɔːft scoffing/ly 'skɒf ɪŋ /li ‖ 'skɑːf-
'skɔːf- scoffs skɒfs ‖ skɑːfs skɔːfs
scoffer 'skɒf ə ‖ 'skɑːf ᵊr 'skɔːf- ~s z
Scofield 'skəʊ fiːᵊld ‖ 'skoʊ-
scold skəʊld →skɒʊld ‖ skoʊld scolded
'skəʊld ɪd →'skɒʊld-, -əd ‖ 'skoʊld əd
scolding/s 'skəʊld ɪŋ/z →'skɒʊld-
‖ 'skoʊld ɪŋ/z scolds skəʊldz →skɒʊldz
‖ skoʊldz
scoliosis ˌskɒl i 'əʊs ɪs ˌskəʊl-, §-əs
‖ ˌskoʊl i 'oʊs əs ˌskɑːl-
scoliotic ˌskɒl i 'ɒt ɪk ◄ ˌskəʊl-
‖ ˌskoʊl i 'ɑːt̬ ɪk ◄ ˌskɑːl-
scollop 'skɒl əp ‖ 'skɑːl əp ~ed t ~ing ɪŋ ~s
s
scombroid 'skɒm brɔɪd ‖ 'skɑːm- ~s z
sconce skɒnᵗs ‖ skɑːnᵗst sconced
skɒnᵗst ‖ skɑːnᵗst sconces 'skɒnᵗs ɪz -əz
‖ 'skɑːnᵗs əz sconcing
'skɒnᵗs ɪŋ ‖ 'skɑːnᵗs ɪŋ

SCONE

BrE 1998

	skɒn		skəʊn		
0	20	40	60	80	100%

---

scone skɒn skəʊn ‖ skoʊn skɑːn —*BrE 1998
poll panel preference:* skɒn 65%, skəʊn 35%.
scones skɒnz skəʊnz ‖ skoʊnz skɑːnz
Scone *place in Tayside* skuːn
scoop skuːp scooped skuːpt scooping
'skuːp ɪŋ scoops skuːps
scooper 'skuːp ə ‖ -ᵊr ~s z
scoot skuːt scooted 'skuːt ɪd -əd ‖ 'skuːt̬ əd
scooting 'skuːt ɪŋ ‖ 'skuːt̬ ɪŋ scoots skuːts
scoot|er 'skuːt ə ‖ 'skuːt̬ ᵊr ~ered əd ‖ ᵊrd
~ering ᵊr ɪŋ ~ers əz ‖ ᵊrz
scope skəʊp ‖ skoʊp scopes skəʊps ‖ skoʊps
scoping 'skəʊp ɪŋ ‖ 'skoʊp ɪŋ
-scope skəʊp ‖ skoʊp — microscope
'maɪk rə skəʊp ‖ -skoʊp
Scopes skəʊps ‖ skoʊps
-scopic 'skɒp ɪk ‖ 'skɑːp ɪk — microscopic
ˌmaɪk rəʊ 'skɒp ɪk ◄ ‖ -rə 'skɑːp ɪk
scopolamine skəʊ 'pɒl ə miːn -mɪn, §-mən
‖ skə 'pɑːl- skoʊ-; ˌskoʊp ə 'læm ən
scopoline 'skəʊp ə liːn -lɪn, §-lən ‖ 'skoʊp-
Scopus 'skəʊp əs ‖ 'skoʊp əs
-scopy *stress-imposing* +skəp i — microscopy
maɪ 'krɒsk əp i ‖ -'krɑːsk-

scorbutic skɔː ˈbjuːt ɪk ‖ skɔːr ˈbjuːt̬ ɪk ~ally
əl_i
scorch skɔːtʃ ‖ skɔːrtʃ scorched
skɔːtʃt ‖ skɔːrtʃt scorches ˈskɔːtʃ ɪz -əz
‖ ˈskɔːrtʃ əz scorching/ly ˈskɔːtʃ ɪŋ /li
‖ ˈskɔːrtʃ ɪŋ /li
,scorched ˈearth, ,scorched ˈearth ,policy
scorcher ˈskɔːtʃ ə ‖ ˈskɔːrtʃ ər ~s z
score skɔː ‖ skɔːr skoʊr scored skɔːd ‖ skɔːrd
skoʊrd scores skɔːz ‖ skɔːrz skoʊrz
scoring ˈskɔːr ɪŋ ‖ ˈskoʊr-
ˈscore draw
scoreboard ˈskɔː bɔːd ‖ ˈskɔːr bɔːrd
ˈskoʊr boʊrd ~s z
scorebook ˈskɔː bʊk §-buːk ‖ ˈskɔːr- ˈskoʊr-
~s s
scorecard ˈskɔː kɑːd ‖ ˈskɔːr kɑːrd ˈskoʊr- ~s
z
scorekeeper ˈskɔː ˌkiːp ə ‖ ˈskɔːr ˌkiːp ər
ˈskoʊr- ~s z
scoreless ˈskɔː ləs -lɪs ‖ ˈskɔːr- ˈskoʊr-
scoreline ˈskɔː laɪn ‖ ˈskɔːr- ˈskoʊr- ~s z
scorer ˈskɔːr ə ‖ -ər ˈskoʊr- ~s z
scoria ˈskɔːr i_ə skə ˈriː_ə ‖ ˈskoʊr-
scoriaceous ˌskɔːr i ˈeɪʃ əs ◀ ‖ ˌskoʊr-
scorn skɔːn ‖ skɔːrn scorned skɔːnd ‖ skɔːrnd
scorning ˈskɔːn ɪŋ ‖ ˈskɔːrn ɪŋ scorns
skɔːnz ‖ skɔːrnz
scornful ˈskɔːn fəl -fʊl ‖ ˈskɔːrn- ~ly _i ~ness
nəs nɪs
Scorpian ˈskɔːp i_ən ‖ ˈskɔːrp- ~s z
Scorpio ˈskɔːp i_əʊ ‖ ˈskɔːrp i oʊ ~s z
scorpion ˈskɔːp i_ən ‖ ˈskɔːrp- ~s z
Scorpius ˈskɔːp i_əs ‖ ˈskɔːrp-
Scorsese skɔː ˈseɪz i ‖ skɔːr-
scorzonera ˌskɔːz ə ˈnɪər ə ‖ ˌskɔːrz ə ˈner ə
Scot, scot skɒt ‖ skɑːt Scots skɒts ‖ skɑːts
Scotcade tdmk ˈskɒt keɪd ‖ ˈskɑːt-
Scotch, s~ skɒtʃ ‖ skɑːtʃ scotched
skɒtʃt ‖ skɑːtʃt scotches ˈskɒtʃ ɪz -əz
‖ ˈskɑːtʃ əz scotching ˈskɒtʃ ɪŋ ‖ ˈskɑːtʃ ɪŋ
,Scotch ˈbroth; ,Scotch ˈegg; ,Scotch ˈmist;
,Scotch ˈpancake; ,Scotch ˈtape tdmk, ˈ• •;
,Scotch ˈwhisky
Scotchgard tdmk ˈskɒtʃ gɑːd ‖ ˈskɑːtʃ gɑːrd
Scotch-Irish ,skɒtʃ ˈaɪər ɪʃ ◀ ‖ ,skɑːtʃ-
Scotch|man ˈskɒtʃ |mən ‖ ˈskɑːtʃ- ~men mən
~woman ,wʊm ən ~women ,wɪm ɪn §-ən
scoter ˈskəʊt ə ‖ ˈskoʊt̬ ər ~s z
scot-free ,skɒt ˈfriː ‖ ,skɑːt-
Scotia, s~ ˈskəʊʃ ə ‖ ˈskoʊʃ ə
Scotland ˈskɒt lənd ‖ ˈskɑːt-
,Scotland ˈYard
scotoma skɒ ˈtəʊm ə skəʊ- ‖ skə ˈtoʊm ə
skoʊ- ~s z
Scots skɒts ‖ skɑːts
,Scots ˈpine
Scots|man ˈskɒts |mən ‖ ˈskɑːts- ~men mən
Scotstoun ˈskɒts tən ‖ ˈskɑːts-
Scots|woman ˈskɒts |ˌwʊm ən ‖ ˈskɑːts-
~women ,wɪm ɪn §-ən
Scott skɒt ‖ skɑːt
Scotticism ˈskɒt ɪ ,sɪz əm -ə- ‖ ˈskɑːt̬ ə- ~s z

Scottie, s~ ˈskɒt i ‖ ˈskɑːt̬ i ~s z
Scottish ˈskɒt ɪʃ ‖ ˈskɑːt̬ ɪʃ ~ness nəs nɪs
,Scottish ˈGaelic; ,Scottish ˈterrier
Scottsdale ˈskɒts deɪəl ‖ ˈskɑːts-
Scott|y, s~ ˈskɒt |i ‖ ˈskɑːt̬ |i ~ies, ~y's iz
Scotus ˈskəʊt əs ‖ ˈskoʊt̬ əs
scoundrel ˈskaʊndr əl ~s z
scoundrelly ˈskaʊndr əl i
scour ˈskaʊ_ə ‖ skaʊ_ər scoured
ˈskaʊ_əd ‖ skaʊ_ərd scouring
ˈskaʊ_ər ɪŋ ‖ ˈskaʊ_ər ɪŋ scours
ˈskaʊ_əz ‖ skaʊ_ərz
scourer ˈskaʊ_ər ə ‖ ˈskaʊ_ər ər ~s z
scourge skɜːdʒ ‖ skɜːdʒ scourged
skɜːdʒd ‖ skɜːdʒd scourges ˈskɜːdʒ ɪz -əz
‖ ˈskɜːdʒ əz scourging
ˈskɜːdʒ ɪŋ ‖ ˈskɜːdʒ ɪŋ
Scouse, s~ skaʊs
Scouser ˈskaʊs ə ‖ -ər ~s z
scout, Scout skaʊt scouted ˈskaʊt ɪd -əd
‖ ˈskaʊt̬ əd scouting ˈskaʊt ɪŋ ‖ ˈskaʊt̬ ɪŋ
scouts skaʊts
scouter, S~ ˈskaʊt ə ‖ ˈskaʊt̬ ər ~s z
scoutmaster ˈskaʊt ,mɑːst ə §-,mæst-
‖ -,mæst ər ~s z
scow skaʊ scows skaʊz
scowl skaʊl scowled skaʊld scowler/s
ˈskaʊl ə/z ‖ -ər/z scowling/ly ˈskaʊl ɪŋ /li
scowls skaʊlz
scrabbl|e, S~ tdmk ˈskræb əl ~ed d ~es z
~ing _ɪŋ
scrabbl|y ˈskræb əl_i ~ier i_ə ‖ i_ər ~iest i_ɪst
i_əst
scrag skræg scragged skrægd scragging
ˈskræg ɪŋ scrags skrægz
,scrag ˈend
scraggl|y ˈskræg əl_i ~ier i_ə ‖ i_ər ~iest i_ɪst
i_əst ~iness i nəs i nɪs
scraggly ˈskræg li ~ier i_ə ‖ i_ər ~iest i_ɪst
i_əst ~ily ɪ li əl i ~iness i nəs i nɪs
scram skræm scrammed skræmd
scramming ˈskræm ɪŋ scrams skræmz
scrambl|e ˈskræm bəl ~ed d ~es z ~ing _ɪŋ
,scrambled ˈegg
scrambler ˈskræm blə ‖ -blər ~s z
scran skræn
Scranton ˈskrænt ən ‖ -ən
scrap skræp scrapped skræpt scrapping
ˈskræp ɪŋ scraps skræps
ˈscrap heap; ˈscrap ,iron; ˈscrap
,paper,; ˈ• •
scrapbook ˈskræp bʊk §-buːk ~s s
scrape skreɪp scraped skreɪpt scrapes
skreɪps scraping/s ˈskreɪp ɪŋ/z
scraper ˈskreɪp ə ‖ -ər ~s z
scraperboard ˈskreɪp ə bɔːd ‖ -ər bɔːrd -boʊrd
~s z
scrapheap ˈskræp hiːp ~s s
scrapie ˈskreɪp i
scraping ˈskreɪp ɪŋ ~s z
scrapp... —see scrap
scrapple ˈskræp əl

S

scrapp|y 'skræp |i ~**ier** i‿ə ‖ i‿ᵊr ~**iest** i‿ɪst
i‿əst ~**ily** ɪ li əl i ~**iness** i nəs i nɪs
scratch skrætʃ **scratched** skrætʃt **scratches**
'skrætʃ ɪz -əz **scratching/s** 'skrætʃ ɪŋ/z
'scratch ,paper; 'scratch sheet; 'scratch
test
scratchcard 'skrætʃ kɑːd ‖ -kɑːrd ~**s** z
scratcher 'skrætʃ ə ‖ -ᵊr ~**s** z
scratchpad 'skrætʃ pæd ~**s** z
Scratchwood 'skrætʃ wʊd
scratch|y 'skrætʃ |i ~**ier** i‿ə ‖ i‿ᵊr ~**iest** i‿ɪst
i‿əst ~**ily** ɪ li əl i ~**iness** i nəs i nɪs
scrawl skrɔːl ‖ skrɑːl **scrawled** skrɔːld
‖ skrɑːld **scrawling** 'skrɔːl ɪŋ ‖ 'skrɑːl-
scrawls skrɔːlz ‖ skrɑːlz
scrawler 'skrɔːl ə ‖ -ᵊr 'skrɑːl- ~**s** z
scrawl|y 'skrɔːl |i ‖ 'skrɑːl- ~**ier** i‿ə ‖ i‿ᵊr ~**iest**
i‿ɪst i‿əst ~**iness** i nəs i nɪs
scrawn|y 'skrɔːn |i ‖ 'skrɑːn- ~**ier** i‿ə ‖ i‿ᵊr
~**iest** i‿ɪst i‿əst ~**ily** ɪ li əl i ~**iness** i nəs i nɪs
scream skriːm **screamed** skriːmd
screaming/ly 'skriːm ɪŋ /li **screams** skriːmz
screamer 'skriːm ə ‖ -ᵊr ~**s** z
scree skriː **screes** skriːz
screech skriːtʃ **screeched** skriːtʃt **screeches**
'skriːtʃ ɪz -əz **screeching** 'skriːtʃ ɪŋ
'screech owl
screecher 'skriːtʃ ə ‖ -ᵊr ~**s** z
screech|y 'skriːtʃ |i ~**ier** i‿ə ‖ i‿ᵊr ~**iest** i ɪst
i əst
screed skriːd **screeds** skriːdz
screen skriːn **screened** skriːnd **screening/s**
'skriːn ɪŋ/z **screens** skriːnz
'screen ,printing; 'screen ,saver; 'screen
test
screenplay 'skriːn pleɪ →'skriːm- ~**s** z
screenshot 'skriːn ʃɒt ‖ -ʃɑːt ~**s** s
screenwriter 'skriːn ,raɪt ə ‖ -,raɪt̬ ᵊr ~**s** z
screw skruː **screwed** skruːd **screwing**
'skruː‿ɪŋ **screws** skruːz
'screw cap; 'screw jack; 'screw pine;
'screw thread; 'screw top n, ,·'·
screwball 'skruː bɔːl ‖ -bɑːl ~**s** z
screwdriver 'skruː ,draɪv ə ‖ -ᵊr ~**s** z
screw-top adj ,skruː 'tɒp ◄ '·· ‖ -'tɑːp ◄
,screw-top 'jar
screw-up 'skruː ʌp ~**s** s
screwworm 'skruː wɜːm ‖ -wɜˑːm ~**s** z
screw|y 'skruː‿|i ~**ier** i‿ə ‖ i‿ᵊr ~**iest** i‿ɪst i‿əst
Scriabin skri 'æb ɪn §-ən; 'skriˑəb ɪn ‖ -'ɑːb ən
—Russ ['skrjæ bjin]
scribal 'skraɪb əl
scribbl|e 'skrɪb əl ~**ed** d ~**es** z ~**ing/s** ‿ɪŋ/z
scribbler 'skrɪb əl‿ə ‖ ‿ᵊr ~**s** z
scribe skraɪb **scribed** skraɪbd **scribes** skraɪbz
scribing 'skraɪb ɪŋ
scriber 'skraɪb ə ‖ -ᵊr ~**s** z
Scribner 'skrɪb nə ‖ -nᵊr
scrim skrɪm **scrims** skrɪmz
Scrimgeour, Scrimger 'skrɪm dʒə ‖ -dʒᵊr
scrimmag|e 'skrɪm ɪdʒ ~**ed** d ~**es** ɪz əz ~**ing**
ɪŋ

scrimp skrɪmp **scrimped** skrɪmpt **scrimping**
'skrɪmp ɪŋ **scrimps** skrɪmps
scrimshank 'skrɪm ʃæŋk ~**ed** t ~**er/s** ə/z ‖ ᵊr/
z ~**ing** ɪŋ ~**s** s
scrimshaw 'skrɪm ʃɔː ‖ -ʃɑː ~**ed** d
scrimshawing 'skrɪm ʃɔːr ɪŋ ‖ -ʃɔː ɪŋ -ʃɑː-
~**s** z
scrip skrɪp **scrips** skrɪps
'scrip ,issue
Scripps skrɪps
scripsit 'skrɪps ɪt §-ət
script skrɪpt **scripted** 'skrɪpt ɪd -əd **scripting**
'skrɪpt ɪŋ **scripts** skrɪpts
scriptori|um skrɪp 'tɔːr i‿|əm ‖ -'toʊr- ~**a** ə
~**ums** əmz
scriptural 'skrɪp tʃᵊr əl -ʃᵊr_ ~**ly** i
scripture, S~ 'skrɪp tʃə -ʃə ‖ -tʃᵊr ~**s** z
scriptwriter 'skrɪpt ,raɪt ə ‖ -,raɪt̬ ᵊr ~**s** z
scrivener, S~ 'skrɪv ᵊn_ə ‖ ‿ᵊr ~**s** z
scrod skrɒd ‖ skrɑːd **scrods** skrɒdz ‖ skrɑːdz
scrofula 'skrɒf jʊl ə §-jəl- ‖ 'skrɑːf jəl ə
'skrɔːf-
scrofulous 'skrɒf jʊl əs §-jəl- ‖ 'skrɑːf jəl əs
'skrɔːf- ~**ly** li ~**ness** nəs nɪs
scroggin 'skrɒg ɪn -ən ‖ 'skrɑːg ən
scroll skrəʊl →skrɒʊl ‖ skroʊl **scrolled**
skrəʊld →skrɒʊld ‖ skroʊld **scrolling**
'skrəʊl ɪŋ →'skrɒʊl- ‖ 'skroʊl ɪŋ **scrolls**
skrəʊlz →skrɒʊlz ‖ skroʊlz
scrollwork 'skrəʊl wɜːk →'skrɒʊl-
‖ 'skroʊl wɜˑːk
Scrooby 'skruːb i
Scrooge, s~ skruːdʒ **Scrooges, s~** 'skruːdʒ ɪz
-əz
scrot|um 'skrəʊt |əm ‖ 'skroʊt̬ |əm ~**a** ə ~**al** əl
~**ums** əmz
scrounge skraʊndʒ **scrounged** skraʊndʒd
scrounges 'skraʊndʒ ɪz -əz **scrounging**
'skraʊndʒ ɪŋ
scrounger 'skraʊndʒ ə ‖ -ᵊr ~**s** z
scrub skrʌb **scrubbed** skrʌbd **scrubbing**
'skrʌb ɪŋ **scrubs** skrʌbz
'scrubbing brush, 'scrub brush
scrubber 'skrʌb ə ‖ -ᵊr ~**s** z
scrubb|y 'skrʌb |i ~**ier** i‿ə ‖ i‿ᵊr ~**iest** i‿ɪst
i‿əst ~**iness** i nəs i nɪs
scrubland 'skrʌb lənd -lænd ‖ -lænd
scruff skrʌf **scruffs** skrʌfs
scruff|y 'skrʌf |i ~**ier** i‿ə ‖ i‿ᵊr ~**iest** i‿ɪst i‿əst
~**ily** ɪ li əl i ~**iness** i nəs i nɪs
scrum skrʌm **scrummed** skrʌmd **scrumming**
'skrʌm ɪŋ **scrums** skrʌmz
scrumcap 'skrʌm kæp ~**s** s
scrum|half ,skrʌm |'hɑːf §-'hæf ‖ -'hæf
~**halves** 'hɑːvz §'hævz ‖ 'hævz
scrummag|e 'skrʌm ɪdʒ ~**ed** d ~**es** ɪz əz
~**ing** ɪŋ
scrump skrʌmp **scrumped** skrʌmpt
scrumping 'skrʌmp ɪŋ **scrumps** skrʌmps
scrumptious 'skrʌmp ʃəs ~**ly** li ~**ness** nəs nɪs
scrumpy 'skrʌmp i
scrunch skrʌntʃ **scrunched** skrʌntʃt

S

scrunches 'skrʌntʃ ɪz -əz **scrunching**
'skrʌntʃ ɪŋ
scrunch|ie, scrunch|y 'skrʌntʃ| i ~**ies** iz
scrupl|e 'skru:p əl ~**ed** d ~**es** z ~**ing** ɪŋ
scrupulosit|y ˌskru:p ju 'lɒs ət| i ˌ•jə-
‖ -jə 'lɑ:s ət̬| i ~**ies** iz
scrupulous 'skru:p jʊl əs -jəl- ‖ -jəl əs ~**ly** li
~**ness** nəs nɪs
scrutable 'skru:t əb əl ‖ 'skru:t̬-
scrutator skru 'teɪt ə ‖ -'teɪt̬ ər ~**s** z
scrutineer ˌskru:t ɪ 'nɪə -ə-, -ən 'ɪə
‖ ˌskru:t ən 'ɪər ~**s** z
scrutinis|e, scrutiniz|e 'skru:t ɪ naɪz -ə-,
-ən aɪz ‖ -ən aɪz ~**ed** d ~**es** ɪz əz ~**ing** ɪŋ
scrutin|y 'skru:t ɪn ‖i -ən‿i ‖ -ən‿li ~**ies** iz
Scruton 'skru:t ən
scry skraɪ **scried** skraɪd **scries** skraɪz **scrying**
'skraɪ ɪŋ
Scrymgeour 'skrɪm dʒə ‖ -dʒ³r
SCSI 'skʌz i
scuba 'sku:b ə 'skju:b-
'scuba ˌdiving
scud skʌd **scudded** 'skʌd ɪd -əd **scudding**
'skʌd ɪŋ **scuds** skʌdz
Scudamore 'skju:d ə mɔ: 'sku:d- ‖ -mɔ:r
-mʊər
scuff skʌf **scuffed** skʌft **scuffing** 'skʌf ɪŋ
scuffs skʌfs
scuffl|e 'skʌf əl ~**ed** d ~**es** z ~**ing** ɪŋ
scuffmark 'skʌf mɑ:k ‖ -mɑ:rk ~**s** s
scull skʌl (= skull) **sculled** skʌld **sculling**
'skʌl ɪŋ **sculls** skʌlz
sculler 'skʌl ə ‖ -ər ~**s** z
sculler|y 'skʌl ər‿li ~**ies** iz
Sculley 'skʌl i
Scullin 'skʌl ɪn §-ən
scullion 'skʌl i‿ən ‖ 'skʌl jən ~**s** z
Scully 'skʌl i
sculpsit 'skʌlps ɪt §-ət
sculpt skʌlpt **sculpted** 'skʌlpt ɪd -əd
sculpting 'skʌlpt ɪŋ **sculpts** skʌlpts
sculptor 'skʌlpt ə ‖ -ər ~**s** z
sculptress 'skʌlp trəs -trɪs, -tres ~**es** ɪz əz
sculptural 'skʌlp tʃər‿əl -ʃər- ~**ly** i
sculp|ture 'skʌlp |tʃə -ʃə ‖ -ɪtʃər ~**tured** tʃəd
ʃəd ‖ tʃ³rd ~**tures** tʃəz ʃəz ‖ tʃ³rz ~**turing**
tʃər ɪŋ ʃər‿ɪŋ
sculpturesque ˌskʌlp tʃə 'resk ◂ -ʃə- ~**ly** li
~**ness** nəs nɪs
scum skʌm **scummed** skʌmd **scumming**
'skʌm ɪŋ **scums** skʌmz
scumbag 'skʌm bæg ~**s** z
scumbl|e 'skʌm bəl ~**ed** d ~**es** z ~**ing** ɪŋ
scummy 'skʌm i
scuncheon 'skʌntʃ ən ~**s** z
scunge skʌndʒ
scung|y 'skʌndʒ| i ~**ier** i‿ə ‖ i‿ər ~**ies** iz ~**iest**
i‿ɪst ‿əst
scunner 'skʌn ə ‖ -ər ~**ed** d **scunnering**
'skʌn ər‿ɪŋ ~**s** z
Scunthorpe 'skʌn θɔ:p ‖ -θɔ:rp
scup skʌp

scupper 'skʌp ə ‖ -ər ~**ed** d ~**ering**
'skʌp ər‿ɪŋ ~**s** z
Scuppernong, s~ 'skʌp ə nɒŋ ‖ -ər nɑ:ŋ -nɔ:ŋ
~**s** z
scurf skɜ:f ‖ skɜ˞:f
scurf|y 'skɜ:f ‖i ‖ 'skɜ˞:f li ~**iness** i nəs i nɪs
scurri... —*see* **scurry**
scurrilit|y skə 'rɪl ət i li skʌ-, -ɪt- ‖ -ət̬ li ~**ies** iz
scurrilous 'skʌr əl əs -ɪl- ‖ 'skɜ˞:- ~**ly** li ~**ness**
nəs nɪs
scurr|y 'skʌr ‖i ‖ 'skɜ˞: li ~**ied** id ~**ies** iz
~**ying** i‿ɪŋ
scurv|y 'skɜ:v ‖i ‖ 'skɜ˞:v li ~**ier** i‿ə ‖ i‿ər ~**iest**
i‿ɪst i‿əst ~**ily** ɪ li əl i ~**iness** i nəs i nɪs
'scuse skju:z
scut skʌt **scuts** skʌts
scuta —*see* **scutum**
Scutari 'sku:t ər i sku 'tɑ:r i ‖ 'sku:t̬ ər i —*It*
['sku: ta ri]
scutch skʌtʃ **scutched** skʌtʃt **scutches**
'skʌtʃ ɪz -əz **scutching** 'skʌtʃ ɪŋ
scutcheon 'skʌtʃ ən ~**s** z
scute skju:t sku:t **scutes** skju:ts sku:ts
scutell|um skju 'tel ləm sku- ~**a** ə
scutt|er 'skʌt| ə ‖ 'skʌt̬| ³r ~**ered** əd ‖ -³rd
~**ering** ³r ɪŋ ‖ ³r ɪŋ ~**ers** əz ‖ -³rz
scuttl|e 'skʌt əl ‖ 'skʌt̬ əl ~**ed** d ~**es** z ~**ing**
ɪŋ
scuttlebutt 'skʌt əl bʌt ‖ 'skʌt̬- ~**s** s
scut|um, S~ 'skju:t |əm 'sku:t- ‖ 'skju:t̬ |əm
'sku:t̬- ~**a** ə
scuzz|y 'skʌz ‖i ~**ier** i‿ə ‖ i‿³r ~**iest** i‿ɪst i‿əst
Scylla 'sɪl ə
scythe saɪð §saɪθ **scythed** saɪðd §saɪθt
scythes saɪðz §saɪθs **scything** 'saɪð ɪŋ
§'saɪθ-
Scythi|a 'sɪð i‿ə 'sɪθ- ‖ 'sɪθ- ~**an/s** ən/z
SDI ˌes di ‿'aɪ
SDLP ˌes di el 'pi:
SDP ˌes di: 'pi:
se *in Latin expressions* seɪ si:, *in French*
expressions sə —*see also phrases with this*
word
SE ˌes 'i: ◂ —*see* southeast, southeastern
sea si: (= *see*) **seas** si:z
'sea a,nemone; 'sea breeze; ˌ• '•; 'sea
ˌcaptain; 'sea change; 'sea cow; 'sea dog;
ˌsea 'green◂; ˌsea ˌisland 'cotton; 'sea
king; 'sea legs; 'sea ˌlevel; 'sea ˌlion; 'sea
mile; 'sea mist; 'sea ˌpower; 'Sea Scout;
'sea ˌserpent; 'sea slug; 'sea ˌurchin
seabed 'si: bed
seabird 'si: bɜ:d ‖ -bɜ˞:d ~**s** z
seaboard 'si: bɔ:d ‖ -bɔ:rd -boʊrd
Seaborg 'si: bɔ:g ‖ -bɔ:rg
seaborne 'si: bɔ:n ‖ -bɔ:rn -boʊrn
seacoast 'si: kəʊst ‖ -koʊst ~**s** s
seafarer 'si: ˌfeər ə ‖ -ˌfer ³r -ˌfær- ~**s** z
seafaring 'si: ˌfeər ɪŋ ‖ -ˌfer ɪŋ -ˌfær-
seafood 'si: fu:d
Seaford (i) 'si:f əd ‖ -³rd, (ii) ˌsi: 'fɔ:d ‖ -'fɔ:rd
-'foʊrd —*Both (i) and (ii) are used for the*

S

place in East Sussex; the place in Long Island, NY is (i)

Seaforth 'si: fɔːθ ‖ -fɔːrθ -fouθ

seafront 'si: frʌnt ~s s

Seaga si 'ɑːg ə

seagirt 'si: gɜːt ‖ -gɜːt

seagoing 'si: ˌgəu ɪŋ ‖ -ˌgou ɪŋ

seagull 'si: gʌl ~s z

seahors|e 'si: hɔːs ‖ -hɔːrs **~es** ɪz əz

seakale 'si: keɪəl

seal, Seal si:əl **sealed** si:əld **sealing** 'si:əl ɪŋ **seals** si:əlz
  'sealing wax

sealant 'si:əl ənt ~s s

Seale si:əl

sealer 'si:əl ə ‖ -ər ~s z

Sealey 'si:l i

Sealink *tdmk* 'si: lɪŋk

sealskin 'si:əl skɪn

Sealyham 'si:l i ̩əm‖ -hæm **~s** z

seam si:m *(= seem)* **seamed** si:md **seaming** 'si:m ɪŋ **seams** si:mz

sea|man, S~ 'si: ˌmən **~men** mən men

seaman|like 'si: mən ‖laɪk **~ship** ʃɪp

Seamas 'ʃeɪm əs

seamen 'si: mən -men

seamer, S~ 'si:m ə ‖ -ər ~s z

seamless 'si:m ləs -lɪs **~ly** li **~ness** nəs nɪs

seamstress 'semʲs trəs 'si:mʲs-, -trɪs ‖ 'si:mʲs- **~es** ɪz əz

Seamus 'ʃeɪm əs

seam|y 'si:m i **~ier** i ə ‖ i ʲr **~iest** i ɪst i ̩əst **~iness** i nəs i nɪs

Sean ʃɔːn ‖ ʃɑːn —*Irish* Seán [ʃɑːn]

Seanad 'ʃæn əd -əð —*Irish* ['ʃa nəd]

seanc|e, séanc|e 'seɪ ɒ̃s -ɑːnᵗs, -ɒnᵗs ‖ -ɑːnᵗs —*Fr* [se ɑ̃ːs] **~es** ɪz əz

seaplane 'si: pleɪn **~s** z

seaport 'si: pɔːt ‖ -pɔːrt -pourt ~s s

sear sɪə ‖ sɪʲr **seared** sɪəd ‖ sɪʲrd **searing/ly** 'sɪər ɪŋ /li ‖ 'sɪr ɪŋ /li **sears** sɪəz ‖ sɪʲrz

search sɜːtʃ ‖ sɜːtʃ **searched** sɜːtʃt ‖ sɜːtʃt **searches** 'sɜːtʃ ɪz -əz ‖ 'sɜːtʃ əz **searching/ly** 'sɜːtʃ ɪŋ /li ‖ 'sɜːtʃ ɪŋ /li **'search ˌparty; 'search ˌwarrant**

searchlight 'sɜːtʃ laɪt ‖ 'sɜːtʃ- ~s s

Searcy *(i)* 'sɪəs i ‖ 'sɪrs i, *(ii)* 'sɜːs i ‖ 'sɜ·s i —*The place in AL is (ii)*

Searle sɜːl ‖ sɜ·l

Sears sɪəz ‖ sɪʲrz

Seascale 'si: skeɪəl

seascape 'si: skeɪp ~s s

seashell 'si: ʃel ~s z

seashore 'si: ʃɔː ‖ -ʃɔːr -ʃour ~s z

seasick 'si: sɪk

seasickness 'si: sɪk nəs -ˌsɪk-, -nɪs

seaside 'si: saɪd ̩•'•

season 'si:z ən **~ed** d **~ing** ˌɪŋ **~s** z
  'season ˌticket ‖ ̩•'••

seasonab|le 'si:z ən̩_əb |əl **~ly** li

seasonal 'si:z ən̩_əl **~ly** i

seasoning 'si:z ən̩ɪŋ **~s** z

seat si:t **seated** 'si:t ɪd -əd ‖ 'si:t̬ əd **seating** 'si:t ɪŋ ‖ 'si:t̬ ɪŋ **seats** si:ts
  'seat belt

SEAT *tdmk* 'seɪ æt -ət ‖ -ɑːt

-seater 'si:t ə ‖ 'si:t̬ ʲr — **three-seater** ̩θri: 'si:t ə ◂ ‖ -'si:t̬ ʲr ◂

Seathwaite 'si: θweɪt

seating 'si:t ɪŋ ‖ 'si:t̬ ɪŋ **~s** z

SEATO 'si:t əu ‖ -ou

Seaton 'si:t ən

Seattle si 'æt əl ‖ -'æt̬ əl

seawall ̩si: 'wɔːl '•• ‖ -'wɑːl ~s z

seaward 'si: wəd ‖ -wʲrd ~s z

seawater 'si: ˌwɔːt ə ‖ -ˌwɔːt̬ ʲr -ˌwɑːt̬-

seaway 'si: weɪ ~s z

seaweed 'si: wi:d

seaworth|y 'si: ˌwɜːð li i ‖ -ˌwɜ·ð li i **~iness** i nəs i nɪs

Seb seb

sebaceous sə 'beɪʃ əs sɪ-

Sebastian sə 'bæst i ̩ən sɪ- ‖ sə 'bæs tʃən

Sebastopol sə 'bæst ə pɒl sɪ-, -pəl ‖ -poul —*Russ* Sevastopol [sʲɪ vʌ 'sto pəlʲ]

Sebba 'seb ə

seborrhea, seborrhoea ̩seb ə 'ri: ̩ə

Sebring 'si:b rɪŋ

sebum 'si:b əm

sec sek

SECAM 'si: kæm

secant 'si:k ənt 'sek- ‖ -ænt ~s s

secateurs 'sek ət əz -ə tɜːz, ̩sek ə 'tɜːz ‖ ̩sek ə 'tɜ·z

Secaucus sɪ 'kɔːk əs sə- ‖ -'kɑːk-

secco 'sek əu ‖ -ou —*It* ['sek ko] ~s z

Seccotine *tdmk* 'sek ə ti:n

seced|e sɪ 'si:d sə- **~ed** ɪd əd **~es** z **~ing** ɪŋ

secession sɪ 'seʃ ən sə- **~ism** ̩ɪz əm **~ist/s** ɪst/s §əst/s ‖ əst/s **~s** z

sech *'hyperbolic secant'* seʃ setʃ, ʃek —*or as* sec h

Secker 'sek ə ‖ -ʲr

seclud|e sɪ 'klu:d sə- **~ed** ɪd əd **~es** z **~ing** ɪŋ

seclud|ed|ly sɪ 'klu:d ɪd |li -əd- **~ness** nəs nɪs

seclusion sɪ 'klu:ʒ ən sə-

seclusive sɪ 'klu:s ɪv sə-, §-'klu:z- **~ly** li **~ness** nəs nɪs

Secombe 'si:k əm

second *adj; n; pronoun; determiner; v 'support'* 'sek ənd △-ənt **~ed** ɪd əd **~ing** ɪŋ **~s** z
  ̩second 'best ◂; ̩second 'childhood; ̩second 'class; ̩Second 'Coming; ̩second 'cousin; 'second hand *(on a clock)*; at ̩second 'hand *'indirectly'* ; ̩second 'helping; ̩second lieu'tenant ◂; ̩second 'mortgage; ̩second 'nature; ̩second 'person ◂, ̩second ̩person 'plural; ̩second 'sight; ̩second 'thoughts; ̩second 'wind; ̩Second ̩World 'War

second *v 'move to special duty'* sɪ 'kɒnd sə- ‖ -'kɑːnd **~ed** ɪd əd **~ing** ɪŋ **~s** z

secondarily 'sek ənd_ʲr əl i, ̩•ən 'der əl i, '•••• ‖ ̩sek ən 'der əl i '••••

secondar|y 'sek ənd‿ər ‖i §-ən der- ‖ -ən der ‖i
  ~ies iz **~iness** i nəs i nɪs
  ˌsecondary 'modern; ˌsecondary 'accent,
  ˌsecondary 'stress
second-class ˌsek ənd 'klɑːs ◄ →-ŋ-, §-'klæs
  ‖ -'klæs ◄
  ˌsecond-class 'citizen
second-degree ˌsek ənd dɪ 'griː ◄ →ˌ•'ŋ-,
  -də'•, §-diː'•
  ˌsecond-deˌgree 'burn
seconder 'sek ənd ə ‖ -ər **~s** z
second-generation ˌsek ənd ˌdʒen ə 'reɪʃ ən ◄
  →ˌ•'ŋ-
  ˌsecond-geneˌration Au'stralian
second-guess ˌsek ənd 'ges →-ŋ- **~ed** t **~er/s**
  ə/z ‖ ər/z **~es** ɪz əz **~ing** ɪŋ
secondhand, second-hand *adj* ˌsek ənd
  'hænd ◄
  ˌsecond-hand 'furniture
second-in-command ˌsek ənd ɪn kə 'mɑːnd
  →-ɪŋ•'•, §-'mænd ‖ -'mænd **~s** z
secondly 'sek ənd li
secondment sɪ 'kɒnd mənt sə- ‖ -'kɑːnd- **~s** s
second|o se 'kɒnd ləʊ sɪ-, sə- ‖ sɪ 'koʊnd loʊ
  -'kɑːnd- **~i** iː
second-rate ˌsek ənd 'reɪt ◄ →-ŋ- **~ness** nəs
  nɪs
  ˌsecond-rate per'formance
second-rater ˌsek ənd 'reɪt ə ‖ -'reɪt ər **~s** z
second-string ˌsek ənd 'strɪŋ ◄ →-ŋ-
secrecy 'siːk rəs i -rɪs-
secret 'siːk rət -rɪt **~s** s
  ˌsecret 'agent; ˌsecret po'lice; ˌsecret
  'service
secretaire ˌsek rə 'teə -rɪ- ‖ -'teər **~s** z
secretarial ˌsek rə 'teər i‿əl ◄ ˌ•'rɪ- ‖ -'ter-
secretariat ˌsek rə 'teər i‿ət ˌ•rɪ-, -æt ‖ -'ter-
  ~s s
secretar|y 'sek rət‿ər ‖i '•rɪt, △'•jʊt‿,
  △'•ət‿; -rə ter ‖i, -rɪ••, △-ju••, △-ə••
  ‖ -rə ter ‖i △-ə•• **~ies** iz
secretary-general ˌsek rət‿ər i 'dʒen ər‿əl
  ˌ•rɪt‿, △ˌ•jʊt‿, △ˌ•ət‿; ˌ•rə ter i-, ˌ•rɪ-,
  △ˌ•ju-, △ˌ•ə-, ˌ•rə ter ə- **~s** z
secrete sɪ 'kriːt sə- **secreted** sɪ 'kriːt ɪd sə-,
  -əd; △'siːk rət-, △-rɪt- ‖ -'kriːt əd **secretes**
  sɪ 'kriːts sə- **secreting** sɪ 'kriːt ɪŋ sə-;
  △'siːk rət ɪŋ, △-rɪt- ‖ -'kriːt ɪŋ
secretion sɪ 'kriːʃ ən sə- **~s** z
secretive 'siːk rət ɪv -rɪt-; sɪ 'kriːt ɪv, sə-
  ‖ 'siːk rət̮ ɪv sɪ 'kriːt̮ ɪv **~ly** li **~ness** nəs nɪs
secretor|y sɪ 'kriːt‿ər ‖i sə- **~ies** iz
sect sekt **sects** sekts
sectarian sek 'teər i‿ən ‖ -'ter- **~ism** ˌɪz əm
  ~s z
sectar|y 'sekt ər ‖i **~ies** iz
section 'sek ʃən **~ed** d **~ing** ˌɪŋ **~s** z
sectional 'sek ʃən‿əl **~ly** i
sectionalis... —*see* **sectionaliz...**
sectionalism 'sek ʃən‿əl ˌɪz əm
sectionalization ˌsek ʃən‿əl aɪ 'zeɪʃ ən -ɪ'•-
  ‖ -ə'•-

sectionaliz|e 'sek ʃən‿ə laɪz **~ed** d **~es** ɪz əz
  ~ing ɪŋ
sector 'sekt ə ‖ -ər **~s** z
sectoral 'sekt ər əl
secular 'sek jʊl ə -jəl- ‖ -jəl ər **~ly** li **~s** z
secularis... —*see* **seculariz...**
secularism 'sek jʊl ə ˌrɪz əm -jəl ə- ‖ -jəl ə-
secularist 'sek jʊl ər ɪst -jəl ər-, §-əst ‖ -jəl ər-
secularity ˌsek ju 'lær ət i ˌ•jə-, -ɪt i
  ‖ -jə 'lær ət̮ i -'ler-
secularization ˌsek jʊl ər aɪ 'zeɪʃ ən ˌ•jəl-,
  -ɪ'•- ‖ -jəl ər ə-
seculariz|e 'sek jʊl ə raɪz -jəl ə- ‖ -jəl ə- **~ed**
  d **~es** ɪz əz **~ing** ɪŋ
secure sɪ 'kjʊə sə-, -'kjɔː ‖ -'kjʊər **~d** d **~s** z
  securing sɪ 'kjʊər ɪŋ sə-, -'kjɔːr- ‖ -'kjʊr ɪŋ
securely sɪ 'kjʊə li sə-, -'kjɔː- ‖ -'kjʊər li
Securicor *tdmk* sɪ 'kjʊər ɪ kɔː sə-, -'kjɔːr-, -ə-
  ‖ -'kjʊr ə kɔːr
securitis... —*see* **securitiz...**
securitization sɪ ˌkjʊər ɪt aɪ 'zeɪʃ ən sə-,
  -ˌkjɔːr-, -ˌ•ət-, -ɪ'•- ‖ -ˌkjʊr ət̮ ə-
securitiz|e sɪ 'kjʊər ɪ taɪz sə-, -'kjɔːr-, -ə-
  ‖ -'kjʊr ə taɪz **~ed** d **~es** ɪz əz **~ing** ɪŋ
securit|y sɪ 'kjʊər ət ‖i sə-, -'kjɔːr-, -ɪt i
  ‖ -'kjʊr ət̮ ‖i **~ies** iz
  se'curity ˌblanket; se'curity ˌclearance;
  Se'curity ˌCouncil; se'curity risk
Sedaka sə 'dɑːk ə sɪ-
sedan, Sedan sɪ 'dæn sə- —*Fr* [sə dɑ̃] **~s** z
  se,dan 'chair ‖ •'• •
sedate *adj, v* sɪ 'deɪt sə- **sedated** sɪ 'deɪt ɪd
  sə-, -əd ‖ -'deɪt̮ əd **~ly** li **~ness** nəs nɪs **~s** s
  sedating sɪ 'deɪt ɪŋ sə- ‖ -'deɪt̮ ɪŋ
sedation sɪ 'deɪʃ ən sə- **~s** z
sedative 'sed ət ɪv ‖ -ət̮ ɪv **~s** z
Sedbergh 'sed bə →'seb-, -bɜːg, 'sed bər‿ə
  ‖ -bɝːg
Seddon 'sed ən
sedentarily 'sed ənt‿ər əl i 'sed ən ter əl i, -ɪ li,
  ˌ••'•••; §sɪ 'dent‿, sə- ‖ ˌsed ən 'ter əl i
sedentar|y 'sed ənt‿ər ‖i §-ən ter li; §sɪ 'dent
  ər ‖i, §sə- ‖ -ən ter li **~iness** i nəs i nɪs
Seder 'seɪd ə ‖ -ər
sedge sedʒ **sedges** 'sedʒ ɪz -əz
Sedgefield 'sedʒ fiːəld
Sedgemoor 'sedʒ mɔː -mʊə ‖ -mʊr
Sedgewick, Sedgwick 'sedʒ wɪk
sedgy 'sedʒ i
sedilia sɪ 'dɪl i‿ə -'diːl-, -'daɪl-
sediment 'sed ɪ mənt -ə- **~s** s
sedimentary ˌsed ɪ 'ment‿ər i ◄ ˌ•ə-
  ‖ -'ment̮ ər i ◄ →-'mentr i
sedimentation ˌsed ɪ men 'teɪʃ ən ˌ•ə-,
  -mən'•-
sedition sɪ 'dɪʃ ən sə-
seditious sɪ 'dɪʃ əs sə- **~ly** li **~ness** nəs nɪs
Sedlescombe 'sed əlz kəm
Sedley 'sed li
seduc|e sɪ 'djuːs sə-, →§-'dʒuːs ‖ -'duːs -'djuːs
  ~ed t **~er/s** ə/z ‖ -ər/z **~es** ɪz əz **~ing** ɪŋ
seduction sɪ 'dʌk ʃən sə- **~s** z
seductive sɪ 'dʌkt ɪv sə- **~ly** li **~ness** nəs nɪs

S

S

seductress sɪ 'dʌk trəs sə-, -trɪs **~es** ɪz əz
sedulity sɪ 'djuːl ət i sə-, →§-'dʒuːl-, -ɪt-
  ‖ -'duːl ət̬ i -'djuːl-
sedulous 'sed jʊl əs §-jəl-; 'sedʒ ʊl-
  ‖ 'sedʒ əl əs **~ly** li **~ness** nəs nɪs
sedum 'siːd əm **~s** z
see siː **saw** sɔː ‖ sɑː **seeing** 'siː ɪŋ **seen** siːn
  sees siːz
  ˌSeeing 'Eye dog
Seear 'siːˌə ‖ _ər
Seebeck 'siː bek —Ger ['zeː bɛk]
  'Seebeck efˌfect
seed, Seed siːd **seeded** 'siːd ɪd -əd **seeding**
  'siːd ɪŋ **seeds** siːdz
seedbed 'siːd bed →'siːb- **~s** z
seedcake 'siːd keɪk →'siːg- **~s** s
seedcorn 'siːd kɔːn →'siːg- ‖ -kɔːrn
seed-eater 'siːd ˌiːt ə ‖ -ˌiːt̬ ər **~s** z
seeder 'siːd ə ‖ -ər **~s** z
seedless 'siːd ləs -lɪs
seedling 'siːd lɪŋ **~s** z
seeds|man 'siːdz |mən **~men** mən men
seedtime 'siːd taɪm **~s** z
seed|ly 'siːd li **~ier** iˌə ‖ iˌər **~iest** iˌɪst iˌəst
  ~ily ɪ li əl i **~iness** i nəs i nɪs
Seeger 'siːg ə ‖ -ər
seek siːk **seeking** 'siːk ɪŋ **seeks** siːks **sought**
  sɔːt ‖ sɑːt
seeker 'siːk ə ‖ -ər **~s** z
Seeley, Seely 'siːl i
seem siːm **seemed** siːmd **seeming/ly**
  'siːm ɪŋ /li **seems** siːmz
seem|ly 'siːm |li **~lier** liˌə ‖ liˌər **~liest** liˌɪst
  liˌəst **~liness** li nəs li nɪs
seen siːn
seep siːp **seeped** siːpt **seeping** 'siːp ɪŋ
  seeps siːps
seepag|e 'siːp ɪdʒ **~es** ɪz əz
seer sɪə 'siːˌə ‖ sɪər 'siː ˈr **seers** sɪəz 'siːˌəz
  ‖ sɪərz 'siː rz
seersucker 'sɪə ˌsʌk ə ‖ 'sɪr ˌsʌk ər
seesaw 'siː sɔː ‖ -sɑː **~ed** d **seesawing**
  'siː sɔːr ɪŋ ‖ -sɔː ɪŋ -sɑː- **~s** z
seethe siːð **seethed** siːðd **seethes** siːðz
  seething 'siːð ɪŋ
see-through 'siː θruː
Seferis se 'feər ɪs sɪ-, sə-, §-əs —Greek [sɛ 'fɛ
  rɪs]
Sefton 'seft ən
Sega tdmk 'siːg ə 'seɪg ə
Segal 'siːg əl
Seggie 'seg i
segment n 'seg mənt **~s** s
seg|ment v ₍ᵢ₎seg |'ment sɪg-, səg- ‖ ' • •
  ~mented ment ɪd -əd ‖ ment̬ əd **~menting**
  ment ɪŋ ‖ ment̬ ɪŋ **~ments** ments
segmental seg 'ment əl sɪg-, səg- ‖ -'ment̬-
  ~ly i **~s** z
segmentation ˌseg men 'teɪʃ ən -mən- **~s** s
segno 'seg nəʊ 'sen jəʊ, 'seɪn- ‖ 'seɪn joʊ —It
  ['seɲ ɲo]
sego 'siːg əʊ ‖ -oʊ **~s** z
  ˌsego 'lily

Segovia sɪ 'gəʊv iˌə sə-, se- ‖ -'goʊv- —Sp
  [se 'ɣo βja]
Segrave 'siː greɪv
segre|gate 'seg rɪ |geɪt -rə- **~gated** geɪt ɪd
  -əd ‖ geɪt̬ əd **~gates** geɪts **~gating**
  geɪt ɪŋ ‖ geɪt̬ ɪŋ
segregation ˌseg rɪ 'geɪʃ ən -rə- **~ist/s** ɪst/s
  §əst/s ‖ əst/s
segue 'seg weɪ 'seɪg-, -wi —It ['seː gwe] **~d** d
  ~ing ɪŋ **~s** z
seguidilla ˌseg i 'diːl jə -'diː- —Sp [se ɣi 'ði ʎa,
  -ja] **~s** z
sei seɪ (= say)
  'sei whale
seiche seɪʃ **seiches** 'seɪʃ ɪz -əz
Seidlitz 'sed lɪts §-ləts
Seifert 'siːf ət ‖ -ərt
seigneur sen 'jɜː seɪn-; 'seɪn jə ‖ seɪn 'jɝː
  siːn- —Fr [sɛ njœːʁ] **~s** z
seigneurial sen 'jɜːr iˌəl seɪn- ‖ seɪn 'jɝː-
  -'jʊr-
seignior 'seɪn jə ‖ -jɔːr • ' • **~s** z
seigniorage 'seɪn jər ɪdʒ
seigniorial ₍ᵢ₎seɪn 'jɔːr iˌəl ‖ -'joʊr-
seignior|y 'seɪn jər |i **~ies** iz
Seiko tdmk 'seɪk əʊ 'siːk- ‖ -oʊ —Jp [se,i koo,
  se,e-]
seine, Seine seɪn —Fr [sɛn] **seined** seɪnd
  seines seɪnz **seining** 'seɪn ɪŋ
  'seine net
Seinfeld 'saɪn feld
Seiriol 'saɪˈr i ɒl ˌəl ‖ -aːl -ɔːl —Welsh
  ['səɪr jɔl]
seise siːz (= seize, sees, seas) **seised** siːzd
seisin 'siːz ɪn §-ən
seismic 'saɪz mɪk **~ally** ᵊl_i
seismicity ₍ᵢ₎saɪz 'mɪs ət i -ɪt i ‖ -ət̬ i
seismograph 'saɪz mə grɑːf -græf ‖ -græf **~s** s
seismographic ˌsaɪz mə 'græf ɪk ◄ **~ally** ᵊl_i
seismography saɪz 'mɒg rəf i ‖ -'mɑːg-
seismologist saɪz 'mɒl ədʒ ɪst -əst ‖ -'mɑːl-
  ~s s
seismology saɪz 'mɒl ədʒ i ‖ -'mɑːl-
seismometer ₍ᵢ₎saɪz 'mɒm ɪt ə -ət ə
  ‖ -'mɑːm ət̬ ər **~s** z
seize siːz (= sees, seas) **seized** siːzd **seizes**
  'siːz ɪz -əz **seizing** 'siːz ɪŋ
seizure 'siːʒ ə 'siːz jə ‖ -ər **~s** z
sejant 'siːdʒ ənt
Sejanus sɪ 'dʒeɪn əs sə-
selah, Selah 'siːl ə -aː
Selangor sə 'læŋ ə sɪ-, -ɔː ‖ -ər -'lɑːŋ-, -ɔːr,
  -gɔːr
Selassie sə 'læs i sɪ- ‖ -'lɑːs i
Selborne, Selbourne 'sel bɔːn ‖ -bɔːrn -boʊrn
Selby 'sel bi
Selden 'seld ən
seldom 'seld əm
select sə 'lekt sɪ- **~ed** ɪd əd **~ing** ɪŋ **~ness**
  nəs nɪs **~s** s
  seˌlect comˈmittee
selectee sə ˌlek 'tiː sɪ- **~s** z
selection sə 'lek ʃᵊn sɪ- **~s** z

selective sə 'lekt ɪv sɪ- ~ly li ~ness nəs nɪs
selectivity sə ‚lek 'tɪv ət i sɪ-, ‚sɪl ek-, ‚si:l ek-,
‚sel ek-, -ɪt i ‖ -əṭ i
selector sə 'lekt ə sɪ- ‖ -ər ~s z
Selena sə 'li:n ə sɪ-
Selene sə 'li:n i sɪ-
selenic sə 'li:n ik sɪ-, -'len-
selenite 'sel ə naɪt -ɪ-
selenium sə 'li:n i‿əm
seleno- comb. form
  with stress-neutral suffix sə ‚li:n əʊ sɪ- ‖ -oʊ -ə
  — selenographic sə ‚li:n əʊ
  'græf ɪk ◄ ‖ -oʊ- -ə-
  with stress-imposing suffix ‚si:l ə 'nɒ+ -ɪ-
  ‖ ‚sel ə 'nɑ:+ — selenology ‚si:l ə 'nɒl ədʒ i
  -ɪ- ‖ ‚sel ə 'nɑ:l-
Seles 'sel ez -əs —Serbian Seleš ['sɛ lɛʃ]
Seleucia sə 'lu:s i‿ə sɪ-, -'lu:ʃ-, -'lju:s-, -'lju:ʃ-
Seleucid sə 'lu:s ɪd sɪ-, -'lju:s-, §-əd ~s z
Seleucus sə 'lu:k əs sɪ-, -'lju:k-
self, Self self selves selvz
self- ‚self —Words with this prefix normally have
  late stress. — self-abasement
  ‚self ə 'beɪs mənt
self-abnegation ‚self ‚æb nɪ 'geɪʃ ᵊn -ne'•-,
  -nə'•-
self-absorbed ‚self əb 'sɔ:bd ◄ -æb-, -'zɔ:bd
  ‖ -'sɔ:rbd ◄ -'zɔ:rbd
self-acting ‚self 'ækt ɪŋ ◄
self-addressed ‚self ə 'drest ◄
self-appointed ‚self ə 'pɔɪnt ɪd ◄ -əd
  ‖ -'pɔɪnṭ əd ◄
self-assembly ‚self ə 'sem bli
self-assertion ‚self ə 'sɜ:ʃ ᵊn ‖ -'sɜ:ʃ ᵊn
self-assertive ‚self ə 'sɜ:t ɪv ‖ -'sɜ:ṭ ɪv ~ly li
  ~ness nəs nɪs
self-assurance ‚self ə 'ʃɔ:r ᵊnᵗs -'ʃʊər-
  ‖ -'ʃʊr ᵊnᵗs -'ʃɝ:-
self-assured ‚self ə 'ʃɔ:d ◄ -'ʃʊəd ‖ -'ʃʊᵊrd ◄
  -'ʃɝ:d
self-catering ‚self 'keɪt‿ər ɪŋ ‖ -'keɪṭ-
self-centered, self-centred
  ‚self 'sent əd ‖ -'senṭ ᵊrd ~ly li ~ness nəs
  nɪs
self-command ‚self kə 'mɑ:nd §-'mænd
  ‖ -'mænd
self-confessed ‚self kən 'fest ◄ §-kɒn-
  ‚self-con‚fessed 'liar
self-confid|ence ‚self 'kɒn fɪd ᵊnᵗs §-fəd-
  ‖ -'kɑ:n- ~ent/ly ᵊnt /li
self-congratulatory ‚self kən ‚grætʃ u 'leɪt
  ər i ◄ →‚•kəŋ-, §,•kɒn-, -,•ə-, -,græt ju-;
  ,••'••lət‿ər i ‖ ‚self kən 'grætʃ əl‿ə tɔ:r i
  ⚠-'grædʒ-, -tour i
self-conscious ‚self 'kɒnᵗʃ əs ◄ ‖ -'kɑ:nᵗʃ əs ◄
  ~ly li ~ness nəs nɪs
self-contained ‚self kən 'teɪnd ◄ §-kɒn-
self-contradictory ‚self ‚kɒntr ə 'dɪkt ər‿i
  ‖ -‚kɑ:ntr-
self-control ‚self kən 'trəʊl §-kɒn-, →-'trɒʊl
  ‖ -'troʊl ~led d
self-defeating ‚self dɪ 'fi:t ɪŋ ◄ -də-, §-di:-
  ‖ -'fi:ṭ ɪŋ ◄

self-defence, self-defense ‚self dɪ 'fenᵗs -də-
self-denial ‚self dɪ 'naɪ‿əl -də-, §-di:- ~s z
self-destruct ‚self dɪ 'strʌkt -də-, §-di:- ~ed ɪd
  əd ~ing ɪŋ ~s s
self-destruction ‚self dɪ 'strʌk ʃᵊn -də-, §-di:-
self-destructive ‚self dɪ 'strʌkt ɪv ◄ -də-, §-di:-
  ~ly li ~ness nəs nɪs
self-determination ‚self dɪ ‚tɜ:m ɪ 'neɪʃ ᵊn
  ,•də-, §,•di:-, -ə'•- ‖ -,tɝ:m-
self-discipline ‚self 'dɪs ə plɪn -ɪ-, §,•dɪ 'sɪp lɪn
  ~d d ◄
self-|doubt ‚self |'daʊt ~doubting
  'daʊt ɪŋ ‖ 'daʊṭ ɪŋ
self-drive ‚self 'draɪv ◄
self-educated ‚self 'ed ju keɪt ɪd ◄ -'edʒ u-,
  §-'edʒ ə- ‖ -'edʒ ə keɪṭ əd ◄
self-effac|ement ‚self ɪ 'feɪs |mənt -ə- ~ing
  ɪŋ ◄
self-em|ployed ‚self ɪm |'plɔɪd ◄ §-əm-
  ~ployment 'plɔɪ mənt
self-esteem ‚self ɪ 'sti:m §-ə-
self-evident ‚self 'ev ɪd ᵊnt ◄ -əd-, §-ə dent
  ~ly li
self-examination ‚self ɪg ‚zæm ɪ 'neɪʃ ᵊn ,•eg-,
  ,•əg-, ,•ɪk-, ,•ek-, ,•ək-, -ə'•-
self-explanatory ‚self ɪk 'splæn ət‿ər i ◄ ,•ek-,
  ,•ək- ‖ -ə tɔ:r i -tour i
self-expression ‚self ɪk 'spreʃ ᵊn -ek-, -ək-
self-fulfilling ‚self fʊl 'fɪl ɪŋ ◄
  ‚self-ful‚filling 'prophecy
self-government ‚self 'gʌv ᵊn mənt →-ᵊm-
  ‖ -ᵊrn-
selfheal 'self hi:ᵊl ~s z
self-help ‚self 'help
selfhood 'self hʊd
self-imag|e ‚self 'ɪm ɪdʒ ~es ɪz əz
self-import|ance ‚self ɪm 'pɔ:t ᵊnᵗs
  ‖ -'pɔ:rt ᵊnᵗs ~ant/ly ᵊnt /li
self-imposed ‚self ɪm 'pəʊzd ◄ ‖ -'poʊzd ◄
  ‚self-im‚posed 'task
self-indulg|ence ‚self ɪn 'dʌldʒ ᵊnᵗs ~ent/ly
  ᵊnt /li
self-interest ‚self 'ɪntr əst -ɪst, -est;
  'ɪnt ə rest ‖ 'ɪnṭ ə rest ~ed ɪd əd
selfish 'self ɪʃ ~ly li ~ness nəs nɪs
self-knowledge ‚self 'nɒl ɪdʒ ‖ -'nɑ:l-
selfless 'self ləs -lɪs ~ly li ~ness nəs nɪs
self-locking ‚self 'lɒk ɪŋ ◄ ‖ -'lɑ:k ɪŋ ◄
self-made ‚self 'meɪd ◄
  ‚self-made 'man
self-pity ‚self 'pɪt i ‖ -'pɪṭ i ~ing/ly ɪŋ /li
self-possessed ‚self pə 'zest ◄ ~ly li
self-possession ‚self pə 'zeʃ ᵊn
self-preservation ‚self ‚prez ə 'veɪʃ ᵊn ‖ -ᵊr-
self-raising ‚self 'reɪz ɪŋ
  ‚self-'raising ‚flour, ,•'•• '••
self-reli|ance ‚self rɪ 'laɪ‿ᵊnᵗs -rə-, §-ri:-
  ~ant/ly ᵊnt /li
self-respect ‚self rɪ 'spekt -rə-, §-ri:- ~ing ɪŋ ◄
Selfridg|e 'self rɪdʒ ~es ɪz əz
self-righteous ‚self 'raɪtʃ əs ◄ -'raɪt i‿əs ~ly li
  ~ness nəs nɪs
self-rising ‚self 'raɪz ɪŋ ◄

self-rule ˌself 'ruːl
self-sacrific|e ˌself 'sæk rɪ faɪs -rə- **~ing** ɪŋ
selfsame 'self seɪm ˌ•'•
self-satisfied ˌself 'sæt ɪs faɪd ◂ -əs- ‖ -'sæt̬ əs-
self-seek|er/s ˌself 'siːk |ə/z ‖ -|ᵊr/z **~ing** ɪŋ ◂
self-service ˌself 'sɜːv ɪs ◂ §-əs ‖ -'sɝːv əs ◂
self-starter ˌself 'stɑːt ə ‖ -'stɑːrt̬ ᵊr **~s** z
self-styled ˌself 'staɪᵊld ◂
self-suffici|ency ˌself sə 'fɪʃ |ᵊnˢts i **~ent/ly**
  ᵊnt /li
self-supporting ˌself sə 'pɔːt ɪŋ ‖ -'pɔːrt̬ ɪŋ
  -'pʊərt̬-
self-will ˌself 'wɪl **~ed** d ◂
self-winding ˌself 'waɪnd ɪŋ ◂
Selhurst 'sel hɜːst ‖ -hɝːst
Seligman, Seligmann 'sel ɪg mən
Selina sə 'liːn ə sɪ-
Seljuk ˌsel 'dʒuːk '••
Selkirk 'sel kɜːk ‖ -kɝːk
sell sel **selling** 'sel ɪŋ **sells** selz **sold** səʊld
  →sɒʊld ‖ soʊld
  'selling point
Sellafield 'sel ə fiːᵊld
Sellar 'sel ə ‖ -ᵊr
Sellars 'sel əz ‖ -ᵊrz
sell-by date 'sel baɪ deɪt
seller 'sel ə ‖ -ᵊr **~s** z
  ˌseller's 'market
Sellers 'sel əz ‖ -ᵊrz
Sellick 'sel ɪk
Sellinge 'sel ɪndʒ
sellotap|e, S~ tdmk 'sel əʊ teɪp ‖ -ə- **~ed** t **~es**
  s **~ing** ɪŋ
sell-out 'sel aʊt **~s** s
Selly 'sel i
Selma 'selm ə
Selous sə 'luː
Selsey 'sels i
seltzer, S~ 'selts ə ‖ -ᵊr **~s** z
selvag|e, selvedg|e 'selv ɪdʒ **~es** ɪz əz
selves selvz
Selwyn 'sel wɪn
Selznick 'selz nɪk
semanteme sə 'mænt iːm sɪ- **~s** z
semantic sə 'mænt ɪk sɪ- ‖ -'mænt̬ ɪk **~ally** ᵊl̩i
  ~s s
semantician ˌsem ən 'tɪʃ ᵊn sɪ- **~s** z
semanticist sə 'mænt əs ɪst sɪ-, -ɪs-, §-əst
  ‖ -'mænt̬- **~s** s
semaphore 'sem ə fɔː ‖ -fɔːr -foʊr **~d** d **~s** z
  semaphoring 'sem ə fɔːr ɪŋ ‖ -foʊr ɪŋ
semaphoric ˌsem ə 'fɒr ɪk ◂ ‖ -'fɔːr ɪk ◂ -'fɑːr-
  ~ally ᵊl̩i
semasiology sə ˌmeɪz i 'ɒl ədʒ i sɪ-, -ˌmeɪs-
  ‖ -'ɑːl-
sematic sə 'mæt ɪk sɪ- ‖ -'mæt̬ ɪk
semblanc|e 'sem blənˢts **~es** ɪz əz
semeio... —see **semio...**
Semele 'sem əl i -ɪl-; -ə leɪ
sememe 'siːm iːm **~s** z
semen 'siːm ən -en (= seamen)
Semer Water 'sem ə ˌwɔːt ə ‖ -ᵊr ˌwɔːt̬ ᵊr
  -ˌwɑːt̬-

semester sə 'mest ə sɪ- ‖ -ᵊr **~s** z

SEMI

■-i ▢-aɪ

AmE 1993

0 20 40 60 80 100%

semi 'sem i ‖ -aɪ **~s** z
semi- ˌsem i ‖ -aɪ —Words with this prefix mostly
  have late stress; certain exceptions are found in
  the list below. —AmE 1993 poll panel
  preference: -i 60%, -aɪ 40%. — **semiblind**
  ˌsem i 'blaɪnd ◂ ‖ -aɪ-
semiautomatic
  ˌsem i ˌɔːt ə 'mæt ɪk ◂ ‖ -ˌɔːt̬ ə 'mæt̬ ɪk ◂
  ˌ•aɪ- **~ally** ᵊl̩i
semibreve 'sem i briːv ‖ -aɪ-, -brev **~s** z
semicircle 'sem i ˌsɜːk ᵊl ‖ -ˌsɝːk ᵊl **~s** z
semicircular ˌsem i 'sɜːk jʊl ə ◂ -jəl ə
  ‖ -'sɝːk jəl ᵊr ◂
semicolon ˌsem i 'kəʊl ən -ɒn, '••ˌ••
  ‖ 'sem i ˌkoʊl ən **~s** z
semiconduct|ing ˌsem i kən 'dʌkt ɪŋ
  §-kɒn'•- ‖ ˌ•aɪ- **~or/s** ə/z ‖ -ᵊr/z
semidetached ˌsem i dɪ 'tætʃt ◂ -də'•,
  §-diː'•' ‖ ˌ•aɪ-
  ˌsemide̩tached 'bungalow
semifinal ˌsem i 'faɪn ᵊl ◂ ‖ -aɪ- **~s** z
semifinalist ˌsem i 'faɪn ᵊl ɪst §-əst ‖ ˌ•aɪ- **~s** s
semillon, S~ 'sem i ɒ̃ 'seɪm- ‖ ˌ•'i 'joʊn —Fr
  Sémillon [se mi jɔ̃]
seminal 'sem ɪn ᵊl 'siːm-, -ən- **~ly** i
seminar 'sem ɪ nɑː -ə- ‖ -nɑːr **~s** z
seminarian ˌsem ɪ 'neər i_ən ˌ•ə- ‖ -'ner- **~s** z
seminarist 'sem ɪn ər ɪst '•ən-, §-əst **~s** s
seminar|y 'sem ɪn ər_i '•ən- ‖ -ə ner li **~ies** iz
Seminole 'sem ɪ nəʊl -ə-, →-nɒʊl ‖ -noʊl **~s** z
semiolog|ist/s ˌsem i 'ɒl ədʒ |ɪst/s ˌsiːm-,
  §-əst/s ‖ -'ɑːl- ˌ•aɪ- **~y** i
semiology ˌsem i 'ɒl ədʒ i ˌsiːm- ‖ -'ɑːl- ˌ•aɪ-
semiotic ˌsem i 'ɒt ɪk ◂ ˌsiːm- ‖ -'ɑːt̬ ɪk ◂ -aɪ-
  ~s s
semiotician ˌsem i_ə 'tɪʃ ᵊn ˌsiːm- **~s** z
Semipalatinsk ˌsem i pə 'læt ɪnsk ‖ -'lɑːt-
  —Russ [sʲɪ mʲi pə 'ɫa tʲinsk]
semiprecious ˌsem i 'preʃ əs ◂ -aɪ-
semiprofessional ˌsem i prə 'feʃ ᵊn_əl ◂ ˌ•aɪ-
  ~s z
semiquaver 'sem i ˌkweɪv ə ‖ -ᵊr -aɪ- **~s** z
Semiramide ˌsem i 'rɑːm ɪd i -əd i; -ɪ deɪ
Semiramis sə 'mɪr ə mɪs sɪ-, se-, §-əm əs
semiskilled ˌsem ɪ 'skɪld ◂ ‖ -aɪ-
Semite 'siːm aɪt 'sem- ‖ 'sem aɪt **~s** s
Semitic sə 'mɪt ɪk sɪ- ‖ -'mɪt̬ ɪk **~s** s
semitone 'sem ɪ təʊn -toʊn -aɪ- **~s** z
semitropical ˌsem i 'trɒp ɪk ᵊl ◂ ‖ -'trɑːp- ˌ•aɪ-
semivocalic ˌsem i vəʊ 'kæl ɪk ◂ ‖ -voʊ'•-
semivowel 'sem i ˌvaʊ_əl '••ˌvaʊl **~s** z
semiweek|ly ˌsem i 'wiːk |li ◂ ‖ -aɪ- **~lies** liz
semolina ˌsem ə 'liːn ə
  ˌsemo̩lina 'pudding
Semper, s~ 'semp ə ‖ -ᵊr
sempiternal ˌsemp ɪ 'tɜːn ᵊl ◂ -ə- ‖ -'tɝːn ᵊl ◂
  ~ly i

S

Semple 'semp əl
semplice 'semp lɪtʃ i -lɪ tʃeɪ —*It* ['sem pli tʃe]
sempre 'semp ri -reɪ —*It* ['sɛm pre]
sempstress 'sem*p*s trəs -trɪs **~es** ɪz əz
Semtex *tdmk* 'sem teks
SEN ˌes iː 'en **~s** z
sen *unit of currency* sen
Sen., sen. —*see* **senator, senior**
senary 'siːn ər i 'sen-
senate, S~ 'sen ət -ɪt **~s** s
senator, S~ 'sen ət ə ‖ -ət ər —*In AmE, as a title
    also* 'sent ər **~s** z
senatorial ˌsen ə 'tɔːr i‿əl ◀ ‖ -'toʊr- **~ly** i
send, Send send **sending** 'send ɪŋ **sends**
    sendz **sent** sent
Sendai 'send aɪ —*Jp* ['sen daɪ]
Sendak 'send æk
sender 'send ə ‖ -ər **~s** z
send-off 'send ɒf -ɔːf ‖ -ɔːf -ɑːf **~s** s
send-up 'send ʌp **~s** s
Senec|a 'sen ɪk ‿ə -ək- **~an** ən **~as** əz
    ˌSeneca 'Falls; ˌSeneca 'Lake
Senegal ˌsen ɪ 'gɔːl -ə-, -'gɑːl
Senegalese ˌsen ɪg ə 'liːz ◀ -ɔː' •
Senegambia ˌsen ɪ 'gæm bi‿ə ˌ•ə-
senescence sɪ 'nes ᵊnts sə-
senescent sɪ 'nes ᵊnt sə-
seneschal 'sen ɪʃ əl -əʃ-; -ɪ ʃɑːl, -ə- **~s** z
Senghenydd seŋ 'hen ɪð
Senhor, s~ sen 'jɔː ‖ seɪn 'jɔːr —*Port* [sɪ 'ɲor]
Senhora, s~ sen 'jɔːr ə ‖ seɪn- -'joʊr- —*Port*
    [sɪ 'ɲo rɐ]
Senhorita, s~ ˌsen jɔː 'riːt ə -jə-
    ‖ ˌseɪn jə 'riːt̮ ə —*Port* [sɪ ɲo 'ri tɐ] **~s** z
senile 'siːn aɪᵊl ‖ 'sen-, -ᵊl **~ly** li
senility sə 'nɪl ət i sɪ-, -ɪt- ‖ -ət̮ i
senior, S~ 'siːn i‿ə ‖ 'siːn jᵊr **~s** z
    ˌsenior 'citizen
seniorit|y ˌsiːn i 'ɒr ət i -ɪt i ‖ siːn 'jɔːr ət̮ i
    -'jɑːr- **~ies** iz
Senlac 'sen læk
senna 'sen ə
Sennacherib se 'næk ər ɪb sə-, sɪ-, §-əb
sennet 'sen ɪt §-ət **~s** s
Sennett 'sen ɪt §-ət
sennight, se'nnight 'sen aɪt **~s** s
Senor, Señor, s~ sen 'jɔː ‖ seɪn 'jɔːr —*Sp*
    [se 'ɲor]
Senora, Señora, s~ sen 'jɔːr ə ‖ seɪn- -'joʊr-
    —*Sp* [se 'ɲo ra]
Senorita, Señorita, s~ ˌsen jɔː 'riːt ə -jə-
    ‖ ˌseɪn jə 'riːt̮ ə —*Sp* [se ɲo 'ri ta] **~s** z
sensate 'sen*t*s eɪt -ət, -ɪt
sensation sen 'seɪʃ ᵊn sᵊn- **~s** z
sensational sen 'seɪʃ ᵊn‿əl sᵊn- **~ly** i
sensationalis|e, sensationaliz|e sen 'seɪʃ ᵊn‿ə
    laɪz sᵊn- **~ed** d **~es** ɪz əz **~ing** ɪŋ
sensational|ism sen 'seɪʃ ᵊn‿əl‖, ˌɪz əm sᵊn-
    ~ist/s ɪst/s §əst/s ‖ əst/s
sense sen*t*s **sensed** sen*t*st **senses** 'sen*t*s ɪz -əz
    sensing 'sen*t*s ɪŋ
    'sense ˌorgan
senseless 'sen*t*s ləs -lɪs **~ly** li **~ness** nəs nɪs

sensibilit|y ˌsen*t*s ə 'bɪl ət li ˌ•ɪ-, -ɪt i ‖ -ət̮ li
    ~ies iz
sensib|le 'sen*t*s əb |ᵊl -ɪb- **~leness** ᵊl nəs -nɪs
    ~ly li
Sensimetrics *tdmk* ˌsen*t*s ɪ 'metr ɪks -ə-
sensitis... —*see* **sensitiz...**
sensitive 'sen*t*s ət ɪv -ɪt- ‖ -ət̮ ɪv **~ly** li **~ness**
    nəs nɪs **~s** z
sensitivit|y ˌsen*t*s ə 'tɪv ət li ˌ•ɪ-, -ɪt i ‖ -ət̮ li
    ~ies iz
sensitization ˌsen*t*s ət aɪ 'zeɪʃ ᵊn, ˌ•ɪt-, -ɪ' •-
    ‖ -ət̮ ə- **~s** z
sensitiz|e 'sen*t*s ə taɪz -ɪ- **~ed** d **~es** ɪz əz
    ~ing ɪŋ
Sensodyne *tdmk* 'sen*t*s əʊ daɪn ‖ -ə-
sensor 'sen*t*s ə ‖ -ᵊr (= *censor*) **~s** z
sensorimotor ˌsen*t*s ər‿i 'məʊt ə ◀
    ‖ -'moʊt̮ ᵊr ◀
sensory 'sen*t*s ər‿i
sensual 'sen*t*s ju‿əl 'sentʃ u‿əl ‖ 'sentʃ u‿əl
    'sentʃ əl **~ism** ˌɪz əm **~ist/s** ɪst/s §əst/s
    ‖ əst/s **~ly** i
sensualit|y ˌsen*t*s ju 'æl ət li ˌsentʃ u-, -ɪt i
    ‖ ˌsentʃ u 'æl ət̮ i **~ies** iz
sensuous 'sen*t*s ju‿əs 'sentʃ u‿əs ‖ 'sentʃ u‿əs
    ~ly li **~ness** nəs nɪs
sent sent
sentenc|e 'sent ᵊn*t*s ‖ -ᵊn*t*s **~ed** t **~es** ɪz əz
    ~ing ɪŋ
    'sentence ˌstructure
sentential sen 'tentʃ ᵊl **~ly** i
sententious sen 'tentʃ əs **~ly** li **~ness** nəs nɪs
sentience 'sentʃ ᵊn*t*s 'sentʃ i‿ᵊn*t*s;
    'sent i‿ᵊn*t*s ‖ 'sentʃ i‿ᵊn*t*s
sentient 'sentʃ ᵊnt 'sentʃ i‿ᵊnt;
    'sent i‿ᵊnt ‖ 'sentʃ i‿ᵊnt **~ly** li **~s** s
sentiment 'sent ɪ mənt -ə- ‖ 'sent̮ ə- **~s** s
sentimental ˌsent ɪ 'ment ᵊl ◀ -ə-
    ‖ ˌsent̮ ə 'ment̮ ᵊl ◀
sentimentalis... —*see* **sentimentaliz...**
sentimentalism ˌsent ɪ 'ment ə ˌlɪz əm ˌ•ə-,
    -ᵊl ˌɪz- ‖ ˌsent̮ ə 'ment̮ ᵊl ˌɪz əm
sentimentalist ˌsent ɪ 'ment ᵊl ɪst ˌ•ə-
    ‖ ˌsent̮ ə 'ment̮- **~s** s
sentimentality ˌsent ɪ men 'tæl ət i ˌ•ə-,
    -mən' •-, -ɪt i ‖ ˌsent̮ ə men 'tæl ət̮ i -mən' •-
sentimentalization ˌsent ɪ ˌment əl aɪ 'zeɪʃ ᵊn
    ˌ•ə-, -ɪ' •- ‖ ˌsent̮ ə ˌment̮ ᵊl ə-
sentimentaliz|e ˌsent ɪ 'ment ə laɪz ˌ•ə-, -ᵊl aɪz
    ‖ ˌsent̮ ə 'ment̮ ᵊl aɪz **~ed** d **~es** ɪz əz **~ing**
    ɪŋ
sentimentally ˌsent ɪ 'ment ᵊl i ˌ•ə-
    ‖ ˌsent̮ ə 'ment̮ ᵊl i
sentinel 'sent ɪn ᵊl -ən- ‖ 'sent̮ ᵊn‿əl **~s** z
sentr|y 'sentr li **~ies** iz
    'sentry box
sentry-go 'sentr i gəʊ ‖ -goʊ
senza 'sen*t*s ə -aː: —*It* ['sent tsa]
Seonaid ʃə 'neɪd —*ScG* ['ʃo nɪdʒ]
Seoul səʊl →sɒʊl ‖ soʊl —*Korean* ['sə ul]
sepal 'sep ᵊl 'siːp- **~s** z
-sepalous 'sep əl əs — polysepalous
    ˌpɒl i 'sep əl əs ◀ ‖ ˌpɑːl-

-sepaly 'sep əl i — **polysepaly** ˌpɒl i 'sep əl i
‖ ˌpɑːl-

separability ˌsep ər‿ə 'bɪl ət i -ɪt i ‖ -əţ i

separab|le 'sep ər‿əb |ᵊl ~**ly** li

separate *adj, n* 'sep ᵊr‿ət ‿ɪt ~**ly** li ~**ness** nəs
nɪs ~**s** s

sepa|rate *v* 'sep ə |reɪt ~**rated** reɪt ɪd -əd
‖ reɪţ əd ~**rates** reɪts ~**rating**
reɪt ɪŋ ‖ reɪţ ɪŋ

separation ˌsep ə 'reɪʃ ᵊn ~**s** z

separatism, S~ 'sep ᵊr‿ət ˌɪz əm ‿ɪt,ˈ- ‖ ‿əţ ˌˈ-

separatist, S~ 'sep ᵊr‿ət ɪst ‿ɪt ɪst, §-əst
‖ ‿əţ əst ~**s** s

separative 'sep ᵊr‿ət ɪv ‖ ‿əţ ɪv -ə reɪţ ɪv

separator 'sep ə reɪt ə ‖ -reɪţ ᵊr ~**s** z

Sephard|i sɪ 'fɑːd |iː sə-, se-, -i ‖ -'fɑːrd |i ~**ic**
ɪk ~**im** ɪm §əm ‖ əm

sepia 'siːp i‿ə ~**s** z

sepiolite 'siːp i‿ə laɪt

sepoy 'siːp ɔɪ ~**s** z

sepsis 'seps ɪs §-əs

sept sept **septs** septs

September sep 'tem bə sɪp-, səp- ‖ -bᵊr ~**s** z

septennial sep 'ten i‿əl ~**ly** i

septet, septette ₍ₗ₎sep 'tet ~**s** s

septic 'sept ɪk
ˌseptic 'tank, ˈ• • •

septicaemia, septicemia ˌsept ɪ 'siːm i‿ə §, •ə-

Septimus 'sept ɪm əs -əm-

septuagenarian ˌsept juˌə dʒə 'neər i‿ən ◄
ˌsep tʃuˌ, -dʒɪˈ• - ‖ ˌsep tʃuˌ ə dʒə 'ner-
ˌsept uˌ, ˌsept juˌ ~**s** z

Septuagesima ˌsept juˌə 'dʒes ɪm ə ˌsep tʃuˌ,
-əm ə ‖ ˌsep tʃuˌ ˌsept uˌ, ˌsept juˌ

Septuagint 'sept juˌə dʒɪnt 'sep tʃuˌ ‖ -uˌə-
'sep tʃuˌ, 'sept juˌ

sept|um 'sept |əm ~**a** ə

sepulcher 'sep ᵊlk ə ‖ -ᵊr ~**s** z

sepulchral sə 'pʌlk rəl sɪ-, se- ~**ly** i

sepulchre 'sep ᵊlk ə ‖ -ᵊr ~**s** z

sepulture 'sep ᵊltʃ ə -ᵊl tjuə ‖ -ᵊltʃ ᵊr -ᵊl tʃur

Sepulveda sə 'pʌlv əd ə -'pʊlv- —*Also,*
inappropriately, ˌsep ᵊl 'veɪd ə

sequel 'siːk wᵊl ~**s** z

sequel|a sɪ 'kwiːl |ə sə-, se-, -'kwel- ~**ae** iː

sequenc|e 'siːk wən¹s ~**ed** t ~**er/s** ə/z ‖ ᵊr/z
~**es** ɪz əz ~**ing** ɪŋ

sequent 'siːk wənt ~**s** s

sequential sɪ 'kwen¹ʃ ᵊl sə- ~**ly** i

sequester sɪ 'kwest ə sə- ‖ -ᵊr ~**ed** d
sequestering sɪ 'kwest ᵊr‿ɪŋ ~**s** z

sequestrant 'siːk wəs trənt 'sek-, -wɪs-, -wes-;
sɪ 'kwes-, sə- ~**s** s

seque|strate 'siːk wə |streɪt 'sek-, -wɪ-, -we-;
sɪ 'kwes treɪt, sə- ~**strated** streɪt ɪd -əd
‖ streɪţ əd ~**strates** streɪts ~**strating**
streɪt ɪŋ ‖ streɪţ ɪŋ

sequestration ˌsiːk wə 'streɪʃ ᵊn ˌsek-, -wɪ-,
-we- ~**s** z

seques|trum sɪ 'kwes trəm sə- ~**tra** trə

sequin 'siːk wɪn §-wən ~**ed, ~ned** d ~**s** z

sequoia, S~, Sequoya sɪ 'kwɔɪ ə sə-, se- ~**s** z

sera 'sɪər ə ‖ 'sɪr ə

seraglio sə 'rɑːl i‿əʊ sɪ-, se- ‖ -'ræl joʊ -'rɑːl-
~**s** z

serape sə 'rɑːp i sɪ-, se-, -'ræp-, -eɪ ~**s** z

ser|aph 'ser |əf ~**aphim** ə fɪm ~**aphs** əfs

seraphic sə 'ræf ɪk sɪ-, se- ~**ally** ᵊl‿i

seraphim 'ser ə fɪm

Seraphina ˌser ə 'fiːn ə

Serapis 'ser əp ɪs §-əs ‖ sə 'reɪp-

Serb sɜːb ‖ sɝːb **Serbs** sɜːbz ‖ sɝːbz

Serbi|a 'sɜːb i‿ə ‖ 'sɝːb- ~**an/s** ən/z

Serbo-Croat ˌsɜːb əʊ
'krəʊ æt ◄ ‖ ˌsɝːb oʊ 'kroʊ æt ◄

Serbo-Croatian ˌsɜːb əʊ
krəʊ 'eɪʃ ᵊn ◄ ‖ ˌsɝːb oʊ kroʊ 'eɪʃ ᵊn ◄

sere sɪə ‖ sɪᵊr (= *sear*)

Serena sə 'riːn ə sɪ-, se-, -'reɪn-

serenad|e ˌser ə 'neɪd -ɪ-, '• • • ~**ed** ɪd əd ~**es**
z ~**ing** ɪŋ

serendipitous ˌser ən 'dɪp ət əs ˌ•en-, -ɪt əs
‖ -əţ əs ~**ly** li

serendipity ˌser ən 'dɪp ət i ˌ•en-, -ɪt i ‖ -əţ i

serene sə 'riːn sɪ- ~**ly** li ~**ness** nəs nɪs

Serengeti ˌser ən 'get i →-əŋ-, -ɪn-, →-ɪŋ-
‖ -'geţ i

serenit|y sə 'ren ət |i sɪ-, -ɪt- ‖ -əţ |i ~**ies** iz

serf sɜːf ‖ sɝːf (= *surf*) **serfs** sɜːfs ‖ sɝːfs

serf|dom 'sɜːf |dəm ‖ 'sɝːf- ~**hood** hʊd

serge sɜːdʒ ‖ sɝːdʒ

Serge sɜːdʒ ‖ sɝːdʒ —*Fr* [sɛʁʒ]

sergeant 'sɑːdʒ ᵊnt ‖ 'sɑːrdʒ ᵊnt ~**s** s
ˌsergeant 'major◄

sergeant|-at-arms ˌsɑːdʒ ᵊnt| ət 'ɑːmz
‖ ˌsɑːrdʒ ᵊnţ| əţ 'ɑːrmz **sergeants~** ˌ•ənts

Sergei 'seə geɪ 'sɜːg-, •'• ‖ ser 'geɪ —*Russ*
['sʲɪr gʲej]

Sergio 'sɜːdʒ i əʊ ‖ 'sɝːdʒ i oʊ —*It* ['ser dʒo]

serial 'sɪər i‿əl ‖ 'sɪr- ~**s** z
'serial ˌnumber; ˌserial moˈnogamy; 'serial
ˌrights

serialis... —*see* **serializ...**

serialization ˌsɪər i‿əl aɪ 'zeɪʃ ᵊn -ɪˈ• -
‖ ˌsɪr i‿əl ə- ~**s** z

serializ|e 'sɪər i‿ə laɪz ‖ 'sɪr- ~**ed** d ~**es** ɪz əz
~**ing** ɪŋ

serially 'sɪər i‿əl i ‖ 'sɪr-

seriatim ˌsɪər i 'eɪt ɪm ˌser-, -'ɑːt-, §-əm
‖ ˌsɪr ɪ 'eɪţ əm -'æţ-

sericulture 'sɪər ɪ ˌkʌltʃ ə 'ser-, §-ə-
‖ 'ser ə ˌkʌltʃ ᵊr

seriema ˌser i 'iːm ə ~**s** z

series *sing., pl* 'sɪər iːz -ɪz ‖ 'sɪr iːz —*Some BrE*
speakers pronounce the sing. with -ɪz, the pl
with -iːz

serif 'ser ɪf -əf ~**s** s

serin 'ser ɪn §-ən ~**s** z

Seringapatam sə ˌrɪŋ gə pə 'tɑːm sɪ-, -'tæm

seriocomic ˌsɪər i əʊ 'kɒm ɪk ◄
‖ ˌsɪr i oʊ 'kɑːm ɪk ◄ ~**ally** ᵊl‿i

serious 'sɪər i‿əs ‖ 'sɪr- ~**ly** li ~**ness** nəs nɪs

serjeant 'sɑːdʒ ᵊnt ‖ 'sɑːrdʒ ᵊnt ~**s** s

serjeant|-at-arms ˌsɑːdʒ ᵊnt| ət 'ɑːmz
‖ ˌsɑːrdʒ ᵊnţ| əţ 'ɑːrmz **serjeants~** ˌ•ənts

Serle sɜːl ‖ sɝːl

sermon 'sɜːm ən ‖ 'sɝːm ən **~s** z
sermonette ˌsɜːm ə 'net ‖ ˌsɝːm- **~s** s
sermonis|e, sermoniz|e 'sɜːm ə naɪz ‖ 'sɝːm-
  ~ed d **~er/s** ə/z ‖ ᵊr/z **~es** ɪz əz **~ing** ɪŋ
serocon|vert ˌsɪər əʊ kən |'vɜːt §-kɒn|•
  ‖ ˌsɪr oʊ kən |'vɝːt **~verted** 'vɜːt ɪd -əd
  ‖ 'vɝːt̬ əd **~verting** 'vɜːt ɪŋ ‖ 'vɝːt̬ ɪŋ
  ~verts 'vɜːts ‖ 'vɝːts
serological ˌsɪər ə 'lɒdʒ ɪk ᵊl ◄ ‖ ˌsɪr ə 'lɑːdʒ-
  ~ly _i
serology sɪ 'rɒl ədʒ i sɪə- ‖ -'rɑːl-
seronegative ˌsɪər əʊ 'neg ət ɪv ◄
  ‖ ˌsɪr oʊ 'neg ət̬ ɪv ◄
seropositive ˌsɪər əʊ 'pɒz ət ɪv ◄ -ɪt ɪv
  ‖ ˌsɪr oʊ 'pɑːz ət̬ ɪv ◄
seropositivity ˌsɪər əʊ ˌpɒz ə 'tɪv ət i -ɪ'••-, -ɪt i
  ‖ ˌsɪr oʊ ˌpɑːz ə 'tɪv ət̬ i
Serota sə 'rəʊt ə sɪ- ‖ -'roʊt̬ ə
serotine 'ser əʊ taɪn ‖ -ə- -tɪn **~s** z
serotonin ˌsɪər əʊ 'təʊn ɪn ˌser-, §-ən
  ‖ ˌsɪr ə 'toʊn ən ˌser-
serous 'sɪər əs ‖ 'sɪr əs
serow 'ser əʊ ‖ -oʊ sə 'roʊ **~s** z
Serpell 'sɜːp ᵊl ‖ 'sɝːp ᵊl
Serpens 'sɜːp enz -ᵊnz ‖ 'sɝːp-
serpent 'sɜːp ənt →-mt ‖ 'sɝːp- **~s** s
serpentine, S~ 'sɜːp ən taɪn →-m-
  ‖ 'sɝːp ən tiːn -taɪn
SERPS sɜːps ‖ sɝːps
Serra 'ser ə —Sp ['se rra]
serrated sə 'reɪt ɪd sɪ-, se-, -əd ‖ -'reɪt̬ əd
serration sə 'reɪʃ ᵊn sɪ-, se- **~s** z
serried 'ser id
ser|um 'sɪər |əm ‖ 'sɪr |əm **~a** ə **~ums** əmz
serval 'sɜːv ᵊl ‖ 'sɝːv ᵊl **~s** z
servant 'sɜːv ᵊnt ‖ 'sɝːv ᵊnt **~s** s
serve sɜːv ‖ sɝːv **served** sɜːvd ‖ sɝːvd
  serves sɜːvz ‖ sɝːvz **serving**
  'sɜːv ɪŋ ‖ 'sɝːv ɪŋ
server 'sɜːv ə ‖ 'sɝːv ᵊr **~s** z
server|y 'sɜːv ᵊr li ‖ 'sɝːv- **~ies** iz
servic|e, S~ 'sɜːv ɪs §-əs ‖ 'sɝːv əs **~ed** t **~es**
  ɪz əz **~ing** ɪŋ
  'service charge; 'service flat; 'service road;
  'service ˌstation
serviceab|le 'sɜːv ɪs əb |ᵊl §'••əs- ‖ 'sɝːv əs-
  ~leness ᵊl nəs -nɪs **~ly** li
serviceberr|y 'sɜːv ɪs ˌber li -əs- ‖ 'sɝːv əs-
  ~ies iz
service|man 'sɜːv ɪs |mæn §-əs- ‖ 'sɝːv əs-
  -men mən men **~woman** ˌwʊm ən
  ~women ˌwɪm ɪn §-ən
serviette ˌsɜːv i 'et ‖ ˌsɝːv- **~s** s
servile 'sɜːv aɪl ‖ 'sɝːv ᵊl -aɪᵊl **~ly** li **~ness**
  nəs nɪs
servility sɜː 'vɪl ət i -ɪt- ‖ sɝː 'vɪl ət̬ i
serving 'sɜːv ɪŋ ‖ 'sɝːv ɪŋ **~s** z
  'serving spoon
Servis tdmk 'sɜːv ɪs §-əs ‖ 'sɝːv-
Servite 'sɜːv aɪt ‖ 'sɝːv- **~s** s
servitor 'sɜːv ɪt ə -ət- ‖ 'sɝːv ət̬ ᵊr **~s** z
servitude 'sɜːv ɪ tjuːd -ə-, →§-tʃuːd
  ‖ 'sɝːv ə tuːd -tjuːd

servo 'sɜːv əʊ ‖ 'sɝːv oʊ **~s** z
servomechanism 'sɜːv əʊ ˌmek ə nɪz əm
  ‖ 'sɝːv oʊ- **~s** z
servomotor
  'sɜːv əʊ ˌməʊt ə ‖ 'sɝːv oʊ ˌmoʊt̬ ᵊr **~s** z
sesame 'ses əm i
  'sesame seeds
Sesotho sɪ 'suːt uː sə-, se-
sesqui- ˌsesk wi— **sesquioxide**
  ˌsesk wi 'ɒks aɪd ‖ -'ɑːks-
sesquicentennial ˌsesk wi sen 'ten i_əl **~s** z
sesquipedalian ˌsesk wi pɪ 'deɪl i_ən ◄, •wə-,
  -pə'••-, -pe'•- **~s** z
sessile 'ses aɪᵊl -ᵊl, -ɪl
session 'seʃ ᵊn **~s** z
sessional 'seʃ ᵊn_ᵊl **~ly** i **~s** z
Sessions 'seʃ ᵊnz
sest|erce 'sest |ɜːs ‖ -|ɝːs **~erces** ɜːs ɪz əs-,
  -əz; ə siːz ‖ ɝːs əz
sesterti|um se 'stɜːt i_|əm -'stɜːʃ- ‖ -'stɝːʃ-
  -'stɝːʃ |əm **~a** ə
sestet ₍ₙ₎ses 'tet **~s** s
set set **sets** sets **setting** 'set ɪŋ ‖ 'set̬ ɪŋ
  ˌset 'book; ˌset 'piece; ˌset 'point; 'set
  ˌtheory
seta 'siːt ə ‖ 'siːt̬ ə **setae** 'siːt iː -eɪ, -aɪ
setaceous sɪ 'teɪʃ əs sə-, siː-
setaside 'set ə ˌsaɪd ‖ 'set̬-
setback 'set bæk **~s** s
set-down 'set daʊn
se-tenant sə 'ten ənt sɪ-, siː- ‖ ˌset ᵊn 'ɑːn —Fr
  [sə tə nɑ̃]
Seth seθ —but as an Indian name, seɪt
Seton, s~ 'siːt ᵊn
setscrew 'set skruː **~s** z
setsquare 'set skweə ‖ -skwer -skwær **~s** z
sett set **setts** sets
settee se 'tiː sə- **~s** z
setter, S~ 'set ə ‖ 'set̬ ᵊr **~s** z
setting 'set ɪŋ ‖ 'set̬ ɪŋ **~s** z
settl|e 'set ᵊl ‖ 'set̬ ᵊl **~ed** d **~es** z **~ing** ɪŋ
settlement 'set ᵊl mənt **~s** s
settler 'set ᵊl_ə ‖ 'set̬ ᵊl_ᵊr **~s** z
set-to 'set tuː ˌ•'• **~s** z
Setubal, Setúbal sə 'tuːb ᵊl se-, -æl —Port
  [sə 'tu βɐl]
set-up 'set ʌp ‖ 'set̬ ʌp **~s** s
Seumas 'ʃuːm əs —ScG ['ʃu məs]
Seurat 'sɜːr ɑː ‖ sʊ 'rɑː —Fr [sœ ʁa]
Seuss sjuːs suːs ‖ suːs
Sevastopol sə 'væst ə pɒl sɪ-, -pᵊl ‖ -poʊl
  —Russ Sevastopol [sʲɪ vʌ 'sto pəlʲ]
seven 'sev ᵊn —In casual speech also →'seb m
  (not before a vowel sound) **~s** z
sevenfold 'sev ᵊn fəʊld →'seb m-, →fɒʊld
  ‖ -foʊld
sevenish 'sev ᵊn ɪʃ
Sevenoaks 'sev ᵊn əʊks ‖ -oʊks
seventeen ˌsev ᵊn 'tiːn ◄ —In casual speech
  also →ˌseb m- **~s** z
seventh 'sev ᵊntθ —Casually also →'seb mᵖθ
  ~s s
  ˌseventh 'heaven

seventieth 'sev ᵊnt i_əθ ɪθ ‖ 'sev ᵊnt̬-
—*Casually also* →'seb mᵖt i_əθ ~s s
sevent|y 'sev ᵊnt li ‖ -ᵊnt̬ li —*Casually also*
→'seb mᵖt li ~ies iz
seventy-eight ˌsev ᵊnt i 'eɪt ◄ ‖ ˌsev ᵊnt̬-
—*Casually also* →ˌseb mᵖt- ~s s
Seven-Up, 7-Up *tdmk* ˌsev ᵊn 'ʌp ~s s
seven-year ˌsev ᵊn 'jɪə ◄ -'jɜː ‖ -'jɪᵊr ◄
—*Casually also* →ˌseb m-
ˌseven-year 'itch
sever 'sev ə ‖ -ᵊr ~ed d severing 'sev ᵊr_ɪŋ
~s z
several 'sev rəl 'sev ᵊr_əl ~ly i
severanc|e 'sev ᵊr_ᵊnˈs ~es ɪz əz
'severance pay
severe sɪ 'vɪə sə- ‖ -'vɪᵊr severer sɪ 'vɪər ə sə-
‖ -'vɪr ᵊr severest sɪ 'vɪər ɪst sə-, -əst
‖ -'vɪr əst -ly li ~ness nəs nɪs
severed 'sev əd ‖ -ᵊrd
severit|y sɪ 'ver ət li sə-, -ɪt i ‖ -ət̬ li ~ies iz
Severn 'sev ᵊn ‖ -ᵊrn
Severus sɪ 'vɪər əs sə- ‖ -'vɪr əs
seviche sɪ 'viːtʃ eɪ sə-, seɪ-, -i —*AmSp*
[se 'vi tʃe]
Seville sə 'vɪl sɪ-, se- —*Sp* Sevilla [se 'βi ʎa,
-ja] —*but usually* 'sev ᵊl, -ɪl *in the expression*
ˌSeville 'orange
Sevres, Sèvres 'seɪv rə 'sev- ‖ 'sev rə —*Fr*
[sɛːvʁ]
sew səʊ ‖ soʊ (= *so*) sewed səʊd ‖ soʊd
sewing 'səʊ ɪŋ ‖ 'soʊ ɪŋ sews səʊz ‖ soʊz
'sewing ma,chine
sewage 'suː ɪdʒ 'sjuː‿
'sewage farm
Seward (i) 'siː wəd ‖ -wᵊrd, (ii) 'sjuː‿əd 'suː‿
‖ 'suː ᵊrd
Sewell 'sjuː‿əl 'suː‿; 'sjuːl, 'suːl ‖ 'suː əl
sewer '*drain*'; '*servant*' 'suː‿ə 'sjuː‿ ‖ -ᵊr ~s z
sewer '*one that sews*' 'səʊ ə ‖ 'soʊ ᵊr ~s z
sewerage 'suː‿ᵊr ɪdʒ 'sjuː‿
sewn səʊn ‖ soʊn
sex seks sexed sekst (= *sext*) sexes 'seks ɪz
-əz sexing 'seks ɪŋ
'sex ap,peal; 'sex ,hormone; 'sex ,object;
'sex 'organ
sexagenarian ˌseks ə dʒə 'neər i_ən ◄ -dʒɪ'•-,
-dʒe'•- ‖ -'ner- ~s z
Sexagesima ˌseks ə 'dʒes ɪm ə -əm ə
-sexed 'sekst — highly-sexed ˌhaɪ li 'sekst ◄
sexi... —*see* sexy
sexism 'seks ˌɪz əm
sexist 'seks ɪst §-əst ~s s
sexless 'seks ləs -lɪs ~ly li ~ness nəs nɪs
sex-linked ˌseks 'lɪŋkt ◄ '••
sexological ˌseks ə 'lɒdʒ ɪk ᵊl ◄ ‖ -'lɑːdʒ-
sexologist sek 'sɒl ədʒ ɪst §-əst ‖ -'sɑːl- ~s s
sexology sek 'sɒl ədʒ i ‖ -'sɑːl-
sexploitation ˌseks plɔɪ 'teɪʃ ᵊn
sexpot 'seks pɒt ‖ -pɑːt ~s s
sex-starved 'seks stɑːvd ,•'• ‖ -stɑːrvd
sext, Sext sekst
Sextans 'sekst ᵊnz
sextant 'sekst ᵊnt ~s s

sextet ₍ₗ₎seks 'tet ~s s
sextile 'sekst aɪᵊl
sextodecimo ˌsekst əʊ 'des ɪ məʊ -ə•
‖ -oʊ 'des ə moʊ
sexton, S~ 'sekst ᵊn ~s z
sextupl|e 'sekst ʊp ᵊl -jəp-; sek 'stjuːp-
‖ sek 'stuːp ᵊl -'stʊp-, -'stʌp-; 'sekst əp- ~ed
d -es z ~ing ɪŋ
sextuplet 'seks tjʊp lət seks 'tjuːp-, §-'tʌp-,
-lɪt, -let ‖ sek 'stʌp- -'stuːp-, -'stjuːp-;
'sekst əp- ~s s
sexual 'sek ʃu_əl 'seks ju_əl, 'sek ʃᵊl ~ly i
ˌsexual 'intercourse
sexualit|y ˌsek ʃu 'æl ət i ‖ ˌseks ju-, -ɪt i ‖ -ət̬ li
~ies iz
sex|y 'seks li ~ier i_ə ‖ i_ᵊr ~iest i_ɪst i_əst
~ily ɪ li əl i ~iness i nəs i nɪs
Seychelles ₍ₗ₎seɪ 'ʃelz -'ʃel, '••
Seychellois ˌseɪ ʃel 'wɑː ◄
Seyfert 'saɪf ət 'siːf- ‖ -ᵊrt
Seymour (i) 'siː mɔː ‖ -mɔːr -moʊr, (ii)
'siːm ə ‖ -ᵊr, (iii) 'seɪm ə ‖ -ᵊr
sez *non-standard spelling of* says sez
sforzand|o
₍ₗ₎sfɔːt 'sænd ləʊ ‖ ₍ₗ₎sfɔːrt 'sɑːnd loʊ -'sænd-
~i iː
sgian-dhu ˌskiːʼ ən 'duː ˌskiːn'•
sgraffit|o skræ 'fiːt əʊ ‖ -oʊ —*It* [zgraf 'fiː to]
~i iː i
Sgurr skʊə ‖ skʊᵊr —*ScG* [skur]
sh, shh, ssh ʃ
Shaanxi ˌʃɑːn 'ʃiː —*Chi* Shǎnxī [³ʂan ¹ɕi]
shabb|y 'ʃæb li ~ier i_ə ‖ i_ᵊr ~iest i_ɪst i_əst
~ily ɪ li əl i ~iness i nəs i nɪs
shack ʃæk shacked ʃækt shacking 'ʃæk ɪŋ
shacks ʃæks
shackl|e 'ʃæk ᵊl ~ed d ~es z ~ing ɪŋ
Shackleton 'ʃæk ᵊl tən ~s, ~'s z
shad ʃæd shads ʃædz
Shadbolt 'ʃæd bəʊlt →'ʃæb-, →-bɒʊlt ‖ -boʊlt
shadbush 'ʃæd bʊʃ ~es ɪz əz
shaddock, S~ 'ʃæd ək ~s s
shade ʃeɪd shaded 'ʃeɪd ɪd -əd shades ʃeɪdz
shading/s 'ʃeɪd ɪŋ/z
shadoof ʃə 'duːf ʃæ- ~s s
shadow 'ʃæd əʊ ‖ -oʊ ~ed d ~ing ɪŋ ~s z
ˌshadow 'cabinet; 'shadow play
shadowbox 'ʃæd əʊ bɒks ‖ -oʊ bɑːks ~ed t
~es ɪz əz ~ing ɪŋ
shadow|y 'ʃæd əʊ li ‖ -oʊ li ~ier i_ə ‖ i_ᵊr
~iest i_ɪst i_əst ~iness i nəs i nɪs
Shadrach 'ʃædr æk 'ʃeɪdr-, -ɑːx
Shadwell 'ʃæd wel -wəl
shad|ly 'ʃeɪd li ~ier i_ə ‖ i_ᵊr ~iest i_ɪst i_əst
~ily ɪ li əl i ~iness i nəs i nɪs
SHAEF ʃeɪf
Shafaye ʃə 'feɪ
Shaeffer 'ʃeɪf ə ‖ -ᵊr
Shaffer 'ʃæf ə ‖ -ᵊr
shaft ʃɑːft §ʃæft ‖ ʃæft shafted 'ʃɑːft ɪd
§'ʃæft-, -əd ‖ 'ʃæft əd shafting/s 'ʃɑːft ɪŋ/z
§'ʃæft- ‖ 'ʃæft ɪŋ/z shafts ʃɑːfts §ʃæfts
‖ ʃæfts

Shaftesbury 'ʃɑːfts bər_i §'ʃæfts-
‖ 'ʃæfts ˌber i
Shafto, Shaftoe 'ʃɑːft əʊ §'ʃæft- ‖ 'ʃæft oʊ
shag ʃæg shagged ʃægd shagging 'ʃæg ɪŋ
shags ʃægz
ˌshagged 'out
shagbark 'ʃæg bɑːk ‖ -bɑːrk ~s s
shagger 'ʃæg ə ‖ -ᵊr ~s z
shagg|y 'ʃæg |i ~ier i_ə ‖ i_ᵊr ~iest i_ɪst i_əst
~ily ɪ li əl i ~iness i nəs i nɪs
shaggy-dog ˌʃæg i 'dɒg ‖ -'dɔːg -'dɑːg
ˌshaggy-'dog ˌstory
shagreen ʃə 'griːn ʃæ-
shah, Shah ʃɑː shahs ʃɑːz
Shairp (i) ʃɑːp ‖ ʃɑːrp, (ii) ʃeəp ‖ ʃeᵊrp
Shaka 'ʃɑːk ə 'ʃɑːg-
shake ʃeɪk shaken 'ʃeɪk ən shakes ʃeɪks
shaking/s 'ʃeɪk ɪŋ/z shook ʃʊk §ʃuːk
shakedown 'ʃeɪk daʊn ~s z
shaken 'ʃeɪk ən
shake-out, shakeout 'ʃeɪk aʊt ~s s
shaker, S~ 'ʃeɪk ə ‖ -ᵊr ~s z
Shakerley 'ʃæk ə li ‖ -ᵊr-
Shakeshaft 'ʃeɪk ʃɑːft §-ʃæft ‖ -ʃæft
Shakespear, Shakespeare 'ʃeɪk spɪə ‖ -spɪr
Shakespearean ₍ᵢ₎ʃeɪk 'spɪər i_ən ‖ -'spɪr- ~s z
Shakespeareana ʃeɪk ˌspɪər i 'ɑːn ə
ˌʃeɪk spɪər i'•- ‖ -'æn ə -'ɑːn-, -'eɪn-
Shakespearian ₍ᵢ₎ʃeɪk 'spɪər i_ən ‖ -'spɪr- ~s z
Shakespeariana ʃeɪk ˌspɪər i 'ɑːn ə
ˌʃeɪk spɪər i'•- ‖ -'æn ə -'ɑːn-, -'eɪn-
shake-up 'ʃeɪk ʌp ~s s
shako 'ʃæk əʊ 'ʃeɪk-, 'ʃɑːk- ‖ -oʊ ~s z
shak|y 'ʃeɪk |i ~ier i_ə ‖ i_ᵊr ~iest i_ɪst i_əst
~ily ɪ li əl i ~iness i nəs i nɪs
Shalden, Shaldon 'ʃɔːld ən 'ʃɒld- ‖ 'ʃɑːld-
shale ʃeɪᵊl shales ʃeɪᵊlz
Shalford 'ʃæl fəd ‖ -fᵊrd
shall strong form ʃæl, weak form ʃᵊl —There are
also weak forms ʃə, ʃ, used only before a
following word beginning with a consonant.
shallop 'ʃæl əp ~s s
shallot ʃə 'lɒt ‖ -'lɑːt 'ʃæl ət ~s s
shallow 'ʃæl əʊ ‖ -oʊ ~ed d ~er ə ‖ ᵊr ~est
ɪst əst ~ing ɪŋ ~ly li ~ness nəs nɪs ~s z
shalom ʃæ 'lɒm ʃə-, -'ləʊm ‖ ʃɑː 'loʊm ʃə-
sha,lom a'leichem ə 'leɪx əm
shalt strong form ʃælt, weak form ʃᵊlt
sham ʃæm shammed ʃæmd shamming
'ʃæm ɪŋ shams ʃæmz
shaman 'ʃæm ən 'ʃeɪm-, 'ʃɑːm- ‖ 'ʃɑːm ən
'ʃeɪm-, 'ʃæm- ~ism ˌɪz əm ~s z
shamanistic ˌʃæm ə 'nɪst ɪk ◄ ˌʃɑːm-, ˌʃeɪm-
‖ ˌʃɑːm-, ˌʃeɪm-, ˌʃæm-
shamateur 'ʃæm ət ə -ə tʃʊə, -tʃə, -tjʊə;
ˌʃæm ə 'tɜː ◄ ‖ 'ʃæm ə tʃʊr -əʈ ᵊr, -ə tjʊr ~s
z
shamateurism 'ʃæm ət ər ˌɪz əm -ətʃ ᵊr-,
-ə tɜːr-, -ə tʃʊər-, -ə tjʊər- ‖ 'ʃæm ə tʃʊr-
-əʈ ᵊr-, -ə tjʊr-
shambl|e 'ʃæm bᵊl ~ed d ~es z ~ing ˌɪŋ
shambolic ʃæm 'bɒl ɪk ‖ -'bɑːl ɪk ~ally ᵊl_i

shame ʃeɪm shamed ʃeɪmd shames ʃeɪmz
shaming 'ʃeɪm ɪŋ
shamefaced ˌʃeɪm 'feɪst ◄
shamefaced|ly ˌʃeɪm 'feɪst |li -'feɪs ɪd li, -əd-
~ness nəs nɪs
shameful 'ʃeɪm fᵊl -fʊl ~ly _i ~ness nəs nɪs
shameless 'ʃeɪm ləs -lɪs ~ly li ~ness nəs nɪs
shaming 'ʃeɪm ɪŋ ~ly li
shamisen 'ʃæm ɪ sen ‖ 'ʃɑːm- —Jp
[ça ˌmi seɴ] ~s z
shamm... —see sham
shamm|y 'ʃæm |i ~ies iz
shampoo ₍ᵢ₎ʃæm 'puː ~ed d ~ing ɪŋ ~s z
shamrock 'ʃæm rɒk ‖ -rɑːk ~s s
shamus 'ʃɑːm əs 'ʃeɪm- ~es ɪz əz
Shan ʃɑːn —and for the people and language,
also ʃæn Shans ʃɑːnz ʃænz
Shandong ˌʃæn 'dɒŋ ‖ ˌʃɑːn 'dɔːŋ —Chi
Shāndōng [¹ʂan ¹tʊŋ]
shand|y 'ʃænd |i ~ies iz
shandygaff 'ʃænd i gæf ~s s
Shane ʃeɪn
Shang dynasty ʃæŋ ‖ ʃɑːŋ —Chi Shāng [¹ʂaŋ]
Shangaan ʃæn 'gɑːn ~s z
Shanghai, s~ ˌʃæŋ 'haɪ '•• —Chi Shànghǎi
[⁴ʂaŋ ³xai] ~ed d ~ing ɪŋ ~s z
Shango 'ʃæŋ gəʊ ‖ -goʊ
Shangri-La ˌʃæŋ gri 'lɑː
Shanita ʃə 'niːt ə ‖ -'niːt ə
shank ʃæŋk shanks ʃæŋks
ˌshank's 'mare
Shankill 'ʃæŋk ɪl -ᵊl
Shanklin 'ʃæŋk lɪn §-lən
Shankly 'ʃæŋk li
Shanks ʃæŋks
shanks's 'ʃæŋks ɪz -əz
ˌshanks's 'pony
Shannon 'ʃæn ən
shan't ʃɑːnt ‖ ʃænt
Shantou ˌʃæn 'təʊ ‖ ˌʃɑːn 'toʊ —Chi Shàntóu
[⁴ʂan ²tʰou]
shantung, S~ ˌʃæn 'tʌŋ —Chi Shāndōng [¹ʂan
¹tʊŋ]
shant|y 'ʃænt |i ‖ 'ʃænʈ li ~ies iz
shanty-town 'ʃænt i taʊn ‖ 'ʃænʈ- ~s z
Shanxi ˌʃæn 'ʃiː —Chi Shānxī [¹ʂan ¹çi]
Shap ʃæp
shape ʃeɪp shaped ʃeɪpt shapes ʃeɪps
shaping 'ʃeɪp ɪŋ
SHAPE ʃeɪp
-shaped ʃeɪpt — pear-shaped
'peə ʃeɪpt ‖ 'per-
shapeless 'ʃeɪp ləs ~ly li ~ness nəs nɪs
shape|ly 'ʃeɪp |li ~lier li_ə ‖ li_ᵊr ~liest li_ɪst
əst ~liness li nəs -nɪs
Shapiro ʃə 'pɪər əʊ ‖ -'pɪr oʊ
shard ʃɑːd ‖ ʃɑːrd shards ʃɑːdz ‖ ʃɑːrdz
share ʃeə ‖ ʃeᵊr ʃæᵊr shared ʃeəd ‖ ʃeᵊrd
ʃæᵊrd shares ʃeəz ‖ ʃeᵊrz ʃæᵊrz sharing
'ʃeər ɪŋ ‖ 'ʃer ɪŋ 'ʃær-
'share cer,tificate
sharecropper 'ʃeə krɒp ə ‖ 'ʃer krɑːp ᵊr 'ʃær-
~s z

shareholder 'ʃeə ˌhəʊld ə →-ˌhɒʊld-
‖ 'ʃer ˌhoʊld ᵊr 'ʃær- ~s z
shareholding 'ʃeə ˌhəʊld ɪŋ →-ˌhɒʊld-
‖ 'ʃer ˌhoʊld ɪŋ 'ʃær- ~s z
share-out 'ʃeᵊr aʊt ‖ 'ʃer aʊt 'ʃær- ~s s
shareware 'ʃeə weə ‖ 'ʃer wer 'ʃær wær
sharia, shari'ah ʃə 'riː_ə ʃɑː- —Ar [ʃa 'riː ʕa]
Sharif, s~ ʃə 'riːf ʃɑː-, ʃæ-
Sharjah 'ʃɑːdʒ ɑː 'ʃɑːʒ-, -ə ‖ 'ʃɑːrdʒ-
shark ʃɑːk ‖ ʃɑːrk sharks ʃɑːks ‖ ʃɑːrks
sharkskin 'ʃɑːk skɪn ‖ 'ʃɑːrk-
Sharman 'ʃɑː mən ‖ 'ʃɑːr-
Sharon personal name 'ʃær ən ‖ 'ʃer-
Sharon place name; (rose of ~) 'ʃeᵊr ən 'ʃɑːr-,
'ʃær-, -ɒn ‖ 'ʃær ən 'ʃer-
'Sharon fruit
Sharon Israeli politician ʃə 'rɒn -'rəʊn ‖ -'roʊn
sharp ʃɑːp ‖ ʃɑːrp sharped ʃɑːpt ‖ ʃɑːrpt
sharper 'ʃɑːp ə ‖ 'ʃɑːrp ᵊr sharpest
'ʃɑːp ɪst -əst ‖ 'ʃɑːrp əst sharping
'ʃɑːp ɪŋ ‖ 'ʃɑːrp ɪŋ sharps ʃɑːps ‖ ʃɑːrps
'sharp end; ˌsharp 'practice
Sharp, Sharpe ʃɑːp ‖ ʃɑːrp
sharpen 'ʃɑːp ən ‖ 'ʃɑːrp ən ~ed d ~ing ɪŋ
~s z
sharpener 'ʃɑːp nə 'ʃɑːp ən_ə ‖ 'ʃɑːrp ən_ᵊr
sharper 'ʃɑːp ə ‖ 'ʃɑːrp ᵊr ~s z
Sharpeville 'ʃɑːp vɪl ‖ 'ʃɑːrp-
sharp-eyed ˌʃɑːp 'aɪd ◄ ‖ ˌʃɑːrp-
sharpie 'ʃɑːp i ‖ 'ʃɑːrp i ~s z
sharpish 'ʃɑːp ɪʃ ‖ 'ʃɑːrp ɪʃ ~ly li
Sharples 'ʃɑːp əlz ‖ 'ʃɑːrp əlz
sharp|ly 'ʃɑːp |li ‖ 'ʃɑːrp |li ~ness nəs nɪs
Sharpness ˌʃɑːp 'nes ‖ ˌʃɑːrp-
sharp-set ˌʃɑːp 'set ◄ ‖ ˌʃɑːrp-
sharpshooter 'ʃɑːp ˌʃuːt ə ‖ 'ʃɑːrp ˌʃuːt̬ ᵊr ~s z
Sharwood 'ʃɑː wʊd ‖ 'ʃɑːr-
shashlik 'ʃæʃ lɪk 'ʃɑːʃ- ‖ 'ʃɑːʃ- ˌ•'• ~s s
Shasta 'ʃæst ə
ˌShasta 'daisy
shat ʃæt
shatter 'ʃæt ə ‖ 'ʃæt̬ ᵊr ~ed d shattering/ly
'ʃæt̬_ər ɪŋ /li ‖ 'ʃæt̬ ər ɪŋ /li ~s z
shatterproof 'ʃæt ə pruːf §-prɒf ‖ 'ʃæt̬ ᵊr-
Shaughnessy 'ʃɔːn əs i ‖ 'ʃɑːn-
Shaun ʃɔːn ‖ ʃɑːn
shave ʃeɪv shaved ʃeɪvd shaves ʃeɪvz
shaving 'ʃeɪv ɪŋ
'shaving cream; 'shaving foam
shaveling 'ʃeɪv lɪŋ ~s z
shaven 'ʃeɪv ən
shaver 'ʃeɪv ə ‖ -ᵊr ~s z
Shavian 'ʃeɪv i_ən ~s z
Shaw, shaw ʃɔː ‖ ʃɑː
Shawcross 'ʃɔː krɒs -krɔːs ‖ -krɑːs 'ʃɑː krɑːs
shawl ʃɔːl ‖ ʃɑːl shawls ʃɔːlz ‖ ʃɑːlz
shawm ʃɔːm ‖ ʃɑːm shawms ʃɔːmz ‖ ʃɑːmz
Shawn ʃɔːn ‖ ʃɑːn
Shawnee ˌʃɔː 'niː ₍₀₎ʃɑː- ~s z
shay ʃeɪ shays ʃeɪz
Shayler 'ʃeɪl ə ‖ -ᵊr
she strong form ʃiː, weak form ʃi
she- 'ʃi: — she-cat 'ʃi: kæt

s/he ˌʃiː ɔː 'hiː ‖ -ᵊr-
shea tree ʃiː 'ʃiː_ə
'shea nut
Shea name ʃeɪ
sheaf ʃiːf sheaves ʃiːvz
Sheaffer 'ʃeɪf ə ‖ -ᵊr
shear ʃɪə ʃɪᵊr (= sheer) sheared ʃɪəd ‖ ʃɪᵊrd
shearing 'ʃɪᵊr ɪŋ ‖ 'ʃɪr ɪŋ shears ʃɪəz ‖ ʃɪᵊrz
shorn ʃɔːn ‖ ʃɔːrn ʃoʊrn
Sheard (i) ʃeəd ‖ ʃeᵊrd, (ii) ʃɪəd ‖ ʃɪᵊrd, (iii)
ʃɜːd ‖ ʃɜːd
shearer, S~ 'ʃɪər ə ‖ 'ʃɪr ᵊr ~s z
shearling 'ʃɪə lɪŋ ‖ 'ʃɪr- ~s z
Shearman 'ʃɪə mən ‖ 'ʃɪr-
shears ʃɪəz ‖ ʃɪᵊrz
shearwater 'ʃɪə ˌwɔːt ə ‖ 'ʃɪr ˌwɔːt̬ ᵊr -ˌwɑːt̬-
~s z
sheath n ʃiːθ sheaths ʃiːðz ʃiːθs
'sheath knife
sheathe v ʃiːð sheathed ʃiːðd sheathes ʃiːðz
sheathing 'ʃiːð ɪŋ
sheave ʃiːv sheaved ʃiːvd sheaves ʃiːvz
sheaving 'ʃiːv ɪŋ
Sheba 'ʃiːb ə
shebang ʃɪ 'bæŋ ʃə-
she-bear 'ʃiː beə ‖ -ber ~s z
shebeen ʃɪ 'biːn ʃə- ~s z
Sheboygan ʃɪ 'bɔɪg ən ʃə-
shed ʃed shedding 'ʃed ɪŋ sheds ʃedz
she'd strong form ʃiːd, occasional weak form ʃid
she-devil 'ʃiː ˌdev əl -ɪl ~s z
Sheehan 'ʃiː hən
Sheelagh 'ʃiːl ə
sheen, Sheen ʃiːn
Sheena, Sheenagh, Sheenah 'ʃiːn ə
Sheene ʃiːn
sheep ʃiːp sheep's ʃiːps
'sheep's eyes; 'sheep tick
sheepdip 'ʃiːp dɪp ~s s
sheepdog 'ʃiːp dɒg ‖ -dɔːg -dɑːg ~s z
sheepfold 'ʃiːp fəʊld →-fɒʊld -foʊld ~s z
sheepish 'ʃiːp ɪʃ ~ly li ~ness nəs nɪs
sheepmeat 'ʃiːp miːt
sheepsbit 'ʃiːps bɪt ~s s
sheepshank 'ʃiːp ʃæŋk ~s s
sheepskin 'ʃiːp skɪn ~s z
sheer ʃɪə ‖ ʃɪᵊr sheered ʃɪəd ‖ ʃɪᵊrd sheerer
'ʃɪər ə ‖ 'ʃɪr ᵊr sheerest 'ʃɪər ɪst -əst
‖ 'ʃɪr əst sheering 'ʃɪər ɪŋ ‖ 'ʃɪr ɪŋ sheers
ʃɪəz ‖ ʃɪᵊrz
Sheerness ˌʃɪə 'nes ◄ ‖ ˌʃɪr-
sheesh ʃiːʃ
sheet ʃiːt sheeting 'ʃiːt ɪŋ ‖ 'ʃiːt̬ ɪŋ sheets
ʃiːts
'sheet ˌanchor; 'sheet ˌfeeder; ˌsheet
'lightning, '• ˌ•'•; 'sheet ˌmusic, ˌ• '••
Sheetrock tdmk 'ʃiːt rɒk ‖ -rɑːk
Sheffer 'ʃef ə ‖ -ᵊr
Sheffield 'ʃef iːᵊld
ˌSheffield 'plate
Shefford 'ʃef əd ‖ -ᵊrd
sheikh, sheik, S~ ʃeɪk ʃiːk sheikhs, sheiks
ʃeɪks ʃiːks

sheikhdom, sheikdom 'ʃeɪk dəm 'ʃiːk- ~s z
Sheila, s~ 'ʃiːl ə ~s, ~'s z
shekel 'ʃek əl ~s z
Shelagh 'ʃiːl ə
Shelburne 'ʃel bən -bɜːn ‖ -bɜːːn
Shelby 'ʃel bi
Sheldon 'ʃeld ən
Sheldonian ʃel 'dəʊn i‿ən ‖ -'doʊn-
sheldrake, S~ 'ʃel dreɪk ~s s
shelduck 'ʃel dʌk ~s s
shelf ʃelf **shelves** ʃelvz
  'shelf life
Shelford 'ʃel fəd ‖ -fᵊrd
shell, Shell ʃel **shelled** ʃeld **shelling** 'ʃel ɪŋ
  shells, Shell's ʃelz
she'll *strong form* ʃiːᵊl, *occasional weak form* ʃil
shellac ʃə 'læk ʃe-; 'ʃel æk **~ked** t **~king** ɪŋ
  ~s s
shellback 'ʃel bæk ~s s
Shelley 'ʃel i
shellfire 'ʃel ˌfaɪ‿ə ‖ -ˌfaɪ‿ᵊr
shellfish 'ʃel fɪʃ **~es** ɪz əz
shell-like 'ʃel laɪk
Shell-Mex *tdmk* ˌʃel 'meks
shellshock 'ʃel ʃɒk ‖ -ʃɑːk **~ed** t
Shelta 'ʃelt ə
shelter 'ʃelt ə ‖ -ᵊr **~ed** d **sheltering**
  'ʃelt‿ᵊr ɪŋ ~s z
shelt|ie, shelt|y 'ʃelt li **~ies** iz
Shelton 'ʃelt ən
shelve ʃelv **shelved** ʃelvd **shelves** ʃelvz
  shelving 'ʃelv ɪŋ
Shem ʃem
shemozzle ʃɪ 'mɒz əl ʃə- ‖ -'mɑːz-
Shena 'ʃiːn ə
Shenandoah ˌʃen ən 'dəʊ ə ◄ ‖ -'doʊ ə ◄
  ˌShenanˌdoah 'Valley
shenanigan ʃɪ 'næn ɪg ən ʃə-, §-əg- ~s z
Shenfield 'ʃen fiːᵊld
Shenyang ˌʃen 'jæŋ ˌʃʌn- ‖ -'jɑːŋ —*Chi*
  Shěnyáng [³ʂən ²jaŋ]
Shenzhen ˌʃen 'dʒen ˌʃʌn 'dʒʌn —*Chi*
  Shēnzhèn [¹ʂən ⁴tʂən]
Sheol, She'ol 'ʃiː ɒl -əʊl ‖ -oʊl •'•
Shepard 'ʃep əd ‖ -ᵊrd
shepherd, S~ 'ʃep əd ‖ -ᵊrd **~ed** ɪd əd **~ing** ɪŋ
  ~s z
  ˌshepherd's 'pie
shepherdess ˌʃep ə 'des '•••, -dɪs
  ‖ 'ʃep ᵊrd əs **~es** ɪz əz
shepherd's-purse ˌʃep ədz 'pɜːs ‖ -ᵊrdz 'pɜːːs
Sheppard 'ʃep əd ‖ -ᵊrd
  ˌSheppard's cor'rection
Sheppey 'ʃep i
Shepreth 'ʃep rəθ
Shepshed 'ʃep ʃed
Shepton 'ʃept ən
  ˌShepton 'Mallet
Sher *(i)* ʃɜː ‖ ʃɜːː, *(ii)* ʃeə ‖ ʃeᵊr
Sheraton 'ʃer ət ən ‖ -ᵊn ~s z
sherbert, sherbet 'ʃɜːb ət ‖ 'ʃɜːːb- -ᵊrt ~s s
Sherborne, Sherbourne 'ʃɜː bən -bɔːn
  ‖ 'ʃɜːː bɔːrn

Sherbrooke 'ʃɜː brʊk ‖ 'ʃɜːː-
sherd ʃɜːd ‖ ʃɜːːd **sherds** ʃɜːdz ‖ ʃɜːːdz
Shere ʃɪə ‖ ʃɪᵊr
Sheree, Sheri 'ʃer i
sheria ʃə 'riː‿ə
Sheridan 'ʃer ɪd ən -əd- ‖ -ᵊn
sheriff 'ʃer ɪf -əf ~s s
Sheringham 'ʃer ɪŋ əm
Sherlaw 'ʃɜː lɔː ‖ 'ʃɜːː- -lɑː
Sherley 'ʃɜːl i ‖ 'ʃɜːːl i
Sherlock 'ʃɜː lɒk ‖ 'ʃɜːː lɑːk
  ˌSherlock 'Holmes
Sherlockian ʃɜː 'lɒk i‿ən ‖ ʃɜːː 'lɑːk- ~s z
Sherman 'ʃɜː mən ‖ 'ʃɜːː mən
Sherpa, s~ 'ʃɜːp ə ‖ 'ʃɜːːp ə ~s z
Sherratt 'ʃer ət
Sherree, Sherri 'ʃer i
Sherrin 'ʃer ɪn §-ən
Sherrington 'ʃer ɪŋ tən
sherr|y, S~ 'ʃer li **~ies** iz
Sherwin 'ʃɜː wɪn -wən ‖ 'ʃɜːː-
Sherwood 'ʃɜː wʊd ‖ 'ʃɜːː-
  ˌSherwood 'Forest
Sheryl 'ʃer ɪl -əl
she's *strong form* ʃiːz, *occasional weak form* ʃiz
Shetland 'ʃet lənd ~s z
  ˌShetland 'pony
Shetlander 'ʃet lənd ə ‖ -ᵊr ~s z
Shettleston 'ʃet əls tən ‖ 'ʃet̬-
Shevardnadze ˌʃev əd 'nɑːd zeɪ -zi ‖ -ᵊrd-
Shevington 'ʃev ɪŋ tən
Shevon, Shevonne ʃə 'vɒn ʃɪ- ‖ -'vɑːn
shew... —*see* **show...**
Shew ʃuː
shewbread 'ʃəʊ bred ‖ 'ʃoʊ-
Shewell 'ʃuː‿əl ʃuːl
she-|wolf 'ʃi: wʊlf **~wolves** wʊlvz
shh *interjection* ʃ
Shia, Shi'a, Shi'a, Shiah 'ʃiː ə
shiatsu ʃi 'æts uː -'ɑːts- ‖ -'ɑːts- —*Jp*
  [ɕi ˌa tsu]
shibboleth 'ʃɪb ə leθ -əl əθ, -əl ɪθ ~s s
shicker 'ʃɪk ə ‖ -ᵊr **~ed** d
shie... —*see* **shy**
shield ʃiːᵊld **shielded** 'ʃiːᵊld ɪd -əd **shielding**
  'ʃiːᵊld ɪŋ **shields** ʃiːᵊldz
Shields ʃiːldz
shieling 'ʃiːl ɪŋ ~s z
shift ʃɪft **shifted** 'ʃɪft ɪd -əd **shifting** 'ʃɪft ɪŋ
  shifts ʃɪfts
  'shift key; 'shift stick; 'shift ˌworker; 'shift
  ˌworking
shifter 'ʃɪft ə ‖ -ᵊr ~s z
shiftless 'ʃɪft ləs -lɪs **~ly** li **~ness** nəs nɪs
shiftwork 'ʃɪft wɜːk ‖ -wɜːːk **~er/s** ə/z ‖ -ᵊr/z
shift|y 'ʃɪft li **~ier** i‿ə ‖ i‿ᵊr **~iest** i‿ɪst i‿əst
  ~ily ɪ li əl i **~iness** i nəs i nɪs
shigell|a ʃɪ 'gel ə **~ae** iː **~as** əz
shigellosis ˌʃɪg ə 'ləʊs ɪs -e-, §-əs ‖ -'loʊs əs
shih-tzu, shih tzu, S~ ˌʃɪt 'tsuː ˌʃɪ-, ˌʃiː-
  —*Chinese* shīzī [¹ʂʊr ¹dzi] ~s z
Shiism 'ʃiː ˌɪz əm
shiitake ʃɪ 'tɑːk eɪ ˌʃiːˌɪ'•• -i —*Jp* [ɕii ta ke]

Shiite, Shi'ite, Shi'ite 'ʃiː aɪt ~s s

Shijiazhuang ˌʃiː dʒiːˌə dʒu 'æŋ ‖ -ˈɑːŋ —Chi Shíjiāzhuāng [²ʂɰ ¹tɕja ¹tʂwaŋ]

shikaree, shikari ʃɪ 'kɑːr i ʃə-, -ˈkær- ~s z

Shikoku 'ʃiːk əʊ kuː ‖ -oʊ- —Jp [ɕi̥ 'ko kɯ]

shiksa, shikse 'ʃɪks ə ~s z

shillelagh ʃɪ 'leɪl ə ʃə-, -i ~s z

Shillibeer 'ʃɪl ɪ bɪə -ə- ‖ -bɪr

shilling, S~ 'ʃɪl ɪŋ ~s z

Shillong ʃɪ 'lɒŋ ‖ -ˈlɔːŋ -ˈlɑːŋ

Shilluk ʃɪ 'lʊk ‖ -ˈluːk ~s s

shilly-shall|y 'ʃɪl i ˌʃæl i ~ied id ~ies iz ~ying i‿ɪŋ

Shiloh 'ʃaɪl əʊ ‖ -oʊ

Shilton 'ʃɪlt ən

shim ʃɪm shimmed ʃɪmd shimming 'ʃɪm ɪŋ shims ʃɪmz

shimmer 'ʃɪm ə ‖ -ᵊr ~ed d shimmering 'ʃɪm ər_ɪŋ ~s z

shimm|y 'ʃɪm i ~ied id ~ies iz ~ying i‿ɪŋ

shin ʃɪn shinned ʃɪnd shinning 'ʃɪn ɪŋ shins ʃɪnz

shinbone 'ʃɪn bəʊn →'ʃɪm- ‖ -boʊn ~s z

shindig 'ʃɪn dɪg ~s z

shind|y 'ʃɪnd i ~ies iz

shine ʃaɪn shined ʃaɪnd shines ʃaɪnz shining 'ʃaɪn ɪŋ shone ʃɒn ‖ ʃoʊn (*)

shiner 'ʃaɪn ə ‖ -ᵊr ~s z

shingl|e 'ʃɪŋ gᵊl ~ed d ~es z ~ing _ɪŋ

shingly 'ʃɪŋ gli

shining 'ʃaɪn ɪŋ ~ly li

shinn|y 'ʃɪn i ~ied id ~ies iz ~ying i‿ɪŋ

Shinto 'ʃɪnt əʊ ‖ -oʊ —Jp ['ɕin to] ~ism ˌɪz əm ~ist/s ɪst/s §əst/s ‖ əst/s

shinty 'ʃɪnt i ‖ 'ʃɪnt̬ i

Shinwell 'ʃɪn wel -wəl

shin|y 'ʃaɪn i ~ier i‿ə ‖ i‿ᵊr ~iest i‿ɪst i‿əst ~ily ɪ li əl i ~iness i nəs i nɪs

ship ʃɪp shipped ʃɪpt shipping 'ʃɪp ɪŋ ships ʃɪps
    'ship ˌbiscuit; 'ship caˌnal; ˌship's 'chandler

-ship ʃɪp — workmanship 'wɜːk mən ʃɪp ‖ 'wɜːk-

shipboard 'ʃɪp bɔːd ‖ -bɔːrd -boʊrd

shipbroker 'ʃɪp ˌbrəʊk ə ‖ -ˌbroʊk ᵊr ~s z

shipbuild|er/s 'ʃɪp ˌbɪld ə/z ‖ -ᵊr/z ~ing ɪŋ

Shiplake 'ʃɪp leɪk

Shipley 'ʃɪp li

shipload 'ʃɪp ləʊd ‖ -loʊd ~s z

Shipman 'ʃɪp mən

shipmate 'ʃɪp meɪt ~s s

shipment 'ʃɪp mənt ~s s

shipowner 'ʃɪp ˌəʊn ə ‖ -ˌoʊn ᵊr ~s z

Shippam 'ʃɪp əm

shipper 'ʃɪp ə ‖ -ᵊr ~s z

shipping 'ʃɪp ɪŋ
    'shipping ˌforecast; 'shipping lane

shipshape 'ʃɪp ʃeɪp

Shipston 'ʃɪpst ən

Shipton 'ʃɪpt ən

ship-to-shore ˌʃɪp tə 'ʃɔː ◂ -tu- ‖ -'ʃɔːr ◂ -'ʃoʊr

shipway 'ʃɪp weɪ ~s z

shipworm 'ʃɪp wɜːm ‖ -wɜ̞ːm ~s z

shipwreck 'ʃɪp rek ~ed t ~ing ɪŋ ~s s

shipwright 'ʃɪp raɪt ~s s

shipyard 'ʃɪp jɑːd ‖ -jɑːrd ~s z

Shiraz, s~ ʃɪ 'ræz ʃɪə-, -'rɑːz ‖ -'rɑːz

shire 'ʃaɪ‿ə ‖ 'ʃaɪ‿ᵊr shires 'ʃaɪ‿əz ‖ 'ʃaɪ‿ᵊrz
    'shire ˌcounties; 'shire horse

-shire ʃə ʃɪə ‖ ʃᵊr ʃɪr — Lincolnshire 'lɪŋk ən ʃə -ʃɪə ‖ -ʃᵊr -ʃɪr

Shire, Shiré river and region in Malawi 'ʃɪər eɪ -ə ‖ 'ʃɪr-

shirk ʃɜːk ‖ ʃɜ̞ːk shirked ʃɜːkt ‖ ʃɜ̞ːkt shirking 'ʃɜːk ɪŋ ‖ 'ʃɜ̞ːk ɪŋ shirks ʃɜːks ‖ ʃɜ̞ːks

shirker 'ʃɜːk ə ‖ 'ʃɜ̞ːk ᵊr ~s z

Shirley 'ʃɜːl i ‖ 'ʃɜ̞ːl i

shirr ʃɜː ‖ ʃɜ̞ː shirred ʃɜːd ‖ ʃɜ̞ːd shirring 'ʃɜːr ɪŋ ‖ 'ʃɜ̞ː ɪŋ shirrs ʃɜːz ‖ ʃɜ̞ːz

shirt, Shirt ʃɜːt ‖ ʃɜ̞ːt shirts ʃɜːts‖ ʃɜ̞ːts

shirtfront 'ʃɜːt frʌnt ‖ 'ʃɜ̞ːt- ~s s

shirting 'ʃɜːt ɪŋ ‖ 'ʃɜ̞ːt̬ ɪŋ ~s z

shirtsleeve 'ʃɜːt sliːv ‖ 'ʃɜ̞ːt- ~d d ~s z

shirttail 'ʃɜːt teɪᵊl ‖ 'ʃɜ̞ːt- ~s z

shirtwaist 'ʃɜːt weɪst ˌ•'• ‖ 'ʃɜ̞ːt- ~er/s ə/z ‖ ᵊr/z ~s s

shirt|y 'ʃɜːt i ‖ 'ʃɜ̞ːt̬ i ~ier i‿ə ‖ i‿ᵊr ~iest i‿ɪst i‿əst ~iness i nəs i nɪs

shish kebab ˌʃɪʃ kə 'bæb ˌʃiː-ʃ-, -kɪ-, '•• ‖ 'ʃɪʃ kə bɑːb ~s z

shit ʃɪt shat ʃæt shits ʃɪts shitted 'ʃɪt ɪd -əd ‖ 'ʃɪt̬ əd shitting 'ʃɪt ɪŋ ‖ 'ʃɪt̬ ɪŋ

shitake, shitaki ʃɪ 'tɑːk i ˌʃiːˌɪ'••, -eɪ —Jp ['ɕii ta ke]

shitbag 'ʃɪt bæg ~s z

shite ʃaɪt

shitfaced 'ʃɪt feɪst

shithead 'ʃɪt hed ~s z

shithouse 'ʃɪt haʊs

shitless 'ʃɪt ləs -lɪs

Shittim, s~ 'ʃɪt ɪm §-əm ‖ 'ʃɪt̬ əm

shitt|y 'ʃɪt i ‖ 'ʃɪt̬ i ~ier i‿ə ‖ i‿ᵊr ~iest i‿ɪst i‿əst ~ily ɪ li əl i ~iness i nəs i nɪs

shiv ʃɪv shivs ʃɪvz

Shiva 'ʃiːv ə 'ʃɪv- —Hindi [ʃɪʋ]

shivaree ˌʃɪv ə 'riː '••• ~s z

shiver 'ʃɪv ə ‖ -ᵊr ~ed d shivering/ly 'ʃɪv ər_ɪŋ /li ~s z

shivery 'ʃɪv ər_i

shl... —see schl...

Shloer tdmk ʃlɜː ‖ ʃlɜ̞ː

shmuck ʃmʌk shmucks ʃmʌks

shmutter, schmatte 'ʃmʌt ə ‖ 'ʃmɑːt̬ ə

Shoah 'ʃəʊ ɑː ‖ 'ʃoʊ-

shoal ʃəʊl →ʃʊʊl ‖ ʃoʊl shoaled ʃəʊld →ʃʊʊld ‖ ʃoʊld shoaling 'ʃəʊl ɪŋ →'ʃʊʊl- ‖ 'ʃoʊl ɪŋ shoals ʃəʊlz →ʃʊʊlz ‖ ʃoʊlz

shoat ʃəʊt ‖ ʃoʊt shoats ʃəʊts ‖ ʃoʊts

shock ʃɒk ‖ ʃɑːk shocked ʃɒkt ‖ ʃɑːkt shocking/ly 'ʃɒk ɪŋ /li ‖ 'ʃɑːk ɪŋ /li shocks ʃɒks ‖ ʃɑːks
    'shock abˌsorber; ˌshocking 'pink◂; 'shock ˌtreatment; 'shock troops; 'shock wave

shocker 'ʃɒk ə ‖ 'ʃɑːk ᵊr ~s z

Shockey 'ʃɒk i ‖ 'ʃɑːk i
shockheaded ˌʃɒk 'hed ɪd ◄ -əd ‖ ˌʃɑːk-
shockproof 'ʃɒk pruːf §-pruf ‖ 'ʃɑːk-
shod ʃɒd ‖ ʃɑːd
shodd|y 'ʃɒd |i ‖ 'ʃɑːd |i ~ier i‿ə ‖ i‿ᵊr ~ies iz
  ~iest i‿ɪst i‿əst ~ily ɪ li əl i ~iness i nəs i nɪs
shoe ʃuː *(= shoo)* **shod** ʃɒd ‖ ʃɑːd **shoed** ʃuːd
  shoeing 'ʃuː ɪŋ **shoes** ʃuːz
shoebill 'ʃuː bɪl ~s z
shoeblack 'ʃuː blæk ~s s
Shoeburyness ˌʃuː bər‿i 'nes
shoehorn 'ʃuː hɔːn ‖ -hɔːrn ~ed d ~ing ɪŋ ~s
  z
shoelace 'ʃuː leɪs ~es ɪz əz
shoeless 'ʃuː ləs -lɪs
shoemaker 'ʃuː ˌmeɪk ə ‖ -ᵊr ~s z
shoeshine 'ʃuː ʃaɪn
shoestring 'ʃuː strɪŋ ~s z
shoetree 'ʃuː triː ~s z
shogun 'ʃəʊ ɡʌn -ɡuːn, -ɡən ‖ 'ʃoʊ- —*Jp*
  [ço̜o̜ ŋɯɴ, -ɡɯɴ] ~s z
shogunate 'ʃəʊ ɡə neɪt -ɡu-, -ɡʌ-; -ɡən ət, -ɪt
  ‖ 'ʃoʊ- ~s z
Sholokhov 'ʃɒl ə kɒf ‖ 'ʃɔːl ə kɔːf 'ʃɑːl ə kɑːf
  —*Russian* ['ʃo lə xəf]
Sholto 'ʃɒlt əʊ ‖ 'ʃɑːlt oʊ
Shona *personal name* 'ʃəʊn ə ‖ 'ʃoʊn ə
Shona *Zimbabwean language and people* 'ʃɒn ə
  'ʃəʊn- ‖ 'ʃoʊn ə ~s z
shone ʃɒn ‖ ʃoʊn *(*)*
shonk|y 'ʃɒŋk| i ‖ 'ʃɑːŋk| i ~ier i‿ə ‖ i‿ᵊr
  ~iest i‿ɪst ‿əst
shoo ʃuː **shooed** ʃuːd **shooing** 'ʃuː ɪŋ **shoos**
  ʃuːz
shoofly 'ʃuː flaɪ
  ˌshoofly 'pie ‖ '•‿•
shoo-in 'ʃuː ɪn ~s z
shook ʃʊk §ʃuːk
shoot ʃuːt **shooting/s** 'ʃuːt ɪŋ/z ‖ 'ʃuːt̬ ɪŋ/z
  shoots ʃuːts **shot** ʃɒt ‖ ʃɑːt
  'shooting box; 'shooting brake; 'shooting
  ˌgallery; 'shooting match; ˌshooting 'star;
  'shooting stick
shooter, S~ 'ʃuːt ə ‖ 'ʃuːt̬ ᵊr ~s z
-shooter ˌʃuːt ə ‖ ˌʃuːt̬ ᵊr — duck-shooter
  'dʌk ˌʃuːt ə ‖ -ˌʃuːt̬ ᵊr
shoot-out 'ʃuːt aʊt ‖ 'ʃuːt̬- ~s s
shop ʃɒp ‖ ʃɑːp **shopped** ʃɒpt ‖ ʃɑːpt
  shopping 'ʃɒp ɪŋ ‖ 'ʃɑːp ɪŋ **shops**
  ʃɒps ‖ ʃɑːps
  'shop as,sistant; ˌshop 'floor, '• •;
  'shopping ˌbasket; 'shopping ˌcentre;
  'shopping mall; ˌshop 'steward ‖ '• •, • ••;
  ˌshop 'window
shopfitt|er 'ʃɒp ˌfɪt| ə ‖ 'ʃɑːp ˌfɪt̬| ᵊr ~ers
  əz ‖ -ᵊrz ~ing ɪŋ
shopfront 'ʃɒp frʌnt ‖ 'ʃɑːp- ~s s
shophar 'ʃəʊf ɑ ‖ 'ʃoʊf ɑːr -ᵊr ~s z
shopkeeper 'ʃɒp ˌkiːp ə ‖ 'ʃɑːp ˌkiːp ᵊr ~s z
shoplift 'ʃɒp lɪft ‖ 'ʃɑːp- ~ed ɪd əd ~er/s
  ə/z ‖ ᵊr/z ~ing ɪŋ ~s s
shoppe ʃɒp ‖ ʃɑːp —*jocularly also*
  'ʃɒp i ‖ 'ʃɑːp i

shopp... —*see* **shop**
shopper 'ʃɒp ə ‖ 'ʃɑːp ᵊr ~s z
shopsoiled 'ʃɒp sɔɪᵊld ‖ 'ʃɑːp-
shopwalker 'ʃɒp ˌwɔːk ə ‖ 'ʃɑːp ˌwɔːk ᵊr
  -ˌwɑːk- ~s z
shopworn 'ʃɒp wɔːn ‖ 'ʃɑːp wɔːrn -woʊrn
shore, Shore ʃɔː ‖ ʃɔːr ʃoʊr **shored**
  ʃɔːd ‖ ʃɔːrd ʃoʊrd **shores** ʃɔːz ‖ ʃɔːrz ʃoʊrz
  shoring 'ʃɔːr ɪŋ ‖ 'ʃoʊr-
  'shore leave
Shoreditch 'ʃɔː dɪtʃ ‖ 'ʃɔːr- 'ʃoʊr-
Shoreham 'ʃɔːr əm ‖ 'ʃoʊr-
shoreline 'ʃɔː laɪn ‖ 'ʃɔːr- 'ʃoʊr- ~s z
shorn ʃɔːn ‖ ʃɔːrn ʃoʊrn

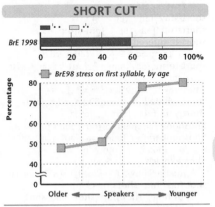

SHORT CUT

BrE 1998

short, Short ʃɔːt ‖ ʃɔːrt **shorted** 'ʃɔːt ɪd -əd
  ‖ 'ʃɔːrt̬ əd **shorter** 'ʃɔːt ə ‖ 'ʃɔːrt̬ ᵊr
  shortest 'ʃɔːt ɪst -əst ‖ 'ʃɔːrt̬ əst **shorting**
  'ʃɔːt ɪŋ ‖ 'ʃɔːrt̬ ɪŋ **shorts** ʃɔːts ‖ ʃɔːrts
  ˌshort ˌback and 'sides; ˌshort 'circuit;
  'short cut, ˌ• '• —*BrE 1998 poll panel
  preference:* '•• *59%,* ˌ•'• *41%;* 'short list;
  ˌshort 'shrift; ˌshort 'story; ˌshort 'term;
  ˌshort 'time; ˌshort 'wave
shortag|e 'ʃɔːt ɪdʒ ‖ 'ʃɔːrt̬- ~es ɪz əz
shortbread 'ʃɔːt bred ‖ 'ʃɔːrt- ~s z
shortcake 'ʃɔːt keɪk ‖ 'ʃɔːrt- ~s s
short-chang|e ˌʃɔːt 'tʃeɪndʒ ‖ ˌʃɔːrt- ~ed d
  ~es ɪz əz ~ing ɪŋ
short-circu|it ˌʃɔːt 'sɜːk ɪt §-ət
  ‖ ˌʃɔːrt 'sɜːk ət ~ited ɪt ɪd §ət-, -əd ‖ ət̬ əd
  ~iting ɪt ɪŋ §ət- ‖ ət̬ ɪŋ ~its ɪts §əts ‖ əts
shortcoming 'ʃɔːt ˌkʌm ɪŋ ,•'•• ‖ 'ʃɔːrt- ~s z
shortcrust 'ʃɔːt krʌst ‖ 'ʃɔːrt-
short-dated ˌʃɔːt 'deɪt ɪd ◄ -əd
  ‖ ˌʃɔːrt 'deɪt̬ əd ◄
short-eared ˌʃɔːt 'ɪəd ◄ ‖ 'ʃɔːrt̬ ɪrd
shorten 'ʃɔːt ᵊn ‖ 'ʃɔːrt ᵊn ~ed d ~ing ‿ɪŋ ~s
  z
Shorter 'ʃɔːt ə ‖ 'ʃɔːrt̬ ᵊr
shortfall 'ʃɔːt fɔːl ‖ 'ʃɔːrt- -fɑːl ~s z
shorthand 'ʃɔːt hænd ‖ 'ʃɔːrt-
  ˌshorthand 'typist
shorthanded ˌʃɔːt 'hænd ɪd ◄ -əd ˌʃɔːrt-
short-haul 'ʃɔːt hɔːl ,•'• ‖ 'ʃɔːrt- -hɑːl
shorthold 'ʃɔːt həʊld →-hɒʊld ‖ 'ʃɔːrt hoʊld
  ~s z

S

shorthorn, S~ 'ʃɔːt hɔːn ‖ 'ʃɔːrt hɔːrn ~s z
shortie 'ʃɔːt i ‖ 'ʃɔːrt̮ i ~s z
shortish 'ʃɔːt ɪʃ ‖ 'ʃɔːrt̮ ɪʃ
Shortland 'ʃɔːt lənd ‖ 'ʃɔːrt-
short-list 'ʃɔːt lɪst ‖ 'ʃɔːrt- ~ed ɪd əd ~ing ɪŋ
~s s
short-lived ˌʃɔːt 'lɪvd ◄ ‖ ˌʃɔːrt 'laɪvd ◄ -'lɪvd
short|ly 'ʃɔːt |li ‖ 'ʃɔːrt |li ~ness nəs nɪs
Shorto 'ʃɔːt əʊ ‖ 'ʃɔːrt̮ oʊ
short-order 'ʃɔːt ˌɔːd ə ˌ•'•• ‖ 'ʃɔːrt ˌɔːrd ər
short-range ˌʃɔːt 'reɪndʒ ◄ ‖ ˌʃɔːrt-
shortsighted ˌʃɔːt 'saɪt ɪd ◄ -əd
‖ ˌʃɔːrt 'saɪt̮ əd ◄ ~ly li ~ness nəs nɪs
short-staffed ˌʃɔːt 'staːft ◄ §-'stæft
‖ ˌʃɔːrt 'stæft ◄
short-stay ˌʃɔːt 'steɪ ◄ ‖ ˌʃɔːrt-
shortstop 'ʃɔːt stɒp ‖ 'ʃɔːrt staːp ~s s
short-tempered
ˌʃɔːt 'temp əd ◄ ‖ ˌʃɔːrt 'temp ərd ◄
short-term ˌʃɔːt 'tɜːm ◄ ‖ ˌʃɔːrt 'tɜːm ◄ ~ism
ˌɪz əm
shortwave ˌʃɔːt 'weɪv ◄ '•• ‖ ˌʃɔːrt-
short-winded ˌʃɔːt 'wɪnd ɪd ◄ -əd ‖ ˌʃɔːrt-
short|y 'ʃɔːt li ‖ 'ʃɔːrt̮ li ~ies iz
Shoshone ʃəʊ 'ʃəʊn i ‖ ʃoʊ 'ʃoʊn i ʃə- ~s z
Shoshonean ʃəʊ 'ʃəʊn i‿ən ˌʃəʊʃ ə 'niː‿ən
‖ ʃoʊ 'ʃoʊn i‿ən ˌʃoʊʃ ə 'niː ən
Shostakovich ˌʃɒst ə 'kəʊv ɪtʃ
‖ ˌʃaːst ə 'koʊv ɪtʃ —Russ [ʃi stʌ 'kɔ vʲɪtʃ]
shot ʃɒt ‖ ʃaːt shots ʃɒts ‖ ʃaːts
'shot hole; 'shot put; ˌshot 'silk; 'shot
ˌtower
shotgun 'ʃɒt ɡʌn ‖ 'ʃaːt- ~s z
ˌshotgun 'wedding
shot-putter 'ʃɒt ˌpʊt ə ‖ 'ʃaːt ˌpʊt̮ ər ~s z
shott ʃɒt ‖ ʃaːt (= shot) shotts ʃɒts ‖ ʃaːts
Shotton 'ʃɒt ən ‖ 'ʃaːt ən
Shotts ʃɒts ‖ ʃaːts
Shotwick 'ʃɒt wɪk ‖ 'ʃaːt-
should strong form ʃʊd, occasional weak forms
ʃəd ʃd, ʃt (!)
shoulder 'ʃəʊld ə →'ʃɒʊld- ‖ 'ʃoʊld ər (!) ~ed
d shouldering 'ʃəʊld_ər ɪŋ →'ʃɒʊld_
‖ 'ʃoʊld_ər ɪŋ ~s z
'shoulder bag; 'shoulder blade; 'shoulder
strap
shouldn't 'ʃʊd ənt
shouldst strong form ʃʊdst ʃʊtst, occasional
weak form ʃədst ʃətst
shout ʃaʊt shouted 'ʃaʊt ɪd -əd ‖ 'ʃaʊt̮ əd
shouting 'ʃaʊt ɪŋ ‖ 'ʃaʊt̮ ɪŋ shouts ʃaʊts
shove ʃʌv shoved ʃʌvd shoves ʃʌvz
shoving 'ʃʌv ɪŋ
shove-halfpenny, shove-ha'penny
ˌʃʌv 'heɪp ni
shovel 'ʃʌv əl ~ed, ~led d ~ing, ~ling _ɪŋ ~s
z
shovelboard 'ʃʌv əl bɔːd ‖-bɔːrd -boʊrd
shoveler, shoveller 'ʃʌv əl_ə ‖ _ər ~s z
shovelful 'ʃʌv əl fʊl ~s z
show ʃəʊ ‖ ʃoʊ showed ʃəʊd ‖ ʃoʊd
showing 'ʃəʊ ɪŋ ‖ 'ʃoʊ ɪŋ shown
ʃəʊn ‖ ʃoʊn shows ʃəʊz ‖ ʃoʊz

'show ˌbusiness; 'show ˌjumper; 'show
ˌjumping; ˌshow of 'hands; 'show ˌtrial
showband 'ʃəʊ bænd ‖ 'ʃoʊ- ~s z
showbiz 'ʃəʊ bɪz ‖ 'ʃoʊ-
showboat 'ʃəʊ bəʊt ‖ 'ʃoʊ boʊt ~s s
showcas|e 'ʃəʊ keɪs ‖ 'ʃoʊ- ~es ɪz əz
showdown 'ʃəʊ daʊn ‖ 'ʃoʊ- ~s z
shower v; n 'sudden rain; ~ bath; etc.'
'ʃaʊ_ə ‖ 'ʃaʊ_ər ~ed d showering
'ʃaʊ_ər ɪŋ ‖ 'ʃaʊ_ər ɪŋ ~s z
'shower bath; 'shower gel
shower 'one that shows' 'ʃəʊ ə ‖ 'ʃoʊ ər ~s z
showerproof 'ʃaʊ_ə pruːf -§prʊf
‖ 'ʃaʊ_ər pruːf ~ed t ~ing ɪŋ ~s s
showery 'ʃaʊ_ər i ‖ 'ʃaʊ_ər i
showgirl 'ʃəʊ ɡɜːl ‖ 'ʃoʊ ɡɜːl ~s z
showground 'ʃəʊ ɡraʊnd ‖ 'ʃoʊ- ~s z
showi... —see showy
show|man 'ʃəʊ |mən ‖ 'ʃoʊ- ~manship
mən ʃɪp ~men mən men
shown ʃəʊn §'ʃəʊ ən ‖ ʃoʊn
show-off 'ʃəʊ ɒf -ɔːf ‖ 'ʃoʊ ɔːf -aːf ~s s
showpiec|e 'ʃəʊ piːs ‖ 'ʃoʊ- ~es ɪz əz
showplac|e 'ʃəʊ pleɪs ‖ 'ʃoʊ- ~es ɪz əz
showroom 'ʃəʊ ruːm -rʊm ‖ 'ʃoʊ- ~s z
show-stopper 'ʃəʊ ˌstɒp ə ‖ 'ʃoʊ ˌstaːp ər ~s z
show-stopping 'ʃəʊ ˌstɒp ɪŋ ‖ 'ʃoʊ ˌstaːp ɪŋ
show|y 'ʃəʊ li ‖ 'ʃoʊ li ~ier i_ə ‖ i_ər ~iest
i_ɪst i_əst ~ily ɪ li əl i ~iness i nəs i nɪs
shoyu 'ʃɔɪ uː —Jp [ço,o ɟɯ]
shrank ʃræŋk
shrapnel, S~ 'ʃræp nəl
shred ʃred shredded 'ʃred ɪd -əd shredding
'ʃred ɪŋ shreds ʃredz
shredder 'ʃred ə ‖ -ər ~s z
Shreveport 'ʃriːv pɔːt ‖ -pɔːrt -poʊrt
shrew ʃruː shrews ʃruːz
'shrew mole
shrewd ʃruːd shrewder 'ʃruːd ə ‖ -ər
shrewdest 'ʃruːd ɪst -əst shrewdly 'ʃruːd li
shrewdness 'ʃruːd nəs -nɪs
shrewish 'ʃruː ɪʃ ~ly li ~ness nəs nɪs
Shrewsbury (i) 'ʃrəʊz bər_i ‖ 'ʃroʊz- -ˌber i,
(ii) 'ʃruːz- —The place in England is usually
(i), though locally also (ii). The places in the US
are (ii).
shriek ʃriːk shrieked ʃriːkt shrieking/ly
'ʃriːk ɪŋ /li shrieks ʃriːks
shrift ʃrɪft
shrike ʃraɪk shrikes ʃraɪks
shrill ʃrɪl shrilled ʃrɪld shriller 'ʃrɪl ə ‖ -ər
shrillest 'ʃrɪl ɪst -əst shrilling 'ʃrɪl ɪŋ shrills
ʃrɪlz
shrilly adv 'ʃrɪl li -i
shrillness 'ʃrɪl nəs -nɪs
shrimp ʃrɪmp shrimped ʃrɪmpt shrimping
'ʃrɪmp ɪŋ shrimps ʃrɪmps
shrimper 'ʃrɪmp ə ‖ -ər ~s z
Shrimpton 'ʃrɪmpt ən
shrine ʃraɪn shrines ʃraɪnz
Shriner 'ʃraɪn ə ‖ -ər ~s z
shrink ʃrɪŋk shrank ʃræŋk shrinking/ly
'ʃrɪŋk ɪŋ /li shrinks ʃrɪŋks shrunk ʃrʌŋk

Short vowel, long vowel

A. SPELLING

1 To each vowel letter in English spelling there correspond two vowel sounds, the vowel letter then traditionally being known as 'short' or 'long' respectively (see **a, e, i, o, u**). (There are also other possibilities that have no traditional names.) The following guidelines are to help you decide whether the short or long pronunciation is likely to be appropriate.

2 A single vowel letter generally counts as **short**
- in a word of one syllable, ending in a consonant (**back, red, tip, rod, cut, hymn**)
- in a stressed penultimate syllable, where the vowel is followed by two or more consonant letters (**battle, jelly, middle, doctor, system**).

3 A single vowel letter generally counts as **long**
- before one consonant letter plus silent **e** (**take, complete, time, rope, rude, type**). However, there are several exceptions, including **have, give, one, come, love**.
- in a word of one syllable, where the vowel is not followed by a consonant (**me, hi, go, flu, try**).
- in a stressed penultimate syllable, where the vowel is followed by only one consonant letter, or by a vowel letter (**potato, thesis, item, over, tribunal, asylum; chaos, neon, triumph, heroic, ruin, dying**).

4 There are many cases not covered by these guidelines. Furthermore, the guidelines have exceptions. That is why you need a pronunciation dictionary.

B. PHONETICS

5 The English vowels can also be divided into short and long on the basis of their pronunciation. Other things being equal, a long vowel has greater duration than a short vowel. However, vowel duration is strongly influenced by the phonetic environment. In general, the difference between short and long vowels is less noticeable in AmE than in BrE.

6 The **short** vowels are ɪ, e, æ, ɒ, ʊ, ʌ, together with the WEAK vowels ə, i, u. Of these, æ is a special case: it is not similar in quality to any long vowel, and many speakers lengthen it (particularly before certain consonants, notably b and d).

7 The **long** vowels are iː, uː, ɑː, ɔː, together with BrE ɜː and AmE ɜ˞ː. In the phonetic transcription system used in LPD, long vowels are always written with the length mark ː, in accordance with the PHONEME principle; but long vowels may in certain environments be phonetically quite short (see CLIPPING).

8 The duration of **diphthongs** is like that of long vowels.

S

> ▶ *Short vowel, long vowel*

9 With one exception, the 'short' vowels of spelling correspond to phonetically short vowels. The exception is AmE ɑː, which is phonetically long, yet is associated with the traditional 'short O'. (The corresponding BrE ɒ is phonetically short.) The 'long vowels' of spelling correspond to three phonetic diphthongs (eɪ, aɪ, əʊ‖oʊ), one long vowel (iː), and one sequence of semivowel plus long vowel (juː).

S

shrunken 'ʃrʌŋk ən
  ˌshrinking 'violet
shrinkag|e 'ʃrɪŋk ɪdʒ ~es ɪz əz
shrink-wrap 'ʃrɪŋk ræp ˌ•'• ~ped t ~ping ɪŋ
  ~s s
shrive ʃraɪv shrived ʃraɪvd shriven 'ʃrɪv ən
  (!) shrives ʃraɪvz shriving 'ʃraɪv ɪŋ shrove
  ʃrəʊv ‖ ʃroʊv
shrivel 'ʃrɪv əl ~ed, ~led d ~ing, ~ling ɪŋ ~s
  z
shriven 'ʃrɪv ən
Shrivenham 'ʃrɪv ən_əm
shroff ʃrɒf ‖ ʃrɑːf shroffed ʃrɒft ‖ ʃrɑːft
  shroffing 'ʃrɒf ɪŋ ‖ 'ʃrɑːf ɪŋ shroffs
  ʃrɒfs ‖ ʃrɑːfs
Shropshire 'ʃrɒp ʃə -ʃɪə ‖ 'ʃrɑːp ʃər -ʃɪr
shroud ʃraʊd shrouded 'ʃraʊd ɪd -əd
  shrouding 'ʃraʊd ɪŋ shrouds ʃraʊdz
shrove, S~ ʃrəʊv ‖ ʃroʊv
  ˌShrove 'Tuesday
Shrovetide 'ʃrəʊv taɪd ‖ 'ʃroʊv-
shrub ʃrʌb shrubs ʃrʌbz
shrubber|y 'ʃrʌb ər i ~ies iz
shrubb|y 'ʃrʌb |i ~ier i_ə ‖ i_ər ~iest i_ɪst i_əst
  ~iness i nəs i nɪs
shrug ʃrʌg shrugged ʃrʌgd shrugging
  'ʃrʌg ɪŋ shrugs ʃrʌgz
shrunk ʃrʌŋk
shrunken 'ʃrʌŋk ən
shtick ʃtɪk shticks ʃtɪks
shtook, shtuck ʃtʊk
shtup ʃtʊp shtupped ʃtʊpt shtupping
  'ʃtʊp ɪŋ shtups ʃtʊps
shubunkin ʃu 'bʌŋk ɪn §-ən ~s z
shuck ʃʌk shucked ʃʌkt shucking 'ʃʌk ɪŋ
  shucks ʃʌks
Shuckburgh 'ʃʌk bər_ə ‖ 'ʃʌk bɜˑg
shudder 'ʃʌd ə ‖ -ər ~ed d shuddering/ly
  'ʃʌd_ər ɪŋ /li ~s z
shuffl|e 'ʃʌf əl ~ed d ~es z ~ing ˌɪŋ
shuffleboard 'ʃʌf əl bɔːd ‖ -bɔːrd -boʊrd
Shufflebottom 'ʃʌf əl ˌbɒt əm ‖ -ˌbɑːt əm
Shufflewick 'ʃʌf əl wɪk
shufti, shufty 'ʃʊft i shuftis 'ʃʊft iz
Shughie 'ʃuː i
shul ʃuːl ʃʊl shuln ʃuːln ʃʊln
Shulamite 'ʃuːl ə maɪt ~s s
Shulman 'ʃuːl mən

shun ʃʌn shunned ʃʌnd shunning 'ʃʌn ɪŋ
  shuns ʃʌnz
'shun *military command: 'attention'* ʃʌn
shunt ʃʌnt shunted 'ʃʌnt ɪd -əd ‖ 'ʃʌnt̬ əd
  shunting 'ʃʌnt ɪŋ ‖ 'ʃʌnt̬ ɪŋ shunts ʃʌnts
  'shunting ˌengine
shush ʃʊʃ ʃʌʃ shushed ʃʊʃt ʃʌʃt shushes
  'ʃʊʃ ɪz 'ʃʌʃ-, -əz shushing 'ʃʊʃ ɪŋ 'ʃʌʃ-
Shuster 'ʃʊst ə 'ʃuːst- ‖ -ər
Shuswap 'ʃʊs wɒp 'ʃʊʃ- ‖ -wɑːp
shut ʃʌt shuts ʃʌts shutting 'ʃʌt ɪŋ ‖ 'ʃʌt̬ ɪŋ
shutdown 'ʃʌt daʊn ~s z
Shute ʃuːt
Shuter 'ʃuːt ə ‖ 'ʃuːt̬ ər
shut-eye 'ʃʌt aɪ ‖ 'ʃʌt̬ aɪ
shut-in *n* 'ʃʌt ɪn ‖ 'ʃʌt̬- ~s z
shut-in *adj* ˌʃʌt 'ɪn ◄ ‖ ˌʃʌt̬-
shutoff *n* 'ʃʌt ɒf -ɔːf ‖ 'ʃʌt̬ ɔːf -ɑːf ~s s
shutout *n* 'ʃʌt aʊt ‖ 'ʃʌt̬- ~s z
shutter 'ʃʌt ə ‖ 'ʃʌt̬ ər ~ed d shuttering
  'ʃʌt_ər ɪŋ ‖ 'ʃʌt̬ ər ɪŋ ~s z
shuttl|e 'ʃʌt əl ‖ 'ʃʌt̬ əl ~ed d ~es z ~ing ˌɪŋ
  'shuttle diˌplomacy
shuttlecock 'ʃʌt əl kɒk ‖ 'ʃʌt̬ əl kɑːk ~s s
Shuttleworth 'ʃʌt əl wɜːθ -wəθ ‖ 'ʃʌt̬ əl wɜːθ
Shuy ʃaɪ
shwa ʃwɑː ʃvɑː shwas ʃwɑːz ʃvɑːz
shy ʃaɪ shied ʃaɪd shier, shyer 'ʃaɪ_ə ‖ 'ʃaɪ_ər
  shies ʃaɪz shiest, shyest 'ʃaɪ ɪst -əst
  shying 'ʃaɪ ɪŋ
-shy ʃaɪ — work-shy 'wɜːk ʃaɪ ‖ 'wɜːk-
Shylock 'ʃaɪ lɒk ‖ -lɑːk
shy|ly 'ʃaɪ |li ~ness nəs nɪs
shyster 'ʃaɪst ə ‖ -ər ~s z
si siː
SI ˌes 'aɪ
sial 'saɪ_əl
sialagogue, sialogogue saɪ 'æl ə gɒg 'saɪ_əl-
  ‖ -gɑːg ~s z
Siam ˌsaɪ 'æm '••
siamang 'siː_ə mæŋ 'saɪ_ ~s z
Siamese ˌsaɪ_ə 'miːz ◄ ‖ -'miːs
  ˌSiamese 'cat; ˌSiamese 'twin
Sian, Siân ʃɑːn
sib sɪb sibs sɪbz
Sibelius sɪ 'beɪl i_əs sə- —*Swed, Finnish*
  [si 'beː li us]
Siberi|a saɪ 'bɪər i_ə ‖ -'bɪr- ~an/s ən/z
sibilanc|e 'sɪb ɪl ənts -əl- ~y i

sibilant 'sɪb ɪl ənt -əl- ~**ly** li ~**s** s
sibil|late 'sɪb ɪ |leɪt -ə- ~**lated** leɪt ɪd -əd
‖ leɪt̮ əd ~**lates** leɪts ~**lating** leɪt ɪŋ ‖ leɪt̮ ɪŋ
sibilation ˌsɪb ɪ 'leɪʃ ᵊn -ə- ~**s** z
Sibley 'sɪb li
sibling 'sɪb lɪŋ ~**s** z
sibyl, Sibyl 'sɪb ɪl -ᵊl ~**s**, ~'**s** z
sibylline, S~ 'sɪb ɪ laɪn -ə-; sɪ 'bɪl aɪn, sə- ‖ -liːn
sic sɪk siːk —*see also phrases with this word*
siccative 'sɪk ət ɪv ‖ -ət̮- ~**s** z
Sichuan ˌsɪtʃ 'waːn —*Chi* Sìchuān [⁴sɨ ¹tṣʰwɑn]
Sicilian sɪ 'sɪl i‿ən sə- ~**s** z
Sicil|y 'sɪs əl i -ɪl- ~**ies** iz
sick sɪk **sicker** 'sɪk ə ‖ 'sɪk ᵊr **sickest** 'sɪk ɪst
-əst
    'sick call; ˌsick 'headache; 'sick leave; 'sick
    paˌrade; 'sick pay
sickbay 'sɪk beɪ ~**s** z
sickbed 'sɪk bed ~**s** z
sicken 'sɪk ᵊn ~**ed** d ~**ing/ly** ‿ɪŋ /li ~**s** z
Sickert 'sɪk ət ‖ -ᵊrt
sickl|e 'sɪk ᵊl ~**ed** d ~**es** z ~**ing** ‿ɪŋ
sickle-cell 'sɪk ᵊl sel
    ˌsickle-cell a'naemia
sick|ly 'sɪk |li ~**lier** li‿ə ‖ li‿ᵊr ~**liest** li‿ɪst li‿əst
    ~**liness** li nəs li nɪs
sickness 'sɪk nəs -nɪs ~**es** ɪz əz
    'sickness ˌbenefit
sicko 'sɪk əʊ ‖ -oʊ ~**s** z
sickroom 'sɪk ruːm -rʊm ~**s** z
sic transit gloria mundi ˌsɪk 'trænz ɪt
    ˌglɔːr i‿ə 'mʊnd i ˌsiːk-, -'trænts-, -'trɑːnz-,
    -'trɑːnts-, §-'• ət-, -i ɑː -iː ‖ -ˌgloʊr-
Sid sɪd
Sidcup 'sɪd kʌp →'sɪg-, -kəp
Siddall 'sɪd ɔːl ‖ -ɑːl
Siddeley 'sɪd ᵊl‿i
Siddhartha sɪ 'dɑːt ə ‖ -'dɑːrt̮ ə
Siddons 'sɪd ᵊnz
side saɪd **sided** 'saɪd ɪd -əd **sides** saɪdz
    siding 'saɪd ɪŋ
    'side dish; 'side efˌfect; 'side ˌissue; 'side
    ˌorder; 'side street
sidearm 'saɪd ɑːm ‖ -ɑːrm ~**s** z
sideband 'saɪd bænd →'saɪb-
sidebar 'saɪd bɑː →'saɪb- ‖ -bɑːr ~**s** z
sideboard 'saɪd bɔːd →'saɪb- ‖ -bɔːrd -boʊrd
    ~**s** z
Sidebotham, Sidebottom 'saɪd ˌbɒt əm
    →'saɪb- ‖ -ˌbɑːt̮ əm —*Some bearers of these
    names insist on fanciful pronunciations such as*
    'siːd-, -ˌbəʊθ əm ‖ -ˌboʊθ-, *or even*
    ˌsɪd ɪ bə 'tɑːm, -'təʊm ‖ -'toʊm
sideburn 'saɪd bɜːn →'saɪb- ‖ -bɝːn ~**s** z
sidecar 'saɪd kɑː →'saɪg- ‖ -kɑːr ~**s** z
-sided 'saɪd ɪd -əd — **many-sided**
    ˌmen i 'saɪd ɪd ◄ -əd
sidekick 'saɪd kɪk →'saɪg- ~**s** s
sidelight 'saɪd laɪt ~**s** s
sidelin|e 'saɪd laɪn ~**ed** d ~**es** z ~**ing** ɪŋ
sidelong 'saɪd lɒŋ ‖ -lɔːŋ -lɑːŋ
side|man 'saɪd |mən →'saɪb-, -mæn ~**men**
    men mən

side-on ˌsaɪd 'ɒn ◄ ‖ -'ɑːn ◄ -'ɔːn
sidereal saɪ 'dɪər i‿əl sɪ- ‖ -'dɪr-
siderite 'saɪd ə raɪt 'sɪd- ‖ 'sɪd-
siderostat 'sɪd ᵊr əʊ stæt ‖ -ə • ~**s** s
sidesaddle 'saɪd ˌsæd ᵊl ~**s** z
sideshow 'saɪd ʃəʊ ‖ -ʃoʊ ~**s** z
sideslip 'saɪd slɪp ~**ped** t ~**ping** ɪŋ ~**s** s
sides|man 'saɪdz |mən ~**men** mən men
sidesplitting 'saɪd ˌsplɪt ɪŋ ‖ -ˌsplɪt̮ ɪŋ ~**ly** li
sidestep 'saɪd step ~**ped** t ~**ping** ɪŋ ~**s** s
sidestroke 'saɪd strəʊk ‖ -stroʊk
sideswip|e 'saɪd swaɪp ~**ed** t ~**es** s ~**ing** ɪŋ
sidetrack 'saɪd træk ~**ed** t ~**ing** ɪŋ ~**s** s
sidewalk 'saɪd wɔːk ‖ -wɑːk ~**s** s
    'sidewalk ˌartist
sidewall 'saɪd wɔːl ‖ -wɑːl ~**s** z
sideward 'saɪd wəd ‖ -wᵊrd ~**s** z
sideways 'saɪd weɪz
side-wheeler 'saɪd ˌwiːᵊl ə -hwiːᵊl- ‖ -ˌhwiːᵊl ᵊr
sidewinder 'saɪd ˌwaɪnd ə ‖ -ᵊr ~**s** z
Sidgwick 'sɪdʒ wɪk
siding 'saɪd ɪŋ ~**s** z
sidl|e 'saɪd ᵊl ~**ed** d ~**es** z ~**ing** ‿ɪŋ
Sidmouth 'sɪd məθ →'sɪb-
Sidney 'sɪd ni
Sidon 'saɪd ᵊn
Sidonian saɪ 'dəʊn i‿ən ‖ -'doʊn- ~**s** z
Sidonie sɪ 'dəʊn i ‖ -'doʊn i
Sieff siːf
siege siːdʒ siːʒ **sieges** 'siːdʒ ɪz 'siːʒ-, -əz
Sieg Heil ˌsiːg 'haɪᵊl —*Ger* [ˌziːk 'haɪl]
Siegfried 'siːg friːd —*Ger* ['ziːk fʀiːt]
Sieglinde sɪ 'glɪnd ə sɪ- —*Ger* ['ziːk 'lɪn də]
Siemens, s~ 'siːm ᵊnz —*Ger* ['ziː mᵊns]
Siena si 'en ə —*It* ['sjɛː na]
Sienese ˌsi: e 'niːz ◄ -ə- ‖ -'niːs
sienna si 'en ə
sierra, S~ si 'er ə -'eᵊr-; 'sɪər ə —*Sp* ['sjɛ ʀʀa]
    ~**s** z —*see also phrases with this word*
    Siˌerra Ne'vada
Sierra Leone si ˌer ə li 'əʊn -ˌeᵊr-, -'əʊn i;
    ˌsɪər•• ‖ -'oʊn -'oʊn i
Sierra Leonian si ˌer ə li 'əʊn i‿ən ◄ -ˌeᵊr-;
    ˌsɪər••'•- ‖ -'oʊn- ~**s** z
Sierra Madre si ˌer ə 'mɑːdr eɪ -ˌeᵊr-, -i —*Sp*
    ['maðɾ re]
siesta si 'est ə ~**s** z
sieve sɪv (*!*) **sieved** sɪvd **sieves** sɪvz **sieving**
    'sɪv ɪŋ
sievert, S~ 'siːv ət ‖ -ᵊrt ~**s** s
sift sɪft **sifted** 'sɪft ɪd -əd **sifting/s** 'sɪft ɪŋ/z
    sifts sɪfts
Sifta *tdmk* 'sɪft ə
sifter 'sɪft ə ‖ -ᵊr ~**s** z
Sigal 'siːg ᵊl
sigh saɪ **sighed** saɪd (= *side*) **sighing** 'saɪ ɪŋ
    sighs saɪz (= *size*)
sight saɪt (= *site, cite*) **sighted** 'saɪt ɪd -əd
    ‖ 'saɪt̮ əd **sighting** 'saɪt ɪŋ ‖ 'saɪt̮ ɪŋ **sights**
    saɪts
-sighted 'saɪt ɪd -əd ‖ 'saɪt̮ əd — **far-sighted**
    ˌfɑː 'saɪt ɪd ◄ -əd ‖ ˌfɑːr 'saɪt̮ əd ◄
sightless 'saɪt ləs -lɪs ~**ly** li ~**ness** nəs nɪs

sightline 'saɪt laɪn ~**s** z
sight|ly 'saɪt |li ~**lier** li‿ə ‖ li‿ªr ~**liest** li‿ɪst
  li‿əst
sight-|read pres 'saɪt |riːd ~**read** past & pp red
  ~**reader/s** riːd ə/z ‖ -ªr/z ~**reading** riːd ɪŋ
  ~**reads** riːdz
sightscreen 'saɪt skriːn ~**s** z
sightseeing 'saɪt ˌsiː ɪŋ
sightseer 'saɪt ˌsiː‿ə ‖ ªr ~**s** z
sigint, SIGINT 'sɪg ɪnt
Sigismond, Sigismund 'sɪg ɪs mənd 'sɪdʒ-, -ɪz-
sig|lum 'sɪg |ləm ~**la** lə
sigma 'sɪg mə ~**s** z
sigmatic sɪg 'mæt ɪk ‖ -'mæt̬ ɪk
sigmoid 'sɪg mɔɪd
Sigmund 'sɪg mənd —Ger ['ziːk mʊnt]
sign saɪn (= sine) **signed** saɪnd **signing**
  'saɪn ɪŋ **signs** saɪnz
  '**sign** ˌlanguage
signage 'saɪn ɪdʒ
signal 'sɪg nªl ~**ed, ~led** d ~**ing, ~ling** ɪŋ ~**s**
  z
  '**signal** box; '**signal** ˌtower
signaler 'sɪg nªl ə ‖ -ªr ~**s** z
signalis|e, signaliz|e 'sɪg nə laɪz -nªl aɪz ~**ed**
  d ~**es** ɪz əz ~**ing** ɪŋ
signaller 'sɪg nªl ə ‖ -ªr ~**s** z
signally 'sɪg nªl i
signal|man 'sɪg nªl |mən -mæn ~**men** mən
  men
signalment 'sɪg nªl mənt ~**s** s
signal-to-noise ˌsɪg nªl tə 'nɔɪz
  ˌsignal-to-'noise ˌratio
signator|y 'sɪg nət‿ªr li ‖ -nə tɔːr li -tour i
  ~**ies** iz
signature 'sɪg nətʃ ə -nɪtʃ- ‖ -ªr -nə tʃʊr ~**s** z
  '**signature** tune
signboard 'saɪn bɔːd →'saɪm- ‖ -bɔːrd -bourd
  ~**s** z
signer 'saɪn ə ‖ -ªr ~**s** z
signet 'sɪg nɪt -nət ~**s** s
  '**signet** ring
significance sɪg 'nɪf ɪk ən⁀s -ək-
significant sɪg 'nɪf ɪk ənt -ək- ~**ly** li
signification ˌsɪg nɪf ɪ 'keɪʃ ªn ˌ•nəf-, §-ə'•-
  ~**s** z
significative sɪg 'nɪf ɪk ət ɪv -'•ək-; -ɪ keɪt-,
  -ə keɪt- ‖ -ə keɪt̬ ɪv ~**ly** li ~**ness** nəs nɪs
signi|fy 'sɪg nɪ |faɪ -nə- ~**fied** faɪd ~**fier/s**
  faɪ‿ə/z ‖ faɪ‿ªr/z ~**fies** faɪz ~**fying** faɪ ɪŋ
Signor, s~ 'siːn jɔː •'• ‖ -jɔːr —It [siɲ 'ɲor]
Signora, s~ siːn 'jɔːr ə —It [siɲ 'ɲoː ra]
Signorina, s~ ˌsiːn jɔː 'riːn ə ◂ -jə- —It
  [siɲ ɲo 'ri: na]
signpost 'saɪn pəʊst →'saɪm- ‖ -poʊst ~**ed** ɪd
  əd ~**ing** ɪŋ ~**s** s
signwrit|er 'saɪn raɪt |ə ‖ -raɪt̬ |ªr ~**ers**
  əz ‖ -ªrz ~**ing** ɪŋ
Sigourney sɪ 'gɔːn i -'gʊən- ‖ -'gʊrn i
Sigurd 'sɪg ʊəd 'siːg-, -3ːd ‖ -ªrd
Sihanouk 'siː‿ə nuːk
sika 'siːk ə ~**s** z
sike, Sike saɪk **sikes, Sikes** saɪks

Sikh siːk sɪk —Hindi [sɪkʰ] **Sikhs** siːks sɪks
Sikhism 'siːk ˌɪz əm 'sɪk-
Sikkim 'sɪk ɪm sɪ 'kɪm
Sikkimese ˌsɪk ɪ 'miːz ◂ -'miːs
Sikorsky sɪ 'kɔːsk i ‖ -'kɔːrsk-
silage 'saɪl ɪdʒ
silane 'sɪl eɪn 'saɪl-
Silas 'saɪl əs
Silbury 'sɪl bªr‿i ‖ -ˌber i
  ˌSilbury 'Hill
Silchester 'sɪltʃ ɪst ə -əst-; 'sɪl tʃest ə ‖ -ªr
Silcox 'sɪl kɒks ‖ -kɑːks
sild sɪld **silds** sɪldz
Sile, Síle personal name 'ʃiːl ə
Sileby 'saɪªl bi
silenc|e 'saɪl ən⁀s ~**ed** t ~**es** ɪz əz ~**ing** ɪŋ
silencer 'saɪl ən⁀s ə ‖ -ªr ~**s** z
silent 'saɪl ənt ~**ly** li ~**ness** nəs nɪs
  ˌsilent 'partner
Silenus saɪ 'liːn əs sɪ-, -'leɪn-
Silesia, s~ saɪ 'liːz i‿ə sɪ-, -'liːs-; -'liːʒ ə, -'liːʃ-
  ‖ saɪ 'liːʒ ə sɪ-, -'liːʃ-
Silesian saɪ 'liːz i‿ən sɪ-, -'liːs-; -'liːʒ ªn, -'liːʃ-
  ‖ saɪ 'liːʒ ªn sɪ-, -'liːʃ- ~**s** z
silex 'saɪl eks
silhou|ette ˌsɪl u 'et -ju-, '••• ~**etted** et ɪd
  -əd ‖ et̬ əd ~**ettes** ets ~**etting** et ɪŋ ‖ et̬ ɪŋ
silica 'sɪl ɪk ə
silicate 'sɪl ɪ keɪt -ə-; -ɪk ət, -ɪt ~**s** s
silicic sɪ 'lɪs ɪk sə-
silicon 'sɪl ɪk ən -ək-; -ɪ kɒn, -ə-,
  ⚠-kəʊn ‖ -ɪ kɑːn
  ˌsilicon 'chip; ; ˌSilicon 'Valley
silicone 'sɪl ɪ kəʊn -ə- ‖ -koʊn ~**s** z
silicosis ˌsɪl ɪ 'kəʊs ɪs -ə-, §-əs ‖ -'koʊs əs
silicotic ˌsɪl ɪ 'kɒt ɪk ◂ -ə- ‖ -'kɑːt̬- ~**s** s
silk, Silk sɪlk **silks** sɪlks
silken 'sɪlk ən
silki... —see **silky**
Silkin 'sɪlk ɪn §-ən
silkscreen 'sɪlk skriːn
silkworm 'sɪlk wɜːm ‖ -wɜ˞ːm ~**s** z
silk|y 'sɪlk |i ~**ier** i‿ə ‖ i‿ªr ~**iest** i‿ɪst i‿əst
  ~**ily** ɪ li əl i ~**iness** i nəs i nɪs
sill sɪl **sills** sɪlz
sillabub 'sɪl ə bʌb ~**s** z
Sillars 'sɪl əz ‖ -ªrz
Sillery 'sɪl ər i
silli... —see **silly**
sillimanite 'sɪl ɪm ə naɪt '•əm-
Sillito, Sillitoe 'sɪl ɪ təʊ -ə- ‖ -toʊ
Silloth 'sɪl əθ
Sills sɪlz
sill|y 'sɪl |i ~**ier** i‿ə ‖ i‿ªr ~**ies** iz ~**iest** i‿ɪst
  i‿əst ~**iness** i nəs i nɪs
  ˌsilly 'billy, '••, •••; 'silly ˌseason
silo 'saɪl əʊ ‖ -oʊ ~**s** z
Siloam saɪ 'ləʊ əm sɪ-, -æm ‖ -'loʊ-
siloxane sɪ 'lɒks eɪn saɪ-, sə- ‖ -'lɑːks-
Silsoe 'sɪls əʊ ‖ -oʊ
silt sɪlt **silted** 'sɪlt ɪd -əd **silting** 'sɪlt ɪŋ **silts**
  sɪlt s
siltation sɪl 'teɪʃ ªn

silty 'sɪlt i

Silures saɪ 'lʊər iːz sɪ-, -'ljʊər-, -'ljɔːr-
∥ 'sɪl jər-

Silurian saɪ 'lʊər i‿ən sɪ-, -'ljʊər-, -'ljɔːr-
∥ -'lʊr-

Silva 'sɪlv ə

silvan 'sɪlv ən

Silvanus sɪl 'veɪn əs

silver, S~ 'sɪlv ə ∥ -ᵊr ~ed d silvering
'sɪlv ər‿ɪŋ ~s z
,silver 'birch; 'silver foil, ,·· '·; ,silver
'jubilee, ,·· ,··'·; ,silver 'medal; ,silver
'nitrate; ,silver 'paper; ,silver 'plate◂;
,silver 'wedding, ,silver 'wedding
anni,versary

silverfish 'sɪlv ə fɪʃ ∥ -ᵊr- ~es ɪz əz

silveri... —see silvery

Silverman 'sɪlv ə mən ∥ -ᵊr-

Silvers 'sɪlv əz ∥ -ᵊrz

silverside 'sɪlv ə saɪd ∥ -ᵊr- ~s z

silversmith 'sɪlv ə smɪθ ∥ -ᵊr- ~ing ɪŋ ~s s

Silverstone 'sɪlv ə stəʊn ∥ -ᵊr stoʊn

silver-tongued ,sɪlv ə 'tʌŋd ◂ §-'tɒŋd ∥ -ᵊr-

Silvertown 'sɪlv ə taʊn ∥ -ᵊr-

silverware 'sɪlv ə weə ∥ -ᵊr wer -wær

silverweed 'sɪlv ə wiːd ∥ -ᵊr-

silver|y 'sɪlv ər‿li ~iness i nəs i nɪs

silver-Y ,sɪlv ə 'waɪ ∥ -ᵊr-
,silver-'Y moth

Silvester sɪl 'vest ə ∥ -ᵊr

Silvia 'sɪlv i‿ə

silviculture 'sɪlv ɪ ‚kʌltʃ ə §-ə- ∥ -ᵊr

Silvie 'sɪlv i

Silvikrin tdmk 'sɪlv ɪ krɪn -ə-

s'il vous plait, s'il vous plaît ‚siː vuː 'pleɪ ‚siːᵊl-
—Fr [sil vu plɛ]

Sim sɪm

sima 'saɪm ə

simazine 'saɪm ə ziːn

simba, Simba 'sɪm bə

Simca tdmk 'sɪm kə ~s z

Simcox 'sɪm kɒks ∥ -kɑːks

Simenon 'siːm ə nɒ̃ 'sɪm-, -nɒn ∥ ‚siːm ə 'nɔːn
-'noʊn, -'nɑːn —Fr [sim nɔ̃]

Simeon 'sɪm i‿ən

Simes saɪmz

Simey 'saɪm i

Simi sɪ 'miː 'siːm i

simian 'sɪm i‿ən ~s z

similar 'sɪm əl‿ə -ɪl ə ∥ -ᵊl‿ər

similarit|y ‚sɪm ə 'lær ət li ,·ɪ-, -ɪt li ∥ -əṱ li
-'ler- ~ies ɪz

similarly 'sɪm əl‿ə li -ɪl ə li ∥ -ᵊl‿ər li

simile 'sɪm əl i -ɪl- ~s z

similitude sɪ 'mɪl ɪ tjuːd sə-, -ə-, →§-tʃuːd
∥ -ə tuːd -tjuːd ~s z

Simla 'sɪm lə

Simm sɪm

simmer 'sɪm ə ∥ -ᵊr ~ed d simmering
'sɪm ər‿ɪŋ ~s z

Simmonds 'sɪm əndz

Simmons 'sɪm ənz

Simms sɪmz

simnel, S~ 'sɪm nᵊl

Simon 'saɪm ən —but as a French name,
siː 'mɒ̃ ∥-'moʊn —Fr [si mɔ̃]
,Simon 'says

Simonds (i) 'sɪm əndz, (ii) 'saɪm əndz

Simone sɪ 'məʊn sə- ∥ -'moʊn

simoniacal ‚saɪm ə 'naɪ‿ək ᵊl ◂

Simonides saɪ 'mɒn i diːz -ə- ∥ -'mɑːn-

simon-pure ‚saɪm ən 'pjʊə ◂ -'pjɔː ∥ -'pjʊᵊr ◂

Simons 'saɪm ənz

Simonsbath 'sɪm ənz bɑːθ §-bæθ ∥ -bæθ

Simonstown 'saɪm ənz taʊn

simony 'saɪm ən i 'sɪm-

simoom sɪ 'muːm §sə- ~s z

simpatico sɪm 'pæt ɪ kəʊ -'pɑːt- ∥ -'pɑːṱ ɪ koʊ
-'pæt- —It [sim 'pa: ti ko]

simper 'sɪmp ə ∥ -ᵊr ~ed d simpering/ly
'sɪmp ər‿ɪŋ /li ~s z

Simpkin 'sɪmp kɪn

Simpkins 'sɪmp kɪnz

Simpkinson 'sɪmp kɪn sən

simple 'sɪmp ᵊl simpler 'sɪmp lə ∥ -lᵊr
simples 'sɪmp ᵊlz simplest 'sɪmp lɪst -ləst
,simple 'fracture; ,simple 'interest; ,simple
'life; ,simple ma'chine; ,simple 'time

simple-hearted ‚sɪmp ᵊl 'hɑːt ɪd ◂ -əd
∥ -'hɑːrṱ əd ◂

simple-minded ‚sɪmp ᵊl 'maɪnd ɪd ◂ -əd ~ly li
~ness nəs nɪs

simpleness 'sɪmp ᵊl nəs -nɪs

simpleton 'sɪmp ᵊl tən ~s z

simplex 'sɪm pleks

simplicit|y sɪm 'plɪs ət li -ɪt- ∥ -əṱ li ~ies ɪz

simplification ‚sɪmp lɪf ɪ 'keɪʃ ᵊn ,·ləf-, §-ə'·-
~s z

simpli|fy 'sɪmp lɪ |faɪ -lə- ~fied faɪd ~fier/s
faɪ‿ə/z ∥ faɪ‿ᵊr/z ~fies faɪz ~fying faɪ ɪŋ

simplistic sɪm 'plɪst ɪk ~ally ᵊl‿i

Simplon 'sæm plɒn 'sɪm- ∥ -plɑːn —Fr
[sæ̃ plɔ̃]

simply 'sɪmp li

Simpson 'sɪmps ᵊn
,Simpson 'Desert

Sims sɪmz

Simson 'sɪmᵖ sᵊn

simulac|rum ‚sɪm ju 'leɪk |rəm §-jə-, -'læk-
∥ ‚sɪm jə- ~ra rə

simu|late 'sɪm ju |leɪt -jə- ∥ -jə- ~lated leɪt ɪd
-əd ∥ leɪṱ əd ~lates leɪts ~lating
leɪt ɪŋ ∥ leɪṱ ɪŋ

simulation ‚sɪm ju 'leɪʃ ᵊn -jə- ∥ -jə- ~s z

simulator 'sɪm ju leɪt ə '·jə- ∥ -jə leɪṱ ᵊr ~s z

simulcast 'sɪm ᵊl kɑːst §-kæst 'saɪm ᵊl kæst
(*) ~ed ɪd əd ~ing ɪŋ ~s s

simultaneity ‚sɪm ᵊl tə 'neɪ ət i -'niː‿, -ɪt i
∥ ‚saɪm ᵊl tə 'niː‿ əṱ i (*)

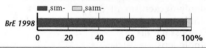

SIMULTANEOUS

	,sɪm-	,saɪm-
BrE 1998		
0	20 40 60	80 100%

simultaneous ‚sɪm ᵊl 'teɪn i‿əs ◂ ∥ ‚saɪm- (*)

—BrE 1998 poll panel preference: ˌsɪm- 97%,
ˌsaɪm- 3%. **~ly** li **~ness** nəs nɪs
sin *'do wrong'* sɪn **sinned** sɪnd **sinning** ˈsɪn ɪŋ
sins sɪnz
sin *in trigonometry* saɪn
Sinai ˈsaɪn aɪ ˈsaɪn iˌaɪ, ˈsaɪn eɪ aɪ
Sinatra sɪ ˈnɑːtr ə sə-
Sinbad ˈsɪn bæd →ˈsɪm-
sin-bin ˈsɪn bɪn →ˈsɪm- **~s** z
since sɪnᵗs
sin|cere sɪn ǀˈsɪə sᵊn- ‖ -ǀˈsɪᵊr **~cerely**
ˈsɪə li ‖ ˈsɪr li **~cerer** ˈsɪər ə ‖ ˈsɪr ᵊr **~cerest**
ˈsɪər ɪst -əst ‖ ˈsɪr əst
sincerity sɪn ˈser ət i sᵊn-, -ɪt i ‖ -əți
Sinclair *(i)* ˈsɪn kleə →ˈsɪŋ-, §-klə ‖ -kler -klær,
(ii) sɪn ˈkleə →sɪŋ-‖ -ˈkleᵊr -ˈklæᵊr
Sind, Sindh sɪnd *—Hindi* [sɪn̩dʰ]
Sinden ˈsɪnd ən
Sindhi ˈsɪnd i -hi *—Hindi* [sɪn̩ d̪ʰi] **~s** z
Sindy *tdmk* ˈsɪnd i
sine *n, in trigonometry* saɪn **sines** saɪnz
ˈsine wave
sine *prep, Latin* ˈsɪn i ˈsaɪn-, ˈsiːn-, -eɪ *—see also
phrases with this word*
Sinead, Sinéad ʃɪ ˈneɪd -ˈneəd
sinecure ˈsɪn ɪ kjʊə ˈsaɪn-, -§ə-, -kjɔː ‖ -kjʊr
~s z
sine die ˌsaɪn i ˈdaɪ iː -i; ˌsɪn i ˈdiː eɪ, -eɪ-;
⚠ˌsaɪn i ˈdaɪ
sine qua non ˌsɪn i ˌkwɑː ˈnɒn ˌsiːn-, -eɪ-,
-ˈnəʊn; ˌsaɪn i ˌkweɪ- ‖ -ˈnɑːn -ˈnoʊn
sinew ˈsɪn juː **~s** z
sinewy ˈsɪn juːˌi
sinfonia, S~ ˌsɪn fə ˈnɪə sɪn ˈfəʊn iˌə
‖ ˌsɪn fə ˈniː ə -foʊ- **~s** z
sinfonietta ˌsɪn fəʊn i ˈet ə ˌ•fən-, ˌ•fɒn-;
ˌ•ˈjet ə ‖ ˌsɪn fən ˈjeț ə -foʊn- **~s** z
sinful ˈsɪn fᵊl -fʊl **~ly** i **~ness** nəs nɪs
sing sɪŋ **sang** sæŋ **singing** ˈsɪŋ ɪŋ **sings** sɪŋz
sung sʌŋ
ˈSing Sing
singable ˈsɪŋ əb ᵊl
singalong ˈsɪŋ ə lɒŋ ‖ -lɔːŋ -lɑːŋ **~s** z
Singapore ˌsɪŋ ə ˈpɔː ◄ -gə-, ˈ••• ‖ ˈsɪŋ gə pɔːr
-ə-, -poʊr
Singaporean ˌsɪŋ ə ˈpɔːr iˌən ◄ -gə-,
-pɔː ˈriːˌən ‖ -ˈpoʊr- **~s** z
singe sɪndʒ **singed** sɪndʒd **singeing** ˈsɪndʒ ɪŋ
singes ˈsɪndʒ ɪz -əz
singer, S~ ˈsɪŋ ə ‖ -ᵊr **~s** z
Singh sɪŋ
Singhalese ˌsɪŋ ə ˈliːz ◄ -hə-, -gə- ‖ -gə- -ˈliːs
singing ˈsɪŋ ɪŋ
singl|e ˈsɪŋ gᵊl **~ed** d **~es** z **~ing** ɪŋ
ˌsingle ˈfile; ˌsingle ˈparent
single-action ˌsɪŋ gᵊl ˈæk ʃᵊn ◄
single-breasted ˌsɪŋ gᵊl ˈbrest ɪd ◄ -əd
single-decker ˌsɪŋ gᵊl ˈdek ə ◄ ‖ -ᵊr ◄ **~s** z
single-handed ˌsɪŋ gᵊl ˈhænd ɪd ◄ -əd **~ly** li
~ness nəs nɪs
single-lens ˌsɪŋ gᵊl ˈlenz ◄
ˌsingle-lens ˈreflex (ˌcamera)

single-minded ˌsɪŋ gᵊl ˈmaɪnd ɪd ◄ -əd **~ly** li
~ness nəs nɪs
singleness ˈsɪŋ gᵊl nəs -nɪs
single-sex ˌsɪŋ gᵊl ˈseks ◄
singlestick ˈsɪŋ gᵊl stɪk **~s** s
singlet ˈsɪŋ glət -glɪt **~s** s
singleton, S~ ˈsɪŋ gᵊl tən **~s** z
single-track ˌsɪŋ gᵊl ˈtræk ◄
single-user ˌsɪŋ gᵊl ˈjuːz ə ◄ ‖ -ᵊr ◄
singly ˈsɪŋ gli
singsong ˈsɪŋ sɒŋ ‖ -sɔːŋ -sɑːŋ **~s** z
singular ˈsɪŋ gjʊl ə -gjəl- ‖ -gjəl ᵊr **~ly** li
~ness nəs nɪs **~s** z
singularit|y ˌsɪŋ gju ˈlær ət i li, ˌ•gjə-, -ɪt i
‖ -gjə ˈlær əț li -ˈler- **~ies** iz
singulary ˈsɪŋ gjʊl ər i ‖ -gjə ler i
sinh ʃaɪn sɪnᵗʃ, ˌsaɪn ˈeɪtʃ ‖ sɪnᵗʃ
Sinhalese ˌsɪn hə ˈliːz ◄ ˌsɪŋ-, -ə- ‖ -ˈliːs
sinister ˈsɪn ɪst ə §-əst- ‖ -ᵊr **~ly** li **~ness** nəs
nɪs
sinistral ˈsɪn ɪs trᵊl -əs- **~ly** i **~s** z
sinistrorse ˈsɪn ɪ strɔːs -ə-, ˌ•ˈ• ‖ -strɔːrs **~ly**
li
Sinitic saɪ ˈnɪt ɪk sɪ- ‖ -ˈnɪț-
Sinitta sɪ ˈniːt ə sə- ‖ -ˈniːț-
sink sɪŋk **sank** sæŋk **sinking** ˈsɪŋk ɪŋ **sinks**
sɪŋks **sunk** sʌŋk **sunken** ˈsʌŋk ᵊn
ˈsinking ˌfeeling; ˈsinking fund
sinkable ˈsɪŋk əb ᵊl
sinker ˈsɪŋk ə ‖ -ᵊr **~s** z
sinkhole ˈsɪŋk həʊl →-hɒʊl -hoʊl **~s** z
sinless ˈsɪn ləs -lɪs **~ly** li **~ness** nəs nɪs
Sinnatt ˈsɪn ət
sinner ˈsɪn ə ‖ -ᵊr **~s** z
Sinn Fein ˌʃɪn ˈfeɪn *—Ir* Sinn Féin [ˌʃiːnʲ ˈheːnʲ]
~er/s ə/z ‖ ᵊr/z
Sinnott ˈsɪn ət
Sino- ˌsaɪn əʊ ‖ -oʊ — **Sino-Japanese**
ˌsaɪn əʊ ˌdʒæp ə ˈniːz ‖ ˌ•oʊ- -ˈniːs
sinological ˌsaɪn əʊ ˈlɒdʒ ɪk ᵊl ◄ ˌsɪn-
‖ -ə ˈlɑːdʒ-
sinologist saɪ ˈnɒl ədʒ ɪst sɪ-, §sə-, §-əst
‖ -ˈnɑːl- **~s** s
sinologue ˈsaɪn əʊ lɒg ˈsɪn-, -ᵊl ɒg ‖ -ᵊl ɔːg -ɑːg
~s z
sinology saɪ ˈnɒl ədʒ i sɪ-, §sə- ‖ -ˈnɑːl-
Sino-Tibetan ˌsaɪn əʊ tɪ ˈbet ᵊn ◄ ˌsɪn-, -tə•-
‖ ˌ•oʊ-
sinter ˈsɪnt ə ‖ ˈsɪnț ᵊr **~ed** d **sintering**
ˈsɪnt ᵊr ɪŋ ‖ ˈsɪnț- **~s** z
sinuosit|y ˌsɪn ju ˈɒs ət i li -ɪt i ‖ -ˈɑːs əț li **~ies**
iz
sinuous ˈsɪn juˌəs **~ly** li **~ness** nəs nɪs
sinus ˈsaɪn əs **~es** ɪz əz
sinusitis ˌsaɪn ə ˈsaɪt ɪs §-əs ‖ -ˈsaɪț əs
sinusoid ˈsaɪn ə sɔɪd **~s** z
sinusoidal ˌsaɪn ə ˈsɔɪd ᵊl ◄ **~ly** i
Siobhan, Siobhán ʃə ˈvɒːn ʃɪ- ‖ -ˈvɑːn
Sion *'Zion'* ˈsaɪ ən ˈzaɪ
Sion, Siôn *male personal name, Welsh* ʃɔːn
‖ ʃɑːn
Sion *place in Switzerland* si ˈɒ̃ ‖ -ˈɔːn -ˈɑːn,
-ˈoʊn *—Fr* [sjɔ̃]

Siouan 'suː‿ən
Sioux *sing.* suː   Sioux *pl* suːz suː
Siouxsie 'suːz i
sip sɪp **sipped** sɪpt **sipping** 'sɪp ɪŋ **sips** sɪps
siphon 'saɪf ən **~ed** d **~ing** ‿ɪŋ **~s** z
siphonic saɪ 'fɒn ɪk ‖ -'fɑːn-
siphonophore saɪ 'fɒn ə fɔː 'sɪf ən ə-
   ‖ -'fɑːn ə fɔːr -four **-s** z
Siple 'saɪp əl
sir, Sir *strong form* sɜː ‖ sɜˑ, *weak form* sə ‖ sᵊr
   —*The weak form is customary in BrE whenever*
   this word is used with a name, as Sir John; Sir
   Peter Smith. *Otherwise the strong form is usual:*
   yes, sir. *In AmE the weak form is little used.*
   sirs sɜːz ‖ sɜˑːz —*There is no weak form of the*
   plural.
sirdar, S~ 'sɜːd ɑː sɜː 'dɑː ‖ 'sɜˑːd ɑːr **~s** z
sire 'saɪ‿ə ‖ 'saɪ‿ᵊr **sired** 'saɪ‿əd ‖ 'saɪ‿ᵊrd
   sires 'saɪ‿əz ‖ 'saɪ‿ᵊrz **siring**
   'saɪ‿ər ɪŋ ‖ 'saɪ‿ᵊr ɪŋ
siren 'saɪᵊr ən -ɪn **~s** z
sirenian saɪᵊ 'riːn i‿ən **~s** z
Sirhowy sɜː 'haʊ‿i ‖ sɜˑː-
Sirius 'sɪr i‿əs 'saɪᵊr-
sirloin 'sɜː lɔɪn ‖ 'sɜˑː- **~s** z
   ˌsirloin 'steak
sirocco sɪ 'rɒk əʊ sə- ‖ -'rɑːk oʊ **~s** z
Siros 'sɪᵊr ɒs ‖ 'sɪr ɑːs —*Gk* ['si ros]
sirrah 'sɪr ə
sirree ˌsɜː 'riː sə- ‖ sə 'riː ˌsɜˑː 'iː
sis sɪs
sisal 'saɪs əl 'saɪz-
siskin 'sɪsk ɪn §-ən **~s** z
Sisley 'sɪz li
Sissie 'sɪs i
sissified 'sɪs ɪ faɪd -ə-
Sissinghurst 'sɪs ɪŋ hɜːst ‖ -hɜˑːst
Sisson 'sɪs ən
Sissons 'sɪs ᵊnz
siss|y 'sɪs li **~ies** iz
sister, S~ 'sɪst ə ‖ -ᵊr **~s** z
sisterhood 'sɪst ə hʊd ‖ -ᵊr- **~s** z
sister-|in-law 'sɪst ər‿ɪn ˌlɔː 'sɪs tə-, §‿ən, •
   ‖ -ᵊr- -ˌlɑː **sisters-~** 'sɪst əz ‖ 'sɪst ᵊrz
sist|erly 'sɪst ə li -ləl i ‖ -lᵊr li **~erliness**
   ə li nəs ᵊl i-, -nɪs ‖ ᵊr li nəs
Sistine 'sɪst iːn -aɪn
sis|trum 'sɪs |trəm **~tra** trə **~troid** trɔɪd
   ~trums trəmz
siSwati sɪ 'swɑːt i
Sisyphean ˌsɪs ɪ 'fiːˑən ◄ -ə-
Sisyphus 'sɪs ɪf əs -əf-
sit sɪt **sat** sæt **sits** sɪts **sitting** 'sɪt ɪŋ ‖ 'sɪt̬ ɪŋ
sitar sɪ 'tɑː 'sɪt ɑː ‖ sɪ 'tɑːr —*Hindi* [sɪ t̬aːr] **~s**
   z
sitcom 'sɪt kɒm ‖ -kɑːm **~s** z
sit-down 'sɪt daʊn
site saɪt (= *sight, cite*) **sited** 'saɪt ɪd -əd
   ‖ 'saɪt̬ əd **sites** saɪts **siting** 'saɪt ɪŋ ‖ 'saɪt̬ ɪŋ
sit-in 'sɪt ɪn ‖ 'sɪt̬ ɪn **~s** z
Sitka, sitka 'sɪt kə
sitrep 'sɪt rep **~s** s
sitter 'sɪt ə ‖ 'sɪt̬ ᵊr **~s** z

sitting 'sɪt ɪŋ ‖ 'sɪt̬ ɪŋ **~s** z
   ˌSitting 'Bull; ˌsitting 'duck; 'sitting room;
   ˌsitting 'target; ˌsitting 'tenant
Sittingbourne 'sɪt ɪŋ bɔːn ‖ 'sɪt̬ ɪŋ bɔːrn
   -boʊrn
situ|ate *v* 'sɪtʃ u eɪt 'sɪt ju-, §'sɪt u- **~ated**
   eɪt ɪd -əd ‖ eɪt̬ əd **~ates** eɪts **~ating**
   eɪt ɪŋ ‖ eɪt̬ ɪŋ
situate *adj* 'sɪtʃ u eɪt 'sɪt ju-, §'sɪt u-, -ət, -ɪt

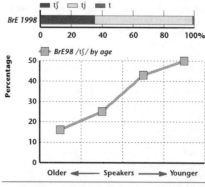

SITUATION

	tʃ	tj	t
BrE 1998			

0   20   40   60   80   100%

BrE98 /tʃ/ by age

Percentage (50, 40, 30, 20, 10, 0)

Older ◄———— Speakers ————► Younger

situation ˌsɪtʃ u 'eɪʃ ən ˌsɪt ju-, §ˌsɪt u- —*BrE*
   1998 poll panel preference: tʃ *35%,* tj *64%,* t
   1%. **~al** əl **~ally** əl‿i **~s** z
   ˌsitu,ation 'comedy, ˌ•••ˈ•••, ˈ•••;
   ˌsitu'ation room
sit-up 'sɪt ʌp ‖ 'sɪt̬ ʌp **~s** s
sit-upon 'sɪt ə ˌpɒn ‖ 'sɪt̬ ə ˌpɑːn -pɔːn **~s** z
Sitwell 'sɪt wəl -wel **~s** z
sitz sɪts (= *sits*)
   'sitz bath
Siva 'ʃiːv ə 'ʃɪv-, 'siːv-, 'sɪv- —*Hindi* [ʃɪʋ]
Siwash, s~ 'saɪ wɒʃ ‖ -wɑːʃ -wɔːʃ
six sɪks **sixes** 'sɪks ɪz -əz
   ˌSix 'Counties; ˌSix ˌDay 'War
sixer 'sɪks ə ‖ -ᵊr **~s** z
sixfold 'sɪks fəʊld →-fɒʊld ‖ -foʊld
six-footer ˌsɪks 'fʊt ə ‖ -'fʊt̬ ᵊr **~s** z
sixgun 'sɪks gʌn **~s** z
sixish 'sɪks ɪʃ
six-pack 'sɪks pæk **~s** s
sixpenc|e 'sɪks pən¦s **~es** ɪz əz
sixpenny 'sɪks pən i
six-shooter 'sɪks ˌʃuːt ə →-'sɪkʃ-, ˌ•'••
   ‖ -ˌʃuːt̬ ᵊr **~s** z
sixte sɪkst
sixteen ˌsɪks 'tiːn ◄ **~s** z
sixteenmo, 16mo ˌsɪks 'tiːn məʊ →-'tiːm-
   ‖ -moʊ
sixteenth ˌsɪks 'tiːntθ ◄ **~ly** li **~s** s
   ˌsix'teenth note
sixth sɪksθ sɪkstθ, △sɪkθ **sixths** sɪksθs
   sɪkstθs, △sɪkθs —*but in casual speech both*
   sing. and pl are sometimes sɪks *or* sɪkst
   'sixth form; ˌsixth 'sense
sixties 'sɪkst iz
sixtieth 'sɪkst i‿əθ ‿ɪθ **~s** s
Sixtus 'sɪkst əs

S

sixt|y 'sıkst |i ~ies iz
sixty-four ˌsıkst i 'fɔː ◄ ‖ -'fɔːr ◄ -'foʊr
  ˌsixty-four ˌthousand ˌdollar 'question,
  ˌ-'•• ˌ••
sixty-fourth ˌsıkst i 'fɔːθ ◄ ‖ -'fɔːrθ ◄ -'foʊrθ
  ~s s
sixty-nine ˌsıkst i 'naın
sizab|le 'saız əb |əl ~leness əl nəs -nıs ~ly li
sizar 'saız ə ‖ -ər ~s z
size saız sized saızd sizes 'saız ız -əz sizing
  'saız ıŋ
sizeab|le 'saız əb |əl ~leness əl nəs -nıs ~ly li
-sized 'saızd saızd — medium-sized
  ˌmiːd i_əm 'saızd ◄
Sizer, Sizergh 'saız ə ‖ -ər
Sizewell 'saız wəl -wel
sizzl|e 'sız əl ~ed d ~es z ~ing/ly ˌıŋ /li
sizzler 'sız əl_ə ‖ ˌər ~s z
sjambok 'ʃæm bɒk -bʌk ‖ ʃæm 'bɑːk -'bʌk
  —Afrikaans ['ʃam bok] ~s s
ska skɑː
skag skæg
Skagerrak 'skæg ə ræk —Danish ['sgaː ɣə ʁak,
  'sga-]
Skagway 'skæg weı
skank skæŋk
Skara Brae ˌskær ə 'breı ‖ ˌsker-
skat skæt ‖ skɑːt skæt —Ger [skaːt]
skate skeıt skated 'skeıt ıd -əd ‖ 'skeıt̬ əd
  skates skeıts skating 'skeıt ıŋ ‖ 'skeıt̬ ıŋ
skateboard 'skeıt bɔːd ‖ -bɔːrd -boʊrd ~er/s
  ə/z ‖ ər/z ~ing ıŋ ~s z
skater 'skeıt ə ‖ 'skeıt̬ ər ~s z
skatole 'skæt əʊl →-ɒʊl ‖ -oʊl
skean skiːn 'skiː_ən skeans skiːnz 'skiː_ənz
  ˌskean 'dhu duː
Skeat skiːt
skedaddl|e skı 'dæd əl skə- ~ed d ~es z ~ing
  ˌıŋ
skeet skiːt
  'skeet ˌshooting
Skeffington 'skef ıŋ tən
skeg skeg skegs skegz
Skegness ˌskeg 'nes ◄
skein skeın skeins skeınz
skeletal 'skel ıt əl -ət-; skı 'liːt-, skə-
  ‖ 'skel ət̬ əl skə 'liːt̬ əl ~ly i
skeleton 'skel ıt ən -ət-, △-ınt- ‖ -ən ~s z
  'skeleton key
Skelmersdale 'skelm əz deıəl ‖ -ərz- —locally
  also 'skem-
Skelton 'skelt ən
skep skep skeps skeps
skeptic, S~ 'skept ık ~s s
skeptical 'skept ık əl ~ly i ~ness nəs nıs
skepticism 'skept ı ˌsız əm -ə-
Skerritt 'sker ıt §-ət
skerr|y 'sker |i ~ies iz
sketch sketʃ sketched sketʃt sketches
  'sketʃ ız -əz sketching 'sketʃ ıŋ
sketchbook 'sketʃ bʊk §-buːk
sketchi... —see sketchy
Sketchley 'sketʃ li

sketchpad 'sketʃ pæd ~s z
sketch|y 'sketʃ |i ~ier i_ə ‖ i_ər ~iest i_ıst
  i_əst ~ily ı li əl i ~iness i nəs i nıs
skew skjuː skewed skjuːd skewing 'skjuː ıŋ
  skews skjuːz
skewbald 'skjuː bɔːld ‖ -bɑːld ~s z
Skewen 'skjuː_ın §_ən
skewer 'skjuː_ə ‖ _ər ~ed d skewering
  'skjuː_ər ıŋ ~s z
skewness 'skjuː nəs -nıs
skew-whiff ˌskjuː 'wıf ◄ -'hwıf
ski skiː —In 1935 BBC announcers were
  recommended to say ʃiː. Yet this form is now
  entirely obsolete. skied skiːd skiing 'skiː ıŋ
  skis skiːz
  'ski jump; 'ski ˌjumping; 'ski lift; 'ski plane;
  'ski pole; 'ski stick
skibob 'skiː bɒb ‖ -bɑːb ~ber/s ə/z ‖ ər/z
  ~bing ıŋ ~s z
skid skıd skidded 'skıd ıd -əd skidding
  'skıd ıŋ skids skıdz
  ˌskid 'row
Skiddaw 'skıd ɔː ‖ -ɑː
skiddoo skı 'duː ~ed d ~ing ıŋ ~s z
skidlid 'skıd lıd ~s z
Skidmore 'skıd mɔː ‖ -mɔːr
skidoo skı 'duː ~ed d ~ing ıŋ ~s z
skidpan 'skıd pæn →'skıb- ~s z
skied past of ski skiːd
skied past of sky skaıd
skier 'skiː_ə ‖ _ər ~s z
skies skaız
skiff skıf skiffs skıfs
skiffle 'skıf əl
skijoring 'skiː ˌdʒɔːr ıŋ ˌ•'•• ‖ -ˌdʒoʊr-
skilful 'skıl fəl -fʊl ~ly _i ~ness nəs nıs
skill skıl skilled skıld skills skılz
skillet 'skıl ıt -ət ~s s
skillful 'skıl fəl -fʊl ~ly _i ~ness nəs nıs
skilly 'skıl i
skim skım skimmed skımd skimming/s
  'skım ıŋ/z skims skımz
  ˌskimmed 'milk, ˌskim 'milk
skimmer 'skım ə ‖ -ər ~s z
skimmia 'skım i_ə ~s z
skimp skımp skimped skımpt skimping
  'skımp ıŋ skimps skımps
skimp|y 'skımp |i ~ier i_ə ‖ i_ər ~iest i_ıst
  i_əst ~ily ı li əl i ~iness i nəs i nıs
skin skın skinned skınd skinning 'skın ıŋ
  skins skınz
  'skin ˌdiver; 'skin ˌdiving; 'skin flick; 'skin
  graft
skincare 'skın keə →'skıŋ- ‖ -ker
skin-deep ˌskın 'diːp ◄
skin-|dive 'skın |daıv ~dived daıvd ~dives
  daıvz ~diving daıv ıŋ ~dove dəʊv ‖ doʊv
skinflint 'skın flınt ~s s
skinful 'skın fʊl ~s z
skinhead 'skın hed ~s z
skink skıŋk skinks skıŋks
skinless 'skın ləs -lıs
skinlike 'skın laık

-skinned 'skınd — thick-skinned ˌθık 'skınd ◂
skinn... —see skin
Skinner, s~ 'skın ə ‖ -ᵊr ~s, ~'s z
Skinnerian skı 'nıər i ˌən ‖ -'nır- -'ner- ~s z
skinn|y 'skın |i ~ier i ə ‖ i ᵊr ~iest i ˌıst i ˌəst
  ~iness i nəs i nıs
skinny-dip 'skın i dıp ~ped t ~per/s ə/z ‖ ᵊr/z
  ~ping ıŋ ~s s
skint skınt
skin-tight ˌskın 'taıt ◂
skip skıp skipped skıpt skipping 'skıp ıŋ
  skips skıps
skipjack 'skıp dʒæk ~s s
skipper 'skıp ə ‖ -ᵊr ~ed d skippering
  'skıp ᵊr ıŋ ~s z
skipping-rope 'skıp ıŋ rəʊp ‖ -roʊp ~s s
Skipton 'skıp tən
skirl skɜːl ‖ skɜˑːl skirled skɜːld ‖ skɜˑːld
  skirling 'skɜːl ıŋ ‖ 'skɜˑːl ıŋ skirls
  skɜːlz ‖ skɜˑːlz
skirmish 'skɜːm ıʃ ‖ 'skɜˑːm- ~ed t ~er/s
  ə/z ‖ -ᵊr/z ~es ız əz ~ing ıŋ
skirret 'skır ıt -ət
skirt skɜːt ‖ skɜˑːt skirted 'skɜːt ıd -əd
  ‖ 'skɜˑːt̬ əd skirting/s 'skɜːt ıŋ/z ‖ 'skɜˑːt̬ ıŋ/
  z skirts skɜːts ‖ skɜˑːts
  'skirting board
skis skiːz
skit skıt skits skıts
skite skaıt skited 'skaıt ıd -əd ‖ 'skaıt̬-
  skites skaıts skiting 'skaıt ıŋ ‖ 'skaıt̬-
skitter 'skıt ə ‖ 'skıt̬ ᵊr ~ed d skittering
  'skıt ᵊr ıŋ ‖ 'skıt̬ ᵊr ıŋ ~s z
skittish 'skıt ıʃ ‖ 'skıt̬ ıʃ ~ly li ~ness nəs nıs
skittl|e 'skıt ᵊl ‖ 'skıt̬ ᵊl ~ed d ~es z ~ing ˌıŋ
skive skaıv skived skaıvd skives skaıvz
  skiving 'skaıv ıŋ
skiver 'skaıv ə ‖ -ᵊr ~s z
skivv|y 'skıv |i ~ied id ~ies ız ~ying i ˌıŋ
skiwear 'ski: weə ‖ -wer -wær
skoal skəʊl →skɒʊl ‖ skoʊl
Skoda, Škoda tdmk 'skəʊd ə 'ʃkəʊd-
  ‖ 'skoʊd ə —Czech ['ʃko da] ~s z
Skokholm 'skɒk həʊm 'skəʊk əm
  ‖ 'ska:k hoʊm
Skokie 'skəʊk i ‖ 'skoʊk i
skol, Skol tdmk skɒl skəʊl ‖ skoʊl
Skomer 'skəʊm ə ‖ 'skoʊm ᵊr
Skopje 'skɒp ji -jeı ‖ 'ska:p- 'skɔ:p-, 'skoʊp-
  —Macedonian ['skɔp jɛ], Serbian Skoplje
  ['skɔp ljɛ]
Skrine (i) skri:n, (ii) skraın
skua 'skju: ə ~s z
Skues skju:z
skulduggery skʌl 'dʌg ᵊr i
skulk skʌlk skulked skʌlkt skulking 'skʌlk ıŋ
  skulks skʌlks
skull skʌl skulls skʌlz
skullcap 'skʌl kæp ~s s
skullduggery skʌl 'dʌg ᵊr i
skunk skʌŋk skunks skʌŋks
  'skunk ˌcabbage

sky skaı skied skaıd skies skaız skying
  'skaı ıŋ
sky-blue ˌskaı 'blu: ◂
skycap 'skaı kæp ~s s
skydiver/s 'skaı ˌdaıv ə/z ‖ -ᵊr/z ~ing ıŋ
Skye skaı
sky-high ˌskaı 'haı ◂
skyhook 'skaı hʊk ~s s
skyjack 'skaı dʒæk ~ed t ~er/s ə/z ‖ ᵊr/z
  ~ing ıŋ ~s s
Skylab 'skaı læb
skylark 'skaı la:k ‖ -la:rk ~ed t ~ing ıŋ ~s s
skylight 'skaı laıt ~s s
skyline 'skaı laın
skyrock|et 'skaı ˌrɒk |ıt §-ət ‖ -ˌra:k |ət ~eted
  ıt ıd §ət-, -əd ‖ ət əd ~eting ıt ıŋ §ət-
  ‖ ət ıŋ ~ets ıts §əts ‖ əts
skyscape 'skaı skeıp ~s s
skyscraper 'skaı ˌskreıp ə ‖ -ᵊr ~s z
skyward 'skaı wəd ‖ -wᵊrd ~s z
skywriting 'skaı ˌraıt ıŋ ‖ -ˌraıt̬ ıŋ
slab slæb slabbed slæbd slabbing 'slæb ıŋ
  slabs slæbz
  'slab cake
Slabbert 'slæb ət ‖ -ᵊrt
slack, Slack slæk slacked slækt slacker
  'slæk ə ‖ -ᵊr slackest 'slæk ıst -əst slacking
  'slæk ıŋ slacks slæks
slacken 'slæk ᵊn ~ed d ~ing ˌıŋ ~s z
slacker 'slæk ə ‖ -ᵊr ~s z
slack|ly 'slæk |li ~ness nəs nıs
Slade sleıd
slag slæg slagged slægd slagging 'slæg ıŋ
  slags slægz
slagg|y 'slæg |i ~ier i ə ‖ i ᵊr ~iest i ˌıst i ˌəst
slagheap 'slæg hi:p ~s s
slain sleın
slainte, slàinte 'sla:nt ʃ ə 'sla:ndʒ ə, 'sla:n jə
  —ScG ['sɫa: ɲə]
  ˌslàinte 'mhath va: —ScG [va]
Slaithwaite 'slæθ weıt —locally also 'slaʊ ıt
slake sleık slaked sleıkt slakes sleıks
  slaking 'sleık ıŋ
slalom 'sla:l əm ~s z
slam slæm slammed slæmd slamming
  'slæm ıŋ slams slæmz
slam-bang ˌslæm 'bæŋ
slammer 'slæm ə ‖ -ᵊr ~s z
slander 'sla:nd ə §'slænd- ‖ 'slænd ᵊr ~ed d
  slandering 'sla:nd ᵊr ıŋ §'slænd ‖ 'slænd ᵊr ıŋ ~s z
slanderous 'sla:nd ᵊr əs §'slænd
  ‖ 'slænd ᵊr əs ~ly li ~ness nəs nıs
slang slæŋ slanged slæŋd slanging 'slæŋ ıŋ
  slangs slæŋz
  'slanging match
slang|y 'slæŋ |i ~ily ı li əl i ~iness i nəs i nıs
slant sla:nt §slænt ‖ slænt slanted 'sla:nt ıd
  §'slænt-, -əd ‖ 'slænt̬ əd slanting/ly
  'sla:nt ıŋ /li §'slænt- ‖ 'slænt̬ ıŋ /li slants
  sla:nts §slænts ‖ slænts
slant|ways 'sla:nt weız §'slænt- ‖ 'slænt-
  ~wise waız

S

slap slæp **slapped** slæpt **slapping** 'slæp ɪŋ
  slaps slæps
slap-bang ˌslæp 'bæŋ
slapdash 'slæp dæʃ ˌ•'•
slaphapp|y 'slæp ˌhæp |i ˌ•'•• ~**ier** i‿ə ‖ i‿ᵊr
  ~**iest** i‿ɪst i‿əst
slaphead 'slæp hed ~**s** z
slapjack 'slæp dʒæk ~**s** s
slapstick 'slæp stɪk ~**s** s
slap-up 'slæp ʌp ˌ•'•
slash slæʃ **slashed** slæʃt **slashes** 'slæʃ ɪz -əz
  slashing 'slæʃ ɪŋ
  'slash mark
slasher 'slæʃ ə ‖ -ᵊr ~**s** z
slat slæt **slats** slæts **slatted** 'slæt ɪd -əd
  ‖ 'slæt̬ əd **slatting** 'slæt ɪŋ ‖ 'slæt̬ ɪŋ
slate sleɪt **slated** 'sleɪt ɪd -əd ‖ 'sleɪt̬ əd **slates**
  sleɪts **slating** 'sleɪt ɪŋ ‖ 'sleɪt̬ ɪŋ
slater, S~ 'sleɪt ə ‖ 'sleɪt̬ ᵊr ~**s** z
slather 'slæð ə ‖ -ᵊr ~**ed** d **slathering**
  'slæð ᵊr‿ɪŋ ~**s** z
slattern 'slæt ᵊn -ɜːn ‖ 'slæt̬ ᵊrn ~**liness** li nəs
  -nɪs ~**ly** li ~**s** z
Slattery 'slæt ᵊr i ‖ 'slæt̬-
slaty 'sleɪt i ‖ 'sleɪt̬ i
slaughter, S~ 'slɔːt ə ‖ 'slɔːt̬ ᵊr 'slɑːt̬- ~**ed** d
  slaughtering 'slɔːt‿ᵊr ɪŋ ‖ 'slɔːt̬ ᵊr ɪŋ 'slɑːt̬-
  ~**s** z
slaughterer 'slɔːt ᵊr ə ‖ 'slɔːt̬ ᵊr ᵊr 'slɑːt̬- ~**s** z
slaughter|house 'slɔːt ə |haʊs ‖ 'slɔːt̬ ᵊr-
  'slɑːt̬- ~**houses** ˌhaʊz ɪz -əz
Slav slɑːv ‖ slæv **Slavs** slɑːvz ‖ slævz
slave sleɪv **slaved** sleɪvd **slaves** sleɪvz
  slaving 'sleɪv ɪŋ
  'slave ˌdriver; 'slave ˌlabour; 'slave trade;
  'slave ˌtraffic
slaver v 'drool'; n 'saliva' 'slæv ə 'sleɪv-
  ‖ 'slæv ᵊr 'sleɪv-, 'slɑːv- ~**ed** d **slavering**
  'slæv ᵊr‿ɪŋ 'sleɪv- ‖ 'sleɪv-, 'slɑːv- ~**s** z
slaver n 'one dealing in slaves' 'sleɪv ə ‖ -ᵊr ~**s** z
slavery 'sleɪv ᵊr‿i
slavey 'sleɪv i ~**s** z
Slavic 'slɑːv ɪk 'slæv-
slavish 'sleɪv ɪʃ ~**ly** li ~**ness** nəs nɪs
Slavo- ˌslɑːv əʊ ˌslæv- ‖ -oʊ — **Slavophile**
  'slɑːv əʊ faɪᵊl 'slæv-, -fɪl ‖ -oʊ-
Slavonia slə 'vəʊn i‿ə ‖ -'voʊn-
Slavonic slə 'vɒn ɪk slæ- ‖ -'vɑːn ɪk
slaw slɔː ‖ slɑː
slay sleɪ **slain** sleɪn **slayed** sleɪd **slaying**
  'sleɪ ɪŋ **slays** sleɪz **slew** sluː
slayer 'sleɪ ə ‖ -ᵊr ~**s** z
Slazenger tdmk 'slæz ɪndʒ ə -əndʒ- ‖ -ᵊr
Sleaford 'sliː fəd ‖ -fᵊrd
sleaze sliːz
sleaze|bag/s 'sliːz| bæg/z ~**ball/s** bɔːl/z
  ‖ bɑːl/z
sleaz|y 'sliːz |i ~**ier** i‿ə ‖ i‿ᵊr ~**iest** i‿ɪst i‿əst
  ~**ily** ɪ li əl i ~**iness** i nəs i nɪs
sled sled **sledded** 'sled ɪd -əd **sledding**
  'sled ɪŋ **sleds** sledz
sledge sledʒ **sledged** sledʒd **sledges**
  'sledʒ ɪz -əz **sledging** 'sledʒ ɪŋ

sledgehammer 'sledʒ ˌhæm ə ‖ -ᵊr ~**s** z
sleek sliːk **sleeked** sliːkt **sleeker** 'sliːk ə ‖ -ᵊr
  sleekest 'sliːk ɪst -əst **sleeking** 'sliːk ɪŋ
  sleeks sliːks
sleek|ly 'sliːk |li ~**ness** nəs nɪs
sleep sliːp **sleeping** 'sliːp ɪŋ **sleeps** sliːps
  slept slept
  'sleeping bag; 'sleeping car; 'sleeping
  draught; ˌsleeping 'partner 'inactive
  business partner' ; 'sleeping pill; ˌsleeping
  po'liceman; 'sleeping ˌsickness
Sleepeezee tdmk ˌsliːp 'iːz i
sleeper 'sliːp ə ‖ -ᵊr ~**s** z
sleepi... —see **sleepy**
sleepless 'sliːp ləs -lɪs ~**ly** li ~**ness** nəs nɪs
sleepwalk|er/s 'sliːp ˌwɔːk ə/z ‖ -ᵊr/z -ˌwɑːk|-
  ~**ing** ɪŋ
sleep|y 'sliːp |i ~**ier** i‿ə ‖ i‿ᵊr ~**iest** i‿ɪst i‿əst
  ~**ily** ɪ li əl i ~**iness** i nəs i nɪs
sleepyhead 'sliːp i hed ~**s** z
sleet sliːt **sleeted** 'sliːt ɪd -əd ‖ 'sliːt̬ əd
  sleeting 'sliːt ɪŋ ‖ 'sliːt̬ ɪŋ **sleets** sliːts
sleety 'sliːt i ‖ 'sliːt̬ i
sleeve sliːv **sleeved** sliːvd **sleeves** sliːvz
  sleeving 'sliːv ɪŋ
-sleeved 'sliːvd — short-sleeved
  ˌʃɔːt 'sliːvd ◄ ‖ ˌʃɔːrt-
sleeveless 'sliːv ləs -lɪs
sleigh sleɪ (= slay) **sleighed** sleɪd **sleighing**
  'sleɪ ɪŋ **sleighs** sleɪz
sleighbell 'sleɪ bel ~**s** z
sleight slaɪt (= slight)
slend|er 'slend |ə ‖ -|ᵊr ~**erer** ᵊr ə ‖ ᵊr ər
  ~**erest** ᵊr ɪst -əst
slenderis|e, slenderiz|e 'slend ə raɪz ~**ed** d
  ~**es** ɪz əz ~**ing** ɪŋ
slender|ly 'slend ə |li ‖ -ᵊr- ~**ness** nəs nɪs
slept slept
Slessor 'sles ə ‖ -ᵊr
sleuth sluːθ sljuːθ **sleuthed** sluːθt sljuːθt
  sleuthing 'sluːθ ɪŋ 'sljuːθ- **sleuths** sluːθs
  sljuːθs
sleuthhound 'sluːθ haʊnd 'sljuːθ- ~**s** z
slew sluː sljuː **slewed** sluːd sljuːd **slewing**
  'sluː ɪŋ 'sljuː:- **slews** sluːz sljuːz
slice slaɪs **sliced** slaɪst **slices** slaɪs ɪz -əz
  slicing 'slaɪs ɪŋ
  ˌsliced 'bread
slice-of-life ˌslaɪs əv 'laɪf
slicer 'slaɪs ə ‖ -ᵊr ~**s** z
slick slɪk **slicked** slɪkt **slicker** 'slɪk ə ‖ 'slɪk ᵊr
  slickest 'slɪk ɪst -əst **slicking** 'slɪk ɪŋ **slicks**
  slɪks
slickenside 'slɪk ᵊn saɪd →-ŋ- ~**s** z
slicker 'slɪk ə ‖ -ᵊr ~**s** z
slide slaɪd **slid** slɪd **slides** slaɪdz **sliding**
  'slaɪd ɪŋ
  'slide rule; 'slide valve; ˌsliding 'door;
  ˌsliding 'scale
Slieve sliːv
slight slaɪt **slighted** 'slaɪt ɪd -əd ‖ 'slaɪt̬ əd
  slighter 'slaɪt ə ‖ 'slaɪt̬ ᵊr **slightest** 'slaɪt ɪst

-əst ‖ 'slaɪt̬ əst **slighting/ly** 'slaɪt ɪŋ /li
‖ 'slaɪt̬ ɪŋ /li **slights** slaɪts
slightly 'slaɪt li
Sligo 'slaɪg əʊ ‖ -oʊ
slily 'slaɪ li
slim, Slim slɪm **slimmed** slɪmd **slimmer**
'slɪm ə ‖ -ᵊr **slimmest** 'slɪm ɪst -əst
slimming 'slɪm ɪŋ **slims** slɪmz
Slimbridge 'slɪm brɪdʒ
Slimcea tdmk 'slɪm si‿ə
slime slaɪm **slimed** slaɪmd **slimes** slaɪmz
sliming 'slaɪm ɪŋ
slimi... —see **slimy**
slimline 'slɪm laɪn
slim|ly 'slɪm |li ~**ness** nəs nɪs
slimm... —see **slim**
slimmer 'slɪm ə ‖ -ᵊr ~**s** z
slim|y 'slaɪm |i ~**ier** i‿ə ‖ i‿ᵊr ~**iest** i‿ɪst i‿əst
~**ily** ɪ li əl i ~**iness** i nəs i nɪs
sling slɪŋ **slinging** 'slɪŋ ɪŋ **slings** slɪŋz **slung**
slʌŋ
slingback 'slɪŋ bæk ~**s** s
slinger 'slɪŋ ə ‖ -ᵊr ~**s** z
slingshot 'slɪŋ ʃɒt ‖ -ʃɑːt ~**s** s
slink slɪŋk **slinking** 'slɪŋk ɪŋ **slinks** slɪŋks
slunk slʌŋk
slink|y 'slɪŋk |i ~**ier** i‿ə ‖ i‿ᵊr ~**iest** i‿ɪst i‿əst
~**ily** ɪ li əl i ~**iness** i nəs i nɪs
slip slɪp **slipped** slɪpt **slipping** 'slɪp ɪŋ **slips**
slɪps
ˌslipped 'disc; 'slip road
slipcas|e 'slɪp keɪs ~**es** ɪz əz
slipcover 'slɪp ˌkʌv ə ‖ -ᵊr ~**s** z
slipknot 'slɪp nɒt ‖ -nɑːt ~**s** s
slip-on 'slɪp ɒn ‖ -ɑːn -ɔːn ~**s** z
slipover 'slɪp ˌəʊv ə ‖ -ˌoʊv ᵊr ~**s** z
slippag|e 'slɪp ɪdʒ ~**es** ɪz əz
slipp... —see **slip**
slipper 'slɪp ə ‖ -ᵊr ~**s** z
slipper|y 'slɪp ᵊr‿|i ~**ier** i‿ə ‖ i‿ᵊr ~**iest** i‿ɪst
i‿əst ~**ily** əl i ɪ li ~**iness** i nəs i nɪs
slipp|y 'slɪp |i ~**ier** i‿ə ‖ i‿ᵊr ~**iest** i‿ɪst i‿əst
~**iness** i nəs i nɪs
slipshod 'slɪp ʃɒd ‖ -ʃɑːd
slipstitch 'slɪp stɪtʃ ~**ed** t ~**es** ɪz əz ~**ing** ɪŋ
slipstream 'slɪp striːm ~**s** z
slip-up 'slɪp ʌp ~**s** s
slipway 'slɪp weɪ ~**s** z
slit slɪt **slits** slɪts **slitting** 'slɪt ɪŋ ‖ 'slɪt̬ ɪŋ
slither 'slɪð ə ‖ -ᵊr ~**ed** d **slithering** 'slɪð ᵊr‿ɪŋ
~**s** z
slithery 'slɪð ᵊr‿i
sliver 'slɪv ə ‖ -ᵊr —but in some rare technical
senses 'slaɪv- ~**ed** d **slivering** 'slɪv ᵊr‿ɪŋ ~**s**
z
slivovitz 'slɪv ə vɪts 'sliːv-
Sliwa 'sliː wə
Sloan, Sloane sləʊn ‖ sloʊn **Sloanes, Sloan's**
sləʊnz ‖ sloʊnz
ˌSloane 'Ranger; ˌSloane 'Square
slob slɒb ‖ slɑːb **slobs** slɒbz ‖ slɑːbz
slobber 'slɒb ə ‖ 'slɑːb ᵊr ~**ed** d **slobbering**
'slɒb ᵊr‿ɪŋ ‖ 'slɑːb- ~**s** z

slobberer 'slɒb ᵊr ə ‖ 'slɑːb ᵊr ᵊr ~**s** z
slobber|y 'slɒb ᵊr |i ‖ 'slɑːb- ~**iness** i nəs i nɪs
slobbish 'slɒb ɪʃ ‖ 'slɑːb-
Slocombe, Slocum 'sləʊk əm ‖ 'sloʊk-
sloe sləʊ ‖ sloʊ (= slow) **sloes** sləʊz ‖ sloʊz
sloe-eyed ˌsləʊ 'aɪd ◂ ' • • ‖ ˌsloʊ-
slog slɒg ‖ slɑːg **slogged** slɒgd ‖ slɑːgd
slogging 'slɒg ɪŋ ‖ 'slɑːg ɪŋ **slogs**
slɒgz ‖ slɑːgz
slogan 'sləʊg ᵊn ‖ 'sloʊg ᵊn ~**s** z
sloganeer ˌsləʊg ə 'nɪə ‖ ˌsloʊg ə 'nɪᵊr ~**ed** d
sloganeering ˌsləʊg ə 'nɪər ɪŋ
‖ ˌsloʊg ə 'nɪr ɪŋ ~**s** z
slogger 'slɒg ə ‖ 'slɑːg ᵊr ~**s** z
Sloman 'sləʊ mən ‖ 'sloʊ-
sloop sluːp **sloops** sluːps
slop slɒp ‖ slɑːp **slopped** slɒpt ‖ slɑːpt
slopping 'slɒp ɪŋ ‖ 'slɑːp ɪŋ **slops**
slɒps ‖ slɑːps
slope sləʊp ‖ sloʊp **sloped** sləʊpt ‖ sloʊpt
slopes sləʊps ‖ sloʊps **sloping/ly**
'sləʊp ɪŋ /li ‖ 'sloʊp ɪŋ /li
slopp|y 'slɒp |i ‖ 'slɑːp |i ~**ier** i‿ə ‖ i‿ᵊr ~**iest**
i‿ɪst i‿əst ~**ily** ɪ li əl i ~**iness** i nəs i nɪs
slosh slɒʃ ‖ slɑːʃ **sloshed** slɒʃt ‖ slɑːʃt
sloshes 'slɒʃ ɪz -əz ‖ 'slɑːʃ əz **sloshing**
'slɒʃ ɪŋ ‖ 'slɑːʃ ɪŋ
slosh|y 'slɒʃ |i ‖ 'slɑːʃ |i ~**ier** i‿ə ‖ i‿ᵊr ~**iest**
i‿ɪst i‿əst ~**ily** ɪ li əl i ~**iness** i nəs i nɪs
slot slɒt ‖ slɑːt **slots** slɒts ‖ slɑːts **slotted**
'slɒt ɪd -əd ‖ 'slɑːt̬ əd **slotting**
'slɒt ɪŋ ‖ 'slɑːt̬ ɪŋ
'slot maˌchine
sloth sləʊθ §slɒθ ‖ slɔːθ slɑːθ, sloʊθ **sloths**
sləʊθs §slɒθs ‖ slɔːθs slɑːθs, sloʊθs
slothful 'sləʊθ fᵊl 'slɒθ-, -fʊl ‖ 'slɔːθ- 'slɑːθ-,
'sloʊθ- ~**ly** ‿i ~**ness** nəs nɪs
slouch slaʊtʃ **slouched** slaʊtʃt **slouches**
'slaʊtʃ ɪz -əz **slouching/ly** 'slaʊtʃ ɪŋ /li
ˌslouch 'hat
slouch|y 'slaʊtʃ |i ~**ily** ɪ li əl i ~**iness** i nəs
i nɪs
slough n 'mud, marsh, swamp' slaʊ ‖ sluː slaʊ
(*)—Some Americans make a distinction
between sluː in the literal sense and slaʊ in the
figurative (ˌslough of de'spond). **sloughs**
slaʊz ‖ sluːz slaʊz
slough v; n 'cast-off skin' slʌf **sloughed** slʌft
sloughing 'slʌf ɪŋ **sloughs** slʌfs
Slough place in Berks (formerly Bucks) slaʊ
Slovak 'sləʊv æk -ɑːk ‖ 'sloʊv- ~**s** s
Slovakia sləʊ 'væk i‿ə -'vɑːk- ‖ sloʊ-
sloven 'slʌv ᵊn ~**s** z
Slovene 'sləʊv iːn sləʊ 'viːn ‖ 'sloʊv- ~**s** z
Sloveni|a sləʊ 'viːn i‿ə ‖ sloʊ- ~**an/s** ᵊn/z
sloven|ly 'slʌv ᵊn |li ~**liness** li nəs -nɪs
slow sləʊ ‖ sloʊ **slowed** sləʊd ‖ sloʊd **slower**
'sləʊ ə ‖ 'sloʊ ᵊr **slowest** 'sləʊ ɪst -əst
‖ 'sloʊ əst **slowing** 'sləʊ ɪŋ ‖ 'sloʊ ɪŋ **slows**
sləʊz ‖ sloʊz
ˌslow 'motion
slowcoach 'sləʊ kəʊtʃ ‖ 'sloʊ koʊtʃ ~**es** ɪz əz
slowdown 'sləʊ daʊn ‖ 'sloʊ- ~**s** z

S

slowly 'sləʊ li ‖ 'sloʊ li
slow-motion ˌsləʊ 'məʊʃ ᵊn ◄
  ‖ ˌsloʊ 'moʊʃ ᵊn ◄
slowness 'sləʊ nəs -nɪs ‖ 'sloʊ nəs
slowpoke 'sləʊ pəʊk ‖ 'sloʊ poʊk ~s s
slowworm 'sləʊ wɜːm ‖ 'sloʊ wɝːm ~s z
slub slʌb slubbed slʌbd slubbing 'slʌb ɪŋ
  slubs slʌbz
sludge slʌdʒ
sludgy 'slʌdʒ i
slue sluː slued sluːd slues sluːz sluing
  'sluː ɪŋ
slug slʌg slugged slʌgd slugging 'slʌg ɪŋ
  slugs slʌgz
sluggard 'slʌg əd ‖ -ᵊrd ~ly li ~s z
slugger 'slʌg ə ‖ -ᵊr ~s z
sluggish 'slʌg ɪʃ ~ly li ~ness nəs nɪs
sluice sluːs sluiced sluːst sluices 'sluːs ɪz -əz
  sluicing 'sluːs ɪŋ
sluicegate 'sluːs geɪt ~s s
sluiceway 'sluːs weɪ ~s z
slum slʌm slummed slʌmd slumming
  'slʌm ɪŋ slums slʌmz
  'slum ˌclearance; 'slum ˌdweller
slumber 'slʌm bə ‖ -bᵊr ~ed d slumbering
  'slʌm bᵊr_ɪŋ ~s z
slumberer 'slʌm bᵊr_ə ‖ -bᵊr ər ~s z
slumberland, S~ tdmk 'slʌm bə lænd ‖ -bᵊr-
slumberwear 'slʌm bə weə ‖ -bᵊr wer
slumberous 'slʌm bᵊr_əs ~ly li ~ness nəs nɪs
slumbrous 'slʌm brəs ~ly li ~ness nəs nɪs
slumlord 'slʌm lɔːd ‖ -lɔːrd ~s z
slumm|y 'slʌm li ~ier i_ə ‖ i_ᵊr ~iest i_ɪst i_əst
  ~iness i nəs i nɪs
slump slʌmp slumped slʌmpt slumping
  'slʌmp ɪŋ slumps slʌmps
slung slʌŋ
slunk slʌŋk
slur slɜː ‖ slɝː slurred slɜːd ‖ slɝːd slurring
  'slɜːr ɪŋ ‖ 'slɝː ɪŋ slurs slɜːz ‖ slɝːz
slurp slɜːp ‖ slɝːp slurped slɜːpt ‖ slɝːpt
  slurping 'slɜːp ɪŋ ‖ 'slɝːp ɪŋ slurps
  slɜːps ‖ slɝːps
slurr... —see slur
slurr|y 'slʌr li ‖ 'slɝː li ~ies iz
slush slʌʃ slushed slʌʃt slushes 'slʌʃ ɪz -əz
  slushing 'slʌʃ ɪŋ
  'slush fund
slush|y 'slʌʃ li ~ier i_ə ‖ i_ᵊr ~iest i_ɪst i_əst
  ~ily ɪ li əl i ~iness i nəs i nɪs
slut slʌt sluts slʌts
sluttish 'slʌt ɪʃ ‖ 'slʌt̬ ɪʃ ~ly li ~ness nəs nɪs
sly, Sly slaɪ slier, slyer 'slaɪ_ə ‖ 'slaɪ_ᵊr sliest,
  slyest 'slaɪ ɪst -əst
sly|ly 'slaɪ lli ~ness nəs nɪs
slype slaɪp slypes slaɪps
smack smæk smacked smækt smacking/s
  'smæk ɪŋ/z smacks smæks
smack-dab ˌsmæk 'dæb
smacker 'smæk ə ‖ -ᵊr ~s z
smackeroo ˌsmæk ə 'ruː ~s z
Smail, Smale smeɪᵊl
Smails, Smales smeɪᵊlz

small smɔːl ‖ smɑːl smaller 'smɔːl ə ‖ -ᵊr
  'smɑːl- smallest 'smɔːl ɪst -əst ‖ 'smɑːl-
  smalls smɔːlz ‖ smɑːlz
  'small ad; 'small arms ‖ ˌ· '·; ˌsmall 'beer;
  ˌsmall 'capital; ˌsmall 'change; ˌsmall
  'fortune; 'small fry; 'small hours; ˌsmall
  in'testine; ˌsmall 'print, '· ·; ˌsmall
  'screen, '· ·; ˌsmall 'talk
Smalley 'smɔːl i ‖ 'smɑːl-
smallholder 'smɔːl ˌhəʊld ə →-ˌhɒʊld-
  ‖ -ˌhoʊld ᵊr 'smɑːl- ~s z
smallholding 'smɔːl ˌhəʊld ɪŋ →-ˌhɒʊld-
  ‖ -ˌhoʊld ɪŋ 'smɑːl- ~s z
smallish 'smɔːl ɪʃ ‖ 'smɑːl-
small-minded ˌsmɔːl 'maɪnd ɪd ◄ -əd ‖ ˌsmɑːl-
  ~ly li ~ness nəs nɪs
smallness 'smɔːl nəs -nɪs ‖ 'smɑːl-
Smallpiece 'smɔːl piːs ‖ 'smɑːl-
smallpox 'smɔːl pɒks ‖ -pɑːks 'smɑːl-
small-scale ˌsmɔːl 'skeɪᵊl ◄ ‖ ˌsmɑːl-
small-tim|e ˌsmɔːl 'taɪm ◄ ‖ ˌsmɑːl- ~er/s
  ə/z ‖ ᵊr/z
  ˌsmall-time 'gangsters
small-town ˌsmɔːl 'taʊn ◄ ‖ ˌsmɑːl-
Smallwood 'smɔːl wʊd ‖ 'smɑːl-
smalt smɔːlt smɒlt ‖ smɑːlt
smaltite 'smɔːlt aɪt 'smɒlt- ‖ 'smɑːlt-
Smarden 'smɑːd ᵊn -en ‖ 'smɑːrd ᵊn
smarm smɑːm ‖ smɑːrm smarmed
  smɑːmd ‖ smɑːrmd smarming
  'smɑːm ɪŋ ‖ 'smɑːrm ɪŋ smarms
  smɑːmz ‖ smɑːrmz
smarm|y 'smɑːm li ‖ 'smɑːrm li ~ier i_ə ‖ i_ᵊr
  ~iest i_ɪst i_əst
smart, Smart smɑːt ‖ smɑːrt smarted
  'smɑːt ɪd -əd ‖ 'smɑːrt̬ əd smarter
  'smɑːt ə ‖ 'smɑːrt̬ ᵊr smartest 'smɑːt ɪst
  -əst ‖ 'smɑːrt̬ əst smarting
  'smɑːt ɪŋ ‖ 'smɑːrt̬ ɪŋ smarts
  smɑːts ‖ smɑːrts —see also phrases with this
  word
  'smart card
smart aleck 'smɑːt ˌæl ɪk -ek, ˌ·'·· ‖ 'smɑːrt̬-
  -ˌel- ~s s
smart-alecky 'smɑːt ˌæl ɪk i ◄ -ek i, -ək i,
  ˌ·'··· ‖ 'smɑːrt̬- -ˌel-
smart-arse, smart-ass 'smɑːt ɑːs -æs
  ‖ 'smɑːrt̬ æs
smarten 'smɑːt ᵊn ‖ 'smɑːrt ᵊn ~ed d ~ing
  ɪŋ ~s z
Smartie tdmk 'smɑːt i ‖ 'smɑːrt̬ i ~s z
smartish 'smɑːt ɪʃ ‖ 'smɑːrt̬ ɪʃ
smart|ly 'smɑːt lli ‖ 'smɑːrt lli ~ness nəs nɪs
smarty-pants 'smɑːt i pænts ‖ 'smɑːrt̬-
smash smæʃ smashed smæʃt smashes
  'smæʃ ɪz -əz smashing 'smæʃ ɪŋ
smash-and-grab ˌsmæʃ ᵊnd 'græb →-ᵊŋ-
  ˌsmash-and-'grab raid
smasher 'smæʃ ə ‖ -ᵊr ~s z
smash-up 'smæʃ ʌp ~s s
smatana 'smæt ᵊn ə
smattering 'smæt_ᵊr ɪŋ ‖ 'smæt̬ ᵊr ɪŋ ~s z

S

smear smɪə ‖ smɪᵊr **smeared** smɪəd ‖ smɪᵊrd
  smearing 'smɪər ɪŋ ‖ 'smɪr ɪŋ **smears**
  smɪəz ‖ smɪᵊrz
  'smear test
smeary 'smɪər i ‖ 'smɪr i
Smeaton 'smiːt ᵊn
smectic 'smekt ɪk ~s s
Smedley 'smed li
Smee smiː
smegma 'smeg mə
smell smel **smelled** smeld **smelling** 'smel ɪŋ
  smells smelz **smelt** smelt
  'smelling salts
Smellie 'smel i
smell|ly 'smel |i ~**ier** i‿ə ‖ i‿ᵊr ~**iest** i‿ɪst i‿əst
  ~**iness** i nəs i nɪs
smelt smelt **smelted** 'smelt ɪd -əd **smelting**
  'smelt ɪŋ **smelts** smelts
smelter 'smelt ə ‖ -ᵊr ~s z
Smetana 'smet ᵊn ə —Czech ['sme ta na]
Smethurst 'smeθ ɜːst -hɜːst ‖ -hɝːst
Smethwick 'smeð ɪk
smew smjuː **smews** smjuːz
smidgen, smidgin 'smɪdʒ ᵊn -ɪn ~s z
Smike smaɪk
smilax 'smaɪl æks
smile smaɪᵊl **smiled** smaɪᵊld **smiles** smaɪᵊlz
  smiling/ly 'smaɪl ɪŋ /li
Smiles smaɪᵊlz
smiley 'smaɪl i ~s z
Smiley, Smily 'smaɪl i
smirch smɜːtʃ ‖ smɝːtʃ **smirched**
  smɜːtʃt ‖ smɝːtʃt **smirches** 'smɜːtʃ ɪz -əz
  ‖ 'smɝːtʃ əz **smirching**
  'smɜːtʃ ɪŋ ‖ 'smɝːtʃ ɪŋ
smirk smɜːk ‖ smɝːk **smirked**
  smɜːkt ‖ smɝːkt **smirking/ly** 'smɜːk ɪŋ /li
  ‖ 'smɝːk- **smirks** smɜːks ‖ smɝːks
Smirke smɜːk ‖ smɝːk
Smirnoff tdmk 'smɜːn ɒf ‖ 'smɝːn ɔːf 'smɪrn-,
  -ɑːf
smite smaɪt **smit** smɪt **smites** smaɪts
  smiting 'smaɪt ɪŋ ‖ 'smaɪt̬ ɪŋ **smitten**
  'smɪt ᵊn **smote** sməʊt ‖ smoʊt
smith, Smith smɪθ **smiths, Smith's** smɪθs
smithereens ˌsmɪð ə 'riːnz
Smithers 'smɪð əz ‖ -ᵊrz
Smithfield 'smɪθ fiːᵊld
Smithson 'smɪθ sən
Smithsonian smɪθ 'səʊn i‿ən ‖ -'soʊn-
smithsonite 'smɪθ sə naɪt
smith|ly 'smɪð li ‖ 'smɪθ- ~**ies** iz
smitten 'smɪt ᵊn
smock smɒk ‖ smɑːk **smocked**
  smɒkt ‖ smɑːkt **smocking**
  'smɒk ɪŋ ‖ 'smɑːk ɪŋ **smocks**
  smɒks ‖ smɑːks
smog smɒg ‖ smɑːg smɔːg **smogs**
  smɒgz ‖ smɑːgz smɔːgz
smogg|ly 'smɒg li ‖ 'smɑːg li 'smɔːg- ~**ier**
  i‿ə ‖ i‿ᵊr ~**iest** i‿ɪst i‿əst
smoke sməʊk ‖ smoʊk **smoked**
  sməʊkt ‖ smoʊkt **smokes** sməʊks ‖ smoʊks

smoking 'sməʊk ɪŋ ‖ 'smoʊk ɪŋ
  'smoking ˌjacket; 'smoking comˌpartment
smokeless 'sməʊk ləs -lɪs ‖ 'smoʊk-
smoker, S~ 'sməʊk ə ‖ 'smoʊk ᵊr ~s z
smokescreen 'sməʊk skriːn ‖ 'smoʊk- ~s z
smokestack 'sməʊk stæk ‖ 'smoʊk- ~s s
  'smokestack ˌindustry
smoko 'sməʊk əʊ ‖ 'smoʊk oʊ ~s z
smok|ly 'sməʊk |i ‖ 'smoʊk |i ~**ier** i‿ə ‖ i‿ᵊr
  ~**iest** i‿ɪst i‿əst ~**ily** ɪ li əl i ~**iness** i nəs i nɪs
smold|er 'sməʊld |ə →'smoʊld- ‖ 'smoʊld |ᵊr
  ~**ered** əd ‖ ᵊrd ~**ering** ᵊr ɪŋ ~**ers** əz ‖ ᵊrz
Smolensk smɒ 'lenᵗsk smə- ‖ smoʊ- —Russ
  [smʌ 'ljensk]
Smollett 'smɒl ɪt §-ət ‖ 'smɑːl-
smolt smɒʊlt →smɒʊlt ‖ smoʊlt **smolts**
  smɒʊlts →smɒʊlts ‖ smoʊlts
smooch smuːtʃ **smooched** smuːtʃt
  smooches 'smuːtʃ ɪz -əz **smooching**
  'smuːtʃ ɪŋ
smooth smuːð **smoothed** smuːðd **smoother**
  'smuːð ə ‖ -ᵊr **smoothes** smuːðz
  smoothest 'smuːð ɪst -əst **smoothing**
  'smuːð ɪŋ
smoothbore 'smuːð bɔː ‖ -bɔːr -boʊr ~s z
smoothe smuːð **smoothed** smuːðd
  smoothes smuːðz **smoothing** 'smuːð ɪŋ
smoothie 'smuːð i ~s z
smooth|ly 'smuːð |li ~**ness** nəs nɪs
smooth|y 'smuːð |i ~**ies** iz
smorgasbord 'smɔːg əs bɔːd 'smɝːg-, -əz-
  ‖ 'smɔːrg əs bɔːrd -boʊrd —Swedish
  smörgåsbord ['smœr gɔs buɖ]
smote sməʊt ‖ smoʊt
smother 'smʌð ə ‖ -ᵊr ~**ed** d **smothering**
  'smʌð ᵊr ɪŋ ~s z
smould|er 'sməʊld |ə →'smoʊld- ‖ 'smoʊld |ᵊr
  ~**ered** əd ‖ ᵊrd ~**ering** ᵊr ɪŋ ~**ers** əz ‖ ᵊrz
smudge smʌdʒ **smudged** smʌdʒd **smudges**
  'smʌdʒ ɪz -əz **smudging** 'smʌdʒ ɪŋ
smudgepot 'smʌdʒ pɒt ‖ -pɑːt ~s s
smudg|ly 'smʌdʒ |i ~**ily** ɪ li əl i ~**iness** i nəs
  i nɪs
smug smʌg **smugger** 'smʌg ə ‖ -ᵊr
  smuggest 'smʌg ɪst -əst
smuggl|e 'smʌg ᵊl ~**ed** d ~**er/s** ə/z ‖ ᵊr/z
  ~**es** z ~**ing** ‿ɪŋ
smug|ly 'smʌg |li ~**ness** nəs nɪs
smurf smɜːf ‖ smɝːf **smurfs** smɜːfs ‖ smɝːfs
smut smʌt **smuts, Smuts** smʌts
smutt|ly 'smʌt |i ‖ 'smʌt̬ |i ~**ier** i‿ə ‖ i‿ᵊr ~**iest**
  i‿ɪst i‿əst ~**ily** ɪ li əl i ~**iness** i nəs i nɪs
Smyrna 'smɜːn ə ‖ 'smɝːn ə —Turkish zmir
  ['iz mir]
Smyth (i) smɪθ, (ii) smaɪθ, (iii) smaɪð
Smythe (i) smaɪð, (ii) smaɪθ
snack snæk **snacked** snækt **snacking**
  'snæk ɪŋ **snacks** snæks
  'snack bar
Snaefell ˌsneɪ 'fel
snaffl|e 'snæf ᵊl ~**ed** d ~**es** z ~**ing** ‿ɪŋ
  'snaffle bit
snafu snæ 'fuː ~**ed** d ~**ing** ɪŋ ~s z

S

snag snæg **snagged** snægd **snagging**
'snæg ɪŋ **snags** snægz
Snagge snæg
snaggletooth 'snæg ᵊl tuːθ §-tʊθ **~ed** t
snail sneɪᵊl **snails** sneɪᵊlz
'snail's pace
Snaith sneɪθ
snake, Snake sneɪk **snaked** sneɪkt **snakes**
sneɪks **snaking** 'sneɪk ɪŋ
'snake ˌcharmer; ˌsnakes and 'ladders
snakebite 'sneɪk baɪt **~s** s
snakeroot 'sneɪk ruːt ‖ -rʊt **~s** s
snakeskin 'sneɪk skɪn **~s** z
snak|y 'sneɪk |i **~ier** i‿ə ‖ i‿ᵊr **~iest** i‿ɪst i‿əst
~ily ɪ li ᵊl i **~iness** i nəs i nɪs
snap snæp **snapped** snæpt **snapping**
'snæp ɪŋ **snaps** snæps
'snap ˌfastener
snapdragon 'snæp ˌdræg ᵊn **~s** z
Snape sneɪp
snapper 'snæp ə ‖ -ᵊr **~s** z
snappish 'snæp ɪʃ **~ly** li **~ness** nəs nɪs
Snapple tdmk 'snæp ᵊl
snapp|y 'snæp |i **~ier** i‿ə ‖ i‿ᵊr **~iest** i‿ɪst i‿əst
~ily ɪ li ᵊl i **~iness** i nəs i nɪs
snapshot 'snæp ʃɒt ‖ -ʃɑːt **~s** s
snare sneə ‖ sneᵊr **snared** sneəd ‖ sneᵊrd
snares sneəz ‖ sneᵊrz **snaring**
'sneər ɪŋ ‖ 'sner ɪŋ
'snare drum
snark snɑːk ‖ snɑːrk **snarks** snɑːks ‖ snɑːrks
snarl snɑːl ‖ snɑːrl **snarled** snɑːld ‖ snɑːrld
snarling/ly 'snɑːl ɪŋ /li ‖ 'snɑːrl ɪŋ /li **snarls**
snɑːlz ‖ snɑːrlz
snarl-up 'snɑːl ʌp ‖ 'snɑːrl- **~s** z
snatch snætʃ **snatched** snætʃt **snatches**
'snætʃ ɪz -əz **snatching** 'snætʃ ɪŋ
snatcher 'snætʃ ə ‖ -ᵊr **~s** z
snazz|y 'snæz |i **~ier** i‿ə ‖ i‿ᵊr **~iest** i‿ɪst i‿əst
~ily ɪ li ᵊl i **~iness** i nəs i nɪs
sneak sniːk **sneaked** sniːkt **sneaking**
'sniːk ɪŋ **sneaks** sniːks **snuck** snʌk
ˌsneak 'preview; 'sneak thief
sneaker 'sniːk ə ‖ -ᵊr **~s** z
sneaking 'sniːk ɪŋ **~ly** li **~ness** nəs nɪs
sneak|y 'sniːk |i **~ier** i‿ə ‖ i‿ᵊr **~iest** i‿ɪst i‿əst
~ily ɪ li ᵊl i **~iness** i nəs i nɪs
sneer snɪə ‖ snɪᵊr **sneered** snɪəd ‖ snɪᵊrd
sneering/ly 'snɪər ɪŋ /li ‖ 'snɪr ɪŋ /li **sneers**
snɪəz ‖ snɪᵊrz
sneeze sniːz **sneezed** sniːzd **sneezes**
'sniːz ɪz -əz **sneezing** 'sniːz ɪŋ
sneezeweed 'sniːz wiːd **~s** z
sneezewort 'sniːz wɜːt §-wɔːt ‖ -wɝːt -wɔːrt
~s s
Sneezum 'sniːz əm
Sneinton 'snent ən ‖ -ᵊn
snell, Snell snel
Snelgrove, Snellgrove 'snel grəʊv ‖ -groʊv
Snetterton 'snet ət ən ‖ 'snet̬ ᵊrt ᵊn
Sneyd sniːd
snib snɪb **snibbed** snɪbd **snibbing** 'snɪb ɪŋ
snibs snɪbz

snick snɪk **snicked** snɪkt **snicking** 'snɪk ɪŋ
snicks snɪks
snicker 'snɪk ə ‖ -ᵊr **~ed** d **snickering/ly**
'snɪk ᵊr‿ɪŋ /li **~s** z
Snickers tdmk 'snɪk əz ‖ -ᵊrz
snickersnee ˌsnɪk ə 'sniː: '• • • ‖ -ᵊr- **~s** z
snicket 'snɪk ɪt §-ət **~s** s
snide snaɪd **snider** 'snaɪd ə ‖ -ᵊr **snidest**
'snaɪd ɪst -əst
snide|ly 'snaɪd |li **~ness** nəs nɪs
sniff snɪf **sniffed** snɪft **sniffing** 'snɪf ɪŋ **sniffs**
snɪfs
sniffer 'snɪf ə ‖ -ᵊr **~s** z
'sniffer dog
sniffl|e 'snɪf ᵊl **~ed** d **~es** z **~ing** ɪŋ
sniffl|y 'snɪf |i **~ier** i‿ə ‖ i‿ᵊr **~iest** i‿ɪst i‿əst
~ily ɪ li ᵊl i **~iness** i nəs i nɪs
snifter 'snɪft ə ‖ -ᵊr **~s** z
snigger 'snɪg ə ‖ -ᵊr **~ed** d **sniggering/ly**
'snɪg ᵊr‿ɪŋ /li **~s** z
snip snɪp **snipped** snɪpt **snipping** 'snɪp ɪŋ
snips snɪps
snipe snaɪp **sniped** snaɪpt **snipes** snaɪps
sniping 'snaɪp ɪŋ
sniper 'snaɪp ə ‖ -ᵊr **~s** z
snipper 'snɪp ə ‖ -ᵊr **~s** z
snippet 'snɪp ɪt §-ət **~s** s
snit snɪt **snits** snɪts
snitch snɪtʃ **snitched** snɪtʃt **snitches** 'snɪtʃ ɪz
-əz **snitching** 'snɪtʃ ɪŋ
snivel 'snɪv ᵊl **~ed, ~led** d **~er/s, ~ler/s** ə/z
‖ ᵊr/z **~ing, ~ling** ɪŋ **~s** z
snob snɒb ‖ snɑːb **snobs** snɒbz ‖ snɑːbz
snobbery 'snɒb ər i ‖ 'snɑːb-
snobbish 'snɒb ɪʃ ‖ 'snɑːb- **~ly** li **~ness** nəs
nɪs
snobbism 'snɒb ˌɪz əm ‖ 'snɑːb-
snobb|y 'snɒb |i ‖ 'snɑːb |i **~ier** i‿ə ‖ i‿ᵊr **~iest**
i‿ɪst i‿əst **~ily** ɪ li ᵊl i **~iness** i nəs i nɪs
SNOBOL 'snəʊb ɒl ‖ 'snoʊb ɔːl -ɑːl
Sno-Cat tdmk 'snəʊ kæt ‖ 'snoʊ- **~s** s
Snodgrass 'snɒd grɑːs §-græs ‖ 'snɑːd græs
Snodland 'snɒd lənd ‖ 'snɑːd-
snoek snuːk snʊk (= snook)
snog snɒg ‖ snɑːg **snogged** snɒgd ‖ snɑːgd
snogging 'snɒg ɪŋ ‖ 'snɑːg ɪŋ **snogs**
snɒgz ‖ snɑːgz
snood snuːd snʊd **snoods** snuːdz snʊdz
snook 'gesture of defiance' snuːk snʊk ‖ snʊk
snuːk **snooks** snuːks snʊks ‖ snʊks snuːks
snook fish snuːk snʊk
snooker 'snuːk ə ‖ 'snʊk ᵊr (*) **~ed** d
snookering 'snuːk ᵊr‿ɪŋ ‖ 'snʊk ᵊr‿ɪŋ **~s** z
snoop snuːp **snooped** snuːpt **snooping**
'snuːp ɪŋ **snoops** snuːps
snooper 'snuːp ə ‖ -ᵊr **~s** z
Snoopy, snoop|y 'snuːp |i **~ier** i‿ə ‖ i‿ᵊr **~iest**
i‿ɪst i‿əst
snoot snuːt **snoots** snuːts
snoot|y 'snuːt |i ‖ 'snuːt̬ |i **~ier** i‿ə ‖ i‿ᵊr **~iest**
i‿ɪst i‿əst **~ily** ɪ li ᵊl i **~iness** i nəs i nɪs
snooze snuːz **snoozed** snuːzd **snoozes**
'snuːz ɪz -əz **snoozing** 'snuːz ɪŋ

snore snɔː ‖ snɔːr snoʊr **snored**
snɔːd ‖ snɔːrd snoʊrd **snores** snɔːz ‖ snɔːrz
snoʊrz **snoring** 'snɔːr ɪŋ ‖ 'snoʊr-
snorer 'snɔːr ə ‖ -ᵊr 'snoʊr- ~s z
snorkel 'snɔːk ᵊl ‖ 'snɔːrk ᵊl ~ed, ~led d
~ing, ~ling ɪŋ ~s z
snort snɔːt ‖ snɔːrt **snorted** 'snɔːt ɪd -əd
‖ 'snɔːrt̬ əd **snorting** 'snɔːt ɪŋ ‖ 'snɔːrt̬ ɪŋ
snorts snɔːts ‖ snɔːrts
snorter 'snɔːt ə ‖ 'snɔːrt̬ ᵊr
snot snɒt ‖ snɑːt
snott|y 'snɒt li ‖ 'snɑːt̬ li ~ier i‿ə ‖ i‿ᵊr ~iest
i‿ɪst i‿əst ~ily ɪ li əl i ~iness i nəs i nɪs
snotty-nosed ˌsnɒt i 'nəʊzd ◂ '•••
‖ ˌsnɑːt̬ i 'noʊzd
snout snaʊt **snouts** snaʊts
snow, Snow snəʊ ‖ snoʊ **snowed**
snəʊd ‖ snoʊd **snowing** 'snəʊ ɪŋ ‖ 'snoʊ ɪŋ
snows snəʊz ‖ snoʊz
  'snow ˌblindness; ˌSnow 'White
snowball, S~ 'snəʊ bɔːl ‖ 'snoʊ- -bɑːl ~ed d
~ing ɪŋ ~s z
snowberr|y 'snəʊ bᵊr‿li '•ˌber li ‖ 'snoʊ ˌber li
~ies iz
snowbird 'snəʊ bɜːd ‖ 'snoʊ bɜ˞ːd ~s z
snow-blind 'snəʊ blaɪnd ‖ 'snoʊ-
snowblower 'snəʊ ˌbləʊ ə ‖ 'snoʊ ˌbloʊ ᵊr ~s
z
snowbound 'snəʊ baʊnd ‖ 'snoʊ-
snow-capped 'snəʊ kæpt ‖ 'snoʊ-
  ˌsnow-capped 'peaks
Snowcem *tdmk* 'snəʊ sem ‖ 'snoʊ-
snow-clad 'snəʊ klæd ‖ 'snoʊ-
Snowden, Snowdon 'snəʊd ᵊn ‖ 'snoʊd ᵊn
Snowdonia snəʊ 'dəʊn i‿ə ‖ snoʊ 'doʊn-
Snowdown 'snəʊ daʊn ‖ 'snoʊ-
snowdrift 'snəʊ drɪft ‖ 'snoʊ- ~s s
snowdrop 'snəʊ drɒp ‖ 'snoʊ drɑːp ~s s
snowfall 'snəʊ fɔːl ‖ 'snoʊ- -fɑːl ~s z
snowfield 'snəʊ fiːᵊld ‖ 'snoʊ- ~s z
snowflake 'snəʊ fleɪk ‖ 'snoʊ- ~s s
snowline 'snəʊ laɪn ‖ 'snoʊ- ~s z
snow|man 'snəʊ |mæn ‖ 'snoʊ- ~men men
snowmobile 'snəʊ mə ˌbiːᵊl -moʊ- ‖ 'snoʊ-
-moʊ- ~s z
snowplough, snowplow 'snəʊ plaʊ ‖ 'snoʊ-
~s z
snowshoe 'snəʊ ʃuː ‖ 'snoʊ- ~s z
snowstorm 'snəʊ stɔːm ‖ 'snoʊ stɔːrm ~s z
snow-white ˌsnəʊ 'waɪt ◂ -'hwaɪt
‖ ˌsnoʊ 'hwaɪt ◂
snow|y, Snowy 'snəʊ li ‖ 'snoʊ li ~ier
i‿ə ‖ i‿ᵊr ~iest i‿ɪst i‿əst ~ily ɪ li əl i ~iness
i nəs i nɪs
  ˌSnowy 'Mountains
SNP ˌes en 'piː →-em-
snr, Snr —*see* **senior**
snub snʌb **snubbed** snʌbd **snubbing**
'snʌb ɪŋ **snubs** snʌbz
snubb|y 'snʌb li ~ier i‿ə ‖ i‿ᵊr ~iest i‿ɪst i‿əst
~iness i nəs i nɪs
snub-nosed ˌsnʌb 'nəʊzd ◂ '•• ‖ -'noʊzd ◂
snuck snʌk

snuff snʌf **snuffed** snʌft **snuffing** 'snʌf ɪŋ
snuffs snʌfs
snuffbox 'snʌf bɒks ‖ -bɑːks ~es ɪz əz
snuffer 'snʌf ə ‖ -ᵊr ~s z
snuffl|e 'snʌf ᵊl ~ed d ~er/s ̩ə/z ‖ ̩ᵊr/z ~es
z ~ing ̩ɪŋ
snug, Snug snʌg **snugger** 'snʌg ə ‖ -ᵊr
snuggest 'snʌg ɪst -əst
snugger|y 'snʌg ᵊr li ~ies iz
snuggl|e 'snʌg ᵊl ~ed d ~es z ~ing ̩ɪŋ
snug|ly 'snʌg |li ~ness nəs nɪs
so səʊ ‖ soʊ —*There is an occasional weak form*
sə
soak səʊk ‖ soʊk **soaked** səʊkt ‖ soʊkt
soaking 'səʊk ɪŋ ‖ 'soʊk ɪŋ **soaks**
səʊks ‖ soʊks
soakage 'səʊk ɪdʒ ‖ 'soʊk-
soakaway 'səʊk ə ˌweɪ ‖ 'soʊk- ~s z
Soames səʊmz ‖ soʊmz
so-and-so 'səʊ ən səʊ -ənd- ‖ 'soʊ ən soʊ ~s
z
Soane səʊn ‖ soʊn
soap səʊp ‖ soʊp **soaped** səʊpt ‖ soʊpt
soaping 'səʊp ɪŋ ‖ 'soʊp ɪŋ **soaps**
səʊps ‖ soʊps
  'soap ˌbubble; 'soap ˌopera
soapberr|y 'səʊp ˌber li ‖ 'soʊp- ~ies iz
soapbox 'səʊp bɒks ‖ 'soʊp bɑːks ~es ɪz əz
soapi... —*see* **soapy**
soapstone 'səʊp stəʊn ‖ 'soʊp stoʊn
soapsuds 'səʊp sʌdz ‖ 'soʊp-
soapwort 'səʊp wɜːt §-wɔːt ‖ 'soʊp wɜ˞ːt
-wɔːrt ~s s
soap|y 'səʊp li ‖ 'soʊp li ~ier i‿ə ‖ i‿ᵊr ~iest
i‿ɪst i‿əst ~ily ɪ li əl i ~iness i nəs i nɪs
soar sɔː ‖ sɔːr soʊr (= *sore*) **soared**
sɔːd ‖ sɔːrd soʊrd **soaring/ly** 'sɔːr ɪŋ /li
‖ 'soʊr- **soars** sɔːz ‖ sɔːrz soʊrz
Soar *river* sɔː ‖ sɔːr soʊr
Soar *place in Wales* 'səʊ ɑː ‖ 'soʊ ɑːr
soaraway 'sɔːr ə ˌweɪ ‖ 'soʊr-
Soares 'swɑːr eʃ —*Port* ['swa rɪʃ]
SOAS 'səʊ æs -æz; ˌes əʊ eɪ 'es ‖ 'soʊ-
Soay 'səʊ eɪ -ə ‖ 'soʊ-
sob sɒb ‖ sɑːb **sobbed** sɒbd ‖ sɑːbd **sobbing**
'sɒb ɪŋ ‖ 'sɑːb ɪŋ **sobs** sɒbz ‖ sɑːbz
  'sob ˌstory
sobeit səʊ 'biː ɪt ‖ soʊ-
Sobell 'səʊ bel ‖ 'soʊ-
sober 'səʊb ə ‖ 'soʊb ᵊr **sobered**
'səʊb əd ‖ 'soʊb -ᵊrd **soberer** 'səʊb ᵊr‿ə
‖ 'soʊb ᵊr‿ᵊr **soberest** 'səʊb ᵊr‿ɪst ̩əst
‖ 'soʊb- **sobering/ly** 'səʊb ᵊr ɪŋ /li ‖ 'soʊb-
~ly li ~ness nəs nɪs
Sobers 'səʊb əz ‖ 'soʊb ᵊrz
Sobranie *tdmk* səʊ 'brɑːn i ‖ soʊ-
sobriety səʊ 'braɪ‿ət i ̩ɪt i ‖ soʊ 'braɪ ət̬ i
sobriquet 'səʊb rɪ keɪ -rə- ‖ 'soʊb- ˌ•••◂ ~s
z
soca 'səʊk ə ‖ 'soʊk ə
socage 'sɒk ɪdʒ ‖ 'sɑːk-
so-called ˌsəʊ 'kɔːld ◂ ‖ ˌsoʊ- -'kɑːld ◂
soccer 'sɒk ə ‖ 'sɑːk ᵊr

S

sociability ˌsəʊʃ ə 'bɪl ət i -ɪt i ‖ ˌsoʊʃ ə 'bɪl ət̬ i
sociab|le 'səʊʃ əb |ᵊl ‖ 'soʊʃ- ~leness ᵊl nəs
-nɪs ~ly li
social 'səʊʃ ᵊl ‖ 'soʊʃ ᵊl ~s z
  ˌsocial ˌanthro'pology; ˌsocial 'climber;
  ˌSocial 'Democrat; 'social diˌsease; ˌsocial
  'distance; ˌSocial 'Register tdmk; ˌsocial
  'science; ˌsocial se'curity; ˌsocial
  'services; ˌsocial ˌstudies; ˌsocial work
socialis... —see socializ...
socialism 'səʊʃ ə ˌlɪz əm -ᵊl ˌɪz- ‖ 'soʊʃ-
socialist 'səʊʃ ᵊl ɪst §-əst ‖ 'soʊʃ- ~s s
socialistic ˌsəʊʃ ə 'lɪst ɪk ◂ ‖ ˌsoʊʃ- ~ally ᵊl_i
socialite 'səʊʃ ə laɪt ‖ 'soʊʃ- ~s s
socialization ˌsəʊʃ ᵊl aɪ 'zeɪʃ ᵊn -ɪ' • -
  ‖ ˌsoʊʃ ᵊl ə-
socializ|e 'səʊʃ ə laɪz ‖ 'soʊʃ- ~ed d ~es ɪz əz
  ~ing ɪŋ
  ˌsocialized 'medicine
socially 'səʊʃ ᵊl i ‖ 'soʊʃ-
societal sə 'saɪ_ət ᵊl ‖ -ət̬ ᵊl ~ly i
societ|y sə 'saɪ_ət li ‖ -ət̬ i ~ies iz
Socinian səʊ 'sɪn i_ən ‖ soʊ- sə- ~s z
Socinus səʊ 'saɪn əs ‖ soʊ- sə-
socio- comb. form
  with stress-neutral suffix ˌsəʊʃ i_əʊ ˌsəʊs-
  ‖ ˌsoʊs i_oʊ — sociobiology
  ˌsəʊʃ i_əʊ baɪ 'ɒl ədʒ i ˌsəʊs-
  ‖ ˌsoʊs i_oʊ baɪ 'ɑːl-
  with stress-imposing suffix ˌsəʊs i 'ɒ+ ˌsəʊʃ-
  ‖ ˌsoʊs i 'ɑː+ — sociometry ˌsəʊs i 'ɒm ətr i
  ˌsəʊʃ-, -ɪtr i ‖ ˌsoʊs i 'ɑːm-
socioeconomic ˌsəʊʃ i_əʊ ˌiːk ə 'nɒm ɪk ˌsəʊs-,
  -ˌek- ‖ ˌsoʊs i_oʊ ˌek ə 'nɑːm ɪk -ˌiːk- ~ally
  ᵊl_i
sociolect 'səʊʃ i_əʊ lekt 'səʊs- ‖ 'soʊs i_oʊ-
  ~s s
sociolectal ˌsəʊʃ i_əʊ 'lekt ᵊl ◂ ˌsəʊs-
  ‖ ˌsoʊs i_oʊ-
sociolinguist ˌsəʊʃ i_əʊ 'lɪŋ gwɪst ˌsəʊs-
  ‖ ˌsoʊs i_oʊ- ~s s
sociolinguistic ˌsəʊʃ i_əʊ lɪŋ 'gwɪst ɪk ◂ ˌsəʊs-
  ‖ ˌsoʊs i_oʊ- ~ally ᵊl_i ~s s
sociological ˌsəʊʃ i_ə 'lɒdʒ ɪk ᵊl ◂ ˌsəʊs-
  ‖ ˌsoʊs i_ə 'lɑːdʒ- ~ly _i
sociologist ˌsəʊʃ i 'ɒl ədʒ ɪst ˌsəʊs-, §-əst
  ‖ ˌsoʊs i 'ɑːl- ~s s
sociology ˌsəʊʃ i 'ɒl ədʒ i ˌsəʊs- ‖ ˌsoʊs i 'ɑːl-
sociopath 'səʊʃ i_əʊ pæθ 'səʊs- ‖ 'soʊs i_oʊ-
  ~s s
sociopolitical ˌsəʊʃ i_əʊ pə 'lɪt ɪk ᵊl ◂ ˌsəʊs-
  ‖ ˌsoʊs i_oʊ pə 'lɪt̬-
sock sɒk ‖ sɑːk socked sɒkt ‖ sɑːkt socking
  'sɒk ɪŋ ‖ 'sɑːk ɪŋ socks sɒks ‖ sɑːks
sockdolager, sockdologer
  ˌsɒk 'dɒl ədʒ ə ‖ sɑːk 'dɑːl ɪdʒ ᵊr ~s z
sock|et 'sɒk |ɪt §-ət ‖ 'sɑːk |ət ~eted ɪt ɪd
  §ət-, -əd ‖ ət̬ əd ~eting ɪt ɪŋ §ət- ‖ ət̬ ɪŋ
  ~ets ɪts §əts ‖ əts
sockeye 'sɒk aɪ ‖ 'sɑːk aɪ ~s z
Socotra səʊ 'kəʊtr ə sɒ- ‖ soʊ 'koʊtr ə sə-
Socrates 'sɒk rə tiːz ‖ 'sɑːk-

Socratic sɒ 'kræt ɪk səʊ- ‖ sə 'kræt̬ ɪk soʊ-
  ~ally ᵊl_i
sod sɒd ‖ sɑːd sods sɒdz ‖ sɑːdz
  ˌsod's 'law, ' • •
soda 'səʊd ə ‖ 'soʊd ə ~s z
  'soda bread; 'soda ˌfountain; 'soda ˌwater
sodality səʊ 'dæl ət i -ɪt- ‖ soʊ 'dæl ət̬ i ~ies
  iz
sodden 'sɒd ᵊn ‖ 'sɑːd ᵊn ~ed d ~ing ˌɪŋ ~ly
  li ~ness nəs nɪs ~s z
sodding 'sɒd ɪŋ ‖ 'sɑːd ɪŋ
Soddy 'sɒd i ‖ 'sɑːd i
sodium 'səʊd i_əm ‖ 'soʊd-
  ˌsodium 'chloride
Sodom 'sɒd əm ‖ 'sɑːd əm
sodomis|e 'sɒd ə maɪz ‖ 'sɑːd- ~ed d ~es ɪz
  əz ~ing ɪŋ
sodomite 'sɒd ə maɪt ‖ 'sɑːd- ~s s
sodomiz|e 'sɒd ə maɪz ‖ 'sɑːd- ~ed d ~es ɪz
  əz ~ing ɪŋ
sodomy 'sɒd əm i ‖ 'sɑːd-
Sodor 'səʊd ə ‖ 'soʊd ᵊr
soever səʊ 'ev ə ‖ soʊ 'ev ᵊr
sofa 'səʊf ə ‖ 'soʊf ə ~s z
sofabed 'səʊf ə bed ‖ 'soʊf- ~s z
Sofer 'səʊf ə ‖ 'soʊf ᵊr
soffit 'sɒf ɪt §-ət ‖ 'sɑːf ət ~s s
Sofia 'səʊf i_ə 'sɒf-; səʊ 'fiː_ə, -'faɪ_ə
  ‖ 'soʊf i_ə —Bulgarian ['so fi ja]
soft sɒft sɔːft ‖ sɔːft sɑːft softer 'sɒft ə
  'sɔːft- ‖ 'sɔːft ᵊr 'sɑːft- softest 'sɒft ɪst
  'sɔːft-, -əst ‖ 'sɔːft əst 'sɑːft-
  ˌsoft 'fruit; ˌsoft 'furnishings; ˌsoft
  'landing; ˌsoft 'option; ˌsoft 'palate; ˌsoft
  'sell; ˌsoft 'soap; 'soft spot; ˌsoft 'touch
softball 'sɒft bɔːl 'sɔːft- ‖ 'sɔːft- 'sɑːftbɑːl ~s
  z
soft-boiled ˌsɒft 'bɔɪᵊld ◂ ˌsɔːft- ‖ ˌsɔːft-
  ˌsɑːft-
  ˌsoft-boiled 'eggs
soft-centered, soft-centred ˌsɒft 'sentəd ◂
  ˌsɔːft- ‖ ˌsɔːft 'sent̬ ᵊrd ◂ ˌsɑːft-
soft-core ˌsɒft 'kɔː ◂ ˌsɔːft- ‖ ˌsɔːft 'kɔːr ◂
  ˌsɑːft-, -'koʊr
  ˌsoft-core 'porn
soft-cover ˌsɒft 'kʌv ə ˌsɔːft- ‖ ˌsɔːft 'kʌv ᵊr ◂
  ˌsɑːft-
soften 'sɒf ᵊn 'sɔːf- ‖ 'sɔːf ᵊn 'sɑːf- ~ed d
  ~ing ˌɪŋ ~s z
softener 'sɒf ᵊn_ə 'sɔːf- ‖ 'sɔːf ᵊn_ᵊr 'sɑːf- ~s
  z
softhearted ˌsɒft 'hɑːt ɪd ◂ ˌsɔːft-, §-əd
  ‖ ˌsɔːft 'hɑːrt̬ əd ◂ ˌsɑːft- ~ness nəs nɪs
softie 'sɒft i ‖ 'sɔːft i 'sɑːft- ~s z
softish 'sɒft ɪʃ 'sɔːft- ‖ 'sɔːft- 'sɑːft-
soft|ly 'sɒft |li 'sɔːft- ‖ 'sɔːft |li 'sɑːft- ~ness
  nəs nɪs
softly-softly ˌsɒft li 'sɒft li ˌsɔːft li 'sɔːft-
  ‖ ˌsɔːft li 'sɔːft li ˌsɑːft li 'sɑːft-
soft-pedal ˌsɒft 'ped ᵊl ˌsɔːft- ‖ ˌsɔːft- ˌsɑːft-
  ~ed, -led d ~ing, ~ling ˌɪŋ ~s z
soft-soap ˌsɒft 'səʊp ˌsɔːft- ‖ ˌsɔːft 'soʊp
  ˌsɑːft- ~ed t ~ing ɪŋ ~s s

soft-spoken ˌsɒftˈspəʊk ən ◄ ˌsɔːft- ‖ ˌsɔːft ˈspəʊk ən ◄ ˌsɑːft-

software ˈsɒft weə ˈsɔːft- ‖ ˈsɔːft wer ˈsɑːft-, -wær
ˈsoftware house

softwood ˈsɒft wʊd ˈsɔːft- ‖ ˈsɔːft- ˈsɑːft- ~s z

soft|y ˈsɒft li ˈsɔːft- ‖ ˈsɔːft li ˈsɑːft- ~ies iz

SOGAT ˈsəʊ gæt ‖ ˈsoʊ-

Sogdian ˈsɒgd i_ən ‖ ˈsɑːgd- ~s z

Sogdiana ˌsɒgd iˈɑːn ə -ˈeɪn ə ‖ ˌsɑːgd iˈæn ə

sogg|y ˈsɒg li ‖ ˈsɑːg li ˈsɔːg- ~ier i_ə ‖ i_ər
~iest i_ɪst i_əst ~ily ɪ li əl i ~iness i nəs i nɪs

soh səʊ ‖ soʊ (= so)

Soham ˈsəʊ əm ‖ ˈsoʊ-

Soho, SoHo ˈsəʊ həʊ ˌ•ˈ• ‖ ˈsoʊ hoʊ
ˌSoho ˈSquare

soi-disant ˌswɑː ˈdiːz ɒ̃ ◄ -diː ˈzɒ̃ ‖ -diː ˈzɑːn ◄
—Fr [swa di zɑ̃]

soigne, soigné, soignee, soignée ˈswɑːn jeɪ
•ˈ• ‖ swɑːn ˈjeɪ —Fr [swan je]

soil sɔɪəl **soiled** sɔɪəld **soiling** ˈsɔɪəl ɪŋ **soils**
sɔɪəlz

soilpipe ˈsɔɪəl paɪp ~s s

soiree, soirée ˈswɑːr eɪ ‖ swɑː ˈreɪ —Fr
[swa ʁe] ~s z

soixante-neuf ˌswæs ɒnt ˈnɜːf ˌswʌs-
‖ ˌswɑːs ɑːnt ˈnɜːf -ˈnʌf —Fr [swa sɑ̃t nœf]

sojourn ˈsɒdʒ ən ˈsʌdʒ-, -ɜːn ‖ soʊ ˈdʒɜːn ˈ••
(**)—Some speakers of AmE make a stress
difference between the noun ˈ•• and the verb
•ˈ• ~ed d ~ing ɪŋ ~s z

sojourner ˈsɒdʒ ən ə ˈsʌdʒ-, -ɜːn-
‖ soʊ ˈdʒɜːn ər ˈ••• ~s z

soke səʊk ‖ soʊk (= soak)

Sokoto ˈsəʊk ə təʊ ‖ ˈsoʊk oʊ toʊ

sol, Sol sɒl ‖ sɑːl sɔːl —but as the name of a
coin, in AmE also soʊl **sols** sɒlz ‖ sɑːlz

sola ˈsəʊl ə ‖ ˈsoʊl ə
ˌsola ˈtopi

solac|e ˈsɒl əs -ɪs ‖ ˈsɑːl əs ~ed t ~es ɪz əz
~ing ɪŋ

solan ˈsəʊl ən ‖ ˈsoʊl ən ~s z

solanaceous ˌsɒl əˈneɪʃ əs ◄ ˌsəʊl- ‖ ˌsoʊl-

solanum səʊ ˈleɪn əm ‖ sə-

solar, Solar ˈsəʊl ə §-ɑː ‖ ˈsoʊl ər
ˌsolar ˈcell; ˌsolar ˈpanel; ˌsolar ˈplexus;
ˈsolar ˌsystem; ˌsolar ˈwind; ˌsolar ˈyear

solari|um sə ˈleər i_əm səʊ- ‖ -ˈler- soʊ-,
-ˈlær- ~a ə ~ums əmz

solati|um səʊ ˈleɪʃ i_əm -ˈleɪʃ ləm ‖ soʊ- ~a ə
~ums əmz

sold səʊld →sɒʊld ‖ soʊld (= soled)

sold|er ˈsɒld lə ˈsəʊld-, §ˈsɒd-, §ˈsɔːd-
‖ ˈsɑːd lər (**) ~ered əd ‖ ərd ~ering ər ɪŋ
~ers əz ‖ ərz
ˈsoldering ˌiron

soldier ˈsəʊldʒ ə →ˈsɒʊldʒ- ‖ ˈsoʊldʒ ər
—There is also an occasional spelling
pronunciation ˈsəʊld i_ə ‖ ˈsoʊld i_ər ~ed d
soldiering ˈsəʊldʒ ər_ɪŋ →ˈsɒʊldʒ-
‖ ˈsoʊldʒ ər_ɪŋ ~s z
ˌsoldier of ˈfortune

soldierlike ˈsəʊldʒ ə laɪk →ˈsɒʊldʒ-
‖ ˈsoʊldʒ ər-

soldierly ˈsəʊldʒ ə li →ˈsɒʊldʒ- ‖ ˈsoʊldʒ ər-

soldier|y ˈsəʊldʒ ər li →ˈsɒʊldʒ- ‖ ˈsoʊldʒ-
~ies iz

sole səʊl →sɒʊl ‖ soʊl **soled** səʊld sɒʊld
‖ soʊld **soles** səʊlz →sɒʊlz ‖ soʊlz **soling**
ˈsəʊl ɪŋ →ˈsɒʊl- ‖ ˈsoʊl ɪŋ

solecism ˈsɒl ɪ ˌsɪz əm ˈsəʊl-, -ə- ‖ ˈsɑːl- ˈsoʊl-
~s z

Soledad ˈsɒl ɪ dæd -ə- ‖ ˈsɑːl- —Sp
[so le ˈðað]

solely ˈsəʊl li →ˈsɒʊl- ‖ ˈsoʊl li

solemn ˈsɒl əm ‖ ˈsɑːl əm ~ly li ~ness nəs nɪs

solemnis... —see **solemniz...**

solemnit|y sə ˈlem nət li sɒ-, -nɪt i ‖ -nət̬ li
~ies iz

solemnization ˌsɒl əm naɪ ˈzeɪʃ ən -nɪ ˈ•-
‖ ˌsɑːl əm nə- ~s z

solemniz|e ˈsɒl əm naɪz ‖ ˈsɑːl- ~ed d ~es ɪz
əz ~ing ɪŋ

solenoid ˈsɒl ə nɔɪd ˈsəʊl-, -ɪ- ‖ ˈsoʊl- ˈsɑːl-
~s z

Solent ˈsəʊl ənt ‖ ˈsoʊl-

solera sə ˈleər ə -ˈlɪər- ‖ -ˈler- -ˈlær- —Sp
[so ˈle ra]

Soley ˈsəʊl i ‖ ˈsoʊl i

sol-fa ˌsɒl ˈfɑː §ˌsəʊl- ‖ ˌsoʊl-

solfatara ˌsɒlf əˈtɑːr ə ‖ ˌsoʊlf- ~s z

solfegg|io sɒl ˈfedʒ li əʊ -ˈfedʒ ləʊ
‖ sɑːl ˈfedʒ loʊ ~i i:

solferino, S~ ˌsɒlf əˈriːn əʊ ‖ ˌsɑːlf əˈriːn oʊ

solic|it sə ˈlɪs lɪt §səʊ-, §-ət ‖ -lət ~ited ɪt ɪd
§ət-, -əd ‖ ət̬ əd ~iting ɪt ɪŋ §ət- ‖ ət̬ ɪŋ ~its
ɪts §əts ‖ əts

solicitation sə ˌlɪs ɪ ˈteɪʃ ən §səʊ-, -, ˈ•ə- ~s z

solicitor sə ˈlɪs ɪt ə §səʊ-, -ət- ‖ -ət̬ ər ~s z
soˌlicitor ˈGeneral

solicitous sə ˈlɪs ɪt əs §səʊ-, -ət- ‖ -ət̬ əs ~ly li
~ness nəs nɪs

solicitude sə ˈlɪs ɪ tjuːd §səʊ-, -ə-, →§-tʃuːd
‖ -tuːd -tjuːd

solid ˈsɒl ɪd §-əd ‖ ˈsɑːl əd ~s z

solidago ˌsɒl ɪ ˈdeɪg əʊ -ə- ‖ ˌsɑːl ə ˈdeɪg oʊ

solidarity ˌsɒl ɪ ˈdær ət i ˌ•ə-, -ɪt i
‖ ˌsɑːl ə ˈdær ət̬ i -ˈder-

solidi ˈsɒl ɪ daɪ -ə-, -diː ‖ ˈsɑːl-

solidification sə ˌlɪd ɪf ɪ ˈkeɪʃ ən sɒ-, -, ˈ•əf-,
§-ə ˈ•-

solidify sə ˈlɪd ɪ faɪ sɒ-, -ˈ•ə-

solidity sə ˈlɪd ət i sɒ-, -ɪt i ‖ -ət̬ i

solid|ly ˈsɒl ɪd lli §-əd- ‖ ˈsɑːl əd- ~ness nəs
nɪs

solid-state ˌsɒl ɪd ˈsteɪt ◄ §-əd- ‖ ˌsɑːl əd-

sol|idus ˈsɒl lɪd əs -əd- ‖ ˈsɑːl ləd əs ~idi ɪ daɪ
-ə-, -diː

Solignum tdmk səʊ ˈlɪg nəm ‖ soʊ-

Solihull ˌsəʊl iˈhʌl ˌsɒl- ‖ ˌsoʊl-

soliloquis|e, soliloquiz|e sə ˈlɪl ə kwaɪz səʊ-,
sɒ- ~ed d ~es ɪz əz ~ing ɪŋ

soliloq|uy sə ˈlɪl ək lwi səʊ-, sɒ- ~uies wiz

solipsism ˈsɒl ɪp ˌsɪz əm ˈsəʊl-, -əp- ‖ ˈsɑːl əp-

solipsist 'sɒl ɪp sɪst 'səʊl-, -əp-, §-səst
‖ 'saːl əp səst ~s s
solipsistic ˌsɒl ɪp 'sɪst ɪk ◄ ˌsəʊl-, -əp-
‖ ˌsaːl əp- ~ally ᵊl i
solitaire ˌsɒl ɪ 'teə -ə-, '••• ‖ 'saːl ə ter -tær
~s z
solitarily 'sɒl ə‿tər əl i '•ɪ-, -ɪ li; ˌ••'teər ə-
‖ ˌsaːl ə 'ter əl i
solitar|y 'sɒl ə‿tər li '•ɪ‿ ‖ 'saːl ə ter li ~ies iz
~iness i nəs i nɪs
ˌsolitary con'finement
solitude 'sɒl ə tjuːd -ɪ-, →§-tʃuːd ‖ 'saːl ə tuːd
-tjuːd ~s z
solleret ˌsɒl ə 'ret ‖ ˌsaːl- ~s s
solo 'səʊl əʊ ‖ 'soʊl oʊ ~s z
soloist 'səʊl əʊ ɪst §-əst ‖ 'soʊl oʊ- ~s s
Solomon 'sɒl əm ən ‖ 'saːl-
Solomons 'sɒl əm ənz ‖ 'saːl-
Solon 'səʊl ɒn -ən ‖ 'soʊl ən -aːn
solstic|e 'sɒlst ɪs -əs ‖ 'saːlst əs 'soʊlst- ~es ɪz
əz
Solti 'sɒlt i ‖ 'soʊlt i —Hung ['ʃol ti]
solubility ˌsɒl ju 'bɪl ət i ˌ•jə- -ɪt i
‖ ˌsaːl jə 'bɪl ət̬ i
solub|le 'sɒl jub |ᵊl -jəb- ‖ 'saːl jəb |ᵊl
~leness ᵊl nəs -nɪs ~ly li
solus 'səʊl əs ‖ 'soʊl əs
solute 'sɒl juːt sɒ 'luːt, -'ljuːt ‖ 'saːl- ~s s
solution sə 'luːʃ ᵊn -'ljuːʃ- ~s z
Solutrean sə 'luːtr i‿ən
solvability ˌsɒlv ə 'bɪl ət i -ɪt i ‖ ˌsaːlv ə 'bɪl ət̬ i
solvable 'sɒlv əb ᵊl ‖ 'saːlv-
solvate n 'sɒlv eɪt ‖ 'saːlv- ~s s
solv|ate v sɒl 'v|eɪt 'sɒlv |eɪt ‖ 'saːlv eɪt
~ated eɪt ɪd -əd ‖ eɪt̬ əd ~ates eɪts ~ating
eɪt ɪŋ ‖ eɪt̬ ɪŋ
solvation sɒl 'veɪʃ ᵊn ‖ saːl-
Solvay 'sɒlv eɪ ‖ 'saːlv- —Fr [sɔl vɛ]
ˈSolvay ˌprocess
solve sɒlv §səʊlv ‖ saːlv solved sɒlvd §səʊlvd
‖ saːlvd solves sɒlvz §səʊlvz ‖ saːlvz
solving 'sɒlv ɪŋ §'səʊlv- ‖ 'saːlv ɪŋ
solvency 'sɒlv ᵊnᵗs i §'səʊlv- ‖ 'saːlv-
solvent 'sɒlv ᵊnt §'səʊlv- ‖ 'saːlv- ~s s
ˈsolvent aˌbuse
solver 'sɒlv ə §'səʊlv- ‖ 'saːlv ᵊr ~s z
Solway 'sɒl weɪ ‖ 'saːl-
ˌSolway 'Firth
Solzhenitsyn ˌsɒl ʒə 'nɪts ɪn -ʒɪ-, -'niːts-, §-ən
‖ ˌsoʊl- —Russ [səɫ ʒɨ 'nʲi tsɨn]
soma 'səʊm ə ‖ 'soʊm ə
Somali, s~ sə 'maːl i səʊ- ‖ soʊ- ~s z
Somali|a sə 'maːl i‿ə səʊ- ‖ soʊ- ~an/s ən/z
~land lænd
somatic səʊ 'mæt ɪk soʊ ‖ soʊ 'mæt̬ ɪk sə-
somato- comb. form
with stress-neutral suffix ˌsəʊm ət ə
ˌˌsəʊm ə təʊ; səʊ ˌmæt ə ‖ ˌsoʊm ət̬ ə
sə 'mæt ə — somatoplasm 'səʊm ət əʊ
ˌplæz əm səʊ 'mæt ə- ‖ sə 'mæt̬ ə-
'soʊm ət̬ ə-
with stress-imposing suffix
ˌsəʊm ə 'tɒ+ ‖ ˌsoʊm ə 'taː+ —

somatology
ˌsəʊm ə 'tɒl ədʒ i ‖ ˌsoʊm ə 'taːl-
somatotype 'səʊm ət əʊ taɪp səʊ 'mæt-
‖ sə 'mæt̬ ə- 'soʊm ət̬ ə- ~s s
somber, sombre 'sɒm bə ‖ 'saːm bᵊr ~ly li
sombrero sɒm 'breər əʊ ‖ saːm 'brer oʊ səm-
~s z
some strong form sʌm, weak form səm —In
stranded (exposed) position only the strong form
is used: I've found some. aɪv 'faʊnd sʌm.
Otherwise the weak form is usual if the word is
unstressed: I've found some coins
aɪv ˌfaʊnd səm 'kɔɪnz
-some səm— burdensome
'bɜːd ᵊn səm ‖ 'bɜːd- — eightsome
'eɪt səm —With this pronunciation, -some
forms adjectives or collective numerals:
compare the following.
-some in biology, 'body' səʊm ‖ soʊm —
chromosome
'krəʊm ə səʊm ‖ 'kroʊm ə soʊm —This
-some is used with combining forms and means
'body': compare the preceding.
somebody 'sʌm bəd i -ˌbɒd- ‖ -ˌbaːd- —There
is also a casual form 'sʌm di
someday 'sʌm deɪ
somehow 'sʌm haʊ —There is also a casual
form 'sʌm aʊ
someone 'sʌm wʌn §-wɒn
ˌsomeone 'clever; ˌsomeone 'else
—Compare the phrase ˌsome 'one, as in ˌSome
'one of us will ˌhave to ˌdo it
someplace 'sʌm pleɪs —Compare the phrase
ˌsome 'place
Somerfield 'sʌm ə fiːᵊld ‖ -ᵊr-
Somerleyton 'sʌm ə ˌleɪt ᵊn ‖ -ᵊr-
Somers 'sʌm əz ‖ -ᵊrz
somersault 'sʌm ə sɔːlt -sɒlt ‖ -ᵊr- -saːlt ~ed
ɪd əd ~ing ɪŋ ~s s
Somerset 'sʌm ə set -sɪt ‖ -ᵊr-
Somerton 'sʌm ət ᵊn ‖ -ᵊrt ᵊn
Somerville 'sʌm ə vɪl ‖ -ᵊr-
something 'sʌm θɪŋ △-θɪŋk; 'sʌmᵖθ ɪŋ,
→'sʌnᵗθ-, △-ɪŋk ‖ →'sʌmp m —There are
casual forms 'sʌm hɪŋ, 'sʌm ɪŋ
ˌsomething 'else
sometime 'sʌm taɪm (NB not '•) —Compare
the phrase some 'time səm 'taɪm, as in I ˌneed
some ˌtime to 'think
sometimes 'sʌm taɪmz (NB not '•)
someway 'sʌm weɪ
somewhat 'sʌm wɒt -hwɒt, §-ət ‖ -hwʌt
-hwaːt, -hwət
somewhere 'sʌm weə -hweə ‖ -hweᵊr
ˌsomewhere 'else
somite 'səʊm aɪt ‖ 'soʊm- ~s s
Somme sɒm ‖ saːm sʌm —Fr [sɔm]
sommelier sɒ 'mel i‿ə sʌ-, -eɪ; ˌsʌm ᵊl 'jeɪ,
ˌsɒm-, '••• ‖ ˌsʌm ᵊl 'jeɪ —Fr [sɔ mə lje] ~s
z
somnambulant sɒm 'næm bjʊl ᵊnt -bjəl ᵊnt
‖ saːm 'næm bjəl ᵊnt ~s s

somnambu|late sɒm 'næm bju ‖eɪt -bjə leɪt
‖ saːm 'naːm bjə- **~lated** leɪt ɪd -əd ‖ leɪt̬ əd
~lates leɪts **~lating** leɪt ɪŋ ‖ leɪt̬ ɪŋ
somnambulation sɒm ˌnæm bju 'leɪʃ ᵊn
ˌ•••'••, -bjə'•- ‖ saːm ˌnæm bjə-
somnambulism sɒm 'næm bju ˌlɪz əm -'•bjə-
‖ saːm 'næm bjə-
somnambulist sɒm 'næm bjʊl ɪst -'•bjəl-,
§-əst ‖ saːm 'næm bjəl əst **~s** s
somniferous sɒm 'nɪf ər əs ‖ saːm-
somnolence 'sɒm nəl ənᵗs ‖ 'saːm-
somnolent 'sɒm nəl ənt ‖ 'saːm- **~ly** li
Somoza sə 'məʊz ə ‖ -'moʊz- -'moʊs- —
AmSp [so 'mo sa]
Sompting 'sɒmpt ɪŋ 'sʌmpt- ‖ 'saːmpt-
son *'male child'* , **Son** sʌn *(= sun)* **sons** sʌnz
son *French word, 'sound'*, sɒn ‖ sɔːn soʊn —*Fr*
[sɔ̃] —*see also phrases with this word*
sonagram 'səʊn ə græm 'sɒn- ‖ 'soʊn- 'saːn-
~s z
sonagraph, S~ *tdmk* 'səʊn ə graːf 'sɒn-, -græf
‖ 'soʊn ə græf 'saːn- **~s** s
sonant 'səʊn ənt 'sɒn- ‖ 'soʊn- **~s** s
sonar 'səʊn aː ‖ 'soʊn aːr **~s** z
sonata sə 'naːt ə ‖ -'naːt̬- **~s** z
sonatina ˌsɒn ə 'tiːn ə ‖ ˌsaːn- **~s** z
sonde sɒnd ‖ saːnd **sondes** sɒndz ‖ saːndz
Sondheim 'sɒnd haɪm ‖ 'saːnd-
sone səʊn ‖ soʊn **sones** səʊnz ‖ soʊnz
son et lumiere, son et lumière
ˌsɒn eɪ 'luːm i eə ˌ••,••'•
‖ ˌsaːn eɪ luːm 'jeᵊr ˌsoʊn- —*Fr*
[sɔ̃ nɛ ly mjɛːʁ]
song sɒŋ ‖ sɔːŋ saːŋ **songs** sɒŋz ‖ sɔːŋz saːŋz
ˌsong and 'dance; 'song thrush
songbird 'sɒŋ bɜːd ‖ 'sɔːŋ bɜːd 'saːŋ- **~s** z
songbook 'sɒŋ bʊk §-buːk ‖ 'sɔːŋ- 'saːŋ- **~s**
s
Songhai ₍ₗ₎sɒŋ 'gaɪ ‖ ₍ₗ₎sɔːŋ- ₍ₗ₎saːŋ- **~s** z
songster 'sɒŋ stə 'sɒŋᵏst ə ‖ 'sɔːŋᵏst ᵊr
'saːŋᵏst- **~s** z
songstress 'sɒŋ strəs -strɪs, -stres
‖ 'sɔːŋks trəs 'saːŋᵏs- **~es** ɪz əz
songwriter 'sɒŋ ˌraɪt ə ‖ 'sɔːŋ ˌraɪt̬ ᵊr 'saːŋ- **~s**
z
Sonia 'sɒn i_ə 'səʊn- ‖ 'soʊn jə
sonic 'sɒn ɪk ‖ 'saːn ɪk **~s** s
ˌsonic 'boom
son-in-law ˌsʌn ɪn ˌlɔː §-ən- ‖ -ˌlaː: **sons-in-
law** ˌsʌnz ɪn ˌlɔː §-ən- ‖ -ˌlaː
Sonja 'sɒn jə 'səʊn- ‖ 'soʊn-
sonnet 'sɒn ɪt -ət ‖ 'saːn ət **~s** s
sonneteer ˌsɒn ɪ 'tɪə -ə- ‖ ˌsaːn ə 'tɪᵊr **~s** z
Sonning 'sɒn ɪŋ 'sʌn- ‖ 'saːn-
sonn|y, Sonn|y 'sʌn li *(= sunny)* **~ies, ~y's** iz
son-of-a-bitch ˌsʌn əv ə 'bɪtʃ **~es** ɪz əz
sons-of-bitches ˌsʌnz əv 'bɪtʃ ɪz -əz
son-of-a-gun ˌsʌn əv ə 'gʌn **sons-of-guns**
ˌsʌnz əv 'gʌnz
sonogram 'səʊn ə græm 'sɒn- ‖ 'soʊn- 'saːn-
~s z
sonograph 'səʊn ə graːf 'sɒn-, -græf
‖ 'soʊn ə græf 'saːn- **~s** s

Sonoma sə 'nəʊm ə ‖ -'noʊm-
sonometer səʊ 'nɒm ɪt ə sɒ-, -ət ə
‖ soʊ 'naːm ət̬ ᵊr sə- **~s** z
Sonor|a sə 'nɔːr |ə ‖ -'noʊr- **-an** ən
sonorant 'sɒn ər ənt 'səʊn- ‖ 'soʊn- 'saːn-;
sə 'nɔːr-, soʊ-, -'noʊr- **~s** s
sonority sə 'nɒr ət i səʊ-, -ɪt i ‖ sə 'nɔːr ət̬ i
sə 'naːr-
sonorous 'sɒn ər əs sə 'nɔːr- ‖ sə 'nɔːr əs
-'noʊr-; 'saːn ər- **~ly** li
sons-... —*see* **son-...**
sonsy, sonsie 'sɒnᵗs i ‖ 'saːnᵗs i
Sontag 'sɒn tæg ‖ 'saːn-
Sony *tdmk* 'səʊn i 'sɒn- ‖ 'soʊn i —*Jp* ['so ɲii]
Sonya 'sɒn jə ‖ 'soʊn-
soon suːn §sʊn **sooner** 'suːn ə §'sʊn- ‖ -ᵊr
soonest 'suːn ɪst §'sʊn-, -əst

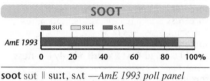

SOOT

| ■ sʊt | □ suːt | ■ sʌt |

AmE 1993

| 0 | 20 | 40 | 60 | 80 | 100% |

soot sʊt ‖ suːt, sʌt —*AmE 1993 poll panel
preference:* sʊt 89%, suːt 10%, sʌt 1%.
sooth suːθ
soothe suːð **soothed** suːðd **soothes** suːðz
soothing 'suːð ɪŋ
soother 'suːð ə ‖ -ᵊr **~s** z
soothing 'suːð ɪŋ **~ly** li **~ness** nəs nɪs
soothsay|er/s 'suːθ ˌseɪ ə/z ‖ -ᵊr/z **~ing** ɪŋ
soot|y, Sooty 'sʊt li ‖ 'sʊt̬ li 'suːt̬-, 'sʌt̬- **~ier**
i_ə ‖ i_ᵊr **~iest** i_ɪst i_əst **~iness** i nəs i nɪs
sop sɒp ‖ saːp **sopped** sɒpt ‖ saːpt **sopping**
'sɒp ɪŋ ‖ 'saːp ɪŋ **sops** sɒps ‖ saːps
Soper 'səʊp ə ‖ 'soʊp ᵊr
Sophia səʊ 'faɪ_ə -'fiː_ə ‖ soʊ 'fiː ə sə-
Sophie 'səʊf i ‖ 'soʊf i
sophism 'sɒf ˌɪz əm ‖ 'saːf-
sophist 'sɒf ɪst §-əst ‖ 'saːf əst **~s** s
sophister 'sɒf ɪst ə §-əst- ‖ 'saːf əst ᵊr **~s** z
sophistic sə 'fɪst ɪk sɒ- ‖ saː- **~al** ᵊl **~ally** ᵊl_i
sophisti|cate *v* sə 'fɪst ɪ ˌkeɪt §-ə keɪt **~cated**
keɪt ɪd -əd ‖ keɪt̬ əd **~cates** keɪts **~cating**
keɪt ɪŋ ‖ keɪt̬ ɪŋ
sophisticate *n* sə 'fɪst ɪ keɪt §-ə-; -ɪk ət, §-ək-,
-ɪt **~s** s
sophistication sə ˌfɪst ɪ 'keɪʃ ᵊn §-ə-
sophis|try 'sɒf ɪs |tri -əs- ‖ 'saːf- **~tries** triz
Sophoclean ˌsɒf ə 'kliː_ən ‖ ˌsaːf-
Sophocles 'sɒf ə kliːz ‖ 'saːf-
sophomore 'sɒf ə mɔː ‖ 'saːf ə mɔːr -moʊr;
'saːf mɔːr, -moʊr **~s** z
Sophronia səʊ 'frəʊn i_ə ‖ sə 'froʊn-
Sophy 'səʊf i ‖ 'soʊf i
-sophy *stress-imposing* səf i — **philosophy**
fɪ 'lɒs əf i ‖ -'laːs-
soporific ˌsɒp ə 'rɪf ɪk ◄ ˌsəʊp- ‖ ˌsaːp- ˌsoʊp-
~s s
sopping 'sɒp ɪŋ ‖ 'saːp ɪŋ
ˌsopping 'wet◄
sopp|y 'sɒp li ‖ 'saːp li **~ier** i_ə ‖ i_ᵊr **~iest**
i_ɪst i_əst **~ily** ɪ li əl i **~iness** i nəs i nɪs

S

sopranino ˌsɒp rə 'niːn əʊ ‖ ˌsoʊp rə 'niːn oʊ
　~s z
sopran|o sə 'prɑːn ləʊ ‖ -'præn loʊ -'prɑːn- ~i
　-iː ~os əʊz ‖ oʊz
Sopwith 'sɒp wɪθ ‖ 'sɑːp-
Soraya sə 'raɪ‿ə
sorb, Sorb sɔːb ‖ sɔːrb **sorbs, Sorbs**
　sɔːbz ‖ sɔːrbz
sorbet 'sɔːb eɪ -ət, -ɪt ‖ 'sɔːrb ət sɔːr 'beɪ
　sorbets 'sɔːb eɪz -əts, -ɪts ‖ 'sɔːrb əts
　sɔːr 'beɪz
Sorbian 'sɔːb i‿ən ‖ 'sɔːrb- ~s z
sorbic 'sɔːb ɪk ‖ 'sɔːrb-
sorbitol 'sɔːb ɪ tɒl -ə- ‖ 'sɔːrb ə tɔːl -tɑːl, -toʊl
sorbo, Sorbo *tdmk* 'sɔːb əʊ ‖ 'sɔːrb oʊ
Sorbonne ₍ˌ₎sɔː 'bɒn ‖ sɔːr 'bɑːn -'bɑːn —*Fr*
　[sɔʁ bɔn]
sorbose 'sɔːb əʊz -əʊs ‖ 'sɔːrb oʊs
sorcerer 'sɔːs ər‿ə ‖ 'sɔːrs ər‿ər ~s z
sorceress 'sɔːs ə res -ər‿əs, _ɪs, ˌsɔːs ə 'res
　‖ 'sɔːrs ər‿əs ~es ɪz əz
sorcer|y 'sɔːs ər‿li i ‖ 'sɔːrs- ~ies iz
sordid 'sɔːd ɪd §-əd ‖ 'sɔːrd əd ~ly li ~ness
　nəs nɪs
sordin|o sɔː 'diːn |əʊ ‖ sɔːr 'diːn |oʊ ~i iː
sore sɔː ‖ sɔːr soʊr *(= soar)* **sorer**
　'sɔːr ə ‖ 'sɔːr ər 'soʊr- **sores** sɔːz ‖ sɔːrz
　soʊrz **sorest** 'sɔːr ɪst-əst ‖ 'soʊr-
　ˌsore 'throat
sorehead 'sɔː hed ‖ 'sɔːr- 'soʊr- ~s z
sore|ly 'sɔː |li ‖ 'sɔːr- 'soʊr- ~ness nəs nɪs
Sorensen 'sɒr ən sən ‖ 'sɔːr- 'sɑːr-
sorghum 'sɔːg əm ‖ 'sɔːrg əm
sorites sɒ 'raɪt iːz sə- ‖ soʊ-
Soroptimist, s~ sə 'rɒpt ɪm ɪst -əm-, §-əst
　‖ -'rɑːpt- ~s s
sororit|y sə 'rɒr ət li sɒ-, -ɪt i ‖ -'rɔːr ət̬ li -'rɑːr-
　~ies iz
Soros 'sɔːr ɒs 'sɒr-, 'ʃɒr-, -ɒʃ, -əs, -əʃ ‖ -ɑːs
　-oʊs
soros|is sɒ 'rəʊs| ɪs §-əs ‖ -'roʊs|- ~es iːz
sorrel 'sɒr əl ‖ 'sɔːr əl 'sɑːr- ~s z
Sorrel, Sorrell *(i)* 'sɒr əl ‖ 'sɔːr əl 'sɑːr-, *(ii)*
　sə 'rel
Sorrento sə 'rent əʊ ‖ -oʊ —*It* [sor 'rɛn to]
sorri|ly 'sɒr |əl i -ɪ li ‖ 'sɔːr- 'sɑːr- ~iness
　i nəs i nɪs
sorrow 'sɒr əʊ ‖ 'sɔːr oʊ 'sɑːr- ~ed d ~ing/ly
　ɪŋ /li ~s z
sorrowful 'sɒr əʊ f‿əl -fʊl ‖ 'sɔːr ə- 'sɑːr-, -oʊ-
　~ly ‿i ~ness nəs nɪs

SORRY

　　　■ 'sɑːr-　　▢ 'sɔːr-
AmE 1993
　　　0　　20　　40　　60　　80　　100%

sorr|y 'sɒr |i ‖ 'sɑːr |i 'sɔːr- —*AmE 1993 poll
panel preference:* 'sɑːr- 68%, 'sɔːr- 32%.
　~ier i‿ə ‖ i‿ər ~iest i‿ɪst i‿əst
sort sɔːt ‖ sɔːrt **sorted** 'sɔːt ɪd -əd ‖ 'sɔːrt̬ əd
　sorting 'sɔːt ɪŋ ‖ 'sɔːrt̬ ɪŋ **sorts**
　sɔːts ‖ sɔːrts
sorta 'sɔːt ə ‖ 'sɔːrt̬ ə

sortal 'sɔːt ‿əl ‖ 'sɔːrt̬ ‿əl ~s z
sorter 'sɔːt ə ‖ 'sɔːrt̬ ər ~s z
sortie 'sɔːt i -iː ‖ 'sɔːrt̬ i sɔːr 'tiː ~s z
sortilege 'sɔːt ɪl ɪdʒ -əl- ‖ 'sɔːrt̬ ‿əl-
sort-out 'sɔːt aʊt ‖ 'sɔːrt̬- ~s s
sorus 'sɔːr əs ‖ 'soʊr-
SOS ˌes əʊ 'es ‖ -oʊ- ~s, ~'s ɪz əz
Soskice 'sɒsk ɪs §-əs ‖ 'sɑːsk-
so-so 'səʊ səʊ ‖ 'soʊ soʊ
sostenut|o ˌsɒst ə 'nuːt |əʊ -ɪ-, -'njuːt-
　‖ ˌsɑːst ə 'nuːt |oʊ ˌsoʊst- ~i iː ~os
　əʊz ‖ oʊz
sot sɒt ‖ sɑːt **sots** sɒts ‖ sɑːts
soteriology səʊ ˌtɪər i 'ɒl ədʒ i sɒ-
　‖ soʊ ˌtɪr i 'ɑːl-
Sotheby 'sʌð ə bi ~'s z
Sothic 'səʊθ ɪk 'sɒθ- ‖ 'soʊθ ɪk 'sɑːθ-
Sotho 'suːt u: 'səʊt əʊ ‖ 'soʊt oʊ ~s z
sottish 'sɒt ɪʃ ‖ 'sɑːt̬ ɪʃ ~ly li ~ness nəs nɪs
sotto voce ˌsɒt əʊ 'vəʊtʃ i ‖ ˌsɑːt̬ oʊ 'voʊtʃ i
　—*It* [ˌsot to 'vo: tʃe]
sou suː **sous** suːz
soubise su 'biːz
soubrette su 'bret ~s s
soubriquet 'suːb rɪ keɪ -rə-, ˌ•'•
souchong ˌsuː 'tʃɒŋ ◂ -'ʃɒŋ ‖ -'tʃɑːŋ ◂ ˌsoʊ-,
　-'ʃɑːŋ, '••
souffle *'egg dish'*, **soufflé** 'suːf leɪ ‖ su 'fleɪ
　~s z
souffle *'blowing sound'* 'suːf ‿əl ~s z
Soufriere, Soufrière su 'frɪə 'suːf ri eə ‖ -'frɪ‿ər
sough *'sigh, murmur'* saʊ sʌf **soughed** saʊd
　sʌft **soughing** 'saʊ ɪŋ 'sʌf- **soughs** saʊz
　sʌfs
sought sɔːt ‖ sɑːt
sought-after 'sɔːt ˌɑːft ə §-ˌæft- ‖ 'sɔːt̬ ˌæft ər
　'sɑːt̬-
souk suːk **souks** suːks
soul, Soul səʊl →sɒʊl ‖ soʊl *(= sole)* **souls**
　səʊlz →sɒʊlz ‖ soʊlz
　'soul ˌbrother; 'soul mate; 'soul ˌmusic;
　'soul ˌsister
Soulbury 'səʊl bər‿i →'sɒʊl- ‖ 'soʊl ˌber i
Soulby 'səʊl bi →'sɒʊl- ‖ 'soʊl bi
soul-destroying 'səʊl dɪ ˌstrɔɪ ɪŋ də-, §-diː-
　‖ 'soʊl-
soulful 'səʊl f‿əl →'sɒʊl-, -fʊl ‖ 'soʊl- ~ly ‿i
　~ness nəs nɪs
soulless 'səʊl ləs →'sɒʊl-, -lɪs ‖ 'soʊl- ~ly li
　~ness nəs nɪs
soul-searching 'səʊl ˌsɜːtʃ ɪŋ →'sɒʊl-
　‖ 'soʊl ˌsɜːtʃ ɪŋ
sound saʊnd **sounded** 'saʊnd ɪd -əd
　sounding/s 'saʊnd ɪŋ/z **sounds** saʊndz
　'sound ˌbarrier; 'sound efˌfects; 'sounding
　board; 'sound ˌsystem; 'sound wave
soundboard 'saʊnd bɔːd →'saʊm- ‖ -bɔːrd
　-boʊrd ~s z
soundless 'saʊnd ləs -lɪs ~ly li
soundproof 'saʊnd pruːf →'saʊm-, §-prʊf
　~ed t ~ing ɪŋ ~s s
soundtrack 'saʊnd træk ~s s
Souness 'suːn əs -ɪs

soup suːp **soups** suːps
'soup ˌkitchen; 'soup spoon
soupcon, soupçon 'suːps ɒn -ɒ̃ ‖ -ɑːn
suːp 'soʊn —*Fr* [sup sɔ̃] ~s z
soupy 'suːp i **soupier** 'suːp iˌə ‖ ˌ_ər **soupiest**
'suːp iˌɪst ˌ_əst
sour 'saʊ_ə ‖ 'saʊ_ᵊr **soured** 'saʊ_əd ‖ 'saʊ_ᵊrd
sourer 'saʊ_ər ə ‖ 'saʊ_ᵊr ᵊr **sourest**
'saʊ_ər ɪst -əst ‖ 'saʊ_ᵊr əst **souring**
'saʊ_ər ɪŋ ‖ 'saʊ_ᵊr ɪŋ **sours**
'saʊ_əz ‖ 'saʊ_ᵊrz
ˌsour 'cream; ˌsour 'grapes
source sɔːs ‖ sɔːrs soʊrs **sourced**
sɔːst ‖ sɔːrst soʊrst **sources** 'sɔːs ɪz -əz
‖ 'sɔːrs əz 'soʊrs- **sourcing**
'sɔːs ɪŋ ‖ 'sɔːrs ɪŋ 'soʊrs-
sourceless 'sɔːs ləs -lɪs ‖ 'sɔːrs- 'soʊrs-
sourdine ₍ₗ₎soʊə 'diːn ‖ sʊr- ~s z
sourdough 'saʊ_ə dəʊ ‖ 'saʊ_ᵊr doʊ ~s z
sour|ly 'saʊ_ə ‖li ‖ 'saʊ_ᵊr ‖li ~**ness** nəs nɪs
sourpuss 'saʊ_ə pʊs ‖ 'saʊ_ᵊr pʊs ~**es** ɪz əz
soursop 'saʊ_ə sɒp ‖ 'saʊ_ᵊr sɑːp ~s s
Sousa 'suːz ə
sousaphone 'suːz ə fəʊn ‖ -foʊn ~s z
sous-chef 'suː ʃef ~s s
souse saʊs **soused** saʊst **souses** 'saʊs ɪz -əz
sousing 'saʊs ɪŋ
Sousse suːs
soutach|e su 'tæʃ ~**es** ɪz əz
soutane su 'tɑːn -'tæn ~s z
Soutar, Souter 'suːt ə ‖ 'suːt̬ ᵊr
south, South saʊθ
₍ₗ₎South 'Africa; ˌSouth A'merica; ˌSouth
Au'stralia; ˌSouth ˌCaro'lina; ˌSouth
Da'kota; ˌSouth Gla'morgan; ˌSouth 'Pole;
ˌSouth Sea 'Bubble; ˌSouth 'Yorkshire
Southall *place in London* 'saʊθ ɔːl 'saʊð- ‖ -ɑːl
Southall *family name* 'sʌð ɔːl -ᵊl ‖ -ɑːl
Southam 'saʊð əm
Southampton ₍ₗ₎saʊθ 'hæmpt ən saʊ 'θæmpt-,
sə-; sə 'ðæmpt-
Southborough 'saʊθ bᵊr_ə ‖ -ˌbɜː oʊ
southbound 'saʊθ baʊnd
Southcott 'saʊθ kɒt -kət ‖ -kɑːt
Southdown 'saʊθ daʊn
southeast, S~ ˌsaʊθ 'iːst ◂
ˌSoutheast 'Asia
southeaster ˌsaʊθ 'iːst ə ‖ -ᵊr ~s z
southeaster|ly ₍ₗ₎saʊθ 'iːst ə ‖li -ᵊ‖l i ‖ -ᵊr ‖li
~**lies** liz
southeastern ₍ₗ₎saʊθ 'iːst ən ‖ -ᵊrn
southeastward ₍ₗ₎saʊθ 'iːst wəd ‖ -wᵊrd ~s z
Southend ˌsaʊθ 'end
ˌSouthend-on-'Sea
souther|ly 'sʌð ə ‖li ‖ -ᵊr- *(!)* ~**lies** liz
southern, S~ 'sʌð ən ‖ -ᵊrn *(!)*
ˌSouthern 'Cross; ˌsouthern 'lights
Southerndown 'sʌð ən daʊn ‖ -ᵊrn-
southerner, S~ 'sʌð ən_ə ‖ -ᵊrn_ər -ən_ ~s z
southernmost 'sʌð ən məʊst →-ᵊm-
‖ -ᵊrn moʊst
southernwood 'sʌð ən wʊd ‖ -ᵊrn-
Southey *(i)* 'saʊð i, *(ii)* 'sʌð i

Southgate 'saʊθ geɪt -gɪt
southing 'saʊð ɪŋ 'saʊθ- ~s z
southland 'saʊθ lænd
southpaw 'saʊθ pɔː ‖ -pɑː ~s z
Southport 'saʊθ pɔːt ‖ -pɔːrt -poʊrt
Southron, s~ 'sʌð rən ~s z
Southsea 'saʊθ siː
southward 'saʊθ wəd ‖ -wᵊrd —*also naut*
'sʌð əd ‖ -ᵊrd ~s z
Southwark 'sʌð ək ‖ -ᵊrk *(!)*
Southwell *(i)* 'sʌð ᵊl, *(ii)* 'saʊθ wəl
southwest, S~ ˌsaʊθ 'west ◂ —*also naut* ₍ₗ₎saʊ-
southwester ₍ₗ₎saʊθ 'west ə ‖ -ᵊr —*also naut*
₍ₗ₎saʊ- ~s z
southwester|ly ₍ₗ₎saʊθ 'west ə ‖li -ᵊ‖l i ‖ -ᵊr ‖li
—*also naut* ₍ₗ₎saʊ- ~**lies** liz
southwestern, S~ ₍ₗ₎saʊθ 'west ən ‖ -ᵊrn —*also
naut* ₍ₗ₎saʊ-
southwestward ₍ₗ₎saʊθ 'west wəd ‖ -wᵊrd
—*also naut* ₍ₗ₎saʊ- ~s z
Southwick 'saʊθ wɪk —*But the places in
Northants and Hants are sometimes* 'sʌð ɪk
Southwold 'saʊθ wəʊld →-wɒʊld ‖ -woʊld
Souttar, Soutter 'suːt ə ‖ 'suːt̬ ᵊr
souvenir ˌsuːv ə 'nɪə ◂ '••• ‖ -'nɪᵊr ~s z
souvlaki su 'vlɑːk i —*ModGk* [su 'vla ci] ~**a** _ə
~s z
sou'wester saʊ 'west ə ‖ -ᵊr ~s z
sovereign 'sɒv rɪn -rən ‖ 'sɑːv rən 'sɑːv ᵊr ən
~s z
sovereign|ty 'sɒv rən ‖ti -rɪn- ‖ 'sɑːv-
'sɑːv ᵊr ən ‖ti ~**ties** tiz

SOVIET

		'saʊv-	'sɒv-
BrE 1988			

| 0 | 20 | 40 | 60 | 80 | 100% |

soviet, S~ 'saʊv iˌət 'sɒv-, -et ‖ 'soʊv i et
'sɑːv-, ˌ_ət —*BrE 1988 poll panel preference:*
'saʊv- *73%*, 'sɒv- *27%*. ~s s
ˌSoviet 'Union
sovran 'sɒv rən ‖ 'sɑːv-
sow *v 'place (seeds)'* səʊ ‖ soʊ *(= so)* **sowed**
səʊd ‖ soʊd **sowing** 'səʊ ɪŋ ‖ 'soʊ ɪŋ **sown**
səʊn ‖ soʊn **sows** səʊz ‖ soʊz
sow *n 'female pig'* saʊ **sows** saʊz
sowbread 'saʊ bred
sower 'səʊ ə ‖ 'soʊ ᵊr ~s z
Sowerbutts 'saʊ_ə bʌts ‖ 'saʊ_ᵊr bʌts
Sowerby *(i)* 'saʊ_ə bi ‖ 'saʊ_ᵊr-, *(ii)*
'səʊ ə bi ‖ 'soʊ ᵊr-
Soweto sə 'wet əʊ -'weɪt- ‖ -oʊ —*Xhosa/Zulu*
[sɔ 'wɛː tɔ]
sown səʊn ‖ soʊn
sox sɒks ‖ sɑːks *(= socks)*
soy sɔɪ
ˌsoy 'sauce, '• •
soya 'sɔɪ ə
'soya bean
soybean 'sɔɪ biːn ~s z
Soyinka sɔɪ 'ɪŋk ə
Soyuz sɔɪ 'uːz —*Russ* [sʌ 'jus]
sozzled 'sɒz ᵊld ‖ 'sɑːz-

S

spa, Spa spɑː spas spɑːz
space speɪs spaced speɪst spaces 'speɪs ɪz
-əz spacing 'speɪs ɪŋ
'space ˌcapsule; ˌspaced 'out◄; 'space
flight; 'space ˌheater; 'space probe; 'space
ˌshuttle; 'space ˌstation
space-age 'speɪs eɪdʒ
space-bar 'speɪs bɑː ‖ -bɑːr ~s z
spacecraft 'speɪs krɑːft §-kræft ‖ -kræft ~s s
spacelab 'speɪs læb ~s z
space|man 'speɪs |mæn -mən ~men men mən
spacer 'speɪs ə ‖ -ər ~s z
spaceship 'speɪs ʃɪp →'speɪʃ- ~s s
spacesuit 'speɪs suːt -sjuːt ~s s
space-time ˌspeɪs 'taɪm
spacewalk 'speɪs wɔːk ‖ -wɑːk
space|woman 'speɪs |ˌwʊm ən ~women
ˌwɪm ɪn -ən
spac|ey 'speɪs i ~ier i‿ə ‖ i‿ər ~iest i‿ɪst ‿əst
spacing 'speɪs ɪŋ ~s z
spacious 'speɪʃ əs ~ly li ~ness nəs nɪs
spackle 'spæk əl
spade speɪd spades speɪdz
spadeful 'speɪd fʊl ~s z
spadework 'speɪd wɜːk ‖ -wɝːk
spadix 'speɪd ɪks spadices 'speɪd ɪ siːz -ə-
spaghetti spə 'get i ‖ -'geṯ-
spahi 'spɑː hiː ~s z
Spain speɪn
spake speɪk
Spalding 'spɔːld ɪŋ ‖ 'spɑːld-
spall spɔːl ‖ spɑːl spalled spɔːld ‖ spɑːld
spalling 'spɔːl ɪŋ ‖ 'spɑːl- spalls spɔːlz
‖ spɑːlz
spallation spɔː 'leɪʃ ən ‖ spɑː- ~s z
spalpeen spæl 'piːn 'spælp iːn ~s z
spam, Spam tdmk spæm spammed spæmd
spamming 'spæm ɪŋ spams spæmz
spammer 'spæm ə ‖ -ər ~s z
span spæn spanned spænd spanning
'spæn ɪŋ spans spænz
Spandau 'spænd aʊ —Ger ['ʃpan daʊ]
spandex 'spænd eks
spandrel 'spændr əl ~s z
spangl|e 'spæŋ ɡəl ~ed d ~es z ~ing ‿ɪŋ
Spaniard 'spæn jəd ‖ -jərd ~s z
spaniel 'spæn jəl ~s z
Spanier 'spæn jeɪ -jə ‖ -jər
Spanish 'spæn ɪʃ
ˌSpanish 'Main; ˌSpanish 'onion
spank spæŋk spanked spæŋkt spanking/s
'spæŋk ɪŋ/z spanks spæŋks
spanker 'spæŋk ə ‖ -ər ~s z
spanner 'spæn ə ‖ -ər ~s z
spar spɑː ‖ spɑːr sparred spɑːd ‖ spɑːrd
sparring 'spɑːr ɪŋ spars spɑːz ‖ spɑːrz
'sparring ˌpartner
sparaxis spə 'ræks ɪs §-əs
spare speə ‖ speər spæər spared
speəd ‖ speərd spæərd spares speəz ‖ speərz
spæərz sparing 'speər ɪŋ ‖ 'sper ɪŋ 'spær-
ˌspare 'part; ˌspare-part 'surgery; ˌspare
'tyre

sparerib 'speə rɪb ˌ•'•‖ 'sper- 'spær-, -əb ~s
z
sparing|ly 'speər ɪŋ ‖li ‖ 'sper- 'spær- ~ness
nəs nɪs
spark spɑːk ‖ spɑːrk sparked spɑːkt ‖ spɑːrkt
sparking 'spɑːk ɪŋ ‖ 'spɑːrk ɪŋ sparks
spɑːks ‖ spɑːrks
'sparking plug, 'spark plug
Spark, Sparke spɑːk ‖ spɑːrk Sparkes
spɑːks ‖ spɑːrks
sparkl|e 'spɑːk əl ‖ 'spɑːrk əl ~ed d ~es z
~ing ‿ɪŋ
sparkler 'spɑːk lə ‖ 'spɑːrk lər ~s z
Sparklet tdmk 'spɑːk lət -lɪt ‖ 'spɑːrk- ~s s
sparkling adj 'spɑːk lɪŋ ‖ 'spɑːrk- ~ly li
spark|y 'spɑːk| i ‖ 'spɑːrk| i ~ier i‿ə ‖ i‿ər
~iest i‿ɪst i‿əst ~iness i nəs i nɪs
sparr... —see spar
sparrow, S~ 'spær əʊ ‖ -oʊ 'sper- ~s z
sparrowhawk 'spær əʊ hɔːk ‖ -oʊ- 'sper-,
-hɑːk ~s s
sparse spɑːs ‖ spɑːrs sparser
'spɑːs ə ‖ 'spɑːrs ər sparsest 'spɑːs ɪst -əst
‖ 'spɑːrs-
sparse|ly 'spɑːs ‖li ‖ 'spɑːrs ‖li ~ness nəs nɪs
sparsity 'spɑːs ət i -ɪt- ‖ 'spɑːrs əṯ i
Spart spɑːt ‖ spɑːrt
Sparta 'spɑːt ə ‖ 'spɑːrṯ ə
Spartacist 'spɑːt əs ɪst §-əst ‖ 'spɑːrṯ- ~s s
Spartacus 'spɑːt ək əs ‖ 'spɑːrṯ-
spartan, S~ 'spɑːt ən ‖ 'spɑːrt ən ~s z
Spartist 'spɑːt ɪst §-əst ‖ 'spɑːrṯ- ~s s
spasm 'spæz əm ~s z
spasmodic spæz 'mɒd ɪk ‖ -'mɑːd- ~ally əl‿i
spastic 'spæst ɪk ~ally əl‿i ~s s
spasticity spæ 'stɪs ət i -ɪt- ‖ -əṯ i
spat spæt spats spæts
spatchcock 'spætʃ kɒk ‖ -kɑːk ~ed t ~ing ɪŋ
~s s
spate speɪt spates speɪts
spathe speɪð spathes speɪðz
spathic 'spæθ ɪk
spatial 'speɪʃ əl 'speɪʃ i‿əl ~ly i
spatiotemporal ˌspeɪʃ i‿əʊ 'temp ər‿əl ◄
‖ -i‿oʊ- ~ly i
Spätlese 'ʃpeɪt ˌleɪz ə —Ger ['ʃpɛːt leːz ə,
'ʃpeːt-]
spatter 'spæt ə ‖ 'spæṯ ər ~ed d spattering
'spæt‿ər ɪŋ ‖ 'spæṯ ər ɪŋ ~s z
spatterdash 'spæt ə dæʃ ‖ 'spæṯ ər- ~es ɪz əz
spatterdock 'spæt ə dɒk ‖ 'spæṯ ər dɑːk ~s s
spatula 'spæt jʊl ə §'spætʃ əl ə ‖ 'spætʃ əl‿ə
~s z
spavin 'spæv ɪn -ən ~ed d
spawn spɔːn ‖ spɑːn spawned spɔːnd
‖ spɑːnd spawning 'spɔːn ɪŋ ‖ 'spɑːn-
spawns spɔːnz ‖ spɑːnz
spay speɪ spayed speɪd (= spade) spaying
'speɪ ɪŋ spays speɪz
SPE ˌes piː 'iː
Speaight speɪt
speak spiːk speaking 'spiːk ɪŋ speaks spiːks
spoke spəʊk ‖ spoʊk spoken 'spəʊk ən

‖ 'spoʊk ən
,speaking 'clock; 'speaking tube
-speak spiːk — doublespeak 'dʌb əl spiːk
speakeas|y 'spiːk ˌiːz li ~ies iz
speaker, S~ 'spiːk ə ‖ -ər ~s z
,Speaker's 'Corner
speakership 'spiːk ə ʃɪp ‖ -ər-
-speaking ˌspiːk ɪŋ — English-speaking
'ɪŋ glɪʃ ˌspiːk ɪŋ
Spean 'spiːˌ ən
spear spɪə ‖ spɪər speared spɪəd ‖ spɪərd
spearing 'spɪər ɪŋ ‖ 'spɪr ɪŋ spears
spɪəz ‖ spɪərz
spearhead 'spɪə hed ‖ 'spɪr- ~ed ɪd əd ~ing
ɪŋ ~s z
spear|man, S~ 'spɪə |mən ‖ 'spɪr- ~men mən
men
spearmint 'spɪə mɪnt ‖ 'spɪr-
spearwort 'spɪə wɜːt §-wɔːt ‖ 'spɪr wɜ:t
-wɔːrt ~s s
spec spek (= speck) specs speks
special 'speʃ əl ~s z
'Special Branch; ,special de'livery; ,special
'drawing rights; ,special 'licence; ,special
'pleading; 'special school
specialis... —see specializ...
specialism 'speʃ əl ˌɪz əm -ə ˌlɪz- ~s z
specialist 'speʃ əl ɪst §-əst ~s s
specialit|y ˌspeʃ i 'æl ət li -ɪt i ‖ -əṭ li ~ies iz
specialization ˌspeʃ əl ˌaɪ 'zeɪʃ ən -əl ɪ- ‖ -əl ə-
~s z
specializ|e 'speʃ ə laɪz -əl aɪz ~ed d ~es ɪz əz
~ing ɪŋ
specially 'speʃ əl i
special|ty 'speʃ əl |ti ~ties tiz
speciation ˌspiːs i 'eɪʃ ən ˌspiːʃ-
specie 'spiːʃ i -iː
species 'spiːʃ iːz 'spiːs-, -ɪz —Some speakers
pronounce the sing. with -ɪz, the pl with -iːz
speciesism 'spiːʃ iːz ˌɪz əm 'spiːs-, '•ɪz-
specifiable 'spes ə faɪˌəb əl '•ɪ-, ˌ•ɪ'•••
specific spə 'sɪf ɪk spɪ- ~ally əlˌi ~s s
spe,cific 'gravity
specification ˌspes əf ɪ 'keɪʃ ən ˌ•ɪf-, §-ə'•- ~s
z
specificity ˌspes ə 'fɪs ət i ˌ•ɪ-, -ɪt i ‖ -əṭ i
speci|fy 'spes ə |faɪ -ɪ- ~fied faɪd ~fier/s
faɪˌə/z ‖ faɪˌər/z ~fies faɪz ~fying faɪ ɪŋ
specimen 'spes ə mɪn -ɪ-, -mən ~s z
specious 'spiːʃ əs ~ly li ~ness nəs nɪs
speck speck specked spekt specks speks
speckl|e 'spek əl ~ed d ~es z ~ing ˌɪŋ
speckless 'spek ləs -lɪs ~ly li ~ness nəs nɪs
specs speks
spectacle 'spekt ək əl -ɪk- ~d d ~s z
spectacular spek 'tæk jʊl ə -jəl ə ‖ -jəl ər ~ly
li ~s z
spect|ate spek 't|eɪt 'spekt eɪt ‖ 'spekt eɪt
~ated eɪt ɪd -əd ‖ eɪṭ əd ~ates eɪts ~ating
eɪt ɪŋ ‖ eɪṭ ɪŋ
spectator, S~ spek 'teɪt ə 'spekt eɪt ə
‖ 'spekt eɪṭ ər —BrE 1988 poll panel
preference •'•• 91%, '••• 9%. ~s z

BrE 1988

0 20 40 60 80 100%

specter 'spekt ə ‖ -ər ~s z
Spector 'spekt ə ‖ -ər
spectra 'spek trə
spectral 'spek trəl ~ly i
spectre 'spekt ə ‖ -ər ~s z
spectro- comb. form
with stress-neutral suffix ¦spek trəʊ
‖ ¦spek troʊ — spectrophotometer
ˌspek trəʊ fəʊ 'tɒm ɪt ə -ət ə
‖ -troʊ fə 'taːm əṭ ər
with stress-imposing suffix
spek 'trɒ+ ‖ spek 'traː+ — spectrometer
spek 'trɒm ɪt ə -ət ə ‖ -'traːm əṭ ər
spectrogram 'spek trəʊ græm ‖ -trə- ~s z
spectrograph 'spek trəʊ graːf -græf
‖ -trə græf ~s s
spectrographic ˌspek trəʊ 'græf ɪk ◄ ‖ -trə-
~ally əlˌi
spectrography spek 'trɒg rəf i ‖ -'traːg-
spectroscape 'spek trəʊ skeɪp ‖ -trə- ~s s
spectroscope 'spek trə skəʊp ‖ -trə skoʊp ~s
s
spectroscopic ˌspek trə 'skɒp ɪk ◄ ‖ -'skaːp-
~ally əlˌi
spectroscopy spek 'trɒsk əp i ‖ -'traːsk-
spec|trum 'spek |trəm ~tra trə
specu|late 'spek jʊ |leɪt -jə- ‖ -jə- ~lated
leɪt ɪd -əd ‖ leɪṭ əd ~lates leɪts ~lating
leɪt ɪŋ ‖ leɪṭ ɪŋ
speculation ˌspek jʊ 'leɪʃ ən -jə- ‖ -jə- ~s z
speculative 'spek jʊl ət ɪv '•jəl-; -ju leɪt-,
-jə leɪt- ‖ -jə leɪṭ- -jə ləṭ- ~ly li ~ness nəs
nɪs
speculator 'spek jʊ leɪt ə '•jə- ‖ -jə leɪṭ ər ~s
z
specu|lum 'spek jʊl |əm -jəl- ‖ -jəl- ~a ə
~ums əmz
sped sped
speech spiːtʃ speeches 'spiːtʃ ɪz -əz
'speech com,munity; 'speech day; 'speech
de,fect, '• ,•••; ,speech pa'thology;
,speech 'synthesis, '• ,••••; ,speech
'synthesizer, '• ,•••••; 'speech ,therapist,
ˌ•' '•••; ,speech 'therapy, '• ,•••
speechification ˌspiːtʃ ɪf ɪ 'keɪʃ ən §ˌ•əf-,
§-ə'•-
speechi|fy 'spiːtʃ ɪ |faɪ §-ə- ~fied faɪd ~fier/s
faɪˌə/z ‖ faɪˌər/z ~fies faɪz ~fying faɪ ɪŋ
speechless 'spiːtʃ ləs -lɪs ~ly li ~ness nəs nɪs
speed spiːd sped sped speeded 'spiːd ɪd -əd
speeding 'spiːd ɪŋ speeds spiːdz
'speed ,limit; 'speed ,merchant; 'speed
trap
speedball 'spiːd bɔːl ‖ -baːl ~s z
speedboat 'spiːd bəʊt →'spiːb- ‖ -boʊt ~s s

S

speedo 'spiːd əʊ ‖ -oʊ ~s z
speedometer spɪ 'dɒm ɪt ə ₍ₗ₎spiːd 'ɒm-, -ət ə
‖ -'dɑːm ət ər ~s z
speedster 'spiːd stə ‖ -stər ~s z
speed-up 'spiːd ʌp ~s s
speedway 'spiːd weɪ ~s z
speedwell 'spiːd wel ~s z
Speedwriting *tdmk* 'spiːd ˌraɪt ɪŋ ‖ -ˌraɪt̬-
speed|y 'spiːd |i ~ier i‿ə ‖ i‿ər ~iest i‿ɪst i‿əst
~ily ɪ li əl i ~iness i nəs i nɪs
Speight speɪt
Speir spɪə ‖ spɪər
speiss spaɪs (= *spice*)
Speke spiːk
spelae... —*see* **spele...**
speleological ˌspiːl i‿ə 'lɒdʒ ɪk əl ◂ ˌspel-
‖ -'lɑːdʒ- ~ly ‿i
speleologist ˌspiːl i 'ɒl ədʒ ɪst ˌspel-, §-əst
‖ -'ɑːl- ~s s
speleology ˌspiːl i 'ɒl ədʒ i ˌspel- ‖ -'ɑːl-
spell spel **spelled** speld **spelling/s** 'spel ɪŋ/z
spells spelz **spelt** spelt
'spelling bee; 'spelling pronunci,ation,
ˌ• • •ˌ• • •◂
spellbind 'spel baɪnd ~er/s ə/z ‖ ər/z ~ing ɪŋ
~s z **spellbound** 'spel baʊnd
spellcheck 'spel tʃek ~ed t ~er/s ə/z ‖ -ər/z
~ing ɪŋ ~s s
speller, S~ 'spel ə ‖ -ər ~s z
Spellman 'spel mən
spelt spelt
spelter 'spelt ə ‖ -ər
spelunker spɪ 'lʌŋk ə spə-, spiː- ‖ -ər ~s z
Spen spen
Spenborough 'spen bər‿ə →'spem- ‖ -ˌbɜː oʊ
Spence spents
Spencer, s~ 'spents ə ‖ -ər ~s z
spend spend **spending** 'spend ɪŋ **spends**
spendz **spent** spent
'spending ˌmoney
spender, S~ 'spend ə ‖ -ər ~s z
spendthrift 'spend θrɪft ~s s
Spengler 'speŋ lə -glə ‖ -glər —*Ger* ['ʃpɛŋ lɐ]
Spennymoor 'spen i mɔː -mʊə ‖ -mɔːr -mʊər,
-mʊr
Spens spenz
Spenser 'spents ə ‖ -ər
Spenserian spen 'sɪər i‿ən ‖ -'sɪr- -'ser-
spent spent
sperm spɜːm ‖ spɜˑːm **sperms**
spɜːmz ‖ spɜˑːmz
'sperm bank; 'sperm count; 'sperm oil;
'sperm whale
-sperm spɜːm ‖ spɜˑːm — **gymnosperm**
'dʒɪm nəʊ spɜːm ‖ -nə spɜˑːm
spermaceti ˌspɜːm ə 'set i -'siːt i
‖ ˌspɜˑːm ə 'set̬ i -'siːt̬ i
spermatic spɜː 'mæt ɪk ‖ spɜˑː 'mæt̬ ɪk
spermato- *comb. form*
with stress-neutral suffix ¦spɜːm ət əʊ
spɜː ¦mæt- ‖ spɜˑː ¦mæt̬ ə — **spermatocyte**
'spɜːm ət əʊ saɪt spɜː 'mæt- ‖ spɜˑː 'mæt̬ ə-
with stress-imposing suffix

ˌspɜːm ə 'tɒ+ ‖ ˌspɜˑːm ə 'tɑː+ —
spermatolysis ˌspɜːm ə 'tɒl əs ɪs ɪs -ɪs ɪs, §-əs
‖ ˌspɜˑːm ə 'tɑːl-
spermatozo|on ˌspɜːm ət ə 'zəʊ |ɒn -ən
‖ ˌspɜˑːm ət̬ ə 'zoʊ |ɑn spɜˑː, ˌmæt̬-, -ˌɑːn ~a ə
~al əl ~an ən ~ic ɪk
spermicidal ˌspɜːm ɪ 'saɪd əl ◂, •ə- ‖ ˌspɜˑːm-
spermicide 'spɜːm ɪ saɪd -ə saɪd ‖ 'spɜˑːm- ~s
z
Sperry 'sper i
spew spjuː **spewed** spjuːd **spewing** 'spjuː ɪŋ
spews spjuːz
Spey speɪ
sphagnum 'sfæg nəm
sphalerite 'sfæl ə raɪt 'sfeɪl-
sphene sfiːn
sphenoid 'sfiːn ɔɪd ~s z
sphere sfɪə ‖ sfɪər **spheres** sfɪəz ‖ sfɪərz
-sphere sfɪə ‖ sfɪr — **biosphere** 'baɪ əʊ sfɪə
‖ -ə sfɪr
-spheric 'sfer ɪk 'sfɪər ɪk ‖ 'sfɪr ɪk —
biospheric ˌbaɪ əʊ 'sfer ɪk ◂ -'sfɪər ɪk ‖ -ə-
-'sfɪr ɪk
spherical 'sfer ɪk əl ‖ 'sfɪr- ~ly ‿i ~ness nəs
nɪs
spheroid 'sfɪər ɔɪd ‖ 'sfɪr- 'sfer- ~s z
spheroidal sfɪə 'rɔɪd əl ‖ sfɪ- sfe- ~ly i
sphincter 'sfɪŋkt ə ‖ -ər ~s z
sphinx, S~ sfɪŋks **sphinxes, Sphinx's**
'sfɪŋks ɪz -əz
sphragistic sfrə 'dʒɪst ɪk ~s s
sphygmo- *comb. form*
with stress-neutral suffix ¦sfɪg məʊ ‖ -mə —
sphygmogram 'sfɪg məʊ græm ‖ -mə-
with stress-imposing suffix sfɪg 'mɒ+ ‖ -'mɑː+
— **sphygmography**
sfɪg 'mɒg rəf i ‖ -'mɑːg-
sphygmomanometer ˌsfɪg məʊ mə 'nɒm ɪt ə
-ət ə ‖ -moʊ mə 'nɑːm ət ər ~s z
spic spɪk **spics** spɪks
spica, Spica 'spaɪk ə 'spiːk-
spiccato spɪ 'kɑːt əʊ ‖ -'kɑːt̬ oʊ —*It*
[spik 'ka: to]
spice spaɪs **spiced** spaɪst **spices** 'spaɪs ɪz -əz
spicing 'spaɪs ɪŋ
spicebush 'spaɪs bʊʃ ~es ɪz əz
spick-and-span ˌspɪk ən 'spæn ◂ →-ŋ-
spicule 'spɪk juːl 'spaɪk- ~s z
spic|y 'spaɪs |i ~ier i‿ə ‖ i‿ər ~iest i‿ɪst i‿əst
~ily ɪ li əl i ~iness i nəs i nɪs
spider 'spaɪd ə ‖ -ər ~s z
'spider plant
spider|man, S~ 'spaɪd ə |mæn ‖ -ər- ~men
men
spiderweb 'spaɪd ə web ‖ -ər- ~s z
spiderwort 'spaɪd ə wɜːt -wɔːt ‖ -ər wɜˑːt
-wɔːrt ~s s
spidery 'spaɪd ər i
spie... —*see* **spy**
spiegeleisen 'spiːg əl aɪz ən
Spiegl 'spiːg əl
spiel ʃpiːəl spiːəl **spiels** ʃpiːəlz spiːəlz
Spielberg 'spiːl bɜːg ‖ -bɜˑːg

Spelling pronunciation

1 A **spelling pronunciation** of a word is a pronunciation that, unlike the traditional pronunciation, corresponds closely to the spelling.

2 Examples of spelling pronunciations often heard from native speakers of English include **ate** eɪt (rather than et), **envelope** ˈen və ləʊp ‖ -loʊp (rather than ˈɒn- ‖ ˈɑːn-), and **synod** ˈsɪn ɒd ‖ -ɑːd (rather than -əd— compare **method**). People whose first encounter with the word **awry** is as a written form sometimes fail to recognize its analysis as prefix **a-** plus stem **wry**, and infer a spelling pronunciation ˈɔːr i rather than the proper ə ˈraɪ.

3 Learners of EFL should avoid using spelling pronunciations that native speakers do not use. Do not, for example, use a strong vowel ɔː in the second syllable of **effort** ˈef ət ‖ -ərt, **information** ˌɪnf ə ˈmeɪʃ ən ‖ -ər-, **Oxford** ˈɒks fəd ‖ ˈɑːks fərd. Do not use ɑː in the first and last syllables of **particular** pə ˈtɪk jʊl ə ‖ pər ˈtɪk jəl ər. Do not pronounce a b in **climb** klaɪm or **debt** det.

4 British place-names are especially difficult. Spelling pronunciations of **Gloucester**, **Southwark** and **Harwich** sound absurd and would possibly not be understood.

S

Spier *(i)* spɪə ‖ spɪər, *(ii)* ˈspaɪ‿ə ‖ ˈspaɪ‿ər
spiff spɪf **spiffed** spɪft **spiffing** ˈspɪf ɪŋ
  spiffs spɪfs
spiffli|cate ˈspɪf lɪ |keɪt -lə- ~**cated** keɪt ɪd -əd
  ‖ keɪt̬ əd ~**cates** keɪts ~**cating**
  keɪt ɪŋ ‖ keɪt̬ ɪŋ
spiff|ly ˈspɪf |li ~**ier** i‿ə ‖ i‿ər ~**iest** i‿ɪst i‿əst
  ~**ily** ɪ li əl i ~**iness** i nəs i nɪs
spignel ˈspɪg nəl
spigot ˈspɪg ət ~**s** s
spik spɪk **spiks** spɪks
spike spaɪk **spiked** spaɪkt **spikes** spaɪks
  spiking ˈspaɪk ɪŋ
spikelet ˈspaɪk lət -lɪt ~**s** s
spikenard ˈspaɪk nɑːd ˈspaɪk ə nɑːd ‖ -nɑːrd
spik|y ˈspaɪk |li ~**ier** i‿ə ‖ i‿ər ~**iest** i‿ɪst i‿əst
  ~**ily** ɪ li əl i ~**iness** i nəs i nɪs
spile spaɪəl **spiled** spaɪəld **spiles** spaɪəlz
  spiling ˈspaɪəl ɪŋ
spill spɪl **spilled** spɪld **spilling** ˈspɪl ɪŋ **spills**
  spɪlz **spilt** spɪlt
spillag|e ˈspɪl ɪdʒ ~**es** ɪz əz
Spillane spɪ ˈleɪn §spə-
Spiller ˈspɪl ə ‖ -ər
spillikin ˈspɪl ɪk ɪn §-ək-, §-ən ~**s** z
spillover ˈspɪl ˌəʊv ə ‖ -ˌoʊv ər ~**s** z
spillway ˈspɪl weɪ ~**s** z
Spilsbury ˈspɪlz bər‿i ‖ -ˌber i
spilt spɪlt
spin spɪn **span** spæn **spinning** ˈspɪn ɪŋ **spins**
  spɪnz **spun** spʌn
  ˌspin ˈbowler; ˈspin ˌdoctor
spina bifida ˌspaɪn ə ˈbɪf ɪd ə -ˈbaɪf-, -əd ə
spinach ˈspɪn ɪdʒ -ɪtʃ ‖ -ɪtʃ

spinal ˈspaɪn əl ~**ly** i
  ˌspinal ˈcord ‖ˈ• • •
spindle ˈspɪnd əl ~**s** z
spindleberry ˈspɪnd əl ˌber i
spindleshanks ˈspɪnd əl ʃæŋks
spindling ˈspɪnd lɪŋ
spind|ly ˈspɪnd |li ~**lier** li‿ə ‖ li‿ər ~**liest** li‿ɪst
  li‿əst
spindrift ˈspɪn drɪft
spin-|dry ˌspɪn ˈdraɪ ˈ• • ~**dried** draɪd ~**dries**
  draɪz ~**drying** draɪ ɪŋ
spin-dryer ˌspɪn ˈdraɪ‿ə ˈ• • • ‖ -ˈdraɪ‿ər ~**s** z
spine spaɪn **spined** spaɪnd **spines** spaɪnz
spine-chiller ˈspaɪn ˌtʃɪl ə ‖ -ər ~**s** z
spine-chilling ˈspaɪn ˌtʃɪl ɪŋ
spinel spɪ ˈnel §spə-
spineless ˈspaɪn ləs -lɪs ~**ly** li ~**ness** nəs nɪs
spinet spɪ ˈnet §spə-; ˈspɪn et, -ɪt, §-ət
  ‖ ˈspɪn ət ~**s** s
spinifex ˈspɪn ɪ feks -ə-
Spink spɪŋk
spinnaker ˈspɪn ək ə -ɪk- ‖ -ər ~**s** z
spinner ˈspɪn ə ‖ -ər ~**s** z
spinneret ˈspɪn ə ret ˌ• • •ˈ• ~**s** s
spinney ˈspɪn i ~**s** z
spinning ˈspɪn ɪŋ
  ˌspinning ˈjenny, ˈ• • ˌ• •; ˈspinning wheel
spin-off ˈspɪn ɒf -ɔːf ‖ -ɔːf -ɑːf ~**s** s
spinose ˈspaɪn əʊs spaɪ ˈnəʊs ‖ -oʊs
spinous ˈspaɪn əs
Spinoza spɪ ˈnəʊz ə §spə- ‖ -ˈnoʊz- —*Dutch*
  [spi ˈnoː zaː]
spinster ˈspɪntst ə ‖ -ər ~**hood** hʊd ~**s** z
spinsterish ˈspɪntst ər ɪʃ ~**ness** nəs nɪs

spinthariscope spɪn ˈθær ɪ skəʊp -ə- ‖ -skoʊp
-ˈθer- ~s s
spinule ˈspaɪn juːl ˈspɪn- ~s z
spin|y ˈspaɪn |i ~ier i_ə ‖ i_ər ~iest i_ɪst i_əst
~iness i nəs i nɪs
Spion Kop ˌspaɪ_ən ˈkɒp →ˌ_əŋ- ‖ -ˈkɑːp
spiracle ˈspaɪ²r ək ³l ˈspɪr-, -ɪk- ~s z
spiraea spaɪ² ˈrɪə -ˈriː_ə
spiral ˈspaɪ²r ³l ~ed, ~led d ~ing, ~ling ɪŋ ~s
z
spirant ˈspaɪ²r ənt ~s s
spirantisation, spirantization ˌspaɪ²r
ənt aɪ ˈzeɪʃ ³n -ɪˈ•- ‖ -əˈ•- ~s z
spire ˈspaɪ_ə ‖ ˈspaɪ_ər spires
ˈspaɪ_əz ‖ ˈspaɪ_ərz
spirea spaɪ² ˈrɪə -ˈriː_ə
Spirella tdmk spaɪ² ˈrel ə
spirill|um spaɪ² ˈrɪl |əm ~a ə
spir|it, S~ ˈspɪr |ɪt -ət ‖ -lət ~ited ɪt ɪd -ət-, -əd
‖ ət əd ~iting ɪt ɪŋ ət- ‖ ət ɪŋ ~its ɪts əts
‖ əts
ˈspirit ˌlevel
spirited|ly ˈspɪr ɪt ɪd |li ˈ•ət-, -əd• ‖ -ət əd |li
~ness nəs nɪs
-spirited ˈspɪr ɪt ɪd -ət-, -əd ‖ -ət əd —
public-spirited ˌpʌb lɪk ˈspɪr ɪt ɪd ◄ -ət-, -əd
‖ -ət əd
spiritism ˈspɪr ɪt ˌɪz əm -ət- ‖ -ət-
spiritist ˈspɪr ɪt ɪst -ət-, §-əst ‖ -ət- ~s s
spiritless ˈspɪr ɪt ləs -ət-, -lɪs ~ly li ~ness
nəs nɪs
spiritous ˈspɪr ɪt əs -ət- ‖ -ət-
spiritual ˈspɪr ɪtʃ u_əl ˈ•ətʃ-; -ɪt ju_,
-ət ju_ ‖ ˈspɪr ɪtʃ ³l ~s z
spiritualis... —see spiritualiz...
spiritualism ˈspɪr ɪtʃ u ˌlɪz əm ˈ•ətʃ-, ˈ•••ə-;
ˈ•••_ə, ••, ˈ•ɪt ju_, ˈ•ət-
spiritualist ˈspɪr ɪtʃ ʊl ɪst ˈ•ətʃ-, -əl•, §-əst;
ˈ••u_əl•, ˈ•ɪt ju_, ˈ•ət- ~s s
spiritualistic ˌspɪr ɪtʃ u ˈlɪst ɪk ◄ , ˈ•ətʃ-, ˌ••ə-;
ˌ•••_ə ◄ ••, ˌ•ɪt ju_, ˌ•ət-
spiritualit|y ˌspɪr ɪtʃ u ˈæl ət |i -ətʃ u-, -ɪt ju-,
-ət ju-, -ɪt i ‖ -ət |i ~ies iz
spiritualization ˌspɪr ɪtʃ ʊl aɪ ˈzeɪʃ ³n ˈ•ətʃ-,
-ɪˈ••; ˌ••u_əl•ˈ••, ˌ•ɪt ju_, ˌ•ət•-
spiritualiz|e ˈspɪr ɪtʃ u laɪz -ətʃ u-; ˈ•ɪtʃ u_ə•,
ˈ•ɪt ju_, ˈ•ət- ~ed d ~es ɪz əz ~ing ɪŋ
spirituous ˈspɪr ɪtʃ u_əs -ətʃ u_, -ɪt ju_, -ət ju_
~ness nəs nɪs
spiritus ˈspɪr ɪt əs -ət- ‖ -ət-
spirochaete ˈspaɪ²r əʊ kiːt ‖ -ə- ~s s
spirograph ˈspaɪ²r əʊ grɑːf -græf ‖ -ə græf ~s
s
spirogyra ˌspaɪ²r əʊ ˈdʒaɪ²r ə ‖ -ə-
spirt spɜːt ‖ spɜ˞ːt spirted ˈspɜːt ɪd -əd
‖ ˈspɜ˞ːt əd spirting ˈspɜːt ɪŋ ‖ ˈspɜ˞ːt ɪŋ
spirts spɜːts ‖ spɜ˞ːts
spirula ˈspaɪ²r ʊl ə -əl ə ‖ -jəl ə
spit spɪt spat spæt spits spɪts spitted
ˈspɪt ɪd -əd ‖ ˈspɪt əd spitting
ˈspɪt ɪŋ ‖ ˈspɪt ɪŋ
ˌspit and ˈpolish; ˌspitting ˈimage
Spital ˈspɪt ³l ‖ ˈspɪt ³l

Spitalfields ˈspɪt ³l fiːˀldz ‖ ˈspɪt-
spitball ˈspɪt bɔːl ‖ -bɑːl ~s z
spite spaɪt spited ˈspaɪt ɪd -əd ‖ ˈspaɪt əd
spites spaɪts spiting ˈspaɪt ɪŋ ‖ ˈspaɪt ɪŋ
spiteful ˈspaɪt fəl -fʊl ~ly _i ~ness nəs nɪs
spitfire, S~ ˈspɪt ˌfaɪ_ə ‖ -ˌfaɪ_ər ~s z
Spithead ˌspɪt ˈhed ◄
Spitsbergen ˈspɪts ˌbɜːg ³n , •ˈ•• ‖ -ˌbɜ˞ːg-
Spittal ˈspɪt ³l ‖ ˈspɪt ³l
spitt... —see spit
spittle ˈspɪt ³l ‖ ˈspɪt ³l
spittoon spɪ ˈtuːn §spə- ~s z
spitz, Spitz spɪts —Ger [ʃpɪts] spitzes
ˈspɪts ɪz -əz
spiv spɪv spivs spɪvz
spivvy ˈspɪv i
splanchnic ˈsplæŋk nɪk
splash splæʃ splashed splæʃt splashes
ˈsplæʃ ɪz -əz splashing ˈsplæʃ ɪŋ
ˈsplash guard
splashback ˈsplæʃ bæk ~s s
splashdown ˈsplæʃ daʊn ~s z
splash|y ˈsplæʃ |i ~ier i_ə ‖ i_ər ~iest i_ɪst
i_əst ~ily ɪ li əl i ~iness i nəs i nɪs
splat splæt splats splæts
splatter ˈsplæt ə ‖ ˈsplæt ²r ~ed d splattering
ˈsplæt_ər ɪŋ ‖ ˈsplæt ²r ɪŋ
splay spleɪ splayed spleɪd splaying ˈspleɪ ɪŋ
splays spleɪz
splay|foot ˈspleɪ |fʊt ~feet fiːt
splayfooted ˌspleɪ ˈfʊt ɪd ◄ -əd ‖ -ˈfʊt- ~ly li
~ness nəs nɪs
spleen spliːn
spleenwort ˈspliːn wɜːt §-wɔːt ‖ -wɜ˞ːt -wɔːrt
splendid ˈsplend ɪd -əd ~ly li ~ness nəs nɪs
splendiferous (ˌ)splen ˈdɪf ²r əs ~ly li ~ness
nəs nɪs
splendor, splendour ˈsplend ə ‖ -²r ~s z
splendrous ˈsplendr əs ~ly li
splenetic splə ˈnet ɪk splɪ- ‖ -ˈnet ɪk ~ally ³l_i
splenic ˈsplen ɪk ˈspliːn-
spleno- comb. form
with stress-neutral suffix ˈspliːn əʊ ‖ -oʊ —
splenomegaly ˌspliːn əʊ ˈmeg ³l i ‖ ˌ•oʊ-
with stress-imposing suffix splɪ ˈnɒ+ ‖ -ˈnɑː+
— splenography splɪ ˈnɒg rəf i ‖ -ˈnɑːg-
splice splaɪs spliced splaɪst splices ˈsplaɪs ɪz
-əz splicing ˈsplaɪs ɪŋ
spliff splɪf spliffs splɪfs
spline splaɪn splined splaɪnd splines splaɪnz
splining ˈsplaɪn ɪŋ
splint splɪnt splinted ˈsplɪnt ɪd -əd ‖ ˈsplɪnt əd
splinting ˈsplɪnt ɪŋ ‖ ˈsplɪnt ɪŋ splints
splɪnts
splinter ˈsplɪnt ə ‖ ˈsplɪnt ²r ~ed d
splintering ˈsplɪnt_ər ɪŋ ‖ ˈsplɪnt ²r ɪŋ ~s z
ˈsplinter group
splintery ˈsplɪnt ²r i
split, Split splɪt splits splɪts splitting
ˈsplɪt ɪŋ ‖ ˈsplɪt ɪŋ
ˌsplit ˈend; ˌsplit inˈfinitive; ˌsplit ˈpea;
ˌsplit ˌперсоˈnality; ˌsplit ˈring; ˌsplit
ˈsecond

split-level ˌsplɪt ˈlev əl ◄
split-second ˌsplɪt ˈsek ənd ◄ ⚠-ənt
split-up ˈsplɪt ʌp ‖ ˈsplɪt̬ ʌp ~s s
splodge splɒdʒ ‖ splɑːdʒ splodges ˈsplɒdʒ ɪz
-əz ‖ ˈsplɑːdʒ əz
splodg|y ˈsplɒdʒ |i ‖ ˈsplɑːdʒ |i ~ier i‿ə ‖ i‿ər
~iest i‿ɪst i‿əst ~iness i nəs i nɪs
splosh splɒʃ ‖ splɑːʃ sploshed splɒʃt ‖ splɑːʃt
sploshes ˈsplɒʃ ɪz -əz ‖ ˈsplɑːʃ əz sploshing
ˈsplɒʃ ɪŋ ‖ ˈsplɑːʃ ɪŋ
splotch splɒtʃ ‖ splɑːtʃ splotched
splɒtʃt ‖ splɑːtʃt splotches ˈsplɒtʃ ɪz -əz
‖ ˈsplɑːtʃ əz
splotch|y ˈsplɒtʃ |i ‖ ˈsplɑːtʃ |i ~ier i‿ə ‖ i‿ər
~iest i‿ɪst i‿əst ~iness i nəs i nɪs
Splott splɒt ‖ splɑːt
splurge splɜːdʒ ‖ splɝːdʒ splurged
splɜːdʒd ‖ splɝːdʒd splurges ˈsplɜːdʒ ɪz -əz
‖ ˈsplɝːdʒ əz splurging
ˈsplɜːdʒ ɪŋ ‖ ˈsplɝːdʒ ɪŋ
splutter ˈsplʌt ə ‖ ˈsplʌt̬ ər ~ed d spluttering
ˈsplʌt_ər ɪŋ ‖ ˈsplʌt̬ ər ɪŋ ~s z
Spock spɒk ‖ spɑːk
Spode, spode spəʊd ‖ spoʊd
spodumene ˈspɒd ju miːn §ˈspɒdʒ ə-
‖ ˈspɑːdʒ ə-
Spofforth ˈspɒf əθ -ɔːθ ‖ ˈspɑːf ər̩θ
Spohr spɔː ‖ spɔːr spour —Ger [ʃpoːɐ]
spoil spɔɪəl spoiled spɔɪəld spoiling ˈspɔɪəl ɪŋ
spoils spɔɪəlz spoilt spɔɪəlt
spoilage ˈspɔɪəl ɪdʒ
spoiler ˈspɔɪəl ə ‖ -ər ~s z
spoilsport ˈspɔɪəl spɔːt ‖ -spɔːrt -spoʊrt ~s s
spoilt spɔɪəlt
Spokane spəʊ ˈkæn ‖ spoʊ- (!)
spoke spəʊk ‖ spoʊk spokes spəʊks ‖ spoʊks
spoken ˈspəʊk ən ‖ ˈspoʊk ən —
-spoken ˈspəʊk ən ‖ -ˈspoʊk ən — nicely-
spoken ˌnaɪs li ˈspəʊk ən ◄ ‖ -ˈspoʊk-
spokeshave ˈspəʊk ʃeɪv ‖ ˈspoʊk- ~s z
spokes|man ˈspəʊks |mən ‖ ˈspoʊks- ~men
mən men ~people ˌpiːp əl ~person/s
ˌpɜːs ən/z ‖ ˌpɝːs ən/z ~woman ˌwʊm ən
~women ˌwɪm ɪn -ən
spoliation ˌspəʊl i ˈeɪʃ ən ‖ ˌspoʊl-
spondaic spɒn ˈdeɪ ɪk ‖ spɑːn-
spondee ˈspɒnd iː ‖ ˈspɑːnd iː ~s z
Spondon ˈspɒnd ən ‖ ˈspɑːnd ən
spondulicks, spondulix spɒn ˈduːl ɪks -ˈdjuːl-
‖ spɑːn ˈduːl-
spondylitis ˌspɒnd ɪ ˈlaɪt ɪs -ə-, §-əs
‖ ˌspɑːnd ə ˈlaɪt̬ əs
Spong spɒŋ ‖ spɑːŋ
spong|e spʌndʒ sponged spʌndʒd sponges
ˈspʌndʒ ɪz -əz sponging ˈspʌndʒ ɪŋ
ˈsponge bag; ˈsponge cake; ˌsponge
ˈpudding; ˌsponge ˈrubber
sponger ˈspʌndʒ ə ‖ -ər ~s z
spongiform ˈspʌndʒ ɪ fɔːm ‖ -fɔːrm
spong|y ˈspʌndʒ |i ~ier i‿ə ‖ i‿ər ~iest i‿ɪst
i‿əst ~iness i nəs i nɪs
sponsion ˈspɒnʃ ən ‖ ˈspɑːntʃ ən
sponson ˈspɒns ən ‖ ˈspɑːns ən ~s z

sponsor ˈspɒns ə ‖ ˈspɑːns ər ~ed d
sponsoring ˈspɒns ər_ɪŋ ‖ ˈspɑːns ər ɪŋ ~s
z ~ship ʃɪp
spontaneity ˌspɒnt ə ˈneɪ ət i -ˈniːˌ, -ɪt i
‖ ˌspɑːnt ən ˈiː ət̬ i -ˈeɪ-
spontaneous ˌspɒn ˈteɪn i‿əs spən- ‖ spɑːn-
~ly li ~ness nəs nɪs
Spontex tdmk ˈspɒnt eks ‖ ˈspɑːnt-
spoof spuːf spoofed spuːft spoofing
ˈspuːf ɪŋ spoofs spuːfs
spook spuːk spooked spuːkt spooking
ˈspuːk ɪŋ spooks spuːks
spook|y ˈspuːk |i ~ier i‿ə ‖ i‿ər ~iest i‿ɪst i‿əst
~ily ɪ li əl i ~iness i nəs i nɪs
spool spuːl spooled spuːld spooling ˈspuːl ɪŋ
spools spuːlz
spoon spuːn spooned spuːnd spooning
ˈspuːn ɪŋ spoons spuːnz
spoonbill ˈspuːn bɪl →ˈspuːm- ~s z
Spooner ˈspuːn ə ‖ -ər
spoonerism ˈspuːn ə ˌrɪz əm ~s z
spoon|feed ˈspuːn |fiːd ~fed fed ~feeding
fiːd ɪŋ ~feeds fiːdz
spoonful ˈspuːn fʊl ~s z spoonsful
ˈspuːnz fʊl
spoor spʊə spɔː ‖ spʊər spɔːr, spoʊr spoors
spʊəz spɔːz ‖ spʊərz spɔːrz, spoʊrz
Sporades ˈspɒr ə diːz spə ˈrɑːd iːz ‖ ˈspɔːr-
sporadic spə ˈræd ɪk spɒ- ~ally əl_i
sporangi|um spə ˈrændʒ i‿əm ~a ə
spore spɔː ‖ spɔːr spoʊr spores spɔːz ‖ spɔːrz
spoʊrz
sporo- comb. form
with stress-neutral suffix ˈspɔːr əʊ ˈspɒr-
‖ ˈspɔːr ə ˈspoʊr- — sporocyst ˈspɔːr əʊ sɪst
ˈspɒr- ‖ -ə- ˈspoʊr-
sporogeny spɔː ˈrɒdʒ ən i spə- ‖ spə ˈrɑːdʒ-
sporogony spɔː ˈrɒg ən i spə-, -ˈrɒdʒ-
‖ spə ˈrɑːg-
sporran ˈspɒr ən ‖ ˈspɔːr ən ˈspɑːr- ~s z
sport spɔːt ‖ spɔːrt spoʊrt sported ˈspɔːt ɪd
-əd ‖ ˈspɔːrt̬ əd ˈspoʊrt̬- sporting/ly
ˈspɔːt ɪŋ /li ‖ ˈspɔːrt̬ ɪŋ /li ˈspoʊrt̬- sports
spɔːts ‖ spɔːrts spoʊrts
ˈsports car; ˈsports day; ˈsports ˌjacket
sporti... —see sporty
sportive ˈspɔːt ɪv ‖ ˈspɔːrt̬ ɪv ˈspoʊrt̬- ~ly li
~ness nəs nɪs
sportscast ˈspɔːts kɑːst §-kæst ‖ ˈspɔːrts kæst
ˈspoʊrts- ~er/s ə/z ‖ ər/z ~ing ɪŋ
sports|man ˈspɔːts |mən ‖ ˈspɔːrts- ˈspoʊrts-
~manlike mən laɪk ~manship mən ʃɪp
~men mən
sportswear ˈspɔːts weə ‖ ˈspɔːrts wer
ˈspoʊrts-, -wær
sports|woman ˈspɔːts |ˌwʊm ən ‖ ˈspɔːrts-
ˈspoʊrts- ~women ˌwɪm ɪn -ən
sport|y ˈspɔːt |i ‖ ˈspɔːrt̬ |i ˈspoʊrt̬- ~ier
i‿ə ‖ i‿ər ~iest i‿ɪst i‿əst ~ily ɪ li əl i ~iness
i nəs i nɪs
sporule ˈspɒr uːl -juːl ‖ ˈspɔːr juːl ˈspoʊr- ~s z
s'pose nonstandard version of suppose

S

spəuz ‖ spouz **s'posing**
'spəuz ıŋ ‖ 'spouz ıŋ
spot spɒt ‖ spaːt **spots** spɒts ‖ spaːts
spotted 'spɒt ıd -əd ‖ 'spaːt̮ əd **spotting**
'spɒt ıŋ ‖ 'spaːt̮ ıŋ
،spot 'check ‖ '• •; ،spotted 'dick
spot-check ،spɒt 'tʃek '•• ‖ 'spaːt tʃek ~ed t
~ing ıŋ ~s s
spotless 'spɒt ləs -lıs ‖ 'spaːt- ~ly li ~ness
nəs nıs
spot|light 'spɒt |laıt ‖ 'spaːt- ~lighted laıt ıd
-əd ‖ laıt̮ əd ~lighting laıt ıŋ ‖ laıt̮ ıŋ
~lights laıts ~lit lıt
spot-on ،spɒt 'ɒn ◂ ‖ ،spaːt̮ 'aːn ◂ -'ɔːn
Spotsylvania ،spɒt sıl 'veın i‿ə ،•sˀl- ‖ ،spaːt-
spott... —see spot
spotter 'spɒt ə ‖ 'spaːt̮ ˀr ~s z
'spotter plane
Spottiswoode (i) 'spɒts wud ‖ 'spaːts-; (ii)
'spɒt ıs wud -ız-, -əs- ‖ 'spaːt̮-
spott|y 'spɒt li i ‖ 'spaːt̮ li ~ier i‿ə ‖ i‿ˀr ~iest
i‿ıst i‿əst ~ily ı li əl i ~iness i nəs ı nıs
spot-weld 'spɒt weld ‖ 'spaːt- ~ed ıd əd
~ing ıŋ ~s z
spousal 'spauz ˀl ~s z
spouse spaus spauz **spouses** 'spaus ız
'spauz-, -əz
spout spaut **spouted** 'spaut ıd -əd ‖ 'spaut̮ əd
spouting 'spaut ıŋ ‖ 'spaut̮ ıŋ **spouts**
spauts
sprachgefuhl, sprachgefühl, S~
'ʃpraːx gə ،fjuːl 'ʃpraːk-, -fuːl —Ger
['ʃpʀaːx gə ،fyːl]
sprag spræg **spragged** sprægd **spragging**
'spræg ıŋ **sprags** sprægz
Spragge spræg
Sprague spreıg
sprain spreın **sprained** spreınd **spraining**
'spreın ıŋ **sprains** spreınz
spraint spreınt **spraints** spreınts
sprang spræŋ
sprat spræt **sprats** spræts
Spratt spræt
sprawl sprɔːl ‖ spraːl **sprawled** sprɔːld
‖ spraːld **sprawling/ly** 'sprɔːl ıŋ /li ‖ 'spraːl-
sprawls sprɔːlz ‖ spraːlz
spray spreı **sprayed** spreıd **spraying**
'spreı ıŋ **sprays** spreız
'spray gun
spraycan 'spreı kæn ~s z
sprayer 'spreı ə ‖ -ˀr ~s z
spray-on 'spreı ɒn ‖ -aːn -ɔːn
،spray-on de'odorant
spread spred **spreading** 'spred ıŋ **spreads**
spredz
spreadable 'spred əb ˀl
spread-eagl|e (i)spred 'iːg ˀl ‖ 'spred ،iːg ˀl (**)
~ed d ~es z ~ing ،ıŋ
spreader 'spred ə ‖ -ˀr ~s z
spreadsheet 'spred ʃiːt ~s s
sprechgesang, S~ 'ʃprex gə ،zæŋ 'ʃprek-,
-،zʌŋ —Ger ['ʃpʀeç gə ،zaŋ]

sprechstimme, S~ 'ʃprex ،ʃtım ə 'ʃprek-
—Ger ['ʃpʀeç ،ʃtım ə]
spree spriː **sprees** spriːz
sprig sprıg **sprigged** sprıgd **sprigging**
'sprıg ıŋ **sprigs** sprıgz
Sprigg sprıg
spright|ly 'spraıt |li ~lier li‿ə ‖ li‿ˀr ~liest
li‿ıst li‿əst ~liness li nəs -nıs
spring, S~ sprıŋ **sprang** spræŋ **springing**
'sprıŋ ıŋ **springs** sprıŋz **sprung** sprʌŋ
،spring 'balance; ،spring 'chicken; ،spring
'fever; ،spring 'onion; ،spring 'roll; ،spring
'tide
springboard 'sprıŋ bɔːd ‖ -bɔːrd -bourd ~s z
springbok, S~ 'sprıŋ bɒk ‖ -baːk ~s s
Springburn 'sprıŋ bɜːn ‖ -bɝːn
spring-clean v ،sprıŋ 'kliːn ◂ ~ed d ~ing ıŋ
~s z
spring-clean n 'sprıŋ kliːn ،•'• ~s z
springe sprındʒ **springes** 'sprındʒ ız -əz
springer, S~ 'sprıŋ ə ‖ -ˀr ~s z
Springfield 'sprıŋ fiːˀld
springlike 'sprıŋ laık
spring-loaded ،sprıŋ 'ləud ıd ◂ -əd ‖ -'loud-
Springs sprıŋz
Springsteen 'sprıŋ stiːn
springtail 'sprıŋ teıˀl ~s z
springtime 'sprıŋ taım
spring|y 'sprıŋ li ~ier i‿ə ‖ i‿ˀr ~iest i‿ıst i‿əst
~ily ı li əl i ~iness i nəs ı nıs
sprinkl|e 'sprıŋk ˀl ~ed d ~es z ~ing ،ıŋ
sprinkler 'sprıŋk lə 'sprıŋk ˀl‿ə ‖ -lˀr ~s z
sprinkling n 'sprıŋk lıŋ ~s z
sprint sprınt **sprinted** 'sprınt ıd -əd
‖ 'sprınt̮ əd **sprinting** 'sprınt ıŋ ‖ 'sprınt̮ ıŋ
sprints sprınts
sprinter 'sprınt ə ‖ 'sprınt̮ ˀr ~s z
sprit sprıt **sprits** sprıts
sprite spraıt **sprites** spraıts
spritsail 'sprıt sˀl -seıˀl ~s z
spritz sprıts ʃprıts **spritzed** sprıtst ʃprıtst
spritzes 'sprıts ız 'ʃprıts-, -əz **spritzing**
'sprıts ıŋ 'ʃprıts-
spritzer 'sprıts ə 'ʃprıts- ‖ -ˀr ~s z
Sproat sprəut ‖ sprout
sprocket 'sprɒk ıt §-ət ‖ 'spraːk ət ~s s
sprog sprɒg ‖ spraːg **sprogs** sprɒgz ‖ spraːgz
Sprot, Sprott sprɒt ‖ spraːt
Sproughton 'sprɔːt ˀn ‖ 'spraːt-
Sproule (i) sprəul ‖ sproul, (ii) spruːl
sprout spraut **sprouted** 'spraut ıd -əd
‖ 'spraut̮ əd **sprouting**
'spraut ıŋ ‖ 'spraut̮ ıŋ **sprouts** sprauts
spruce spruːs **spruced** spruːst **sprucer**
'spruːs ə ‖ 'spruːs ˀr **spruces** 'spruːs ız -əz
sprucest 'spruːs ıst -əst **sprucing** 'spruːs ıŋ
spruce|ly 'spruːs |li ~ness nəs nıs
sprue spruː **sprues** spruːz
spruik spruːk **spruiked** spruːkt **spruiker/s**
'spruːk ə/z ‖ -ˀr/z **spruiking** 'spruːk ıŋ
spruiks spruːks
sprung sprʌŋ

spry, Spry spraɪ **spryer** 'spraɪ_ə ‖ 'spraɪ_ᵊr
  spryest 'spraɪ ɪst -əst **spryly** 'spraɪ li
  spryness 'spraɪ nəs -nɪs
spud spʌd **spuds** spʌdz
spumante spu: 'mænt i ‖ -'mɑːnt eɪ —*It*
  [spu 'man te]
spume spjuːm **spumed** spjuːmd **spumes**
  spjuːmz **spuming** 'spjuːm ɪŋ
spun spʌn
spunk spʌŋk
spunk|y 'spʌŋk |i ~**ier** i_ə ‖ i_ᵊr ~**iest** i_ɪst
  i_əst ~**ily** ɪ li əl i ~**iness** i nəs i nɪs
spur spɜː ‖ spɜ·: **spurred** spɜːd ‖ spɜ·:d
  spurring 'spɜːr ɪŋ ‖ 'spɜ·: ɪŋ **spurs**
  spɜːz ‖ spɜ·:z
spurge spɜːdʒ ‖ spɜ·:dʒ **spurges** 'spɜːdʒ ɪz
  -əz ‖ 'spɜ·:dʒ əz
Spurgeon 'spɜːdʒ ən ‖ 'spɜ·:dʒ ən
spurious 'spjʊər i_əs 'spjɔ:r- ‖ 'spjʊr- ~**ly** li
  ~**ness** nəs nɪs
Spurling 'spɜːl ɪŋ ‖ 'spɜ·:l ɪŋ
spurn, Spurn spɜːn ‖ spɜ·:n **spurned**
  spɜːnd ‖ spɜ·:nd **spurning**
  'spɜːn ɪŋ ‖ 'spɜ·:n ɪŋ **spurns**
  spɜːnz ‖ spɜ·:nz
   Spurn 'Head
spur-of-the-moment ˌspɜːr əv ðə 'məʊm ənt ◂
  -ə ðə- ‖ ˌspɜ·: əv ðə 'moʊm-
Spurrell 'spʌr əl ‖ 'spɜ·:_əl
spurrey 'spʌr i ‖ 'spɜ·: i ~**s** z
Spurrier, s~ 'spʌr i_ə ‖ 'spɜ·: i_ᵊr ~**s** z
spurr|y 'spʌr |i ‖ 'spɜ·: |i ~**ies** iz
spurt spɜːt ‖ spɜ·:t **spurted** 'spɜːt ɪd -əd
  ‖ 'spɜ·:t̬ əd **spurting** 'spɜːt ɪŋ ‖ 'spɜ·:t̬ ɪŋ
  spurts spɜːts ‖ spɜ·:ts
sputnik 'spʊt nɪk 'spʌt- ‖ 'spuːt- ~**s** s
sputter 'spʌt ə ‖ 'spʌt̬ ᵊr ~**ed** d **sputtering**
  'spʌt_ər ɪŋ ‖ 'spʌt̬ ᵊr ɪŋ ~**s** z
sputum 'spjuːt əm ‖ 'spjuːt̬ əm
Spuyten Duyvil ˌspaɪt ᵊn 'daɪv ᵊl ◂
  ˌSpuyten ˌDuyvil 'Creek
spy spaɪ **spied** spaɪd **spies** spaɪz **spying**
  'spaɪ ɪŋ
spycatcher 'spaɪ ˌkætʃ ə ‖ -ᵊr ~**s** z
spyglass 'spaɪ glɑːs §-glæs ‖ -glæs ~**es** ɪz əz
spyhole 'spaɪ həʊl →-hɒʊl ‖ -hoʊl ~**s** z
spymaster 'spaɪ ˌmɑːst ə §-ˌmæst- ‖ -ˌmæst ᵊr
  ~**s** z
sq —*see* **square**
Sqezy *tdmk* 'skwiːz i
squab skwɒb ‖ skwɑːb **squabs**
  skwɒbz ‖ skwɑːbz
squabbl|e 'skwɒb ᵊl ‖ 'skwɑːb ᵊl ~**ed** d ~**er/s**
  _ə/z ‖ _ᵊr/z ~**es** z ~**ing**_ɪŋ
squacco 'skwæk əʊ ‖ 'skwɑːk oʊ ~**s** z
squad skwɒd ‖ skwɑːd **squads**
  skwɒdz ‖ skwɑːdz
   'squad car
squaddie, squadd|y 'skwɒd |i ‖ 'skwɑːd |i
  ~**ies** iz
squadron 'skwɒdr ən ‖ 'skwɑːdr ən ~**s** z
  ˌsquadron 'leader◂, '•• ˌ••

squalid 'skwɒl ɪd §-əd ‖ 'skwɑːl əd 'skwɔːl-
  ~**ly** li ~**ness** nəs nɪs
squalidity skwɒ 'lɪd ət i -ɪt- ‖ skwɑː 'lɪd ət̬ i
  skwɔː-
squall skwɔːl ‖ skwɑːl **squalled** skwɔːld
  ‖ skwɑːld **squalling** 'skwɔːl ɪŋ ‖ 'skwɑːl-
  squalls skwɔːlz ‖ skwɑːlz
squally 'skwɔːl i ‖ 'skwɑːl-
squalor 'skwɒl ə ‖ 'skwɑːl ᵊr 'skwɔːl-
squam|a 'skweɪm |ə ‖ 'skwɑːm- ~**ae** iː
Squamish 'skwɑːm ɪʃ ‖ 'skwɔːm-
squamous 'skweɪm əs ~**ly** li ~**ness** nəs nɪs
squander 'skwɒnd ə ‖ 'skwɑːnd ᵊr ~**ed** d
  squandering 'skwɒnd_ər ɪŋ ‖ 'skwɑːnd ᵊr ɪŋ
  ~**s** z
squanderer 'skwɒnd_ər ə ‖ 'skwɑːnd ᵊr ᵊr ~**s**
  z
square skweə ‖ skweᵊr skwæᵊr **squared**
  skweəd ‖ skweᵊrd skwæᵊrd **squares**
  skweəz ‖ skweᵊrz skwæᵊrz **squaring**
  'skweər ɪŋ ‖ 'skwer ɪŋ 'skwær-
  ˌsquare 'bracket; 'square dance; 'square
  knot; ˌsquare 'leg, ˌsquare leg 'umpire;
  ˌsquare 'meal; ˌsquare 'one; ˌsquare 'root
square-bashing 'skweə ˌbæʃ ɪŋ ‖ 'skwer-
  'skwær-
square-danc|e 'skweə dɑːnts §-dænts
  ‖ 'skwer dænts 'skwær- ~**er/s** ə/z ‖ ᵊr/z
  ~**ing** ɪŋ
squarely 'skweə li ‖ 'skwer li 'skwær-
squareness 'skweə nəs -nɪs ‖ 'skwer- 'skwær-
square-rigged ˌskweə 'rɪgd ◂ ‖ ˌskwer-
  ˌskwær-
squarish 'skweər ɪʃ ‖ 'skwer ɪʃ 'skwær-
squash skwɒʃ ‖ skwɑːʃ skwɔːʃ **squashed**
  skwɒʃt ‖ skwɑːʃt skwɔːʃt **squashes**
  'skwɒʃ ɪz -əz ‖ 'skwɑːʃ əz 'skwɔːʃ-
  squashing 'skwɒʃ ɪŋ ‖ 'skwɑːʃ ɪŋ 'skwɔːʃ-
squash|y 'skwɒʃ |i ‖ 'skwɑːʃ |i 'skwɔːʃ- ~**ier**
  i_ə ‖ i_ᵊr ~**iest** i_ɪst i_əst ~**ily** ɪ li əl i ~**iness**
  i nəs i nɪs
squat skwɒt ‖ skwɑːt **squats**
  skwɒts ‖ skwɑːts **squatted** 'skwɒt ɪd -əd
  ‖ 'skwɑːt̬ əd **squatting**
  'skwɒt ɪŋ ‖ 'skwɑːt̬ ɪŋ
squatter 'skwɒt ə ‖ 'skwɑːt̬ ᵊr ~**s** z
squaw skwɔː ‖ skwɑː **squaws** skwɔːz
  ‖ skwɑːz
squawk skwɔːk skɔːk ‖ skwɑːk **squawked**
  skwɔːkt skɔːkt ‖ skwɑːkt **squawking**
  'skwɔːk ɪŋ 'skɔːk- ‖ 'skwɑːk- **squawks**
  skwɔːks skɔːks ‖ skwɑːks
squeak skwiːk **squeaked** skwiːkt **squeaking**
  'skwiːk ɪŋ **squeaks** skwiːks
squeaker 'skwiːk ə ‖ -ᵊr ~**s** z
squeak|y 'skwiːk |i ~**ier** i_ə ‖ i_ᵊr ~**iest** i_ɪst
  i_əst ~**ily** ɪ li əl i ~**iness** i nəs i nɪs
squeaky-clean ˌskwiːk i 'kliːn ◂
squeal skwiːᵊl **squealed** skwiːᵊld **squealing**
  'skwiːᵊl ɪŋ **squeals** skwiːᵊlz
squealer 'skwiːᵊl ə ‖ -ᵊr ~**s** z
squeamish 'skwiːm ɪʃ ~**ly** li ~**ness** nəs nɪs
squeegee 'skwiː dʒiː ˌ•'• ~**d** d ~**ing** ɪŋ ~**s** z

Squeers skwɪəz ‖ skwɪᵊrz
squeeze skwiːz **squeezed** skwiːzd **squeezes**
  'skwiːz ɪz -əz **squeezing** 'skwiːz ɪŋ
squeezebox 'skwiːz bɒks ‖ -baːks **~es** ɪz əz
squeezer 'skwiːz ə ‖ -ᵊr **~s** z
squelch skwelt∫ **squelched** skwelt∫t
  squelches 'skwelt∫ ɪz -əz **squelching/ly**
  'skwelt∫ ɪŋ /li
squelchy 'skwelt∫ i
squib skwɪb **squibs** skwɪbz
squid skwɪd **squids** skwɪdz
squidg|y 'skwɪdʒ| i ~**ier** i̯_ə ‖ i̯_ᵊr ~**iest** i̯_ɪst
  _əst ~**ily** ɪ li əl i ~**iness** i nəs i nɪs
squiff|y 'skwɪf| i ~**ier** i̯_ə ‖ i̯_ᵊr ~**iest** i̯_ɪst
  _əst ~**ily** ɪ li əl i ~**iness** i nəs i nɪs
squiggl|e 'skwɪg ᵊl ~**ed** d ~**es** z ~**ing** ɪŋ
squiggly 'skwɪg ᵊl_i
squill skwɪl **squills** skwɪlz
squillion 'skwɪl jən ~**s** z
squinch skwɪnt∫ **squinched** skwɪnt∫t
  squinches 'skwɪnt∫ ɪz -əz **squinching**
  'skwɪnt∫ ɪŋ
squint skwɪnt **squinted** 'skwɪnt ɪd -əd
  ‖ 'skwɪnt̬ əd **squinting** 'skwɪnt ɪŋ
  ‖ 'skwɪnt̬ ɪŋ **squints** skwɪnts
squinty 'skwɪnt i ‖ 'skwɪnt̬ i
squirarch|y, squirearch|y
  'skwaɪ_ər aːk |i ‖ 'skwaɪ_ᵊr aːrk |i ~**ies** iz
squire, Squire 'skwaɪ_ə ‖ 'skwaɪ_ᵊr **squired**
  'skwaɪ_əd ‖ 'skwaɪ_ᵊrd **squires**
  'skwaɪ_əz ‖ 'skwaɪ_ᵊrz **squiring**
  'skwaɪ_ər ɪŋ ‖ 'skwaɪ_ᵊr ɪŋ
Squires 'skwaɪ_əz ‖ 'skwaɪ_ᵊrz
squirm skwɜːm ‖ skwɜˈːm **squirmed**
  skwɜːmd ‖ skwɜˈːmd **squirming**
  'skwɜːm ɪŋ ‖ 'skwɜˈːm ɪŋ **squirms**
  skwɜːmz ‖ skwɜˈːmz
squirm|y 'skwɜːm| i ‖ 'skwɜˈːm| i ~**ier**
  i̯_ə ‖ i̯_ᵊr ~**iest** i̯_ɪst _əst ~**ily** ɪ li əl i
  ~**iness** i nəs i nɪs
squirrel 'skwɪr əl ‖ 'skwɜˈː_əl (*) ~**ed**, ~**led** d
  ~**ing**, ~**ling** ɪŋ ~**s** z
squirt skwɜːt ‖ skwɜˈːt **squirted** 'skwɜːt ɪd
  -əd ‖ 'skwɜˈːt̬ əd **squirting**
  'skwɜːt ɪŋ ‖ 'skwɜˈːt̬ ɪŋ **squirts**
  skwɜːts ‖ skwɜˈːts
squish skwɪ∫ **squished** skwɪ∫t **squishes**
  'skwɪ∫ ɪz -əz **squishing** 'skwɪ∫ ɪŋ
squish|y 'skwɪ∫| i ~**ier** i̯_ə ‖ i̯_ᵊr ~**iest** i̯_ɪst
  i̯_əst ~**ily** ɪ li əl i ~**iness** i nəs i nɪs
squit skwɪt **squits** skwɪts
squitters 'skwɪt əz ‖ 'skwɪt̬ ᵊrz
Sr —*see* **Senior; Señor**
Sranan 'sraːn ən
Srebrenica ˌsreb rə 'niːts ə
Sri, sri sriː ∫riː —*see also phrases with this word*
Sri Lank|a srɪ 'læŋk |ə ∫rɪ-, ˌsriː-, ˌ∫riː-
  ‖ -'laːŋk |ə ~**an/s** ən/z
Srinagar srɪ 'nʌg ə ∫rɪ-, ₍ₒ₎sriː-, ₍ₒ₎∫riː-, ˌsɪr i'••,
  -'naːg- ‖ -ᵊr —*Hindi* [sɪ riː nə gər]
SS ˌes 'es ◀
  ˌSS 'Kittiwake
ssh ∫

-**st** *superlative* ɪst -əst — **finest** 'faɪn ɪst -əst
  —*see* -**est**
St, St. '*Street*' striːt —*In names of thoroughfares,*
  unstressed: 'Oxford St
St, St. '*Saint*' sənt sən ‖ seɪnt —*In RP the*
  strong form seɪnt *is not customary when* St *is*
  prefixed to a name; and of the two weak forms
  listed sən *tends to be restricted to cases where*
  the following name begins with a consonant. In
  GenAm there is no weak form. In French names
  St *may be pronounced* sæn, sæ *(Fr* [sæ]).
  —*Proper names beginning* St *are listed in this*
  dictionary alphabetically as St-, *not as* Saint-.
  St 'Anthony; St 'Lawrence, St ˌLawrence
  'Seaway
Staaten *Australian river* 'stæt ᵊn
stab stæb **stabbed** stæbd **stabbing** 'stæb ɪŋ
  stabs stæbz
Stabat Mater ˌstaːb æt 'maːt ə ˌstæb-, -ət-
  ‖ -aːt 'maːt̬ ᵊr
stabb... —*see* **stab**
stabber 'stæb ə ‖ -ᵊr **~s** z
St Abb's sənt 'æbz §sᵊn- ‖ seɪnt̬ 'æbz
stability stə 'bɪl ət i -ɪt i ‖ -ət̬ i
stabilis... —*see* **stabiliz...**
stabilization ˌsteɪb əl aɪ 'zeɪ∫ ᵊn ₍ₒ₎ɪl-, -ɪ'•-
  ‖ -ᵊ'•- ~**s** z
stabiliz|e 'steɪb ə laɪz -ɪ-; -ᵊl aɪz ~**ed** d ~**es** ɪz
  əz ~**ing** ɪŋ
stabilizer 'steɪb ə laɪz ə '•ɪ-; -ᵊl aɪz- ‖ -ᵊr ~**s** z
stabl|e 'steɪb ᵊl ~**ed** d ~**er** _ə ‖ _ᵊr ~**es** z
  ~**est** _ɪst _əst ~**ing** _ɪŋ
  'stable boy; ˌstable 'door
stablemate 'steɪb ᵊl meɪt ~**s** s
stablish 'stæb lɪ∫ ~**ed** t ~**es** ɪz əz ~**ing** ɪŋ
staccato stə 'kaːt əʊ stæ- ‖ -oʊ ~**s** z
Stacey, Stacie 'steɪs i
stack stæk **stacked** stækt **stacking** 'stæk ɪŋ
  stacks stæks
Stackhouse 'stæk haʊs
Stacpoole 'stæk puːl
stacte 'stækt i -iː
Stacy 'steɪs i
stade steɪd **stades** steɪdz
stadia 'steɪd i̯_ə
stadiometer ˌsteɪd i 'ɒm ɪt ə -ət ə ‖ -'aːm ət̬ ᵊr
  ~**s** z
stadi|um 'steɪd i̯_əm ~**a** ə ~**ums** əmz
staff staːf §stæf ‖ stæf **staffed** staːft §stæft
  ‖ stæft **staffing** 'staːf ɪŋ §'stæf- ‖ 'stæf ɪŋ
  staffs staːfs §stæfs ‖ stæfs
  'staff college; 'staff nurse; 'staff ˌofficer;
  'staff ˌsergeant
Staffa 'stæf ə
staffer 'staːf ə ‖ 'stæf ᵊr ~**s** z
Stafford 'stæf əd ‖ -ᵊrd ~**shire** ∫ə ∫ɪə ‖ ∫ᵊr ∫ɪr
Staffs, Staffs. stæfs
stag stæg **stagged** stægd **stagging** 'stæg ɪŋ
  stags stægz
  'stag ˌbeetle; 'stag ˌparty
stage steɪdʒ **staged** steɪdʒd **stages** 'steɪdʒ ɪz
  -əz **staging/s** 'steɪdʒ ɪŋ/z
  'stage diˌrection; ˌstage 'door◀; ˌstage

door 'Johnny; 'stage ef‚fect; 'stage fright;
‚stage 'manager ‖ '• ‚• • •; 'stage name;
‚stage 'whisper ‖ '• ‚• •; 'staging post
stagecoach 'steɪdʒ kəʊtʃ ‖ -koʊtʃ ~es ɪz əz
stagecraft 'steɪdʒ krɑːft §-kræft ‖ -kræft
stagehand 'steɪdʒ hænd ~s z
stage-manag|e ‚steɪdʒ 'mæn ɪdʒ '•‚• •
   ‖ 'steɪdʒ ‚mæn ɪdʒ ~ed d ~es ɪz əz ~ing ɪŋ
stager 'steɪdʒ ə ‖ -ər ~s z
stagestruck 'steɪdʒ strʌk
stag|ey 'steɪdʒ |i ~ier i‿ə ‖ i‿ər ~iest i‿ɪst
i‿əst ~ily ɪ li əl i ~iness i nəs i nɪs
stagflation ‚stæg 'fleɪʃ ən
Stagg stæg
stagger 'stæg ə ‖ -ər ~ed d staggering/ly
   'stæg ər‿ɪŋ /li ~s z
staghorn 'stæg hɔːn ‖ -hɔːrn
staghound 'stæg haʊnd ~s z
staging —see stage
Stagira stə 'dʒaɪ⁼r ə 'stædʒ ɪr ə, -ər ə
Stagirite 'stædʒ ɪ raɪt -ə- ~s s
stagnancy 'stæg nən⁼s i
stagnant 'stæg nənt ~ly li
stag|nate ₍ᵢ₎stæg 'neɪt '• • ‖ 'stæg |neɪt
   ~nated neɪt ɪd -əd ‖ neɪt̬ əd ~nates neɪts
   ~nating neɪt ɪŋ ‖ neɪt̬ ɪŋ
stagnation ₍ᵢ₎stæg 'neɪʃ ən
St Agnes sənt 'æg nɪs §sən-, -nəs ‖ seɪnt̬-
stag|ly 'steɪdʒ |i ~ier i‿ə ‖ i‿ər ~iest i‿ɪst i‿əst
~ily ɪ li əl i ~iness i nəs i nɪs
staid steɪd (= stayed) staidly 'steɪd li
staidness 'steɪd nəs -nɪs
stain steɪn stained steɪnd staining 'steɪn ɪŋ
   stains steɪnz
   ‚stained 'glass◄, ‚stained glass 'window
Stainby 'steɪn bi →'steɪm-
stainer, S~ 'steɪn ə ‖ -ər
Staines steɪnz
Stainforth 'steɪn fɔːθ -fəθ ‖ -fɔːrθ -foʊrθ
stainless 'steɪn ləs -lɪs ~ly li ~ness nəs nɪs
   ‚stainless 'steel◄, ‚stainless steel 'cutlery
Stainton 'steɪnt ən ‖ -ᵊn
stair steə ‖ steᵊr stæᵊr stairs steəz ‖ steᵊrz
   stæᵊrz
   'stair rod
staircas|e 'steə keɪs ‖ ster- stær- ~es ɪz əz
stairway 'steə weɪ ‖ ster- 'stær- ~s z
stairwell 'steə wel ‖ ster- 'stær- ~s z
staithe steɪð staithes, S~ steɪðz
stake steɪk staked steɪkt stakes steɪks
   staking 'steɪk ɪŋ
stakeholder 'steɪk ‚həʊld ə →-‚hɒʊld-
   ‖ -‚hoʊld ᵊr ~s z
stakeout 'steɪk aʊt ~s s
stakhanovism stə 'kæn ə ‚vɪz əm stæ-, -'kɑːn-
   ‖ -'kɑːn-
stakhanovite stə 'kæn ə vaɪt stæ-, -'kɑːn-
   ‖ -'kɑːn- ~s s
stalactite 'stæl ək taɪt ‖ stə 'lækt aɪt (*) ~s s
Stalag 'stæl æg -əg ‖ 'stɑːl ɑːg 'stæl əg —Ger
   ['ʃta lak]
stalagmite 'stæl əg maɪt ‖ stə 'læg- (*) ~s s

St Albans sənt 'ɔːlb ənz §sən-, -'ɒlb- ‖ seɪnt̬-
   -'ɑːlb-
St Aldate's sənt 'ɔːld əts -'ɒld-, -ɪts, -eɪts
   ‖ seɪnt̬- -'ɑːld-
stale steɪᵊl staler 'steɪᵊl ə ‖ -ər stalest
   'steɪᵊl ɪst -əst stalely 'steɪᵊl li
stale|mate 'steɪᵊl |meɪt ~mated meɪt ɪd -əd
   ‖ meɪt̬ əd ~mates meɪts ~mating
   meɪt ɪŋ ‖ meɪt̬ ɪŋ
staleness 'steɪᵊl nəs -nɪs
Stalin 'stɑːl ɪn 'stæl-, §-ən ‖ -iːn —Russ
   ['sta lʲɪn]
Stalingrad 'stɑːl ɪn græd 'stæl-, →-ɪŋ-, §-ən-
   —Russ [stə lʲɪn 'grat]
Stalinism 'stɑːl ɪ ‚nɪz əm 'stæl-, -ə-
Stalinist 'stɑːl ɪn ɪst 'stæl-, -ən-, §-əst ~s s
stalk stɔːk ‖ stɑːk stalked stɔːkt ‖ stɑːkt
   stalking 'stɔːk ɪŋ ‖ 'stɑːk- stalks stɔːks
   ‖ stɑːks
stalker, S~ 'stɔːk ə ‖ -ər 'stɑːk- ~s z
stalking-hors|e 'stɔːk ɪŋ hɔːs ‖ -hɔːrs 'stɑːk-
   ~es ɪz əz
Stalky, s~ 'stɔːk i ‖ 'stɑːk-
stall stɔːl ‖ stɑːl stalled stɔːld ‖ stɑːld
   stalling 'stɔːl ɪŋ ‖ 'stɑːl- stalls stɔːlz ‖ stɑːlz
stallage 'stɔːl ɪdʒ
stallholder 'stɔːl ‚həʊld ə →-‚hɒʊld-
   ‖ -‚hoʊld ᵊr 'stɑːl- ~s z
stallion 'stæl jən ~s z
Stallone stə 'ləʊn stæ- ‖ -'loʊn
Stallybrass 'stæl i brɑːs §-bræs ‖ -bræs
stalwart 'stɔːl wət 'stɒl- ‖ -wᵊrt 'stɑːl- ~ly li
   ~ness nəs nɪs ~s s
Stalybridge 'steɪl i brɪdʒ ‚•'•'•
Stamboul, Stambul ₍ᵢ₎stæm 'buːl
stamen 'steɪm en -ən ~s z
Stamford 'stæmp fəd ‖ -fᵊrd
stamina 'stæm ɪn ə -ən-
stammer 'stæm ə ‖ -ər ~ed d stammering/ly
   'stæm ər‿ɪŋ /li ~s z
stamp, Stamp stæmp stamped stæmpt
   stamping 'stæmp ɪŋ stamps stæmps
   'stamp col‚lection; 'stamp ‚duty;
   'stamping ground
stamped|e ₍ᵢ₎stæm 'piːd ~ed ɪd əd ~es z
   ~ing ɪŋ
stamper 'stæmp ə ‖ -ər ~s z
Stan stæn
Stanbury 'stæn bər_i →'stæm- ‖ -‚ber i
stance stæn⁼s stɑːn⁼s stances 'stæn⁼s ɪz
   'stɑːn⁼s-, -əz
stanch stɑːntʃ §stæntʃ ‖ stɔːntʃ stanched
   stɑːntʃt §stæntʃt ‖ stɔːntʃt stanching
   'stɑːntʃ ɪŋ §'stæntʃ- ‖ 'stɔːntʃ- stanches
   'stɑːntʃ ɪz §'stæntʃ-, -əz ‖ 'stɔːntʃ-
stanchion 'stɑːntʃ ən 'stæntʃ- ‖ 'stæntʃ ən ~s
   z
Stancliffe 'stæn klɪf →'stæŋ-
stand stænd standing 'stænd ɪŋ stands
   stændz stood stʊd
   ‚standing 'order; ‚standing o'vation;
   'standing room
stand-alone 'stænd ə ‚ləʊn ‚• •'•◄ ‖ -‚loʊn

S

standard 'stænd əd ‖ -ərd ~s z
,standard ,devi'ation; 'standard lamp;
,standard of 'living; ,standard 'time
standard-bearer 'stænd əd ,beər ə →-əb-
‖ -ərd ,ber ər -,bær- ~s z
standardis... —see standardiz...
standardization ,stænd əd aɪ 'zeɪʃ ən -ɪ'•-
‖ -ərd ə- ~s z
standardiz|e 'stænd ə daɪz ‖ -ər- ~ed d ~es ɪz
əz ~ing ɪŋ
standby 'stænd baɪ →'stæmb- ~s z
Standedge 'stæn edʒ 'stænd-
standee stæn 'diː ~s z
Standen 'stænd ən
stand-in 'stænd ɪn ~s z
Standish 'stænd ɪʃ
standoff 'stænd ɒf -ɔːf ‖ -ɔːf -ɑːf ~s s
,standoff 'half, '• • •
standoffish ,stænd 'ɒf ɪʃ -'ɔːf- ‖ -'ɔːf- -'ɑːf-
~ly li ~ness nəs nɪs
standpipe 'stænd paɪp →'stæmb- ~s s
standpoint 'stænd pɔɪnt →'stæmb- ~s s
St Andrews sənt 'ændr uːz §sən- ‖ seɪnt̩
—locally sɪn 'tændr-
standstill 'stænd stɪl ~s z
stand-up 'stænd ʌp
Stanfield 'stæn fiːəld
Stanford 'stæn fəd ‖ -fərd
Stanford-Binet ,stæn fəd 'biːn eɪ,•• bɪ 'neɪ
‖ ,•fərd bɪ 'neɪ
,Stanford-Bi'net test
Stanford-le-Hope
,stæn fəd lɪ 'həʊp ‖ -fərd lɪ 'hoʊp
stang stæŋ
Stanhope, s~ 'stæn əp -həʊp ‖ -hoʊp ~s, ~'s s
Stanislas 'stæn ɪs ləs -əs-; -ɪ slæs, -ə-, -slɑːs
Stanislaus 'stæn ɪ slaʊs -ə-, -slɔːs ‖ -slɔːs -slɑːs
Stanislavski, Stanislavsky ,stæn ɪ 'slæv ski -ə-
‖ -'slɑːv ski —Russ [stə nʲɪ 'sɫaf skʲɪj]
stank stæŋk
Stanley 'stæn li
,Stanley 'Falls; 'Stanley knife
Stanmore 'stæn mɔː →'stæm- ‖ -mɔːr -moʊr
Stannard 'stæn əd ‖ -ərd
stannar|ly 'stæn ər li ~ies iz
St Anne's sənt 'ænz §sən- ‖ seɪnt̩-
stannic 'stæn ɪk
stannous 'stæn əs
Stansfield 'stænz fiːəld 'stæn̩ts-
Stansgate 'stænz geɪt
Stansted 'stæn sted 'stæn̩tst ɪd, -əd
St Anthony sənt 'ænt ən i §sən- ‖ seɪnt̩
'ænt ən i -'ænt̩θ ən i
Stanton 'stænt ən ‖ -ən
Stanway 'stæn weɪ
Stanwell 'stæn wel -wəl
Stanwick, Stanwyck (i) 'stæn ɪk, (ii) -wɪk
stanza 'stænz ə ~s z
stanzaic stæn 'zeɪ ɪk
stapelia stə 'piːl i̯ə ‖ -'piːl jə
stapes 'steɪp iːz
staph stæf

staphylo- comb. form
with stress-neutral suffix ¦stæf ɪl əʊ -əl- ‖ -ə
-oʊ — staphyloplasty 'stæf ɪl əʊ ,plæst i
'•əl- ‖ -ə,•-, -oʊ,•-
with stress-imposing suffix ,stæf ɪ 'lɒ+ -ə-
‖ -'lɑː+ — staphylorrhaphy ,stæf ɪ 'lɒr əf i
,•ə- ‖ -'lɑːr- -'lɔːr-
staphylo|coccus ,stæf ɪl əʊ |'kɒk əs ,•əl-
‖ -ə |'kɑːk əs -oʊ|•- ~coccal
'kɒk əl ◄ ‖ -'kɑːk əl ◄ ~cocci 'kɒks aɪ 'kɒk-,
'kɒs-, -iː ‖ 'kɑːks aɪ 'kɑːk-, -iː
stapl|e 'steɪp əl ~ed d ~es z ~ing ͜ɪŋ
Stapleford 'steɪp əl fəd ‖ -fərd —but the place
in Leics is 'stæp-
Staplehurst 'steɪp əl hɜːst ‖ -hɝːst
stapler 'steɪp lə ‖ -lər ~s z
Stapleton 'steɪp əl tən
star stɑː ‖ stɑːr starred stɑːd ‖ stɑːrd
starring 'stɑːr ɪŋ stars stɑːz ‖ stɑːrz
,star 'chamber ‖ '•,••; ,Stars and 'Stripes;
'star sign; 'star wars
star-apple ,stɑːr 'æp əl '•,•• ‖ 'stɑːr ,æp əl ~s
z
starboard 'stɑː bəd -bɔːd ‖ 'stɑːr bərd
Starbuck 'stɑː bʌk ‖ 'stɑːr-
starburst 'stɑː bɜːst ‖ 'stɑːr bɝːst ~s s
starch stɑːtʃ ‖ stɑːrtʃ starched
stɑːtʃt ‖ stɑːrtʃt starches 'stɑːtʃ ɪz -əz
‖ 'stɑːrtʃ əz starching
'stɑːtʃ ɪŋ ‖ 'stɑːrtʃ ɪŋ
starch-reduced ,stɑːtʃ rɪ 'djuːst ◄ -rə-, §-riː-,
→§-'dʒuːst, '••,• ‖ ,stɑːrtʃ rɪ 'duːst ◄
-'djuːst
,starch-re,duced 'crispbread
starch|y 'stɑːtʃ li ‖ 'stɑːrtʃ li ~ier i̯ə ‖ i̯ər
~iest i̯ɪst i̯əst ~ily ɪ li əl i ~iness i nəs i nɪs
star-crossed 'stɑː krɒst -krɔːst, ,•'•
‖ 'stɑːr krɒst -krɑːst
stardom 'stɑː dəm ‖ 'stɑːr-
stardust 'stɑː dʌst ‖ 'stɑːr-
stare steə ‖ steər stæər stared steəd ‖ steərd
stæərd stares steəz ‖ steərz stæərz staring
'steər ɪŋ ‖ 'ster ɪŋ 'stær-
starfish 'stɑː fɪʃ ‖ 'stɑːr- ~es ɪz əz
stargazer 'stɑː ,geɪz ə ‖ 'stɑːr ,geɪz ər ~s z
stargazing 'stɑː ,geɪz ɪŋ ‖ 'stɑːr-
staring 'steər ɪŋ ‖ 'ster ɪŋ 'stær- ~ly li
stark, Stark stɑːk ‖ stɑːrk starker
'stɑːk ə ‖ 'stɑːrk ər starkest 'stɑːk ɪst -əst
‖ 'stɑːrk əst
starkers 'stɑːk əz ‖ 'stɑːrk ərz
Starkey, Starkie 'stɑːk i ‖ 'stɑːrk i
starkly 'stɑːk li ‖ 'stɑːrk li
stark-naked ,stɑːk 'neɪk ɪd ◄ -əd ‖ ,stɑːrk-
starkness 'stɑːk nəs -nɪs ‖ 'stɑːrk-
starless 'stɑː ləs -lɪs ‖ 'stɑːr-
starlet 'stɑː lət -lɪt ‖ 'stɑːr- ~s s
starlight 'stɑː laɪt ‖ 'stɑːr-
starling, S~ 'stɑːl ɪŋ ‖ 'stɑːrl- ~s z
starlit 'stɑː lɪt ‖ 'stɑːr-
Starr stɑː ‖ stɑːr
starr... —see star
star-studded 'stɑː ,stʌd ɪd-əd ‖ 'stɑːr-

starr|y 'stɑːr i ~ier i_ə ‖ i_ər ~iest i_ɪst i_əst
  ~iness i nəs i nɪs
starry-eyed ˌstɑːr i 'aɪd ◂
star-spangled 'stɑː ˌspæŋ gəld ˌ•'• •
  ‖ ˌstɑːr 'spæŋ gəld ◂
  ˌStar-ˌSpangled 'Banner
starstruck 'stɑː strʌk ‖ 'stɑːr-
star-studded 'stɑː ˌstʌd ɪd -əd ˌ•'• • ‖ 'stɑːr-
start, Start stɑːt ‖ stɑːrt started 'stɑːt ɪd -əd
  ‖ 'stɑːrt̬ əd starting 'stɑːt ɪŋ ‖ 'stɑːrt̬ ɪŋ
  starts stɑːts ‖ stɑːrts
  'starting block; 'starting gate; 'starting
  ˌpistol; 'starting price
starter 'stɑːt ə ‖ 'stɑːrt̬ ər ~s z
Startin 'stɑːt ɪn §-ən ‖ 'stɑːrt ən
startl|e 'stɑːt əl ‖ 'stɑːrt̬ əl ~ed d ~es z
  ~ing/ly _ɪŋ /li
Start-rite tdmk 'stɑːt raɪt ‖ 'stɑːrt-
start-up 'stɑːt ʌp ‖ 'stɑːrt̬ ʌp ~s s
starvation ₍ᵢ₎stɑː 'veɪʃ ən ₍ᵢ₎stɑːr-
  star'vation ˌwages, •ˌ•• '• •
starve stɑːv ‖ stɑːrv starved stɑːvd ‖ stɑːrvd
  starves stɑːvz ‖ stɑːrvz starving
  'stɑːv ɪŋ ‖ 'stɑːrv ɪŋ
starveling 'stɑːv lɪŋ ‖ 'stɑːrv- ~s z
starwort 'stɑː wɜːt §-wɔːt ‖ 'stɑːr wɜːrt -wɔːrt
  ~s s
St Asaph sənt 'æs əf §sən- ‖ seɪnt̬-
stash stæʃ stashed stæʃt stashes 'stæʃ ɪz -əz
  stashing 'stæʃ ɪŋ
Stasi 'stɑːz i —Ger ['ʃtɑː zi]
stas|is 'steɪs ɪs 'stæs-, §-əs ~es iːz
Stassen 'stæs ən
-stat stæt — thermostat 'θɜːm əʊ stæt
  ‖ 'θɜːm ə-
state, State steɪt stated 'steɪt ɪd -əd
  ‖ 'steɪt̬ əd states, States steɪts stating
  'steɪt ɪŋ ‖ 'steɪt̬ ɪŋ
  'State De,partment; ˌstate's 'evidence
statecraft 'steɪt krɑːft §-kræft ‖ -kræft
statehood 'steɪt hʊd
state|house, S~ 'steɪt ǀhaʊs ~houses haʊz ɪz
  -əz
stateless 'steɪt ləs -lɪs ~ness nəs nɪs
state|ly 'steɪt ǀli ~lier li_ə ‖ li_ər ~liest li_ɪst
  _əst ~iness li nəs -nɪs
  ˌstately 'home
statement 'steɪt mənt ~ed ɪd əd ~ing ɪŋ ~s
  s
Staten 'stæt ən
  ˌStaten 'Island
state-of-the-art ˌsteɪt əv ði 'ɑːt ◂ ˌ•ə-
  ‖ ˌsteɪt̬ əv ði 'ɑːrt ◂
stater 'steɪt ə ‖ 'steɪt̬ ər ~s z
stateroom 'steɪt ruːm -rʊm ~s z
stateside 'steɪt saɪd
states|man 'steɪts ǀmən ~men mən
statesman|like 'steɪts mən ǀlaɪk ~ship ʃɪp
statewide ˌsteɪt 'waɪd ◂
Statham (i) 'steɪθ əm, (ii) 'steɪð əm
St Athan sənt 'æθ ən §sən- ‖ seɪnt̬-
static 'stæt ɪk ‖ 'stæt̬ ɪk ~ally əl_i ~s s

statice 'stæt ɪs i -əs i; 'stæt ɪs, §-əs ‖ 'stæt̬ əs i
  'stæt̬ əs
station 'steɪʃ ən ~ed d ~ing _ɪŋ ~s z
  'station break; 'station house; ˌstations of
  the 'Cross; 'station ˌwagon
stationary 'steɪʃ ən ər_i -ən_ər i ‖ -ə ner i
stationer 'steɪʃ ən_ə ‖ _ər ~s z
stationery 'steɪʃ ən ər_i -ən_ər i ‖ -ə ner i (=
  stationary)
stationmaster 'steɪʃ ən ˌmɑːst ə §-ˌmæst-
  ‖ -ˌmæst ər ~s z
statism 'steɪt ˌɪz əm ‖ 'steɪt̬- ˌ
statist 'advocate of state power' 'steɪt ɪst §-əst
  ‖ 'steɪt̬ əst ~s s
statist 'statistician' 'stæt ɪst -əst ‖ 'stæt̬ əst ~s
  s
statistic stə 'tɪst ɪk ~s s
statistical stə 'tɪst ɪk əl ~ly _i
statistician ˌstæt ɪ 'stɪʃ ən -ə- ‖ ˌstæt̬- ~s z
Statius 'steɪʃ i_əs 'steɪt-
stative 'steɪt ɪv ‖ 'steɪt̬- ~s z
stato- comb. form
  with stress-neutral suffix ǀstæt əʊ ‖ ǀstæt̬ ə —
  statolith 'stæt əʊ lɪθ ‖ 'stæt̬ ə- -əl ɪθ
  with stress-imposing suffix stæ 'tɒ+ ‖ -'tɑː+ —
  statometer stæ 'tɒm ɪt ə -ət ə ‖ -'tɑːm ət̬ ər
Staton 'steɪt ən
stator 'steɪt ə ‖ 'steɪt̬ ər ~s z
stats 'statistics' stæts
statuar|y 'stæt ʃ u_ər i ‖ 'stæt ju_ -er i ~ies iz
statue 'stæt ʃ uː 'stæt juː ~s z
statuesque ˌstæt ʃ u 'esk ◂ ˌstæt ju- ~ly li
statuette ˌstæt ʃ u 'et ˌstæt ju- ~s z
stature 'stæt ʃ ə ‖ -ər ~s z
status 'steɪt əs 'stæt- ‖ 'steɪt̬ əs 'stæt̬- ~es ɪz
  əz
  ˌstatus 'quo
statute 'stæt ʃ uːt 'stæt juːt ~s s
  'statute book; 'statute law
statutor|y 'stæt ʃ ʊt_ər i ǀ•uːt_; 'stæt jʊt_,
  ǀ•ˌjuːt_; §stə 'tjuːt ər i ‖ 'stæt ʃ ə tɔːr i ǀ•u-,
  -toʊr i ~ily əl i -ɪ li
St Aubyn sənt 'ɔːb ɪn §sən-, §-ən ‖ seɪnt̬-
  -'ɑːb-
Staughton 'stɔːt ən ‖ 'stɑːt-
St Augustine sənt ɔː 'gʌst ɪn §sən-, ˌseɪnt-,
  §-ən ‖ ˌseɪnt̬ ɔː- ˌ, •ˈɑː-
staunch adj stɔːntʃ ‖ stɑːntʃ —in RP formerly
  also stɑːntʃ stauncher 'stɔːntʃ ə ‖ -ər
  'stɑːntʃ- staunchest 'stɔːntʃ ɪst -əst ‖
  'stɑːntʃ-
staunch v stɔːntʃ stɑːntʃ, §stæntʃ staunched
  stɔːntʃt stɑːntʃt, §stæntʃt staunches
  'stɔːntʃ ɪz 'stɑːntʃ-, §'stæntʃ-, -əz
  staunching 'stɔːntʃ ɪŋ 'stɑːntʃ-, §'stæntʃ-
staunch|ly 'stɔːntʃ ǀli ‖ 'stɑːntʃ- ~ness nəs nɪs
Staunton (i) 'stɔːnt ən ‖ 'stɑːnt-, (ii)
  'stænt ən ‖ -ən —The English family name is
  (i), as is the place in IL; the place in VA is (ii)
staurolite 'stɔːr ə laɪt ~s s
stauroscope 'stɔːr ə skəʊp ‖ -skoʊp ~s s
stauroscopic ˌstɔːr ə 'skɒp ɪk ◂ ‖ -'skɑːp-
  ~ally əl_i

S

St Austell sənt 'ɔːst əl §sən-, -'ɒst-, -'ɔːs-
‖ seɪnt̬- -'aːst-
Stavanger stə 'væŋ ə ‖ staː 'vɑːŋ ər —*Norw*
[sta 'vaŋ ər]
stave steɪv **staved** steɪvd **staves** steɪvz
staving 'steɪv ɪŋ **stove** stəʊv ‖ stoʊv
Staveley 'steɪv li
Staverton 'stæv ət ən ‖ -ərt ən
staves *pl of* **staff** steɪvz
stavesacre 'steɪvz ,eɪk ə ‖ -ər ~s z
Stawell stɔːl ‖ staːl
stay **stayed** steɪd (= *staid*) **staying**
'steɪ ɪŋ **stays** steɪz
'staying ,power
stay-at-home 'steɪ ət ,həʊm ‖ -,hoʊm ~s z
stayer 'steɪ ə ‖ -ər ~s z
Stayman 'steɪ mən
staysail 'steɪ sᵊl -seɪᵊl ~s z
St Barts sənt 'baːts ‖ seɪnt 'baːrts
St Bernard sənt 'bɜːn əd →səm-
‖ ,seɪnt bər 'naːrd —*Fr* [sæ bɛʁ naːʁ] ~s z
St ,Bernard 'Pass ‖ ,St Ber,nard 'Pass
St Briavels sənt 'brev əlz →səm- ‖ seɪnt-
St Christopher sənt 'krɪst əf ə →səŋ-
‖ seɪnt 'krɪst əf ər
St Clair sənt 'kleə →səŋ- ‖ seɪnt 'kleᵊr -'klæᵊr
—*but as a family name also* 'sɪŋ kleə,
'sɪn- ‖ -kler, -klær
St Cloud sæŋ 'kluː —*Fr* [sæ klu] —*but the*
place in MN is seɪnt 'klaʊd
St Croix sənt 'krɔɪ ‖ seɪnt-
STD ,es tiː 'diː
St David's sənt 'deɪv ɪdz §-ədz ‖ seɪnt-
St 'David's day
St Dogmaels sənt 'dɒg mᵊlz ‖ seɪnt 'dɔːg-
-'daːg-
St Denis sənt 'den ɪs §-əs ‖ seɪnt- —*but for the*
places in Paris and Réunion ,sæn də 'niː, —*Fr*
[sæd ni]
St Donat's sənt 'dɒn əts ‖ seɪnt 'daːn-
stead sted
Stead (i) sted, (ii) stiːd
steadfast 'sted faːst -fəst, §-fæst ‖ -fæst ~ly li
~ness nəs nɪs
steading 'sted ɪŋ ~s z
Steadman 'sted mən →'steb-
stead|y 'sted |i ~ier i‿ə ‖ i‿ər ~iest i‿ɪst i‿əst
~ily ɪ li əl i ~iness i nəs i nɪs
,steady 'state, ,steady 'state ,theory
steak steɪk (= *stake*) **steaks** steɪks
,steak tar'tare
steak|house 'steɪk |haʊs ~houses haʊz ɪz -əz
steal stiːᵊl (= *steel*) **stealing** 'stiːᵊl ɪŋ **steals**
stiːᵊlz **stole** stəʊl →stɒʊl ‖ stoʊl **stolen**
'stəʊl ən →'stɒʊl- ‖ 'stoʊl ən
stealer 'stiːᵊl ə ‖ -ər ~s z
stealth stelθ
stealth|y 'stelθ |i ~ier i‿ə ‖ i‿ər ~iest i‿ɪst
i‿əst ~ily ɪ li əl i ~iness i nəs i nɪs
steam stiːm **steamed** stiːmd **steaming**
'stiːm ɪŋ **steams** stiːmz
'steam ,iron; 'steam ,shovel
steamboat 'stiːm bəʊt ‖ -boʊt ~s s

steamed-up ,stiːmd 'ʌp ◂
steam-engine 'stiːm ,endʒ ɪn §-,ɪndʒ-, -ən ~s
z
steamer 'stiːm ə ‖ -ər ~s z
steamroll 'stiːm ,rəʊl →-,rɒʊl ‖ -,roʊl ~ed d
~ing ɪŋ ~s z
steamroll|er 'stiːm ,rəʊl ə →-,rɒʊl- ‖ -,roʊl |ər
~ered əd ‖ ərd ~ering ər ɪŋ ~ers əz ‖ ərz
steamship 'stiːm ʃɪp ~s s
steam|y 'stiːm |i ~ier i‿ə ‖ i‿ər ~iest i‿ɪst i‿əst
~ily ɪ li əl i ~iness i nəs i nɪs
stearate 'stɪər eɪt ‖ 'stiː ə reɪt 'stɪr eɪt ~s s
stearic sti 'ær ɪk ‖ -'er-; 'stɪr ɪk
stearin 'stɪər ɪn §-ən ‖ 'stiː ər ən 'stɪr ən
stearoptene ,stɪə 'rɒpt iːn ‖ ,stiː ə 'raːpt-
Stearn, Stearne stɜːn ‖ stɜːrn
steatite 'stiː‿ə taɪt
steatolysis ,stiː‿ə 'tɒl əs ɪs -ɪs ɪs, §-əs ‖ -'taːl-
steatopygia ,stiː‿ət əʊ 'paɪdʒ i‿ə -'pɪdʒ-
‖ sti ,æt̬ ə- ,stiː əṭ ə-
steatopygous ,stiː‿ət əʊ 'paɪg əs ◂
,stiː‿ə 'tɒp ɪg əs, §-əg əs ‖ sti ,æt̬ ə-
,stiː əṭ ə-; ,stiː ə 'taːp əg əs
steatorrhea, steatorrhoea
,stiː‿ət ə 'riː‿ə ‖ sti ,æt̬ ə- ,stiː əṭ ə-
Stebbing 'steb ɪŋ
Stechford 'stetʃ fəd ‖ -fᵊrd
stedfast 'sted faːst -fəst, §-fæst ‖ -fæst ~ly li
~ness nəs nɪs
Stedman 'sted mən →'steb-
St Edmunds sənt 'ed məndz §sən-, →-'eb-
‖ seɪnt̬-
steed, Steed stiːd **steeds, Steed's** stiːdz
steel stiːᵊl **steeled** stiːᵊld **steeling** 'stiːᵊl ɪŋ
steels stiːᵊlz
'steel band; ,steel 'wool
Steel, Steele stiːᵊl
steeli... —*see* **steely**
steelworker 'stiːᵊl ,wɜːk ə ‖ -,wɜːk ᵊr ~s z
steelworks 'stiːᵊl wɜːks ‖ -wɜːks
steel|y 'stiːᵊl |i ~ier i‿ə ‖ i‿ər ~iest i‿ɪst i‿əst
~iness i nəs i nɪs
steelyard 'stiːᵊl jaːd 'stɪl-, -jəd ‖ 'stiːᵊl jaːrd
'stɪl jᵊrd ~s z
Steen stiːn —*but as a Dutch name* steɪn,
—*Dutch* [steːn]
steenbok 'stiːn bɒk →'stiːm-, 'steɪn-, 'stɪən-,
-bʌk ‖ -baːk ~s s
steep stiːp **steeper** 'stiːp ə ‖ -ər **steepest**
'stiːp ɪst -əst
steepen 'stiːp ən ~ed d ~ing ‿ɪŋ ~s z
steeple 'stiːp ᵊl ~s z
steeplechas|e 'stiːp ᵊl tʃeɪs ~er/s ə/z ‖ -ᵊr/z
~es ɪz əz ~ing ɪŋ
steeplejack 'stiːp ᵊl dʒæk ~s s
steep|ly 'stiːp |li ~ness nəs nɪs
steer stɪə ‖ stɪᵊr **steered** stɪəd ‖ stɪᵊrd
steering 'stɪər ɪŋ ‖ 'stɪr ɪŋ **steers**
stɪəz ‖ stɪᵊrz
'steering com,mittee; 'steering wheel
steerage 'stɪər ɪdʒ ‖ 'stɪr- ~way weɪ
steers|man 'stɪəz |mən ‖ 'stɪrz- ~men mən
men

Stefan 'stef ᵊn -æn
Stefanie 'stef ᵊn i
Steffens 'stef ᵊnz
stegodon 'steg ə dɒn ‖ -dɑːn ~s z
stegosaur 'steg ə sɔː ‖ -sɔːr ~s z
stegosaurus ˌsteg ə 'sɔːr əs ~es ɪz əz
Steiger 'staɪg ə ‖ -ᵊr
stein staɪn—Ger [ʃtain] steins staɪnz
Stein (i) staɪn, (ii) stiːn—but as a German
   name, ʃtaɪn —Ger [ʃtain]
Steinbeck 'staɪn bek→'staɪm-
Steinberg 'staɪn bɜːg→'staɪm- ‖ -bɝːg
steinbock, steinbok 'staɪn bɒk→'staɪm-, -bʌk
   ‖ -bɑːk ~s s
Steine place in Brighton, Sx stiːn
Steinem 'staɪn əm
Steiner 'staɪn ə ‖ -ᵊr—Ger ['ʃtai nɐ]
Steinway tdmk 'staɪn weɪ ~s z
Stelazine tdmk 'stel ə ziːn
stel|a 'stiːl |ə ~ae iː
stele (i) 'stiːl i -iː (ii) stiːᵊl—in archaeology
   usually (i), in botany usually (ii)   steles (i)
   'stiːl iz -iːz (ii) stiːᵊlz
Stella 'stel ə
stellar 'stel ə ‖ -ᵊr
stellate adj 'stel eɪt -ət, -ɪt
Steller 'stel ə ‖ -ᵊr ~'s z
   ˌSteller's 'jay
St Elmo sᵊnt 'elm əʊ §sᵊn- ‖ seɪnt 'elm oʊ ~'s
   z
   St ˌElmo's 'fire
stem stem stemmed stemd stemming
   'stem ɪŋ stems stemz
stemm|a 'stem| ə ~ata ət ə ‖ əṱ ə
-stemmed 'stemd— long-stemmed
   ˌlɒŋ 'stemd ◄ ‖ ˌlɔːŋ- ˌlɑːŋ-
stemware 'stem weə ‖ -wer -wær
Sten sten
   'Sten gun
stench stentʃ stenches 'stentʃ ɪz -əz
stencil 'stenᵗs ᵊl -ɪl ~ed, ~led d ~ing, ~ling
   ɪŋ ~s z
Stendhal 'stɒnd ɑːl ‖ sten 'dɑːl—Fr [stɑ̃ dal],
   though popularly believed in Britain to be [stɒ̃-]
Stenhousemuir ˌsten haʊs 'mjʊə -əs-, -'mjɔː
   ‖ -'mjʊᵊr
steno 'sten əʊ ‖ -oʊ ~s z
steno- comb. form
   with stress-neutral suffix ˌsten əʊ ‖ -ə —
   stenothermal ˌsten əʊ 'θɜːm ᵊl ◄ ‖ -ə 'θɝːm-
   with stress-imposing suffix ste 'nɒ+ stə-
   ‖ -'nɑː+ — stenophagous ste 'nɒf əg əs
   stə- ‖ -'nɑːf-
stenograph 'sten ə grɑːf -græf ‖ -græf ~ed t
   ~ing ɪŋ ~s s
stenographer stə 'nɒg rəf ə ste-
   ‖ -'nɑːg rəf ᵊr ~s z
stenographic ˌsten ə 'græf ɪk ◄ ~ally ᵊl_i
stenography stə 'nɒg rəf i ste- ‖ -'nɑːg-
stenos|is ste 'nəʊs |ɪs stɪ-, stə-, §-əs ‖ -'noʊs-
   ~es iːz
stenotype, S~ tdmk 'sten əʊ taɪp ‖ -ə- ~s s
stenotypist 'sten əʊ taɪp ɪst §-əst ‖ '•ə- ~s s

stenotypy 'sten əʊ taɪp i ‖ '•ə-
stent stent
Stentor, S~ 'stent ɔː -ə ‖ 'stent ɔːr 'stenṱ ᵊr ~s
   z
stentorian sten 'tɔːr i_ən ‖ -'toʊr-
step step stepped stept stepping 'step ɪŋ
   steps steps
step- ˌstep—Compounds of step- not listed below
   mostly have late stress, thus ˌstep'grandson.
stepbrother 'step ˌbrʌð ə ‖ -ᵊr ~s z
step-by-step ˌstep baɪ 'step ◄
step|child 'step ˌtʃaɪᵊld ~children ˌtʃ ɪldr ən
stepdaughter 'step ˌdɔːt ə ‖ -ˌdɔːṱ ᵊr -ˌdɑːṱ- ~s
   z
step-down 'step daʊn ~s z
stepfather 'step ˌfɑːð ə ‖ -ᵊr ~s z
Stepford 'step fəd ‖ -fᵊrd
Stephanie 'stef ᵊn i
stephanotis ˌstef ə 'nəʊt ɪs §-əs ‖ -'noʊṱ əs
Stephen 'stiːv ᵊn
Stephens 'stiːv ᵊnz
Stephenson 'stiːv ᵊn sᵊn
step-in 'step ɪn ~s z
Stepinac 'step ɪ næts -ə- —Croatian
   [ˌstɛ 'pi nats]
stepladder 'step ˌlæd ə ‖ -ᵊr ~s z
stepmother 'step ˌmʌð ə ‖ -ᵊr ~s z
Stepney 'step ni
   ˌStepney 'Green
stepparent 'step ˌpeər ənt ‖ -ˌper- -ˌpær- ~s s
steppe step (= step) steppes steps
stepper 'step ə ‖ -ᵊr ~s z
stepping-stone 'step ɪŋ stəʊn ‖ -stoʊn ~s z
stepsister 'step ˌsɪst ə ‖ -ᵊr ~s z
stepson 'step sʌn ~s z
Steptoe 'step təʊ ‖ -toʊ
step-up 'step ʌp ~s s
stepwise 'step waɪz
-ster stress-neutral stə ‖ stᵊr— songster
   'sɒŋᵏst ə 'sɒŋ stə ‖ 'sɔːŋᵏst ᵊr 'sɑːŋᵏst-;
   'sɔːŋ stᵊr, 'sɑːŋ-
Steradent tdmk 'ster ə dent
steradian stə 'reɪd i_ən ~s z
stercoraceous ˌstɜːk ə 'reɪʃ əs ◄ ‖ ˌstɝːk-

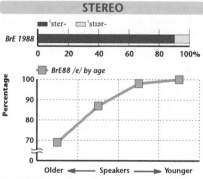

STEREO

	'ster-	'stɪər-
BrE 1988		

0   20   40   60   80   100%

BrE88 /e/ by age

Percentage
100
90
80
70
0

Older ◄———— Speakers ————► Younger

stereo 'ster i əʊ 'stɪər- ‖ 'ster i oʊ 'stɪr-
   —BrE 1988 poll panel preference: 'ster- 90%,
   'stɪər- 10%. ~s z

stereo- *comb. form*
  with stress-neutral suffix ˌster i əʊ ˌstɪər-
  ‖ ˌster i oʊ ˌstɪr- — **stereoisomer**
  ˌster i əʊ ˈaɪs əʊm ə ˌstɪər-
  ‖ ˌster i oʊ ˈaɪs əm ᵊr ˌstɪr-
  with stress-imposing suffix ˌster i ˈɒ+ ˌstɪər-
  ‖ ˌster i ˈɑː+ ˌstɪr- — **stereography**
  ˌster i ˈɒg rəf i ˌstɪər- ‖ ˌster i ˈɑːg- ˌstɪr-
stereobate ˈster i əʊ beɪt ˈstɪər- ‖ ˈster i oʊ-
  ˈstɪr- ~**s** s
stereophonic ˌster i‿ə ˈfɒn ɪk ◂ ˌstɪər-, -i əʊ-
  ‖ ˌster i‿ə ˈfɑːn ɪk ◂ ˌstɪr- ~**ally** ᵊl‿i
stereoscope ˈster i‿ə skəʊp ˈstɪər-, -i əʊ-
  ‖ ˈster i‿ə skoʊp ˈstɪr- ~**s** s
stereoscopic ˌster i‿ə ˈskɒp ɪk ◂ ˌstɪər-, -i əʊ-
  ‖ ˌster i‿ə ˈskɑːp ɪk ◂ ˌstɪr- ~**ally** ᵊl‿i
stereotyp|e ˈster i‿ə taɪp ˈstɪər- ‖ ˈstɪr- ~**ed** t
  ~**er/s** ə/z ‖ ᵊr/z ~**es** s ~**ing** ɪŋ
stereotypical ˌster i‿ə ˈtɪp ɪk ᵊl ◂ ˌstɪər-,
  -i əʊ- ‖ ˌstɪr- ~**ly** ‿i
stereotypy ˈster i‿ə taɪp i ˈstɪər- ‖ ˈstɪr-
Stergene *tdmk* ˈstɜːdʒ iːn ‖ ˈstɜ˞ːdʒ-
steric ˈster ɪk ˈstɪər- ‖ ˈstɪr-
sterilant ˈster əl ənt -ɪl- ~**s** s
sterile ˈster aɪᵊl ‖ ˈster əl (*) ~**ly** li ~**ness** nəs
  nɪs
sterility stə ˈrɪl ət i ste-, -ɪt i ‖ -ət̬ i
sterilis... —*see* **steriliz...**
sterilization ˌster əl aɪ ˈzeɪʃ ᵊn ˌˌɪl-, -ɪˈ•-
  ‖ -əˈ•- ~**s** z
steriliz|e ˈster ə laɪz -ɪ- ~**ed** d ~**es** ɪz əz ~**ing**
  ɪŋ
sterling, S~ ˈstɜːl ɪŋ ‖ ˈstɜ˞ːl ɪŋ
stern stɜːn ‖ stɜ˞ːn **sterner** ˈstɜːn ə ‖ ˈstɜ˞ːn ᵊr
  sternest ˈstɜːn ɪst -əst ‖ ˈstɜ˞ːn əst
Stern stɜːn ‖ stɜ˞ːn —*but as a German name,*
  ʃteən ‖ ʃtern —*Ger* [ʃtɛʁn]
sterna ˈstɜːn ə ‖ ˈstɜ˞ːn ə
Sterne stɜːn ‖ stɜ˞ːn
sternly ˈstɜːn li ‖ ˈstɜ˞ːn li
sternmost ˈstɜːn məʊst →ˈstɜːm-
  ‖ ˈstɜ˞ːn moʊst
sternness ˈstɜːn nəs -nɪs ‖ ˈstɜ˞ːn-
sternpost ˈstɜːn pəʊst →ˈstɜːm-
  ‖ ˈstɜ˞ːn poʊst ~**s** s
stern|um ˈstɜːn |əm ‖ ˈstɜ˞ːn |əm ~**a** ə
sternutation ˌstɜːn ju ˈteɪʃ ᵊn ‖ ˌstɜ˞ːn jə- ~**s** z
sternutator|y ˌstɜːn ju ˈteɪt ᵊr li
  stɜː ˈnjuːt ət‿ᵊr li ‖ stᵊr ˈnuːt̬ ə tɔːr li -ˈnjuːt̬-,
  -toʊr i ~**ies** iz
steroid ˈstɪər ɔɪd ˈster- ‖ ˈstɪr- ~**s** z
sterol ˈstɪər ɒl ˈster- ‖ ˈstɪr ɔːl -ɑːl, -oʊl ~**s** z
stertor ˈstɜːt ə ‖ ˈstɜ˞ːt̬ ᵊr
stertorous ˈstɜːt ᵊr əs ‖ ˈstɜ˞ːt̬- ~**ly** li ~**ness**
  nəs nɪs
stet stet **stets** stets **stetted** ˈstet ɪd -əd
  ‖ ˈstet̬ əd **stetting** ˈstet ɪŋ ‖ ˈstet̬ ɪŋ
stethoscope ˈsteθ ə skəʊp ‖ -skoʊp ~**s** s
stethoscopic ˌsteθ ə ˈskɒp ɪk ◂ ‖ -ˈskɑːp- ~**ally**
  ᵊl‿i
stethoscopy ste ˈθɒsk əp i ‖ -ˈθɑːsk-
stetson, S~ ˈstets ᵊn ~**s** z
Steuart ˈstjuː‿ət →§ˈstʃuː‿ ‖ ˈstuː ᵊrt ˈstjuː-

Steuben ˈstjuːb ən →§ˈstʃuːb- ‖ ˈstuːb ən
  ˈstjuːb-; stu ˈben, stju-
Stevas ˈstiːv əs -æs
Steve stiːv
stevedore ˈstiːv ə dɔː -ɪ- ‖ -dɔːr -doʊr ~**d** d
  ~**s** z **stevedoring** ˈstiːv ə dɔːr ɪŋ
  ˈ•ɪ- ‖ -doʊr ɪŋ
Stevenage ˈstiːv ᵊn ɪdʒ
Steven ˈstiːv ᵊn
Stevens ˈstiːv ᵊnz
Stevenson ˈstiːv ᵊn sᵊn
Steventon ˈstiːv ᵊn tən
Stevie ˈstiːv i
stew stjuː →§stʃuː ‖ stuː stjuː **stewed** stjuːd
  →§stʃuːd ‖ stuːd stjuːd **stewing** ˈstjuː‿ɪŋ
  →§ˈstʃuː‿ ‖ ˈstuː ɪŋ ˈstjuː- **stews** stjuːz
  →§stʃuːz ‖ stuːz stjuːz
steward, S~ ˈstjuː‿əd →§ˈstʃuː‿ ‖ ˈstuː ᵊrd
  ˈstjuː ~**ed** ɪd əd ~**ing** ɪŋ ~**s** z
stewardess ˌstjuː‿ə ˈdes →§ˌstʃuː‿, ˈ•••,
  ‿ə dɪs, §‿ə dəs ‖ ˈstuː ᵊrd əs ~**es** ɪz əz
stewardship ˈstjuː‿əd ʃɪp →§ˈstʃuː‿
  ‖ ˈstuː ᵊrd ʃɪp ˈstjuː ~**s** s
Stewart ˈstjuː‿ət →§ˈstʃuː‿ ‖ ˈstuː ᵊrt ˈstjuː
stewpan ˈstjuː pæn →§ˈstʃuː- ‖ ˈstuː- ˈstjuː-
  ~**s** z
Steyn *family name* staɪn
Steyne *place name* stiːn
Steyning ˈsten ɪŋ
St Fagan's sᵊnt ˈfæg ənz ‖ seɪnt-
St George sᵊnt ˈdʒɔːdʒ ‖ seɪnt ˈdʒɔːrdʒ ~**'s** ɪz
  əz
     St ˌGeorge's ˈChannel
St Gotthard sᵊnt ˈgɒt əd -ɑːd ‖ seɪnt ˈgɑːt̬ ᵊrd
  —*Ger* [zaŋkt ˈgɔt haʁt]
St Helena *name of saint* sᵊnt ˈhel ən ə §sᵊn-,
  -ɪn ə; -hɪ ˈliːn ə, -hə'•- ‖ seɪnt-
St Helena *name of island* ˌsent hɪ ˈliːn ə sᵊnt-,
  -hə-, -ˈleɪn ə
St Helens sᵊnt ˈhel ənz §sᵊn-, -ɪnz ‖ seɪnt-
St Helier sᵊnt ˈhel i‿ə §sᵊn- ‖ seɪnt ˈhel jᵊr
sthenic ˈsθen ɪk
stibine ˈstɪb aɪn ‖ -iːn
stibnite ˈstɪb naɪt
Stich ʃtiːk —*Ger* [ʃtɪç]
stichometry stɪ ˈkɒm ətr i §stə-, -ɪtr i
  ‖ -ˈkɑːm-
stichomythia ˌstɪk əʊ ˈmɪθ i‿ə ‖ ˌ•ə-
stick stɪk **sticking** ˈstɪk ɪŋ **sticks** stɪks **stuck**
  stʌk
  ˈsticking ˌplaster; ˈsticking point; ˈstick
  ˌinsect; ˈstick shift
sticker ˈstɪk ə ‖ -ᵊr ~**s** z
stick-in-the-mud ˈstɪk ɪn ðə ˌmʌd §ˈ•ən-
  ‖ ˈstɪk ən- ~**s** z
stickleback ˈstɪk ᵊl bæk ~**s** s
Sticklepath ˈstɪk ᵊl pɑːθ §-pæθ ‖ -pæθ
stickler ˈstɪk lə ‖ -lᵊr ~**s** z
stick-on ˈstɪk ɒn ‖ -ɑːn -ɔːn
stickpin ˈstɪk pɪn ~**s** z
stickum ˈstɪk əm ~**s** z
stick-up ˈstɪk ʌp ~**s** s

stick|y 'stɪk |i **~ier** i‿ə ‖ i‿ər **~iest** i‿ɪst i‿əst
~ily ɪ li əl i **~iness** i nəs i nɪs
ˌsticky 'end; ˌsticky 'wicket

stie... —*see* **sty**

stiff stɪf **stiffer** 'stɪf ə ‖ -ər **stiffest** 'stɪf ɪst
-əst
ˌstiff ˌupper 'lip

stiffen 'stɪf ən **~ed** d **~ing** ɪŋ **~s** z

stiffener 'stɪf ən‿ə ‖ ‿ər **~s** z

Stiffkey 'stɪf ki: —*formerly also* 'stjuːk i,
'stuːk i

stiffly 'stɪf li

stiffie 'stɪf i **~s** z

stiff-necked ˌstɪf 'nekt ◄

stiffness 'stɪf nəs -nɪs **~es** ɪz əz

stifl|e 'staɪf əl **~ed** d **~es** z **~ing/ly** ɪŋ /li

stigma 'stɪg mə **~s** z **stigmata** 'stɪg mət ə
stɪg 'maːt ə ‖ stɪg 'maːt ə 'stɪg mət ə

stigmatic stɪg 'mæt ɪk ‖ -'mæt- **~s** s

stigmatis... —*see* **stigmatiz...**

stigmatization ˌstɪg mət aɪ 'zeɪʃ ən -ɪ'•-
‖ -mət ə- **~s** z

stigmatiz|e 'stɪg mə taɪz **~ed** d **~es** ɪz əz
~ing ɪŋ

stilb stɪlb

stilbene 'stɪlb iːn

stilbestrol stɪl 'biːs trɒl -'bes-, -trəl
‖ -'bes trɔːl -traːl, -troʊl

stilbite 'stɪlb aɪt

stilboestrol stɪl 'biːs trɒl -'bes-, -trəl
‖ -'bes trɔːl -traːl, -troʊl

stile staɪəl (= *style*) **stiles** staɪəlz

Stiles staɪəlz

stiletto stɪ 'let əʊ stə- ‖ -'let oʊ **~s** z
stiˌletto 'heel

Stilgoe 'stɪlg əʊ ‖ -oʊ

Stilicho 'stɪl i kəʊ ‖ -koʊ

still stɪl **stilled** stɪld **stiller** 'stɪl ə ‖ 'stɪl ər
stillest 'stɪl ɪst -əst **stilling** 'stɪl ɪŋ **stills**
stɪlz
ˌstill 'life

stillbirth 'stɪl bɜːθ ˌ•'• ‖ -bɝːθ **~s** s

stillborn 'stɪl bɔːn ˌ•'• ‖ -bɔːrn

stillness 'stɪl nəs -nɪs **~es** ɪz əz

stillroom 'stɪl ruːm -rʊm **~s** z

Stillson 'stɪls ən
'Stillson wrench *tdmk*

stilly *adj* 'stɪl i

stilly *adv* 'stɪl li

stilt stɪlt **stilts** stɪlts

stilted 'stɪlt ɪd -əd **~ly** li **~ness** nəs nɪs

Stilton, s~ 'stɪlt ən

Stimson 'stɪmps ən

stimulant 'stɪm jʊl ənt -jəl- ‖ -jəl- **~s** s

stimu|late 'stɪm ju |leɪt -jə- ‖ -jə- **~lated**
leɪt ɪd -əd ‖ leɪt əd **~lates** leɪts **~lating**
leɪt ɪŋ ‖ leɪt ɪŋ

stimulation ˌstɪm ju 'leɪʃ ən -jə- ‖ -jə- **~s** z

stimulative 'stɪm jʊl ət ɪv -ju leɪt ɪv
‖ -jə leɪt ɪv

stimulator 'stɪm ju leɪt ə ˌ•'• jə- ‖ -jə leɪt ər **~s**
z

stimulus 'stɪm |jʊl əs -jəl əs ‖ -|jəl əs **~uli**
ju laɪ jə-, -liː ‖ jə-

stimy 'staɪm i **stimied** 'staɪm id **stimies**
'staɪm iz **stimying** 'staɪm i ɪŋ

sting stɪŋ **stinging** 'stɪŋ ɪŋ **stings** stɪŋz
stung stʌŋ
'stinging ˌnettle

stinger 'stɪŋ ə ‖ -ər **~s** z

stingi... —*see* **stingy**

stingo 'stɪŋ gəʊ ‖ -goʊ

stingray 'stɪŋ reɪ **~s** z

sting|y *'ungenerous'* 'stɪndʒ |i **~ier** i‿ə ‖ i‿ər
~iest i‿ɪst i‿əst **~ily** ɪ li əl i **~iness** i nəs i nɪs

stingy *'having a sting'* 'stɪŋ i

stink stɪŋk **stank** stæŋk **stinking/ly**
'stɪŋk ɪŋ /li **stinks** stɪŋks **stunk** stʌŋk

stink-bomb 'stɪŋk bɒm ‖ -baːm **~s** z

stinker 'stɪŋk ə ‖ -ər **~s** z

stinkhorn 'stɪŋk hɔːn ‖ -hɔːrn **~s** z

stinkpot 'stɪŋk pɒt ‖ -paːt **~s** s

stint stɪnt **stinted** 'stɪnt ɪd -əd ‖ 'stɪnt əd
stinting 'stɪnt ɪŋ ‖ 'stɪnt ɪŋ **stints** stɪnts

stipe staɪp **stipes** staɪps

stipend 'staɪp end -ənd **~s** z

stipendiar|y staɪ 'pend i‿ər i stɪ-,
⚠-'pend ər i ‖ -i er i **~ies** iz
stiˌpendiary 'magistrate

stipes *sing.* 'staɪp iːz

stippl|e 'stɪp əl **~ed** d **~es** z **~ing** ɪŋ

stipu|late *v* 'stɪp ju |leɪt -jə- ‖ -jə- **~lated**
leɪt ɪd -əd ‖ leɪt əd **~lates** leɪts **~lating**
leɪt ɪŋ ‖ leɪt ɪŋ

stipulation ˌstɪp ju 'leɪʃ ən -jə- ‖ -jə- **~s** z

stipulatory 'stɪp jʊl ət‿ər i ˌstɪp ju 'leɪt ər i
‖ 'stɪp jəl ə tɔːr i -toʊr i

stipule 'stɪp juːl **~s** z

stir stɜː ‖ stɝː **stirred** stɜːd ‖ stɝːd **stirring/
ly** 'stɜːr ɪŋ /li ‖ 'stɝː- **stirs** stɜːz ‖ stɝːz

stir-crazy ˌstɜː 'kreɪz i ‖ ˌstɝː-

stir-|fry ˌstɜː |'fraɪ ‖ ˌstɝː- **~fried** 'fraɪd ◄
~fries 'fraɪz **~frying** 'fraɪ ɪŋ

Stirling 'stɜːl ɪŋ ‖ 'stɝːl ɪŋ

stirps stɜːps ‖ stɝːps **stirpes**
'stɜːp iːz ‖ 'stɝːp iːz

stirr... —*see* **stir**

stirrer 'stɜːr ə ‖ 'stɝː ər **~s** z

stirrup 'stɪr əp ‖ 'stɝː əp 'stɪr- (*) **~s** s
'stirrup cup; 'stirrup pump

stitch stɪtʃ **stitched** stɪtʃt **stitches** 'stɪtʃ ɪz
-əz **stitching** 'stɪtʃ ɪŋ

stitchwort 'stɪtʃ wɜːt §-wɔːt ‖ -wɝːt -wɔːrt
~s s

St Ivel *tdmk* sənt 'aɪv əl §sən- ‖ seɪnt-

St Ives sənt 'aɪvz §sən- ‖ seɪnt-

Stivichall 'staɪtʃ əl -ɔːl (!)

St James sənt 'dʒeɪmz §sənt- **St James's** sənt
'dʒeɪmz ɪz -əz; sənt 'dʒeɪmz ‖ seɪnt-

St John sənt 'dʒɒn ‖ seɪnt 'dʒaːn —*but as a
surname also* 'sɪndʒ ən

St John's sənt 'dʒɒnz ‖ seɪnt 'dʒaːnz
St 'John's wort

St Kilda sənt 'kɪld ə →sən- ‖ seɪnt-

St Kitts sənt 'kɪts →sən- ‖ seɪnt-

St Kitts-Nevis sənt ˌkɪts ˈniːv ɪs →sᵊŋ-, §-əs
‖ seɪnt-
St Laurent ˌsæn lɒ ˈrɒ̃ -lɔː:-, -lə-, -ˈrɑːnt
‖ -loʊ ˈrɑːn -lɔː:-, -lɑː- —*Fr* [sæ̃ lɔ ʁɑ̃]
St Leger sənt ˈledʒ ə ‖ seɪnt ˈledʒ ᵊr —*but as a
surname also* ˈsel ɪndʒ ə, -əndʒ- ‖ -ᵊr
St Louis sənt ˈluːˌɪs ˌi, §_əs ‖ seɪnt-
St Lucia sənt ˈluːʃ ə -ˈluːʃ i_ə, -ˈluːs- ‖ seɪnt-
St Malo sæ ˈmɑːl əʊ sæn-, sᵊnt-
‖ ˌsæn mɑː ˈloʊ —*Fr* [sæ̃ ma lo]
St Mary Axe sənt ˌmeər i ˈæks ‖ seɪnt ˌmer i-
-ˌmær- —*formerly* ˌsɪm ᵊr i ˈæks
St Moritz ˌsæn mə ˈrɪts →sæm-; sənt ˈmɒr ɪts
‖ -moʊ- —*Ger* Sankt Moritz [zaŋkt ˈmoː ʁɪts,
-mo ˈʁɪts]
St Neots sənt ˈniːˌəts -ˈniːts ‖ seɪnt-
stoa ˈstəʊ ə ‖ ˈstoʊ ə ~s z
stoat stəʊt stoʊt **stoats** stəʊts ‖ stoʊts
Stobart ˈstəʊb ɑːt ‖ ˈstoʊb ɑːrt
Stobie ˈstəʊb i ‖ ˈstoʊb i
stochastic stə ˈkæst ɪk stɒ- ‖ stoʊ- **~ally** ᵊl_i
stock, Stock stɒk ‖ stɑːk **stocked**
stɒkt ‖ stɑːkt **stocking** ˈstɒk ɪŋ ‖ ˈstɑːk ɪŋ
stocks stɒks ‖ stɑːks
ˈstock cerˌtificate; ˈstock cube; ˈstock
exˌchange; ˈstock ˌmarket
stockad|e stɒ ˈkeɪd ‖ stɑː- **~ed** ɪd əd **~es** z
~ing ɪŋ
stockbreeder ˈstɒk ˌbriːd ə ‖ ˈstɑːk ˌbriːd ᵊr
~s z
Stockbridge ˈstɒk brɪdʒ ‖ ˈstɑːk-
stockbroker ˈstɒk ˌbrəʊk ə ‖ ˈstɑːk ˌbroʊk ᵊr
~s z
ˈstockbroker belt
stockbrokerage ˈstɒk ˌbrəʊk ᵊr ɪdʒ
‖ ˈstɑːk ˌbroʊk ᵊr_ɪdʒ
stockbroking ˈstɒk ˌbrəʊk ɪŋ ‖ ˈstɑːk ˌbroʊk ɪŋ
stockcar ˈstɒk kɑː ‖ ˈstɑːk kɑːr ~s z
Stockdale ˈstɒk deɪᵊl ‖ ˈstɑːk-
stockfish ˈstɒk fɪʃ ‖ ˈstɑːk-
Stockhausen ˈʃtɒk ˌhaʊz ᵊn ˈstɒk- ‖ ˈʃtɑːk-
—*Ger* [ˈʃtɔk haʊ zᵊn]
stockholder ˈstɒk ˌhəʊld ə →-ˌhɒʊld-
‖ ˈstɑːk ˌhoʊld ᵊr ~s z
Stockholm ˈstɒk həʊm §-həʊlm ‖ ˈstɑːk hoʊm
-hoʊlm —*Swed* [ˈstɔk hɔlm]
stockinet, stockinette ˌstɒk ɪ ˈnet -ə- ‖ ˌstɑːk-
stocking ˈstɒk ɪŋ ‖ ˈstɑːk ɪŋ **~ed** d ~s z
stocking-filler ˈstɒk ɪŋ ˌfɪl ə ‖ ˈstɑːk ɪŋ ˌfɪl ᵊr
~s z
stock-in-trade ˌstɒk ɪn ˈtreɪd §-ən- ‖ ˌstɑːk
ən- ⋅•⋅, ⋅•
stockist ˈstɒk ɪst §-əst ‖ ˈstɑːk əst ~s s
stockjobber ˈstɒk ˌdʒɒb ə ‖ ˈstɑːk ˌdʒɑːb ᵊr ~s
z
Stockley ˈstɒk li ‖ ˈstɑːk li
stock|man ˈstɒk |mən -mæn ‖ ˈstɑːk- **~men**
mən men
stockpil|e ˈstɒk paɪᵊl ‖ ˈstɑːk- **~ed** d **~es** z
~ing ɪŋ
Stockport ˈstɒk pɔːt ‖ ˈstɑːk pɔːrt -poʊrt
stockpot ˈstɒk pɒt ‖ ˈstɑːk pɑːt ~s s
stockroom ˈstɒk ruːm -rʊm ‖ ˈstɑːk- ~s z

Stocks stɒks ‖ stɑːks
Stocksbridge ˈstɒks brɪdʒ ‖ ˈstɑːks-
stock-still ˌstɒk ˈstɪl ◂ ‖ ˌstɑːk-
stocktaking ˈstɒk ˌteɪk ɪŋ ‖ ˈstɑːk-
Stockton ˈstɒkt ən ‖ ˈstɑːkt ən
Stockton-on-Tees
ˌstɒkt ən ɒn ˈtiːz ‖ ˌstɑːkt ən ɑːn- -ɔːn'⋅
Stockwell ˈstɒk wel -wəl ‖ ˈstɑːk-
Stockwood ˈstɒk wʊd ‖ ˈstɑːk-
stock|y ˈstɒk |i ‖ ˈstɑːk |i **~ier** i_ə ‖ i_ᵊr **~iest**
i_ɪst i_əst **~ily** ɪ li əl i **~iness** i nəs i nɪs
stockyard ˈstɒk jɑːd ‖ ˈstɑːk jɑːrd ~s z
Stoddard ˈstɒd əd ‖ ˈstɑːd ᵊrd
Stoddart ˈstɒd ət ‖ ˈstɑːd ᵊrt
stodge stɒdʒ ‖ stɑːdʒ **stodged**
stɒdʒd ‖ stɑːdʒd **stodges** ˈstɒdʒ ɪz -əz
‖ ˈstɑːdʒ əz **stodging** ˈstɒdʒ ɪŋ ‖ ˈstɑːdʒ ɪŋ
stodg|y ˈstɒdʒ |i ‖ ˈstɑːdʒ |i **~ier** i_ə ‖ i_ᵊr
~iest i_ɪst i_əst **~ily** ɪ li əl i **~iness** i nəs i nɪs
stoep stuːp stʊp **stoeps** stuːps stʊps
stog|ey, stog|y ˈstəʊg |i ‖ ˈstoʊg |i **~ies** iz
Stogumber stə ˈgʌm bə stəʊ-; ˈstɒg əm-
‖ -bᵊr
Stogursey stə ˈgɜːz i stəʊ- ‖ -ˈgɜ˞ːz i
stoic, Stoic ˈstəʊ ɪk ‖ ˈstoʊ ɪk ~s s
stoical ˈstəʊ ɪk ᵊl ‖ ˈstoʊ- **~ly** _i
stoichiometric ˌstɔɪk i_ə ˈmetr ɪk ◂
-əʊ-⋅•- ‖ -oʊ-⋅•- **~ally** ᵊl_i
stoichiometry ˌstɔɪk i ˈɒm ətr i -ɪtr i ‖ -ˈɑːm-
stoicism ˈstəʊ ɪ ˌsɪz əm -ə- ‖ ˈstoʊ ə-
stoke, Stoke stəʊk ‖ stoʊk **stoked**
stəʊkt ‖ stoʊkt **stokes** stəʊks ‖ stoʊks
stoking ˈstəʊk ɪŋ ‖ ˈstoʊk ɪŋ
ˌStoke ˈd'Abernon ˈdæb ən ən ‖ ˈdɑːb-
‖ -ᵊrn-; ˌStoke ˈMandeville; ˌStoke ˈPoges
ˈpəʊdʒ ɪz -əz ‖ ˈpoʊdʒ əz
stokehold ˈstəʊk həʊld →-hɒʊld
‖ ˈstoʊk hoʊld ~s z
stokehole ˈstəʊk həʊl →-hɒʊl ‖ ˈstoʊk hoʊl
~s z
Stoke-on-Trent
ˌstəʊk ɒn ˈtrent ◂ ‖ ˌstoʊk ɑːn- -ɔːn-
stoker ˈstəʊk ə ‖ ˈstoʊk ᵊr ~s z
Stokes stəʊks ‖ stoʊks **Stokes'** stəʊks
ˈstəʊks ɪz, -əz ‖ stoʊks ˈstoʊks əz
Stokowski stə ˈkɒf ski -ˈkɒv- ‖ -ˈkɔːf- -ˈkɑːf-;
-ˈkaʊsk i
STOL, stol stɒl ˈest ɒl ‖ stɑːl stɔːl; ˈest ɔːl, -ɑːl
St Olaves sənt ˈɒl əvz §sən-, -ɪvz ‖ seɪnt ˈɑːl-
stole stəʊl →stɒʊl ‖ stoʊl **stoles** stəʊlz
→stɒʊlz ‖ stoʊlz
stolen ˈstəʊl ən →ˈstɒʊl- ‖ ˈstoʊl ən
stolid ˈstɒl ɪd §-əd ‖ ˈstɑːl əd **~ly** li **~ness** nəs
nɪs
stolidity stə ˈlɪd ət i stɒ-, -ɪt i ‖ -əɾ i stɑː-
Stoll *(i)* stɒl ‖ stɑːl stɔːl, *(ii)* stəʊl →stɒʊl
‖ stoʊl
stollen ˈstɒl ən ‖ ˈstoʊl ən ˈstɔːl-, ˈstɑːl-, ˈstʌl-
—*Ger* [ˈʃtɔl ən] ~s z
stolon ˈstəʊl ɒn -ən ‖ ˈstoʊl ən -ɑːn ~s z
Stolport, STOLport ˈstɒl pɔːt ‖ ˈstɔːl pɔːrt
ˈstɑːl-, -poʊrt ~s s

stoma 'stəʊm ə ‖ 'stoʊm ə ~s z **stomata**
'stəʊm ət ə 'stɒm-; stəʊ 'maːt ə
‖ 'stoʊm ət ə 'staːm-; stoʊ 'maːt ə

stomach 'stʌm ək §-ɪk ~**ed** t ~**s** s ~**ing** ɪŋ
'stomach pump

stomachache 'stʌm ək eɪk §-ɪk- ~**s** s

stomacher 'stʌm ək ə §-ɪk- ‖ -ᵊr —*formerly*
-ətʃ-, -ədʒ- ~**s** z

stomachful 'stʌm ək fʊl §-ɪk- ~**s** z

stomachic stə 'mæk ɪk stəʊ-; 'stʌm ək-

stomata 'stəʊm ət ə 'stɒm-; stəʊ 'maːt ə
‖ 'stoʊm ət ə 'staːm-; stoʊ 'maːt ə

stomatitis ˌstəʊm ə 'taɪt ɪs ˌstɒm-, §-əs
‖ ˌstoʊm ə 'taɪt əs ˌstaːm-

stomato- *comb. form*
with stress-neutral suffix ¦stəʊm ət ə ¦stɒm-
‖ ¦stoʊm ət ə stoʊ ¦mæt ə — **stomatoplasty**
'stəʊm ət ə ˌplæst i 'stɒm- ‖ 'stoʊm ət-
stoʊ 'mæt-
with stress-imposing suffix ˌstəʊm ə 'tɒ+
ˌstɒm- ˌstoʊm ə 'taː+ ˌstaːm- —
stomatology ˌstəʊm ə 'tɒl ədʒ i ˌstɒm-
‖ ˌstoʊm ə 'taːl- ˌstaːm-

-stome stəʊm ‖ stoʊm — **cyclostome**
'saɪk ləʊ stəʊm ‖ -lə stoʊm

-stomous *stress-imposing* stəm əs —
monostomous mɒ 'nɒst əm əs mə-
‖ maː 'naːst-

stomp stɒmp ‖ staːmp **stomped**
stɒmpt ‖ staːmpt **stomping**
'stɒmp ɪŋ ‖ 'staːmp ɪŋ **stomps**
stɒmps ‖ staːmps

-stomy *stress-imposing* stəm i — **colostomy**
kə 'lɒst əm i ‖ -'laːst-

stone, Stone stəʊn ‖ stoʊn **stoned**
stəʊnd ‖ stoʊnd **stones** stəʊnz ‖ stoʊnz
stoning 'stəʊn ɪŋ ‖ 'stoʊn ɪŋ
'Stone Age; 'stone fruit; 'stone ˌmarten ;
'stone's throw

stone-blind ˌstəʊn 'blaɪnd ◄ →ˌstəʊm-
‖ ˌstoʊn-

stonebreaker 'stəʊn ˌbreɪk ə →'stəʊm-
‖ 'stoʊn ˌbreɪk ᵊr ~**s** z

Stonebridge 'stəʊn brɪdʒ →'stəʊm- ‖ 'stoʊn-

stonechat 'stəʊn tʃæt ‖ 'stoʊn- ~**s** s

stone-cold ˌstəʊn 'kəʊld ◄ →ˌstəʊŋ-, →-'kʊld
‖ ˌstoʊn 'koʊld ◄

stonecrop 'stəʊn krɒp →'stəʊŋ-
‖ 'stoʊn kraːp ~**s** s

stonecutter 'stəʊn ˌkʌt ə →'stəʊŋ-
‖ 'stoʊn ˌkʌt ᵊr ~**s** z

stone-dead ˌstəʊn 'ded ◄ ‖ ˌstoʊn-

stone-deaf ˌstəʊn 'def ◄ ‖ ˌstoʊn-

stonefish 'stəʊn fɪʃ ‖ 'stoʊn- ~**es** ɪz əz

stone-ground 'stəʊn graʊnd →'stəʊŋ-, ˌ•'•
‖ 'stoʊn-

Stonehaven ˌstəʊn 'heɪv ᵊn ‖ ˌstoʊn- —*There
is also a local pronunciation* ˌsteɪn 'haɪ.

Stonehenge ˌstəʊn 'hendʒ ◄ ‖ 'stoʊn hendʒ

Stonehouse 'stəʊn haʊs ‖ 'stoʊn-

Stoneleigh ˌstəʊn 'liː ‖ ˌstoʊn-

stoneless 'stəʊn ləs -lɪs ‖ 'stoʊn-

stonemason 'stəʊn ˌmeɪs ᵊn →'stəʊm-
‖ 'stoʊn- ~**s** z

stonewall, S~ ˌstəʊn 'wɔːl ◄'•• ‖ 'stoʊn wɔːl
-waːl ~**ed** d ~**er/s** ə/z ‖ ᵊr/z ~**ing** ɪŋ ~**s** z

stoneware 'stəʊn weə ‖ 'stoʊn wer -wær

stonewashed 'stəʊn wɒʃt ˌ•'• ‖ 'stoʊn wɔːʃt
-waːʃt

stonework 'stəʊn wɜːk ‖ 'stoʊn wɝːk

stonk stɒŋk ‖ staːŋk **stonked** stɒŋkt ‖ staːŋkt
stonking 'stɒŋk ɪŋ ‖ 'staːŋk ɪŋ **stonks**
stɒŋks ‖ staːŋks

stonker 'stɒŋk ə ‖ 'staːŋk ᵊr ~**ed** d ~**s** z

stonking 'stɒŋk ɪŋ ‖ 'staːŋk ɪŋ ~**ly** li

Stonor *(i)* 'stəʊn ə ‖ 'stoʊn ᵊr, *(ii)*
'stɒn ə ‖ 'staːn ᵊr

ston|y 'stəʊn |i ‖ 'stoʊn |i ~**ier** i‿ə ‖ i‿ᵊr ~**iest**
i‿ɪst i‿əst ~**ily** ɪ li əl i ~**iness** i nəs i nɪs
ˌstony 'broke; 'Stony Brook *NY*;
ˌStony'Point

stood stʊd

Stoodley 'stuːd li

stooge stuːdʒ **stooged** stuːdʒd **stooges**
'stuːdʒ ɪz -əz **stooging** 'stuːdʒ ɪŋ

stook stuːk stʊk **stooks** stuːks stʊks

stool stuːl **stools** stuːlz

stoolie 'stuːl i ~**s** z

stoolpigeon 'stuːl ˌpɪdʒ ᵊn -ɪn ~**s** z

stoop stuːp **stooped** stuːpt **stooping**
'stuːp ɪŋ **stoops** stuːps

stop stɒp ‖ staːp **stopped** stɒpt ‖ staːpt
stopping 'stɒp ɪŋ ‖ 'staːp ɪŋ **stops**
stɒps ‖ staːps
ˌstop 'press◄

stopcock 'stɒp kɒk ‖ 'staːp kaːk ~**s** s

stope stəʊp ‖ stoʊp **stoped** stəʊpt ‖ stoʊpt
stopes stəʊps ‖ stoʊps **stoping**
'stəʊp ɪŋ ‖ 'stoʊp ɪŋ

Stopes stəʊps ‖ stoʊps

Stopford 'stɒp fəd ‖ 'staːp fᵊrd

stopgap 'stɒp gæp ‖ 'staːp- ~**s** s

stop-go ˌstɒp 'gəʊ ◄ ‖ ˌstaːp 'goʊ ◄

stoplight 'stɒp laɪt ‖ 'staːp- ~**s** s

stoploss 'stɒp lɒs -lɔːs ‖ 'staːp lɔːs -laːs

stopoff 'stɒp ɒf -ɔːf ‖ 'staːp ɔːf -aːf ~**s** s

stopover 'stɒp ˌəʊv ə ‖ 'staːp ˌoʊv ᵊr ~**s** z

stoppag|e 'stɒp ɪdʒ ‖ 'staːp- ~**es** ɪz əz

Stoppard 'stɒp aːd -əd ‖ 'staːp aːrd -ᵊrd

stopper 'stɒp ə ‖ 'staːp ᵊr ~**ed** d **stoppering**
'stɒp ᵊr ɪŋ ‖ 'staːp ᵊr ɪŋ ~**s** z

stopwatch 'stɒp wɒtʃ ‖ 'staːp waːtʃ ~**es** ɪz əz

storage 'stɔːr ɪdʒ ‖ 'stoʊr-
'storage de,vice; 'storage ,heater

storax 'stɔːr æks ‖ 'stoʊr-

store stɔː ‖ stɔːr stoʊr **stored** stɔːd ‖ stɔːrd
stoʊrd **stores** stɔːz ‖ stɔːrz stoʊrz **storing**
'stɔːr ɪŋ ‖ 'stoʊr-
'store de,tective

storefront 'stɔː frʌnt ‖ 'stɔːr- 'stoʊr- ~**s** s

store|house 'stɔː |haʊs ‖ 'stɔːr- 'stoʊr-
~**houses** haʊz ɪz -əz

storekeeper 'stɔː ˌkiːp ə ‖ 'stɔːr ˌkiːp ᵊr 'stoʊr-
~**s** z

S

storeroom 'stɔː ruːm -rʊm ‖ 'stɔːr- 'stoʊr- ~s z

storey, S~ 'stɔːr i ‖ 'stoʊr i *(= story)* ~s z

-storeyed, -storied 'stɔːr id ‖ 'stoʊr id — **three-storeyed, three-storied** ˌθriː 'stɔːr id ◄ ‖ -'stoʊr-

stori... —*see* **story**

stori|ate 'stɔːr i| eɪt ‖'stoʊr- **~ated** eɪt ɪd -əd ‖ -eɪt̬ əd **~ates** eɪts **~ating** eɪt ɪŋ ‖ eɪt̬ ɪŋ

storiation ˌstɔːr i 'eɪʃ ən ˌstoʊr-

stork, Stork stɔːk ‖ stɔːrk **storks** stɔːks ‖ stɔːrks

storksbill 'stɔːks bɪl ‖ 'stɔːrks- ~s z

storm, Storm stɔːm ‖ stɔːrm **stormed** stɔːmd ‖ stɔːrmd **storming** 'stɔːm ɪŋ ‖ 'stɔːrm ɪŋ **storms** stɔːmz ‖ stɔːrmz
  'storm cloud; 'storm cone; 'storm ˌpetrel; 'storm ˌtrooper

stormbound 'stɔːm baʊnd ‖ 'stɔːrm-

Stormont 'stɔː mənt -mɒnt ‖ 'stɔːr- -maːnt

stormproof 'stɔːm pruːf §-prʊf ‖ 'stɔːrm- ~ed t ~ing ɪŋ ~s s

storm|y 'stɔːm |i ‖ 'stɔːrm |i **~ier** i‿ə ‖ i‿ər **~iest** i‿ɪst i‿əst **~ily** ɪ li əl i **~iness** i nəs i nɪs ˌstormy 'petrel

Stornoway 'stɔːn ə weɪ ‖ 'stɔːrn-

Storr stɔː ‖ stɔːr

Storrington 'stɒr ɪŋ tən ‖ 'stɔːr- 'staːr-

Storrs stɔːz ‖ stɔːrz

Stortford 'stɔːt fəd 'stɔː- ‖ 'stɔːrt fərd

Storthing, Storting 'stɔː tɪŋ ‖ 'stɔːr-

story 'stɔːr i ‖ 'stoʊr- **storied** 'stɔːr id ‖ 'stoʊr- **stories** 'stɔːr iz ‖ 'stoʊr- 'story line

storyboard 'stɔːr i bɔːd ‖ -bɔːrd 'stoʊr i boʊrd ~s z

storybook 'stɔːr i bʊk §-buːk ‖ 'stoʊr- ~s s

storyteller 'stɔːr i ˌtel ə ‖ -ər 'stoʊr- ~s z

Storyville 'stɔːr i vɪl ‖ 'stoʊr-

stoss stɒs ʃtɒs ‖ stoʊs staːs, stɔːs —*Ger* [ʃtoːs]

St Osyth sənt 'əʊz ɪθ §sən-, -'əʊs- ‖ seɪnt 'oʊz əθ

stot stɒt ‖ staːt **stots** stɒts ‖ staːts **stotted** 'stɒt ɪd -əd ‖ 'staːt̬ əd **stotting** 'stɒt ɪŋ ‖ 'staːt̬ ɪŋ

stotious 'stəʊʃ əs ‖ 'stoʊʃ əs

Stott stɒt ‖ staːt

Stouffer 'stəʊf ə ‖ 'stoʊf ər (!)

Stoughton (i) 'staʊt ən ‖ 'stoʊt ən, (ii) 'staʊt ən, (iii) 'stɔːt ən ‖ 'staːt- —*For the publishers* Hodder & ~, *(i) is appropriate, although (ii) is probably more often heard.*

stoup stuːp (= stoop) **stoups** stuːps

Stour (i) stʊə ‖ stʊər, (ii) staʊ ə ‖ staʊ ər, (iii) 'staʊ ə ‖ 'stoʊ ər —*The river in Suffolk and Essex is (i), as, usually, is that in Kent. That in Warwickshire is (ii) or (iii). Others are mostly (ii).*

Stourbridge 'staʊ‿ə brɪdʒ 'stəʊ ə- ‖ 'staʊ‿ər-

Stourhead (i) ˌstɔː 'hed ‖ ˌstɔːr- ˌstoʊr-, (ii) ˌstaʊ‿ə 'hed ‖ ˌstaʊ‿ər-

Stourmouth 'staʊ‿ə maʊθ 'stʊə maʊθ ‖ 'staʊ‿ər-

Stourport 'staʊ‿ə pɔːt 'stʊə pɔːt ‖ 'staʊ‿ər pɔːrt -poʊrt

Stourton (i) 'stɜːt ən ‖ 'stɜːt ən, (ii) 'stɔːt ən ‖ 'stɔːrt ən 'stoʊrt-

stoush staʊʃ **stoushed** staʊʃt **stoushes** 'staʊʃ ɪz -əz **stoushing** 'staʊʃ ɪŋ

stout, Stout staʊt **stouter** 'staʊt ə ‖ 'staʊt̬ ər **stoutest** 'staʊt ɪst -əst ‖ 'staʊt̬ əst

stouthearted ˌstaʊt 'haːt ɪd ◄ -əd ‖ -'haːrt̬- ~ly li ~ness nəs nɪs

stoutish 'staʊt ɪʃ ‖ 'staʊt̬ ɪʃ

stout|ly 'staʊt |li ~ness nəs nɪs

stove stəʊv ‖ stoʊv **stoves** stəʊvz ‖ stoʊvz

stovepipe 'stəʊv paɪp ‖ 'stoʊv- ~s s ˌstovepipe 'hat

stover 'stəʊv ə ‖ 'stoʊv ər

stow, Stow stəʊ ‖ stoʊ **stowed** stəʊd ‖ stoʊd **stowing** 'stəʊ ɪŋ ‖ 'stoʊ ɪŋ **stows** stəʊz ‖ stoʊz

stowage 'stəʊ ɪdʒ ‖ 'stoʊ-

stowaway 'stəʊ ə ˌweɪ ‖ 'stoʊ- ~s z

Stowe stəʊ ‖ stoʊ

Stowell 'stəʊ əl ‖ 'stoʊ əl

Stowey 'stəʊ i ‖ 'stoʊ i

Stowmarket 'stəʊ ˌmaːk ɪt §-ət ‖ 'stoʊ ˌmaːrk ət

Stow-on-the-Wold ˌstəʊ ɒn ðə 'wəʊld →-'wɒʊld ‖ ˌstoʊ aːn ðə 'woʊld -ɔːn •-

St Pancras sənt 'pæŋk rəs →səm- ‖ seɪnt-

St Paul sənt 'pɔːl ‖ seɪnt- -'paːl -'s z

St Peter sənt 'piːt ə ‖ seɪnt 'piːt̬ ər ~s z St ˌPeter 'Port

St Petersburg sənt 'piːt əz bɜːg ‖ seɪnt 'piːt̬ ərz bɜːg —*Russ* Sankt Peterburg [ˌsankt pjɪ tjɪr 'burk]

Strabane strə 'bæn

strabismus strə 'bɪz məs stræ-

Strabo 'streɪb əʊ ‖ -oʊ

Strabolgi strə 'bəʊg i ‖ -'boʊg i

Strachan (i) strɔːn ‖ straːn, (ii) 'stræk ən 'stræx-

Strachey 'streɪtʃ i ‖ 'stræx-

Strad stræd **Strads** strædz

Strada *tdmk* 'straːd ə ~s z

Stradbroke 'stræd brʊk →'stræb-, -brəʊk ‖ -broʊk

straddl|e 'stræd əl ~ed d ~es z ~ing ɪŋ

Stradey 'streɪd i

Stradivari ˌstræd ɪ 'vaːr i -ə- ‖ ˌstraːd-

Stradivari|us ˌstræd ɪ 'veər i‿əs ˌ•ə-, -'vaːr- ‖ -'ver- -'vær- ~i aɪ

Stradling 'stræd lɪŋ

strafe straːf streɪf ‖ streɪf **strafed** straːft streɪft ‖ streɪft **strafes** straːfs streɪfs ‖ streɪfs **strafing/s** 'straːf ɪŋ/z 'streɪf- ‖ 'streɪf ɪŋ/z

Strafford 'stræf əd ‖ -ərd

straggl|e 'stræg əl ~ed d ~er/s ə/z ‖ ər/z ~es z ~ing ɪŋ

straggl|y 'stræg əl‿i ~ier i‿ə ‖ i‿ər ~iest i‿ɪst i‿əst

straight streɪt (= *strait*) **straighter**
'streɪt ə ‖ 'streɪt̬ ər **straightest** 'streɪt ɪst
-əst ‖ 'streɪt̬ əst **straights** streɪts
ˌstraight and 'narrow; ˌstraight 'fight;
'straight man
straightaway ˌstreɪt ə 'weɪ ‖ ˌstreɪt̬-
straightedg|e 'streɪt edʒ ‖ 'streɪt̬- **~ed** d **~es**
ɪz əz
straighten 'streɪt ən **~ed** d **~er/s** ə/z ‖ ər/z
~ing ɪŋ **~s** z
straight-faced ˌstreɪt 'feɪst ◄
straightforward ˌstreɪt 'fɔː wəd ◄
‖ -'fɔːr wərd ◄ **~ly** li **~ness** nəs nɪs
straight-out ˌstreɪt 'aʊt ◄ ‖ ˌstreɪt̬-
ˌstraight-out 'answer
straightway 'streɪt weɪ ˌ•'•
strain streɪn **strained** streɪnd **straining**
'streɪn ɪŋ **strains** streɪnz
'strain gauge
strainer 'streɪn ə ‖ -ər **~s** z
strait streɪt **straits** streɪts
straitened 'streɪt ənd
straitjacket 'streɪt ˌdʒæk ɪt §-ət **~s** s
straitlaced ˌstreɪt 'leɪst ◄
strake streɪk **strakes** streɪks
Straker 'streɪk ə ‖ -ər
stramonium strə 'məʊn i_əm ‖ -'moʊn-
strand, Strand strænd **stranded** 'strænd ɪd
-əd **stranding** 'strænd ɪŋ **strands** strændz
Strang stræŋ
strange, Strange streɪndʒ **stranger**
'streɪndʒ ə ‖ -ər **strangest** 'streɪndʒ ɪst -əst
strange|ly 'streɪndʒ |li **~ness** nəs nɪs
stranger 'streɪndʒ ə ‖ -ər **~s** z
Strangeways 'streɪndʒ weɪz
Strangford 'stræŋ fəd ‖ -fərd
strangl|e 'stræŋ gəl **~ed** d **~es** z **~ing** ɪŋ
stranglehold 'stræŋ gəl həʊld →-hɒʊld
‖ -hoʊld **~s** z
strangu|late 'stræŋ gju |leɪt -gjə- ‖ -gjə-
~lated leɪt ɪd -əd ‖ leɪt̬ əd **~lates** leɪts
~lating leɪt ɪŋ ‖ leɪt̬ ɪŋ
strangulation ˌstræŋ gju 'leɪʃ ən -gjə- ‖ -gjə-
~s z
strangury 'stræŋ gjər i -gju³r-
Stranraer ₍ᵢ₎stræn 'rɑː strən- ‖ -'rɑːr
strap stræp **strapped** stræpt **strapping**
'stræp ɪŋ **straps** stræps
straphanger 'stræp ˌhæŋ ə ‖ -ər **~s** z
straphanging 'stræp ˌhæŋ ɪŋ
strapless 'stræp ləs -lɪs
strapline 'stræp laɪn **~s** z
strapper 'stræp ə ‖ -ər **~s** z
strappy 'stræp i
Strasbourg, Strassburg 'stræz bɜːg -bʊəg,
-bɔːg ‖ 'strɑːs bɜːg 'strɑːz-, -bʊrg —*Fr*
[stʁaz buːʁ] —*Ger* Straßburg ['stʁaːs bʊʁk]
strass stræs
strata 'strɑːt ə 'streɪt- ‖ 'streɪt̬ ə 'stræt̬- **~s** z
stratagem 'stræt ədʒ əm -ɪdʒ-; -ə dʒem, -ɪ-
‖ 'stræt̬- **~s** z
stratal 'strɑːt əl 'streɪt- ‖ 'streɪt̬ əl 'stræt̬-
strategic strə 'tiːdʒ ɪk **~al** əl **~ally** əl_i

strategist 'stræt ədʒ ɪst -ɪdʒ-, §-əst ‖ 'stræt̬-
~s s
strateg|y 'stræt ədʒ |i -ɪdʒ- ‖ 'stræt̬- **~ies** iz
Stratford 'stræt fəd ‖ -fərd
Stratford-atte-Bowe ˌstræt fəd ˌæt i 'bəʊ -ə'•
‖ -fərd ˌæt̬ i 'boʊ
Stratford-on-Avon
ˌstræt fəd ɒn 'eɪv ən ‖ -fərd ɑːn 'eɪv ɑːn
-ɔːn'•-
Stratford-upon-Avon
ˌstræt fəd ə ˌpɒn 'eɪv ən ‖ -fərd ə ˌpɑːn 'eɪv ɑːn
-ˌpɔːn-
strath, Strath stræθ strɑːθ **straths** stræθs
Strath- stræθ strəθ —*For many speakers,* stræθ
*functions as the strong form of this prefix, used
in unfamiliar names or careful style, and* strəθ
*as the weak form, appropriate for familiar
names and casual style. This applies in the
entries that follow.*
Strathaven *place in Strathclyde* 'streɪv ən *(!)*
Strathclyde ₍ᵢ₎stræθ 'klaɪd strəθ-
Strathcona stræθ 'kəʊn ə strəθ- ‖ -'koʊn ə
Strathearn stræθ 'ɜːn strəθ- ‖ -'ɜːn
Stratheden stræθ 'iːd ən strəθ-
Strathleven stræθ 'liːv ən strəθ-
Strathmore stræθ 'mɔː strəθ- ‖ -'mɔːr -'moʊr
Strathpeffer stræθ 'pef ə strəθ- ‖ -ər
strathspey, S~ stræθ 'speɪ strəθ- ‖ '•• **~s** z
Strathtay stræθ 'teɪ strəθ-
stratification ˌstræt ɪf ɪ 'keɪʃ ən ˌ•əf-, §-ə'•-
‖ ˌstræt̬- **~al** əl **~ally** əl_i **~s** z
stratiform 'stræt ɪ fɔːm -ə- ‖ 'stræt̬ ə fɔːrm
strati|fy 'stræt ɪ |faɪ -ə- ‖ 'stræt̬- **~fied** faɪd
~fies faɪz **~fying** faɪ ɪŋ
stratigraphic ˌstræt ɪ 'græf ɪk ◄ §-ə- ‖ ˌstræt̬-
~ally əl_i
stratigraphy strə 'tɪg rəf i
stratocum|ulus ˌstreɪt əʊ 'kjuːm |jʊl əs
ˌstræt-, -jəl əs ‖ ˌstreɪt̬ oʊ 'kjuːm |jəl əs
ˌstræt̬-, **~uli** ju laɪ jə laɪ ‖ jə laɪ
stratopause 'stræt əʊ pɔːz ‖ 'stræt̬ ə- -pɑːz
stratosphere 'stræt ə sfɪə -əʊ- ‖ 'stræt̬ ə sfɪr
stratospheric ˌstræt ə 'sfer ɪk ◄ -əʊ- ‖ ˌstræt̬-
-'sfɪr-
Stratton 'stræt ən
strat|um 'strɑːt |əm 'streɪt- ‖ 'streɪt̬ |əm
'stræt̬- **~a** ə
stratus 'streɪt əs ‖ 'streɪt̬ əs 'stræt̬-
Strauli 'strɔːl i ‖ 'strɑːl-
Strauss straʊs —*Ger* [ʃtʁaʊs]
Stravinsky strə 'vɪntˢ ski —*Russ*
[stra 'vjin skjɪj]
straw strɔː ‖ strɑː **straws** strɔːz ‖ strɑːz
ˌstraw 'man; ˌstraw 'poll ‖ '• •; ˌstraw
'vote ‖ '• •
strawberr|y, S~ 'strɔː bər_|i ‖ 'strɔː ˌber li
-bər_li **~ies** iz
ˌstrawberry 'blonde; 'strawberry mark
strawboard 'strɔː bɔːd ‖ -bɔːrd 'strɑː-, -boʊrd
straw-colored, straw-coloured
'strɔː ˌkʌl əd ‖ -ərd 'strɑː-
Strawson 'strɔːs ən ‖ 'strɑːs-
strawy 'strɔːr i ‖ 'strɔː i 'strɑː i

S

stray streɪ **strayed** streɪd **straying** 'streɪ ɪŋ
 strays streɪz
streak striːk **streaked** striːkt **streaking**
 'striːk ɪŋ **streaks** striːks
streaker 'striːk ə ‖ -ᵊr ~s z
streak|y 'striːk |i ~ier i‿ə ‖ i‿ᵊr ~iest i‿ɪst i‿əst
 ~ily ɪ li əl i ~iness i nəs i nɪs
stream striːm **streamed** striːmd **streaming**
 'striːm ɪŋ **streams** striːmz
streamer 'striːm ə ‖ -ᵊr ~s z
streamlet 'striːm lət -lɪt ~s s
streamlin|e 'striːm laɪn ~ed d ~es z ~ing ɪŋ
Streatfeild, Streatfield 'stret fiːᵊld
Streatham 'stret əm ‖ 'streṭ əm
Streatley place in Berks 'striːt li
Streep striːp
street, Street striːt **streets** striːts —Unlike all
 other words referring to thoroughfares, street is
 usually not accented in names: 'Oxford Street,
 'Regent Street (compare ˌOxford 'Road,ˌRegent
 'Crescent)
 ˌstreet ˌcredi'bility; 'street light; 'street
 smarts; 'street ˌvalue
streetcar 'striːt kɑː ‖ -kɑːr ~s z
street-cred ˌstriːt 'kred
Streeter 'striːt ə ‖ 'striːṭ ᵊr
streetwalker 'striːt ˌwɔːk ə ‖ -ᵊr -ˌwɑːk- ~s z
streetwise 'striːt waɪz
Streisand 'straɪ sænd -zænd, -sənd
strelitzia stre 'lɪts i‿ə strə- ~s z
strength streŋᵏθ §strenᵗθ **strengths** streŋᵏθs
 §strenᵗθs
strengthen 'streŋᵏθ ᵊn §'strenᵗθ- ~ed d ~er/s
 ˌə/z ‿ᵊr/z ~ing ˌɪŋ ~s z
strenuous 'stren ju‿əs ~ly li ~ness nəs nɪs
strep strep
strepto|coccal ˌstrept ə ‖'kɒk ᵊl ◄ -‖'kɑːk ᵊl ◄
 ~cocci 'kɒks aɪ 'kɒk-, 'kɒs-, -iː ‖ 'kɑːks aɪ
 'kɑːk-, -iː ~coccus 'kɒk əs ‖ 'kɑːk əs
streptomycin ˌstrept ə 'maɪs ɪn §-ᵊn
streptothricin, streptothrysin
 ˌstrept ə 'θraɪs ɪn -əʊ-, -'θrɪs-, §-ᵊn
stress stres **stressed** strest **stresses** 'stres ɪz
 -əz **stressing** 'stres ɪŋ
 'stress mark
-stress strəs strɪs, stres — **songstress**
 'sɒŋks trəs -trɪs, -tres; 'sɒŋ strəs, -strɪs,
 -stres ‖ 'sɔːŋks trəs 'sɑːŋks-; 'sɔːŋ strəs,
 'sɑːŋ-
stressful 'stres fᵊl -fʊl ~ly ‿i ~ness nəs nɪs
stretch stretʃ **stretched** stretʃt **stretches**
 'stretʃ ɪz -əz **stretching** 'stretʃ ɪŋ
stretch|er 'stretʃ |ə ‖ -ᵊr ~ered əd ‖ ᵊrd
 ~ering ᵊr ɪŋ ~ers əz ‖ ᵊrz
 'stretcher ˌparty
stretcher-bearer 'stretʃ ə ˌbeər ə ‖ -ᵊr ˌber ᵊr
 -ˌbær- ~s z
stretchmark 'stretʃ mɑːk ‖ -mɑːrk ~s s
stretchy 'stretʃ i
Stretford 'stret fəd ‖ -fᵊrd
stretto 'stret əʊ ‖ -oʊ —It ['stret to] ~s z
Stretton 'stret ᵊn
Strevens 'strev ᵊnz

strew struː **strewed** struːd **strewing** 'struː ɪŋ
 strewn struːn §'struːˌən **strews** struːz
strewth struːθ
stria 'straɪˌə **striae** 'straɪ iː
striated straɪ 'eɪt ɪd -əd ‖ 'straɪ eɪṭ əd (*)
striation straɪ 'eɪʃ ᵊn ~s z
Strick, strick strɪk
stricken 'strɪk ᵊn
Strickland 'strɪk lənd
strickl|e 'strɪk ᵊl ~ed d ~es z ~ing ˌɪŋ
strict strɪkt **stricter** 'strɪkt ə ‖ -ᵊr **strictest**
 'strɪkt ɪst -əst
strict|ly 'strɪkt |li ~ness nəs nɪs
stricture 'strɪk tʃə -tʃᵊr ~s z
stride, Stride straɪd **stridden** 'strɪd ᵊn
 strides straɪdz **striding** 'straɪd ɪŋ **strode**
 strəʊd ‖ stroʊd
stridency 'straɪd ᵊnts i
strident 'straɪd ᵊnt ~ly li
stridor 'straɪd ɔː -ə ‖ -ᵊr -ɔːr
stridu|late 'strɪd ju ‖leɪt -jə- ‖ 'strɪdʒ ə ‖leɪt
 ~lated leɪt ɪd -əd ‖ leɪṭ əd ~lates leɪts
 ~lating leɪt ɪŋ ‖ leɪṭ ɪŋ
stridulation ˌstrɪd ju 'leɪʃ ᵊn -jə- ‖ ˌstrɪdʒ ə-
 ~s z
strife straɪf
strigil 'strɪdʒ ɪl -ᵊl ~s z
strike straɪk **strikes** straɪks **striking** 'straɪk ɪŋ
 struck strʌk
 'strike pay
strikebound 'straɪk baʊnd
strikebreaker 'straɪk ˌbreɪk ə ‖ -ᵊr ~s z
strikebreaking 'straɪk ˌbreɪk ɪŋ
strikeout 'straɪk aʊt ~s s
striker 'straɪk ə ‖ -ᵊr ~s z
striking 'straɪk ɪŋ ~ly li ~ness nəs nɪs
 'striking ˌdistance
strim strɪm **strimmed** strɪmd **strimming**
 'strɪm ɪŋ **strims** strɪmz
strimmer, S~ tdmk 'strɪm ə ‖ -ᵊr ~s z
Strindberg 'strɪnd bɜːg →'strɪmb- ‖ -bɜːg
 —Swed ['strɪnd bærj]
Strine straɪn
string strɪŋ **stringing** 'strɪŋ ɪŋ **strings** strɪŋz
 strung strʌŋ
 ˌstring 'bean, '· ·; ˌstringed 'instrument
stringency 'strɪndʒ ᵊnts i
stringent 'strɪndʒ ᵊnt ~ly li
stringer, S~ 'strɪŋ ə ‖ -ᵊr ~s z
Stringfellow 'strɪŋ ˌfel əʊ ‖ -oʊ
string|y 'strɪŋ |i ~ier i‿ə ‖ i‿ᵊr ~iest i‿ɪst i‿əst
 ~ily ɪ li əl i ~iness i nəs i nɪs
strip strɪp **stripped** strɪpt **stripping** 'strɪp ɪŋ
 strips strɪps
 ˌstrip car'toon; 'strip club; 'strip ˌlighting;
 'strip ˌmining; ˌstrip 'poker
stripe straɪp **striped** straɪpt **stripes** straɪps
 striping 'straɪp ɪŋ
stripling 'strɪp lɪŋ ~s z
stripp... see **strip**
strippagram 'strɪp ə græm ~s z
stripper 'strɪp ə ‖ -ᵊr ~s z
stripperama ˌstrɪp ə 'rɑːm ə ~s z

S

Stress

1 A **stressed** syllable is one that carries a **rhythmic beat**. It is marked by greater loudness than unstressed syllables, and often by pitch-prominence, or greater duration, or more clearly defined vowel qualities.

2 An **accent** is the placement of intonational pitch-prominence (= higher or lower pitch than the surroundings) on a word. Speakers choose to accent certain words (or to de-accent others) because of the particular meaning they wish to convey in a particular situation. Accents can be located only on stressed syllables. Thus to accent the word **collapse** kə 'læps the pitch-prominence goes on the syllable læps, but in **tumble** 'tʌm bᵊl on the syllable tʌm.

3 The stresses marked in LPD are **lexical** (= potential) stresses. Whether they are realized as accents depends on intonation.

4 LPD recognizes two levels of stress:

primary stress (ˈ)   When a word is said in isolation, this is where the nuclear tone (= sentence accent) goes. A word or phrase has only one primary stress.

secondary stress (ˌ)   In a word or phrase that potentially has more than one stress, this symbol marks the place of a stress other than the primary one. If this syllable is **before** the primary stress, it may also bear an accent. See STRESS SHIFT.

5 In the first edition of LPD, a distinction was made between secondary (ˌ) and tertiary (ˏ) stress. In this second edition the distinction has been abandoned. We continue to regard as unstressed the STRONG-vowelled syllables at the end of words such as **hesitate** 'hez ɪ teɪt, **acorn** 'eɪk ɔːn ‖ 'eɪk ɔːrn.

6 If the primary stress is located on the third or later syllable of a word, then there must also be a secondary stress on one or other of the first two syllables. Thus ˌorganiˈzation has the same stress pattern as ˌExeter ˈstation; asˌsociˈation has the same stress pattern as aˌnother ˈnation.

S

---

strip-search ˌstrɪp 'sɜːtʃ 'ꞏ ꞏ ‖ 'strɪp sɜːtʃ
~**ed** t ~**es** ɪz əz ~**ing** ɪŋ
striptease 'strɪp tiːz ˌꞏꞏ
strip|y 'straɪp li ~**ier** iᵊ ‖ iᵊr ~**iest** i‿ɪst i‿əst
~**iness** i nəs i nɪs
strive straɪv **striven** 'strɪv ᵊn (!) **strives**
straɪvz **striving/s** 'straɪv ɪŋ/z **strove**
strəʊv ‖ stroʊv
striver 'straɪv ə ‖ -ᵊr ~**s** z
strobe strəʊb ‖ stroʊb **strobes**
strəʊbz ‖ stroʊbz
'**strobe light**
stroboscope 'strəʊb ə skəʊp ‖ 'stroʊb ə skoʊp
~**s** s
stroboscopic ˌstrəʊb ə 'skɒp ɪk ◄ ˌstrɒb-
‖ ˌstroʊb ə 'skɑːp ɪk ◄ ~**ally** ᵊl‿i
strode, Strode strəʊd ‖ stroʊd

stroganoff 'strɒg ə nɒf ‖ 'stroʊg ə nɔːf
'strɔːg-, 'strɑːg-, -nɑːf
stroke strəʊk ‖ stroʊk **stroked**
strəʊkt ‖ stroʊkt **strokes** strəʊks ‖ stroʊks
stroking 'strəʊk ɪŋ ‖ 'stroʊk ɪŋ
stroll strəʊl →strɒʊl ‖ stroʊl **strolled** strəʊld
→strɒʊld ‖ stroʊld **strolling** 'strəʊl ɪŋ
→'strɒʊl- ‖ 'stroʊl ɪŋ **strolls** strəʊlz
→strɒʊlz ‖ stroʊlz
stroller 'strəʊl ə →'strɒʊl- ‖ 'stroʊl ᵊr ~**s** z
strom|a 'strəʊm |ə ‖ 'stroʊm |ə ~**ata**
ət ə ‖ ət̬ ə
stromatolite strəʊ 'mæt ə laɪt -ᵊl aɪt
‖ stroʊ 'mæt̬ ᵊl aɪt ~**s** s
Stromboli 'strɒm bᵊl i ‖ 'strɑːm- —*It*
['strom bo li]
Stromness 'strɒm nes 'strʌm- ‖ 'strɑːm-

Stress shift

1 Some words seem to change their stress pattern in connected speech. Although in isolation we say **fundamental** with the primary stress on ment and **Japanese** with the primary stress on niːz, in connected speech these words often have a different pattern. For example, there might be greater stress on fʌnd than on ment, or greater stress on dʒæp than on niːz. This phenomenon is known as **stress shift**.

2 A phrase usually receives late stress (see COMPOUNDS AND PHRASES). The placing of primary stress on the last element of the phrase means that the basic stress of the first element is weakened: combining ˈweekly and ˈlessons gives the phrase ˌweekly ˈlessons. So you might expect that ˌfundaˈmental plus miˈstake would give fundaˌmental miˈstake, and that ˌJapaˈnese plus ˈlanguage would give Japaˌnese ˈlanguage.

3 But these stress patterns are unbalanced. To balance them, native speakers of English usually switch round the stress levels in the first element, and say ˌfundamental miˈstake, ˌJapanese ˈlanguage.

4 The same thing happens in a phrase such as ˌvery ˈlazy plus ˈpeople. Stress shift produces ˌvery lazy ˈpeople.

5 In principle, stress shift can apply to any word that has a secondary stress before its primary stress. In practice, though, it is most likely to apply to those which are regularly followed in a phrase by a more strongly stressed word: most adjectives, but only certain nouns. As a helpful reminder, LPD attaches the symbol ◄ to the words in which stress shift is most likely.

6 Conversely, the decision whether or not to mark a secondary stress sometimes depends on whether or not stress shift can occur. In some cases usage is divided, and then LPD writes the secondary stress mark in parentheses: **antique** is written ₍ˌ₎ænˈtiːk because in a phrase such as **an antique chair** some speakers stress-shift, saying an ˌantique ˈchair, but others do not, saying an anˌtique ˈchair.

S

strong, Strong strɒŋ ‖ strɔːŋ straːŋ **stronger**
 ˈstrɒŋ ɡə ‖ ˈstrɔːŋ ɡ°r ˈstraːŋ- **strongest**
 ˈstrɒŋ ɡɪst -ɡəst ‖ ˈstrɔːŋ ɡəst ˈstraːŋ-
 ˌstrong ˈlanguage
strongarm ˈstrɒŋ ɑːm ‖ ˈstrɔːŋ ɑːrm ˈstraːŋ-
strongbox ˈstrɒŋ bɒks ‖ ˈstrɔːŋ baːks ˈstraːŋ-
 ~es ɪz əz
stronghold ˈstrɒŋ həʊld ‖ ˈstrɔːŋ hoʊld
 ˈstraːŋ- ~s z
strongly ˈstrɒŋ li ‖ ˈstrɔːŋ li ˈstraːŋ-
strong|man ˈstrɒŋ |mæn ‖ ˈstrɔːŋ- ˈstraːŋ-
 ~men men
strong-minded ˌstrɒŋ ˈmaɪnd ɪd ◄ -əd
 ‖ ˌstrɔːŋ- ˌstraːŋ- ~ly li ~ness nəs nɪs
strongpoint, strong point
 ˈstrɒŋ pɔɪnt ‖ ˈstrɔːŋ- ˈstraːŋ- ~s s
strongroom ˈstrɒŋ ruːm -rʊm ‖ ˈstrɔːŋ-
 ˈstraːŋ- ~s z
strong-willed ˌstrɒŋ ˈwɪld ◄ ‖ ˌstrɔːŋ- ˌstraːŋ-

Stronsay ˈstrɒnz eɪ ‖ ˈstraːnz eɪ
strontia ˈstrɒnt i̯ə ˈstrɒntʃ- ‖ ˈstraːntʃ i̯ə
 ˈstraːnt̯-
Strontian place in Highland
 ₍ˌ₎strɒn ˈtiː ən ‖ ₍ˌ₎straːn-
strontium ˈstrɒnt i̯əm ˈstrɒntʃ-
 ‖ ˈstraːntʃ i̯əm ˈstraːnt̯-
 ˌstrontium ˈ90
Strood struːd
strop strɒp ‖ straːp **stropped** strɒpt ‖ straːpt
 stropping ˈstrɒp ɪŋ ‖ ˈstraːp ɪŋ **strops**
 strɒps ‖ straːps
strophanth|in strəʊ ˈfæntθ |ɪn strɒ-, §-ən
 ‖ stroʊ- ~us əs
strophe ˈstrəʊf i ˈstrɒf-, -iː ‖ ˈstroʊf i ~s z
strophic ˈstrɒf ɪk ˈstrəʊf- ‖ ˈstroʊf ɪk ˈstraːf-
stropp|y ˈstrɒp |i ‖ ˈstraːp |i ~ier i̯ə ‖ i̯°r
 ~iest i̯ɪst i̯əst ~ily ɪ li əl i ~iness i nəs i nɪs
Stroud, stroud straʊd

Stroudley 'straʊd li
strove straʊv ‖ stroʊv
Strowger 'straʊdʒ ə ‖ -ʲr
struck strʌk
structural 'strʌk tʃʳ‿əl -ʃʳ‿ ~ly i
structuralism 'strʌk tʃʳ‿ə ‚lɪz əm '•ʃʳ‿,
‿əl ‚ɪz-
structuralist 'strʌk tʃʳ‿əl ɪst '•ʃʳ‿, §-əst ~s s
structure 'strʌk tʃə -ʃə ‖ -tʃʳ ~d d ~s z
structuring 'strʌk tʃʳ‿ɪŋ -ʃʳ‿
strudel 'struːd əl —Ger ['ʃtʁuː dəl] ~s z
struggl|e 'strʌg əl ~ed d ~er/s ‿ə/z ‖ ‿ər/z
~es z ~ing/ly ‿ɪŋ /li
strum strʌm strummed strʌmd strumming
'strʌm ɪŋ strums strʌmz
struma, S~ 'struːm ə ~s z
Strumble 'strʌm bəl
strumpet 'strʌmp ɪt §-ət ~s s
strung strʌŋ
strung-out ‚strʌŋ 'aʊt ◄
strung-up ‚strʌŋ 'ʌp ◄
strut strʌt struts strʌts strutted 'strʌt ɪd -əd
‖ 'strʌt̬ əd strutting/ly 'strʌt ɪŋ /li
‖ 'strʌt̬ ɪŋ /li
struth struːθ
Struthers 'strʌð əz ‖ -ʲrz
Strutt strʌt
Struwwelpeter ‚struː‿əl 'piːt ə '••,••;
‚struː'l••, '•,•• ‖ -'piːt̬ ʲr —Ger
['ʃtʁʊv əl ‚pe: tɐ]
strychnine 'strɪk niːn -nɪn, -naɪn, §-nən ‖ -naɪn
-nən, -niːn
Strymon 'straɪm ən
Strzelecki Australian name strez 'lek i —Polish
[st-ʃe 'lets ki]
St Thomas sənt 'tɒm əs ‖ seɪnt 'tɑːm əs
St Tropez ‚sæn trəʊ 'peɪ ‖ -troʊ- ——Fr Saint-
Tropez [sæ̃ tʁɔ pe]
Stu stjuː → §stʃuː ‖ stuː stjuː
Stuart 'stjuː‿ət → §'stʃuː‿ ‖ 'stuː ʲrt 'stjuː
stub stʌb stubbed stʌbd stubbing 'stʌb ɪŋ
stubs stʌbz
stubble 'stʌb əl
stubbly 'stʌb əl‿i
stubborn 'stʌb ən ‖ -ʲrn ~ly li ~ness nəs nɪs
Stubbs stʌbz
stubb|y 'stʌb li ~ier i‿ə ‖ i‿ʲr ~ies iz ~iest
i‿ɪst i‿əst ~ily ɪ li əl i ~iness i nəs i nɪs
stucco 'stʌk əʊ ‖ -oʊ ~ed d ~es, ~s z ~ing ɪŋ
stuck stʌk
stuck-up ‚stʌk 'ʌp ◄
stud stʌd studded 'stʌd ɪd -əd studding
'stʌd ɪŋ studs stʌdz
‚stud 'poker
studbook 'stʌd bʊk →'stʌb-, §-bʊːk ~s s
studdingsail 'stʌd ɪŋ seɪ‿əl —also naut 'stʌn‿s əl
~s z
Studebaker 'stuːd ə beɪk ə 'stjuːd-, '•ɪ- ‖ -ʲr
~s z
student 'stjuːd ənt §'stuːd-, →§'stʃuːd-
‖ 'stuːd ənt 'stjuːd- —AmE 1993 poll panel
preference: 'stuːd- 88%, 'stjuːd- 12%. ~s s

STUDENT

■ 'stuːd- □ 'stjuːd-

AmE 1993

0 20 40 60 80 100%

~ship/s ʃɪp/s
‚students' 'union
studied 'stʌd id ~ly li ~ness nəs nɪs
studio 'stjuːd i‿əʊ §'stuːd-, →§'stʃuːd-
‖ 'stuːd i oʊ 'stjuːd- ~s z
'studio couch
studious 'stjuːd i‿əs 'stuːd-, →§'stʃuːd-
‖ 'stuːd- 'stjuːd- ~ly li ~ness nəs nɪs
Studland 'stʌd lənd
Studley 'stʌd li
study 'stʌd i studied 'stʌd id studies 'stʌd iz
studying 'stʌd i‿ɪŋ
stuff stʌf stuffed stʌft stuffing/s 'stʌf ɪŋ/z
stuffs stʌfs
‚stuffed 'shirt, '• •
stuff|y 'stʌf li ~ier i‿ə ‖ i‿ʲr ~iest i‿ɪst i‿əst
~ily ɪ li əl i ~iness i nəs i nɪs
Stuka 'stuːk ə ~s z —Ger ['ʃtuː ka, 'ʃtʊ-]
stultification ‚stʌlt ɪf ɪ 'keɪʃ ən '‚əf-, §-ə'•-
stulti|fy 'stʌlt ɪ |faɪ -ə- ~fied faɪd ~fies faɪz
~fying/ly faɪ ɪŋ /li
stum 'grape juice' stʌm
stum, stumm 'silent' ʃtʊm
stumbl|e 'stʌm bəl ~ed d ~es z stumbling/
ly 'stʌm blɪŋ /li
'stumbling block
stumblebum 'stʌm bəl bʌm ~s z
stumbler 'stʌm blə ‖ -blʲr ~s z
stumer 'stjuːm ə →§'stʃuːm- ‖ 'stuːm ʲr
'stjuːm- ~s z
stumm ʃʊm
stump stʌmp stumped stʌmpt stumping
'stʌmp ɪŋ stumps stʌmps
stumpage 'stʌmp ɪdʒ
stump|y 'stʌmp li ~ier i‿ə ‖ i‿ʲr ~iest i‿ɪst
i‿əst ~iness i nəs i nɪs
stun stʌn stunned stʌnd stunning/ly
'stʌn ɪŋ /li stuns stʌnz
'stun gun
stung stʌŋ
stunk stʌŋk
stunn... —see stun
stunner 'stʌn ə ‖ -ʲr ~s z
stunsail, stuns'l 'stʌn səl ~s z
stunt stʌnt stunted 'stʌnt ɪd -əd ‖ 'stʌnt̬ əd
stunting 'stʌnt ɪŋ ‖ 'stʌnt̬ ɪŋ stunts stʌnts
'stunt man, 'stunt ‚woman
stupa 'stuːp ə ~s z
stupe stjuːp ‖ stuːp stjuːp stupes
stjuːps ‖ stuːps stjuːps
stupefaction ‚stjuːp ɪ 'fæk ʃən ‚stʊp-,
§‚stuːp-, →§‚stʃuːp-, -ə- ‖ ‚stuːp- ‚stjuːp-
stupe|fy 'stjuːp ɪ |faɪ 'stʊp-, §'stuːp-,
→§'stʃuːp-, -ə- ‖ 'stuːp- 'stjuːp- ~fied faɪd
~fier/s faɪ‿ə/z ‖ faɪ‿ʲr/z ~fies faɪz ~fying
faɪ ɪŋ
stupendous stjuː 'pend əs §stuː-, →§stʃuː-
‖ stuː- stjuː- ~ly li ~ness nəs nɪs

stupid 'stjuːp ɪd 'stjʊp-, →§'stʃuːp-,
§-əd ‖ 'stuːp əd 'stjuːp- **~er** ə ‖ ᵊr **~est** ɪst
əst

stupidit|y stju 'pɪd ət i §stu-, →§stʃu-, -ɪt i
‖ stu 'pɪd ət̬ i stju- **~ies** iz

stupid|ly 'stjuːp ɪd |li 'stjʊp-, §'stuːp-,
→§'stʃuːp-, §-əd- ‖ 'stuːp əd |li 'stjuːp-
~ness nəs nɪs

stupor 'stjuːp ə §'stuːp-, →§'stʃuːp-
‖ 'stuːp ᵊr 'stjuːp- **~s** z

sturd|y 'stɜːd |i ‖ 'stɝːd |i **~ier** i_ə ‖ i_ᵊr **~iest**
i_ɪst i_əst **~ily** ɪ li əl i **~iness** i nəs i nɪs

Sturge stɜːdʒ ‖ stɝːdʒ

sturgeon, S~ 'stɜːdʒ ən ‖ 'stɝːdʒ ən **~s** z

Sturm und Drang ˌʃtʊəm ʊnt 'dræŋ
‖ ˌʃtʊrm ʊnt 'drɑːŋ —*Ger* [ˌʃtʊʁm ʊnt 'dʁaŋ]

Sturmer 'stɜːm ə ‖ 'stɝːm ᵊr

Sturminster 'stɜː ˌmɪnt st ə ‖ 'stɝː ˌmɪnt st ᵊr

Sturridge 'stʌr ɪdʒ ‖ 'stɝː ɪdʒ

Sturrock 'stʌr ək ‖ 'stɝː ək

Sturt stɜːt ‖ stɝːt

Sturtevant, Sturtivant 'stɜːt ɪv ənt -əv-
‖ 'stɝːt̬-

Sturton 'stɜːt ən ‖ 'stɝːt ən

Stuttaford 'stʌt ə fəd ‖ 'stʌt̬ ə fᵊrd

Stuttard 'stʌt əd ‖ 'stʌt̬ ᵊrd

stutter 'stʌt ə ‖ 'stʌt̬ ᵊr **~ed** d **stuttering**
'stʌt ᵊr ɪŋ ‖ 'stʌt̬ ᵊr ɪŋ **~s** z

stutterer 'stʌt_ᵊr ə ‖ 'stʌt̬ ᵊr ᵊr →'stʌtr ᵊr **~s** z

Stuttgart 'ʃtʊt gɑːt ‖ -gɑːrt 'ʃtuːt- —*Ger*
['ʃtʊt gaʁt]

Stuyvesant 'staɪv əs ənt -ɪs-

St Vincent sənt 'vɪnˀs ənt ‖ seɪnt-

St Vitus sənt 'vaɪt əs ‖ seɪnt 'vaɪt̬ əs **St Vitus',**
St Vitus's sənt 'vaɪt əs ɪz -əz; -'•əs
‖ seɪnt 'vaɪt̬ əs əz -'•əs
St ˌVitus' 'dance

St Weonards sənt 'wen ədz ‖ seɪnt 'wen ᵊrdz

sty staɪ **sties** staɪz

Styal 'staɪ_əl staɪᵊl

stye staɪ *(= sty)* **styes** staɪz

Stygian, s~ 'stɪdʒ i_ən

style staɪᵊl **styled** staɪᵊld **styles** staɪᵊlz
styling 'staɪᵊl ɪŋ

-style staɪᵊl — **peristyle** 'per ɪ staɪᵊl -ə-, -i-

Styles staɪᵊlz

stylet 'staɪl ət 'staɪᵊl-, -ɪt **~s** s

stylis... —*see* **styliz...**

stylish 'staɪl ɪʃ 'staɪᵊl- **~ly** li **~ness** nəs nɪs

stylist 'staɪl ɪst 'staɪᵊl-, -əst **~s** s

stylistic staɪ 'lɪst ɪk **~ally** ᵊl_i **~s** s

stylite 'staɪl aɪt 'staɪᵊl- **~s** s

Stylites staɪ 'laɪt iːz

stylization ˌstaɪl aɪ 'zeɪʃ ᵊn ˌstaɪᵊl-, -ɪ- ‖ -ə- **~s**
z

styliz|e 'staɪl aɪz 'staɪᵊl- **~ed** d **~es** ɪz əz **~ing**
ɪŋ

stylo 'staɪl əʊ ‖ -oʊ **~s** z

stylo- *comb. form*
with stress-neutral suffix ¦staɪl əʊ ‖ -oʊ —
stylohyoid ˌstaɪl əʊ 'haɪ ɔɪd ◀ ‖ -oʊ-
with stress-imposing suffix staɪ 'lɒ+ ‖ -'lɑː+ —
stylography staɪ 'lɒg rəf i ‖ -'lɑːg-

stylobate 'staɪl ə beɪt -əʊ- ‖ -oʊ- **~s** s

stylograph 'staɪl əʊ grɑːf -græf ‖ -ə græf **~s** s

styloid 'staɪl ɔɪd

stylus 'staɪl əs **~es** ɪz əz

stymie, stymy 'staɪm i **stymied** 'staɪm id
stymies 'staɪm iz **stymieing, stymying**
'staɪm i ɪŋ

styptic 'stɪpt ɪk **~s** s

styrax 'staɪᵊr æks

styrene 'staɪᵊr iːn

Styri|a 'stɪr i_ə **~an/s** ən/z

styrofoam, S~ *tdmk* 'staɪᵊr ə fəʊm ‖ -foʊm

Styx stɪks

Su suː

suasion 'sweɪʒ ᵊn

suave swɑːv —*Formerly also* sweɪv

suave|ly 'swɑːv |li 'sweɪv- **~ness** nəs nɪs

suavity 'swɑːv ət i 'sweɪv-, -ɪt i ‖ -ət̬ i

sub sʌb —*but as a Latin word also* sʊb **subbed**
sʌbd **subbing** 'sʌb ɪŋ **subs** sʌbz —*see also*
phrases with this word

sub- səb, ¦sʌb —*As a productive prefix,* ¦sʌb
('subcom,mittee, ˌ•• ' ••); *as a fossilized prefix,*
usually səb, §sʌb *if the following syllable is*
stressed (sub'stantial), ¦sʌb *if not* ('substance).

subacute ˌsʌb ə 'kjuːt ◀ **~ly** li

subalpine ˌsʌb 'ælp aɪn ◀

subaltern 'sʌb ᵊlt ən ‖ sə 'bɔːlt ᵊrn -'bɑːlt- *(*)*
~s z

subaqua, sub-aqua ˌsʌb 'æk wə ‖ -'ɑːk-

subarachnoid ˌsʌb ə 'ræk nɔɪd ◀

Subaru *tdmk* 'suːb ə ruː ˌ••'• —*Jp* ['sɯ ba rɯ]
~s z

subassem|bly 'sʌb ə ˌsem |bli ˌ••'•• **~blies**
bliz

subatomic ˌsʌb ə 'tɒm ɪk ◀ ‖ -'tɑːm-
ˌsubaˌtomic 'particles

subb... —*see* **sub**

subbuteo, S~ *tdmk* sə 'buːt i əʊ sʌ-, -'bjuːt-
‖ -'buːt̬ i oʊ

subclass 'sʌb klɑːs §-klæs ‖ -klæs **~ed** t **~es**
ɪz əz **~ing** ɪŋ

subclinical ˌsʌb 'klɪn ɪk ᵊl ◀

subcommittee 'sʌb kə ˌmɪt i ˌ••'•• ‖ -ˌmɪt̬-
~s z

subcompact ˌsʌb kəm 'pækt ◀ §-kɒm-;
-'kɒm pækt ‖ (ˌ)sʌb 'kɑːm pækt **~s** s

subconscious (ˌ)sʌb 'kɒntʃ əs ‖ -'kɑːntʃ- **~ly** li
~ness nəs nɪs

subcontinent ˌsʌb 'kɒnt ɪn ənt -ən-, '•,•••
‖ -'kɑːnt ᵊn_ənt **~s** s

subcontinental ˌsʌb ˌkɒnt ɪ 'nent ᵊl -ə-
‖ -ˌkɑːnt ᵊn 'ent̬ ᵊl

subcontract *v* ˌsʌb kən 'trækt §-kɒn-,
-'kɒn trækt ‖ -'kɑːn trækt **~ed** ɪd əd **~ing**
ɪŋ **~s** s

subcontract *n* (ˌ)sʌb 'kɒn trækt '•,•• ‖ -'kɑːn-
~s s

subcontractor ˌsʌb kən 'trækt ə §-kɒn-,
'•,••, ••; ˌsʌb 'kɒn trækt ə
‖ (ˌ)sʌb 'kɑːn trækt ᵊr '•,•••, ˌ•kən'•• **~s** z

subculture 'sʌb ˌkʌltʃ ə ‖ -ᵊr **~s** z

subcutaneous ˌsʌb kju 'teɪn i_əs ◀ **~ly** li

subdivid|e ˌsʌb dɪ ˈvaɪd -də-, §-diː-; ˈ••• **~ed**
ɪd əd **~es** z **~ing** ɪŋ

subdivision ˈsʌb dɪ ˌvɪʒ ᵊn -də-, §-diː-, ˌ••ˈ••
—*The stressing* ˌ••ˈ••• *is mostly restricted to
the sense 'act of subdividing'; a portion
resulting from this act is a* ˈ••ˌ••. **~s** z

subdominant ˌsʌb ˈdɒm ɪn ənt -ən_ ‖ -ˈdɑːm-
~s s

subduct səb ˈdʌkt ₍ᵢ₎sʌb- **~ed** ɪd əd **~ing** ɪŋ
~s s

subduction səb ˈdʌk ʃᵊn ₍ᵢ₎sʌb- **~s** z
subˈduction zone

subdu|e səb ˈdjuː §sʌb-, →§ˈdʒuː ‖ -ˈduː -ˈdjuː
~ed d **~es** z **~ing** ɪŋ

subdural ₍ᵢ₎sʌb ˈdjʊər əl →§-ˈdʒʊər-, -ˈdjɔːr-
‖ -ˈdʊr- -ˈdjʊr-

subed|it ˌsʌb ˈed ɪt §-ət, ˈ•ˌ•• ‖ -lət **~ited**
ɪt ɪd §ət-, -əd ‖ ət̬ əd **~iting** ɪt ɪŋ §ət- ‖ ət̬ ɪŋ
~its ɪts §əts ‖ əts

subeditor ˌsʌb ˈed ɪt ə §-ət ə, ˈ•ˌ••• ‖ -ət̬ ər
~s z

subfamil|y ˈsʌb ˌfæm əl_i -ɪl i **~ies** iz

subfusc ˈsʌb fʌsk ˌ•ˈ•

subglottal ˌsʌb ˈglɒt əl ◄ ‖ -ˈglɑːt̬-

subgroup ˈsʌb gruːp **~s** s

subharmonic ˌsʌb hɑː ˈmɒn ɪk ‖ -hɑːr ˈmɑːn-
~s s

subhead ˈsʌb hed, ˌ•ˈ• **~ing/s** ɪŋ/z **~s** z

subhuman ˌsʌb ˈhjuːm ən §-ˈjuːm-

subjacency ₍ᵢ₎sʌb ˈdʒeɪs ᵊn_ts i

subjacent ₍ᵢ₎sʌb ˈdʒeɪs ᵊnt **~ly** li

subject *n, adj* ˈsʌb dʒekt -dʒɪkt **~s** s
ˈsubject ˌmatter

subject *v* səb ˈdʒekt sʌb-; ˈsʌb dʒekt, -dʒɪkt
~ed ɪd əd **~ing** ɪŋ **~s** s

subjection səb ˈdʒek ʃᵊn sʌb-

subjectival ˌsʌb dʒɪk ˈtaɪv əl ◄ -dʒek-

subjectiv|e səb ˈdʒekt ɪv ₍ᵢ₎sʌb- **~ely** li **~eness**
nəs nɪs **~ism** ˌɪz əm

subjectivity ˌsʌb dʒek ˈtɪv ət i -ɪt i ‖ -ət̬ i

subject-raising ˈsʌb dʒekt̬ ˌreɪz ɪŋ -dʒɪkt̬-

subjoin ˌsʌb ˈdʒɔɪn **~ed** d **~ing** ɪŋ **~s** z

sub judice ˌsʌb ˈdʒuːd əs i ˌsʊb-, -ˈjuːd-, -ɪs i;
-ə seɪ, -ɪ-, -keɪ

subju|gate ˈsʌb dʒu ˌɡeɪt -dʒə- ‖ -dʒə-
~gated ɡeɪt ɪd -əd ‖ ɡeɪt̬ əd **~gates** ɡeɪts
~gating ɡeɪt ɪŋ ‖ ɡeɪt̬ ɪŋ

subjugation ˌsʌb dʒu ˈɡeɪʃ ᵊn -dʒə- ‖ -dʒə-

subjugator ˈsʌb dʒu ɡeɪt ə ˌ•ˈ•dʒə-
‖ -dʒə ɡeɪt̬ ər **~s** z

subjunct ˈsʌb dʒʌŋkt **~s** s

subjunctive səb ˈdʒʌŋkt ɪv §sʌb- **~ly** li **~s** z

subleas|e *n* ˈsʌb liːs, ˌ•ˈ• **~es** ɪz əz

subleas|e *v* ˌsʌb ˈliːs ˈ•• **~ed** t **~es** ɪz əz
~ing ɪŋ

sub|let ˌsʌb ‖ˈlet **~lets** ˈlets **~letting**
ˈlet ɪŋ ‖ ˈlet̬ ɪŋ

sublieutenant ˌsʌb lef ˈten ənt -ləf- ‖ -luː- **~s**
s

subli|mate *v* ˈsʌb lɪ ˌmeɪt -lə- **~mated** meɪt ɪd
-əd ‖ meɪt̬ əd **~mates** meɪts **~mating**
meɪt ɪŋ ‖ meɪt̬ ɪŋ

sublimate *n* ˈsʌb lɪm ət -ləm-, -ɪt; -lɪ meɪt, -lə-
~s s

sublimation ˌsʌb lɪ ˈmeɪʃ ᵊn -lə-

sublim|e sə ˈblaɪm **~ed** d **~ely** li **~eness** nəs
nɪs **~es** z **~ing** ɪŋ

subliminal ˌsʌb ˈlɪm ɪn əl sə ˈblɪm-, -ən- **~ly** i

sublimity sə ˈblɪm ət i -ɪt i ‖ -ət̬ i

sublunary ₍ᵢ₎sʌb ˈluːn ər i ‖ ˈsʌb luː ner i

submachine gun ˌsʌb mə ˈʃiːn ɡʌn →-ˈʃiːŋ-
~s z

SUBMARINE

	ˈ•••	ˌ•ˈ•
BrE 1988		
AmE 1993		

0   20   40   60   80   100%

submarin|e *n, adj* ˈsʌb mə riːn, ˌ••ˈ• —*Poll
panel preferences: BrE 1988,* ˈ••• *42%,* ˌ••ˈ•
58%; AmE 1993, ˌ••ˈ• *61%,* ˌ••ˈ• *39%.* **~ing**
ɪŋ **~es** z

submariner ₍ᵢ₎sʌb ˈmær ɪn ə -ən-
‖ ˈsʌb mə riːn ər, ˌ••ˈ•• (*) **~s** z

submediant ₍ᵢ₎sʌb ˈmiːd i_ənt **~s** s

submerg|e səb ˈmɜːdʒ sʌb- ‖ -ˈmɜːdʒ **~ed** d
~es ɪz əz **~ing** ɪŋ

submergence səb ˈmɜːdʒ ᵊn_ts sʌb- ‖ -ˈmɜːdʒ-

submerse səb ˈmɜːs sʌb- ‖ -ˈmɜːs **~d** t

submersible səb ˈmɜːs əb əl sʌb-, -ɪb-
‖ -ˈmɜːs- **~s** z

submersion səb ˈmɜːʃ ᵊn sʌb-, -ˈmɜːʒ-
‖ -ˈmɜːʒ- -ˈmɜːʃ- **~s** z

submission səb ˈmɪʃ ᵊn §sʌb- **~s** z

submissive səb ˈmɪs ɪv §sʌb- **~ly** li **~ness** nəs
nɪs

sub|mit səb ‖ˈmɪt §sʌb- **~mits** ˈmɪts **~mitted**
ˈmɪt ɪd -əd ‖ ˈmɪt̬ əd **~mitting**
ˈmɪt ɪŋ ‖ ˈmɪt̬ ɪŋ

subnormal ˌsʌb ˈnɔːm əl ◄ -ˈnɔːrm- **~ly** i **~s**
z

subnormality ˌsʌb nɔː ˈmæl ət i -ɪt i
‖ -nɔːr ˈmæl ət̬ i

suborbital ₍ᵢ₎sʌb ˈɔːb ɪt əl §-ət- ‖ -ˈɔːrb ət̬ əl

subordi|nate *v* sə ˈbɔːd ɪ ˌneɪt -ə-; -ᵊn eɪt
‖ -ˈbɔːrd ᵊn eɪt **~nated** neɪt ɪd -əd ‖ neɪt̬ əd
~nates neɪts **~nating** neɪt ɪŋ ‖ neɪt̬ ɪŋ

subordinate *adj, n* sə ˈbɔːd ɪn ət -ᵊn_ət, -ɪt
‖ -ˈbɔːrd- **~ly** li **~s** s
suˌbordinate ˈclause

subordination sə ˌbɔːd ɪ ˈneɪʃ ᵊn -ə-; -ᵊn ˈeɪʃ-
‖ -ˌbɔːrd ᵊn ˈeɪʃ ᵊn

subordinative sə ˈbɔːd ɪn ət ɪv -ˈ•ᵊn-
‖ -ˈbɔːrd ᵊn eɪt̬ ɪv

suborn sə ˈbɔːn sʌ- ‖ -ˈbɔːrn **~ed** d **~ing** ɪŋ
~s z

subornation ˌsʌb ɔː ˈneɪʃ ᵊn -ɔːr- -ᵊr-

Subotica ˈsuːb ɒ tiːts ə ‖ ˈ•oʊ- —*Serbian*
[ˈsu bɔ ti tsa]

subpen|a sə ˈpiːn ə səb-, ˌsʌb- **~aed** əd
~aing ᵊr ɪŋ ‖ ə ɪŋ **~as** əz

subplot ˈsʌb plɒt ‖ -plɑːt **~s** s

subpoen|a sə ˈpiːn ə səb-, ˌsʌb- **~aed** əd
~aing ᵊr ɪŋ ‖ ə ɪŋ **~as** əz

S

sub-post offic|e ˌsʌb 'pəʊst ˌɒf ɪs §-əs
‖ -'poʊst ˌɔːf əs -ˌɑːf- **~es** ɪz əz
sub rosa ˌsʌb 'rəʊz ə ‖ -'roʊz ə
subroutine 'sʌb ruː ˌtiːn **~s** z
subscrib|e səb 'skraɪb §sʌb- **~ed** d **~er/s** ə/z
‖ ər/z **~es** z **~ing** ɪŋ
subscript 'sʌb skrɪpt
subscription səb 'skrɪp ʃən §sʌb- **~s** z
subsection 'sʌb ˌsek ʃən **~s** z
subsequenc|e *'sequence that is subordinate'*
'sʌb ˌsiːk wənts **~es** ɪz əz
subsequence *'being subsequent'* 'sʌb sɪk wənts
-sək-
subsequent 'sʌb sɪk wənt -sək- **~ly** li
subservienc|e səb 'sɜːv i̯ənts sʌb- ‖ -'sɝːv-
~y i
subservient səb 'sɜːv i̯ənt sʌb- ‖ -'sɝːv- **~ly**
li
subset 'sʌb set **~s** s
subsid|e səb 'saɪd §sʌb- **~ed** ɪd əd **~es** z
~ing ɪŋ

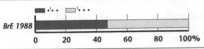

SUBSIDENCE

BrE 1988						
0	20	40	60	80	100%	

subsidenc|e səb 'saɪd ənts §sʌb-; 'sʌb sɪd ənts,
-səd- —*BrE 1988 poll panel preference:* •'••
47%, '••• *53%.* **~es** ɪz əz
subsidiarity səb ˌsɪd i 'ær ət i ˌsʌb sɪd-, -ɪt i
‖ -ət̬ i -'er-
subsidiar|y səb 'sɪd i̯ər i §sʌb-; ⚠-'sɪd ər‿li
‖ səb 'sɪd i er li **~ies** iz **~ily** əl i ɪ li
subsidis... —*see* **subsidiz...**
subsidization ˌsʌb sɪd aɪ 'zeɪʃ ən, •səd-, -ɪ'•-
‖ -ə'• **~s** z
subsidiz|e 'sʌb sɪ daɪz -sə- **~ed** d **~es** ɪz əz
~ing ɪŋ
subsid|y 'sʌb səd li -sɪd- **~ies** iz
subsist səb 'sɪst §sʌb- **~ed** ɪd əd **~ing** ɪŋ **~s** s
subsistence səb 'sɪst ənts §sʌb-
sub'sistence crop; sub'sistence ˌfarmer
subsoil 'sʌb sɔɪəl **~s** z
subsonic ˌsʌb 'sɒn ɪk ‖ -'sɑːn- **~ally** əl‿i
subspecies 'sʌb ˌspiːʃ iːz -ˌspiːs-, -ɪz —*see note
at* species
substanc|e 'sʌb stənts **~es** ɪz əz
substandard ˌsʌb 'stænd əd ◄ ‖ -ərd ◄

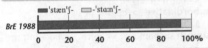

SUBSTANTIAL

■ 'stæn'ʃ- □ -'staːn'ʃ-					
BrE 1988					
0	20	40	60	80	100%

substantial səb 'stænʧ əl §sʌb-, -'staːnʧ-
—*BrE 1988 poll panel preference:* -'stænʧ-
93% (southerners 90%), -'staːnʧ- *7%
(southerners 10%). In AmE always* -'stænʧ-.
~ly i
substanti|ate səb 'stænʧ i eɪt §sʌb-,
-'staːnʧ-, -'stænts- **~ated** eɪt ɪd -əd ‖ eɪt̬ əd
~ates eɪts **~ating** eɪt ɪŋ ‖ eɪt̬ ɪŋ

substantiation səb ˌstænʧ i 'eɪʃ ən §sʌb-,
-ˌstaːnʧ-, -ˌstæn'ts-
substantival ˌsʌb stən 'taɪv əl ◄
substantive *adj* səb 'stænt ɪv §sʌb-;
'sʌb stənt- ‖ 'sʌb stənt ɪv **~ly** li **~ness** nəs
nɪs
substantive *n* 'sʌb stənt ɪv səb 'stænt ɪv,
§sʌb- **~s** z
substation 'sʌb ˌsteɪʃ ən **~s** z
substitutable 'sʌb stɪ tjuːt əb əl '•stə-,
→§-tʃuːt••, ˌ•'•• ‖ -tuːt̬ əb əl -tjuːt̬••
substitutability ˌsʌb stɪ tjuːt ə 'bɪl ət i ˌ•stə-,
→§, ••tʃuːt-, -ɪt i ‖ -tuːt̬ ə 'bɪl ət̬ i -tjuːt̬•'•-
substi|tute *v, n* 'sʌb stɪ tjuːt -stə-, →§-tʃuːt
‖ -ǀtuːt -tjuːt **~tuted** tjuːt ɪd →§tʃuːt-, -əd
‖ tuːt̬ əd tjuːt̬- **~tutes** tjuːts →§tʃuːts
‖ tuːts tjuːts **~tuting** tjuːt ɪŋ →§tʃuːt-
‖ tuːt̬ ɪŋ tjuːt̬-
substitution ˌsʌb stɪ 'tjuːʃ ən -stə-, →§-'tʃuːʃ-
‖ -'tuːʃ- -'tjuːʃ- **~s** z
substitutive 'sʌb stɪ tjuːt ɪv '•stə-, →§tʃuːt •
‖ -tuːt̬ ɪv -tjuːt̬•
substrate 'sʌb streɪt **~s** s
substrat|um 'sʌb ˌstraːt ləm -, streɪt-, ˌ•'••
‖ -ˌstreɪt̬ ləm -ˌstræt̬- **~a** ə
substructure 'sʌb ˌstrʌk tʃə -ʃə ‖ -tʃ ʃ ər **~s** z
subsum|e səb 'sjuːm §sʌb-, -'suːm ‖ -'suːm
~ed d **~es** z **~ing** ɪŋ
subsystem 'sʌb ˌsɪst əm -ɪm
subteen ˌsʌb 'tiːn ◄
subtenanc|y ˌsʌb 'ten ənts li '•,••• **~ies** iz
subtenant ˌsʌb 'ten ənt '•,•• **~s** s
subtend səb 'tend §sʌb- **~ed** ɪd əd **~ing** ɪŋ
~s z
subterfug|e 'sʌb tə fjuːdʒ -fjuːʒ ‖ -tər- **~es** ɪz
əz
subterranean ˌsʌb tə 'reɪn i̯ən ◄ **~ly** li
subtext 'sʌb tekst **~s** s
subtitl|e 'sʌb ˌtaɪt əl ‖ -ˌtaɪt̬ əl **~ed** d **~es** z
~ing ɪŋ
subtle 'sʌt əl ‖ 'sʌt̬ əl *(!)* **~ness** nəs nɪs **~er**
ə ‖ ər **~est** ɪst əst
subtle|ty 'sʌt əl ǀti ‖ 'sʌt̬- **~ties** tiz
subtly 'sʌt əl‿i ‖ 'sʌt̬ əl i →'sʌt li
subtonic ˌsʌb 'tɒn ɪk ◄ ‖ -'taːn- **~s** s
subtopi|a sʌb 'təʊp i̯ə ‖ -'toʊp- **~an** ən
subtotal 'sʌb ˌtəʊt əl ˌ•'•• ‖ -ˌtoʊt̬ əl **~ed,
~led** d **~ing, ~ling** ɪŋ **~s** z
subtract səb 'trækt §sʌb- **~ed** ɪd əd **~ing** ɪŋ
~s s
subtraction səb 'træk ʃən §sʌb- **~s** z
subtractive səb 'trækt ɪv §sʌb- **~ly** li
subtrahend 'sʌb trə hend **~s** z
subtropic ˌsʌb 'trɒp ɪk ‖ -'traːp- **~al** əl ◄ **~s** s
subtype 'sʌb taɪp **~s** s
suburb 'sʌb ɜːb §-əb ‖ -ɝːb **~s** z
suburban sə 'bɜːb ən ‖ -'bɝːb-
suburbanite sə 'bɜːb ə naɪt ‖ -'bɝːb- **~s** s
suburbia sə 'bɜːb i̯ə ‖ -'bɝːb-
subvariet|y 'sʌb və ˌraɪ̯ət li ˌɪt li ‖ -ˌraɪ ət̬ li
~ies iz
subvention səb 'venʧ ən sʌb- **~s** z

subversion səb ˈvɜːʃ ᵊn sʌb-, §-ˈvɜːʒ-
  ‖ -ˈvɜˑʒ ᵊn -ˈvɜːʃ-
subversive səb ˈvɜːs ɪv sʌb-, §-ˈvɜːz- ‖ -ˈvɜˑːs-
  ~ly li ~ness nəs nɪs ~s z
sub|vert səb |ˈvɜːt sʌb- ‖ -|ˈvɝːt ~verted
  ˈvɜːt ɪd -əd ‖ ˈvɝːt̬ əd ~verting
  ˈvɜːt ɪŋ ‖ ˈvɝːt̬ ɪŋ ~verts ˈvɜːts ‖ ˈvɝːts
subway ˈsʌb weɪ ~s z
Suby ˈsuːb i
subzero ˌsʌb ˈzɪər əʊ ◄ ‖ -ˈzɪr oʊ ◄ -ˈziː roʊ
  ˌsub ˌzero ˈtemperatures
succeed sək ˈsiːd §sʌk- ~ed ɪd əd ~ing ɪŋ ~s
  z
succes, succès ˌsuk ˈseɪ ◄ sək-. —Fr [syk sɛ]
  ˌsuccès de scanˈdale, sucˌcès-
  də skɒn ˈdɑːl ‖ -skɑːn◄ —Fr [də skɑ̃ dal];
  ˌsuccès dʼeˈstime, sucˌcès- de ˈstiːm —Fr
  [dɛs tim]; ˌsuccès ˈfou, sucˌcès- fu: —Fr [fu]
success sək ˈses §sʌk- ~es ɪz əz
  sucˈcess ˌstory
successful sək ˈses fᵊl §sʌk-, -fʊl ~ly ˌi
succession sək ˈseʃ ᵊn §sʌk- ~al ᵊl ~ally ᵊl i
  ~s z
successive sək ˈses ɪv §sʌk- ~ly li ~ness nəs
  nɪs
successor sək ˈses ə §sʌk- ‖ -ᵊr ~s z
succinate ˈsʌks ɪ neɪt -ə-
succinct sək ˈsɪŋkt sʌk-, sə- ~ly li ~ness nəs
  nɪs
succinic sʌk ˈsɪn ɪk sək-
succ|or ˈsʌk| ə ‖ -ᵊr (= sucker) ~ored əd ‖ ᵊrd
  ~oring ər ɪŋ ~ors əz ‖ ᵊrz
succory ˈsʌk ər i
succotash ˈsʌk ə tæʃ
Succoth ˈsuk əs ˈsʌk-; su ˈkɒt ‖ su ˈkoʊs
succ|our ˈsʌk| ə ‖ -ᵊr (= sucker) ~oured
  əd ‖ ᵊrd ~ouring ər ɪŋ ~ours əz ‖ ᵊrz
succ|uba ˈsʌk |jub ə -jəb- ‖ -|jəb ə ~ubae
  ju biː jə-, -baɪ ‖ jə- ~ubi ju baɪ jə-, -biː ‖ jə-
  ~ubus jub əs jəb- ‖ jəb-
succulence ˈsʌk jul ənᵗs -jəl- ‖ -jəl-
succulent ˈsʌk jul ənt -jəl- ‖ -jəl- ~ly li
succumb sə ˈkʌm ~ed d ~ing ɪŋ ~s z
such strong form sʌtʃ, occasional weak form sətʃ
  ˈsuch and ˌsuch
Suchard tdmk ˈsuːʃ ɑːd -ɑː ‖ su ˈʃɑːrd —Fr
  [sy ʃaːʁ]
Suchet ˈsuːʃ eɪ
suchlike ˈsʌtʃ laɪk
suck sʌk **sucked** sʌkt **sucking** ˈsʌk ɪŋ **sucks**
  sʌks
  ˈsucking pig
sucker ˈsʌk ə ‖ -ᵊr ~s z
suckl|e ˈsʌk ᵊl ~ed d ~es z ~ing ˌɪŋ
suckling n, S~ ˈsʌk lɪŋ ~s z
sucre, Sucre ˈsuːk reɪ —Sp [ˈsuk re] ~s z
sucrose ˈsuːk rəʊs ˈsjuːk-, -rəʊz ‖ -roʊs
suction ˈsʌk ʃᵊn ~ed d ~ing ˌɪŋ ~s z
  ˈsuction pump
Sudan su ˈdɑːn -ˈdæn ‖ -ˈdæn
Sudanese ˌsuːd ə ˈniːz ◄, ˌsud-, -ᵊn ˈiːz ◄
  ‖ ˌsuːd ᵊn ˈiːz ◄ -ˈiːs ◄
Sudanic su ˈdæn ɪk

sudari|um su ˈdeər i_ləm sju- ‖ -ˈder- -ˈdær-
  ~a ə
sudatori|um ˌsuːd ə ˈtɔːr i_ləm ˌsjuːd- ‖ -ˈtoʊr-
  ~a ə
sudator|y ˈsuːd ət ᵊr i ˈsjuːd- ‖ ˈsuːd ə tɔːr li
  -toʊr i ~ies iz
Sudbury ˈsʌd bər i →ˈsʌb- ‖ -ˌber i
Suddaby ˈsʌd əb i
sudden ˈsʌd ᵊn ~ly li ~ness nəs nɪs
  ˌsudden ˈdeath
Sudeten su ˈdeɪt ᵊn ~land lænd
sudorific ˌsuːd ə ˈrɪf ɪk ◄ ˌsjuːd-, -ɒ-, -ɔː- ~s s
suds sʌdz
sudsy ˈsʌdz i
sue sjuː suː ‖ suː **sued** sjuːd suːd ‖ suːd **sues**
  sjuːz suːz ‖ suːz **suing** ˈsjuːˌɪŋ ˈsuːˌ
  ‖ ˈsuːˌɪŋ
Sue suː
suede, suède sweɪd (= swayed)
  ˈsuede ˌshoes
suet ˈsuːˌɪt ˈsjuːˌ, §-ət
  ˈsuet ˌpudding
Suetonius ˌsuːˌ ɪ ˈtəun i_əs ˌsjuːˌ, əˈ•-, swiːˈ•-
  ‖ -ˈtoun-
Suez ˈsuːˌɪz ˈsjuːˌ ‖ ˌsu ˈez ◄ ˈsu ez (*)
  ˈSuez Caˈnal
suffer ˈsʌf ə ‖ -ᵊr ~ed d **suffering** ˈsʌf ər_ɪŋ
  ~s z
sufferab|le ˈsʌf ər_əb ᵊl ~ly li
sufferance ˈsʌf ər_ᵊnᵗs
sufferer ˈsʌf ər_ə ‖ -ᵊr ~s z
suffic|e sə ˈfaɪs ~ed t ~es ɪz əz ~ing ɪŋ
sufficiency sə ˈfɪʃ ᵊnᵗs i
sufficient sə ˈfɪʃ ᵊnt ~ly li
suffix n ˈsʌf ɪks ~es ɪz əz
suffix v ˈsʌf ɪks sə ˈfɪks, sʌ- ~ed t ~es ɪz əz
  ~ing ɪŋ
suffixal ˈsʌf ɪks ᵊl sə ˈfɪks ᵊl, sʌ-
suffixation ˌsʌf ɪk ˈseɪʃ ᵊn
suffo|cate ˈsʌf ə |keɪt ~cated keɪt ɪd -əd
  ‖ keɪt̬ əd ~cates keɪts ~cating/ly keɪt ɪŋ /li
  ‖ keɪt̬ ɪŋ /li
suffocation ˌsʌf ə ˈkeɪʃ ᵊn
Suffolk ˈsʌf ək
suffragan ˈsʌf rəg ᵊn △-rədʒ- ~s z
suffrag|e ˈsʌf rɪdʒ ~es ɪz əz
suffragette ˌsʌf rə ˈdʒet -rɪ- ~s s
suffragist ˈsʌf rədʒ ɪst -rɪdʒ-, §-əst ~s s
suffus|e sə ˈfjuːz sʌ- ~ed d ~es ɪz əz ~ing ɪŋ
suffusion sə ˈfjuːʒ ᵊn sʌ- ~s z
Sufi ˈsuːf i ~s z
Sufism ˈsuːf ˌɪz əm
sugar ˈʃug ə ‖ -ᵊr (!) ~ed d **sugaring** ˈʃug
  ər_ɪŋ ~s z
  ˌsugar ˈbeet,ˈ•• •; ˈsugar bowl; ˈsugar
  ˌdaddy
sugarcane ˈʃug ə keɪn ‖ -ᵊr-
sugarcoated ˌʃug ə ˈkəut ɪd ◄ -əd
  ‖ -ᵊr ˈkout̬ əd ◄
sugariness ˈʃug ər_i nəs -nɪs
sugarloaf ˈʃug ə ləuf ‖ -ᵊr louf
sugarplum ˈʃug ə plʌm ‖ -ᵊr- ~s z
sugary ˈʃug ər i

S

Sugden 'sʌg dən

SUGGEST

■ with g ▭ without g

AmE 1993

0 20 40 60 80 100%

suggest sə 'dʒest ‖ səg 'dʒest sə- —*AmE 1993 poll panel preference: with g 77%, without g 23%.* ~ed ɪd əd ~ing ɪŋ ~s s
suggestibility sə ˌdʒest ə 'bɪl ət i -ˌ•ɪ-, -ɪt i ‖ səg ˌdʒest ə 'bɪl ət̬ i sə-
suggestible sə 'dʒest əb əl -ɪb- ‖ səg- sə-
suggestion sə 'dʒes t∫ən →-'dʒeʃ- ‖ səg- sə- ~s z
suggestive sə 'dʒest ɪv ‖ səg- sə- ~ly li ~ness nəs nɪs
Sugrew, Sugrue 'suː gruː
Suharto su 'haːt əʊ ‖ -'haːrt oʊ
sui 'suː aɪ 'sjuː-, -iː
 ˌsui 'generis 'dʒen ər ɪs 'gen-; ˌsui 'juris 'dʒʊər ɪs 'jʊər-
Sui *dynasty* 'suː i sweɪ —*Chi Suí [²sweɪ]*
suicidal ˌsuː ɪ 'saɪd əl ◄ ˌsjuː-, ˌ-ə- ~ly i
suicide 'suː ɪ saɪd 'sjuː-, ˌ-ə- ~s z
suint swɪnt 'suː ɪnt, 'sjuː-

SUIT

■ suːt ▭ sjuːt

BrE 1988

0 20 40 60 80 100%

■ BrE88 without /j/, by age

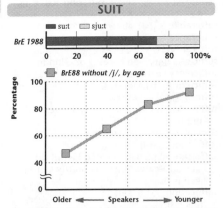

Percentage

100

80

60

40

0

Older ◄— Speakers —► Younger

suit suːt sjuːt —*BrE 1988 poll panel preference:* suːt 72%, sjuːt 28%. *AmE always* suːt.
 suited 'suːt ɪd 'sjuːt-, -əd ‖ 'suːt̬ əd
 suiting/s 'suːt ɪŋ/z 'sjuːt- ‖ 'suːt̬ ɪŋ/z suits suːts sjuːts ‖ suːts
suitability ˌsuːt ə 'bɪl ət i ˌsjuːt-, -ɪt i ‖ ˌsuːt̬ ə 'bɪl ət̬ i
suitab|le 'suːt əb əl 'sjuːt- ‖ 'suːt̬- ~leness əl nəs -nɪs ~ly li
suitcas|e 'suːt keɪs 'sjuːt- ~es ɪz əz
suite swiːt (= *sweet*) —*but in AmE sometimes* suːt *in the sense 'suite of furniture'* suites swiːts
suitor 'suːt ə 'sjuːt- ‖ 'suːt̬ ər ~s z
Sukey, Sukie 'suːk i
sukiyaki ˌsuːk i 'jaːk i ˌsʊk- —*Jp* [sɯ̥ˌki ja ki]
Sulawesi ˌsuːl ə 'weɪs i
sulcal 'sʌlk əl ~ly i
sulcalis... *see* sulcaliz...

sulcalization ˌsʌlk ə laɪ 'zeɪʃ ən -lɪ'•• ‖ ˌ•əl ə-
sulcaliz|e 'sʌlk ə laɪz ~ed d ~es ɪz əz ~ing ɪŋ
sulcate *adj* 'sʌlk eɪt
sulcus 'sʌlk əs sulci 'sʌls aɪ 'sʌlk-, -iː
Suleiman ˌsʊl i 'maːn ˌsuːl-, -eɪ-, '•••
sulfa 'sʌlf ə
 'sulfa ˌdrug
sulfadiazine ˌsʌlf ə 'daɪˌə ziːn
sulfaguanidine ˌsʌlf ə 'gwaːn ɪ diːn -'•ə-
sulfamic sʌl 'fæm ɪk
sulfanilamide ˌsʌlf ə 'nɪl ə maɪd
sulfate 'sʌlf eɪt ~s s
sulfathiazole ˌsʌlf ə 'θaɪˌə zəʊl →-zɒʊl ‖ -zoʊl
sulfide 'sʌlf aɪd ~s z
sulfite 'sʌlf aɪt ~s s
sulfonamide sʌl 'fɒn ə maɪd ‖ -'faːn- -'foʊn-
sulfo|nate 'sʌlf ə |neɪt ~nated neɪt ɪd -əd ‖ neɪt̬ əd ~nates neɪts ~nating neɪt ɪŋ ‖ neɪt̬ ɪŋ
sulfone 'sʌlf əʊn ‖ -oʊn ~s z
sulfonic sʌl 'fɒn ɪk ‖ -'faːn- -'foʊn-
sulfur 'sʌlf ə ‖ -ər
sulfureous sʌl 'fjʊər iˌəs -'fjɔːr- ‖ -'fjʊr-
sulfu|ret 'sʌlf jʊ |ret -jə-, -ə-; ˌ••'• ‖ -ə- ~reted, ~retted ret ɪd -əd ‖ ret̬ əd ~reting, ~retting ret ɪŋ ‖ ret̬ ɪŋ ~rets rets
sulfuric sʌl 'fjʊər ɪk -'fjɔːr- ‖ -'fjʊr- sulˌfuric 'acid
sulfurous 'sʌlf ər əs -jʊr- ~ly li ~ness nəs nɪs
Sulgrave 'sʌl greɪv
sulk sʌlk sulked sʌlkt sulking 'sʌlk ɪŋ sulks sʌlks
sulk|y 'sʌlk |i ~ier iˌə ‖ iˌər ~iest iˌɪst iˌəst ~ily ɪ li əl i ~iness i nəs i nɪs
Sulla 'sʌl ə 'sʊl-
sullage 'sʌl ɪdʒ
sullen 'sʌl ən ~ly li ~ness nəs nɪs
sulli... —*see* sully
Sullivan 'sʌl ɪv ən -əv-
Sullom Voe ˌsʊl əm 'vəʊ ˌsʌl- ‖ -'voʊ
sully, Sully 'sʌl i sullied 'sʌl id sullies 'sʌl iz sullying 'sʌl i ɪŋ
sulpha 'sʌlf ə
 'sulpha ˌdrug
sulphadiazine ˌsʌlf ə 'daɪˌə ziːn
sulphaguanidine ˌsʌlf ə 'gwaːn ɪ diːn -'•ə-
sulphamic sʌl 'fæm ɪk
sulphanilamide ˌsʌlf ə 'nɪl ə maɪd
sulphate 'sʌlf eɪt ~s s
sulphathiazole ˌsʌlf ə 'θaɪˌə zəʊl →-zɒʊl ‖ -zoʊl
sulphide 'sʌlf aɪd ~s z
sulphite 'sʌlf aɪt ~s s
sulphonamide sʌl 'fɒn ə maɪd ‖ -'faːn- -'foʊn-
sulpho|nate 'sʌlf ə |neɪt ~nated neɪt ɪd -əd ‖ neɪt̬ əd ~nates neɪts ~nating neɪt ɪŋ ‖ neɪt̬ ɪŋ
sulphone 'sʌlf əʊn ‖ -oʊn ~s z
sulphonic sʌl 'fɒn ɪk ‖ -'faːn- -'foʊn-
sulphur 'sʌlf ə ‖ -ər
sulphureous sʌl 'fjʊər iˌəs -'fjɔːr- ‖ -'fjʊr-

S

sulphu|ret 'sʌlf juə |ret -jə-, -ə-; ˌ•'•'• ‖ -ə-
  ~reted, ~retted ret ɪd -əd ‖ reţ əd **~reting,**
  ~retting ret ɪŋ ‖ reţ ɪŋ **~rets** rets
sulphuric sʌl 'fjʊər ɪk -'fjɔːr- ‖ -'fjʊr-
  sul͵phuric 'acid
sulphurous 'sʌlf ər əs -jʊr- **~ly** li **~ness** nəs
  nɪs
sultan 'sʌlt ən ‖ -ᵊn **~s** z
sultana sʌl 'tɑːn ə səl- ‖ -'tæn- **~s** z
sultanate 'sʌlt ən ət -ɪt; -ə neɪt, -ᵊn eɪt
  ‖ -ᵊn eɪt **~s** s
sultr|y 'sʌltr |i **~ier** i‿ə ‖ i‿ᵊr **~iest** i‿ɪst i‿əst
  ~ily əl i ɪ li **~iness** i nəs i nɪs
Sulu 'suːl uː
Sulwen 'sɪ:ᵊl wen -wən —*Welsh* ['sɪl wen, 'sɪl-]
Sulwyn 'sɪ:ᵊl wɪn —*Welsh* ['sɪl wɪn, 'sɪl-]
sum sʌm **summed** sʌmd **summing** 'sʌm ɪŋ
  sums sʌmz
  ͵sum 'total
sumac, sumach 'ʃuːm æk 'suːm-, 'sjuːm- **~s** s
Sumatr|a su 'mɑːtr |ə sju-, sə- **~an/s** ən/z
Sumburgh 'sʌm bər‿ə
Sumer 'suːm ə ‖ -ᵊr
Sumerian su 'mɪər i‿ən sju-, sə-, -'meər-
  ‖ -'mer- -'mɪr- **~s** z
Sumitomo ˌsuːm i 'təʊm əʊ ‖ -'toʊm oʊ —*Jp*
  [sɯ ˌmi to mo]
summa 'sʌm ə 'sʊm-, -ɑː
  ͵summa cum 'laude
summaris|e, summariz|e 'sʌm ə raɪz **~ed** d
  ~es ɪz əz **~ing** ɪŋ
summar|y 'sʌm ər‿|i **~ies** iz
summat 'sʌm ət —*Since this is mainly a North*
  of England dialect word, in practice it is more
  usually 'sʊm-
summation sʌ 'meɪʃ ᵊn sə- **~s** z
summer 'sʌm ə ‖ -ᵊr **~s** z
  'summer school
Summerfield 'sʌm ə fiːᵊld ‖ -ᵊr-
Summerhayes 'sʌm ə heɪz ‖ -ᵊr-
Summerhill 'sʌm ə hɪl ‖ -ᵊr-
summer|house 'sʌm ə |haʊs ‖ -ᵊr- **~houses**
  haʊz ɪz -əz
summeriness 'sʌm ər i nəs -nɪs
Summers 'sʌm əz ‖ -ᵊrz
Summerscale 'sʌm ə skeɪᵊl ‖ -ᵊr-
Summerskill 'sʌm ə skɪl ‖ -ᵊr-
summertime 'sʌm ə taɪm ‖ -ᵊr-
summery 'sʌm ər i
summing-up ˌsʌm ɪŋ 'ʌp **summings-up**
  ˌsʌm ɪŋz 'ʌp
summit 'sʌm ɪt §-ət **~s** s
  'summit ͵conference
summiteer ˌsʌm ɪ 'tɪə -ə- ‖ -'tɪᵊr **~s** z
summitry 'sʌm ɪtr i §-ətr-
summon 'sʌm ən **~ed** d **~ing** ɪŋ **~s** z
summons 'sʌm ənz **~ed** d **~es** ɪz əz **~ing** ɪŋ
summum bonum ˌsʌm əm 'bəʊn əm ˌsʊm-,
  -ʊm-, -'bɒn-, -ʊm ‖ -'boʊn-
Sumner 'sʌm nə ‖ -nᵊr
sumo 'suːm əʊ ‖ -oʊ —*Jp* [sɯ ˌmoo]
sump sʌmp **sumps** sʌmps
sumptuary 'sʌmp tʃu‿ər i -tju‿ər- ‖ -er i

sumptuous 'sʌmp tʃu‿əs -tju‿ **~ly** li **~ness**
  nəs nɪs
Sumter 'sʌmpt ə ‖ -ᵊr
sun sʌn **sunned** sʌnd **sunning** 'sʌn ɪŋ **suns**
  sʌnz
  'sun god; 'sun lounge; 'sun parlor; 'sun
  porch; 'sun ͵visor
sunbaked 'sʌn beɪkt →'sʌm-
sunbath|e 'sʌn beɪð →'sʌm- **~ed** d **~er/s**
  ə/z ‖ ᵊr/z **~es** z **~ing** ɪŋ
sunbeam, S~ 'sʌn biːm →'sʌm- **~s** z
sunbed 'sʌn bed →'sʌm- **~s** z
sunbelt, S~ 'sʌn belt →'sʌm-
sunbird 'sʌn bɜːd →'sʌm- ‖ -bɜːd **~s** z
sunblind 'sʌn blaɪnd →'sʌm- **~s** z
sunblock 'sʌn blɒk →'sʌm- ‖ -blɑːk **~s** s
sunbonnet 'sʌn ˌbɒn ɪt →'sʌm-, §-ət
  ‖ -ˌbɑːn ət **~s** s
sunburn 'sʌn bɜːn →'sʌm- ‖ -bɜːn **~ed** d
sunburnt 'sʌn bɜːnt →'sʌm- ‖ -bɜːnt
sunburst 'sʌn bɜːst →'sʌm- ‖ -bɜːst **~s** s
Sunbury 'sʌn bər‿i →'sʌm- ‖ -ˌber i
Sunda 'sʌnd ə 'sʊnd-, 'suːnd-
sundae 'sʌnd eɪ -i **~s** z
Sundanese ˌsʌnd ə 'niːz ◄ ˌsʊnd-,
  ˌsuːnd- ‖ -'niːs
Sunday 'sʌn deɪ 'sʌnd i —*see note at* -day **~s** z
  ͵Sunday 'best; 'Sunday school
sundeck 'sʌn dek **~s** s
sunder 'sʌnd ə ‖ -ᵊr **~ed** d **sundering**
  'sʌnd‿ər ɪŋ **~s** z
Sunderland 'sʌnd ə lənd→-ᵊl ənd ‖ -ᵊr-
sundew 'sʌn djuː →§-dʒuː ‖ -duː -djuː **~s** z
sundial 'sʌn ˌdaɪ‿əl **~s** z
sundown 'sʌn daʊn **~s** z
sundowner 'sʌn daʊn ə ‖ -ᵊr **~s** z
sundrenched 'sʌn drenʧt
sundress 'sʌn dres **~es** ɪz əz
Sundridge 'sʌndr ɪdʒ
sun-dried 'sʌn draɪd ˌ•'•◄
sundr|y 'sʌndr |i **~ies** iz
sunfish 'sʌn fɪʃ **~es** ɪz əz
sunflower 'sʌn ˌflaʊ‿ə ‖ -ˌflaʊ‿ᵊr **~s** z
sung sʌŋ
sunglasses 'sʌn ˌglɑːs ɪz →'sʌŋ-, §-ˌglæs-, -əz
  ‖ -ˌglæs əz
sunhat 'sʌn hæt **~s** s
sunk sʌŋk
sunken 'sʌŋk ən
sunkissed, Sunkist *tdmk* 'sʌn kɪst→'sʌŋ-
sunlamp 'sʌn læmp **~s** s
sunless 'sʌn ləs -lɪs **~ly** li **~ness** nəs nɪs
sunlight, S~ 'sʌn laɪt
sunlit 'sʌn lɪt
sunlounger 'sʌn ˌlaʊndʒ ə ‖ -ᵊr **~s** z
Sunna 'sʊn ə 'sʌn-
Sunni 'sʊn i 'sʌn- **~s** z
Sunningdale 'sʌn ɪŋ deɪᵊl
Sunnite 'sʌn aɪt 'sʌn- **~s** s
sunn|y, Sunn|y 'sʌn |i **~ier** i‿ə ‖ i‿ᵊr **~iest**
  i‿ɪst i‿əst **~ily** i li əl i **~iness** i nəs i nɪs
Sunnyside 'sʌn i saɪd
sunny-side up ˌsʌn i saɪd 'ʌp

S

sunray 'sʌn reɪ ~s z
sunris|e 'sʌn raɪz ~es ɪz əz
  'sunrise ˌindustry
sunroof 'sʌn ruːf -rʊf ~s s
sunscreen 'sʌn skriːn ~s z
sunset 'sʌn set ~s s
sunshade 'sʌn ʃeɪd ~s z
sunshine 'sʌn ʃaɪn
sunspot 'sʌn spɒt ‖ -spɑːt ~s s
sunstroke 'sʌn strəʊk ‖ -stroʊk
suntan 'sʌn tæn ~ned d ~ning ɪŋ ~s z
Suntory tdmk 'sʌn tɔːr i •'•• —Jp ['san to rii]
suntrap 'sʌn træp ~s s
sun-up 'sʌn ʌp ~s s
Sun Yatsen ˌsʌn jæt 'sen ‖ -jɑːt- —Chi Sūn
  Zhōngshān [¹swən ¹tʂʊŋ ¹ʂan]
sup sʌp **supped** sʌpt **supping** 'sʌp ɪŋ **sups**
  sʌps
super 'suːp ə 'sjuːp- ‖ -ər ~s z
super- ˌsuːp əˌsjuːp ə ‖ -ər— **superpower**
  'suːp ə ˌpaʊ̯ əˈsjuːp- ‖ 'suːp ər ˌpaʊ̯ ər
superabundance ˌsuːp ər̯ ə 'bʌnd ən¹s ˌsjuːp-,
  -ə ə-
superabundant ˌsuːp ər̯ ə 'bʌnd ənt ◂ ˌsjuːp-,
  -ə ə- ~ly li
superannu|ate ˌsuːp ər 'æn ju eɪt ˌsjuːp-
  ‖ ˌ•ər- ~ated eɪt ɪd-əd ‖ eɪt̯ əd ~ates eɪts
  ~ating eɪt ɪŋ ‖ eɪt̯ ɪŋ
superannuation ˌsuːp ər ˌæn ju 'eɪʃ ən ˌsjuːp-,
  ‖ ˌ•ər- ~s z
superb su 'pɜːb sju-, sə- ‖ -'pɝːb ~ly li ~ness
  nəs nɪs
Superbowl 'suːp ə bəʊl 'sjuːp-, →-bɒʊl
  ‖ -ər boʊl
supercargo ˌsuːp ə 'kɑːg əʊ ˌsjuːp-, '•••
  ‖ -ər 'kɑːrg oʊ ~s z
supercharged 'suːp ə tʃɑːdʒd 'sjuːp-, ˌ••'•
  ‖ -ər tʃɑːrdʒd
supercharger 'suːp ə ˌtʃɑːdʒ ə 'sjuːp-, ˌ••'•••
  ‖ -ər ˌtʃɑːrdʒ ər ~s z
supercilious ˌsuːp ə 'sɪl i̯ əs ◂ ˌsjuːp- ‖ ˌ•ər-
  ~ly li ~ness nəs nɪs
superconduction ˌsuːp ə kən 'dʌk ʃən ˌsjuːp-,
  §-kɒn'• ‖ ˌ•ər-
superconductivity ˌsuːp ə ˌkɒn dʌk 'tɪv ət i
  ˌsjuːp-, -ɪt i ‖ -ər ˌkɑːn dʌk 'tɪv ət̯ i
superconductor ˌsuːp ə kən 'dʌkt ə ˌsjuːp-,
  §-kɒn'• ‖ -ər kən 'dʌkt ər ~s z
supercool ˌsuːp ə 'kuːl ◂ ˌsjuːp-, '••• ‖ ˌ•ər-
  ~ed d ~ing ɪŋ ~s z
superduper ˌsuːp ə 'duːp ə ◂ ˌsjuːp-
  ‖ -ər 'duːp ər
superego ˌsuːp ər 'iːg əʊ ˌsjuːp-, -ə-, -'eg-
  ‖ -'iːg oʊ ~s z
superelevation ˌsuːp ərˌel ɪ 'veɪʃ ən, ˌ•ə-, -ə'•-
supererogatory ˌsuːp ər ɪ 'rɒg ət ər i ˌsjuːp-,
  ˌ•ə'•-, -e'• ‖ -'rɑːg ə tɔːr i-toʊr i
supererogation ˌsuːp ər er ə 'geɪʃ ən ˌsjuːp-,
  ˌ•ə-
superficial ˌsuːp ə 'fɪʃ əl ◂ ˌsjuːp- ‖ -ər- ~ly i
  ~ness nəs nɪs
superficiality ˌsuːp ə ˌfɪʃ i 'æl ət i ˌsjuːp-, -ɪt i
  ‖ -ər ˌfɪʃ i 'æl ət̯ i

superficies ˌsuːp ə 'fɪʃ iːz ˌsjuːp-, -'fɪʃ i iːz
  ‖ -ər-
superfine ˌsuːp ə faɪn 'sjuːp-, ˌ••'• ‖ -ər-
  ~ness nəs nɪs
superfix 'suːp ə fɪks 'sjuːp- ‖ -ər- ~es ɪz əz
superfluid 'suːp ə ˌfluː̯ ɪd 'sjuːp-, §ˌ•əd ‖ -ər-
  ~s z
superfluidity ˌsuːp ə flu 'ɪd ət i ˌsjuːp-, -ɪt i
  ‖ -ər flu 'ɪd ət̯ i
superfluit|y ˌsuːp ə 'fluː̯ ət i ˌsjuːp-, ˌ•t i
  ‖ -ər 'fluː ət̯ li ~ies iz
superfluous su 'pɜːf lu̯ əs sju- ‖ -'pɝːf- (!)
  ~ly li ~ness nəs nɪs
supergiant 'suːp ə ˌdʒaɪ̯ ənt 'sjuːp- ‖ -ər- ~s s
superglue, Super Glue tdmk 'suːp ə gluː
  'sjuːp- ‖ -ər- ~d d
supergrass 'suːp ə grɑːs 'sjuːp-, §-græs
  ‖ -ər græs ~es ɪz əz
superhero 'suːp ə ˌhɪər əʊ 'sjuːp-, ˌ••'••
  ‖ -ər ˌhɪr oʊ-ˌhiː roʊ ~es z
superhet 'suːp ə het 'sjuːp- ‖ -ər- ~s s
superhighway ˌsuːp ə 'haɪ weɪ ˌsjuːp-, '••,••
  ‖ -ər- ~s z
superhuman ˌsuːp ə 'hjuːm ən ◂ ˌsjuːp-,
  §-'juːm- ‖ -ər-
  ˌsuper ˌhuman 'efforts
superimpos|e ˌsuːp ər ɪm 'pəʊz ˌsjuːp-, ˌ•ə-
  ‖ -'poʊz ~ed d ~es ɪz əz ~ing ɪŋ
superimposition ˌsuːp ər ˌɪmp ə 'zɪʃ ən ˌsjuːp-,
  ˌ•ə-
superintend ˌsuːp ər ɪn 'tend ˌsjuːp-, ˌ•ə-,
  §ˌ•ən'• ~ed ɪd əd ~ency ən¹s i ~ing ɪŋ ~s z
superintendent ˌsuːp ər ɪn 'tend ənt ˌsjuːp-,
  ˌ•ə-, §ˌ•ən'•- ~s s
superior, S~ su 'pɪər i̯ əs sju- ‖ su 'pɪr i̯ ər sə-
  ~ly li ~s z
superiority su ˌpɪər i 'ɒr ət i sju-, -ɪt i
  ‖ su ˌpɪr i 'ɔːr ət̯ i sə-, -'ɑːr-
  su ˌperi'ority ˌcomplex
superlative su 'pɜːl ət ɪv sju- ‖ su 'pɝːl ət̯ ɪv
  ~ly li ~ness nəs nɪs ~s z
super|man, S~ 'suːp ə ˌmæn 'sjuːp- ‖ -ər-
  ~men men
supermarket 'suːp ə ˌmɑːk ɪt 'sjuːp-, §-ət
  ‖ -ər ˌmɑːrk ət ~s s
supermen 'suːp ə men 'sjuːp- ‖ -ər-
supermodel 'suːp ə ˌmɒd əl 'sjuːp-
  ‖ -ər ˌmɑːd əl ~s z
supernal su 'pɜːn əl sju- ‖ -'pɝːn- ~ly i
supernatural ˌsuːp ə 'nætʃ ər əl ◂ ˌsjuːp-
  ‖ ˌ•ər- ~ly i ~ness nəs nɪs
supernormal ˌsuːp ə 'nɔːm əl ◂ ˌsjuːp-
  ‖ -ər 'nɔːrm- ~ly i
supernov|a ˌsuːp ə 'nəʊv ə ˌsjuːp- ‖ -ər 'noʊv-
  ~ae iː ~as əz
supernumerar|y ˌsuːp ə 'njuːm ər̯ ər li ◂
  ˌsjuːp-, △-'•ər li ‖ ˌsuːp ər 'nuːm ə rer li ◂
  -'njuːm-, △-'•ər li ~ies iz
superordinate adj, n ˌsuːp ər 'ɔːd ən̯ ət ◂
  ˌsjuːp-, ˌ•t, -ɪn ət, -ɪn ɪt; -ə neɪt, -ən eɪt,
  -ɪ neɪt ‖ -ər 'ɔːrd- ~s s
superphosphate ˌsuːp ə 'fɒs feɪt ˌsjuːp-
  ‖ -ər 'fɑːs- ~s s

superpower 'suːp ə ˌpaʊ‿ə 'sjuːp-, ˌ•‿•'••
‖ -ʳr ˌpaʊ‿ʳr ~s z
supersatu|rate ˌsuːp ə 'sætʃ ə ˌreɪt ˌsjuːp-,
-'sætʃ u-, -'sæt juː- ‖ ˌ•'ʳr- ~**rated** reɪt ɪd-əd
‖ reɪt̬ əd ~**rates** reɪts ~**rating**
reɪt ɪŋ ‖ reɪt̬ ɪŋ
superscript 'suːp ə skrɪpt 'sjuːp- ‖ -ʳr- ~s s
superscription ˌsuːp ə 'skrɪp ʃən ˌsjuːp- ‖ -ʳr-
~s z
supersed|e ˌsuːp ə 'siːd ˌsjuːp- ‖ -ʳr- ~**ed** ɪd
əd ~**es** z ~**ing** ɪŋ
supersession ˌsuːp ə 'seʃ ən ˌsjuːp- ‖ -ʳr- ~s z
superset 'suːp ə set 'sjuːp- ‖ -ʳr- ~s s
supersonic ˌsuːp ə 'sɒn ɪk ◄ ˌsjuːp- ‖ -ʳr 'sɑːn-
~**ally** ᵊl i ~s s
superstar 'suːp ə stɑː 'sjuːp- ‖ -ʳr stɑːr ~**dom**
dəm ~s z
superstition ˌsuːp ə 'stɪʃ ən ˌsjuːp- ‖ -ʳr- ~s z
superstitious ˌsuːp ə 'stɪʃ əs ◄ ˌsjuːp- ‖ -ʳr-
~**ly** li ~**ness** nəs nɪs
superstore 'suːp ə stɔː 'sjuːp- ‖ -ʳr stɔːr
-stoʊr ~s z
superstrate 'suːp ə streɪt 'sjuːp- ‖ -ʳr- ~s s
superstring 'suːp ə strɪŋ 'sjuːp- ‖ -ʳr- ~s z
superstructure 'suːp ə ˌstrʌk tʃə 'sjuːp-, -ʃə
‖ -ʳr ˌstrʌk tʃʳr ~s z
supertanker 'suːp ə ˌtæŋk ə 'sjuːp-
‖ -ʳr ˌtæŋk ʳr ~s z
supertax 'suːp ə tæks 'sjuːp- ‖ -ʳr-
supertonic ˌsuːp ə 'tɒn ɪk ◄ ˌsjuːp-, '••, ••
‖ -ʳr 'tɑːn- ~s s
superven|e ˌsuːp ə 'viːn ˌsjuːp- ‖ -ʳr- ~**ed** d
~**es** z ~**ing** ɪŋ
supervis|e 'suːp ə vaɪz 'sjuːp- ‖ -ʳr- ~**ed** d
~**es** ɪz əz ~**ing** ɪŋ
supervisee ˌsuːp ə vaɪ 'ziː ˌsjuːp- ‖ ˌ•'ʳr- ~s z
supervision ˌsuːp ə 'vɪʒ ən ˌsjuːp- ‖ -ʳr- ~s z
supervisor 'suːp ə vaɪz ə 'sjuːp- ‖ -ʳr vaɪz ʳr
~s z
supervisory ˌsuːp ə 'vaɪz ər i ◄ ˌsjuːp-, -'vɪz-;
'••••• ‖ ˌ•'ʳr-
super|woman 'suːp ə ˌwʊm ən 'sjuːp- ‖ -ʳr-
~**women** ˌwɪm ɪn §-ən
supi|nate 'suːp ɪ ˌneɪt 'sjuːp-, -ə- ~**nated**
neɪt ɪd-əd ‖ neɪt̬ əd ~**nates** neɪts ~**nating**
neɪt ɪŋ ‖ neɪt̬ ɪŋ
supination ˌsuːp ɪ 'neɪʃ ən ˌsjuːp-, -ə-
supinator 'suːp ɪ neɪt ə 'sjuːp-, '•ə- ‖ -neɪt̬ ʳr
~s z
supine *'lying on the back'; 'lazy'* 'suːp aɪn
'sjuːp-; ˌsuː 'paɪn, ˌsjuː:- ~**ly** li ~**ness** nəs nɪs
supine *grammatical term* 'suːp aɪn 'sjuːp- ~s z
Suppé 'suːp eɪ ‖ su 'peɪ—*Ger* [zʊ 'peː]
supper 'sʌp ə ‖ -ʳr ~s z
suppertime 'sʌp ə taɪm ‖ -ʳr- ~s z
sup|plant sə ‖'plɑːnt §-'plænt ‖ -‖'plænt
~**planted** 'plɑːnt ɪd §'plænt-, -əd ‖ 'plænt̬ əd
~**planting** 'plɑːnt ɪŋ §'plænt- ‖ 'plænt̬ ɪŋ
~**plants** 'plɑːnts §'plænts ‖ 'plænts
supple, S~ 'sʌp ᵊl ~**ly** li ~**ness** nəs nɪs
supplejack 'sʌp ᵊl dʒæk
supplement *n* 'sʌp lɪ mənt -lə- ~s s

supple|ment *v* 'sʌp lɪ ‖ment -lə-, ˌ••'•• —*see
note at* -ment ~**mented** ment ɪd-əd
‖ ment̬ əd ~**menting** ment ɪŋ ‖ ment̬ ɪŋ
~**ments** ments
supplemental ˌsʌp lɪ 'ment ᵊl ◄ -lə- ‖ -'ment̬ ᵊl
~**ly** i
supplementar|y ˌsʌp lɪ 'ment ʳr li ◄, •lə-
‖ -'ment̬ ʳr li◄-'mentr li ~**ies** iz
ˌsupple ˌmentary 'benefit
supplementation ˌsʌp lɪ men 'teɪʃ ən, •lə-,
-mən'•-
suppletion sə 'pliːʃ ən
suppletive sə 'pliːt ɪv 'sʌp lət ɪv, -lɪt-
‖ sə 'pliːt̬ ɪv 'sʌp lət̬ ɪv ~s z
suppliant 'sʌp li ənt ~**ly** li ~s s
supplicant 'sʌp lɪk ənt -lək- ~s s
suppli|cate 'sʌp lɪ ˌkeɪt -lə- ~**cated** keɪt ɪd-əd
‖ keɪt̬ əd ~**cates** keɪts ~**cating**
keɪt ɪŋ ‖ keɪt̬ ɪŋ
supplication ˌsʌp lɪ 'keɪʃ ən-lə- ~s z
supplicatory ˌsʌp lɪ 'keɪt ʳr i ◄'•••-;
'sʌp lɪk ət ʳr i ‖ 'sʌp lɪk ə tɔːr i-toʊr i (*)
supplier sə 'plaɪ‿ə ‖ -'plaɪ‿ʳr ~s z
sup|ply *v, n* sə ‖'plaɪ ~**plied** 'plaɪd ~**plies**
'plaɪz ~**plying** 'plaɪ ɪŋ
sup ˌply and de'mand; sup ply 'teacher
supply *adv of* **supple** 'sʌp ᵊl li-ᵊl i
supply-sid|e sə 'plaɪ saɪd ~**er/s** ə/z ‖ -ʳr/z
sup|port *v, n* sə ‖'pɔːt ‖ -‖'pɔːrt -'poʊrt
~**ported** 'pɔːt ɪd-əd ‖ 'pɔːrt̬ əd'poʊrt-
~**porting** 'pɔːt ɪŋ ‖ 'pɔːrt̬ ɪŋ'poʊrt- ~**ports**
'pɔːts ‖ 'pɔːrts 'poʊrts
sup'porting ˌpart; sup'porting
'programme; sup'porting 'role
supportab|le sə 'pɔːt əb ᵊl ‖ -'pɔːrt̬- -'poʊrt̬-
~**ly** li
supporter sə 'pɔːt ə ‖ -'pɔːrt̬ ʳr-'poʊrt̬- ~s z
sup'porters' ˌclub
supportive sə 'pɔːt ɪv ‖ -'pɔːrt̬- -'poʊrt̬- ~**ness**
nəs nɪs
suppos|e sə 'pəʊz ‖ -'poʊz—*but the phrase* I
suppose *is often* aɪ 'spəʊz ‖ -'spoʊz ~**es** ɪz əz
~**ing** ɪŋ
supposed *in* (be) supposed to *'ought to'*
sə 'pəʊst→'spəʊst; sə'pəʊzd ‖ -'poʊzd
supposed *past and pp of* **suppose**
sə 'pəʊzd ‖ -'poʊzd
supposed *adj* sə 'pəʊzd-'pəʊz ɪd, -əd
‖ -'poʊzd-'poʊz əd
supposedly sə 'pəʊz ɪd li-əd- ‖ -'poʊz-
supposition ˌsʌp ə 'zɪʃ ən ~s z
suppositional ˌsʌp ə 'zɪʃ ən ᵊl ~**ly** i
suppositious ˌsʌp ə 'zɪʃ əs ◄
supposititious sə ˌpɒz ɪ 'tɪʃ əs ◄-ə- ‖ -ˌpɑːz-
~**ly** li ~**ness** nəs nɪs
suppositive sə 'pɒz ət ɪv-ɪt- ‖ -'pɑːz ət̬- ~**ly** li
~s z
suppositor|y sə 'pɒz ɪt ʳr i-'•ət̬
‖ sə 'pɑːz ə tɔːr i-toʊr i ~**ies** iz
suppress sə 'pres ~**ed** t ~**es** ɪz əz ~**ing** ɪŋ
suppressant sə 'pres ᵊnt ~s s
suppression sə 'preʃ ən ~s z
suppressive sə 'pres ɪv ~**ly** li

S

suppressor sə 'pres ə ‖ -ᵊr **~s** z
suppu|rate 'sʌp juə |reɪt -jə- ‖ -jə- **~rated**
  reɪt ɪd -əd ‖ reɪt̬ əd **~rates** reɪts **~rating**
  reɪt ɪŋ ‖ reɪt̬ ɪŋ
suppuration ˌsʌp juə 'reɪʃ ᵊn -jə- ‖ -jə-
suppurative 'sʌp jʊr ət ɪv '•jər-; -ju reɪt ɪv,
  -jə•• ‖ 'sʌp jər ət̬ ɪv -jə reɪt̬-; 'sʌp rət̬ ɪv **~s**
  z
supra 'su:p rə 'sju:p-, -rɑː
supra- ˌsu:p rə ˌsju:p- — **suprarenal**
  ˌsu:p rə 'ri:n ᵊl ◂ ˌsju:p-
supraglottal ˌsu:p rə 'glɒt ᵊl ◂ ˌsju:p- ‖ -'glɑːt̬-
  ˌsupra ˌglottal 'tract
supralapsarian ˌsu:p rə læp 'seər i‿ən ◂ ˌsju:p-
  ‖ -'ser- -'sær- **~ism** ˌɪz əm
supranational ˌsu:p rə 'næʃ ᵊn ᵊl ◂ ˌsju:p-
suprasegmental ˌsu:p rə seg 'ment ᵊl ◂ ˌsju:p-
  ‖ -'ment̬- **~s** z
supremacist su 'prem əs ɪst sju-, §-əst **~s** s
supremac|y su 'prem əs |i sju- **~ies** iz
supreme 'highest', 'greatest', 'ultimate'
  su 'pri:m sju-, ˌsu:-, ˌsju:- **~ly** li **~ness** nəs
  nɪs **S~s** z
  Su,preme 'Being; Su,preme 'Court
supreme French word, cooking term, **suprême**
  su ˌpri:m sju-, -'prem, -'preɪm —Fr
  [sy pʀɛm]
supremo su 'pri:m əʊ sju- ‖ -oʊ **~s** z
sur- ˌsɜː ‖ ˌsɝː: but in certain words sə ‖ sᵊr —
  surrejoinder ˌsɜː rɪ 'dʒɔɪnd ə -rə-, §-ri:-
  ‖ ˌsɝː rɪ 'dʒɔɪnd ᵊr
sura 'sʊər ə ‖ 'sʊr ə **~s** z
Surabaya ˌsʊər ə 'baɪ‿ə ‖ ˌsʊr ə 'baː jə
surah 'sʊər ə ‖ 'sʊr ə **~s** z
sural 'sjʊər ᵊl 'sʊər- ‖ 'sʊr ᵊl
Surbiton 'sɜːb ɪt ən §-ət- ‖ 'sɝː:b ət ᵊn
surceas|e ₍ᵢ₎sɜː 'si:s '•• ‖ ₍ᵢ₎sɝː:- **~ed** t **~es** ɪz
  əz **~ing** ɪŋ
surcharg|e n, v 'sɜː tʃɑːdʒ ₍ᵢ₎sɜː 'tʃɑːdʒ
  ‖ 'sɝː: tʃɑːrdʒ **~ed** d **~es** ɪz əz **~ing** ɪŋ
surcingle 'sɜː ˌsɪŋ gᵊl ‖ 'sɝː:- **~s** z
surcoat 'sɜː kəʊt ‖ 'sɝː: koʊt **~s** s
surd sɜːd ‖ sɝː:d **surds** sɜːdz ‖ sɝː:dz

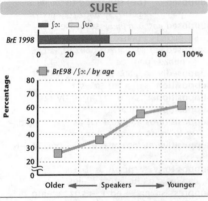

sure ʃɔː ʃʊə ‖ ʃʊᵊr ʃɝː: —BrE 1998 poll panel
preference: ʃɔː 46% (born since 1973: 60%),
ʃʊə 54%. **surer** 'ʃɔːr ə 'ʃʊər ə ‖ 'ʃʊr ᵊr 'ʃɝː:-

surest 'ʃɔːr ɪst 'ʃʊər-, -əst ‖ 'ʃʊr əst 'ʃɝː:-
  ˌsure 'thing
surefire 'ʃɔː ˌfaɪ‿ə 'ʃʊə- ‖ 'ʃʊr ˌfaɪ‿ᵊr 'ʃɝː:-
surefooted ˌʃɔː 'fʊt ɪd ◂ ˌʃʊə-, -əd
  ‖ ˌʃʊr 'fʊt̬ əd ◂ ˌʃɝː:-, '••, •• **~ness** nəs nɪs
sure|ly 'ʃɔː |li 'ʃʊə- ‖ 'ʃʊr |li 'ʃɝː:- **~ness** nəs
  nɪs
suret|y 'ʃɔːr ət i 'ʃʊər-, -ɪt- ‖ 'ʃʊr ət̬ i 'ʃɝː:-;
  'ʃʊrt̬ li, 'ʃɝː:t̬ i —in RP formerly also 'ʃʊət li
  ~ies iz **~yship/s** i ʃɪp/s
surf sɜːf ‖ sɝː:f **surfed** sɜːft ‖ sɝː:ft **surfing**
  'sɜːf ɪŋ ‖ 'sɝː:f ɪŋ **surfs** sɜːfs ‖ sɝː:fs
surfac|e n, v, adj 'sɜːf ɪs -əs ‖ 'sɝː:f əs **~ed** t
  ~es ɪz əz **~ing** ɪŋ
  'surface mail; 'surface noise; 'surface
  ˌstructure; ˌsurface 'tension
surface-to-air ˌsɜːf ɪs tu 'eə ◂ '•əs-
  ‖ ˌsɝː:f əs tu 'eᵊr ◂ -tə'•, -'æᵊr
surfactant sɜː 'fækt ᵊnt sə-; 'sɜː fækt ᵊnt
  ‖ sɝː:- **~s** s
surfboard 'sɜːf bɔːd ‖ 'sɝː:f bɔːrd -boʊrd
  ~er/s ə/z ‖ ᵊr/z **~ing** ɪŋ **~s** z
surfboat 'sɜːf bəʊt ‖ 'sɝː:f boʊt **~s** s
surf|eit n, v 'sɜːf |ɪt -ət, -iːt ‖ 'sɝː:f |ət **~eited**
  ɪt ɪd ət-, iːt-, -əd ‖ ət̬ əd **~eiting** ɪt ɪŋ ət-, iːt-
  ‖ ət̬ ɪŋ **~eits** ɪts əts, iːts ‖ əts
surfer 'sɜːf ə ‖ 'sɝː:f ᵊr **~s** z
surfie 'sɜːf i ‖ 'sɝː:f i **~s** z
surfing 'sɜːf ɪŋ ‖ 'sɝː:f ɪŋ
surfrid|ing 'sɜːf ˌraɪd ɪŋ ‖ 'sɝː:f- **~er/s** ə/z
  ‖ ᵊr/z
surge sɜːdʒ ‖ sɝː:dʒ **surged** sɜːdʒd ‖ sɝː:dʒd
  surges 'sɜːdʒ ɪz -əz ‖ 'sɝː:dʒ əz **surging**
  'sɜːdʒ ɪŋ ‖ 'sɝː:dʒ ɪŋ
surgeon 'sɜːdʒ ᵊn ‖ 'sɝː:dʒ ᵊn **~s** z
surger|y 'sɜːdʒ ᵊr‿|i ‖ 'sɝː:dʒ- **~ies** iz
surgical 'sɜːdʒ ɪk ᵊl ‖ 'sɝː:dʒ- **~ly** ‿i
  ˌsurgical 'spirit
suricate 'sʊər ɪ keɪt 'sjʊər-, -ə- ‖ 'sʊr- **~s** s
Surinam, Suriname ˌsʊər ɪ 'næm ˌsjʊər-, -ə-;
  '••• ‖ 'sʊr ə nɑːm -næm —Dutch
  [sy ri 'nɑː mə]
Surinamese ˌsʊər ɪ næ 'mi:z ◂ ˌsjʊər-, ˌ•ə-,
  -nəˈ• ‖ ˌsʊr ə nə 'mi:z ◂ -'mi:s
surly 'sɜːl i ‖ 'sɝː:l i **surlier** 'sɜːl i‿ə ‖ 'sɝː:l i‿ᵊr
  surliest 'sɜːl i‿ɪst ‿əst ‖ 'sɝː:l- **surlily**
  'sɜːl ɪl i -əl- ‖ 'sɝː:l- **surliness** 'sɜːl i nəs -nɪs
  ‖ 'sɝː:l-
surmis|e v, n sə 'maɪz sɜː-; 'sɜː maɪz ‖ sᵊr-
  ~ed d **~es** ɪz əz **~ing** ɪŋ
sur|mount sə |'maʊnt sɜː- ‖ sᵊr- **~mounted**
  'maʊnt ɪd -əd ‖ 'maʊnt̬ əd **~mounting**
  'maʊnt ɪŋ ‖ 'maʊnt̬ ɪŋ **~mounts** 'maʊnts
surname 'sɜː neɪm ‖ 'sɝː:- **~d** d **~s** z
surpass sə 'pɑːs sɜː-, §-'pæs ‖ sᵊr 'pæs **~ed** t
  ~es ɪz əz **~ing/ly** ɪŋ /li
surplic|e 'sɜːp ləs -lɪs ‖ 'sɝː:p- **~ed** t **~es** ɪz əz
surplus 'sɜːp ləs ‖ 'sɝː: plʌs 'sɜːp ləs **~es** ɪz əz
surpris|e sə 'praɪz ‖ sᵊr- sə- **~ed** d **~es** ɪz əz
  ~ing/ly ɪŋ /li
  sur'prise ˌparty
surreal sə 'rɪəl -'ri:ᵊl ‖ -'ri:əl **~ly** i

surrealism sə 'rɪəl ˌɪz əm -'riːəl-
‖ sə 'riː ə ˌlɪz əm
surrealist sə 'rɪəl ɪst -'riːəl-, §-əst ‖ sə 'riː əl əst
~s s
surrealistic sə ˌrɪə 'lɪst ɪk ◄ sjʊ-, -ˌriː ə '•-
‖ sə ˌriː ə 'lɪst ɪk ◄ ~**ally** əl_i
surrebutter ˌsʌr ɪ 'bʌt ə -ə- ‖ ˌsɝː ɪ 'bʌt̬ ər -ɪ-
~s z
surrejoinder ˌsʌr ɪ 'dʒɔɪnd ə -ə-
‖ ˌsɝː rɪ 'dʒɔɪnd ər -ɪ- ~s z
surrender sə 'rend ə ‖ -ər ~**ed** d
surrendering sə 'rend_ər ɪŋ ~s z
sur'render ˌvalue
surreptitious ˌsʌr əp 'tɪʃ əs ◄ -ɪp-, -ep- ‖ ˌsɝː-
~**ly** li ~**ness** nəs nɪs
Surrey, s~ 'sʌr i ‖ 'sɝː i ~s z
Surridge 'sʌr ɪdʒ ‖ 'sɝː-
surrogacy 'sʌr əg əs i ‖ 'sɝː-
surrogate n, adj 'sʌr əg ət -ɪt, -ə geɪt ‖ 'sɝː-
~s z ~**ship** ʃɪp
surround sə 'raʊnd ~**ed** ɪd əd ~**ing/s** ɪŋ/z ~s
z
sursum corda ˌsɜːs əm 'kɔːd ə -ʊm-
‖ ˌsʊrs əm 'kɔːrd ə -'koʊrd-, -ɑː
surtax 'sɜː tæks ‖ 'sɝː- ~**ed** t ~**es** ɪz əz ~**ing**
ɪŋ
Surtees 'sɜː tiːz ‖ 'sɝː-
surtitle 'sɜː ˌtaɪt əl ‖ 'sɝː ˌtaɪt̬ əl ~**ed** d ~**ing**
_ɪŋ ~s z
Surtsey 'sɜːts i -eɪ ‖ 'sɝːts i —Icelandic
['sʏr̥ts eɪ]
surveil sə 'veɪəl ~**led** d ~**ling** ɪŋ ~s z
surveillance sə 'veɪl ənts sɜː- ‖ sər- -jənts;
-'veɪ-
survey v sə 'veɪ sɜː-; 'sɜː veɪ ‖ sər- ~**ed** d
~**ing** ɪŋ ~s z
survey n 'sɜː veɪ ˌ•'•, sə 'veɪ ‖ 'sɝː veɪ sər 'veɪ
~s z
surveyor sə 'veɪ ə ‖ sər 'veɪ ər ~s z
survivable sə 'vaɪv əb əl ‖ sər-
survival sə 'vaɪv əl ‖ sər- ~s z
**sur'vival kit; sur'vival of the 'fittest;
sur'vival ˌvalue**
survivalist sə 'vaɪv əl ɪst §-əst ‖ sər- ~s s
surviv|e sə 'vaɪv ‖ sər- ~**ed** d ~**es** z ~**ing** ɪŋ
survivor sə 'vaɪv ə ‖ sər 'vaɪv ər ~s z ~**ship**
ʃɪp
sus sʌs **sussed** sʌst **susses** 'sʌs ɪz -əz
sussing 'sʌs ɪŋ
Susa 'suːz ə 'suːs-
Susan 'suːz ən
Susann su 'zæn
Susanna, Susannah su 'zæn ə
susceptance sə 'sept ənts
susceptibilit|y sə ˌsept ə 'bɪl ət i -ɪ-, ˌ•ɪ-, -ɪt i
‖ -ət̬ li ~**ies** iz
susceptib|le sə 'sept əb əl -ɪb- ~**leness** əl nəs
-nɪs ~**ly** li
susceptive sə 'sept ɪv ~**ness** nəs nɪs
susceptivity ˌsʌs ep 'tɪv ət i -ɪt i ‖ -ət̬ i
sushi 'suːʃ i 'sʊʃ-, -iː —Jp [sɯ ꜛɕi]
Susie 'suːz i
suslik 'sʊs lɪk 'sʌs-, 'suːs- ~s s

suspect n, adj 'sʌsp ekt ~s s
suspect v sə 'spekt ~**ed** ɪd əd ~**ing** ɪŋ ~s s
suspend sə 'spend ~**ed** ɪd əd ~**ing** ɪŋ ~s z
su,spended 'sentence
suspender sə 'spend ə ‖ -ər ~s z
su'spender belt
suspense sə 'spen̩ts ~**ful** fəl fʊl
suspension sə 'spen̩tʃ ən ~s z
su'spension bridge
suspensive sə 'spen̩ts ɪv ~**ly** li ~**ness** nəs nɪs
suspensor|y sə 'spen̩ts ər_li ~**ies** iz
suspicion sə 'spɪʃ ən ~s z
suspicious sə 'spɪʃ əs ~**ly** li ~**ness** nəs nɪs
Susquehanna ˌsʌsk wɪ 'hæn ə -wə-
suss sʌs **sussed** sʌst **susses** 'sʌs ɪz -əz
sussing 'sʌs ɪŋ
Sussex 'sʌs ɪks §-əks
Susskind 'sʊs kɪnd 'sʌs-
sustain sə 'steɪn ~**ed** d ~**ing** ɪŋ ~s z
sustainability sə ˌsteɪn ə 'bɪl ət i -ɪt i ‖ -ət̬ i
sustainable sə 'steɪn əb əl
sustainer sə 'steɪn ə ‖ -ər ~s z
sustainment sə 'steɪn mənt →-'steɪm-
sustenance 'sʌst ən_ən̩ts -ɪn-
sustentation ˌsʌst en 'teɪʃ ən -ən-
sustention sə 'sten̩tʃ ən
Sutch sʌtʃ
Sutcliff, Sutcliffe 'sʌt klɪf
Sutherland 'sʌð ə lənd ‖ -ər-
Sutlej 'sʌt lɪdʒ -ledʒ
sutler 'sʌt lə ‖ -lər ~s z
sutra, Sutra 'suːtr ə ~s z
Sutro 'suːtr əʊ ‖ -oʊ
suttee 'sʌt iː sʌ 'tiː —Hindi [sə t̪iː] ~s z
Sutter 'sʌt ə ‖ 'sʌt̬ ər —but the 19th-century
German-born owner of ˌSutter's 'Mill, CA, (Ger
Suter ['zuː tɐ]) is sometimes referred to as
'suːt ə ‖ 'suːt̬ ər
Sutton 'sʌt ən
ˌSutton 'Coldfield 'kəʊld fiːəld →-'kɒʊld-;
ˌSutton 'Hoo
Suttor 'sʌt ə ‖ 'sʌt̬ ər
suture 'suːtʃ ə ‖ 'suːtʃ ər —There are also very
careful or precious variants 'sjuːt jʊə, 'suːt-,
-jə ‖ -jʊr, -jər ~**d** d ~s z **suturing** 'suːtʃ
ər ɪŋ
Suva 'suːv ə
Suwannee sə 'wɒn i su- ‖ -'wɑːn- -'wɔːn-
Suzanna, Suzannah su 'zæn ə
Suzanne su 'zæn
suzerain 'suːz ə reɪn 'sjuːz-, -ər_ən ~s z
suzerain|ty 'suːz ə reɪn ti 'sjuːz-, -ər_ən ti
~**ties** tiz
Suzette su 'zet
Suzhou ˌsu: 'dʒəʊ ‖ -'dʒoʊ —Chi Sūzhōu ['su
ꜛtʂou]
Suzie 'suːz i
Suzman (i) 'sʊz mən, (ii) 'suːz mən
Suzuki tdmk sə 'zuːk i su- —Jp [sɯ ˌdzɯ ki]
~s z
Suzy 'suːz i
Svalbard 'svæl bɑːd 'svɑːl-, -bɑː ‖ 'svɑːl bɑːrd
-bɑːr —Norw ['svɑːl bɑr]

S

svarabhakti ˌsfʌr ə ˈbʌkt i ˌsfɑːr-;
ˌsfær ə ˈbækt i —*Hindi* [svər bfiək t̪i]
svelte sfelt svelt **svelter** ˈsfelt ə ˈsvelt- ‖ -ᵊr
sveltest ˈsfelt ɪst ˈsvelt-, -əst
Svengali, s~ sfen ˈgɑːl i sven-, →sfeŋ-
Sverdlovsk ˌsfeəd ˈlɒfsk -ˈlɒvsk; '••
‖ ˌsferd ˈlɔːfsk -ˈlɑːfsk —*Russ* [svjɪr ˈdɫɔfsk]
swab swɒb ‖ swɑːb **swabbed**
swɒbd ‖ swɑːbd **swabbing**
ˈswɒb ɪŋ ‖ ˈswɑːb ɪŋ **swabs** swɒbz ‖ swɑːbz
swabber ˈswɒb ə ‖ ˈswɑːb ᵊr ~s z
Swabi|a ˈsweɪb i‿ə ~an/s ən/z
Swaby ˈsweɪb i
swaddie ˈswɒd i ‖ ˈswɑːd i ~s z
swaddl|e ˈswɒd ᵊl ‖ ˈswɑːd ᵊl ~ed d ~es z
~ing ‿ɪŋ
ˈswaddling clothes
swadd|y ˈswɒd li ‖ ˈswɑːd li ~ies iz
Swadlincote ˈswɒd lɪn kəʊt →-lɪŋ-, §-lən-
‖ ˈswɑːd lən koʊt
Swaffer ˈswɒf ə ‖ ˈswɑːf ᵊr
Swaffham ˈswɒf əm ‖ ˈswɑːf-
Swaffield ˈswɒf iːᵊld ‖ ˈswɑːf-
swag swæg
swage sweɪdʒ **swaged** sweɪdʒd **swages**
ˈsweɪdʒ ɪz -əz **swaging** ˈsweɪdʒ ɪŋ
Swaggart ˈswæg ət ‖ -ᵊrt
swagger ˈswæg ə ‖ -ᵊr ~ed d **swaggering/ly**
ˈswæg ᵊr_ɪŋ /li ~s z
ˈswagger stick
swaggerer ˈswæg ᵊr ə ‖ -ᵊr ᵊr ~s z
swag|man ˈswæg |mæn -mən ~men men mən
—*in Australia*, -mən
Swahili swə ˈhiːl i swɑː- ~s z
swain, Swain sweɪn **swains, Swain's** sweɪnz
Swainson ˈsweɪn sən
Swalcliffe ˈsweɪ klɪf
Swale, swale sweɪᵊl **swales** sweɪᵊlz
Swaledale ˈsweɪᵊl deɪᵊl
Swales sweɪᵊlz
swallow, S~ ˈswɒl əʊ ‖ ˈswɑːl oʊ ~ed d ~er/s
ə/z ‖ ᵊr/z ~ing ɪŋ ~s z
ˈswallow dive
swallowtail ˈswɒl əʊ teɪᵊl ‖ ˈswɑːl oʊ- -ə- ~ed
d ~s z
swam swæm
swami, Swami ˈswɑːm i —*Hindi* [svɑː mi] ~s z
swamp swɒmp ‖ swɑːmp swɔːmp **swamped**
swɒmpt ‖ swɑːmpt swɔːmpt **swamping**
ˈswɒmp ɪŋ ‖ ˈswɑːmp ɪŋ ˈswɔːmp- **swamps**
swɒmps ‖ swɑːmps swɔːmps
swamper ˈswɒmp ə ‖ ˈswɑːmp ᵊr ˈswɔːmp- ~s
z
swampland ˈswɒmp lænd ‖ ˈswɑːmp-
ˈswɔːmp- ~s z
swamp|y, S~ ˈswɒmp li ‖ ˈswɑːmp li ˈswɔːmp li
~ier i‿ə ‖ i‿ᵊr ~iest i‿ɪst i‿əst ~iness i nəs
i nɪs
swan, Swan swɒn ‖ swɑːn **swanned**
swɒnd ‖ swɑːnd **swanning**
ˈswɒn ɪŋ ‖ ˈswɑːn ɪŋ **swans** swɒnz ‖ swɑːnz
ˈswan dive
Swanage ˈswɒn ɪdʒ ‖ ˈswɑːn-

Swanee ˈswɒn i ‖ ˈswɑːn i ˈswɔːn i
swank swæŋk **swanked** swæŋkt **swanking**
ˈswæŋk ɪŋ **swanks** swæŋks
swank|y ˈswæŋk li ~ier i‿ə ‖ i‿ᵊr ~iest i‿ɪst
i‿əst ~ily ɪ li əl i ~iness i nəs i nɪs
Swanley ˈswɒn li ‖ ˈswɑːn-
Swann swɒn ‖ swɑːn
swanner|y ˈswɒn ᵊr li ‖ ˈswɑːn- ~ies iz
Swanscombe ˈswɒnz kəm ‖ ˈswɑːnz-
swansdown, swan's-down
ˈswɒnz daʊn ‖ ˈswɑːnz-
Swansea *place in Wales* ˈswɒnz i ‖ ˈswɑːn siː
ˈswɑːnz i
Swanson ˈswɒnᵗs ən ‖ ˈswɑːnᵗs ən
swansong ˈswɒn sɒŋ ‖ ˈswɑːn sɔːŋ -sɑːŋ ~s z
Swanton ˈswɒnt ən ‖ ˈswɑːnt ᵊn
swan-upping ˌswɒn ˈʌp ɪŋ '•,•• ‖ ˌswɑːn-
Swanwick ˈswɒn ɪk ‖ ˈswɑːn-
swap swɒp ‖ swɑːp **swapped** swɒpt ‖ swɑːpt
swapping ˈswɒp ɪŋ ‖ ˈswɑːp ɪŋ **swaps**
swɒps ‖ swɑːps
ˈswap meet
SWAPO ˈswɑːp əʊ ˈswɒp- ‖ -oʊ
Swarbrick ˈswɔː brɪk ‖ ˈswɔːr-
sward swɔːd ‖ swɔːrd **swards**
swɔːdz ‖ swɔːrdz
sware sweə ‖ sweᵊr swæᵊr
swarf swɔːf swɑːf ‖ swɔːrf
Swarfega *tdmk* swɔː ˈfiːg ə swɑː- ‖ swɔːr-
Swarkeston, Swarkestone ˈswɔːkst ən
‖ ˈswɔːrkst-
swarm swɔːm ‖ swɔːrm **swarmed**
swɔːmd ‖ swɔːrmd **swarming**
ˈswɔːm ɪŋ ‖ ˈswɔːrm ɪŋ **swarms**
swɔːmz ‖ swɔːrmz
swart, Swart swɔːt ‖ swɔːrt
swarth|y ˈswɔːð li ‖ ˈswɔːrð li ~ier i‿ə ‖ i‿ᵊr
~iest i‿ɪst i‿əst ~ily ɪ li əl i ~iness i nəs i nɪs
swash swɒʃ ‖ swɑːʃ swɔːʃ **swashed**
swɒʃt ‖ swɑːʃt swɔːʃt **swashes** ˈswɒʃ ɪz -əz
‖ ˈswɑːʃ əz ˈswɔːʃ- **swashing**
ˈswɒʃ ɪŋ ‖ ˈswɑːʃ ɪŋ ˈswɔːʃ-
swashbuckl|er
ˈswɒʃ ˌbʌk ᵊl‿ə ‖ ˈswɑːʃ ˌbʌk ᵊl‿ᵊr ˈswɔːʃ-
~ers əz ‖ ᵊrz ~ing ɪŋ
swastika ˈswɒst ɪk ə ‖ ˈswɑːst- ~s z
swat, Swat swɒt ‖ swɑːt *(= swot)* **swats**
swɒts ‖ swɑːts **swatted** ˈswɒt ɪd-əd
‖ ˈswɑːt̬ əd **swatting** ˈswɒt ɪŋ ‖ ˈswɑːt̬ ɪŋ
swatch, Swatch *tdmk* swɒtʃ ‖ swɑːtʃ
swatches ˈswɒtʃ ɪz -əz ‖ ˈswɑːtʃ əz
swath swɒθ swɔːθ ‖ swɑːθ swɔːθ **swaths**
swɒθs swɔːθs, swɔːðz ‖ swɑːθs swɔːθs
swathe sweɪð **swathed** sweɪðd **swathes**
sweɪðz **swathing** ˈsweɪð ɪŋ
Swatow ˌswɑː ˈtaʊ —*Chi* Shàntóu [⁴ʂan ²tʰou]
swatter ˈswɒt ə ‖ ˈswɑːt̬ ᵊr ~s z
Swavesey ˈsweɪvz i ‖ ˈsweɪv əz i
sway, Sway sweɪ **swayed** sweɪd **swaying/ly**
ˈsweɪ ɪŋ /li **sways** sweɪz
swayback ˈsweɪ bæk ~ed t
Swazi ˈswɑːz i ~s z
Swaziland ˈswɑːz i lænd

swear sweə ‖ sweᵊr **swearing**
'sweər ɪŋ ‖ 'swer ɪŋ **swears** sweəz ‖ sweᵊrz
swore swɔː ‖ swɔːr swour

swearer 'sweər ə ‖ 'swer ᵊr ~s z

swearword 'sweə wɜːd ‖ 'swer wɜːd ~s z

sweat swet **sweated** 'swet ɪd -əd ‖ 'swet̮ əd
sweating 'swet ɪŋ ‖ 'swet̮ ɪŋ **sweats** swets
'sweat gland

sweatband 'swet bænd ~s z

sweater 'swet ə ‖ 'swet̮ ᵊr ~s z

sweatshirt 'swet ʃɜːt ‖ -ʃɜ˞ːt ~s s

sweatshop 'swet ʃɒp ‖ -ʃɑːp ~s s

sweatsuit 'swet suːt -sjuːt ~s s

sweat|y 'swet |i ‖ 'swet̮ |i ~ier i_ə ‖ i_ᵊr ~iest
i_ɪst i_əst ~ily ɪ li əl i ~iness i nəs i nɪs

Swede, swede swiːd **Swedes**, swedes swiːdz

Sweden 'swiːd ᵊn

Swedenborg 'swiːd ᵊn bɔːg ‖ -bɔːrg —*Swedish*
['sveː dən bɔrj]

Swedenborgian ˌswiːd ᵊn 'bɔːdʒ i_ən ◂ -'bɔːg-
‖ -'bɔːrdʒ- -'bɔːrg- ~s z

Swedish 'swiːd ɪʃ

Sweeney 'swiːn i
ˌSweeney 'Todd

sweeny 'swiːn i

sweep swiːp **sweeping** 'swiːp ɪŋ **sweeps**
swiːps **swept** swept

sweeper 'swiːp ə ‖ -ᵊr ~s z

sweeping 'swiːp ɪŋ ~ly li ~s z

sweepstake 'swiːp steɪk ~s s

sweet, Sweet swiːt **sweeter**
'swiːt ə ‖ 'swiːt̮ ᵊr **sweetest** 'swiːt ɪst -əst
‖ 'swiːt̮ əst
ˌsweet 'gum; ˌsweet 'nothings; ˌsweet
'pea ‖ '• •; ˌsweet po'tato ‖ '• •, • •;
'sweet talk; ˌsweet 'tooth ‖ '• •; ˌsweet
'william

sweet-and-sour ˌswiːt ᵊn 'sau_ə ◂ -ᵊnd-
‖ -'sau_ᵊr

sweetbread 'swiːt bred ~s z

sweetbriar, sweetbrier 'swiːt ˌbraɪ_ə
‖ -ˌbraɪ_ᵊr ~s z

sweetcorn 'swiːt kɔːn ‖ -kɔːrn

sweeten 'swiːt ᵊn ~ed d ~er/s _ə/z ‖ _ᵊr/z
~ing _ɪŋ ~s z

Sweetex *tdmk* 'swiːt eks

sweetheart 'swiːt hɑːt ‖ -hɑːrt ~s s

sweetie 'swiːt i ‖ 'swiːt̮ i ~s z

sweeting, S~ 'swiːt ɪŋ ‖ 'swiːt̮ ɪŋ

sweetish 'swiːt ɪʃ ‖ 'swiːt̮ ɪʃ

sweetlip 'swiːt lɪp ~s s

sweetly 'swiːt li

sweetmeal 'swiːt miːᵊl

sweetmeat 'swiːt miːt ~s s

sweetness 'swiːt nəs -nɪs

sweetshop 'swiːt ʃɒp ‖ -ʃɑːp ~s s

sweetsop 'swiːt sɒp ‖ -sɑːp ~s s

sweet-talk 'swiːt tɔːk ˌ•'• ‖ -tɑːk ~ed t ~ing
ɪŋ ~s s

swell swel **swelled** sweld **swelling/s**
'swel ɪŋ/z **swells** swelz **swollen**
'swəʊl ən ‖ 'swoul ən

swelter 'swelt ə ‖ -ᵊr ~ed d **sweltering/ly**
'swelt_ər ɪŋ /li ~s z

swept swept

swept-back ˌswep*t* 'bæk ◂ '• •

swept-wing ˌswept 'wɪŋ ◂

swerve swɜːv ‖ swɜ˞ːv **swerved**
swɜːvd ‖ swɜ˞ːvd **swerves** swɜːvz ‖ swɜ˞ːvz
swerving 'swɜːv ɪŋ ‖ 'swɜ˞ːv ɪŋ

Swetenham, Swettenham 'swet ᵊn_əm

swift, Swift swɪft **swifter** 'swɪft ə ‖ -ᵊr
swiftest 'swɪft ɪst -əst **swifts** swɪfts

swiftlet 'swɪft lət -lɪt ~s s

swift|ly 'swɪft |li ~ness nəs nɪs

swig swɪg **swigged** swɪgd **swigging** 'swɪg ɪŋ
swigs swɪgz

swill swɪl **swilled** swɪld **swilling** 'swɪl ɪŋ
swills swɪlz

swim swɪm **swam** swæm **swimming**
'swɪm ɪŋ **swims** swɪmz **swum** swʌm
'swimming bath; 'swimming ˌcostume;
'swimming pool; 'swimming trunks

swimathon 'swɪm ə θɒn ‖ -θɑːn ~s z

swimmer 'swɪm ə ‖ -ᵊr ~s z

swimmeret 'swɪm ə ret ˌ• •'• ~s s

swimmingly 'swɪm ɪŋ li

swimsuit 'swɪm suːt -sjuːt ~s s

swimwear 'swɪm weə ‖ -wer -wær

Swinbourne 'swɪn bɔːn →'swɪm- ‖ -bɔːrn
-bourn

Swinburn, Swinburne 'swɪn bɜːn →'swɪm-
‖ -bɜ˞ːn

Swindells (i) 'swɪnd ᵊlz, (ii) ₍ᵢ₎swɪn 'delz

swindl|e 'swɪnd ᵊl ~ed d ~er/s _ə/z ‖ _ᵊr/z
~es z ~ing _ɪŋ

Swindon 'swɪnd ən

swine swaɪn
'swine ˌfever

swineherd 'swaɪn hɜːd ‖ -hɜ˞ːd ~s z

Swiney (i) 'swaɪn i, (ii) 'swɪn i

swing swɪŋ **swinging** 'swɪŋ ɪŋ **swings** swɪŋz
swung swʌŋ
'swing ˌdoor

swingeing 'swɪndʒ ɪŋ ~ly li

swinger 'swɪŋ ə ‖ -ᵊr ~s z

swingl|e 'swɪŋ gᵊl ~ed d ~es z ~ing _ɪŋ

Swingler 'swɪŋ glə ‖ -glᵊr

swingletree 'swɪŋ gᵊl triː ~s z

swingometer ₍ᵢ₎swɪŋ 'ɒm ɪt ə -ət ə ‖ -'ɑːm ət̮ ᵊr
~s z

swing-wing ˌswɪŋ 'wɪŋ ◂

swinish 'swaɪn ɪʃ ~ly li ~ness nəs nɪs

Swinley 'swɪn li

Swinnerton 'swɪn ət ən ‖ -ᵊrt ᵊn

Swinton 'swɪnt ən ‖ -ᵊn

swipe swaɪp **swiped** swaɪpt **swipes** swaɪps
swiping 'swaɪp ɪŋ

Swire 'swaɪ_ə ‖ 'swaɪ_ᵊr

swirl swɜːl ‖ swɜ˞ːl **swirled** swɜːld ‖ swɜ˞ːld
swirling 'swɜːl ɪŋ ‖ 'swɜ˞ːl ɪŋ **swirls**
swɜːlz ‖ swɜ˞ːlz

swish swɪʃ **swished** swɪʃt **swishes** 'swɪʃ ɪz
-əz **swishing** 'swɪʃ ɪŋ

swish|y 'swɪʃ |i ~**ier** i_ə ‖ i_ᵊr ~**iest** i_ɪst i_əst
 ~**ily** ɪ li əl i ~**iness** i nəs i nɪs
Swiss swɪs
 ,Swiss 'chard; ,Swiss 'cheese; ,swiss 'roll,
 ' • •
Swissair *tdmk* 'swɪs eə ,•'• ‖ -er -ær
switch swɪtʃ **switched** swɪtʃt **switches**
 'swɪtʃ ɪz -əz **switching** 'swɪtʃ ɪŋ
switchable 'swɪtʃ əb əl
switchback 'swɪtʃ bæk ~**s** s
switchblade 'swɪtʃ bleɪd ~**s** z
switchboard 'swɪtʃ bɔːd ‖ -bɔːrd -boʊrd ~**s** z
switched-on ,swɪtʃt 'ɒn ◀ ‖ -'ɑːn ◀ -'ɔːn
switchgear 'swɪtʃ gɪə ‖ -gɪr
switch-|hit ,swɪtʃ |'hɪt ~**hits** 'hɪts ~**hitter/s**
 'hɪt ə/z ‖ 'hɪt̬ ᵊr/z ~**hitting** 'hɪt ɪŋ ‖ 'hɪt̬ ɪŋ
switch|man 'swɪtʃ |mən ~**men** mən men
switchover 'swɪtʃ ,əʊv ə ‖ -,oʊv ᵊr ~**s** z
Swithin, Swithun 'swɪð ᵊn 'swɪθ-, -ɪn ~'**s** z
Switzerland 'swɪts ə lənd -əl_ənd ‖ -ᵊr-
swive swaɪv **swived** swaɪvd **swives** swaɪvz
 swiving 'swaɪv ɪŋ
swivel 'swɪv əl ~**ed**, ~**led** d ~**ing**, ~**ling** _ɪŋ
 ~**s** z
swiz, swizz swɪz
swizzle 'swɪz əl
 'swizzle stick
swob —*see* **swab**
swollen 'swəʊl ən →'swɒʊl- ‖ 'swoʊl-
 ,swollen 'head
swollen-headed ,swəʊl ən 'hed ɪd ◀ →,swɒʊl-,
 -əd ‖ ,swoʊl- ~**ly** li ~**ness** nəs nɪs
swoon swuːn **swooned** swuːnd **swooning**
 'swuːn ɪŋ **swoons** swuːnz
swoop swuːp **swooped** swuːpt **swooping**
 'swuːp ɪŋ **swoops** swuːps
swoosh swuːʃ swʊʃ **swooshed** swuːʃt swʊʃt
 swooshes 'swuːʃ ɪz 'swʊʃ-, -əz **swooshing**
 'swuːʃ ɪŋ 'swʊʃ-
 a 'swooshing noise
swop swɒp ‖ swɑːp **swopped** swɒpt ‖ swɑːpt
 swopping 'swɒp ɪŋ ‖ 'swɑːp ɪŋ **swops**
 swɒps ‖ swɑːps
sword sɔːd ‖ sɔːrd soʊrd *(!)* **swords**
 sɔːdz ‖ sɔːrdz soʊrdz
 'sword dance, 'sword ,dancer; ,sword of
 'Damocles
swordbearer 'sɔːd ,beər ə →'sɔːb-
 ‖ 'sɔːrd ,ber ᵊr 'soʊrd- ~**s** z
swordfish 'sɔːd fɪʃ ‖ 'sɔːrd- 'soʊrd- ~**es** ɪz əz
swordplay 'sɔːd pleɪ →'sɔːb- ‖ 'sɔːrd- 'soʊrd-
 ~**er/s** ə/z ‖ ᵊr/z
swords|man 'sɔːdz |mən ‖ 'sɔːrdz- 'soʊrdz-
 ~**manship** mən ʃɪp ~**men** mən
swordstick 'sɔːd stɪk ‖ 'sɔːrd- 'soʊrd- ~**s** s
sword-swallower 'sɔːd ,swɒl əʊ ə
 ‖ 'sɔːrd ,swɑːl oʊ ᵊr 'soʊrd- ~**s** z
swore swɔː ‖ swɔːr swoʊr
sworn swɔːn ‖ swɔːrn swoʊrn
swot swɒt ‖ swɑːt **swots** swɒts ‖ swɑːts
 swotted 'swɒt ɪd -əd ‖ 'swɑːt̬ əd **swotting**
 'swɒt ɪŋ ‖ 'swɑːt̬ ɪŋ
swum swʌm

swung swʌŋ
 ,swung 'dash
Swyer, Swyre 'swaɪ_ə ‖ 'swaɪ_ᵊr
Sybaris 'sɪb ər ɪs §-əs; sɪ 'bɑːr-
sybarite 'sɪb ə raɪt ~**s** s
sybaritic ,sɪb ə 'rɪt ɪk ◀ ‖ -'rɪt̬- ~**ally** ᵊl_i
Sybil 'sɪb ᵊl -ɪl
sycamore 'sɪk ə mɔː ‖ -mɔːr -moʊr ~**s** z
syce saɪs **syces** 'saɪs ɪz -əz
sycophanc|y 'sɪk əf ᵊnts |i 'saɪk-, -ə fænts |i
 ~**ies** iz
sycophant 'sɪk əf ᵊnt 'saɪk-, -ə fænt ~**s** s
sycophantic ,sɪk əʊ 'fænt ɪk ◀ ,saɪk-
 ‖ -ə 'fænt̬- ~**ally** ᵊl_i
Sydenham 'sɪd ᵊn_əm
Sydney 'sɪd ni
Sydneysider 'sɪd ni saɪd ə ‖ -ᵊr ~**s** z
syenite 'saɪ_ə naɪt
Sykes saɪks
Sylheti sɪl 'het i sɪ 'let i ~**s** z
syllabar|y 'sɪl əb ᵊr_li ‖ -ə ber li ~**ies** iz
syllabi 'sɪl ə baɪ -biː
syllabic sɪ 'læb ɪk sə- ~**ally** ᵊl_i ~**s** s
 syl,labic 'consonant
syllabi|cate sɪ 'læb ɪ |keɪt sə-, §-ə- ~**cated**
 keɪt ɪd -əd ‖ keɪt̬ əd ~**cates** keɪts ~**cating**
 keɪt ɪŋ ‖ keɪt̬ ɪŋ
syllabication sɪ ,læb ɪ 'keɪʃ ᵊn sə-, -ə- ~**s** z
syllabicity ,sɪl ə 'bɪs ət i -ɪt i ‖ -ət̬ i
syllabification sɪ ,læb ɪf ɪ 'keɪʃ ᵊn sə-, -,•əf-,
 §-ə'•- ~**s** z
syllabi|fy sɪ 'læb ɪ |faɪ sə-, -ə- ~**fied** faɪd ~**fies**
 faɪz ~**fying** faɪ ɪŋ
syllable 'sɪl əb ᵊl ~**s** z
 'syllable ,boundary; 'syllable ,structure
syllabub 'sɪl ə bʌb ~**s** z
syll|abus 'sɪl |əb əs ~**abi** ə baɪ -biː ~**abuses**
 əb əs ɪz -əz
syleps|is sɪ 'leps |ɪs sə-, -'liːps-, §-əs ~**es** iːz
syllogism 'sɪl ə ,dʒɪz əm ~**s** z
syllogistic ,sɪl ə 'dʒɪst ɪk ◀ ~**ally** ᵊl_i
sylph sɪlf **sylphs** sɪlfs
Sylphides sɪl 'fiːd ‖ —*Fr* [sil fid]
sylphlike 'sɪlf laɪk
sylvan 'sɪlv ᵊn ~**s** z
sylvatic sɪl 'væt ɪk sᵊl- ‖ -'væt̬-
Sylvester sɪl 'vest ə sᵊl- ‖ -ᵊr
Sylvia 'sɪlv i_ə
Sym sɪm
sym- sɪm, ¦sɪm — **sympatric** sɪm 'pætr ɪk
symbiont 'sɪm baɪ ɒnt -bi- ‖ -ɑːnt ~**s** s
symbiosis ,sɪm baɪ 'əʊs ɪs -bi-, §-əs ‖ -'oʊs-
symbiotic ,sɪm baɪ 'ɒt ɪk ◀ -bi- ‖ -'ɑːt̬- ~**ally**
 ᵊl_i
symbol 'sɪm bᵊl ~**s** z
symbolic sɪm 'bɒl ɪk ‖ -'bɑːl- ~**al** ᵊl ~**ally** ᵊl_i
 ~**alness** ᵊl nəs -nɪs
symbolis... —*see* **symboliz...**
symbolism 'sɪm bə ,lɪz əm -bʊ- ~**s** z
symbolist 'sɪm bᵊl ɪst -bʊl-, §-əst ~**s** s
symbolization ,sɪm bᵊl aɪ 'zeɪʃ ᵊn ,•bʊl-, -ɪ'•-
 ‖ -ə'•- ~**s** z

Syllabic consonants

1 Most syllables contain an obvious vowel sound. Sometimes, though, a syllable consists phonetically only of a consonant or consonants. If so, this consonant (or one of them) is a nasal (usually n) or a liquid (l or, especially in AmE, r). For example, in the usual pronunciation of **suddenly** ˈsʌd n li, the second syllable consists of n alone. Such a consonant is a **syllabic consonant**.

2 Instead of a syllabic consonant it is always possible to pronounce a vowel ə plus an ordinary (non-syllabic) consonant. Thus it is possible, though not usual, to say ˈsʌd ən li rather than ˈsʌd n li.

3 Likely syllabic consonants are shown in LPD with the symbol ᵊ, thus **suddenly** ˈsʌd ᵊn li. LPD's regular principle is that a raised symbol indicates a sound whose inclusion LPD does not recommend (see OPTIONAL SOUNDS). Hence this notation implies that LPD prefers bare n in the second syllable. Since there is then no proper vowel in this syllable, the n must be syllabic.

4 Similarly, in **middle** ˈmɪd ᵊl LPD recommends a pronunciation with syllabic l, thus ˈmɪd l. In **father** ˈfɑːð ə ‖ ˈfɑːð ᵊr LPD recommends for AmE a pronunciation with syllabic r, thus ˈfɑːð r.

S

5 The IPA provides a special diacritic [ˌ] to show syllabicity. If syllabification is not shown in a transcription, then syllabic consonants need to be shown explicitly, thus n̩. For the syllabic r of AmE, the special symbol ɚ is sometimes used. Because LPD uses spaces to show syllabification, it does not need these conventions. Any nasal or liquid in which there is no other vowel must automatically be syllabic.

6 Syllabic consonants are also sometimes used where LPD shows italic ə plus a nasal or liquid, thus **distant** ˈdɪst ənt. Although there is a possible pronunciation ˈdɪst nt, LPD recommends ˈdɪst ənt. (In some varieties of English or styles of speech, a syllabic consonant may in fact arise from almost any sequence of ə and a nasal or liquid.)

7 When followed by a weak vowel, a syllabic consonant may lose its syllabic quality, becoming a plain non-syllabic consonant: see COMPRESSION. For example, **threatening** ˈθret ᵊn_ɪŋ may be pronounced with three syllables, including syllabic n, thus ˈθret.n̩.ɪŋ; or compressed into two syllables, with plain n, thus ˈθret.nɪŋ.

---

symbolizǀe ˈsɪm bə laɪz -bʊ- **~ed** d **~es** ɪz əz
~ing ɪŋ
symbology sɪm ˈbɒl ədʒ i ‖ -ˈbɑːl-
Syme saɪm
Symington (i) ˈsaɪm ɪŋ tən, (ii) ˈsɪm-
symmetric sɪ ˈmetr ɪk sə-
symmetrical sɪ ˈmetr ɪk ᵊl sə- **~ly** ‿i
symmetrǀy ˈsɪm ətr i ‖ -ɪtr- **~ies** iz
Symon ˈsaɪm ən

Symonds (i) ˈsɪm əndz, (ii) ˈsaɪm əndz
ˌSymonds ˈYat ˌsɪm əndz ˈjæt
Symons (i) ˈsɪm ənz, (ii) ˈsaɪm ənz
sympathectomǀy ˌsɪmp ə ˈθekt əm i ‖ **~ies** iz
sympathetic ˌsɪmp ə ˈθet ɪk ◄ ‖ -ˈθeţ- **~ally** ᵊl‿i
ˌsympaˌthetic ˈmagic
sympathisǀe, sympathizǀe ˈsɪmp ə θaɪz **~ed** d
~er/s ə/z ‖ ᵊr/z **~es** ɪz əz **~ing** ɪŋ
sympathǀy ˈsɪmp əθ i ‖ **~ies** iz
symphonic sɪm ˈfɒn ɪk ‖ -ˈfɑːn-

Syllables

1 In phonetics, a **syllable** is a group of sounds that are pronounced together. Every English word consists of one or more complete syllables.
glad consists of one syllable: glæd
coming consists of two syllables: ˈkʌm and ɪŋ
So does **valley**: ˈvæl and i
tobacco consists of three syllables: tə, ˈbæk, and əʊ or oʊ.

Each syllable contains exactly one vowel. This vowel may be preceded or followed by one or more consonants. The vowel itself may be a short vowel, a long vowel, or a diphthong; or, if it is the weak vowel ə, it may be combined with a nasal or liquid to give a SYLLABIC CONSONANT.

2 **Phonetic** (spoken) syllables must not be confused with **orthographic** (written) syllables. An orthographic syllable is a group of letters in spelling. When a word is split across two lines of writing, it should be broken at an orthographic syllable boundary. (Word processors do this automatically with a **hyphenation** program.) In some cases an orthographic boundary may not correspond exactly to a phonetic syllable boundary. For example, in the word **happen** the spelling includes two **p**s, and the orthographic syllabification is **hap.pen**. But the pronunciation has only a single p, and the syllables are ˈhæp and ᵊn.

3 LPD shows the phonetic syllabification of words by putting spaces between successive syllables.

S

symphonist ˈsɪmpf ən ɪst §-əst ~s s
symphon|y ˈsɪmpf ən li ~ies iz
 ˈsymphony ˌorchestra
symph|ysis ˈsɪmpf lɪs ɪs -əs-, §-əs ~yses ɪ siːz
 -ə-
symposia sɪm ˈpəʊz i_ə ‖ -ˈpoʊz-
symposiac sɪm ˈpəʊz i æk ‖ -ˈpoʊz-
symposiarch sɪm ˈpəʊz i ɑːk ‖ -ˈpoʊz i ɑːrk ~s
 s
symposiast sɪm ˈpəʊz i æst ‖ -ˈpoʊz- ~s s
symposi|um sɪm ˈpəʊz i_əm ‖ -ˈpoʊz- ~a ə
symptom ˈsɪmpt əm ~s z
symptomatic ˌsɪmpt ə ˈmæt ɪk ◄ ‖ -ˈmæt̬-
 ~ally əl_i
syn- sɪn, ¦sɪn— synonym ˈsɪn ə nɪm
synaer|esis sɪ ˈnɪər ləs ɪs sə-, -ɪs-, §-əs ‖ -ˈnɪr-
 ~eses ə siːz -ɪ-
synaesthesia ˌsɪn iːs ˈθiːz i_ə, •ɪs-, §, •əs-,
 -ˈθiːʒ ə ‖ ˌsɪn əs ˈθiːʒ ə -ˈ•i_ə
synagogue ˈsɪn ə ɡɒɡ ‖ -ɡɑːɡ ~s z
synalepha, synaloepha ˌsɪn ə ˈliːf ə -ˈlef- ~s z
synaps|e ˈsaɪn æps ˈsɪn-; sɪ ˈnæps ‖ ˈsɪn æps
 sə ˈnæps ~es ɪz əz
synaps|is sɪ ˈnæps lɪs ɪs ~es iːz
synaptic sɪ ˈnæpt ɪk ~ally əl_i
synarthros|is ˌsɪn ɑː ˈθrəʊs lɪs §-əs
 ‖ -ɑːr ˈθroʊs- ~es iːz
synax|is sɪ ˈnæks lɪs sə-, §-əs ~es iːz

sync, synch sɪŋk (= sink)
synchro ˈsɪŋk rəʊ ‖ -roʊ ~s z
synchroflash ˈsɪŋk rəʊ flæʃ ‖ -roʊ- ~es ɪz əz
synchromesh ˈsɪŋk rəʊ meʃ ‖ -roʊ- ~es ɪz əz
synchronic sɪn ˈkrɒn ɪk→sɪŋ- ‖ -ˈkrɑːn- ~ally
 əl_i
synchronicity ˌsɪŋ krə ˈnɪs ət i ˌsɪn-, ˌ•krɒ-,
 -ɪt i ‖ -ət̬ i ˌ•krɑː-
synchronis... —see synchroniz...
synchronism ˈsɪŋk rə ˌnɪz əm
synchronistic ˌsɪŋk rə ˈnɪst ɪk ◄ ~ally əl_i
synchronization ˌsɪŋk rən aɪ ˈzeɪʃ ᵊn -ɪ ˈ•-
 ‖ -ə ˈ•- ~s z
synchroniz|e ˈsɪŋk rə naɪz ~ed d ~es ɪz əz
 ~ing ɪŋ
synchronous ˈsɪŋk rən əs ~ly li ~ness nəs nɪs
synchron|y ˈsɪŋk rən li ~ies iz
synchrotron ˈsɪŋk rəʊ trɒn ‖ -rə trɑːn ~s z
synclinal ˌ(ˌ)sɪŋ ˈklaɪn ᵊl ˌ(ˌ)sɪn- ~ly i
syncline ˈsɪŋ klaɪn ‖ ˈsɪn- ~s z
synco|pate ˈsɪŋk ə ¦peɪt ~pated peɪt ɪd-əd
 ‖ peɪt̬ əd ~pates peɪts ~pating
 peɪt ɪŋ ‖ peɪt̬ ɪŋ
syncopation ˌsɪŋk ə ˈpeɪʃ ᵊn ~s z
syncope ˈsɪŋk əp i ~s z
syncretic ˌ(ˌ)sɪŋ ˈkret ɪk ˌ(ˌ)sɪn- ‖ -ˈkret̬-
syncretism ˈsɪŋk rə ˌtɪz əm -rɪ- ~s z
syncretistic ˌsɪŋk rə ˈtɪst ɪk ◄ -rɪ-

syncretiz|e 'sɪŋk rə taɪz -rɪ- **~ed** d **~es** ɪz əz
~ing ɪŋ
syndactyl sɪn 'dækt ɪl -əl, -aɪəl **~y** i
syndesis 'sɪnd ɪs ɪs -əs-, §-əs; sɪn 'diːs-
syndesmosis ˌsɪn dez 'məʊs ɪs -des-, §-əs
‖ -'moʊs əs
syndetic sɪn 'det ɪk ‖ -'deṭ-
syndic 'sɪnd ɪk **~s** s
syndicalism 'sɪnd ɪk ə ˌlɪz əm -əl ˌɪz-
syndicalist 'sɪnd ɪk əl ɪst §-əst **~s** s
syndicate n 'sɪnd ɪk ət -ək-, -ɪt; -ɪ keɪt, -ə- **~s**
s
syndi|cate v 'sɪnd ɪ |keɪt -ə- **~cated** keɪt ɪd
-əd ‖ keɪṭ əd **~cates** keɪts **~cating**
keɪt ɪŋ ‖ keɪṭ ɪŋ
syndication ˌsɪnd ɪ 'keɪʃ ən -ə- **~s** z
syndiotactic ˌsɪn daɪ̯ə 'tækt ɪk ◂ -di̯ə-
Syndonia sɪn 'dəʊn i̯ə ‖ -'doʊn-
syndrome 'sɪn drəʊm -drəm ‖ -droʊm
—*Formerly also* -drəʊm i **~s** z
syndyotactic ˌsɪn daɪ̯ə 'tækt ɪk ◂ -di̯ə-
syne saɪn zaɪn
synecdoche sɪ 'nek dək i **~s** z
synecious sɪ 'niːʃ əs
syner|esis sɪ 'nɪər |əs ɪs sə-, -ɪs-, §-əs ‖ -'ner-
-'nɪr- **~eses** ə siːz ɪ-
synergic sɪ 'nɜːdʒ ɪk sə- ‖ -'nɜːdʒ-
synergism 'sɪn ə ˌdʒɪz əm -ɜː-; sɪ 'nɜːdʒ ˌɪz
əm, sə- ‖ -ər- **~s** z
synergist 'sɪn ədʒ ɪst -ɜːdʒ-, §-əst; sɪ 'nɜːdʒ-,
sə- ‖ -ərdʒ- **~s** s
synergistic ˌsɪn ə 'dʒɪst ɪk ◂ -ɜː- ‖ -ər- **~ally**
əl i
synerg|y 'sɪn ədʒ |i -saɪn-, -ɜːdʒ- ‖ -ərdʒ- **~ies**
iz
synesis 'sɪn ɪs ɪs -əs-, §-əs
synesthesia ˌsɪn iːs 'θiːz i̯ə ˌ•ɪs-, §, •əs-,
-'θiːʒ ə ‖ ˌsɪn əs 'θiːʒ ə -'•i̯ə
Synge sɪŋ
synizes|is ˌsɪn ɪ 'ziːs |ɪs -ə-, §-əs **~es** iːz
synod 'sɪn əd -ɒd ‖ -ɑːd **~s** z
synodal 'sɪn əd əl -ɒd- ‖ -ɑːd-
synodic sɪ 'nɒd ɪk sə- ‖ -'nɑːd- **~al** əl
synoecious sɪ 'niːʃ əs
synonym 'sɪn ə nɪm **~s** z
synonymous sɪ 'nɒn əm əs sə-, -ɪm- ‖ -'nɑːn-
~ly li
synonym|y sɪ 'nɒn əm |i sə-, -ɪm-‖ -'nɑːn- **~ies**
iz
synops|is sɪ 'nɒps |ɪs sə-, §-əs ‖ -'nɑːps- **~es**
iːz
synoptic sɪ 'nɒpt ɪk sə- ‖ -'nɑːpt- **~ally** əl i
sy, noptic 'gospels
synovi|a saɪ 'nəʊv i̯ə sɪ-, sə- ‖ -'noʊv- **~al** əl
synovitis ˌsaɪn əʊ 'vaɪt ɪs ˌsɪn-, §-əs
‖ -ə 'vaɪṭ əs
syntactic sɪn 'tækt ɪk **~al** əl **~ally** əl i **~s** s
syntagm 'sɪn tæm **~s** z
syntag|ma sɪn 'tæg |mə **~mata** mət ə ‖ məṭ ə
syntagmatic ˌsɪnt æg 'mæt ɪk ◂ ‖ -'mæṭ- **~ally**
əl i

syntax 'sɪnt æks **~es** ɪz əz
synth sɪntθ **synths** sɪntθs
synth|esis 'sɪntθ |əs ɪs -ɪs-, §-əs **~eses** ə siːz ɪ-
ˌsynthesis-by-'rule
synthesis|e, synthesiz|e 'sɪntθ ə saɪz -ɪ- **~ed** d
~er/s ə/z ‖ ər/z **~es** ɪz əz **~ing** ɪŋ
synthetic sɪn 'θet ɪk ‖ -'θeṭ- **~al** əl **~ally** əl i
~s s
Syon 'saɪ̯ən
syphilis 'sɪf əl ɪs -ɪl-, §-əs
syphilitic ˌsɪf ə 'lɪt ɪk ◂ -ɪ- ‖ -'lɪṭ- **~s** s
syphon 'saɪf ən **~ed** d **~ing** ɪŋ **~s** z
Syracusan ˌsaɪ̯ər ə 'kjuːz ən ◂ ˌsɪr- **~s** z
Syracuse *place in Sicily* 'saɪ̯ər ə kjuːz 'sɪr-
Syracuse *place in NY* 'sɪr ə kjuːs -kjuːz
Syria 'sɪr i̯ə
Syriac 'sɪr i æk
Syrian 'sɪr i̯ən **~s** z
syringa sɪ 'rɪŋ gə sə- **~s** z
syring|e n, v sɪ 'rɪndʒ sə-; 'sɪr ɪndʒ **~ed** d **~es**
ɪz əz **~ing** ɪŋ
syrinx, S~ 'sɪr ɪŋks **~es** ɪz əz
syrphid 'sɜːf ɪd §-əd ‖ 'sɜːf- 'sɪrf- **~s** z
Syrtis 'sɜːt ɪs §-əs ‖ 'sɜːṭ əs

SYRUP

AmE 1993	■ 'sɪr-	□ 'sɜː-			
0	20	40	60	80	100%

syrup 'sɪr əp ‖ 'sɜː:- —*AmE 1993 poll panel
preference:* 'sɪr- 50%, 'sɜː:- 50%. **~s** s
syrupy 'sɪr əp i ‖ 'sɜː:-
sysop 'sɪs ɒp ‖ -ɑːp **~s** s
systaltic sɪ 'stælt ɪk sə-
system 'sɪst əm -ɪm **~s** z
'systems ˌanalyst, ˌ•• ' •••
systematic ˌsɪst ə 'mæt ɪk ◂ -ɪ- ‖ -'mæṭ- **~al** əl
~ally əl i **~s** s
systematis... —*see* **systematiz...**
systematist 'sɪst əm ət ɪst sɪ 'stem-, sə-, §-əst
‖ -əṭ əst **~s** s
systematization ˌsɪst əm ət aɪ 'zeɪʃ ən ˌ•ɪm-,
-ɪ'•-; sɪ ˌstem-, sə- ‖ -əm əṭ ə- **~s** z
systematiz|e 'sɪst əm ə taɪz ˌ'•ɪm- sɪ 'stem-,
sə-, -'stiːm- **~ed** d **~es** ɪz əz **~ing** ɪŋ
systemic sɪ 'stiːm ɪk -'stem- ‖ -'stem- **~ally**
əl i **~s** s
systole 'sɪst əl i 'sɪst əʊl
systolic sɪ 'stɒl ɪk ‖ -'staːl-
Syston 'saɪst ən
syzyg|y 'sɪz ədʒ |i -ɪdʒ- **~ies** iz
Szczecin 'ʃtʃetʃ iːn —*Polish* ['ʃtʃe tɕin],
German Stettin [ʃtɛ 'tiːn]
Szechuan, Szechwan ˌsetʃ 'waːn ˌseɪtʃ-
—*Chi* Sìchuān [⁴sɿ ¹tʂʰwan]
Szeged 'seg ed —*Hung* ['sɛ gɛd]
Szerelmy sə 'relm i
Szold zəʊld →zɒʊld ‖ zoʊld

T t

t	Spelling-to-sound

1 Where the spelling is **t**, the pronunciation is regularly
   t, as in **tent** tent.
   Less frequently, it is regularly
   tʃ, as in **nature** 'neɪtʃ ə ‖ 'neɪtʃ ʳr, or
   ʃ, as in **nation** 'neɪʃ ᵊn.
   t may also be part of the digraph **th**.

2 In AmE, t has the variant ţ in certain positions (see T VOICING). This is
   shown explicitly in the LPD transcriptions, for example **atom** 'æt əm ‖
   'æţ əm.

3 Where the spelling is double **tt**, the pronunciation is again t, as in **button**
   'bʌt ᵊn, **better** 'bet ə ‖ 'beţ ʳr.

4 The pronunciation is tʃ in most words ending **-ture**, for example **departure**
   dɪ 'pɑːtʃ ə ‖ dɪ 'pɑːrtʃ ʳr, **picture** 'pɪk tʃə ‖ 'pɪk tʃʳr. Historically, this
   pronunciation came about through yod coalescence (see ASSIMILATION). More
   generally, the pronunciation is usually tʃ wherever the spelling is **t** followed
   by weak **u**, as **actual** 'æk tʃu̬_əl, **situated** 'sɪtʃ u eɪt ɪd ‖ -eɪţ əd. In some
   words of this type, however, there is an older or more careful pronunciation
   with t j, and this is regularly the case where the **u** is strong, as in **attitude**
   'æt ɪ tjuːd ‖ 'æţ ə tuːd. In this latter type, AmE prefers plain t.
   In much BrE, the pronunciation is also tʃ wherever conservative RP would
   have t j, as in **Tuesday, tune**.

5 Where **t** at the end of a stressed syllable is followed by **i** plus a vowel within
   a word, the pronunciation is regularly ʃ, as in **partial** 'pɑːʃ ᵊl ‖ 'pɑːrʃ ᵊl,
   action 'æk ʃᵊn, **superstitious** ˌsuːp ə 'stɪʃ əs ‖ -ʳr-. When the following
   vowel is weak, as in the examples just given, the **i** is silent; but when it is
   strong, the pronunciation is i, as in **initiate** ɪ 'nɪʃ i eɪt. Sometimes there is an
   alternative possibility with s, particularly if the word already contains a ʃ, as
   in **negotiation**.

6 **t** is usually silent in two groups of words:
   • in **-sten, -stle**, as **listen** 'lɪs ᵊn, **thistle** 'θɪs ᵊl; also in **Christmas, soften**
     and sometimes in **often**;
   • at the end of words recently borrowed from French, as **chalet** 'ʃæl eɪ ‖
     ʃæ 'leɪ.
   The sound t is often elided (see ELISION), giving further silent **t**s in words
   such as **postman**.

th — Spelling-to-sound

1 Where the spelling is the digraph **th**, the pronunciation is regularly
θ, as in **thick** θɪk, or
ð, as in **mother** 'mʌð ə ‖ 'mʌð ər.
Exceptionally, it is also
t, as in **Thomas** 'tɒm əs ‖ 'tɑːm əs.

2 At the beginning of a word, the pronunciation is θ or ð depending on the grammatical class to which the word belongs. In the definite article and other determiners, and in pronouns, conjunctions and pronominal adverbs, it is ð, as in **this** ðɪs, **they** ðeɪ, **though** ðəʊ ‖ ðoʊ, **thus** ðʌs. Otherwise it is θ, as in **three** θriː, **thing** θɪŋ, **thread** θred.

3 In the middle of a word (provided that **th** is not at the end of a stem), the pronunciation is generally
θ in words of Greek or Latin origin, as **method, author, ether**;
ð in words of Germanic origin, as **father, together, heathen**.

4 At the end of a word or stem, the pronunciation is usually
θ, as in **breath** breθ, **truth** truːθ, but
ð in **smooth** smuːð and one or two other words.
In **with**, RP prefers ð, GenAm θ.
Before silent **e**, and in inflected forms of the stems concerned, the pronunciation is regularly
ð, as in **breathe** briːð, **soothing** 'suːð ɪŋ (from **soothe**).

5 Several stems switch from θ to ð on adding the plural ending (**mouth** maʊθ, **mouths** maʊðz), on adding **-ern** or **-erly** (**northern, southerly**), or on converting from noun to verb (to **mouth** maʊð).

6 The pronunciation is t in **thyme** taɪm and certain proper names, including **Chatham, Streatham, Thames, Thomas**. In some cases, however, t has been or is being displaced by θ because of the influence of the spelling.

7 **th** is sometimes silent in **asthma, clothes, isthmus**. It is not a digraph in **hothouse, apartheid**.

T, t tiː *(= tea, tee)* **t's, Ts, T's** tiːz
 —*Communications code name:* Tango
 'T cell
't t —*see* 'tain't, 'tis, 'twas, 'twere, 'twill, 'twould
ta *'thank you'* tɑː
Taaffe tæf
Taal *'Afrikaans'* tɑːl
Taal *volcano in Philippines* tɑː 'ɑːl
tab tæb **tabbed** tæbd **tabbing** 'tæb ɪŋ **tabs** tæbz
tabard 'tæb ɑːd -əd ‖ -ərd ~s z
tabasco, T~ *tdmk* tə 'bæsk əʊ ‖ -oʊ
 ta,basco 'sauce
Tabatha 'tæb əθ ə
tabbouleh tə 'buːl ə -i, -eɪ

tabb|y 'tæb |i ~**ies** iz
tabernacle 'tæb ə næk əl ‖ '•ər- ~s z
Taberner *(i)* 'tæb ən ə ‖ -ərn ər; *(ii)* tə 'bɜːn ə ‖ -'bɜːn ər
tabes 'teɪb iːz
 ,tabes dor'salis dɔː 'seɪl ɪs -'sɑːl-, §-əs ‖ dɔːr 'seɪl- -'sæl-
Tabitha 'tæb ɪθ ə -əθ-
tabla 'tæb lə ‖ 'tɑːb- —*Hindi* [t̪əb lɑː] ~s z
tablature 'tæb lətʃ ə -lɪtʃ-; -lə tjʊə, -lɪ- ‖ -lə tʃʊr -lətʃ ər ~s z
table 'teɪb əl —*see also phrases with this word*
 tabled 'teɪb əld **tables** 'teɪb əlz **tabling** 'teɪb əl‿ɪŋ

tableau	762	tailboard

'table ˌlinen; 'table ˌmanners; 'table talk;
'table ˌtennis; 'table wine
tableau 'tæb ləʊ ‖ 'tæb loʊ tæ 'bloʊ ~s, ~x z
—or as sing.
table|cloth 'teɪb əl ǀklɒθ -klɔːθ ‖ -ǀklɔːθ -klɑːθ
~cloths klɒθs klɒðz, klɔːðz, klɔːθs ‖ klɔːðz
klɔːθs, klɑːðz, klɑːθs
table d'hote, table d'hôte
ˌtɑːb əl 'dəʊt ‖ -'doʊt ˌtæb- —Fr [ta blə dot]
tableland 'teɪb əl lænd ~s z
tablemat 'teɪb əl mæt ~s s
tablespoon 'teɪb əl spuːn ~s z
tablespoonful 'teɪb əl spuːn fʊl ~s z
tablespoonsful 'teɪb əl spuːnz fʊl
tablet 'tæb lət -lɪt ~s s
tableware 'teɪb əl weə ‖ -wer -wær
tabloid 'tæb lɔɪd ~s z
taboo tə 'buː ₍ₜ₎tæ- ~ed d ~ing ɪŋ ~s z
tabor 'teɪb ə -ɔː ‖ -ər ~s z
Tabor 'teɪb ɔː -ə ‖ -ər
tabouli tə 'buːl i
tabular 'tæb jʊl ə -jəl- ‖ -jəl ər ~ly li
tabula rasa ˌtæb jʊl ə 'rɑːz ə ˌ•jəl-, -'rɑːs ə
‖ -jəl ə-
tabu|late 'tæb ju ǀleɪt -jə- ‖ -jə- ~lated leɪt ɪd
-əd ‖ leɪt̬ əd ~lates leɪts ~lating
leɪt ɪŋ ‖ leɪt̬ ɪŋ
tabulation ˌtæb ju 'leɪʃ ən -jə- ‖ -jə- ~s z
tabulator 'tæb ju leɪt ə ˌ•ˈjə- ‖ -jə leɪt̬ ər ~s z
tacamahac 'tæk əm ə hæk ~s s
tache 'moustache' tæʃ tɑːʃ taches 'tæʃ ɪz
'tɑːʃ-, -əz
tachism 'tæʃ ˌɪz əm —Fr tachisme [ta ʃism]
tachistoscope tə 'kɪst ə skəʊp ‖ -skoʊp ~s s
tachistoscopic tə ˌkɪst ə 'skɒp ɪk ◄ ‖ -'skɑːp-
~ally əl i
tachograph 'tæk ə grɑːf -græf ‖ -græf ~s s
tachometer tæ 'kɒm ɪt ə -ət ə ‖ -'kɑːm ət̬ ər
~s z
tachycardia ˌtæk i 'kɑːd i ə ‖ -'kɑːrd-
tachymeter tæ 'kɪm ɪt ə -ət ə ‖ -ət̬ ər ~s z
tacit 'tæs ɪt §-ət ~ly li ~ness nəs nɪs
taciturn 'tæs ɪ tɜːn -ə- ‖ -tɜːn ~ly li
taciturnity ˌtæs ɪ 'tɜːn ət i ˌ•ə-, -ɪt i
‖ -'tɜːn ət̬ i
Tacitus 'tæs ɪt əs -ət- ‖ -ət̬ əs
tack tæk tacked tækt (= tact) tacking 'tæk ɪŋ
tacks tæks (= tax)
tacki... —see tacky
tack|le 'tæk əl —but as a nautical term, often
'teɪk əl ~ed d ~es z ~ing ˌɪŋ
tack|y 'tæk li ~ier i ə ‖ i ər ~iest i ɪst i əst
~ily ɪ li əl i ~iness i nəs i nɪs
taco 'tæk əʊ 'tɑːk- ‖ 'tɑːk oʊ ~s s
Tacolneston 'tæk əl stən (!)
Tacoma tə 'kəʊm ə ‖ -'koʊm-
Taconic tə 'kɒn ɪk ‖ -'kɑːn-
taconite 'tæk ə naɪt
tact tækt
tactful 'tækt fəl -fʊl ~ly i ~ness nəs nɪs
tactic 'tækt ɪk ~s s
-tactic 'tækt ɪk — morphotactic ˌmɔːf əʊ
'tækt ɪk ◄ ‖ ˌmɔːrf ə-

tactical 'tækt ɪk əl ~ly i
tactician tæk 'tɪʃ ən ~s z
tactile 'tækt aɪəl ‖ 'tækt əl -aɪəl
tactless 'tækt ləs -lɪs ~ly li ~ness nəs nɪs
tactual 'tæk tʃu_əl 'tækt ju_əl ~ly i
tad, Tad tæd tads, Tad's tædz
Tadcaster 'tæd ˌkæst ə -kəst-, -ˌkɑːst-
‖ -ˌkæst ər
Tadema 'tæd ɪm ə -əm-
Tadley 'tæd li
tadpol|e 'tæd pəʊl →'tæb-, →-pɒʊl ‖ -poʊl
~es z ~ing ɪŋ
Tadzhik ta: 'dʒiːk 'tɑːdʒ ɪk ~s s
Tadzhikistan ta: ˌdʒiːk ɪ 'stɑːn -ˌdʒɪk-, -ə-,
-'stæn ‖ •ˈ•••
Taegu ˌteɪ 'guː —Korean ['dɛ gu]
tae kwon do, taekwondo ˌtaɪ kwɒn 'dəʊ ˌteɪ-,
-'kwɒn dəʊ ‖ ˌtaɪ kwɑːn 'doʊ —Korean
[tʰɛ gwɒn do]
tael teɪəl (= tail, tale) taels teɪəlz
ta'en teɪn
taeni|a 'tiːn i_ə ~ae iː
Taff tæf
taffeta 'tæf ɪt ə -ət- ‖ -ət̬ ə ~s z
taffia, T~ 'tæf i_ə
taffrail 'tæf reɪəl -rəl, -rɪl ~s z
taff|y, Taff|y 'tæf li ~ies iz
tafia 'tæf i_ə
Taft tæft tɑːft
tag tæg tagged tægd tagging 'tæg ɪŋ tags
tægz
'tag ˌwrestling
Tagalog tə 'gɑːl ɒg -'gæl-, -əg ‖ -əg -ɔːg, -ɑːg
~s z
Tagamet tdmk 'tæg ə met ~s s
tagetes tæ 'dʒiːt iːz
Taggart 'tæg ət ‖ -ərt
tagg... —see tag
tagliatelle ˌtæl jə 'tel i ˌtæg li_ə 'tel i ‖ ˌtɑːl-
tagmeme 'tæg miːm ~s z
tagmemic tæg 'miːm ɪk ~s s
Tagore tə 'gɔː ‖ -'gɔːr —Bengali [tʰa kur]
tagua 'tɑːg wə
Tagus 'teɪg əs
tahini tə 'hiːn i tɑː-
Tahiti tə 'hiːt i tɑː- ‖ -'hiːt̬ i
Tahitian tə 'hiːʃ ən tɑː-, -'hiːt i_ən ~s z
Tahoe 'tɑː həʊ ‖ -hoʊ
tahr tɑː ‖ tɑːr (= tar) tahrs tɑːz ‖ tɑːrz
Tai taɪ
tai chi, t'ai chi ˌtaɪ 'tʃiː ◄ -'dʒiː —Chi tàijí [⁴tʰai
²tɕi]
t'ai chi ch'uan tʃu 'æn ‖ -'ɑːn —Chi quán
[²tɕʰɥɛn]
Taichung, T'ai-chung ˌtaɪ 'tʃʊŋ —Chi
Táizhōng [²tʰai ¹tʂʊŋ]
taig, Taig teɪg taigs, Taigs teɪgz
taiga 'taɪg ə -aː —Russ [tʌj 'ga]
tail teɪəl tailed teɪəld tailing/s 'teɪəl ɪŋ/z tails
teɪəlz
ˌtail 'end; 'tail pipe
tailback 'teɪəl bæk ~s s
tailboard 'teɪəl bɔːd ‖ -bɔːrd -boʊrd ~s z

T-voicing

1 For most Americans and Canadians the phoneme t is sometimes pronounced as a voiced sound. Where this is the usual AmE pronunciation it is shown in LPD by the symbol ţ.

2 Phonetically, ţ is a voiced alveolar tap (flap). It sounds like a quick English d, and also like the r of some languages. For many Americans, it is actually identical with their d in the same environment, so that AmE **shutter** 'ʃʌţ ᵊr may sound just the same as **shudder** 'ʃʌd ᵊr.

3 Learners of English as a foreign language who take AmE as their model are encouraged to use ţ where appropriate.

4 After n, AmE ţ can optionally be ELIDED. Accordingly, it is shown in LPD in italics, as *ţ*. Thus AmE **winter** 'wɪnţ ᵊr can sound exactly the same as **winner** 'wɪn ᵊr. Some Americans, though, consider this pronunciation incorrect.

5 In connected speech, t at the **end of a word** may change to ţ if **both** the following conditions apply:
- the sound before the t is a vowel sound or r
- the next word begins with a vowel sound and follows without a pause.

Thus in AmE **right** raɪt may be pronounced raɪţ in the phrases **right away** ˌraɪţ ə 'weɪ, **right out** ˌraɪţ 'aʊt. But in **right now** ˌraɪt 'naʊ no ţ is possible; nor in **left over** ˌleft 'oʊv ᵊr.

6 Under the same conditions, if the sound before a t at the end of a word is n, the t may change to *ţ* (and therefore possibly disappear): **paint** peɪnt, but **paint it** 'peɪnţ ɪt. Again, some people consider this incorrect.

T

tailcoat ˌteɪᵊl 'kəʊt '•• ‖ -'koʊt ~s s
-tailed 'teɪᵊld — **long-tailed** ˌlɒŋ 'teɪᵊld ◂ ‖ ˌlɔːŋ- ˌlɑːŋ-
tail-end ˌteɪᵊl 'end ~er/s ə/z ‖ ᵊr/z ~s z
tail|gate 'teɪᵊl |geɪt ~gated geɪt ɪd -əd ‖ geɪţ əd ~gater/s geɪt ə/z ‖ geɪţ ᵊr/z ~gates geɪts ~gating geɪt ɪŋ ‖ geɪţ ɪŋ
tailless 'teɪl ləs -lɪs ~ness nəs nɪs
taillight 'teɪᵊl laɪt ~s s
tailor 'teɪl ə ‖ -ᵊr ~ed d **tailoring** 'teɪl ᵊr ɪŋ ~s z
tailor-made ˌteɪl ə 'meɪd ◂ ‖ -ᵊr-
tailpiec|e 'teɪᵊl piːs ~es ɪz əz
tailpipe 'teɪᵊl paɪp ~s s
tailplane 'teɪ ᵊl pleɪn ~s z
tailrac|e 'teɪᵊl reɪs ~es ɪz əz
tailskid 'teɪᵊl skɪd ~s z
tailspin 'teɪᵊl spɪn ~s z
tailwind 'teɪᵊl wɪnd ~s z
Tain, tain teɪn
Taine teɪn —*Fr* [tɛn]
Taino 'taɪn əʊ taɪ 'iːn-, tɑː 'iːn- ‖ -oʊ ~s z
taint teɪnt **tainted** 'teɪnt ɪd -əd ‖ 'teɪnţ əd **tainting** 'teɪnt ɪŋ ‖ 'teɪnţ ɪŋ **taints** teɪnts
'taint, 'tain't teɪnt

taipan 'taɪp æn ~s z
Taipei, T'aipei ˌtaɪ 'peɪ —*Chi* Táiběi [²tʰai ³pei]
Taiping ˌtaɪ 'pɪŋ —*Chi* Tàipíng [⁴tʰai ²pʰiŋ]
Taishan ˌtaɪ 'ʃæn ‖ -'ʃɑːn —*Chi* Tàishān[⁴tʰai ¹san]
Tait teɪt
Taiwan, T'aiwan ˌtaɪ 'wɑːn -'wɒn, -'wæn —*Chi* Táiwān [²tʰai ¹wan]
Taiwanese ˌtaɪ wə 'niːz ◂ -wɑː- ‖ -'niːs
Tajik tɑː 'dʒiːk 'tɑːdʒ ɪk ~s s
Tajikistan tɑː ˌdʒiːk ɪ 'stɑːn -ˌdʒɪk-, -ə-, -'stæn •ˈ•••
Taj Mahal ˌtɑːdʒ mə 'hɑːl ˌtɑːʒ- —*Hindi* [tɑːdʒ mə həl]
takahe 'tɑːk ə hiː -ɑː- ~s z
take teɪk △tek **taken** 'teɪk ən △'tek- **takes** teɪks △teks **taking** 'teɪk ɪŋ △'tek- **took** tʊk §tuːk
takeaway 'teɪk ə ˌweɪ ~s z
take-home pay ˌteɪk həʊm peɪ ˌ•• '•, ˌˌ•'•• ‖ -hoʊm-
take-it-or-leave-it ˌteɪk ɪt ɔː 'liːv ɪt -ə'•-, §ˌ•ət-, -ət- ‖ ˌteɪk əţ ᵊr 'liːv ət
taken 'teɪk ən
takeoff 'teɪk ɒf -ɔːf ‖ -ɔːf -ɑːf ~s s

takeout 'teɪk aʊt ~**s** s
takeover 'teɪk ˌəʊv ə ‖ -ˌoʊv ᵊr ~**s** z
taker 'teɪk ə ‖ -ᵊr ~**s** z
take-up, takeup 'teɪk ʌp
takin 'taːk iːn ~**s** z
taking 'teɪk ɪŋ ~**ly** li ~**ness** nəs nɪs ~**s** z
Talacre *place in Clwyd* tæ 'læk reɪ tə-, -ə
—*Welsh* [ta 'lak re]
talapoin 'tæl ə pɔɪn ~**s** z
Talbot, t~ *(i)* 'tɔːlb ət 'tɒlb- ‖ 'taːlb-, *(ii)*
'tælb ət —*In BrE usually (i), in AmE usually
(ii).* ~**s, ~'s** s
talc tælk **talced, talcked** tælkt **talcing,
talcking** 'tælk ɪŋ **talcs** tælks
Talcott 'tɔːlk ət 'tɒlk-, 'tælk-, -ɒt ‖ 'tɔːl kaːt
'taːl-, 'tæl-
talcum 'tælk əm
'talcum ˌpowder
tale teɪᵊl (= *tail*) **tales** teɪᵊlz
talebear|er/s 'teɪᵊl ˌbeər |ə/z ‖ -ˌber |ᵊr/z -ˌbær-
~**ing** ɪŋ
talent 'tæl ənt **talented** 'tæl ənt ɪd -əd
‖ -ənt̬ əd ~**s** s
'talent ˌscout; 'talent ˌspotter
talentless 'tæl ənt ləs -lɪs
tales *pl of* **tale** teɪᵊlz
tales *'group summoned for jury service'* 'teɪl iːz
~**man** mən mæn ~**men** mən men
taleteller 'teɪᵊl ˌtel ə ‖ -ᵊr ~**s** z
Talfan 'tælv ən —*Welsh* ['tal van]
Talgarth 'tæl gaːθ ‖ -gaːrθ
tali —*see* **talus**
Taliban 'tæl ɪ bæn 'taːl-, -ə-, -baːn, ˌ•••
‖ 'taːl ə baːn tæl-
Taliesin ˌtæl i 'es ɪn ˌtæl 'jes ɪn, §-ᵊn —*Welsh*
[tal 'jes in]
talipes 'tæl ɪ piːz -ə-
talipot 'tæl ɪ pɒt -ə- ‖ -paːt ~**s** s
talisman 'tæl ɪz mən -əz-, -ɪs-, -əs- ‖ -əs- -əz-
~**s** z
talismanic ˌtæl ɪz 'mæn ɪk ◀ -əz-, -ɪs-, -əs-
‖ -əs- -əz-
Talitha 'tæl ɪθ ə -əθ-
talk tɔːk ‖ taːk **talked** tɔːkt ‖ taːkt **talking**
'tɔːk ɪŋ ‖ 'taːk- **talks** tɔːks ‖ taːks
ˌtalking 'head; 'talking ˌpoint; 'talking
ˌshop; 'talk ˌshow
talkathon 'tɔːk ə θɒn ‖ -θaːn 'taːk- ~**s** z
talkative 'tɔːk ət ɪv ‖ -ət̬ ɪv 'taːk- ~**ly** li ~**ness**
nəs nɪs
talkback 'tɔːk bæk ‖ 'taːk- ~**s** s
talker 'tɔːk ə ‖ -ᵊr 'taːk- ~**s** z
talkie 'tɔːk i ‖ 'taːk- ~**s** z
talking-to 'tɔːk ɪŋ tuː -tu ‖ 'taːk- ~**s** z
talktime 'tɔːk taɪm ‖ 'taːk-
tall tɔːl ‖ taːl **taller** 'tɔːl ə ‖ -ᵊr 'taːl- **tallest**
'tɔːl ɪst -əst ‖ 'taːl-
ˌtall 'story
tallage 'tæl ɪdʒ
Tallahassee ˌtæl ə 'hæs i
tallboy 'tɔːl bɔɪ ‖ 'taːl- ~**s** z
Talleyrand 'tæl i rænd —*Fr* [ta lɛ ʁɑ̃]

Tallin, Tallinn 'tæl ɪn tæ 'lɪn, -'liːn ‖ 'taːl ɪn
—*Estonian* ['tal lin]
Tallis 'tæl ɪs §-əs
tallish 'tɔːl ɪʃ ‖ 'taːl-
tallith 'tæl ɪθ 'taːl-, -ɪs —*Hebrew* [ta 'liːt]
tallness 'tɔːl nəs -nɪs ‖ 'taːl-
tallow 'tæl əʊ ‖ -oʊ
tallowy 'tæl əʊ i ‖ -oʊ-
Tallulah tə 'luːl ə
tally 'tæl i **tallied** 'tæl id **tallies** 'tæl iz
tallying 'tæl i ɪŋ
tallyho ˌtæl i 'həʊ ‖ -'hoʊ
tally|man 'tæl i |mən ~**men** mən men
Talmud 'tæl mʊd -məd, -mʌd ‖ 'taːl-
talmudic tæl 'mʊd ɪk -'mjuːd-, -'mʌd- ‖ taːl-
~**al** ᵊl
talon 'tæl ən ~**ed** d ~**s** z
talus *'slope'* 'teɪl əs 'tæl- ~**es** ɪz əz
talus *'anklebone'* 'teɪl əs **tali** 'teɪl aɪ
Talybont, Tal-y-bont ˌtæl i 'bɒnt -ə- ‖ -'baːnt
—*Welsh* [tal ə 'bɔnt] —*see note at* -y-
Tal-y-llyn ˌtæl i 'lɪn -ə-, -'θlɪn —*Welsh*
[tal ə 'ɬin, -'ɬɪn] —*see note at* -y-
Tam, tam tæm —*see also phrases with this word*
tams, Tam's tæmz
tamable 'teɪm əb ᵊl
tamagotchi ˌtæm ə 'gɒtʃ i i ˌtaːm ə 'goʊtʃ i
-'gaːtʃ i — Jp [ta ˌma'got tɕi]
tamale tə 'maːl i -eɪ ~**s** z
tamandua ˌtæm ən 'duː ˌə ‖ tə 'mænd u ˌə
•ˌ••'aː ~**s** z
Tamar 'teɪm aː -ə ‖ -ᵊr —*the river in Devon and
Cornwall is locally* -ə, §-ᵊr
Tamara *(i)* tə 'maːr ə -'mær-, *(ii)* 'tæm ər ə
tamarack 'tæm ə ræk ~**s** s
tamarillo ˌtæm ə 'rɪl əʊ ‖ -oʊ ~**s** z
tamarin 'tæm ər ɪn §-ən; -ə ræn ~**s** z
tamarind 'tæm ər ɪnd §-ənd ~**s** z
tamarisk 'tæm ər ɪsk §-əsk ~**s** s
tamber 'tæm bə ‖ -bᵊr ~**s** z
tambour 'tæm bʊə -bɔː ‖ -bʊr •ˈ• ~**s** z
tamboura tæm 'bʊər ə -'bɔːr- ‖ -'bʊr- ~**s** z
tambourin 'tæm bə rɪn ~**s** z
tambourine ˌtæm bə 'riːn ~**s** z
Tamburlaine 'tæm bə leɪn ‖ -bᵊr-
tame, Tame teɪm **tamed** teɪmd **tamer**
'teɪm ə ‖ -ᵊr **tames** teɪmz **tamest** 'teɪm ɪst
-əst **taming** 'teɪm ɪŋ
tameable 'teɪm əb ᵊl
tame|ly 'teɪm |li ~**ness** nəs nɪs
tamer 'teɪm ə ‖ -ᵊr ~**s** z
Tamerlane 'tæm ə leɪn ‖ -ᵊr-
Tameside 'teɪm saɪd
Tamika 'tæm ɪk ə
Tamil 'tæm ɪl -ᵊl ‖ 'taːm- ~**s** z
ˌTamil 'Nadu 'naːd uː
Tamla Motown ˌtæm lə 'məʊ taʊn ‖ -'moʊ-
Tammany 'tæm ən i
Tammie, Tammy, t~ 'tæm i
Tam O'Shanter, tam-o'-shanter
ˌtæm ə 'ʃænt ə ‖ -'ʃænt̬ ᵊr ~**s, ~'s** z
tamoxifen tə 'mɒks ɪ fen tæ-, -ə-
‖ -'maːks əf ən

tamp tæmp **tamped** tæmpt **tamping**
'tæmp ɪŋ **tamps** tæmps
Tampa 'tæmp ə
Tampax *tdmk* 'tæmp æks
tamper 'tæmp ə ‖ -ʳr **~ed** d **tampering**
'tæmp ər_ɪŋ **~s** z
Tampere 'tæmp ə reɪ ‖ 'taːmp- —*Finnish*
['tam pe re]
tamper-evident ˌtæmp ər 'ev ɪd ənt ◂-əd•,
§-ɪ dent, §-ə dent ‖ ,•ʳr-
tamper-proof 'tæmp ə pruːf §-pruf ‖ -ʳr-
Tampico tæm 'piːk əʊ ‖ -oʊ taːm- —*Sp*
[tam 'pi ko]
tampion 'tæmp i_ən **~s** z
tampon 'tæmp ɒn -ən ‖ -aːn **~s** z
tamponade ˌtæmp ə 'neɪd **~s** z
Tamsin, Tamsyn *(i)* 'tæm sɪn, *(ii)* -zɪn
Tamworth, t~ 'tæm wɜːθ -wəθ, §-əθ ‖ -wɝːθ
~s, ~'s s
tan tæn **tanned** tænd **tanning** 'tæn ɪŋ **tans**
tænz
tana, Tana 'taːn ə
tanager 'tæn ədʒ ə -ɪdʒ- ‖ -ʳr **~s** z
Tanagra 'tæn əg rə
Tanami 'tæn ə maɪ
Tancock 'tæn kɒk →'tæŋ- ‖ -kaːk
Tancred 'tæŋk rɪd -red, §-rəd
tandem 'tænd əm **~s** z
tandoor 'tænd ʊə -ɔː; tæn 'dʊə, -'dɔː
‖ taːn 'dʊʳr **~s** z
tandoori, tanduri tæn 'dʊər i tʌn-, -'dɔːr-
‖ taːn 'dʊr- -'dɝː-
Tandy 'tænd i
Taney 'tɔːn i ‖ 'taːn- *(!)*
tang tæŋ **tangs** tæŋz
Tang, T'ang *dynasty* tæŋ tʌŋ ‖ taːŋ —*Chi* Táng
[²tʰaŋ]
tanga, Tanga 'tæŋ gə **~s** z
Tanganyika ˌtæŋ gən 'jiːk ə ,•gæn-
tangelo 'tændʒ ə ləʊ ‖ -loʊ **~s** z
tangent 'tændʒ ənt **~s** s
tangential tæn 'dʒen↑ʃəl **~ly** i
tangerine, T~ ˌtændʒ ə 'riːn '••• **~s** z
tangibility ˌtændʒ ə 'bɪl ət i ,•ɪ-, -ɪt i ‖ -əti i
tangib|le 'tændʒ əb |əl -ɪb- **~ly** li
Tangier ₍₎tæn 'dʒɪə ‖ -'dʒɪʳr
Tangiers ₍₎tæn 'dʒɪəz ‖ -'dʒɪʳrz
tangl|e 'tæŋ gəl **~ed** d **~es** z **~ing** _ɪŋ
Tanglewood 'tæŋ gəl wʊd
tangly 'tæŋ gli
Tangmere 'tæŋ mɪə ‖ -mɪr
tango 'tæŋ gəʊ ‖ -goʊ **~ed** d **~ing** ɪŋ **~s** z
tangram 'tæn græm →'tæŋ- **~s** z
Tangshan ˌtæŋ 'ʃæn ‖ ˌtaːŋ 'ʃaːn —*Chi*
Tángshān [²tʰaŋ ¹ʂan]
Tanguy 'tæŋ gi ‖ taːn 'gi: —*Fr* [tɑ̃ gi]
tangy 'tæŋ i
Tangye 'tæŋ gi
tanh θæn tæn↑ʃ, ˌtæn 'eɪtʃ
Tania 'taːn i_ə
tank tæŋk **tanked** tæŋkt **tanking** 'tæŋk ɪŋ
tanks tæŋks
ˌtanked 'up; 'tank ˌengine; 'tank top

tanka 'tæŋk ə 'taːŋk- ‖ 'taːŋk ə —*Jp* ['taŋ ka]
~s z
tankage 'tæŋk ɪdʒ
tankard 'tæŋk əd ‖ -ʳrd **~s** z
tanker 'tæŋk ə ‖ -ʳr **~s** z
tankful 'tæŋk fʊl **~s** z
tannate 'tæn eɪt
tann... —*see* **tan**
tanner, T~ 'tæn ə ‖ -ʳr **~s** z
tanner|y 'tæn ər |i **~ies** iz
Tannhauser, Tannhäuser 'tæn ˌhɔɪz ə -ˌhaʊz-
‖ 'taːn ˌhɔɪz ʳr —*Ger* ['tan hɔy zɐ]
tannic 'tæn ɪk
tannin 'tæn ɪn §-ən **~s** z
tannoy, T~ *tdmk* 'tæn ɔɪ **~s** z
Tanoan tə 'nəʊ ən 'taːn əʊ- ‖ tə 'noʊ ən
'taːn oʊ-
Tanqueray 'tæŋk ʳr i-ə reɪ
Tansey 'tænz i
tans|y, Tansy 'tænz |i **~ies** iz
tantalic tæn 'tæl ɪk
tantalis|e, tantaliz|e 'tænt ə laɪz -ʳl aɪz
‖ 'tænt ʳl aɪz **~ed** d **~es** ɪz əz **~ing** ɪŋ
tantalous 'tænt əl əs ‖ 'tænt-
tantalum 'tænt əl əm ‖ 'tænt-
tantalus, T~ 'tænt əl əs ‖ 'tænt-
tantamount 'tænt ə maʊnt ‖ 'tænt-
tantara ˌtænt ə 'raː 'tænt ʳr ə,
tæn 'taːr ə ‖ tæn 'tær ə
tantiv|y tæn 'tɪv |i **~ies** iz
Tantr|a, t~ 'tæntr| ə 'tʌntr| ə ‖ 'tʌntr| ə
'taːntr| ə, 'tæntr| ə **~ic** ɪk **~ism** ɪz əm
tantrum 'tæntr əm **~s** z
Tanya 'taːn jə 'tæn-, -i_ə
Tanzani|a ˌtæn zə 'niː_|ə tæn 'zeɪn i_|ə **~an/s**
ən/z
Tao taʊ daʊ —*Chi* Dào [⁴tɐu]
ˌTao Te 'Ching teɪ 'tʃɪŋ də 'dʒɪŋ —*Chi*
Dàodéjīng [⁴tau ²tɤ ¹tɕɪŋ]
Taoism 'taʊ ˌɪz əm 'daʊ-; 'teɪ əʊ ,••, 'taː-
Taoiseach 'tiːʃ ək -əx —*Ir* ['tˠiː ʃəx]
Taoist 'taʊ ɪst 'daʊ-, §-əst; 'teɪ əʊ-; 'taː- **~s** s
Taos taʊs
tap tæp **tapped** tæpt **tapping** 'tæp ɪŋ **taps**
tæps
'tap dance; 'tap ˌdancer; 'tap ˌdancing
tapa 'taːp ə
tapas 'tæp æs -əs ‖ 'taːp- —*Sp* ['ta pas]
tape teɪp **taped** teɪpt **tapes** teɪps **taping**
'teɪp ɪŋ
'tape deck; 'tape ˌmeasure; 'tape
re,corder
tapenade, tapénade ˌtæp ə 'naːd ‖ ˌtaːp- **~s**
z —*Fr* [ta pe nad]
taper 'teɪp ə ‖ -ʳr **~ed** d **tapering/ly**
'teɪp ər_ɪŋ /li **~s** z
tape-record 'teɪp rɪ ˌkɔːd -rə-, §-riː- ‖ -kɔːrd
~ed ɪd əd **~er/s** ə/z ‖ ʳr/z **~ing** ɪŋ **~s** z
tapes|try 'tæp ɪs |tri -əs- **~tries** triz
tapeworm 'teɪp wɜːm ‖ -wɝːm **~s** z
tapioca ˌtæp i 'əʊk ə ‖ -'oʊk ə
tapir 'teɪp ə -ɪə ‖ -ʳr **~s** z
tapis 'tæp i -iː ‖ tæ 'piː —*Fr* [ta pi]

Taplin 'tæp lɪn §-lən
Taplow 'tæp ləʊ ‖ -loʊ
Tapp tæp
tapp... —*see* **tap**
tapper 'tæp ə ‖ -ᵊr ~s z
tappet 'tæp ɪt §-ət ~s s
taproom 'tæp ruːm -rʊm ~s z
taproot 'tæp ruːt ~s s
Tapscott 'tæps kɒt ‖ -kɑːt
Tapsell 'tæps ᵊl
tapster 'tæpst ə ‖ -ᵊr ~s z
tar tɑː ‖ tɑːr **tarred** tɑːd ‖ tɑːrd **tarring**
    'tɑːr ɪŋ **tars** tɑːz ‖ tɑːrz
Tara 'tɑːr ə 'tær ə ‖ 'tær ə 'ter ə, 'tɑːr ə
ta-ra tə 'rɑː
taradiddle 'tær ə dɪd ᵊl ‖ 'ter-, ͵•••'•• ~s z
taramasalata, taramosalata
    ͵tær əm ə sə 'lɑːt ə tə ͵rɑːm-, tə ͵ræm-
    ‖ 'tɑːr əm ə sə ͵lɑːt ə ͵•••'•• —*ModGk*
    [ta ra mɔ sa 'la ta]
Taranaki ͵tær ə 'næk i
tarantella ͵tær ən 'tel ə ~s z
Tarantino ͵tær ən 'tiːn əʊ ‖ -oʊ -ter-
Taranto tə 'rænt əʊ ‖ -oʊ -'rɑːnt-; 'tɑːr ənt-
    —*It* ['tɑː ran to]
tarantula tə 'rænt jʊl ə -jəl ə; -'rænt ʃ əl-
    ‖ -'rænt ʃ əl ə -'rænt ʃ ᵊl ə ~s z
taraxacum, T~ tə 'ræks ək əm
Tarbert 'tɑːb ət ‖ 'tɑːrb ᵊrt
Tarbet 'tɑːb ɪt -ət ‖ 'tɑːrb ət
tarboosh ͵tɑː 'buːʃ ‖ tɑːr- '•• ~es ɪz əz
Tarbuck 'tɑː bʌk ‖ 'tɑːr-
tardigrade 'tɑːd ɪ greɪd §-ə- ‖ 'tɑːrd- ~s z
Tardis 'tɑːd ɪs §-əs ‖ 'tɑːrd-
tard|ly 'tɑːd li ‖ 'tɑːrd li ~ier i ə ‖ i ᵊr ~iest
    i ɪst i əst ~ily ɪ li əl i ~iness i nəs i nɪs
tare teə ‖ teᵊr tæᵊr **tares** teəz ‖ teᵊrz tæᵊrz
Tarentum tə 'rent əm
targ|et 'tɑːg ɪt §-ət ‖ 'tɑːrg ət ~eted ɪt ɪd
    §ət-, -əd ‖ ət əd ~eting ɪt ɪŋ §ət- ‖ ət ɪŋ
    ~ets ɪts §əts ‖ əts
    'target ͵language
tariff 'tær ɪf §-əf ‖ 'ter- ~s s
Tariq 'tær ɪk 'tɑːr-
Tarka 'tɑːk ə ‖ 'tɑːrk ə
Tarkington 'tɑːk ɪŋ tən ‖ 'tɑːrk-
Tarleton 'tɑːl tən ‖ 'tɑːrl-
tarmac, T~ *tdmk* 'tɑː mæk ‖ 'tɑːr- ~ked t
    ~king ɪŋ ~s s
tarmacadam ͵tɑː mə 'kæd əm ‖ ͵tɑːr-
tarn, Tarn tɑːn ‖ tɑːrn **tarns** tɑːnz ‖ tɑːrnz
tarnation tɑː 'neɪʃ ᵊn ‖ tɑːr-
tarnish 'tɑːn ɪʃ ‖ 'tɑːrn ɪʃ ~ed t ~es ɪz əz
    ~ing ɪŋ
taro 'tɑːr əʊ ‖ -oʊ 'tær-, 'ter- ~s z
taroc, tarok 'tær ək -ɒk ‖ -ɑːk 'ter- ~s s
tarot 'tær əʊ ‖ -oʊ 'ter- ~s z
tarp tɑːp ‖ tɑːrp **tarps** tɑːps ‖ tɑːrps
tarpaper 'tɑː ͵peɪp ə ‖ 'tɑːr ͵peɪp ᵊr
tarpaulin ₍₎tɑː 'pɔːl ɪn §-ən ‖ tɑːr- -'pɑːl-;
    'tɑːrp əl- ~s z
Tarpeian tɑː 'piː ən ‖ tɑːr-
tarpon 'tɑːp ɒn -ən ‖ 'tɑːrp ɑːn -ən ~s z

Tarporley 'tɑːp əl i ‖ 'tɑːrp ᵊr li
Tarquin 'tɑːk wɪn §-wən ‖ 'tɑːrk-
Tarquinius tɑː 'kwɪn i əs ‖ tɑːr-
Tarr tɑː ‖ tɑːr
tarradiddle 'tær ə dɪd ᵊl ‖ 'ter-, ͵•••'•• ~s z
tarragon 'tær əg ən ‖ 'ter-
Tarragona ͵tær ə 'gəʊn ə ‖ -'goʊn- ͵ter-, ͵tɑːr-
    —*Sp* [ta ra 'ɣo na]
Tarrant 'tær ənt ‖ 'ter-
tarr... —*see* **tar**
Tarring *place in West Sussex; family name*
    'tær ɪŋ ‖ 'ter-
tarr|y *v 'delay'* 'tær li ‖ 'ter- ~ied id ~ies iz
    ~ying i ɪŋ
tarry *adj 'tar-covered, tar-like'* 'tɑːr i
Tarrytown 'tær i taʊn ‖ 'ter-
tarsal 'tɑːs ᵊl ‖ 'tɑːrs ᵊl ~s z
Tarshish 'tɑːʃ ɪʃ ‖ 'tɑːrʃ ɪʃ
tarsier 'tɑːs i ə ‖ 'tɑːrs i ᵊr -eɪ ~s z
tars|us, T~ 'tɑːs ləs ‖ 'tɑːrs- ~i aɪ
tart tɑːt ‖ tɑːrt **tarted** 'tɑːt ɪd -əd ‖ 'tɑːrt̬ əd
    tarting 'tɑːt ɪŋ ‖ 'tɑːrt̬ ɪŋ **tarts** tɑːts ‖ tɑːrts
tartan 'tɑːt ᵊn ‖ 'tɑːrt ᵊn ~s z
tartar, T~ 'tɑːt ə -ɑː- ‖ 'tɑːrt̬ ᵊr ~s z
    ͵tartar 'sauce,'••
tartare tɑː 'tɑː- ‖ tɑːr 'tɑːr △-'teə ‖ tɑːr 'tɑːr
Tartarean tɑː 'teər i ən ‖ tɑːr ter- -'tær-
tartaric tɑː 'tær ɪk ‖ tɑːr- -'ter-
    tar͵taric 'acid
Tartarus 'tɑːt ər əs ‖ 'tɑːrt̬-
Tartary 'tɑːt ər i ‖ 'tɑːrt̬-
tartlet 'tɑːt lət -lɪt ‖ 'tɑːrt- ~s s
tart|ly 'tɑːt li ‖ 'tɑːrt li ~ness nəs nɪs
tartrate 'tɑːtr eɪt ‖ 'tɑːrtr- ~s s
tartrazine 'tɑːtr ə ziːn ‖ 'tɑːrtr-
Tartuffe ₍₎tɑː 'tuːf -'tuf ‖ ₍₎tɑːr- —*Fr* [taʁ tyf]
tart|y 'tɑːt̬ i ‖ 'tɑːrt̬ i ~ier i ə ‖ i ᵊr ~iest
    i ɪst i əst ~ily ɪ li əl i ~iness i nəs i nɪs
Tarvin 'tɑːv ɪn §-ən ‖ 'tɑːrv ᵊn
Tarzan 'tɑːz ᵊn -æn ‖ 'tɑːrz æn -ᵊn
Tasha 'tæʃ ə ‖ 'tɑːʃ ə
Tashkent ͵tæʃ 'kent ‖ ͵tɑːʃ- —*Russ* [taʃ 'kjent]
task tɑːsk §tæsk ‖ tæsk **tasked** tɑːskt §tæskt
    ‖ tæskt **tasking** 'tɑːsk ɪŋ §'tæsk- ‖ 'tæsk ɪŋ
    tasks tɑːsks §tæsks ‖ tæsks
    'task force
taskbar 'tɑːsk bɑː ‖ 'tæsk bɑːr ~s z
Tasker 'tæsk ə ‖ -ᵊr
taskmaster 'tɑːsk ͵mɑːst ə §'tæsk ͵mæst ə
    ‖ 'tæsk ͵mæst ᵊr ~s z
taskmistress 'tɑːsk ͵mɪs trəs §'tæsk-, -trɪs
    ‖ 'tæsk- ~es ɪz əz
Tasman 'tæz mən
Tasmani|a tæz 'meɪn i ə ~an/s ən/z
Tass tæs ‖ tɑːs
tassel 'tæs ᵊl ~ed, ~led d ~s z
tassie *'cup'* 'tæs i ~s z
Tassie *'Tasmanian'* 'tæz i ~s z
Tasso 'tæs əʊ ‖ -oʊ 'tɑːs- —*It* ['tas so]
taste teɪst **tasted** 'teɪst ɪd -əd **tastes** teɪsts
    tasting 'teɪst ɪŋ
    'taste bud
tasteful 'teɪst fᵊl -fʊl ~ly _i ~ness nəs nɪs

tasteless 'teɪst ləs -lɪs ~ly li ~ness nəs nɪs
taster 'teɪst ə ‖ -ər ~s z
tast|y 'teɪst |i ~ier i‿ə ‖ i‿ər ~iest i‿ɪst i‿əst
  ~ily ɪ li əl i ~iness i nəs i nɪs
tat tæt tats tæts tatted 'tæt ɪd -əd ‖ 'tæt̬ əd
  tatting 'tæt ɪŋ ‖ 'tæt̬ ɪŋ
tata, ta-ta ͵ˌtæ 'tɑː tə-
tatami tə 'tɑːm i tɑː-, tæ- —Jp [ta ͵ta mi] ~s z
Tatar 'tɑːt ə ‖ 'tɑːt̬ ər ~s z
Tatchell 'tætʃ əl
Tate teɪt
tater 'teɪt ə ‖ 'teɪt̬ ər ~s z
Tatham (i) 'tæt əm ‖ 'tæt̬ əm, (ii) 'teɪθ əm, (iii)
  'teɪð əm
Tati tæ 'tiː: tɑː- ‖ tɑː- —Fr [ta ti]
Tatiana ͵tæt i 'ɑːn ə ‖ tɑːt i 'jɑːn ə
tatie 'teɪt i ‖ 'teɪt̬ i ~s z
Tatler tdmk 'tæt lə ‖ -lər
Tatra 'tɑːtr ə 'tætr ə
tatter 'tæt ə ‖ 'tæt̬ ər ~ed d ~s z
tatterdemalion ͵tæt ə dɪ 'meɪl i‿ən -də'•-,
  -'mæl- ‖ ͵tæt̬ ər-
Tattersall, t~ 'tæt ə sɔːl -sᵊl ‖ 'tæt̬ ər- -saːl ~s,
  ~'s z
tattl|e 'tæt əl ‖ 'tæt̬ əl ~ed d ~es z ~ing/ly
  ɪŋ /li
tattler 'tæt əl‿ə ‖ 'tæt̬ əl‿ər ~s z
Tatton 'tæt ən
tattoo tæ 'tuː tə- ~ed d ~ing ɪŋ ~s z
tattooist tæ 'tuː ɪst tə-, §-əst ~s s
tatt|y 'tæt i ‖ 'tæt̬ i ~ier i‿ə ‖ i‿ər ~iest i‿ɪst
  i‿əst ~ily ɪ li əl i ~iness i nəs i nɪs
Tatum 'teɪt əm ‖ 'teɪt̬ əm
Tatung tdmk 'tɑː tʊŋ
tau tɔː tau ‖ tau tɔː, tɑː
taught tɔːt ‖ tɑːt (= taut)
taunt tɔːnt ‖ tɑːnt taunted 'tɔːnt ɪd -əd
  ‖ 'tɔːnt̬ əd 'tɑːnt̬- taunting/ly 'tɔːnt ɪŋ /
  li ‖ 'tɔːnt̬- 'tɑːnt̬- taunts tɔːnts ‖ tɑːnts
Taunton 'tɔːnt ən ‖ 'tɔːnt ən 'tɑːnt- —in
  Somerset, locally also 'tɑːnt-
Taunus 'tɔːn əs 'taʊn- ‖ 'taʊn- —Ger
  ['tau nʊs]
taupe təʊp ‖ toʊp (= tope)
Taurean, t~ 'tɔːr i‿ən tɔː 'riː‿ən ~s z
taurine adj 'bovine' 'tɔːr aɪn
taurine n 'C₂H₇NO₃S' 'tɔːr iːn -ɪn
Taurus 'tɔːr əs
taut tɔːt ‖ tɑːt tauter 'tɔːt ə ‖ 'tɔːt̬ ər 'tɑːt̬-
  tautest 'tɔːt ɪst -əst ‖ 'tɔːt̬ əst 'tɑːt̬-
tauten 'tɔːt ən ‖ 'tɑːt- ~ed d ~ing ɪŋ ~s z
taut|ly 'tɔːt |li ‖ 'tɑːt- ~ness nəs nɪs
tauto- comb. form
  with plain suffix ͵tɔːt əʊ ‖ ͵tɔːt ə ͵tɑːt̬ —
  tautomeric ͵tɔːt ə 'mer ɪk ◄ ‖ ͵tɔːt̬- ͵tɑːt̬-
  with stress-imposing suffix tɔː 'tɒ+ ‖ tɔː 'tɑː+
  tɑː- — tautomerism tɔː 'tɒm ər ͵ɪz əm
  ‖ -'tɑːm- tɑː-
tautological ͵tɔːt ə 'lɒdʒ ɪk əl ◄ ‖ ͵tɔːt ə 'lɑːdʒ-
  ͵tɑːt̬- ~ly‿i
tautologous tɔː 'tɒl əg əs △-ədʒ əs ‖ -'tɑːl-
  tɑː-
tautolog|y tɔː 'tɒl ədʒ |i ‖ -'tɑːl- tɑː- ~ies iz

tautomer 'tɔːt əm ə ‖ 'tɔːt̬ əm ər 'tɑːt̬- ~s z
tautonym 'tɔːt ə nɪm -ᵊn ɪm ‖ 'tɔːt̬ ᵊn ɪm 'tɑːt̬-
  ~s z
tautosyllabic ͵tɔːt əʊ sɪ 'læb ɪk ◄ -sə'•-
  ‖ ͵tɔːt̬ oʊ- ͵tɑːt̬-
Tavare, Tavaré 'tæv ə reɪ
Tavener 'tæv ᵊn ə ‖ -ər
tavern 'tæv ən ‖ -ᵊrn ~s z
taverna tə 'vɜːn ə tæ- ‖ -'vɜ˞ːn- —ModGk
  [ta 'vɛr na] ~s z
Taverne tə 'vɜːn ‖ -'vɜ˞ːn
Taverner 'tæv ᵊn ə ‖ -ᵊrn ər
Tavistock 'tæv ɪ stɒk -ə- ‖ -stɑːk
Tavy 'teɪv i
taw tɔː ‖ tɑː tawed tɔːd ‖ tɑːd tawing
  'tɔːr ɪŋ ‖ 'tɔː ɪŋ 'tɑː- taws tɔːz ‖ tɑːz
tawdr|y 'tɔːdr |i ‖ 'tɑːdr- ~ier i‿ə ‖ i‿ər ~iest
  i‿ɪst i‿əst ~ily əl i i li ~iness i nəs i nɪs
Tawe river 'tau‿i -eɪ —Welsh ['ta we]
Tawney 'tɔːn i ‖ 'tɑːn-
tawn|y 'tɔːn |i ‖ 'tɑːn- ~ier i‿ə ‖ i‿ər ~iest
  i‿ɪst i‿əst ~iness i nəs i nɪs
tawse tɔːz ‖ tɑːz
tax tæks taxed tækst taxes 'tæks ɪz -əz
  taxing/ly 'tæks ɪŋ /li
  'tax e͵vasion; 'tax ͵exile; 'tax ͵haven; 'tax
  re͵turn; 'tax ͵shelter; 'tax year
taxa 'tæks ə
taxability ͵tæks ə 'bɪl ət i -ɪt i ‖ -əṯ i
taxable 'tæks əb əl ~ness nəs nɪs
taxation tæk 'seɪʃ ən ~s z
tax-deductible ͵tæks dɪ 'dʌkt əb əl ◄ ͵•də-,
  §͵•diː-, -ɪb əl; '• •, • • •
taxeme 'tæks iːm ~s z
taxemic tæk 'siːm ɪk ~s s
tax-exempt ͵tæks ɪg 'zempt ◄ -eg-, -əg-, -ɪk-,
  -ek-, -ək-
tax-free ͵tæks 'friː ◄
taxi 'tæks i ~ed d ~ing ɪŋ ~es, ~s z
  'taxi ͵driver; 'taxi rank; 'taxi stand
taxicab 'tæks i kæb ~s z
taxiderm|al ͵tæks ɪ 'dɜːm |əl ◄ -ə- ‖ -'dɜ˞ːm-
  ~ic ɪk
taxidermist 'tæks ɪ dɜːm ɪst '•ə-, §-əst,
  ͵• •'• •; tæk 'sɪd əm- ‖ 'tæks ə dɜ˞ːm əst ~s
  s
taxidermy 'tæks ɪ dɜːm i '•ə- ‖ -dɜ˞ːm i
taximeter 'tæks i ͵miːt ə ‖ -͵miːt̬ ər ~s z
taxis sing. n, Taxis 'tæks ɪs §-əs
taxis pl of taxi 'tæks iz
-taxis 'tæks ɪs §-əs — thermotaxis ͵θɜːm əʊ
  'tæks ɪs §-əs ‖ ͵θɜ˞ːm ə-
taxiway 'tæks i weɪ ~s z
tax|man 'tæks |mæn ~men men
taxon 'tæks ɒn ‖ -ɑːn ~s z taxa 'tæks ə
taxonomic ͵tæks ə 'nɒm ɪk ◄ ‖ -'nɑːm- ~al əl
  ~ally əl‿i
  ͵taxo͵nomic pho'nemics
taxonomist tæk 'sɒn əm ɪst §-əst ‖ -'sɑːn- ~s
  s
taxonom|y tæk 'sɒn əm |i ‖ -'sɑːn- ~ies iz
taxpayer 'tæks ͵peɪ ə ‖ -ər ~s z
taxying 'tæks i ɪŋ

Tay teɪ

tayberr|y 'teɪ bər_|i -ˌber |i -ˌber |i **~ies** iz

Tayler, Taylor 'teɪl ə ‖ -ᵊr

Taylorian teɪ 'lɔːr i_ən

Taylour 'teɪl ə ‖ -ᵊr

Tayport 'teɪ pɔːt ‖ -pɔːrt -poʊrt

tayra 'taɪᵊr ə **~s** z

Tay-Sachs ˌteɪ 'sæks
ˌTay 'Sachs diˌsease

Tayside 'teɪ saɪd

Taz tæz

TB ˌtiː 'biː

T-bar 'tiː bɑː ‖ -bɑːr **~s** z

Tbilisi tə 'bliːs i tə bɪ 'liːs i, -bə-

T-bone 'tiː bəʊn ‖ -boʊn **~s** z

T-cell 'tiː sel **~s** z

Tchaikovsky tʃaɪ 'kɒf ski ‖ -'kɔːf- -'kɑːf-
—*Russ* [tʃɪj 'kɔf skʲɪj]

TCP *tdmk* ˌtiː siː 'piː

te tiː —*see also phrases with this word*

tea tiː (= *tee*) **teas** tiːz (= *tease*)
'tea break; 'tea ˌcaddy; 'tea chest; 'tea
cloth; 'tea ˌcosy; 'tea ˌparty; 'tea ˌservice;
'tea ˌtowel; 'tea ˌtrolley; 'tea ˌwagon

teabag 'tiː bæg **~s** z

teabread 'tiː bred

teacake 'tiː keɪk **~s** s

teach, Teach tiːtʃ **taught** tɔːt ‖ tɑːt **teaches**
'tiːtʃ ɪz -əz **teaching/s** 'tiːtʃ ɪŋ/z
'teaching ˌpractice; 'teaching ˌhospital

teachability ˌtiːtʃ ə 'bɪl ət i -ɪt i ‖ -ət̬ i

teachable 'tiːtʃ əb ᵊl

teacher, T~ 'tiːtʃ ə ‖ -ᵊr **~s** z
ˌteacher 'training ˌcollege

teach-in 'tiːtʃ ɪn **~s** z

teacup 'tiː kʌp 'tiː kʌp **~s** s

teacupful 'tiː kʌp fʊl 'tiː kʌp- **~s** z
teacupsful 'tiː kʌps fʊl 'tiː kʌps-

teagarden, T~ 'tiː ˌgɑːd ᵊn ‖ -ˌgɑːrd- **~s** z

Teague tiːg

tea|house 'tiː |haʊs **~houses** haʊz ɪz -əz

teak tiːk

teakettle 'tiː ˌket ᵊl ‖ -ˌket̬- **~s** z

teal, Teal tiːᵊl **teals** tiːᵊlz

tea|leaf 'tiː |liːf **~leaves** liːvz

team tiːm (= *teem*) **teamed** tiːmd **teaming**
'tiːm ɪŋ **teams** tiːmz
ˌteam 'spirit

tea-maker 'tiː ˌmeɪk ə ‖ -ᵊr **~s** z

team-mate 'tiːm meɪt **~s** s

teamster 'tiːmᵖst ə ‖ -ᵊr **~s** z

teamwork 'tiːm wɜːk ‖ -wɜːk

Tean tiːn

teapot 'tiːp ɒt 'tiː pɒt ‖ 'tiː pɑːt **~s** s

teapoy 'tiːp ɔɪ **~s** z

tear '*liquid from the eye*' tɪə ‖ tɪᵊr **tears**
tɪəz ‖ tɪᵊrz
'tear duct; 'tear gas

tear '*rip*', '*rush*' teə ‖ teᵊr tæᵊr (= *tare*)
tearing 'teər ɪŋ ‖ 'ter ɪŋ 'tær- **tears**
teəz ‖ teᵊrz tæᵊrz **tore** tɔː ‖ tɔːr toʊr **torn**
tɔːn ‖ tɔːrn toʊrn

tearaway 'teər ə ˌweɪ ‖ 'ter- 'tær- **~s** z

teardrop 'tɪə drɒp ‖ 'tɪr drɑːp **~s** s

tearful 'tɪəf ᵊl ‖ 'tɪrf ᵊl **~ly** _i **~ness** nəs nɪs

teargas 'tɪə gæs ‖ 'tɪr- **~sed** t **~ses** ɪz əz
~sing ɪŋ

tearing 'teər ɪŋ ‖ 'ter ɪŋ 'tær-

tearjerker 'tɪə ˌdʒɜːk ə ‖ 'tɪr ˌdʒɜːk ᵊr **~s** z

Tearlach 'tʃaːl əx -ək ‖ 'tʃɑːrl- —*Ir* ['tʲaːr ləx]

tearless '*unweeping*' 'tɪə ləs -lɪs ‖ 'tɪr- **~ly** li
~ness nəs nɪs

tearoff 'teər ɒf -ɔːf ‖ 'ter ɔːf 'tær-, -ɑːf

tearoom 'tiː ruːm -rʊm **~s** z

tearstained 'tɪə steɪnd ‖ 'tɪr-

Teasdale 'tiːz deɪᵊl

tease tiːz **teased** tiːzd **teases** 'tiːz ɪz -əz
teasing/ly 'tiːz ɪŋ /li

teasel 'tiːz ᵊl **~ed, ~led** d **~ing, ~ling** ɪŋ **~s** z

teaser 'tiːz ə ‖ -ᵊr **~s** z

teashop 'tiː ʃɒp ‖ -ʃɑːp **~s** s

Teasmade *tdmk* 'tiːz meɪd

teaspoon 'tiːsp uːn 'tiː spuːn **~s** z

teaspoonful 'tiːsp uːn fʊl 'tiː spuːn- **~s** z
teaspoonsful 'tiːsp uːnz fʊl 'tiː spuːnz-

teat tiːt **teats** tiːts

teatime 'tiːt aɪm 'tiː taɪm

tea-tree 'tiː triː **~s** z

tea-urn 'tiː ɜːn ‖ -ɜːn **~s** z

teazel, teazle 'tiːz ᵊl **teazeled, teazelled,
teazled** 'tiːz ᵊld **teazeling, teazelling,
teazling** 'tiːz ᵊl ɪŋ **teazels, teazles** 'tiːz ᵊlz

Tebay *place in Cumbria* 'tiːb eɪ —*but locally* -i

Tebbit, Tebbitt 'teb ɪt §-ət

tec tek **tecs** teks

tech tek

techie 'tek i **~s** z

technetium tek 'niːʃ i_əm -'niːs-; -'niːʃ əm

technical 'tek nɪk ᵊl
'technical ˌcollege; ˌtechnical 'knockout

technicalit|y ˌtek nɪ 'kæl ət |i ˌ•nə-, -ɪt i ‖ -ət̬ |i
~ies iz

technically 'tek nɪk ᵊl_i

technician tek 'nɪʃ ᵊn **~s** z

Technicolor *tdmk*, **t~, technicolour**
'tek nɪ ˌkʌl ə -nə- ‖ -ᵊr

technics, T~ 'tek nɪks

technique ₍₎tek 'niːk **~s** s

techno 'tek nəʊ ‖ -noʊ

techno- *comb. form*
with stress-neutral suffix ˌtek nəʊ ‖ -noʊ —
technophobia ˌtek nəʊ
'fəʊb i_ə ‖ -noʊ 'foʊb-
with stress-imposing suffix tek 'nɒ+ ‖ -'nɑː+ —
technography tek 'nɒg rəf i ‖ -'nɑːg-

technocrac|y tek 'nɒk rəs |i ‖ -'nɑːk- **~ies** iz

technocrat 'tek nə kræt **~s** s

technocratic ˌtek nə 'kræt ɪk ◄ ‖ -'kræt̬- **~ally**
ᵊl_i

technological ˌtek nə 'lɒdʒ ɪk ᵊl ◄ ‖ -'lɑːdʒ-
~ly _i

technologist tek 'nɒl ədʒ ɪst §-əst ‖ -'nɑːl- **~s**
s

technolog|y tek 'nɒl ədʒ |i ‖ -'nɑːl- **~ies** iz

technophobe 'tek nəʊ fəʊb ‖ -noʊ foʊb **~s** z

tech|y '*technical enthusiast*' 'tek| i **~ies** iz

Teck tek
tectonic tek 'tɒn ɪk ‖ -'tɑːn- ~s s
Tecumseh tɪ 'kʌmᵖs ə tə-, -i
Tecwyn 'tek wɪn
ted, Ted ted tedded 'ted ɪd -əd tedding
    'ted ɪŋ teds tedz
Tedder, t~ 'ted ə ‖ -ᵊr ~s z
Teddie 'ted i
Teddington 'ted ɪŋ tən
tedd|y, Tedd|y 'ted |i ~ies, ~y's iz
    'teddy bear; 'teddy boy
Te Deum ˌtiː 'diː‿əm ˌteɪ 'deɪ-, -ʊm ~s z
tedious 'tiːd i‿əs §'tiːdʒ əs -ly li ~ness nəs
    nɪs
tedium 'tiːd i‿əm
tee tiː teed tiːd teeing 'tiː ɪŋ tees tiːz
    'tee shirt
teehee ˌtiː 'hiː
teem tiːm teemed tiːmd teeming 'tiːm ɪŋ
    teems tiːmz
teen tiːn teens tiːnz
Teena 'tiːn ə
teenage 'tiːn eɪdʒ ~d d
teenager 'tiːn eɪdʒ ə ‖ -ᵊr ~s z
teens|y 'tiːnz |i ~ier i‿ə ‖ i‿ᵊr ~iest i‿ɪst i‿əst
    ˌteensy 'weensy◄
teen|y 'tiːn |i ~ier i‿ə ‖ i‿ᵊr ~iest i‿ɪst i‿əst
    ˌteeny 'weeny◄
teenybopper 'tiːn i ˌbɒp ə ‖ -ˌbɑːp ᵊr ~s z
teepee 'tiːp iː ~s z
Tees tiːz
Teesdale 'tiːz deɪᵊl
Teesside 'tiː saɪd 'tiːz-
teeter 'tiːt ə ‖ 'tiːt̬ ᵊr ~ed d teetering
    'tiːt ᵊr ɪŋ ‖ 'tiːt̬ ᵊr ɪŋ ~s z
teeterboard 'tiːt ə bɔːd ‖ 'tiːt̬ ᵊr bɔːrd -boʊrd
    ~s z
teeter-totter 'tiːt ə ˌtɒt ə ‖ 'tiːt̬ ᵊr ˌtɑːt̬ ᵊr ~s z
teeth tiːθ
teethe tiːð teethed tiːðd teethes tiːðz
    teething 'tiːð ɪŋ
    'teething ring; 'teething troubles
teetotal ˌtiː 'təʊt ᵊl ◄ ‖ -'toʊt̬ ᵊl ◄ '•ˌ••
teetotaler, teetotaller ₍ˌ₎tiː 'təʊt ᵊl‿ə ‖
    -'toʊt̬ ᵊl ᵊr ~s z
tef, t'ef, teff tef
TEFL 'tef ᵊl
Teflon tdmk, t~ 'tef lɒn ‖ -lɑːn
teg teg tegs tegz
Tegucigalpa te ˌguːs ɪ 'gælp ə -ə- ‖ -'gɑːlp-, -ɑː
    —AmSp [te ɣu si 'ɣal pa]
tegument 'teg ju mənt ‖ -jə- ~s s
Teheran, Tehran ˌteə 'rɑːn -'ræn; ˌte hə '•
    ‖ te 'rɑːn -'ræn; ˌteɪ ə '•
Teifi 'taɪv i —Welsh ['təi vi]
Teign tiːn tɪn
Teignmouth 'tɪn məθ 'tiːn-, →'tɪm-
Teilhard de Chardin ˌteɪ ɑː də 'ʃɑːd æn •, ••-,
    •ˌjɑː-, -ˌʃɑː; 'dæ ‖ ˌteɪ jɑːr də ʃɑːr 'dæn —Fr
    [tɛ jaʁ də ʃaʁ dæ̃]
Te Kanawa ti 'kɑːn ə wə tə-
tektite 'tekt aɪt ~s s
telamon, T~ 'tel əm ən -ə mɒn ‖ -ə mɑːn ~s z

Tel Aviv ˌtel ə 'viːv -'vɪv
telco 'tel kəʊ ‖ -koʊ ~s z
tele 'tel i
tele- comb form
    with stress-neutral suffix ¦tel ɪ -ə —but when an
    independent prefix ¦tel i ‖ ¦tel ə — telephone
    'tel ɪ fəʊn -ə- ‖ -ə foʊn
    with stress-imposing suffix tə 'le+ tɪ-, te- —
    telescopy tə 'lesk əp i tɪ-, te-
telecast v, n 'tel i kɑːst -ə-, §-kæst ‖ -ə kæst
    ~ed ɪd əd ~ing ɪŋ ~s s
telecom, T~ 'tel i kɒm -ə- ‖ -ə kɑːm ~s z
telecommunication ˌtel i kə ˌmjuːn ɪ 'keɪʃ ᵊn
    ˌ•ə-, -ˌ•ə- ‖ ˌtel ə- ~s z
telecom|mute ˌtel i kə |'mjuːt ‖ 'tel ə•¦ˌ•
    ~muted 'mjuːt ɪd -əd ‖ -ˌmjuːt̬ əd
    ~muter/s 'mjuːt ə/z ‖ ˌmjuːt̬ ᵊr/z ~mutes
    'mjuːts ‖ ˌmjuːts ~muting
    'mjuːt ɪŋ ‖ ˌmjuːt̬ ɪŋ
teleconferenc|e 'tel i ˌkɒn fᵊr‿ᵊnts ˌ••'•••
    ‖ -ə ˌkɑːn- ~es ɪz əz ~ing ɪŋ
teledu 'stinking badger' 'tel ɪ du: -ə- —but the
    Welsh word for 'television', also spelt like this,
    is [te 'le di, -di] ~s z
telegenic ˌtel i 'dʒen ɪk ◄ ‖ ˌtel ə-
Telegonus tɪ 'leg ᵊn əs tə-
telegony tɪ 'leg ᵊn i tə-
telegram 'tel i græm -ə- ~s z
telegraph n, v 'tel ɪ grɑːf -ə-, -græf ‖ -ə græf
    ~ed t ~ing ɪŋ ~s s
    'telegraph pole; 'telegraph post
telegrapher tə 'leg rəf ə tɪ-, te- ‖ -ᵊr ~s z
telegraphese ˌtel ɪ grɑːf 'iːz ˌ•ə-, -græf'•,
    -grəf'• ‖ -ə græf 'iːz -'iːs
telegraphic ˌtel ɪ 'græf ɪk ◄ -ə- ~ally ᵊl‿i
telegraphist tə 'leg rəf ɪst tɪ-, te-, §-əst ~s s
telegraphy tə 'leg rəf i tɪ-, te-
telekinesis ˌtel ɪ kaɪ 'niːs ɪs ˌ•ə-, -kɪ'•-,
    §-kə'•-, §-əs
Telemachus tə 'lem ək əs tɪ-, te-
Telemann 'teɪl ə mæn 'tel- ‖ -mɑːn —Ger
    ['teː lə man]
telemark, T~ 'tel i mɑːk -ə- ‖ -ə mɑːrk ~s s
telemarketing 'tel i ˌmɑːk ɪt ɪŋ '•ə-, §-ət ɪŋ,
    ˌ••'••• ‖ -ə ˌmɑːrk ət̬ ɪŋ
Telemessag|e tdmk, t~ 'tel i ˌmes ɪdʒ ‖ -ə-
    ~es ɪz əz
telemeter tə 'lem ɪt ə tɪ-, te-, §-ət ə;
    'tel ɪ ˌmiːt ə, -ə- ‖ tə 'lem ət̬ ᵊr 'tel ə ˌmiːt̬ ᵊr
    ~ed d ~s z
telemetry tə 'lem ətr i tɪ-, te-, -ɪtr i
teleological ˌtiːl i‿ə 'lɒdʒ ɪk ᵊl ◄ ˌtel- ‖ -'lɑːdʒ-
    ~ly ‿i
teleologist ˌtiːl i 'ɒl ədʒ ɪst ˌtel-, §-əst ‖ -'ɑːl-
    ~s s
teleolog|y ˌtiːl i 'ɒl ədʒ |i ˌtel- ‖ -'ɑːl- ~ies iz
teleost 'tiːl i ɒst 'tel- ‖ -ɑːst ~s s
telepathic ˌtel ɪ 'pæθ ɪk ◄ -ə- ~ally ᵊl‿i
telepathist tə 'lep əθ ɪst tɪ-, te-, §-əst ~s s
telepathy tə 'lep əθ i tɪ-, te-
telepherique, téléphérique ˌtel ɪ fə 'riːk ˌ•ə-,
    ˌ•eɪ-, -fe'• —Fr [te le fe ʁik] ~s s

telephon|e *n, v* 'tel ɪ fəʊn -ə- ‖ -ə foʊn ~ed d
~es z ~ing ɪŋ
'telephone book; 'telephone booth;
'telephone box; 'telephone di,rectory;
'telephone ex,change; 'telephone ,kiosk;
'telephone ,number
telephonic ,tel ɪ 'fɒn ɪk ◄ -ə- ‖ -ə 'fɑːn- ~ally
əl_i
telephonist tə 'lef ən ɪst tɪ-, te-,
§-əst ‖ 'tel ə foʊn- ~s s
telephony tə 'lef ən i tɪ-, te-
telephoto, Telephoto *tdmk* ,tel i 'fəʊt əʊ ◄ -ə-
‖ -ə 'foʊt oʊ ◄ ~s z
,tele,photo 'lens
telephotograph ,tel i 'fəʊt ə grɑːf ,•ə-, -græf
‖ ,tel ə 'foʊt ə græf ~s s
telephotographic ,tel i ,fəʊt ə 'græf ɪk ,•ə-
‖ -ə ,foʊt̬ ə- ~ally əl_i
telephotography ,tel i fə 'tɒg rəf i ,•ə-
‖ -ə fə 'tɑːg-
telepoint 'tel i pɔɪnt ‖ -ə- ~s s
tele|port 'tel i |pɔːt -ə- ‖ -ə |pɔːrt -poʊrt
~ported pɔːt ɪd -əd ‖ pɔːrt̬ əd poʊrt̬ əd
~porting pɔːt ɪŋ ‖ pɔːrt̬ ɪŋ poʊrt̬ ɪŋ ~ports
pɔːts ‖ pɔːrts poʊrts
teleprinter 'tel i ,prɪnt ə -ə- ‖ -ə ,prɪnt̬ ər ~s z
teleprompter, TelePrompTer *tdmk*
'tel ɪ ,prɒmpt ə -ə- ‖ -ə ,prɑːmpt ər ~s z
Teleri tə 'ler i tɪ- —*Welsh* [te 'le ri]
telesales 'tel i seɪəlz ‖ -ə-
telescop|e *n, v* 'tel ɪ skəʊp -ə- ‖ -ə skoʊp ~ed
t ~es s ~ing ɪŋ
telescopic ,tel ɪ 'skɒp ɪk ◄ -ə- ‖ -ə 'skɑːp-
~ally əl_i
telescopist tɪ 'lesk əp ɪst tə-, te-, §-əst ~s s
telescopy tɪ 'lesk əp i tə-, te-
teleselling 'tel i ,sel ɪŋ -ə-, ,•'•|'•• ‖ -ə-
teleshopping 'tel i ,ʃɒp ɪŋ ‖ -ə ,ʃɑːp-
teletex, T~ *tdmk* 'tel i teks -ə-
teletext 'tel i tekst -ə-
telethon 'tel ə θɒn -ɪ- ‖ -θɑːn ~s z
Teletubb|y 'tel i ,tʌb| i -ə- ~ies iz
teletyp|e, T~ *tdmk* 'tel i taɪp -ə- ‖ -ə- ~ed t
~es s ~ing ɪŋ
televangelist ,tel ɪ 'vænʤ əl ɪst ,•ə-, -ɪl•,
§-əst ‖ ,•ə- ~s s
teleview|er/s 'tel i vjuː_ə/z ‖ -ə ,vjuː ər/z
~ing ɪŋ
televis|e 'tel ɪ vaɪz -ə- ‖ -ə- ~ed d ~es ɪz əz
~ing ɪŋ
television 'tel ɪ ,vɪʒ ən -ə-, ,••'•• ‖ -ə- ~s z
'television set, ,••'••• •
televisual ,tel ɪ 'vɪʒ u_əl ◄ ,•ə-, -'vɪz ju_əl
‖ -ə 'vɪʒ əl ◄ ~ly i
telework|er/s 'tel i ,wɜːk| ə/z ‖ -ə ,wɜːk ər/z
~ing ɪŋ
telex *n, v* 'tel eks ~ed t ~es ɪz əz ~ing ɪŋ
telfer, T~ 'telf ə ‖ -ər ~s z
Telford 'telf əd ‖ -ərd
telic 'tel ɪk 'tiːl-
tell, Tell tel telling/ly 'tel ɪŋ /li tells telz told
təʊld →tɒʊld ‖ toʊld
teller, T~ 'tel ə ‖ -ər ~s z

telling-off ,tel ɪŋ 'ɒf -'ɔːf ‖ -'ɔːf -'ɑːf
tellings-off ,tel ɪŋz 'ɒf -'ɔːf ‖ -'ɔːf -'ɑːf
telltale 'tel teɪəl ~s z
tellurian te 'lʊər i_ən tɪ-, tə-, -'ljʊər- ‖ -'lʊr-
~s z
telluric te 'lʊər ɪk tɪ-, tə-, -'ljʊər- ‖ -'lʊr-
telluride, T~ 'tel juə raɪd ‖ -jə-
tellurium te 'lʊər i_əm tɪ-, tə-, -'ljʊər- ‖ -'lʊr-
telly 'tel i tellies 'tel iz
tell|net 'tel| net ~nets nets ~netted net ɪd
-əd ‖ net̬ əd ~netting net ɪŋ ‖ net̬ ɪŋ
telomerase 'tiːl ə mɪər eɪz 'tel-
‖ 'tel əm ə reɪz
telomere 'tiːl əʊ mɪə 'tel- ‖ 'tel ə mɪr ~s z
telpher 'telf ə ‖ -ər ~s z
telpherage 'telf ər ɪʤ
Telscombe 'tels kəm
telson 'tels ən ~s z
Telstar *tdmk* 'tel stɑː ‖ -stɑːr
Telstra 'tel strə
Telugu 'tel ə guː -u- ~s z
temazepam tɪ 'mæz ɪ pæm te-, tə-, -'meɪz-, -ə-
temblor ,tem 'blɔː: '••, '•blə ‖ -'blɔːr -'bloʊr,
'••, '•blər ~s z
temerarious ,tem ə 'reər i_əs ◄ ‖ -'rer- -'rær-
temerity tə 'mer ət i tɪ-, te-, -ɪt i ‖ -ət̬ i
Temne 'tem ni
temp temp temped tempt temping 'temp ɪŋ
temps temps
Tempe 'temp i
tempe, tempeh 'temp eɪ
temper 'temp ə ‖ -ər ~ed d tempering
'temp ər_ɪŋ ~s z
tempera 'temp ər ə
temperament 'temp ər_ə mənt ~s s
temperamental ,temp ər_ə 'ment əl ◄
‖ -'ment̬ əl ◄ ~ly i
temperance 'temp ər_ənts
temperate 'temp ər_ət _ɪt ~ly li ~ness nəs
nɪs
temperature 'temp ər_ətʃ ə _ɪtʃ ə ‖ _ətʃ ər
_ə tʃʊr ~s z
-tempered 'temp əd ‖ -ərd — even-tempered
,iːv ən 'temp əd ◄ ‖ -ərd ◄
Temperley 'temp ə li ‖ -ər-
Temperton 'temp ət ən ‖ -ərt ən
tempest 'temp ɪst -əst ~s s
tempestuous tem 'pes tʃu_əs təm-, →-'peʃ-;
-'pest ju_əs ~ly li ~ness nəs nɪs
tempi 'temp iː
Templar 'temp lə ‖ -lər ~s z
template 'tem pleɪt 'temp lət, -lɪt ~s s
temple, T~ 'temp əl ~s z
templet 'temp lət -lɪt ~s s
Templeton 'temp əl tən
templ|o 'temp ləʊ ‖ -loʊ ~i iː: ~os əʊz ‖ oʊz
temporal 'temp ər_əl ~ly i
temporalit|y ,temp ə 'ræl ət li -ɪt i ‖ -ət̬ li ~ies
iz
temporarily 'temp ər_ər əl i -ɪ li; ,temp ə 'rer-,
-'reər-; ⚠'temp rəl i ‖ ,temp ə 'rer-
temporar|ly 'temp ər_ər li §-ə reər i ‖ -ə rer li

—*in casual speech also* 'temp r|i ~**ies** iz
~**iness** i nəs i nıs
temporis|e, temporiz|e 'temp ə raız ~**ed** d
~**es** ız əz ~**ing** ıŋ
tempt tempt **tempted** 'tempt ıd -əd
tempting/ly 'tempt ıŋ /li **tempts** tempts
temptation temp 'teıʃ ən ~**s** z
tempter 'tempt ə ‖ -ər ~**s** z
temptress 'temp trəs -trıs ~**es** ız əz
tempura tem 'puər ə 'temp ər ə ‖ tem 'pur ə
-'pɜː- —*Jp* [te̞m pɯ ɾa]
tempus fugit ˌtemp əs 'fjuːdʒ ıt -'fjuːg-,
-'fuːg-, §-ət
ten ten **tens** tenz
tenability ˌten ə 'bıl ət i ˌtiːn-, -ıt i ‖ -ət̬ i
tenab|le 'ten əb |əl 'tiːn- ~**leness** əl nəs -nıs
~**ly** li
tenac|e 'ten eıs -əs, -ıs; te 'neıs ~**es** ız əz
tenacious tı 'neıʃ əs tə-, te- ~**ly** li ~**ness** nəs
nıs
tenacity tı 'næs ət i tə-, te-, -ıt i ‖ -ət̬ i
Tenafly 'ten ə flaı
tenanc|y 'ten ənts |i ~**ies** iz
tenant 'ten ənt ~**s** s
ˌtenant 'farmer
tenantr|y 'ten əntr |i ~**ies** iz
Tenbury 'ten bər_i →-'tem-
Tenby 'ten bi →-'tem-
tench, Tench tentʃ **tenches** 'tentʃ ız -əz
tend tend **tended** 'tend ıd -əd **tending**
'tend ıŋ **tends** tendz
tendenc|y 'tend ənts |i ~**ies** iz
tendentious ten 'dentʃ əs ~**ly** li ~**ness** nəs nıs
tender 'tend ə ‖ -ər **tendered** 'tend əd ‖ -ərd
tenderer/s 'tend ər_ə/z ‖ -ər_ər/z **tenderest**
'tend ər_ıst _əst **tendering** 'tend_ər ıŋ
tenders 'tend əz ‖ -ərz
tender|foot 'tend ə |fut ‖ -ər- ~**feet** fiːt
tenderhearted ˌtend ə 'hɑːt ıd ◄-əd
‖ 'tend ər ˌhɑːrt̬ əd ~**ly** li ~**ness** nəs nıs
tenderis|e, tenderiz|e 'tend ə raız ~**ed** d
~**er/s** ə/z ‖ ər/z ~**es** ız əz ~**ing** ıŋ
tenderloin 'tend ə lɔın ‖ -ər-
tenderly 'tend ə li -əl i ‖ -ər li
tenderness 'tend ə nəs -nıs ‖ -ər- ~**es** ız əz
tendinitis ˌtend ı 'naıt ıs -ə-, §-əs ‖ -ə 'naıt̬ əs
tendon 'tend ən ~**s** z
tendonitis ˌtend ə 'naıt ıs §-əs ‖ -'naıt̬ əs
tendril 'tendr əl-ıl ~**s** z
tenebrae, T~ 'ten ə breı-ı-, -briː, -braı
tenebrous 'ten ə brəs-ı-
Tenedos 'ten ı dɒs-ə- ‖ -dɑːs-dous
tenement 'ten ə mənt-ı- ~**s** s
Tenerife, Teneriffe ˌten ə 'riːf—*Sp*
[te ne 'ri fe]
tenesmus tı 'nez məs tə-
tenet 'ten ıt 'tiːn-, -et, §-ət ~**s** s
tenfold 'ten fəuld →-fɒuld ‖ -fould
ten-gallon hat ˌten ˌgæl ən 'hæt →ˌteŋ- ~**s** s
tenia 'tiːn i_ə
Teniers 'ten ıəz ‖ -jərz—*Dutch* [tə 'niːrs]
Tenison 'ten ıs ən-əs-
Tenko 'teŋk əu ‖ -ou

Tennant 'ten ənt
tenner 'ten ə ‖ -ər ~**s** z
Tennessee ˌten ə 'siː ◄-ı- —*locally also* '•• əs i,
-ıs i
Tennessean, Tennesseean ˌten ə 'siː_ən ◄-ı-
~**s** z
Tenniel 'ten i_əl
tennis 'ten ıs §-əs
'tennis ball; ˌtennis 'elbow; 'tennis match;
'tennis ˌplayer; 'tennis ˌracquet
Tennison, Tennyson 'ten ıs ən-əs-
Tennysonian ˌten ı 'səun i_ən ˌ•ə-
‖ -'soun jən ~**s** z
tenon 'ten ən ~**s** z
'tenon saw
tenor 'ten ə ‖ -ər (= *tenner*) ~**s** z
tenpin 'ten pın →'tem- ~**s** z
ˌtenpin 'bowling
tenrec 'ten rek ~**s** s
tense tents **tensed** tentst **tensely** 'tents li
tenseness 'tents nəs -nıs **tenser**
'tents ə ‖ -ər **tenses** 'tents ız -əz **tensest**
'tents ıst -əst **tensing** 'tents ıŋ
ˌtensed 'up
tensile 'tents aıəl ‖ -əl (*)
tensility ten 'sıl ət i -ıt i ‖ -ət̬ i
tension 'tentʃ ən ~**ed** d ~**ing** ıŋ ~**s** z
tensity 'tents ət i -ıt i ‖ -ət̬ i
tensor 'tents ə -ɔː ‖ -ər -ɔːr ~**s** z
tent tent **tented** 'tent ıd -əd ‖ 'tent̬ əd
tenting 'tent ıŋ ‖ 'tent̬ ıŋ **tents** tents
tentacle 'tent ək əl-ık- ‖ 'tent̬- ~**d** d ~**s** z
tentacular ten 'tæk jul ə-jəl- ‖ -jəl ər
tentative 'tent ət ıv ‖ 'tent̬ ət̬ ıv ~**ly** li ~**ness**
nəs nıs
Tenterden 'tent ə dən ‖ 'tent̬ ər-
tenterhook 'tent ə huk ⚠'tend-, §-huːk
‖ 'tent̬ ər- ~**s** s
tenth tentθ **tenthly** 'tentθ li **tenths** tentθs
→tents
tenu|is 'ten ju|_ıs §-əs ~**es** iːz eız
tenuity te 'njuː_ət i tə-, tı-, _ıt i ‖ -'nuː ət̬ i
-'njuː-
tenuous 'ten ju_əs ~**ly** li ~**ness** nəs nıs
tenure 'ten jə-juə ‖ -jər ~**d** d ~**s** z
Tenzing 'tenz ıŋ
teosinte ˌteı əu 'sınt i ‖ -ou 'sınt̬ i
tepal 'tep əl 'tiːp- ~**s** z
tepee 'tiːp iː ~**s** z
tephra 'tef rə
tephrite 'tef raıt
tepid 'tep ıd §-əd ~**ly** li ~**ness** nəs nıs
tepidity te 'pıd ət i -ıt i ‖ -ət̬ i
tequila tı 'kiːl ətə-, te- ‖ teı-
tera- ˌter ə— **terahertz** 'ter ə hɜːts ‖ -hɝːts
teraph 'ter əf **teraphim** 'ter ə fım
teratogenic ˌter ət əu 'dʒen ık ◄ ‖ -ət̬ ə-
teratology ˌter ə 'tɒl ədʒ i ‖ -'tɑːl-
teratoma ˌter ə 'təum ə ‖ -'toum ə ~**s** z
terbium 'tɜːb i_əm ‖ 'tɝːb-
terce tɜːs ‖ tɝːs (= *terse*)
tercel 'tɜːs əl ‖ 'tɝːs əl ~**s** z
Tercel 'tɜːs el tər 'sel ~**s** z

tercentenar|y ˌtɜː sen 'tiːn ər li ˌ•ˈsǝn-, -ˈten-
‖ ˌtɜː sen 'ten ər li ˌ•ˈsent ǝn er i ~ies iz
tercentennial ˌtɜː sen 'ten i_ǝl ◄ ˌ•ˈsǝn- ‖ ˌtɜː-
~s z
tercet 'tɜːs ɪt -et, §-ǝt; ₍ₒ₎tɜː 'set ‖ 'tɜːs ǝt ~s s
terebene 'ter ǝ biːn -ɪ-
terebinth 'ter ǝ bɪntθ -ɪ- ~s s
teredo tǝ 'riːd ǝʊ tɪ-, te-, -'reɪd- ‖ -oʊ ~s z
Terence 'ter ǝnts
Teresa (i) tǝ 'riːz ǝ tɪ-, te-, (ii) -'reɪz-, (iii)
-'riːs-, (iv) -'reɪs- —(iii) and (iv) are AmE, but
not usually BrE
Terese (i) tǝ 'riːz tɪ-, te-, -'riːs, (ii) -'reɪz
tergivers|ate 'tɜːdʒ ɪ vɜːs eɪt -vǝ sleɪt
‖ tɜː 'dʒɪv ər sleɪt -'gɪv-; ˌtɜːdʒ ǝ 'vɜːs eɪt
(*) ~ated eɪt ɪd -ǝd ‖ eɪt̬ ǝd ~ates eɪts
~ating eɪt ɪŋ ‖ eɪt̬ ɪŋ
tergiversation ˌtɜːdʒ ɪ vɜː 'seɪʃ ǝn §, •ǝ-, -vǝˈ•-
‖ tɜː ˌdʒɪv ər- -ˌgɪv-; ˌtɜːdʒ ǝ vɜː- ~s z
teriyaki ˌter i 'æk i ‖ -ˈjɑːk i —Jp [te ˌri ja ki]
term tɜːm ‖ tɜːm **termed** tɜːmd ‖ tɜːmd
  terming 'tɜːm ɪŋ ‖ 'tɜːm ɪŋ **terms**
  tɜːmz ‖ tɜːmz
  ˌterms of 'reference
termagant 'tɜːm ǝg ǝnt ‖ 'tɜːm- ~s s
terminable 'tɜːm ɪn ǝb ǝl -ǝn_ǝb- ‖ 'tɜːm-
~ness nǝs nɪs
terminal 'tɜːm ɪn ǝl -ǝn- ‖ 'tɜːm ǝn_ǝl ~ly i
~s z
  ˌTerminal 'Four
termi|nate 'tɜːm ɪ ǀneɪt -ǝ- ‖ 'tɜːm- ~nated
  neɪt ɪd -ǝd ‖ neɪt̬ ǝd ~nates neɪts ~nating
  neɪt ɪŋ ‖ neɪt̬ ɪŋ
termination ˌtɜːm ɪ 'neɪʃ ǝn -ǝ- ‖ ˌtɜːm- ~s z
terminative 'tɜːm ɪn ǝt ɪv -ǝn-; -ɪ neɪt ɪv, -ǝ••
‖ 'tɜːm ǝ neɪt̬ ɪv ~ly li
terminator 'tɜːm ɪ neɪt ǝ '•ǝ- ‖ 'tɜːm ǝ neɪt̬ ǝr
~s z
termini 'tɜːm ɪ naɪ -ǝ- ‖ 'tɜː-
terminological ˌtɜːm ɪn ǝ 'lɒdʒ ɪk ◄ ˌ•ǝn-,
-ǝl 'ɒdʒ- ‖ ˌtɜːm ǝn ǝl 'ɑːdʒ- ~ly_i
terminolog|y ˌtɜːm ɪ 'nɒl ǝdʒ li ˌ•ǝ-
‖ ˌtɜːm ǝ 'nɑːl- ~ies iz
term|inus 'tɜːm ɪn ǝs -ǝn- ‖ 'tɜːm- ~ini ɪ naɪ
ǝ-
  ˌterminus ad 'quem æd 'kwem ‖ ɑːd-;
  ˌterminus a 'quo ɑː 'kwǝʊ ‖ ɑː 'kwoʊ
termite 'tɜːm aɪt ‖ 'tɜːm- ~s s
termly 'tɜːm li ‖ 'tɜːm-
termtime 'tɜːm taɪm ‖ 'tɜːm-
tern tɜːn ‖ tɜːn (= turn) **terns** tɜːnz ‖ tɜːnz
ternar|y 'tɜːn ǝr li ‖ 'tɜːn- ~ies iz
terpene 'tɜːp iːn ‖ 'tɜːp- ~s z
Terpsichore tɜːp 'sɪk ǝr i ‖ tɜːp-
terpsichorean, T~ ˌtɜːps ɪk ǝ 'riː_ǝn ◄ -ɒˈ•-;
ˌ•ɪ 'kɔːr i_ǝn ‖ ˌtɜːps-
terra, Terra 'ter ǝ
  ˌterra 'cotta 'kɒt ǝ ‖ 'kɑːt̬ ǝ; ˌterra 'firma
  'fɜːm ǝ ‖ 'fɜːm ǝ; ˌterra inˈcognita
  ɪn ˈkɒg nɪt ǝ →ɪŋ-; ˌɪŋ kɒg 'niːt ǝ
  ‖ ˌɪn kɑːg 'niːt̬ ǝ ɪn 'kɑːg nǝt̬ ǝ, ˌterra 'nullius
  'nʊl i_ǝs
terrac|e 'ter ǝs -ɪs ~ed t ~es ɪz ǝz ~ing ɪŋ

terracotta ˌter ǝ 'kɒt ǝ ◄ ‖ -ˈkɑːt̬ ǝ ◄
terrain tǝ 'reɪn te-, tɪ-; 'ter eɪn
terramycin, T~ ˌter ǝ 'maɪs ɪn §-ǝn
terrapin 'ter ǝ pɪn §-ǝp ǝn
terrari|um tǝ 'reǝr i_ǝm te-, tɪ- ‖ -'rer- -'rær-
~a ǝ ~ums ǝmz
terrazzo te 'ræts ǝʊ tǝ-, tɪ- ‖ -'ræz oʊ -'rɑːts-
Terre Haute ˌter ǝ 'hǝʊt ‖ -'hoʊt -'hʌt
terrene 'ter iːn te 'riːn
terrestrial tǝ 'res tri_ǝl tɪ-, te- ~ly i ~s z
terret 'ter ɪt -ǝt ~s s
Terri 'ter i
terrible 'ter ǝb ǝl -ɪb- ~ness nǝs nɪs
terribly 'ter ǝb li -ɪb-
terrier 'ter i_ǝ ‖ -_ǝr ~s z
terrific tǝ 'rɪf ɪk —casually also 'trɪf ɪk ~ally
ǝl_i
terri|fy 'ter ǝ ǀfaɪ -ɪ- ~fied faɪd ~fies faɪz
~fying/ly faɪ ɪŋ /li
terrine te 'riːn tǝ-; 'ter iːn ~s z
territorial ˌter ǝ 'tɔːr i_ǝl ◄ ˌ•ɪ- ‖ -'toʊr- ~ly i
~s z
  ˌTerriˌtorial 'Army; ˌterriˌtorial 'waters
territoriality ˌter ǝ ˌtɔːr i 'æl ǝt i ˌ•ɪ-, -ɪt i
‖ -ǝt̬ i -ˌtoʊr-
territor|y 'ter ǝ_tǝr li '•ɪ- ‖ -tɔːr li -toʊr i (*)
~ies iz
terror 'ter ǝ ‖ -ǝr ~s z
terroris... —see **terroriz...**
terrorism 'ter ǝr ˌɪz ǝm
terrorist 'ter ǝr ɪst §-ǝst ~s s
terroriz|e 'ter ǝ raɪz ~ed d ~es ɪz ǝz ~ing ɪŋ
terror-stricken 'ter ǝ ˌstrɪk ǝn ‖ -ǝr-
terror-struck 'ter ǝ strʌk ‖ -ǝr-
terry, Terry 'ter i
terrycloth 'ter i klɒθ -klɔːθ ‖ -klɔːθ -klɑːθ
terse tɜːs ‖ tɜːs **tersely** 'tɜːs li ‖ 'tɜːs li
  terseness 'tɜːs nǝs -nɪs ‖ 'tɜːs nǝs **terser**
  'tɜːs ǝ ‖ 'tɜːs ǝr **tersest** 'tɜːs ɪst -ǝst
  ‖ 'tɜːs ǝst
tertian 'tɜːʃ ǝn 'tɜːʃ i_ǝn ‖ 'tɜːʃ ǝn
tertiar|y, T~ 'tɜːʃ ǝr i i -i_ǝr- ‖ 'tɜːʃ i er li
'•ǝr li ~ies iz
  ˌtertiary ˌeduˈcation; ˌtertiary 'stress
tertium quid ˌtɜːʃ i_ǝm 'kwɪd 'tɜːt- ‖ ˌtɜːʃ-
ˌtɜːt̬-
Tertius 'tɜːʃ i_ǝs ‖ 'tɜːʃ-
Tertullian tǝ 'tʌl i_ǝn tǝ- ‖ tǝr-
terylene, T~ tdmk 'ter ǝ liːn -ɪ-
terza rima ˌteǝts ǝ 'riːm ǝ ˌtɜːts- ‖ ˌterts- —It
[ˌter tsa 'riː ma]
Tesco tdmk 'tesk ǝʊ ‖ -oʊ
TESL 'tes ǝl
Tesla, tesla 'tes lǝ ~s z
TESOL 'tiːs ɒl ‖ -ɑːl 'tes ǝl
Tess tes
Tessa, TESSA 'tes ǝ
tesse|late 'tes ǝ ǀleɪt -ɪ- ~lated leɪt ɪd -ǝd
‖ leɪt̬ ǝd ~lates leɪts ~lating leɪt ɪŋ ‖ leɪt̬ ɪŋ
tesselation ˌtes ǝ 'leɪʃ ǝn -ɪ- ~s z
tesser|a 'tes ǝr| ǝ ~ae i:
tesseract 'tes ǝ rækt ~s s
Tessie 'tes i

tessitura ˌtes ɪ 'tʊər ə -ə-, -'tjʊər ə ‖ -'tʊr ə
—*It* [tes si 'tu: ɾa]
test, Test test **tested** 'test ɪd -əd **testing**
'test ɪŋ **tests** tests
'test ban; 'test card; 'test case; 'testing
ground; 'test match; 'test ˌpaper; 'test
ˌpilot; 'test tube
testability ˌtest ə 'bɪl ət i -ɪt i ‖ -ət̬ i
testable 'test əb əl
testament 'test ə mənt ~s s
testamentary ˌtest ə 'ment̬_ər i ◂
‖ -'ment̬ ər i ◂ →-'mentr i
testamur te 'steɪm ə ‖ -ər ~s z
testate 'test eɪt -ət, -ɪt
testator te 'steɪt ə ‖ 'test eɪt̬ ər te 'steɪt̬ ər ~s z
testatr|ix te 'steɪtr |ɪks ‖ 'test eɪtr- ~**ices**
ɪ siːz ə-
test-bed 'test bed
test-|drive 'test |draɪv ~**driven** drɪv ən
~**drives** draɪvz ~**driving** draɪv ɪŋ ~**drove**
drəʊv ‖ droʊv
tester, T~ 'test ə ‖ -ər ~s z
testes 'test iːz
testicle 'test ɪk əl ~s z
testicular te 'stɪk jʊl ə -jəl- ‖ -jəl ər
testi|fy 'test ɪ |faɪ -ə- ~**fied** faɪd ~**fier/s**
faɪ_ə/z ‖ faɪ_ər/z ~**fies** faɪz ~**fying** faɪ ɪŋ
testimonial ˌtest ɪ 'məʊn i_əl ◂ , •ə- ‖ -'moʊn-
~s z
testimon|y 'test ɪ mən li ' • ə- ‖ -ə moʊn li (*)
~**ies** iz
test|is 'test |ɪs §-əs —**es** iːz
testosterone te 'stɒst ə rəʊn ‖ -'stɑːst ə roʊn
test-tube 'test tjuːb §-tʃuːb ‖ -tuːb -tjuːb
~s z
ˌtest-tube 'baby
testud|o te 'stjuːd |əʊ →§-'stʃuːd-
‖ -'stuːd |oʊ -'stjuːd- ~**ines** ɪ niːz ə-, -neɪz
~**os** əʊz ‖ oʊz
test|y 'test li ~**ier** i_ə ‖ i_ər ~**iest** i_ɪst i_əst
~**ily** ɪ li əl i ~**iness** i nəs i nɪs
Tet tet
tetanic te 'tæn ɪk tɪ-, tə-
tetanus 'tet ən_əs
tetany 'tet ən i
Tetbury 'tet bər_i ‖ -ˌber i
tetch|y 'tetʃ li ~**ier** i_ə ‖ i_ər ~**iest** i_ɪst i_əst
~**ily** ɪ li əl i ~**iness** i nəs i nɪs
tete-a-tete, tête-à-tête ˌteɪt ə 'teɪt ˌtet-, -ɑː-,
-'tet ‖ ˌteɪt̬ ə 'teɪt ˌtet̬ ə 'tet; ' • • • —*Fr*
[tɛ ta tɛt] ~s s
tete-beche, tête-bêche ˌteɪt 'beʃ ˌtet-, -'beɪʃ
—*Fr* [tɛd beʃ]
tether 'teð ə ‖ -ər ~**ed** d **tethering** 'teð ər_ɪŋ
~s z
Tethys 'tiːθ ɪs 'teθ-, §-əs
Tetley 'tet li
Teton 'tiːt ən -ɒn ‖ -ɑːn -ən ~s z
tetra 'tetr ə ~s z
tetra- *comb form*
with stress-neutral suffix ˌtetr ə —
tetrachloride ˌtetr ə 'klɔːr aɪd ‖ -'kloʊr-

with stress-imposing suffix te 'træ+ —
tetramerous te 'træm ər əs
tetrabrik 'tetr ə brɪk ~s s
tetrachord 'tetr ə kɔːd ‖ -kɔːrd ~s z
tetracycline ˌtetr ə 'saɪk liːn -lɪn, -laɪn
tetrad 'tetr æd ~s z
tetraethyl ˌtetr ə 'iːθ aɪəl -'eθ ɪl, -əl ‖ -əl
tetragrammaton, T~ ˌtetr ə 'græm ət ən
-ə tɒn ‖ -ə tɑːn
tetrahedr|on ˌtetr ə 'hiːdr |ən -'hedr- ~**a** ə
~**al** əl ~**ons** ənz
tetralog|y te 'træl ədʒ li ‖ -'trɑːl- ~**ies** iz
tetrameter te 'træm ɪt ə -ət ə ‖ -ət̬ ər ~s z
tetrarch 'tetr ɑːk ‖ -ɑːrk ~s s
tetravalent ˌtetr ə 'veɪl ənt
tetrode 'tetr əʊd ‖ -oʊd ~s z
Tettenhall 'tet ən hɔːl ‖ -hɑːl
tetter 'tet ə ‖ 'tet̬ ər
Teucer 'tjuːs ə →§'tʃuːs- ‖ 'tuːs ər 'tjuːs-
Teucrian 'tjuːk ri_ən →§'tʃuːk- ‖ 'tuːk-
'tjuːk- ~s z
Teuton 'tjuːt ən →§'tʃuːt- ‖ 'tuːt ən 'tjuːt- ~s
z
Teutonic tju 'tɒn ɪk →§tʃu- ‖ tu 'tɑːn ɪk tju-
Teversham 'tev əʃ əm ‖ -ərʃ-
Teviot 'tiːv i_ət 'tev-
Tew tjuː →§tʃuː ‖ tuː tjuː
Tewa 'teɪ wə 'tiː- ~s z
Tewkesbury 'tjuːks bər_i →§'tʃuːks-
‖ 'tuːks ˌber i 'tjuːks- —*but locally* -bər_i *in
MA, just as in Gloucs.*
Tex teks
TEX, TₑX *software* tek —*although its author
Knuth insists on* tex
Texaco *tdmk* 'teks ə kəʊ ‖ -koʊ -ɪ-
Texan 'teks ən ~s z
Texas 'teks əs
ˌTexas 'Ranger
Texel 'teks əl
Tex-Mex ˌteks 'meks ◂
text tekst **texts** teksts
text-based 'tekst beɪst , • ' • ◂
textbook 'tekst bʊk §-buːk ~s s
textile 'tekst aɪəl ‖ -əl ~s z
textual 'tekst ʃu_əl 'tekst ju_ ~**ly** i
textuality ˌtekst ju 'æl ət i -tʃu' • -, -ɪt i
‖ ˌtekst ʃu 'æl ət̬ i
texture 'teks tʃə ‖ -tʃər -**d** d **texturing**
'teks tʃər ɪŋ ~s z
ˌtextured ˌvegetable 'protein
-**textured** 'teks tʃəd ‖ -tʃərd — **even-
textured** ˌiːv ən 'teks tʃəd ◂ ‖ -tʃərd ◂
Tey teɪ
-th θ — **fourth** fɔːθ ‖ fɔːrθ foʊrθ
Thabo 'tɑːb əʊ ‖ -oʊ —*Xhosa* ['tʰɑː ɓo]
Thackeray 'θæk ər i -ə reɪ
Thad θæd
Thaddeus 'θæd i_əs θæ 'diː_əs
Thai taɪ **Thais** taɪz
Thailand 'taɪ lænd -lənd
Thais, Thaïs *personal name* 'θeɪ ɪs §-əs
Thais *pl of* **Thai** taɪz
thal|amus 'θæl əm əs ~**ami** ə maɪ -miː

thalassaemia, thalassemia ˌθæl ə ˈsiːm i‿ə
thalassic θə ˈlæs ɪk
thalassotherapy θə ˌlæs əʊ ˈθer əp i θæ-
‖ •ˌ•ə-
thaler ˈtɑːl ə ‖ -ᵊr ~s z
Thales ˈθeɪl iːz
Thalia θə ˈlaɪ‿ə ˈθeɪl i‿ə, ˈθæl-
thalidomide θə ˈlɪd ə maɪd
thallium ˈθæl i‿əm
thall|us ˈθæl |əs ~i aɪ ~uses əs ɪz -əz
Thame teɪm *(!)*
Thames *(i)* temz *(!)*, *(ii)* θeɪmz —*The rivers in England, Canada and NZ are* (i), *the one in CT usually* (ii).
than *strong form* ðæn, *weak form* ðən
Thanatos ˈθæn ə tɒs ‖ -tɑːs
thane θeɪn **thanes** θeɪnz
thaneship ˈθeɪn ʃɪp ~s s
Thanet ˈθæn ɪt -ət
thank θæŋk **thanked** θæŋkt **thanking**
ˈθæŋk ɪŋ **thanks** θæŋks
thank you ˈθæŋk ju —*There are also casual forms such as* ˈhæŋk ju, ŋk ju
thankful ˈθæŋk fᵊl -fʊl ~ly ‿i ~ness nəs nɪs
thankless ˈθæŋk ləs -lɪs ~ly li ~ness nəs nɪs
thanksgiving, T~ ˈθæŋks ˌgɪv ɪŋ ˌ•ˈ•ˈ•
‖ ˌθæŋks ˈgɪv ɪŋ ~s z
Thanks'giving Day
thankyou *n, adj* ˈθæŋk ju: ~s z
Thapsus ˈθæps əs
that *determiner (demonstrative adj), demonstrative pronoun, and adverb* ðæt
—*There is no weak form for* that *in this sense:* that (ðæt) man, stop that, not that bad.
that *complementizer (conjunction and relative pronoun): strong form* ðæt, *weak form* ðət
—*Normally, the weak form is used:* say that (ðət) she's right, the one that I chose.
thataway ˈðæt ə weɪ ‖ ˈðæt̬-
thatch θætʃ **thatched** θætʃt **thatches**
ˈθætʃ ɪz -əz **thatching** ˈθætʃ ɪŋ
Thatcham ˈθætʃ əm
thatcher, T~ ˈθætʃ ə ‖ -ᵊr ~s z
Thatcherism ˈθætʃ ər ˌɪz əm
that'll *strong form* ˈðæt ᵊl ‖ ˈðæt̬ ᵊl, *weak form* ðət ᵊl ‖ ðət̬ ᵊl —*see entries at* that: I think that'll (ðæt ᵊl) please you, a thing that'll (ðət ᵊl) please you
that's *strong form* ðæts, *weak form* ðəts —*see entries at* that: I think that's (ðæts) right, a thing that's (ðəts) wrong
thaumatology ˌθɔːm ə ˈtɒl ədʒ i ‖ -ˈtɑːl-
ˌθɑːm-
thaumaturg|e ˈθɔːm ə tɜːdʒ ‖ -tɜːdʒ ˈθɑːm-
~es ɪz əz
thaumaturgic ˌθɔːm ə ˈtɜːdʒ ɪk ◂ ‖ -ˈtɜːdʒ-
ˌθɑːm- ~al ᵊl
thaumaturgy ˈθɔːm ə tɜːdʒ i ‖ -tɜːdʒ i ˈθɑːm-
thaw, Thaw θɔː ‖ θɑː **thawed** θɔːd ‖ θɑːd
thawing ˈθɔːʳ ɪŋ ‖ ˈθɔː ɪŋ ˈθɑː- **thaws** θɔːz
‖ θɑːz
Thawpit *tdmk* ˈθɔːp ɪt §-ət ‖ ˈθɑːp-
Thayer ˈθeɪ ə θeə ‖ ˈθeɪ ᵊr θeᵊr, θæᵊr

the *strong form* ðiː, *weak forms* ði, ðə —*The EFL learner is advised to use* ðə *before a consonant sound* (the boy, the house), ði *before a vowel sound* (the egg, the hour). *Native speakers, however, sometimes ignore this distribution, in particular by using* ðə *before a vowel (which in turn is usually reinforced by a preceding* [ʔ]), *or by using* ði *in any environment, though especially before a hesitation pause. Furthermore, some speakers use stressed* ðə *as a strong form, rather than the usual* ðiː.
Thea ˈθiːˌə
Theale θiːᵊl
theater, theatre ˈθɪət ə θi ˈet ə ‖ ˈθiː ət̬ ᵊr ~s z
ˌtheatre in the 'round
theatergoer, theatregoer ˈθɪət ə ˌgəʊ ə
θi ˈet ə ˌgəʊ ə ‖ ˈθiː ət̬ ᵊr ˌgoʊ ᵊr ~s z
theaterland, theatreland ˈθɪət ə lænd
θi ˈet ə lænd ‖ ˈθiː ət̬ ᵊr lænd
theatrical θi ˈætr ɪk ᵊl §-ˈetr- ~ly ‿i ~ness nəs
nɪs ~s z
theatricality θi ˌætr ɪ ˈkæl ət i §-ˌetr-, -ˌ•ə-,
-ɪt i ‖ -ət̬ i
theatrics θi ˈætr ɪks §-ˈetr-
Thebaid ˈθiːb eɪ ɪd -i-, §-əd
Theban ˈθiːb ᵊn ~s z
Thebes θiːbz
theca ˈθiːk ə **thecae** ˈθiːs iː ˈθiːk-
thecodont ˈθiːk əʊ dɒnt ‖ -ə dɑːnt ~s s
thee *strong form* ðiː, *weak form* ði
theft θeft **thefts** θefts
thegn θeɪn (= *thane*) **thegns** θeɪnz
their ðeə §ˈðeɪ ə ‖ ðeᵊr ðæᵊr —*In GenAm there is also a weak form* ðᵊr. *In RP there is either no weak form, or just an occasional weak form* ðər *used only before a following vowel.*
theirs ðeəz §ˈðeɪ əz ‖ ðeᵊrz ðæᵊrz
theism ˈθiː ˌɪz əm
theist ˈθiː ɪst §-əst ~s s
theistic θi ˈɪst ɪk ~al ᵊl ~ally ᵊl‿i
Thelma ˈθelm ə
Thelwall ˈθel wɔːl ‖ -wɑːl
Thelwell ˈθel wᵊl -wel
them *strong form* ðem, *weak form* ðəm
thematic θɪ ˈmæt ɪk θiː- ‖ -ˈmæt̬ ɪk ~ally ᵊl‿i
theme θiːm **themes** θiːmz
ˈtheme park; ˈtheme song; ˈtheme tune
Themis ˈθem ɪs ˈθiːm-, §-əs
Themistocles θə ˈmɪst ə kliːz θɪ-, θe-
themselves ðəm ˈselvz —*occasionally also, with contrastive stress,* ˈðem selvz
then ðen
thenar ˈθiːn ɑː -ə ‖ -ᵊr -ɑːr ~s z
thence ðen̊s ‖ θen̊s
thenceforth ˌðen̊s ˈfɔːθ ‖ -ˈfɔːrθ ˌθen̊s-,
-ˈfoʊrθ
thenceforward ˌðen̊s ˈfɔː wəd ‖ -ˈfɔːr wᵊrd
ˌθen̊s-, -ˈfoʊr- ~s z
Theo ˈθiːˌəʊ ‖ -oʊ
theo- *comb. form*
with stress-neutral suffix ˌθiː əʊ ‖ -ə —
theocentric ˌθiː əʊ ˈsentr ɪk ◂ ‖ -ə-

with stress-imposing suffix θi ˈɒ+ ‖ -ˈɑː+ —
theophagy θi ˈɒf ədʒ i ‖ -ˈɑːf-
Theobald ˈθiː_ə bɔːld ‖ -bɑːld —*Formerly also*
ˈtɪb əld ~s z
theobromine ˌθiː əʊ ˈbrəʊm iːn -ɪn
‖ -ə ˈbroʊm-
theocrac|y θi ˈɒk rəs |i ‖ -ˈɑːk- ~ies iz
theocratic ˌθiː_ə ˈkræt ɪk ◄ ‖ -ə ˈkræt̬- ~ally
əl_i
Theocritus θi ˈɒk rɪt əs -rət- ‖ -ˈɑːk-
theodic|y θi ˈɒd əs |i -ɪs- ‖ -ˈɑːd- ~ies iz
theodolite θi ˈɒd ə laɪt -əl aɪt ‖ -ˈɑːd əl aɪt ~s s
Theodora ˌθiː_ə ˈdɔːr ə ‖ -ˈdoʊr-
Theodorakis ˌθiː_ə dɔː ˈrɑːk ɪs -də'•-, §-əs
—*ModGk* [θε ɔ ðɔ ˈra cis]
Theodore ˈθiː_ə dɔː ‖ -dɔːr -doʊr
Theodoric θi ˈɒd ər ɪk ‖ -ˈɑːd-
Theodosi|us ˌθiː_ə ˈdəʊs i_əs ‖ -ˈdoʊʃ- ~an
ən
theogon|y θi ˈɒg ən |i ‖ -ˈɑːg- ~ies iz
theologian ˌθiː_ə ˈləʊdʒ i_ən -ˈ•ən ‖ -ˈloʊdʒ-
~s z
theological ˌθiː_ə ˈlɒdʒ ɪk əl ◄ ‖ -ˈlɑːdʒ- ~ly _i
theolog|y θi ˈɒl ədʒ |i ‖ -ˈɑːl- ~ies iz
theomachy θi ˈɒm ək i ‖ -ˈɑːm-
theomancy ˈθiː əʊ ˌmæn's i ‖ -oʊ-
theophan|y θi ˈɒf ən |i ‖ -ˈɑːf- ~ies iz
Theophilus θi ˈɒf ɪl əs -əl- ‖ -ˈɑːf-
Theophrastus ˌθiː_ə ˈfræst əs
theophylline ˌθiː_ə ˈfɪl iːn -ɪn, -aɪn; θi ˈɒf ɪ liːn,
-ə-, -lɪn, -laɪn
theorbo θi ˈɔːb əʊ ‖ -ˈɔːrb oʊ ~s z
theorem ˈθɪər əm §ˈθiː ər əm ‖ ˈθiː ər əm.
ˈθɪr əm ~s z
theoretic ˌθɪə ˈret ɪk ◄ §ˌθiː ə'•-
‖ ˌθiː ə ˈret̬ ɪk ◄ θɪ'•- ~al əl ~ally əl_i ~s s
theoretician ˌθɪər ə ˈtɪʃ ən -e-, -ɪ-
‖ ˌθiː ər ə ˈtɪʃ ən ˌθɪr ə'•• ~s z
theorie... —*see* **theory**
theoris... —*see* **theoriz...**
theorist ˈθɪər ɪst §ˈθiː ər-, §-əst ‖ ˈθiː ər əst
ˈθɪr əst ~s s
theoriz|e ˈθɪər aɪz §ˈθiː ə raɪz ‖ ˈθiː ə raɪz ~ed
d ~es ɪz əz ~ing ɪŋ
theor|y ˈθɪər |i ‖ ˈθiː ər |i ‖ ˈθiː ər |i ˈθɪr |i ~ies iz
theosophical ˌθiː_ə ˈsɒf ɪk əl ◄ ‖ -ˈsɑːf- ~ly _i
theosophist θi ˈɒs əf ɪst §-əst ‖ -ˈɑːs- ~s s
theosoph|y θi ˈɒs əf |i ‖ -ˈɑːs- ~ies iz
Thera ˈθɪər ə ‖ ˈθɪr ə —*ModGk* [ˈθi ra]
therapeutic ˌθer ə ˈpjuːt ɪk ◄ ‖ -ˈpjuːt̬ ɪk ◄
~ally əl_i ~s s
therapie... —*see* **therapy**
therapist ˈθer əp ɪst §-əst ~s s
therapsid θə ˈræps ɪd θɪ-, θe-, §-əd ~s z
therap|y ˈθer əp |i ~ies iz
Theravada ˌθer ə ˈvɑːd ə
there *existential pronoun (adv): strong form*
ðeə ‖ ðer ðær, *weak form* ðə ‖ ðɚ —*Some*
speakers hardly use the weak form, even though
the word is never stressed; others hardly use the
strong form
there *adv of place; interj* ðeə ‖ ðeər ðæər
thereabout ˌðeər ə ˈbaʊt ˈ•••,• ‖ ˌðer- ˌðær-

thereabouts ˌðeər ə ˈbaʊts ˈ••,• ‖ ˌðer- ˌðær-
thereafter ˌˌðeər ˈɑːft ə §-ˈæft- ‖ ˌˌðer ˈæft ər
ˌˌðær-
thereat ˌðeər ˈæt ‖ ˌðer-
thereby ˌðeə ˈbaɪ ˈ•• ‖ ˌðer- ˌðær-
there'd *strong form* ðeəd ‖ ðerd ðærd, *weak*
form ðəd ‖ ðɚd —*See note at* there
therefor ˌðeə ˈfɔː ‖ ˌðer ˈfɔːr ˌðær-
therefore ˈðeə fɔː §-fə ‖ ˈðer fɔːr ˈðær-, -foʊr
therefrom ˌðeə ˈfrɒm ‖ ˌðer ˈfrʌm -ˈfrɑːm
therein ˌðeər ˈɪn ‖ ˌðer- ˌðær-
thereinafter ˌðeər ɪn ˈɑːft ə §-ˈæft-
‖ ˌðer ɪn ˈæft ər ˌðær-
there'll *strong form* ðeəl ðeər əl ‖ ðerl ðærl,
ðer əl, ðær əl, *weak form* ðəl ðər əl ‖ ðɚl
ðɚr əl —*See note at* there
theremin, thérémin, T~ ˈθer əm ɪn §-ən ~s z
thereof ˌðeər ˈɒv ‖ ˌðer ˈʌv, ðær-, -ˈɑːv
thereon ˌðeər ˈɒn ‖ ˌðer ˈɑːn, ðær-, -ˈɔːn
there's *strong form* ðeəz ‖ ðerz ðærz, *weak form*
ðəz ‖ ðɚz —*See note at* there
Theresa tə ˈriːz ə tɪ-, -ˈreɪz- ‖ -ˈriːs- (!)
Therese, Thérèse tə ˈreɪz —*Fr* [te ʁɛːz]
thereto ˌðeə ˈtuː ‖ ˌðer- ˌðær-
thereunder ˌðeər ˈʌnd ə ‖ ˌðer ˈʌnd ər ˌðær-
thereupon ˌðeər ə ˈpɒn ˈ••,• ‖ ˌðer ə ˈpɑːn
ˌðær-, -ˈpɔːn
there've *strong form* ðeəv ‖ ðerv ðærv, *weak*
form ðəv ðər əv ‖ ðɚv ðɚr əv —*See note at*
there
therewith ˌðeə ˈwɪð -ˈwɪθ ‖ ˌðer- ˌðær-
therewithal ˈðeə wɪð ɔːl -wɪθ-, ,••ˈ• ‖ ˌðer-
ˈðær-, -ɑːl
therm θɜːm ‖ θɜ·ːm **therms** θɜːmz ‖ θɜ·ːmz
thermal ˈθɜːm əl ‖ ˈθɜ·ːm əl ~ly i ~s z
thermic ˈθɜːm ɪk ‖ ˈθɜ·ːm ɪk
Thermidor ˈθɜːm ɪ dɔː §-ə- ‖ ˈθɜ·ːm ə dɔːr
—*Fr* [tɛʁ mi dɔːʁ]
thermion ˈθɜːm i_ən ‖ ˈθɜ·ːm- -ɑːn ~s z
thermionic ˌθɜːm i ˈɒn ɪk ◄ ‖ ˌθɜ·ːm i ˈɑːn ɪk ◄
~s s
  ˌthermiˌonic ˈvalve
thermistor θɜː ˈmɪst ə ˈθɜːm ɪst ə
‖ θɜ·ː ˈmɪst ər ˈθɜ·ːm ɪst- ~s z
thermite ˈθɜːm aɪt ‖ ˈθɜ·ːm-
thermo- *comb. form*
  with stress-neutral suffix ˌθɜːm əʊ ‖ ˌθɜ·ːm ə —
    thermographic ˌθɜːm əʊ
    ˈgræf ɪk ◄ ‖ ˌθɜ·ːm ə-
  with stress-imposing suffix
    θɜː ˈmɒ+ ‖ θɜ·ː ˈmɑː+ — **thermography**
    θɜː ˈmɒg rəf i ‖ θɜ·ː ˈmɑːg-
thermocouple ˈθɜːm əʊ ˌkʌp əl ‖ ˈθɜ·ːm ə- ~s
z
thermodynamic ˌθɜːm əʊ daɪ ˈnæm ɪk ◄
‖ ˌθɜ·ːm oʊ- ~ally əl_i ~s s
thermoelectric ˌθɜːm əʊ ɪ ˈlek trɪk ◄ -ə'•-
‖ ˌθɜ·ːm oʊ- ~ally əl_i
thermometer θə ˈmɒm ɪt ə -ət-
‖ θər ˈmɑːm ət̬ ər ~s z
thermonuclear ˌθɜːm əʊ ˈnjuːk li_ə ◄ §-ˈnuːk-
‖ ˌθɜ·ːm oʊ ˈnuːk li_ər -ˈnjuːk-, △-jəl ər

thermoplastic ˌθɜːm əʊ 'plæst ɪk ◄ -'plɑːst-
‖ ˌθɜːm ə- ~s s
Thermopylae θə 'mɒp əl i θɜː-, -ɪl-, -iː
‖ θər 'mɑːp-
thermos, T~ *tdmk* 'θɜːm əs -ɒs ‖ 'θɜ˞ːm əs ~es
ɪz əz
'thermos flask
thermosetting 'θɜːm əʊ ˌset ɪŋ ˌ••'••
‖ 'θɜ˞ːm oʊ ˌset̬ ɪŋ
thermostat 'θɜːm əʊ stæt ‖ 'θɜ˞ːm ə- ~s s
thermostatic ˌθɜːm əʊ 'stæt ɪk ◄
‖ ˌθɜ˞ːm ə 'stæt̬ ɪk ◄ ~ally əl i
-thermy ˌθɜːm i ‖ ˌθɜ˞ːm i — diathermy
'daɪ‿ə ˌθɜːm i ‖ -ˌθɜ˞ːm i
Theroux θə 'ruː
Thersites θɜː 'saɪt iːz ‖ θɜ˞r-
thesaur|us θɪ 'sɔːr |əs θə- ~i aɪ ~uses əs ɪz
-əz
these ðiːz
theses 'θiːs iːz
Theseus 'θiːs juːs 'θiːs i‿əs ‖ 'θiːs i‿əs 'θiːs uːs
Thesiger 'θes ɪdʒ ə ‖ -ər
thesis 'θiːs ɪs §-əs —*but as a metrical term,*
sometimes 'θes- theses 'θiːs iːz
thespian, T~ 'θesp i‿ən ~s z
Thespis 'θesp ɪs §-əs
Thessalian θe 'seɪl i‿ən θɪ-, θə- ~s z
Thessalonian ˌθes ə 'ləʊn i‿ən ◄ ‖ -'loʊn- ~s z
Thessalonica ˌθes ə 'lɒn ɪk ə §-ək ə ‖ -'lɑːn-
—*ModGk* Thessaloniki [θɛ sa lɔ 'ni ci]
Thessaly 'θes əl i
theta 'θiːt ə ‖ 'θeɪt̬ ə 'θiːt̬- ~s z
Thetford 'θet fəd ‖ -fərd
thetic 'θet ɪk ‖ 'θet̬ ɪk
Thetis (i) 'θet ɪs §-əs ‖ 'θet̬-, (ii) 'θiːt ɪs -əs
‖ 'θiːt̬- —*The Greek sea goddess is usually (i),*
the personal name (ii)
thew θjuː ‖ θuː θjuː thews θjuːz ‖ θuːz θjuːz
they ðeɪ
they'd ðeɪd
Theydon Bois ˌθeɪd ən 'bɔɪz
they'd've ðeɪd əv
they'll ðeɪəl ðeəl
they're ðeə §'ðeɪ ə ‖ ðer (= *there*) —*In GenAm*
there is also a weak form ðər. *There is no RP*
weak form.
they've ðeɪv
thiamine 'θaɪ‿ə miːn -mɪn; §-ə mən
thiazine 'θaɪ‿ə ziːn -zaɪn
thiazole 'θaɪ‿ə zəʊl →-zɒʊl ‖ -zoʊl
thick θɪk thicker 'θɪk ə ‖ -ər thickest 'θɪk ɪst
-əst
thicken 'θɪk ən ~ed d ~ing ꞏɪŋ ~s z
thickener 'θɪk ən‿ə ‖ -ən‿ər ~s z
thicket 'θɪk ɪt §-ət ~s s
thickhead 'θɪk hed ~s z
thickheaded ˌθɪk 'hed ɪd ◄ -əd ‖ '•ꞏ,•• ~ly li
~ness nəs nɪs
thickie 'θɪk i ~s z
thickish 'θɪk ɪʃ
thickly 'θɪk li
thickness 'θɪk nəs -nɪs ~es ɪz əz
thickset ˌθɪk 'set ◄ ‖'••

thick-skinned ˌθɪk 'skɪnd ◄ ‖'••
thick-witted ˌθɪk 'wɪt ɪd ◄ -əd ‖ -'wɪt̬ əd ◄
'•ꞏ,•• ~ly li ~ness nəs nɪs
thief θiːf thief's θiːfs thieves θiːvz
thieve θiːv thieved θiːvd thieves θiːvz
thieving 'θiːv ɪŋ
thievery 'θiːv ər i
thievish 'θiːv ɪʃ ~ly li ~ness nəs nɪs
thigh θaɪ thighs θaɪz
thighbone 'θaɪ bəʊn ‖ -boʊn ~s z
thigmo- *comb. form*
with stress-neutral suffix ˌθɪg məʊ ‖ -mə —
thigmotaxis ˌθɪg məʊ 'tæks ɪs §-əs ‖ -mə-
with stress-imposing suffix θɪg 'mɒ+ ‖ -'mɑː+
— thigmotropism θɪg 'mɒtr ə ˌpɪz əm
‖ -'mɑːtr- (*also* ˌθɪg məʊ 'trəʊp ˌɪz əm
‖ -mə 'troʊp-)
thill θɪl thills θɪlz
thimble 'θɪm bəl ~s z
thimbleful 'θɪm bəl fʊl ~s z
thimblerig 'θɪm bəl rɪg ~ged d ~ging ɪŋ ~s z
thimerosal θaɪ 'mer ə sæl
thin θɪn thinned θɪnd thinner 'θɪn ə ‖ -ər
thinnest 'θɪn ɪst -əst thinning 'θɪn ɪŋ
thins θɪnz
ˌthin 'air
thine ðaɪn
thing θɪŋ things θɪŋz
thingama... —*see* thingummy...
thingie 'θɪŋ i ~s z
thinguma... —*see* thingummy...
thingumm|y 'θɪŋ əm |i ~ies iz
thingummybob 'θɪŋ əm i bɒb -ə bɒb ‖ -ə bɑːb
~s z
thingummyjig 'θɪŋ əm i dʒɪg -ə dʒɪg ~s z
thing|y 'θɪŋ |i ~ies iz
think θɪŋk thinking 'θɪŋk ɪŋ thinks θɪŋks
thought θɔːt ‖ θɑːt
'think piece; 'think tank
thinkable 'θɪŋk əb əl
thinker 'θɪŋk ə ‖ -ər ~s z
thinly 'θɪn li
thinn... —*see* thin
thinner 'θɪn ə ‖ -ər ~s z
thinness 'θɪn nəs -nɪs
thin-skinned ˌθɪn 'skɪnd ◄ ‖'••
thio 'θaɪ əʊ ‖ -oʊ
thio- *comb. form*
with stress-neutral suffix ˌθaɪ əʊ ‖ -ə —
thiosulfate, thiosulphate
ˌθaɪ əʊ 'sʌlf eɪt ‖ -ə-
thiokol, T~ *tdmk* 'θaɪ‿ə kɒl ‖ -kɑːl -kɔːl, -koʊl
thiol 'θaɪ ɒl ‖ -ɑːl -ɔːl, -oʊl ~s z
thionate 'θaɪ‿ə neɪt
thiouracil ˌθaɪ əʊ 'jʊər ə sɪl ‖ -oʊ 'jʊr-
third θɜːd ‖ θɜ˞ːd thirds θɜːdz ‖ θɜ˞ːdz
ˌthird de'gree; ˌthird 'party; ˌthird
'person; ˌthird 'reading; ˌThird 'World◄
third-class ˌθɜːd 'klɑːs ◄→ˌθɜːg-, §-'klæs
‖ ˌθɜ˞ːd 'klæs ◄
third-degree ˌθɜːd dɪ 'griː ◄ -də-, §-diː-
‖ ˌθɜ˞ːd-
ˌthird-deˌgree 'burns

thirdhand ˌθɜːd ˈhænd ◀ ‖ ˌθɜ·ːd-
thirdly ˈθɜːd li ‖ ˈθɜ·ːd li
third-rate ˌθɜːd ˈreɪt ◀ ‖ ˌθɜ·ːd-
Thirkell ˈθɜːk əl ‖ ˈθɜ·ːk əl
Thirlmere ˈθɜːl mɪə ‖ ˈθɜ·ːl mɪr
Thirsk θɜːsk ‖ θɜ·ːsk
thirst θɜːst ‖ θɜ·ːst **thirsted** ˈθɜːst ɪd -əd
‖ ˈθɜ·ːst əd **thirsting** ˈθɜːst ɪŋ ‖ ˈθɜ·ːst ɪŋ
thirsts θɜːsts ‖ θɜ·ːsts
thirst|y ˈθɜːst li ‖ ‖ ˈθɜ·ːst li ~**ier** i‿ə ‖ i‿ər ~**iest**
i‿ɪst i‿əst ~**ily** ɪ li əl i ~**iness** i nəs i nɪs
thirteen ˌθɜː ˈtiːn ◀ §ˌθɜːt- ‖ ˌθɜ·ː- ˌθɜ·ːt- ~**s** z
thirteenth ˌθɜː ˈtiːntθ ◀ §ˌθɜːt- ‖ ˌθɜ·ː- ˌθɜ·ːt-
~**s** s
thirtieth ˈθɜːt i‿əθ §-ti-, -ɪθ ‖ ˈθɜ·ːt i əθ ~**s** s
thirt|y ˈθɜːt li §ˈθɜːt tli ‖ ˈθɜ·ːt̬ li ~**ies** iz
ˌThirty ₍ₒ₎**Years' War**
thirtyfold ˈθɜːt i fəʊld →-fɒʊld ‖ ˈθɜ·ːt̬ i foʊld
thirty-nine ˌθɜːt i ˈnaɪn ◀ §-ti- ‖ ˌθɜ·ːt̬- ~**s** z
ˌThirty-nine **'Articles**
this ðɪs —*Some speakers use a weak form* ðəs *in
the expressions* ~ *afternoon,* ~ *evening,* ~
*morning. In GenAm, this weak form is used
more widely.* **these** ðiːz
Thisbe ˈθɪz bi
thistle ˈθɪs əl ~**s** z
thistledown ˈθɪs əl daʊn
Thistlethwaite ˈθɪs əl θweɪt
thistly ˈθɪs əl‿i
thither ˈðɪð ə §ˈθɪð- ‖ ˈθɪð ər ˈðɪð- ~**ward/s**
wəd/z ‖ wərd/z
thixotropic ˌθɪks ə ˈtrɒp ɪk ◀ ‖ -ˈtrɑːp-
thixotropy θɪk ˈsɒtr əp i ‖ -ˈsɑːtr-
tho, tho' ðəʊ §θəʊ ‖ ðoʊ
Thoday ˈθəʊd eɪ ‖ ˈθoʊd eɪ
Thody ˈθəʊd i ‖ ˈθoʊd i
thon ðɒn ‖ ðɑːn
-thon θɒn ‖ θɑːn — **singathon**
ˈsɪŋ ə θɒn ‖ -θɑːn —*See note at* -on.
thong θɒŋ ‖ θɔːŋ θɑːŋ **thongs** θɒŋz ‖ θɔːŋz
θɑːŋz
Thor θɔː ‖ θɔːr
Thora ˈθɔːr ə
thoraces ˈθɔːr ə siːz θɔː ˈreɪs iːz ‖ ˈθoʊr-
thoracic θɔː ˈræs ɪk θɒ-, θə- ‖ θə-
thoraco- *comb. form*
with stress-neutral suffix ˈθɔːr ə kəʊ
θɔː ˈræk əʊ ‖ -koʊ ˈθoʊr- — **thoracoplasty**
ˈθɔːr ə kəʊ ˌplæst i θɔː ˈræk- ‖ -koʊ, •-
ˈθoʊr-
with stress-imposing suffix
ˌθɔːr ə ˈkɒ+ ‖ -ˈkɑː+ ˌθoʊr- — **thoracotomy**
ˌθɔːr ə ˈkɒt əm i ‖ -ˈkɑːt̬- ˌθoʊr-

thorax ˈθɔːr æks ‖ ˈθoʊr- **thoraces** ˈθɔːr ə siːz
θɔː ˈreɪs iːz ‖ ˈθoʊr- ~**es** ɪz əz
Thorazine *tdmk* ˈθɔːr ə ziːn ‖ ˈθoʊr-
Thorburn ˈθɔː bɜːn ‖ -bɜ·ːn
Thoreau ˈθɔːr əʊ θɔː ˈrəʊ, θə- ‖ θə ˈroʊ θɔː-;
ˈθɔː oʊ
thorite ˈθɔːr aɪt ‖ ˈθoʊr-
thorium ˈθɔːr i‿əm ‖ ˈθoʊr-
Thorley ˈθɔːl i ‖ ˈθɔːrl i
thorn, Thorn θɔːn ‖ θɔːrn **thorns**
θɔːnz ‖ θɔːrnz
ˈthorn ˌapple
Thornaby ˈθɔːn əb i ‖ ˈθɔːrn-
thornbill ˈθɔːn bɪl →ˈθɔːm- ‖ ˈθɔːrn- ~**s** z
Thorndike ˈθɔːn daɪk ‖ ˈθɔːrn-
Thorne θɔːn ‖ θɔːrn
Thorner ˈθɔːn ə ‖ ˈθɔːrn ər
Thorneycroft ˈθɔːn i krɒft ‖ ˈθɔːrn i krɑːft
-krɑːft
Thornham ˈθɔːn əm ‖ ˈθɔːrn-
Thornhill ˈθɔːn hɪl ‖ ˈθɔːrn-
thornless ˈθɔːn ləs -lɪs ‖ ˈθɔːrn-
Thornley ˈθɔːn li ‖ ˈθɔːrn-
Thornton ˈθɔːn tən ‖ ˈθɔːrn t̬ən
thorn|y ˈθɔːn li ‖ ˈθɔːrn li ~**ier** i‿ə ‖ i‿ər ~**iest**
i‿ɪst i‿əst ~**iness** i nəs i nɪs
Thorogood ˈθɒr ə gʊd ‖ ˈθɜ·ː-
Thorold ˈθɒr əld ˈθʌr-, -əʊld ‖ ˈθɔːr əld ˈθɑːr-
thoron ˈθɔːr ɒn ‖ -ɑːn ˈθoʊr-
thorough ˈθʌr ə ‖ ˈθɜ·ː oʊ (*)
thoroughbred ˈθʌr ə bred ‖ ˈθɜ·ː oʊ- -ə- ~**s** z
thoroughfare ˈθʌr ə feə ‖ ˈθɜ·ː oʊ fer -ə-, -fær
~**s** z
thoroughgoing
ˌθʌr ə ˈgəʊ ɪŋ ◀ ‖ ˌθɜ·ː oʊ ˈgoʊ ɪŋ ◀ -ə-
thorough|ly ˈθʌr ə ‖ li ‖ ˈθɜ·ː oʊ ‖li ~**ness** nəs
nɪs
Thorp, Thorpe θɔːp ‖ θɔːrp
Thorpeness ˌθɔːp ˈnes ‖ ˌθɔːrp-
those ðəʊz ‖ ðoʊz
Thoth θəʊθ təʊt, θɒθ ‖ θoʊθ toʊt
thou *pronoun* ðaʊ —*In dialectal speech there
may also be a weak form such as* ðə
thou *'thousand'; 'thousandth'* θaʊ **thous** θaʊz
though ðəʊ §θəʊ ‖ ðoʊ
thought θɔːt ‖ θɑːt **thoughts** θɔːts ‖ θɑːts
thoughtful ˈθɔːt fəl -fʊl ‖ ˈθɑːt- ~**ly** ‿i ~**ness**
nəs nɪs
thoughtless ˈθɔːt ləs -lɪs ‖ ˈθɑːt- ~**ly** li ~**ness**
nəs nɪs
thought-out ˌθɔːt ˈaʊt ◀ ‖ ˌθɔːt̬- ˌθɑːt̬-
thought-provoking ˈθɔːt prə ˌvəʊk ɪŋ
‖ -ˌvoʊk- ˈθɑːt-
thought-reader ˈθɔːt ˌriːd ə ‖ -ər ˈθɑːt- ~**s** z
Thouless ˈθaʊ ləs
thousand ˈθaʊz ənd ~**s** z
ˌThousand **'Islands;** ˌThousand ˌIsland
'dressing
thousandfold ˈθaʊz ənd fəʊld →-fɒʊld ‖ -foʊld
thousandth ˈθaʊz əntθ -ənd̬θ ~**s** s
Thrace θreɪs
Thracian ˈθreɪʃ ən ˈθreɪʃ i‿ən ~**s** z
Thraco-Phrygian ˌθreɪk əʊ ˈfrɪdʒ i‿ən ◀ ‖ ˌ•oʊ-

thraldom 'θrɔːl dəm ‖ 'θrɑːl-
Thrale θreɪəl
thrall θrɔːl ‖ θrɑːl
thralldom 'θrɔːl dəm ‖ 'θrɑːl-
thrang θræŋ
thrash θræʃ thrashed θræʃt thrashes
'θræʃ ɪz -əz thrashing 'θræʃ ɪŋ
thrasher 'θræʃ ə ‖ -ər ~s z
thread θred threaded 'θred ɪd -əd threading
'θred ɪŋ threads θredz
threadbare 'θred beə →'θreb- ‖ -ber -bær
~ness nəs nɪs
threadlike 'θred laɪk
Threadneedle ˌθred 'niːd əl '•‚••
threadworm 'θred wɜːm ‖ -wɝːm ~s z
threat θret threats θrets
threaten 'θret ən ~ed d ~ing/ly ˌɪŋ /li ~s z
three θriː threes θriːz
ˌthree 'R's
three-cornered ˌθriː 'kɔːn əd ◄ ‖ -'kɔːrn ərd ◄
three-D, 3-D ˌθriː 'diː ◄
three-day ˌθriː 'deɪ ◄
ˌthree-day 'week
three-decker ˌθriː 'dek ə ◄ ‖ -ər ~s z
three-dimensional ˌθriː daɪ 'mentʃ ən_əl ◄
‚•dɪ-, ‚•də-
threefold 'θriː fəʊld →-fɒʊld, ‚•'• ‖ -foʊld
three-halfpence ˌθriː 'heɪp ənts →-mps
threeish 'θriː ɪʃ
three-legged ˌθriː 'leg ɪd ◄ -əd; ‚•'legd
ˌthree-'legged race
three-line ˌθriː 'laɪn ◄
ˌthree-line 'whip
threepence n '3d' 'θrep ənts 'θrʌp-, 'θrɪp-,
'θrʊp-, →-mps —but meaning '3p', in modern
currency, usually three pence ˌθriː 'pents
threepenny adj '3d' 'θrep ən_i 'θrʌp-, 'θrɪp-,
'θrʊp- —but meaning '3p', in modern
currency, usually three-penny ˌθriː 'pen i ◄
ˌthreepenny 'bit
three-piece ˌθriː 'piːs ◄
ˌthree-piece 'suite
three-ply 'θriː plaɪ, ‚•'•
three-point ˌθriː 'pɔɪnt ◄
ˌthree-point 'turn
three-quarter ˌθriː 'kwɔːt ə ◄ -'kɔːt-
‖ -'kwɔːrt ər ◄ ~s z
three-ring ˌθriː 'rɪŋ ◄
ˌthree-ring 'circus
threescore ˌθriː 'skɔː ◄ ‖ -'skɔːr ◄ -'skoʊr
threesome 'θriː səm ~s z
three-star ˌθriː 'stɑː ◄ ‖ -'stɑːr ◄
ˌthree-star ho'tel
three-way ˌθriː 'weɪ ◄
three-wheeler ˌθriː 'wiːəl ə -'hwiːəl-
‖ -'hwiːəl ər ~s z
Threlfall 'θrel fɔːl ‖ -fɑːl
Threlkeld 'θrel keld
threnod|y 'θren əd |i 'θriːn- ~ies iz
thresh θreʃ threshed θreʃt threshes 'θreʃ ɪz
-əz threshing 'θreʃ ɪŋ
thresher, T~ 'θreʃ ə ‖ -ər ~s z

threshold 'θreʃ həʊld -əʊld, →-hɒʊld ‖ -oʊld
-hoʊld ~s z
threw θruː (= through)
Thribb θrɪb
thrice θraɪs
thrift θrɪft thrifts θrɪfts
thriftless 'θrɪft ləs -lɪs ~ly li ~ness nəs nɪs
thrift|y 'θrɪft |i ~ier i_ə ‖ i_ər ~iest i_ɪst i_əst
~ily ɪ li əl i ~iness i nəs i nɪs
thrill θrɪl thrilled θrɪld thrilling/ly 'θrɪl ɪŋ /li
thrills θrɪlz
thriller 'θrɪl ə ‖ -ər ~s z
Thring θrɪŋ
thrips θrɪps
thrive θraɪv thrived θraɪvd thriven 'θrɪv ən
(!) thrives θraɪvz thriving/ly 'θraɪv ɪŋ /li
throve θrəʊv ‖ θroʊv
thro, thro' θruː
throat θrəʊt ‖ θroʊt throats θrəʊts ‖ θroʊts
throaty 'θrəʊt |i ‖ 'θroʊt̬ |i ~ier i_ə ‖ i_ər ~iest
i_ɪst i_əst ~ily ɪ li əl i ~iness i nəs i nɪs
throb θrɒb ‖ θrɑːb throbbed θrɒbd ‖ θrɑːbd
throbbing/ly 'θrɒb ɪŋ /li ‖ 'θrɑːb ɪŋ /li
throbs θrɒbz ‖ θrɑːbz
throes θrəʊz ‖ θroʊz (= throws)
Throgmorton ˌ‚ˌθrɒɡ 'mɔːt ən '•••
‖ θrɑːɡ 'mɔːrt ən
thrombi 'θrɒm baɪ ‖ 'θrɑːm-
thrombin 'θrɒm bɪn §-bən ‖ 'θrɑːm-
thrombo- comb. form
with stress-neutral suffix
¦θrɒm bəʊ ‖ ¦θrɑːm boʊ — thromboplastic
ˌθrɒm bəʊ 'plæst ɪk ◄ ‖ ˌθrɑːm boʊ-
with stress-imposing suffix
θrɒm 'bɒ+ ‖ θrɑːm 'bɑː+ — thrombolysis
θrɒm 'bɒl əs ɪs -ɪs-, §-əs ‖ θrɑːm 'bɑːl-
thrombos|e 'θrɒm bəʊz -bəʊs, ‚•'• ‖ -boʊz
-boʊs ~ed d ~es ɪz əz ~ing ɪŋ
thrombos|is θrɒm 'bəʊs |ɪs §-əs
‖ θrɑːm 'boʊs ləs ~es iːz
thrombotic θrɒm 'bɒt ɪk ‖ θrɑːm 'bɑːt̬ ɪk
throm|bus 'θrɒm |bəs ‖ 'θrɑːm |bəs ~bi baɪ
throne θrəʊn ‖ θroʊn throned
θrəʊnd ‖ θroʊnd thrones θrəʊnz ‖ θroʊnz
throning 'θrəʊn ɪŋ ‖ 'θroʊn ɪŋ
throng θrɒŋ ‖ θrɔːŋ θrɑːŋ thronged
θrɒŋd ‖ θrɔːŋd θrɑːŋd thronging
'θrɒŋ ɪŋ ‖ 'θrɔːŋ ɪŋ 'θrɑːŋ- throngs
θrɒŋz ‖ θrɔːŋz θrɑːŋz
throstle 'θrɒs əl ‖ 'θrɑːs əl ~s z
throttl|e 'θrɒt əl ‖ 'θrɑːt̬ əl ~ed d ~es z ~ing
ɪŋ
through θruː
throughout θru 'aʊt
throughput 'θruː pʊt
throughway 'θruː weɪ ~s z
throve θrəʊv ‖ θroʊv
throw θrəʊ ‖ θroʊ threw θruː throwing
'θrəʊ ɪŋ ‖ 'θroʊ ɪŋ thrown θrəʊn §'θrəʊ ən
‖ θroʊn throws θrəʊz ‖ θroʊz
throwaway 'θrəʊ ə ˌweɪ ‖ 'θroʊ- ~s z
throwback 'θrəʊ bæk ‖ 'θroʊ- ~s s
thrower, T~ 'θrəʊ ə ‖ 'θroʊ ər ~s z

throw-in ˈθrəʊ ɪn ‖ ˈθroʊ- ~s z
thrown θrəʊn §ˈθrəʊ ən ‖ ˈθroʊn *(usually =* **throne***)*
thru θruː
thrum θrʌm **thrummed** θrʌmd **thrumming** ˈθrʌm ɪŋ **thrums** θrʌmz
thrush θrʌʃ **thrushes** ˈθrʌʃ ɪz -əz
thrust θrʌst **thrusting/ly** ˈθrʌst ɪŋ /li **thrusts** θrʌsts
thruster ˈθrʌst ə ‖ -ᵊr ~s z
thruway ˈθruː weɪ ~s z
Thucydidean θju ˌsɪd ə ˈdiː ən ◂ -ɪ- ‖ θu-
Thucydides θju ˈsɪd ə diːz -ɪ- ‖ θu-
thud θʌd **thudded** ˈθʌd ɪd -əd **thudding** ˈθʌd ɪŋ **thuds** θʌdz
thug θʌg **thugs** θʌgz
thuggery ˈθʌg ər i
thuggish ˈθʌg ɪʃ ~**ly** li ~**ness** nəs nɪs
thuja ˈθjuːdʒ ə ˈθuːdʒ-; ˈθjuː jə, ˈθuː- ‖ ˈθuːdʒ ə ~s z
Thule θjuːl ˈθjuːl i, ˈθuːl-, -iː ‖ ˈθuːl i —*but the base in Iceland is* ˈtuːl i
thulium ˈθjuːl i‿əm ˈθuːl- ‖ ˈθuːl-
thumb θʌm **thumbed** θʌmd **thumbing** ˈθʌm ɪŋ **thumbs** θʌmz
ˌthumbs ˈdown; ˌthumbs ˈup
thumbnail ˈθʌm neɪᵊl ~s z
thumbprint ˈθʌm prɪnt ~s s
thumbscrew ˈθʌm skruː ~s z
thumbtack ˈθʌm tæk ~**ed** t ~**ing** ɪŋ ~s s
thummim ˈθʌm ɪm ˈθʊm-, ˈtʊm-
thump θʌmp **thumped** θʌmpt **thumping/ly** ˈθʌmp ɪŋ /li **thumps** θʌmps
thumper ˈθʌmp ə ‖ -ᵊr ~s z
thunbergia θʌn ˈbɜːdʒ i‿ə θʊn-, •ˈ•ə ‖ -ˈbɝːdʒ- ~s z
thunder ˈθʌnd ə ‖ -ᵊr ~**ed** d **thundering/ly** ˈθʌnd ᵊr ɪŋ /li ~s z
ˌThunder ˈBay
thunderbird, T~ ˈθʌnd ə bɜːd ‖ -ᵊr bɝːd ~s z
thunderbolt ˈθʌnd ə bəʊlt →-bɒʊlt ‖ -ᵊr boʊlt ~s s
thunderclap ˈθʌnd ə klæp ‖ -ᵊr- ~s s
thundercloud ˈθʌnd ə klaʊd ‖ -ᵊr- ~s z
thunderer ˈθʌnd ᵊr ə ‖ -ᵊr ər
thunder|fly ˈθʌnd ə| flaɪ ‖ -ᵊr|- ~**flies** flaɪz
thunderhead ˈθʌnd ə hed ‖ -ᵊr- ~z z
thunderous ˈθʌnd ᵊr əs ~**ly** li
thundershower ˈθʌnd ə ˌʃaʊ‿ə ‖ ˈθʌnd ᵊr ˌʃaʊ‿ᵊr ~s z
thunderstorm ˈθʌnd ə stɔːm ‖ -ᵊr stɔːrm ~s z
thunderstruck ˈθʌnd ə strʌk ‖ -ᵊr-
thundery ˈθʌn dᵊr i
Thurber ˈθɜːb ə ‖ ˈθɝːb ᵊr
Thurgarton ˈθɜːg ət ən ‖ ˈθɝːg ᵊrt ən
Thurgood ˈθɜː gʊd ‖ ˈθɝː-
thurible ˈθjʊər ɪb ᵊl -əb- ‖ ˈθʊr- ˈθɝː- ~s z
thurifer ˈθjʊər ɪf ə -əf- ‖ ˈθʊr əf ᵊr ˈθɝː- ~s z
Thuringi|a θjʊᵊ ˈrɪndʒ i‿ə tuᵊ-, -ˈrɪŋ gi‿; •ˈ•ə ‖ θu- ~**an/s** ən/z
Thurleigh *place in Bedfordshire* ˌθɜː ˈlaɪ ‖ ˌθɝː-
Thurlestone ˈθɜːl stən ‖ ˈθɝːl-
Thurloe, Thurlow ˈθɜːl əʊ ‖ ˈθɝːl oʊ

Thurrock ˈθʌr ək ‖ ˈθɝː ək
Thursday ˈθɜːz deɪ -di ‖ ˈθɝːz- —*See note at* -**day** ~s z
Thurso ˈθɜːs əʊ ‖ ˈθɝːs oʊ
Thurston ˈθɜːst ən ‖ ˈθɝːst ən
thus ðʌs **thusly** ˈðʌs li
thwack θwæk **thwacked** θwækt **thwacking** ˈθwæk ɪŋ **thwacks** θwæks
Thwaite θweɪt **Thwaites** θweɪts
thwart θwɔːt ‖ θwɔːrt **thwarted** ˈθwɔːt ɪd -əd ‖ ˈθwɔːrt̬ əd **thwarting** ˈθwɔːt ɪŋ ‖ ˈθwɔːrt̬ ɪŋ **thwarts** θwɔːts ‖ θwɔːrts
thy ðaɪ
Thyestean θaɪ ˈest i‿ən
Thyestes θaɪ ˈest iːz
thylacine ˈθaɪl ə siːn -saɪn ~s z
thyme taɪm *(! =* **time***)*
-thymia ˈθaɪm i‿ə— **cyclothymia** ˌsaɪk ləʊ ˈθaɪm i‿ə ‖ -ˈlə-
thymidine ˈθaɪm ɪ diːn -ə-
thymine ˈθaɪm iːn
thymol ˈθaɪm ɒl ‖ -oʊl -ɔːl, -ɑːl
thymus ˈθaɪm əs ~**es** ɪz əz
Thynne θɪn
thyratron ˈθaɪᵊr ə trɒn ‖ -traːn ~s z
thyristor θaɪᵊ ˈrɪst ə ‖ -ᵊr ~s z
thyro- *comb. form*
   with stress-neutral suffix ¦θaɪᵊr əʊ ‖ -oʊ — **thyrohyoid** ˌθaɪᵊr əʊ ˈhaɪ ɔɪd ◂ ‖ -oʊ-
   with stress-imposing suffix θaɪᵊ ˈrɒ+ ‖ -ˈraː+ — **thyropathy** ˌθaɪᵊ ˈrɒp əθ i ‖ -ˈraːp-
thyroid ˈθaɪᵊr ɔɪd ~s z
thyroxine θaɪᵊ ˈrɒks iːn -ɪn, §-ᵊn ‖ -ˈraːks-
thyrs|us ˈθɜːs |əs ‖ ˈθɝːs |əs ~**i** aɪ
thyself ðaɪ ˈself
Thyssen ˈtiːs ᵊn —*Ger* [ˈtʏs ᵊn]
ti *'musical note'; 'Cordyline tree'* tiː: **tis** tiːz
TI ˌtiː ˈaɪ
Tia Maria *tdmk* ˌtiː‿ə mə ˈriː‿ə ~s z
Tiananmen ti ˌæn ən ˈmen ◂ ˌtiː‿ən•ˈ•, -ˈmɪn ‖ -ˌɑːn- -ˌæn-; ˈtjen əm ən —*Chi* Tiān'ānmén [¹tʰjæn ¹an ²mən]
Tiˌananmen ˈSquare
Tianjin ti ˌæn ˈdʒɪn -ˌen- ‖ -ˌɑːn- —*Chi* Tiānjīn [¹tʰjæn ¹tɕɪn]
tiara ti ˈɑːr ə ‖ -ˈær ə -ˈer-, -ˈɑːr- ~s z
Tibbenham ˈtɪb ᵊn‿əm
Tibbett ˈtɪb ɪt §-ət
Tibbitts ˈtɪb ɪts §-əts
Tibbles ˈtɪb ᵊlz
Tibbs tɪbz
Tibenham ˈtɪb ᵊn‿əm
Tiber ˈtaɪb ə ‖ -ᵊr
Tiberias taɪ ˈbɪər i æs -əs ‖ -ˈbɪr-
Tiberius taɪ ˈbɪər i‿əs ‖ -ˈbɪr-
Tibet tɪ ˈbet §tə- —*Chi* Xīzàng [¹ɕi ⁴tsaŋ]
Tibetan tɪ ˈbet ᵊn §tə- ~s z
Tibeto-Burman tɪ ˌbet əʊ ˈbɜːm ən ◂ §tə- ‖ tə ˌbet̬ oʊ ˈbɝːm ən ◂
tibi|a ˈtɪb i‿ə ~**ae** iː ~**as** əz
Tibullus tɪ ˈbʌl əs §tə-, -ˈbʊl-

tic tɪk *(= tick)* **tics** tɪks
  ˌtic ˌdoulouˈreux ˌduːl ə ˈrɜː ‖ -ˈruː —*Fr*
  [tik du lu ʁø]
tice taɪs **tices** ˈtaɪs ɪz -əz
Ticehurst ˈtaɪs hɜːst ‖ -hɝːst
Tichborne ˈtɪtʃ bɔːn ‖ -bɔːrn -boʊrn
Ticino tɪ ˈtʃiːn əʊ ‖ -oʊ —*It* [ti ˈtʃiː no]
tick tɪk **ticked** tɪkt **ticking** ˈtɪk ɪŋ **ticks** tɪks
  ˌticking ˈoff *n*
ticker ˈtɪk ə ‖ -ər ~**s** z
tickertape ˈtɪk ə teɪp ‖ -ər-
tick|et ˈtɪk |ɪt §-ət ‖ -|ət ~**eted** ɪt ɪd §ət-, -əd
  ‖ əţ əd ~**eting** ɪt ɪŋ §ət- ‖ əţ ɪŋ ~**ets** ɪts
  §əts ‖ əts
  ˈticket ˌagency; ˈticket colˌlector; ˈticket
  ˌoffice; ˈticket tout
tickety-boo ˌtɪk ət i ˈbuː ˌ•ɪt- ‖ -əţ i-
ticking ˈtɪk ɪŋ
tickl|e ˈtɪk əl ~**ed** d ~**es** z ~**ing** _ɪŋ
tickler ˈtɪk əl ə ‖ _ər ~**s** z
ticklish ˈtɪk əl_ɪʃ ~**ly** li ~**ness** nəs nɪs
tick-over ˈtɪk ˌəʊv ə ‖ -ˌoʊv ər
ticktack ˈtɪk tæk
tick-tack-toe, tic-tac-toe ˌtɪk tæk ˈtəʊ ‖ -ˈtoʊ
ticktock ˈtɪk tɒk ˌ•ˈ• ‖ -tɑːk ~**ed** t ~**ing** ɪŋ ~**s**
  s
Ticonderoga ˌtaɪ kɒnd ə ˈrəʊg ə •ˌ••ˈ••
  ‖ ˌtaɪ kɑːnd ə ˈroʊg ə
tidal ˈtaɪd əl
  ˌtidal ˈwave,ˈ•••
tidbit ˈtɪd bɪt →ˈtɪb- ~**s** s
tiddledywink ˈtɪd əld i wɪŋk ~**s** s
tiddler ˈtɪd əl ə ‖ _ər ~**s** z
Tiddles ˈtɪd əlz
tiddley, tiddly ˈtɪd əl_i
tiddleywink, tiddlywink ˈtɪd əl_i wɪŋk ~**s** s
tide taɪd **tided** ˈtaɪd ɪd -əd **tides** taɪdz **tiding**
  ˈtaɪd ɪŋ
  ˈtide ˌtable
tideland ˈtaɪd lænd ~**s** z
tidemark ˈtaɪd mɑːk →ˈtaɪb- ‖ -mɑːrk ~**s** s
Tidenham ˈtɪd ən_əm
Tideswell ˈtaɪdz wel —*Locally also* ˈtɪdz əl
tidewater ˈtaɪd ˌwɔːt ə ‖ -ˌwɔːţ ər -ˌwɑːţ-
tideway ˈtaɪd weɪ
tidi... —*see* **tidy**
tidily ˈtaɪd ɪ li -əl i
tidiness ˈtaɪd i nəs -nɪs
tidings ˈtaɪd ɪŋz
Tidmarsh ˈtɪd mɑːʃ →ˈtɪb- ‖ -mɑːrʃ
tidy, Tidy ˈtaɪd i **tidied** ˈtaɪd id **tidier**
  ˈtaɪd i_ə ‖ _ər **tidies** ˈtaɪd iz **tidiest**
  ˈtaɪd i_ɪst _əst **tidying** ˈtaɪd i_ɪŋ
tie taɪ **tied** taɪd **ties** taɪz **tying** ˈtaɪ ɪŋ
  ˈtie clip; ˌtied ˈcottage; ˌtied ˈhouse
tiebreak ˈtaɪ breɪk ~**s** s
tiebreaker ˈtaɪ ˌbreɪk ə ‖ -ər ~**s** z
tie-dye ˈtaɪ daɪ ~**d** d ~**s** z ~**ing** ɪŋ
tie-in ˈtaɪ ɪn ~**s** z
tie-on ˈtaɪ ɒn ‖ -ɑːn -ɔːn ~**s** z
tiepin ˈtaɪ pɪn ~**s** z
Tiepolo ti ˈep ə ləʊ ‖ -loʊ —*It* [ˈtjɛː po lo]

tier *'rank, row'* tɪə ‖ tɪ°r *(= tear 'eye-water')*
  tiered tɪəd ‖ tɪ°rd **tiering** ˈtɪər ɪŋ ‖ ˈtɪr ɪŋ
  tiers tɪəz ‖ tɪ°rz
tier *'one that ties'* ˈtaɪ_ə ‖ ˈtaɪ_°r **tiers**
  ˈtaɪ_əz ‖ ˈtaɪ_°rz
tierce tɪəs ‖ tɪ°rs —*but in cards also* tɜːs ‖ tɝːs
tiercel ˈtɪəs əl ˈtɜːs- ‖ ˈtɪrs əl ~**s** z
Tierney ˈtɪən i ‖ ˈtɪrn i
Tierra del Fuego ti ˌeər ə del ˈfweɪg əʊ -ˌer-;
  ˌtɪər••ˈ•• ‖ ti ˌer ə del ˈfweɪg oʊ —*Sp*
  [ˌtje rra ðel ˈfwe ɣo]
tie-up ˈtaɪ ʌp ~**s** s
tiff tɪf **tiffs** tɪfs
Tiffan|y, t~ ˈtɪf ən |i ~**ies, y's** iz
tiffin, T~ ˈtɪf ɪn §-ən ~**s** z
Tiflis ˈtɪf lɪs §-ləs
tig tɪg
Tigellinus ˌtɪdʒ ə ˈlaɪn əs
tiger ˈtaɪg ə ‖ -ər ~**s** z
  ˈtiger cat; ˈtiger ˌlily; ˈtiger moth; ˈtiger
  shark
tigerish ˈtaɪg ər ɪʃ ~**ly** li
Tigger ˈtɪg ə ‖ -ər
Tiggy-Winkle ˈtɪg i ˌwɪŋk əl ˌ••ˈ••
Tighe taɪ
tight taɪt **tighter** ˈtaɪt ə ‖ ˈtaɪţ ər **tightest**
  ˈtaɪt ɪst -əst ‖ ˈtaɪţ əst **tights** taɪts
tighten ˈtaɪt ən ~**ed** d ~**ing** _ɪŋ ~**s** z
tightfisted ˌtaɪt ˈfɪst ɪd ◄ -əd
tightknit ˌtaɪt ˈnɪt ◄ ‖ ˈ••
tight-lipped ˌtaɪt ˈlɪpt ◄ ‖ ˈ••
tight|ly ˈtaɪt |li ~**ness** nəs nɪs
tightrope ˈtaɪt rəʊp ‖ -roʊp ~**s** s
  ˈtightrope ˌwalker
tightwad ˈtaɪt wɒd ‖ -wɑːd ~**s** z
Tiglath-pileser ˌtɪg læθ paɪ ˈliːz ə -pɪˈ•-, -pəˈ•-
  ‖ -ər
tiglic ˈtɪg lɪk
Tignes tiːn —*Fr* [tiɲ]
tigon ˈtaɪg ən ~**s** z
Tigray, Tigre, Tigré ˈtɪg reɪ ‖ tiː ˈgreɪ
tigress ˈtaɪg rəs -rɪs, -res ~**es** ɪz əz
Tigrinya tɪ ˈgrɪn jə -ˈgriːn-
Tigris ˈtaɪg rɪs -rəs
Tijuana ti ˈwɑːn ə ˌtiː_ə ˈwɑːn-, -ˈhwɑːn-
  ‖ ˌtiː ə ˈwɑːn ə —*Sp* [ti ˈxwa na]
tike taɪk **tikes** taɪks
tiki ˈtiːk i ~**s** z
tikka ˈtiːk ə ˈtɪk-
  ˌtikka maˈsala mə ˈsɑːl ə
til *'sesame'* tɪl
'til tɪl *see also* **till**
tilak ˈtɪl æk ~**s** s
tilapia tɪ ˈlæp i_ə tə-, -ˈleɪp- ‖ -ˈlɑːp- ~**s** z
Tilbury, t~ ˈtɪl bər_i ‖ -ber i
tilde ˈtɪld ə -i, -eɪ; tɪld ~**s** z
Tilden ˈtɪld ən
tile taɪ°l **tiled** taɪ°ld **tiles** taɪ°lz **tiling** ˈtaɪl ɪŋ
Tilehurst ˈtaɪ°l hɜːst ‖ -hɝːst
till tɪl *Note: for the prep and conj (not for the*
  noun and verb) there is also an occasional weak
  form t°l **tilled** tɪld **tilling** ˈtɪl ɪŋ **tills** tɪlz
tillage ˈtɪl ɪdʒ

Tillamook 'tɪl ə mʊk
tiller, T~ 'tɪl ə ‖ -ᵊr ~s z
Tilley 'tɪl i
  'Tilley lamp
Tillicoultry ˌtɪl ɪ 'kuːtr i -ə-
Tillie, Tilly 'tɪl i
Tilsit, t~ 'tɪls ɪt 'tɪlz-, §-ət —*Ger* ['tɪl zɪt]
tilt tɪlt **tilted** 'tɪlt ɪd -əd **tilting** 'tɪlt ɪŋ **tilts** tɪlts
tilth tɪlθ
Tilton 'tɪlt ən
Tim tɪm
timbale 'tɪm bᵊl tæm 'bɑːl, tɪm- —*Fr* [tæ̃ bal] ~s z
timber 'tɪm bə ‖ -bᵊr ~ed d **timbering** 'tɪm bər ɪŋ ~s z
Timberlake 'tɪm bə leɪk ‖ -bᵊr-
timberland, T~ 'tɪm bə lænd ‖ -bᵊr-
timberline 'tɪm bə laɪn ‖ -bᵊr-
timberyard 'tɪm bə jɑːd ‖ -bᵊr jɑːrd ~s z
timbre 'tæm bə 'tɪm- ‖ -bᵊr —*Fr* [tæ̃ːbʁ] ~s z
timbrel 'tɪm brəl ~s z
Timbuctoo, Timbuktu ˌtɪm bʌk 'tuː: -bək-
time taɪm **timed** taɪmd **times** taɪmz **timing** 'taɪm ɪŋ
  ˌtime and a 'half; ˌtime-and-'motion ˌstudy; 'time bomb; 'time ˌcapsule; 'time clock; 'time exˌposure; 'time fuse; ˌtime immeˈmorial; 'time lag; 'time ˌlimit; 'time lock; 'time maˌchine; ˌtime 'off; 'time sheet; 'time ˌsignal; 'time ˌsignature; 'time span; 'time switch; 'time ˌtrial; 'time warp; 'time zone
time-consuming 'taɪm kən ˌsjuːm ɪŋ §-kɒn-, -,suːm- ‖ -,suːm-
time-honored, time-honoured 'taɪm ˌɒn əd ‖ -ˌɑːn ᵊrd
timekeep|er/s 'taɪm ˌkiːp ə/z ‖ -ᵊr/z ~ing ɪŋ
time-lapse 'taɪm læps
timeless 'taɪm ləs -lɪs ~ly li ~ness nəs nɪs
time|ly 'taɪm |li ~lier li_ə ‖ li_ᵊr ~liest li_ɪst li_əst ~liness li nəs -nɪs
timeous 'taɪm əs ~ly li
timeout, time-out, time out ˌtaɪm 'aʊt
timepiec|e 'taɪm piːs ~es ɪz əz
timer 'taɪm ə ‖ -ᵊr ~s z
Times taɪmz
  ˌTimes 'Roman
timesaving 'taɪm ˌseɪv ɪŋ
timescale 'taɪm skeɪᵊl ~s z
timeserver 'taɪm ˌsɜːv ə ‖ -,sɝːv ᵊr ~s z
timeserving 'taɪm ˌsɜːv ɪŋ ‖ -,sɝːv-
timeshare 'taɪm ʃeə ‖ -ʃer -ʃær ~s z
time-sharing 'taɪm ˌʃeər ɪŋ ‖ -ʃer ɪŋ -ˌʃær-
time-shift 'taɪm ʃɪft ~ed ɪd əd ~ing ɪŋ ~s s
timetabl|e 'taɪm ˌteɪb ᵊl ~ed d ~es z ~ing ɪŋ
timework 'taɪm wɜːk ‖ -wɝːk ~er/s ə/z ‖ ᵊr/z
timeworn 'taɪm wɔːn ‖ -wɔːrn -woʊrn
Timex *tdmk* 'taɪm eks
timid 'tɪm ɪd §-əd ~ly li ~ness nəs nɪs
timidity tɪ 'mɪd ət i -ɪt i ‖ -əṭ i

timing 'taɪm ɪŋ ~s z
  'timing chain
Timisoara ˌtɪm i 'ʃwɑːr ə ˌtiːm- —*Romanian* Timişoara [ti mi 'ʃöa ɾa]
Timmie, Timmy 'tɪm i
Timon 'taɪm ən -ɒn
Timor 'tiːm ɔː 'tɪm- ‖ -ɔːr
Timorese ˌtɪm ə 'riːz◄ ‖ -'riːs
timorous 'tɪm ər_əs ~ly li ~ness nəs nɪs
Timotei *tdmk* 'tɪm ə teɪ
Timothy, t~ 'tɪm əθ i
timpani 'tɪmp ən i -ə niː
timpanist 'tɪm pən ɪst §-əst ~s s
Timpson 'tɪmps ᵊn
tin tɪn **tinned** tɪnd **tinning** 'tɪn ɪŋ **tins** tɪnz
  ˌtin 'can; ˌtin 'god; ˌtin 'hat; 'tin ˌopener; ˌtin pan 'alley; ˌtin 'whistle
Tina 'tiːn ə
Tinbergen 'tɪn ˌbɜːg ən →'tɪm- ‖ -ˌbɝːg- —*Dutch* ['tɪn bɛr xə]
tinctorial tɪŋk 'tɔːr i_əl ‖ -'toʊr-
tincture 'tɪŋk tʃə -ʃə ‖ -tʃᵊr ~d d **tincturing** 'tɪŋk tʃər ɪŋ -ʃər_ ~s z
Tindal 'tɪnd ᵊl
Tindale 'tɪnd ᵊl -eɪᵊl
Tindall 'tɪnd ᵊl -ɔːl
Tindell 'tɪnd ᵊl 'tɪn del
tinder 'tɪnd ə ‖ -ᵊr
tinderbox 'tɪnd ə bɒks ‖ -ᵊr bɑːks ~es ɪz əz
tine taɪn **tines** taɪnz
tinea 'tɪn i_ə
tinfoil 'tɪn fɔɪᵊl
ting, Ting *tdmk* tɪŋ **tinged** tɪŋd **tinging** 'tɪŋ ɪŋ **tings** tɪŋz
tingaling ˌtɪŋ ə 'lɪŋ ~s z
tinge tɪndʒ **tinged** tɪndʒd **tinges** 'tɪndʒ ɪz -əz **tingeing, tinging** 'tɪndʒ ɪŋ
tinged *past & pp of* **ting** tɪŋd
tinged *past & pp of* **tinge** tɪndʒd
Tingewick 'tɪndʒ wɪk
tingl|e, T~ 'tɪŋ gᵊl ~ed d ~es z ~ing _ɪŋ ~y _i
tingly 'tɪŋ gli **tinglier** 'tɪŋ gli_ə ‖ _ᵊr **tingliest** 'tɪŋ gli_ɪst _əst
Tingwall 'tɪŋ wəl
tinhorn 'tɪn hɔːn ‖ -hɔːrn ~s z
tini... —*see* **tiny**
tinker, T~ 'tɪŋk ə ‖ -ᵊr ~ed d **tinkering** 'tɪŋk ᵊr_ɪŋ ~s z
Tinkerbell 'tɪŋk ə bel ‖ -ᵊr-
Tinkertoy *tdmk* 'tɪŋk ə tɔɪ ‖ -ᵊr-
tinkl|e 'tɪŋk ᵊl ~ed d ~es z ~ing _ɪŋ
Tinky-Winky ˌtɪŋk i 'wɪŋk i
tinn... —*see* **tin**
Tinney 'tɪn i
tinnitus tɪ 'naɪt əs tə-; 'tɪn ɪt əs, -ət- ‖ tə 'naɪt əs 'tɪn əṭ əs
tinny 'tɪn i **tinnier** 'tɪn i_ə ‖ _ᵊr **tinnies** 'tɪn iz **tinniest** 'tɪn i_ɪst _əst **tinnily** 'tɪn ɪ li -ᵊl i **tinniness** 'tɪn i nəs -nɪs
tinplate 'tɪn pleɪt →'tɪm-
tinpot, tin-pot 'tɪn pɒt →'tɪm- ‖ -pɑːt

tinsel 'tɪnᵗs ᵊl ~ed, ~led d ~ing, ~ling ɪŋ ~s
z
tinselly 'tɪnᵗs ᵊl i
Tinseltown 'tɪnᵗs ᵊl taʊn
Tinsley 'tɪnz li
tinsmith 'tɪn smɪθ ~s s
tint tɪnt tinted 'tɪnt ɪd -əd ‖ 'tɪnt̬ əd tinting
'tɪnt ɪŋ ‖ 'tɪnt̬ ɪŋ tints tɪnts
tintack 'tɪn tæk ~s s
Tintagel tɪn 'tædʒ əl
tinter 'tɪnt ə ‖ 'tɪnt̬ ər ~s z
Tintern 'tɪnt ən ‖ -ᵊrn
Tintin 'tɪn tɪn
tintinnabulation ˌtɪn tɪ ˌnæb jʊ 'leɪʃ ᵊn ˌ•tə-
‖ -ˌ•jə- ~s z
Tintoretto ˌtɪnt ə 'ret əʊ ‖ ˌtɪn tə 'ret̬ oʊ —It
[tin to 'ret to] ~s z
tiny 'taɪn i tinier 'taɪn i‿ə ‖ ᵊr tiniest
'taɪn i‿ɪst əst
-tion stress-imposing ʃᵊn — solution sə 'luːʃ ᵊn
-'ljuːʃ-
Tio Pepe tdmk ˌtiː əʊ 'pep eɪ -i ‖ -oʊ-
-tious stress-imposing ʃəs — fictitious
fɪk 'tɪʃ əs
tip tɪp tipped tɪpt tipping 'tɪp ɪŋ tips tɪps
tip-and-run ˌtɪp ən 'rʌn →-m-
tipcat 'tɪp kæt
tip-off 'tɪp ɒf -ɔːf ‖ -ɔːf -ɑːf ~s s
Tippecanoe ˌtɪp i kə 'nuː ˌ•ə-
tipper 'tɪp ə ‖ -ᵊr ~s z
'tipper truck
Tipperary ˌtɪp ə 'reər i ‖ -'rer i -'rær i
tippet, T~, Tippett 'tɪp ɪt §-ət ~s s
Tippex, Tipp-Ex tdmk 'tɪp eks ~ed t ~es ɪz əz
~ing ɪŋ
tippl|e 'tɪp ᵊl ~ed d ~es z ~ing ɪŋ
tippler 'tɪp ᵊl‿ə ‖ ‿ər ~s z
tipstaff 'tɪp stɑːf §-stæf ‖ -stæf ~s s
tipstaves 'tɪp steɪvz
tipster 'tɪp stə ‖ -stᵊr ~s z
tips|y 'tɪps li ~ier i‿ə ‖ i‿ər ~iest i‿ɪst i‿əst
~ily ɪ li əl i ~iness i nəs i nɪs
tiptoe 'tɪp təʊ ‖ -toʊ ~d d ~ing ɪŋ ~s z
Tipton 'tɪpt ən
tip-top ˌtɪp 'tɒp ◄ ‖ -'tɑːp ◄
Tiptree 'tɪp triː
tip-up 'tɪp ʌp
tirade ₍ₒ₎taɪᵊ 'reɪd tə-, tɪ- ‖ 'taɪᵊr eɪd ~s z
tiramisu ˌtɪr əm ɪ 'suː ‖ -ə 'miː suː —It tiramisù
[ti ra mi 'su]
Tirana tɪ 'rɑːn ə —Albanian Tiranë [ti 'ra nə]
tire 'taɪᵊ ‖ 'taɪᵊr tired 'taɪᵊd ‖ 'taɪᵊrd tires
'taɪᵊz ‖ 'taɪᵊrz tiring 'taɪᵊr ɪŋ ‖ 'taɪᵊr ɪŋ
tired 'taɪᵊd ‖ 'taɪᵊrd ~ly li ~ness nəs nɪs
Tiree ₍ₒ₎taɪᵊ 'riː
tireless 'taɪᵊ ləs -lɪs ‖ 'taɪᵊr ləs ~ly li ~ness
nəs nɪs
Tiresias taɪᵊ 'riːs i æs -'res-, -əs
tiresome 'taɪᵊ səm ‖ 'taɪᵊr səm ~ly li ~ness
nəs nɪs
tiro 'taɪᵊr əʊ ‖ -oʊ ~s z
Tirol tɪ 'rəʊl tə-, →-'rɒʊl; 'tɪr əl, -əʊl ‖ -'roʊl
—Ger [ti 'ʁoːl]

Tirolean ˌtɪr əʊ 'liː‿ən ◄ tɪ 'rəʊl i‿ən, tə- ‖ -ə-
~s z
Tirolese ˌtɪr əʊ 'liːz ◄ ‖ -ə- -'liːs
Tirpitz 'tɜːp ɪts §-əts ‖ 'tɜːp- —Ger ['tɪʁ pɪts]
'tis tɪz
tisane tɪ 'zæn tiː- ‖ -'zɑːn ~s z
Tishbite 'tɪʃ baɪt ~s s
Tisiphone taɪ 'sɪf ən i tɪ-
Tissot 'tiːs əʊ ‖ tiː 'soʊ —Fr [ti so] ~s z
tissue 'tɪʃ u: 'tɪs juː, 'tɪʃ juː ~s z
'tissue ˌculture; 'tissue ˌpaper
tit tɪt tits tɪts
ˌtit for 'tat
titan, Titan 'taɪt ᵊn ~s z
titanate 'taɪt ə neɪt -ᵊn eɪt ‖ -ᵊn eɪt
Titania, t~ tɪ 'tɑːn i‿ə taɪ-, -'teɪn- ‖ -'teɪn-
titanic, T~ taɪ 'tæn ɪk ~ally ᵊl‿i
titanium taɪ 'teɪn i‿əm tɪ-
titbit 'tɪt bɪt ~s s
titch tɪtʃ titches 'tɪtʃ ɪz -əz
titch|y 'tɪtʃ li ~ier i‿ə ‖ i‿ᵊr ~iest i‿ɪst i‿əst
~iness i nəs i nɪs
titer 'tiːt ə 'taɪt- ‖ 'taɪt̬ ᵊr 'tiːt̬ ᵊr ~s z
titfer 'tɪt fə ‖ -fᵊr ~s z
tithe taɪð tithed taɪðd tithes taɪðz tithing/s
'taɪð ɪŋ/z
Tithonus tɪ 'θəʊn əs taɪ- ‖ -'θoʊn-
titi tree 'tiː tiː 'taɪ taɪ ~s z
titi monkey tɪ 'tiː 'tiː tiː ~s z
Titian, t~ 'tɪʃ ᵊn 'tɪʃ i‿ən ~s z
Titicaca ˌtɪt ɪ 'kɑːk ə -'kɑː kɑː —Sp
[ti ti 'ka ka]
titill|ate 'tɪt ɪ lleɪt -ə-, -ᵊl eɪt ‖ 'tɪt̬ ᵊl eɪt
~ated eɪt ɪd -əd ‖ eɪt̬ əd ~ates eɪts ~ating
eɪt ɪŋ ‖ eɪt̬ ɪŋ
titillation ˌtɪt ɪ 'leɪʃ ᵊn -ə-, ˌtɪt ᵊl 'eɪʃ-
‖ ˌtɪt̬ ᵊl 'eɪʃ ᵊn ~s z
titi|vate 'tɪt ɪ |veɪt -ə- ‖ 'tɪt̬- ~vated veɪt ɪd
-əd ‖ veɪt̬ əd ~vates veɪts ~vating
veɪt ɪŋ ‖ veɪt̬ ɪŋ
titivation ˌtɪt ɪ 'veɪʃ ᵊn -ə- ‖ ˌtɪt̬- ~s z
titlark 'tɪt lɑːk ‖ -lɑːrk ~s s
titl|e 'taɪt ᵊl ‖ 'taɪt̬ ᵊl ~ed d ~es z ~ing ɪŋ
'title ˌdeed,ˌ • • ' •; 'title ˌpage; 'title
ˌrole,ˌ • • ' •
titleholder 'taɪt ᵊl ˌhəʊld ə →-ˌhɒʊld-
‖ 'taɪt̬ ᵊl ˌhoʊld ᵊr ~s z
Titmarsh 'tɪt mɑːʃ ‖ -mɑːrʃ
tit|mouse 'tɪt |maʊs ~mice maɪs
Titmus 'tɪt məs
Tito 'tiːt əʊ ‖ -oʊ ~ism ˌɪz əm
titrant 'taɪtr ənt ~s s
titr|ate taɪ 'treɪt tɪ-; 'taɪtr eɪt ‖ 'taɪtr eɪt
~ated eɪt ɪd -əd ‖ eɪt̬ əd ~ates eɪts ~ating
eɪt ɪŋ ‖ eɪt̬ ɪŋ
titration taɪ 'treɪʃ ᵊn tɪ- ~s z
titre 'tiːt ə 'taɪt- ‖ 'taɪt̬ ᵊr 'tiːt̬ ᵊr ~s z
Tittensor 'tɪt ᵊn sə -sɔː ‖ -sᵊr -sɔːr
titter 'tɪt ə ‖ 'tɪt̬ ᵊr ~ed d tittering 'tɪt ᵊr ɪŋ
‖ 'tɪt̬ ᵊr ɪŋ ~s z
tittiv... —see titiv...
tittle 'tɪt ᵊl ‖ 'tɪt̬ ᵊl ~s z

tittle-tattl|e *n, v* 'tɪt ³l ˌtæt ³l ˌ•• • •
‖ 'tɪt̬ ³l ˌtæt̬ ³l **~ed** d **~es** z **~ing** ˌɪŋ
tittup 'tɪt əp ‖ 'tɪt̬ əp **~ed, ~ped** t **~ing,**
~ping ɪŋ **~s** s
titt|y 'tɪt i ‖ 'tɪt̬ i **~ies** iz
titubation ˌtɪt ju 'beɪʃ ³n §ˌtɪtʃ ə- ‖ ˌtɪtʃ ə-
titular 'tɪtʃ ʊl ə §-³l-; 'tɪt jʊl ə, -jəl-
‖ 'tɪtʃ ³l_ər **~ly** li **~s** z
titular|y 'tɪtʃ ʊl ər li §'•³l-; 'tɪt jʊl-, '•jəl-
‖ 'tɪtʃ ə ler li **~ies** iz
Titus 'taɪt əs ‖ 'taɪt̬ əs
Tiv tɪv
Tiverton 'tɪv ət ³n ‖ -³rt ³n
Tivoli 'tɪv əl i —*It* ['ti: vo li]
Tivy 'taɪv i
Tizard *(i)* 'tɪz ɑːd ‖ -ɑːrd, *(ii)* -əd ‖ -³rd
Tizer *tdmk* 'taɪz ə ‖ -³r
tiz, tizz tɪz
tizzwazz, tizzwoz 'tɪz wɒz ‖ -wɑːz
tizz|y 'tɪz i **~ies** iz
T-junction 'tiː ˌdʒʌŋk ʃ³n **~s** z
TLC ˌtiː el 'siː
Tlingit 'tlɪŋ gɪt -kɪt, §-gət **~s** s
T-lymphocyte 'tiː ˌlɪmᵖf ə saɪt **~s** s
tmesis 'tmiːs ɪs 'miːs-, §-əs; tə 'miːs-
TNT ˌtiː en 'tiː
to *strong form* tuː, *weak forms* tu, tə —*The BrE-*
oriented EFL learner is advised to use tə *before*
a consonant sound, tu *before a vowel sound.*
Native speakers, however, sometimes ignore this
distribution, in particular by using tə *before a*
vowel (usually reinforced by a preceding [ʔ] —
see HARD ATTACK) *or, in very formal speech,*
by using tu *even before a consonant. In AmE*
the weak form tə *is used before both consonants*
and vowels. In got to, ought to, used to, want to,
one t *may be elided.*
toad təʊd ‖ toʊd **toads** təʊdz ‖ toʊdz
toadflax 'təʊd flæks ‖ 'toʊd- **~es** ɪz əz
toad-in-the-hole ˌtəʊd ɪn ðə 'həʊl ˌ•³n-,
→ˌ•-'hɒʊl ‖ ˌtoʊd ³n ðə 'hoʊl
toadstool 'təʊd stuːl ‖ 'toʊd- **~s** z
toad|y 'təʊd i ‖ 'toʊd i **~ied** id **~ies** iz **~ying**
i ɪŋ
to-and-fro ˌtuː_ən 'frəʊ ‖ -'froʊ
toast təʊst ‖ toʊst **toasted** 'təʊst ɪd -əd
‖ 'toʊst əd **toasting** 'təʊst ɪŋ ‖ 'toʊst ɪŋ
toasts təʊsts ‖ toʊsts
'**toasting fork**; '**toast rack**
toaster 'təʊst ə ‖ 'toʊst ³r **~s** z
toastmaster 'təʊst ˌmɑːst ə §-ˌmæst-
‖ 'toʊst ˌmæst ³r **~s** z
tobacco tə 'bæk əʊ ‖ -oʊ **~es, ~s** z
tobacconist tə 'bæk ³n ɪst §-əst **~s** s
Tobago tə 'beɪg əʊ ‖ -oʊ
Tobagonian ˌtəʊb ə 'gəʊn i_ən
‖ ˌtoʊb ə 'goʊn- **~s** z
-to-be tə 'biː tu- — **mother-to-be**
ˌmʌð ə tə 'biː -'tu'• ‖ -ˌ•³r-
Tobermory ˌtəʊb ə 'mɔːr i ‖ ˌtoʊb ³r-
Tobey 'təʊb i ‖ 'toʊb i
ToBI 'təʊb i ‖ 'toʊb i
Tobias tə 'baɪ_əs

Tobin 'təʊb ɪn §-ən ‖ 'toʊb-
Tobit 'təʊb ɪt §-ət ‖ 'toʊb-
Toblerone *tdmk* ˌtəʊb lə 'rəʊn '•••
‖ ˌtoʊb lə 'roʊn
toboggan tə 'bɒg ³n ‖ -'bɑːg- **~ed** d **~er/s**
ə/z ‖ ³r/z **~ing** ɪŋ **~ist/s** ɪst/s §əst/s ‖ əst/s
~s z
Tobruk tə 'brʊk
Tob|y, tob|y 'təʊb |i ‖ 'toʊb |i **~ies, ~y's** iz
'**toby jug**
toccata tə 'kɑːt ə tɒ- ‖ -'kɑːt̬ ə —*It*
[tok 'ka: ta] **~s** z
Toc H ˌtɒk 'eɪtʃ §-'heɪtʃ ‖ ˌtɑːk-
Tocharian tɒ 'kɑːr i_ən tə-, -'keər-
‖ toʊ 'ker i_ən -'kær- **~s** z
tocopherol tɒ 'kɒf ə rɒl tə- ‖ toʊ 'kɑːf ə rɔːl
-rɑːl, -roʊl
Tocqueville 'tɒk vɪl 'təʊk- ‖ 'toʊk- —*Fr*
[tɔk vil]
tocsin 'tɒks ɪn §-ən ‖ 'tɑːks ən (= *toxin*) **~s** z
tod, Tod tɒd ‖ tɑːd
today tə 'deɪ tu- ~'**s** z
Todd tɒd ‖ tɑːd
toddl|e 'tɒd ³l ‖ 'tɑːd ³l **~ed** d **~es** z **~ing** ɪŋ
toddler 'tɒd ³l_ə ‖ 'tɑːd ³l_ər **~s** z
todd|y 'tɒd i ‖ 'tɑːd i **~ies** iz
todger 'tɒdʒ ə ‖ 'tɑːdʒ ³r **~s** z
Todhunter 'tɒd ˌhʌnt ə ‖ 'tɑːd ˌhʌnt̬ ³r
Todman 'tɒd mən→'tɒb- ‖ 'tɑːd-
Todmorden 'tɒd məd ³n -mɔːd-
‖ 'tɑːd mɔːrd ³n
to-do tə 'duː tu- **~s** z
tody 'təʊd i ‖ 'toʊd i **~ies** iz
toe təʊ ‖ toʊ **toed** təʊd ‖ toʊd **toeing**
'təʊ ɪŋ ‖ 'toʊ ɪŋ **toes** təʊz ‖ toʊz
'**toe cap**
toehold 'təʊ həʊld→-hɒʊld ‖ 'toʊ hoʊld **~s** z
toe-in 'təʊ ɪn ‖ 'toʊ- **~s** z
toenail 'təʊ neɪ³l ‖ 'toʊ- **~s** z
toerag 'təʊ ræg ‖ 'toʊ- **~s** z
toff tɒf ‖ tɑːf **toffs** tɒfs ‖ tɑːfs
toffee 'tɒf i ‖ 'tɑːf i 'tɔːf- **~s** z
'**toffee ˌapple**, ˌ• • '••
toffee-nosed 'tɒf i nəʊzd ˌ•• '•
‖ ˌtɑːf i 'noʊzd ◄ ˌtɔːf-
toff|y 'tɒf i ‖ 'tɑːf i 'tɔːf- **~ies** iz
Toft, toft tɒft ‖ tɑːft tɔːft
Tofts tɒfts ‖ tɑːfts tɔːfts
tofu 'təʊf uː ‖ 'toʊf uː —*Jp* [to,o 'ɸɯ]
tog tɒg ‖ tɑːg tɔːg **togs** tɒgz ‖ tɑːgz tɔːgz
toga 'təʊg ə ‖ 'toʊg ə **~ed** d **~s** z
together tə 'geð ə tu- ‖ -³r **~ness** nəs nɪs
toggl|e 'tɒg ³l ‖ 'tɑːg ³l **~ed** d **~es** z **~ing** ɪŋ
Togo 'təʊg əʊ ‖ 'toʊg oʊ **~land** lænd
Togolese ˌtəʊg əʊ 'liːz ◄ ‖ ˌtoʊg ə- -oʊ-, -'liːs
toil tɔɪ³l **toiled** tɔɪ³ld **toiling** 'tɔɪ³l ɪŋ **toils**
tɔɪ³lz
toile twɑːl
toiler 'tɔɪ³l ə ‖ -³r **~s** z
toil|et 'tɔɪl ət -ɪt ‖ -lət **~eted** ɪt ɪd §ət-, -əd
‖ ət̬ əd **~eting** ɪt ɪŋ §ət- ‖ ət̬ ɪŋ **~ets** ɪts
§əts ‖ əts

'toilet ,paper; 'toilet roll; 'toilet ,training; 'toilet ,water

toiletr|y 'tɔɪl ətr |i -ɪtr- **~ies** iz

toilette twɑː 'let —*Fr* [twa lɛt]

toilet-trained 'tɔɪl ət traɪnd -ɪt-

toilsome 'tɔɪᵊl səm **~ly** li **~ness** nəs nɪs

toilworn 'tɔɪᵊl wɔːn ‖ -wɔːrn -woʊrn

to-ing and fro-ing
,tuː_ɪŋ ən 'frəʊ ɪŋ ‖ -'froʊ ɪŋ **to-ings and fro-ings** ,tuː_ɪŋz ən 'frəʊ ɪŋz ‖ -'froʊ ɪŋz

tokamak 'təʊk ə mæk 'tɒk- ‖ 'toʊk- 'tɑːk- **~s** s

Tokay, tokay təʊ 'keɪ tɒ-, -'kaɪ, '•• ‖ toʊ- —*Hung* ['to kɒj] **~s** z

toke təʊk ‖ toʊk **tokes** təʊks ‖ toʊks

Tokelau 'təʊk ə laʊ 'tɒk- ‖ 'toʊk-

token 'təʊk ᵊn ‖ 'toʊk ᵊn **~ed** d **~ing** _ɪŋ **~ism** ,ɪz ᵊm **~s** z

Tokharian tɒ 'kɑːr i_ən tə-, -'keər- ‖ toʊ 'ker i_ən -'kær- **~s** z

Toklas 'tɒk ləs 'təʊk- ‖ 'toʊk-

Tok Pisin ,tɒk 'pɪz ɪn §-ᵊn ‖ ,tɑːk- ,tɔːk-

Tokyo 'təʊk i_əʊ ‖ 'toʊk i_oʊ —*Jp* [to,o kjoo]

tola 'təʊl ə ‖ 'toʊl ə **~s** z

tolbutamide tɒl 'bjuːt ə maɪd ‖ tɑːl 'bjuːt̬-

told təʊld →tɒʊld ‖ toʊld

tole təʊl →tɒʊl ‖ toʊl —*Fr* tôle [toːl]

Toledo (i) tə 'liːd əʊ ‖ -oʊ, (ii) tɒ 'leɪd əʊ tə- ‖ toʊ 'leɪd oʊ —*The place in OH is (i), as is the trade name for a car. The place in Spain is usually (ii) in BrE.* —*Sp* [to 'le ðo]

tolerab|le 'tɒl ər_əb |ᵊl ‖ 'tɑːl- **~leness** ᵊl nəs -nɪs **~ly** li

toleranc|e 'tɒl ər ənts -ᵊr_ənts ‖ 'tɑːl- **~es** ɪz əz

tolerant 'tɒl ər ənt -ᵊr_ənt ‖ 'tɑːl- **~ly** li

tole|rate 'tɒl ə |reɪt ‖ 'tɑːl- **~rated** reɪt ɪd -əd ‖ reɪt̬ əd **~rates** reɪts **~rating** reɪt ɪŋ ‖ reɪt̬ ɪŋ

toleration ,tɒl ə 'reɪʃ ᵊn ‖ ,tɑːl-

Tolkien 'tɒl kiːn ‖ 'toʊl- 'tɑːl-

toll təʊl →tɒʊl, §tɒl ‖ toʊl **tolled** təʊld →tɒʊld, §tɒld ‖ toʊld (*usually = told*) **tolling** 'təʊl ɪŋ →'tɒʊl-, §'tɒl- ‖ 'toʊl ɪŋ **tolls** təʊlz →tɒʊlz, §tɒlz ‖ toʊlz
'toll bridge

toll|booth 'təʊl |buːð →'tɒʊl-, 'tɒl-, -buːθ ‖ 'toʊl |buːθ **~booths** buːðz buːθs ‖ buːðz buːθs

Tollemache 'tɒl mæʃ -mɑːʃ ‖ 'tɑːl-

Tolleshunt 'təʊlz hʌnt →'tɒʊlz- ‖ 'toʊlz- ,Tolleshunt 'd'Arcy 'dɑːs i ‖ 'dɑːrs i

toll-free ,təʊl 'friː ◄ →,tɒʊl- ‖ ,toʊl-

tollgate 'təʊl geɪt →'tɒʊl-, §'tɒl- ‖ 'toʊl- **~s** s

toll|house 'təʊl |haʊs →'tɒʊl-, §'tɒl- ‖ 'toʊl- **~houses** haʊz ɪz -əz

Tolman 'təʊl mən →'tɒʊl- ‖ 'toʊl-

Tolpuddle 'tɒl ,pʌd ᵊl ‖ 'tɑːl- —*locally also* -,pɪd-

Tolstoy 'tɒl stɔɪ ‖ 'toʊl- 'tɑːl-, ,•'• —*Russ* [tʌɫ 'stɔj]

Toltec 'tɒl tek ‖ 'toʊl- 'tɑːl-

tolu tɒ 'luː təʊ-, -'ljuː ‖ tɔː 'luː tɑː-, tə-

toluene 'tɒl ju iːn ‖ 'tɑːl-

toluic tɒ 'ljuː ɪk təʊ-, -'luː- ‖ tə 'luː ɪk

Tolworth 'tɒl wəθ 'təʊl-, -wɜːθ ‖ 'tɑːl wɜ˞θ

Tom, tom tɒm ‖ tɑːm **toms, Tom's** tɒmz ‖ tɑːmz
,Tom 'Collins; ,Tom, ,Dick, and 'Harry; ,Tom 'Thumb

tomahawk 'tɒm ə hɔːk ‖ 'tɑːm- -hɑːk **~s** s

Tomalin 'tɒm əl ɪn §-ən ‖ 'tɑːm-

tomato tə 'mɑːt əʊ ‖ tə 'meɪt̬ oʊ (*) **~es** z

tomb tuːm (!) **tombs** tuːmz

tombac 'tɒm bæk ‖ 'tɑːm-

tombola tɒm 'bəʊl ə 'tɒm bəl ə ‖ tɑːm 'boʊl ə

tomboy 'tɒm bɔɪ ‖ 'tɑːm- **~s** z

Tombs tuːmz

tombstone, T~ 'tuːm stəʊn ‖ -stoʊn **~s** z

tomcat 'tɒm kæt ‖ 'tɑːm- **~s** s

tome təʊm ‖ toʊm **tomes** təʊmz ‖ toʊmz

-tome təʊm ‖ toʊm — **microtome** 'maɪk rəʊ təʊm ‖ -rə toʊm

tomentose tə 'ment əʊs -əʊz; 'təʊm ən təʊs ‖ toʊ 'ment oʊs 'toʊm ən toʊs

tomfool ,tɒm 'fuːl ◄ ‖ ,tɑːm-

tomfooler|y (i)tɒm 'fuːl ər |i ‖ ,tɑːm- **~ies** iz

-tomical 'tɒm ɪk ᵊl ‖ 'tɑːm- — **anatomical** ,æn ə 'tɒm ɪk ᵊl ◄ ‖ -'tɑːm-

Tomintoul ,tɒm ɪn 'taʊl -ən- ‖ ,tɑːm-

Tomkins 'tɒmᵖ kɪnz ‖ 'tɑːmᵖ-

Tomlin 'tɒm lɪn §-lən ‖ 'tɑːm-

Tomlinson 'tɒm lɪn sᵊn §-lən- ‖ 'tɑːm-

Tommie, Tommy, tommie, tommy 'tɒm i ‖ 'tɑːm i **tommies, Tommy's** 'tɒm iz ‖ 'tɑːm iz
'tommy gun

tommyrot 'tɒm i rɒt ‖ 'tɑːm i rɑːt

tomogram 'təʊm ə græm 'tɒm- ‖ 'toʊm- **~s** z

tomography təʊ 'mɒg rəf i ‖ toʊ 'mɑːg-

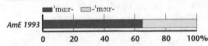

TOMORROW

	-'mɑːr-	-'mɔːr-			
AmE 1993					
0	20	40	60	80	100%

tomorrow tə 'mɒr əʊ tu- ‖ tə 'mɑːr oʊ -'mɔːr- —*In* ~ morning, ~ night *also* -ə, -u; *in* ~ afternoon, ~ evening *also* -u —*AmE 1993 poll panel preference:* -'mɑːr- 65%, -'mɔːr- 35%. **~s, ~'s** z
to,morrow ,after'noon; to,morrow 'evening; to,morrow 'morning; to,morrow 'night

Tompion 'tɒmp i_ən ‖ 'tɑːmp-

Tomp|kin 'tɒmᵖ| kɪn ‖ 'tɑːmᵖ|- **~kins** kɪnz **~kinson** kɪn sᵊn

Toms tɒmz ‖ tɑːmz

Tomsk tɒmᵖk ‖ tɔːmᵖsk tɑːmᵖsk —*Russ* [tɔmsk]

tomtit 'tɒm tɪt ,•'• ‖ 'tɑːm- **~s** s

tom-tom 'tɒm tɒm ‖ 'tɑːm tɑːm **~s** z

-tomy *stress-imposing* təm i — **anatomy** ə 'næt əm i ‖ -'næt̬-

ton *'unit of weight, displacement, or speed'* tʌn (*= tun*) **tons** tʌnz

ton *French word 'style'* tɒ̃ ‖ tɔːn toʊn —*Fr* [tɔ̃]

tonal 'təʊn ᵊl ‖ 'toʊn ᵊl **~ly** i

tonalit|y təʊ 'næl ət |i -ɪt i ‖ toʊ 'næl əṭ |i ~**ies**
ɪz

Tonbridge 'tʌn brɪdʒ →'tʌm-

Ton-du *place in MidGlam* ˌtɒn 'diː ‖ ˌtɔːn-

tone, Tone təʊn ‖ toʊn **toned** təʊnd ‖ toʊnd
tones təʊnz ‖ toʊnz **toning**
'təʊn ɪŋ ‖ 'toʊn ɪŋ

'**tone** ˌlanguage; '**tone** ˌpoem

tone-deaf ˌtəʊn 'def ◄ ‖ 'toʊn def ~**ness** nəs
nɪs

toneless 'təʊn ləs -lɪs ‖ 'toʊn- ~**ly** li ~**ness**
nəs nɪs

tonematic ˌtəʊn ɪ 'mæt ɪk ◄ -iː-, -ə-
‖ ˌtoʊn ə 'mæṭ ɪk ◄

toneme 'təʊn iːm ‖ 'toʊn- ~**s** z

tonemic təʊ 'niːm ɪk ‖ toʊ- ~**ally** ᵊl_i ~**s** s

toner 'təʊn ə ‖ 'toʊn ᵊr ~**s** z

tonetic təʊ 'net ɪk ‖ toʊ 'neṭ ɪk ~**ally** ᵊl_i ~**s** s

ton|ey 'təʊn| i ‖ 'toʊn| i ~**ier** i_ə ‖ i_ᵊr ~**iest**
i_ɪst i_əst

Tonfanau tɒn 'væn aɪ ‖ tɑːn- —*Welsh*
[ton 'va nai, -nai, -ne, -na]

tong, Tong tɒŋ ‖ tɑːŋ tɔːŋ **tongs** tɒŋz ‖ tɑːŋz
tɔːŋz

tonga 'tɒŋ gə ‖ 'tɑːŋ- ~**s** z

Tonga *place in Polynesia* 'tɒŋ ə -gə ‖ 'tɑːŋ-

Tonga *African people and language*
'tɒŋ gə ‖ 'tɑːŋ-

Tongan 'tɒŋ ən -gən ‖ 'tɑːŋ- ~**s** z

Tonge *surname (i)* tɒŋ ‖ tɑːŋ, *(ii)*
tɒndʒ ‖ tɑːndʒ, *(iii)* tʌŋ

Tonge *placename* tɒŋ ‖ tɑːŋ

tongs tɒŋz ‖ tɑːŋz tɔːŋz

tongue, T~ tʌŋ §tɒŋ **tongued** tʌŋd §tɒŋd
tongues tʌŋz §tɒŋz **tonguing** 'tʌŋ ɪŋ
§'tɒŋ-

'**tongue** ˌtwister

tongue-tied 'tʌŋ taɪd §'tɒŋ-

Toni 'təʊn i ‖ 'toʊn i

Tonia 'təʊn i_ə ‖ 'toʊn i_ə

Tonibell *tdmk* 'təʊn i bel ‖ 'toʊn-

tonic 'tɒn ɪk ‖ 'tɑːn ɪk ~**s** s

ˌtonic ˌsol-'fa; 'tonic ˌwater

tonicit|y təʊ 'nɪs ət |i tɒ-, -ɪt i ‖ toʊ 'nɪs əṭ |i
~**ies** ɪz

tonight tə 'naɪt tu- ~'**s** s

tonite *n 'explosive'* 'təʊn aɪt ‖ 'toʊn-

tonite *'tonight'* tə 'naɪt

tonka, Tonka 'tɒŋk ə ‖ 'tɑːŋk ə

'**tonka** bean

Tonkin *part of Vietnam* ˌtɒn 'kɪn →ˌtɒŋ-
‖ ˌtɑːn- →ˌtɑːŋ-

Tonkin *family name* 'tɒŋk ɪn §-ən ‖ 'tɑːŋk-

Tonks tɒŋks ‖ tɑːŋks

tonnag|e 'tʌn ɪdʒ ~**es** ɪz əz

tonne tʌn tɒn **tonnes** tʌnz tɒnz

tonneau 'tɒn əʊ ‖ tə 'noʊ 'tɑːn oʊ ~**s, ~x** z

tonogenesis ˌtəʊn əʊ 'dʒen əs ɪs -ɪs ɪs, §-əs
‖ ˌtoʊn oʊ-

tonology təʊ 'nɒl ədʒ i ‖ toʊ 'nɑːl-

tonsil 'tɒnᵗs ᵊl -ɪl ‖ 'tɑːnᵗs ᵊl ~**s** z

tonsillectom|y ˌtɒnᵗs ə 'lekt əm |i ˌ•ɪ-
‖ ˌtɑːnᵗs- ~**ies** ɪz

tonsillitis ˌtɒnᵗs ə 'laɪt ɪs -ɪ-, §-əs
‖ ˌtɑːnᵗs ə 'laɪṭ əs

tonsorial tɒn 'sɔːr i_əl ‖ tɑːn- -'soʊr-

tonsure 'tɒnᵗʃ ə 'tɒnᵗs jʊə ‖ 'tɑːnᵗʃ ᵊr ~**d** d

tonsuring 'tɒnᵗʃ ᵊr ɪŋ 'tɒnᵗs jʊər ɪŋ
‖ 'tɑːnᵗʃ ᵊr ɪŋ ~**s** z

tontine 'tɒnt aɪn -iːn; ˌtɒn 'tiːn ‖ 'tɑːnt iːn
tɑːn 'tiːn ~**s** z

Tonto 'tɒnt əʊ ‖ 'tɑːnṭ oʊ

ton-up ˌtʌn 'ʌp ◄

tonus 'təʊn əs ‖ 'toʊn-

Tony 'təʊn i ‖ 'toʊn i **Tonies, Tony's**
'təʊn iz ‖ 'toʊn iz

ton|y 'təʊn| i ‖ 'toʊn| i ~**ier** i_ə ‖ i_ᵊr ~**iest**
i_ɪst i_əst

Tonypandy ˌtɒn ə 'pænd i ˌtəʊn-, -i- ‖ ˌtɑːn-
—*Welsh* [ton ə 'pan di]

Tonyrefail ˌtɒn i 'rev aɪ³l ‖ ˌtɑːn- —*Welsh*
[ton ər 'e vail]

too tuː —*NB this word has no weak form*

toodle-oo ˌtuːd ᵊl 'uː

toodle-pip ˌtuːd ᵊl 'pɪp

Toogood 'tuː gʊd

took tʊk §tuːk

Took, Tooke tʊk §tuːk

tool tuːl **tooled** tuːld **tooling** 'tuːl ɪŋ **tools**
tuːlz

toolbox 'tuːl bɒks ‖ -bɑːks ~**es** ɪz əz

Tooley 'tuːl i

tool-maker 'tuːl ˌmeɪk ə ‖ -ᵊr ~**s** z

toolshed 'tuːl ʃed ~**s** z

toon tuːn **toons** tuːnz

toot *'sound (horn)'; 'spree'* tuːt **tooted** 'tuːt ɪd
-əd ‖ 'tuːṭ əd **tooting** 'tuːt ɪŋ ‖ 'tuːṭ ɪŋ
toots tuːts

toot *'toilet'; 'paper bag'* tʊt **toots** tʊts

Tootal *tdmk* 'tuːt ᵊl ‖ 'tuːṭ ᵊl

tooth, Tooth tuːθ §tʊθ **teeth** tiːθ **toothed**
tuːθt tuːðd, §tʊθt **toothing** 'tuːθ ɪŋ §'tʊθ-
tooths tuːθs §tʊθs

'**tooth** ˌpowder

toothache 'tuːθ eɪk §'tʊθ- ~**s** s

toothbrush 'tuːθ brʌʃ §'tʊθ- ~**es** ɪz əz

toothcomb 'tuːθ kəʊm §'tʊθ- ‖ -koʊm ~**s** z

toothed *adj* tuːθt tuːðd, §tʊθt ‖ 'tuːθ əd

Toothill 'tuːt hɪl

toothless 'tuːθ ləs §'tʊθ-, -lɪs ~**ly** li ~**ness**
nəs nɪs

toothmug 'tuːθ mʌg §'tʊθ- ~**s** z

toothpaste 'tuːθ peɪst §'tʊθ- ~**s** s

toothpick 'tuːθ pɪk §'tʊθ- ~**s** s

toothsome 'tuːθ səm §'tʊθ- ~**ly** li ~**ness** nəs
nɪs

toothwort 'tuːθ wɜːt §'tʊθ-, §-wɔːt ‖ -wɜːt
-wɔːrt ~**s** s

tooth|y 'tuːθ |i §'tʊθ- ~**ier** i_ə ‖ i_ᵊr ~**iest** i_ɪst
i_əst ~**ily** ɪ li ᵊl i ~**iness** i nəs i nɪs

Tooting 'tuːt ɪŋ ‖ 'tuːṭ ɪŋ

tootl|e 'tuːt ᵊl ‖ 'tuːṭ ᵊl ~**ed** d ~**es** z ~**ing** _ɪŋ

toots tuːts tʊts

toots|ie, toots|y 'tʊts i ‖ 'tuːts- ~**ies** ɪz

Toowoomba tə 'wʊm bə tu-

T

top tɒp ‖ tɑːp **topped** tɒpt ‖ tɑːpt **topping**
'tɒp ɪŋ ‖ 'tɑːp ɪŋ **tops** tɒps ‖ tɑːps
ˌtop 'brass; ˌtop 'dog; ˌtop 'drawer; ˌtop
'hat

topaz 'təʊp æz ‖ 'toʊp- **~es** ɪz əz

topcoat 'tɒp kəʊt ‖ 'tɑːp koʊt **~s** s

Topcliff, Topcliffe 'tɒp klɪf ‖ 'tɑːp-

top-down ˌtɒp 'daʊn ◄ ‖ ˌtɑːp-

top-dress ˌtɒp 'dres ' • • ‖ 'tɑːp dres **~ed** t
~es ɪz əz **~ing/s** ɪŋ/z

tope, Tope təʊp ‖ toʊp **toped** təʊpt ‖ toʊpt
topes təʊps ‖ toʊps **toping**
'təʊp ɪŋ ‖ 'toʊp ɪŋ

topee 'təʊp iː -i ‖ 'toʊp iː toʊ 'piː **~s** z

Topeka təʊ 'piːk ə ‖ tə-

top-flight ˌtɒp 'flaɪt ◄ ‖ ˌtɑːp-

topgallant tɒp 'gæl ənt tə- ‖ ˌtɑːp- —*naut* tə-

Topham 'tɒp əm ‖ 'tɑːp-

top-heav|y ˌtɒp 'hev li ◄ ‖ 'tɑːp ˌhev li **~iness**
i nəs i nɪs

Tophet 'təʊf et ‖ 'toʊf-

toph|us 'təʊf ləs ‖ 'toʊf- **~i** aɪ

topi 'təʊp iː -i ‖ 'toʊp iː toʊ 'piː **~s** z

topiar|y 'təʊp i‿ər li ‖ 'toʊp i er li **~ies** iz

topic 'tɒp ɪk ‖ 'tɑːp ɪk **~s** s

topical 'tɒp ɪk əl ‖ 'tɑːp- **~ly** _i

topicalis... —*see* **topicaliz...**

topicality ˌtɒp ɪ 'kæl ət i §, • ə-, -ɪt i
‖ ˌtɑːp ə 'kæl ət̬ i

topicalization ˌtɒp ɪk əl aɪ 'zeɪʃ ən -ɪ' • •
‖ ˌtɑːp ɪk əl ə-

topicaliz|e 'tɒp ɪk ə laɪz -əl aɪz ‖ 'tɑːp- **~ed** d
~es ɪz əz **~ing** ɪŋ

topknot 'tɒp nɒt ‖ 'tɑːp nɑːt **~s** s

Toplady 'tɒp ˌleɪd i ‖ 'tɑːp-

top-level ˌtɒp 'lev əl ◄ ‖ ˌtɑːp-

topless 'tɒp ləs -lɪs ‖ 'tɑːp-

topmast 'tɒp mɑːst -məst, §-mæst
‖ 'tɑːp mæst

topmost 'tɒp məʊst ‖ 'tɑːp moʊst

topnotch ˌtɒp 'nɒtʃ ◄ ‖ ˌtɑːp 'nɑːtʃ ◄

topo 'tɒp əʊ ‖ 'tɑːp oʊ **~s** z

topo- *comb. form*
   with stress-neutral suffix ˌtɒp ə ‖ ˌtɑːp ə—
   toponymic ˌtɒp ə 'nɪm ɪk ◄ ‖ ˌtɑːp-
   with stress-imposing suffix tə 'pɒ+ tɒ-
   ‖ tə 'pɑː+ — **toponymy** tə 'pɒn əm i tɒ-,
   -ɪm i ‖ -'pɑːn-

topographer tə 'pɒg rəf ə tɒ- ‖ tə 'pɑːg rəf ər
~s z

topographical ˌtɒp ə 'græf ɪk əl ◄ ‖ ˌtɑːp- **~ly**
   _i

topograph|y tə 'pɒg rəf li tɒ- ‖ -'pɑːg- **~ies** iz

topological ˌtɒp ə 'lɒdʒ ɪk əl ◄ ‖ ˌtɑːp ə 'lɑːdʒ-
~ly _i

topologist tə 'pɒl ədʒ ɪst tɒ-, §-əst ‖ -'pɑːl- **~s**
   s

topolog|y tə 'pɒl ədʒ li tɒ- ‖ -'pɑːl- **~ies** iz

Topolsky tə 'pɒl ski ‖ -'pɑːl-

toponym 'tɒp ə nɪm ‖ 'tɑːp- **~s** z

toponymy tə 'pɒn əm i tɒ-, -ɪm i ‖ -'pɑːn-

top|os 'tɒp lɒs ‖ 'toʊp lɑːs **~oi** ɔɪ

topper, T~ 'tɒp ə ‖ 'tɑːp ər **~s** z

topping, T~ 'tɒp ɪŋ ‖ 'tɑːp ɪŋ **~s** z

toppl|e 'tɒp əl ‖ 'tɑːp əl **~ed** d **~es** z **~ing** _ɪŋ

topsail 'tɒp seɪəl -səl ‖ 'tɑːp- —*naut* -səl **~s** z

top-secret ˌtɒp 'siːk rət ◄ -rɪt ‖ ˌtɑːp-

Topsham 'tɒps əm 'tɒpʃ- ‖ 'tɑːps-

topside 'tɒp saɪd ‖ 'tɑːp-

Topsider *tdmk* 'tɒp saɪd ə ‖ 'tɑːp saɪd ər **~s** z

topsoil 'tɒp sɔɪəl ‖ 'tɑːp- **~s** z

topspin 'tɒp spɪn ‖ 'tɑːp-

topspinner 'tɒp spɪn ə ‖ -ər **~s** z

Topsy 'tɒps i ‖ 'tɑːps i

topsy-turv|y
   ˌtɒps i 'tɜːv li ◄ ‖ ˌtɑːps i 'tɝːv li ◄ **~idom**
   i dəm **~iness** i nəs i nɪs

top-up *n* 'tɒp ʌp ‖ 'tɑːp- **~s** s

toque təʊk ‖ toʊk (= *toke*) **toques**
   təʊks ‖ toʊks

tor tɔː ‖ tɔːr **tors** tɔːz ‖ tɔːrz

Torah 'tɔːr ə 'təʊ rə; tɔː 'rɑː ‖ 'toʊr- —*Hebrew*
   [tɔ 'ra]

Torbay ˌtɔː 'beɪ ◄ ‖ ˌtɔːr-

torch tɔːtʃ ‖ tɔːrtʃ **torched** tɔːtʃt ‖ tɔːrtʃt
torches 'tɔːtʃ ɪz -əz ‖ 'tɔːrtʃ əz **torching**
'tɔːtʃ ɪŋ ‖ 'tɔːrtʃ ɪŋ

torchlight 'tɔːtʃ laɪt ‖ 'tɔːrtʃ-

Torcross ˌtɔː 'krɒs -'krɔːs ‖ ˌtɔːr 'krɔːs -'krɑːs

Tordoff 'tɔːd ɒf ‖ 'tɔːrd ɑːf

tore tɔː ‖ tɔːr toʊr

toreador 'tɒr i‿ə dɔː ‖ 'tɔːr i‿ə dɔːr **~s** z

torero tɒ 'reər əʊ tə- ‖ tə 'rer oʊ **~s** z

Torfaen ˌtɔː 'vaɪn ‖ ˌtɔːr- —*Welsh* [tɔr 'vain,
   -'vaɪn]

tori 'tɔːr aɪ ‖ 'toʊr-

toric 'tɒr ɪk 'tɔːr- ‖ 'tɔːr ɪk 'tɑːr-, 'toʊr-

Torie... —*see* **Tory**

torii 'tɔːr i iː ‖ 'toʊr- —*Jp* [to ˌɾii]

Torino tɒ 'riːn əʊ ‖ -oʊ —*It* [to 'riː no]

tor|ment *v* ₍ˌ₎tɔː 'ment ‖ ₍ˌ₎tɔːr 'ment ' • •
~mented/ly 'ment ɪd -əd ‖ 'ment̬- **~menting/ly** 'ment ɪŋ /li ‖ 'ment̬- **~ments**
'ment*s*

torment *n* 'tɔː ment ‖ 'tɔːr- **~s** s

tormentil 'tɔːm ən tɪl ‖ 'tɔːrm- **~s** z

tormentor ₍ˌ₎tɔː 'ment ə ‖ ₍ˌ₎tɔːr 'ment̬ ər ' • • •
~s z

torn tɔːn ‖ tɔːrn toʊrn

tornado tɔː 'neɪd əʊ ‖ tɔːr 'neɪd oʊ **~es, ~s** z

toroid 'tɔːr ɔɪd ‖ 'toʊr- **~s** z

toroidal tɔː 'rɔɪd əl ‖ toʊ-

Toronto tə 'rɒnt əʊ ‖ -'rɑːnt̬ oʊ

torpedo tɔː 'piːd əʊ ‖ tɔːr 'piːd oʊ **~es** z
tor'pedo boat

Torpenhow 'tɔːp ən haʊ ‖ 'tɔːrp- —*locally
also* trɪ 'pen ə, trə-

torpid 'tɔːp ɪd §-əd ‖ 'tɔːrp əd **~ly** li **~ness**
nəs nɪs **~s** z

torpidity tɔː 'pɪd ət i -ɪt i ‖ tɔːr 'pɪd ət̬ i

Torpoint ˌtɔː 'pɔɪnt ‖ ˌtɔːr-

torpor 'tɔːp ə ‖ 'tɔːrp ər

Torquay ˌtɔː 'kiː ◄ ‖ ˌtɔːr-

torque tɔːk ‖ tɔːrk **torques** tɔːks ‖ tɔːrks

Torquemada ˌtɔːk wɪ 'mɑːd ə -ɪ-, -wə-
‖ ˌtɔːrk ə- —*Sp* [tor ke 'ma ða]

Torquil 'tɔːk wɪl -wəl ‖ 'tɔːrk-
torr tɔː ‖ tɔːr **torrs** tɔːz ‖ tɔːrz
Torrance 'tɒr ənts ‖ 'tɔːr- 'tɑːr-
torrefaction ˌtɒr ɪ 'fæk ʃən -ə- ‖ ˌtɔːr- ˌtɑːr-
torre|fy 'tɒr ɪ |faɪ -ə- ‖ 'tɔːr- 'tɑːr- **~fied** faɪd
~**fies** faɪz **~fying** faɪ ɪŋ
Torremolinos ˌtɒr ɪm ə 'liːn ɒs ˌ•əm-
‖ ˌtɔːr əm ə 'liːn oʊs —*Sp* [ˌrre mo 'li nos]
Torrens 'tɒr ənz ‖ 'tɔːr ənz 'tɑːr-
torrent 'tɒr ənt ‖ 'tɔːr ənt 'tɑːr- **~s** s
torrential tə 'rentʃ əl tɒ- ‖ tɔː- tə- **~ly** i
Torres 'tɒr ɪs 'tɔːr-, -ɪz, §-əs ‖ 'tɔːr əs
Torrey 'tɒr i ‖ 'tɔːr i 'tɑːr-
torrid 'tɒr ɪd §-əd ‖ 'tɔːr əd 'tɑːr- **~ly** li **~ness**
nəs nɪs
Torrington 'tɒr ɪŋ tən ‖ 'tɔːr- 'tɑːr-
torsion 'tɔːʃ ən ‖ 'tɔːrʃ ən **~al** əl
torso 'tɔːs əʊ ‖ 'tɔːrs oʊ **~s** z
tort tɔːt ‖ tɔːrt **torts** tɔːts ‖ tɔːrts
torte tɔːt ‖ tɔːrt —*Ger* T~ ['tɔʁ tə]
Tortelier tɔː 'tel i eɪ ‖ ˌtɔːrt el 'jeɪ —*Fr*
[tɔʁ tə lje]
tortellini ˌtɔːt ə 'liːn i -əl 'iːn- ‖ ˌtɔːrt əl 'iːn i
—*It* [tor tel 'li: ni]
tort-feasor ˌtɔːt 'fiːz ə ‖ ˌtɔːrt 'fiːz ər **~s** z
torticollis ˌtɔːt ɪ 'kɒl ɪs §-ə-, §-əs
‖ ˌtɔːrt ə 'kɑːl əs
tortilla tɔː 'tiː ə -jə; -'tɪl ə ‖ tɔːr- —*Sp*
[tor 'ti ʎa, -ja] **~s** z
tortious 'tɔːʃ əs ‖ 'tɔːrʃ əs **~ly** li
tortois|e 'tɔːt əs §'tɔː tɔɪs, §-tɔɪz ‖ 'tɔːrt əs
~es ɪz əz
tortoiseshell 'tɔːt əs ʃel→-əʃ-, -ə- ‖ 'tɔːrt-
Tortola tɔː 'təʊl ə ‖ tɔːr 'toʊl ə
Tortuga tɔː 'tuːɡ ə ‖ tɔːr-
tortuosit|y ˌtɔːtʃ u 'ɒs ət i ˌtɔːt ju-, -ɪt i
‖ ˌtɔːrtʃ u 'ɑːs ət̬ li **~ies** iz
tortuous 'tɔːtʃ u_əs 'tɔːt ju_əs ‖ 'tɔːrtʃ u_əs
~ly li **~ness** nəs nɪs
torture *v, n* 'tɔːtʃ ə ‖ 'tɔːrtʃ ər **~d** d **torturing**
'tɔːtʃ ər_ɪŋ ‖ 'tɔːrtʃ ər_ɪŋ **~s** z
torturer 'tɔːtʃ ər_ə ‖ 'tɔːrtʃ ər_ər **~s** z
torturous 'tɔːtʃ ər_əs ‖ 'tɔːrtʃ- **~ly** li
Torun 'tɔːr uːn 'tɒr- —*Pol* Toruń ['tɔ ruɲ]
tor|us 'tɔːr |əs ‖ 'toʊr- **~i** aɪ
Torvill 'tɔː vɪl ‖ 'tɔːr-
Tor|y 'tɔːr li ‖ 'toʊr- **~ies** iz **~yism** i ˌɪz əm
Tosa, tosa 'təʊz ə 'təʊs ə ‖ 'toʊs ə **~s** z—*Jp*
['to sa]
Toscanini ˌtɒsk ə 'niːn i ‖ ˌtɑːsk- —*It*
[to ska 'ni: ni]
tosh, Tosh tɒʃ ‖ tɑːʃ
Toshack 'tɒʃ æk ‖ 'tɑːʃ-
Toshiba *tdmk* tɒ 'ʃiːb ə tə- ‖ tə- toʊ- —*Jp*
[to̞ o̞ ɕi ba]
toss tɒs tɔːs ‖ tɔːs tɑːs **tossed** tɒst tɔːst
‖ tɔːst tɑːst **tosses** 'tɒs ɪz 'tɔːs-, -əz
‖ 'tɔːs əz 'tɑːs- **tossing** 'tɒs ɪŋ 'tɔːs-
‖ 'tɔːs ɪŋ 'tɑːs-
tosspot 'tɒs pɒt ‖ 'tɔːs pɑːt 'tɑːs- **~s** s
toss-up 'tɒs ʌp 'tɔːs- ‖ 'tɔːs- 'tɑːs- **~s** s
tot tɒt ‖ tɑːt **tots** tɒts ‖ tɑːts **totted** 'tɒt ɪd
-əd ‖ 'tɑːt̬ əd **totting** 'tɒt ɪŋ ‖ 'tɑːt̬ ɪŋ

total 'təʊt əl ‖ 'toʊt̬ əl **~ed, ~led** d **~ing, ~ling**
ɪŋ **~s** z
totalis... —*see* **totaliz...**
totalitarian təʊ ˌtæl ɪ 'teər i_ən ◂ ˌtəʊ tæl-,
-ə-'•- ‖ toʊ ˌtæl ə 'ter- ˌtoʊ tæl- **~ism** ˌɪz
əm
totalit|y təʊ 'tæl ət i-ɪt i ‖ toʊ 'tæl ət̬ li **~ies**
iz
totalizator 'təʊt əl aɪ zeɪt ə-ɪ•
‖ 'toʊt̬ əl ə zeɪt̬ ər **~s** z
totaliz|e 'təʊt ə laɪz-əl aɪz ‖ 'toʊt̬ əl aɪz **~ed** d
~er/s ə/z ‖ ər/z **~es** ɪz əz **~ing** ɪŋ
totally 'təʊt əl i ‖ 'toʊt̬ əl i
totaquine 'təʊt ə kwiːn ‖ 'toʊt̬-
tote təʊt ‖ toʊt **toted** 'təʊt ɪd-əd ‖ 'toʊt̬ əd
totes təʊts ‖ toʊts **toting** 'təʊt ɪŋ ‖ 'toʊt̬ ɪŋ
'tote bag
totem 'təʊt əm ‖ 'toʊt̬- **~ism** ˌɪz əm **~s** z
'totem pole
totemic təʊ 'tem ɪk ‖ toʊ-
tother, t'other 'tʌð ə ‖ -ər
Tothill 'tɒt hɪl-ɪl ‖ 'tɑːt-
Totley 'tɒt li ‖ 'tɑːt-
Totnes 'tɒt nɪs-nəs ‖ 'tɑːt-
toto 'təʊt əʊ ‖ 'toʊt oʊ
Totpak *tdmk* 'tɒt pæk ‖ 'tɑːt- **~s** s
tott... —*see* **tot**
Tottenham 'tɒt ən_əm ‖ 'tɑːt-
ˌTottenham ˌCourt 'Road; ˌTottenham
'Hotspur
totter 'tɒt ə ‖ 'tɑːt̬ ər **~ed** d **tottering/ly**
'tɒt ər ɪŋ /li ‖ 'tɑːt̬ ər ɪŋ /li **~s** z
Totteridge 'tɒt ər ɪdʒ ‖ 'tɑːt̬-
tottery 'tɒt ər i ‖ 'tɑːt̬-
tott|ie, tott|y 'tɒt li ‖ 'tɑːt̬ li **~ies** iz
Totton 'tɒt ən ‖ 'tɑːt ən
toucan 'tuːk ən-æn, -ɑːn ‖ -æn -ɑːn; tuː 'kɑːn
~s z
touch tʌtʃ(!) **touched** tʌtʃt **touches** 'tʌtʃ ɪz
-əz **touching/ly** 'tʌtʃ ɪŋ /li
'touch judge
Touch *family name* taʊtʃ
Touch *place in Fife* tuːx
touch-and-go ˌtʌtʃ ən 'ɡəʊ ◂→-əŋ- ‖ -'ɡoʊ ◂
touchdown 'tʌtʃ daʊn **~s** z
touche, touché 'tuːʃ eɪ ‖ tuː 'ʃeɪ
Touche tuːʃ
touchi... —*see* **touchy**
touchline 'tʌtʃ laɪn **~s** z
touch-me-not 'tʌtʃ mi nɒt ‖ -nɑːt **~s** s
touchpad 'tʌtʃ pæd **~s** z
touchpaper 'tʌtʃ ˌpeɪp ə ‖ -ər
touchstone 'tʌtʃ stəʊn ‖ -stoʊn **~s** z
touch-tone 'tʌtʃ təʊn ‖ -toʊn
touch-typ|e 'tʌtʃ taɪp **~ed** t **~es** s **~ing** ɪŋ
ist/s ɪst/s §əst/s
touch-up *n* 'tʌtʃ ʌp **~s** s
touchwood 'tʌtʃ wʊd
touch|y 'tʌtʃ li **~ier** i_ə ‖ i_ər **~iest** i_ɪst i_əst
~ily i lɪ əl i **~iness** i nəs i nɪs
touchy-feel|ie, ~y ˌtʌtʃ i 'fiːəl i ◂ **~ies** iz
tough tʌf(!) (= *tuff*) **tougher** 'tʌf ə ‖ -ər

toughest 'tʌf ɪst -əst
‚tough 'luck
Tough *family name* (i) tʌf, (ii) tuːx
Tough *place in Grampian* tuːx
toughen 'tʌf ən ~ed d ~ing ɪŋ ~s z
toughie 'tʌf i ~s z
toughly 'tʌf li
tough-minded ‚tʌf 'maɪnd ɪd ◄ -əd ~ly li
~ness nəs nɪs
toughness 'tʌf nəs -nɪs
Toulon ₍ₒ₎tuː 'lɒ̃ ‖ -'lɔːn -'lɑːn —*Fr* [tu lɔ̃]
Toulouse ₍ₒ₎tuː 'luːz tə- —*Fr* [tu luːz]
Toulouse-Lautrec ‚tuː luːz ləʊ 'trek •, ••'•, tə-
‖ tuː ‚luːz lə 'trek —*Fr* [tu luz lo tʁɛk]
toupee, toupée 'tuːp eɪ ‚tuː 'peɪ ‖ tuː 'peɪ
—*Fr* toupet [tu pe] ~s z
tour tʊə tɔː ‖ tʊᵊr **toured** tʊəd tɔːd ‖ tʊᵊrd
touring 'tʊər ɪŋ 'tɔːr- ‖ 'tʊr ɪŋ **tours** tʊəz
tɔːz ‖ tʊᵊrz
‚tour de 'force —*Fr* [tuʁ də fɔʁs]; ‚Tour de
'France —*Fr* [tuʁ də fʁɑ̃ːs]; 'tour ‚operator
tourer 'tʊər ə 'tɔːr- ‖ 'tʊr ᵊr ~s z
Tourette tʊ 'ret ~'s s
tourism 'tʊər ‚ɪz əm 'tɔːr- ‖ 'tʊr-
tourist 'tʊər ɪst 'tɔːr-, §-əst ‖ 'tʊr əst ~s s
'tourist ‚class
touristic ₍ₒ₎tʊə 'rɪst ɪk ₍ₒ₎tɔː- ‖ tʊ- ~ally ᵊl_i
touristy 'tʊər ɪst i 'tɔːr-, -əst- ‖ 'tʊr-
tourmaline 'tʊəm ə liːn 'tɜːm-, -lɪn ‖ 'tʊrm-
tournament 'tʊən ə mənt 'tɔːn-, 'tɜːn-
‖ 'tʊrn- 'tɔːrn-, 'tɜːn- ~s s
tournedos *sing.* 'tʊən ə dəʊ 'tɔːn-, 'tɜːn-
‖ ‚tʊrn ə 'doʊ ~ *pl* z
tourney 'tʊən i 'tɔːn-, 'tɜːn- ‖ 'tʊrn i 'tɔːrn-,
'tɜːn- ~ed d ~ing ɪŋ ~s z
tourniquet 'tɔːn ɪ keɪ 'tʊən-, 'tɜːn-, -ə-
‖ 'tɜːn ək ət 'tʊrn-, -ɪk- (*) ~s z ‖ s
Tours *place in France* tʊə tʊəz, tɔːz ‖ tʊᵊr —*Fr*
[tuːʁ]
Tours *English family name* tʊəz tɔːz ‖ tʊᵊrz
tousl|e 'taʊz ᵊl ~ed d ~es z ~ing ɪŋ
tout *v, n* taʊt **touted** 'taʊt ɪd -əd ‖ 'taʊt əd
touting 'taʊt ɪŋ ‖ 'taʊt ɪŋ **touts** taʊts
tout *adj, adv, in French expressions* tuːt —*but
before consonants* tuː
‚tout 'court ‚tuː 'kʊə-'kɔː: ‖ -'kʊᵊr —*Fr*
[tu kuːʁ]; ‚tout en'semble
‚tuːt ɒn 'sɒm bᵊl ‖ -ɑːn 'sɑːm- —*Fr*
[tu tɑ̃ sãːbl]
Tovell 'təʊv ᵊl ‖ 'toʊv-
Tovey (i) 'təʊv i ‖ 'toʊv i, (ii) 'tʌv i
tow təʊ §taʊ ‖ toʊ *(usually = toe)* **towed** təʊd
§taʊd ‖ toʊd *(usually = toad)* **towing** 'təʊ ɪŋ
§'taʊ- ‖ 'toʊ ɪŋ **tows** təʊz §taʊz ‖ toʊz
'tow truck
Tow Law ‚taʊ 'lɔː ‖ -'lɑː
towage 'təʊ ɪdʒ ‖ 'toʊ-
toward *prep* tə 'wɔːd tu-; tɔːd ‖ tɔːrd toʊrd;
tə 'wɔːrd, twɔːrd, twoʊrd
toward *adj* 'təʊ əd tɔːd ‖ tɔːrd toʊrd ~liness
li nəs -nɪs ~ly li ~ness nəs nɪs
towards tə 'wɔːdz tu-; tɔːdz ‖ tɔːrdz toʊrdz;
tə 'wɔːrdz, twɔːrdz, twoʊrdz

towaway 'təʊ ə ‚weɪ ‖ 'toʊ-
towbar 'təʊ bɑː ‖ 'toʊ bɑːr ~s z
Towcester 'təʊst ə ‖ 'toʊst ᵊr
towel 'taʊ_əl taʊl ‖ 'taʊ_əl **toweled, towelled**
'taʊ_əld taʊld ‖ 'taʊ_əld **toweling,
towelling** 'taʊ_əl ɪŋ 'taʊl ɪŋ ‖ 'taʊ_əl ɪŋ
towels 'taʊ_əlz taʊlz ‖ 'taʊ_əlz
towelette ‚taʊ ə 'let ‚taʊ 'let ~s s
tower, Tower 'taʊ_ə ‖ 'taʊ_ᵊr ~ed d
towering 'taʊ_ᵊr ɪŋ ‖ 'taʊ_ᵊr ɪŋ ~s z
'tower ‚block; ‚Tower 'Bridge◄, ‚Tower
‚Bridge 'Road; ‚Tower 'Hamlets; ‚tower of
'strength
Towers 'taʊ_əz ‖ 'taʊ_ᵊrz
tow-haired ‚təʊ 'heəd ◄ ‖ ‚toʊ 'heᵊrd ◄ -'hæᵊrd
towhead 'təʊ hed ‖ 'toʊ- ~ed ɪd əd ~s z
towline 'təʊ laɪn §'taʊ- ‖ 'toʊ- ~s z
town taʊn **towns** taʊnz
‚town 'clerk; ‚town 'crier; ‚town 'hall;
'town house; ‚town 'planning
Towne taʊn
Townes taʊnz
townie 'taʊn i ~s z
Townley 'taʊn li
townscape 'taʊn skeɪp ~s s
Townsend 'taʊnz end
‚Townsend 'Thoresen *tdmk* 'tɒr əs ən -ɪs-
‖ 'tɔːr-
townsfolk 'taʊnz fəʊk ‖ -foʊk
Townshend 'taʊnz end
township 'taʊn ʃɪp ~s s
towns|man 'taʊnz |mən ~men mən men
~people ‚piːp ᵊl
Townsville 'taʊnz vɪl -vᵊl
towns|woman 'taʊnz |‚wʊm ən ~women
‚wɪm ɪn §-ən
tow|path 'təʊ |pɑːθ §'taʊ-, §-pæθ ‖ 'toʊ |pæθ
~paths pɑːðz §pæðz, §pɑːθs, §pæθs ‖ pæðz
pæθs
towrope 'təʊ rəʊp §'taʊ- ‖ 'toʊ roʊp ~s s
Towy 'təʊ i —*Welsh* ['tə wi, 'to-]
Towyn 'taʊ ɪn 'təʊ- —*Welsh* ['tə wɪn, 'to-,
-wɪn]
toxaemia, toxemia tɒk 'siːm i‿ə ‖ tɑːk-
toxic 'tɒks ɪk ‖ 'tɑːks ɪk ~ally ᵊl_i
‚toxic 'shock ‚syndrome
toxicit|y tɒk 'sɪs ət i‿ɪt i i ‖ tɑːk 'sɪs əṭ li ~ies
iz
toxicological ‚tɒks ɪk əʊ 'lɒdʒ ɪk ᵊl ◄
‖ ‚tɑːks ɪk ə 'lɑːdʒ- ~ly _i
toxicologist ‚tɒks ɪ 'kɒl ədʒ ɪst ‚•ə-, §-əst
‖ ‚tɑːks ɪ 'kɑːl- ~s s
toxicology ‚tɒks ɪ 'kɒl ədʒ i ‚•ə-
‖ ‚tɑːks ɪ 'kɑːl-
toxin 'tɒks ɪn §-ən ‖ 'tɑːks ən ~s z
toxocariasis ‚tɒks əʊ kə 'raɪ_əs ɪs §-əs
‖ ‚tɑːks ə-
toxoid 'tɒks ɔɪd ‖ 'tɑːks- ~s z
toxophilite tɒk 'sɒf ə laɪt -ɪ- ‖ tɑːk 'sɑːf- ~s s
toxoplasmosis ‚tɒks əʊ plæz 'məʊs ɪs -əs
‖ ‚tɑːks ə plæz 'moʊs əs, ‚•oʊ-
Toxteth 'tɒkst əθ -ɪθ, -eθ ‖ 'tɑːkst-

toy tɔɪ **toyed** tɔɪd **toying** 'tɔɪ ɪŋ **toys** tɔɪz
 'toy ˌfactory *where toys are made,* ˌtoy
 'factory *for a child to play with;* ˌtoy 'gun;
 ˌtoy 'poodle; ˌtoy 'soldier
Toya, Toyah 'tɔɪ ə
toyboy 'tɔɪ bɔɪ ~s z
Toye tɔɪ
Toynbee 'tɔɪn bi →'tɔɪm-, -biː
Toyota *tdmk* tɔɪ 'əʊt ə ‖ -'oʊt̬ ə ~s z —*Jp*
['to jo ta]
toyshop 'tɔɪ ʃɒp ‖ -ʃɑːp ~s s
Tozer 'təʊz ə ‖ 'toʊz ər
T'Pau tə 'paʊ
Trabant *tdmk* 'træb ænt -ənt —*Ger* [tʁa 'bant]
trace treɪs **traced** treɪst **traces** 'treɪs ɪz -əz
 tracing 'treɪs ɪŋ
 'trace ˌelement
traceable 'treɪs əb əl
tracer 'treɪs ə ‖ -ər ~s z
tracer|y 'treɪs ər_li ~ies iz
Tracey 'treɪs i
trache|a trə 'kiː_|ə ‖ 'treɪk i_|ə ‖ 'treɪk i_|ə ~ae
iː ~al əl ~as əz
tracheitis ˌtreɪk i 'aɪt ɪs ˌtræk-, §-əs ‖ -'aɪt̬ əs
tracheo- *comb. form*
 with stress-neutral suffix ˌtreɪk i əʊ ˌtræk-
 ‖ -oʊ — **tracheocele** 'treɪk i əʊ siːəl 'træk-
 ‖ -i oʊ-
 with stress-imposing suffix ˌtreɪk i 'ɒ+ ˌtræk-
 ‖ -'ɑː+ — **tracheostomy** ˌtreɪk i 'ɒst əm i
 ˌtræk- ‖ -'ɑːst-
tracheotom|y ˌtræk i 'ɒt əm |i ˌtreɪk-
 ‖ ˌtreɪk i 'ɑːt̬- ~ies iz
trachoma trə 'kəʊm ə ‖ -'koʊm-
tracing 'treɪs ɪŋ ~s z
 'tracing ˌpaper
track træk **tracked** trækt *(= tract)* **tracking**
 'træk ɪŋ **tracks** træks
 'track eˌvent; 'tracking ˌstation; 'track
 ˌrecord; 'track rod
trackage 'træk ɪdʒ
tracker 'træk ə ‖ -ər ~s z
tracklay|er/s 'træk ˌleɪ |ə/z ‖ -|ər/z ~ing ɪŋ
trackless 'træk ləs -lɪs
track|suit 'træk |suːt -sjuːt ~suited suːt ɪd
sjuːt-, -əd ‖ suːt̬ əd ~suits suːts sjuːts
tract trækt **tracts** trækts
tractability ˌtræk t̬ə 'bɪl ət i -ɪt i ‖ -ət̬ i
tractab|le 'træk t̬əb |əl ~leness əl nəs -nɪs ~ly
li
Tractarian træk 'teər i_ən ‖ -'ter- ~s z
tractate 'træk teɪt ~s s
tractile 'træk taɪəl ‖ -əl -aɪəl
traction 'træk ʃən
 'traction ˌengine
tractive 'trækt ɪv
tractor 'trækt ə ‖ -ər ~s z
tractorfeed 'trækt ə fiːd ‖ -ər-
Tracy 'treɪs i
trad træd
trade treɪd **traded** 'treɪd ɪd -əd **trades** treɪdz
 trading 'treɪd ɪŋ
 'trade gap; 'trade name; 'trade price;

'trade route; ˌtrade 'secret; ˌTrades ˌUnion
 'Congress; ₍₎ˌtrade 'union; 'trade wind;
 'trading eˌstate; 'trading post; 'trading
 stamp; ˌtrade(s) 'union ‖ '• , ••
trade-in 'treɪd ɪn ~s z
trademark 'treɪd mɑːk →'treɪb- ‖ -mɑːrk ~ed
t ~ing ɪŋ ~s s
trade-off 'treɪd ɒf -ɔːf ‖ -ɔːf -ɑːf ~s s
trader 'treɪd ə ‖ -ər ~s z
Tradescant trə 'desk ənt
tradescantia ˌtræd ɪ 'skænt i_ə ˌtreɪd-, ˌ•e-,
 ˌ•ə-, -'skæntʃ- ‖ -'skæntʃ- ~s z
trades|man 'treɪdz |mən ~men mən men
 ~people ˌpiːp əl
tradition trə 'dɪʃ ən ~s z
traditional trə 'dɪʃ ən_əl ~ism ˌɪz əm ~ist/s
ɪst/s §əst/s ‖ əst/s ~ly i
traduc|e trə 'djuːs →§-'dʒuːs ‖ -'duːs -'djuːs
 ~ed t ~es ɪz əz ~ing ɪŋ
Trafalgar trə 'fælg ə ‖ -ər -'fɑːlg- —*But the
pronunciation* ˌtræf əl 'gɑː ◄ ‖ -'gɑːr ◄ *was
formerly used for the viscountcy and is still
sometimes used for* T~ *House near Salisbury.*
—*Sp* [tra fal 'ɣar]
traffic 'træf ɪk ~ked t ~king ɪŋ ~s s
 'traffic ˌcircle; 'traffic ˌisland; 'traffic jam;
 'traffic light; 'traffic ˌsignal; 'traffic
 ˌwarden
trafficator 'træf ɪ keɪt ə §'••ə- ‖ -keɪt̬ ər ~s z
trafficker 'træf ɪk ə ‖ -ər ~s z
Trafford 'træf əd ‖ -ərd
tragacanth 'træg ə kæntθ 'trædʒ-
tragedian trə 'dʒiːd i_ən ~s z
tragedienne trə ˌdʒiːd i 'en ~s z
traged|y 'trædʒ əd |i -ɪd i ~ies iz
Trager 'treɪg ə ‖ -ər
tragic 'trædʒ ɪk ~ally əl_i
tragicomed|y ˌtrædʒ i 'kɒm əd |i ‖ -'kɑːm-
 ~ies iz
tragicomic ˌtrædʒ i 'kɒm ɪk ◄ ‖ -'kɑːm- ~ally
əl_i
tragopan 'træg ə pæn ~s z
tragus 'treɪg əs **tragi** 'treɪdʒ aɪ 'treɪg-
Traherne trə 'hɜːn ‖ -'hɝːn
trail treɪəl **trailed** treɪəld **trailing** 'treɪəl ɪŋ
 trails treɪəlz
 'trail bike; ˌtrailing 'edge; '••
trailblaz|er/s 'treɪəl ˌbleɪz |ə/z ‖ -|ər/z ~ing ɪŋ
trailer 'treɪl ə ‖ -ər ~s z
 'trailer camp; 'trailer park
Traill treɪəl
train, Train treɪn **trained** treɪnd **training**
 'treɪn ɪŋ **trains** treɪnz
 'training ˌcollege; 'training course; 'train
 set
trainbearer 'treɪn ˌbeər ə →'treɪm- ‖ -ˌber ər
 -ˌbær- ~s z
trainee ˌtreɪ 'niː ~s z ~ship/s ʃɪp/s
trainer 'treɪn ə ‖ -ər ~s z
train|man 'treɪn |mən →'treɪm- ~men mən
men
train-spott|er/s 'treɪn spɒt| ə/z ‖ -spɑːt̬ | ər/z
 ~ing ɪŋ

T

traipse treɪps **traipsed** treɪpst **traipses**
'treɪps ɪz -əz **traipsing** 'treɪps ɪŋ
trait treɪ treɪt ‖ treɪt **traits** treɪz treɪts ‖ treɪts
traitor 'treɪt ə ‖ 'treɪt̬ ər ~**s** z
traitorous 'treɪt ər_əs ‖ 'treɪt̬ ər əs →'treɪtr əs
~**ly** li ~**ness** nəs nɪs
Trajan 'treɪdʒ ən
trajector|y trə 'dʒek tər_li 'trædʒ ɪk-, '·ək-
~**ies** iz
tra-la traː trə-
tra-la-la ˌtraːl aː 'laː -ə-
Tralee trə 'liː
tram træm **trams** træmz
tramcar 'træm kaː ‖ -kaːr ~**s** z
tramline 'træm laɪn ~**s** z
trammel 'træm əl ~**ed, ~led** d ~**ing, ~ling** ɪŋ
~**s** z
tramontane trə 'mɒnt eɪn ‖ -'maːnt- ~**s** z
tramp træmp **tramped** træmpt **tramping**
'træmp ɪŋ **tramps** træmps
trampl|e 'træmp əl ~**ed** d ~**es** z ~**ing** ˌɪŋ
trampolin|e 'træmp ə liːn -lɪn, ˌ··'· ~**ed** d
~**es** z ~**ing** ɪŋ
tramway 'træm weɪ ~**s** z
trance traːnts §trænts ‖ trænts **trances**
'traːnts ɪz §'trænts-, -əz ‖ 'trænts əz
tranche traːntʃ trɔːntʃ, træntʃ **tranches**
'traːntʃ ɪz 'trɔːntʃ-, 'træntʃ-, -əz
trank træŋk **tranks** træŋks
Tranmere 'træn mɪə →'træm- ‖ -mɪr
trann|ie, ~y 'træn li ~**ies** iz
tranquil 'træŋk wɪl -wəl ~**ly** li
tranquility, tranquillity træŋ 'kwɪl ət i -ɪt i
‖ træn 'kwɪl ət̬ i →træŋ-
tranquiliz|e, tranquillis|e, tranquilliz|e
'træŋk wə laɪz -wɪ- ~**ed** d ~**er/s** ə/z ‖ -ər/z
~**es** ɪz əz ~**ing** ɪŋ
trans- trænts trænz, traːnts, traːnz —*For EFL
learners, the form* træns *is acceptable in all
contexts in all kinds of English. Actual usage
preferences are fairly complex. —In the choice
between* s *and* z *forms we can distinguish
various phonetic contexts according to the
sound with which the stem begins, as follows.
(1) Before a voiceless sound* (trans'form), s *is
usual. (2) Before* l (trans'late) *and before an
unstressed vowel sound* ('transit), s *is usual
though a minority use* z. *(3) Before other
consonants* (trans'gress, trans'mit), *and before a
stressed vowel sound* (trans'act), *the tendency is
for BrE to prefer* z, *but AmE to prefer* s. *This
also applies in any word where the prefix is felt
as separate* (ˌtransˌconti'nental). —*For the
vowel, RP prefers* æ, *although a substantial
minority use* aː, *and some words have variants
with* ə; *AmE always has* æ. —*Before a stem
beginning with* s *the final consonant sound is
often lost* (trans + scribe *giving* transcribe
træn 'skraɪb).
transact træn 'zækt traːn-, trən-, -'sækt;
ˌtrænts 'ækt ‖ -'sækt -'zækt ~**ed** ɪd əd ~**ing**
ɪŋ ~**s** s

transactinide ˌtrænts 'ækt ɪ naɪd ˌtraːnts-,
ˌtrænz-, §-ə- ~**s** z
transaction træn 'zæk ʃən traːn-, trən-, -'sæk-;
ˌtrænts 'æk- ‖ -'sæk- -'zæk- ~**al** əl ~**s** z
transalpine ₍ₜ₎trænz 'ælp aɪn ₍ₜ₎traːnz-,
₍ₜ₎trænts- ‖ ₍ₜ₎trænts- ₍ₜ₎traːnz-, -ən ~**s** z
transatlantic ˌtrænz ət 'lænt ɪk ◂ ˌtraːnz-,
§ˌtrænts-, -æt- ‖ ˌtrænts ət 'lænt̬ ɪk ◂ ˌtrænz-
Transcarpathian ˌtrænz kaː 'peɪθ i_ən ◂
ˌtraːnz-, ˌtrænts- ‖ ˌtrænts kaːr-
Transcaucasia ˌtrænz kɔː 'keɪz i_ə ˌtraːnz-,
ˌtrænts-, -'keɪʒ ə ‖ ˌtrænts kɔː 'keɪʒ ə -kaː-,
-'keɪʃ ə
transceiver træn 'siːv ə traːn- ‖ -ər ~**s** z
transcend træn 'send traːn- ~**ed** ɪd əd ~**ing**
ɪŋ ~**s** z
transcendenc|e træn 'send ənts traːn- ~**y** i
transcendent træn 'send ənt traːn- ~**ly** li
transcendental ˌtrænts en 'dent əl ◂ ˌtraːnts-,
-ən- ‖ -'dent̬ əl ◂ ~**ism** ˌɪz əm ~**ly** i
ˌtranscenˌdental ˌmedi'tation
transcontinental ˌtrænz ˌkɒnt ɪ 'nent əl
ˌtraːnz-, ˌtrænts-, -ə-
‖ ˌtrænts ˌkaːnt ən 'ent̬ əl
transcrib|e ₍ₜ₎træn 'skraɪb ₍ₜ₎traːn-;
₍ₜ₎trænts 'kraɪb ~**ed** d ~**er/s** ə/z ‖ ər/z ~**es** z
~**ing** ɪŋ
transcript 'trænts krɪpt 'traːnts- ~**s** s
transcriptase ₍ₜ₎træn 'skrɪpt eɪz ₍ₜ₎traːn-, -eɪs;
₍ₜ₎trænts 'krɪpt-
transcription ₍ₜ₎træn 'skrɪp ʃən ₍ₜ₎traːn-;
₍ₜ₎trænts 'krɪp- ~**al** əl ~**ally** əl i ~**s** z
transducer ₍ₜ₎trænz 'djuːs ə ₍ₜ₎traːnz-, ₍ₜ₎trænts-,
₍ₜ₎traːnts-, →§-'dʒuːs- ‖ ₍ₜ₎trænts 'duːs ər
-'djuːs- ~**s** z
transept 'trænts ept 'traːnts- ~**s** s
transeunt 'trænts i_ənt 'traːnts-
transexual træn 'sek ʃu_əl traːn-, ˌtrænz-,
ˌtraːnz-, ˌtrænts-, ˌtraːnts-, -'seks ju_əl,
-'sek ʃəl ‖ trænts- ~**ism** ˌɪz əm ~**s** z
trans|fer v trænts |'fɜː traːnts-, trənts-, '··
‖ trænts |'fɝː '·· ~**ferred** 'fɜːd ‖ 'fɝːd
~**ferring** 'fɜːr ɪŋ ‖ 'fɝː ɪŋ ~**fers** 'fɜːz ‖ 'fɝːz
transfer n trænts fɜː 'traːnts- ‖ -fɝː ~**s** z
'transfer fee
transferability trænts ˌfɜːr ə 'bɪl ət i traːnts-,
ˌ··-, ˌ·fər_ə-, -ɪt i ‖ -ˌfɝː ə 'bɪl ət̬ i

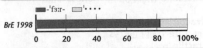

BrE 1998						
0	20	40	60	80		100%

transferable trænts 'fɜːr əb əl traːnts-, ˌ·'·-,
trənts-; 'trænts fər_əb əl, 'traːnts- ‖ -'fɝː-
—*BrE 1998 poll panel preference:* -'fɜːr- 82%,
'···· 18%.
transferal, transferral trænts 'fɜːr əl traːnts-,
trənts- ‖ trænts 'fɝː əl ~**s** z
transferas|e 'trænts fə reɪz 'traːnts-, -reɪs ~**es**
ɪz əz
transferee ˌtrænts fɜːr 'iː -fər- ‖ -fɝː- ~**s** z
transferenc|e 'trænts fər_ənts 'traːnts-;

ₒtræntˈfɜːr ənts, ₒtrɑːnts-, trənts-
‖ trænts ˈfɜː ənts ˈ•fᵊr_• ~es ɪz əz
transferor, transferrer trænts ˈfɜːr ətrɑːnts-
‖ -ˈfɜː ᵊr ~s z
transfiguration, T~ ˌtrænts ˌfɪg ə ˈreɪʃ ᵊn
ˌtrɑːnts-, •, • • ˈ • •, -jə-, -juᵊ- ‖ -jə- ~s z
transfigure trænts ˈfɪg ətrɑːnts- ‖ -jᵊr(*) ~d
d ~s z **transfiguring** trænts ˈfɪg_ᵊr ɪŋ
trɑːnts- ‖ -jᵊr ɪŋ
transfinite trænts ˈfaɪn aɪt trɑːnts-
transfix trænts ˈfɪks trɑːnts- ~ed t ~es ɪz əz
~ing ɪŋ
transform v trænts ˈfɔːm trɑːnts-, trənts-;
ˈtrænts fɔːm, ˈtrɑːnts- ‖ -ˈfɔːrm ~ed d ~ing
ɪŋ ~s z
transform n ˈtrænts fɔːm ˈtrɑːnts- ‖ -fɔːrm ~s
z
transformable trænts ˈfɔːm əb ᵊltrɑːnts-,
trənts- ‖ -ˈfɔːrm-
transformation ˌtrænts fə ˈmeɪʃ ᵊn ˌtrɑːnts-,
-fɔː- ‖ -fᵊr- -fɔːr- ~al _ᵊl ◄ ~ally ᵊl_i ~s z
ˌtransfor͵mational ˈgrammar
transformer trænts ˈfɔːm ətrɑːnts-, trənts-
‖ -ˈfɔːrm ᵊr ˈ • • • ~s z
transfus|e trænts ˈfjuːz trɑːnts-, trənts- ~ed d
~es ɪz əz ~ing ɪŋ
transfusion trænts ˈfjuːʒ ᵊn trɑːnts-, §trənts-
~s z
transgenic ˌtrænts ˈdʒen ɪk ◄ ˌtrɑːnz-, ˌtrænts-,
ˌtrɑːnts- ‖ ˌtrænts- ˌtrænz-
transgress trænz ˈgres trɑːnz-, trænts-,
trɑːnts-, §trɒnz- ‖ trænts- trænz- ~ed t
~es ɪz əz ~ing ɪŋ
transgression trænz ˈgreʃ ᵊn trɑːnz-, trænts-,
trɑːnts-, §trɒnz- ‖ trænts- trænz- ~s z
transgressor trænz ˈgres ətrɑːnz-, trænts-,
trɑːnts-, §trɒnz- ‖ trænts ˈgres ᵊr trænz- ~s
z
tranship trænts ˈʃɪp trɑːnts-, →trænᵗʃ-,
→trɑːnᵗʃ-, træn-, trɑːn-, trænz-, trɑːnz-,
§trɒnts-, →§trɒnᵗʃ-, §trɒn-, §trɒnz- ‖ trænts-
→trænᵗʃ- ~ped t ~ping ɪŋ ~s s
transhumance trænts ˈhjuːm ənts trɑːnts-,
§-ˈjuːm-
transienc|e ˈtrænz i_ənts ˈtrɑːnz-, ˈtrænts-,
ˈtrɑːnts- ‖ ˈtrænᵗʃ ənts, ˈtrænʒ- ~y i
transient ˈtrænz i_ənt ˈtrɑːnz-, ˈtrænts-,
ˈtrɑːnts- ‖ ˈtrænᵗʃ ənt, ˈtrænʒ- ~ly li ~ness
nəs nɪs

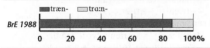
transistor træn ˈzɪst ə trɑːn-, §trɒn-, -ˈsɪst-
‖ -ᵊr —BrE 1988 poll panel preferences: træn-
86% (southerners 84%), trɑːn- 14%
(southerners 16%); -ˈzɪst- 63%, -ˈsɪst- 37%.
~s z
tran͵sistor ˈradio
transistoris|e, transistoriz|e træn ˈzɪst ə raɪz
trɑːn-, §trən-, -ˈsɪst- ~ed d ~es ɪz əz ~ing
ɪŋ

trans|it ˈtrænts ɪt ˈtrɑːnts-, ˈtrænz-, ˈtrɑːnz-,
§-ət ‖ ˈtrænts ət ˈtrænz- ~ited ɪt ɪd§ət-, -əd
‖ ət əd ~iting ɪt ɪŋ§ət- ‖ ət ɪŋ ~its ɪts§əts
‖ əts
transit lounge; transit passengers;
transit ͵visa

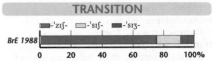
transition træn ˈzɪʃ ᵊn trɑːn-, trən-, -ˈsɪʃ-,
-ˈsɪʒ- —BrE 1988 poll panel preference: -ˈzɪʃ-
75%, -ˈsɪʃ- 16%, -ˈsɪʒ- 9%. ~al _ᵊl ~ally _ᵊl i
~s z
transitive ˈtrænts ət ɪv ˈtrɑːnts-, ˈtrænz-,
ˈtrɑːnz-, -ɪt ɪv ‖ ˈtrænts ət̬ ɪv ˈtrænz- ~ly li
~ness nəs nɪs ~s z
transitivity ˌtrænts ə ˈtɪv ət i ˌtrɑːnts-, ˌtrænz-,
ˌtrɑːnz-, , • ɪ-, -ɪt i ‖ -ət̬ i
transitor|y ˈtrænts ət_ᵊr li ˈtrɑːnts-, ˈtrænz-,
ˈtrɑːnz-, ˈ • ɪt̬_ ‖ ˈtrænts ə tɔːr li ˈtrænz-,
-toʊr i (*) ~ily ᵊl i ɪ li ~iness i nəs i nɪs
Transkei ˌtrænts ˈkaɪ trɑːnts-, ˌtrænz-, ˌtrɑːnz-

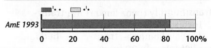
trans|late trænts ‖ˈleɪt trɑːnts-, trænz-, trɑːnz-,
trənts-, trənz- ‖ ˈtrænts ‖leɪt ˈtrænz-, • ˈ •
—AmE 1993 poll panel preference: ˈ • • 83%,
• ˈ • 17%. ~lated ˈleɪt ɪd-əd ‖ leɪt̬ əd ~lates
ˈleɪts ‖ leɪts ~lating ˈleɪt ɪŋ ‖ leɪt̬ ɪŋ
translation trænts ˈleɪʃ ᵊn trɑːnts-, trænz-,
trɑːnz-, trənts-, trənz- ‖ trænz- ~s z
translator trænts ˈleɪt ə trɑːnts-, trænz-,
trɑːnz-, trənts-, trənz- ‖ trænts ˈleɪt̬ ᵊr
trænz-, ˈ • • • ~s z
translite|rate trænts ˈlɪt ə ˌreɪt trɑːnts-, trænz-,
trɑːnz-, , • -, trənts-, trənz- ‖ trænts ˈlɪt̬-
trænz- ~rated reɪt ɪd -əd ‖ reɪt̬ əd ~rates
reɪts ~rating reɪt ɪŋ ‖ reɪt̬ ɪŋ
transliteration trænts ˌlɪt ə ˈreɪʃ ᵊn trɑːnts-,
trænz-, trɑːnz-, , • , • -, trənts-, trənz-
‖ trænts ˌlɪt̬- trænz-, , • , • - ~s z
translo|cate ˈtrænts ləʊ ˌkeɪt ˈtrɑːnts-, ˈtrænz-,
ˈtrɑːnz-, , • • ˈ • ‖ ˈtrænz loʊ- ˈtrænts-, , • ˈ • •
~cated keɪt ɪd -əd ‖ keɪt̬ əd ~cates keɪts
~cating keɪt ɪŋ ‖ keɪt̬ ɪŋ
translocation ˌtrænts ləʊ ˈkeɪʃ ᵊn trɑːnts-,
ˌtrænz-, ˌtrɑːnz- ‖ ˌtrænz loʊ- ˌtrænts-
translucenc|e trænts ˈluːs ᵊnts trɑːnts-, trænz-,
trɑːnz-, -ˈljuːs- ~y i
translucent trænts ˈluːs ᵊnt trɑːnts-, trænz-,
trɑːnz-, -ˈljuːs- ~ly li
transmig|rate ˌtrænz maɪ ˈgreɪt ˌtrɑːnz-,
ˌtrænts-, ˌtrɑːnts- ‖ ˈtrænts ˈmaɪg ˌreɪt
ˌtrænz-, ˈ • , • • (*) ~rated reɪt ɪd -əd ‖ reɪt̬ əd
~rates reɪts ~rating reɪt ɪŋ ‖ reɪt̬ ɪŋ
transmigration ˌtrænz maɪ ˈgreɪʃ ᵊn ˌtrɑːnz-,
ˌtrænts-, ˌtrɑːnts- ‖ ˌtrænts- ˌtrænz- ~s z

T

transmissibility trænz ˌmɪs ə 'bɪl ət i trɑːnz-,
træn^ts-, trɑːn^ts-, ˌ•ˌ•-, -ɪ'•-, -ɪt i
‖ træn^ts ˌmɪs ə 'bɪl ət̬ i trænz-, ˌ•ˌ•-

transmissible trænz 'mɪs əb əl trɑːnz-, træn^ts-,
trɑːn^ts-, -ɪb əl ‖ træn^ts- trænz-

transmission trænz 'mɪʃ ən trɑːnz-, træn^ts-,
trɑːn^ts- ‖ træn^ts- trænz- ~s z

transmissive trænz 'mɪs ɪv trɑːnz-, træn^ts-,
trɑːn^ts- ‖ træn^ts- trænz-

transmissivity ˌtrænz mɪ 'sɪv ət i ˌtrɑːnz-,
ˌtræn^ts-, ˌtrɑːn^ts-, -ɪt i ‖ ˌtræn^ts mɪ 'sɪv ət̬ i
ˌtrænz-

trans|mit trænz |'mɪt trɑːnz-, træn^ts-, trɑːn^ts-
‖ træn^ts- trænz- **~mits** 'mɪts **~mitted**
'mɪt ɪd -əd ‖ 'mɪt̬ əd **~mitting**
'mɪt ɪŋ ‖ 'mɪt̬ ɪŋ

transmittal trænz 'mɪt əl trɑːnz-, træn^ts-,
trɑːn^ts- ‖ træn^ts 'mɪt̬ əl trænz- **~s** z

transmittanc|e trænz 'mɪt ən^ts trɑːnz-,
træn^ts-, trɑːn^ts- ‖ træn^ts- trænz- **~y** i

transmitter trænz 'mɪt ə trɑːnz-, træn^ts-,
trɑːn^ts- ‖ træn^ts 'mɪt̬ ər trænz-, '••• **~s** z

transmogrification trænz ˌmɒg rɪf ɪ 'keɪʃ ən
trɑːnz-, træn^ts-, trɑːn^ts-, ˌ•ˌ•-, -rəf •'•-,
§-ə'•- ‖ træn^ts ˌmɑːg rəf ə- trænz-, ˌ•ˌ•- **~s**
z

transmogri|fy trænz 'mɒg rɪ |faɪ trɑːnz-,
træn^ts-, trɑːn^ts-, ˌ•-, -rə faɪ
‖ træn^ts 'mɑːg rə- trænz-, ˌ•- **~fied** faɪd
~fies faɪz **~fying** faɪ ɪŋ

transmutation ˌtrænz mju 'teɪʃ ən ˌtrɑːnz-,
ˌtræn^ts-, ˌtrɑːn^ts- ‖ træn^ts- ˌtrænz- **~s** z

trans|mute trænz |'mjuːt trɑːnz-, træn^ts-,
trɑːn^ts- ‖ træn^ts- trænz- **~muted** 'mjuːt ɪd
-əd ‖ 'mjuːt̬ əd **~mutes** 'mjuːts **~muting**
'mjuːt ɪŋ ‖ 'mjuːt̬ ɪŋ

transnational ˌtrænz 'næʃ ən əl ◂ ˌtrɑːnz-,
ˌtræn^ts-, ˌtrɑːn^ts- ‖ ˌtræn^ts- ˌtrænz- **~s** z

transoceanic ˌtrænz ˌəʊʃ i 'æn ɪk ˌtrɑːnz-,
ˌtræn^ts-, ˌtrɑːn^ts-, -ˌəʊs- ‖ ˌtræn^ts ˌoʊʃ-
ˌtrænz-

transom 'træn^ts əm **~ed** d **~s** z

transparenc|y træn^ts 'pær ən^ts |i trɑːn^ts-,
trænz-, trɑːnz-, ˌ•-, trɒn^ts-, trɒnz-,
-'peər- ‖ -'per- **~ies** iz

transparent træn^ts 'pær ənt trɑːn^ts-, trænz-,
trɑːnz-, ˌ•-, trɒn^ts-, trɒnz-, -'peər- ‖ -'per-
~ly li **~ness** nəs nɪs

transpiration ˌtræn^ts pə 'reɪʃ ən ˌtrɑːn^ts-, -pɪ-

tran|spire træn |'spaɪ ə trɑːn-, §trən-
‖ -'spaɪ ər **~spired** 'spaɪ əd ‖ 'spaɪ ərd
~spires 'spaɪ əz ‖ 'spaɪ ərz **~spiring**
'spaɪ ər ɪŋ ‖ 'spaɪ ər ɪŋ

trans|plant v ˌtræn^ts |'plɑːnt ˌtrɑːn^ts-, §-'plænt
‖ ˌtræn^ts |'plænt **~planted** 'plɑːnt ɪd
§'plænt-, -əd ‖ 'plænt̬ əd **~planting**
'plɑːnt ɪŋ §'plænt- ‖ 'plænt̬ ɪŋ **~plants**
'plɑːn_ts §'plæn_ts ‖ 'plæn_ts

transplant n 'træn^ts plɑːnt 'trɑːn^ts-, §-plænt
‖ 'træn^ts plænt **~s** s

transplantation ˌtræn^ts plɑːn 'teɪʃ ən ˌtrɑːn^ts-,
-plæn- ‖ ˌtræn^ts plæn- **~s** z

transpolar ˌtrænz 'pəʊl ə ◂ ˌtrɑːnz-, ˌtræn^ts-,
ˌtrɑːn^ts- ‖ ˌtræn^ts 'poʊl ər ◂

transponder træn 'spɒnd ə trɑːn-
‖ træn 'spɑːnd ər træn^ts 'pɑːnd- **~s** z

transpontine ˌtrænz 'pɒnt aɪn ◂ ˌtrɑːnz-,
ˌtræn^ts-, ˌtrɑːn^ts- ‖ ˌtræn^ts 'pɑːnt-

trans|port v træn^ts |'pɔːt trɑːn^ts-
‖ træn^ts |'pɔːrt -'poʊrt, '•• **~ported** 'pɔːt ɪd
-əd ‖ 'pɔːrt̬ əd 'poʊrt- **~porting**
'pɔːt ɪŋ ‖ 'pɔːrt̬ ɪŋ 'poʊrt- **~ports**
'pɔːts ‖ 'pɔːrts 'poʊrts

transport n 'træn^ts pɔːt 'trɑːn^ts-
‖ 'træn^ts pɔːrt -poʊrt **~s** z
'transport ˌcafe

transportable træn^ts 'pɔːt əb əl trɑːn^ts-
‖ træn^ts 'pɔːrt̬- -'poʊrt̬-

transportation ˌtræn^ts pɔː 'teɪʃ ən ˌtrɑːn^ts-,
-pə- ‖ ˌtræn^ts pər-

transporter træn^ts 'pɔːt ə trɑːn^ts-
‖ træn^ts 'pɔːrt̬ ər -'poʊrt̬-, '••• **~s** z
trans'porter ˌbridge

transpos|e træn^ts 'pəʊz trɑːn^ts-
‖ træn^ts 'poʊz **~al** əl **~ed** d **~es** ɪz əz **~ing**
ɪŋ

transposition ˌtræn^ts pə 'zɪʃ ən ˌtrɑːn^ts- **~s** z

transputer træn^ts 'pjuːt ə trɑːn^ts-, trænz-,
trɑːnz- ‖ træn^ts 'pjuːt̬ ər **~s** z

transsexual træn 'sek ʃu əl trɑːn-, trænz-,
trɑːnz-, ˌtræn^ts-, ˌtrɑːn^ts-, -'seks ju əl,
-'sek ʃəl ‖ træn^ts- **~ism** ˌɪz əm **~s** z

transship træn^ts 'ʃɪp trɑːn^ts-, →træn^tʃ-,
→trɑːn^tʃ-, træn-, trɑːn-, trænz-, trɑːnz-,
§trən-, →§trɒn^tʃ-, §trɒn-, §trɒnz- ‖ træn^ts-
→træn^tʃ- **~ped** t **~ping** ɪŋ **~s** s

Trans-Siberian ˌtrænz saɪ 'bɪər i‿ən ◂ ˌtrɑːnz-
‖ ˌtræn^ts saɪ 'bɪr-

transubstanti|ate ˌtræn^ts əb 'stæn^tʃ i |eɪt
ˌtrɑːn^ts-, §,•ʌb-, -'stɑːn^tʃ-, -'stæn^ts- **~ated**
eɪt ɪd -əd ‖ eɪt̬ əd **~ates** eɪts **~ating**
eɪt ɪŋ ‖ eɪt̬ ɪŋ

transubstantiation ˌtræn^ts əb stæn^tʃ i 'eɪʃ ən
ˌtrɑːn^ts-, §,•ʌb-, -ˌstɑːn^tʃ-, -ˌstæn^ts-

transudate 'træn^ts ju deɪt 'trɑːn^ts-, 'trænz-,
'trɑːnz-, -u- **~s** s

transudation ˌtræn^ts ju 'deɪʃ ən ˌtrɑːn^ts-,
trænz-, ˌtrɑːnz-, -u- **~s** z

transud|e træn 'sjuːd trɑːn-, -'suːd, -'zjuːd,
-'zuːd **~ed** ɪd əd **~es** z **~ing** ɪŋ

transuranic ˌtrænz juə 'ræn ɪk ◂ ˌtrɑːnz-,
ˌtræn^ts-, ˌtrænz- ‖ ˌtræn^ts- ˌtrænz-,
→ˌtræn^tʃ-, →ˌtrænʒ-, -ə-

Transvaal 'trænz vɑːl 'trɑːnz-, 'træn^ts-,
'trɑːn^ts-, ˌ•'• ‖ ˌtræn^ts 'vɑːl trænz-
—locally also ˌ•'fɑːl **~er/s** ə/z ‖ -ər/z

transvers|e (ˌ)trænz 'vɜːs (ˌ)trɑːnz-, (ˌ)træn^ts-,
(ˌ)trɑːn^ts-, '•• ‖ (ˌ)træn^ts 'vɜːs (ˌ)trænz-, '••
~al əl **~ally** əl‿i **~ely** li

transvestism trænz 'vest ˌɪz əm trɑːnz-,
træn^ts-, trɑːn^ts- ‖ træn^ts- trænz-

transvestite trænz 'vest aɪt trɑːnz-, træn^ts-,
trɑːn^ts- ‖ træn^ts- trænz- **~s** s

Transworld tdmk ˌtrænz 'wɜːld ◂ ˌtrɑːnz-,
ˌtræn^ts-, ˌtrɑːn^ts- ‖ ˌtræn^ts 'wɜːld ◂ ˌtrænz-

Transylvani|a ˌtræn⁀ts ɪl 'veɪn i‿ə ˌtrɑːn⁀ts-, ˌ•əl-
~an/s ən/z
Trant trænt
Tranter 'trænt ə ‖ 'træn⁀t ər
trap træp trapped træpt trapping 'træp ɪŋ
traps træps
trapdoor ˌtræp 'dɔː '•• ‖ -'dɔːr -'doʊr ~s z
trapes treɪps trapesed treɪpst trapeses
'treɪps ɪz -əz trapesing 'treɪps ɪŋ
trapez|e trə 'piːz ‖ træ- ~es ɪz əz
tra'peze ˌartist
trapezi|um trə 'piːz i‿əm ~a ə ~i aɪ ~ums
əmz ~us/es əs /ɪz -əz
trapezoid 'træp ɪ zɔɪd -ə- ~s z
Trapp træp
trapp... —see trap
trapper 'træp ə ‖ -ər ~s z
trappings 'træp ɪŋz
Trappist 'træp ɪst §-əst ~s s
trapshooting 'træp ˌʃuːt ɪŋ ‖ -ˌʃuːt̬-
trash træʃ trashed træʃt trashes 'træʃ ɪz -əz
trashing 'træʃ ɪŋ
trashcan 'træʃ kæn ~s z
trash|man 'træʃ |mæn -mən ~men men mən
trash|y 'træʃ |i ~ier i‿ə ‖ i‿ər ~iest i‿ɪst i‿əst
~ily ɪ li əl i ~iness i nəs i nɪs
Trasimene 'træz ɪ miːn -ə-
trass træs
trattoria ˌtræt ə 'riː‿ə ‖ ˌtrɑːt̬- —It
trattoría [trat to 'ri: a] ~s z
traum|a 'trɔːm |ə 'traʊm- ‖ 'traʊm |ə 'trɔːm-,
'trɑːm- ~as əz ~ata ət ə ‖ ət̬ ə
traumatic trɔː 'mæt ɪk traʊ- ‖ trə 'mæt̬ ɪk
traʊ-, trɔː-, trɑː- ~ally əl‿i
traumatis... —see traumatiz...
traumatism 'trɔːm ə ˌtɪz əm 'traʊm- ‖ 'traʊm-
'trɔːm-, 'trɑːm- ~s z
traumatization ˌtrɔːm ət aɪ 'zeɪʃ ən ˌtraʊm-,
-ɪ'•- ‖ ˌtraʊm ət̬ ə- ˌtrɔːm-, ˌtrɑːm-
traumatiz|e 'trɔːm ə taɪz 'traʊm- ‖ 'traʊm-
'trɔːm-, 'trɑːm- ~ed d ~es ɪz əz ~ing ɪŋ
travail 'træv eɪəl trə 'veɪəl ~ed d ~ing ɪŋ ~s z
Travancore ˌtræv ən 'kɔː →-əŋ- ‖ 'træv ən kɔːr
-koʊr
travel 'træv əl ~ed, ~led d ~ing, ~ling ɪŋ ~s
z
'travel ˌagency; 'travel ˌagent;
'travel((l)ing ex,penses; ˌtravel(l)ing
'salesman
travelator 'træv ə leɪt ə -əl eɪt- ‖ -əl eɪt̬ ər ~s z
Travelcard 'træv əl kɑːd ‖ -kɑːrd ~s z
traveler, traveller 'træv əl‿ə ‖ ˌ_ər ~s z
ˌtraveller's 'cheque ‖ 'traveler's check
Travelodge tdmk 'træv ə lɒdʒ ‖ -lɑːdʒ
travelog, travelogue 'træv ə lɒg ‖ -lɔːg -lɑːg
~s z
travelsick 'træv əl sɪk ~ness nəs nɪs
Travers 'træv əz ‖ -ərz
travers|e v trə 'vɜːs træ-, 'træv ɜːs, -əs
‖ trə 'vɜːs træ-, 'træv ərs ~ed t ~es ɪz əz
~ing ɪŋ
travers|e n 'træv ɜːs -əs; trə 'vɜːs, træ-
‖ 'træv ɜːs trə 'vɜːs, træ- ~es ɪz əz

travertine 'træv ət ɪn §-ən; -ə tiːn ‖ -ər tiːn
travest|y 'træv əst li -ɪst i ~ies iz
Traviata ˌtræv i 'ɑːt ə ‖ ˌtrɑːv- —It
[tra 'vja: ta]
Travis 'træv ɪs §-əs
travois sing. trə 'vɔɪ 'træv ɔɪ travois pl
trə 'vɔɪz 'trav ɔɪz
travolator 'træv ə leɪt ə -əl eɪt- ‖ -əl eɪt̬ ər ~s z
Travolta trə 'vɒlt ə -'vəʊlt- ‖ -'voʊlt ə
trawl trɔːl ‖ trɑːl trawled trɔːld ‖ trɑːld
trawling 'trɔːl ɪŋ ‖ 'trɑːl- trawls trɔːlz
‖ trɑːlz
'trawl line
trawler 'trɔːl ə ‖ -ər 'trɑːl- ~man mən ~men
mən men ~s z
Trawsfynydd ˌtraʊs 'van ɪð ˌtrɔːz-, -'fɪn-, -ɪd
—Welsh [traus 'və nɪð, -nɪð]
tray treɪ trays treɪz
Treacher 'triːtʃ ə ‖ -ər
treacherous 'tretʃ ər‿əs ~ly li ~ness nəs nɪs
treacher|y 'tretʃ ər i ~ies iz
treacle 'triːk əl ~s z
treacly 'triːk əl‿i
tread tred treading 'tred ɪŋ treads tredz
trod trɒd ‖ trɑːd trodden
'trɒd ən ‖ 'trɑːd ən
treadle 'tred əl ~s z
treadmill 'tred mɪl →'treb- ~s z
treason 'triːz ən ~s z
treasonab|le 'triːz ən_əb |əl ~leness əl nəs -nɪs
~ly li
treasonous 'triːz ən_əs ~ly li
treas|ure 'treʒ ə ‖ -|ər 'treɪʒ- ~ured əd ‖ ərd
~ures əz ‖ ərz ~uring ər_ɪŋ
'treasure hunt; 'treasure trove
treasure-house 'treʒ ə haʊs ‖ -ər-
treasurer 'treʒ ər_ə ‖ -ər_ər 'treɪʒ- ~ship/s
ʃɪp/s ~s z
treasur|y, T~ 'treʒ ər_i ‖ 'treɪʒ- ~ies iz
'treasury bill; 'treasury note
treat triːt treated 'triːt ɪd -əd ‖ 'triːt̬ əd
treating 'triːt ɪŋ ‖ 'triːt̬ ɪŋ treats triːts
treatis|e 'triːt ɪz -ɪs, §-əz, §-əs ‖ 'triːt̬ əs ~es ɪz
əz
treatment 'triːt mənt ~s s
treat|y 'triːt |i ‖ 'triːt̬ |i ~ies iz
'treaty port
Trebizond 'treb ɪ zɒnd -ə- ‖ -ə zɑːnd
treble 'treb əl ~d d ~s z trebling 'treb əl_ɪŋ
ˌtreble 'chance; ˌtreble 'clef
Treblinka tre 'blɪŋk ə trə-
Trebor tdmk 'triː bɔː ‖ -bɔːr
trebuchet 'treb ju ʃet -ə-, -ʃeɪ, ˌ••'•
Tredegar trɪ 'diːg ə trə- ‖ -ər
tree, Tree triː treed triːd treeing 'triː ɪŋ
trees triːz
'tree ˌdiagram; 'tree fern; 'tree frog; 'tree
ˌsurgeon
treecreeper 'triː ˌkriːp ə ‖ -ər ~s z
treeless 'triː ləs -lɪs
treeline 'triː laɪn ~d d
treen triːn
treetop 'triː tɒp ‖ -tɑːp ~s s

T

Trefdraeth 'trev draιθ
Trefeglwys trιv 'eg lu‿ιs
Trefgarne 'tref gɑːn ‖ -gɑːrn
trefoil 'tref ɔιᵊl 'triː fɔιᵊl ~**ed** d ~**s** z
Trefor 'trev ə ‖ -ᵊr —*Welsh* ['tre vor]
Trefusis trι 'fjuːs ιs trə-, §-əs
Tregaron trι 'gær ən trə- ‖ -'ger-
Treharris trι 'hær ιs trə-, §-əs ‖ -'her-
Trehearne, Treherne trι 'hɜːn trə- ‖ -'hɝːn
trek trek **trekked** trekt **trekking** 'trek ιŋ
 treks treks
trekker 'trek ə ‖ -ᵊr ~**s** z
trekkie, T~ 'trek i ~**s** z
Trelawney trə 'lɔːn i trι- ‖ -'lɑːn-
trellis 'trel ιs §-əs ~**ed** t ~**es** ιz əz ~**ing** ιŋ
 ~**work** wɜːk ‖ wɝːk
Tremain trι 'meιn trə-
trematode 'trem ə təʊd 'triːm- ‖ -toʊd ~**s** z
tremble 'trem bᵊl ~**d** d ~**s** z **trembling/ly**
 'trem blιŋ /li
trembler 'trem blə ‖ -blᵊr ~**s** z
trem|bly 'trem| bli ~**blier** bli‿ə ‖ bli‿ᵊr
 ~**bliest** bli‿ιst ‿əst
tremendous trə 'mend əs trι-, △-'mendʒ- ~**ly**
 li ~**ness** nəs nιs
Tremlett 'trem lət -lιt
tremolo 'trem ə ləʊ ‖ -loʊ ~**s** z
tremor 'trem ə ‖ -ᵊr —*as a medical term, also*
 'triːm- ~**s** z
tremulant 'trem jʊl ənt -jəl- ‖ -jəl-
tremulous 'trem jʊl əs -jəl- ‖ -jəl- ~**ly** li
 ~**ness** nəs nιs
trench, T~ trenʃ **trenched** trenʃt **trenches**
 'trenʃ ιz -əz **trenching** 'trenʃ ιŋ
 trench coat
trenchancy 'trenʃ ᵊnᵗs i
trenchant 'trenʃ ənt ~**ly** li
Trenchard 'trenʃ ɑːd -əd ‖ -ɑːrd -ᵊrd
trencher 'trenʃ ə ‖ -ᵊr ~**s** z
trencher|man 'trenʃ ə |mən ‖ -ᵊr- ~**men** mən
 men
trend trend **trended** 'trend ιd -əd **trending**
 'trend ιŋ **trends** trendz
trendsett|ing 'trend ,set |ιŋ ‖ -,seţ ιŋ ~**er/s**
 ə/z ‖ ᵊr/z
trend|y 'trend li ~**ier** i‿ə ‖ i‿ᵊr ~**iest** i‿ιst i‿əst
 ~**ily** ι li əl i ~**iness** i nəs i nιs
Trengganu treŋ 'gɑːn uː
Trent trent
Trentham 'trent əm
Trenton 'trent ən ‖ -ᵊn
Treorchy tri 'ɔːk i ‖ -'ɔːrk i
trepan trι 'pæn trə- ~**ned** d ~**ning** ιŋ ~**s** z
trepang trι 'pæŋ trə-; 'triː pæŋ ~**s** z
trephination ,tref ι 'neιʃ ᵊn §-ə- ~**s** z
trephin|e trι 'fiːn trə-, tre-, -'faιn ~**ed** d ~**es** z
 ~**ing** ιŋ
trepidation ,trep ι 'deιʃ ᵊn §-ə-
treponem|a ,trep ə 'niːm |ə ~**ata** ət ə ‖ əţ ə
Tresco 'tresk əʊ ‖ -oʊ
Tresillian trι 'sιl i‿ən trə-
trespass 'tresp əs §'tres pɑːs,

§-pæs ‖ 'tres pæs ~**ed** t ~**er/s** ə/z ‖ ᵊr/z ~**es**
 ιz əz ~**ing** ιŋ
tress tres **tresses** 'tres ιz -əz
trestle 'tres ᵊl ~**s** z
Tretchikoff 'tretʃ ι kɒf ‖ -kɔːf -kɑːf
Trethowan trι 'θaʊ‿ən trə-, -'θəʊ-
trevall|y trι 'væl| i trə- ~**ies** iz
Trevelyan *(i)* trι 'vιl jən trə-, *(ii)* -'vel- —*In*
 Cornwall, (i).
Trevethick trι 'veθ ιk trə-
Trevino trə 'viːn əʊ trι- ‖ -oʊ
Trevor 'trev ə ‖ -ᵊr
trews truːz
trey treι *(= tray)* **treys** treιz
tri- *as a productive prefix* ¦traι — *but in certain*
 established words trι *(see entries) —*
 trichromatic ,traι krəʊ 'mæt ιk ◄
 ‖ -kroʊ 'mæţ-
triable 'traι‿əb ᵊl
triad, Triad 'traι æd 'traι‿əd ~**s** z
triage 'triː ɑːʒ 'traι-, -ιdʒ ‖ tri 'ɑːʒ
trial 'traι‿əl ‖ 'traι‿əl ~**ed, ~led** d ~**ing, ~ling**
 ιŋ ~**s** z
 'trial court; ,**trial 'run**
triangle 'traι æŋ gᵊl ~**s** z
triangular traι 'æŋ gjʊl ə -gjəl- ‖ -gjəl ᵊr ~**ly**
 li
triangularity traι ,æŋ gju 'lær ət i ,•,••-,-gjə-,
 -ιt i ‖ -gjə 'lær əţ i -'ler-
triangu|late traι 'æŋ gju |leιt -gjə- ‖ -gjə-
 ~**lated** leιt ιd -əd ‖ leιţ əd ~**lates** leιts
 ~**lating** leιt ιŋ ‖ leιţ ιŋ
triangulation traι ,æŋ gju 'leιʃ ᵊn ,•,••-, -gjə-
 ‖ -gjə- ~**s** z
triassic, T~ traι 'æs ιk
triathlete ₍ₜ₎traι 'æθ liːt ~**s** s
triathlon ₍ₜ₎traι 'æθ lən -lɒn ‖ -lɑːn
tribade 'trιb əd ~**s** z
tribadism 'trιb əd ,ιz əm
tribal 'traιb ᵊl ~**ly** i ~**s** z
tribalism 'traιb ə ,lιz əm -ᵊl ,ιz-
tribalistic ,traιb ə 'lιst ιk ◄
tribe traιb **tribes** traιbz
Tribeca traι 'bek ə
tribes|man 'traιbz |mən ~**men** mən men
 ~**people** ,piːp ᵊl ~**woman** ,wʊm ən
 ~**women** ,wιm ιn §-ən
tribo- *comb. form*
 with stress-neutral suffix ¦traιb əʊ ¦trιb- ‖ -oʊ
 — **triboluminescent**
 ,traιb əʊ ,luːm ι 'nes ᵊnt ,trιb-, -,ljuːm-, -ə'••-
 ‖ ,•oʊ-
 with stress-imposing suffix traι 'bɒ+ trι-
 ‖ -'bɑː+ — **tribology** traι 'bɒl ədʒ i trι-
 ‖ -'bɑːl-
tribrach 'trιb ræk 'traι bræk ~**s** s
tribulation ,trιb ju 'leιʃ ᵊn -jə- ‖ -jə- ~**s** z
tribunal traι 'bjuːn ᵊl trι- ‖ -ᵊl
tribune 'trιb juːn ‖ trι 'bjuːn ~**s** z
tributar|y 'trιb jʊt ᵊr i ‖ -jə ter i ~**ies** iz
tribute 'trιb juːt ‖ -jət ~**s** s
trice traιs
Tricel *tdmk* 'traι sel

triceps ˈtraɪs eps
triceratops ˌ₍ˌ₎traɪ ˈser ə tɒps ‖ -tɑːps
trichin|a trɪ ˈkaɪn |ə trə- ~ae iː ~as əz
trichinosis ˌtrɪk ɪ ˈnəʊs ɪs -ə-, §-əs ‖ -ˈnoʊs-
trichloroethylene ˌtraɪ ˌklɔːr əʊ ˈeθ ə liːn
   -ˌklɒr-, -ɪ liːn, -əl iːn ‖ -oʊˈ•- -ˌkloʊr-
trichological ˌtrɪk ə ˈlɒdʒ ɪk əl ◂ ‖ -ˈlɑːdʒ- ~ly
   i
trichologist trɪ ˈkɒl ədʒ ɪst §-əst ‖ -ˈkɑːl- ~s s
trichology trɪ ˈkɒl ədʒ i ‖ -ˈkɑːl-
trichomoniasis ˌtrɪk əʊ məʊ ˈnaɪ_əs ɪs -məˈ•-,
   §-əs ‖ ˌtrɪk əm ə-
trichotom|y ˌtraɪ ˈkɒt əm |i ‖ -ˈkɑːt̬- ~ies iz
Tricia ˈtrɪʃ ə ‖ ˈtriːʃ-
Tricity tdmk ˈtrɪs ət i -ɪt i ‖ -ət̬ i
tri-city ˌtraɪ ˈsɪt i ◂ ˈ•ˌ•• ‖ -ˈsɪt̬-
trick trɪk tricked trɪkt tricking ˈtrɪk ɪŋ tricks
   trɪks
   ˌtrick or ˈtreat
tricker|y ˈtrɪk ər |i ~ies iz
trickl|e ˈtrɪk əl ~ed d ~es z ~ing ˌɪŋ
trickledown ˈtrɪk əl daʊn
trickster ˈtrɪk stə ‖ -stər ~s z
tricksy ˈtrɪks i
trick|y ˈtrɪk |i ~ier i_ə ‖ i_ər ~iest i_ɪst i_əst
   ~ily ɪ li əl i ~iness i nəs i nɪs
triclini|um trɪ ˈklɪn i_|əm trə-, -ˈklaɪn- ~a ə
tricolor, tricolour ˈtrɪk əl ə ˈtraɪ ˌkʌl ə
   ‖ ˈtraɪ ˌkʌl ər ~s z
tricorn ˈtraɪ kɔːn ‖ -kɔːrn ~s z
tricot ˈtrɪk əʊ ˈtriːk- ‖ ˈtriːk oʊ ~s z
tricuspid ₍ˌ₎traɪ ˈkʌsp ɪd §-əd ~s z
tricycl|e ˈtraɪs ɪk əl -ək- ~ed d ~es z ~ing ˌɪŋ
trident, T~ ˈtraɪd ənt ~s s
Tridentine traɪ ˈdent aɪn trɪ-, trə-, -iːn, -ɪn
tried traɪd
triennial traɪ ˈen i_əl ~ly i
trienni|um traɪ ˈen i_əm ~a ə ~ums əmz
trier ˈtraɪ_ə ‖ ˈtraɪ_ər ~s z
Trier place in Germany trɪə ‖ trɪər —Ger [tʁiːɐ]
trierarch ˈtraɪ_ə rɑːk ‖ -rɑːrk ~s s
tries traɪz
Trieste tri ˈest —It [tri ˈɛs te]
triffid ˈtrɪf ɪd §-əd ~s z
trifid ˈtraɪf ɪd §-əd
trifl|e ˈtraɪf əl ~ed d ~es z ~ing ˌɪŋ
trifler ˈtraɪf lə ‖ -lər ~s z
trifling adj ˈtraɪf lɪŋ ~ly li ~ness nəs nɪs
trifori|um traɪ ˈfɔːr i_əm ‖ -ˈfoʊr- ~a ə
trig, Trig trɪg
trigeminal ₍ˌ₎traɪ ˈdʒem ɪn əl -ən əl
trigger, T~ ˈtrɪg ə ‖ -ər ~ed d triggering
   ˈtrɪg ər ɪŋ ~s z
trigger-happy ˈtrɪg ə ˌhæp i ‖ -ər-
triglyceride traɪ ˈglɪs ə raɪd ~s z
triglyph ˈtraɪg lɪf ˈtraɪ glɪf ~s s
trigonal ˈtrɪg ən əl ~ly i
trigonometric ˌtrɪg ən ə ˈmetr ɪk ◂ ~al əl
   ~ally əl_i
   ˌtrigono ˌmetric ˈfunction
trigonometry ˌtrɪg ə ˈnɒm ətr i -ɪtr i ‖ -ˈnɑːm-
trigraph ˈtraɪ grɑːf -græf ‖ -græf ~s s
trijet ˈtraɪ dʒet ~s s

trike traɪk trikes traɪks
trilateral ˌtraɪ ˈlæt ər əl ◂ ‖ -ˈlæt̬ ər əl ◂
   →-ˈlætr əl ~ly i
trilb|y, T~ ˈtrɪlb |i ~ies iz
   ˈtrilby ˈhat
trilingual ˌtraɪ ˈlɪŋ gwəl ◂ -gju_əl ~ly i ~s z
triliteral ˌtraɪ ˈlɪt_ər əl ◂ ‖ -ˈlɪt ər əl ◂ →-ˈlɪtr əl
   ~s z
trill trɪl trilled trɪld trilling ˈtrɪl ɪŋ trills trɪlz
Trilling ˈtrɪl ɪŋ
trillion ˈtrɪl jən ˈ•i_ən ~s z
trillionth ˈtrɪl jəntθ ˈ•i_əntθ ~s s
trillium ˈtrɪl i_əm
trilobite ˈtraɪl əʊ baɪt ‖ -ə- ~s s
trilog|y ˈtrɪl ədʒ |i ~ies iz
trim, Trim trɪm trimmed trɪmd trimming/s
   ˈtrɪm ɪŋ/z trims trɪmz
trimaran ˈtraɪm ə ræn ˌ••ˈ• ~s z
Trimble ˈtrɪm bəl
trimester traɪ ˈmest ə trɪ- ‖ -ər ˈ••• ~s z
trimeter ˈtrɪm ɪt ə -ət- ‖ -ət̬ ər ~s z
trimly ˈtrɪm li
trimm... —see trim
trimmer ˈtrɪm ə ‖ -ər ~s z
trimness ˈtrɪm nəs -nɪs
Trina ˈtriːn ə
Trincomalee ˌtrɪŋk əʊ mə ˈliː ‖ -ə mə-
Trinculo ˈtrɪŋk ju ləʊ -jə- ‖ -jə loʊ
Trinder ˈtrɪnd ə ‖ -ər
trine traɪn trines traɪnz
Tring trɪŋ
Trinidad ˈtrɪn ɪ dæd -ə-, ˌ••ˈ•
Trinidadian ˌtrɪn ɪ ˈdæd i_ən ◂ ˌ•ə-, -ˈdeɪd- ~s
   z
trinitarian, T~ ˌtrɪn ɪ ˈteər i_ən ◂ ˌ•ɪ- ‖ -ˈter-
   ~ism ˌɪz əm ~s z
trinitrotoluene ˌtraɪ ˌnaɪtr əʊ ˈtɒl ju iːn •ˌ•-
   ‖ -oʊ ˈtɑːl-
trinity, T~ ˈtrɪn ət i -ɪt i ‖ -ət̬ i
   ˌTrinity ˈCollege, ˌTrinity ˌCollege
   ˈCambridge; ˌTrinity ˈHouse; ˌTrinity
   ˈSunday
trinket ˈtrɪŋk ɪt §-ət ~s s
trinomial traɪ ˈnəʊm i_əl ‖ -ˈnoʊm- ~s z
trio ˈtriː əʊ ‖ -oʊ ~s z
triode ˈtraɪ əʊd ‖ -oʊd ~s z
triolet ˈtriː_ə let ˈtraɪ_, -əʊ-, -lət, -lɪt ~s s
trioxide ₍ˌ₎traɪ ˈɒks aɪd ‖ -ˈɑːks- ~s z
trip trɪp tripped trɪpt tripping/ly ˈtrɪp ɪŋ /li
   trips trɪps
tripartite ₍ˌ₎traɪ ˈpɑːt aɪt ‖ -ˈpɑːrt-
tripe traɪp tripes traɪps
triphammer ˈtrɪp ˌhæm ə ‖ -ər ~s z
triphthong ˈtrɪf θɒŋ ˈtrɪp- ‖ -θɔːŋ -θɑːŋ ~s z
triphthongal ˌtrɪf ˈθɒŋ gəl ◂ ˌtrɪp- ‖ -ˈθɔːŋ-
   -ˈθɑːŋ- ~ly i
tripl|e ˈtrɪp əl ~ed d ~es z ~ing ˌɪŋ
   ˌTriple Alˈliance; ˈtriple jump,ˌ ,••ˈ•
triplet ˈtrɪp lət -lɪt ~s s
triplex, T~ tdmk ˈtrɪp leks
triplicate adj, n ˈtrɪp lɪk ət -lək-, -ɪt
tripli|cate v ˈtrɪp lɪ |keɪt -lə- ~cated keɪt ɪd

-əd ‖ 'keɪt̬ əd **~cates** keɪts **~cating**
keɪt ɪŋ ‖ 'keɪt̬ ɪŋ
triploid 'trɪp lɔɪd **~s** z
tripod 'traɪ pɒd ‖ -pɑːd **~s** z
Tripoli, t~ 'trɪp əl i
Tripolis 'trɪp əl ɪs §-əs
Tripolitania ˌtrɪp əl ɪ 'teɪn i‿ə -ə'•-
tripos 'traɪp ɒs ‖ -ɑːs **~es** ɪz əz
Tripp trɪp
tripp... —*see* **trip**
tripper 'trɪp ə ‖ -ər **~s** z
triptane 'trɪpt eɪn
Triptolemus trɪp 'tɒl ɪm əs -əm- ‖ -'tɑːl-
triptych 'trɪpt ɪk **~s** s
triptyque trɪp 'tiːk **~s** s
Tripura 'trɪp ʊr ə -ər-
tripwire 'trɪp ˌwaɪ‿ə ‖ -ˌwaɪ‿ər **~s** z
trireme 'traɪə riːm **~s** z
trisect ˌ(ˌ)traɪ 'sekt **~ed** ɪd əd **~ing** ɪŋ **~s** s
Trisha 'trɪʃ ə
trishaw 'traɪ ʃɔː ‖ -ʃɑː **~s** z
triskaidekaphobia ˌtrɪs kaɪ ˌdek ə 'fəʊb i‿ə
•ˌ•'•- ‖ -'foʊb-
triskeli|on trɪ 'skel i |ɒn ˌ(ˌ)traɪ-, ˌ‿ən ‖ -|ɑːn **~a**
ə
trismus 'trɪz məs
Tristan 'trɪst ən
ˌTristan da 'Cunha də 'kuːn ə -jə
Tri-Star *tdmk* 'traɪ stɑː ‖ -stɑːr **~s** z
Tristram 'trɪs trəm
trisyllabic ˌtraɪ sɪ 'læb ɪk ◀ -sə- **~ally** əl‿i
trisyllable ˌtraɪ 'sɪl əb əl '•ˌ•- **~s** z
trite traɪt **triter** 'traɪt ə ‖ 'traɪt̬ ər **tritest**
'traɪt ɪst -əst ‖ 'traɪt̬ əst
trite|ly 'traɪt |li **~ness** nəs nɪs
triticale ˌtrɪt ɪ 'keɪl i -ə- ‖ ˌtrɪt̬ ə-
tritium 'trɪt i‿əm ‖ 'trɪt̬- 'trɪʃ-
Triton '*sea god*', '*mollusc*', '*satellite of Neptune*',
t~ 'traɪt ən -ɒn ‖ -ɑːn
triton '*nucleus of a tritium atom*' 'traɪt ɒn -ən
‖ -ɑːn
tritone 'traɪ təʊn ‖ -toʊn **~s** z
triumph *n, v,* **T~** 'traɪ ʌmᵖf 'traɪ‿əmᵖf **~ed** t
~ing ɪŋ **~s** s
triumphal traɪ 'ʌmᵖf əl
triumphant traɪ 'ʌmᵖf ənt **~ly** li
triumvir traɪ 'ʌm və tri-, 'traɪ‿əm-, -vɜː ‖ -vər
~s z
triumvirate traɪ 'ʌm vər ət tri-, -vɪr-, -ɪt **~s** s
triune 'traɪ juːn
trivalent ˌ(ˌ)traɪ 'veɪl ənt 'trɪv əl-
Trivandrum trɪ 'vændr əm
trivet 'trɪv ɪt §-ət **~s** s
trivia 'trɪv i‿ə
trivial 'trɪv i‿əl **~ly** i
trivialis... —*see* **trivializ...**
trivialit|y ˌtrɪv i 'æl ət i -ɪt i ‖ -ət̬ li **~ies** iz
trivialization ˌtrɪv i‿əl ən 'zeɪʃ ən -ɪ'•- ‖ -ə'•-
trivializ|e 'trɪv i‿ə laɪz **~ed** d **~es** ɪz əz **~ing**
ɪŋ
trivium 'trɪv i‿əm
triweek|ly ˌ(ˌ)traɪ 'wiːk |li **~ies** iz
Trixie 'trɪks i

Troad 'trəʊ æd ‖ 'troʊ-
Troas 'trəʊ æs ‖ 'troʊ-
Trobriand 'trəʊb ri‿ənd -ænd ‖ 'troʊb-
Trocadero ˌtrɒk ə 'dɪər əʊ ‖ ˌtrɑːk ə 'der oʊ
trocar 'trəʊk ɑː ‖ 'troʊk ɑːr **~s** z
trochaic trəʊ 'keɪ ɪk ‖ troʊ- **~s** s
trochanter trəʊ 'kænt ə ‖ troʊ 'kænt̬ ər **~s** z
troche trəʊʃ 'trəʊk iː ‖ 'troʊk iː **troches**
'trəʊʃ ɪz -əz; 'trəʊk iːz ‖ 'troʊk iːz
trochee 'trəʊk iː -i ‖ 'troʊk- **~s** z
trochle|a 'trɒk li‿|ə ‖ 'trɑːk- **~ae** iː
trochlear 'trɒk li‿ə ‖ 'trɑːk li‿ər
trochoid 'trəʊk ɔɪd 'trɒk- ‖ 'troʊk- 'trɑːk- **~s**
z
trod trɒd ‖ trɑːd
trodden 'trɒd ən ‖ 'trɑːd ən
trog trɒg ‖ trɑːg trɔːg
troglodyte 'trɒg lə daɪt ‖ 'trɑːg- **~s** s
troglodytes *sing. 'wren'*, ˌtrɒg lə 'daɪt iːz
trɒ 'glɒd ə tiːz, -ɪ- ‖ ˌtrɑːg-
troglodytic ˌtrɒg lə 'dɪt ɪk ◀ ‖ ˌtrɑːg lə 'dɪt̬ ɪk ◀
trogon, T~ 'trəʊg ɒn ‖ 'troʊg ɑːn **~s** z
troika 'trɔɪk ə 'trəʊ ɪk ə **~s** z
troilism 'trɔɪ ˌlɪz əm
Troilus 'trɔɪl əs 'trəʊ ɪl əs, §-əl- ‖ 'troʊ əl-
Trojan 'trəʊdʒ ən ‖ 'troʊdʒ ən **~s** z
ˌTrojan 'horse; ˌTrojan 'War
troll trɒl trəʊl ‖ troʊl —*In BrE both*
pronunciations shown appear to be in use for all
the various meanings (both n and v) of the word.
trolled trɒld trəʊld ‖ troʊld **trolling** 'trɒl ɪŋ
'trəʊl- ‖ 'troʊl ɪŋ **trolls** trɒlz trəʊlz ‖ troʊlz
trolley 'trɒl i ‖ 'trɑːl i **~s** z
trolleybus 'trɒl i bʌs ‖ 'trɑːl- **~es** ɪz əz
trollop 'trɒl əp ‖ 'trɑːl əp **~s** s
Trollope 'trɒl əp ‖ 'trɑːl əp
trombone trɒm 'bəʊn ‖ trɑːm 'boʊn '•• **~s** z
trombonist trɒm 'bəʊn ɪst §-əst
‖ trɑːm 'boʊn- '••• **~s** s
tromp trɒmp ‖ trɑːmp **tromped**
trɒmpt ‖ trɑːmpt **tromping**
'trɒmp ɪŋ ‖ 'trɑːmp ɪŋ **tromps**
trɒmps ‖ trɑːmps
trompe l'oeil ˌtrɒmp 'lɔɪ -'ləʊ i, -'lɜː
‖ ˌtrɔːmp-, ˌtrɑːmp-, -'leɪ —*Fr* [tʀɔ̃ plœj]
Trondheim 'trɒnd haɪm 'trɒn- ‖ 'trɑːn heɪm
—*Norw* ['trɔn hɛim]
Troon truːn
troop truːp **trooped** truːpt **trooping**
'truːp ɪŋ **troops** truːps
'troop ˌcarrier
trooper 'truːp ə ‖ -ər **~s** z
troopship 'truːp ʃɪp **~s** s
trope trəʊp ‖ troʊp **tropes** trəʊps ‖ troʊps
-trope trəʊp ‖ troʊp — **heliotrope**
'hiːl i‿ə trəʊp ‖ -troʊp
trophic 'trɒf ɪk ‖ 'troʊf ɪk 'trɑːf- **~ally** əl‿i
-trophic 'trɒf ɪk ‖ 'troʊf ɪk 'trɑːf- —
hypertrophic ˌhaɪp ə 'trɒf ɪk ◀ ‖ -ər 'troʊf-
-'trɑːf-
tropho- *comb. form*
with stress-neutral suffix ˌtrɒf əʊ ‖ ˌtroʊf ə
ˌtrɑːf ə — **trophoplasm** 'trɒf əʊ ˌplæz əm

‖ 'trəʊf ə- 'trɑːf-
with stress-imposing suffix trəʊ 'fɒ+ trɒ-
‖ trɒʊ 'fɑː+ — **trophology** trəʊ 'fɒl ədʒ i
trɒ- ‖ trɒʊ 'fɑːl-
troph|y 'trəʊf li ‖ 'trɒʊf li ~**ies** iz
-trophy *stress-imposing* trəf i — **hypertrophy**
haɪ 'pɜːtr əf i ‖ -'pɜ˞ːtr-
tropic 'trɒp ɪk ‖ 'trɑːp ɪk ~**s** s
-tropic 'trɒp ɪk ‖ 'trɒʊp ɪk — **heliotropic**
ˌhiːl i‿əʊ 'trɒp ɪk ◄ ‖ ə 'trɒʊp-
tropical 'trɒp ɪk ᵊl ‖ 'trɑːp- ~**ly** ‿i
ˌtropical 'storm
tropicalis|e, tropicaliz|e 'trɒp ɪk ə laɪz -ᵊl aɪz
‖ 'trɑːp- ~**ed** d ~**es** ɪz əz ~**ing** ɪŋ
tropism 'trəʊp ˌɪz əm ‖ 'trɒʊp- ~**s** z
-tropism trə ˌpɪz əm 'trəʊp ˌɪz əm, ˌ•••
—*Usage varies as to whether this suffix is
stress-imposing or stress-neutral.* —
heliotropism ˌhiːl i 'ɒtr ə ˌpɪz əm ˌ‿əʊ
'trəʊp ˌɪz əm, '••• ‖ -'ɑːtr ə ˌpɪz əm
ˌ‿ə 'trɒʊp ˌɪz əm
tropo- *comb. form*
with stress-neutral suffix ˌtrɒp əʊ ‖ ˌtrɒʊp ə
'trɑːp- — **tropophyte** 'trɒp əʊ faɪt
‖ 'trɒʊp ə- 'trɑːp-
with stress-imposing suffix trɒ 'pɒ+ trə-
‖ trɒʊ 'pɑː+ — **tropophilous** trɒ 'pɒf ɪl əs
trə-, -ᵊl əs ‖ trɒʊ 'pɑːf-
tropopause 'trɒp ə pɔːz ‖ 'trɒʊp- 'trɑːp-,
-pɑːz
troposphere 'trɒp ə sfɪə ‖ 'trɒʊp ə sfɪr 'trɑːp-
-tropous *stress-imposing* trəp əs —
heterotropous
ˌhet ə 'rɒtr əp əs ◄ ‖ ˌhet ə 'rɑːtr-
troppo 'trɒp əʊ ‖ 'trɑːp ɒʊ —*It* ['trɔp po]
Trossachs 'trɒs əks -æks, -əxs ‖ 'trɑːs-
trot, Trot trɒt ‖ trɑːt **trots** trɒts ‖ trɑːts
trotted 'trɒt ɪd -əd ‖ 'trɑːt̬ əd **trotting**
'trɒt ɪŋ ‖ 'trɑːt̬ ɪŋ
troth trəʊθ trɒθ ‖ trɔːθ trɑːθ, trɒʊθ
Trotsky 'trɒt ski ‖ 'trɑːt- ~**ism** ˌɪz əm
Trotskyist 'trɒt ski ɪst §-əst ‖ 'trɑːt- ~**s** s
Trotskyite 'trɒt ski aɪt ‖ 'trɑːt- ~**s** s
Trott trɒt ‖ trɑːt
trott... —*see* **trot**
trotter, T~ 'trɒt ə ‖ 'trɑːt̬ ᵊr ~**s** z
Trottiscliffe 'trɒz li ‖ 'trɑːz- *(!)*
troubadour 'truːb ə dʊə -dɔː ‖ -dɔːr -dʊər,
-dʊr ~**s** z
troubl|e 'trʌb ᵊl *(!)* ~**ed** d ~**es** z ~**ing** ɪŋ
ˈtrouble spot
troublemak|er/s 'trʌb ᵊl ˌmeɪk| ə/z ‖ -ᵊr/z
~**ing** ɪŋ
troubleshoot|er/s 'trʌb ᵊl ˌʃuːt| ə/z
‖ -ˌʃuːt̬| -ᵊr/z ~**ing** ɪŋ
troublesome 'trʌb ᵊl səm ~**ly** li ~**ness** nəs nɪs
troublous 'trʌb ləs
Troubridge 'truː brɪdʒ
trough trɒf trɔːf ‖ trɔːf trɑːf **troughs** trɒfs
trɔːfs ‖ trɔːfs trɑːfs
Troughton 'traʊt ᵊn
trounce traʊnts **trounced** traʊntst **trounces**
'traʊnts ɪz -əz **trouncing** 'traʊnts ɪŋ

troupe truːp *(= troop)* **troupes** truːps
trouper 'truːp ə ‖ -ᵊr ~**s** z
troupial 'truːp i‿əl ~**s** z
trouser 'traʊz ə ‖ -ᵊr ~**ed** d
ˈtrouser press; ˈtrouser suit
trousers 'traʊz əz △-ɪz ‖ -ᵊrz
trousseau 'truːs əʊ truː 'səʊ ‖ truː 'soʊ
'truːs oʊ ~**s**, ~**x** z
trout traʊt **trouts** traʊts
Troutbeck 'traʊt bek
trove trəʊv ‖ trɒʊv
trow trəʊ traʊ ‖ trɒʊ
Trowbridge 'trəʊ brɪdʒ ‖ 'trɒʊ-
trowel 'traʊ‿əl traʊl ‖ 'traʊ‿əl **troweled,**
trowelled 'traʊ‿əld traʊld ‖ 'traʊ‿əld
troweling, trowelling 'traʊ‿əl ɪŋ 'traʊl ɪŋ
‖ 'traʊ‿əl ɪŋ **trowels** 'traʊ‿əlz traʊlz
‖ 'traʊ‿əlz
Trowell *(i)* 'traʊ‿əl traʊl ‖ 'traʊ‿əl,
(ii) 'trəʊ əl ‖ 'trɒʊ‿əl
Troy, troy trɔɪ
ˈtroy weight
truanc|y 'truː‿ənᵗs li ~**ies** iz
tru|ant 'truː‿|ənt ~**anted** ənt ɪd -əd ‖ ənt̬ əd
~**anting** ənt ɪŋ ‖ ənt̬ ɪŋ ~**ants** ənts
Trubenised, Trubenized *tdmk* 'truːb ə naɪzd
Trubetzkoy ˌtruːb ets 'kɔɪ -ɪts-, -əts- —*Russ*
[tru bits 'kɔj]
Trubner, Trübner 'truːb nə ‖ -nᵊr —*Ger*
['tʁyːb nɐ]
Trubshaw 'trʌb ʃɔː ‖ -ʃɑː
truce truːs **truces** 'truːs ɪz -əz
trucial, T~ 'truːʃ ᵊl 'truːs i‿əl
truck trʌk **trucked** trʌkt **trucking** 'trʌk ɪŋ
trucks trʌks
ˈtruck farm; ˈtruck stop
truckage 'trʌk ɪdʒ
Truckee 'trʌk i
trucker 'trʌk ə ‖ -ᵊr ~**s** z
truckl|e 'trʌk ᵊl ~**ed** d ~**es** z ~**ing** ‿ɪŋ
truckload 'trʌk ləʊd ‖ -loʊd ~**s** z
truculence 'trʌk jʊl ənts -jəl- ‖ -jəl-
truculent 'trʌk jʊl ənt -jəl- ‖ -jəl- ~**ly** li
Trudeau 'truːd əʊ ‖ truː 'doʊ —*Fr* [tʁy do]
trudge trʌdʒ **trudged** trʌdʒd **trudges**
'trʌdʒ ɪz -əz **trudging** 'trʌdʒ ɪŋ
Trudgen, t~ 'trʌdʒ ən
Trudgill 'trʌd gɪl →'trʌg-, §-gᵊl
Trudi, Trudy 'truːd i
true truː **trued** truːd **trueing, truing** 'truː‿ɪŋ
truer 'truː‿ə ‖ -ᵊr **trues** truːz **truest**
'truː‿ɪst ‿əst
ˌtrue 'north
true-blue ˌtruː 'bluː ◄ ~**s** z
trueborn ˌtruː 'bɔːn ◄ ‖ -'bɔːrn ◄
truehearted ˌtruː 'hɑːt ɪd ◄ -əd ‖ -'hɑːrt̬ əd ◄
'•••
true-life ˌtruː 'laɪf ◄
truelove, T~ 'truː lʌv ~**s** z
trueness 'truː nəs -nɪs
TrueType *tdmk* 'truː taɪp

Truffaut 'trɒf əʊ 'truːf- ‖ truː 'foʊ —*Fr*
[tʁy fo]

truffle 'trʌf ᵊl ~s z

trug trʌɡ trugs trʌɡz

truism 'truː ˌɪz əm ~s z

Trujillo tru 'hiː jəʊ -'hiːl- ‖ -joʊ —*Sp*
[tru 'xi ʎo, -jo]

Truk trʌk trʊk

truly 'truː li

Truman 'truːm ən

trump, Trump trʌmp trumped trʌmpt
trumping 'trʌmp ɪŋ trumps trʌmps
'trump card

trumped-up ˌtrʌmpt 'ʌp ◄
ˌtrumped-up 'charges

trumper|y 'trʌmp ər li ~ies iz

trump|et 'trʌmp ɪt §-ət ‖ -ət ~eted ɪt ɪd
§ət-, -əd ‖ ət əd ~eting ɪt ɪŋ §ət- ‖ ət ɪŋ
~ets ɪts §əts ‖ əts

trumpeter 'trʌmp ɪt ə §-ət- ‖ -ət ər ~s z

trun|cate trʌŋ 'keɪt 'trʌŋ|k eɪt ‖ 'trʌŋ|k eɪt
'trʌn |keɪt ~cated keɪt ɪd -əd ‖ keɪt əd
~cates keɪts ~cating keɪt ɪŋ ‖ keɪt ɪŋ

truncation trʌŋ 'keɪʃ ᵊn ~s z

truncheon 'trʌntʃ ᵊn 'trʌndʒ- ~ed d ~ing ɪŋ
~s z

trundl|e 'trʌnd ᵊl ~ed d ~es z ~ing ˌɪŋ

trunk trʌŋk trunks trʌŋks
'trunk call; 'trunk road; 'trunk route

trunnel 'trʌn ᵊl ~s z

trunnion 'trʌn i‿ən ~ed d ~s z

Truro 'trʊər əʊ ‖ 'trʊr oʊ

Truscott 'trʌsk ət -ɒt ‖ -ɑːt

truss trʌs trussed trʌst (= *trust*) trusses
'trʌs ɪz -əz trussing 'trʌs ɪŋ

trust trʌst trusted 'trʌst ɪd -əd trusting
'trʌst ɪŋ trusts trʌsts
'trust fund; 'trust ˌterritory

trustee ˌtrʌ 'stiː ◄ ~s z

trusteeship ˌtrʌ 'stiː ʃɪp ~s s

trustful 'trʌst fᵊl -fʊl ~ly i

Trusthouse 'trʌst haʊs

trustworth|y 'trʌst ˌwɜːð li ‖ -ˌwɜːð li ~ily ɪ li
əl i ~iness i nəs i nɪs

trust|y 'trʌst li ~ier i‿ə ‖ i‿ər ~ies iz ~iest
i‿ɪst i‿əst ~ily ɪ li əl i ~iness i nəs i nɪs

truth truːθ truths truːðz truːθs
'truth drug; 'truth ˌtable

truthful 'truːθ fᵊl -fʊl ~ly ‿i ~ness nəs nɪs

try traɪ tried traɪd tries traɪz trying 'traɪ ɪŋ
—*see note at* trying

Tryfan 'trɪv ᵊn 'trɪf-, 'trʌv- —*Welsh* ['trə van]

trying 'traɪ ɪŋ ~ly li ~ness nəs nɪs —*As a
close-knit expression*, trying to *has casual weak
forms* 'traɪ‿ənt ə, 'ˌtraɪ‿ən ə ‖ 'traɪ ən ə *(or
with final* u *for* ə *before a following vowel
sound)*

Tryon 'traɪ‿ən

try-on 'traɪ ɒn ‖ -ɑːn -ɔːn ~s z

try-out 'traɪ aʊt ~s s

trypanosome 'trɪp ən ə səʊm trɪ 'pæn-
‖ -soʊm ~s z

trypanosomiasis ˌtrɪp ən əʊ səʊ 'maɪ‿əs ɪs
trɪ ˌpæn-, §-əs ‖ -ə sə' •-

trypsin 'trɪps ɪn §-ᵊn

tryptophan 'trɪpt əʊ fæn ‖ -ə-

tryst trɪst traɪst trysted 'trɪst ɪd 'traɪst-, -əd
trysting 'trɪst ɪŋ 'traɪst- trysts trɪsts traɪsts

tsar zɑː tsɑː ‖ zɑːr tsɑːr tsars zɑːz tsɑːz
‖ zɑːrz tsɑːrz

tsarevich, tsarevitch 'zɑːr ə vɪtʃ 'tsɑːr- ~es ɪz
əz

tsarina zɑː 'riːn ə tsɑː- ~s z

tsar|ism 'zɑːr ˌɪz əm 'tsɑːr- ~ist/s ɪst/s §əst/s

TSB ˌtiː es 'biː

tsetse 'tets i 'tsets-
'tsetse fly

Tshiluba tʃi 'luːb ə

T-shirt, t-shirt 'tiː ʃɜːt ‖ -ʃɝːt ~s s

tsk ‖ —*This is a conventional spelling for the
alveolar* CLICK.

tsotsi 'tsɒts i ‖ 'tsɑːts i ~s z

T-square 'tiː skweə ‖ -skwer -skwær ~s z

tsunami tsu 'nɑːm i su-, -'næm- —*Jp*
[tsɯ ˌna mi] ~s z

tsutsugamushi ˌtsuːts əɡ ə 'muːʃ i ˌtsʊts-,
ˌsuːts-, • ʊːɡ-, • ʊɡ-, -'mʊʃ i —*Jp*
[tsɯ̥ ˌtsɯ 'ŋa mɯ ɕi, -'ga-]
ˌtsutsuga'mushi di ˌsease

Tswana 'tswɑːn ə 'swɑːn- ~s z

Tuamotu ˌtuːˌə 'məʊt uː ‖ -'moʊt-

Tuareg 'twɑːr eɡ ~s z

tuatara ˌtuːˌə 'tɑːr ə ~s z

tub tʌb tubbed tʌbd tubbing 'tʌb ɪŋ tubs
tʌbz

tuba 'tjuːb ə →§'tʃuːb- ‖ 'tuːb ə 'tjuːb- ~s z

tubal 'tjuːb ᵊl →'tʃuːb- ‖ 'tuːb ᵊl 'tjuːb-

tubb|y 'tʌb li ~ier i‿ə ‖ i‿ər ~iest i‿ɪst i‿əst
~iness i nəs i nɪs

TUBE

■ tuːb ▫ tjuːb					
AmE 1993					
0	20	40	60	80	100%

tube tjuːb →§tʃuːb ‖ tuːb tjuːb —*AmE 1993
poll panel preference:* tuːb 91%, tjuːb 9%.
tubed tjuːbd →§tʃuːbd ‖ tuːbd tjuːbd
tubes tjuːbz →§tʃuːbz ‖ tuːbz tjuːbz
tubing 'tjuːb ɪŋ →§'tʃuːb- ‖ 'tuːb ɪŋ 'tjuːb-

tubeless 'tjuːb ləs →§'tʃuːb-, -lɪs ‖ 'tuːb-
'tjuːb-

tuber 'tjuːb ə →§'tʃuːb- ‖ 'tuːb ər 'tjuːb- ~s z

tubercle 'tjuːb ək ᵊl →§'tʃuːb- ‖ 'tuːb ərk ᵊl
'tjuːb- ~s z

tubercular tju 'bɜːk jʊl ə tə-, tu-, →§tʃu-, -jəl-
‖ tu 'bɜ̃ːk jəl ər tju-, tə-

tuberculin tju 'bɜːk jʊl ɪn tə-, tu-, →§tʃu-,
-jəl-, §-ᵊn ‖ tu 'bɜ̃ːk jəl ən tju-, tə-

tuberculosis tju ˌbɜːk ju 'ləʊs ɪs tə-, tu-,
→§tʃu-, -jə-, §-əs ‖ tu ˌbɜ̃ːk jə 'loʊs əs tju-,
tə-

tuberculous tju 'bɜːk jʊl əs tə-, tu-, →§tʃu-,
-jəl- ‖ tu 'bɜ̃ːk jəl əs tju-, tə-

tuberos|e *n* 'tjuːb ə rəʊz →§'tʃuːb-, • • •
‖ 'tuːb ə roʊz 'tjuːb- —*Also, by folk*

etymology, △ˈtjuːb rəʊz, ˈtʃuːb- ‖ ˈtuːb roʊz,
ˈtjuːb- **~es** ɪz əz
tuberose _adj_ ˈtjuːb ə rəʊs →§ˈtʃuːb-
‖ ˈtuːb ə roʊs ˈtjuːb-
tuberosit|y ˌtjuːb ə ˈrɒs ət i →§ˌtʃuːb-, -ɪt i
‖ ˌtuːb ə ˈrɑːs ət̬ i ˌtjuːb- **~ies** iz
tuberous ˈtjuːb ər əs →§ˈtʃuːb- ‖ ˈtuːb-
ˈtjuːb-
tubful ˈtʌb fʊl **~s** z
tubifex ˈtjuːb ɪ feks →§ˈtʃuːb-, §-ə- ‖ ˈtuːb-
ˈtjuːb- **~es** ɪz əz
tubiform ˈtjuːb ɪ fɔːm →ˈtʃuːb-, §-ə-
‖ ˈtuːb ə fɔːrm ˈtjuːb-
tubing ˈtjuːb ɪŋ →§ˈtʃuːb- ‖ ˈtuːb ɪŋ ˈtjuːb-
Tubingen ˈtjuːb ɪŋ ən ˈtuːb- ‖ ˈtuːb- —_Ger_
Tübingen [ˈtyː bɪŋ ən]
Tubman ˈtʌb mən
tub-thump|ing ˈtʌb ˌθʌmp ɪŋ **~er/s** ə/z ‖ ər/z
tubular ˈtjuːb jʊl ə →§ˈtʃuːb-, -jəl-
‖ ˈtuːb jəl ər ˈtjuːb-
tubule ˈtjuːb juːl →§ˈtʃuːb- ‖ ˈtuːb- ˈtjuːb-
~s z
TUC ˌtiː juː ˈsiː
tuck, Tuck tʌk **tucked** tʌkt **tucking** ˈtʌk ɪŋ
tucks tʌks
ˈtuck box; ˈtuck shop
tuckahoe ˈtʌk ə həʊ ‖ -hoʊ **~s** z
tucker, T~ ˈtʌk ə ‖ -ər **~ed** d **~s** z
tuckerbag ˈtʌk ə bæg ‖ -ər- **~s** z
tuckeroo ˌtʌk ə ˈruː **~s** z
tuck-in ˈtʌk ɪn
Tucson ˈtuː sɒn ˌ•ˈ• ‖ -sɑːn (!)
-tude tjuːd →§tʃuːd ‖ tuːd tjuːd —
amplitude ˈæmp lɪ tjuːd -lə-, →§-tʃuːd
‖ -tuːd -tjuːd
Tudor ˈtjuːd ə →§ˈtʃuːd- ‖ ˈtuːd ər ˈtjuːd- **~s**
z
Tudur ˈtɪd ɪə ‖ -ɪr —_Welsh_ [ˈtɨ dɪr, ˈti dɪr]
Tue tjuː →§tʃuː ‖ tuː tjuː
Tuesday ˈtjuːz di →§ˈtʃuːz-, -deɪ ‖ ˈtuːz-
ˈtjuːz- —_see note at_ -day **~s** z
tufa ˈtjuːf ə →§ˈtʃuːf-, ˈtuːf- ‖ ˈtuːf ə ˈtjuːf-
tufaceous tjuː ˈfeɪʃ əs →tʃuː-, tu- ‖ tuː- tjuː-
tuff tʌf
tuffet ˈtʌf ɪt §-ət **~s** s
Tuffnell, Tufnell ˈtʌf nəl
ˌTufnell ˈPark
tuft tʌft **tufted** ˈtʌft ɪd -əd **tufting** ˈtʌft ɪŋ
tufts tʌfts
Tufts tʌfts
tuft|y ˈtʌft li **~ier** i‿ə ‖ i‿ər **~iest** i‿ɪst i‿əst
~iness i nəs i nɪs
tug tʌg **tugged** tʌgd **tugging** ˈtʌg ɪŋ **tugs**
tʌgz
tugboat ˈtʌg bəʊt ‖ -boʊt **~s** s
Tugendhat ˈtuːg ən hɑːt
tugg... —_see_ tug
tug-of-love ˌtʌg əv ˈlʌv ◄
tug-of-war ˌtʌg əv ˈwɔː -ə- ‖ -ˈwɔːr
tugrik ˈtuːg rɪk **~s** s
Tuileries ˈtwiːl ər i -iz —_Fr_ [tɥil ʁi]
Tuite (i) tjuːt →§tʃuːt ‖ tuːt tjuːt, (ii) ˈtjuːˌ ɪt
→§ˈtʃuːˌ, §-ət ‖ ˈtuːˌ ət ˈtjuː-

tuition tjuː ˈɪʃ ən →§tʃuː- ‖ tu- tjuː-
Tuitt ˈtjuːˌ ɪt →§ˈtʃuːˌ, §-ət ‖ ˈtuːˌ ət ˈtjuː-
Tuke tjuːk →§tʃuːk ‖ tuːk tjuːk
Tulare tu ˈleər i -ˈleə ‖ tu ˈler i -ˈlær-; -ˈleᵊr,
-ˈlæᵊr
tularaemia, tularemia ˌtuːl ə ˈriːm i‿ə ˌtjuːl-
Tule, tule ˈtuːl i
tulip ˈtjuːl ɪp →§ˈtʃuːl-, §-əp ‖ ˈtuːl əp ˈtjuːl-
~s s
ˈtulip tree
Tull tʌl
Tullamarine ˌtʌl ə mə ˈriːn
tulle tjuːl →§tʃuːl ‖ tuːl —_Fr_ [tyl] **tulles**
tjuːlz →§tʃuːlz ‖ tuːlz
Tulloch ˈtʌl ək -əx
Tully ˈtʌl i
Tulsa ˈtʌls ə
Tulse tʌls
ˌTulse ˈHill
tum tʌm **tums** tʌmz
tumbl|e ˈtʌm bəl **~ed** d **~es** z **~ing** ‿ɪŋ
tumbledown ˈtʌm bəl daʊn
tumble-drier, tumble-dryer ˌtʌm bəl ˈdraɪ‿ə
ˈ•ˌ•• ‖ -ˈdraɪ‿ər **~s** z
tumble-|dry ˌtʌm bəl ˈdraɪ ˈ••• **~dried** ˈdraɪd
~dries ˈdraɪz **~drying** ˈdraɪ ɪŋ
tumbler ˈtʌm blə ‖ -blər **~s** z
tumbleweed ˈtʌm bəl wiːd **~s** z
tumbrel, tumbril ˈtʌm brəl -brɪl **~s** z
tumefacient ˌtjuːm ɪ ˈfeɪʃ i‿ənt ◄ §→ˌtʃuːm-,
§ˌ•ə-, -ˈfeɪs-, -ˈfeɪʃ ənt ‖ ˌtuːm- ˌtjuːm-
tumefaction ˌtjuːm ɪ ˈfæk ʃən §→ˌtʃuːm-, §-ə-
‖ ˌtuːm- ˌtjuːm-
tume|fy ˈtjuːm ɪ faɪ →§ˈtʃuːm-, -ə- ‖ ˈtuːm-
ˈtjuːm- **~fied** faɪd **~fies** faɪz **~fying** faɪ ɪŋ
tumescence tjuː ˈmes ənts →§tʃuː- ‖ tu- tjuː-
tumescent tjuː ˈmes ənt →§tʃuː- ‖ tu- tjuː-
tumid ˈtjuːm ɪd →§ˈtʃuːm-, §-əd ‖ ˈtuːm əd
ˈtjuːm- **~ly** li **~ness** nəs nɪs
tumidity tjuː ˈmɪd ət i →§tʃuː-, -ɪt-
‖ tu ˈmɪd ət̬ i tjuː-
Tummel ˈtʌm əl
tumm|y ˈtʌm li **~ies** iz
tumor, tumour ˈtjuːm ə →§ˈtʃuːm- ‖ ˈtuːm ər
ˈtjuːm- **~s** z
tump tʌmp **tumps** tʌmps
tumuli ˈtjuːm ju laɪ →§ˈtʃuːm-, -jə-
‖ ˈtuːm jə laɪ ˈtjuːm-
tumult ˈtjuːm ʌlt →§ˈtʃuːm-, -əlt ‖ ˈtuːm-
ˈtjuːm- **~s** s
tumultuous tjuː ˈmʌltʃ u‿əs →§tʃuː-, -ˈmʌlt ju‿
‖ tu- tjuː- **~ly** li **~ness** nəs nɪs
tum|ulus ˈtjuːm |jʊl əs →§ˈtʃuːm-, -jəl-
‖ ˈtuːm |jəl əs ˈtjuːm- **~uli** ju laɪ jə- ‖ jə laɪ
tun tʌn **tuns** tʌnz
tuna ˈtjuːn ə ˈtuːn-, →ˈtʃuːn- ‖ ˈtuːn ə ˈtjuːn-
~s z
ˈtuna fish; ˌtuna ˈsalad
Tunbridge ˈtʌn brɪdʒ →ˈtʌm-
ˌTunbridge ˈWells
tundish ˈtʌn dɪʃ **~es** ɪz əz
tundra ˈtʌndr ə

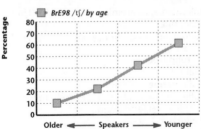

TUNE

■ tjuːn ■ tʃuːn ■ tuːn

BrE 1998

0 20 40 60 80 100%

BrE98 /tʃ/ by age

Percentage

80
70
60
50
40
30
20
10
0

Older ◀— Speakers —▶ Younger

tune tjuːn →§'tʃuːn ‖ tuːn tjuːn —*BrE 1998 poll panel preference:* tjuːn *64%,* tʃuːn *35%,* tuːn *1%.* **tuned** tjuːnd →§'tʃuːnd ‖ tuːnd tjuːnd **tunes** tjuːnz →§'tʃuːnz ‖ tuːnz tjuːnz **tuning** 'tjuːn ɪŋ →§'tʃuːn- ‖ 'tuːn ɪŋ 'tjuːn-
  'tuning fork; 'tuning peg
tuneful 'tjuːn fəl →§'tʃuːn-, -fʊl ‖ 'tuːn- 'tjuːn- ~**ly** i ~**ness** nəs nɪs
tuneless 'tjuːn ləs →§'tʃuːn-, -lɪs ‖ 'tuːn- 'tjuːn- ~**ly** li ~**ness** nəs nɪs
tuner 'tjuːn ə →§'tʃuːn- ‖ 'tuːn ər 'tjuːn- ~**s** z
tunesmith 'tjuːn smɪθ →§'tʃuːn- ‖ 'tuːn- 'tjuːn- ~**s** s
tune-up 'tjuːn ʌp →§'tʃuːn- ‖ 'tuːn- 'tjuːn- ~**s** s
tung tʌŋ
tungsten 'tʌŋkst ən
Tungus 'tʊŋ gʊs tʊŋ 'guːz ~**es** ɪz əz
Tungusic tʊŋ 'gʊs ɪk -'guːz-
tunic 'tjuːn ɪk →§'tʃuːn- ‖ 'tuːn ɪk 'tjuːn- ~**s** s
tunicate 'tjuːn ɪk ət →§'tʃuːn-, §-ək-, -ɪt; -ɪ keɪt, -ə- ‖ 'tuːn- 'tjuːn- ~**s** s
tunicle 'tjuːn ɪk əl →§'tʃuːn-, §-ək- ‖ 'tuːn- 'tjuːn- ~**s** z
Tunis 'tjuːn ɪs §→'tʃuːn-, §-əs ‖ 'tuːn əs 'tjuːn-
Tunisi|a tju 'nɪz i‿ə →§tʃu-, -'nɪs- ‖ tu 'niːʒ ə tju-, -'niːʃ-, -'nɪʒ-, -'nɪʃ- *(*)* ~**an/s** ən/z ‖ ən/z
tunnel 'tʌn əl ~**ed**, ~**led** d ~**ing**, ~**ling** ɪŋ ~**s** z
  ,tunnel 'vision, '•• ,••
tunneler, tunneller 'tʌn əl ə ‖ -ər ~**s** z
Tunney 'tʌn i
Tunnicliff, Tunnicliffe 'tʌn i klɪf
tunn|y 'tʌn |i ~**ies** ɪz
Tunstall 'tʌnˀst əl 'tʌn stɔːl
Tuohey, Tuohy 'tuː i -hi
Tuolumne tu 'ɒl əm i ‖ -'ɑːl-
tup tʌp **tupped** tʌpt **tupping** 'tʌp ɪŋ **tups** tʌps
Tupamaro ,tuːp ə 'mɑːr əʊ ‖ -oʊ ~**s** z —*Sp* [tu pa 'ma ro, -s]
tupelo, T~ 'tjuːp ə ləʊ →§'tʃuːp- ‖ 'tuːp ə loʊ 'tjuːp- ~**s** z
Tupi tu 'piː 'tuːp i ~**s** z

-tuple tjuːp əl tjʊp əl, tʌp əl, →tʃuːp-, →tʃʊp-; '•• ‖ tuːp əl tjuːp əl, tʌp əl —*usually unstressed*
tuppenc|e 'tʌp ən^ts →-mps ~**es** ɪz əz
tuppenny 'tʌp ən i
  ,tuppenny 'ha'penny◀
Tupper 'tʌp ə ‖ -ər
Tupperware *tdmk* 'tʌp ə weə ‖ -ər wer -wær
tu quoque ,tu: 'kwɒk wi -'kwəʊk-, -weɪ ‖ -'kwoʊk-
Turandot 'tjʊər ən dɒt 'tʊər-, →§'tʃʊər-, -dəʊ ‖ 'tʊr ən dɑːt -doʊ —*It* [tu ran 'dɔt]
Turanian tjuə 'reɪn i‿ən →§tʃuə- ‖ tu- tju- ~**s** z
turban 'tɜːb ən ‖ 'tɜːːb ən ~**ed** d ~**s** z
turbar|y 'tɜːb ər |i ‖ 'tɜːːb- ~**ies** iz
turbid 'tɜːb ɪd §-əd ‖ 'tɜːːb- ~**ly** li ~**ness** nəs nɪs
turbidity tɜː 'bɪd ət i -ɪt- ‖ tɜːː 'bɪd ət i
turbinate 'tɜːb ɪn ət -ən-, -ɪt; -ɪ neɪt, -ə- ‖ 'tɜːːb-
turbine 'tɜːb aɪn -ɪn, §-ən ‖ 'tɜːːb- ~**s** z
turbo 'tɜːb əʊ ‖ 'tɜːːb oʊ ~**s** z
turbo- ¦tɜːb əʊ ‖ ¦tɜːːb oʊ — **turboelectric** ,tɜːb əʊ ɪ 'lek trɪk ◀ -ə'•- ‖ ,tɜːːb oʊ-
turbocharg|e 'tɜːb əʊ tʃɑːdʒ ‖ 'tɜːːb oʊ tʃɑːrdʒ ~**ed** d ~**er/s** ə/z ‖ ər/z ~**es** ɪz əz ~**ing** ɪŋ
turbofan 'tɜːb əʊ fæn ,••'• ‖ 'tɜːːb oʊ- ~**s** z
turbojet 'tɜːb əʊ dʒet ‖ 'tɜːːb oʊ- ~**s** s
turboprop 'tɜːb əʊ prɒp ‖ 'tɜːːb oʊ prɑːp ~**s** s
turbot 'tɜːb ət ‖ 'tɜːːb ət ~**s** s
turbulenc|e 'tɜːb jʊl ən^ts -jəl- ‖ 'tɜːːb jəl- ~**y** i
turbulent 'tɜːb jʊl ənt -jəl- ‖ 'tɜːːb jəl- ~**ly** li
Turco- ¦tɜːk əʊ ‖ ¦tɜːːk oʊ — **Turco-Greek** ,tɜːk əʊ 'griːk ◀ ‖ ,tɜːːk oʊ-
turd tɜːd ‖ tɜːːd **turds** tɜːdz ‖ tɜːːdz
tureen tjuə 'riːn ,tjʊə-, tu-ə-, §→tʃuə, §→,tʃʊə-, tjə-, tə- ‖ tə- tju-, tu- ~**s** z
turf tɜːf ‖ tɜːːf **turfed** tɜːft ‖ tɜːːft **turfing** 'tɜːf ɪŋ ‖ 'tɜːːf ɪŋ **turfs** tɜːfs ‖ tɜːːfs **turves** tɜːvz ‖ tɜːːvz
  'turf ac,countant
Turgenev tʊə 'geɪn jev tɜː-, -'gen- ‖ tʊr- tɜːː- —*Russ* [tur 'gʲe nʲɪf]
turgid 'tɜːdʒ ɪd §-əd ‖ 'tɜːːdʒ- ~**ly** li ~**ness** nəs nɪs
turgidity tɜː 'dʒɪd ət i -ɪt- ‖ tɜːː 'dʒɪd ət i
turgor 'tɜːg ə ‖ 'tɜːːg ər
Turin ,tjʊə 'rɪn tjuː-; 'tʊər ɪn ‖ tu 'rɪn 'tʊr ən, 'tjʊr-, 'tɜːː-
  the ,Turin 'shroud
Turing 'tjʊər ɪŋ →§'tʃʊər- ‖ 'tʊr ɪŋ 'tjʊr-, 'tɜːː-
  'Turing ma,chine
Turk tɜːk ‖ tɜːːk **Turks** tɜːks ‖ tɜːːks
  ,Turks and 'Caicos 'keɪk ɒs ‖ -oʊs
Turkestan ,tɜːk ɪ 'stɑːn -ə-, -'stæn ‖ ,tɜːːk-
Turkey, t~ 'tɜːk i ‖ 'tɜːːk i ~**s** z
turkeycock 'tɜːk i kɒk ‖ 'tɜːːk i kɑːk ~**s** s
Turkic 'tɜːk ɪk ‖ 'tɜːːk-

Turkish 'tɜːk ɪʃ ‖ 'tɜːk-
   Turkish 'bath; Turkish de'light
Turkmen 'tɜːk men -mən ‖ 'tɜ˞ːk-
Turkmeni|a tɜːk 'miːn iｰə ‖ tɜ˞ːk- ~an/s ｰən/
  z
Turkmenistan ˌtɜːk men ɪ 'staːn •, •-, -ə-,
  -'stæn ‖ ˌtɜ˞ːk-
Turkoman 'tɜːk əm ən -ə mæn, -ə maːn
  ‖ 'tɜ˞ːk- ~s z
Turku 'tʊək uː ‖ 'tʊrk uː —Finnish ['tur ku]
Turl, Turle tɜːl ‖ tɜ˞ːl
turmeric 'tɜːm ər ɪk ‖ 'tɜ˞ːm-
turmoil 'tɜːm ɔɪəl ‖ 'tɜ˞ːm-
turn tɜːn ‖ tɜ˞ːn turned tɜːnd ‖ tɜ˞ːnd
  turning 'tɜːn ɪŋ ‖ 'tɜ˞ːn ɪŋ turns
  tɜːnz ‖ tɜ˞ːnz
  'turning ˌcircle; 'turning point
turnabout 'tɜːn ə ˌbaʊt ‖ 'tɜ˞ːn- ~s s
turnaround 'tɜːn ə ˌraʊnd ‖ 'tɜ˞ːn- ~s z
Turnberry 'tɜːn bər_i →'tɜːm- ‖ 'tɜ˞ːn ˌber i
turnbuckle 'tɜːn ˌbʌk əl →'tɜːm- ‖ 'tɜ˞ːn- ~s z
Turnbull 'tɜːn bʊl →'tɜːm- ‖ 'tɜ˞ːn-
turncoat 'tɜːn kəʊt →'tɜːŋ- ‖ 'tɜ˞ːn koʊt ~s s
turncock 'tɜːn kɒk →'tɜːŋ- ‖ 'tɜ˞ːn kɑːk ~s s
turndown 'tɜːn daʊn ‖ 'tɜ˞ːn-
turner, T~ 'tɜːn ə ‖ 'tɜ˞ːn ər ~s z
turner|y 'tɜːn ər |i ‖ 'tɜ˞ːn- ~ies iz
Turnham 'tɜːn əm ‖ 'tɜ˞ːn-
Turnhouse 'tɜːn haʊs ‖ 'tɜ˞ːn-
turning 'tɜːn ɪŋ ‖ 'tɜ˞ːn ɪŋ ~s z
  'turning point
turnip 'tɜːn ɪp §-əp ‖ 'tɜ˞ːn əp ~s s
turnkey 'tɜːn kiː →'tɜːŋ- ‖ 'tɜ˞ːn- ~s z
turn-off 'tɜːn ɒf -ɔːf ‖ 'tɜ˞ːn ɔːf -ɑːf ~s s
turn-on 'tɜːn ɒn ‖ 'tɜ˞ːn ɑːn -ɔːn ~s z
turnout 'tɜːn aʊt ‖ 'tɜ˞ːn- ~s s
turnover 'tɜːn ˌəʊv ə ‖ 'tɜ˞ːn ˌoʊv ər ~s z
turnpike 'tɜːn paɪk →'tɜːm- ‖ 'tɜ˞ːn- ~s s
turnround 'tɜːn raʊnd ‖ 'tɜ˞ːn- ~s z
turnstile 'tɜːn staɪəl ‖ 'tɜ˞ːn- ~s z
turnstone 'tɜːn stəʊn ‖ 'tɜ˞ːn stoʊn ~s z
turntable 'tɜːn ˌteɪb əl ‖ 'tɜ˞ːn- ~s z
turn-up 'tɜːn ʌp ‖ 'tɜ˞ːn- ~s s
turpentine 'tɜːp ən taɪn →-m-, -ɪn- ‖ 'tɜ˞ːp-
Turpin 'tɜːp ɪn §-ən ‖ 'tɜ˞ːp ən
turpitude 'tɜːp ɪ tjuːd -ə-, →§-tʃuːd
  ‖ 'tɜ˞ːp ə tuːd -tjuːd
turps tɜːps ‖ tɜ˞ːps
turquoise 'tɜːk wɔɪz -waːz ‖ 'tɜ˞ːk- -ɔɪz
turr|et 'tʌr |ɪt -ət ‖ 'tɜ˞ː |ət ~eted ɪt ɪd §ət-,
  -əd ‖ ət əd ~ets ɪts §əts ‖ əts
Turriff 'tʌr ɪf -əf ‖ 'tɜ˞ː əf
turtle 'tɜːt əl ‖ 'tɜ˞ːt əl ~s z
turtledove 'tɜːt əl dʌv ‖ 'tɜ˞ːt- ~s z
turtleneck 'tɜːt əl nek ‖ 'tɜ˞ːt- ~s s
Turton 'tɜːt ən ‖ 'tɜ˞ːt ən
turves tɜːvz ‖ tɜ˞ːvz
Turvey 'tɜːv i ‖ 'tɜ˞ːv i
Tuscan 'tʌsk ən ~s z
Tuscany 'tʌsk ən i
Tuscarora ˌtʌsk ə 'rɔːr ə ‖ -'roʊr-
tush interj; n 'tusk' tʌʃ
tush n 'buttocks' tʊʃ tushes 'tʊʃ ɪz -əz

tushery 'tʌʃ ər i
tushie 'tʊʃ i ~s z
tusk tʌsk tusked tʌskt tusks tʌsks
tusker 'tʌsk ə ‖ -ər ~s z
tussah 'tʌs ə
Tussaud's tə 'sɔːdz tu-, -'səʊdz; 'tuːs ɔːdz,
  -əʊdz ‖ tu 'soʊz —The Tussaud family call
  themselves 'tuːs əʊ
tussl|e 'tʌs əl ~ed d ~es z ~ing _ɪŋ
tussock 'tʌs ək ~s s
tussore 'tʌs ə -ɔː ‖ -ər -ɔːr, -oʊr
tut name of interj tʌt —The interj itself is [ǀ], an
  alveolar CLICK. tuts tʌts tutted 'tʌt ɪd -əd
  ‖ 'tʌt əd tutting 'tʌt ɪŋ ‖ 'tʌt ɪŋ
Tutankhamen ˌtuːt ən 'kaːm en -əŋ-,
  -æŋ- ‖ -aːŋ-
Tutbury 'tʌt bər_i
tutee ˌtjuː 'tiː →§ˌtʃuː- ‖ ˌtuː- ˌjuː- ~s z
tutelage 'tjuːt əl ɪdʒ →§'tʃuːt-, -ɪl- ‖ 'tuːt əl-
  'tjuːt-
tutelar 'tjuːt əl ə →§'tʃuːt-, -ɪl- ‖ 'tuːt əl ər
  'tjuːt-, -aːr
tutelary 'tjuːt əl ər i →§'tʃuːt-, '•ɪl-
  ‖ 'tuːt əl er i 'tjuːt-
Tutin 'tjuːt ɪn →§'tʃuːt-, §-ən ‖ 'tuːt ən 'tjuːt-
tutor 'tjuːt ə →§'tʃuːt- ‖ 'tuːt ər 'tjuːt- ~ed d
  tutoring 'tjuːt ər ɪŋ →§'tʃuːt- ‖ 'tuːt-
  'tjuːt- ~s z
tutorage 'tjuːt ər ɪdʒ →§'tʃuːt- ‖ 'tuːt- 'tjuːt-
tutorial tjuː 'tɔːr iｰəl →§'tʃuː- ‖ tu- -'toʊr- ~s
  z
tutorship 'tjuːt ə ʃɪp →§'tʃuːt- ‖ 'tuːt ər-
  'tjuːt- ~s s
tutsan 'tʌts ən
Tutsi 'tʊts i 'tuːts-
tutti 'tʊt i 'tuːt-, -iː —It ['tut ti] ~s z
tutti-frutti ˌtuːt i 'fruːt i ‖ ˌtuːt i 'fruːt i ~s z
Tuttle 'tʌt əl ‖ 'tʌt əl
tut-|tut name of interj; v ˌtʌt 'tʌt —The interj
  itself is [ǀ ǀ], a repeated alveolar CLICK. ~tuts
  'tʌts ~tutted 'tʌt ɪd -əd ‖ 'tʌt əd ~tutting
  'tʌt ɪŋ ‖ 'tʌt ɪŋ
tutty 'tʌt i ‖ 'tʌt i
tutu, Tutu 'tuːt uː ~s z
Tuva 'tuːv ə —Russ [tu 'va]
Tuvalu tu 'vaːl uː ˌtuːv ə 'luː
tu-whit tu-whoo tə ˌwɪt tə 'wuː tu ˌwɪt tu-,
  -,hwɪt-, -'hwuː ‖ tə ˌhwɪt tə 'hwuː
tux tʌks tuxes 'tʌks ɪz -əz
tuxedo, T~ tʌk 'siːd əʊ ‖ -oʊ ~s z
Tuxford 'tʌks fəd ‖ -fərd
Tuzla 'tʊz lə 'tuːz- ‖ 'tuːz- —SCr ['tuz la]
TV ˌtiː 'viː ◄ TVs, TV's ˌtiː 'viːz
  ˌTV 'dinner; ˌT'V ˌprogram(me)
Twaddell (i) 'twɒd əl ‖ 'twaːd əl, (ii)
  twɒ 'del ‖ twaː-
twaddle 'twɒd əl ‖ 'twaːd əl
twain, Twain tweɪn
twang twæŋ twanged twæŋd twanging
  'twæŋ ɪŋ twangs twæŋz
Twankey, Twanky 'twæŋk i
'twas strong form twɒz ‖ twʌz twaːz, weak form
  twəz

T

twat twɒt twæt ‖ twɑːt **twats** twɒts twæts
‖ twɑːts
twayblade 'tweɪ bleɪd ~s z
tweak twiːk **tweaked** twiːkt **tweaking**
'twiːk ɪŋ **tweaks** twiːks
twee twiː **tweer** 'twiː ə ‖ -ᵊr **tweest** 'twiː ɪst
-əst
tweed, Tweed twiːd **tweeds** twiːdz
Tweeddale 'twiːd deɪᵊl
Tweedie 'twiːd i
Tweedledee ˌtwiːd ᵊl 'diː
Tweedledum ˌtwiːd ᵊl 'dʌm
Tweedsmuir 'twiːdz mjʊə -mjɔː ‖ -mjʊr
tweed|y 'twiːd |i ~ier iˌə ‖ iˌᵊr ~iest iˌɪst
iˌəst ~iness i nəs i nɪs
'tween, tween twiːn **tweening** 'twiːn ɪŋ
tween|y 'twiːn |i ~ies iz
tweet twiːt **tweeted** 'twiːt ɪd -əd ‖ 'twiːt̬ əd
tweeting 'twiːt ɪŋ ‖ 'twiːt̬ ɪŋ **tweets** twiːts
tweeter 'twiːt ə ‖ 'twiːt̬ ᵊr ~s z
tweeze twiːz **tweezed** twiːzd **tweezes**
'twiːz ɪz -əz **tweezing** 'twiːz ɪŋ
tweezer 'twiːz ə ‖ -ᵊr ~s z
twelfth twelfθ twelθ **twelfthly** 'twelfθ li
'twelθ- **twelfths** twelfθs twelθs
ˌTwelfth 'Night ‖ ' ˌ ˌ
twelve twelv **twelves** twelvz
twelvemonth 'twelv mʌnθ ~s s
twelve-tone ˌtwelv 'təʊn ◄' ˌ ˌ ‖ -'toʊn ◄
twelvish 'twelv ɪʃ
twentieth 'twent iˌəθ △'twen-, ˌ ˌɪθ ‖ 'twent̬-
~s s
twent|y 'twent |i △'twen i ‖ 'twent̬ li ~ies iz
twenty-first ˌtwent i 'fɜːst ◄ △ˌtwen-
‖ ˌtwent̬ i 'fɜːst ◄ ~s s
twentyfold 'twent i fəʊld △'twen-, →-fɒʊld
‖ 'twent̬ i foʊld
twenty-one ˌtwent i 'wʌn ◄ △ˌtwen-
‖ ˌtwent̬- ~s z
twenty-twenty ˌtwent i 'twent i ◄
△ˌtwen i 'twen i ‖ ˌtwent̬ i 'twent̬ i ◄
ˌtwenty-ˌtwenty 'vision
'twere strong form twɜː tweə ‖ twɜˑɪ, weak form
twə ‖ twᵊr
twerp twɜːp ‖ twɜˑp **twerps** twɜːps ‖ twɜˑps
Twi twiː —Twi [tɕ ɥi]
twice twaɪs
twice-told ˌtwaɪs 'təʊld ◄→-'tɒʊld ‖ -'toʊld ◄
Twickenham 'twɪk ən əm
Twickers 'twɪk əz ‖ -ᵊrz
twiddl|e 'twɪd ᵊl ~ed d ~er/s ˌə/z ‖ ˌᵊr/z ~es
z ~ier iˌə ‖ iˌᵊr ~iest iˌɪst -əst ~ing ˌɪŋ
~y ˌi
twig twɪg **twigged** twɪgd **twigging** 'twɪg ɪŋ
twigs twɪgz
Twigg twɪg
twigg|y, T~ 'twɪg |i ~ier iˌə ‖ iˌᵊr ~iest iˌɪst
iˌəst
twilight 'twaɪ laɪt
twilit 'twaɪ lɪt
twill twɪl **twilled** twɪld **twilling** 'twɪl ɪŋ
twills twɪlz
'twill twɪl —sometimes with a weak form twᵊl

twin twɪn **twinned** twɪnd **twinning** 'twɪn ɪŋ
twins twɪnz
ˌtwin 'bed; 'twin set
twin-bedded ˌtwɪn 'bed ɪd ◄ -əd
twine twaɪn **twined** twaɪnd **twines** twaɪnz
twining 'twaɪn ɪŋ
twinge twɪndʒ **twinged** twɪndʒd **twinges**
'twɪndʒ ɪz -əz **twingeing, twinging**
'twɪndʒ ɪŋ
Twining 'twaɪn ɪŋ
twink twɪŋk **twinks** twɪŋks
Twinkie tdmk 'twɪŋk i ~s z
twinkl|e 'twɪŋk ᵊl ~ed d ~es z ~ing ˌɪŋ
twinkling n 'twɪŋk lɪŋ 'twɪŋk ᵊlˌɪŋ ~s z
Twinn twɪn
twinset 'twɪn set ~s s
twin-tub ˌtwɪn 'tʌb ◄' ˌ ˌ
twirl twɜːl ‖ twɜˑl **twirled** twɜːld ‖ twɜˑld
twirling 'twɜːl ɪŋ ‖ 'twɜˑl ɪŋ **twirls**
twɜːlz ‖ twɜˑlz
twirp twɜːp ‖ twɜˑp **twirps** twɜːps ‖ twɜˑps
Twisleton 'twɪs ᵊl tən
twist twɪst **twisted** 'twɪst ɪd -əd **twisting**
'twɪst ɪŋ **twists** twɪsts
'twist grip
twister 'twɪst ə ‖ -ᵊr ~s z
twist|y 'twɪst| i ~ier iˌə ‖ iˌᵊr ~iest iˌɪst ˌəst
twit twɪt **twits** twɪts **twitted** 'twɪt ɪd -əd
‖ 'twɪt̬ əd **twitting** 'twɪt ɪŋ ‖ 'twɪt̬ ɪŋ
twitch twɪtʃ **twitched** twɪtʃt **twitches**
'twɪtʃ ɪz -əz **twitching/s** 'twɪtʃ ɪŋ/z
twitcher 'twɪtʃ ə ‖ -ᵊr ~s z
twitch|y 'twɪtʃ |i ~ier iˌə ‖ iˌᵊr ~iest iˌɪst
iˌəst ~iness i nəs i nɪs
Twitchett 'twɪtʃ ɪt §-ət
twite twaɪt **twites** twaɪts
twitter 'twɪt ə ‖ 'twɪt̬ ᵊr ~ed d **twittering/ly**
'twɪt ᵊr ɪŋ /li ‖ 'twɪt̬ ᵊr ɪŋ /li ~s z
twittery 'twɪt ᵊr i ‖ 'twɪt̬-
twixt, 'twixt twɪkst
two tuː (= too) **twos** tuːz
ˌtwo 'bits
two-bit 'tuː bɪt
two-by-four ˌtuː bə 'fɔː -bi-, -baɪ- ‖ -'fɔːr
-'four
two-dimensional ˌtuː daɪ 'mentʃ ᵊnˌᵊl ◄, •dɪ-,
ˌ•də- ~ly i
two-edged ˌtuː 'edʒd ◄
two|faced ˌtuː 'feɪst ◄ ~facedly 'feɪs ɪd li
-əd-; 'feɪst li ~facedness 'feɪs ɪd nəs -əd-,
-nɪs; 'feɪst nəs, -nɪs
twofold 'tuː fəʊld→-fɒʊld ‖ -foʊld
two-handed ˌtuː 'hænd ɪd ◄ -əd ~ly li ~ness
nəs nɪs
Twohy 'tuːˌi
two-ish 'tuː ɪʃ
two-legged ˌtuː 'legd◄-'leg ɪd, -əd
Twomey 'tuːm i
twopenc|e n '2d' 'tʌp ənᵗs→-mᵖs —but
meaning '2p', in modern currency, usually two
pence ˌtuː 'penᵗs ~es ɪz əz
twopenn|y adj '2d', and in figurative senses
'tʌp ənˌli—but meaning '2p', in modern

currency, usually two-penny‚tuː ˈpen li ◂ ~**ies**
iz
twopenny-halfpenny ‚tʌp ən‚i ˈheɪp ən‚i ◂
two-piece ˈtuː piːs
two-ply ˈtuː plaɪ
two-seater ‚tuː ˈsiːt ə ‖ -ˈsiːt̬ ər ~**s** z
two-sided ‚tuː ˈsaɪd ɪd ◂-əd ~**ness** nəs nɪs
twosome ˈtuː səm ~**s** z
two-star ˈtuː stɑː, ˌ•ˈ• ‖ -stɑːr
two-step ˈtuː step ~**s** s
two-stroke ˈtuː strəʊk ‖ -stroʊk ~**s** s
two-tim|e ˈtuː taɪm ~**ed** d ~**es** z ~**ing** ɪŋ
two-tone ˈtuː təʊn ‖ -toʊn
'twould twʊd
two-way ‚tuː ˈweɪ ◂
‚two-way ˈradio
Twyford ˈtwaɪ fəd ‖ -fərd
Ty taɪ —*but in Welsh place names,* tiː —*Welsh*
Tŷ [tiː, tiː]
‚Ty ˈCoch ‚tiː ˈkəʊk -ˈkəʊx ‖ -ˈkoʊk —*Welsh*
[‚tiː ˈkoːχ, ‚tiː-]
-ty ti— **sixty** ˈsɪkst i —*The pronunciation* taɪ *is*
occasionally used in order to avoid the danger
of confusion resulting from the near-homophony
of-ty and -teen, thus ˈsɪks taɪ
Tybalt ˈtɪb əlt
Tyburn ˈtaɪ bən -bɜːn ‖ -bərn
Tyche ˈtaɪk i
Tycho ˈtaɪk əʊ ‖ -oʊ —*Danish* [ˈty go]
tycoon ₍ˌ₎taɪ ˈkuːn ~**s** z
Tye taɪ
tying ˈtaɪ ɪŋ
tyke taɪk **tykes** taɪks
Tyldesley ˈtɪldz li
Tyler ˈtaɪl ə ‖ -ər
tympan ˈtɪmp ən ~**s** z
tympana ˈtɪmp ən ə
tympani ˈtɪmp ən i
tympanic tɪm ˈpæn ɪk
tympanist ˈtɪmp ən ɪst §-əst ~**s** s
tympan|um ˈtɪmp ən |əm ~**a** ə ~**ums** əmz
~**y** i
Tynan ˈtaɪn ən
Tyndale ˈtɪnd əl ˈtɪn deɪəl
Tyndall ˈtɪnd əl
Tyndrum ₍ˌ₎taɪn ˈdrʌm
Tyne taɪn
‚Tyne and ˈWear ˈwɪə ‖ ˈwɪər
Tynemouth ˈtaɪn maʊθ→ˈtaɪm-, ˈtɪn-, -məθ
Tynesid|e ˈtaɪn saɪd ~**er/s** ə/z ‖ ər/z
Tynwald ˈtɪn wəld ˈtaɪn-
type taɪp **typed** taɪpt **types** taɪps **typing**
ˈtaɪp ɪŋ
-type taɪp— **prototype** ˈprəʊt əʊ
taɪp ‖ ˈproʊt̬ ə-
typebar ˈtaɪp bɑː ‖ -bɑːr ~**s** z
typecast ˈtaɪp kɑːst §-kæst ‖ -kæst ~**ing** ɪŋ
~**s** s
typefac|e ˈtaɪp feɪs ~**es** ɪz əz
typescript ˈtaɪp skrɪpt ~**s** s
type|set ˈtaɪp |set ~**sets** sets ~**setting**
set ɪŋ ‖ set̬ ɪŋ
typesetter ˈtaɪp ‚set ə ‖ -‚set̬ ər ~**s** z

typewriter ˈtaɪp ‚raɪt ə ‖ -‚raɪt̬ ər ~**s** z
typewriting ˈtaɪp ‚raɪt ɪŋ ‖ -‚raɪt̬-
typewritten ˈtaɪp ‚rɪt ən
Typhoeus taɪ ˈfiː‚əs -ˈfəʊ juːs
typhoid ˈtaɪf ɔɪd
‚typhoid ˈfever
Typhon ˈtaɪf ən -əʊn, -ɒn ‖ -ɑːn
typhonic taɪ ˈfɒn ɪk ‖ -ˈfɑːn-
Typhoo *tdmk* ₍ˌ₎taɪ ˈfuː
typhoon ₍ˌ₎taɪ ˈfuːn ~**s** z
typhus ˈtaɪf əs
-typic ˈtɪp ɪk— **autotypic** ‚ɔːt əʊ ˈtɪp ɪk ◂
‖ ‚ɔːt̬ ə- ‚ɑːt̬-
typical ˈtɪp ɪk əl ~**ness** nəs nɪs
typicality ‚tɪp ɪ ˈkæl ət i, ‚•ə-, -ɪt i ‖ -ət̬ i
typically ˈtɪp ɪk əl_i
typi|fy ˈtɪp ɪ |faɪ -ə- ~**fied** faɪd ~**fier/s** faɪ ə/z
‖ faɪ ər/z ~**fies** faɪz ~**fying** faɪ ɪŋ
typing ˈtaɪp ɪŋ
ˈtyping pool
typist ˈtaɪp ɪst §-əst ~**s** s
typo ˈtaɪp əʊ ‖ -oʊ ~**s** z
typographer taɪ ˈpɒg rəf ə ‖ -ˈpɑːgr əf ər ~**s** z
typographic ‚taɪp ə ˈgræf ɪk ◂ ~**al** əl ~**ally** əl_i
typograph|y taɪ ˈpɒg rəf li ‖ -ˈpɑːg- ~**ies** iz
typological ‚taɪp ə ˈlɒdʒ ɪk əl ◂ ‖ -ˈlɑːdʒ- ~**ly** _i
typolog|y taɪ ˈpɒl ədʒ li i ‖ -ˈpɑːl- ~**ies** iz
-typy ‚taɪp i —*sometimes treated as stress-*
imposing, tɪp i, təp i — **autotypy**
ˈɔːt əʊ ‚taɪp i ɔː ˈtɒt ɪp i, -əp i ‖ ˈɔːt̬ oʊ ‚taɪp i
ˈɑːt̬-; ɔː ˈtɑːt əp i, ɑː-
Tyr tɪə tjʊə ‖ tɪər
tyramine ˈtaɪər ə miːn ˈtɪr-
tyrannical tɪ ˈræn ɪk əl tə-, taɪ-, taɪə- ~**ly** _i ~**ness**
nəs nɪs
tyrannicide tɪ ˈræn ɪ saɪd tə-, taɪ-, -ə- ~**s** z
tyrannis|e, tyranniz|e ˈtɪr ə naɪz ~**ed** d ~**es** ɪz
əz ~**ing** ɪŋ
tyrannosaur tɪ ˈræn ə sɔː tə-, taɪ- ‖ -sɔːr ~**s** z
tyrannosaurus tɪ ‚ræn ə ˈsɔːr əs ◂tə-, taɪə-
~**es** ɪz əz
Ty‚ranno‚saurus ˈrex
tyrannous ˈtɪr ən əs ~**ly** li
tyrann|y ˈtɪr ən li ~**ies** iz
tyrant ˈtaɪər ənt ~**s** s
tyre, Tyre ˈtaɪ‚ə ‖ ˈtaɪ‚ər *(= tire)* **tyres**
ˈtaɪ‚əz ‖ ˈtaɪ‚ərz
Tyrian ˈtɪr i‚ən
Tyrie ˈtɪr i
tyro ˈtaɪər əʊ ‖ -oʊ ~**s** z
Tyrol tɪ ˈrəʊl tə-, →-ˈrɒl; ˈtɪr əl, -əʊl ‖ -ˈroʊl
—*Ger* Tirol [ti ˈʁoːl]
Tyrolean ‚tɪr əʊ ˈliː‚ən ◂tɪ ˈrəʊl i‚ən, tə- ‖ -ə-
~**s** z
Tyrolese ‚tɪr əʊ ˈliːz ◂ ‖ -ə- -ˈliːs ◂
Tyrolienne tɪ ‚rəʊl i ˈen tə-, ‚tɪr əʊl- ‖ -‚roʊl-
~**s** z
Tyrone *county in N.Ireland* tɪ ˈrəʊn tə- ‖ -ˈroʊn
Tyrone *personal name* ˈtaɪər əʊn ‚taɪə ˈrəʊn, tɪ-,
tə- ‖ -oʊn
tyrosine ˈtaɪər əʊ siːn ˈtɪr-, -sɪn ‖ -ə-
tyrothricin ‚taɪər əʊ ˈθraɪs ɪn §-ən ‖ -ə-
Tyrozets *tdmk* ˈtaɪ‚ər ə zets ˈtɪr-

T

Tyrrell 'tɪr əl
Tyrrhenian tɪ 'riːn iˌən tə-
Tyson 'taɪs ᵊn
Tyte taɪt
Tywyn 'taʊ ɪn —*Welsh* ['tə wɪn, -wɪn]
Tyzack *(i)* 'taɪz æk -ək, *(ii)* 'tɪz-

tzar zɑː tsɑː ‖ zɑːr tsɑːr **tzars** zɑːz tsɑːz
‖ zɑːrz tsɑːrz
tzarina zɑː 'riːn ə tsɑː- ~**s** z
tzar|ism 'zɑːr ˌɪz əm 'tsɑːr- ~**ist/s** ɪst/s §əst/s
tzatziki tæt 'siːk i tsæt- ‖ taːt- —*ModGk*
[dza 'dzi ci]

U u

u   Spelling-to-sound

1 Where the spelling is **u**, the pronunciation differs according to whether the vowel is short or long, followed or not by **r**, and strong or weak.

2 The 'strong' pronunciation is regularly
ʌ, as in **cup** kʌp ('short U'), or
juː, as in **music** 'mjuːz ɪk ('long U').

3 Less frequently, it is
ʊ, as in **push** pʊʃ (especially before **sh, l**).

4 Where the spelling is **ur**, the 'strong' pronunciation is
ɜː ‖ ɜˑ, as in **turn** tɜːn ‖ tɜˑn, or
jʊə ‖ jʊr, as in **pure** pjʊə ‖ pjʊr (in BrE ʊə is often replaced by ɔː, thus pjɔː);
or, indeed, there may be the regular 'short' pronunciation
ʌ ‖ ɜˑ, as in **hurry** 'hʌr i ‖ 'hɜˑr i (in most AmE, the ʌ and r coalesce into ɜˑ).

5 In the case of expected juː, jʊə, jʊ, the j drops out as follows:
 • after the consonant sounds tʃ, dʒ, ʃ, r, j, as in **jury** 'dʒʊər i ‖ 'dʒʊr i, **rude** ruːd;
 • sometimes in BrE, and always in AmE, after l, θ, s, z, as in **assume** ə 's(j)uːm ‖ ə 'suːm;
 • usually in AmE, but not in BrE, after t, d, n, as in **tune** tjuːn ‖ tuːn (see also ASSIMILATION for the BrE possibility of tʃuːn).

6 Note the exceptional words **busy** 'bɪz i, **business** 'bɪz nəs, **bury** 'ber i.

7 The 'weak' pronunciation is
jʊ ‖ jə as in **stimulus** 'stɪm jʊl əs ‖ 'stɪm jəl əs (but in BrE at the end of a syllable the vowel may be tenser, and LPD writes ju, thus **stimulate** 'stɪm ju leɪt ‖ 'stɪm jə leɪt),
ə, as in **album** 'ælb əm, **Arthur** 'ɑːθ ə ‖ 'ɑːrθ ər, or
jə, as in **failure** 'feɪl jə ‖ 'feɪl jər.
In the ending **-ure** the vowel is usually weak. Note also **minute** (noun) 'mɪn ɪt ‖ 'mɪn ət, **lettuce** 'let ɪs ‖ 'let̬ əs, where the BrE vowel sound is ɪ rather than ə.

8 **u** also forms part of the digraphs **au, eu, ou, ue, ui, uy**.

ue   Spelling-to-sound

1 Where the spelling is the digraph **ue**, the pronunciation is regularly

 juː, as in **cue** kjuː, or
uː, as in **blue** bluː.
(For the dropping of j, see **u** 5 above.)

2 **ue** is not a digraph in **duet, cruel, pursuer**.

ui   Spelling-to-sound

1 Where the spelling is the digraph **ui**, the pronunciation is regularly
juː, as in **nuisance** ˈnjuːs ᵊnᵗs (AmE usually ˈnuːs-), or
uː, as in **fruit** fruːt.
(For the dropping of j, see **u** 5 above.)

2 Less frequently, the pronunciation is
ɪ, as in **build** bɪld, or
aɪ, as in **guide** ɡaɪd; also
ɪ ‖ ə, as in **biscuit** ˈbɪsk ɪt ‖ ˈbɪsk ət (when weak).

3 Note the exceptional case **suite** swiːt.

4 **ui** is not a digraph in **fluid, tuition**, nor in **quick, quite** (where the digraph **qu** is followed by **i**).

uy   Spelling-to-sound

In the rare cases where the spelling is the digraph **uy**, the pronunciation is regularly
aɪ, as in **buy** baɪ.

U

U, u juː *(= you)* **U's, u's, Us** juːz
  —*Communications code name:* Uniform
UAE ˌjuː eɪ ˈiː
UART ˈjuː ɑːt ‖ -ɑːrt
UB40 ˌjuː ˌbiː ˈfɔːt i ‖ -ˈfɔːrt̬ i
U-bend ˈjuː bend ~s z
ubermensch, übermensch ˈuːb ə menᵗʃ ˈjuːb-
  ‖ -ᵊr- —*Ger* Ü~ [ˈyː bɐ menʃ]
ubiquitous ju ˈbɪk wɪt əs -wət- ‖ -wət̬ əs ~ly
li ~ness nəs nɪs
ubiquity ju ˈbɪk wət i -wɪt- ‖ -wət̬ i
U-boat ˈjuː bəʊt ‖ -boʊt ~s s
Ubu Roi ˌuːb uː ˈrwɑː
UC ˌjuː ˈsiː
UCAS ˈjuːk æs
  ˈUCAS form
Uccello uː ˈtʃel əʊ ‖ -oʊ —*It* [ut ˈtʃɛl lo]
Uckfield ˈʌk fiːᵊld
UCL ˌjuː siː ˈel
UCLA ˌjuː siː el ˈeɪ
UDA ˌjuː diː ˈeɪ
Udall *(i)* ˈjuːd ᵊl -ɔːl, -æl ‖ ˈjuːd ɔːl -ɑːl, *(ii)*
ju ˈdæl -ˈdɔːl ‖ -ˈdɔːl, -ˈdɑːl
udder ˈʌd ə ‖ -ᵊr ~s z
UDI ˌjuː diː ˈaɪ

Udimore ˈjuːd ɪ mɔː ˈʌd-, -ə- ‖ -mɔːr -moʊr
Udmurt ˈʊd mʊət •ˈ• ‖ -mʊrt ~s s
UDR ˌjuː diː ˈɑː ‖ -ˈɑːr
UEFA ju ˈeɪf ə -ˈiːf-; ˈjuːf ə
UFC ˌjuː ef ˈsiː
Uffizi ʊ ˈfɪts i uː-, -ˈfiːts- —*It* [uf ˈfit tsi]
UFO ˌjuː ef ˈəʊ ˈjuːf əʊ ‖ ˌjuː ef ˈoʊ ˈjuːf oʊ ~s
z
ufolog|y ˌjuː ˈfɒl ədʒ| i ‖ -ˈfɑːl- ~ist/s ɪst/s
əst/s
Ugand|a ju ˈɡænd |ə ‖ u ˈɡɑːnd |ə ~an/s ən/z
Ugaritic ˌuːɡ ə ˈrɪt ɪk ◂ ˌjuːɡ- ‖ -ˈrɪt̬-
UGC ˌjuː dʒiː ˈsiː
ugh ʊx ʌɡ, jʌx, ʊə, uː —*and various other
non-speech exclamations typically involving a
vowel in the range* [ɯ, u, ʌ, ɜ] *and sometimes a
consonant such as* [x, ɸ, h]
ugli ˈʌɡ li ~s z
uglification ˌʌɡ lɪf ɪ ˈkeɪʃ ᵊn ˌ•ləf-, §-ə'•-
ugli|fy ˈʌɡ lɪ |faɪ -lə- ~fied faɪd ~fies faɪz
 ~fying faɪ ɪŋ
ugly ˈʌɡ li **uglier** ˈʌɡ li ə ‖ -ᵊr **ugliest**
ˈʌɡ li ɪst ᵊst **ugliness** ˈʌɡ li nəs -nɪs
  ˌugly ˈduckling
Ugrian ˈjuːɡ ri ən ˈuːɡ- ~s z

Ugric 'juːg rɪk   'uːg-

UHF ˌjuː eɪtʃ 'ef §-heɪtʃ-

uh huh, uh-huh *'yes'* 'ʌ̃ hʌ̃ 'ə̃ hə̃, 'm m̩m,
  'n n̩n; •'• ‖ • '• —*usually with a low-rise tone*

uhlan 'uːl ɑːn 'juːl-, -ən; u 'lɑːn, ju-   ~s z

uh oh *said when you have made a mistake or
something bad has happened* '?ʌ? əʊ -ɜː
  ‖ '?ʌ? oʊ •'• —*usually with the first syllable
on a high level tone, the second on a mid or
low-rising tone*

UHT ˌjuː eɪtʃ 'tiː ◂ §-heɪtʃ-

Uhu *tdmk* 'juː huː 'uː-

uh uh, uh-uh *'no'* '?ʌ̃? ʌ̃ '?ə̃? ə̃, '?m? m
  —*always with a falling tone*

Ui 'uːˌi

Uig 'uː ɪg 'juː-

Uighur, Uigur 'wiːg ʊə ‖ -ʊr   ~s z

Uinta ju 'ɪnt ə ‖ -'ɪnt̬ ə

Uist 'juː ɪst

Uitenhage 'juːt ən heɪg

UK ˌjuː 'keɪ ◂

ukas|e ju 'keɪz -'keɪs   ~es ɪz əz

ukelele ˌjuːk ə 'leɪl i   ~s z

Ukiah *place in CA* ju 'kaɪˌə

Ukraine ju 'kreɪn

Ukrainian ju 'kreɪn iˌən   ~s z

Ukridge 'juːk rɪdʒ

ukulele ˌjuːk ə 'leɪl i   ~s z

Ulaanbaatar, Ulan Bator ˌuːl ɑːn 'bɑːt ɔː
  u ˌlɑːn '•• ‖ -ɔːr

-ular *stress-imposing* jʊl ə jəl ə ‖ jəl ər —
  mandibular mæn 'dɪb jʊl ə -jəl- ‖ -jəl ər

ulcer 'ʌls ə ‖ -ər   ~s z

ulce|rate 'ʌls ə ˌreɪt   ~rated reɪt ɪd -əd
  ‖ reɪt̬ əd   ~rates reɪts   ~rating
  reɪt ɪŋ ‖ reɪt̬ ɪŋ

ulceration ˌʌls ə 'reɪʃ ən   ~s z

ulcerative 'ʌls ər_ət ɪv -ə reɪt- ‖ -ə reɪt̬-
  -ər_ət̬-

ulcerous 'ʌls ər_əs   ~ly li

Uldall 'ʊl dɔːl

-ule juːl — **globule** 'glɒb juːl ‖ 'glɑːb-

ulema 'uːl ɪm ə -əm-; -ɪ mɑː, -ə-, ˌ••'•   ~s z

-ulence *stress-imposing* jʊl ən̩ts jəl- ‖ jəl- —
  opulence 'ɒp jʊl ən̩ts -jəl- ‖ 'ɑːp jəl ən̩ts

-ulent *stress-imposing* jʊl ənt jəl- ‖ jəl- —
  corpulent 'kɔːp jʊl ənt -jəl- ‖ 'kɔːrp jəl ənt

Ulfilas 'ʊlf ɪ læs -ə-; -ɪl əs, -əl-

Ulick 'juːl ɪk

ullage 'ʌl ɪdʒ

Ullapool 'ʌl ə puːl

Ullman, Ullmann 'ʊl mən

Ullswater 'ʌlz ˌwɔːt ə ‖ -ˌwɔːt̬ ər -ˌwɑːt̬-

Ulm ʊlm

ulna 'ʌln ə   **ulnae** 'ʌln iː   **ulnas** 'ʌln əz

ulnar 'ʌln ə ‖ -ər -ɑːr

ulpan 'ʊlp æn -ɑːn

Ulpian 'ʌlp iˌən

Ulrich 'ʊl rɪk -rɪx —*Ger* ['?ʊl ʁɪç]

Ulrika ʊl 'riːk ə

Ulster, u~ 'ʌlst ə ‖ -ər   ~s, ~'s z

Ulster|man 'ʌlst ə |mən ‖ -ər-   ~**men** mən men
  ~**woman** ˌwʊm ən   ~**women** ˌwɪm ɪn §-ən

ult, ult. ʌlt

ulterior ʌl 'tɪər iˌə ‖ -'tɪr iˌər   ~ly li

ultima 'ʌlt ɪm ə -əm-

ultimate 'ʌlt ɪm ət -əm-, -ɪt   ~ly li   ~ness nəs
  nɪs

ultimat|um ˌʌlt ɪ 'meɪt əm -ə- ‖ -'meɪt̬ əm
  -'mɑːt-   ~a ə   ~ums əmz

ultimo 'ʌlt ɪ məʊ -ə- ‖ -moʊ

ultra 'ʌltr ə 'ʊltr-, -ɑː   ~s z

  ˌultra 'vires 'vaɪər iːz 'vɪər-, -eɪz

ultra- ˌʌltr ə — **ultramodern**
  ˌʌltr ə 'mɒd ən ◂ ‖ -'mɑːd ərn ◂

ultrahigh ˌʌltr ə 'haɪ ◂

  ˌultrahigh 'frequency

ultramarine ˌʌltr ə mə 'riːn ◂

ultramontane ˌʌltr ə 'mɒnt eɪn ◂ -mɒn 'teɪn
  ‖ -'mɑːnt eɪn ◂ -mɑːn 'teɪn

ultrasonic ˌʌltr ə 'sɒn ɪk ◂ ‖ -'sɑːn-   ~**ally** əlˌi
  ~s s

ultrasound 'ʌltr ə saʊnd ˌ••'•

ultraviolet ˌʌltr ə 'vaɪˌəl ət ◂ -ɪt

ULU 'juːl u:

ulu|late 'juːl ju lleɪt 'ʌl-, -jə- ‖ -jə-   ~**lated**
  leɪt ɪd -əd ‖ leɪt̬ əd   ~**lates** leɪts   ~**lating**
  leɪt ɪŋ ‖ leɪt̬ ɪŋ

ululation ˌjuːl ju 'leɪʃ ən ˌʌl-, -jə- ‖ -jə-   ~s z

Uluru ˌuːl ə 'ruː ◂

  ˌUluru ˌNational 'Park

Ulverston, Ulverstone 'ʌlv əst ən ‖ -ərst-

Ulysses ju 'lɪs iːz 'juːl ɪ siːz, -ə-

um *hesitation noise* ʌm əm, ɜːm, ə̃ —*usually with
a level tone*

umbel 'ʌm bəl   ~s z

umbellifer ʌm 'bel ɪf ə -əf- ‖ -ər   ~s z

umbelliferae ˌʌm bə 'lɪf ə riː ˌ•be-

umbelliferous ˌʌm bə 'lɪf ər_əs ◂ ˌ•be-

umber 'ʌm bə ‖ -bər   ~s z

Umberto ʊm 'beət əʊ -'bɜːt- ‖ -'bert oʊ —*It*
  [um 'ber to]

umbilical ʌm 'bɪl ɪk əl -ək-; ˌʌm bɪ 'laɪk əl ◂,
  -bə-

umbilicus ʌm 'bɪl ɪk əs -ək-; ˌʌm bɪ 'laɪk əs,
  -bə-   **umbilici** ʌm 'bɪl ə saɪ -ɪ-;
  ˌʌm bɪ 'laɪs aɪ, -bə-

umble 'ʌm bəl   ~s z

umbo 'ʌm bəʊ ‖ -boʊ   **umbones**
  ʌm 'bəʊn iːz ‖ -'boʊn-   **umbos**
  'ʌm bəʊz ‖ -boʊz

um|bra 'ʌm |brə   ~**brae** briː   ~**bras** brəz

umbrage 'ʌm brɪdʒ

UMBRELLA

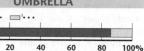

	AmE 1993				
0	20	40	60	80	100%

umbrella ʌm 'brel ə ‖ '•'•• —*AmE 1993 poll
panel preference:* •'•• *86%,* '••• *14%.*   ~s z

Umbria 'ʌm bri_ə

Umbrian 'ʌm bri_ən   ~s z

Umbriel 'ʌm bri_əl

Umbro *tdmk* 'ʌm brəʊ ‖ -broʊ

umiak 'uːm i æk   ~s s

UMIST 'juːm ɪst

U

um|laut 'ʊm ‖laʊt ~lauted laʊt ɪd -əd ‖ laʊt̬ əd
~lauting laʊt ɪŋ ‖ laʊt̬ ɪŋ ~lauts laʊts
umpire 'ʌmp aɪ‿ə ‖ -aɪ‿ᵊr ~d d ~s z
umpiring 'ʌmp aɪ‿ər ɪŋ ‖ 'ʌmp aɪ‿ər ɪŋ
umpteen ˌʌmp 'tiːn ◂
umpteenth ˌʌmp 'tiːntθ ◂
'un nonstandard weak form of one ən, ⁿn — a
big 'un ə 'bɪg ən
un- ʌn, ˌʌn —This prefix may lexically be
stressed or unstressed. It is unstressed
particularly where it is not a true prefix
(un'wieldy); it is stressed particularly (a) where
the initial syllable of the stem does not bear the
primary stress (ˌunaˈshamed), and (b) in verbs
(ˌun'coil). In some words usage is divided or
uncertain (ˌ₍ᵢ₎un'bearable).
UN ˌjuː 'en ◂
ˌUN 'troops
Una 'juːn ə
unabashed ˌʌn ə 'bæʃt ◂
unabated ˌʌn ə 'beɪt ɪd ◂ -əd ‖ -'beɪt̬ əd ◂
unable ʌn 'eɪb əl , •-
unabridged ˌʌn ə 'brɪdʒd ◂
unaccented ˌʌn ək 'sent ɪd ◂ -æk-, -əd
‖ ˌʌn æk 'sent̬ əd ◂
unacceptability ˌʌn ək ˌsept ə 'bɪl ət i , •æk-,
, •ɪk-, , •ɪk- ‖ -ət̬ i
unacceptab|le ˌʌn ək 'sept əb əl ◂ , •ɪk- ~ly li
unaccompanied ˌʌn ə 'kʌmp ən‿id ◂
ˌunacˌcompanied 'children
unaccountable ˌʌn ə 'kaʊnt əb əl ◂ ‖ -'kaʊnt̬-
unaccounted-for ˌʌn ə 'kaʊnt ɪd fɔː ◂ -əd •
‖ -'kaʊnt̬ əd fɔːr
unaccusative ˌʌn ə 'kjuːz ət ɪv ◂ ‖ -ət̬ ɪv ◂ ~s
z
unaccusativity ˌʌn ə ˌkjuːz ə 'tɪv ət i -ɪt i
‖ -ət̬ i
unaccustomed ˌʌn ə 'kʌst əmd ◂
ˌunacˌcustomed 'duty
unadopted ˌʌn ə 'dɒpt ɪd ◂ -əd ‖ -'dɑːpt-
unadulterated ˌʌn ə 'dʌlt ə reɪt ɪd ◂ -əd
‖ -reɪt̬ əd
unadvised ˌʌn əd 'vaɪzd ◂ §-æd-
unadvised|ly ˌʌn əd 'vaɪz ɪd|li §-æd-, -əd •
~ness nəs nɪs
unaffected ˌʌn ə 'fekt ɪd ◂ -əd
unaided ˌ₍ᵢ₎ʌn 'eɪd ɪd -əd
unaligned ˌʌn ə 'laɪnd ◂
unalloyed ˌʌn ə 'lɔɪd ◂
unalterab|le ʌn 'ɔːlt‿ər əb əl ◂ ˌʌn-,
-'ɒlt‿ ‖ -'ɑːlt̬‿ ~ly li
unambiguous ˌʌn æm 'bɪg juː‿əs ◂
un-American ˌʌn ə 'mer ɪk ən ◂ -ək ən
unanalysable, unanalyzable
ˌʌn 'æn ə laɪz əb əl ◂ ‖-'æn əl aɪz-; , •, • •¹• •••
unanimity ˌjuːn ə 'nɪm ət i , •æ-, -ɪt i ‖ -ət̬ i
unanimous juː 'næn ɪm əs -əm əs ~ly li ~ness
nəs nɪs
unannounced ˌʌn ə 'naʊntst ◂
unanswerable ˌ₍ᵢ₎ʌn 'ɑːnts ‿ər əb əl §-'ænts-
‖ -'ænts-
unapproachable ˌʌn ə 'prəʊtʃ əb əl ◂
‖ -'proʊtʃ-

unappropriated ˌʌn ə 'prəʊp ri eɪt ɪd ◂ -əd
‖ -'proʊp ri eɪt̬ əd ◂
unarmed ˌʌn 'ɑːmd ◂ ‖ -'ɑːrmd ◂
ˌunarmed 'combat
unary 'juːn ər i
unashamed ˌʌn ə 'ʃeɪmd ◂
unashamed|ly ˌʌn ə 'ʃeɪm ɪd |li -'• əd-;
-'ʃeɪmd |li ~ness nəs nɪs
unasked ˌʌn 'ɑːskt ◂ §-'æskt ‖ -'æskt ◂
unaspirated ˌ₍ᵢ₎ʌn 'æsp ə reɪt ɪd -'•ɪ-, -əd
‖ -reɪt̬ əd
unassailable ˌʌn ə 'seɪl əb əl ◂
unassuming ˌʌn ə 'sjuːm ɪŋ ◂ -'suːm-, §-'ʃuːm-
‖ -'suːm- ~ly li ~ness nəs nɪs
unattached ˌʌn ə 'tætʃt ◂
unattended ˌʌn ə 'tend ɪd ◂ -əd
unauthorised, unauthorized
ʌn 'ɔːθ ə raɪzd ‖ -'ɑːθ-
unavailing ˌʌn ə 'veɪl ɪŋ ◂
unavoidab|le ˌʌn ə 'vɔɪd əb əl ◂ ~leness
əl nəs -nɪs ~ly li
unaware ˌʌn ə 'weə ‖ -'weᵊr -'wæᵊr ~s z
unbalanc|e ˌʌn 'bæl ənts →ˌʌm- ~ed t ~es ɪz
əz ~ing ɪŋ
unbar ˌʌn 'bɑː ◂ →ˌʌm- ‖ -'bɑːr ◂ ~red d
unbarring ˌʌn 'bɑːr ɪŋ →ˌʌm- ~s z
unbearab|le ˌ₍ᵢ₎ʌn 'beər əb əl ◂ →ˌ₍ᵢ₎ʌm- ‖ -'ber-
-'bær- ~leness əl nəs -nɪs ~ly li
unbeatab|le ˌ₍ᵢ₎ʌn 'biːt əb əl ◂ →ˌ₍ᵢ₎ʌm- ‖ -'biːt̬-
~ly li
unbeaten ˌ₍ᵢ₎ʌn 'biːt ən
unbecoming ˌʌn bɪ 'kʌm ɪŋ ◂ →ˌʌm-, -bə-,
-biː- ~ly li ~ness nəs nɪs
unbeknown ˌʌn bɪ 'nəʊn ◂ →ˌʌm-, -bə-, §-biː-
‖ -'noʊn ◂
unbeknownst ˌʌn bɪ 'nəʊntst →ˌʌm-, -bə-,
§-biː- ‖ -'noʊntst
unbelief ˌʌn bɪ 'liːf →ˌʌm-, -bə-, §-biː-
unbelievab|le ˌʌn bɪ 'liːv əb əl ◂ →ˌʌm-, , •bə-,
§, •biː- ~leness əl nəs -nɪs ~ly li
unbeliever ˌʌn bɪ 'liːv ə →ˌʌm-, -bə-, §-biː-
‖ -ᵊr ~s z
unbelieving ˌʌn bɪ 'liːv ɪŋ ◂ →ˌʌm-, -bə-, §-biː-
~ly li
unbend ˌʌn 'bend →ˌʌm- ~ing ɪŋ ~s z
unbent ˌʌn 'bent ◂ →ˌʌm-
unbending adj 'inflexible' ʌn 'bend ɪŋ →ʌm-
~ly li ~ness nəs nɪs
unbent ˌʌn 'bent ◂ →ˌʌm-
unbiased, unbiassed ˌ₍ᵢ₎ʌn 'baɪ‿əst →ˌ₍ᵢ₎ʌm-
~ly li ~ness nəs nɪs
unbidden ˌʌn 'bɪd ən →ˌʌm-
unbind ˌʌn 'baɪnd →ˌʌm- ~ing ɪŋ unbound
ˌʌn 'baʊnd ◂
unblemished ʌn 'blem ɪʃt →ʌm, , •-
unblinking ˌʌn 'blɪŋk ɪŋ →ˌʌm- ~ly li
unblushing ˌʌn 'blʌʃ ɪŋ ◂ →ˌʌm- ~ly li
unbolt ˌʌn 'bəʊlt ◂ →ˌʌm-, →-'bɒʊlt
‖ -'boʊlt ◂ ~ed ɪd əd ~ing ɪŋ ~s s
unborn ˌʌn 'bɔːn ◂ →ˌʌm- ‖ -'bɔːrn ◂
unbosom ˌʌn 'bʊz əm →ˌʌm-, §-'buːz- ~ed d
~ing ɪŋ ~s z
unbound ˌʌn 'baʊnd ◂ →ˌʌm-

unbounded ₍ᵢ₎ʌn 'baʊnd ɪd -əd ~**ly** li ~**ness**
nəs nɪs
unbowed ˌʌn 'baʊd ◄ →ˌʌm-
unbridled ₍ᵢ₎ʌn 'braɪd əld →₍ᵢ₎ʌm-
unbroken ₍ᵢ₎ʌn 'brəʊk ən →₍ᵢ₎ʌm- ‖ -'brəʊk-
~**ly** li ~**ness** nəs nɪs
unbuckl|e ˌʌn 'bʌk əl →ˌʌm- ~**ed** d ~**es** z
~**ing** _ɪŋ
unburden ˌʌn 'bɜːd ən →ˌʌm- ‖ -'bɜːːd- ~**ed** d
~**ing** _ɪŋ ~**s** z
unbutton ˌʌn 'bʌt ən ◄ →ˌʌm- ~**ed** d ~**ing** _ɪŋ
~**s** z
uncalled-for ₍ᵢ₎ʌn 'kɔːld fɔː →₍ᵢ₎ʌŋ- ‖ -fɔːr
-'kɑːld-
uncann|y ʌn 'kæn li →ʌŋ- ~**ily** ɪ li əl i ~**iness**
i nəs i nɪs
uncap ˌʌn 'kæp →ˌʌŋ- ~**ped** t ◄ ~**ping** ɪŋ ~**s**
s
uncared-for ₍ᵢ₎ʌn 'keəd fɔː →₍ᵢ₎ʌŋ-
‖ -'kerd fɔːr -'kærd-
unceasing ʌn 'siːs ɪŋ ˌ•- ~**ly** li ~**ness** nəs nɪs
unceremonious ˌʌn ˌser ɪ 'məʊn i̯_əs -ˌ•ə-
‖ -'məʊn- ~**ly** li ~**ness** nəs nɪs
uncertain ʌn 'sɜːt ən ˌ•-, -ɪn ‖ -'sɜːːt ən ~**ly** li
uncertain|ty ʌn 'sɜːt ən ti -ɪn- ‖ -'sɜːːt- ~**ties**
tiz
un**'certainty ˌprinciple**
unchain ˌʌn 'tʃeɪn ~**ed** d ~**ing** ɪŋ ~**s** z
uncharitab|le ₍ᵢ₎ʌn 'tʃær ɪt əb əl -'•ət-
‖ -'tʃær ət̬- -'tʃer- ~**leness** əl nəs -nɪs ~**ly** li
uncharted ˌʌn 'tʃɑːt ɪd ◄ -əd ‖ -'tʃɑːrt̬ əd ◄
unchecked ˌʌn 'tʃekt ◄
unchristian ₍ᵢ₎ʌn 'krɪst jən →₍ᵢ₎ʌŋ-, -'krɪs tʃən,
-'krɪst i̯_ən ~**ly** li
unci 'ʌnts aɪ
uncial 'ʌnts i̯_əl 'ʌntʃ-; 'ʌntʃ əl ‖ 'ʌntʃ əl -i̯_əl
~**s** z
unciform 'ʌnts ɪ fɔːm -ə- ‖ -fɔːrm
uncinate 'ʌnts ɪn ət -ən-, -ɪt; -ɪ neɪt, -ə-
uncircumcised ˌʌn 'sɜːk əm saɪzd ◄ ‖ -'sɜːːk-
uncircumcision ˌʌn ˌsɜːk əm 'sɪʒ ən ‖ -ˌsɜːːk-
uncivilised, uncivilized ₍ᵢ₎ʌn 'sɪv ə laɪzd -ɪ-,
-əl aɪzd
unclad ˌʌn 'klæd ◄ →ˌʌŋ-
unclasp ˌʌn 'klɑːsp →ˌʌŋ-, §-'klæsp ‖ -'klæsp
~**ed** t ~**ing** ɪŋ ~**s** s
unclassified ˌʌn 'klæs ɪ faɪd ◄ →ˌʌŋ-, -ə-
uncle 'ʌŋk əl ~**s** z
ˌUncle **'Sam**; ˌUncle **'Tom**
unclean ˌʌn 'kliːn ◄ →ˌʌŋ- ~**er** ə ‖ ər ~**est** ɪst
əst ~**ly** li ~**ness** nəs nɪs
unclean|ly *adj* ˌʌn 'klen |li →ˌʌŋ- ~**liness** li nəs
-nɪs
unclear ˌʌn 'klɪə ◄ →ˌʌŋ- ‖ -'klɪr ◄ ~**ly** li
unclench ˌʌn 'klentʃ ◄ →ˌʌŋ- ~**ed** t ~**es** ɪz əz
~**ing** ɪŋ
unclog ˌʌn 'klɒg ◄ →ˌʌŋ- ‖ -'klɑːg ◄ ~**ged** d
~**ging** ɪŋ ~**s** z
unclouded ₍ᵢ₎ʌn 'klaʊd ɪd ◄ →₍ᵢ₎ʌŋ-, -əd
unco 'ʌŋk ə -əʊ ‖ -oʊ
uncoil ˌʌn 'kɔɪl ◄ →ˌʌŋ- ~**ed** d ~**ing** ɪŋ ~**s** z
uncolored, uncoloured ˌʌn 'kʌl əd ◄ →ˌʌŋ-
‖ -ərd ◄

uncomfortab|le ʌn 'kʌmᵖft əb |əl →ˌʌŋ-,
-'kʌmᵖf ət əb |əl ‖ -əᵇb |əl; -'kʌmᵖf ət̬ əb |əl,
-'•ərt̬- ~**leness** əl nəs -nɪs ~**ly** li
uncommitted ˌʌn kə 'mɪt ɪd ◄ →ˌʌŋ-, -əd
‖ -mɪt̬ əd ◄
uncommon ʌn 'kɒm ən →ʌŋ-, ˌ•- ‖ -'kɑːm-
~**ly** li ~**ness** nəs nɪs
uncommunicative ˌʌn kə 'mjuːn ɪk ət ɪv ◄
→ˌʌŋ-, §-'•ək-, -eɪt ɪv ‖ -ə keɪt̬ ɪv -ək ət̬- ~**ly**
li ~**ness** nəs nɪs
uncompetitive ˌʌn kəm 'pet ət ɪv ◄ →ˌʌŋ-,
§ˌ•kɒm-, -'•ɪt- ‖ -'pet̬ ət̬- ~**ness** nəs nɪs
uncomplaining ˌʌn kəm 'pleɪn ɪŋ ◄ →ˌʌŋ-,
§-kɒm- ~**ly** li
uncompromising ʌn 'kɒmp rə maɪz ɪŋ →ʌŋ-
‖ -'kɑːmp- ~**ly** li ~**ness** nəs nɪs
unconcern ˌʌn kən 'sɜːn →ˌʌŋ-, §-kɒn-
‖ -'sɜːːn ~**ed** d
unconcerned|ly ˌʌn kən 'sɜːn ɪd |li -'•əd-;
-'sɜːnd |li ‖ -'sɜːːn- ~**ness** nəs nɪs
unconditional ˌʌn kən 'dɪʃ ən_əl ◄ →ˌʌŋ-,
§ˌ•kɒn- ~**ly** li
unconnected ˌʌn kə 'nekt ɪd ◄ →ˌʌŋ-, -əd ~**ly**
li ~**ness** nəs nɪs
unconquerab|le ʌn 'kɒŋk ər_əb| əl →ʌŋ-
‖-'kɑːŋk- ~**ly** li
unconscionab|le ʌn 'kɒntʃ ən_əb |əl →ʌŋ-
‖-'kɑːntʃ- ~**leness** əl nəs -nɪs ~**ly** li
unconscious ʌn 'kɒntʃ əs →ʌŋ-, ˌ•- ‖ -'kɑːntʃ-
~**ly** li ~**ness** nəs nɪs
unconsidered ˌʌn kən 'sɪd əd ◄ →ˌʌŋ-, §-kɒn-
‖ -ərd ◄
ˌuncon.sidered **'trifles**
unconstitutional ˌʌn ˌkɒntst ɪ 'tjuːʃ ən_əl
→ˌʌŋ-, -ˌ•ə-, →§-'tʃuːʃ- ‖ -ˌkɑːntst ə 'tuːʃ-
-'tjuːʃ- ~**ly** i
uncontrollab|le ˌʌn kən 'trəʊl əb| əl ◄ →ˌʌŋ-,
§ˌ•kɒn-, →-'trʊʊl- ‖ -'troʊl-
unconventional ˌʌn kən 'ventʃ ən_əl ◄ →ˌʌŋ-,
§ˌ•kɒn- ~**ly** i
unconvinced ˌʌn kən 'vɪntst →ˌʌŋ-
unconvincing ˌʌn kən 'vɪnts ɪŋ →ˌʌŋ- ~**ly** li
uncork ˌʌn 'kɔːk ◄ →ˌʌŋ- ‖ -'kɔːrk ◄ ~**ed** t
~**ing** ɪŋ ~**s** s
uncountable ˌʌn 'kaʊnt əb əl ◄ →ˌʌŋ-
‖ -'kaʊnt̬-
uncounted ₍ᵢ₎ʌn 'kaʊnt ɪd →₍ᵢ₎ʌŋ-, -əd
‖ -'kaʊnt̬ əd
uncoupl|e ˌʌn 'kʌp əl →ˌʌŋ- ~**ed** d ~**es** z
~**ing** _ɪŋ
uncouth ʌn 'kuːθ →ʌŋ-, ˌ•- ~**ly** li ~**ness** nəs
nɪs
uncover ʌn 'kʌv ə →ʌŋ-, ˌ•- ‖ -ər ~**ed** d
uncovering ʌn 'kʌv ər_ɪŋ →ʌŋ-, ˌ•- ‖ -ər_ɪŋ ~**s** z
uncritical ₍ᵢ₎ʌn 'krɪt ɪk əl →₍ᵢ₎ʌŋ- ‖ -'krɪt̬- ~**ly** _i
uncrowned ˌʌn 'kraʊnd ◄ →ˌʌŋ-
ˌuncrowned **'king**
uncrushable ₍ᵢ₎ʌn 'krʌʃ əb əl
unction 'ʌŋk ʃən
unctuous 'ʌŋk tʃu_əs -tju_əs ~**ly** li ~**ness** nəs
nɪs
uncurl ˌʌn 'kɜːl ◄ →ˌʌŋ- ‖ -'kɜːːl ◄ ~**ed** d
~**ing** ɪŋ ~**s** z

U

uncus 'ʌŋk əs **unci** 'ʌnⁱs aɪ
uncut ˌʌn 'kʌt ◄→,ʌŋ-
undamaged ₍ᵢ₎ʌn 'dæm ɪdʒd
undamped ˌʌn 'dæmpt ◄
undaunted ₍ᵢ₎ʌn 'dɔːnt ɪd -əd ‖ -'dɔːnʈ əd
-'dɑːnʈ- **~ly** li **~ness** nəs nɪs
undecagon ʌn 'dek əg ən -ə gɒn ‖ -ə gɑːn **~s**
z
undeceiv|e ˌʌn dɪ 'siːv -də- **~ed** d **~es** z **~ing**
ɪŋ
undecided ˌʌn dɪ 'saɪd ɪd ◄ -də-, -əd **~ly** li
~ness nəs nɪs
undeclared ˌʌn dɪ 'kleəd ◄ -də- ‖ -'kleᵊrd ◄
-'klæᵊrd
undemonstrative ˌʌn dɪ 'mɒnⁱs trət ɪv ◄ ,•də-,
§,•diː- ‖ -'mɑːnⁱs trət- **~ly** li **~ness** nəs nɪs
undeniab|le ˌʌn dɪ 'naɪˍəb |ᵊl ◄ ,•də- **~ly** li
undenominational ˌʌn dɪ ˌnɒm ɪ 'neɪʃ ən‿ᵊl
,•də-, §,•diː-, -,-ə- ‖ -ˌnɑːm- **~ly** i
under 'ʌnd ə ‖ -ᵊr
under- ˌʌnd ə ‖ -ᵊr —*but before a vowel sound*
ˌʌnd ər ‖ -ᵊr
underachiev|e ˌʌnd ər ə 'tʃiːv ‖ ,•ər- **~ed** d
~er/s ə/z ‖ ᵊr/z **~es** z **~ing** ɪŋ
underact ˌʌnd ər 'ækt ‖ -ər- **~ed** ɪd əd **~ing**
ɪŋ **~s** s
underage ˌʌnd ər 'eɪdʒ ‖ -ər-
ˌunderage 'drinking
underarm 'ʌnd ər ɑːm ‖ -ər ɑːrm
underbell|y 'ʌnd ə ˌbel |i ‖ -ᵊr- **~ies** iz
underbid ˌʌnd ə 'bɪd ‖ -ᵊr- **~ding** ɪŋ **~s** z
underbrush 'ʌnd ə brʌʃ ‖ -ᵊr-
undercapitalis|e, undercapitaliz|e
ˌʌnd ə 'kæp ɪt ə laɪz §-'•ət-, -ᵊl aɪz
‖ -ᵊr 'kæp ət̬- **~ed** d **~es** ɪz əz **~ing** ɪŋ
undercarriag|e 'ʌnd ə ˌkær ɪdʒ ‖ -ᵊr- -ˌker-
~es ɪz əz
undercart 'ʌnd ə kɑːt ‖ -ᵊr kɑːrt **~s** s
undercharg|e v ˌʌnd ə 'tʃɑːdʒ ‖ -ᵊr 'tʃɑːrdʒ
~ed d **~es** ɪz əz **~ing** ɪŋ
undercharg|e n 'ʌnd ə tʃɑːdʒ ,•'•
‖ -ᵊr tʃɑːrdʒ **~es** ɪz əz
underclass 'ʌnd ə klɑːs §-klæs ‖ -ᵊr klæs **~es**
ɪz əz
underclothes 'ʌnd ə kləʊðz -kləʊz ‖ -ᵊr kloʊz
-kloʊðz
underclothing 'ʌnd ə ˌkləʊð ɪŋ ‖ -ᵊr ˌkloʊð-
undercoat 'ʌnd ə kəʊt ‖ -ᵊr koʊt **~s** s
undercook ˌʌnd ə 'kʊk §-'kuːk ‖ -ᵊr- **~ed** t ◄
~ing ɪŋ **~s** s
undercover ˌʌnd ə 'kʌv ə ◄ '•• ,••
‖ -ᵊr 'kʌv ᵊr ◄
undercroft 'ʌnd ə krɒft ‖ -ᵊr krɔːft -krɑːft **~s**
s
undercurrent 'ʌnd ə ˌkʌr ənt ‖ -ᵊr ˌkɝː- **~s** s
under|cut v ˌʌnd ə |'kʌt ‖ -ᵊr- **~cuts** 'kʌts
~cutting 'kʌt ɪŋ ‖ 'kʌt̬ ɪŋ
undercut n 'ʌnd ə kʌt ‖ -ᵊr- **~s** s
underdevelop ˌʌnd ə dɪ 'vel əp -də-'••, §-diː-'••
‖ ,•ᵊr- **~ed** t ◄ **~ing** ɪŋ **~ment** mənt **~s** s
ˌunderdeˌveloped 'countries
underdog 'ʌnd ə dɒg ‖ -ᵊr dɔːg -dɑːg **~s** z

underdone ˌʌnd ə 'dʌn ◄ ‖ -ᵊr-
ˌunderdone 'meat
underemployed ˌʌnd ər ɪm 'plɔɪd ◄ -əm'•
‖ ,•ᵊr-
underemployment ˌʌnd ər ɪm 'plɔɪ mənt
-əm'•- ‖ ,•ᵊr-
underesti|mate v ˌʌnd ər 'est ɪ |meɪt -ə•
‖ ,•ᵊr- **~mated** meɪt ɪd -əd ‖ meɪt̬ əd
~mates meɪts **~mating** meɪt ɪŋ ‖ meɪt̬ ɪŋ
underestimate n ˌʌnd ər 'est ɪm ət -əm ət, -ɪt;
-ɪ meɪt, -ə meɪt ‖ ,•ᵊr- **~s** s
underexpos|e ˌʌnd ər ɪk 'spəʊz -ək'•, -ek'•
‖ -ᵊr ɪk 'spoʊz **~ed** d **~es** ɪz əz **~ing** ɪŋ
underexposure ˌʌnd ər ɪk 'spəʊʒ ə -ək'•-,
-ek'•- ‖ -ᵊr ɪk 'spoʊʒ ᵊr **~s** z
under|feed ˌʌnd ə |'fiːd ‖ -ᵊr- **~fed** 'fed ◄
~feeding 'fiːd ɪŋ **~feeds** 'fiːdz
underfelt 'ʌnd ə felt ‖ -ᵊr- **~s** s
underfloor ˌʌnd ə 'flɔː ◄ ‖ -ᵊr 'flɔːr ◄ -'floʊr
ˌunderfloor 'heating
underfoot ˌʌnd ə 'fʊt ‖ -ᵊr-
underfund ˌʌnd ə 'fʌnd ‖ -ᵊr- **~ed** ɪd əd
~ing ɪŋ **~s** z
undergarment 'ʌnd ə ˌgɑːm ənt ‖ -ᵊr ˌgɑːrm-
~s s
under|go ˌʌnd ə |'gəʊ ‖ -ᵊr |'goʊ **~goes**
'gəʊz ‖ 'goʊz **~gone** 'gɒn §'gɑːn ‖ 'gɔːn
'gɑːn **~went** 'went
undergrad 'ʌnd ə græd ,•'• ‖ -ᵊr- **~s** z
undergraduate ˌʌnd ə 'grædʒ u‿ət ◄
-'græd ju‿ət, -ˌɪt, -eɪt ‖ ,•ᵊr- **~s** s
underground adj, adv ˌʌnd ə 'graʊnd ◄ '•••
‖ -ᵊr-
ˌunderground 'passages
underground n, U~ 'ʌnd ə graʊnd ‖ -ᵊr- **~s** z
undergrowth 'ʌnd ə grəʊθ ‖ -ᵊr groʊθ
underhand ˌʌnd ə 'hænd ◄ '••• ‖ -ᵊr-
underhanded ˌʌnd ə 'hænd ɪd ◄ -əd ‖ -ᵊr- **~ly**
li **~ness** nəs nɪs
Underhill 'ʌnd ə hɪl ‖ -ᵊr-
underhung ˌʌnd ə 'hʌŋ ◄ ‖ -ᵊr-
underinsured ˌʌnd ər ɪn 'ʃʊəd -'ʃɔːrd
‖ -ᵊr ɪn 'ʃʊᵊrd -'ʃɝːd
underlaid ˌʌnd ə 'leɪd ‖ -ᵊr-
underlain ˌʌnd ə 'leɪn ‖ -ᵊr-
underlay n 'ʌnd ə leɪ ‖ -ᵊr- **~s** z
under|lie ˌʌnd ə |'laɪ ‖ -ᵊr- **~lay** 'leɪ **~lies** 'laɪz
~lying/ly 'laɪ ɪŋ /li
ˌunderˌlying 'form
underlin|e v ˌʌnd ə 'laɪn '••• ‖ -ᵊr- **~ed** d **~es**
z **~ing** ɪŋ
underline n 'ʌnd ə laɪn ,•'• ‖ -ᵊr- **~s** z
underling 'ʌnd ə lɪŋ ‖ -ᵊr- **~s** z
underlying ˌʌnd ə 'laɪ ɪŋ ◄ ,•ᵊr- **~ly** li
undermanned ˌʌnd ə 'mænd ◄ ‖ -ᵊr-
undermentioned ˌʌnd ə 'menʈʃ ənd ◄ ‖ -ᵊr-
undermin|e ˌʌnd ə 'maɪn ‖ -ᵊr- **~ed** d **~es** z
~ing ɪŋ
underneath ˌʌnd ə 'niːθ ◄ ‖ -ᵊr-
undernourish ˌʌnd ə 'nʌr ɪʃ ‖ -ᵊr 'nɝː- **~ed** t
~es ɪz əz **~ing** ɪŋ
underpaid ˌʌnd ə 'peɪd ◄ ‖ -ᵊr-
underpants 'ʌnd ə pænⁱs ‖ -ᵊr-

U

underpass 'ʌnd ə pɑːs §-pæs ‖ -ᵊr pæs **~es** ɪz
əz
under|pay ˌʌnd ə |'peɪ ‖ -ᵊr- **~paid** 'peɪd
~paying 'peɪ ɪŋ **~payment/s** 'peɪ mənt/s
~pays 'peɪz
underpin ˌʌnd ə 'pɪn ‖ -ᵊr- **~ned** d **~ning** ɪŋ
~s z
underpinning n ˌʌnd ə 'pɪn ɪŋ '••,•• ‖ -ᵊr- **~s**
z
underplay v ˌʌnd ə 'pleɪ ‖ -ᵊr- **~ed** d **~ing** ɪŋ
~s z
underpric|e v ˌʌnd ə 'praɪs ‖ -ᵊr- **~ed** t **~es** ɪz
əz **~ing** ɪŋ
underprivileged ˌʌnd ə 'prɪv əl ɪdʒd ◄ -ɪl ɪdʒd
‖ ˌ•ᵊr-
underproof ˌʌnd ə 'pruːf ‖ -ᵊr-
under|quote ˌʌnd ə |'kwəʊt ‖ -ᵊr |'kwəʊt
~quoted 'kwəʊt ɪd -əd ‖ 'kwəʊt̬ əd **~quotes**
'kwəʊts ‖ 'kwəʊts **~quoting**
'kwəʊt ɪŋ ‖ 'kwəʊt̬ ɪŋ
under|rate ˌʌnd ə |'reɪt ‖ -ᵊr- **~rated** 'reɪt ɪd
-əd ‖ 'reɪt̬ əd **~rates** 'reɪts **~rating**
'reɪt ɪŋ ‖ 'reɪt̬ ɪŋ
under|run ˌʌnd ə |'rʌn ‖ -ᵊr- **~ran** 'ræn
~running 'rʌn ɪŋ **~runs** 'rʌnz
underscore v ˌʌnd ə 'skɔː '••• ‖ ˌʌnd ᵊr skɔːr
-skoʊr **~d** d **~s** z **underscoring**
ˌʌnd ə 'skɔːr ɪŋ '•••• ‖ ˌʌnd ᵊr skɔːr ɪŋ
-skoʊr ɪŋ
underscore n 'ʌnd ə skɔː ‖ -ᵊr skɔːr -skoʊr **~s**
z
undersea ˌʌnd ə 'siː ◄ '••• ‖ -ᵊr-
underseal n, v 'ʌnd ə siːᵊl ‖ -ᵊr- **~ed** d **~ing** ɪŋ
~s z
undersecretar|y ˌʌnd ə 'sek rət̬ ᵊr i -'•rɪt̬ˌ,
⚠-'•jʊt̬ˌ, ⚠-'•ət̬ˌ; -'sek rə ter li, -'•rɪ-,
⚠-'•ju-, ⚠-'•ə- ‖ ˌʌnd ᵊr 'sek rə ter li **~ies**
iz
under|sell ˌʌnd ə |'sel ‖ -ᵊr- **~selling** 'sel ɪŋ
~sells 'selz **~sold** 'səʊld→'sɒʊld ‖ 'soʊld
undersexed ˌʌnd ə 'sekst ◄ ‖ -ᵊr-
Undershaft 'ʌnd ə ʃɑːft §-ʃæft ‖ -ᵊr ʃæft
undershirt 'ʌnd ə ʃɜːt ‖ -ᵊr ʃɜːt **~s** s
under|shoot v ˌʌnd ə |'ʃuːt '••• ‖ -ᵊr-
~shooting ʃuːt ɪŋ ‖ ʃuːt̬ ɪŋ **~shoots** ʃuːts
~shot ʃɒt ‖ ʃɑːt
undershoot n 'ʌnd ə ʃuːt ‖ -ᵊr-
undershorts 'ʌnd ə ʃɔːts ‖ -ᵊr ʃɔːrts
underside 'ʌnd ə saɪd ‖ -ᵊr-
undersigned ˌʌnd ə 'saɪnd ◄'••• ‖ -ᵊr-
undersize ˌʌnd ə 'saɪz ◄ ‖ -ᵊr- **~d** d
underslung ˌʌnd ə 'slʌŋ ◄ ‖ -ᵊr-
undersold ˌʌnd ə 'səʊld→-'sɒʊld ‖ -ᵊr 'soʊld
under|spend ˌʌnd ə |'spend ‖ -ᵊr- **~spending**
'spend ɪŋ **~spends** 'spendz **~spent** 'spent
understaffed ˌʌnd ə 'stɑːft §-'stæft ‖ -ᵊr 'stæft
understand ˌʌnd ə 'stænd ‖ -ᵊr- **~ing** ɪŋ **~s** z
understood ˌʌnd ə 'stʊd ‖ -ᵊr-
understandab|le ˌʌnd ə 'stænd əb |əl ‖ ˌ•ᵊr-
~ly li
understanding ˌʌnd ə 'stænd ɪŋ ‖ -ᵊr- **~ly** li
~s z

under|state ˌʌnd ə |'steɪt ‖ -ᵊr- **~stated**
'steɪt ɪd -əd ‖ 'steɪt̬ əd **~states** 'steɪts
~stating 'steɪt ɪŋ ‖ 'steɪt̬ ɪŋ
understatement ˌʌnd ə 'steɪt mənt '••,••
‖ -ᵊr-
understeer n 'ʌnd ə stɪə ‖ -ᵊr stɪr
understeer v ˌʌnd ə 'stɪə '••• ‖ -ᵊr 'stɪᵊr **~ed**
d **understeering**
ˌʌnd ə 'stɪᵊr ɪŋ ‖ -ᵊr 'stɪr ɪŋ **~s** z
understood ˌʌnd ə 'stʊd ‖ -ᵊr-
understrapper 'ʌnd ə ˌstræp ə ‖ -ᵊr ˌstræp ᵊr
~s z
understud|y v, n ˌʌnd ə ˌstʌd li ‖ -ᵊr- **~ied** id
~ies iz **~ying** i ɪŋ
under|take ˌʌnd ə |'teɪk ‖ -ᵊr- **~taken** 'teɪk ən
~takes 'teɪks **~taking** 'teɪk ɪŋ **~took** 'tʊk
§'tuːk
undertaker 'funeral director'
'ʌnd ə teɪk ə ‖ -ᵊr teɪk ᵊr **~s** z
undertaking n 'task'; 'promise' ˌʌnd ə 'teɪk ɪŋ
'•••• ‖ -ᵊr- **~s** z
undertaking n 'funeral direction'
'ʌnd ə teɪk ɪŋ ‖ -ᵊr-
under-the-counter
ˌʌnd ə ðə 'kaʊnt ə ◄ ‖ -ᵊr ðə 'kaʊnt̬ ᵊr ◄
undertone 'ʌnd ə təʊn ‖ -ᵊr toʊn **~s** z
undertook ˌʌnd ə 'tʊk §-'tuːk ‖ -ᵊr-
undertow 'ʌnd ə təʊ ‖ -ᵊr toʊ **~s** z
underused ˌʌnd ə 'juːzd ◄ ‖ -ᵊr-
undervalu|e ˌʌnd ə 'væl juː ‖ -ᵊr- **~ed** d **~es** z
~ing ɪŋ
underwater ˌʌnd ə 'wɔːt ə ◄ ‖ -ᵊr 'wɔːt̬ ᵊr ◄
-'wɑːt̬-
underwear 'ʌnd ə weə ‖ -ᵊr wer -wær
underweight ˌʌnd ə 'weɪt ◄ ‖ -ᵊr-
underwent ˌʌnd ə 'went ‖ -ᵊr-
underwhelm ˌʌnd ə 'welm -'hwelm
‖ -ᵊr 'ʰwelm **~ed** d **~ing** ɪŋ **~s** z
underwing 'ʌnd ə wɪŋ ‖ -ᵊr- **~s** z
Underwood, u~ 'ʌnd ə wʊd ‖ -ᵊr-
underworld, U~ 'ʌnd ə wɜːld ‖ -ᵊr wɜːld **~s** z
under|write ˌʌnd ə |'raɪt '••• ‖ -ᵊr- **~writes**
'raɪts **~written** 'rɪt ᵊn **~wrote** 'rəʊt ‖ 'roʊt
underwriter 'ʌnd ə raɪt ə ‖ -ᵊr raɪt̬ ᵊr **~s** z
undesirability ˌʌn dɪ ˌzaɪ_ᵊr ə 'bɪl ət i ˌ•də-,
§ˌ•diː-, -ɪt i ‖ -ˌzaɪ_ᵊr ə 'bɪl ət̬ i
undesirable ˌʌn dɪ 'zaɪ_ᵊr əb əl ◄ ˌ•də-, §ˌ•diː-
‖ -'zaɪ_ᵊr- **~s** z
undeveloped ˌʌn dɪ 'vel əpt ◄ ˌ•də-, ˌ•diː-
undeviating ₍ᵢ₎ʌn 'diːv i eɪt ɪŋ ‖ -eɪt̬ ɪŋ **~ly** li
undid ₍ᵢ₎ʌn 'dɪd
undies 'ʌnd iz
undiluted ˌʌn daɪ 'luːt ɪd ◄-dɪ-, §-də-, -'ljuːt-,
-əd ‖ -'luːt̬ əd ◄
Undine, u~ 'ʌnd iːn ʌn 'diːn, ʊn- **~s** z
undischarged ˌʌn dɪs 'tʃɑːdʒd ◄ ‖ -'tʃɑːrdʒd ◄
ˌundischarged 'bankrupt
undistinguished ˌʌn dɪ 'stɪŋ gwɪʃt ◄, •də-,
-wɪʃt
undivided ˌʌn dɪ 'vaɪd ɪd ◄, •də-, -əd
un|do ₍ᵢ₎ʌn |'duː **~did** 'dɪd **~does** 'dʌz
~doing 'duː_ɪŋ **~done** 'dʌn

undomesticated ˌʌn də 'mest ɪ keɪt ɪd ◂ -'•ə-,
-əd ‖ -keɪt̬ əd ◂
undone ˌ(ˌ)ʌn 'dʌn
undoubted ʌn 'daʊt ɪd -əd ‖ -'daʊt̬ əd
undreamed-of ʌn 'driːmd ɒv ˌʌn-, -'dremᵖt-,
-əv ‖ -ʌv -ɑːv
undreamt-of ʌn 'dremᵖt ɒv ˌʌn-, -əv ‖ -ʌv -ɑːv
undress v, n ʌn 'dres ˌʌn- ~ed t ~es ɪz əz
~ing ɪŋ
undue ˌʌn 'dju: ◂ §→-'dʒu: ‖ -'du: ◂ -'dju:
undulant 'ʌnd jʊl ənt 'ʌndʒ ʊl- ‖ 'ʌndʒ əl-
'ʌnd jəl-, -əl-
undu|late 'ʌnd ju ǀleɪt 'ʌndʒ u- ‖ 'ʌndʒ ə-
'ʌnd jə-, -ə- ~lated leɪt ɪd -əd ‖ leɪt̬ əd
~lates leɪts ~lating leɪt ɪŋ ‖ leɪt̬ ɪŋ
undulation ˌʌnd ju 'leɪʃ ən ˌʌndʒ u- ‖ ˌʌndʒ ə-
ˌʌnd jə-, -ə- ~s z
undulatory 'ʌnd jʊl ət_ər i 'ʌndʒ ʊl-;
ˌʌnd ju 'leɪt ər i, ˌʌndʒ u- ‖ 'ʌndʒ əl ə tɔːr i
'ʌnd jəl-, •əl-, -toʊr i
unduly ˌ(ˌ)ʌn 'dju: li §→-'dʒu:- ‖ -'du:- -'dju:-
undying ˌ(ˌ)ʌn 'daɪ ɪŋ ~ly li
unearned ˌʌn 'ɜ:nd ◂ ‖ -'ɜ:nd ◂
ˌunearned 'income
unearth ˌ(ˌ)ʌn 'ɜ:θ ‖ -'ɜ:θ ~ed t ~ing ɪŋ ~s s
unearth|ly ʌn 'ɜ:θ ǀli ‖ -'ɜ:θ- ~lier li_ə ‖ li_ər
~liest _li_ɪst _əst ~liness li nəs -nɪs
unease ʌn 'iːz ˌʌn-
uneas|y ʌn 'iːz |i ˌʌn- ~ier i_ə ‖ i_ər ~iest i_ɪst
i_əst ~ily ɪ li əl i ~iness i nəs i nɪs
uneconomic ˌʌn ˌi:k ə 'nɒm ɪk ◂ -,ek-
‖ -'nɑːm- ~al əl ~ally əl_i
unedifying ʌn 'ed ɪ faɪ ɪŋ -'•ə- ~ly li
uneducated ˌ(ˌ)ʌn 'ed ju keɪt ɪd -'edʒ u-, -əd
‖ -'edʒ ə keɪt̬ əd
unemployable ˌʌn ɪm 'plɔɪ əb əl ◂ -,em-,
-,•əm- ~s z
unemployed ˌʌn ɪm 'plɔɪd ◂ -em-, -əm-
unemployment ˌʌn ɪm 'plɔɪ mənt -em-, -əm-
ˌunem'ployment ˌbenefit
unending ʌn 'end ɪŋ -,•- ~ly li
unenlightened ˌʌn ɪn 'laɪt ənd ◂ -en-, -ən-
unenviab|le ˌ(ˌ)ʌn 'en vi_əb əl ~ly li
unequal ˌ(ˌ)ʌn 'i:k wəl ~ed, ~led d ~ly i ~s z
unequivocal ˌʌn ɪ 'kwɪv ək əl ◂ -,•ə- ~ly _i
unerring ˌ(ˌ)ʌn 'ɜ:r ɪŋ §-'er- ‖ -'er- -'ɜ:- ~ly li
Unesco, UNESCO ju 'nesk əʊ ‖ -oʊ
unethical ʌn 'eθ ɪk əl ~ly _i
uneven ˌ(ˌ)ʌn 'i:v ən ~ly li ~ness nəs nɪs
uneventful ˌʌn ɪ 'vent fəl ◂ -ə-, -fʊl ~ly li
~ness nəs nɪs
unexampled ˌʌn ɪg 'zɑːmp əld ◂ -eg-, -əg-,
-ɪk-, -ek-, -ək-, §-'zæmp- ‖ -'zæmp-
unexceptionab|le ˌʌn ɪk 'sep ʃən_əb əl ◂
-,•ek-, -,•ək- ~leness əl nəs -nɪs ~ly li
unexceptional ˌʌn ɪk 'sep ʃən_əl -,ek-, -,•ək-
~ly i
unexpected ˌʌn ɪk 'spekt ɪd ◂ -ek-, -ək-, -əd
~ly li ~ness nəs nɪs
unexpurgated ˌ(ˌ)ʌn 'eks pə geɪt ɪd -'•pɜ:-, -əd
‖ -pər geɪt̬ əd
unfailing ʌn 'feɪl ɪŋ ~ly li

unfair ˌʌn 'feə ◂ ‖ -'feʳr ◂ -'fæʳr ~ly li ~ness
nəs nɪs
unfaithful ˌ(ˌ)ʌn 'feɪθ fəl -fʊl ~ly i ~ness nəs
nɪs
unfaltering ˌ(ˌ)ʌn 'fɔːlt_ər ɪŋ -'fɒlt- ‖ -'fɑːlt̬_
~ly li
unfamiliar ˌʌn fə 'mɪl i_ə ◂ ‖ -,•'mɪl jər ◂ ~ly
li
unfamiliarity ˌʌn fə ˌmɪl i 'ær ət i -ɪt i
‖ -,• 'jær ət̬ i -'jer-; -,•i 'ær-, -,•i 'er-
unfasten ˌ(ˌ)ʌn 'fɑːs ən §-'fæs- ‖ -'fæs- ~ed d
~ing ɪŋ ~s z
unfathomab|le ʌn 'fæð əm_əb əl ~leness
əl nəs -nɪs ~ly li
unfathomed ˌ(ˌ)ʌn 'fæð əmd
unfavorab|le, unfavourab|le
ˌ(ˌ)ʌn 'feɪv ər_əb əl ~leness əl nəs -nɪs ~ly li
unfeeling ʌn 'fiːl ɪŋ ~ly li ~ness nəs nɪs
unfettered ˌʌn 'fet əd ◂ ‖ -'fet̬ ərd ◂
unfinished ˌʌn 'fɪn ɪʃt ◂
un|fit v, adj ˌ(ˌ)ʌn |'fɪt ~fitly 'fɪt li ~fitness
'fɪt nəs -nɪs ~fits 'fɪts ~fitted 'fɪt ɪd -əd
‖ 'fɪt̬ əd ~fitting/ly 'fɪt ɪŋ /li ‖ 'fɪt̬ ɪŋ /li
unflagging ˌʌn 'flæg ɪŋ ~ly li
unflappab|le ˌ(ˌ)ʌn 'flæp əb əl ~ly li
unflinching ˌ(ˌ)ʌn 'flɪntʃ ɪŋ ~ly li
unfold ʌn 'fəʊld ˌʌn-, →-'fɒʊld ‖ -'foʊld ~ed
ɪd əd ~ing ɪŋ ~s z
unforeseen ˌʌn fɔː 'siːn ◂ -fə- ‖ -fɔːr- -foʊr-,
-fər-
ˌunforeseen 'circumstances
unforgettab|le ˌʌn fə 'get əb əl ◂ ‖ -fər 'get̬-
~ly li
unfortunate ʌn 'fɔːtʃ ən_ət -ɪt ‖ -'fɔːrtʃ- ~ly li
~s s
unfounded ˌ(ˌ)ʌn 'faʊnd ɪd -əd
unfrequented ˌʌn frɪ 'kwent ɪd ◂ -frə-, -əd
‖ -'kwent̬ əd ◂
ˌunfreˌquented 'byways
unfriend|ly ˌ(ˌ)ʌn 'frend ǀli ~liness li nəs -nɪs
unfrock ˌʌn 'frɒk ‖ -'frɑːk ~ed t ~ing ɪŋ ~s s
unfurl ˌʌn 'fɜːl ‖ -'fɜ:l ~ed d ~ing ɪŋ ~s z
ungain|ly ˌ(ˌ)ʌn 'geɪn ǀli →(ˌ)ʌŋ- ~liness li nəs
-nɪs
Ungava ʌŋ 'gɑːv ə -'geɪv-
ungenerous ˌ(ˌ)ʌn 'dʒen ər_əs ~ly li
ungetatable ˌʌn get 'æt əb əl ◂ →,ʌŋ-
‖ -get̬ 'æt̬-
ungod|ly ʌn 'gɒd ǀli →,ʌŋ-, ˌʌn- ‖ -'gɑːd-
~liness li nəs -nɪs
Ungoed (i) 'ɪŋ gɔɪd, (ii) 'ʌŋ gɔɪd
ungovernab|le ˌ(ˌ)ʌn 'gʌv ən_əb əl →(ˌ)ʌŋ-
‖ -ᵊrn əb- ~leness əl nəs -nɪs ~ly li
ungracious ˌ(ˌ)ʌn 'greɪʃ əs →(ˌ)ʌŋ- ~ly li ~ness
nəs nɪs
ungrammatical ˌʌn grə 'mæt ɪk əl ◂ →,ʌŋ-
‖ -'mæt̬- ~ly _i
ungrammaticality ˌʌn grə ˌmæt ɪ 'kæl ət i
→,ʌŋ-, §-,•-, -ɪt i ‖ -,mæt̬ ə 'kæl ət̬ i
ungrateful ʌn 'greɪt fəl →ʌŋ-, ˌʌn-, -fʊl ~ly _i
~ness nəs nɪs
ungrudging ˌ(ˌ)ʌn 'grʌdʒ ɪŋ →(ˌ)ʌŋ- ~ly li

unguarded (ˌ)ʌn ˈgɑːd ɪd →(ˌ)ʌŋ-, -əd ‖ -ˈgɑːrd-
~ly li **~ness** nəs nɪs
unguent ˈʌŋ gwənt ˈʌŋ gju‿ənt, Δˈʌndʒ ənt
~s s
un|gula ˈʌŋ |gjʊl ə -gjəl- ‖ -|gjəl ə **~gulae**
gju liː gjə- ‖ gjə liː
ungulate ˈʌŋ gju leɪt -gjʊl ət, -gjəl-, -ɪt ‖ -gjə-
~s s
unhallowed (ˌ)ʌn ˈhæl əʊd ‖ -oʊd
unhand ˌʌn ˈhænd **~ed** ɪd əd **~ing** ɪŋ **~s** z
unhapp|y ʌn ˈhæp li ˌʌn- **~ily** ɪ li əl i **~iness**
i nəs i nɪs
unhealth|y ʌn ˈhelθ li ˌʌn- **~ily** ɪ li əl i **~iness**
i nəs i nɪs
unheard (ˌ)ʌn ˈhɜːd ‖ -ˈhɜ˞ːd
unheard-of (ˌ)ʌn ˈhɜːd ɒv -əv ‖ -ˈhɜ˞ːd ʌv -ɑːv
unhesitating ʌn ˈhez ɪ teɪt ɪŋ -ˈ•ə- ‖ -teɪt̬ ɪŋ
~ly li
unhing|e (ˌ)ʌn ˈhɪndʒ **~ed** d **~es** ɪz əz **~ing** ɪŋ
unhol|y (ˌ)ʌn ˈhəʊl li i ‖ -ˈhoʊl li **~iness** i nəs
i nɪs
    un,holy al'liance
unhook (ˌ)ʌn ˈhʊk §-ˈhuːk **~ed** t **~ing** ɪŋ **~s** s
unhoped-for (ˌ)ʌn ˈhəʊpt fɔː ‖ -ˈhoʊpt fɔːr
unhors|e (ˌ)ʌn ˈhɔːs ‖ -ˈhɔːrs **~ed** t **~es** ɪz əz
~ing ɪŋ
uni ˈjuːn i **unis** ˈjuːn iz
uni- ¦juːn i —but in certain established words
¦juːn ɪ, -ə — **unilingual** ˌjuːn i ˈlɪŋ gwəl ◂
Uniat ˈjuːn i æt
Uniate ˈjuːn i‿ət ˌɪt, -eɪt
unicameral ˌjuːn ɪ ˈkæm ər‿əl ◂
UNICEF ˈjuːn ɪ sef -ə-
unicellular ˌjuːn i ˈsel jʊl ə ◂ -jəl ə ‖ -jəl ər ◂
Unichem tdmk ˈjuːn i kem
Unicode ˈjuːn i kəʊd ‖ -koʊd
unicorn ˈjuːn ɪ kɔːn -ə- ‖ -kɔːrn **~s** z
unicycle ˈjuːn i ˌsaɪk əl **~s** z
unidentified ˌʌn aɪ ˈdent ɪ faɪd ◂ -ˈ•ə-
‖ -ˈdent̬-
unification ˌjuːn ɪf ɪ ˈkeɪʃ ən ˌ•əf-, §-əˈ•- **~s** z
unifie... —see **unify**
uniform ˈjuːn ɪ fɔːm -ə- ‖ -fɔːrm —The adj is
occasionally stressed ˌ•• ◂ˈ• **~ed** d **~ly** li
~ness nəs nɪs **~s** z
uniformity ˌjuːn ɪ ˈfɔːm ət i ˌ•ə-, -ɪt i
‖ -ˈfɔːrm ət̬ i
uni|fy ˈjuːn ɪ |faɪ -ə- **~fied** faɪd **~fier/s** faɪ‿ə/z
‖ faɪ‿ər/z **~fies** faɪz **~fying** faɪ ɪŋ
Unigate tdmk ˈjuːn i geɪt
unilateral ˌjuːn i ˈlæt ˌər əl ◂ ˌ•ə- ‖ -ˈlæt̬ ər əl ◂
→-ˈlætr əl **~ism** ˌɪz əm **~ist/s** ɪst/s §əst/s
‖ əst/s **~ly** li
Unilever tdmk ˈjuːn i ˌliːv ə -ə- ‖ -ər
unimpeachab|le ˌʌn ɪm ˈpiːtʃ əb |əl ◂ **~ly** li
unimproved ˌʌn ɪm ˈpruːvd ◂
uninformed ˌʌn ɪn ˈfɔːmd ◂ ‖ -ˈfɔːrmd ◂
uninhabitable ˌʌn ɪn ˈhæb ɪt əb əl §-ˈ•ət-
‖ -ˈ•ət̬-
uninhibited ˌʌn ɪn ˈhæb ɪt ɪd ◂ §-ət ɪd, -əd
‖ -ət̬ əd ◂ **~ly** li **~ness** nəs nɪs
uninitiated ˌʌn ɪ ˈnɪʃ i eɪt ɪd -əd ‖ -eɪt̬ əd
uninspired ˌʌn ɪn ˈspaɪ‿əd ◂ ‖ -ˈspaɪ‿ərd ◂

uninspiring ˌʌn ɪn ˈspaɪ‿ər ɪŋ ‖ -ˈspaɪ‿ər- **~ly** li
uninterested (ˌ)ʌn ˈɪntr əst ɪd -ɪst-, -əd;
-ˈɪnt ə rest- ‖ -ˈɪnt̬ ə rest-, -ər əst- **~ly** li
~ness nəs nɪs
uninterrupted ˌʌn ˌɪnt ə ˈrʌpt ɪd -əd ‖ -ˌɪnt̬ ə-
~ly li **~ness** nəs nɪs
union ˈjuːn i‿ən ‖ ˈjuːn jən **~s** z
    'union card; 'Union flag, ˌ•• '•; **,Union
    'Jack** ‖ '•• •
unionis... —see **unioniz...**
Unionism ˈjuːn i‿ə ˌnɪz əm ən ˌɪz-
‖ ˈjuːn jə ˌnɪz əm
unionist, U~ ˈjuːn i‿ən ɪst §-əst ‖ ˈjuːn jən əst
~s s
unionization ˌjuːn i‿ən aɪ ˈzeɪʃ ən -ɪˈ•-
‖ ˌjuːn jən ə ˈzeɪʃ ən
unioniz|e ˈjuːn i‿ə naɪz ‖ ˈjuːn jə naɪz **~ed** d
~es ɪz əz **~ing** ɪŋ
Unipart tdmk ˈjuːn i pɑːt ‖ -pɑːrt
unique ju ˈniːk ˌju:- **~ly** li **~ness** nəs nɪs
Uniroyal tdmk ˈjuːn i ˌrɔɪ əl
unisex ˈjuːn i seks -ə-
unisexual ˌjuːn i ˈsek ʃu‿əl ◂ -ˈseks ju‿əl,
-ˈsek ʃəl **~ly** i
unison ˈjuːn ɪs ən -ɪz-, -əs-, -əz-
unit ˈjuːn ɪt §-ət **~s** s
    ,unit 'trust
UNITA ju ˈniːt ə
unitard ˈjuːn ɪ tɑːd -ə- ‖ -tɑːrd **~s** z
Unitarian, u~ ˌjuːn ɪ ˈteər i‿ən ◂ ˌ•ə- ‖ -ˈter-
-ˈtær- **~s** z
unitary ˈjuːn ɪt ˌər i ‖ '•ət̬‿ ‖ -ə ter i
Unitas tdmk ˈjuːn ɪ tæs -ə-
u|nite ju |ˈnaɪt ˌju:- **~nited** ˈnaɪt ɪd -əd
‖ ˈnaɪt̬ əd **~nites** ˈnaɪts **~niting**
ˈnaɪt ɪŋ ‖ ˈnaɪt̬ ɪŋ
    **U,nited ,Arab 'Emirates; U,nited
    'Kingdom; U,nited 'Nations, U,nited
    'Nations Associ,ation; U,nited Re'formed
    Church; U,nited 'States◂, U,nited ,States
    of A'merica**
unit-linked ˌjuːn ɪt ˈlɪŋkt ◂ §-ət-
unit|y, Unity ˈjuːn ət li -ɪt- ‖ -ət̬ li **~ies** iz
Univac tdmk ˈjuːn ɪ væk -ə-
univalve ˈjuːn i vælv **~s** z
universal ˌjuːn ɪ ˈvɜːs əl ◂ ˌ•ə- ‖ -ˈvɜ˞ːs- **~s** z
    ,uni,versal 'joint; ,uni,versal 'language
universalism, U~ ˌjuːn ɪ ˈvɜːs ə ˌlɪz əm ˌ•ə-,
-əl ˌɪz- ‖ -ˈvɜ˞ːs-
universalist, U~ ˌjuːn ɪ ˈvɜːs əl ɪst ˌ•ə-, §-əst
‖ -ˈvɜ˞ːs- **~s** s
universality ˌjuːn ɪ vɜː ˈsæl ət i ˌ•ə-, -ɪt i
‖ -vɜ˞ː ˈsæl ət̬ i
universal|ly ˌjuːn ɪ ˈvɜːs əl li ˌ•ə- ‖ -ˈvɜ˞ːs-
~ness nəs nɪs
univers|e ˈjuːn ɪ vɜːs -ə- ‖ -vɜ˞ːs **~es** ɪz əz
universit|y ˌjuːn ɪ ˈvɜːs ət li ˌ•ə-, -ɪt i
‖ -ˈvɜ˞ːs ət̬ li **~ies** iz
Unix, UNIX tdmk ˈjuːn ɪks
unjust ˌʌn ˈdʒʌst ◂ **~ly** li **~ness** nəs nɪs
unjustifiab|le ˌʌn ˌdʒʌst ɪ ˈfaɪ əb |əl ◂ -ə-ˈ•-,
(ˌ)•ˈ•••• **~ly** li
unjustified ʌn ˈdʒʌst ɪ faɪd ˌʌn-, -ə- **~ly** li

unkempt ˌʌn 'kempt ◄→ˌʌŋ- **~ly** li **~ness** nəs nıs

unkind ˌʌn 'kaınd ◄→ˌʌŋ-, ʌn- **~er** ə ‖ ᵊr **~est** ıst əst **~ly** li **~ness** nəs nıs

unkind|ly (ˌ)ʌn 'kaınd |li→(ˌ)ʌŋ- **~lier** li_ə ‖ li_ᵊr **~liest** li_ıst li_əst **~liness** li nəs -nıs

un|knit ˌʌn |'nıt **~knits** 'nıts **~knitted** 'nıt ıd -əd ‖ 'nıt̮ əd **~knitting** 'nıt ıŋ ‖ 'nıt̮ ıŋ

un|knot ˌʌn |'nɒt ‖ -'nɑːt **~knots** 'nɒts ‖ 'nɑːts **~knotted** 'nɒt ıd -əd ‖ 'nɑːt̮ əd **~knotting** 'nɒt ıŋ ‖ 'nɑːt̮ ıŋ

unknowab|le (ˌ)ʌn 'nəʊ əb |ᵊl ‖ -'noʊ- **~leness** ᵊl nəs -nıs **~les** ᵊlz **~ly** li

unknowing (ˌ)ʌn 'nəʊ ıŋ ‖ -'noʊ- **~ly** li

unknown ˌʌn 'nəʊn ◄ ‖ -'noʊn ◄ **~ness** nəs nıs **~s** z

ˌunknown 'quantity; ˌUnknown 'Soldier

unlac|e ˌʌn 'leıs **~ed** t **~es** ız əz **~ing** ıŋ

unlawful (ˌ)ʌn 'lɔː fᵊl -fʊl ‖ -'lɑː- **~ly** _i **~ness** nəs nıs

unleaded (ˌ)ʌn 'led ıd ◄ -əd

unlearn ˌʌn 'lɜːn ‖ -'lɝːn **~ed** d **~ing** ıŋ **~s** z

unleash (ˌ)ʌn 'liːʃ **~ed** t **~es** ız əz **~ing** ıŋ

unleavened (ˌ)ʌn 'lev ᵊnd ◄

unless ən 'les ʌn- —occasionally also, for emphasis, ˌʌn-

unlettered ˌʌn 'let əd ◄ ‖ -'let̮ ᵊrd ◄

unlicensed (ˌ)ʌn 'laıs ᵊn'st

unlike ˌʌn 'laık ◄ **~ness** nəs nıs

unlike|ly ʌn 'laık |li ˌʌn- **~liness** li nəs -nıs

unlimited ʌn 'lım ıt ıd ˌ•-, §-ət ıd, -əd ‖ -ət̮ əd **~ly** li **~ness** nəs nıs

unlisted ʌn 'lıst ıd ˌ•-, -əd

unlit ˌʌn 'lıt ◄

unload (ˌ)ʌn 'ləʊd ‖ -'loʊd **~ed** ıd əd **~ing** ıŋ **~s** z

unlock (ˌ)ʌn 'lɒk ‖ -'lɑːk **~ed** t **~ing** ıŋ **~s** s

unlooked-for (ˌ)ʌn 'lʊkt fɔː ‖ -fɔːr

unloos|e (ˌ)ʌn 'luːs **~ed** t **~es** ız əz **~ing** ıŋ

unloosen (ˌ)ʌn 'luːs ᵊn **~ed** d **~ing** _ıŋ **~s** z

unluck|y (ˌ)ʌn 'lʌk |i **~ier** i_ə ‖ i_ᵊr **~iest** i_ıst i_əst **~ily** ı li əl i **~iness** i nəs i nıs

unmade ˌʌn 'meıd ◄→ˌʌm-

unman ˌʌn 'mæn →ˌʌm- **~ned** d **~ing** ıŋ **~s** z

unman|ly ˌʌn 'mæn |li→ˌʌm- **~lier** li_ə ‖ li_ᵊr **~liest** li_ıst əst **~liness** li nəs -nıs

unmanner|ly ʌn 'mæn ə |li→ʌm- ‖ -ᵊr- **~liness** li nəs -nıs

unmarked ˌʌn 'mɑːkt ◄→ˌʌm- ‖ -'mɑːrkt ◄ ˌunmarked 'car

unmarried ˌʌn 'mær id ◄→ˌʌm- ‖ -'mer- **~s** z

unmask ˌʌn 'mɑːsk →ˌʌm-, §-'mæsk ‖ -'mæsk **~ed** t **~ing** ıŋ **~s** s

unmatched ˌʌn 'mætʃt ◄→ˌʌm-

unmeasured (ˌ)ʌn 'meʒ əd →(ˌ)ʌm- ‖ -ᵊrd -'meʒ-

unmentionab|le ʌn 'menʧ ᵊn_əb |ᵊl →ˌʌm- **~leness** ᵊl nəs -nıs **~les** ᵊlz **~ly** li

unmerciful ʌn 'mɜːs ı fᵊl ˌ•-, -ə-, -fʊl ‖ -'mɝːs- **~ly** _i **~ness** nəs nıs

unmindful (ˌ)ʌn 'maınd fᵊl →(ˌ)ʌm-, -fʊl **~ly** i **~ness** nəs nıs

unmistakab|le, unmistakeab|le ˌʌn mı 'steık əb |ᵊl ◄→ˌʌm-, ˌ•mə- **~leness** ᵊl nəs -nıs **~ly** li

unmitigated ʌn 'mıt ı geıt ıd→ʌm-, §-'•ə-, -əd ‖ -'mıt̮ ə geıt̮ əd **~ly** li

unmixed ˌʌn 'mıkst ◄→ˌʌm-

unmoved (ˌ)ʌn 'muːvd→(ˌ)ʌm-

unnamed ˌʌn 'neımd ◄

unnatural (ˌ)ʌn 'nætʃ ᵊr_əl **~ly** i **~ness** nəs nıs

unnecessarily ʌn 'nes əs ᵊr_əl i ˌʌn-, -'•ıs-, ı li; ˌʌn ˌnes ə 'ser əl i, ʌn,•-, -ı'•-, -ı li ‖ ˌʌn ˌnes ə 'ser əl i

unnecessar|ly ʌn 'nes əs ᵊr_|i ˌʌn-, -'•ıs-; -ə ser i, -'•ı- ‖ -ə ser li **~iness** i nəs i nıs

unnerv|e ʌn 'nɜːv ‖ -'nɝːv **~ed** d **~es** z **~ing** ıŋ

unnumbered ˌʌn 'nʌm bəd ◄ ‖ -bᵊrd

UNO 'juːn əʊ ‖ -oʊ

Uno tdmk, car model 'uːn əʊ'juːn- ‖ -oʊ

unobtrusive ˌʌn əb 'truːs ıv ◄ -ɒb-, §-'truːz- **~ly** li **~ness** nəs nıs

unoccupied (ˌ)ʌn 'ɒk ju paıd ◄ ‖ -'ɑːk jə-

unofficial ˌʌn ə 'fıʃ ᵊl ◄ §-əʊ- **~ly** i

unopposed ˌʌn ə 'pəʊzd ◄ ‖ -'poʊzd ◄

unorthodox ʌn 'ɔːθ ə dɒks ˌʌn- ‖ -'ɔːrθ ə dɑːks **~ly** li

unorthodox|y ʌn 'ɔːθ ə dɒks li ˌʌn- ‖ -'ɔːrθ ə dɑːks li **~ies** iz

unpack ˌʌn 'pæk →ˌʌm- **~ed** t **~ing** ıŋ **~s** s

unpaid ˌʌn 'peıd ◄→ˌʌm- ˌunpaid 'bills

unpalatable ʌn 'pæl ət əb ᵊl →ˌʌm-, ˌ•- ‖ -'•ət̮-

unparalleled (ˌ)ʌn 'pær ə leld -əl əld ‖ -'per-

unparliamentary ˌʌn ˌpɑːl ə 'ment ər i →ˌʌm-, -,•ı-, -,•i_ə'•- ‖ -ˌpɑːrl ə 'ment̮ ər i →-'mentr i

unpeg ˌʌn 'peg →ˌʌm- **~ged** d **~ging** ıŋ **~s** z

unperson ˌʌn 'pɜːs ᵊn →ˌʌm-, '•,•• ‖ -'pɝːs- **~s** z

unpick ˌʌn 'pık →ˌʌm- **~ed** t **~ing** ıŋ **~s** s

unplaced ˌʌn 'pleıst ◄→ˌʌm-

unplayable (ˌ)ʌn 'pleı əb ᵊl →(ˌ)ʌm-

unpleasant ʌn 'plez ᵊnt →ʌm- **~ly** li

unpleasantness ʌn 'plez ᵊnt nəs →ʌm-, -nıs **~es** ız əz

unplug ˌʌn 'plʌg →ˌʌm- **~ged** d **~ging** ıŋ **~s** z

unplumbed ˌʌn 'plʌmd ◄→ˌʌm- ˌunplumbed 'depths

unpopular (ˌ)ʌn 'pɒp jʊl ə →(ˌ)ʌm-, -jəl ə ‖ -'pɑːp jəl ᵊr **~ly** li

unpopularity ˌʌn ˌpɒp ju 'lær ət i →ʌm-, -,•jə-, -ıt i ‖ -ˌpɑːp jə 'lær ət̮ i -'ler-

unpracticed, unpractised (ˌ)ʌn 'prækt ıst →(ˌ)ʌm-, §-əst

unprecedented ʌn 'pres ı dent ıd →ʌm-, ˌ•-, -'priːs-, -'•ə-, -ıd ənt-, -əd ənt-, -əd; •,•'•dent•,ˌ•,•- ‖ -'pres ə dent̮ əd **~ly** li

unpredictability ˌʌn prı ˌdıkt ə 'bıl ət i →ˌʌm-, ˌ•prə-, §,•priː-, -ıt i ‖ -ət̮ i

unpredictab|le ˌʌn prı 'dıkt əb |ᵊl ◄→ˌʌm-, ˌ•prə-, §,•priː- **~leness** ᵊl nəs -nıs **~ly** li

unprejudiced (ˌ)ʌn 'predʒ ʊd ɪst →(ˌ)ʌm-,
-'•əd-, §-əst, §-aɪst ‖ -əd əst

unpremeditated ˌʌn priː 'med ɪ teɪt ɪd ◄
→ˌʌm-, ˌ•priː-, -əd ‖ -teɪt̬ əd ◄

unprepared ˌʌn prɪ 'peəd ◄→ˌʌm-, -prə-,
§-priː- ‖ -'peᵊrd ◄-'pæᵊrd

unprepared|ly ˌʌn prɪ 'peər ɪd ‖li →ˌʌm-,
ˌ•prə-, §ˌ•priː-, -əd• ‖ -'per əd ‖li -'pær-
~**ness** nəs nɪs

unprepossessing ˌʌn ˌpriː pə 'zes ɪŋ →ˌʌm-;
•ˌ•-; (ˌ)•ˈ••• ~**ly** li

unpretentious ˌʌn prɪ 'ten̩ʧ əs ◄→ˌʌm-, -prə-,
§-priː- ~**ly** li ~**ness** nəs nɪs

unprincipled (ˌ)ʌn 'prɪn̩ts əp ᵊld →(ˌ)ʌm-, -ɪp-

unprintable (ˌ)ʌn 'prɪnt əb ᵊl →(ˌ)ʌm- ‖ -'prɪn̩t-

unprofessional ˌʌn prə 'feʃ ᵊn_əl ◄→ˌʌm- ~**ly**
i

Unprofor 'ʌn prə fɔː →'ʌm- ‖ -fɔːr

unprompted (ˌ)ʌn 'prɒmpt ɪd →(ˌ)ʌm-, -əd
‖ -'prɑːmpt əd

unpronounceable ˌʌn prə 'naʊn̩ts əb ᵊl →ˌʌm-

unprovoked ˌʌn prə 'vəʊkt ◄→ˌʌm-
‖ -'voʊkt ◄

unpunctual ˌʌn 'pʌŋk tʃu_əl →ˌʌm-, -tju_əl
~**ly** i

unpunctuality ˌʌn ˌpʌŋk tʃu 'æl ət i -ˌ•tju-,
-ɪt i ‖ -ət̬ i

unpunished (ˌ)ʌn 'pʌn ɪʃt (ˌ)ʌm-

unputdownable ˌʌn pʊt 'daʊn əb ᵊl →ˌʌm-

unqualified 'downright, not limited'
ʌn 'kwɒl ɪ faɪd →ʌŋ-, -ə- ‖ -'kwɑːl-

unqualified 'lacking qualifications'
ˌʌn 'kwɒl ɪ faɪd ◄→ˌʌŋ-, -ə- ‖ -'kwɑːl-

unquestionab|le (ˌ)ʌn 'kwes tʃən_əb ᵊl
→(ˌ)ʌŋ-, →-'kweʃ-, -'•tʃən- ~**leness** ᵊl nəs
-nɪs ~**ly** li

unquestioned (ˌ)ʌn 'kwes tʃənd →(ˌ)ʌŋ-,
→-'kweʃ-, -tʃənd

unquestioning (ˌ)ʌn 'kwes tʃən ɪŋ →(ˌ)ʌŋ-,
→'kweʃ-, -tʃən- ~**ly** li

unquiet ˌʌn 'kwaɪ_ət ◄→ˌʌŋ- ~**ly** li ~**ness** nəs
nɪs

unquote ˌʌn 'kwəʊt →ˌʌŋ-, -'kəʊt ‖ 'ʌn kwoʊt

unravel (ˌ)ʌn 'ræv ᵊl ~**ed**, ~**led** d ~**ing**, ~**ling**
ɪŋ ~**s** z

unread ˌʌn 'red ◄

unreadab|le (ˌ)ʌn 'riːd əb ᵊl ~**leness** ᵊl nəs
-nɪs ~**ly** li

unread|y ˌʌn 'red li ~**ily** ɪ li əl i ~**iness** i nəs
i nɪs

unreal (ˌ)ʌn 'rɪəl -'riː_ᵊl ‖ -'riː_əl

unreality ˌʌn ri 'æl ət i -ɪt i ‖ -ət̬ i

unreasonab|le (ˌ)ʌn 'riːz ᵊn_əb ᵊl ~**leness**
ᵊl nəs -nɪs ~**ly** li

unreasoning (ˌ)ʌn 'riːz ᵊn_ɪŋ ~**ly** li

unrecognisab|le, unrecognizab|le
ˌʌn 'rek əg naɪz əb ᵊl -'•ə-; ˌ•ˌ•ˈ••'•- ~**ly** li

unregenerate ˌʌn rɪ 'dʒen ᵊr_ət ˌ•rə-, §ˌ•riː-,
_ɪt, -ə reɪt ~**ly** li

unrelenting ˌʌn rɪ 'lent ɪŋ ◄-rə-, §-riː-
‖ -'lent̬ ɪŋ ◄ ~**ly** li ~**ness** nəs nɪs

unreliability ˌʌn rɪ ˌlaɪ_ə 'bɪl ət i ˌ•rə-, §ˌ•riː-,
-ɪt i ‖ -ət̬ i

unreliab|le ˌʌn rɪ 'laɪ_əb ᵊl ◄, •rə-, §ˌ•riː-
~**leness** ᵊl nəs -nɪs ~**ly** li

unrelieved ˌʌn rɪ 'liːvd ◄-rə-, §-riː-
ˌunrelieved 'boredom

unremitting ˌʌn rɪ 'mɪt ɪŋ ◄-rə-, §-riː-
‖ -'mɪt̬ ɪŋ ◄ ~**ly** li ~**ness** nəs nɪs
ˌunre mitting 'efforts

unrequited ˌʌn rɪ 'kwaɪt ɪd ◄-rə-, §-riː-, -əd
‖ -'kwaɪt̬ əd ◄
ˌunre quited 'love

unre|served ˌʌn rɪ ‖'zɜːvd ◄-rə-, §-riː-
‖ -‖'zɜːvd ~**servedly** 'zɜːv ɪd li -əd- ‖ 'zɜːv-

unresisting ˌʌn rɪ 'zɪst ɪŋ -rə-, §-riː- ~**ly** li

unrest (ˌ)ʌn 'rest

unrestrained ˌʌn rɪ 'streɪnd ◄-rə-, §-riː-

unrestrainedly ˌʌn rɪ 'streɪn ɪd li ˌ•rə-, §ˌ•riː-,
-əd li

unrip (ˌ)ʌn 'rɪp ~**ped** t ~**ping** ɪŋ ~**s** s

unripe ˌʌn 'raɪp ◄ ~**ness** nəs nɪs

unrivaled, unrivalled ʌn 'raɪv ᵊld ˌʌn-

unroll (ˌ)ʌn 'rəʊl →-'rɒʊl ‖ -'roʊl ~**ed** d ~**ing**
ɪŋ ~**s** z

unround ˌʌn 'raʊnd ◄ ~**ed** ɪd əd ~**ing** ɪŋ ~**s** z

unruffled (ˌ)ʌn 'rʌf ᵊld

unrul|y ʌn 'ruːl li ~**iness** i nəs i nɪs

UNRWA 'ʌn rə

unsaddl|e (ˌ)ʌn 'sæd ᵊl ~**ed** d ~**es** z ~**ing** _ɪŋ

unsafe (ˌ)ʌn 'seɪf ~**ly** li ~**ness** nəs nɪs

unsaid (ˌ)ʌn 'sed

unsaturated (ˌ)ʌn 'sætʃ ə reɪt ɪd -'•ʊ, -əd;
-'sæt jʊ- ‖ -reɪt̬ əd

unsavor|y, unsavour|y (ˌ)ʌn 'seɪv ᵊr_li ~**iness**
i nəs i nɪs

un|say ˌʌn ‖'seɪ —but as contrasted with say, '••
~**said** 'sed ~**saying** 'seɪ ɪŋ ~**says** 'sez 'seɪz

unscathed (ˌ)ʌn 'skeɪðd

unscheduled ˌʌn 'ʃed juːld ◄-'sked-
‖ -'skedʒ uːld ◄-əld

unschooled ˌʌn 'skuːld

unscientific ˌʌn ˌsaɪ_ən 'tɪf ɪk ~**ally** ᵊl_i

Unscom, UNSCOM 'ʌn skɒm ‖ -skɑːm

unscrambl|e (ˌ)ʌn 'skræm bᵊl ~**ed** d ~**es** z
~**ing** _ɪŋ

unscrew (ˌ)ʌn 'skruː ~**ed** d ~**ing** ɪŋ ~**s** z

unscripted ˌʌn 'skrɪpt ɪd ◄ ʌn-, -əd

unscrupulous ʌn 'skruːp jʊl əs ˌʌn-, -jəl-
‖ -jəl əs ~**ly** li ~**ness** nəs nɪs

unseal ˌʌn 'siː_ᵊl ~**ed** d ~**ing** ɪŋ ~**s** z

unseasonab|le ʌn 'siːz ᵊn_əb ᵊl ˌʌn- ~**leness**
ᵊl nəs -nɪs ~**ly** li

un|seat ˌʌn ‖'siːt ~**seated** 'siːt ɪd -əd ‖ 'siːt̬ əd
~**seating** 'siːt ɪŋ ‖ 'siːt̬ ɪŋ ~**seats** 'siːts

unsecured ˌʌn sɪ 'kjʊəd ◄-sə-, §-siː-, -'kjɔːd
‖ -'kjʊᵊrd ◄
ˌunsecured 'loan

unseeded ˌʌn 'siːd ɪd -əd

unseeing ˌʌn 'siː_ɪŋ ◄

unseem|ly ʌn 'siːm ‖li ~**liness** li nəs -nɪs

unseen ˌʌn 'siːn ◄ ~**s** z

unselfish (ˌ)ʌn 'self ɪʃ ~**ly** li ~**ness** nəs nɪs

unserviceab|le (ˌ)ʌn 'sɜːv ɪs əb ᵊl §-'•əs-
‖ -'sɜːv əs- ~**leness** ᵊl nəs -nɪs ~**ly** li

U

unsettl|e ₍ᵢ₎ʌn 'set ᵊl ‖ -'seţ ᵊl **~ed** d **~es** z
~ing _ɪŋ
unsettled *adj* ˌʌn 'set ᵊld ◄ ‖ -'seţ ᵊld ◄ **~ness**
nəs nɪs
unsex ₍ᵢ₎ʌn 'seks **~ed** t **~es** ɪz əz **~ing** ɪŋ
unshakab|le, unshakeab|le ʌn 'ʃeɪk əb |ᵊl
~leness ᵊl nəs -nɪs **~ly** li
unshaven ˌʌn 'ʃeɪv ᵊn ◄
unsheath|e ₍ᵢ₎ʌn 'ʃiːð **~ed** d **~es** z **~ing** ɪŋ
unshockable ˌʌn 'ʃɒk əb ᵊl ◄ ‖ -'ʃɑːk-
unshod ˌʌn 'ʃɒd ◄ ‖ -'ʃɑːd ◄
unsight|ly ʌn 'saɪt |li **~liness** li nəs -nɪs
unsigned ˌʌn 'saɪnd ◄
unskilled ˌʌn 'skɪld ◄
unsociab|le ₍ᵢ₎ʌn 'səʊʃ əb |ᵊl ‖ -'souʃ- **~leness**
ᵊl nəs -nɪs **~ly** li
unsocial ˌʌn 'səʊʃ ᵊl ◄ ‖ -'souʃ- **~ly** i
ˌun͵social 'hours
unsolicited ˌʌn sə 'lɪs ɪt ɪd ◄ §-ət •, -əd
‖ -əţ əd ◄
unsold ˌʌn 'səʊld ◄ →-'sɒʊld ‖ -'sould ◄
unsophisticated ˌʌn sə 'fɪst ɪ keɪt ɪd ◄ §-'•ə-,
-əd ‖ -ə keɪţ əd ◄
unsound ˌʌn 'saʊnd ◄
unsparing ʌn 'speər ɪŋ ‖ -'sper- -'spær- **~ly**
li **~ness** nəs nɪs
unspeakab|le ʌn 'spiːk əb |ᵊl **~leness** ᵊl nəs
-nɪs **~ly** li
unspoiled ˌʌn 'spɔɪld ◄ -'spɔɪᵊlt
unspoilt ˌʌn 'spɔɪᵊlt ◄
unspoken ₍ᵢ₎ʌn 'spəʊk ən ‖ -'spouk ən
unspotted ˌʌn 'spɒt ɪd ◄ -əd ‖ -'spɑːţ əd ◄
~ness nəs nɪs
Unst ʌnᵗst
unstab|le ₍ᵢ₎ʌn 'steɪb |ᵊl **~leness** ᵊl nəs -nɪs
~ly li
unstead|y ₍ᵢ₎ʌn 'sted |i **~ied** id **~ier** i_ə ‖ i_ᵊr
~ies iz **~iest** i_ɪst i_əst **~ily** ɪ li əl i **~iness**
i nəs i nɪs **~ying** i_ɪŋ
unstick ˌʌn 'stɪk **~ing** ɪŋ **~s** s **unstuck**
ˌʌn 'stʌk
unstinted ʌn 'stɪnt ɪd -əd ‖ -'stɪnţ əd
unstinting ʌn 'stɪnt ɪŋ ‖ -'stɪnţ ɪŋ **~ly** li
unstop ˌʌn 'stɒp ‖ -'stɑːp **~ped** t **~ping** ɪŋ
~s s
unstoppab|le ʌn 'stɒp əb |ᵊl ˌʌn- ‖ -'stɑːp-
~leness ᵊl nəs -nɪs **~ly** li
unstreamed ˌʌn 'striːmd ◄
unstressed ˌʌn 'strest ◄
ˌunstressed 'syllables
unstructured ₍ᵢ₎ʌn 'strʌk tʃəd -ʃəd ‖ -tʃᵊrd **~ly**
li **~ness** nəs nɪs
unstrung ˌʌn 'strʌŋ
unstuck ˌʌn 'stʌk ◄
unstudied ˌʌn 'stʌd id ◄
unsubtle ˌʌn 'sʌt ᵊl ‖ -'sʌţ ᵊl
unsuccessful ˌʌn sək 'ses fᵊl ◄ §-sʌk-, -fʊl **~ly**
_i **~ness** nəs nɪs
unsuitab|le ₍ᵢ₎ʌn 'suːt əb |ᵊl ‖ -'sjuːt- ‖ -'suːţ-
~leness ᵊl nəs -nɪs **~ly** li
unsullied ˌʌn 'sʌl id ◄
unsung ˌʌn 'sʌŋ ◄
ˌunsung 'hero

unsupervised ˌʌn 'suːp ə vaɪzd -'sjuːp-
‖ -ᵊr vaɪzd
unsupported ˌʌn sə 'pɔːt ɪd ◄ -əd ‖ -'pɔːrţ əd ◄
-'poʊrţ-
unsure ˌʌn 'ʃʊə ◄ -'ʃɔː ‖ -'ʃʊᵊr ◄ -'ʃɝː **~ly** li
~ness nəs nɪs
unsurpassed ˌʌn sə 'pɑːst ◄ -§'pæst
‖ -sᵊr 'pæst ◄
unsuspected ˌʌn sə 'spekt ɪd ◄ -əd **~ly** li
unsuspecting ˌʌn sə 'spekt ɪŋ ◄ **~ly** li
unsweetened ˌʌn 'swiːt ᵊnd ◄
unswerving ʌn 'swɜːv ɪŋ ˌʌn- ‖ -'swɝːv ɪŋ
~ly li
Unsworth 'ʌnz wɜːθ -wəθ ‖ -wɝːθ
unsystematic ˌʌn ˌsɪst ə 'mæt ɪk -ɪ- ‖ -'mæţ ɪk
~ally ᵊl_i
untalented ₍ᵢ₎ʌn 'tæl ənt ɪd -əd ‖ -ənţ əd
untamable, untameable ˌʌn 'teɪm əb ᵊl ◄
untamed ˌʌn 'teɪmd ◄
untangl|e ₍ᵢ₎ʌn 'tæŋ gᵊl **~ed** d **~es** z **~ing** _ɪŋ
untapped ˌʌn 'tæpt ◄
untarnished ₍ᵢ₎ʌn 'tɑːn ɪʃt ‖ -'tɑːrn ɪʃt
untaught ˌʌn 'tɔːt ◄ ‖ -'tɑːt
untenable ʌn 'ten əb ᵊl ˌʌn-, -'tiːn-
Unthank 'ʌn θæŋk
unthinkab|le ʌn 'θɪŋk əb |ᵊl **~leness** ᵊl nəs
-nɪs **~ly** li
unthinking ₍ᵢ₎ʌn 'θɪŋk ɪŋ **~ly** li **~ness** nəs nɪs
unthought-of ʌn 'θɔːt ɒv -əv ‖ -'θɑːţ-, ʌv
-'θɑːţ-, -əv
unthought-out ˌʌn θɔːt 'aʊt ◄ ‖ -θɔːţ- -θɑːţ-
untid|y ₍ᵢ₎ʌn 'taɪd |li **~ied** id **~ier** i_ə ‖ i_ᵊr **~ies**
iz **~iest** i_ɪst i_əst **~ily** ɪ li əl i **~iness** i nəs
i nɪs **~ying** i_ɪŋ
untie ˌʌn 'taɪ **~d** d **~s** z **untying** ʌn 'taɪ ɪŋ
until ən 'tɪl ₍ᵢ₎ʌn- —*also occasionally, in*
STRESS SHIFT environments (ˌuntil 'now),
'ʌn tᵊl
untime|ly ₍ᵢ₎ʌn 'taɪm |li **~liness** li nəs -nɪs
untinged ˌʌn 'tɪndʒd ◄
untiring ʌn 'taɪᵊr ɪŋ ‖ -'taɪ_ᵊr ɪŋ **~ly** li
unto 'ʌn tu —*also, esp before a consonant,* -tə
untold ˌʌn 'təʊld ◄ ʌn-, →-'tɒʊld ‖ -'tould ◄
ˌuntold 'suffering
untouchability ʌn ˌtʌtʃ ə 'bɪl ət i ˌʌn,•-, -ɪt i
‖ -əţ i
untouchable ₍ᵢ₎ʌn 'tʌtʃ əb ᵊl ◄ **~s** z
untoward ˌʌn tə 'wɔːd ◄ -tu-; ˌʌn 'təʊ əd
‖ ʌn 'tɔːrd -'tourd (*) **~ly** li **~ness** nəs nɪs
untrammeled, untrammelled ₍ᵢ₎ʌn 'træm ᵊld
untrue ₍ᵢ₎ʌn 'truː
un|truth ₍ᵢ₎ʌn |'truːθ '•• **~truths** 'truːðz
'truːθs
untruthful ₍ᵢ₎ʌn 'truːθ fᵊl -fʊl **~ly** _i **~ness** nəs
nɪs
untuck ˌʌn 'tʌk **~ed** t **~ing** ɪŋ **~s** s
untutored ˌʌn 'tjuːt əd →-§-'tʃuːt-
‖ -'tuːţ ᵊrd ◄ -'tjuːţ-
unused *'not made use of'* ˌʌn 'juːzd ◄
unused *'unaccustomed'* ₍ᵢ₎ʌn 'juːst
unusual ʌn 'juːʒ u_əl i ˌʌn-, -ju_əl; -'juːʒ ᵊl
unusually ʌn 'juːʒ u_əl i ˌʌn-, -'•ju_; -'juːʒ ᵊl i

U

unutterab|le ʌn 'ʌt̬‿ər əb |ºl || -'ʌt̬ ər- **~leness**
ºl nəs -nɪs **~ly** li
unvarnished ˌʌn 'vɑːn ɪʃt ◄ ʌn- || -'vɑːrn ɪʃt ◄
unveil ˌʌn 'veɪºl **~ed** d **~ing** ɪŋ **~s** z
unversed ⁽ˌ⁾ʌn 'vɜːst || -'vɜːst
unvoic|e ˌʌn 'vɔɪs ◄ **~ed** t **~es** ɪz əz **~ing** ɪŋ
unwaged ˌʌn 'weɪdʒd ◄
unwarrantab|le ʌn 'wɒr ənt əb |ºl || -'wɔːr ənt̬-
-'wɑːr- **~ly** li
unwarranted ʌn 'wɒr ənt ɪd-əd || -'wɔːr ənt̬
əd -'wɑːr-
unwar|y ⁽ˌ⁾ʌn 'weər |i || -'wer |i-'wær- **~ily** əl i
ɪ li **~iness** i nəs i nɪs
unwashed ˌʌn 'wɒʃt ◄ || -'wɔːʃt ◄-'wɑːʃt
unwed ˌʌn 'wed ◄
unwelcome ʌn 'welk əm ˌʌn-
unwell ⁽ˌ⁾ʌn 'wel
unwholesome ⁽ˌ⁾ʌn 'həʊl səm→-'hɒʊl-
|| -'hoʊl- **~ly** li **~ness** nəs nɪs
unwield|y ʌn 'wiːºld |i **~ily** ɪ li əl i **~iness**
i nəs i nɪs
unwilling ⁽ˌ⁾ʌn 'wɪl ɪŋ **~ness** nəs nɪs
unwillingly ʌn 'wɪl ɪŋ li
Unwin 'ʌn wɪn
unwind ˌʌn 'waɪnd **~ing** ɪŋ **~s** z **unwound**
ˌʌn 'waʊnd
unwise ˌʌn 'waɪz ◄ **~ly** li
unwished-for ⁽ˌ⁾ʌn 'wɪʃt fɔː || -fɔːr
unwitting ⁽ˌ⁾ʌn 'wɪt ɪŋ || -'wɪt̬ ɪŋ **~ly** li
unwonted ʌn 'wəʊnt ɪd-əd || -'wɔːnt̬ əd
-'wɑːnt̬-, -'woʊnt̬-, -'wʌnt̬- (*) **~ly** li **~ness**
nəs nɪs
unworkable ⁽ˌ⁾ʌn 'wɜːk əb ºl || -'wɜːk-
unworld|ly ⁽ˌ⁾ʌn 'wɜːld |li || -'wɜːld- **~liness**
li nəs -nɪs
unworried ʌn 'wʌr id,•- || -'wɜː id
unworth|y ⁽ˌ⁾ʌn 'wɜːð |i || -'wɜːð |i **~ily** ɪ li əl i
~iness i nəs i nɪs
unwound ˌʌn 'waʊnd
unwritten ˌʌn 'rɪt ºn ◄
ˌun written 'law
unyok|e ˌʌn 'jəʊk ʌn- || -'joʊk **~ed** t **~es** s
~ing ɪŋ
Unzen 'ʊn zen—*Jp* ['ʊn *dzen*]
unzip ˌʌn 'zɪp **~ped** t **~ping** ɪŋ **~s** s
up ʌp **upped** ʌpt **upping** 'ʌp ɪŋ **ups** ʌps
ˌups and 'downs
up- ˌ'ʌp— **upgrowth** 'ʌp grəʊθ || -groʊθ
up-and-coming ˌʌp ən 'kʌm ɪŋ ◄-ənd-, →-m-,
→-əŋ-
up-and-down ˌʌp ən 'daʊn-ənd-, →-m-
up-and-up ˌʌp ən 'ʌp-ənd-
Upanishad u 'pʌn ɪʃ əd ju-, -'pæn-, -əʃ•;
-ɪ ʃæd || u 'pɑːn ɪ ʃɑːd **~s** z
upas 'juːp əs **~es** ɪz əz
upbeat 'ʌp biːt **~s** s
upbraid ʌp 'breɪd **~ed** ɪdəd **~ing** ɪŋ **~s** z
upbringing 'ʌp ˌbrɪŋ ɪŋ
upcast 'ʌp kɑːst §-kæst || -kæst **~s** s
upchuck 'ʌp tʃʌk **~ed** t **~ing** ɪŋ **~s** s
upcoming 'ʌp ˌkʌm ɪŋ,•'••
up-country ˌʌp 'kʌntr i ◄

up|date v ˌʌp |'deɪt **~dated** 'deɪt ɪd-əd
|| 'deɪt̬ əd **~dates** 'deɪts **~dating**
'deɪt ɪŋ || 'deɪt̬ ɪŋ
update n 'ʌp deɪt,•'• **~s** s
Updike 'ʌp daɪk
updraft, updraught 'ʌp drɑːft §-dræft
|| -dræft **~s** s
upend ʌp 'end **~ed** ɪdəd **~ing** ɪŋ **~s** z
upfront ˌʌp 'frʌnt **~ness** nəs nɪs
upgrad|e v ˌʌp 'greɪd'•• **~ed** ɪdəd **~ing** ɪŋ
~es z
upgrade n 'ʌp greɪd,•'• **~s** s
upheaval ʌp 'hiːv ºl **~s** z
upheld ʌp 'held
uphill ˌʌp 'hɪl ◄
ˌuphill 'struggle
uphold ʌp 'həʊld→-'hɒʊld || -'hoʊld **upheld**
ʌp 'held **~er/s** ə/z || ər/z **~ing** ɪŋ **~s** z
upholst|er ʌp 'həʊlst ə əp-, →-'hɒʊlst-
|| ʌp 'hoʊlst ºr ə 'poʊlst- **~ered** əd || ºrd
~ering ər ɪŋ **~ers** əz || ºrz
upholsterer ʌp 'həʊlst ər‿ə əp-, →-'hɒʊlst-
|| ʌp 'hoʊlst ºr‿ər ə 'poʊlst- **~s** z
upholster|y ʌp 'həʊlst ər‿li əp-, →-'hɒʊlst-
|| ʌp 'hoʊlst- ə 'poʊlst- **~ies** iz
UPI ˌjuː piː 'aɪ
Upjohn 'ʌp dʒɒn || -dʒɑːn
upkeep 'ʌp kiːp
upland 'ʌp lənd-lænd **~s** z
uplift v ⁽ˌ⁾ʌp 'lɪft'•• **~ed** ɪdəd **~ing** ɪŋ **~s** s
uplift n 'ʌp lɪft **~s** s
uplighter 'ʌp ˌlaɪt ə || -ˌlaɪt̬ ºr **~s** z
up-market ˌʌp 'mɑːk ɪt §-ət || -'mɑːrk ət ◄
Upminster 'ʌp mɪnt stə || -ºr
upmost 'ʌp məʊst || -moʊst
upon ə 'pɒn | ə 'pɑːn-'pɔːn —*There is also an*
occasional weak form əp ən
upper 'ʌp ə || -ºr **~s** z
ˌupper 'case ‡ ˌUpper 'Chamber; ˌupper
'class ‡ ˌupper 'crust ‡ ˌupper 'hand;
ˌUpper 'House
upper-class ˌʌp ə 'klɑːs ◄§-'klæs || -ºr 'klæs ◄
an ˌupper-class 'accent
uppercut 'ʌp ə kʌt || -ºr- **~s** s
uppermost 'ʌp ə məʊst || -ºr moʊst
Uppingham 'ʌp ɪŋ əm
uppish 'ʌp ɪʃ **~ly** li **~ness** nəs nɪs
uppity 'ʌp ət i-ɪt- || -ət̬ i
Uppsala ʊp 'sɑːl əʌp-, '••• —*Swedish*
['ʊp sɑː la]
up|rate v ⁽ˌ⁾ʌp |'reɪt **~rated** 'reɪt ɪd-əd
|| 'reɪt̬ əd **~rates** 'reɪts **~rating**
'reɪt ɪŋ || 'reɪt̬ ɪŋ
Uprichard ʌp 'rɪtʃ əd ju 'prɪtʃ-, -aːd || -ºrd
upright 'ʌp raɪt,•'• **~ly** li **~ness** nəs nɪs **~s** s
uprising 'ʌp ˌraɪz ɪŋ,•'•• **~s** z
upriver ˌʌp 'rɪv ə ◄ || -ºr
uproar 'ʌp rɔː || -rɔːr-roʊr **~s** z
uproarious ʌp 'rɔːr i‿əs || -'roʊr- **~ly** li **~ness**
nəs nɪs
up|root ⁽ˌ⁾ʌp |'ruːt'•• || -'rʊt **~rooted** 'ruːt ɪd
-əd || 'ruːt̬ əd'rʊt- **~rooting** 'ruːt ɪŋ || 'ruːt̬ ɪŋ
'rʊt- **~roots** 'ruːts || 'rʊts

U

uprush 'ʌp rʌʃ ~es ɪz əz
UPS ˌjuː piː 'es
upsadaisy ˌʌps ə 'deɪz i
upscale ˌʌp 'skeɪəl ◄
up|set v ʌp |'set ~sets 'sets ~setting
'set ɪŋ ‖ 'seṭ ɪŋ
upset adj ˌʌp 'set ◄
ˌupset 'stomach
upset n 'ʌp set •' • ~s s
Upshire 'ʌp ˌʃaɪ̯ə 'ʌp ʃə ‖ -ˌʃaɪ̯ʳr 'ʌp ʃʳr
upshot 'ʌp ʃɒt ‖ -ʃɑːt
upside down, upside-down ˌʌp saɪd 'daʊn
-saɪ-
upsilon juːp 'saɪl ən uːp-, ʊp-, -ɒn; 'juːps ɪl ən,
'ʌps-, -ɒn ‖ 'juːps ə lɑːn 'ʌps-, -əl ən (*) ~s z
upstag|e ˌʌp 'steɪdʒ ~ed d ~es ɪz əz ~ing ɪŋ
upstairs ˌʌp 'steəz ◄ ‖ -'steʳrz ◄ -'stæʳrz
upstanding ˌʌp 'stænd ɪŋ ◄ ʌp- ~ness nəs nɪs
upstart 'ʌp stɑːt ‖ -stɑːrt ~s s
upstate ˌʌp 'steɪt ◄
upstream ˌʌp 'striːm ◄
upstretched ˌʌp 'stretʃt ◄
upstroke 'ʌp strəʊk ‖ -stroʊk ~s s
upsurg|e n 'ʌp sɜːdʒ ‖ -sɝːdʒ ~es ɪz əz
upswept ˌʌp 'swept ◄ '••
upswing n 'ʌp swɪŋ ~s z
upsy-daisy ˌʌps i 'deɪz i
uptake n 'ʌp teɪk ~s s
up-tempo ˌʌp 'temp əʊ ◄ ‖ -oʊ ◄
upthrust n 'ʌp θrʌst ~s s
uptick 'ʌp tɪk ~s s
uptight 'ʌp taɪt, •'• ~ness nəs nɪs
up-to-date ˌʌp tə 'deɪt ◄ ~ness nəs nɪs
Upton 'ʌpt ən
up-to-the-minute ˌʌp tə ðə 'mɪn ɪt ◄ §-ət
uptown ˌʌp 'taʊn ◄
an ˌuptown 'bus
upturn n 'ʌp tɜːn ‖ -tɝːn ~s z
upturned ˌʌp 'tɜːnd ◄ ‖ -'tɝːnd ◄
ˌupturned 'cars
upward, U~ 'ʌp wəd ‖ -wʳrd ~ly li
upwardly-mobile
ˌʌp wəd li 'məʊb aɪ̯əl ◄ ‖ -wʳrd li 'moʊb əl ◄
-iːəl, -aɪ̯əl
upwards 'ʌp wədz ‖ -wʳrdz
upwind ˌʌp 'wɪnd ◄
Ur ancient city 3ː ʊə ‖ 3ːʳ ʊʳr
ur- 'primeval' |ʊə |3ː ‖ |ʊr —Ger [ʔuːɐ] —
Ursprache 'ʊə ˌʃprɑːx ə '3ː- ‖ 'ʊr ˌʃprɑːk ə
'3ːʳ- —Ger ['ʔuːɐ ˌʃpʁɑː xə]
uracil 'jʊər ə sɪl
uraemia jʊə 'riːm iˍə
Ural 'jʊər əl 'jɔːr- ‖ 'jʊr əl —Russ [u 'ralʲ] ~s z
Ural-Altaic ˌjʊər əl æl 'teɪ ɪk ◄ ˌjɔːr- ‖ ˌjʊr-
Uralian jʊə 'reɪl iˍən
Uralic jʊə 'ræl ɪk
Urani|a jʊə 'reɪn iˍə ~an/s ən/z
uranic jʊə 'ræn ɪk
uranium jʊə 'reɪn iˍəm
uˌranium 023'5
uranographic ˌjʊər ən əʊ 'græf ɪk ◄ ˌjɔːr-
‖ jʊr ən ə-

uranography ˌjʊər ə 'nɒg rəf i ˌjɔːr-
‖ ˌjʊr ə 'nɑːg-
uranous 'jʊər ən əs 'jɔːr- ‖ 'jʊr-
Uranus 'jʊər ən əs 'jɔːr-; jʊə 'reɪn- ‖ 'jʊr-
urban, Urban '3ːb ən ‖ '3ːb ən
Urbana 3ː 'bæn ə -'bɑːn- ‖ 3ː-
urbane 3ː 'beɪn ‖ 3ː- ~ly li ~ness nəs nɪs
urbanis... —see urbaniz...
urbanite '3ːb ə naɪt ‖ '3ːb- ~s s
urbanit|y 3ː 'bæn ət i -ɪt- ‖ 3ː 'bæn əṭ i ~ies
ɪz
urbanization ˌ3ːb ən aɪ 'zeɪʃ ən -ɪ'•-
‖ ˌ3ːb ən ə-
urbaniz|e '3ːb ə naɪz ‖ '3ːb- ~ed d ~es ɪz əz
~ing ɪŋ
urbi et orbi ˌ3ːb i et 'ɔːb i ˌʊəb-
‖ ˌ3ːb i et 'ɔːrb i
urchin '3ːtʃ ɪn §-ən ‖ '3ːtʃ ən ~s z
Urdd Gobaith Cymru ˌɪəð ˌgɒb aɪθ 'kʌm ri
-ˌgəʊb- ‖ ˌɪrð ˌgoʊb- —Welsh
[ˌɪrð ˌgo baɪθ 'kəm ri, ˌɪrð-, -ri]
Urdu 'ʊəd uː '3ːd- ‖ 'ʊrd uː —Hindi-Urdu
[ʊr ḍuː]
Ure jʊə ‖ jʊʳr
-ure jə jʊə ‖ jʳr jʊr —The j normally coalesces
with a preceding t, d, s, z, to give tʃ, dʒ, ʃ, ʒ
respectively — closure 'kləʊʒ ə ‖ 'kloʊʒ ʳr
urea jʊə 'riːˍə 'jʊər iˍə, 'jɔːr-
ureide 'jʊər i aɪd 'jɔːr- ‖ 'jʊr- ~s z
uremia jʊə 'riːm iˍə
Uren jʊə 'ren
ureter jʊə 'riːt ə 'jʊər ɪt ə, -ət- ‖ 'jʊr əṭ ʳr
ju 'riːṭ ʳr ~s z
urethane 'jʊər ə θeɪn 'jɔːr-, -ɪ-, ⚠-θiːn ‖ 'jʊr-
ureth|ra jʊə 'riːθ |rə ~rae riː ~ras rəz
urethritis ˌjʊər ə 'θraɪt ɪs ˌjɔːr-, -ɪ-, §-əs
‖ ˌjʊr ə 'θraɪṭ əs
Urey 'jʊər i ‖ 'jʊr i
urge 3ːdʒ ‖ 3ːdʒ urged 3ːdʒd ‖ 3ːdʒd urges
'3ːdʒ ɪz -əz ‖ '3ːdʒ əz urging/s '3ːdʒ ɪŋ/z
‖ '3ːdʒ ɪŋ/z
urgency '3ːdʒ ənᵗs i ‖ '3ːdʒ-
urgent '3ːdʒ ənt ‖ '3ːdʒ- ~ly li
-urgy 3ːdʒ i ‖ 3ːdʒ i — thaumaturgy
'θɔːm ə t3ːdʒ i ‖ -t3ːdʒ i 'θɑːm- —but see
also metallurgy
-uria 'jʊər iˍə 'jɔːr- ‖ 'jʊr iˍə — polyuria
ˌpɒl i 'jʊər iˍə -'jɔːr- ‖ ˌpɑːl i 'jʊr iˍə
Uriah jʊə 'raɪˍə
uric 'jʊər ɪk 'jɔːr- ‖ 'jʊr ɪk
uridine 'jʊər ɪ diːn -ə-, -daɪn ‖ 'jʊr-
uridylic ˌjʊər ɪ 'dɪl ɪk ◄ ˌjɔːr-, -ə- ‖ ˌjʊr-
Uriel 'jʊər iˍəl 'jɔːr- ‖ 'jʊr-
urim, Urim 'jʊər ɪm 'jɔːr-, §-əm ‖ 'jʊr əm
urinal jʊə 'raɪn əl 'jʊər ɪn əl, 'jɔːr-, -ən-
‖ 'jʊr ən əl ~s z
urinalysis ˌjʊər ɪ 'næl əs ɪs ˌjɔːr-, •'ə-, -ɪs•,
§-əs ‖ ˌjʊr-
urinary 'jʊər ɪn ərˍi 'jɔːr-, '•ən- ‖ 'jʊr ə ner i
uri|nate 'jʊər ɪ neɪt 'jɔːr-, -ə- ‖ 'jʊr ə-
~nated neɪt ɪd -əd ‖ neɪṭ əd ~nates neɪts
~nating neɪt ɪŋ ‖ neɪṭ ɪŋ

urination ˌjʊər ɪ 'neɪʃ ᵊn ˌjɔːr-, -ə- ‖ ˌjʊr ə- **~s** z

urine 'jʊər ɪn 'jɔːr-, §-ən, §-aɪn ‖ 'jʊr ən

URL ˌjuː ɑːr 'el ‖ -ɑːr-

Urmston 'ɜːmᵖst ən ‖ 'ɝːmᵖst-

urn ɜːn ‖ ɝːn (= *earn*) **urns** ɜːnz ‖ ɝːnz

uro- *comb. form*
  with stress-neutral suffix ˌjʊər əʊ ˌjɔːr-
  ‖ ˌjʊr əʊ — **urogenital** ˌjʊər əʊ 'dʒen ɪt ᵊl ◄
  ˌjɔːr-, -ət ᵊl ‖ ˌjʊr əʊ 'dʒen əṭ ᵊl ◄
  with stress-imposing suffix jʊə 'rɒ+ ‖ -'rɑː+ —
  uroscopy jʊə 'rɒsk əp i ‖ -'rɑːsk-

urologist jʊə 'rɒl ədʒ ɪst §-əst ‖ jə 'rɑːl- **~s** s

urology jʊə 'rɒl ədʒ i ‖ -'rɑːl-

Urquhart 'ɜːk ət ‖ 'ɝːk ᵊrt

Ursa 'ɜːs ə ‖ 'ɝːs ə
  ˌUrsa 'Major

ursine 'ɜːs aɪn ‖ 'ɝːs-

Ursula 'ɜːs jʊl ə -jəl- ‖ 'ɝːs əl ə

Ursuline 'ɜːs ju laɪn 'ɜːʃ-, -jə-, -lɪn ‖ 'ɝːs əl ən
  -ə laɪn, -ə liːn **~s** z

urticaria ˌɜːt ɪ 'keər i‿ə §ˌ•ə- ‖ ˌɝːt̬ ə 'ker i‿ə
  -'kær-

Uruguay 'jʊər ə gwaɪ 'ʊər-, 'ʊr-, 'jɔːr-, -ʊ-,
  ˌ•'• ‖ 'jʊr- 'ʊr-, -gweɪ —*Sp* [u ɾu 'ɣwaɪ]

Uruguayan ˌjʊər ə 'gwaɪ ən ◄ ˌʊər-, ˌʊr-, ˌjɔːr-,
  -ʊ- ‖ ˌjʊr- ˌʊr-, -'gweɪ- **~s** z

Urumqi, Ürümqi ʊ 'rʊm tʃiː —*Chi* Wūlǔmùqí
  [¹wu ³lu ⁴mu ²tɕʰi]

urus 'jʊər əs 'jɔːr- ‖ 'jʊr əs **~es** ɪz əz

Urwin 'ɜː wɪn ‖ 'ɝː-

us *strong form* ʌs §ʌz, *weak form* əs §əz —*see*
  also **'s**

US ˌjuː 'es ◄
  ˌUS 'Navy

USA ˌjuː es 'eɪ

usab|le 'juːz əb |ᵊl **~leness** ᵊl nəs -nɪs **~ly** li

USAF ˌjuː es eɪ 'ef

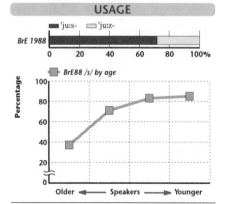

USAGE

■ 'juːs-   ☐ 'juːz-

BrE 1988 | 0   20   40   60   80   100%

■ *BrE88 /s/ by age*

Percentage — 100 / 80 / 60 / 40 / 20 / 0

Older ◄——— Speakers ———► Younger

usag|e 'juːs ɪdʒ 'juːz- —*BrE 1988 poll panel*
  preference: 'juːs- 72%, 'juːz- 28%. **~es** ɪz əz

usanc|e 'juːz ᵊnts **~es** ɪz əz

Usborne 'ʌz bɔːn ‖ -bɔːrn -bʊərn

USDAW 'ʌs dɔː 'ʌz- ‖ -dɑː

use *n* juːs **uses** 'juːs ɪz -əz

use *v* juːz (= *yews*) **used** juːzd **uses** 'juːz ɪz
  -əz **using** 'juːz ɪŋ —*See also* **used to**

used *'made use of* juːzd

used *adj 'accustomed'* juːst

used *'was/were accustomed'* (*expressing a former
fact or state*): **used to** *final or before a vowel*
  'juːst tu, *before a cons* 'juːst tə

usedn't 'juːs ᵊnt 'juːst-

useful 'juːs fᵊl -fʊl **~ly** ‿i **~ness** nəs nɪs

useless 'juːs ləs -lɪs **~ly** li **~ness** nəs nɪs

usen't 'juːs ᵊnt

user 'juːz ə ‖ -ᵊr **~s** z

user-defined ˌjuːz ə dɪ 'faɪnd ◄ -də'•, §-diː'•
  ‖ ˌ•ᵊr-

user-friend|ly ˌjuːz ə 'frend |li ◄ ‖ -ᵊr- **~liness**
  li nəs -nɪs

userid 'juːz ər aɪ ˌdiː **~s** z

username 'juːz ə neɪm ‖ -ᵊr- **~s** z

Ushant 'ʌʃ ᵊnt

usher, Usher 'ʌʃ ə ‖ -ᵊr **~ed** d **ushering**
  'ʌʃ ᵊr ɪŋ **~s** z

usherette ˌʌʃ ə 'ret **~s** s

Usk ʌsk

USN ˌjuː es 'en

usquebaugh 'ʌsk wɪ bɔː -wə- ‖ -bɑː

Ussher 'ʌʃ ə ‖ -ᵊr

USSR ˌjuː es es 'ɑː ‖ -'ɑːr

Ustinov 'juːst ɪ nɒf 'uːst-, -ə-, -nɒv ‖ -nɔːf
  -nɑːf —*Russ* [u 'sitji nəf]

usual 'juːʒ u‿əl -ju‿; 'juːʒ ᵊl **~ness** nəs nɪs

usually 'juːʒ u‿əl i '•ju‿; 'juːʒ ᵊl‿i

usufruct 'juːs ju frʌkt 'juːz- ‖ -ə-

usurer 'juːʒ ər‿ə ‖ -ᵊr ər **~s** z

usurious ju 'zjʊər i‿əs -'ʒʊər-, -'zjɔːr- ‖ -'ʒʊr-
  -'zʊr- **~ly** li **~ness** nəs nɪs

usurp ju 'zɜːp -'sɜːp ‖ ju 'sɝːp -'zɝːp **~ed** t
  ~ing ɪŋ **~s** s

usurpation ˌjuːz ɜː 'peɪʃ ᵊn ˌjuːs- ‖ ˌjuːs ᵊr-
  ˌjuːz- **~s** z

usur|y 'juːʒ ər‿|i -ʊər-, -jʊər-, -ʊr- **~ies** iz

ut ʊt ʌt, uːt

Utah 'juːt ɑː -ɔː ‖ -ɑː

Utahan, Utahn 'juːt ɑːn -ɔːn ‖ -ɔːn -ɑːn **~s** z

Ute juːt **Utes** juːts 'juːt iz

utensil ju 'tenᵗs ᵊl -ɪl **~s** z

uterine 'juːt ə raɪn -rɪn, -rən ‖ 'juːt̬-

ut|erus 'juːt|‿ər əs ‖ 'juːt̬ |- **~eri** ə raɪ

Uther 'juːθ ə ‖ -ᵊr
  ˌUther Pen'dragon

Utica 'juːt ɪk ə ‖ 'juːt̬-

utilis... —*see* **utiliz...**

utilitarian ju ˌtɪl ɪ 'teər i‿ən ◄ ˌjuːt ɪl-, -ə'•-
  ‖ -'ter- **~s** z

utilit|y ju 'tɪl ət i -ɪt- ‖ -əṭ li **~ies** iz
  u'tility room

utilizable 'juːt ɪ laɪz əb ᵊl '•ə-, '•ᵊl aɪz-, ˌ•'•-
  ‖ 'juːt̬ ᵊl aɪz-

utilization ˌjuːt ɪl aɪ 'zeɪʃ ᵊn ˌ•əl-, -ɪ'•-
  ‖ ˌjuːt̬ ᵊl ə- **~s** z

utiliz|e 'juːt ɪ laɪz -ə-, -ᵊl aɪz ‖ 'juːt̬ ᵊl aɪz **~ed**
  d **~es** ɪz əz **~ing** ɪŋ

utmost 'ʌt məʊst -məst ‖ -moʊst

Uto-Aztecan ˌjuːt əʊ 'æz tek ən ◄ -•'••
  ‖ ˌjuːt̬ oʊ- **~s** z

U

utopi|a, U~ ju 'təʊp i‿ə ‖ -'toup- **~an/s** ən/z
~anism ən ˌɪz *ə*m **~as** əz
Utrecht 'juːtr ekt -ext; ˌjuː 'trekt, -'trext
—*Dutch* ['yː trɛxt]
utricle 'juːtr ɪk *ə*l **~s** z
Utrillo ju 'trɪl əʊ ‖ -oʊ—*Fr* [y tʁi jo] **~s** z
Utsira uːt 'sɪər ə ‖ -'sɪr ə—*Norw* ["uːt siː ra]
Uttar Pradesh ˌʊt ə prə 'deʃ-'deɪʃ ‖ ˌʊʈ ər-
—*Hindi* [ʊʈ ʈər prə ɖeːʃ]
utter 'ʌt ə ‖ 'ʌʈ ər uttered 'ʌt əd ‖ 'ʌʈ ərd
uttering 'ʌt‿ər ɪŋ ‖ 'ʌʈ ər ɪŋ utters
'ʌt əz ‖ 'ʌʈ ərz
utteranc|e 'ʌt‿ər ənts ‖ 'ʌʈ ər ənts **~es** ɪz əz
utterly 'ʌt ə li-əl i ‖ 'ʌʈ ər li
uttermost 'ʌt ə məʊst ‖ 'ʌʈ ər moʊst
Uttoxeter ju 'tɒks ɪt ə ʌ-, -ət-; 'ʌks ɪt ə, -ət-
‖ ju 'tɑːks əʈ ər
U-turn 'juː tɜːn ˌ•'• ‖ -tɝːn **~s** z
uuencod|e ˌjuː juː juː ɪn 'kəʊd ◂-en'•, -ən'•
‖ -'koʊd ◂ **~ed** ɪd əd **~es** z **~ing** ɪŋ
uvea 'juːv i‿ə
UVF ˌjuː viː 'ef

uv|ula 'juːv ˌjʊl ə-jəl- ‖ -jəl ə **~ulae** ju liː jə-
‖ jə liː **~ulas** jʊl əz jəl- ‖ jəl əz
uvular 'juːv jʊl ə-jəl- ‖ -jəl ər **~s** z
uvularis... —*see* uvulariz...
uvularity ˌjuːv ju 'lær ət i, • jə-, -ɪt i
‖ -jə 'lær əʈ i-'ler-
uvularization ˌjuːv jʊl ər aɪ 'zeɪʃ ən, • jəl-,
-ɪ'•- ‖ ˌ• jəl ər ə-
uvulariz|e 'juːv jʊl ə raɪz'• jəl- ‖ '• jəl- **~ed** d
~es ɪz əz **~ing** ɪŋ
UWIST 'juː wɪst
Uxbridge 'ʌks brɪdʒ
uxorial ʌk 'sɔːr i‿əl ‖ -'soʊr-; ʌg 'zɔːr-, -'zoʊr-
uxoricide ʌk 'sɔːr ɪ saɪd §-ə- ‖ -'soʊr-;
ʌg 'zɔːr-, -'zoʊr- **~s** z
uxorious ʌk 'sɔːr i‿əs ‖ -'soʊr-; ʌg 'zɔːr-,
-'zoʊr- **~ly** li **~ness** nəs nɪs
Uzbek 'ʊz bek 'ʌz- **~s** s
Uzbekistan ˌʊz bek ɪ 'stɑːn ˌʌz-, -ə'•, -'stæn
‖ ʊz 'bek ə stæn-ɪ stæn
Uzi *tdmk* 'uːz i

U

V v

Spelling-to-sound

1 Where the spelling is **v**, the pronunciation is regularly v, as in **very** 'ver i.

2 v is also occasionally written **vv**, as in **skivvy** 'skɪv i; **ph**, as in **Stephen** 'stiːv ən; and **f** in the single word **of** ɒv, əv ‖ ʌv, ɑːv, əv.

V, v viː **V's, v's, Vs** viːz —*Communications code name:* Victor
  ˌV and ˈA; ˌVˈO ˌlanguage; ˌVˈU ˌmeter
v *'versus'* 'vɜːs əs viː ‖ 'vɝːs-
V-1 ˌviː 'wʌn §-'wɒn ~**s** z
V-2 ˌviː 'tuː ~**s** z
Vaal vɑːl
vac væk **vacs** væks
vacanc|y 'veɪk ənts li →-ŋts- ~**ies** iz
vacant 'veɪk ənt →-ŋt **~ly** li ~**ness** nəs nɪs
vacate və 'keɪt veɪ- ‖ 'veɪk eɪt *(*)* **vacated**
  və 'keɪt ɪd veɪ-, -əd ‖ 'veɪk eɪt̬ əd **vacates**
  və 'keɪts veɪ- ‖ 'veɪk eɪts **vacating**
  və 'keɪt ɪŋ veɪ- ‖ 'veɪk eɪt̬ ɪŋ

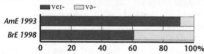

VACATION

	veɪ-	və-
AmE 1993		
BrE 1998		

0   20   40   60   80   100%

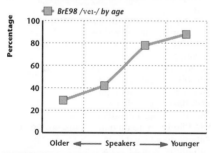

🔲 BrE98 /veɪ-/ by age

Older ◀— Speakers —▶ Younger

vacation veɪ 'keɪʃ ən və- —*Poll panel preferences: AmE 1993,* veɪ- *91%,* və- *9%; BrE 1998,* veɪ- *61%,* və- *39%.* **~er/s** ə/z ‖ ˌ-ər/z **~ist/s** ɪst/s §ˌ-əst/s ‖ ˌ-əst/s ~**s** z
vacci|nate 'væks ɪ |neɪt -ə- ~**nated** neɪt ɪd -əd ‖ neɪt̬ əd ~**nates** neɪts ~**nating** neɪt ɪŋ ‖ neɪt̬ ɪŋ
vaccination ˌvæks ɪ 'neɪʃ ən -ə- ~**s** z
vaccinator 'væks ɪ neɪt ə -ə- ‖ -neɪt̬ ər ~**s** z
vaccine 'væks iːn -ɪn ‖ væk 'siːn *(*)* ~**s** z
vaccinia væk 'sɪn i_ə
Vachel, Vachell *(i)* 'veɪtʃ əl, *(ii)* 'vætʃ əl
Vacher 'væʃ ə ‖ -ər
vacherin 'væʃ ə ræ̃ -ɪn ~**s** z —*Fr* [vaʃ ʀæ̃]

vacil|late 'væs ɪ |leɪt -ə- ~**lated** leɪt ɪd -əd ‖ leɪt̬ əd ~**lates** leɪts ~**lating** leɪt ɪŋ ‖ leɪt̬ ɪŋ
vacillation ˌvæs ɪ 'leɪʃ ən -ə- ~**s** z
Vaclav, Václav 'vɑːt slɑːv 'væt-, -slæv, -slɑːf, -slæf —*also, by those unfamiliar with the name,* 'vɑːk lɑːv, 'væk-, -læv —*Czech* ['vaːts laf]
vacua 'væk ju_ə
vacuit|y væ 'kjuːˌət li və-, ˌɪt i ‖ -ət̬ li ~**ies** iz
vacuole 'væk ju əʊl →-ɒʊl ‖ -oʊl ~**s** z
vacuous 'væk ju_əs **~ly** li ~**ness** nəs nɪs
vacuum 'væk ju_əm 'væk jʊm, -juːm ~**s** z
  'vacuum ˌcleaner; 'vacuum flask; 'vacuum pump
vacuum-packed ˌvæk ju_əm 'pækt ◀ ˌ•jʊm'•, ˌ•juːm'•, '•••
  ˌvacuum-packed 'cheese
vade mecum ˌvɑːd i 'meɪ kəm ˌwɑːd-, ˌ•eɪ-, -kʊm; ˌveɪd i 'miː-, -kʌm ~**s** z
Vaduz vɑː 'duːts —*Ger* [fa 'dʊts, va 'duːts]
vagabond 'væg ə bɒnd ‖ -bɑːnd ~**s** z
vagabondage 'væg ə bɒnd ɪdʒ ‖ -bɑːnd ɪdʒ
vagal 'veɪg əl
vagar|y 'veɪg ər li ‖ və 'ger li, -'gær- —*in BrE formerly also* və 'geər li ~**ies** iz
vagin|a və 'dʒaɪn |ə ~**ae** iː ~**as** əz
vaginal və 'dʒaɪn əl 'vædʒ ɪn əl, -ən- ‖ 'vædʒ ən əl ~**ly** li
vaginismus ˌvædʒ ɪ 'nɪz məs -ə-, -'nɪs-
vagotom|y veɪ 'gɒt əm li və-, væ- ‖ -'gɑːt̬- ~**ies** iz
vagrancy 'veɪg rənts i
vagrant 'veɪg rənt ~**s** s
vague veɪg **vaguely** 'veɪg li **vagueness** 'veɪg nəs -nɪs **vaguer** 'veɪg ə ‖ -ər **vaguest** 'veɪg ɪst -əst
vagus 'veɪg əs **vagi** 'veɪdʒ aɪ 'veɪg-
Vail, vail veɪəl (= *veil*) **vailed** veɪəld **vailing** 'veɪəl ɪŋ **vails** veɪəlz
vain veɪn **vainer** 'veɪn ə ‖ -ər **vainest** 'veɪn ɪst -əst
vainglorious ˌ(ˌ)veɪn 'glɔːr i_əs ‖ -'gloʊr- **~ly** li ~**ness** nəs nɪs
vainglor|y ˌ(ˌ)veɪn 'glɔːr li ‖ -'gloʊr-; '•ˌ•• ~**ies** iz
vain|ly 'veɪn |li ~**ness** nəs nɪs
Vaizey 'veɪz i
Val væl

valanc|e 'væl ənts **~ed** t **~es** ɪz əz
Valda 'væld ə
Valdemar 'væld ə maː -ɪ- ‖ 'vɑːld ə maːr 'væld-
Valderrama ˌvæl də 'rɑːm ə ‖ ˌvɑːl- —Sp [bal de 'rra ma]
Valderma tdmk væl 'dɜːm ə ‖ -'dɝːm-
Valdez place in AK væl 'diːz
vale n 'valley' veɪəl **vales** veɪəlz
vale Latin interj, n 'farewell' 'vɑːl eɪ 'væl-, 'veɪl-, -i
valediction ˌvæl ɪ 'dɪk ʃən -ə- **~s** z
valedictorian ˌvæl ɪ dɪk 'tɔːr i_ən ˌ•ə- ‖ -'toʊr- **~s** z
valedictor|y ˌvæl ɪ 'dɪk tər_|i ◂ ˌ•ə- **~ies** iz
valenc|e 'veɪl ənts **~es** ɪz əz
Valencia və 'lentʃ i_ə -'lents-, -'lentʃ ə —Sp [ba 'len θja]
Valenciennes ˌvæl ənts i 'en ˌ•ɒs-; və ˌlents- ‖ -'enz —Fr [va lɑ̃ sjɛn]
valenc|y 'veɪl ənts |i **~ies** iz
Valency river; family name və 'lents i
valentine, V~ 'væl ən taɪn -tɪn **~s** z
Valentinian ˌvæl ən 'tɪn i_ən
Valentino ˌvæl ən 'tiːn əʊ ‖ -oʊ
Valera və 'lɪər ə -'leər- ‖ 'ler- -'lɪr-
valerian, V~ və 'lɪər ɪ_ən -'leər- ‖ -'lɪr- **~s** z
valeric və 'lɪər ɪk -'leər-, -'ler- ‖ -'lɪr- -'ler-
Valerie 'væl ər_i
Valéry ˌvæl ə 'riː -eə-, '••• ‖ ˌvɑːl-, -e- —Fr [va le ʁi]
valet 'væl ɪt -ət, -eɪ ‖ væ 'leɪ The traditional form with t is rivalled by an imitated French form in -eɪ. **valeted** 'væl ɪt ɪd -ət-, -əd; 'væl eɪd ‖ 'væl ət̮ əd væ 'leɪd **valeting** 'væl ɪt ɪŋ -ət-, -eɪ- ‖ 'væl ət̮ ɪŋ væ 'leɪ ɪŋ **valets** 'væl ɪts -əts, -eɪz ‖ væ 'leɪz
valetudinarian ˌvæl ɪ ˌtjuːd ɪ 'neər i_ən ˌ•ə-, →§-ˌtʃuːd-, -ə'••-, -ən 'eər- ‖ -ˌtuːd ən 'er- -ˌtjuːd- **~s** z
valetudinary ˌvæl ɪ 'tjuːd ɪn ər_i ◂ ˌ•ə-, →§-'tʃuːd-, -'•ən- ‖ -'tuːd ən er i -'tjuːd-
valgus 'vælg əs **~es** ɪz əz
Valhalla væl 'hæl ə ‖ vɑːl 'hɑːl ə
valiant 'væl i_ənt ‖ 'væl jənt **~ly** li **~ness** nəs nɪs
valid 'væl ɪd §-əd **~ly** li **~ness** nəs nɪs
vali|date 'væl ɪ |deɪt -ə- **~dated** deɪt ɪd -əd ‖ deɪt̮ əd **~dates** deɪts **~dating** deɪt ɪŋ ‖ deɪt̮ ɪŋ
validation ˌvæl ɪ 'deɪʃ ən -ə- **~s** z
validit|y və 'lɪd ət li væ-, -ɪt i ‖ -ət̮ li **~ies** iz
valis|e və 'liːz væ-, -'liːs ‖ -'liːs **~es** ɪz əz
valium, V~ tdmk 'væl i_əm **~s** z
Valkyrie 'vælk ər i -ɪr-, -ɪər-; væl 'kɪr i, -'kɪər-, -'kaɪər- ‖ væl 'kɪr i 'vælk ər i **~s** z
Valladolid ˌvæl ə dəʊ 'lɪd ‖ -doʊ '• —Sp [ba ʎa ðo 'lið, •ja-]
Vallance, Vallans 'væl ənts
Valle Crucis ˌvæl i 'kruːs ɪs
Vallee 'væl i
Vallejo place in CA və 'leɪ əʊ væ-, -həʊ ‖ -oʊ -hoʊ

Valletta və 'let ə
valley, V~ 'væl i **~s** z
Vallins 'væl ɪnz §-ənz
vallum 'væl əm
Valois 'væl wɑː ‖ væl 'wɑː —Fr [va lwa] —but the place in NY is və 'lɔɪs
valor, Valor tdmk 'væl ə ‖ -ər
valoris... —see valoriz...
valorization ˌvæl ər aɪ 'zeɪʃ ən -ɪ' • ‖ -ə' •-
valoriz|e 'væl ə raɪz **~ed** d **~es** ɪz əz **~ing** ɪŋ
valorous 'væl ər əs **~ly** li **~ness** nəs nɪs
valour 'væl ə ‖ -ər
Valparaiso place in Chile ˌvæl pə 'raɪz əʊ -'reɪz- ‖ -oʊ —Sp Valparaíso [bal pa ɾa 'i so]
Valparaiso place in IN ˌvæl pə 'reɪz əʊ ‖ -oʊ
Valpeda tdmk væl 'piːd ə
Valpolicella, v~ ˌvæl pɒl ɪ 'tʃel ə ‖ ˌvɑːl poʊl- —It [val po li 'tʃɛl la]
valse vɑːls væls, vɔːls **valses** 'vɑːls ɪz 'væls-, 'vɔːls-, -əz
valuable 'væl jʊb əl -juˌəb əl ‖ -jəb- **~ness** nəs nɪs **~s** z
valuation ˌvæl ju 'eɪʃ ən **~s** z
value 'væl juː -ju **~d** d **~s** z **valuing** 'væl juːˌɪŋ
 'value ˌjudgment
value-added ˌvæl juː 'æd ɪd ◂ -əd
 ˌvalue-'added ˌtax, ˌ•ˌ•• '•
valueless 'væl ju ləs -lɪs
valuer 'væl juˌə ‖ -ər **~s** z
Valujet tdmk 'væl ju dʒet
valvate 'vælv eɪt
valve vælv **valved** vælvd **valves** vælvz
Valvoline tdmk 'vælv ə liːn
valvular 'vælv jʊl ə -jəl- ‖ -jəl ər
vamoos|e və 'muːs væ- **~ed** t **~es** ɪz əz **~ing** ɪŋ
vamp væmp **vamped** væmpt **vamping** 'væmp ɪŋ **vamps** væmps
vampire 'væmp aɪ_ə ‖ -aɪ_ər **~s** z
 'vampire ˌbat
vampirism 'væmp aɪ_ər ˌɪz əm ‖ -aɪ_ər-
vampish 'væmp ɪʃ **~ness** nəs nɪs
van, Van væn **vans** vænz
vanadate 'væn ə deɪt **~s** s
vanadic və 'næd ɪk -'neɪd-
vanadinite və 'næd ɪ naɪt -'neɪd-, -ə-, -ən aɪt
vanadium və 'neɪd i_əm
vanadous 'væn əd əs və 'neɪd-
Van Allen væn 'æl ən
Vananchal və 'nɑːntʃ əl
Vanbrugh 'væn brə →'væm- ‖ væn 'bruː
Van Buren væn 'bjʊər ən ‖ -'bjʊr- -'bjɝː-
Vance vænts vɑːnts
Vancouver væn 'kuːv ə →væŋ- ‖ -ər
vandal, V~ 'vænd əl **~s** z
Vandalia væn 'deɪl i_ə ‖ -'deɪl jə
vandalis... —see vandaliz...
vandalism 'vænd ə ˌlɪz əm -əl ˌɪz-
vandaliz|e 'vænd ə laɪz -əl aɪz **~ed** d **~es** ɪz əz **~ing** ɪŋ
Van de Graaff ˌvæn də 'grɑːf ◂ -'græf ‖ -'græf
 ˌVan de ˌGraaff 'generator

Vandenberg, Van den Bergh 'vænd ən bɜːg
→-əm- ‖ -bɝːg

Vanden Plas ˌvænd ən 'plæs →-əm-, -'plɑːs

Vanderbilt 'vænd ə bɪlt ‖ -ər-

Vanderbyl 'vænd ə baɪəl ‖ -ər-

van der Post ˌvænd də 'pɒst ‖ -dər 'pɑːst

Van der Waals ˌvæn də 'wɑːlz ◂ ‖ -'wɔːlz
—*Dutch* [vɑn dər 'waːls]
ˌVan der ˌWaals 'forces

Van Diemen ₍ᵢ₎væn 'diːm ən

Van Dyck, Vandyke, v~ ₍ᵢ₎væn 'daɪk

vane, Vane veɪn *(= vain)* **vanes** veɪnz

Vanessa və 'nes ə

Van Eyck væn 'aɪk

vang væŋ **vangs** væŋz

Van Gogh væn 'gɒf →væŋ-, -'gɒx ‖ -'goʊ
—*Dutch* [vɑn 'xɔx]

vanguard 'væn gɑːd →'væŋ- ‖ -gɑːrd ~s z

vanilla və 'nɪl ə ‖ -'nel- ~s z

vanillin və 'nɪl ɪn §-ən; 'væn əl-, -ɪl-

vanish 'væn ɪʃ ~ed t ~es ɪz əz ~ing ɪŋ
'vanishing point

vanitory, V~ *tdmk* 'væn ət ər i ‖•ɪt ‖ -ə tɔːr i
-toʊr i

vanit|y 'væn ət i -ɪt- ‖ -ət̬ i ~ies iz

Van Nuys væn 'naɪz

vanquish 'væŋk wɪʃ ‖ 'væn kwɪʃ ~ed t ~es ɪz
əz ~ing ɪŋ

Vansittart væn 'sɪt ət ‖ -'sɪt̬ ərt

van Straubenzee ˌvæn strɔː 'benz i ‖ -strɑː-

vantage 'vɑːnt ɪdʒ §'vænt- ‖ 'vænt̬ ɪdʒ

vantagepoint 'vɑːnt ɪdʒ pɔɪnt §'vænt-
‖ 'vænt̬- ~s s

Vanuatu ˌvæn u 'ɑːt uː -'æt-; ˌvæn ə 'wɑːt uː;
'• • • • ‖ ˌvɑːn-

Van Wyck væn 'waɪk ‖ -'wɪk
Van ˌWyck Ex'pressway

Vanya 'vɑːn jə 'væn-

Vanzetti væn 'zet i ‖ -'zet̬ i

vapid 'væp ɪd §-əd ~ly li ~ness nəs nɪs

vapidity væ 'pɪd ət i və-, -ɪt- ‖ -ət̬ i

vapor... —*see* **vapour...**

vaporett|o ˌvæp ə 'ret ləʊ ‖ -loʊ—*It*
[va po 'ret to] ~i iː ~os əʊz ‖ oʊz

vaporis... —*see* **vaporiz...**

vaporization ˌveɪp ər aɪ 'zeɪʃ ən -ɪ'• ‖ -ə'•-

vaporiz|e 'veɪp ə raɪz ~ed d ~es ɪz əz ~ing
ɪŋ

vaporous 'veɪp ər əs ~ly li ~ness nəs nɪs

vapour 'veɪp ə ‖ -ər ~ed d **vapouring/s**
'veɪp ər ɪŋ/z ~s z
ˈvapour trail

vapourer 'veɪp ər ə ‖ -ər ər ~s z

vapoury 'veɪp ər i

Varah 'vɑːr ə

Varangian və 'rændʒ i ən ~s z

Varden 'vɑːd ən ‖ 'vɑːrd ən

varec 'vær ek -ɪk

Varèse və 'rez

varia 'veər i ə ‖ 'ver- 'vær-

variability ˌveər i ə 'bɪl ət i -ɪt i
‖ ˌver i ə 'bɪl ət̬ i ˌvær-

variab|le 'veər i əb ləl ‖ 'ver- 'vær- ~les əlz
~ly li

varianc|e 'veər i ənts ‖ 'ver- 'vær- ~es ɪz əz

variant 'veər i ənt ‖ 'ver- 'vær- ~s s

variate 'veər i ət ɪt, -eɪt ‖ 'ver- 'vær- ~s s

variation ˌveər i 'eɪʃ ən ‖ ˌver- ˌvær- ~s z

variational ˌveər i 'eɪʃ ən əl ◂ ‖ ˌver- ˌvær-
~ly i

variationist ˌveər i 'eɪʃ ən ɪst §ˌ_əst ‖ ˌver-
ˌvær- ~s s

varicella ˌvær i 'sel ə ‖ ˌver-

varices 'vær i siːz 'veər-, -ə- ‖ 'ver-

varicocele 'vær ɪ kəʊ siːəl '•ə- ‖ -ə koʊ siːəl
'ver- ~s z

varicolored, varicoloured
'veər i ˌkʌl əd ‖ 'ver i ˌkʌl ərd 'vær-

varicose 'vær ɪ kəʊs -ə-, -kəʊz, -kəs ‖ -ə koʊs
'ver-
ˌvaricose 'veins

varicosit|y ˌvær ɪ 'kɒs ət i ˌ•ə-, -ɪt i
‖ -ə 'kɑːs ət̬ i ˌver- ~ies iz

varicotom|y ˌvær ɪ 'kɒt əm li ˌ•ə- ‖ -ə 'kɑːt̬-
ˌver- ~ies iz

varied 'veər id ‖ 'ver id 'vær- ~ly li

variegated 'veər i ə geɪt ɪd '•ɪ•••, -əd;
'•ɪ geɪt•, '•ə- ‖ 'veər ɪ geɪt̬ əd 'vær-, '•ɪ ə••

variegation ˌveər i ə 'geɪʃ ən ˌ•ɪ ɪ'••; ˌ•ɪ'••,
ˌ•ə'•• ‖ ˌver i 'geɪʃ ən ˌvær-, ˌ•ɪ ə'••

varietal və 'raɪ ət əl ɪt- ‖ -ət̬ əl ~ly i

variet|y və 'raɪ ət i ɪt- ‖ -'raɪ ət̬ i ~ies iz
va'riety show; va'riety store

varifocal 'veər i fəʊk əl ˌ••'•• ‖ 'ver i foʊk əl
'vær-' ˌ••'•• ~s z

variform 'veər ɪ fɔːm -ə- ‖ 'ver i fɔːrm 'vær-

Varig *tdmk* 'vær ɪg ‖ 'ver-

variola və 'raɪ əl ə ‖ ˌver i 'oʊl ə

variolate 'veər i ə leɪt ‖ 'ver- 'vær-

variolite 'veər i ə laɪt ‖ 'ver- 'vær-

variometer ˌveər i 'ɒm ɪt ə -ət ə
‖ ˌver i 'ɑːm ət̬ ər ˌvær- ~s z

variorum ˌveər i 'ɔːr əm ˌvær- ‖ ˌver- ˌvær-,
-'oʊr-

various 'veər i əs ‖ 'ver i əs 'vær- ~ly li
~ness nəs nɪs

variphone 'veər i fəʊn ‖ 'ver i foʊn 'vær- ~s z

Varityper *tdmk* 'veər i taɪp ə ‖ 'ver i taɪp ər
'vær- ~s z

varix 'veər ɪks ‖ 'ver- 'vær- **varices** 'vær ɪ siːz
'veər-, -ə- ‖ 'ver-

varlet 'vɑːl ət -ɪt ‖ 'vɑːrl ət ~s s

Varley 'vɑːl i ‖ 'vɑːrl i

varmint 'vɑːm ɪnt -ənt ‖ 'vɑːrm- ~s s

Varney 'vɑːn i ‖ 'vɑːrn i

varnish 'vɑːn ɪʃ ‖ 'vɑːrn ɪʃ ~ed t ~es ɪz əz
~ing ɪŋ

Varro 'vær əʊ ‖ -oʊ 'ver-

varroa və 'rəʊ ə 'vær əʊ ə ‖ -'roʊ-

varsit|y 'vɑːs ət i -ɪt- ‖ 'vɑːrs ət̬ i ~ies iz

Varteg 'vɑːt eg ‖ 'vɑːrt-

varus 'veər əs ‖ 'ver əs 'vær- ~es ɪz əz

varve vɑːv ‖ vɑːrv **varves** vɑːvz ‖ vɑːrvz

var|y 'veər li ‖ 'ver li 'vær- ~ied id ~ies iz
~ying i ɪŋ

V

vas væs vɑːs **vasa** 'veɪz ə 'vɑːz-, 'veɪs-, 'vɑːs-
ˌvas 'deferens 'def ə renz
Vasco da Gama ˌvæsk əʊ də 'gɑːm ə
‖ ˌvɑːsk oʊ- -'gæm- —*Port*
[ˌvaʃ ku ðɐ 'ɣɐ mɐ]
vascul|um 'væsk jʊl əm -jəl- ‖ -jəl ləm **~a** ə
~ar ə ‖ ᵊr
vase vɑːz ‖ veɪs veɪz *(*)* —*in BrE formerly also*
vɔːz **vases** 'vɑːz ɪz -əz ‖ 'veɪs əz 'veɪz-
vasectom|y və 'sekt əm li væ- **~ies** iz
vaseline, V~ *tdmk* 'væs ə liːn 'væz-, -ɪ-, -ᵊl iːn,
ˌ•·ˈ•
Vashti 'væʃt aɪ
vasoconstriction ˌveɪz əʊ kən 'strɪk ʃᵊn
§-kɒn'•- ‖ ˌ•ˌoʊ-
vasoconstrictor ˌveɪz əʊ kən 'strɪkt ə §-kɒn'•-
‖ -oʊ kən 'strɪkt ᵊr **~s** z
vasodilator ˌveɪz əʊ daɪ 'leɪt ə ‖ -oʊ daɪ 'leɪt̬ ᵊr
-də'•-; -'daɪl eɪt̬ ᵊr **~s** z
vasomotor ˌveɪz əʊ 'məʊt ə ◂ ‖ -ə 'moʊt̬ ᵊr ◂
ˌvæs-, ˌ•ˈoʊ-
vasopressin ˌveɪz əʊ 'pres ɪn §-ᵊn ‖ -oʊ- ˌvæs-
vassal, V~ 'væs ᵊl **~s** z
vassalage 'væs ᵊl ɪdʒ
Vassar 'væs ə ‖ -ᵊr
vast vɑːst §væst ‖ væst **vaster** 'vɑːst ə
§'væst- ‖ 'væst ᵊr **vastest** 'vɑːst ɪst §'væst-,
-əst ‖ 'væst əst
vast|ly 'vɑːst lli §'væst- ‖ 'væst lli **~ness/es**
nəs ɪz nɪs-, -əz
vat væt **vats** væts
VAT ˌviː eɪ 'tiː væt —*But as an informal verb,*
always væt **VAT'd** 'væt ɪd -əd ‖ 'væt̬ əd
VAT'ing 'væt ɪŋ ‖ 'væt̬ ɪŋ **VAT's** væts
VATable 'væt əb ᵊl ‖ 'væt̬-
Vatersay 'væt ə seɪ ‖ 'væt̬ ᵊr-
Vathek 'vɑːθ ek 'væθ-
vatic 'væt ɪk ‖ 'væt̬ ɪk
Vatican 'væt ɪk ən ‖ 'væt̬-
ˌVatican 'City
vatici|nate væ 'tɪs ɪ ˌneɪt -ə-, -ᵊl n eɪt ‖ -ᵊl n eɪt
~nated neɪt ɪd -əd ‖ neɪt̬ əd **~nates** neɪts
~nating neɪt ɪŋ ‖ neɪt̬ ɪŋ
vaticination ˌvæt ɪs ɪ 'neɪʃ ᵊn ˌ• əs-; væ ˌtɪs-,
və- ‖ və ˌtɪs- ˌvæt̬ əs- **~s** z
VAT|man 'væt mæn **~men** men
Vaucluse vəʊ 'kluːz ‖ voʊ- —*Fr* [vo klyːz]
vaudeville 'vɔːd ə vɪl 'vəʊd-; ˈ•ˈvɪl, -vᵊl ‖ 'vɑːd-
Vaughan, Vaughn vɔːn ‖ vɑːn
ˌVaughan 'Williams
vault vɔːlt vɒlt ‖ vɑːlt **vaulted** 'vɔːlt ɪd 'vɒlt-,
-əd ‖ 'vɑːlt- **vaulting** 'vɔːlt ɪŋ 'vɒlt- ‖ 'vɑːlt-
vaults vɔːlts vɒlts ‖ vɑːlts
'vaulting horse
vaunt vɔːnt ‖ vɑːnt **vaunted** 'vɔːnt ɪd -əd
‖ 'vɔːnt̬ əd 'vɑːnt̬- **vaunting/ly** 'vɔːnt ɪŋ /li
‖ 'vɔːnt̬ ɪŋ /li 'vɑːnt̬- **vaunts** vɔːnts ‖ vɑːnts
Vaux *(i)* vɔːks ‖ vɑːks, *(ii)* vəʊ ‖ voʊ, *(iii)*
vɒks ‖ vɑːks
Vauxhall 'vɒks ɔːl -hɔːl; ˌvɒk 'sɔːl, ˌvɒks 'hɔːl
‖ 'vɑːks- 'vɔːks-, -ɑːl, -hɔːl, -hɑːl
vavasor, vavasour, V~ 'væv ə sɔː -sʊə; -əs ə
‖ -sɔːr -sʊər **~s** z

Vavasseur ˌvæv ə 'sɜː ‖ -'sɝː
VAX *tdmk* væks
Vaz væz
VC ˌviː 'siː **~s, ~'s** z
VCR ˌviː siː 'ɑː ‖ -'ɑːr **~s, ~'s** z
VD ˌviː 'diː
VDU, vdu ˌviː diː 'juː **~s, ~'s** z
've əv —*but after a pronoun ending in a vowel*
sound, v — *some've done it* ˌsʌm əv 'dʌn ɪt,
they've tried ðeɪv 'traɪd
veal, Veal viːᵊl
Veblen 'veb lən
Vectis 'vekt ɪs §-əs
vector 'vekt ə ‖ -ᵊr **~ed** d **vectoring**
'vekt ᵊr ɪŋ **~s** z
vectorial vek 'tɔːr i ᵊl ‖ -'toʊr-
Vectra *tdmk* 'vek trə
Veda 'veɪd ə 'viːd-
Vedanta vɪ 'dɑːnt ə ve-, veɪ-, və-, -'dænt-
—*Hindi* [veː ɖaːn̪t̪]
Vedda 'ved ə **~s** z
vedette vɪ 'det və- **~s** s
Vedic 'veɪd ɪk 'viːd-
veep viːp **veeps** viːps
veer vɪə ‖ vɪᵊr **veered** vɪəd ‖ vɪᵊrd **veering**
'vɪər ɪŋ ‖ 'vɪr ɪŋ **veers** vɪəz ‖ vɪᵊrz
veg vedʒ
Vega *name of star* 'viːg ə 'veɪg-
Vega *Spanish name* 'veɪg ə —*Sp* ['be ɣa]
vegan 'viːg ən **~ism** ˌɪz əm **~s** z
Veganin *tdmk* 'vedʒ ən ɪn §-ən
Vegas 'veɪg əs
vegeburger 'vedʒ i ˌbɜːg ə ‖ -bɜːg ᵊr **~s** z
vegemite, V~ *tdmk* 'vedʒ ə maɪt -ɪ-
vegetable 'vedʒ təb ᵊl 'vedʒ ət əb ᵊl,
'•ɪt- ‖ -'•ət̬ əb ᵊl **~s** z
'vegetable knife; ˌvegetable 'marrow
vegetal 'vedʒ ɪt ᵊl -ət- ‖ -ət̬ ᵊl
vegetarian ˌvedʒ ə 'teər i ən ◂ ˌ•ɪ- ‖ -'ter-
-'tær- **~s** z
vege|tate 'vedʒ ə teɪt -ɪ- **~tated** teɪt ɪd -əd
‖ teɪt̬ əd **~tates** teɪts **~tating**
teɪt ɪŋ ‖ teɪt̬ ɪŋ
vegetation ˌvedʒ ə 'teɪʃ ᵊn -ɪ-
vegetative 'vedʒ ət ət ɪv -'•ɪt-; -ə teɪt-, -ɪ teɪt-
‖ -ə teɪt̬ ɪv **~ly** li **~ness** nəs nɪs
veggie, veggy, vegie 'vedʒ i **~s** z
veggieburger 'vedʒ i ˌbɜːg ə ‖ -bɜːg ᵊr **~s** z
vehemence 'viːˌəm ənᵗs 'veɪ-, ˌɪm-, -həm-,
-hɪm-
vehement 'viːˌəm ənt 'veɪ-, ˌɪm-, -həm-, -hɪm-
~ly li

VEHICLE			
	■'viː ək- ▨'viː hɪk- ▬-'hɪk-		
AmE 1993			
0	20 40	60	80 100%

vehicle 'viːˌɪk ᵊl ˌ•ək-, §-hɪk- ‖ 'viː ək ᵊl -hɪk-,
•'hɪk• —*AmE 1993 poll panel preference:*
'viː ək- *62%,* 'viː hɪk- *33%;* -'hɪk- *5%.* **~s** z
vehicular vɪ 'hɪk jʊl ə və-, viː-, -jəl-
‖ viː 'hɪk jəl ᵊr

veil veɪᵊl *(= vale)* veiled veɪᵊld veiling
'veɪᵊl ɪŋ veils veɪlz
vein veɪn *(= vain)* veined veɪnd veining
'veɪn ɪŋ veins veɪnz
vela, Vela 'viːl ə
velar 'viːl ə ‖ -ᵊr ~s z
velaric viː 'lær ɪk vɪ- ‖ -'ler-
velaris... —*see* velariz...
velarity viː 'lær ət i vɪ-, -ɪt- ‖ -əti̯ -'ler-
velarization ˌviːl ər aɪ 'zeɪʃ ᵊn -ɪ'•- ‖ -ə'•
velariz|e 'viːl ə raɪz ~ed d ~es ɪz əz ~ing ɪŋ
Velasquez, Velásquez, Velázquez
vɪ 'læsk wɪz və-, ve-, -ɪz, -wez, -wɪθ
‖ və 'lɑːsk eɪs -'læsk-, -əs —*Sp* [be 'laθ keθ,
-'las-]
Velcro *tdmk,* v~ 'vel krəʊ ‖ -krəʊ ~ed d
veld, veldt velt felt
veleta və 'liːt ə vɪ- ‖ -'liːt̯ ə ~s z
Velia 'viːl i_ə
velic 'viːl ɪk
Velindre ve 'lɪn dreɪ -'lɪndr ə
velleit|y ve 'liː_ət i li və-, -ɪt- ‖ -ət̯ li ~ies iz
vellum 'vel əm
Velma 'velm ə
velocipede və 'lɒs ə piːd vɪ-, -ɪ- ‖ -'lɑːs- ~s z
velociraptor və ˌlɒs ɪ 'ræpt ə vɪ-, -ə-
‖ -ˌlɑːs ə 'ræpt ᵊr ~s z
velocit|y və 'lɒs ət i li vɪ-, -ɪt- ‖ -'lɑːs ət̯ li ~ies
iz
velodrome 'vel ə drəʊm 'viːl- ‖ -drəʊm ~s z
velour, velours və 'lʊə ve- ‖ -'lʊᵊr
veloute, velouté və 'luːt eɪ ve- ‖ və ˌluː 'teɪ
velum 'viːl əm vela 'viːl ə
velvet 'velv ɪt §-ət ~s s
velveteen ˌvelv ə 'tiːn -ɪ-, '••• ~s z
velvety 'velv ət i -ɪt- ‖ -ət̯ i
vena 'viːn ə venae 'viːn iː
ˌvena 'cava 'keɪv ə
Venable 'ven əb ᵊl
Venables 'ven əb ᵊlz
venal 'viːn ᵊl ~ly i
venality viː 'næl ət i vɪ-, -ɪt- ‖ -ət̯ i
vend vend vended 'vend ɪd -əd vending
'vend ɪŋ vends vendz
'vending maˌchine
Venda 'vend ə
vendace 'vend ɪs -əs, -eɪs
vendee ˌven 'diː ~s z
vender 'vend ə ‖ -ᵊr ~s z
vendetta ven 'det ə ‖ -'det̯ ə ~s z
vendor 'vend ə ‖ -ᵊr —*for contrast also*
-ɔː ‖ -ɔːr, *or* ˌven 'dɔː ‖ -'dɔːr ~s z
veneer və 'nɪə vɪ- ‖ -'nɪᵊr ~ed d veneering
və 'nɪər ɪŋ vɪ- ‖ -'nɪr ɪŋ ~s z
venerab|le 'ven ər_əb ᵊl ~leness ᵊl nəs -nɪs
~ly li
vene|rate 'ven ə ǀreɪt ~rated reɪt ɪd -əd
‖ reɪt̯ əd ~rates reɪts ~rating
reɪt ɪŋ ‖ reɪt̯ ɪŋ
veneration ˌven ə 'reɪʃ ᵊn
venerator 'ven ə reɪt ə ‖ -reɪt̯ ᵊr ~s z
venereal və 'nɪər i_əl vɪ- ‖ -'nɪr-
veˌnereal di'sease, •'••• •ˌ•

venereologist və ˌnɪər i 'ɒl ədʒ ɪst vɪ-, §-əst
‖ -ˌnɪr i 'ɑːl- ~s s
venereology və ˌnɪər i 'ɒl ədʒ i vɪ-
‖ -ˌnɪr i 'ɑːl-
venery 'ven ər i ‖ -'viːn-
Veness və 'nes vɪ-
Venetia və 'niːʃ ə vɪ-, -'niːʃ i_ə
Venetian, v~ və 'niːʃ ᵊn vɪ-, -'niːʃ i_ən ~s z
veˌnetian 'blind
Venetic və 'net ɪk vɪ-, ve- ‖ -'net̯ ɪk
Venezuel|a ˌven ə 'zweɪl ǀə -ɪ-, -e- —*AmSp*
[be ne 'swe la] ~an/s ən/z
vengeance 'vendʒ ᵊnts
vengeful 'vendʒ fᵊl -fʊl ~ly _i ~ness nəs nɪs
veni, vidi, vici ˌveɪn iː ˌviːd iː 'viːk iː -'viːtʃ iː;
ˌweɪn i ˌwiːd i 'wiːk i
venial 'viːn i_əl ~ly i ~ness nəs nɪs
veniality ˌviːn i 'æl ət i -ɪt i ‖ -ət̯ i
Venice 'ven ɪs §-əs
venison 'ven ɪs ᵊn -əs-, -ɪz-, -əz-; 'venz ᵊn
Venite və 'naɪt ə vɪ-, ve-, -'niːt eɪ ‖ -'naɪt̯ i
-'niːt eɪ
Venn ven
Venner 'ven ə ‖ -ᵊr
venom 'ven əm
venomous 'ven əm əs ~ly li ~ness nəs nɪs
Veno's *tdmk* 'viːn əʊz ‖ -əʊz
venous 'viːn əs ~ly li
vent vent vented 'vent ɪd -əd ‖ 'vent̯ əd
venting 'vent ɪŋ ‖ 'vent̯ ɪŋ vents vents
Vent-Axia *tdmk* ˌvent 'æks i_ə
venti|late 'vent ɪ ǀleɪt -ə-, -ᵊl eɪt ‖ 'vent̯ ᵊl eɪt
~lated leɪt ɪd -əd ‖ leɪt̯ əd ~lates leɪts
~lating leɪt ɪŋ ‖ leɪt̯ ɪŋ
ventilation ˌvent ɪ 'leɪʃ ᵊn -ə-, -ᵊl 'eɪʃ-
‖ ˌvent̯ ᵊl 'eɪʃ ᵊn
ventilator 'vent ɪ leɪt ə -ə-, -ᵊl eɪt-
‖ 'vent̯ ᵊl eɪt ᵊr ~s z
Ventnor 'vent nə ‖ -nᵊr
Ventolin *tdmk* 'vent əʊ lɪn -ᵊl ɪn, §-ᵊn
‖ 'vent̯ ᵊl ən
ventral 'ventr əl ~ly i
ventricle 'ventr ɪk ᵊl ~s z
ventricular ven 'trɪk jʊl ə və-, -jəl- ‖ -jəl ᵊr
ventriloquial ˌventr ɪ 'ləʊk wi_əl ◂ ˌ•ə-
‖ -'loʊk-
ventriloquism ven 'trɪl ə ˌkwɪz əm
ventriloquist ven 'trɪl ək wɪst §-wəst ~s s
ventriloquy ven 'trɪl ək wi
Ventris 'ventr ɪs §-əs
venture, V~ 'ventʃ ə ‖ -ᵊr ~d d ~s z
venturing 'ventʃ ər_ɪŋ
'venture ˌcapital
venturer 'ventʃ ər ə ‖ -ᵊr_ᵊr ~s z
venturesome 'ventʃ ə səm ‖ -ᵊr- ~ly li ~ness
nəs nɪs
Venturi, v~ ven 'tjʊər i →§-'tʃʊər i ‖ -'tʊr i ~s
z
venˌturi tube
venturous 'ventʃ ər_əs ~ly li ~ness nəs nɪs
venue 'ven juː ~s z
venule 'ven juːl 'viːn- ~s z

Venus 'vi:n əs ~es, ~'s ɪz əz
ˌVenus('s) 'flytrap
Venusian və 'nju:z i_ən vɪ-, -'nju:s- ‖ -'nu:ʒ ən
-'nu:ʃ-, -'nju:ʒ-, -'nju:ʃ-, -'•i_ən ~s z
Vera 'vɪər ə ‖ 'vɪr ə
veracious və 'reɪʃ əs vɪ-, ve- ~ly li ~ness nəs
nɪs
veracit|y və 'ræs ət li vɪ-, ve-, -ɪt- ‖ -əṭ li ~ies
ɪz
Veracruz, Vera Cruz ˌvɪər ə 'kru:z ˌver-, ˌveər-
‖ ˌver- —AmSp [ˌbe ɾa 'krus]
veranda, verandah və 'rænd ə ~ed d ~s z
verb vɜ:b ‖ vɝ:b verbs vɜ:bz ‖ vɝ:bz
verbal 'vɜ:b əl ‖ 'vɝ:b əl ~ed, ~led d ~ing,
~ling ɪŋ ~ly i ~s z
ˌverbal 'noun
verbalis... —see verbaliz...
verbalism 'vɜ:b ə ˌlɪz əm -əl ˌɪz- ‖ 'vɝ:b-
verbalization ˌvɜ:b əl aɪ 'zeɪʃ ən -ɪ'•-
‖ ˌvɝ:b əl ə- ~s z
verbaliz|e 'vɜ:b ə laɪz -əl aɪz ‖ 'vɝ:b- ~ed d
~es ɪz əz ~ing ɪŋ
verbatim vɜ: 'beɪt ɪm -'bɑ:t-, §-əm
‖ vɝ: 'beɪṭ əm -ɪm
verbena vɜ: 'bi:n ə və- ‖ vɝ:-
verbiage 'vɜ:b i_ɪdʒ ‖ 'vɝ:b-
verbose vɜ: 'bəʊs ‖ vɝ: 'boʊs ~ly li ~ness
nəs nɪs
verbosity vɜ: 'bɒs ət i -ɪt- ‖ vɝ: 'bɑːs əṭ i
verboten fə 'bəʊt ən və- ‖ fər 'boʊt ən vər-
—Ger [fɛɐ 'boː tən]
Vercingetorix ˌvɜːs ɪn 'dʒet ə rɪks ˌ•ən-, -'get-
‖ ˌvɝ:s ɪn 'dʒeṭ- -'get-
verd vɜ:d ‖ vɝ:d
verdancy 'vɜ:d ənts i ‖ 'vɝ:d-
verdant 'vɜ:d ənt ‖ 'vɝ:d- ~ly li
Verde (i) vɜ:d veəd ‖ vɝ:d, (ii) 'vɜ:d i 'veəd i
‖ 'vɝ:d i 'verd i — Cape Verde and its islands
are (i), or an imitation of the Portuguese form;
the river in AZ is (ii). —Port ['veɾ də]
Verdean 'vɜːd i_ən 'veəd- ‖ 'vɝːd- ~s z
verderer 'vɜːd ər ə ‖ 'vɝːd ər ər ~s z
Verdi 'veəd i ‖ 'verd i —It ['ver di]
verdict 'vɜːd ɪkt ‖ 'vɝːd- ~s s
verdigris 'vɜːd ɪ gri: -ə-, -griːs, -grɪs
‖ 'vɝːd ə grɪs -griːs
Verdun vɜ: 'dʌn ‖ vɝ:- —Fr [vɛʁ dœ̃, -dæ̃]
verdure 'vɜːdʒ ə 'vɜːd jə, -jʊə ‖ 'vɝːdʒ ər
(usually = verger)
Vere vɪə ‖ vɪ²r
verge vɜːdʒ ‖ vɝːdʒ verged vɜːdʒd ‖ vɝːdʒd
verges 'vɜːdʒ ɪz -əz ‖ 'vɝːdʒ əz verging
'vɜːdʒ ɪŋ ‖ 'vɝːdʒ ɪŋ
verger 'vɜːdʒ ə ‖ 'vɝːdʒ ²r ~s z
Vergil 'vɜːdʒ ɪl -²l ‖ 'vɝːdʒ əl
Vergilian vɜ: 'dʒɪl i_ən və- ‖ vɝ:-
veridical və 'rɪd ɪk ²l ve-, vɪ- ~ly_i
veridicality və ˌrɪd ɪ 'kæl ət i ve-, vɪ-, §-ˌ•ə-,
-ɪt i ‖ -əṭ i
veriest 'ver i_ɪst ˌ_əst
verifiab|le 'ver ɪ faɪˌəb ²l '•ə-, ˌ•'•••• ~ly li
verification ˌver ɪf ɪ 'keɪʃ ən ˌ•əf-, §-ə'•- ~s z

veri|fy 'ver ɪ ˌfaɪ -ə- ~fied faɪd ~fier/s faɪˌə/z
‖ faɪˌ²r/z ~fies faɪz ~fying faɪ ɪŋ
verily 'ver əl i -ɪ li
verisimilitude ˌver ɪ sɪ 'mɪl ɪ tjuːd ˌ•ə-, ˌˌ•i-,
-sə'•-, -'•ə-, -ɪ tʃuːd ‖ -§-tʃuːd -tuːd -tjuːd
verismo ve 'rɪz məʊ və-, -'riːz- ‖ -moʊ —It
[ve 'riz mo]
veritab|le 'ver ɪt əb ²l '•ət- ‖ '•əṭ- ~leness
²l nəs -nɪs ~ly li
verit|y, V~ 'ver ət i -ɪt- ‖ -əṭ i ~ies ɪz
verjuice 'vɜː dʒuːs ‖ 'vɝː-
verkrampte fə 'kræmpt ə ‖ fər- —Afrikaans
[fər 'kram tə] ~s z
Verlaine və 'leɪn veə- ‖ v²r- ver- —Fr
[vɛʁ lɛn]
verligte fə 'lɪxt ə ‖ fər 'lɪkt ə —Afrikaans
[fər 'ləx tə] ~s z
Vermeer və 'mɪə vɜː-, -'meə ‖ v²r 'mɪ²r
—Dutch [vər 'meːr] ~s z
vermeil 'vɜːm eɪ²l -ɪl, §-²l ‖ 'vɝːm-
vermicelli ˌvɜːm ɪ 'tʃel i -ə-, -'sel- ‖ ˌvɝːm-
vermicide 'vɜːm ɪ saɪd -ə- ‖ 'vɝːm- ~s z
vermiculate vɜː 'mɪk ju leɪt və-, -jə-
‖ vɝː 'mɪk jə-
vermiculite vɜː 'mɪk ju laɪt və-, -jə-
‖ vɝː 'mɪk jə-
vermiform 'vɜːm ɪ fɔːm §-ə- ‖ 'vɝːm ə fɔːrm
ˌvermiform ap'pendix
vermifug|e 'vɜːm ɪ fjuːdʒ §-ə- ‖ 'vɝːm- ~es
ɪz əz
vermilion və 'mɪl i_ən vɜː- ‖ v²r 'mɪl jən ~ed
d ~s z
vermin 'vɜːm ɪn §-ən ‖ 'vɝːm ən
verminous 'vɜːm ɪn əs §-ən- ‖ 'vɝːm ən əs
~ly li ~ness nəs nɪs
Vermont və 'mɒnt vɜː- ‖ v²r 'mɑːnt
Vermonter və 'mɒnt ə və vɜː- ‖ v²r 'mɑːnṭ ²r ~s
z
vermouth 'vɜːm əθ -uːθ; və 'muːθ, vɜː-
‖ v²r 'muːθ ~s s
Verna 'vɜːn ə ‖ 'vɝːn ə
vernacular və 'næk jʊl ə -jəl- ‖ v²r 'næk jəl ²r
və- ~ly li ~s z
vernal 'vɜːn ²l ‖ 'vɝːn ²l ~ly i
ˌvernal 'equinox
vernalis... —see vernaliz...
vernalization ˌvɜːn ²l aɪ 'zeɪʃ ən -ɪ'•-
‖ ˌvɝːn ²l ə-
vernaliz|e 'vɜːn ə laɪz -²l aɪz ‖ 'vɝːn ²l aɪz
~ed d ~es ɪz əz ~ing ɪŋ
Verne vɜːn veən ‖ vɝːn —Fr [vɛʁn]
Verner 'vɜːn ə 'veən- ‖ 'vɝːn ²r —Dan
['vɛʁʔ nɐ] ~'s z
'Verner's law
Verney 'vɜːn i i ‖ 'vɝːn i
vernier 'vɜːn i_ə ‖ 'vɝːn i_²r ~s z
vernissag|e ˌvɜːn ɪ 'sɑːʒ ‖ ˌvɝːn- ~es ɪz əz
Vernon 'vɜːn ən ‖ 'vɝːn ən
Verona və 'rəʊn ə ve-, vɪ- ‖ -'roʊn- —It
[ve 'roː na]
veronal, V~ tdmk 'ver ən ²l ~s z
Veronese ˌver əʊ 'neɪz i ‖ -ə- -'neɪs- —It
[ve ɾo 'ne ze]

veronica, V~ və ˈrɒn ɪk ə ve-, vɪ- ‖ -ˈrɑːn- ~s,
~ˈs z

Verrazano ˌver ə ˈzɑːn əʊ ‖ -oʊ —*It*
[ver rat ˈtsaː no]
ˌVerraˌzano ˈNarrows

ver|ruca və ˈruːk ə ve-, vɪ- ~rucae ˈruːs iː
ˈruːk-, -aɪ ~rucas ˈruːk əz

versa ˈvɜːs ə ‖ ˈvɝːs ə

Versace və ˈsɑːtʃ i vɜː- ‖ vɚ-

Versailles veə ˈsaɪ vɜː- ‖ ver- —*Fr* [vɛʁ saj]

versant ˈvɜːs ənt ‖ ˈvɝːs- ~s s

versatile ˈvɜːs ə taɪəl ‖ ˈvɝːs ət əl (*) ~ly li
~ness nəs nɪs

versatility ˌvɜːs ə ˈtɪl ət i -ɪt- ‖ ˌvɝːs ə ˈtɪl ət i

verse vɜːs ‖ vɝːs versed vɜːst ‖ vɝːst verses
ˈvɜːs ɪz -əz ‖ ˈvɝːs əz

versicle ˈvɜːs ɪk əl ‖ ˈvɝːs-

versification ˌvɜːs ɪf ɪ ˈkeɪʃ ən ˌ•əf-, §-ə•-
‖ ˌvɝːs- ~s z

versi|fy ˈvɜːs ɪ ˈfaɪ -ə- ‖ ˈvɝːs- ~fied faɪd
~fier/s faɪ_ə/z ‖ faɪ_ɚr/z ~fies faɪz ~fying
faɪ ɪŋ

version ˈvɜːʃ ən ˈvɜːʒ- ‖ ˈvɝːʒ ən ˈvɝːʃ- ~s z

verso ˈvɜːs əʊ ‖ ˈvɝːs oʊ ~s z

versus ˈvɜːs əs ‖ ˈvɝːs əs

vert vɜːt ‖ vɝːt

vert|ebra ˈvɜːt ɪb rə -əb- ‖ ˈvɝːt- ~ebrae
ɪ breɪ ə-, -briː ~ebras ɪb rəz əb-

vertebral ˈvɜːt ɪb rəl -əb- ‖ ˈvɝːt- vɝː ˈtiːb-

Vertebrata, v~ ˌvɜːt ɪ ˈbrɑːt ə -ə-, -ˈbreɪt-
‖ ˌvɝːt ə ˈbrɑːt ə -ˈbreɪt-

vertebrate ˈvɜːt ɪb rət -əb-, -rɪt; -ɪ breɪt, -ə-
‖ ˈvɝːt- ~s s

vertex ˈvɜːt eks ‖ ˈvɝːt- vertices ˈvɜːt ɪ siːz
-ə- ‖ ˈvɝːt-

vertical ˈvɜːt ɪk əl ‖ ˈvɝːt- ~ly _i ~s z

verticality ˌvɜːt ɪ ˈkæl ət i ˌ•ə-, -ɪt i
‖ ˌvɝːt ə ˈkæl ət i

vertices ˈvɜːt ɪ siːz -ə- ‖ ˈvɝːt-

vertiginous vɜː ˈtɪdʒ ɪn əs -ən əs ‖ vɝː- ~ly li
~ness nəs nɪs

vertigo ˈvɜːt ɪ gəʊ -ə- ‖ ˈvɝːt ɪ goʊ ~s z

Verulam ˈver ʊl əm -jʊl- ‖ -jəl-

Verulamium ˌver ʊ ˈleɪm i_əm ˌ•ju- ‖ ˌ•jə-

vervain ˈvɜːv eɪn ‖ ˈvɝːv-

verve vɜːv ‖ vɝːv

vervet ˈvɜːv ɪt §-ət ‖ ˈvɝːv ət ~s s

Verwoerd fə ˈvʊət feə- ‖ fɚ ˈvʊərt —*Afrikaans*
[fər ˈvuːrt]

very ˈver i —*Some speakers use a casual weak
form* vər i **veriest** ˈver i_ɪst _əst
ˌvery ˌhigh ˈfrequency

Very ˈvɪər i ˈver- ‖ ˈver i ˈvɪr-
ˈVery light

Veryan ˈver i_ən

Vesalius və ˈseɪl i_əs vɪ-

Vesey ˈviːz i

vesic|a ˈves ɪk lə vɪ ˈsaɪk lə, və- ~al əl ~ant/s
ənt/s ~as əz

vesicle ˈves ɪk əl ‖ ˈviːs- ~s z

vesicular və ˈsɪk jʊl ə ve-, vɪ-, -jəl ə ‖ -jəl ɚr
~ly li

Vespa *tdmk* ˈvesp ə ~s z

Vespasian ves ˈpeɪʒ ən -ˈ•i_ən; -ˈpeɪz i_ən

vesper, V~ ˈvesp ə ‖ -ɚr ~s z

vespertine ˈvesp ə taɪn ‖ -ɚr-

vespine ˈvesp aɪn

Vespucci ve ˈspuːtʃ i —*It* [ve ˈsput tʃi]

vessel ˈves əl ~s z

vest vest vested ˈvest ɪd -əd vesting ˈvest ɪŋ
vests vests
ˌvested ˈinterest

Vesta, vesta ˈvest ə ~s, ~ˈs z

vestal ˈvest əl ~s z
ˌvestal ˈvirgin

vestibular ve ˈstɪb jʊl ə -jəl- ‖ -jəl ɚr

vestibule ˈvest ɪ bjuːl -ə- ~s z

vestig|e ˈvest ɪdʒ ~es ɪz əz

vestigial ves ˈtɪdʒ i_əl -ˈtɪdʒ əl ~ly i

vestment ˈvest mənt ~s s

vest-pocket ˌvest ˈpɒk ɪt ◂ §-ət ‖ -ˈpɑːk-

ves|try ˈves |tri ~tries triz

vestry|man ˈves tri |mən ~men mən men

vesture ˈves tʃə ‖ -tʃɚr ~d d ~s z

Vesuvianite və ˈsuːv i_ə naɪt vɪ-, -ˈsjuːv-

Vesuvius və ˈsuːv i_əs vɪ-, -ˈsjuːv-

vet vet vets vets vetted ˈvet ɪd -əd ‖ ˈveṭ əd
vetting ˈvet ɪŋ ‖ ˈveṭ ɪŋ

vetch vetʃ vetches ˈvetʃ ɪz -əz

vetchling ˈvetʃ lɪŋ ~s z

veteran ˈvet_ər ən ‖ ˈveṭ ɚr ən →ˈvetr ən ~s z
ˈVeterans Day

veterinarian ˌvet_ər ɪ ˈneər i_ən -ə•-;
ˌvet ə ˈneər i_ən ‖ ˌveṭ ɚr ə ˈner i_ən
→ˌvetr ə ˈner- ~s z

veterinar|y ˈvet_ər ən ər_li -ɪn ər_i; ˈvet ɪn ər_li,
ˈvet ən ər_li ‖ ˈveṭ ɚr ə ner li →ˈvetr ə ner li,
ˈvet ən er li ~ies iz
ˌveterinary ˈsurgeon

vetiver ˈvet ɪv ə ‖ -ɚr

veto ˈviːt əʊ ‖ ˈviːṭ oʊ ˈviːt- ~ed d ~es z ~ing
ɪŋ

vex veks vexed vekst vexes ˈveks ɪz -əz
vexing ˈveks ɪŋ

vexation vek ˈseɪʃ ən ~s z

vexatious vek ˈseɪʃ əs ~ly li ~ness nəs nɪs

vexillology ˌveks ɪ ˈlɒl ədʒ i ˌ•ə- ‖ -ˈlɑːl-

VHF ˌviː eɪtʃ ˈef §-heɪtʃ-

VH1 ˌviː eɪtʃ ˈwʌn §-heɪtʃ-, §-ˈwɒn

VHS *tdmk* ˌviː eɪtʃ ˈes §-heɪtʃ-

Vi vaɪ

via ˈvaɪ_ə ˈviː_ə —*see also phrases with this word*

viability ˌvaɪ_ə ˈbɪl ət i -ɪt i ‖ -əṭ i

viab|le ˈvaɪ_əb |əl ~ly li

Viacom *tdmk* ˈvaɪ_ə kɒm ‖ -kɑːm

Via Dolorosa, via d~ ˌviː_ə ˌdɒl ə ˈrəʊs ə
‖ -ˌdɑːl ə ˈroʊs- -ˌdoʊl-

viaduct ˈvaɪ_ə dʌkt ~s s

Viagra *tdmk* vaɪ ˈæg rə vi- ‖ -ˈɑːg-

vial ˈvaɪ_əl ‖ ˈvaɪ_əl ~s z

via media ˌvaɪ_ə ˈmiːd i_ə ˌviː_ə ˈmeɪd-

viand ˈvaɪ_ənd ˈviː_ ~s z

viatic|al vaɪ ˈæt ɪk |əl vi- ‖ -ˈæṭ- ~a ə ~um/s
əm/z

vibes vaɪbz

vibist ˈvaɪb ɪst §-əst ~s s

vibraharp 'vaɪb rə hɑːp ‖ -hɑːrp ~s s
Vibram *tdmk* 'vaɪb rəm
vibrancy 'vaɪb rənˡs i
vibrant 'vaɪb rənt ~ly li ~s s
vibraphone 'vaɪb rə fəʊn ‖ -foʊn ~s z
vib|rate vaɪ 'b|reɪt ‖ 'vaɪb |reɪt *(*)* ~rated
reɪt ɪd -əd ‖ reɪt̬ əd ~rates reɪts ~rating
reɪt ɪŋ ‖ reɪt̬ ɪŋ
vibratile 'vaɪb rə taɪˀl ‖ -rət̬ ˀl
vibration vaɪ 'breɪʃ ən ~s z
vibrational vaɪ 'breɪʃ ən̩ əl
vibrationless vaɪ 'breɪʃ ən ləs -lɪs
vibrative vaɪ 'breɪt ɪv 'vaɪb rət- ‖ 'vaɪb rət̬ ɪv
vibrato vɪ 'brɑːt əʊ §və-, vaɪ-, viː- ‖ -oʊ ~s z
vibrator vaɪ 'breɪt ə ‖ 'vaɪb reɪt̬ ᵊr *(*)* ~s z
vibratory vaɪ 'breɪt ər i 'vaɪb rət‿ər i
‖ 'vaɪb rə tɔːr i -toʊr i *(*)*
vibrio 'vɪb ri əʊ ‖ -oʊ ~s z
vibriss|a 'brɪs lə ~ae iː
vibro- ¦vaɪb rəʊ ‖ -roʊ — vibromassage
'vaɪb rəʊ ˌmæs ɑːʒ ˌ•• '••• ‖ -roʊ mə ˌsɑːʒ
ˌ•••'•
viburnum vaɪ 'bɜːn əm ‖ -'bɝːn- ~s z
Vic vɪk
vicar 'vɪk ə ‖ -ᵊr ~s z
vicarag|e 'vɪk ər‿ɪdʒ ~es ɪz əz
vicarial vɪ 'keər i‿əl və-, vaɪ- ‖ -'ker- -'kær-
vicarious vɪ 'keər i‿əs və-, vaɪ- ‖ -'ker- -'kær-
~ly li ~ness nəs nɪs
vice *n* vaɪs vices 'vaɪs ɪz -əz
'vice squad
vice *prep, Latin* 'vaɪs i -ə; vaɪs, 'viːs eɪ
ˌvice 'versa 'vɜːs ə ‖ 'vɝːs ə
vice- ¦vaɪs — vice-presidency
ˌvaɪs 'prez ɪd ənˡs i -'•əd- ‖ -ə denˡs i
vice-chair ˌvaɪs 'tʃeə ‖ -'tʃeᵊr -'tʃæᵊr ~man
mən ~men mən ~person/s ˌpɜːs ᵊn/z
‖ ˌpɝːs ᵊn/z ~woman ˌwʊm ən ~women
ˌwɪm ɪn §-ən
vice-chancellor ˌvaɪs 'tʃɑːnⁱs əl‿ə §-'tʃænⁱs-
‖ -'tʃænⁱs əl‿ᵊr ~ship ʃɪp ~s z
vicegerant ˌvaɪs 'dʒer ənt -'dʒɪər- ‖ -'dʒɪr- ~s
s
vicelike 'vaɪs laɪk
viceregal ˌvaɪs 'riːg ᵊl ◄ ~ly i
vicereine ˌvaɪs 'reɪn '•• ~s z
viceroy 'vaɪs rɔɪ ~s z
Vichy 'viːʃ i 'vɪʃ- —*Fr* [vi ʃi]
'Vichy ˌwater
Vichyite 'viːʃ i aɪt 'vɪʃ- ~s s
vichyssoise ˌviːʃ i 'swɑːz ˌvɪʃ- —*Fr*
[vi ʃi swɑːz]
vicinal 'vɪs ɪn ᵊl -ən‿ᵊl
vicinit|y və 'sɪn ət li vɪ-, -ɪt- ‖ -ət̬ li ~ies ɪz
vicious 'vɪʃ əs ~ly li ~ness nəs nɪs
ˌvicious 'circle
vicissitude vaɪ 'sɪs ɪ tjuːd və-, vɪ-, →§-tʃuːd
‖ və 'sɪs ə tuːd vaɪ-, -tjuːd ~s z
Vick vɪk
Vickers 'vɪk əz ‖ -ᵊrz
Vickery 'vɪk ər i
Vicki, Vickie 'vɪk i
Vicksburg 'vɪks bɜːg ‖ -bɝːg

Vicky 'vɪk i
victim 'vɪkt ɪm §-əm ~hood hʊd ~s z
victimis... —*see* victimiz...
victimization ˌvɪkt ɪm aɪ 'zeɪʃ ᵊn ˌ•əm-, -ɪˈ•-
‖ -əˈ•- ~s, ~'s z
victimiz|e 'vɪkt ɪ maɪz -ə- ‖ -ə- ~ed d ~es ɪz
əz ~ing ɪŋ
victor, V~ 'vɪkt ə ‖ -ᵊr ~s z
ˌvictor lu'dorum lu 'dɔːr əm
Victoria, v~ vɪk 'tɔːr i‿ə ‖ -'toʊr- —*but the
London railway terminus is sometimes double-
stressed,* ˌ•ˈ•••◄ ~s, ~'s z
Vicˌtoria 'Cross; Vicˌtoria 'Falls; vicˌtoria
'plum; Vicˌtoria 'Station, ˌ•ˌ•ˈ•-
Victorian vɪk 'tɔːr i‿ən ‖ -'toʊr- ~ism ˌɪz əm
~s z
Victoriana vɪk ˌtɔːr i 'ɑːn ə ˌ•••'••◄ ‖ -ˌtoʊr-,
-'æn-
victorious vɪk 'tɔːr i‿əs ‖ -'toʊr- ~ly li ~ness
nəs nɪs
victor|y 'vɪkt ər li →'vɪk trli ~ies iz
Victory-V *tdmk* ˌvɪk tri 'viː
Victrola *tdmk* vɪk 'trəʊl ə ‖ -'troʊl ə
victual 'vɪt ᵊl *(!)* ~s z
victualer, victualler 'vɪt ᵊl‿ə ‖ ‿ᵊr —*Also
sometimes a spelling pronunciation*
'vɪk tʃu‿əl ə ‖ -ᵊr ~s z
vicuna, vicuña vɪ 'kjuːn ə və-, vaɪ-, -'kuːn-, -jə
—*Sp* [bi 'ku ɲa] ~s z
Vidal *(i)* vɪ 'dɑːl və-, ˌviː-, -'dæl, *(ii)* 'vaɪd ᵊl
—*The writer Gore Vidal is (i).*
vide 'vaɪd i 'vɪd-, 'viːd-, -eɪ
videlicet vɪ 'diːl ɪ set və-, vaɪ-, -'deɪl-, -'del-,
-ə-, -ket
video 'vɪd i əʊ ‖ -oʊ ~ed d ~ing ɪŋ ~s z
'video ˌcamera; ˌvideo cas'sette, ˌ•••ˈ•, •ˈ•;
ˌvideo cas'sette reˌcorder ‖ '•••ˈ•ˌ•ˈ•, •ˈ•;
'video ˌgame; 'video ˌlink; 'video reˌcorder
videoconferenc|e 'vɪd i əʊ ˌkɒn fᵊr‿ənⁱs
‖ -oʊ ˌkɑːn- ~ing ɪŋ
videodisc 'vɪd i əʊ dɪsk ‖ -oʊ dɪsk ~s s
videofit 'vɪd i əʊ fɪt ‖ -oʊ• ~s s
videograph|er/s ˌvɪd i 'ɒg rəf| ᵊ/z
‖ -'ɑːg rəf| ᵊr/z ~y i
videophone, V~ *tdmk* 'vɪd i əʊ fəʊn ‖ -oʊ foʊn
~s z
videotap|e 'vɪd i əʊ teɪp ‖ -oʊ teɪp ~ed t ~es
s ~ing ɪŋ
'videotape reˌcorder
videotex 'vɪd i əʊ teks ‖ -oʊ teks
videotext 'vɪd i əʊ tekst ‖ -oʊ tekst
vidicon 'vɪd i kɒn ‖ -kɑːn ~s z
Vidler 'vɪd lə ‖ -lᵊr
vie vaɪ vied vaɪd vies vaɪz vying 'vaɪ ɪŋ
Vienna vi 'en ə
Viennese ˌviː‿ə 'niːz ◄ ‖ -'niːs ◄
Vietcong, Viet Cong ˌvi: et 'kɒŋ ◄ -ɪt-, vi‿ˌet-
‖ -'kɑːŋ ◄ -'kɔːŋ
Vietminh, Viet Minh ˌviː et 'mɪn ◄ -ɪt-, vi‿ˌet-
Vietnam, Viet Nam ˌvi: et 'næm ◄ -ɪt-, vi‿ˌet-,
-'nɑːm ‖ -'nɑːm
Vietnamese vi ˌet nə 'miːz ◄ ˌviː et-,
ˌviː ɪt- ‖ -'miːs

view vjuː **viewed** vjuːd **viewing** 'vjuː ɪŋ
  views vjuz
viewdata, V~ 'vjuː ˌdeɪt ə -ˌdɑːt- ‖ -ˌdeɪt̬ ə
  -ˌdæt̬-, -ˌdɑːt̬-
viewer 'vjuːˌ_ə ‖ _ʳr ~**s** z
viewfinder 'vjuː ˌfaɪnd ə ‖ -ʳr ~**s** z
Viewgraph *tdmk* 'vjuː grɑːf -græf ‖ -græf ~**s** s
viewpoint 'vjuː pɔɪnt ~**s** s
Vigar 'vaɪg ə -ɑː ‖ -ʳr -ɑːr
vigesimal vaɪ 'dʒes ɪm ᵊl -əm-
vigil 'vɪdʒ ɪl -ᵊl ~**s** z
vigilance 'vɪdʒ əl ənts -ɪl-
  'vigilance comˌmittee
vigilant 'vɪdʒ əl ənt -ɪl- ~**ly** li
vigilante ˌvɪdʒ ɪ 'lænt i -ə- ‖ -'læn̬t̬ i -'lɑːn̬t̬- ~**s**
  z
vigilantism ˌvɪdʒ ɪ 'læn ˌtɪz əm -ə-
vignette vɪn 'jet viːn- —*Fr* [vi ɲɛt] ~**s** s
Vigo (i) 'viːg əʊ ‖ -oʊ, (ii) 'vaɪg- —*Sp* ['bi ɣo].
  —*For the place in Spain, usually (i); as a*
  personal, place or street name in English-
  speaking countries, often (ii).
vigor 'vɪg ə ‖ -ʳr
vigorous 'vɪg ər_əs ~**ly** li ~**ness** nəs nɪs
vigour 'vɪg ə ‖ -ʳr
Viking, v~ 'vaɪk ɪŋ ~**s** z
Vikki 'vɪk i
vile vaɪᵊl **viler** 'vaɪᵊl ə ‖ -ʳr **vilest** 'vaɪᵊl ɪst
  -əst
Vileda *tdmk* vaɪ 'liːd ə
vile|ly 'vaɪᵊl |li ~**ness** nəs nɪs
vilification ˌvɪl ɪf ɪ 'keɪʃ ᵊn ˌ•əf-, §-ə'•-
vili|fy 'vɪl ɪ |faɪ -ə- ~**fied** faɪd ~**fier/s** faɪ_ə/z
  ‖ faɪ_ʳr/z ~**fies** faɪz ~**fying** faɪ ɪŋ
villa, Villa 'vɪl ə ~**s** z
Villa *Spanish name* 'viːl jə 'viː ə —*Sp* ['bi ʎa,
  -ja]
village 'vɪl ɪdʒ ~**es** ɪz əz
villager 'vɪl ɪdʒ ə §-ədʒ- ‖ -ʳr ~**s** z
villain 'vɪl ən ~**s** z
villainous 'vɪl ən əs ~**ly** li ~**ness** nəs nɪs
villain|y 'vɪl ən |i ~**ies** iz
Villa-Lobos ˌviːl ə 'ləʊb ɒs ˌviː-, -jə-
  ‖ -'loʊb oʊs -əs, -oʊʃ —*BrPort* [ˌvi la 'lo bus]
villanella ˌvɪl ə 'nel ə ~**s** z
villanelle ˌvɪl ə 'nel ~**s** z
Villanovan ˌvɪl ə 'nəʊv ən ◄ ‖ -'noʊv-
-ville vɪl — **dullsville** 'dʌlz vɪl
villein 'vɪl eɪn -ɪn, -ən ~**s** z
villeinage, villenage 'vɪl ən ɪdʒ -eɪn-, -ɪn-
Villeneuve 'viːᵊl nɜːv ‖ ˌviːᵊl 'nuːv —*Fr*
  [vil nœːv]
villi 'vɪl aɪ
Villiers (i) 'vɪl əz ‖ -ʳrz, (ii) 'vɪl i_əz ‖ _ʳrz
Villon 'viː ɒ̃ 'vɪl ən —*Fr* [vi jɔ̃, -lɔ̃]
villosit|y vɪ 'lɒs ət |i -ɪt- ‖ vɪ 'lɑːs ət̬ |i ~**ies** iz
villous 'vɪl əs ~**ly** li
vill|us 'vɪl |əs ~**i** aɪ iː
Vilnius, Vilnyus 'vɪl ni_əs -ʊs
vim, Vim *tdmk* vɪm
Vimto *tdmk* 'vɪm təʊ ‖ -toʊ
vin væ̃ væn —*Fr* [væ̃]
  ˌvin 'blanc blɒ̃ blɒŋ ‖ blɑːn —*Fr* [blɑ̃]

Viña del Mar ˌviːn jə del 'mɑː ‖ -'mɑːr —*AmSp*
  [ˌbi ɲa ðel 'maɾ]
vinaceous vaɪ 'neɪʃ əs vɪ-, §və-
vinaigrette ˌvɪn eɪ 'gret -ɪ-, -ə- ~**s** s
vinca 'vɪŋk ə ~**s** z
Vince vɪnts
Vincennes (i) væn 'sen væ- —*Fr* [væ̃ sɛn]; (ii)
  vɪn 'senz —*In France, (i); in Indiana, (ii).*
Vincent 'vɪnts ᵊnt
Vincentian vɪn 'sentʃ ᵊn ~**s** z
Vinci 'vɪntʃ i —*It* ['vin tʃi]
vinculum 'vɪŋk jʊl əm -jəl- ‖ -jəl-
vindaloo ˌvɪnd ə 'luː ~**s** z
vindi|cate 'vɪnd ɪ |keɪt §-ə- ~**cated** keɪt ɪd -əd
  ‖ keɪt̬ əd ~**cates** keɪts ~**cating**
  keɪt ɪŋ ‖ keɪt̬ ɪŋ
vindication ˌvɪnd ɪ 'keɪʃ ᵊn §-ə-
vindictive vɪn 'dɪkt ɪv ~**ly** li ~**ness** nəs nɪs
vin du pays ˌvæn du peɪ 'iː, ˌvæ̃-, ˌ•dju- —*Fr*
  [væ̃ dy pe i]
vine, Vine vaɪn **vines** vaɪnz
vinegar 'vɪn ɪg ə §-əg- ‖ -ʳr ~**s** z
vinegary 'vɪn ɪg ər_i §'•əg-
Vineland 'vaɪn lənd
Viner 'vaɪn ə ‖ -ʳr
viner|y 'vaɪn ər |i ~**ies** iz
vineyard 'vɪn jəd -jɑːd ‖ -jᵊrd ~**s** z
vingt-et-un ˌvænt eɪ 'ɜ̃ː, ˌvæt-, -'ɜːn ‖ -'ʊn -'ʌn
  —*Fr* [væ̃ te œ̃, -æ̃]
vinho verde ˌviːn əʊ 'vɜːd i ‖ -oʊ 'vɝːd i
  —*Port* [ˌvi ɲu 'veɾ di]
vinic 'vaɪn ɪk 'vɪn-
viniculture 'vɪn i ˌkʌltʃ ə 'vaɪn-, §'•ə- ‖ -ʳr
Vinland 'vɪn lənd -lænd
vino 'viːn əʊ ‖ -oʊ
vin ordinaire ˌvæn ˌɔːd ɪ 'neə -ə-
  ‖ -ˌɔːrd ᵊn 'eʳr —*Fr* [væ̃ nɔʁ di nɛːʁ]
vinosity vaɪ 'nɒs ət i vɪ-, §və-, -ɪt- ‖ -'nɑːs ət̬ i
vinous 'vaɪn əs
vin rouge ˌvæn 'ruːʒ ˌvæ̃- —*Fr* [væ̃ ʁuʒ]
vintage 'vɪnt ɪdʒ ‖ 'vɪn̬t̬ ɪdʒ ~**es** ɪz əz
  ˌvintage 'car; ˌvintage 'year
vintner 'vɪnt nə ‖ -nʳr ~**s** z
vinyl 'vaɪn ᵊl -ɪl ~**s** z
  ˌvinyl 'chloride
vinylidene vaɪ 'nɪl ɪ diːn -ə-
viol 'vaɪ_əl ‖ 'vaɪ_ᵊl -oʊl ~**s** z
viola *'kind of flower'*, **Viola** *personal name*
  'vaɪ_əl ə 'viːˌ_, -əʊl ə; vi 'əʊl ə, vaɪ-
  ‖ vaɪ 'oʊl ə vi-; 'vaɪ əl ə ~**s**, ~**'s** z
viola *'musical instrument'* vi 'əʊl ə vaɪ-; 'viːˌ_əl ə
  ‖ vi 'oʊl ə ~**s** z
  viˌola da 'gamba də 'gæm bə ‖ -'gɑːm-;
  viˌola d'a'more dæ 'mɔːr i -eɪ ‖ dɑː 'mɔːr eɪ
vio|late 'vaɪ_ə |leɪt ~**lated** leɪt ɪd -əd ‖ leɪt̬ əd
  ~**lates** leɪts ~**lating** leɪt ɪŋ ‖ leɪt̬ ɪŋ
violation ˌvaɪ_ə 'leɪʃ ᵊn ~**s** z
violator 'vaɪ_ə leɪt ə ‖ -leɪt̬ ʳr ~**s** z
violence 'vaɪ_əl ənts §'vaɪl ənts
violent 'vaɪ_əl ənt §'vaɪl ənt ~**ly** li
violet, V~ 'vaɪ_əl ət -ɪt; §'vaɪl ət, -ɪt ~**s** s
violin ˌvaɪ_ə 'lɪn '••• ~**s** z
violinist ˌvaɪ_ə 'lɪn ɪst §-əst, '•••• ~**s** s

violist *'viola player'* vi 'əʊl ıst §-əst ‖ -'oʊl- ~s
s
violist *'viol player'* 'vaɪ_əl ıst §-əst ~s s
violoncellist ˌvaɪ_əl ən 'tʃel ıst §-əst ~s s
violoncello ˌvaɪ_əl ən 'tʃel əʊ ‖ -oʊ ~s z
violone 'vaɪ_ə ləʊn 'viː_; ˌviː_ə 'ləʊn eɪ
‖ ˌviː ə 'loʊn eɪ ~s z
VIP ˌviː aɪ 'piː ~s, ~'s z
viper 'vaɪp ə ‖ -ər ~s z
viperine 'vaɪp ə raın
viperish 'vaɪp ər_ıʃ
viperous 'vaɪp ər_əs
virago və 'rɑːg əʊ vɪ- ‖ -oʊ ~es, ~s z
viral 'vaɪər əl
vire 'vaɪ_ə vɪə ‖ 'vaɪ_ər vɪər vired 'vaɪ_əd
vɪəd ‖ 'vaɪ_ərd vɪərd vires 'vaɪ_əz vɪəz
‖ 'vaɪ_ərz vɪərz viring 'vaɪ_ər ıŋ 'vɪər ıŋ
‖ 'vaɪ_ər ıŋ 'vɪr ıŋ
virement 'vaɪ_ə mənt 'vɪə mɒ̃ ‖ 'vaɪ_ər mənt
vɪr 'mɑːn —Fr [viʁ mɑ̃]
vireo 'vɪr i əʊ ‖ -oʊ ~s z
vires *Latin, 'powers'* 'vaɪər iːz
vires *3 sing of vire* 'vaɪ_əz vɪəz ‖ 'vaɪ_ərz vɪərz
Virgil 'vɜːdʒ ıl -əl ‖ 'vɝːdʒ əl
Virgilian vɜː 'dʒɪl i_ən və- ‖ vɝː-
virgin, V~ 'vɜːdʒ ın §-ən ‖ 'vɝːdʒ ən ~s z
ˌvirgin 'birth; 'Virgin ˌIslands ‖ ˌ• • '• • •;
ˌVirgin 'Mary; ˌVirgin 'Queen
virginal 'vɜːdʒ ın əl -ən- ‖ 'vɝːdʒ- ~s z
Virginia, v~ və 'dʒɪn i_ə ‖ vər 'dʒɪn jə
Vir,ginia 'Beach; vir,ginia 'creeper;
Vir,ginia 'reel
Virginian və 'dʒɪn i_ən ‖ vər 'dʒɪn jən ~s z
virginity və 'dʒɪn ət i vɜː-, -ıt- ‖ vər 'dʒɪn ət̬ i
Virgo 'vɜːg əʊ ‖ 'vɝːg oʊ ~s z
ˌvirgo in'tacta ın 'tækt ə
virgule 'vɜːg juːl ‖ 'vɝːg- ~s z
viridescence ˌvɪr ı 'des ənts ˌ•ə-
viridescent ˌvɪr ı 'des ənt ◄ ˌ•ə-
viridian və 'rɪd i_ən vɪ-
virile 'vɪr aɪəl ‖ -əl (*)
virility və 'rɪl ət i vɪ-, -ıt- ‖ -ət̬ i
virion 'vaɪər i_ən 'vɪr-, -ɒn ‖ -i ɑːn ~s z
viroid 'vaɪər ɔɪd 'vɪr-
Virol *tdmk* 'vaɪər ɒl ‖ -ɑːl -ɔːl, -oʊl
virologist vaɪə 'rɒl ədʒ ıst §-əst ‖ -'rɑːl- ~s s
virology vaɪə 'rɒl ədʒ i ‖ -'rɑːl-
virtu vɜː 'tuː ‖ vɝː-
virtual 'vɜːtʃ u_əl 'vɜːt ju_ ‖ 'vɝːtʃ u_əl '•_əl
~ly i
virtue 'vɜːtʃ uː 'vɜːt juː ‖ 'vɝːtʃ uː ~s z
virtuosic ˌvɜːtʃ u 'ɒs ık ◄ ˌvɜːt ju-, -'əʊs-
‖ ˌvɝːtʃ u 'ɑːs ık ◄
virtuosity ˌvɜːtʃ u 'ɒs ət i ˌvɜːt ju-, -ıt i
‖ ˌvɝːtʃ u 'ɑːs ət̬ i
virtuoso ˌvɜːtʃ u 'əʊs əʊ ◄ ˌvɜːt ju-, -'əʊz-
‖ ˌvɝːtʃ u 'oʊs oʊ ◄ -'oʊz- ~s z
virtuous 'vɜːtʃ u_əs 'vɜːt ju_ ‖ 'vɝːtʃ- ~ly li
~ness nəs nıs
virulenc|e 'vɪr ʊl ənts -jʊl-, -jəl-, -əl- ‖ -əl-
-jəl- ~y i

virulent 'vɪr ʊl ənt -jʊl-, -jəl-, -əl- ‖ -əl- -jəl-
~ly li
virus 'vaɪər əs ~es ız əz
vis vıs

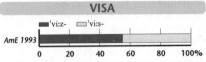

visa, Visa *tdmk* 'viːz ə ‖ 'viːs- —*AmE 1993 poll
panel preference:* 'viːz- 55%, 'viːs- 45%.
~ed d visaing 'viːz ər ıŋ ‖ 'viːz ə ıŋ 'viːs-
~s z
visag|e 'vız ıdʒ ~es ız əz
-visaged 'vız ıdʒd — grim-visaged
ˌgrım 'vız ıdʒd ◄
visagist 'vız ədʒ ıst §-əst ~s s
visagiste ˌviːz ɑː 'ʒiːst ~s s
Visalia vı 'seıl i_ə vaı-
vis-a-vis, vis-à-vis ˌviːz ə 'viː ◄ ˌvız-, -ɑː-, -æ-
viscacha vı 'skɑːtʃ ə -'skætʃ ə ~s z
viscera 'vıs ər ə
visceral 'vıs ər əl
viscid 'vıs ıd §-əd ~ly li ~ness nəs nıs
Visconti vı 'skɒnt i ‖ -'skɔːnt i -'skɑːnt- —*It*
[vis 'kon ti]
viscose 'vısk əʊs -əʊz ‖ -oʊs -oʊz
viscosit|y vı 'skɒs ət |i -ıt- ‖ -'skɑːs ət̬ |i ~ies
iz
viscount 'vaı kaʊnt ~s s
viscount|cy 'vaı kaʊnt |si ~sies siz
viscountess ˌvaı kaʊn 'tes ◄ 'vaı kaʊnt ıs, -əs
‖ 'vaı kaʊnt̬ əs ~es ız əz
viscous 'vısk əs ~ly li ~ness nəs nıs
vise vaıs (= *vice*) vises 'vaıs ız -əz
Vise-Grips *tdmk* 'vaıs grıps
Vishnu 'vıʃ nuː
visibilit|y ˌvız ə 'bıl ət |i ˌ•ı-, -ıt i ‖ -ət̬ |i ~ies
iz
visib|le 'vız əb |əl -ıb- ~les əlz ~ly li
ˌvisible 'speech
VisiCalc *tdmk* 'vız i kælk
Visigoth 'vız i gɒθ 'vıs- ‖ -gɑːθ ~s s
vision 'vıʒ ən ~s z
visionar|y 'vıʒ ən ər_|i ‖ -ə ner |i ~ies iz
vis|it 'vız ıt §-ət ‖ -ət ~ited ıt ıd §ət-, -əd
‖ ət̬ əd ~iting ıt ıŋ §ət- ‖ ət̬ ıŋ ~its ıts §əts
‖ əts
'visiting card; ˌvisiting 'fireman; ˌvisiting
pro'fessor
visitant 'vız ıt ənt §-ət- ~s s
visitation ˌvız ı 'teıʃ ən §-ə- ~s z
visitor 'vız ıt ə §-ət- ‖ -ət̬ ər ~s z
'visitors' book
visna 'vız nə 'vıs-
visor 'vaız ə ‖ -ər ~s z
vista 'vıst ə ~s z
Vistula 'vıst jʊl ə 'vıs tʃəl ə ‖ 'vıs tʃʊl ə
—*Polish* Wisła ['vis wa]
visual 'vıʒ u_əl 'vız ju_, 'vıʒ ju_ ~ly i ~s z
ˌvisual 'aid; ˌvisual di'splay ˌunit
visualis... —*see* visualiz...

visualization ˌvɪʒ u‿əl aɪ 'zeɪʃ ən ˌvɪz ju‿,
ˌvɪʒ ju‿, -ɪ'•- ‖ -ə 'zeɪʃ ən ˌvɪʒ əl ə'•• ~s z
visualiz|e 'vɪʒ u‿ə laɪz 'vɪz ju‿, 'vɪʒ ju‿
‖ 'vɪʒ ə laɪz ~ed d ~es ɪz əz ~ing ɪŋ
vita 'viːt ə 'vaɪt- ‖ 'viːt̬ ə 'vaɪt̬- ~s z
Vitaglass *tdmk* 'vaɪt ə glɑːs ‖ 'vaɪt̬ ə glæs
vital 'vaɪt ᵊl ‖ 'vaɪt̬ ᵊl ~ly i ~s z
ˌvital ca'pacity; ˌvital 'signs; ˌvital
sta'tistics
vitalis... *see* **vitaliz...**
vitality vaɪ 'tæl ət i -ɪt- ‖ -ət̬ i
vitaliz|e 'vaɪt ə laɪz -ᵊl aɪz ‖ 'vaɪt̬ ᵊl ɪz ~ed d
~es ɪz əz ~ing ɪŋ
vitally 'vaɪt ᵊl i ‖ 'vaɪt̬ ᵊl i
vitamin 'vɪt əm ɪn 'vaɪt-, §-ən ‖ 'vaɪt̬- ~s z
ˌvitamin 'C
VitBe *tdmk* 'vɪt bi
vitelline vɪ 'tel aɪn -ɪn, §-ən
viti|ate 'vɪʃ i |eɪt ~ated eɪt ɪd-əd ‖ eɪt̬ əd
~ates eɪts ~ating eɪt ɪŋ ‖ eɪt̬ ɪŋ
vitiation ˌvɪʃ i 'eɪʃ ən
viticulture 'vɪt i ˌkʌltʃ ə 'vaɪt-, §'•ə-
‖ 'vɪt̬ ə ˌkʌltʃ ər
Viti Levu ˌviːt i 'lev uː
vitiligo ˌvɪt ɪ 'laɪg əʊ -ə-, ˌvɪt ᵊl 'aɪg-
‖ ˌvɪt̬ ᵊl 'aɪg oʊ
vitreous 'vɪtr i‿əs ~ness nəs nɪs
vitrifaction ˌvɪtr ɪ 'fæk ʃᵊn-ə-
vitrification ˌvɪtr ɪf ɪ 'keɪʃ ᵊn, •əf-, §-ə'•-
vitri|fy 'vɪtr ɪ |faɪ -ə- ~fied faɪd ~fies faɪz
~fying faɪ ɪŋ
vitriol 'vɪtr i‿əl-ɒl
vitriolic ˌvɪtr i 'ɒl ɪk ◂ ‖ -'ɑːl- ~ally ᵊl‿i
vitro 'viːtr əʊ ‖ -oʊ
Vitruvius vɪ 'truːv i‿əs və-
Vittel *tdmk* vɪ 'tel
vitupe|rate vaɪ 'tjuːp ə |reɪt vɪ-, §və-,
→§-'tʃuːp- ‖ -'tuːp- -'tjuːp-
vituperation vaɪ ˌtjuːp ə 'reɪʃ ᵊn vɪ-, §və-,
→§-ˌtʃuːp- ‖ -ˌtuːp- -ˌtjuːp-
vituperative vaɪ 'tjuːp ᵊr‿ət ɪv vɪ-, §və-,
→§-'tʃuːp-, -ə reɪt- ‖ -'tuːp ᵊr‿ət̬ ɪv -'tjuːp-,
-ə reɪt̬-
Vitus 'vaɪt əs ‖ 'vaɪt̬ əs
viva *'oral examination'* 'vaɪv ə ~ed d **vivaing**
'vaɪv ᵊr‿ɪŋ ‖ 'vaɪv ə ɪŋ ~s z
viva *'long live'* , **Viva** *tdmk* 'viːv ə ~s z
vivace vɪ 'vɑːtʃ i §və-, -eɪ
vivacious vɪ 'veɪʃ əs §və-, vaɪ- ~ly li ~ness
nəs nɪs
vivacity vɪ 'væs ət i §və-, -ɪt- ‖ -ət̬ i
Vivaldi vɪ 'væld i ‖ -'vɑːld- —*It* [vi 'val di]
vivari|um vaɪ 'veər i‿|əm vɪ-, §və- ‖ -'ver-
-'væər- ~a ə ~ums əmz
vivat 'vaɪv æt 'viːv- ‖ -ɑːt ~s s
viva voce ˌvaɪv ə 'vəʊtʃ i ˌviːv-, -'vəʊs-
‖ -'voʊtʃ- -'voʊs-
vivax 'vaɪv æks
Vivian 'vɪv i‿ən
vivid 'vɪv ɪd §-əd ~ly li ~ness nəs nɪs
Vivien 'vɪv i‿ən
Vivienne *(i)* 'vɪv i‿ən, *(ii)* ˌvɪv i 'en
vivification ˌvɪv ɪf ɪ 'keɪʃ ᵊn §, •əf-, §-ə'•-

vivi|fy 'vɪv ɪ |faɪ §-ə- ~fied faɪd ~fier/s faɪ‿ə/z
‖ faɪ‿ər/z ~fies faɪz ~fying faɪ ɪŋ
viviparous vɪ 'vɪp ᵊr əs vaɪ-, §və- ~ly li
vivisect 'vɪv ɪ sekt -ə-, ˌ•• '• ~ed ɪd əd ~ing
ɪŋ ~s s
vivisection ˌvɪv ɪ 'sek ʃᵊn §-ə-
vivisectionist ˌvɪv ɪ 'sek ʃᵊn‿ɪst §, •ə-, §‿əst
~s s
vixen 'vɪks ən ~s z
vixenish 'vɪks ən ɪʃ
Viyella *tdmk* vaɪ 'el ə
viz, viz. vɪz —*Usually read aloud as* namely
'neɪm li
vizier vɪ 'zɪə §və-; 'vɪz ɪə ‖ və 'zɪər ~s z
vizsla 'vɪʒ lə —*Hung* ['viʒ lɒ] ~s z
Vlach vlɑːk **Vlachs** vlɑːks
Vlad vlæd —*Romanian* [vlad]
Vladimir 'vlæd ɪ mɪə -ə- ‖ -ə mɪr —*Russ*
[vɫʌ 'dʲi mʲɪr], *Czech* Vladimír ['vla dʲɪ miːr]
Vladivostok ˌvlæd ɪ 'vɒst ɒk §-ə- ‖ -'vɑːst ɑːk
—*Russ* [vɫə dʲɪ vʌ 'stɔk]
VLSI ˌviː el es 'aɪ
Vltava 'vʊlt əv ə —*Czech* ['vl ta va]
V-neck 'viː nek, •'• ~ed t ~s s
vocab 'vəʊk æb ‖ 'voʊk-
vocabular|y vəʊ 'kæb jʊl ər li-ɪ-'•jəl-; §-ju ler i,
§-'•jə-, §-'•ə- ‖ voʊ 'kæb jə ler li və- ~ies
ɪz
vocal 'vəʊk ᵊl ‖ 'voʊk ᵊl ~ly i ~s z
ˌvocal 'cords, '••• ‖ '••• •; ˌvocal 'folds
‖ '•• •
vocalic vəʊ 'kæl ɪk ‖ voʊ- və-
vocalis... —*see* **vocaliz...**
vocalism 'vəʊk ə ˌlɪz əm-ᵊl ˌɪz- ‖ 'voʊk-
vocalist 'vəʊk ᵊl ɪst §-əst ‖ 'voʊk- ~s s
vocalization ˌvəʊk ᵊl aɪ 'zeɪʃ ᵊn -ɪ'•-
‖ ˌvoʊk ᵊl ə- ~s z
vocaliz|e 'vəʊk ə laɪz-ᵊl aɪz ‖ 'voʊk- ~ed d
~es ɪz əz ~ing ɪŋ
vocally 'vəʊk ᵊl i ‖ 'voʊk-
vocation vəʊ 'keɪʃ ᵊn ‖ voʊ- ~s z
vocational vəʊ 'keɪʃ ᵊn‿ᵊl ‖ voʊ- ~ly i
vocative 'vɒk ət ɪv ‖ 'vɑːk ət̬ ɪv ~s z
Voce vəʊs ‖ voʊs
vocife|rate vəʊ 'sɪf ə |reɪt ‖ voʊ- ~rated
reɪt ɪd-əd ‖ reɪt̬ əd ~rates reɪts ~rating
reɪt ɪŋ ‖ reɪt̬ ɪŋ
vociferation vəʊ ˌsɪf ə 'reɪʃ ᵊn ‖ voʊ- ~s z
vociferous vəʊ 'sɪf ᵊr‿əs ‖ voʊ- ~ly li ~ness
nəs nɪs
vocoder ˌvəʊ 'kəʊd ə ‖ ˌvoʊ 'koʊd ər ~s z
vocoid 'vəʊk ɔɪd ‖ 'voʊk- ~s z
vocoidal vəʊ 'kɔɪd ᵊl ‖ voʊ-
Vodafone *tdmk* 'vəʊd ə fəʊn ‖ 'voʊd ə foʊn ~s
z
vodka 'vɒd kə ‖ 'vɑːd kə ~s z
voe, Voe vəʊ ‖ voʊ **voes** vəʊz ‖ voʊz
Vogt *(i)* vəʊkt ‖ voʊkt, *(ii)* vəʊt ‖ voʊt, *(iii)*
vɒt ‖ vɑːt
vogue vəʊg ‖ voʊg **vogues** vəʊgz ‖ voʊgz
voguish 'vəʊg ɪʃ ‖ 'voʊg- ~ness nəs nɪs
Vogul 'vəʊg ʊl -ᵊl ‖ 'voʊg- ~s z

voice vɔɪs **voiced** vɔɪst **voices** 'vɔɪs ɪz -əz
　voicing 'vɔɪs ɪŋ
　'**voice box**
-voiced 'vɔɪst — **gruff-voiced** ˌɡrʌf 'vɔɪst ◄
voiceless 'vɔɪs ləs -lɪs **~ly** li **~ness** nəs nɪs
voice-mail 'vɔɪs meɪəl
voice-over 'vɔɪs ˌəʊv ə ˌˈ▪ˈ▪▪ ‖ -ˌoʊv ər **~s** z
voiceprint 'vɔɪs prɪnt **~s** s
void vɔɪd **voided** 'vɔɪd ɪd -əd **voiding**
　'vɔɪd ɪŋ **voids** vɔɪdz
voidable 'vɔɪd əb əl **~ness** nəs nɪs
voidance 'vɔɪd ənts
Voight, Voigt vɔɪt
voila, voilà vwæ 'lɑː vwʌ-, vwɑː- ‖ vwɑː-
　—Fr [vwa la]
voile vɔɪəl vwɑːl *—Fr* [vwal]
voix vwɑː *—Fr* [vwa]
　ˌvoix ce'leste, ˌvoix cé'leste sɪ 'lest sə-
　—Fr [se lɛst]
Vojvodina ˌvɔɪv ə 'diːn ə *—S-Cr*
　["vɔj vɔ di na]
vol, vol. vɒl ‖ vɑːl *—or as* volume
volant 'vəʊl ənt ‖ 'voʊl-
Volapuk, Volapük 'vɒl ə puːk 'vəʊl-, -pʊk,
　ˌ▪▪'▪ ‖ 'voʊl- 'vɑːl- *—Volapük* ['vo la pyk]
volatile 'vɒl ə taɪəl ‖ 'vɑːl ət əl *(*)* **~s** z *—but
　see also* **sal volatile**
volatilis... *—see* **volatiliz...**
volatility ˌvɒl ə 'tɪl ət i -ɪt i ‖ ˌvɑːl ə 'tɪl ət i
volatilization və ˌlæt ɪl aɪ 'zeɪʃ ən vɒ-, vəʊ-,
　-ˌ▪əl-, -ɪ'▪▪; ˌvɒl ət- ‖ ˌvɑːl ət əl‿ə 'zeɪʃ ən
volatiliz|e və 'læt ɪ laɪz vɒ-, vəʊ-, 'vɒl ət-,
　-ə laɪz, -əl aɪz ‖ 'vɑːl ət əl aɪz **~ed** d **~es** ɪz
　əz **~ing** ɪŋ
vol-au-vent 'vɒl ə vɒ̃ 'vəʊl-, -əʊ-, -vɒn, -vɒŋ,
　ˌ▪▪'▪ ‖ ˌvɔːl oʊ 'vɑːn ˌvɑːl- *—Fr* [vɔ lo vɑ̃]
　~s z
volcanic vɒl 'kæn ɪk ‖ vɑːl- **~ally** əl‿i
volcanism 'vɒlk ə ˌnɪz əm
volcano vɒl 'keɪn əʊ ‖ vɑːl 'keɪn oʊ **~s** z
volcanological ˌvɒlk ən ə 'lɒdʒ ɪk əl ◄
　‖ ˌvɑːlk ən ə 'lɑːdʒ- **~ly** ‿i
volcanologist ˌvɒlk ə 'nɒl ədʒ ɪst §-əst
　‖ ˌvɑːlk ə 'nɑːl- **~s** s
volcanology ˌvɒlk ə 'nɒl ədʒ i ‖ ˌvɑːlk ə 'nɑːl-
vole vəʊl →vɒʊl ‖ voʊl **voles** vəʊlz →vɒʊlz
　‖ voʊlz
volenti non fit injuria vəʊ ˌlent i ˌnəʊn fɪt
　ɪn 'dʒʊər i‿ə vɒ-, -ˌnɒn-, -'jʊər-
　‖ voʊ ˌlent i ˌnɑːn fɪt ɪn 'dʒʊr i‿ə
Volga 'vɒlɡ ə ‖ 'vɑːlɡ ə *—Russ* ['vɔɫ ɡə]
Volgograd 'vɒlɡ əʊ ɡræd ‖ 'vɑːlɡ ə- *—Russ*
　[vəɫ ɡʌ 'ɡrat]
volitant 'vɒl ɪt ənt -ət- ‖ 'vɑːl-
volition və 'lɪʃ ən ‖ voʊ- və-
volitional və 'lɪʃ ən‿əl ‖ voʊ- və- **~ly** i
volitive 'vɒl ət ɪv -ɪt- ‖ 'vɑːl ət ɪv
Volk *family name (i)* vɒlk ‖ vɑːlk, *(ii)* vəʊlk
　→vɒʊlk ‖ voʊlk
Volk *German, 'people'* fɒlk vɒlk ‖ fɔːlk fɑːlk
　—Ger [fɔlk]
Volkswagen *tdmk* 'vɒlks ˌwæɡ ən 'vəʊks-,

'fɒlks-, -ˌwɑːɡ-, -ˌvɑːɡ- ‖ 'voʊks- -ˌwɑːɡ-
　—Ger ['fɔlks ˌvɑːɡ ən] **~s** z
volley 'vɒl i ‖ 'vɑːl i **~ed** d **~ing** ɪŋ **~s** z
volleyball 'vɒl i bɔːl ‖ 'vɑːl- -bɑːl
volplan|e 'vɒl pleɪn ‖ 'vɑːl- **~ed** d **~es** z **~ing**
　ɪŋ
Volpone vɒl 'pəʊn i ‖ vɑːl 'poʊn i vɔːl-
Volsci 'vɒls ki -aɪ, -iː ‖ 'vɑːls-
Volscian 'vɒls ki‿ən ‖ 'vɑːls- **~s** z
Volstead 'vɒl sted ‖ 'vɑːl-
volt vəʊlt →vɒʊlt, vɒlt ‖ voʊlt **volts** vəʊlts
　→vɒʊlts, vɒlts ‖ voʊlts
volta *dance, piece of music, 'time, turn'*
　'vɒlt ə ‖ 'voʊlt ə 'vɑːlt- *—It* ['vɔl ta] **~s** z
Volta *lake and river* 'vɒlt ə ‖ 'voʊlt ə
Volta *physicist* 'vəʊlt ə 'vɒlt- ‖ 'voʊlt ə *—It*
　['vɔl ta]
voltag|e 'vəʊlt ɪdʒ →'vɒʊlt-, 'vɒlt- ‖ 'voʊlt-
　~es ɪz əz
voltaic, V~ vɒl 'teɪ ɪk vəʊl- ‖ vɑːl- voʊl-
Voltaire vɒl 'teə vəʊl-, '▪▪ ‖ voʊl 'teər *—Fr*
　[vɔl tɛːʁ]
volte-fac|e ˌvɒlt 'fɑːs -'fæs ‖ ˌvɔːlt 'fɑːs ˌvɑːlt-,
　ˌvoʊlt- *—Fr* [vɔl tə fas] **~es** ɪz əz *—or as
　sing.*
voltmeter 'vəʊlt ˌmiːt ə 'vɒlt- ‖ 'voʊlt ˌmiːt ̮ər
　~s z
volubility ˌvɒl ju 'bɪl ət i, ˌ▪jə-, -ɪt i
　‖ ˌvɑːl jə 'bɪl ət i
volub|le 'vɒl jub əl §-jəb- ‖ 'vɑːl jəb əl
　~leness əl nəs -nɪs **~ly** li
volume 'vɒl juːm -jʊm ‖ 'vɑːl jəm -jʊm -juːm
　~s z
volumetric ˌvɒl ju 'metr ɪk ◄ §-jə- ‖ ˌvɑːl jə-
　~ally əl‿i
voluminous və 'luːm ɪn əs vɒ-, -'ljuːm-, -ən-
　~ly li **~ness** nəs nɪs

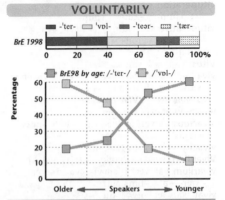

VOLUNTARILY

■ -'ter-　☐ 'vɒl-　■ -'teər-　▨ -'tær-

BrE 1998

0　20　40　60　80　100%

BrE98 by age: /-'ter-/　/'vɒl-/

Percentage
60
50
40
30
20
10
0

Older ◄——— Speakers ———► Younger

voluntarily ˌvɒl ən 'ter əl i -'teər-, -'tær-, -ɪ li;
　'vɒl ənt ̮ər əl i, -ɪ li ‖ ˌvɑːl ən 'ter əl i -'tær-;
　'▪▪▪▪▪ *—BrE 1998 poll panel preference:*
　-'ter- 40%, 'vɒl- 32%, -'teər- 15%, -'tær-
　12%.
voluntar|y 'vɒl ənt ̮ər |i -ən ter-
　‖ 'vɑːl ən ter li **~ies** iz **~iness** i nəs i nɪs
volunteer ˌvɒl ən 'tɪə ‖ ˌvɑːl ən 'tɪər **~ed** d

Voiced and voiceless

1 Voiced sounds are produced with the vocal folds vibrating – opening and closing rapidly, producing **voice**. **Voiceless** sounds are made with the vocal folds apart, allowing the air to pass freely between them.

2 The sounds p, t, k, tʃ, f, θ, s, ʃ, h are normally voiceless, while the remaining English sounds are classified as voiced.

3 There is a difficulty with this classification, since it refers to PHONEMES – yet in reality a given English phoneme may have both voiced and voiceless ALLOPHONEs. For example, in AmE the 'voiceless' phoneme /t/ includes the voiced allophone [t̬], which is so noticeable that LPD gives it a separate symbol (see T-VOICING).

4 Another difficulty arises with b, d, g, dʒ, v, ð, z, ʒ. It is only when they are between other voiced sounds that these consonants are reliably voiced. In other positions there is often little or no actual vibration of the vocal folds during their production. Hence they are sometimes classified as **lenis** rather than as voiced. The corresponding term for p, t, k, tʃ, f, θ, s, ʃ is **fortis**, rather than voiceless.

5 A **devoiced** lenis does not sound quite like a fortis. Quite apart from differences such as those described in the notes at ASPIRATION and CLIPPING, b, d, g etc. have less articulatory force than p, t, k etc. This may be due to the vocal folds, which in the case of a devoiced lenis sound probably remain in the narrowed ''whisper'' configuration, distinct from their wide open configuration for a true voiceless (fortis) sound.

volunteering ˌvɒl ən ˈtɪər ɪŋ ‖ ˌvɑːl ən ˈtɪr ɪŋ
~**s** z
voluptuar|y və ˈlʌp tʃu‿ər |i -ˈlʌp tju‿,
-ˈlʌp tʃər |i ‖ -tʃu er |i ~**ies** iz
voluptuous və ˈlʌp tʃu‿əs -tju‿əs ~**ly** li ~**ness**
nəs nɪs
volute və ˈluːt vɒ-, vəʊ-, -ˈljuːt ~**s** s
voluted və ˈluːt ɪd vɒ-, vəʊ-, -ˈljuːt-, -əd
‖ -ˈluːt̬ əd
volution və ˈluːʃ ən vɒ-, vəʊ-, -ˈljuːʃ-
volv|a ˈvɒlv |ə ‖ ˈvɑːlv |ə ~**ae** iː
Volvic tdmk ˈvɒlv ɪk ‖ ˈvɑːlv- ˈvoʊlv-
Volvo tdmk ˈvɒlv əʊ ‖ ˈvɑːlv oʊ ˈvoʊlv- ~**s** z
volvox ˈvɒlv ɒks ‖ ˈvɑːlv ɑːks
vomer ˈvəʊm ə ‖ ˈvoʊm ər ~**s** z
vom|it ˈvɒm |ɪt §-ət ‖ ˈvɑːm |ət ~**ited** ɪt ɪd
§ət-, -əd ‖ ət̬ əd ~**iting** ɪt ɪŋ §ət- ‖ ət̬ ɪŋ ~**its**
ɪts §əts ‖ əts
vomitori|um ˌvɒm ɪ ˈtɔːr i‿əm ˌ•ə- ‖ ˌvɑːm ə-
-ˈtoʊr- ~**a** ə ~**ums** əmz
vomitor|y ˈvɒm ɪ‿tər |i ˈ•ə‿ ‖ ˈvɑːm ə tɔːr |i
-toʊr i ~**ies** iz
von, Von in family names vɒn fɒn ‖ vɑːn —Ger
[fɔn]
Vonnegut ˈvɒn ɪ ɡʌt -ə- ‖ ˈvɑːn- ˈvɔːn-
Vono tdmk ˈvəʊn əʊ ‖ ˈvoʊn oʊ
voodoo ˈvuːd uː ~**ism** ˌɪz əm

Voortrekker ˈfʊə ˌtrek ə ˈvʊə-, ˈfɔː-, ˈvɔː-
‖ ˈfɔːr ˌtrek ər ˈfoʊr- —Afrikaans
[ˈfoːr ˌtrek ər] ~**s** z
voracious və ˈreɪʃ əs vɒ- ~**ly** li ~**ness** nəs nɪs
voracity və ˈræs ət i vɒ-, -ɪt- ‖ -ət̬ i
-**vorous** stress-imposing vər əs— **omnivorous**
ɒm ˈnɪv ər əs ‖ ɑːm-
Vorsprung durch Technik
ˌvɔː sprʌŋ ˌdɜːx ˈtex nɪk -tek ˈniːk
‖ ˌvɔːr sprʌŋ dɜːx- —Ger
[ˌfoːɐ ʃpʁʊŋ dʊʁç ˈtɛç nɪk]
vortex ˈvɔːt eks ‖ ˈvɔːrt- ~**es** ɪz əz **vortices**
ˈvɔːt ɪ siːz -ə- ‖ ˈvɔːrt̬-
vorticism ˈvɔːt ɪ ˌsɪz əm -ə- ‖ ˈvɔːrt̬-
Vortigern ˈvɔːt ɪ ɡɜːn -ɪg ən ‖ ˈvɔːrt̬ ɪ ɡɜːn
Vosburgh ˈvɒs bə‿rə ‖ ˈvɑːs-
Vosene tdmk ˈvəʊz iːn ‖ ˈvoʊz-
Vosges vəʊʒ ‖ voʊʒ —Fr [voːʒ]
Voss vɒs ‖ vɑːs vɔːs
Vostok ˈvɒst ɒk ‖ ˈvɑːst ɑːk —Russ [vʌ ˈstɔk]
votaress ˈvəʊt ə res -ər əs, -ər ɪs ‖ ˈvoʊt̬ ər əs
~**es** ɪz əz
votar|y ˈvəʊt ər |i ‖ ˈvoʊt̬- ~**ies** iz
vote vəʊt ‖ voʊt **voted** ˈvəʊt ɪd -əd ‖ ˈvoʊt̬ əd
votes vəʊts ‖ voʊts **voting**
ˈvəʊt ɪŋ ‖ ˈvoʊt̬ ɪŋ
ˌvote of ˈthanks; ˈvoting maˌchine

V

voteless 'vəʊt ləs -lɪs ‖ 'voʊt-
voter 'vəʊt ə ‖ 'voʊt̬ ᵊr ~s z
votive 'vəʊt ɪv ‖ 'voʊt̬ ɪv
Votyak 'vɒt jæk 'vəʊt-, '·i æk ‖ 'voʊt jɑːk
 -jæk
vouch vaʊtʃ vouched vaʊtʃt vouches
 'vaʊtʃ ɪz -əz vouching 'vaʊtʃ ɪŋ
voucher 'vaʊtʃ ə ‖ -ᵊr ~s z
vouchsaf|e ₍ᵢ₎vaʊtʃ 'seɪf '·· ~ed t ~es s ~ing
 ɪŋ
Vouvray 'vuːv reɪ ‖ vuː 'vreɪ —Fr [vu vʁɛ]
vow vaʊ vowed vaʊd vowing 'vaʊ ɪŋ vows
 vaʊz
vowel 'vaʊ‿əl vaʊl ‖ 'vaʊ‿əl voweled,
 vowelled 'vaʊ‿əld vaʊld ‖ 'vaʊ‿əld
 voweling, vowelling 'vaʊ‿əl ɪŋ 'vaʊl ɪŋ
 ‖ 'vaʊ‿əl ɪŋ vowels 'vaʊəlz vaʊlz ‖ 'vaʊ‿əlz
vowelless 'vaʊ‿əl ləs 'vaʊl ləs; -lɪs ‖ 'vaʊ‿əl-
vowel-like 'vaʊ‿əl laɪk 'vaʊl laɪk ‖ 'vaʊ‿əl-
Vowles (i) vəʊlz →vɒʊlz ‖ voʊlz, (ii) vaʊᵊlz
vox vɒks ‖ vɑːks
 ˌvox hu'mana hju 'mɑːn ə; ˌvox 'pop; ˌvox
 'populi 'pɒp ju laɪ -jə-, -liː ‖ 'pɑːp jə-
voyag|e 'vɔɪ ɪdʒ ~ed d ~es ɪz əz ~ing ɪŋ
voyager, V~ 'vɔɪ ɪdʒ ə -ədʒ- ‖ -ᵊr ~s z
voyeur ₍ᵢ₎vwaɪ 'ɜː ₍ᵢ₎vɔɪ-; ₍ᵢ₎vwɑː 'jɜː; 'vɔɪ ə,
 'vwɔɪ- ‖ vwɑː 'jɜː —Fr [vwa jœːʁ] ~s z
voyeurism ₍ᵢ₎vwaɪ 'ɜːr ˌɪz əm ₍ᵢ₎vɔɪ-;
 ₍ᵢ₎vwɑː 'jɜːr-; 'vɔɪ ər-, 'vwɔɪ- ‖ vwɑː 'jɜːr-
voyeuristic ˌvwaɪ ɜː 'rɪst ɪk ◄ ˌvɔɪ-, ˌvwɔɪ-, -ə-;
 ˌvwɑː jɜː- ‖ ˌvwɑː jə- ~ally ᵊl‿i
VRML 'vɜːm ᵊl ‖ 'vɝːm ᵊl
vroom vruːm vrʊm
V-shaped 'viː ʃeɪpt
V-sign 'viː saɪn ~s z
vs, vs. 'vɜːs əs ‖ 'vɝːs əs
VSO ˌviː es 'əʊ ‖ -'oʊ
 ˌVS 'O ˌlanguage
VTOL 'viː tɒl ˌviː tiː əʊ 'el ‖ 'viː tɔːl -tɑːl
VTR ˌviː tiː 'ɑː ‖ -'ɑːr ~s, ~'s z
vug, vugg, vugh vʌg vuggs, vughs, vugs
 vʌgz
Vuitton tdmk 'vjuː ɪ tɒn -ɪt ᵊn, §-ət-; 'vwiːt ɒ̃
 ‖ 'vjuː ə tɑːn —Fr [vɥi tɔ̃]

Vukovar 'vuːk ə vɑː ‖ -vɑːr —S-Cr
 [vu "kɔ vaːr]
Vulcan 'vʌlk ən
vulcanis... —see vulcaniz...
vulcanism 'vʌlk ə ˌnɪz əm
vulcanite 'vʌlk ə naɪt
vulcanization ˌvʌlk ən aɪ 'zeɪʃ ᵊn -ɪ'·- ‖ -ə'·-
vulcaniz|e 'vʌlk ə naɪz ~ed d ~es ɪz əz ~ing
 ɪŋ
vulcanological ˌvʌlk ən ə 'lɒdʒ ɪk ᵊl ◄ ‖ -'lɑːdʒ-
 ~ly‿i
vulcanologist ˌvʌlk ə 'nɒl ədʒ ɪst §-əst
 ‖ -'nɑːl- ~s s
vulcanology ˌvʌlk ə 'nɒl ədʒ i ‖ -'nɑːl-
vulgar 'vʌlg ə ‖ -ᵊr ~ly li ~ness nəs nɪs
 ˌvulgar 'fraction; ˌVulgar 'Latin
vulgarian vʌl 'geər i‿ən ‖ -'ger- -'gær- ~s z
vulgaris... —see vulgariz...
vulgarism 'vʌlg ə ˌrɪz əm ~s z
vulgarit|y vʌl 'gær ət i -ɪt- ‖ -ət̬ i -'ger- ~ies
 iz
vulgarization ˌvʌlg ər aɪ 'zeɪʃ ᵊn -ɪ'·- ‖ -ə'·-
vulgariz|e 'vʌlg ə raɪz ~ed d ~es ɪz əz ~ing
 ɪŋ
Vulgate 'vʌlg eɪt -ət, -ɪt
Vulliamy 'vʌl jəm i
vulnerability ˌvʌln ər ə 'bɪl ət i ˌvʌn-, -ɪt i
 ‖ -ət̬ i
vulnerab|le 'vʌln ər əb ᵊl 'vʌn- ~leness ᵊl nəs
 -nɪs ~ly li
vulnerary 'vʌln ər ər i ‖ -ə rer i
Vulpecula vʌl 'pek jʊl ə -jəl- ‖ -jəl ə
vulpine 'vʌlp aɪn
vulture 'vʌltʃ ə ‖ -ᵊr ~s z
vulv|a 'vʌlv ə ~ae iː ~as əz
vulvitis vʌl 'vaɪt ɪs §-əs ‖ -'vaɪt̬ əs
vulvovaginitis ˌvʌlv əʊ ˌvædʒ ɪ 'naɪt ɪs -ə'·-,
 §-əs ‖ -oʊ ˌvædʒ ə 'naɪt̬ əs
VW tdmk ˌviː 'dʌb ᵊl juː -ju ‖ -jə
vying 'vaɪ ɪŋ
Vyrnwy 'vɜːn wi 'vɜːn u i ‖ 'vɝːn-
Vyvyan 'vɪv i‿ən

W w

w | Spelling-to-sound

1 Where the spelling is **w**,
- either the pronunciation is w, as in **swim** swɪm, **away** ə 'weɪ, or else
- the **w** forms part of one of the digraphs **aw, ew, ow** (see under **a, e, o** respectively), as in **few** fjuː.

2 **w** is always silent in **wr** at the beginning of a word or stem, as in **wreck** rek, **rewrite** (noun) 'riː raɪt; also in the exceptionally spelled words **two** tuː, **answer** 'ɑːnᵗs ə ‖ 'ænᵗs ᵊr.

3 **w** is also regularly written **u**, as in **persuade** pə 'sweɪd ‖ pᵊr-, and as part of the digraph **qu**, as in **quite** kwaɪt.

wh | Spelling-to-sound

1 Where the spelling is the digraph **wh**, the pronunciation in most cases may be either w or hw, depending on regional, social and stylistic factors. In RP and other accents of England, and in Australian English, it is usually w, as in **white** waɪt; but in GenAm usually, and in Scottish and Irish English almost always, it is hw, as in **white** hwaɪt. (In England and Australia the pronunciation with hw tends to be considered 'better', and so is used by some people in specially formal styles only.) Learners of EFL are recommended to use plain w if they are following the RP model, hw if they are following the GenAm model.

2 Occasionally, the pronunciation is h, as in **whole** həʊl ‖ hoʊl, **who** huː.

W, w 'dʌb ᵊl juː -ju ‖ -jə —*in AmE sometimes reduced to* 'dʌb jə **W's, w's, Ws** 'dʌb ᵊl juːz —*Communications code name:* Whisky
ˌW'C; ˌW'H ˌquestion; ˌW,H'O; ˌW,P'C
WAAC wæk
WAAF, Waaf wæf **Waafs** wæfs
Wabash 'wɔː bæʃ ‖ 'wɑː-
WAC, Wac wæk **Wacs** wæks
Wace weɪs
wack wæk
wacko 'wæk əʊ ‖ -oʊ
wack|y 'wæk li ~**ier** i_ə ‖ i_ᵊr ~**iest** i_ɪst i_əst ~**ily** ɪ li əl i ~**iness** i nəs i nɪs
Waco 'weɪk əʊ ‖ -oʊ
wad wɒd ‖ wɑːd **wadded** 'wɒd ɪd -əd ‖ 'wɑːd əd **wadding** 'wɒd ɪŋ ‖ 'wɑːd ɪŋ **wads** wɒdz ‖ wɑːdz
Waddell (i) 'wɒd ᵊl ‖ 'wɑːd ᵊl, (ii) wɒ 'del wə- ‖ wɑː-

Waddesdon 'wɒdz dən ‖ 'wɑːdz-
wadding 'wɒd ɪŋ ‖ 'wɑːd ɪŋ
Waddington 'wɒd ɪŋ tən ‖ 'wɑːd-
waddl|e 'wɒd ᵊl ‖ 'wɑːd ᵊl ~**ed** d ~**es** z ~**ing** _ɪŋ
Waddon 'wɒd ᵊn ‖ 'wɑːd ᵊn
waddl|y 'wɒdl i ‖ 'wɑːdl i ~**ies** iz
wade, Wade weɪd **waded** 'weɪd ɪd -əd **wades** weɪdz **wading** 'weɪd ɪŋ 'wading bird; 'wading pool
Wadebridge 'weɪd brɪdʒ →'weɪb-
Wade-Giles ˌweɪd 'dʒaɪᵊlz ˌWade-'Giles ˌsystem
wader 'weɪd ə ‖ -ᵊr ~**s** z
wadge, Wadge wɒdʒ ‖ wɑːdʒ **wadges** 'wɒdʒ ɪz -əz ‖ 'wɑːdʒ əz
Wadham 'wɒd əm ‖ 'wɑːd-
Wadhurst 'wɒd hɜːst ‖ 'wɑːd hɝːst
wadi 'wɒd i 'wɑːd i ‖ 'wɑːd i ~**s** z

W

wading —*see* **wade**
Wadsworth 'wɒdz wəθ -wɜːθ ‖ 'waːdz wərθ
wad|ly 'wɒd li ‖ 'waːd li ~ies iz
wafer 'weɪf ə ‖ -ər ~s z
wafer-thin ,weɪf ə 'θɪn ◄ ‖ -ər-
waffl|e 'wɒf əl ‖ 'waːf əl ~ed d ~er/s ə/z ‖ ər/
z ~es z ~ing ɪŋ
' waffle ,iron
waffler 'wɒf əl_ə ‖ 'waːf əl_ər ~s z
waffly 'wɒf əl i ‖ 'waːf əl i
waft waːft wɒft, wɔːft, §wæft ‖ wæft wafted
'waːft ɪd 'wɒft-, 'wɔːft-, §'wæft-,
-əd ‖ 'wæft- wafting 'waːft ɪŋ 'wɒft-,
'wɔːft-, §'wæft- ‖ 'wæft- wafts waːfts
wɒfts, wɔːfts, §wæfts ‖ wæfts
wag wæg wagged wægd wagging 'wæg ɪŋ
wags wægz
wage weɪdʒ waged weɪdʒd wages 'weɪdʒ ɪz
-əz waging 'weɪdʒ ɪŋ
' wage ,earner; ' wage ,packet; ' wage rate;
' wage rise; ' wage slave
wager 'weɪdʒ ə ‖ -ər ~ed d wagering
'weɪdʒ ər_ɪŋ ~s z
Wagg wæg
wagga, Wagga 'wɒg ə ‖ 'waːg ə
Wagga Wagga ' •• ,•• ,• •'••
waggery 'wæg ər i
waggish 'wæg ɪʃ ~ly li ~ness nəs nɪs
waggl|e 'wæg əl ~ed d ~es z ~ing ɪŋ
waggly 'wæg əl_i
waggon 'wæg ən ~s z
waggoner 'wæg ən ə ‖ -ən ər ~s z
waggonette ,wæg ə 'net ~s s
waggonload 'wæg ən ləʊd ‖ -loʊd ~s z
Waghorn 'wæg hɔːn ‖ -hɔːrn
Wagnall 'wæg nəl
Wagner *English or American family name*
'wæg nə ‖ -nər
Wagner *German name, composer* 'vaːg nə ‖ -nər
—*Ger* ['vaːg nɐ]
Wagnerian vaːg 'nɪər i_ən ‖ -'nɪr- -'ner- ~s z
wagon 'wæg ən ~s z
' wagon train
wagoner 'wæg ən ə ‖ -ən ər ~s z
wagonette ,wæg ə 'net ~s s
wagon-lit ,wæg ɒn 'liː -ð̃- ‖ ,vaːg ɒn- -ɔːn-,
-oʊn- —*Fr* [va gɔ̃ li] ~s *same as sing., less
commonly* z
wagonload 'wæg ən ləʊd ‖ -loʊd ~s z
Wagstaff 'wæg staːf §-stæf ‖ -stæf
wagtail 'wæg teɪəl ~s z
Wahabi, Wahhabi wə 'haːb i waː-
wahoo waː 'huː '•• ~s z
wah-wah 'waː waː ~s z
waif weɪf waifs weɪfs
Waikato waɪ 'kæt əʊ -'kaːt- ‖ -'kaːt oʊ
Waikiki ,waɪk ɪ kiː, ,• •'•
wail weɪəl wailed weɪəld wailing 'weɪəl ɪŋ
wails weɪəlz
wain weɪn wains weɪnz
Wain, Waine weɪn
Wainfleet 'weɪn fliːt

wainscot 'weɪn skət -skɒt ‖ -skaːt, -skoʊt
wainscoted, wainscotted 'weɪn skət ɪd
-skɒt-, -əd ‖ -skət̬ əd -skaːt̬-, -skoʊt̬-
wainscoting, wainscotting 'weɪn skət ɪŋ
-skɒt- ‖ -skət̬ ɪŋ -skaːt̬-, -skoʊt̬- ~s s
Wainwright, w~ 'weɪn raɪt ~s s
waist weɪst (= *waste*) waisted 'weɪst ɪd -əd
waists weɪsts
waistband 'weɪst bænd ~s z
waistcoat 'weɪs kəʊt 'weɪst-; 'wesk ət, -ɪt
‖ 'wesk ət 'weɪst koʊt ~s s
waist-deep ,weɪst 'diːp ◄
waist-high ,weɪst 'haɪ ◄
waistline 'weɪst laɪn ~s z
wait weɪt waited 'weɪt ɪd -əd ‖ 'weɪt̬ əd
waiting 'weɪt ɪŋ ‖ 'weɪt̬ ɪŋ waits weɪts
' waiting game; ' waiting list; ' waiting
room
wait-and-see ,weɪt ən 'siː -ənd-
Waitangi (ı)waɪ 'tæŋ i
Waite weɪt
waiter 'weɪt ə ‖ 'weɪt̬ ər ~s z
Waites weɪts
wait|person 'weɪt ,pɜːs ən ‖ -,pɝːs ən
~people ,piːp əl
waitress 'weɪtr əs -ɪs ~es ɪz əz
Waitrose *tdmk* 'weɪt rəʊz ‖ -roʊz
waive weɪv (= *wave*) waived weɪvd waives
weɪvz waiving 'weɪv ɪŋ
waiver 'weɪv ə ‖ -ər (= *waver*) ~s z
Wajda 'vaɪd ə —*Polish* ['vai da]
wake, Wake weɪk waked weɪkt wakes weɪks
waking 'weɪk ɪŋ woke wəʊk ‖ woʊk
woken 'wəʊk ən ‖ 'woʊk ən
Wakefield 'weɪk fiːəld
wakeful 'weɪk fəl -fʊl -ly_i ~ness nəs nɪs
Wakeham 'weɪk əm
Wakehurst 'weɪk hɜːst ‖ -hɝːst
Wakelin 'weɪk lɪn §-lən
waken 'weɪk ən ~ed d ~ing ɪŋ ~s z
Wakering 'weɪk ər ɪŋ
wake-robin 'weɪk ,rɒb ɪn §-ən ‖ -,raːb-
wakey 'weɪk i
, wakey 'wakey!
waking —*see* **wake**
Wakley (i) 'wæk li, (ii) 'weɪk li
Walachi|a wɒ 'leɪk i_ə wə- ‖ waː- ~an/s ən/z
Walberswick 'wɔːlb əz wɪk 'wɒlb- ‖ -ərz-
'waːlb-
Walbrook 'wɔːl brʊk 'wɒl- ‖ 'waːl-
Walcot, Walcott 'wɔːl kət 'wɒl-, -kɒt ‖ 'waːl-,
-kaːt
Waldegrave (i) 'wɔːld greɪv 'wɒld- ‖ 'waːld-,
(ii) 'wɔːld ɪ greɪv 'wɒld-, -ə- ‖ 'waːld-
Waldemar 'væld ə maː 'wɔːld-, -ɪ-
‖ 'vaːld ə maːr —*Ger* ['val də maʁ], *Swed*
[-mar]
Walden 'wɔːld ən 'wɒld- ‖ 'waːld-
Waldens|es wɒl 'dents iːz wɒl- ‖ waːl-
~ian/s i_ən/z
Waldheim 'vaːld haɪm ‖ 'wɔːld- —*Ger*
['valt haɪm]
Waldo 'wɔːld əʊ 'wɒld- ‖ -oʊ 'waːld-

Waldorf 'wɔːld ɔːf 'wɒld- ‖ -ɔːrf 'wɑːld-
 ,Waldorf 'salad
Waldron 'wɔːldr ən 'wɒldr- ‖ 'wɑːldr-
Waldstein (i) 'væld staɪn 'vɑːld-, 'vɒld-
 ‖ 'vɑːld-, (ii) 'wɔːld staɪn 'wɒld- ‖ 'wɑːld-
—For the Beethoven sonata, and as a German
name, (i) —Ger ['valt ʃtaɪn]; as an American
family name, (ii).
wale weɪəl **wales** weɪəlz
Wales weɪəlz
Walesa, Wałęsa vaː 'wenˢts ə və-, wə-, -'wenz-,
 -'lenˢts- ‖ waː 'lenˢts ə —Polish [va 'wew̃ sa]
Waley 'weɪl i
Walford 'wɔːl fəd 'wɒl- ‖ -fᵊrd 'wɑːl-
Walgreens tdmk 'wɔːl griːnz 'wɒl- ‖ 'wɑːl-
Walham 'wɒl əm ‖ 'wɑːl-
Walian 'weɪl i‿ən
walk wɔːk ‖ wɑːk **walked** wɔːkt ‖ wɑːkt
 walking 'wɔːk ɪŋ ‖ 'wɑːk- **walks** wɔːks
 ‖ wɑːks
 'walking ˌpapers; 'walking shoes; 'walking
stick; 'walking tour; ˌwalk of 'life
walkabout 'wɔːk ə ˌbaʊt ‖ 'wɑːk-
walkathon 'wɔːk ə θɒn ‖ -θɑːn 'wɑːk- ~s z
walkaway 'wɔːk ə ˌweɪ ‖ 'wɑːk- ~s z
Walkden 'wɔːk dən ‖ 'wɑːk-
walker, W~ 'wɔːk ə ‖ -ᵊr 'wɑːk- ~s z
walkies 'wɔːk iz ‖ 'wɑːk-
walkie-talkie ˌwɔːk i 'tɔːk i ‖ ˌwɑːk i 'tɑːk i ~s
 z
walk-in 'wɔːk ɪn ‖ 'wɑːk- ~s z
Walkman tdmk, w~ 'wɔːk mən ‖ 'wɑːk- ~s z
walk-on 'wɔːk ɒn ‖ -ɑːn 'wɑːk-, -ɔːn ~s z
walkout 'wɔːk aʊt ‖ 'wɑːk- ~s s
walkover 'wɔːk ˌəʊv ə ‖ -ˌoʊv ᵊr 'wɑːk- ~s z
walk-up 'wɔːk ʌp ‖ 'wɑːk- ~s s
walkway 'wɔːk weɪ ‖ 'wɑːk- ~s z
walky-talk|y ˌwɔːk i 'tɔːk| i ‖ ˌwɑːk i 'tɑːk| i
 ~ies iz
wall, Wall wɔːl ‖ wɑːl **walled** wɔːld ‖ wɑːld
 walling 'wɔːl ɪŋ ‖ 'wɑːl- **walls** wɔːlz ‖ wɑːlz
 'wall ˌpainting; 'Wall Street, ˌWall Street
'Journal
walla, Walla 'wɒl ə ‖ 'wɑːl ə
wallab|y 'wɒl əb |i ‖ 'wɑːl- ~ies iz
Wallace 'wɒl ɪs -əs ‖ 'wɑːl əs 'wɔːl-
Wallachi|a wɒ 'leɪk i‿|ə wə- ‖ wɑː- ~an/s ən/z
wallah 'wɒl ə ‖ 'wɑːl ə ~s z
wallaroo, W~ ˌwɒl ə 'ruː ‖ ˌwɑːl- ~s z
Wallasey 'wɒl əs i ‖ 'wɑːl-
wallboard 'wɔːl bɔːd ‖ -bɔːrd 'wɑːl-, -boʊrd
 ~s z
wallchart 'wɔːl tʃɑːt ‖ -tʃɑːrt 'wɑːl- ~s s
Waller (i) 'wɒl ə ‖ 'wɑːl ᵊr, (ii) 'wɔːl ə ‖ -ᵊr
 'wɑːl-
Wallerawang wə 'leər ə wæŋ ‖ -'ler-
wallet 'wɒl ɪt -ət ‖ 'wɑːl ət ~s s
walleye 'wɔːl aɪ ‖ 'wɑːl- ~s z
wall-eyed 'wɔːl aɪd ˌ·'· ‖ 'wɑːl-
wallflower 'wɔːl ˌflaʊ‿ə ‖ -ᵊr 'wɑːl- ~s z
wallie... —see **wally**
Walliker 'wɒl ɪk ə -ək- ‖ 'wɑːl ək ᵊr
Wallingford 'wɒl ɪŋ fəd ‖ 'wɑːl ɪŋ fᵊrd

Wallington 'wɒl ɪŋ tən ‖ 'wɑːl-
Wallis 'wɒl ɪs §-əs ‖ 'wɑːl əs 'wɔːl-
Wallonia wɒ 'ləʊn i‿ə wə- ‖ wɑː 'loʊn-
Walloon wɒ 'luːn wə- ‖ wɑː- ~s z
wallop, W~ 'wɒl əp ‖ 'wɑːl əp ~ed t ~ing/s
 ɪŋ/z ~s s
wallow 'wɒl əʊ ‖ 'wɑːl oʊ ~ed d ~er/s ə/z
 ‖ ᵊr/z ~ing ɪŋ ~s z
wallpaper 'wɔːl ˌpeɪp ə ‖ -ᵊr 'wɑːl- ~ed d
 wallpapering 'wɔːl ˌpeɪp ᵊr‿ɪŋ ‖ 'wɑːl- ~s z
Walls wɔːlz ‖ wɑːlz
Wallsend 'wɔːlz end ‖ 'wɑːlz-
wall-to-wall ˌwɔːl tə 'wɔːl ◀
 -tu- ‖ ˌwɑːl tə 'wɑːl
 ˌwall-to-wall 'carpeting
wallum 'wɒl əm ‖ 'wɑːl-
Wallwork 'wɔːl wɜːk 'wɒl- ‖ -wɜ˞ːk 'wɑːl-
wall|y n, **Wally** 'wɒl i ‖ 'wɑːl i ~ies iz
Wal-Mart tdmk 'wɒl mɑːt 'wɔːl- ‖ 'wɔːl mɑːrt
 'wɑːl-
Walmer 'wɔːlm ə 'wɒlm- ‖ -ᵊr 'wɑːlm-
Walmesley, Walmisley, Walmsley 'wɔːmz li
 ‖ 'wɑːmz-
Walney 'wɔːln i 'wɒln- ‖ 'wɑːln-
walnut 'wɔːl nʌt ‖ 'wɑːl- ~s s
Walpamur tdmk 'wɔːl pə mjʊə 'wɒl-, -mɜː
 ‖ -mjʊr 'wɑːl-
Walpole 'wɔːl pəʊl 'wɒl-, →-pɒʊl ‖ -poʊl
 'wɑːl-
Walpurgis væl 'pʊəg ɪs vɑːl-, -'pɜːg-, §-əs
 ‖ vɑːl 'pʊrg əs
walrus 'wɔːl rəs 'wɒl-, -rʌs ‖ 'wɑːl- ~es ɪz əz
 ˌwalrus mou'stache ‖ -'··
Walsall 'wɔːl sɔːl 'wɒl-, -sᵊl ‖ 'wɑːl sɑːl
 —locally also 'wɔːs ᵊl
Walsh wɔːlʃ wɒlʃ ‖ wɑːlʃ
Walsham 'wɔːlʃ əm 'wɒlʃ- ‖ 'wɑːlʃ- —locally
also 'wɒls əm
Walsingham (i) 'wɔːls ɪŋ əm 'wɒls- ‖ 'wɑːls-,
 (ii) 'wɔːlz- 'wɒlz- ‖ 'wɑːlz- —the personal
name is (i), but the place in Nfk is (ii)
Walt wɔːlt wɒlt ‖ wɑːlt
Walter 'wɔːlt ə 'wɒlt- ‖ -ᵊr 'wɑːlt- —but as a
German name, 'vɑːlt ə ‖ -ᵊr, Ger ['val tɐ]
 ˌWalter 'Mitty 'mɪt i ‖ 'mɪt̬ i
Walters 'wɔːlt əz 'wɒlt- ‖ -ᵊrz 'wɑːlt-
Waltham 'wɔːlθ əm 'wɒlθ- ‖ 'wɑːlθ- —but
Great W~ and Little W~ in Essex are
traditionally 'wɔːlt-; W~ in MA is locally
'wɔːl θæm
 ˌWaltham 'Forest
Walthamstow 'wɔːlθ əm stəʊ 'wɒlθ- ‖ -stoʊ
 'wɑːlθ- —previously 'wɔːlt-, 'wɒlt-
Walton 'wɔːlt ən 'wɒlt- ‖ 'wɑːlt-
Walton-le-Dale ˌwɔːlt ən li 'deɪᵊl
 ˌwɒlt- ‖ ˌwɑːlt-
Walton-on-the-Naze ˌwɔːlt ən ˌɒn ðə 'neɪz
 ˌwɒlt- ‖ -ˌɑːn- ˌwɑːlt-, -ˌɔːn-
waltz wɔːls wɒls, wɔːlts, wɒlts ‖ wɔːlts wɑːlts,
 wɔːls, wɑːls **waltzed** wɔːlst wɒlst, wɔːltst,
wɒltst ‖ wɔːltst wɑːltst, wɔːlst, wɑːlst
waltzes 'wɔːls ɪz 'wɒls-, 'wɔːlts-, 'wɒlts-, -əz
 ‖ 'wɔːlts əz 'wɑːlts-, 'wɔːls-, 'wɑːls-

W

waltzing 'wɔːls ɪŋ 'wɒls-, 'wɔːlts-, 'wɒlts-
 ‖ 'wɔːlts ɪŋ 'wɑːlts-, 'wɔːls-, 'wɑːls-
waltzer 'wɔːls ə 'wɒls-, 'wɔːlts-, 'wɒlts-
 ‖ 'wɔːlts ᵊr 'wɑːlts-, 'wɔːls-, 'wɑːls- ~s z
Walvis Bay ˌwɔːlv ɪs 'beɪ §-əs- ‖ ˌwɑːlv-
Walworth 'wɔːl wəθ 'wɒl-, -wɜːθ ‖ -wᵊrθ
 'wɑːl-
wampum 'wɒmp əm ‖ 'wɑːmp-
wan *'pale'* wɒn ‖ wɑːn **wanner**
 'wɒn ə ‖ 'wɑːn ᵊr **wannest** 'wɒn ɪst -əst
 ‖ 'wɑːn əst
WAN, wan *'wide area network'* wæn
Wanamaker 'wɒn ə meɪk ə ‖ 'wɑːn ə meɪk ᵊr
Wanchai ˌwɒn 'tʃaɪ ‖ ˌwɑːn- —*Cantonese*
 [¹waːn ²tsɐj]
wand wɒnd ‖ wɑːnd **wands** wɒndz ‖ wɑːndz
Wanda 'wɒnd ə ‖ 'wɑːnd ə
wander 'wɒnd ə ‖ 'wɑːnd ᵊr **~ed** d
 wandering/s 'wɒnd_ᵊr ɪŋ/z ‖ 'wɑːnd_ᵊr ɪŋ/z
 ~s z
 ˌWandering 'Jew
wanderer 'wɒnd_ᵊr ə ‖ 'wɑːnd_ᵊr ᵊr ~s z
wanderlust 'wɒnd ə lʌst ‖ 'wɑːnd ᵊr- —*Ger*
 W~ ['van dɐ lʊst]
Wandle 'wɒnd ᵊl ‖ 'wɑːnd ᵊl
Wandsworth 'wɒndz wəθ -wɜːθ
 ‖ 'wɑːndz wᵊrθ -wɜːθ
wane waned weɪnd **wanes** weɪnz
 waning 'weɪn ɪŋ
Wang *tdmk* wæŋ ‖ wɑːŋ
Wanganui ˌwɒŋ ə 'nuː i -gə- ‖ ˌwɑːŋ-
Wangaratta ˌwæŋ gə 'ræt ə ‖ -'ræt̮-
wangl|e 'wæŋ gᵊl **~ed** d **~es** z **~ing** ɪŋ
wanigan 'wɒn ɪg ᵊn ‖ 'wɑːn- ~s z
wank wæŋk **wanked** wæŋkt **wanking**
 'wæŋk ɪŋ **wanks** wæŋks
Wankel, w~ 'wæŋk ᵊl ‖ 'wɑːŋk ᵊl —*Ger*
 ['van kᵊl]
wanker 'wæŋk ə ‖ -ᵊr ~s z
wanly 'wɒn li ‖ 'wɑːn li
wanna *casual form of* **want to, want a**
 'wɒn ə ‖ 'wɑːn ə 'wɔːn ə —*not standard in*
 BrE; the RP equivalent is 'wɒnt ə
wannabe, wannabee 'wɒn əb i -ə biː ‖ 'wɑːn-
 'wɔːn- ~s z
wanne... —*see* **wan**
wanness 'wɒn nəs -nɪs ‖ 'wɑːn nəs
Wansbeck 'wɒnz bek ‖ 'wɑːnz-
Wanstead 'wɒn stɪd -sted, §-stəd ‖ 'wɑːn-
want wɒnt ‖ wɑːnt wɔːnt **wanted** 'wɒnt ɪd
 -əd ‖ 'wɑːnt̮ əd 'wɔːnt̮- **wanting**
 'wɒnt ɪŋ ‖ 'wɑːnt̮ ɪŋ 'wɔːnt̮- **wants**
 wɒnts ‖ wɑːnts wɔːnts —*In the close-knit*
 phrase want to *before a verb, the consonants*
 are often simplified to 'wɒnt ə,
 §'wɒn ə ‖ 'wɑːn ə, 'wɔːn ə. *See also* wanna.
 'want ad
Wantage, w~ 'wɒnt ɪdʒ ‖ 'wɑːnt̮ ɪdʒ 'wɔːnt̮-
Wantagh 'wɒnt ɔː ‖ 'wɑːnt- -ɑː
wanton 'wɒnt ᵊn ‖ 'wɑːnt ᵊn **~ly** li **~ness** nəs
 nɪs ~s z
wapentake 'wɒp ᵊn teɪk 'wæp- ‖ 'wɑːp- ~s s
wapiti 'wɒp ət i -ɪt- ‖ 'wɑːp ət̮ i ~s z

Waple 'weɪp ᵊl
Wapner 'wɒp nə ‖ 'wɑːp nᵊr
Wapping 'wɒp ɪŋ ‖ 'wɑːp ɪŋ
Wappingers Falls ˌwɒp ɪndʒ əz 'fɔːlz
 ‖ ˌwɑːp əndʒ ᵊrz- -'fɑːlz
war wɔː ‖ wɔːr **warred** wɔːd ‖ wɔːrd **warring**
 'wɔːr ɪŋ **wars** wɔːz ‖ wɔːrz
 'war bride; 'war clouds; 'war
 corre‚spondent; 'war crime; 'war cry; 'war
 dance; 'war game; ˌwar of 'nerves; 'war
 paint
waratah 'wɒr ə tɑː ˌ•• '• ‖ 'wɔːr- ~s z
Warbeck 'wɔː bek ‖ 'wɔːr-
warbl|e 'wɔːb ᵊl ‖ 'wɔːrb ᵊl **~ed** d **~es** z **~ing**
 ɪŋ
 'warble fly
warbler 'wɔːb lə ‖ 'wɔːrb lᵊr ~s z
Warboys 'wɔː bɔɪz ‖ 'wɔːr-
Warburg 'wɔː bɜːg ‖ 'wɔːr bɝːg
Warburton 'wɔːb ət ᵊn 'wɔː ˌbɜːt ᵊn
 ‖ 'wɔːr ˌbɝːt ᵊn
ward, Ward wɔːd ‖ wɔːrd **warded** 'wɔːd ɪd
 -əd ‖ 'wɔːrd əd **warding**
 'wɔːd ɪŋ ‖ 'wɔːrd ɪŋ **wards** wɔːdz ‖ wɔːrdz
-ward wəd ‖ wᵊrd — **heavenward**
 'hev ᵊn wəd ‖ -wᵊrd
Wardell wɔː 'del ‖ wɔːr-
warden, W~ 'wɔːd ᵊn ‖ 'wɔːrd ᵊn ~s z ~ship
 ʃɪp
warder 'wɔːd ə ‖ 'wɔːrd ᵊr ~s z
Wardian 'wɔːd i_ən ‖ 'wɔːrd-
Wardle 'wɔːd ᵊl ‖ 'wɔːrd ᵊl
Wardour 'wɔːd ə ‖ 'wɔːrd ᵊr
wardress 'wɔːdr əs -ɪs, -es ‖ 'wɔːrdr- **~es** ɪz əz
wardrobe 'wɔːdr əub ‖ 'wɔːrdr oub ~s z
wardroom 'wɔːd ruːm -rʊm ‖ 'wɔːrd- ~s z
-wards wədz ‖ wᵊrdz — **seawards**
 'siː wədz ‖ -wᵊrdz
wardship 'wɔːd ʃɪp ‖ 'wɔːrd- ~s s
ware, Ware weə ‖ weᵊr wæᵊr **wares**
 weəz ‖ weᵊrz wæᵊrz
-ware weə ‖ wer wær — **silverware**
 'sɪlv ə weə ‖ -ᵊr wer -wær
Wareham 'weər əm ‖ 'wer əm 'wær-
ware|house *n* 'weə |haʊs ‖ 'wer- 'wær-
 ~houses haʊz ɪz -əz
ware|house *v* 'weə |haʊz -haʊs ‖ 'wer- 'wær-
 ~housed haʊzd haʊst **~houses** haʊz ɪz
 haʊs-, -əz **~housing** haʊz ɪŋ haʊs-
warehouse|man 'weə haʊs |mən ‖ 'wer-
 'wær- **~men** mən men
Wareing 'weər ɪŋ ‖ 'wer ɪŋ 'wær-
warfare 'wɔː feə ‖ 'wɔːr fer -fær
warfarin 'wɔːf ᵊr ɪn §-ᵊn ‖ 'wɔːrf-
Wargrave 'wɔː greɪv ‖ 'wɔːr-
warhead 'wɔː hed ‖ 'wɔːr- ~s z
Warhol 'wɔː həʊl →-hɒʊl ‖ 'wɔːr hoʊl
warhors|e 'wɔː hɔːs ‖ 'wɔːr hɔːrs **~es** ɪz əz
wari... —*see* **wary**
Waring 'weər ɪŋ ‖ 'wer ɪŋ 'wær-
Warks —*see* **Warwickshire**
Warkworth 'wɔːk wəθ -wɜːθ ‖ 'wɔːrk wɜːθ
 'wɑːrk-

Warley 'wɔːl i ‖ 'wɔːrl i
warlike 'wɔː laɪk ‖ 'wɔːr-
Warlingham 'wɔːl ɪŋ əm ‖ 'wɔːrl-
warlock, W~ 'wɔː lɒk ‖ 'wɔːr lɑːk ~s s
warlord 'wɔː lɔːd ‖ 'wɔːr lɔːrd ~ism ˌɪz əm ~s
z
warm wɔːm ‖ wɔːrm warmed
wɔːmd ‖ wɔːrmd warmer
'wɔːm ə ‖ 'wɔːrm ər warmest 'wɔːm ɪst -əst
‖ 'wɔːrm əst warming 'wɔːm ɪŋ ‖ 'wɔːrm ɪŋ
warms wɔːmz ‖ wɔːrmz
'warming pan
warm-blooded ˌwɔːm 'blʌd ɪd ◂ -əd ‖ ˌwɔːrm-
~ness nəs nɪs
warmer 'wɔːm ə ‖ 'wɔːrm ər ~s z
warm-hearted ˌwɔːm 'hɑːt ɪd ◂ -əd
‖ ˌwɔːrm 'hɑːrt əd ◂ ~ly li ~ness nəs nɪs
Warmington 'wɔːm ɪŋ tən ‖ 'wɔːrm-
Warminster 'wɔː mɪntˢt ə ‖ 'wɔːr mɪntˢt ər
warmly 'wɔːm li ‖ 'wɔːrm li
warmonger 'wɔː ˌmʌŋ gə ‖ 'wɔːr ˌmʌŋ gər
-ˌmɑːŋ- ~s z
warmongering 'wɔː ˌmʌŋ gər_ɪŋ ‖ 'wɔːr-
-ˌmɑːŋ-
warmth wɔːmᵖθ ‖ wɔːrmᵖθ
warm-up 'wɔːm ʌp ‖ 'wɔːrm- ~s s
warn wɔːn ‖ wɔːrn warned wɔːnd ‖ wɔːrnd
warning/ly 'wɔːn ɪŋ /li ‖ 'wɔːrn- warns
wɔːnz ‖ wɔːrnz
Warne wɔːn ‖ wɔːrn
Warner 'wɔːn ə ‖ 'wɔːrn ər
Warnham 'wɔːn əm ‖ 'wɔːrn-
warning 'wɔːn ɪŋ ‖ 'wɔːrn ɪŋ ~s z
Warninglid 'wɔːn ɪŋ lɪd ‖ 'wɔːrn-
Warnock 'wɔːn ɒk ‖ 'wɔːrn ɑːk
warp wɔːp ‖ wɔːrp warped wɔːpt ‖ wɔːrpt
warping 'wɔːp ɪŋ ‖ 'wɔːrp ɪŋ warps
wɔːps ‖ wɔːrps
warpath 'wɔː pɑːθ §-pæθ ‖ 'wɔːr pæθ
warplane 'wɔː pleɪn ‖ 'wɔːr- ~s z
Warr wɔː ‖ wɔːr
Warragamba ˌwɒr ə 'gæm bə ‖ ˌwɔːr-
warr|ant 'wɒr |ənt ‖ 'wɔːr |ənt 'wɑːr- ~anted
ənt ɪd-əd ‖ ənt̬ əd ~anting ənt ɪŋ ‖ ənt̬ ɪŋ
~ants ənts
'warrant ˌofficer
warrantab|le 'wɒr ənt əb| əl ‖ 'wɔːr- 'wɑːr-
~ly li
warrantee ˌwɒr ən 'tiː ‖ ˌwɔːr- ˌwɑːr- ~s z
warrantor 'wɒr ən tɔː, •'•• ‖ 'wɔːr ən tɔːr
'wɑːr-, ˌ•'•• ~s z
warrant|y 'wɒr ənt |i ‖ 'wɔːr ənt̬ |i'wɑːr- ~ies
iz
Warre wɔː ‖ wɔːr
warren, W~ 'wɒr ən ‖ 'wɔːr ən'wɑːr-
—formerly also -ɪn ~s z
Warrender 'wɒr ənd ə-ɪnd- ‖ 'wɔːr ənd ər
'wɑːr-
warrigal 'wɒr ɪg əl-əg- ‖ 'wɔːr- 'wɑːr- ~s z
warring 'wɔːr ɪŋ
Warrington 'wɒr ɪŋ tən ‖ 'wɔːr- 'wɑːr-
warrior 'wɒr i_ə ‖ 'wɔːr i_ər'wɑːr- ~s z
Warriss 'wɒr ɪs§-əs ‖ 'wɔːr əs'wɑːr-

Warrumbungle ˌwɒr əm 'bʌŋ gəl ‖ ˌwɔːr-
Warsaw 'wɔː sɔː ‖ 'wɔːr- -sɑː
ˌWarsaw 'Pact
warship 'wɔː ʃɪp ‖ 'wɔːr- ~s s
Warsop 'wɔː sɒp ‖ 'wɔːr sɑːp
Warspite 'wɔː spaɪt ‖ 'wɔːr-
wart wɔːt ‖ wɔːrt warts wɔːts ‖ wɔːrts
Wartburg tdmk 'wɔːt bɜːg 'vɑːt- ‖ 'wɔːrt bɜːg
—Ger ['vaʁt buʁk]
warthog 'wɔːt hɒg ‖ 'wɔːrt hɔːg -hɑːg ~s z
wartime 'wɔː taɪm ‖ 'wɔːr-
Warton 'wɔːt ən ‖ 'wɔːrt ən
war-torn 'wɔː tɔːn ‖ 'wɔːr tɔːrn -toʊrn
wart|y 'wɔːt li ‖ 'wɔːrt̬ li ~ier i_ə ‖ i_ər ~iest
i_ɪst i_əst ~iness i nəs i nɪs
war-wear|y 'wɔː ˌwɪər i, •'•• ‖ 'wɔːr ˌwɪr i
~iness i nəs i nɪs
Warwick (i) 'wɒr ɪk ‖ 'wɔːr ɪk 'wɑːr-, (ii)
'wɔː wɪk ‖ 'wɔːr- —The English name and the
places in Warks and Queensland are (i); the
place in RI and the American name are usually
(ii).
Warwickshire 'wɒr ɪk ʃə-ʃɪə ‖ 'wɔːr ɪk ʃər
'wɑːr-, -ʃɪr
war|y 'weər |i ‖ 'wer |i'wær- ~ier i_ə ‖ i_ər
~iest i_ɪst i_əst ~ily əl i li ~iness i nəs i nɪs
was strong form wɒz ‖ wʌz wɑːz, weak form
wəz
wasabi 'wɑːs ə biː -ɑː-; wə 'sɑːb i —Jp
['ɰa sa bi]
Wasatch 'wɔː sætʃ ‖ 'wɑː-
Wasdale 'wɒs dəl-deɪəl ‖ 'wɑːs-
wash, Wash wɒʃ ‖ wɑːʃ wɔːʃ —There are also
non-standard AmE forms wɔːrʃ, wɑːrʃ
washed wɒʃt ‖ wɑːʃt wɔːʃt washes 'wɒʃ ɪz
-əz ‖ 'wɑːʃ əz'wɔːʃ- washing
'wɒʃ ɪŋ ‖ 'wɑːʃ ɪŋ'wɔːʃ-
wash ˌdrawing; 'washing day; 'washing
ma chine; 'washing powder
washable 'wɒʃ əb əl ‖ 'wɑːʃ- 'wɔːʃ-
washbasin 'wɒʃ ˌbeɪs ən ‖ 'wɑːʃ- 'wɔːʃ- ~s z
washboard 'wɒʃ bɔːd ‖ 'wɑːʃ bɔːrd'wɔːʃ-,
-boʊrd ~s z
Washbourn, Washbourne
'wɒʃ bɔːn ‖ 'wɑːʃ bɔːrn'wɔːʃ-, -boʊrn
washbowl 'wɒʃ bəʊl→-bɒʊl ‖ 'wɑːʃ boʊl
'wɔːʃ- ~s z
Washbrook 'wɒʃ brʊk ‖ 'wɑːʃ- 'wɔːʃ-
Washburn 'wɒʃ bɜːn ‖ 'wɑːʃ bɜˑn'wɔːʃ-
wash|cloth 'wɒʃ |klɒθ-klɔːθ ‖ 'wɑːʃ |klɔːθ
'wɔːʃ-, -klɑːθ ~cloths klɒθs klɔːθs, klɒðz,
klɔːðz ‖ klɔːðzklɑːðz, klɔːθs, klɑːθs
washday 'wɒʃ deɪ ‖ 'wɑːʃ- 'wɔːʃ- ~s z
washed-out ˌwɒʃt 'aʊt ◂ ‖ ˌwɑːʃt- ˌwɔːʃt-
washed-up ˌwɒʃt 'ʌp ◂ ‖ ˌwɑːʃt- ˌwɔːʃt-
washer 'wɒʃ ə ‖ 'wɑːʃ ər'wɔːʃ- ~s z
washer-dryer ˌwɒʃ ə 'draɪ_ə ‖ ˌwɑːʃ ər 'draɪ_ər
ˌwɔːʃ- ~s z
washer-up ˌwɒʃ ər 'ʌp ‖ ˌwɑːʃ ər 'ʌp,wɔːʃ-
washers-up ˌwɒʃ əz 'ʌp ‖ ˌwɑːʃ ərz 'ʌp
ˌwɔːʃ-
washer|woman 'wɒʃ ə ˌwʊm ən ‖ 'wɑːʃ ər-
'wɔːʃ- ~women ˌwɪm ɪn-ən

W

washer|y 'wɒʃ ər li ‖ 'wɑːʃ- 'wɔːʃ- ~ies iz
wash|house 'wɒʃ |haʊs ‖ 'wɑːʃ- 'wɔːʃ-
~houses haʊz ɪz -əz
Washington 'wɒʃ ɪŋ tən ‖ 'wɑːʃ- 'wɔːʃ-
Washingtonian ˌwɒʃ ɪŋ 'təʊn i‿ən ◂
‖ ˌwɑːʃ ɪŋ 'toʊn- ˌwɔːʃ- ~s z
washing-up ˌwɒʃ ɪŋ 'ʌp ‖ ˌwɑːʃ- ˌwɔːʃ-
washleather 'wɒʃ ˌleð ə ‖ 'wɑːʃ ˌleð ər 'wɔːʃ-
~s z
Washoe 'wɒʃ əʊ ‖ 'wɑːʃ oʊ
washout 'wɒʃ aʊt ‖ 'wɑːʃ- 'wɔːʃ- ~s s
washpot 'wɒʃ pɒt ‖ 'wɑːʃ pɑːt 'wɔːʃ- ~s s
washrag 'wɒʃ ræg ‖ 'wɑːʃ- 'wɔːʃ- ~s z
washroom 'wɒʃ ruːm -rʊm ‖ 'wɑːʃ- 'wɔːʃ- ~s z
washstand 'wɒʃ stænd ‖ 'wɑːʃ- 'wɔːʃ- ~s z
washtub 'wɒʃ tʌb ‖ 'wɑːʃ- 'wɔːʃ- ~s z
wash-up 'wɒʃ ʌp ‖ 'wɑːʃ- 'wɔːʃ- ~s s
wash-wipe ˌwɒʃ 'waɪp ‖ ˌwɑːʃ- ˌwɔːʃ-
wash|woman 'wɒʃ ˌwʊm ən ‖ 'wɑːʃ- 'wɔːʃ-
~women ˌwɪm ɪn -ən
wash|y 'wɒʃ li ‖ 'wɑːʃ li 'wɔːʃ- ~ier i‿ə ‖ i‿ər
~iest i‿ɪst i‿əst ~iness i nəs i nɪs
wasn't 'wɒz ənt ‖ 'wʌz ənt 'wɑːz-
wasp, WASP, Wasp wɒsp ‖ wɑːsp wasps,
WASPs, Wasps wɒsps ‖ wɑːsps
waspish 'wɒsp ɪʃ ‖ 'wɑːsp ɪʃ ~ly li ~ness nəs
nɪs
wasp-waisted ˌwɒsp 'weɪst ɪd ◂ -əd, '•ˌ••
‖ 'wɑːsp ˌweɪst əd
wasp|y, Wasp|y, WASP|y 'wɒsp li ‖ 'wɑːsp li
~ier i‿ə ‖ i‿ər ~iest i‿ɪst i‿əst ~ily ɪ li əl i
~iness i nəs i nɪs
wassail 'wɒs eɪəl -əl ‖ 'wɑːs- ~ed d ~ing ɪŋ
~s z
Wassermann 'wæs ə mən 'væs-, 'vɑːs-
‖ 'wɑːs ər- —Ger ['vas ɐ man]
'Wassermann test
Wasson 'wɒs ən ‖ 'wɑːs ən
wast strong form wɒst ‖ wɑːst , weak form wəst
wastag|e 'weɪst ɪdʒ ~es ɪz əz
Wastdale 'wɒs dəl 'wɒst-, -deɪəl ‖ 'wɑːst-
waste weɪst (= waist) wasted 'weɪst ɪd -əd
wastes weɪsts wasting 'weɪst ɪŋ
ˌwaste 'paper, '•ˌ••; ˌwaste 'paper
ˌbasket, '•ˌ••ˌ•• ‖ '•ˌ••ˌ••; 'waste pipe;
'waste ˌproduct
wastebasket 'weɪst ˌbɑːsk ɪt §-ˌbæsk-, §-ət
‖ -ˌbæsk ət ~s s
wasteful 'weɪst fəl -fʊl ~ly i ~ness nəs nɪs
wasteland 'weɪst lænd -lənd ~s z
wastepaper ˌweɪst 'peɪp ə '•ˌ••
‖ 'weɪst ˌpeɪp ər
wastepipe 'weɪst paɪp ~s s
waster 'weɪst ə ‖ -ər ~s z
wastrel 'weɪs trəl ~s z
Wastwater 'wɒst ˌwɔːt ə ‖ 'wɑːst ˌwɔːt ər
-ˌwɑːt-
Wat, wat wɒt ‖ wɑːt
watch wɒtʃ ‖ wɑːtʃ wɔːtʃ watched
wɒtʃt ‖ wɑːtʃt wɔːtʃt watches 'wɒtʃ ɪz -əz
‖ 'wɑːtʃ əz 'wɔːtʃ- watching

'wɒtʃ ɪŋ ‖ 'wɑːtʃ ɪŋ 'wɔːtʃ-
ˌwatching 'brief; 'watch night
watchable 'wɒtʃ əb əl ‖ 'wɑːtʃ- 'wɔːtʃ-
watchband 'wɒtʃ bænd ‖ 'wɑːtʃ- 'wɔːtʃ- ~s z
watchcas|e 'wɒtʃ keɪs ‖ 'wɑːtʃ- 'wɔːtʃ- ~es
ɪz əz
watchdog 'wɒtʃ dɒg ‖ 'wɑːtʃ dɔːg 'wɔːtʃ-,
-dɑːg ~s z
watcher 'wɒtʃ ə ‖ 'wɑːtʃ ər 'wɔːtʃ- ~s z
Watchet 'wɒtʃ ɪt §-ət ‖ 'wɑːtʃ ət
watchful 'wɒtʃ fəl -fʊl ‖ 'wɑːtʃ- 'wɔːtʃ- ~ly i
~ness nəs nɪs
watchmaker 'wɒtʃ ˌmeɪk ə ‖ 'wɑːtʃ ˌmeɪk ər
'wɔːtʃ- ~s z
watch|man 'wɒtʃ |mən ‖ 'wɑːtʃ- 'wɔːtʃ-
~men mən men
watchnight 'wɒtʃ naɪt ‖ 'wɑːtʃ- 'wɔːtʃ-
watchstrap 'wɒtʃ stræp ‖ 'wɑːtʃ- 'wɔːtʃ- ~s s
watchtower 'wɒtʃ ˌtaʊ‿ə ‖ 'wɑːtʃ ˌtaʊ‿ər
'wɔːtʃ- ~s z
watchword 'wɒtʃ wɜːd ‖ 'wɑːtʃ wɜːd 'wɔːtʃ-
~s z
Watendlath wɒ 'tend ləθ ‖ wɑː-
water 'wɔːt ə ‖ 'wɔːt ər 'wɑːt- ~ed d
watering 'wɔːt_ər ɪŋ ‖ 'wɔːt ər ɪŋ 'wɑːt- ~s z
'water bird; 'water ˌbiscuit; 'water
ˌbuffalo; 'water butt; 'water ˌcannon;
ˌwater 'chestnut ‖ '•ˌ• ˌ•ˌ•; 'water ˌcloset;
'water ˌcooler; ˌwatered 'silk; 'water ice;
'watering can; 'watering hole; 'watering
place; 'water jump; 'water ˌlevel; 'water
ˌlily; 'water main; 'water ˌmeadow; 'water
pipe; 'water ˌpolo; 'water rat; 'water rate;
'water ˌsoftener; 'water supˌply; 'water
ˌtable; 'water ˌtower; 'water ˌvapour;
'water vole
waterborne 'wɔːt ə bɔːn ‖ 'wɔːt ər bɔːrn
'wɑːt-, -boʊrn
waterbuck 'wɔːt ə bʌk ‖ 'wɔːt ər- 'wɑːt-
Waterbury 'wɔːt ə bər_i ‖ 'wɔːt ər ˌber i 'wɑːt-,
-bər_i
watercolor, watercolour 'wɔːt ə ˌkʌl ə
‖ 'wɔːt ər ˌkʌl ər 'wɑːt- ~s z
watercolorist, watercolourist
'wɔːt ə ˌkʌl ər ɪst §-əst ‖ 'wɔːt ər ˌkʌl ər ɪst
'wɑːt- ~s s
water-cool 'wɔːt ə kuːl ‖ 'wɔːt ər- 'wɑːt- ~ed
d ~ing ɪŋ ~s z
watercours|e 'wɔːt ə kɔːs ‖ 'wɔːt ər kɔːrs
'wɑːt-, -koʊrs ~es ɪz əz
watercraft 'wɔːt ə krɑːft §-kræft
‖ 'wɔːt ər kræft 'wɑːt- ~s s
watercress 'wɔːt ə kres ‖ 'wɔːt ər- 'wɑːt-
watered-down ˌwɔːt əd 'daʊn ◂ ‖ ˌwɔːt ərd-
ˌwɑːt-
waterfall 'wɔːt ə fɔːl ‖ 'wɔːt ər- 'wɑːt-, -fɑːl
~s z
Waterford 'wɔːt ə fəd ‖ 'wɔːt ər fərd 'wɑːt-
waterfowl 'wɔːt ə faʊl ‖ 'wɔːt ər- 'wɑːt- ~s z
waterfront 'wɔːt ə frʌnt ‖ 'wɔːt ər- 'wɑːt- ~s
s
Watergate 'wɔːt ə geɪt ‖ 'wɔːt ər- 'wɑːt-

waterhole 'wɔːt ə həʊl →-hɒʊl ‖ 'wɔːt̬ ər hoʊl
　'wɑːt̬- ~s z
Waterhouse 'wɔːt ə haʊs ‖ 'wɔːt̬ ər- 'wɑːt̬-
wateriness 'wɔːt̬ ər i nəs -nıs ‖ 'wɔːt̬- 'wɑːt̬-
waterless 'wɔːt ə ləs -lıs; -əl əs, -ıs
　‖ 'wɔːt̬ ər ləs 'wɑːt̬-
waterline 'wɔːt ə laın -əl aın ‖ 'wɔːt̬ ər laın
　'wɑːt̬- ~s z
waterlog 'wɔːt ə lɒg -əl ɒg ‖ 'wɔːt̬ ər lɔːg
　'wɑːt̬-, -lɑːg ~ged d ~ging ıŋ ~s z
Waterloo ˌwɔːt ə 'luː ◂ -əl 'uː ‖ ˌwɔːt̬ ər 'luː
　ˌwɑːt̬-, '•••
　ˌWaterloo 'Road; ˌWaterloo 'Station
Waterlooville ˌwɔːt ə ˌluː 'vıl ‖ ˌwɔːt̬ ər- ˌwɑːt̬-
water|man, W~ 'wɔːt ə |mən ‖ 'wɔːt̬ ər- 'wɑːt̬-
　~men mən men
watermark 'wɔːt ə mɑːk ‖ 'wɔːt̬ ər mɑːrk
　'wɑːt̬- ~ed t ~ing ıŋ ~s s
watermelon 'wɔːt ə ˌmel ən ‖ 'wɔːt̬ ər- 'wɑːt̬-
　~s z
watermill 'wɔːt ə mıl ‖ 'wɔːt̬ ər- 'wɑːt̬- ~s z
waterpower 'wɔːt ə ˌpaʊ_ə ‖ 'wɔːt̬ ər ˌpaʊ_ər
　'wɑːt̬-
waterproof 'wɔːt ə pruːf §-prʊf ‖ 'wɔːt̬ ər-
　'wɑːt̬- ~ed t ~ing ıŋ ~s s
water-repellent ˌwɔːt ə rı 'pel ənt ◂ -rə'•-,
　§-riː'•-, '•••,•• ‖ 'wɔːt̬ ər rı ˌpel ənt 'wɑːt̬-
water-resistant ˌwɔːt ə rı 'zıst ənt ◂ -rə'•-,
　§-riː'•-, '•••,•• ‖ 'wɔːt̬ ər rı ˌzıst ənt 'wɑːt̬-
Waters 'wɔːt ə əz ‖ 'wɔːt̬ ərz 'wɑːt̬-
watershed 'wɔːt ə ʃed ‖ 'wɔːt̬ ər- 'wɑːt̬- ~s z
Watership 'wɔːt ə ʃıp ‖ 'wɔːt̬ ər- 'wɑːt̬-
　ˌWatership 'Down
waterside 'wɔːt ə saıd ‖ 'wɔːt̬ ər- 'wɑːt̬-
water-ski 'wɔːt ə skiː ‖ 'wɔːt̬ ər- 'wɑːt̬- ~ed d
　~er/s ə/z ‖ ər/z ~ing ıŋ ~s z
Waterson 'wɔːt ə əs ən ‖ 'wɔːt̬ ərs ən 'wɑːt̬-
waterspout 'wɔːt ə spaʊt ‖ 'wɔːt̬ ər- 'wɑːt̬- ~s
　s
Waterstone 'wɔːt ə stəʊn ‖ 'wɔːt̬ ər stoʊn
　'wɑːt̬-
watertight 'wɔːt ə taıt ‖ 'wɔːt̬ ər- 'wɑːt̬-
Waterton 'wɔːt ət ən ‖ 'wɔːt̬ ərt ən 'wɑːt̬-
Watertown 'wɔːt ə taʊn ‖ 'wɔːt̬ ər- 'wɑːt̬-
waterway 'wɔːt ə weı ‖ 'wɔːt̬ ər- 'wɑːt̬- ~s z
waterweed ˌwɔːt ə wiːd ‖ 'wɔːt̬ ər- 'wɑːt̬- ~s z
waterwheel 'wɔːt ə wiː əl -hwiː əl
　‖ 'wɔːt̬ ər hwiː əl 'wɑːt̬- ~s z
waterwings 'wɔːt ə wıŋz ‖ 'wɔːt̬ ər- 'wɑːt̬-
waterworks 'wɔːt ə wɜːks ‖ 'wɔːt̬ ər wɜ˞ːks
　'wɑːt̬-
watery 'wɔːt ər i ‖ 'wɔːt ər i 'wɑːt̬-
Wates weıts
Watford 'wɒt fəd ‖ 'wɑːt fərd
Wath wɒθ ‖ wɑːθ
Watkin 'wɒt kın ‖ 'wɑːt-
Watkins 'wɒt kınz ‖ 'wɑːt-
Watkinson 'wɒt kın sən ‖ 'wɑːt-
Watling 'wɒt lıŋ ‖ 'wɑːt-
　'Watling Street
Watney 'wɒt ni ‖ 'wɑːt ni
WATS wɒts ‖ wɑːts
Watson 'wɒts ən ‖ 'wɑːts ən

watt, Watt wɒt ‖ wɑːt watts wɒts ‖ wɑːts
wattag|e 'wɒt ıdʒ ‖ 'wɑːt ıdʒ ~es ız əz
Watteau 'wɒt əʊ ‖ wɑː 'toʊ —Fr [va to]
watt-hour ˌwɒt 'aʊ_ə ‖ ˌwɑːt 'aʊ_ər ~s z
wattle 'wɒt əl ‖ 'wɑːt əl ~d d ~s z
　ˌwattle and 'daub
wattlebird 'wɒt əl bɜːd ‖ 'wɑːt əl bɜ˞ːd ~s z
wattmeter 'wɒt ˌmiːt ə ‖ 'wɑːt ˌmiːt̬ ər ~s z
Watts wɒts ‖ wɑːts
Watusi wə 'tuːs i wɑː-, -'tuːz-
Wauchope (i) 'wɔːk əp 'wɒx- ‖ 'wɑːk-, (ii)
　'wɔː həʊp ‖ -hoʊp 'wɑː-
Waugh (i) wɔː ‖ wɑː, (ii) wɒf wɑːf, wɒx ‖ wɑːf
　—The writers Evelyn Waugh and Auberon
　Waugh are (i).
Waunfawr 'waın vaʊ_ə ‖ -vaʊ_ər —Welsh
　['wain vaur, 'wain-]
wave weıv waved weıvd waves weıvz
　waving 'weıv ıŋ
　'wave band; ˌwave me'chanics
waveform 'weıv fɔːm ‖ -fɔːrm ~s z
waveguide 'weıv gaıd ~s z
wavelength 'weıv leŋᵏθ §-lenᵗθ ~s s
wavelet 'weıv lət -lıt ~s s
Wavell 'weıv əl
Waveney 'weıv ən_i
waver 'weıv ə ‖ -ər ~ed d wavering/ly
　'weıv ər_ıŋ /li ~s z
waverer 'weıv ər_ə ‖ -ər_ər ~s z
Waverley 'weıv ə li ‖ -ər-
Wavertree 'weıv ə triː ‖ -ər-
waving 'weıv ıŋ
wav|ly 'weıv |li ~ier i_ə ‖ i_ər ~iest i_ıst i_əst
　~ily ı li əl i ~iness i nəs i nıs
Wawona wɔː 'wəʊn ə ‖ -'woʊn- wɑː-
wax, Wax wæks waxed wækst waxes
　'wæks ız -əz waxing 'wæks ıŋ
　'waxed ˌpaper; 'wax ˌpaper
waxbill 'wæks bıl ~s z
waxen 'wæks ən
waxplant 'wæks plɑːnt §-plænt ‖ -plænt ~s s
waxwing 'wæks wıŋ ~s z
waxwork 'wæks wɜːk ‖ -wɜ˞ːk ~s s
wax|y 'wæks |li ~ier i_ə ‖ i_ər ~iest i_ıst i_əst
　~iness i nəs i nıs
way, Way weı ways weız
　ˌway 'in; ˌway 'out
waybill 'weı bıl ~s z
wayfarer 'weı ˌfeər ə ‖ -ˌfer ər -ˌfær- ~s z
wayfaring 'waı ˌfeər ıŋ ‖ -ˌfer ıŋ -ˌfær-
　'wayfaring tree
waylaid ₍ᵢ₎weı 'leıd
Wayland 'weı lənd
waylay ₍ᵢ₎weı 'leı waylaid ₍ᵢ₎weı 'leıd ~ing ıŋ
　~s z
wayleave 'weı liːv ~s z
waymark 'weı mɑːk ‖ -mɑːrk ~ed t ~ing ıŋ
　~s s
Wayne weın
Waynflete 'weın fliːt
way-out adj ˌweı 'aʊt ◂
　ˌway-out 'fashions
-ways weız — sideways 'saıd weız

W

wayside 'weɪ saɪd ~s z
wayward 'weɪ wəd ‖ -wərd ~ly li ~ness nəs nɪs
Waziristan wə ˌzɪər ɪ 'stɑːn -ə- ‖ -ˌzɪr-
we *strong form* wiː, *weak form* wi
weak wiːk (= *week*) **weaker** 'wiːk ə ‖ -ər
  weakest 'wiːk ɪst -əst
  'weaker ˌsex, ˌ•• '•
weaken 'wiːk ən ~ed d ~ing _ɪŋ ~s z
weak-kneed ˌwiːk 'niːd ◄
weakling 'wiːk lɪŋ ~s z
weakly 'wiːk li
weak-minded ˌwiːk 'maɪnd ɪd ◄ -əd ~ly li
  ~ness nəs nɪs
weakness 'wiːk nəs -nɪs -es ɪz əz
weal wiːəl **weals** wiːəlz
Weald, weald wiːəld
wealden, W~ 'wiːəld ən
Wealdstone 'wiːəld stəʊn ‖ -stoʊn
wealth welθ
wealth|y 'welθ |i ~ier i_ə ‖ i_ər ~iest i_ɪst i_əst
  ~ily ɪ li əl i ~iness i nəs i nɪs
wean wiːn **weaned** wiːnd **weaning** 'wiːn ɪŋ
  weans wiːnz
weaner 'wiːn ə ‖ -ər ~s z
weapon 'wep ən ~s z
weaponry 'wep ən ri
wear weə ‖ weᵊr wæᵊr **wearing**
  'weᵊr ɪŋ ‖ 'wer ɪŋ 'wær- **wears**
  weəz ‖ weᵊrz wæᵊrz **wore** wɔː ‖ wɔːr woʊr
  worn wɔːn ‖ wɔːrn woʊrn
  ˌwear and 'tear
Wear *river* wɪə ‖ wɪᵊr
wearability ˌweər ə 'bɪl ət i -ɪt i
  ‖ ˌwer ə 'bɪl əṭ i ˌwær-
wearable 'weər əb ᵊl ‖ 'wer- 'wær-
Weardale 'wɪə deɪᵊl ‖ 'wɪr-
wearer 'weər ə ‖ 'wer ᵊr 'wær- ~s z
weari... —*see* **weary**
wearisome 'wɪər i səm ‖ 'wɪr- ~ly li ~ness
  nəs nɪs
Wearmouth 'wɪə maʊθ -məθ ‖ 'wɪr-
wear|y 'wɪər li ‖ 'wɪr li ~ied id ~ier i_ə ‖ i_ər
  ~ies iz ~iest i_ɪst i_əst ~ily əl i i li ~iness
  i nəs i nɪs ~ying i ɪŋ
weasel 'wiːz ᵊl ~ed d ~ing _ɪŋ ~s z
weaselly 'wiːz ᵊl i
weather 'weð ə ‖ -ər ~s z
  'weather balˌloon; 'weather ˌforecast;
  'weather map; 'weather ship; 'weather
  ˌstation; 'weather vane
Weatherall 'weð ər ɔːl ‖ -ɑːl
weather-beaten 'weð ə ˌbiːt ən ‖ -ər-
weatherboard 'weð ə bɔːd ‖ -ər bɔːrd -boʊrd
  ~ing ɪŋ ~s z
weather-bound 'weð ə baʊnd ‖ -ər-
weathercock 'weð ə kɒk ‖ -ər kɑːk ~s s
weatherglass 'weð ə glɑːs §-glæs ‖ -ər glæs
  ~es ɪz əz
Weatherhead 'weð ə hed ‖ -ər-
weather|man, W~ 'weð ə |mæn ‖ -ər- ~men
  men

weatherproof 'weð ə pruːf §-prʊf ‖ -ər- ~ed t
  ~ing ɪŋ ~s s
weathertight 'weð ə taɪt ‖ -ər-
weave wiːv **weaved** wiːvd **weaves** wiːvz
  weaving 'wiːv ɪŋ **wove** wəʊv ‖ woʊv
  woven 'wəʊv ᵊn ‖ 'woʊv ᵊn
weaver, W~ 'wiːv ə ‖ -ər ~s z
weaverbird 'wiːv ə bɜːd ‖ -ər bɝːd ~s z
web web **webbed** webd **webbing** 'web ɪŋ
  webs webz
  ˌweb 'offset; 'web page
Webb web
Webber 'web ə ‖ -ər
webbing 'web ɪŋ
webcam, W~ 'web kæm ~s z
webding, W~ 'web dɪŋ ~s z
weber *unit of magnetic flux* 'veɪb ə 'web- ‖ -ər
  ~s z
Weber *English family name (i)* 'web ə ‖ -ər, *(ii)*
  'wiːb ə ‖ -ər, *(iii)* 'weɪb ə ‖ -ər
Weber *German family name; composer,*
  sociologist 'veɪb ə ‖ -ər —*Ger* ['veː bɐ]
Webern 'veɪb ɜːn -ən ‖ -ɝːn —*Ger* ['veː bɐn]
web|foot 'web |fʊt ~feet fiːt
web-footed ˌweb 'fʊt ɪd ◄ -əd, '•ˌ••
  ‖ -'fʊṭ əd ◄
Webley 'web li
webmaster 'web ˌmɑːst ə §-ˌmæst-
  ‖ -ˌmæst ər ~s z
website 'web saɪt ~s s
Webster 'web stə ‖ -stᵊr ~'s z
web-toed ˌweb 'təʊd ◄ ‖ -'toʊd ◄
Wechsler 'weks lə ‖ -lᵊr
wed wed **wedded** 'wed ɪd -əd **wedding**
  'wed ɪŋ **weds** wedz
we'd *strong form* wiːd, *weak form* wid
Wed —*see* **Wednesday**
wedded 'wed ɪd -əd
Weddell *(i)* 'wed ᵊl, *(ii)* wɪ 'del wə- —*For the*
  W~ Sea, (i)
Wedderburn 'wed ə bɜːn ‖ -ər bɝːn
wedding 'wed ɪŋ ~s z
  'wedding ˌbreakfast; 'wedding cake;
  'wedding day; 'wedding march; 'wedding
  ring
wedel 'veɪd ᵊl ~ed, ~led d ~ing, ~ling _ɪŋ
  ~s z
wedeln 'veɪd ᵊln ~ing ɪŋ
wedge wedʒ **wedged** wedʒd **wedges**
  'wedʒ ɪz -əz **wedging** 'wedʒ ɪŋ
Wedgewood, Wedgwood 'wedʒ wʊd
wedlock 'wed lɒk ‖ -lɑːk
Wedmore 'wed mɔː →'web- ‖ -mɔːr
Wednesbury 'wenz bər_i —*There is also a*
  spelling pronunciation 'wed nɪz bər_i,
  'wed nəz-; *locally also* 'wedʒ bər_i
Wednesfield 'wen|s fiːᵊld —*There is also a*
  spelling pronunciation 'wed nɪs fiːᵊld, -nəs-;
  locally also 'wedʒ fiːᵊld
Wednesday 'wenz deɪ -di; 'wed ᵊnz deɪ, -di
  —*see note at* -day ~s z
Weds —*see* **Wednesday** —*sometimes spoken*
  as wedz

Weak forms

1 Many English function words (= articles, pronouns, prepositions, auxiliaries, modals, etc.) have more than one pronunciation. In particular, they have a **strong form**, containing a **strong** vowel, and a **weak form**, containing a **weak** vowel. An example is **at**, with the strong form æt and the weak form ət.

2 The weak form is generally used if the word is unstressed (as is usually the case with function words). The strong form is used only when the word is stressed, usually because it is accented (see STRESS).
Jim's ət lunch. He'll be back ət one.
We say "æt home', not 'in home'.
I'll invite ðəm round.
Tell me how they 'wɜː ‖ 'wɜ·ː.
They wə ‖ wəʳ delighted.

3 Nevertheless, the strong form is used for unaccented function words in certain positions:
• usually, for a preposition when it is between a weak syllable and a pronoun, to help the rhythm:
I'm 'looking æt ju. (Compare: Don't 'look ət mi.)
• always, when a function word is **stranded** (= left exposed by a syntactic operation involving the movement or deletion of the word on which it depends):
Where does she 'kʌm frɒm ‖ frʌm? (...from X)
'aɪ kən speak English better than 'juː kæn. (= than you can speak)
It was 'eɪmd æt but not achieved. (= they aimed at it)

4 It is important for learners of English to use weak forms appropriately. Otherwise, listeners may think they are emphasizing a word where this is not really so. Equally, native speakers should not be misled into supposing that careful or declamatory speech demands strong forms throughout. One exception is the pronunciation style used for **singing**, where strong forms are often used. Even here, though, articles are usually weak.

---

wee wiː **weed** wiːd **weeing** 'wiː ɪŋ **wees** wiːz
Weech wiːtʃ
weed wiːd **weeded** 'wiːd ɪd -əd **weeding** 'wiːd ɪŋ **weeds** wiːdz
weeder 'wiːd ə ‖ -ʳr ~s z
weedi... —see **weedy**
weedkiller 'wiːd ˌkɪl ə →'wiːg- ‖ -ʳr ~s z
Weedon 'wiːd ən
weed|y 'wiːd li ~ier i_ə ‖ i_ʳr ~iest i_ɪst i_əst ~ily ɪ li əl i ~iness i nəs i nɪs
Weehawken wiː 'hɔːk ən ‖ -'hɑːk-
Weejuns *tdmk* 'wiːdʒ ənz
week wiːk **weeks** wiːks
weekday 'wiːk deɪ ~s z
weekend ˌwiːk 'end ◄ '·· ‖ '·· ~ed ɪd əd ~ing ɪŋ ~s z
weekender ˌwiːk 'end ə ‖ 'wiːk end ʳr ~s z
Weekes wiːks
Weekley 'wiːk li
week|ly 'wiːk lli ~lies liz
weeknight 'wiːk naɪt ~s s
Weeks wiːks
ween wiːn
weenie 'wiːn i ~s z
weensy 'wiːnz i
ween|y 'wiːn li ~ier i_ə ‖ i_ʳr ~ies iz ~iest i_ɪst i_əst
weenybopper 'wiːn i ˌbɒp ə ‖ -ˌbɑːp ʳr ~s z
weep wiːp **weeping** 'wiːp ɪŋ **weeps** wiːps
wept wept
ˌweeping 'willow
weeper 'wiːp ə ‖ -ʳr ~s z

Weak vowels

1 Among unstressed syllables it is useful to distinguish between those that nevertheless contain a strong vowel and those that have a weak vowel. This distinction has implications for syllabification (as shown in LPD) and for rhythm.

2 A stressed syllable (shown in words of more than one syllable by one of the marks ' and ˌ) must always contain a **strong** vowel (= any vowel or diphthong except ə, i, u). All the syllables in the following words, whether stressed or unstressed, are strong-vowelled: **red** red, **hope** həʊp ‖ hoʊp, **bedtime** 'bed taɪm, **undone** ˌʌn 'dʌn, **acorn** 'eɪk ɔːn ‖ 'eɪk ɔːrn, **butane** 'bjuːt eɪn.

3 The vowels ə, i, u are always weak. The vowel ɪ, too, is weak in many cases, and also sometimes ʊ in BrE and oʊ in AmE. The unstressed syllables in the following words are all **weak**-vowelled: **allow** ə 'laʊ, **happy** 'hæp i, **situation** ˌsɪtʃ u 'eɪʃ ᵊn, **carelessness** 'keə ləs nəs -lɪs -nɪs ‖ 'ker-, **remember** rɪ 'mem bə rə- ‖ rɪ 'mem bᵊr, **standard** 'stænd əd ‖ 'stænd ᵊrd, **stimulus** 'stɪm jʊl əs ‖ 'stɪm jəl əs. The weak vowel ə may be realized in the form of a SYLLABIC CONSONANT, as in **suddenly** 'sʌd ᵊn li. If a diphthong is created through the COMPRESSION of weak syllables, it remains weak, as in **annual** 'æn ju‿əl.

4 The distinction between weak ɪ and ə has the power of distinguishing words in RP. For example, **V.I.Lenin** is 'len ɪn, but **John Lennon** is 'len ən. The words **rabbit** 'ræb ɪt and **abbot** 'æb ət do not rhyme. In certain other kinds of English, however, this distinction may be NEUTRALIZED, with ə used instead of weak ɪ in virtually all positions, or with the choice between ə and ɪ dependent upon the phonetic context. Accordingly, at **rabbit** LPD shows a secondary pronunciation §'ræb ət.

5 Even in RP and in other kinds of English that maintain the distinction between weak ɪ and ə, many words may be heard with either pronunciation, and this is shown in LPD. For example, **carelessness, civil, private** are nowadays more usually pronounced 'keə ləs nəs, 'sɪv ᵊl, 'praɪv ət. A conservative minority say 'keə lɪs nɪs, 'sɪv ɪl, 'praɪv ɪt, and these are given in LPD as secondary pronunciations.

W

weep|ie, weep|y 'wiːp |i ~**ier** i‿ə ‖ i‿ᵊr ~**ies** iz
~**iest** i‿ɪst i‿əst ~**iness** i nəs i nɪs
Weetabix *tdmk* 'wiːt ə bɪks ‖ 'wiːt̬- ~**es** ɪz əz
weever 'wiːv ə ‖ -ᵊr ~**s** z
weevil 'wiːv ᵊl -ɪl ~**s** z
wee-wee 'wiː wiː ~**d** d ~**ing** ɪŋ ~**s** z
weft weft
Wehrmacht 'veə mɑːxt -mɑːkt, -mæxt, -mækt
‖ 'ver- —*Ger* ['veːɐ maxt]
Weidenfeld 'vaɪd ᵊn felt 'waɪd-
Weidman 'waɪd mən →'waɪb-
weigela waɪ 'dʒiːl ə wɪ-, wə-, -'dʒel-, -'giːl-;
⚠•'•i‿ə; 'waɪg ɪl ə, -ᵊl- ~**s** z

weigh weɪ (= *way*) **weighed** weɪd (= *wade*)
weighing 'weɪ ɪŋ **weighs** weɪz
weighbridg|e 'weɪ brɪdʒ ~**es** ɪz əz
Weighell *(i)* wiːᵊl, *(ii)* 'weɪ‿əl
weigh-in 'weɪ ɪn
weight, W~ weɪt (= *wait*) **weighted** 'weɪt ɪd
-əd ‖ 'weɪt̬ əd **weighting/s** 'weɪt ɪŋ/z
‖ 'weɪt̬ ɪŋ/z **weights** weɪts
weightless 'weɪt ləs -lɪs ~**ly** li ~**ness** nəs nɪs
weightlift|ing 'weɪt ˌlɪft ɪŋ ~**er/s** ə/z ‖ ᵊr/z
Weighton 'wiːt ᵊn
weightwatch|er/s, WeightWatchers *tdmk*
'weɪt ˌwɒtʃ ə/z ‖ -ˌwɑːtʃ ᵊr/z ~**ing** ɪŋ

weight|y 'weɪt |i ‖ 'weɪt̬ |i **~ier** i‿ə ‖ i‿ər **~iest** i‿ɪst i‿əst **~ily** ɪ li əl i **~iness** i nəs i nɪs

Weil, Weill (i) vaɪəl, (ii) wiːəl —Ger, Fr [vail]

Weimar 'vaɪm ɑː ‖ -ɑːr —Ger ['vai maʁ]

Weimaraner, w~ 'vaɪm ə rɑːn ə 'waɪm-, ˌ•••• ‖ -ər **~s** z

Weinberger 'waɪn bɜːg ə →'waɪm- ‖ -bɝːg ər

Weinstock 'waɪn stɒk ‖ -stɑːk

weir, Weir wɪə ‖ wɪər **weirs** wɪəz ‖ wɪərz

weird wɪəd ‖ wɪərd **weirder** 'wɪəd ə ‖ 'wɪrd ər **weirdest** 'wɪəd ɪst -əst ‖ 'wɪrd əst

weirdie 'wɪəd i ‖ 'wɪrd i **~s** z

weird|ly 'wɪəd |li ‖ 'wɪrd |li **~ness** nəs nɪs

weirdo 'wɪəd əu ‖ 'wɪrd ou **~es** z

Weismann 'vaɪs mən ‖ -mɑːn —Ger ['vais man]

Weiss (i) vaɪs, (ii) weɪs —Ger [vais]

Weissmuller 'waɪs mʌl ə 'vaɪs-, -mul- ‖ -ər

Weizmann 'vaɪts mən ‖ -mɑːn —Ger ['vaits man]

Welbeck 'wel bek

Welbourne 'wel bɔːn ‖ -bɔːrn -bourn

Welby 'wel bi

Welch (i) weltʃ, (ii) welʃ

welch weltʃ welʃ **welched** weltʃt welʃt **welches** 'weltʃ ɪz 'welʃ-, -əs **welching** 'weltʃ ɪŋ 'welʃ-

welcom|e 'welk əm **~ed** d **~es** z **~ing** ɪŋ **~eness** nəs nɪs **~er/s** ə/z ‖ ər/z

weld, Weld weld **welded** 'weld ɪd -əd **welding** 'weld ɪŋ **welds** weldz

welder 'weld ə ‖ -ər **~s** z

Weldon 'weld ən

welfare, W~ 'wel feə ‖ -fer -fær ˌwelfare 'state ‖ '•••

welfarism 'wel feər ˌɪz əm ‖ -fer- -fær-

Welford 'wel fəd ‖ -fərd

welkin 'welk ɪn §-ən

well wel **welled** weld **welling** 'wel ɪŋ **wells** welz —When used as an interjection (but not otherwise) this word has an occasional weak form wəl.

we'll strong form wiːəl, weak form wil

well-adjusted ˌwel ə 'dʒʌst ɪd ◂ -əd

well-advised ˌwel əd 'vaɪzd ◂ §-æd-

Welland 'wel ənd

well-appointed ˌwel ə 'pɔɪnt ɪd ◂ -əd ‖ -'pɔɪnt̬ əd ◂

well-balanced ˌwel 'bæl ənᵗst ◂

well-behaved ˌwel bi 'heɪvd ◂ -bə-

wellbeing ˌwel 'biː ɪŋ '•, ••

Wellbeloved 'wel bi lʌvd -bə-

wellborn ˌwel 'bɔːn ◂ ‖ -'bɔːrn ◂

well-bred ˌwel 'bred ◂

well-built ˌwel 'bɪlt ◂

well-chosen ˌwel 'tʃəuz ən ◂ ‖ -'tʃouz-

Wellcome 'welk əm

well-connected ˌwel kə 'nekt ɪd ◂ -əd

well-cooked ˌwel 'kukt ◂ §-'kuːkt

well-defined ˌwel dɪ 'faɪnd ◂ -də-, §-diː-

well-disposed ˌwel dɪ 'spəuzd ◂ -də- ‖ -'spouzd ◂

well-done ˌwel 'dʌn ◂

well-earned ˌwel 'ɜːnd ◂ ‖ -'ɝːnd ◂

Weller 'wel ə ‖ -ər

Welles welz

Wellesbourne 'welz bɔːn ‖ -bɔːrn -bourn

Wellesley 'welz li

well-established ˌwel ɪ 'stæb lɪʃt ◂ -ə-

well-favoured ˌwel 'feɪv əd ◂ ‖ -ərd ◂

well-fed ˌwel 'fed ◂

well-formed ˌwel 'fɔːmd ◂ ‖ -'fɔːrmd ◂

well-formedness ˌwel 'fɔːm ɪd nəs -əd-, -nɪs ‖ -'fɔːrm-

well-found ˌwel 'faund ◂

well-founded ˌwel 'faund ɪd ◂ -əd

well-groomed ˌwel 'gruːmd ◂ -'grumd

well-grounded ˌwel 'graund ɪd ◂ -əd

wellhead 'wel hed **~s** z

well-heeled ˌwel 'hiːəld ◂

well-hung ˌwel 'hʌŋ ◂

wellie 'wel i **~s** z

well-informed ˌwel ɪn 'fɔːmd ◂ ‖ -'fɔːrmd ◂

Welling 'wel ɪŋ

Wellingborough 'wel ɪŋ bər_ə ‖ -ˌbɝː ou

Wellington, w~ 'wel ɪŋ tən —but in New Zealand, locally usually 'wæl- **~s, ~'s** z ˌwellington 'boot

wellingtonia ˌwel ɪŋ 'təun i‿ə ‖ -'toun- **~s** z

well-intentioned ˌwel ɪn 'tenᵗʃ ənd ◂

well-knit ˌwel 'nɪt ◂

well-known ˌwel 'nəun ◂ ‖ -'noun ◂

well-liked ˌwel 'laɪkt ◂

well-lined ˌwel 'laɪnd ◂

well-made ˌwel 'meɪd ◂

well-meaning ˌwel 'miːn ɪŋ ◂

well-meant ˌwel 'ment ◂

well-nigh ˌwel 'naɪ ◂

well-off ˌwel 'ɒf ◂ -'ɔːf ‖ -'ɔːf ◂ -'ɑːf

well-oiled ˌwel 'ɔɪəld ◂

well-ordered ˌwel 'ɔːd əd ◂ ‖ -'ɔːrd ərd ◂

well-preserved ˌwel prɪ 'zɜːvd ◂ -prə-, §-priː- ‖ -'zɝːvd ◂

well-proportioned ˌwel prə 'pɔːʃ ənd ◂ ‖ -'pɔːrʃ- -'pourʃ-

well-read ˌwel 'red ◂

well-rounded ˌwel 'raund ɪd ◂ -əd

Wells welz

well-set ˌwel 'set ◂

well-spoken ˌwel 'spəuk ən ◂ ‖ -'spouk-

wellspring 'wel sprɪŋ **~s** z

well-tempered ˌwel 'temp əd ◂ ‖ -ərd ◂

well-thought-of ˌwel 'θɔːt ɒv ◂ -əv ‖ -'θɔːt̬ ʌv -'θɑːt̬-, -ɑːv

well-thought-out ˌwel θɔːt 'aut ◂ -θɔːt̬- -θɑːt̬-

well-thumbed ˌwel 'θʌmd ◂

well-timed ˌwel 'taɪmd ◂

well-to-do ˌwel tə 'duː ◂ -tu-

well-tried ˌwel 'traɪd ◂

well-turned ˌwel 'tɜːnd ◂ ‖ -'tɝːnd ◂

well-versed ˌwel 'vɜːst ◂ ‖ -'vɝːst ◂

well-wisher 'wel ˌwɪʃ ə, •'•• ‖ -ər **~s** z

well-worn ˌwel 'wɔːn ◂ ‖ -'wɔːrn ◂ -'wourn

well|y 'wel |i **~ies** iz

W

Welsh, welsh welʃ **welshed** welʃt **welshes**
'welʃ ɪz -əz **welshing** 'welʃ ɪŋ
,**Welsh 'rabbit,** ,**Welsh 'rarebit**
welsher 'welʃ ə ‖ -ᵊr ~**s** z
Welsh|man 'welʃ |mən ~**men** mən men
~**ness** nəs nɪs
Welshpool 'welʃ puːl ,•'•
Welsh|woman 'welʃ |,wʊm ən ~**women**
,wɪm ɪn §-ən
welt welt **welted** 'welt ɪd -əd **welting**
'welt ɪŋ **welts** welts
weltanschauung 'velt æn ,ʃaʊ ʊŋ -ən-, ,•••'••
‖ -ɑːn- —*Ger* W~ ['vɛlt ,an ʃaʊ ʊŋ]
welter 'welt ə ‖ -ᵊr ~**ed** d **weltering**
'welt ᵊr ɪŋ ~**s** z
welterweight 'welt ə weɪt ‖ -ᵊr- ~**s** s
Welthorpe 'wel θɔːp ‖ -θɔːrp
weltschmerz 'velt ʃmeəts ‖ -ʃmerts —*Ger* W~
['vɛlt ʃmɛʁts]
Welty 'welt i
welwitschia wel 'wɪtʃ i‿ə ~**s** z
Welwyn 'wel ɪn §-ən
Wem wem
Wembley 'wem bli
Wemmick 'wem ɪk
Wemyss wiːmz
wen wen **wens** wenz
Wenceslas, Wenceslaus 'wenᵗs əs ləs -ɪs-,
⚠-ləs-, -læs ‖ -lɔːs, -lɑːs
wench wenʃ **wenched** wenʃt **wenches**
'wenʃ ɪz -əz **wenching** 'wenʃ ɪŋ
wend, Wend wend **wended** 'wend ɪd -əd
wending 'wend ɪŋ **wends, Wends** wendz
Wendell 'wend ᵊl
Wenden 'wend ən
Wendish 'wend ɪʃ
Wendon 'wend ən
Wendover 'wend əʊv ə ‖ -oʊv ᵊr
Wendy 'wend i
'**Wendy house**
Wenham 'wen əm
Wenlock 'wen lɒk ‖ -lɑːk
,**Wenlock 'Edge**
Wensley 'wenz li 'wenᵗs-
Wensleydale, w~ 'wenz li deɪᵊl 'wenᵗs-
Wensum 'wenᵗs əm
went went
wentletrap 'went ᵊl træp ~**s** s
Wentworth 'went wəθ -wɜːθ ‖ -wɜːθ
Wenvoe 'wen vəʊ ‖ -voʊ
Weobley 'web li
wept wept
were *strong forms* wɜː weə ‖ wɜːː, *weak form*
wə ‖ wᵊr
we're wɪə ‖ wɪᵊr (= *weir*)
weren't wɜːnt weənt ‖ wɜːnt
were|wolf 'weə 'wʊlf 'wɪə-, 'wɜː- ‖ 'wer-
'wɪr-, 'wɜːː- ~**wolves** wʊlvz
Werner 'veən ɪk ‖ 'wɜːn ᵊr —*Ger* ['vɛʁ nɐ]
Wernicke 'veən ɪk ə ‖ 'vern- -i —*Ger*
['vɛʁ nɪk ə]
'**Wernicke's ,area**

wert *strong form* wɜːt ‖ wɜːːt, *weak form*
wət ‖ wᵊrt
Weser 'veɪz ə ‖ -ᵊr —*Ger* ['veː zɐ]
Wesker 'wesk ə ‖ -ᵊr
Wesley (i) 'wes li, (ii) 'wez li —*The founder of
Methodism was actually* (i), *though often
pronounced as* (ii). ~**s**, ~'**s** z
Wesleyan 'wez li‿ən 'wes- ~**s** z
Wessex 'wes ɪks §-əks
Wesson 'wes ᵊn
west, West west
,**West 'Bank;** ,**West 'Coast◄;** 'West
,**Country,** ,• '•••◄; ,**West 'End◄;** ,**West
Gla'morgan;** ₍ᵢ₎**West 'Indian,** ₍ᵢ₎**West
'Indies;** ,**West 'Midlands;** ,**West Vir'ginia;**
,**West 'Yorkshire**
westbound 'west baʊnd
Westbourne 'west bɔːn -bən ‖ -bɔːrn -boʊrn
Westbrook 'west brʊk
Westbury 'west bər‿i ‖ -,ber i
Westbury-on-Trym ,west bər‿i ɒn 'trɪm
‖ -ɑːn'• -ɔːn'•
Westclox *tdmk* 'west klɒks ‖ -klɑːks
Westcott 'west kət
wester, W~ 'west ə ‖ -ᵊr ~**ed** d **westering**
'west ᵊr ɪŋ ~**s** z
Westerham 'west ᵊr əm →'wes trəm
wester|ly 'west ə |li -ᵊl i ‖ -ᵊr |li ~**lies** liz
western, W~ 'west ən ‖ -ᵊrn ~**s** z
,**Western Au'stralia;** ,**Western 'Isles**
westerner, W~ 'west ən ə ‖ -ᵊrn ᵊr -ᵊn ər ~**s** z
westernis... —*see* **westerniz...**
westernization ,west ən aɪ 'zeɪʃ ᵊn -ɪ'•-
‖ -ᵊrn ə-
westerniz|e 'west ə naɪz ‖ -ᵊr- ~**ed** d ~**es** ɪz
əz ~**ing** ɪŋ
westernmost 'west ən məʊst →-əm-
‖ -ᵊrn moʊst
Westfield 'west fiːᵊld
Westgate 'west geɪt -gɪt, -gət
Westhoughton ,west 'hɔːt ᵊn ‖ -'hɑːt-
Westin 'west ɪn §-ən
Westinghouse 'west ɪŋ haʊs
Westlake 'west leɪk
Westland *tdmk* 'west lənd ~'**s** z
Westmeath ,west 'miːð
Westminster 'west mɪnᵗst ə ,•'•••;
⚠,•'mɪn ɪst ə, ⚠-əst ə ‖ -ᵊr
,**Westminster 'Abbey**
Westmoreland, Westmorland
'west mə lənd ‖ -mɔːr- -moʊr-
west-northwest ,west nɔːθ 'west ‖ -nɔːrθ-
—*also naut* -nɔː- ‖ -nɔːr-
Westoby (i) 'west əb i, (ii)
we 'stəʊb i ‖ -'stoʊb-
Weston 'west ᵊn
Westoning 'west ᵊn ɪŋ
Weston-super-Mare ,west ᵊn ,suːp ə 'meə
-,sjuːp-; ,•••'••• ‖ -ᵊr 'meᵊr -'mæᵊr
Westphali|a west 'feɪl i‿ə ~**an/s** ən/z
Westray 'wes treɪ -tri
west-southwest ,west saʊθ 'west —*also naut*
-saʊ-

westward 'west wəd ‖ -wərd **~s** z
,Westward 'Ho!
Westwood 'west wʊd
wet wet **wets** wets **wetted** 'wet ɪd -əd
‖ 'weṭ əd **wetter** 'wet ə ‖ 'weṭ ər **wettest**
'wet ɪst -əst ‖ 'weṭ əst **wetting**
'wet ɪŋ ‖ 'weṭ ɪŋ
,wet 'blanket ‖ '•‚•••; ,wet 'dream; 'wet
nurse; 'wet suit; 'wetting ,agent
wetback 'wet bæk **~s** s
wether 'weð ə ‖ -ər (= weather) **~s** z
Wetherall 'weð ər ɔːl -ər‚əl ‖ -ɑːl
Wetherby 'weð ə bi ‖ -ər-
wetland 'wet lænd -lənd **~s** z
wet-look 'wet lʊk §-luːk
Wetmore 'wet mɔː ‖ -mɔːr
wett... —see **wet**
Wetton 'wet ən
Wetzel 'wets əl
we've strong form wiːv, weak form wiv
Wexford 'weks fəd ‖ -fərd
Wexler 'weks lə ‖ -lər
Wey wei
Weybridge 'wei brɪdʒ
Weyman (i) 'wai mən, (ii) 'wei mən
Weymouth 'wei məθ
whack wæk hwæk ‖ hwæk **whacked** wækt
hwækt ‖ hwækt **whacking/s** 'wæk ɪŋ/z
'hwæk- ‖ hwæk ɪŋ/z **whacks** wæks hwæks
‖ hwæks
,whacked 'out
whacko ‚wæk 'əʊ ‚hwæk- ‖ 'hwæk oʊ
whale weiəl hweiəl ‖ hweiəl **whales** weiəlz
hweiəlz ‖ hweiəlz
'whale of a ,time
whaleboat 'weiəl bəʊt 'hweiəl- ‖ 'hweiəl boʊt
~s s
whalebone 'weiəl bəʊn 'hweiəl-
‖ 'hweiəl boʊn
whaler 'weiəl ə 'hweiəl- ‖ 'hweiəl ər **~s** z
Whaley 'weil i 'hweil- ‖ 'hweil i
whaling 'weiəl ɪŋ 'hweiəl- ‖ 'hweiəl ɪŋ
Whalley (i) 'wɒl i 'hwɒl- ‖ 'hwaːl i, (ii) 'wɔːl i
'hwɔːl- ‖ 'hwɔːl i 'hwaːl-, (iii) 'weil i 'hweil-
‖ 'hweil i —The place near Blackburn, Lancs.,
is (ii), but W~ Range in Manchester is (i).
wham, Wham wæm hwæm ‖ hwæm
whammed wæmd hwæmd ‖ hwæmd
whamming 'wæm ɪŋ 'hwæm- ‖ 'hwæm ɪŋ
whams wæmz hwæmz ‖ hwæmz
whammo 'wæm əʊ 'hwæm- ‖ 'hwæm oʊ
whamm|y 'wæm i 'hwæm- ‖ 'hwæm i **~ies** iz
whang wæŋ hwæŋ ‖ hwæŋ **whanged** wæŋd
hwæŋd ‖ hwæŋd **whanging** 'wæŋ ɪŋ
'hwæŋ- ‖ 'hwæŋ ɪŋ **whangs** wæŋz hwæŋz ‖
hwæŋz
whangee ‚wæŋ 'iː ‚hwæŋ-, -'giː ‖ ‚hwæŋ- **~s** z
whare 'wɒr i 'hwɒr i ‖ 'hwaːr i **~s** z
wharf wɔːf hwɔːf ‖ hwɔːrf **wharfs** wɔːfs
hwɔːfs ‖ hwɔːrfs **wharves** wɔːvz hwɔːvz ‖
hwɔːrvz
wharfage 'wɔːf ɪdʒ 'hwɔːf- ‖ 'hwɔːrf ɪdʒ
Wharfe wɔːf hwɔːf ‖ hwɔːrf

Wharfedale 'wɔːf deiəl 'hwɔːf- ‖ 'hwɔːrf-
wharfinger 'wɔːf ɪndʒ ə 'hwɔːf-, §-əndʒ-
‖ 'hwɔːrf əndʒ ər **~s** z
Wharton 'wɔːt ən 'hwɔːt- ‖ 'hwɔːrt ən
wharve wɔːv hwɔːv ‖ hwɔːrv **wharves** wɔːvz
hwɔːvz ‖ hwɔːrvz
what wɒt hwɒt ‖ hwʌt hwaːt —Also, when
followed by weak do/does/did, sometimes wɒ ‖
hwʌ, hwaː — as What do you do?
‚wɒd ə ju 'duː ‖ ‚hwʌd-
‚what 'for
what-d'you-call-it 'wɒdʒ u ‚kɔːl ɪt 'wɒdʒ ə-,
'wɒt dʒu-, 'wɒt dʒə-, §-ət ‖ 'hwʌdʒ-
'hwaːdʒ-, -‚kaːl-
whate'er wɒt 'eə hwɒt- ‖ hwʌt 'eər hwaːt-
whatever wɒt 'ev ə hwɒt- ‖ hwʌt 'ev ər hwaːt-
Whatmore 'wɒt mɔː 'hwɒt- ‖ 'hwaːt mɔːr
Whatmough 'wɒt məʊ 'hwɒt-, -mʌf
‖ 'hwaːt moʊ
whatnot 'wɒt nɒt 'hwɒt- ‖ 'hwʌt naːt 'hwaːt-
~s s
what's wɒts hwɒts ‖ hwʌts hwaːts
what's-her-name 'wɒts ə neim ‖ 'hwʌts ər-
'hwaːts-
what's-his-name 'wɒts ɪz neim -əz- ‖ 'hwʌts-
'hwaːts-
whatsit, what's it 'wɒts ɪt 'hwɒts-, §-ət
‖ 'hwʌts ət 'hwaːts- **~s** s
whatsitsname, what's its name
'wɒts ɪts neim 'hwɒts-, §-əts- ‖ 'hwʌts-
'hwaːts-
whatsoe'er ‚wɒt səʊ 'eə ‚hwɒt-
‖ ‚hwʌt soʊ 'eər ‚hwaːt-
whatsoever ‚wɒt səʊ 'ev ə ‚hwɒt-
‖ ‚hwʌt soʊ 'ev ər ‚hwaːt-
Whatton 'wɒt ən 'hwɒt- ‖ 'hwaːt ən
what-you-may-call-it 'wɒdʒ ə mə ‚kɔːl ɪt
'wɒtʃ-, 'hwɒdʒ-, 'hwɒtʃ-, '••i-, §-ət ‖ 'hwʌtʃ-
'hwaːtʃ-, -‚kaːl-
Wheal, wheal wiːəl hwiːəl ‖ hwiːəl **wheals**
wiːəlz hwiːəlz ‖ hwiːəlz
wheat wiːt hwiːt ‖ hwiːt
'wheat germ
Wheatcroft 'wiːt krɒft 'hwiːt- ‖ 'hwiːt krɔːft
-kraːft
wheatear 'wiːt ɪə 'hwiːt- ‖ 'hwiːṭ ɪr **~s** z
wheaten 'wiːt ən 'hwiːt- ‖ 'hwiːt ən
Wheathampstead 'wiːt əmp sted 'hwiːt-,
'wet-, 'hwet- ‖ 'hwiːṭ-
Wheatley 'wiːt li 'hwiːt- ‖ 'hwiːt li
wheatmeal 'wiːt miːəl 'hwiːt- ‖ 'hwiːt-
Wheatstone 'wiːt stən 'hwiːt-, -stəʊn
‖ 'hwiːt stoʊn
whee wiː hwiː ‖ hwiː —usually uttered on a
prolonged high-fall tone
wheedl|e 'wiːd əl 'hwiːd- ‖ 'hwiːd əl **~ed** d
~es z **~ing/ly** ɪŋ/li
wheel wiːəl hwiːəl ‖ hwiːəl **wheeled** wiːəld
hwiːəld ‖ hwiːəld **wheeling** 'wiːəl ɪŋ 'hwiːəl-
‖ 'hwiːəl ɪŋ **wheels** wiːəlz hwiːəlz ‖ hwiːəlz
wheelbarrow 'wiːəl ‚bær əʊ 'hwiːəl-
‖ 'hwiːl ‚bær oʊ -‚ber- **~s** z

W

wheelbas|e 'wiːᵊl beɪs 'hwiːᵊl- ‖ 'hwiːᵊl- **~es**
ɪz əz

wheelchair 'wiːᵊl tʃeə 'hwiːᵊl-; ˌ•'•
‖ 'hwiːᵊl tʃer -tʃær **~s** z

Wheeler, w~ 'wiːl ə 'hwiːl- ‖ 'hwiːᵊl ᵊr **~s** z

-wheeler 'wiːl ə 'hwiːᵊl- ‖ 'hwiːᵊl ᵊr —
three-wheeler ˌθriː 'wiːl ə -'hwiːᵊl ə
‖ -'hwiːᵊl ᵊr

wheeler-dealer ˌwiːl ə 'diːl ə ˌhwiːl-
‖ ˌhwiːᵊl ᵊr 'diːl ᵊr **~s** z

wheel|house 'wiːᵊl |haʊs 'hwiːᵊl- ‖ 'hwiːᵊl-
~houses haʊz ɪz -əz

wheelie 'wiːᵊl i 'hwiːᵊl- ‖ 'hwiːᵊl i **~s** z

wheelwright 'wiːᵊl raɪt 'hwiːᵊl- ‖ 'hwiːᵊl- **~s** s

Wheen wiːn hwiːn ‖ hwiːn

wheez|e wiːz hwiːz ‖ hwiːz **wheezed** wiːzd
hwiːzd ‖ hwiːzd **wheezes** 'wiːz ɪz 'hwiːz-,
-əz ‖ 'hwiːz əz **wheezing/ly** 'wiːz ɪŋ /li
'hwiːz- ‖ 'hwiːz ɪŋ /li

wheez|y 'wiːz li 'hwiːz- ‖ 'hwiːz li **~ier**
i_ə ‖ i_ᵊr **~iest** i_ɪst i_əst **~ily** ɪ li əl i **~iness**
i nəs i nɪs

Whelan 'wiːl ən 'hwiːl- ‖ 'hwiːᵊl ən

whelk welk hwelk —*An initial hw in
the sense 'shellfish' is not supported by the
etymology.* **whelks** welks hwelks ‖ hwelks

whelp welp hwelp ‖ hwelp **whelped** welpt
hwelpt ‖ hwelpt **whelping** 'welp ɪŋ 'hwelp-
‖ 'hwelp ɪŋ **whelps** welps hwelps ‖ hwelps

when wen hwen ‖ hwen

whence wenᵗs hwenᵗs ‖ hwenᵗs

whene'er wen 'eə hwen-, wən- ‖ hwen 'eᵊr

whenever wen 'ev ə hwen-, wən- ‖
hwen 'ev ᵊr

where weə hweə ‖ hweᵊr hwæᵊr

whereabouts *interrogative adv* ˌweər ə 'baʊts ◀
ˌhweər- ‖ 'hwer ə baʊts 'hwær-

whereabouts *n* 'weər ə baʊts 'hweər- ‖ 'hwer-
'hwær-

whereas weər 'æz hweər-, ˌ•'•, wer- ‖ hwer-
hwær-

whereat weər 'æt hweər-, ˌ•'•, wer- ‖ hwer-
hwær-

whereby weə 'baɪ hweə-, ˌ•'• ‖ hwer- hwær-

where'er weər 'eə hweər-, ˌ•'•, wer- ‖
hwer 'eᵊr hwær-

wherefore 'weə fɔː 'hweə- ‖ 'hwer fɔːr
'hwær-, -four **~s** z

wherein weər 'ɪn hweər-, ˌ•'•, wer- ‖ hwer-
hwær-

whereof weər 'ɒv hweər-, ˌ•'•, wer- ‖
hwer 'ʌv hwær-, -'ɑːv

whereon weər 'ɒn hweər-, ˌ•'•, wer- ‖
hwer 'ɑːn hwær-, -'ɔːn

where's weəz hweəz ‖ hweᵊrz hwæᵊrz

wheresoever ˌweə səʊ 'ev ə ˌhweə-
‖ ˌhwer soʊ 'ev ᵊr ˌhwær-

whereto weə 'tuː hweə- ‖ hwer- hwær-

whereunto weər 'ʌn tu hweər-, ˌ•'••; ˌ••'tuː:
‖ hwer- hwær-

whereupon ˌweər ə 'pɒn ˌhweər-, '•••
‖ ˌhwer ə 'pɑːn ˌhwær-, -'pɔːn

wherever weər 'ev ə hweər-, ˌ•'•• ‖
hwer 'ev ᵊr hwær-

wherewithal *n* 'weə wɪð ɔːl 'hweə-, §-wɪθ-,
ˌ••'• ‖ 'hwer- 'hwær-, -wɪθ-, -ɑːl

Whernside 'wɜːn saɪd 'hwɜːn- ‖ 'hwɝːn-

wherr|y 'wer li 'hwer- ‖ 'hwer li **~ies** iz

whet wet hwet ‖ hwet **whets** wets hwets ‖
hwets **whetted** 'wet ɪd 'hwet-, -əd
‖ 'hwet̬ əd **whetting** 'wet ɪŋ 'hwet-
‖ 'hwet̬ ɪŋ

whether 'weð ə 'hweð- ‖ 'hweð ᵊr

whetstone, W~ 'wet stəʊn 'hwet-
‖ 'hwet stoʊn **~s** z

whew fjuː hwjuː —*and non-speech sounds such
as* [ʍ, ʍu, ɸ, pɸː, yu̜]

Wheway 'wiː weɪ 'hwiː- ‖ 'hwiː-

Whewell 'hjuː_əl hjuːl

whey weɪ hweɪ ‖ hweɪ

wheyfaced 'weɪ feɪst 'hweɪ- ‖ 'hweɪ-

which wɪtʃ hwɪtʃ ‖ hwɪtʃ

Whicher 'wɪtʃ ə 'hwɪtʃ- ‖ 'hwɪtʃ ᵊr

whichever wɪtʃ 'ev ə hwɪtʃ-, ˌ•'•• ‖
hwɪtʃ 'ev ᵊr

whicker, W~ 'wɪk ə 'hwɪk- ‖ 'hwɪk ᵊr **~ed** d
whickering 'wɪk ᵊr ɪŋ 'hwɪk- ‖ 'hwɪk- **~s** z

whiff wɪf hwɪf ‖ hwɪf **whiffed** wɪft hwɪft ‖
hwɪft **whiffing** 'wɪf ɪŋ 'hwɪf- ‖ 'hwɪf ɪŋ
whiffs wɪfs hwɪfs ‖ hwɪfs

Whiffen 'wɪf ɪn 'hwɪf-, §-ᵊn ‖ 'hwɪf ᵊn

whiffl|e 'wɪf ᵊl 'hwɪf- ‖ 'hwɪf ᵊl **~ed** d **~es** z
~ing _ɪŋ

whiffl|y 'wɪf li 'hwɪf- ‖ 'hwɪf li **~ier** i_ə ‖ i_ᵊr
~iest i_ɪst i_əst **~iness** i nəs i nɪs

Whig wɪg hwɪg ‖ hwɪg **Whigs** wɪgz hwɪgz ‖
hwɪgz

Whigg|ery 'wɪg| ᵊr i 'hwɪg- ‖ 'hwɪg- **~ish** ɪʃ
~ism ɪz əm

while waɪᵊl hwaɪᵊl ‖ hwaɪᵊl **whiled** waɪᵊld
hwaɪᵊld ‖ hwaɪᵊld **whiles** waɪᵊlz hwaɪᵊlz ‖
hwaɪᵊlz **whiling** 'waɪᵊl ɪŋ 'hwaɪᵊl-
‖ 'hwaɪᵊl ɪŋ

whilst waɪᵊlst hwaɪᵊlst ‖ hwaɪᵊlst

whim wɪm hwɪm ‖ hwɪm **whims** wɪmz hwɪmz
‖ hwɪmz

whimbrel 'wɪm brᵊl 'hwɪm- ‖ 'hwɪm- **~s** z

whimper 'wɪmp ə 'hwɪmp- ‖ 'hwɪmp ᵊr **~ed** d
whimpering/ly 'wɪmp ᵊr_ɪŋ /li 'hwɪmp-
‖ 'hwɪmp- **~s** z

whimsey 'wɪmz i 'hwɪmz- ‖ 'hwɪmz i **~s** z

whimsical 'wɪmz ɪk ᵊl 'hwɪmz- ‖ 'hwɪmz- **~ly**
i

whimsicalit|y ˌwɪmz ɪ 'kæl ət li ˌhwɪmz-, §,•ə-,
-ɪt i ‖ ˌhwɪmz ə 'kæl ət̬ li **~ies** iz

whims|y 'wɪmz li 'hwɪmz- ‖ 'hwɪmz li **~ies** iz

whin wɪn hwɪn ‖ hwɪn

whinchat 'wɪn tʃæt 'hwɪn- ‖ 'hwɪn- **~s** s

whine waɪn hwaɪn ‖ hwaɪn **whined** waɪnd
hwaɪnd ‖ hwaɪnd **whines** waɪnz hwaɪnz ‖
hwaɪnz **whining/ly** 'waɪn ɪŋ /li 'hwaɪn-
‖ 'hwaɪn ɪŋ /li

whiner 'waɪn ə 'hwaɪn- ‖ 'hwaɪn ᵊr **~s** z

whinge wɪndʒ hwɪndʒ ‖ hwɪndʒ **whinged**
wɪndʒd hwɪndʒd ‖ hwɪndʒd **whinges**

'wɪndʒ ɪz 'hwɪndʒ-, -əz ‖ 'hwɪndʒ əz
whingeing, whinging 'wɪndʒ ɪŋ 'hwɪndʒ-
‖ 'hwɪndʒ ɪŋ
whinger 'wɪndʒ ə 'hwɪndʒ- ‖ 'hwɪndʒ ər ~s z
whinn|y 'wɪn |i 'hwɪn- ‖ 'hwɪn |i ~**ied** id ~**ies**
iz ~**ying** i ɪŋ
whinstone 'wɪn stəʊn 'hwɪn- ‖ 'hwɪn stoʊn
whin|y 'waɪn |i 'hwaɪn- ‖ 'hwaɪn |i ~**ier**
i‿ə ‖ i‿ər ~**iest** i ɪst -əst ~**iness** i nəs -nɪs
whip wɪp hwɪp ‖ hwɪp **whipped** wɪpt hwɪpt ‖
hwɪpt **whipping/s** 'wɪp ɪŋ/z 'hwɪp-
‖ 'hwɪp ɪŋ/z **whips** wɪps hwɪps ‖ hwɪps
'whip hand, ‚• '•; 'whipping boy;
'whipping cream
whipcord 'wɪp kɔːd 'hwɪp- ‖ 'hwɪp kɔːrd
whiplash 'wɪp læʃ 'hwɪp- ‖ 'hwɪp- ~**es** ɪz əz
whipp... —*see* **whip**
whipp|er-in ‚wɪp |ər 'ɪn ‚hwɪp- ‖ ‚hwɪp |ər 'ɪn
~**ers-in** əz 'ɪn ‖ ərz-
whippersnapper 'wɪp ə ‚snæp ə 'hwɪp-
‖ 'hwɪp ər ‚snæp ər ~**s** z
whippet 'wɪp ɪt 'hwɪp-, §-ət ‖ 'hwɪp ət ~**s** s
whippoorwill 'wɪp ə wɪl 'hwɪp-, -ʊə-, -pʊə-,
‚•• '• ‖ 'hwɪp ər- ~**s** z
whipp|y 'wɪp |i 'hwɪp- ‖ 'hwɪp |i ~**ier** i‿ə ‖ i‿ər
~**iest** i‿ɪst i‿əst
whip-round 'wɪp raʊnd 'hwɪp- ‖ 'hwɪp- ~**s** z
whipsaw 'wɪp sɔː 'hwɪp- ‖ 'hwɪp- -sɑː ~**s** z
Whipsnade 'wɪp sneɪd 'hwɪp- ‖ 'hwɪp-
whir wɜː hwɜː ‖ hwɝː **whirred** wɜːd hwɜːd ‖
hwɝːd **whirring** 'wɜːr ɪŋ 'hwɜːr- ‖ 'hwɝː ɪŋ
whirs wɜːz hwɜːz ‖ hwɝːz
whirl wɜːl hwɜːl ‖ hwɝːl **whirled** wɜːld
hwɜːld ‖ hwɝːld **whirling** 'wɜːl ɪŋ 'hwɜːl-
‖ 'hwɝːl ɪŋ **whirls** wɜːlz hwɜːlz ‖ hwɝːlz
whirligig 'wɜːl i gɪg 'hwɜːl- ‖ 'hwɝːl- ~**s** z
whirlpool 'wɜːl puːl 'hwɜːl- ‖ 'hwɝːl- ~**s** z
whirlwind 'wɜːl wɪnd 'hwɜːl- ‖ 'hwɝːl- ~**s** z
whirlybird 'wɜːl i bɜːd 'hwɜːl- ‖ 'hwɝːl i bɝːd
~**s** z
whirr wɜː hwɜː ‖ hwɝː **whirred** wɜːd hwɜːd ‖
hwɝːd **whirring** 'wɜːr ɪŋ 'hwɜːr- ‖ 'hwɝː ɪŋ
whirr's wɜːz hwɜːz ‖ hwɝːz
whisk wɪsk hwɪsk ‖ hwɪsk **whisked** wɪskt
hwɪskt ‖ hwɪskt **whisking** 'wɪsk ɪŋ 'hwɪsk-
‖ 'hwɪsk ɪŋ **whisks** wɪsks hwɪsks ‖ hwɪsks
Whiskas *tdmk* 'wɪsk əz 'hwɪsk- ‖ 'hwɪsk əz
whisker 'wɪsk ə 'hwɪsk- ‖ 'hwɪsk ər ~**ed** d ~**s**
z
whiskey 'wɪsk i 'hwɪsk- ‖ 'hwɪsk i ~**s** z
whisk|y 'wɪsk |i 'hwɪsk- ‖ 'hwɪsk |i ~**ies** iz
whisper 'wɪsp ə 'hwɪsp- ‖ 'hwɪsp ər ~**ed** d
whispering/s 'wɪsp ər_ɪŋ/z 'hwɪsp-
‖ 'hwɪsp- ~**s** z
'whispering cam‚paign
whisperer 'wɪsp ər ə 'hwɪsp- ‖ 'hwɪsp ər ər
~**s** z
whist wɪst hwɪst ‖ hwɪst
'whist drive
whistl|e 'wɪs əl 'hwɪs- ‖ 'hwɪs əl ~**ed** d ~**es** z
~**ing** _ɪŋ
'whistle stop

whistle-blower 'wɪs əl ‚bləʊ ə 'hwɪs-
‖ 'hwɪs əl ‚bloʊ ər ~**s** z
whistler, W~ 'wɪs lə 'hwɪs- ‖ 'hwɪs lər ~**s**, ~'**s**
z
whistle-stop 'wɪs əl stɒp 'hwɪs-
‖ 'hwɪs əl stɑːp ~**ped** t ~**ping** ɪŋ ~**s** s
‚whistle-stop 'tour
whit, Whit wɪt hwɪt ‖ hwɪt
‚Whit 'Monday; ‚Whit 'Sunday
Whitaker 'wɪt ək ə 'hwɪt-, -ɪk- ‖ 'hwɪt̬ ək ər
Whitbread 'wɪt bred 'hwɪt- ‖ 'hwɪt-
Whitby 'wɪt bi 'hwɪt- ‖ 'hwɪt bi
Whitchurch 'wɪt tʃɜːtʃ 'hwɪt- ‖ 'hwɪt tʃɝːtʃ
—*in Wales usually* 'wɪtʃ ɜːtʃ, -ətʃ
Whitcut, Whitcutt 'wɪt kʌt 'hwɪt- ‖ 'hwɪt-

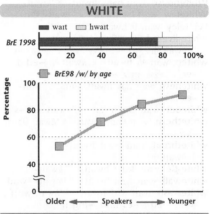

WHITE

	■ waɪt	□ hwaɪt

BrE 1998

0   20   40   60   80   100%

BrE98 /w/ by age

Percentage: 100, 80, 60, 40, 0

Older ◄——— Speakers ———► Younger

white, White waɪt hwaɪt ‖ hwaɪt —*BrE 1998
poll panel preference:* waɪt 77%, hwaɪt 23%.
whited 'waɪt ɪd 'hwaɪt-, -əd ‖ 'hwaɪt̬ əd
whiter 'waɪt ə 'hwaɪt- ‖ 'hwaɪt̬ ər **whites**
waɪts hwaɪts ‖ hwaɪts **whitest** 'waɪt ɪst -əst
‖ 'hwaɪt̬ əst **whiting** 'waɪt ɪŋ 'hwaɪt-
‖ 'hwaɪt̬ ɪŋ
‚white 'ant; ‚white 'blood cell; ‚white
'corpuscle, - cor'puscle; ‚whited
'sepulchre; ‚white 'dwarf; ‚white
'elephant; ‚white 'flag; 'white goods;
‚white 'heat; 'White House —*This is the
AmE stress pattern for the President's official
residence. In BrE it is sometimes stressed* ‚• '•;
‚white 'knight; ‚white 'lead led; ‚white 'lie;
‚white 'magic; ‚white 'man; ‚white 'meat;
‚white 'metal; a ‚white 'paper; ‚white
'pepper; ‚white ‚people; ‚white 'sauce
‖ ‚• '•; ‚white 'slavery; ‚white 'spirit; ‚white
'tie; ‚white 'trash; ‚white 'water; ‚white
'wedding
whitebait 'waɪt beɪt 'hwaɪt- ‖ 'hwaɪt̬-
whitebeam 'waɪt biːm 'hwaɪt- ‖ 'hwaɪt̬- ~**s** z
whiteboard 'waɪt bɔːd 'hwaɪt- ‖ 'hwaɪt̬ bɔːrd
-boʊrd
whitecap 'waɪt kæp 'hwaɪt- ‖ 'hwaɪt̬- ~**s** s
Whitechapel 'waɪt ‚tʃæp əl 'hwaɪt- ‖ 'hwaɪt̬-
white-collar ‚waɪt 'kɒl ə ◄ ‚hwaɪt-
‖ ‚hwaɪt 'kɑːl ər ◄

W

Whitefield *(i)* 'wɪt fiːˤld 'hwɪt-‖ 'hwɪt-, *(ii)*
'waɪt- 'hwaɪt- ‖ 'hwaɪt- —*The family name
may be (i) or (ii); the Methodist evangelist was
(i). The place in Manchester is (ii).*

whitefish 'waɪt fɪʃ 'hwaɪt- ‖ 'hwaɪt-

white|fly 'waɪt lflaɪ 'hwaɪt- ‖ 'hwaɪt- **~flies**
flaɪz

Whitefriars 'waɪt ˌfraɪˌəz 'hwaɪt-, ˌ•'••
‖ 'hwaɪt ˌfraɪˌərz

Whitehall 'waɪt hɔːl 'hwaɪt-, ˌ•'• ‖ 'hwaɪt-
-hɑːl

Whitehaven 'waɪt ˌheɪv ³n 'hwaɪt- ‖ 'hwaɪt-

Whitehead 'waɪt hed 'hwaɪt- ‖ 'hwaɪt-

Whitehorn 'waɪt hɔːn 'hwaɪt- ‖ 'hwaɪt hɔːrn

Whitehorse 'waɪt hɔːs 'hwaɪt- ‖ 'hwaɪt hɔːrs

white-hot ˌwaɪt 'hɒt ◄ ˌhwaɪt- ‖ ˌhwaɪt 'hɑːt ◄

Whitehouse 'waɪt haʊs 'hwaɪt- ‖ 'hwaɪt-

Whitelaw 'waɪt lɔː 'hwaɪt- ‖ 'hwaɪt- -lɑː

Whiteley 'waɪt li 'hwaɪt- ‖ 'hwaɪt li

white-livered ˌwaɪt 'lɪv əd ◄ ˌhwaɪt-
‖ ˌhwaɪt 'lɪv ³rd ◄

whiten 'waɪt ³n 'hwaɪt- ‖ 'hwaɪt ³n **~ed** d
~er/s ˌə/z ‖ ˌər/z **~ing** ˌɪŋ **~s** z

whiteness 'waɪt nəs 'hwaɪt-, -nɪs ‖ 'hwaɪt-
~es ɪz əz

whiteout 'waɪt aʊt 'hwaɪt- ‖ 'hwaɪt aʊt **~s** s

whitethorn 'waɪt θɔːn 'hwaɪt- ‖ 'hwaɪt θɔːrn
~s z

whitethroat 'waɪt θrəʊt 'hwaɪt-
‖ 'hwaɪt θroʊt **~s** s

white-tie ˌwaɪt 'taɪ ◄ ˌhwaɪt- ‖ ˌhwaɪt-

whitewall 'waɪt wɔːl 'hwaɪt- ‖ 'hwaɪt- -wɑːl

whitewash 'waɪt wɒʃ 'hwaɪt- ‖ 'hwaɪt wɑːʃ
-wɔːʃ **~ed** t **~es** ɪz əz **~ing** ɪŋ

whitewater, W~ 'waɪt ˌwɔːt ə 'hwaɪt-
‖ 'hwaɪt ˌwɔːt̮ ³r -ˌwɑːt̮-

whitewood 'waɪt wʊd 'hwaɪt- ‖ 'hwaɪt-

whitey 'waɪt i 'hwaɪt- ‖ 'hwaɪt̮ i **~s** z

Whitfield 'wɪt fiːˤld 'hwɪt- ‖ 'hwɪt-

Whitgift 'wɪt gɪft 'hwɪt- ‖ 'hwɪt-

whither 'wɪð ə 'hwɪð- ‖ 'hwɪð ³r

whithersoever ˌwɪð ə səʊ 'ev ə ˌhwɪð-
‖ ˌhwɪð ³r soʊ 'ev ³r

Whithorn 'wɪt hɔːn 'hwɪt- ‖ 'hwɪt hɔːrn

whiting, W~ 'waɪt ɪŋ 'hwaɪt- ‖ 'hwaɪt̮ ɪŋ **~s** z

whitish 'waɪt ɪʃ 'hwaɪt- ‖ 'hwaɪt̮ ɪʃ **~ness** nəs
nɪs

Whitlam 'wɪt ləm 'hwɪt- ‖ 'hwɪt-

Whitley 'wɪt li 'hwɪt- ‖ 'hwɪt li

Whitlock 'wɪt lɒk 'hwɪt- ‖ 'hwɪt lɑːk

whitlow 'wɪt ləʊ 'hwɪt- ‖ 'hwɪt loʊ **~s** z

Whitman 'wɪt mən 'hwɪt- ‖ 'hwɪt mən

Whitmore 'wɪt mɔː 'hwɪt- ‖ 'hwɪt mɔːr

Whitney 'wɪt ni 'hwɪt- ‖ 'hwɪt ni

Whitstable 'wɪt stəb ³l 'hwɪt- ‖ 'hwɪt-

Whitsun 'wɪt s³n 'hwɪt- ‖ 'hwɪt- **~s** z

Whitsuntide 'wɪt s³n taɪd 'hwɪt- ‖ 'hwɪt- **~s** z

Whittaker 'wɪt ək ə 'hwɪt-, -ɪk- ‖ 'hwɪt̮ ək ³r

Whittall 'wɪt 'hwɪt-, -ɔːl ‖ 'hwɪt ³l

Whittier 'wɪt i ə 'hwɪt- ‖ 'hwɪt̮ i ³r

Whittington 'wɪt ɪŋ tən 'hwɪt- ‖ 'hwɪt̮-

whittl|e, W~ 'wɪt ³l 'hwɪt- ‖ 'hwɪt̮ ³l **~ed** d
~es z **~ing** ˌɪŋ

Whittle-le-Woods ˌwɪt ³l lə 'wʊdz ˌhwɪt-, -li'•
‖ ˌhwɪt̮-

Whittlesford 'wɪt ³lz fəd 'hwɪt-
‖ 'hwɪt̮ ³lz f³rd

Whitton 'wɪt ³n 'hwɪt- ‖ 'hwɪt ³n

Whitty 'wɪt i 'hwɪt- ‖ 'hwɪt̮ i

Whitworth 'wɪt wɜːθ 'hwɪt-, -wəθ
‖ 'hwɪt wɜːθ

whit|ly 'waɪt li 'hwaɪt- ‖ 'hwaɪt̮ li **~ies** iz

whiz, whizz wɪz hwɪz ‖ hwɪz **whizzed** wɪzd
hwɪzd ‖ hwɪzd **whizzes** 'wɪz ɪz 'hwɪz-, -əz
‖ 'hwɪz əz **whizzing** 'wɪz ɪŋ 'hwɪz-
‖ 'hwɪz ɪŋ

'whiz kid, 'whizz kid

whizbang, whizzbang 'wɪz bæŋ 'hwɪz-
‖ 'hwɪz- **~s** z

who *strong form* huː, *occasional weak forms*
hu, u —*The weak forms are used, if at all, only
for the relative (not the interrogative).*

Who *name of pop group* huː

whoa wəʊ hwəʊ, həʊ ‖ hwoʊ hoʊ

Whoberley 'wəʊb ə li ‖ 'hwoʊb ³r-

who'd *strong form* huːd, *occasional weak forms*
hud, ud —*The weak forms are used, if at all,
only for the relative (not the interrogative).*

whodunit, whodunnit ˌhuː 'dʌn ɪt §-ət **~s** s

whoe'er hu 'eə ‖ -'eᵊr

whoever hu 'ev ə ‖ -³r —*also* u- *when not
clause-initial* **~'s** z

whole həʊl →hɒʊl, §huːl ‖ hoʊl *(= hole)*
wholes həʊlz →hɒʊlz, §huːlz ‖ hoʊlz
'whole note; ˌwhole 'number ‖ '• ˌ••

wholefood 'həʊl fuːd →'hɒʊl-, §'huːl- ‖ 'hoʊl-
~s z

wholegrain 'həʊl greɪn →'hɒʊl-, §'huːl-
‖ 'hoʊl-

whole-hearted ˌhəʊl 'hɑːt ɪd ◄→ˌhɒʊl-,
§ˌhuːl-, -əd ‖ ˌhoʊl 'hɑːrt̮ əd ◄ **~ly** li **~ness**
nəs nɪs

wholemeal 'həʊl miːˤl →'hɒʊl-, §'huːl-
‖ 'hoʊl-

wholeness 'həʊl nəs →'hɒʊl-, §'huːl-, -nɪs
‖ 'hoʊl-

wholesale 'həʊl seɪ³l →'hɒʊl-, §'huːl- ‖ 'hoʊl-

wholesaler 'həʊl seɪ³l ə →'hɒʊl-, §'huːl-
‖ 'hoʊl seɪ³l ³r **~s** z

wholesome 'həʊl səm →'hɒʊl-, §'huːl-
‖ 'hoʊl- **~ly** li **~ness** nəs nɪs

wholewheat 'həʊl wiːt →'hɒʊl-, §'huːl-, -hwiːt
‖ 'hoʊl hwiːt

wholistic həʊ 'lɪst ɪk ‖ hoʊ- **~ally** ³l_i

who'll *strong form* huːl, *occasional weak forms*
hul, ul —*The weak forms are used, if at all,
only for the relative (not the interrogative).*

wholly 'həʊl li →'hɒʊl-; 'həʊl i, §'huːl-
‖ 'hoʊl li -i

whom *strong form* huːm, *occasional weak forms*
hum, um —*The weak forms are used, if at all,
only for the relative (not the interrogative).*

whomever huːm 'ev ə ‖ -³r

whomsoever ˌhuːm səʊ 'ev ə ‖ -soʊ 'ev ³r

whoop wuːp huːp, wʊp ‖ huːp hʊp, hwʊp,
hwuːp **whooped** wuːpt huːpt, wʊpt ‖ huːpt

hʊpt, ʜwʊpt, ʜwuːpt **whooping** 'wuːp ɪŋ
'huːp-, 'wʊp- ‖ 'huːp ɪŋ 'hʊp-, 'ʜwʊp-,
'ʜwuːp- **whoops** wuːps huːps, wʊps ‖ huːps
hʊps, ʜwʊps, ʜwuːps
whoopee *interj* wʊ 'piː hʊ-, ˌwuː- ‖ 'ʜwʊp iː
ʜwʊ 'piː, ʜwuː-
whoopee *n*, **Whoopi** 'wʊp iː 'wuːp-, -i
‖ 'ʜwʊp i 'ʜwuː-p-
whooping cough 'huːp ɪŋ kɒf §'wuːp-, -kɔːf
‖ 'huːp ɪŋ kɔːf 'hʊp-, -kɑːf
whoops wʊps wuːps, hwʊps, hwuːps ‖ ʜwʊps
ʜwuːps
whoops-a-daisy ˌwʊps ə 'deɪz i ˌhwʊps-;
'•• , •• ‖ ˌhwʊps- ˌhwuːps-
whoosh wʊʃ wuːʃ, hwʊʃ, hwuːʃ ‖ ʜwuːʃ ʜwʊʃ
whop wɒp hwɒp ‖ ʜwɑːp **whopped** wɒpt
hwɒpt ‖ ʜwɑːpt **whopping** 'wɒp ɪŋ 'hwɒp-
‖ 'ʜwɑːp ɪŋ **whops** wɒps hwɒps ‖ ʜwɑːps
whopper 'wɒp ə 'hwɒp- ‖ 'ʜwɑːp ᵊr **~s** z
whopping 'wɒp ɪŋ 'hwɒp- ‖ 'ʜwɑːp ɪŋ
whore hɔː ‖ hɔːr hoʊr, hʊᵊr *(= hoar)* **whored**
hɔːd ‖ hɔːrd hoʊrd, hʊᵊrd *(= hoard)* **whores**
hɔːz ‖ hɔːrz hoʊrz, hʊᵊrz **whoring** 'hɔːr ɪŋ
‖ 'hoʊr-, 'hʊr-
who're 'huːˌə ‖ ˌᵊr
whoredom 'hɔː dəm ‖ 'hɔːr- 'hoʊr-, 'hʊr-
whore|house 'hɔː |haʊs ‖ 'hɔːr- 'hoʊr-, 'hʊr-
~houses haʊz ɪz -əz
whoremaster 'hɔː ˌmɑːst ə §-ˌmæst-
‖ 'hɔːr ˌmæst ᵊr 'hoʊr-, 'hʊr- **~s** z
whoremonger 'hɔː ˌmʌŋ gə §-ˌmɒŋ-
‖ 'hɔːr ˌmʌŋ gᵊr 'hoʊr-, -ˌmɑːŋ- **~s** z
whoreson 'hɔː sən ‖ 'hɔːr- 'hoʊr-, 'hʊr- **~s** z
Whorf wɔːf hwɔːf ‖ ʜwɔːrf
whorish 'hɔːr ɪʃ ‖ 'hoʊr-, 'hʊr- **~ly** li **~ness**
nəs nɪs
whorl wɜːl hwɜːl, §wɔːl, §hwɔːl ‖ ʜwɝːl ʜwɔːrl
whorled wɜːld hwɜːld, §wɔːld, §hwɔːld ‖
ʜwɝːld ʜwɔːrld **whorls** wɜːlz hwɜːlz,
§wɔːlz, §hwɔːlz ‖ ʜwɝːlz ʜwɔːrlz
whortleberr|y 'wɜːt ᵊl ˌber i 'hwɜːt-, -bᵊr_i
‖ 'ʜwɝːt̬ ᵊl ˌber i **~ies** iz
who's *strong form* huːz, *occasional weak forms*
huz, uz —*The weak forms are used, if at all,*
only for the relative (not the interrogative).
whose *strong form* huːz, *occasional weak forms*
huz, uz —*The weak forms are used, if at all,*
only for the relative (not the interrogative).
whoso 'huː səʊ ‖ -soʊ
whosoever ˌhuː səʊ 'ev ə ◀ ‖ -soʊ 'ev ᵊr ◀
who've *strong form* huːv, *occasional weak forms*
huv, uv —*The weak forms are used, if at all,*
only for the relative (not the interrogative).
whump wʌmp hwʌmp **whumped** wʌmpt
hwʌmpt **whumping** 'wʌmp ɪŋ 'hwʌmp-
whumps wʌmps hwʌmps
why waɪ hwaɪ ‖ ʜwaɪ **whys** waɪz hwaɪz ‖
ʜwaɪz
Whyalla waɪ 'æl ə hwaɪ- ‖ ʜwaɪ-
Whyatt 'waɪˌət 'hwaɪˌ ‖ 'ʜwaɪ ət
why'd waɪd waɪd ‖ ʜwaɪd
whydah, W~ 'wɪd ə ‖ 'hwɪd ə **~s** z
why'll 'waɪˌəl 'hwaɪˌ ‖ 'ʜwaɪˌəl

why're 'waɪˌə 'hwaɪˌ ‖ 'ʜwaɪˌᵊr
why's waɪz hwaɪz ‖ ʜwaɪz
Whyte waɪt hwaɪt ‖ ʜwaɪt
Whyteleaf 'waɪt liːf 'hwaɪt- ‖ 'ʜwaɪt-
Whythorne 'waɪt hɔːn 'hwaɪt- ‖ 'ʜwaɪt hɔːrn
why've waɪv hwaɪv ‖ ʜwaɪv
Wibberley 'wɪb ə li ‖ -ᵊr-
Wibsey 'wɪb si -zi —*The place in WYks is locally*
also →'wɪp si
Wicca, wicca 'wɪk ə
Wichita 'wɪtʃ ɪ tɔː -ə- ‖ -tɑː
Wichnor 'wɪtʃ nɔː -nə ‖ -nɔːr
wick, Wick wɪk **wicks** wɪks
wicked 'wɪk ɪd §-əd **~er** ə ‖ ᵊr **~est** ɪst əst
~ly li **~ness** nəs nɪs
Wicken 'wɪk ən -ɪn **~s** z
wicker, W~ 'wɪk ə ‖ -ᵊr
wickerwork 'wɪk ə wɜːk ‖ -ᵊr wɝːk
wicket 'wɪk ɪt §-ət **~s** s
   'wicket gate; 'wicket ˌkeeper
Wickham 'wɪk əm
Wickins 'wɪk ɪnz §-ənz
wickiup 'wɪk i ʌp **~s** s
Wicklow 'wɪk ləʊ ‖ -loʊ
Wicks wɪks
Widdecombe, Widdicombe 'wɪd ɪ kəm -ə-
widdershins 'wɪd ə ʃɪnz ‖ -ᵊr-
widdl|e 'wɪd ᵊl **~ed** d **~es** z **~ing** ɪŋ
Widdowes, Widdows 'wɪd əʊz ‖ -oʊz
Widdowson 'wɪd əʊ sᵊn ‖ -oʊ-
wide waɪd **wider** 'waɪd ə ‖ -ᵊr **wides** waɪdz
widest 'waɪd ɪst -əst
   'wide boy
wide-angle ˌwaɪd 'æŋ gᵊl ◀
wide-awake *adj* ˌwaɪd ə 'weɪk ◀
wide-awake *n* 'waɪd ə ˌweɪk **~s** s
wide-bod|y 'waɪd ˌbɒd li 'waɪb- ‖ -ˌbɑːd-
~ied id **~ies** iz
Widecombe 'wɪd ɪ kəm -ə-
wide-eyed ˌwaɪd 'aɪd ◀
Wideford 'waɪd fəd ‖ -fᵊrd
widely 'waɪd li
Widemouth 'wɪd məθ →'wɪb-
widen 'waɪd ᵊn **~ed** d **~ing** ɪŋ **~s** z
wideness 'waɪd nəs -nɪs
wide-open ˌwaɪd 'əʊp ᵊn ◀ ‖ -'oʊp-
Wideopen 'waɪd ˌəʊp ᵊn ‖ -ˌoʊp-
wide-screen ˌwaɪd 'skriːn ◀ ' • •
widespread 'waɪd spred , • ' •
widgeon 'wɪdʒ ᵊn -ɪn **~s** z
Widgery 'wɪdʒ ᵊr i
widget 'wɪdʒ ɪt §-ət **~s** s
widish 'waɪd ɪʃ
Widlake 'wɪd leɪk
Widmark 'wɪd mɑːk →'wɪb- ‖ -mɑːrk
Widmerpool 'wɪd mə puːl ‖ -mᵊr-
Widnes 'wɪd nɪs -nəs
widow 'wɪd əʊ ‖ -oʊ **~ed** d **~ing** ɪŋ **~s** z
widower 'wɪd əʊ ə ‖ -oʊ ᵊr **~s** z
widowhood 'wɪd əʊ hʊd ‖ -oʊ-
width wɪdθ wɪtθ **widths** wɪdθs wɪtθs
wield wiːᵊld **wielded** 'wiːᵊld ɪd -əd **wielding**
'wiːᵊld ɪŋ **wields** wiːᵊldz

wielder 'wiːᵊld ə ‖ -ᵊr ~s z

wiener, W~ 'wiːn ə ‖ -ᵊr -i —*but as a German name*, 'viːn- —*Ger* W~ ['viː nɐ] ~s z

Wiener schnitzel ˌviːn ə 'ʃnɪts ᵊl △-'snɪtʃ-
‖ 'viːn ᵊr ˌ•• 'wiːn-, -ˌsnɪts- ~s z

Wiesbaden 'viːs ˌbɑːd ᵊn 'viːz- —*Ger*
['viːs ba: dᵊn]

Wiesenthal 'wiːz ᵊn tɑːl 'viːz-, -θɒːl —*Ger*
['viː zᵊn ta:l]

wife waɪf wife's waɪfs wives waɪvz
'wife ˌswapping

wife|hood 'waɪf hʊd ~less ləs lɪs ~like laɪk
~ly li

Wiffle *tdmk* 'wɪf ᵊl
'Wiffle ball

wig wɪg wigged wɪgd wigging/s 'wɪg ɪŋ/z
wigs wɪgz

Wigan 'wɪg ᵊn §-ɪn

wigeon 'wɪdʒ ᵊn -ɪn ~s z

Wigg wɪg

wigg... —*see* wig

Wiggin 'wɪg ɪn §-ᵊn

Wiggins 'wɪg ɪnz §-ᵊnz

wiggl|e 'wɪg ᵊl ~ed d ~es z ~ing ɪŋ

Wigglesworth 'wɪg ᵊlz wɜːθ -wəθ ‖ -wɝːθ

wiggly 'wɪg ᵊlˌi

Wight, wight waɪt

Wightman 'waɪt mən

Wightwick 'wɪt ɪk

Wigley 'wɪg li

Wigmore 'wɪg mɔː ‖ -mɔːr

Wigoder 'wɪg əd ə ‖ -ᵊr

Wigram 'wɪg rəm

Wigston 'wɪg stən

Wigton 'wɪg tən

Wigtown 'wɪg taʊn -tən

wigwag 'wɪg wæg ~ged d ~ging ɪŋ ~s z

wigwam 'wɪg wæm ‖ -wɑːm ~s z

Wike waɪk

Wilberforce 'wɪlb ə fɔːs ‖ -ᵊr fɔːrs -foʊrs

Wilbert 'wɪlb ət ‖ -ᵊrt

Wilbraham 'wɪlb rə həm -hæm; 'wɪlb rəm

Wilbur 'wɪlb ə ‖ -ᵊr

Wilby, Wilbye 'wɪl bi

wilco 'wɪl kəʊ ˌ•'• ‖ -koʊ

Wilcock 'wɪl kɒk ‖ -kɑːk

Wilcocks, Wilcox 'wɪl kɒks ‖ -kɑːks

Wilcoxon wɪl 'kɒks ᵊn ‖ -'kɑːks-

wild, Wild waɪᵊld wilder 'waɪᵊld ə ‖ -ᵊr
wildest 'waɪᵊld ɪst -əst wilds waɪᵊldz
ˌwild 'boar; 'wild ˌflower; ˌwild 'oats; ˌwild
'rice; ˌWild 'West

Wildblood 'waɪᵊld blʌd

wild|cat 'waɪᵊld |kæt ~cats kæts ~catted
kæt ɪd -əd ‖ kæt̬ əd ~catting kæt ɪŋ ‖ kæt̬ ɪŋ
ˌwildcat 'strike

wildcatter 'waɪᵊld kæt ə ‖ -kæt̬ ᵊr ~s z

Wilde waɪᵊld

Wildean 'waɪᵊld i ˌən

wildebeest 'vɪld ə biːst 'wɪld-, -ɪ-, -bɪəst ~s s

Wildenstein 'wɪld ᵊn staɪn —*Ger*
['vɪl dᵊn ʃtaɪn]

Wilder 'waɪᵊld ə ‖ -ᵊr

wilderness, W~ 'wɪld ə nəs -nɪs ‖ -ᵊr- ~es ɪz
əz

wild-eyed ˌwaɪᵊld 'aɪd ◂ '••

Wildfell 'waɪld fel

wildfire 'waɪᵊld ˌfaɪ_ə ‖ -ˌfaɪ_ᵊr

wildfowl 'waɪᵊld faʊl ~ed d ~er/s ə/z ‖ ᵊr/z
~ing ɪŋ ~s z

wild-goose chase ˌwaɪᵊld 'guːs tʃeɪs

Wilding, w~ 'waɪᵊld ɪŋ ~s z

wildlife 'waɪᵊld laɪf

wild|ly 'waɪᵊld |li ~ness nəs nɪs

wildwood 'waɪᵊld wʊd ~s z

wile waɪᵊl wiled waɪᵊld (= *wild*) wiles waɪᵊlz
wiling 'waɪᵊl ɪŋ

Wiley 'waɪl i

Wilf wɪlf

Wilford 'wɪl fəd ‖ -fᵊrd

Wilfred, Wilfrid 'wɪlf rɪd §-rəd

wilful 'wɪl fᵊl -fʊl ~ly ˌi ~ness nəs nɪs

Wilhelmina ˌwɪl hel 'miːn ə -ə-

wili... —*see* wily

wiliness 'waɪl i nəs -nɪs

Wilkes wɪlks

Wilkes-Barre *place in PA* 'wɪlks ˌbær i -ˌber-, -ə

Wilkie 'wɪlk i

Wilkins 'wɪlk ɪnz §-ᵊnz

Wilkinson 'wɪlk ɪn's ᵊn §-ᵊn-

Wilks wɪlks

will *modal v strong form* wɪl, *occasional weak
forms* wᵊl, ᵊl —*see also* 'll

will *v* 'wish, intend', 'bequeath'; *n* wɪl willed
wɪld willing 'wɪl ɪŋ wills wɪlz

Will wɪl

Willa 'wɪl ə

Willamette wɪ 'læm ɪt wə-, §-ət

Willandra wɪ 'lændr ə

Willard 'wɪl ɑːd ‖ -ᵊrd

Willcock 'wɪl kɒk ‖ -kɑːk

Willcocks, Willcox 'wɪl kɒks ‖ -kɑːks

-willed 'wɪld — strong-willed
ˌstrɒŋ 'wɪld ◂ ‖ ˌstrɔːŋ- ˌstrɑːŋ-

Willenhall 'wɪl ən hɔːl ‖ -hɑːl

Willesden 'wɪlz dən

willet 'wɪl ɪt -ət ~s s

Willey 'wɪl i

willful 'wɪl fᵊl -fʊl ~ly ˌi ~ness nəs nɪs

William 'wɪl jəm

Williams 'wɪl jəmz

Williamsburg 'wɪl jəmz bɜːg ‖ -bɝːg

Williamsport 'wɪl jəmz pɔːt ‖ -pɔːrt -poʊrt

Williamson 'wɪl jəm sən

Willie, w~ 'wɪl i ~s z

willing 'wɪl ɪŋ ~ly li ~ness nəs nɪs

Willis 'wɪl ɪs §-əs

williwaw 'wɪl i wɔː ‖ -wɑː ~s z

Willmott 'wɪl mət -mɒt

Willock 'wɪl ək

will-o'-the-wisp ˌwɪl ə ðə 'wɪsp ~s s

Willoughby 'wɪl ə bi

willow 'wɪl əʊ ‖ -oʊ ~s z
'willow ˌpattern

willowherb 'wɪl əʊ hɜːb ‖ -oʊ ɝːb ~s z

willowy 'wɪl əʊ i ‖ -oʊ-

W

willpower 'wɪl ˌpaʊ‿ə ‖ -ˌpaʊ‿ər
Wills wɪlz
Willy, willly 'wɪl li ~**ies** iz
willy-nilly ˌwɪl i 'nɪl i
Wilma 'wɪlm ə
Wilmcote 'wɪlm kəʊt ‖ -koʊt
Wilmer 'wɪlm ə ‖ -ər
Wilmette wɪl 'met
Wilmington 'wɪlm ɪŋ tən
Wilmot, Wilmott 'wɪl mət -mɒt
Wilmslow 'wɪlmz ləʊ ‖ -loʊ
Wilsher 'wɪl ʃə ‖ -ʃər
Wilson 'wɪls ən
Wilsonian wɪl 'səʊn i ˌən ‖ -'soʊn-
wilt '_wither, droop_' wɪlt **wilted** 'wɪlt ɪd -əd
  wilting 'wɪlt ɪŋ **wilts** wɪlts
wilt _archaic_ thou-_form of_ will: _strong form_ wɪlt
  weak form wəlt
Wilton 'wɪlt ən ~**s** z
Wilts wɪlts
Wiltshire 'wɪlt ʃə -ʃɪə ‖ -ʃər -ʃɪr
willy 'waɪl li ~**ier** i‿ə ‖ i‿ər ~**iest** i‿ɪst i‿əst
wimble 'wɪm bəl ~**s** z
Wimbledon 'wɪm bəl dən
Wimborne, Wimbourne 'wɪm bɔːn ‖ -bɔːrn
  -boʊrn
Wimbush 'wɪm bʊʃ
wimin, wimmin 'wɪm ɪn §-ən
Wimmera 'wɪm ər ə
Wimoweh 'wɪm ə weɪ
wimp wɪmp **wimps** wɪmps
Wimpey 'wɪmp i
wimpish 'wɪmp ɪʃ ~**ly** li ~**ness** nəs nɪs
wimple, W~ 'wɪmp əl ~**s** z
Wimpole 'wɪm pəʊl →-pɒʊl ‖ -poʊl
wimpy, Wimpy _tdmk_ 'wɪmp i
  '**Wimpy bar**
Wimsey 'wɪmz i
Wimshurst 'wɪmz hɜːst ‖ -hɝːst
win wɪn **winning** 'wɪn ɪŋ **wins** wɪnz **won**
  wʌn
Winalot _tdmk_ 'wɪn ə lɒt -lɑːt
Wincanton wɪn 'kænt ən →wɪŋ- ‖ -ən
Wincarnis _tdmk_ wɪn 'kɑːn ɪs →wɪŋ-, §-əs
  ‖ -'kɑːrn-
wince wɪnts **winced** wɪntst **winces** 'wɪnts ɪz
  -əz **wincing/ly** 'wɪnts ɪŋ /li
wincey 'wɪnts i ~**s** z
winceyette ˌwɪnts i 'et
winch, Winch wɪntʃ **winched** wɪntʃt
  winches 'wɪntʃ ɪz -əz **winching** 'wɪntʃ ɪŋ
Winchelsea 'wɪntʃ əl siː
Winchester, w~ 'wɪntʃ ɪst ə -əst-,
  §'wɪn ˌtʃest ə ‖ 'wɪn ˌtʃest ər ~**s** z
Winchmore 'wɪntʃ mɔː ‖ -mɔːr
wind _n_ '_breeze, moving air_' wɪnd **winds** wɪndz
  '**wind** ˌ**instrument**; '**wind gauge**; '**wind**
  ˌ**tunnel**; '**wind** ˌ**turbine**
wind _n_ '_bend_' waɪnd **winds** waɪndz
wind _v_ '_turn_'; '_blow on horn_' waɪnd **winded**
  'waɪnd ɪd -əd **winding/s** 'waɪnd ɪŋ/z **winds**
  waɪndz **wound** waʊnd

wind _v_ '_make breathless_', '_give respite to_', '_smell_'
  wɪnd **winded** 'wɪnd ɪd -əd **winding**
  'wɪnd ɪŋ **winds** wɪndz
windagle 'wɪnd ɪdʒ ~**es** ɪz əz
windbag 'wɪnd bæg →'wɪmb- ~**s** z
windblown 'wɪnd bləʊn →'wɪmb- ‖ -bloʊn
wind-borne 'wɪnd bɔːn →'wɪmb- ‖ -bɔːrn
  -boʊrn
windbreak 'wɪnd breɪk →'wɪmb- ~**s** s
windbreaker, W~ _tdmk_ 'wɪnd ˌbreɪk ə
  →'wɪmb- ‖ -ər ~**s** z
windburn 'wɪnd bɜːn →'wɪmb- ‖ -bɝːn
windcheater 'wɪnd ˌtʃiːt ə ‖ -ˌtʃiːt ər ~**s** z
wind-chill 'wɪnd tʃɪl
winder 'waɪnd ə ‖ -ər ~**s** z
Windermere 'wɪnd ə mɪə ‖ -ər mɪr
Windeyer 'wɪnd i‿ə ‖ -ər
windfall 'wɪnd fɔːl ‖ -fɑːl ~**s** z
windflower 'wɪnd ˌflaʊ‿ə ‖ -ˌflaʊ‿ər ~**s** z
Windhoek 'wɪnd hʊk 'vɪnd-, 'wɪnt-, 'vɪnt-
windhover 'wɪnd ˌhɒv ə -ˌhʌv- ‖ -ˌhʌv ər
  -ˌhɑːv- ~**s** z
windi... —_see_ **windy**
Windies 'wɪnd iz
winding _adj, n_ 'waɪnd ɪŋ ~**ly** li ~**s** z
  '**winding sheet**
winding-up ˌwaɪnd ɪŋ 'ʌp
windjammer 'wɪnd ˌdʒæm ə ‖ -ər ~**s** z
windlass 'wɪnd ləs ~**es** ɪz əz
Windlesham 'wɪnd əl ʃəm
windless 'wɪnd ləs -lɪs
windmill 'wɪnd mɪl →'wɪmb- ~**ed** d ~**ing** ɪŋ
  ~**s** z
Windolene _tdmk_ 'wɪnd əʊ liːn ‖ -oʊ-
window 'wɪnd əʊ ‖ -oʊ ~**ed** d ~**ing** ɪŋ ~**s** z
  '**window box**; '**window** ˌ**dressing**; '**window**
  seat; '**window shade**
windowpane 'wɪnd əʊ peɪn ‖ -oʊ- -ə- ~**s** z
Windows _tdmk_ 'wɪnd əʊz ‖ -oʊz
  ˌ**Windows** ˌ9ˈ7
window-shop 'wɪnd əʊ ʃɒp ‖ -oʊ ʃɑːp -ə-
  ~**ped** t ~**ping** ɪŋ ~**s** s
windowsill 'wɪnd əʊ sɪl ‖ -oʊ- -ə- ~**s** z
windpipe 'wɪnd paɪp →'wɪmb- ~**s** s
windrow 'wɪnd rəʊ ‖ -roʊ ~**s** z
Windrush 'wɪnd rʌʃ
Windscale 'wɪnd skeɪəl
windscreen 'wɪnd skriːn ~**s** z
  '**windscreen** ˌ**wiper**
windshear 'wɪnd ʃɪə ‖ -ʃɪr
windshield 'wɪnd ʃiːəld ~**s** z
  '**windshield** ˌ**wiper**
windsock 'wɪnd sɒk ‖ -sɑːk ~**s** s
Windsor 'wɪnz ə 'wɪndz- ‖ -ər
  ˌ**Windsor** '**Castle**
windstorm 'wɪnd stɔːm ‖ -ˌstɔːrm ~**s** z
windsurf 'wɪnd sɜːf ‖ -sɝːf ~**ed** t ~**er/s** ə/z
  ‖ ər/z ~**ing** ɪŋ ~**s** s
windswept 'wɪnd swept
wind-up 'waɪnd ʌp ~**s** s
Windus 'wɪnd əs
windward, W~ 'wɪnd wəd §'wɪn- ‖ -wərd ~**s**
  z

W

wind|y 'wɪnd |i ~**ier** i‿ə ‖ i‿ər ~**iest** i‿ɪst i‿əst
  ~**ily** ɪ li əl i ~**iness** i nəs i nɪs
wine waɪn **wined** waɪnd **wines** waɪnz
  wining 'waɪn ɪŋ
  'wine bar; 'wine ˌbottle
winebibber 'waɪn ˌbɪb ə →'waɪm- ‖ -ər ~**s** z
winebibbing 'waɪn ˌbɪb ɪŋ →'waɪm- ~**s** z
wineglass 'waɪn glɑːs →'waɪŋ-, §-glæs ‖ -glæs
  ~**es** ɪz əz
winegrow|er/s 'waɪn ˌgrəʊ ə/z →'waɪŋ-
  ‖ -ˌgroʊ ər/z ~**ing** ɪŋ
winepress 'waɪn pres →'waɪm- ~**es** ɪz əz
winer|y 'waɪn ər |i ~**ies** iz
wineskin 'waɪn skɪn ~**s** z
Winfield 'wɪn fiːəld
Winford 'wɪn fəd ‖ -fərd
Winfred 'wɪn frɪd §-frəd
Winfrey 'wɪn fri
Winfrith 'wɪn frɪθ §-frəθ
wing, Wing wɪŋ **winged** wɪŋd **winging**
  'wɪŋ ɪŋ **wings** wɪŋz
  'wing comˌmander; 'wing nut
Wingate 'wɪn geɪt →'wɪŋ-, -gɪt, -gət
wingding 'wɪŋ dɪŋ ~**s** z
winge 'complain' —see **whinge**
winged adj 'having wings'; pp of **wing** wɪŋd
  —but formerly, and sometimes in verse still,
  also 'wɪŋ ɪd, -əd
winger 'wɪŋ ə ‖ -ər ~**s** z
-winger 'wɪŋ ə ‖ -ər — **left-winger** ˌleft
  'wɪŋ ə ‖ -ər
Wingfield 'wɪŋ fiːəld
wingless 'wɪŋ ləs -lɪs ~**ness** nəs nɪs
winglet 'wɪŋ lət -lɪt ~**s** s
wingspan 'wɪŋ spæn ~**s** z
wingspread 'wɪŋ spred ~**s** z
wingtip 'wɪŋ tɪp ~**s** s
Winifred 'wɪn ɪf rɪd -əf-, §-rəd
wink wɪŋk **winked** wɪŋkt **winking** 'wɪŋk ɪŋ
  winks wɪŋks
winker 'wɪŋk ə ‖ -ər ~**s** z
winkl|e 'wɪŋk əl ~**ed** d ~**es** z ~**ing** ˌɪŋ
winkle-picker 'wɪŋk əl ˌpɪk ə ‖ -ər ~**s** z
Winn wɪn
Winnebago ˌwɪn ɪ 'beɪg əʊ -ə- ‖ -oʊ ~**s** z
winner, W~ 'wɪn ə ‖ -ər ~**s** z
Winnie 'wɪn i
Winnie-the-Pooh ˌwɪn ɪ ðə 'puː
winning 'wɪn ɪŋ ~**ly** li ~**ness** nəs nɪs ~**s** z
  'winning post
Winnipeg 'wɪn ɪ peg §-ə-
Winnipegosis ˌwɪn ɪ pɪ 'gəʊs ɪs -§, • ə-, -pə' • -,
  §-əs ‖ -'goʊs əs
Winnipesaukee ˌwɪn ɪp ə 'sɔːk i ˌ • əp- ‖ -'sɑːk-
winnow 'wɪn əʊ ‖ -oʊ ~**ed** d ~**er/s** ə/z ‖ ər/z
  ~**ing** ɪŋ ~**s** z
wino 'waɪn əʊ ‖ -oʊ ~**s** z
Winona wɪ 'nəʊn ə wə- ‖ -'noʊn ə
Winsford 'wɪnz fəd 'wɪnts- ‖ -fərd
Winslade 'wɪn sleɪd
Winslet 'wɪnz lɪt -lət
Winslow 'wɪnz ləʊ ‖ -loʊ
winsome, W~ 'wɪnts əm ~**ly** li ~**ness** nəs nɪs

Winstanley (i) 'wɪntst ən li, (ii) wɪn 'stæn li
  —The place in Greater Manchester is (i); the
  family name is usually (ii)
Winston 'wɪntst ən
Winston-Salem ˌwɪntst ən 'seɪl əm
winter, W~ 'wɪnt ə ‖ 'wɪnt̬ ər ~**ed** d
  wintering 'wɪnt̬ ˌər ɪŋ ‖ 'wɪnt̬ ərɪŋ
  →'wɪntr ɪŋ ~**s** z
  ˌwinter 'sports
Winterbotham, Winterbottom
  'wɪnt ə ˌbɒt əm ‖ 'wɪnt̬ ər ˌbɑːt̬ əm
Winterbourn, Winterbourne, w~
  'wɪnt ə bɔːn ‖ 'wɪnt̬ ər bɔːrn -boʊrn ~**s** z
wintergreen 'wɪnt ə griːn ‖ 'wɪnt̬ ər- ~**s** z
winterization ˌwɪnt ər aɪ 'zeɪʃ ən -ɪ' • -
  ‖ ˌwɪnt̬ ər ə-
winteriz|e 'wɪnt ər aɪz ‖ 'wɪnt̬ ər- ~**ed** d ~**es**
  ɪz əz ~**ing** ɪŋ
Winters 'wɪnt əz ‖ 'wɪnt̬ ərz
Winterthur 'vɪnt ə tʊə ‖ 'vɪnt̬ ər tʊr —Ger
  ['vɪn tɐ tuːɐ]
wintertime 'wɪnt ə taɪm ‖ 'wɪnt̬ ər-
Winterton 'wɪnt ət ən ‖ 'wɪnt̬ ərt ən
wintery 'wɪnt ər‿i ‖ 'wɪnt̬ ər i →'wɪntr i
Winthrop 'wɪn θrɒp 'wɪntθ rəp ‖ 'wɪntθ rəp
Winton 'wɪnt ən ‖ -ən
Wintour 'wɪnt ə ‖ 'wɪnt̬ ər
wintr|y 'wɪntr |i ~**ier** i‿ə ‖ i‿ər ~**iest** i‿ɪst i‿əst
  ~**ily** əl i ɪ li ~**iness** i nəs i nɪs
Winwick 'wɪn ɪk
wipe waɪp **wiped** waɪpt **wipes** waɪps
  wiping 'waɪp ɪŋ
  ˌwiped 'out
wipeout 'waɪp aʊt ~**s** s
wiper 'waɪp ə ‖ -ər ~**s** z
wire 'waɪ‿ə ‖ 'waɪ‿ər ~**d** d ~**s** z **wiring**
  'waɪ‿ər ɪŋ ‖ 'waɪ‿ər ɪŋ
  ˌwire 'netting; ˌwire 'wool
wirecutters 'waɪ‿ə ˌkʌt əz ‖ 'waɪ‿ər ˌkʌt̬ ərz
wire|draw 'waɪ‿ə |drɔː ‖ 'waɪ‿ər- -drɑː
  ~**drawing** drɔː‿r ɪŋ ‖ drɔː ɪŋ drɑː- ~**drawn**
  drɔːn ‖ -drɑːn ~**draws** drɔːz ‖ drɑːz ~**drew**
  druː
wire-haired ˌwaɪ‿ə 'heəd ◄ ‖ 'waɪ‿ər herd
  -hærd
wireless 'waɪ‿ə ləs -lɪs ‖ 'waɪ‿ər- ~**ed** d ~**es** ɪz
  əz ~**ing** ɪŋ
wirepuller 'waɪ‿ə ˌpʊl ə ‖ 'waɪ‿ər ˌpʊl ər ~**s** z
wiretap 'waɪ‿ə tæp ‖ 'waɪ‿ər- ~**s** s
wire-tapping 'waɪ‿ə ˌtæp ɪŋ ‖ 'waɪ‿ər-
wireworm 'waɪ‿ə wɜːm ‖ 'waɪ‿ər wɜːm ~**s** z
wiri... —see **wiry**
wiring 'waɪ‿ər ɪŋ ‖ 'waɪ‿ər ɪŋ ~**s** z
Wirksworth 'wɜːks wəθ -wɜːθ ‖ 'wɜːks wɜːθ
Wirral 'wɪr əl ‖ 'wɜː-
wir|y 'waɪ‿ər |i ‖ 'waɪ‿ər |i ~**ier** i‿ə ‖ i‿ər ~**iest**
  i‿ɪst i‿əst ~**ily** əl i ɪ li ~**iness** i nəs i nɪs
Wisbech 'wɪz biːtʃ
Wisconsin wɪ 'skɒnts ɪn §-ən ‖ -'skɑːnts-
Wisconsinite wɪ 'skɒnts ɪ naɪt §-ə- ‖ -'skɑːnts-
  ~**s** s
Wisden 'wɪz dən

wisdom, W~ 'wɪz dəm
  'wisdom tooth
wise, Wise waɪz **wised** waɪzd **wiser**
  'waɪz ə ‖ -ᵊr **wises** 'waɪz ɪz -əz **wisest**
  'waɪz ɪst -əst **wising** 'waɪz ɪŋ
  'wise guy
-wise waɪz — **timewise** 'taɪm waɪz
wiseacre 'waɪz ˌeɪk ə ‖ -ᵊr ~s z
wisecrack 'waɪz kræk ~ed t ~ing ɪŋ ~s s
wisely 'waɪz li
Wiseman 'waɪz mən
wisent 'viːz ent 'wiːz-, -ᵊnt ~s s
wish wɪʃ **wished** wɪʃt **wishes** 'wɪʃ ɪz -əz
  wishing 'wɪʃ ɪŋ
Wishart 'wɪʃ ət ‖ -ᵊrt
Wishaw 'wɪʃ ɔː ‖ -ɑː
wishbone 'wɪʃ bəʊn ‖ -boʊn ~s z
wishful 'wɪʃ fᵊl -fʊl ~ly i ~ness nəs nɪs
  ˌwishful 'thinking
wishing-well 'wɪʃ ɪŋ wel ~s z
wishy-wash|y 'wɪʃ i ˌwɒʃ |i ˌ•'•• ‖ -ˌwɑːʃ |i
  -ˌwɔːʃ- ~iness i nəs i nɪs
Wisley 'wɪz li
wisp wɪsp **wisps** wɪsps
Wispa tdmk 'wɪsp ə
wispy 'wɪsp i
wist wɪst
wistaria, wisteria wɪ 'stɪər i_ə -'steər- ‖ -'stɪr-
  ~s z
wistful 'wɪst fᵊl -fʊl ~ly i ~ness nəs nɪs
Wiston 'wɪst ən
Wistow 'wɪst əʊ ‖ -oʊ
Wistrich 'wɪs trɪtʃ
Wisty 'wɪst i
wit wɪt **wits** wɪts
witch wɪtʃ **witched** wɪtʃt **witches** 'wɪtʃ ɪz
  -əz **witching/ly** 'wɪtʃ ɪŋ /li
  'witching ˌhour
witchcraft 'wɪtʃ krɑːft §-kræft ‖ -kræft
witchdoctor 'wɪtʃ ˌdɒkt ə ‖ -ˌdɑːkt ᵊr ~s z
witcher|y 'wɪtʃ ᵊr |i ~ies iz
witchetty 'wɪtʃ ət i -ɪt- ‖ -əṭ i
witch-hazel 'wɪtʃ ˌheɪz ᵊl ~s z
witch-hunt 'wɪtʃ hʌnt ~s s
witenagemot 'wɪt ᵊn_ə gɪ ˌməʊt -gə, •,
  ˌ•••'• ‖ -gə ˌmoʊt

with wɪð §wɪθ ‖ wɪθ wɪð —*Poll panel*
preferences: AmE 1993, wɪθ *84%,* wɪð *16%;*
BrE 1998, wɪð *85%,* wɪθ *15%. —In Britain,*
wɪθ is nevertheless frequent in Scotland
(preferred by 82% of Scottish respondents). —In
some varieties, including GenAm but not RP,
there may also be a weak form wəð*,* wəθ
withal wɪð 'ɔːl §wɪθ- ‖ -'ɑːl
Witham *family name; place in Essex*
  'wɪt əm ‖ 'wɪṭ-
Witham *river* 'wɪð əm
with|draw wɪð 'drɔː wɪθ|- ‖ -'drɑː ~drawing
  'drɔːʳ ɪŋ ‖ 'drɔː ɪŋ -'drɑː ɪŋ ~drawn 'drɔːn
  ‖ 'drɑːn ~draws 'drɔːz ‖ 'drɑːz ~drew 'druː
withdrawal wɪð 'drɔːʳ əl wɪθ-, -'drɔːl
  ‖ -'drɔːˌəl -'drɑːˌəl ~s z
  with'drawal ˌsymptoms
withdrawn wɪð 'drɔːn wɪθ- ‖ -'drɑːn
withdrew wɪð 'druː wɪθ-
withe wɪθ waɪð, wɪð **withes** wɪθs waɪðz, wɪðz
wither 'wɪð ə ‖ -ᵊr ~ed d **withering/ly**
  'wɪð ᵊr_ɪŋ /li ~s z
Withernsea 'wɪð ᵊn siː ‖ -ᵊrn-
Withers, w~ 'wɪð əz ‖ -ᵊrz
Witherspoon 'wɪð ə spuːn ‖ -ᵊr-
with|hold wɪð |'həʊld wɪθ-, →-'hɒʊld
  ‖ -|'hoʊld ~held 'held ~holding 'həʊld ɪŋ
  →'hɒʊld- ‖ 'hoʊld ɪŋ ~holds 'həʊldz
  →'hɒʊldz ‖ 'hoʊldz
  with'holding tax
within wɪð 'ɪn §wɪθ-
Withington 'wɪð ɪŋ tən
without wɪð 'aʊt §wɪθ-
withstand wɪð 'stænd wɪθ- ~ing ɪŋ ~s z
  withstood wɪð 'stʊd wɪθ-
with|y, Withy 'wɪð |i §'wɪθ- ~ies iz
Withycombe 'wɪð i kəm
witless 'wɪt ləs -lɪs ~ly li ~ness nəs nɪs
Witley 'wɪt li
witness 'wɪt nəs -nɪs ~ed t ~es ɪz əz ~ing ɪŋ
  'witness box; 'witness stand
Witney 'wɪt ni
-witted 'wɪt ɪd -əd ‖ 'wɪṭ əd — **slow-witted**
  ˌsləʊ 'wɪt ɪd ◂ -əd ‖ ˌsloʊ 'wɪṭ əd ◂
Wittenberg 'wɪt ᵊn bɜːg ‖ -bɝːg —*Ger*
  ['vɪt ᵊn bɛʁk]
witter 'wɪt ə ‖ 'wɪṭ ᵊr ~ed d **wittering**
  'wɪt_ᵊr ɪŋ ‖ 'wɪṭ ᵊr ɪŋ ~s z
Wittgenstein 'vɪt gən ʃtaɪn -staɪn
witticism 'wɪt ɪ ˌsɪz əm -ə- ‖ 'wɪṭ ə- ~s z
witti... —*see* **witty**
witting 'wɪt ɪŋ ‖ 'wɪṭ ɪŋ ~ly li
Witton 'wɪt ᵊn
witt|y, Witty 'wɪt |i ‖ 'wɪṭ |i ~ier i_ə ‖ i_ᵊr
  ~iest i_ɪst i_əst ~ily ɪ li əl i ~iness i nəs i nɪs
Witwatersrand wɪt 'wɔːt əz rænd ˌ•-, -'wɑːt-,
  -rɑːnd, -rɒnt, -rɑːnt, ˌ•, ••'•, '••••
  ‖ 'wɪt wɔːṭ ᵊrz- -'•wɑːṭ- —*Afrikaans*
  [ˌvɪt ˌvɑt ᵊrs 'rɑnt]
Wiveliscombe 'wɪv ə lɪs kəm —*locally also*
  'wɪls kəm
Wivelsfield 'wɪv ᵊlz fiːᵊld
Wivenhoe 'wɪv ᵊn həʊ ‖ -hoʊ

wives waɪvz
Wix wɪks
wiz wɪz
wizard 'wɪz əd ‖ -ᵊrd **~s** z
wizardry 'wɪz əd ri ‖ -ᵊrd-
wizened 'wɪz ᵊnd
woad wəʊd ‖ woʊd
wobbl|e 'wɒb ᵊl ‖ 'wɑːb ᵊl **~ed** d **~es** z **~ing** _ɪŋ
wobb|ly, W~ 'wɒb |li ‖ 'wɑːb- **~lier** li_ə ‖ li_ᵊr **~lies** liz **~liest** li_ɪst _əst
Wobegon 'wəʊ bɪ gɒn -bə- ‖ 'woʊ bɪ gɔːn -gɑːn
Woburn 'wəʊ bɜːn 'wuː-, -bən ‖ 'woʊ bɝːn
Wodehouse 'wʊd haʊs §-əs
Woden 'wəʊd ᵊn ‖ 'woʊd ᵊn
wodge wɒdʒ ‖ wɑːdʒ **wodges** 'wɒdʒ ɪz -əz ‖ 'wɑːdʒ əz
woe wəʊ ‖ woʊ **woes** wəʊz ‖ woʊz
woebegone 'wəʊ bɪ gɒn -bə- ‖ 'woʊ bɪ gɔːn -gɑːn
woeful 'wəʊ fᵊl -fʊl ‖ 'woʊ- **~ly** _i **~ness** nəs nɪs
wog wɒg ‖ wɑːg wɔːg **wogs** wɒgz ‖ wɑːgz wɔːgz
Wogan 'wəʊg ᵊn ‖ 'woʊg ᵊn
woggle 'wɒg ᵊl ‖ 'wɑːg ᵊl **~s** z
Wojtyla vɔɪ 'tɪl ə —Polish Wojtyła [vɔj 'tɪ wa]
wok wɒk ‖ wɑːk —Cantonese [⁶wɔːk] **woks** wɒks ‖ wɑːks
woke wəʊk ‖ woʊk
woken 'wəʊk ᵊn ‖ 'woʊk ᵊn
Woking 'wəʊk ɪŋ ‖ 'woʊk ɪŋ
Wokingham 'wəʊk ɪŋ əm ‖ 'woʊk-
wold wəʊld →wɒʊld ‖ woʊld **wolds, Wolds** wəʊldz →wɒʊldz ‖ woʊldz
Woldingham 'wəʊld ɪŋ əm →'wɒʊld- ‖ 'woʊld-
Woledge 'wəʊl ɪdʒ
wolf wʊlf **wolfed** wʊlft **wolfing** 'wʊlf ɪŋ **wolfs** wʊlfs **wolves** wʊlvz
   'wolf cub; 'wolf ˌwhistle
Wolf wʊlf —but as a German name, also vɒlf ‖ vɔːlf, vɑːlf —Ger [vɔlf]
Wolfe wʊlf
Wolfenden 'wʊlf ᵊn dən
Wolff wʊlf —Ger, Fr [vɔlf]
Wolfgang 'wʊlf gæŋ —Ger ['vɔlf gaŋ]
wolfhound 'wʊlf haʊnd **~s** z
wolfish 'wʊlf ɪʃ **~ly** li **~ness** nəs nɪs
Wolfit 'wʊlf ɪt §-ət
wolflike 'wʊlf laɪk
Wolford 'wʊl fəd ‖ -fᵊrd
wolfram 'wʊlf rəm
wolframite 'wʊlf rə maɪt
wolfsbane 'wʊlfs beɪn
Wollaston 'wʊl əst ᵊn
wollastonite 'wʊl əst ə naɪt
Wollongong 'wʊl ən gɒŋ →-əŋ- ‖ -gɔːŋ -gɑːŋ
Wollstonecraft 'wʊlst ᵊn krɑːft §-kræft ‖ -kræft
Wolmer 'wʊlm ə ‖ -ᵊr
Wolof 'wɒl ɒf ‖ 'woʊl ɑːf

Wolseley 'wʊlz li
Wolsey 'wʊlz i
Wolsingham 'wʊlz ɪŋ əm 'wɒls- ‖ 'wɑːls-
Wolstenholme 'wʊlst ᵊn həʊm ‖ -hoʊm
Wolverhampton ˌwʊlv ə 'hæmpt ᵊn '•••,•• ‖ -ᵊr-
wolverine 'wʊlv ə riːn **~s** z
Wolverton 'wʊlv ət ᵊn ‖ -ᵊrt ᵊn
wolves wʊlvz
woman 'wʊm ən **woman's** 'wʊm ənz **women** 'wɪm ɪn §-ən **women's** 'wɪm ɪnz §-ənz
   ˌWomen's 'Instutute; ˌwomen's 'lib; ˌwomen's ˌlibe'ration; 'women's ˌmovement; 'women's ˌstudies
womanhood 'wʊm ən hʊd
womanis... —see **womaniz...**
womanish 'wʊm ən ɪʃ **~ly** li **~ness** nəs nɪs
womaniz|e 'wʊm ə naɪz **~ed** d **~er/s** ə/z ‖ ᵊr/z **~es** ɪz əz **~ing** ɪŋ
womankind ˌwʊm ən kaɪnd →-əŋ-, ˌ•••
woman|ly 'wʊm ən |li **~liness** li nəs -nɪs
womb wuːm (!) **wombs** wuːmz
wombat 'wɒm bæt -bət ‖ 'wɑːm- **~s** s
wombl|e, W~ 'wɒm bᵊl ‖ 'wɑːm- **~ed** d **~es** z **~ing** _ɪŋ
Wombourne 'wɒm bɔːn ‖ 'wɑːm bɔːrn -boʊrn
Wombwell 'wʊm wel 'wuːm-, 'wɒm-, -wᵊl
women 'wɪm ɪn §-ən
womenfolk 'wɪm ɪn fəʊk -ən-, §-fɔʊlk ‖ -foʊk
womyn 'wɪm ɪn §-ən
won past & pp of **win** wʌn
won Korean currency wɒn ‖ wɑːn
wonder, W~ 'wʌnd ə ‖ -ᵊr **~ed** d **wondering/ly** 'wʌnd_ᵊr ɪŋ /li **~s** z
wonderful 'wʌnd ə fᵊl -fʊl ‖ -ᵊr- —In casual AmE also 'wʌn ᵊr- **~ly** _i **~ness** nəs nɪs
wonderland 'wʌnd ə lænd ‖ -ᵊr- **~s** z
wonderment 'wʌnd ə mənt ‖ -ᵊr-
wondrous 'wʌndr əs **~ly** li **~ness** nəs nɪs
Wonersh 'wɒn ɜːʃ ‖ 'wɑːn ɝːʃ
Wong wɒŋ ‖ wɑːŋ wɔːŋ —Cantonese [⁴wɔːŋ]
wonga-wonga 'wɒŋ gə ˌwɒŋ gə ,••'•• ‖ 'wɑːŋ gə ˌwɑːŋ gə
wonk|y 'wɒŋk |i ‖ 'wɑːŋk |i **~ier** i_ə ‖ i_ᵊr **~iest** i_ɪst i_əst
wont wəʊnt wɒnt ‖ wɔːnt wɑːnt, woʊnt
won't wəʊnt ‖ woʊnt wʊnt —Also, esp. before a consonant, wəʊn ‖ woʊn. This word has no weak form.
wonted 'wəʊnt ɪd -əd ‖ 'wɔːnt̬ əd 'wɑːnt̬-, 'woʊnt̬-
wonton ˌwɒn 'tɒn ◄ '•• ‖ 'wɑːn tɑːn ˌwonton 'soup
woo wuː **wooed** wuːd **wooing** 'wuː_ɪŋ **woos** wuːz
Woo wuː —Chi Wú [²wu], Cantonese [⁴wuː]
wood, Wood wʊd **wooded** 'wʊd ɪd -əd **wooding** 'wʊd ɪŋ **woods** wʊdz
   ˌwood 'alcohol; 'wood ˌpulp
Woodall 'wʊd ɔːl ‖ -ɑːl
woodbine 'wʊd baɪn →'wʊb- **~s** z
woodblock 'wʊd blɒk →'wʊb- ‖ -blɑːk **~s** s

Woodbridge 'wʊd brɪdʒ →'wʊb-
Woodburn 'wʊd bɜːn →'wʊb- ‖ -bɜːn
Woodbury 'wʊd bər_i →'wʊb- ‖ -,ber i
woodcarv|er/s 'wʊd ,kɑːv| ə/z →'wʊg-
‖ -,kɑːrv ər/z ~ing/s ɪŋ/z
woodchip 'wʊd tʃɪp
woodchuck 'wʊd tʃʌk ~s s
woodcock, W~ 'wʊd kɒk →'wʊg- ‖ -kɑːk ~s
s
woodcraft 'wʊd krɑːft →'wʊg-, §-kræft
‖ -kræft ~s s
woodcut 'wʊd kʌt →'wʊg- ~s s
woodcutter 'wʊd ,kʌt ə →'wʊg- ‖ -,kʌt̬ ər ~s
z
wooded 'wʊd ɪd -əd
wooden 'wʊd ən ~ly li ~ness nəs nɪs
,wooden 'spoon
woodenheaded ,wʊd ən 'hed ɪd ◀ -əd
Woodford 'wʊd fəd ‖ -fərd
Woodhall 'wʊd hɔːl ‖ -hɑːl
Woodhead 'wʊd hed
Woodhouse 'wʊd haʊs
woodland, W~ 'wʊd lənd -lænd ~s z
woodlark 'wʊd lɑːk ‖ -lɑːrk ~s s
Woodlesford 'wʊd əlz fəd ‖ -fərd
Woodley 'wʊd li
Woodliff 'wʊd lɪf
wood|louse 'wʊd |laʊs ~lice laɪs
wood|man, W~ 'wʊd |mən →'wʊb- ~men
mən
woodnote 'wʊd nəʊt ‖ -noʊt ~s s
Woodnutt 'wʊd nʌt
woodpecker 'wʊd ,pek ə →'wʊb- ‖ -ər ~s z
woodpile 'wʊd paɪəl →'wʊb- ~s z
Woodrow 'wʊd rəʊ ‖ -roʊ
woodruff, W~ 'wʊd rʌf ~s s
Woods wʊdz
woodscrew 'wʊd skruː ~s z
woodshed 'wʊd ʃed ~s z
woodsia 'wʊdz i_ə ~s z
Woodside ,wʊd 'saɪd ˈ··
woods|man 'wʊdz |mən ~men mən
Woodstock 'wʊd stɒk ‖ -stɑːk
woods|y 'wʊdz |i ~ier i_ə ‖ i_ər ~iest i_ɪst
i_əst
Woodward 'wʊd wəd ‖ -wərd
woodwind 'wʊd wɪnd
woodwork 'wʊd wɜːk ‖ -wɜːk
woodworm 'wʊd wɜːm ‖ -wɜːm
wood|y, Woody 'wʊd |i ~ier i_ə ‖ i_ər ~iest
i_ɪst i_əst ~iness i nəs i nɪs
wooer 'wuː_ə ‖ _ər ~s z
woof 'threads' wuːf ‖ wʊf wuːf woofs
wuːfs ‖ wʊfs wuːfs
woof 'dog's bark' wʊf woofs wʊfs
woofer 'wʊf ə 'wuːf- ‖ -ər ~s z
Woofferton 'wʊf ət ən ‖ -ərt ən
woofter 'wʊft ə ‖ -ər ~s z
Wookey 'wʊk i
wool, Wool wʊl wools wʊlz
Woolacombe 'wʊl ə kəm
Woolard 'wʊl ɑːd ‖ -ɑːrd
woolen 'wʊl ən ~s z

Wooler 'wʊl ə ‖ -ər
Woolf wʊlf
Woolford 'wʊl fəd ‖ -fərd
woolgather|ing 'wʊl ,gæð ər_ɪŋ ‖ -ər_ɪŋ
~er/s _ə/z ‖ _ər/z
Woolite tdmk 'wʊl aɪt
Woollard 'wʊl ɑːd ‖ -ɑːrd
Woollcott 'wʊl kət -kɒt ‖ -kɑːt
woollen 'wʊl ən ~s z
Woolley 'wʊl i
Woolloomooloo ,wʊl əm ə 'luː
wooll|y 'wʊl |i ~ier i_ə ‖ i_ər ~ies iz ~iest
i_ɪst i_əst ~iness i nəs i nɪs
woolly-headed ,wʊl i 'hed ɪd ◀ -əd
woolpack 'wʊl pæk ~s s
woolsack 'wʊl sæk ~s s
Woolton 'wʊlt ən
Woolwich 'wʊl ɪdʒ -ɪtʃ
Woolworth 'wʊl wəθ -wɜːθ ‖ -wɜːθ ~'s s
Woomera, w~ 'wʊm ər ə 'wuːm- ~s z
Woon wuːn
Woonsocket wuːn 'sɒk ɪt §-ət ‖ -'sɑːk-
Woore wɔː ‖ wɔːr wʊər
Woosnam 'wuːz nəm
Wooster 'wʊst ə 'wuːst- ‖ -ər
Wootten, Wootton 'wʊt ən
wooz|y 'wuːz |i 'wʊz- ~ier i_ə ‖ i_ər ~iest i_ɪst
i_əst ~ily ɪ li əl i ~iness i nəs i nɪs
wop wɒp ‖ wɑːp wops wɒps ‖ wɑːps
Worcester 'wʊst ə ‖ -ər ~shire ʃə ʃɪə ‖ ʃər ʃɪr
,Worcester(shire) 'sauce ‖ '··(·) ·
Worcestershire 'wʊst ə ʃə -ʃɪə ‖ -ər ʃər -ʃɪr
Worcs —see Worcestershire
word wɜːd ‖ wɜːd worded 'wɜːd ɪd -əd
‖ 'wɜːd əd wording/s 'wɜːd ɪŋ/z
‖ 'wɜːd ɪŋ/z words wɜːdz ‖ wɜːdz
'word ,blindness; 'word class; 'word
count; 'word ,order; 'word ,processing;
'word ,processor; 'word square
wordag|e 'wɜːd ɪdʒ ‖ 'wɜːd- ~es ɪz əz
wordbreak 'wɜːd breɪk →'wɜːb- ‖ 'wɜːd- ~s
s
wordless 'wɜːd ləs -lɪs ‖ 'wɜːd ləs ~ly li
~ness nəs nɪs
word-perfect, WordPerfect tdmk
,wɜːd 'pɜːf ɪkt ◀ →,wɜːb-, -ekt, §-əkt
‖ ,wɜːd 'pɜːf ɪkt ◀ ~ly li
wordplay 'wɜːd pleɪ →'wɜːb- ‖ 'wɜːd-
wordsmith 'wɜːd smɪθ ‖ 'wɜːd- ~s s
Wordstar, WordStar tdmk 'wɜːd stɑː
‖ 'wɜːd stɑːr
Wordsworth 'wɜːdz wəθ -wɜːθ ‖ 'wɜːdz wɜːθ
~'s s
Wordsworthian ,wɜːdz 'wɜːð i_ən -'wɜːθ-
‖ ,wɜːdz 'wɜːθ- -'wɜːð- ~s z
wordwrap 'wɜːd ræp ‖ 'wɜːd-
word|y 'wɜːd |i ‖ 'wɜːd |i ~ier i_ə ‖ i_ər ~iest
i_ɪst i_əst ~ily ɪ li əl i ~iness i nəs i nɪs
wore wɔː ‖ wɔːr wʊər
work wɜːk ‖ wɜːk worked wɜːkt ‖ wɜːkt
working/s 'wɜːk ɪŋ/z ‖ 'wɜːk ɪŋ/z works
wɜːks ‖ wɜːks
,worked 'up; ,working 'class ◀ ‖ '·· ·

ˌ**working ˈday** ‖ ˈ• • •; ˌ**working ˈknowledge;** ˌ**working ˈorder** ‖ ˈ• • ˌ• •; ˈ**working** ˌ**party;** ˌ**working ˈweek** ‖ ˈ• • •
-work wɜːk ‖ wɜ˞ːk — **spadework** ˈspeɪd wɜːk ‖ -wɜ˞ːk
workab|le ˈwɜːk əb |ᵊl ‖ ˈwɜ˞ːk- **~leness** ᵊl nəs -nɪs **~ly** li
workaday ˈwɜːk ə deɪ ‖ ˈwɜ˞ːk-
workaholic ˌwɜːk ə ˈhɒl ɪk ◂ ‖ ˌwɜ˞ːk ə ˈhɑːl ɪk ◂ -ˈhɔːl- **~s** s
workbag ˈwɜːk bæg ‖ ˈwɜ˞ːk- **~s** z
workbasket ˈwɜːk ˌbɑːsk ɪt §-ˌbæsk-, §-ət ‖ ˈwɜ˞ːk ˌbæsk ət **~s** s
workbench ˈwɜːk bentʃ ‖ ˈwɜ˞ːk- **~es** ɪz əz
workbook ˈwɜːk bʊk ‖ ˈwɜ˞ːk- **~s** s
workbox ˈwɜːk bɒks ‖ ˈwɜ˞ːk bɑːks **~es** ɪz əz
workday ˈwɜːk deɪ ‖ ˈwɜ˞ːk-
worker ˈwɜːk ə ‖ ˈwɜ˞ːk ᵊr **~s** z
worker-priest ˌwɜːk ə ˈpriːst ‖ ˌwɜ˞ːk ᵊr- **~s** s
workfare ˈwɜːk feə ‖ ˈwɜ˞ːk fer -fær
workforce ˈwɜːk fɔːs ‖ ˈwɜ˞ːk fɔːrs -fours
workhors|e ˈwɜːk hɔːs ‖ ˈwɜ˞ːk hɔːrs **~es** ɪz əz
work|house ˈwɜːk |haʊs ‖ ˈwɜ˞ːk- **~houses** haʊz ɪz -əz
work-in ˈwɜːk ɪn ‖ ˈwɜ˞ːk- **~s** z
working-class ˌwɜːk ɪŋ ˈklɑːs ◂ §-ˈklæs ‖ ˈwɜ˞ːk ɪŋ klæs
working-out ˌwɜːk ɪŋ ˈaʊt ‖ ˌwɜ˞ːk-
Workington ˈwɜːk ɪŋ tən ‖ ˈwɜ˞ːk-
workload ˈwɜːk ləʊd ‖ ˈwɜ˞ːk loʊd **~s** z
work|man, W~ ˈwɜːk |mən ‖ ˈwɜ˞ːk- **~manlike** mən laɪk **~manship** mən ʃɪp **~men** mən
workmate, W~ *tdmk* ˈwɜːk meɪt ‖ ˈwɜ˞ːk- **~s** s
workmen ˈwɜːk mən ‖ ˈwɜ˞ːk-
workout ˈwɜːk aʊt ‖ ˈwɜ˞ːk- **~s** s
workpeople ˈwɜːk ˌpiːp ᵊl ‖ ˈwɜ˞ːk-
workplac|e ˈwɜːk pleɪs ‖ ˈwɜ˞ːk- **~es** ɪz əz
workroom ˈwɜːk ruːm -rʊm ‖ ˈwɜ˞ːk- **~s** z
work-sharing ˈwɜːk ˌʃeər ɪŋ ‖ ˈwɜ˞ːk ˌʃer ɪŋ -ˌʃær-
worksheet ˈwɜːk ʃiːt ‖ ˈwɜ˞ːk- **~s** s
workshop ˈwɜːk ʃɒp ‖ ˈwɜ˞ːk ʃɑːp **~s** s
workshy ˈwɜːk ʃaɪ ‖ ˈwɜ˞ːk-
Worksop ˈwɜːk sɒp ‖ ˈwɜ˞ːk sɑːp
workspace ˈwɜːk speɪs ‖ ˈwɜ˞ːk-
workstation ˈwɜːk ˌsteɪʃ ᵊn ‖ ˈwɜ˞ːk- **~s** z
work-study ˈwɜːk ˌstʌd i ‖ ˈwɜ˞ːk-
worktable ˈwɜːk ˌteɪb ᵊl ‖ ˈwɜ˞ːk- **~s** z
worktop ˈwɜːk tɒp ‖ ˈwɜ˞ːk tɑːp **~s** s
work-to-rule ˌwɜːk tə ˈruːl -tu- ‖ ˌwɜ˞ːk-
world wɜːld ‖ wɜ˞ːld **worlds** wɜːldz ‖ wɜ˞ːldz ˌ**World ˈBank;** ˌ**World ˈCup;** ˌ**World ˈHealth Organiˌzation;** ˌ**world ˈpower;** ˌ**World ˈSeries;** ˌ**world ˈwar;** ˌ**World** ˌ**War ˈTwo;** ˌ**World Wide ˈWeb**
world-beater ˈwɜːl*d* ˌbiːt ə ‖ ˈwɜ˞ːl*d* ˌbiːt̬ ᵊr **~s** z
world-class ˌwɜːl*d* ˈklɑːs ◂ §-ˈklæs ‖ ˌwɜ˞ːl*d* ˈklæs ◂
world-famous ˌwɜːl*d* ˈfeɪm əs ◂ ‖ ˌwɜ˞ːld- ˈ• ˌ• •
worldling ˈwɜːld lɪŋ ‖ ˈwɜ˞ːld- **~s** z
world|ly ˈwɜːl*d* |li ‖ ˈwɜ˞ːl*d* |li **~lier** li‿ə ‖ li‿ᵊr **~liest** li‿ɪst ‿əst **~liness** li nəs -nɪs
worldly-wise ˌwɜːl*d* li ˈwaɪz ◂ ‖ ˌwɜ˞ːl*d*- ˈ• • •
worldshaking ˈwɜːld ˌʃeɪk ɪŋ ‖ ˈwɜ˞ːld-
world-wear|y ˌwɜːld ˈwɪər |i ◂ ˈ• ˌ• • ‖ ˈwɜ˞ːld ˌwɪr |i **~ier** i‿ə ‖ i‿ᵊr **~iest** i‿ɪst i‿əst **~ily** əl i ɪ li **~iness** i nəs i nɪs
worldwide ˌwɜːl*d* ˈwaɪd ◂ ‖ ˌwɜ˞ːl*d*-
Worley ˈwɜːl i ‖ ˈwɜ˞ːl i
Worlingham ˈwɜːl ɪŋ əm ‖ ˈwɜ˞ːl-
worm wɜːm ‖ wɜ˞ːm **wormed** wɜːmd ‖ wɜ˞ːmd **worming** ˈwɜːm ɪŋ ‖ ˈwɜ˞ːm ɪŋ **worms** wɜːmz ‖ wɜ˞ːmz ˈ**worm cast;** ˈ**worm gear**
Wormald ˈwɜːm ᵊld ‖ ˈwɜ˞ːm-
wormcast ˈwɜːm kɑːst §-kæst ‖ ˈwɜ˞ːm kæst **~s** s
worm-eaten ˈwɜːm ˌiːt ᵊn ‖ ˈwɜ˞ːm-
wormhole ˈwɜːm həʊl →-hɒʊl ‖ ˈwɜ˞ːm hoʊl **~s** z
Wormold ˈwɜːm əʊld →-ɒʊld, -ᵊld ‖ ˈwɜ˞ːm oʊld
Worms *place in Germany* vɔːmz wɜːmz ‖ wɜ˞ːmz —*Ger* [vɔʁms]
wormwood, W~ ˈwɜːm wʊd ‖ ˈwɜ˞ːm- ˌ**Wormwood ˈScrubs**
worm|y ˈwɜːm |i ‖ ˈwɜ˞ːm |i **~ier** i‿ə ‖ i‿ᵊr **~iest** i‿ɪst i‿əst **~iness** i nəs i nɪs
worn wɔːn ‖ wɔːrn woʊrn
worn-out ˌwɔːn ˈaʊt ◂ ‖ ˌwɔːrn- ˌwoʊrn-
Worple ˈwɔːp ᵊl ‖ ˈwɔːrp ᵊl
Worplesdon ˈwɔːp ᵊlz dən ‖ ˈwɔːrp-
Worrall ˈwɒr əl ‖ ˈwɔːr- ˈwɑːr-
worrie... —*see* **worry**
worriment ˈwʌr i mənt ‖ ˈwɜ˞ː- **~s** s
worrisome ˈwʌr i səm ‖ ˈwɜ˞ː- **~ly** li
worr|it ˈwʌr |ɪt §-ət ‖ ˈwɜ˞ː |ət **~ited** ɪt ɪd §ət-, -əd ‖ ət̬ əd **~iting** ɪt ɪŋ §ət- ‖ ət̬ ɪŋ **~its** ɪts §əts ‖ əts
worr|y ˈwʌr |i ‖ ˈwɜ˞ː |i **~ied/ly** id /li **~ier/s** i‿ə/z ‖ i‿ᵊr/z **~ies** iz **~ying/ly** i‿ɪŋ /li ˈ**worry beads**
worrywart ˈwʌr i wɔːt ‖ ˈwɜ˞ː i wɔːrt **~s** s
worse wɜːs ‖ wɜ˞ːs
worsen ˈwɜːs ᵊn ‖ ˈwɜ˞ːs ᵊn **~ed** d **~ing** ‿ɪŋ **~s** z
worship, W~ ˈwɜːʃ ɪp §-əp ‖ ˈwɜ˞ːʃ əp **~ed, ~ped** t **~ing, ~ping** ɪŋ **~s** s
worshiper, worshipper ˈwɜːʃ ɪp ə §-əp- ‖ ˈwɜ˞ːʃ əp ᵊr **~s** z
worshipful ˈwɜːʃ ɪp fᵊl §-əp-, -fʊl ‖ ˈwɜ˞ːʃ əp- **~ly** i **~ness** nəs nɪs
Worsley ˈwɜːs li ˈwɜːz- ‖ ˈwɜ˞ːs-
Worsnip ˈwɜːs nɪp §-nəp ‖ ˈwɜ˞ːs-
worst wɜːst ‖ wɜ˞ːst **worsted** ˈwɜːst ɪd -əd ‖ ˈwɜ˞ːst əd **worsting** ˈwɜːst ɪŋ ‖ ˈwɜ˞ːst ɪŋ **worsts** wɜːsts ‖ wɜ˞ːsts
worsted *ˈcloth'* ˈwʊst ɪd -əd ‖ ˈwɜ˞ːst əd
Worsthorne ˈwɜːs θɔːn ‖ ˈwɜ˞ːs θɔːrn
wort wɜːt §wɔːt ‖ wɜ˞ːt wɔːrt
worth wɜːθ ‖ wɜ˞ːθ
Worth wɜːθ ‖ wɜ˞ːθ —*but as a French name* vɔːt ‖ vɔːrt —*Fr* [vɔʁt]

-worth wəθ wɜːθ ‖ wɝːθ — **poundsworth**
'paʊndz wəθ -wɜːθ ‖ -wɝːθ
worthi... —*see* **worthy**
Worthing 'wɜːð ɪŋ ‖ 'wɝːð ɪŋ
Worthington 'wɜːð ɪŋ tən ‖ 'wɝːð-
worthless 'wɜːθ ləs -lɪs ‖ 'wɝːθ- **~ly** li **~ness**
nəs nɪs
worthwhile ˌwɜːθ 'waɪəl ◄ -'hwaɪəl
‖ ˌwɝːθ 'hwaɪəl ◄
worth|y, W~ 'wɜːð |i ‖ 'wɝːð |i **~ier** i_ə ‖ i_ər
~ies iz **~iest** i_ɪst i_əst **~ily** ɪ li əl i **~iness**
i nəs i nɪs
-worthy ˌwɜːð i ‖ ˌwɝːð i — **blameworthy**
'bleɪm ˌwɜːð i ‖ -ˌwɝːð-
Wortley 'wɜːt li ‖ 'wɝːt-
Worzel 'wɜːz əl ‖ 'wɝːz əl
wot wɒt ‖ waːt
Wotan 'vəʊt aːn -æn ‖ 'voʊt- —*Ger* ['voː tan]
wotcha, wotcher 'wɒtʃ ə ‖ 'waːtʃ ə -ər
Wotton 'wɒt ən 'wɒt- ‖ 'waːt-
Wotton-under-Edge ˌwɒt ən ˌʌnd ər
'edʒ ‖ -ər' • —*locally also* ˌ• • ʌndr ɪdʒ
would *strong form* wʊd (= *wood*) , *occasional*
weak forms wəd, əd —*see also* 'd
would-be 'wʊd biː →'wʊb-, -bi
wouldn't 'wʊd ənt §'wʊt ənt
wouldst wʊdst wʊtst
Woulfe wʊlf
wound *'injure, injury'* wuːnd **wounded/ly**
'wuːnd ɪd /li -əd /li **wounding/ly**
'wuːnd ɪŋ /li **wounds** wuːndz
wound *past & pp of* **wind** waʊnd
wound-up ˌwaʊnd 'ʌp ◄
woundwort 'wuːnd wɜːt §-wɔːt ‖ -wɝːt -wɔːrt
~s s
wove wəʊv ‖ woʊv
woven 'wəʊv ən ‖ 'woʊv ən
wow waʊ **wowed** waʊd **wowing** 'waʊ ɪŋ
wows waʊz
wowser 'waʊz ə ‖ -ər **~s** z
Wozzeck 'vɒts ek 'vɔɪts- ‖ 'vɔːts- 'vaːts-
WRAC ræk
wrack ræk (= *rack*) **wracked** rækt **wracking**
'ræk ɪŋ **wracks** ræks
Wragg, Wragge ræg
wraith, W~ reɪθ **wraiths** reɪθs
wraithlike 'reɪθ laɪk
Wrangel, Wrangell 'ræŋ gəl
wrangl|e 'ræŋ gəl **~ed** d **~es** z **~ing** ɪŋ
wrangler, W~ *tdmk* 'ræŋ glə ‖ -glər **~s** z
wrap ræp (= *rap*) **wrapped** ræpt **wrapping/s**
'ræp ɪŋ/z **wraps** ræps
wraparound 'ræp ə ˌraʊnd **~s** z
wrapper 'ræp ə ‖ -ər (= *rapper*) **~s** z
wrapround 'ræp raʊnd **~s** z
wrasse ræs **wrasses** 'ræs ɪz -əz
wrath, Wrath rɒθ rɔːθ, §raːθ, §ræθ ‖ ræθ (*)
Wrathall 'rɒθ əl ‖ 'ræθ ɔːl -aːl
wrathful 'rɒθ fəl 'rɔːθ-, §'raːθ-, §'ræθ-, -fʊl
‖ 'ræθ- **~ly** i **~ness** nəs nɪs
Wray reɪ
Wraysbury 'reɪz bər_i

wreak riːk §rek (= *reek*) **wreaked** riːkt
wreaking 'riːk ɪŋ **wreaks** riːks
wreath riːθ **wreaths** riːðz riːθs
wreathe riːð **wreathed** riːðd **wreathes** riːðz
wreathing 'riːð ɪŋ
wreck rek (= *reck*) **wrecked** rekt **wrecking**
'rek ɪŋ **wrecks** reks (= *rex*)
wreckage 'rek ɪdʒ
wrecker 'rek ə ‖ -ər **~s** z
Wrekin 'riːk ɪn §-ən
wren, Wren ren **wrens, Wrens, Wren's** renz
wrench, W~ rentʃ **wrenched** rentʃt
wrenches 'rentʃ ɪz -əz **wrenching** 'rentʃ ɪŋ
Wrenn ren
wrest rest (= *rest*) **wrested** 'rest ɪd -əd
wresting 'rest ɪŋ **wrests** rests
wrestl|e 'res əl ‖ 'ræs- **~ed** d **~es** z **~ing** ɪŋ
wrestler 'res lə ‖ ˌ•əl_ə ‖ 'res lər 'ræs- **~s** z
wretch retʃ **wretches** 'retʃ ɪz -əz
wretched 'retʃ ɪd -əd (!) **~ly** li **~ness** nəs nɪs
Wrexham 'reks əm
wrick rɪk (= *rick*) **wricked** rɪkt **wricking**
'rɪk ɪŋ **wricks** rɪks
wrie... —*see* **ry**
wriggl|e 'rɪg əl **~ed** d **~er/s** _ə/z ‖ _ər/z **~es** z
~ing ɪŋ **~y** _i
wright, Wright raɪt (= *right*) **wrights,**
Wright's raɪts
Wrightington 'raɪt ɪŋ tən
Wrighton 'raɪt ən
Wrigley 'rɪg li **~'s** z
wring rɪŋ (= *ring*) **wringing** 'rɪŋ ɪŋ **wrings**
rɪŋz **wrung** rʌŋ
ˌwringing 'wet◄
wringer 'rɪŋ ə ‖ -ər (= *ringer*) **~s** z
wrinkl|e 'rɪŋk əl **~ed** d **~es** z **~ing** ɪŋ
wrink|ly 'rɪŋk |li **~lies** liz
Wriothesley 'raɪ_əθs li
wrist rɪst **wrists** rɪsts
wristband 'rɪst bænd **~s** z
wristlet 'rɪst lət -lɪt **~s** s
wristwatch 'rɪst wɒtʃ ‖ -waːtʃ **~es** ɪz əz
wristy 'rɪst i
writ rɪt **writs** rɪts
write raɪt (= *right*) **writes** raɪts **writing**
'raɪt ɪŋ ‖ 'raɪt̬ ɪŋ **written** 'rɪt ən **wrote**
rəʊt ‖ roʊt
write-in 'raɪt ɪn ‖ 'raɪt̬ ɪn **~s** z
write-off 'raɪt ɒf -ɔːf ‖ 'raɪt̬ ɔːf -aːf **~s** s
writer 'raɪt ə ‖ 'raɪt̬ ər **~s** z
ˌwriter's 'cramp ‖ ˌ• • •
write-up 'raɪt ʌp ‖ 'raɪt̬ ʌp **~s** s
writhe raɪð **writhed** raɪðd **writhes** raɪðz
writhing 'raɪð ɪŋ
writing 'raɪt ɪŋ ‖ 'raɪt̬ ɪŋ **~s** z
'writing desk; 'writing ˌpaper
written 'rɪt ən
Wroclaw, Wrocław 'vrɒts laːv -læv
‖ 'vrɔːts laːf 'vraːts- —*Polish* ['vrɔts waf]
wrong rɒŋ ‖ rɔːŋ raːŋ **wronged** rɒŋd ‖ rɔːŋd
raːŋd **wronging** 'rɒŋ ɪŋ ‖ 'rɔːŋ ɪŋ 'raːŋ-
wrongs rɒŋz ‖ rɔːŋz raːŋz

W

wrongdoer 'rɒŋ ˌduː‿ə ˌ•'•• ‖ 'rɔːŋ ˌduː ər
'rɑːŋ-; ˌ•'•• ~s z
wrongdoing 'rɒŋ ˌduː‿ɪŋ ˌ•'•• ‖ 'rɔːŋ- 'rɑːŋ-
~s z
wrong-|foot ˌrɒŋ ‖'fʊt ‖ ˌrɔːŋ- ˌrɑːŋ- ~**footed**
'fʊt ɪd -əd ‖ 'fʊt̬ əd ~**footing** 'fʊt ɪŋ ‖ 'fʊt̬ ɪŋ
~**foots** 'fʊts
wrongful 'rɒŋ fəl -fʊl ‖ 'rɔːŋ- 'rɑːŋ- ~**ly** i
~**ness** nəs nɪs
wrongheaded ˌrɒŋ 'hed ɪd ◄ -əd ‖ ˌrɔːŋ-
ˌrɑːŋ- ~**ly** li ~**ness** nəs nɪs
wrong|ly 'rɒŋ |li ‖ 'rɔːŋ |li 'rɑːŋ- ~**ness** nəs nɪs
wrote rəʊt ‖ rout (= *rote*)
wroth rəʊθ rɒθ ‖ rɔːθ rɑːθ (*)
Wrotham *place in Kent* 'ruːt əm ‖ 'ruːt̬-
Wrottesley 'rɒts li ‖ 'rɑːts-
wrought rɔːt ‖ rɑːt
ˌwrought'iron◄
wrought-up ˌrɔːt 'ʌp ◄ ‖ ˌrɔːt̬- ˌrɑːt̬-
Wroxeter 'rɒks ɪt ə ‖ 'rɑːks ət̬ ər
Wroxham 'rɒks əm ‖ 'rɑːks-
wrung rʌŋ (= *rung*)
wry raɪ (= *rye*) **wrier, wryer** 'raɪ ə ‖ 'raɪ ər
wriest, wryest 'raɪ ɪst -əst
wryly 'raɪ li
wryneck 'raɪ nek ~s s
wryness 'raɪ nəs -nɪs
Wrythe raɪð
Wu wuː —*Chi* Wú [²wu], *Cantonese* [⁴wuː]
Wuhan ˌwuː 'hæn ‖ -'hɑːn —*Chi* Wǔhàn [³wu
⁴xan]
wulfenite 'wʊlf ə naɪt -ɪ-
Wulfrun 'wʊlf rən
Wulstan 'wʊlst ən
wunderkind 'wʌnd ə kɪnd 'vʊnd- ‖ -ər- —*Ger*
['vʊn dɐ kɪnt] ~s z
Wuppertal 'vʊp ə tɑːl 'wʊp- ‖ -ər- —*Ger*
['vʊp ɐ taːl]
Wurlitzer 'wɜːl ɪts ə -əts- ‖ 'wɝːl əts ər ~s z
wurst wɜːst wʊəst, vʊəst ‖ wɝːst wʊrst, wʊst
—*Ger* [vʊʁst]
Wurttenberg, Württemberg 'vɜːt əm bɜːg
'wɜːt- ‖ 'wɝːt̬ əm bɝːg —*Ger*
['vʏʁ təm bɛʁk]
Wurzburg, Würzburg 'vɜːts bɜːg 'wɜːts-

‖ 'wɝːts bɝːg —*Ger* ['vʏʁts bʊʁk]
wuss wʊs **wusses** 'wʊs ɪz -əz
wussy 'wʊs i **wussies** 'wʊs iz
wuthering, W~ 'wʌð ər ɪŋ
ˌWuthering'Heights
Wuxi ˌwuː 'ʃiː —*Chi* Wúxī [²wu ¹çi]
Wyandot, wyandotte 'waɪ_ən dɒt ‖ -dɑːt ~s s
Wyatt 'waɪ_ət
wych-elm 'wɪtʃ elm ~s z
Wycherley 'wɪtʃ ə li ‖ -ər-
wych-hazel 'wɪtʃ ˌheɪz əl ~s z
Wychwood 'wɪtʃ wʊd
Wyclif, Wycliffe 'wɪk lɪf
Wycliffite 'wɪk lɪ faɪt -lə- ~s s
Wycombe 'wɪk əm
Wye, wye waɪ (= *Y*) **wyes, Wye's** waɪz (=
wise)
Wyeth 'waɪ_əθ
Wyke waɪk
Wykeham 'wɪk əm
Wykehamist 'wɪk əm ɪst §-əst ~s s
Wyld, Wylde waɪ³ld
Wylfa 'wɪlv ə —*Welsh* ['uɪl va, 'wɪl-]
Wylie, Wyllie, Wylye 'waɪl i
Wyman 'waɪ mən
Wymondham (i) 'waɪm ənd əm, (ii) 'wɪnd əm,
(iii) 'wɪm ənd əm —*The place in Leics is (i),
that in Nfk (ii) or (iii).*
Wyn wɪn
wynd waɪnd **wynds** waɪndz
Wyndham 'wɪnd əm
Wynette wɪ 'net wə-
Wynford 'wɪn fəd ‖ -fərd
Wynn, Wynne wɪn
Wyoming waɪ 'əʊm ɪŋ ‖ -'oʊm-
Wyomingite waɪ 'əʊm ɪŋ aɪt ‖ -'oʊm- ~s s
Wyre 'waɪ_ə ‖ 'waɪ_ər
Wyrley 'wɜːl i ‖ 'wɝːl i
WYSIWYG, wysiwyg 'wɪz i wɪg
Wystan 'wɪst ən
Wytch wɪtʃ
Wythenshawe 'wɪð ən ʃɔː ‖ -ʃɑː
wyvern 'waɪv ən -ɜːn ‖ -ərn ~s z

X x

1 Where the spelling is **x**, the pronunciation is regularly ks, as in **six** sɪks. Less commonly, it is gz, and occasionally z or kʃ.

2 The pronunciation gz is found mainly in words beginning **ex-** before a stressed vowel, for example **exist** ɪg ˈzɪst. There is a variant pronunciation with kz. However, in words beginning **exce-, exci-**, the pronunciation is ks, with the **c** silent, as in **exceed** ɪk ˈsiːd.

3 The pronunciation is regularly z at the beginning of a word, as in **xerox** ˈzɪər ɒks ‖ ˈzɪr ɑːks. Note also **anxiety** æŋ ˈzaɪ̯ət i ‖ -ət̬ i.

4 The pronunciation is kʃ in words ending **xious, xion, xure**, for example **crucifixion, anxious** ˈæŋk ʃəs. In **luxury** and its derivatives some speakers use kʃ, some gʒ.

5 ks is also regularly written
cks, as in **kicks** kɪks,
ks, as in **thanks** θæŋks, and
cc, as in **accident** ˈæks ɪd ənt.

6 **x** is silent in certain names and other words borrowed from French, as in **prix** priː.

X, x eks **X's, x's, Xs** ˈeks ɪz -əz
—*Communications code name:* ˈX-ray
ˈX ˌchromosome
X-acto *tdmk* eks ˈækt əʊ ‖ -oʊ
Xan zæn
Xanadu ˈzæn ə duː ˈgzæn-, ˌ•••• —*Chi* (Yuán)shàngdū [(²ɥɛn) ⁴şaŋ ¹tu]
xanth- *comb. form before vowel*
  with unstressed suffix ˈzænθ ˈgzænθ —
  xanthene ˈzænθ iːn ˈgzænθ-
  with stressed suffix zæn ˈθ+ gzæn ˈθ+ —
  xanthoma zæn ˈθəʊm ə gzæn- ‖ -ˈθoʊm ə
Xanthe ˈzænθ i ˈgzænθ-
xanthelasma ˌzænθ ɪ ˈlæz mə -ə-
xanthic ˈzænθ ɪk
Xanthippe zæn ˈθɪp i gzæn-, -ˈtɪp-
Xantia *tdmk* ˈzænt i̯ə
Xantippe zæn ˈtɪp i gzæn-
xantho- *comb. form*
  with stress-neutral suffix ˈzænθ əʊ ˈgzænθ əʊ
  ‖ -ə — **xanthochroic** ˌzænθ əʊ ˈkrəʊ ɪk ◂
  ˌgzænθ- ‖ -ə ˈkroʊ-
  with stress-imposing suffix zæn ˈθɒ+
  gzæn ˈθɒ+ ‖ -ˈθɑː+ — **xanthochroism**
  zæn ˈθɒk rəʊ ˌɪz əm gzæn- ‖ -ˈθɑːk roʊ-
Xavier ˈzæv i̯ə ˈzeɪv- ‖ ̯ər —*Sp* [xa ˈβjer]

Xavierian zæ ˈvɪər i̯ən zeɪ- ‖ -ˈvɪr- ~s z
x-axis ˈeks ˌæks ɪs §-əs
X-bar ˈeks bɑː ‖ -bɑːr
xebek ˈziːb ek ˈzeɪb- ~s s
Xenia, xenia ˈziːn i̯ə ˈzen-
Xenical *tdmk* ˈzen ɪ kæl -ə-
Xenix *tdmk* ˈziːn ɪks
xeno- *comb. form*
  with stress-neutral suffix ˈzen əʊ ˈziːn əʊ -ə
  — **xenophile** ˈzen əʊ faɪ̯əl ˈziːn- ‖ -ə-
  with stress-imposing suffix ze ˈnɒ+ ziː-, zɪ-
  ‖ -ˈnɑː+ — **xenogamy** ze ˈnɒg əm i ziː-, zɪ-
  ‖ -ˈnɑːg-
xenon ˈziːn ɒn ˈzen-, ˈgziːn-, ˈzen- ‖ ˈziːn ɑːn
  ˈzen-
xenophobe ˈzen ə fəʊb ˈziːn- ‖ -foʊb ~s z
xenophobia ˌzen ə ˈfəʊb i̯ə ˌziːn- ‖ -ˈfoʊb-
xenophobic ˌzen ə ˈfəʊb ɪk ◂ ˌziːn- ‖ -ˈfoʊb-
Xenophon ˈzen əf ən -ə fɒn ‖ -ə fɑːn
xer- *comb. form before vowel*
  with unstressed suffix ˈzɪər ‖ ˈzɪr — **xerarch**
  ˈzɪər ɑːk ‖ ˈzɪr ɑːrk
  with stressed suffix zɪə ˈr+ zɪ ˈr+, zə ˈr+
  ‖ zə ˈr+ zɪ ˈr+ — **xerosis** zɪə ˈrəʊs ɪs zɪ-, zə-
  ‖ zə ˈroʊs əs zɪ-
xeric ˈzɪər ɪk ‖ ˈzɪr ɪk

xero- *comb. form*
 with stress-neutral suffix ˈzɪər əʊ ˈgzɪər əʊ
 ‖ ˈzɪr ə — **xeroderma** ˌzɪər əʊ ˈdɜːm ə
 ˌgzɪər- ‖ ˌzɪr ə ˈdɜːm ə
 with stress-imposing suffix zɪə ˈrɒ+ ze-, zɪ-,
 gzɪə-, gze-, §zi:- ‖ zə ˈrɑː+ zɪ- —
 xerophilous zɪə ˈrɒf ɪl əs ze-, zɪ-, gzɪə-,
 gze-, §zi:-, §-əl- ‖ zə ˈrɑːf əl əs zɪ-
xerographic ˌzɪər ə ˈɡræf ɪk ◂ ‖ ˌzɪr- ~ally əˌli
xerography zɪə ˈrɒg rəf i ze-, zɪ-, §zi:-
 ‖ zə ˈrɑːg- zɪ-
xerophthalmia ˌzɪər ɒf ˈθælm i‿ə ˌ•ɒp-
 ‖ ˌzɪr ɑːf- ˌ•ɑːp-
xerophyte ˈzɪər əʊ faɪt ˈgzɪər- ‖ ˈzɪr ə- ~s s
xerox, Xerox *tdmk* ˈzɪər ɒks ‖ ˈzɪr ɑːks ~ed t
 ~es ɪz əz ~ing ɪŋ
Xerxes ˈzɜːks iːz ‖ ˈzɝːks-
Xhosa ˈkɔːs ə ˈkəʊs-, ˈkɔːz-, ˈkəʊz- ‖ ˈkoʊs ə
 ˈhoʊs- —*Xhosa* [ˈǁhɔː sa] ~s z
xi *name of Greek letter* saɪ ksaɪ, zaɪ, gzaɪ ‖ zaɪ
 xis, xi's saɪz ksaɪz, zaɪz, gzaɪz ‖ zaɪz
Xia *dynasty* ʃi ˈɑː —*Chi* Xià [⁴çja]
Xiamen ˌʃɑː ˈmʌn ʃi ˌɑː- —*Chi* Xiàmén [⁴çja
 ²mən]
Xian, Xi'an ˌʃiː ˈæn ‖ -ˈɑːn —*Chi* Xī'ān [¹çi ¹an]
Ximenes ˈzɪm ə niːz -ɪ- ‖ hɪ ˈmen ez —*Sp*
 [xi ˈme nes]
xing, XING *in road signs* ˈkrɒs ɪŋ ˈkrɔːs-
 ‖ ˈkrɔːs ɪŋ ˈkrɑːs-
Xingu, Xingú ʃɪŋ ˈguː ʃiːŋ-, ˈ•• —*Port*
 [ʃĩ ˈgu]
Xinhua *News Agency* ˌʃɪn ˈʰwɑː —*Chi* Xīnhuá
 [¹çɪn ²xwa]

Xinjiang ˌʃɪn dʒi ˈæŋ ‖ -ˈɑːŋ —*Chi* Xīnjiāng
 [¹çɪn ¹tçjaŋ]
xiphoid ˈzɪf ɔɪd
Xmas ˈkrɪs məs ˈeks-
XP ˌkaɪ ˈrəʊ ‖ -ˈroʊ
x-ray, X-ray ˈeks reɪ ˌ•ˈ•◂ ~ed d ~ing ɪŋ ~s z
Xsara *tdmk* ˈzɑːr ə
xth eksθ
xyl- *comb. form before vowel*
 with unstressed suffix zaɪl gzaɪl — **xylyl**
 ˈzaɪl ɪl ˈgzaɪl-, §-əl
 with stressed suffix zaɪ ˈl+ gzaɪ ˈl+ —
 xylamidine zaɪ ˈlæm ɪ diːn gzaɪ-, §-ə-
xylem ˈzaɪl əm -em
xylene ˈzaɪl iːn ˈgzaɪl-
xylidine ˈzaɪl ɪ diːn -ə-
xylo- *comb. form*
 with stress-neutral suffix ˈzaɪl əʊ ˈgzaɪl- ‖ -ə
 — **xylocarpous** ˌzaɪl əʊ ˈkɑːp əs ◂ ˌgzaɪl-
 ‖ -ə ˈkɑːrp-
 with stress-imposing suffix zaɪ ˈlɒ+ gzaɪ-
 ‖ -ˈlɑː+ — **xylography** zaɪ ˈlɒg rəf i gzaɪ-
 ‖ -ˈlɑːg-
xylol ˈzaɪl ɒl ˈgzaɪl- ‖ -ɔːl -ɑːl, -oʊl
xylonite, X~ *tdmk* ˈzaɪl ə naɪt ˈgzaɪl-
xylophone ˈzaɪl ə fəʊn ˈzɪl-, ˈgzaɪl- ‖ -foʊn ~s
 z
xylophonist zaɪ ˈlɒf ən ɪst ˈzaɪl ə fəʊn-, §-əst
 ‖ ˈzaɪl ə foʊn əst ~s s
xylose ˈzaɪl əʊz ˈgzaɪl-, -əʊs ‖ -oʊs
xyster ˈzɪst ə ˈgzɪst- ‖ -ər ~s z

Y y

Spelling-to-sound

1 At the beginning of a word or syllable, where the spelling is **y**, the pronunciation is
j, as in **yet** jet, **beyond** bɪ 'jɒnd ‖ bɪ 'jɑːnd.

2 Elsewhere, the same pronunciations correspond to **y** as to **i**, namely
ɪ ('short'), as in **crystal** 'krɪst ᵊl,
aɪ ('long'), as in **type** taɪp,
weak i, as in **happy** 'hæp i,
or **y** may be part of one of the digraphs **ay, ey, oy, uy** (see under **a, e, o, u**, respectively).

3 The sound j is also sometimes written **i**, as in **onion** 'ʌn jən. It frequently arises through COMPRESSION of i with a following weak vowel, as in **convenient** kən 'viːn i‿ənt → kən 'viːn jənt. As part of the sequence juː (or one of its derivatives juə, jʊ, jɔː, ju, jə) it is regularly written **eu, ew, u, ue**.

Y, y *name of letter* waɪ **Y's, y's, Ys** waɪz
—*Communications code name:* Yoke
'Y ˌchromosome
Y, y *in Welsh expressions* ə
-y i— **panicky** 'pæn ɪk i
-y- *in Welsh place names* i ə —*Welsh* [ə]
ya '*yes'* jɑː
yabber 'jæb ə ‖ -ᵊr **~ed** d **yabbering**
  'jæb ər‿ɪŋ **~s** z
yabb|ie, yabb|y 'jæb |i **~ies** iz
yacht jɒt ‖ jɑːt **yachted** 'jɒt ɪd -əd ‖ 'jɑːt̬ əd
  yachting 'jɒt ɪŋ ‖ 'jɑːt̬ ɪŋ **yachts**
  jɒts ‖ jɑːts
yachts|man 'jɒts |mən ‖ 'jɑːts- **~men** mən
  ~woman ˌwʊm ən **~women** ˌwɪm ɪn §-ən
yack jæk **yacked** jækt **yacking** 'jæk ɪŋ **yacks**
  jæks
yackety-yak ˌjæk ət i 'jæk ˌ•ɪt- ‖ ˌjæk ət̬-
  ~ked t **~king** ɪŋ **~s** s
yaffle 'jæf ᵊl **~s** z
Yagi, yagi 'jɑːg i 'jæg- —*Jp* ['ja ɲi, -gi, •ˌ•]
  ~s z
yah jɑː
yahoo, Yahoo ₍ₐ₎jɑː 'huː jə-, 'jɑː huː **~s** z
Yahveh 'jɑː veɪ
Yahweh 'jɑː weɪ
yak jæk **yaks** jæks
Yakima 'jæk ɪ mɑː -ə- ‖ -mɔː -mɑː **~s** z
yakitori ˌjæk i 'tɔːr i ‖ ˌjɑːk- ˌjæk- —*Jp*
  [ja ˌki to ri]
yakka 'jæk ə
Yakult *tdmk* 'jæk ᵊlt

Yakut jə 'kʊt jæ-, jɑː- ‖ -'kuːt **~s** s
Yakutsk jə 'kʊtsk jæ-, jɑː- ‖ -'kuːtsk —*Russ*
  [jɪ 'kutsk]
yakuza jə 'kuːz ə 'jæk u zɑː —*Jp* ['ja kɯ dza]
Yalden 'jɔːld ᵊn 'jɒld- ‖ 'jɑːld-
Yale jeɪᵊl
y'all jɔːl ‖ jɑːl
Yalta 'jælt ə 'jɔːlt-, 'jɒlt- ‖ 'jɔːlt ə 'jɑːlt-
  —*Russ* ['jaɫ tə]
yam jæm **yams** jæmz
Yamaha *tdmk* 'jæm ə hɑː -hə ‖ 'jɑːm- **~s** z
  —*Jp* [ja ˌma ha]
Yamani jə 'mɑːn i
yammer 'jæm ə ‖ -ᵊr **~ed** d **yammering**
  'jæm ər‿ɪŋ **~s** z
yang, Yang jæŋ ‖ jɑːŋ jæŋ
Yangtse, Yangtze 'jæŋkt si ‖ 'jɑːŋkt si —*Chi*
  Yángzǐ [²jaŋ ³tsɨ]
  ˌYangtse Ki'ang, -'Kiang ki 'æŋ kjæŋ ‖ -'ɑːŋ
  —*Chi* Jiāng [¹tɕjaŋ]
Yangzhou ˌjæŋ 'dʒəʊ ‖ ˌjɑːŋ 'dʒoʊ —*Chi*
  Yángzhōu [²jaŋ ¹tʂoʊ]
yank, Yank jæŋk **yanked** jæŋkt **yanking**
  'jæŋk ɪŋ **yanks, Yanks** jæŋks
Yankee 'jæŋk i **~dom** dəm **~ism/s** ˌɪz əm/z
  ~s z
  ˌYankee 'Doodle
Yaounde, Yaoundé jɑː 'ʊnd eɪ ‖ ˌjɑː ʊn 'deɪ
  —*Fr* [ja un de]
yap jæp **yapped** jæpt **yapping/ly** 'jæp ɪŋ /li
  yaps jæps
Yap *island* jæp jɑːp ‖ jɑːp

yapok jə 'pɒk ‖ -'pɑːk ~s s
yapp, Yapp jæp
yapper 'jæp ə ‖ -ər ~s z
Yaqui 'jɑːk i ~s z
Yarborough, y~ 'jɑː bər_ə ‖ 'jɑːr ˌbɜː oʊ ~s z
yard jɑːd ‖ jɑːrd **yards** jɑːdz ‖ jɑːrdz
yardag|e 'jɑːd ɪdʒ ‖ 'jɑːrd- ~es ɪz əz
yardarm 'jɑːd ɑːm ‖ 'jɑːrd ɑːrm ~s z
yardbird 'jɑːd bɜːd →'jɑːb- ‖ 'jɑːrd bɜːd ~s z
yardie, Y~ 'jɑːd i ‖ 'jɑːrd i ~s z
Yardley 'jɑːd li ‖ 'jɑːrd-
yardstick 'jɑːd stɪk ‖ 'jɑːrd- ~s s
Yare, yare jeə ‖ jeər jæər, jɑːr
Yarm jɑːm ‖ jɑːrm
Yarmouth 'jɑː məθ ‖ 'jɑːr-
yarmulka, yarmulke 'jɑːm ʊlk ə 'jʌm-, -əlk-
 ‖ 'jɑːrm- 'jɑːm-, -ək- ~s z
yarn jɑːn ‖ jɑːrn **yarned** jɑːnd ‖ jɑːrnd
 yarning 'jɑːn ɪŋ ‖ 'jɑːrn ɪŋ **yarns**
 jɑːnz ‖ jɑːrnz
Yarra 'jær ə
Yarralumla ˌjær ə 'lʌm lə
yarrow, Y~ 'jær əʊ ‖ -oʊ 'jer- ~s z
Yarwood 'jɑː wʊd ‖ 'jɑːr-
yashmak 'jæʃ mæk ‖ 'jɑːʃ mɑːk ~s s
Yasmin, Yasmine 'jæs mɪn 'jæz-, 'jɑːs-
Yasser, Yassir 'jæs ə ‖ 'jɑːs ər —*Arabic*
 ['jɑː sir]
yataghan 'jæt əg ən ‖ 'jæt̬ ə gæn -əg ən ~s z
Yates jeɪts
yatter 'jæt ə ‖ 'jæt̬ ər ~ed d **yattering**
 'jæt_ər ɪŋ ‖ 'jæt̬ ər ɪŋ ~s z
Yaunde ja: 'ʊnd eɪ ‖ ˌjɑː ʊn 'deɪ —*Fr* Yaoundé
 [ja un de]
yaw jɔː ‖ jɑː **yawed** jɔːd ‖ jɑːd **yawing/s**
 'jɔː ɪŋ/z ‖ 'jɔː ɪŋ/z 'jɑː- **yaws** jɔːz ‖ jɑːz
yawl jɔːl ‖ jɑːl **yawls** jɔːlz ‖ jɑːlz
yawn jɔːn ‖ jɑːn **yawned** jɔːnd ‖ jɑːnd
 yawning/ly 'jɔːn ɪŋ /li ‖ 'jɑːn- **yawns** jɔːnz
 ‖ jɑːnz
yawp jɔːp ‖ jɑːp **yawped** jɔːpt ‖ jɑːpt
 yawping 'jɔːp ɪŋ ‖ 'jɑːp- **yawps** jɔːps
 ‖ jɑːps
yaws jɔːz ‖ jɑːz
y-axis 'waɪ ˌæks ɪs §-əs
yclept ɪ 'klept iː-
ye *pronoun strong form* jiː, *weak form* ji
ye *'the'* jiː —*or* →the
yea jeɪ **yeas** jeɪz
Yeading 'jed ɪŋ
Yeadon (i) 'jiːd ən, (ii) jeɪd ən, (iii) 'jed ən
 —*The place in WYks is (i), that in PA (ii). The
 family name may be any of the three.*
yeah jeə ‖ 'je ə

‖ jɪərz
ˌyear 'dot
yearbook 'jɪə bʊk 'jɜː- ‖ 'jɪr- ~s s
yearling 'jɪə lɪŋ 'jɜː- ‖ 'jɪr- ~s z
yearlong ˌjɪə 'lɒŋ ◂ ˌjɜː- ‖ ˌjɪr 'lɔːŋ ◂ -'lɑːŋ
yearly 'jɪə li 'jɜː- ‖ 'jɪr li
yearn jɜːn ‖ jɜːn **yearned** jɜːnd ‖ jɜːnd
 yearning 'jɜːn ɪŋ ‖ 'jɜːn ɪŋ **yearns**
 jɜːnz ‖ jɜːnz
yearning 'jɜːn ɪŋ ‖ 'jɜːn ɪŋ ~ly li ~s z
year-round ˌjɪə 'raʊnd ◂ ˌjɜː- ‖ ˌjɪr-
yeast jiːst **yeasts** jiːsts
yeast|y 'jiːst |i ~ier i_ə ‖ i_ər ~iest i_ɪst i_əst
 ~ily ɪ li əl i ~iness i nəs i nɪs
Yeates, Yeats jeɪts (!)
yecch, yech jex jek, jʌx, jʌk
Yehudi jɪ 'huːd i jə-, je-
yell, Yell jel **yelled** jeld **yelling** 'jel ɪŋ **yells**
 jelz
Yelland 'jel ənd
yellow 'jel əʊ ‖ -oʊ ~ed d ~ing ɪŋ ~s z
 ˌyellow 'fever; ˌYellow 'Pages ‖ '• • , • • ;
 'yellow ˌrattle; ˌYellow 'Sea
yellowhammer 'jel əʊ ˌhæm ə ‖ -oʊ ˌhæm ər
 -ə- ~s z
yellowish 'jel əʊ ɪʃ ‖ -oʊ-
Yellowknife 'jel əʊ naɪf ‖ -oʊ- -ə-
yellow|ly 'jel əʊ |li ‖ -oʊ- ~ness nəs nɪs
Yellowstone 'jel əʊ stəʊn ‖ -oʊ stoʊn -ə-
yellowwood 'jel əʊ wʊd ‖ -oʊ -ə- ~s z
yellowy 'jel əʊ i ‖ -oʊ-
yelp jelp **yelped** jelpt **yelping** 'jelp ɪŋ **yelps**
 jelps
Yeltsin 'jelts ɪn -ən —*Russ* ['jelʲ tsin]
Yelverton 'jelv ət ən ‖ -ərt ən
Yemen 'jem ən 'jeɪm-
Yemeni 'jem ən i 'jeɪm- ~s z
yen *'long(ing)'* jen **yenned** jend **yenning**
 'jen ɪŋ **yens** jenz
yen *'Japanese currency'* jen —*Jp* ['eɴ]
Yenisei, Yenisey ˌjen ɪ 'seɪ -ə- —*Russ*
 [jɪ nʲɪ 'sʲej]
Yeo jəʊ ‖ joʊ (!)
yeo|man 'jəʊ |mən ‖ 'joʊ- ~manly mən li
 ~manry mən ri ~men mən
 ˌyeoman 'service ‖ '• • , • •
Yeovil 'jəʊ vɪl -vəl ‖ 'joʊ-
yep jep —*usually said with no audible release of
 the* [p]
yer *'weak vowel in Slavonic languages'* jɜː ‖ jɜː
 yers jɜːz ‖ jɜːz
yer *informal spelling of the weak form of 'your' or
 'you're'* jə ‖ jər
yer *informal spelling of the weak form of 'you'
 (BrE only)* jə ‖ —
yer *informal 'yes' (BrE only)* jeə jɜː ‖ —
Yerba Buena ˌjeəb ə 'bweɪn ə ˌjɜːb- ‖ ˌjerb-
 ˌjɜːb-
Yerevan ˌjer ə 'væn -vɑːn, -ɪ-, '• • • ‖ -'vɑːn
 —*Russ* [jɪ rʲɪ 'van]
Yerkes 'jɜːk iːz ‖ 'jɜːk-
yes jes —*Casual variants include* yah, yeah, yep,
 yup *(see).* **yeses** 'jes ɪz -əz

Y

YEAR					
■ jɪə □ jɜː					
BrE 1988					
0	20	40	60	80	100%

year jɪə jɜː ‖ jɪər —*BrE 1988 poll panel
preference:* jɪə 80%, jɜː 20%. **years** jɪəz jɜːz

yeshiva, yeshivah jə 'ʃiːv ə ~s z
yes-|man 'jes |mæn ~men men
yes/no question ˌjes 'nəʊ ˌkwes tʃən -ˌkweʃ-
‖ -'noʊ- ~s z
yesterday 'jest əd i -ə deɪ; §,••'deɪ ‖ -ərd i
-ər deɪ ~s, ~'s z
yesteryear 'jest ə jɪə -jɜː, ,••'• ‖ -ər jɪr
yet jet
Yetholm 'jet əm ‖ 'jet̬-
yeti 'jet i ‖ 'jet̬ i ~s z
Yevtushenko ˌjev tu 'ʃeŋk əʊ -tə- ‖ -oʊ
—*Russ* [jɪf tu 'ʃeŋ kə]
yew juː *(= you, ewe, U)* **yews** juːz *(= use v.)*
Y-front *tdmk* 'waɪ frʌnt ~s s
Ygdrasil, Yggdrasil 'ɪg drə sɪl
YHA ˌwaɪ eɪtʃ 'eɪ §-heɪtʃ-
yid jɪd **yids** jɪdz
Yiddish 'jɪd ɪʃ
yiddisher, Y~ 'jɪd ɪʃ ə ‖ -ər ~s z
yield jiːəld **yielded** 'jiːəld ɪd -əd **yielding/ly**
'jiːəld ɪŋ /li **yields** jiːəldz
yin, Yin jɪn
yip jɪp **yipped** jɪpt **yipping** 'jɪp ɪŋ **yips** jɪps
yippee ˌ(ˌ)jɪ 'piː ‖ 'jɪp i
-yl əl ɪl, aɪəl ‖ -iːəl —*in BrE there is an
inconsistent preference for* aɪəl *in* butyl *but* əl *in*
methyl
ylang-ylang ˌiːl æŋ 'iːl æŋ ‖ ˌiːl ɑːŋ 'iːl ɑːŋ
YMCA ˌwaɪ em si: 'eɪ
-yne aɪn — **alkyne** 'ælk aɪn
Ynys 'ʌn ɪs △'ɪn- —*Welsh* ['ə nis, -nis]
ˌYnys 'Mon, ˌYnys 'Môn mɔːn —*Welsh*
[moːn]
Ynys-ddu ˌʌn ɪs 'diː- -'ðiː —*Welsh* [ˌə nis 'ðiː]
Ynysybwl ˌʌn ɪs ə 'bʊl —*Welsh* [ˌə nis ə 'bʊl]
yo jəʊ ‖ joʊ
yob jɒb ‖ jaːb **yobs** jɒbz ‖ jaːbz
yobbish 'jɒb ɪʃ ‖ 'jaːb- **~ly** li **~ness** nəs nɪs
yobbism 'jɒb ˌɪz əm ‖ 'jaːb-
yobbo 'jɒb əʊ ‖ 'jaːb oʊ ~s z
yod jɒd ‖ jaːd jɔːd, jʊd **yods** jɒdz ‖ jaːdz
jɔːdz, jʊdz
yodel 'jəʊd əl ‖ 'joʊd əl **~ed, ~led** d **~ing,
~ling** ˌɪŋ **~s** z
yoga 'jəʊg ə ‖ 'joʊg ə
yogh jɒg jəʊg ‖ joʊg joʊx, joʊx **yoghs** jɒgz
jəʊgz ‖ joʊgz joʊks, joʊxs
yoghourt, yoghurt 'jɒg ət -ʊət ‖ 'joʊg ərt *(*)*
~s s
yogi 'jəʊg i ‖ 'joʊg i ~s z
yogic 'jəʊg ɪk ‖ 'joʊg-
yogurt 'jɒg ət -ʊət ‖ 'joʊg ərt *(*)* **~s** s
yo-heave-ho ˌjəʊ ˌhiːv 'həʊ ‖ ˌjoʊ ˌhiːv 'hoʊ
yohimbine jəʊ 'hɪm biːn ‖ joʊ-
yo-ho ˌ(ˌ)jəʊ 'həʊ ‖ ˌ(ˌ)joʊ 'hoʊ
yo-ho-ho ˌjəʊ ˌhəʊ 'həʊ ‖ ˌjoʊ ˌhoʊ 'hoʊ
yoicks jɔɪks
yoke jəʊk ‖ joʊk **yoked** jəʊkt ‖ joʊkt **yokes**
jəʊks ‖ joʊks **yoking** 'jəʊk ɪŋ ‖ 'joʊk ɪŋ
yokel 'jəʊk əl ‖ 'joʊk əl ~s z
Yoknapatawpha ˌjɒk nə pə 'tɔːf ə ‖ ˌjaːk-
-'tɑːf-
Yoko 'jəʊk əʊ ‖ 'joʊk oʊ —*Jp* ['joo ko]

Yokohama ˌjəʊk əʊ 'hɑːm ə ‖ ˌjoʊk ə- —*Jp*
[jo ˌko ha ma]
Yolanda jəʊ 'lænd ə ‖ joʊ- -'lɑːnd-
yolk jəʊk ‖ joʊk joʊlk, jelk *(= yoke)* **yolks**
jəʊks ‖ joʊks joʊlks, jelks
Yom Kippur ˌjɒm kɪ 'pʊə •'kɪp ə
‖ ˌjoʊm 'kɪp ər ˌjɒːm-, ˌjaːm-, -kɪ 'pʊər
yomp jɒmp ‖ jaːmp **yomped** jɒmpt ‖ jaːmpt
yomping 'jɒmp ɪŋ ‖ 'jaːmp ɪŋ **yomps**
jɒmps ‖ jaːmps
yon jɒn ‖ jaːn
yond jɒnd ‖ jaːnd
yonder 'jɒnd ə ‖ 'jaːnd ər
Yonge jʌŋ
yoni 'jəʊn i ‖ 'joʊn i ~s z
Yonkers 'jɒŋk əz ‖ 'jaːŋk ərz
yonks jɒŋks ‖ jaːŋks
yoof *non-standard variant of* youth juːf
yoo-hoo ˌju: 'hu: '•• ‖ 'ju: hu:
YOP jɒp ‖ jaːp
Yorba Linda ˌjɔːb ə 'lɪnd ə ‖ ˌjɔːrb- —*Sp* [ˌjor
βa 'lin da]
yore, Yore jɔː ‖ jɔːr joʊr
Yorick 'jɒr ɪk ‖ 'jɔːr ɪk 'jaːr-
York, york, Yorke jɔːk ‖ jɔːrk **yorked**
jɔːkt ‖ jɔːrkt **yorking** 'jɔːk ɪŋ ‖ 'jɔːrk ɪŋ
yorks, York's jɔːks ‖ jɔːrks
yorker 'jɔːk ə ‖ 'jɔːrk ər ~s z
yorkie, Y~ *tdmk* 'jɔːk i ‖ 'jɔːrk i ~s z
Yorkist 'jɔːk ɪst §-əst ‖ 'jɔːrk- ~s s
Yorks. jɔːks ‖ jɔːrks
Yorkshire 'jɔːk ʃə -ʃɪə ‖ 'jɔːrk ʃər -ʃɪr **~man**
mən **~men** mən men **~s** z **~woman**
ˌwʊm ən **~women** ˌwɪm ɪn §-ən
ˌYorkshire 'pudding; ˌYorkshire 'terrier
Yorktown 'jɔːk taʊn ‖ 'jɔːrk-
Yoruba 'jɒr ʊb ə ‖ 'jɔːr əb ə ~s z
Yosemite jəʊ 'sem ət i -ɪt- ‖ joʊ 'sem ət̬ i
Yossarian jɒ 'seər i_ən -'saːr- ‖ joʊ 'ser-
-'saːr-
Yost jəʊst ‖ joʊst
you *strong form* juː, *weak forms* ju jə, *before a
vowel also* §j —*(1) Learners of BrE are advised
not to use weak forms other than* ju; jə *is
unusual in RP, while* j *is clearly non-RP. In
GenAm, on the other hand, the weak form* jə *is
acceptable.* —*(2) The initial* j *of this word
readily coalesces with the final* t *or* d *of a
preceding word to give* tʃ *or* dʒ *respectively:*
don't you 'dəʊntʃ u ‖ 'doʊntʃ ə, did you
'dɪdʒ u ‖ -ə
you-all ju 'ɔːl jɔːl ‖ jɔːl, ju 'aːl, jaːl
you'd *strong form* juːd, *weak forms* jud jəd
—*See note (1) at* you
Youel, Youell 'juːˌəl juːl
Youens 'juːˌɪnz ˌənz
Youghal jɔːl ‖ jaːl
you'll *strong forms* juːl juːˌəl, *weak forms* jul jəl
—*See note (1) at* you
young, Young jʌŋ **younger** 'jʌŋ gə ‖ -gər
youngest 'jʌŋ gɪst -gəst
ˌyoung 'man; ˌyoung 'woman
Younger 'jʌŋ gə ‖ -gər

Younghusband 'jʌŋ ˌhʌz bənd
youngish 'jʌŋ ɪʃ -gɪʃ
youngling 'jʌŋ lɪŋ ~s z
youngster 'jʌŋᵏst ə ‖ -ᵊr ~s z
Youngstown 'jʌŋz taʊn
your *strong forms* jɔː juə ‖ juᵊr jɔːr, juʊr, *weak form* jə ‖ jᵊr —*Learners of BrE are advised not to use the weak form* jə, *which is fairly unusual in RP.*
you're *strong forms* jɔː juə ‖ juᵊr, *weak form* jə ‖ jᵊr —*Learners of BrE are advised not to use the weak form* jə, *which is fairly unusual in RP. (= your)*

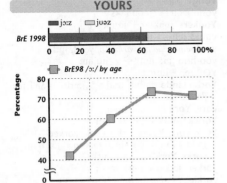

YOURS

BrE 1998 ▮ jɔːz ▭ juəz

0   20   40   60   80   100%

BrE98 /ɔː/ by age

Percentage
80
70
60
50
40
0

Older ◀—— Speakers ——▶ Younger

yours jɔːz juəz ‖ juᵊrz jɔːrz, juʊrz —*BrE 1998 poll panel preference:* jɔːz 64%, juəz 36%.
ˌyours ˈtruly
your|self jɔː ‖'self juə-, jə- ‖ jʊr- jɔːr-, jᵊr-, juʊr- ~**selves** 'selvz
yous, youse *strong form* juːz, *weak forms* jəz, jɪz —*This second person pl pronoun, being non-standard, has no standard pronunciation.*

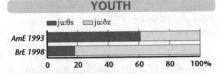

YOUTH

AmE 1993 ▮ juːθs ▭ juːðz
BrE 1998

0   20   40   60   80   100%

youth juːθ **youths** juːðz juːθs ‖ juːθs juːðz —*Poll panel preferences: AmE 1993,* juːθs 61%, juːðz 39%; *BrE 1998,* juːðz 82%, juːθs 18%. **youth's** juːθs
'youth club; 'youth ˌhostel
youthful 'juːθ fᵊl -fʊl ~**ly** i ~**ness** nəs nɪs
you've *strong form* juːv, *weak forms* juv jəv —*See note (1) at* you
yowl jaʊl **yowled** jaʊld **yowling** 'jaʊl ɪŋ **yowls** jaʊlz

yoyo, yo-yo, Yo-Yo *tdmk* 'jəʊ jəʊ ‖ 'joʊ joʊ ~s z
Ypres 'iːp rə -rəz, -əz; iːp; 'waɪp əz —*Fr* [ipχ]
Yr, yr *in Welsh expressions* ər
Ystalyfera ˌʌst əl ə 'ver ə —*Welsh* [ˌəs dal ə 've ra]
Ystrad 'ʌs trəd —*Welsh* ['əs drad]
Ystradgynlais ˌʌs trəd 'gʌn laɪs -træd- —*Welsh* [ˌəs drad 'gən lais]
Ystwyth 'ʌst wɪθ —*Welsh* ['əs duiθ, -duiθ]
Ythan 'aɪθ ᵊn
YTS ˌwaɪ tiː 'es
ytterbium ɪ 'tɜːb iˌəm ‖ -'tɜːːb-
yttrium 'ɪtr iˌəm
Yu juː —*Cantonese* [⁴jyː]
yuan, Yuan ju 'æn -'ɑːn ‖ -'ɑːn —*Chi* yuán [²ɥæn]
Yucatan, Yucatán ˌjʊk ə 'tɑːn ˌjuːk-, -'tæn ‖ ˌjuːk ə 'tæn -'tɑːn —*Sp* [ju ka 'tan]
yucca 'jʌk ə 'juːk- ~s z
yuck jʌk
yuck|y 'jʌk |i ~**ier** iˌə ‖ iˌᵊr ~**iest** iˌɪst iˌəst
Yudkin 'juːd kɪn
Yue *(i)* ju 'eɪ —*Chi* Yuè [⁴ɥɛ]; *(ii)* juː —*Cantonese* [⁴jyː]
Yugoslav 'juːg əʊ slɑːv ˌ•'•' ‖ ˌjuːg oʊ 'slɑːv ◀ -'slæv ~s z
Yugoslavi|a ˌjuːg əʊ 'slɑːv iˌ|ə ‖ ˌ•oʊ- ~**an/s** ən/z
yuk jʌk
yukk|y 'jʌk |i ~**ier** iˌə ‖ iˌᵊr ~**iest** iˌɪst iˌəst
Yukon 'juːk ɒn ‖ -ɑːn
Yul juːl
yule, Yule juːl
'yule log
yuletide, Y~ 'juːl taɪd
Yuma 'juːm ə ~s z
Yuman 'juːm ən
yumm|y 'jʌm |i ~**ier** iˌə ‖ iˌᵊr ~**iest** iˌɪst iˌəst
yum-yum, Yum-Yum ˌjʌm 'jʌm
Yunnan ˌju 'næn ˌjʊn- ‖ -'nɑːn —*Chi* Yúnnán [²jyn ²nan]
yup jʌp —*usually said with no audible release of the* [p]
Yupik 'juːp ɪk ~s s
yuppie, Y~ 'jʌp i ~s z
yuppification ˌjʌp ɪf ɪ 'keɪʃ ᵊn ˌ•əf-, §-ə'•-
yuppi|fy 'jʌp ɪ |faɪ §-ə- ~**fied** faɪd ~**fies** faɪz ~**fying** faɪ ɪŋ
yupp|y, Yupp|y 'jʌp |i ~**ies** iz
Yuri 'jʊər i ‖ 'jʊr i 'jɜː- —*Russ* ['ju rʲi]
yurt jʊət jɜːt ‖ juᵊrt **yurts** jʊəts jɜːts ‖ juᵊrts
Yussuf 'jʊs ʊf -əf
Yves iːv —*Fr* [iːv]
Yvette ɪ 'vet ₍ᵢ₎iː-
Yvonne ɪ 'vɒn ₍ᵢ₎iː- ‖ -'vɑːn

Y

Zz

| **z** | Spelling-to-sound |

1 Where the spelling is **z**, the pronunciation is regularly z, as in **lazy** 'leɪz i.

2 Where the spelling is double **zz**, the pronunciation is again z, as in **dazzle** 'dæz əl.

3 Because of yod coalescence (see ASSIMILATION), the pronunciation is occasionally ʒ, as in **seizure** 'siːʒ ə ‖ 'siːʒ ər.

4 In certain words borrowed from foreign languages, spelling with **z**, **zz** or the foreign digraph **tz**, the pronunciation is ts, as in **Nazi** 'nɑːts i, **pizza** 'piːts ə, **quartz** kwɔːts ‖ kwɔːrts.

5 The sound z is also regularly written **s**, as in **choose** tʃuːz.

Z, z zed ‖ ziː: (*) **Z's, z's, Zs** zedz ‖ ziːz
—*Communications code name:* Zulu
zabaglione ˌzæb əl 'jəʊn i -æl-, -eɪ
‖ ˌzɑːb əl 'joʊn i —*It* [tsa baʎ 'ʎoː ne] **~s** z
Zachariah ˌzæk ə 'raɪ‿ə
Zachary 'zæk ər i
Zadok 'zeɪd ɒk ‖ -ɑːk
Zagreb 'zɑːg reb 'zæg-, ˌzɑː 'greb —*Serbo-Croat* ['za greb]
Zaire, Zaïre, zaire ⑴zaɪ 'ɪə zɑː:- ‖ zɑː 'ɪər 'zɑː ɪr
Zairean, Zaïrean zaɪ 'ɪər i‿ən zɑː:- ‖ zɑː 'ɪr- **~s** z
Zak zæk
Zambezi ⑴zæm 'biːz i
Zambia 'zæm bi‿ə
Zambian 'zæm bi‿ən **~s** z
zambuck, Z~, Zam-Buk *tdmk* 'zæm bʌk **~s** s
Zamenhof 'zæm ən hɒf -en- ‖ 'zɑːm ən hoʊf
Zander, z~ 'zænd ə ‖ -ər **~s** z
Zandra 'zɑːndr ə 'zændr-
Zane zeɪn
Zangwill 'zæŋ wɪl -wəl, -gwɪl, -gwəl
Zantac *tdmk* 'zænt æk
Zante 'zænt i
ZANU 'zɑːn uː 'zæn-
Zanuck 'zæn ək
zan|y 'zeɪn li **~ier** i‿ə ‖ i‿ər **~ies** iz **~iest** i‿ɪst i‿əst **~ily** ɪ li əl i **~iness** i nəs i nɪs
Zanzibar 'zænz ɪ bɑː: -ə-, ˌ••'• ‖ -bɑːr
Zanzibari ˌzænz ɪ 'bɑːr i ◄ -ə- **~s** z
zap zæp **zapped** zæpt **zapping** 'zæp ɪŋ **zaps** zæps
Zapata zə 'pɑːt ə zæ- ‖ -'pɑːt̬- —*AmSp* [sa 'pa ta]
Zapotec 'zæp ə tek 'zɑːp-, ˌ••'•
zapp... —*see* **zap**

Zappa 'zæp ə
zapper 'zæp ə ‖ -ər **~s** z
Zara 'zɑːr ə
Zaragoza ˌsær ə 'ɡɒs ə ‖ ˌzær ə 'ɡoʊz ə —*Sp* [θa ɾa 'ɣo θa]
Zarathustra ˌzær ə 'θuːs trə ‖ ˌzer-
Zaria 'zɑːr i‿ə
Zatopek 'zæt ə pek ‖ 'zæt̬- —*Czech* Zátopek ['za to pek]
zax zæks **zaxes** 'zæks ɪz -əz
z-axis 'zed ˌæks ɪs §-əs ‖ 'ziː-
zeal, Zeal ziːəl
Zealand 'ziː lənd
zealot 'zel ət **~s** s
zealotry 'zel ət ri
zealous 'zel əs **~ly** li **~ness** nəs nɪs
Zebedee 'zeb ə diː -ɪ-

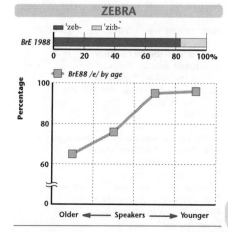

ZEBRA

| ■ 'zeb- | ▨ 'ziːb- |

BrE 1988

0 — 20 — 40 — 60 — 80 — 100%

▨ BrE88 /e/ by age

Percentage

100

80

60

0

Older ◄— Speakers —► Younger

Z

zebra 'zeb rə 'zi:b- ‖ 'zi:b- —*BrE 1988 poll
panel preference:* 'zeb- *83%,* 'zi:b- *17%.* ~s z
,zebra 'crossing

zebu 'zi:b u: -ju: ~s z

Zebulon, Zebulun 'zeb jʊl ən ze 'bju:l-, zə-

Zechariah ,zek ə 'raɪ ə

zed zed **zeds** zedz

Zedekiah ,zed ɪ 'kaɪ ə -ə-

zedoary 'zed əʊ ər i zə 'dəʊ- ‖ -oʊ er i

zee zi: **zees** zi:z

Zeebrugge ,zeɪ 'brʊg ə ,zi:-, '•·,•• , zɪ'••;
'zeɪ bru:ʒ —*Dutch* ['ze: ,bryx ə]

Zeeland 'zi: lənd —*Dutch* ['ze: lɑnt]

Zeeman 'zi: mən —*Dutch* ['ze: mɑn]

Zeffirelli ,zef ə 'rel i -ɪ- —*It* [tsɛf fi 'rel li]

Zeiss zaɪs —*Ger* [tsaɪs]

zeitgeist 'zaɪt gaɪst —*Ger* Z~ ['tsaɪt gaɪst]

zek, Zek zek **zeks** zeks

Zelda 'zeld ə

Zeldin 'zeld ɪn §-ən

zelkova 'zelk əv ə zel 'kəʊv ə ‖ zel 'koʊv ə ~s
z

Zelotes zɪ 'ləʊt i:z zə-, ze- ‖ -'loʊt-

Zen zen —*Jp* ['dzeɴ, dze,ɴ]
,Zen 'Buddhism

Zena 'zi:n ə

zenana ze 'nɑ:n ə zɪ-, zə- ~s z

Zend zend

Zenda 'zend ə

Zeneca *tdmk* 'zen ɪk ə -ək-

Zener 'zi:n ə 'zen- ‖ -ᵊr
,Zener 'diode

zenith 'zen ɪθ 'zi:n-, §-əθ ‖ 'zi:n əθ ~s s

zenithal 'zen ɪθ ᵊl 'zi:n-, §-əθ- ‖ 'zi:n əθ ᵊl

Zennor 'zen ə ‖ -ᵊr

Zeno 'zi:n əʊ ‖ -oʊ

Zenobia zɪ 'nəʊb i ə zə-, ze- ‖ -'noʊb-

zeolite 'zi: ə laɪt ~s s

Zephaniah ,zef ə 'naɪ ə

zephyr 'zef ə ‖ -ᵊr ~s z

Zephyrus 'zef ər əs -ɪr-

zeppelin, Z~ 'zep əl ɪn §-ən —*Ger* ['tsɛp ə li:n]
~s z

Zermatt 'zɜː mæt ‖ tser 'mɑːt —*Ger*
[tsɛʁ 'mat]

zero 'zɪər əʊ 'zɪr- ‖ 'zɪr oʊ 'zi: roʊ ~ed d
~es, ~s z ~ing ɪŋ
,zero 'gravity; 'zero ,hour

zero-rated ,zɪər əʊ 'reɪt ɪd ◄ ,zɪr-, -əd, '•• ,••
‖ ,zɪr oʊ 'reɪt̬ əd ◄ ,zi: roʊ-

zeroth *ordinal numeral* 'zɪər əʊθ 'zɪr-
‖ 'zɪ roʊθ 'zi: roʊθ

zest zest

zestful 'zest fᵊl -fʊl

zest|y 'zest li ~ier i ə ‖ i ᵊr ~iest i ɪst i əst

zeta, Zeta 'zi:t ə ‖ 'zeɪt̬ ə 'zi:t̬- ~s z

Zetland 'zet lənd

Zetters 'zet əz ‖ 'zet̬ ᵊrz

zeugma 'zju:g mə 'zu:g- ‖ 'zu:g- ~s z

Zeus zju:s zu:s; 'zi: əs ‖ zu:s

Zeuxis 'zju:ks ɪs 'zu:ks-, §-əs ‖ 'zu:ks-

Zewe 'zi: wi

Zhang dʒæŋ ‖ dʒɑ:ŋ
,Zhang Xueli'ang ,dʒæŋ ʃweɪl i 'æŋ
‖ ,dʒɑ:ŋ-, -'ɑ:ŋ —*Chi* Zhāng Xuéliáng [¹tʂaŋ
²ɕɥe ²ljaŋ]

Zhejiang ,dʒɜː dʒi 'æŋ ‖ ,dʒʌdʒ i 'ɑ:ŋ —*Chi*
Zhèjiāng [⁴tʂɤ ¹tɕjaŋ]

Zhirinovsky ,ʒɪr ɪ 'nɒf ski -ə- ‖ -'nɑ:f- —*Russ*
[ʒɨ rʲɪ 'nɔf skʲi]

Zhivago ʒɪ 'vɑ:g əʊ ʒə- ‖ -oʊ

Zhou *dynasty* dʒəʊ tʃəʊ ‖ dʒoʊ tʃoʊ —*Chi*
Zhōu [¹tʂoʊ]
,Zhou En'lai ,tʃəʊ en 'laɪ -ən- ‖ ,tʃoʊ-
—*Chi* Zhōu Ēnlái [¹tʂoʊ ¹ən ²laɪ]

Zhuhai ,dʒu: 'haɪ —*Chi* Zhūhǎi [¹tʂu ³xai]

Zhukov 'ʒu:k ɒv -ɒf ‖ -ɔ:f -ɑ:f —*Russ* ['ʒu kəf]

zibeline, zibelline 'zɪb ə laɪn -ᵊl aɪn, -ɪn,
§-ən ‖ -ə li:n

Ziegfeld 'zɪg feld 'zi:g-, -fi:ᵊld

Ziegler 'zi:g lə ‖ -lᵊr —*Ger* ['tsi: glɐ]

ziggurat 'zɪg ʊ ræt -ə- ‖ -ə- ~s s

Ziggy 'zɪg i

zigzag *n, v, adv* 'zɪg zæg ~ged d ~ging ɪŋ ~s
z

zilch zɪltʃ

zillion 'zɪl jən '•i ən ~s z

Zimbabwe zɪm 'bɑ:b wi -'bæb-, -weɪ

Zimbabwean zɪm 'bɑ:b wi ən -'bæb-, -weɪ-
~s z

zimmer, Z~ *tdmk* 'zɪm ə ‖ -ᵊr ~s z

zinc zɪŋk **zinced, zincked** zɪŋkt **zincing,
zincking** 'zɪŋk ɪŋ **zincs** zɪŋks
,zinc 'oxide

zincite 'zɪŋk aɪt

zine zi:n **zines** zi:nz

zineb 'zɪn eb 'zaɪn-

zinfandel, Z~ 'zɪn fən del ,••'• ~s z

zing zɪŋ **zinged** zɪŋd **zinging** 'zɪŋ ɪŋ **zings**
zɪŋz

zinjanthropus zɪn 'dʒænᵗθ rəp əs
,zɪndʒ æn 'θrəʊp- ‖ ,zɪndʒ æn 'θroʊp-

zinkenite 'zɪŋk ə naɪt

zinnia 'zɪn i ə ~s z

Zinoviev zɪ 'nəʊv i ev zə- ‖ -'noʊv- —*Russ*
[zʲɪ 'no vʲɪf]

Zion 'zaɪ ən

Zionism 'zaɪ ə ,nɪz əm

Zionist 'zaɪ ən ɪst §-əst ~s s

zip zɪp **zipped** zɪpt **zipping** 'zɪp ɪŋ **zips** zɪps
'zip code; ,zip 'fastener

zip-on 'zɪp ɒn ‖ -ɑ:n -ɔ:n

zipper 'zɪp ə ‖ -ᵊr ~s z

Zippo *tdmk* 'zɪp əʊ ‖ -oʊ

Zipporah 'zɪp ər ə

zipp|y 'zɪp li ~ier i ə ‖ i ᵊr ~iest i ɪst i əst

zip-up 'zɪp ʌp

zircon 'zɜː kɒn -ən ‖ 'zɝː k ɑːn ~s z

zirconium zɜː 'kəʊn i əm ‖ zɝː 'koʊn-

zit zɪt **zits** zɪts

zither 'zɪð ə ‖ -ᵊr 'zɪθ- ~s z

zizz zɪz

zloty 'zlɒt i ‖ 'zlɔːt̬ i 'zlɑːt- —*Polish* ['zwɔ ti]
~s z

-zoa 'zəʊ ə ‖ 'zoʊ ə — **spermatozoa**
  ˌspɜːm ət ə 'zəʊ ə ‖ ˌspɜːm ət̬ ə 'zoʊ ə
zodiac 'zəʊd i æk ‖ 'zoʊd-
zodiacal zəʊ 'daɪ̯ək ᵊl ‖ zoʊ-
Zoe, Zoë 'zəʊ i ‖ 'zoʊ i zoʊ
zoetrope 'zəʊ i trəʊp ‖ 'zoʊ i troʊp **~s** s
Zoff *tdmk* zɒf ‖ 'zɔːf zɑːf
Zoffany 'zɒf ən i ‖ 'zɑːf-
Zog zɒg ‖ zɔːg zɑːg —*Albanian* Zogu ['zɔ gu]
-zoic 'zəʊ ɪk ‖ 'zoʊ ɪk — **paleozoic** ˌpæl i əʊ
  'zəʊ ɪk ◂ ˌpeɪl- ‖ ˌpeɪl i̯ə 'zoʊ ɪk ◂
zoisite 'zɔɪs aɪt
Zola 'zəʊl ə ‖ 'zoʊl ə —*Fr* [zɔ la]
Zollner, Zöllner 'zɒl nə ‖ 'zɑːl nᵊr **~'s** z —*Ger*
  ['tsœl nɐ]
  ˌZollner's 'lines
Zomba 'zɒm bə ‖ 'zɑːm-
zombi, zombie 'zɒm bi ‖ 'zɑːm- **~s** z
zonal 'zəʊn ᵊl ‖ 'zoʊn ᵊl **~ly** i
zonation zəʊ 'neɪʃ ᵊn ‖ zoʊ- **~s** z
zone zəʊn ‖ zoʊn **zoned** zəʊnd ‖ zoʊnd
  zones zəʊnz ‖ zoʊnz **zoning**
  'zəʊn ɪŋ ‖ 'zoʊn ɪŋ
zonk zɒŋk ‖ zɑːŋk zɔːŋk **zonked**
  zɒŋkt ‖ zɑːŋkt zɔːŋkt **zonking**
  'zɒŋk ɪŋ ‖ 'zɑːŋk ɪŋ 'zɔːŋk- **zonks**
  zɒŋks ‖ zɑːŋks zɔːŋks
Zonta 'zɒnt ə ‖ 'zɑːnt̬ ə
Zontian 'zɒnt i̯ən ‖ 'zɑːnt̬ i̯ən **~s** z
zonule 'zɒn juːl 'zəʊn- ‖ 'zoʊn- **~s** z
zoo zuː **zoos** zuːz
zoo- *comb. form*
  with stress-neutral suffix ˌzəʊ ə ˌzuːˌə ‖ ˌzoʊ ə
  — **zoophile** 'zəʊ ə faɪᵊl 'zuːˌ ‖ 'zoʊ-
  with stress-imposing suffix zəʊ 'ɒ+ zu 'ɒ+
  ‖ zoʊ 'ɑː+ — **zoophilous** zəʊ 'ɒf ɪl əs zu-,
  -əl- ‖ zoʊ 'ɑːf-
zooid 'zəʊ ɔɪd ‖ 'zoʊ- **~s** z
zoological ˌzəʊ ə 'lɒdʒ ɪk ᵊl ◂ ˌzuːˌə-, zu 'lɒdʒ-
  ‖ ˌzoʊ ə 'lɑːdʒ- **~ly** i
  ˌzooˌlogical 'gardens
zoologist zəʊ 'ɒl ədʒ ɪst zu-, §-əst ‖ zoʊ 'ɑːl-
  ~s s
zoology zəʊ 'ɒl ədʒ i zu- ‖ zoʊ 'ɑːl-
zoom zuːm **zoomed** zuːmd **zooming**
  'zuːm ɪŋ **zooms** zuːmz
  'zoom lens
zoometry zəʊ 'ɒm ətr i -ɪtr- ‖ zoʊ 'ɑːm-
-zoon zəʊ ɒn -ən ‖ 'zoʊ ɑːn —
  spermatozoon ˌspɜːm ət ə 'zəʊ ɒn -ən
  ‖ ˌspɜːm ət̬ ə 'zoʊ ɑːn
zoophyte 'zəʊ ə faɪt 'zuːˌ ‖ 'zoʊ- **~s** s
zoospore 'zəʊ ə spɔː 'zuːˌ ‖ 'zoʊ ə spɔːr
  -spoʊr **~s** z
zoot zuːt
  'zoot suit
Zora, Zorah 'zɔːr ə ‖ 'zoʊr-
Zoroaster ˌzɒr əʊ 'æst ə '•••
  ‖ 'zɔːr oʊ æst ᵊr 'zoʊr-
Zoroastrian ˌzɒr əʊ 'æs tri̯ən ◂ ‖ ˌzɔːr oʊ-
  ˌzoʊr- **~ism** ˌɪz əm **~s** z
Zorro 'zɒr əʊ ‖ 'zɔːr oʊ —*Sp* ['θo rro, 'so-]

zoster 'zɒst ə ‖ 'zɑːst ᵊr
zouave, Z~ zu 'ɑːv 'zuː ɑːv, zwɑːv **zouaves,**
  Z~ zu 'ɑːvz 'zuː ɑːvz, zwɑːvz
zounds zaʊndz zuːndz
Zsa Zsa 'ʒɑː ʒɑː
Zubes *tdmk* zuːbz zjuːbz
zucchetto zu 'ket əʊ ‖ -'ket̬ oʊ **~s** z
zucchini zu 'kiːn i
Zuckerman 'zʊk ə mən ‖ -ᵊr-
Zugspitze 'zʊg ˌʃpɪts ə —*Ger* ['tsuːk ˌʃpɪts ə]
zugzwang 'zuːg zwæŋ —*Ger* ['tsuːk tsvaŋ]
Zuider Zee ˌzaɪd ə 'ziː ‖ -ᵊr- —*Dutch*
  [ˌzœy dər 'zeː]
Zuleika zu 'leɪk ə -'laɪk-
Zulu 'zuːl u **~s** z
Zululand 'zuːl u: lænd
Zuni, Zuñi 'zuːn i -ji —*AmSp* ['su ɲi] **~s** z
Zurich, Zürich 'zʊər ɪk 'zjʊər- ‖ 'zʊr ɪk —*Ger*
  ['tsyː ʁɪç]
Zutphen 'zʌt fən —*Dutch* ['zʏt fən]
Zuyder Zee ˌzaɪd ə 'ziː ‖ -ᵊr- —*Dutch*
  [ˌzœy dər 'zeː]
Zwemmer 'zwem ə ‖ -ᵊr
zwieback 'zwiː bæk -bɑːk ‖ 'zwaɪ- 'swiː-,
  'swaɪ-, 'zwiː **~s** s
Zwingli 'zwɪŋ gli -li —*Ger* ['tsvɪŋ li]
Zwinglian 'zwɪŋ gli̯ən -li̯ **~s** z
zwitterion 'zwɪt ər ˌaɪ̯ən 'tsvɪt-, -ɒn
  ‖ 'zwɪt̬ ə ˌraɪ̯ən -aːn **~s** z
zyg- *comb. form before vowel*
  with unstressed suffix ˌzaɪg — **zygote**
  'zaɪg əʊt ‖ -oʊt
  with stressed suffix zaɪ 'g+ zɪ 'g+ — **zygosis**
  zaɪ 'gəʊs ɪs zɪ-, §-əs ‖ -'goʊs-
zygo- *comb. form*
  with stress-neutral suffix ˌzaɪg əʊ 'zɪg əʊ ‖ -ə
  — **zygospore** 'zaɪg əʊ spɔː 'zɪg- -ə spɔːr
  -spoʊr
  with stress-imposing suffix zaɪ 'gɒ+ zɪ-
  ‖ -'gɑː+ — **zygopteran** zaɪ 'gɒpt ər ən zɪ-
  ‖ -'gɑːpt-
zygoma zaɪ 'gəʊm ə zɪ- ‖ -'goʊm ə **~s** z
zygomatic ˌzaɪg əʊ 'mæt ɪk ◂ ˌzɪg- ‖ -ə 'mæt̬-
zygote 'zaɪg əʊt 'zɪg- ‖ -oʊt **~s** s
zygotic zaɪ 'gɒt ɪk zɪ- ‖ -'gɑːt̬- **~ally** ᵊl̯i
zym- *comb. form before vowel*
  with unstressed suffix ˌzaɪm — **zymurgy**
  'zaɪm ɜːdʒ i ‖ -ɜːdʒ-
  with stressed suffix zaɪ 'm+ — **zymoma**
  zaɪ 'məʊm ə ‖ -'moʊm-
zymase 'zaɪm eɪs -eɪz
zymo- *comb. form*
  with stress-neutral suffix ˌzaɪm əʊ ‖ -ə —
  zymolytic ˌzaɪm əʊ 'lɪt ɪk ◂ ‖ -ə 'lɪt̬-
  with stress-imposing suffix zaɪ 'mɒ+ ‖ -'mɑː+
  — **zymolysis** zaɪ 'mɒl əs ɪs -ɪs-, §-əs
  ‖ -'mɑːl-
zymosis zaɪ 'məʊs ɪs §-əs ‖ -'moʊs-
zymotic zaɪ 'mɒt ɪk ‖ -'mɑːt̬ ɪk **~ally** ᵊl̯i
Zyrian, Zyryan 'zɪr i̯ən **~s** z
zzz —*sometimes said aloud as* [zː]

Z

Abbreviations

adj	adjective	*n*	noun
adv	adverb	*N*	North
AK	Alaska	*naut*	nautical
AL	Alabama	*NB*	Nebraska; nota bene, note well
AmE	American English	*NC*	North Carolina
AmSp	American Spanish	*Nfk*	Norfolk
AR	Arkansas	*NH*	New Hampshire
AZ	Arizona	*NJ*	New Jersey
BBC	British Broadcasting Corporation	*NM*	New Mexico
Berks	Berkshire	*Norw*	Norwegian
BrE	British English	*Notts*	Nottinghamshire
Bucks	Buckinghamshire	*NSW*	New South Wales
CA	California	*N. Terr*	Northern Territories
Chi	Chinese	*NY*	New York
Co.	County	*NYC*	New York City
comb.	combining	*NYks*	North Yorkshire
conj	conjunction	*OH*	Ohio
CT	Connecticut	*OR*	Oregon
DE	Delaware	*PA*	Pennsylvania
E	East	*pl*	plural
EFL	English as a foreign language	*Port*	Portuguese
e.g.	for example	*pp*	past participle
esp.	especially	*PR*	Puerto Rico
Fr	French	*prep*	preposition
GA	Georgia; General American	*pres*	present
GenAm	General American	*RI*	Rhode Island
Glam	Glamorgan	*RP*	Received Pronunciation
Gloucs	Gloucestershire	*Russ*	Russian
H&W	Hereford & Worcester	*S*	South
Hung	Hungarian	*SC*	South Carolina
IA	Iowa	*ScG*	Scottish Gaelic
IL	Illinois	*S-Cr*	Serbo-Croat
IN	Indiana	*SD*	South Dakota
interj	interjection	*sing.*	singular
It	Italian	*Skt*	Sanskrit
Jp	Japanese	*Sp*	Spanish
KS	Kansas	*Staffs*	Staffordshire
Lancs	Lancashire	*StdEng*	Standard English
Leics	Leicestershire	*Swed*	Swedish
LI	Long Island	*Sx*	Sussex
LPD	Longman Pronunciation Dictionary	*SYks*	South Yorkshire
		tdmk	trademark, trade name, proprietary name*
MA	Massachusetts		
MD	Maryland	*TX*	Texas
ME	Maine	*UK*	United Kingdom
med	medical(ly)	*US*	United States
MI	Michigan	*v*	verb
MN	Minnesota	*VA*	Virginia
MO	Missouri	*VT*	Vermont
ModGk	Modern Greek	*W*	West
MT	Montana	*Warks*	Warwickshire
mus	musically, in music	*WYks*	West Yorkshire

* Dictionary entries that we believe to constitute trademarks have been designated *tdmk*. However, neither the presence nor the absence of this designation should be regarded as affecting the legal status of any trademark.